A Dictionary of the Bible

A Dictionary of the Bible

Dealing with its Language, Literature, and Contents
Including the Biblical Theology

Edited by

James Hastings, M.A., D.D.

With the assistance of

John Selbie, M.A., D.D.
A. B. Davidson, D.D., LL.D.
S. R. Driver, D.D., Litt.D.
H. B. Swete, D.D., Litt.D.

Volume 2
FEIGN – KINSMAN

HENDRICKSON
PUBLISHERS
PEABODY, MASSACHUSETTS 01961-3473

A DICTIONARY OF THE BIBLE, 5 Volume set

Hendrickson Publishers, Inc. edition

ISBN: 0-943575-07-9

reprinted from the edition
originally published by T. & T. Clark, Edinburgh, 1898

First printing — November 1988

Printed in the United States of America

PREFACE

'GIVE heed to . . . teaching.' Perhaps the Church of Christ has never given sufficient heed to teaching since the earliest and happiest days. In our own day the importance of teaching, or, as we sometimes call it, expository preaching, has been pressed home through causes that are various yet never accidental; and it is probable that in the near future more heed will be given by the Church to teaching than has ever been given before.

As a contribution towards the furnishing of the Church for that great work, this DICTIONARY OF THE BIBLE is published. It is a Dictionary of the Old and New Testaments, together with the Old Testament Apocrypha, according to the Authorized and Revised English Versions, and with constant reference to the original tongues. Every effort has been used to make the information it contains reasonably full, reliable, and accessible.

As to fulness. In a Dictionary of the Bible one expects that the words occurring in the Bible, which do not explain themselves, will receive some explanation. The present Dictionary more nearly meets that expectation than any Dictionary that has hitherto been published. Articles have been written on the names of all Persons and Places, on the Antiquities and Archæology of the Bible, on its Ethnology, Geology, and Natural History, on Biblical Theology and Ethic, and even on the obsolete or archaic words occurring in the English Versions. The greater number of the articles are of small compass, for care has been exercised to exclude vague generalities as well as unaccepted idiosyncrasies; but there are many articles which deal with important and difficult subjects, and extend to considerable length. Such, for example, is the article in the first volume on the Chronology of the New Testament, and the article in the present volume on Jesus Christ.

As to reliability. The names of the authors are appended to their articles, except where the article is very brief or of minor importance; and these names are the best guarantee that the work may be relied on. So far as could be ascertained, those authors were chosen for each particular subject who had made a special study of that subject, and might be able to speak with authority upon it. Then, in addition to the work of the Editor and his Assistant, every sheet has passed through the hands of the three distinguished scholars whose names are found on the title-page. Those scholars are not responsible for errors of any kind, if such should be discovered in the Dictionary, but the time and care they have spent upon it may be taken as a good assurance that the work as a whole is reliable and authoritative.

As to accessibility. While all the articles have been written expressly for this work, so they have been arranged under the headings one would most naturally turn to. In a very few cases it has been found necessary to group allied subjects together. But even then, the careful system of black-lettering and cross-reference adopted should enable the reader to find the subject wanted without delay. And so important has it seemed to the Editor that each subject should be found under its own natural title, that he has allowed a little repetition here and there (though not in identical terms) rather than distress the reader by sending him from one article to another in search of the information he desires. The Proper Names will be found under the spelling adopted in the Revised Version, and in a few very familiar instances the spelling of the Authorized Version is also given, with a cross-reference to the other. On the Proper Names generally, and particularly on the very difficult and unsettled questions of their derivation, reference may be made to the article NAMES (PROPER), which will be found in the third volume. The Hebrew, and (where it seemed to be of consequence for the identification of the name) the Greek of the Septuagint, have been given for all proper and many common names. It was found impracticable to record all the variety of spelling discovered in different manuscripts of the Septuagint; and it was considered unnecessary, in view of the great Edition now in preparation in Cambridge, and the Concordance of Proper Names about to be published at the Clarendon Press. The Abbreviations, considering the size and scope of the work, will be seen to be few and easily mastered. A list of them, together with a simple and uniform scheme of transliterating Hebrew and Arabic words, will be found on the following pages.

The Editor has pleasure in recording his thanks to many friends and willing fellow-workers, including the authors of the various articles. In especial, after those whose names are given on the title-page, he desires to thank the Rev. W. SANDAY, D.D., LL.D., Lady Margaret Professor of Divinity in the University of Oxford, who has again read many of the articles and given valuable assistance in other ways; next, the Rev. G. M. MACKIE, M.A., of Beyrout, whose knowledge of modern Syrian life is both intimate and sympathetic; also Professor MAHAFFY of Dublin, who kindly read some articles in proof; Professor RYLE of Cambridge; Principal SALMOND of Aberdeen; Principal STEWART of St. Andrews; and Principal FAIRBAIRN and Mr. J. VERNON BARTLET, M.A., of Mansfield College, Oxford. The Editor regrets to have to record the death, since the issue of the first volume, of Dr. D. Shearer and the Rev. H. A. White, M.A., New College, Oxford.

SCHEME OF TRANSLITERATION

ARABIC.		HEBREW.	
'	أ	'	א
b	ب	b	ב
t	ت	g	ג
th	ث	d	ד
j	ج	h	ה
ḥ	ح	u, w	ו
kh	خ	z	ז
d	د	ḥ	ח
dh	ذ	ṭ	ט
r	ر	i, y	י
z	ز	k	כ ל
s	س	l	ל
sh	ش	m	מ
ṣ	ص	n	נ
ḍ	ض	ṣ	ס
ṭ	ط	'	ע
ẓ	ظ	p	פ
'	ع	ẓ	צ
gh	غ	ḳ	ק
f	ف	r	ר
ḳ	ق	s, sh	שׁ שׂ
k	ك	t	ת
l	ل		
m	م		
n	ن		
h	ه		
u, w	و		
i, y	ي		

LIST OF ABBREVIATIONS

I. GENERAL

Alex. = Alexandrian.
Apoc. = Apocalypse.
Apocr. = Apocrypha.
Aq. = Aquila.
Arab. = Arabic.
Aram. = Aramaic.
Assyr. = Assyrian.
Bab. = Babylonian.
c. = *circa*, about.
Can. = Canaanite.
cf. = compare.
ct. = contrast.
D = Deuteronomist.
E = Elohist.
edd. = editions or editors.
Egyp. = Egyptian.
Eng. = English.
Eth. = Ethiopic.
f. = and following verse or page; as Ac 10$^{34f.}$
ff. = and following verses or pages; as Mt 11$^{28ff.}$
Gr. = Greek.
H = Law of Holiness.
Heb. = Hebrew.
Hel. = Hellenistic.
Hex. = Hexateuch.
Isr. = Israelite.
J = Jahwist.
J" = Jehovah.
Jerus. = Jerusalem.
Jos. = Josephus.

LXX = Septuagint.
MSS = Manuscripts.
MT = Massoretic Text.
n. = note.
NT = New Testament.
Onk. = Onkelos.
OT = Old Testament.
P = Priestly Narrative.
Pal. = Palestine, Palestinian.
Pent. = Pentateuch.
Pers. = Persian.
Phil. = Philistine.
Phœn. = Phœnician.
Pr. Bk. = Prayer Book.
R = Redactor.
Rom. = Roman.
Sam. = Samaritan.
Sem. = Semitic.
Sept. = Septuagint.
Sin. = Sinaitic.
Symm. = Symmachus.
Syr. = Syriac.
Talm. = Talmud.
Targ. = Targum.
Theod. = Theodotion.
TR = Textus Receptus.
tr. = translate or translation
VSS = Versions.
Vulg. = Vulgate.
WH = Westcott and Hort's text.

II. BOOKS OF THE BIBLE

Old Testament.

Gn = Genesis.
Ex = Exodus.
Lv = Leviticus.
Nu = Numbers.
Dt = Deuteronomy.
Jos = Joshua.
Jg = Judges.
Ru = Ruth.
1 S, 2 S = 1 and 2 Samuel.
1 K, 2 K = 1 and 2 Kings.
1 Ch, 2 Ch = 1 and 2 Chronicles.
Ezr = Ezra.
Neh = Nehemiah.
Est = Esther.
Job.
Ps = Psalms.
Pr = Proverbs.
Ec = Ecclesiastes.

Ca = Canticles.
Is = Isaiah.
Jer = Jeremiah.
La = Lamentations.
Ezk = Ezekiel.
Dn = Daniel.
Hos = Hosea.
Jl = Joel.
Am = Amos.
Ob = Obadiah.
Jon = Jonah.
Mic = Micah.
Nah = Nahum.
Hab = Habakkuk.
Zeph = Zephaniah.
Hag = Haggai.
Zec = Zechariah.
Mal = Malachi.

Apocrypha.

1 Es, 2 Es = 1 and 2 Esdras.
To = Tobit.
Jth = Judith.

Ad. Est = Additions to Esther.
Wis = Wisdom.
Sir = Sirach or Ecclesiasticus.
Bar = Baruch.
Three = Song of the Three Children.

Sus = Susanna.
Bel = Bel and the Dragon.
Pr. Man = Prayer of Manasses.
1 Mac, 2 Mac = 1 and 2 Maccabees.

New Testament.

Mt = Matthew.
Mk = Mark.
Lk = Luke.
Jn = John.
Ac = Acts.
Ro = Romans.
1 Co, 2 Co = 1 and 2 Corinthians.
Gal = Galatians.
Eph = Ephesians.
Ph = Philippians.
Col = Colossians.

1 Th, 2 Th = 1 and 2 Thessalonians.
1 Ti, 2 Ti = 1 and 2 Timothy.
Tit = Titus.
Philem = Philemon.
He = Hebrews.
Ja = James.
1 P, 2 P = 1 and 2 Peter.
1 Jn, 2 Jn, 3 Jn = 1, 2, and 3 John.
Jude.
Rev = Revelation.

III. English Versions

Wyc. = Wyclif's Bible (NT *c.* 1380, OT *c.* 1382, Purvey's Revision *c.* 1388).
Tind. = Tindale's NT 1526 and 1534, Pent. 1530.
Cov. = Coverdale's Bible 1535.
Matt. or Rog. = Matthew's (*i.e.* prob. Rogers') Bible 1537.
Cran. or Great = Cranmer's 'Great' Bible 1539.
Tav. = Taverner's Bible 1539.
Gen. = Geneva NT 1557, Bible 1560.

Bish. = Bishops' Bible 1568.
Tom. = Tomson's NT 1576.
Rhem. = Rhemish NT 1582.
Dou. = Douay OT 1609.
AV = Authorized Version 1611.
AVm = Authorized Version margin.
RV = Revised Version NT 1881, OT 1885.
RVm = Revised Version margin.
EV = Auth. and Rev. Versions.

IV. For the Literature

AHT = Ancient Hebrew Tradition.
AT = Altes Testament.
BL = Bampton Lecture.
BM = British Museum.
BRP = Biblical Researches in Palestine.
CIG = Corpus Inscriptionum Græcarum.
CIL = Corpus Inscriptionum Latinarum.
CIS = Corpus Inscriptionum Semiticarum.
COT = Cuneiform Inscriptions and the OT.
DB = Dictionary of the Bible.
EHH = Early History of the Hebrews.
GAP = Geographie des alten Palästina.
GGA = Göttingische Gelehrte Anzeigen.
GGN = Nachrichten der königl. Gesellschaft der Wissenschaften zu Göttingen.
GVI = Geschichte des Volkes Israel.
HCM = Higher Criticism and the Monuments.
HE = Historia Ecclesiastica.
HGHL = Historical Geog. of Holy Land.
HI = History of Israel.
HJP = History of the Jewish People.
HPM = History, Prophecy, and the Monuments.
IJG = Israelitische und Jüdische Geschichte.
JBL = Journal of Biblical Literature.
JDTh = Jahrbücher für deutsche Theologie.
JQR = Jewish Quarterly Review.
JRAS = Journal of the Royal Asiatic Society.
JRL = Jewish Religious Life after the Exile.
KAT = Die Keilinschriften und das Alte Test.
KIB = Keilinschriftliche Bibliothek.
LCBl = Literarisches Centralblatt.
LOT = Introd. to the Literature of the Old Test.
NHWB = Neuhebräisches Wörterbuch.

NTZG = Neutestamentliche Zeitgeschichte.
ON = Otium Norvicense.
OTJC = The Old Test. in the Jewish Church.
PB = Polychrome Bible.
PEF = Palestine Exploration Fund.
PEFSt = Quarterly Statement of the same.
PSBA = Proceedings of Soc. of Bibl. Archæology.
PRE = Real-Encyclopädie für protest. Theologie und Kirche.
QPB = Queen's Printers' Bible.
REJ = Revue des Études Juives.
RP = Records of the Past.
RS = Religion of the Semites.
SBOT = Sacred Books of Old Test.
SK = Studien und Kritiken.
SP = Sinai and Palestine.
SWP = Memoirs of the Survey of W. Palestine.
ThL or *ThLZ* = Theol. Literaturzeitung.
ThT = Theol. Tijdschrift.
TSBA = Transactions of Soc. of Bibl. Archæology.
TU = Texte und Untersuchungen.
WAI = Western Asiatic Inscriptions.
WZKM = Wiener Zeitschrift für Kunde des Morgenlandes.
ZA = Zeitschrift für Assyriologie.
ZAW or *ZATW* = Zeitschrift für die Alttest. Wissenschaft.
ZDMG = Zeitschrift der Deutschen Morgenländischen Gesellschaft.
ZDPV = Zeitschrift des Deutschen Palästina-Vereins.
ZKSF = Zeitschrift für Keilschriftforschung.
ZKW = Zeitschrift für kirchliche Wissenschaft.

A small superior number designates the particular edition of the work referred to, as *KAT*², *LOT*⁶.

AUTHORS OF ARTICLES IN VOL. II

Rev. WALTER F. ADENEY, M.A., D.D., Principal of the Lancashire Independent College, Manchester.

Ven. A. S. AGLEN, M.A., D.D., Archdeacon of St. Andrews.

Rev. WILLOUGHBY C. ALLEN, M.A., Chaplain, Fellow, and Lecturer in Theology and Hebrew, Exeter College, Oxford.

Rev. BENJAMIN WISNER BACON, M.A., D.D., Professor of New Testament Criticism and Interpretation in Yale University, New Haven.

Rev. JOHN S. BANKS, D.D., Professor of Systematic Theology in the Headingley College, Leeds.

Rev. W. EMERY BARNES, M.A., D.D., Hulsean Professor of Divinity and Fellow of Peterhouse, Cambridge.

JAMES VERNON BARTLET, M.A., Professor of Church History, Mansfield College, Oxford.

Rev. LLEWELLYN J. M. BEBB, M.A., Principal of St. David's College, Lampeter; formerly Fellow and Tutor of Brasenose College, Oxford.

Rev. WILLIS JUDSON BEECHER, D.D., Professor of Hebrew Language and Literature in Auburn Theological Seminary, New York.

Rev. WILLIAM HENRY BENNETT, D.D., Litt.D., Professor of Old Testament Exegesis in Hackney and New Colleges, London; sometime Fellow of St. John's College, Cambridge.

Very Rev. JOHN HENRY BERNARD, D.D., Fellow of Trinity College, and Dean of St. Patrick's, Dublin.

Rev. J. F. BETHUNE-BAKER, M.A., Fellow and Dean of Pembroke College, Cambridge.

FREDERICK J. BLISS, B.A., Ph.D., late Director of the Palestine Exploration Fund in Jerusalem.

The late Rev. ALEXANDER BALMAIN BRUCE, M.A., D.D., Professor of Apologetics and New Testament Exegesis in the Free Church College, Glasgow.

Rev. CHARLES FOX BURNEY, M.A., Lecturer in Hebrew, and Fellow of St. John Baptist's College, Oxford.

Rev. WINFRID O. BURROWS, M.A., Vicar of Holy Trinity, Leeds.

Rev. GEORGE G. CAMERON, M.A., D.D., Professor of Hebrew in the United Free Church College, Aberdeen

The late Rev. JAMES S. CANDLISH, M.A., D.D., Professor of Systematic Theology in the Free Church College, Glasgow.

Rev. WILLIAM CARSLAW, M.A., M.D., of the Lebanon Schools, Beyrout, Syria.

Rev. ARTHUR THOMAS CHAPMAN, M.A., Fellow, Tutor, and Hebrew Lecturer, Emmanuel College, Cambridge.

Rev. ROBERT HENRY CHARLES, D.D., Professor of Biblical Greek in the University of Dublin.

Rev. FREDERIC HENRY CHASE, M.A., D.D., Norrisian Professor of Divinity, President of Queens' College, and Vice-Chancellor of the University of Cambridge.

Col. CLAUDE REIGNIER CONDER, R.E., LL.D., M.R.A.S.

FRED. C. CONYBEARE, M.A., formerly Fellow of University College, Oxford.

Rev. G. A. COOKE, M.A., The Parsonage, Dalkeith.

Rev. HENRY COWAN, M.A., D.D., Professor of Church History in the University of Aberdeen.

W. E. CRUM, M.A., of the Egypt Exploration Fund.

Rev. EDWARD LEWIS CURTIS, Ph.D., D.D., Professor of Hebrew Language and Literature in the Divinity School of Yale University, New Haven.

The late Rev. ANDREW BRUCE DAVIDSON, D.D., LL.D., Professor of Hebrew in the New College, Edinburgh.

Rev. T. WITTON DAVIES, B.A., Ph.D., M.R.A.S., Professor of Hebrew and Old Testament Literature in the Baptist College, Bangor, and Lecturer in Semitic Languages in University College, Bangor.

Rev. W. T. DAVISON, M.A., D.D., Professor of Systematic Theology in the Handsworth Theological College, Birmingham.

Rev. JAMES DENNEY, M.A., D.D., Professor of Systematic Theology in the United Free Church College, Glasgow.

Rev. MARCUS DODS, M.A., D.D., Professor of Exegetical Theology in the New College, Edinburgh.

Rev. SAMUEL ROLLES DRIVER, D.D., Litt.D., Canon of Christ Church, and Regius Professor of Hebrew in the University of Oxford.

Rev. DAVID EATON, M.A., D.D., Glasgow.

Rev. WILLIAM K. EDDY, of the American Mission, Sidon, Syria.

Rev. WILLIAM EWING, M.A., Glasgow, formerly of Tiberias, Palestine.

Rev. GEORGE FERRIES, M.A., D.D., Cluny, Aberdeenshire.

Rev. ALFRED ERNEST GARVIE, M.A., D.D., Professor of Philosophy and Ethics in Hackney College, London.

Rev. G. BUCHANAN GRAY, M.A., D.D., Professor of Hebrew in Mansfield College, Oxford.

Rev. ALEXANDER GRIEVE, M.A., Ph.D., Forfar.

FRANCIS LLEWELLYN GRIFFITH, M.A., F.S.A., of the British Museum ; Superintendent of the Archæological Survey of the Egypt Exploration Fund.

Rev. GEORGE HARFORD, M.A., Balliol College, Oxford ; Vicar of Mossley Hill, Liverpool.

J. RENDEL HARRIS, M.A., Litt.D., Fellow and Librarian of Clare College, and Lecturer in Palæography in the University of Cambridge.

Rev. ARTHUR CAYLEY HEADLAM, M.A., B.D., Principal of King's College, London ; formerly Fellow of All Souls College, Oxford.

FRITZ HOMMEL, Ph.D., LL.D., Ord. Professor of Semitic Languages in the University of Munich.

EDWARD HULL, M.A., LL.D., F.R.S., F.R.G.S., late Director of the Geological Survey of Ireland, and Professor of Geology in the Royal College of Science, Dublin.

FRANK BYRON JEVONS, M.A., Litt.D., Principal of Bishop Hatfield's Hall, Durham.

Rev. ARCHIBALD R. S. KENNEDY, M.A., D.D., Professor of Hebrew and Semitic Languages in the University of Edinburgh.

Rev. JAMES HOUGHTON KENNEDY, M.A., D.D., Assistant Lecturer in the Divinity School of Dublin University.

EDUARD KÖNIG, Ph.D., D.D., Professor of Old Testament Exegesis in the University of Bonn.

Rev. JOHN LAIDLAW, M.A., D.D., Professor of Systematic Theology in the New College, Edinburgh.

Rev. WALTER LOCK, M.A., D.D., Warden of Keble College, and Dean Ireland's Professor of New Testament Exegesis in the University of Oxford.

ALEXANDER MACALISTER, LL.D., M.D., F.R.S., F.S.A., Fellow of St. John's College, and Professor of Anatomy in the University of Cambridge.

Rev. J. A. M'CLYMONT, M.A., D.D., Aberdeen.

Rev. GEORGE M. MACKIE, M.A., D.D., Chaplain to the Church of Scotland at Beyrout, Syria.

The late Rev. JOHN MACPHERSON, M.A., Edinburgh.

Rev. D. S. MARGOLIOUTH, M.A., Fellow of New College, and Laudian Professor of Arabic in the University of Oxford.

Rev. JOHN TURNER MARSHALL, M.A., Principal of the Baptist College, Manchester.

Rev. ALEXANDER MARTIN, M.A., D.D., Professor of Apologetic Theology in the New College, Edinburgh.

JOHN MASSIE, M.A., D.D., late Yates Professor of New Testament Exegesis in Mansfield College, Oxford ; formerly Scholar of St. John's College, Cambridge.

JOSEPH BICKERSTETH MAYOR, M.A., Litt.D., Emeritus Professor of King's College, London, and Hon. Fellow of St. John's College, Cambridge.

Rev. SELAH MERRILL, D.D., LL.D., U.S. Consul at Jerusalem.

Rev. JAMES MILLAR, M.A., B.D., New Cumnock.

Rev. GEORGE MILLIGAN, M.A., B.D., Caputh, Perthshire.

Rev. R. WADDY MOSS, Professor of Classics in the Didsbury College, Manchester.

Rev. WILLIAM MUIR, M.A., B.D., B.L., Blairgowrie.

W. MAX MÜLLER, Ph.D., LL.D., Professor of Old Testament Literature in the Reformed Episcopal Church Seminary, Philadelphia.

Rev. J. O. F. MURRAY, M.A., Vice-Principal of St. Augustine's College, Canterbury ; late Fellow of Emmanuel College, Cambridge.

EBERHARD NESTLE, Ph.D., D.D., Professor at Maulbronn.

Rev. THOMAS NICOL, M.A., D.D., Professor of Divinity and Biblical Criticism in the University of Aberdeen.

Rev. JAMES ORR, M.A., D.D., Professor of Apologetics and Theology in the United Free Church College, Glasgow.

Rev. ROBERT LAWRENCE OTTLEY, M.A., successively Student of Christ Church and Fellow of Magdalen College ; sometime Principal of the Pusey House, Oxford.

Rev. WILLIAM P. PATERSON, M.A., D.D., Professor of Systematic Theology in the University of Aberdeen.

Rev. JAMES PATRICK, M.A., B.D., B.Sc., Examiner for Degrees in Divinity in the University of St. Andrews.

ARTHUR S. PEAKE, M.A., Professor in the Primitive Methodist College, Manchester, and Lecturer in Lancashire Independent College ; sometime Fellow of Merton and Lecturer in Mansfield College, Oxford.

WILLIAM FLINDERS PETRIE, D.C.L., Litt.D., LL.D., Ph.D., F.R.S., Professor of Egyptology in University College, London.

I. A. PINCHES, Sippar House, London.

THEOPHILUS GOLDRIDGE PINCHES, LL.D., M.R.A.S., of the Egyptian and Assyrian Department in the British Museum.

Rev. ALFRED PLUMMER, M.A., D.D., late Master of University College, Durham.

Rev. FRANK CHAMBERLIN PORTER, M.A., Ph.D., D.D., Professor of Biblical Theology in the Divinity School of Yale University, New Haven.

Rev. GEORGE POST, M.D., F.L.S., Professor in the American College, Beyrout, Syria.

IRA MAURICE PRICE, M.A., B.D., Ph.D., Professor of Semitic Languages and Literatures in the University of Chicago.

Rev. CYRIL HENRY PRICHARD, M.A., late Classical Scholar of Magdalene College, Cambridge, and Lecturer at St. Olave's, Southwark.

The late Rev. GEORGE T. PURVES, D.D., LL.D., Professor of New Testament Literature and Exegesis in Princeton Theological Seminary, New Jersey.

WILLIAM M. RAMSAY, D.C.L., LL.D., Litt.D., Professor of Humanity in the University of Aberdeen, Honorary Fellow of Exeter and Lincoln Colleges, Oxford.

The late Rev. HENRY ROBERT REYNOLDS, D.D., Principal of Cheshunt College, Herts.

Right Rev. ARCHIBALD ROBERTSON, M.A., D.D., LL.D., Bishop of Exeter.

Very Rev. J. ARMITAGE ROBINSON, M.A., Ph.D., D.D., D.Th., Dean of Westminster.

Right Rev. HERBERT EDWARD RYLE, M.A., D.D., Bishop of Winchester.

Rev. STEWART DINGWALL FORDYCE SALMOND, M.A., D.D., F.E.I.S., Principal and Professor of Systematic Theology in the United Free Church College, Aberdeen.

Rev. WILLIAM SANDAY, D.D., LL.D., D.Sc., Lady Margaret Professor of Divinity, and Canon of Christ Church, Oxford.

Rev. ARCHIBALD HENRY SAYCE, M.A., D.D., Fellow of Queen's College, and Professor of Assyriology in the University of Oxford.

Rev. JOHN A. SELBIE, M.A., D.D., Maryculter, Kincardineshire.

Rev. DAVID W. SIMON, M.A., D.D., Principal of the United College, Bradford.

Rev. JOHN SKINNER, M.A., D.D., Professor of Hebrew and Old Testament Exegesis in Westminster College, Cambridge.

Rev. GEORGE ADAM SMITH, M.A., D.D., LL.D., Professor of Hebrew in the United Free Church College, Glasgow.

Rev. VINCENT HENRY STANTON, M.A., D.D., Fellow of Trinity College, and Ely Professor of Divinity in the University of Cambridge.

JOHN F. STENNING, M.A., Fellow and Lecturer in Hebrew and Theology, Wadham College, Oxford.

Rev. GEORGE B. STEVENS, Ph.D., D.D., Professor of Systematic Theology in Yale University.

Rev. ALEXANDER STEWART, M.A., D.D., Principal of St. Mary's College, and Professor of Systematic Theology in the University of St. Andrews.

Rev. JAMES STRACHAN, M.A., St. Fergus.

Very Rev. THOMAS B. STRONG, D.D., Dean of Christ Church, Oxford.

Rev. HENRY BARCLAY SWETE, M.A., D.D., Litt.D., Regius Professor of Divinity, Cambridge.

Rev. JOHN TAYLOR, M.A., D.Lit., Vicar of Winchcombe.

HENRY ST. JOHN THACKERAY, M.A., Examiner in the Board of Education, formerly Divinity Lecturer in Selwyn College, Cambridge.

Rev. G. W. THATCHER, M.A., B.D., Hebrew Tutor and Lecturer on Old Testament History and Literature in Mansfield College, Oxford.

The late Rev. JOSEPH HENRY THAYER, M.A., D.D., Litt.D., Bussey Professor of New Testament Criticism and Interpretation in the Divinity School of Harvard University.

Rev. GEERHARDUS VOS, D.D., Professor of Biblical Theology in Princeton Theological Seminary, New Jersey.

Rev. GEORGE WALKER, M.A., B.D., Aberdeen.

Lieut.-General Sir CHARLES WARREN, G.C.M.G., K.C.B., F.R.S., Royal Engineers.

Rev. ADAM C. WELCH, M.A., B.D., Glasgow.

The late Rev. HENRY ALCOCK WHITE, M.A., Tutor in the University of Durham, and formerly Fellow of New College, Oxford.

Rev. NEWPORT J. D. WHITE, M.A., B.D., Librarian of Archbishop Marsh's Library, and Assistant Lecturer in Divinity and Hebrew in the University of Dublin.

Rev. OWEN C. WHITEHOUSE, M.A., D.D., Principal and Professor of Biblical Exegesis and Theology, Cheshunt College, Herts.

Rev. A. LUKYN WILLIAMS, M.A., Vicar of Guilden Morden, late Tyrwhitt and Crosse Scholar of the University of Cambridge.

Major-General Sir CHARLES WILLIAM WILSON, R.E., K.C.B., K.C.M.G., D.C.L., LL.D., F.R.S.

Rev. FRANCIS HENRY WOODS, M.A., B.D., Vicar of Chalfont St. Peter, and late Fellow and Theological Lecturer of St. John's College, Oxford.

Rev. JOHN WORTABET, M.A., M.D., Beyrout, Syria.

DICTIONARY OF THE BIBLE

FEIGN (Lat. *fingĕre*, to mould, invent ; Old Fr. *feindre*, ptcp. *feignant*).—**1.** To devise, invent : Neh 6[8] 'There are no such things done as thou sayest, but thou feignest them out of thine own heart' (בָּדָא, only here and 1 K 12[33] EV 'devise') ; 2 P 2[3] 'And through covetousness shall they with feigned words make merchandise of you' (πλαστοῖς λόγοις, only here in NT ; Salmond 'made up or craftly constructed speeches'). Cf. Lk 24[11] Tind. 'their wordes seemed vnto them fayned thinges' ; and Knox, *Hist.* p. 177, 'Which reports are all (God knoweth) most vain, fained, and untrue.' **2.** To put on an appearance, pretend : 1 K 14[5] 'she shall feign herself *to be* another *woman*' (מִתְנַכֵּרָה) ; so 14[6] ; 1 S 21[13] 'he changed his behaviour before them, and feigned himself mad in their hands' (וַיְתְהֹלֵל) ; 2 S 14[2] 'feign thyself to be a mourner' (הִתְאַבְּלִי־נָא) ; Ps 17[1] 'give ear unto my prayer, *that goeth* not out of feigned lips' (שִׂפְתֵי מִרְמָה, lit. 'lips of guile'). Cf. Knox, *Hist.* 101, 'yet was every head so fully answered, and especially one. . . . To wit, That Paul at the commandment of James, and of the Elders of Jerusalem, passed to the Temple, and fained himself to pay his vow with others' ; and Elyot, *The Governour*, ii. 432, 'Unto euery man disclose nat thy harte, leest perauenture he wyl gyue to the a fained thanke, and after reporte rebukefully of the' ; Barlowe, *Dialogue*, ed. 1897, p. 48, 'Then beganne he [Luther] stoutly to fortefy his fayned fayth voyde of good workes' ; Tindale, *Works*, i. 94, 'For where right faith is, there bringeth she forth good works ; if there follow not good works, it is (no doubt) but a dream and an opinion or feigned faith' ; also Tind. *Expositions*, 163, 'And for them that would not receive such pardons feigned they purgatory, and for them that received them feigned they pardon, turning binding and loosing, with preaching God's word, unto buying and selling sin for money.'

Feignedly=with pretence, deceitfully : Jer 3[10] 'Judah hath not turned unto me with her whole heart, but feignedly' (בְּשֶׁקֶר 'in falsehood,' as AVm) ; 2 Es 8[28] 'Think not upon those that have walked feignedly before thee' (*false conversati sunt*). So Tindale, *Works*, i. 177, 'the children of the devil, in time of adversity, fly from Christ, whom they followed feignedly.'

J. HASTINGS.

FELIX, Antonius, procurator of Judæa (Ac 23[25f.]–24[27]) at the time of St. Paul's last visit to Jerusalem and arrest there. The military tribune **Claudius Lysias** sends Paul under escort to Cæsarea, with a letter to Felix reciting, in a light favour-able to his own conduct, the circumstances of the arrest. Arrived at Cæsarea, the apostle, after a purely formal interview, is remanded by Felix for trial, and detained in the government house (præ-torium), originally a palace of Herod the Great, until the arrival of his accusers. On the fifth day the proceedings begin. The case against the prisoner is opened by an advocate (see TERTULLUS). Evidence is given by the Jews, and, upon a sign from the procurator, Paul makes a speech in defence. Felix, perhaps interested in the matter by his Jewish wife (Ac 24[22]), then adjourns the trial till the arrival of Lysias, and Paul is again remanded as a prisoner, but under lenient conditions. We hear nothing of any resumption of the trial. But after some days Felix, accompanied by **Drusilla** (and, according to some authorities for the Western text, at her special request), sends for Paul and gives him audience concerning the belief 'in Christ' (or 'Jesus as Christ'). The apostle (taking, as usual, common ground with his hearer) addresses him upon broad moral truths, and the judgment (looked for by heathens as well as Jews) after death. Felix becomes alarmed, and sends him away till a future occasion. He sends for him ('secretly,' Gig.) 'somewhat often' for further con-versation, excited mainly by the hope of a bribe (cf. Ramsay, *St. Paul the Trav.* p. 310 ff.). Two years after St. Paul's arrest Felix is recalled, and, to ingratiate himself with the Jews (or, according to some Western sources, for the sake of Drusilla), leaves Paul a prisoner.

The dubious light in which the character of Felix appears in the NT narrative is bright com-pared with that shed upon it by the other histories of the time. Felix was the (apparently) younger brother of Pallas, the well-known and all-powerful favourite of Claudius. That An-tonius, not Claudius, was the *nomen* borne by Felix (Tac. *Hist.* v. 9 ; the nomen Claudius for Felix is based on a probably corrupt reading in Suidas, *s.v.*) suggests that Felix was a freedman of Antonia, mother of Claudius (so also probably Pallas ; see Jos. *Ant.* XVIII. vi. 6 ; cf. Schürer, *HJP* I. ii. 175). The brothers claimed descent, as Tacitus ironically mentions, from ancient kings of Arcadia (*Ann.* xii. 53).

We first hear of Felix in connexion with the disorders in Samaria under his predecessor Ven-tidius Cumanus. The latter refusing to punish the Samaritans for the murder of some Galilæan pilgrims, the Zealots massacred many Samaritans, and were in turn massacred by Cumanus. Both sides appealed to Ummidius Quadratus, legate of

Syria, who intervened with great severity and sent Cumanus to Rome (Jos. *BJ* II. xii. 3 ff.; *Ant.* xx. vi. 1–3). According to Josephus, Felix was now, at the request of the high priest Jonathan, who had been sent to Rome with Cumanus, sent as successor to the latter; and Jos. proceeds to relate how, upon completing his twelfth year (Jan. 24, A.D. 53), Claudius gave certain territories to Agrippa. Coupled with the fact that Tacitus places the deposition of Cumanus in the year 52, this fairly fixes Felix' appointment to the latter year. A difficulty arises, however, from the fact that Tacitus, in his account (*Ann.* xii. 54) of what led to the deposition of Cumanus, speaks of Felix as '*iam pridem* Iudaeae impositus . . . ut [Cumano] Galilaeorum natio, Felici Samaritae parerent.' It has been attempted to combine the latter statement with the 'many years' of Ac 24[10] by the hypothesis that before his appointment as procurator Felix had held some subordinate appointment in Samaria. But Josephus clearly intimates that Felix was first appointed to the province on this occasion; and on the whole, in spite of the authority of Mommsen and the arguments of Blass (*Act. Apost.* p. 21), we join Schürer in following Josephus here, as likely to be the better informed.

Felix received from his patron the (for a freedman) unprecedented honour of military command as well as civil jurisdiction ('cohortibus et alis prouinciaeque' . . . Suet. *Claud.* 28). His character as governor was that of a man raised from a low origin to unfitting eminence — 'per omnem saeuitiam et libidinem ius regium seruili ingenio exercuit' (Tac. *Hist.* v. 9). The general results of his rule are aptly summed up by the same writer, 'intempestiuis remediis delicta accendebat' (*Ann.* xii. 54, and see TERTULLUS). His ferocity against the 'Zealots' and their supposed partisans gave birth, or new strength, to the Sicarii,—a more numerous and extreme class of fanatics,—who were in turn used by fanatical rebels (cf. Ac 21[38]) until half the nation was in the wildest disaffection. St. Paul probably came into contact with Felix as stated above from two to four years after the accession of Nero (54), by whom Felix must have been confirmed in office. The πολλὰ ἔτη of Ac 24[10] are hardly, therefore (as Harnack, *Chron.* 253, contends), compatible with a date earlier than the last named. During the last two years of Felix' tenure of office, and therefore during Paul's imprisonment at Cæsarea, fall the serious riots between the Jewish and Syrian inhabitants of the latter town about ἰσοπολιτεία. Felix, whose customary methods had failed to quell the disturbances, sent the heads of both parties to Rome for the emperor to decide the case. But before any final decision Felix was recalled. The violence with which he had interfered in this matter partly explains his anxiety to do the Jews a parting favour (Ac 24[27]; see Jos *BJ* II. xiii. 7; *Ant.* XX. viii. 7). The Jews, however (Jos. *Ant.* XX. viii. 9), lodged an indictment against him, which failed only through the influence of Pallas. Of Felix' later history nothing is known (see Schürer, *HJP* I. ii. 174 ff., and the authorities cited by him. For the chronological questions involved, see FESTUS, and art. CHRONOLOGY OF NT, p. 417 f.).   A. ROBERTSON.

FELLOW (from *fé* = property, money, and *lag* to lay; hence 'one who lays down money in a joint undertaking with others'). In AV two easily separated meanings are found.

1. *Partner, companion.* The Heb words are (*a*) רֵעַ *rêa'*, Ex 2[13], Jg 7[13. 14. 22], 1 S 14[20], 2 S 2[16 bis], Is 34[14], Jon 1[7], Zec 3[8]; RV adds 1 K 20[35] for AV 'neighbour,' as the word is generally tr[d] elsewhere in AV and RV. Once the fem. of this word (רַעְיָה *

     * For the reading see Moore, *in loc.*

rê'âh) is tr[d] 'fellow,' Jg 11[37], though in the next verse it is 'companion' as in Ps 45[14], its only remaining occurrence. RV has 'companion' in all three places. (*b*) חָבֵר *hâbhêr*, Ps 45[7], Ec 4[10], Is 44[11], Ezk 37[19]; RV in Ezk 'companion,' as the word is elsewhere tr[d] in AV and RV, except Jg 20[11] (כְּאִישׁ אֶחָד חֲבֵרִים, EV 'knit together as one man'); and Aram. forms חֲבַר *hâbhar*, Dn 2[13. 18] (in v.[17] 'companion' as RV in all), and חַבְרָה *habhrâh*, Dn 7[20]. (*c*) עָמִית *'âmîth*, Zec 13[7] (גֶּבֶר עֲמִיתִי, EV 'the man that is my fellow'). The word is in form abstract, hence lit. 'the man of my fellowship'; but elsewhere it occurs only in Lv and in the concrete sense of 'neighbour.'

The Gr. words are (*a*) ἡ πλησίον, only once and fem., Bar 6[43] 'she reproacheth her fellow' (cf. Jg 11[37] above, where, however, the LXX is συνεταιρίς). The commonest word for 'neighbour' in NT is ὁ πλησίον. (*b*) ἑταῖρος, Mt 11[16]. (*c*) μέτοχος, He 1[9], a quotation from Ps 45[7], where LXX has μ. (*d*) οἱ περί, Three [26].

This meaning of 'fellow' may be illustrated by the foll. paragraph from T. Adams, *II Peter* (Sherman's ed. p. 42):—'As fellows, in due measure, with God himself: "Truly our fellowship is with the Father, and with his Son Jesus Christ," 1 Jn 1[3]. We may have a society with man, this is requisite, for we are all of one mould; but to God, what, all fellows? Yes, we have a fellowship with God; such is his mercy, not our merits. The proud gallant scorns the poor mechanic: What, are you my fellow? Yet, *mors sceptra ligonibus æquat*, Death takes away difference between king and beggar, tumbles both the knight and the pawn into one bag. Well, let the world despise us, it is enough the Lord doth not disdain our fellowship.' Again (on p. 43) Adams says, 'Thus we partake of the Divine nature (with all reverence be it spoken) as fellows. But, not to deny the King his supremacy, we are fellows with Christ in his joy, reserving the throne to himself.' Cf. also Ac 4[23] Wyc. (1388), 'thei camen to her *felowis*, and telden to hem, hou grete thingis the princis of preestis and the eldre men hadden seid to hem'; He 1[033] Wyc. (1388), 'ye weren maad felowis of men lyuynge so.' Shaks. *Tempest*, III. i. 84—

     ' To be your fellow
     You may deny me; but I'll be your servant.'

2. *Person,* first without and then with contempt; for the word has a history. Melvill (*Diary*, Wod. p. 78), can say of John Dury, 'He was a verie guid fallow, and tuk delyt, as his speciall comfort, to haiff his table and houss filled with the best men,' and thereby express reverence for him. But Adams (*II Peter*, p. 43) says, 'There is a generation of men that lavish their estates,—as we say, fling the house out at the windows,—that call themselves good fellows,' where the meaning is still 'companion,' but the glory is departing. The word was used to express easy familiarity, then by a superior in condescension to an inferior, and finally as the utterance of contempt. In Gn 39[2] Tindale has, 'And the LORDE was with Ioseph, and he was a luckie fellowe,' where 'fellow' is simply 'man'; nor is contempt expressed in Mk 4[41] 'what felowe is this? For booth winde and see obey him' (= Lk 8[25]); and even in Mk 2[7] 'how doeth this felowe so blaspheme?' (οὗτος), or Jn 6[52] 'How can this felowe geve us his flesshe to eate?' (οὗτος) the sense is probably no more than 'this man,' or at least than we should express by 'this person.'

The Heb. words so translated in AV are (*a*) אִישׁ *'ish*, 1 S 29[4] 'Make this fellow return' (RV 'the man'); and in plu. 'fellows,' Jg 18[25] (אֲנָשִׁים מָרֵי נֶפֶשׁ, lit. 'men, bitter of soul,' as RVm; Moore, 'men of acrid temper'). RV adds Jg 9[4] (AV 'persons') 11[3] (AV 'men'). In these places neither the Heb. nor probably the Eng. means more than 'person.' And even when 'this fellow' is the tr[n] of (*b*) זֶה *zeh*, 'this' (1 S 21[15 bis] 25[21], 1 K 22[27] = 2 Ch 18[26], 2 K 9[11]; to which RV adds 1 S 29[4]), there is at least less contempt expressed than the words now carry. The Greek words correspond to the Hebrew. (*a*) ἀνήρ, 1 Mac 10[61] 'certain pestilent fellows' (ἄνδρες λοιμοί); Ac 17[5] 'took unto them certain lewd fellows' (τινὰς ἄνδρας πονηρούς). (*b*) οὗτος, Sir 13[23],

1 Mac 4⁵, Mt 12²⁴ 26⁶¹·⁷¹, Lk 22⁵⁹ 23², Jn 9²⁹, Ac 18¹³. RV prefers 'man' except in Sir, where 'fellow' is simply omitted. (c) ὁ τοιοῦτος, Ac 22²².

Perhaps the strongest expression of contempt is given when 'fellow' is added to an adj. The examples are (a) רֵקִים *rēḳîm*, 2 S 6²⁰ 'vain fellows'; (b) τολμηρός, Sir 8¹⁵ 'bold fellow'; and (c) λοιμός, Ac 24⁵ 'pestilent fellow' (cf. ἄνδρες λοιμοί, 'pestilent fellows,' 1 Mac 10⁶¹ above).

The Amer. RV prefers '*base* fellow' to AV 'son (man) of Belial,' and '*base* fellows' to sons (men, children) of Belial.' See BELIAL.

In composition 'fellow' always means partner or companion. The foll. compounds occur in AV: (1) **Fellowcitizen** (συνπολίτης), Eph 2¹⁹, RV adds He 8¹¹, reading ὁ πολίτης with edd. for ὁ πλησίον of TR which gave AV 'neighbour.' (2) **Fellowdisciple** (συνμαθητής), Jn 11¹⁶. (3) **Fellowheir** (συνκληρονόμος), Eph 3⁶. (4) **Fellowhelper** (συνεργός, see 'fellow-worker'), 2 Co 8²³, 3 Jn ⁸. (5) **Fellowlabourer** (συνεργός, see 'fellow-worker'), Ph 4³, 1 Th 3², Philem ¹·²⁴. (6) **Fellowprisoner** (συναιχμάλωτος), Ro 16⁷, Col 4¹⁰, Philem ²³. (7) **Fellowservant** (σύνδουλος), Mt 18²⁸·²⁹·³¹·³³ 24⁴⁹, Col 1⁷ 4⁷ (= 'fellow-worker' in Col), Rev 6¹¹ 19¹⁰ 22⁹. (8) **Fellowsoldier** (TR συστρατιώτης, edd. συνστρ.), Ph 2²⁵, Philem ². (9) **Fellow worker** (so 1611, συνεργός), Col 4¹¹. RV adds 'fellow-worker,' Ro 16³·⁹ (AV 'helper'), 1 Co 3⁹ 'we are God's fellow-workers' (AV 'labourers together with God'), 2 Co 8²³ (AV 'fellowhelper'), Ph 2²⁵ (AV 'companion in labour') 4³, Philem ¹·²⁴ (AV 'fellowlabourer'), 3 Jn ⁸ (AV 'fellowhelper'). (10) **Workfellow** (συνεργός), Ro 16²¹. (11) **Yokefellow** (TR σύζυγος, edd. σύνζυγος), Ph 4³. To those RV adds (12) **Fellow-elder** (συμπρεσβύτερος, T. WH, συνπρ.), 1 P 5¹ (AV 'also an elder'). (13) **Fellow-member of the body** (TR, σύσσωμος, edd. σύνσωμος), Eph 3⁶ (AV 'of the same body'). (14) **Fellow-partaker** (συμμέτοχος, T. WH, συνμ.), Eph 3⁶ (AV 'partaker').

For **Fellowship**, see COMMUNION.

J. HASTINGS.

FENCE.—This Eng. word is not used in NT. In AV of OT it translates various Hebrew words. In the case of three of these, the tr. is a mistake, and is changed in RV (Is 5², 2 S 23⁷, Job 10¹¹). The words from the stems *ẓûr* and *bâẓar*, צוּר and בָּצַר, denote fortifications or fortified places (*e.g.* 2 Ch 8⁵ 11²³, Dt 3⁵ etc.) Those from the stem *gâdar*, גָּדַר, denote a stone wall (Ps 62³, Job 19⁸). RV tr. the words of this stem by 'fence' in many places where we find 'wall' or 'hedge' in AV. A fence is properly that which fends or defends. The fence described in the Heb. words of this group is ordinarily the enclosure defending a field or vineyard or sheepfold. See HEDGE.

W. J. BEECHER.

FENCED CITIES (עָרֵי מִבְצָר, properly 'cut off' from outside, and hence inaccessible; RV generally substitutes 'fortified' for 'fenced').—Collections of houses in ancient times may be classed under three heads: (1) Cities, walled or fenced. (2) Unwalled towns and villages, with towers for resort of villagers in times of danger. (3) Unwalled towns and villages.

The number or size of the houses did not affect the question. A city might be of very small extent. Gn 19²⁰ 'Behold now, this city is near to flee unto, and it is a little one: Oh! let me escape thither (is it not a little one?) and my soul shall live.' On the other hand, the suburbs of a city might become so extensive that it became equivalent to a town without walls. Zec 2⁴ 'Jerusalem shall be inhabited as villages without walls, for the multitude of men and cattle therein.'

Towns and villages that were without walls were a prey to any hostile foraging party, and were considered of no account. Lv 25²⁹·³¹ 'If a man sell a dwelling-house in a walled city, then he may redeem it. . . . But the houses of the villages, which have no wall round about them, shall be reckoned with the fields of the country.' As a village or town prospered and more solid houses were built, they would for purposes of defence be joined together, and the town would thus become a walled city. Towns and villages appear to have been dependent upon fenced cities both for administrative purposes and for protection of the inhabitants. Jos 15⁴⁷ 'Ashdod with her towns and her villages; Gaza with her towns and her villages.' As an indication of absolute security, a land of safety is pictured as 'a land of unwalled villages . . . dwelling without walls, and having neither bars nor gates' (Ezk 38¹¹). The suburbs of the cities were occupied by cattle (Jos 14⁴ 21²). The villages, however, were not wholly without protection. The Israelites could not drive out the inhabitants of the valley or low country because they had chariots of iron (Jg 1¹⁹, Jos 17¹⁶). Both at Jericho and Damascus houses were built on the city walls (Jos 2¹⁵, 2 Co 11³³).

Sufficient still exists of the remains of the ancient cities of Palestine, together with the historical accounts, to give us a clear idea of the positions and the general configuration of their walls. They were built in commanding positions both in the hill-country and the plains, and on the seashore they were generally on promontories. In many cases most inaccessible positions were taken advantage of, so that the battering-ram might be of no avail. Dt 1²⁸ 'The cities are great, and fenced up to heaven.' Cisterns were cut in the rock for the supply of rain-water, so as to be independent of water from without (2 Ch 26¹⁰, Neh 9²⁵, Jos. *BJ* v. iv. 3, VII. viii. 3).

There are many remains of ancient cities still exposed to view in various parts of Palestine, inhabited by nomadic tribes, where the system of defence can yet be observed: as an example, Masada, built by Jonathan Maccabæus, and strengthened by Herod the Great, may be mentioned. None of the remains, however, can be accurately ascribed to the time of Joshua, though the sites may not have changed, and it is doubtful whether at that early date the walls of fenced cities were of the same solid type as that which necessarily obtained when the battering-ram came into use. Some of the fenced cities mentioned in the Book of Joshua were taken by stratagem, but others were taken by assault by a nation which did not possess the mechanical contrivances required for the capture of cities with strong walls. From what remains of the ruins of Jericho (assumed to be near 'Ain es-Sultân), it may be inferred that these walls were built from the earliest date of sun-burnt bricks; and from the knowledge we now possess of the walls about Jerusalem, it may be considered that at the time of the capture of the city by Joab the walls were built of small stones.

The stones of the ancient towers and walls of Jerusalem still existing are of considerable size, some of those in the wall of the temple enclosure weighing nearly 90 tons. At Baalbek the great temple stands on a massive wall, with courses of stone averaging 3 ft. 9 in. in height. Thirty feet in advance of this, N., S., and W., is a protecting wall, 10 ft. thick, of monoliths weighing 600 to 800 tons each, three of them being estimated to weigh over 1000 tons each.

The bulwarks of the fenced cities of Palestine, so far back as the time of the Jewish kings, appear to have consisted of a solid masonry wall of cut stone, with parapets and battlements, and with towers at intervals from which the foot of the wall could be seen (2 Ch 32⁵, Jer 31³⁸). In the walls were watchmen (2 K 9[17], 2 S 18[26], Is 62[6]). Within the city was usually a citadel or acropolis (Jg 9[51]), and without were walls, outworks, and towers (2 Ch 14[7] 'Let us build these cities, and make about them walls and towers, gates and bars'; 2 S 20[15], Is 26[1], Nah 3[8], 2 Ch 26[6]).

The protracted resistance offered by many of the fenced cities of Palestine may have been due as much to the strength of their position as to their walls; Samaria resisted the king of Assyria for three years, and Jerusalem successfully resisted the power of Rome, and only fell before Titus owing to the internal dissensions of the Jewish leaders.

The whole subject connected with the attack and defence of cities and fortified places is treated of under WAR, and special cases for reference will be found under JERUSALEM, SAMARIA, JERICHO, GATH, GAZA, and other strongholds of Philistia. See also GATE.　　　　　　　　　C. WARREN.

FERRET (אֲנָקָה 'ănâḳah, Lv 11[30] AV).—The ferret is not found in Palestine or Syria, and cannot be the animal intended. It is probably, as in RV, the gecko. See GECKO.　　　　　　G. E. POST.

FERVENCY, FERVENT. — Fervency is found only in Jth 4[9] 'every man of Israel cried to God with great fervency' (ἐκτένεια [B -ία], which in the same verse is tr[d] 'vehemency,' as it is tr[d] in 2 Mac 14[38]; RV always 'earnestness.' The Gr. word occurs also 3 Mac 6[41], and in NT Ac 26[7] ἐν ἐκτενείᾳ, AV 'instantly,' RV 'earnestly'). Knox (*Hist.* 132) says that after the martyrdom of Walter Mill 'began a new fervency among the whole people'; and *Works* (ed. Laing, iii. 289), 'Peter, in a fervencie, firste left his bote, and yet after feared.' The adj. *fervent* is twice applied literally in the sense of 'intense,' 2 P 3[10] 'the elements shall melt with fervent heat' (καυσούμενα λυθήσεται), and 3[12] (καυσούμενα τήκεται). 'With fervent heat' (lit. 'being burned up') is the Bishops' tr[n], and is retained in RV; most of the other VSS have simply 'shall melt with heat.' Cf. Elyot, *The Governour*, ii. 322, 'beynge sore chaufed with fervent heate and the lengthe of his iournay'; and Dt 28[22] Gen. 'The Lord shall smite thee with a consumption, and with the feauer, and with a burning ague, and with feruent heat.' The word is also applied to cold, as R. Fox, *Chron.* 116, 'Hit was a fervent coolde weder'; Stewart, *Cron. Scot.* ii. 337, 'The fervent frost so bitter wes.'　　　　　　J. HASTINGS.

FESTIVAL.—See FEASTS AND FASTS.

FESTUS, Porcius, succeeded Felix as procurator of Judæa. On his arrival he visited Jerusalem, whither the priests endeavoured unsuccessfully to induce him to send for Paul. His reply (Ac 25[16]), that to hand over a man unheard was 'not customary with Romans' (whatever it might be for Jews), has a touch of disdainful dignity. Endeavouring to induce Paul to consent to a trial at Jerusalem, he provokes and allows the appeal to Cæsar. Then follows the hearing before Festus and Agrippa, the latter of whom is there as an expert assessor. The attitude of Festus is throughout (25[19] 26[24. 31]) one of official impartiality, touched with good-natured indifference to the technicalities of Jewish controversies.

The gens Porcia is not otherwise known to have comprised a family of Festi, nor is this Festus known to us apart from the NT and Josephus. According to the latter, the first important event of Festus' governorship was the decision of the emperor in favour of the Syrians at Cæsarea (FELIX, *sub fin.*). This was effected by Beryllus (so all MSS in Jos. *Ant.* XX. viii. 9; *vulgo* 'Burrus'), Greek secretary to the emperor, whom the Syrians

had won by corruption. This decision provoked the Jews to riots, in which Josephus sees the first simmerings of the war of 66. This point must not be forgotten when we come to the question of dates. The other principal occurrences of Festus' tenure of office mentioned by Josephus were, *firstly*, the putting down of the Sicarii, and especially of one dangerous rebel, similar to the one of Ac 21[38] (*Ant.* XX. viii. 10; cf. *BJ* II. xiv. 1); *secondly*, the disturbances at Jerusalem in consequence of the wall erected at the temple to intercept the view from the new wing of Agrippa's palace. Festus took the side of Agrippa, but allowed the priests to appeal to Rome. Before the result of this appeal was known Festus died.

The important question connected with the name of Festus is that of chronology (see art. CHRONOLOGY of NT, p. 417 ff.). According to Eusebius and Jerome (Eus. *Chron.*, Schöne ii. 148 f.; Hier. *de vir. illustr.*), Felix became procurator in the eleventh year of Claudius (51), Festus in the second year of Nero (56), Albinus succeeded Festus in the sixth or seventh year of Nero (60 cr 61), and the Acts bring us (so Euthal. *Praef. in epp. Pauli*) to the fourth year of Nero (58). There has been a tendency lately, *e.g.* on the part of Blass and Harnack, to revert to this chronology. But apart from the fact that had Festus governed Judæa for four or five years, Josephus would surely have had more to tell us in connexion with his procuratorship, the authority of Eusebius in this matter is more than precarious. Eusebius, doubtless, made use of Julius Africanus, who in turn used Justus of Tiberias, who stated the death-year of Agrippa II. But that Justus stated the years of the procuratorships there is not a word of evidence to prove. Eusebius may be as far from the truth here as when he places the outbreak of the Neronian persecution in 67-68. At the same time the question is worth reconsidering, and the recent discussion of Harnack (*Chronol. d. altchr. Lit.* p. 233 ff.) deserves more minute discussion than the limits of this article allow. The chronology of Eusebius has the merit, be it what it may, of fitting in with Clemen's date for St. Paul's arrest, namely, A.D. 54 (1 CORINTHIANS, § 6). But that the rule of Festus was a short one, everything goes to prove; and, as we saw above, the disturbances which then began were viewed by Josephus as the first mutterings of the great storm of the year 66. But it would help us much if we could fix the date of the arrival of Albinus, which was separated by only a few stormy months from the death of Festus. Unfortunately, we have only the *terminus ad quem* firmly fixed, namely, the summer of 62 (Schürer, *HJP* I. ii. 183, note 47). That his successor Gessius Florus was procurator only from 64-66 may be taken as proved (*ib.* note 58). But we have only inferential evidence, though it amounts to high probability, that the rule of Albinus was short. Perhaps the date furnished by ARETAS, with which Harnack fails to deal satisfactorily, coupled with the general data of St. Paul's life (1 CORINTHIANS, § 6, small print), may suffice to make us pause before putting the arrival of Festus anything like as early as 56. On the other hand, as Albinus cannot have arrived later than 62, and the events of Festus' procuratorship, together with those which follow his death and precede the arrival of Albinus, though insufficient to fill five years, are yet too many for one year, it is hardly possible to place the arrival of Festus later than 60. The system adopted *s.v.* CHRONOLOGY may be right in going back two years further (60 to 58). On the whole this variation may be taken, upon a full review of all our materials, as the most probable limit of doubt as regards this important date. It may be remarked that if Festus arrived in 60, the διετία ὅλη of Ac 28[30] ends about February 63 ; between this and the Neronian persecution of midsummer 64, to which Harnack would again bring back St. Paul's death, there is sufficient though hardly ample time for the events presupposed in the Epp. to Timothy and Titus (see Schürer, as quoted above, esp. note 38 ; Harnack, as quoted above ; Blass, *Acta Apost. Ed. Philol.* p. 23, and the authorities for CHRONOLOGY OF NT).

A. ROBERTSON.

FETCH.—To fetch is to *cause to come*, as Fuller, *Holy Warre*, 230, 'If they should say the Templars were burned wrongfully, they may be fetched over the coals themselves for charging his Holinesse so deeply'; and this meaning is easily seen in most of its phrases. **1.** *Fetch up*, 1 S 6[21] 7[1]. So Shaks. *Ant. and Cleop.* IV. xv. 35—

'Had I great Juno's power,
The strong-wing'd Mercury should fetch thee up,
And set thee by Jove's side.'

2. *Fetch again, i.e.* cause to come back (see AGAIN): 1 Es 4[34] 'Swift is the sun in his course, for he compasseth the heavens round about, and fetcheth his course again to his own place in one day' (πάλιν ἀποτρέχει). Cf. Bunyan, *Holy Citie*, 252, 'Revivings that (like Aquaviæ) do fetch again, and chear up the soul'; and Tindale, *Expositions*, 165, 'He wil return again unto his mercy, and fetch his power home again, which he lent to vex thee.' **3.** *Fetch about*: 2 S 14[20] 'To fetch about this form of speech hath thy servant Joab done this thing' (לְבַעֲבוּר סַבֵּב אֶת־פְּנֵי הַדָּבָר, lit. 'for the purpose of bringing round the face of the business,' or as RV 'to change the face of the matter'). See ABOUT, and cf. Shaks. *K. John*, IV. ii. 24—

'Like a shifted wind unto a sail,
It makes the course of thoughts to fetch about.'

Bacon, *Essays*, 'Of Cunning' (Gold. Treas. ed. p. 95, l. 5), 'It is strange, how long some men will lie in wait, to speake somewhat they desire to say : and how farre about they will fetch ; and how many other Matters they will beat over to come near it.' **4.** *Fetch a compass, i.e.* 'make a circuit,' instead of going in a straight line. Thus Fuller, *Pisgah Sight*, IV. ii. 43, 'Wicked men may for a time retard, not finally obstruct our access to happiness. It is but fetching a compass, making two steps for one ; a little more pains and patience will do the deed.' The Heb. is simply the verb סָבַב *ṣâbhabh*, which means to make a turning or a circuit. RV gives 'turn about' in Nu 34[5], Jos 15[3], and 'make a circuit' in 2 S 5[23], 2 K 3[9]. The Gr. is περιέρχομαι, go round about, Ac 28[13] (RV 'make a circuit').* In 'fetch a compass' as in 'fetch about' the idea of the circuitous route is not in the verb, but in its complement.† See COMPASS. Similar phrases are found, as T. Adams, *II Peter*, 54, 'Merchants would give much to know a short cut to those remote places of traffic, without passing straits or fetching bouts'; Fuller, *Holy Warre*, p. 29, 'As if sensible of his sad fate, and desirous to deferre what he cannot avoid, he [the Jordan] fetcheth many turnings and windings, but all will not excuse him from falling into the Dead sea.' **5.** *Fetch a stroke*, Dt 19[5] 'his hand fetcheth a stroke with the axe.' So Fuller, *Holy Warre*, 219, 'Being about to fetch another stroke, the Prince with his foot gaue him such a blow that he felled him to the ground'; and Bunyan, *Holy*

*Lightfoot (*Fresh Revision*[2] 193) says, 'We have heard how the inquiring schoolboy has been perplexed at reading that St. Paul and his companions "fetched a compass" when they set sail from Syracuse (Ac 28[13]), not being able to reconcile this statement with the date given for the invention of this instrument.'

† Fuller, *Holy Warre*, p. 119, says, 'His navie he sent about by Spain'; then on p. 120, 'behold his navie there safely arriving, which with much difficultie and danger had fetched a compass about Spain.'

War (Clar. Press ed. p. 47, l. 20), 'If I fetch my blow, *Mansoul*, down you go.' **6.** *Fetch one's breath*, Sir 31[19] 'he fetcheth not his wind short upon his bed' (οὐκ ἀσθμαίνει, RV 'he doth not breathe hard'). Cf. Shaks. 1 *Henry IV.* II. iv. 579, 'Hark, how hard he fetches breath.' Search his pockets'; and *Troilus*, III. ii. 23, 'She does so blush, and fetches her wind so short, as if she were frayed with a sprite : I'll fetch her. It is the prettiest villain : she fetches her breath so short as a new-ta'en sparrow.'

In Old English there were two distinct verbs, *fet* and *fetch*. Fet seems to have been the older of the two. Indeed, Bradley (*Oxf. Eng. Dict. s.v.* 'Fetch') believes that Platt and Sievers are right in deriving fetch from fet by a singular series of changes. The *i* of the oldest form *feti-an* became a consonantal *y*, then this *ty* being sounded as *cc* became written so, and *cc* easily passed into the spelling *ch*. Cf. *ort-yeard*, in Old Eng. *orceard*, now *orchard*.

Fet and Fetch were synonymous in meaning, as we may see from Tindale, whose trⁿ (1534) of Mt 24[17.18] is, 'And let him which is on the housse toppe not come downe to fet (ἆραι) eny thinge out of his housse. Nether let him which is in the felde returne backe to fetche (ἆραι) his clothes.' Fet gradually gave way to fetch. In the Geneva version of 1560 it is found in the imperat., 1 S 20[31] 'wherefore now send and fet him vnto me, for he shal surely dye,' and in the indic., Dt 19[12] 'Then the Elders of his citie shal send and fet him thence.' And even in AV of 1611 the infin. is once employed, Jer 36[21] 'So the king sent Iehudi to fet the roule.' But after the Old Eng. period the word was used chiefly in the past tense and past ptcp., as an alternative with 'fetcht' or 'fetched,' and that is its use elsewhere in AV.

In the 1611 ed. of AV 'fet' occurs 9 times (2 S 9[5] 11[27], 1 K 7[13] 9[28], 2 K 11[4], 2 Ch 12[11], Jer 26[23] 36[21], Ac 28[13]) ; 'fetcht' 5 times (Gn 18[7], 1 S 7[1], 2 S 14[2], 2 K 3[9], 2 Ch 1[17]) ; and 'fetched' 6 times (Gn 18[4] 27[14], Jos 15[3], Jg 18[18], 1 S 10[22], 2 S 4[6]). In course of time, chiefly through the influence of Dr. Paris (1762) and Dr. Blayney (1769), 'fet' was banished from AV. In his *Camb. Paragraph Bible* of 1873, Scrivener restored it to all its original places, and Scrivener's text is used in the *Camb. Bible for Schools and Colleges*. But the Camb. and Oxf. Parallel Bibles do not use it once. They use even 'fetcht' only once, Gn 18[7]; elsewhere always 'fetched.'

J. HASTINGS.

FETTER.—Three Heb. words are translated fetter. **1.** נְחֹשֶׁת, Arab. *naḥâs*, copper. In La 3[7] this word is rendered chain, in Jer 39[7] 52[11] (RV) fetters, also in Jg 16[21], 2 S 3[34], 2 K 25[7], 2 Ch 33[11] 36[6]. In the Arab. tr. by Van Dyck, נְחֻשְׁתַּיִם is rendered *silâsil naḥâs*, copper chains, or *silsilatain min naḥâs*, two chains of copper. It is still the custom in Syria to attach a chain to each of the rings put round a prisoner's ankles, the middle of the chain being fastened to his girdle. A prisoner is thus, according to the Arabic way of speaking, bound with two chains. **2.** כֶּבֶל, Syr. *kĕbel* (a late word borrowed from Aramaic. The Arab. *kabal* is probably a loan-word from the Aramaic). There are two passages in which this word is used, both referring to fetters of iron, Ps 105[18] and Ps 149[8]. **3.** זֵק, זִקִּים (Is 45[14], Nah 3[10] fetters of captives, Job 36[8] fig.). Horses and other animals are usually tethered by ropes fastened to the fore foot and the hind foot on one side.

W. CARSLAW.

FEVER.—See MEDICINE.

FIELD.—See AGRICULTURE.

FIERY SERPENT.—See SERAPHIM and SERPENT.

FIGS (תְּאֵנִים *tĕ'ênîm*, the fruit of the *fig tree*, which is תְּאֵנָה *tĕ'ênâh*; in NT συκῆ is the *fig tree*, and σῦκον the *fig*).—The fig tree, *Ficus Carica*, L., is cultivated everywhere in the Holy Land, and also grows spontaneously in many places. It is a tree of moderate size, seldom attaining a height of 15 ft., but its spreading branches often cover a circle with a diameter of 25 to 30 ft. Fig trees are habitually planted near houses, and the people sit in their shade, and that of the vines which grow over the trellises. This familiar sight did not fail to be noted in OT and Apocr. as an emblem of peace and prosperity (1 K 4[25], Mic 4[4], Zec 3[10],

1 Mac 14¹²). There are numerous varieties of figs cultivated, some of which bear a tart, blackish fruit, others a sweet, greenish or whitish one. The branches are straggling and naked in winter, but when the rains are nearly or quite over, small green knobs appear at the ends of the twigs. They are the young fruits, פַּג *pag*, 'green figs' (Ca 2¹³). The leaf-bud now expands, and the new pale green leaves soon more or less overshadow the little figs. This is a familiar sign of early summer (Mt 24³²). Hence a fig tree with leaves must already have young fruits, or it will be barren for the season. The first figs ripen late in May or early in June. They are called in Heb. בִּכּוּרָה *bikkûrâh*, in Arab. *bâkûrah*, that is, *first ripe*, Is 28⁴ (AV *hasty fruit*), Jer 24², Hos 9¹⁰, Mic 7¹.

When our Lord came to the fig tree near Bethany (Mk 11¹³), just before the passover, *i.e.* from late in March to the middle of April, 'the time of figs was not yet,' that is, the season for ripe figs had not come. Among the various explanations of Christ's action which may be given, the only ones which seem to us worthy of consideration are the following: (1) That being hungry, and seeing from a distance that the tree had leaves, and therefore was not dead, he came, not to find *new figs*, but to find and eat any figs of the last season which might have remained over on the tree. The expression 'if haply he might find anything thereon' implies that he did not expect to find much. One or two figs will often stay an empty stomach marvellously. According to this opinion, the offence of the fig tree was the fact of not having what must have been a very exceptional relic of a former harvest. (2) That, finding leaves, he knew that there should be young fruit, and hoped that there might, even at that early period, be 'the first ripe figs,' *bikkûrâh*. According to this interpretation, the fault of the fig tree was in not having a precocious fig or two before the time, 'for the time of figs was not yet.' We will not dispute the possibility of finding a winter fig or two on a tree (although during a residence of thirty-three years in Syria we have searched and inquired in vain for them), or of the exceptionally early maturing of some variety of figs, perhaps not now cultivated. Neither of these theories, however, accords with our conception of Christ's justice. In neither case would the fig tree be blameworthy. We are not held accountable for *extraordinary* attainments in religion. (3) Christ was at the moment hungry. Orientals do not eat early in the morning. Labourers and artificers come fasting to their work, and often toil an hour or two before eating. So it is presumable that our Saviour, in his morning walk of two miles from Bethany to Jerus., had not broken his fast. The physical sensation of hunger as a basis gave direction to his thoughts, as he happened to see a most familiar spectacle, a fig tree, at a distance, with fresh, young foliage. The fact that it is mentioned that 'the time of figs was not yet' (AV), or 'it was not the season of figs' (RV), would seem to prove that Christ would not have thought it strange that he had not found *winter figs* or *precocious first fruits*. It is hardly conceivable that he could have condemned the tree for that. But, when he arrived, he found *no fruit at all*. Immediately the disappointment of unsatisfied hunger was lost in the moral lesson which flashed across his mind. A fig tree with leaves should have at least green fruit. This one had none. There was *pretension*, which, in the moral sphere, is *hypocrisy*. Having leaves and no fruit, it was a *deceiver*. The *ripeness* of the fruit is not the point. If it had had *unripe* fruit, it would not have been condemned. It was condemned because it had *nothing but leaves*.

The failure of the fig and vine was a sign of great distress (Jer 5¹⁷ 8¹³, Jl 1⁷·¹², Hab 3¹⁷·¹⁸). Figs were dried and pressed into cakes for food (1 S 25¹⁸). These were used as poultices (2 K 20⁷, Is 38²¹). Fig leaves are thick, palmately lobed, and often a span or more across. There is no good reason to doubt the identity of the leaves which Adam and Eve used to make aprons (Gn 3⁷).

           G. E. POST.

FIGURE.—**1.** Dt 4¹⁶ 'Lest ye corrupt yourselves, and make you a graven image, the similitude of any figure' (סֶמֶל *sēmel*, Driver 'statue.' The word is found also 2 Ch 33⁷·¹⁵ EV 'idol,' and Ezk 8³·⁵ EV 'image.' The meaning 'statue' is confirmed by the Phœn. inscriptions. See Driver on Dt 4¹⁶ and Davidson on Ezk 8³). The Eng. word seems to be used in the obsolete sense of the distinctive shape or appearance of a person or thing. The Gen. version has 'a graven image or representacion of anie figure'; the Bishops', 'a graven image and picture of any maner of figure.' Cf. Chaucer, *Monk's Tale*, 232—

'And thanne had god of him [Nebuchadnezzar] compassioun,
And him restored his regne and his figure'—

i.e. his proper shape as a man. So Shaks. *Hamlet*, I. i. 41—

'In the same figure, like the king that's dead.'

2. 1 K 6²⁹ 'he carved all the walls of the house round about with carved figures of cherubims' (מִקְלָעוֹת *miklā'ôth* occurs only in this ch. and the next: 6¹⁸ EV 'was carved,' *i.e.* 'was carving of'; 6³² EV 'carvings'; 7³¹ EV 'gravings'). These 'carved figures' (as the single Heb. word is here tr⁴) were representations of cherubim cut in relief on the wood of the doors. See CARVING. For this use of the Eng. word, cf. Caxton, *Cato*, A iii. b, 'to adoure the ymages and other fygures humayn'; and Milton, *Lycidas*, 105—

'Next Camus, reverend sire, went footing slow,
His mantle hairy, and his bonnet sedge,
Inwrought with figures dim.'

3. Is 44¹³ 'The carpenter . . . maketh it [the image] after the figure of a man' (תַּבְנִית *tabhnîth*). The Heb. is frequent for the outward appearance of a person or thing. It occurs long with *sēmel* (above) in Dt 4¹⁶ and is tr⁴ 'likeness.' The Eng. word is used in the same sense as **1** above. Cf. He 1³ Wyc. 'he is the schynynge of glorie, and figure of his substaunce'; and Mk 16¹² Tind. 'After that, he appered unto two of them in a straunge figure.' **4.** Ac 7⁴³ 'figures which ye made to worship them'; and Ro 5¹⁴ 'who is the figure of him that was to come' (τύπος). Sanday-Headlam's note on the Greek word is as follows—

τύπος (τύπτω): (1) the 'impression' left by a sharp blow (τὸν τύπον τῶν ἥλων, 'the print of the nails,' Jn 20²⁵), in particular the 'stamp' struck by a die; (2) inasmuch as such a stamp bears the figure on the face of the die, 'copy,' 'figure,' or 'representation'; (3) by a common transition from effect to cause, 'mould,' 'pattern,' 'exemplar'; (4) hence in the special sense of the word type which we have adopted from the Greek of NT, 'an event or person in history corresponding in certain characteristic features to another event or person.'

In Ac 7⁴³ the meaning is 'representations' or 'images of gods' (the second meaning above); in Ro 5¹⁴ it is 'type' (the fourth meaning above). **5.** He 9²⁴ 'Christ is not entered into the holy places made with hands, *which are* the figures of the true; but into heaven itself' (ἀντίτυπα τῶν ἀληθινῶν, RV 'like in pattern to the true'); and 1 P 3²¹ 'The like figure whereunto *even* baptism doth also now save us' (ὃ καὶ ἡμᾶς ἀντίτυπον νῦν σώζει βάπτισμα, RV 'which also after a true likeness doth now save you [reading ὑμᾶς with edd.], *even* baptism,' RVm 'in the antitype'). The antitype (τὸ ἀντίτυπον) is the event or person in history that corresponds with the type (ὁ τύπος) — see Sanday-Headlam above. The one that occurs first in history is the type, the second the antitype. Hence in He 9[24] heaven is the type, the holy place in the tabernacle the antitype ; but in 1 P 3[21] the water of the deluge is the type, of which baptism is the antitype. See TYPE, and cf. Cartwright, *Cert. Relig.* (1651) i. 222, 'The Rock . . . was a Type and a Figure of Christ.' **6.** He 9[9] 'a figure for the time then present,' and 11[19] 'Accounting that God *was* able to raise *him* up, even from the dead ; from whence also he received him in a figure' (παραβολή, RV 'parable,' in both). The meaning of 9[9] is clear, but 11[19] is much disputed.

There are two favourite interpretations: (1) 'As a parable,' *sc.* of the resurrection. Wyclif ('in to a parable') and the Rhemish ('for a parable') decline to commit themselves.* Tind. in ed. of 1534 translates 'for an ensample,' and is followed by Coverdale ; but in 1526 ed. he had boldly 'as an ensample of the resurrection,' and this was adopted by Cranmer, and very nearly by the Bishops ('in a *certaine* similitude *of the resurrection*'). This trn gives a well-recognized sense to παραβολή. The objection felt against it is that Isaac was actually *not* raised from the dead. Hence the favourite interpretation at present is that of AV 'in a figure,' *i.e.* figuratively ; Isaac was not really dead, but he was as good as dead, and so figuratively was raised from the dead (see Westcott, *ad loc.*). Cf. Geneva 'in a sort.' The objection is that παραβολή has not elsewhere this meaning.

7. 1 Co 4[6] 'And these things, brethren, I have in a figure transferred to myself and to Apollos' (μετεσχημάτισα). The Gr. verb tr[d] 'in a figure transferred' elsewhere means to change one's form or appearance (σχῆμα) into some other form, 2 Co 11[13. 14. 15] (AV 'transform,' RV 'fashion into' or 'fashion as') and Ph 3[21] (AV 'change,' RV 'fashion anew'). Here it is the truth stated that is to change its application : applied by the apostle to himself and Apollos, it really applies to the Corinthians.† **8.** Sir 49[9] 'he made mention of the enemies under *the figure* of the rain' (ἐν ὄμβρῳ, RV 'he remembered the enemies in storm,' RVm 'in rain').

RV gives 'figure' for AV 'interpretation' in Pr 1[6], but with 'interpretation' in marg. (מְלִיצָה), elsewhere only Hab 2[6] (EV 'proverb,' RVm 'riddle') ; and for AV 'fashion,' Ac 7[44] τύπος (see FASHION). RV also introduces the verb 'to figure,' not in AV text, Lv 26[1] ('figured stone' as AVm, Heb. אֶבֶן מַשְׂכִּית, AV 'image of stone') ; and Nu 33[52] ('figured *stones*,' Heb. מַשְׂכִּיֹּת, AV 'pictures'). See IDOLATRY and STONE. This meaning of the verb (evidently 'adorned with figures or designs') **may** be illustrated from Shaks. *Rich. II.* III. iii. 150—

> 'I'll give my jewels for a set of beads, . . .
> My figured goblets for a dish of wood.'

J. HASTINGS.

FILL.—As a subst., meaning a full supply, fill is used of *food*, Lv 25[19], Dt 23[24] ; of *drink*, 2 Es 1[20], Jth 7[21] ; and metaphorically of *love*, Pr 7[18] 'Come, let us take our fill of love until the morning.' Cf. S. Rutherford, *Letters*, xxxv., 'those who live long, and get a heavy fill of this life' ; and Shaks. *Troil. and Cress.* V. viii. 4—

> 'Rest, sword ; thou hast thy fill of blood and death.'

The verb to fill is frequently used by Wyclif (and other early writers) in the sense of execute, accomplish, modern *fulfil*. Thus Gn 27[5] (1388) 'he hadde go in to the feeld to fille the comaundment of the fadir' (1382 'that he fulfille the heest of the fader') ; Lk 9[31] (1380) 'forsothe Moyses and Elye weren seyn in mageste ; and thei seyden his goynge out, which he was to fillinge in Jerusalem' (1388 'which he should fulfille'). So once in AV, 2 Es 4[36] 'when the number of seeds is filled in you' (*impletus fuerit* ; RV 'fulfilled').

---

* But the Rhem. NT has a marginal note, 'That is, in figure and mysterie of Christ dead, and aliue againe.' This margin probably gave AV the word 'figure.'

† Field (*ON, ad loc.*) suggests ' by a fiction ' for EV ' in a figure.' In illustration of the Gr. verb he quotes 1 S 28[8] 'Saul disguised himself' (Sym. μετεσχημάτισεν ἑαυτόν) ; and 1 K 14[2] 'Arise, I pray thee, and disguise thyself' (Theod. μετασχημάτισον σεαυτόν).

To 'fill up' is to fill to the full, the prep. *up*, like Gr. κατά, intensifying the verb : as Mt 23[32] 'Fill ye up then the measure of your fathers' (πληρώσατε) ; * 1 Th 2[16] 'to fill up their sins alway' (εἰς τὸ ἀναπληρῶσαι) ; Col 1[24] 'Who now rejoice in my sufferings for you, and fill up that which is behind of the afflictions of Christ in my flesh for his body's sake, which is the church' (ἀνταναπληρῶ, RV 'fill up on my part,' which is Lightfoot's tr.) † ; Mt 9[16] 'No man putteth a piece of new cloth unto an old garment, for that which is put in to fill it up taketh from the garment, and the rent is made worse' (τὸ πλήρωμα αὐτοῦ, lit. 'its filling' ; RV 'that which should fill it up') ; so Mk 2[21] ; Rev 15[1] 'in them is filled up the wrath of God' (ἐτελέσθη, RV 'is finished'). Cf. Shaks. 1 *Henry IV.* III. ii. 116—

> 'To fill the mouth of deep defiance up
> And shake the peace and safety of our throne.'

J. HASTINGS.

FILLET.—Two words are tr[d] so : (1) חוּט *hût*, Jer 52[21] of that which would 'compass' the pillars which king Solomon had made in the house of the LORD, and which the Chaldæans brake to carry the brass away ; AVm 'thread' ; RV 'line,' which is the translation in 1 K 7[15] of both AV and RV. See PILLAR and TEMPLE. The same word is used for the scarlet 'thread' which Rahab placed in her window (Jos 2[18]), and for the threefold 'cord' which cannot be broken of Ec 4[12]. (2) [חֲשֻׁקִים] *hâshûk*, only found in plu. and with suffixes, Ex 27[10. 11] 36[38] 38[10. 11. 12. 17. 19], of that which clasped the pillars in the tabernacle, those of the pillars of the court being overlaid with silver, those of the pillars at the door with gold. See PILLAR and TABERNACLE. The verb חָשַׁק *hishshak*, to furnish with fillets, is tr[d] 'fillet' where it occurs, Ex 27[17] 'the pillars . . . shall be filleted with silver,' 38[18] 'the pillars . . . were filleted with silver,' 38[28] '[Bezalel] filleted them' (RV 'made fillets for them').

A fillet is a little thread (Lat. *fīlum*, a thread, Fr. *fil*, dim. *filet*). Its oldest and commonest application is to a ribbon for binding the hair. Thus Spenser, *FQ* I. iii. 4—

> 'From her faire head her fillet she undight';

and Fuller, *Holy Warre*, 125, 'They pleaded that the Crown was tied on Guy's head with a woman's fillet.' But it came to be used early, and is still in use, for any narrow strip of binding material.

J. HASTINGS.

FINE. — For the subst. *Fine* see CRIMES AND PUNISHMENTS. The adj. 'fine' is of frequent occurrence, but only in a few cases does it represent a Heb. or Gr. word. These are : (1) טוֹב *tôbh*, 2 Ch 3[5. 8] 'fine gold,' Ezr 8[27] 'fine copper,' La 4[1] 'most fine gold' (in Gn 2[12] it is tr[d] 'good,' its usual tr[n], 'the gold of that land is good'). Aram. טָב *tâbh*, Dn 2[32] 'fine gold.' (2) שָׂרִיק *sârîk*, Is 19[9] 'fine flax,' lit. 'combed flax,' as RV. (3) פָּז *pâz*, Ca 5[11] 'most fine gold,' Ges. 'refined gold.' (4) חֵלֶב

---

* Cf. Shaks. *K. John*, II. i. 556—
> 'I trust we shall,
> If not fill up the measure of her will,
> Yet in some measure satisfy her.'

† This is the only occurrence of the particular compound ἀντανα-πληρόω in biblical Greek. Lightfoot gives classical quotations, in order to bring out that the special force of ἀντί is 'from another quarter.' That is what is sought to be expressed by 'on my part.' But T. K. Abbott ('Intern. Crit. Com.' *in loc.*) points out that ἀναπληρόω itself, in the two instances where in NT it is used with ὑστέρημα (1 Co 16[17], Ph 2[30]), expresses a supply coming from a different quarter from the deficiency. He finds the idea of *balance* in the ἀντί, and hopes it is not an over-refinement to suggest that ἀνταναπληρόω is more unassuming than ἀναπληρόω, 'since part of the force of the word is thrown on the idea of correspondence.' Christ's afflictions are incomplete till Paul brings his quota of affliction to add to them. And every Christian must bring his quota of affliction to add to them before they are complete. For the afflictions are not those of the Redeemer, but of His Body the Church. They are His afflictions just because the Church is His Body.

hêlebh, Ps 81¹⁶ 147¹⁴ 'the finest of the wheat,' lit. as AVm and RVm 'fat of wheat': the fuller phrase 'kidney-fat of wheat' is found in Dt 32¹⁴. (5) καθαρός, Jth 10⁵ 'fine bread' (RVm 'pure').

In all other cases 'fine' goes with its subst. in order to bring out the full meaning of the subst. in the Heb. or Greek. It is used (1) along with *linen* for שֵׁשׁ *shêsh*, Gn 41⁴² , Ex 25⁴ etc., Ezk 16¹⁰· ¹³ 27⁷ ; for בּוּץ *bûz*, 1 Ch 4²¹ 15²⁷ , 2 Ch 2¹⁴ 3¹⁴ , Est 1⁶ 8¹⁵ , Ezk 27¹⁶ ; for סָדִין *sâdhîn*, Pr 31²⁴ (RV 'linen garments'), Is 3²³ ; for אֵטוּן *'êṭûn*, Pr 7¹⁶ (RV 'linen of the yarn'); for βύσσος, Lk 16¹⁹ , Rev 18¹² ; for (adj.) βύσσινος, 1 Es 3⁶ , Rev 18¹⁶ 19⁸ ᵇⁱˢ· ¹⁴ ; and for σινδών, Mk 15⁴⁶ (RV 'a linen cloth'). (2) With *flour* for סֹלֶת *sôleth*, Lv 2¹ etc., Nu 6¹⁵ etc., 1 K 4²² , 2 K 7¹· ¹⁶· ¹⁸ , 1 Ch 9²⁹ 23²⁹ , Ezk 16¹³· ¹⁹ 46¹⁴ ; and for σεμίδαλις, Sir 35² 38¹¹ , Bel³ , 2 Mac 1⁸ 15³⁹ , Rev 18¹³ . (3) With *gold* for פָּז *pâz*, Job 28¹⁷ , Ps 19¹⁰ 119¹²⁷ , Pr 8¹⁹ , Ca 5¹⁵ , Is 13¹² , La 4² ; for כֶּתֶם *kethem*, Job 31²⁴ , Pr 25¹² , Dn 10⁵ (RV 'pure gold'); and for חָרוּץ *hârûz* Pr 3¹⁴ , Zec 9³ . (4) With *brass* for χαλκολίβανον [-ος], Rev 1¹⁵ 2¹⁸ (RV 'burnished'). Thus the adj., which was introduced to mark a distinction in the Heb. and Greek words, has been used so freely as to obliterate any distinction, and RV has done little to restore it. 'Fine' means '*finished*' (Lat. *finitus*, Old Fr. *fin*), and hence of superior quality, and that is its meaning in all those places. RV, however, has introduced the word in the sense of 'broken small,' 'of minute particles,' Dt 9²¹ 'as fine as dust' (לְעָפָר, דַּק, AV 'small as dust').

The verb *to fine* (mod. 'refine') is derived from the adj., and signifies to make pure. It occurs only Job 28¹ 'Surely there is a vein for silver, and a place for gold where they fine it' (יָזֹקּוּ, RV 'which they refine'). 'Fining' is used twice, Pr 17³ 'the fining pot is for silver' (מַצְרֵף, Amer. RV 'refining pot'), so 27²¹ . 'Finer' occurs only Pr 25⁴ 'a vessel for the finer' (צֹרֵף, Amer. RV 'refiner').

J. HASTINGS.

FIR (בְּרוֹשׁ *bĕrôsh*; once בְּרוֹתִים *bĕrôthîm*, Ca 1¹⁷ ; ἄρκευθος, κέδρος, πίτυς, κυπάρισσος, πεύκη; *abies, cupressus*). From the numerous words by which the LXX has tr⁴ the Heb. original, it is clear that the learned men of that day were not agreed as to the identity of the tree intended. In a considerable number of passages the trⁿ is not the name of a tree at all. The conditions required in the tree are—(1) That it could supply boards and planks and timber for doors (LXX πεύκιναι, 1 K 6¹⁵· ³⁴). (2) That it could supply beams (LXX κέδρινοι, 2 Ch 3⁵) for the roofing of the temple. These must have been large, and very strong. (3) That it was useful in shipbuilding (Ezk 27⁵). The LXX in this passage has transposed the words for *cedar* and *fir*, giving as follows: 'The cedar from Senir was built for thee, the planks of the decks were taken off the cypress of Lebanon, of which to make for thee pine masts.' It uses here κυπάρισσος for the transposed word. It is not clear why the word *pine* in the last clause was added. Perhaps it refers to the resinous quality of the wood. (4) It was suitable for musical instruments (2 S 6⁵). The LXX, however, in this passage renders the word *bĕrôshîm* by ἐν ἰσχύϊ, *in strength*, and not by the name of any tree. This corresponds with the parallel passage 1 Ch 13⁸ 'with all their might,' where the Heb. text is בְּכָל־עֹז instead of וּבִשִׁרִים בְּכָל עֲצֵי בְרוֹשִׁים. If we adopt the reading of 1 Ch in 1 S, the abruptness and apparent unseasonableness of the mention of the wood of which the musical instruments were made is avoided, and the two passages satisfactorily reconciled. The slight clerical error which would thus be corrected is obvious on a comparison of the two texts side by side. Budde has adopted this amended reading in his new edition of the text

of Samuel. Should we also adopt it, there would no longer be any necessity to consider the adaptation of the *bĕrôsh* to the manufacture of musical instruments (see Wellh. and Driver, *ad loc.*).

Pinus Halepensis, Mill., has been proposed as the equivalent of *bĕrôsh*. But its wood is not durable, and would hardly have been chosen for the beams of the temple. Two other trees have been proposed as the equivalent of *bĕrôsh*, either of which would meet all the requirements: *Juniperus excelsa*, M.B., and *Cupressus sempervirens*, L. The former is called in Arab. *lizzâb* and

'JUNIPERUS EXCELSA.' TALL JUNIPER.

sherbîn. It grows in the alpine and sub-alpine regions of Lebanon and Antilebanon, up to an altitude of 9000 ft. Its comus, when not hacked by the woodman, is ovate-lanceolate. Its trunk is straight, and its wood very solid and durable. It has dense ascending branches, small appressed leaves, and black berries as large as a marrowfat pea. The wood is well stored with resin—a fact which threatens the tree with extinction, as the remaining forests are fast being cut down by the tar smelters. Its trunks make solid and indestructible beams, and its wood, which is reddish and fragrant, is suitable for boards, planks, ship timber, and other purposes. But, notwithstanding the suitableness of the juniper as a tree to the requirements of the case, the weight of evidence is in favour of the *cypress, Cupressus sempervirens*, L. This tree has qualities resembling those of the last named. It has a straight trunk, horizontal, somewhat straggling branches, forming an ovate-oblong comus, small appressed leaves, and globular galbules, about an inch in diameter, composed of woody, shield-shaped scales. Its wood is useful for all the purposes indicated for the fir. Its name, κυπάρισσος, is one of the most frequent translations of it in the LXX. It is called in Arab. *saru* and *sherbîn*, both of which are the equivalent of *cypress* in that language. Contrary to an opinion cited in *Oxf. Heb. Lex.*, under the head בְּרוֹשׁ, it is found in abundance in Lebanon and Antilebanon. A variety of it, with ascend-

'CUPRESSUS SEMPERVIRENS.' WILD CYPRESS.

ing branches, forming a lanceolate comus, is the familiar *cemetery cypress*, so common in the neighbourhood of Oriental cities. Many of these have tall straight trunks, which would make massive beams and ship timbers.   G. E. POST.

FIRE (in OT most commonly אֵשׁ, πῦρ, πυρισμός, also אֶשָּׁה, אֲעֵרָה, אוּר; in Dn occurs Aram. נוּר; in NT πῦρ, also πυρά, φῶς) denotes primarily the ordinary process of combustion, with its accompaniments of light and heat. The Scripture references to it are too numerous to classify exhaustively. Those which deserve special attention fall into two groups, according as the word is used in a literal or in a figurative sense.

I. LITERAL USAGE.—Here we may distinguish —**1. Fire accompanying God's presence.** Besides numerous metaphorical allusions in connexion with theophanies, there are several references to fire as a physical phenomenon appearing on such occasions. See Gn 15[17], Ex 3[2] (the burning bush), Ex 19[18], Dt 4[36] (Mt. Sinai), Ex 40[38], Nu 9[15], Dt 1[33], Ps 78[14] 105[39] (the guiding pillar). **2. Sacrificial fire.** (*a*) Sacrifice by fire was a primitive mode of worship (Gn 8[20] 22[6]). (*b*) Under the Mosaic law fire was a most important means of offering the various prescribed sacrifices, which are described as 'offerings made by fire unto J".' For this purpose a fire was kept continually burning on the altar of burnt-offering (Lv 6[13], 1 Es 6[24]). Accord-

ing to Lv 9[24] it had a miraculous origin, and it was similarly rekindled in Solomon's temple (2 Ch 7[1-3]). Some find a reference to this perpetual fire in Is 31[9] (but see Cheyne, Delitzsch, *in loc.*), and in the name Ariel (the hearth of God?) applied to Jerus. in Is 29[1. 2. 7]. In 2 Mac 1[19-22] there is a legend about the hiding of the sacred fire at the fall of Jerus., and its discovery by Nehemiah after the Exile. For the story of a later rekindling see 2 Mac 10[3]. (*c*) Mention is made of special answers by fire when sacrifices were offered elsewhere than at the regular sanctuary, as in the cases of Gideon (Jg 6[21]), Elijah (1 K 18[38]), and David (1 Ch 21[26]). (*d*) Fire was used for offering incense. It was carried in censers (Lv 16[12. 13]), or placed on the altar of incense (Ex 30[7. 8]), and the incense sprinkled upon it. To use any other than the sacred fire for this purpose was to offer 'strange fire,' the offence for which Nadab and Abihu perished (Lv 10[1], Nu 3[4] 26[61]). (*e*) Human sacrifice, especially child sacrifice, by fire was practised by certain of Israel's neighbours (Dt 12[31], 2 K 17[31]). It was strictly forbidden in the law (Lv 18[21], Dt 18[10]), but is repeatedly mentioned as a sin of Israel (2 K 17[17], Jer 7[31] 19[5] 32[35], Ezk 16[21] 20[26. 31]), being carried on in particular by Ahaz (2 K 16[3], 2 Ch 28[3]) and Manasseh (2 K 21[6], 2 Ch 33[6]). The scene of these rites was Topheth in the valley of Hinnom (Jer 7[31]). See W. R. Smith, *RS*, pp. 352, 353, and Driver, *Deut.* p. 222. **3. Lightning.** In such expressions as 'fire from heaven,' 'the fire of God,' etc., which describe at times a destructive agency (Lv 10[2], 2 K 1[10. 12], Job 1[16]), and at times the token by which sacrifice was approved (2 *c*, above), some such phenomenon as lightning is evidently to be understood, as also when 'fire and hail' are mentioned together (Ex 9[23. 24], Ps 105[32] 148[8]). **4. Fire for domestic purposes.** Its use in this respect was twofold. (*a*) For the preparation of food, as for roasting flesh (Ex 12[8], 2 Ch 35[13], Is 44[16], 1 Es 1[12]), for broiling fish (Jn 21[9]), for baking (1 K 17[12], Jer 7[18]). (*b*) For warmth, as in Is 44[16], Jer 36[22], Mk 14[54], Lk 22[55], Jn 18[18], Ac 28[2]. In Pal. fire is only occasionally used for heating, and there are no regular fireplaces except in kitchens, but portable braziers or 'fire-pans' are employed. The larger houses have special 'winter rooms' (Jer 36[22], Am 3[15]). In these a cavity is made in the middle of the floor, in which the 'stove' (אָח) is placed. When the fire has burnt out a wooden frame is placed over it, and this is covered with a carpet so as to retain the heat (Keil, *Bib. Arch.* ii. 107 ; Nowack, *Heb. Arch.* 141 ; Benzinger, *Heb. Arch.* 124). The Arabs in the desert use as a hearth a hole lined with stones (Niebuhr, *Travels in Arabia*, i. 209). The use of fire on the Sabbath for domestic purposes was forbidden in the law (Ex 35[3] ; Jos. *Wars*, II. viii. 9). **5. Fire in metallurgy.** Fire has been employed from the earliest times for refining, casting, and forging metals. Among the Scripture allusions to this use are Ex 32[24] (the golden calf), the various references to 'molten images,' and also Is 44[12] 54[16], 2 Es 16[73], Sir 2[5], 1 P 1[7]. **6. Fire as a destroying agent.** Among the effects of fire destruction is naturally prominent. Death by fire (or possibly burning *after* execution by another method) was the penalty for certain offences (Lv 20[14] 21[9], Jos 7[15. 25]), and was also a mode of inflicting vengeance (2 S 12[31] [?], Jer 29[22], Dn 3[11. 15], 2 Mac 7[5]). Conquerors burned the idols of vanquished nations (2 K 19[18], Is 37[19]), and the Israelites were specially enjoined so to destroy those of the Canaanites (Dt 7[5], 1 Mac 5[68]). Fire was a common means of destroying cities and property taken in war ; and hence 'a fire shall go forth,' 'I will send (or kindle) a fire,' are formulæ which occur frequently in the prophetical books. Setting a crop on fire was one way of provoking a quarrel (Jg 15[4. 5], 2 S 14[30]), and provision was made in the law (Ex 22[6]) for making good the damage done by fire accidentally raised. Fire was a convenient method of destroying obnoxious writings (Jer 36[23], 1 Mac 1[56]). The disposal of human bodies by burning was quite exceptional among the Hebrews (1 S 31[12], Am 6[10]), but the refuse of the bodies of animals used in sacrifice was destroyed by fire (Lv 4[12] 6[30] 16[27], He 13[11]). Garments infected by 'leprosy' were to be burnt (Lv 13[52. 57]), and it was also common to burn rubbish of various kinds, as stubble (Is 5[24]), chaff (Mt 3[12], Lk 3[17]), and tares (Mt 13[30]). Topheth (2 e, above) is said to have become in later times a receptacle and burning-place of rubbish. (This is doubted by Robinson; see *BRP*[2] i. 274.) Fire is contemplated as the means by which the visible universe is to be destroyed (2 P 3[7-12]). **7.** Fire as a purifying agent. This use arises from the previous one in cases where impurities are of a combustible nature while the material to be purified is not so (Nu 31[23]).

II. METAPHORICAL USAGE.—Many of the foregoing properties and uses of fire have suggested fig. applications of the word. Thus we find it employed as a symbol—**1.** Of God Himself. (*a*) Of His glory, in such visions as those described in Ezk 1[4. 13] 10[6. 7], Dn 7[9] 10[6]. (*b*) Of His protecting presence (2 K 6[17], Zec 2[5]). (*c*) Of His holiness (Dt 4[24], He 12[29]). **2.** Of God's righteous judgment, which tests the deeds of men (Zec 13[9], Mal 3[2], 1 Co 3[13]). **3.** Of God's wrath against sin (Is 66[15. 16], Jer 4[4] 21[12], La 2[3. 4], Ezk 21[31] 22[21], Am 5[6] 7[4] etc.). **4.** Of the punishment of the wicked (Ps 68[2] 97[3], Is 47[14], Ezk 28[18], Mt 13[42. 50], 2 Th 1[8]). Topheth or Gehenna (I. **6** above) suggests the language in Is 66[24], Jth 16[17], Sir 7[17], Mt 18[9], Mk 9[43-48]. Fire is the emblem of the danger which the saved escape (Zec 3[2], Jude [23]). 'Eternal fire' and 'the lake of fire' are images of the punishment of the lost (Mt 25[41], Jude [7], Rev 19[20] 20[10. 14. 15] 21[8]). **5.** Of sin (Is 9[18] 65[5]), and particularly of lust (Hos 7[6], Sir 23[16]), and of the mischief of the tongue (Pr 16[27], Ja 3[6]). **6.** Of trouble and affliction (Ps 66[12], Is 43[2], Jer 51[58], Hab 2[13]). **7.** Of religious emotion (Ps 39[3]), and especially of prophetic inspiration, as 'the word of the Lord' (Jer 5[14] 20[9] 23[29]). **8.** Of the law (2 Es 13[38]). **9.** Of the Holy Spirit (Mt 3[11], Lk 3[16], Ac 2[3]).

Reference is apparently made in 2 Mac 10[3] to the method of procuring fire by striking steel against flint. With regard to *fuel*, the material used for the sacrificial fire, both in primitive and in later times, was wood (Gn 22[3. 6], Lv 6[12]). Special arrangements were made for supplying the altar fire. The Gibeonites were made 'hewers of wood' for the house of the Lord (Jos 9[23]), and after the Exile a special wood-offering was appointed for the temple (Neh 10[34] 13[31]). It is called by Josephus the festival of Xylophoria (*Wars*, II. xvii. 6). For ordinary purposes the staple fuel was charcoal (see COAL), but other materials were also used, such as thorns (Ps 58[9] 118[12], Ec 7[6], Is 33[12]) and grass (Mt 6[30], Lk 12[28]). The asphaltum found near the Dead Sea is combustible, as is also the 'stink-stone' found in the same neighbourhood, which is burnt along with camel's dung (Burckhardt, *Travels in Syria*, p. 394). The last mentioned, as well as other kinds of dung (Ezk 4[15]), is also used alone as fuel (Niebuhr, *Travels in Arabia*, ii. 232; Wright, *Palmyra and Zenobia*, p. 369).

JAMES PATRICK.

FIREBRAND.—See BRAND. **FIREPAN.**—See CENSER.

FIRKIN.—See WEIGHTS AND MEASURES.

FIRMAMENT.—See COSMOGONY.

FIRSTBORN.—See FAMILY.

FIRST-FRUITS (בִּכּוּרִים, in Lv 23[20] בִּכְּרִים, LXX πρωτογεννήματα; ראשׁית ἀπαρχή).—The custom of offering first-fruits was shared by the Isr. with many other ancient nations, and it is also found in many savage religions. Frazer (*Golden Bough*, ii. 68–90) cites many examples to show that the new corn was eaten sacramentally in order that the worshippers might share in the divine life of the corn-spirit, with which it was assumed that the grain was instinct. The eating of the first-fruits is, then, similar to the earliest form of animal sacrifice, in which the victim was regarded as divine, and the essence of the sacrifice lies in the communal feast and the participation of all the worshippers in the divine life. The two still remain separated by an important difference. The divine animal probably belonged to the kin of the worshippers, and the sacrificial meal strengthened the bond of kinship by a distribution of the common life. There is no reason for assuming this in the case of the corn-spirit. He gives, further, several instances of the offering of the first-fruits to the deity, in which the sacramental idea is absent (*Golden Bough*, ii. 373–384). The offering is in these cases of the nature of tribute or thank-offering. It is considered unsafe to eat of the new crops till the god has received his share, and the rite thus falls into the same category as numerous others familiar to the student of ritual and custom. The offering of the first-fruits does not sanctify the rest of the crop, but it makes it lawful food (W. R. Smith, *RS*,[2] 241).

The Heb. first-fruits belong to the latter class; they are tribute, not the staple of a sacramental meal. The history is not in all points clear, partly owing to the shifting sense of the terminology. It is essential, if confusion is to be avoided, to keep the regulations of the codes distinct, and take them in their chronological order.

(*a*) In the oldest legislation (JE) the first-fruits of the harvest are required (Ex 23[16] 34[22]). Twice the curious phrase occurs, 'the first of the first-fruits' (רֵאשִׁית בִּכּוּרֵי) Ex 23[19] 34[26], so in Ezk 44[30]. This is taken by some to mean the first-ripe, by others the choicest, of the first-fruits. But probably 'of the first-fruits' is added to explain 'the first,' the first, that is, the first-fruits. It seems probable that in Ex 22[29] first-fruits are referred to in the words מְלֵאָתְךָ וְדִמְעֲךָ (lit. 'thy fulness and thy tear,' paraphrased in RV as 'the abundance of thy fruits and of thy liquors'), on account of the mention of the firstborn in the parallel clause. If so, the first-fruits can hardly be confined to cereals, but will include wine and oil ('thy liquors'). The LXX gives ἀπαρχαὶ ἅλωνος καὶ ληνοῦ ('first-fruits of thy threshing-floor and wine-press'). A feast was connected with the offering, 'the feast of harvest, the first-fruits of thy labour' (Ex 23[16]), 'the feast of weeks, *even* of the first-fruits of wheat harvest' (Ex 34[22]). The amount to be offered is not stated; it seems to have been left to the discretion of the offerer. It is interesting to observe that a man brought Elisha as a gift 'bread of the first-fruits, twenty loaves of barley, and fresh ears of corn' (2 K 4[42]).

(*b*) In Deuteronomy (D) the Isr. is ordered to bring of his first-fruits in a basket to the central sanctuary and present it to the priest, with a profession of gratitude to God for deliverance from Egyp. bondage and the possession of the fruitful land of Palestine. A feast then follows, in which the Levite and the stranger are to share the offerer's hospitality (Dt 26[1-11]). According to 18[4] the priest is to receive the first-fruits of corn, wine, and oil, and the first of the fleece. The two regulations seem to be in conflict, and it has been supposed that 18[4] is a later addition. Possibly there is no discrepancy. The basket of first-fruits may be only a portion, and this may be the first-fruits meant in 18[4], the rest being kept for the feast, or it may be the whole and the feast not made of the first-fruits at all. (See Driver, *Deut.* p. 290. He decides for the latter alternative.) It is not clear what was the relation of the first-fruits to the Tithe. Several scholars regard them as really identical, but this is not certain. See TITHE.

(*c*) As Dt 18[4] claims the first - fruits for the Levitical priests, so *Ezekiel*, whose legislation forms the transition to the Priestly Code, claims for the priests (*i.e.* the sons of Zadok) 'the first of all the first-fruits of everything,' and, in addition, the first of the dough (44[30]).

(*d*) In the small code known as the Law of Holiness (H) it is enjoined that on the day after the Sabbath a sheaf of the first-fruits of the harvest should be brought to the priest, who should wave it before the Lord. A burnt-offering and a meal-offering are to accompany this ceremony, and, till it is accomplished, no bread, parched corn, or fresh ears must be eaten (Lv 23[10-14]). Seven weeks later two wave loaves of two-tenths of an ephah of fine flour and leavened are to be offered as first-fruits (Lv 23[17]. The additional regulations in 23[18-20] are for the most part a later insertion interpolated from Nu 28[27-29]).

(*e*) In the Priestly Code (P) the *rêshîth* and the *bikkûrîm* seem to be distinguished. In Nu 18[12] the best of the corn, wine, and oil, that is, the *rêshîth*, belongs to the priest. In the next verse the *bikkûrîm* of all that is in their land also belong to the priest. Probably, the *bikkûrîm* should be interpreted as the first ripe raw fruits, while the *rêshîth* will be the prepared oil and wine and corn. (So Wellhausen, Nowack, and RV.) Accordingly, we find in Neh 10[35] that the *bikkûrîm* of the ground and of the fruit trees were brought into the house of the Lord, while the *rêshîth* of dough, heave-offerings, fruit, wine, and oil were brought into the store-rooms of the temple (10[37] 12[44]). The distinction is observed in LXX and by Philo and Josephus. In Nu 15[20, 21] it is enacted that the first of the dough also shall be given as a heave-offering. According to Lv 2[12] leaven and honey might be included in the first-fruits, though they could not be part of any offering made by fire. The meal-offering of first-fruits consisted of parched corn in the ear with oil and frankincense. Part of the corn and oil with all the frankincense was to be burnt (Lv 2[14-16]). An interesting law, which rests on the same principle as the law of first-fruits, is that of Lv 19[23-25], which ordains that the fruit of a tree shall not be used for the first three years after it is planted ('three years shall they be as uncircumcised unto you'), and shall be consecrated to God in the fourth year. In the fifth year it may be eaten.

(*f*) In the later period a distinction was made between the *bikkûrîm* and the *tĕrûmôth* (תְּרוּמוֹת oblations); the fullest treatment of the subject is in the two tracts of the Mishna which bear these names. The *bikkûrîm* were taken from wheat, barley, grapes, figs, pomegranates, olives, and honey. The fruits were offered fresh by those who dwelt near Jerus., and dried by those who came from a distance. The companies came in a procession headed by the ox for the sacrifice, and marched to the music of pipes. They were met in Jerus. by the chief priests. The offerers then carried their wreathed baskets on their shoulders to the temple courts, and were welcomed by the Levites with the singing of Ps 30. Then the baskets were given to the priests, and the formula (Dt 26[5-10]) was repeated. The *tĕrûmôth* were a tax for the support of the priests, and used only by them, and were levied on every kind

of fruit of the ground and of trees. The choicest of the fruits were to be given; not more than $\frac{1}{40}$ or less than $\frac{1}{60}$ of the crop was expected. There was also the *Ḥallah* (חַלָּה), which was the first of the dough, $\frac{1}{24}$ of the whole piece in the case of private individuals, and $\frac{1}{48}$ in that of public bakers.

LITERATURE.—Nowack, *Heb. Archäol.* ii. pp. 255–257; Wellhausen, *Prolegom.* pp. 157, 158; Schürer, *HJP* ii. i. 237–242. See also Philo, *De festo cophini* and *De præmiis sacerdotum.*

A. S. PEAKE.

FIRSTLING.—A firstling * is the first (in time) of its kind, Pr 3[9] Cov. 'Honoure the LORDE with thy substaunce, and with the firstlinges of all thine encrease.' In *Macbeth*, IV. i. 147, Shaks. uses the word of the first thoughts of the heart and the first acts of the hand—

'From this moment
The very firstlings of my heart shall be
The firstlings of my hand.'

In EV it is used only of the firstborn of beasts, though the Heb. words so tr[d] (בְּכוֹר or בְּכוֹרָה, and פֶּטֶר) are used also of the firstborn of women.

FISH.—Fishes are very abundant in the inland waters of Pal. and Syria, except the Dead Sea, as well as in the adjacent Mediter. and the Nile. Even the intensely salt springs by the Dead Sea swarm with certain kinds of fish, while the water of that sea, which contains a large percentage of chloride of magnesium, is fatal to all animal life. Thousands of fish are borne by the rapid current of the Jordan into that sea, and, as soon as they reach its waters, are stupefied, and fall a prey to cormorants and kingfishers, or their bodies are washed up on the shore and feed the ravens and vultures. Tristram mentions forty-three species of fish found in inland waters. Of these the large number of twenty-two are peculiar to Pal. and Syria, and of this number fourteen are peculiar to the Jordan Valley and one to the mountain lake of Yamûni, S.E. of the cedars, and three inhabit only the Damascus lakes. Many of the species swarm in immense shoals in the Sea of Galilee and in the warm fountains by its shores, as well as in the Jordan and its affluents, the Leontes, the Orontes, and the lakes of Antioch, Ḥems, etc. Fresh - water fishes are also very abundant in all the perennial streams which flow into the Mediter., often ascending long distances, and not infrequently leaping up the rapids and cascades to reach their spawning places. The adjacent Mediter. is also well stocked with a large number of species of fish.

The large number and great fecundity of fish is expressed in the Heb. name דָּג *dâg*, from דָּגָה to *multiply abundantly.* They were taken from the earliest times, and many of them used as food (Gn 9[2, 3]). Not a few of them are highly specialized in form and aspect; yet, while a considerable number of land animals and birds and even insects had names in Heb., not a single species of fish is named in the Scriptures. The only attempt at classification was into *clean* and *unclean* (Lv 11[9, 10]). The former comprised those which had fins and scales; the latter, all others. This distinction was recognized in ancient Egypt (Wilkinson, *Anc. Egyp.* iii. 58, 59), and under el-Ḥâkim, who prohibited the use of unclean fish (Lane, *Mod. Egyp.* i. 132). The good and bad fish (Mt 13[48]) may have referred to this distinction, or to some other standard of excellence. The writer has seen a fisherman on the Mediter. coast in his anger beat to a jelly the head of a fish to which he objected.

* From *first* and *ling* a suffix with varying force but generally dimin., seen also in changeling, darling, fatling, fondling, foundling, gosling, hireling, inkling, nestling, nurseling, seedling, stripling, starveling, underling, worldling.

At other times they cast them away on the shore, or back into the water.

The Hebrews seem to have classified together all creatures living in the waters, whether 'whales' AV, or 'sea-monsters' RV (Gn 1²¹; Heb. *tannínîm*), or 'great fish' (Jon 1¹⁷ דָּג גָּדוֹל *dâg gâdhôl*), or the 'living creature that moveth' (Gn 1²¹), or 'fish' (v.²⁸).

The fish was an object of idolatry in all the ancient world. The Philistines worshipped Dagon, the Fish-god (1 S 5⁴), who was represented with the body of a man and the tail of a fish (but see DAGON, p. 544ᵃ). Hence it was forbidden to make an image of a fish (Dt 4¹⁸), which to the Heb. included, as before said, all living creatures in the water (Ex 20⁴).   G. E. POST.

FISHER.—Fisher, says Bradley (*Oxf. Eng. Dict.*), is now archaic, being superseded in ordinary use by 'fisherman.' AV has followed previous versions in giving 'fisher' in Is 19⁸, Jer 16¹⁶, Ezk 47¹⁰ (דַּיָּג, only plu.), Mt 4¹⁸·¹⁹, Mk 1¹⁶·¹⁷ (ἁλιεύς), though it has 'fisherman' after Tind. and the others (except Wyc. and Rhem.) in Lk 5² (ἁλιεύς). For the 'fisher's coat' of Jn 21⁷ see COAT.

FISHING.—The natural history of Palestine fish has been little studied. Along the coast there are the usual Mediterranean varieties, with an undue proportion of mullet. Some 33 varieties of fresh-water fish have been counted in the Jordan Valley, where fish swarm in Galilee as remarked by Tristram, and in the waters of Merom one may see tons taken in one day by a drag-net. The fact that the fish of this basin resemble African species was first observed by Josephus. 'There are several kinds of fish in it (Galilee), different both to the taste and sight from those elsewhere.' Also he says of the Capharnaum fountain, 'it produces the Coracin fish' (*BJ* III. x. 8). Several Nilotic species abound. The Chromides, carp-like, are called by the Arabs 'combs,' from their flat shape and projecting spines. Of the Siluridæ, sheat fish (*Clarias Macracanthus*, Arab. *Berboot*) grows to the size of 3 or 4 ft.; its flesh is much prized. Most abundant are the barbel and bream, while dace, bleak, and loaches are found. Eels are in many streams, and swarm in the Orontes. Near Tripoli is a pool full of sacred fish. Fossil fish, beautifully preserved in the Lebanon limestone, are of existing genera. While not strictly fish, we may mention that along the coast are dolphins, seals, and whales—the two latter very rare. The 'badger skins'(AV Ex 26¹⁴) were probably of the Red Sea dugong, a marine mammal, whose skin is used now; and the Hebrew term תַּחַשׁ corresponds to Arab. *tuḥas*, which includes this animal.

Fishes technically are not mentioned in the *creative* acts of the fifth period except as included in the terms שֶׁרֶץ, lit. 'swarmer' (AV 'moving creature'), and הַתַּנִּינִם הַגְּדֹלִים (AV 'great whales,' RV 'great sea-monsters'). The first of these terms occurs more specifically Lv 11¹⁰ שֶׁרֶץ הַמַּיִם. The dominion of man, however, is interesting to note, is given over fish, דְּגֵי הַיָּם (Gn 1²⁸, renewed Gn 9², cf. Ps 8⁸).

Fish were a staple article of diet in Egypt, and their loss part of the plague (Ex 7¹⁸·²¹). The Israelites murmured, 'we remember the fish we did eat freely' (Nu 11⁵). The ceremonial law declared all that had not 'fins and scales' an 'abomination' (Lv 11⁹⁻¹²). The repeated prohibition of worship of anything 'that is in the water under the earth' (Ex 20⁴), 'the likeness of any fish that is in the waters beneath the earth' (Dt 4¹⁸), was needed, for the Philistines worshipped Dagon = 'little fish' (1 S 5²; but see art. DAGON). It has also been alleged (but see Baethgen, *Rel.-ges.*

60) that 'Sîdon was the fish goddess of Phœnicia' (Tristram). This cult existed both in Assyria and India. Solomon, in his wisdom, 'spake of the fishes' (1 K 4³³). In the time of Nehemiah, fish, probably cured, were brought by the Tyrians to Jerusalem (Neh 13¹⁶), where we know there was a 'Fish-gate.' See JERUSALEM.

The 'great fish' (דָּג גָּדוֹל Jon 1¹⁷) prepared' for Jonah has been supposed to be a shark or whale. Both AV and RV tr. κῆτος in Mt 12⁴⁰ 'whale' (RVm 'sea-monster'). The fact that a killer-whale, 21 ft. long, can swallow porpoises and seals would imply that a much larger whale *might* swallow a man. Part of the skeleton of a whale, 43 ft. long, is in the museum of the Syr. Prot. College, Beirût. The carcass of this whale was cast by a storm on the coast near Tyre.

As a type of restoration, Ezk 47⁹·¹⁰ tells us that in the Dead Sea 'shall be a very great multitude of fish.' 'These fish shall be according to their kinds, as the fish of the great sea, exceeding many.'

Fish in NT brought a livelihood to the apostles; they are one of the 'good gifts' (Mt 7¹⁰) twice miraculously multiplied to the multitudes (Mt 17¹⁷ff. 15³⁴ff.). Broiled fish was eaten by our Saviour (Lk 24⁴²) and given by Him to the disciples (Jn 21⁹·¹³). The discrimination between good and bad fish is used as a type of final separation of classes of men (Mt 13⁴⁸). To the early Christians the fish became a sacred symbol, the Greek word ἰχθύς being formed by the initial letters of the four Gr. words used in the confession, 'Jesus Christ, Son of God, Saviour' (Ἰησοῦς Χριστός, Θεοῦ υἱός, Σωτήρ). See *D.C.A. s.v.* Ἰχθύς.

As formerly, so now, in the East fishing is the occupation of the simple and poor, and wholly unknown as a pastime. The methods and means have likewise changed but little. These were principally—

(1) The small net cast by hand, חֵרֶם (Ezk 26⁵·¹⁴ 32³ 47¹⁰, Hab 1¹⁵·¹⁷, Mic 7², Ec 7²⁶), δίκτυον (Mt 4²⁰ etc.), ἀμφίβληστρον (Mt 4¹⁸, Mk 1¹⁶). This is very commonly employed still. The present writer has watched its use at Tabigha (probably Bethsaida), where fish gather at the outlet of streams into the lake.

(2) The seine, מִכְמֹרֶת (Is 19⁸) or מִכְמֶרֶת (Hab 1¹⁵), σαγήνη. This was used in two ways—either let down into the deep and drawn together in a narrowing circle and then drawn into the boat or boats (Lk 5⁴⁻⁹), or as a semicircle drawn to the shore (Mt 13⁴⁸). Both these methods are seen daily.

(3) The hook, חַכָּה (Is 19⁸, Job 41¹), צִנָּה, סִיר (Am 4²), ἄγκιστρον (Mt 17²⁷). This was used with a line, חֶבֶל, but no mention is made of a rod, as fly-fishing is unknown. Hab 1¹⁵ mentions all the three methods we have described.

(4) The harpoon or spear (Job 41⁷), EV 'barbed irons' (שֻׂכּוֹת), 'fish spears' (צִלְצַל דָּגִים). This is a method depicted on Egyptian and Assyrian monuments. At present it is practised only at night by torchlight.

In spite of the mistranslations 'fish pools' (Ca 7⁴ AV), 'ponds for fish' (Is 19¹⁰ AV), there is no evidence that the pools of the Bible were used for fish culture.

The Turkish Government now taxes fishing as an occupation, and also takes 20 per cent. of the price of the fish sold in the seaports, and collects this again if the fish are taken to another port. The fisheries of Merom and Galilee are farmed out to contractors, who forbid all others to engage in the trade.

As an occupation fishing has been honoured by the selection of its followers as apostles; by being the object of Jesus' special favour on two occasions

(Lk 5[1ff.], Jn 21); and chosen as the type of earnest, skilful soul-saving (Mk 1[17], Lk 5[10]).

W. K. EDDY.

FISH-GATE.—See JERUSALEM.

FISH-POOL occurs in AV of Ca 7[4] 'Thine eyes are [like] the fish-pools of Heshbon,' but the exact translation is simply 'pools' (so RV; Heb. בְּרֵכוֹת, LXX λίμναι). See Hitzig, *ad loc.*, and art. HESH-BON. Equally unwarrantable is the introduction of 'fish' in Is 19[10], where AV, following Ibn Ezra, tr. כָּל־עֹשֵׂי שֶׂכֶר אַגְמֵי־נָפֶשׁ 'all that make sluices [and] ponds for fish.' The passage is obscure (see Skinner, *ad loc.*), but probably the correct tr[n] is that of RV, 'all they that work for hire shall be grieved in soul.'* It is possible that the elsewhere unexampled אַגְמֵי (for עֲגַם) was a play suggested by the employment of the 'workers for hire' in the construction of water-tanks (אֲגַמִּים; so Del. quoting Ehrentreu, *ad loc.*). The LXX, while agreeing with this tr[n] of אַגְמֵי־נָפֶשׁ (λυπηθήσονται καὶ τὰς ψυχὰς πονέσουσιν), gives 'manufacturers of strong drink' (ποιοῦντες τὸν ζῦθον),† instead of 'workers for hire.' They must have read שֵׁכָר for שֶׂכֶר.

J. A. SELBIE.

FITCHES.—AV gives fitches in the text in two places. **1.** Ezk 4[9]. Here the Heb. is כֻּסֶּמֶת *kuṣṣemeth*, tr[d] in AVm and RV *spelt*. We believe the plant intended is the *kirseneh* or *kirsenneh* of the Arabs, *Vicia Ervilia*, L. The same Heb. word is used in two other places (Ex 9[32], Is 28[25]), where AV has *rye* and RV *spelt* (see RYE). **2.** Is 28[25. 27]. Here the Heb. is קֶצַח *keẓaḥ*. This is the *nutmeg flower, Nigella sativa*, L., a Ranunculaceous plant, cultivated everywhere in the East for its black seeds, which are used as a condiment and a medicine. It is called in Arab. *shûniz*, or *shihnîz*, and *habbat el-barakah*, *i.e.* the *seed of blessing*, or *el-habbat es-sauda*, *i.e.* the *black seed*. An Arab. proverb says, 'in the black seed is the medicine for every disease.' Avicenna recommends it in dyspepsia, and for bronchial and other affections. Orientals often put a pinch of the seeds on the middle of the upper surface of the flat loaves of bread before baking. In baking they adhere. Pliny alludes to their use by bakers (*Nat. Hist.* xix. 52). They are believed to assist digestion. They have a warm aromatic flavour and carminative properties. Like other seeds produced in small quantities, as *cummin*, they are often beaten out with a stick, as mentioned in Is 28[27], instead of being threshed out with the *môrag*.

G. E. POST.

FLAG.—Two Heb. words are tr[d] by *flag*. **1.** אָחוּ ('âḥu; ἄχει [in LXX of Sir 40[16] this was supposed till 1896 to represent the Heb. 'âḥû] βούτομον) occurs in three connexions. (*a*) Where the kine feed in an 'âḥu (Gn 41[2. 18]). (*b*) Where Bildad asks, 'Can the *rush* (גֹּמֶא, πάπυρος) grow up without mire? can the *flag* (אָחוּ, βούτομον) grow without water?' (Job 8[11]). (*c*) In a passage (Hos 13[15]) where both AV and RV, following the LXX, give *brethren* for אַחִים 'âḥim, which the *Oxf. Heb. Lex.* regards as a plural of אָח, abbreviated from אֲחָוִים 'âḥâwim, the context seeming to point to a water plant, withering before the E. wind, which dries up its spring. In the passage in Job the *gôme* and the 'âḥu occur in the two members of a parallelism. RVm gives for *gôme* 'papyrus,' and for 'âḥu 'reed-grass' (cf. Ebers, *Egypten u. die Bücher Moses*, 338 f.). The latter is no more definite than *flag*, and therefore only confuses the question of identity by another term. We

---

have the authority of the LXX that the *gôme* was the πάπυρος, *papyrus*, and the 'âḥu, βούτομον, which some believe to be *Cyperus esculentus*, L., the edible galingale, and others *Butomus umbellatus*, L., the flowering rush, both swamp plants. אָחוּ (Gn 41[2. 18]) should be rendered 'in the flowering rushes,' or 'in the sedges,' or 'in the fens.' Similarly, the doubtful אָחִים 'âḥîm (Hos 13[15]). The same indefiniteness is found in the Arab. term *rabi*', which means literally 'spring,' and refers to 'spring herbage,' and *half*, which refers to *Gramineæ* and *Cyperaceæ* in general. It is also found in the English 'grass.'

2. סוּף (*ṣûph*, ἕλος, *carectum*) is used (*a*) of the *sedgy* or *reedy* plants on a river's bank (Ex 2[3. 5], Is 19[6]); (*b*) of *weeds* (Jn 2[5]), meaning *sea-weeds*. From the presence of these, and perhaps of other marine growths, as of coral, the Red Sea was named יַם־סוּף (*yam-ṣûph*).

G. E. POST.

FLAGON occurs five times in AV, but in only one of these instances is the tr[n] retained by RV, namely Is 22[24], where both VSS tr. כְּלֵי הַנְּבָלִים by 'vessels of flagons.' נֶבֶל or נֵבֶל (when not used for a musical instrument) generally means a leather pitcher. Here it is perhaps an earthenware bottle. On the other hand, RV introduces 'flagons' in two instances where it is not found in AV, namely Ex 25[39] 37[16] (in both קָשׂוֹת). This tr[n] is probably correct (see CUP), although RV gives 'cups' for the same Heb. word in Nu 4[7]. In all these three passages AV has 'covers.' In the remaining four instances where AV gives 'flagons,' the Heb. is אֲשִׁישָׁה (2 S 6[19], 1 Ch 16[3], Hos 3[1] [אֲשִׁישֵׁי עֲנָבִים], Ca 2[5] [אֲשִׁישׁוֹת]; cf. אֲשִׁישֵׁי קִיר חֲרָשֶׂת 'the raisin-cakes [AV 'foundations'] of Kir-hareseth,' Is 16[7]). The meaning of this word is a 'pressed cake . . . composed of meal, oil, and *dibs*' (W. R. Smith, *OTJC*[1] 434, n. 7). Hence in 2 S 6[19], 1 Ch 16[3], RV gives 'cake of raisins' for AV 'flagon [of wine],' in Hos 3[1] 'cakes of raisins' for 'flagons of wine,' and in Ca 2[5] 'raisins' (RVm 'cakes of raisins') for 'flagons.' The LXX has in 2 S 6[19] λάγανον ἀπὸ τηγάνου, in 1 Ch 16[3] ἀμορείτην, in Hos 3[1] πέμματα μετὰ σταφίδος, and in Ca 2[5] μύροι. Luther, who like AV adopted a false Rabbinical derivation and interpretation of אֲשִׁישָׁה, tr. in 2 S 6[19] and 1 Ch 16[3] *ein Nössel Wein*, and in Hos 3[1] *eine Kanne Weins*. In Ca 2[5] he has *Blumen*. In Kautzsch's *AT* we find for 2 S 6[19] and 1 Ch 16[3] *Rosinenkuchen*, and for Hos 3[1] and Ca 2[5] *Traubenkuchen*. See further under FOOD, p. 32[b].

J. A. SELBIE.

FLAX (פִּשְׁתָּה *pishtâh*, λίνον, *linum*).—The Heb. and its equivalents in Gr., Lat., and Eng. are used (1) for the *growing plant* (Ex 9[31]); (2) for the *stalks* when cut (Jos 2[6] פִּשְׁתֵּי הָעֵץ, λινοκάλαμη, *stipulæ lini*); (3) for a *wick* made of the fibres (Is 42[3] 43[17], AV 'tow,' RV 'flax,' marg. 'a wick'). The root form פֵּשֶׁת *pêsheth*, with suffix פִּשְׁתִּי *pishti*, LXX ὀθόνιά μου, is also used for the flax fibres (Hos 2[5. 9]). The plural of the same, פִּשְׁתִּים *pishtîm*, is used for the *hackled fibres* (Pr 31[13], Is 19[9]); these are twisted into *cords* (Jg 15[14]) or woven into stuff (Dt 22[11]). The shorter fibres are called נְעֹרֶת *nĕ'ôreth* = *tow* (Jg 16[9], Is 1[31]). The plural *pishtîm* is also used for *linen* (Lv 13[48. 52]), as well as for *linen garments* (vv.[47. 59], LXX ἱματίῳ στιππυίνῳ, Ezk 44[17] στολὰς λινᾶς).

Flax, *Linum sativum*, L., is a plant of the order *Linaceæ*, which has been cultivated from the earliest periods of the world's history. It is a perennial, with slender stalks, 2 to 3 ft. high, linear-lanceolate leaves, and showy blue flowers. Its stalks produce the strong fibres out of which linen is manufactured. These stalks were dried on the flat roofs of the houses (Jos 2[6]), then steeped in water to cause the decay of the pulp,

---

* Rashi has 'ponds of *rest*,' where the waters rest and are retained! Ibn Ezra gives 'where are the souls of the fish'; this is also adopted by Kimchi in his *Lexicon* ('pools in which they hunt fish'); in his *Comm.* he mentions it, but he himself offers the same explanation as the RV.

† Properly 'beer,' which was a favourite Egyptian beverage.

then hackled (Is 19[9]) to straighten the fibres and comb out the shorter ones, which are *tow* (Jg 16[9], Is 1[31]). It was regarded as a crop of importance (Ex 9[31], Hos 2[9]). Linen garments were used by the priests, etc. (Lv 13[47. 59]); the material is usually spoken of as שֵׁשׁ *shêsh* (a name still retained in the Arab. *shâsh*, which is used for the grade of cotton cloth known in English as *cheese-cloth*). The mummies of Egypt were swathed in linen bandages.

G. E. POST.

FLAYING.—See CRIMES AND PUNISHMENTS.

FLEA (פַּרְעֹשׁ *par'ôsh*, ψύλλος, *pulex*).—An insect, *Pulex irritans*, L., universal in warm climates, and a great pest to man and the animals which it infests. Insignificant as it is, its bite is very irritating, often causing considerable swelling and intolerable itching, which robs its victim of many an hour of sleep, and makes him ridiculous in his frequently vain efforts to catch his tormentor. The habit of the natives of the East of sleeping in the same clothes which they wear by day, and spreading their beds on the mats on which they sit, contributes much to the multiplication of the insect in their houses and camps. Fleas swarm esp. in the filthy tents of the Bedawîn, and in stables and dog kennels. The flea is mentioned by David (1 S 24[14]),* who compares himself to this contemptible insect, in order to ridicule the insensate character of Saul's persecution by likening it to the vain hunt above alluded to. In Ex 8[16] RVm has 'fleas' for 'lice' (wh. see).

G. E. POST.

FLESH, represented by בָּשָׂר, שְׁאֵר in OT, and by σάρξ and κρέας in NT. שְׁאֵר occurs very seldom in comp. with the constant word בָּשָׂר, but seems to cover some of the same meanings, particularly flesh for food, and flesh of consanguinity. Cf. Ps 73[26] 78[20. 27], Pr 11[17], Jer 51[35], Lv 25[49]. κρέας is only used twice in NT, and each time in the phrase κρέα φαγεῖν, Ro 14[21], 1 Co 8[13]. It is impossible to do justice to the biblical uses of this term *Flesh* without clearly distinguishing at least the following five meanings :—

1. *Substance of an animal body*, whether of beast or of man (*e.g.* Gn 41[2], Lv 4[11], Job 31[31], 1 Co 15[39]). For this use of the term in its application to FOOD and to SACRIFICES, see under these words. It denotes the living human body in such places as Ex 4[7], Lv 13[10] 17[14]. Indeed, through a great part of OT flesh is equivalent to the whole human BODY, on the principle mentioned *s.v.*, in which application, it is to be noted, that the LXX often renders בָּשָׂר (sing.), in accordance with Gr. idiom, by the plural σάρκες (*e.g.* Gn 40[19], Nu 12[12], Job 32[25]), and even by σῶμα (*e.g.* Lv 15[2], 1 K 21[27]).

2. *Relation, of consanguinity or by marriage* (*e.g.* Gn 2[24] 37[27], Neh 5[5], Is 58[7], Mt 19[5], 1 Co 10[18]). The literal word is used in the orig. in places where the versions, our own included, employ a periphrasis 'near of kin' (*e.g.* Lv 18[6] 25[49]). In the same significance, the fuller phrase 'flesh and bones' is peculiarly biblical (*e.g.* Gn 2[23] 29[14], Jg 9[2], 2 S 5[1] 19[12. 13], Eph 5[30], cf. Lk 24[39]).

3. *Creature nature generally, human nature* particularly. In this use it can denote all terrestrial beings possessing life (Gn 7[21]); especially the finite earthly creature in contrast with God and with the spirit which immediately comes from God. 'The Egyptians are men, and not God; and their horses flesh, and not spirit' (Is 31[3]). The frailness and dependence of man is the thing marked by this contrast (*e.g.* Gn 6[3], Job 34[15], Ps 56[4] 78[39], Is 40[6-8] quoted 1 P 1[24]). There is a persistent tendency in translators and commentators to ignore this peculiarly biblical antithesis, and

* Its mention in 1 S 26[20] is due to corruption in MT (see
Driver, Wellh., Budde, *ad loc.*).

confound it with the Greek antithesis between material and immaterial. Further, though finite and creaturely weakness is implied in it, there is not necessarily any moral disparagement, *e.g.* 'all flesh' is used for the 'whole human race' in connexions that are most honourable, *e.g.* Ps 65[2] 145[21], Is 40[5], Jl 2[28]. Conclusive as to this is the use of 'flesh' for the human nature of our Lord (Jn 1[14], Ro 1[3] 9[5], 1 Ti 3[16]). In the same line with this stands the more expanded phrase 'flesh and blood' for human nature on its earthly side in contrast with something greater than itself (Mt 16[17], 1 Co 15[50], Gal 1[16], Eph 6[12], He 2[14], to which should perhaps be added Jn 1[13]). This phrase is peculiar to the NT, though germane to the OT idea 'the life of the flesh is in the blood,' and the beginning of the usage can be traced to the OT Apocr. writers (cf. Sir 14[18] 17[31]). It is common in Rabbinical literature. This whole biblical use of the term 'flesh' in application to man means that he is so called from his creaturely nature, or from his nature on its creaturely side.

4. As *one constituent of human nature* (the corporeal) combined or contrasted with the others. OT usage presents a variety of such combinations. The whole of man is expressed as 'flesh' and 'soul' in Ps 63[1], Job 13[14] 14[22]; as 'flesh' and 'heart' in Ps 73[26], Ezk 44[7. 9], Ec 11[10], Pr 14[30]; as 'flesh,' 'heart,' and 'soul,' Ps 84[2], in all which a duality of outer and inner, or lower and higher in man, is plainly intended. But so far is 'flesh' from being despised in these contrasts that it is joined with the higher elements in the relation of the whole man to God and to his future (?) hopes, as in Ps 63[1] 16[9] 84[2], Job 19[26]. In the NT its use in this sense for the lower element in man, without any ethical disparagement, though not very frequent, is still clear. In a sufficient number of passages it occurs coupled with 'spirit,' in the Pauline writings as well as others, to show that these two are the natural elements of which man is made up, exactly as 'flesh' and 'soul,' 'flesh' and 'heart' are in the OT (*e.g.* Mt 26[41], Ro 2[28. 29], 1 Co 5[5]). 'Flesh' is used by St. Paul of corporeal presence, cognizable by the senses, in contrast to fellowship in 'spirit' (2 Co 5[16], Col 2[1. 5]), indeed of man's earthly or bodily life without moral qualification (Gal 2[20], Ph 1[22]). Even when man's sinful state is the topic, the dual nature is sometimes expressed in the usual terms; 'desires of the flesh and of the mind' (Eph 2[3]), 'defilement of the flesh and spirit' (2 Co 7[1]), seem to mean that man's nature, in both its constituent parts, is affected by sin. There is a use of this antithesis, between flesh and spirit, in application to Christ, which points to lower and higher elements in His personality quite peculiar to Himself (*e.g.* Ro 1[3. 4], 1 Ti 3[16], 1 P 3[18]).

5. Its *ethical* or *doctrinal sense*. Besides the morally indifferent applications of flesh already discussed, there is in the NT, and esp. in the Pauline writings, a use of it which is charged with ethical or doctrinal content. It is thus used once in contrast with 'mind' (Ro 7[25]), more frequently with 'spirit' (Ro 8[4. 5. 6. 7] RV 8. 9. 12. 13, Gal 5[16-25] 6[8]). In the same manner the adjectives 'fleshly,' 'carnal' are contrasted with 'spiritual' in Ro 7[14], 1 Co 3[1. 3. 4], 2 Co 1[12], Col 2[18] 'fleshly mind,' orig. 'mind of the flesh.'* That in the connexions cited above flesh with its adjective has reference to the principle of sin and its seat in man's fallen nature, while 'spirit' and 'spiritual' refer to the principle of the regenerate or divine life in man,

* There occurs in the same writings a quite unethical use of
'carnal' as equivalent to 'corporeal' or 'earthly,' *e.g.* Ro 15[27],
1 Co 9[11], 2 Co 3[3] 10[4], He 7[16]; for the complications both of reading and rendering in these passages, created by the use of
σαρκικός or σάρκινος, see Trench, *N.T. Synonyms, s.v.*

will hardly be questioned. But various have been the accounts given of the *rationale* of this metaphorical or indirect use of flesh and 'fleshly' in a theological or doctrinal sense. Writers like Holsten, Pfleiderer, Schenkel make strenuous efforts, without much success, to derive this peculiarly Pauline application of the term from the older sense of it as denoting the weakness and frailty of man's nature. The only account which seems to satisfy all the ideas involved is that the 'carnal' denotes the sinful element in man's nature, because that element entering his nature now in the ordinary course of human production is an inheritance of the flesh; whereas the 'spiritual' is that which comes into it from above, or is given in the New Birth. This explanation is confirmed by our Lord's words, reported in Jn 3[6]. For some further remarks on this question and on the possible connexion of all the meanings of flesh here noted, see PSYCHOLOGY.   J. LAIDLAW.

FLESH-HOOK.—See FOOD.

FLESHLY, FLESHY.—Modern editions of AV have retained the distinction between 'fleshly' and 'fleshy' of 1611. Fleshly is that which belongs to the flesh and not the spirit, *carnal*. It occurs in NT 2 Co 1[12], 1 P 2[11] (σαρκικόs), Col 2[18] 'fleshly mind' (νοῦs τῆs σαρκόs, 'mind of the flesh'). In Ad. Est 14[10] the meaning is apparently simply *mortal* (σάρκινοs). Fleshy is that which is made of flesh (and not of stone), soft, *tender*, Sir 17[16], 2 Co 3[3] (σάρκινοs). The distinction did not appear in the earlier versions: Wyc. Tind. Gen. Bish. have 'fleshly' in 2 Co 3[3], Cov. has 'fleshy.' Nor was it observed by Eng. writers of the day: T. Wright (1604), *Passions*, v. iv. 212, says, 'Fleshy concupiscence deserveth rather the name of Mercenarie Lust then Love,' and Culpepper and Cole, *Anat.* I. xvii. 45, 'Such as are given to fleshy desires have larger Kidneys than ordinary.' But once made it is well worth maintaining.   J. HASTINGS.

FLESH-POT.—See FOOD.

FLIES.—See FLY and PLAGUE.

FLINT (in OT חַלָּמִישׁ, ἀκρότομοs, στερεὰ πέτρα; צֹר, ἀκρότομοs, πέτρα, ψῆφοs; צֻר, στερεὰ πέτρα; in Apocr. ἀκρότομοs, κόχλαξ) is the term by which the foregoing Heb. words are rendered, in AV generally, and in RV uniformly. The reference in every case is to a rock or stone whose characteristic quality is hardness or sharpness. The Gr. equivalents have a general rather than a definite meaning, ἀκρότομοs being elsewhere (Sir 40[15] 48[17]) tr[d] 'hard' (RV sheer) rock,' while in Is 2[21] 51[1] στερεὰ πέτρα stands for צוּר (rock); though, on the other hand, in Job 22[24] צוּר is represented in Vulg. by *silex*. On the whole, flint is the substance which best fulfils the conditions stated, and in the passages where small stones rather than masses of rock are referred to it is probably the true rendering.

חַלָּמִישׁ corresponds to Assyr. *elmēšu* (ZDMG xl. 728), which seems to mean any hard stone used for striking fire, even rock crystal or diamond. According to Hommel (PSBA, xv. 291), *elmēšu* is abbreviated from *algamišu* (Heb. אַלְגָּבִישׁ Ezk 13[11. 13] 38[22]), both being variants of *gilgamish* or *gibilgamish*, which is a synonym of *Gišdubar*, an ancient Bab. fire deity.

Flint is the name given to the rock from which Moses brought water in the wilderness (Dt 8[15], Ps 114[8], Wis 11[4]). Flints were the primitive instruments of circumcision (Ex 4[25] RV, Jos 5[2. 3] RV). In the latter passage LXX expands חֻרְבוֹת צֻרִים into μαχαίραs πετρίναs ἐκ πέτραs ἀκροτόμου. The LXX additions to Joshua relate how these knives of flint were preserved as a memorial in

Timnath-serah, and were buried with Joshua there (21[42d] 24[30a]). In 1 Mac 10[73] the absence of flints in a plain is given as a reason why cavalry should not be encountered there, as slingers would thus be at a disadvantage. The word used is κόχλαξ, and it is found in a similar connexion in the LXX of 1 S 14[14], which, however, does not correspond with the MT (Wellhausen, *Text der BB. Sam.* 87, 88; Driver, *Heb. Text of Sam.* 82, 83). In the Song of Moses 'oil from the rocky flint' (Dt 32[13]) is a poetical way of describing olives growing on rocky soil (see Job 29[6]). In Job 28[9], to illustrate man's power and skill, it is said that the miner puts forth his hand upon the flinty rock, and overturns the mountains. The hoofs of the Assyrian horses are compared to flint (Is 5[28]), which is also an emblem of prophetic resoluteness (Is 50[7], Ezk 3[9]).

Flint is a form of silica, a mineral which occurs in its purest condition as quartz. Flint is found in bands and nodules in certain calcareous rocks, notably in chalk, in various parts of the world. It is exceedingly hard, and breaks with a glassy fracture and sharp edges. When pieces of it are struck together, or against steel, sparks are emitted, and this method of obtaining fire has been used from the earliest times. It is probably alluded to in 2 Mac 10[3]. Flints are often dark coloured owing to impurities. Their origin is one of the problems of geology not yet completely solved, but it is supposed that the siliceous framework of certain marine organisms was dissolved, and afterwards deposited in cavities, or actually substituted for the material of other organic remains.

A great part of Palestine and the Sinaitic peninsula is composed of Cretaceous strata, which pass on the W. into Nummulitic (Eocene) limestone. In both of these formations flints are found; and in some of the strata, especially those which line the Jordan Valley, they are particularly abundant (Green, *Physical Geology*, 231–33; Hull, *SWP* 61).   JAMES PATRICK.

FLOCK. — Four Heb. words are tr[d] flock:— 1. עֵדֶר *'ēder*, ποίμνιον, ἀγέλη. This word, when used alone (Gn 29[3. 8], Jg 5[16], 1 S 17[34], Ps 78[52], Ca 1[7] etc.), usually signifies a *flock* of sheep or goats, or both mingled. It corresponds to the Arab. *katị'*. The exception to this is in Gn 32[16. 19], where it is tr[d] *drove*. צֹאן (עֶדְרֵי Gn 29[2], Jl 1[18], Mic 5[8]) signifies *flocks of sheep*, and עֶדְרֵי בָקָר, in the same sentence in Jl, is *herds of cattle*, and עֵדֶר הָעִזִּים (Ca 4[1] 6[5]) *flock of goats*. עֵדֶר יהוה (Jer 13[17]) is the *flock of J"*, that is, *God's people* (cf. Zec 10[3]), and עֵדֶר הָרֹחֲלִים (Ca 6[6]) a *flock of ewes*. מִגְדַּל עֵדֶר the *tower of 'eder (flock)* (Gn 35[21]) is a place near Bethlehem, mentioned again (Mic 4[8]) as the 'hill' (marg. 'Heb. Ophel') of the daughter of Zion. Some suppose it to have been a tower on the hill Ophel at Jerusalem. If Ophel be Zion, the allusion would be perfect in its details. See HERD.

2. צֹאן *zō'n*. This word, which means *sheep*, is the original of most of the passages in OT tr[d] *flock*. It corresponds to the Arab. *dân*, but *dân* refers to *sheep* as distinguished by having wool, from *goats*, which are known by the name of *ma'z*. *Zō'n* may include both, Gn 38[17] RV (cf. AV) 'I will send thee a kid of the goats from the flock' (*zō'n*). In some cases the context makes it clear that it does not include both, as in 1 S 25[2] 'he had three thousand sheep (*zō'n*), and a thousand goats (*'izzîm*), and he was shearing his sheep (*zō'n*) in Carmel.' Where *zō'n* and *bâkâr* are mentioned together, they are always tr[d] *flocks* and *herds*. It would be better, in every case where the context does not clearly demand the rendering *flock*, to translate *zō'n* sheep.

3. מִקְנֵה הַצֹּאן *mikneh hazzō'n* (Gn 47[17]), is tr[d] AV, RV 'flocks,' RVm 'cattle of flocks.' It would

have been better rendered *possession of sheep*, and *miḳneh habbâḳâr*, in the same verse, *possession of oxen* (cf. Ec 2⁷).

4. צֹאן *miḳneh* (Ps 78⁴⁸), is trᵈ AV, RV 'flocks.' It is elsewhere generally rendered 'cattle'; once 'possessions' (Ec 2⁷).

The NT words for flock are ποίμνη and ποίμνιον, the latter of which is used exclusively in a fig. sense of the Church (Lk 12³², Ac 20²⁸, 1 P 5² etc.).

G. E. POST.

FLOOD (Gn 6–9¹⁷).—A story connected with the early history of man, which tells how, in consequence of their sins, especially those of violence, God destroyed by a flood the whole race, excepting only Noah and his family and two (or seven) pairs of every animal. These were saved in a huge ark or chest, which Noah had been directed to make when first warned of the coming flood. As the waters were abating, Noah sent forth a raven which did not return, and afterwards a dove twice at a week's interval, in order to ascertain whether the ground was dry. This was shown to be so by the dove returning the second time with an olive leaf in her mouth. The ark finally settled on Mt. Ararat. On leaving the ark, Noah offered up a sacrifice which appeased God, who promised never again to destroy the earth with a flood.

Simple and uniform as this story appears, it is a fact admitting of no reasonable doubt that the account of Genesis is really composed of two Flood stories, which, while agreeing in general purport, differ considerably both in character and detail. One belongs to the early source of the Hexateuch known as J, the other to the post-exilic P. They may be clearly distinguished here by the names of God and other well-known characteristics of these documents. The sections ascribed to J in Kautzsch's *AT* are 6¹⁻⁸ 7¹⁻⁵. ⁷⁻¹⁰. ¹². ¹⁶ᵇ⁻¹⁷. ²²⁻²³ 8²ᵇ⁻³ᵃ. ⁶⁻¹². ¹³ᵇ. ²⁰⁻²², to P 6⁹⁻²² 7⁶. ¹¹. ¹³⁻¹⁶ᵃ. ¹⁸⁻²¹ 7²⁴ᵃ⁻⁸²ᵃ 8³ᵇ⁻⁵. ¹³ᵃ. ¹⁴⁻¹⁹ 9¹⁻¹⁷ (on 7⁸. ⁹ see below). It will be sufficient to notice that in P we find the minute directions regarding the construction and size of the ark, the blessing of Noah, the laws against murder and eating blood, the covenant of the rainbow; in J only we have the picturesque narrative of sending out the raven and the dove, and the sacrifice of Noah, which so pleased J″ that He determined never again to curse the ground. In some respects the accounts of J and P contradict each other. (*a*) According to P one pair of *every* kind of animals is to be selected (6¹⁸⁻²⁰), according to J seven pairs of clean and two of unclean (7². ³). But in 7⁸. ⁹, where the actual entry is made, a reviser has, it would seem, combined the statements of J and P so as to agree with P. As it stands, the distinction between clean and unclean animals in that verse is purposeless, and indeed has the effect of emphasizing what appears like an act of disobedience on Noah's part, who took only one instead of seven pairs of clean animals as directed in 7². In J this verse must have run much as follows: 'Of clean beasts, seven and seven, and, of unclean beasts, two and two, went unto Noah into the ark.' In P the statement was probably, 'Of the fowl after its kind, and of the cattle after its kind, and of everything that creepeth upon the ground after its kind, two of every (sort) did he bring into the ark, as God commanded Noah.' (*b*) According to P it was 150 days before the waters began to subside (8³), and it was 8 months and 13 days before the tops of the mountains were visible (cf. 7¹¹ and 8⁵), and a whole year and 10 days before the earth was perfectly dry (8¹⁴). According to J the duration of the Flood was only 40 days (7¹² 8⁶), and even before this the water had considerably abated (8²ᵇ. ³ᵃ. ⁶⁻¹⁰. ¹². ¹³ᵇ). (*c*). What is in P a covenant with Noah that the waters should 'no more become a flood to destroy all flesh' (9¹⁵), is in J the self-deliberation of

J″ in consequence of Noah's sweet-smelling sacrifice (8²¹. ²²). See HEXATEUCH.

I. HISTORICITY OF THE FLOOD.—Until comparatively recent times the belief in a deluge covering the whole world and destroying all men and animals except those providentially preserved in the ark was practically universal among Christians. The fossil remains of marine animals, and the Flood traditions common to people in so many different parts of the world, were confidently appealed to as establishing the truth of the Bible story. Our increased knowledge of geology on the one hand and of comparative mythology on the other have now shown the little value of such evidence, and on these and other grounds this belief has been now surrendered by most biblical scholars as untenable. (*a*) It has been frequently pointed out that the whole quantity of moisture contained in the world, whether in an aqueous or vaporous form, if all reduced to water, would not be nearly enough to cover the highest mountains, supposing that the earth's surface was in anything like its present condition. But there is no evidence or scientific probability that the whole surface was ever so contracted or so levelled as to admit such a possibility. (*b*) Again, a thorough examination and a comparison of the numerous Flood myths make it impossible to refer them all to one single event. (*c*). Anthropological science points in the same direction. The diversity of the human race and of language alike makes it extremely improbable that men were derived from a single pair, and this, together with what we know of the early civilization of man, makes it impossible that a universal Flood should have occurred within at least many centuries of the time assigned by biblical chronology. The early relics of primitive man found in caves, ancient graves, etc., all over the world, point to an unbroken succession of human beings, their advance in civilization developing by gradual stages, and the whole extending over many thousands of years.

(*d*) But, after all, the most obvious difficulties are those which lie on the surface in the narrative itself, supposing that it describes a flood extending over the whole world *as we now know it*. Noah is said to have collected together animals of every kind, one pair at least of each. Let us try to imagine the long journeys necessary to different parts of the world, including the Tropics and the Arctic Regions, and that in an age when the difficulties and dangers of travelling must have made it almost impossible, and the difficulty of capturing and bringing home the animals when captured. How many years will it still take the Royal Zoological Society, with all the resources of modern civilization, to collect even *single* specimens of all the known larger animals of the world, to say nothing of the hundreds of species still unknown, nothing of the myriads of insects, *crustaceæ*, etc., included in the 'creeping things' of the Bible! Again, the dimensions of the ark could not possibly have allowed room for the housing of all the creatures; for, supposing that they were shut up in separate cells ('nests,' Gn 6¹⁴ RVm), almost as much space would have been required for passages to get at them as for the cells themselves. We have also to take into account the immense amount of room required for the storage of food, especially that needed for the larger animals, such as hay for the elephants, and animals of different sorts for the *carnivoræ*, besides all the food necessary for some time after the Flood, before revived vegetation should make fresh food procurable. Even if we could suppose that the dimensions of the ark permitted all this, how would it have been possible to keep all these animals alive? The polar bear would have required very different conditions from the tiger or the boa-constrictor. How, again, is it conceivable that eight persons should have been sufficient to attend to the wants of all these animals, as well as to their own ? But besides all this, there is no provision for making the ark seaworthy. It is merely a huge wooden box liable to capsize, and quite incapable of weathering a storm. The difficulties here pointed out readily suggest the true answer. The Flood was not in the writer's view universal, as we should understand a universal Flood, simply because the world he is writing of is a totally different world from ours. It is a very little world. Men and animals are all living within easy reach of each other. Man is still the lord of creation. He can gather together the animals to be saved, whether beast of the field or fowl of the air, at his will. No difficulties, even such as would have occurred in the writer's own day, have any place in that ideal world of the distant past, where holy men walked with God, and there was no need of miracles, because everything was of course so different. That the writers and compilers of Genesis sincerely believed the story we need have no doubt, but in the light of scientific and historical criticism it must be frankly recognized as one of those many stories or legends which are found in the folk-lore and early literature of all peoples.

II. THE RELATION OF THE BIBLE FLOOD STORIES TO SIMILAR STORIES OF OTHER PEOPLES.—It was formerly supposed that the many Flood stories found in different parts of the world were all traditions of the Bible Deluge brought by various peoples from the ancient cradle of the human race. A comparison, however, of the stories with one another and with the Bible narrative makes it quite clear that they stand severally in a very different relation to the latter, and are due to many different causes. We may roughly divide these stories, according to their resemblance to the Flood story of Genesis, into the following classes :—

i. First and foremost stands the *Babylonian or Accadian* account of the Deluge. This is so like the Bible story, both in its general drift and many of its details, that it cannot be other than a different version of the same. The Babylonian legend itself exists in two forms. One is contained in the fragments of Berosus, an Egyptian priest of the 3rd cent. B.C., who wrote a history of Babylon. The second is contained in a cuneiform inscription on tablets preserved in the British Museum, and first deciphered by George Smith in 1872.

(*a*) Of these the first is very short and of comparatively little importance, except that some differences of detail in comparison with the other prove that the Babylonian story had a wide currency. The main differences are the clay which Xisuthros, the hero of the Flood, finds on the legs of the birds when they return for the second time, and the translation of Xisuthros' daughter and the pilot of the ship, as well as that of Xisuthros himself and his wife.

(*b*) The story of Berosus is altogether thrown into the shade by the far fuller and more circumstantial account found on the Accadian tablets. These contain an epic poem in 12 parts. Each part is connected with a sign of the Zodiac, and the 11th, containing the Flood story, has the sign corresponding to Aquarius, 'the water-bearer.' In this part the deified Sît-napišti, or, as the name is sometimes written, Khasisadra (Xisuthros), communicates the history of the Flood at the mouth of the Euphrates to his grandson Gisdubar (the Nimrod of Genesis). Ea, the god of wisdom, reveals to Sît-napišti the intention of the gods of Surippak—Anu, Bel, etc.—to bring a Flood, and commands him to build a ship, and save what he can of the germ of life. Sît-napišti

expostulates on the absurdity of building a ship on dry land, but finally consents. The making of the ship is then given in some detail, among other things its dimensions (according to G. Smith, 600 cubits long, 60 broad, 60 high ; omitted by Sayce), *and the pouring of bitumen over its sides, inside and out.* Food was brought into the ship, including beer and wine, and also all that he had of gold and silver. 'Slaves and concubines, the cattle of the field, the beasts of the field, the sons of the people : all of these did I bring up.' The ship was built by the help of the sun-god Samas, who fixed the season for the Flood on the evening before Sît-napišti *shut the door.* A highly poetical description is then given of the storm, brought about by the direct agency of the gods of wind, water, etc., so terrible that even the gods trembled and sought refuge in the heaven of Anu, where they crowded in a heap 'like a dog in his kennel,' and gods and goddesses wept for pity. For six days and nights the storm continues, and subsides on the seventh. The sea begins to dry. Sît-napišti opens the windows and sees the corpses floating on the water. On the horizon he sees land, and the ship is steered for the mountain of Nizir, which it reaches the second day. *On the seventh day after this he sends forth a dove, which finds no resting-place and returns* ; then a swallow, which does the same ; and lastly *a raven, which feeds on the carrion and does not return.* The animals are sent forth to the four winds, and *a sacrifice is offered on an altar which he builds* on the peak of the mountain. The gods *smelt the savour,* and 'gathered like flies over the sacrifice.' Thereupon the great goddess *lighted up the rainbow* which Anu had created. Bel, angry with the gods that his will had not been fully carried out, alone refused to come to the altar. He stayed by the ship and would have stopped the exit of the survivors ; but Adar explained that Ea had revealed the counsel of the gods to Sît-napišti. Then Ea himself expostulates with Bel for wishing to destroy the faithful with the sinners. Better at any rate to send wild beasts, or famine, or plague. After all, it was only by a dream that he had revealed the determination of the gods. Then Bel enters the ship and very graciously *makes a covenant with Sît-napišti,* saying that henceforth he and his wife are to be as gods, and Sît-napišti is to dwell at the mouth of the river. (Sayce, *Fresh Light,* ch. ii.)

This story is said by experts to be as old at least as 3000 years B.C. That the early Hebrews derived the story from Babylonia, and not *vice versâ,* may be considered a practical certainty. While Babylonia from the days of the Patriarchs was highly advanced in civilization, the Jews, even far down into their history, were comparatively simple and far less civilized even than the Canaanitish tribes, who themselves derived their culture from Babylon. The Babylonian language and script had already before the Exodus become naturalized in Palestine, and been made, as the Tel el-Amarna tablets show, the official means of communication between the Babylonian court and the various Canaanitish tribes. Thus there was more than one channel by which a popular story of Babylonia might become part of Jewish folk-lore. At the same time the variations in the story suggest that it is likely to have passed through many mouths before it reached its Bible form. Even the differences in its religious character are more probably due to gradual changes of thought and feeling than to a single literary process. It is, however, quite possible that if several variations of the story were, as is probable, current, some few particulars in the Bible story may be actually more original than in the Accadian version. The sending out of the birds in the latter is rather pointless, as the non-return of the raven, which fed upon the corpses, proved nothing. Both the J and P stories are derived from the Babylonian, each document selecting for the most part, and sometimes enlarging upon, those details which best accorded with its own character and aim.

ii. A very large number of Flood stories bear only a very general and probably accidental resemblance to the biblical or Accadian Deluge. The mere fact that a legend has to do with a flood, even though it be a universal one, is not enough to constitute any real relationship to the Bible Deluge-story. For such legends can be proved to have arisen from several different causes. These causes may be roughly divided into three classes : **1.** Some theory of Creation which connects it with water as perhaps a creative element. Flood stories dealing with Creation bear comparison with 'the deep' of Gn 1[2] rather than with Noah's Flood. Thus the Binnas in the Malay Peninsula held that the earth was originally completely covered with a hard crust. God in early ages broke through the crust, so that the water covered the whole world. Out of the water He afterwards let rise Mt. Lulumet and other hills, as well as the plain on which the Binnas now live. This conception of the centre of the world as a vast body of water we find again in a Flood story of the Acawoio (British Guiana), and is probably to be understood in the biblical phrase 'the water under the earth' (Ex 20[4]), the idea being that the land floated on the water. **2.** Most frequently, however, the Flood story is the highly coloured tradition of some historical event or extraordinary natural phenomenon.

A. *Among island and coastland peoples* (a) the early settlement of their ancestors, who came in boats across the ocean. In such stories the particular land in which they live was the land of refuge from the great Deluge. In the story of the Binnas this tradition is combined with the notion of Creation. The primeval man and woman were created in a boat, which moved over the waters until at last it stranded on dry land. (b) The appearance or disappearance of an island by a volcanic eruption. Thus the inhabitants of the Minahassa (the northern volcanic peninsula of Celebes) relate that the land originally rose out of a flood ; and the stories of the Fiji and Pelew islanders appear to have originated from the disappearance of islands by volcanic action. (c) A tidal wave resulting from an earthquake. The Flood story current among the Eskimo in the Prince of Wales Peninsula is expressly connected with an earthquake. In a story of the Makah Indians (Washington Territory) it is related how the water flowed into the land from the Pacific, until Cape Flattery became an island. Similar features are found in the stories of some other Indian tribes—among them the Araucanians (in Chili), with whom the Flood is the result of an earthquake accompanied by volcanic eruptions. B. *Among inland peoples* the causes of Flood stories are (a) very frequently the overflow of some river, especially where, by the bursting of its banks, a large plain is inundated. This is the case in China, where, however, the Flood stories have hardly passed out of the region of sober history into that of myth, and deal with floods similar to those which have been known to have taken place,—the last two during the 19th cent. in 1852 and 1881. In the second of these no fewer than two millions are said to have perished. The Chinese Flood stories, then, are evidently not derived from Babylonia, and we should avoid yielding to the temptation of appealing to the early connexion in language and script between China and Baby-

lonia.[*] (b) The formation of a lake or inland sea, or its disappearance by the water eating out a channel for itself through soft rock, such as limestone. Livingstone tells a legend describing how the Dilolo Lake in Central Africa (on the southern border of the Congo State) came into existence as the consequence of a woman's curse pronounced upon a native chieftain who refused hospitality. The inhabitants of Thibet relate how once a flood covered the whole country and destroyed the ape-like inhabitants. By the compassion of a god the waters were drained off, and the new people taught civilization. In Santa Fé de Bogotá in Colombia there is a story that there was once a huge flood brought about by the witchery of a wicked woman, who caused the Rio de Bogotá to overflow and fill the basin-like plain of Cundinamarca. Her good husband changed her into the moon. and opened the present outlet through the limestone rock by which the water now flows down over the Falls of Tequendama (cf. Schwarz, *Sintfluth*, noticed in *Expos. Times*, viii., 1897, 271 f.). (c) The melting of the winter snows. In the district of the Indian tribe of the Chippewas there is a story telling how a mouse once gnawed through the bag which held the heat, and this escaping, the melting snow became a flood, which covered the whole world.

3. Not infrequently, and sometimes in connexion with one or more of the causes already mentioned, the Flood story appears to have originated in an attempt to account for some otherwise unexplained fact, as—(a) The dispersion of peoples and difference of language. This is especially frequent among, if not indeed peculiar to, the Indian tribes of N. America. Among the Thlinkeets in the North West the difference of speech between them and the rest of mankind is naïvely accounted for by the breaking of the ark in two, their ancestors having been in one half, those of all other races in the other ! More frequently, the dispersion is the result of the boats drifting away in the waters of the Deluge, as, *e.g.*, with the Bella Coola Indians (between 52° and 53° N. lat. on the coast of the Pacific). The ancient rock-carvings found among the aborigines of Mexico, in which, as it is said, a dove is depicted distributing gifts of speech in the form of tongues to the survivors of the Flood, would be a striking illustration of this kind of Flood story, could we be certain that this interpretation of it is correct ; but it is at least doubtful. (b) The red colour of some of the N. American tribes. This colour is, according to the Crees, the direct consequence of the Flood, the Red Indians of to-day being the descendants of the single woman who was rescued, when the waters had all but covered her (see below, III. 9). On the other hand, the Herero, a native tribe of South Africa, relate that it was the Flood that brought to their ancient home the white man and woman from whom they are descended ; hence their pale colour. (c) The existence of fossil remains on dry land, and even on hills. It is curious that the same evidence which, from the days of Tertullian at any rate, has been frequently adduced as evidence of the Bible Flood has been appealed to by several different peoples as evidence of their own Flood stories ; and if the remains did not in every, or perhaps in any, case actually give rise to the story, they certainly helped to give it credence and permanence. With the Leeward islanders the mussels and corals on their hills are a standing proof of an ancient flood, in which all but one small coral island were immersed. The Samoan islanders call attention to the fish which have been turned into stone; and the central Eskimos of N. America can still see the outer shells of many mussels, fish, sea-dogs, and whales which were left upon the dry land by the Flood. (d) The same Eskimo tribes give a similar explanation of glaciers. They are the icebergs left on the tops of the mountains by the receding waters.

It is also important to observe that the cause of the Flood story has very often a special connexion with the locality to which it belongs. Thus we notice that the melting of the ice is a frequent cause with the extreme northernly tribes of N. American Indians. Earthquakes are a common feature in the Flood legends of tribes on those coastlands of America where they frequently occur. The submergence or emergence of islands accounts for those of tribes inhabiting volcanic districts. In China the Flood stories are associated with the bursting of the banks of the great rivers where such events occur, and are accompanied with great loss of life and property. Still more remarkable is it, on the other hand, that in Africa, where the overflow of the great rivers is a regular and expected phenomenon, and, in fact, has become necessary to cultivation, and therefore cannot be considered as the result of *special* divine agency, Flood stories are singularly rare, and never of this kind.

iii. Very frequently an old myth has become mixed up with, or at any rate coloured by, the Babylonian or Bible story. Thus the account of the Grecian Flood (Deucalion's) as given in the *de Deâ Syrâ* of the pseudo-Lucian, a writer of the 2nd cent. A.D., differs from the earlier form of the story as contained in Ovid (*Met.* i. 163–437), for instance, by the addition of several details belonging to the Babylonian and biblical stories, such as the name Sisythes (=Xisuthros), the building of a chest, the saving in it of Deucalion's family and pairs of every animal. Plutarch similarly introduces Deucalion's sending out the dove to ascertain the *weather* (!), according as it returned or remained behind. This colouring is probably, however, in most cases due to the teaching of Christian missionaries, who would naturally emphasize and unconsciously, or perhaps even intentionally, exaggerate points of resemblance between native folk-lore and Bible stories. Andree (see *Literature* below) quotes a story to show how easily the Bible Flood could find its way into the folk-lore of an imaginative people. A missionary heard a Flood story from a native Hottentot which bore a suspicious resemblance to that of the Bible, and yet he was assured that it had been handed down from early ages. Shortly after he met another missionary, who told him that he had himself taught the native the Bible story. It is not always easy to say positively that a legend has been influenced by the Bible Flood, but in the following cases it may be considered highly probable :—(a) When the legend resembles the Bible story in one or more definite particulars, but in general drift or in its more important features differs widely from it. In that of the Mandari (a branch of the Kohls, East India), the flood out of which a brother and sister only had been rescued under a tree, is put an end to by the serpent Lurbing, *in connexion with whom appears the rainbow.* In the Lithuanian story the rainbow is sent to comfort a pair of wretched survivors, and counsels them to obtain offspring by jumping over the bones of the earth. The Lummi Indians (north of Washington Territory) have a story that an old man escaped on a raft to a mountain, and *thence* twice sent forth a crow, which returned the second time with a leaf. (b) When the parts

corresponding with the Bible story break the context, and do not fit in well with the rest. This is obviously the case with a story of the Algonquins (an Indian tribe of N. America), preserved in a very curious pictographic document, where, in the middle of a passage describing how some of the people were rescued on Turtle Island, the mention of a boat, as though an independent means of rescue, is very awkwardly introduced. (c) Where two forms of the story exist, in one of which the biblical features occur and in the other are absent. When, as with Deucalion's Flood, the former is known to be later, the probability of interpolation may be considered a certainty. Among the Mandans, an Indian tribe on the Missouri River, according to a current Flood legend the ark is a tower-like building, and the supposed model of the building, which is preserved as a relic in a public place, is in shape like a wooden cylinder. But not only is this model called 'the great canoe,' but, in the festival which commemorates the Flood, the representative of 'the First Man,' who was saved therein, tells how 'the great canoe' stranded on a high mountain. Moreover, the festival is always arranged to take place when the willows are in leaf, because, so they say, it was a branch of that tree, with all its leaves on, which the bird brought back to the ark. It is clear that we have here a confusion between two stories—an ancient legend according to which the survivors were saved in a tower, and the Bible Flood. (d) Where the Flood legend is mixed up with other stories from the Bible. Thus in that of the Papagos (an Indian tribe, east of California), Montezuma, the hero of the Flood, is so ungrateful to his deliverer, that he presumes to build a house whose top is to reach to heaven, whereupon the great Spirit sends his thunder and destroys the building. This evident borrowing from the Tower of Babel story makes us suspect that his sending out the jackal after the Flood to see how far the land extended, originated in the sending forth of birds from Noah's ark. In one of the Mexican legends, current in the neighbourhood of Cholulu, an artificial mountain, raised as a memento of the mountain in the caves of which the seven giants were saved from the Flood, threatened to reach to heaven, whereupon the gods sent down fire and destroyed several of the builders. This legend, connected with a half-finished pyramid, shows how readily Bible stories found their way among the aborigines of Mexico, and explains why features of the Bible Flood so often occur in the Flood myths of various Mexican tribes. In the story of the Mandari, above referred to as giving special prominence to the Bible feature of the rainbow, the creation of man *out of earth* stands in close connexion with the Flood. Similarly, the Flood story of the Macoushi (near British Guiana) relates how the first man found, on waking out of a deep sleep, a woman standing by his side. After this we can feel very little confidence in the originality of the statement that after the Flood the rat sent out by a survivor returned with an ear of maize in its mouth. This is evidently nothing else but a local adaptation of the dove and the olive branch. (e) The stories of the Papagos and Macoushi give another ground for suspecting biblical influence, namely, where some well-known features of a class of Flood legends appear so changed as to agree with the Noachian Deluge. The object of the sending forth of animals in the Indian stories is, as a rule, to obtain earth to create dry ground for the survivors. A rat is sent forth as well as other animals for this purpose in the legend of the Ojibways and the Chippewas, a fish in those of the Sac and Fox Indians. But in the stories of the Papagos and Macoushi the object is, as in the Bible, to discover the extent of dry land.

In some cases, however, the appearance of biblical details may be after all a mere coincidence. The likelihood of such coincidence becomes far greater than we might have thought when we take into account the very large number of Flood stories and the singular variety of detail. The following is an attempt to give as shortly as is practicable some idea of the extraordinary extent of this variety.

III. VARIETY OF DETAILS IN DIFFERENT FLOOD LEGENDS.—(1) *The Beings destroyed by the Flood* are often described as strange or unnatural beings, such as baneful monsters (Persian *Bundehesh*); ape-like men (Thibet); descendants of a primeval man and woman, who were drowned in the sea and became a whale and a crab; the descendants appear, however, to have been human in form, at any rate capable of religious and moral delinquency (Andamanese); giants (later Scandinavian *Edda*); men, one tribe of whom consisted only of women, another of men with dog-like tails (Fiji islanders); gods of the earth upon whom the Flood was sent at the request of the nether gods (the Sac and Fox Indians); a demigod (Ojibways, see above); imperfect men (Quiché Indians of Guatemala); the descendants of gods and men (Miztecs of Mexico, cf. Gn 6$^{1-4}$).

(2) *The reasons for the Flood* are differently given. Very frequently to get rid of these monstrous forms of life (in the *Bundehesh* a second Flood is necessary to purify the world of the poison which the monsters still left behind them); as in the Bible, to punish men for their wickedness (Andamanese); or, more frequently, for some definite crime or offence, as the refusal to wash and work (Mandari); killing and eating a huge serpent (Dyaks of Borneo); cooking a fish in violation of a sacred promise (Gipsies of the Sieben Gebirge); the crime of the demigod Menaboshu against the water-serpents in killing their king and three sons in revenge for the destruction of his little pet wolf (Ojibways); the inhospitality of a local S. African chieftain towards a woman who, in consequence, brought about a local flood through her incantation (Dilolo Lake); the insult perpetrated on a sea-god by a fisherman who fished in sacred waters and caught the god by his hair (Leeward Islands); the injury done to the raven by 'the wise man,' who had punished it by throwing it into the fire (Hare Indians, North America). In one case, as already noticed, the Flood is the result of a quarrel between the gods of the nether and upper world (the Sac and Fox Indians).

(3) The *direct cause of the Flood* is usually the rise and overflow of the sea, or of some river or lake; rather less frequently a prodigious storm and rainfall. An exceptional case is the melting of the winter snow (Chippewas, see above, II. 2 B c). Once it is occasioned by the blood flowing from a slaughtered giant (later *Edda*). Occasionally, the Flood consists of hot water (Finns). In the legend of the Quiché there is a second Flood of resin after one of water, and occasionally fire takes the place of water (so with the Yuracarés in Bolivia, among whom a legend of this sort has many parallels with the Flood stories of other peoples). In an Eskimo story the people are destroyed by heat as well as by the water. In one case the Flood is caused by the accidental breaking of a jar (examined through curiosity) containing the waters of the ocean (Haiti Island). Similarly, a flood is caused by an inquisitive ape taking away the mat placed in a hollow tree to stop up the water which communicated with the water beneath the earth (Acawoio, British Guiana).

(4) The Flood generally seems to have come

unexpectedly; but sometimes *the survivors were forewarned*, as a rule by a god, but occasionally through the medium of animals. In the sacred books of India it is the fish, which is no other than the incarnate Vishnu, or, in one form of the legend, even the great Brahma himself. In the legend of the Cherokee Indians (N. America) it is a dog which tells his master, having first attracted his attention by standing up to his neck in the water and refusing to stir. In one of the Peruvian stories it is the llamas which warn their shepherd. He had noticed that they looked sad and gazed at the stars, upon which he inquired the cause, and was told of the coming Flood.

(5) The Flood is generally represented as *universal*, though originating in some definite place; but sometimes it is purely *local*.

(6) Men are usually *drowned*, but in one legend some of them are devoured by sea-monsters (Algonquins). In several of the Peruvian Flood stories they are changed into fish, and in one instance the dead bodies become salmon and frogs (Maidu, near Sacramento).

(7) The *number of survivors* varies very greatly in the different stories. Where the inhabitants of the world are monsters, they are, of course, all destroyed. Sometimes even men are all destroyed, and a new set of men created. Sometimes, on the other hand, they appear to have all escaped (Kabadi, a south-east district of New Guinea). As a rule, the survivors are very few, most frequently a single family, or even less; in several cases only one man or woman. Once it is only the coyote (prairie-wolf) of all living beings (Wappo, California); in another story it is the coyote and the demigod Montezuma (Papagos); in another the raven and his mother (Thlinkeets, Indian tribe of N. America, see below, III. 9).

(8) *The reason why the particular survivors were permitted to escape* is generally left unexplained. But when it is explained, it is usually, of course, because they had no part in the cause for which the Flood was sent. Thus in the Gipsy legend (see above, III. 2), while the wife who cooked the fish is struck by the first lightning flash of the storm which preceded the Flood, the husband, who was faithful to his promise, was saved. In the legend of the Leeward Islands (see above, III. 2), however, by a strange want of poetic justice, the penitent fisherman succeeds in appeasing the wrath of the god, and he and his family alone escape.

(9) The *methods of escape* exhibit also great variety. In many cases it is by fleeing to a mountain or an island, the latter generally being left unimmersed by the rising water, not so much from its elevation as from its sacred character (Algonquins, Victoria, Leeward Islands, Greece, etc.). Sometimes the place of refuge is the top of a tree (Karens in Burmah, Tupi in Brazil, Acawoio in British Guiana), or underneath (!) a tree (Mandari), or in caves (Mexicans of Cholula); once in the hole of a huge crawfish in a rice field (Uraus, a branch of Kohls); in a tower expressly built for the purpose (Mandans, see above, II. iii. c). The most usual method of escape, however, is by a boat or raft of some kind. In one of the Fiji stories, two gods themselves come in a boat, and fish the drowning bodies out of the water. The raft or ship is usually allowed to drift, but sometimes, as in the Accadian story, it is regularly steered. In the legends of India it is towed by the god-fish with a rope tied to his horn. Sometimes, to prevent its drifting away, it is secured by a rope, fastened either to a stone acting as an anchor (Kamtschatka), or, more frequently, to a tree (Pelew islanders, Twanas of Puget Sound, Washington Territory). Occasionally, as in the Bible story, the means of escape is a floating chest (Banar in Cambodia); in one legend

a nut-shell, which conveniently fell from a god, who was eating nuts in heaven during the Flood, on to the topmost peak of a mountain, whither men had fled for refuge (Lithuanians). Usually, as in the Accadian and Bible stories, the ark lands on a mountain; but, curiously enough, in some of the Persian legends the mountain of refuge itself floats like a boat. Other means of escape are still more quaint. In one legend the raven and his mother, presumably in a pre-raven state of existence, put on birds' skins and fly up to heaven, which the former, in his impetuosity, hits so violently that his beak gets stuck. In this predicament he is obliged to wait till the waters reach him (Thlinkeets). In another the single surviving maiden succeeds in catching hold of a bird, which flies up with her to a rock of safety (Crees).

(10) The Flood usually *disappears* by subsidence or evaporation; but, in isolated instances, it flows away down a hole (Deucalion's Flood, Tinney Indians), or into a rift in a mountain, and so finds its way into the sea (Maidu).

(11) The survivors in several legends *send out animals* from their various retreats, usually to dive down into the waters, that they may get earth, out of which new land is created. Of this we have a characteristic example in the story of the Ojibways, in which the surviving Menaboshu, after having stood on the topmost peak of a mountain for five days, with the water up to his mouth, in despair prays a passing sea-gull to dive down and discover whether the land has been entirely washed away. After the gull has dived several times to no purpose, Menaboshu sees the stiffened body of a musk-rat floating by. Having restored it to life, he sends it down on a similar quest. After a long while the dead body of the musk-rat appears on the surface with a few grains of sand in its claws. These Menaboshu throws on the water, and they become little islands, which grow and join together until they form habitable earth. In the stories of the Sac and Fox Indians, it is a fish which returns with its huge mouth full of earth; in that of the Chippewas, the beaver, otter, musk-rat, and northern diver, all dive down, and the last returns with mud in its webbed feet. Sometimes, as in the Bible, and presumably the Accadian stories, the animals are sent forth to discover whether or where the land is dry (Papagos, etc., see above, II. iii. *e*).

(12) The survivors, *hard put to it for food*, sometimes feed on fish, which they either cook by putting them under their armpits (!) (Tolowa in California), or with fire procured by rubbing sticks together, at which the god is angry, and turns the fish into dogs (an old Mexican story in the Codex Chimalpopoca). Fire is obtained in a similar way in the legend of the Dyaks of Borneo. In the Andamanesian story an arctic bird sends down a firebrand from heaven. In one of the Peruvian legends, meals are provided for the two surviving brothers by two parrots.

(13) There is a very curious variety with regard to the *methods by which the world was re-peopled after the Deluge*. When all the inhabitants were destroyed, there was, of necessity, a new creation. Most frequently, as in the Bible, the new men were simply the offspring of the few survivors, but in several legends they appear as propagated in some strange and miraculous manner, as by stones thrown over the survivors' heads (Deucalion's Flood, Acawoio and other Indian tribes on the Upper Orinoco). In one story cocoa-nuts are thrown with a similar result (Maypuri and neighbouring tribes of S. America). In the Lithuanian story men come into being by the survivors leaping over the bones of the earth. According to the Pelew islanders, it was by intercourse of the gods with a

woman whose dead body was brought to life, and indwelt for a time by a goddess. Another legend ascribes it to the union between the single surviving maiden and a great eagle (Crees). Still more curious is the legend of the Wappo, who ascribe the re-peopling of the world to the coyote, which planted the tail feathers of various birds in the places where wigwams formerly stood. According to the Tinney Indians, it was brought about by the gods changing animals into men.

(14) The deification of Xisuthros after the Flood in the Accadian story has hardly a parallel in the myths of other peoples. Sometimes the survivor is already a sort of god (Papagos). In the story of the Pelew islanders the gods wish to deify the last woman, whom they had already restored to life, but are prevented by the malice of the bird Tariit (*Rallus pectoralis*).

If we now examine these legends in connexion with their locality, we shall find that features which repeat themselves (leaving out of consideration what has been borrowed from the Bible story) in several legends are of two kinds: (*a*) those which characterize the legends of neighbouring or related tribes; and (*b*) those which appear sporadically, so to speak, in far separated peoples. As examples of the first we may notice, generally, the tendency to combine Flood stories with animal fables common to almost all tribes of American Indians, and more especially the fables of the coyote, the jackal, and the raven, each of which marks off a definite group of tribes. We may instance also the floating mountain, which is confined to the neighbourhood of Peru. In many cases the second class belongs to the form which the legend would be most likely to take. It is more likely that men would escape a flood by going up into a mountain, or by means of a boat or raft, than in any other way, and therefore we find this to be most frequently the case. But when we consider the great multiplicity of stories, it is not at all surprising that, in a few isolated cases, the imagination of different peoples should independently hit upon the same idea. Where so many methods of escape suggested themselves, it might easily have occurred to more than one people that the boat of safety was like a chest, or, again, that the boat was tied by a rope. In the same way we may account for the really far stranger incident, the subsequent creation of men out of stones.

It is of the greatest importance to notice that this second class of similarities is by no means confined to features contained in the Bible story. Those who argue for the truth of the latter on the ground that several of its details are confirmed by other legends, are in danger of proving too much. The same argument makes equally for the truth of other details not found in the Bible. If all these stories are really the traditions of one single event, does not the evidence point to a boat rather than an ark, if indeed the survivors did not merely ascend a mountain; and is not the statement of the boat being moored by a rope, which appears in legends so widely scattered, at least as probable as that of the sending out of animals, on the presence of which, in different legends, so much stress is often laid? For, as a matter of fact, the stories which contain this feature are often liable to the suspicion of a Christian colouring on the grounds above given, and indeed it is just this picturesque touch which would inevitably most strike the imagination, and most easily find its way into the popular stories of a people. It must also be borne in mind that there is a vast difference between *sending out* animals to ascertain how far the waters were dry, and *begging them to dive down* under the water to obtain earth for making dry land. The clay on the feet of the birds in the

Babylonian story is connected with the first, that on the feet of the diver in the story of the Chippewas with the second. In a word, all that the multifarious Flood stories really can be said to prove is, that there was among a very large number of ancient peoples the belief in a Flood, and often, though by no means so frequently, in a universal Deluge ; but this alone does not prove that they all describe one real event, still less that the one true account of that event is the Bible Flood. It is rather the case that a thorough study and comparison of these stories make both these hypotheses extremely improbable.

IV. THE CAUSE OF THE ACCADIAN FLOOD STORY. —Four theories as to the origin of the Flood story are possible. That it was originally (1) a mere product of the fancy, (2) a nature myth, (3) a cosmogonic fable, (4) the poetical presentation of some natural occurrence. The first is contrary to the analogy of similar legends among all peoples, and hardly needs serious discussion. The second has in its favour the connexion of the Flood story with Aquarius, and possibly, perhaps, the location of Sît-napišti at the mouth of the Euphrates ; but, on the other hand, this watery subject, supposing the story to be already in existence, was specially suited for this particular zodiacal sign ; and the mouth of the Euphrates might be deemed a fitting place for the deified hero of the Flood. The third finds some analogy among the Flood legends of other nations, but the analogy of the great majority of Flood stories is strongly in favour of the fourth, and there can be no doubt that it is correct.

The question then arises, 'What event is likely to have given rise to the Accadian story?' (a) That it was a universal Deluge is, for reasons already given, quite out of the question. (b) Writers have, however, still maintained (and founded their arguments on scientific grounds) that this Flood was much more than a local flood, and really covered a very considerable area. Among these is the late Professor Prestwich, a man who, on account of his geological researches, is entitled to the highest respect (see Literature). He maintains the view, that long after the appearance of palæolithic man there was a submergence of the crust of the earth, chiefly in Western Europe, but extending to the N.W. of Africa, though probably not as far as Egypt, causing a great inundation of the sea, which rose (relatively speaking) at its highest to about 1500 ft. on the Continent, and 1000 ft. in England. It seems to have risen suddenly and to have subsided soon ; that is to say, the inundation did not probably last more than a year or two at most. It destroyed a vast amount of animal and some human life, so that some species of animals became extinct in regions which they formerly inhabited : for example, the lion, panther, spotted hyæna, caffir cat, hippopotamus, African elephant in Europe and N. Africa, and all the then existing mammalia in Malta. The proofs of this inundation are : (1) the various forms of what the Professor calls distinctively Rubble Drift (distinct in character from the Glacial Drift in its various forms of breccia, etc.), and (2) a sedimentary deposit (loess) found on mountains (distinct from all valley deposits left by rivers). It seems probable to him that, when the Flood rose, animals of all sorts were driven to the mountains, where some escaped, from which the submerged districts were again re-stocked after the Flood. In one instance (at Palermo) it would appear that the light-footed animals, which would have had little difficulty in making their escape, survived, whereas the hippopotamus became extinct. Without attempting to call in question the geological arguments on which this view is maintained, it will be readily seen that it is extremely difficult to make it square with the evidence of the Flood traditions of different peoples, to which Professor Prestwich himself appeals to fortify his case. Had this view been correct, we should certainly have expected to find wide recollections of the Flood throughout the region where it occurred, and more faint traditions in other parts. But this is by no means the case, and the district of Babylonia, from which the most important and graphic Flood story originates, is, according to our present knowledge, wanting in those geological phenomena on which the Professor depends (indeed they have not yet been discovered even in the east of Europe), and therefore is apparently beyond the region of the supposed Deluge. On the other hand, in Europe Flood legends are comparatively scarce, and usually of a very mythical type (Edda, Lithuanians, etc.) ; in N.W. Africa they are altogether absent. Again, they are most frequent by far in Northern and Central America, regions far removed from the supposed locality of the Flood. The same objection, though not to the same extent, lies to the view that the Accadian Flood story is to be referred to geological changes in Thibet, by which what was once a great inland sea became a plain (see above, II. 2 B b).

Judging from the genesis of similar legends, this Accadian story is far more likely to have originated in Babylonia itself, and to be due to some local cause. The same analogy, if we take also into account the character of the country, suggests that our choice lies between a great overflow of the Tigris and Euphrates caused by an extraordinary rainfall, and the incursion of a tidal wave through an earthquake somewhere in the south. Edward Süss, whose views are mentioned by Andree, is inclined to think that both these causes were at work. He argues from the description of the Accadian story, which speaks not only of the earth trembling, and the breaking out of the floods below the earth, and the waves of the storm-god reaching up to heaven—expressions which point to an earthquake accompanied by a tidal wave—but also of the whirlwind, and the thunder, and the overflow of the canals. Del. (Gen. 1887, p. 164), Haupt (Amer. Journ. Philol. ix. 423 f.), and esp. Huxley (Essays on Controverted Questions, 586 ff., 619), agree with Süss, and Dillm. (Gen.⁶ p. 175) inclines to the same view. Andree gives several instances, recorded in history, showing to what an enormous distance an earthquake affects the movement of the sea. For example, an earthquake which took place in Peru on the 13th of August 1868, caused a great wave which struck the Sandwich Islands on the following day, and on the day after washed the coastlands of Australia and New Zealand. How terrible the destruction wrought by a local inundation may be, is shown by the cyclone which struck the coast of India on Nov. 1st, 1864, and involved the loss of 60,000 lives. It is not so very surprising that in Babylonia, as in many other countries, such a flood should by long oral tradition have been magnified into a universal Deluge, from which only a few survived.

It has been necessary in this article to lay considerable stress on points of resemblance between the Flood story of the Bible and the numerous Flood legends of other peoples. We have shown that, looked at from a merely historical point of view, they stand on a similar footing, and, in fact, that the Bible story is merely a later variant of one of them. Here, however, the resemblance ends. In tone and religious character the Bible story is immeasurably above all others. It is true, indeed, that the God of the Flood, Who took pleasure in the sweet smell of Noah's sacrifice, stands far below the God of the psalmist, Who delighted not in burnt-offerings and sacrifice, but in a broken and troubled spirit. But for all that, it is a God who hated iniquity, transgression, and sin as utterly unworthy of His own creation, not a deity avenging a merely personal insult, far less, as in the original story, a troop of gods wrangling with each other in jealous rivalry. Even though it be true that the Israelites found this Flood story handed down from the religious mists of a far distant past, a religious student of Scripture will have no difficulty in recognizing that divinely guided religious feeling and insight by which an ancient legend became the vehicle of religious and spiritual truth.

LITERATURE.—George Smith, *The Chaldean Account of Genesis*, new ed. by Sayce; *KAT*[2], 55–79; Sayce, *HCM*, 107 ff.; J. Prestwich, *On Certain Phenomena belonging to the close of the last Geological Period, and on their bearing upon the Tradition of the Flood*, Macmillan, 1895; Andree, *Die Flutsagen, ethnographisch betrachtet*, Brunswick, 1891,—an excellent work giving a summary of the Flood legends of a large number of races, and made much use of in this article; Charles Hardwick, *Christ and other Masters*, Cambridge, contains some Flood legends, see esp. pt. II. iii. 3, pt. III. ii. pp. 162–164; F. Lenormant, *Origines de l'histoire d'après la Bible*, Paris; see also in this *DB* the art. BABYLONIA, p. 221.

F. H. WOODS.

FLOOD.—A flood is a *flow* of water. In early Eng. (as in late) it is used of the flow of the tide, as *Trin. Coll. Hom.* (1200) 177, 'For swiche flode, and for swich ebbinge the prophete nemmeth this woreld se.' But in the earliest quotation in *Oxf. Eng. Dict.* it is applied to a stream,—an application which has long since dropped out of prose, though it is still in use poetically. In this sense 'flood' is of frequent occurrence in AV. The following is a complete list of the passages in which the word is found.

1. A stream: Job 14[11] (*nâhâr*, usual word for 'river,' RV 'river'); 20[17] 'the floods, the brooks of honey and butter' (*nâhâr*, RV 'the flowing streams'); 28[11] 'he bindeth the floods from overflowing' (*nâhâr*, RV 'the streams that they trickle not,' RVm '*Heb.* from weeping,' the allusion is to the use of lime or clay to prevent water percolating into the mine—Davidson); Ps 98[8] (*nâhâr*); Job 28[4] 'the flood breaketh out from the inhabitant' (*nahal*, usual word for 'brook,' here understood of the miner's 'shaft,' RV 'he breaketh open a shaft away from where men sojourn'); Ps 74[15] 'Thou didst cleave the fountain and the flood' (*nahal*, in ref. to the stream from the rock in the wilderness); Is 44[3] 'I will pour water upon him that is thirsty, and floods upon the dry ground' (*nôzĕlîm*, ptcp. of *nâzal*, to flow, RV 'streams'). In Apocr., 2 Es 16[60] (*flumen*, RV 'river'), Ad. Est 11[10] 'a great flood' (*ποταμὸς μέγας*, distinguished from *μικρὰ πηγή*, 'a little fountain'; RV 'river'); Sir 21[13] 39[22] (*κατακλυσμός*). This meaning is found in Shaks., but more rarely: *Much Ado*, I. i. 318—

'What need the bridge much broader than the flood?'

2. A special river: (*a*) The *Euphrates*, Jos 24[2] 'Your fathers dwelt on the other side of the flood in old time' (בְּעֵבֶר הַנָּהָר, RV 'beyond the River'); so 24[3] (מֵעֵבֶר 'from,' etc.), 24[14. 15]. In Apocr., 2 Es 13[44] 'the most High . . . held still the flood, till they were passed over' (*statuit venas fluminis*, RV 'stayed the springs of the River'); 1 Mac 7[8] 'Bacchides . . . who ruled beyond the flood' (*ἐν τῷ πέραν τοῦ ποταμοῦ*, RV 'in the country beyond the river'). Cf. Rev 9[14] Wyc. 'Vnbynde foure aungels, that ben bounde in the great flood Eufrates'; Milton, *PL* i. 419—

'With these came they who from the bordering flood
Of old Euphrates to the brook that parts
Egypt from Syrian ground, had general names
Of Baälim and Ashtaroth.'

(*b*) The *Nile*: Ps 78[44] (נוֹזְלֵיהֶם, RV 'their streams'); Am 8[8 *bis*] 9[5 *bis*]; the Heb. is *ye'ôr*, the word for the Nile, *the* River, as RV; in 8[5b] and 9[5b] *Miẓraim* 'of Egypt' is added, but that is quite exceptional.

Sometimes RV translates boldly by 'Nile,' Is 19[7 *ter.* 8] (AV 'brook'), 23[3. 10] (AV 'river'), Jer 46[7. 8] (AV 'flood'), Zec 10[11] (AV 'river'). Cf. Ac 7[21] Wyc. 'whanne he was put out *in the flood*, the daughter of Farao took hym up.' (*c*) The *Jordan*: Ps 66[6] 'they went through the flood on foot' (*nâhâr*, RV 'river'). Cf. Pr. Bk. 1549, 'by the Baptism of thy well-beloved Son Jesus Christ, thou didst sanctify the flood Jordan, and all other waters, to this mystical washing away of sin' (so 1552, 1559, and Scot. Liturgy, 1604; but in 1662 changed to 'the river Jordan').

3. An overflow of water, a torrent: Job 22[16] 'whose foundation was overthrown with a flood' (lit., as Dav., 'was poured away *and became* a flood,' RV 'was poured out as a stream,' Heb. *nâhâr*); Ps 32[6] 'in the floods of great waters' (שֶׁטֶף), מַיִם רַבִּים, RV 'when the great waters overflow'); 69[2] (שִׁבֹּלֶת *shibbôleth*, the word which baffled the Ephraimites to pronounce, see SHIBBOLETH); 69[15] 'waterflood' (*shibbôleth mayim*, 1611 'water flood'); 90[5] 'Thou carriest them away as with a flood' (וְרַמְתָּם, lit., as Cheyne, 'thou stormest upon them'); Is 28[2] 'a flood of mighty waters overflowing' (*zerem*, properly a flood of *rain*, a downpour; RV 'tempest'); Jer 47[2] 'an overflowing flood' (*nahal*, RV 'stream,' Cheyne 'torrent,' who says, 'It is in autumn-time that the torrents of Palestine become dangerous, and water-courses, dry or almost dry in summer, become filled with a furiously rushing stream'); Dn 9[26] 11[22], Nah 1[8] (*shêṭeph*). In Apocr., Wis 5[22] 'the floods shall cruelly drown them' (*ποταμοί*, RV 'the rivers shall sternly overwhelm them'). In NT, Mt 7[25. 27] (*ποταμοί*), Lk 6[48] (*πλήμμυρα*, fr. root of *πίμπλημι*, to fill); Rev 12[15. 16] (*ποταμός*, RV 'river'; and 12[15] 'that he might cause her to be carried away of the flood' (*ποταμοφόρητον*, RV 'carried away by the stream').

4. Noah's flood is always designated in Heb. *mabbûl*, in LXX *κατακλυσμός*, and in Vulg. *diluvium* (whence Eng. 'deluge'). The reff. in OT are Gn 6[17] 7[6. 7. 10. 17] 9[11 *bis*. 15. 28] 10[1. 32] 11[10], Ps 29[10]; in Apocr., 2 Es 3[9. 10], Wis 10[4], Sir 40[10 * 44[17. 18]; and in NT, Mt 24[38. 39], Lk 17[27], 2 P 2[5]. See preceding article.

The only doubtful ref. is Ps 29[10] 'The LORD sitteth upon the flood' (לַמַּבּוּל יָשָׁב), RV 'sat *as king* at the Flood'). The majority of recent commentators take it with RV to be a ref. to Noah's Flood. 'The storm,' says Kirkpatrick, 'reminds the poet of the great typical example of judgment and mercy, in which Jehovah's judicial severity was exhibited.' The chief argument in favour is the use of the word (observe that it has the article '*the* Flood'). Against is the unexpectedness of the reference to the Flood, and the prep. (?) 'at,' 'to,' or 'on.' Kirkpatrick says of the prep.: 'we may render, *Sat for the Flood*; with His seat on His throne in order to execute that memorable judgment (Ps 97).' The tr[n] of AV (which is that of Geneva Bible) makes the ref. to be to a flood of water in the storm itself. This is clear from the note in the Gen. Bible. Johnson (*Speaker's Com.*) agrees. But the storm is a storm of wind, not of water; for in any case there is no mention in the psalm, although it may be argued that it is presupposed. Cheyne carries the psalmist's mind beyond the Noachic Flood to the original meaning of the word. That is 'destruction'; 'a wasting flood' being only secondary. He therefore boldly ignores the Flood and any ref. to water, and tr. 'At the storm Jehovah sat enthroned' (*Book of Psalms*, p. 81, and Crit. Note on p. 380).†

5. It is only in poetic parallelism that 'flood' is used of the *sea*: Ps 24[2]—

'He hath founded it [the earth] upon the seas,
And established it upon the floods';

Ps 93[3 *ter*], Jon 2[3] (all *nâhâr*); and Ex 15[8] (*nôzĕlîm*, of the waters of the Red Sea). In Apocr., 2 Es 4[15. 17. 19. 21] (*fluctus*, RV 'waves').

<hr>

* So plainly in AV, since the marg. ref. is to Gn 7[11]; and the Gr. is *κατακλυσμός*: but RV omits the ref., and prints 'flood,' not 'Flood,' and the recently discovered Heb. text gives 'river' (Cowley and Neubauer).

† This cancels the 'Parchment' tr[n] 'Jehovah has seated himself above the flood,' and its note, 'either the deluge or the heavenly ocean already referred to in v.[3].'

6. Finally, the word is thrice used metaphorically : 2 S 22⁵ = Ps 18⁴ 'the floods of ungodly men made me afraid' (נַחֲלֵי בְלִיַּעַל, lit. 'streams of Belial'; RV 'floods of ungodliness'; see Selbie, Cheyne, and Hommel in *Expos. Times*, viii. [1897] 360, 423, 472; and Baudissin, Cheyne, Jensen, *ib*. ix. 40, 91, 283, 332). Cf. Shaks. *Timon of Athens*, I. i. 42—

'You see this conference, this great flood of visitors.'

Also 1 Mac 6¹¹ 'a flood of *misery*' (ποταμός, RV simply 'a flood'). Cf. Milton, *On Time*, 13—

'And joy shall overtake us as a flood.'

J. HASTINGS.

FLOOR.—The word 'floor' is now most familiar as the part we tread on in a room; but it once as readily suggested the platform on which corn was threshed. Hence in AV (after earlier VSS) 'floor' stands as the trⁿ of גֹּרֶן *gôren*, fourteen times, which elsewhere is mostly trᵈ 'threshing-floor.'

The Heb. word occurs altogether 36 times : it is trᵈ 'threshing-floor' (1611 two sep. words) 19 times (Gn 50¹⁰, Nu 15²⁰ 18²⁷·³⁰, Ru 3², 1 S 23¹, 2 S 6⁶ 24¹⁸·²¹·²⁴, 1 Ch 13⁹ 21¹⁵·¹⁸·²¹·²²·²⁸, 2 Ch 3¹, Jer 51³³), and 'floor' 11 times (Gn 50¹¹, Dt 15¹⁴, Jg 6³⁷, Ru 3³·⁶·¹⁴, Is 21¹⁰, Hos 9² 13³, Jl 2²⁴, Mic 4¹²). RV gives 'threshing-floor' everywhere except Gn 50¹¹, Is 21¹⁰, and Jl 2²⁴, retaining 'floor' in these places. Elsewhere *gôren* is trᵈ 'barn-floor' 2 K 6²⁷ (1611 'barn floor'; RV 'threshing-floor'); 'threshingplace' 2 S 24¹⁶ (1611 'threshing place,' RV 'threshing-floor'); 'a void place' 1 K 22¹⁰ = 2 Ch 18⁹ (RV 'an open place'), 'barn' Job 39¹² (RV 'threshing-floor'), 'corn' Dt 16¹³ ('after that thou hast gathered in thy corn and thy wine,' RV 'after that thou hast gathered in from thy threshing-floor and from thy wine-press'), and in Hos 9¹ [all] the fuller phrase *kol-gornôth dâgân* is trᵈ 'cornfloor' (1611 'corn floor').

The only other OT word is אִדַּר *'iddar*, which occurs only Dn 2³⁵ and is trᵈ 'threshing-floor' (אִדְּרֵיכֹם, EV 'summer threshing-floors'). In NT ἅλων occurs only Mt 3¹², Lk 3¹⁷ and is trᵈ 'floor,' RV 'threshing-floor.' In Apocr. *area* is trᵈ 'floor' 2 Es 4³² (so RV), 4³⁵·³⁹ (RV 'threshing-floor'). See AGRICULTURE.

For the floor of a room see HOUSE.

J. HASTINGS.

FLOTE.—The timber for the temple, being cut in Lebanon, was conveyed by sea to Joppa in flotes : 1 K 5⁹ (דֹּבְרוֹת, RV 'rafts'), 2 Ch 2¹⁶ (רַפְסֹדוֹת). The logs themselves would form the raft; hence in 1 Es 5⁵⁵ it is said that for the building of the second temple the timber was brought to the haven of Joppa, not '*by* rafts' (AV, as if σχεδίαις), but '*in* rafts' (RV, cf. LXX σχεδίας). In 1 K 5⁹ LXX reads σχεδίας, in 2 Ch 2¹⁶ σχεδίαις. AV 1611 spells 'flotes' at each occurrence. Modern editions give 'flotes' in 2 Ch 2¹⁶ * and 1 Es 5⁵⁵, but 'floats' 1 K 5⁹. Scrivener restores 'flotes,' and is followed in *Camb. Bible for Schools and Colleges*.

FLOUR.—See FOOD.

FLOURISH.—Two stages may be marked in the use of the verb to flourish : 1. To flower, blossom, said (*a*) literally or (*b*) metaphorically, as (*a*) Lyte (1578), *Dodoens*, II. xx. 117, 'It beginneth to floure at the toppe of the stalke, and so goeth florishing downewarde.' So in AV Ec 12⁵ 'the almond tree shall flourish' (יָנֵאץ, RV 'shall blossom'); Ca 6¹¹ 7¹² of the vine (פָּרַח, RV 'bud'; cf. Chaucer, *Parsonnes Tale*, § 43, Student's ed. 697, 'To smelle the sote savour of the vyne whanne it florissheth'); Is 17¹¹ 'in the morning shalt thou make thy seed to flourish' (תַּפְרִיחִי, RV 'thou makest thy seed to blossom'); Ps 90⁶ of the grass (יָצִיץ, Del., Cheyne 'blossoms'). (*b*) Metaphorically of persons or things : Ps 103¹⁵ 'As for man, his days are as

* Why was *flotes* left in 2 Ch ? Because less read, and reckoned of less consequence ? So in the Heb. Bible some explain the presence of *Esh-baal*, 1 Ch 8³³ 9³³, when the name was changed in 2 S into *Ish-bosheth*.

grass : as a flower of the field so he flourisheth' (צִיץ הַשָּׂדֶה כֵּן יָצִיץ, lit. 'as the flower of the field so he flowereth' : so Ps 72¹⁶ 92⁷ 132¹⁸, all *ġûz* [in Hiph.], which means to bring forth flowers, and is trᵈ 'blossom' in Is 27⁶ as well as [in Qal] Ezk 7¹⁰); Sir 39¹⁴ 'flourish as a lily' (ἀνθήσατε ἄνθος; RV 'put forth flowers'). 2. To shoot up quickly, or grow vigorously, again said literally of plants and metaphorically of persons and things. Thus Ezk 17²⁴ in the Wyclifite version of 1388 is 'Y made the drie tree to brynge forth boowis,' but the earlier version has 'Y made the drye tree for to florisshe,' which is retained in AV. In this sense are all the remaining instances of the word, the Heb. being some part of פָּרַח, or (in Ps 92¹⁴) the adj. רַעֲנָן (Aram. רַעֲנַן Dn 4⁴); the Greek ἀναθάλλειν, Sir 1¹⁸ 11²² 46¹² 49¹⁰, Ph 4¹⁰; and the Lat. *flôrêre*, 2 Es 6²⁸.

J. HASTINGS.

FLOWERS.—Visitors to Palestine unite in their enthusiasm over the flowers. Everywhere they brighten the landscape with their brilliant colours, white, yellow, blue, violet, purple, maroon, crimson, scarlet, brown, and even black. Fields, many acres in extent, are aglow with anemones, ranunculi, poppies, chorisporas, silenes, clovers, milk vetches, chamomiles, groundsels, crocuses, colchicums, irises, ixiolirions, gladioli, and tulips. The hedges are gay with their wealth of broom, roses, and brambles. The sandstone is clothed with pink and white rock - roses, and dainty little heaths. The hillsides are adorned with the lavish blossoms of the styrax, the redbud, the arbutus, and the myrtle. Even the bleak shingle of alpine Lebanon, 10,000 ft. above the sea, is covered with large patches of *Vicia canescens*, Lab., and *V. gregaria*, Boiss. et Held., with their beautiful racemes of blue and white flowers. The tableland of Moab is gorgeous with deep purple irises. Finally, the deserts have a rich and varied flora, numbering over 400 species, not found in other localities. Flowers are an emblem of beauty (Mt 6²⁸ᶠ·), but at the same time of frailty and instability (Job 14², Ps 103¹⁵, Is 28¹ 40⁶, Ja 1¹⁰ etc.). The coming of flowers is a sign of spring (Ca 2¹²). 'The flower of her age' is the bloom of a maiden's youth (1 Co 7³⁶).

G. E. POST.

FLOWERS in Lv 15²⁴·³³ signifies the menstrual discharge (נִדָּה, RV 'impurity'). So Andrew, *Brunswyke's Distyll-Waters*, A iii. 'the same water . . . causeth women to have their flowers, named menstruum.' In the same sense Fr. *fleurs*; but both are now obsolete.

FLUE-NET.—In Hab 1¹⁵ m 'flue-net' is given as an alternative for 'drag' of the text (Heb. מִכְמֶרֶת). The form *flu* is found in French, and *fluwe* for a fishing-net in Dutch. The flue (together with the 'trammel or hooped net whatsoever') is forbidden to river fishermen in early laws. The word is still in occasional use, as *Three in Norway* (1882), vi. 44, 'Seven boats . . . were out with a huge flue net.' Coverdale has 'yarne' in this and the foll. verse, and is followed by the Geneva and Bishops' Bibles.

FLUTE.—See MUSIC.

FLUX.—Ac 28⁸ 'the father of Publius lay sick of a fever and of a bloody flux,' *i.e*. lit. a flow of blood (from *fluxus*, ptcp. of *fluĕre*, to flow, through Fr. *flux*; the spelling in 1611 is 'flixe' ['bloody-flixe'], a spelling derived from the Fr. pronunciation with ü—Bradley); Gr. δυσεντερία in TR, but edd. prefer the later form δυσεντέριον; RV 'dysentery.' The AV trⁿ comes from Wyclif, who in ed. 1380 has 'Sothli þe bifel, þe fadir of Puplius for to ligge trauelid with feueres and dissenterie, or flix,' thus using 'flix' without the adj., for it often stood alone in early Eng. as a synonym for dysentery. But the ed. of 1388 has 'blodi flux.' So in Mt 9²⁰ Wyclif (1380) gives 'And loo! a womman that suffride the flix, or rennynge of blood (Gr. αἱμορροοῦσα) twelve yeer, cam to byhynde and touchide the hemme of his clothe,' but ed. 1388 'the blodi flux.' And so T. Fuller, *Holy Warre* (ed. 1640), p. 216, 'The siege was no sooner begun but the plague seised on the Christian armie: whereof thousands died; amongst others, Tristram, King Lewis his sonne: And he himself of a flux followed after.' But p. 94, 'King Almerick himself, wearied with whole volleys of miseries, ended his life of a bloudy flux.' See MEDICINE.   J. HASTINGS.

FLY.—In 1 S 14³² (reading וַיַּעַט with Ḳerê, for Kethîbh וַיַּעַשׂ) and 15¹⁹ (וַתַּעַט) AV gives (and RV retains) 'fly upon the spoil,' a more forcible rendering than that of the previous versions 'turn to' (the Bishops' have 'gate them to' in 14³²). In 1 S 25¹⁴ 'flew upon' (AV 'railed on') is used figuratively: עַיִט 'bird of prey' comes from the same root. In Lv 11²¹·²³ occurs the curious combination 'flying creeping thing' (שֶׁרֶץ הָעוֹף). As Driver points out (art. CREEPING THINGS, see also *Com.* on Dt 14¹⁹ where the phrase is 'every creeping thing that flieth'), the Heb. word here used does not describe *creeping* but *swarming* creatures; so that the trⁿ should be 'winged swarming things,' not as in RV 'winged creeping things,' the reference being to insects like the locust.

FLY, FLIES.—Two Hebrew words are translated *fly* :—**1.** זְבוּב *zĕbhûbh*, μυῖα, *musca*. This word is found only in two places (Ec 10¹, Is 7¹⁸). It corresponds to the Arab. *dhubâb*, which is specially applied to *house flies*, but is also understood in the general sense of insects resembling them. It is used in Arab. as an emblem of *weakness*, 'he is more frail than the fly'; and of *contemptibleness*, 'he is more contemptible to me than the buzzing of the fly.' 'The refuge of the fly' is a proverb, applied to him who is protected by his ignobleness. 'The father of the fly' signifies a person with a stinking breath (cf. Ec 10¹). It is also said of such a person that he is 'more stinking in breath than the father of the fly.' From these qualities *dhubâb* has come to signify *evil* or *mischief*. An unlucky man is 'a fly man.' The same expression is also used to denote *demoniacal possession*, or *insanity*, or *ignorance*. More or fewer of these various significations in the Arab. may have obtained also in the Heb. word, which would account for the god of Ekron being called Baal-zebub (2 K 1²), 'the *god of flies*.' See BAAL-ZEBUB.
2. עָרֹב *'ârôbh*, κυνόμυια, *omne genus muscarum*, EV Ex 8²¹⁻³¹ *swarms of flies*, AV Ps 78⁴⁵ 105³¹ *divers sorts of flies*, RV *swarms of flies*. In all three passages LXX gives κυνόμυια, *dog-fly*, a word the significance of which in Greek is not clear. The Rabbins interpret *'ârôbh* as referring to a mixture of noxious insects, as if from עָרַב *'ârab*, to mix. Some have argued from Ex 8³¹ 'there remained not one,' that the fly referred to must be a definite species, which was sent as a plague, and totally destroyed at its close. But even if the expression 'not one' is to be pressed to its literal interpretation, it would not necessarily imply that the swarms were all of one kind. They might have been 'divers sorts.' The fact that the swarms of flies 'devoured' the Egyptians, has been supposed to imply that they were flies that bit them. But, apart from the fact that a biting fly could hardly be said to devour its victim, the true interpretation is to be sought in the comparison of the two members of the parallelism, 'flies which devoured them, and frogs which destroyed them.'

Both are strong expressions of the ruinous nature of the plague, and in both the reference is probably more to the corruption of their food and drink than to the destruction of their bodies. As it is impossible to determine whether a particular insect, or a mixture of insects, is intended, we may accept *swarms of flies* as conveying the essential meaning in the passages in question. See PLAGUE.
A resident in the cooler parts of Europe and America can hardly realize the number and persistence of the flies which swarm in Egypt and Syria. They not only defile food, but convey contagion, particularly that of *ophthalmia, diphtheria*, and, one kind of fly, that of *malignant pustule*. They also deposit their eggs in wounds and sores, and sometimes in the nose and ears of filthy people, and their larvæ hatch out, and fill these cavities, to the great distress and injury of the unfortunate patient.
                                                G. E. POST.
FODDER occurs only once in AV (Job 6⁵ as trⁿ of בְּלִיל, strictly *mixed food, farrago* [see *Oxf. Heb. Lex.*]). RV not only retains the term here, but introduces it in Jg 19²¹, where the denom. vb. בָּלַל ('give fodder,' AV 'give provender') occurs. The same Heb. word בְּלִיל occurs in Job 24⁶, but here RV has 'provender' (AV 'corn'), and in Is 30²⁴ (AV and RV 'provender'). This last term (see PROVENDER) is more frequently the trⁿ of מִסְפּוֹא Gn 24²⁵·³² 42²⁷ 43²⁴, Jg 19¹⁹. See further under AGRICULTURE.

FOLD. — (A) IN OT. — **1.** גְּדֵרָה (only in plur.), properly the walls or fences erected to shelter and defend the flock, Nu 32¹⁶·³⁴·³⁶, Zeph 2⁶. **2.** דֹּבֶר Is 5¹⁷ Mic 2¹² prob. means 'pasture' (so RV), but both the text and the meaning of this passage are doubtful (see Nowack, *ad loc.*). **3.** מִכְלָה, a transcriptional error for מִכְלָא (from כָּלָא 'shut up') in Hab 3¹⁷. The correct form appears in Ps 50⁹ 78⁷⁰. **4.** נָוֶה 'farm' or 'homestead' (2 S 7⁸), including both farm-house and lands; often used in connexion with sheep and shepherds (Is 65¹⁰, Jer 33¹²), and also poetical for 'habitation,' whether of men or flocks (Is 23²⁰, Jer 31²³ of Jerus.; Pr 3³³ of the righteous; Ex 15¹³, 2 S 15²⁵ of J''). **5.** [נָאָה] only in pl. const. נְאוֹת 'pastures' (Jl 2²², Ps 65¹², Jer 23¹⁰, Am 1², where see Driver's note). **6.** שְׁפַתַּיִם, which in AV of Ps 68¹³ is trᵈ 'pots,' prob. means 'sheepfolds' (so RV), like **7.** מִשְׁפְּתַיִם Gn 49¹⁴ (of Issachar 'couching between the sheepfolds' [RV], 'between two burdens' [AV]), Jg 5¹⁶ (of Reuben; see Moore's note). **8.** In Is 13²⁰ where AV has 'neither shall the shepherds make their fold there,' it is a verb that is used, הִרְבִּיץ, which RV accurately tr. 'make their flocks to lie down.' **9.** In 2 Ch 32²⁸ עֲדָרִים לָאֲוֵרוֹת cannot mean as in RV 'flocks in folds'; the AV 'cotes for flocks' is prob. correct, although this involves a transposition and the reading אֻדֹרוֹת לָעֲדָרִים (see Kittel in *SBOT, ad loc.*).
(B) IN NT.—**1.** αὐλή, the enclosed space or court within which the sheep were penned, Jn 10¹·¹⁶. **2.** ποιμνή. In Jn 10¹⁶ AV has 'there shall be one *fold*,' a mistranslation which suggests an erroneous doctrine of the Church. The meaning is correctly given by RV 'they shall become one *flock*' (cf. Mt 26³¹, Lk 2⁸, 1 Co 9⁷).
Folds were used mainly as a protection at night from wild beasts (cf. Gn 31³⁹, 1 S 17³⁴). They consisted of an enclosure surrounded by a stone wall (Nu 32¹⁶), by preference near a well (Ex 2¹⁶ᶠ·, Ps 23²), and had often the extra protection of a tower (Gn 35²¹ (?), 2 Ch 26¹⁰, Mic 4⁸). The flocks were carefully counted as they passed in and out (Jer 33¹³). Sometimes a number of flocks might be kept in one fold under the charge of a 'porter' (θυρωρός), who opened to each shepherd as he came to reclaim his flock (Jn 10³). See further under SHEEP, SHEPHERD.   J. A. SELBIE.

FOLDEN.—This earlier ptcp. of the verb to fold is found in Nah 1[10] 'while they be folden together as thorns' (RV 'like tangled [Amer. RV entangled] thorns'). The meaning is that the thorns are intertwined so as to form an impenetrable hedge. The tr[n] comes from the Geneva Bible, 'For *he shall come as* unto thornes folden one in another,' with the marginal gloss, 'Thogh the Assyrians thinke them selves like thornes that pricke on all sides, yet the Lord wil set fyre on them.' For this sense of the verb to fold cf. Mt 27[29] Wyc. 'thei foldynge a crowne of thornis,' and Ca 7[5] Cov. 'The hayre of thy heade is like the kynges purple folden up in plates.' The Heb. (סְרֻכִים) is used in Job 8[17] of roots entwined round a heap of stones, EV 'His roots are wrapped about the heap.'

J. HASTINGS.

FOLK was at one time used as equivalent to 'nation'(Ger. *Volk*). Thus Ac 10[35] Wyc. 'in eche folk he that dredith God and worchith rightwisnesse is accepte to hym'; Ps 33[12] Cov. 'Blessed are the people that holde the LORDE for their God, and blessed are the folke whom he hath chosen to be his heritage' (a tr[n] preferred by 'Four Friends': see *Psalms Chron. Arranged*, 1891, p. 387) ; 2 Es 5[26] Cov. 'Amonge all ye multitudes of folkes thou hast gotten the one people.' So in AV Jer 51[58] 'the people shall labour in vain, and the folk in the fire' (לְאֻמִּים ; RV 'the nations for the fire'). So in Pr 30[26] the meaning is 'nation,' though the application is to the 'conies,' after Cov. 'the conyes are but a feeble folk' (Heb. עַם). But in Gn 33[15] (עַם) the word is used of a chieftain's followers or retainers, a special sense which is now only Scottish.* Cf. G. Pettie (1581), Tr[n] of Guazzo's *Civ. Conv.* iii. 170, 'The maister of the house . . . ought . . . to shewe himselfe more seuere towards his owne folke, then towards others.' In NT the word is thrice used for people or persons indefinitely (Mk 6[5], Jn 5[3], Ac 5[16]), and there is no corresponding Greek word. In the last passage a plural form is employed ('sicke folkes' in 1611), which is now used only of relatives, esp. in the phrase 'young folks,' the word 'folk' being itself collective. See KINSFOLK.

J. HASTINGS.

FOLLOW, FOLLOWER.—In the OT 'follow' is sometimes the tr[n] of the adv. אַחַר *ahar* (often in plur. constr. אַחֲרֵי), *after*, with some verb meaning to go or walk, thrice with הָיָה to be (Ex 23[2], 2 S 2[10], 1 K 16[21]). This verb is often omitted, however, a pregnant Heb. idiom being the result, as 1 S 13[7] 'all the people followed him trembling' (חָרְדוּ אַחֲרָיו literally, as AVm 'trembled after him') ; Am 7[15] 'the Lord took me as I followed the flock' (מֵאַחֲרֵי הַצֹּאן, lit. as AVm 'from behind the flock,' RV 'from following'). Still more idiomatically, the verb 'to fill' is used with this adv., and then the Eng. is 'follow fully' or 'wholly,' as Dt 1[36] 'he hath wholly followed the LORD' (מִלֵּא אַחֲרֵי יהוה, lit. 'he hath filled up after the LORD,' or as AVm 'fulfilled [to go] after').

Occasionally, the meaning is to follow so as to overtake, to pursue, when the Heb. is רָדַף, as Ps 38[20] 'I follow the thing that good is.' Then the Eng. is most often 'follow after,' as Gn 44[4] 'Up, follow after the men ; and when thou dost overtake them, say unto them.' The force of these passages is probably lost to the modern Eng. reader. Thus in Is 5[11] 'Woe unto them that rise up early in the morning, that they may follow

* Cf. Kethe's version of Ps 100[3] (as it first appeared in Daye's Psalter, 1560–61)—

'The Lord ye know is God in dede
with out our aide, he did us make :
We are his folck, he doth us fede,
and for his shepe, he doth us take.'

Modern editors have altered 'folck,' which represents 'people' in the prose versions, into 'flock,' which represents nothing.

strong drink,' though RV retains 'follow,' the word conveys the sense of determined pursuit (LXX διώκειν, Vulg. *sectari*, Luther *sich befleissigen*). Cf. Shaks. *Coriol.* IV. v. 104—

'Since I have ever followed thee with hate.'

In Ps 23[6] 'Surely goodness and mercy shall follow me all the days of my life,' the Heb. is the same (יִרְדְּפוּנִי), but the Eng. is probably rather 'accompany me,' as 1 Co 10[13] Tind. 'There hath none other temptacion taken you, but soche as foloweth the nature of men.'

To the Heb. text רָדְפוּ, *i.e.* 'pursue' of Jg 3[28] (EV 'Follow after me'), Moore prefers רְדוּ, *i.e.* 'follow down,' after LXX Κατάβητε ὀπίσω μου, and the Heb. of the next clause.

Another Heb. phrase tr[d] 'follow' is lit. 'at the feet of,' as Jg 8[5] 'the people that follow me' (בְּרַגְלַי, lit. 'at my feet') ; so Ex 11[8], 1 S 25[27], 1 K 20[10], 2 K 3[9]. Finally, the Heb. verb דָּבֵק *to cleave to* is occasionally translated 'follow close after,' Jer 42[16], or 'f. hard after,' Ps 63[8] (and in Hiph. 1 S 14[22], 2 S 1[6], 1 Ch 10[2]) ; or 'f. hard upon,' 1 S 31[2] (Hiph.) 'And the Philistines followed hard upon Saul and upon his sons.' Cf. Job 13[25] Cov. 'Wilt thou be so cruell and extreme unto a flyenge leaf, and folowe upon drye stubble?' and Bingham (1623), *Xenophon*, 115, 'They dare and will be readie to follow upon us if we retire.' RV adds Jg 20[42] 'the battle followed hard after them' (AV 'overtook them').

In 2 Mac 4[48] προαγορεύω in its solitary occurrence in bibl. Greek is tr[d] in AV 'followed the matter' (οἱ προηγορήσαντες, RV 'they that were spokesmen'). The word is common enough in class. Greek in the sense here intended, viz. to speak for, or claim a right, in public. The Eng. of AV means to pursue the matter to its accomplishment, to prosecute the affair ; for which cf. *Hum. Town* (1693), i. 30, 'giving his lawyer double Fees, that his Cause may be well followed'; and Shaks. *2 Henry IV.* I. i. 21—

'O ! such a day,
So fought, so followed, and so fairly won,
Came not till now to dignify the times,
Since Cæsar's fortunes.'

No other obsolete or unusual expression seems to be used in the Apocr. which is not represented in OT or NT. But the variety of words tr[d] in AV 'follow' is instructive. The foll. are found : ἀκολουθέω, Jth 15[13], Sir 23[28] (RV omits), 2 Mac 4[17] 8[36] ; ἐξακολουθέω, Sir 5[2], Three 18 ; ἐπακολουθέω, Ad. Est 15[4], Sir 46[6] ; κατακολουθέω, Jth 11[6] ; παρακολουθέω, 2 Mac 8[11] ; διώκω, Sir 11[10] (RV 'pursue') 27[8] 29[19] (Gr. διώκων ἐργολαβείας, AV 'he that undertaketh and followeth other men's business for gain,' RV 'undertaketh contracts for work') 31[5] 34[2] ; καταδιώκω, Sir 27[17] (RV 'pursue') ; πορεύομαι, To 4[5] ; πορεύομαι ὀπίσω, Sir 46[10], RV 'walk after'; ἐπιπορεύομαι, 2 Mac 2[28] (Gr. τὸ δὲ ἐπιπορεύεσθαι τοῖς ὑπογραμμοῖς τῆς ἐπιτομῆς ἀτονοῦντες, AV 'labouring to follow the rules of an abridgement,' RV 'and again having no strength [marg. 'making no effort'] to fill in [marg. 'enlarge on'] the outlines of our abridgement) ; ἐξέρχομαι ὀπίσω, Mac 227 (RV 'come forth after') ; γίνομαι πρός, 2 Mac 11[29] ; ζηλόω, Sir 51[18] (AV 'earnestly I followed,' RV 'I was zealous for'), 2 Mac 4[16] (AV 'followed so earnestly,' RV 'earnestly followed') ; σύνειμι, 2 Mac 9[4] (RV 'accompany'). Besides those verbs there are the expressions τὴν ὑπογεγραμμένην ἐπιστολήν, 1 Es 2[16], AV 'these letters following,' RV 'the letter following'; τὰ ὑπογεγραμμένα, 'as followeth'; τῇ ἐχομένῃ, 'on the day following'; and in 2 Es *sequor* 6[7. 9] 11[13], *subsequor* 7[35].

In NT the most frequent word is the simple verb ἀκολουθέω, which is used 77 times in the Gospels of following Jesus, and only once otherwise (Mk 14[13]) of following the man with the pitcher of water. We find also 5 of its compounds tr[d] either 'follow' or 'follow after' : (1) ἐξακολουθέω, to follow out or to the end, 2 P 1[16] 2[2. 15] ; (2) ἐπακολουθέω, to follow close upon, Mk 16[20], 1 Ti 5[10] (EV 'diligently followed'), 5[24] ('Some men's sins are open beforehand, going before to judgment ; and some men they follow after,' *i.e.* may be undetected by man, but follow them hard to God's judgment-seat), 1 P 2[21] ; (3) κατακολουθέω, to follow behind, used only of women in NT, Lk 23[55], Ac 16[17] ; (4) παρακολουθέω, to follow close, to follow up, tr[d] 'follow' in AV only in 'Mk' 16[17] 'these signs shall follow them that believe,' but the same vb. is used in Lk 1³ of following up the details of a narrative (AV 'having had understanding,' RV 'having traced the course'), also in 1 Ti 4⁶ of closely following Paul's teaching, so as to teach alike (AV 'good doctrine whereunto thou hast attained,' RV 'which thou hast followed *until now*), and in 2 Ti 3¹⁰ so as to practise it (AV 'hast fully known my doctrine,' RV 'didst follow my teaching') ; (5) συνακολουθέω, to follow by one's side, to accompany a leader, Mk 5³⁷ 14⁵¹, Lk 23⁴⁹.

As *rādhaph* in OT is almost invariably trᵈ by διώκω in LXX, so διώκω itself is sometimes trᵈ in NT by 'follow,' He 12¹⁴ 'Follow peace with all men,' 1 Th 5¹⁵ 'f. that which is good,' 2 Ti 2²² 'f. righteousness,' and Lk 17²³ ; or 'follow after,' Ro 9³⁰· ³¹ 14¹⁹, 1 Co 14¹, Ph 3¹², 1 Ti 6¹¹. RV has 'follow after' throughout, except Ph 3¹² 'press on.' The compound καταδιώκω is used in Mk 1³⁶, its only occurrence, and trᵈ in EV 'followed after' ; but, as Gould says, that trⁿ is inadequate, since the κατά gives the idea of hard, persistent search, as in our phrase 'to hunt down,' hence rather 'pursued him closely.' In all those passages, however, the Eng. 'follow,' even with the addition of 'after,' is now inadequate.

In the trⁿ of some of the compounds of ἀκολουθέω the sense of 'follow' is very nearly 'imitate.' This is unmistakably the meaning where the Gr. is μιμεῖσθαι, 2 Th 3⁷· ⁹, He 13⁷, 3 Jn ¹¹. Thus in He 13⁷ 'whose faith follow.' RV has always 'imitate.' Cf. T. Adams (1615), *Spirit. Navig.* 41, 'Glasse among stones is as a foole amongst men ; for it followes precious stones in colour, not in virtue.' So μιμητής in all its occurrences (1 Co 4¹⁶ 11¹, Eph 5¹, 1 Th 1⁶ 2¹⁴, He 6¹²) is rendered by 'follower' in AV, by 'imitator' in RV ; and συνμιμητής, Ph 3¹⁷, is in AV 'followers together,' in RV 'imitators together.' Cf. Burke (1781), *Corresp.* ii. 437, 'We, who ought to have taken the lead in so noble a work, are but ill followers even of the examples which are set to us.'

In 1 P 3¹³ the edd. prefer ζηλωταί after the best MSS to μιμηταί of TR, hence 'zealous' in RV for AV 'followers.'

                     J. HASTINGS.

FOLLY.—See FOOL.

FOOD.—I. The material eaten for the sustenance of the body is often mentioned in the Bible, in AV most commonly as *bread*, but often as *meat*, occasionally as *food* or *victuals*. מַאֲכָל *ma'ăkhāl*, or victual in general, is used about 29 times, always in its literal sense ; לֶחֶם *leḥem*, literally bread, is used for food in general about 230 times, and is often used figuratively (see BREAD). אֹכֶל *'ōkhel* is used 42 times for food or victuals in the literal sense, and the cognate *'okhlah* is used by Ezekiel for fuel, in the sense of food for the fire. In the NT βρῶμα is the word used 17 times, and τροφή 16 times. βρῶσις is used 4 times by St. John and 5 times in the Epistles, often in a metaphorical sense. The commonest metaphorical uses are (1) that which refreshes the soul, doing the will of God, Jn 4³² ; and in a cognate sense Christ our Saviour is the food of the soul, Jn 6⁵⁵ ; (2) advanced doctrinal teaching, 1 Co 3², He 5¹⁴ ; (3) mere ceremonial observances, He 9¹⁰ 13⁹ (for other uses see BREAD).

II. FOOD-STUFFS.—According to Gn 1²⁹ the original food of mankind consisted of fruits and seeds which the earth produced naturally. In this respect man resembled those of the higher mammals which are most nearly allied to him in structure, which are for the most part herbivorous and frugivorous. After the primary dispersion the spoils of the chase were added to the primitive dietary even from the earliest times, for the broken bones of wild animals and the shells of molluscs which have served as food are among the earliest traces of

primeval man as yet discovered. There were mighty hunters even before Nimrod (Gn 6¹¹ 10⁹), and implements of the chase were among the first of man's inventions.

In process of time, as agricultural and pastoral industries developed, the produce of the tilled field and of the herd and flock supplied men with additional food-stuffs (Gn 4². ³· ⁴· ²⁰). The expression of the divine sanction for these additions, recorded in Gn 9³, seems to have for its special object the injunction of the taboo concerning the eating of blood.

A. The inhabitants of the Bible lands lived chiefly on *vegetable food*. At the present day, bread, olives and oil, butter, milk, and cheese, fruit and vegetables, with meat on special occasions, or in particularly wealthy households, make up the dietary of most of their descendants in the East (Thomson, i. 98). The staff of life was, and is, bread made of cereal grains, especially wheat, millet, dhūrah, and barley, to which is now added rice, unknown in Bible times (see BREAD).

(*a*) **Parched corn** is 5 times mentioned as an article of diet, and is coupled with bread in Lv 23¹⁴. One form of this, called קָלִי (*ḳālī*), was made of the common, nearly ripe wheat by heating the grain on an iron 'girdle' (Lane, i. 251 ; Robinson, ii. 50), or by binding the ears into wisps and roasting them over the fire (*ib.* iii. 393). In Arabic *ḳali* means anything done in the frying-pan, and the material of the parched corn may be meal, or polenta, or flour, or else the unground grain. It is a common food of labourers (Ru 2¹⁴), and is sold ready prepared in Eastern towns as a convenient food for travellers. David brought 3 pecks of it to his brethren at Elah (1 S 17¹⁷) ; and Abigail brought 5 pecks to David's men (1 S 25¹⁸). In Lv 2¹⁴ 'green ears of corn dried by the fire' are mentioned, and in Lv 23¹⁴ these are coupled with parched corn. This form is made, according to Abu'l Walid, of finer garden wheat, which is called כַּרְמֶל *karmel* (2 K 4⁴²). In RV this is called 'bruised corn of the fresh ear,' alluding to its being beaten in a mortar (Pr 27²²). When this bruised corn was dried in the sun it was called רִיפוֹת *riphôth* (Pr 27²², 2 S 17¹⁹), Grain of this kind was used to cover the well in which Ahimaaz and Jonathan were hidden at Bahurim (LXX ἀραφώθ, Vulg. *siccans ptisana*). The flour and parched corn of 2 S 17²⁸ is called ἄλευρον καὶ ἄλφιτον, flour and polenta or meal in LXX (see Herod. vii. 119). Ἄλφιτον is used in Homer for barley-meal only, but Hippocrates uses this word for meal in general. For classic and Hebrew usage of polenta see Gruner, *de oblatione Primitiarum*, in Ugolini, vol. xvii. Royle has contended that *ḳali* is not corn, but some leguminous plant, as *ḳalee* is the Hindi for pulse ; but R. Salomon in his Commentary on *Aboda Zara* says there are two kinds—one of corn and one of cicer or lentiles. For mention of parched peas see Plautus, *Bacch.* iv. 5. 7, and Horace, *de art. poet.* 249. Robinson speaks of a variety of this parched corn which is first boiled, then bruised in a mill to take off the husk, then dried ; this is named *burgoul* (ii. 394). According to Burckhardt, *burgoul* is wheat boiled with leaven and dried in the sun, cooked by being boiled with butter and oil. It is the common dish with all classes in Syria (*Notes*, i. 59).

(*b*) The leguminous plants, beans and lentiles, form an important part of the diet of the Western Asiatics. These were probably included in the זֵרֹעִים *zērō'îm*, or pulse of Dn 1¹², which was despised but sufficient nourishment (v.¹⁰· ¹⁵) ; in Theod. the word is σπέρματα (LXX ὄσπρια, RVm herbs), which meant any vegetable food ; see the name of the herbseller in Aristoph. *Lysist.* 457. In 2 S 17²⁸ the word pulse is not in the Hebrew.

Lentiles (עֲדָשִׁים *'ădāshîm*, LXX φακός), the seeds

of *Ervum lens*, which is still, as formerly (2 S 23[11]), cultivated in Palestine, and used as food (Thomson, i. 253; Burckhardt, *Arabia*, i. 65). There are two varieties, one pale red the other dark brown, and the pottage made by boiling either of these is savoury (Gn 25[34]), pleasant to the taste, and red, hence Esau called it 'the red, this red' (see incident in Diog. Laert. vii. 3). In Egypt lentiles were called *ārsāna* (*Pap. Anastasi*, iv. 15), and in Assyria *a'ssu*. In Greece they were used as food by the poor (Aristoph. *Plutus*, 1004–5; and Pherecrates, *ap. Athen.* iv. p. 159). The Romans regarded lentiles as an Egyptian plant (Virg. *Georg.* i. 228; and Martial, *Epig.* xiii. 9), and they were sometimes used as a bread-stuff (Athenæus, *Deipnos*, iv. 158; see also Ezk 4[9]). An allied species of vicia is used as a camel-food by the Arabs, and called *kersenna* (Robinson, ii. 83). Lentile flour is sold in this country under the name 'revalenta.' Lentiles were brought by Barzillai to David in exile (2 S 17[28]). Pottage is sometimes made by boiling the lentiles with meat, more commonly a little suet is added to the water when boiling (Kitto).

Beans (פּוֹל *pol*, LXX κύαμος), the seeds of the common bean, *Faba vulgaris*, are also used in Palestine for food, especially by the poor. The bean is originally a native of Persia, and was sometimes used as a bread-stuff, as it is still in Savoy and other parts of Europe (Ezk 4[9]; Pliny, xviii. 12); it is sometimes eaten parched or roasted (Theocritus, *Id.* 7. 65; Robinson, iii. 87). Food of this kind was brought to David in exile (2 S 17[28], but LXX omits the parched pulse). More commonly, beans are boiled in oil with garlic (Shaw, *Travels*, i. 257) or in water, and made into pottage, with or without meat; sometimes they are eaten with butter and pepper. Robinson describes raw beans, soaked in water until they sprout, as part of the Lenten fare of the monks at Mount Sinai (i. 259). In Egypt beans were used, and have been found sometimes in mummy cases; they were called *kat'a*, *ari*, and sometimes *pir*, but the last was probably the bean of the *Nelumbium lotus*, and *kat'a* is tr. by Lieblein the Opuntia fruit. Birch and Eisenlohr tr. *khep* in the Harris papyrus as 'bean'; if so, they formed a part of the offering to Ptah; although Herodotus says that they were not eaten in Egypt, and were accounted impure (ii. 37). For similar prejudices against beans, see Porphyry, *De Abstinentia*, i. 26; Diog. Laert. viii. 19; Clement Alex. *Strom.* iii., and other authors. The high priest was forbidden to eat beans and lentiles on the day before the great Day of Atonement (Gemara, *Joma*, i. § 4), and the Flamen Dialis was forbidden to eat them also, as they were thought to dull the senses and cause disturbing dreams. For other superstitions concerning beans see Pliny, xviii. 12.

Husks (κεράτια) in the parable of the Prodigal Son (Lk 15[16]) are the dark purple horn-like pods of *Ceratonia siliqua*, the charrub tree of the Arabs and of the Talmud. This is a large handsome spreading tree common in Mediterranean countries, whose sweet, fleshy pods, the caroba beans of the Italians, are used as food by the poor (Robinson, ii. 250). In Greece and Italy they were used by the Stoics as a disciplinary food for youths (Persius, iii. 55; Juv. xi. 58), and Horace's reference, *Ep.* II. i. 123, is well known. In Palestine, where the tree is fairly common, the beans are used as cattle food (*Shabbath*, xxiv. § 2), and are occasionally mentioned in the Talmud (see Maimon. in *Demai*, ii. § 1, and Buxtorf, *s.v.*). Pliny refers to their use in feeding swine (xv. 24; see Columella, vii. 9), and in Italy they are thought to give a sweet taste to the animal's flesh. They are imported into this country, and are sometimes called 'locust-beans' or St. John's bread, from a mistaken notion that they were the ἀκρίδες of Mt 3[4]. Steeped in water

they are used to make a pleasant, sweetish drink (see Pliny, xiii. 16 and xxiii. 8).

Fitches in Ezk 4[9] (*kussemoth*) were cereal grains, probably spelt (see BREAD). The same word in AV of Is 28[25-27] is in Heb. קֶצַח *ḳezaḥ*, LXX μελάνθιον, and signifies the black cummin, which is the seed of a ranunculaceous plant, *Nigella sativa*, a native of the Eastern Mediterranean countries. These seeds are beaten out of the pod-like follicles with a *matteh* or staff, and sprinkled on bread as a carminative, as we use caraway seeds (Pliny, xix. 7). They have a hot but not unpleasant taste. The plant is called *ḳizah* by the Arabs and *kuzatu* in the Assyr. plant list, and in Vulg. is named *git*. For references to the use of these seeds, see Plautus, *Rudens*. v. 2, 39; Ausonius, 344, 8; Dioscorides, iii. 83; Pliny, xix. 8, xx. 17, etc.

(*c*) Of cucurbitaceous plants, melons, cucumbers, and gourds are mentioned in the Bible. The two former are fruits much relished in Egypt (Nu 11[5]).

Cucumbers (קִשֻּׁאִים *kishshu'im*, LXX σίκυοι) are the fruit of *Cucumis chate* (the *khata* of the Arabs) and *C. sativus*, the common cucumber. Both species grow freely in Egypt (Nu 11[5]) and in Palestine, and, according to Kitto, is eaten by all classes to an extent that would scarcely be credible in this country; and Forskål says this is the commonest fruit in Egypt (*Fl. Ægypt.* 168). Finn speaks of Arabs eating cucumbers by the wayside for refreshment (*Byeways in Palestine*, 2). Robinson saw fields of them (iii. 344), and Thomson describes a garden of cucumbers with a booth for a watchman (Is 1[8]). As birds do not eat them, a scarecrow is useless in such a place (Bar 6[70]). In Assyr. they are called *kissu* and in Egyptian *skheptu*. Hippocrates speaks of them as eaten when green (*de Vict. Ratione*, ii.). The fruit of the *chaté* is longer and greener than the common cucumber. They are often eaten with vinegar or bread, or filled with mince-meat and spices. Tristram notes Arab children bringing to school as their dinner barley-bread and cucumber, which they ate rind and all. Forskål describes the method whereby a delicious drink is made from its juice.

Melons (אֲבַטִּחִים *'ăbaṭṭiḥim*, LXX πέπονες, Nu 11[5]), called by the Arabs *baṭṭikh*, are grown and used abundantly both in Egypt and Palestine. Both the water-melon (*Citrullus vulgaris*) and the flesh-melon (*Cucumis melo*) are cultivated, and both were probably included under this name. The Talmudists distinguish these, calling the former *melapepon* and the latter *'ăbaṭṭihim* (*Maaseroth*, i. § 4; *Terumoth*, viii. § 6; *Chilaim*, i. § 2), but in *Aruch* they are both known by their Heb. name. It is singular that in Coptic they are called by their Greek name.

Wild Gourd (פַּקֻּעַת), in plural *pēḳāim*, 1 K 6[18] 7[24], or *paḳḳuōth*, 2 K 4[39], tr. in former passage 'knops,' in the latter 'wild gourd,' is the fruit of the vine-like *Citrullus colocynthis*, which is common in the Jordan Valley. 'To human nature it is of so mortal bitterness that little indeed, and even the leaf, is a most vehement purgative. They say that it will leave a man half dead, and he may only recover his strength by eating flesh meat' (Doughty, i. 132). It is very rare in the hill-country of Ephraim, hence the son of the prophet who gathered it did not know the plant, but mistook it for the non-poisonous *Cucumis prophetarum* or globe cucumber common in Samaria. In an Arabic version of La 3[15] the text is rendered 'he hath sated me with colocynth,' so proverbial is its bitterness. Its elegant shape suggested its imitation in the ornamenting of the carved panelling of the temple and of the edge of the molten sea. In Assyr. it is *pikkuti*.

Jonah's Gourd (קִיקָיוֹן *ḳiḳāyōn*, LXX κολοκύνθη)

was supposed from the likeness of the name to the Egyptian *kiki* (Herod. ii. 94) to be the *Ricinus communis*, the *Palma Christi* or castor-oil plant, a rapidly-growing herb which Pliny describes as becoming almost tree-like and capable of affording shade; even in our gardens its growth under favourable conditions is extraordinarily rapid. It is not quite clear what the *kiki* of the hieroglyphic texts was, as *ricinus* is in Coptic called *jismis*, which represents the ancient form *kesmes* or *kesbet*. Maimonides in *Shabbath*, ii. 1, says, however, the oil of kik is from a plant called by the Arabs *kherua*, which is *ricinus*. Tristram objects to this identification, as the *ricinus* is not a climbing plant, but the passage in Jon 4⁶ does not describe it as such; he supposes the plant to have been the roof-gourd or *Lagenaria vulgaris* of which Pliny states that 'shooting upwards with the greatest rapidity it soon covers the arched roofs of houses and trellises' (xix. 24). The Vulg. renders it *hedera* or ivy, and this occasioned a controversy between Jerome and Augustine (see Hieron. in Jon 4⁶ and *Epist.* 89). In early Christian art the plant is fancifully represented as a trailing melon-like plant covering a trellis-work, as on the sarcophagus in the Lateran from St. Peter's crypt (Parker's *Photog.* No. 2905; see also Bellorius, *de Antiq. Lucernis*, pl. iii. fig. 30, for a representation on a lamp). An undetermined species of climbing plant in Assyrian was called *ḳaḳulla*.

(*d*) Of alliaceous vegetables there are three mentioned as favourite foods of the Israelites in Egypt—onions, leeks, and garlic (Nu 11⁵). All these are still much cultivated in Bible lands, and are in constant use among Orientals either raw or cooked.

Onions (בְּצָלִים *bĕzālim*, LXX κρόμμυον), the bulbs of *Allium cepa*. These are commonly eaten raw as a relish with bread, or boiled with meal (Robinson, ii. 211), or with lentiles (*Terumoth*, x. 1; Martial, *Epig.* iii. 376), or with beef (Apicius, 224). By the Assyrians the onion was called *sursu*, and by the Egyptians *het* (Copt. *mejol*). Herodotus tells that on the casing of the great pyramid was inscribed the value of the onions, garlic, and radishes eaten by the builders (ii. 25). The later Latin writers say that the onion was deified by the Egyptians (Juv. xv. 9; Plut. *de Iside*, 353). Pliny (xix. 6) says that garlic and onions are invoked by them when taking an oath; and Lucian (*Jup. Trag.* 42) says that the inhabitants of Pelusium were especially devoted to this cultus. There is, however, no native evidence for this. Among the Greeks onions were highly esteemed, and Homer speaks of Hecamede giving Patroclus an onion as a relish (*Il.* xi. 630); but Lucian describes them as food for the poor (*Dial.* Mer. 14. 2; *Ep. Sat.* 28).

Leeks (חָצִיר *ḥāzir*, LXX πράσα). The Heb. name used in Nu 11⁵ literally means 'green herb,' and is rendered grass, hay, or green herb in 15 other passages; but as these are not human food, the translators have here followed the LXX, leeks being supposed to resemble grass in habit and colour. Leeks are eaten raw with bread, or sliced and put into vinegar, or boiled in pottage (Artemidorus, i. 67). Nero is said to have on stated days fed only on leeks and oil to improve his voice (Pliny, xix. 6). The Egyptian leek was particularly esteemed by the Romans. It was known as *āga* (Copt. *ēgi*), while the Assyrians called it *ezallu usuratti*. Ludolf translates *ḥāzir* 'lettuce,' and Scheuchzer says that it probably means the *Nelumbium lotus*; but the balance of evidence is in favour of the common leek (*Allium porrum*).

Garlic (שׁוּם *shûm*, LXX σκόρδον). The cloves or bulbs of *Allium sativum* were so commonly used as flavouring that the Jews were reproached for their liking for these strongly-scented herbs. In *Shabbat Jehuda* they are said to smell foully of garlic; and Salomon Levi defends their taste in *Theriac. Jud.* i. § 20. In Egypt this plant was, and is still, much used (Herod. ii. 125; Wilkinson, i. 169; Lane, i. 257). Garlic was supposed to have the power of neutralizing the poison of the asp, and its use by penitent criminals was believed to purify them and absolve them of guilt. In *Maaser sheni*, v. § 8, garlic is called the 'Lord of tears.' At the present day it is much prized in the East as a remedy for many ailments and as an antidote for many poisons; Pliny enumerates 61 ways in which it was recommended medicinally, and Prudentius speaks of an altar to the garlic as being erected at Pelusium. The Egyptians called it *ṣeṣen* (Copt. *ṣeṣen*).

Bitter Herbs (מְרֹרִים *mĕrōrim*, LXX πικρίδες, Vulg. *lactucæ agrestes*) are mentioned in Ex 12⁸, Nu 9¹¹, and referred to in La 3¹⁵ (EV 'bitterness'). Bitter salads are often eaten with meat in Egypt, Syria, and elsewhere, the commonest plant used for this purpose being the lettuce (*Lactuca sativa*), the *āfa* of the Egyptians, called by the Hebrews *ḥazereth* (probably the Assyrian *haserottu*). According to the rabbinical writers (*Pesachim*, ii. § 6), there were five bitter herbs which might be eaten with the paschal lamb: the endive (*Lactuca endivia*) was the second of these, called by them *ulshin* (probably the Assyr. *harussu*); it also is common in Egypt. The third is called *thamkah*, described by Maimonides as a garden endive, the *cichorium* of Pliny (xix. 6), but said in *Aruch* to be a *carduus*, in the Gemara to be a *gingidium*, probably the *Artedia squamata* of botanists, a bitter aromatic umbelliferous plant. In *Zemaṭẓ David* it is said to be a kind of helminthia which grows near date palms. The fourth, *ḥarḥabina*, was probably *marrubium*, or the horehound, but according to Lightfoot the beet; and the fifth, *maror*, is called in *Aruch* a pot-herb, possibly *Inula Helenium* or *Elecampane*, which was a plant highly esteemed as a stomachic in the *Regimen sanitatis* of Salernum. Maimonides says it was a bitter coriander, which, according to Varro, was often pounded, mixed with vinegar, and sprinkled over meat; but Lightfoot thinks that *maror* is horehound (*Ministerium Templi*, XIII. v. 2).

It is probable that the words of the ordinance of the passover were not meant to specify any particular bitter herb. According to *Pesachim*, ii. § 6, the herbs might be eaten fresh or dried, but must not be soaked, stewed, or boiled. Delitzsch gives *marru* and *muraru* as the names of bitter garden plants (*Assyr. Handwörterbuch*, 427).

For **Mandrakes** see MEDICINE.

(*e*) The fruits mentioned in the Bible are not very numerous.

Almonds (שָׁקֵד *shāḳēd*, LXX κάρυον) are mentioned in Gn 43¹¹ as part of the present sent by Jacob to the Egyptian viceroy. They are said not to be common in Egypt, and the Egyptian name of the fruit is doubtful. Brugsch believes it to be the tree called *net'*; but the Coptic uses the Greek name, which means any nut. According to Heracleon, Epicharmos, and Philyllius, κάρυον is specially used for the almond, the bitter almond being distinguished in Greek as κάρυα πικρά or ἀμυγδάλα (see Athenæus, *Deipnos*, ii. 38). The almond was supposed to prevent the intoxicating effect of wine, and was consequently taken at wine banquets (Pliny, xxiii. 8; Plutarch, *Quæst. Conviv.* vi. 4). This tree grows wild on Carmel and in Moab, and is cultivated extensively in Palestine. The Heb. name means 'hastener' in reference to its early blossoming, hence the paronomasia in Jer 1¹². The blossoms, which look white at a distance, are compared to grey hair in Ec 12⁵, and their shape was the pattern from which the cups of the seven-branched candlestick were made (Ex 25³³). Aaron's rod was probably an almond branch

(Nu 17[8]); but there was an old tradition that it was of storax wood, and that its bearing almonds was miraculous (see the verses falsely attributed to Tertullian, contra Marcion. iv. 117). In Gn 30[37] the almond tree is named לוּז lûz, the word from which the old name of Bethel was derived. Robinson notes a sweetmeat made of a mixture of almonds and dates as a present given to distinguished guests (i. 115). The ancient Medes mixed almonds with their bread.

Apples (תַּפּוּחַ tappûaḥ, LXX μῆλον), mentioned in Ca 2[3-5] 7[8] 8[5], Pr 25[11], Jl 1[12], cannot be the fruit to which we give this name, as it does not grow freely in Palestine, of which country it is not a native (see H. C. Hart, PEFSt, 1885, 282). Thomson says that he has seen it growing luxuriantly (i. 172), but Tristram believes that he has mistaken the tree (N.H. of Bible, 334). Robertson Smith, on philological grounds, has defended the claims of the common apple (Pyrus malus) to be identified with the tappûaḥ, but its scarcity renders this very improbable (Journal of Philology, xiii. 1885, p. 65). Kitto believed it to be the citron, which now grows freely in Palestine, and is described in Jos. (Ant. XIII. xiii. § 5) as one of the trees whose boughs were used at the feast of Tabernacles; but the citron is a native of N. India and China, and was probably of late introduction. Tristram has claimed the apricot as the apple of Canticles. It is a very widely cultivated tree, but is a native of Armenia (hence called by Dioscorides μῆλον Ἀρμενιακόν, HP i. 160), and is probably also a late import. The characteristics suggested by the texts are—(1) a shady tree, (2) with golden coloured fruit, (3) which is fragrant, (4) and pleasant to taste, (5) and which is the symbol of love. All these conditions are fulfilled by the quince. The tree is not very large, but it is one under whose shade one could sit or lie, as in the texts, and it is as suitable for this purpose as the vine or fig tree. Its fruit is extremely fragrant, and some varieties might be called golden by contrast if gathered in a silver filigree basket (Pr 25[11]). It is pre-eminently the fruit of love (see the mass of evidence on this gathered in Celsius' Hierobotanicon, i. 255 ff.). The quince is called μῆλον without any adjective by some of the Greek authors (see, however, Il. ix. 542, where the μῆλον tree is called tall), and is the first of the apples described by Pliny (xxiii. 6). In the light of the description in the passage in Ca 8[5] the weight of evidence is in favour of regarding this tree as the quince, which, though unpleasing to the taste of most Europeans, is yet eaten with relish by many in the East, and esteemed most wholesome. Athenæus says that full ripe quinces are better food than any other kind of apple (Deipnos, iii. 20). For a discussion on the nature of the tappûaḥ, see Houghton, PSBA, 1889, 42. The quince has a special name in the Talmud, parish (see Kelaim, i. 4), and in Arabic, which forms the basis of Robertson Smith's argument; but in Jerus. Talmud, according to Abu'l Walid, parishim means asparagus; see Guisius, in loco, Chilaim (I. iii.). A common tradition identifies the quince with the tree of the knowledge of good and evil.

Dates, the fruit of the date-palm, Phœnix dactylifera, though given in the AVm 2 Ch 31[5] as a possible translation of דְּבַשׁ debash (elsewhere rendered 'honey'), are not otherwise mentioned in the Bible. This is remarkable considering how frequently palms are referred to, and it has been supposed that the word honey in the phrase so often used in the Pentateuch descriptive of Palestine may refer to dibs or date-honey made by boiling down the fruit. This sweetmeat was made in Babylonia where palms abounded (Herodotus, i. 193), and was also made at Jericho (Jos. BJ IV. viii.

§ 3). LXX translates קֵן in 2 S 16[1] φοίνικες, 'dates,' and the palm is put among the fruit trees in Jl 1[12]. As a cultivated tree the palm is little grown now in Palestine west of the Jordan. In Egypt the date-palm was called ám and bà, and dates benrà. In Assyria the date-palm was gisimmaru, and date-honey dispu. According to Doughty (i. 148), there is no worse food than the date, and he reports the Arabs as saying that when the date is eaten alone human nature decays. For references to the palm in classical and Oriental literature, see Celsius, Hierobot. ii. 445 ff.

Figs (תְּאֵנָה teʾēnâh, LXX συκή), the fruit of Ficus carica, next to the grape the most highly prized of all the fruits of Bible lands, and 53 times mentioned in the Bible. Mohammed says of it that if any fruit has really come from Paradise it must have been the fig. Botanically speaking, what is called the fruit is the soft fleshy receptacle within which are the flowers and later the grain-like, hard, dry achenes. Hence the ancient authors speak of the fig tree as bearing fruit without flowers (Macrobius, Saturnalia, ii. 16); but as the fig itself is the inflorescence, the language of Hab 3[17] is strictly correct. The buds or young figs appear before the leaves, hence a fig tree in full leaf should have its fruit developed. The precocious tree of Mt 21[19] and Mk 11[13] was therefore unnaturally barren. The fig tree bears every year (Thomson, ii. 101), but the Rabbinists speak of a variety called benoth shuaḥ, which only brings forth fruit each third year (Maimon. Demai, i. 1, and Bartenora in Shebiith, v. v. 1), and it has been supposed that this is referred to in Mk 11[13]. The manuring of such an unpromising tree is alluded to by Cato, as in the parable, Lk 13[6].

The first crop, called בְּכּוּרָה bikkûrâh, πρόδρομοι, begins to redden in March and is ripe by June; unripe figs are called פַּגִּים paggim (hence the place-name Bethphage, 'house of green figs'). LXX calls the unripe figs in Ca 2[13] ὄλυνθοι; but according to Theophrastus (vi. 8) and Hippocrates (574. 23) these are winter figs, which grow under the leaves and do not ripen. The early figs are the most delicious and refreshing (Is 28[4], Jer 24[2], Mic 7[1], Hos 9[10]), and are easily shaken off (Nah 3[12]). See Macrobius, ii. 16. The untimely figs of Rev 6[13] are olynthi.

The summer figs, קַיִץ (2 S 16[1]), ripen in August and September (see also Mic 7[1], Am 8[1]). These are either eaten fresh or dried in the sun (Shabbath, viii. § 6), or made into cakes called דְּבֵלִים debēlim (1 S 25[18] 30[12], 2 K 20[7], 1 Ch 12[40], Is 38[21]). In making these the figs are sometimes first beaten in a mortar, then pressed into a cake (Taanith, xxviii. 1). These cakes, called by LXX παλάθη, were either round or square (see Terumoth, iv. § 8; Baba mesia, ii.). Herodotus uses the name παλάθη of other fruit cakes (iv. 23), but Athenæus distinguishes fig cakes as π. Συριακη. Such cakes are still used by the Arabs (Burckhardt, i. 51), and with barley-bread are the common food of poor travellers in the East. The town Beth-diblathaim means the house of the two cakes of figs. On the two crops of figs see the διφόρου συκῆς of Arist. Eccles. 708.

A third crop of winter figs appears in August, and ripens at the end of November. These sometimes hang on the tree when the leaves are shed, unless the tree be exposed to frost.

Figs are liable to disease, both from parasitic fungi and from insects. There are several species of both, which attack the fruit and cause it to be shed prematurely, or to shrivel and become uneatable (Jer 24[8] 29[17]). For reflections on this vision see Hieron. Comment. in Jer., on 5[24].

Sycomore Figs (שִׁקְמָה, pl. shikmim or shikmôth in Ps 78[47]) are the small fig of the Ficus sycomorus, a bluish-purple fruit eaten by the poorer classes, but considered unwholesome and indigestible (Dioscor. i. 182). The tree grows to a large size, and is found in Palestine in the lower lands from Joppa to Egypt (1 K 10²⁷, 2 Ch 1¹⁵; see Bartenora in *Shebiith*, ix. 2). Jerome notes that they are easily killed by frost, and so they were destroyed by the storm-plague in Egypt (Ps 78⁴⁷). As in the hollow receptacle the flowers which bear stamens are at the upper and those bearing pistils at the lower part, it ensures fertilization to pinch or incise them, thereby facilitating the entrance of the insects whose movements in the plant promote fertilization; this is known as caprification (Pliny, xiii. 14; Theophrastus, iv. 2). Amos calls himself a בּוֹלֵם *bôleṣ*, or scratcher of sycomore fruit, in allusion to this (LXX κνίζων συκάμινα, RV 'dresser of sycomore trees'). The superintendence of this was probably the function of Baal-hanan (1 Ch 27²⁸). This tree is abundant in Egypt, and of its wood most mummy coffins are made; as its branches generally arise from the trunk low down, it is easily climbed (Lk 19⁴). The fruit was free from tithing among the Jews (*Demai*, i. 1).

Mulberries (בָּכָא *baca*, LXX συκάμινος) are not mentioned as fruit; but as the tree is common in Palestine, and as the berries are now eaten freely, they were probably used in Bible times. The trees are named in 2 S 5²³ᶠ· and 1 Ch 14¹⁵, and the place named from them 'Baca's vale' in Ps 84⁶. Our Lord refers to the tree under the name sycamine in His lesson on faith (Lk 17⁶). For a description of the marvels of this tree see Pliny, xvi. 41, where it is described as being as remarkable as a creature possessed of animation (see also xxiii. 7).

Nuts (בָּטְנִים *boṭnîm*, LXX τερέβινθος) are the fruit of the *Pistacia vera*. This tree is a native of Syria, although not very abundant, and was brought into Europe by the Romans. The nut is the stone in the centre of the greenish drupe, and its kernel is oily, soft, and not unpleasant to taste. It is mentioned only in Gn 43¹¹. The tree is often mentioned, but its name אֵלָה *'ēlâh* or *'ēlôn* is translated oak or teil tree, as Is 6¹³ (RV terebinth tree).

Olives (וַיִת *zayith*, LXX ἐλαία), the same name for both tree and fruit. These are often mentioned in Scripture (37 times in OT and 18 in NT), and the *Olea Europæa* is a native of Palestine, and much cultivated for the sake of the oil extracted from its drupes. In Egypt the tree was called *degam*, and was esteemed in early days as a specific for all ailments (see *Papyrus Ebers*, p. 47; in the *Harris Pap.* it is called *degetu*). The tree is small, slow of growth, and irregularly branched. Its wood is hard and fine-grained, and its leaves like those of a large privet, but whitish beneath. It has a small white flower growing in racemes, and its fruit is well known. The wild plants of the olive are sometimes used as stocks on which to graft cultivated varieties with larger fruit (Ro 11¹⁷). The low size of the tree made the olive leaf brought by the dove to Noah significant (Gn 8¹¹). These trees are cultivated in orchards or olive yards (Ex 23¹¹); when ripe they are beaten (Dt 24²⁰) in order to strike off the fruit (in Is 17⁶ and 24¹⁸ badly tr. 'shaken'), and the fruit is brought to the oil mills, which consist of circular stone basins in which the drupes are crushed by a heavy stone wheel that is rolled over them. The mass is then put into small wicker baskets, which are piled over each other in a *m'aẓerah* or handpress, in which they are squeezed either by means of a long lever or a screw. The ancient presses were all lever presses. After the first pressing the pulp is put into copper pans, sprinkled with water and heated, and then pressed again. Where there is water-power the press is larger, and the mill is called a *mutrûf*; in this the olives are pressed in a stone cylinder, within which an iron-shod shaft

rotates. In old presses the pressure of the lever was supplemented by heavy stones (Thomson, i. 286). The oil is allowed to stand until the sediment subsides, and it is then poured off; sometimes salt is used to clarify it. Among those who have no oil presses the pulp is put in hot water and the oil skimmed off. The fruit is sometimes kept until soft and black before crushing. It is possible that in this state it may sometimes have been trodden by the feet, but that is never done now (Mic 6¹⁵). The oil is kept in cisterns of stone or cement (1 Ch 27²⁸), or in jars (*khawabies*) kept in cellars. For a description of the oil presses see Robinson, *BRP* iii. 365; and Thomson, *Land and Book*, ii. 286 ff. Gethsemane means an oil press.

The oil of the olive was one of the most important products of the Holy Land: corn, wine, and oil were its three staple crops. 'Certe oleo et vino gaudebat Palæstina præ Ægypto' (Reland, *Palæstina*, ccclvii.). The oil is used in cookery (Lv 2⁴), and is spread on bread (Ex 29²³), or burnt in lamps for lighting (Ex 25⁶), or used externally for anointing. This use is referred to in Jotham's parable (Jg 9⁹). The excessive use of oil was a luxury which brought men to poverty (Pr 21¹⁷). Olive oil is called שֶׁמֶן וַיִת *shemen zayith*; the finer oil which runs out of pounded olives without compression is distinguished as כָּתִית *kāthîth* (Ex 27²⁰, Lv 24² etc.). Olive oil was one of the exports from Judah to Tyre (Ezk 27¹⁷). Oil was occasionally carried as a part of their provisions by travellers (Lk 10³⁴).

The olive tree is liable to a parasitic mould disease, a mildew which causes it to cast its fruit or makes its flower to shrivel (Dt 28⁴⁰, Job 15³³). It is also liable to be attacked by insects (Am 4⁹). The olive tree is used as a type of heavenly favour (Ps 52⁸, Hos 14⁶, Jer 11¹⁶), and of family prosperity (Ps 128³). Oil is used metaphorically as expressive of divine grace (see ANOINTING); or the salutary reproof of the righteous (Ps 141⁵). The oil of joy is spoken of in Is 61³, see Erman, p. 231. The oil tree, *ēẓ shemen* of Neh 8¹⁵, 1 K 6²³, Is 41¹⁹, is generally believed to be the *zackum* or *Balanites Ægyptiaca*, a native of the Jordan Valley, and one whose oil is esteemed as a useful medicine.

Pomegranates (רִמּוֹן *rimmôn*, LXX ῥόα), used both for the tree and the fruit. This is also an abundant fruit in Palestine, of which it is a native, and is mentioned 32 times in the Bible. Pomegranates were among the fruits brought back by the spies from Eshcol (Nu 13²³). The tree (*Punica granatum*) grows to about 20 ft. in height, and has myrtle-like leaves and scarlet flowers, which come out early in the spring (Ca 6¹¹). The fruit is well known, and was a favourite with the Jews; its bright colour is referred to in Ca 4³. Its sour juice was, and is, used in cookery (Russell, i. 85; Thomson, i. 286) and in making cooling sherbet, as we use lemons. The juice is sometimes fermented (Dioscorides, v. 34), but the wine is rather tasteless unless spiced (Ca 8²). 'In this fruit Nature has shown to us a grape, and indeed not must, but wine ready made' (Pliny, xxiii. 6). The pomegranate supplied a pattern for ornament (1 K 7²⁰, Ex 28³³). In RV 'pomegranates' in 1 K 7¹⁸ is tr. 'pillars').

Vines (גֶּפֶן *gephen*; in Nu 6⁴, Jg 13¹⁴ גֶּפֶן הַיַּיִן *gephen hayyayin*, the wine-vine). The *Vitis vinifera* was the fruit tree most abundantly cultivated in Palestine and Egypt in ancient times. It is a native of the hilly countries north of Syria, but early spread along the shores of the Mediterranean. Grape kernels have been found in mummy cases of the 11th dynasty in Egypt, dating from about B.C. 2000. A special variety with dark red grapes is called שֹׂרֵק *sôrēk* (Is 5², Jer 2²¹, Gn 49¹¹); these grapes have very small kernels. Figuratively, the unpruned vine in the sabbatic year and jubilee is called נָזִיר *nāzîr*, being compared to the untrimmed hair of the Nazirite. The colocynth plant in 2 K 4[39] is called *gephen sādeh*, a vine of the fields. A wild grape-vine bearing worthless grapes is called *gephen nokri* in Jer 2[21], 'the degenerate plant of a strange vine.' Palestine, especially in its hilly parts, is well suited for vine-growing—'Apertos Bacchus amat colles' (Virgil, *Georg.* ii. 113). The valley of Eshcol, named from its bunches of grapes, produced the great cluster which the two spies carried home between them on a staff, Nu 13[24] (see Wagenseil, *Sota*, 709[a]). Modern travellers have seen bunches of 10 to 12 lb. in weight; still larger bunches up to 19 lb. have been grown in this country under glass. The hills about Jezreel, where Naboth's vineyard was situated, were famous for their vines, as were the grapes of Ephraim (Jg 8[2]). The Moabite hills of Sibmah (Is 16[8. 9], Jer 48[32]), and those of Heshbon and Elealeh, were also renowned, and those of Engedi (Ca 1[14]) in Judah. It was in the hill-country of Judah that the *sōrēḳ* grew (Gn 49[11]), and the valleys of Sorek and Eshcol were named from these, as was Beth-haccherem, 'the house of vines,' near Tekoa (Jer 6[1]). A bottle of Bethlehem wine was a present fit for a king (1 S 16[20]). The wines of Lebanon (Hos 14[7]) and of Helbon (Aleppo *) (one of the exports from Syria to Tyre, Ezk 27[18]) are also named (Robinson, *BRP* iii. 472).

In preparing the vineyard, the stones had to be gathered out of the soil (Is 5[2]). This is noticed by Cato (*De Re Rustica*, 46), who says that the vineyard should be 'bipalio delapidato.' It needed also to be fenced with a hedge (Mt 21[33]), a stone wall (Nu 22[24]), or a ditch, to protect it from the wild beasts, such as jackals (Ca 2[15], Ezk 13[4]), boars (Ps 80[13]), and from robbers (Jer 49[9]). The favourite site was a hillside (Is 5[1], Jer 31[5], Am 9[13]), and the plants are set about three paces from each other in rows (Robinson, ii. 80 f.). When the vines grew up they were sustained on stout stakes, over which the branches were trained (Ezk 19[11. 12]). This was also the practice in Egypt; see Lepsius, *Denkmäler*, ii. 53, 61. All these conditions may be observed to this day, although the Mohammedan rule has discouraged viticulture in Palestine. There is usually a tower (πύργος) in a large vineyard, as described in Mt 21[33], in which the watchers of the vineyard stay. Vineyards were called in Heb. כֶּרֶם *kerem*. In Am 5[11] this is coupled with חֶמֶר *ḥemed*, 'pleasant,' in Is 27[2] with חֶמֶר *ḥemer*, 'of wine,' but Targ. reads *ḥemed* here also, and LXX καλός. The towers in the vineyards for the keepers or vine-dressers (פֹּרְמִים) (Ca 1[6]) are mentioned in *Chilaim*, v. § 3, but in smaller vineyards they lived in booths (Is 1[8]). The vineyard must not be sown with two kinds of seed, else the whole produce was forfeited as a קֹדֶשׁ *ḳodesh*, or sanctified thing (Dt 22[9]); but trees of other sorts, as fig trees, might be planted in a vineyard (Lk 13[6], Mic 4[4]). Ramses III. had olive trees in his large vineyard, which he called the 'spirit of Egypt,' *Pap. Harris*, i. 8. 7.

The vine-buds appear in March, and send out new branches, which are called שָׂרִיגִים *sarigim*. These are not tendrils, for in Gn 40[10] they are described as bearing fruit; when living, these new branches are green, but when the surface is eaten by locusts the skeleton branch looks white (Jl 1[7]). The tendrils are called זַלְזַלִּים *zalzallim* in Is 18[5], or *ṣalṣillôth* in Jer 6[9] (see BASKET). The flowers appear in early April, and have a slight fragrance (Ca 2[11. 13]). This was the time when the vines were pruned, hence it is said in the passage that in the spring-time the period of the זָמִיר or pruning of vines (RVm) has come (so LXX, Aq. Symm. Targ. Vulg.). AV follows Parchon and Kimchi in rendering it 'the time of the singing of birds is come.' The reference to the pruning of vines in Jn 15[9] is familiar.

* But Schrader (*COT*[2] ii. 121) disputes the identification.

The grape (עֵנָב *'ēnāb*) grows in clusters, which are named אֶשְׁכֹּל *'eshkól*, LXX σταφυλή. The fruit-bearing branch is in Nu 13[23] called זְמוֹרָה *zĕmôrâh*, which is the word used in the phrase descriptive of the worship of the sun in Ezk 8[17] 'they put the branch to the nose,' usually taken as referring to an old Persian custom of holding a bundle of vine-rods, called *barsom*, before the face of the priest when praying to the unextinguished fire of the Pyrætheia (Strabo, ed. Casaubon, xv. 733). For a different meaning see Tract *Joma*, 77[a].

The ripening grapes are called בֹּסֶר *bōṣer* in Is 18[5], and nearly the same word is used in Job 15[33]. These are sour and set the teeth on edge (Ezk 18[2]). Sickly vines sometimes drop their grapes in this stage (as in Job 15[33]), the result of a blight. In June or July the early grapes are ripe (Is 18[5]), and in September the vintage (בָּצִיר *bāẓîr*) begins. This is a season of rejoicing, and during the grape-harvest the people live in booths in the midst of the vineyards. It has been conjectured that the ordinance of the Feast of Tabernacles was a mode of turning this custom to the service of religion. This vintage season was celebrated at Shechem (Jg 9[27]). The grapes are cut with a מַזְמֵרָה *mazmērâh*, or pruning hook (Is 2[4], Jl 3[10]), which is called מַגָּל *maggâl*, or sickle in Jl 3[13], and are collected in baskets. There was no vine-harvest in the sabbatic or jubilee year. For particulars on viticulture see Thomson, *The Grape Vine*; and Barron, *Vine Culture*.

The best grapes were dried in the sun into raisins, which were compressed into צִמּוּק *zimmûḳ*, or cakes (Kimchi). Abigail brought 100 such cakes to David (1 S 25[18]), and David refreshed the fainting Egyptian with two such cakes (1 S 30[12]). Similar cakes were brought by Ziba to David (2 S 16[1]; see also 1 Ch 12[40]). These raisins, as well as fresh grapes, were forbidden to the Nazirite while under his vow. To him all that comes of the grape, from the חַרְצַנִּים *ḥarzannîm*, or kernels, to the זָג *zāg*, or husks, was taboo (see Jg 13[14]). The אֲשִׁישׁוֹת *'ăshî-shôth*, given by David to those who accompanied him in bringing the ark to Jerusalem (2 S 6[19], 1 Ch 16[3]), and tr. in AV 'flagons of wine,' were probably **cakes of raisins**, as in RV, which has made a similar change in Ca 2[5]. The reading in the AV is supported on Talmudic authority, but this rests on a very doubtful etymology. For the use of these fruit-cakes by travellers see Russell, i. 82. Cakes of this kind were used as offerings to Baal (Hos 3[1]).

The grape gatherers were forbidden to glean, the עֹלֵלוֹת *'ōlēlôth* or gleanings being left for the stranger, the widow, and the fatherless. In the prophetic picture of rebellious Jerusalem as a vine, the fruit is described as being completely gleaned, the gatherer turning his hand back into the tendrils of the vine (Jer 6[9]; see also Jer 49[9]).

A portion of the grape-harvest is used in making artificial honey or *dibs*, the juice expressed from the grape being boiled into a syrup, 'dulcis musti Vulcano decoquit humorem, et foliis undam trepidi despumat aheni' (Virg. *Georg.* i. 295). The Heb. name is דְּבַשׁ *dĕbash*, or honey, and it was an article of commerce exported from Palestine to Tyre (Ezk 27[17]), and sent by Jacob to Egypt (Gn 43[11]). (See **Dates**, above.) *Dibs* forms 'a part of the food of the present inhabitants of Palestine' (Thomson, i. 279; Russell, i. 82). It was, and is, the ordinary sweetener of cakes and pastry (Lv 2[11], Robinson, iii. 381).

Most of the crop was carried in baskets by girls and children to the wine-presses (see description of the shield of Achilles, *Il.* xviii. 562 ff.). These were cavities either hollowed out of the rock or built on the ground, and lined with masonry and cement (Mt 21[33]). Each press, called

גּת gath, LXX ληνός, was made of two parts. The upper was the פּוּרָה pûrâh (LXX προλήνιον), or wine-press proper (Is 63³ 5²). From the bottom of this a pipe, צִנּוֹר zinnôr, leads into the lower receptacle or יֶקֶב yekeb (LXX ὑπολήνιον, the 'fat' or vat of Jl 2²⁴ and 3¹³ as in Mk 12¹ AV, wine-press RV). The names yekeb or gath are used, however, for the whole wine-press. In Hag 2¹⁶ the pûrâh is called the press-fat (AV) or wine-fat (RV, see Aboda Zara, iv. 8). In these presses the grapes were trodden. The whole process is shown in several Egyptian pictures (Lepsius, ii. 13, 53, 96, iii. 11ᵃ; Wilkinson, i. 385), in one of which the treaders are represented holding by cords from the roof over the pûrâh. Sometimes flat stones are put over the grapes to assist the treading. The garments and feet of those treading are dyed with the 'blood of the grape' (Dt 32¹⁴, Is 63³). As they trod they shouted (Jer 48³³) and sang their vintage songs (Is 16¹⁰). It has been supposed that there is a line of one of these preserved in Is 65⁸ (see Smith, OTJC² 209). The same customs are still observed wherever wine is made in the East (Robinson, i. 431 and ii. 81). The wine-press is a favourite figure with the prophets, typifying God's judgments on sin (Is 63³, La 1¹⁵, Rev 14²⁰).

The first part of the juice which entered the yekeb was the first-fruits (Ex 22²⁹), and was offered to God. In Egypt the residuum from the press is put into a sack and squeezed by wringing; see Lepsius, ii. 53.

There is no mention in the Bible of the subsequent processes of wine-making, but probably the expressed juice was left in the 'fats' until fermentation had set in (Hag 2⁶), or put, as represented in the Egyptian picture (Wilkinson, i. 385), into jars, or, when fermented, it was transferred for storage to large ox-skins. These at the present day are kept ranged around the storehouse or cellar, which is called in 1 Ch 27²⁷ אוֹצְרוֹת הַיַּיִן 'ôzar hayyayin. Bruce speaks of ox-skins capable of holding 60 gallons, and greased on the outside to prevent evaporation (Travels, iv. 334; see Athenæus, ii. 28. Herodotus speaks of camel-skin vessels, iii. 9). When the deposit of the tartarous matter or lees שְׁמָרִים shĕmârîm, LXX τρυγίας, δόξα, or φύλαγμα) had taken place, the clear supernatant wine was poured off into a new vessel (Jer 48¹¹), and this is the well-refined wine of Is 25⁶. In this passage shĕmârîm is used in alliteration with shĕmânîm, 'fat things,' in the earlier clause. Drinking the lees is used allegorically in the sense of the bitter penal consequences of sin (Ps 75⁸; see also Zeph 1¹², Jer 48¹¹).

Wine is known by nine names in the OT, but these do not necessarily mean different kinds. The varieties of wines are named from the locality of their production. Thus we read of the wines of Kerotim, Tolim, Bethrima, Bethlaba, and Signa as those suited for the service of the sanctuary (Menachoth, viii. 6). Other well-known wines were those of En-gedi, Acco, and Gaza. In Egypt the wines of Bubastis (Herod. ii. 126), of Sebennytus, and of Mareotis (Strabo, xvii. 779; Athenæus, i. 33) were highly esteemed. Saronitic wine was so strong that it needed two parts of water to dilute it (Shabbath, lxxvii. 1), and Babylonian wine needed also to be diluted (Berachoth, i.). See Kimchi (Comm. on Hos 14⁸).

The commonest word used for wine is יַיִן yayin, a loan word from a non-Semitic root. This occurs 143 times, being first mentioned in connexion with Noah's drunkenness. It is the word used for wine in the blessing of Jacob (Gn 49¹¹·¹²); it is said to cheer God and man (Jg 9¹³), and to make glad the heart of man (Ps 104¹⁵). Repentant and returning Israel is to be rewarded by again drinking the wine of her vineyards (Am 9¹⁴), as she had done before (Ec 9⁷). It was to be given to them of heavy heart (Pr 31⁶), but its use had to be limited, for it was intoxicating, as in the cases of Nabal (1 S 25³⁷), Lot (Gn 19³²), Amnon (2 S 13²⁸), the drunkards of Ephraim (Is 28¹). It was the wine used by Job's family (Job 1¹³); but king Lemuel was dissuaded from its use, because it is said to prevent judgment (Pr 31⁵), and to cause vomiting (Is 28⁷ 5¹¹, Hos 7⁵). It is called a mocker (Pr 20¹; see also Jer 23⁹). It was this form of wine with which Melchizedek welcomed Abraham's return (Gn 14¹⁸). It is usually rendered οἶνος by LXX. In general, this word is used when wine is spoken of as a beverage.

תִּירוֹשׁ tîrôsh occurs 38 times, and is rendered by LXX by οἶνος, ῥώξ (Is 65⁸), or μέθυσμα (1 S 1¹⁵, Jer 13¹³, Hos 4¹¹). It is so called because it takes possession of the brain and inebriates (Gesenius; but most moderns reject this etymology). In enumerating the products of the land, corn and wine (tîrôsh) are mentioned 21 times, and oil is coupled with tîrôsh 15 times. The Targumists, Onkelos, and Jonathan render it by ḥamer. It is said to take away the understanding in Hos 4¹¹, and its intoxicating qualities are referred to by the Talmudists, 'Tirosh easily takes possession of (יוֹרֵשׁ, a play upon the word) the mind,' Sanhedrin, lxxvi. § 1. In Joma, lxxvi. 2, it is said, 'If thou abuse it thou shalt be poor (רָשׁ), if thou rightly use it thou shalt be head (רֹאשׁ)'; and in the Gemara on this, 'Wherefore is it called tirosh? Because all taken by it shall be poor.' In Jer 40¹⁰·¹² the words yayin and tîrôsh are used as synonyms, and in general tîrôsh is translated 'new wine' in AV. It has been argued that tîrôsh meant grapes, because the phrase is used 'to gather tîrôsh'; but the same is used of yayin, and both are spoken of as trodden out, yayin in Is 16¹⁰, tîrôsh in Mic 6¹⁵. Collating all the references, it seems as if tîrôsh was especially used for wine as the produce of the vineyard. See further, Driver, Joel and Amos, 79 f.

שֵׁכָר shêkâr, LXX σίκερα, is the word tr. in general 'strong drink,' which occurs 23 times in OT. It was used for the drink-offering (Nu 28⁷), and was permitted to be bought with the tithe money and consumed at the temple (Dt 14²⁶). In excess it caused merriment (Is 24⁹, Ps 69¹²) and intoxication (Is 56¹²); it is often coupled with wine, as if another intoxicating fluid; Ibn Ezra says it was made from palm-juice or wheat, Kimchi says from fruit juice, Jerome from grain, grapes, or honey (Epist. ad Nepotianum, ii. 11), so it may have been like the barley wine of the Egyptians (Herod. ii. 77), or like arrack, which is at present often used in Palestine (Robinson, iii. 195). It is mentioned, among other places, in Lv 10⁹, Nu 6³, Dt 29⁶, Jg 13⁴·⁷·¹⁴, 1 S 1¹⁵, Mic 2¹¹. Strong drink was to be given to those ready to perish (Pr 31⁶), which has been supposed to refer to the practice of giving intoxicants to deaden the pain of execution. Lightfoot says that it was the practice of wealthy women in Jerusalem to provide the strong drink for this purpose (Hor. Heb. xi. 366). The vinegar given to our Lord may have been intended for this purpose. Shêkâr seems to be named from its effects (שָׁכַר 'to be drunk').

חֶמֶר ḥemer, used twice in Heb. (Dt 32¹⁴, Is 27², but last probably mistake for חֶמֶד) and six times in Aram. (Ezr 6⁹ 7²², Dn 5¹·²·⁴·²³), seems to be derived from the sparkling, foaming appearance of fermenting wine. In Is 27² the clause in which it occurs appears to be another line from a vintage song. It was wine of this kind that Cyrus gave for the temple use (Ezr 6⁹). In Dt 32¹⁴ it is called the pure blood of the grape, i.e. not mixed with water; but RV has tr. it the blood of the grape, wine. It is red wine in Is 27², and it was the wine which Belshazzar drank out of the temple vessels (Dn 5¹).

עָסִיס 'âṣîṣ, a poetical synonym meaning that which is trodden out. It is the new wine of Ca 8²: the sweet intoxicating wine of Is 49²⁶, the sweet wine lamented by the drunkards in Jl 1⁵, and that which is supplied to the restored remnant of Israel as a blessing (Jl 3¹⁸). It is rendered in LXX νᾶμα, γλυκασμός, but the sweet wine of Am 9¹³ is μέθη. It is probably the same as 'the sweet' of Neh 8¹⁰, where it is called מַמְתַּקִּים *mamtakḳim*, or sweetnesses.

אבָס *ṣōbe'*, intoxicating drink in general, the wine of Is 1²², which was spoiled by mixture with water, or that in Hos 4¹⁸, which had become sour, or that which drenched the drunkard to helplessness (Nah 1¹⁰).

מֶסֶךְ *meṣek*, in Ca 8² מֶזֶג *mezeg*, LXX κέρασμα, is mixed wine, to which spices have been added to make it hotter and improve its flavour. In Pr 23³⁰, Ps 75⁸, Is 65¹¹ it is called *mimṣāk*. In Pr 9². ⁵ it is used metaphorically for the inspiring drink supplied by wisdom, and in Is 5²² for the strong drink which warps the judgment. In Pr 23³⁰ it is a parallel synonym for *yayin*.

חֹמֶץ *ḥōmez*, or vinegar, is sour wine, the common refreshing drink for labourers, forbidden to the Nazirite while under his vow (Nu 6³), used in the harvest field (Ru 2¹⁴), and prophetically mentioned in Ps 69²¹. In Pr 10²⁶ LXX renders it ὄμφαξ, an unripe grape.

In NT the word commonly used is οἶνος, as at the marriage feast at Cana. This wine in excess produced μεθύσις (Jn 2¹⁰). New wine was regarded as inferior to old (Lk 5³⁹). Γλεῦκος, 'new sweet wine,' is mentioned in Ac 2¹³ as that by which the Jews thought the apostles were intoxicated at Pentecost. It cannot have been unfermented, as that would not have produced the effect, and Pentecost was eight months after the vintage.

The collecting of juice from the grapes, which the chief butler in his dream squeezed into the cup, was plainly only a symbol, as in the dream he saw the whole process of budding, blossoming, and fruiting taking place. There is no evidence of any such custom as squeezing grapes into a cup for royal or guest refreshment. There are several figurative names for wine: 'the fruit of the vine' (Lk 22¹⁸), 'the blood of the grape' (Dt 32¹⁴); the former reminds us of Pindar's δρόσος ἀμπέλου (vii. 3), or of the name of the vine οἴνου μήτηρ in Æschylus (*Persæ*, 614).

The study of the names applied to wine shows that they are, for the most part, evidently synonyms, and that the substance indicated by them all was one which, if used to excess, was liable to cause intoxication. An attempt has been made to obtain a textual support for total abstinence by differentiating intoxicating from unfermented wine in the biblical terminology; but it is only special pleading without adequate foundation. The teaching of Scripture as to the pernicious effects of intemperance in any form is clear and explicit, and the Apostle Paul has stated the case for total abstinence in Ro 14 in a way which does not require the treacherous aid of doubtful exegesis for its support.

The wine stored in the large skins in the cellar was drawn for use into smaller skins, the bottles of Scripture, called חֵמֶת *ḥēmeth* in Gn 21¹⁴ff., נֵבֶל *nêbel*, 1 S 1²⁴ 10³, 2 S 16¹ (this word is used figuratively for the clouds in Job 38³⁷), or נֹאד *nôd*, Jos 9⁴⁻¹³, Jg 4¹⁹, 1 S 16²⁰. This word is also used figuratively in Ps 56⁸ in alliteration with *nôd*, 'wandering,' for there is no evidence of the use of lacrymatories among the Jews. The *nôd* was liable to shrivel if hung up in the heat (Ps 119⁸³). In LXX and NT bottle is ἀσκός. These were made of goatskins, prepared by cutting off the head, tail, and feet, and then drawing off the skin from the body without other cutting, and stuffing it with straw, into which wooden wedges were then driven, to stretch it to its fullest capacity. The hair was

left on the outer surface, the tail and limb holes were closely sewn up, and the neck hole left open. The skin was thereafter tanned with oak or acacia bark. These skins are prepared in this manner at the present day, and are called *zumzammim* or *mattaru*. When filled, the neck hole is tied round with a thong. Robinson saw about 500 of these bottles in one tanyard (ii. 75). The larger bottles are of he-goat skins, the smallest of the skins of kids. This variety of size is alluded to in Is 22²⁴. When active fermentation is in progress these skins become much distended, and are liable to burst. This is especially liable to occur with new skins of young animals, which are called אוֹב, as in Job 32¹⁹. These are called in Vulg. *lagunculæ*. Skins which are old are liable to crack, and cannot bear the tension of the carbonic acid produced during fermentation. This is referred to in Mt 9¹⁷, Mk 2²², Lk 5³⁷. The preservation of the wine did not mean keeping it from fermentation,—for, with the total absence of antiseptic precautions characteristic of Orientals, it would have been impossible to do so,—but the storing of it in a bottle which could resist the strain. One of these bottles was a load for a man (1 S 10³).

Wine was largely used in Egypt, and the figures of drinking feasts, and the painting of an inebriated female from a tomb of the New Empire, are well known (see Wilkinson, i. 392, 424, etc.). There is an interesting letter written by the scribe Amenem-apt to Penta-ur, in which the evils of intemperance are graphically described (*Pap. Sallier*, I. ix. 9, etc.). The commonest beverage in Egypt was beer, made from barley, and called *heḳ*. The wine made from the grape, also commonly used, was called *arp*, and date wine was called *baḳ*. Among the presents to Ptah enumerated in the *Harris Papyrus* were 2366 wine vessels of one form and 820 of another; and in the inventory of presents on pl. 72 of that papyrus are 486,303 vessels of beer. The Persians were also much addicted to wine (Herod. i. 133), and the royal wine of Est 1⁷ is referred to by Athenæus (*Deipnos.* i. 51); it was called Chalybonian, and Posidonius says that it is made in Damascus. Figuratively, the washing of garments in wine means plenty and prosperity (Gn 49¹¹). Wine of astonishment, Ps 60³ (RV staggering), is a figure of God's judgment on sin, making its objects helpless, as if intoxicated. This is called the cup of staggering in Is 51¹⁷.

The **Vine of Sodom** (Dt 32³²) is probably, as Seetzen and Robinson have supposed, the *'ôsher* or *Calotropis procera*, an asclepiadaceous plant, whose fruit looks attractive, but is full of dry cottony hairs. These are the 'grapes of gall.' Pococke supposed that it referred to diseased pomegranates, and Hooker conjectures that the colocynth may have been meant; but its fruit has no resemblance to grapes (see **Wild Gourd,** above). Elliot suggests oak galls as referred to, and Hasselquist the egg plant, either *Solanum melongena* or *S. Sodomæum*; but the first identification is most probably correct, more especially as the *Calotropis*, while not very common, grows abundantly in one locality by the Dead Sea.

Walnut (אֱגוֹז *'ĕgōz*, καρύα) is not mentioned as a fruit; but a garden of nuts, which is mentioned in Ca 6¹¹, is taken by the rabbinical authorities as meaning a garden of walnuts. The Arabs call the tree *gyaus*, and it is very common in Palestine. The common walnut, *Juglans regia*, is too well known to need description.

Fruit is referred to metaphorically in the sense of (1) the result of a course of conduct (Ro 6²¹); (2) the work of the Holy Spirit in the conduct (Gal 5²², Eph 5⁹); (3) children (Ps 127³); (4) praise (Is 57¹⁹); (5) the results of industry (Pr 31¹⁶. ³¹), etc.

Mallows (מַלּוּחַ *mallûaḥ*, LXX ἅλιμον, Vulg. *Ar-*

borum cortices) are spoken of in Job 30⁴ as plants eaten by starving outcasts. They have been variously identified as nettles by R. Levi, as possibly a mesembryanthemum by Kitto, as mallows (*malva*) by Thomson (*L. and B.* i. 291), as *Corchorus olitorius* by Sprengel ; but are most probably the saltwort, as in the RV, the *Atriplex halimus* or seapurslain, which is called by the Arabs *mulluah*, and grows on the shores of the Dead Sea and of the Gulf of Akabah. It is a plant with sour leaves, and has been known to form a part of the diet of the people in periods of scarcity. Thomson saw poor people cutting coarse green food of this kind as a relish for bread (ii. 345). The mallow in Arabic is called *khŭbbarzeh*. In a parallel passage in Job 24⁵ the poor are said to cut בְּלִיל for their children, which may be cattle food (Is 30²⁴) or coarse vegetables in general, and probably the אלח or greens which the prophet went to gather were of the same nature (2 K 4³⁹). The Syriac uses this name *mallûah* for the חָרוּל or ʻnettleʼ of Zeph 2⁹.

Juniper roots (רֹתֶם *rôthem*). This occurs along with the last as part of the food of the outcast in Job 30⁴, but the word occurs also as the name of the tree under which Elijah sheltered (1 K 19⁴ᶠ·), and in the phrase ʻcoals of juniperʼ in Ps 120⁴. LXX renders it ʼΡαθμέν or ʼΡαμάθ, and in Job ῥίζας ξύλων. Symm. tr. it ῥίζαν σίτων ἀγρίων, and Josephus does not name the tree, but calls it ʻa certain treeʼ (*Ant.* VIII. xiii. 7). The Syriac VS calls it a terebinth, and Clement a *Paliurus* (*Pædagog.* iii. 236). The later Jewish authorities, however, recognized it as the desert broom, *Retama retem*, which the Arabs call *retama*. It is a shrub with pale pink flowers and very bitter roots. It grows about 10 ft. high, and in many places in the desert is the only shrub under which one could shelter. Robinson describes it in such places ; and one of the wilderness stations of Israel was called Rithmah =broomy (Nu 33¹⁸). The roots were used as fuel (Ps 120⁴), and the Revisers have put ʻto warm themʼ in marg. of Job 30⁴, which, considering the uneatable nature of the roots, is a more intelligible rendering. The word לַחְמָם may be regarded as a derivative of the verb חָמַם ʻto heat,ʼ in which sense the same word occurs in Is 47¹⁴. This sense is taken by some Heb. commentators, as R. Levi ben-Gerson (*in loc.*), but the rendering of the text is that in the Gemara, *Aboda Zara*, i. Juniper roots are often used for fuel in the wilderness (Thomson, i. 345).

B. Animal food consisted either of flesh or of animal products, such as milk, eggs, and honey. Flesh was habitually used only in royal or great houses, and among ordinary people was chiefly used at feasts. Its sources were restricted by law among the Jews, by custom among the neighbouring nations. The word שְׁאֵר, which literally means flesh meat (Ps 78²⁰·²⁷), was sometimes used for food in general (Ex 21¹⁰).

The division of beasts into clean and unclean, mentioned in the story of the Deluge (Gn 7²), was written in the light of later legislation, but embodies a distinction which can be traced back to a very early period of human history. The two lists of clean and unclean animals (Lv 11³ᶠᶠ· and Dt 14⁴ᶠᶠ·) are practically identical. The mammals permitted to be eaten were the ruminants proper, except the camel, which, with the *hyrax*, hare, and swine, are prohibited by name. There is reason to believe that this selection is of more than arbitrary value, and that the danger of the transmission of parasitic diseases by the flesh of these is less than in the case of the excluded forms (see Guéneau de Mussy, *Etude sur l'hygiène de Moïse*). For fanciful representations of the forbidden animals as types of vices, see Eusebius, *Præp. Evang.* viii. 9 ; Clement, *Pædag.* ii. 10 ; Novatianus, *de cibis Judæorum*, iii.

The permitted mammals named in Dt are ten. (*a*) The three domestic groups, **oxen**, **sheep**, and **goats.** The first group was called in general בְּהֵמָה *běhēmâh*, or cattle (Dt 14⁴), neat cattle being distinguished as בָּקָר *bāḳār*, LXX βόες, tr. the herd, as distinguished from the flock. The calf is in Heb. עֵגֶל *ʼēgel* (Is 27¹⁰) ; an *ʼēgel marbēḳ* or fatted calf was killed for Saul by the witch (1 S 28²⁴) ; see also Gn 18⁷ (where the calf is *ben bāḳār*, ʻthe son of the herdʼ) and ὁ σιτευτὸς μόσχος of Lk 15³⁰. שׁוֹר *shôr* (LXX μόσχος) is used for a bullock, as in Lv 22²⁷, Neh 5¹⁸, or else פַּר *par*, as in Nu 8⁸, Ps 22¹² ; and a heifer is called *ʼeglath bāḳār* (Gn 15⁹, Dt 21³) or *pārāh* (Gn 41², Nu 19²). Bulls are named (poet.) אַבִּירִים *ʼabbîrîm* (Is 34⁷, Ps 22¹²), and cows or cattle in general אֲלָפִים *ʼǎlāphîm*. The commonest breed were black or brown, short limbed and small, and they were principally kept in the valleys and in the low country. Fat oxen were part of Solomon's daily provision (1 K 4²³) ; these were fed in a אֵבוּס or stall, and hence are called stalled oxen (Pr 15¹⁷) ; Solomon had also pasture-fed oxen (1 K 4²³, see also Elisha, 1 K 19²¹). The aurochs or wild bull (the Hebrew רְאֵם *rěʼēm*) was probably seldom captured, even in nets (Is 51²⁰). The buffalo was not originally a native, but has been imported into Palestine since Bible times.

From the flock צֹאן *ʼzōn* (Gn 4²) the food animals were טָלֶה *ṭāleh*, or sucking lambs (LXX ἀρνός γαλαθηνός), as in 1 S 7⁹. A hogget or lamb from one to three years old was named כֶּבֶשׂ *kebes* (Nu 7¹⁵) or כֶּשֶׂב *keseb* (Lv 3⁷), LXX ἀμνός or ἀρνός. In Aramaic a young sheep is called אִמַּר *ʼimmar*, as in Ezr 6⁹ ; a ewe is רָחֵל *rāḥēl* (Gn 31³⁸) ; and a fatted sheep כַּר *kar* (2 K 3⁴) ; while sheep in general are called שֶׂה *seh* (Jg 6⁴). The commonest breed of sheep in Palestine is the fat-tailed variety, whose tail is wide and flat, and may weigh 10 lb., most of which is pure fat. This fat tail (RV) is the אַלְיָה *ʼalyâh* or rump (AV) of Ex 29²² (see Herod. iii. 113). In Northern Palestine and Syria there is also a short-woolled small sheep, resembling the merino ; both are varieties of the one species *Ovis Aries*. The lamb was the commonest of all meats for feasts, and is still the animal often killed for a guest (Doughty, i. 16). The ram, אַיִל *ʼayil*, possibly the *beden* or wild-goat (Gn 15⁹), was also used as food (Gn 31³⁸). For the use of lambs see 2 S 12⁴, Is 53⁷, and the paschal lamb (Ex 12³).

The goat (שָׂעִיר *sāʼîr*) was commonly kept in flocks in the more mountainous districts, while the sheep was fed in the lower pastures ; the two species of goat, *Capra hircus* and *C. mambrica*, were not apparently differentiated by name ; the former is the common goat, the latter has a sheep-like head and long pendulous, flapping ears. The male or he-goat of the former breed is the תַּיִשׁ *tayish* (Gn 30³⁵, Pr 30³¹, and of the latter עַתּוּד *ʼattûd* (Gn 31¹⁰), or in Aramaic צְפִיר *zěphîr*, as Ezr 6¹⁷. The עֵז *ʼēz* may have been the *Capra Ægagrus* or *Sinaitica*, both of which are natives of Bible lands, and probably the source of Esau's savoury meat. The kid, גְּדִי *gědî* (Dt 14²¹), is mentioned as the material for a small feast (Jg 6¹⁹ 13¹⁵). Compare the ἔριφος of the parable (Lk 15²⁹), and the elder brother's implied comparison between the kid and the calf. As the lamb is useful for his fleece as well as his flesh (Pr 27²⁶), the kid is commonly used by the poorer or more economical classes (see 1 Es 1⁷). Rebekah used it for making Isaac's savoury meat (Gn 27⁹).

The thrice-repeated taboo concerning seething a kid in its mother's milk (Ex 23¹⁹ 34²⁶, Dt 14²¹) has been interpreted : (1) As a prohibition of the slaughter of the mother and offspring at the same time (as in Lv 22²⁸). (2) As forbidding the killing of the young animal before it was eight days old ; we learn from the passage just quoted that an animal was not allowed to be sacrificed until it had reached that age, and it has been thought that it was also unclean as food. (3) The most probable explanation is that it had reference to some custom among the surrounding nations, such as that described by Cudworth and Spencer (*de legibus Hebr. ritual.* ii. 335), in which a kid was boiled in its mother's milk, and the broth sprinkled on the ground as a sacrifice to propitiate the harvest gods and ensure fruitfulness. (4) Michaelis has supposed that mother's milk is a euphemism for butter, and that the food forbidden was meat drenched with butter. For other views on this תּוֹעֵבָה *to'ēbâh*, or abomination, see Tract *Chullin*, viii. § 4, and Maimonides, *More nebochim*, iii. 48.

Milk and its derivatives formed an important element of the food of the Bible peoples, Palestine is described as a land flowing with milk and honey (Ex 3⁸ and eighteen other places). חָלָב *ḥālāb*, LXX γάλα, is used for fresh milk (Ca 5¹², Is 28⁹), or of cream from which butter is made (Pr 30³³). Milk of goats was esteemed the best (Pr 27²⁷), then that of sheep (Dt 32¹⁴). Cow's milk is rarely as good as either of the others, on account of the unsuitability of the pasture, and is not often specified in the Bible. Camel's milk was probably used by the patriarchs, as we infer from Gn 32¹⁵; but it sours more quickly than other milk, and often pains strangers when they first take it (Doughty, i. 216).

Milk is used as a drink with meals (Gn 18⁸, Ezk 25⁴), and so is coupled with wine (Ca 5¹, Is 55¹). When the pasturage is good, sweet milk is still handed round after an Arab meal. It is also offered as refreshment to travellers. Jael opened for Sisera a *nōd*, or leathern bottle of milk (Jg 4¹⁹), which Deborah (Jg 5²⁵) calls a *sēphel 'addîrîm*, 'a cup of the nobles' (EV a lordly dish). Goat's milk is spoken of as the staple drink of servants (Pr 27²⁷); and, as the Hebrew children were mother-nursed, milk was their sole sustenance until they were weaned, hence the metaphorical sense of milk-feeding in 1 Co 3², He 5¹². The comparison of the law to milk was used by the Jews; thus Kimchi on Is 55¹ says, 'As milk feeds and nourishes a child, so the law feeds and nourishes the soul.' Milk mixed with flour or rice, and eaten with salad, or occasionally with meat, forms a large part of the food of the poor in Aleppo (Russell, i. 118) and elsewhere. Among some Jews milk is not eaten with meat, on account of their interpretation of Ex 23¹⁹ (see above).

Butter (חֶמְאָה *ḥem'âh*, LXX βούτυρον) is used for cream and thick preparations of it, as well as for butter proper. In Is 7²² it probably means cream, and in Jg 5²⁵ the milk which was called *ḥālāb* in Jg 4¹⁹ is named *ḥem'âh*; but it was liquid enough to be kept in a skin bottle, and was used to quench thirst. The 'butter' of Gn 18⁸ was probably soured milk, which is now much used in the East, and called *leben* (Burckhardt, *Bedouins*, i. 240). The process of churning is called מִיץ *mîz*, or 'pressure,' in Pr 30³³. It is now performed by rocking a skin of milk upon the knees (Doughty, i. 221), or by beating with a stick a skin of milk hung up in a frame, or jerking a skin thus suspended to and fro (Robinson, i. 485). The milk used is that of goats (Robinson, iii. 69) or cows (Dt 32¹⁴); some forms of butter are semi-fluid, and hence the figurative language of Job 20¹⁷ 29⁶. The amount of butter eaten by Arabs is large, when it can be procured. Kitto says that all well-prepared Arab food swims in it; and Burckhardt describes the Arabs as taking a cupful of butter as breakfast in the morning (see Robinson, i. 449). Melted butter is used, poured over bread in a bowl, as a breakfast dish, and is called *samen* (cf. Doughty, ii. 67 f., 208 f., 655 f.). Metaphorically, the smoothness of hypocritical words is compared to butter (Ps 55²¹).

Cheese (חָרִיץ *ḥārîz*) is mentioned as a delicacy sent by Jesse to the captain of the troop in which his sons were (1 S 17¹⁸), the expression used there meaning ten slices of curd. The [שְׁפָה] *shāphâh* (pl. *shāphôth*) of 2 S 17²⁹ was probably the *leben*, which here was made of cow's milk. Cheese is often made of the milk of the ewe or of the goat.

A third word, גְּבִינָה *gĕbînâh*, means a clot, and is compared (Job 10¹⁰) with the material out of which the body develops (cf. גֹּלֶם *gôlem* of Ps 139¹⁶).

The Arabs use dried milk, which they rub up with water when wanted (Doughty, i. 262); this they call *mereesy*. It is also mentioned by Burckhardt (i. 60).

(*b*) Besides the three domestic groups, seven forms of large game were allowed to be eaten; these were the **fallow deer**, *Dama vulgaris* (אַיָּל, LXX ἔλαφος, the hart of RV and AV, as in Ps 42¹, La 1⁶); the **gazelle**, *Gazella dorcas* (צְבִי *zĕbî*, LXX δορκάς, AV roebuck, 2 S 2¹⁸), called by the Egyptians *gahs*, and often used as a sacrifice; the **wild cow antelope**, *Bubalus boselaphus* (יַחְמוּר *yaḥmûr*, LXX πύγαργος, Vulg. *bubalus*, AV fallow deer, RV roebuck), called *shes* by the Egyptians.

These three were hunted (Dt 12¹⁵. ²², Pr 6⁵), and formed elements in Solomon's daily provision (1 K 4²³). The other large game were: the **ibex** or **wild goat**, *Capra beden*, the *n'eafu* of Egypt; the Sinaitic ibex is also called יָעֵל (Job 39¹, Ps 104¹⁸), hence the name of Heber's wife Jg 4¹⁷. ¹⁸ (אַקּוֹ *'akkô*, AV and RV wild goat); the **addax**, *Antilope addax* (דִּישׁוֹן *dîshôn*, AV and RV 'pygarg,' the ancient Egyptian *nudu*), an antelope with lyrate horns and white hinder part, not uncommon in some parts of Western Asia, and found in Palestine; the **oryx**, *Oryx beatrix* (תְּאוֹ *tĕ'ô*, LXX ὄρυξ, AV wild ox, RV antelope), a straight-horned antelope, extending in distribution from N. Africa to Persia; the African form, called in Egyptian *maud*, differs from the Asiatic in some respects, and is called *O. leucoryx*; it is very commonly represented as being sacrificed in Egyptian pictures; and lastly, the kibisch or **mouflon**, *Ovis tragelaphus* (זֶמֶר *zemer*, LXX καμηλοπάρδαλις, AV and RV chamois). This is a mountain sheep which is found in Lebanon, Moab, and the Taurus, as well as in Corsica. Neither the chamois nor the giraffe is a native of Palestine.

(*c*) The law of clean *birds* is one of exclusion. All carnivorous or predaceous birds and seabirds, together with the ostrich, raven, heron, and stork, are declared unclean. On the positive side, the birds named as articles of diet were six: (1) the **pigeon** (*Columba livia*, יוֹנָה *yônâh*, LXX περιστερά); (2) the **turtle dove** (*Turtur communis*, תּוֹר *tôr*, LXX τρυγών). These two were the commonest birds used for food in Palestine, and the only ones admitted as sacrifices. (3) The **partridge**, of which two species are found in Palestine, *Caccabis chukar*, the large Indian partridge, and *Ammoperdix Heyi*, the small partridge of Judæa (1 S 26²⁰). This bird is *hunted*, as it runs when pursued, and is slow to rise in flight (Robinson, iii. 403). Its nest is sought after on account of the eggs, which are favourite articles of food (Jer 17¹¹, Sir 11³⁰). LXX renders it νυκτικόραξ, which is a kind of heron. The place-name Beth-hoglah means the house of the partridge. Partridges as food are represented on an Assyrian sculpture in the British Museum. (4) The **quail** (*Coturnix communis*, שְׂלָו *sĕlâv*, LXX ὀρτυγομήτρα), which furnished meat to the Israelites in their wilderness journey (Ex 16¹³). These are common in Egypt, where they are salted and eaten raw (Herodotus, ii. 77). The quail annually migrates in immense bevies across the desert nearly along the line of the Israelites' march (Robinson, i. 260). (5) Fatted fowl, which were prepared for Solomon's table (1 K 4²³), are called בַּרְבֻּרִים. They were probably **ducks** or **geese**, so largely used in Egypt, where they are called *aptiu* and *terpu*. They were apparently not domesticated, but caught in nets, fattened and eaten (Lepsius, ii. 46 and 132). (6) Fowl in Neh 5[18] צִפֳּרִים *zippŏrîm*, were probably **domestic fowl** introduced from Babylonia, to which they had been brought from India, their native country. In NT times they had become domesticated in Palestine. It is said in the Mishna that fowl were not allowed in Jerusalem (*Baba Kama*, vii. 7) ; but this is a mistake (see Mt 26[75] and parallel passages). Our Lord was familiar with them and their habits, see Mt 23[37], where He quotes from 2 Es 1[30].

Eggs as articles of food in early times were those of wild birds (Dt 22[6], Is 10[14] 59[5]) ; but with the introduction of geese from Egypt and domestic fowl from India they became much more important as a part of the diet, and now are very largely used (Lk 11[12]). There is no reference to the ancient modes of cooking them, but at the present day they are boiled, or eaten swimming in hot butter and with honey (Finn. 141), or eaten with olives (*ib.* 272), or boiled with rice (Robinson, i. 91), or fried in fat.

The *white of an egg* (רִיר חַלָּמוּת *rîr ḥallāmûth*) of Job 6[6] may be either the material literally expressed, see Tract *Chull.* 64*a*, or curdled milk ; but is understood by some as a succulent, tasteless plant like purslain, *Portulaca oleracea*, as in the RVm. This plant is common in most places in Palestine, and is in Arabic associated with imbecility. Golius quotes the proverb '*more* foolish than purslain,' *Sentent. Arab.* 81. For other meanings see Gesenius, *Thesaurus, sub voce.*

Dove's dung, mentioned in connexion with the famine during the siege of Samaria, has been variously understood by commentators. It is said (2 K 6[25]) that one imperial pint of it was sold for about 12s. 6d. חֲרֵייֹנִים *ḥărîyōnîm*, or as it is in Ḳerê דִּבְיֹנִים *dibyōnîm*, is understood by Josephus literally, and he supposes it to have been used as a condiment in place of salt (*Ant.* IX. iv. 4). The threat in Rabshakeh's appeal to the Jews (2 K 18[27]) is in favour of this view. Others have supposed that this material was used for fuel, as the cow dung in Ezk 4[12] ; and Harmer thinks it was used to manure melons and other vegetables grown within the city (*Obs.* iii. 185 ; see Morier's *Second Journey,* p. 141). Fuller surmised that it might be the contents of the pigeon's crop. Linnæus and Smith identify it as the root of a liliaceous plant, the *Ornithogalum umbellatum* or star of Bethlehem ; but this as well as Bochart's conjecture, that it was a chick-pea or small species of *cicer*, and the view that it was a small species of *sorghum*, are without foundation, as there is no reason why the price of these rare foods should be specified. On the whole, there is as much evidence for the literal interpretation as for any of these guesses.

(*d*) No *reptile* was permitted to be eaten ; of *fishes* all that have fins and scales were clean ; but it is a remarkable fact that no species of fish is mentioned in the Bible, nor is there any discrimination except good or bad (Mt 13[48]), and big and little (Jon 1[17], Jn 21[11], Mk 8[7]). The Sea of Galilee abounds in fishes, which are delicate and well flavoured (Robinson, ii. 386). Altogether 43 species have been found by Lortet, Tristram, and others, of which 14 are peculiar to the lake and to the Jordan. One of the largest of these, *Clarias macracanthus*, being scaleless, was unclean (κορακῖνος, Jos. *BJ* III. x. 8). The largest of the clean fishes are species of *Chromis*, which resemble the carp, and have large scales. One of these, *Chromis Niloticus*, called *Moncht* by the fishermen of Tiberias, has been found up to 5 lb. in weight ; another, *C. Tiberiadis*, is peculiar to the lake, and very plenti-

ful ; *C. Andreæ* and *C. Simonis* are also peculiar, as is the *C. Flavii Josephi*. There are also four species of barbel of the genera *Barbus, Scaphiodon* and *Capoeta*, as well as one species each of dace, loach, and bleak, and two blennies, *B. Lupulus* and *B. varius.* Sea fishery was carried on at Tyre (Ezk 26[5]), and from thence preserved fish were imported into Jerusalem (Neh 13[16]), probably dried and cured. It was likely some dried fishes which formed part of the food with which the 5000 were fed. The fish-market at Jerusalem was probably at the fish-gate (2 Ch 33[14]). The fishpools of Heshbon (Ca 7[4]) have been regarded as indicating that the Jews kept fish in them for use ; but the word 'fish' is here an interpolation. Abundance of fish was one of the elements in the prosperity of Joseph, according to his blessing, Gn 49[25]. Fish was one of the staple foods in Egypt (Nu 11[5]). See picture of fishing in Baedeker's *Egypt*, p. 411, and Wilkinson, ii. 102.

(*e*) Four *insects* were allowed to be eaten according to the list in Lv ; these were: (1) אַרְבֶּה *'arbeh*, LXX βροῦχος, the swarming locust, *Ædipoda migratoria*; (2) סָלְעָם *ṣol'âm*, LXX ἀττάκης, probably *Acrydium peregrinum*, the bald locust of AV ; (3) חַרְגֹּל *hargôl*, LXX ὀφιομάχος (AV beetle), a leaping animal, and therefore not a beetle, probably the *khardjala* of the Arabs, which the Rabbins supposed to be a grasshopper, more probably the largest of the locusts, *Ædipoda cristata* ; and (4) חָגָב *hāgâb*, LXX ἀκρίς, probably the little black locust found in the Sinaitic desert which the Arabs call *Faras el-jundi* or soldiers' horses, recalling the description of the locusts in Rev 9[7]. It is, however, not possible precisely to identify these two latter forms. Locusts formed part of the food of the Baptist (Mt 3[4], Mk 1[6]). Doughty describes them as being prepared by salting, and then being stived into a leathern sack in which they kept good a long while. They mingle them, brayed small, with butter-milk. The best is the fat spring locust ; the later brood is dry and unwholesome (i. 203). Burckhardt says they are put alive into boiling brine, then dried in the sun, the head, legs, and wings being plucked off and then stored in bags. They are sometimes mixed with butter and spread on bread. They taste not unlike shrimps. On one of the Assyrian sculptures in the British Museum two slaves are represented with long *sticks* of locusts.

Honey took the place of sugar in cookery, either the natural product (1 S 14[25], Mt 3[4], Lk 24[42], AV, not RV) or the artificial *dibs* made of grapes or dates, described above. True honey is collected by the bee, *Apis fasciata* (see BEE). It is found in hollows in rocks (Dt 32[13], Ps 81[16]) or in hollow trees (1 S 14[26]), from which it drops on the ground. A shrub or tree on which was a honeycomb was called יַעַר, a word used for honeycomb in Ca 5[1]. Birds, jackals, and ants would soon reduce a lion to a dry skeleton, so that in a few days a swarm of bees might take possession of it (Jg 14[8]). Herodotus tells us that the head of Onesilus, suspended over the gate of Amathus, became filled with honeycomb (v. 114). See also the account of the Egyptian practice of killing a calf and placing it in a favourable place, when in nine days bees swarm within the carcase (Virgil, *Georg.* iv. 300 ff.). Compare with this Pythagoras' theory of the origin of bees, Ovid, *Metamorph.* xv. 27.

As honey is liable to ferment, it was forbidden to be used in any offering to God (Lv 2[11]), the preservative material salt being used instead. Honey was one of the exports of Palestine to Tyre. Along with it is named the substance PANNAG, supposed by some to be a sweetmeat. LXX translates it 'cassia,' and the Vulgate 'balsam.' In the Syriac it is said to be millet.

At the present day honey is used by the Arabs

to sweeten cakes (Ex 16³¹) as we use sugar. It is sometimes, but not often, eaten by itself from the comb (Jg 14⁹), or as it drops from the comb (1 S 14²⁷). The liquid honey as it has dropped, called צוּף *zûph* (Pr 16²⁴, Ps 19¹⁰), is the best, and a cruse of this was part of the present brought by Jeroboam's wife to Ahijah (1 K 14³). Honey was brought with the other provisions to David in exile (2 S 17²⁹), and wild honey (μέλι ἄγριον) was part of the Baptist's diet (Mt 3⁴). Butter and honey is expressive of a rich diet, see Burckhardt, *Arabia*, i. 54, but not Is 7¹⁵·²². Milk and honey are the products of a fertile land (*Odyss*. xx. 68). The effects of a surfeit of honey are graphically described in Pr 25¹⁶. Honey is still stored in jars or skins as of old (Jer 41⁸).

Salt (מֶלַח), eaten with food as a condiment to flavour it (Job 6⁶, Sir 39²⁶), used to preserve food, and given to cattle (Is 30²⁴), was extracted from the salt beds by the Dead Sea, or made by evaporation from sea water. There are masses of rock salt several miles in extent on the S.E. of the Dead Sea (Robinson, ii. 108), and the salt of Sodom is named in a Gemara; see also Josephus, *Ant*. XII. iii. 3, XIII. iv. 9. Much of this salt was very impure, hence it sometimes lost its savour as well as its preserving power, and was cast out on the land as waste (Mt 5¹³, Lk 14³⁵). This was due to the rain washing out the salt and leaving only the earthy dross. Too much salt rendered the land barren, and to sow with salt meant to doom to perpetual desolation (Dt 29²³, Jg 9⁴⁵, Zeph 2⁹, Jer 17⁶, Job 39⁶). Salt was to be used with all the sacrifices (Lv 2¹³, Ezk 43²⁴, Mk 9⁴⁹ TR). See *Il*. i. 449, and *Æneid*, ii. 133. For this purpose salt was sold in the temple market; see Maii, *de usu Salis Symbol. in rebus sacris Dissert*., Giessen, 1692; *Middoth*, v. 3. The addition of salt to the animal sacrifice was probably a later arrangement. See Philo, ii. 255; Hottinger, *Jur. Heb. Leg*. p. 168, and *de Usu Salis in Cultu sacro*, Marburg, 1706; Wokenius, *de Salitura Oblationum*, 1747. Salted incense is referred to in Ex 30³⁵. Salt is much prized, both in Syria and Egypt. A Bedawi prefers salt to sugar when both are offered to him. It is an emblem of hospitality; to eat bread and salt with one is to be bound to him by ties of hospitality, a covenant of salt (Lv 2¹³, Nu 18¹⁹, 2 Ch 13⁵). A similar alliance is expressed in Ezr 4¹⁴. See Niebuhr, *Beschreibung*, 48; Bæhrdt, *de Fœdere Salis*. For the washing of infants in salt see MEDICINE. It is possible that the Sidonian Misrephoth-maim of Jos 11⁸ 13⁶ may have been a place of salt-pans where sea water was evaporated.

Hyssop (אֵזוֹב), which may be mentioned as an accessory to the feast of Passover, though in itself not a food-stuff, is a labiate herb of inconspicuous size, which was used by the Egyptian priests for food (Porphyry, *de Abstinentia*, iv. 7), but is mentioned in the Bible only as a means of aspersion, considered by Celsius to be the *Hyssopus officinalis*, a thyme-like plant. In *Negaim*, xiv. 6, there are five kinds recognized—the Greek (*Origanum Smyrnæum*), the Egyptian (*Origanum Ægyptiacum*), the wild (*O. Syriacum*), the Cochali (*Origanum maru*), and the Roman (*Satureja Juliana*). As the hyssop had a firm stem and could be tied in a bundle, it was probably the *O. maru*. Kitto conjectures that it is the poke (*Phytolocca decandra*); but this is not a native of Palestine. Royle, Tristram, and Stanley believe it to be the caper (*Capparis spinosa*); but this does not fulfil the conditions; it is soft, smooth, and irregularly branched, besides it is mentioned under another name as אֲבִיּוֹנָה *'ăbîyōnāh* (Ec 12⁵, 'desire' AV, 'caperberry' RV). The flower-buds of the caper are supposed to stimulate passion and appetite, and were eaten with vinegar along with meat as they are still; hence the metaphorical use in the passage, whose

real meaning is better conveyed by the AV than by the RV literal reading.

The following fruits or herbs are used with meats as condiments :—

Anise or dill (Mt 23²³), an umbelliferous plant, *Anethum graveolens*, whose fruits were used as a carminative. It is a native of Palestine. The allied *Pimpinella anisum* is the anise of Pliny; but the dill is called by Hippocrates ἄνηθον, and by Dioscorides ἄνικητον, the word used in the text. Its properties are much the same as those of the caraway seed. For an account of references in classical literature see Pliny, xx. 17; and for a figure see Woodville's *Med. Botany*. In *Maaseroth*, iv. § 5, Rabbi Eliezer says the seeds, leaves, and stem of the *shabath* or anise are liable to tithe. Dill is called in Arabic *shibt*. At the present day the fruit of *Anethum* is called dill, and that of *Pimpinella* is anise-seed.

Coriander, the small round fruit of *Coriandrum sativum* to which the manna was compared, used in the same way as anise, especially in Egypt (Ex 16³¹, Nu 11⁷). It is an umbelliferous plant, and grows in Syria and Egypt (see Pliny, xx. 20; and for figures of this and the following plants see Woodville).

Cummin, also an umbelliferous plant (*Cuminum sativum*), whose fruit was cultivated as a carminative, and was beaten with a rod off the plant when it was ripe (Is 28²⁵, Mt 23²³). In Heb. it is called כַּמֹּן, *kammôn*, and in Gr. κύμινον. For its use see Pliny, xix. 8. As to the doubt of its being tithed see *Demai*, ii. § 1.

Mint (ἡδύοσμον, Heb. מִינְתָא), the well-known aromatic labiate plant *Mentha sylvestris*, mentioned with the last in Mt 23²³. For its use among the Jews see Celsius, *Hierobot*. i. 546, and Pliny, xix. 47. See *Uketzin*, i. § 2; also *Nedarim*, 51b; *Shebiith*, vii. §§ 1, 2.

Mustard (σίναπι), the small seed of the common *Sinapis nigra*, which grows to a very large size in Palestine as the 'greatest of herbs' (Mt 13³² 17²⁰, Lk 13¹⁹ 17⁶), and is used as a condiment. See Thomson, *Land and Book*, i. 453. The pungent seeds of a small tree, *Salvadora persica*, have been supposed by Dr. Royle to be the mustard of the parable; but this is rarely, if at all, found in Palestine, and is not an herb, but a tree. The only claim is, that it is called in India *kharjal*, while *khardal* is the Arabic for mustard (see Royle, *Journ. Asiatic Soc*. 1844, No. xv., and Lambert, *Trans. Linn. Soc*. xvii. 449).

To the miraculous food by which the Israelites were fed, the name **Manna** is given. This has been supposed to be the gummy exudation of the *Tamarix mannifera*, a shrub which grows in the wilderness; but the whole description indicates that it was a miraculous food.

III. TABOOS.—There are certain prohibitions specially mentioned in the Pentateuch. One of these, the kid in mother's milk, has been already discussed. **Blood** is one of the most ancient of these taboos, and in connexion with it all animals which died of themselves or were killed otherwise than by being bled, were forbidden. Any such נְבֵלָה, *nĕbēlâh*, or carcase, might be given to strangers, or sold to foreigners, but was an abomination to the Jews (Dt 14²¹). The eater of it was rendered unclean (Lv 17¹⁵ 22⁸). Likewise that which was torn of beasts (Ex 22³¹), while it might be eaten by the stranger, was not allowed to the Israelite (Lv 17¹⁵). Hunting by dogs was therefore not practised. The observance of this taboo of פִּגּוּל *piggûl*, or abominable flesh, is referred to in Ezk 4¹⁴ and Ac 10¹⁴ (πᾶν κοινὸν καὶ ἀκάθαρτον), and it was one of the four 'necessary things' prohibited to the Gentile converts by the Jerusalem Council, Ac 15²⁸ ('things strangled'). The eating of blood, which is one of the most ancient prohibitions (Gn 9⁴) re-enacted in the Mosaic law in which it is frequently repeated, had not only a hygienic basis, but had reference probably to the drink-offerings of blood which were parts of the heathen rituals (Ps 16⁴). It was thus a law of demarcation, and in Lv 19²⁶ eating with the blood and auguries are bracketed together. The poisonous effects of bull's blood are referred to by several authors; Midas (Strabo, I. xi. § 21) and Psammenitus (Herodotus, iii. 15) are said to have been killed by it.

The **Fat** of animals was also forbidden (Lv 7³⁰) as food, and in the sacrificed victims this is called 'the food of the burnt-offering' Lv 3¹¹. 'All the fat is the Lord's' (v.¹⁶), see 1 S 2¹⁶, 2 Ch 7⁷, Gn 4⁴. What is specially referred to is the thick subcutaneous layer, and that around the kidneys and other viscera, as well as the fatty tails of the sheep. The 'fat things' of the promised spiritual feast in Is 25⁶ as well as in Neh 8¹⁰ are מַשְׁמַנִּים mashmannim, delicate things, not חֵלֶב ḥēleb, suet.

The **Sinew that shrank** (Gn 32³²), which it was the custom of the Jews to avoid, was a tribal taboo although not specially interdicted by statute. It is not known what part is particularized by the name גִּיד gîd, as the word is a general one, used of the sinews of the whole body in the vision of dry bones, Ezk 37⁶. Some have supposed it to be the great sciatic nerve at the back of the hip (Josephus, Ant. I. xx. 2), but that is not situated in the hollow of the thigh. This region, kaph hayyerek, evidently means the groin, which was facing his antagonist when Jacob was wrestling. There are two sinews there which if cramped cause lameness—one the tendon of the psoas, which exactly fits the description, but is very seldom cramped; the other, that of the adductor longus, is exceedingly liable to cramp when the thigh is twisted, and this causes agonizing pain and lameness, and would effectually disable a wrestler. I have known it to be severely strained in athletic exercises, causing lameness for several weeks. Some Jews have recommended that the hind legs of animals should not be eaten, lest by accident this sinew should be partaken of by mistake. This was not the practice in early times, for Samuel's cook set the thigh of the animal before Saul as the piece of honour (1 S 9²⁴. AV and RVm tr. שׁוֹק here 'shoulder'). See Tract Chullin, 7.

Swine, forbidden as food to the Jews, were eaten by the surrounding peoples in general. The Egyptians also considered the pig unclean (Herod. ii. 47), for a reason the Greek author forbears to mention, but which we learn from the Book of the Dead, as the demon Set once appeared in the form of a pig. Hence they are never represented in the older monuments, but appear in those of the New Empire (Wilkinson, ii. 100). The foul habits and coarse feeding of swine, their supposed liability to glandular disease [which has given us the Latin name of such swellings 'scrofula' (Celsus, v. xxviii. 7), and its Greek equivalent χοιράς (Hippoc. Aph. 1248)], and the notion that leprosy followed the eating of swine's flesh, contributed to this dislike. After the Captivity, however, especially under Syrian and Roman domination, the keeping of swine was practised for commercial purposes if not for food, hence our Lord's references Mt 7⁶, Lk 15¹⁵, Mt 8³⁰ (see Thomson, i. 355 ff.). Swine's flesh is taboo to the Mohammedan as well as to the Jew. For a detailed consideration of this prohibition see Spencer, de legibus Hebræorum ritualibus, Cambridge, 1727, i. p. 131.

The **Camel,** which is eaten by the Bedawin, was forbidden by the Levitical code. It is coarse and rather dry meat. The milk, however, was used in patriarchal times (see above). It was probably camel's milk which Jael gave to Sisera.

The **Hare** (אַרְנֶבֶת), only mentioned as being unclean because it is not cloven-footed, was common in the hilly regions. In the North the commonest species is Lepus Syriacus, in the South L. Ægyptiacus, and in the Arabah and Dead Sea district L. Sinaiticus. It is said to chew the cud from its habit of sitting in its form, but it is not a true ruminant. The same is the case with the shaphan or coney, which is the Hyrax Syriacus.

The oldest taboo is that of the fruit of the tree הַדַּעַת טוֹב וָרָע ' of the knowledge of good and evil.' Conjecture as to the actual tree meant is useless, but it is worth noting that the banana was identified with it by many mediæval writers; see Brocard's Descript. Terra Sancta, xi. See also Celsius, Hierobot., in which it is supposed to be the quince.

In the NT there is added the taboo of things offered to idols (Ac 21²⁶, 1 Co 8¹). The early ecclesiastics increased the stringency of the apostle's ordinance, and by the Council of Ancyra (c. 7) it was forbidden to a Christian to eat in any place which was connected with idolatrous worship, even if he brought his own food. On the other hand, Gregory, in writing to Augustine (Ep. xi. 76), recommends that the heathen sacrifices of oxen should be allowed to be continued in the English temples to accustom the people gradually to the change of ritual, but that they should be made on saints' days. For the tabooed vineyard on account of mixed seeds see above; and for rabbinical comments on taboos see Aboda Zara, especially v. § 9.

The **Ass,** though an unclean animal, was eaten during periods of famine. In 2 K 6²⁵ it is said that during the siege of Samaria a רֹאשׁ־חֲמוֹר rōsh-ḥāmôr, or ass's head, was sold for about £10. It has been supposed that this meant a measure of corn, but this is unlikely. In periods of dearth, distinctions of food are impracticable (Ezk 4¹³); for parallels see Plutarch (vit. Artax. Mnemon, i. 1023, and Xenophon, Anab. i. § 5). Even human flesh was eaten in such straits, see 2 K 6²⁹, La 4¹⁰, Ezk 5¹⁰.

IV. FOOD PREPARATION.—In primitive times the field, the flock, and the herd supplied all that was needful to the family, who procured it directly when wanted as in Gn 18⁵; but with the growth of towns and the consequent division of labour, food became a matter of merchandise. It was so in time of famine (Gn 42⁴), or to those on journeys (Dt 2⁶·²⁸). Markets or bazaars became established in the towns (Jer 37²¹), and merchants and shopmen (1 K 10¹⁵) supplied the wants of the town-dwellers. We read of such sellers of victual in Jerusalem (Neh 13¹⁵) and Samaria (Jn 4⁸). In this way, bread, water, fruit, milk, and flesh are purveyed to the people of the cities of the East.

Cookery was practised or supervised by the wife (Gn 18⁶), or by a slave (Gn 18⁷). At set feasts there was a cook employed (1 S 9²³) who killed the animals, and hence was called טַבָּח ṭabbâh, a word also applied to soldiers or executioners (Jer 39⁹). Some of these were female cooks (1 S 8¹³) who dressed the meats, and differed from the אֹפֶה or bakers, and the רַקָּחוֹת who were perfumers or spice mixers (1 S 8¹³ AV and RV ' confectionaries').

The animals were killed immediately before being cooked (Gn 18⁷, Lk 15²³); the throat was cut and the blood poured out in accordance with Lv 7²⁶ (see 1 S 14³²ff.); they were then flayed (Mic 3³) and cut up into joints, except in the case of small animals such as lambs, which were cooked whole (Ex 12⁴⁶). With larger animals the flesh was separated from the bones, and these broken when the flesh was to be boiled (Mic 3³). The doubtful ἅπ. λεγ. פִּימָה is tr. in Job 15²⁷ collops.

Boiling was the ordinary method of cooking, hence בָּשַׁל bāshal, to boil, is used of cooking in general (2 S 13⁸). The vessels used for this purpose were pots or caldrons of different kinds, which are called by six different names (see below). Some of the sacrifices were boiled, having first been flayed, the fat alone being burned (2 Ch 35[13]). This was especially the case with the sacrificial feasts, peace-offering, or *hostia honorifica*. In boiling, the caldron was first partly filled with water, and the flesh put in (Ezk 24[3]); sometimes milk was used, as Burckhardt describes being done at the present day (i. 63), and occasionally the bones were used to make the fire burn briskly, as Ezekiel describes. When the scum rises it is taken off (Ezk 24[6], but RV tr. חֶלְאָה *hel'âh*, as 'the rust of the pot,' not scum, LXX ἰός). In Ezk 24[10] AV tr. הַרְקַח *harkîah*, 'spice it well," as if derived from רָקַח to mix spices, but LXX has it ἐλαττώθη ὁ ζωμός, and RV renders it 'make thick the broth.' Spicing, that is, mixing with savoury or carminative herbs, was used to render meat savoury (Gn 27[4]), and such food was called 'dainty meat' (Pr 23[3·6] מַטְעַם *mat'am*, but called *man'am* in Ps 141[4]). Salt was also added, and when boiled the broth, מָרָק *mârak* (Is 65[4] *Ḳerê*, but the *Kethib* *paraḳ*, which means a stew or a mess of mincemeat in broth), was served separately (Jg 6[19. 20]). In modern Hebrew, soup is רַקְרֶקֶת *raḳreḳeth*. The broth may be used as a sauce for meat (Burckhardt, i. 63), or eaten with bread and butter (Gn 18[6]). Vegetables or rice or meal may be boiled in it or eaten mixed with it. Vegetable food was also boiled in water, with butter or with milk, to make pottage (Gn 25[29], 2 K 4[38]), which was of the consistence of thick Scotch broth or thin porridge.

Roasting was practised with small animals, such as the paschal lamb, which was cooked whole (Ex 12[46]) over an open fire (Ex 12[8], 2 Ch 35[13]), which was of wood (Is 44[16]). Animals taken in the chase were also roasted (חָרַךְ *hârak*, Pr 12[27]). Or the meat was baked in an oven, which may have been sunk in the ground (see BREAD). The paschal lamb was flayed before being roasted (2 Ch 35[11]). Eli's sons (1 S 2[12ff.]) sinned in that they took part of the flesh, which should have been boiled, and roasted it. They also seem not to have been content with the priestly share, which was ultimately fixed as the breast of the peace-offering and the right shoulder (Lv 7[31-32]). The only method of cooking fish mentioned in the Bible is broiling (ὀπτός, Lk 24[42], see Jn 21[9]) on the coals. In the Gizeh Museum there is a representation of shepherds broiling fish over the fire, and wiping the ashes from them with little bundles of straw (see Perrot-Chipiez, *Hist. de l'Art dans l'antiquité*, i.).

V. VESSELS used in the conveyance and cooking of food. There were several kinds of **basket** (see BASKET). The **pots** were of six kinds: **1.** סִיר *sîr*, LXX λέβης, called in Jer 1[13] a *sîr nâphûah* or boiling caldron. Of this kind were the flesh-pots of Egypt (Ex 16[3]) and the great pot used by the sons of the prophets (2 K 4[38]), as well as the caldron of Ezekiel's visions (11[3·7] 24[6]), and of Zechariah (14[20. 21]). In the list of temple furniture this word is tr. 'pot' in 1 K 7[45] and 'pan' in Ex 27[3], in which cases it was a brazen vessel for ashes, not for boiling. It is tr[d] 'washpot' in Ps 60[8] and 'caldrons' in Jer 52[18] (RV pots). **2.** דּוּד *dûd*, usually tr. basket (which see), is the kettle of 1 S 2[14] and the caldron of 2 Ch 35[13], tr. λέβης by LXX in the latter case. **3.** The pan of 1 S 2[14], 1 K 7[38], and 2 Ch 4[6] is כִּיּוֹר *kiyyor*, LXX λέβης. This word is variously tr. 'torch' (Zec 12[6], RV 'pan'), 'laver,' or washing vessel (Ex 30[18] etc.), and seems to have been a shallow, wide-mouthed utensil. The כִּירַיִם of Lv 11[35], which like the *tannûr* or oven could be broken down, was probably, as AV and RV render it in the text, a firehearth or range for pots (RVm has 'stewpan'), perhaps of two sides as the dual indicates, LXX χυτρόποδες. **4.** The caldron of Mic 3[3] is קַלַּחַת *ḳallahath*, similarly tr. in 1 S 2[14], LXX χύτρα, an earthenware vessel for

boiling. These were slightly glazed by means of salt and litharge. This may be referred to in the סִינִים or silver dross of Pr 26[23]. **5.** The pot of 1 S 2[14] is פָּרוּר *pârûr*, tr. 'pan' in Nu 11[8] (RV pots); in Jg 6[19] it was a pot for holding broth, LXX χυτρά. **6.** The pan of 2 Ch 35[13] is צֵלָחָה *zêlâhâh*. This is the word tr. 'cruse' in 2 K 2[20], and 'dish' in 2 K 21[13] and Pr 19[24] (AV tr. it here 'bosom' as LXX κόλπος).

The caldron of AV Job 41[20] is properly translated 'rushes' in RV. The figure being that leviathan's snortings make the pool in which he swims to boil like a caldron and the reeds to seem as if on fire.

The מַזְלֵג or **flesh hook** was a brazen fork (Ex 27[3]), which had three teeth (1 S 2[13]). The hooks of Ezk 40[43] for hanging up the slaughtered carcases of the offered animals are called שְׁפַתַּיִם *shĕphattaim*.

The **firepan** or chafing dish of 2 K 25[15] מַחְתָּה *mahtâh* was used for carrying burning coals. These vessels were of gold in the first temple.

The dishes or trays or other vessels in which food and drink were served are known by various names. Pottage was eaten out of the pot in which it was boiled (2 K 4[40]). Thomson describes the Bedawin sitting around a large saucepan and doubling their bread spoon-fashion to eat their lentil pottage (i. 253). Many of the vessels named were employed only in the temple service.

אֲגַרְטָל *'ăgartâl*, LXX ψυκτήρ, Vulg. *phiala*, only used in Ezr 1[9] and tr. 'charger,' was a gold bowl or basin, said by Ibn Ezra to be the same as that called *mizrâḳ*.

אַגָּן *'aggân*, LXX κρατήρ, used in Ex 24[6] for a wash-vessel or basin for sacrificial blood, made of gold, silver, or brass. Its plural is tr. *cups* in Is 22[24]; see also Ca 7[2].

אָסוּךְ *'âsûk*, an oil vessel 2 K 4[2] tr. 'pot,' after Kimchi, but more probably a flask or bottle.

אַרְגָּז *'argâz*, a coffer or box, which could be slung to the side of a cart, such as that in which the votive offerings of the Philistines were sent (1 S 6[11]).

בַּקְבֻּק *baḳbuḳ*, a wide-mouthed bottle or cruse for carrying honey (1 K 14[3]). It was of earthenware, and so was easily broken (Jer 19[1. 10]); LXX renders it βικός, which is the name given by Herodotus to the Babylonian casks of palm wine (i. 194). Athenaeus uses it for a drinking vessel (784 D). In Maltese a large vessel of this kind is called *bakbyka*.

גָּבִיעַ *gâbia'*, wine bowls (as Jer 35[5], LXX κεράμιον), of earthenware, from which wine was poured into goblets. A silver cup used for drinking and divination Gn 44[2]; LXX κόνδυ, said to be a Persian word. It is used for the pots of wine out of which Jeremiah filled the *ḳôṣôth* for the Rechabites, Jer 35[5].

גֻּלָּה *gullâh*, LXX στρεπτὸν ἀνθέμιον, a round vessel for holding oil in a lamp Zec 4[3], the golden cruse of Ec 12[6], used also for the rounded bowls above the capitals of the temple-pillars in 1 K 7[41] and 2 Ch 4[12. 13], possibly volutes such as those shown on the tablet of Samas in the Brit. Museum.

כַּד *kad*, a pail or barrel to hold meal 1 K 17[14], or water 1 K 18[33]. This name is given to Rebekah's pitcher Gn 24[14. 15ff.], and to Gideon's men's pitchers Jg 7[16]; see also Ec 12[6].

כְּלִי *kĕlî*, a vessel in general, of gold and silver Gn 24[53], or of clay Lv 11[33], apparently so called irrespective of shape, used for the vessels of the temple Is 52[11], Ezr 1[7], Nu 4[15].

כּוֹס *kôs*, a wine cup as in Gn 40[11. 13. 21]. Pharaoh's wine chalice, the cup which passed around the circle at a meal 2 S 12[3]. See also Pr 23[31], used metaphorically Ps 11[6] 116[13], Is 51[17-22], Hab 2[16] etc.

כֹּר *kor* and קַב *ḳab* were vessels of measurement, the former about 8 bushels, the latter about 4 pints. סְאָה, also a measure, nearly equals the English peck, and is a little greater than the μόδιος or 'bushel' of Mt 5[15]. See WEIGHTS AND MEASURES.

כְּפוֹר *kĕphôr*, a deep cup or chalice as 1 Ch 28¹⁷, Ezr 1¹⁰, and 8²⁷, probably a cup with a cover.

מַחֲבַת *maḥăbath*, a flat plate(?) for frying or baking bread Lv 6¹⁴ 7⁹, 1 Ch 23²⁹, Ezk 4³. See BREAD.

מַחְתָּה *maḥtâh*, a firepan 2 K 25¹⁵, or an incense bowl Lv 16¹², a coalpan Ex 27³ 25³⁸, LXX πυρεῖον.

מְנַקִּיָּה *mĕnakkiyâh*, a sacrificial dish Ex 25²⁹ 37¹⁶, Nu 4⁷, Jer 52¹⁹, probably a libation vessel.

מְדֹכָה *mĕdôkâh*, a mortar in which *e.g.* the manna was beaten before being baked Nu 11⁸.

מִזְרָק a bowl; of these Hiram made a hundred 2 Ch 4⁸, 1 K 7⁴⁵· ⁴⁶. See Ex 25²⁹, 1 Ch 28¹⁴· ¹⁷, Nu 7¹³, Zec 9¹⁵. For the numbers of these φιάλαι and σπονδεῖα see Jos. *Ant.* VIII. iii. 7, 8. It is a sacrificial bowl for dashing (זָרַק) the blood in a volume against the altar (see Driver's note on Am 6⁶).

נֹאד *nôd*, a skin bottle, see above under **Wine**.

נֶבֶל *nebel*, a skin of wine 1 S 1²⁴ 10³, 2 S 16¹; this word is also used for an earthen vessel as in Is 22²⁴ 30¹⁴. It is also the name of a musical instrument, a lute (RV) or psaltery or viol Is 5¹².

סַף *ṣaph*, a basin or bowl for blood Ex 12²², Jer 52¹⁹, for wine Is 51¹⁷, Zec 12².

סֵפֶל *sĕphel*, a bowl Jg 5²⁵ 6³⁸; LXX λεκάνη; also in 1 K 7⁵⁰ and 2 K 12¹³.

פַּךְ *pak*, a vial or flask of oil 1 S 10¹, 2 K 9¹⁻³; LXX φακός, probably the same as the *bakbuk*.

צַפַּחַת *zappaḥath*, a water bottle 1 S 26¹², 1 K 19⁶, or an oil bottle 1 K 17¹²; an oryballus or round vessel with a narrow neck, see Thomson, ii. 21. See 2 K 9¹⁻³ for box of ointment.

צֵלָחָה *zēlāḥâh*, a dish or bowl in which sacrifices were boiled as in 2 Ch 35¹³, or a flat saucer for salt 2 K 2²⁰ 21¹³, Pr 19²⁴ 26¹⁵.

צִנְצֶנֶת *zinzeneth*, in Ex 16³³, was the pot in which the manna was laid up, a vase or jar according to Abu'l Walid and Sa'adya.

'Αλάβαστρον of Mt 26⁷ was a vessel made of satin spar or Oriental alabaster, which is a variegated kind of marble of calcium carbonate, not the gypsum or calcium sulphate now called alabaster. Vessels of this kind are described by Theophrastus (*de Odoribus*, 41) and by Pliny (ix. 56) as elongated or pear-shaped with fairly narrow necks. Some alabastra were made of glass, gold (Plutarch, *Vit. Alex.*), or earthenware (Epiphanius, *de mensuris et ponderibus*, xxiv. 182).

Πίναξ, the charger in which the Baptist's head was sent (Mt 14⁸· ¹¹), was a flat dish. Finn refers to a case in which some Bedawin sent the head of an enemy on a dish on the top of a pillau of rice (p. 35). The παροψίς of Mt 23²⁵ was a smaller dish on which dainty food was served.

Of other NT vessels, ποτήριον is the drinking cup of Mk 7⁴, and that used at the Last Supper Mk 14²³ etc. ξέστης in Mk 7⁴ is a Latinism, a corruption of *sextarius*, a pint measure. The word is used by Sicilian writers. χάλκιον in the same passage is a copper or bronze vessel of any shape. ὑδρίαι λίθιναι at the feast at Cana (Jn 2⁶) were stone pitchers of considerable capacity. Early figures of these from sarcophagi and from the well-known ivory plaque in Ravenna are published by Bottari and Bandini, and an ancient *hydria* is shown as one of these in the Ch. of St. Ursula in Cologne; for others see Didron, *Annales Archéol.* xiii. 2.

VI. The usual MEALS in ordinary life were two—a mid-day meal or dinner, and an evening meal or supper, which was the more important. Breakfast was, and still is, an informal repast. That in Jn 21¹³ was a meal after a night of toil, so 'dine' in AV is replaced in RV by 'break your fast' (ἀριστήσατε). The meal at the Pharisee's house in Lk 11³⁷ is also, as in RVm, a breakfast or early meal. Peter, defending the apostles, points out that they could not be drunken, as it was only 9 o'clock in the morning (Ac 2¹⁵). Early drinking of wine at such a time was a sign of degradation (Is 5¹¹), and eating in the morning is deprecated as culpable luxury (Ec 10¹⁶) and out of due season.

It is still the custom in the East to make the morning repast a very slight one—a cup of milk, a piece of butter. Robinson describes melted butter (*semen*), or oil poured over bread, as a breakfast dish (ii. 70), or cakes baked on the ashes and broken up and mixed with butter in a dish (ii. 18). The morning meal of the Bedawi is about 9 or 10 o'clock (Burckhardt, *Notes*, i. 69). Drummond notices how his negro bearers in tropical Africa rose from sleep and began their day's work without food (*Tropical Africa*, p. 100).

The mid-day meal or dinner in Egypt was at noon (Gn 43¹⁶), and probably was at the same time in Palestine (Ru 2¹⁴). Abstinence from this is called fasting (Jg 20²⁶, 1 S 14²⁴, 2 S 11² 3³⁵). From these passages it is evident that the people were accustomed to 'eat bread' at mid-day. God promised to Israel bread in the morning and flesh in the evening (Ex 16¹²). This early meal is the ἄριστον of Lk 14¹². St. Peter's intended meal, interrupted by Cornelius' messengers, was at 12 o'clock. This meal took some time to prepare, so the good housewife began to make ready this פַת while it was yet night (Pr 31¹⁵). The meal is called אֲרֻחָה *'aruḥâh*, as in Jer 40⁵ 52³⁴, 2 K 25³⁰, and Pr 15¹⁷. The noon meal is described in Lane's *Modern Egyptians*, p. 156 ff. (Gardner's ed.). It sometimes was a period of excess (1 K 20¹⁶).

The supper after the day's work is done (Ru 3⁷) is, and was, the more important meal (see Burckhardt's *Notes*, i. 69), and the one at which flesh meat was more commonly used. At these meals the whole family was gathered together. According to Josephus, the law required dinner to be at the sixth hour on the Sabbath day (*Life*, 54), *i.e.* at 12 o'clock ; but in § 44 he speaks of feasting with his friends at the second hour of the night=8 p.m. See also *BJ* I. xvii. 4, and the great supper of Lk 14¹⁵ff.

In the patriarchal days they seem to have sat on the ground as they do at present. Abraham's guests probably thus sat while he stood and served (Gn 18⁸). Jacob says to his father 'sit and eat of my venison,' but that was probably because the blind old man was recumbent (Gn 27¹⁹). Jacob's sons also sat down to eat (Gn 37²⁵), as the Egyptian shepherds are represented in a painting from Sakkarah, now in the Gizeh Museum. The Levite and his concubine sat down to eat (Jg 19⁶). Saul also sat at meat (1 S 20⁵· ²⁴), as did Samuel when he brought Saul to feast with him (1 S 9²²), and Jesse and his family (1 S 16¹¹). The old prophet and his guest likewise took the forbidden meal sitting at a table (1 K 13²⁰). Sitting at meat is mentioned in Pr 23¹, Jer 16⁸, Ezk 44³. Sitting, however, might have in some of these cases meant reclining, for Oholibah is described as sitting on a stately bed with a table prepared before it (Ezk 23⁴¹), and the guests at Esther's banquet reclined on couches (Est 7⁸). The table is also mentioned in Ps 23⁵. Sitting on the ground was, however, regarded as a sign of humiliation and abasement in prophetic times, as in Is 3²⁶ 47¹ 52², Jer 13¹⁸ RVm, La 2¹⁰, Ezk 26¹⁶.

In NT times the usual attitude was reclining and resting on the left elbow ; as at the supper described in Jn 13²³, John reclined in front of our Lord, and so when he leant back to speak to Him John's head was on Jesus' breast. It has been supposed from these expressions that the patriarchal custom changed, and that the practice of sitting as the Egyptians did was adopted by early Israel, the fashion changing in later time into the Græco-Roman custom of reclining on a couch with a cushion for the left elbow, and the right arm free ; but it is probable that these changes were slight, and that the phrase sitting at meat does not specify a posture such as that to which we give the name. Thus our Lord uses the phrase of the attitude in His own time (Lk 14⁸ 17⁷ 22²⁷), and the multitude whom He miraculously fed sat down on the ground (Jn 6¹⁰). Of the tables, we have preserved a figure in the shewbread table on the Arch of Titus. They must have been high enough in the days of Adonibezek for the 70 captive kings to sit on a lower level (Jg 1⁷); but the same phrase is used in NT times of the crumbs falling to the dogs under the table (Mt 15²⁷, Mk 7²⁸), and Lazarus is said to have sat at table at the feast (Jn 12²). The couches or mattresses on which the eaters sat or reclined are never mentioned except in the cases given above, and the stool in the prophet's chamber is the only material seat specified in the OT, except royal thrones. At ordinary meals it is probable that the family squatted around the dish, out of which they all helped themselves, even as is done at the present day by the Bedawin. For an account of the ancient tables see Athenæus, *Deipnosophistæ*, especially ii. 32. The costly couches for reclining, with ivory corners, are mentioned in Am 3¹² and 6⁴. Homer refers to sitting at food, *Il.* x. 578; *Odyss.* i. 145.

The food at an ordinary meal at present consists of messes of lentile-pottage (נָזִיד *nāzîd*) eaten with bread or wooden spoons (Robinson, ii. 86; Gn 25³⁴). Sometimes this is thickened with vegetables, or pillaus of rice with or without meat, thin sheets of bread serving for plates, and used to sop up the gravy (Finn, 24). Sometimes bread, cheese, olives, and *leben* make up the repast (Finn, 272). Doughty describes an Arab meal in which the family surrounded a vast trencher heaped with boiled mutton 'and great store of girdle bread.' Pieces torn off with the hand from the meat were lapped in the thin cakes of bread and handed to those who could not reach the dish (i. 46). Robinson saw, likewise, the guests surrounding a circular tray on which was a mountain of pillau of rice boiled with butter, and small pieces of meat strewed through it. Other dishes used are sausages stuffed with rice and chopped meat. Burckhardt gives a graphic account of the discomforts of such a feast to one unaccustomed to Eastern habits, *Notes*, i. 63. The poorer classes of Bedawin live chiefly on bread, eaten with raw leeks or radishes for flavouring, which is the 'dinner of herbs' (Pr 15¹⁷; see Ro 14², Dn 1¹²). For such a meal the son of the prophets went out to collect the '*ôrôth* or herbs (2 K 4³⁹). The Bedawi meal described in Ezk 25⁵ consisted of bread, dates, and milk. For an ordinary meal there is generally one dish, so that the member of the family who cooks, when it is brought in, has no further work. Hence our Lord's remonstrance with Martha, that one dish alone was needful (Lk 10⁴²). It was the duty of the cook to bring in the dishes when prepared (1 S 9²³), and that of the head of the family to distribute the portions (1 S 1⁵), whose size might be varied according to his affection for the members of the circle. So Joseph gave Benjamin a fivefold mess, and Elkanah gave Hannah a double portion (but LXX says that he gave her only μερίδα μίαν, 'a single portion,' *because* she had no child). Very often, however, the circle help themselves when they can reach the dish, and as the meat has been cut up before being cooked it does not need any carving. At the present day the Mussulmans drink water or milk or *leben* with their meals, but probably in earlier times wine was used as a drink. In ancient times barley or polenta was used as rice is now, and the pillau was the ἠλφιτωμένα κρέα of the classics (see Gruner, *de Primit. Oblatione*). The food carried on journeys consisted of bread, cakes of figs or raisins, parched corn, and water. The good

Samaritan carried also wine and oil. Dough is sometimes carried tied in a wallet or cloth (see Doughty, i. 231).

VII. FEASTS, or special meals, were provided on particular occasions, and are frequently mentioned. These were of various kinds—(1) Feasts of hospitality for the entertainment of strangers (Gn 18²ff.). These might be at any time—Abraham's was at the heat of the day, Lot's (Gn 19¹⁻³) was in the evening. For such feasts at the present day see Burckhardt, Robinson, Doughty, etc. (2) Entertainments of friends specially invited (Lk 14¹⁶ and many other passages). These were usually evening feasts. (3) Religious or sacrificial feasts, non-Jewish or Jewish, 'eating bread before God' (Ex 18¹²), eating of sacrifices (Ex 34¹⁵ 29³², Lv 19⁵·⁶, Nu 29¹²ff., Dt 12⁷ 27⁶·⁷, 1 S 9¹³, 2 S 6¹⁹, 1 K 19 3¹⁵, Zeph 1⁷); also at the offering of tithes (Dt 14²⁶). Closely allied were the (4) anniversary feasts, such as Passover (Ex 12¹⁴), Purim (Est 9²²), and the Lord's Supper. (5) Celebrations of the completion of a great work, such as the building of the temple (2 Ch 7⁸), the carrying home of the ark (2 S 6¹⁹), a great deliverance (Jg 16²³), or the ratification of a treaty (Gn 26³⁰ and 31⁵⁴). (6) At the beginning of a great work or laying a foundation. A reference to such a feast is in Pr 9¹⁻⁵. (7) Harvesthomes (Ex 23¹⁶), sheepshearing (1 S 25³⁶, 2 S 13²³), vintage (Jg 9²⁷), and other agricultural events, were likewise the occasions of feasting. (8) Family events were celebrated by feasts of relatives and friends: circumcision (Lk 2⁵⁸⁻⁵⁹), weaning (Gn 21⁸), marriage (Jn 2¹, Gn 29²², To 8¹⁹, Jg 14¹⁰, Mt 22²), the return of a wandering member (Lk 15²³), funerals (2 S 3³⁵, Jer 16⁷, Hos 9⁴, To 4¹⁷). Birthday feasts were not common among Jews, some of whom thought them profane (Lightfoot, Iselius), probably because other nations, such as the Persians, honoured them so conspicuously (see Herod. i. 133). Birthday feasts are mentioned in Gn 40²⁰, Job 1⁴, Mt 14⁶⁻⁹). Among modern Jews the circumcision feast is an important occasion (see CIRCUMCISION).

Any such feast was called מִשְׁתֶּה *mishteh*, the primary meaning of which is a banquet of wine, such as that given by queen Esther (Est 5⁶ 7⁷). Abraham's feast at Isaac's weaning is called a *mishteh gādôl*, or great drinking. Job feared lest his sons should be led into excess at their periodic feasts (1⁵) Such drinking feasts are specially mentioned in 1 S 25³⁶, 2 S 13²⁸, Dn 5¹, and reprobated by the prophets Amos (6⁶) and Isaiah (5¹¹). In the NT κῶμοι are spoken of in Ro 13¹³, Gal 5²¹, and 1 P 4³. The feast in 2 K 6²³ is named כֵּרָה *kērâh*, perhaps because the prisoner guests sat in a ring (cf. סָבַב in 1 S 16¹¹).

For these banquets the food animals were slain early in the day (Is 22¹³, Pr 9², Mt 22⁴), and a second invitation sent to remind just before the feast (Est 6¹⁴, Pr 9³, Mt 22³). The guests on arrival were sometimes welcomed with a kiss (To 7⁶, Lk 7⁴⁵; see Goezius, *de Osculo*, in Ugolini, xxx.), and provided with water to wash their hands, as they put their hands in the common dish (Mk 7³; see *Odyss.* i. 136). These washings were made burdensome by traditional rituals (Mk 7²⁻¹³). When the visitors came from a distance they were supplied with water to wash their feet. So Abraham did for the angels at their noontide feast (Gn 18⁴), and Lot for their evening feast (Gn 19²). So the old man at Gibeah did for the Levite and his concubine (Jg 19²¹). See our Lord's rebuke to Simon (Lk 7⁴⁴), His own practice (Jn 13⁴), and apostolic reference (1 Ti 5¹⁰). The anointing of guests is referred to in Ps 23⁵, Am 6⁶, Lk 7³⁸, Jn 12³ (see ANOINTING; and in addition to the literature quoted there, see Weymar, *de Unctione Sacra Heb.*, in Ugolini, xii.; Reinerus and Verwey, *de*

Unctionibus, and Graberg, *de unctione Christi in Bethania*, in Ugolini, xxx.). The crowning of guests with garlands is mentioned in Is 28[1], Wis 2[8], Jos. *Ant.* XIX. ix. 1. See Plutarch, *Symp.* III. i. 3, and Martial, x. 19. After these preliminaries they sat down, males and females together (Ru 2[14], 1 S 1[4], Job 1[4], Lk 10[40]); and grace was said in Jewish feasts (Mt 14[19], Lk 9[16], Jn 6[11]). The guests were arranged in order of rank (Gn 43[33], 1 S 9[22] 20[25], Lk 14[8], Mk 12[39], Jos. *Ant.* xv. ii. 4), the highest occupying the 'chief room,' the seat on the *protoklisia*. In Assyr. feasts they are represented as sitting (Layard, *Nineveh*, ii. 411). For Jewish practice see above. According to the Tosaphoth to *Berachoth*, vi., each guest had a separate table, but Pr 23[1] speaks of sitting at meat with the host; and David says that he sat at table with Saul (1 S 20[5]). The food was distributed either by the cook or by the head of the house (2 S 6[19], Gn 43[24]), and the most honoured guest received the largest portion (Gn 43[34]; see Herod. vi. 57), or else the tit-bit (1 S 9[24]). To guests who could not come, presents of food were sometimes sent (2 S 11[8], Neh 8[10], Est 9[19-22]).

At a feast in NT times the guests reclined on a *triclinium*, the couches being arranged on three sides of a square, the fourth side being open for serving, and strangers might stand around on the outer side (see Rashi, *ad Berachoth*, 46*b*. 16; *Pesachim*, vii. 13). A wine cup was passed round containing wine mixed with three parts of water (*Shabbath*, viii. 1); to this there are many metaphorical allusions in which the cup in the hand of the Lord is spoken of (Ps 75[8], Jer 25[15]; see Buxtorf, *Synagog. Jud.* xii. 242, and Werner, *de Poculo Benedictionis*). The guests were entertained with music (2 S 19[35], Is 5[12], Am 6[4. 5], Lk 15[25]; see Maimonides, *de Jejuniis*, 5), dancing (Mt 14[6]), and riddles (Jg 14[12]). After the feast the hands were washed, as they were soiled by eating. Finn saw a guest taking handfuls of buttered rice from the dish, out of which he squeezed the butter between his fingers and licked it as it flowed down (*Byeways*, 171; Burckhardt, *Notes*, i. 63). Grace was said at the close of the meal (Dt 8[10], Ro 14[6]; see *Berachoth*, vi. § 8). Wedding feasts were given by the bridegroom (Jg 14[10]), but the arrangements were carried out under the direction of a *symposiarch* or ruler of the feast, and they sometimes lasted seven days (Jn 2[9], To 7[8]; see Selden, *de Uxor. Heb.* ii. 11). Wedding garments given to guests are mentioned in Mt 22[11].

The giver of the feast sometimes marked distinguished guests by giving them a sop of bread held between the thumb and finger. A ψωμίον of this kind dipped in the *ḥarôseth* was given by our Lord to Judas. Sops are used to catch and convey pieces of meat (Lane, i. 193; Burckhardt, i. 63). In Proverbs the laziness of the sluggard is said to be such that he will not even lift up a sop (19[24] 26[15]).

For metaphorical allusions to feasts see Is 25[6]; the feast of angels at the finishing of creation is referred to in Job 38[7]. For Jewish feasts in general see Buxtorf, *de conviviis vet. Hebræorum*.

LITERATURE. — For food-stuffs see Bochart, *Hierozoicon*, Frankf. 1675; Tristram, *Nat. Hist. of Palestine*; Post, *Flora of Palestine*; Erman, *Life in Ancient Egypt*, 1894; Celsius, *Hierobotanicon*, Amst. 1748; Hiller, *Hierophyton*, Tübingen, 1723; Rosenmüller, *Botany of the Bible*, Edinburgh, 1840. For customs, Burckhardt, *Reisen in Syrien, Palästina*, etc. (ed. Gesenius), Weimar, 1823, the same writer's *Notes on the Bedouins and Wahâbys*, Lond. 1830, and his *Travels in Arabia*, Lond. 1829; Robinson, *BRP* (3 vols. 1867); Thomson, *Land and Book* (3 vols. 1881–86); Doughty, *Arabia Deserta* (2 vols. 1888); Finn, *Byeways in Palestine*. Talmudic quotations in the above article are from Surenhusius (Amsterdam edition).   A. MACALISTER.

FOOL.—*A.* IN OT. The words tr[d] by 'fool,' 'folly,' 'foolishness,' are the following: **1.** נָבָל‎, נְבָל‎ (opp. חָכָם‎ in Dt 32[6], see Driver, *ad loc.*, and on 22[21] 32[15. 21]).

2. כְּסִיל‎, סָכָל‎, סֶכֶל‎, כְּסִילוּת‎, כְּסָלָה‎, כֶּסֶל‎, סָכָל‎, סֶכֶל‎, סִכְלוּת‎ (the root כסל‎ means possibly 'to be thick, plump, sluggish'). **3.** אֱוִיל‎, אֱוֶלֶת‎ (root-conception possibly the same as in the preceding). **4.** מְהוֹלָל‎, הוֹלֵלוּת‎, הוֹלֵלוֹת‎ (from a root suggesting the idea of wild frantic folly). **5.** תָּפֵל‎, תִּפְלָה‎ (from a root 'to be insipid'), only in Job 1[22] 24[12], Jer 23[13]. **6.** תַּהֲלָה‎ (supposed by Dillm. to be connected with Eth. *tahala*, 'to err'), Job 4[18].

All these terms denote something distinct from imbecility on the one hand and insanity on the other hand. It is in the forms under **4** only that the notions of 'folly' and 'madness' come together (cf. Job 12[17], Is 44[25] with 1 S 21[13], Jer 25[16]). As a rule, different words (derivatives from שָׁגַע‎) are used for 'madman' and 'madness.' The OT idea of 'folly' can be best understood from the antithesis it forms to 'wisdom.' Wisdom is not a theoretical or abstractly scientific apprehension of things, but such a practical immediate insight into their reality and manner of action as enables one to use them to advantage. Correspondingly, a fool is not one who is deficient in the power of logical thought, but one who lacks the natural discernment and tact required for success in life. Both wisdom and folly are teleological conceptions, and rest on the principle of adjustment to a higher law for some practical purpose. This general idea is, however, applied with considerable variety as to particular shades of meaning.

(*a*) In the widest sense folly is lack of common-sense in ordinary affairs (Gn 31[28], 1 S 25[25] [נְבָלָה‎], 26[21] [הִסְכַּלְתָּ‎], 2 S 15[31] [סִכֵּל‎]). Here the element of unreasonableness and inexpediency is most prominent.

(*b*) A moral and religious element enters into the conception where it expresses flagrantly sinful conduct such as offends against the fundamental principles of natural law and usage. In this sense fools are great sinners—impious, reprobate people. But the original idea is retained in so far as the thought of sudden divine retribution lies in the background, it being considered the height of folly, by violating the elementary rules of religion and morality, to expose one's self to the untimely end which frequently befalls the fool (Jos 7[15], 2 S 3[33] (cf. Driver, *in loco*), Job 2[10] 30[8] 5[2. 3] [all נְבָלָה‎, נָבָל‎], Ps 107[17] [אֱוִיל‎]). A profounder and more spiritualized turn is given to this idea in some of the psalms, where it is applied to sin as such (Ps 38[5] 69[5] [אִוֶּלֶת‎], cf. 2 S 24[10] [נִסְכַּלְתִּי‎]). This whole usage, with its identification of what is sensible and right, bespeaks a high development of the popular moral sense in Israel.

(*c*) A special usage connected with the foregoing characterizes as folly sexual sins of various kinds (Gn 34[7], Dt 22[21], Jg 19[22. 23. 24] 20[6. 10], Jer 29[23]). The standing phrase is 'folly in Israel,' 'which ought not to be done,' the implication being that such offences go against all reason in undermining the foundations of society as well as destroying the holiness of Israel. נָבָל‎ and נְבָלָה‎ are regularly used in this meaning; a synonym is זִמָּה‎ 'lewdness'; cf. further the sense of נְבָלוּת‎ in Hos 2[12], and of the verb in passages like Jer 14[21], Mic 7[6], Nah 3[6]; further, נְבָלָה‎ in Job 42[8].

(*d*) Inasmuch as in the Mosaic law a special norm has been given for the wise guidance of Israel's life, disregard of this law is equivalent to foolishness. Apostate Israel is 'a foolish (נָבָל‎) people and unwise' (Dt 32[6]); the Gentiles, not possessed of such a revelation, are 'a foolish nation,' 'a no-people' (Dt 32[21]; cf. Dt 4[6], Jer 4[22] [סָכָל‎]). The heathen diviners stand revealed as fools when the divinely-guided course of history foretold by Israel mocks their prognostications (Is 19[11. 13] 44[25], Ezk 13[3]). Especially the higher classes among Israel might be expected to have profited by this wisdom (Jer 5[4]).

(*e*) A more specialized meaning is assumed by the term 'fool' in the so-called Ḥokhma-literature of the OT (Job, Proverbs, Ecclesiastes, and some psalms and prophetic passages). Here also foolishness is the opposite of wisdom. But wisdom has developed, out of the unreflecting instinctive gift of seeing right and doing right, into the conscious art of successfully ordering the whole of individual life and conduct in harmony with the teleological principles of the divine government of the world, especially as embodied in the revealed law. Hence wisdom and folly are here introduced as personifications; and the divine wisdom, as the archetypal source of every teleological arrangement, is distinguished from human wisdom. Wisdom in this sense is 'practical virtuosity in the entire domain of ethics' (Riehm); it is equivalent to methodically applied religion and morality, as appears from the frequent interchange between it and the terms denoting piety and righteousness. Folly, as its contrast, is presented under two aspects, being either confined to a simple disregard of the rules of wisdom, or proceeding to open denial of the principle of divine government on which these rules are based. In the former character the fool is elaborately depicted in Proverbs. While wisdom consists primarily in circumspect behaviour, self-control, self-restraint, and teachableness, the fool is he who lets his undisciplined nature have free play—the self-reliant, self-pleased, arrogant, indocile, hasty with words, contentious, envious, quick to anger, intemperate, credulous, sluggish, given to pursuit of vain things, unable to conceal his own folly and shame. As easily seduced, he is called פְּתִי 'simple,' as unreceptive of instruction either by counsel or experience כְּסִיל, as by nature stupid בַּעַר, as insensible to the claims of God or man ; cf. the definition of נָבָל in Is 32⁶ (in Pr נָבָל occurs only 17⁷· ²¹ 30²², אֱוִיל 19 t., כְּסִיל 49 t.).

Folly, in the most advanced sense of a systematically conceived and applied theory of life opposed to that of wisdom, is equivalent to practical atheism. The fool (נָבָל) is he who has said in his heart, 'There is no God'; by which, not a theoretical denial of the divine existence, but a practical negation of God's moral government is meant (Ps 14¹ 53¹ 39⁸, Is 9¹⁷). Synonymous with נָבָל in this meaning is לֵץ 'mocker.'

B. IN NT. Analogies for most of the above meanings may be found in NT, usually with a somewhat larger admixture of the intellectual element.

(a) Foolishness appears as the lack of common-sense perception of the reality of things natural and spiritual, or as the imprudent ordering of one's life in regard to salvation; ἄφρων, μωρός, ἀνόητος (Mt 7²⁶ 23¹⁷ 25²ᶠᶠ·, Lk 11⁴⁰ 12²⁰ 24²⁵, Gal 3¹· ³).

(b) The OT נָבָל as a moral reprobate reappears in the μωρέ of Mt 5²², a term of opprobrium distinguished by its ethical import from the Aramaic 'Ρακά, occurring in the same verse and expressing merely intellectual imbecility.

(c) Of the natural foolishness belonging to the heathen mind, the only remedy for which lies in the wisdom supplied by revelation, we read in Ro 2²⁰, Tit 3³. The counterpart of the OT idea of the law as an institution for the wise guidance of Israel is furnished by St. Paul, who represents the gospel as a teleological arrangement in which the highest wisdom is manifested and recognized by the believer (Ro 11³³). Inasmuch, however, as the Gentile mind sustains a radically wrong relation to the moral world, it fails to see this marvellous adaptation and decries the gospel as foolishness. Even the converted Greek is under temptation to justify its reasonableness from the worldly point of view by such a presentation as will materially alter its character. Hence the sharp antithesis, 1 Co 1²¹⁻²⁵ 2¹⁴ 3¹⁸⁻²³ 4¹⁰, the wisdom of the world is foolishness to God, the foolishness of Christ crucified is the wisdom of God.

(d) In Ro 16¹⁹, Eph 5¹⁵· ¹⁷ we are reminded of the Ḥokhma usage. The fool under whose mask St. Paul speaks 2 Co 11¹⁶ᶠᶠ· corresponds in a formal sense to the boasting fool of Proverbs.

LITERATURE.—Bruch, *Weisheitslehre der Hebräer*; Cheyne, *Job and Solomon*; Cremer, *Wörterb. der NT Gr.*, *s.vv.* σοφός, σοφία; Delitzsch, *Proverbs* (Introduction); Kuyper, *Encycl.* ii. 65–71; Oehler, *Theol. of OT*, part iii.; Riehm, *Alttest. Theologie*, 350–359; Siegfried, *Philo von Alexandrien*; Smend, *Lehrb. der alttest. Religionsgeschichte*, 508–525.

GEERHARDUS VOS.

FOOLERY.—Sir 22¹³ 'Talk not much with a fool . . . and thou shalt never be defiled with his fooleries' (οὐ μὴ μολυνθῇς ἐν τῷ ἐντιναγμῷ αὐτοῦ BS, -γματι A ; RV 'thou shalt not be defiled in his onslaught'). The form in A, ἐντίναγμα, is found in Aq. at Is 28² 32², and in Symm. Theod. at Is 28²; neither form elsewhere in Greek. The verb from which the subst. is derived, ἐντινάσσω, is used in LXX, 1 Mac 2³⁶ and 2 Mac 4⁴¹ of casting stones, and in 2 Mac 11¹¹ of charging an enemy. It is probably with the last passage in mind that RV renders 'onslaught.' Edersheim (*Speaker's Com.*) prefers the more etymological trⁿ 'that which he throws out,' but understands that either *saliva* is meant literally, or that it is used figuratively for foolish words; Bissell follows Fritzsche and Bunsen, and renders *slaver*, 'which, of course, is used for low and foolish words.' For the Eng. word, cf. Shaks. *Winter's Tale*, III. ii. 185—

    'Thy tyranny
Together working with thy jealousies,—
Fancies too weak for boys, too green and idle
For girls of nine,—O, think, what they have done,
And then run mad, indeed; stark mad! for all
Thy bygone fooleries were but spices of it.'

J. HASTINGS.

FOOT (רֶגֶל, πούς).—There are various ideas connected with the foot due to its position as the lowest part of the human body.

1. *Subjection*, Jos 10²⁴, 2 S 22³⁹, Is 49²³, 1 Co 15²⁵· ²⁷. The foot on the neck is seen on the Egyptian monuments. The promise made to Joshua of possessing every place that the sole of his foot should tread upon, is literally claimed and acted upon by Islam. The Sultan is *the Shadow of God*, the token of the Almighty's presence and power; military conquest is therefore a triumph of the faith and an inalienable possession. After the war with Greece in 1897, this article of belief created a religious dilemma with regard to withdrawing from conquered Thessaly.

2. *Humility*, as in the relationship of disciple sitting at the feet of master (Dt 33³, Lk 10³⁹, Ac 22³), and generally of inferior to superior in the act of obeisance and worship (Nu 16⁴, Ru 2¹⁰, Ezk 11¹³, Mt 18²⁹, Rv 5¹⁴ etc.). Such prostration forms part of the ordinary Moslem devotions.

3. *Defilement*, Ex 3⁵. Contact with the common earth was considered defiling, and gave rise to the Oriental rule about removing the shoe, and on certain occasions washing the feet before entering sacred places, such as buildings devoted to worship, shrines, and in houses the carpeted rooms where prayer is offered. Shaking the dust from the feet is an easy and often-repeated act on the dusty roads of the East. The shoe or slipper is not usually removed, but the foot is held out and shaken with the shoe hanging down from the toes, until the dust falls out. It was a symbol of scornful and complete rejection (Mt 10¹⁴, Ac 13⁵¹). The same thought is now more commonly expressed by shaking the collar of the coat (cf. Ac 18⁶).

The feet were put in stocks (Job 13²⁷), fastened with fetters (Ps 105¹⁸; see CHAIN). They were also adorned with anklets (Is 3¹⁸).

When the word of God is called *a lamp to the feet* (Ps 119¹⁰⁵), the reference is to village or town life, with ditches, refuse, and dogs in the pathway. A lantern was carried in the hand, or by a servant walking in front. Until recently, before the streets began to be lit by lamps at distant intervals, any one found walking at night without a lantern was liable to be arrested as a thief. In the journeys of the desert the direction is by the stars; or where there is a path the horse or baggage animal is trusted to keep it.

Washing the feet was rendered necessary by the heat and dust of the road, and by the open sandals or loose shoes that were worn. As an attention rendered to a guest, both on account of the humility of the service and the comfort to the traveller, it belonged to the inner graces of hospitality (Lk 7³⁸, Jn 13⁵, 1 Ti 5¹⁰).

For 'foot-breadth,' Dt 2⁵, RV gives 'for the sole of the f. to tread upon.' For 'foot' of laver Ex 38⁸ RV gives 'base' (בֵּן). By the *lex talionis* (Ex 21²⁴, Dt 19²¹) 'foot for foot' was exacted. In Dt 11¹⁰ a contrast is drawn between the climate and the methods of cultivation characteristic of Palestine and of Egypt. When Israel was in the last-named country they 'sowed their seed and *watered it with the foot*.' The reference here appears to be to the use of some machine by which water was raised and distributed for irrigation purposes (see Lane, *Modern Egyptians*, ed. 1871, ii. 25 ff.), but the precise method is doubtful (cf. the full and interesting note in Driver's *Deut*. p. 129, and in 2nd ed. p. xxi).*

G. M. MACKIE.

FOOTMAN.—This word is used in two different senses: **1.** A foot-soldier, always in plu. 'footmen,' foot-soldiers, infantry. The Heb. is either רַגְלִי *raglî* (always sing. except Jer 12⁵, where the meaning is, however, not foot-soldiers but foot-runners; see below), or more fully אִישׁ רַגְלִי *'îsh raglî* (Jg 20², 2 S 8⁴, 1 Ch 18⁴ 19¹⁸). The Greek is mostly πεζοί (1 Es 8⁵¹, Jth 1⁴ 2⁵·¹⁹·²² 7²⁰ 9⁷, 2 Mac 11⁴ 13²), but we also find ἄνδρές 1 Mac 9⁴, φάλαγξ 1 Mac 10⁸², δυνάμεις 1 Mac 12⁴⁹, and πεζικοί (א¹ -ή) 1 Mac 16⁵. Footmen probably composed the whole of the Isr. forces (1 S 4¹⁰ 15⁴) before the time of David. From Solomon's day onwards Israel certainly possessed also chariots and cavalry (1 K 4²⁶ EV). See ARMY. The Eng. word is used freely in old writers in this sense, as Malory, *Morte Darthur*, I. ix. 'And when he came to the sea he sent home the footmen again, and took no more with him but ten thousand men on horseback'; I. xiv. 'ever in saving of one of the footmen we lose ten horsemen for him.'

2. A runner on foot: 1 S 22¹⁷ 'And the king said unto the footmen that stood about him, Turn, and slay the priests of the LORD' (רָצִים *razîm*; AVm 'or *guard*,' Heb. *runners*'; RV 'guard,' RVm 'Heb. *runners*'). 'Runners' would be the literal, and at the same time the most appropriate trⁿ. The king had a body of runners about him, not so much to guard his person as to run his errands and do his bidding. They formed a recognized part of the royal state (1 S 8¹¹, 2 S 15¹); they served as executioners (1 S 22¹⁷, 2 K 10²⁵); and, accompanying the king or his general into battle, they brought back official tidings of its progress or event (2 S 18¹⁹, and see AHIMAAZ). Out of this running messenger the Persian kings developed a regular postal system (Est 3¹³, and see POST).

Runners were at one time in England an essential part of a nobleman's train. Thus Prior (1718), *Alma*, i. 58—

'Like Footmen running before Coaches
To tell the Inn what Lord approaches.'

But the *Bee* (1791) says 'their assistance was often wanted to support the coach on each side, to prevent it from being overturned.' The modern footman has a different function, but he is the lineal descendant of the 'running footman,' as he came to be called, of an earlier day.

In Jer 12⁵ both the Heb. (רַגְלִים) and the Eng. (footmen) seem to be used in the more general sense of racers *on foot*: 'If thou hast run with the footmen, and they have wearied thee, then how canst thou contend with horses?' Cf. Webster (1654), *Appius and Virg*. I. i.—

'I have heard of cunning footmen that have worn
Shoes made of lead, some ten days 'fore a race,
To give them nimble and more active feet.'

J. HASTINGS.

FOOTSTOOL.—Although this word occurs repeatedly in the Bible, it is remarkable that only twice at most is it used in its literal sense. In OT it appears in 2 Ch 9¹⁸ as trⁿ of כֶּבֶשׂ (fr. כָּבַשׁ 'tread under foot'), the golden footstool of Solomon's throne, but here Kittel (see his note in Haupt's *OT*) would read כֶּבֶשׂ 'lamb.' The one clear reference to a literal footstool is in Ja 2³ 'sit under my footstool' (ὑποπόδιόν μου). Everywhere else, both in OT (1 Ch 28², Is 66¹, La 2¹, Ps 99⁵ 110¹ 132⁷, in all of which it is trⁿ of הֲדֹם רַגְלַיִם, the word הֲדֹם being poet. or late) and NT (Mt 5³⁵, Mk 12³⁶, Lk 20⁴³, Ac 2³⁵ 7⁴⁹, He 1¹³ 10¹³, all ὑποπόδιον τῶν ποδῶν, trⁿ by RV with strict accuracy 'footstool of my [thy, his] feet' instead of AV 'my [thy, his] footstool '),* it is used metaphorically. Originally הֲדֹם רַגְ, spoken of God, seems to have designated the *ark*, 1 Ch 28², but was naturally extended to include the whole of the *temple*, La 2¹ (see notes of Thenius and Löhr), Ps 99⁵ 132⁷ (cf. Is 60¹³, Ezk 43⁷). In Ps 110¹ the vanquished foes of the Messianic King are put as a footstool under His feet. In Is 66¹ earth is the footstool of Him whose throne is heaven.

J. A. SELBIE.

FOR.—Both as prep. and as conj. 'for' has some archaic or obscure uses that deserve attention.

1. When the meaning is *on account of*, as Gn 20³ 'Behold thou art but a dead man, for the woman which thou hast taken' (עַל, RV 'because of'). The RV has changed 'for' into 'because of' in Ezk 6¹¹ (Heb. אֶל); Gn 20³, Est 9²⁶, Hos 9¹⁵ (Heb. עַל); Lv 16³⁴, La 4¹³, Dn 5¹⁹ (Heb. מִן); 2 S 13² (Heb. בַּעֲבוּר); 2 K 16¹⁸, Jer 9⁷ 38⁹ (Heb. מִפְּנֵי); Jer 11¹⁷ (Heb. בִּגְלַל): and into 'by reason of' in Lv 17¹¹† (Heb. בְּ); Dt 28⁴⁷, Is 31⁹, Ezk 27¹⁸, Hos 8¹⁰, Zec 2⁴ (Heb. מִן). In NT ἀπό, ἐν, ἕνεκα, ἐπί with dat. and διά with acc. are all used in this sense, and trⁿ 'for.' When the Gr. is διά, with acc., RV changes 'for' into 'because of' in Jn 4³⁹, Ro 3²⁵ 13⁵, 1 Co 7⁵, Col 1⁵, He 2⁹, Rev 4¹¹; and into 'by reason of' in 1 Co 7²⁶, 2 Co 9¹⁴, He 5¹². For this meaning cf. Chaucer, *Romaunt*, A 1564—

'Abouten it is gras springing,
For moiste so thikke and wel lyking,
That it ne may in winter dye,
No more than may the see be drye.'

Sometimes the meaning approaches that of *against*, as 2 K 16¹⁸ 'the king's entry without, turned he from the house of the LORD for the king of Assyria' (מִפְּנֵי, RV 'because of'); so Ps 27¹¹ Wyc. 'dresse thou me in thi path for myn enemyes'; and Is 32² Cov. 'He shalbe unto men, as a defence for the wynde, and as a refuge for the tempeste.'

2. For means *instead of*, or *in exchange for*, as in Dn 8⁸ 'the great horn was broken; and for it came up four notable ones' (תַּחַת, RV 'instead of it'); Is 61⁷ 'For your shame ye shall have double; and for confusion they shall rejoice in their portion' (תַּחַת); so Nu 8¹⁸ (תַּחַת, RV 'instead of');

---

* In modern Syria, where level irrigated ground like that of Egypt is planted with vegetables or mulberry trees in rows, the field or patch is laid out in shallow drills, and, as each receives its sufficiency of water, a little earth is taken from the end of the next drill and patted by the naked foot into a dam, so that the water may pass to the drill next in order.

* In Mt 22⁴⁴ for AV 'till I make thine enemies thy footstool' RV gives 'till I put thine enemies under thy feet' (ἕως ἂν θῶ τοὺς ἐχθρούς σου ὑποκάτω [TR ὑποπόδιον] τῶν ποδῶν σου).

† On the translation and meaning of this important passage see especially Kalisch, *in loc*.

Gn 47[17] (בְּ, RV 'in exchange for'); Pr 21[18] (לֹ, RV 'in the stead of'); Nu 18[31] (חֵלֶף, RV 'in return for'). Cf. Philem [16] Wyc. 'now not as a servaunt, but for a servaunt a most dere brother.'

3. For is occasionally equivalent to *as*: Is 43[3] 'I gave Egypt for thy ransom' (כְּפָרְךָ, RV 'as thy ransom'); Mt 21[46] 'they took him for a prophet' (ὡς); 1 P 2[16] 'not using your liberty for a cloke of maliciousness' (ὡς). Cf. *Merlin* (E.E.T.S.), iii. 642, 'Thei clayme Bretaigne for thiers, and I clayme Rome for myne'; Defoe, *Rob. Crusoe* (Gold Treas. ed. p. 522), 'I was never pursued for a Thief before.'

4. For, as a conj., is used to introduce the cause or reason. Sometimes modern usage would prefer 'because' or 'seeing that,' as in Wyclif, *Select Works*, iii. 105, 'And for God made alle thinges to help of mankynde, therfore we sholde axe thes thynges of God'; and p. 110, 'And ones they reprovede Crist, for his disciples wesche nought here hondes whanne they sholde eete, as here custome was'; and Tindale's tr[n] of 1 Jn 3[12] in *Expositions*, 191, 'And wherefore slew he him? For his deeds were evil, and his brother's righteous' (in edd. of NT 1526 and 1534 'because'). So in some places of AV, as Jn 11[47] 'What do we? for this man doeth many miracles.' In the foll. passages RV changes 'for' into 'because': Nu 21[7] 27[14] 32[12], Dt 14[7], 1 S 9[24], Job 15[25] 32[16], Jer 20[11] 51[11], Ezk 36[18], Dn 9[19], Mt 23[13], Lk 1[13] 4[41] 6[48] 21[28], Ac 22[18], Eph 5[30], Ph 1[29], 1 P 4[14], 1 Jn 3[9], Rev 12[12]: to which Amer. RV adds Jer 3[21], 1 Jn 3[20]. Some of these changes, however, are due to a change in the construction of the sentence, especially Ezk 36[18]. There is, indeed, no glaringly obsolete example of 'for' in this sense in AV, such as we find so often in Shaks. Cf. *Tempest*, I. ii. 272—

> 'And, for thou wast a spirit too delicate
> To act her earthy and abhorred commands,
> Refusing her grand hests, she did confine thee,
> . . . .
> Into a cloven pine.'

5. The foll. phrases are archaic or obsolete: (1) *For all*, Ps 78[32] 'For all this they sinned still' (בְּכָל־זֹאת); Jn 21[11] 'for all there were so many, yet was not the net broken' (τοσούτων ὄντων). Cf. Chaucer, *Knightes Tale*, 1162—

> 'The sowe freten the child right in the cradel;
> The cook y-scalded, for al his longe ladel.'

(2) *For because*, Gn 22[16] 'By myself have I sworn, saith the LORD, for because thou hast done this thing . . . that in blessing I will bless thee' (כִּי יַעַן אֲשֶׁר, RV 'because'); Jg 6[22] 'Alas, O Lord God! for because I have seen an angel of the LORD face to face' (כִּי־עַל־כֵּן, RV 'forasmuch as'). So Knox, *Hist.* 110, 'Let him be judged of you both foolish, and your mortall enemie: Foolish, for because he understood nothing of Gods approued wisdome; and enemie unto you, because he laboured to separate you from Gods favour'; and p. 159, 'One of the Bishops sons thrust thorow with a Rapier one of Dundie, for because hee was looking in at the Girnel door'; Barlowe, *Dialoge*, 76, '*W*. Why do ye then despise the vniuersall churche, because some of them be noughte. *N*. Mary for because the more somme of the euyll, surmountethe the lesse number of the good.' (3) *For that* = 'because,' Ex 16[7. 8] (בְּ), [29] 'See, for that the LORD hath given you the Sabbath, therefore he giveth you on the sixth day the bread of two days' (בְּ); 1 Es 7[15] (ὅτι), 1 Mac 4[58] (καὶ, RV 'and'); Jn 12[18], 2 Co 1[24] (RV 'that'), 1 Ti 1[12] (all ὅτι); He 7[15] (εἰ, RV 'if') 5[2] (ἐπεί), 2 Co 5[4] (TR ἐπειδή, edd. ἐφ' ᾧ), Ro 5[12] (ἐφ' ᾧ), Ja 4[15] 'For that ye ought to say' (ἀντὶ τοῦ λέγειν, RVm 'Instead of your saying'). RV shows a fondness for this phrase, omitting it from AV only where marked above, and adding Jg 5[2] *bis*, Ezk 16[5]

23[30] (Heb. בְּ); Nu 12[11] *bis*, Neh 2[10], Is 19[25] (Heb. אֲשֶׁר); Jn 2[24] (διὰ τό with inf.); 2 Th 2[13] (ὅτι). Cf. Shaks. *Mer. of Venice*, I. iii. 43—

> 'I hate him for he is a Christian,
> But more for that in low simplicity,
> He lends out money gratis.'

(4) *For to*: The infinitive of purpose used often to be strengthened by *for*, an idiom that is still in use locally. Thus Gn 43[30] Tind. (1530), 'Joseph made hast (for his hert dyd melt upon his brother) and soughte for to wepe' (changed in Matthew's Bible of 1537 into 'where'); Pr. Bk. 1549 (Keeling, p. 33), 'To be a light for to lighten the Gentiles' (the 'for' is omitted in the 1552 ed. and afterwards); Fuller, *Holy Warre*, 215, 'As for his good father, he was content to let go the staff of his age for to be a prop to the Church.' Although in AV this 'for' seems always to express purpose, it was formerly added to the infin. even when no purpose was expressed, as Berners, *Froissart*, I. cxxvi., 'The king of England being at Airaines wist not where for to pass the river of Somme.' The 'for' is retained or omitted in AV at the mere good pleasure of the translators. Moon (*Eccles. English*, 117) gives a curious list: Gn 31[18] 'for to go,' Ru 1[18] 'to go'; Is 41[22] 'for to come,' Jer 40[4] 'to come'; Gn 41[57] 'for to buy,' 42[7] 'to buy'; and so on through a list of fifteen couples. The RV for the most part leaves these inconsistencies alone; but it adds some of its own. Thus in AV ἵνα is tr[d] 'for to' in Mk 3[10], Jn 10[10] 11[53], Ac 17[15] 22[5], Eph 2[15], Rev 9[15] 12[4]; RV changes all into 'that' with subj. except Ac 22[5], which it leaves untouched. Again, in Mt 11[8] RV retains 'for to see,' but in the parallel passage, Lk 7[21], omits the 'for,' though the Greek is the same.

6. 'For' as the tr[n] of ἀντί, περί, or ὑπέρ (and it is the frequent rendering of each of these prepositions) assumes considerable theological importance. The RV has been particularly careful and discriminating in this case. Beyond that, the English reader must consult the exegetical commentaries, and such articles as ATONEMENT, PROPITIATION.

J. HASTINGS.

FORAY occurs once in RV (2 S 3[22] 'from a foray,' AV 'from [pursuing] a troop'). The Heb. word גְּדוּד, which frequently means *a marauding band* (*e.g.* 1 S 30[8. 15. 23], 1 K 11[24]), seems in this instance to bear the transferred but natural sense of an expedition of such a band.

FORBEAR, FORBEARANCE.—In the still common meanings of *abstain from*, *refrain*, or *desist*, forbear is used in AV both absolutely and with an infin. following. Thus absolutely, 1 K 22[6] 'Shall I go against Ramoth-gilead to battle, or shall I forbear?'; Zec 11[12] 'If ye think good, give me my price; and if not, forbear' (both חֲדָל, the usual word so tr[d]); 2 Co 12[6] (φείδομαι). Or with foll. infin., Pr 24[11] 'If thou forbear to deliver them that are drawn unto death, and those that are ready to be slain' (אִם־תִּתְחַשָּׂךְ); RV 'Deliver them that are carried away unto death, and those that are ready to be slain see that thou hold back,' taking אִם as a particle expressing a wish, not as a conj. 'if'; so *Oxf. Heb. Lex.* and most edd.; RVm 'forbear thou not to deliver'); Ezk 24[17] 'Forbear to cry' (הֵאָנֵק דֹּם, lit. 'sigh, be silent'; RV 'Sigh, but not aloud'; Skinner, 'Sigh in silence': the Geneva Bible gives 'Cease from sighing'; Bishops', 'Mourne in silence'; Douay, 'Sigh holding thy peace'; Segond, 'Soupire en silence'; Siegfried, 'Seufze still'); 1 Co 9[6] 'Have not we power to forbear working?' ([τοῦ] μὴ ἐργάζεσθαι); Eph 6[9] 'forbearing threatening' (ἀνιέντες τὴν ἀπειλήν; T. K. Abbott, 'giving up your threatening,' which they had been accustomed to use before they were Christians).

Forbear is used once in AV (and retained in RV)

reflexively, a construction which is very rare: 2 Ch 35²¹ 'forbear thee from meddling with God, who is with me, that he destroy thee not' (חֲדַל־לְךָ מֵאֱלֹהִים, Oxf. Lex. 'leave off provoking God'). Here forbear means restrain thyself, refrain: cf. Ad. Est 16¹¹ Cov., 'he coude not forbeare him self from his pryde.'

But the most noticeable use of 'forbear' is as a *transitive* verb, in the sense of *bear with, be patient with*. The examples are, Neh 9³⁰ 'Yet many years didst thou forbear them' (וַתִּמְשֹׁךְ עֲלֵיהֶם, lit. as AVm, 'didst protract over them'; LXX εἵλκυσας [A ἤλ-] ἐπ' αὐτούς; Vulg. 'protraxisti super eos'); 2 Es 1⁹ 'How long shall I forbear them, unto whom I have done so much good?' (*usquequo eos sustinebo*); Eph 4²=Col 3¹³ 'forbearing one another' (ἀνεχόμενοι ἀλλήλων). So Tindale's tr. of Rev 2² 'thou cannest not forbeare them which are evyll'; T. Adams, *II Peter*, on 1¹, 'Rotten kernels under fair shells, full of Herod's and Naaman's exceptives: in this forbear us'; Livingstone, *Memorable Characteristics* (Wodrow, *Select Biog.* i. 324), 'somewhat forborn for their non-conformity'; and Shaks. *Othello*, I. ii. 10—

> 'with the little godliness I have,
> I did full hard forbear him.'

RV introduces 'forbearing' in this sense into the text of 2 Ti 2²⁴ from AVm, the text of AV being 'patient' (Gr. ἀνεξίκακος, lit. 'patient of wrong,' from fut. of ἀνέχομαι to bear, and κακόν wrong); and it is in this sense only that **Forbearance** occurs, Ro 2⁴ 3²⁵ (ἀνοχή), both of God's forbearance with men; and in RV, Ph 4⁵ 'Let your forbearance be known unto all men' (τὸ ἐπιεικές; AV 'moderation,' RVm 'gentleness': Vincent, 'From εἰκός, reasonable, hence *not unduly rigorous*'; Wyc. 'pacience,' Tind. 'softenes,' so Cov. Cran. Gen. 'patient mind,' so Bish.; Rhem. 'modestie,' after Vulg. *modestia*, Luther 'Gelindigkeit,' Weizsäcker 'Lindigkeit,' the French VSS 'douceur.' The idea, says Vincent, is 'Do not make a rigorous and obstinate stand for what is your just due.' See next article.   J. HASTINGS.

FORBEARANCE, LONG-SUFFERING. — Forbearance is the tr. in AV of NT of ἀνοχή, and longsuffering of μακροθυμία. Their close connexion in meaning is shown by their combination in various passages. Thus in Ro 2⁴ the wealth of God's 'forbearance and long-suffering' is mentioned as designed to lead men to repentance. In Ro 3²⁵ the f. of God is the ground, not of the forgiveness of sins, but of their pretermission; not of the annulling, but of the suspension of His punishment. The same combination is required of Christians in Eph 4²; they are to walk worthy of their calling, 'with long-suffering, forbearing one another in love,' where the last words interpret the first. In OT ἀνοχή seems to occur only in 1 Mac 12²⁵ in the technical sense of 'truce'; the corresponding verb is used in a wide range of meanings, which, however, are easily connected with each other. Μακρόθυμος, again, in the LXX is the regular rendering of the Heb. אֶרֶךְ אַפַּיִם. It is most frequently used of God, and in combination with such words as πολυέλεος, οἰκτίρμων, ἐλεήμων. It designates that attribute of God in virtue of which He bears long with that which provokes His anger, and does not proceed at once to execute judgment upon it.

Where μακροθυμία is used of men, the meaning is sometimes rather different. It becomes akin to patience as well as to forbearance. Thus it is combined with ὑπομονή in Col 1¹¹ and with κακοπάθεια (-ία WH) in Ja 5¹⁰; cf. also 2 Ti 3¹⁰. These examples, as well as those in He 6¹⁵, Ja 5⁷ᵗ·, Sir 2⁴, prove that Trench's distinction is hardly accurate, viz. that μακροθυμία will be found to express

patience in respect of persons, ὑπομονή patience in respect of things. In the passages just quoted μακροθυμία is shown in bravely enduring the pressure of what seem adverse circumstances, the trials of the good life, and is better reproduced by 'patience' or 'endurance' than by 'long-suffering.' A real parallel to this use is found in 1 Mac 8⁴, where we are told how the Romans subdued all Spain by their counsel and their μακροθυμία; where the word evidently means their stubborn persistence, that quality in virtue of which, though sometimes defeated in battle, they were always victorious in war. But though this sense of μακροθυμία is represented in NT, the prevailing one is that which is akin, not to endurance but to forbearance; it is a slowness, like that of God, in avenging wrongs, a restraint of anger, a gentleness and meekness in dealing with those who treat us unjustly. The synonymous word in this direction is rather πραότης than ὑπομονή. There is a difficult passage about God's long-suffering in Lk 18⁷. If we compare Sir 32²² ὁ κύριος οὐ μὴ βραδύνῃ οὐδὲ μὴ μακροθυμήσει ἐπ' αὐτοῖς, ἕως ἂν συντρίψῃ ὀσφὺν ἀνελεημόνων, it can hardly seem doubtful that the evangelist meant by his last words, 'though he shows long indulgence to them,' *i.e.* to the enemies of the elect; if, however, ἐπ' αὐτοῖς must refer to the elect, then there seems no clear meaning to be got but by confining the force of the οὐ to the first clause, and saying that God surely does not exercise longsuffering (this would be the effect of the interrogative μή) where the interests of His elect are at stake, but avenges them speedily. But whatever we make of this case, there is no doubt that longsuffering and forbearance are characteristically and conspicuously qualities both of the divine and of the Christian character. As distinguished from each other, ἀνοχή suggests that it is merely a temporary restraint that is being practised; this may be the case with μακροθυμία also, indeed it is the case, and hence such warnings as we have in Ro 2⁴ᵗ·, but it is not suggested by the word itself.   J. DENNEY.

FORBID. — To forbid is to order one not to do a thing, and the proper construction is a personal object and an infin., as 1 Th 2¹⁶ 'Forbidding us to speak to the Gentiles that they might be saved.' But custom allows the omission of the person, as Lk 23² 'We found this fellow perverting the nation, and forbidding to give tribute to Cæsar'; or of the infin., as Nu 11²⁸ 'My lord Moses, forbid them,' Mt 3¹⁴ 'But John forbad him.' But when 'forbid' is found with an impers. object and that alone, the construction is quite irregular. There are two instances, 2 P 2¹⁶ 'a dumb ass speaking with man's voice forbad the madness of the prophet' (RV 'stayed'),* and Ac 10⁴⁷ 'Can any man forbid water that these should not be baptized?' In both cases the Greek verb (κωλύειν) is that usually translated 'forbid,' and in Greek writers it has the meanings of 'restrain' (as 2 P 2¹⁶) and 'refuse' (as Ac 10⁴⁷), but the Eng. verb 'forbid' has not properly these meanings, and should not have been used. In both places 'forbid' is as old as Wyclif, who, following the Vulg. *prohibere*, used the word very freely: compare its use in Ac 11¹⁷ 'Who was Y, that myghte forbeede the Lord, that he gyue not the Hooli Goost to hem that bileueden in the name of Jhesu Crist?'

From Wyclif also comes **God forbid**, the strong and striking translation of חָלִלָה *hâlîlâh* and of μὴ γένοιτο.

Hâlîlâh is a subst. formed from the verb *hâlal* to pollute or (ceremonially) profane, the suffix being locative. It is used

---

* Cf. Paraphrase 62¹⁰ (1775)—
'The contrite race he counts his friends,
Forbids the suppliant's fall.'

only as an exclamation, *Ad profanum*! Away with it! Far be it! Twice it stands alone in the sentence, 1 S 14⁴⁵ 20² חָלִילָה לֹּא חָמוּת, EV 'God forbid; thou shalt not die'. Sometimes a pronoun accompanies it, 1 S 2³⁰ לִי חָלִילָה, EV 'Be it far from me'), so Gn 18²⁵ᵇ, 1 S 20⁹ 22¹⁵. But most frequently it is connected with the sentence by a conjunction, כִּן with infin. Gn 18²⁵ 447.¹⁷, Jos 24¹⁶, 1 S 12²³, 2 S 23¹⁷, 1 Ch 11¹⁹, and (attached to the 'profane' thing) Job 34¹⁰ חָלִלָה לָאֵל מֶרֶשַׁע, EV 'Far be it from God that he should do wickedness'); or אִם 1 S 14⁴⁵ 247, 2 S 20²⁰, Job 27⁵. The exclamation tended to assume the form of an oath, and in four places the name of J″ is added, 1 S 247 26¹¹, 28 23¹⁷, 1 Ch 11¹⁹. The shorter form חָלִלָה is used Gn 18²⁵ ᵇⁱˢ, Job 34¹⁰.

The LXX translates the word variously : by μὴ γένοιτο Gn 447.¹⁷, Jos 22²⁹ 24¹⁶, 1 K 21³ ; by μηδαμῶς (with or without μοι, σοι) Gn 18²⁵ ᵇⁱˢ, 1 S 2³⁰ 12²³ 202.9 22¹⁵ 246 26¹¹ ; by ἵλεώς μοι [ὁ θεος] 2 S 23¹⁷, 1 Ch 11¹⁹ ; by ζῇ Κύριος 1 S 14⁴⁵ ; and by μή μοι εἴη Job 27⁵.

The Vulg. is more uniform, rendering by *Absit* (hoc) *a me* (*te*, etc.) in all places except Gn 18²⁵ᵇ *nequaquam*, 447 where *absit* of Old Lat. may have dropped out, 1 S 14⁴⁵ *Hoc nefas est*, and *Propitius sit mihi Dominus* in 1 S 24⁷ 26¹¹, 2 S 23¹⁷, 1 K 21³. Wyclif followed the Vulgate, the later version having 'Fer be it fro me, thee,' etc., wherever Vulg. has *Absit* (hoc) *a me, te*, etc., and 'The Lord be merciful to me' in 1 S 246 26¹¹, 2 S 23¹⁷, 1 K 21³ ; while Gn 447 is 'Whi speketh oure Lord so,' and 1 S 14⁴⁵ 'This is unleueful.' The earlier version is less uniform, thus Jos 22²⁹ 'God shilde fro us this hidows gilt,' 1 Ch 11¹⁹ 'God sheelde,' 1 S 14⁴⁵ 'that is felony.' So, wherever μὴ γένοιτο occurs in NT the earlier Wyc. vers. has 'Fer be it,' but the later has always 'God forbede.' And this phrase was accepted by Tindale, and after him by nearly all the Versions both in OT for *hălîlâh* and in NT for μὴ γένοιτο.

AV and RV translate *hălîlâh* by 'God forbid' ('The Lord forbid' 1 S 246 26¹¹, 1 K 21³, and 'My God forbid it me' 1 Ch 11¹⁹) everywhere except Gn 18²⁵ ᵇⁱˢ, 1 S 2³⁰ 20⁹ 22¹⁵, 2 S 20²⁰ 23¹⁷, where the Wyclifite phrase 'Far be it from' or 'Be it far from' has been retained. This phrase Amer. RV prefers throughout OT.

As we have seen, μὴ γένοιτο is only one of the renderings of *hălîlâh* in LXX. Of the others μηδαμῶς occurs twice in NT, Ac 10¹⁴ 11⁸ (EV 'Not so, Lord'), and ἵλεώς σοι once, Mt 16²² (EV 'Be it far from thee, Lord'). But μὴ γένοιτο is found fifteen times, all but Lk 20¹⁶ being in St. Paul's Epistles, and in twelve of St. Paul's fourteen instances it is used to express the apostle's abhorrence of an inference which he fears may be falsely drawn from his argument. See Burton, *NT Moods and Tenses*², p. 79. EV translates everywhere by 'God forbid,' a phrase which is undoubtedly more forcible than the original, and for which Lightfoot suggests 'Nay, verily,' or 'Away with the thought.'

'God forbid' occurs also in Apocr., 1 Mac 2²¹ 'God forbid that we should forsake the law and the ordinances' (Ἵλεως ἡμῖν καταλιπεῖν, RVm 'Heaven forbid,' RVm 'Gr. *May* he be propitious. Cf. 2 S 23¹⁷ Sept.'); 9¹⁰ 'Then Judas said, God forbid that I should do this thing' (Μή μοι γένοιτο ποιῆσαι, RV 'Let it not be so that I should do this thing').   J. HASTINGS.

FORCE.—The subst. 'force' has become restricted in meaning since 1611. It then signified a man's personal *might*, as Jer 23¹⁰ 'their course is evil, and their force is not right' (גְבוּרָה, Cheyne 'their might or heroism'); even *physical strength*, as Dt 34⁷ 'his eye was not dim, nor his natural force abated' (לֵחַ, only here, but adj. לַח is *moist, fresh*, of fruit, Nu 6³, or of growing or freshly-cut wood, Ezk 17²⁴, Gn 30³⁷, hence 'neither had his freshness fled'—Driver); Job 40¹⁶ 'his force is in the navel (RV muscles) of his belly' (אוֹן, here of behemoth, in 18⁷·¹² of man's strength); Am 2¹⁴ 'the strong shall not strengthen his force' (כֹּחַ). Cf. Ps 102²³ (Sternhold and Hopkins)—

'My wonted strength and force he hath abated in the way.'

Force as a personal attribute is now restricted to strength in action or application, as it is in Ezk 34⁴ 'with force and with cruelty have ye ruled them' (חָזְקָה); and in the phrase 'take by force,' which in Mt 11¹², Jn 6¹⁵, Ac 23¹⁰ is the trⁿ of the single verb ἁρπάζειν, to seize.

The phrase 'of force' is now replaced by 'in force.' It occurs He 9¹⁷ 'a testament is of force after men are dead' (βέβαιος); and in a slightly different sense, 2 Es 7³⁵ 'the good deeds shall be of force, and wicked deeds shall bear no rule' (*iustitiæ vigilabunt*, RV 'shall awake'): cf. 9³⁷ 'the law perisheth not, but remaineth in his force' (*permansit in suo honore*, RV 'in its honour'). The phrase was also used in the sense of 'by com-

pulsion,' as we still use 'perforce'; so often in Shaks. as *I Henry IV*. II. iii. 120—

'Will this content you, Kate?
It must, of force';

Jul. Cæs. IV. iii. 203—

'Good reasons must, of force, give place to better';

Milton, *PL* iv. 813—

'No falsehood can endure
Touch of celestial temper, but returns
Of force to its own likeness';

and i. 144—

'Our conqueror (whom I now
Of force believe almighty)'—

though Craik thinks 'of force' in the last passage may mean 'in power.'

For Force, Forces=military strength, see ARMY.
J. HASTINGS.

FORD (מַעֲבָר, מַעֲבָרָה. In Jg 12⁵·⁶ AV needlessly substitutes 'passages' for 'fords'; in 2 S 15²⁸ 17¹⁶ RV has 'fords' (עברות) where AV has 'plains' (ערבות). See Driver's note, *ad loc*.)—Fords were important landmarks in early OT times, when there were no bridges across rivers. There seem to have been two principal fords across the Jordan—(1) that opposite Jericho (Jos 2⁷, Jg 3²⁸, 2 S 19¹⁵), used to this day for crossing from Pal. into Moab, except in early summer when the river is in flood (Jos 3¹⁵); (2) Bethabara (the reading of TR and AV, but WH and RV have Bethany) where John baptized (Jn 1²⁸). The site has been identified by the officers of the Ordnance Survey, and described by Conder as the spot called *'Abârah*, where the Jalūd river, flowing down the Valley of Jezreel, debouches into the Jordan (*Tent Work in Pal*. p. 229). Some of the fords of the Jordan, of which about forty were identified by the *Pal. Survey*, are impassable in spring or early summer, as the waters, swollen by the melting of the snows of the Lebanon and adjoining regions, rise and overflow their banks, covering the alluvial plains on either side. Such was the case when the Isr. under Joshua crossed on dry ground by command of J″ to besiege Jericho (Jos 3¹⁵). Amongst the other fords mentioned in Scripture are those of the Jabbok (Gn 32²²) and the Arnon, a river descending from the tableland on the east of the Jordan Valley, and at the time of the Isr. invasion forming the boundary between the Moabites and the Amorites (Nu 21¹³), also referred to in Is 16². The Romans were probably the first great bridge-builders over the streams of Palestine. (See, further, G. A. Smith, *Hist. Geog*. 266, 337 n. ; Moore, *Judges*, 102 f. 214 ; Driver, *Text of Sam*. 245, 257.)   E. HULL.

FORECAST.—In the phrase 'forecast devices,' Dn 11²⁴·²⁵ חָשַׁב מַחֲשָׁבָה, RV 'devise devices'), the meaning is 'contrive beforehand,' as Golding (1587), *De Mornay*, xiii. 203, 'At the first sight the thing which was forecast by good order, seemeth to happen by adventure.' In Wis 17¹¹ the word occurs in the sense of 'think beforehand,' 'forebode': 'Wickedness . . . always forecasteth grievous things' (אᶜ·ᵃ προείληφεν, but B προσείληφεν, whence RVm 'hath added').

FOREFRONT.—In earlier use the 'forefront' was opposed to the 'backfront,' as Evelyn (1659), *To R. Boyle*, 3 Sept. 'To the entry fore front of this a court, and at the other back front a plot walled in of a competent square,' and Leoni (1726), *Alberti's Archit*. I. xxxix. 2, 'From the . . . Forefront of the Work I draw a Line quite thro' to the Back-front.' But the 'back' being no longer called a 'front,' 'forefront' is mostly replaced by 'front.' It is used in AV as trⁿ of (1) פָּנִים *face*, 2 K 16¹⁴, Ezk 40¹⁹ ᵇⁱˢ 47¹ ; (2) מוּל פָּנִים *overagainst the face*, Ex 26⁹ 28³⁷, Lv 8⁹, 2 S 11¹⁵; (3) שֵׁן *tooth*,

1 S 14⁵ ; (4) רֹאשׁ *head*, 2 Ch 20²⁷ ; and πρόσωπον *face*, 1 Mac 4⁵⁷. RV changes Lv 8⁹ ' upon the mitre, even upon his forefront,' into ' upon the mitre, in front' ; and 1 S 14⁵ ' The forefront of the one was situate northward' into ' The one crag rose up on the north.' RV also adds Jos 22¹¹ ' in the fore-front of the land of Canaan' (אֶל־מוּל, AV ' over against') ; and Ezk 40¹⁵ *bis* ' And from the forefront of the gate at the entrance unto the forefront of the inner porch' (עַל־פְּנֵי אֵלָם הַשַּׁעַר הַיֵּאתוֹן עַל־לִפְנֵי, AV ' from the face . . . unto the face').

FOREGO.—Sir 7¹⁹ ' Forego not a wise and good woman : for her grace is above gold' (μὴ ἀστόχει γυναικὸς σοφῆς καὶ ἀγαθῆς, RV ' Forgo not a wise and good wife'). The Gr. verb occurs elsewhere in LXX only in 8⁹ ' Miss not the discourse of the elders' (RV ' aged'). In NT it is found only in the Pastoral Epistles, 1 Ti 1⁶ (EV ' swerve '), 6²¹ (EV ' err '), 2 Ti 2¹⁸ (EV ' err '), and at each occurrence RVm gives 'miss the mark,' which is its lit. meaning (ἁ and στόχος, *a mark*). The meaning here is almost certainly that suggested by Wahl *noli separari ab uxore sapiente*, ' do not separate yourself from, *i.e.* do not divorce a wise wife.' And that is probably the meaning of AV, which seems to be a new trⁿ, the earlier Versions having uniformly ' Depart not from a discreet and good woman,'* with the addition, ' that is fallen unto thee for thy portion in the fear of the LORD,' after Vulg. *quam sortitus es in timore Domini*. For in earlier Eng. ' forgo' had the meaning of *forsake*, as *Cursor Mundi* (1340), 13,280, ' Petur and andrew . . . with o word haue thei ship forgone' ; and Shaks. *Henry VIII*. III. ii. 422—

'*Crom.*   O my lord,
Must I then leave you ? Must I needs forgo
So good, so noble, and so true a master ? '

And this sense is still in use poetically, as in Mrs. Browning, *Catarina to Camoens*, iv.—

' And if they looked up to you,
All the light which has forgone them
Would be gathered back anew.'

The spelling of modern editions of AV is *forego*, but *forgo*, which is the spelling of 1611 (' forgoe'), is the correct form. Forego is a different word, and means ' to go before,' as Fotherby (1619), *Atheom*. II. iii. 2. 214, ' The cause doth alwayes his effect fore-goe.' The prep. in ' forgo' is *for* (Ger. *ver*), not *fore*, and reverses the meaning of the verb, as in forbid, fordo, forget, forswear, forspent, forspoke. In forbear and forgive it adds force to the simple verb.

J. HASTINGS.

FOREHEAD (מֵצַח, μέτωπον).—This word occurs repeatedly in the Bible, both in a literal and in a metaphorical sense. It was upon his forehead that the high priest wore the plate of gold inscribed ' Holy to the LORD' (Ex 28³⁸) ; the stone slung by David entered the forehead of Goliath (1 S 17⁴⁹) ; leprosy broke out in the forehead of Uzziah when he sought to burn incense (2 Ch 26¹⁹ff.). In Jer 3³ ' a harlot's forehead ' is the type of shamelessness ; in Ezk 3⁷·⁸·⁹ the people in their obstinacy are described as ' of an hard forehead,' but the prophet's forehead is to be made hard against them, his determination is to be equal to their own. In Ezk 9⁴ff. a mark is directed to be put on the forehead of the faithful in Jerusalem. The name for this mark is תָּו *tav*, a letter (ת) which may have been used in much the same way as a X amongst ourselves (cf. Job 31³⁵, where, however, the sense appears to be somewhat different ; see Davidson's and Dillmann's notes, *ad loc*.). It is even possible that the reference in Ezk is to practices such as that described in Is 44⁵ ' Another shall mark on his hand, Unto the LORD.' See CUTTINGS IN THE FLESH, vol. i. p. 538ᵇ. These OT passages suggested the NT usage (Rev 7³ 9⁴ 13¹⁶ 14¹·⁹ 17⁵ 20⁴ 22⁴).

* Except Wyclif (1382), ' Wile thou not gon awei fro a wel felende womman, and a good.'

In Ezk 16¹², where AV has ' I put a jewel on thy forehead,' RV gives more correctly ' I put a ring upon thy nose' (וָאֶתֵּן נֶזֶם עַל־אַפֵּךְ).

For Lv 13⁴¹ff. (' forehead bald') see BALDNESS.

J. A. SELBIE.

FOREIGNER occurs four times in AV. It is the trⁿ in Ex 12⁴⁵ of תּוֹשָׁב (RV more accurately ' so-journer'), in Dt 15³ and Ob ¹¹ of נָכְרִי, and in Eph 2¹⁹ of πάροικος (RV ' sojourner'). RV sub-stitutes ' foreigner' for AV ' stranger' as trⁿ of בֶּן־נֵכָר in Lv 22²⁵, and of נָכְרִי in Dt 17¹⁵ 23²⁰ 29²². Amer. RV makes the same change in Ru 2¹⁰, 2 S 15¹⁹, where the Heb. word is the same.

A cognate term is **alien(s)**, which occurs in AV of Ex 18³ as trⁿ of גֵּר (RV correctly ' sojourner'), of בְּנֵי נֵכָר in Is 61⁵, and of נָכְרִי in Dt 14²¹ (RV ' foreigner'), Job 19¹⁵, Ps 69⁸, La 5². RV adds Ex 12⁴³, Ezk 44⁷·⁹, Pr 5¹⁰, where AV has ' stranger,' and Ps 144⁷·¹¹, where AV has ' strange children' (Heb. in all these בְּנֵי נֵכָר).

Strangers is the favourite rendering in AV, not only of נָכְרִי or בֶּן־נֵכָר, or זָר (see below), but also of גֵּר and תּוֹשָׁב. The latter circumstance is specially unfortunate, because it obscures to the Eng. reader the distinction between the *foreigner* and the *gēr*, which in Heb. is marked clearly enough, and on which not a little depends for the understanding of many passages. The *gēr* is indeed a foreigner by birth, but he resides in Israel and is protected by the community ; whereas the foreigner proper (נָכְרִי) is not only an alien by birth, but has neither home nor rights in Israel. It would have been well if RV had uniformly, instead of occasionally, substituted ' sojourner' for ' stranger' as the trⁿ of גֵּר, and left ' stranger,' ' foreigner,' ' alien ' to represent such words as נָכְרִי and זָר.

We shall now examine the linguistic usage of the last two Heb. words and their equivalents in LXX and NT.

(*a*) זָר (*zâr*) in its root meaning appears scarcely to differ from *gēr*, although ultimately the two words have very different connotations. The orig. sense of both is *one who turns aside from the way* (*sc.* to lodge somewhere). It is easy to connect this with the idea of a *stranger* or *alien*. Amongst other applications זָר is used to designate one who is not of a priestly family, Ex 29³³ 30³³, Nu 3¹⁰·³⁸ 18⁷ (all P), Lv 22¹⁰·¹²·¹³ (H), or who does not belong to the tribe of Levi, Nu 15¹ 18⁴ (P). The plur. זָרִים is a frequent designation of foreign (generally hostile) peoples in contrast to Israel, Hos 7⁹ 8⁷, Is 17, Ezk 7²¹, Jl 3¹⁷, Ob ¹¹ etc. The LXX equivalents are ἀλλότριος and ἀλλογενής, the former of which occurs not infrequently in NT, the latter only once (Lk 17¹⁸ of the Samaritan leper).

(*b*) נָכְרִי (*nokhri*) or בֶּן־נֵכָר (*ben-nēkhâr*). If the root idea here is *strangeness*, perhaps ' stranger' might with advantage be reserved as the special trⁿ of these two equivalent terms. נָכְרִי is ‖ גָּלָה ' exile' in 2 S 15¹⁹ (of Ittai the Gittite) ; it is opposed to a ' brother' (אָח), *i.e.* a fellow-Israelite, in Dt 15³ 17¹⁵ ; it is used of the stranger who directs his prayer towards the temple of Israel's God, 1 K 8⁴¹ = 2 Ch 6³² ; of the foreign wives (נָכְרִיּוֹת), Ezr 10² ; of foreign garb (מַלְבּוּשׁ נָכְרִי) perhaps referring to the uniform of the foreign body-guard), Zeph 1⁸ (cf. כָּל־נֵכָר ' every-thing foreign,' Neh 13³⁰). The commonest LXX equivalent is ἀλλότριος (cf. Ac 7⁶, He 11⁹·³⁴). ἀλλογενής also occurs (*e.g.* Gn 17²⁷, Ex 12⁴³, Lv 22²⁵, Is 56³·⁶) and ἀλλόφυλος (Is 26 61⁵). This last, which is the favourite LXX trⁿ of פְּלִשְׁתִּים (Philistines), occurs only once in NT (Ac 10²⁸ of Cornelius). Another favourite LXX rendering of נָכְרִי is ξένος (*e.g.* 2 S 15¹⁹ of Ittai). It is the exact opposite of ἐπιχώριος. The only instances of its occurrence in NT are Mt 25³⁵·³⁸·⁴³ 27⁷, Ac 17²¹, Eph 2¹²·¹⁹, He 11¹³, 3 Jn⁵.

As in olden times *foreigner* and *enemy* were almost convert-ible terms, we find both זָר and נָכְרִי used so as to include the idea of hostility or barbarism (cf. Is 17, Ps 54³, Ezk 11⁹, Hos 7⁹ [all זָרִים], Ps 144⁴·⁴⁵ [בְּנֵי נֵכָר]). The same meaning of *hostile* is contained in the ἀλλότριοι of He 11³⁴, 1 Mac 1³⁸ 2⁷, Sir 45¹⁸ etc.).

PRESENCE AND POSITION OF FOREIGNERS IN ISRAEL.—In the early stages of their history, the relations of Israel to foreigners did not differ essen-tially from those of other nations. As the law, however, was gradually introduced, the attitude of Israelites to non-Israelites underwent a material change, until ultimately the ' nations' outside

Israel became the 'heathen,' while the stranger domiciled in Israel, the '*gēr*,' became the 'proselyte' (Bertholet).

(a) *The pre-Deuteronomic Period.*—Our earliest sources contain abundant references to foreigners, whether passing strangers or residents in Israel. Trade was frequently the motive of their visits. The two words for 'merchant,' סֹחֵר and רֹכֵל, both mean originally 'traveller'; in Pr 31²⁴ and Job 41⁶ 'Canaanite' is synonymous with 'trader,' showing that in early times the travelling merchantmen in Palestine had been, not Israelites, but Canaanites. The danger of travelling alone (Jg 5⁶) was avoided by caravans, some of the most important of whose trade-routes traversed Palestine (Gn 37²⁵, 1 K 10², Is 8²³ [Eng. 9¹] 60⁶·⁷, Ezk 26²). It must never be forgotten that from the occupation of Canaan downwards Israel was in constant contact with foreigners in the shape of the large remnants of the original inhabitants of the land. Our different sources offer different explanations of the survival of the Canaanites, but they all agree as to the fact (Ex 23²⁹, Dt 7²², Jg 2²³ 3¹ff.). We have the well-known story of the Gibeonites (Jos 9), as well as a whole list of Can. towns enumerated amongst the various Isr. tribes (Jg 1²⁷ff.); in 1³²f. it is the Isr. that dwell among the Can., while Issachar is actually tributary to the latter (Gn 49¹⁴f.). In Jg 5¹⁴ (cf. 12¹⁵) we hear of Amalekite remnants, in Jg 5²⁴ (cf. Ex 18¹³ff.), Nu 10³¹, 1 S 15⁶ of Kenites, Midianites, etc. The Jerahmeelites, the clans of Caleb, Othniel, Kenaz, etc. (1 S 30¹⁴·²⁹), appear to have been of Arabian or Edomite origin. Even at the era of the Exodus the early narrative JE speaks of a 'mixed multitude' which attached itself to Israel (Ex 12³⁸, Nu 11⁴). Shechem was still a Can. city in the time of Abimelech (Jg 9); Jerus. continued in the possession of the Jebusites down to the time of David (2 S 5⁶ff.), and even after its conquest by the latter we find Araunah the Jebusite still in possession of property there (2 S 24; cf. Jos 15⁶³, Jg 1²¹); Rahab's descendants dwell in Israel 'to this day' (Jos 6²⁵, JE); Gezer is first taken from the Can. by the Pharaoh who was Solomon's father-in-law (1 K 9¹⁶).

The general attitude to foreigners was one of hostility, where some special agreement or safeguard was not present. Driven out from his old settlement, Cain protests, 'Whosoever findeth me shall slay me' (Gn 4¹⁴). The Song of Deborah (Jg 5), the story of Samuel and Agag (1 S 15³²f.), the cruelties of David to his prisoners (2 S 8² 12³¹), illustrate the prevailing temper towards a foreign foe. Conduct passes uncensured when non-Israelites are concerned, which would have been considered improper towards a fellow-countryman (Gn 12 Abraham and Pharaoh, Gn 26 Isaac and Abimelech, Gn 30³⁷ff. Jacob and Laban, Ex 3²² the 'spoiling' of the Egyptians).

The position of the foreigner being so precarious, people were slow to leave their own country, esp. as this implied also abandoning the service and losing the protection of their ancestral gods (1 S 26¹⁹). Amongst the most frequent causes that led to such self-expatriation were famine (Gn 12¹⁰ Abraham, 26¹ Isaac, 47⁴ Jacob and his sons, Ru 1¹ff. Elimelech and his family, 2 K 8¹ff. the Shunammite), blood-feud (Gn 4¹⁶ Cain, Ex 2¹⁵ Moses, 2 S 13³⁴ Absalom) or political reasons (1 S 27² David, 1 K 11⁴⁰ Jeroboam, 11¹⁷ Hadad).

There were, however, three circumstances that helped to mitigate the lot of the stranger in a strange land—(1) The hospitality to strangers, which is one of the noblest virtues of ancient peoples: 'the stranger did not lodge in the street, but I opened my doors to the traveller' (Job 31³²; cf. Gn 18. 19. 24. 43, Jg 13. 19, 2 S 12⁴, 1 K 17). Public inns in the modern sense (the Eastern *khan*

is something quite different) were unknown and unneeded. In Lk 10³⁴ we first hear of an inn (πανδοχεῖον) where the host (πανδοχεύς) takes payment for accommodating travellers. While spies naturally received no consideration (Gn 42⁹, Jos 2³ff.), the narratives of Gn 19 and Jg 19 show how scrupulously the old Israelites guarded their guests. In an age when the altar was universally an asylum (see ALTAR, p. 76ᵇ), the helpless stranger was frequently considered to be under the special protection of the god of the land, hence the 'fear of God' (Gn 20¹¹ 42¹⁸) was an extra safeguard to him. (2) The alliances with other nations of which we read must have exercised a considerable influence upon Israel's attitude towards foreigners (1 K 15¹⁸ff. Asa with Benhadad, 2 K 16⁵ Is 7¹ Pekah with Rezin, 2 K 16⁸ Ahaz with Tiglath-pileser, 2 K 17⁴ Hosea with So, 2 K 20¹²ff. Is 39 Hezekiah with Merodach-baladan, Ezk 17¹⁵ Zedekiah with Egypt). Those who had fought shoulder to shoulder against a common foe would not be strangers in each other's country. One of the most familiar results of this intercourse is seen in the syncretism in religious matters, against which the prophets protest (Is 17¹⁰, Ezk 8⁷ff. etc.). (3) Israel's own trading enterprises, which carried her citizens beyond the confines of Palestine (Ezk 27¹¹ to Tyre, 1 K 9²⁸ 10¹¹ 22⁴⁸ to Ophir, 20³⁴ to Damascus), taught the Israelites to sympathize with the feelings of a stranger who came to sojourn in their land (Ex 23⁹).

In Israel, as in most Oriental nations, the king encouraged the presence of foreigners at his court, and depended upon their fidelity more than upon that of his own subjects (1 S 21⁷ 22⁹ Doeg the Edomite, 2 S 15¹⁸ 20⁷ 1 K 1³⁸·⁴⁴ Cherethites and Pelethites, 2 S 15¹⁹ Ittai the Gittite, 2 K 11⁴·¹⁹ Carites). By foreign marriages the Isr. king also sought to strengthen his position. Amongst David's wives were Abigail a Kalibbite, Maacah a Geshurite (1 S 25⁴², 2 S 3³), while his sister was married to Ithra an Ishmaelite (1 Ch 2¹⁷, not *Israelite* 2 S 17²⁵). Solomon's harem included, besides Pharaoh's daughter, Moabites, Ammonites, Edomites, Zidonians, and Hittites (1 K 11¹). The wife of Ahab was Jezebel, daughter of Ethbaal king of the Zidonians (1 K 16³¹). Intermarriages with the Can. are forbidden in Ex 34¹⁵f. (JE), and there were doubtless many in Israel who disliked mixed marriages (Gn 29¹⁹ 24³·³⁷, Nu 12¹, Jg 14³); yet these must have been quite common. Unfortunately, the story of Dinah and Shechem (Gn 34), which is of composite origin (Wellh. *Comp.* 47 f., 312 f.; Kuenen, *Abhandl.* 255 ff.; see also artt. SHECHEM, SIMEON), has been so often worked over that it is impossible to draw inferences from it with certainty, but Jg 3⁵ff. doubtless gives a true picture of the condition of things (cf. Gn 38², Jg 8³¹, 1 K 7¹⁴). It was really more through amalgamation than by war that the Can. were subdued. The tribe of Judah confessedly contained a large admixture of Can. elements (see CALEB), and Ed. Meyer goes the length of maintaining (*ZAW*, 1886, pp. 1 ff.) that Joseph was originally a Can. tribe. It is this process of amalgamation that helps to account for the rapid increase in the number of Israel's warriors between the time of the judges and the early days of the monarchy (cf. Jg 5⁸ with 2 S 24⁹).

Besides foreign traders and resident *gērim*, there must always have been in Israel a number of foreign *slaves*, either taken captive in war, or bought from Phœn. or other traders (Gn 17¹², Lv 25⁴⁴f., Nu 31²⁶ff.). See SLAVES.

(b) *The Period of the Deuteronomic Legislation.*—To protest against religious syncretism had always been a chief part of the prophet's work. The worship of the Tyrian Baal, and the corrupting influences of foreign civilization, were specially distasteful to Elijah, whose feelings were shared by Elisha and the usurper Jehu (2 K 9. 10). It is significant that Jehonadab the son of Rechab is associated with Jehu (2 K 10[15ff.]), for the whole *raison d'être* of the Rechabite movement lay in opposition to Can. civilization and in attachment to the primitive simplicity, alike in religious and secular matters (Jer 35, cf. W. R. Smith, *Proph. of Isr.* 84 f.). The attitude of the prophets who have left us their *writings* is equally clear (Am 2[11] 3[15] 5[11. 25] 6[8] 8[5], Hos 2[19] 8[14] 9[10] 10[13] 12[7ff.] 14[4]). Specially noteworthy is Hos 9[1] 'Rejoice not, O Israel, like the peoples,' where already 'peoples' is almost = 'heathen.' The same disinclination to foreigners appears in Is 2[6] 10[4] 17[10] 28[15] 30[1-5] (protest against foreign alliances), Zeph 1[8. 11], Jer 2[36f.] 10[25] (although this last may be a late interpolation) 35[1ff.] 37[6f.]. These feelings find expression in the highest degree in the Deuteronomic 'law-book' of Josiah's reign (2 K 22). Israel is a 'holy people' (Dt 7[6]), and the land must not be 'defiled' (21[23]) or 'caused to sin' (24[4]). The relation of Israelites to non-Israelites is henceforth *determined by law*. The watchword is *separation*. The old injunction of Ex 23[31f.] (JE) is repeated in much stronger terms in Dt 7[1-5] 20[16-18] (where the *present* aversion takes the form of a *past* command to exterminate the Can.), and special stress is laid upon the prohibition of inter-marriages with Can. (Dt 7[3], Jos 23[12]). Further, in Dt 15[3] and 23[20], the foreigner (*nokhri*) is expressly excluded from participation in two of the Israelite's privileges—that of having a creditor's claims waived every seventh year, and that of borrowing without having to pay interest. In Dt 14[21] he is allowed to use for food the flesh of an animal that has died of itself, a concession which, although made in the same passage to the *gēr*, is ultimately withdrawn from the latter, and pronounced to be improper for any *dweller* in the land of Israel (Lv 17[15]). See GER.

It is well to remember that universalism as well as particularism may be traced in the conduct and the teaching of the early prophets (cf. 1 K 17[8ff.] Elijah and the widow of Zarephath, 2 K 5 Elisha and Naaman, Is 2[2-4] = Mic 4[1-3] the oracle of the mountain of the Lord's house). This element found expression, however, in the direction of proselytizing the *gēr*, not in that of cultivating friendly relations with foreigners proper. For the development of this subject see GER.

(*c*) *The Exilic and Post-Exilic Periods.*—If an approximation of *gēr* to Israelite was fostered by the Deut. legislation, and grew as time went on, upon the other hand the gulf between Israelite and *foreigner* became always wider. Even in the 'unclean' land of their exile (Ezk 4[13f.]), where sacrifice could not be offered, Israel could cling to her Sabbaths and to circumcision, and probably meetings akin to those of the later synagogue contributed to the maintaining of her separate existence and manner of life. The legislative programme of Ezekiel is specially instructive for our subject. The uncircumcised foreigners who kept guard in the temple (2 K 11[4ff.]), and probably performed other services (see CHERETHITES), are henceforward to be strictly excluded (Ezk 44[6-10]), and such functions are to be discharged by the Levites (cf. 44[22] priests to marry only virgins of the seed of the house of Israel or the widow of a priest).

The exiles who returned from Babylon had to solve the problem of their relations with the other inhabitants of Judæa and with their neighbours. A large number of the original inhabitants had never been carried captive at all, Edomites and others had taken possession of unoccupied settlements, and the colonists planted by the Assyr. king in Samaria (2 K 17[24ff.]) had probably also encroached on Judæa. The majority of the old

inhabitants, and a section of the returned exiles, were quite willing to coalesce with their neighbours (Neh 13[24], Mal 2[11]), but, thanks to the fiery zeal of Ezra and Nehemiah, such an incorporating union was prevented. The unsparing rigour with which the two reformers carried out their work is matter of history. See EZRA, NEHEMIAH. It was a veritable crisis. Weapons of various kinds were used on both sides. It may be that literature was pressed into the service. If Dt 23[4-6] be, as Wellhausen and Cornill think, a later interpolation, it may date from this period, while the Book of Ruth may have been a manifesto issued by the party of toleration. The triumph of the puritan party was completed when the covenant was sealed (Neh 10[30]), 'that we would not give our daughters unto the peoples of the land, nor take their daughters for our sons,' and when the Torah (P) was accepted as the norm of Israel's conduct (Neh 8). The ideal of P, even more than of D, is a holy people dwelling in a holy land, and serving God according to the prescriptions of His law (Nu 35[34], cf. Lv 19[26-31]). The narrative portions of P carefully omit or modify what does not tally with this conception (*e.g.* no mention of Moses' sojourn in Midian, or his relations with the priest of that people; Balaam, again, could not be a prophet of J", but becomes a Midianite counsellor, by whose instrumentality Israel was led into immorality). In accordance with the above conceptions, Ezra deliberately sought to erect a hedge, not only around the law, but around Israel, and thus to prevent all contact, except what was absolutely unavoidable, with those outside the pale of Judaism. If the *gēr* had become the *proselyte* to be welcomed, the *nokhri* had become the *heathen* to be shunned. For the further development of the subject see GENTILES, HEATHEN.

LITERATURE.—Bertholet's monograph, *Die Stellung d. Isr. u. d. Jud. zu d. Fremden* (to which the above article has special obligations); Driver, *Deut.* xxxi f., 98, 239; W. R. Smith, *OTJC*[2] 279, 364 f.; Cheyne, *Jeremiah*, 67; Schürer, *HJP* II. i. 51–56; Benzinger, *Heb. Arch.* 339 f., 350, 479; Thayer, *NT Lex.*, and Cremer, *Bib.-Theol. Lex. s.* ἀλλογενής, ἀλλότριος.

J. A. SELBIE.

FOREKNOW, FOREORDAIN—Both these words translate the same Greek verb προγινώσκειν, the former in Ro 8[29], the latter in 1 P 1[20]. 'Foreordain' does not appear before 1611, but Tindale introduced 'ordain before' in 1 P 1[20], which was the more surprising that in Ro 8[29] he translated both verbs correctly, οὓς προέγνω καὶ προώρισεν, 'those which he knewe before, he also ordeyned before.' Both verbs are rare in English, the earliest certain example of 'foreordain' found by *Oxf. Eng. Dict.* being Norton's tr[n] of Calvin's *Institutes* (1561), iii. 202, 'Some to be foreordeined to saluation, other some to destruction,' though the ptcp. is found in the Prol. to Wyclif's Mark (1420), 'The for-ordenede John.' RV tr. 1 P 1[20] correctly 'was foreknown,' and retains 'foreordain' for προορίζειν wherever it occurs, Ac 4[28] (AV 'determine before'), Ro 8[29. 30] (AV 'predestinate'), 1 Co 2[7] (AV 'ordain'), Eph 1[5. 11] (AV 'predestinate').

FOREKNOWLEDGE.—As an attribute of God, foreknowledge is simply a special case or aspect of omniscience. God knows all things, therefore not only the present and the past, but the future also, must lie open to His sight. This is implied in all His *promises*, whether they refer to the individual only, as where offspring is promised to Abraham (Gn 18[14]), or are on a national scale, as when the glory of Abraham's descendants is foretold (Gn 18[18]). It is implied also in the *warnings* which God gives, or causes to be given, as in the story of Lot and Sodom (Gn 19), or in that of Moses before Pharaoh (Ex 8–11). To an earlier Pharaoh God shows in a dream 'what he is about to do' (Gn 41[25]), and similarly, at a later period, to Nebuchadnezzar 'what shall be in the latter days' (Dn $2^{28.\ 29}$). In all such cases, however, it may be objected that they are less examples of foreknowledge than declarations regarding His own future action on the part of One who has full power of doing what He wills; that they illustrate therefore omnipotence rather than omniscience. This close association of the two attributes must always be allowed for in the usage of Scripture. Where all events are referred to the direct action of the Deity, it is not strange that He should know and foretell what He is about to do. It may be the sense that thus to foreknow and bring about events demonstrates the existence and activity of the divine, or it may be that the course of the world was already regarded as possessing a relative independence, which forms the ground of the appeal to the foreknowledge of God as proving His superiority to the idols of the nations. Such an appeal occurs more than once in Deutero-Isaiah, e.g. Is 42^9 'Behold, the former things are come to pass, and new things do I declare; before they spring forth I tell you of them'; 46^{10} 'Declaring the end from the beginning, and from ancient times things that are not yet done; saying, My counsel shall stand'; cf. also 44^{6-8} $48^{3.\ 5.\ 6}$. In the NT Jesus asserts foreknowledge on the part of God of what is yet hidden even from the Son (Mk 13^{32}); and St. James (Ac 15^{18}), quoting the words of Amos ($9^{11.\ 12}$), substitutes for 'the LORD that doeth this,' 'the LORD who maketh these things known from the beginning of the world.' All the references, indeed, to the fulfilment of prophecy, which are so frequently found in the NT, are intelligible only on the assumption that they are taken as evidencing the foreknowledge of God.

It is, however, in its application, not to events generally, but to *salvation*, and that both of the individual and of the community, that the question of the divine foreknowledge has arrested the attention, engaged the thoughts, and sometimes tried the hearts of men. True piety refers all things to God, and rejoices to see in the individual life of faith and love the manifestation of divine activity. It seems to it that, were the case otherwise, there could be no assurance of salvation, and the peace which is the most priceless possession of God's children would be impossible to them. It is argued that, as God is both able and willing to bring about the salvation of the individual, He must know beforehand, not only His purpose to do so, but its fulfilment. We refer salvation, along with all other events, to the Divine Will; but, as God is not only Supreme Will but Supreme Intelligence, before, or accompanying the forthputting of that will there must be an act of knowledge. Thus foreknowledge comes to be associated with ELECTION and PREDESTINATION (which see) as a constitutive element in the ultimate ground of the salvation made known in Christ. But in proportion as this conclusion removes difficulties on the one side, it raises them on the other. While theoretically admitting the determinative influence of the divine action upon the course of events in general, we recognize that to us they are contingent, and we are not perplexed by a difficulty which we scarcely feel. But with the question of personal salvation it is different. Foreknowledge here implies a determinative action which seems to leave no room for choice, or moral freedom. Further, experience shows that there are gradations in the extent of spiritual privileges accorded, and infinite variations in the degree to which men avail themselves of these. Are we then to argue a limitation of the divine power, or of the divine will, to save? The interests of piety and morality, the facts of religion and experience, seem incompatible here, the one demanding an absoluteness of determination

which the other cannot admit. It is the difficulty which has divided schools of earnest men and powerful thinkers, like the Augustinian and the Pelagian, the Calvinist and the Arminian, which in various forms and degrees enters into and moulds men's whole conception of the religious life. Into its later phases we cannot here enter; we must confine ourselves to stating the data of the problem as they are presented in Scripture.

In the OT the question in this special form scarcely occurs. The prophets regard Israel as having been chosen from among the peoples of the earth to be God's special heritage (Dt 7^{6-8}, Neh $9^{7.\ 8}$, Is $41^{8.\ 9}$ $44^{1.\ 2}$); but the thought of a decree affecting the eternal destiny of individuals could not present itself to those who had only a dim conception of the future life, and who regarded religious blessings as coming to the individual only through his membership of the elect nation. In the NT the difficulty is for the most part not acutely felt, the two sides of the problem being in turn referred to without any apparent sense of antagonism or incompatibility. Thus Jesus recognizes the Father's action in revealing to babes what is hidden from the wise and prudent (Mt $11^{25.\ 26}$), declares that to some it is given to know the mysteries of the kingdom of heaven, while from others it is withheld (Mt 13^{11-16}), says that many are called, but few chosen (Mt 22^{14}; cf. Jn 6^{44} 12^{40}). On the other hand, He preaches the gospel of repentance (Mt 4^{17}), and laments over Jerusalem for neglecting or abusing her opportunities (Mt 23^{37}). Nowhere is it made an excuse for the rejection of salvation that any one has not been included in the saving purpose of God.

It is in connexion with certain passages in the writings of St. Paul that the questions in regard to foreknowledge definitely arise. These are two. How far does foreknowledge imply predestination, decision of the fate of an individual anterior to his personal existence and therefore to his own moral choice? and, What is the relation of foreknowledge to the ground of salvation; is there anything foreknown which accounts for the saving choice falling upon one and passing by another? In Ro $8^{29.\ 30}$ we read: 'For whom he foreknew (οὓς προέγνω), he also foreordained (AV did predestinate) to be conformed to the image of his Son, . . . and whom he foreordained, them he also called; and whom he called, them he also justified; and whom he justified, them he also glorified.' Here the process of salvation is represented as a chain, as a succession of stages, of which the origin was a divine purpose based upon a divine foreknowledge. The word προγινώσκω in its ordinary classical use means simply 'to know previously,' 'to have knowledge of beforehand,' and hence, since 'all demonstration depends on previously existing knowledge' (ἐκ προγινωσκομένων πᾶσα διδασκαλία, Arist. *Eth. Nic.* vi. 3), present knowledge leads to forecasting the future by tracing out the probable course of events; cf. 2 P 3^{17} 'Ye therefore, beloved, knowing these things beforehand, beware.' But, with men, the course of events can at best be foreknown only with a high degree of probability, it is never more than an inference founded on experience; but God's foreknowledge must, we argue, be absolute, and involves the actual occurrence of that which is the object of it,—if it refers to time πρόγνωσις seems inevitably to involve πρόθεσις. There is, however, a certain vagueness in the way in which προέγνω is used in Ro 8^{29}, which is still more apparent in Ro 11^2 'God did not cast off his people which he foreknew.' There is something wanting to fill up the conception. Cremer (*Bibl.-Theol. Lex.*) therefore suggests taking these passages in connexion with another class of passages, where the simple verb is used, of which 1 Co 8^3 may be taken as an example:

'If any man loveth God, the same is known of him' (ἔγνωσται ὑπ' αὐτοῦ). The union between God and man thus expressed is represented in προέγνω as anticipated and determined upon 'in the divine counsels before their manifestation in history.' Another shade of meaning which προγινώσκειν in these texts appears to bear is that in the chain of events leading to salvation it denotes the *self-determination* of God to that work. With the προ-ορίζειν the first active step to its fulfilment has been taken, but the foreknowledge of God implies His own adoption of the plan. It thus, as Cremer remarks, ideally precedes even the ἐκλέγεσθαι of Eph 1⁴·⁵ 'Even as he chose (ἐξελέξατο) us in him before the foundation of the world . . . having foreordained (προορίσας) us unto adoption as sons,' ἐκλέγεσθαι expressing 'a determination directed to the objects of the fellowship' into which God has resolved to enter with His people. Πρόγνωσις thus 'denotes the foreordained fellowship between God and the objects of His saving counsels, God's self-determination to enter into such fellowship preceding the realization thereof.' This definition establishes the place of foreknowledge in the order of the saving acts, but does not free it of the difficulty which its connexion with that order involves. In the self-determination of God to save, if this has an individual application, the whole problem is raised. It is evident that the apostle, anxious to establish the Christian's faith upon a sure foundation, overlooks for the moment the bearing of his explanation upon the question of moral choice. There is no reason to think that he would ignore the latter. His Epistles are full of appeals which recognize the moral nature and responsibilities of man. But the key to his attitude is probably to be found in that personal experience which he describes in Gal 1¹⁵, where, as Lightfoot remarks, he heaps up words to emphasize the point he is maintaining ('the sole agency of God as distinct from his own efforts'), 'the *good pleasure* of God, who *separated me* (set me apart, devoted me to a special purpose), even from my mother's womb, and *called* me through his *grace.*' As he felt that he had been destined and was being prepared for his high office, even when he had been unconscious of it, and had been making in the opposite direction, so it was with humanity in general; man was moving towards the goal prepared for him, and God's purpose in spite of human recalcitrancy was being realized. But neither in the one case nor in the other did the leadings of Providence mean that the human will was being set aside.

But now, turning to the other question, has the προέγνω of Ro 8²⁹ 11² any special qualitative import? God knows, foreknows, His people—what constitutes them His people, is there anything in them or about them which accounts for foreknowledge becoming foreordination, which explains the ground of election? Here opinions differ, and it is probable that each exegete will read into the word what agrees with his general doctrinal standpoint. Thus, to take one or two examples, Cremer appears to think there is no such import, the conception being complete in itself, and the word not indicating 'a decision come to concerning any one'; Grimm (*NT Lex.*, Thayer's ed.) holds the meaning to be that 'God foreknew that they would love him, or (with reference to what follows) he foreknew them to be fit to be conformed to the likeness of his Son.' This explanation (that of foreseen love) is adopted also by Weiss (*NT Theology*, § 88), while Godet (*Romans*, Eng. tr. ii. 109) takes 'faith' to be the other object of foreknowledge, the condition of salvation which God foreknew that His people would fulfil. It is doubtful, however, whether St. Paul had followed out his thought on this side into a definite form. He was concerned with the purpose of God, not with the ground of that purpose. Both in Gal 1¹⁵,

as we have seen, in reference to himself, and in Eph 1⁵·¹¹ in reference to the Church, he lays stress upon the fact that God's action is 'according to the good pleasure of his will, to the praise of the glory of his grace'—'according to the purpose of him who worketh all things after the counsel of his own will.'

To these indications from the Pauline writings, the occurrences of προγινώσκειν and πρόγνωσις in other parts of NT (Ac 2²³ 26⁵, 1 P 1²·²⁰, 2 P 3¹⁷) add nothing in regard to the questions we have been considering. St. Paul founds upon election, as the method appointed by Providence for the education of humanity, his religious philosophy of history. Some are set apart for special privilege, but have also laid upon them special duty. The Jews are set aside until the Gentiles be come in; salvation is extended to the Gentiles in order that the Jews might come to share its blessings; but 'God does not cast off his people which he foreknew'; His purpose is not abandoned, but worked out according to the dictates of infinite wisdom and perfect love. It has been suggested (Plumptre, *Epp. of St. Peter*, in 'Cambridge Bible for Schools') that in the words 'the foreknowledge of God *the Father*' (1 P 1²) 'we find, perhaps, the secret of their (the apostles') acceptance of this aspect of the divine government. The choice and the knowledge were not those of an arbitrary sovereign will, capricious as are the sovereigns of earth, in its favours and antipathies, seeking only to manifest its power, but of a Father whose tender mercies were over all His works, and who sought to manifest His love to all His children.' 'In what way,' says the same writer, 'the thought of man's freedom to will was reconcilable with that of God's electing purpose, the writers of NT did not care to discuss.' They felt, we may believe, instinctively, half-unconsciously, that the problem was insoluble, and were content to accept the two beliefs, which cannot logically be reconciled.' In this condition of unsolved antinomy the Bible leaves all such doctrines as those of grace and election, a heritage of discussion and speculation to age after age of the Church; yet, however difficult to the intellect, constantly receiving its practical solution and reconciliation in the Christian experience of the soul, which is at once conscious of its own moral responsibility and of its dependence upon God.

LITERATURE.—In addition to the authorities cited above, see Sanday-Headlam, *Romans*, *ll.cc.*; the *Biblical Theologies* of Beyschlag, Bovon, and Schmid; Cunningham, *Historical Theology*, ii. 441 ff.; K. Müller, *Die göttliche Zuvorersehung und Erwählung*; Bruce, *Providential Order of the World* (1897), Lect. x.; and the Literature at end of articles ELECTION, PREDESTINATION.   A. STEWART.

FOREPART.—The forepart (always one word in 1611) is either the front portion of a thing (Heb. פָּנִים *face*), Ex 28²⁷ 39²⁰ (of the 'ephod'), 1 K 6²⁰ (of the 'oracle'), Ezk 42²⁷ (of the 'chambers' of Ezekiel's temple, RV 'before'); or specifically the prow or bow of a vessel (πρῶρα), Ac 27⁴¹, where it is opposed to the 'hinder part' (so 1611) or stern (πρύμνα). RV gives 'foreship' in the last passage, so as to correspond with v.³⁰ (the only other occurrence of the Gr. word), where AV and RV have 'foreship.' The *Oxf. Eng. Dict.* queries if 'forepart' is obsolete in this sense; it has found no later instance than Dampier (1699), *Voyages*, II. i. 74, 'The head or fore-part is not altogether so high as the Stern.' For illustration of 'forepart,' meaning generally the front, take T. Adams, *II Peter*, on 1² 'There is a helmet for the head, a corselet for the breast, a shield for the foreparts; but no guard, no regard for the back'; and Bunyan, *Holy War* (Clar. Pr. ed. p. 224, l. 35), 'Every door also was filled with persons who had adorned every one their fore-part against their house with something of variety and singular excellency, to entertain him withal as he passed in the streets,' where the 'fore-part' is explained by the editor as ' the space lying between a house and the public street or highway, the plot of ground forming a garden or fore-court.'

J. HASTINGS.

FORERUNNER (πρόδρομος) occurs once in Apocr. and once in NT. Wis 12⁸ 'Thou sentest hornets as forerunners of thy host'; He 6²⁰ 'whither as a forerunner Jesus entered for us.' The meaning of both these passages is illustrated by the classical usage of πρόδρομος as a military term (Herod. i. 60, iv. 121, 122 ; Æsch. *Theb.* 80 ; Thuc. ii. 22, etc.). It was applied especially to the light-armed soldiers who were sent in advance of an army as scouts. A special corps of πρόδρομοι was attached to the Macedonian army (Arrian, *Anab.* i. 12; Diod. xvii. 17). When a king was to travel, a forerunner was sent to see that the way was in good order (Is 40³ff.; cf. Mal 3¹). Both these OT passages are applied in NT to John the Baptist as the forerunner of Jesus (Mt 11¹⁰, Mk 1², Lk 7²⁷). In Lk 9⁵² Jesus sends 'messengers before his face to make ready for him.' Cf. Jn 14² 'I go to prepare a place for you.' The kings of Israel had runners before their chariots (1 S 8¹¹); Doeg the Edomite was the mightiest of Saul's runners (1 S 21⁷, reading רָצִים for רֹעִים); Absalom and Adonijah prepared fifty men to run before them (2 S 15¹, 1 K 1⁵); Elijah ran before the chariot of Ahab (1 K 18⁴⁶). See further under GUARD, RUNNERS.

J. A. SELBIE.

FORESHIP.—In AV, Ac 27³⁰ only, ' under colour as though they would have cast anchors out of the foreship' (1611 'fore-ship', Gr. πρώρα, the bow of a ship). RV adds v.⁴¹. See FOREPART. It was Tindale that gave 'forshippe' as the trⁿ of πρώρα in v.³⁰ and 'foore parte' in v.⁴¹. The translators of AV retained the variety according to their precept, ' that nicenesse in wordes was alwayes counted the next step to trifling' (*The Translators to the Reader*). 'Foreship' is still in use. For the anchorage of ships see Smith, *Voyage and Shipwreck of St. Paul*, 132, and art. SHIP.

FORESKIN.—See CIRCUMCISION.

FOREST.—There are five Heb. words for collections of trees and shrubs :—**1.** יַעַר *ya'ar*, δρυμός. This word, which is by far the most common, is tr. sometimes *forest* (Jer 46²³, Mic 3¹²), more frequently *wood* (Dt 19⁵ RV 'forest,' 2 K 2²⁴, Ps 96¹² etc.). Its Arab. equivalent, *wa'r*, signifies *difficult*, and is used for rugged and stony regions, whether wooded or not. The expression 'thickets of the forest' (Is 9¹⁸) refers to a forest with tangled undergrowth. **2.** חֹרֶשׁ *ḥoresh* is used twice for collections of trees :—(*a*) *Wood* (1 S 23¹⁵ etc.), where (reading חֹרֶשׁ) LXX has the proper name Καινη. RV text has *wood*, marg. the proper name *Ḥoresh* (wh. see, and cf. Driver, *Text of Samuel, ad loc.*). Many believe that the reference here is to a town and not to a forest. (*b*) *Forest* (2 Ch 27⁴), where it is trᵈ in LXX by δρυμός. The same word is used for *dense foliage* (Ezk 31³ 'shadowing shroud'). It is also used for a 'bough' (RV 'wood') Is 17⁹. The LXX here tr. 'of the Amorites and the Hivites,' and this is probably correct. In every instance of the genuine occurrence of this word, the proper meaning appears to be 'wooded height.' **3.** סְבַךְ *sĕbhak*, *thicket* (Is 9¹⁸ 10³⁴, Jer 4⁷). This word is given as a proper name in LXX (Gn 22¹³ Σαβέκ). It is also trᵈ by δρυμός, Ps 74⁵ (AV 'thick trees,' RV 'a thicket of trees'). **4.** עֲבִים *'ăbhim*, ἄλση, 'thickets' (Jer 4²⁹), called so on account of the *darkness* of such places.

5. פַּרְדֵּס *pardés*, παράδεισος. This is a word of Persian origin, found in Sanskrit, *paradeza*; Armenian, *pardes*; Syriac, *pardaysâ*; Arab. *firdaus*. It is used once (Neh 2⁸) of a royal (AV) 'forest' or (RVm) 'park,' under the care of an officer, whose permission had to be obtained in order to fell wood within its limits. It is twice used for *orchards* (Ca 4¹³, Ec 2⁵ pl. RV 'parks ').

Pal. and Syria were doubtless much more heavily wooded in ancient times than now. Numerous forests are mentioned in Scripture. (1) The wood lands of the Canaanites and Rephaim clothed the mountains of Samaria and Galilee, and extended apparently to Beth-shean (Jos 17¹⁵⁻¹⁸). Tabor is a representative of this *wood of Ephraim*. For another ' wood of Ephraim' see (9) below. (2) There was a forest near Bethel, clothing the sides of the ravines coming up from the Jordan Valley (2 K 2²³. ²⁴). (3) The ' forest of Hareth' was on the W. slopes of the Judæan hills (1 S 22⁵). (4) A forest in the hill-country, probably near Aijalon (1 S 14²⁵. ²⁶, cf. v.³¹), where Jonathan ate the honey. (5) The ' fields of the wood ' (Ps 132⁶) refer to the region of Kiriath-jearim, the 'village of the woods' (1 S 7²). (6) The forests where Jotham 'built castles and towers' (2 Ch 27⁴) were in the mountains of Judah. (7) If ḥoresh (1 S 23¹⁵ etc.) refers to a *wood*, then there was a forest at the edge of the Judæan desert, near Ziph. The LXX seems to regard it as a place, Καινη. Conder located it at *Khurbet-Khureisa*. Tristram, however, thinks that a forest was intended. (8) The latter opinion is strengthened by the allusion (Ezk 20⁴⁶. ⁴⁷) to the ' forest of the south field' and ' forest of the south' (AV), and ' forest of the field in the south' (Negeb), ' forest of the south' (RV). These must have been forests of S. Judæa, overlooking the Judæan wilderness and et-Tîh. (9) There were extensive forests in Bashan (Is 2¹³) and Gilead (2 S 18⁶ 'the wood [RV 'forest'] of Ephraim'). (10) Lebanon was noted for its forests (1 K 7²), as also Carmel (2 K 19²³). RV trᵈ כַּרְמִלּוֹ in this passage 'fruitful field' (*sc.* of Lebanon, which seems demanded by the context). Forests are mentioned in Apocr. (1 Mac 4³⁸).

Forests were an emblem of *pride* (Zec 11²). They were contrasted with cultivated ground, as an emblem of *neglect* (Is 29¹⁷).

Notwithstanding the ravages of conquerors, and the improvidence of the people, there are still considerable wooded regions, even in W. Palestine. The slopes of the hills, and not a few of the sides of the ravines, are clothed with thickets, and in a few places there are groves of trees, as on the flanks of Carmel and Tabor. Gilead and Bashan have quite extensive open woods of oak, terebinth, arbutus, and pine. There are still traces of the old cedar groves of Lebanon, and large open groves of pine, oak, cypress, juniper, and spruce. There are also many scrubs of dwarf oaks and carobs. Willows and poplars and plane trees are abundant along the watercourses, and tamarisks along the seashore and in the deserts. Acacias are fairly numerous in the valleys around the Dead Sea, and southward to Sinai. Terebinths, carobs, evergreen oaks, ash, hackberry, and Pride of India are scattered freely over the whole country. Large forests of full-grown trees are found in N. Lebanon, and in the heart of Amanus in N. Syria. In the latter chain are large districts, wholly occupied by forests of cedar of Lebanon, beech, pine, oak, hornbeam, cypress, spruce, and yew.

G. E. POST.

FORETELL.—Thrice 'foretell' occurs in AV, each time for a different Gr. verb, and twice in the sense of 'tell beforehand,' not specially prophesy or prognosticate : Mk 13²³ 'Behold, I have foretold you all things' (προείρηκα, RV 'I have told you all things beforehand'); 2 Co 13² 'I told you before, and foretell you, as if I were present, the second time' (προείρηκα καὶ προλέγω, RV 'I have said beforehand, and I do say beforehand,' RVm 'plainly' for *beforehand*). For this meaning see Shaks. *Tempest*, IV. i. 149—

> 'These our actors,
> As I foretold you, were all spirits';

and *III Henry VI.* IV. vii. 12—

> 'For many men that stumble at the threshold
> Are well foretold that danger lurks within.'

In the third instance the meaning is prophesy, predict, Ac 3[24] 'all the prophets . . . have likewise foretold of these days' (TR προκατήγγειλαν, but edd. κατήγγειλαν, whence RV 'they also told of these days'). [προκαταγγέλλω is accepted by edd. in Ac 3[18] (AV 'God before had shewed,' RV 'God foreshewed'), and 7[52] (EV 'shewed before')].   J. HASTINGS.

FOREWARD.—In 1 Mac 9[11] it is said of the army of Bacchides, 'they that marched in the foreward were all mighty men.' The Gr. for 'they that marched in the foreward' is οἱ πρωταγωνισταί, whence comes our 'protagonist.' The same word occurs in 2 Mac 15[30], where Judas is called ὁ πρωταγωνιστὴς ὑπὲρ τῶν πολιτῶν, AV 'the chief defender of the citizens,' RV 'the foremost champion of his fellow-citizens.' It signified first the principal actor in a play, and then the person taking a leading part in any enterprise, the one who 'plays first fiddle,' in fact, as Liddell and Scott suggest. The Eng. phrase 'in the foreward' comes from Geneva, 'they that foght in the forewarde were all valiant men.' The *foreward* (='front-guard') was the foremost line of an army, its vanguard; thus Caxton (1489), *Sonnes of Aymon*, i. 41, 'Fyrste of alle came the forewarde wyth the Oryflame'; and Shaks. *Rich. III.* v. iii. 293—

> 'My foreward shall be drawn out all in length,
> Consisting equally of horse and foot.'

RV translates, 'the mighty men that fought in the front of the battle'; which is almost a return to Wyclif (1382), 'the first of the bateil al the mighty.'   J. HASTINGS.

FORFEIT.—From Old French *forfait* or *forfet* after late Latin *forisfactum*, a trespass, or fine (Lat. *foris* without, and *facere* to do), a 'forfeit' was originally an act outside of righteousness, and 'to forfeit' was to act unrighteously, to sin. Thus Berners, *Froissart*, I. ccccxxxi. 'Sir, ye know well the Flemings that be yonder have done us no forfeit'; and Chaucer, *Parsones Tale*, 275 (Student's ed. p. 682ᵃ), 'And al this suffred Jesu Crist, that neuere forfeited.' From this the meaning passed early into the expression of a penalty due for transgression, a fine; and the verb came to signify to lose, or lose the right to, something, a meaning in which both subst. and vb. are still used. But in its only occurrence in AV the vb. 'forfeit' (the subst. is not found) is used with direct reference to the authority or executive power to confiscate; and in that sense it is marked by *Oxf. Eng. Dict.* as obsolete: Ezr 10[8] 'And that whosoever would not come within three days, according to the counsel of the princes and the elders, all his substance should be forfeited' (חֵ֫רֶם, AVm and RVm 'devoted'). Cf. Dn 2[5] Wyc. (1382), 'your housis shuln be maad commoun *or forfetid*.'

RV introduces 'forfeit' into Dt 22[9] 'Thou shalt not sow thy vineyard with two kinds of seed; lest the whole fruit be forfeited' (תִּקְדַּשׁ, AV 'defiled,' RVm 'consecrated'; Driver, 'lit. *become holy* or *sacred, i.e.* be forfeited to the sanctuary'); Mt 16[26], Mk 8[36] 'forfeit his life' (ζημιωθῇ τὴν ψυχὴν αὐτοῦ, AV 'lose his own soul');

and Lk 9[25] 'and lose or forfeit his own self' (ἑαυτὸν δὲ ἀπολέσας ἢ ζημιωθείς, AV 'be cast away'). In the remaining occurrences of ζημιοῦν (1 Co 3[15], 2 Co 7[9], Ph 3[8]), RV renders 'suffer loss.'   J. HASTINGS.

FORGE, FORGER.—Forge and fabricate come both from Lat. *fabricare*, the former through the Old French *forgier*, the latter directly. To 'forge' is therefore to make or shape, as Ex 4[11], Wyc. (1382), 'Who made the mouth of man, or who forgide (1388 'made') the dowmbe and the deef, the seer and the blynde?'; Tindale, *Works* (ed. Russell, 1831), i. 93, 'The power of God . . . altereth him, changeth him clean, fashioneth and forgeth him anew.' It is especially used of shaping metals by fire and hammer; and in this sense RV uses the subst. *forger*, Gn 4[22] 'Tubal-cain, the forger of every cutting instrument of brass and iron' (לֹטֵשׁ כָּל־חֹרֵשׁ, AV 'an instructer [m. 'whetter'] of every artificer in brass and iron'; so RVm). The passage is difficult, perhaps corrupt; it is fully discussed in Dillmann and in Spurrell. But in AV 'forge' and 'forger' are used only in the metaphorical sense of framing or inventing lies: Job 13[4] 'ye are forgers of lies' (טֹפְלֵי־שָׁקֶר); Ps 119[69] 'The proud have forged a lie against me' (טָפְלוּ עָלַי שֶׁקֶר); and Sir 51[2] 'lips that forge lies' (ἐργαζομένων ψεῦδος). The Geneva tr. of Lk 19[8] is, 'If I have taken from any men by forged cauillation, I restore hym foure folde.' And Shaks. *Rich. II.* IV. i. 40, gives—

> 'If thou deny'st it twenty times, thou liest;
> And I will turn thy falsehood to thy heart,
> Where it was forged, with my rapier's point.'

     J. HASTINGS.

FORGETFULNESS.—Forgetful in the sense of *heedless*, *neglectful*, is perhaps still in use colloquially, but in literary English we should not now say as AV after Tindale in He 13[2] 'Be not forgetful to entertain strangers' (τῆς φιλοξενίας μὴ ἐπιλανθάνεσθε, RV 'Forget not to show love unto strangers'). 'A forgetful hearer' (Ja 1[25]) is more modern, but RV prefers 'a hearer that forgetteth' (ἀκροατὴς ἐπιλησμονῆς, lit. 'a hearer of forgetfulness,' as in 2[4] 'judges of evil thoughts' = evil-thoughted judges').

In Sir 23[14] the meaning is again, probably, *heedless* and so unmannerly, 'Remember thy father and thy mother, when thou sittest among great men. Be not forgetful before them, and so thou by thy custom become a fool' (μή ποτε ἐπιλάθῃ). But the passage is obscure. Wyclif has it, 'Lest perauenture God forgete thee in the sighte of hem,' after Vulg. *Ne forte obliviscatur te Deus in conspectu illorum*; and he (or the Vulg.) is followed by Rogers', Coverdale's, the Bishops', and the Douay versions; the Geneva has 'lest thou be forgotten in their sight.' RV slightly alters the construction of the sentence, and so gets a new meaning—

> 'Remember thy father and thy mother,
> For thou sittest in the midst of great men;
> That thou be not forgetful before them,
> And become a fool by thy custom.'

The great men are presumably the father and mother; if so, 'great ones' would have been better; the Gr. is simply ἀνὰ μέσον μεγιστάνων. Ball, in *QPB*, follows Fritzsche and AV, and explains, 'Low language reflects upon one's upbringing.'

Forgetfulness occurs in Ps 88[12] 'Shall thy wonders be known in the dark? and thy righteousness in the land of forgetfulness?' (אֶרֶץ נְשִׁיָּה), where 'forgetfulness' is not the condition of losing all recollection, but of being forgotten, *oblivion*,—a meaning which Bradley (*Oxf. Eng. Dict.*) marks as probably obsolete. The condition of losing recollection might be represented as a blessed one, as in Shaks. *II Henry IV.* III. i. 8—

> 'O sleep! O gentle sleep!
> Nature's soft nurse, how have I frighted thee,
> That thou no more wilt weigh my eyelids down,
> And steep my senses in forgetfulness?'

But the Psalmist's thought is rather as in Norton (1561), *Calvin's Inst.* IV. xviii. 704, 'This Masse

... shamefully ... putteth his death in forget-fulnesse'; and Gray, *Elegy*, l. 85—

> ' For who, to dumb Forgetfulness a prey,
>   This pleasing anxious being e'er resigned,
>   Left the warm precincts of the cheerful day,
>   Nor cast one longing ling'ring look behind?'

This is the meaning also of Wis 17³ 'they were scattered under a dark vail of forgetfulness' (ἀφεγγεῖ λήθης παρακαλύμματι, Vulg. *tenebroso oblivionis velamento*'); but in 14²⁶ 16¹¹, Sir 11²⁵, the word is used in its usual sense of a tendency to forget.   J. HASTINGS.

FORGIVENESS.—In OT three words especially are used to express the idea of forgiveness—כָּפַר* 'cover' or 'pacify'; סָלַח (root meaning unknown); נָשָׂא 'lift up' or 'away.' AV and RV render all three usually 'forgive,' sometimes 'pardon.' The first and second are always used of divine forgiveness—the first, rarely (Ps 78³⁸, Jer 18²³, Dt 21⁸, 2 Ch 30¹⁸), the second, frequently (*e.g.* 1 K 8³⁰ᶠ·, Lv 4²⁰ᶠ·); the third is in common use of ordinary human forgiveness as well (*e.g.* Gn 50¹⁷, Ex 10¹⁷, 1 S 15²⁵ 25²⁸). In nearly all instances the context implies repentance for the offence, and an intention to avoid a repetition of it, as a condition of the forgiveness; and as a result of it, that the offender is placed again in the position which he occupied before the offence, in the old covenant relation to God, or in the same friendly relation as before to the person affected. Under the sacrificial system the repentance and the amends are represented by the sacrifice which is offered by the offender through the priest (see Oehler, *Theology of the OT*, § 139); but in other cases in the Psalms and the Prophets there is no suggestion of more than acknowledgment of sin, repentance, and that intention of amendment which is expressed by the phrase 'turning to the Lord.' Forgiveness is a free act on the part of God or of man; it restores the offender to the state in which there is no obstacle to his communion with him from whom he has been alienated; it gives peace of mind (Ps 32), a consciousness of the divine mercy (Ps 103); it removes the fear of punishment and quickens love (2 S 12¹³, Job 33²⁸, Ps 103²). Nor is it only an individual matter; the whole nation may be alienated from God through neglect of his will, and may by forgiveness be restored,—such is the burden of many a prophetic exhortation.

It has been said that 'no permanent state of reconciliation' was established under the old covenant; that there was only such forgiveness for the past as might enable men to begin again to seek justification through the works of the law. It has also been maintained that the old covenant furnished only a 'passing over' of sin, a 'closing the eyes' to it on the part of God—by which, though satisfaction was not made, though there was no real remission of sin, punishment was forgone. The consideration of these questions involves the whole subject of ATONEMENT (wh. see); but it may be stated here that neither the national and individual experiences recorded in the OT, nor the words and general language used, seem to suggest any fundamental difference in the idea of forgiveness from that which we find in the NT. When St. Paul in a particular passage (Ro 3²⁵) uses, with reference to sins committed by men living under the old covenant, a word (πάρεσις) different from that (ἄφεσις) which is in common use in the NT to express 'forgiveness,' he has in mind a different thought. He is arguing that because in former ages God had not exacted from men the punishment which was due for their sins (cf. Ac

* On this important term see *Oxf. Heb. Lex. s.v.*, also Driver, *Deut.* 243, 425 f., and art. PROPITIATION.

14¹⁶, 17³⁰), his forbearance had been misunderstood; he had 'passed by sins till the world was in danger of forgetting that he was a God of righteousness; and the time had come for a signal exhibition of his hatred of sin in the propitiation made in Christ Jesus (see Ro 3²⁵· ²⁶ RV, the sense of the argument is lost in AV). With men such 'passing by' might involve forgetting, it could not be the same as 'forgiving'; with God it would be neither (see Trench, *Synonyms*, § xxxiii.). No argument with regard to the nature of forgiveness under the old covenant can be drawn from the passage. Indeed, so far as the relation between the individual and God is concerned, there is nothing to indicate that the forgiveness granted by God in the experience of his people before the coming of Christ was different in kind from that which Christ proclaimed. A difference in the requirement of it from men in their relations with one another, no doubt, may readily be detected between the teaching of the OT and the NT. It is here that the real development is in the ethical teaching of the NT on the subject is to be found. The duty of forgiving injuries and wrongs committed against oneself or others cannot be said to occupy the prominent place in the OT that it has in the teaching of Jesus. It must be recognized that in this respect there is a real distinction to be drawn. But true as it is that the revelation of the divine will and of the ideal of human life and character, the power of the whole revelation made in Christ, has immeasurably facilitated the individual's opportunity of conscious enjoyment of the divine forgiveness, and stimulated his readiness to bestow forgiveness in his measure upon others; yet it is none the less true that the same forgiveness of sin was offered to previous generations of men—'they are not to be heard, which feign that the old fathers did look only for transitory promises.' The materials for determining the idea of forgiveness are, however, so much richer in the NT than in the OT, that we turn to it rather than to the OT for the elaboration of the idea.

So closely, indeed, is the principle associated with the teaching and work of Christ, that forgiveness has been called 'Christ's most striking innovation in morality,' and the phrase a 'Christian' spirit is commonly regarded as synonymous with a disposition of readiness to forgive an injury. The pagan ideal of manly life was to succeed in doing as much good to your friends and as much injury to your enemies as possible; and if it be not true that forgiveness was a virtue unknown in the ancient world, it was at all events not one that was demanded or proclaimed as a duty by any ethical system. Indeed it is clear that without a sense of the need of personal holiness and the consciousness of guilt, without—in the widest meaning of the phrase—a conviction of sin, there could be no true repentance, no sense of the need of forgiveness. And such a conviction of sin neither Greek nor Roman religion produced.

The words which are used in the NT are the Gr. representatives of the Heb. words in the OT. We have, though rarely, the word (καλύπτω) meaning 'cover' or 'hide' (Ro 4⁷, 1 P 4⁸, Ja 5²⁰, all quoted from LXX); and once, with reference to former times, the word for 'passing by' (Ro 3²⁵); but by far the commonest word is that which expresses the idea of 'sending away,' or 'letting go' or 'releasing' (ἄφεσις), which is rendered in this connexion either 'forgive,' 'forgiveness,' or 'remit,' 'remission.' The noun occurs in this sense eleven times in the synoptic Gospels (not at all in Jn) and Ac (Mt 26²⁸, Mk 1⁴ 3²⁹, Lk 17⁷ 3³ 24⁴⁷, Ac 2³⁸ 5³¹ 10⁴³ 13³⁸ 26¹⁸; eight times in Lk and Ac, a favourite word of St. Luke), and four times elsewhere (Eph 1⁷, Col 1¹⁴, He 9²² 10¹⁸). In eleven of these instances there is added 'of sins,' in one ' of trespasses,' in one the same words are in the immediate context, and in the two remaining instances the word stands absolutely. (AV renders nine times 'remission,' six times 'forgiveness.') The verb with the same meaning occurs about forty times in the synoptic Gospels, once in Ac (8[22]), three times in Jn [Gospel once (20[23]), 1 Ep. twice (1[9] 2[12])], and twice elsewhere (Ro 4[7], Ja 5[15]). It is found predominantly with the usual word for 'sin' (ἁμαρτία) or 'sins' expressed or implied in the context, but other words—'debt,' 'trespasses,' 'iniquities'—are also used. The verb implies the complete removal of the cause of offence. The sin is taken out of the way, out of sight. The debt is cancelled, the debtor released from his obligation (cf. Mt 18[23-35]). As far as the offender is concerned, the trespass is done away. He no longer has the sense of sin, of guilt and liability to punishment; he is restored to the harmonious relations which existed before. (It is noticeable that though this is the favourite word of the Gospels and Acts, it is scarcely found in the NT outside them: the idea of forgiveness is merged in the wider ones of justification and salvation). Instead of this word St. Paul uses one (χαρίζεσθαι ten times) which has the special sense 'confer a favour on,' 'be gracious to'—of men towards one another and of Christ in relation to them (2 Co 2[7. 10] 12[13], Eph 4[32], Col 2[13] 3[13]). St. Luke has this word twice (Lk 7[42. 43]), each time of a debt (AV 'frankly forgave'), and twice he has also a word (ἀπολύω, 6[37 bis]), meaning to 'loose from,' 'release,' 'set at liberty.' In the Apocalypse the nearest equivalent is found probably in the idea of the blood 'loosing' from sin and 'cleansing' (e.g. Rev 1[5] 7[14]; cf. 1 Jn 1[7. 9]).

The teaching of the NT as to forgiveness is sufficiently represented by (1) the sayings of Christ which led up to it (Lk 17[3. 4], Mt 18[15-17] and 18[21. 22]), and St. Peter's question and the answer to it (Lk 17[3. 4], Mt 18[15-17] and 18[21. 22]), and the Parables of the Prodigal and of the great Debtor (Lk 15[11-32], Mt 18[23-35]); (2) the clause in the Lord's Prayer (with the comment which is added Mt 6[14. 15], cf. Mk 11[25. 26]); and (3) the allusion to blasphemy against the Holy Spirit (Mt 12[31] and parallels), and St. John's mention of sin 'unto death' (1 Jn 5[17]).

(1) The teaching is given much more fully in Mt than in Lk, but the full essence of it is in the words of Lk, 'If thy brother trespass against thee, rebuke him; and if he repent, forgive him. And if he trespass against thee seven times in a day, and seven times in a day turn again to thee, saying, I repent; thou shalt forgive him.' It is clear at once that, if certain conditions are satisfied, the teaching of Christ admits of no limitations to the law of forgiveness. The account in Mt more vividly enforces this point. It represents Christ as at first only enunciating the general principle. St. Peter seeks for further guidance, wishing to reduce the principle to the compass of a definite rule, and asking, 'Lord, how oft shall my brother sin against me, and I forgive him? till seven times?' and it is in answer to his question that the words are elicited which raise the duty out of the sphere of mere numerical calculation—'I say not unto thee, Until seven times: but, Until seventy times seven.' There is to be no limit whatever to the readiness of a follower of Christ to forgive. On the other hand, it is equally clear that something is required on the part of the offender before he can be the recipient of forgiveness. 'If thy brother . . . turn again to thee, saying, I repent' —this is the condition: there must be the consciousness of sin, the free avowal of error (cf. Lk 15[21]), the recognition of wrong-doing and the turning away from it, and, it seems, the willingness to make amends (cf. Lk 19[8]). That there must be

such repentance * (change of mind, acceptance of a new ideal of life) is still more plainly shown in the account of Mt: the Christian is not to remain passive till the offender of his own accord comes to him penitent and begging reconciliation—he is, on the contrary, to adopt all rational means he can to bring home to him the error and evil of his conduct; and should he still remain inpenitent and obdurate, there is no forgiveness for him—he places himself outside the pale of Christian life— 'Let him be unto thee as a heathen man and a publican.'

The Parable of the Prodigal Son shows the same relation between forgiveness and repentance. The wish to leave the father—the revolt against his will, his plan of life—was the sin: the return is in itself sufficient proof of repentance, even though it was prompted by the sense of failure and physical hunger; the father recognizes it as such, and hastens to meet and welcome the offender, and forgives him before he has had time to put into words his confession of sin; the son is in that moment restored to the position in his father's household which he had forfeited. (The teaching of the apostles as described in Ac lays similar emphasis on repentance as a first condition of salvation [e.g. Ac 2[38]], baptism being from one point of view the outward mark of repentance). So, too, the publican goes down to his house 'justified' because penitent (Lk 18[14]).

Similarly, a readiness to forgive others is laid down as a condition for a man's own forgiveness (cf. Mt 6[12], Mk 11[25. 26], Mt 5[7]). The Parable of the great Debtor shows that the absence of a forgiving spirit in men prevents their being themselves forgiven.

(2) The instances of Christ's teaching which have been cited might be interpreted as having reference only to relations between men, though it is scarcely conceivable that the parables are not intended to be significant of the relations of mankind as sons to God the Father, the ideal of character. The clause in the Lord's Prayer (Mt 6[12], Lk 11[4]) makes it evident that human forgiveness and divine forgiveness are represented as strictly analogous. There is indeed no indication of any fundamental difference between the forgiveness which the Christian wins from God and that which he in turn bestows upon his 'brother.' It is the same phrase which is used throughout—a phrase denoting actual 'remission' of sin; and it is used by Christ of his own action, and alike of God's and of man's part in the mysterious process. If it were not so, it would be mockery to offer up the petition, 'Forgive us our trespass, as we forgive them that trespass against us.' The comment on the clause, which Mt appends to the Prayer, and the similar saying, which Mk introduces in connexion with the exhortation to faith in praying, forbid any differentiation (cf. Col 3[13]). The statements are quite general. Forgiveness is to be won by repentance and confession, whatever the nature of the offence, whoever the persons concerned may be. (In view of the indisputably general application of the Parable of the Prodigal Son and the other references to forgiveness, it seems impossible to accept the interpretation of Mt 18[15-17] which would limit its teaching to relations between Christians).

(3) There are, however, two references which seem to set a limit to the possibility of divine forgiveness. One is the case of the blasphemy against the Holy Spirit; the other is St. John's

---

* Two words are used which imply change of mind (involving regret for the course pursued and change of conduct for the future) Mt 4[17], Mk 1[15], Lk 15[7. 10], and change of will Mt 21[29] (on the question whether the distinction holds or not, see Trench, *Synonyms*, § lxix.); and there are also words which mean 'turning' or 'conversion,' Lk 22[32], Mt 18[3].

allusion to 'sin unto death.' The first of these references declares that there is a supreme sin for which no man can ever hope to be forgiven— 'All their sins shall be forgiven unto the sons of men, and their blasphemies wherewith soever they shall blaspheme' (Mk 3²⁸); but with these sins and blasphemies there is pointedly contrasted one—'Whosoever shall blaspheme against the Holy Spirit hath never forgiveness, but is guilty of an eternal sin,' and it 'shall not be forgiven him, neither in this world, nor in that which is to come' (Mt 12³²). All that can be said with certainty as to the nature of this sin is that the opposition of the scribes and Pharisees to Christ was a sign and indication of it, and that the Pharisaic charge that it was by the powers of evil that he was enabled to perform his works of healing, was the immediate occasion of his denunciation of it. Augustine regarded the sin as deliberate persistence in evil (for other interpretations see Westcott, note on 1 Jn 5¹⁷). It would appear from the rest of Christ's teaching on forgiveness that it was in any case of such a character as to deaden and destroy the spiritual sense in him who yielded himself up to its influence, so that repentance would become impossible to him. The idea of unpardonable sin is further suggested by St. John's exception of 'sin unto death' from the subjects of intercessory prayer (1 Jn 5¹⁶). To one who thus sins the way of forgiveness is closed; at least it is not to be opened through the intercession of his brethren, which in other cases would avail.

There remains to be considered the problem of the significance of Christ's cry from the Cross, 'Father, forgive them; for they know not what they do' (Lk 23³⁴). It is evident that it is a prayer for the forgiveness of those who have not repented, who have not even come to knowledge of their guilt. It cannot, however, be regarded as limited in its scope to the Roman soldiers, and excluding any reference to the share in the final tragedy taken by the party of the scribes and Pharisees. The soldiers could not be thought of as in any real sense needing forgiveness for carrying out their orders in what they could only consider an ordinary execution: even Pilate was treated as comparatively guiltless. The cry must therefore be the supreme expression of the human sympathy and love of Christ, of the great principle which he had always inculcated. The sin embodied in the conduct of the Pharisaic party he had condemned in burning words; towards it there could not be any change of feeling; but they might be brought to repentance late though it was, and the words which are under consideration are a prayer for that result, a loving hope for the enlightenment of those blind leaders of the blind. It may be a hope against hope, but the cry does not constitute an exception to the principles and conditions of forgiveness which are to be drawn from other parts of the NT. It is a crowning example of 'forgivingness,' if so be that the divine mercy may transcend the usual conditions of the bestowal of the boon. Such a spirit of 'forgivingness' may be present (it has been noticed that it is required in all cases from the individual who has been injured, whether 'forgiven-ness' (the remission of the offence as regards the person who has offended) ensues or not. The word 'forgiveness' is capable of the active and of the passive sense. In the active sense it is clear that it is an ordinary Christian duty; in the passive sense, before it can be realized the conditions which have been elicited must be fulfilled.

LITERATURE.—Oehler, Theol. of OT; Schmid, Bib. Theol. of NT; Martensen, Christian Ethics; Seeley, Ecce Homo; Dorner, System of Christian Doctrine. See also Literature under arts. ATONEMENT, PROPITIATION.   J. F. BETHUNE-BAKER.

FORM.—Numerous as are the Heb. and Gr. words trᵈ 'form,' the meanings of the word in AV and RV may be reduced to the following: **1.** Shape, as an orderly arrangement of parts, Gn 1² 'The earth was without form' (תֹּהוּ, RV 'waste'; so in Jer 4²³); Wis 11¹⁷ 'thy Almighty hand, that made the world of matter without form' (ἐξ ἀμόρφου ὕλης, RV 'out of formless matter'). Cf. Shaks. K. John, III. i. 253—

'All form is formless, order orderless.'

2. Such orderly arrangement as produces *beauty, comeliness,* Is 52¹⁴ 53² 'he hath no form nor comeliness' (תֹּאַר); Wis 15⁵ 'they desire the form of a dead image, that hath no breath' (εἶδος; Farrar, 'he yearns for the unbreathing beauty of a dead image'). For this meaning see Shaks. *Mids. Night's Dream,* I. ii. 233—

'Things base and vile, holding no quantity, Love can transpose to form and dignity.'

3. The special or characteristic shape of a person or thing, Ezk 8³ 'And he put forth the form of an hand, and took me by a lock of mine head' (תַּבְנִית; so 10⁸); Dn 3¹⁹ 'Then was Nebuchadnezzar full of fury, and the form of his visage was changed' (צְלֵם); Mk 16¹², Ph 2⁶·⁷ (μορφή, the characteristic form of the Son of God and His characteristic form as the Son of Man; see Gifford, *The Incarnation,* p. 22 ff.; and art. FASHION). Cf. Shaks. Com. of Errors, II. ii. 200—

'Thou hast thine own form.
        No, I am an ape.
If thou art changed to aught, 'tis to an ass.'

Milton, Comus, l. 70—

'Their human countenance,
Th' express resemblance of the gods, is chang'd
Into some brutish form of wolf or bear.'

And Par. Reg. iv. 599—

'True image of the Father, whether thron'd
In the bosom of bliss, and light of light
Conceiving, or remote from Heav'n, enshrin'd
In fleshly tabernacle, and human form,
Wand'ring the wilderness.'

4. The representation or pattern of anything, Ezk 8¹⁰ 'And behold, every form of creeping things . . . pourtrayed upon the wall round about' (תַּבְנִית); 2 Ch 4⁷ 'he made ten candlesticks of gold according to their form' (מִשְׁפָּט, RV 'according to the ordinance concerning them'); Ezk 43¹¹ quater (צוּרָה); Ro 6¹⁷ 'that form of doctrine which was delivered you' (τύπος, RVm 'pattern'); 2 Ti 1¹³ 'Hold fast the form of sound words which thou hast heard of me' (ὑποτύπωσις, RV 'pattern'). So Wyclif's tr. of 1 Th 1⁷ 'so that ye ben maad fourme, or ensaumple, to alle men bileuynge'; and Locke, Human Underst. III. iii. 230, 'To make abstract general Ideas, and set them up in the Mind, with Names annexed to them, as Patterns, or Forms (for in that sense the word Form has a very proper signification).' **5.** Outward aspect (a); often the mere outward appearance as opposed to the inner reality (b): Thus (a) Job 4¹⁶ 'It stood still, but I could not discern the form thereof' (מַרְאֶה, RV 'appearance'); 1 S 28¹⁴ 'And the woman said unto Saul, I saw gods ascending out of the earth. And he said unto her, What form is he of?' (תֹּאַר); Dn 2³¹ 3²⁵ (רֵו, RV 'aspect'). So Shaks. Coriol. III. iii. 109—

'Art thou a man? thy form cries out thou art';

and Henry V. III. vi. 72, 'Why, 'tis a gull, a fool, a rogue: that now and then goes to the wars, to grace himself at his return unto London under the form of a soldier.' (b) 2 S 14²⁰ 'To fetch about this form of speech hath thy servant Joab done this thing' (פְּנֵי הַדָּבָר, RV 'to change the face of the matter'); Ro 2²⁰, 2 Ti 3⁵ 'Having a form of godliness, but denying the power thereof' (both μόρφωσις, which is not so purely as σχῆμα the mere outward form, but seems to be so used in both these passages, esp. 2 Ti 3⁵, and that is clearly the meaning of AV. See Sanday-Headlam on Ro 2²⁰). In illustration, take again Shaks., *Henry V.* II. ii. 116—

> 'And other devils that suggest by treasons,
> Do botch and bungle up damnation
> With patches, colours, and with forms, being fetch'd
> From glistering semblances of piety';

and *Othello*, II. i. 243, 'a knave very voluble, no further consciable than in putting on the mere form of civil and humane seeming, for the better compassing of his salt and most hidden - loose affection.'

The word 'form' has been occasionally introduced into RV when it is not in AV. It is used to tr. (1) Heb. תְּמוּנָה in all its occurrences except one, either for AV 'likeness' (Ex 20⁴, Dt 4²³·²⁵ ⁵⁸), or 'similitude' (Nu 12⁸, Dt 4¹²·¹⁵·¹⁶), or 'image' (Job 4¹⁶). The exception is Ps 17¹⁵ 'I shall be satisfied when I awake with thy likeness,' where RV gives 'form' in marg., Amer. RV in text. (2) חֵצֶב in 1 K 6²⁵ ⁷³⁷ for AV 'size'; but not in the only other occurrence of that word Jon 2⁶ (EV 'bottom'—'I went down to the bottoms of the mountains,' AVm 'Heb. cuttings off'). (3) εἶδος Lk 3²², Jn 5³⁷ (AV 'shape'), 1 Th 5²² (AV 'appearance'). (4) τύπος Ac 23²⁵ (AV 'manner').

J. HASTINGS.

FORMER.—This comparative adj. was at one time freely used to express the more advanced of two positions. Thus Wyclif (1388), after saying that Jacob 'departide (1382 'dyuydide') the puple that was with hym . . . in to twei cumpenyes,' adds (Gn 32¹⁷), 'And he comaundide to the formere (1382 'forther'), and seide, If thou schalt mete my brothir Esau,' etc.; and Knox, *Hist.* 88, 'Fiftie horse and men of the first rank lay dead at once, without any hurt done to the Scottish Armie, except that the Speares of the former two rankes were broken.' In this way 'former' is used in Zec 14⁸ 'Living waters shall go out from Jerusalem; half of them toward the former sea, and half of them toward the hinder sea' (הַיָּם הַקַּדְמוֹנִי, AVm and RV 'the eastern sea'), the 'eastern' sea being the Dead Sea, and the 'hinder' or 'western' sea (הַיָּם הָאַחֲרוֹן) the Mediterranean.

FORNICATION. — See CRIMES AND PUNISH-MENTS.

FORSOMUCH. — Wis 12¹⁵ 'Forsomuch then as thou art righteous thyself' (δίκαιος δὲ ὤν, RV 'But being righteous'); and Lk 19⁹ 'forsomuch as he also is a son of Abraham' (καθότι, RV 'forasmuch as'). The form is rare. Far more common is 'forasmuch,' which occurs forty-three times in AV, and was introduced generally by Tindale (it does not seem to occur in the Wyclifite versions). Tindale always keeps the parts of the word distinct, 'for as moche'; AV always presents an undivided word. It is Rogers (*Matthew's Bible*) that gives 'for so much' in Wis 12¹⁵; but in Lk 19⁹ AV is the first to use that form (perhaps by a slip of the pen or the printer), Tindale and others having 'for as moche.'

FORSWEAR.—To 'forswear' is to undo one's swearing, in accordance with the meaning of *for* (see under FOREGO). In AV it is always used reflexively, 'to forswear oneself,' with the meaning to swear falsely, to perjure oneself: 1 Es 1⁴⁸ 'And after that king Nabuchodonosor had made him to swear by the name of the Lord, he forswore himself, and rebelled' (ἐφιόρκησας ἀπέστη); Wis 14²⁸ 'they . . . lightly forswear themselves' (ἐπιορκοῦσιν ταχέως); and Mt 5³³ 'Thou shalt not forswear thyself, but shalt perform unto the Lord thine oaths' (οὐκ ἐπιορκήσεις; AV is Tindale's trⁿ, Wyclif has the intrans. form, 'Thou shalt not forswere': with which we may compare T. Adams,

II Peter, on 1⁴ 'Peter swore like a ruffian, and forswore like a renegade, till Christ looked on him, and then he wept'). For the AV trⁿ cf. Shaks. *III Henry VI.* v. v. 75—

> '*Clarence.* Did'st thou not hear me swear I would not do it?
> *Q. Margaret.* Ay, but thou usest to forswear thyself:
> 'Twas sin before, but now 'tis charity.'

FORT.—See WAR.

FORTH.—As Germ. *fort* from *vor*, so 'forth' is an adverb formed from 'fore'; and its general meaning is 'to the front.' When used with such verbs as 'bring' or 'come' it means *forward into view*, as Pr 25⁶ 'Put not forth thyself in the presence of the king' (RV 'put not thyself forward,' RVm '*Heb.* glorify not thyself'); Jn 8⁴² 'I proceeded forth, and came from God' (ἐξῆλθον, RV 'I came forth'). In this, its most characteristic meaning, it is used both literally and figuratively, and accompanies a great many different verbs, as *bring*, Gn 1¹¹ 'Let the earth bring forth grass,' Is 41²¹ 'bring forth your strong reasons'; *come*, Job 14² 'He cometh forth like a flower, and is cut down'; *put*, Mt 13²⁴ 'Another parable put he forth unto them' (παρέθηκεν αὐτοῖς, RV 'set he before them'); *stretch*, Ex 25²⁰ 'the cherubims shall stretch forth their wings on nigh' (RV 'spread out'); *shoot*, Gn 40¹⁰ 'her blossoms shot forth'; *send*, Ex 15⁷ 'Thou sentest forth thy wrath'; *show*, Mt 14² 'mighty works do show forth themselves in him' (αἱ δυνάμεις ἐνεργοῦσιν, RV 'these powers work'); and in like manner: *set*, Lk 1¹; *stand*, Jer 46⁴, Mk 3³; *call*, Is 31⁴; *bud*, Ca 7¹²; *spring*, Job 38²⁷; *creep*, Ps 104²⁰; *reach*, Pr 31²⁰; *shed*, Ac 2³³.

Sometimes the idea expressed is motion from a confined place to a more open, as 2 S 22²⁰ = Ps 18¹⁹ 'He brought me forth also into a large place'; Nu 24⁶ 'As the valleys are they spread forth'; 2 S 11¹ 'at the time when kings go forth to war.' This meaning is also expressed by 'abroad.' When 'forth' is used, it is always with a verb of motion; never as in Shaks. *Comedy of Errors*, II. ii. 212—

> 'Sirrah, if any ask for your master,
> Say, he dines forth, and let no creature enter.'

Then 'forth' expresses generally *movement away from a place*, as Gn 3²³ 'God sent him forth from the garden'; and more particularly movement *onwards from a given point*, as Jos 18¹¹ 'the coast of their lot came forth between the children of Judah and the children of Joseph' (RV 'the border of their lot went out'); Mt 9⁹ 'Jesus passed forth from thence' (RV 'by'); Ph 3¹³ 'forgetting those things which are behind, and reaching forth unto those things which are before' (RV 'stretching forward'). Cf. Ezk 6¹⁴ Cov. 'from the wildernesse off Deblat forth'; and Ps 72⁸ (Stern. and Hopk.) 'His large and great dominion shall from sea to sea extend: it from the river shall reach forth unto earth's utmost end.'

It is in this last sense only—'forward from a given point'—that 'forth' is used with expressions of time. These are: (1) 'from this time forth' (מֵעַתָּה Ps 113² 115¹⁸ 121⁸); (2) 'from that time forth' (מִן־הַיּוֹם הַהוּא Neh 4¹⁶; מֵהָעֵת הַהִיא 13²¹; ἀπὸ τότε, Mt 16²¹ [RV omits 'forth']); and (3) 'from that day forth' (ἀπ' ἐκείνης τῆς ἡμέρας, Mt 22⁴⁶, Jn 11⁵³).

In many of the foregoing expressions modern usage would prefer 'forward' or 'out.' In the following examples 'out' is distinctly the modern word: with *put*, Ac 9⁴⁰ 'Peter put them all forth' (so Gn 8⁹, Jg 6²¹, Mt 9²⁵); with *break*, 2 S 5²⁰ 'The LORD hath broken forth upon mine enemies'; with *give*, Ezk 18⁸·¹³ 'He that hath not given forth upon usury';* with *set*, Ezk 27¹⁰ 'they set forth thy

---

* Cf. Pref. to AV 1611, 'He gaue foorth, that hee had not seene any profit.'

comeliness'; with *spread*, Ezk 47[10] 'a place to spread forth nets' (RV 'for the spreading of nets'); with *cast*, Jon 1[5. 12. 15]; *let*, Lk 20[9] 'A certain man planted a vineyard, and let it forth to husbandmen' (RV 'out'); *look*, Ca 2[9] 'he looketh forth at the windows' (RV 'in,' Heb. מִן); or omitted altogether, as in Jn 2[11] 'Jesus . . . manifested forth his glory.'

The phrase 'forth of,' which occurs in AV Gn 8[16] 9[18], Jg 11[31], 2 Ch 23[14], Job 5[6], Am 7[17], Jth 2[21], has sometimes been taken to be a prep., as by Abbott (*Shaks. Grammar*, § 156). It seems, however, to be a contracted form of 'forth out of,' which is found Gn 8[19] 'Every beast . . . went forth out of the ark.' Thus Gn 8[16] 'Go forth of the ark'; Jg 11[31] 'whatsoever cometh forth of the doors of my house to meet me'; Am 7[17] 'Israel shall surely go into captivity forth of his land' (RV 'out of'); and even 2 Ch 23[14] 'Have her forth of the ranges' (RV 'forth between the ranks'). In illustration of the phrase, cf. Knox, *Hist.* 365, 'Herewith was the Queen more offended; and commanded the said *John* to passe forth of the Cabinet, and to abide further of her pleasure in the Chamber'; and his tr[n] of Ps 18[16] (*Works*, iii. 320), 'he hath drawen me forth of many waters'; and so Bacon, *Essays* ('Of Prophecies,' Gold. Treas. ed. p. 150, l. 13), 'In *Vespasians* Time, there went a *Prophecie* in the East: That those that should come forth of Iudea, should reigne over the World.' A further ellipsis sometimes takes place, the 'of' being omitted (not in AV), as Shaks. *Mids. Night's Dream*, I. i. 164—

> 'If thou lov'st me then,
> Steal forth thy father's house to-morrow night.'
>   J. HASTINGS.

FORTIFICATION, FORTRESS.—See WAR.

FORTUNATUS (Φορτούνατος), a member of the Church at Corinth, is mentioned in the first Epistle to that Church (16[17]) as having visited St. Paul at Ephesus, along with Stephanas and Achaicus. They had gone as deputies to seek the apostle's help and advice regarding certain ethical questions, and especially regarding marriage, meats offered to idols, and spiritual gifts, and to strengthen the tie between him and the Corinthians. The state of affairs which their statements disclosed is dealt with at length in the Epistle in which they are mentioned, and which most likely they carried back with them, perhaps in company with Titus. Weiss suggests that the way in which the names are mentioned, seems to show that F. and Achaicus in some way belonged to the house of Stephanas. The name F., which is Roman, was a very common one, and hence it is precarious to identify St. Paul's visitor, as some have proposed to do, with the F. mentioned by Clement of Rome (*Ep.* 59).   W. MUIR.

FORTY.—See NUMBER.

FORUM.—Only in *Appii forum* (so 1611, not *Forum* as in mod. ed.) Ac 28[15], one of the stages in St. Paul's journey to Rome. The Gr. 'Αππίου φόρον is a transliteration of the Lat., which has been taken directly into English. Wyclif translated the word: 'the cheping of Appius'; so did the Geneva translators, 'the Market of Appius,' whom RV follows. But the other versions present various forms of the Lat.: Tind. 'Apiphorum' (though he translates the other name 'the thre taverns'), so the Great Bible; Cov. 'Apiforum'; the Rhemish 'Apij-forum'; Matthew's Bible, the Bishops' Bible, and AV 'Appii forum.' See APPIUS (MARKET OF).

FORWARD, FORWARDNESS.—Forward is used both as adj. and as adv. in AV, but the adj.,

though independent in early Eng., seems to have been lost, and afterwards re-formed from the adverb. So the adv. properly comes first.

As an adv. 'forward' means 'towards the front,' as opposed to 'backward,' as Job 23[8] 'Behold I go forward, but he is not there; and backward, but I cannot perceive him,' and Nu 32[19] 'For we will not inherit with them on yonder side Jordan, or forward, because our inheritance has fallen to us on this side Jordan eastward' (הָלְאָה, 'further on,' as 1 S 20[22] 'the arrows are beyond thee,' הֶמָּה וָהָלְאָה, lit. 'from thee and onwards'). So Berners, *Froissart*, I. xvii. 18, 'All his barones went out of the cite, and the first nyght they lodged vi. myle forwarde.' In the same sense it is applied to time, as Ezk 39[22] 'from that day and forward'; 43[27] 'upon the eighth day, and *so* forward.' Cf. Stubbes, *Anat. Abus.* ii. 34, 'If sixtie would serue, they must have an hundred, and so forward.' A bold expression is found in 2 Es 3[6] 'before ever the earth came forward,' that is, into existence (*antequam terra adventaret*), a tr[n] retained in RV, though it is perhaps unique in Eng. literature.

When used figuratively with certain verbs 'forward' has the meaning of 'advance the interests of, help the progress of an undertaking.' The verbs in AV are (1) *set*, 1 Ch 23[4] 'to set forward the work of the house of the LORD' (נַצַּח, RV as AVm 'to oversee': so in Ezr 3[8. 9] RV changes AV 'set forward' into 'have the oversight,' though in 2 Ch 34[12] 'to set it forward' is accepted for the same * Heb. with RVm 'to preside over it'; and in 34[13] 'overseers' of AV is changed into 'set forward,' for Heb. מְנַצְּחִים). The phrase is applied to evil works as well as to good, Job 30[13] 'they set forward my calamity' (יֹעִילוּ); Wis 14[18] 'the singular diligence of the artificer did help to set forward the ignorant to more superstition' (προέτρεψατο, RV 'urged forward by the ambition of the artificer'). To those examples RV adds 1 Co 16[6] 'that ye may set me forward on my journey,' and 2 Co 1[16], 3 Jn 6 (all προπέμπω), where the meaning is somewhat different, to start one upon a journey. Shakespeare often uses the phrase intransitively (never trans. as here), as *I Henry IV*. II. iii. 38, 'We are prepared. I will set forward to-night.' The expression 'set forward' in this literal sense is also found in AV, but only in Nu, where it occurs 15 times of the marching of the Israelites in the Wilderness. (2) *Help*, only Zec 1[15] 'they helped forward the affliction' (עָזְרוּ לְרָעָה, RVm 'helped the evil'), that is, the heathen not only acted as God's instruments in chastising Israel, but went further. (3) *Haste*, only 1 Es 1[27] 'the Lord is with me hasting me forward' (ἐπισπεύδων). (4) *Bring*, only 3 Jn 6 'whom if thou bring forward on their journey after a godly sort, thou shalt do well' (RV 'set forward,' as above). The same meaning is found *intransitively* with *go* in Gn 26[13] 'waxed great, and went forward' (וַיֵּלֶךְ הָלוֹךְ וְגָדֵל, lit. as AVm, 'went going'; RV 'grew more and more'); and Ad. Est 13[4]. The literal sense occurs in Nu 2[24] 10[5] and ('go on forward') 1 S 10[3]. Cf. Goldsmith, *Vicar*, xi. (Globe ed. p. 21[a] l. 3), 'Mr. Burchell, who was of the party, was always fond of seeing some innocent amusement going forward'; and Shaks. *Mids. Night's Dream*, IV. ii. 17, 'If our sport had gone forward, we had all been made men.'

In modern English 'forward' as an adj. means presumptuous, impertinent. This meaning is found as early as the beg. of the 17th cent.; thus, Warner, *Alb. Eng.* IX. xlvii. 221, 'They tould how forward Maidens weare, how proude if in request.' But it

---

* The only remaining occurrence of the infin. is 1 Ch 15[21], where AV has 'to excel,' AVm 'to oversee,' and RV 'to lead.' The meaning is undoubtedly always 'to preside over,' whether workmen or more especially a choir of singers. The ptcp. seen in 2 Ch 34[13] is found in the title of many psalms and translated 'the chief (RV Chief) Musician.'

does not occur in AV. There the adj. means either *ready*, 2 Co 8[10] 'to be forward a year ago' (τὸ θέλειν, RV 'to will'), or *zealous*, 2 Co 8[17] 'being more forward, of his own accord he went unto you' (σπουδαιότερος, RV 'very earnest'); Gal 2[10] 'which I also was forward to do' (ἐσπούδασα, RV 'was zealous'); and 1 Mac 1[13], where the zeal is in a bad cause (προεθυμήθησάν τινες). Cf. Hall, *Contemplations* (*Works*, ed. 1634, ii. 52), 'What marvell is it if God bee not forward to give, where we care not to aske, or aske as if we cared not to receive?' and (for the meaning 'ready') Livingstone (*Select Biographies*, Wod. i. 229), 'Mr. James went back with him, and finding him forward to go in with him . . . believed him.'

Forwardness occurs once in Shakespeare, and then in later writers frequently in the mod. sense of over-confidence, presumption. *As You Like It*, I. ii. 159—

'Since the youth will not be intreated,
His own peril on his forwardness.'

But in AV the only meaning is readiness or zeal. Once it is in a bad cause, Wis 14[17] (σπουδή; RV 'zeal'); elsewhere only 2 Co 8[8] (σπουδή, RV 'earnestness'), and 9[2] 'I know the forwardness of your mind' (τὴν προθυμίαν ὑμῶν, RV 'your readiness'). So Hall (*Works*, ii. 16), referring to the Wise Men from the East, says, 'God encourages their holy forwardnesse from heaven.'

J. HASTINGS.

FOUL (Old Eng. *fúl*) is of the same root (Sanskrit *pū*, to stink) as Gr. πύον and Lat. *pūs*, purulent matter, as from a sore, and its earliest meaning is *loathsome*, whether to sight or smell. It is applied, for example, to blood, Wis 11[16] 'a perpetual running river troubled with foul blood,' in reference to the Egyptian plague (αἵματι λυθρώδει, the only occurrence of this adj. in bibl. Greek, lit. 'with blood like gore,' RV 'with clotted blood'). In this sense 'foul' is applied to disease, as Shaks. *Hamlet*, IV. i. 21—

'But, like the owner of a foul disease,
To keep it from divulging, let it feed
Even on the pith of life';

and *Lear*, I. i. 167—

'Kill thy physician, and the fee bestow
Upon thy foul disease.'

2. From this to *moral uncleanness* the step was easily and early made. In AV it is so applied only to unclean spirits, and only twice, Mk 9[25], Rev 18[2] (both ἀκάθαρτος).

The adj. ἀκάθαρτος is used 22 times in NT with πνεῦμα (Mt 2, Mk 11, Lk 5, Ac 2, Rev 2) and once with πνεῦμα δαιμονίου (Lk 4[33]). Tindale translates by 'unclean spirit' generally, but he gives 'foul spirit' in Mk 12[7] 5[8] 7[25], Lk 4[36] 6[18] 8[29], and is always followed by Cov., Cran., Gen., and (except in Mk 7[25]) Bish. Wyclif., and the Rhem. NT, after Vulg. *spiritus immundus*, have 'unclean spirit' everywhere. AV seems quite accidentally to retain 'foul' in Mk 9[25]; but in Rev 18[2] it is probably retained for variety, the same Gr. word as applied to birds being tr[d] 'unclean' in the same verse. RV gives 'unclean' everywhere.

Since ἀκάθαρτος is properly ceremonially unclean, the moral element is less prominent than when πονηρός is applied to πνεῦμα (Mt 12[45], Lk 7[21] 8[2] 11[26], Ac 19[12. 13. 15. 16], AV 'evil' or 'wicked,' RV always 'evil'), and consequently 'foul' with its suggestion of separation through loathsomeness is a very appropriate tr[n], and is frequently used of evil spirits, or their abode, in English literature. Thus Shaks. *Tam. of Shrew*, Induc. ii. 17—

'O, that a mighty man of such descent,
Of such possessions and so high esteem,
Should be infused with so foul a spirit.'

Cf. Watts, *Ps* cxxi. (L. M.) 25—

'On thee foul spirits have no power.'

Shaks. has 'foul devil' (*Rich. III.* I. ii. 50), and often 'foul fiend' (14 times, of which 11 are in K.)

Lear and always in the mouth of 'Edgar'), as *Rich. III.* I. iv. 58—

'With that, methoughts, a legion of foul fiends
Environed me.'

3. 'Foul' is often set in opposition to fair, and that (1) in the sense of *ugly*. Thus Chaucer, *Clerk-Merchant* (E. 1209)—

'If thou be fair, ther folk ben in presence
Shew thy thy visage and thyn apparaille;
If thou be foul, be fre of thy dispence,
To gete thee frendes ay do thy travaille.'

This is the meaning of Job 16[16] 'My face is foul with weeping,' though RVm gives 'defiled,' as if a closer rendering of the Heb. (חֳמַרְמַר); but the Heb. root is to be red, and the most probable tr[n] 'my face is red with weeping.' So Livingstone, *Select Biog.* 306, 'When he came out all his face was foul with weeping.' (2) As applied to weather: 1 Es 9[6] (χειμών), 9[11] (ὥρα χειμερινή), and Mt 16[3] (χειμών).

4. Foul is twice found in AV with the meaning of *disgraceful*: Sir 5[14] 'a foul shame is upon the thief' (αἰσχύνη; RV 'upon the thief there is shame'); 20[24] 'A lie is a foul blot in a man' (μῶμος πονηρός). Examples of both phrases are found in Shaks. Thus *Rich. III.* I. iii. 249—

'*Hast.*   False-boding woman, end thy frantic curse,
          Lest to thy harm thou move our patience.'
Q. Marg. Foul shame upon you! you have all moved mine';

and *Much Ado*, III. i. 64—

'Nature, drawing an antick,
Made a foul blot.'

5. The Amer. RV introduces 'foul' in the mod. sense of *dirty*: Is 19[6] 'And the rivers shall become foul' (AV 'And they shall turn the rivers far away'; RV 'And the rivers shall stink'). So Job 30[6] Cov. 'Their dwellings was beside foule brokes.' This is the meaning of the verb 'to foul' in Ezk 32[2] 34[18. 19], its only occurrences, where it refers to the polluting of running water.

J. HASTINGS.

FOUNDATION.—In the OT the words 'found' and 'foundation' are for the most part tr[n] of יָסַד and its derivatives, which are freely used in a metaphorical as well as a literal sense. The foundation stones of some of Solomon's buildings are described as huge and costly (1 K 7[10]). In connexion with the laying of the foundation stone various superstitious rites were widely practised, the offering of a human victim being a not infrequent accompaniment of the ceremony (see Trumbull, *Threshold Covenant*, 22, 51, 55; Strack, *Der Blutaberglaube*, 68). It is possible that the record of such an incident was embodied in the original form of the tradition preserved about Hiel the Bethelite, 'He laid the foundation [of Jericho] on (? בְּ) Abiram his firstborn, and set up the gates thereof on his youngest son Segub' (1 K 16[34]).

In NT 'foundation' is used in two distinct senses, an active and a passive. In the former sense it represents καταβολή (properly 'founding'), which (except in He 11[11] καταβολὴ σπέρματος, used of Sarah) is confined to the collocation καταβολὴ κόσμου, 'the foundation of the world,' Mt 13[35] 25[34], Lk 11[50], Jn 17[24], Eph 1[4], He 4[3] 9[26], 1 P 1[20], Rev 13[8] 17[8]. In the passive sense 'the foundations of the earth' (מוֹסְדֵי אֶרֶץ), once Job 38[6] אֲדָנִים 'pedestals,' once Ps 104[5] מְכוֹנוֹת 'bases') frequently appears in OT, Mic 6[2], Is 24[18] 40[21], Jer 31[37], Ps 82[5], Pr 8[29]. The passive sense of the word is in NT represented by θεμέλιος (both literal and metaphorical). This word is used, *e.g.*, in our Lord's simile of the two buildings (Lk 6[48f.]), as well as in St. Paul's simile of the building tested by fire (1 Co 3[10ff.]). In 1 Co 3[11] the Church's foundation is Christ, in Eph 2[20] she is built upon the foundation of (the gospel of) the apostles and (NT) prophets, Jesus Christ being the chief corner-stone.

In Jer 50[15], where AV has 'foundations,' the

meaning of אֲשִׁיה is prob. 'bulwarks' (RV) or 'buttresses' (see *Oxf. Heb. Lex.*). In Is 16⁷ 'raisin-cakes' seems to be the meaning, not 'foundations' (see FLAGON). The 'gate of the foundation' (שַׁעַר הַיְסוֹד) in 2 Ch 23⁵ is obscure. Perhaps we should read שַׁ׳ סוּר 'the gate Sur,' as in 2 K 11⁶, or שַׁ׳ הַסּוּסִים 'the horse gate' (see *Oxf. Heb. Lex. s.* יְסוֹד). In 2 Ch 3³ for AV 'these are the things wherein Solomon was instructed,' RV substitutes 'these are the foundations which Sol. laid' (taking הוּסַד as Hoph. infin. of יָסַד). RV further gives 'foundations' for 'posts' in Is 6⁴ as tr. of אַמּוֹת, a derivative from אֵם in metaph. sense. Finally, in two instances (Ps 89¹⁴ 97²) where AV tr. מָכוֹן 'habitation,' RV gives the correct sense 'foundation.'

J. A. SELBIE.

FOUNTAIN.—1. A fountain is a natural outflow, or spring, of water, and is in this way distinguished from a well of artificial construction (see WELL). Palestine, owing to its physical structure, is especially rich in fine springs of water. Remarkably appropriate is the statement (Dt 8⁷), 'For the Lord thy God bringeth thee into a good land, a land of brooks of water, of fountains (עֲיָנוֹת) and depths springing forth in valleys and hills.'

2. The Cretaceous limestone of which W. Palestine is mainly composed being open and porous, the rain (or snow) which falls during the winter months percolates downwards and forms underground reservoirs in the strata, which burst forth along the sides of the Jordan depression, as also on the western flanks of the central table-land.* Equally favourable is the geological structure of the eastern sides of the Jordanic depression for the production of springs; for the heavy falls of snow which cover the Lebanon and Hermon ranges in winter give rise to copious fountains which supply the head waters of the Litany, the Jordan, and the rivers of Damascus. Not less remarkable are some of the fountains of the region of Trachonitis and the Peræa, which have their sources in the volcanic mountains of the Hauran, and their outlets into the Jordan by the Hieromax and the Jabbok. Fine springs are also numerous along the western shore of the L. of Tiberias, scattering verdure and fertility along their course. Amongst the Edomite mountains and those of the Sinaitic peninsula the most important fountains are those of the Wady Musâ, which flows down through the city of Petra; the 'Ain Abu Werideh (or el-Weibeh), and 'Ain Ghurundel in the Arabah; the Wady el-'Ain at the entrance to the grand gorge of es-Sûḳ, between Jebel Musâ and 'Aḳabah; † and those which descend from the flanks of Jebel Mûsa (Mount Sinai) itself. The spring of 'Ain Ḳadis, which issues forth at the base of a limestone cliff in the Badiet et-Tîh (Wilderness of Paran), has been identified, with much probability, as the site of Kadesh-Barnea.‡

3. *Thermal Springs.*—Many of the springs which flow directly into the Dead Sea and the lower waters of the Jordan have a high temperature, due partly to the existence of volcanic rocks (basalt), still highly heated, with which the waters come in contact; and partly to the depth below the surface to which the underground waters descend before issuing forth into day.

The following are the most important thermal springs § :—

1. *Ḥammam* (or *Ḥammath*), situated on the W.

side of the Sea of Tiberias, near to which Herod the tetrarch built the city of that name.* Temp. 143·3° Fahr., water sulphurous.† **2.** *Yarmuk*, N. of Umm Ḳeis (Gadara). Temp. 109° Fahr., water sulphurous.‡ **3.** *Zerḳa Ma'in* (Callirrhoë), ten principal warm and sulphurous springs, of which the lowest reaches a temperature of 143° Fahr.§ Here Herod the Great bathed during his last illness.‖ **4.** *'Ain Zara* enters the Dead Sea on the E. side. Temp. 109° Fahr.¶ **5.** *'Ain es-Sulṭân*, in the Plain of Jericho (el-Ghôr), W. of the Jordan. Temp. 71° Fahr. (See ARABAH, JERICHO.) **6.** *'Ain el-Beida* enters the Wady el-Jeib S. of Jebel Usdum. Temp 91° Fahr. **7.** *'Ain el-Khubarah*, W. of the Dead Sea, water sulphurous. Temp. 88–93° Fahr.** **8.** *'Ain Feshkhah*, W. of the Dead Sea. Temp. 82° Fahr.†† **9.** The springs of Ænon ('*Ainun*) near to Salim in Samaria, where John baptized (Jn 3²³). According to Conder the head springs issue from an open valley, surrounded by desolate hills; but the water gushes forth over a stony bed and rapidly produces a fine perennial stream surrounded by oleanders.‡‡ **10.** *Kishon.* The springs forming the head waters of the Kishon are remarkable for their copiousness. Stanley describes them as 'full-grown from their birth.' They rise at the foot of Mt. Tabor and form a chain of pools and springs, together with quagmires and swamps, which were fatal to many of Sisera's army §§ (Jg 5²¹). The river enters the Mediterranean at the northern base of Mt. Carmel. **11.** *Baniâs.* The springs at the head of the Jordan at Baniâs (Cæsarea Philippi) issue from a cavern above the town, constituting the 'upper sources,' and are augmented by a still larger fountain below, which is known as 'the lower springs'; so that the Jordan is full-grown from its birth.‖‖ **12.** *The Jerusalem fountains.* Jerus. in former times was supplied from several sources; but we are here concerned only with the natural fountains. Of these the most remarkable are the *Upper Springs of Gihon*,¶¶ which are intermittent, and break out underground in the Kidron Valley (Wady en-Nar), forming the chief source of this stream, from whence the water is carried by an underground conduit to a pool, now known as the 'Fountain of the Virgin' ('*Ain Umm ed-Deraj*), to the west side of the City of David. This conduit, 1760 feet (or 1200 cubits) in length, was constructed by Hezekiah on the approach of the Assyrian army (2 K 20²⁰, 2 Ch 32³⁰). In 1880 a pupil of Schick observed an inscription which was afterwards deciphered by Sayce and Guthe. It contains in old Heb. characters a record of the construction.*** This fount is the only natural spring of water at Jerusalem, and is the chief source of supply of pure water at the present day. The *pools of Solomon*, near Bethlehem, were formerly the chief sources of supply for Jerus., and were conducted into the city by an upper and lower conduit hewn in stone, now fallen into disuse. The pools are supplied by a fine spring which issues

along the line of the great 'fault,' by which the valley is traversed. (See ARABAH.)

* Jos. *Ant.* XVIII. ii. 3.   † Lynch, *Off. Rep.* p. 202.
‡ Robinson, *Phys. Geog. Holy Land*, 24.
§ Tristram, *Land of Moab*, xiii. 247; Conder, *Heth and Moab*, 145, 149.
‖ Jos. *Ant.* XVII. vi. 5. This spring is also supposed to be that called 'En-eglaim' (spring of the calves), Ezk 47¹⁰.
¶ Lartet, *Voy. d'Explor.* 291.
** Tristram, *Land of Israel*, 305.   †† *Ib.* pp. 252–255.
‡‡ *Tent-Work in Palestine*, p. 50.   §§ *Ib.* pp. 69, 97.
‖‖ The springs rise at a level of about 1000 feet above the Mediterranean, and are joined by the waters of the Hasbany coming down from the western slopes of Hermon (Conder, *Tent-Work*, 215; Tristram, *Land of Israel*, 584).
¶¶ Explored by Robinson in 1838, and by Warren and Conder, *SWP* pt. II. 346 (1886), also *Recovery of Jerusalem*, 257.
*** Generally known as the Siloam Tablet; *SWP* ii. 346 (1886); *Recovery of Jerusalem*, 257; *ZDMG* (1882), pp. 725–750; Sayce, *HCM* 377 ff.; Driver, *Heb. Text of Sam.* xv.; Pilcher, *PSBA*, xix. 165 ff.

* The average rainfall at Jerus. is about 30 inches, nearly the whole of which falls between Nov. and Feb.; in the Lebanon it is probably considerably greater. See Glaisher, 'Meteorological Observations at Jerus.' in *PEFSt*, 1887–98.
† Described by Rüppell, Miss Martineau, Dean Stanley, and Major Kitchener (*Mount Seir*, App. 208).
‡ This fountain was discovered by Rowlands, and his identification of it with Kadesh-Barnea has been supported by Holland and Trumbull after personal inspection of the spot (*Kadesh-Barnea*, 1884).
§ Some of the Jordan Valley springs appear to burst forth

forth from the limestone rock above the upper pool. The water is still carried by a conduit to Bethlehem, and also fertilizes 'the gardens of Solomon' in the valley below.   E. HULL.

FOUNTAIN GATE.—See GATE and JERUSALEM.

FOUR.—See NUMBER.

FOURSQUARE.—Now that 'square' is confined to that which has *four* equal sides, 'foursquare' is looked upon as redundant, though writers like Ruskin, steeped in biblical phraseology, use it still. Formerly 'square' meant simply equal-sided, and the number of sides had to be expressed. Thus 'fivesquare,'1 K 6³¹ᵐ, taken from the text of the Geneva Bible, 'the upper poste and side postes were fiue square.' 'Foursquare' is used of the altar of burnt-offering (Ex 27¹ 38¹), of the incense-altar (Ex 30² 37²⁵), and of the high priest's breastplate (28¹⁶ 39⁹), the meaning being clearly expressed in 30² 'A cubit shall be the length thereof, and a cubit the breadth thereof; foursquare shall it be' (רָבֻעַ). It is also used of the borders of the brazen bases in Solomon's temple (1 K 7³¹ מְרֻבָּע); of the inner court of Ezekiel's temple (Ezk 40⁴⁷) and of the 'holy oblation' (48²⁰); and, finally, of the holy city, new Jerusalem (Rev 21¹⁶, τετράγωνος).

FOWL.—The word 'fowl,' now restricted to the domestic cock and hen, 'the barn-door fowl,' was formerly applied to all feathered animals, and occasionally even to all winged creatures. Thus Sir 11³ in Wyclif's trⁿ of 1382 is 'Short in foules (Vulg. *in volatilibus*) is a bee,' though Purvey's Revision of 1388 gives, 'A bee is litil among briddis.' Indeed, when Wyclif has to make a distinction between feathered and unfeathered creatures that fly, he uses 'fowl' of the latter : Ezk 39¹⁷ 'Saye thou to eche bryd, and to alle foulis' (אֱמֹר לְצִפּוֹר כָּל־כָּנָף, Vulg. *dic omni volucri et universis avibus*), though Rogers and Coverdale reverse the order, 'Speake unto alle the foules and euery byrde.' * And AV uses 'fowls' of unfeathered winged creatures in Lv 11²⁰ 'All fowls that creep, going upon all four, shall be an abomination unto you' (כֹּל שֶׁרֶץ הָעוֹף). This is Wyclif's trⁿ 'Alle of foules (1388, 'Al thing of foulis') that goth on foure feete'; after Vulg. *Omne de volucribus quod graditur super quatuor pedes*; and Tindale's, 'all foules that crepe and goo upon all iiii. shalbe an abhominacion unto you.' The LXX has πάντα τὰ ἑρπετὰ τῶν πετεινῶν; RV 'All winged creeping things' (see art. CREEPING THINGS).† T. Adams (*Works*, i. 13) distinguishes 'fowls' from 'flies': 'the eagles hunt no flies so long as there be fowls in the air.' He thus uses 'fowls' exactly as we now use 'birds,' and that was its commonest use by far. Thus Bacon, *Essays* (Gold. Treas. ed. p. 181, l. 22), 'Why, doe you not think me as wise, as some Fowle are, that ever change their Aboad towards the Winter?'

RV accepts the AV rendering 'fowl' or 'fowls' throughout OT, except Lv 11²⁰, Ezk 39¹⁷, already noted, and in the three passages in which the Heb. is עַיִט 'ayit, a bird of prey: Gn 15¹¹ (RV 'birds of prey'), Job 28⁷ (RV 'bird of prey'), Is 18⁶ (RV 'ravenous birds'). Cf. Bacon, *Essays* (p. 240, l. 2), 'But now, if a Man can tame this *Monster*, and bring her to feed at the hand, and govern her,

* The Geneva Bible of 1560 translated more accurately (as LXX Εἰπὸν παντὶ ὀρνέῳ πτεινῷ), 'Speake to euerie feathered foule.' This was accepted by AV, with marg. 'to the fowl of every wing.' RV has 'Speak unto the birds of every sort'; Siegfried, *Sprich zu den mannigfach beschwingten Vögeln.*

† This use was either unknown to or ignored by Shakespeare when he wrote, *Comedy of Errors*, III. i. 79—

'I pray thee, let me in.
Ay, when fowls have no feathers, and fish have no fin.

and with her fly other ravening Fowle, and kill them, it is somewhat worth'; and Milton, *PL* x. 274—

'A flock of ravenous fowl.'

In Wis 19¹¹ 'a new generation of fowls' (νέαν γένεσιν ὀρνέων) is changed into 'a new race of birds.' In NT the Gr. (always plu.) is either ὄρνεον (Rev 19¹⁷·²¹) or πετεινόν (Mt 6²⁶ 13⁴, Mk 4⁴·³², Lk 8⁵ 12²⁴ 13¹⁹, Ac 10¹² 11⁶), and, except in the two places in Ac, RV changes into 'birds.'   J. HASTINGS.

FOWL.—Neither in AV nor in RV has any system been followed in the rendering of the various words for birds in the Heb. original. These words are—**1.** עוֹף 'ôph. This word signifies collectively birds or winged creatures, It is often in the construct state with הַשָּׁמַיִם *the skies*. It corresponds with the Arab. *ṭair*, the root of which seems to signify to *fly*. It ought to be trᵈ everywhere *birds*. It is, however, more generally trᵈ *fowl*, but also often *birds* (Jer 4²⁵). It is usually collective (Ezk 31⁶·¹³), but sometimes singular (?) (Gn 1²¹·³⁰, Lv 17¹³). It is sometimes used for *carrion birds* (2 S 21¹⁰).

2. עַיִט 'ayit, usually collective (in Is 46¹¹ singular, applied to Cyrus) for *birds of prey*, is, however, trᵈ in AV *fowls* (Gn 15¹¹), RV *birds of prey*; also AV *fowls* (Job 28⁷, Is 18⁶), RV *birds of prey* and *ravenous birds*, AV and RV צִפּוֹר עַיִט *ravenous birds* (Ezk 39⁴).

3. צִפּוֹר *zippôr* is in many places a collective term for birds, from the root צָפַר *zāphar*, to 'twitter,' or 'chirp,' or 'whistle' (cf. Arab. *ṣafar*, to 'whistle'). It is used collectively, Gn 15¹¹, Lv 14⁴·⁵³, Dt 14¹¹, etc., where it is trᵈ AV and RV 'birds'; Dt 4¹⁷, Neh 5¹⁸, Ps 8⁸, where it is trᵈ EV 'fowl.' It is sometimes in construct state with כָּל־כָּנָף (Ezk 17²³ etc.), at others with כָּנָף (Ps 148¹⁰). *Zippôr*, like its Arab. equivalent *'uṣfûr*, is also used for the smaller twittering birds, particularly the sparrow (Ps 84³ etc.).

The *zippor* is said to nest in the cedar (Ps 104¹⁷), to flee to the mountains (Ps 11¹), to be taken in nets and snares (Ps 124⁷, Pr 6⁵, Am 3⁵). Four different ways of taking animals and birds are alluded to in a single passage (Job 18⁸⁻¹⁰). In all there are seven different Heb. words for the various sorts of traps. The 'cage full of birds' (Jer 5²⁷) may refer to the custom of hanging cages of birds on the trees, on which birdlime or snares are placed, or near which the sportsman lies concealed, to entice the birds by the singing of the captives (but see CAGE). The voice of the *zippôr* (Ec 12⁴) is the morning song, announcing the dawn.

4. בַּעַל כָּנָף *ba'al-kānâph* (Pr 1¹⁷), the 'possessor of a wing,' is a figurative expression for a bird.

5. In NT (and Sir 43¹⁴) πετεινά (or τὰ π.) is general for *birds*, by which it is trᵈ in RV, while AV gives *fowls* (Mt 13⁴, Lk 13¹⁹). When birds of prey are intended ὄρνεα is used (Rev 19¹⁷).

Birds are divided into *clean* and *unclean* (Dt 14¹¹⁻²⁰). Lv gives the list only of the unclean birds (11¹³⁻²⁰). The 'fowls that creep' or 'creeping thing that flieth,' RV 'winged creeping things' (Lv 11²⁰·²³, Dt 14¹⁹), may refer to such as the bats, and the insects that do not leap as well as fly (see full discussion in art. CREEPING THINGS). The birds allowed in sacrifice were *turtle-doves* and *pigeons* (Lv 1¹⁴⁻¹⁷), and *zippôrîm* (Lv 14⁴⁻⁵³). The last were prob. any twitterers or clean birds except the two above mentioned. Among the birds mentioned as having been used as food are *quails*, *partridges*, *fatted fowls* (barburîm, 1 K 4²³, see COCK), and *fowl* (zippôr, Neh 5¹⁸). The last may refer to small birds. It is prob. that the *sparrows*, sold two for a farthing and five for two farthings (Mt 10²⁹, Lk 12⁶), were for food. They and other small birds are caught and sold in immense numbers at this day, and at prices similar to those of our Saviour's day. **Cocks** and **hens** are mentioned in NT, and were doubtless used for food.

The *migrations of birds* are especially noteworthy in the Holy Land, as a country midway between the tropics and cooler regions of the north. They are noted in Scripture (Ca 2[11. 12], Jer 8[7]).

Their *singing* is also alluded to (Ec 12[4], Ps 104[12]), and their *flight* (Ex 19[4], Dt 32[11. 12]).

Eggs were eaten (Lk 11[12]). The eggs of wild birds, on which the hen was sitting, could be taken, but not the hen at the same time (Dt 22[6]). Ostrich eggs are mentioned (Job 39[14], see OSTRICH). 'Eggs that are left' (Is 10[14]) may refer to the supplementary eggs of the ostrich, or to the nests that have been deserted owing to fright of the parent birds. Eggs of serpents are alluded to (Is 59[5]). For the expression 'sitteth on eggs' (Jer 17[11] RV, AVm 'gathereth young'), see PARTRIDGE. Birds' nests are often found in places of worship (Ps 84[3]). For general subject of birds, their habits, etc., see NATURAL HISTORY.   G. E. POST.

FOWLER is marked by the *Oxf. Eng. Dict.* as 'now rare,' the more commonplace 'bird-catcher' being its substitute. It is found in AV, Ps 124[7] (יָקוֹשׁ, ptcp. of [יָקַשׁ] to lay snares); Hos 9[8] (יָקוּשׁ [all]); Ps 91[3], Pr 6[5] (יָקוּשׁ, found also in Jer 5[26], AV 'he that setteth snares'; RV 'fowlers,' which is Wyclif's word). Shaks. has the word but once—*Mids. Night's Dream*, III. ii. 20—

> 'As wild geese that the creeping fowler eye.'

For **Fowling** see under HUNTING.

FOX (שׁוּעָל *shû'âl*, ἀλώπηξ, *vulpes*).—There can be no doubt that *shû'âl* meant both *jackal* and *fox*. It is used in the sing. only once in OT (Neh 4[3]), where the intention is doubtless to refer to a small animal, and *fox* is more likely to be meant than *jackal*. The plural *shû'âlim* is used in a number of places in OT. AV has tr[d] it in all of them *foxes*. In two of these (Jg 15[4], Ps 63[10]) the context makes it pretty certain that the *jackal* is intended. In the first passage Samson is said to have caught 300 *shû'âlim*. This would be well-nigh impossible in the case of foxes, which are shy, solitary animals, but not difficult in that of jackals, which are gregarious. In the second the expression 'they shall be a portion for foxes' implies a carrion-eater. Foxes may sometimes join other animals in feasting on the slain, but it is jackals that share with vultures the carcase of a battlefield. In the other passages of OT *shû'âlim* may mean either animal, though the context points rather to the habits of the fox than to those of the jackal. Thus La 5[18] represents *shû'âlim* as walking on the ruins of Zion, and Ezk 13[4] '*shû'âlim* in the deserts' (RV 'waste places'), and Ca 2[15] speaks of 'the foxes, the little foxes that spoil the vines' (RV 'vineyards'). A special word for *jackals* occurs in OT אִיִּים (see DRAGON under תַּנִּים, and JACKAL).

The Gr. ἀλώπηξ means the fox only. In NT the sing. occurs once (Lk 13[32]), where Herod is spoken of as a fox. Here the reference is to the well-known cunning of this animal. It occurs twice in the plu. (Mt 8[20], Lk 9[58]) 'foxes have holes.'

The fox of Syria does not differ essentially from the common fox of Europe, *Vulpes vulgaris*, L. Its body is about 14 in. long, and its bushy tail almost as long. It is of a grey colour, has a long pointed snout, and small cunning eyes. It is a nocturnal animal, prowling about houses and encampments. It captures poultry, and small birds and animals. It is also very fond of grapes, and both it and the jackal do much mischief in vineyards.   G. E. POST.

FRAGMENT.—The word κλάσμα (from κλάειν, to break) is used in the plu. (κλάσματα) of the remains of the loaves and fishes in the account of the Feeding of the Five Thousand (Mt 14[20], Mk 6[43], Lk 9[17], Jn 6[12. 13]), the Four Thousand (Mt 15[37], Mk 8[8]), and in the reference to these miracles (Mk 8[19. 20]), and it is used nowhere else in NT.[*]

The Versions have offered a great variety of trⁿ. Wyclif varies between 'broken gobbets' (Mt 14[20]), 'relefis' (Mt 15[37], Mk 8[8], Jn 6[12. 13]), and 'broken meat' or 'metis.' Tind. has 'gobbets' in Mt 14[20] and Mk 6[43], elsewhere 'broken meate' (1526 ed. in Mk 8[20] 'levinges'). Rogers (Matthew's Bible) introduces 'scrappes' (Mt 14[20]), has 'gobbettes' in Mk 6[43], and 'broken meate' in the rest. Coverdale gives 'broken meate' everywhere except Mk 6[43] 'broken peces.' The Great Bible offers 'fragments' as a new trⁿ (Mt 14[20]), and 'leauinges' (Mk 8[20]), says simply 'baskettes full of' in Mk 6[43], and for the rest has 'broken meate.' The Geneva and Bishops' Bibles follow the Great Bible in all places except Mk 6[43] 'fragments,' and (Gen. 1560 only) Mt 15[37] 'fragments' again. The Rhemish NT prefers 'fragments' everywhere except Mt 14[20] 'leauings.' AV accepts 'fragments' in all but the two passages which refer to the miracle of the Four Thousand, where it falls back on the rendering 'broken meat.' RV chooses 'broken pieces' (which has appeared only once before, Mk 6[43] Cov.), and uses it consistently throughout.

Why were the Revisers not content with AV 'fragments'? 'For some mysterious reason,' says Sir Edmund Beckett (*Should the Revised New Test. be Authorised?* 1882, p. 91), 'they prefer "broken pieces" to "fragments that remained over" of the two sets of loaves and fishes. We have all heard of "broken victuals"; but the victuals were once whole, and had been broken. Each piece of bread or fish is a piece, and not broken, though broken off, if they will be so precise. But a fragment is a piece broken off. So here is another miserable bit of pedantry of some kind, and for some unknown reason, which only turns right into wrong for nothing; for the AV is certainly quite as accurate a translation: indeed the Durham Greek professor said more so.'

But there are two good reasons. In the first place the word 'fragment' carries, and has always carried, a sense of contempt. Shaks. uses the word seven times, and this is always present, mostly prominent. The aptest instance is perhaps *Troil. and Cress.* v. ii. 159—

> 'The fragments, scraps, the bits, and greasy reliques
> Of her o'er-eaten faith, are bound to Diomed.'

Cf. T. Fuller, *Holy Warre*, iv. 16 (p. 195), 'Yea, now full willingly would the Christians have accepted the terms formerly offered them; and now their hungrie stomachs would make dainties of those conditions which before, when full of pride, they threw away as fragments.' In the second place the 'broken pieces' were not fragments of larger pieces; all that the disciples gave to the multitude were 'broken pieces,' and these which were gathered up were the broken pieces that were in excess of the requirements.   J. HASTINGS.

FRAME.—To 'frame' (from Old Eng. *framian*, to profit, succeed) is primarily to make good progress, to prosper, as Melville, *Diary*, p. 272, 'The Bischope haid lurked a yeir or twa lyk a tod in his holl, as his custom was when things framed nocht with him.' Then it is used in a neutral sense, to get on well or ill as the case may be, as Rutherford, *Letters*, No. xxxii., 'But let us, however matters frame, cast over the affairs of the bride upon the Bridegroom.' And then come the various transitive meanings of preparing, fitting for use. In AV the verb is used with a direct object, except once with a foll. infinitive.

1. To contrive, to manage, Jg 12[6] 'he could not frame to pronounce it right' (יָכִין לְדַבֵּר כֵּן, lit. 'fix to speak so,' perhaps 'fix the mind,' *i.e.* catch the slight difference in the pronunciation).

[*] Its occurrences in LXX are Lv 26 6[21], Jg 9[53] 19[5], 1 S 30[12], 2 S 11[21. 22], Ezk 13[19]; where EV give 'piece,' except Jg 19[6] 'morsel' (of bread), and Ezk 13[19] 'handful' (of barley).

Cf. *Return from Parnass.* IV. v. 62 (2nd pt.), 'Schollers must frame to liue at a low sayle.'

2. To direct, Hos 5[4] 'They will not frame their doings to turn unto their God' (לֹא יִתְּנוּ, lit. as AVm 'they will not give'; RV as AVm. 'Their doings will not suffer them to turn unto their God,' with AV text in marg.). Cf. Rutherford, *Letters*, No. clxxxvii., 'Frame yourself for Christ, and gloom not upon his Cross': Ps 145[21] (L. M.), Stern. and Hopk.—

    'Therefore my mouth and lips I'll frame
      To speak the praises of the Lord.'

3. To form, Is 29[16] 'Shall the thing framed say of him that framed it, He had no understanding?' (אָמַר לְיֹצְרוֹ יֵצֶר; Amer. RV 'formed'); and in RV, Job 10[8] 'Thine hands have framed me and fashioned me' (עִצְּבוּנִי; AV 'made me'). So Ps 106[19], Stern. and Hopk.—

    'Upon the hill of Horeb they an idol-calf did frame';

and Shaks. *Merch. of Venice*, I. i. 51—

    'Nature hath framed strange fellows in her time.'

4. To fit together, make, Eph 2[21] 'all the building fitly framed together' (συναρμολογουμένη); He 11[3] 'the worlds were framed by the word of God' (κατηρτίσθαι); and in RV, Eph 4[16] 'all the body fitly framed and knit together' (συναρμολογούμενον). Cf. Spenser, *FQ* II. ii. 30—

    'And, thinking of those branches green to frame
    A girlond for her dainty forehead fit,
    He pluckt a bough; out of whose rift there came
    Smal drops of gory bloud, that trickled down the same.'

5. To devise, Ps 50[19] 'thy tongue frameth deceit' (תַּצְמִיד); 94[20] 'which frameth mischief' (יֹצֵר); Jer 18[11] 'Behold, I frame evil against you' (יוֹצֵר); and in Amer. RV, Dt 31[21] 'I know their imagination which they frame' (עֹשֶׂה, lit. 'do,' EV 'go about'). So Barclay (1514), *Cyt.* (Percy Soc.) 23—

    'Than frame they fraudes men slyly to begyle';

and Ps 10[2], Stern. and Hopk.—

    'In these devices they have framed
    Let them be taken sure.'

6. To express, embody, 2 Mac 15[39] 'speech finely framed delighteth the ears of them that read the story' (τὸ τῆς κατασκευῆς τοῦ λόγου; RV 'the fashioning of the language'). AV is a modification of the Geneva tr[n], 'the setting out of the matter,' and may be illustrated from Milton, *PL* v. 460—

    'His wary speech
    Thus to th' empyreal minister he framed.'

As a subst. 'frame' occurs twice in AV, and means something constructed. 1. The structure of the body, Ps 103[14] 'he knoweth our frame; he remembereth that we are dust' (יִצְרֵנוּ). To this RV adds Ps 139[15] 'My frame was not hidden from thee, when I was made in secret' (עָצְמִי, AV 'my substance,' AVm 'or, strength; or, body'); and Amer. RV, Job 41[12] 'his [leviathan's] goodly frame' (עֶרְכּוֹ חִין, EV 'his comely proportion'). So frequently in *Paraphrases in Verse* (1775), as 57[4]—

    'With sympathetic feelings touch'd
    He knows our feeble frame';

and 51[4]—

    'We know, that when the soul uncloath'd
    Shall from this body flie,
    Twill animate a purer frame
    With life that cannot die.'

2. The structure of a city, Ezk 40[2] 'a very high mountain, by which was as the frame of a city' (כְּמִבְנֵה־עִיר, Davidson, 'a building of a city, that is, a city-like or citadel-like building').

3. RV adds Nu 4[10. 12], a frame *fitted together* for carrying things upon (מוֹט, AV 'bar').

                           J. HASTINGS.

FRANKINCENSE (לְבֹנָה *lĕbhônâh*, λίβανος, λιβαν-ωτός).—*Lebhônâh* is erroneously tr[d] in some places in AV 'incense' (Is 43[23] 60[6], Jer 6[20] etc. In RV it is correctly rendered *frankincense*). Incense, however, is the proper rendering of another word קְטֹרָה *kĕṭôrâh*. This substance was compounded of f. and other aromatic gums, and *seasoned with salt* (Ex 30[34. 35]), or *sweet*, *i.e.* not so seasoned (Ex 25[6], Lv 16[12]). All incense not so made was a strange incense, and could not be offered (Ex 30[9], cf. 'strange fire' Lv 10[1]).

F. is the fragrant resin of an Indian tree, *Boswellia serrata*, Stackh., procured by slitting the bark. It is imported through Arabia (Is 60[6], Jer 6[20]). It is known in Arabia by a name kindred to the Heb., *i.e. lubân*. It was one of the gifts offered by the Magi (Mt 2[11]). The 'incense' of both AV and RV (Rev 8[3]) should be 'frankincense.'

                           G. E. POST.

FRANKISH VERSION.—See VERSIONS.

FRANKLY.—In Lk 7[42] the verb ἐχαρίσατο is tr[d] 'he frankly forgave.' The older VSS have simply 'he forgave' (except Wyclif, 1380, 'he gaf frely'), and RV returns to that. The purpose of the AV translators was, no doubt, to bring out on a special occasion the special force of this word, which, as Bruce says (*Expos. Gr. Test. ad loc.*), is a warmer word than ἀφιέναι, and was welcome to St. Luke as containing the idea of grace (χάρις). It occurs only in the writings of St. Luke (Lk 7[21. 42. 43], Ac 3[14] 25[11. 16] 27[24]) and St. Paul (Ro 8[32], 1 Co 2[12], 2 Co 2[7. 10] 12[13], Gal 3[18], Eph 4[32], Ph 1[29] 2[9], Col 2[13] 3[13 bis], Philem 22]).

The Eng. word 'frankly' is used, not in the mod. sense of *candidly, openly*, but in the old and literal sense of *freely, unrestrainedly*, as in Elyot, *The Governour*, ii. 234, 'puttynge out of their citie their women and all that were of yeres unhabill for the warres, that they mought more frankely sustayne famyne'; and in Shaks. *Meas. for Meas.* III. i. 106—

    'O, were it but my life,
    I'ld throw it down for your deliverance
    As frankly as a pin.'

                           J. HASTINGS.

FRANTICK.—Sir 4[30] 'Be not as a lion in thy house, nor frantick among thy servants' (φαντασιοκοπῶν, lit. 'conceiving fancies,' RV 'fanciful': Fritzsche understands 'suspicious,' 'mistrustful,' *argwöhnisch*, and is followed by Ball [*QPB*]; but Bissell thinks the AV tr. suits the context best, and translates 'as a crazy man'). Tindale has 'frantick' for AV 'lunatick' in Mt 17[15] 'Master have mercy on my soune for he is franticke'; and Sir T. More (*Workes*, p. 270) uses the word in nearly the same sense of Luther, 'And therfore among many folishe wordes of Luther, as foolishe as euer heretyke spake, he neuer spake a more frantike, than in that he saith that God hath nede of our faith.'

FRAY occurs in Zec 1[21] of the terrifying of the 'horns' of the Gentiles, and 'fray away' in Dt 28[26], Jer 7[33] of the driving away of wild beasts from a dead body (all as tr[n] of הֶחֱרִיד). Amer. RV prefers 'frighten.' 'Fray' is also found in 1 Mac 14[12] 'every man sat under his vine and his fig tree, and there was none to fray them' (οὐκ ἦν ὁ ἐκφοβῶν αὐτούς, RV 'to make them afraid'); and 'fray away' in Sir 22[20] 'whoso casteth a stone at the birds frayeth them away' (ἀποσοβεῖ αὐτά).

Fray is what philologists call an aphetic form of 'affray.' That is to say, the old vb. 'affray' lost its unaccented initial vowel by aphesis [ἀφίεναι], as 'esquire' became 'squire,' and the like; and this happened to 'affray' while still spelt 'afray,' a spelling preserved in its past ptcp. 'afraid' (='afrayed'). To 'fray' is therefore originally to 'disturb' (Anglo-Fr. *afrayer*, late Lat. *ex-fridare*, from *ex* and *fridus* [Old High Ger. *fridu*], 'peace'), a meaning well illustrated by the examples in AV.

In Hos 10[11] Cov. uses both forms, 'Yee as a lyon roareth he, that they maye be afrayed, like the children of the see: that they may be scarred awaye from Egipte, as men scarre byrdes: and frayed awaye (as doues use to be) from the Assirians londe.' The only occurrence of the vb. in Shaks. is *Troil. and Cress.* III. ii. 24 : 'She does so blush, and fetches her wind so short, as if she were frayed with a sprite.'   J. HASTINGS.

FRECKLE.—In Lv 13[39] Tindale uses this word as tr[n] of Heb. *bôhak̦*, which occurs only in this place : 'Yf there appeare in their flesh a glisterynge white somewhat blackesh, then it is but frekels growen upp in the skynne : and he is cleane.' Wyclif's tr[n] (1382) was 'a wemme of whijt colour,' (1388) 'a spotte of whijt colour' (after Vulg. *macula coloris candidi*, whence also Douay, 'a spotte of white colour'). Cov. preferred 'a whyte scabbe,' Gen. 'a white spot.' But the Bishops' restored 'freckle' (in sing. 'a freckle'), and that was accepted by AV, 'a freckled spot.' RV prefers 'a tetter,' for the Heb. means more than we now understand by 'freckle,' though that word formerly described an eruption on the skin, as in Whitehead, *Goat's Beard*—

'The freckles, blotches, and parch'd skins,
The worms, which, like black-headed pins,
Peep through the damask cheek, or rise
On noses bloated out of size,
Are things which females ought to dread.'

The word occurs also in Preface to AV 1611, 'A man may be counted a vertuous man, though hee haue made many slips in his life (els, there were none vertuous, for *in many things we offend all*), also a comely man and louely, though hee haue some warts vpon his hand, yea, not onely freakles vpon his face, but also skarres'—where also the word probably means more than it does now. See TETTER.   J. HASTINGS.

FREE, FREEDOM, FREELY.—The adj. *free* 'has been a chief heirloom from Saxon times, and has made a figure in all stages of the national story. Perhaps no other Saxon adj. is comparable for length and variety of career. Originally meaning lordly, noble, gentle, it has with each change of the national aim so changed its usage as still to take a prominent place. In the growth of the municipal bodies the privileged members were designated *free-men*; in the constitutional struggles it managed to represent the idea of liberty; and in these latter days, when social equality is the universal pretension, it signifies the manners thereon attendant in the modern coupling *free and easy.*'—Earle, *Philology of the Eng. Tongue*[5], 413.

The most modern meaning to be found in AV is also the most common, and it may be best to begin with that and work backwards.

1. *At liberty, not fettered,* whether physically, as Milton, *Samson Agonistes*, 1235—

'My heels are fetter'd, but my fist is free';

or morally, as Locke, *Human Underst.* II. xxi. 8, 'So far as a man has a power to think or not to think, to move or not to move, according to the preference or direction of his own mind, so far is a man free.' So Job 3[19] 'The small and great are there; and the servant is free from his master' (שָׁפְחִי, the common Heb. word), and 1 P 2[16] 'As free, and not using your liberty for a cloke of maliciousness, but as the servants of God' (ἐλεύθερος, the common Gr. word).

Passages deserving attention are : (1) Ps 88[5] 'Free among the dead' (חׇפְשִׁי בַּמֵּתִים, RV 'cast off among the dead,' RVm 'cast away'). Hitzig, Ewald, and others tr. 'among the dead is my couch' (taking חׇפְשִׁי from חׇפַשׁ, something spread, a couch, after the doubtful occurrence in Ezk 27[20]); but most edd. now, as AV or RV (taking the word as the adj. usually tr[d] 'free'). Cheyne in 'Parchment' *Psalms* (1884) gives, 'I am one turned adrift among the dead'; but in *Book of Psalms* (1888), 'I am a freedman among the dead,' remarking there, 'The psalmist

alludes to the grim eulogy of death in his favourite poem Job 3[19] [see above]. But he gives a new turn to the phrase. Unlike Job, he regards such freedom as the reverse of a benefit'— which Kirkpatrick describes as 'a far-fetched interpretation.' There is no question, however, that the phrase recalls Job 3[19] to our minds, and yet that the word is used here, and here only, in a bad sense. It means either separated from human friendship, or more probably from divine protection. Delitzsch's interpretation, *set free, discharged,* from the responsibilities of life, like Lat. *defunctus,* is less appropriate to the context. The cognate subst. חׇפְשׁוּת [חׇפְשִׁית] is used in 2 K 15[5]=2 Ch 26[21] of the *separate* house or lazaretto to which Uzziah was confined. (2) Ac 22[28] 'And Paul said, But I was *free* born.' The Gr. is simply Ἐγὼ δὲ καὶ γεγέννημαι, 'But I was even born'; the word to be supplied is, however, Ῥωμαῖος, 'Roman,' from the previous verse : so RV 'But I am a Roman born.'

RV adds Is 45[13] 'he shall let my exiles go free' for AV 'let go my captives' (גׇּלוּתִי).

2. *Unhindered, unimpeded,* as Shaks. *Love's Labour's Lost*, v. ii. 732, 'For mine own part, I breathe free breath.' So 1 Es 4[53] 'And that all they that went from Babylon to build the city should have free liberty' (ὑπάρχειν τὴν ἐλευθερίαν, RV 'should have their freedom'); 2 Th 3[1] 'Pray for us, that the word of the Lord may have free course' (τρέχῃ, lit. 'may run,' as AVm and RV). The AV tr[n] is a combination of Tind. 'maye have fre passage' and Rhem. 'may have course'; RV is a return to Wyclif's 'that the word of God renne.' RV adds with this sense 1 Co 7[39] 'If the husband be dead, she is free to be married to whom she will' (ἐλευθέρα, AV 'at liberty').

3. *Exempt,* Dt 24[5] 'When a man hath taken a new wife he shall not go out to war, neither shall he be charged with any business; but he shall be free at home one year' (נׇקִי), *i.e.* exempt from public duties. 1 Ch 9[33] 'the Levites, who remaining in the chambers were free' (פְּטוּרִים, RV 'free from service'); 1 Mac 15[7] 'And as concerning Jerusalem and the sanctuary, let them be free' (ἐλεύθερα, *sc.* from tribute); Mt 15[6]=Mk 7[11] 'he shall be free' —words added *in italics* to complete the sense without equivalent in Greek; they are omitted by RV; Mt 17[26] 'Then are the children free.' RV adds He 13[5] 'Be ye free from the love of money' (ἀφιλάργυρος ὁ τρόπος, AV 'Let your conversation be without covetousness'; RVm 'Let your turn of mind be free': Vaughan is more modern and literal, 'Let your disposition be unavaricious').

4. *Acquitted* after trial, often equivalent to *innocent,* as Shaks. *Hamlet,* II. ii. 590—

'He would drown the stage with tears,
And cleave the general ear with horrid speech;
Make mad the guilty, and appal the free,
Confound the ignorant; and amaze, indeed,
The very faculty of eyes and ears.'

In AV, Nu 5[19. 28. 31 RV]; and the verb Ro 6[7] 'For he that is dead is freed from sin' (δεδικαίωται, RV 'is justified'), *i.e.* is acquitted from the guilt of sin.

5. *Voluntary, gratuitous,* Ex 21[11] 'then shall she go out free without money' (חִנׇּם, RV 'for nothing'). So the phrase 'free gift,' 1 Es 2[9] (εὐχαῖς, *i.e.* votive offerings, RV 'gifts that were vowed'); Jth 4[14] (ἑκούσια δόματα), 1 Mac 10[39] (δόμα, RV 'a gift'); Ro 5[15. 16. 18] (χάρισμα [not in v.[18], but understood there also], a word which is almost peculiar to St. Paul, occurring elsewhere only in 1 P 4[10], and 'is used of those special endowments which come to every Christian as the result of God's free favour (χάρις) to men, and of the consequent gift of faith'—Sanday-Headlam, *Romans,* p. 358 ff. It is tr[d] 'free gift' only in Ro 5[15. 16], to which RV adds 6[23]; elsewhere simply 'gift'). So again we find 'free offering' for the usual 'freewill offering' in Ex 36[3], Am 4[5], Jth 16[18].

6. *Generous* or even *noble,* the earliest meaning of the word according to Earle (as above), who quotes Shaks. *Troil. and Cress.* IV. v. 139—

'I thank thee, Hector :
Thou art too gentle and too free a man.'

This is Chaucer's meaning also in *Nonne Preestes Tale*, 94—

> 'For certes, what so any womman seith,
> We alle desyren, if it mighte be,
> To han housbondes hardy, wyse, and free.'

This sense occurs twice in AV, 2 Ch 29³¹ 'And the congregation brought in sacrifices and thank offerings; and as many as were of a free heart burnt offerings' (RV 'willing'), and Ps 51¹² 'uphold me with thy free spirit' (RV 'with a free spirit,' Amer. RV and RVm 'willing'; both דְרִיב, which as a subst. means 'prince,' 'noble,' in Pr 25⁷ and elsewhere).

On Ps 51¹² Earle (*The Psalter of* 1539, p. 290) says, 'So 1535 [Coverdale's Bible] after the Vulg. *et spiritu principali confirma me*'—which, again, is after Sept. πνεύματι ἡγεμονικῷ στήρισόν μι. Here there can be no doubt that 'free' was used, not in any of its lower senses, as when it is the equivalent of *liber* as opposed to *servus*; or even in the sense of liberal, bounteous in gifts; but (inclusive perhaps of this latter) with special eye to that higher sense of lordly, noble, generous, princely, royal; which is conspicuous in the best mediæval usage of the word, and which qualified it to represent *principalis* and ἡγεμονικόν. Keble brought this out well—

> 'With that free Spirit blest,
> Who to the contrite can dispense
> The princely heart of innocence.'

Keble, it should be added, has also suggested the correct translation. What the psalmist prays for is not, as AV, that he may be upheld by God's free Spirit, but, as RV, that under the influence of the Spirit of God his own spirit may become willing or spontaneous in the right.

Freedom in Ac 22²⁸ 'With a great sum obtained I this freedom,' is Roman citizenship (πολιτεία, RV 'citizenship'). See CITIZENSHIP. RV has changed 'liberty' of AV into 'freedom' for Gr. ἐλευθερία in Gal 5¹·¹³ *bis*, 1 P 2¹⁶, though retaining 'liberty' for the same Gr. word in Ro 8²¹, 1 Co 10²⁹, 2 Co 3¹⁷, Gal 2⁴, Ja 1²⁵ 2¹², 2 P 2¹⁹. In every case but the last it is the freedom of those who are not under law but under grace; 'freedom' is therefore the best word, and might have been used throughout. See LIBERTY.

Freely is found in the sense of (1) *unrestrainedly*, as in Lv 14⁵³ Wyc. 'And whanne he had left the sparewe to fle in to the feeld frely'; and in AV Gn 2¹⁶ 'Of every tree of the garden thou mayest freely eat' (אָכֹל הֹאכֵל, lit. 'eating thou shalt eat,' as AVm; so 1 S 14³⁰); Ad. Est 16¹⁹ 'that the Jews may freely live after their own laws' (χρῆσθαι, RV 'live'); Ac 2²⁹ 'let me freely speak unto you' (ἐξὸν εἰπεῖν μετὰ παρρησίας, RV 'I may say unto you freely'); 26²⁶ 'I speak freely' (παρρησιαζόμενος λαλῶ); to which RV adds Jn 2¹⁰ 'when men have drunk freely' (ὅταν μεθυσθῶσιν), lit. 'when they are drunken,' as Lk 12⁴⁵, and as Vulg. here 'cum inebriati fuerint.' Wyclif has 'whanne men ben fulfillid' (1382 'filled'); Tind. 'when men be dronke,' so Matthew's and the Great Bibles; Cov. 'whan they are dronken'; but the Geneva preferred 'when men have wel droncke,' and it was followed by Bish., Rhem., and AV. RV is a compromise between the two older translations.

(2) *For nothing, gratuitously*: the most common meaning. It occurs in Nu 11⁵ 'We remember the fish, which we did eat in Egypt freely' (חִנָּם 'gratis,' or as RV 'for nought'). 'Freely' was Wyclif's trⁿ [1388, but 1382 'gladly'], and he no doubt used the word in the sense of 'for nothing' after LXX δωρεάν and especially Vulg. *gratis*, which gave the Douay 'gratis'; 'freely' is the Bishops' word also; but all others 'for nought' (Tind., Rog.), or 'for naught' (Cov., Gen.). Also in 1 Mac 10³³ 'I freely set at liberty every one of the Jews' (ἀφίημι ἐλευθέραν δωρεάν, RV 'I set at liberty without price'); cf. Lk 4¹⁸ Tind. 'frely to set at liberty them that are bruised' (an attempt to express the pregnant phrase ἀποστεῖλαι τεθραυσμένους ἐν ἀφέσει, lit. 'to send away the shattered [so as to be] in release'). And in NT δωρεάν 'as a gift,' from δωρεά, a gift, is so rendered in Mt 10⁸ *bis*, Ro 3²⁴,

2 Co 11⁷, Rev 21⁶ 22¹⁷, where the prominent thought is the *grace* (gratis) of the giver, as Mt 10⁸ 'freely ye received, freely give.' And this is no doubt the meaning in Ro 8³² and 1 Co 2¹² where χαρίζομαι is trᵈ 'freely give.' Illustrations are Ex 21¹¹ Wyc. 'sche schal go out freli without money' (AV 'free,' RV 'for nothing'); Is 52⁵ Cov. 'my people is frely caried awaye' (EV 'for nought'); and Shaks. *Winter's Tale*, I. i. 19, 'You pay a great deal too dear for what's given freely.'

(3) *Voluntarily, spontaneously*, approaching the meaning of 'generous,' 'noble' given last for 'free': Ps 54⁶ 'I will freely sacrifice unto thee' (בִּנְדָבָה, RV 'with a freewill offering,' after most commentators, but Cheyne prefers 'with a free will' both here and at Nu 15³); Hos 14⁴ 'I will heal their backsliding, I will love them freely' (נְדָבָה, LXX ὁμολόγως, Vulg. *spontanee*, Wyc. [1382] 'of my free will,' [1388] 'wilfuli'; Rog. 'wyth al my heart,' Gen. 'frely,' Dou. 'voluntarily,' Cheyne 'spontaneously'). And this is the meaning of 'freely' in Ezr 2⁶⁸ (RV 'willingly') 7¹⁵, where it is used to bring out the force of the Heb. verb. This is Milton's meaning (*PL* viii. 443) where God addresses Adam—

> 'My image, not imparted to the brute;
> Whose fellowship therefore, unmeet for thee,
> Good reason was thou freely shouldst dislike.'

Freeman: 1 Es 3¹⁹ (ἐλεύθερος); 1 Co 7²² 'the Lord's freeman' (ἀπελεύθερος, RV 'freedman,' so as to bring out the spiritual emancipation and to distinguish from the natural 'freeman' (ἐλεύθερος) following. RV adds Col 3¹¹ (ἐλεύθερος, AV 'free').

Freewoman: 1 Mac 2¹¹, Gal 4²²·²³·³⁰, all ἐλευθέρα, of the natural condition, and directly opposed to 'bond-slave' (1 Mac) or 'bondmaid' (Gal). RV adds Gal 4³¹.   J. HASTINGS.

FREEWILL OFFERING.—See SACRIFICE.

FREQUENT.—In the sense of crowded, well-attended, 'frequent' is common in writers of the 17th cent. and earlier, as a 'frequent assembly'—Sanderson, *Works*, ii. 242, 258, a 'frequent college'; 'the College was sa frequent as the roumes war nocht able to receaue them'—Melvill, *Diary*, 50. The sense in which the word occurs in AV is akin to this, but more exactly *well-acquainted, conversant*: 2 Co 11²³ 'in prisons more frequent,' exactly as Knox, *Works*, iv. 139, 'Be frequent in the prophetis and in the epistillis of St. Paul.' The Gr. is περισσοτέρως, and RV follows Bish. and Rhem. 'more abundantly,' the other VSS having 'more plenteously.' Amer. RV and RVm give 'frequent' in 1 S 3¹ for 'open' of AV, 'the word of the Lord was precious in those days; there was no open vision' (אֵין חָזוֹן נִפְרָץ).

FRET.—To 'fret' is primarily to eat up, consume (*for*, intensive prefix, and *etan* to eat, like Ger. *ver-essen*), as in Alisaunder of Macedoine (E.E.T.S.) i. 1159—

> 'Fayre handes and feete freaten too the bonne.'

But a very early meaning and very common is to *eat into, gnaw, corrode*, as of a disease, and the word being used in this sense by Tind. in Lv 13⁵¹·⁵²·⁵⁵ 14⁴⁴, it was retained in AV. The uses in AV, then, are—

1. Transitively: 1. Literally to *eat away, corrode*, Lv 13⁵¹·⁵² 14⁴⁴ 'a fretting leprosy' (רָעַ), and 13⁵⁵ 'it is fret * inward' (פְּחָתָת). So

* It will be observed that in Lv 13⁵⁵ it is fret inward, *fret* is the past ptcp. Cf. More, *Utopia*, i. (Lumby, p. 46, l. 14), 'For he (and that no marvele) beynge so touched on the quicke, and hit on the gaule, so fret, so fumed, and chafed at it, and was in such a rage that he could not refraine himselfe from chidinge, skolding, railing, and reviling.' Similar forms are 'lift' Gn 7¹⁷, Lk 16²³; 'whet' Ps 64³ Pr. Bk.

Fuller says of the death of Godfrey (*Holy Warre*, Bk ii. ch. 6, p. 51), 'It may be the plague took him out of the hands of that lingring disease, and quickly cut off what that had been long in fretting'; and Shaks. makes Lear in the bitterness of his soul say of his daughter Goneril (*Lear*, I. iv. 276)—

> 'If she must teem,
> Create her child of spleen; that it may live
> And be a thwart disnatured torment to her!
> Let it stamp wrinkles in her brow of youth;
> With cadent tears fret channels in her cheeks.'

The trn of Ps 39[12] in the Great Bible of 1539 was 'When thou with rebukes dost chasten man for sinne, thou makest his bewtye to consume awaye, like as it were a mothe.' In 1540 the explanatory phrase 'fretting a garment' was added, which being thereafter adopted into the text appears in the Pr. Bk. version. Cf. Bacon, *Advancement of Learning*, II. ii. 5, 'As for the corruptions and moths of history, which are epitomes, the use of them deserveth to be banished, as all men of sound judgment have confessed, as those that have fretted and corroded the sound bodies of many excellent histories, and wrought them into base and unprofitable dregs.'

2. Figuratively, in two senses. (1) To *vex*. Tindale says (*Expos.*, Parker Soc. p. 31), 'And the nature of salt is to bite, fret, and make smart'; whence Adams passes to the fig. sense (*II Peter*, p. 47 on 1[4]) 'Do we cut, and fret, and trouble you: remember we are salt, the sharper the better.' So in AV, Ezk 16[43] 'Because thou hast not remembered the days of thy youth, but hast fretted me in all these things' (וַתִּרְגְּזִי־לִי; Amer. RV 'raged against'). (2) To *disquiet oneself*, Ps 37[1] 'Fret not thyself because of evildoers' (אַל־תִּתְחַר, so 37[7, 8], Pr 24[19]); Is 8[21] 'when they shall be hungry they shall fret themselves' (הִתְקַצֵּף, Del. 'it is roused to anger'; Cheyne, 'he shall be deeply angered'; Skinner, 'he shall break out in anger').

The AV trn is partly from the Gen. 'he shal euen freat him self,' and partly from the Bish. 'they will bee out of patience.' 'He is out of pacience' is Coverdale's; Wyc. [1382] 'it shal wrathen,' [1388] 'it schal be wrooth,' and the Douay 'he will be angrie,' are both nearer the meaning of the verb, being both after the Vulg. 'irascetur'; but both miss the force of the special form [Hithpael], which is found only here. The LXX gives λυπηθήσεσθε; Luther, 'werden sie zürnen.' A very close parallel occurs in Sir Thomas Wiat (Skeat's *Specimens*, p. 225)—

> 'And whilst they claspe their lustes in armes a-crosse,
> Graunt them, good Lord, as thou maist of thy myght,
> To freate inward, for losyng such a losse.'

2. Intransitively, *be irritable, chafe, grieve*, the modern meaning: 1 S 1[6] 'And her adversary also provoked her sore, for to make her fret' (בַּעֲבוּר הַרְּעִמָהּ), and Pr 19[3] 'his heart fretteth against the LORD' (יִזְעַף). So Shaks. *Jul. Cæs.* IV. iii. 42—

> 'Fret till your proud heart break.'

J. HASTINGS.

FRIEND.—Heb. history has supplied the world with an example of true friendship, as romantic and beautiful as any in Grecian story; and Heb. literature, though it contains no treatise *de Amicitiâ*, abounds in proverbs, setting forth, as eloquently as Laelius himself, the nature of this fine human relation, the claims which it makes, and the blessings which it brings. If Jonathan and David are the Pylades and Orestes of the Bible, the pithy sayings of the Ḥokhma Lit. contain the philosophy of friendship. A genuine attachment is possible only between the virtuous—this is implied in all the directions given in the Book of Pr to the young man for his guidance in life, and expressly indicated in the warnings of 13[20] 28[7], where the word (רֵעֶה) rendered *companion* is that elsewhere often translated *friend*. That even natural ties cannot compare with the bond of friendship for strength and endurance, is said, not without a touch of satire, in 18[24] 'He that maketh many friends doeth it to his own destruction; but there is a friend that sticketh closer than a brother.' David, in his lament, describes the affection

of Jonathan for him as 'passing the love of women.' That, as Lord Bacon puts it in his Essay, the principal fruits of friendship are healthful and sovereign, both for the affections and the understanding, comes out in the striking proverb (27[17]), 'Iron sharpeneth iron; so a man sharpeneth the countenance of his friend'; while the anguish inflicted on a true heart when one trusted and loved proves false or unkind, is exhibited in a concrete form in the behaviour of Job's three friends, and in many a passionate cry wrung from that patriarch (Job 6[14. 27] 19[21]), or from a psalmist under similar provocation (Ps 41[9]).

Among the duties of friendship Cicero places high that of frankness in reproof and counsel; and this could not fail of characteristic recognition in the proverbs of Israel, 'Faithful are the wounds of a friend; but the kisses of an enemy are deceitful' (Pr 27[6]), while in 17[9] are indicated the tact and delicacy necessary in the discharge of this duty.

Pr 27[10] is the Heb. equivalent for the saying that 'old friends are best'; and that poverty and trouble are, like length of time, tests of the genuineness of friendly profession, in contrast with the pretended attachment of flatterers and parasites, is the theme of proverbs like 14[20] 19[4. 7]. True friends are rare with the great and powerful, yet, as Bacon says, they set a higher rate than others on the rare possession, and the Bible gives many instances of the confidence of intimacy between kings and subjects, *e.g.* David and Hushai; prophets and apostles and their disciples, *e.g.* Elijah and Elisha, Paul and Timothy.

But, while the Bible presents an ideal of friendship equal to that demanded by other literature, it does not leave it there. It elevates it in a manner all its own to a transcendent height. It presents it, not only as a human relationship, but one possible between God and man. Abraham was the friend of God (2 Ch 20[7], Is 41[8], Ja 2[23]). With Moses, too, J″ spake 'face to face as a man speaketh unto his friend' (Ex 33[11]), and the Son of God used the name *friend* in preference to *servant*, not only of the apostles, but also of all for whom He laid down His life (Jn 15[13. 14. 15]).

There are nine Heb. words or phrases rendered *friend* in the AV. Those of most frequent occurrence are connected with the roots אָהֵב, expressing *affection*, and רָעָה *sociability*, the most common being רֵעַ, rendered 41 times *friend*, 104 times *neighbour*, and sometimes *companion* and *fellow*. The most usual equivalents in LXX and Vulg. are φίλος and *amicus*. As a term of salutation the vocative ἑταῖρε is three times in NT rendered *friend* (Mt 20[13] 22[12] 26[50]).

Of course the term *friends* sometimes implies no more than political associates or allies, *e.g.* 1 S 30[26], Jer 20[4. 6]. A. S. AGLEN.

FRINGES (Heb. צִיצִית *ẓiẓith*).—In the time of our Lord, the Jews, especially those of the Pharisaic party (cf. esp. Mt 23[5]), attached the greatest importance to three material reminders or 'sensible signs' of their obligations under the Law. These were the *ẓiẓith* (EV 'fringes'), the *tĕphillîn* or phylacteries (wh. see), and the *mĕzûzah* (Dt 6[9] 11[20]) on the doorpost. Of these the first-named was the sign to which the greatest virtue was ascribed. Its observance is first required by the law of Dt (22[12]), where we read 'Twisted cords (גְּדִלִים, LXX στρεπτά: AV, RV incorrectly 'fringes,' but RVm 'twisted threads') shalt thou make thee upon the four corners ('arba' kanphôth, AV 'four quarters,' RV 'four borders') of thy mantle (lit. 'covering' as Ex 22[27] [Heb. 26], see below) wherewith thou coverest thyself.' The object here termed *gĕdilîm* acquired later the special designation *ẓiẓith* צִיצִת, it is so rendered by the Targum *Jerus.* i. (pseudo-

Jonathan) in Dt 22[12],—for there can be no doubt that we meet the same enactment in an expanded form in the priestly legislation : 'And the LORD spake unto Moses saying, Speak unto the children of Israel, and bid them that they make them fringes * in the borders (so AV, RV ; more correctly 'tassels upon the corners'; cf. RVm) of their garments throughout their generations, and that they put upon the fringe of each border (*i.e.* the tassel of each corner) a cord of blue' (Nu 15[37. 38]). There can be no question that the interpretation suggested by the EV, that a fringe attached to the hem of the garment is intended, is quite erroneous. We have only to turn to Hag 2[12], where a still common Eastern practice is referred to, to see that *kānāph* applied to an article of dress can only mean 'corner' or loose flowing end of a garment.† Now, the Hebrews seem to have worn as an outer garment a large piece of cloth of the shape of a Scotch plaid (generally called *simlah*, see DRESS), which also served as a covering (כְּסוּת) by night (Ex 22[26]).‡ To the four corners of this garment, then, the 'twisted cords' of Dt were clearly intended to be fastened. The more extended enactment of the Priestly Code, however, evidently contemplates a more elaborate arrangement of a tassel attached to each corner by a cord of blue. To these tassels the Greek translators give the name κράσπεδα, the term exclusively used by the NT writers. It has even found its way into Targ. Onk. (כרוספרין) (cf. Dalm. *Gram. Aram.* 149) in both passages from the Pentateuch. The *simlah* was worn like the Greek *himation*, which is its NT equivalent, the loose end being thrown over the left shoulder. It was the *zizith* attached to this corner (τ. κρασπέδου τ. ἱματίου) that was reached with comparative ease by the woman with the issue of blood approaching our Lord in the crowd from behind (Mt 9[20], Lk 8[44]).

When we attempt to go behind the prescription of the Torah, there is reason to believe that we have here an ancient custom,§ perhaps with originally magical or superstitious associations (see W. R. Smith, *RS* 416, note ; Nowack, *Heb. Arch.* ii. 123) taken up and impressed with a new significance by the Hebrew legislation. Even so late as NT times a special virtue was supposed to be attached to the 'tassels on the four corners' (Mt 14[36], Mk 6[56]; cf. the special sanctity of the four horns of the altar, Lv 4[7ff.], 1 K 1[50f.]). To the more spiritually minded, however, they were, as they were intended to be, continual reminders of the obligation resting on J'''s people to walk in His Law, and to keep all His commandments (see esp. Nu 15[39. 40]).

With the change in the fashion of the outer garments of the Jews, and with the increasing frequency and cruelty of heathen and Christian persecution, the Jews gradually ceased to wear the tassels in the way prescribed by the original legislation. A special article of clothing was devised of the shape of a modern chest-protector— one part covering the breast, the other the back— with the necessary aperture in the centre for the head to pass through. This garment, to which the names of *tallith* (טַלִּית) and '*arba' kanphôth* (Dt 22[12]) were given, had the tassels attached to its four corners, and was worn as an undergarment, a practice still observed by all orthodox Jews. The more zealous, however, wear it so that one or

more of the tassels may be visible. The *tallith* now described came, later, to be known as *tallith katôn* or 'small tallith,' to distinguish it from the *tallith gadôl*, 'large tallith' or prayer-shawl. The latter more nearly corresponds in shape to the ancient *simlah*, being a quadrangular piece of white woollen (or silken) cloth to which the tassels are attached in the manner about to be described. It is worn universally by the Jews during the daily service in the synagogue, either thrown over the head or round the shoulders, but always so that the tassels shall be visible in front. Special prayers are said before and during the act of adjusting the *tallith*.

The rabbinical prescriptions with regard to the ציצית or tassels have been elaborated with characteristic detail, and fill many pages of the Jewish codes (see literature at end of art.). Only a very few of these need be cited here. From a reference in the Mishna (*Menakh.* iv. 1) it would appear that the former practice of making the *zizîth* by twisting three white threads with one of blue (or blue-purple) was falling into desuetude, perhaps owing to the increasing difficulty of procuring the expensive dye required ; and that it was henceforth permissible to use white threads alone so long as the numbers were complete (see Levy, *Wörterb. s. voc.* עכב). Somewhat later we learn from the curious, and in part obscure, paraphrase of Nu 15[38] in the Targum *Jerus.* i. (pseudo-Jonathan) apparently based on Talmudic decision, that the threads must be spun expressly for the purpose, not made of the refuse of the loom, and that they must be tied with five knots (קיטרין). According to the prescription still in force, it is required that four (white) threads (חוטים) shall be taken, of which one —technically called the *shammesh* or 'servant'— shall be considerably longer than the rest. A small hole or eyelet (נקב) is made in each corner of the *tallith* three thumb-breadths (גודלים) from each margin ; through this the four threads are drawn and the ends brought together. A double knot is tied close to the margin of the *tallith*, the *shammesh* is then twisted tightly 9 times round the remaining 7 threads and another double knot is tied ; then round 9 times and a knot ; then round 11 times and a knot ; and finally round 13 times and a knot, and the *zizîth* is complete. Various mystic significations are attached to the number of knots and twistings. The most interesting, perhaps, is that which deduces from the whole a symbol of the complete Torah : thus the numerical value of the letters of the word ציצית is 90 + 10 + 90 + 10 + 400 = 600, which with the 8 threads and the 5 knots makes a total of 613, the exact number, according to rabbinic calculation, of the positive (248) and negative (365) precepts of the Torah. This has led to the exaggerated statement that the wearing of the *zizîth* is of equal merit with the observance of the whole Law.

Males only are to wear the *tallith* (so already Targum pseudo-Jonathan on Dt 22[5]). This is compulsory after the 13th year, when the Jewish boy becomes a *bar-mizvah*, but the small *tallith* may be worn earlier. The size of the latter is said by Maimonides to be such that a boy, just able to walk alone, shall be completely covered by it. It is not necessary to wear the *tallith* at night ; this is inferred from the words of the Law, 'that ye may *look* upon it and remember' (Nu 15[39]), an injunction impossible of fulfilment in the darkness of the night.* As an illustration of the importance attached to the wearing of the *zizîth*, the following anecdote is frequently quoted. The son of a famous Rabbi was asked which of the commandments above all others his father had especially

---

* The MT has here ציצת in the singular, but probably we ought to read with the Samaritan ציצית ; cf. LXX κράσπεδα.

† Cf. 1 S 15[27] 24. 5. 11 where the LXX renders כָּנָף by the exact terms τὸ πτερύγιον τῆς διπλοΐδος, for which see Jevons and Gardner, *Manual of Gr. Antiq.* 52.

‡ That one and the same garment is intended in Dt and Nu is confirmed by the Targum of Onkelos, which in both passages has כסותה.

§ The practice of wearing tassels was known to the ancient Persians, as appears from the monuments of Persepolis.

* This question was one of the differences between the schools of Hillel and Shammai (*Ediyyoth*, iv. 10).

charged him to keep. His reply was: 'The law concerning the *ẓiẓith*. On descending a ladder my father stepped on one of the threads and tore it off. He refused to move from the spot till it was replaced' (*Shabb.* 118*b*). See also DRESS.

LITERATURE.—The rabbinical prescriptions are found in the authoritative codes of Maimonides (*Yad Ha-ḥazakah, Hilkoth Ẓiẓith*) and Joseph Caro (*Shulḥan 'Aruk Yoré De'a*, ch. viii.–xxiv.). A convenient compendium of the latter work is the ספר חיי אדם על־שלחן ערוך אורח חיים, Wilna, 1888 (rules concerning the *ẓiẓith*, pp. 33–38). Also in the tractate *Ẓiẓith* in Raph. Kircheim, *Septem libri Talmudici parvi Hierosolymitani*, Frankfort, 1851; Hiller, *De vestibus fimbriatis Hebrœorum*, in Ugolini *Thesaurus*, vol. xxi. More easily accessible is Bodenschatz, *Kirchliche Verfassung d. heutigen Juden*, 1748, pt. iv. pp. 9–15; Buxtorf, *Synagoga Judaica*, pp. 160–170. Art. 'Fringes' in Kitto's *Biblical Cyclopædia*[3]. See also Driver on Dt 22[12].   A. R. S. KENNEDY.

FROCK.—'A linen frock' is named in Sir 40[4] as the dress of the poor in contrast to the 'purple' of the rich (ὠμόλινον, lit. 'raw linen'; RV 'a hempen frock'; the word occurs only here in bibl. Greek). The 'frock' was once the coverall of the English labourer, and still remains as 'smock-frock.' See DRESS.

FROG (צְפַרְדֵּעַ *ẓĕphardēa'*, βάτραχος, *rana*). — An amphibious animal, noted in two connexions in the Bible. **1.** As one of the plagues of Egypt (Ex 8[2-14], Ps 78[45] etc.). **2.** As a form assumed by unclean spirits (Rev 16[13. 14]). It is also mentioned in Wis 19[10]. The frog referred to in the story of the plagues is the *Ranula esculenta*, L., the *edible frog*. It is found in all stagnant waters in the Holy Land. The Arab. name for the frog, *dufda'*, bears a strong resemblance to the Hebrew.
G. E. POST.

FROM.—Following the Gen. Bible, 'from' is used in 1 Es 3[23] as equivalent to 'away from': 'But when they are from the wine, they remember not what they have done.' This is the only occurrence of a meaning that is common in Shaks. Thus *Macbeth*, III. i. 132—

'For 't must be done to-night,
And something from the palace';

and *Jul. Cæs.* I. iii. 35—

'But men may construe things after their fashion,
Clean from the purpose of the things themselves.'

FRONTLETS.—See PHYLACTERIES.

FROWARD.—Froward is the Northern form of 'fromward,' as we have 'to and fro' for 'to and from.' Cf. Sidney, *Arcadia*, ii., 'As cheerfully going towards, as Pyrocles went frowardly fromward his death.' Froward is thus the opposite of 'toward,' and is used by Spenser (*FQ* VI. x. 24) in the literal sense of *turned from*—

'And eeke them selves so in their daunce they bore,
That two of them still froward seem'd to bee,
But one still towards shew'd her selfe afore.'

In AV 'froward' is always figurative, *turned from* in sympathy, *opposed, hostile*, as in Ps 18[26] 'with the froward thou wilt show thyself froward' (עִם־עִקֵּשׁ תִּתְפַּתָּל, RV 'with the perverse thou wilt show thyself froward'). Then, by an easy transition, that which goes the wrong way to accomplish its ends, twisted, tortuous, not straightforward. Thus Dt 32[5] Tind., 'The frowarde and overthwarte generation hath marred them selues to himward' (עִקֵּשׁ), EV 'perverse,' which does not adequately express the sense, says Driver. Tindale's 'froward' is better than 'perverse,' for its meaning is just what Driver gives as the meaning of the Heb. here, 'the opposite of what is sincere, straightforward, and frank,' denoting 'a character which pursues devious and questionable courses for the purpose of compassing its ends.' Thus Latimer (*Sermons before Edw. VI.*, Arber's ed. p. 115), 'The herte of man is naughti, a croked, and a froward pece of worke.' Still, 'froward' was frequently used in the sense of obstinate, as T. Lever, *Sermons* (1550, Arber's ed. p. 103), 'The father draweth not by force violentlye them that be stubborne and frowarde, but by loue them that be gentyll, and come wyllyngly.' And the union of the crooked with the obstinate gives perversity. RV prefers 'perverse' in 2 S 22[27] = Ps 18[26] (as above), Pr 2[15] (not Amer. RV) 3[32] 11[20]; and Amer. RV further in Dt 32[20], Pr 2[12] 6[12] 8[13] 10[31] 16[28. 30] 22[5]. RV gives 'crooked' in Pr 8[8] 21[8], and Amer. RV 'wayward' in Pr 2[15] 4[24] 17[20], and 'cunning' in Job 5[13]. But 'froward' is introduced in 2 S 22[27] (AV 'unsavoury'), Pr 23[33] (AV 'perverse'). It will be observed that the ideas represented by this word refer to conduct, especially in public life; it is therefore of most frequent occurrence in Pr, where 'froward' is found 14 times, elsewhere only 7 times.

Wyclif rarely uses the word; not in any of the places where it occurs in AV, his words being 'shrewd,' 'perverted,' or 'wayward.' But it is found in Dt 21[18] (1382), 'If a man gete a rebel sone, and a fraward (1388 'overthewert'), that herith not the fadres and modres heest'; and as a various reading in 2 Ti 3[4]. The introduction of the word so freely into Pr was made by Rogers and Coverdale. Its single occurrence in NT is from Tindale, 1 P 2[18] 'Servauntes obey youre masters with all feare, not only yf they be good and courteous; but also though they be frowarde' (1526 and 1534). The Gr. is σκολιός, which means *tortuous* as of a river, and then ethically *not straightforward*. Here, says Salmond, it means not exactly 'capricious' (as Luther), or 'wayward' (as Rhem.), or even 'froward' (as Tind. Cov. Rog. Cran. Gen. Bish. AV, RV), but 'harsh' or 'perverse,' the disposition that lacks the reasonable and considerate, and makes a tortuous use of the lawful.

The adv. **frowardly** occurs only Is 57[17] 'and he went on frowardly in the way of his heart' (וַיֵּלֶךְ שׁוֹבָב, lit. 'he walked turning away,' as AVm and RVm; Amer. RV 'backsliding'). For the Eng. word cf. Knox, *Hist.* 137, 'Then began she to frowne, and to look frowardly to all such as she knew did favour the Gospel of Jesus Christ.'

Frowardness is used only in Pr 2[14] 6[14] 10[32], תַּהְפֻּכוֹת, a word which is found only in the plu. and means lit. 'turnings about,' *i.e.* 'lines of action, or modes of speech, adopted for the sake of escaping unpleasant realities, or evading the truth, *perversions* of truth or right'—Driver on Dt 32[20]; see his note. The word is tr[d] by the adj. 'froward' in Pr 8[13] ('the froward mouth,' lit. 'the mouth of evasions') 10[31] 16[28]; by 'very froward' in Dt 32[20]; and by 'froward things' in Pr 2[12] 16[30]. Cf. Barlowe, *Dialoge* (Lunn's ed. p. 106), 'And no meruell, thoughe Saull fared the worse for hys people, wher as Moyses the most fayhtfull seruaunte of god was partely by their frowardnes debarred fro the pleasaunt lande of behest.'
J. HASTINGS.

FRUIT. — Palestine is always described as a fruitful land (Ps 107[34], Is 5[1]). The number of 'kindly fruits of the earth' produced here is very large. The great diversity of climate makes possible the cultivation of plants from almost every quarter of the globe. The following list of the products of the soil may be taken as an index, not exhaustive but illustrative of the capabilities of this 'land of promise' :—Fitches (Is 28[25. 27]), opium poppy, mustard, cabbage, cauliflower, turnip, cress, radish, flax, sorrel, rue, vine, Indian fig, jujube, lemon, orange, citron, lupine, beans, horsebeans, peas, lentils, chick peas, mâsh (*Vigna Nilotica*, L.), carob, strawberry, blackberry, peach, plum, almond, apricot, nectarine, apple, quince, medlar, Photinia Japonica, hawthorn, pomegranate, myrtle, watermelon, cantelope, squash, pumpkin, cucumber, coriander, dill, fennel, caraway, anise, celery, parsley, parsnip, carrot, carthamus (bastard saffron), chicory, lettuce, artichokes, potato, tobacco, tomato, eggplant, henbane, nightshade, castor oil, sesame, olive, fig, sycomore, mulberry, hemp, walnut, edible pine, saffron, banana, date, colocasia, maize, wheat, barley, sorghum, sugar cane.   G. E. POST.

FRUIT. — The figurative, and indeed all the literal uses of the word 'fruit,' except the primary one of the fruit of fruit-bearing trees, are suggested by the Hebrew idioms, and belong to what may be called biblical English. Thus it is used of the general products of the earth, Ex 23¹⁰ 'And six years thou shalt sow thy land, and shalt gather in the fruits thereof' (תְּבוּאָה, RV 'increase'). It is also used of the offspring of animals, including man, as Ps 127³ 'Lo, children are an heritage of the LORD : and the fruit of the womb is his reward' (פְּרִי, the common word for 'fruit'). In this sense notice La 2²⁰ 'Shall the women eat their fruit, and children of a span long?' (פְּרִי).

It has been maintained (*Psalms Chron. Arranged*, pp. 150, 446) that 'fruit' in Ps 72¹⁶ has this meaning in AV, 'There shall be an handful of corn in the earth upon the top of the mountains ; the fruit thereof shall shake like Lebanon' (פְּרִי). This might be true of Wyclif's trⁿ (1388), 'Stidefastnesse schal be in the erthe, in the higheste places of mounteyns ; the fruyt therof schal be enhaunsid aboue the Liban' ; and more confidently of Coverdale's, 'There shalbe an heape of corne in the earth hye vpon the hilles, his frute shal shake like Libanus,' though the 'his' probably refers to 'corn.' But the Geneva trⁿ is 'An handful of corne shalbe sowen in the earth, euen in the top of the mountaines, and the frute thereof shal shake like the trees of Lebanon : and the children shal florish out of the citie like the grasse of the earth,' with the marg. note, 'Vnder suche a King shalbe moste great plentie, bothe of frute and also of the increase of mankinde.' And there is little doubt that AV followed the Gen. Bible here. Whether in the *Heb.* 'fruit' refers to the fruit of the earth or of the King's body is another matter. Ewald takes it to be the King's offspring, his posterity, as in Ps 21¹⁰ ; so also Burgess, 'Let His fruit be abundant, on the top of the hills, like (the cedars of) Lebanon,' who compares Ps 92¹² and Hos 14⁵. Cheyne refers the 'fruit' to the people, 'May abundance of corn be in the land, upon the top of the mountains may it wave ; [and the people]—like Lebanon be its fruit.'

Figuratively four meanings are found : 1. The product of effort, as Pr 31³¹ 'Give her of the fruit of her hands' (פְּרִי) ; Ro 1¹³ 'I purposed to come unto you, (but was let hitherto,) that I might have some fruit among you also, even as among other Gentiles' (καρπός). 2. Benefit, profit, Jn 4³⁶ 'And he that reapeth receiveth wages, and gathereth fruit unto life eternal' (καρπός, cf. Eng. 'harvest,' the same word philologically). Ro 6²¹ 'What fruit had ye then in those things whereof ye are now ashamed?' (καρπός). 3. By a strongly idiomatic Heb. phrase, 'The fruit of the lip,' that is, *praise*, Is 57¹⁹ 'I create the fruit of the lips' (נוּב, cf. vb. in Pr 10³¹), an idiom that was accepted into bibl. Gr., He 13¹⁵ 'By him, therefore, let us offer the sacrifice of praise to God continually, that is, the fruit of our lips giving thanks to his name' (καρπός from LXX of Hos 14² [³], פְּרִי for פָּרִים). 4. Of *moral* consequences of action, Is 3¹⁰ 'the fruit of their doings,' cf. Jer 17¹⁰ 21¹⁴ etc. This differs from (1), for it is often undesigned, and from (2), for it is often used of punishment.   J. HASTINGS.

FRUSTRATE.—2 Es 10³⁴ 'Forsake me not, lest I die frustrate of my hope' (*ut non frustra moriar*), and Jth 11¹¹ 'That my lord be not defeated and frustrate of his purpose' (ἄπρακτος). So Hooker, *Eccl. Polity*, I. xi. 4, 'It is an axiom of nature that natural desire cannot utterly be frustrate'; and Knox, *Hist.* 29, 'King Henry frustrate returned to London, and after his indignation declared, began to fortify with men his frontiers toward Scotland.' Such past participles, formed in imitation of the Latin, are common in Elizabethan English. Shaks. uses this form still more boldly as an adj., *Tempest*, III. iii. 10—

'The sea mocks
Our frustrate search on land.'

The meaning is 'defeated,' 'baulked.' The same sense is found with the infin. in Ezr 4⁵ 'Hired counsellors against them to frustrate their purpose' (לְהָפֵר) ; and with the finite verb in Is 44²⁵ '[the LORD] that frustrateth the tokens of the liars' (מֵפֵר, Wyc. [1382], 'voide makende tocnes of deuynoures'; Cov. 'I destroy the tokens of witches'; Del. 'who brings to nought the signs of the lying prophets'). And in the same sense RV adds, Job 5¹² 'He frustrateth the devices of the crafty' (מֵפֵר, AV 'He disappointeth'). But in Gal 2²¹ the meaning is different, 'I do not frustrate the grace of God' (ἀθετῶ, RV 'make void'), *i.e.* not 'baulk,' 'thwart,' or 'disappoint,' but 'nullify,' 'render inoperative,' 'make of no avail or value.' So Elyot, *The Governour*, ii. 385, 'To suche persones as do contemne auncient histories . . . it may be sayd, that in contemnynge histories they frustrate Experience.'

Goodwin, therefore (*Works*, i. pt. 2, p. 205), misses the point when he says, 'It was God's great design to advance grace, and therefore he calls their stepping aside from the doctrine thereof, a frustrating of the grace of God, Gal. ii. ult., which men do by mingling anything with it ; it is a frustrating of the grace of God, because it frustrateth the great design of God, for to frustrate is to make void a design.' Dr. Gwynne (*in loc.*) brings out the meaning thus : 'I do not make void the *atoning* grace of God *by seeking to justify myself* ; for if righteousness *come* by law, then, *indeed*, Christ died needlessly, *and the grace of God is made of none effect*.' The older versions are inaccurate or inadequate, Wyc. 'cast not awei' (after Vulg. *non abiicio*), so Cov. Rhem. ; Tind. 'despyse,' so Rog. Cran. ; Gen. better 'abrogate'; Bish. 'reject.' Augustine is right—*non irritam facio.*

     J. HASTINGS.

FRYING-PAN.—See FOOD.

FUEL. — The Hebrews indicated fuel by a figure as the '*food* of fire' (Is 9⁵· ¹⁹ [Heb. ⁴· ¹⁸] מַאֲכֹלֶת אֵשׁ, EV 'fuel of fire'; Ezk 15⁴· ⁶ 21³² אָכְלָה). In ancient as in modern times, wood was no doubt the principal fuel, either in its natural state or prepared as charcoal. There is no sufficient evidence of the use of mineral coal as fuel. With regard to the use of wood as fuel, we may assume that the variety of woods employed for this purpose was as great as it is in Syria to-day (see the list prepared by Post in *PEF St*, 1891, p. 118 ff.). The term עֵצִים (lit. *woods*) is applied equally to the 'sticks' or twigs gathered by individuals (Nu 15³²· ³³, 1 K 17¹⁰· ¹²), and to the faggots or logs prepared by felling and cutting up the trees of the forest (Lv 1⁷ff· 4¹²). A few of such trees are named in Is 44¹⁴⁻¹⁶. Shrubs of every variety were used for the same purpose, such as the *rôthem* (רֹתֶם Ps 120⁴ 'coals of *juniper*,' more correctly as RVm 'coals of *broom* '), a shrub very largely used as fuel by the Arabs of the present day (Palmer, Doughty). Reduced to charcoal (see below), the *rôthem* (Arab. *ritm*) is said to throw out an intense heat. References to thorns (קוֹצִים, סִירִים) as fuel are numerous in Scripture ; the '*âṭâd* (אָטָד Ps 58¹⁰ [Eng. ⁹]), probably the buck-thorn (see THORNS AND THISTLES), is mentioned in particular. The use of chaff, which includes the chopped straw (*tibn*) from the threshing-floor, is likewise referred to (Mt 3¹²), as also of withered herbage (χόρτος, EV 'grass') in general (Mt 6³⁰, Lk 12²⁸).

The Hebrews, as we have remarked above, were familiar with the advantage, as fuel, of wood in the form of charcoal, for such, without doubt, was the 'coal' of Scripture (see COAL). The ancient Egyptians, acc. to Wilkinson (ed. 1878, ii. 35, 36), used faggots of wood for heating water and boiling meat, but preferred charcoal for roasting. However this may have been among the Hebrews, the fuel used for the brasier (אָח Jer 36²²ff· AV 'hearth,' RV 'brasier') or chafing-dish (כִּיּוֹר אֵשׁ Zec 12⁶, RV 'pan of fire'), by which the houses of the upper classes were warmed in winter, was undoubtedly charcoal (cf. Jn 18¹⁸ 21⁹). No such luxury would be found in the houses of the poor, who had to content themselves with a fire of logs or twigs placed in a depression in the floor of the living-room. The smoke from such a hearth (perhaps מוֹקְדָה—although this word is in our extant literature used only of the altar-hearth, Lv 6² [Eng. 6⁹]—mod. Arab. the same) escaped as best it could through the door or the latticed window (Hos 13³, EV 'chimney'). Chimneys in our sense were not known, although, by a corruption of the text, 2 Es 6⁴ is made to speak of 'the chimneys of Zion.'

It is uncertain to what extent the Hebrews were familiar with the use of animal dung as fuel. This form of fuel, as is well known, is very extensively used in the East, both by the nomads and the fellahin. The dung of the camel is the favourite fuel of the Bedawin, while the Syrian peasant carefully collects the droppings of his cattle, which he uses either in the natural state when sufficiently dry, or mixed with straw. From the incident recorded in Ezk 4¹²⁻¹⁵ we may at least infer that this form of fuel was not unknown (see esp. v.¹⁵), although, as the country was more extensively wooded then than now, there would not be the same necessity as now exists for having recourse to it.   A. R. S. KENNEDY.

FUGITIVE.—**1.** Simply one who flees, as from danger or punishment (the modern, as it is also the earliest, meaning of the word, after Lat. *fugitivus*). So Is 15⁵ 'His fugitives shall flee unto Zoar' (RV 'Her nobles flee unto Zoar,' with 'fugitives' in marg. The reading is doubtful and difficult, see the Comm.); Ezk 17²¹ 'And all his fugitives with all his bands shall fall by the sword' (so RV and *Oxf. Heb. Lex.*, but reading again doubtful). **2.** A *deserter* from duty. This sense belongs to *fugitivus* also. So Jg 12⁴ 'Ye Gileadites are fugitives of Ephraim'; Cov. 'runnagates.' That this is the meaning of EV is certain, but Moore holds that it is a misinterpretation, the Heb. word (פְּלִיטִים) meaning not 'runagate,' but 'survivor' (see his note); 2 K 25¹¹ 'the fugitives that fell away to the king of Babylon' (אֲשֶׁר הַנֹּפְלִים, פָלוּ עַל, RV 'those that fell away, that fell to the king'); Jth 16¹² 'as fugitives' children' (ὡς παῖδας αὐτομολούντων, RV 'as runagates' children'); 2 Mac 8³⁵ (the only example of the adj. in AV) 'He came like a fugitive servant through the midland unto Antioch' (δραπέτου τρόπον, RV 'like a fugitive slave'). So Shaks. *Ant. and Cleop.* IV. ix. 22—

> 'But let the world rank me in register
> A master-leaver, and a fugitive.'

3. A *Wanderer*, as Foxe, *Act. and Mon.*, iii. 747, 'If thou wert an honest Woman, thou wouldest not . . . run about the Country like a Fugitive.' This is the meaning of Gn 4¹²·¹⁴ 'a fugitive and a vagabond' (נָע וָנָד, ptcp. of נוּע to wander; LXX στένων καὶ τρέμων [preserving the paronomasia], Vulg. *vagus et profugus*; Luther, 'unstät und flüchtig'; Wyc. [1382] 'vagaunt and fer fugitif,' [1338] 'unstable of dwellyng and fleynge aboute'; Cov. 'a vagabunde and a rennagate'; Bish. 'a fugitive and a vagabond'). Shaks. presents a close parallel in *I Henry VI.* III. iii. 67—

> 'When Talbot hath set footing once in France,
> And fashion'd thee that instrument of ill,
> Who then but English Henry will be lord,
> And thou be thrust out like a fugitive?'

J. HASTINGS.

FULLER.—The fuller's art is mentioned in both OT and NT only in connexion with itself. In the former the **fuller's field** (2 K 18¹⁷, Is 7³ 36²) is the only word used, and indicated an open field on the west of Jerus. where cloths were fulled and spread out in the sun to dry. The process of

fulling in those times is unknown to us except indirectly, partly from the etymology of the word (כּוֹבֵס, γναφεύς), and partly from an Egyp. picture. It seems to have consisted in washing the material with some preparation of lye, beating or rubbing it, and exposing it to the rays of the sun. This ensured a considerable amount of cleaning and bleaching; and the remains of ancient Egyp. linen show that the result of the art, rude as it may have been, was highly satisfactory. In NT the only reference to it (Mk 9³) is where the garments of Jesus at His transfiguration are said to have become 'glistering, exceeding white; so as no fuller on earth can whiten them' (RV); and this description shows that the reader was familiar with the fuller's art and its beautifying effects. The dress of Egyp. and Jewish priests was made of white linen, and among their higher classes of very fine material, whose lustre was enhanced by art. Fulling is still carried on in the E., probably very much as it was practised in ancient times, and is often employed before dyeing cloth and yarn, to remove impurities and improve the process of colouring; but it is rapidly being superseded by the modern mode of bleaching.   J. WORTABET.

FULLER'S FIELD, THE (שְׂדֵה כוֹבֵס, ὁ ἀγρὸς γναφέως, *ager fullonis*), was the scene of Rabshakeh's interview with Eliakim and others (2 K 18¹⁷, Is 36²), and of that between Ahaz, Isaiah, and his son (Is 7³). In each case it is named in connexion with the phrase 'conduit of the Upper Pool,' which is 'in' or 'on' 'the highway of the Fuller's Field.' The conduit apparently crossed the highway at a point close to the city, as conversation carried on there could be heard by the people on the walls (2 K 18²⁶). The place cannot now be identified with certainty. En-rogel we know was a resort of the fullers; whence probably its name was derived. The same is true of Birket Mamilla, in the vale west of the city. The former, lying in the bottom of the valley S.E., would have been difficult of approach, and hearing from the walls impossible. The higher aqueduct from Solomon's Pools crosses the valley a little above Birket Mamilla, and seems to have entered the city close by the tower Psaphinus, at the N.W. angle. This, however, could hardly be called 'the conduit of the Upper Pool.' From Birket Mamilla a conduit takes water to the Pool of Hezekiah, passing under the wall northward of the Jaffa gate. Birket Mamilla being the 'upper' of the two pools in the valley, there is at least a possibility that the Fuller's Field was located here. On the N., however, an ancient conduit entered the city E. of the Damascus gate. Its course without the wall has not been traced. It may have come from the large pool some distance out, to the left of the Nâblûs road. On this side the city was easiest of approach; the land here would perhaps best suit the description implied in שָׂדֶה 'arable land'; Josephus (*BJ* v. iv. 2) speaks of 'The Fuller's Monument,' at the E. corner of the N. wall; and Arculf mentions a gate west of the Damascus gate, which at the time of his visit (towards the end of the 7th cent.) was called *Porta Villæ Fullonis*, 'Gate of the Fuller's Farm' (cf. Euseb. *HE* ii. 23). These considerations point to the location of the Fuller's Field on the N. of the city. But there is no evidence to warrant any certain conclusion.

W. EWING.

FULNESS.—See PLEROMA.

FUNERAL.—See BURIAL.

FURLONG.—See WEIGHTS AND MEASURES.

FURNACE.—In OT five words are tr⁴ furnace

in EV. **1.** כִּבְשָׁן, a kiln for burning limestone into lime, or for smelting ore, chiefly iron. The former was constructed of lime-stones arranged in concentric layers in the form of a dome, with an opening at the top for the escape of air and smoke, and another at the bottom for supplying the hollow of the dome with fuel. In this case, as well as in furnaces for smelting, great and long-continued heat was required, and the combustion caused a thick and dark column of smoke to ascend. It is this appearance that is referred to in the account of the destruction of Sodom and Gomorrah : ' and, lo, the smoke of the land went up as the smoke of a furnace ' (Gn 19²⁸). **2.** אַתּוּן, an Aram. word still in use in Syria (Arab. *attun*) for the lime-kiln described above. It occurs only in Dn 3, but there repeatedly as the ' furnace ' into which Shadrach, Meshach, and Abed-nego were cast. **3.** עֲלִיל, Ps 12⁶, but the text here is quite uncertain. (See Cheyne, *ad loc.* and *Expos. Times*, viii. 170, 287, 336, 379.) **4.** כּוּר (Arab. *kûr*, a blacksmith's fireplace), a smelting furnace, for iron (Dt 4²⁰, 1 K 8⁵¹, Jer 11⁴), but especially for gold (Pr 17³ 27²¹), used metaphorically (Is 48¹⁰, furnace of affliction). **5.** תַּנּוּר, sometimes tr. ' furnace ' (Gn 15¹⁷), and sometimes ' oven ' (Lv 26²⁶)—the latter being probably the correct trⁿ. The Arab. word *tannur* is still in use on the Lebanon for a special kind of oven in which women bake bread. A pit is dug in the earth, and a hollow cylinder of pottery, about two feet in diameter, is let down into it. Fire is kindled at the bottom, and, when the smoke subsides and the cylinder is sufficiently heated, a thin circular layer of dough, spread out on a pad, is deftly stuck to the inner side of the cylinder. The cakes, which are about a foot in diameter, are considered a very good kind of bread.

The same word in Gr. of NT (Mt 13⁴²) and in Arab. (κάμινος, *kamin*) means a furnace. In Syria the word is still in use for furnaces employed in heating public baths, and the heat generated in them is very great.   J. WORTABET.

FURNITURE.—In Gn 31³⁴ it is said that Rachel had taken the images (RV ' teraphim ') belonging to her father, and put them ' in the camel's furniture.' The Heb. [כַּר] occurs only here (בְּכַר־הַגָּמָל), and designates a basket-shaped palanquin which was placed on the camel's saddle, chiefly for carrying the women. See Dillmann, *in loc.*, who quotes Knobel and refers to Burckhardt, *Bedouins*, ii. 85 ; W. G. Brown, *Travels*, 453 ; Ker Porter, *Travels*, ii. 232 ; Jahn, *Bibl. Arch.* 54 ; see also art. CAMEL. The Eng. word is apparently original to AV. The older Eng. VSS were misled by the Vulg. *stramenta cameli*, and Luther's *die streu der Kamel* (mod. edd. *die Streu der Kameele*), and render ' straw ' or ' litter,' though Gen. Bible has ' saddle ' in marg. (Wyc. 1382 ' the literyng of a camele,' 1388 ' the strewyngis of the camel '). The AV and RV word ' furniture ' is used in the general sense of equipment, accoutrement, as in Bunyan, *Holy War* (Clar. Press ed. p. 112), ' Wherefore, let it please thee to accept of our Palace for thy place of residence, and of the Houses of the best men in our Town for the reception of thy Soldiers and their Furniture.'

The same word is given in AV 7 times (Ex 31⁷· ⁸ ᵇⁱˢ· ⁹ 35¹⁴ 39³³, Nah 2⁹) as the tr. of כְּלִי *kĕlî*, which is usually trᵈ ' vessel.' RV prefers ' vessel ' in Ex 31⁸ᵇ· ⁹ and 35¹⁴, but gives ' furniture ' as the tr. of the same Heb. in Ex 25⁹, Nu 3⁸ 7¹, 2 S 24²² (AV all ' instrument ') ; Ex 40⁹, Nu 1⁵⁰ᵇ 4¹⁵· ¹⁶, 1 Ch 9²⁹ (AV all ' vessel ').

For an account of the furniture of an Eastern house, see HOUSE.   J. HASTINGS.

FURROW.—This is the trⁿ in AV of the follow-

ing Heb. words. **1.** גְּדוּד Ps 65¹⁰ (RV ' ridges '). This word, which is most familiar to us in the sense of a ' troop ' (*e.g.* 1 S 30⁸· ¹⁵· ²³ and oft.), means literally a ' cutting,' and (in plur. fem. גְּדֻדוֹת) appears in Jer 48³⁷ in connexion with cuttings in the flesh as a sign of mourning. **2.** מַעֲנָה or מַעֲנָה Ps 129³, where the word is used metaphorically, ' The plowers plowed upon my back, they made long their furrows ' (מַעֲנוֹתָם *Kethibh*, מַעֲנִיתָם *Kerê*). The only other occurrence of this word is in the obscure expression in 1 S 14¹⁴ כְּבַחֲצִי מַעֲנָה צֶמֶד שָׂדֶה, which is trᵈ in AV ' within as it were an half acre of land [which] a yoke [of oxen might plow]' ; AVm ' half a furrow of an acre of land,' RV ' within as it were half a furrow's length in an acre of land,' RVm ' half an acre of land.' There is the strongest reason to suspect the originality of MT. LXX has ἐν βολίσι καὶ κόχλαξιν τοῦ πεδίου, and it is not improbable that the Heb. expression originally specified the *weapons* used by Jonathan and his armour-bearer, although in that case we have probably here a gloss transferred from v.¹⁹ (see Wellhausen and Driver's notes, *ad loc.*, also Budde in *SBOT*). **3.** עֲרוּגָה Ezk 17⁷· ¹⁰, where RV rightly substitutes ' beds,' as in Ca 5¹³ 6² [all]. **4.** תֶּלֶם Job 31³⁸ 39¹⁰, Hos 10⁴ 12¹¹. The same word (in plur.) is trᵈ by RV ' furrows ' in Ps 65¹¹, where AV has ' ridges.' **5.** In Hos 10¹⁰ the *Kethibh* has עינתם, *Kerê* עוֹנֹתָם ' furrows.' Many modern scholars (following LXX, Vulg. and Pesh.) would read עֲוֺנֹתָם ' transgressions.' The passage appears to be hopelessly corrupt. AV (text) ' when they shall bind themselves in their two furrows,' is of course meaningless. RV proposes ' when they are bound to their two transgressions ' ; but even this fails to yield a satisfactory sense. Probably Nowack is not far wrong in his conjectural trⁿ *um sie zu züchtigen wegen ihrer beiden Vergehungen*, ' to punish them for both their transgressions.' Similarly Guthe (in Kautzsch's *AT*), *wenn sie für ihre zwei Verschuldungen Züchtigung empfangen*, ' when they receive punishment for their two transgressions.' The latter will be their wrong choice of a king and their idolatry, or perhaps the reference may be to the two calves at Bethel and Dan (see Nowack and Wellh. *ad loc.*, and cf. Siegfried-Stade, *s.* עָוֺן). See further under AGRICULTURE.   J. A. SELBIE.

FURTHER.—To ' further ' in the sense of ' help forward ' is used of *persons* in Ezr 8³⁶ ' they furthered the people, and the house of God ' (נִשְּׂאוּ). So Chaucer, *Hous of Fame*, 2023—

> ' And gaf expres commaundement,
> To whiche I am obedient,
> To furthre thee with al my might.'

Furtherance occurs in Ph 1¹²· ²⁵ as tr. of προκοπή, which in 1 Ti 4¹⁵, its only other occurrence, is trᵈ ' profiting.' RV gives ' progress ' in all. On the other hand RV introduces ' furtherance ' into Ph 1⁵ 2²² to express the force of εἰς with the acc. (εἰς τὸ εὐαγγέλιον, ' in furtherance of the gospel,' AV ' in the gospel.' Cf. Healey (1610), *St. Aug. Citie of God*, I. xi. 19, ' The pompes of the funeralls are rather solaces to the living then furtherances to the dead.'

FURY.—The Heb. word חֵמָה *hêmâh*, which is once (Est 1¹²) trᵈ ' anger,' and often ' wrath,' is 66 (חֵמָא of Dn 11⁴⁴ and Aram. חֱמָא, חֱמָא of 3¹³· ¹⁹ make 69) times trᵈ ' fury.' Of these occurrences 61 refer to God, and then Amer. RV prefers ' wrath,' except in Is 42²⁵ 66¹⁵ ' fierceness.' Fury is also the tr. in AV of חָרוֹן *hârôn* in Job 20²³ ; RV ' fierceness,' as the word is a few times trᵈ in AV. In the Apocr. ' fury ' occurs as the tr. of θυμός Sir 1²² 45¹⁸ 48¹⁰, Bar 1¹³ (RV always ' wrath ') ; of θυμοί Wis 7²⁰ (AV ' furies,' RV ' ragings ') 10⁵, 2 Mac 4²⁵ (both AV ' fury,' RV ' rage ') ; **and of**

ἀλάστωρ 2 Mac 7⁹ 'And when he was at the last gasp, he said, Thou like a fury takest us out of this present life' (Σὺ μέν, ἀλάστωρ; the only occurrence of the word in biblical Greek, though it is found also in 4 Mac 9²⁴ 11²³ 18²²; RV 'Thou, miscreant'). See ANGER.　　　　　J. HASTINGS.

FUTURE.—See ESCHATOLOGY.

G

GAAL (גַּעַל, acc. to Wellh. *Isr. u. jüd. Geschichte*, p. 26='beetle,' cf. Arab. *ja'ul*; see Gray, *Hebr. Prop. Names*, p. 110), Jg 9²⁶⁻⁴¹ son of Ebed (עֶבֶד, LXX, A Ἄβεδ, B Ἰωβηλ, prob. error for 'Ἰωβήδ, *Obed* עוֹבֵד; cf. LXX 1 Ch 2³⁷ 11⁴⁷ 26⁷, 2 Ch 23¹. Less prob. 'Ἰώβηλ, i.e. יובל=יבעל 'J" is Baal,' altered to Ebed to avoid offence).—Gaal, apparently a Canaanite and a new-comer to Shechem, was the ringleader of a revolt against Abimelech, son of Gideon. He first ingratiated himself with the Shechemites, and then adroitly seized the occasion of the popular vintage-festival to incite them to revolt and make himself their leader. Zebul, Abimelech's officer in Shechem, heard of the plot, and sent a warning to his chief. Following Zebul's advice, Abimelech marched against the town and surrounded it with ambuscades under cover of night. Gaal, from the entrance of the gate, noticed the approach of Abimelech's men, and pointed them out to Zebul, who replied first with an ironical answer and then with an open taunt, bidding him go forth and fight with them. In the battle which followed, Abimelech completely defeated the rebels, and Zebul drove out Gaal and his brethren from the city. The context suggests that the revolt was one of 'native Shechemites against the half-Israelite Abimelech' (Moore). Gaal poses as their champion. It is by no means clear that Gaal was an Israelite, and that his object was to rouse the Israelite population against the Shechemite ruler. W. R. Smith, *Th. T.* xx. 1886, p. 195 ff., would place v.²⁸ after v.²²; and Budde, *Richt. u. Sam.* p. 118, after v.²⁵. But no transposition is needed. In v.²⁸ read with LXX עַבְדוּ for עֶבֶד 'Do not the son of Jerubbaal and Zebul . . . make slaves of the men of Hamor?' Another simple alteration is עָבְדוּ (perf.) proposed by Moore, 'Were not . . . subject to Hamor?' V.²⁹ for וַיֹּאמֶר read וָאֹמֵר 'and I would say.' V.³¹ for בְּתָרְמָה 'deceitfully' (?) read בָּאֲרֻמָה 'in Arumah,' cf. v.⁴¹. צְרִים can hardly be right: Stade suggests הַם מְצֵרִים; but the text is doubtful. See further under ABIMELECH.　　　　　　　　　G. A. COOKE.

GAASH (גַּעַשׁ).—A mountain in Ephraim, S. of Timnath-serah or Timnath-heres (wh. see), Jos 24³⁰, Jg 2⁹. The torrent-valleys (נַחֲלֵי) of G. are mentioned in 2 S 23³⁰=1Ch 11³².

GABAEL (B Γαβαήλ, A Γαμαήλ).—1. A distant ancestor of Tobit (To 1¹). 2. A friend and kinsman of Tobit, residing at Rages in Media. To him Tobit, when purveyor to the king of Assyria, once entrusted, as a deposit, 10 talents of silver (Vulg. only: 'lent it under a bond, because G. was needy'), To 1¹⁴. For years the money was not claimed. The reason for this is given with great variety in the VSS (1¹⁵). When, however, blindness and poverty came on Tobit in Nineveh, he recollected, after prayer, the long-forgotten treasure (To 4¹), and wished his son Tobias to fetch it (4²¹). Tobias found a guide, Raphael in disguise, who said he had lodged with G. (5⁶). When Tobias married Sarah in Ecbatana he sent Raphael for the deposit (9²). G. welcomed him, and brought forth the bags with seals unbroken, returning with Raphael to the wedding feast. All the VSS, except B and Heb. of Fagius, tell of a hearty blessing which G. gave the bridegroom when he met him (9⁶). Instead of this, B (so EV) says, 'Tobias blessed his wife,' and Heb. Fag. 'Tobias was blessed still more, with Sarah his wife.'

Heb. Fag. uses the form עֲבִיאֵל, except in ch. 10, where we have גַּבְאֵל, as always in Munster's Heb. Itala preserves the form most accurately, 'Gabahel,' גַּבְהָאֵל='God is high.'　　　　　J. T. MARSHALL.

GABATHA (Γαβάθα). — One of two eunuchs whose plot against Artaxerxes (the Ahasuerus, *i.e.* Xerxes of canonical Est) was discovered and frustrated by Mardocheus (Mordecai), Ad. Est 12¹. In Est 2²¹ he is called BIGTHAN and in 6² BIGTHANA.

GABBAI (גַּבָּי, cf. Talm. גַּבַּי 'tax-gatherer').—A Benjamite (Neh 11⁸), but text doubtful (see Smend, *Listen*, p. 7).

GABBATHA occurs only in Jn 19¹³ 'And he [Pilate] brought Jesus out and sat down (ἐκάθισεν, not—according to Justin, *Apol.* i. 35, and the *Gospel of Peter*, ἐκάθισαν αὐτὸν ἐπὶ καθέδραν κρίσεως—'set him') on the judgment-seat at a place called the Pavement (Λιθόστρωτον), but in Hebrew Gabbatha' ('Εβραϊστὶ δὲ Γαββαθά).

The passage offers serious philological and topographical difficulties.

(*a*) Λιθόστρωτον is clearly 'pavement,' especially of mosaic work (*tessellatum*); cf. in the OT, Est 1⁶, Ca 3¹⁰, 2 Ch 1³, but especially Aristeas (ed. Schmidt, p. 30, 3), where on the temple of Jerusalem it is said: Τὸ δὲ πᾶν ἔδαφος λιθόστρωτον καθέστηκε.

(*b*) This particular Pavement was called in Hebrew 'Gabbatha.' It is not necessary or possible, though it is generally attempted, to seek in Gabbatha the exact equivalent of the *appellativum* λιθόστρωτον (*Onomastica sacra*, ed. Lag. 189, 87. 202, 62, Γαββαθὰ λιθόστρωτον).

(*c*) The Greek MSS offer scarcely any variety; some uncials have Γαβαθα; so also the Harclensian VS in the edition of White; but according to Barhebræus it had נאבבאתא; a few minuscules have Καπφαθα. Interesting in this connexion is the spelling of the Peshiṭta, גְּפִיפְתָא, with the remark of Barhebræus, that the ב is to be pronounced hard like פ and the פ both times soft (cf. Duval, *Gr. Syr.* p. 30); the Cureton and Lewis MSS are unhappily defective, but the Arabic Tatian has كَفِيفْتا *Kafiftâ* (thus cod. A, the text of Ciasca كبيتا; in the translation Ciasca and Hogg retained *Gabbatha*). The Evangeliarium Hierosolymitanum shows ניבחא, but codex C (in the forthcoming edition of Mrs. Lewis) נבחא. On the deformations of the word in the MSS of the Latin Bible, see Wordsworth-White. The confusion with *Golgotha* (first hand of cod. Sinaiticus) is found elsewhere (Oliverus, *Descriptio terræ sanctæ*, p. 20, 9, codd. DX *Golgatha*, U *Grabata*).

In this state of the evidence it is safest to presuppose an Aramaic גַּבְּתָא, as st. emph. of a feminine noun גַּב from the root גבב. But the origin and meaning of נבחא is disputed.

1. In Mt 26²³ we find נבחא in the Evang. Hier.

for τρύβλιον ; cf. Ethiopic *gab(b)atâ=patella*, Dillm. *Lex.* 1168, and Latin *gabata*, Martial, 7. 47, 11. 3. Schwally (*Idioticon*) identified this with our Gabbatha. But this נבחא seems to be a dialectic form of בַּפְתָא (fem. of כך), *Thesaur. Syr.* 1791 ; cf. כֻּפְתָא and אָבְפְתָא, *ib.* 766, 1792.

2. Neither can it be=בַּפְתָא (כיפחא) ‘vault,’ καμάρα, ἐξέδρα, ψαλὶς (Vogüé, *Inscr. Sémit.* i. p. 50, n. 70, *ib.* n. 50 ; Targ. Jer. xx. 2, 3, Naz. 56ᵃ), because of the vowel *i* in the first syllable, though the meaning would be very appropriate : an arch, niche, or cupola, under which the tribunal was placed on a mosaic pavement.

3. Generally it is derived from גַּב ‘back’ ; but neither for the form nor for the meaning (*Anhöhe*, ‘height’ ; Kautzsch, *Gramm. des Bibl. Aram.* p. 10) can examples be given. In the OT we have גַּבְתֻן ; in the Mishna the plural גַּבּוֹת ; for ניבבא Targ. Ps 68¹⁶, Lagarde printed ניבנא ; Levy, p. 123, has ניבנא ; Gesen. r. 98, 96ᵃ we have ראש ניבבא הרים ; more frequent is גובבא, Dalman, *Gr. des Aram.* § 25. i. β, where also an example of spelling with פ is given.

4. Others thought of the root נבע, *i.e.* of an Aramaized *נבעתא ‘hill’ (comp. שָׁפָה=שָׁעָה, שָׁבָּת if =*שָׁבְעַת). (The roots נב, נף, and כף are closely allied ; cf. further גֵּב Lv 21²⁰ = ‏ܟܽܘܒ̈ܳܐ‎ ; ‏ܟܽܘܒ̈ܳܐ‎ is explained *caverna* by Barsalibi; ‏ܡܰܟܒܳܐ ܡܶܟܒ̈ܶܐ‎, *spelunca fornicata*, Julian, ed. Hoffm. 139. 21). The exact form and meaning must therefore be left in suspense.

(*d*) No place called Λιθόστρωτον or Gabbatha is mentioned by Josephus, or in any other known source besides the NT. But frequently we hear of a place called גָּזִּית (=Ξυστός), especially of the לְשִׁפּ הַגָּזִית ‘the hall of hewn quaders,’ where the Sanhedrin assembled (Schürer, *HJP* ii. i. 190). It has been attempted to identify these two places. Tradition seeks Gabbatha near the so-called ‘Ecce homo Arch.’ Compare the articles JERUSALEM, PILATE, PRÆTORIUM, TEMPLE. For the sitting of the judge on the *sella*, see Schürer, I. ii. 15 n. 8, and the literature there quoted, especially Josephus, *Ant.* XVIII. iv. 6, where Philippus is praised : τοῦ θρόνου εἰς ὃν κρίνειε καθεζόμενος ἐν ταῖς ὁδοῖς ἐπομένου . . . ἐκ τοῦ ὀξέος ἱδρύσεως τοῦ θρόνου ᾗ καὶ τύχοι γενομένης καθεζόμενος ἠκροᾶτο.

EB. NESTLE.

GABBE (Α Γάββη, Β Κάββη ; AV Gabdes), 1 Es 5²⁰.—In Ezr 2²⁶ Geba.

GABRIAS (Β Γαβρίας, א Γαβρεί, indecl. Greek forms of גַּבְרִי [Aram. גַּבְרִי], shortened form of גַּבְרִיאֵל ‘man of God’ ; omitting, as was customary, the name of the deity. Syr. and Heb. Fagii preserve the complete form).—Acc. to 1¹⁴ Gabrias was the *brother* of the Gabael to whom Tobit entrusted 10 talents of silver. In To 4²⁰ the Gr. reads Γαβαήλῳ τῷ τοῦ Γαβρία, א Γαβρεί, which AV and RV render ‘the son of Gabrias,’ thereby introducing an apparent contradiction, probably gratuitously. Compare Ἰούδας Ἰακώβου, Ac 1¹³, with Jude¹.

J. T. MARSHALL.

GABRIEL (גַּבְרִיאֵל, in LXX and NT Γαβριήλ, *vir Dei*, ‘man of God’) appears in both OT and NT. In Dn 8¹⁵ᶠ· G. is the ‘man’ who interprets Daniel's vision of the ram and the he-goat ; in 9²¹ᶠ· he explains to Daniel Jeremiah's prophecy about the 70 years (Jer 25¹¹ 29¹⁰) as 70 weeks of years, and amplifies details. In NT G. is named by Lk alone ; he foretells the birth of John to Zacharias (1¹¹ᶠ·), and acts as the angel of Annunciation to Mary (1²⁶). Different in some ways as the later is from the earlier presentation, yet both can be

---

easily united as parts, not only of one character, but even of one aspect of it, viz. that of bearing divine sympathy and comforting promise to those in need. These appearances are quite in accordance with the notion of G.'s character afforded by the later and more developed Jewish angelology. The developed angelology of Dn is indeed used as an argument for the later date of that book (Driver, *LOT⁶* p. 508). If the ‘one like the appearance of a man’ (Dn 10¹⁸) be G., as would appear from the fact that his message resembles, even in its words, that of G. in 8 and 9, then G. is a companion of Michael, and both are members of a class, the ‘princes’ or guardian-angels of the nations. In Enoch 9, G. is one of four great archangels ; but, comparing this with Lk 1¹⁹ and other references, he is one of seven (Rev 8²) who present the prayers of the saints and go in and out before God (To 12¹⁵). The Targums add G. as a gloss to other parts of Scripture ; according to pseudo-Jonathan, the ‘man’ who showed Joseph the way towards his brethren (Gn 37¹⁵) was G. ; again, with Michael and others G. takes part in the burial of Moses (Dt 34⁶) ; G. is also the angel whom the Lord sent to destroy the host of Sennacherib (2 Ch 32²¹). About the name Gabriel there is nothing distinctive, but it was probably a proper name from its first use : the personality, however, is very definite. Assuming that the supra-natural beings of the earlier books of the Bible are either the shrivelled-up descendants of the nature-spirits of primitive Semitic superstition (אֱלֹהִים) or subordinate personal beings fully representing God at a definite time and place (מַלְאָכִים) (Schultz, *OT Theol.* ii. 215 f. ; W. R. Smith, *Ency. Brit.⁹* art. ‘Angel’), it is clear that G. belongs to the latter rather than the former. Nor has his connexion with, far less his derivation from, any of the seven Amshaspands of Zoroastrianism, the seven Babylonian planets, or the seven councillors at the Persian court (Ezr 7¹⁴), been made out. He is the messenger of J″: a characteristic Jewish idea, though the number of the archangels—seven— may have been derived from foreign sources. We possess but little description of the special form under which he presented himself ; to Daniel he is simply ‘the man G.,’ though an elaborate and striking picture is drawn of the ‘man’ (G. ?) in Dn 10⁵· ⁶. St. Luke is equally reticent, but calmness and sublimity are added : ‘I am G. that stand in the presence of God.’ In Dn 9²¹ G. is ‘caused to fly swiftly,’ but the passage is not clear ; RVm ‘sore wearied’ seems somewhat inept ; ‘gleaming in splendour’ (Schultz, *OT Theol.* ii. 226 n. 2) is more likely, though it proposes an emendation of the original.

G. appropriates to himself the function of revealing God. He brings the divine into the phenomenal world. In this he is contrasted with Michael, who fights for God and the chosen people. Yet in G.'s character there is also a stern element. Mohammed asserts him to have been the revealer of the Koran, —probably in opposition to the later Jews, whose prince was Michael,—but Mohammed also represents G. as fighting for him, *e.g.* at the head of 3000 angels against the idolatrous Meccans. But, comparing Lk 1²⁰ (also perhaps Dn 10¹³· ²⁰· ²¹) with this, we see that these sterner aspects were not wanting even in the Jewish conception of Gabriel.

A. GRIEVE.

GAD.—Gad is another form of goad, and the gadfly (so correctly RVm for קֶרֶץ in Jer 46²⁰ ; AV, RV ‘destruction’) is the goad-fly, the fly that stings. Hence the favourite derivation for the verb to ‘gad’ (though it is not very certain) is to rush about like animals stung by the gadfly. Perhaps better and more simply (after Skeat), to drive about (which was the orig. sense), *goad* ; then rush

---

about as goaded. Cf. Dryden, *Virgil's Georgics*, iii.—

> 'their stings draw blood
> And drive the cattle gadding through the wood.'

Bacon expresses the usual meaning of the word clearly in *Essays* 'Of Envy' (Gold. Treas. ed. p. 30, l. 21)—'For Envy is a Gadding Passion, and walketh the Streets, and doth not keepe home.' With which cf. T. Adams, *II Peter* (on 1⁴), 'Man's knowledge should not be a gadding harlot, whose feet cannot keep within doors; but a good housewife to stay at home.' In AV we find, Jer 2³⁶ 'Why gaddest thou about so much to change thy way?' (מַה־תֵּזְלִי, lit. 'why goest thou?' mostly poetic in Heb., but in Aram. the usual word for 'to go away'); Sir 25²⁵ 'Give the water no passage; neither a wicked woman liberty to gad abroad' (after Vulg. *veniam prodeundi*, which again follows the reading παρρησίαν ἐξόδου; B has simply ἐξουσίαν; אA παρρησίαν, whence RV 'freedom of speech').

Gadder occurs Sir 26⁸ 'A drunken woman and a gadder abroad causeth great anger' (after the reading καὶ ῥεμβάς, but not Vulg., which has no corresp. words, but to the Gr. [ὀργὴ μεγάλη γυνὴ μέθυσος] adds *et contumelia*; RV follows Gr. 'A drunken woman *causeth* great wrath'). Cf. Grafton, *King John*, An. 13, 'In the mean while the priestes within England had prouided them a false and counterfeated prophet called Peter Wakefielde, a Yorkshireman, who was a hermite, an idle gadder about, and a pratlyng marchant.'

J. HASTINGS.

GAD (גָּד, δαιμόνιον, δαίμων; *Fortuna*; also, probably, גַּד, τύχη).—Properly, the word should be used with the article הַגַּד 'the gad,' *i.e.* 'the (god of) good luck'; that being the meaning of the word, which is apparently the same as גַּד *gād*, 'fortune,' Arab. *jadd*, Aram. גַּדָּא *gaddâ*, Syr. *gadā*. Gad was, therefore, originally an appellative, and its use as a divine name is due to its meaning. Examples of its appellative use are גַּד בִּישׁ 'the unlucky' (Buxtorf, 387); גַּדְעָתָא 'the fortune of Athe' (de Vogüé, *Palm.* 143); גרנעמת and גדנעמנר, etc., in Carthag. inscriptions. The god Gad as Τύχη, 'Fortune,' seems to illustrate the origin of the Old Pers. word for 'God,' *baga*,* which may be traced back to the Sanskrit *bhaga*, 'fortune,' and Baethgen quotes in this connexion the Syr. phrase 'I swear by the Fortune (גַּדָּא) of the king' (P. Smith, *s.v.*), 'fortune' becoming thus a protective divinity, to whom temples were built and statues erected. The worship of this divinity became greatly extended in ancient times, and numerous Gr. inscriptions in the Hauran give the Gr. equivalent word (Τύχη), the identity of which with Gad, notwithstanding the difference of gender (Gad being masc., Tyche fem.), does not admit of doubt. A trace of the Syr. worship of Gad is regarded as being indicated by the exclamation of Leah when Zilpah, her maid, bore Jacob a son (Gn 30¹¹). The expression used is בְּגַד, which is translated in AV (following the Kĕrê, בָּא גָד *bā gād*) 'a troop cometh,' or 'fortune is come.' If, however, the Kethîbh be followed (with pointing בְּגָד *bĕgād*), the word may be translated 'with Gad '† (in RV 'fortunate,' m. 'with fortune'), a rendering favoured by many scholars. As the name of Gad is not met with in Bab. literature, it would seem to have been a native Can. word, retained by the Israelites in consequence of the tendency to polytheism which existed among them as late as the time of the Bab. captivity, when they 'pre-

* Also the Phrygian name of Zeus, Βαγαῖος.
† The Targ. of the pseudo-Jonathan and that of Jerus. both read 'a lucky planet cometh.' (Cf. also Ball's note, *ad loc.*, in Haupt's *OT*).

pared a table for Fortune [לַגַּד],' and filled up 'mingled wine unto Destiny [לַמְנִי]' (Is 65¹¹ RV), as did also the Babylonians and Assyrians for their gods (cf. Bel³, also Jer 51⁴⁴). * By the astrologers Gad was identified with the planet Jupiter, called by the Arabs 'Great Fortuna,' and the question naturally arises whether the Assyrian *Manu rabû*,† 'great Manu,' identified by Lenormant with Meni or 'Destiny,' may not in reality be identical with Gad, Meni being, with the Arabs, 'Lesser Fortuna.' The Assyrians also worshipped a god named Ḳibî-dunḳi, ‡ a name meaning 'Bespeak thou my good fortune,' with whom Gad may also have been identified. The identification of Gad with the star of good fortune (כּוֹכַב צֶדֶק *kôkab ẓedeḳ*), the planet Jupiter, is regarded as being of late date.

Further testimony to the worship of Gad in Canaan is to be found in the place-names Baal-gad (Jos 11¹⁷ 12⁷ 13⁵), where Baal was worshipped as god of fortune, and Migdal-gad (Jos 15³⁷), 'the tower of Gad.' The Hebrews also were so accustomed to regard the worship of Gad as a natural thing, that the words addressed by Isaac to his father, 'let my father arise' (Gn 27³¹), are explained in *Bereshith Rabba*, p. 65, as an invocation to Gada or Fortune.

LITERATURE.—Dillm., Del., and G. A. Smith on Is 65¹¹, Del. on Gn 30¹¹; Lenormant, *Chaldæan Magic*, p. 120; Baethgen, *Beitr. z. Semit. Rel.* 76 ff.; Nöldeke in *ZDMG* (1888), p. 479 ff.; Siegfried in *Jahrb. f. prot. Theol.* (1875), pp. 356–367.

T. G. PINCHES.

GAD (גָּד, Γάδ).—Son of Jacob by his concubine Zilpah, Leah's slave-girl. Gn 30¹¹ RV, 'Leah said, Fortunate! and she called his name Gad,' follows the LXX, εἶπεν Λεία, Ἐν τύχῃ, and Vulg. *Dixit feliciter*. Field mentions the Greek rendering, εὐτύχηκα, 'I have had good fortune,' reading בְּגַד or בְּגַּד. Perhaps we should tr. 'With the help of Gad' (Ball, *Sacred Books of OT*). Dillm. has 'Glückskind.' So *Kethîbh*; the Ḳerê, punctuating differently, has בָּא גָד 'Gad *or* Fortune comes.' So Symm. (ἦλθεν Γάδ) Onk. and Syr. Aq. has ἦλθεν εὐζωΐα ('well-living'), which Field, on the authority of Jerome, etc., corrects to εὐζωνία ('the being well-girded'). The view taken by these authorities suggests that Gad here is either the divine name found in Is 65¹¹ (see preceding art.), or is connected with that name. The AV 'a troop cometh' treats גַּד as equivalent to גְּדוּד, probably on account of Gn 49¹⁹, which, however, is rather a play upon words than a serious etymology. Similar translations are given by the Sam. Version (Dillm.) and the Gr.-Ven. ἥκει στράτευμα.

W. H. BENNETT.

GAD (Tribe); for *Name*, see preceding article.

i. EARLY HISTORY.—The relation of Gad to the other tribes is indicated genealogically by the statement, Gn 30¹¹ (J), 35²⁶ (P), that Gad and Asher were the sons of Zilpah, Rachel's slave, *i.e.* probably, that Gad and Asher were closely connected, and either occupied a secondary position in, or were late accessions to, Israel. The separation of the Palestinian territories of the two tribes shows that this statement refers to a period before the completion of the conquest of Canaan. It is noteworthy that the names Gad and possibly also Asher are connected with the names of Semitic deities. P (Gn 46¹⁶, Nu 26¹⁵⁻¹⁷) enumerates the sons or families of Gad, and states (Nu 1¹⁴ 2¹⁴ 7⁴² 10²⁰ 13¹⁵) that, at the Exodus, the prince of Gad was Eliasaph

* These *lectisternia* or tables for the gods are also referred to in connexion with 'the queen of heaven' in Jer 7¹⁸.
† *WAI* iii. pl. 66. obv. l. 2 c.
‡ *Ib.* obv. 30c, rev. 29f., the latter passage reading 'Ḳibî-dunḳi of Assur (and) Istar (or, of the god and goddess) of Suti' (probably the people Suti transported by Ḳadišman-Muruš 'from east to west,' *i.e.* to Amurri or Phœnicia). Ḳibî-dunḳi is probably the same as the deity Iḳbi-dunḳi, who is described as *mušĕrib damāti*, 'the dispenser of favours.'

ben-Deuel (or Reuel), and that the Gadite amongst the twelve spies was Geuel ben-Machi. Buchanan Gray (*Heb. Proper Names*, 205) considers Eliasaph pre-exilic ; but places Deuel and Geuel in a list of which he says, 'The probability appears to me great that the following seventeen are of late origin, and, probably, also of artificial character' (p. 210). P also tells us that Gad numbered 45,650 at the first census (Nu 1²⁵ 2¹⁵), and at the second 40,500 (MT Nu 26¹⁸), or 44,500 (LXX Nu 26²⁷) ; and that Gad marched in the wilderness in the 'Camp of Reuben' with Reuben and Simeon on the south side of Israel (Nu 2¹⁰⁻¹⁶). In Nu 1⁵⁻¹⁶ Gad occupies the eleventh place, beween Asher and Naphtali ; in 1²⁴ MT and 26¹⁵ MT, the third place after Reuben and Simeon, but in the corresponding 1³⁶ LXX, the ninth place, between Benjamin and Dan, and in 26²⁷ LXX, the sixth place, between Zebulun and Asher. In Nu 2¹⁴ 7⁴² Gad occupies the sixth place, also after Reuben and Simeon.

ii. THE CONQUEST.—In Nu 32 Reuben and Gad receive E. Palestine from Moses on condition of aiding in the conquest of W. Palestine. Although this chapter owes its present form to P, the main

the Arnon, and possibly farther north. Nu 32³⁷· ³⁸ (JE) assigns to Reuben, Heshbon, Elealeh, Kiriathaim, Nebo, and Baal-meon—cities lying in a district about midway between the Jabbok and the Arnon. This suggests that Reuben held an *enclave* in the territory of Gad. See Map, in which the names of the above Reubenite cities are printed in italics. (*b*) Jos 13. Though this chapter comes to us from P, it is probably based on earlier sources. P knows less about the E. than about the W. tribes, and this ch. is obscure and self-contradictory; but it clearly locates Gad north of a line drawn from the north end of the Dead Sea, a little to the N. of Heshbon, and places Reuben south of the same line. This chapter is followed in the ordinary maps of Palestine.

As to the northern boundary of Gad, the statements as to the division of Gilead between Gad and E. Manasseh are contradictory ; and the term Gilead was probably very elastic. The data are too obscure to determine any clear boundary between Gad and E. Manasseh, even as representing any single account. In Nu 32²⁹ (P ?) Moses gives the land of Gilead to Gad and Reuben ; in Nu 32³⁹ (JE), Dt 3¹⁵, Gilead belongs to Machir

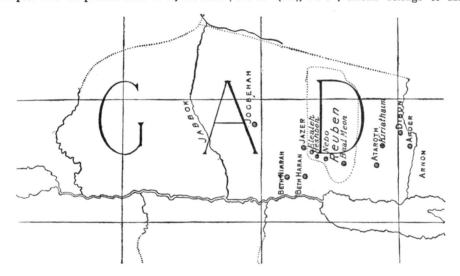

facts were probably contained in J or E or both; but the references to 'half Manasseh' are editorial additions to the original narrative. Similar statements are made in Dt 3¹²⁻¹⁷ 29⁸, Jos 12⁶ (D²) 13⁸⁻²⁸ (D² P). Further, Jos 1¹²⁻¹⁸ 4¹² (D²) tell us that Reuben and Gad fulfilled their promise, and Jos 22¹⁻⁸ (D²) that they afterwards returned home.

Jos 22⁹⁻³⁴ tells how Reuben and Gad on their return erected a great altar by the Jordan—it is not clear on which side ; how the other tribes supposed it to be a schismatic altar and prepared for war, but were appeased on learning that it had been erected as a token of the unity of Reuben and Gad with the other tribes (see ED.). The narrative as it stands is one of the latest additions to P ; but it seems to be based on JE, though it has been so entirely reconstructed by a late editor that we cannot recover the original story. Here again the references to 'half Manasseh' are editorial additions.

iii. THE TERRITORY OF GAD.—Besides minor references, we have two main accounts of the territory : (*a*) Nu 32³⁴⁻³⁶ (JE) assigns to Gad Beth-haran, Beth-nimrah, Dibon, Jogbehah, Jazer, Ataroth, Atroth-shophan, and Aroer, cities scattered over the district between the Jabbok and

ben-Manasseh ; in Dt 3¹² Moses gives half Mt. Gilead to Reuben and Gad ; while in Dt 3¹⁶ Reuben and Gad receive 'from Gilead.' Apparently in Jg 5¹⁷ Gilead=Gad. In Jos 13²⁵· ³¹ (P) G. has all the cities of Gilead, and Machir ben-Manasseh has half Gilead. In the list of Levitical cities in Jos 21³⁸· ³⁹ (P), 1 Ch 6⁸⁰· ⁸¹, Heshbon, which is given to Reuben in Jos 13¹⁷, is reckoned as belonging to Gad. Ramoth-gilead is given to Gad in Jos 20⁸ (P) 21³⁸· ³⁹ (P), Dt 4⁴³, 1 Ch 6⁸⁰· ⁸¹. See Table, p. 78.

iv. HISTORY AFTER THE CONQUEST.—First we may notice the general relation of Gad to the other eastern tribes. Apparently, the strength of Reuben was broken at some early date (see REUBEN), and this tribe became dependent on Gad, much as Simeon on Judah. Hence the situation in JE, in which Reuben occupies a group of cities in the territory of Gad. P's arrangement in Jos 13 is probably a conjectural restoration, after Reuben and Gad had disappeared, embodying the general idea that Reuben lay to the south of Gad. Further, P's idea in Jos of the close early confederation of Reuben and Gad with E. Manasseh is also late. It is doubtful whether the eastern settlement of Manasseh was made before Israel crossed the Jordan, or later by Manassite clans, who recrossed the river from the West (cf. MANASSEH). But, in any case, the interests of Gad and E. Manasseh were separate and often conflicting; and the contradictory statements, some of which assign Gilead to Gad, while others make Gilead a clan of Manasseh, probably indicate that at an early date Gad (with its dependent Reuben) was practically Israel east of the Jordan, and that clans of Manasseh afterwards encroached upon Gad's territory and occupied part of Gilead. According to Jg 5[17] neither Gad nor Reuben had any share in the victory over Sisera. Gad must have been involved in the Ammonite invasion, the deliverance by Jephthah, and the quarrel with Ephraim in Jg 11. 12. 'Gileadite,' used of Jephthah and his followers, may equal 'Gadite,' or be a general term for 'E. Israelite.' The genealogies, if pressed, make Jephthah a member of E. Manasseh; Jg 12[4] may perhaps suggest that his followers belonged to clans of Ephraim and Manasseh, which had migrated to the east of Jordan; but the verse is corrupt and obscure, cf. 11[29]. In any case, this Ammonite war illustrates the border raids and more serious invasions to which Gad, in common with Reuben and E. Manasseh, was exposed throughout the

country into twelve districts, 'which provided victuals for the king and his household.' The description of the districts is vague and obscure, but it is clear that they do not coincide with tribal territories; and it is sometimes held that this new arrangement marks the close of the old tribal system. But Gad at any rate, having by this time absorbed Reuben, stood for S.E. Palestine, and continued to do so; see below on Moabite Stone.

At the disruption Gad fell to the N. kingdom; and Penuel, apparently Jeroboam's capital (1 K 12[25]), probably lay within its territory. Jeroboam's interest in the district would add to its prosperity, but tend to abolish distinct tribal organization, and to merge E. Palestine in the N. kingdom. Probably, as the Moabite Stone speaks of cities taken from Moab by Omri, Moab recovered its independence at or soon after the disruption. Such recovery of Moab may have been chiefly at the expense of Reuben; but Gad also must have suffered through the gains of Moab, and profited by the conquests of Omri. Elijah, and probably (G. A. Smith, *Hist. Geog.* p. 580) the brook Cherith, are of Gilead, *i.e.* probably Gad.

In the long wars between Israel and Aram, E. Palestine was the battle-ground, and the brunt

TABLE OF CITIES ASSIGNED TO GAD.

	ASSIGNED TO									
	GAD.						REUBEN.	MOAB.		REMARKS.
	Nu 32 34-36.	Jos 13 24-28.	Jos 20[8].	Jos 21 38. 39.	1 Ch 6 80. 81.	Nu 33 45-46.	Is	Jer	Stone.	
Dibon . . .	*	..	..	..	..	*	Jos 13[17]	15[2]	48[18]	*	cf. Nu 21[30].
Ataroth . .	*	..	..	..	..	..		..	...	e*	eTaken from Gad.
Aroer . . .	*	*	..	..	..	..	1 Ch 5[8]	..	48[19]	*	
Atroth-shophan .	*	?a	..	..	..	..		..	..	..	a Zaphon.
Jazer . . .	*	*	..	..	*	*		16[8]	48[32]	..	
Jogbehah . .	*	..	..	..	..	..		..	...	..	
Beth-nimrah . .	*	*	..	..	..	...		15[6]d	48[34]d	..	d Waters of Nimrim.
Beth-haran . .	*	*b	..	..	..	...		..	..	..	b haram.
Succoth . .	..	*	..	..	..	..		..	..	..	
Ramoth-gilead .	..	..	*	*	*	..		..	..	..	
Heshbon . .	..	?c	..	*	*	..	{ Nu 32[37] Jos 13[17] }	15[4]	48[34]	..	{ cf. Nu 21[30] and Jer 48[2].
Mahanaim . .	..	?c	..	*	*	..		..	..	..	c '*from*' H. & M.

history. Such a situation, Gad raided and raiding, but more than holding its own, is well described in Gn 49[19], the blessing of Jacob (J from older source)—

> 'Gad, the raiders shall raid him,
> But he shall raid upon their heel.'

In Jg 20. 21 (late post-ex. Midrash on earlier basis, possibly J, or J and E, see Moore and Budde, *in loc.*) the eastern tribes took part in the war against Benjamin; Jabesh-gilead, the only city which furnished no contingent, was sacked, and its inhabitants massacred, only the virgins being saved as wives for the Benjamites.

During the wars with the Philistines, Gad was a stronghold and refuge of the Isr. (1 S 13[7]). After Saul's death it became the main part of Eshbaal's kingdom (2 S 2[8]). Later on it afforded a rallying point for David's adherents during the revolt of Absalom (2 S 17[27]). Amongst David's mighty men was Bani the Gadite (2 S 23[36]). Apparently, Gad was still strong and intact. It would profit by the strength of Israel under David and Solomon. In 1 Ch 12[8-15] Gadites come to David when a fugitive from Saul; and in 12[37] Reuben, Gad, and E. Manasseh come to David at Hebron to make him king. 1 K 4[7-19] tells us that Solomon divided the

fell upon E. Manasseh. Even under Ahab the point of contact was at Ramoth-gilead. Probably E. Manasseh had practically disappeared in these wars, and Gilead again became synonymous with Gad. Gad itself also suffered (Am 1[3. 13]). About the same time Moab revolted and captured Gadite cities in the South (*Moabite Stone*). Gad or Gilead shared in the renewed prosperity of Israel under Jeroboam II., but shortly after, in B.C. 734, E. Palestine was carried captive by Tiglath-pileser (2 K 15[29]), and thus Gad disappears from history. Apparently, the territory was occupied by Ammon (Jer 49[1]). Ezk 48[27. 34] makes provision for Gad in the restored Israel. On the other hand, in Ob [19] the E. tribes are so completely forgotten that Gilead is promised to Benjamin. In Rev 7[5] Gad is enumerated among the tribes of Israel.

LITERATURE.—Buhl, *Geog. d. alt. Palästina*, 79; G. A. Smith, *HGHL*, 566-568, 575-590; Budde, *Richter*, 45 f.; Stade, *GVI*, i. 145 ff.; Driver, *Deut.* 54 f., 410 f.; Moore, *Judges*, 150 f., 154 f.

W. H. BENNETT.

GAD (גָּד) is entitled the seer (חֹזֶה 1 Ch 29[29]), David's or the king's seer (1 Ch 21[9], 2 Ch 29[25], 2 S 24[11]), or the prophet (נָבִיא, 1 S 22[5], 2 S 24[11]). His activity seems to have lain chiefly in the early period of the king's life, at least it is not he but Nathan who appears prominently in that palace intrigue which resulted in the accession of Solomon (1 K 1¹¹ff.). The name might suggest that he belonged to the tribe of Gad; but the only additional support for this view is found in the fact that several of David's chiefs came from that tribe (1 Ch 12⁸). As for Ewald's suggestion, that Gad drew his inspiration from the school of Samuel, while this would agree well with his appearing immediately after David's rupture with Saul (1 S 22⁵), it cannot be considered certain, so long as the existence of 'a school' of Samuel is merely a conjecture.

Gad is represented as having announced the divine condemnation on the royal census, and as having advised the erection of an altar on Araunah's threshing-floor (2 S 24¹¹ff. = 1 Ch 21⁹ff.). The Chronicler again (1 Ch 29²⁹) names him as having written an account of some part of his master's reign. A late conception associated him with the prophet Nathan (2 Ch 29²⁵) in the task of planning some of the king's regulations with reference to the musical part of the service, while (1 S 22⁵) he is also stated to have acted as David's counsellor in peril during the period when the two dwelt together in 'the hold.'   A. C. WELCH.

GAD, VALLEY OF (נַחַל גָּד ['torrent-valley'], AV 'river of Gad').—2 S 24⁵. Taken in connexion with Jos 13²⁵ this passage would indicate that the river or valley of Gad was close to Rabbath-Ammon in the land of Gad; but, on the other hand, 'the city that lieth in the valley' is mentioned in connexion with Aroer on the river Arnon (now el-Mojib), Jos 13⁹. ¹⁶, Dt 2³⁶. It appears to be certain that in 2 S 24⁵, instead of 'and they pitched in Aroer, on the right side of the city that is in the middle of the valley of Gad' (וַיַּחֲנוּ בַעֲרוֹעֵר יְמִין הָעִיר אֲשֶׁר בְּתוֹךְ־הַנַּחַל הַגָּד), we ought to read, 'and they began from Aroer, and from the city that is in the middle of the torrent-valley, towards Gad' (וַיָּחֵלּוּ מֵעֲרוֹעֵר וּמִן הָעִיר וגֹ). This emendation, originally due to Wellhausen (Text d. B. Sam. 217), was afterwards confirmed by Luc. καὶ ἤρξαντο ἀπὸ Ἀροὴρ καὶ ἀπὸ, κ.τ.λ., and is accepted by Driver, Budde, etc. 'The city in the torrent-valley' was possibly 'Ar. See for a full discussion, both of the text and the topography, Driver, Text of Sam. 285 f., Deuteronomy, 45.   C. WARREN.

GADARA, GADARENES.—The country of the Gadarenes is mentioned in the Bible only in connexion with one incident, viz. the miracle concerning the legion of demons who were allowed to enter the herd of swine (Mt 8²⁸, Mk 5¹, Lk 8²⁶), and it is improbable that the city on the seashore mentioned in the account of that incident can be identified with the city of Gadara, which was situated at least 6 miles from the Lake of Gennesaret, and separated from it by a broad plain and the gorge of the river Hieromax. It is possible, however, that the eastern side of the lake at the spot where the miracle actually occurred, which can be located with some certainty (see GERASENES), was situated in the sub-district under the jurisdiction of Gadara. Against this view is the statement of Josephus (BJ IV. vii. 3), that Gadara was the capital of Peræa, which is not supposed to have extended farther north than the Hieromax, the territory beyond that being Gaulanitis.

It has been suggested (Wordsworth's Commentary) that the incident took place on the boundary-line of the jurisdiction of the cities of Gadara and Gergesa, and that the swine owners of these Greek cities belonged to both places. Thomson (The Land and the Book, ii. p. 36) points out that St. Matthew was from this region and personally knew the localities, and that his rendering of Gergesa is most likely to be correct; while St. Mark and St. Luke, being strangers to this part of the country, may possibly have intended by mentioning the country of the Gadarenes to point out to their distant Greek and Roman readers the general position of the place where the miracle occurred; Gergesa, or Gerasa, or Chersa, however pronounced, being small and unknown, while Gadara was a Greek city of importance, celebrated for its temples, theatres, and warm baths. See further under GERASENES.

The city of Gadara has thus no known connexion with biblical history; it was, however, a fortress of great strength, and took a leading part in the struggles between the Seleucidæ and the Ptolemies, and, from the strength of its position and its Hebrew name, it probably existed in early times, and according to the Mishna (Erubhin ix.) was fortified by Joshua. The name does not appear in history until Antiochus the Great, king of Syria, overcame Scopas, the general of the Egyptian king Ptolemy Epiphanes, at Paneas, near the fountain of the Jordan (B.C. 198), and recovered territory previously lost, including Gadara (Ant. XII. iii. 3; Polyb. v. 71). It was again taken from the Syrians by Alexander Jannæus the Hasmonæan king of the Jews, who, acting on a league of mutual defence with Cleopatra queen of Egypt, invaded Cœle-Syria and the territory adjoining and took Gadara after a siege of ten months (c. B.C. 100; Ant. XIII. xiii. 3; BJ I. iv. 2), and enslaved the inhabitants, and compelled them to receive the law of Moses as proselytes of justice (Ant. XIV. xv. 4). The defeat of Alexander Jannæus by Obidas king of the Arabians, is related to have occurred at Gadara, a village of Gilead or Golan (Ant. XIII. xiii. 5; BJ I. iv. 4), probably not the same as the fortress of Gadara.

Gadara was demolished by the Jews and rebuilt by Pompey the Great (B.C. 63) to gratify Demetrius of Gadara, who was one of his own freedmen, when he established the Roman supremacy in Phœnicia, Cœle-Syria, and Palestine; he left the inhabitants in a state of freedom and joined the city to the province of Syria (Ant. XIV. iv. 4; BJ I. vii. 7). It counted from the era of Pompey, and became the seat of one of the five councils which Gabinius, proconsul of Syria (B.C. 57–55), instituted for the government of the Jews (Ant. XIV. v. 4; BJ I. viii. 5). Augustus Cæsar added Gadara to the kingdom of Herod the Great (Ant. XV. vii. 3). The inhabitants subsequently accused Herod to Cæsar of maladministration and plunderings, but Cæsar would not hear them (Ant. XV. x. 2 and 3). On the death of Herod (B.C. 4), Gadara was transferred to the province of Syria (Ant. XVII. xi. 4; BJ II. vi. 3). On the revolt of the Jews against the Roman dominion, they ravaged the country about Gadara, and the Greek inhabitants rose up against the Jews and put the boldest of them to death and imprisoned others (BJ II. xviii. 5). Gadara was taken by Vespasian, on which occasion the inhabitants pulled down its walls to show that they wished for peace. It appears, however, to have still existed for many centuries as an important city, for bishops of Gadara are mentioned as having been present at the general councils of the Church. The style of the existing ruins indicates its having flourished during the time of the Antonines, and the coins extant extend over the period from the rebuilding by Pompey to A.D. 239. Gadara was a fortress of considerable strength (Ant. XIII. iii. 3; BJ IV. vii. 3), situated near the Hieromax (Pliny, HN 16), east of the Sea of Galilee and over-against Scythopolis and Tiberias (Euseb. Onom. s.v.). It was situated on the top of a hill, at the foot of which, at 3 miles' distance, on the bank of the Hieromax, were warm springs and baths called Amatha (Onom. s.v. 'Gadara'; Itin. Ant. Martyr.). It had a district attached called Gadaris (*BJ* III. iii. 1 ; Strabo, XVI. ii. 45). It was one of the cities of Decapolis, and is called by Josephus the capital of Peræa (*BJ* IV. vii. 3), though in another passage (*BJ* III. iii. 3) he gives the bounds of Peræa from north to south as from Pella to Machærus. It is frequently mentioned by Josephus in connexion with Cœle-Syria (*Ant.* XIII. xiii. 3). The main roads from Scythopolis and Tiberias to Damascus and Gerasa passed through it. Josephus calls it a Greek town (*Ant.* XVII. xi. 4 ; *BJ* II. vi. 3), but it is evident from the historical accounts that many Jews were living in and around the city (*BJ* II. xviii. 5), and it is probable that the number of Jews living around may have fluctuated from time to time and have depended on the friendly nature of the government.

The site of Gadara has been recognized at the ruins of *Umm Ḳeis*, which extend over the summit of a high hill, 1200 ft. above the Mediterranean, east of the Jordan on the southern side of the gorge of the *Sheri'at el-Mandhûr* (Jarmûk or Hieromax), about 6 miles south-east of the southern side of the Lake of Gennesaret. At the foot of the hill, about 3 miles north of *Umm Ḳeis* on the right or north bank of the *Sheri'at*, in a flat space below the cliffs, are the remains of the celebrated hot springs, baths, and buildings of Amatha, described by Eusebius, Antoninus Martyr, and Strabo. There are several hot springs along the bank of the river, but those clustered together at this spot are the most copious. The largest spring gives off more water than that of Tiberias ; the temperature is 110° Fahrenheit. The water is strongly impregnated with sulphur. These springs are much resorted to by the Bedawîn for various diseases. The ruins about the baths are very extensive, giving the impression that this spot was also used as a favourite watering-place by the inhabitants of Gadara during inclement weather (Wilson, *Recovery of Jerusalem*).

Umm Ḳeis is situated at the extreme north-western border of the high land of Northern '*Ajlûn*, and commands a magnificent view of the Sea of Tiberias, Southern *Jaulân*, the Jordan Valley, Galilee, and Mount Tabor. There could hardly be a second point in this part of '*Ajlûn*, which combines so perfectly the advantages due to a magnificent soil and a commanding position (*Northern 'Ajlûn*).

The ruins of *Umm Ḳeis* contain the remains of a very handsome and extensive city, with buildings of great magnificence, which appear to have been overthrown by an earthquake, many of the buildings remaining as perfect in their ruin as though the shock had taken place yesterday. Josephus records an earthquake having occurred which devastated the country, B.C. 31 (*Ant.* XV. v. 2), and the ruins of Umm Ḳeis may be due to an earthquake equally severe at a later period. There are to be seen among the ruins two large theatres, a basilica, a temple, the main street running east and west, with colonnades, the columns lying just as they fell, and many large private buildings, the whole surrounded by a city wall with gates. There is a large reservoir, and an aqueduct brought water into the city. The columns are surmounted by Corinthian capitals. The basalt paving is in places quite perfect, and retains traces of the marks of chariot wheels. The eastern theatre is in an almost perfect state of preservation ; the approach to it would have been extremely grand, passing from the main street over a great platform surrounded by columns. A very interesting feature is the large Necropolis on the east and north-east side of the town, in which there are both rock-hewn tombs and sarcophagi ; the former are cut in the limestone rock without any attempt at concealment. A flight of steps leads down to a small

court, from which two or three doors give access to the chambers : the doors are of stone, many of them still perfect, with stone hinges similar to those found in the Hauran. These tombs are inhabited by the present dwellers at *Umm Ḳeis*. Outside the town, to the east, the ancient name Gadara is still preserved in the name of the ruins, *Jedûr Umm Ḳeis* (Wilson, *Recovery of Jerusalem* ; Schumacher, *Northern 'Ajlûn* ; Macgregor, *Rob Roy on the Jordan*). The Christians of Nazareth were in the habit of holding a fair at *Umm Ḳeis*, until in recent years, the Bedawîn having overrun the country, they were obliged to desist.

C. WARREN.

GADDI (גַּדִּי 'my fortune').—The Manassite sent as one of the twelve spies, Nu 13[11] P.

GADDIEL (גַּדִּיאֵל 'God is my fortune'[*]).—The Zebulunite sent as one of the twelve spies, Nu 13[10] P.

GADDIS (Καδδίς, otherwise Γαδδίς, A ; Γαδδεί, א ; *Gaddis*, Vulg. ; ‸ᵣ‸ = *Gadi*, Syr. ; 1 Mac 2²), the surname of Johanan or John, the eldest brother of Judas Maccabæus. The name perhaps represents the Heb. גַּדִּי, *Gaddi* (Nu 13[11]), meaning 'my fortune.'

H. A. WHITE.

GADI (גָּדִי ; cf. Nabatæan נדי (?גדו), Euting, No. 25 ; Palmyrene גדיא, de Vogüé, No. 32 ; Γαδδεί B, Γεδδεί, Γαλλεί A, Γαδδί Luc.).—Father of Menahem king of Israel (2 K 15[14. 17]).

C. F. BURNEY.

GADITES.—See GAD (Tribe).

GAHAM (גַּחַם).—The eponym of a Nahorite clan whose identity has not been established, Gn 22[24]. Gaham is described as a son of Nahor by his concubine Reumah.

GAHAR (גַּחַר).—A family of Nethinim who returned with Zerub. (Ezr 2[47], Neh 7[49]), called in 1 Es 5[30] Geddur. See GENEALOGY.

GAI (גַּיְא) is given as a proper name in RV of 1 S 17[52] 'until thou comest to Gai,' where AV has 'until thou comest to the valley.' This last, however, would demand הַגָּיְא as in v.[3]. In any case, the valley (ravine) referred to in v.[52] must be different from that which separated the opposing forces. See ELAH (VALLEY OF). The LXX, as is noted in RVm, has Γέθ (Gath), and this would suit the context (cf. Wellhausen, Budde, and Driver, *ad loc.*). Wellh. further proposes to treat Shaaraim not as a proper name, but, inserting the article (הַשְּׁעָרִים), as = 'in the gateway.' That is to say, the Israelites pursued the Philistines to the gates of Ekron, and the wounded fell down in the gateway of both Gath and Ekron. An alternative, he suggests, is to view the two expressions, 'until thou comest to Gath and to the gates of Ekron,' and 'even unto Gath and unto Ekron,' as doublets due perhaps to the names of these two cities being in the former clause written indistinctly or incorrectly, in consequence of which an explanatory gloss was added on the margin and afterwards introduced into the text.

J. A. SELBIE.

GAINSAY.—To gainsay is to speak against, as Udal, *Erasmus' Paraphrase* on 1 Jn 1, 'And yf we wyll say, that wee have no sinne in us, we make God a lyar, and say agaynst hym : and he that gayne sayeth hym, must needs lye' ; *Rhem. NT* on Jn 6[49], 'The discontented and incredulous murmured and gainsaid it [the manna].' Wyclif

---

[*] According to Hommel (*Ancient Heb. Tradition*, 1897, p. 300), from the Arabic, 'my grandfather is God.'

has the older form *agenseyen* frequently, as Lk 21¹⁵ (1380) 'I schal gyue to you mouth and wysdom, to whiche alle youre aduersaries schulen not mowe agenstonde, and agenseye.' Sometimes the meaning is rather wider and almost the same as oppose or resist generally. Thus Job 11¹⁰ Wyc. (1382) 'If he turne vpso doun alle thingus, or in to oon drawe togidere, who shal agensein to hym?' (EV 'hinder'); and Pref. to AV 1611, 'For, was there euer any thing proiected, that sauoured any way of newnesse or renewing, but the same endured many a storme of gaine-saying, or opposition?' So in AV we have Jth 8²⁸ 'there is none that may gainsay thy words,' where the Gr. is ὃς ἀντιστήσεται τοῖς λόγοις σου, lit. 'withstand,' Geneva 'resist'; and Ad. Est 13⁹ 'The whole world is in thy power, and if thou hast appointed to save Israel, there is no man that can gainsay thee' (ὃς ἀντιτάξεται σοι; lit. 'range in battle against thee'; Cov. 'withstonde ner lett the'). And even when the orig. word expresses *speaking* against, the general sense of resist is often evident.

The verb occurs in Lk 21¹⁵ 'I will give you a mouth and wisdom, which all your adversaries shall not be able to gainsay nor resist' (after Wyc., as above, who has the order 'agenstonde and agensaye,' as Vulg. *resistere et contradicere*, and as L, T, WH ἀντιστῆναι οὐδὲ [T, WH ἢ] ἀντειπεῖν, while AV follows TR ἀντειπεῖν οὐδὲ ἀντιστῆναι); 2 Es 5²⁹ 'they which did gainsay thy promises' (*qui contradicebant sponsionibus tuis*); Jth 12¹⁴ 'Who am I now, that I should gainsay my lord?' (ἀντεροῦσα τῷ κυρίῳ μου); and 1 Mac 14⁴¹ 'to gainsay his words' (ἀντειπεῖν τοῖς ὑπ' αὐτοῦ ῥηθησομένοις); RV 'to gainsay the words that he should speak,' *i.e.* resist his commands. To these instances RV adds Ac 19³⁶ 'Seeing then that these things cannot be gainsaid' (ἀναντιρρήτων [WH ἀναντιρήτων] οὖν ὄντων τούτων, the only occurrence of this adj., though the adv. occurs Ac 10²⁹, as below; AV 'spoken against'); Tit 2⁹ 'not gainsaying' (μὴ ἀντιλέγοντας, AV 'not answering again,' AVm 'gainsaying').

The adj. is found in Ro 10²¹ 'a disobedient and gainsaying people' (ἀντιλέγοντα). The subst. occurs in Ac 10²⁹ 'Therefore came I unto you without gainsaying' (ἀναντιρρήτως [WH ἀναντιρήτως]); Jude ¹¹ 'and perished in the gainsaying of Core' (καὶ τῇ ἀντιλογίᾳ τοῦ Κορὲ ἀπόλοντο; cf. LXX ὕδωρ ἀντιλογίας = Heb. מְרִיבָה = Eng. 'water of Meribah' of Nu 20¹³); to which RV adds He 12³ 'For consider him that hath endured such gainsaying (AV 'contradiction') of sinners against himself' (ἀντιλογίαν, which in the other two occurrences, He 6¹⁶ 7⁷, RV tr. 'dispute'). The personal subst. 'gainsayer' is found Tit 1⁹ 'to convince (RV 'convict') the gainsayers' (τοὺς ἀντιλέγοντας ἐλέγχειν; Wyc. [1380] 'to reproue hem that agen seyn' [1388 'agenseien'], but in *Prefatory Epistles of St. Jerome*, ch. iii. [1388] Wyc. has 'He comaundide also to Tite, among othere vertues of a bishop . . . to withstonde agenseyeris').   J. HASTINGS.

GAIUS (Γάϊος).—The person to whom the Third Ep. of St. John is addressed. He is spoken of in terms of affection and respect as 'beloved' (vv.¹·²·⁵·¹¹), walking 'in the truth' (v.³), acting well to brethren and to strangers (v.⁵). But beyond this we know nothing of him. Some have thought to identify him with a Caius who is mentioned in the *Apostolic Constitutions* (vii. 46) as having been appointed bishop of Pergamum by John. Others have attempted to identify him with one or other of the men who bear the same name in the NT— the G. of Macedonia (Ac 19²⁹), the G. of Derbe (Ac 20⁴), the G. of Corinth (1 Co 1¹⁴, Ro 16²³). But these are all associated with the Apostle Paul, and

there is nothing in the Epistle itself or elsewhere to help us to an identification. S. D. F. SALMOND.

GALAL (גָּלָל).—The name of two Levites, 1 Ch 9¹⁵·¹⁶, Neh 11¹⁷. See GENEALOGY.

GALATIA (Γαλατία) is understood by different scholars as the name of two distinct countries; and, as the important associated questions are still under discussion, it is necessary to treat the term under two headings, and describe the history and geography of the two different countries which the term is said to denote. The fundamental question is this: Are the Churches of G., to which St. Paul addressed an Epistle, certain congregations in the northern part of the great inner plateau of Asia Minor variously enumerated by different advocates of 'the North-Galatian Theory,' or are they the congregations of Pisidian Antioch, Iconium, Derbe, and Lystra, in the southern part of the plateau, according to 'the South-Galatian Theory'? Each of the related terms *Galatians* and *Region of Galatia* is in like manner demands double treatment. St. Paul mentions the Churches of G. in Gal 1², 1 Co 16¹; and they are addressed with others in 1 P 1¹. Finally, there is a doubt whether in 2 Ti 4¹⁰ Galatia or Gallia should be read, and, if Galatia is read, whether it does not denote Gaul (the modern France).

While the opinions fall into two classes on the crucial question, there are varieties in each class. The South-Galatian theory is held both by those who can see no good reason to think that St. Paul ever was in North Galatia, and by those who consider that he travelled in North Galatia but made no important foundation there. The latter view is held by Zahn (*Einleitung in das Neue Testament*). The North-Galatian theory in its common form maintains that the Epistle was addressed to the Churches of Ancyra, Tavium, Pessinus, and possibly other cities; but the most vigorous argument that St. Paul never was in Ancyra or Tavium is urged by Zöckler (*SK*, 1895, p. 79 f.),* who, approximating to Zahn's view, holds that St. Paul travelled little in Galatia, only in the extreme western and south-western parts, *ib.* p. 59 ff., but maintains, unlike Zahn, that he founded several Churches in that obscure district and addressed his Epistle to them. Salmon (*Introduction to NT*, and arts. in Smith, *DB*) seems to come very close to Zöckler's view,† though he translates the critical passage in Ac 16⁶ in quite a different way (GALATIA, REGION OF). But these minor differences are comparatively unimportant, relating to points of translation and antiquarian research; ‡ it is only the crucial question that is of fundamental consequence: To what group of Churches did St. Paul write his Epistle?

I. GALATIA PROPER, as used in the popular and ordinary Greek way (Roman *Gallogræcia*), was the name applied to a large tract of country in the interior of Asia Minor, after it was taken possession of in the 3rd cent. B.C. by certain warrior tribes who had migrated from Gaul towards the east. Irruptions of Gallic tribes into the eastern parts of Europe are first recorded in B.C. 281, when a small army under Cambaules attacked Thrace. In the following year (280) three large Gallic armies

---

* So Findlay in *Expository Times*, vii. (1896) p. 23€. Zöckler takes Chase for the originator of this view; but the latter informs me that this is a misunderstanding of his words, and that he does not hold the view.

† 'St. Luke's narrative does not warrant us to conclude with any certainty that St. Paul made any prolonged stay in Galatia Proper, or did much work in founding Churches there' (Smith, *DB*² i. 1105).

‡ Sometimes agreement in construction and translation results in total disagreement as to interpretation (GALATIA, REGION OF).

advanced—one under Cerethrius against Thrace, a second under Brennus * and Acichorius against Paeonia, the third under Belgius against Macedonia and Illyria. The young king of Macedonia, Ptolemy Ceraunus, was defeated and slain when he rashly gave battle with a small army. In 279 Brennus and other chiefs marched south into Greece ; but a quarrel arose on the way, and two chiefs, Leonnorius and Lutarius, led away 20,000 Gauls into Thrace. Brennus' attempt was unsuccessful, and his army seems to have scattered in its retreat ; and part of it probably joined the Gauls who had invaded Thrace. Many of the invaders of Thrace went on into Asia, Lutarius crossing the Hellespont in some Macedonian ships which he seized ; Leonnorius crossing the Bosphorus at the invitation of Nikomedes, king of Bithynia, who wanted aid in his wars : the date of these events, so calamitous for Asia, was 278–277.

No certainty is attainable as to the exact events and dates that followed. The Gauls ranged through most of western and central Asia Minor, a terror to all the inhabitants, plundering, slaying, burning. Antiochus I., king of Syria A.D. 281–261, was the first to offer any serious resistance ; from his victories he is said to have gained his title Soter (saviour) ; but his success was far from complete. During the uncertain wars of the following years, the Gauls were often hired as mercenaries by the contending kings and generals, usually by the weaker against the stronger. 'Alternately the scourge and the allies of each Asiatic prince in succession, as passion or interest dictated, they for a time indulged their predatory instincts unchecked' (Lightfoot).

But Attalus I., king of Pergamos B.C. 241–197, checked their power in a series of campaigns about B.C. 232, and confined them to a certain fixed country (previously part of Phrygia and of Cappadocia or even of Paphlagonia), which was called henceforth Galatia. They had, however, probably occupied parts of that country long before,† finding it more open to actual settlement than the districts where many strong cities existed ; and the result of Attalus' operations was to circumscribe their territory, and to fix definite limits.

In the sketch which Strabo (p. 567) gives of the Galatian constitution, he records the interesting fact that each tribe was divided into four cantons or tetrarchies, an old Gaulish custom mentioned among the Helvetii by Julius Cæsar.‡ Originally each tetrarchy had a chief or tetrarch ; § and there was a common council of 300 meeting in a grove called Drynemeton (Perrot thinks that it was situated near Assarli-Kaya, about 7 hours S.W. from Ancyra),‖ and judging all cases of murder. This old system had wholly disappeared before the time of Strabo ; the monarchy of Deiotarus and of Amyntas (44–25 B.C.) had destroyed the last traces of the original Gallic constitution, and the Roman provincial organization was hostile to it. Even in early time, when war broke out, a single chief seems to have been chosen in each tribe (Livy, xxxviii. 19).

The defeat of the Gauls by a Roman army in B.C. 189 (Livy, xxxviii. 18 ff., who uses Polybius as his authority) broke their strength. They were placed between three powers, Pontus, Cappadocia, and Pergamos, and were pressed on by all. They were worsted by Ariarathes, king of Cappadocia, about 164 ; and they seem to have fallen under the influence of the Pontic kings in the latter part of the 2nd century, for Phrygia was

given by Rome to Mithridates IV. in 129, and he could not well rule over Phrygia if divided from it by the great independent country of Galatia (Van Gelder, p. 277).* The Mithridatic wars set free the Gauls from this yoke ; and their eagerness to aid the Roman arms against Pontus exposed them to a massacre ordered by Mithridates in 86. In 64, after the war was ended, Pompey appointed or recognized three tetrarchs,† Castor probably among the Tektosages, Brogitarus of the Trokmi, and Deiotarus of the Tolistobogii : Deiotarus also received Armenia Minor with part of Pontus, and, being much the most powerful, gradually made himself master of the Tektosages and Trokmi, and, finally, as the climax of a career of successful treachery and murder, he was recognized as king of Galatia by the Romans. He died at an advanced age in 40 B.C. His kingdom was given by Antony to the younger Castor, along with inner Paphlagonia, which Pompey in 64 had assigned to Attalus (Dion, xlviii. 33). Castor soon died ; and in 36 Antony gave Galatia to Amyntas, and Paphlagonia to Deiotarus Philadelphus, son of Castor (probably the elder), who reigned till B.C. 5, when his kingdom was incorporated in the province Galatia (see II.).‡

According to our authorities, the Gauls entered Asia as an army, not separately in distinct tribes ; but afterwards they appear as divided into three tribes, who arrogated to themselves three distinct districts, the Trokmi claiming the Hellespontine coast, the Tolistobogii Aeolis and Ionia, i.e. the Ægean coastlands, and the Tektosages the lands of the interior (Livy, xxxviii. 16, where note the word postremo). This tribal classification persisted throughout later history, proving that either the original army was formed mainly from these three tribes, or that three successive swarms, each mainly recruited from one tribe, entered Asia Minor. It seems, however, to be certain that contingents from a number of different tribes swelled the armies that invaded Greece, Thrace, and Asia : similarly, in Gaul certain great tribes, e.g. the Aedui, had smaller tribes as dependants or clients (Cæsar, Bell. Gall. vii. 75, iv. 6). From the ancient arrangement it would appear that the Tektosages were the first to seize Galatia, and that when the bounds were drawn by Attalus I. the Tektosages were forced into the centre and north of Galatia, with Ancyra as capital, the Trokmi were concentrated round Tavium on the east, and the Tolistobogii round Pessinus on the west. In this position we find the tribes in all later time.

The boundaries of the country called Galatia varied greatly at different periods. Thus the chief centre of a people Troknades, at the modern village Kaimaz (between Eski-Sheher and Sivri-Hissar, on the ancient road from Dorylaion to Pessinus), was part of the Roman province Asia (CIL iii. No. 6997) ; and yet the name Troknades is undoubtedly Gallic, so that the place must have been at an earlier time included in the territory of the Galatæ. That is perhaps the most westerly point to which the territory owned by the settled Gauls ever extended ; and both it and even Orkistos, which lies farther east, were probably taken from the Galatian state by Attalus I.,§

<hr/>

* Phrygia Magna was given to Mithridates II. (Justin, 38. 6) about B.C. 240 ; but it then included the country which soon after became Galatia. Moreover, the gift was perhaps a mere Pontic claim, never realized in fact.
† See note § above.
‡ See Niese, Rhein. Museum, 1883, p. 584 ff. ; T. Reinach, Revue Numism. 1891, p. 383 ff. ; Ramsay, Revue des Ét. Gr. 1894, p. 251.
§ It was perhaps at this time that Orkistos was placed under the control of Nakoleia (CIL iii. No. 7000) ; the Pergamenian system was favourable to the growth of powerful cities exerting authority over a large territory.

<hr/>

* Brennus is perhaps a title, not a personal name.
† Perhaps by permission of the Pontic kings (Meyer).
‡ Bell. Gall. i. 12 ; see Mommsen in Hermes, 1884, p. 316.
§ Hence the title tetrarch was wrongly given to the three chiefs nominated by Pompey in B.C. 64.
‖ Dry-, intensive prefix (Holder), not (with Perrot) 'oak.'

and passed along with the rest of the Pergamenian kingdom into the hands of the Romans (see ASIA). In late Roman time, probably when the province G. Secunda was created about 390, the name was extended so far to the west as to include the old Phrygian city Amorium, which was after this called a metropolis of Galatia (so Hierocles and most *Notitiæ Episc.*).*

On the north the dividing line between Galatia to the south and Bithynia and Paphlagonia to the north is indeterminable. Close to the north-western corner lay the city Juliopolis, which was in the 1st and 2nd centuries a Bithynian city † (Pliny, *Epist. ad Traj.* 77; Ptolemy, v. 1), but about A.D. 297 was made a city of Galatia. Near the north-eastern corner lay Gangra (Tchangri) and Andrapa (probably Iskelib), which were Paphlagonian cities, and Eukhaita (probably Tchorum), a Pontic city, famous for the worship of St. Theodorus Stratiotes.

On the east and south-east the dividing line between Galatia on the one hand, and Pontus and Cappadocia on the other hand, was also a varying one, running east of Tavium (Nefez-Keui), capital of the Galatian tribe Trokmi, and west of the Pontic city Sebastopolis-Heracleopolis (Sulu-Serai). It is mentioned by Polybius that a certain territory, long disputed between the Gauls and the Cappadocian kings, passed definitely into the possession of Ariarathes about B.C. 164. Basilika Therma (Terzili-Hammam) was well within Cappadocian territory in later time, and the disputed territory perhaps extended from it to the Halys or even as far as Lake Tatta. In the 4th century after Christ, the frontier between Galatia and Cappadocia lay between the Galatian Galea (a village subject to Aspona) and the Cappadocian Andrapa (subject to Parnassos).

The southern limit was, doubtless, always quite vague, running across the level, treeless, sparsely populated plain of the Axylon, south of Amorium, north of Laodiceia-Katakekaumene, and touching or intersecting the large, shallow salt lake Tatta. The limit between Lycaonia on the south and Galatia on the north was probably never fixed very narrowly in this valueless plain; and, moreover, we know that certain large districts were sometimes held by the Gauls, and sometimes separated from their country. A considerable tract of country lying along the west side of Lake Tatta, and stretching west towards Amorium and Laodiceia, is assigned by Ptolemy to Galatia under the name Proseilemmene, *i.e.* προσειλημμένη (χώρα), the 'Added Territory.' The date when this territory was added to G. is uncertain. The opinion has been expressed doubtfully that it was separated from Lycaonia by Antoninus Pius (or possibly Hadrian) when the triple eparchy, Cilicia-Lycaonia-Isauria, was constituted a Roman province (Ramsay, *Histor. Geogr. of As. Min.* pp. 251, 377); but that event seems not sufficiently important to have given a new name to the country, and the analogy of the similar name Epiktetos, *i.e.* ἐπίκτητος Φρυγία, the 'Acquired Phrygia,' suggests that the transference of territory took place as a permanent and real change of rule at a much earlier period. Now, according to Pliny (*Nat. Hist.* v. 95), the part of Lycaonia that adjoined Galatia was given to it as a tetrarchy. This Lycaonian tetrarchy was certainly close to Ptolemy's Proseilemmene, and probably another name for it. Pliny says that the tetrarchy contained 14 cities, with Iconium as capital, and distinguishes it from Lycaonia Proper

(*ipsa Lycaonia*), which extended along the front of Mt. Taurus. Ptolemy, indeed, does not make Proseilemmene extend so far west as Iconium; but he is incorrect about the extent of all the divisions of this whole region. Lycaonia as a whole had been added to the Pergamenian kingdom by Rome in B.C. 190; but the kings were not strong enough to hold this distant territory, and part of it was probably taken by the Gauls about 160; and this part afterwards passed under the power of the Pontic kings along with Galatia. Hence Eumachus, Mithridates' general, who conquered Pisidia, Isauria, and parts of Cilicia, evidently used Lycaonia as his basis of operations. Another possibility is that the part of Lycaonia held by Amyntas (see II.) was styled by him the Tetrarchy; but that is, for several reasons, less probable. Amyntas' part of Lycaonia, however, must have been nearly the same in extent as the Tetrarchy. In any case, the name Tetrarchy must have originated before the Roman provincial organization was instituted; and thus Iconium had an old connexion with Galatia (*Studia Biblica*, iv. p. 46 ff.).

As to the relation between the immigrant Gauls and the older Phrygian inhabitants in Galatia, evidence fails; but the analogy of similar conquests and the general facts of this case warrant some probable conclusions. It is not to be supposed that the older population was exterminated or expelled. The Gaulish invaders were few. The total number that first entered Asia under Leonnorius and Lutarius is stated as 20,000, of whom only half were fighting men; the rest were women and children (Livy, xxxviii. 16, borrowing from Polybius). Doubtless, other swarms followed, encouraged by the success of the first; but that was the main army. In the continual wars and marches and raids of the following 46 years, the number of deaths was probably larger than the number of births; and the total Gallic population that was settled in Galatia, when its bounds were fixed by Attalus about 232, cannot have been numerous. In a country nearly 200 miles long, such a population must have been merely a small dominant caste amidst a much larger subject population; and Van Gelder expresses the general opinion of historical investigators, that the Gallic invaders did not live in cities, or become agriculturists, but employed the natives as cultivators of the land, on condition of paying to the Gauls as lords of the soil a proportion of the produce, while the conquerors occupied themselves in war and in pasturage, taking according to the usual practice one-third of the land, and leaving two-thirds to the older population (Cæsar, *Bell. Gall.* i. 31). As Lightfoot, in his edition of the Epistle, p. 9, rightly declares, the population consisted of Phrygians, Gauls, and Greeks, to whom were afterwards added a considerable sprinkling of Romans and a smaller number of Jews; and Van Gelder rightly points out that the cities were mainly populated by the Phrygians, who practised the arts of peace and conducted all trade, while the Gallic chiefs dwelt in their fortified villages (φρούρια, *castella*), keeping up a rude barbaric magnificence, and the mass of the Gauls led a pastoral and half-nomadic life when they were not engaged in war. As late as B.C. 189 the priests of the temple of Pessinus were opposed to the Gauls, and welcomed the Roman army of Manlius as deliverers; but that would hardly have been possible, unless the city had been really Phrygian and not Gaulish.* Van Gelder,

---

* Marquardt, *Röm. Staatsalt.* i. p. 359, errs in counting Amorium, Aizanoi, and Orkistos as cities of Galatia in the Roman period.
† Wrongly mentioned as perhaps the seat of one of the Churches of Galatia by many scholars.

* Körte (*Athenische Mittheilungen des Inst.* 1897, pp. 16 and 39) shows that Pessinus was not conquered by the Gauls till some year between 189 and 164; and he publishes an inscription of about A.D. 80-90, which shows that of the ten leading priests at Pessinus five were Gauls and five belonged to the original

p. 183, says of such cities as Tavium, Pessinus, Ancyra, 'those cities were in Galatia, but were not Galatian cities; they preserved Phrygian character and Phrygian customs, now affected with a Grecian tinge.' All Jews, Greeks, and resident Romans would certainly be dwellers in the cities. In the governing cities, Ancyra, Tavium, Pessinus, a number of Gaulish families doubtless settled, and formed an aristocracy. Ancyra and Tavium, especially, were Gaulish strongholds from 250 onwards (Manlius occupied Ancyra in 189); but Pessinus was more purely Phrygian. But, even in Ancyra, indubitably, the mass of the lower and trading classes was Phrygian or Greek.

In B.C. 189 the Galatian tribes are pictured by Polybius and Livy as barbarians, devoid of any trace of Greek culture, fighting naked, without order or tactics, armed with swords and large wooden or wicker shields; and their pastoral life, remote from cities and intercourse, long preserved their native customs. As the military power and the vigour of the Gaulish conquerors declined in the 2nd and 1st centuries B.C., they perhaps began to mix more freely with the older population; and the opinion has been expressed that they even adopted the native religion, on the ground that certain Gallic names occur at the great native sanctuaries, implying that Gallic families began to hold priesthoods: in the 2nd century the high priest of Pessinus, bearing the holy official Phrygian title Atis, had a brother Aiorix, and in the 1st century Brogitarus was priest at Pessinus, while Dyteutus, son of Adiatorix, was priest at Comana Pontica under Augustus. But although some Gaulish nobles assumed the place and swayed the enormous power that lay in the hands of the priest-kings of the great native temples,* it does not follow that the mass of the Gaulish people adopted the Phrygian religion.

Further, it has even been asserted by some recent scholars that the Gauls adopted to a large extent the manners and customs of the Græco-Phrygian population, retaining not very much of their Gallic ways and habits in the 1st century after Christ; but this opinion seems contrary to the evidence, and against natural probability.† The Gauls, though readily civilizable, have not been quick to throw off national character and put on foreign characteristics. Moreover, they seem to have long retained the Gallic language, for Strabo mentions that all three tribes spoke the same language and had the same manners; and so late as the 4th century after Christ, Jerome declares that they were bilingual, speaking Greek and a dialect like that used by the Treveri in Gaul (though changes had occurred).‡ Now, it is difficult to believe that a small caste amid a larger population could have adopted entirely the religion and customs of the surrounding population and yet retained their separate language. The first step in Hellenization was always the adoption of the Greek language. Moreover, Strabo, in speaking of their uniformity of character, evidently does not mean that they had all adopted the Græco-Phrygian manners and ways, but distinctly implies that there was a common Gallic character among the various tribes. The ambition of their chiefs, who found that the shortest way to power lay in adopting the civilized

methods of Greece and Rome, probably caused the first steps in change to be made. The chiefs connected themselves with the powerful priesthood, became priests themselves, and gradually the freer old Gaulish system was replaced by the tyranny of kings. The general opinion among those scholars who hold the North-Galatian theory seems to be right, that these Gauls, even in A.D. 50, retained much of the Gallic character; and they vainly seek to support that theory by finding Gallic characteristics in the congregations to which St. Paul wrote his Epistle. When Livy (xxxvii. 8) speaks of *exoleta stirpe gentis*, as the fact of his own time, he refers to the decay of their warlike character rather than to any change of manners and customs.* Lightfoot (p. 12) rightly says, ' the tough vitality of the Celtic character maintained itself comparatively unimpaired.'

No trace remains in local inscriptions (chiefly A.D. 100–250) of Gallic manners or language, and little of Gallic names; but that does not prove that the Gallic manners and language had been lost. A Gaul who received any education learned Greek; and all who wrote, wrote in Greek. The Gaulish language was a proof of barbarism, and a reason for shame (whence the contempt for Galatians which appears in the Cappadocian Fathers, see Ramsay, *Historical Geography*, p. 288); no one would blazon his want of education to the world, and it may be doubted whether any one could write who spoke only Gaulish. Moreover, the inscriptions almost all belong to the great cities, which were civilized seats of Græco-Roman culture, inhabited by Greeks, Romans, Phrygians, Jews, and Romanized Gauls (the latter forming a small aristocracy). Ancyra was quite a Romanized city, civilized and rich; and Pessinus was so in a less degree. The native languages of Asia Minor, Phrygian, Lycaonian, etc., persisted through the Roman period, until destroyed by the language of the NT, but no traces of them remain in inscriptions (except a few execrations on tombs in the Phrygian language).

In the time of St. Paul, therefore, there was probably a great and marked difference between the rustic Gaulish population of Galatia, who retained much of the old ruder barbarian character, and were probably little affected by Greek manners or language,† and the population of the cities, who spoke Greek, and the majority of whom were not of Gaulish origin.‡ But, while continuing Gauls in feeling, the Galatian tribes in A.D. 50 must have been to some extent affected in habits and standard of life during three centuries spent as a conquering caste amid more civilized peoples. The chief point to notice is that they were an aristocracy among inferiors; and the effect produced by that long experience on a race always proud, free, and bold, must be estimated.

It is not justifiable in any case to select one or two of the long list of vices in Gal 5[19. 21], and quote some passage in which a similar fault is charged against Gauls; the list in these verses is chargeable against human nature, not specially against Gaulish nature. In 6[6. 7] niggardliness is a characteristic of the Galatians, and in 1[6] they change their religion quickly. It may be doubted whether either fact was characteristic of the Gauls; though fickle in some respects, they never were quick to change their religion, but rather the con-

---

priestly families (*Woch. f. klass. Phil.* 1898, p. 3); the arrangement was probably made B.C. 189–164. Gordium, a great emporium in 189, must have been Phrygian; later, it was conquered by Gauls, and disappeared from history.

* On the priestly power see Hennig, *As. Min. Reges Sacerdotes*; Ramsay, *Cities and Bishoprics*, i. pp. 10 f., 101 f., 130 ff., 292 ff.

† The name Gallogræcia is appealed to as evidence of the Hellenization of the Gauls; but this name is Roman in origin, and had no such implication among its originators.

‡ Mommsen (*Röm. Gesch.* v. p. 92) accepts the testimony of Jerome, which Perrot and Van Gelder try to discredit.

---

* The speech of Manlius, xxxviii. 17, is apparently Livy's free invention, and contains a similar sentiment.

† Similarly, Mommsen (*Röm. Gesch.* v. 92) shows that in Gaul the Gallic language continued in common use at least as late as the 4th century.

‡ Salmon fully recognizes that the Christians of the North-Galatian Churches were not as a rule the Gauls, but the Phrygians; and that the attempt to find Celtic characteristics in those whom St. Paul addresses is a failure (Smith, *DB²* i. p. 1106).

trary ; * greedy to seek money they were said to be, but at the same time the fault to which they tend is to be too apt to spend even to ostentation. The further quality, that the Galatians are 'a superstitious people given to ritual observances,' was peculiarly characteristic of the type of religion widely spread over Asia Minor, with its great seats at places like Pessinus, Pisidian Antioch, Comana, Ephesus, etc. We may say that the characteristics of the Galatian congregations are those of the general native population of Asia Minor, and not those of the Gauls.

After the Roman imperial centre was transferred first to Nikomedia, and afterwards to Constantinople, the Hellenization of Galatia proceeded much more rapidly, for the north side of the plateau then rapidly advanced in civilization and importance (Ramsay, *Histor. Geogr.* pp. 74, 197 ff.), while the south side, which had previously lain on the line of the greatest routes, declined. Christianity spread the knowledge of Greek in the 4th cent. ; and hence we find expressions like that of Themistius (p. 360), that Galatia is almost wholly Greek. That, however, is a rhetorician's phrase ; Jerome and the contempt expressed by Basil and Gregory show that it is probably exaggerated ; but, even if it be near the truth, it must not be applied to the 1st cent.

Galatia Proper, as it was in the 1st or 2nd cent., was a rough oval in shape, extending about 200 miles in length (east to west), and 100 miles in breadth at the most. It is probably the most monotonous and least picturesque country of Asia Minor, so far as it is known ; but its north-eastern and eastern and southern parts are hardly explored. The climate is severe in the long winter ; and the want of trees over great part of the district (especially near the lines of road, except part of that leading to Constantinople) makes the heat of summer great. There is a considerable extent of fertile soil (with much more pasture land, and barren undulating hilly ground) producing grain, fruits, cotton, tobacco, opium, etc. ; but, owing to difficulties in transport, the only important products for commerce are wool and mohair (the fleece of the beautiful Angora goat). In the Byzantine period, after being ravaged by Persians and Arabs, Ancyra with Galatia in general (west of the Halys) passed into the hands of the Seljuk Turks, was held by the Latins for a short time, taken by Tartars, and finally captured in 1354 by the Turks under Suleiman.

The earliest reference to Christianity in North Galatia is at Ancyra, where the local church (ἡ κατὰ τόπον ἐκκλησία, cf. Ramsay, *Cities and Bishoprics of Phr.* i. p. 272 f. No. 192) is mentioned about A.D. 192 in an anti-Montanist treatise as having been affected by Montanism and saved by the writer (Euseb. *HE* v. 16). Many martyrs suffered there under Diocletian, some of whom may have been brought from other parts of Galatia for trial at the capital ; the dates are not recorded, and only the names of most are known, but probably all may be placed in the great persecution (Clemens, Donatus, Papias, etc., 23rd Jan. ; Theodotus, etc., 18th May ; Plato, etc., 22nd July ; Gaianus, Julianus, Rufinus, etc., 31st Aug. ; Marcellus, Silvanus, Gaianus, etc., 4th Sept. ; Seleucus, Valerius, etc., 15th Sept. ; Eusebius episcopus, 16th Sept. ; children, 23rd Sept. ; Theodorus episc., 3rd Nov. or 6th Apr. ; Eutychus, Domitianus, 28th Dec.). Any other early Churches in North Galatia have been overwhelmed in oblivion, and hardly a trace of them survives. At Juliopolis, the martyrs Plato (22nd July, see above), Heuretos, and Gemellus

were venerated in the 6th cent., but their connexion is uncertain.* At the Ancyran Council (A.D. 314) a full muster of Galatian bishops might be expected, but only Ancyra and Juliopolis were represented. The following bishoprics also can be traced in the 4th cent. : Kinna, 325 ; Tavium, 325 ; Aspona, 344 ; Pessinus, 403.† But in the 5th cent. there come into our knowledge Mnizos, 451 ; Orkistos, 431‡ ; Petenissos, 451 ; Eudoxias, 451 ; Amorion, 431 ; Myrikion, 451 ; and in the 6th or later, Verinopolis, 680 ; Kaloumne, 879 ; Klaneos, 680 ; Germa, 553. We cannot conclude with certainty that a bishopric did not exist in the 4th cent., though it was not represented at the early Councils ; but, remembering that Galatia was situated so conveniently for the early Councils of Ancyra, Nicæa, and Constantinople, we must see in this list, when compared with those of the more distant Byzantine provinces Lycaonia and Pisidia, a proof that Galatia was late in taking its proper rank in the Christian world. Ancyra and the road to Constantinople are the early home of Galatian Christianity ; and from thence it spreads. Above all, it is clear that western and south-western Galatia (where Zöckler and Salmon place the Pauline Churches, and where Zahn, etc., believe that St. Paul preached) are latest of all in being thoroughly christianized, Germa, Klaneos, Myrikion, Eudoxias, Petenissos (only Pessinus, Orkistos, and Troknades [the latter two in Roman Asia] can be traced to the 4th cent.). The inference drawn from the bishops' lists is confirmed by epigraphic evidence, which points to the conclusion that (except in Pessinus, where 4th cent. Christian inscriptions occur) Christianity was late in taking root in south-western Galatia (*Zeitschr. f. vergl. Sprachf.* 1887, p. 383). There are a considerable number of Christian inscriptions in Tavium and other parts of East Galatia ; but all are of late date.

The Galatian Jews have left few memorials. A rather bold speculation (Ramsay, *Cities and Bishoprics of Phr.* i. pp. 648 ff., 673) assigns Jewish origin to some noble families of Ancyra ; and a report is spread that a highly important Jewish inscription has been found there, but it is not yet published. Jewish names occur in several late inscriptions, probably of Jewish Christians, *e.g.* at Pessinus, Matatas (according to Lightfoot, p. 11, but the text is untrustworthy, *CIG* 4088) ; at Eudoxias (Yürme), Jacob the deacon [δ]ειάκωνος and Esther ; at Tavium, Daniel, etc. *CIG* 4129, which is Jewish, is wrongly assigned to Galatia by Schürer (*Jüd. Volk.* i. p. 690), Franz, etc. ; it belongs to Asia, being found near Dorylaion. The decree of Augustus, quoted as giving special privileges to Jews at Ancyra by Lightfoot, Schürer, and many others, depends on an error ; it was addressed to the Koinon of Asia (*Studia Biblica,* iv. p. 41 f.). The Jews settled in the Seleucid colonies of Phrygia (GALATIA II.) spread gradually to the great cities of Galatia Proper.

II. GALATIA PROVINCIA is a complicated subject, and the mass of details is unintelligible, unless we observe the force which guided all the changes, viz. the Roman frontier policy, which sought to educate barbarous tribes up to the Roman standard by a gradual process, first placing them under a dependent and allied king, who could control them

---

* On 15th April, martyrs *in Taudia Galaciæ* probably belong to Gallæcia. A martyr, Dikasios of Tavium, of unknown date, is mentioned ; a Dikasios was bishop there in 325.
† Lagania is added by Le Quien ; but Erechtius, the bishop in question, was more probably of Egdaumana or Glavama, a Lycaonian see on the Galatian frontier, as appears from the forms Damanitanus, Gadanitanus, Gatmaneas, Planathon, etc.
‡ Orkistos in A.D. 331 claimed to be wholly Christian in a petition to Constantine, *CIL* iii. 7000 : it was at that time subject to Nakoleia in Asia, and could not therefore be a bishopric. Amorion, Orkistos, and Troknades were joined to Galatia about 386–395, *Hist. Geogr. As. Min.* p. 221.

by his presence and armies (Strab. p. 671), and then receiving them into the Empire as they became civilized and orderly. During the 1st cent. A.D. the province G. embodied the Roman spirit in central Asia Minor, as opposed to the native kingdoms bordering on it; and the history of *G. Provincia* is the history of Roman policy in its advance towards the Euphrates frontier—a long slow process, in which the Roman genius undoubtedly was exerted to the utmost to influence and impress, to educate and discipline, the population of the various countries taken into the province Galatia (see also GALATIANS).

The South-Galatian theory, then, takes the foundation of the Galatian Churches as an episode in the political and social history of the province; and inasmuch as several questions in Acts turn on the exact boundaries of the province, it is necessary to be minute and accurate as regards its growth (which is nowhere described fully).

Amyntas, formerly a secretary of Deiotarus, was made king of Pisidia by Antony in 39, at the same time as Darius, grandson of Mithridates, was granted the kingdom of Pontus, and Polemon (son of Zenon, the rhetor of Laodiceia) that of a part of Cilicia (*i.e.* either Ketis, or more probably the whole of Cilicia Tracheiotis). All were dependent on Rome, and paid tribute (Appian, *Bell. Civ.* v. 75). Amyntas' kingdom included Apollonia and Antioch (a district which had been set free by Rome in B.C. 190, Strab. pp. 569, 577).

In the interval between 39 and 36 Darius died or was disgraced. Polemon was his successor, and in 36, as king of Pontus, accompanied Antony to the Parthian war; and as a reward for his services therein Armenia Minor was added to his kingdom in 35 (Dion Cass. xlix. 33; cf. Plutarch, *Ant.* 38). Polemon lost his Cilician kingdom early in 36, and probably Pontus was given him in compensation.* Antony, returning from Tarentum, gave all Tracheiotis except Seleukeia to Cleopatra (Strab. pp. 671, 669) as part of a great Asiatic kingdom;† and a Cleopatran era was instituted, of which the year 1 ended 31st Aug. B.C. 36 (Porphyrius, *ap.* Müller, *Fragm. Hist. Græc.* iii. 724).

In 36 Amyntas received from Antony a large accession of territory, viz. Galatia Proper with parts of Lycaonia and Pamphylia (Dion Cass. xlix. 32). His kingdom included most of the great plains between Lake Tatta and Taurus (Strab. p. 568). The gift of part of Lycaonia was evidently intended to make his territory continuous, so that the Galatian portion should not be divided from the Pisidian portion by alien territory. Iconium, therefore, was necessarily included in it, as otherwise continuity could hardly be attained.‡

Amyntas and Polemon supported Antony at Actium, B.C. 31, but were confirmed in their kingdoms by Augustus in 30. Amyntas received

Tracheiotis in addition, including Isaura (Strab. p. 569), and he was permitted freely to enlarge his kingdom out of non-Roman territory. Part of Lycaonia, including Derbe and Laranda, had been seized by Antipater, once a friend of Cicero (*ad Fam.* xiii. 73); this was conquered by Amyntas (Strab. p. 569), but he soon afterwards perished, in B.C. 25, in attempting to reduce the Homonades, a people on the borders of Lycaonia, Pisidia, and Isauria (in the country south and east of Bey-Sheher lake).

The kingdom of Amyntas passed with his whole property to the Romans, and a new Roman province was constituted, called Galatia, doubtless because Amyntas had been since 36 currently known to the Romans as king of Galatia (compare ASIA). The sudden death of Amyntas caused great confusion; months must have elapsed before news reached Rome, and instructions came back after deliberation. Lollius was named as first governor of Galatia Provincia. He needed an army to carry out the change. Thus time elapsed, and only in B.C. 20 was the question of frontier and bounds settled. Pamphylia was apparently not included in the new province, though sometimes the old attachment remained (Tacitus, *Hist.* ii. 9). Tracheiotis was given to Archelaos, king of Cappadocia, being tacked on to Eastern Lycaonia (*i.e.* Kybistra, etc.) * as an eleventh or 'added' *Strategia* of Cappadocia (ἐνδεκάτη or ἐπίκτητος, Strab. pp. 535, 537; cf. Appian, *Bell. Mithr.* 105, 114). Strabo (p. 671) says emphatically that the same extent of Cilicia Tracheiotis was ruled by Archelaos as had been held previously by Cleopatra (36–31) and Amyntas (30–25);† cf. also the inscription *CIA* iii. 545. Archelaos in A.D. 17 was summoned to Rome and degraded. He had been a weak prince, and when he, a few years previously, became temporarily insane, Augustus had appointed a *tutor*, and had also taken from him part of Tracheiotis, permitting Ajax about A.D. 11–12‡ to become high priest of Kennatis and Lalassis with right of coinage. Cappadocia became a province in A.D. 17, but apparently Archelaos, son of the old king, was allowed to retain Eastern Lycaonia and part of Cilicia, while M. Antonius Polemon became dynast of Olba, Kennatis, and Lalassis,§ and reigned at least 11 years. In 36 Archelaos II. was king in Tracheiotis, and his attempt to take a *census* after the Roman style caused a revolt in Ketis, which seems to imply that Antonius Polemon's rule had passed to Archelaos (Tacitus, *Ann.* vi. 41; *Expositor*, April 1897, p. 281). In 37 Tracheiotis and Eastern Lycaonia were given to Antiochus, king of Commagene; and though he was disgraced soon, yet Claudius in 41 restored his kingdom.‖ He struck coins with the legend ΛΤΚΑΟΝΩΝ, implying probably that Laranda was added to his kingdom (it had been in the province since

---

* It is beyond doubt (Raillard, *Numismat. Zeitschrift*, 1895, p. 23 ff.) that Strabo, pp. 493, 495, 499, 556, 560, 568, 578, is always alluding to the same Polemon, the famous king of his own country Pontus, and the trusted ally of Rome; it is inadmissible to separate one of these allusions from the rest as denoting some otherwise unknown Polemon. Strabo everywhere assumes that his readers recognize the one famous Polemon. But, as Mommsen clearly shows (*Ephem. Epigraph.* ii. p. 259 ff.), it is impossible to suppose that this Greek king was the Roman M. Antonius Polemon; the coins with that name on them belong probably to the period about A.D. 17–28. See above, note §.

† On the date, see Kromayer in *Hermes*, 1894, p. 574 f.; Gardthausen, *Augustus und seine Zeit*, i. pt. 1, p. 293. Plutarch, *Ant.* 36 (cf. 54), and Dion Cass. xlix. 32. 3-5 (who omits Tracheiotis), are decisive as to the year, and Josephus (who gives 34, *Ant. Jud.* xv. iii. 5–iv. 1) has made a mere error.

‡ Moreover, Amyntas proceeded to conquer Derbe, implying that he already had Iconium to start from. Previously Polemon's Cilician kingdom had included Iconium (Strab. p. 568); and hence in the *Acta Pauli et Theclæ* his descendant Tryphaina had estates in the region of which Antioch was the governing centre (Ramsay, *Church in Rom. Emp.* p. 396), and which included Iconium.

* This Lycaonian *strategia*, originally extending up to Derbe, was given by Pompey to Ariobarzanes, king of Cappadocia, in B.C. 64; but Antipater seized Derbe and Laranda, defying the Roman policy (apparently in the troubles following 50, Strab. p. 535). The Roman governors of Phrygia and Cilicia, B.C. 60-50, retained the right of passage across by Kybistra from Iconium to Tarsus (Cicero, *Fam.* xv. ii. 2, iv. 4; *Att.* v. xviii. 1, xx. 2).

† Ketis must be included in this kingdom, and cannot therefore have been under separate dynasts with right of coinage, as some scholars have thought, at any period between B.C. 36 and the disgrace of Archelaos; but Aba ruled Olba under Cleopatra as overlord till 31 (Strab. p. 672).

‡ Coins of his second year name Augustus, of his fifth year Tiberius (Waddington, *Mélanges de Numism.* ii. p. 126).

§ He is mentioned by Strabo (p. 556), who makes him grandson of Polemon, king of Pontus; but probably the text is falsely arranged, and Strabo refers to the son of Polemon (who first held rule without title under his mother, queen Pythodoris, after Polemon died, and then about A.D. 17 or 18 was made dynast of Olba; see Ramsay, *Church in Rom. Emp.* p. 427 f.).

‖ But he gave Olba, Kennatis, and Lalassis to Polemon II. king of Pontus (see below, Waddington, *l.c.* p. 129).

B.C. 25, but it was the key to Tracheiotis, and necessary for successful administration of the kingdom). Thus Derbe came to be the frontier city of the Roman Province; and it was probably this important position that led to its receiving the honorary title Claudio-Derbe.

G. Provincia had meanwhile been enlarged also on the north-east, and contained, when St. Paul visited it, the following districts in addition to G. Proper (all are mentioned in inscriptions of the 1st century under these names): (1) *Paphlagonia*, incorporated B.C. 5 (probably on death of Deiotarus Philadelphus).* (2) Parts of *Pontus*, incorporated at various dates (Sebastopolis, Amaseia, and probably Gazelonitis in B.C. 2-1, Comana in A.D. 34-35), and called as a whole *Pontus Galaticus*, *i.e.* Pontus belonging to G. as distinguished from *Pontus Polemoniacus*, which was governed by Polemon II. (that kingdom was ruled by Polemon II. A.D. 37-63, his mother Tryphæna being associated with him until 54: † in 63 it also was incorporated in Galatia, but retained the distinguishing name Polemoniacus). (3) *Phrygia*, including Apollonia, Antioch, and Iconium (wh. see): as contrasted with *Phrygia Asiana* (Galen, π. τρ. δυν. iv. p. 312, vi. p. 515 Kuhn), it would naturally be termed *Phrygia Galatica* (a title preserved only in a note of martyrdom, *Acta Sanctorum*, 28th Sept., p. 563, where *Galaciæ* is printed): see PHRYGIA. (4) *Pisidia*, Ac 14²⁴. (5) Part of *Lycaonia*, including the cities Lystra and Derbe, and some other places not yet organized as cities (such as Hyde, Barata, Perta, etc., summed up in Ac 14⁶ as ἡ περίχωρος). In contrast to *Lycaonia ipsa* (Pliny, *NH* v. 95), *i.e.* the non-Roman country governed by Antiochus and styled *Lycaonia Antiochiana* (*CIL* x. 8660), it was doubtless called *Lycaonia Galatica*, like *Pontus Galaticus*, *Phrygia Galatica*. (6) *Isauria*, the territory attached to the city Isaura, and called Ἰσαυρικὴ (χώρα) by Strabo, pp. 568, 569. It has been maintained that the name G. was never employed in correct official usage to denote this large composite province, and that the proper and technical usage was to designate the province by enumerating its component parts. This position is untenable, and has been frankly abandoned by one of its champions, Prof. E. Schürer (*Theolog. Litteraturztg.* 30th Sept. 1893). The following arguments are decisive against it.

(*a*) Ptolemy devotes the successive chapters of his Book V. to the Roman provinces of Asia Minor: ch. 1. Πόντου καὶ Βιθυνίας (the official name was strictly double, and so was the constitution in some respects); 2. τῆς ἰδίας Ἀσίας (as distinguished from Asia the continent); 3. Λυκίας; 4. Γαλατίας (containing Paphlagonia, and parts of Pisidia, Lycaonia, and Isauria, with the cities Antioch, Lystra, Isaura); 5. Παμφυλίας (which he says is bounded by Galatia on the north).

(*b*) Pliny (who often uses G. in the narrower sense of G. Proper) defines in v. 146, 147, Galatia (*i.e.* the province) as reaching to Cabalia of Pamphylia and to the Milyæ, and as containing Lystra and various cities in the Phrygian, Pisidian, and Paphlagonian territories, altogether 195 peoples.‡

(*c*) Tacitus (*Hist.* ii. 9) mentions Galatia and Pamphylia as being governed by Calpurnius Asprenas, implying that the two formed one great continuous district. Eutropius (vii. 10) and Syncellus (i. p. 592) apply the name G. to the whole province formed in B.C. 25; and they simply reproduce an old authority, using G. in a sense which it no longer bore in their time.

* On the date, see *Revue des Ét. Grecques*, 1894, p. 251.
† Imhoof Blumer, *Zft. f. Numism.* 1897, p. 269.
‡ Paphlagonia Galatica and Pontus Galaticus are called Γαλατία, Dion, 48, 33, 5 (see Holder, *Altk. Sprachschatz*, p. 1591), and Steph. Byz. *s.v.* Κάρανα (Strab. p. 560).

(*d*) A practical people like the Romans would never use as the strictly technical and official title of a province 'Galatia, Paphlagonia, Pisidia Phrygia, Lycaonia, Pontus Galaticus.' That accumulation of names was used for the sake of clearness on milestones, enumerating the *Viæ* of the various districts of the province (*CIL* iii. 312, 318), and on honorary inscriptions to give additional dignity to the governor of so many vast regions. These inscriptions belong to the later years of the century, when the constructive effort was exhausted, and the national spirit was reviving (Hadrian, at last, frankly recognized it).

It is, however, clear that it was not the current and popular Greek usage to designate G. Provincia by the name Galatia. The Greek-speaking natives, so far as evidence survives, called it the Galatic Province (*CIG* 3991), or enumerated the parts. It was only those who adopted fully the Roman point of view that employed the simple name Galatia; and the use of that name must be taken as a sign that the person who uses it speaks as a Roman, and deliberately follows the Roman provincial divisions, and would destroy those national distinctions which were opposed to the organized Roman unity. It is implied in the South-Galatian theory that St. Paul took that view (see GALATIANS II.). The author of Acts, however, did not take that view; and he never speaks of the province as Galatia, but mentions its parts (see GALATIA, REGION OF, IV.).

No information has been preserved to enable us to sketch the constitution of this vast province, except that it was governed by a prætorian *legatus Augusti pro prætore*, and had no legions stationed in it. The name Γαλατικὴ Ἐπαρχία, which the people of Iconium employed to designate the province about A.D. 54 (*CIG* 3991), clearly implies that the intention was to work the province into a unity, like *Asia Provincia*, and to override the national distinctions of Lycaonian, Phrygian, etc. Undoubtedly, this attempt ultimately proved a failure: the national characteristics were too strong, and revived after a time. But in the period of growth (B.C. 25 to A.D. 63) a vigorous effort was made to impose a Roman unity, expressed by the Roman title G. *Provincia*, on the various races. If we could trust a rather bold interpretation of an inscription, which seems to make Apollonia a part of the Trokmi (*Studia Biblica*, iv. p. 53 f.), it would even appear that the attempt was made to enrol the various parts in one or other of the three Gaulish tribes of G. Proper (τὰ τρία ἔθνη), just as Asia with its equally great variety of peoples was 'the nation Asia' (ἡ Ἀσία τὸ ἔθνος, Dion Cass. liv. 30); so the term ἔθνος is frequently applied in inscriptions to designate any entire province, however varied its population was. Unfortunately, inscriptions other than epitaphs are very rare in the province Galatia.

Ancyra was the capital of the province G.; and it is probable that Colonia Cæsareia Antiochia (see ANTIOCH) was a sort of secondary metropolis, being the centre of a system of Roman garrison towns (*coloniæ*) and military or imperial roads (ὁδοὶ βασιλικαί, Ramsay, *Church in Rom. Emp.* p. 32), and a place where ceremonies of the provincial cultus were held (*op. cit.* p. 396). Probably, the various parts of the province retained some separate individuality, though its nature is uncertain. Even after Pontus Galaticus and Pontus Polemoniacus had been merged in G. Provincia, they retained their separate names (in inscriptions and in Ptolemy), which implies that these artificial divisions of purely Roman origin had some real political distinction to preserve their separate existence. So also St. Luke seems to indicate some distinction between the districts of the province (see GALATIA, REGION OF). Metropoleis of various districts are known from coins or inscriptions (Pompeiopolis of Paphlagonia, Laranda of Lycaonia, Sagalassos of Pisidia, Isaura of Isaurica, Amaseia and Neocæsareia of the Pontic divisions); but the titles appear only in the 2nd or 3rd century, and are no argument for the Pauline period. Whether the Koinon of G. was a provincial institution or confined to Galatia Proper, cannot be determined; but the Koinon of Lycaonia (which has been quoted as a similar institution) was not founded till Lycaonia was incorporated (probably by Pius) in the new province of the Three Eparchiai (Ramsay, *Histor. Geogr.* p. 377).

The number of Roman foundations made in G. Provincia between B.C. 20 and A.D. 50 is an index of the vigour with which the imperial policy was urged on in that region. Augustus founded seven colonies—Germa in North Galatia, and Antioch, Lystra, Parlais, Cremna, Comama, Olbasa in South Galatia, besides a system of roads and milestones measured from Antioch. Nothing comparable in scale to this was done by him in any other part of the East. Under the succeeding emperors, we find several cities remodelled and Romanized in character and name: Pappa-Tiberiopolis, Claudio - Seleuceia, Claudio - Derbe, Claudio-Iconium, all in South Galatia.

Owing to the enormous extent of the Province G., the greatest variety of soil and scenery and products are found in it, from the dead - level plains on the Lycaonian and Cappadocian frontier, with their vast herds of sheep (alike now and in ancient times, Strab. p. 570), to the picturesque mountains and deep glens of Pisidia. On the northern half, see I.; the southern half was a highly cultivated and rich country in the 1st century, containing many great cities, traversed by the two important roads from east to west—one from Cilicia through Iconium and Antioch to Apameia and the Ægean coast, one from Commagene through Cæsareia Capp. and Laodiceia Katakekaumene to Apameia.[*] All intercourse by land between inner Asia and the west passed through the great Roman cities of South Galatia. Hence the great stream of intercourse backwards and forwards between Rome and the East, which played such an important part in moulding Christian history, affected these cities very strongly and developed them rapidly. Questions of doctrine and ritual were debated there at an early time, and called for decision. Jewish emissaries from Jerusalem (Gal 1⁷ 4¹⁷ etc.) would naturally pass through them and affect them first. On the other hand, as Rome was the magnet that attracted all intercourse, it is not so easy to see how Jewish emissaries should affect Ancyra very early; and utterly improbable that they should affect the towns in the western parts of Galatia Proper.

That Jews in large numbers dwelt in the cities of Phrygia Galatica is well known. They were greatly favoured as colonists by the Seleucid kings; and their presence may be confidently looked for in all Seleucid foundations. Seleucus I. and his successors found them loyal and trusty settlers in their garrison cities, such as Antioch, Apameia, etc., cities which served to maintain the Seleucid power in a foreign land. The Jewish colonists had the right of citizenship, along with various special privileges of a kind which their religious ideas required, as regards burial, money grants in place of oil-distribution, etc.; and their privileges and rights seemed to have been summed up in a body of city law, called in an Apamean inscription νόμος τῶν Ἰουδαίων (Ramsay, *Cities and Bishoprics of Phrygia*, pp. 538 f., 668 f.). Seleucus I.

granted them citizenship in all his colonies, implying that there were Jews in all, and his successors carried out the same policy (Jos. *Ant. Jud.* XII. iii. 1, § 119, 125); and Antiochus the Great about 200 B.C. brought 2000 Jewish families from Babylonia to the cities of Phrygia and Lydia (*id. ib.* § 148 ff.). These Seleucid colonies were almost all planted on the southern side of the plateau, and chiefly on the great lines of communication leading east and west; and the mass of Jewish colonists are to be expected in the cities along these routes. They penetrated farther north in the course of trade; but their settlement in North Galatia belongs to a period later than their establishment in the south.

The Jewish colonists undoubtedly exercised great influence on the development of Asia Minor in the Roman period; but they have left few conspicuous traces of their presence. They adopted Greek and Roman names (at least in public life), and it is doubtful how far they retained any knowledge of Hebrew; hence they are hardly to be distinguished from the ordinary citizens, and the attempt to do so in ch. xv. (also xiv.) of *Cities and Bishoprics of Phrygia* is very speculative. But they seem to have taken part in public life, and to have exercised great influence through their wealth and ability, as well as through the power of their peculiar and impressively pure religion. Even the marked analogy which existed in point of ceremonial between the Asianic and the Judaic religion increased the influence of the latter (see GALATIANS II.).

Few Jewish or Jewish-Christian inscriptions can be detected in South-Galatian cities, because the names are usually unrecognizable and few emblems or Jewish formulæ are employed: in Antioch, Sterrett, *Epigr. Journ.* No. 138 (cf. *Cities and Bish. of Phrygia*, p. 525 n. 1); and at Apollonia, *Bull. Corr. Hell.* 1893; in Iconium, *CIG* 4001*b*, 3998, 3995*b*, 9270; and in Laodiceia Combusta, *CIG* 3989*d*, and *Athen. Mitth.* xiii. pp. 241, 254, 255, 258, 260. Among the few known inscriptions of Lystra and Derbe none have any Jewish appearance, except one with the name Mouisas at a village a little west of Derbe (Sterrett, *Wolfe Exped.* No. 46).

Christian inscriptions are comparatively numerous in Galatic Phrygia and Lycaonia, especially in the country that lies north and north-west of Iconium; and, though none are dated, yet style indicates that some must be as early as the 3rd century. Besides the Jewish-Christian ones just mentioned, others certainly or probably Christian (some perhaps Jewish-Christian) and early (omitting all that are later), are *A. E. Mitth. Oesterr.* 1896, p. 36 f., Nos. 20, perhaps 19, 24; Sterrett, *Epigr. Journ.* 142, *Wolfe Exped.* 555 (see *Expositor*, Oct. 1888, p. 263), *Journ. of Hell. Stud.* 1890, p. 165, No. 23 (cross above omitted by editor), *Athen. Mitth.* xiii. p. 249 ff. Nos. 44, 49, 53, 54, etc., with others unpublished. As is pointed out in *Cities and Bishoprics of Phrygia*, i. pp. 511, 715 f., epigraphic evidence would suggest that this district is one of those where Christianity took the earliest and strongest hold. Little is known about the later history of the Churches of Galatic Phrygia and Lycaonia. It is suggested that St. Mark carried on evangelization in the eastern districts after about 60 A.D.;[*] and his name is commoner than any other except Paul and John in the Christian inscriptions of the district (*Athen. Mitth.* xiii. p. 252 ff. Nos. 55, 56, 61, 92, 99; *St. Paul the Trav.* p. 351). Round Iconium, Antioch, and to a less degree Lystra, clings a great body of

---

[*] On the roads, see *Histor. Geogr.* pp. 43 f., 49 f. etc.

[*] Bartholomew, the apostle of the Lycaonians, is probably to be connected with the Inner Lycaones of the province Asia (*Cities and Bishoprics*, i. 709).

early tradition ; but Derbe is as little prominent in tradition as in the narrative of Ac, and the earliest known bishop seems to be Daphnus, 381.

III. In 2 Ti 4[10] Tischendorf with א reads εἰς Γαλλίαν, WH εἰς Γαλατίαν. The former reading would necessitate a new article containing an account of Gaul (Γαλλία) : even the latter reading, as many contend, refers to that country (cf. Theod. Mops, *ad loc.*). Gaul is called Γαλατία by many Greek * writers ; and, beyond doubt, that was the current Greek name in the 1st and 2nd cents. ; but it may be doubted whether St. Paul, whose usage in names geographical is thoroughly Roman,[†] would not here also employ the Roman term, if he meant Gaul. Moreover, it could not escape him that Γαλατία would be ambiguous, and would naturally be understood as Galatia by Timothy, who was resident in Asia ; and it is highly probable that he would not use that term to signify Gaul without employing some of the various ways of distinguishing. We must conclude that either St. Paul meant the same country which he elsewhere calls Galatia, or the true reading is ΓΑΛΛΙΑΝ, which would readily be corrupted into ΓΑΛΑΤΙΑΝ. Manuscript authority, however, is generally considered decisive in favour of Γαλατίαν, though Tischendorf thinks otherwise. Against Tischendorf's reading it has been stated that Γαλλία or Γάλλοι is first used in Greek by Epictetus (or rather Arrian), *Dissert.* ii. 20. 17 (Lightfoot, *Gal.* p. 3 note) ; but Strabo (p. 195) has Γαλλικόν, used in a way suggesting that he recognized it to be the Roman equivalent to the Greek Γαλατικόν.

Fourth century tradition says that Crescens was sent to Gaul ; and the Churches of Vienne and Mayence claimed him as their founder ; but the latter claim is certainly improbable, and the whole tradition may be founded on a false interpretation of 2 Ti 4[10]. There was a natural desire to connect the Gaulish Church with apostolic times ; this would lead to the interpretation of G. in that passage as Gaul ; the name Γαλλίαν would be written as a gloss on the margin, and this false reading finally crept into a few manuscripts. Tillemont's argument (*Mémoires pour servir* etc., i. art. 52, note 81, pp. 133, 263), that the evangelization of Gaul did not take place so early as this supposed mission of Crescens, has never been seriously shaken, and remains the most probable view.

Even more improbable is the view that in 1 Mac 8[2] the reference is to Roman victories in Gaul. At the period in question, about B.C. 160, the Romans had recently conquered Cisalpine Gaul ; but there is no reason to think that this not specially important event would produce any effect on the mind of the Jews. On the other hand, the Galatians were a terror in Asia for nearly a century ; and even the victories of Attalus had only restrained the range of their power, but not broken it. But Manlius marched at will through their land, and defeated them in the heart of their country ; and this event would be noised through the Seleucid dominions, and would naturally suggest to the Jews the desirability of entering into friendly relations with a government that could exercise such power on the Seleucid frontier.

LITERATURE. — Van Gelder, *de Gallis in Græcia et Asia* (1888) ; Droysen, *Gesch. des Hellenismus* ; Zwintcher, *de Galatarum Tetrarchis* ; Perrot, *de Galatia Prov. Romana*, also *Exploration Archéologique de la Galatie*, etc., and *Mém. d'Archéol.* p. 229 ff. ; Robiou, *Hist. des Gaulois d'Orient*, Paris, 1866 ; Contzen, *Die Wanderungen der Kelten*, Leipzig 1861 ; Thierry, *Hist. des Gaulois* (very poor) ; the elabor-

* Γαλατία and Γαλάται are so used in Diodorus, Strabo, Josephus, Plutarch, Appian, Pausanias, Dio. Cass., Athenæus, etc.
† Zahn, *Einleitung*, § 11, A 4, and GALATIANS II.

ate and useful Wernsdorff, *de Republica Galatarum*, 1743 ; Clemen, *Chronologie d. Paulin. Briefe*, 201 ff. ; Zahn, *Einleitung in das Neue Testament* ; the Introductions to the editions of the Epistle ; Ramsay, *Historical Geography of Asia Minor*, Ch. H. K., *Church in the Roman Empire*, chs. ii.-vi., *St. Paul the Traveller*, chs. v. vi. viii. ; Th. Reinach, *Revue Numismatique*, 1891, p. 377 ff.; Niese, *Rhein. Mus.* 1883, p. 583 ff. On the Galatian controversy the most recent articles are : North-Galatian side, Schürer, *Jahrb. f. protest. Theol.* 1892, p. 471, *Theol. Litterztg.* Sept. 30, 1893 ; Chase, *Expositor*, Dec. 1893, May 1894 ; Zöckler, *SK*, 1895, p. 51 ff. ; Findlay, *Expository Times*, vii. pp. 54, 235. South-Galatian side, Gifford, *Expositor*, July 1894 ; Rendall, *Expositor*, Nov. 1893, Apr. 1894 ; Holtzmann, *Zft. f. Kirchl. Gesch.* 1893, p. 336 ff. ; Ramsay, *Expositor*, Jan. Feb. Apr. Aug. 1894, July, Aug. 1895, *Expository Times*, vii. pp. 142, 285, *Studia Biblica*, iv. p. 17 ff. ; Clemen, *Zft. f. wiss. Theol.* xxxvii. p. 396 ff. On the *Quellenkritik*, see Schmidt, *de fontibus veterum auctorum in enarr. expedit. a Gallis susceptis* (Berlin, 1834) ; Müller, *Fragm. Hist. Græc.* iv. p. 640 ; Nissen, *Kritische Untersuchungen* (Berl. 1863), as well as Van Gelder, etc. (Stähelin, *d. Gal. in Kleinasien*, subsequently published, is in agreement).   W. M. RAMSAY.

GALATIA, REGION OF, more strictly rendered Galatic Region (ἡ Γαλατικὴ χώρα, Ac 18[23] ; ἡ Φρυγία καὶ Γαλατικὴ χώρα, Ac 16[6]), is a phrase difficult to explain, because it takes us into the popular topographical terminology of a district and a period that are utterly obscure.

I. According to the North-Galatian theory, and also according to Zahn, who holds the South-Galatian view in all essentials, this term is merely a synonym for Γαλατία in the common sense of G. Proper. The difficulty in accepting this apparently simple interpretation is that the use of the term Γαλατικὴ χώρα, where Γαλατία should be expected, is not supported by analogy. The only analogy quoted is ἐπὶ Ἀγκύρας τῆς Γαλατικῆς, Arrian, *Anab.* ii. 4. 1 ; but this denotes, not 'Ancyra of the Galatic country,' as is assumed, but 'Ancyra the Galatic' as distinguished from Ancyra the Phrygian (τῇ Φρυγιακῇ, Strab. p. 567) ; Arrian, in describing the period of Alexander the Great, uses the word by anticipation. If the reference in Ac 16[6] 18[23] is to G. Proper, all Greek usage, earlier and later alike, demands that the noun Γαλατία should be used ; and this is all the more necessary if (as is maintained on this view) it is coupled with the noun Φρυγία. The defenders of this interpretation can hardly plead that the obscurity of the subject should be accepted as an excuse for their failure to explain the reason of this perplexing and unnecessary deviation from common nomenclature ; because the adj. Γαλατικός is used with comparative frequency in the topographical terminology of that period, and always in a well-marked and characteristic way. This point needs careful study. There is a regular tendency to distinguish the scope of the derived adjective in -ικός from the simple word : thus, for example, οἱ Ἀτταλικοὶ βασιλεῖς are the whole dynasty of which the Attali were the most prominent members (Strab. p. 288) ; ἔργα Γαλατικά are deeds perpetrated by anybody similar to ἔργα τῶν Γαλατῶν : Γαλατικὸς κόλπος, Σικελικὸν πέλαγος, etc., are the bodies of water adjoining or pertaining to Galatia, Sicily, etc.: ἡ Ἰσαυρικὴ χώρα was the whole region of which Isaura was the leading city, but it did not all belong to Isaura. Many examples might be quoted ; but the closest parallel to the pair of terms Γαλατικὴ χώρα and Γαλατία is Λακωνικὴ γῆ and Λακωνία. Λακωνία is the old historic land of Lacedæmonia ; but Λακωνικὴ γῆ comprises the entire region which had passed under Spartan rule and been added to Laconia, including Messenia and the land near Pylos (Thuc. ii. 25, iv. 41, v. 34 ; Xen. *Hell.* vi. 2. 9 and 31). As Spartan power dwindled, γῆ Λακωνικὴ shrank in extent till it practically coincided with Laconia. The distinction is analogous to that between 'British territory' and 'Britain' ; the former being enormously wider than the latter. There are cases in which, for some special purpose, the wider term may be used about the smaller country; but in ordinary expression the wider term is used only about the enlarged country. It is not safe to say more than that a tendency exists to observe this distinction; as time goes on, its delicacy often leads to its being blurred.* In the adj. Γαλατικός the distinction is well observed. In an Iconian inscription of A.D. 54, the enlarged Galatia Provincia is Γαλατικὴ ἐπαρχεία (CIG 3991); the part of Pontus included in the province is called Γαλατικός in many inscriptions and in Ptolemy: similarly, the corresponding term Phrygia Galatica once occurs. If St. Luke used Γαλατικὴ χώρα where Γαλατία would have been the simple and clear term, he contradicts all that we know of contemporary usage, and yet attains no conceivable purpose thereby. The Greek-speaking population of Asia Minor ordinarily called Galatia Proper Γαλατία, and Enlarged Galatia Γαλατική (usually with some noun): only when they adopted the Roman point of view, Greek-speaking persons occasionally and for some special purpose used Γαλατία in the Roman sense of the Province. Analogy points to the conclusion that the Greek Luke would use Γαλατικὴ χώρα to indicate the Province, which the Roman Paul calls Γαλατία.

II. Lightfoot argued that in Ac 16⁶ τὴν Φρυγίαν καὶ Γαλατικὴν χώραν must denote a single territory to which two epithets are applied, 'the region which in ancient time was Phrygian and afterwards Galatian.' This explains why an unusual term was adopted; but such antiquarian lore is quite out of keeping with the style of Acts. We require here a current term in popular speech, for that is the character of Lukan expression. Zahn, who, like many other scholars, holds that Φρυγίαν here must be a noun, demands some case analogous to the double topographic epithet. Lightfoot gave only Lk 3¹: we add some from Strabo, p. 195, τὸ φῦλον ὁ νῦν Γαλλικόν τε καὶ Γαλατικὸν καλοῦσι; p. 788 (of the Nile mouths) τὸ μὲν Πηλουσιακὸν καλεῖται, τὸ δὲ Κανωβικὸν καὶ Ἡρακλειωτικόν; † p. 802 (Xois is defined as) ὑπὲρ τοῦ Σεβεννυτικοῦ καὶ Φατνιτικοῦ στόματος, i.e. above the Sebennytic-Phatnitic branch in the upper part, where these two branches are still joined, and which may bear either name; p. 97, τὴν Σκυθικὴν καὶ Κελτικήν, the (northern) zone that may be called either Scythian or Celtic (after the two chief races that inhabit its eastern and western parts); p. 670, τοῦ Κιλικίου καὶ Παμφυλίου τρόπου. The Greek καί is used to connect alternative names (Latin sive, seu, English or, alias);‡ and the grammatical character of Lightfoot's construction seems clearly established by these examples. In Ac 18²³ Γαλατικὴ χώρα on his interpretation must be used needlessly for Galatia Proper.

III. Gifford (Expositor, July 1894, p. 12) accepts Lightfoot's construction, but interprets 'the borderlands of Phrygia and Galatia.' Then Ac 18²³ mentions 'the Galatic Province (Region) and Phrygia.' This view has much to recommend it. It gives in 16⁶ a route leading direct from Iconium by Dorylaion

to Bithynia, making St. Paul turn direct towards that country when forbidden to preach in Asia; then, when he came to Dorylaion over-against Mysia,* he was forbidden to cross the Bithynian frontier, and turned west. It then becomes, however, almost necessary to suppose that the prohibition 16⁶ was given in Iconium or Lystra, and that St. Paul, abandoning his previous intention (15³⁶) of going over all the Churches, omitted Antioch. Salmon interprets much in this way, but is clear that Paul went to Antioch, and translates Ac 16⁶ as in next section, IV. (Smith's Bib. Dict.² i. p. 1105).

IV. Another explanation takes us into the obscure minutiæ of the Galatic Province. The various parts of the province retained a certain distinction (see GALATIA II.), and were probably termed Regiones or χῶραι. The term Regio occurs in one inscription, mentioning a centurion charged with duty in the Regio of which Antioch was centre, i.e. Phrygia Galatica,† while χώρα is understood in Strabo, pp. 568, 569, ἡ Ἰσαυρικὴ (χώρα), and in Ptolemy, v. 6, 17, ἡ Ἀντιοχειανὴ (χώρα).‡

The route taken by St. Paul in Ac 16¹⁻⁶ and 18²³ led across two of the regions (χῶραι) of the Galatic Province, viz. the Galatic part of Lycaonia and the Galatic part of Phrygia; the former contained Derbe and Lystra, the latter Iconium and Antioch. In 18²³ two regions are mentioned, τὴν Γαλατικὴν χώραν καὶ Φρυγίαν: here it is grammatically equally possible to take Φρυγίαν as noun and as adj.; for when two different names, expressed by two adjs. agreeing with the same noun, are coupled by καί, the regular usage is to express the noun only with the first (so in Strabo,§ τὴν Ἀκυιτανὴν μερίδα καὶ τὴν Ναρβωνῖτιν, p. 191; τὸ Μενδήσιον στόμα καὶ τὸ Τανιτικόν, p. 802; τοῦ Αἰγαίου πελάγους καὶ τοῦ Παμφυλικοῦ καὶ τοῦ Ἰσσικοῦ, p. 121; in Epiphanius (Hæres. 19), τῆς Ναβατικῆς χώρας καὶ Ἰτουραίας καὶ Μωαβίτιδος καὶ Ἀρηλίτιδος; and others innumerable ‖). The two regions intended ought to be the χώρα Λυκαονία and the χώρα Φρυγία. Now, Roman Lycaonia was naturally always designated with reference to the other half, non-Roman Lycaonia. One pair of terms would be Lycaonia Antiochiana (found CIL x. 8660) and Lycaonia Galatica (not actually found, but it may be assumed confidently on the analogy of Pontus Galaticus, Phrygia Galatica); another pair of terms would be Ἀντιοχιανὴ (χώρα) as in Ptolemy, and Γαλατικὴ χώρα as in Ac 18²³. The latter pair would be naturally used by a person speaking inside the country and not requiring to name it,¶ the former by a person outside the country. The Phrygian region of the Galatic Province was called Φρυγία χώρα by St. Luke, who seems to have always used this form of designating the various regions of the province (but those who prefer to treat Φρυγία as a noun in 18²³ may take the same sense from the noun as from

---

* So sometimes with γῆ Λακωνική or χώρα Λ. But in such cases a purpose can often be detected. Aristophanes stands alone in using Λακωνικαί as 'Laconian women'; but that was undoubtedly an Athenian slang term, perhaps in the sense of 'women of Laconian type' (cf. Λακωνικά, shoes of Laconian style). Such usages as πόλις Γαλατική, city belonging to the Γαλάται, i.e. Galatian city, πόλεμος Θεσσαλικός, war in which the Thessali take one side, are of a different class.

† An exactly equivalent form is used by Ptolemy, iv. 5, Ἡρακλειωτικὸν στόμα τὸ καὶ Κανωβικόν (on the sense of τὸ καί in names, see Ramsay, Cities and Bishoprics, i. p. 637 f.).

‡ In Greek, esp. of later period, καί often means 'or,' Thuc. vi. 60, 1; II. 35. 2; 42, 3; Ar. Eq. 256 (Neil); Aesch. Sept. 414 f., 1058; Eur. Supp. 895; Iph. Aul. 643; Plut. Q. Conv. iv. 2, 655c; Postgate on Propert. v. 6, 51. The Roman sive is often used to connect alternative names, where the Greek form is either ὁ καί or ἐπικαλούμενος; see Marquardt, Röm. Privalterth.² p. 27; Cagnat, Manuel d'Epigraphie Lat.² p. 57.

* κατά as in Ac 27²; Thuc. vi. 65 and 104; Herod. i. 76.

† ἑκατοντάρχην βηγεωνάριον, Sterrett, Epigraphic Journey, No. 92, who wrongly alters to [λ]εγ.; Prof. O. Hirschfeld accepts the reading given above (and in the copy), see Berlin Akad. Sitzungsber. 1893, p. 421.

‡ In that passage the two parts of Lycaonia (Galatica and Antiochiana) are opposed to each other under the names Lycaonia and Antiochiana; they retained distinct names in the 2nd century, but evidently great variety existed in the way of designating them, and Ptolemy selects an ill-fitting pair of names.

§ Strabo, who very rarely uses the common article to hold two nouns together (an example, however, in p. 388), repeats the article with the second member.

‖ Strabo has two other forms, much rarer, κόλπους τόν τι Ἀδριατικὸν καὶ τὸν Τυρρηνικόν, p. 92; τὸ Κρητικὸν καὶ Σικελικὸν καὶ Σαρδῷον πέλαγος βαθία ἐστί, p. 59. In the latter class we can usually see the intention to treat the whole as a unity made up of several parts; and the example quoted is so harsh as to be suspicious in text (if correct, the grammar is much worse than Strabo's average).

¶ The author of Ac 18²³ speaks from the point of view of a person in the country, placing himself alongside of St. Paul.

Φρυγία with χώρα understood, for in the inscriptions of Antioch the noun is often used to designate Galatic Phrygia [*CIL* iii. Suppl. 6818, 6819], and St. Luke may be allowed to speak as the people of Antioch wrote). Ac 18²³, then, implies 'he made a mission tour * through the Galatic region (Derbe and Lystra) and the Phrygian (Iconium and Antioch), stablishing all the disciples (in all the Galatian Churches).' †

Ac 16⁶ is more complicated. It describes the journey from Lystra onwards, *i.e.* through Galatic Phrygia. Had the expression been τὴν Φρυγίαν χώραν, there would have been less doubt; but the author, wishing to bring out with minute accuracy that his meaning was restricted to the Galatic part of the large country of Phrygia, added a second adjective to express 'the Region that is Phrygian and Galatic,' *i.e.* 'which was geographically Phrygia, but politically Galatia.' ‡ The verse, then, implies 'they made a mission tour * through the Phrygo-Galatic Region (Iconium and Antioch), [but no farther], because they were forbidden to speak the word in Asia (which they entered immediately on going onward from Antioch).'

It is objected that this view is too complicated and artificial; but the complicacy arises from our being forced to write a lost page of history concerning an obscure corner of the empire, before we can interpret the language of an author who assumes that we are as familiar as he was with the terminology of his own time. Asterius, bishop of Amasia in Pontus Galaticus 400 A.D., understood 18²³ exactly in this way, for in paraphrasing it he uses the words, τῶν Λυκαονίαν καὶ τὰς τῆς Φρυγίας πόλεις (*Hom.* viii., Migne, *Patrolog. Græc.* vol. xl.). This testimony of a man familiar with the topography of Asia Minor should have great weight; and Zahn is not justified in setting it aside as a false inference, into which Asterius was betrayed by taking Antioch in Ac 18²² as Pisidian Antioch. Asterius places the journey through Lycaonia and Phrygia immediately before the visit to Asia (Ac 19¹), and therefore evidently understood τὴν Γαλατικὴν χώραν καὶ Φρυγίαν in that sense. No mere error about Antioch explains such a rendering of 18²³. We have here a distinct testimony by an ancient authority in favour of the view stated in this section.   W. M. RAMSAY.

GALATIANS (Γαλάται), used only in Gal 3¹.

I. According to the majority of scholars, it denotes the people of Galatia Proper, a mixed population, consisting of a minority descended from the three Gaulish tribes, and a large majority of the ancient population, Phrygians west of the Halys, Cappadocians east of that river, with an intermixture of Greeks, Romans, and Jews. In the great cities, such as Ancyra, the Phrygians, etc., probably constituted the overwhelming majority, while Gauls were found there only as a small aristocratic caste; but in country parts the Gauls were more numerous. That is the usual sense of the term G., and needs no proof. On the character of these Gauls, their position as a small conquering caste of barbarians among a more numerous and more educated population, and their relation to that older population, see GALATIA I.

The general population of North Galatia was summed up as *Galatai* in ordinary ancient usage. But this term had no ethnological implication; it did not mean that the people so designated were all of Gallic descent, for it is doubtful whether so much as five per cent. of the total population was of Gallic origin, and it is practically certain that, in the great cities, an even smaller proportion of the population was of Gallic descent.* The name Galatai meant really no more than 'people of Galatia,' though the usual ethnological fiction crept in, and Phrygians and Greeks were feigned to be of the three tribes, just as the composite province Asia was called an ἔθνος (see p. 87ᵇ). It is quite unjustifiable to suppose that the Churches addressed by St. Paul, even if they were situated in North-Galatian cities, consisted of persons of Gallic blood to any important extent: the probability is that such Galatian Christians would be to a very large extent free from any mixture of Gallic blood. Only in that form of the North-Galatian theory which is advocated by Dr. Zöckler is it admissible to suppose that the Christian Galatians were to some extent Gauls (see p. 81, 84 f.). The historical review given under GALATIA, and the authorities quoted there, furnish the proof of the statements here made.

The origin of the peculiar Greek word Γαλάτης is doubtful; it probably arose among the Greek settlers on the Gallic coast at Massalia or Massilia, and means, according to Holder (*Sprachschatz*), 'noble,' while Galli means 'warlike.' Three terms occur in Greek writers, and it was only at a later period and in a half-hearted way that a distinction was drawn between Γαλάται as the people of Galatia in Asia, Γάλλοι as the people of Gaul or France, and Κέλται as the generic name of all cognate tribes whether found in these two countries or elsewhere; the last of these distinctions, which is universal among modern writers, can hardly be traced, even in embryo, among the ancients (though the use of Κελτικός in Strab. vii. 5. 2, p. 314, approximates to it); but the Romans began sooner to appreciate the convenience of the distinction between *Galli* and *Galatæ* in political usage, and the geographers adopted it from them by degrees (traces of it appear in Strabo).

II. It is maintained by other scholars, that, corresponding to the term *Galatia Provincia*, there was a Roman term *Galatæ*, indicating the body of provincials. It was necessary in official and legal usage to have a term designating the entire population of a province; and the term was always the ethnic derived from the official name of the province. Thus all the inhabitants of Africa were *Afri* (*e.g.* Juvenal, viii. 120; Pliny, *Epist.* ii. 11. 2), of Hispania Bætica *Bætici* (Pliny, *Epist.* iii. 9. 3, etc.), and so on, even though several nations inhabited each province, some of which, *e.g.* Carthaginians or Greeks, regarded themselves as far superior to barbarian Afri, etc. The Romans used these generic terms when it was necessary to describe as a class the whole population; but 'the same writer who at one time and from one point of view summed up the population of *Sicilia Provincia* as *Siculi*, would at another time and for another purpose pointedly emphasize the Greek character and origin of the people of Syracuse or Messana,' and would distinguish them from the Siculi as a different race.† Similarly, the term *Galatæ* was for purposes of generalization employed by the Romans to sum up the entire population of the province Galatia; ‡ but its use in this way is determined by the pur-

---

* On this sense of διῆλθεν, see *Expositor*, May 1895, p. 385 ff.
† Such is the reading of RV, Tischendorf, Westcott and Hort, etc. But probably Lightfoot was right (*Biblical Essays*, p. 235), that the TR and AV represent the correct reading here.
‡ This cannot justly be interpreted as describing any other country than the region of Antioch, Apollonia, and Iconium; but Salmon, while translating by these words, interprets them as describing part of Galatia Proper (Smith, *DB* p. 1105).

* Slaves Sosias, Maiphateis, etc., called Γαλάται in Delphic inscriptions, are by race Phrygian (*Expositor*, August 1898).
† See *Studia Biblica*, iv. p. 26 ff., for a fuller discussion (which, according to Zahn [*Einleitung*, p. 130], 'ausführlich und überzeugend handelt hievon').
‡ For example, Tacitus speaks of levies from the provinces of Galatia and Cappadocia, sometimes as *habiti per Galatiam Cappadociamque dilectus* (*Ann.* xiii. 35), sometimes, with his usual love of variation in language, as *Galatarum Cappa-*

pose and views of the speaker. Three points are involved in this use of the term: (1) the speaker or writer is generalizing about a set of inhabitants of the province; (2) he has not in mind any thought of the racial character—as Phrygians, Pisidians, Galatians, etc.—of the persons addressed; (3) he is speaking from the Roman point of view. All these three points are united in Gal 3¹. (1) St. Paul is addressing in a generalizing style people of two cities in Phrygia and two in Lycaonia, viz. the members of the four 'Churches of Galatia.' If it is possible to speak of the 'Churches of Galatia,' it must from the same point of view be possible to classify the members as 'Galatians.' (2) There is here no thought of racial character, only of classifying a group of towns by their common character, and no common characteristic lies so near as their common Roman relation. The policy of Rome was to prevent the subject cities from uniting with one another, and to unite them all closely to herself; and their Roman relationship exists only in virtue of their forming part of a Roman province. Hence analogies from modern divisions, such as English counties, which opponents of this interpretation of the term G. bring forward, are inapposite: a native of an English county does not rank as a Briton in virtue of his belonging to the county, but a native of the province Galatia ranked as a member of the Roman Empire in virtue of his belonging to the province. Similarly, a modern governor might sum up members of a Society with branches in New Brunswick and Ontario as 'Canadians,' though even here the parallel is not complete, for New Brunswick was a part of the British Empire before it was federated with Canada, but Lycaonia was governed by a native prince before it was incorporated in the province Galatia. (3) Paul, the *civis Romanus*, naturally spoke from the Roman point of view. His whole career shows how thoroughly he accepted the existing political facts and inculcated loyal submission to the reigning power. He classified his Churches according to the provinces, Achaia, Macedonia, Asia, Galatia. Especially after the decision in favour of religious freedom pronounced by Gallio, he recognized, also, that the liberal Roman administration was his ally against the Jews.* But, from the outset, the Pauline teaching was, as a practical force in society, tending to produce certain results, which the Roman policy also aimed at, viz. (1) spread of the Greek language as being used in the Christian books; (2) revolt against the power of the great religious centres with their colleges of priests; (3) education of the people; (4) development of a feeling of unity among members of different nations, *i.e.* destruction of national separation.†

But would the people of Pisidia and Lycaonia be willing to accept the title Galatæ? It has been maintained that this is incredible, and that the burden of proof lies with those who assert that the names Lycaonian or Pisidian or Phrygian would ever be disowned by natives of that country. But two of the four Churches were in Roman cities, *Coloniæ Romanæ*; to judge from the analogy of *colonia* Corinth with its numerous Roman names (see CORINTH, p. 480ᵇ), there were almost certainly some Romans in the Churches: could these be addressed as Lycaonians? And the non-Roman population of a *colonia* shared in the honour of

their city. The provincials, with Oriental facility, adopted the Roman ideas and titles, and learned to contemn the uneducated barbarians outside the pale of the empire, to pride themselves on being civilized and Romanized, and to adopt as marks of honour Roman names: thus the four Pauline Churches were at Claudio-Derbe, Colonia Julia Felix Gemina Lystra (sometimes with exaggerated Roman feeling, Lustra), Claudio-Iconium,* and Colonia Cæsarea Antiochia. To cities which were proud of titles like these, it is surely beyond dispute that the national names, Phrygian or Lycaonian or Pisidian, were far less honourable than the provincial title. Among the Romans a national designation, Phryx, Afer, Syrus, etc., was a slave's name; and among both Greeks and Romans the Phrygians were known as a race of slaves.† The Roman Empire, moreover, which brought peace and fair government after centuries of war and oppression, was immensely popular in the Asiatic provinces.

Accordingly, the possibility that St. Paul should address a group of Christians in two Roman colonies and two half-Romanized cities of the province Galatia as 'Galatians,' must be admitted. Whether he actually did so, is a matter of interpretation of Gal and Acts.

The general type of religion and manners among the population of the Phrygian and Lycaonian cities seems to have been much the same: it was found also in the great North-Galatian cities like Ancyra and Pessinus (see GALATIA I.); and the Gentiles addressed in Gal, Eph, Col are of that type. A highly elaborate religious system reigned over the country. Superstitious devotion to an artificial system of rules, and implicit obedience to the directions of the priests (cf. Gal 4³⁻¹¹), were universal among the uneducated native population. The priestly hierarchy at the great religious centres, *hiera*, expounded the will of the god to his worshippers.‡ Thus the government was a theocracy; and the whole system, with its prophets, priests, religious law, punishments inflicted by the god for infractions of the ceremonial law, warnings and threats, and the set of superstitious minutiæ, presented a remarkable and real resemblance in external type to the old Jewish ceremonial and religious rule. It is not until this is properly apprehended that Gal 4³⁻¹¹ becomes clear and natural. Paul in that passage implies that the Judaizing movement of the Christian Galatians is a recurrence to their old heathen type. After being set free from the bonds of a hard ceremonial law, they were putting themselves once more into the bonds of another ceremonial law, equally hard. In their action they were showing themselves senseless (ἀνόητοι, Gal 3¹), devoid of the educated mind that could perceive the real nature of things. There is an intentional emphasis in the juxtaposition of ἀνόητοι with Γαλάται, for it was the more educated party, opposed to the native superstition, that would most warmly welcome the provincial title; hence the address, 'senseless G.,' already anticipates the longer expostulation (4³⁻¹¹), 'G. who are sinking from the educated standard to the ignorance and superstition of the native religion.'

Further, the great strength of the Jews in the cities of South Galatia and South Phrygia had produced a peculiar mixed type of religion. The Phrygian religion of Sabazios formed the foundation on which this mixed type was built up.

---

documque auxilia (*Ann.* xv. 6); and Syncellus, depending on an older authority, after mentioning the province Galatia, says that Augustus imposed taxes on the G., obviously meaning the whole people of the province.

* From this point of view, the composition of Gal should be placed after the trial before Gallio, rather than (as Zahn, *Einleitung*, § 12, puts it) before that event: perhaps at Antioch (Ac 18²²).

† See **Zahn**, *Einleitung*, § 11, A 4 (*St. Paul the Trav.* p. 130 ff.).

* Created a *colonia* by Hadrian; older authorities say it was made a *colonia* by Claudius, and Zahn (*Einleitung*, p. 136) wrongly follows them.

† As Mommsen points out, the national designation as Lycaonian or Phrygian was the servile designation applied to slaves, horses, and marines (*classiarii*), who were originally servile (*Hermes*, 1884, p. 33 ff.).

‡ *Cities and Bishoprics of Phrygia*, i. 134 ff., 147 ff., 94 ff., etc.

Sabazios was identified with the Jewish Sabaoth; and the Most High God ($\theta\epsilon\dot{o}\varsigma$ $\H{\upsilon}\psi\iota\sigma\tau o\varsigma$) was adored in a form strongly influenced by Jewish elements, but yet in many cases indubitably pagan. Purely Jewish references to the $\theta\epsilon\dot{o}\varsigma$ $\H{\upsilon}\psi\iota\sigma\tau o\varsigma$ also occur, and are to be distinguished from the mixed worship. Considerable sections of the Phrygian people, especially in the centre and south, were affected by the semi-Jewish, semi-pagan cult; and, as M. Cumont observes in his admirable paper, *Hypsistos* (*Supplément à la Revue de l'instruction publ. en Belg.* 1897): 'ces milieux, tout pénétrés d'idées bibliques sans être étroitement attachés à la loi judaïque, constituaient un terrain fécond pour la prédication chrétienne, et l'on s'explique mieux, en tenant compte de cette situation, que la foi nouvelle, ait opéré plus de conversions en Asie Mineure, que dans toute autre région.' The remark which M. Cumont makes about Asia Minor in general applies with most force to those districts where the Jews were specially strong. See also *Cities and Bishoprics of Phrygia*, i. pp. 667–676, also pp. 388, 533, 538, 566, etc.; Schürer in *Theol. Littztg.* 1897, p. 506.   W. M. RAMSAY.

GALATIANS, EPISTLE TO THE.—i. AUTHORSHIP.—The Pauline origin of this Epistle has never been called in question by a critic of first-rate importance, and until recently has never been questioned at all. In the early part of the 2nd cent. it formed a part of Marcion's *Apostolicon*. A little later it was included in the Syr. and Old Lat. VSS, and was recognized by the Muratorian Canon. It is cited as the work of St. Paul by Irenæus (III. vi. 5, III. xvi. 3, v. xxi. 1), by Clement of Alexandria (*Strom.* iii. 16); and it is quoted by Justin Martyr (*Dial.* c. 95; *Oratio*, 5) and by Athenagoras (*Legatio*, c. 16). And while the echoes of its language which have been detected in Clement, Barnabas, Ignatius, and Hermas, are somewhat dull and doubtful, a clear reference to the Ep. occurs in Polycarp (*Phil.* 5), $\epsilon\dot{\iota}\delta\acute{o}\tau\epsilon\varsigma$ $o\dot{\upsilon}\nu$ $\H{o}\tau\iota$ $\dot{o}$ $\theta\epsilon\dot{o}\varsigma$ $o\dot{\upsilon}$ $\mu\upsilon\kappa\tau\eta\rho\acute{\iota}\zeta\epsilon\tau\alpha\iota$ (Gal 6[7]), and almost certainly in the words (c. 3), $\H{\eta}\tau\iota\varsigma$ $\dot{\epsilon}\sigma\tau\dot{\iota}\nu$ $\mu\acute{\eta}\tau\eta\rho$ $\pi\acute{\alpha}\nu\tau\omega\nu$ $\dot{\eta}\mu\tilde{\omega}\nu$ (cf. Gal 4[26]).

The internal evidence is irresistible. It has been felt that it is a real person who speaks in the Ep., a person engaged with earnestness and vehemence in a critical conflict. A Paulinist of the 2nd cent. would not be likely to dwell upon the fact that his master's apostleship had been called in question, or to represent some of his earliest and most highly prized conquests from heathenism as slipping through his fingers. Esp. does the subject discussed in the Ep. speak for its early date. It is a polemical tract, a contribution to a controversy which was raging at the time of its appearance. As Gloël says, it is not a sermon, it is not a treatise, it is a sword-cut, delivered in the hour of greatest danger by a combatant who is assaulted by determined foes. The question, then, is, When was there any risk of Gentile Christians being compelled to submit to circumcision? It is idle to look for such a danger in any generation subsequent to the year A.D. 70. Before that time there already existed throughout the empire strong Gentile churches of uncircumcised members. And if this letter is part of a conflict against real and not imaginary dangers, a place must be found for it in the earliest years of Gentile admission to the Christian Church. It can surprise no one that this admission should have been won only by conflict. To discard Mosaism might well seem to the Jews to be equivalent to discarding religion. The surprising thing is that the Gentiles were led to liberty by a Hebrew of the Hebrews. But what brought St. Paul to the front was not merely that he had been appointed Apostle and Defender of the Faith to the Gentiles, but much more that he perceived that this was a conflict involving the very existence of Christianity. Was Christ sufficient for salvation, or must other things be added? This was the question which St. Paul saw to be involved in the question of circumcision. To his eye it was an alternative, Circumcision *or* the Cross. And this Ep. bears upon it the marks of having been written in the very heat of this conflict. But if so, then it can have proceeded from no other hand than that of the man whose life was spent in the service and defence of the Gentiles.

The first assault upon its authenticity was made by Bruno Bauer in 1850 (*Kritik der Paul. Briefe*). This critic maintained that it was a compilation from Ro and Co, intended to correct the false impression of St. Paul conveyed by the Acts. In 1886 Pierson and Naber published their *Verisimilia. Laceram conditionem NT exemplis illustrarunt et ab origine repetierunt* (Amstelodami), which has been well rendered 'The NT in Tatters.' They allege that the Epistles known as Pauline were really compiled by Paulus Episcopus (Paul the Bishop), who made use of letters or parts of letters which had already been addressed to Gentile churches by a missionary of reformed and spiritualized Judaism. This theory discredited its authors rather than the Epp. of Paul. (See Steck, *Der Galaterbrief*; Kuenen, *ThT*, xx. (1886) 491 ff., included in the *Gesammelte Abhandlungen*, tr[d] by Budde, 1894, pp. 330–369; Van Manen in the *Jahrbücher für Protest. Theol.* 1887; Zahn in *Zeitschrift f. Kirchliche Wissenschaft*, 1889). Loman (*Quæstiones Paulinæ*, Amsterdam, 1882–86) supposed that the four great Epistles of St. Paul were written in his name to recommend universalistic Christianity in opp. to the original Christianity, which had been a Jewish Messianic movement centring in a mythical Jesus. Paul was not wholly mythical, but the canonical Paul was.

Scarcely more serious or plausible than those assaults was that of Rudolf Steck of Bern, who, in 1888, published at Berlin his small volume, entitled *Der Galaterbrief nach seiner Echtheit untersucht nebst kritischen Bemerkungen zu den paulinischen Hauptbriefen*. In this publication Steck aimed at proving that the sketch of primitive church history offered by the Tübingen school was as little in correspondence with fact as the outline given in the Bk of Ac, and that the four principal Epp. of St. Paul are as little entitled to be considered genuine as the smaller Epp. Baur had contented himself with saying, 'There has never been the slightest suspicion cast upon these four Epp. They bear on themselves so incontestably the character of Pauline originality that it is not possible for critical doubt to be exercised upon them with any show of reason.' Very good, says Steck, but where does Baur learn the marks of 'Pauline originality'? Is he not perilously near a *petitio principii*? He rejects Ac as a true picture of Paul's character: whence, then, does he receive the true impression? Accordingly, Steck applies to Gal the Tübingen method, and finds that it is not genuine. Much has been derived from Ro, but it betrays a more fully developed Paulinism; and the borrowed expressions appear in Gal as stones from an old house built into a new wall. The date must be subsequent to A.D. 70, because Jerus. is said to be in bondage (!). The inviting of attention to the large letters in which Paul writes is a manifest attempt to palm off the Ep. as Pauline. This criticism was answered from the Tübingen side by Holsten and Holtzmann; but by far the most effective reply is to be found in Gloël's *Die jüngste Kritik des Galaterbriefes auf ihre Berechtigung geprüft* (Erlangen, 1890). See also Lindemann's *Die Echtheit der Paulinischen Hauptbriefe gegen Steck's Umsturzversuch vertheidigt*. Steck was followed by Völter, who attempted to show (*Die Komposition d. Paul. Hauptbriefe*, Tübingen, 1890) that Gal is spurious and dependent on Ro and 1 and 2 Co. [A full account of these assaults upon the genuineness and integrity of Gal is given by Knowling in his *Witness of the Epistles*, pp. 133–243. See also Clemen, *Die Einheitlichkeit der Paul. Briefe* (Göttingen, 1894), pp. 100–125; and, on the other side, van Manen in *Expos. Times*, Feb., March, April, 1898].

ii. THE PERSONS ADDRESSED.—These are designated (1[2]) 'the churches of Galatia.' Alone among the Epp. of St. Paul this is addressed, not to an individual or to any single church, but to a group of churches. Where are we to look for these churches? For the name 'Galatia' has a wider and a narrower application (see GALATIA). Are 'the churches of G.' to be sought for in the geographically limited district inhabited by the Celtic Galatians, or in the wider region comprehended in the Rom. province, G.? The majority of critics hold that as in the Bk of Ac the term G. is used in the narrower sense to denote the district of G. proper, or original, so this Ep. is addressed to the churches of that remote country, which probably existed in the towns of Ancyra, Pessinus, Germa, and Tavium in the N., and not to the churches of Antioch, Iconium, Lystra, and Derbe in the S. Such is the opinion, *e.g.*, of Weiss, Lipsius, Sieffert, Lightfoot, Davidson, and Godet. On the other hand, the claims of provincial G. have been advocated by such critics as Renan and Perrot in France; Mynster, Weizsäcker, Hausrath, Zahn, and Pfleiderer in Germany. And this opinion has recently been reinforced by the adhesion of Prof. W. M. Ramsay, whose personal knowledge of Asia Minor and acquaintance with its history lend great weight to his judgment.

There are three sources from which light upon this question may be sought : the Bk of Ac, the other Pauline Epp., and this Epistle itself. In the Bk of Ac (13¹⁴–14²⁴) we possess a pretty full account of the foundation of churches in S. G., although it is to be noted that the writer uses the ethnographical names, Lycaonia and Pisidia, and not the political designation of the district, G. On the other hand, no account is given nor any notice taken of the founding of churches in N. G. And this silence is not sufficiently accounted for by the fact that at the time of the presumed founding of these churches St. Luke was not St. Paul's companion, for other events of which St. Luke was not an eye-witness are fully described. But if St. Luke joined St. Paul immediately after the apostle had been so warmly received and so successfully engaged in N. G., as by the hypothesis he had been, then certainly it is strange that no notice should be taken of so remarkable a mission. No sure conclusion can be based on this silence, but it is more likely that a letter should have been addressed to churches regarding which we have some information than to those of which St. Luke tells us nothing. For it is to be considered that St. Luke must have known the intense interest which St. Paul took in the churches thus addressed, and would naturally have informed himself and others about them.

The passage in the Bk of Ac (16⁴⁻⁸) in which St. Paul's route from Derbe and Lystra to Troas is described, has been claimed both by the advocates of the N. G. and by the upholders of the S. G. theory. According to Ramsay (*Church in Rom. Emp.* pp. 74–111), this journey was described by one who wrote under the immediate influence of St. Paul himself. It must therefore be accepted as exact and intelligible. Antioch in Pisidia may be taken as the starting-point, for probably it was while in that city, and while he was making arrangements for passing westwards through Asia to Ephesus, that it was made plain to him that he must not at this time proclaim Christ in Asia. Instead of going W., therefore, he turned to the N. 'And they passed through Phrygia and the region of G.,' and so reached Mysia. Now, it is not to be denied that if any one was so minded it was possible to go from Antioch to Pessinus in G., and from Pessinus to Germa, and at that point to form the design of entering Bithynia. But in this case the force of the topographical notice, that it was when they had come over against Mysia that they proposed to enter Bithynia, is entirely lost.

Accordingly, Prof. Ramsay proposes another route, following the road which runs N.W., and not the road which runs N.E. This road would have led St. Paul and his party into Bithynia, but when they came so far N. as to be opposite Mysia, that is to say, as to have it lying to their left, 'the Spirit of Jesus suffered them not' to enter Bithynia, and therefore, turning to the W., they skirted the southern border of Mysia, and so came to Troas. Certainly, this gives a route that has great probability in its favour. For (1) any one proposing to go from Lystra and Derbe to Bithynia would naturally go by the road passing through Dorylaion, and from this road, or any part of it, it would be out of the way to enter G. proper. And (2) to use Prof. Ramsay's words, 'From N. G. no possible route to Bithynia could be said to bring a traveller to a point 'over against Mysia,' still less 'to the frontier of Mysia.' Another strong point in favour of this route and undelayed journey is this, that in vv.⁶·⁷ (Ac 16) a single definite journey is described. The statement, 'They passed through Phrygia . . . and when they came opposite Mysia,' seems to leave no room for any such mission in G. as is required by the N. Gal. theory. It is not easily credible that had St. Paul intercalated into this journey a digression eastwards of about 300 miles into N. G., so important a mission would have been passed over in silence.

This theory, however, implies a rendering and a construction of Ac 16⁶ to which exception has been taken. This verse, as it stands in modern editions, reads thus: διῆλθον δὲ τὴν Φρυγίαν καὶ Γαλατικὴν χώραν, κωλυθέντες ὑπὸ τοῦ Ἁγίου Πνεύματος λαλῆσαι τὸν λόγον ἐν τῇ Ἀσίᾳ. Prof. Ramsay contends that Φρυγίαν is here an adj., not a substantive, and that the designation τὴν . . . χώραν means 'the country to which the epithets Phrygian and Galatic apply,' 'the Phrygo-Galatic territory.' This country, Phrygia-Galatica, lies in the southern part of the Rom. province G., and includes Iconium, Lystra, and Antioch of Pisidia. But in the only other passages in which St. Luke mentions Phrygia (Ac 2¹⁰ and 18²³) he uses Φρυγία as a substantive. In the latter of these passages the expression τὴν Γαλατικὴν χώραν καὶ Φρυγίαν throws light on 16⁶. It may be inferred that in both passages he had the same tract of country in view, and that as in 18²³ Φρυγία is a substantive, so it is in 16⁶. And as it is grammatically possible to render the disputed phrase 'Phrygia and the Gal. country,' it becomes very doubtful whether Prof. Ramsay's rendering is tenable.

It has also been supposed that the use of the phrase 'the Gal. country,' and the avoidance of the simple 'Galatia,' implies or

suggests that St. Luke may have wished thus to indicate that he was speaking of the whole land that could be called 'Galatian,' rather than of the smaller country which originally was known as G. This is plausible. But it may be that the writer wished to indicate that rural districts as well as cities were evangelized by St. Paul (see 14⁶).

Again, Prof. Ramsay's construction requires a somewhat unusual and difficult relation of the participle κωλυθέντες to the main verb διῆλθον. The natural construction undoubtedly is that which RV has adopted, involving that St. Paul and the rest passed through Phrygia and G. in consequence of having been prevented from preaching in Asia. But Prof. Ramsay maintains that the sequence of the verbs *as they stand in the sentence* is the sequence of time : '(1) they went through the Phrygo-Galatic land ; (2) they were forbidden to speak in Asia ; (3) they came over against Mysia ; (4) they essayed to go into Bithynia ; (5) the Spirit suffered them not ; (6) they passed through Mysia ; (7) they came to Troas.'

In this uncertainty the suggestion of Dr. Gifford (*Expositor*, July 1894) is worthy of consideration. He supposes that the Phrygian and Gal. country is the borderland between the two countries, the E. edge of Phrygia and the W. strip of G. Leaving Antioch, St. Paul, instead of going W. to Ephesus in Asia as apparently he had intended, went northwards through the Phrygian-Gal. borderland with the purpose of entering Bithynia ; but when he came opposite Mysia he was compelled to turn W. to the coast.

In the other Epp. of St. Paul we find one significant allusion to 'the churches of G.,' 1 Co 16¹ 'Concerning the collection for the saints as I gave order unto the churches of G., so do ye.' Now, if by this designation we are to understand the churches of N. G. exclusively, then how is it that the churches of the S., which he so repeatedly visited and cherished, were not included in this great scheme of beneficence? On this allusion to 'the churches of G.' Dr. Plummer has the following just observation : 'We are not entitled to conclude that because St. Luke, when historically relating the course of St. Paul's journeys, describes the places visited by their precise geographical designations, St. Paul may not have used the word G. in a wide sense when in want of a word to include all the churches which he had founded in the Rom. province of G. In fact, if he had wished to include under one designation the churches of Antioch, Iconium, Derbe, and Lystra, together possibly with others in the adjacent district, it is hard to say what other term he could have used. There is . . . no certain evidence that St. Paul founded churches in G. proper ; if he did, these, of course, would be included among the churches of G. But the question is whether we are bound to understand St. Paul's use of the word as excluding all churches save those of G. proper? Now, it is not likely either that when he was organizing a collection for the poor Christians of Jerus., he would omit to appeal to the churches in the Gal. province with which his relations were so intimate, or that he would leave those churches unmentioned when writing to Corinth.'

In the Ep. itself (4¹³⁻¹⁵) there occurs an allusion to the circumstances in which he first preached the gospel to the churches now addressed, οἴδατε ὅτι δι' ἀσθένειαν τῆς σαρκὸς εὐηγγελισάμην ὑμῖν τὸ πρότερον, which can only mean, 'you know that it was on account of an infirmity of my flesh I formerly preached to you.' This statement implies that he was weak and ill when in the district referred to, and that but for this weakness he would not have preached in it. Prof. Ramsay ingeniously construes the situation thus: While on his first journey St. Paul caught a fever at Perga, and as its natural cure a change to the higher and purer air of Antioch was prescribed. He reached Antioch with traces of illness upon him, and with liability to its recurrence. This is possible ; but may not the 'weakness' have been connected with the stoning he suffered at Lystra? It was after this stoning, which must have left very obvious marks upon him, that he preached in Derbe, Lystra itself, Iconium, and Antioch (Ac 14¹⁹⁻²³). In this case, as in the course of events suggested by Prof. Ramsay, τὸ πρότερον receives its proper sense, 'on the former of my two visits.' *

But whatever the weakness was, and however incurred, the fact remains that it afforded him an opportunity of preaching in a district where he had no intention of preaching : a district, therefore, which lay on the road to some more attractive field of operation. Now, it will scarcely do to say that G. proper lay on the road to nowhere, for, as we have seen, St. Paul had a desire to enter Bithynia, and might, because debarred from Asia, have chosen to pass through the western edge of G. on his way to the more northern province. It seems, therefore, as easy to construe this expression in keeping with the N. Galatian theory as with the S. Galatian.

We find from the Ep. itself that emissaries from Jerus. had appeared among the Gal. churches, and it has been argued that such persons would scarcely have penetrated so far into the interior of Asia Minor as the N. Gal. theory supposes. But this is both to misconceive the accessibility of the region and to underrate the eager propagandism of the Jew and the antipathy to St. Paul. It is more to the purpose to point to 5¹¹ and to find in it an allusion to the circumcision of Timothy, which was well known among the S. Gal. churches, and might naturally be used as a handle against St. Paul, and a ground of charging him with inconsistency.

---

* The Greek interpreters understood the ἀσθενεία of persecution. Theodoret, *e.g.*, says : καίτοι πολλὴν ἔφερον ἐπὶ τοῦ σώματος ἀτιμίαν, αἰκιζόμενος καὶ στρεβλούμενος καὶ μυρία ὑπομένων δεινά.

The internal evidence which the Ep. bears, that it was addressed to Celts, cannot be regarded as trustworthy. Lightfoot and others have collected very interesting notices of the Celtic character, their sensuousness and impulsiveness, and so forth, and have adduced from the Ep. illustrations of these qualities which are certainly striking. But although these might serve as corroborative evidence to an otherwise strong argument, the insecurity of founding upon them is at once apparent when it is considered how difficult it is to grasp national character, and when we reflect that the Celtic character produces types so diverse as the Irish, the Welsh, and the Highlanders of Scotland.

iii. OCCASION OF THE EPISTLE.—The Galatians had received St. Paul with extraordinary demonstrations of friendliness (4^15). They had felicitated themselves on their good fortune in having him for their guest, and they had received his gospel as a message from heaven, or as if Christ Jesus Himself had come among them (4^14). Churches had been formed, and they 'ran bravely' (5^7). That a second visit had been paid to these churches before this letter was written, is the natural inference from some expressions which occur in it. The τὸ πρότερον of 4^13 might merely mean 'formerly,' and not definitely 'on the former of two occasions'; neither is the expression of the 16th verse decisive (ὥστε ἐχθρὸς ὑμῶν γέγονα ἀληθεύων ὑμῖν), for it is possible that in these words he might be merely alluding to the change of feeling towards him produced by the representations of his enemies, or anticipating the resentment this letter itself might occasion. But when he uses such expressions as those which occur in 1^9 and 5^3, and which point to emphatic warnings uttered when he was among them, it would appear that such warnings are incongruous with the circumstances of his first visit, and must be referred to a second, when he perceived symptoms of defection from the gospel he had proclaimed.

The symptoms he had observed rapidly developed. They were moving away from the free standing of faith to the bondage of the law; they were being circumcised, observing days and new moons and other seasons, and returning to the weak and beggarly elements from which St. Paul believed they had escaped (1^6 4^9. 10 5^3). In this retrograde movement St. Paul sees a renunciation of grace, a virtual renunciation of Christ (5^4). He still tried to persuade himself that irreparable damage had not yet been done (5^10); but assuredly the evil leaven was working among them, and 'a little leaven leaveneth the whole lump' (5^9).

This sad change had been wrought by the Judaizing party, and apparently in great part by one individual. This individual seems to have been a personage of some distinction. He exerted a fascinating power over the Galatians (3^1), and apparently claimed to speak with authority (1^8). Whether St. Paul actually knew him is doubtful (see 5^9 ὅστις ἐὰν ᾖ, and 5^7 and 3^1): that he knew him by name may be taken for granted.

No special reason need be sought to account for the Judaizing party having emissaries in G. The question of the relation of Gentile Christians to the Jewish law was sure, sooner or later, to emerge in every church in which there were any Jewish Christians. Must a Gentile enter Christianity through Judaism? and to what extent is the Mosaic law binding on Gentiles?—these questions must be answered, and the battle between legalism and liberty fought through to the end. Superficially, the Judaizers, who maintained that to become a Christian a man must also become a Jew, had a great deal to say for themselves. The law was a divine institution. The promises had been given to Abraham and his seed. The Messiah was the Messiah of the Jews. Jesus Himself had been circumcised, and had kept the whole law. The original apostles did the same. Was not this an obvious and infallible example? Besides, if the Gentile converts were not to keep the law, how were they to escape from the immoralities in which they had been brought up? And who was this Paul who taught them to neglect the law? What claim had he to be considered an apostle? He did not keep company with Christ while on earth, as the others had done; he was not called, as they had been, to the apostolate by the Lord in His lifetime; he had no external authentication of himself, like their letters of commendation from the mother-church at Jerusalem. The Judaizers did not scruple even to speak slightingly of his appearance, and to insinuate that his motives were impure and his conduct inconsistent with his teaching. When it suited him he practised circumcision, as in the case of Timothy. If, therefore, he had not enjoined it on the Galatians, it was through a desire to please men (5^11 1^10).

All personal abuse and calumny St. Paul could no doubt have overlooked; what he could not overlook was the Judaizing adulteration or subversion of the gospel of Christ. And the very speciousness of the arguments used, and the characteristic zeal for the law displayed by the Judaizers, all the more emphatically inspired St. Paul with the feeling that the crisis was of tremendous moment, and that his life-work among the Gentiles hung in the balance. For not only was he aware that to demand circumcision and impose the whole Mosaic law on the Gentile world, was to undertake a hopeless task, but also he perceived that it would obscure the gospel of Christ. He saw, as apparently no other man of influence saw, that to represent anything else than the cross of Christ as *essential* to salvation, was really to affirm that the cross alone was not sufficient. St. Paul recognized that it was *either* the law or Christ; that a man could not be justified by both. 'Behold, I Paul say unto you, that if ye receive circumcision, Christ will profit you nothing' (5^2); 'ye are severed from Christ, ye who would be justified by the law: ye are fallen away from grace' (5^4 κατηργήθητε ἀπὸ Χριστοῦ οἵτινες ἐν νόμῳ δικαιοῦσθε, τῆς χάριτος ἐξεπέσατε). The importance of the crisis cannot be over-estimated. 'It really seemed as if the mighty enthusiasm of Pentecost might sink into respectable legalism, as if Christianity might be strangled in its cradle by the iron hand of the law, as if it might sink into an obscure Jewish sect, and disappear in the national ruin, instead of breaking its fetters, spreading its mighty spiritual pinions, and claiming the universal heaven as its home' (Bishop Moorhouse, *Dangers of the Apostolic Age*, p. 21).

DATE OF THE EPISTLE.—The date of the Ep. has been, and still is, contested. It has been assigned by different critics to the beginning, to the close, and to every intermediate stage of its author's epistolary activity. It stands first in the canon of Marcion; but there is reason to believe that this canon was not arranged in chronological order (Tertul. *adv. Marcion.* v. 2). One or two modern scholars, as Michaelis, Koppe, Zahn, have placed it earliest among the Epp. of St. Paul; while Koehler and Schrader consider it the latest (Davidson, *Introd.* i. 73). Calvin held that it was written before the Council at Jerus., and that the visit to Jerus., which St. Paul relates in Gal 2, is the same as that which is mentioned in Ac 11^30, and is not that of Ac 15. This view has received the powerful advocacy of Prof. Ramsay (*Expositor*, Aug. 1895), who argues that the account of the journey in Ac 11. 12 is 'in the most singular agreement' with the narrative of Gal 2. Hausrath dogmatically pronounces that the Ep. was written in the autumn of 53, and on the following ingeniously discovered ground: 'As the Gal. are on the point of joining with the synagogue in celebrating the beginning of the sabbatical year (Gal 4[10]), lasting from Sept. 53 to Sept. 54, the Ep. must date from the autumn of 53, in which St. Paul crossed into Macedonia' (*Time of the Apostles*, iii. 188. Hausrath, of course, holds the S. Gal. theory). Renan, again, places the Ep. between the second and third missionary journeys, and dates it from Antioch.

The majority of continental critics, however, such as Weiss, Holtzmann, Sieffert, Lipsius, and Godet, place it very early in the Ephesian residence, and consequently first of the four great Epp. In this finding they are considerably influenced by the οὕτως ταχέως of 1[6]. This expression, it is supposed, involves that no long time can have elapsed between St. Paul's second visit to the Gal. churches and this letter. Lightfoot, however, has shown (*Gal.* pp. 41, 42) that this conclusion rests on two erroneous assumptions: (1) that 'so soon' means 'so soon after I left you'; whereas it rather refers to the time of their conversion ; and (2) that a period so indicated cannot embrace more than a few months ; whereas 'quickness and slowness are relative terms,' and the expression might have been used 'though a whole decade of years had passed since they were first brought to the knowledge of Christianity.' Warfield, irrespective of the οὕτως ταχέως, finds reasons for placing the Ep. before the other three which belong to this period, 'only a few weeks at most before 1 Co,' *i.e.* 'about or somewhat earlier than the passover time of the year A.D. 57.' His strongest argument is drawn from 1 Co 9[2] 'If to others I am not an apostle, yet to you at least I am,' in which he finds an allusion to the recent disparagement of St. Paul's apostleship among the Galatians. (*Journ. of Exegetical Soc.* Paper read in Dec. 1884).

Lightfoot and Salmon bring the Ep. down a few months later, and date it from Corinth early in the year A.D. 58. The resemblances between Gal and 2 Co and Ro are obvious. The ideas suggested in Gal 3 and 4 regarding the Spirit as the promise of the Father, and as the true emancipator and sign of sonship, are elaborated in Ro 8. The impossibility of salvation by works, or of finding anything but a curse in the law, is taken up again in Ro and expounded at large. But neither can there be any doubt regarding the priority of the Ep. to the Galatians. The similarity and dissimilarity between the two Epp. are of that kind which tends to show that the Ep. to the Gal. could not have been written either after or contemporary with the Ep. to the Rom., and that it was not, therefore, a compendium of it ; nor is it probable that it was written very long before it. See Jowett, *St. Paul's Epp.*[1] i. 240 (2nd ed. om.).

The similarity to 2 Co is also apparent. There is the same self-defensive tone and the same invective against those teachers who interfered with his work. In Corinth as well as in G. emissaries from Jerus. were at work ; but in the Cor. Ep. no elaborate exposure of their doctrinal error is given. The conflict between himself and the Judaizers has not reached the doctrinal stage. And hence it is argued that the Ep. to the Gal., in which this stage is reached, and in which, together with a defence of his apostolic authority, there is also an elaborate exposure of the error of the Judaizers, must be later than the 2nd to the Corinthians. This conclusion, though not certain, is highly probable.

Recently, however, fresh indications of date have been pointed out by Ramsay and McGiffert. The former in his illuminating papers on the Ep. (*Expositor*, 1898) argues with much force that it was written from Antioch at the close of the

second missionary journey (Ac 18[22]). It was on that journey St. Paul had circumcised Timothy (Ac 16[1-3]), and this gave plausibility to the insinuation of the Judaizers that when it suited him he preached circumcision (Gal 5[11]). It was on that journey also he delivered to the Galatians the decrees ordained at Jerus. (Ac 16[4]), and this might seem to give colour to the allegation that he was the mere messenger of the higher officials and not himself an apostle (Gal 1. 2). McGiffert, on the other hand, thinks it is unquestionable that in Gal 2 St. Paul is relating events about which the Galatians had no previous knowledge, at least from him ; while it is incredible that he should have visited G. subsequent to these events without speaking of them. On these and other grounds, therefore, McGiffert (*Apostol. Age*, pp. 227–8) thinks it probable that the Ep. was written from Antioch previous to his departure on the second missionary journey. Subsequently, the Judaizers, while they might, as at Antioch, refuse to eat with the Gentiles, could scarcely urge their circumcision without seeming to break with the mother-church.

CONTENTS OF THE EPISTLE.—The Epistle divides itself into three almost equal portions—a personal, a doctrinal, and a practical. In the first two chapters St. Paul disposes of the insinuations which the Judaizers had made against his authority and standing as an apostle. In the two following chapters he explains the relation of the law to Christ, or of Mosaism to Christianity. And in the closing chapters he refutes the allegation that liberty and licence are the same.

To the disparagement of his apostolic standing, and consequently of the gospel he preached, he makes a threefold reply : (1) He declares himself to be an apostle, not sent merely from a Christian community, or commissioned by a human authority, but by Jesus Christ ; and this he proves by a brief narrative of his movements subsequent to his conversion, by which it is made apparent that his gospel could not have been learned from men (ch. 1). (2) It was only after he had been preaching for many years that he went at length to confer with the apostles at Jerus. ; and even then, so far from receiving additional light or being reprimanded, he received from them acknowledgment and encouragement (2[1-10]). (3) Instead of being instructed by the older apostles, or being obliged to occupy a subordinate place, he himself had occasion to rebuke St. Peter and assume the position of instructor (2[11-21]).

Next, St. Paul examines the dogmatic significance of the demand that the Gentiles should keep the whole law. And first he appeals to their own experience. As Christian men they had received the Spirit. Had this all-comprehending gift become theirs by the observance of the law? They knew it was not so ; they had received the Spirit as a gift. Believing God's offer of the Spirit, they had accepted what God gave (3[1-5]). Nor was this an exceptional or novel experience. It was the same with the typical justified man, Abraham. Whatever he enjoyed of God's favour he had by faith (3[6-9]). Indeed, so far from the law having power to bless, it has only power to curse, and on this account and from this curse Christ came to redeem us (3[10-14]). Moreover, hundreds of years before the law was heard of, the promise had been given to Abraham, and could not be made of none effect by any subsequently introduced institution. The promise held the field. It was given irrespective of the law, and could not be annulled by it. And yet the law was not superfluous. It had its use. It was added to instruct the conscience, that men might know their sin to be transgression, and might learn to crave righteousness. It was meant to stimulate men to crave the coming of the Spirit.

And thus it served the purpose of a schoolmaster, or of the guardian who took charge of boys under age. But when the fulness of time is come the guardian is no more needed, the full-grown son having received the spirit of his father (3^{15}–4^7). Lastly, out of the law itself St. Paul brings proof that there is a better thing than law, even liberty. This he does by allegorizing the story of Ishmael and Isaac.

In the third division of the Ep. (5. 6) St. Paul proceeds to vindicate Christian liberty against all aspersions. First of all (5^{1-12}), he exhorts the Gal. to stand fast in their liberty, and to beware of coming under bondage to minute observances. On the other hand, he warns them against using this liberty as an occasion to the flesh (5^{13}–6^{10}). In a brief conclusion, written with his own hand in the large characters which distinguished it from the more clerkly writing of his amanuensis, he contrasts his own devotedness and affectionate attitude towards them with the selfish aims of the Judaizers.

Hence, as Godet says, 'This Ep. marks an epoch in the history of man ; it is the ever-precious document of his spiritual emancipation.'

DIFFICULTIES RAISED BY THE EPISTLE.—1. *Its discrepancy with the Acts of the Apostles.*—Baur (*Paul*, c. v.) maintains that the autobiographical statements made by St. Paul in Gal 2 shed an unfavourable light on the Ac, 'the statements in which can only be looked at as intentional deviations from hist. truth in the interest of the special tendency which they possess.' Weizsäcker (*Das Apostol. Zeitalter*, p. 87 ff., Eng. tr. i. 102) follows in Baur's steps with pedantic rigour.

(1) The first discrepancy which is discovered by a comparison of the two narratives is that whereas St. Paul says that three years elapsed after his conversion before he returned to Jerus., St. Luke says (Ac 9^{23}), ὡς δὲ ἐπληροῦντο ἡμέραι ἱκαναί (which Weizsäcker inaccurately renders 'nur einige Tage,' 'only a few days'), he was compelled to leave Damascus. To find here a discrepancy damaging to the trustworthiness of Ac, is to neglect the consideration that St. Paul had a reason for giving the exact time, while St. Luke had no occasion to be definite and rigidly exact. (2) A second discrepancy urged by Baur has more weight. St. Luke says (9^{26}) that when St. Paul came to Jerus. he sought to attach himself to the disciples, but they feared him. How was it possible that the Christians of Jerus. should not have heard of his conversion ? There was constant communication between the two places, and St. Paul was so outstanding a figure that it is difficult to believe that his adhesion to the Christian Church should not have been known to all Jerusalem. It has been urged that his absence in Arabia may have withdrawn him from attention ; that he may not have occupied the outstanding position at that time which subsequent events suggest, and, indeed, although commissioned to Damascus, it seems to have been at his own request, and not because he was selected by the Sanhedrin. Besides, even in St. Paul's own account (Gal 1^{23}), it appears that he was still known rather as the persecutor than as a convert. And, on the other hand, even in Luke's account, it is apparent that some, *e.g.* Barnabas, knew of his conversion. The introduction by Barnabas has certainly the air of truth. No doubt difficulties remain ; but not such as discredit the account in Ac, considering the very different points of view of the two writers. (3) A third discrepancy is found in the statement of St. Paul, that he saw none of the apostles but Peter ; whereas St. Luke says that Barnabas 'brought him to *the apostles . . .* and he was with them going in and going out at Jerus., preaching boldly in the name of the Lord' (Ac $9^{27.\,28}$). Weizsäcker is here again inaccurate in alleging that St. Paul himself assures us that he got to know no one in the Church, and that he continued for years to be personally unknown to the members. This is not what St. Paul says. He states that he saw no other apostle besides Peter, and that he remained unknown to the Churches of Judæa. Whether he became acquainted with Christians who were not apostles, and whether he preached in Jerus. or not, he does not say. The discrepancy really amounts to this, that in the one account he is represented as being introduced to the apostles as a body, in the other to St. Peter alone. (4) The difficulties which Baur raises, and which Weizsäcker inherits, regarding the visit to Jerus. which Luke interpolates between the two mentioned by St. Paul, are trifling and fictitious. Weizsäcker's ground for rejecting this visit is that 'Paul assures us he was seen by no one in Jerus.' during the fourteen years which elapsed between the first and second visits mentioned in Gal. Where St. Paul makes this statement we do not know. (5) The discrepancies which the Tübingen school at one time found between Gal 2 and Ac 15 have been rather thrown into the background by the living members of

that school. Pfleiderer, *e.g.*, says (*Hibbert Lect.* p. 103, cf. p. 111), 'the agreement as to the chief points is in any case greater than the discrepancies in the details, and these discrepancies can be for the most part explained simply by the difference of the standpoint of the relaters.'

It is further objected that the conduct ascribed to St. Paul in the Ac is inconsistent with the attitude he assumes and the principles he maintains in Gal. In Ac he is represented as circumcising Timothy (16^3), as shaving his head in fulfilment of a vow (18^{18}), as attending the Jewish feasts (20^{16}), and as being at charges for four men who had a vow on them ($21^{23.\,24}$). Such acts of conformity to the law are, it is thought, incompatible with the principle St. Paul lays down in the Ep., 'If ye be circumcised, Christ shall profit you nothing.' The solution is obvious. When St. Paul makes this strong statement, what he means is, If you observe the ordinances of Moses because you believe them to be necessary to salvation, Christ shall profit you nothing. Together with this fundamental principle he held also as an ethical maxim, that it is right to become all things to all men, a Jew to the Jew if need be. And when he observes the Mosaic ordinances in the temple, it is not because he believes they have any virtue for salvation, but because he wishes to give no offence to his Jewish brethren. These Jewish observances have become to him matters of indifference, and only when they are lifted out of their proper position and considered essentials do they become dangerous. 'Neither is circumcision anything, *nor uncircumcision*' (Gal 6^{15}, cf. 1 Co 7^{18}). That he did not yield when it was demanded of him as a matter of principle that he should circumcise Titus, is perfectly consistent with his circumcising Timothy as a concession to expediency. No doubt St. Paul's principle carried with it the inference that as circumcision and the keeping of the whole ceremonial law were unnecessary for the Gentiles they were unnecessary for Jews also. But if the Jew clung to the temple service, the stated hours of prayer, and other observances, while at the same time he recognized that Christ alone was sufficient for salvation, St. Paul rather defended than denounced his position. So long as the observances of the law were treated as matters of indifference, St. Paul was content to leave the Jewish conscience to the education which time must bring. His attitude towards things indifferent is fully explained in 1 Co 8, 10^{23-33}.

2. *Collision with St. Peter at Antioch.*—In Gal 2^{11-14} we find a description of a scene which is certainly derogatory to the dignity of St. Peter, and which casts suspicion even on his authority. Naturally, this has quickened in the interpreting mind a desire in some way to shield the great apostle. Clement of Alex. held that the Cephas of Gal 2 was not the apostle, but 'one of the seventy disciples, a man who bore the same name' (Euseb. *HE* I. xii. 2). Although many persons adopted this view, it was so manifestly untenable that the idea was started that the two apostles arranged the scene for the edification of the people, who might thus more clearly see the folly of Judaizing. The champion of this idea was Jerome, who, however, says that it was first broached by Origen. A somewhat angry correspondence followed between Augustine and Jerome, in which the former found it easy to expose the lameness of the proposed interpretation. He maintained that 'to speak well of a falsehood uttered in God's behalf was a crime not less, perhaps even greater, than to speak ill of His truth' (see Augustine's *Letters*, esp. 28 and 40). Strangely enough, the idea seemed to attract many minds. Chrysostom advocated it, and Theodore speaks of it as at any rate a

possible view ['sive consensu ipsam controversiam inter se simulaverunt pro aliorum utilitate, sunt vere quidem mirandi, eo quod omnia ad aliorum utilitatem facere adquieverunt']. The point is treated with fulness in Lightfoot, *Gal.*, 127–131.

LITERATURE.—The four great Greek commentators, Chrysostom, Theodore of Mopsuestia, Theodoret, and Theophylact, are always lucid and sensible, although the two last named are for the most part reproductions of the two first mentioned. The late Bishop Lightfoot in his Commentary on the Epistle devoted several pages (pp. 223–232) to an account and estimate of the patristic and mediæval writers who have dealt with it. To this nothing need be added except that the com. of Theodore can now be consulted in the convenient ed. of Dr. Swete published by the Camb. Univ. Press in 1880–1882. Among the Latin Fathers, Jerome and Augustine have both left expositions of this Epistle, the former esp. being of value. Among the Reformers, Luther, Calvin, and Beza may be consulted with advantage. Estius, Bengel, and Wetstein contribute much from their special points of view. Among more recent expositions the following are worthy of mention: Usteri, *Komm. über d. Gal.* (1833); Schott, *Epistolæ P. ad Thess. et Gal.* (1834); Windischmann (Roman Cath.), *Erklärung d. Gal.* (1843); Hilgenfeld, *Der Galaterbrief* (1852); Ellicott, *Crit. and Gram. Comment. on Gal.* (1854); Jowett, *The Epistles of Paul* (1859, 2nd ed. 1894); Bisping (Rom. Cath.), *Gal.* (2nd ed. 1863); Hofmann, *Die heil. Schrift NT*, ii. 1 (1863); Lightfoot, *St. Paul's Ep. to Gal.* (1865); Meyer, *Crit. and Exegetical Handbook* (1870); Sanday in Ellicott's *NT* (1879); Holsten, *Das Evangelium d. Paulus* (1880); Philippi, *Gal. erklärt* (1884); Sieffert in the re-edited Meyer (1886); Palmieri (Rom. Cath.), *Gal.* (1886); Schaff in *Illustr. Popular Com.* (1881); Beet, *Com. on St. Paul's Ep. to Gal.* (1885); Findlay in *Expositor's Bible* (1888); Goebel, *Neutest. Schriften* (1889); Cornely (Rom. Cath.), *Gal.* (1890); Lipsius in *Hand-comm.* (2nd ed. 1892); Zöckler in Strack and Zöckler's *Kgf. Comm.* (2nd ed. 1894); B. Weiss, *Die Paulin. Briefe* (1896); Zahn, *Einleit. in d. NT* (1897). [Useful bibliographical lists will be found in Meyer, Sieffert, and Lipsius.]

MARCUS DODS.

GALBANUM (חֶלְבְּנָה *ḥelbĕnâh*, χαλβάνη, *galbanum*). —A gum resin, *Ferula galbaniflua*, Boiss. et Buhse; and *F. rubricaulis*, Boiss. It is known in Arab. by the name ḳinnah, and in Persian as *birzed*. It occurs in the form of *tears* and *lumps*. The *tears* are round, yellow to brownish-yellow, translucent, and not larger than a pea. The *lump galbanum* is more common, and consists of irregular masses of a brownish or brownish-yellow colour, composed of agglutinated tears. Fruits with bits of stem and other impurities are mixed with the resin. The odour is balsamic. Pliny (*Nat. Hist.* xii. 56) declares it to be a product of a kind of giant fennel, growing in Amanus. There are many species of *Ferula*, *Ferulago*, *Colladonia*, and other large Umbelliferæ in Amanus, but no such gum is now extracted from any of them, and none of the plants reputed to yield galbanum grow there. Pliny (*l.c.*) and Virgil (*Georg.* iii. 415) say that its smoke drives away serpents. G. is imported from India and the Levant. It is mentioned only once in the OT (Ex 30³⁴) as an ingredient of the sacred incense, and once in Apocr. (Sir 24¹⁵).   G. E. POST.

GALEED (גַּלְעֵד 'cairn of witness,' LXX Βουνὸς μαρτυρεῖ, E -ίου).—The name which, according to Gn 31⁴⁷, was given by Jacob to the cairn erected on the occasion of the compact between him and Laban. There is evidently a characteristic attempt also to account in this way for the name *Gilead*. The respective proceedings of Jacob and of Laban are uncertain, for the narrative is not only of composite origin, but has suffered through the introduction of glosses into the text. Kautzsch-Socin remark that even if v.⁴⁷ belonged originally to E (which Wellh. strongly denies, setting it down as a gloss due to pure pedantry), it is certainly introduced by R in the wrong place. A similar remark applies to v.⁴⁸ 'Therefore was the name of it called Galeed,' which probably was derived from J. There is a confusion in the present text due to the attempt to harmonize E's account of the erection of a *maṣṣēbāh* with the statement of J that it was a 'cairn' (גַּל) that was erected. It is pretty certain that we should read 'Laban' in-

stead of 'Jacob' in v.⁴⁵ (so Wellh., Dillm.). The LXX seeks unsuccessfully to reduce the narrative to order by means of transpositions.

LITERATURE.—Commentaries of Del. and Dillm. *ad loc.*; Ball in Haupt's *SBOT*; Kautzsch-Socin, *Genesis*² 73; Wellhausen, *Comp. d. Hex.* 42 f.; Kittel, *Hist. of Heb.* i. 143, 156; Driver, *LOT*⁶ 17.   J. A. SELBIE.

GALILÆAN (Γαλιλαῖος).—An inhabitant of Galilee. The apostles, who spoke with divers tongues on the day of Pentecost, were said by the crowd to be Galilæans, which made the matter all the more surprising (Ac 2⁷); a massacre of Galilæans by Pilate was reported to Jesus (Lk 13¹); Pilate spoke of Jesus as a Galilæan (Lk 23⁶); Peter was told, when trying to conceal the fact that he was a Galilæan, that it was useless for him to do so, as his speech * betrayed him (Mk 14⁷⁰); the attitude of the Galilæans towards Jesus is contrasted with that of the Jerusalemites (Jn 4⁴⁵). In the article GALILEE some traits of the inhabitants are mentioned, to which very much might be added. They were healthy, brave, and industrious; they developed the resources of their province in a wonderful manner; they were skilful merchants, and added to their wealth by shipping their commodities to other parts of the world; from a religious point of view, they were the most liberal-minded people of Palestine; they were enterprising, intelligent, and possessed a poetical talent of very high order; and in the great struggle with Rome, A.D. 66–70, they were the strongest defenders of liberty of whom the Jewish nation could boast.

S. MERRILL.

GALILEE (גָּלִיל הַגּוֹיִם, הַגָּלִילָה, הַגָּלִיל, Γαλειλαία).—It is singular that a province so well known as Galilee was in NT times, and occupying the place it did in the history of the Jewish nation, is mentioned but six times in OT (Dillm. also in Jos 12²³). Three of these being identical (Jos 20⁷ 21³², 1 Ch 6⁷⁶)—a mere statement of the fact that Kedesh, the city of refuge, was in Galilee—the number is reduced to four. When Kedesh is mentioned (in these three passages), also the invasion of Tiglath-pileser (2 K 15²⁹), and Solomon's present of twenty cities to Hiram (1 K 9¹¹), Galilee is spoken of in the same familiar manner that it is in NT and in Josephus. There remains one instance only which attracts our attention, namely, Is 9¹ 'Galilee of the nations.'† This has always been admitted to be a difficult passage. The only biblical commentary is the historical notice of Tiglath-pileser's invasion (2 K 15²⁹), 'he took Ijon, and Abel-beth-maacah, and Janoah, and Kedesh, and Hazor, and Gilead, and Galilee, all the land of Naphtali.' Here Galilee appears to be as well known as Gilead; and no hint is furnished as to its extent or character. The same can be said of the transaction between Hiram and Solomon (1 K 9¹¹ᶠᶠ·); for whatever meaning the word 'Cabul' may have, it is evident that Solomon considered the twenty cities a proper and ample compensation for the favours he had received from Hiram.

Thus far we have gained little except to learn that the Bible gives us no account of the origin of the word Galilee, of how large an area it embraced at first, or of how it came to be applied to all the northern part of Palestine.

Palestine west of the Jordan was, in the time of our Lord, divided into three provinces, Judæa, Samaria, and Galilee. The latter was the most northern, and occupied in general the territory that had been assigned by Joshua to the four tribes, Asher, Naphtali, Zebulun, and Issachar.

---

* Alluding probably to a Galilæan habit of confounding the gutturals (Smith, *HGHL* 423 n.; Dalm., *Gram. d. Aram.* 5, 42 f.).

† The word, which has regularly the art., 'the *gālīl*,' appears to mean 'circle' or 'district.' Apparently, Is 9¹ gives the full title.

It extended to the Jordan on the E., the Leontes, *Litany*, on the N., the territory of Tyre, which was then a narrow strip of seacoast on the W., and below the territory of Tyre it touched the Mediterranean and included Ptolemais (*Accho*) and Mount Carmel, and on the S. the line, which was irregular, passed near Ginea (*Jenin*), included Scythopolis or Bethshean to the E., Taanach and Megiddo to the W., and followed the Carmel ridge to the Mediterranean. Its extent in miles was about sixty from north to south, and about thirty from east to west.

Josephus divides the province into Upper and Lower Galilee. Lower Galilee extended east and west from Carmel to the Jordan; the S. line would be that already indicated as passing near Jenin, and the N. boundary included Arbela on the west of the Sea of Galilee, and also Jotapata (*Jefat*). Tarichea, Tiberias, Sepphoris (the capital of Galilee during a large portion of Christ's life), Cana, and Nazareth were all in Lower Galilee. The boundaries of Upper Galilee are given by Josephus (*Wars*, III. iii. 1; *Life*, 37), and were no doubt well understood by his readers; but it is difficult for us to indicate its limits, since the places noted still remain unidentified. The district extended from Bersabe on the S. to Baca on the N., and from Thella, a place bordering on the Jordan, to Meroth on the west.

In the year B.C. 47 Galilee had as military governor a young man then but twenty-five years of age, who subsequently became known to the world as Herod the Great. He had been appointed to this position by his father, Antipater, and proved a successful ruler. After his death, in B.C. 4, his son Antipas was made tetrarch of Galilee, and, since he was not banished by Caligula till A.D. 39, he governed the province during the entire life of our Lord. During the reign of Antipas, Galilee was bounded on the E. by the dominions of his half-brother Herod Philip II. After the removal of Antipas, Galilee came under the rule of Herod Agrippa I., who died in A.D. 44 as described in Ac 12. Although these men ruled by the favour of Rome, they were still native rulers, and in that fact the inhabitants felt a degree of pride, because their dependent state was thereby made less apparent and no doubt far less galling.

In comparing Galilee with other portions of the Holy Land, there are certain respects in which it can claim to be unique. In fact it would be difficult to find anywhere else on the globe another district of equal size whose natural characteristics are so wonderfully diversified as are those of Galilee.

The white dome of Hermon was ever present to the inhabitants as much as if that mountain had risen from their own soil, and the same was true of the wide expanse of the Mediterranean to the west. The long line of seacoast with its cities of wealth and its composite life must be taken into the account, and on the other side the depression of the Jordan Valley, in which, 700 ft. below the level of the Mediterranean, lay the Sea of Galilee. In Lower Galilee the group of Nazareth hills was picturesque; isolated Tabor had a grandeur and a beauty of its own, while in Upper Galilee but a single peak, Jebel Jermuk, reached a height of 4000 ft.; 2000 to 2500 ft. being the general elevation. Nowhere were the mountains rugged, their gradual slopes and the intervening valleys were always attractive. The Esdraelon plain was of inexhaustible fertility, and so was the region about Lakes Merom and Tiberias. The climate was all that could be desired; the temperature was mild on the seacoast, hot in the Jordan Valley, and always cool in the highlands. The air was invigorating, and no doubt it was owing partly to

this fact that the Galilæans were always noted for being healthy, hardy, and brave. The forests, meadows, and pastures, the tilled fields and gardens, the vineyards and olive orchards, the broad acres covered with wheat and barley, the fountains, streams, lakes, and rivers, the prosperous cities and towns which dotted the land, made the aspect of the country singularly varied and attractive.

In the Blessing of Moses (Dt 33) upon the tribes occupying this territory there are suggestive hints as to its natural features and the peculiar productions of its fertile soil. Special characteristics of these highlanders are brought out in other portions of OT which are fully confirmed and illustrated by what we learn from other sources, regarding both country and people. The NT, Josephus, the Talmud, and modern research present attractive, not to say fascinating, pictures of this highly favoured land.

How frequently in the Gospels are the 'cities and villages' of Galilee mentioned, leading us to suppose that its surface was thickly covered with flourishing centres of life. While Josephus praises the fertility and populousness of the entire province, he rises to enthusiasm when he describes the Plain of Gennesaret, 'that unparalleled garden of God' (*Wars*, III. iii. 2, 3; x. 8). 'For sixteen miles about Sepphoris,' says the Talmud, 'the region is fertile, flowing with milk and honey.' 'The land of Naphtali is everywhere covered with fruitful fields and vines, and its fruits are renowned for their wonderful sweetness' (Talm. Bab. *Megilla* 6[a]). Five of Solomon's commissariat officers were assigned to this region, who furnished for the royal table fine flour, meal and barley, great numbers of fat oxen, also pasture-fed oxen, sheep, harts, gazelles, roebucks, and fatted fowl (1 K 4[22. 23]).

In early times the forests of Galilee were extensive, and even in the country's present degradation they are deserving of notice, for there, besides many flowering trees, shrubs, and aromatic plants, we find the vine, the olive, and the fig, the oak, the hardy walnut, the terebinth, and the hot-blooded palm, the cedar, cypress, and balsam, the fir tree, the pine, the sycomore, the bay tree, the mulberry, the almond, the pomegranate, the citron, and the beautiful oleander. And, among other productions of the soil, Galilee can still boast of wheat, barley, millet, pulse, indigo, rice, sugar cane, oranges, pears, apricots, and some other fruits, besides vegetables in great variety (Merrill, *Galilee in the Time of Christ*, pp. 14–21).

But a fine climate, a rich forest growth, great fertility of soil, and a wealth of vegetation presuppose an abundant supply of water, and in this respect Galilee was notably favoured. One might almost say that the lawgiver had this province specially in mind when he promised the Hebrews that they were to enter a 'land of brooks of water, of fountains and depths, springing forth in valleys and hills' (Dt 8[7]). Lake Merom and Lake Tiberias both belonged to Galilee, and the latter was justly the pride of the nation. The Jordan flowed through them both, and the water of both was sweet and clear.

All of the Jordan north of the Sea of Galilee and one-third of its length to the south of that was reckoned to Galilee. The sources of this river at Banias and Dan are remarkable for their natural features and for the volume of water which in each bursts forth from the ground. From the eastern side of the watershed of Galilee numerous small streams flow into the Jordan, while those on the west side make their way into the Mediterranean. Of the latter one of the most celebrated was the Kishon (*Nahr Muḳaṭṭa*), which took its rise near the foot of Tabor, and after a winding course across the plain of Esdraelon entered the sea near the base of Carmel. This stream had a number of feeders from the north, from Mount Gilboa and the region of En-gannim, and also from the south. This is 'that ancient river' famed in the triumph song of Deborah and Barak (Jg 5).

Near Acre another stream entered the Mediterranean, the Belus (*Nahr Naman*), regarded as the Shihor-libnath of Jos 19²⁶, with which is connected the interesting tradition that from its fine sand the Phœnicians first made glass. It is a fact that this sand was so highly prized that numerous ships came here to convey it to the glass shops of Tyre and Sidon, then the most famous in the world. The supply was thought to be inexhaustible (Pliny, *HN* xxxvi. 65).

All vegetation in Galilee would be affected by the 'dew of Hermon' which is praised in Ps 133³, and snow from this mountain was carried as a luxury to Tyre and Sidon, and to Sepphoris and Tiberias the capitals of Herod Antipas. Springs and fountains were so abundant in Galilee that it would be next to impossible to count them. In addition to these, notice must be taken of the Hot Springs of this province, which had a worldwide fame as resorts for health and pleasure. Those at Tiberias were probably the most celebrated, and their medicinal advantages were known even in Rome (Pliny, *HN* v. 15). The benefit to be derived from bathing in this hot sulphur water was so great that not only the common people but people of learning and rank came hither, seeking by this means to restore their health (Jos. *Life*, 16; Jer. Talmud, *Shab.* 3ª). These springs had a rival in those of Gadara, about two hours S.E. of the Sea of Galilee, where still existing ruins of a small theatre, bath houses, paved courts, beautifully carved stone seats or chairs, dressing rooms, etc., indicate the luxurious provision that was made for the guests (Merrill, *East of the Jordan*, pp. 150–153).

One would hardly expect to find that Galilee, directly under the perpetual snows of Hermon, would be subject to earthquakes; still such is the fact, and several very severe calamities are on record as having visited that country. In 1759 Safed was destroyed by an earthquake, and another in 1837 killed five thousand people out of a total population of about nine thousand. Chasms opened in the earth, and the houses being built on a steep hillside fell one upon another, and the ruin was terrible. Tiberias at the same time was visited in like manner, and half its inhabitants killed. The ravages then caused are still evident in ruined houses and in the cracked and twisted walls of the city, which have never been repaired.

Although there had been a large deportation of its inhabitants by Tiglath-pileser, and no doubt much destruction of life in other wars, Galilee seems to have entirely recovered from these calamities, for there is abundant evidence that in our Lord's time the country was densely populated. The conditions of life there—climate, soil, enterprise, and industry, and a ready market for all products—favoured such a result. The exact number of its inhabitants at any given time may be a matter of speculation; it has been reckoned from two millions to three millions at the beginning of our era; but since it was then customary for people to congregate in cities and towns, we shall be aided in our judgment if we turn our attention briefly to them. When the division of the land took place among the four tribes, sixty-nine cities at least are mentioned by name. Josephus in his account of Galilee mentions by name about forty cities and villages. It is interesting to note that of the nineteen cities assigned to Naphtali sixteen were 'fenced' (עָרֵי מִבְצָר), Jos 19³⁵. About the Sea of Galilee there were ten or twelve flourishing towns. Were not this fact corroborated by historical evidence, it might be disputed were one to judge solely by the present ruined condition of that region.

Beginning at Tiberias and going round by the S. we come first to *Bethmaus*, where was a synagogue, and which consequently ranked as a city. Beyond that was *Tarichea*, famous for its shipbuilding and its fisheries, of whose inhabitants six thousand young men were sent by Vespasian to Corinth to work on the Isthmus canal, and thirty thousand more were sold as slaves (*Wars*, III. x. 10). A fine bridge crossed the Jordan where it leaves the Lake, and beyond that on the E. side was *Gergesa*, the scene of the demoniacs and the herd of swine (Mt 8²⁸⁻³⁴). On the brow of the mountain E. of Gergesa was *Gamala*, 'the strongest city in that part' (*Wars*, II. xx. 4), which withstood a siege of seven months, and was subdued only when Vespasian led against it three of his legions. Near Gamala was *Hippos*, one of the cities of the Decapolis. At the N.E. corner of the Lake was *Julias*, which previous to our era bore the name of Bethsaida, and which Herod Philip II. transformed into a beautiful and flourishing city, where he himself in A.D. 34 was buried in a costly tomb. On the W. side we have *Chorazin*, not far from the Lake, and *Capernaum*, *Bethsaida*, and *Magdala* directly on the shore. Capernaum was called Christ's 'own city' (Mt 9¹); Bethsaida was the home of Philip, Andrew, and Peter, possibly also of Zebedee and his sons James and John; and Magdala is memorable for the touching story of Mary and her connexion with our Lord. Close to Magdala, just above the famous robber-caves of Wady Haman, was *Beth-arbel*, a stronghold from the earliest times (Hos 10¹⁴). We have now reached our starting-point, *Tiberias*, which was a city of great political importance, having been rebuilt in magnificent style by Herod Antipas not long before Christ began His public ministry, when it became the capital of the province.

No more than a glance at the country itself is needed to convince one that this province possessed an unusual number of large towns, to some of which was attached special historic interest. There may be mentioned *Safed*, visible from the shore of the Sea of Galilee, 'a city set upon a hill,' one of the sacred cities of the Jews; *Hazor*, the royal city of king Jabin (Jg 4²); *Cana*, where our Lord's first miracle was performed (Jn 2); *Sepphoris*, the capital of the province till it was removed to Tiberias,—it was a strong place, where was a royal magazine of arms, and where the public archives were kept; *Kedesh*, one of the cities of refuge, and, under Tyrian rule, a centre of pagan worship; *Jotapata*, where one of the longest and most desperate sieges during the war with Rome took place; *Tabor*, conspicuous and beautiful in its position, and strongly fortified from the earliest times; *Japha*, which 'had very strong walls and a large number of inhabitants' (Jos. *Life*, 45); *Zabulon*, whose houses were built after the model of those of Tyre, Sidon, and Beirût, that is, with great elegance and of unusual height; *Gabara*, mentioned with Tiberias and Sepphoris as one of the largest cities of Galilee (Jos. *Life*, 25); *Gadara*, where Vespasian's first blow was struck in his campaign in Galilee (*Wars*, III. vii. 1); *Bethshean*, interesting in its ancient history, and still more famous under its new name Scythopolis; *Ptolemais*, where the Roman fleet and army gathered that had come to destroy the Jews as a nation; and, finally, *Cæsarea Philippi*, which under the name Banias was a seat of idol-worship ten centuries before it was known to the Greeks, and by these people in turn transformed into a shrine of Pan under the name Paneas, adorned by Herod the Great, and still more by his son Herod Philip II., a place visited by Vespasian as the guest of Herod Agrippa II., and later by Titus, wonderfully attractive in its situation, but chiefly interesting to the Christian from its connexion with our Lord. This rapid review, which embraces only a few of the better-known places of Galilee, indicates that wherever we turn our eyes, on hillside or plain, we look upon town, city, or village of prosperous Galilee, and the conclusion is forced upon us that its population was dense.

Among the productions of Galilee, the olive was perhaps the most prominent. In the Blessing of Moses it is said of Asher, 'let him dip his foot in oil' (Dt 33²⁴). The Rabbis said, 'In Asher oil flows like a river,' and ' It is easier to raise a legion of olive trees in Galilee than to raise one child in Judæa.' Both Syrians and Phœnicians, and frequently people from a greater distance, obtained their main supply of oil from this province. Great stores of it existed in Jotapata, so that in the siege of that place by the Romans oil was heated and poured over the soldiers who were crowding up to the walls, and, as it was at the same time set on fire, the effect was terribly disastrous. Of the vast quantity of oil which Solomon gave yearly to king Hiram, 150,000 or 200,000 gallons, a large proportion was supplied from Galilee (2 Ch 2¹⁰). It is needless to add that the amount of revenue derived from this source was great.

Next to the oil, the amount of wheat raised in Galilee was equally surprising. For this article the demand of Phœnicia, whose ships went over the world, was enormous. In Ac 12²⁰, when war was on the point of breaking out between Herod Agrippa I. and the people of Tyre and Sidon, the latter succeeded in appeasing Herod's anger, which for them was most fortunate, since without the supplies of various kinds which they derived from his country they could not live.

Not only oil, wheat, and barley, but large quantities of dried figs, grapes, wine, pomegranates, honey, were raised and sent abroad, as well as numberless fatted fowl, sheep, and cattle. Flax also was produced in large quantities, which the weaving establishments and dye-houses of the seacoast towns transformed into useful or costly and beautiful fabrics.

Moreover, the fisheries of the Sea of Galilee must be mentioned as one of the chief industries of this province. Choice kinds of fish were abundant, and when properly prepared were sent over the world. Both Tarichea and Bethsaida seem to have derived their names from the fish factories for which they were famous.

The Phœnician coast lying so near Galilee, all its industries, manufactures, commerce, and luxurious living would only increase the market facilities of Galilee, of which her industrious inhabitants were ever ready to avail themselves. The prosperity of Galilee was enhanced by the network of roads which covered it (see Smith, *HGHL* 425 f.). These roads help to explain also the facility with which the ὄχλος assembled, which so often thronged our Lord.

Besides its natural attractions, its varied productions and commercial facilities, its populousness and wealth, Galilee appeals to us more strongly than in any other way by its unique place in the religious history of the world. It was the cradle of the Christian faith. Joseph and Mary belonged to Nazareth, and there Jesus lived the larger part of His life. The peculiar influences of this mountain city, and its wonderful outlook over land and sea, no doubt had their effect upon the mind of Christ during His boyhood and youth. When He desired larger opportunities for reaching His fellow-men, He did not go out of His province

to Jerusalem, Rome, or elsewhere, but removed to Capernaum on the shore of the Lake (Mt 9¹). A large proportion of the apostles, the men who helped to shape early Christianity, were from Galilee—namely, Peter, Philip, Andrew, James, John, all of whom were from Bethsaida ; Matthew from Capernaum ; besides Bartholomew or Nathanael, and James the Less, son of Alphæus and Mary, and possibly others, for even those who were not born there could by virtue of residence and labours be classed as Galilæans (Ac 1¹¹). There is a tradition that the parents of the Apostle Paul came from Gischala in Galilee, which is not at all improbable when we remember how large a number of Jews in the days of Herod went forth from Palestine to seek their fortunes in the distant commercial centres of the Roman world. Salome the wife of Zebedee, Anna the prophetess who joined in the welcome to the infant Jesus, furnish hints as to the piety and intelligence of the women of this province.

It is scarcely necessary to look back to the pre-Israelitish period. Still even then the Baal worshippers from the seacoast, who sought out the most attractive spots for their degrading rites, had crowded in and set up their altars in the most beautiful groves and on many of the hills of Galilee—Kedesh, Dan, and Cæsarea Philippi being some of the best-known of these idolatrous centres.

It is a significant fact that the Jews, after the destruction of Jerusalem, should have chosen Galilee as their religious centre. This becomes indeed a matter of great surprise when we consider the relations of the orthodox Jews to the Founder of Christianity and His followers as these are portrayed to us in the Gospels. They must have considered it a congenial atmosphere for their libraries, schools, and learned men, for here these flourished in a remarkable manner. During the long period of three or more centuries many synagogues were erected, and remains of some of these are still found at different places, those at Biram, Chorazin, and Tell Hum being familiar to everybody. Here, before A.D. 200, the Mishna had been compiled, *i.e.* the oral or traditional law to which Christ so often referred was given a fixed form by being written down, and also the commentary on this, known as the Palestinian Talmud, was made, having been completed about two centuries later. Tiberias, like Safed, became one of the sacred cities of the Jews, and here the great Maimonides and some other of their famous Rabbis were buried.

Among the famous personages of Galilee may be mentioned Barak, one of Israel's heroes ; Deborah, the author of a triumph song ; the judges Ibzan, Elon, and Tola, who judged Israel forty years ; the prophets Hosea (?), Jonah the son of Amittai, and Elisha the successor of Elijah. This was not Elijah's birthplace, still he can be said to belong to Galilee, because this was the scene of a large part of his labours.

The fascinating and inspiring natural objects so abundant in Galilee — vine-clad slopes, plains brilliant with flowers, and the beautiful lake deep within the bosom of the hills—could hardly fail to awaken the spirit of poetry ; and besides the well-known examples in proof of this, some eminent scholars, as Gesenius and others, would locate here the Song of Songs.

Not only did our Lord, and also His disciples by birth or residence, belong to Galilee, but it is surprising to find so large a proportion of the Gospels picturing Galilæan scenes and life : places, people, parables, miracles, healing ; rulers, soldiers, merchants, beggars ; everything so vivid that we seem to be walking with the Master along the shore and from village to village of His native land.

The Sermon on the Mount (Mt 5), the raising of the widow's son (Lk 7¹¹⁻¹⁵), stilling the tempest (Mt 8²⁶), feeding the five thousand (Mk 6⁴⁴), the transfiguration (Mk 9²), the marriage feast (Jn 2¹), the custom house (Lk 5²⁷), the draught of fishes (Lk 5⁶), the mountain refuge for secret prayer (Mt 14²³), the little child in the Saviour's arms Mk 9³⁶), and the marvellous explanation of the bread of life (Jn 6),—these and a multitude of other sayings and incidents which make up the Gospels take us at once to Galilee. The number and variety of natural objects which Christ introduces so frequently in His utterances, illustrate the extent and correctness of His habit of observation. Nothing escapes His notice,—sky, earth, sea, fields, flowers, grass, grain, fruits, trees, fish, birds, and animals,—the salient facts of the world immediately about Him were grasped and made the basis of beautiful lessons. A very exhaustive article on this subject, entitled 'Christ as a Practical Observer of Nature, Persons, and Events,' may be found in the *Bibliotheca Sacra*, July 1872, pp. 510-531, by the present writer.

The part played by Galilee in the war with Rome will always command the admiration of the world. It was a life-and-death struggle, and her people rallied with the utmost enthusiasm to the defence of their fatherland. The fact that during the first year of the war Galilee stood alone has not received the attention it deserves. The forces that were, or might have been, gathered in Judæa were not sent to her aid. From their camp at Ptolemais four veteran legions with their engines of war marched towards the hills of Galilee; but it proved to be no holiday expedition on which they had started. The campaign was long and bloody; the highland patriots resisted with almost superhuman energy; the Romans were successful at last, but their victory was a costly one. The hardest fighting of the war was done on the soil of Galilee, and in that terrible year one hundred and fifty thousand of her people perished. From the days of Joshua to those of Bar-Cochba no Jewish army had shown greater valour than did the compatriots of Jesus of Nazareth—the men from the home-land of Christ.

LITERATURE.—For a full account of this province in all its historical phases of interest, see the present writer's *Galilee in the Time of Christ*, Boston (U.S.) 1881, London 1885; cf. also his *East of the Jordan*; G. A. Smith, *HGHL* 413 ff.; Neubauer, *Géog. du Talmud*, 180 ff.; Reland, *Palest.*; Robinson, *BRP²* ii.; Stanley, *Sinai and Palestine*, 361 ff.; Conder, *Handbk. to Bible*, 301 ff.; Guérin, *Galilée*; Buhl, *Geog. Alt. Paläst.*; Baedeker-Socin, *Paläst.*; Schürer, *HJP* (Index).

S. MERRILL.

GALILEE, MOUNTAIN IN.—After our Lord's resurrection, the eleven disciples went away from Jerusalem 'into Galilee, unto the mountain where Jesus had appointed them (εἰς τὴν Γαλιλαίαν εἰς τὸ ὄρος οὗ ἐτάξατο αὐτοῖς ὁ Ἰησοῦς).' There the disciples saw and worshipped Him, and received His final commission (Mt 28¹⁶⁻²⁰). No record or hint indicates to us what mountain is meant. For harmonistic reasons the theory that the Galilæan hill was the Mt. of Olives, whose north point is said to have borne the name 'Galilee,' has found favour in some quarters. This opinion scarcely needs refutation (see Keim, *Jesus of Nazara*, vi. 380 n.).

S. MERRILL.

GALILEE, SEA OF.—This appears in the Bible under several different names, which must first be noticed. Modern writers not infrequently speak of the 'Lake of Tiberias,' but this term is never used in NT. Moreover, Lk 5¹ is the only place where the name 'Lake of Gennesaret' (λίμνη Γεννησαρέτ) occurs. In four instances it is referred to as 'the Lake' (λίμνη), Lk 5² 8²². ²³. ³³, and in several others as 'the sea' (θάλασσα), Jn 6¹¹⁻²⁵. Twice John employs 'Sea of Tiberias' (θάλασσα τῆς Τιβεριάδος),

6¹ 21¹, but in the first case he had already mentioned in a natural way the Sea of Galilee, and immediately added as an explanation for his Gentile readers that it was the same as the Sea of Tiberias. This reduces the use of the latter name to a single instance. 'Sea of Galilee' (θάλασσα τῆς Γαλιλαίας) would seem to be the best known and most appropriate name, and this is used five times (Mt 4¹⁸ 15²⁹, Mk 1¹⁶ 7³¹, Jn 6¹). Glancing at the OT we find for this body of water two names, or properly one name spelled in different ways. The 'Sea of Chinnereth' (כִּנֶּ֫רֶת יָם) appears in defining the boundary of the land (Nu 34¹¹), and again in defining the border of the territory of Gad (Jos 13²⁷). 'Sea of Chinneroth' is given in describing the territory of Sihon that was conquered by Moses (Jos 12³). Chinnereth (כִּנֶּ֫רֶת) is used once alone (Dt 3¹⁷) and Chinneroth (כִּנְּר֫וֹת) also (Jos 11²), both referring to the Sea of Galilee. Once Chinneroth is used for a district conquered by Benhadad (1 K 15²⁰), and Chinnereth appears in Jos 19³⁵ as a 'fenced city.' It is perfectly consistent with Oriental usage for a city, a district, and a body of water adjoining it to be called by the same name, although it is quite possible that Dt 3¹⁷ (see Driver, *ad loc.*), Jos 11² 19³⁵ all refer to the *city* Chinnereth or Chinneroth.

To this brief survey of biblical names for this lake we may add that Gennesar (τὸ ὕδωρ τοῦ Γεννησάρ, RV 'the water of **Gennesareth**') is given in 1 Mac 11⁶⁷. Josephus had occasion to refer to this lake many times, and he always uses the name Gennesar (e.g. *Ant.* XIII. v. 7). The change from the Heb. Kinnereth to Gennesar was a natural one (but see G. A. Smith, *HGHL* 443 n.). Josephus adhered to the OT name in its changed form, while the NT writers, as we have seen, used the title 'Sea of Galilee.'

As to the meaning of these names, Galilee is obviously derived from the province of that name, and Tiberias from the city on the west shore of the lake. *Chinnereth* may be from כִּנּוֹר, 'harp.' Benzinger (*Heb. Arch.* 23) thinks this improbable; and Fuerst suggests 'basin.' *Gennesaret* may have the same meaning as *Chinnereth* if we allow that it was simply transferred from the Hebrew; or it may be from *gan* and *sâr*, 'prince's garden,' applied, of course, to the Land of Gennesaret, from which the Sea of Galilee is once called the 'Lake of Gennesaret' (Lk 5¹).

The Sea of Galilee is 13 miles long and a little less than 7 miles wide in its widest part. Its greatest depth is less than 200 ft. It is not quite oval in form, although it appears to be so when looked at from the surrounding heights. It is more properly pear-shaped, having the small end at the south. Its level below the Mediterranean is about 700 ft. On the east side the mountain rises from its shore to an elevation of 2000 ft., the same as that of the great plateau of Bashan beyond. On the west side there is also a mountain wall, but towards the north the slopes are very gradual, and on the south the lake touches the plain of the Jordan Valley. To the eye it is a most attractive object, a beautiful body of water set deep in a vast basin among the hills. Not only the Jews, but people of many other races who were not natives of the soil, have praised the beauty of the Sea of Galilee. 'Although God has created seven seas,' said the Rabbis, 'yet He has chosen this one as His special delight.' They speak of its 'gracefully flowing' or 'gliding waters.' The mountains, the peaceful shore at their base, the blue water overarched by the blue sky, form a landscape picture that has kindled the enthusiasm of many hearts. It is seen at present at its worst estate; but in the time of our Lord this shore was a continuous garden, and even the matter-of-fact Pliny declared that this lake was 'surrounded by pleasant towns' (*HN* v. 15).

These towns have been described briefly in the article GALILEE, but the list at least may be repeated :—Tiberias, and south of it Bethmaus, Tarichea, Sinnabris, Gergesa, Gamala, Hippos, Julias, Bethsaida, Chorazin, Capernaum, Magdala, and Beth-arbel. On the mountain to the S.E. was Gadara, Safed on its lofty summit to the N.W., and a castle was perched directly above Tiberias almost overhanging the lake. Through Wady Hamam the Horns of Hattin appeared, and to the north rose the magnificent dome of Hermon. This famous mountain is not one of a cluster, it is not hemmed in and dwarfed by surrounding peaks, but it stands alone, revealing its full grandeur. From the shore of the Sea of Galilee, if we add its depression of 700 ft. to the elevation of Mount Hermon, we look up to its summit a sheer height of over 10,000 ft. Among all the mountains of the world, such a view is seldom surpassed.

The hills, which appear to surround the lake, recede from the shore a distance varying from a few hundred yards to half a mile or more, and this belt is generally level, so that, without cutting or filling, a carriage road could readily be constructed entirely round the lake ; with a horse and carriage the circuit could be made in four or five hours. At two points, where the recession of the mountain is greatest, two charming plains are formed, namely, *el-Batiha* on the N.E. of the lake, and Gennesaret on the N.W. They resemble each other, are equally fertile, but it is Gennesaret that has always received the most praise. See GENNESARET (LAND OF).

The river Jordan enters the lake at the northern end, and passes out at the southern end. It brings down so much sediment at times that it appears like a very dirty stream : still the water of the lake itself is always clear ; it is also sweet and cool.

The steep mountain wall on the E. side, already referred to, is volcanic, a part of the great lava formation which includes the Bashan plain and the Hauran mountains, where exist a score or more of extinct craters. The hot springs of Gadara, within 5 miles of the S.E. corner of the lake, those at Tiberias on the W. shore, and likewise the earthquakes which visit that region from time to time, are indications that internal fires still exist. The latest recorded earthquake from which Tiberias suffered severely was in 1837, vividly described by the American missionary Rev. Wm. M. Thomson, well known as the author of *The Land and the Book*. The region to the N. of the lake through which the Jordan passes, extending to Chorazin and Tell Hum, is simply a mass of large basalt boulders, packed so closely that it is next to impossible to get through them.

The hot springs near Tiberias have been famous from the earliest history of the country, and the inhabitants still prize them for their medicinal uses. The volume of water is large, and, could they be properly cared for and managed by other than their present degraded owners, there is no reason why these springs should not become one of the most famous health resorts in the world. Except in midsummer the climate is delightful—in fact, tropical ; and when a person is chilled by the strong winds of mountain or tableland, the sensation of going down to the warm, even balmy, atmosphere of the lake shore is one of extreme pleasure.

Equally with the hot baths, the fish of this lake have always been held in highest estimation. Laws traditionally dating from the time of Joshua (Bab. Talm. *Baba Kama*, 80*b*) regulated this industry, and, with certain limitations, made this fishing ground free to all. There were several choice varieties, and the inhabitants of the region boasted that some of them were the same as those found in the Nile. There seems, moreover, to have been an inexhaustible supply of fish. Bethsaida on the north was a 'house of fish' ; Tarichea on the south was 'a fish factory,' and the trade in this commodity had enriched its citizens. On the part of the Jews there was not only a choice in kind but in quality as well, for they distinguished sharply between 'clean' and 'unclean,' a fact no doubt alluded to in our Lord's parable of the net, where the 'good were gathered into baskets, and the bad were cast away' (Mt 13[47.48]).

The lake is subject to violent storms, owing partly to the difference of temperature about it from that of the mountains or tableland so far above it, so that the event recorded in Mt 8[24], when Christ stilled the waves, was of no infrequent occurrence. From an eminence the writer has several times seen the clouds gather above the lake, a dense black mass, not covering a great area, and sink lower and lower towards the water as if about to smite the surface ; and even should they not actually do so, they disturb it so that the waves are strong and boats are placed in great peril.

From the way in which the NT speaks of boats and ships on the Sea of Galilee, we infer that it was covered with them. There seem to have been numbers of them ready at any given point. Given ten or twelve flourishing cities on or near the shore of the lake between which there was constant communication, it could not be otherwise than that the number should be great. These boats were engaged in fishing or traffic, or in carrying travellers or parties of pleasure from shore to shore. Some writers are slow to admit that there were ships of any size on the lake, although the Greek word for ship (πλοῖον) is used in the NT, whether the Sea of Galilee or the Mediterranean is the body of water referred to. So far as this evidence goes, the boats might be as large in one case as in the other. On one occasion during the Jewish war, when a movement was planned against Tiberias, Josephus in a short time got ready two hundred and forty ships from Tarichea and its vicinity alone (*Wars*, II. xxi. 8 ; *Life*, 32). In this city shipbuilding was a lucrative industry. At a later period during that war many of the soldiers and citizens of Tarichea took refuge from the Romans in ships, and four thousand to six thousand of them were slain—showing that the boats, to have held such a multitude, must have been of considerable size. Josephus speaks of 'climbing up into the ships' (*Wars*, III. x. 5), which implies quite a different craft than would be meant had he said 'they stepped from the shore into their boats.' In Jn 21[8] is found a reference to the small boat (πλοιάριον) which always accompanies, being frequently towed after, a large ship the same as now. From all that we can learn of the facts, we certainly have a right to picture the Sea of Galilee in Christ's time as dotted with white sails, just as we know that the shore was lined with cities and the whole basin full of life. Between its present state and its former prosperity the contrast is extremely painful.

The Sea of Galilee was praised by the Romans and was the pride of the Jews, but it appeals to the Christian far more strongly than it could possibly have done to them, because of its connexion with Jesus of Nazareth. It is He that has made it immortal. Everywhere about this lake we trace His footsteps, and at every point locate some act of His blessed ministry. The memories of His life linger here as nowhere else in Palestine. He made one of its beautiful cities (Capernaum) His home

(Mt 4¹³). Here He called the fishermen Peter, Andrew, James, and John to be fishers of men (Mt 4¹⁸⁻²²), also for the same purpose Matthew was called from the receipt of custom (Mk 2¹³⁻¹⁷). Here 'multitudes' came to Him 'to be healed of their diseases,' and 'he healed them all' (Lk 6¹⁷⁻¹⁹). Out of the large number of such cases we readily recall that of the nobleman's son (Jn 4⁴⁶⁻⁵⁴), the centurion's servant (Mt 8⁵⁻¹³), the raising of Jairus' daughter (Mt 9¹⁸⁻²⁶), the paralytic who was let down through the uncovered roof (Mk 2¹⁻¹²), the demoniac in the synagogue at Capernaum (Mk 1²¹⁻²⁸), the demoniac of Gadara on the eastern shore (Lk 8²⁶⁻⁴⁰), the blind man at Bethsaida (Mk 8²²⁻²⁶), and the curing of Peter's wife's mother of the fever (Mt 8¹⁴⁻¹⁷). Of another class of incidents which illustrate our Lord's character and His life in Galilee, a few may be mentioned, as His walking on the water and stilling the tempest (Mt 14²²⁻³⁶), and His feeding of the five thousand (Mt 14¹³⁻²¹). Still another illustrative class comes under the head of conversations, lessons, and warnings. In the leaven of the Pharisees hypocrisy was rebuked (Lk 12¹); in the innocence of childhood humility was inculcated (Lk 9⁴⁶⁻⁴⁸); the feast with Levi showed that social courtesies are to be observed (Mk 2¹⁵); that both patriotism and religion have their claims upon the individual is made clear in the paying of the tribute money (Mt 17²⁴⁻²⁷); the signs in the sky as well as the sower in the field teach valuable truths (Mt 13¹⁻¹⁵ and ch. 16); and it was here in Galilee that the foundation principles of the New Religion were first promulgated and the nature of the Bread of Life unfolded (Mt 5¹⁻²⁴, Jn 6). It is to some or all of these facts that Christ Himself alludes as 'mighty works' (Mt 11²⁰⁻²⁴), which would have moved the people of Tyre, or even those of Sodom, could they have witnessed them.

Of the cities about the Sea of Galilee attention should be directed to Capernaum. There was some special reason why our Lord chose this as His residence. Its importance was not wholly commercial; more than any other city of the north, one might say with truth of Palestine, with the single exception of Jerusalem, it was a centre of news. Roads led thence to Damascus and the Euphrates; to the cities of the Mediterranean coast which were in touch with Europe; to the S.W. by Gaza and thence to Egypt; to the S. along the great mountain range to Shechem, Jerusalem, and Hebron; to the Jordan Valley and the rich and populous country of Peræa. Sailors, soldiers, merchants, travellers, messengers, officers, princes, men of many classes and from many parts of the world, passed through this place on business or pleasure. The fame of some startling event, some great healer, some teacher of unusual wisdom, would be carried thence with rapidity and in every direction. While this fact serves to illustrate further the busy life of this lake shore at a single point, we cannot help feeling at the same time that it makes more significant the other fact that Christ took up here His residence. The record is very simple, 'leaving Nazareth ... he dwelt in Capernaum' (Mt 4¹³). Could it have been said, 'Jesus shut himself up in a cloister,' how widely different would have been the history of Christianity!

Additional Note.—It seems necessary to add the following note on the depth of the Sea of Galilee. In 1875 Lortet made soundings which corresponded in general with those already known and accepted by Palestinian scholars. He also found, as he supposed, near the north end of the lake where the Jordan enters, a hole '250 metres in depth,' which would be over 800 ft. Having crossed the lake at or near this point many times,

and made soundings of his own, the present writer was certain that Lortet was wrong. The bottom of the hole would be 100 ft. lower than the surface of the Dead Sea. Moreover, had such a hole ever existed, it would very soon have been filled by mud brought down by the Upper Jordan. These facts were laid before the public. In 1890 another Frenchman, Th. Barrois, made soundings, but found nothing to corroborate Lortet's impossible figures. Soon after, Lortet admitted that he was in error. The mischief having been done, the mistake is perpetuated because people quote Lortet without being aware of the corrections. Lortet's book, *La Syrie d'Aujourd'hui*, was published in 1884 (see pp. 505, 506), and Barrois' notes may be found in the *PEFSt* for July 1894, pp. 211-220.

LITERATURE.—In addition to what has been cited in the article, the reader may consult the following: Merrill, *Galilee in the Time of Christ*, also his *East of the Jordan*; Neubauer, *Géog. du Talm.* 25, 45, 214 f.; G. A. Smith, *HGHL* 439 ff.; Robinson, *BRP²* ii.; De Saulcy, *Journey round the Dead Sea*, etc. ii. 392 ff.; Buhl, *Geog.* 113, 229; Tristram, *Nat. Hist. of Bible*, 285; Reland, *Pal.* i. 239, 240; Baedeker-Socin, *Pal.*; Guérin, *Galilée*.

S. MERRILL.

GALL.—The Eng. rendering for two Heb. words. 1. מְרֵרָה *mĕrêrâh*, or מְרֹרָה *mĕrôrâh*, denotes 'bitterness,' corresponding to the Arab. *mĕrârah*. It is used in this sense (Job 13²⁶), 'thou writest bitter things against me,' *mĕrôrôth*. The expression אֶשְׁכְּלֹת מְרֹרֹת 'clusters of bitternesses' (AV and RV 'clusters are bitter'), Dt 32³², is a parallelism with *grapes of gall*, עֲנָבֵימוֹ־רֹשׁ *'innĕbhê-rôsh*, *i.e.* poppy-heads (see below). This meaning led to its application to the *bile* (Job 16¹³), and the *gall bladder*, as its receptacle (Job 20²⁵, To 6⁶ etc.). The ancients supposed that the poison of serpents lay in the gall (Pliny, *Nat. Hist.* xi. 62; Job 20¹⁴).

2. רֹאשׁ or רוֹשׁ *rôsh*.—A plant characterized by its bitterness, 'a root that beareth (*rôsh*) gall and wormwood' (Dt 29¹⁸), 'the wormwood and the (*rôsh*) gall' (La 3¹⁹). Jer (8¹⁴ 9¹⁵) speaks of 'water of (*rôsh*) gall.' Figuratively, one in affliction is described as 'compassed with (*rôsh*) gall and travail' (La 3⁵). Judgment is said to spring up as *hemlock* (*rôsh*) 'in the furrows of the field' (Hos 10⁴), and is said to be 'turned into (*rôsh*) gall' (Am 6¹²). It is impossible to tell with certainty what plant is intended. Some have supposed the poison hemlock, *Conium maculatum*, L., but this is not a field plant. Others have supposed the colocynth, *Citrullus Colocynthis*, L. This, although it has a bitter fruit, is not a plant of ploughed ground. Others, again, have supposed the darnel, *Lolium temulentum*, L. This, however, is not bitter. The more probable view is that the poppy, *Papaver*, is intended, perhaps *P. rheas*, L., or *P. somniferum*, L., the *opium* plant. A head of this plant is called in Arab. *rás el-khishkhash*, 'head of khish-khâsh,' the word *ras* being the same as the Hebrew *rôsh*, a *head*. They are called in Eng. poppy-heads.

What was the (χολή) *gall* that was mingled with *vinegar* (Mt 27³⁴, cf. *Ev. Petr.* 5, χολὴν μετὰ ὄξους; RV 'wine,' cf. Ps 69²¹), and the *myrrh* mingled with *wine* (Mk 15²³ ἐσμυρνισμένον οἶνον)? Both of these evangelists add that, at a later period in the crucifixion day, a man soaked a sponge in vinegar, and put it on a reed, and gave it to Jesus to drink (Mt 27⁴⁸, Mk 15³⁶). Jesus evidently partook of it. John doubtless alludes to the same (19²⁹·³⁰), showing how our Saviour called for it by saying 'I thirst' (v.²⁸). John adds that the sponge dipped in vinegar was 'put upon hyssop.' It is probable that the soldiers who mocked Christ by offering Him vinegar (Lk 23³⁶), did so only to aggravate His thirst, and did not give it to Him, and that this refinement of cruelty led to the *bonâ fide* offer which our Saviour accepted. How was it that He called for this draught after He had refused the one at first offered before His crucifixion? It is well known that a cup of wine with frankincense in it was given to criminals, just before their execution, to alleviate their pain. Myrrh would have properties similar to those of frankincense. It is possible that the *gall* of Mt was the same as the *myrrh* of Mk, the word *myrrh* being of the same root as the Heb. original of *gall* (Ps 69²¹), and, like it, signifying primarily *bitter*. Mt, according to Hengstenberg, gives the word χολή, which agrees textually with the LXX of the psalm, that he may point out the prophetic character of the latter, and its fulfilment in Christ, while Mk gives the name of the substance used. This substance is said by Mt to have been given in ὄξος, which means both *sour wine* and *vinegar*, and by Mk in οἶνος, which is the ordinary word for wine. Here again, acc. to Hengstenberg, Mt aims at textual conformity with the psalmist, while Mk gives the more familiar name. Jn also notes the prophecy of thirst (19²⁸, cf. Ps 69²¹), and its fulfilment in Christ. The motive of our Saviour, in refusing the potent anæsthetic offered before His sacrifice was complete, would seem to have been His desire to endure all that was appointed for Him, in full consciousness of the purpose in view. He only consented to moisten His parched lips and tongue at the last, not to soothe His anguish, but to gain strength enough to enable Him to cry, 'with a loud voice,' 'It is finished,' that is, 'my work is done, and the world is saved,' and then He bowed His head and gave up the ghost.   G. E. POST.

GALLANT.—In Is 33²¹ as adj., and in Nah 2⁵ᵐ, Zec 11²ᵐ as subst., 'gallant' is employed to tr. the Heb. word אַדִּיר *'addîr*, which is also both an adj. and a subst. As an adj. *'addîr* signifies magnificent or majestic; and as a subst. a great one, a noble. In Is 33²¹ the adj. is applied to a ship, and it is to be observed that in the same verse the word is used of J" (AV 'glorious,' RV 'in majesty'). In this sense of magnificent the Eng. word 'gallant' is nearly obsolete. Bunyan (*Holy War*, Clar. Press ed. p. 8) uses it of a country (as *'addîr* is applied to a nation in Ezk 32¹⁸, EV 'famous'), 'Now, there is in this gallant country of Universe, a fair and delicate town, a Corporation, called Mansoul.'   J. HASTINGS.

GALLERY.—1. AV in Ca 7⁵ reads 'The king is held in the galleries.' The Heb. is רְהָטִים, which, there is no reasonable doubt, means 'in the tresses' (so RV). The king is captivated, that is to say, by the tresses of this 'prince's daughter.' רְהָטִים, prob. of Aramaic origin (Dillm., Siegfried-Stade), is found elsewhere only in Gn 30³⁸ and Ex 2¹⁶, in the sense of 'watering troughs.' In Ca 1¹⁷ the *Ḳerê* has רְהִיטֵנוּ (AVm 'galleries'), but the *Kethibh* רַהִיטֵנוּ appears preferable (AV and RV 'rafters'; Siegfried - Stade, and Baethgen in Kautzsch's *AT*, 'Getäfel,' *i.e.* 'panelling'). 2. אַתִּיק, a word whose etymology and meaning are both obscure. It is found only in the description of Ezekiel's temple, Ezk 41¹⁵·¹⁶ 42³·⁵. In the first of these passages the *Kethibh* has אַתּוּק; Cornill substitutes קִירוֹתֶיהָ 'its walls,' and this meaning, if not reading, appears to be demanded by the context (cf. notes of Davidson and Bertholet, *ad ll.citt.*). The trⁿ 'colonnade' (Siegfried - Stade, *Säulengänge* (?), AVm 'walks with pillars') would suit some of the other passages. See further, under TEMPLE.   J. A. SELBIE.

GALLEY occurs once in OT (Is 33²¹ AV and RV), where it is said of the (metaphorical) waters defending Jerusalem 'that no galley with oars' shall enter them. The Heb. is אֳנִי שַׁיִט, which would be more correctly trᵈ 'no fleet [אֳנִי being

a collective noun, אֳנִיָּה denoting a single ship] with oars.'

The galley of mediæval times was the successor or representative of the war-galleys (*naves longæ*) of the Romans, Greeks, and Carthaginians. (See SHIPS). It consisted of a long narrow open boat worked by oars, but carrying one or two masts with lateen sails to be used when the wind was favourable. There was a short deck at the prow for carrying the fighting men, and another at the stern for the captain, knights, and gentlemen. The largest of these vessels were called *galleasses*, and were formerly employed by the Venetians, Spaniards, and Portuguese. These last in the Spanish Armada carried each 110 soldiers and 222 galley slaves. The Venetian galleasses were about 162 ft. long above, and 133 ft. by the keel; 32 ft. wide, with 23 ft. length of sternpost. They were furnished with three masts and thirty-two banks of oars; each bank having two oars worked by six or seven slaves, generally chained to the oar. In the prow were three small batteries of cannon, together with guns on each quarter, and the complement reached 1000 or 1200 men. Along with these war-vessels of the largest size were the *half-galleys*, from 120 to 130 ft. in length, furnished with two masts and sails, to be used as required, and carrying five pieces of cannon. Of a size still smaller were the *quarter-galleys*, provided with twelve to sixteen banks of oars. Galleys were in use on the Thames down to the beginning of the century; and a common punishment for criminals in England and France was to be 'sent to the galleys' for life or for shorter periods.

The life of galley slaves in mediæval times was miserable in the extreme. They were generally chained to their benches or oars, and compelled to work by boatswains, who occupied a bridge running along the centre of the boat, and were armed with long whips, which they applied mercilessly to the bare backs of the oarsmen. Their food consisted of biscuit, with sometimes a little rice or vegetables; their drink was water often foul, but containing a little vinegar or oil. A galley slave when condemned in perpetuity was, in a civil sense, dead; he could not dispose of his effects, nor inherit; if married, his marriage was null; and his widow could not have any of her dower out of his goods, which were confiscated. Amongst the Mediterranean nations, galley slaves were generally prisoners of war.   E. HULL.

GALLIM (גַּלִּים 'heaps').—A place near Jerusalem, 1 S 25⁴⁴. It is personified, along with Anathoth and other towns, in Is 10³⁰. It is generally placed to the N. of Jerus., but may have been to the S., at the modern *Beit Jala*, near which are remarkable stone cairns. See *SWP* vol. iii. sheet xvii.

GALLIO (Γαλλίων, Ac 18).—Son of M. Annæus Seneca, a Roman eques and rhetorician, brother of Seneca the philosopher, and uncle of Lucan the poet. He was born at Cordova, but came with his father to Rome in the reign of Tiberius. Originally called M. Annæus Novatus, he was adopted by, and took the name of, L. Junius Gallio (Dio C. lx. 35). Under Claudius he became proconsul * of Achaia, probably through the influence of Seneca, who was Nero's tutor, and also perhaps, as Renan suggests, on account of his 'haute culture hellénique.' He entered on office at Corinth during St. Paul's first visit to the city, *c.* A.D. 52–53. An attack

* The title indicates that Achaia was a senatorial province, and illustrates the writer's accuracy; for under Tiberius and Caligula it had been imperially governed (Tac. *Ann.* 76), and under Nero it received temporary 'liberty' in 66 or 67 A.D. (Suet. *Nero*, 24). Claudius transferred the province to the Senate in 44 A.D.

of fever, which he attributed to the climate, led
to his departure, and to a sea-voyage for his health
(Sen. *Ep.* 104); eventually he returned to Rome
(Dio C. lxi. *s.f.*). Seneca's high position after Nero's
accession in 54 would secure for G. a continuance
of court favour, and he may be the L. Junius to
whom a wax tablet found at Pompeii refers as
consul under that emperor. Pliny (*HN* xxxi.
33) remembered a voyage of G. 'post consulatum,'
on account of blood-expectoration. When Nero
constrained Seneca to kill himself (A.D. 65), G.
begged for his own life (Tac. *Ann.* xv. 73), and
was spared at the time; but afterwards he and his
brother Mela (Lucan's father) became victims.[*]
With apparent timidity G. united singular amia-
bility. Seneca (who dedicates to G. his *De ira* and
De vita beata) writes: 'Nemo mortalium uni tam
dulcis est quam hic omnibus'; he eulogizes him,
also, as free from vice, impervious to flattery, and
one whom to love to the utmost was to love too
little (*Q.N.* iv. Pr.). His reputation for wit is
attested by Dio, who refers (lx. 35), about 160
years after G.'s death, to a 'jocus urbanissimus'
of his † as still current.

Soon after G.'s arrival at Corinth, a band of
Jews, provoked by the conversion of Crispus, the
ruler of their synagogue, and relying, probably,
on the new proconsul's complaisance, dragged St.
Paul before his tribunal, clamouring for judgment
against a man who 'persuaded men to worship
God contrary to the (Mosaic) law.' Judaism was
a 'religio licita,' and entitled to protection; but
G. saw in St. Paul's alleged offence only the outcome of some internal religious disputation among
the Jews, and neither a civil wrong done to the
complainers (ἀδίκημα) nor an outrage against public
morality (ῥᾳδιούργημα πονηρόν). He declined to hear
St. Paul's defence in a case which called for no
judicial intervention, and contemptuously drove
the accusers from his judgment-seat. When the
Greek by-standers,‡ without special interest, probably, in the apostle, but readily showing their
animus against the unpopular Jews, seized and
beat Sosthenes, the successor of Crispus and the
ringleader presumably of the disturbance, G. refrained from interposing; the Jews, he doubtless
considered, would not be the worse for being thus
taught to keep their religious disputes to themselves. To this assault on Sosthenes, not to the
Christian faith, the statement 'G. cared for none
of these things' directly refers; but it is not likely
that he interested himself further in St. Paul or his
doctrine; and it is no more than possible that a
report about the apostle by G. to Seneca helped
afterwards to lead to a personal connexion, itself
doubtful, between Seneca and St. Paul (Lightf.
Phil. Exc. ii.). G.'s Roman justice protected, but
his Roman pride would ignore, the man to whose
incidental association with him his own notability
is mainly due.

LITERATURE.—Add to reff. above, Hausrath, art. 'Gallio,' in
Schenkel's *Bib.-Lex.* v. ii.; Farrar, *Seekers after God*, pp. 16–21;
Ramsay, *St. Paul the Traveller*, pp. 257–261. On Gallio as a
possible link of connexion between St. Paul and Seneca,
Gelpke, *De Familiaritate P. et S.*; Aubertin, *Sénèque et St.
Paul.*   H. COWAN.

GALLOWS.—See HANGING, and CRIMES AND
PUNISHMENTS, vol. i. p. 525a.

---

[*] So Dio C. lxii. 25. Jerome places G.'s death (by compulsory
suicide) prior to Seneca's (*Add. to Chron. Euseb.* p. 161, ed.
Scal.).

† When Claudius was poisoned by his wife Agrippina, G.,
alluding to the deification of emperors, and to the custom of
dragging criminals by a hook to the Tiber, spoke of Claudius as
'unco in cœlum raptum.'

‡ The word 'Greeks' is not in the oldest MSS, but is probably a correct gloss. Ewald, however (*Hist. Isr.* vii. 380), refers
to the Jews the assault on Sosthenes, whom he identifies with
the Sosthenes of 1 Co 1, and regards as already in sympathy
with St. Paul.

GAMAEL (A Γαμαήλ, B Γάμηλος), 1 Es 8²⁹.—In
Ezr 8² DANIEL (which see, No. 2).

GAMALIEL (גַּמְלִיאֵל, Γαμαλιήλ = *Reward of God*).
—**1.** The son of Pedahzur, and 'prince of the
children of Manasseh' (Nu 1¹⁰ 2²⁰ 7⁵⁴·⁵⁹ 10²³). **2.** 'A
Pharisee . . . a doctor of the law, had in honour of
all the people,' who intervened in the Sanhedrin
on behalf of Peter and the other apostles (Ac 5³⁴⁻³⁹),
and the instructor of Saul of Tarsus (Ac 22³). This
Gamaliel is generally identified with the famous
Rabbi Gamaliel, the grandson of Hillel the
founder of the more liberal of the two schools into
which the Pharisees were divided. He is known in
Jewish writings as Gamaliel *ha-zāḳēn*, i.e. *the older*,
to distinguish him from his grandson Gamaliel II.,
and from his high character and learning was the
first of the seven Jewish doctors who were honoured
with the title of *Rabban* (our Rabbi or Master).
All that we can learn of Gamaliel proves him to
have been an open-minded, liberal man, though
some of the anecdotes usually cited in support of
this, such as the story of the Statue and the Bath
quoted by Conybeare and Howson, are now known
to refer to his grandson Gamaliel II. How far,
however, he was in advance of his times is shown
by his studies in Greek literature, which by the
narrower Rabbis was put on the same level as
Egyptian thaumaturgy, and by various humane
enactments. Thus he laid it down that the poor
heathen should have the same rights as the poor
Jews in gathering the gleanings after harvest, and
that the Jews on meeting the heathen should
extend to them the customary greeting, 'Peace
be with you,' even on their feast days, when
they were mostly engaged in worshipping their
idols; while to him are also ascribed certain laws
to protect wives against unprincipled husbands,
and widows against unscrupulous children (see
Ginsburg in *Kitto's Bibl. Cycl.*, art. 'Gamaliel').
In view of all this, it is easy to understand the
attitude which Gamaliel adopted in the Sanhedrin
on the occasion of the apostles' trial; although
even there his conduct must be traced rather to a
prudential dread of violent measures than to a
spirit of systematic tolerance. There is nothing
certainly to prove that he had at any time a
decided leaning towards Christianity, and the
traditions that he was a secret disciple (Clement,
Recogn. i. 65), and was baptized by Peter and Paul
(Phot. *Cod.* 171, p. 199), are now universally rejected. He died, as he had lived, a strict Jew; and
so great was his reputation that, according to the
Mishna (*Sota*, ix. 15), 'with the death of Gamaliel
the reverence for the law ceased, and purity and
abstinence died away.' It is right to add that
Baur and the Tübingen school find it so difficult
to reconcile Gamaliel's attitude in Ac 5 with the
persecuting spirit afterwards shown by Saul, then
his pupil, that they pronounce the whole passage
unhistorical. But do pupils never in later years
diverge from their teachers' doctrines? And may
not special circumstances have arisen in connexion
with the appearance of Stephen which called forth
a fanatic zeal in Saul little in accord with his early
training?

LITERATURE.—Lechler, *Apost. and Post-Apost. Times*, i. 76,
n. 1; Farrar, *Life and Work of St. Paul*, i., Excursus v. 'Gamaliel
and the School of Tübingen'; Schürer, *HJP* II. i. 183, 323,
363 f. For the Jewish references to G., Ginsburg, in the art.
above cited, refers specially to Frankel, *Hodegetica in Mischnam*,
Lipsiæ, 1859, p. 57 ff.   G. MILLIGAN.

GAMES do not appear in the Scriptures of the
Jewish people with anything like the same
frequency as on the monuments and in the ancient
literature of Egypt and Greece and Rome. Of
public games like those of ancient Greece there is
no mention in the OT, although in the Maccabæan

period we read that Jason the high priest (2 Mac 4⁷⁻¹⁷), in his zeal for the introduction of Greek customs, obtained the authority of Antiochus Epiphanes to set up a Greek place of exercise, and form a body of youths to be trained therein. His conduct in this is severely condemned, for it is said of him and of the priests under his influence that 'they had no more any zeal for the services of the altar, but, despising the sanctuary and neglecting the sacrifices, they hasten to enjoy that which was unlawfully provided in the palæstra, after the summons of the discus; thinking of no account the honours of their fathers, and thinking the glories of the Greeks best of all' (2 Mac 4¹⁴· ¹⁵).

Of children's games there are but few traces. It is given by the prophet Zechariah as a token of the peace and prosperity that should one day bless Jerusalem, that the 'streets of the city shall be full of boys and girls playing in the streets thereof' (Zec 8⁵). What their games might be the prophet does not say. One of the diversions of Jewish children, we know from the Talmud, was imitating the doings of their elders; and Jesus has made us familiar with children playing at marriages and funerals, 'calling one to another, and saying, We have piped unto you, and ye have not danced; we have mourned to you, and ye have not wept' (Mt 11¹⁷, Lk 7³²). The children seem also to have amused themselves with living creatures. 'Wilt thou play with him as with a bird; or wilt thou bind him for thy maidens?' is God's remonstrance addressed to Job (Job 41⁵), where He asks the patriarch if he could make a plaything of the crocodile, as the child does of a bird. *Dancing* was a diversion of children as well as of grown-up people (Job 21¹¹). The Talmud speaks of games in which the children played with nuts, and, taking this in connexion with the proverbial Latin expression *relinquere nuces*, we may have a reference to it in St. Paul's words, 'When I was a child, I spake as a child, I understood as a child, I thought as a child; but when I became a man, I put away childish things' (1 Co 13¹¹).

Of manly sports among the Jews the traces are likewise few. *Archery* seems to have been practised as a sport as well as cultivated for the requirements of war. The uncertainty of the rendering in 2 S 1¹⁸ does not allow us to use it as evidence, but Job seems to have it in mind when he complains (Job 16¹²· ¹³), 'God hath set me up for his mark; his arrows compass me round about'; and we find the same image in La 3¹² 'He hath bent his bow, and set me as a mark for the arrow.' The use of the *sling*, which played an important part in the military training of the Israelite (Jg 20¹⁶, 1 S 17¹⁹, 1 Ch 12², 2 Ch 26¹⁴), must have demanded considerable practice, especially in the case of the left-handed Benjamites, who 'could sling stones at an hairbreadth and not miss.' A sport which was common among the youths of Palestine in the time of Jerome is described by him as consisting of raising stones of great weight to the knees, to the shoulders and the head, and above the head, according to their strength, wrestlers being matched against each other according to this test. It has been supposed by Ewald and others that 'the burdensome stone' of Zec 12³ is to be explained by the practice thus described by Jerome, being something like the 'putting stone' of Highland games in Scotland; but the allusion may be simply to a weight that is too heavy to be borne, and dangerous to those who meddle with it (compare Dn 2³⁴, Mt 21⁴⁴). The *discus*, as we have seen, was introduced with other Grecian exercises by Jason the high priest in the Maccabæan times (2 Mac 4¹⁴· ¹⁵). It was a flat, circular slab of stone, or of wood, or of bronze, of considerable weight. A specimen in the British Museum is said to weigh about 12

pounds. The throwing of the *discus* was one of the essential exercises of the pentathlic contests. It was thrown from a low platform known as the βαλβίς, and the man who threw it the greatest distance was the winner. A skilful athlete, by putting all his weight into the throw, would sometimes hurl it more than a hundred feet. The attitude of the player and the manner of holding the discus is seen in Myron's celebrated statue of the δισκοβόλος, shown in books of Greek antiquities. Their devotion to this sport and the other exercises of the Grecian pentathlon, even to the neglect of the services of the altar, brought great unpopularity to Jason the high priest and his brethren of the priesthood, and Jason has been handed down to us as 'that ungodly man, and no high priest.'

Hunting, as a diversion, was not pursued till the days of Herod, who greatly favoured the introduction of Greek and Roman customs; and the Talmud gives strong warning against it. The *theatre*, too, was condemned as sternly by the Talmud as by Tertullian; and it was a hope of the days of Messiah that the buildings devoted by the Romans to theatrical representations would be turned into seminaries for the study of the law. Josephus (*Ant.* xv. viii. 1), speaking of the theatre and the amphitheatre built by Herod at Jerusalem, declares both of them to be in direct antagonism to the sentiment of the Jewish people.

Music and *song* fall to be treated rather in connexion with worship, but they were largely cultivated, as was also the *dance*, as a source of enjoyment. At the vintage merrymakings (Jg 9²⁷ 21²¹), at the gatherings of the young men in the city gate (La 5¹⁴), at triumphal processions (Jg 11³⁴, 1 S 18⁶), at celebrations of victory (Ex 15²⁰f.), at the accession of kings (1 K 1⁴⁰), and at domestic rejoicings (Jer 31⁴, Lk 15²⁵), music and singing, and oftentimes dancing, were called in to give expression to the gladness of such occasions.

Story-telling and *riddles* were a common diversion of the ancient Hebrews, as they are of the Arabs to this day (Jg 14¹², Ezk 17², 1 K 10¹). Feasts and wedding-parties were enlivened by such amusements. Samson's riddle (Jg 14¹²), with his wager that the guests will not be able to answer it within a week, is a specimen of the kind of thing that was common. As to *games of chance and of skill*, the Jews seem not to have known them till they learned them from the Greeks. The soldiers who, perhaps by means of the dice, cast lots for the seamless robe of Jesus, were Roman soldiers. There was a game among the ancient Hebrews (see Liddell and Scott under κολλαβίζω), in which one person covered his eyes and guessed which of his companions struck him; and a similar game among the ancient Egyptians (Wilkinson, ii. 59), in which a man knelt with his face to the ground and had to guess who struck him on the back. Was this the idea of the insult offered, when the men that held Jesus blindfolded Him, and struck Him on the face and blasphemously asked Him, 'Prophesy, who is it that smote thee?' (Lk 22⁶⁴).

In NT, especially in the Acts and in the Epistles of St. Paul, the allusions are almost exclusively to the games and athletic contests of ancient Greece. We do read in the Epistle of St. James of 'the crown of life which the Lord hath promised to them that love him' (Ja 1¹²), but the allusion can be explained from Jewish ideas without reference to Greek games. In the Epistle to the Hebrews (12¹· ²) we have the imagery of the assembly (νέφος μαρτύρων), of the contest (ἀγών), of the race (τρέχωμεν), of the training (ὄγκον ἀποθέμενοι πάντα), of the absorbed and eager racers (ἀφορῶντες), all most vividly set before us. It is in connexion with St. Paul, however, that these allusions are most frequent and distinct. Wherever the great apostle travelled among the cities of the Greeks, at Corinth, at Ephesus, at Athens, the athletic contests in which all the kindreds of the Grecian people took pride met his eye, and furnished him with his aptest and most effective illustrations of the Christian life. The gymnasium or place of training, and the stadium or racecourse, were conspicuous and familiar in every considerable city.

The *foot-race* occupies the largest place in the imagery of the apostle, as it was the contest which of all the Grecian games aroused the deepest interest and the keenest excitement. In his addresses reported in the Acts of the Apostles, St. Paul alludes to the foot-race,—describing John the Baptist as 'fulfilling his course' (δρόμος, Ac 13²⁵), and speaking of himself as counting not even life dear unto him that he may finish his course (δρόμος) with joy (Ac 20²⁴). In his Epistles the image occurs again and again. In his very first Epistles he asks the prayers of the Thessalonians that the word of 'the Lord may run (τρέχῃ) and be glorified' (2 Th 3¹ RV). In his last, when the crown is full in view, he writes to Timothy, saying, 'I have fought the good fight (τὸν καλὸν ἀγῶνα); I have finished the course' (τὸν δρόμον) (2 Ti 4⁷·⁸). His whole career as an apostle and as a follower of Christ, and that of his converts, is a race; he is anxious 'lest by any means he should run, or had run, in vain' (Gal 2²); he hopes to rejoice 'in the day of Christ that he had not run in vain' (Ph 2¹⁶); 'ye did run well,' is his remonstrance to the Galatians; 'who hath hindered you, that ye should not obey the truth?' (Gal 5⁷).

In the Epistles to the Philippians and the Corinthians his employment of the imagery of the games reaches its highest point: 'Not as though I had already attained, either were already perfect; but this one thing I do, forgetting those things which are behind, and reaching forth (ἐπεκτεινόμενος) unto those things which are before, I press (διωκῶ) toward the mark (σκοπόν), for the prize (βραβεῖον) of the high calling (τῆς ἄνω κλήσεως) of God in Christ Jesus' (Ph 3¹²⁻¹⁴); 'Know ye not that they which run in a race (οἱ ἐν σταδίῳ τρέχοντες) run all, but one obtaineth the prize? So run, that ye may obtain. And every man that striveth in the games (πᾶς ὁ ἀγωνιζόμενος) is temperate in all things (ἐγκρατεύεται πάντα). Now they do it that they may obtain a corruptible crown, but we an incorruptible (φθαρτὸν στέφανον . . . ἄφθαρτον). I therefore so run, as not uncertainly; so fight I (πυκτεύω, passing from the racer to the boxer), as not beating the air: but I buffet (ὑπωπιάζω) my body, and bring it into bondage (δουλαγωγῶ); lest by any means, after that I have preached to others (κηρύξας, having summoned others to the contest), I myself should be rejected (ἀδόκιμος, driven in disgrace from the games as not having contended in accordance with the rules)' (1 Co 9²⁴⁻²⁷ RV). The imagery in these passages is unusually full and rich. The strenuous, exciting, and definite purpose of the racer, the self-control imposed during the period of training, with the punishment of the body to make it more fit, the prize, the crown, the reward of the victor, the call to the contest, and the proclamation of the conditions, the chance of final disgrace if these are not properly observed (compare 2 Ti 2¹⁵), are all set forth with a vividness that must have brought home powerfully and impressively, to those who were familiar with the Isthmian and Olympian games, the lessons of Christian instruction which the apostle wished to convey.

In other passages there are allusions to the onlookers (1 Co 4⁹), to the umpire or judge (Col 3¹⁵ βραβευέτω; cf. καταβραβευέτω of Col 2¹⁸ and notes of Lightfoot and Abbott; 2 Ti 4⁸ ὁ δίκαιος κριτής), to the joy of victory (Ac 20²⁴). To the gladiatorial spectacles of the amphitheatre, St. Paul makes what

we may take to be a figurative reference (1 Co 15³²
ἐθηριομάχησα ἐν Ἐφέσῳ). At Ephesus St. Paul came in contact with the directors of the games held in the city of Diana. The Asiarchs (Ac 19³¹ τινὲς καὶ τῶν Ἀσιαρχῶν ὄντες αὐτῷ φίλοι) mentioned as friendly to the apostle have long been one of the puzzles of commentators, but it is now certain (see Hicks in his *Ancient Greek Inscriptions in the BM*, iii. 2, p. 81; and Ramsay, *The Church in the Roman Empire*, ch. vii., and art. ASIARCH) that those officials were the high priests of the worship offered to the Roman emperors within the province of Asia. The cities of the province joined together in an association for the worship of the emperors, and the head of the association was styled high priest and Asiarch. In this capacity he had to furnish every year funds for the celebration of the provincial games in honour of the reigning Cæsar, and it appears that as the cult of the Cæsars and the worship of Diana were in close alliance, the games in honour of both would coincide, and be held in the month Artemision—the month of May, sacred to Diana.

LITERATURE.—Löw, *Die Lebensalter in der Jüdischen Literatur*, 1875; Howson, *Metaphors of St. Paul*, ch. iv.; Percy Gardner, *New Chapters in Greek History*, ch. ix.; Kitto, Smith, Herzog, art. 'Games.'   THOMAS NICOL.

GAMMADIM (גַּמָּדִים).—A term of very doubtful meaning, occurring in Ezk 27¹¹ 'The Gammadim (AV -ims) were in thy towers.' No place of the name of Gammad is known, but a proper name is what the context seems to demand. Probably, Cornill's conjecture צְמָרִים (Zemarites, Gn 10¹⁸) is as good as any. Lagarde (*Onom. Sacr.* ii. 95) proposes גֹּמְרִים (they of Gomer, *Cappadocians* [?]). RVm 'valorous men,' although supported by Gesenius (*Thes.* 292), has not commended itself to the majority of scholars. LXX has φύλακες; Symm. appears to have read גַּם פָּרַס, 'and also Medes.'

GAMUL (גָּמוּל 'weaned').—A chief of the Levites, and head of the 24th course of priests, 1 Ch 24¹⁷. See GENEALOGY.

GARDEN (גַּן, properly 'enclosure'; גַּנָּה, const. גִּנַּת in Ca 6¹¹, Est 1⁵ ⁷·⁸; κῆπος).—These terms appear to have been practically equivalent to the Armenian *pardes* (פַּרְדֵּס, Neh 2⁸, Ca 4¹³, Ec 2⁵ [all]), which in Asia Minor to-day is applied equally to flower and vegetable gardens, orchards, parks, and pleasure grounds. The garden planted eastward in Eden (Gn 2⁸) combined the features of all; and these were present in the Jewish idea of paradise, παράδεισος (Lk 23⁴³), which in rabbinical language was פַּרְדֵּס. They figure again in Mohammed's descriptions of *el-Janneh*, 'the garden,' the Moslem paradise, wherein flowing fountains, full rivers, shady trees, and abundant fruits are constantly named as attractions to 'the faithful.'

Gardens are usually enclosed by hedges, drystone dykes with a layer of thorns built in near the top, or by walls of compressed mud, dried in the sun, as are the celebrated gardens that encircle Damascus. The cactus, or prickly pear, is a common hedge in the warmer districts. Its multitudinous sharp spines offer a splendid defence against intruders; but it is apt soon to become a harbour for venomous things. If one break through such a fence, he need not be surprised (a serpent bite him (Ec 10⁸). A mud-built hut, or booth of wattled twigs, is erected for the watchman within the enclosure. The *nâtûr*, or 'watchman,' is the modern representative of the נֹצֵר (Job 27¹⁸). He is not the gardener, but one who guards the fruits and vegetables from pillage. The gardener is named only once directly in Scripture, κηπουρός (Jn 20¹⁵). But gardening as a means of livelihood has always been a popular calling in the East.

Patches of land thus enclosed were cultivated by most families in ancient times. Now, in Palestine, they are found only in the environs of larger towns. In some parts of Asia Minor every house has its own garden.

Kings and men of wealth had extensive and beautiful gardens adjoining or near to their residences. 'The king's gardens' at Jerusalem (2 K 25⁴, Neh 3¹⁵) lay in the fat valley S.E., close by the Pool of Siloam. Recent excavation shows that the western wall of the pool may have been the parapet of 'the stairs that go down from the city of David,' Neh 3¹⁵ (*PEFSt*, Jan. 1897, p. 13; Oct. 1897, p. 264). The gate Gennath (Jos. *BJ* v. iv. 2) possibly took its name from the fact that it led to the gardens outside the city. It seems to have stood some distance E. of the Jaffa gate, where Uzziah once erected a tower of defence (2 Ch 26⁹). With the exception of the rose gardens, which had existed from the days of the prophets (Is 35¹), no gardens were found in later Jerusalem, on account of the evil odour arising from decaying weeds and the manure employed. They crept up, however, close to the walls. Titus, incautiously venturing near to view the city, was surprised by the Jews, and escaped with difficulty, being entangled among the garden trenches and hedges which ran out from the walls (Jos. *BJ* v. ii. 2). Ḳoheleth speaks of planting great gardens and making pools for watering them (Ec 2⁵). Tradition locates these in *Wady Artâs*, S. of Bethlehem. Three gigantic reservoirs, lying in the head of the vale, are supplied by a series of springs. From these the gardens below were watered; a supply also being carried to Jerusalem in conduits. These seem to be indicated by Josephus (*Ant.* VIII. vii. 3) when he speaks of a place Etham, about 50 furlongs from the city, with fine gardens, abounding in rivulets of water, whither Solomon used to drive in state in the early morning. The floor of the valley is still cultivated by the villagers of *Artâs*, and yields richly, but the surrounding slopes are rocky and bare. Possibly, there is a trace of the ancient delights of this neighbourhood in the name of a contiguous height, called by the Arabs *Jebel el-Fureidis*, '|Mount of the little Paradise.' From the Targum on Ec 2⁵ we learn that Solomon indulged his splendid tastes by cultivating in these gardens foreign trees and plants, 'which the goblins and demons brought out of India.' But the Targumist seems to identify these with 'the king's gardens' mentioned above. 'The boundary,' he says, ' was from the wall that is in Jerusalem, by the bank of the waters of Siloam.' The growing of exotics is paralleled by the monks of Sinai, but for a different reason. They are Greeks, not Arabs. And so, as Dean Stanley says (*Sinai and Palestine*, p. 52), one ' sees in the gardens the produce, not of the desert or of Egypt, but of the isles of Greece; not the tamarisk, or the palm, or the acacia, but the olive, the almond tree, the apple tree, the poplar, and the cypress of Attica and Corcyra.'

Ahasuerus is said to have entertained all the notables of his empire with many and varied splendours, for seven days, in the garden attached to his palace (Est 1¹·⁸). For the pleasure of his queen, the king of Babylon constructed the renowned 'hanging gardens,' the κρεμαστὸς παράδεισος of Berosus (quoted by Jos. *c. Ap.* i. 19). Joakim, a rich Jew of the Captivity, 'had a fair garden joining unto his house' (Sus ⁴), in the seclusion of which were all conveniences for bathing (v.¹⁵). Of gardens on this princely scale there is an excellent illustration in *el-Bahjeh*, the palace built for himself by Abdullah Pasha near Acre. It is surrounded by a great extent of ground, beautifully laid out, wherein are reservoirs of water, and multitudinous conduits to all parts of the enclosure. Flowers of every hue brighten the soil; fruit trees vie with each other in season, offering their tempting burdens; the homelier vegetables also have their place. The pleasant pathways, and retired and shady nooks, under embowering greenery, make a very paradise amid the exposed plain.

Egypt was compared to 'a garden of herbs,' watered ʲᶜwith the foot'; Palestine was a land ' which drinketh water of the rain of heaven' (Dt 11¹¹). Gardens could be made in Egypt wherever water could be led from the river. The ground was divided into compartments by little banks of earth, along which ran the water channels. One side of the bank was broken down with the foot, allowing the water to flow into the division: the breach repaired with the foot, the stream was led into the next division, and so on until all were refreshed. This process may be seen to-day. In Palestine, for the most part, the presence of a spring, or a capacious cistern, was essential to the existence of a garden. In the Jordan Valley the river afforded abundant streams, which, carrying beauty and fertility with them, made the plain as 'the garden of the LORD' (Gn 13¹⁰). But such gardens as those of Hebron, Nablûs, and Jenîn—wherein we have a reminiscence of old *En-gannim* (Ca 4¹⁵)—are created by the springs that gurgle up from under the mountains. The luxuriant groves around Jaffa depend upon deep wells, whence the water is raised by a chain of buckets revolving on a wheel, turned usually by a span of mules. The wheels are of rude construction, the pinions often being formed of broken branches, and the creaking they make is not charming. The water is stored in a large tank, connected with the gardens by a network of cemented channels. Towards evening the outflow is opened, and throughout the orchards is heard the musical ripple of running water, and light figures dart among the trees, guiding the streams whither they will. This familiar scene is reflected in the proverb, 'the king's heart· is in the hand of the LORD as the watercourses. He turneth it whithersoever he will' (Pr 21¹). Wisdom in her beneficent power is compared to a 'stream from a river,' and 'a conduit into a garden' (Sir 24³⁰). Gardens, with plentiful supplies of water, were to the Oriental suggestive symbols of prosperity. Balaam likens the spreading tents of Israel to 'gardens by the river side' (Nu 24⁶). The house of Jacob restored to favour shall be 'like a watered garden' (Is 58¹¹, Jer 31¹²). By foul idolatries the sap of manhood is dried up, and men become 'as a garden that hath no water' (Is 1³⁰).

Cucumbers, melons, leeks, onions, and garlic, so common in Egypt (Nu 11⁵), and probably also lettuce and endive, were grown in Palestine, together with such plants as coriander (Ex 16³¹, Nu 11⁷), caper (Ec 12⁵ RV), camphire or henna (Ca 1¹⁴), cummin (Is 28²⁵·²⁷, Mt 23²³), mustard (Mt 13³¹·³²), anise (Mt 23²³), and rue (Lk 11⁴²). Vines clung to almost every hillside. In olden times the mulberry, olive, fig, pomegranate, almond, and walnut (Ca 6¹¹) were well known. The *tappûaḥ* (Ca 2³·⁵ 7⁸) was probably the apricot. To these the Mishna adds the quince, the citron, the medlar, and the service (*Chilaim*, i. 4). To-day the orange, lemon, and peach grow luxuriantly in the groves, *e.g.* at Jaffa, Sidon, and Damascus. The banana flourishes at Sidon; while apples and pears are cultivated with moderate success. The egg plant, the tomato, and the potato, together with the homely cabbage, are found in almost every garden. See further under FOOD.

The gardens, with their shady foliage, have always been a favourite retreat for the people during the hotter seasons. It was reckoned a token of public peace and security, when a man could sit without fear under his vine and fig tree, the two often growing together (Mic 4⁴, Zec 3¹⁰). Many family meals are eaten under the shelter of spreading fig and mulberry. In the cool of the day companies assemble in the gardens; as darkness falls, the light of a lamp swung on a bough twinkles through the greenery; and sounds of laughter and song, accompanied by the twanging of the 'oud, or the shrill voice of the pipe, are borne far upon the quiet air. When the fruits are ripening, and until they are safely gathered, many make their beds under the fruit trees.

The secluded recesses among clustering trees and bushes made the gardens a popular resort for purposes of devotion. They were often the haunts of idolatrous worship (Is 1²⁹ 65³ 66¹⁷). Baruch (6⁷⁰) compares the idols, 'gods of wood,' set up in the gardens, with the 'scarecrow,' προβασκάνιον, 'in a garden,' which 'keepeth nothing.' An abiding charm clings to the slopes of Olivet, because Jesus 'ofttimes resorted . . . with his disciples' to a garden there (Jn 18², Lk 22³⁹), where linger the deathless memories of GETHSEMANE. The Moslem who spreads his little carpet, and solemnly prays to Allah under the shade of the trees he tends, is true heir to the ancient tradition of the Orient.

The garden sometimes contained the family tomb or burial-cave. In the garden of Uzza both Manasseh and his son Amon found sepulture (2 K 21¹⁸ 21²⁶). Nor can we forget that in the place where Jesus 'was crucified there was a garden, and in the garden a new tomb, wherein was never man yet laid. There . . . they laid Jesus' (Jn 19⁴¹·⁴²)   W. EWING.

GAREB (גָּרֵב).—One of David's 'Thirty' (2 S 23³⁸, 1 Ch 11⁴⁰). Like Ira, in the same verse, he is described as an Ithrite (הַיִּתְרִי), i.e. a member of one of the families of Kiriath-jearim (1 Ch 2⁵³). In notices of this kind, however, it is more usual to give the name of the locality to which the warrior belonged, and we should probably read with Wellh., in both cases, 'of Yattir' (הַיַּתִּרִי), a town in the hill-country of Judah (Jos 15⁴⁸ 21¹⁴, cf. 1 S 30²⁷). See IRA.   J. F. STENNING.

GAREB (גָּרֵב).—A hill near Jerusalem, Jer 31³⁹. Its situation is uncertain, being located by some, e.g. Riehm and Graf, to the S.W., while others place it to the N. of the capital. At the present day there is a Wady Gourab to the W. of Jerusalem. (See Neubauer, Géog. du Talmud, p. 150).

GARLAND.—See CROWN.

GARLIC (שׁוּם shûm, τὰ σκόρδα, allia).—The bulblets of Allium sativum, L., still known in Arabic by the cognate thûm. It is now, as in the days of the ancient Egyptians (Nu 11⁵), a favourite addition to the complex stews and the roasts of the Orientals. It is cultivated everywhere in the East. Too often the natives reek with its stale, penetrating odour.   G. E. POST.

GARMENT.—See DRESS.

GARMITE (הַגַּרְמִי).—A gentilic name applied in a totally obscure sense to Keilah in 1 Ch 4¹⁹. The text in the LXX is hopelessly confused (cf. Swete's ed., and see Kittel's note in Haupt's Sacred Bks. of OT).

GARNER.—Garner, which is now archaic if not obsolete, and granary, the form now in use, both come from Lat. granaria, a storehouse for grain (itself from granum, a grain, corn), the former through the Fr. gernier, a variant of grenier, the latter directly. Garner occurs in plu. Ps 144¹³ (מְזָוִים, the only occurrence); Jl 1¹⁷ (אֹצָרוֹת, a common word, used both of stores of any kind and of storehouses for any purpose; the Eng. word 'garner' is narrower in meaning); and Sir 1¹⁷ (τὰ ἀποδοχεῖα [Bᵃᵇℵ, -ια B*ᶜ]; a word peculiar to Sir, where it occurs also 39¹⁷ EV 'receptacles,' Cowley and Neubauer 'treasure'; and 50³ EV 'cistern': it is also of wider use than 'garner,' being applied in the last two cases to receptacles for water). In NT 'garner' is used in the sing., Mt 3¹²=Lk 3¹⁷ (ἀποθήκη, elsewhere in NT tr⁴ 'barn,' Mt 6²⁶ 13³⁰, Lk 12¹⁸·²⁴). Chaucer (Prol. to Cant. Tales, 592) says of the Reve, 'Wel coude he kepe a gerner and a binne'; and T. Adams, Works, i. 87, says, 'The Lord sends grain, and the devil sends garners.'

RV retains the subst. in all those occurrences, and introduces the verb, Is 62⁹ 'They that have garnered it shall eat it' (מְאַסְפָיו; AV 'gathered,' which RV uses for the verb יְקַבְּצוּ, which occurs in the same verse).   J. HASTINGS.

GARRISON.—See WAR.

GAS (Γάς, AV Gar), 1 Es 5³⁴.—His sons were among the 'temple servants.' The last nine names in this list, of whom Gas is one, have no corresponding names in the lists of Ezra and Nehemiah. The AV form is derived from the Aldine text.

GASHMU (גַּשְׁמוּ, Γόσεμ, Neh 6⁶).—A form of the name GESHEM (which see), probably representing the pronunciation of N. Arabian dialect. Proper names with the termination u (ו) are found in Nabatæan inscriptions. The words 'and Gashmu saith' do not occur in the older MSS of LXX (ABℵ*).   H. A. WHITE.

GATAM (גַּעְתָּם).—The son of Eliphaz (Gn 36¹¹ = 1 Ch 1³⁶), and 'duke' of an Edomite clan (Gn 36¹⁶) which has not been identified.

GATE.—**1.** שַׁעַר, root שָׁעַר 'cleave,' 'divide' (?); a gate or entrance of a camp (Ex 32²⁶), city (Jos 20⁴), palace (Est 2¹⁹), or temple (2 Ch 23²⁰); πύλη, porta. **2.** פֶּרַע Aram., only in Daniel. A gate or mouth as of a furnace (3²⁶). Gate of the King or Royal Court (2⁴⁹). Corresponding terms in Arabic and Turkish are used of the califs and Turkish emperors, and of the Persian court (Gesen.); cf. θύρα, fores. פֶּרַע 'porter,' 'doorkeeper' (of the Temple), occurs in Ezr 7²⁴. The usual Heb. term is שׁוֹעֵר. **3.** פֶּתַח, root פָּתַח 'open.' The entrance of the gate of a city (Jos 20⁴, Jg 9³⁵). **4.** דֶּלֶת, root דָּלָה 'hang down'; the leaf of a door, dual, folding doors such as the gates of a city; κλισίας, valva. For Doorway and Door, and distinction between דֶּלֶת and שַׁעַר, see HOUSE.

City gateways among the Greeks and Romans in later days appear to have been principally used for making secure the city, but in early times among the Greeks and at all times in Syria they have been used for many public purposes, and were important positions in the economy of the state. Jerome says that as the Hebrews were for the most part employed in labouring in the field, it was wisely provided that assemblies should be held at the city gates, and justice administered there in a summary manner, that those labouring men who were busy at their work might lose no time, and that the country people might not be obliged to enter and spend their time there (Cruden, Conc. s. 'Gate').

The gate of the city in the early dawn of civilization was the ordinary place of public resort for the transaction of business and administration of justice, and for discussing the news, just as the doorway of the house was the place where private business was despatched and friendly greetings exchanged. It was also the place of the markets, where goods were exposed for sale.

Gesenius gives the foll. explanation (*s.v.* שַׁעַר). 'At the gates of cities there was the *forum* (רְחֹב), where trials were held, and the citizens assembled, some of them for business and some to sit at leisure to look on and converse (Gn 19¹, Ru 4¹¹, Pr 31²³, La 1⁴); whence "in the gate," often for "in the forum," "in judgment," Dt 25⁷, Job 5⁴ 31²¹, Ps 127⁵, Pr 22²², Is 29²¹, Am 5¹⁰· ¹²· ¹⁸.' Cf. further Driver on Am 5¹⁰. The word רְחֹב is rendered by Gesenius —(1) *a street*, (2) *open place, forum*, *i.e.* an ample space at the gate of Oriental cities where trials were held, and wares set forth for sale, 2 Ch 32⁶; cf. Neh 8¹· ³· ¹⁶, Ezr 10⁹. In RV '*broad place*' has been substituted in several instances for 'street'; the trⁿ proposed in *QPB* is '*public place.*'

In the earliest days the city gate is mentioned as the place of public resort, where people met for business and to discuss news. Gn 19¹ 'And Lot sat in the gate of Sodom'; Gn 23¹⁰ 'Ephron the Hittite answered Abraham in the audience of the children of Heth at the gate of his city'; Gn 34²⁰ 'And Hamor and Shechem his son came unto the gate of their city, and communed with the men of their city'; 1 S 4¹³ 'Eli sat upon his seat by the side of the gate watching the way'; 2 S 15²· ⁶ 'Absalom stole the hearts of the men of Israel at the gate of the city'; Neh 8¹ 'Ezra the scribe read the law to the people gathered together into the broad place (*forum*) before the water gate.'

The gate was also used for administration of justice, deliberation, and audience for kings, etc. Dt 21¹⁹ the stubborn and rebellious son is to be brought before the elders of the city at the gate; Dt 25⁷ if the man does not like to take his brother's wife, she shall go up to the gate unto the elders; Jos 20⁴ the manslayer shall declare his cause before the elders of the city of refuge at the entering in of the gate; Ru 4¹ Boaz consulted the elders at the gate concerning Ruth's property; 2 S 19⁸ king David sat in the gate, and the people came before him; 1 K 22¹⁰ the kings of Israel and Judah sat in an open place at the entrance of the gate of Samaria, and all the prophets prophesied before them; Jer 38⁷ king Zedekiah sat in the gate of Benjamin; La 5¹⁴ 'The elders have ceased from the gate'; Am 5¹² 'Ye that afflict the just, that take a bribe, and that turn aside the needy in the gate from their right'; Zec 8¹⁶ 'Judge truth and the judgment of peace in your gates'; Ps 69¹² 'They that sit in the gate speak against me.'

Until the battering-ram was perfected with its machinery, so as to be serviceable against heavy stone walls, the gate was the only point in a well-built city wall where a successful assault could be made, and there is constant reference in the Bible to 'war in the gates' (Jg 5⁸), and to them that turn the battle to the gate (Is 28⁶), and shall speak with the enemies in the gate (Ps 127⁵, where, however, the enemies are perhaps only forensic).

In the account of the assault on Abel-beth-maacah in the time of David, EV says that the people that were with Joab 'battered the wall to throw it down' (2 S 20¹⁵); but the meaning of the Hebrew מַשְׁחִיתִם לְהַפִּיל הַחוֹמָה is doubtful. See Driver, *Text of Sam.* 265. Mention is made in Deuteronomy (20¹⁹ᶠ·) of building bulwarks (מָצוֹר, lit. 'siege,' *i.e.* siegeworks) against a city in war; yet, even as late as the final taking of Jerusalem by the Assyrians (B.C. 588), the battering-ram was used

against the gates (Ezk 21²²), though Ezekiel (4²) also appears to speak of the ram being used round about, against the walls. Among the Macedonians the ram first became an important military engine in the time of Philip and Alexander the Great (cf. Thuc. ii. 76).

At the siege of Rabbah (*c.* B.C. 1000) the garrison made a sortie, and the army of Israel was 'upon them even unto the entering of the gate' (2 S 11²³). In the attack on the strong tower within the city of Thebez (*c.* B.C. 1170), Abimelech went hard unto the door of the tower to burn it with fire (Jg 9⁵²). Nehemiah (B.C. 444) also speaks of the city gates being burnt with fire (Neh 1³ 2³· ¹³· ¹⁷); and Jeremiah prophesies that the high gates of Babylon shall be burned with fire (Jer 51⁵⁸). The breaking of gates of brass and cutting in sunder the bars of iron is spoken of (Ps 107¹⁶, Is 45²).

City gateways, in order to be secure against these various forms of attack, required flanking towers (2 Ch 14⁷ 26⁹ 32⁵, Ps 48¹², Ca 8¹⁰, Ezk 26⁴) to protect the entrance, and galleries above (2 S 18²⁴· ³³), from which the defenders could throw boiling pitch and oil upon the assailants: there were probably two sets of gates, one to each entrance, with a courtyard or barbican between. 'And David sat between the two gates, and the watchman went up to the roof of the gate unto the wall' (2 S 18²⁴). There was a chamber over the gate (2 S 18³³). Possibly, at the outer entrance there was a portcullis or *cataracta*, which is described by Vegetius as an *ancient* contrivance; and it has been suggested ('Cataracta,' in Smith's *Dic. Gr. and Rom. Antiquities*) that it is alluded to in the passage, 'Lift up your heads, O ye gates; and be ye lift up, ye everlasting doors' (Ps 24⁷· ⁹; cf. Jer 20² 51⁵⁸).

Rooms would be required for the guard of the gate, for the porters, and for the watchmen, and the entrance gateway would require to be of considerable dimensions, where the people of the city could readily congregate. Being of so great importance from a defensive point of view, the chief officer of the city would naturally take great interest in its secure condition; and being on the high road from the country the traders would bring their wares there, and would be detained there before entry for examination and toll. Thus the vicinity of the gate would naturally become the public place of resort for business and pleasure, where also justice could be administered and punishment meted out.

As civilization and luxury increased, the gateways seem to have been less used among the Greeks and Romans, the Agora or Basilica, or forum and portico, being placed near the royal palace, or, in a seaport town, near the harbour; and the markets were divided up according to the articles sold there (Polyb. ix. 47, x. 19). Some articles, such as salt fish, seem to have been sold outside the gates (Aristoph. *Equit.* 1246). But even in late days among the Greeks and Romans the gates were surmounted by towers (Virg. *Aen.* vi. 552), and Polybius (xv. 29) calls a building at Alexandria 'the gatehouse at the palace used for the transaction of public business.' The entrances to military camps (*castra*) were, when necessity arose, defended by towers (Cæsar, *B. G.* viii. 9). The gateway at Treves, so late as the time of the emperor Constantine, was built in such a style as shows that it was intended to be used during peace for the object of civil government.

In Syria the vicinity of the gate has always been the focus of business transactions, but as Greek and Roman influences prevailed, no doubt the gate did not occupy, for a time, so important a position in the social life of the people; and markets were constructed in various parts of the city apart from the gates. In the latter days of Jerusalem the upper city is called by Josephus (*Wars*, v. iv. 1) the Agora or market place ; the sheep market was on the north side of the temple, near the pool of Bethesda (Jn 5²) ; and a place is mentioned outside the second wall where were the merchants of wool, the braziers, and the market of cloth (Jos. *Wars*, v. viii. 1). In early days, however, the markets were probably close to the gates, 'To-morrow about this time shall a measure of fine flour be sold for a shekel, and two measures of barley for a shekel, in the gate of Samaria (2 K 7¹ ; cf. Neh 13¹⁶· ¹⁹).

In the Assyrian cities the gateways were either arched or had flat stone lintels, with flanking towers and overhead galleries, as at Khorsabad (Layard, *Nineveh*, ii. 388, 395, and bas-relief in British Museum, 'Assyria,' 25, 26, 49). Herodotus (i. 179) and Ctesias state that the walls of Babylon were furnished with 100 brazen gates, with lintels and sideposts of the same material, and with 250 towers to protect the weaker parts. Jeremiah (51⁵³· ⁵⁸) speaks of burning these gates. In Nebuchadrezzar's account of Babylon, stamped on the bricks, the great gates are described as made of cedarwood covered with copper, with thresholds of bronze.

In the later Egyptian temples the gates appear to have been fortified (Wilkinson, *Anc. Egyp.* i. 409). At Pompeii may be seen a gateway protected by a portcullis, with a barbican, within which again were gates of wood and iron.

Besides the open space or forum at the entrance of the city gate, there was evidently an open place of assembly near the entrance to the temple and before the gate of the royal palace. At Jerusalem there was the broad place before the water gate, which appears to have been on the south side of the outer court of the temple (Neh 8¹ᶠ·). At Shushan, Mordecai went to the broad place of the city before the king's gate ; and queen Esther made her petition to king Ahasuerus at the king's gate (Est 4⁶ 5²; cf. Herod. iii. 120, 140). Daniel sat in the gate of the king (Dn 2⁴⁹). It is not improbable that in Est and Dn 'gate' is used by metonymy for 'palace' or 'king's court.' Cf. the modern 'Sublime Porte.'

The gates were closed and guarded by night. Jos 2⁵· ⁷ 'About the time of the shutting of the gate, when it was dark'; Neh 7³ 'Let not the gates of Jerusalem be opened till the sun be hot: and while they stand on guard let them shut the doors, and bar ye them'; Is 60¹¹ 'Thy gates also shall be open continually, they shall not be shut day nor night'; Rev 21²⁵ 'And the gates thereof shall in no wise be shut by day (for there is no night there)'; Neh 13¹⁹ 'When the gates of Jerusalem began to be dark before the sabbath, I commanded that the doors should be shut.' The gateways of palaces and temples were highly ornamented—those of Nimroud (B.C. 884), Persepolis, and Khorsabad (Fergusson, *Archit.* pp. 154, 160, 174) were flanked by colossal figures of animals, winged bulls at Nimroud and Khorsabad. The doors of city gates were usually plated with iron or copper, to prevent their being easily burnt or broken (Ps 107¹⁶, Is 45²). In the temple of Solomon (1 K 6³¹) the doors leading to the Holy of Holies were of olive wood, with carvings of cherubim and palm trees, and overlaid with gold. The doors to the temple were of cypress wood, carved in like manner, and overlaid with gold, with doorposts of olive wood (1 K 6³⁴ᶠ·, 2 K 18¹⁶, Ezk 41²³ᶠ·). Josephus (*Wars*, v. v. 3) speaks of nine of the gates of the temple courts being covered with gold and silver, while the east gate of the inner court (the **Beautiful Gate** of Ac 3²) was of Corinthian brass, and greatly excelled the others. These gates were 30 cubits

high and 15 broad, while the doors of the east gate were 40 cubits high and required 20 men to close them, and had bolts fastened deeply into the solid stone threshold (Jos. *Wars*, v. v. 3, VI. v. 3).

The bars, bolts, locks, etc., of doors of gateways were the same as those used for doors of houses, but larger in proportion (see HOUSE).

In some cities of Syria the doors were made of massive pieces of stone. Buckingham (*Arab Tribes*, p. 221) describes ponderous doors of stone in the *Hauran*, 15 in. thick, closed on the inside with bars. Burckhardt (*Syria*, p. 90) mentions doors of the city gate at *Kuffir*, 10 ft. high, of single pieces of stone ; he also mentions doors at *Ezra*, of one piece, 4 in. thick, some upwards of 9 ft. in height, turning upon hinges worked out of the stone.

Maundrell (*Early Travels*, p. 447, A.D. 1697) mentions large stone doors to tombs at Jerusalem, 6 in. thick, turning on hinges of the same piece with the door. Schumacher (*Northern Ajlûn*, p. 71) gives a sketch of a basalt door to a tomb at *Umm Keis* (Gadara), 4 ft. high, 7 in. thick, with stone hinges, and a lock and bolt which can be pushed home and withdrawn from the outside. Gates of single precious stones are mentioned poetically (Is 54¹², Rev 21²¹).

At the present day the people of the East have reverted to their primitive customs regarding the uses of the gate, and many business and social duties are carried out there. Thomson (*Land and the Book*, i. p. 31) mentions having seen at Jaffa the *Kâdi* and his court sitting at the entrance of the gate, hearing and adjudicating all sorts of cases in the audience of all that went in and out thereat. At Suakin in 1886 the present writer found it necessary to sit at the gate to transact official business in order that the public might freely approach and relate their grievances. Bertrandon de la Broquére (*Early Travels*, p. 349, A.D. 1433) gives an interesting account of his reception at the court of the Turks, the 'Sublime Porte,' at Constantinople. The ambassadors were received at the gate of the palace, and all business was transacted there. Chardin relates (vii. 368) that the principal gate of the royal palace of Ispahan was held sacred, and used by criminals as a place of refuge. The present writer conducted all his business transactions with the governors of Al-Arish, Nukl, and Akabah in 1882 at the gate, where there were arched roofs giving protection from the sun and rain, and seats for the administration of justice. At Nukl the council chamber was immediately over the gate. The city gateways of the present day have usually flanking towers and overhead galleries, with an arched passage within, so that a second set of gates may be erected inside the barbican or courtyard. 'Frequently in the gates of cities, as at Mosul, these recesses are used as shops for the sale of wheat and barley, bread and grocery' (Layard, *Nineveh and Babylon*, p. 57 note). Morier (*Second Journey through Persia*, p. 189) speaks of the market for mules, asses, and camels held every morning outside the gate of Teheran, and also states that temporary shops and tents of sellers of all sorts of goods were erected there. Denham and Clapperton (*Discoveries in Africa*, i. 216, 217) speak of the markets for slaves, sheep and cattle, wheat, rice, etc., outside one of the principal gates of a town. At Jerusalem there is an extensive temporary market outside the Jaffa gate on a Sunday morning, and here also is the principal place of public execution.

The gate of a city is necessarily the place for the collector of local customs to sit to receive the moneys due for commodities entering the city (Mt 9⁹).

These gateways are often very highly ornamented, sentences from the Korân being inscribed on the doorways and on the doors (cf. Dt 6⁹, Is 54¹², Rev 21²¹). Maundrell (*Early Travels*, p. 488, A.D. 1697), speaking of Damascus, says, 'In these walls you find the gates and doors adorned with marble portals, carved and inlaid with great beauty and variety.' The city gates of the present day are usually two-leaved, of wood studded with iron nails, and often covered with iron or copper plates. As in olden times, the gates of walled cities, such as Jerusalem, Damascus, Cairo, etc., are closed at night (Robinson, *BRP* iii. 455 ; Lane, *Mod. Egyp.* i. 25).

Burying places were outside the gate (Lk 7¹²) ; so was the προσευχή at Philippi (Ac 16¹³) ; Jesus suffered 'without the gate,' He 13¹² (cf. Lv 24¹⁴, Nu 15³⁶, 1 K 21¹⁰·¹³ etc.).

The word 'gate' is used, in a figurative sense, in a variety of ways. It is used, esp. in Dt, to denote the city itself, 'And thy seed shall possess the gate of his enemy' (Gn 22¹⁷ 24⁶⁰, Dt 12¹²). We read also of the gate of heaven (Gn 28¹⁷) ; the gate of the Lord (Ps 118²⁰) ; the gates of death (Ps 9¹³) ; the gates of the grave (Is 38¹⁰) ; the gates of Hades (Mt 16¹⁸). The gate from its importance and defensive strength becomes the synonym for strength, power, and dominion. 'Thou shalt call thy walls Salvation, and thy gates Praise' (Is 60¹⁸) ; 'The Lord loveth the gates of Zion' (Ps 87²) ; 'Lift up your heads, O ye gates' (Ps 24⁷) ; in time of calamity the gates howl and languish, lament and mourn (Is 14³¹ 3²⁶, Jer 14²). By metonymy 'the gates' meant those who administered justice at the gates and held government (Hom. *Il.* ix. 312 ; cf. Mt 16¹⁸).

To keep and watch over the temple, city, and palace gates were porters (doorkeepers) and watchmen (שׁוֹעֵר, θυρωρός, πυλωρός, *portarius, janitor*). In the temple of Jerusalem the duties of keeping the gates ultimately devolved upon the Levites (1 Ch 9¹⁸ᶠ· 15²³ᶠ·, 2 Ch 31¹⁴, Jer 35⁴). In the time of the Chronicler 4000 of the Levites were porters (doorkeepers) about the temple (1 Ch 23⁵), and the porters waited at every gate (2 Ch 35¹⁵). The location of the porters at the gates is given in 1 Ch 26.

In the palace of Shushan (Est 2²¹ 6²) the king's chamberlains kept the door. In the time of our Lord it is mentioned that a maid kept the door of the court of the high priest at Jerus. (Jn 18¹⁶, cf. Ac 12¹³). There were also porters and watchmen in the city gates. David sat between the two gates at Mahanaim, and the watchman went up over the gate and called unto the porter (2 S 18²⁶). The lepers called to the porters of the city of Samaria (2 K 7¹⁰). Nehemiah on rebuilding the walls of Jerusalem speaks of appointing the porters, and appointing watches of the inhabitants (Neh 7²ᶠ·) ; he also set his servants over the gates when they were shut on the Sabbath (Neh 13¹⁹). There were also guards to the gates (2 K 11⁶) and guard chambers (1 K 14²⁸). Keepers of prison doors are spoken of (Ac 5²³ 12⁶).

The porter or doorkeeper (θυρωρός) of a fold is spoken of as opening to the shepherd (Jn 10³). In private houses there were doorkeepers to watch the entrance (Mk 13³⁴). In Greek and Roman houses there was a small room (θυρών, *cella*) for the porter and also for his dog, which was usually kept in the hall to guard the house (Aristot. *Oecon.* i. 6 ; Plato, *Protag.* p. 314 ; Aristoph. *Equit.* 1025 ; Tibull. i. l. 56).   C. WARREN.

GATH (גַּת 'wine-press'; LXX Γέθ ; Jos. Γίττα ; Vulg. *Geth*), one of the five royal cities of the Philistines (Jos 13³, 1 S 6¹⁷), the site of which is still uncertain, though its position can be located, within a radius of a few miles, from the various references to it in Scripture. The preponderance of opinion is in favour of its identity with the village of *Tell es-Sâfi*, the Blanchegarde of the Crusaders ; while some

authorities give reasons for identifying it with the village of *Beit Jibrîn*, which is also identified as Eleutheropolis. These two sites are about 8 miles apart, within that portion of the Shephelah or undulating country which was allotted to the tribe of Judah, and is recognized as being within the border of the Philistines. According to Josephus, however (*Ant.* v. i. 22), Gath was in the territory of Dan, and is coupled with Jamnia as though in its vicinity on the southern border of the territory.

Gath is not mentioned in Jos as having been allotted to either the tribe of Judah or Dan, but all the references to it indicate that it was close to the border separating these two tribes : in common with Ashdod and Gaza, it remained in possession of the Anakim after Joshua had destroyed them out of all the other cities of Palestine (Jos 11²²).

Gath was a fenced city of considerable importance, and was constantly the scene of struggles between the Philistines and Israelites, and was taken and retaken by either side (1 S 7¹⁴ 17⁴·⁵², 2 S 21²⁰, 2 K 12¹⁷, 1 Ch 7²¹ 8¹³ 18¹ 20⁶, 2 Ch 11⁸ 26⁶).

The journey of the ark of God from Ashdod to Gath (1 S 5), and thence by Ekron to Beth-shemesh and Kiriath-jearim, indicates the site of Gath to have been near the boundary-line between Dan and Judah. The account of the flight of the Philistines on the death of Goliath, 'by the way to Shaaraim, even unto Gath, and unto Ekron' (1 S 17⁵²), gives the same indication.

Gath remained a stronghold of the Philistines during the reigns of Saul and David, and the latter twice (but see DAVID, i. 564ᵃ) took refuge there : first, when he fled from Saul at Gibeah (1 S 21¹⁰) he went to Achish the king of Gath, and being discovered, feigned himself mad in their hands ; secondly, when he again fled from Saul at the head of 600 men, he dwelt with Achish at Gath, and formed a friendship with him (1 S 27⁵) and with the Gittites, 600 of whom came after him from Gath when he reigned in Jerusalem, and accompanied him under Ittai the Gittite on his flight from Jerusalem over Jordan (2 S 15¹⁸ᶠᶠ·), when his son Absalom conspired and stole the hearts of the men of Israel.

Rehoboam fortified Gath (2 Ch 11⁸), but it seems to have fallen again into the hands of the Philistines, as Uzziah 'brake down the wall of Gath' (2 Ch 26⁶) when he went forth and warred against the Philistines. Amos about this time speaks of 'Gath of the Philistines' (Am 6²; see Driver's note). The last reference to Gath as an existing (?) city is in the Bk. of Micah (1¹⁰), in the days of Hezekiah king of Judah, 'Declare ye it not at Gath.' Both Ashdod and Ekron are referred to in the times of Josiah (Zeph 2⁴) and after the Exile (Zec 9⁵), but Gath has disappeared from history. It may have been destroyed when Hezekiah smote the Philistines even unto Gaza (2 K 18⁸), or when Sennacherib 'came up against all the fenced cities of Judah and took them' (2 K 18¹³), as it plays no further part in history.

Little is learned concerning the site of Gath by reference to Eusebius and Jerome. Gath is stated to have been 5 Roman miles north of Eleutheropolis towards Diospolis (Lydda), while Gath-rimmon, a Levitical city in the tribe of Dan, is stated as about 12 miles from Diospolis towards Eleutheropolis : this would in each case indicate a site close to *Tell es-Sâfi*, which is situated within the boundary of the tribe of Judah, and is nowhere near the site which Gath-rimmon is supposed to have occupied in Dan, not far from Joppa and Lydda. It may, then, be assumed that both these references are to the royal Gath of the Philistines and not to Gath-rimmon (*Onomast. s.* 'Gath'). Jerome in another work (*Comm. in Mic* 1¹¹) states that Gath, one of the five cities of the Philistines, was situated near the borders of Judah on the way from Eleutheropolis to Gaza, and was then a very large village. There is obviously a mistake in the word 'Gaza,' as the way indicated does not go near the borders of Judah. Eusebius further mentions the Gath to which the ark was taken from Ashdod on the way to Ekron as lying between Antipatris (*Ras el-'Aïn*) and Jamnia (*Yebna*); this line lies within the tribe of Dan, and the Gath thus located appears to be Gath-rimmon and not the royal Gath.

The Crusaders considered Gath to be identical with Jamnia (*Yebna*), and erected there the castle of Ibelin, which Benjamin of Tudela (*Early Travels*, p. 37) identifies with Jabneh, now *Yebna* (Will. Tyr. 15. 24. 25).

The view that Gath, Bethgabra, Eleutheropolis, and *Beit Jibrîn* are all one and the same city is based by Thomson (*Land and Book*) and Canon Tristram (*Bible Places*) on the ground that Bethgabra and *Beit Jibrîn* may be rendered 'house of the giants' (Anakim), and on the finding of the name *Kherbet Gat* among the ruined heaps at *Beit Jibrîn*, and also on the assumption that Mareshah was a suburb of Gath (2 Ch 11[8], Mic 1[14]), from the connexion of the words in those two passages. As, however, the word Gath in Hebrew signifies 'wine-press,' and as the Anakim at one time occupied all the territory round about, this proposal cannot be pressed home.

The view generally accepted is that proposed by Porter in 1857, viz. that Gath is represented by the site of the modern village of *Tell es-Sâfi*. The position generally satisfies all the geographical references so far as they go, and for a fenced city it is naturally a very strong site, having precipitous sides towards the west. The only difficulty is that the sites of Ekron, Ashdod, Ashkelon, Gaza, and other Philistine fenced cities do not present any natural features capable of defence; they are simply mounds on the undulating plain, and it may be that Gath may yet be discovered as a mound somewhere near *Tell es-Sâfi*. If it had such pronounced natural features for defence as the hill in question has, it is difficult to understand how its existence can have so completely disappeared from history after the time of king Hezekiah.

Tell es-Sâfi (*BRP*[2] ii. pp. 29–32) is an isolated oblong hill or ridge stretching from north to south between the Shephelah to the east and the plains of Philistia to the west, Wady es - Sunt (the valley of Elah) passing by on the north. It stands out conspicuously towards the north, south, and west, about 300 ft. above the plain and 700 above the Mediterranean; and, presenting on three sides many hundred feet of white precipices, would as a fenced city have been remarkably strong. There are many caves and excavations on the northern scarps; water is obtained to the west at the foot of the hill. The name signifies 'the white hill,' and it can be seen at several hours' distance to north and west.

On the top is a modern village of mud huts with a sacred *wely*. There are still remains of drafted stones visible, remnants of the old castle of Blanchegarde (*Alba Specula*), erected in A.D. 1144 by Fulke of Anjou as a check against the incursions of the Saracens from Ashkelon. It was taken by Saladin in A.D. 1191 and dismantled, but was again fortified by Richard of England in the following year. It continued for some centuries as a place of importance in the hands of the Moslems. (See, in addition to the authorities cited above, G. A. Smith, *HGHL* 194 ff.; Gautier, *Souvenirs de Terre-Sainte*, 93). C. WARREN.

GATH-HEPHER (גַּת הַחֵפֶר 'wine-press of digging'; in Jos 19[13] with ה *locale* גִּתָּה חֵפֶר which AV mis-

takenly tr. Gittah-hepher).—The home of the prophet Jonah (2 K 14[25]), and on the border of Zebulun and Naphtali near Japhia and Rimmon (Jos 19[12. 13]), which have been identified in the villages of *Yâfa* and *Rummâneh*.

There is a general concurrence in the identification of Gath-hepher with the present village of *el-Meshhed* (*SWP* i. pp. 363–367), the site of one of the many Moslem tombs of Neby Yûnas, the prophet Jonah. This village is regarded by both Christians and Moslems as being the home of the prophet Jonah, and there appears to be a chain of tradition supporting this view. About 2½ miles to the west of *el-Meshhed* is the village of *Seffûrieh*, where there are still the remains of a castle and church identified by Robinson (*BRP* ii. 345) as the site of the Sepphoris of Josephus, the Tsippori of the Rabbins, a place not mentioned in Scripture, but afterwards called by the Romans Diocæsarea. Jerome says (*Proœm. in Jonam*) that the home and tomb of the prophet Jonah were shown at a small village 2 miles from Sepphoris or Diocæsarea on the road to Tiberias. Benjamin of Tudela in the 12th cent. states that the tomb of the prophet Jonah was shown in his time near Sepphoris (*Early Travels in Palestine*, p. 89). Isaac Chelo in the 14th cent. states that the name of Gath-hepher was Meshad (Carmoly, *Itin.* p. 256). The rabbinical writers state that the tomb of Jonah the prophet was shown at Gath-hepher on a hill near Sepphoris. The *wely* or *makân* has two domes, and is very conspicuous, dominating the plain on the north at a height of 1250 ft. above the Mediterranean.

LITERATURE.—Besides the authorities cited above, see Baedeker-Socin, *Pal.* 252; Reland, *Pal.* ii. 786; Neubauer, *Géog. du Talm.* 200 f. C. WARREN.

GATH-RIMMON (גַּת־רִמּוֹן).—There are perhaps two places mentioned of this name.

1. A Levitical city in the territory of Dan (Jos 21[24], 1 Ch 6[69]), situated near Jehud, Bene-berak, and Me-jarkon, not far from Joppa (Jos 19[45]). The site has not been ascertained. This is probably the Gath mentioned by Eusebius as lying between Antipatris and Jamnia (*Onom. s.* 'Gath'). A Gath-rimmon is mentioned as lying between Diospolis and Eutheropolis, but this reference is probably to the royal city of Gath. See GATH.

2. A town of Manasseh, west of Jordan (Jos 21[25]), assigned to the Levites. It is only once mentioned, with no indication whatever of its situation within the tribe of Manasseh. It follows immediately after Gath-rimmon of Dan in the previous verse; and as the LXX has Ἰεβαθά (B) or Βαιθσά (A), and the parallel passage in 1 Ch 6[70] has Bileam (בִּלְעָם), it is possibly an error of the transcribers. *Oxf. Heb. Lex.* would read in Jos 21[25] בִּלְעָם, and identify this with the place referred to in 1 Ch 6[70] (so also Bennett in *SBOT* on Jos *ad loc.*). See further IBLEAM. C. WARREN.

GAULANITIS (Γαυλανῖτις).—The name of a district east of the Sea of Galilee, and frequently mentioned by Josephus, together with Trachonitis, Auranitis, and Batanæa. It is from *Gaulôn*, Γαυλών, which is the Gr. form of the Heb. word Golan, גּוֹלָן, of which the modern Arab. representative is *Jaulân*. Could we locate with certainty Golan, which was the northernmost of the three cities of refuge east of the Jordan, we should have the central or chief city of the district in question, and thus be able, no doubt, to determine its geographical limits more definitely.

After the death of Herod the Great, Gaulanitis fell to his son Philip, and during his long reign was a portion of his dominions (*Ant.* XVIII. iv. 6). It was divided into two parts, Upper and Lower, and belonged to Agrippa II., from whom it revolted to the Romans in A.D. 66–70 (Josephus, *Life*, 37;

Wars, III. iii. 5, IV. i. 1). The province could not have been of great extent; it was free from hills, having some portions rocky and others exceedingly fertile. It is a part of the great east-Jordan plateau, and rises some 2000 ft. above the sea-level. Judging from existing ruins, this region was once densely populated. See on the whole subject Schumacher, *The Jaulân*. S. MERRILL.

GAULS (Γαλάται) are mentioned in 1 Mac 8² as conquered by the Romans, and in 2 Mac 8²⁰ as defeated in Babylonia by the Jews (RVm in the second passage and AV in both read 'Galatians'). The historical allusions are doubtful, although probably the former passage refers to the victories of Manlius in Asia Minor (B.C. 189). See further under GALATIA, p. 89ᵃ.

GAZA (עזּה Gn 10¹⁹, Dt 2²³, Arab. *Ghŭzzeh*).— One of the five chief cities of Philistia, situated on a slight eminence amidst trees and gardens at a distance of 2 miles from the shore of the Mediterranean, and on the high road from Egypt to Jaffa and the East (lat. 31–30° N.; long. 34–33° E.). Between the present town and the coast rises a high range of sandhills,[*] which protects the town from the westerly winds of winter, but is a constant source of danger and loss, as the sands, impelled by the winds from the sea, are ever advancing inland; and it is supposed, with much probability, that the city of the time of the judges (*c.* B.C. 1100) is buried beneath these immense mounds. To the east of the town rises a ridge, 270 feet high, called el-Muntâr, or 'the watch-tower,' supposed to be the mount, 'in the direction of Hebron,' to which Samson carried the gates of the city (Jg 16³); and on the coast are some traces of ruins, Tell et-Tîneh and el-Mineh, which are considered to mark the position of the former harbour. There is, however, no natural harbour, or safe anchorage, at any part of this coast for many miles from Gaza, and the place could never have been a seaport town. One of the most interesting objects about Gaza is the forest of ancient olive trees extending for 3 miles along the Jaffa road, somewhat resembling a forest of ancient oaks in the gnarled and wrinkled character of their bark, and the girth of their corrugated trunks.[†] The country around is rich and well cultivated, or else laid out in pasturage for sheep, goats, and herds of cattle; and the Arabs from the neighbouring desert assemble here in the market-place to buy and sell commodities. They belong to the Azazimeh and Terabîn tribes inhabiting the districts to the N. and S. of the Wady es-Seba (here called the Wady Ghŭzzeh), and stretching southwards into the sterile region of the Badiet et-Tih.

History.—Gaza is one of the most ancient cities named in the Bible. We find it mentioned, along with the cities of the plain, as lying along the border of the Canaanites (Gn 10¹⁹,[‡] and it was captured, but not retained, by the tribe of Judah on the invasion of Pal. by the Israelites (Jg 1¹⁸. ¹⁹). The special interest of its early history is connected with the exploits of Samson during the wars between Israel and the Philistines (Jg 13–16), at which time G. seems to have risen to a position of great importance, and to have become the capital of the Philistine confederacy; a position which it retained down to the time of Alexander the Great.

In the year B.C. 710, when joined in alliance with Sabako king of Egypt, and ruled by Hanno, it was attacked by Sargon and the army of Assyria. A great battle was fought at Raphia (the modern Rafeh), about half-way between Gaza and the Wady el-'Arîsh ('River of Egypt'), in which the allies were defeated by Sargon. Hanno was deprived of his crown, and carried captive to Assyria by the conqueror. This was the first trial of strength between the two great powers of Egypt and Assyria.[*] Still later (B.C. 332) G. was strong enough to resist for a period of two months a siege by Alexander the Great, after the battle of Issus, but was ultimately taken by storm. The city at this time is described as 20 stadia distant from the sea, and very difficult of access owing to the height of the sandhills. The city itself was wide, and placed on a lofty hill and strongly fortified by a wall.[†]

But the ultimate decay of G. foretold by the prophets (Jer 47, Am 1⁶, Zeph 2⁴, Zec 9⁵) was hastening towards fulfilment. G. suffered greatly (1 Mac 11⁶¹. ⁶² 13⁴³) in the wars between Ptolemy IX. and Alexander Jannæus, a prince of the Maccabæan line (B.C. 105–78). By Augustus it was assigned to the kingdom of Herod along with the neighbouring maritime cities. This brings us to the first event recorded in NT history in which the name of G. comes prominently into view, namely, the conversion and baptism of the Ethiopian eunuch, which took place near the city (Ac 8²⁶). The precise spot where he was baptized by Philip cannot be determined with certainty; but it may be inferred to have been at the crossing of either the brook Wady el-Hessy or Wady el-Ḥalib by the road from Jaffa to Gaza.‡ Henceforth G. almost disappears from the page of history, till in A.D. 634 it was captured by the generals of the first calif, Abu Bekr. During the crusades it was garrisoned by the Knights Templars, but finally fell into the hands of Saladin after the disastrous battle of Hattin (A.D. 1170). Since then it has remained a Mohammedan city. (For a full account of Gaza and its history see G. A. Smith, *HGHL* 181 ff., and cf. Gautier, *Souvenirs de Terre-Sainte*, 116 ff.; Clermont-Ganneau, *Arch. Researches in Pal.* (1896), p. 279 ff.). E. HULL.

GAZARA (Γαζάρα, Γάζαρα, Γαζηρά, Γάσηρα).—An important stronghold often mentioned during the Maccabæan struggle, 1 Mac 4¹⁵ 7⁴⁵ 9⁵² 13⁵³ (in this last all MSS have Γάζαν, *Gaza*, but the context and the parallel passage in Jos. *Ant.* XIII. vi. 7 show that the correct reading is Γαζάραν, see RVm) 13⁵³ 14⁷. ³⁴ 15²⁸ 16¹, 2 Mac 10³². In *Ant.* XII. vii. 4, XIV. v. 4, *Wars*, I. viii. 5, it is called *Gadara*. There seems to be no doubt that it is the OT GEZER (which see). See further, Schürer, *HJP* I. i. 261 f., 372, and G. A. Smith, *HGHL* 215 ff. J. A. SELBIE.

GAZELLE (צְבִי *zĕbhî*, δορκάς).—AV renders *zĕbhî* in the poetical books, and in 2 S 2¹⁸ 1 Ch 12⁸ by *roe*. RV gives the same rendering, but adds in the marg. in all but three places (2 S 2¹⁸, Ca 3⁵ 7³) *gazelle*. In the lists of animals used as food AV renders *zĕbhî* by *roebuck*, while RV renders it inconsistently with itself in the other passages, *gazelle*. The latter is undoubtedly the correct rendering for all, instead of *roe* and *roebuck*. The Arabic word *zabî*, the exact counterpart of *zĕbhî*, is one of the names of the gazelle in that tongue;

---

[*] Survey Map of Palestine.
[†] One of these trees was found to be 19 feet in circumference at 4 feet from the ground when measured by the present writer in 1884; and many of them may be a thousand years of age and upwards.
[‡] It does not necessarily follow that Gaza was in existence at that time, but only in the time of the writer of the Book of Genesis.

[*] Rawlinson, *Anc. Mon.* vol. ii. 144.
[†] Arrian, ii. 26, where an account of the siege is given. During its progress Alexander received a wound in the shoulder.
[‡] The Hessy is crossed by the road at a distance of 12 miles from Gaza, the Ḥalib at 5 miles. Either of these spots fits in with the narrative. The ruins of el-Mineh on the seacoast mark the site of a town and episcopal see of the 5th cent called 'Constantia' or 'Limena Gazæ.'

the other is *ghazál*, from which our word *gazelle* is derived. It was expressly permitted as food (Dt 12¹⁵ 14⁵ 15²²). It was daily served on Solomon's table (1 K 4²³). Asahel and the Gadites were as fleet as *zĕbhîs* (2 S 2¹⁸, 1 Ch 12⁸). The *zĕbhî* was much hunted (Pr 6⁵, Is 13¹⁴). It is frequently alluded to in Ca (2⁷·⁹·¹⁷ 3⁵ 4⁵ 7³ 8¹⁴). The fem. form צְבִיָה *zĕbhiyyâh* became (by law of interchange) Aram. *ṭabitha*, which was translated δορκάς = *gazelle* (cf. Ac 9³⁶).

The gazelle, *Gazella Dorcas*, L., is one of the most beautiful of the antelopes. It is abundant throughout the country, but especially in the remoter mountain districts and in the deserts. It is often met with in herds, which sometimes number as many as a hundred. The general colour is fawn, with white and dark stripes down the face, and a white mark on the hind quarters. A local variety, called the *ariel gazelle*, *Gazella Arabica*, Ehr., is found in Gilead. It is of a darker fawn colour than the type.

Gazelles are hunted by lying in wait for them at the springs, or by chasing them with greyhounds and falcons. They are very fleet, however, and often 'deliver themselves from the hand of the hunter' (Pr 6⁵). They are often taken in large numbers by driving them into an enclosure, with a pitfall at either side. As many as fifty may thus be taken at one time. When taken young the gazelle is easily tamed, and becomes very affectionate.   G. E. POST.

GAZERA (A Γαζηρά, B Καζηρά), 1 Es 5³¹.—His sons were among the 'temple servants.' In Ezr 2⁴⁸ GAZZAM.

GAZEZ (גָּזֵז, Wellh., *de gent. et fam. Jud.* 26, would write גָּזֵז).—1. A son of Ephah, Caleb's concubine, 1 Ch 2⁴⁶. 2. In same verse a second G. is mentioned as a son of Haram, who was another of Ephah's sons. Smith's *DB* ² incorrectly states that this second G. is omitted in B. The latter MS reads both times Γεζούε; Luc. has in second instance Γαζάς.

GAZINGSTOCK.—Men are no longer punished by being exposed to public gaze, whether in the stocks or otherwise, and 'gazing-stock' has gone out of use. It is one of several compounds of 'stock' which have become obsolete. We find 'mocking stock' in 2 Mac 7⁷; and Tindale uses 'gestyngestocke' in Dt 28³⁷ for EV 'byword.' The only compound still in use is 'laughing-stock.'

Gazingstock (1611 'gazing stocke') occurs Nah 3⁶ 'I . . . will set thee as a gazingstock'; Heb. רֹאִי [in pause], lit. 'as a sight' (from רָאָה 'to look upon'; the word is found also in Gn 16¹³ אֵל רֳאִי, AV 'Thou God seest me,' RV 'Thou art a God that seeth,' RVm 'God of seeing'—which is probably nearest the mark, *rôî* being a subst. here); in 1 S 16¹² of David (EV 'goodly to look to'); and in Job 33²¹ (רְאִי, of the wasting away of Job's flesh, EV 'that it cannot be seen'). For the *thought* of Nah 3⁶ Davidson refers to Ezk 28¹⁷·¹⁸, Mt 1¹⁹, 1 Co 4⁹; to which may be added the other example of 'gazingstock,' He 10³³ (cf. also Moab. Stone, l. 12, 'a g. to Chemosh and to Moab'). Here the ptcp. θεατριζόμενοι is tr⁴ in AV 'whilst ye were made a gazingstock,' in RV 'being made a g.,' a tr. which comes from the Bishops' Bible; Wyc. and Rhem. having 'spectacle,' after Vulg. *spectaculum facti*. This is the only occurrence of the Gr. verb, but θέατρον γίνομαι is found in 1 Co 4⁹, already referred to, in a precisely similar meaning, EV 'We are made a spectacle unto the world,' which is Wyclif's and the Rhem. tr., again after Vulg. *spectaculum facti*. Tindale's word here is 'gasyngestocke,' and he is followed by the other ver-

sions. Shaks. uses 'gaze' for 'gazing-stock' in *Macbeth*, v. viii. 24—

> 'Then yield thee, coward,
> And live to be the show and gaze o' the time;
> We'll have thee, as our rarer monsters are,
> Painted upon a pole, and underwrit,
> "Here may you see the tyrant."'
>   J. HASTINGS.

GAZITES ([הַ]עַזָּתִי).—The inhabitants of GAZA (wh. see), Jos 13³ (AV Gazathites), Jg 16².

GAZZAM (גַּזָּם).—A family of Nethinim who returned with Zerub. (Ezr 2⁴⁸, Neh 7⁵¹), called in 1 Es 5³¹ Gazera. See GENEALOGY.

GEBA.—1. (גֶּבַע, in pause גָּבַע = *Gaba*, a 'hill') A city of Benjamin—one of those assigned under Joshua to the Levites (Jos 21¹⁷, 1 Ch 6⁶⁰). It was situated on the N.E. border of Benjamin (Jos 18²⁴). It is abundantly clear from the history of the two kingdoms that Geba is to be identified with the modern *Jeba*. The latter lies some 7 miles to the N. of Jerusalem, the road to which joins the main road between Bethel and Jerusalem, just N. of *Tell el-Fûl* (Gibeah). It is situated on the S. side of the steep defile of the *Wady Suweinît*, facing Michmash (*Mŭkhmās*) on the other side (1 S 14⁵ 'The one crag rose up on the north in front of Michmash, and the other on the south in front of Geba'). It was from this spot that Jonathan (1 S 14¹ᶠ·), accompanied only by his armour-bearer, started to descend the precipitous cliffs of the pass, and, in so doing, purposely revealed himself to the garrison of the Philistines on the opposite height. The words of the latter merely served to confirm the two warriors in their resolve, while the very audacity of their undertaking ensured its success. Climbing up on their hands and feet (v.¹³), they fell upon the astonished Philistines with undiminished vigour, and, by their daring, initiated a panic, which quickly spread throughout the Philistine forces, and caused the complete discomfiture of the latter at the hands of Saul. Saul, with but a scanty remnant of his forces, would seem to have been encamped at Gibeah (13¹⁶ Geba must be a mistake for Gibeah; cf v.¹⁵), some 3 miles to the S., so that Jonathan could start on his daring errand without awakening the suspicions of his countrymen as to the object of his expedition. In the reign of Asa king of Judah, this important position on the frontier was fortified with 'the stones of Ramah (*er-Râm*) and the timber thereof, wherewith Baasha (king of Israel) had builded' (1 K 15²² = 2 Ch 16⁶). From this period onwards G. appears to have marked the N. limit of the kingdom of Judah. Hence we find the old formula, 'from Dan to Beersheba,' which denoted the extent of the united kingdom, altered into 'from Geba to Beersheba' (2 K 23⁸, cf. Zec 14¹⁰). The position of Geba, its strategic importance, and its distinction from the similar-sounding Gibeah (for the latter point cf. Jos 18²⁴·²⁸), are once more clearly shown in Isaiah's dramatic picture of the march of Sennacherib's army against Jerusalem from the N. (Is 10²⁸⁻³², see GIBEAH, 2 (4)); while in the times of Ezra and Nehemiah it was still a well-known spot (Neh 11³¹ 12²⁹; cf. 7³⁰, Ezr 2²⁶, 1 Ch 8⁶).

In the following passages the Hebrew text wrongly gives Geba for Gibeah: Jg 20¹⁰·³³, 1 S 13³·¹⁶; for further details see GIBEAH, 2. In Jg 20³¹ (see above) Geba is to be restored in place of Gibeah, while in 2 S 5²⁵ it seems probable that we should restore Gibeon for Geba, in accordance with the parallel passage 1 Ch 14¹⁶.

2. (Γαιβαί) About 3 miles N. of Samaria. It was the southernmost of the three fortresses which commanded the road leading up from Esdraelon, through the pass of En-gannim (*Jenin*),

into Samaria. It was between this fort and Scythopolis that Holofernes pitched his camp preparatory to attacking Judæa (Jth 3[10]).

J. F. STENNING.

GEBAL.—**1.** גְּבָל, Γαιβάλ or Γεβάλ, Ps 83[8] [Eng. [7]]. A mountainous district south of the Dead Sea, which still bears the name of *Jebâl* (Robinson, *BR* ii. 154). Josephus regards Γοβολῖτις as a part of Idumæa (*Ant.* II. i. 2, cf. IX. ix. 1), and Jerome explains Seir by *Gebalena* (Euseb. *Onomast.* 'Seir'). In Ps 83[8] Gebal is named, together with Ammon, Amalek, and other nations, as forming a confederacy against Israel. The date and occasion of the psalm are unknown, but many commentators connect it with the events described in 1 Mac 5.

2. גְּבָל, (οἱ πρεσβύτεροι) Βυβλίων, Ezk 27[9]. GEBALITES הַגִּבְלִים, AV Giblites, but in 1 K 'the stonesquarers,' Jos 13[5], 1 K 5[18]. A Phœnician city, situated on rising ground near the sea, at the foot of Lebanon, and about 20 miles N. of Beirût. The name is found frequently in Phœnician (*CIS* 1) and Assyrian inscriptions in the forms *Gubal* or *Gubli* (cf. Schrader, *COT* i. 174 and Gloss.), and also on the Tel el-Amarna tablets; while to the Greeks the town was well known as Byblus (Βύβλος or Βίβλος, cf. Strabo, xvi. p. 755). The modern name is *Jebeil.* The city was celebrated for the worship of Adonis and Astarte, while its maritime importance is attested by Ezekiel, who speaks of the 'elders and wise men of Gebal' as being the carpenters or 'calkers' of the ships of Tyre (27[9]). According to Jos 13[5] the land of the GEBALITES (AV Giblites) was included within the ideal boundaries of Israel; but it was never occupied by the Israelites, and it seems doubtful whether it could in any sense have been regarded as belonging to the Promised Land. Moreover, the passage is syntactically incorrect (וְהָאָרֶץ הַגִּבְלִי), and the widely different reading of LXX points to an early corruption of the text. It is better to read 'as far as the border of the Gebalites,' עַד גְּבוּל הַגִּבְלִי, omitting the preceding words הָאָרֶץ וְהָאָרֶץ, and to suppose that the territory of Gebal extended inland in a southeasterly direction (see Dillm. *ad loc.*). The Gebalites are mentioned again in 1 K 5[18] [Heb. [32]], where they are said to have fashioned the stones for the building of the temple along with the builders of Solomon and the builders of Hiram. But here, too, the text is probably faulty. Thenius reads, 'and Solomon's builders . . . fashioned them (the stones), and *made a border for them*' (וַיַּגְבִּלוּם for וְהַגִּבְלִים, LXX ἔβαλον). H. A. WHITE.

GEBER (גֶּבֶר 'man' *or* 'mighty man,' Γαβέρ A, om. B Luc. 1 K 4[19]).—One of Solomon's twelve commissariat officers, whose district lay to the E. of Jordan, and perhaps S. of that of the officer mentioned v.[13]. At the end of v.[19] comes a sentence referred by AV and RV to this Geber, and rendered 'and *he was* the only officer which was in the land.' This is usually thought to mean that in this large district more than one officer might have been expected, but that this was not the case, probably because the country was rugged and thinly populated. Such a rendering, however, together with the interpretation put upon it, can by no means be extracted from the Hebrew, which is certainly corrupt. Klostermann by a clever emendation obtains the statement 'and one officer was over all the officers who were in the land,' the reference being, not to Geber, but to Azariah son of Nathan, mentioned v.[5] as 'over the officers.' Cf. the interpretation of Jos. (*Ant.* VIII. ii. 3) ἐπὶ δὲ τούτων εἰς πάλιν ἄρχων ἀποδέδεικτο.

C. F. BURNEY.

GEBIM (הַגֵּבִים 'the trenches').—A place N. of Jerusalem, the inhabitants of which are graphically pictured by the prophet as saving their goods by flight upon the approach of the Assyrian army, Is 10[31] only. In Eusebius (*Onomast. s.* 'Gebin') a Geba 5 Roman miles from Gophna, on the way to Neapolis (Shechem), is noticed. This is the modern *Jebîa*, which, being near the great northern road, is a possible site for Gebim. See *SWP* vol. ii. sh. xiv.

C. R. CONDER.

GECKO (אֲנָקָה 'ănâḳâh, μυγαλή, mygale).—The AV (Lv 11[30]) renders 'ănâḳâh, ferret. This animal, however, is not found in the Holy Land, and is not at all likely to be the one intended here. The LXX μυγαλή signifies the *shrew mouse*, of which several kinds are met with in the Holy Land : (1) *Sorex araneus*, De Selys, Arab. *fâr el-khalâ*, in the hilly districts of N. Galilee ; (2) *S. tetragonurus*, Desm., in Lebanon ; (3) *S. pygmæus*, De Selys, about one-third as large as the first ; (4) *S. crassicaudus*, Licht., a silver-grey species, in the S. deserts ; (5) *S. fodiens*, Schreb., the *water shrew*, by streams in Cœlesyria and Antilebanon. Notwithstanding the above t[rn] of the LXX and the notion of the Rabbins that the *hedgehog* was the animal intended, the position of 'ănâḳâh among the *lizards* has inclined scholars to regard it as one of them. The RV has adopted *gecko* (so Pesh.). This rendering, however, must be regarded as purely conjectural. There are several of the *Geckonidæ* in the Holy Land. The commonest of all is the common gecko, *Ptyodactylus Hasselquistii*, Schneid., which is found everywhere among rocks and in ruins and about houses. It has a fan-shaped foot (whence its generic name), with suckers on the sides of the toes, so that it can walk on smooth walls, and even run inverted like a fly. It moves noiselessly. But it can emit a rapid clucking sound, by vibrating the tongue against the palate. The name *gecko* is an attempted imitation of this sound. There is a popular superstition in the country, that a *gecko*, crawling over the body, will produce leprous sores; hence its name *abu bureis*, 'father of leprosy.' This opinion, which is probably ancient, would add to the lacertine form of the animal a reason for considering it unclean. It has a flattish-triangular head, covered with scales, a wide mouth, large eyes and small teeth, and a broad tail, nearly as long as the body. The general colour is black, but the whole body is spotted with rows of rounded warts or prominences. It is the most repulsive-looking of the lizards in Palestine.

G. E. POST.

GEDALIAH (גְּדַלְיָה, גְּדַלְיָהוּ ' J'' is great').—**1.** Son of Ahikam, who had protected Jeremiah from the anti-Chaldæan party (Jer 26[24]), and probably grandson of Shaphan, the pious scribe (2 K 22). G. naturally shared the views of Jeremiah. This commended him to Nebuchadnezzar, who made him governor over 'the poor of the people that were left in the land.' His two months' rule and treacherous murder are detailed in Jer 40, 41 (2 K 25[22-25]). At Mizpah in Benjamin the scattered elements of the national life gathered round G. First came Jeremiah, then the remnant of the army, and finally the Jews that had been dispersed in the adjacent countries. At G.'s bidding they began to settle in the deserted towns, and to gather in the now ownerless crops. Meanwhile Baalis, king of the Ammonites, resolved, by the assassination of G., to destroy 'the remnant of Judah' (Jer 40[15]). He found a tool in Ishmael 'of the seed royal,' formerly a high officer under Zedekiah, but now a bandit in the service of Ammon (41[10]). Disbelieving the warnings which he received, G. entertained Ishmael and ten followers at Mizpah. G. and the small garrison of Jews and Chaldæans were slain, probably while at table (Jos. *Ant.* X. ix. 4), and their bodies cast promiscuously (41⁹) into the ancient cistern of Asa. The plot of Baalis succeeded but too well; for the Jewish captains, fearing lest they might be held responsible for the audacious murder of the great king's representative (41². ¹⁸), fled into Egypt, carrying with them Jeremiah and 'all the remnant of Judah.' 'It seemed to be the revocation of the advantages of the Exodus' (Stanley). The anniversary of G.'s murder—the third day of the seventh month, Tisri (Zec 7⁵ 8¹⁹)—has been ever since observed as one of the four Jewish fasts. Grätz (see Cheyne on Jer 41¹) argues that G.'s government lasted five years, but his reasons do not seem conclusive.

2. 1 Ch 25³·⁹ eldest 'son' of Jeduthun, leader of the second course of temple musicians. **3.** Ezr 10¹⁸ (1 Es 9¹⁹ Joadanus), a priest 'of the sons of Jeshua,' who 'had married a strange woman.' **4.** Jer 38¹ son of Pashhur (Jer 20¹⁻⁶), a prince in the reign of Zedekiah. **5.** Zeph 1¹ grandfather of the prophet Zephaniah.   N. J. D. WHITE.

GEDDUR (A Γεδδούρ, B Κεδδούρ), 1 Es 5³⁰.—In Ezr 2⁴⁷ Neh 7⁴⁹ GAHAR. נחר was perhaps read גדור.

GEDER (גֶּדֶר). — An unidentified Canaanitish town, whose king was amongst those conquered by Joshua, Jos 12¹³ (only). While LXX A has Γαδέρ, B has 'Ασεί. It is very probably identical with **Beth-gader** of 1 Ch 2⁵¹. In 1 Ch 27²⁸ Baal-hanan, who had charge of David's olives and sycomores, is called the **Gederite** (הַגְּדֵרִי), which may be a gentilic name derived from Geder, although some prefer to derive it from GEDERAH (wh. see).

GEDERAH. — AV of 1 Ch 4²³ᵇ reads, 'Those that dwelt among plants (RVm plantations) and hedges,' but RV gives 'the inhabitants of Netaim and Gederah,' and this is probably the correct trⁿ of יֹשְׁבֵי נְטָעִים וּגְדֵרָה. In that case the Gederah referred to would probably be the city of that name located by Jos 15³⁶ in the Shephelah, the modern *Jedireh* (SWP vol. iii. sh. xx.) and the Gedour of Eusebius (Onomast. p. 254, Lagarde, 2nd ed.). The gentilic name **Gederathite** (הַגְּדֵרָתִי) occurs in 1 Ch 12⁴.   J. A. SELBIE.

GEDEROTH (גְּדֵרוֹת, in 2 Ch 28¹⁷ הַגְּ).—A town of Judah in the Shephelah, Jos 15⁴¹, 2 Ch 28¹⁸, noticed with Beth-dagon, Makkedah, and Naamah. It appears to be the modern *Katrah* near Yebna, where a Jewish colony is now established. Possibly it is also the **Kidron** of 1 Mac 15³⁹·⁴¹ 16⁹. See SWP vol. iii. sh. xvi.   C. R. CONDER.

GEDEROTHAIM (גְּדֵרֹתַיִם) occurs in Jos 15³⁶ as one of the fourteen cities of Judah that lay in the Shephelah. There are, however, fourteen cities without it, and it is probable that the name has arisen by dittography from the preceding Gederah (Nöldeke, Krit. d. AT, 101). The names of the cities in the LXX show several divergences from the MT; in v.³⁶ Adithaim is omitted, and after Γαδηρά we read καὶ αἱ ἐπαύλεις αὐτῆς, which is evidently intended to be the trⁿ of גְּדֵרֹתַיִם ('sheep-folds'). Both the Oxf. Heb. Lex. and Siegfried-Stade are surely in error in stating that the name is omitted in the LXX. The subterfuge of the AVm 'Gederah or Gederothaim' is, of course, not permissible.   J. A. SELBIE.

GEDOR (גְּדוֹר).—**1.** A town of Judah, named along with Halhul and Beth-zur, Jos 15⁵⁸; cf. 1 Ch 4⁴·¹⁸ 12⁷ (in this last גְּדוֹר, Baer and Kittel גְּדוּר). It is generally identified with the modern *Jedûr* (Robinson, BRP² ii. 13) north of Beit Sur. **2.** The district from which the Simeonites are said

to have expelled the Hamite settlers, 1 Ch 4³⁹ᶠᶠ. The LXX, however, reads Γέραρα (Gerar), and Gerar 'suits admirably as to direction' (Kittel in SBOT). This reading is adopted also by Ewald (Gesch. Isr. i. 344), Bertheau (Chron. 51), Hitzig (on Mic 1¹⁵), Graf (Der Stamm Simeon, 25), Oxf. Heb. Lex., Siegfried-Stade, etc.

GEDOR (גְּדוֹר, גְּדֹר 'wall').—**1.** A Benjamite, an ancestor of king Saul, 1 Ch 8³¹ 9³⁷. **2. 3.** The eponym of two Judahite families, 1 Ch 4⁴·¹⁸. See GENEALOGY.

GE-HARASHIM (גֵּיא חֲרָשִׁים), 'valley of craftsmen,' 1 Ch 4¹⁴, Neh 11³⁵. In the latter passage it occurs with Lod and Ono. The name may survive at the ruin *Hirsha*, E. of Lydda. See SWP vol. ii. sh. xiv.

GEHAZI (גֵּחֲזִי, except in 2 K 5²⁵ 8⁴·⁵, where it is גֵּיחֲזִי, 'valley of vision'; LXX Γιεζεί, Vulg. Giezi) is four times called the *servant* (נַעַר, lit. 'boy') of Elisha, a term which indicates a lower kind of service than Elisha's 'ministry' to Elijah. He may, however, be the person called in 2 K 4⁴³ Elisha's *minister* (מְשָׁרֵת), the word which is applied to Elisha himself in 1 K 19²¹. Gehazi is one of those Bible characters—Achan, Judas, Ananias, Demas, etc.—whose crimes and apostasy point the moral that the love of money is a root of all sorts of evil. What is known of him is told in three narratives.

1. In the story of the lady of Shunem (2 K 4⁸⁻³⁷) he appears as a man of shrewd practical sense, but incapable of understanding the impulses of deep feeling. His moral quality is scarcely defined. Elisha having failed to persuade his benefactress to ask any favour, turns in perplexity to consult his servant (4¹⁴). G. has penetrated the good lady's thoughts, and tells the prophet of her secret longing for a son. Elisha perceives that his servant's insight has surpassed his own, and, recalling the Shunammite, promises that the desire of her heart will be granted. In the sequel to the story, when the lady, bereft of this child of promise, comes in haste to the retreat at Carmel and casts herself at the prophet's feet in a passion of grief, G.'s commonplace mind is shocked at this liberty taken by a woman. He would rudely thrust her away; but the prophet, pitying her unknown sorrow, reproves his servant for adding to the bitterness of her soul. When she has told the cause of her grief, G. is directed to hasten to Shunem, saluting no man by the way (cf. Lk 10⁴), and lay the prophet's staff on the face of the child.

2. In the story of Naaman G. appears as a finished example of covetousness (2 K 5²⁰⁻²⁷). His baseness is in startling contrast to the high-mindedness of his master. In vain does Naaman press his treasure on the acceptance of Elisha; he has to depart with it intact (5¹⁶). To the sordid mind of G. this situation of affairs presents a temptation which he cannot resist. His passion for gain, probably long nourished in secret, suddenly overmasters him. The voice of reason and religion is stifled, and blasphemy, lying, sacrilege, and fraud come to serve his master passion. Elisha's refusal to take the stranger's gold seems to him madness. 'As J" liveth,' he will secure a portion of it for himself—thus lightly does he use the same oath with which Elisha solemnly refused the filthy lucre (5¹⁶⁻²⁰). Running to overtake the Syrian cavalcade, G. invents a clever story of two poor young sons of the prophets having just come to Samaria, whose wants Elisha has bethought himself of supplying out of the treasure which he had refused for himself. G. begs for them a talent of silver (£400!) and two changes of raiment.

Plausible though the story was, it could hardly fail to lower the prophet in the estimation of the Syrians. They would reflect that he was like other men, after all. But G.'s request is at once granted, and two of Naaman's servants return to Samaria laden with the changes of raiment and twice as much silver as had been asked. When they come to the hill (לֶפֶל, LXX εἰς τὸ σκοτεινόν, *to the secret place*, from a reading לָפֵל; Vulg. *jam vesperi*) G. dismisses the men and conceals his prize. He then boldly presents himself before his master, and in answer to a question assures him with an air of innocence that he has been nowhere. But the prophet has at last discovered his servant's true character, and with searching interrogations lays bare his guilt, and reads the very thoughts and intents of his heart. G. is utterly confounded. Pale and speechless he hears the curse of Naaman's leprosy entailed, with awful appropriateness, on himself and his family for ever, and goes from Elisha's presence a leper, white as snow.

3. In the third narrative (2 K 8¹⁻⁶) G. appears engaged in conversation with king Jehoram, who has called him to recite the story of Elisha's wonderful deeds. G. is telling of the restoration of the Shunammite's son to life, when the lady herself comes on the scene to petition the king to reinstate her in the house and land which she had lost in a recent famine. The difficulty of imagining the king talking to a leper and G. glorifying Elisha has led some critics to suppose that this narrative is misplaced, and should appear before 2 K 5. But it reads quite naturally as it stands. Conversation with lepers was not forbidden. The story certainly shows G. in a more favourable light than the previous narrative. The notice taken of him by the king, and the truthfulness and respect with which he recounts the deeds of his former master, may be charitably taken to indicate that affliction had at last made him a wiser and better man.

Elisha's choice of this covetous man to be his follower presents a difficulty of the same kind, though not so great, as Christ's choice of a covetous disciple. It appears that the prophet's insight, though often marvellous, was sometimes quite ordinary (2 K 4¹⁴). He confesses his inability to read the mind of the Shunammite: ' J" hath hid it from me, and hath not told me' (4²⁷). In the same way he was evidently mistaken with regard to the character of his servant. He probably chose him for his ready wit and practical sense; and if he detected in him a love of money, he may have hoped that the force of example would wean him from it. But to minds steeped in avarice the means of grace are often a savour of death rather than of life, and a holy example may not change the heart. 'Happy was it for Gehazi,' says Bishop Hall, 'if, while his skin was snow-white with leprosy, his humbled soul was washed white as snow with the water of true repentance.'

J. STRACHAN.

GEHENNA. — The word Gehenna, Γέεννα in Tischendorf and WH (or Γέεννα according to other scholars, on the ground of its derivation from the Aram. גֵּיהִנָּם), is derived ultimately from the Hebrew expression גֵּי הִנֹּם = 'valley of Hinnom,' Jos 15⁸ 18¹⁶, Neh 11³⁰, which is an abbreviated form of גֵּי־בֶן־הִנֹּם = 'valley of the son of Hinnom,' Jos 15⁸ 18¹⁶, 2 Ch 28³ 33⁶, Jer 7³¹. ³² 19². ⁶, or in the *Kethib* of 2 K 23¹⁰ בְּנֵי־הִנֹּם. But this place became so notorious through its evil associations that it was simply called 'the valley' κατ' ἐξοχήν, Jer 2²³ 31⁴⁰, and the gate of Jerusalem leading to it 'the valley-gate,' 2 Ch 26⁹, Neh 2¹³. ¹⁵ 3¹³. This valley lay to the S. and S.W. of Jerusalem (Robinson, *BRP* ii. 273, 274). The derivation of הִנֹּם is quite uncertain. In the LXX this name appears variously as φάραγξ

Ὀνόμ (B : Ἐννόμ A), Jos 15⁸; (B) νάπη Σοννάμ (B : υἱοῦ Ἐννόμ A), Jos 18¹⁶; Γαίεννα (B : Γαὶ Ὀννόμ A), Jos 18¹⁶; Γαιβενθόμ (B : Γηβεεννόμ A), 2 Ch 28³; γὲ βανὲ Ἐννόμ (B : γη Βεεννομ A), 2 Ch 33⁶. Elsewhere we find generally φάραγξ (υἱοῦ) Ἐννόμ.

This term is used in a variety of meanings in the course of Israelitish and Jewish history. These we shall consider separately according as they appear in OT, Apocalyptic literature, the NT, or in later Judaism.

I. ITS USE IN THE OT falls under three heads. (*a*) It is used in a merely *topographical sense*. Thus it formed the boundary between Judah and Benjamin, Jos 15⁸ 18¹⁶, and the northern limit of the district occupied by the tribe of Judah after the Captivity, Neh 11³⁰, and lay in front of the gate Harsith of Jerusalem, Jer 19². See further under HINNOM (VALLEY OF).

(*b*) It is used in a *religious significance as implying a place of idolatrous and inhuman sacrifices*. These were first offered by Ahaz and Manasseh, who made their children to 'pass through the fire' to Molech in this valley, 2 K 16³, 2 Ch 28³, and 2 K 21⁶, 2 Ch 33⁶. These sacrifices were probably made on the 'high places of Topheth, which is in the valley of the son of Hinnom,' Jer 7³¹; cf. Jer 32¹⁵. In order to put an end to these abominations, Josiah polluted it with human bones and other corruptions, 2 K 23¹⁰. ¹³. ¹⁴. But this worship of Molech was revived under Jehoiakim, Jer 11¹⁰⁻¹³, Ezk 20³⁰. In consequence of these idolatrous practices in the Valley of Hinnom, Jeremiah prophesied that one day it would be called the 'Valley of Slaughter,' and that they should 'bury in Topheth till there be no place to bury,' Jer 7³² 19¹¹. Many scholars have accepted the statement of Kimchi (*c.* 1200 A.D.) on Ps 27 : 'Gehennam fuit locus spretus, in quem abjecerunt sordes et cadavera, et fuit ibi perpetuo ignis ad comburendum sordes illas et ossa; propterea parabolice vocatur judicium impiorum Gehennam.' But this is denied by Robinson, i. 274, who writes that 'there is no evidence of any other fires than those of Molech having been kept up in this valley' (Rosenmüller, *Biblisch. Geogr.* II. i. 156, 164).

(*c*) It signifies the *place of punishment for rebellious or apostate Jews in the presence of the righteous*. Gehinnom or Gehenna is not actually mentioned with this signification in the OT, but it is it and no other place that is implied in Is 50¹¹ 'in a place of pain shall ye lie down,' and 66²⁴ with this new connotation. Both these passages are very late, and probably from the same hand—not earlier than the 3rd cent. B.C. (see Cheyne, *Introd. to the Bk. of Isaiah*, p. 380 ; Smend, *Alttestamentliche Religionsgeschichte*, p. 506). Further, the punishment of the apostate Jews in Is 66²⁴ is conceived as eternal : 'They shall look upon the carcases of the men that have transgressed against me ; for their worm shall not die, neither shall their fire be quenched, and they shall be an abhorring to all flesh.' The punishment of Gehenna is implied also in Dn 12² 'some to shame and everlasting abhorrence.' We should observe that the same word דְּרָאוֹן 'abhorrence' occurs in these two passages, and in these only, and the reference in both is to Gehenna.

II. ITS MEANING AND FURTHER DEVELOPMENT IN APOCALYPTIC LITERATURE.* In this literature

---

* There is no actual mention of the word Gehenna in biblical Apocryphal literature ; but in Jth 16¹⁷—

οὐαὶ ἔθνεσιν ἐπανιστανομένοις τῷ γένει μου.
Κύριος Παντοκράτωρ ἐκδικήσει αὐτοὺς ἐν ἡμέρᾳ κρίσεως,
δοῦναι πῦρ καὶ σκώληκας εἰς σάρκας αὐτῶν,
καὶ κλαύσονται ἐν αἰσθήσει ἕως αἰῶνος.

the reference to Gehenna is undeniable. In Sir 7¹⁷, however, the text ἐκδίκησις ἀσεβοῦς πῦρ καὶ σκώληξ is probably corrupt, being without the support of the Syriac Version and the best MSS of the Ethiopic. Sheol, moreover, has become synonymous with Gehenna in the Similitudes. Thus : 'Sheol will devour the sinners in the presence of the elect,' 56⁸, cf. 63¹⁰.

this conception underwent further development. (*a*) Thus Gehenna was conceived as *a place of corporal and spiritual punishment for apostate Jews in the presence of the righteous for ever.* (See Eth. En. 27[2. 3] 90[26. 27]). In the Similitudes of that book, *i.e.* chs. 37–70, there is a slight modification of the above idea. Thus, though the punishment is everlasting, only its initial stages will be executed in the presence of the righteous. On the expiration of these, the wicked will be swept for ever from the presence of the righteous, 48[9] 62[12. 13].

(*b*) *A place of spiritual punishment for apostate Jews in the presence of the righteous.* Heretofore Gehenna was always conceived as a place of both corporal and spiritual punishment. This new development is attested in the Eth. En. 91–104 (*c.* 134–95 B.C.). Thus in 98[3] 'their spirits will be cast into the furnace of fire.' Cf. also 103[8]. From 99[11] 103[7. 8] it is clear that Sheol and Gehenna have become equivalent terms in this writer also. See also 100[9]. The same conception is found in an Essene writing, *i.e.* Eth. En. 108[6] and in the Assumpt. Mos. 10[10]. In the latter passage Gehenna or rather 'the valley' is mentioned by name (see Charles, *Assumption of Moses*, pp. 43, 44). It is noteworthy that in all these books only a blessed immortality of the souls of the righteous is taught.

(*c*) *A place of corporal and spiritual punishment for all the wicked in the presence of the righteous.* We arrive at this stage of development in 2 Es 7[36-38] 'Et apparebit locus tormenti, et contra illum erit locus requietionis: clibanus gehennæ ostendetur, et contra eum jocunditatis paradisus. Et dicet tunc Altissimus ad excitatas gentes—— "Videte contra et in contra; hic jocunditas et requies, et ibi ignis et tormenta."'

III. ITS MEANING IN THE NT.—In the NT Gehenna is always the final place of punishment into which the wicked are cast after the last judgment. It is a place of torment both for body and soul. Thus Mt 5[29] 'It is profitable for thee that one of thy members should perish, and not thy whole body go into Gehenna.' So also in 5[30]. Some have argued that Christ has here only the living in view; but this limitation appears unwarranted. It is not till after the final judgment that the wicked are cast into Gehenna. At the resurrection, soul and body are united. Both are punished in Gehenna. Gehenna as the last punishment was conceived also as the worst. It slew both soul and body—not, indeed, in an absolute sense, but relatively. Thus Mt 10[28] 'Fear him which is able to destroy both soul and body in Gehenna.' Cf. Lk 12[5]. This final stage of retribution is carefully distinguished in Eth. En. 22[11-13]. There the souls in the third division of Sheol are raised in order to be delivered over to their worst penalty, but of the sinners in the fourth division it is said: 'Their souls will not be slain on the day of judgment, nor will they be raised from thence.' For the phrase 'slaying of the soul' in this connexion, compare also Eth. En. 108[3-6]. Gehenna is conceived as a fire, Mt 5[22] 18[9]; an unquenchable fire, Mk 9[45]; as a place where 'their worm dieth not, and the fire is not quenched,' Mk 9[48]; a 'furnace of fire,' Mt 13[42. 50]; 'the outer darkness,' Mt 8[12] 22[13] 25[30]. It is the 'lake of fire' in Rev 19[20] 20[10. 14. 15] 21[8]. Hades is finally cast into it, Rev 20[14]. In the NT Hades and Gehenna seem never to be confused together.

IV. IN LATER JUDAISM.—Here Gehenna is conceived as a *Purgatory for faithless Jews*, who were afterwards to be admitted into paradise, but still remained the place of eternal perdition for the Gentiles (cf. Weber, *Jüdische Theologie*[2], pp. 341, 342; Driver, *Sermons on OT*, 79 f., 87, 89 f., 97).

R. H. CHARLES.

GELILOTH (גְּלִילוֹת, Γαλιαώθ, A Ἀγαλλιλώθ).—One of the places mentioned in Jos 18[17] as defining the S. boundary of Benjamin. The border, it is said, after leaving the valley of the son of Hinnom, 'went out' first to En-shemesh (probably *'Ain Ḥaud*, about 2 miles E. of Jerusalem), and afterwards to G. 'in front of the ascent of Adummim,' and so passed on into the Jordan Valley. The 'ascent of Adummim' is in all probability the ascent, some 5 miles long, leading up from the plain of Jericho to *Tala'at ed-Dumm*, about 6 miles E.N.E. of Jerusalem, on the regular route between Jerusalem and Jericho. The place G. has not, however, been identified; and all that can be said about it is that it was some spot on the boundary between Benjamin and Judah, conspicuous as a landmark to a traveller climbing up this steep ascent. In Jos 15[7], where the N. boundary of Judah (in the opposite direction) is described, the place, similarly described, is called *Gilgal* (גִּלְגָּל, LXX B Τααγάδ, A Γαλγάλ). We have no means of determining which is the true reading; the idea that the Gilgal between Jericho and the Jordan can be intended is, of course, quite out of the question; the border, at the point in question, must, as is evident from the terms employed ('went up,' 15[6b. 7a]; 'went down,' 18[17b. 18b]), have been *above* the plain.

Geliloth, in the sense, as it seems, of *circuits* or *districts*, appears also (in the Heb.) as the technical name of the administrative districts of the Philistines (Jos 13[2], Joel 3 (4)[4]; cf 1 Mac 5[15])—perhaps, of those ruled by their five 'lords' (Jos 13[3]). It occurs likewise in the obscure and uncertain expression (Jos 22[10. 11]), 'districts of Jordan' (גְּלִילוֹת הַיַּרְדֵּן), which describes the locality in which the altar 'Ed' was built by the 2½ tribes.

S. R. DRIVER.

GEM.—See STONES (PRECIOUS).

GEMALLI (גְּמַלִּי 'camel-owner,' or 'my rewarder').—Father of the Danite spy, Nu 13[12] P.

GEMARA.—See TALMUD.

GEMARIAH (גְּמַרְיָהוּ, גְּמַרְיָה, 'J" hath accomplished'). —1. A son of Shaphan the scribe, from whose chamber Baruch read the prophecies of Jeremiah in the ears of all the people. He vainly sought to deter king Jehoiakim from burning the roll (Jer 36[10. 11. 12. 25]). 2. A son of Hilkiah who carried a letter from Jeremiah to the captives at Babylon (Jer 29[3]).

GENDER (a clipt form of 'engender,' which comes from Lat. *ingenerare*, through Old Fr. *engendrer*, the *d* being excrescent after *n* as in 'tender' from *tener*) is used in AV with both transitively and intransitively, both literally and figuratively. The trans. and lit. sense 'to beget' is common in Wyclif, as Mt 1[2] (1380) 'Abraham gendride, *or bigate*, Ysaac'; and Ec 6[3] (1388) 'If a man gendrith an hundrid fre sones, and lyveth many yeris, and hath many daies of age, and his soule usith not the goodis of his catel, and wantith biriyng; Y pronounce of this man that a deed borun child is betere than he.' It is from Wyc. (1388) that the AV tr. of Job 38[29] comes, 'The hoary frost of heaven, who hath gendered it?' (יֹלְדוֹ, Gen. 'ingendred'; RVm 'given it birth'). In Zec 13[3] Wyc. uses the word of mother as well as father, 'his fader and moder that gendriden hym,' and in the same verse he speaks of 'his fadir and modir, gendrers of hym'; and then in Gal 4[24] he employs the word of the mother alone = bear, bring forth children, 'gendringe in to seruage.' This has passed into AV (in Tindale's form 'which gendreth unto bondage') through all the intermediate versions (Gr. εἰς δουλείαν γεννῶσα, RV 'bearing children unto bondage).

The Gr. verb γιννάω, like the Eng. verb 'gender,' properly refers to the father, but is used of the mother in Lk 1¹³. ⁵⁷,²³²⁹, Jn 16²¹, and in this passage. The meaning of the passage is well brought out by Lightfoot, 'for these *women* are (represent) two covenants; one of them, *which was given* from Mount Sinai, bearing children unto bondage; inasmuch as she (ἥτις) is Hagar.' Add Gwynne's explanation, 'As Hagar, the bond-woman, brought forth children unto bondage,—for the children follow the condition of their mother,—so likewise did the Sinaitic covenant bring forth children unto bondage; the one is a fit representative of the other.'

This trans. verb is used metaph. in 2 Ti 2²³ 'But foolish and unlearned questions avoid, knowing that they do gender strifes' (γεννῶσι μάχας; Wyc. 'gendren chidingis,' Tind. 'gendre stryfe,' Rhem. 'ingender braules').

The intrans. examples (= 'copulate,' 'breed') are Lv 19¹⁹ and Job 21¹⁰, with which cf. Shaks. *Othello*, IV. ii. 62—

> 'Or keep it as a cistern, for foul toads
>   To knot and gender in.'

                         J. HASTINGS.

GENEALOGY.—Under this title will be considered—*A.* Biblical Genealogy in general; *B.* The Genealogical Lists of the Tribes of Israel and a few other lists of names; *C.* Lists of persons and families associated with the labours of Ezra and Nehemiah.

A. 1. *Definition.* — The word genealogy (sing. and plur.) occurs in OT as a tr. of the Heb. noun יַחַשׂ (ἅπ. λεγ. Neh 7⁵) and of the denom. verb יָחַשׂ (only Hithp. in 1 and 2 Ch, Ezr, and Neh), with the meaning of a family register or a registration by families (1 Ch 4³³ 5¹·⁷·¹⁷ etc.). In connexion with these registrations are often given lines of descent (cf. 1 Ch 1–9), and occasionally the pedigrees of individuals (1 Ch 2¹⁰⁻¹³· ³⁶⁻⁴¹ *et al.*). Tables of genealogical descent appear in OT as an expansion of the word תּוֹלְדוֹת, 'generations' (cf. Gn 5¹ 10¹ 11¹⁰ etc., also Mt 1¹ βίβλος γενέσεως Ἰησοῦ Χριστοῦ, LXX for סֵפֶר תּוֹלְדוֹת, 'The genealogy of Jesus Christ,' RVm). Genealogies appear in two forms—one giving the generations in a descending scale (Gn 5, Ru 4¹⁸⁻²³ etc.), the other in an ascending scale (1 Ch 6³³⁻⁴³, Ezr 7¹⁻⁵ etc.).

2. *The registration of families and individuals.*— Just when the Hebrews began to preserve family registers it is impossible to determine. Lists of families and of citizens for official purposes must have been made very early, in connexion, for example, with the census of David (2 S 24). Familiarity with such enrolments is implied in the reference to 'the book of J''' (Ex 32³², Ps 139¹⁶), 'the book of life' (Ps 69²⁸, cf. Is 4³, Dn 12¹), and they seem to be directly mentioned in Jer 22³⁰, Ezk 13⁹. At the time of the giving of the Deuteronomic law there must have been some way of determining whether one was of pure Isr. descent (Dt 23²⁻⁸). But in the earlier centuries of the pre-exilic period, when marriages probably were freely made with the old Can. inhabitants, and when these inhabitants were being gradually incorporated and amalgamated into Israel, a motive for carefully preserving lines of individual descent is not apparent, and we have no reason to believe that such records were generally made. An exception, which is only probable, may have occurred in the case of royalty, nobility, and perhaps the priesthood. (The laws of inheritance seem not sufficiently complicated to have required the preservation of family genealogies). After the restoration, however, when Israel had become a church, and a sharp line of separation was drawn between the Jews and the other peoples of Palestine, and union with them by marriage had become a grievous trespass (Ezr 9¹⁻⁴), the case was far different. Hence, from the time of reforms introduced by Ezra and Nehemiah (*c.* B.C. 444), the preservation of family genealogies, or records of the descent of individuals, became a matter of special importance. Already,

at that time, certain families were debarred from the office of priests because they could not produce genealogical registers (Ezr 2⁶¹⁻⁶³, Neh 7⁶³⁻⁶⁵). From then onwards care was doubtless exercised for their preservation. Their value is shown by the repeated allusion to them in 1 and 2 Ch, Ezr, and Neh. To become a priest, a prime requisite was an evidence of proper pedigree. From the statement of Josephus that his pedigree was given in the public records (*Vita*, 1; cf. *c. Ap.* i. 7), it is probable that family genealogies were thus kept from their importance in reference to inheritance, marriage, redemption of lands, and service in the temple. Many families at the time of Christ evidently had genealogical registers (Mt 1¹, Lk 2³⁶ 3²³ff., Ac 4³⁶, Ro 11¹, Ph 3⁵).

'Davididæ, or descendants of the house of David, were found among the Jews in the Persian, Grecian, and even as late as the Roman period (comp. Zunz, *Analekten*, No. 5, p. 46, note 18). But, in consequence of the exterminating wars and the Dispersion, the records of old families were lost as early as the first centuries, and even the families of the priests did not remain unpolluted (*Jerus. Kiddushin*, iv. 1)' (Zunz in Asher's *Itinerary of Benj. Tudela*, ii. p. 6). Julius Africanus (*Ep. Aristides*, v.) gives a tradition that Herod I. destroyed the genealogical lists which were kept at Jerus., to deprive Jewish families of the knowledge of their descent. This story is doubtful, though received by some. (See Sachs, *Beiträge*, Heft ii. pp. 155 ff.).

3. *Figurative and artificial genealogies.*—These appear frequently in OT. In Gn 5 an unbroken line of descent of ten generations—from Adam to Noah inclusive—furnishes a chronology for the antediluvian period; in Gn 11¹⁰⁻²⁶ a similar line from Shem to Terah inclusive furnishes the chronology of the period from the Deluge to the birth of Abraham. In Gn 10 is a table of nations, presenting the geographical and political relationships in the form of a genealogy or family tree from the three sons of Noah. From Terah, Abraham, and Isaac is traced the descent of the peoples with whom Israel recognized a close racial union, *i.e.* the Aramæans of N. Mesopotamia (Gn 22²⁰⁻²⁴), the tribes of Arabia (Gn 25¹⁻¹⁸), the Ammonites and Moabites (Gn 19³⁷ᶠ), and Edomites (Gn 36). These peoples, both as wholes and in their various subdivisions, are mentioned as descendants from individual ancestors bearing generally tribal or geographical names, as though peoples and tribes grew out of single households. The same principle is applied to Israel, who is represented as the father of twelve sons, bearing the names of the twelve tribes, from whom in like manner sprang the various clans and families of these tribes (cf. Gn 46⁸⁻²⁷, Nu 26).

This form of representation is not peculiar to OT writers. It is the usual way in which primitive peoples explain their origin and tribal relationships. The Greeks traced their descent from Hellen, who had three sons, Dorus and Aeolus, who gave their names to the Dorians and Aeolians, and Xuthus, who through his two sons, Ion and Achæus, became the forefather of the Ionians and Achæans. But especially is this the method of Sem. people, as is illustrated among Israel's kinsmen, the Arabs. According to their writers, the inhabitants of Arabia are 'patriarchal tribes formed by the subdivision of an original stock on the system of kinship through male descendants. A tribe was but a larger family; the tribal name was the name or nickname of a common ancestor. In process of time it broke up into two or more tribes, each embracing the descendants of one of the great ancestor's sons, and taking its name from him. These tribes were again divided and subdivided on the same principle.' 'Between a nation, a tribe, a sept or sub-tribe and a family, there is no difference on this theory, except in size and distance, from a common ancestor' (W. R. Smith, *Kinship and Marriage in Early Arabia*, pp. 3 f.). This likewise seems to have been the view in Israel, and is especially worked out in P. (Most of the genealogical tables and tribal and family lists in the Hex. belong to this document).

While in some instances tribes, clans, or families take their name from historic persons,—some Arabic clans are thus named (*Kinship*, p. 15; Sprenger, *Mohammed*, iii. p. cxxxvi, *Jour. Bibl. Lit.* vol. xi. 1892, p. 120),—in genealogical lists the founders of tribes, clans, and families are usually to be regarded as eponymous heroes, for countries and cities are frequently mentioned as parents (Mizraim Gn 10[13], Canaan 10[15], Gilead Jg 11[1], Hebron 1 Ch 2[43], *et al.*). Under the form of family experience are given events of tribal life (Gn 38. See G. A. Smith, *Hist. Geog.* p. 289; Stade, *Gesch.* i. pp. 157 f.; Moore on Jg 1[14-15]). Elder sons prob. represent earlier or more powerful tribes and families; marriages their coalitions, the weaker being perhaps the wife, and an inferior a concubine; untimely deaths their disappearances; different relationships of the same person political or geographical changes or different traditions (cf. Stade, *Gesch.* i. p. 30). But many genealogical stories and relationships originated evidently in folk-tales, and hence they present a mingling of fact and fancy, and the relationships of father, mother, wife, son, daughter, etc., cannot be interpreted upon any uniform theory in respect to the precise meaning of each.

Where pedigrees for generations of remote antiquity are given (Gn 5. 11[10-26], 1 Ch 2[9-12] 6[1-48] *et al.*), they probably do not rest upon authentic records, but are artificial.

'Life in the Orient is much too unsafe, and the changes much too great, for one to expect to find family records of several centuries. Moreover, in the desert [and so generally under nomadic conditions which Israel for centuries experienced] family archives are unimaginable, and it is sheer nonsense to believe that all the branches of a family tree could be preserved by memory' (Sprenger, *Mohammed*, iii. p. cxli).

This statement, made in view of Arabian genealogies, is equally applicable to those of early mankind and Israel. These, too, when they present a continuous line of descent from father to son, are the conjectures of later ages (see CHRONOLOGY OF OT). They are, however, not the fruit of a spirit of deception, but of good faith with poetic imagination in vindicating family rights and privileges, and religious institutions, or in glorifying the family and national and religious heroes. The impulse for the formation of such pedigrees is synchronous with the stress laid upon purity of descent and the actual keeping of family genealogies. The names introduced were not usually inventions, but taken from legend and story, representing often historical persons, families, and conditions.

These artificial pedigrees abound in Arabic genealogies (see Sprenger), and also occur in Jewish writings — for example, the *Seder Olam sutta*. (Zunz, *Gottesdienstliche Vorträge*, Berlin, 1892, pp. 142 ff.; Asher, *Itiner. of Benj. of Tudela*, vol. ii. pp. 6 ff.).

B. THE GENEALOGICAL LISTS OF THE TWELVE TRIBES.—These lists are found almost exclusively in Gn 46[8-24], Ex 6[14-26], Nu 26[5-62], 1 Ch 1-9. They exhibit different sources, and have suffered much in transcription, especially those in Chronicles, so that we often have little more than a confused mass of names, which defy any proper genealogical treatment. The genealogies are partially figurative and artificial, and partially genuine family records; but where the exact line is to be drawn between those due to fancy or theory and those due to records cannot always be determined. In some instances there may be a commingling of both elements. The whole history behind these genealogies is very obscure; hence the explanatory notes, when they depart from a recital of mere facts, must be received as tentative. The lists are prepared also primarily for the purpose of locating OT proper names in this Dictionary, and many names are given which probably represent no real persons or families, but have arisen from textual errors.

N.B. The tribes are indicated by Rom. numerals. The various lists under each tribe, grouped by generations, pedigrees, or other classifications given in OT, are numbered with Arabic numerals, providing a means of cross-reference. Heavy

(Clarendon) type indicates the father of the person or persons whose name or names immediately follow. Italics indicate a son of the preceding and the father of the succeeding (a continuous line of descent from father to son is indicated by a succession of names in italics). The child or children of the person named in heavy type or italics immediately preceding are given in ordinary type. Mothers' names are placed in brackets before their children. The following abbreviations are used: d. daughter, f. father or father of, m. mother, s. son of, ss. sons of.

Since these lists are found mainly in 1 Ch, the following abbreviations are used referring to its literature:

Be.=E. Bertheau in *Kgf. Handb.* 1873; Ke. =O. F. Keil in *Bible Comm.* [1872]; Ki.=R. Kittel in the *Sacred Books of the OT*, a critical edition of the Heb. Text, 1895; Kau.=E. Kautzsch in *Die Heilige Schrift d. a. T. übersetzt und herausgegeben*, 1894; Oe.=S. Oettli in *Kgf. Komm.* 1889; Sm.=R. Smend, *Die Listen der Bücher Ezra und Nehemiah*, 1881; We. =J. Wellhausen, *De Gentibus et Familiis Judæis quæ* 1 *Chr.* 2. 4. *enumerantur*, 1870; We. *Prol.*=J. Wellhausen, *Prolegomena to the History of Israel*, 1885; Zoe. =O. Zoeckler in *Lange's Commentary*, 1876. [Unfortunately, Gray's *Studies in Heb. Proper Names* and Hommel's *Anc. Heb. Tradition* both appeared too late for use in the present article].

Jacob: (m. Leah) Reuben (I.), Simeon (II.), Levi (III.), Judah (IV.), Issachar (V.), Zebulun (VI.), d. Dinah; (m. Rachel) Joseph (Manasseh and Ephraim) (VII.[ab]), Benjamin (VIII.); (m. Bilhah) Dan (IX.), Naphtali (X.); (m. Zilpah) Gad (XI.), Asher (XII.), Gn 35[22b-26], cf. 29[31]-30[24] 35[18] 46[8-25] 49[2-27], Ex 1[1-5] etc.

This genealogy is a reflection of a more or less artificial division of Israel into twelve tribes (cf. the twelve sons of Ishmael, Gn 25[13-16]). The history and the sentiment which occasioned such a motherhood, as well as the order of birth of these tribes, and the placing of a daughter among them, is only partially clear (see ISRAEL, and Stade, *Gesch.* i. 145 ff.).

I. 1. REUBEN: Hanoch, Pallu (2), Hezron, Carmi, Gn 46[9], Ex 6[14], Nu 26[5f.], 1 Ch 5[3].

2. Pallu (1): *Eliab*, Nemuel, Dathan, Abiram, Nu 26[8f.].

3. —— *Joel* (4)?, *Shemaiah, Gog, Shimei, Micah, Reaiah, Baal,* Beerah, 1 Ch 5[4ff.].

4. —— *Joel* (3)?, *Shema, Azaz, Bela,* 1 Ch 5[8].

5. —— Jeiel, Zechariah, 1 Ch 5[7].

Hanoch, Pallu, Hezron, and Carmi are names of clans (Nu 26[5]), of which we know nothing further. Hanoch appears also as a clan of Midian (Gn 25[4]), and Hezron as one of Judah (Nu 26[21]); Nemuel is mentioned only in this connexion. For Dathan and Abiram see KORAH. The relation of Joel to any of the four sons of Reuben is not given. Ki., after Sam. and Arab. VSS, removes Joel and inserts Carmi, but the Joel of vv.[4] and [8] may be the same (Be.); Shema (v.[8])=Shemaiah or Shimei. Beerah (1 Ch 5[6]) was a prince of the Reubenites, carried away by Tiglath-pileser. Bela, with whom Jeiel and Zechariah are associated, represented a powerful clan, occupying a wide extent of territory (1 Ch 5[8f.]).

II. 1. SIMEON: Jemuel,* Jamin, Ohad,† Jachin,‡ Zohar,§ (m. Canaanitess) Shaul (2), Gn 46[10], Ex 6[15], Nu 26[12-14], 1 Ch 4[24].

2. Shaul (1): *Shallum, Mibsam, Mishma, Hammuel, Zaccur, Shimei,* sixteen sons and six daughters, 1 Ch 4[25-27].

3. [A list of princes], Meshobab, Jamlech, Joshah, (s. Amaziah) Joel, Jehu, (s. Joshibiah, s. Seraiah, s. Asiel) Elioenai, Jaakobah, Jeshohaiah, Asaiah, Adiel, Jesimiel, Benaiah, Ziza, (s. Shiphi, s. Allon, s. Jedaiah, s. Shimri, s. Shemaiah) 1 Ch 4[34-38].

4. —— *Ishi,* Pelatiah, Neariah, Rephaiah, Uzziel, 1 Ch 4[42].

The descent of Shaul from a Canaanitess mother (Gn 46[10], Ex 6[15]) implies a clan of mixed Isr. and Can. elements. Nothing further than their mention is known of the other clans. (On the early disappearance of Simeon see SIMEON.) Mibsam and Mishma (2) are names also of Ishmael's descendants (Gn 25[14], 1 Ch 1[29]), and suggest a mingling of Simeonites with the Arabians. The princes (3) represent families of shepherds which, in the reign of Hezekiah, had conquered for themselves a dwelling-place near Gerar (1 Ch 4[39-41], Gedor MT, Gerar LXX, Ki.). The sons of Ishi are captains who went to Mt. Seir, and, smiting the Amalekites, abode there (1 Ch 4[42, 43]).

We. (*Prol.* pp. 212 f.) doubts the historicity of the Chronicler's notices of the continued existence of the tribes of Reuben and Simeon during the Heb. monarchy; Stade also, that of Simeon (*Gesch.* i. p. 155). On the other hand, Graf thought that the

---

* Nemuel, Nu 26[12], 1 Ch 4[24].
† Wanting 1 Ch 4[24], Nu 26[12-14].
‡ Jarib, 1 Ch 4[24].   § Zerah, 1 Ch 4[24].

tribes had not entirely died out, and saw historical movements of their remnants in the Chronicler's statements (*Der Stamm Simeon*, pp. 22 ff.). This is more probable.

III. 1. LEVI: Gershon (2) (3),* Kohath (9), Merari (31), Gn 46[11], Ex 6[16], Nu 3[17] 26[57], 1 Ch 6[1. 16] 23[6].

2. Gershon (1) (3): Libni (6), (Ladan (7)), Shimei (8), Ex 6[17], Nu 3[18], 1 Ch 6[17] 23[6].

Libni and Ladan (1 Ch 23[7-9] 26[21]) evidently represent the same clan. Libni is derived from the priestly city Libnah. Why Ladan (לַעְדָּן) should be its equivalent is not clear. Possibly Laadah (לַעְדָּה) (1 Ch 4[21]—if a town—and Libnah were identical, and Ladan (לַעְדָּן) is to be connected with the former. Or Ladan may have been a pure clan or family name, and Libni one taken from place of residence.

3. Gershon (1) (2): *Jahath, Shimei, Zimmah, Ethan, Adaiah, Zerah, Ethni, Malchijah, Baaseiah, Michael, Shimea, Berechiah, Asaph, Zaccur* (4), *Joseph, Nethaniah, Asharelah,*† 1 Ch 6[39-43] 25[2].

The pedigree of Asaph the singer (see ASAPH). His four sons, acc. to the Chronicler, were appointed by David for the service of song in the house of the Lord (1 Ch 25[1f.]). See also (6), and see notes under (22[a,b]).

4. Zaccur (3):‡ *Micaiah,§ Mattaniah* (5), *Shemaiah, Jonathan,* Zechariah, Neh 12[35].

The pedigree of Zechariah, a musician who, with his brethren, *i.e.* fellow musicians, Shemaiah, Azarel, Milalai, Gilalai, Maai, Nethanel, Judah, Hanani, took part in the dedication of the wall of Jerus. (Neh 12[27-36]); Mattaniah in this pedigree evidently corresponds to the M. who was 'chief to begin the thanksgiving in prayer' (Neh 11[17]); mentioned also as a resident of Jerus. (1 Ch 9[15]).

5. Mattaniah (4): *Hashabiah, Bani,* Uzzi, Neh 11[22].

The pedigree of Uzzi, an overseer of the Levites at Jerus. (Neh 11[22]), whose descent is given thus from Mica (Micaiah) (4), of the sons of Asaph. Another line of descent from a Mattaniah of the ss. Asaph is given in 2 Ch 20[14], viz. **Mattaniah:** *Jeiel, Benaiah, Zechariah, Jahaziel. Jahaziel was the Levite who encouraged, by divine inspiration, Jehoshaphat and his people, prior to the battle with the children of Ammon, Moab, and Mt. Seir (2 Ch 20[14ff.]).

6. Libni (2): *Jahath, Zimmah, Joah, Iddo, Zerah,* Jeatherai, 1 Ch 6[20f.].

Jeatherai (יְאָתְרַי), otherwise unknown, is evidently Ethni (אֶתְנִי) (v.[26]), and (6) is a fragment of a pedigree of Asaph (3). (Cf. the similar names ; so Be.; Zoe. rejects this assumption. Iddo (עִדּוֹ) prob.=Adaiah (עֲדָיָה); Joah (יוֹאָח), perhaps through textual corruption=Ethan (אֵיתָן).

7. Ladan (2): Jehiel, Zetham, Joel, (ss. Shimei) Shelomoth, Haziel, Haran, 1 Ch 23[8f.], cf. 26[22].

8. Shimei (2): Jahath, Zina,‖ Jeush, Beriah, 1 Ch 23[10].

These 'sons' (7) and (8) of Ladan and Shimei, acc. to the Chronicler, represented Levitical houses of the time of David. Zetham and Joel (7), as the sons of Jehieli, were placed over the treasuries of the house of the Lord (1 Ch 26[22]). The introduction of ss. Shimei (7) as subordinate to Ladan (1 Ch 23[9]) is difficult of explanation. Probably genealogies varied ; cf. Jahath s. Libni in (6), and Shimei s. Jahath in (3).

9. Kohath (1): Amram (10), Izhar (21), Hebron (27), Uzziel (28), Ex 6[18], Nu 3[19], 1 Ch 6[2. 18] 23[12].

10. Amram (9): (m. Jochebed) Aaron (11), Moses (18), Miriam, Ex 6[20], Nu 26[59], 1 Ch 6[3] 23[12].

11. Aaron (10): Nadab, Abihu, Eleazar (12), Ithamar, Ex 6[23], Nu 26[60], 1 Ch 6[3] 24[1].

12. Eleazar (11): *Phinehas, Abishua, Bukki, Uzzi, Zerahiah, Meraioth, Amariah, Ahitub, Zadok, Ahimaaz, Azariah, Johanan, Azariah, Amariah, Ahitub, Zadok, Shallum, Hilkiah, Azariah, Seraiah,* Jehozadak,¶ 1 Ch 6[4-14], cf. Ezr 7[1-5] *i.e.* (14).

Eleazar, with whom this pedigree starts, was, according to P, Aaron's successor (Nu 20[28]), and priest at the time of the conquest of Canaan (Jos 14[1]). Phinehas is mentioned as his son and successor (Jos 24[33], Jg 20[28]). Seraiah the f. Jehozadak, with whom this pedigree closes, was chief priest at the fall of Jerus. (B.C. 586), and was taken captive and put to death at Riblah (2 K 25[18-21]), while Jehozadak went into captivity (1 Ch 6[15]).

Hence this pedigree, according to the Chronicler's view (that of P) of the origin of Israel's religious institutions, was designed to furnish a list of high priests from the entrance into Canaan until the Captivity.* As such a list, this line of descent presents certain striking features. (1) There is no mention of the line of priesthood, Eli: *Phinehas, Ahitub, Ahimelech,* Abiathar (1 S 14[3] 22[20]), unless Ahitub f. Zadok (v.[8]) is identical with Ahitub f. Ahimelech. This, however, is improbable, since the removal of Abiathar, in whose place Zadok was established, is regarded as a fulfilment of the prophecy of the disestablishment of the house of Eli (1 K 2[27. 35]).†

(2) Jehoiada (2 K 11[9], 2 Ch 22[11], etc.), and Urijah (2 K 16[11ff.]), are not mentioned, and the order of the priests appears incorrect. Amariah was chief priest in the reign of Jehoshaphat (2 Ch 19[11]). The next priests mentioned in the historical books are Azariah in the reign of Uzziah (2 Ch 26[20]), and Hilkiah in the reign of Josiah (2 K 22[4], 2 Ch 34[9]). In this list, however, there is no Azariah between Amariah and Hilkiah.

(3) The number of priests, including Aaron, from the Exodus to the Captivity, is exactly 23. Allowing forty years, or a generation, for each, this gives 40×12+40×11 years. Now, according to the artificial chronology of P, Jg, 1 and 2 K, 1 and 2 Ch (see CHRONOLOGY OF OT), 480 years elapsed from the Exodus to the founding of Solomon's temple (1 K 6[1]), and 480 years from thence to the founding of the second temple, and the Captivity occurred in the eleventh generation of this second period. Hence these 22 names seem chosen to fit exactly into this chronological scheme. This is still further seen in the statement—transferring 10[b] to 9[b] (Be. Oe. Zoe.)—that Azariah the 13th priest (including Aaron) ministered in Solomon's temple.

(4) There is a surprising number of names occurring more than once. Such repetition, while possible in a genuine pedigree, has decidedly a suspicious look, as though the names were used simply to represent so much time.

Hence, in view of these facts, it is evident that this list of names, covering many centuries, does not rest entirely upon historical records, but, as a whole, is artificial. This accords with the modern critical view of the late origin of the Levitical law and institutions (*OTJC*, Lect. ix.–xiii.; *LOT*[6] pp. 126–159). The explanation of Josephus mentioned is not based upon facts, but is a mere surmise. That this list should not be in harmony with statements elsewhere in 1 and 2 Ch shows that it probably did not originate with the author of Chronicles, but represented a notion about the line of priests, varying from that which he elsewhere followed. Ki. assigns it to the subsequent additions of 1 and 2 Ch. (On this list see We. *Prol.* pp. 222 ff.).

13. Jehozadak (12): *Jeshua, Joiakim, Eliashib, Joiada, Jonathan,* Jaddua, Ezr 3[2], Neh 12[10f.].

This genealogy brings the list of high priests down to the time of Alexander the Great (Josephus, *Ant.* XI. viii. 4).

14. Aaron (10): *Eleazar* (11), *Phinehas* (12), *Abishua, Bukki, Uzzi, Zerahiah, Meraioth, Azariah, Amariah, Ahitub, Zadok, Shallum, Hilkiah, Azariah, Seraiah,* Ezra, Ezr 7[1-5].

This ancestry of Ezra, the priest and scribe (see EZRA), is evidently the same as that of Jehozadak (12) given in shorter form. Ezra appears to have been a descendant, probably a great-grandson, of Seraiah f. Jehozadak, through a younger brother. Of similar descent is Azariah (Seraiah, Neh 11[11]) s. Hilkiah, s. Meshullam (=Shallum), s. Zadok, s. Meraioth, s. Ahitub, mentioned among the priests residing in Jerus. (1 Ch 9[11], Neh 11[11]). Seraiah is probably the correct reading, since the substitution of Azariah might be suggested by 1 Ch 6[13], but not the converse. The two names appear, however, elsewhere interchanged (cf. Ezr 2[2] with Neh 7[7]). This Seraiah represented a division of the post-exilic priests in Jerus. (Neh 11[11f.]). That he should belong to the high priest's family has been thought striking (Sm. p. 8).

15. Jehoiarib, Jedaiah, Harim, Seorim, Malchijah (16), Mijamin, Hakkoz, Abijah, Jeshua, Shecaniah, Eliashib, Jakim, Huppah, Jeshebeab, Bilgah, Immer (17), Hezir, Happizzez, Pethahiah, Jehezkel, Jachin, Gamul, Delaiah, Maaziah, 1 Ch 24[7-18].

---

* The observation on Azariah in v.[10] also shows this.

† The Jewish explanation of these facts, given by Josephus, is that the family of Phinehas s. of Aaron, represented in (12), at first held the high priesthood, and afterwards it was transferred in Eli to the family of Ithamar s. Aaron, who held the priesthood until Zadok's establishment, which restored it again to the family of Phinehas, which had in the meantime been in private life (Jos. *Ant.* v. xi. 5, VIII. i. 3). This explanation has usually been received. (Ke. thinks that after the slaughter of the priests at Nob the tabernacle was moved to Gibeon, and the high priesthood intrusted to Zadok's father, and thus, during the reign of David, Zadok was priest at Gibeon [1 Ch 16[39]], and Abiathar at Jerusalem). The Chronicler evidently held to this double line of priests, for he says that both Eleazar and Ithamar executed the priest's office, and places Zadok as the representative of the former and Ahimelech (evidently Abiathar s. Ahimelech) as representing the latter at the time of David (1 Ch 24[1ff.]).

---

* Gershom, 1 Ch 6[16f.].   † Jesharelah, 1 Ch 25[14].
‡ Zabdi, Neh 11[17]; Zichri, 1 Ch 9[15].
§ Mica, Neh 11[22].   ‖ Zizah, 1 Ch 23[11].
¶ Jozadak, Ezr 3[4] *et al.*

These are the names of the heads of the twenty-four courses of priests, sixteen taken from the ss. Eleazar and eight from the ss. Ithamar, who, acc. to the Chronicler, were assigned by David for service in the house of the Lord. Jehoiarib, Jedaiah, and Jachin appear also among the priests or priestly families of the post-exilic inhabitants of Jerus. (1 Ch 9[10], Neh 11[10]).

16. Malchijah (15) : *Pashhur, Jeroham, Adaiah*, 1 Ch 9[12].

17. Immer (15): *Meshillemith, Meshullam, Jahzerah, Adiel, Maasai*, 1 Ch 9[12], cf. Neh 11[12f.].

Adaiah (16) and Maasai (עֲמַשְׁסַי=עֲמַשְׁסַי Amashsai, Neh 11[13]) (17) are among the post-ex. priests or priestly families of Jerusalem. In Neh 11[12f.] the pedigrees are slightly different, *i.e.* **Malchijah**, *Pashhur, Zechariah, Amzi, Pelaliah, Jeroham, Adaiah* ; **Immer**, *Meshillemoth, Ahzai, Azarel*, Amashsai.

18. Moses (10): Gershom (19), Eliezer (20), Ex 18[3t.], 1 Ch 23[15].

19. Gershom (18) : *Shebuel,* * Jehdeiah, 1 Ch 23[16], 24[20].

20. Eliezer (18): *Rehabiah, Isshiah,*† *Joram, Zichri*, Shelomoth, 1 Ch 23[17] 24[21] 26[25].

Of these descendants of Moses, who, acc. to the Chronicler, represented Levites of the time of David, Shebuel (19) and Shelomoth (20) were rulers of the treasuries. A certain confusion appears in the different lengths of descent assigned to each, and in the fact that Isshiah (18) and Isshiah (20) appear as their contemporaries (see ref.). The LXX obviates this by reading Eliezer, Rehabiah, Isshiah, Joram, Zichri, Shelomoth (1 Ch 26[25]).

21. Izhar (9): Korah (22[ab]), Nepheg, Zichri, Ex 6[21].

22[a]. Korah (21): *Assir, Elkanah, Ebiasaph* (24), *Assir, Tahath, Uriel, Uzziah, Shaul* [*Elkanah*], *Amasai, Ahimoth* (ss. *Elkanah*), *Zophai, Nahath, Eliab, Jeroham, Elkanah, Samuel* (LXX), Joel (Syr. RV), Abiah, 1 Ch 6[22-28].

Korah in this list appears as the son of Amminadab (see below).

22[b]. Korah (21): *Ebiasaph* (24), *Assir, Tahath, Zephaniah, Azariah, Joel, Elkanah, Amasai, Mahath, Elkanah, Zuph, Toah, Eliel, Jeroham, Elkanah, Samuel, Joel*, Heman (23), 1 Ch 6[33-38].

These two lines of descent (22[a]) and (22[b]) are evidently the same (Be. Zoe. Oe.), as may be clearly shown by placing the names in parallel columns side by side.

(22[a]).	(22[b]).
Amminadab.	Izhar.
Korah.	Korah.
Assir Elkanah Ebiasaph.	Ebiasaph.
Assir.	Assir.
Tahath.	Tahath.
Uriel.	Zephaniah.
Uzziah.	Azariah.
Shaul.	Joel.
Elkanah.	Elkanah.
Amasai.	Amasai.
Ahimoth.	Mahath.
Elkanah.	Elkanah.
Zophai.	Zuph.
Nahath.	Toah.
Eliab.	Eliel.
Jeroham.	Jeroham.
Elkanah.	Elkanah.
Samuel.	Samuel.
{ Joel.	Joel.
{ Abiah.	Heman.

In respect to the variations : Amminadab appears in Ex 6[23] as the father-in-law of Aaron, and may have been placed for Izhar in (22[a]) through an oversight. Assir and Elkanah are either redundant in (22[a]) through a similar cause or have fallen out from (22[b]). Uriel and Zephaniah are difficult to explain as equivalents. The names Uzziah and Azariah are interchangeable (as in the case of the well-known king of Judah). The differences between the other corresponding names have probably arisen through transcription. The context clearly demands the addition of 'Samuel his son' in v.[27] and 'Joel' in v.[28]. This pedigree is clearly artificial. A portion of its construction comes from 1 S 1[1], where Elkanah is mentioned as s. Jeroham, s. Elihu, s. Tohu, s. Zuph. Zuph is probably a district, and Tohu (Toah Nahath) a family (cf. Tahath 1 Ch 7[20] ; We. *Prol.* p. 220). The story of Samuel shows distinctly that he was not a Levite, for then he would have belonged to the Lord without the gift of his mother (1 S 1[27f.]). He is made a Levite by the Chronicler according to the notions of his own times respecting Samuel's service at the sanctuary.

The motive for this pedigree of Heman, and also those of Asaph (3) and Jeduthun (Ethan) (35), is very apparent. At the

time of the Chronicler there were three guilds of singers, named after Asaph, Heman, and Ethan (1 Ch 6[31ff.]) or Jeduthun (1 Ch 25[1]), reckoned as belonging to the three great Levitical houses of Gershon, Kohath, and Merari. The Chronicler assumes that this organization of singers dated from David, but in reality it was quite modern, for, according to Ezr 2[41] Neh 7[44], ss. Asaph and singers were equivalent, and the singers were distinct from the Levites. (This distinction is held by Sm. p. 26 ; *OTJC*[2] p. 204 ; Baudissin, *Gesch. des A. T. Priesterthums*, p. 142 ff. ; Nowack, *Heb. Arch.* ii. p. 111 ; on the other hand, Torrey claims that no such distinction can be found in Ezr and Neh., *Comp. and Hist. Value of Ezr and Neh*, p. 22 f.). Gradually, however, singers were evolved into Levites and the three guilds. Remains of steps of this evolution and fluctuating traditions appear in the Levitical genealogies. In Ex 6[21] the three ss. Korah are Assir, Elkanah, and Abiasaph (=Ebiasaph), *i.e.* f. Asaph, and hence we should expect to find Asaph a descendant of Korah, but, according to (3), he is not. Also we find Assir and Elkanah placed not co-ordinate but following each other (21[ab]). Different genealogists certainly worked over these names. (22[a]) (22[b]) are assigned by Ki. to different sources ; (22[a]) to the older. The ss. Korah appearing in the titles of the Ps (42. 44-49. 84. 85. 87. 88) probably mark a step in this evolution earlier than the formation of the three guilds. Korah in 1 Ch 2[43] is associated with Tappuah as a son of Hebron. This indicates either a place or Judæan family of that name from whose Levites originated the Levitical Korahites (We. *Is. und Jüd. Gesch.* p. 151 f.).

23. Heman (22[b]) : Bukkiah, Mattaniah, Uzziel,* Shebuel,† Jerimoth, Hananiah, Hanani, Eliathah, Giddalti, Romamti-ezer, Joshbekashah, Mallothi, Hothir, Mahazioth, 1 Ch 25[4].

These fourteen sons of Heman were appointed by David, acc. to the Chronicler, for the service of song in the house of the Lord (1 Ch 25[6. 9-31]). This list of names is most interesting, since prob. from Hananiah (חֲנַנְיָה חָנֵּנִי אֵלִיָּאתָה), certainly from Giddalti (נְּדִלְתִּי וְרֹמַמְתִּי עֶזֶר וְשָׁבְקְשָׁה מַלּוֹתִי הוֹתִיר מַחֲזִיאוֹת), they are a fragment of a hymn or psalm which perhaps originally read : 'Be gracious to me, J″; be gracious to me ! thou art my God. I have magnified and exalted the help of him sitting in distress, I have declared abundantly visions' (חָנֵּנִי יָהּ חָנֵּנִי אֵלִי אַתָּה נִּדַּלְתִּי וְרֹמַמְתִּי עֶזֶר יָשַׁב קָשֶׁה מַלּוֹתִי הוֹתִיר מַחֲזִיאוֹת). There is no doubt about the exact rendering and construction of these lines (cf. Ewald, *Ausführ. Lehrbuch d. Heb. Sprache*, p. 680 ; *ZAW*, 1886, p. 260 ; We. *Prol.* p. 219 ; Oe. Kau. Ki. *in loco*), but none about the names, at least the last six, being fashioned out of such a prayer or meditation.

24. Ebiasaph (22[ab]): *Kore*, Shallum, Meshelemiah‡ (25), 1 Ch 9[19] 26[1].

25. Meshelemiah‡ (24): Zechariah, Jediael, Zebadiah, Jathniel, Elam, Jehohanan, Eliehoenai, 1 Ch 26[2f.].

In (24) (25) we have families of porters or door-keepers assigned by the Chronicler to the time of David. It is possible that Shallum and Meshelemiah or Shelemiah represent the same person or family (Be. Oe.). M.'s descent is given through Kore from Asaph (1 Ch 26[1]), evidently to be read Ebiasaph (LXX B, Ki. RVm). With Shallum are associated Akkub, Talmon, and Ahiman (1 Ch 9[17]). Akkub and Talmon appear as porters in post-exilic Jerus. (Neh 11[19]). Zechariah (25) is mentioned 1 Ch 9[21].

The Chronicler doubtless designed also that Obed-edom the door-keeper, with his sons Shemaiah, Jehozabad, Joah, Sacar, Nethanel, Ammiel, Issachar, and Peullethai, and the ss. Shemaiah, Othni, Rephael, Obed, Elzabad, Elihu, and Semachiah, should be enrolled among the Korahites (1 Ch 26[4-7. 19]) (Ke. Zoe.), although Obed-edom's descent from Jeduthun (1 Ch 16[38]) would suggest that he belonged to the Merarites. That this Obed-edom is intended to represent Obed-edom the Gittite (2 S 6[10f.], 1 Ch 13[13]), transformed, like Samuel (22[ab]), into a Levite, is most probable, although the contrary has been maintained. (Ke. also distinguishes between the singer Obed-edom and the door-keeper Obed-edom (1 Ch 15[21. 24])).

26. ——— : *Shelomoth,*§ Jahath, 1 Ch 24[22].

These are mentioned as Izharites of the time of David. Their descent is not given more specifically.

27. Hebron (9): Jeriah, ‖ Amariah, Jahaziel, Jekameam, 1 Ch 23[19] 24[23].

These Hebronites are mentioned as serving in the house of the Lord at the time of David (1 Ch 23[24]). In the family of Hebron we may have a perpetuation of the old line of priests, subordinated into Levites who originally ministered at the sanctuary of Hebron ; at any rate the name must be associated with Levites residing in Hebron. Jeriah (Jerijah) is mentioned in 1 Ch 26[31ff.] as the chief whose brethren were appointed by David overseers of the Reubenites, Gadites, and the half-tribe of the Manassites 'for every matter pertaining to God and for the affairs of the king.' A Hashabiah of the Hebronites, with

---

Azarel, 1 Ch 25[18].   † Shubael, 1 Ch 25[20].
‡ Shelemiah, 1 Ch 26[14].   § Shelomith, 1 Ch 23[18].
‖ Jerijah, 1 Ch 26[31].

his brethren, is given a similar position of 'oversight of Israel beyond Jordan westward' (v.[30]). Eliel is mentioned as the chief of the Hebronites at the removal of the ark (1 Ch 15[9]).

28. Uzziel (9): Mishael, Elzaphan, Sithri, Ex 6[22]; Micah (29), Isshiah (30), 1 Ch 23[20] 24[24f.].

Sithri is mentioned only in Ex 6[22]. Mishael and Elzaphan in Lv 10[4] are commanded to carry out of the camp the bodies of Nadab and Abihu. Elizaphan (=Elzaphan) in Nu 3[30] is appointed prince of the families of the Kohathites. As a family name it appears in 1 Ch 15[8], 2 Ch 29[13]. To Micah and Isshiah is assigned general Levitical service along with the Hebronites (27) (see above).

29. Micah (28): Shamir, 1 Ch 24[24].

30. Isshiah (28): Zechariah, 1 Ch 24[25].

Nothing special is assigned to these Uzzielites (29) (30), who are given ss. Levi of the time of David (see ref.). An Amminadab was the chief of the Uzzielites at the time of the removal of the ark (1 Ch 15[10]).

31. Merari (1): Mahli (3[2]) (35[ab]), Mushi (34), Jaaziah ? (38), Ex 6[19], Nu 3[20], 1 Ch 6[19] 23[21] 24[26].

It is possible that the family Mushi (מוּשִׁי) derived their name from Moses (מֹשֶׁה) (We. *Is. und Jüd. Gesch.* p. 151 f.). On the appearance of Jaaziah, among ss. Merari, mentioned in 1 Ch 24[26], see below (38).

32. Mahli (31): Eleazar, Kish (33), 1 Ch 23[21].

33. Kish (32): Jerahmeel, 1 Ch 24[29].

34. Mushi (31): Mahli (35), Eder, Jerimoth, 1 Ch 24[30].

These Merarites (31)–(34) are recorded as in general Levitical service at the time of David (see ref. and 1 Ch 23[24] 24[31]).

35[a]. Mahli (34): *Shemer, Bani, Amzi, Hilkiah, Amaziah, Hashabiah, Malluch, Abdi, Kishi,* * Jeduthun (Ethan) (36) (37), 1 Ch 6[44-47].

Instead of Jeduthun we have the name Ethan in 1 Ch 6[47], but both names are undoubtedly designed to indicate one and the same person (Be. Ke. Oe. Zoe.). Cf. on this pedigree the remarks on 22[ab].

35[b]. Mahli (31) or (34): *Libni, Shimei, Uzzah, Shimea, Haggiah,* Asaiah, 1 Ch 6[29f.].

The pedigree of an otherwise unknown Asaiah. Be. regards it as a fragment, in spite of the great difference of names, representing originally the same line of descent as that seen in the first members of 35[a]. Ke. Zoe. and Oe. reject this hypothesis.

36. Jeduthun (35[a]): Gedaliah, Zeri, † Jeshaiah, Hashabiah, Mattithiah, Shimei, 1 Ch 25[3].

These six sons (Shimei is derived from 1 Ch 25[17]), with their father, were assigned by David, acc. to the Chronicler, to the service of song in the house of the Lord (ref.).

37. Jeduthun (35[a]): *Galal, Shemaiah,* ‡ Obadiah, § 1 Ch 9[16], Neh 11[17].

Obadiah is mentioned among the Levites residing in Jerus. after the Exile (ref.).

38. Jaaziah (31), Beno? Shoham, Zaccur, Ibri, 1 Ch 24[27].

Beno (בְּנוֹ 'his son,' LXX, Vulg. RV) arises from a clear misunderstanding of the Heb. text, and should be struck out of the list of sons. It is the common noun (בֵּן) with the pronominal ending, and should be rendered 'his son,' *i.e.* Jaaziah is the son of Merari. The MT is difficult and probably corrupt (see Be. Oe. Ki.). Ke. and Zoe. regard the references to Jaaziah and his sons as a gloss. The name Ibri (עִבְרִי) 'Hebrew,' is noticeable, and shows at once that we are in a post-exilic or relatively late period of Israel's history.

39. Hosah: Shimri, Hilkiah, Tebaliah, Zechariah, 1 Ch 26[10f.].

Hosah of the ss. Merari (closer descent is not given), with his sons and brethren, all of whom numbered 13, is recorded among the door-keepers of the house of the Lord of the time of David. To him and Shuppim (שֻׁפִּים) was given the charge of the gate 'Shallecheth' westward. The name Shuppim, however, is a dittography from the preceding הָאֲסֻפִּים 'the storehouse,' and is to be struck out (Ki.) (1 Ch 26[10-16]).

---

* Kushaiah, 1 Ch 15[17].
‡ Shammua, Neh 11[17].
† Izri, 1 Ch 25[11].
§ Abda, Neh 11[17].

ADDITIONAL LISTS OF LEVITES.

40. Of the reign of David: *a.* Uriel (ss. Kohath), Asaiah (ss. Merari), Joel (ss. Gershom), Shemaiah (ss. Elizaphan), Eliel (ss. Hebron), Amminadab (ss. Uzziel), 1 Ch 15[5-11].

b. Zechariah, Ben, Jaaziel,* Shemiramoth, Jehiel, Unni, Eliab, Benaiah, Maaseiah, Mattithiah, Eliphelehu, Mikneiah, Obed-edom, Jeiel, Azaziah, 1 Ch 15[18-21].

c. Shebaniah, Joshaphat, Nethanel, Amasai, Zechariah, Benaiah, Eliezer, 1 Ch 15[24].

d. Chenaniah, Berechiah, Elkanah, 1 Ch 15[22f.].

The Levites (*a b c d*) are mentioned in connexion with David's removal of the ark to Jerusalem. List *a* were chiefs of the Levitical families; list *b*, the singers or musicians with psalteries and harps under the direction of Heman, Asaph, and Ethan; list *c*, priestly trumpeters. Chenaniah (*d*) was the leader of the song or the carrying up of the ark, and Berechiah and Elkanah were door-keepers, also an Obed-edom and Jehiah (1 Ch 15[24]).

41. Of the reign of Jehoshaphat. Teachers of the law. (*a*) Priests: Elishama, Jehoram. (*b*) Levites: Shemaiah, Nethaniah, Zebadiah, Asahel, Shemiramoth, Jehonathan, Adonijah, Tobijah, Tobadonijah, 2 Ch 17[8].

42. Of the reign of Hezekiah: *a.* Mahath s. Amasai, Joel s. Azariah (ss. Kohath), Kish s. Abdi, Azariah s. Jehallelel (ss. Merari), Joah s. Zimmah, Eden s. Joah (Gershonites), Shimri, Jeuel (ss. Elizaphan), Zechariah, Mattaniah (ss. Asaph), Jehuel, Shimei (ss. Heman), Shemaiah, Uzziel (ss. Jeduthun), 2 Ch 29[12-14].

These Levites are mentioned as employed by Hezekiah in cleansing the temple after its defilement in the reign of Ahaz.

b. Rulers: Conaniah, Shimei (his brother). Overseers: Jehiel, Azaziah, Nahath, Asahel, Jerimoth, Jozabad, Eliel, Ismachiah, Mahath, Benaiah, 2 Ch 31[12f.].

During the reign of Hezekiah, acc. to the Chronicler, the people contributed abundantly of tithes and firstfruits, and these men had charge of the tithes and oblations brought into the chambers of the temple (2 Ch 31[5-13]).

c. Kore s. Imnah, Eden, Miniamin, Jeshua, Shemaiah, Amariah, Shecaniah, 2 Ch 31[14f.].

Kore was the porter at the E. gate of the temple, and had charge of the free-will offerings and the distribution of the portions of the priests. Under him were the others named above, stationed in the cities of the priests to distribute the portions of the priests (2 Ch 31[15-17]).

43. Of the reign of Josiah: *a.* Shaphan s. Azaliah, Maaseiah, Joah s. Joahaz, Jahath, Obadiah (ss. Merari), Zechariah, Meshullam (ss. Kohathites), 2 Ch 34[8, 12].

These persons are all mentioned in connexion with the repair of the temple. The first three, of whom Shaphan was the scribe, Maaseiah was governor of the city, and Joah (or his f. Joahaz) the recorder, seem to have had general superintendence of the work, while the other four oversaw the workmen. The first three were not necessarily Levites, and are grouped here merely for convenience of reference (2 Ch 34[8-13]).

b. Rulers of the Temple: Hilkiah, Zechariah, Jehiel, 2 Ch 35[8].

c. Chiefs of the Levites: Conaniah, Shemaiah, Nethanel, Hashabiah, Jeiel, Jozabad, 2 Ch 35[9].

These had charge of the distribution of the offerings at the celebration of the passover kept by Josiah (2 Ch 35[1-19]).

IV. 1. JUDAH: (m. Shua, Gn 38[2-5]) Er, Onan, Shelah (2) (3); (m. Tamar, Gn 38[6-30]), Perez (4), Zerah (59), Gn 46[12], Nu 26[19f.], 1 Ch 2[3f.].

Er and Onan are represented as dying in Canaan (Gn 38[7-10] 46[12], Nu 26[19]), implying that two of the ancient and original clans of Judah early disappeared. The Canaanite mothers, Shua and Tamar (Gn 38[2, 6ff.]), indicate a union with Canaanites (see art. JUDAH).

2. Shelah (1): Er f. Lecah, Laadah f. Mareshah. Families of Ashbea, Jokim, men of Cozeba, Joash, Saraph, Jashubi-lehem ?, 1 Ch 4[21f.].

* Jahaziel, 1 Ch 16[6]

Er here appears as the son and not the brother of Shelah. A remnant of the clan Er may have united with, and become subordinate to, that of Shelah. Mareshah is the name of a city (see MARESHAH), probably also Lecah. Whether Ashbea is the name of a place or family cannot be determined. Cozeba (כּוֹזֵבָא) may be Chezib (כְּזִיב Gn 38⁵). Jashubi-lehem has arisen from a misunderstanding of the text, וַיָּשָׁבוּ בֵּית לֶחֶם=וְיֹשְׁבֵי לָחֶם 'and they returned to Bethlehem.' The Vulg., following evidently an old Jewish Midrash, renders v.²² et qui stare fecit solem, virique mendacii, et Securus et Incendens, qui principes fuerunt in Moab, et qui reversi sunt in Lahem. The whole passage (vv.²¹⁻²³) is very obscure, and probably preserves the family traditions and relationships of certain weavers and potters of the post-exilic times. The ref. to Moab and a return suggests some story similar to that of Ruth. Ki. assigns the verses to the later additions to Chronicles.

3. Shelah fam.: *Zechariah, Joiarib, Adaiah, Hazaiah, Col-hozeh, Baruch, Maaseiah,* Neh 11⁵.

This is the genealogy of Maaseiah (מַעֲשֵׂיָה), representing a family of the inhabitants of Jerus. after the Return (Neh 11⁴). In 1 Ch 9⁵ the name is Asaiah (עֲשָׂיָה).

4. Perez (1): Hezron (5), Hamul, Gn 46¹², Nu 26²¹, 1 Ch 2⁵.

5. Hezron (4): Jerahmeel (6), Ram (16), Chelubai (Caleb) (29) (35), 1 Ch 2⁹.

Ram as a second son of Hezron is suspicious: (1) Because OT knows of no Judæan clan Ram co-ordinate with Caleb and Jerahmeel. (2) The descendants are given, not in families and cities, but simply in a pedigree of David. This pedigree in 1 Ch 2¹⁰⁻¹⁵ appears taken from Ru 4¹⁸⁻²², where Ram may have stood for Ram the son of Jerahmeel (6), the father's name being omitted (We. p. 17 f.). Yet, while the pedigree of David may be conjectural, the Chronicler is clearly nearer the truth in deriving his descent from Ram s. Hezron than from Ram s. Jerahmeel, since, according to the narrative of 1 and 2 S, David cannot have been a Jerahmeelite. That the Chronicler's Judæan genealogies should principally consist of Calebite and Jerahmeelite families, as we shall see, is probably due to the fact that family names and traditions, along with family or clan life, are held more tenaciously among rural and pastoral peoples than the inhabitants of cities or more highly organized communities.

6. Jerahmeel (5): Ram (7), Bunah, Oren, Ozem, Ahijah? (m. Atarah), Onam (8), 1 Ch 2²⁵ᶠ.

Ahijah (אֲחִיָּה) is either to be struck out, having arisen from a misinterpretation of an original אֶחָיו or אָחִיו 'his brother' (LXX, Ki. אֶחָיו 'his brothers,' We. p. 15), or held to be the mother of the preceding sons (Be. Ke. Zoe. Oe.), the original text having been 'Ozem (and his brothers) from Ahijah' (אֹצֶם מֵאֲחִיָּה). The former is preferable.

7. Ram (6): Maaz, Jamin, Eker, 1 Ch 2²⁷.

8. Onam (6): Shammai (9), Jada (14), 1 Ch 2²⁸.

9. Shammai (8): Nadab (10), Abishur (13), 1 Ch 2²⁸.

10. Nadab (9): Seled, Appaim (11), 1 Ch 2³⁰.

11. Appaim (10): Ishi, *Sheshan* (12), Ahlai, 1 Ch 2³¹.

12. Sheshan (11): *Jarha* (son-in-law), *Attai, Nathan, Zabad, Ephlal, Obed, Jehu, Azariah, Helez, Eleasah, Sismai, Shallum, Jekamiah,* Elishama, 1 Ch 2³⁵⁻⁴¹.

This pedigree of the otherwise unknown Elishama—for he is not to be identified with others of the same name mentioned elsewhere in OT—was derived evidently from another source than that of the preceding, and (in our lists) following descendants of Jerahmeel (Ki. We. p. 18). To remove the discrepancy between the mention of Ahlai (11) and the statement (v.³⁴) that Sheshan had no sons, ignoring the fact of different sources, it has been assumed that Ahlai was a daughter (Ke. Zoe. *et al.*). Jarha is said to have been an Egyptian servant (v.³⁴). Some family represented by Elishama, probably near the time of the Chronicler, evidently traced their descent from the family or clan of Sheshan and an Egyp. individual or family who united with it. The free intercourse between Canaan and Egypt serves to confirm this statement.

13. Abishur (9): (m. Abihail) Ahban, Molid, 1 Ch 2²⁹.

14. Jada (8): Jether, Jonathan (15), 1 Ch 2³².

15. Jonathan (14): Peleth, Zaza, 1 Ch 2³³.

This (15) completes the list of the descendants of Jerahmeel (1 Ch 2²⁵⁻³³). It is evidently a record of the families of the Jerahmeelites, who are mentioned in 1 S 27¹⁰ as inhabiting a Negeb or south country distinct from that of Judah (see JERAHMEEL). The binary form of descent suggests an artistic construction. The names Bunah, Oren, Maaz, Eker, Abishur, Ahban, Molid, Seled, Appaim, Sheshan, and Zaza, occur only

in this connexion, also Ozem, except as that of a brother of David mentioned only in 1 Ch 2¹⁵. Onam is the name of a family of Edom (Gn 36²³); Jamin of Simeon (Gn 46¹⁰); Jether an Ishmaelite name (1 Ch 2¹⁷), or Midianite (Ex 4¹⁸ RVm). (It is equivalent to Jethro). These names suggest a close relationship with these neighbours. The m. Atarah of Onam (6), the most widely extended family, probably arose from their inhabiting Ataroth or protected places (We. p. 15). The Jerahmeelites do not appear in connexion with the restoration, and the 13 generations between Sheshan and Elishama show that their families were thought of as living at least some 500 years before the time of the Chronicler. The list is probably of pre-exilic origin, and historical.

16. Ram (5): *Amminadab, Nahshon, Salma,* * *Boaz, Obed, Jesse*; Eliab,† Abinadab, Shimea,‡ Nethanel, Raddai, Ozem, David (17), d. Zeruiah (27), d. Abigail (28), 1 Ch 2¹⁰⁻¹⁶, cf. Ru 4¹⁸⁻²².

Acc. to 1 S 17¹² Jesse had eight sons (cf. 1 S 16²ᶠᶠ.); Syr. has in our passage eight sons, Elihu (cf. 1 Ch 27¹⁸) being the seventh.

In addition to the descendants of Jesse recorded in (17)–(28) we have **Jesse**, *Eliab*, d. *Abihail* (f. Jerimoth), d. *Mahalath* (f. Rehoboam), Jeush, Shemariah, Zaham, 2 Ch 11¹⁸ᶠ.; or **Jesse**, *Eliab*, d. *Abihail* (f. Rehoboam), Jeush, Shemariah, Zaham, 2 Ch 11¹⁸ RVm. Cf. (18) note.

17. David (16): (m. Ahinoam) Amnon, (m. Abigail) Chileab, (m. Maacah) Absalom (see below), (m. Haggith) Adonijah, (m. Abital) Shephatiah, (m. Eglah) Ithream, (m. Bathsheba) Shammua, Shobab, Nathan (see below), Solomon (18), (m. unknown) Ibhar, Elishua, Nepheg, Japhia, Elishama, Eliada, Eliphelet, 2 S 3²⁻⁵ 5¹⁴⁻¹⁶, cf. 1 Ch 3¹⁻⁹ 14⁴⁻⁷.

The names of the ss. David in 1 Ch 3¹⁻⁹ 14⁴⁻⁷, owing in the main to erroneous transcription, are somewhat diff. from those in the earlier and more authentic source (2 S) given in (17): Daniel (3¹) for Chileab (see DANIEL), Shimea (3⁵) for Shammua (perhaps mere variation of spelling שִׁמְעָא), Elishama (3⁶) for Elishua; Eliphelet (3⁶), or Elpelet (14⁵), Nogah (3⁷ 14⁶), two additional names developed, one from the preceding, and the other from the following names (Ki.); Beeliada (14⁷) for Eliada. The former probably is correct (see BEELIADA). Bath-sheba, written Bathshua, is mentioned as the m. in 1 Ch 3⁵. Jerimoth, f. Mahalath wife of king Rehoboam is mentioned as a s. David (2 Ch 11¹⁸) (16 note) (18 note). Since he does not appear elsewhere, he is thought to have been a. concubine, unless Jerimoth (יְרִימוֹת) is a corruption of Ithream (יִתְרְעָם).

Besides the line of Solomon (18), descendants of David are given in the line of the ancestry of Joseph f. Christ traced back to Nathan (Lk 3²³⁻³¹), see GENEALOGY OF CHRIST; and in Maacah d. (evidently grand d.) of Absalom (1 K 15², 2 Ch 11²²). Since Absalom's ss. must have died without posterity (2 S 14²⁷, 18¹⁸), her mother probably was Tamar d. Absalom and father Uriel of Gibeah (2 Ch 13²). She was a wife of king Rehoboam and m. of king Abijam (see (18) note).

18. Solomon (17): *Rehoboam, Abijah, Asa, Jehoshaphat, Joram, Ahaziah, Joash, Amaziah, Azariah, Jotham, Ahaz, Hezekiah, Manasseh, Amon, Josiah,* Johanan, Jehoiakim (19), Zedekiah, Shallum,§ 1 Ch 3¹⁰⁻¹⁵.

Of these ss. Josiah (1 Ch 3¹⁵) Johanan is mentioned nowhere else. It looks as though he were designed to stand for Jehoahaz, Josiah's immediate successor (2 K 23³⁰), who was followed by Jehoiakim (2 K 23³⁴), and the latter, after the 3 months' reign of his son Jeconiah, by his brother Zedekiah (2 K 24¹⁷). Jehoiakim, however, was older than Jehoahaz (2 K 23³¹·³⁶), while Zedekiah was much younger than either of them, and Shallum was another name for Jehoahaz (Jer 22¹¹). Hence their order of birth is incorrectly given (1 Ch 3¹⁵), and probably the writer made the further mistake, after identifying Johanan with Jehoahaz, of taking Shallum for another son; although it is possible that the eldest s. Josiah was a Johanan who may have died before his father, or with him at the battle of Megiddo.

To (18), which represents the kings of Judah in order of succession from Solomon to Josiah inclusive, the following genealogical particulars may be added here :—

(a) Mothers of Kings.—Of Rehoboam, Naamah the Ammonitess (1 K 14²¹·³¹, 2 Ch 12¹³); of Abijah,‖ Maacah d. Absalom (1 K 15², 2 Ch 11²⁰). In 2 Ch 13² she is called Micaiah d. Uriel of Gibeah, hence, as the intervening time requires, she was a grand d., at least, of Absalom (see (17) note); of Asa—no mother is given, only grandmother Maacah (1 K 15¹⁰, 2 Ch 15¹⁶); of Jehoshaphat, Azubah d. Shilhi (1 K 22⁴², 2 Ch 20³¹); of Joram, Athaliah d. (grand d.) Omri, king of Israel (2 K 8²⁶, 2 Ch 22²); of Joash, Zibiah of Beersheba (2 K 12¹, 2 Ch 24¹); of Amaziah,

---

* Salmon, Ru 4²⁰ᶠ.
† Elihu is mentioned as a brother of David, 1 Ch 27¹⁸. Ki. reads Eliab.
‡ Shammah, 1 S 16⁹; Shimeah, 2 S 13³.
§ 2 K 23³⁰ Jehoahaz, cf. Jer 22¹¹; but see note above.
‖ Abijam, 1 K 15².

Jehoaddin,* of Jerusalem (2 K 14², 2 Ch 25¹); of Azariah,† Jecoliah † (2 K 15², 2 Ch 26³); of Jotham, Jerusha d. Zadok (2 K 15³³,
2 Ch 27¹); of Ahaz, the name is not given; of Hezekiah, Abi‡ d.
Zechariah (2 K 18², 2 Ch 29¹); of Manasseh, Hephzibah (2 K 21¹);
of Amon, Meshullemeth d. Haruz of Jotbah (2 K 21¹⁹); of
Josiah, Jedidah d. Adaiah of Bozkath (2 K 22¹); of Jehoahaz
and Zedekiah, Hamutal d. Jeremiah of Libnah (2 K 23³¹); of
Jehoiakim, Zebidah d. Pedaiah of Rumah (2 K 23³⁶); of Jeconiah
(19), Nehushta d. Elnathan of Jerusalem (2 K 24⁸).

(b) **Additional Sons of Kings.**—Of Rehoboam, (m. Mahalath
or Abihail, see (16) note c) Jeush, Shemariah, Zaham, (m. Maacah)
Attai, Ziza, Shelomith (2 Ch 11¹⁸⁻²⁰); of Jehoshaphat,—Azariah,
Jehiel, Zechariah, Azariah(?), Michael, Shephatiah (2 Ch 21²).
Nothing further is known of these princes. For a d. Joram,
see JEHOSHEBA.

19. Jehoiakim (18): *Jeconiah* § (20), Zedekiah,
1 Ch 3¹⁶.

Some hold this Zedekiah to be identical with s. Josiah (19),
the Chronicler's error or form of statement having arisen
because Z. was Jeconiah's successor on the throne (We. *Prol.*
p. 216).

20. Jeconiah (19): Assir (RVm)? Shealtiel,
Malchiram, Pedaiah (21), Shenazzar, Jekamiah,
Hoshama, Nedabiah, 1 Ch 3¹⁷, ¹⁸.

Assir as a proper name arose from a misunderstanding of the
adj. *'assir* (אַסִּר), meaning captive (see RVm and art. ASSIR).

21. Pedaiah (20): Zerubbabel (22), Shimei, 1 Ch
3¹⁹ᵃ.

In Ezr 3². ⁸ 5², Neh 12¹, Hag 1¹. ¹². ¹⁴ 2². ²³, cf. Mt 1¹², Lk 3²⁷,
Zerubbabel (wh. see) is called the son of Shealtiel. Pedaiah
probably was his real father; but Zerubbabel succeeding Shealtiel, of whom no sons are mentioned, as the head of the family
of David or house of Judah, is called his son.

22. Zerubbabel (21): Meshullam, Hananiah, d.
Shelomith, Hashubah, Ohel, Berechiah, Hasadiah,
Jushab-hesed, 1 Ch 3¹⁹ᵇ, ²⁰.

23. Hananiah (22): Pelatiah, Jeshaiah, ss.
Rephaiah, ss. Arnan, ss. Obadiah, ss. Shecaniah
(24), 1 Ch 3²¹.

This list has been interpreted in two ways: (a) Hananiah was
the father of six sons, whose names follow, before four of whom
'sons' was written because they were founders of distinguished
families of the time of the writer (Be.); (b) From 'sons of
Rephaiah' (21³) to the end of the chapter is a genealogical
fragment representing branches of the family of David, whose
connexion with Zerubbabel was unascertainable (Ke.); LXX,
Vulg. and Syr. read instead of בְּנֵי 'sons' בְּנוֹ 'his son,' and the
genealogy (23) (24), then, is as follows: Hananiah, *Pelatiah,
Jeshaiah, Obadiah, Shecaniah, Shemaiah,* Hattush, Igal, Bariah,
Neariah, Shaphat. This is preferred by Ki. *et al.* and brings
the descendants of David down to nine generations after
Zerubbabel.

24. Shecaniah (23): *Shemaiah,* Hattush, Igal,
Bariah, Neariah (25), Shaphat, 1 Ch 3²².

25. Neariah (24): Elioenai (26), Hizkiah, Azrikam.

26. Elioenai (25): Hodaviah, Eliashib, Pelaiah,
Akkub, Johanan, Delaiah, Anani, 1 Ch 3²⁴.

This completes the list of the descendants of David.

27. Zeruiah (16): Abishai, Joab, Asahel,
1 Ch 2¹⁶.

28. Abigail (16): (f. Jether) Amasa, 1 Ch 2¹⁷.

29. Caleb (5): Mesha f. Ziph, ss. Mareshah f.
Hebron (30), d. Achsah, 1 Ch 2⁴². ⁴⁹ᵇ.

Caleb represents the powerful clan of the Calebites of S.
Judah (see CALEB). The record in (29) is obscure; LXX has
Mareshah for Mesha (also Ki. who thinks an enumeration of
ss. Mareshah must have stood at the end of v.⁴²). Better We.
that ss. M. is written to distinguish the gentilic name Mareshah
from that of the city. On Achsah see art. (cf. Jg 1¹⁴. ¹⁵).

30. Hebron (29): Korah, Tappuah, Rekem (31),
Shema (32), 1 Ch 2⁴³.

31. Rekem (30): *Shammai,* Maon f. Bethzur,
1 Ch 2⁴⁴ᵇ ᵗ.

32. Shema (30): Raham f. Jorkeam, 1 Ch 2⁴⁴.

33. Jahdai (?): Regem, Jotham, Geshan, Pelet,
Ephah, Shaaph (34), 1 Ch 2⁴⁷.

The connexion of Jahdai with the foregoing is not given.
His name evidently has fallen out of the text.

34. Shaaph (33) **f. Madmannah**: Sheva f. Machbena, and f. Gibea, 1 Ch 2⁴⁹ᵃ.

Vv.⁴⁶ and ⁴⁸ are from another source, and to be separated
from vv.⁴⁵. ⁴⁷. ⁴⁹ (We. Ki.), since Ephah, in v.⁴⁶ the name of a
concubine of Caleb, in v.⁴⁷ is the name of a s. Shaaph. Their
contents appears in (35). V.⁴⁹ is an evident continuation of v.⁴⁷.
Instead of 'and she bare' (וַתֵּלֶר) we should read (וַיֵּלֶר) 'and Shaaph
begat.'
In the foregoing lists (29)–(34) Hebron, Tappuah, Maon, Ziph,
Bethzur, Madmannah, and Gibea are well-known cities of Judah
within the probable early domain of the Calebites. To these
probably should be added Shema (שְׁמָע)=Shema (שְׁמַע) (Jos 15²⁶),
Jorkeam (יָרְקְעָם)=Jokdeam (יָרְדְעָם) (Jos 15⁵⁶), Pelet (פֶּלֶט)=Beth-
pelet (בֵּית פֶּלֶט) (Jos 15²⁷), Machbena (מַכְבֵּנָא)=Cabbon (כַּבּוֹן) (Jos
15⁴⁰). These towns suggest the transfer of gentilic names to
localities or the converse. While some of the other names occur
elsewhere (Mesha, a king of Moab, 2 K 3⁴; Shammai, 1 Ch 4¹⁷;
Jotham, Jg 9⁵ *et al.*; Sheva? 2 S 20²⁵), they throw no light on
the history behind these genealogies or the families or places
recorded; unless Korah a s. Esau and district of Edom (Gn
36⁵. ¹⁴. ¹⁶), Rekem, a king of Midian (Nu 31⁸); Ephah, a Midianite tribe;—all serve to confirm the indications found elsewhere
of a close affinity between Caleb and the Edomites and adjoining peoples. Raham (רַחַם), a noun kindred with Jerahmeel
(יְרַחְמְאֵל),—Jahdai, Regem, Geshan, and Shaaph are found only
in this connexion.

35. Caleb (5): *a.* (m. Azubah) *d. Jerioth,* Jesher,
Shobab, Ardon, 1 Ch 2¹⁸.

b. (m.c. Ephah) Haran, Moza, Gazez, 1 Ch 2⁴⁶.

c. (m.c. Maacah) Sheber, Tirhanah, 1 Ch 2⁴⁸.

d. (m. Ephrathah) Hur (36) (42), (Ashhur f.
Tekoa), 1 Ch 2¹⁹. ²⁴.

Caleb in (35) as in (29) represents the clan, and the descendants
given in (35)–(39) unquestionably embody traditions or convey
historical information respecting the families and localities of
the clan during different periods of its history. They are
taken from late material in 1 Ch (Ki.). During the pre-exilic
period the Calebites dwelt in S. Judah (see CALEB). During the
post-exilic period, owing to the aggression of the Edomites,
they seem to have moved farther north (or if taken into
captivity were thus located on their return), and thus dwelt
in the districts of Bethlehem and Kiriath-jearim. This, the
supposition of We., seems clearly proved from the geographical
localities mentioned and indicated in 1 Ch 2⁵⁰⁻⁵⁵, viz. Bethlehem, Kiriath-jearim, Netopha, Bethgader, Zorah, Eshtaol,
Atroth-beth-Joab (We. p. 28ff.) (see also (39)). The children
of Azubah (their names may be enigmatical) represent the
families that belonged to the older place of residence, hence perhaps the mother's name Azubah (עֲזוּבָה, 'abandoned.' Ephah
and Maacah as concubines represent alien or inferior elements
which coalesced with the clan. Ephrathah represents the district of Bethlehem (see EPHRATHAH). The meaning and text
of 1 Ch 2¹⁸ is uncertain. Jerioth is regarded as another name
for Azubah (Be.) or another wife with Azubah (Oe.), or a
daughter of Azubah (Vulg. Ki. Ke. Zoe.), or the mother of
Azubah, *i.e.* Azubah was her daughter (בַּת עֲזוּבָה) (We. p. 33).
The MT of 1 Ch 2²⁴, which yields an Abiah, wife of Hezron
and m. of Ashhur, is plainly corrupt. A few slight changes
give the appropriate rendering, 'And after the death of Hezron,
Caleb came unto Ephrathah, the wife of Hezron his father, and
she bare unto him Ashhur.' The meaning seems to be: The
pre-exilic inhabitants of Ephrathah were Hezronites, represented under E. the wife of Hezron. The later settlement of the
Calebites is represented under the union of C. with Ephrathah.
Ashhur (אַשְׁחוּר = אִישׁ חוּר, We. p. 15) is evidently identical with Hur,
the firstborn of Ephrathah (1 Ch 2⁴⁹). On Gazez (35⁶) see art.

36. Hur (35ᵈ) (*Uri,* Bezalel, 1 Ch 2²⁰): Shobal
(37) f. Kiriath-jearim (38), Salma (39) f. Bethlehem,
Hareph f. Bethgader, 1 Ch 2⁵⁰ᶠ.

The genealogy Hur, *Uri,* Bezalel is an evident insertion from
Ex 31², and is out of place in a series of gentilic and geographical names or relationships.

37. Shobal (36): Haroeh (Reaiah, 2 Ch 4²), half
Menuhoth, 1 Ch 2⁵².

Haroeh (הָרֹאֶה) is prob. textual error for Reaiah (רְאָיָה) s. Shobal
in 1 Ch 4². On half Menuhoth see note on (39). Of these
families nothing further is known.

38. Kiriath-jearim families (36): Ithrites, Puthites, Shumathites, Mishraites, Zorathites, Eshtaol-
ites, 1 Ch 2⁵³.

The Puthites, Shumathites, and Mishraites are not mentioned
elsewhere. To the Ithrites belonged two of David's heroes,
Ira and Gareb (2 S 23³⁸, 1 Ch 11⁴⁰). The Zorathites and Esh-
taolites are properly the gentilic names of the inhabitants
of Zorah and Eshtaol. These are placed subordinate to the
Mishraites or the other families (1 Ch 2⁵³). Zorah is mentioned
in Neh 11²⁹, and its people as Zorites again apparently in
1 Ch 2⁵⁴ (39).

39. Salma (36): Bethlehem, Netophathites, Atroth-beth-Joab, half Manahathites, Zorites, Tirathites, Shimeathites, Sucathites, 1 Ch 2⁵⁴ᵗ.

Salma is evidently identical with the reputed f. Boaz (16). The Netophathites (Neh 12²⁸) were inhabitants of Netophah (Ezr 2²², Neh 7²⁶), probably a village near Bethlehem. Atroth-beth-Joab is probably the same as the valley of the craftsmen (Neh 11³⁵). Of the Manahathites nothing is known. They (מְנֻחֹתִי) are probably the same as the Menuhoth (37) (מְנֻחוֹת) (Ki. has מנחתי in v.⁵²). The statement that the Tirathites (תִּרְעָתִים), Shimeathites (שִׁמְעָתִים), and Sucathites (שׂוּכָתִים) were families of scribes which dwelt at Jabez (v.⁵⁵), clearly proves that we have post-ex. material in our lists, for scribes are unknown before this period. The Vulg. saw in the families three different classes of religious functionaries: *canentes, resonantes, et in tabernaculis commorantes*. Be. allows a similar derivation, except that he regards the first class as door-keepers (Aram. תְּרַע =Heb. שַׁעַר door or gate). We. (p. 30 f.) finds underlying the three names תִּרְעָה a technical term for sacred music, שִׁמְעָה the Halacha or sacred tradition, and שׂוּכָה, which he connects with Vulg., and Be. with סוּכָּה 'booth,' cf. Lv 23³⁴. Ges. *Lex.*¹² derives the last two names from unknown places. Ke. interprets as descendants from Tira, Shimei and Suchah. For their connexion with Kenites see KENITES.

40. Reaiah (37): Jahath, Ahumai, Lahad, 1 Ch 4².

The lists (40)–(55) from 1 Ch 4¹·²⁰ 'look almost like a gathering of genealogical pebbles rolled together from various quarters, consisting of older and younger parts that are kept together only by the common connexion with the tribe of Judah' (Zoe.). Several of the leading 'fathers' are Calebites, *i.e.* Shobal, Hur, Ashhur, Chelub, Kenaz, Othniel, and Caleb. Hence the lists represent members of that clan, and Caleb should be substituted for Carmi in v.¹ (We. Ki. Zoe.). Whether the names and relationships reflect pre-exilic conditions or post-exilic is difficult to determine. Ki. regards the passage, with the exception of v.¹ and a few phrases noted below, as from the older sources of Ch. along with (226-33. 42-45. 47. 49. We.'s view is similar, that in the main pre-ex. conditions are reflected. Be. held, on the other hand, from the mention of a number of the names in the history given in Ezr and Neh, that we have a classification of the tribe of Judah actually made in the time between Zerubbabel and Ezra, so that these apparently broken and incoherent genealogies were plain to the readers of the time of the Chronicler. The view of We. and Ki. is more probable. We have, then, an old list of Calebites edited to bring it into greater harmony with the later times. Reaiah, cf. (37), occurs in a Reubenite pedigree 1 Ch 5⁵, and as a family name among the returned with Zerubbabel Ezr 24⁷, Neh 7⁵⁰. Jahath is a frequent Levite name (1 Ch 6²⁰·⁴³ 23¹⁰ᶠ·²⁴²², 2 Ch 34¹²). Ahumai and Lahad are mentioned only here. These are all called families of the Zorathites (v.²ᵇ acc. to Ki. is from a later hand), cf. (38), 1 Ch 15³.

41. Hur? f. Etam: Jezreel, Ishma, Idbash, d. Hazzelelponi, Penuel f. Gedor, Ezer f. Hushah, 1 Ch 4³ᵗ.

The MT of v.³ᵃ is defective (אֵלֶּה אֲבִי עֵיטָם 'these are f. of Etam'). RV supplies 'sons,' *i.e.* Jezreel, etc., are ss. of father of Etam. Ki. inserts 'sons of Hur' (בְּנֵי חוּר), but the 'sons of Hur' (v.⁴ᵇ) must include (40) as well as (41). LXX (also Kau.) has, 'These are the sons of Etam' (οὗτοι υἱοὶ Αἰταμ). Etam is a village near Bethlehem; possibly another place of the same name may be found near Hebron (see ETAM). Jezreel and Gedor are towns of S. Judah (Jos 15⁵⁶·⁵⁸). Two heroes of David's guard are mentioned as Hushites (2 S 21¹⁸ 23²⁷, 1 Ch 11²⁹ 20⁴ 27¹¹), but the location of Hushah is unknown. Penuel, a personal or gentilic name, is otherwise unknown. It cannot be associated with the Penuel E. of the Jordan. Ezer may be the same as Ezrah (53). Of Ishma and Idbash and Hazzelelponi, mentioned only here, nothing is known. The last should be rendered 'the Zelelponites' (צְלֶלְפּוֹנִי = הַצְלֶלְפּוֹנִי with art.). The words in v.⁴⁶ 'firstborn . . . Bethlehem' are according to Ki. from a later hand.

42. Ashhur (Hur) f. Tekoa (35ᵈ): (m. Naarah) Ahuzzam, Hepher, Temeni, Haahashtari, (m. Helah) Zereth, Izhar (Zohar, RVm) Ethnan, 1 Ch 4⁵⁻⁷.

On Ashhur (=Hur) see under (35ᵈ). F. of Tekoa, acc. Ki. is an annotation, cf. 1 Ch 2²⁴ (35ᵈ). Tekoa is near Bethlehem (see TEKOA). Naarah, evidently not this one, was a town on the borders of Ephraim and Benjamin (Jos 16⁷), but no such locality has yet been identified with Judah. Hepher, mentioned in connexion with Tappuah (Jos 12¹⁷) and Socoh (1 K 4¹⁰), evidently belonged to S. Judah. Temeni (תֵּימְנִי) properly means Southerner, *i.e.* of S. Judah. Cf. Teman (תֵּימָן) patronymic (תֵּימָנִי) of Edom (Gn 36¹¹ *et al.*). Ethnan (אֶתְנָן) is prob. identical with Ithnan (יִתְנָן, Jos 15²³), a city of S. Judah. For Izhar (יִצְהָר, Kt.) must be read Zohar (צֹחַר 'and Zohar'). This was the family name of Ephron of Hebron (Gn 23⁸ 25⁹), and also of a s. Simeon

(Gn 46¹⁰). The other names in (42) occur only in this connexion. For Haahashtari (הָאֲחַשְׁתָּרִי = אֲחַשְׁתְּרִי with art.) should be 'the Ahashtarites.' If this word is of Pers. derivation (Be. *Oxf. Heb. Lex.*), it must be an explanatory gloss referring to the preceding families.

43. Hakkoz (Koz): Anub, Zobebah, families of Aharhel s. Harum, 1 Ch 4⁸.

Koz (wrongly Hakkoz AV and RV, Heb. קוֹץ without art.) is a post-ex. family name (1 Ch 24¹⁰, Ezr 26¹, Neh 3⁴·²¹ 7⁶³; in all these passages the name has the art. הַקּוֹץ Hakkoz). The names of his children occur only here. Anub (עָנוּב) is prob. identical with Anab (עֲנָב), a town near Debir (Jos 15⁵⁰). Jabez, described in vv.⁹ᶠ·, prob. was connected in some way with Koz.

44. Chelub (b. Shuhah): Mehir f. Eshton (45), 1 Ch 4¹¹.

Chelub (כְּלוּב) is clearly another form of the clan name Caleb (כָּלֵב); cf. Chelubai (1 Ch 2⁹) (5). It is possible that for Shuhah (שׁוּחָה) we should read Hushah (חוּשָׁה v.⁴) (41). Of Mehir and Eshton, names occurring only here, nothing is known.

45. Eshton (44): Beth-rapha, Paseah, Tehinnah f. Ir-nahash (city of Nahash, RVm), 1 Ch 4¹².

Beth-rapha is otherwise unknown; a Benjaminite Rapha is mentioned 1 Ch 8², and Rapha 'giant' or the pl. Rephaim 'giants' 1 Ch 20⁴. But these throw no light on Beth-rapha. Paseah is a post-ex. family name of the Nethinim, Ezr 24⁹, Neh 7⁵¹, and is mentioned also in Neh 3⁶. The other names do not occur elsewhere. These ss. of Eshton are called 'the men of Recah' (v.¹²ᵇ), a place also otherwise unknown. The LXX has Rechab.

46. Kenaz: Othniel (47), Seraiah (49), 1 Ch 4¹³ᵃ.

Kenaz was an Edomite tribe (Gn 36¹¹·¹⁵·⁴², 1 Ch 136.53). Caleb, acc. to Nu 32¹², Jos 14⁶·¹⁴, was a Kenizzite. Othniel was the son of Kenaz acc. to Jg 1¹³, where Kenaz is also designated either as the f. or b. of Caleb. These statements clearly prove a close relationship between the Calebites and the Edomites. This is further reflected in Shobal f. Manahah, occurring in the list of Edomites, Gn 36²³, cf. (37). Othniel, like Caleb, prob. is a clan name. Whether the clan derived its name from a distinguished hero Othniel, or whether Othniel is a purely eponymous character, cannot perhaps be determined (see OTHNIEL). The close relationship between the clans of Caleb and Othniel is brought out in the story of Jg 1¹²⁻¹⁵ (see Moore *in loco*). Seraiah, a not infrequent name from the time of David onwards, as the brother of Othniel, is mentioned only here. It smacks so strongly of an individual, and the later period of Israel's history, that it is prob. an artificial link inserted among these names. It is among the names of the companions of Zerubbabel, Ezr 25².

47. Othniel (46): Hathath, 1 Ch 4¹³ᵇ.
48. Meonothai: Ophrah, 1 Ch 4¹⁴ᵃ.

Hathath occurs nowhere else. Perhaps Meonothai should be joined as another s. of Othniel. It also is not found elsewhere, but probably represents the inhabitants of Maon of S. Judah. Of Ophrah, the name also of a city of Benjamin (Jos 18²³, 1 S 13¹⁷) and of one of Manasseh (Jg 6¹¹), nothing is known.

49. Seraiah (46): Joab f. Ge-harashim, 1 Ch 4¹⁴ᵇ.

See (39). Acc. to Ki. 'f. Geharashim, craftsmen' v.¹⁴ is from a later hand.

50. Caleb s. Jephunneh: Iru, Elah (51), Naam, 1 Ch 4¹⁵ᵃ.

On Caleb s. of Jephunneh see CALEB. This additional list of descendants of Caleb shows that the Chronicler's lists contain different groups of Calebites not reduced to a perfect genealogical system, but arranged somewhat independently of each other, reflecting, as already intimated, enumerations of different times, localities, and sources. Many writers (the older commentators generally) wishing to harmonize all of the OT notices of Caleb, and regarding each Caleb as representing an individual, have seen several Calebs in 1 Ch 2 and 4. Neteler (*Die Bücher der biblischen Chronik*, p. 34) gives the following line of descent: Judah, *Perez, Hezron, Caleb Ben-hezron, Hur, Caleb Ben-hur, Salma, Kenaz, Jephunneh*, Caleb Ben-jephunneh. A somewhat similar explanation is given in Zoe. For Iru Elah (עִירוּ אֵלָה), Ir and Elah (עִיר וְאֵלָה) may be read (Ki.). We. (p. 39) finds the name Iru equivalent to Iram, a duke of Edom (1 Ch 1⁵⁴ עִירָם = עִירוּ). One is tempted to join Ir (עִיר) 'city' with Elah (אֵלָה = אֵלָת) Dillmann, Gn 36⁴¹) and find reference to the city Elath (see art.). At all events Elah is an Edomitic name (Gn 36⁴¹), and may be seen also in El-paran (אֵיל פָּארָן), the wilderness south of Judah. Naam is otherwise unknown.

51. Elah (50): Kenaz, 1 Ch 4¹⁵ᵇ.

Kenaz as s. Elah is surprising (assuming that the genealogy is not of persons), unless Elah is the name of the district of Elath or El-paran, which might have been the early home of the Kenizzites, or the name of a tribe to which Kenaz became subordinate. Perhaps a transposition should be made in the Heb. text, and instead of וּבְנֵי אֶלָּה קְנַז we should read אֵלֶּה בְנֵי קְנַז 'And these are the sons of Kenaz,' referring to (46)–(50) (vv.13-15).

52. Jehallelel: Ziph, Ziphah, Tiria, Asarel, 1 Ch 4[16].

Jehallelel only here, and as a personal or family name of ss. Merari, 2 Ch 29[12]. Ziph, the name of a city of S. Judah ; Ziphah, fem. form of the same occurs only here. Tiria and Asarel are not mentioned elsewhere.

53. Ezrah: Jether, Mered (54), Epher, Jalon, 1 Ch 4[17a].

Ezrah possibly is the same as Ezer (41). Jether is not an uncommon name, cf. (14). Mered occurs only in this connexion. Epher is the name of a son of Midian (Gn 25[4], 1 Ch 13[33]), and also of an individual or family of the half-tribe of Manasseh (1 Ch 5[24]). Jalon is found only here.

54. Mered (53): (m. Bithiah) Miriam, Shammai, Ishbah f. Eshtemoa, (m. the Jewess) Jered f. Gedor, Heber f. Soco, Jekuthiel f. Zanoah, 1 Ch 4[17f.].

The present text of v.[17f.] gives no complete sense. Usually the clauses are rearranged. The statement, 'And these are the ss. Bithiah d. Pharaoh which Mered took' (18b), is placed immediately after Jalon (17a) (Be. Ke. Zoe. Oe. Kau.) ; this gives (54). LXX (in 17b) has a different text (Καὶ ἐγέννησεν Ἰεθέρ), which Ki. follows, emending וַתַּהַר אֶת־מִרְיָם to וְיֶתֶר הוֹלִיד אֶת־מִרְיָם, 'And Jether begat Miriam,' etc. This places Jether as the progenitor of the ss. given in (54), and assumes that the ss. Mered and Bithiah, originally enumerated, have fallen out of the text. Miriam, elsewhere in OT only of Moses' sister, is here evidently a man's name. Shammai, also the name of a Jerahmeelite, cf. (8). Ishbah and Jekuthiel occur only here, and also Jered, except as the name of the antediluvian patriarch (Gn 5[15ff.]). Heber is not uncommon. In (41) Penuel is given as f. Gedor. Possibly, the posterity of two families or individuals were the reputed founders of the city. Eshtemoa, Gedor, Soco, and Zanoah are all towns in S. Judah or near Hebron (see arts.). Of the connexion here mentioned of Mered or Jether with Bithiah d. Pharaoh nothing is known. Instead of 'the Jewess,' RVm transliterates, Hajehudijah, and AV Jehudijah.

55. Hodiah: (m. sister of Naham) f. Keilah the Garmite, Eshtemoa the Maacathite, 1 Ch 4[19].

Hodiah is a common name of the time of Ezra and Neh. (AV here wrongly a woman's name, 'his wife Hodiah'). Before Eshtemoa probably f. has fallen out. Keilah and Eshtemoa are the names of Judæan towns (see art.). Maacathite (הַמַּעֲכָתִי) shows probably a connexion with Maacah (מַעֲכָה) (35c). Garmite and Naham occur only here.

56. Shimon: Amnon, Rinnah, Ben-hanan, Tilon, 1 Ch 4[20a].

57. Ishi: Zoheth, Ben-zoheth, 1 Ch 4[20b].

There is nothing to throw light on these names, most of which are mentioned only in this connexion. Ishi is in (11). Probably a name has fallen out before Ben-zoheth, i.e. s. Zoheth.

58. Perez fam.: a. Bani, Imri, Omri, Ammihud, Uthai, 1 Ch 9[4].

b. Mahalalel, Shephatiah, Amariah, Zechariah, Uzziah, Athaiah, Neh 11[4].

The pedigrees of the post-exilic Perezites Uthai (cf. Ezr 8[14]) and Athaiah of the inhabitants of Jerusalem.

59. Zerah (1): Zimri (Zabdi 60), Jos 7[1]), Ethan (61), Heman, Calcol, Dara, 1 Ch 2[6].

Ethan, Heman, Calcol, and Dara (Darda) are probably the names of famous men of the family of Zerah (cf. 1 K 4[31]) (see arts.). Whether Ethan and Heman are to be connected with the Levitical singers of those names is uncertain.

60. Zabdi (59): Carmi, Achan, Jos 7[1]; cf. 1 Ch 2[7].

Pedigree of Achan the trespasser (Achar, 1 Ch 27), see ACHAN.

61. Ethan (59): Azariah, 1 Ch 2[8].

Azariah the Ethanite is otherwise unknown. For another Zerahite see note at end of XXI.

V. 1. ISSACHAR: Tola (2), Puah,* Jashub,† Shimron, Gn 46[13], Nu 26[23f.], 1 Ch 7[1].

2. Tola (1): Uzzi (3), Rephaiah, Jeriel, Jahmai, Ibsam, Shemuel, 1 Ch 7[2].

* Puvah (פֻּוָה) (Gn 46[13]).
† Iob (יוֹב) (Gn 46[13]), a txt. err. (Ball, SBOT, in loc.).

3. Uzzi (2): Izrahiah, Michael, Obadiah, Joel, Isshiah, 1 Ch 7[3].

Of the names in the genealogy of Issachar's descendants, Tola appears as that of one of the minor judges, 's. Puah, s. Dodo, a man of Issachar' (Jg 10[1f.]). This implies that traditions varied in respect to the relationship of the clans of Tola and Puah. Puah may have been the more ancient, but Tola was undoubtedly the principal clan of Issachar, whose seat seems to have been centred at the unknown Shamir (Jg 10[1f.]). Of the other persons and families recorded nothing further is known, beyond that those of (2) and (3) are called 'mighty men of valour' and 'chief men,' and assigned apparently to the time of David, 1 Ch 7[2-5].

VI. 1. ZEBULUN: Sered, Elon, Jahleel, Gn 46[14], Nu 26[26].

Nothing further than their mention is known of these clans. Elon, probably an eponym from the clan, is one of the minor judges of Israel, who was buried in a place of the same name whose locality is unknown (Jg 12[11f.], cf. Moore, in loc.). No genealogy of Zebulun is given by the Chronicler.

VII.[a] 1. MANASSEH: a. Machir, Abiezer (7), Helek, Asriel, Shechem (5), Hepher (6), Shemida (5), Jos 17[1f.].

b. Machir, Gilead, Iezer, Helek, Asriel, Shechem, Shemida, Hepher, Nu 26[29-32].

c. (m. Aramæan concubine) Machir (f. Gilead) ; Zelophehad (6), d. Hammolecheth (7), 1 Ch 7[14f. 18].

2. Machir (1[abc]): (m. Maacah) Peresh, Sheresh (3), 1 Ch 7[16].

3. Sheresh (2): Ulam (1), Rakem, 1 Ch 7[16].

4. Ulam (3): Bedan, 1 Ch 7[17].

5. Shemida (1[ab]): Ahian, Shechem (1[ab]), Likhi, Aniam, 1 Ch 7[19].

6. Hepher (1[b]): Zelophehad (1[c]), dd. Mahlah, Noah, Hoglah, Milcah, Tirzah, Nu 26[33] 27[1].

7. Hammolecheth (1[c]): Ishhod, Abiezer (1[a]), and Mahlah, 1 Ch 7[18].

The genealogy of the tribe of Manasseh appears in different forms. Of the clans'enumerated (1[abc]), Machir is by far the most important. In the Song of Deborah he stands for the tribe of Manasseh (Jg 5[14]), and his home at that time seems to have been W. of the Jordan (Jg 5[14]). But he was especially known and remembered as the f. or conqueror of Gilead (Nu 26[29] 32[39], Jos 17[1], Dt 3[14]). Acc. to many authorities this conquest was made from W. Palestine (Smend, HWB, ed. Riehm ; Stade, Gesch. i. p. 149 ; Budde, Richt. u. Sam. p. 34 ff. ; Moore on Jg 5[15] ; but G. A. Smith, Hist. Geog. p. 577 n., regards the argument as inconclusive). From his pre-eminence and earlier development Machir, then, was regarded as the firstborn of Manasseh, or as the only son. In this latter scheme (1[a]) the other clans of Manasseh are recorded, not as descendants of Machir simply, but also of Gilead, as though their home was E. of the Jordan. But the clan Iezer, i.e. Abi-ezer (Gideon's clan), belonged to the district W. of the Jordan (Jg 6[11. 34] 8[2]). Tirzah, the city, a d. Zelophehad s. Hepher (7), was likewise situated W. of the Jordan (see TIRZAH), and Jos 17[1ff.] plainly implies that all of the ss. Manasseh (1[a]) except Machir dwelt W. of the Jordan. To the author of (1[b]) the name Gilead then either had lost its geographical meaning, or, what is more probable, holding that Gilead was first conquered, as represented in the Hex., he regarded the W. Manassites as offshoots of the E. Manassites. The genealogical scheme of (1[c]) (2) (3) (4) (5) (7), given in 1 Ch 7[14-19], is clearly distinct from (1[a]) or (1[b]), although not without points of connexion. The passage from which (1[c]) is derived is corrupt, and in its present state unintelligible, forbidding any satisfactory reconstruction (Ki. ; see attempts in Be. Oe). Asriel (אַשְׂרִיאֵל), 1 Ch 7[14], is plainly a dittography out of the following words (אֲשֶׁר יָלְדָה). The statement that the m. of Machir was an Aramæan appears likewise in the LXX of Gn 50[23]. The reference to Huppim and Shuppim and the sister (v.[15]) is entirely obscure. In Maacah, the wife of Machir, we may possibly see some connexion between Machirites and their neighbours, the Maacathites (see MAACAH). In 1 Ch 2[21] Hezron s. Perez s. Judah is represented as begetting through a d. of Machir, Segub, who begat Jair, 'who had twenty-three cities in the land of Gilead.' Segub (שְׂגוּב), who is not mentioned elsewhere, probably has arisen in transcription from Argob (אַרְגֹּב), the district given as inhabited by Jair the s. Manasseh (Dt 3[14]). Why Hezron, a clan of Judah (IV. 3), should be connected at all with Machir is entirely obscure. The statement probably has arisen through some misunderstanding. Hepher (1[a]) (6) may be connected with Hepher, the city and district mentioned in Jos 12[17] and 1 K 4[10]. According to Kuenen, Zelophehad was originally the name of a city (Dillm. on Nu 26[29]). The Jewish law of female inheritance is represented as traced to the petition of his daughters (Nu 27[1-11], 36[1-12]). The d. Tirzah, as assumed above, is the well-known city, and perhaps the names of the others should be sought in towns or villages. Of the other names introduced in these lists beyond what has been mentioned we know nothing. Perhaps Likhi (לִקְחִי) (5)=Helek (חֵלֶק) (1b) and Aniam (אֲנִיעָם) (5)=Noah (נֹעָה) (6) (Be.).

8. Epher, Ishi, Eliel, Azriel, Jeremiah, Hodaviah, Jahdiel, 1 Ch 5[24].

These are mentioned as 'mighty men of valour, famous men, heads of their fathers' houses,' of the half-tribe of Manasseh dwelling E. of the Jordan (ref.). Nothing further of them, indicating when they lived or for what they were famous, is given.

VII.[b] 1. EPHRAIM: *a.* Shuthelah (12), Becher, Tahan, Nu 26[35].

b. Shuthelah, Ezer, Elead, Beriah, d. Sheerah, Rephah, Resheph (4), 1 Ch 7[21-25].

2. Shuthelah (1): Eran, Nu 26[36].

3. Shuthelah (1[b]): *Bered, Tahath, Eleadah, Tahath, Zabad,* Shuthelah, 1 Ch 7[20f.].

4. Resheph (1[b]): *Telah, Tahan, Ladan, Ammihud, Elishama, Nun,* Joshua, 1 Ch 7[25-27].

The genealogy of Ephraim (1[b]) (3) (4), preserved in 1 Ch 7[20-27], is of uncertain construction. From the Heb. text it is not clear whether Ezer and Elead are the ss. of Shuthelah (No. 2) (3) or of Ephraim; or Sheerah and Rephah, the children of Beriah or Ephraim. The latter rendering in each case, as in (1[b]), is the better. In the first instance the context clearly demands it. Of special interest is the notice of the slaughter of Ezer and Elead on a cattle raid by the men of Gath (v.[21]). To the older commentators, who regarded Ephraim and his children as historical individuals, this episode was difficult of explanation, because it belonged evidently to the period of the sojourn in Egypt. It was usually interpreted as a foray out of Goshen (Zoe. Oe.)—against the use of the word יָרַד 'go down,' Ew. placed the event in the pre-Egyptian period (*Hist.* i. p. 380). Sayce refers to it as historical, and of the Egyptian period (*Patriarchal Palestine*, p. 202). There is little doubt, however, if an historical collision between Ephraimitic clans and Gittites underlies this notice, that the foray was from Mt. Ephraim (Be.). In the original story, Ephraim mourning (v.[22]) probably was no more thought of as an individual than Rachel in Jer 31[15]. The ss. of Ephraim slain then were two Ephraimitic clans, destroyed in some Phil. war. The connexion of Beriah, another clan, with the event arose either from a play upon the word, Beriah being regarded as the equivalent of 'in evil' = בְּרָעָה (בְּרִיעָה) (v. 23), or, in addition to the play upon the name, since Beriah is mentioned as a Benjam. family of Aijalon, who routed the inhabitants of Gath (1 Ch 8[13]), it is possible that this Benjam. Beriah, having driven back Gittite invaders, received the former home of Ezer and Elead, and thus became incorporated into the tribe of Ephraim (Be.). We. regards the entire episode as of late fabrication (*Prol.* p. 214).

The list of names given in this genealogy has a suspicious look. They appear like a repetition of the same elements. Not only is Shuthelah repeated (4), but there is a striking similarity between the other names.

לערן	of Eran.
לעדן	Laadan.
אלעדה	Eleadah.
אלעד	Elead.
שׁתחלה	Shuthelah.
ותלח	and Telah.
תחת	Tahath.
תחן	Tahan.
בכר	Becher.
וברד	and Bered.
זבד	Zabad.

Tahan (1[a]) (4) and Tahath (3) are without doubt the Tohu (1 S 1[1]) and the Tahath, Nahath, and Toah (III. 22[ab]). Sheerah was the reputed builder of Bethhoron, whose name appears in Uzzen-sheerah (wh. see) (v.[24]). Elishama s. Ammihud (1[a]) appears as the prince of the tribe of Ephraim in Nu 1[10], whence it is easy to see how the pedigree of Joshua was constructed.

VIII. 1. BENJAMIN: *a.* Bela (2), Becher (4), Ashbel, Gera, Naaman, Ehi, Rosh, Muppim, Huppim, Ard, Gn 46[21].

b. Bela (2), Ashbel, Ahiram, Shephupham, Hupham, Nu 26[38f.].

c. Bela (2), Becher (4), Jediael (5), 1 Ch 7[6].

d. Bela (2), Ashbel, Aharah, Nohah, Rapha, 1 Ch 8[1].

We have thus four different lists of ss. Benjamin. Bela is common to all; Ehi, Rosh, Muppim, and Huppim (1[a]) are clearly equivalent to Ahiram, Shephupham, and Hupham (1[b]); cf. the Heb. text, אחי ראש מפים חפים, with אחירם שׁפּים חפם. Hence Rosh (1[a]) should be struck out and Ahiram substituted for Ehi (1[a]), and also probably for Aharah (אַחְרַח) (1[d]). Gn 46[21] LXX

reads **Benjamin,** Bela, Becher, Ashbel; **Bela, Gera,** Naaman, Ehi, Rosh, Muppim, and Huppim. This corresponds with (2[a]) (3) (see below), where Gera, Naaman, and Ard are ss., Bela and Shuppim and Huppim grandsons. Hence the original text of Gn 46[21] may have read Benjamin, Bela, Becher, Ashbel; Bela, Gera, Naaman, Ahiram, Shephupham, Huppim, Ard (Ball, *in loco*, *SBOT*).

In (1[c]) Jediael (וְדִיעָאל) appears as the equivalent of Ashbel (אֶשְׁבֵּל = אִישׁ־בַּעַל) either by corruption or substitution. Whether a textual corruption or an independent tradition underlies Nohah and Rapha (1[d]) it is impossible to determine. The names as Benjaminites occur only here.

2. Bela (1[abcd]): *a.* Ard, Naaman, Nu 26[40].

b. Ezbon, Uzzi, Uzziel, Jerimoth, Iri (3), 1 Ch 7[7].

c. Addar, Gera, Abihud, Abishua, Naaman, Ahoah, Gera, Shephuham, Huram, 1 Ch 8[1f.].

The list (2[b]) appears to be entirely independent of the others. The list (2[c]) corresponds closely with the restored text of Gn 46[21] (see above), since Addar (אַדָּר)=Ard (אַרְדְּ); Gera and Abihud probably were originally one and the same person, *i.e.* Gera f. Ehud (cf. Jg 3[15]); the second Gera is plainly a dittography; Huram (חוּרָם) probably = Huppim (חֻפִּים); and hence the only additional names are Abishua and Ahoah (אֲחוֹחַ); and the latter may be a variation or corruption of Ahiram (אֲחִירָם) or Aharah (אַחְרַח), repeated in transcription from the previous generation (1[d]).

3. Iri (2[b]): Shuppim, Huppim, 1 Ch 7[12].

In the text the name is Ir (v.[12]). Shuppim and Huppim seem identical with Shephupham and Hupham, given elsewhere as ss. Benjamin (1[b]) and ss. Bela (2[c]). Nothing further than their appearance in the genealogical lists is known of these individuals or families. In the text v.[12] appears like an appendix (see also (6) below).

4. Becher (1[ac]): Zemirah, Joash, Eliezer, Elioenai, Omri, Jeremoth, Abijah, Anathoth, Alemeth, 1 Ch 7[8].

The names of these ss. Becher (4), Joash, Eliezer, Elioenai, Omri, Jeremoth, and Abijah occur frequently in the OT; Jeremoth again as a Benjaminite in 1 Ch 7[7] 8[14]. Anathoth and Alemeth are names of Benjaminite towns (see arts.). Zemirah occurs only in this connexion.

5. Jediael (1[c]): *Bilhan,* Jeush, Benjamin, Ehud, Chenaanah, Zethan, Tarshish, Ahishahar, 1 Ch 7[10].

This list (5) is striking in having Benjamin as a subordinate family or personal name, and likewise, in this connexion, Ehud, elsewhere s. Gera (cf. Jg 3[15]). Bilhan and Jeush are also Edomite names (Gn 36[5. 14. 18. 27]), and Jeush, moreover, that of a Levite or Levitical family (1 Ch 23[10f.]), and of a son of Rehoboam (2 Ch 11[19]), and again of a Benjaminite (1 Ch 8[39]). (For refs. on Jeush as an Arab. name of a deity, see Gesenius-Buhl.) Chenaanah (כְּנַעֲנָה) suggests the incorporation of a Can. family with the Benjaminites (Be.). In 1 K 22[24] it is the name of the f. Zedekiah the false prophet. Zethan and Ahishahar are found only here. The latter, however, perhaps appears in the cuneiform inscriptions as the name of a king of Minnai (see Gesen.-Buhl). Tarshish, besides being the name of the well known city, stands elsewhere for a precious stone, derived from Tarshish (Ex 28[20] 39[13] *et al.*, RV 'beryl'), and is the name of a Persian prince (Est 1[14]).

These Belaites, Becherites, and Jediaelites (2[b]) (4) (5) are all called heads of fathers' houses and mighty men of valour, but there is no indication of the period of Israel's pre-ex. history to which they were intended to be assigned (1 Ch 7[7-11]).

6. Aher: Hushim, 1 Ch 7[12b].

This genealogical fragment is enigmatical. Hushim (חֻשִׁים) in Gn 46[23] is a s. Dan. There Dan also stands between Benjamin and Naphtali. The Chronicler has given no genealogy of Dan unless it is found here, between the genealogy of Benjamin, vv.[6-11], and that of Naphtali, v.[13]. Hence Dan has been found hidden in Aher (אַחֵר, 'another'), which occurs nowhere else as a proper name. The tribe of Dan was believed thus to have been indicated, owing to its opprobrium on account of its idolatry (Jg 18). Its name does not appear with the other tribes in 1 Ch 6[54-81]. Cf. also its omission in Rev 7[5-8]. (The name Dan, however, does appear in 1 Ch 2[2] 12[35] 27[22], and the genealogy of Zebulun is missing in 1 Ch as well as that of Dan. If the above hypothesis is accepted, the remainder of v.[12] may be a gloss, Shuppim and Huppim suggested by their similarity to Hushim as the ss. of Benjamin intended (Dan not being recognized in Aher, and these ss. being missed in the preceding vv.). Ir (עִיר), then, from the influence of v.[7], may have been later developed out of Ard (אֶרְדְּ), which follows Muppim and Huppim in Gn 46[21] (see 1[a]) (Be.).

If, however, as we have assumed, Hushim is a Benjam. family or individual, Aher may be identical with Ahiram (1[b]) (RVm) or with the Benjaminite Shaharaim (8) (שַׁחֲרַיִם), who had a wife Hushim (1 Ch 8[8. 11]).

7. Ehud: Uzza, Ahihud, 1 Ch 8[6f.].

The verses from which (7) is taken are difficult of interpretation. Probably the text is corrupt (see Comm. *in loco*). The connexion of Ehud (אֵחוּד) with the sons of Benjamin is not given. It is likely, however, that ח=ה, and that reference here also is to clan Ehud (אֵהוּד), s. Gera or s. Jediael, cf. (5). The ss. Ehud (possibly not those given above, but those whose names have fallen out of the text) were heads of families of the inhabitants of Geba (v.[6]) (see note on 23).

8. Shaharaim: (m. Hodesh) Jobab, Zibia, Mesha, Malcam, Jeuz, Shachia, Mirmah, (m. Hushim) Abitub, Elpaal (9) (13 ?), 1 Ch 8[8-10].

The connexion of Shaharaim with any of the ss. Benjamin is also not given. He is said to have begotten children in the field of Moab after he had sent away two wives, Hushim and Baara (v.[8]). These allusions are entirely obscure. The sons whose m. was Hodesh are said to have been heads of families. Their residence is not given, unless by implication it is the country of Moab.

9. Elpaal (8): Eber, Misham, Shemed,* 1 Ch 8[12].

To Shemed is attributed the building, evidently the rebuilding, of Lod and Ono, for these cities were very ancient, appearing prob. in the list of the places conquered by Tahutmes III. (*RP* (New Series), vol. v. pp. 25–53).

10. —— Beriah (11), Shema (12), Ahio? Elpaal? (13), Shashak (14), Jeremoth (15), 1 Ch 8[13f.].

The connexion of these Benjaminites, as in the cases of (7) and (8), with ss. Benjamin is not given. Their brotherhood is obtained by reading in v.[14], after the analogy of the LXX, אָחִיו 'his brother' (Kau.), or אֲחֵיהֶם 'their brothers' (Ki.), instead of אֲחִיו Ahio, a proper name (a reading certainly to be rejected), and by adding the name Elpaal required by v.[19] (Kau. Ki.). Whether for Jeremoth (יְרֵמוֹת) we should read Jeroham (יְרֹחָם), after v.[27], or there substitute Jeremoth, it is impossible to determine. Both names clearly refer to one person; also Shema (שְׁמַע) (v.[13]) and (שִׁמְעִי) (v.[21]).

Beriah and Shema are called 'heads of fathers' houses of Aijalon who put to flight the inhabitants of Gath,' v.[13]. This flight is otherwise unknown, although it has been connected with the slaughter of the ss. Ephraim (1 Ch 7[21]), and Beriah has been identified with Beriah s. Ephraim (1 Ch 7[23], cf. note on VII[b]. 4). Nothing further is stated concerning these five reputed founders of the families mentioned below.

11. Beriah (10): Zebadiah, Arad, Eder, Michael, Ishpah, Joha, 1 Ch 8[15f.].

12. Shimei (**Shema**) (10): Jakim, Zichri, Zabdi, Elienai, Zillethai, Eliel, Adaiah, Beraiah, Shimrath, 1 Ch 8[19-21].

13. Elpaal (10): Zebadiah, Meshullam, Hizki, Heber, Ishmerai, Izliah, Jobab, 1 Ch 8[17f.].

14. Shashak (10): Ishpan, Eber, Eliel, Abdon, Zichri, Hanan, Hananiah, Elam, Anthothijah, Iphdeiah, Penuel, 1 Ch 8[22-25].

15. Jeroham (**Jeremoth**) (10): Shamsherai, Shehariah, Athaliah, Jaareshiah, Elijah, Zichri, 1 Ch 8[26f.].

These lists (11)–(15) represent five clans or families of postexilic Jerus. (see note below on 23), each member mentioned 'the head of a father's house, a chief man' (1 Ch 8[28]). Nothing further is known of them, although some of their names, representing other persons, occur elsewhere in the OT. Be. identifies Elpaal (13) with the Elpaal (9), and Eber (עֵבֶר), Misham (מִשְׁעָם) and Shemed (שֶׁמֶר) (9), with Heber (חֶבֶר), Meshullam (מְשֻׁלָּם), and Ishmerai (יִשְׁמְרַי) (13).

16. Jeiel: (m. Maacah) Abdon, Zur, Kish (17), Baal, Ner (23), Nadab, Gedor, Ahio, Zechariah,† Mikloth (24), 1 Ch 8[29-31] 9[35-37].

17. Kish (16): *Saul*, Jonathan (18), Malchi-shua, Abinadab, Eshbaal, 1 Ch 8[33] 9[39].

18. Jonathan (17): *Merib-baal*, Micah, Pithon, Melech, Tahrea,‡ Ahaz (19), 1 Ch 8[34] 9[40].

19. Ahaz (18): *Jarah*,§ Alemeth, Azmaveth, Zimri (20).

20. Zimri (19): *Moza, Binea, Rephaiah, Eleasah,* Azel (21), Eshek (22), 1 Ch 8[36bf. 39a] 9[42bf.].

21. Azel (20): Azrikam, Bocheru ?, Ishmael, Sheariah, Obadiah, Hanan, 1 Ch 8[38] 9[44].

* Shemer (ר instead of ד) acc. to Hahn's and Theile's Heb. Text, but Shemed acc. to Baer and Del.
† Zecher, 1 Ch 8[31].   ‡ Tarea, 1 Ch 8[34].
§ Jehoaddah, 1 Ch 8[36].

22. Eshek (20): Ulam, Jeush, Eliphelet, 1 Ch 8[39].
23. Ner (16): Abner ?, 1 Ch 8[33] 9[39].
24. Mikloth (16): Shimeam,* 8[32] 9[28].

This genealogy of the house of Saul (16)–(23) is given twice, the original texts being in each case the same (1 Ch 8[29-38] and 9[35-44]). While the latter passage is perhaps in the better state of preservation, and has been mainly followed above, both have suffered some corruption. In v.[39] Abner has clearly fallen out of the text and should be restored, cf. (23) (Kau. Ki.). In v.[41] Ahaz should be added to the ss. Micah, as in 8[35]. In v.[44] instead of Bocheru (בִּכְרוֹ) we should read 'his firstborn' (בְּכֹרוֹ); another name must be supplied to complete the six sons of Azel (21). In (16) the f. Kish and Ner is Jeiel f. Gibeon. This differs from 1 S 9[1 14][51], where Abiel is f. Kish and Ner. The motive for the introduction of this genealogy clearly arose from the fact that at the time of the Chronicler certain Jewish families claimed descent from Saul. The genealogy furnishes a line of 15 generations. Allowing 12 from the founding of Solomon's temple to that of Zerubbabel (see note on III. 12), these descendants belonged to near the time of Ezra and Nehemiah.

Looking at these lists (7)–(24) as a whole, they evidently were based upon post-ex. conditions, for the following reasons:—(*a*) The places of residence (not mentioning Jerus.) are towns recurring in the post-ex. history,—Geba (v.[6]), cf. Ezr 2[26]; Lod and Ono (v.[12]), cf. Ezr 2[33]; Gibeon (v.[29]), cf. Neh 7[25]. (*b*) Many of the names belong also to that period, viz.: Meshullam (13), Hanan, Elam, Hananiah, Anthothijah (Anathoth) (14), cf. Neh 10[10. 14. 19. 20. 23. 26]. (*c*) The coincidence between the residence in or connexion with Moab (v.[8]) and the name Pahath-moab representing an important family among the post-ex. Jews (Ezr 2[6] 8[4] etc.). (Be. conjectures that the birth of this Pahath-moab, 'prince of Moab,' is referred to in v.[8]). (*d*) The Benjaminites had a considerable part in the post-ex. community along with the children of Judah and the Levites. (*e*) The close union between 1 Ch 8 and 9, which latter from its identity with Neh 11 is recognized at once as describing post-ex. conditions.

25. —— *Jeshaiah, Ithiel, Maaseiah, Kolaiah, Pedaiah, Joed, Meshullam,* Sallu, Neh 11[7], cf. 1 Ch 9[7].

Sallu represents a post-ex. family of Jerus. (see ref.). In 1 Ch 9[7] the descent is, Sallu s. Meshullam, s. Hodaviah, s. Hassenuah.

IX. 1. DAN: Hushim,† Gn 46[23], Nu 26[42].

Only one clan is recorded as having belonged to Dan. The difference of name in Gn and Nu has arisen from the transposition of letters, Hushim (חֻשִׁים), Shuham (שׁוּחָם). Dan is passed over by the Chronicler, unless a reference to the tribe is concealed in 1 Ch 7[12]; cf. VIII. 3, above. Nothing more than the genealogical record is known of Hushim. On a single son or clan representing the tribe, see DAN.

X. 1. NAPHTALI: Jahzeel,‡ Guni, Jezer, Shillem,¶ Gn 46[24], Nu 26[48f.], 1 Ch 7[13].

These ss. or clans of Naphtali are not mentioned in any other connexion in OT, neither do their names occur elsewhere, except that of Guni, which is also the name of a Gadite (XI. 4). No further descendants of Naphtali are given.

XI. 1. GAD: Ziphion,§ Haggi, Shuni, Ezbon,§ Eri, Arodi,§ Areli, Gn 46[16], Nu 26[15-17].
2. —— Joel, Shapham, Janai, Shaphat, 1 Ch 5[12].
3. —— *Buz, Jahdo, Jeshishai, Michael, Gilead, Jaroah, Huri, Abihail,* Michael, Meshullam, Sheba, Jorai, Jacan, Zia, Eber, 1 Ch 5[13f.].
4. —— *Guni, Abdiel,* Ahi, 1 Ch 5[15].

Joel, Shapham, Janai, Shaphat (2), Michael, Meshullam, Sheba, Jorai, Jacan, Zia, Eber (3), all represent families of the tribe of Gad, registered according to the Chronicler in the days of Jotham king of Judah, and Jeroboam king of Israel (1 Ch 5[17]). Their connexion with any of the ss. Gad (1) is not given. Indeed, those clans are not mentioned in 1 Ch. Ahi (4) is given as 'chief of their fathers' houses.' We know of nothing further of value that can be said respecting this genealogy.

XII. 1. ASHER: Imnah, Ishvah,‖ Ishvi,‖ Beriah (2), d. Serah, Gn 46[17], Nu 26[44], 1 Ch 7[30].
2. Beriah (1): Heber (3), Malchiel f. Birzaith,¶ Gn 46[17], Nu 26[45], 1 Ch 7[31].
3. Heber (2): Japhlet (4), Shomer** (5), Hotham (6), d. Shua, 1 Ch 7[32].
4. Japhlet (3): Pasach, Bimhal, Ashvath, 1 Ch 7[33].

* Shimeah, 1 Ch 8[32].   † Shuham, Nu 26[42].
‡ Jahziel, Shallum, 1 Ch 7[13].
§ Zephon, Ozni, Arod, Nu 26[15ff.].
‖ The two names Ishvah (יִשְׁוָה) and Ishvi (יִשְׁוִי) prob. represent a dittography. Nu 26[44] omits the former.
¶ F. Birzaith only in 1 Ch 7[31].
** Shemer (v.[34]), preferred by Ki. The two names represent the same person.

5. Shomer (3): Ahi, Rohgah, Jehubbah,* Aram, 1 Ch 7[34].

6. Helem (Hotham)†(3): Zophah, Imna, Shelesh, Amal, 1 Ch 7[35].

7. Zophah (6): Suah, Harnepher, Shual, Beri, Imrah, Bezer, Hod, Shamma, Shilshah, Ithran (8), Beera, 1 Ch 7[36f.].

8. Jether (Ithran) †(7): Jephunneh, Pispah, Ara, 1 Ch 7[38].

9. Ulla (——?)†: Ara, Hanniel, Rizia, 1 Ch 7[39].

Nothing further than their registration is known of these clans and families of Asher. Ishvah, Serah (1), Malchiel, Birzaith (2), Japhlet, Shua (3), Pasach, Bimhal, Ashvath (4), Rohgah, Hubbah (5), Zophah, Imnah, Shelesh, Amal (6), Suah, Harnepher, Beri, Imrah, Hod, Shilshah, Bera (7), Pispah, Ara (8), Ulla, and Rizia occur as prop. names only in this connexion. The occurrence of the others elsewhere throws no light upon their appearance here. It is an interesting fact that the names of the two clans Heber (Habiri) and Malchiel (2) appear also together in the Amarna tablets, representing, it may be, clans of the ancient seat of Asher (see *Journ. of Bib. Lit.* vol. xi. 1892, p. 120). Birzaith (2) is probably the name of a place (בִּרְיַת = בְּאֵרְוִית, *i.e.* 'Olive-well'). Local names may be seen also in Harnepher, Bezer, Beera (7), and perhaps some other names (Be.).

XIII. ‡ 1. David's Recruits at Ziklag.

(*a*) *Of Benjamin* : Ahiezer and Joash ss. Shemaah the Gibeathite ; Jeziel and Pelet ss. Azmaveth, Beracah, Jehu the Anathothite ; Ishmaiah the Gibeonite, Jeremiah, Jahaziel, Johanan, Jozabad the Gederathite, Eluzai, Jerimoth, Bealiah, Shemariah, Shephatiah the Haruphite ; Elkanah, Isshiah, Azarel, Joezer, Jashobeam Korahites ; Joelah and Zebadiah ss. Jeroham of Gedor, 1 Ch 12[3-7].

In the text these are given as Benjaminites. It seems not improbable, however, that the Chronicler may have fused some Judæans among them, since the Korahites can hardly be others than warriors from the Judæan city or family Korah (1 Ch 2[43]). Gedor and Gederah are likewise found among Judæan towns (Jos 15[36. 58], 1 Ch 4[39]). In v.[16], evidently misplaced, it says, 'and there came of the children of Benjamin and Judah to the hold unto David.'

(*b*) *Of Gad* : Ezer, Obadiah, Eliab, Mishmannah, Jeremiah, Attai, Eliel, Johanan, Elzabad, Jeremiah, Machbannai, 1 Ch 12[9-13].

(*c*) *Of Manasseh* : Adnah, Jozabad, Jediael, Michael, Jozabad, Elihu, Zillethai, 1 Ch 12[20].

All of these recruits are mentioned as mighty men of valour. Those of Gad are said to have had faces like the faces of lions, and to have been as swift as the roes upon the mountains (1 Ch 12[8]).

2. David's Mighty Men.

2 S 23[8-39].	1 Ch 11[11-47].
8. Josheb-basshebeth a Tah-chemonite.	11. Jashobeam s. a Hachmonite.
9. Eleazar s. Dodai s. an Ahohite.	12. Eleazar s. Dodo the Ahohite.
11. Shammah s. Agee a Hararite.	[Names wanting, or portions of names omitted, are identical with those in 2 S].
18. Abishai brother of Joab.	20.
20. Benaiah s. Jehoiada.	22.
24. Asahel brother of Joab. Elhanan s. Dodo of Bethlehem.	26.
25. Shammah the Harodite. Elika the Harodite.	27. Shammoth the Harorite. Wanting.
26. Helez the Paltite. Ira s. Ikkesh the Tekoite.	Pelonite.
27. Abiezer the Anathothite. Mebunnai the Hushathite.	28.
28. Zalmon the Ahohite. Maharai the Netophahite.	29. Sibbecai. Ilai.
29. Heleb s. Baanah the Netophahite.	30.
Ittai s. Ribai of Gibeah.	Heled.
30. Benaiah a Pirathonite. Hiddai of the brooks of Gaash.	31. Ithai.
	32. Hurai.

2 S 23[8-39].	1 Ch 11[11-47].
31. Abi-albon the Arbathite.	Abiel.
Azmaveth the Barhumite.	33.
32. Eliahba the Shaalbonite.	
Ss. Jashen, Jonathan.	
33. Shammah the Hararite.	34. Ss. Hashem the Gizonite.
	Jonathan s. Shage the Hararite.
Ahiam s. Sharar the Ararite.	s. Sacar.
	35.
34. Eliphelet s. Ahasbai s. the Maacathite.	Eliphal s. Ur.
Eliam s. Ahithophel the Gilonite.	36. Hepher the Mecherathite Ahijah the Pelonite.
35. Hezro the Carmelite.	37.
Paarai the Arbite.	Naarai s. Ezbai.
36. Igal s. Nathan of Zobah.	38. Joel the brother of Nathan.
Bani the Gadite.	Mibhar s. Hagri.
37. Zelek the Ammonite.	39.
Naharai the Beerothite.	40.
38. Ira the Ithrite.	41.
Gareb the Ithrite.	Zabad s. Ahlai.
39. Uriah the Hittite.	Adina s. Shiza the Reubenite.
	43. Hanan s. Maacah.
	Jehoshaphat the Mithnite.
	44. Uzzia the Ashterathite.
	Shama and} ss. Hotham
	Jeiel } the Aroerite.
	45. Jediael s. Shimri.
	Joha his brother, the Tizite.
	46. Eliel the Mahavite, Jeribai and Joshaviah ss. Elnaam.
	Ithmah the Moabite.
	47. Eliel, Obed, and Jaasiel the Mezobaite.

The first twelve mighty men, as recorded in 1 Ch 11, appear again also in 1 Ch 27[1-15] as captains, each in course, month by month, commanding a monthly levy of 24,000 soldiers, beginning in the first month with Jashobeam, who is called s. Zabdiel, and reckoned as belonging to ss. Perez (IV. 1). The captain of the second month is Dodai, 'Eleazar s.' evidently having fallen from the text. With him is mentioned Mikloth as ruler. With Benaiah was associated Ammizabad his son ; with Asahel, Zebadiah his son. Shammoth appears as Shamhuth and an Izrahite. Helez is called of Ephraim ; Sibbecai, of the Zerahites (IV. 1) ; also Maharai ; Benaiah, the eleventh captain, a Pirathonite of Ephraim ; Heled appears as Heldai (1 Ch 27[15]), and of Othniel (IV. 46).

The names Zabad to Asiel (1 Ch 11[41b-47]) do not appear in 2 S, and were evidently derived from another source. A comparison of the two lists shows that the names vary in several instances, but it is frequently impossible to determine which form is original, or whether both may not be corrupt. The following observations are confined mainly to the variations which appear in 1 Ch, since the names of the list of 2 S are treated elsewhere (see arts.).

Notes on vv.[11-47] : **11.** Jashobeam (s. Zabdiel, 1 Ch 27[2]) (יָשָׁבְעָם) was originally Jishbaal (יִשְׁבַּעַל) or Ishbaal (אִישְׁבַּעַל) (Ki. *et al.*). The reference in Hachmonite is not known. **12.** Dodai (דּוֹדַי) of 2 S is to be preferred to Dodo (דּוֹדוֹ), cf. 1 Ch 27[4]. Ahohite may be a patronymic of the family or clan Ahoah of Benjamin (VIII. 2[c]). **27.** For Shammoth (שַׁמּוֹת) Ki. reads Shamhuth (שַׁמְהוּת), after LXX and 1 Ch 27[8]. Harodite (חֲרֹדִי) is preferable to Harorite (חֲרוֹרִי), and the reference may be to Harod (Jg 7[1]), (see HAROD). In 1 Ch 27[8] he is called an Izrahite (יִזְרָחִי), but the true reading prob. is Zarhite (זַרְחִי), *i.e.* of ss. Zerah (IV. 1). Instead of Pelonite (פְּלוֹנִי) read Paltite (פַּלְטִי) (2 S) (Ges. *Lex.*[12] Buhl, Ki.), and the reference then, acc. to Driver (*Text of Sam.* p. 283), is to Beth-pelet in S. Judah (Jos 15[27]) ; but acc. to 1 Ch 27[10] Helez belonged to Ephraim. **28.** Sibbecai is generally acknowledged to be the true reading. **29.** Ki. combines, on the support of LXX, the readings of 2 S and 1 Ch, and obtains Aliman (עֲלִימָן). **30. 31.** Heled or Heldai (1 Ch 27[15]) is probably correct, and Ithai is equally as defensible as Ittai of 2 S. **32.** Ki. emends Hurai to Hiddai, but Budde (*Crit. Text*, 1 and 2 S) in 2 S emends Hiddai to Hurai. Abiel is probably correct. **33.** For Baharumite (בַּחֲרֻמִי) read Bahurimite (בַּחוּרִמִי), *i.e.* of Bahurim (wh. see). **34.** The corresponding text of 2 S is clearly defective. Probably we should read Jashen the Gunite, Jonathan s. Shammah the Hararite (Ki. Driver, Budde). On Gunite see XI. 1. The reference in Hararite is not known. **35 f.** Sharar and Eliphelet (2 S) are probably correct (Ki.). Ur and Hepher probably have arisen from the name of the f. Eliphelet. Ahasbai (2 S) is suspicious (Driv.). For Mecherathite (מְכֵרָתִי) read Maacathite (מַעֲכָתִי), and follow 2 S (v.[34b]) for 36[b]. **37.** Which of the two readings is to be preferred cannot be determined. **38.** The choice here seems to be in favour of 2 S. Joel, however, might stand. Mibhar (מִבְחָר) has arisen apparently from ' of Zobah' (מִצֹּבָה). **44.** Ashterathite = from Ashteroth, a city of Bashan, cf. 1 Ch 6[71]. **46.** Mahavite (מַחֲוִים) is suspicious. Be. reads Mahanaimite, *i.e.* of Mahanaim (מַחֲנַיְמִי) (Ges. *Lex.*[12] Buhl) **47.** A corruption also underlies Mezobaite (מְצֹבָיָה).

---

* Jehubbah (יְחֻבָּה)=and Hubbah (וְחֻבָּה).

† Helem (הֵלֶם) clearly=Hotham (הוֹתָם) ; Jether (יֶתֶר)=Ithran (יִתְרָן) ; and Ulla (עֻלָּא) probably is a corruption of one of the previous names, perhaps Shual (שׁוּעָל) (7) or Beera (בְּאֵרָא) (7).

‡ Under XIII. have been grouped, for the sake of reference, certain lists of names found chiefly in 1 and 2 Ch.

3. David's Officers over the Twelve Tribes of Israel—

Of Reuben, Eliezer s. Zichri.
„ Simeon, Shephatiah s. Maacah.
„ Levi, Hashabiah s. Kemuel.
„ Aaron, Zadok.
„ Judah, Elihu * brother of David.
„ Issachar, Omri s. Michael.
„ Zebulun, Ishmaiah s. Obadiah.
„ Naphtali, Jeremoth s. Azriel.
„ Ephraim, Hoshea s. Azaziah.
„ W. Manasseh, Joel s. Pedaiah.
„ E. Manasseh, Iddo s. Zechariah.
„ Benjamin, Jaasiel s. Abner.
„ Dan, Azarel s. Jeroham, 1 Ch 27[16-22].

4. Rulers of David's substance—

Azmaveth s. Adiel, over the king's treasuries.
Jonathan s. Uzziah, over treasuries in cities, castles, villages, and fields.
Ezri s. Chelub, over tillers of the ground.
Shimei the Ramathite, over the vineyards.
Zabdi the Shiphmite, over wine cellars.
Baal-hanan the Gederite, over olive and sycomore trees.
Joash, over cellars of oil.
Shitrai the Sharonite, over herds in Sharon.
Shaphat s. Adlai, over herds in the valleys.
Obil the Ishmaelite, over camels.
Jehdeiah the Meronothite, over asses.
Jaziz the Hagrite, over the flocks, 1 Ch 27[25-31].

On Chelub, v.[26], see IV. 44 note. Shiphmite occurs only here, and cannot be more closely defined. Meronothite refers to Meronoth, a place which seems to have been in the neighbourhood of Gibeon and Mizpah, cf. Neh 37. By a Hagrite we understand a descendant of Hagar or an Arabian tribe (cf. 1 Ch 5[10. 19f.]). On the other appellatives see arts.

5. Princes under Jehoshaphat appointed to teach the Law.—Ben-hail, Obadiah, Zechariah, Nethanel, Micaiah, 2 Ch 17[7].

6. Captains under Jehoshaphat.—Adnah, Jehohanan, Amasiah s. Zichri, Eliada, Jehozabad, 2 Ch 17[14-18].

The first three of these captains were of Judah, the other two of Benjamin. Each is said to have commanded from 180,000 men (Eliada) to 300,000 (Adnah).

7. Captains under the priest Jehoiada.—Azariah s. Jeroham, Ishmael s. Jehohanan, Azariah s. Obed, Maaseiah s. Adaiah, Elishaphat s. Zichri, 2 Ch 23[1].

These were associated with Jehoiada in the overthrow of Athaliah and enthronement of Joash. See ATHALIAH, JEHOIADA, JOASH.

8. Heads of ss. Ephraim.—Azariah s. Johanan, Berechiah s. Meshillemoth, Jehizkiah s. Shallum, Amasa s. Hadlai, 2 Ch 28[12].

These are mentioned as opposing, in the reign of Pekah, the bringing of Judæan captives to Samaria, and are said to have clothed and fed the captives, and then sent them home (2 Ch 28[12-15]).

(C) LISTS OF FAMILIES AND PERSONS RECORDED IN CONNEXION WITH THE RETURN AND THE LABOURS OF EZRA AND NEHEMIAH † : — XIV.‡ Those who returned with Zerubbabel. XV. Those who returned with Ezra. XVI. The repairers of the wall of Jerusalem. XVII. Those who had foreign wives. XVIII. The signers of the Covenant. XIX. Priests and Levites of the days of Zerubbabel and Joiakim. XX. Participants in the promulgation of the Law and Dedication of the Wall. XXI. Residents of Jerusalem.

* Probably Eliab (Ki.). See IV. 16.
† These lists are for reference only, and without textual and historical notes.
‡ This nomenclature XIV. XV. etc. is used to bring these tables, for convenience of reference, into line with the previous ones. Where the names and classifications are identical they frequently represent the same person or family.

XIV. THOSE WHO RETURNED WITH ZERUBBABEL.

1. The Leaders.

Neh 7[7].	Ezr 2[2]	1 Es 5[8].
	[Names omitted are identical with those given in Neh]	
Zerubbabel.		Zorobabel.
Jeshua.		Jesus.
Nehemiah.	Seraiah.	Nehemias.
Azariah.	Reelaiah.	Zaraias.
Raamiah.	om.	Resaias.
Nahamani.		Eneneus.
Mordecai.		Mardocheus.
Bilshan.		Beelsarus.
Mispereth.	Mispar.	Aspharasus.
Bigvai.		Reelias.
Nehum.	Rehum.	Roimus.
Baanah.		Baana.

2. Men of the People of Israel.

Neh 7[8-38].	Ezr 2[3-35].	1 Es 5[9-23].
Sons of Parosh.		Sons of Phoros.
„ Shephatiah.		„ Saphat.
„ Arah.		„ Ares.
„ Pahath-moab.		„ Phaath Moab.
„ Jeshua and Joab.		„ Jesus and Joab.
„ Elam.		„ Elam.
„ Zattu.		„ Zathui.
„ Zaccai.		„ Chorbe.
„ Binnui.		„ Bani.
„ Bebai.		„ Bebai.
„ Azgad.		„ Astad.
„ Adonikam.		„ Adonikam.
„ Bigvai.		„ Bagoi.
„ Adin.		„ Adinu.
„ Ater of Hezekiah.		„ Ater of Ezekias.
„ Hashum.		
		„ Kilan and Azetas.
		„ Azaru.
		„ Annis.
		„ Arom.
„ Bezai.		„ Bassai.
„ Hariph.	Jorah.	„ Arsiphurith.
		„ Baiterus.
„ Gibeon.	Gibbar.	
Men of Bethlehem.		Men of Bethlomon.
„ Netophah.		„ Netophas.
„ Anathoth.		„ Anathoth.
„ Beth-azmaveth.	Azmaveth.	„ Bethasmoth.
„ Kiriath-jearim,	Kiriath-arim.	„ Kariathiarius.
Chephirah, and Beeroth.		„ Caphira.
		„ Beroth.
		„ Chadiasai and Ammidioi.
„ Ramah.		„ Kirama.
„ Geba.		„ Gabbe.
„ Michmas.		„ Macalon.
„ Bethel and Ai.		„ Betolion.
Sons of Nebo.		Sons of Niphis.
	Magbish.	
„ Elam.		
„ Harim.		
„ Jericho.		„ Jerechu (v.[22]).
„ Lod, Hadid, and Ono.		„ Calamolalus and Onus.
„ Senaah.		„ Sanaas.

3. Priests.

Neh 7[39-42].	Ezr 2[36-39].	1 Es 5[24-38].
Sons of Jedaiah of House of Jeshua.		Sons of Jeddu s. Jesus.
		„ Sanasib.
„ Immer.		„ Emmeruth.
„ Pashhur.		„ Phassurus.
„ Harim.		„ Charme.

4. Levites.

Neh 7[43].	Ezr 2[40].	1 Es 5[26].
Sons of Jeshua.		Sons of Jesus.
„ Kadmiel.		„ Kadmiel.
		„ Bannas.
„ Hodevah.	Hodaviah.	„ Sudias.

5. Singers.

Neh 7[44].	Ezr 2[41].	1 Es 5[27].
Sons of Asaph.		Sons of Asaph.

6. Porters.

Neh 7[45].	Ezr 2[42].	1 Es 5[28].
Sons of Shallum.		Sons of Salum.
„ Ater.		„ Atar.
„ Talmon.		„ Tolman.
„ Akkub.		„ Dacubi.
„ Hatita.		„ Ateta.
„ Shobai.		„ Sabi.

7. The Nethinim.

Neh 7 46-56.	Ezr 2 43-54.	1 Es 5 29-32.
Sons of Ziha.		Sons of Esau.
,, Hasupha.	Asipha.	
,, Tabbaoth.		,, Tabbaoth.
,, Keros.		,, Keras.
,, Sia.	Siaha.	,, Sua.
,, Padon.		,, Phaleas.
,, Lebana.		,, Labana.
,, Hagaba.		,, Aggaba.
	Akkub.	,, Acud.
		,, Uta.
		,, Ketab.
		,, Accaba.
,, Salmai.	Shamlai.	,, Subai.
,, Hanan.		,, Anan.
,, Giddel.		,, Cathua.
,, Gahar.		,, Geddur.
,, Reaiah.		,, Jairus.
,, Rezin.		,, Daisan.
,, Nekoda.		,, Noeba.
		,, Chaseba.
,, Gazzam.		,, Gazera.
,, Uzza.		,, Ozias.
,, Paseah.		,, Phinoe.
		,, Asara.
,, Besai.		,, Basthai.
		,, Asana.
,, Meunim.		,, Maani.
,, Nephushesim.	Nephisim.	,, Naphisi.
,, Babbuk.		,, Acub.
,, Hakupha.		,, Achipha.
,, Harhur.		,, Asur.
		,, Pharakim.
,, Bazlith.	Bazluth.	,, Basaloth.
,, Mehida.		,, Meedda.
		,, Cutha.
,, Harsha.		,, Charea.
,, Barkos.		,, Barchus.
,, Sisera.		,, Serar.
,, Temah.		,, Thomei.
,, Neziah.		,, Nasi.
,, Hatiphah.		,, Atipha.

8. Sons of Solomon's Servants.

Neh 7 57-59.	Ezr 2 55-57.	1 Es 5 33f.
Sons of Sotai.		
,, Sophereth.	Hassophereth	Sons of Assaphioth.
,, Perida.	Peruda.	,, Pharida.
,, Jaala.		,, Jeeli.
,, Darkon.		,, Lozon.
,, Giddel.		,, Isdael.
,, Shephatiah.		,, Saphuthi.
,, Hattil.		,, Agia.
,, Pochereth-hazzebaim.		,, Phacareth.
		,, Sabie.
		,, Sarothie.
		,, Masias.
		,, Gas.
		,, Addus.
		,, Subas.
		,, Apherra.
		,, Barodis.
		,, Saphat.
,, Amon.	Ami.	,, Allon.

9. Those without Genealogy from

Neh 7 61-63.	Ezr 2 59-61.	1 Es 5 36-38.
Tel-melah.		Thermeleth.
Tel-harsha.		Thelersas.
Cherub.		Charaathalan.
Addon.	Addan.	
Immer.		Allar.

(a) Men of Israel.

Sons of Delaiah.		Sons of Dalan.
,, Tobiah.		,, Ban.
,, Nekoda.		,, Nekodan.

(b) Priests.

Sons of Hobaiah.	Habaiah.	Sons of Obdia.
,, Hakkoz.		,, Akkos.
,, Barzillai.		,, Jaddus.

XV. Those who returned with Ezra.

Ezr 8 2-14.　　　　　1 Es 8 29-40.

1.

Family.	Person.	Family.	Person.
Sons of		Sons of	
Phinehas, Gershom.		Phinees, Gerson.	
Ithamar, Daniel.		Ithamar, Gamael.	
David, Hattush s. Shecaniah.		David, Attus s. Sechenias.	
Parosh, Zechariah.		Phoros, Zacharias.	
Pahath-moab, Eliehoenai s. Zer-ahiah.		Phaath Moab, Eliaonias s. Zar-aias.	

Ezr 8 2-14.　　　　　1 Es 8 29-40.

Family.	Person.	Family.	Person.
Sons of		Sons of	
Zattu?, Shecaniah s. Jahaziel.		Zathoes, Sechenias s. Jezelus.	
Adin, Ebed s. Jonathan.		Adin, Obeth s. Jonathan.	
Elam, Jeshaiah s. Athaliah.		Elam, Jesias s. Gotholias.	
Shephatiah, Zebadiah s. Michael.		Saphatias, Zaraias s. Michael.	
Joab, Obadiah s. Jehiel.		Joab, Abadias s. Jezelus.	
Bani?, Shelomith s. Josiphiah.		Banias, Salimoth s. Josaphias	
Bebai, Zechariah s. Bebai.		Babi, Zecharias s. Bebai.	
Azgad, Johanan s. Hakkatan.		Astath, Joannes s. Akatan.	
Adonikam, Eliphelet, Jeuel, and Shemaiah.		Adonikam, Eliphalat, Jeuel, and Samaias.	
Bigvai, Uthai and Zabbud.		Bago, Uthi s. Istalcurus.	

For the textual emendations see Kau.

2. Eliezer, Ariel, Shemaiah, Elnathan, Jarib, Elnathan, Nathan, Zechariah, Meshullam (chief men) ; Joiarib, Elnathan (teachers), Ezr 8 16.

These chief men and teachers (2), apparently of the company were sent by Ezra from the encampment near Babylon (see AHAVA) unto Iddo, the chief of a colony of Levites at Casiphia (wh. see), to secure Levites and Nethinim to accompany them to Jerus. for service in the temple. They secured Ishsechel (RVm) and Sherebiah of ss. Mahli, with 18 sons and brethren, and Hashabiah and Jeshaiah ss. Merari, with 20 sons and brethren, and 220 Nethinim. Unto Sherebiah and Hashabiah and ten brethren along with 12 chiefs of the priests, was given the care of the offerings of silver, gold, and brass which were being taken to Jerusalem. On the arrival these gifts of bullion and vessels were delivered unto Meremoth s. Uriah the priest, and Eleazar s. Phineas, Jozabad s. Jeshua, and Noadiah s. Binnui, Levites, Ezr 8 15-35.

XVI. Builders of the Wall of Jerusalem.

Neh 3 1-32.

Eliashib the high priest, v.[1].
Men of Jericho, v.[2a].
Zaccur s. Imri, v.[2b].
ss. Hassenaah, v.[3].
Meremoth s. Uriah, s. Hakkoz, v.[4a].
Meshullam s. Berechiah, s. Meshezabel, v.[4b].
Zadok s. Baana, v.[4c].
Tekoites, i.e. men of Tekoa, vv.[5. 27].
Joiada s. Paseah, and Meshullam s. Besodeiah, v.[6].
Melatiah the Gibeonite, and Jadon the Meronothite, and under them men of Gibeon and of Mizpah, v.[7].
Uzziel s. Harhaiah, having oversight of the goldsmiths (Kau), v.[8a].
Hananiah, an apothecary, v.[8b].
Rephaiah s. Hur, ruler of half the district of Jerusalem, v.[9].
Jedaiah s. Harumaph, v.[10a].
Hattush s. Hashabneiah, v.[10b].
Malchijah s. Harim, and Hasshub s. Pahath-moab, v.[11].
Shallum s. Hallohesh, ruler of half the district of Jerusalem, with his daughter, v.[12].
Hanun and the inhabitants of Zanoah, v.[13].
Malchijah s. Rechab, ruler of the district of Beth-haccherem, v.[14].
Shallum s. Col-hozeh, ruler of the district of Mizpah, v.[15].
Nehemiah s. Azbuk, ruler of half the district of Beth-zur, v.[16]
Rehum s. Bani, a Levite, v.[17a].
Hashabiah, ruler of half the district of Keilah, v.[17b].
Bavvai s. Henadad, ruler of half the district of Keilah, v.[18].
Ezer s. Jeshua, ruler of Mizpah, v.[19].
Baruch s. Zabbai, v.[20].
Meremoth s. Uriah, s. Hakkoz, v.[21].
The Priests, the men of the Plain, v.[22].
Benjamin and Hasshub, v.[23a].
Azariah s. Maaseiah, s. Ananiah, v.[23b].
Binnui s. Henadad, v.[24].
Palal s. Uzzai, v.[25a].
Pedaiah s. Parosh, v.[25b].
The Priests, v.[28].
Zadok s. Immer, v.[29a].
Shemaiah s. Shecaniah, keeper of east gate, v.[29b].
Hananiah s. Shelemiah, and Hanun, sixth s. Zalaph, v.[30a].
Meshullam s. Berechiah, v.[30b].
Malchijah, a goldsmith, v.[31].
Goldsmiths and Merchants, v.[32].

XVII. Those who had Foreign Wives.

1. Priests—

	Ezr 10 18-22.	1 Es 9 19-22.
a.	ss. Jeshua and his brethren.	ss. Jesus and his brethren.
	Maaseiah.	Mathelas.
	Eliezer.	Eleazar.
	Jarib.	Joribus.
	Gedaliah.	Joadanus.
b.	ss. Immer.	ss. Emmer.
	Hanani.	Ananias.
	Zebadiah.	Zabdeus.
c.	ss. Harim.	ss. Manes.
	Maaseiah.	Sameus.
	Elijah.	
	Shemaiah.	
	Jehiel.	Hiereel.
	Uzziah.	Azarias.

PRIESTS—

Ezr 10$^{18-22}$.	1 Es 9$^{19-22}$.
d. ss. **Pashhur.**	ss. **Phaisur.**
Elioenai.	Elionas.
Maaseiah.	Massias.
Ishmael.	Ismael.
Nethanel.	Nathanael.
Jozabad.	Ocidelus.
Elasah.	Saloas.

2. LEVITES—

Ezr 10^{23}.	1 Es 9^{23}.
Jozabad.	Jozabdus.
Shimei.	Semeis.
Kelaiah (Kelita).	Colius (Calitas).
Pethahiah.	Patheus.
Judah.	Judas.
Eliezer.	Jonas.

3. SINGERS—

Ezr 10^{24a}.	1 Es 9^{25a}.
Eliashib.	Eliasibus.
	Bacchurus.

4. PORTERS—

Ezr 10^{24b}.	1 Es 9^{25b}.
Shallum.	Sallumus.
Telem.	Tolbanes.
Uri.	

5. MEN OF ISRAEL—

Ezr 10$^{25-43}$.	1 Es 9$^{26-35}$.
a. ss. **Parosh.**	ss. **Phoros.**
Ramiah.	Hiermas.
Izziah.	Ieddias.
Malchijah.	Melchias.
Mijamin.	Maelus.
Eleazar.	Eleazar.
Malchijah.	Asibias.
Benaiah.	Baneas.
b. ss. **Elam.**	ss. **Ela.**
Mattaniah.	Matthanias.
Zechariah.	Zacharias.
Jehiel.	Jezrielus.
Abdi.	Oabdius.
Jeremoth.	Hieremoth.
Elijah.	Aedias.
c. ss. **Zattu.**	ss. **Zamoth.**
Elioenai.	Eliadas.
Eliashib.	Eliasinus.
Mattaniah.	Othonias.
Jeremoth.	Jarimoth.
Zabad.	Sabathus.
Aziza.	Zardeus.
d. ss. **Bebai.**	ss. **Bebai.**
Jehohanan.	Joannes.
Hananiah.	Ananias.
Zabai.	Jozabdus.
Athlai.	Ematheis.
e. ss. **Bani.**	ss. **Mani.**
Meshullam.	Olamus.
Malluch.	Mamuchus.
Adaiah.	Jedeus.
Jashub.	Jasubus.
Sheal.	Jasaelus.
Jeremoth.	Hieremoth.
f. ss **Pahath-moab.**	ss. **Addi.**
Adna.	Naathus.
Chelal.	Moossias.
Benaiah.	Laccunus.
Maaseiah.	Naidus.
Mattaniah.	Mattanias.
Bezalel.	Sesthel.
Binnui.	Balnuus.
Manasseh.	Manasseas.
g. ss. **Harim.**	ss. **Annas.**
Eliezer.	Elionas.
Isshijah.	Aseas.
Malchijah.	Melchias.
Shemaiah.	Sabbeus.
Shimeon.	Simon Chosameus.
Benjamin.	[From ss. Addi to
Malluch.	Simon Chosameus
Shemariah.	only few names appear to correspond with those in Ezr].
h. ss. **Hashum.**	ss. **Asom.**
Mattenai.	Maltanneus.
Mattattah.	Mattathias.
Zabad.	Sabanneus.
Eliphelet.	Eliphalat.
Jeremai.	
Manasseh.	Manasses.
Shimei.	Semei.
i. ss. **Bani.**	ss. **Baani.**
Maadai.	Jeremias.
Amram.	Momdis.
Uel.	Ismaerus.
Benaiah.	Juel.
Bedeiah.	Mamdai.
Cheluhi.	Pedias.
Vaniah.	Anos.
Meremoth.	Carabasion.
Eliashib.	Enasibus.
Mattaniah.	Mamnitanemus.

MEN OF ISRAEL—

Ezr 10$^{25-43}$.	1 Es 9$^{26-35}$.
Mattenai.	Eliasis.
Jaasu.	
Bani.	Bannus.
Binnui.	Eliali.
Shimei.	Someis.
Shelemiah.	Selemias.
Nathan.	Nathanias.
	ss. **Ezora.**
	Sesis.
Adaiah.	Ezril.
Machnadebai.	Azaelus.
Shashai.	Samatus.
Sharai.	Zambri.
Azarel.	[From Jeremias to
Shelemiah.	Zambri many names
Shemeriah.	do not appear to correspond with those
Shallum.	in Ezr].
Amariah.	
Joseph.	Josephus.
j. ss. **Nebo.**	ss. **Nooma.**
Jeiel.	
Mattithiah.	Mazitias.
Zabad.	Zabadeas.
Zebina.	
Iddo.	Edos.
Joel.	Juel.
Benaiah.	Banaias.

XVIII. THE SIGNERS OF THE COVENANT.
Neh 10$^{1-27}$.

1. *The Governor*:—Nehemiah s. Hacaliah.
2. *Priests* (vv.$^{2-7}$):— Zedekiah, Seraiah, Azariah, Jeremiah, Pashhur, Amariah, Malchijah, Hattush, Shebaniah, Malluch, Harim, Meremoth, Obadiah, Daniel, Ginnethon, Baruch, Meshullam, Abijah, Mijamin, Maaziah, Bilgai, Shemaiah.
3. *Levites* (vv.$^{9-13}$):—Jeshua s. Azaniah, Binnui of the ss. Henadad, Kadmiel; Shebaniah, Hodiah, Kelita, Pelaiah, Hanan, Mica, Rehob, Hashabiah, Zaccur, Sherebiah, Shebaniah, Hodiah, Bani, Beninu.
4. *Chiefs of the People* (vv.$^{14-28}$):— Parosh, Pahath-moab, Elam, Zattu, Bani, Bunni, Azgad, Bebai, Adonijah, Bigvai, Adin, Ater, Hezekiah, Azzur, Hodiah, Hashum, Bezai, Hariph, Anathoth, Nobai, Magpiash, Meshullam, Hezir, Meshezabel, Zadok, Jaddua, Pelatiah, Hanan, Anaiah, Hoshea, Hananiah, Hasshub, Hallohesh, Pilha, Shobek, Rehum, Hashabnah, Maaseiah, and Ahiah, Hanan, Anan, Malluch, Harim, Baanah.

XIX. PRIESTS, LEVITES, AND PORTERS.

1. *Priests who returned with Zerubbabel and Jeshua*:—Seraiah, Jeremiah, Ezra, Amariah, Malluch, Hattush, Shecaniah, Rehum, Meremoth, Iddo, Ginnethoi, Abijah, Mijamin, Maadiah, Bilgah, Shemaiah, Joiarib, Jedaiah, Sallu, Amok, Hilkiah, Jedaiah, Neh 12$^{1-7}$.
2. *Levites*:—Jeshua, Binnui, Kadmiel, Sherebiah, Judah, Mattaniah, Bakbukiah, Unno, Neh 12$^{8. 9}$.
3. *Priests and Priestly Houses in the days of Joiakim s. Jeshua*:—Of Seraiah, Meraiah; of Jeremiah, Hananiah; of Ezra, Meshullam; of Amariah, Jehohanan; of Malluchi, Jonathan; of Shebaniah, Joseph; of Harim, Adna; of Meraioth, Helkai; of Iddo, Zechariah; of Ginnethon, Meshullam; of Abijah, Zichri; of Miniamin, ——; of Moadiah, Piltai; of Bilgah, Shammua; of Shemaiah, Jehonathan; of Joiarib, Mattenai; of Jedaiah, Uzzi; of Sallai, Kallai; of Amok, Eber; of Hilkiah, Hashabiah; of Jedaiah, Nethanel, Neh 12$^{12-21}$.
4. *Chief Levites*:—Hashabiah, Sherebiah, Jeshua s. Kadmiel, Neh 12^{24}.
5. *Porters*:— Mattaniah, Bakbukiah, Obadiah, Meshullam, Talmon, Akkub, Neh 12^{25}.
These 'chief Levites' (4) who were over the service of song (ref.) and the 'porters' (5) belonged also to the time of Joiakim (Neh 12^{26}).

XX. 1. Priests and Levites, Participants in the Promulgation of the Law.

a. Mattithiah, Shema, Anaiah, Uriah, Hilkiah, Maaseiah, Pedaiah, Mishael, Malchijah, Hashum, Hashbaddanah, Zechariah, Meshullam, Neh 8^4.
b. Jeshua, Bani, Sherebiah, Jamin, Akkub, Shabbethai, Hodiah, Maaseiah, Kelita, Azariah, Jozabad, Hanan, Pelaiah, Neh 8^7.
c. Jeshua, Bani, Kadmiel, Shebaniah, Bunni, Sherebiah, Bani, Chenani, Jeshua, Kadmiel, Bani, Hashabneiah, Sherebiah, Hodiah, Shebaniah, Pethahiah, Neh 9$^{4f.}$.
List a stood at the right and left of Ezra upon the platform; list b read and explained the law; list c gave responses on the fast-day in connexion with the reading of the law (see ref.).

2. Princes, Priests, and Levites, Participants in the Dedication of the Wall.

a. Hoshaiah, Azariah, Ezra, Meshullam, Judah, Benjamin, Shemaiah, Jeremiah, Neh 12$^{32-34}$.
b. Zechariah (see III. 4), Shemaiah, Azarel, Milalai, Gilalai, Maai, Nethanel, Judah, Hanani, Neh 12$^{35f.}$.
c. Eliakim, Maaseiah, Miniamin, Micaiah, Elioenai, Zechariah, Hananiah, Neh 12^{41}.

d. Maaseiah, Shemaiah, Eleazar, Uzzi, Jehohanan, Malchijah, Elam, Ezer, Jezrahiah, Neh 1242f..

All the names under *a* have been taken as those of princes of Judah (Crosby, Lange, *Comm.*, Eng. ed. *in loco*). Probably, however, only Hoshaiah was a prince of J., and Judah and Benjamin represent members of those tribes, and the other names different classes of priests (Oe. *in loco*). The names under *b* are those of Levitical musicians, and under *c* and *d* of priestly musicians (see ref.).

XXI. RESIDENTS OF JERUSALEM, Neh 11⁴⁻¹⁹, 1 Ch 9³⁻¹⁷. (The names are those of Neh ; for variations, see ref.).

1. *Of Judah—*
  Athaiah * (see IV. 58ᵇ).
  Uthai † (see IV. 58ᵃ).
  Maaseiah (see IV. 3).
  Jeuel † of Zerah.
2. *Benjaminites—*
  Sallu (see VIII. 24).
  Ibneiah † s. Jeroham.
  Elah † s. Uzzi, s. Michri.
  Meshullam † s. Shephatiah, s. Reuel, s. Ibnijah.
  Gabbai.*
  Sallai.*
  Joel * s. Zichri (the overseer).
  Judah * s. Hassenuah (second over the city).
3. *Priests—*
  Jedaiah.‡
  Joiarib.
  Jachin.
  Seraiah (see III. 14).
  Adaiah (see III. 16).
  Amashsai (see III. 17).
  Zabdiel * s. Haggedolim (the overseer).
4. *Levites.—*
  Shemaiah s. Hasshub, s. Azrikam, s. Hashabiah, s. Bunni * of ss. Merari.†
  Shabbethai.
  Jozabad.
  Bakbakkar.†
  Heresh.†
  Galal.†
  Mattaniah (see III. 5).
  Bakbukiah.
  Abda § s. Shammua,§ s. Galal, s. Jeduthun.
  Berechiah † s. Asa, s. Elkanah.
  Uzzi, Neh 11²² (see III. 5).
5. *The Porters—*
  Shallum (see III. 24).
  Akkub.
  Talmon.
  Ahiman.

ʒn connexion with these residents of Jerus., Pethahiah s. Meshezabel of ss. Zerah is mentioned as being 'at the king's hand,' *i.e.* agent of the Persian king, in all matters concerning the people, Neh 11²⁴.

INDEX TO GENEALOGICAL TABLES. ‖

E. L. CURTIS.

GENEALOGY OF JESUS CHRIST.—The only genealogies of the NT are those of Mt 1¹⁻¹⁷ and Lk 3²³⁻³⁸, two independent pedigrees, each purporting to give the descent of Joseph, reputed father of Jesus. The occasion of their insertion is the desire of the evangelists to set forth Jesus as actual heir-apparent to the throne of David. The attempt to vindicate their simultaneous accuracy by harmonistic devices has been abandoned by nearly all writers of authority as a violation of the text, or of historical credibility. Hence the light which modern research seeks from them falls rather on the century after than the centuries before the birth of Christ—on the history of the doctrine of his Davidic sonship rather than His actual descent.

i. TREATMENT OF THE QUESTION BY JESUS AND THE APOSTLES.—If the progress of critical and exegetical science has shown, on the one side, the futility of all harmonistic theories for rescuing the authority of the pedigrees, it has more than compensated for the loss by establishing with equal certainty the acceptance of the fact of the Davidic descent of Jesus by Himself, His contemporaries, and His immediate followers. That Davidic descent was then considered a prerequisite to the establishment of Messianic claims is apparent from a number of NT passages. The use of the title 'Son of David' in Mt 15²² 20³⁰·³¹ (=9²⁷) 21⁹ and parallels is official, implying no knowledge of Jesus' birth or descent, but only the conviction that He is the Messiah. It indicates, however, that Davidic descent was popularly assumed as an attribute of the Christ. This is much more distinctly implied in Mt 12²³, and by the question put by Jesus to His Pharisaic opponents in the temple, Mt 22⁴¹⁻⁴⁶ 'What think ye of Christ? whose son is he?' Such a question by one whose claims to Davidic descent were open to suspicion would have put a weapon in the hands of His foes. Jesus, on the contrary, is not merely confident that they will answer 'David's son,' but is at least equally confident of their inability to disprove His Davidic descent, though He refuses to base His claims upon it. The same tacit assumption of this as an undisputed fact characterizes the rare allusions of St. Paul, Ro 1³, 2 Ti 2⁸ (cf. He 7¹⁴), the ascriptions of Rev 3⁷ 5⁵ 22¹⁶, and, finally, the distinct appeal to prophecy of Ac 2³⁰ 13²³. The last two passages, as emanating from the same source as one of the pedigrees, and the passages Mt 2⁵, Lk 2⁴, where Bethlehem as the birthplace of David is regarded as the necessary birthplace of the Messiah, should perhaps not be cited as independent witness to the existence of the popular assumption ; but the great number of OT passages pointing to this, especially Ps 132¹¹, which cannot date more than a few centuries before NT times, and the Messianic petition of Ps.-Sol 17²³, written not more than 50 years B.C., 'Raise up unto them, O Lord, their king the Son of David,' should suffice to show that Messianic pretensions absolutely devoid of evidence of Davidic descent could not have passed unchallenged, as those of Jesus seem to have done.*

The continued existence in the family of Jesus of claims to Davidic descent, such as could hardly have originated in His own time, is evidenced by Hegesippus (ap. Eus. HE III. 20 and 32), who tells of repeated attempts to involve His collateral descendants in trouble with the Roman authorities on this account. But the suspicions of even a Domitian were disarmed when two grandsons of Jude, the Lord's brother, were brought before him, confessed their Davidic descent (explaining, however, that the kingdom of Christ was 'not temporal or earthly, but heavenly and angelic, to appear at the end of the world'), gave account of their property,—an undivided 39 acres of land, valued at 9000 denarii,—and showed their hands calloused by labour.

It is a fair inference from these facts that the Davidic descent of Jesus was in His own day practically undisputed, at least among His personal followers. What the evidence was on which this assumption rested, whether mere oral family tradition, or public records, and to what extent the basis was trustworthy, is a wholly different

* Even the passage Jn 7⁴² is no exception to the rule that the objection that He is not of Davidic descent is never raised in NT times to Jesus' Messianic claims. The speakers (at Jerus. according to 7³⁷) are strangers to Jesus (8⁴⁸), and merely infer, from His speech or otherwise, that He is a Galilæan. This is, indeed, contrary to their notion of Davidic origin, but the author presupposes the birth in Bethlehem.

question, which can be settled only by the careful scrutiny of the sources.

ii. TREATMENT IN THE ECCLESIASTICAL PERIOD.—There can be no doubt that from near the beginning of the 2nd cent., when our first and third Gospels began to come into general circulation, the Church believed itself in possession of conclusive documentary evidence. Even the collateral descendants of the Lord, the so-called δεσπόσυνοι, to whom Julius Africanus, the contemporary of Origen, applied on this subject, had no other authority to appeal to than the genealogies of Mt and Lk, though they added an ancestress or two of doubtful historicity, and omitted the names Matthat and Levi, Lk 3²⁴. Had the two Gospels been in agreement, the record would perhaps never have been disputed, but the discrepancy was too glaring to be ignored. Even before the time of Africanus and Origen the incompatibility of the pedigrees (ἡ διαφωνία τῶν γενεαλογιῶν) had been an occasion of derision to many an earlier opponent of Christianity, whom Celsus, according to Origen (Opera, ed. Delarue, i. p. 413), might have named had he been better informed. It is no wonder, then, that from the earliest period to which it can be traced, down to recent times, the Church has treated this subject only defensively, and from the harmonistic standpoint.

The first known harmonist of the Gospels is Tatian, a pupil of Justin Martyr. His Diatessaron, however, avoided the difficulty by omitting the genealogies altogether. Half a century later the problem was courageously confronted by Africanus, a careful scholar, for many years bishop of Nicopolis (previously Emmaus) in Palestine. His Letter to Aristides (see Spitta, Der Brief des Jul. Africanus, Halle, 1877 ; Routh, Rel. Sac. ii. pp. 228–237 ; Ante-Nicene Fathers, vi. p. 125 ; and Eus. HE i. 7) proposed a solution of the difficulty which quickly gained general acceptance in the Church, and for 12 centuries retained undisputed supremacy. The theory was not derived, as Eusebius wrongly inferred, from the desposyni, but is expressly stated by Africanus himself (§ 5) to be 'unsupported by testimony.' It assumes a levirate marriage (Dt 25⁵·⁶) in the case of either Jacob or Heli, Joseph's father according to Mt and Lk respectively, the son of the widow by his surviving brother being reckoned a son of the deceased in one or the other genealogy. This explanation requires the further assumption that the brothers Heli and Jacob had different fathers. The objections are overwhelming.

1. The theory does not exonerate the evangelists, since one pedigree or the other uses terms of filial relationship in a fictitious and illegal sense. 2. Granting, against all probability, the possible continuance of the levirate law, in the case here presupposed—that of uterine brothers—it would not apply (Maimonides, Jabom Ve Chalitza, c. 1). 3. Granting even the applicability of the assumption in the case of Joseph, it cannot reasonably be introduced a second time to account for the fact that Shealtiel, f. of Zerubbabel, is at the same time s. of Jechonias (Mt) and of Neri (Lk). Yet this expedient (so W. H. Mill, Pantheistic Principles, p. 165) is less absurd than to assume, with Augustine (followed by Hottinger and Voss), that at the same period of Jewish history there were two (Hottinger three) different fathers of Davidic lineage, each bearing the rare name Shealtiel, and having each a son bearing the rare name Zerubbabel. 4. If our own certainly more accurate text* be followed, instead of that of Africanus, and Matthan and Matthat, paternal grandfather of Joseph according to Mt and Lk respectively, be identified, as is probable, the expedient of a levirate marriage by uterine brothers must be introduced, not twice only, but three times over.

Under the weight of such inherent and extreme improbabilities the Africanian theory of harmonization, after suffering various modifications at the hands of later harmonists, has long since broken down, and is to-day universally abandoned.

The alternative harmonistic theory owes its currency to Annius of Viterbo, c. A.D. 1490, and

* See WH, Gr. Test. App. p. 57.

was widely accepted in the time of the Reformation. It has still an adherent of high repute in the person of the veteran NT scholar B. Weiss, who in his *Leben Jesu* (i. 205, 2nd ed.) puts it in its most favourable light. It assumes that the pedigree of Lk is that, not of Joseph, but of Mary, overcoming the sense of Lk 3²³ ὢν υἱός, ὡς ἐνομίζετο, Ἰωσήφ τοῦ Ἡλεί, κ.τ.λ., by various expedients. Thus the clause was rendered ' being the son (as was supposed of Joseph) of Heli,' *i.e.* being supposed to be the son of Joseph, but being in reality the *grandson* of Heli; or the τοῦ was translated ' son-in-law' (so Holmes, 'Geneal. of Jesus Christ' in Kitto's *Encycl.*³; Robinson, *Harmony of Gospels*, pp. 183–185, *et al.*), or 'adopted son' (so Wetstein, Delitzsch, *et al.*, following Augustine). Weiss (following F. Gomar, *de Geneal. Christi* ; J. Lightfoot, *Hor. Hebr.* vol. iii. p. 54 [ed. Gandell]; G. J. Voss, *de J. Chr. Geneal.* ; and Yardley, *The Genealogies of Christ*) proposes to regard the names as parallel, not consecutive. The list then would be, not a pedigree at all, but a huge parenthesis between ὢν υἱός (v.²³) and τοῦ θεοῦ (v.³⁸).

The chief objection to this theory in all its forms can hardly be more convincingly expressed than by citing the naïve admission of its advocate, Holmes (in the art. above mentioned, p. 96), of the fatal weakness of 'all theories,' meaning *harmonistic* theories: 'If it be objected that this table [Lk] is made out as literally as the other, *in Joseph's name,*[*] and that we violate the literal statement of the evangelist if we transfer the line *to Mary*, we answer, that as Joseph cannot have had two fathers, which yet the genealogies *seem* literally to assign to him (Mt 1¹⁶, Lk 3²³), *some* explanatory accommodation is necessary to all theories.'

The confession of violence to the text is not without reason. It is incredible that υἱός can mean both 'son' and 'grandson' in the same breath, as in the first of the proposed renderings;[†] equally incredible that in the same connexion τοῦ should stand once for 'son-in-law' and the other 75 times for 'son'; while the suggestion that the genealogy is not intended for a genealogy, but merely a list of names of persons of whom Jesus might have been considered the son, though in reality the Son of God, will convince no candid thinker.

But the proposed theory labours under further difficulties. As Plummer well says (*op. cit.* p. 103): 'It would have been quite out of harmony with either Jewish or Gentile ideas to derive the birthright of Jesus from his mother. In the eye of the law Jesus was the heir of Joseph: and therefore it is Joseph's descent which is of importance.' This doubtless accounts for its general rejection by ancient writers. As early as Justin Martyr and *Protevang. Jacobi*, Mary, for obvious reasons, is represented as also descended from David; but with two exceptions no attempt is made to claim for her either of the pedigrees. *Protev. Jac.*, in fact, makes her the daughter of Joachim and Anna. Irenæus (III. xxi. 5, 9) regards the pedigree of Mt as a line expressly excluded from the Messianic succession (Jer 22²⁴⁻³⁰ 36³⁰. ³¹); but this is Joseph's. Jesus is the Son of David only through Mary, whose pedigree is given by Luke. Victorinus (*c.* 300) curiously inverts this theory by adopting as Mary's the genealogy of Mt.[‡] Cod. D boldly cuts the knot by substituting in Lk 3²⁴⁻³¹ the line of Mt, following, however, a text seemingly older than our Mt (see Resch, *T. u. U.* x. 5, pp. 182–201; and Graefe in *SK*, 1898, 1).

Confessed violence to the text which he assumes to vindicate is the suicide of the harmonist. Hence the only treatment which to-day can come into consideration is the critical.

iii. TREATMENT BY MODERN CRITICISM.—Reconciliation of discrepant sources by suppositions within the limits of loyalty to the text and to historical probability is, *per contra*, the first duty of rational criticism. It being admitted, therefore, that both genealogies are given as Joseph's, and that explanation by resort to the levirate law is impracticable, the theory presented by Lord A. C. Hervey (*Genealogies of our Lord*, and art. 'Geneal. of Jesus Christ' in Smith's *DB*²) has much in its favour, and is, in fact, the prevailing view among English divines. It is also widely accepted in modified form among German commentators. According to this view it was not the intention of both evangelists to give an actual pedigree, but

only of Lk (Meyer, Holtzmann, *et al.*, would say ' the *source* followed by Lk in his opening chs.'). Mt (better, ' the source from which our evangelist derived his genealogy') does not trace the order of actual descent, but only of *throne-succession* (so already Grotius). Thus Solomon, although not the true ancestor of Joseph, is mentioned first as heir of the throne of David; then Shealtiel for the same reason, though he was not actually son of Jechoniah, but of Neri (Lk 3²⁷); then Eliakim, and finally Jacob, though neither was a real ancestor of Joseph. By thus throwing all the burden of inaccuracy upon Mt we may rescue at least the possibility of accuracy for Lk.

In favour of this view it must be allowed that Mt's genealogy is extremely defective, since it omits the names Ahaziah, Joash, Amaziah between Joram and Uzziah, and gives but six generations as against thirteen in Lk between Ἀβιούδ (=Ἰούδα [Lk] =הודַיָהוּ [1 Ch 9³]) and Matthan (=Matthat [Lk]). Barely are the names thus made to cover a period of more than 500 years. It is also manifest that its author simply follows in an uncritical manner the royal succession of the OT from David down to the last poor shadow of a Davidic king, ' Zerubbabel son of Shealtiel' (1 Ch 3¹⁹, Ezr 2² etc., Neh 7⁷ etc., Hag 1¹· ¹². ¹⁴ etc., Zec 4⁶·⁷·⁹·¹⁰). But it cannot be allowed that our evangelist by his ἐγέννησεν means anything else than actual physical descent. Of what significance his edifying comment on Bathsheba as the mother of Solomon, if the reader is not to infer that she is thus an ancestress of the Messiah? That he has embodied in his Gospel a current throne-succession not of his own manufacture is not only *à priori* probable, but is evident from the apparent blunder in vv.¹¹. ¹², by which the ' tesseradecad' from the carrying away into Babylon unto Christ contains not, as stated, ' fourteen generations,' but thirteen. It is, indeed, easy to cite examples from contemporary literature for the counting of a name twice to make out the hebdomad or decad into which genealogies were usually divided (see Mill, *op. cit.*, quoted by Hervey, *op. cit.* p. 886); but in this case more than enough of names were available in 1 Ch 3¹⁷⁻¹⁹ to make the count correspond to that of the first two sections of the table. It is probable, therefore, as was already pointed out by Jerome, that we have here an instance, on the part of the evangelist, of the confusion common in both Gr. and Lat. writers (Clem. Al., Ambrose, Africanus, Epiphanius, also 1 Es 1³⁷. ⁴³) between Jehoiakim and Jehoiachin; for Jehoiachin had no ' brethren' (Mt 1¹¹), but Jehoiakim had three, two of whom did succeed to the throne (Jer 22¹¹). The few texts, however, which insert the clause Ἰεχονίας δὲ ἐγέννησε τὸν Ἰεχονίαν, are certainly corrupt, since the reading is later than Porphyry, who had derided this flaw in the genealogy. We must therefore distinguish between the evangelist, who finds edifying significance in the common genealogical device of double heptads (cf. the genealogies of Gn 4–11 and Budde, *Bibl. Urgeschichte*, p. 90), or in the names of Rahab and Bathsheba (so Rabbinic authorities cited by Wetstein, *in loc.*; cf. He 11³¹, Ja 2²⁵), and his unknown authority. The former certainly supposed himself to be giving an actual and complete pedigree of Joseph (see v.¹⁷ πᾶσαι), not a mere throne-succession; whether the latter so believed, or not, must be left in doubt. The list of ten names which he inserts between Joseph and Zerub., beginning with the last generation mentioned by Ch in much altered form, may represent a current throne-succession, carrying down the line from Zerub. towards the Maccab. period,[*] taken up without more ado as *ipso facto* belonging to

---

[*] Italics in the citation are Dr. Holmes'.

[†] So Plummer, *Com. on Lk.*, Intern. Series, 1896, *ad loc.*

[‡] See his Commentary on Rev 4⁷⁻¹⁰.

[*] Cf. the decad of Davididæ from Hananiah s. of Zerub. to Hodaviah in 1 Ch 3¹⁹⁻²⁵ (Haupt's text).

Jesus. Our judgment as to the probable historical value of such current lists must be formed in the light of ancient testimony (see below).

The genealogy of Lk has every appearance of resting on more carefully prepared data, as we should expect from the evangelist's painstaking method (Lk 1[1-4]); but it is even more certain in this case that our author is adapting earlier material to his own uses. The pedigree, like the story of the infancy to which it probably belonged, must have been derived from Pal. sources. To the occidental mind, it is true, there would seem to be a certain incongruity between the account of the miraculous generation and the introduction of a pedigree of *Joseph*. This feeling is apparent in the evangelist's qualifying insertion in 3[23] ὡς ἐνομίζετο. It has been argued that even the sources used in these preliminary chapters are themselves in conflict on this point, the references to Joseph as the 'father' of Jesus (2[33, 43]), and the genealogy, indicating a point of view different from that of the main course of the story. But recent research has suggested that, to the contemporary Jewish mind, there was no incompatibility. Joseph might be not merely the putative or adoptive, but the real father of Jesus, at the same time that the birth was due solely to 'the power of the Highest' (1[35]). Isaac, in like manner, was spoken of as 'God-begotten' (cf. Ro 4[17-20, 24], He 11[12]), without any idea of denying the reality of his relation to Abraham. The ὡς ἐνομίζετο is therefore to be attributed to the evangelist as against the source.

It is also a fair inference, from the very object of the pedigree, that the source did not carry it back beyond Abraham. Hence the extension back to Adam is due to the humanitarian bent of the evangelist, which is even more apparent in the curious addition τοῦ θεοῦ, by which the divine son-ship of the race is indirectly taught. Moreover, the text followed for these earliest 20 generations (10 from Creation to Noah, 10 from the Flood to Abraham) is manifestly the LXX, which alone gives the second Cainan (3[36]), whereas the source in 1[17] cites from an Aramaic version.

Finally, there is a curious indication in 3[27] that the evangelist has not only (as is probable) changed the place of the genealogy, but inverted its order. On 3[27] we have the following comment from Plummer (*Comm.* p. 104): 'Rhesa, who appears in Lk, but neither in Mt nor in 1 Ch, is probably not a name at all, but a title, which some Jewish copyist (?) mistook for a name. "Zerubbabel Rhesa," or "Zerubbabel the prince," has been made into "Zerubbabel (begat) Rhesa."' This correction brings Lk into harmony with both Mt and 1 Ch. For (1) the Gr. Ἰωανάν represents the Heb. Hananiah (1 Ch 3[19]), a generation omitted by Mt ; and (2) Lk's Ἰούδα is the same as Mt's Ἀβιούδ (Jud-a = Ab-jud). Again, Ἰούδα or Ἀβιούδ may be identified with Hodaviah (1 Ch 3[24]); for this name is interchanged with Judah, as is seen by a comparison of Ezr 3[9] and Neh 11[9] with Ezr 2[40] and 1 Ch 9[7, 11]. To have caused the mistake, the original form of the gene-alogy must of course have been a simple list of names in the order Zerubbabel, Rhesa, Joanan, etc., and not, as now, Ἰωανὰν τοῦ Ῥησὰ τοῦ Ζορο-βάβελ, κ.τ.λ.

Taking this list of names in the most original form to which we can restore it, we observe at once that its form is of the same mnemonic type as Mt's, only, as in the series from Zerub. to Jesus in Mt, the commoner system of (double) decads is followed. There are precisely 40 names in all between David and Christ, of which 20 are pre-exilic and 20 post-exilic. The former series begins with Nathan s. of David, the latter with Salathiel (= Shealtiel) f. of Zerub., ending with Joseph f. of Jesus. The list from Adam to Abraham likewise consists of 20, that from Abraham to David being, of course, a tesseradecad.

Twenty generations is not, indeed, an improbable number for the period from David to the Exile (c. 400 years); but a com-parison of Lk 3[27] with 1 Ch 3[17-24] will show that at least

four[*] generations have been omitted between Joanan and Joda; hence the number of generations at least is artificial.

Do the names themselves give any indication of being drawn from trustworthy sources? Allowance must be made for a probable disposition on the part of 1st cent. scribes to assimilate the older names to those in current use (*e.g.* Ἰουδά = הוֹדַוְיָהוּ, Ἰωανάν = חֲנַנְיָהוּ), and possibly (so Hervey, *Gene-alogies*, pp. 36, 90 ff.) for a disposition in certain families to form names by variations of a common root, though this might, with equal plausibility, be attributed to the pedigree-makers. Neverthe-less, it must be admitted that this list of names presents phenomena unparalleled in any authenti-cated OT pedigree. There is no indication in the names of the OT of the practice referred to in Lk 1[61] (cf. Gray, *Heb. Prop. Names*, 2 ff.). Nor can the practice of giving 'Scripture' names, so mani-festly common in Maccab. times and later, have existed to any extent in the earlier period. Hence, while there may be nothing strange in the names Levi and Joseph, as third and sixth ancestor of Joseph f. of Jesus, the series Joseph, Juda, Simeon, Levi, as contemporaries of Ahaziah, Joash, Amaziah, and Uzziah, is surprising. Add to these the names Matthat (*bis*), Mattathias (*bis*), and Mattatha, variants upon the root of 'Nathan,' the names Na[h]um, Amos, and the fact that out of the total of 42 names in Mt and Lk not directly taken from the OT there are but 16 which have not more or less demonstrable affinity with the later 'scriptural' type, and the result cannot be con-sidered favourable to the historical trustworthi-ness of the sources.

iv. EXTERNAL EVIDENCE.—In the absence of other evidence, the seemingly late character of the names of the supposed Davididæ of Mt and Lk might perhaps be insufficient to justify doubt. But the careful investigations of Africanus (*op. cit.*), when compared with the earliest NT treatment of the subject, and the further knowledge obtainable from Eus. (*Qu. ad Steph.* iii. 2), and the later Jewish theology (see Delitzsch in *Ztschr. f. Luth. Theol.* 1860, iii. p. 460) as to current attempts to determine the Davidic descent of the Messiah, shed a light upon the question of the origin of our pedigrees which should not be less welcome because some-what unfavourable to their historical trustworthi-ness.

Africanus' informants were in possession of the pedigrees of Mt and Lk, but could give him neither the means of reconciling their discrepancies nor of establishing the fact requiring to be proved, because of the non-existence of public records. That such had been kept down to the time of Herod the Great they firmly believed, accounting for their disappearance by a demon-strably apocryphal tale of Herod's burning them in order to conceal his own base lineage.[†] They frankly confessed that the pedigrees in their possession were made up ἐκ τε τῆς βίβλου τῶν ἡμερῶν [καὶ ἐκ μνήμης].[‡] The βίβλος τῶν ἡμερῶν is doubtless the Heb. דִּבְרֵי הַיָּמִים, *i.e.* Book of Days (= Chronicles); but 'memory' in the time of Herod, and later, would hardly be of great service to determine the descendants of Nathan *ben* David. The in-dustry of pedigree-making appears as flourishing then as to-day, and basing itself upon the same foibles. 'A few of the more careful,' says Africanus, immediately after the story of Herod's escapade, 'having procured private records of their own, either by remembering the names, or by getting them in some other way from the registers, pride themselves on preserving the memory of their noble extraction. Among these are those already mentioned, called Desposyni, on account of their con-nexion with the family of the Saviour.'

If the current pedigrees were indeed of this character, we can readily understand the attitude

---

[*] According to LXX, adopted by Kittel in Haupt's critical text, *nine*, *i.e.* one entire decad, including Hodaviah.

[†] Herod's lineage was not base, as represented (Afric. *ad Arist.* § 4), but noble (Jos. *Ant.* XIV. vii. 3). Moreover, the public records (which, however, related only to Aaronic families) were still in existence in Josephus' time (*Vita*, § 1 ; cf. *c. Ap.* i. 7).

[‡] The bracketed words are supplied from the tr. of Rufinus, 'partim memoriter, partim etiam ex dierum libris,' in accord-ance with the context (τε and the statement that the desposyni were among those who made up their pedigree in this way. See text).

of Jesus and the older NT writers toward the question of His Davidic descent. He Himself, in Mt 22⁴¹⁻⁴⁶ and parallels, expressly declines to base His Messianic claims on any such trivial and external, if not indeed unsafe, foundation. To be considered one of the Davididæ was an honour which He shared with his elder and younger contemporaries, Hillel and Gamaliel; but Jesus and His first followers (including St. Paul) on the one side, His opponents on the other, are equally content to let the question of descent fall into the background, which would not have been possible had documentary proof either for or against His heirship been accessible to either side. The earliest of our Gospels, and that which though latest is most loftily apostolic in tone, pass by the question of Jesus' descent. One is tempted to find a trace of the same disposition in the ἀρχιερεὺς ἀγενεαλόγητος of He 7³. It is the Palestinian sources of the latter part of the century, on which the infancy chapters of Mt and Lk are based, which first show traces of the assumption that a formal Davidic pedigree is needful to the demonstration of His Messianic claims. But we have already observed that in these *sources* there is no consciousness of incongruity between tracing the pedigree of Jesus through Joseph and the story of His miraculous birth. Not until the times of Justin Martyr do we find on the side of the orthodox a disposition to claim on this account Davidic descent for Mary, and on the part of the Ebionites to reject the narrative of Jesus' miraculous birth, not from incredulity, but to rescue the doctrine of His Davidic descent.

It is among the Jewish Christians of Palestine in the sub-apostolic age, perhaps among the two branches of the *desposyni* themselves, one of whose seats was at Cochaba, near the centre of Ebionism (Epiphan. xxx. 2, 16), the other at Nazara, perhaps the centre of the other Jewish Christian sect of 'Nazarenes,' that we must look for the origins of our two genealogies. Nor have we far to seek for the explanation of their discrepancy. Among the current Rabbinic disputes of the 1st cent. was the question whether Messiah's descent would be of the royal line, through Solomon and his successors on the throne (Jer 23⁵ 30⁹ 33¹⁵. ¹⁷); or, on account of the denunciation and rejection of Jechoniah and his seed (Jer 22²⁸. ³⁰ 36³⁰), through Nathan (Euseb. *Qu. ad Steph.* iii. 2). The first of our pedigrees represents the older and simpler idea. The second, the later reflection that Messiah's line could not include the series of ungodly kings. Of the component elements of each we can know no more until we have more intimate acquaintance with the methods of the pedigree-makers of the time. We may, however, infer something as to the date of our evangelists' work from the manifest interval between their construction and their final adoption into the story, and from the further fact of their construction in decads framed with either Joseph or Jesus in view, implying their origin in Christian circles. That origin is certainly later than when Jesus and His immediate followers were doing all in their power to detach current expectation from these externalities and fix it upon His spiritual Messianic claim,—to subordinate the title 'Son of David according to the flesh' to that of 'Son of God with power according to the Spirit of Holiness' (Ro 1³. ⁴).
B. W. BACON.

GENEALOGY.—Timothy is warned (1 Ti 1⁴) not to give heed to fables and endless genealogies (μηδὲ προσέχειν μύθοις καὶ γενεαλογίαις ἀπεράντοις), and Titus (3⁹) to avoid foolish questions and genealogies (μωρὰς δὲ ζητήσεις καὶ γενεαλογίας). What were these 'genealogies'? Some Fathers towards the end of the second century understood the word to

refer to the emanations of æons and of angels which formed part of the *gnosis*, or secret knowledge claimed by the Gnostics of their own day (see GNOSTICISM). But a parallel phrase in Polybius (IX. ii. 1, περὶ τὰς γενεαλογίας καὶ μύθους) refers to the mythological stories which earlier historians gathered round the birth and descent of their heroes. Similar legends are found in Philo, Josephus, and the Book of Jubilees, regarding the Jewish patriarchs and their families. And if, with Hort (*Judaistic Christianity*, 135 ff.), we may suppose that such genealogical tales had begun to creep from the Jewish into the Christian communities of Asia Minor, the necessity for such a warning to Timothy and Titus will be sufficiently understood.

GENERAL.—1. Once AV uses 'general' to translate שַׂר, 1 Ch 27³⁴ 'The general of the king's army was Joab.' The most usual trⁿ is 'captain,' which RV prefers, after Gen. and Bishops'. Cov. has 'chefe captayne.' See CAPTAIN.

2. As an adj. 'general' means 'common to all,' 'universal,' as Ad. Est 15¹⁰ (κοινός); 2 Mac 3¹⁸ 'Others ran flocking out of their houses to the general supplication' (ἐπὶ πάνδημον ἱκετίαν, AVm 'to make general supplication'; RV 'to make a universal supplication'). Latimer (*Sermons*, ed. 1584, p. 182) says, 'The promises of God our Saviour are general; they pertain to all mankind. He made a general proclamation, saying, Whosoever believeth in me hath everlasting life. . . . Also consider what Christ saith with his own mouth: Come to me, *all* ye that labour and are laden, and I will ease you. Mark here he saith, Come *all* ye; wherefore then should any man despair to shut himself from these promises of Christ, which be general, and pertain to the whole world?' In He 12²³ the Gr. word πανήγυρις is trᵈ in AV 'general assembly,' and RV retains the rendering. The sense is again 'universal assembly,' the adj. 'general' being intended to represent the πᾶς, 'all,' in the word.

The word πανήγυρις (from which comes 'panegyric,' a speech at a festival) is found only here in NT. In LXX it stands for מוֹעֵד Ezk 46¹¹ (EV 'solemnities,' RVm 'appointed feasts'), Hos 2¹¹ (EV 'season') 9⁵ (AV 'solemn,' RV 'solemn assembly'); and for עֲצָרָה Am 5²¹ (EV 'solemn assemblies'). In classical literature it is in frequent use to denote a national or general gathering for festive (and especially festive and religious) purposes, as at the Olympic, Isthmian, and Nemean games. The ἐκκλησία was also an assembly of the people, but not so distinctively national, and rather for political than festive purposes; while ἑορτή signified a feast or festal gathering, but had no national character attached to it. It is surprising, therefore, that מוֹעֵד, which is a general religious assembly, and even עֲצָרָה, which is a religious though not a national gathering, are not more frequently rendered by πανήγυρις in LXX. Cremer suggests that heathen customs were too closely associated with this Greek word, and he thinks it would not have been used where it has been but for the accumulation of Heb. synonyms in those four passages (see Cremer, *Bibl. Theol. Lex. s.v.*, and Trench, *NT Synonyms*³, p. 5, § 1).

The choice of this word by the writer of the Ep. to the Hebrews is an element in the determination of the meaning of the passage in which it occurs, one of the most difficult problems in the Epistle.

There is practically no difference of reading, μυρίων ἀγίων D₂* and μυριάδων vg., for μυριάσιν, being probably suggestions to simplify the construction. The difficulty lies in the punctuation. There are five possible arrangements—
1. καὶ μυριάσιν, ἀγγέλων πανηγύρει; καὶ ἐκκλησία πρωτοτόκων ἀπογεγραμμένων ἐν οὐρανοῖς.

'And to myriads, a general assembly of angels; and to the Church of the firstborn whose names are written in heaven.'

2. καὶ μυριάσιν ἀγγέλων, πανηγύρει· καὶ, κ.τ.λ.

'And to myriads of angels, a general assembly; and to the Church,' etc.

Moses Stuart, Eager, Edwards, and Farrar distinctly prefer the first arrangement; Chrysostom, Oecumenius, Theophylact, Erasmus, Luther, Calvin, Grotius, Hooker, Weiss, Vaughan, Thayer, Kay, Westcott, Briggs prefer the second. But the meaning is the same, though the punctuation differs; and taking the two together without the comma, καὶ μυριάσιν ἀγγέλων πανηγύρει· καὶ, κ.τ.λ, we get the sense which is adopted by Tisch. after all the Gr. MSS which exhibit the connexion of words (including AC), the Syr. and Lat. VSS, Origen, Eusebius, Basil (multitudinem angelorum frequentem), Vulg. (multorum millium angelorum frequentiam et ecclesiam primitivorum, qui conscripti sunt in cœlis), Wyc. ('and [1388 adds to] the multitude of many thousynd aungels, and to the chirche of the firste men'), Tind. ('and to an innumerable sight of angels, and unto the congregation of the fyrst borne sonnes'), Cov., Matt., Cran., Gen., Bish., Rhem., Oltramare (du chœur joyeux des myriades d'anges, de l'assemblée des premiers-nés), Segond.

3. καὶ μυριάσιν, ἀγγέλων πανηγύρει καὶ ἐκκλησίᾳ πρωτοτόκων.

'And to myriads, a general assembly of angels and a congregation of firstborn.' That is, myriads both of angels and of firstborn. This is the view of Wolf, Rambach, Griesbach, Bengel, Knapp, Böhme, Kuinoel, Tholuck, De Wette, Lachmann, Theile, Bleek, Olshausen, Delitzsch, Trench, Ebrard, Alford, Dale, Maclaren, RVm.

4. καὶ μυριάσιν ἀγγέλων· πανηγύρει καὶ ἐκκλησίᾳ πρωτοτόκων.

'And to myriads of angels; to the general assembly and Church of the firstborn.' This is the order of the Elzevirs, Beza, Calov, Carpzov, Storr, Joannes Gregorius, Matthaei, Alberti, AV, RV, Kurz, Liddon, Saphir ('to the general assembly of the Church of the firstborn ones'), Lünemann, Hofmann, Cremer (who argues that only because πανήγυρις and ἐκκλησία both refer to the same company can the presence of πανήγυρις be accounted for; it is an assembly, yea a festive one —an argument which would have more force if π. followed ἐκ.), Ostervald, Angus, Rendall, WH.

5. καὶ μυριάσιν ἀγγέλων, πανηγύρει καὶ ἐκκλησίᾳ πρωτοτόκων.

'And to myriads of angels, a general assembly and congregation of firstborn.' That is, the angels are both the general assembly and the congregation of firstborn. So Davidson (who argues forcibly), Moulton, Weizsäcker (und 'Myriaden von Engeln, einer Festversammlung und Gemeinde von Erstgeborenen).

The adv. 'generally' means (1) universally in every place, Jer 48³⁸ 'There shall be lamentation generally upon all the housetops of Moab' (כֻּלֹּה, lit. 'all of it' [see Driver on 2 S 2⁹]; RV 'every where'). Cf. Art. XVII. (XXXIX. Articles), 'Furthermore, we must receive God's promises in suchwise, as they be generally set forth to us in Holy Scripture' (ut nobis in sacris literis generaliter propositæ sunt *); Hooker, Eccl. Polity, v. lv. 1, 'God in Christ is generally the medicine, which doth cure the world'; Pr. Bk., Catechism, 'How many Sacraments hath Christ ordained in his Church? Two only, as generally necessary to salvation'; and Chaucer, Troilus and Criseyde, i. 86—

> 'The noyse up roos, whan it was first aspyed,
> Thorugh al the toun, and generally was spoken,
> That Calkas traytor fled was, and allyed
> With hem of Grece.'

(2) Together, as a whole, 2 S 17¹¹ 'Therefore I counsel that all Israel be generally gathered unto thee' (הֵאָסֹף יֵאָסֵף, LXX συναγόμενος συναχθήσεται; Vulg. Congregatur ad te universus populus Israel; RV 'together'). In this sense Tindale uses 'in general' (Expositions, on Mt 6¹⁻⁴), 'For we must have a place to come together, to pray in general.' And from this arose the modern meaning 'on the whole.' Shaks. makes Bottom say 'generally,'

---

* On this passage Gibson remarks (The XXXIX. Articles, ii. [1897] 486): 'The English sounds somewhat ambiguous, but there can be no doubt that "generally" here means "universally," i.e. of God's promises as applying to all men, and not, as the Calvinistic party asserted, only to a particular class, consisting of a few favourites of Heaven. This interpretation is rendered certain by the corresponding passage in the Reformatio Legum, where God's promises to the good, and threats to the evil, are spoken of as generaliter propositæ in Holy Scripture. The same interpretation was pointed out by Baro in his Concio ad Clerum in 1595, in the controversy when the Lambeth articles were first projected; and was also asserted against the Puritans by Bishop Bancroft at the Hampton Court Conference. Thus the clause directly condemns the theory of particular redemption.'

'as a whole,' when he means just the opposite, 'individually,' Mids. Night's Dream, I. ii. 2—

> 'You were best to call them generally, man by man.'

J. HASTINGS.

GENERATION.—i. 'Generation' is used in AV to tr. 1. דּוֹר dôr; Aram. דָּר dâr, Dn 4³; LXX γενεά, etc.; Vulg. generatio, etc. Dôr is used (a) generally for a period, especially in the phrases dôr wādhôr, etc., of limitless duration; past, Is 51⁸; future, Ps 106³; past and future, Ps 102²⁴; (b) of all men living at any given time, Gn 6⁹; (c) of a class of men with some special characteristic, Pr 30¹¹⁻¹⁴ of four generations of bad men; (d) in Is 38¹² and Ps 49¹⁹ dôr is sometimes taken as 'dwelling-place.' 2. תּוֹלְדוֹת, tôledhôth, from yāladh, 'beget' or 'bear children,' LXX γένεσις, γενέσεις; Vulg. generationes. Tôlĕdhôth is used in the sense of (a) genealogies, Gn 5¹, figuratively of the account of creation, Gn 2⁴; also (b) divisions of a tribe, as based on genealogy, tôlĕdhôth occurs only in the Priestly Code, in Ru 4¹⁸, and in 1 Ch. 3. γενεά in same sense as 1. (a), Col 1²⁶; as 1. (b), Mt 24³⁴. 4. γένεσις = 2. (a), Mt 1¹, an imitation of LXX use of γένεσις for תּוֹלְדוֹת. 5. γέννημα, 'offspring' = 1. (c). 6. γένος, race = 1. (c).

ii. Γενεά was also loosely used in Greek as 'generation' in English, of a period of about 30 to 33 years, e.g. 'Three generations of men make a hundred years' (Herod. ii. 142). But there is no probable instance of such usage in the Bible. OT texts, such as Gn 15¹³·¹⁶, Job 42¹⁶, are cited in favour of it only under a misapprehension.

LITERATURE.—Oxf. Heb. Lex. s. דּוֹר and תּוֹלְדוֹת, and Thayer-Grimm, NT Lex. s. γενεά, etc.   W. H. BENNETT.

GENERATION.—In the phrase 'generation of vipers,' which occurs in Mt 3⁷ 12³⁴ 23³³ Lk 3⁷, the Greek tr⁴ 'generation' is γεννήματα (plu. of γέννημα, which in the best texts occurs only in those places, elsewhere γένημα), a totally different word from γενεά, which is so often tr⁴ 'generation' in EV. In fact, γεννήματα means 'offspring'; and as this meaning belonged once to 'generation' also, it could stand as its representative. Thus Bp. Hall, Works (1634), i. 781, 'Of the Deluge'— 'These mariages did not beget men, so much as wickednesse, from hence religions (sic) husbands both lost their piety, and gained a rebellious and godlesse generation'; and Shaks. Lear, I. i. 119—

> 'He that makes his generation messes
> To gorge his appetite.'

'Generation of vipers' comes from Tindale, whom the versions mostly follow. Gen. NT has 'of-springes of vipers' in Lk 3⁷, and Rhem. NT 'vipers broodes' throughout.

In Mt 1¹ 'The book of the generation of Jesus Christ,' the Gr. is γένεσις, which is used also in 1¹⁸ (EV 'birth,' RVm 'generation'), Lk 1¹⁴ (EV 'birth'), as well as Ja 1²³ 3⁶, and the meaning is probably 'birth' here also, though all the versions have 'generation.' Cf. Bp. Hall, Works, ii. 104, 'I cannot blame that philosopher who, undertaking to write of the hidden miracles of nature, spends most of his discourse upon the generation and formation of man; Surely we are fearefully and wonderfully made; but, how much greater is the miracle of our spirituall regeneration'; and White, Selborne, xl., 'The threads sometimes discovered in eels are perhaps their young: the generation of eels is very dark and mysterious.'

Still another word is tr⁴ 'generation' in 1 P 2⁹ 'But ye are a chosen generation' (γένος ἐκλεκτόν, RV 'an elect race'). In this sense Mandeville, Travels, 140, 'This Machomete regned in Arabye, the Zeer of oure Lord Jhesu Crist 610; and was one of the Generacioun of Ysmael.' Wyc. (1388) has 'a chosen kyn.'   J. HASTINGS.

GENESIS.—

Introduction.
 i. Contents.
 ii. Plan and Unity.
 iii. Composite Structure.
 iv. Component Sources of the Narrative.
 v. Historical Value.
 vi. Religious Teaching.
  Literature.

The Jews divided their sacred books into three groups—the Law (or *Torah*), the Prophets (or *Nebiim*), and the Writings (or *Kethubim*). Of these the Law (or *Torah*), which corresponded to our Pentateuch, was divided into *five* portions or books, probably for greater convenience in use and reference; and hence the Rabbis sometimes spoke of these books as 'the five fifths of the Torah.' Their first book was the same as our book 'Genesis,' and was called by a title consisting of its opening word *Berêshith* (= 'In the beginning'). In the Septuagint version it was called 'Genesis,' γένεσις ('begetting,' 'origin,' 'generation'), a word which occurs in the rendering of 2⁴ αὕτη ἡ βίβλος γενέσεως οὐρανοῦ καὶ γῆς. This title was adopted and transliterated in the Lat. translation, and so passed into general use in Western and Eastern Churches alike.

i. CONTENTS.—Genesis begins with an account of the creation of the world. A survey of the whole book shows us a division into two unequal portions, one (chs. 1–11) dealing with *primeval*, the other and longer portion (chs. 12–50) dealing with *patriarchal* history. In both these portions we have mention of *five* distinct 'generations' (*tôlĕdhôth* תולדות), which represent, as it were, successive stages in the progress of the narrative. In the primeval history are the 'generations' of (1) the heaven and the earth, chs. 1–4; (2) Adam, 5–6⁸; (3) Noah, 6⁹–9; (4) the sons of Noah, 10¹–11⁹; (5) Shem, 11¹⁰–²⁶. In the patriarchal history are the 'generations' of (1) Terah, chs. 11²⁷–25¹¹; (2) Ishmael, 25¹²–¹⁸; (3) Isaac, 25¹⁹–35; (4) Esau, 36; (5) Jacob, 37–50. It must not be supposed that the number of these 'generations' is accidentally *ten*. The number ten was regarded as symbolical of completeness; and there can be little doubt that the enumeration of the ten tables of 'generations' was intended to denote the completion of the primitive period. The twelve sons of Jacob, who in Genesis are removed into Egypt, have become in Exodus twelve tribes, and the family of Jacob has grown into the nation of Israel. The Bk. of Genesis gives the traditions respecting the beginnings of the world, of man, of the nations, and of the people of Israel. It brings the people of Israel to the close of the patriarchal age, to the threshold of their history as a nation.

ii. PLAN AND UNITY.—The plan upon which the book is constructed is quite easy to recognize. The history of the Israelite people is traced from the three epochs, (*a*) the Creation, (*b*) the Flood, (*c*) the call of Abraham. An account is given of the three patriarchs, Abraham, Isaac, and Jacob. The story of Abraham is given at some length; that of Isaac is dismissed very briefly; that of Jacob is merged in the life of Joseph, through whose instrumentality the sons of Jacob are brought into Egypt. The end of the book leaves the Israelites sojourning in Egypt, after the death of Joseph. The narrative is continued in the Bk. of Exodus. The Bk. of Genesis contains the first portion of the historical narrative which runs continuously from Genesis to the end of the Bks. of Kings.

The book, therefore, presents an obvious unity of design; and the manner in which parenthetical and subsidiary material is introduced but never permitted seriously to impair the general thread of the work, shows artistic skill and a considerable degree of literary self-control.

iii. COMPOSITE STRUCTURE.—But it would be a mistake to let the unity of plan which distinguishes the book conduce to the supposition that its literary structure is homogeneous. The Hebrew chronicles and histories are all of them composite works. Like many of the mediæval chronicles and histories they are compiled from different sources, from materials of different age. The extracts are woven together so as to produce a consecutive narrative. But it is generally not difficult to distinguish the points at which the different sections are pieced together. The similarity of style, in certain sections of the narrative, combined with marked dissimilarity from the style in other sections, has enabled scholars to class together the portions which may be assigned to one or other literary source. In doing this it is easy to let conjecture run too far, and to exaggerate the importance of *minutiæ* in discriminating between different layers in the strata. But within certain limits the analysis of the distribution of the Bk. of Genesis has now been carried out with a great degree of agreement between the principal scholars of all schools. For while scholars may not be agreed as to the date to which these sources should be assigned, there is no disputing the fact of the family resemblance of certain portions of the book, and the necessity of explaining the resemblances by the supposition of compilatory origin.

From the time (1753) when Astruc, the French physician, first inferred, from the intermittent interchange of the sacred names Elohim and Jahweh, that different documents had been employed in the composition of Genesis, critics have carried on this branch of investigation with the utmost patience and minuteness. It is now generally admitted that the distinctive use of the divine name is only one criterion amongst many by which the vocabulary of certain portions in the book can be shown to differ from that of others; and, further, that a difference of literary treatment and of religious tone can be recognized side by side with that of phraseology and diction.

The idea that such a view is based upon mere theorizing or hair-splitting fancifulness is finally abandoned. So far as the composite character of the literary structure of Genesis is concerned, the main conclusions of criticism may be said to be established. Among the causes which necessitate the hypothesis that different documents were used, may be classed (*a*) *varying accounts of the same thing*, e.g. of the Creation, chs. 1 and 2; the number of animals that went into the ark, and the duration of the Flood, chs. 6 and 7; explanations of the names Beersheba 21³¹ 26³³, Bethel 28¹⁸. ¹⁹ 35¹⁴. ¹⁵, Israel 32²⁹ 35¹⁰; of the sale of Joseph by his brethren to Ishmaelites and Midianites, ch. 37: (*b*) *apparent discrepancies*, e.g. Abraham's family after Sarah's death, in extreme old age 25¹ᶠᶠ., cf. 17¹⁷ 18¹¹; the age of Sarah 17¹⁷ and 12¹¹ 20²; of Isaac as described in 27¹. ². ⁷. ¹⁰. ⁴¹ and 26³⁴ 35²⁸; the names of Esau's wives 26³⁴ 28⁹ and 36². ³; Joseph's Egyptian master in 37³⁶ and 39¹–40⁴: (*c*) *the repetition of the same event, or of different traditions of similar events*, e.g. the origin of Isaac's name 17¹⁷ 18¹² 21⁶, of Edom's 25²⁵ and ³⁰, of Issachar's, Zebulun's, and Joseph's ch. 30; and the similar occurrences in 12¹⁰ᶠᶠ. 20¹ᶠ. 26⁷ᶠᶠ.

There is no need here (see HEXATEUCH) to recapitulate the arguments by which it has been demonstrated that the structure of the first six books of the Old Testament is a compilation from different literary sources. 'There was a time,' says Delitzsch, 'when the horizon of Pentateuch criticism was bounded by Genesis and the beginning of Exodus. We now know that the mode of composition found in Genesis continues to the 34th chapter of Deuteronomy. It extends, moreover, beyond Dt 34, and continues in the Bk. of

Joshua. . . . And this Hexateuch also is only a component part of the great historical work in five parts (viz. Moses, Joshua, Judges, Samuel, Kings), extending from Gn 1 to 2 K 25, of which the Pentateuch forms one' (Delitzsch, *New Comm. on Gen.* vol. i. pp. 46, 47).

The biblical student finds in the composite structure a sufficient and satisfactory means of accounting for the numerous minor discrepancies and difficulties in the Bk. of Genesis which have often given occasion for perplexity and doubt, and have too often led to forced and disingenuous methods of exegesis.

iv. THE COMPONENT SOURCES OF THE NARRA-TIVE.—The following describes roughly the general conclusions of modern criticism. Genesis consists of a consecutive narrative welded together by a compiler designated R, out of three main documentary sources designated by critics P (the Priestly Code), J (the Jahwist), and E (the Elohist).

(a) Of these three principal sources the one most easily distinguished is P. For, though the framework of the narrative preserved from the P source is somewhat meagre, its style and characteristics are very marked. Certain leading events are given by it in great detail, *e.g.* the Creation, the Deluge, the Covenant with Noah, and the Covenant with Abraham. The chronology is carefully observed; periods of most remote times are reckoned in years with precision; and brief summaries of other events are given (*e.g.* 10. 25[12]); or their recollection is preserved by means of genealogies (5. 11[10] 35[22ff.]). 'The history [in P] advances along a well-defined line, marked by a gradually diminishing length of human life; by the revelation of God under three distinct names, *Elohim, El Shaddai,* and *Jahweh*; by the blessing of Adam and its characteristic conditions; and by the subsequent covenants with Noah, Abraham, and Israel, each with its special "sign," the rainbow, the rite of circumcision, and the Sabbath, Gn 9[12. 13] 17[11], Ex 31[13]' (Driver, *LOT*[3] p. 127).

P is also characterized by an avoidance of anthropomorphisms. There is no mention of angels or of visions in sleep. God is described as 'appearing' (Gn 17[1. 22. 23] 35[9. 13] 48[3]), and as 'speaking' (Gn 1[29] 6[13] 7[1] 8[15]–9[1]); but, as compared with the other writers whose materials are incorporated in the Pentateuch, P is conspicuously guarded and scrupulous in his references to the Deity against any approach to familiar or irreverent description.

The narrative of P is somewhat formal and precise. It abounds in phrases and expressions which are not elsewhere found.

The following are some of the interesting traits of the P narrative which may be noted here :—

(1) *Divine Name.*—Except in 17[1] 21[1], Elohim, not Jahweh, is used as the name of God; and these two exceptions are probably due to the compiler or to later copyists. God is revealed to the patriarchs as El Shaddai (Gn 17[1] 28[3] 35[11] 48[3], cf. Ex 6[3]).

(2) *Proper Names.*—In P 'the sons of Heth' (בְּנֵי חֵת) is always used (Gn 23[3. 5. 7. 10. 16] 25[10] 27[46] 49[32]), never 'Hittites' (הַחִתִּים), as in J and E. P has 'Kiriath-arba' for 'Hebron' (Gn 23[2] 35[27]), and Paddan-aram (Gn 25[20] 28[2. 5. 6. 7] 31[18] 33[18] 35[9. 26] 46[15]) for the region called in J (Gn 24[10]) Aram-naharaim. The mention of Machpelah occurs only in the P narrative (Gn 23[9. 17. 19] 25[9] 49[30] 50[13]).

(3) Among *the words and phrases* characteristic of P may be mentioned the following, which are found in Genesis :—

אֲחֻזָּה 'possession,' Gn 17[8] 23[4] 36[43] 47[11] 49[30].

אֲנִי 30 times (אָנֹכִי once, Gn 23[4]).

כָּל־בָּשָׂר (כָּל־בָּשָׂר) 'flesh' ('all flesh'), Gn 6[12. 13] 7[15. 16] 8[17] 9[11. 15-17].

גָּוַע 'expire,' Gn 6[17] 7[21] 25[8] 35[29].

זֶרַע 'seed,' Gn 9[9] 17[7] 35[12] 46[6] 48[4].

מְאֹד מְאֹד 'very exceedingly,' Gn 7[19] 17[2].

מִקְנֶה Gn 17[12. 13] 23[18].

מִשְׁפָּחָה (*e.g.* לְמִשְׁפְּחֹתֵיהֶם 'according to their families'), Gn 8[19] 10[5. 20. 31].

עֶצֶם הַיּוֹם הַזֶּה 'the self-same day,' Gn 7[13] 17[23. 26].

פָּרָה וְרָבָה 'be fruitful and multiply,' Gn 1[22. 28] 8[17] 9[1. 7. 17].

רְכוּשׁ 'possessions,' Gn 12[5] 13[6] 31[18] 36[7].

שָׁרַץ 'swarm,' Gn 1[20. 21] 7[21] 8[17] 9[7].

תּוֹלְדוֹת 'generations.'

There is general agreement among critics as to the passages in Genesis that were taken by the compiler from the P document. These are—

1[1]–2[4a] 5[1-28. 30-32] 6[9-22] 7 (portions) 8[1. 2a. 3b-5. 13a. 14-19] 9[1-17. 28. 29] 10[1-7. 20. 22. 23. 31. 32] 11[10-27. 31. 32] 12[4b. 5] 13[6. 11b. 12a] 16[1a. 3. 15. 16] 17. 19[29] 21[1b. 2b-5] 23. 25[7-11a. 12-17. 19. 20. 26b] 26[34. 35] 27[46]–28[9] 29[24. 29] 31[18b] 33[18a] 34 (portions) 35[9-13. 15. 22b-29] 36 (very largely) 37[1. 2a] 41[46] 46[6-27] 47[5. 6a. 7-11. 27b. 28] 48[3-6. 7] 49[1a. 28b-33] 50[12. 13].

(b) When the P portions have been removed, there remains a large portion of Genesis which critics have called 'prophetic,' as distinguished from 'priestly,' being clearly separable from P in language and in treatment of narrative.

But this large portion of prophetic writing has also been conclusively shown to be, not homogeneous, but to consist of two main threads of narrative which to a great extent must have covered the same ground, and which a compiler combined in the form of a consecutive narrative. There were therefore two original documents (J and E) independent of one another, which, being welded together, formed a distinct work, JE, which was afterwards combined with P by the final redactor. As to the relative priority of these two documents, scholars are hardly yet in absolute agreement. But, at the present day, opinion inclines to the view that the document, which has as one of its characteristics the use of Jahweh (Jehovah) for the divine name, and has therefore been entitled the 'Jahwist' (=J, for short), is the earlier in date; and that the other, which on account of its use of Elohim for the sacred name (until Ex 3[14], when the name was revealed to Moses) is called the Elohist (=E, for short), can be only very slightly later. In determining what that date must have been, we are enabled, by the evidence of the language, to discern that both J and E belong to the best period of Hebrew literature, free from the obscurity of the early and from the insipidity of the later age.

The resemblance of these two documents to one another in their contents, and their difference in style and language, may best be illustrated by a comparison of the parallel narratives in Gn 20 and 26, and in the accounts of the patriarchs Jacob and Joseph.

J contains some of the most striking descriptions in all Genesis; and there is probably no Hebrew writing which in beauty of narrative, vigour, simplicity, and artistic skill can be considered to surpass this document. To it we owe the preservation of the famous stories of the Garden of Eden; of Cain and Abel; of Abraham and the three angelic visitors; of Sodom and Gomorrah; of the mission of Eliezer, the servant of Abraham; of Judah and Tamar; of Judah's intercession with Joseph.

Throughout his narrative, the writer of J keeps prominently in view the spiritual and moral purpose with which he indites his records of old time. It is in this respect that he occupies the position of a 'prophet'; he interprets the truths that underlay the history of the past, and explains God's dealings in the world and with His chosen people.

'He is penetrated by the thought of Jehovah's mercifulness, long-suffering, and covenant faithfulness. He delights to trace the successive stages in the development of faith. It is he who tells how Abraham "believed in the Lord, and He counted it to him for righteousness." . . . The Jahwist appears, in fact, to survey the field of history with the eye of mature spiritual experience; in the lowly beginnings of Hebrew history he discerns the divinely intended consummation—the ultimate purpose which from the first filled the incidents of ordinary life with solemn significance (Gn 19²²ff. 16¹² 19³¹ff. 25²⁵ff. 49⁹ff.).' (Ottley's *Bampton Lectures*, 1897, pp. 119, 120).

Among the characteristic features of J's writing the following deserve special mention :—

(1) *The use of Jahweh* (יהוה) *as the name of God.*—Not, of course, that the word Elohim was not known or used by him; he does use it for the purpose of introducing a comparison between the human and the divine (Gn 32²⁹, ³¹ 33¹⁰), or when he represents a non-Israelite speaking of the Deity to an Israelite, or an Israelite to a non-Israelite (Gn 20¹³ 40⁸ 41¹⁶. 25. 28. 32 42²⁹). He puts it into the mouth of the serpent (Gn 3²). The name Jahweh, on the other hand, in his narrative, is known to the patriarchs and used by them; and the writer is not apparently aware of the tradition that the name was first revealed to Moses, as recorded in Ex 3. To an English reader, his use of the sacred name appears an anachronism, or a not unnatural anticipation of later general usage.

(2) *J's use of words and phrases* may be illustrated by—

בֹּאֲכָה, lit. 'as thou comest to,' Gn 10¹⁹ *bis* etc.

מָצָא חֵן בְּעֵינֵי אֲדֹנִי, 'find favour,' Gn 6⁸ 18³ 32⁶ 33⁸. ¹⁵ etc.

עָשָׂה חֶסֶד, Gn 24¹². ¹⁴. ⁴⁹ (used also by E, Gn 20¹³ 21²³ 40¹⁴).

יָדַע (euphemistic use), Gn 41. ¹⁷. ⁴⁵ 19⁸ 24¹⁶ 38²⁶.

[יָצַן] (Hiph.) Gn 30³⁸ 33¹⁵ 439 47².

כָּלָה ל, Gn 18³³ 24¹⁵. ¹⁹. ²².

לִין, Gn 19² 24²³.

עָתַר, Gn 25²¹ (cf. Ex 8⁹. ²⁸ 9²³ 10¹⁷).

הַפַּעַם, Gn 2²³ 18³² 29³⁴ᶠ. 30²⁰ 46³⁰ ; צָעִיר for 'the younger,' Gn 25²³ 43³³ 48¹⁴.

שִׁפְחָה 'maid-servant' (not אָמָה), Gn 16⁵ 30⁷ etc.

הִשְׁקִיף, Gn 18¹⁶ 19²⁸.

(3) *Grammar.*—A preference for verbal suffixes, instead of אֵת with suffixes.

Phrases such as 'and it came to pass,' וַיְהִי כַּאֲשֶׁר, וַיְהִי כִּי.

Emphatic use of זֶה and זֹאת.

Fondness for particles.

Use of precative נָא.

The portions of Genesis which are generally assigned by critics to J are as follows :—

2⁴ᵇ-4²⁶ 5²⁹ 6¹⁻⁸ 7¹⁻⁵. ¹². ¹⁶ᵇ. ¹⁷. ²². ²³ 8²ᵇ. ³ᵃ. ⁶⁻¹². ¹³ᵇ. ²⁰⁻²² 9¹⁸⁻²⁷ 10⁸⁻¹⁹. ²¹. ²⁴⁻³⁰ 11¹⁻⁹. ²⁸⁻³⁰ 12¹⁻⁴ᵃ. ⁶⁻²⁰ 13¹⁻⁵. ⁷⁻¹¹ᵃ. ¹²ᵇ⁻¹⁶ 16¹ᵇ. ². ⁴⁻¹⁴ 18¹⁻¹⁹ 28. 30-38 21¹ᵃ. ²ᵃ. 33 22²⁰⁻²⁴ 24¹⁻²⁵⁶. ¹¹ᵇ. ¹⁸. ²¹⁻²⁶ᵃ. ²⁷⁻³⁴ 26¹⁻³³ (exc. 16. 18) 27¹⁻⁴⁵ (mainly) 28¹⁰. ¹³⁻¹⁶. ¹⁹ 29²⁻¹⁴. ¹⁹⁻³⁵ (exc. 28ᵇ. 29) 30¹⁻²³ (mainly). ²⁴⁻⁴² 31¹. 3 (25-27. 38-40). 46. 48-50 32⁴⁻¹⁴. ²²⁻³² 33¹⁻¹⁷ 34'(largely) 35²¹. ²²ᵃ [36³¹⁻³⁸] 37¹²⁻³⁵ (partly) 38. 39. 42³⁸⁻⁴⁴ 46²⁸⁻⁴⁷⁵. ¹³⁻²⁶. ²⁷ᵃ. ²⁹⁻³¹ 49¹ᵇ⁻²⁸ᵃ 50¹⁻¹¹. ¹⁴.

The majority of critics incline to the view that J was composed by a dweller in the Southern kingdom ; and it is pointed out in support of this view that the dwelling-place of Abraham, and possibly also of Jacob, is, according to J, Hebron, and that the leader of Joseph's brethren is Judah and not Reuben. Such arguments are obviously precarious ; but the alternative opinion, that the writer belonged to the Northern kingdom, as Kuenen maintains, does not rest on any more convincing proofs.

(*c*) The E document in Genesis, like the J document, has preserved many of the most interesting features of the patriarchal narrative. To use Driver's phrase, its narrative 'is more "objective," less consciously tinged by ethical and theological reflexion than that of J.' We owe to it, however, the mention of many of the most striking details to be found in the book. For instance, the traditions preserved in connexion with particular localities in Palestine are in E chronicled with minuteness, *e.g.* the sacrifice on Mt. Moriah (22), the pillar at Bethel (28¹⁸), and that at Gilead (31⁴⁵), the altar at Bethel (35¹. ³. ⁷), and Rachel's burying-place (35²⁰). The story of Joseph is largely narrated from the sources which E preserved ; and it is to E that we are indebted for the record of the Philistine names Ahuzzath and Phicol (21³²), and the Egyptian names Potiphar (37³⁶), Zaphenath-paneah and Asenath (41⁴⁵).

The most important sections from E embrace Abraham's relations with Abimelech in 20 and 21, the expulsion of Hagar and Ishmael 20⁸⁻²¹, the sacrifice of Isaac 22¹⁻¹⁹, Jacob's flight from Haran and his league with Laban 31, and the story of Joseph as related in 40. 41. 42 and 45.

It may be noticed that **E** makes frequent mention of the *means* of divine revelation, whether by dream (*e.g.* 20⁶ 21¹² 22¹ 28¹¹ 31²⁴ 37⁶ 40) or by the ministration of angels (*e.g.* 21¹⁷ 22¹¹ 28¹²). ' He interprets in a religious spirit what he records, and aims at bringing out the didactic significance of events, *e.g.* Gn 50²⁹' (Ottley, *BL* p. 119).

Among the characteristics of E's style, the following deserve notice :—

(1) *The name for God* is ' Elohim ' (אֱלֹהִים). The sacred name יהוה, according to E, was first revealed to Moses. Accordingly it is not employed by E until after Ex 3¹⁴. Other names are also employed by him, as ' El ' אֵל (Gn 33²⁰ 35⁷ 46³) and ' Adonai ' אֲדֹנָי (Gn 20⁴).

The name ' Jacob ' is preferred by E, even after the narrative in Gn 32 with its account of the origin of the name Israel.

(2) *Use of words and phrases*—

עַל־אֹדוֹת, Gn 21¹¹. ²⁵.

אָסוֹן, Gn 42⁴. ³⁸ 44²⁹.

אָמָה, not שִׁפְחָה, Gn 20¹⁷ 21¹⁰. ¹². ¹³ 30³ 31³³.

בָּעַל (vb. and noun) Gn 20³.

בִּלְבַּל, Gn 45¹¹ 47¹² 50²¹.

לֵבָב, Gn 20⁵. ⁶ 31²⁶.

Archaic words preserved in E—

אָמְנָה Gn 20¹².

כֵּן, subst. = ' position,' Gn 40¹³ 41¹³.

     adj. = ' honest,' Gn 42¹¹. ¹⁹. ³¹⁻³⁴.

מוֹנִים Gn 31⁷. ⁴¹.

פָּתַר Gn 40⁸. ⁹ 41⁸. ⁹.

(3) *Grammatical usages*—

(*a*) A marked preference for the use of אֵת with the pronom. suffix instead of attaching the suffix to the verb.

(*b*) Rare uses of the Infinitive—

רְדָה for רֶדֶת, Gn 46³.

עֲשֹׂה, עָשׂוֹ   Gn 31²⁸ 50²⁰.

רְאֹה   Gn 48¹¹.

(*c*) The connexion of loosely attached passages by such phrases as וַיְהִי אַחַר הַדְּבָרִים הָאֵלֶּה Gn 22¹ 40¹ 48¹.

And the colloquial and somewhat redundant phrases prefixed to the interchange of speech, *e.g.* 'And . . . said (*or*, called), and he answered, Here am I,' etc., Gn 22¹. ⁷. ¹¹ etc.

The chief portions of the narrative assigned to E are the following (and it will be observed that they are first to be identified in the story of Abraham) ; 15 (portions, according to some scholars), *e.g.* parts of vv.¹. ². ³. ⁵ 20¹⁻¹⁷ 21⁸⁻³² 22¹⁻¹⁴. ¹⁹ 28¹¹. ¹². 17. 18. 20-22 29¹. 15-18 30 (portions), 31². 4-47. (exc. 18b) 32³. 13b-22 35⁵ᵇ. 18b-20 35¹⁻⁸. 16-20 37²ᵇ⁻¹¹. 14a. 18. 19. 22-24. 28a. 28c-30. 36 40 (showing some influence of J) 41¹⁻⁴⁵. ⁵⁰⁻⁵⁷ 42¹⁻³⁷ 45¹⁻⁴⁶⁵ 48¹. ². ⁸⁻²² 50¹⁵⁻²⁶.

That E represents an Ephraimitic tradition is the generally accepted opinion. This is based upon the prominence given in its narrative to places and persons with which tradition in the Northern kingdom would presumably be closer in sympathy than tradition in the Southern. Joseph, the father of Ephraim, is the most conspicuous personage in the narrative ; and Reuben, not Judah, is the foremost of his brethren. Bethel and Shechem, both sacred places in the Northern kingdom, are particularly mentioned in E. The sojourn of Abraham is not at Hebron, but at Beersheba and Gerar ; that of Jacob, at Beersheba and Shechem.

(*d*) The work of combining JE and P is attributed to the redactor or redactors (R), who ' chose from his sources what was most suited to the plan of his work.' His method is thus admirably and succinctly described by Spurrell : ' Sometimes he merely takes small extracts from one document (*e.g.* 4¹⁷⁻²⁴ 6¹⁻⁴ 30³²⁻⁴²), merely small portions of fuller accounts), or notices individual points (*e.g.* 11²⁹ Jiska mentioned ; 20¹² the relationship between

Abram and Sarai, cf. 28[22] [see 35[7]] 48[22]). At other times the portions taken from the documents are quoted in full, and for the most part are verbally transferred from the original (*e.g.* the narratives in P up to 11[26]), and sometimes, again, whole passages from one document are omitted, possibly because they were at variance with the accounts given by the others (see in P the brief accounts in 11[27-32]; the omission of the introduction to the history of Abram, previous to ch. 12; of the divine manifestation to Isaac, see 35[12]; of the sojourn of Jacob in Paddan-aram; of all the history of Joseph prior to Jacob's arrival in Egypt). Frequently extracts from J are given in an abridged form, in order that P may be reported more fully (cf. 2[5f.] 4[25f.], the Story of Creation, and the Table of Nations, J), and 16[15f.] 21[2ff.] 25[7ff.], 32[4] 35[28f.] . P. Elsewhere, however, in the story of the patriarchs the extracts from J are abridged in favour of E. With the exception of the history of Joseph, E contains (from ch. 20 onwards) fewer passages which are verbally reported. Usually the portions in E are expanded by notices from J, or anything worth recording in E is incorporated into the narrative of J. When combining his sources, the compiler, as far as possible, or as far as he deemed necessary, appears to have taken the narrative verbally from each and inserted both in his book (cf. ch. 2 f. side by side with 1, ch. 27 side by side with 26[34f.] and 28[1-9]; 48[3-7] side by side with 48[9-22]). Elsewhere, as, for example, where the event need only be quoted from one document (*e.g.* the birth or death of any person), he selects his account from one source, even though the same event be recorded in more than one document. In other cases the compiler found two accounts in the documents before him, agreeing in the main but differing in details; he would then weave one account into the other, omitting from each what could not be reconciled, and choosing from both what best suited the plan of his work (cf. chs. 7f. 10. 16. 25. 27-37. 39-50). It was not always possible, without further revision, to place side by side or to weld together the individual extracts from two or three sources. So it was necessary to eliminate what was contradictory from one or other of the documents (*e.g.* 21[17ff.] explanation of Ishmael's name, 32[8] of Maḥanaim, 33[10] of Peniel, cf. 31[25]), or to insert here and there small additions or remarks in order to fill up gaps and remove contradictions. So 4[25] 10[24] 21[14] 26[1a. 15. 18] 35[9] 37[5b. 8b. 39]. 20 43[14] 46[1]. To the desire to produce a readable whole, may be attributed the accommodation necessary to preserve consistency in the use of the names Abram and Sarai in all passages previous to ch. 17, of the double name Yahweh-Elohim in chs. 2-3; also the change of Elohim into Yahweh in 17[1] 21[1]. Another expedient was frequently employed with the same object in view, viz. transposing entire portions of the narrative (so 11[1-9] 12[10-20] 25[5f. 11b] 25[21ff.] 47[12ff.]), or of brief notices (so 2[4a.] 31[45-50] 37[26] etc.), consequently R was obliged to insert all kinds of small additions; cf. 1[1] 9[18] 13[1. 3f.] 24[62]. In other passages the sources are loosely combined (*e.g.* 7[7-9. 22] 15[7f.] 31[45ff.], ch. 36. 46[8-27]), the compiler now and then making additions of his own to bring the documents into harmony (*e.g.* 21[34] 27[46] 35[5] 46[12-20]). Explanatory glosses are also found (*e.g.* 20[18] 31[47] 35[6], and ch. 14, where they are numerous), some of which may be due to a later corrector. All kinds of little additions occur, which are probably not derived from the sources themselves, but were inserted, either when the sources were welded together into one work, or some time after this. These insertions were added partly to explain the object of the narrative (15[12-16] 22[15-18] 26[3b-5]), partly to make it harmonize with statements occurring elsewhere

(25[18b] 35[22a], perhaps 4[15a]), and partly to introduce new notices, or new phases of tradition which were not mentioned in the three chief documents (10[9] 32[33]; perhaps 2[10-14], and in 10[14]; 11[28b] 31[b] 15[7] 22[2], etc.). Sometimes possibly use was also made of materials taken from other sources than J, E, and P (*e.g.* perhaps in ch. 14).'—Spurrell, *Genesis*[2], pp. lxi-lxiii. Whether the work of combining the narratives of J and E was effected by one writer, or was the result of a gradual process directed and influenced by a group or succession of 'prophetic' men, must be left to conjecture. Some scholars, however, are prepared to give an unhesitating reply. 'That the compiler of JE was a Judæan is clear,' says Fripp, 'from 22[2], where he has substituted "Moriah" for some Ephraimite name; and that he was not far removed from the Deuteronomist we may see in 18[19. 23-33a], in the kindred passages 13[16] 15. 16[10] 18[18] 22[17. 18] 26[4] 32[12] (cf. Dt 1[10] 10[22] 28[62]), and still more plainly in 26[5]' (*The Composition of the Book of Genesis*, p. 18).

v. THE HISTORICAL VALUE OF THE BOOK.—Doubtless, the views that are held upon the historical character of Genesis depend in great measure upon the conception which is entertained of 'inspiration.' The book itself makes no claim to being in any way supernaturally furnished with means of information. The writers and compilers appear to have made use of their materials in the same fashion as other writers of their day. There is no indication in this, or in other books of Scripture, that Revelation communicated to man a knowledge of facts that were ascertainable by human means.

The early narratives of Genesis respecting the Creation, the Fall, and the Flood are based upon myths and traditions which the Israelites inherited in common with other branches of the Semitic family. The labours of Rawlinson, Lenormant, George Smith, Schrader, Sayce, and others have shown indisputably the affinity of the Israelite with the Chaldæan cosmogony. And it has often been pointed out that the Israelite version of the myth is free from the puerilities and superstitions inalienable from the polytheism of the Babylonian version. 'Where the Assyrian or Babylonian poet,' says Sayce, 'saw the action of deified forces of nature, the Hebrew writer sees only the will of the one supreme God' (*HCM* p. 71). This assists us to form a judgment upon the true character of these early chapters. The story of the beginnings of the world and of mankind is told, not with a scientific but with a religious purpose. The old-world myths, or tales of Semitic folk-lore, were employed for the purpose of setting forth in their true light — as discerned through the revealing spirit of J″—the unchanging verities respecting the nature of God, of man, and of the created universe (cf. Ryle, *Early Narratives of Genesis*).

The story of the Flood is doubtless drawn from the reminiscence of a fearful devastation by water at some very remote period. The striking resemblance between it and the so-called 'poem of Izdubar,' contained in the cuneiform texts translated by Geo. Smith (1872), illustrates the similar treatment of semi-mythical, semi-historical material by the Israelite writers. The Genesis account presents many insuperable objections, if it were necessary to accept it as a literally accurate record. But the purpose of the narration is not scientific, but religious; it is obviously intended to depict the divine displeasure against sin, and the divine favour towards the upright and God-fearing. On the other hand, there seems no reason to call in question the occurrence of some terrible overthrow by water that laid waste the Euphrates Valley, or the wonderful deliverance of a few individuals. The reminiscence of these events was variously enshrined in versions of a common Semitic legend.

The narrative of the patriarchs stands midway between the Flood tradition and the Mosaic history. As compared with the former, it marks a great advance in the direction of the historic; relatively to the latter, it still belongs to a prehistoric age. The narrative has come down to us through the medium of documents, whose composition, in the form familiar to us, must have been separated by many centuries from the incidents which they relate. On the other hand, there is no reason to doubt that the stories respecting the Israelite ancestors rest upon a foundation of historic fact. The attempts to resolve the patriarchs, Abraham, Isaac, and Jacob, into abstract personifications of tribes, or into primitive tribal gods, have admittedly failed. Without the patriarchs 'the religious position of Moses,' says Kittel (*Hist. of the Hebrews*, p. 174), 'stands before us unsupported and incomprehensible.' It is very possible, indeed most probable, that the picture which has been preserved of the patriarchs derives much of its colouring from the thought and circumstances of a later period, and in particular from the prophetic treatment of the people's history.

Nor can it be questioned that the relationship of tribes and clans is represented in the patriarchal narrative under the symbol of a family genealogy. The primitive connexion of Israel with the peoples round about—Ammon, Moab, Amalek, Ishmael, Edom—is presented to us under the imagery of incidents occurring in the history of a single family during one or two generations. The stories of common folk-lore, deriving proper names from various incidents, are incorporated along with narratives of didactic purpose and deep spiritual import, *e.g.* the call of Abraham and the visions of Jacob. The memory of the great forefathers of the nation was idealized by the prophetic and priestly writers. But they preserved a living tradition of real men and actual experience.

The difficulty which besets the modern student is how to distinguish the substratum of actual history from the accretion of later legend and from the symbolism of Eastern description. The task is one which will probably defy all the attempts of existing scholarship. Future discoveries may bring fresh light to bear upon the patriarchal narrative. For the present, important as recent discoveries have been in illustrating the Genesis narrative, they have not supplied us with any certain data for its chronology. Thus, while the credibility of an Elamite invasion, as mentioned in Gn 14, has been confirmed, in the opinion of competent scholars, by the evidence of cuneiform inscriptions, we have not yet arrived at any settled conclusion as to the century to which the events should be assigned. While the Babylonian equivalent to the name Abraham has been found in the inscriptions, neither he nor Isaac nor Jacob nor Joseph have yet been identified in the monuments. The identification of Y'ḳb'ar and Y'sp'r, by which some scholars transliterated Nos. 102 and 78 in the list of towns and places conquered by Tahutmes III. in his campaign against Palestine and Syria, with Yaḳobel and Yosephel, Jacob and Joseph, would not, supposing it to be accurate, throw any light upon the historical problem. It would, at the most, afford evidence that the names Jacob and Joseph had been current in Palestine as the names of localities and districts 'centuries before the time of Moses' (cf. Dillmann, *Gen.* ii. 4, Eng. tr.).

Again, while we gather from the Tel el-Amarna tablets that the officials in the towns of Palestine and Phœnicia, as well as of Egypt, were wont, in the 15th cent. B.C., to employ the cuneiform character in their diplomatic and state correspondence, we are brought no nearer to the determination of the question, when the Palestinian (Phœnician-Hebrew) writing was first adopted, or whether the nomad Hebrews employed writing.

To maintain that because cuneiform writing was practised in Palestine in the 15th cent. by official scribes for state correspondence, the existing patriarchal narratives are therefore based upon Hebrew transcriptions of cuneiform chronicles which were *contemporary* with the events, is to leap over several stages of the argument. A comparison of the Tel el-Amarna tablets with the patriarchal narrative confronts us with the fact that no one from reading the Genesis account could form any conception of the political condition of Palestine, as it really was, during the patriarchal period. With the isolated exception of the reference to historical details in Gn 14[1ff.], the lives of the Hebrew patriarchs furnish no clue to the history of the centuries that correspond to the period of patriarchal sojourn in Palestine.

The story of Joseph shows abundant signs of acquaintance with Egyptian life and customs. But there is no appearance of its having been committed to writing in Egypt or by any contemporary. The dynastic name of the king of Egypt is alone given, *i.e.* Pharaoh; but we are nowhere told either his own name or that of the capital in which he resided. Accordingly, while some have contended that the mention of the Egyptian hatred for strangers indicates a period subsequent to the domination of the Hyksos, others have held that the elevation of Joseph, a shepherd by birth, to the highest office in the kingdom could have occurred only under a Hyksos dynasty. The Egyptian monuments have hitherto failed to give the name of Joseph; and the mention of a prolonged famine in the el-Kab inscription illustrates, but cannot with any certainty be identified with, the Genesis narrative. The measures taken by Joseph (Gn 47) in consequence of the famine doubtless correspond to Egyptian institutions known to the writer; but hitherto no account of them has been found in other quarters.

The evidence of the monuments, which has in recent years so copiously illustrated the biblical narrative, has not yet contributed with any certainty to the establishment of the literal historical accuracy of the patriarchal story.

The result may be disappointing; but the evidence at our disposal does not at present justify us in claiming more than that the general outline of the narrative is historical, and that the Mosaic epoch presupposes the patriarchal age. 'The historian may complain with Kuenen (see *The Religion of Israel*, vol. i. p. 113) that the strictly historical kernel which can be safely extracted from such a book as Genesis is vague and more or less indefinite. The fact is that the great figures of the patriarchal period are presented to us in narratives "of which," says Prof. G. A. Smith, "it is simply impossible to say at this time of day to establish the accuracy." We have simply to accept the fact that in the present state of our knowledge there are no clear *criteria* by which to distinguish precisely the historical nucleus contained in the patriarchal narratives from the idealized picture. If there is uncertainty on this point, we can only conclude that knowledge of the precise details of the history is not of vital importance' (Ottley, *BL* p. 130 f.).

vi. THE RELIGIOUS TEACHING OF THE BOOK.— A consideration of the religious value of Genesis reveals to us its true character and purpose. The Scriptures were written for religious instruction; and in no book of the OT are the treasures of theology to be found so close, as it were, beneath the surface *as in the Book of Genesis*.

1. The foundations of a true and spiritual religion are contained in the teaching of the early chapters of Genesis. Through the medium of the prehistoric legend, the Israelite writers communicated to their countrymen that which was revealed to them by the Divine Spirit concerning the Being and Nature of God, the origin and first perfection of the God-created universe, the origin of man, the nature and growth of sin, God's love toward man and His purpose of redemption. The narratives of the Creation and of the Fall present pictorially spiritual truths respecting man's nature, his need of restoration, and his capacity for a progressive development.

2. In the narrative of the patriarchs the redemptive purpose is unfolded by the gradual process of election (Ro 9[11]), the principle of which had already been indicated in the contrast of Cain and Abel, of the Cainites and the Sethites. The well-known stories of Abraham, Isaac, and Jacob were selected and arranged to minister to the purpose of religious teaching; and foremost stood the thought that God's love had alone determined the choice of the man and of the family from which should come the nation destined to be the channel of blessing to the world (Gn 12[3] 13[14] 15[5] 17[5] 18[17-19] 22[16] 26[3. 4] 35[11] 48[16]). This principle of election is pointedly emphasized in the providence which shields Sarai and Rebekah (Gn 12. 20. 26) from harm, and grants to them the gift of children in a quasi-miraculous manner (Gn 17[15-20] 18[11-15] 21[6-8] 25[20. 21. 26]). The narrative, too, lays stress upon the divine choice by disposing of the collateral lines in the chosen family before passing on to the detailed account of the particular person on whom God's favour has rested (*e.g.* the family of Japheth, Ham, and Shem, Gn 10[2. 6. 21]; the generations of Shem and Terah, 11[10. 27]; the story of Lot, 18. 19; the collateral branches of Abraham's family, preceding the story of Isaac, 25[1. 19]; the generations of Esau, preceding the story of Joseph, 36).

3. Akin to this treatment of election is the prominence given to the conception of God as One who was in communion with the children of men, though in an especial manner He revealed Himself to those whom He had chosen. That God showed favour to Abel's sacrifice is thus scarcely more significant than that He held converse with Cain the murderer. That He appeared to Abraham, Isaac, and Jacob was not more suggestive of His relation towards mankind than His appearance to Abimelech (20[3]) and to Laban (31[24]). The honour paid by Abraham to Melchizedek typified the recognition of divine power and love transcending the limits of a national covenant (Gn 14). At the same time, the story of 'the priest of God Most High' (14[18]) illustrated the possession of that basis of instructive national religion, the abiding witness of God within man, upon which alone the structure of revelation could stand. With the people of His choice, God is represented as holding communion under the most anthropomorphic conditions (*e.g.* Gn 16. 18. 28). But the constitution of the covenant with Noah is ratified by the sacrament of the 'bow' (9[8-17]), and the covenant with Abraham by that of 'circumcision' (17). And the lesson was thus conveyed to Israel that the phenomena of the physical world are pledges and emblems of a moral purpose overruling all, and that a common—if not almost universal—rite among Semitic races could be set apart and consecrated for the spiritual purposes of the service of the God of revelation.

4. The principle of progressiveness in the religious teaching of Israel is illustrated in Genesis by the three great stages of divine self-manifestation in the history of mankind, represented by the judgment in the Garden of Eden, by the visitation of the Flood, and by the calling of Abraham. Similarly, the record of God's dealings with the chosen man, the chosen family, and the chosen clan, lead up to the formation of the chosen nation, the history of which commences in the Book of Exodus.

The first anticipations of the Messianic hope are expressed in the promise of victory over the power of evil proclaimed in the so-called Prot-evangelium of Gn 3[15]. These receive a narrower definition in the promise made to Abraham that all the families of the earth should bless themselves in him (Gn 12[3. 4]). In Gn 49[11] the allusion to a *personal* Messiah has been much disputed; but, whatever explanation be given of the words rendered 'until Shiloh come,' the significance of this passage in the ancient 'blessing of Jacob' consists in its identification of the ultimate glory of Israel with the sovereignty impersonated by Judah.

Space forbids us to go further into detail respecting the religious teaching of Genesis. It has been well summed up in the following words: 'The Book of Genesis is the true and original birthplace of all theology. It contains those ideas of God and man, of righteousness and judgment, of responsibility and moral government, of failure and hope, which are presupposed through the rest of the Old Testament, and which prepare the way for the mission of Christ' (Girdlestone, *The Foundations of the Bible*, p. 155).

LITERATURE.—For the structure of Genesis, the English student is now well equipped with the recent literature on the subject: Driver, *LOT*; Addis, *Documents of the Hexateuch*; Fripp, *Composition of the Book of Genesis*; O. J. Ball, 'Book of Genesis,' *SBOT*; and Spurrell, *Notes on the Text of Genesis*. The fullest complete commentaries are those by Dillmann and Delitzsch (both now translated into English; Edinburgh: T. & T. Clark). The foreign books which should be consulted are those on the structure by Holzinger (*Einleitung*), Kautzsch-Socin, Wellhausen (*Die Composition des Hexateuchs*, 1889). On Genesis and the Monuments: Sayce, *HCM*; Schrader, *COT*; and the writings of George Smith, Maspero, Pinches, Haupt, and others. On the Theology of Genesis: the *OT Theology* of Schultz, Oehler, Riehm.

The reader may also consult Miss Wedgwood, *Message of Israel*; Watson, *The Book Genesis*; Ottley, *Aspects of the Old Test.*; Westcott, *Faith of the Gospel*; Ryle, *Early Narratives of Genesis*.   H. E. RYLE.

GENNÆUS, AV GENNEUS (Γενναῖος, Γέννεος A, 2 Mac 12[2]).—The father of Apollonius, who was the Syrian commander (στρατηγός) of a district in Pal. under Antiochus V. Eupator.

GENNESARET, LAKE OF (Lk 5[1]; in 1 Mac 11[67] GENNESARETH).—See GALILEE, SEA OF.

GENNESARET, LAND OF (ἡ γῆ Γεννησαρέτ, Mt 13[34], cf. Mk 6[53]) deserves special attention, (1) because of its connexion with our Lord, (2) because of the estimation in which it was held by the inhabitants of the country, and (3) because of the account which Josephus has given of its wonderful fertility and loveliness. The place referred to was on the W. side of the Sea of Galilee and towards its N. end. Directly opposite to it on the E. side of the lake there is a corresponding plain which, however, lacks the characteristics that have made the one on the W. side widely famous. The miraculous feeding of the five thousand took place on the E. plain (Mt 14[15-21], cf. the other Gospels), immediately after which Christ sent His disciples by ship 'to the other side.' According to Mk they were directed to go towards Bethsaida (6[45]); according to Jn they went, without instructions, 'towards Capernaum' (6[17]); but the storm—at that season the strong current of the Jordan would have carried them in spite of themselves out of their course to the S.—compelled them to anchor 'in the land of G.' Bethsaida, Capernaum, and the land of G. are, in our judgment, mentioned in their natural order. The very next act of our Lord mentioned was at Capernaum, leading us to suppose that that place was nearer 'the land of G.' than Bethsaida.

This plain, which is one of the most charming spots in Pal., is about one mile broad and two and a half miles long, having Khan Minyeh on the N. and Mejdel, the ancient Magdala, on the S. The famous pass of Wady Ḥamam leads up through the mountains on the W. towards the Mediterranean. Josephus says, 'Such is the fertility of the soil that it rejects no plant, and accordingly all are here cultivated by the husbandman, for so genial is the air that it suits every variety. The walnut, which delights beyond other trees in a wintry climate, grows here luxuriantly, together with the palm, which is nourished by the heat, and near to these are figs and olives to which a milder atmosphere has been assigned.' Not only does Nature in her ambition here 'nourish fruits of opposite climes, but she maintains a continual supply of them. Thus she produces those most royal of all, the grape and the fig, during ten months without intermission, while the other varieties ripen the year round.' The 'fertilising spring which irrigates the plain,' according to this author, was prob. the fountain at et-Tabigha, which was led in a rock-cut channel round the ledge at Khan Minyeh. 'Ain Mudawareh, which has been suggested as the fountain referred to, is quite out of the question (*Wars*, III. x. 8).

The Rabbis were as enthusiastic in their praise of this 'garden of princes' as was Josephus. It was to them a veritable 'paradise.' Its fruits were prized for their wonderful sweetness, but they were not found at Jerus. at the feasts, and the reason given was that no one should be tempted to come to the feasts merely for the sake of enjoying those fruits (Bab. Talmud, *Pesachim*, 8*b*; Neubauer, *Géog. du Talm.* 45 f.).

S. MERRILL.

GENTILES is one equivalent of the Heb. *goiim* (גּוֹיִם), which is represented in EV also by such renderings as 'nations' and 'heathen.' RV very frequently replaces AV 'Gentiles' by 'nations.'

גּוֹי (*goi*) has the same root meaning as עַם ('*am*, 'people'), which occurs more than 1500 times in OT. In their primary sense of a *connected body* (cf. Dt 32²¹ and Driver's note), *goi* and '*am* are both applied even to troops or herds of animals (Jl 1⁶, Pr 30²⁵·²⁶). So the plur. forms *goiim* and '*ammim*, like the later *lĕummim*, have the general sense of *nations* or *peoples*. Ultimately, however, linguistic usage confined the application of the sing. '*am*, with rare exceptions (*e.g.* Gn 26¹¹ of the Philistines, Ex 9¹⁶ of the Egyptians), to the *people of Isr.*, while the sing. *goi* was prevailingly, though not exclusively, applied to *other nations* (in Is 1⁴ Zeph 2⁹ *goi* and '*am* are both used to designate Isr.). A similar distinction rules the use in LXX of ἔθνος and λαός, which correspond to גּוֹי and עַם respectively. In NT we find (Lk 2³²) τὰ ἔθνη opposed to τῷ λαῷ θεοῦ Ἰσραήλ, although ἔθνος is pretty frequently used of Isr., and that without any disparaging intention (*e.g.* Lk 7⁵ 23², Jn 11⁴⁸·⁵¹·⁵² 18³⁵, Ac 10²² 24³·¹⁰·¹⁷ 26⁴ 28¹⁹).

Goiim (גּוֹיִם 'nations,' or כָּל־הַגּוֹיִם 'all the nations') occurs very freq. in OT as a designation of *non-Jewish* peoples (1 S 8⁵·²⁰, 2 K 18³³ 19¹⁷, 1 Ch 14¹⁷ 16²⁴, 2 Ch 32²³ 36¹⁴, Neh 5¹⁷, Ps 79¹⁰ 106⁴⁷ etc.). The phrase *gĕlîl haggoiim* (גְּלִיל הַגּוֹיִם 'circle of the nations') was applied to a district in the N. of Pal., whose population contained a large Gentile element. It is most familiar to us under its NT form 'Galilee of the Gentiles' (Mt 4¹⁵). The LXX equivalent of גּוֹיִם is ἔθνη, which is the regular term for *Gentiles* in NT as well as in Apocr. (*e.g.* 1 Es 5⁶⁹ 8⁸⁹, Wis 14¹¹ 15¹⁵). The form ἐθνικός occurs in NT three times (Mt 6⁷ 18¹⁷, and in the correct text of 3 Jn ⁸), the adverbial form ἐθνικῶς ('after the manner of Gentiles') once (Gal 2¹⁴).

Another designation, practically identical with *goiim*, is *hā-'ărāṣôth*, '**the lands**' (הָאֲרָצוֹת, more fully עַמֵּי הָאֲרָצוֹת or מַמְלְכוֹת הָאֲרָצוֹת 'peoples *or* kingdoms of the lands'). This term is characteristic of late Heb. (occurring 23 times in Ezk and 22 times in Ch, cf. Jer 16¹⁵, Dn 9⁷ 11⁴⁰·⁴², Ps 105⁴⁴ 106²⁷ 107³ 116⁹).

In NT Ἕλληνες ('Greeks') is sometimes used, especially by St. Paul, as syn. with *Gentiles* (Ro 2⁹, 1 Co 12¹³ etc.). The same writer employs ἔθνη in a twofold sense, either as = *pagan* Gentiles

in opposition to the Jews (Ro 2¹⁴ 3²⁹, Gal 2⁸) or as = Gentile in opposition to Jewish Christians (Ro 11¹³, Gal 2¹²·¹⁴). This double usage is well illustrated by comparing Eph 3¹ with 4¹⁷, in both of which passages ἔθνη is used; but in the first it is simply a mark of nationality, while in the second it has a moral touch, as is often the case with *goiim* in OT and ἔθνη in the Apocr., where *Gentiles* is sometimes practically equivalent to *heathen* (2 K 16³ 21², Ezr 6²¹, Ps 21·⁸, Jer 10² etc.). From this point of view τὰ ἔθνη, the nations outside Isr., have no part in the covenants of promise (Eph 2¹²), hence the emphasis which NT lays upon the new order of things when the mystery of the gospel (Eph 6¹⁹) is made known (Ac 10⁴⁵ 11¹⁸ 15⁹ etc.), until, finally, the difference between Jew and Gentile having disappeared, the word ἔθνη (heathen) may be simply opposed to the (united) Christian Church (1 Co 5¹ 10²⁰ 12², 1 Th 4⁵, 1 P 2¹²).

Israel's attitude towards other nations, never marked by much cordiality, underwent most important modifications in the post-exilic period. The reformation of Ezra deliberately aimed at fostering that spirit of exclusiveness which gave so much offence to the Gentile world, and which lent not a little colour to the charge of Tacitus (*Hist.* v. 5, cf. 1 Th 2¹⁵) and others, that the Jews were enemies of the human race. Even to enter the house of a Gentile, and much more to eat with him, involved ceremonial uncleanness (Jn 18²⁸, Ac 10²⁸ 11³). In the Talm. (*Aboda Zara*, i. 1, 2) we find it enacted that for three days before and after a heathen festival it was unlawful to transact business with G., to lend to or borrow from them, to pay money to or receive it from them. Side by side, indeed, with this exclusiveness, a proselytizing tendency was developed, to which we find allusions both in Jos. and NT (*Ant.* xx. ii.–iv., Mt 23¹⁵). By what seems at first a strange inconsistency, but which is easily susceptible of explanation, even G. who were not proselytes might have sacrifices offered in the temple. This, which is implied in Lv 22²⁵, is expressly asserted by Jos. (*c. Ap.* ii. 5; *Wars*, II. xvii. 2–4; *Ant.* XI. viii. 5, XIII. viii. 2, XVI. ii. 1, XVIII. v. 3; cf. 1 Mac 7³³). But that the G. could enter into full participation in the blessings of salvation except through the portal of Judaism, was an idea that dawned very slowly upon the minds even of some of the apostles of our Lord. The OT prophets suffered from the same limitations of vision. Even Deutero-Isaiah, who delights to describe the mission of Isr. to be a light to the G. (Is 42⁶ 49⁶), doubtless regarded conformity to Israel's law as necessary on the part of the latter. It is true that Isaiah himself reaches the sublime conception of Egypt and Assyria being, equally with Israel, the object of God's complacency (Is 19²³⁻²⁵), and that something approaching the conception of a universal religion set free from every trammel of national individuality is reached in Is 56⁶⁻⁷ and Zeph 3⁹·¹⁰. But these exceptions simply prove the rule. Even the Hel. Jews did not necessarily through contact with the G. rise superior to the ancestral contempt for everything outside the pale of Judaism. On the contrary, their pride and exclusiveness were sometimes intensified, as we see from the bitter opposition with which they met the work of St. Paul. And in the Christian Church itself there was considerable friction between Jewish and G. Christians—a fact which, in spite of the exaggerated importance attached to it by the Tübingen school, must never be left out of account in our construction of the early history of the Church. See further FOREIGNER, HEATHEN, PAUL, PROPHECY, PROSELYTE.

LITERATURE.—Schürer, *HJP* II. i. 51–56, 299–305, ii. 291–327, iii. 253, 268 f.; Briggs, *Mess. Proph.* 207, 391; W. R. Smith, *Proph. of Isr.* 336; Oehler, *OT Theol.* i. 261, ii. 363, 373, 398; Weiss, *NT Theol.* i. 129, ii. 17, 180, 289 f.; Weizsäcker, *Apost. Age*, i. 92 f.; Reuss, *Théol. Chrét. au siecle apost.* i. 353 f.; Baur, *Paulus*, i. 119 f.; Pfleiderer, *Paulinismus*, 275 f.; Farrar, *St. Paul*, i. 258, 285 f.; Trench, *NT Syn.* 352 f.; Thayer and Cremer *s.* ἔθνος, Ἕλλην, λαός; also Literature of art. FOREIGNER.

J. A. SELBIE.

GENTILES, COURT OF.—See TEMPLE.

GENTLENESS.—The word 'gentle' does not occur in OT except in RV of Jer 11¹⁹, which tr^s כֶּבֶשׂ אַלּוּף 'a gentle lamb,' where AV has 'a lamb or an ox.' It occurs five times in NT (AV). In 1 Th 2⁷ and 2 Ti 2²⁴ it corresponds to ἤπιος; it is the character proper to a nurse among trying children, or a teacher with refractory pupils. The RV keeps 'gentle' in both these passages, and it would be hard to find a better word. In Tit 3², Ja 3¹⁷, 1 P 2¹⁸ 'gentle' is the AV tr. of ἐπιεικής. The difficulty of this word is shown by the fact that in 1 Ti 3³ it is rendered 'patient,' while in Ph 4⁵ τὸ ἐπιεικὲς ὑμῶν is tr. 'your moderation.' Yet RV uniformly renders ἐπιεικής 'gentle,' and in Ph 4⁵, though it displaces 'moderation' by 'forbearance,' it puts 'gentleness' in the margin.

The general idea of the word 'ἐπιεικής' is that which is suggested by equity as opposed to strict legal justice; it expresses the quality of considerateness, of readiness to look humanely and reasonably at the facts of a case. There is a good discussion of it in Trench, *Syn.* § xliii. : he thinks there are no words in English which answer exactly to it, the ideas of equity and fairness, which are essential to its import, usually getting less than justice in the proposed equivalents. As opposed to πραΰτης, 'meekness,' it is not easy to draw any other distinction than that πραΰτης is more inward and passive, a disposition or habit of the mind itself; ἐπιείκεια, 'gentleness,' is shown actively in relation to others. These words are found together, as characteristic of Christ, in 2 Co 10¹; ἐπιείκεια occurs once again in Ac 24⁴, but here both AV and RV render it 'clemency.' 'Gentleness' in Gal 5²² is χρηστότης, a word which rather means 'goodness' or 'kindness.' The corresponding adjective is rendered in various places 'good,' 'kind,' 'gracious,' 'easy.'

The only occurrence of 'gentleness' in OT is 2 S 22³⁶=Ps 18³⁵ 'Thy gentleness hath made me great.' The RV keeps 'gentleness' in the text, but gives 'condescension' in the margin, which is much better. It is properly 'thy lowliness' (עַנְוָתְךָ), *i.e.*, as Cheyne explains it, 'thy fellow-feeling with the lowly.' The key to the meaning is found in comparing such passages as Ps 113^{5f.}, Is 57¹⁵, Zec 9⁹, Mt 11²⁹. The rendering of 2 S 22³⁶ in LXX, ἡ ὑπακοή σου ἐπλήθυνέν με, agrees with the MT עֲנֹתְךָ (עֲנֹת = *respondere* = ὑπακούειν).   J. DENNEY.

GENUBATH (גְּנֻבַת, cf. Palmyrene גנבו, de Vogüé, No. 137, Γανηβάθ AB Luc.).—Son of Hadad, the fugitive Edomite prince, by the sister of Tahpenes queen of the Pharaoh who ruled Egypt at the close of the reign of David and the commencement of that of Solomon. Genubath was weaned by queen Tahpenes, and brought up in the palace among the sons of Pharaoh (1 K 11^{19. 20}).
C. F. BURNEY.

GEOGRAPHY.—See PALESTINE, WORLD.

GEOLOGY OF PALESTINE.—In dealing with this subject the name 'Palestine' will be taken in its widest sense to include both the western and eastern sections of country lying on either side of the Jordan-Arabah depression, as well as the mountainous region of Sinai on the south.

There are few countries in which the physical features more clearly indicate the internal geological structure than that we have now to consider; hence, in dealing with these features under distinct heads, we shall have to explain how they are dependent on the nature and position of the formations of which they are constructed.

I. PHYSICAL DIVISIONS.—The whole region is physically divisible into five sections or tracts of country, which the student of Scripture will find to be curiously interwoven with the historical events and incidents therein recorded. Indeed it may be said that without some knowledge of the features of Palestine it is impossible to understand accurately, or to grasp in their full meaning, many of the most important events of Bible history. Many of the articles in this work will serve to illustrate this statement.

1. *The Maritime Plain.*—The first of these physical tracts is the Maritime Plain, stretching along the Mediterranean coast from the Delta of the Nile to the base of Carmel, and including the land of Philistia and part of Phœnicia. Historically, 'the River of Egypt' (*Wady el-'Arīsh*), a waterless dell emptying into Lake Serbonis, should be regarded as the western border of Palestine, but physically it is not of importance. The Maritime Plain consists of a series of low, undulating hills and wide valleys rising into levels of 300 to 400 ft. above the sea inwards to the base of the central tableland; or, west of Gaza, gradually merging into the elevated plain of the Badiet et-Tîh. It is composed of sand, gravel, and soft calcareous sandstone; but considerable areas are covered by a rich brownish loam with exceedingly fertile properties, capable of producing wheat and other plants in abundance. Throughout almost its whole length the coast is bordered by a range of sandhills—sometimes rising to a height of 150 ft.—which are ever moving inland, impelled by the westerly winds, except where hindered by natural or artificial barriers; the natural barriers being streams. North of Carmel, the plain of Esdraelon (*Sanjak Akka*) is the representative of the Maritime Plain of Philistia, and it extends northwards with a gradually narrowing breadth to the mouth of the Nahr el-Kelb at Beirût. This line of coast was originally decorated with palm trees, and gave rise to the name of Phœnicia, by which it is known in ancient history.

2. *The Tableland of Western Palestine and the Desert of the Tîh.*—This forms the central and largest physical district of Palestine, stretching from the base of the Lebanon to the northern margin of the mountainous region of Sinai. On the west it is bounded by the low-lying Maritime tract just described, except where the bold headland of Mount Carmel thrusts itself out into the very waters of the Mediterranean; and on the east by the deep depression of the Jordan-Arabah Valley. Along its centre it consists of an elevated plateau of limestone; or, more frequently, of a narrow ridge invaded by deep ravines coming up from the Maritime Plain on the one hand, and from the Jordanic Valley on the other. Along this ridge runs the main high road from Syria to Hebron and the Sinaitic peninsula; and most of the important towns, including Safed, Bethel, Jerusalem, Bethlehem, and Hebron, are planted on this saddle. Some of the higher points rise to considerable elevations ranging up to over 3000 ft.; thus, Jerusalem at the temple area reaches 2593 ft., and Hebron 3040 ft. above the level of the Mediterranean. Towards the south (lat. 31° N.) the tableland of southern Judæa broadens out into the arid expanse of the Badiet et-Tîh ('Desert of the wanderings'), which stretches southwards as far as lat. 29°, and is perhaps the least known of any part of N. Palestine. It consists of a vast expanse of Cretaceous and Nummulite limestone breaking off along a high escarpment overlooking the plain of Lower Egypt and the Gulf of Suez towards the west, and in the opposite direction forming the western margin of the Wady el-Arabah along a somewhat indented line of limestone cliffs. Towards the south the Badiet et-Tîh terminates in the lofty escarpment of *Jebel Ejmeh*, which reaches a level of over 5000 ft. above the Red Sea, and is formed of strata of nearly horizontal lime-

stone superimposed on others of Nubian sandstone. To the south of this grand rampart of terraced strata rise the lofty ridges and peaks of the Sinaitic mountains.

The Badiet et-Tîh forms a nearly barren, repulsive, but broken tableland of an average level of 4000 ft., with little pasturage except in the neighbourhood of a few springs, and along the course of the valleys. That it was at a former period well watered we have clear evidence in the existence of these valleys themselves, some of which yield an intermittent supply of water, especially those which connect with the rivers Jeib and Fikreh, which enter the Dead Sea from the south. Kadesh-barnea was doubtless situated near the eastern margin of the Badiet et-Tîh.

The streams which descend on either hand from the tableland of Western Palestine generally have their sources in copious springs rising through the limestone strata — which, being highly porous, readily absorb the rain or snow which falls during the winter months. The rain thus imbibed sinks down and forms underground reservoirs which feed the springs. The valleys are generally bounded by steep, sometimes precipitous, banks of limestone; and, owing to the extraordinary depth of the Jordan Valley and its close proximity to the sources, the streams descending from the central watershed on the east side to enter the Jordan or Dead Sea have a very rapid fall. Thus the Wady el-Aujeh, which has its source at Mezráh esh-Sherkiyeh at a level of about 3000 ft. above the Mediterranean, reaches the Jordan at a depth of 1200 ft. below the same plane, having a fall of 4200 ft. within a distance of 15 miles, that is, at the rate of 280 ft. per mile. The Kelt (brook Cherith?), which rises at Bireh (Beeroth) at a height of 2800 ft. and flows for the most part between lofty walls of rock for a distance of 21 miles, reaches the Jordan at a depth of 1170 ft. below the Mediterranean level, the fall being at the rate of about 190 ft. per mile; and lastly, the Wady en-Nar (brook Kidron) rising to the east of Jerusalem after flowing through the deep gorge of Mar Saba, enters the Dead Sea at a level of 1290 ft. below that of the sea, and has a total fall of about 3692 ft. in 14 miles, being at the rate of 264 ft. per mile. The streams entering the Mediterranean have necessarily a less precipitous course, and flow with a gentle current on reaching the Maritime Plain. Throughout the greater part of their extent the hills of Western Palestine are very bare of soil, the limestone strata of which they are formed being clearly traceable by the eye along their flanks, or cropping out under the feet at the summit. But in the valleys where soil has accumulated, and especially where there is artificial irrigation, the fertility is extraordinary and amply rewards cultivation.

(3) *The Jordan - Arabah Valley.* — The third physical feature is that of the Jordan - Arabah Valley intervening between the tableland of Western Palestine and the high plateau of Edom, Moab, and the Jaulán. Commencing in Cœle-Syria at the base of the Lebanon, it ranges southwards to the Dead Sea, when it descends to its lowest level of 1292 ft. below the surface of the Mediterranean, as determined by the officers of the Ordnance Survey (see DEAD SEA); then continuing southwards, the floor of the valley gradually rises to a level of about 640 ft. above the same plane at er-Rishy, from which it descends with a very gentle slope to the head of the Gulf of 'Akabah, of which it forms the physical prolongation. As already stated (see ARABAH), this great depression coincides with a line of 'fault' (or fracture of the earth's crust), along which the strata have been vertically elevated on the east side, or depressed on the west—a view which can be demonstrated at many points by a comparison of the strata along the opposite sides of the valley. Thus at the saddle of er-Rishy, above referred to, we find the Cretaceous limestone forming the cliffs on the west side of the valley, while on the opposite side the Edomite cliffs are composed of masses of granite, porphyry, and schist surmounted by the Nubian sandstone, which is in turn overlain above Petra, at a level of about 4000 ft., by the same Cretaceous limestone of er-Rishy; being very nearly the amount of the vertical displacement of the strata which occurs along the line of fault at this spot. Somewhat similar are the relations of the rocks at the southern end of the Dead Sea; but along the line of the Jordanic Valley towards the Sea of Tiberias the displacement diminishes considerably, so that Cretaceous limestones are found forming both sides of the valley. The Jordan-Arabah 'fault' generally keeps very close to the base of the cliffs forming the eastern margin of the valley, and numerous branching, or parallel, 'faults' accompany the main line of displacement, at least in the region south of the Dead Sea.

The floor of the Jordan-Arabah Valley is formed of alluvial terraces, gravel, blown sand, and mud flats. The terraces are of various ages, the more ancient occupying higher levels; the more recent being only a little elevated above the waters of the Jordan and Dead Sea. The highest and most ancient of the terraces are those seen at Ayûn Buweirdeh, occupying a position in the centre of the valley about 30 miles S. of the southern end of the Dead Sea, and at a level nearly corresponding to that of the Mediterranean. They are formed of calcareous marls with fresh- or brackish-water shells of the genera *Neritina, Melania, Melanopsis*, etc., and point to a time when the waters of a great lake occupied a position about 1300 ft. above the present surface of the Dead Sea. This lake must have extended northwards, so as to include the whole of the Jordan Valley as far as the Lake of Hûleh, a distance of about 200 miles. Next in importance to the terrace above described is that which may be recognized all round the margin of the Dead Sea hollow, known as the 'Ghor,' rising about 600 ft. above its surface —and formed of saliferous marls with gypsum on the west side, and of gravel and sand on the east. The salt terrace (Khasm Usdum) is referable to this horizon; and besides this, there are two or three distinct terraces at lower levels. The surface of the Sea of Tiberias which lies in the upper part of the Jordan Valley is 682 ft. *below* that of the Mediterranean, while the Lake of Hûleh rises to 7 ft. *above* this level. Still proceeding northwards the Jordan itself has its source in the copious fountains of Banias (Cæsarea Philippi) which burst forth, 'full grown at birth,' from the base of Mount Hermon, fed by the well-nigh perennial snows which crown the dome - shaped summit, which, at a height of 10,000 ft. above the level of the sea, dominates all objects terrestrial as far as the eye can reach.[*]

(4) *The Tableland of Edom, Moab, and the Jaulân.* — This section of country has to some extent been described under the head of the ARABAH (wh. see). Bounded on the west by the deep depression above described, it forms the western margin of the great Arabian Desert, the home of the wandering Bedawîn. Commencing on the north at the base of Mount Hermon, it stretches as a gradually ascending tableland southwards, through the Jaulân and Haurân (Trachonitis), into the ancient kingdoms of Ammon, Moab, and

[*] For an account of these springs, see Tristram, *Land of Israel*[2], 585.

Edom. Breaking off along a steep escarpment or series of scarps on the western side, on overlooking the Dead Sea it reaches a level of 3000 ft. above the Mediterranean, and farther south at Petra rises to still higher levels. In this latter part of its range the escarpment is much broken by ravines which penetrate its sides, and cause repetitions of the features along lines of 'faulting'; but, on approaching the head of the Gulf of 'Aḳabah, the escarpment becomes more consolidated, and the granite walls, penetrated by numerous igneous dykes of porphyry, basalt, and diorite, rise with an abrupt ascent from the Valley of the Arabah to levels of 5000 or 6000 ft. above the surface of the gulf. Here the intensely red colour assumed by the rocks has given rise to the name *Jebel en-Nur* ('mountain of fire') which is applied to the heights above 'Aḳabah. At this point the gorge of the Wady el-Ithem offers the only accessible road by which the Arabian Desert can be reached from the Arabah Valley until we arrive opposite Mount Hor (*Jebel Haroun*) at a distance of 45 miles to the northward, and this must consequently have been the route by which the Israelites circumvented the land of Edom when marching towards the plains of Moab on their way to the Promised Land;—the more direct way having been denied them by the king of Edom (Nu 20^{14-21}). The flanks of the tableland are intersected by numerous channels of mountain torrents—those to the southward near 'Aḳabah being generally dry, except after thunderstorms, when they bring down quantities of stones and shingle which they throw out in fan-shaped ramps at the mouth of each wady. A perennial stream, however, flows through the Wady Mûsa at Petra and along the Wady Haroun. But when we reach the borders of Moab and a region of greater rainfall to the northward, streams become more frequent and copious, and the Hessi, Kerat, the Arnon (*Mojib*), and Zerḳa Ma'in (*Callirhoë*), together with numerous smaller brooks, descend the slopes into the Dead Sea from perennial springs.

The southern portion of this tableland within the limits here imposed is made of very ancient formations, consisting of granite, schist, porphyry, and other igneous rocks which pass, in a northerly direction towards Petra, below great masses of red and variegated sandstone of, perhaps, two geological ages, the Carboniferous and Cretaceous. These sandstones often rise in courses of cyclopian masonry above the granitic base; sometimes forming terraces, sometimes truncated pyramids, or rampart-like breastworks, of which Mount Hor offers a striking example. These sandstone strata line the flanks of the escarpment to some, not well-determined, point in the Jordan Valley north of the Dead Sea; but they are everywhere superimposed by the white calcareous strata of Cretaceous age which gradually descend northwards from the Edomite plateau to the bed of the Jordan itself, and constitute the sides of the Jordanic Valley to the margin of the Sea of Galilee.

The region of the Jaulân and Haurân, which in some sense forms a continuation of the Moabite plateau, is an elevated plain formed altogether of sheets of basaltic lava, from the surface of which rise the truncated cones of extinct volcanoes, generally clothed with forests of oak. It is altogether uncertain at what period the volcanic fires became extinct, but it seems probable that it was not later than the close of the Pleistocene, or Glacial period, and was therefore synchronous with the gradual recession of the waters of the great Jordan Valley lake; the proximity of water being necessary to volcanic activity. On the other hand, the relations of the lava streams, both in this region and in the vicinity of the Dead Sea, to

the Cretaceous strata, make it clear that the period of greatest volcanic action was long posterior to the age of these rocks themselves, and may be referred to that of the Pliocene. There is, moreover, no evidence that these volcanoes were in active eruption during the period of the early occupation of the country by man.

(5) *The Sinaitic Peninsula.*—In marked contrast, both as regards form and colour, to the plateaux and terraces of Western Palestine and the Badiet et-Tîh, characterized by greyish and yellowish tints, is the mountainous region of Sinai lying between the two arms of the Red Sea, and bounded along the northern margin by the escarpment of the Cretaceous and Nummulite limestones of Jebel Ejmeh above described. Here we find ourselves in presence of a group of noble mountains, crowned by peaks and serrated ridges, traversed by broad sinuous valleys which form the highways by which the traveller must find his way, and which are now generally dry, though once the channels of rivers and streams. The Sinaitic mountains are formed of rocks amongst the most ancient in the world, and referable to the Archæan age; and, as they are bare and destitute of verdure, they rise above the valleys in naked walls rich in their natural colouring of red, purple, and blue. It is only along the valleys that the green of verdure is seen, owing to the growth of small scrub and desert flowers, with groups of palms and tamarisks around the springs of water. These rescue the region from the reproach of utter barrenness, and allow the Arab to pitch his camp, and even to pasture his flocks of sheep and goats. The mountain summits rise to high elevations. At the head of the group stands the twin-peaked Jebel Katharina, reaching a height of 8551 ft. above the sea; next, Jebel Umm Shomer, 8449 ft.; then Jebel Mûsa (the traditional Mount Sinai), 7373 ft.; and Jebel Serbâl, which though not the highest is certainly the most striking of the series, because of its isolated position and serried outline; its summit reaches an elevation of 6734 ft. above the Gulf of Suez.* Standing on the summit of Sinai, the scene is most striking and impressive. The tumultuous assemblage of peaks and serrated ridges formed of rocks of granite and porphyry, whose natural reddish tints have been deepened and intensified by the powerful rays of the sun; the profound gorges and valleys walled in by lofty cliffs of naked rock; the absence of trees and verdure, except along the floors of the valleys, —all tend to impress the beholder with the conviction that he is here gazing on the face of nature under one of her most savage forms, in which the ideas of solitude, waste, and desolation contend with those of awe and admiration. This assemblage of peaks and ridges is bounded towards the east and west by the deep depressions of the Gulfs of Suez and 'Aḳabah; towards the north, distant glimpses of the tableland of the Tîh are obtained; while the mountains of Edom, rising beyond the Gulf of 'Aḳabah and the valley of the Arabah, bound the view in the direction of the great Desert of Arabia.

II. GEOLOGICAL FORMATIONS.—The formations of which the above tracts of country are composed range from the most ancient to the most recent;— but with wide gaps in the general succession as determined in other regions. For example, we have no representatives of the Cambrian, Silurian, Devonian, Permian, Triassic, or Jurassic formations, all of which are well developed in the British Islands; and we are therefore driven to the con-

* The elevations were determined by the officers of the Ordnance Survey of Sinai. The height of Jebel Mûsa, calculated by Mr. R. Laurence from Suez by aneroid, was 7585 ft., and from 'Aḳabah was 7595 ft., both over those of the Ordnance Survey, but probably less reliable. (See Hull, *Mount Seir*, 48).

clusion that Palestine presented conditions unsuited to the deposition of strata during these periods ; or else that beds belonging to one or more of these periods having been deposited, had afterwards been removed by denuding agencies ; but this is the less probable supposition.

The general succession of the formations present in Palestine is as follows in descending order :—

GEOLOGICAL FORMATIONS.

Recent .	1. Sandhills and Desert sands.
	2. Alluvial deposits of the Jordan and other streams.
From Pluvial to Pliocene.	1. Raised sea-beaches ; sand and gravel with shells.
	2. Calcareous marls, saliferous beds, sand and gravel forming terraces in the Jordan-Arabah Valley ; old Lake beds in Arabia-Petræa.
More Recent Volcanic rocks .	Basalt, dolerite, tuff, etc.
Eocene .	1. Calcareous Sandstone of Philistia (?).
	2. Nummulite limestone series.
Cretaceous .	1. Cretaceous limestone with marls, etc.
	2. 'Nubian sandstone.'
Lower Carboniferous .	1. Wady Nasb limestone.
	2. Desert sandstone and conglomerate.
Volcanic Series	Agglomerates, beds of lava, ashes, and tuff of indeterminate age.
Archæan .	Granitic gneiss, granite, hornblendic and other schists ; dykes of diorite, porphyry, etc.

(a) *Archæan.* — These rocks are found only amongst the Sinaitic and Edomite mountains, and are considered to be the representatives of the crystalline masses which come to the surface from beneath the Nubian sandstone at the First Cataract of the Nile. They lie at the base of all the formations in this part of the world, and have been referred by Fraas to the Archæan period.[*] They consist of hornblendic, chloritic, and talcose schists of the Wadis Nasb, Sarabit, and Feirân, underlain by reddish and greyish granite and gneiss. These rocks are penetrated by innumerable dykes and ridges of red felstone-porphyry, diorite, and basalt, of later, but indeterminate, age ; except that they are more ancient than the Nubian sandstone of the Cretaceous period, or the Desert sandstone of the Carboniferous.

(b) *Volcanic Series.*—To the period of these dykes may be referable the stratified lavas, tuffs, and agglomerates of the Wady Haroun and Jebel esh-Shomrah (or Shomar) which form the basement beds east of the Dead Sea,[†] and are overlain by the Desert sandstone. Magnificent sections of agglomerate and igneous intrusions are laid open in the Wady el-Hessi, near es-Safieh, but their age is indeterminate beyond the fact that they are later than the Archæan and earlier than the Cretaceous or Carboniferous periods.

(c) *Carboniferous Beds.* — One of the most remarkable discoveries amongst the geological series of Palestine was that of Carboniferous rocks in the Wady Nasb by H. Bauerman in 1868,[‡] afterwards extended to the eastern bank of the Dead Sea at Lebruj, near es-Safieh, by the Expedition of the *PEF* in 1883-84.[§] The formation consists of red, purple, and variegated sandstone, which the writer has named 'the Desert sandstone' below, surmounted by blue limestone containing shells and corals of Carboniferous limestone species, such as *Spirifer striatus, S. attenuatus, Productus scabriculus, Orthis michelini, Syringopora ramulosa, Fenestella plebia* (?), and others. The occurrence of these strata in two widely-separated localities

suggests the idea that they once occupied an extended and connected area, and have subsequently been dissevered by denudation. That the limestone is a marine deposit formed over the floor of the sea during a period of submergence, is shown by the names of the fossils above quoted, which are all of marine species and genera. These fragmental tracts may only be relics of a formation which included the upper division of the Carboniferous system, but which has been subsequently removed by denuding agencies.

(d) *Cretaceous Beds ; Nubian Sandstone* (Russegger).—In the absence of several formations which in Europe and the British Isles succeed the Carboniferous, the Cretaceous strata are found in Arabia Petræa resting on an eroded surface of the older formations above described, whether of Carboniferous or of Archæan age. The formation is, however, only found represented by its upper members; the lower, belonging to the stages Neocomian, Urgonian, Aptian, and Albian not being here represented. Notwithstanding this *hiatus*, the Cretaceous is the most important of all the formations of Palestine, stretching from the southern margin of the Badiet et-Tîh to the Lebanon, and forming large tracts of the great Arabian desert east of the Jordan-Arabah depression. It is represented by two divisions ; the lower or Nubian sandstone (Cenomanian of D'Orbigny) the equivalent of our 'Upper Greensand,' and by the Cretaceous limestone and marl, the equivalents of our Chalk and Chalkmarl (Senonian and Turonian). The Nubian sandstone consists of red and variegated, rather soft sandstone with a conglomerate of small pebbles of quartzite, granite, porphyry, and jasper at its base. Its thickness is exceedingly variable, owing to the irregularities of the floor of older rocks over which it was deposited, and its only fossils are fragments of plants at rare intervals. All along the escarpment of the Tîh from the Wady Hamr to the Gulf of 'Akabah it underlies the white limestones and marls of the upper Cretaceous beds, and along the flanks of the great western escarpment from 'Akabah to the northern end of the Dead Sea and beyond it is interposed between the crystalline rocks and the same calcareous strata.[*] On approaching the Sinaitic mountains, the Nubian and Desert sandstones may be observed in isolated masses capping the Archæan rocks ; sometimes rising from their bases in truncated pyramids ; and in the Wady el-'Ain, which is a continuation of the Wady Zelagah, one of the most remarkable old river courses in the peninsula, the walls of Nubian sandstone rise on either hand to a height of several hundred feet above the floor.[†] But it is in the Wady Mûsa at Petra that this formation is displayed to best advantage. Rising in nearly vertical walls from the floor of the valley and its branches, the sandstone has formed the material out of which the tombs and temples have been sculptured in various forms of architecture, displaying marvellous varieties of colour in yellow, orange, red, and purple shades, which have called forth the admiration of all travellers (see PETRA). These colours are due to the presence of various mineral pigments, of which oxides of iron, manganese, and possibly copper, are the most abundant.

The Nubian sandstone is probably a lacustrine deposit laid down over the floor of a vast inland lake, the boundaries of which, owing to extensive geological changes, it is now impossible to define except at distant intervals. One portion of this boundary was undoubtedly formed of the rocks of the Sinaitic group of mountains ; other portions

---

[*] *Aus dem Orient*, p. 7.
[†] 'Phys. Geol. Arabia Petræa,' *Mem. PEF*, p. 37.
[‡] *Quart. Journ. Geol. Soc.* vol. xxv. p. 17.
[§] *Mem. Geol. Arab. Petr. and Palest.* p. 47.

[*] Except where carboniferous or volcanic beds are present.
[†] A view of this gorge is given in the frontispiece of Hull's *Mount Seir.*

may be discovered in Central Africa ; and the lake itself may have been connected with the Cretaceous ocean in the direction of the Mediterranean.* The formation was accumulated from the waste of granitic and plutonic rocks forming the surrounding lands now partly submerged beneath the waters of the ocean.

(e) *Cretaceous Limestone.*—This great series of calcareous strata immediately succeeds the Nubian sandstone ; and as it is altogether a marine deposit, it must have been formed over the bed of the ocean after a general subsidence and submergence of the region occupied by the lacustrine waters of the previous period. The lower beds are chiefly formed of white calcareous marls succeeded by harder limestone strata with bands of siliceous chert or flint. The following section taken in the Wady el-Hessi, at the S.E. border of the Badiet et-Tîh, will serve to give a general idea of the character of the lower portion of the formation. (1) Lowest beds ; — light-blue calcareous marl, passing downwards into dark-blue clay with selenite, 250 ft. thick ; (2) soft white limestone, with rare bands of chert, 200 ft.; (3) hard siliceous limestone with numerous bands of chert, forming the top of the cliff, about 200 ft. thick. Fine sections are also laid open on ascending the flanks of the escarpment overlooking the basin of the Dead Sea (the ' Ghor ') on the eastern side, of which Lartet gives the details.† The total thickness of the Cretaceous limestone series may reach 800 to 1000 ft., and amongst the fossil forms the following may be cited: *Ammonites Luynesi, A. rhotamargensis, Pholadomya Luynesi, Ostrea Mermeti, O. flabellata, Hippurites,* etc. *Foraminifera,* visible only under the microscope, doubtless are abundantly present.

Building Stone. — The uppermost beds of the Cretaceous limestone yield an excellent building stone which has been used in the construction of the buildings in and about Jerusalem, including the walls of the temple. The stone has been extracted from the large quarries and caverns near the Damascus gate. The rock is hard, compact, and delicately coloured, capable not only of furnishing large blocks such as may be seen at the ' Wailing Place of the Jews,' but of being worked into ornaments and smaller objects of use, and of receiving a polish. Fraas gives the following section ‡ :—

1. Craie blanche (*Senonien*).
2. Étage supérieure des *Hippurites* (' Misseh ').
3. Étage inférieure des *Hippurites* (' Melekeh ').
4. Zone of *Ammonites rhotomargensis* (Turonian).

No. 2 (' Misseh ') of the above section affords the principal building stone, and is 16 ft. in thickness ; and Sir C. W. Wilson has shown that the reservoirs, sepulchres, and cellars under and around the city are excavated in the soft beds of No. 3 (' Melekeh ') underlying the firmer beds of the ' Misseh,' which form the platforms for the buildings.§

(f) *Lower Eocene Beds ; Nummulite Limestone.* —This formation, though belonging to the Tertiary division of the geological series, immediately succeeds the Cretaceous limestone just described, and bears so general a resemblance to it that together they appear to constitute one great calcareous formation, incapable of separation. This apparent continuity is, however, illusory, as has

been shown by Zittel in the case of Egypt and the Nubian Desert ; and a detailed survey would doubtless have the result of showing that the two formations are disconnected by an unconformity, however slight. The latest explorer of the geological features of Palestine, Dr. Blanckenkorn, is clearly of opinion that the two formations are capable of separation ; * and Lartet had previously expressed the same view.

The Nummulite limestone is but sparingly represented in Palestine. It forms the southern slopes of part of the Lebanon,† is found capping Mount Carmel, and occurs in isolated masses at Sebastieh (Samaria), Nablûs (Shechem), and the vicinity of Jerusalem. It also overspreads a large tract of the western Tîh plateau, as it has been identified by its characteristic fossils in the limestone cliffs which overlook the Isthmus of Suez, but its inland limits remain to be determined with any degree of accuracy.

The lower beds of the formation consist of white marls and chalky limestone with *Nummulites,* surmounting the harder beds of Cretaceous age : these are succeeded by white limestones with bands of flint, resembling those of the latter period ; and, as Lartet has pointed out, this general resemblance causes much uncertainty in the discrimination of the two formations on the spot. The Nummulite limestone is an oceanic deposit laid down under similar conditions of deposition to those of the Cretaceous beds, but with an interval of slight disturbance and movement in the floor of the sea. The fossils are distinctly of Tertiary genera and species.

(g) *Upper Eocene ? Calcareous Sandstone of Philistia.*—This formation is frequently laid open in small sections between Beersheba and Jaffa, and in the Plain of Philistia. It consists of soft yellowish calcareous sandstone; but its relations to the Cretaceous and Nummulite beds are unknown, as the junction has not been observed. The writer has provisionally assigned these strata to the Upper Eocene stage, for reasons which are too much involved to be stated at length here.‡ No fossils were noticed in the sandstone ; and it is only right to observe that Blanckenkorn considers it to be of post-Tertiary or Diluvial origin. Its real age is one of those points remaining to be determined by future exploration.

(h) *Miocene Period.*—This epoch in the geological history of Palestine is unrepresented by any known strata ; yet it was one of the greatest importance as regards the development of the physical features of this region, and, it may be added, of that of the whole basin of the Mediterranean and surrounding districts. The Miocene was the great land-forming epoch, during which the general outlines of the existing land surfaces were finally determined, and the relative areas of land and sea were constituted as they exist to this day. Down to the close of the preceding Eocene epoch the whole of Palestine, including the Lebanon and the Great Desert east of the Arabah, formed the bed of the ocean, the only emergent portions being the Sinaitic mountain-tops ; all to the northward, eastward, and westward as far as the borders of the Atlas mountains, was overspread by the waters of the ocean. But with the close of the Eocene period a great physical change set in. Owing to contraction and movements in the crust, the sea-bed was elevated into land in the tracts bordering the Great Sea. Mountains, such as the Lebanon, were upraised ; the strata were bent, folded, and fissured ; and amongst the greatest of these fissures

---

* In North Africa the boundary lay along the northern base of the Ahaggar Mountains in lat. 25° N. and the Morocco Atlas on the north, as the present writer has shown elsewhere ; ' Geological History of Egypt and the Nile Valley,' *Trans. Vict. Inst.* vol. xxiv. p. 307 (with Map).
† *Voyage d'exploration,* p. 70, fig. 6.
‡ *Aus dem Orient,* p. 54.
§ *Ordnance Survey of Jerusalem.*

* ' Entstehung u. Geschichte d. Todten Meeres,' *ZDPV* (1896).
† Carl Diener, *Der Libanon.*
‡ These reasons are stated in the *Mem.* ' Phys. Geol. Arabia Petræa,' p. 64.

was that of the Jordan-Arabah Valley, along which the tableland of Edom and Moab was elevated into land. In a word, all the main physical features of the region here being passed under review had their first inception; and although they have been somewhat modified during succeeding periods, these modifications have not materially altered the main outlines of the land. River channels have been originated and deepened, and the land-surfaces have been somewhat eroded and worn down, but the main features remain as they were at the close of the Miocene period. These terrestrial changes occupied, without doubt, a vast length of geological time.

(i) *Pliocene to Pluvial.*—The deposits referable to this period consist of raised beaches on the areas bordering the Mediterranean and Red Seas, and the terraces of the Jordan-Arabah Valley; these latter having been already described, our observations here will be confined to the old sea-terraces.

After the great emergence and elevation of land areas which had taken place during the preceding Miocene period, there appears to have been a subsidence to the extent of at least 220 or 230 ft. around the shores of the Mediterranean and Red Seas. The escarpments bordering the Delta of the Nile, and those of the Tîh and Western Palestine, again became sea-cliffs, with beaches at their base, while the waters of the Mediterranean and Red Seas commingled along the Isthmus of Suez. The amount of the submergence, as above stated, is demonstrated in the clearest manner by the occurrence of old sea-beaches both in Egypt and Palestine, at or about this level; of which the most remarkable is that known as 'Fraas' beach,' at Jebel Mokattam, above Cairo, and again at the Great Pyramid platform near Ghizeh. This occurs at a level of 220 ft. above the sea, and is characterized by beds of sand and gravel with marine shells, some of which are extinct species, while others are still living in the Red Sea; the cliffs of limestone are also penetrated by numerous borings of *Teredo.* Similar beds of gravel with shells may be observed on the eastern margin of the Gulf of Suez, as well as in the Arabah Valley up to a level of nearly 200 ft. above the Gulf of 'Aḳabah. But the most important case is that occurring in the valley of the Sherîah at Tell Abu Hareireh, east of Gaza, at a level of 200 to 220 ft. above the Mediterranean on both sides of the stream — a level corresponding to that of the raised beach above Cairo. Here the terrace lies in a hollow formed in the 'calcareous sandstone of Philistia,' which is clearly of older date than the shelly gravels of the raised beach: the following is the section in descending order;—

		ft.	in.	
1. Loam	. . . .	5	0	thick.
2. Soft calcareous sandstone in thin layers	10	0	,,
3. Beds of shells (chiefly casts) . . .	0	6	,,
4. Soft calcareous sandstone, with small pebbles of flint and oyster shells	5	0	,,
5. River-bed; hard calcareous sandstone (thickness unknown) . . .	(over) 2	0	,,

The shells in bed No. 3 consist of the genera *Turritella, Dentalium, Artemis, Pecten, Cardium, Ostrea,* and spines of *Echinus.*[*]

All along the lower parts of the Maritime Plain extending for several miles inland from Jaffa, and rising from 200 to 300 ft., shelly sands and beds of gravel may be observed; and again inland from Beirût this ancient sea-bed may be observed at intervals, varying in character and composition, as at Ramleh, Lydda (Ludd) and Lokandel el-Motram in the valley between Beirût and the western spurs of the Lebanon, where it consists of conglomerate of

* 'Geol. Arab. Petræa, etc.,' p. 74. A figure showing the relations of this raised beach to the calcareous sandstone is shown, *ib.* p. 64.

water-worn pebbles of limestone, and may be referable to the later Pliocene age. The more recent sea-beaches, formed during the rising of the beds in the Pleistocene age, occupy lower levels, and are characterized by Mediterranean forms, such as *Pectunculus violascens, Purpura hemastoma,* and *Murex brandaris,* etc.

The submergence of the Palestine and adjoining areas, after the present land-surface had been determined, and subsequent re-elevation to existing levels, is therefore clearly determined by the above instances of old sea-margins. Meanwhile, in the region of the Jordan-Arabah depression, corresponding changes had been going on, resulting in the formation of terraces at various levels from that of the outer sea to the present margins of the inland lakes, but in time extending into the Pleistocene (or Pluvial) period; with some account of which, as far as it concerns the Palestine area, our review of the geological history of this region properly ends.

(j) *Pluvial to Recent.*—The general refrigeration of the climate in the northern hemisphere referable to the Glacial epoch, which was accompanied in the temperate zone by accumulations of snow and the advance of glacial ice, did not leave Palestine altogether unaffected; on the contrary, it has left indelible traces on its physical features. We know through the observations of several travellers, commencing with Sir J. D. Hooker, that there are old glacier moraines in the Lebanon at a level of 4000 ft. above the sea, and that one of the principal groups of old cedars is planted on a large moraine.[*] The presence of glaciers in the Lebanon being thus established, we necessarily infer the existence of a climate resembling rather that of the Caucasus and the Alps than that of the present day; perhaps we may say that the mean annual temperature, which is now about 70° Fahr., was at this epoch of extreme cold about 55° or 60°, and a correspondingly lower temperature extended over all the countries to the south of the Lebanon.[†] A further inference may be drawn, namely, that the rainfall all over Palestine, and extending into the Sinaitic peninsula, was considerably larger than at present, and the evaporation less rapid; and the general result would be that the present rivers and streams would have been larger, and valleys which, like those of the Badiet el-Tîh, are now destitute of streams, were channels for running water. It may be readily conceived that, when the perennial snows of the Lebanon were melting during the spring and summer, the waters of the Jordan were swollen far beyond their present limits, and that the surface of the Dead Sea, now retained at its present low level by the equalization of river supply and evaporation, must have risen to a limit far above that of the present day. We cannot, therefore, feel surprise at the evidences of former greater levels of the 'Jordan-Valley lake' afforded by the terraces rising hundreds of feet above the present surface of the Dead Sea, which have been described; they were the necessary result of greater influx of waters from streams, and of smaller evaporation, due to the humidity of the atmosphere and decreased temperature in the climate as compared with that of the present day. As the glacial conditions of the Pleistocene epoch passed away, and those of the present day gradually came into operation by a corresponding process in an opposite direction, the lakes and streams would naturally assume their present limits, or in some instances actually disappear.   E. HULL.

* 'On the Cedars of Lebanon,' *Nat. Hist. Rev.* 1862; Hooker's original observations have been confirmed by Tristram and Lartet.

† Fraas supposes there were glaciers amongst the mountains of Sinai, but the present writer was unable to recognize any clear evidence in support of this view in 1883–84.

GEORGIAN VERSION.—See VERSION.

GEPHYRUN (Γεφυρούν).—A city captured by Judas Maccabæus, 2 Mac 12¹³. AV, perhaps rightly accentuating γεφυροῦν (infin. of γεφυρόω), tr. 'he went also about to make a bridge to a certain city.' RV has 'he also fell upon a certain city Gephyrun,' and appends marginal note, 'The relation between the names *Gephyrun* and *Caspin* is unknown, and perhaps the Greek text is corrupt. Compare *Gephyrun*, the name of a city of Gilead mentioned by Polybius, v. lxx. 12, and *Caspor*, 1 Mac 5²⁶. ³⁶.' Jos. (*Ant.* XII. viii. 5) gives the name as Ephron. The site is unknown.

GER (גֵּר) is a Heb. term which in AV is generally rendered 'stranger.' The fact that the same trⁿ is adopted also for other words whose proper equivalent is 'foreigner,' creates needless confusion, which might be avoided either by leaving *gêr*, which is a technical term, untranslated, or by translating it 'protected stranger.' Driver (*Deut.* p. 126) suggests that the rendering might be uniformly the '**sojourner**' (so frequently in RV), which would preserve the connexion in EV with the verb 'sojourn' (גּוּר) in such passages as Gn 12¹⁰ 19⁹ 47⁴, Is 52⁴.

In opposition to the *nokhri*, who is often a mere *passing stranger* ('thou camest but yesterday,' 2 S 15²⁰), the *gêr*, while not homeborn, is a temporary *dweller* in the land (Gn 23⁴ [P | תּוֹשָׁב] of Abraham at Hebron ; Ex 2²² [J] of Moses in the desert, 18³ [E] to explain the name Gershom ; fig. of J″, Jer 14⁸ ; of Israel in Egypt, Gn 15¹³, Ex 22²¹ 23⁹ [all JE], Lv 19³⁴ [H], Dt 10¹⁹ 23⁸ ; more frequently of *gêrim* in Israel (*e.g.* 2 S 1¹³ an Amalekite, cf. Jos 8³³. ³⁵ [E] 20⁹ [P], Is 14¹). The LXX, which twice transliterates גֵּר (Aram. גֵּיּוֹר) by γ(ε)ιώρας, Ex 12¹⁹, Is 14¹, uses πάροικος 11 times to tr. גֵּר and 10 times for תּוֹשָׁב. πάροικος answers to the classical μέτοικος (which is not used by LXX except in Jer 20³ and not at all in NT). μέτοικος designated a resident in a community who had not the same rights as a native citizen. As גֵּר occupies a position intermediate between אֶזְרָח (native) and נָכְרִי (foreigner), so does μέτοικος between ἀστός or πολίτης and ξένος. Of course the μέτοικος was from one point of view a foreigner, and might be called ξένος ; hence οἱ ἐπιδημοῦντες ξένοι is in Ac 17²¹ rightly applied to the μέτοικοι at Athens. πάροικος appears in NT in same sense as in LXX (Ac 7⁶. ²⁹, Eph 2¹⁹, 1 P 2¹¹). The ξένοι καὶ πάροικοι of Eph 2¹⁹ is specially instructive ; it answers exactly to the *peregrini atque incolæ* of Cic. *de Offic.* i. 34.

The *gêr* in the oldest time is a stranger who dwells under the protection of a family or a tribe to which he does not belong. He is not necessarily a non-Israelite. In Dt 18⁶ Jg 17⁷⁻⁹ 19¹ the term is applied to Levites (see Driver and Moore, *ad loc.*). The position of the *gêr* in Israel is illustrated by W. R. Smith from the precisely analogous institution of the *jâr* among the Arabs. He lives in the midst of the community personally free, but possessed of no political rights. He has left his own kin, it may be on account of a feud, or simply in order to benefit himself, and has cast himself upon the protection of a powerful chief or clan in his new dwelling-place. The institution is still known in Arabia (*OTJC²* 342 n.).

In return for the protection accorded him the *gêr* had services to render. He was not indeed a slave (Micah's Levite not only enjoyed personal freedom but received wages, Jg 17¹⁰, Gn 29¹⁵, Dt 24¹⁴), but his lot was at times hard enough (cf. Gn 31⁷⁻⁴⁰ Jacob's complaint of his treatment by Laban). Nothing evidences the precarious position of the *gêr* better than the frequent OT exhortations to act justly by him Dt 1¹⁶ 24¹⁷ 27¹⁹, to show him kindness Dt 10¹⁹ 26¹², to refrain from oppressing him Ex 22²¹ 23⁹ (both JE), Lv 19³³ (H), Dt 24¹⁴, Jer 7⁶, Zec 7¹⁰. Hence probably also the repeated injunction that he was to enjoy the Sabbath rest Ex 20¹⁰ 23¹² (both JE), Dt 5¹⁴.

A man might be the *gêr* of a king or of the chief of a clan rather than of the whole community. A typical instance of this is found in David's

relation to Achish of Gath. The Phil. lords will have nothing to do with 'these Hebrews' (1 S 29³). David as the *gêr* of Achish was expected to make the interests of his patron his own (1 S 27¹²), and in particular to go to war along with him even against his native country (28¹ff.).

A whole clan or tribe might be *gêrim* (Jos 9 the Gibeonites, 2 S 4² the Beerothites ; and even Israel in Egypt is described as a *gêr* Gn 15¹³, Ex 22²¹ 23⁹ [all JE], Lv 19³⁴ (H), Dt 10¹⁹ 23⁸). In such cases, also, services had to be rendered in return for protection (*e.g.* by Jacob's family according to their occupation Gn 47⁶, by the Gibeonites in hewing wood and drawing water Jos 9²⁷, by the Israelites in the building of cities Ex 1¹³ff.). It frequently happened that these *gêrim* were ultimately absorbed into the tribe whose protection they had invoked. See FOREIGNER, and cf. Kuenen, *Rel. Isr.* i. 182 f.

There were also *gêrim* of a god or a temple, who acted as ἱερόδουλοι in return for the protection accorded by the deity or the sanctuary. Evidence of this is furnished by such Phœn. proper names as Ger'ashtart (see ASHTORETH, p. 168ª), Germelḳart, etc. (cf. the גּוּר of Ps 5⁴ 15¹ 61⁴, and see Cheyne, *ad loc.*, and W. R. Smith, *RS* p. 77 ff.). The Gibeonites may have belonged to this class, and the list of 'Nethinim' (Ezr 2⁴³ff. = Neh 7⁴⁶ff.) contains many names of unquestionably foreign origin (Wellh. *Proleg.* 225 n.).

The close connexion which subsisted in the popular imagination between each land and its god, demanded that whoever settled there must serve the tutelary deity (2 K 17²⁴ff. the story of the Assyr. colonists of Samaria). Hence the Sabbath rest (Ex 20¹⁰ 23¹², Dt 5¹⁴) is not only a privilege enjoyed by the *gêr*, but an obligation imposed upon him. On the other hand, we read of Solomon (and it corresponds with the cosmopolitan character of his policy) that he built sanctuaries at Jerus. for a number of foreign deities (1 K 11⁷ff.). These were doubtless intended to serve, not only for his wives, but for others belonging to foreign nationalities who had been attracted to his capital, and who may have had, as in later times (Neh 13¹⁶), their own quarter of the city. In like manner, the Israelites who had bazaars at Damascus (1 K 20³⁴) prob. erected altars built of earth from the land of Israel (cf. 2 K 5¹⁷), and maintained the worship of J″ side by side with that of the Syrian gods. Solomon's example was copied by Ahab for the benefit of his wife and of the Tyrians and Zidonians who would frequent his court (1 K 16³²f.).

This syncretism in worship and tolerance of dissent from the national religion, which were greatly favoured by the existence of a multitude of local sanctuaries, received a check through the introduction of the Deuteronomic legislation with its central sanctuary, but far more through the enactments of the Priests' Code (P). The ideas introduced in Dt of Israel as a holy people, and of the land as not to be 'defiled' (21²³), led logically to the conclusion that the *gêr* who sojourned in Israel must conform as far as possible to the same regulations as the covenant people. Accordingly, we meet with an extension both of the privileges and the duties of the *gêr*. In D, indeed, matters are not carried so far as in P. In Dt 14²¹ the *gêr* is allowed to eat the flesh of an animal that has died of itself, acc. to Lv 17¹⁵ he is defiled no less than the Isr. by such an act. On the other hand, no difference is recognized between Isr. and *gêr* in the following particulars :—The *gêr* is to participate in the Feast of Weeks (Dt 16¹⁰f.), of Tabernacles (16¹³f.), in the offering of first-fruits (26¹¹), the Sabbath rest (5¹⁴, cf. Ex 20¹⁰ 23¹², JE), the tithes (14²⁸f.), the gleanings of the field, etc.

(24[19ff.]), and he is to have equal justice done to him (24[14]).

The exile helped to draw the bonds of union closer between Israelite and *gêr*, both alike being now strangers in a strange land. Hence in Ezk 47[22f.] we find the same provision made for both in the ideal division of the land. On the other hand, in addition to the keeping of the Sabbath, we are probably safe to infer that circumcision was considered by Ezekiel to be obligatory for the *gêr* (cf. Ezk 44[6-10] where *uncircumcised* 'in heart' and 'in flesh' are parallel terms). Deutero-Isaiah anticipates the conversion to Israel's God, not only of individuals (44[5]), but of kings and princes (49[7]) as well as their subjects (51[4f.]), nay, he foresees a time when to that God 'every knee shall bow and every tongue shall swear' (45[23]). In bringing about this consummation Israel has its function as a missionary nation (42[6. 19] 43[8. 11] 49[6]). The creed of Deutero-Isaiah is, 'There is no God but J″, and Israel is His prophet' (Wellh. *Gesch.* p. 117).

This universalism, indeed, could, according to the notions of most, realize itself only through the forms of Judaism. Non-Israelites must submit to the yoke of Israel's law. In post-exilic times the exclusion from the community of all who would not adopt the drastic reforms of Ezra and Nehemiah, enabled one and the same standard to be applied to the purified remnant. Hence, 'in P the *gêr* is placed practically on the same footing as the native Israelite ; he enjoys the same rights (Nu 35[15], cf. Ezk 47[22]), and is bound by the same laws, whether civil (Lv 24[22]), moral and religious (18[26] 20[2] 24[16], cf. Ezk 14[7]), or ceremonial (Ex 12[19], Lv 16[29] 17[8. 10. 12. 13. 15] 22[18], Nu 15[14. 26. 30] 19[10]) ; the principle, "One law shall there be for the home-born and for the stranger," is repeatedly affirmed (Ex 12[49], Lv 24[22], Nu 9. 14 15[15. 16. 29]), the only specified distinctions being that the *gêr*, if he would keep the passover' (which under no circumstances is the foreigner [בֶּן־נֵכָר] permitted to do), 'must be circumcised (Ex 12[48]), and that an Israelite in servitude with him may be redeemed before the jubilee (Lv 25[48f.]), a privilege not granted in the case of the master's being an Israelite (v.[40f.])' (Driver, *Deut.* p. 165).

After the definite breach with the Samaritans (Neh 13[28ff.]), and the establishment of the temple on Mt. Gerizim (Jos. *Ant.* XI. viii.), the propagandist activity of Jerus. would be stimulated, and it would be felt that the way was more clear to work. There may be a reminiscence of this policy and its results in what the Chronicler reports to have taken place in the reign of Hezekiah (2 Ch 30[1ff.], cf. 1 Ch 13[2], 2 Ch 15[9]). As Schürer points out, the word *gêr* has already in P advanced far on to its later use as = *proselyte* (προσήλυτος), which frequently in LXX represents גֵּר of MT. This meaning appears completely established in the Mishna, where *gêr* denotes one who by circumcision and complete adoption of Israel's laws has become incorporated with the covenant people. If this last sense was intended to be brought out with special distinctness, the phrase גֵּר צֶדֶק ('righteous stranger') was used. For *gêr* in the original sense of a stranger dwelling in Israel, the Mishnic formula was גֵּר תּוֹשָׁב (in OT these terms are parallel in Gn 23[4], Lv 25[23. 35. 47], 1 Ch 29[15], Ps 39[12]), which in mediæval Judaism became גֵּר הַשַּׁעַר = a stranger dwelling within the gates of Israel (cf. Ex 20[10], Dt 5[14] 14[21] 24[14]). The use of גֵּר to designate a *converted* Gentile became finally so well established that a verb (occurring in the Mishna) was formed from it, נִתְגַּיֵּר 'to become a convert' (Schürer, *HJP* II. ii. 315).

The battle which had been fought and gained by Ezra and Nehemiah had indeed to be fought over again more than once in Jewish history, notably in the Gr. period by the MACCABEES (which see) ; but for the further elucidation of the subject we must refer the reader to such articles as HASIDÆANS, PHARISEE, PROSELYTE.

LITERATURE.—Bertholet's monograph, *Die Stellung d. Isr. u. d. Jud. zu d. Fremden* (to which the same obligations are due as in art. FOREIGNER) ; W. R. Smith, *RS* 75 ff., *Kinship*, etc. 42f., 259, *OTJC*[2] 342 n. ; Driver, *Deut.* 126, 165, 175 ; Kuenen, *Rel. Isr.* i. 182 f., ii. 259 f. ; Schürer, *HJP* II. ii. 315 ; Reuss, *A.T.* ii. 28 f. ; Ellicott on Eph 2[19] ; Cremer, *Bib.-Theol. Lex. s. πάροικος* ; Benzinger, *Heb. Arch.* 339 f.   J. A. SELBIE.

GERA (גֵּרָא).—Mentioned as one of Benjamin's sons in Gn 46[21], omitted in Nu 26[38-40]. Acc. to 1 Ch 8[3. 5. 7] G. is a son of Bela and a grandson of Benjamin. Gera was evidently a well-known Benjamite clan, to which belonged Ehud (Jg 3[15] where see Moore's note) and Shimei (2 S 16[5] 19[16. 18], 1 K 2[8]). See GENEALOGY.

GERAH.—See WEIGHTS AND MEASURES.

GERAR (גְּרָר, Γέραρα).—This place, as identified on existing maps, is about 6 miles from Gaza, a little W. of S., and perhaps 25 miles from Beersheba in a direction N. of W. Gerar is mentioned in OT in the history of the time of king Asa and in that of the patriarchs. In Asa's time it was one of several cities in that region (2 Ch 14[13. 14]). (In 1 Ch 4[39] Gerar should possibly be substituted for Gedor of MT. The LXX reads Γέραρα. See GEDOR). In the earlier time, G. is the region where Abraham and Isaac came into contact with a king or kings named Abimelech. The site as now identified is well within the territory properly known as the land of the Philistines. The region as mentioned in Ch and Gn must have extended far to the S., and far enough to the E. to cover part of what is elsewhere known as the Negeb, or S. country.

Were the people whom Abraham and Isaac met in this region true Philistines? That is, did they belong to the same race that afterwards so often oppressed Israel? Their essentially pastoral character is no argument in the negative, for Israel was then also a pastoral people. The region is called the land of the Philistines (Gn 21[32. 34]), but that is not in itself decisive, for the writer uses the geog. terms belonging to his own time, and not necessarily to the time of Abraham. The people are called Philistines (Gn 26[1. 8. 14. 15. 18]), but even that is not so conclusive as at first it seems, for the term may be merely geographical, describing the people who, in the time of Abraham, lived in the country which the writer knew as Philistine. But Abimelech seems to have been a Phil. name (Ps 34, title). Phichol, the 'captain of his host' (Gn 21[22. 32] 26[26]), is witness to the existence of military organization, such as corresponds with the genius of the later Philistines. Ahuzzath (26[26]) is naturally explained as one of the Phil. names in *ăth*, like Goliath. Add these confirmatory particulars to those above given, and we have proof of considerable strength identifying the Philistines of Isaac with those of later times.

G. was a well-known place in the earlier centuries after Christ. A monastery was located there. The abbot Sylvanus, of the 4th cent., was celebrated ; and Marcion, bishop of G., was one of the signatories of the Council of Chalcedon, A.D. 451. The Talm. writings know the district as *Gerarki* (Euseb. ; Jerome, *Onomast.* ; Sozomen, *Hist. Eccles.* vi. 32, ix. 7 ; Schwarz, *Pal.* p. 109). Travellers of the present cent. have given a good deal of attention to this region, *e.g.* Thomson, *Land and Book*, ii. 350 ; Stanley, *Sin. and Pal.* p. 159 ; Robinson, *Researches*, i. 189, ii. 43, 44. See also *PEFSt*, 1871, p. 84 ; 1875, pp. 162, 164 ; 1881, p. 38 ; and Sayce, *Pat. Pal.* 181, 189.   W. J. BEECHER.

GERASA (Γέρασα, Γερασηνοί).—In the RV 'Gerasenes' takes the place of 'Gadarenes' in Mk 5[1], Lk 8[26]; with these exceptions the expression 'the country of the Gerasenes' does not occur in the Bible. See GADARA, GERASENES.

Jerome (*ad Obad.* 1) states that Gilead was called in his day Gerasa, and it is possible that the term 'country of the Gerasenes' (or Gilead) may have extended as far as the Lake of Gennesaret; but as Gilead is usually supposed to have been terminated on its northern boundary by the Hieromax, it seems more probable that the 'country of the Gerasenes' (Mk 5[1]) refers to a town of the name of Gerasa on the eastern shore of Gennesaret (see GERASENES, and cf. Origen, *Opp.* 4, p. 140). According to Ptolemy (v. 15), Gerasa was a city of Cœle-Syria (which included Gilead), 35 miles from Pella; and Pliny describes it (v. 18), Gerasa being read for Galasa, as one of the cities of the Decapolis which was built or rebuilt, colonized and endowed with privileges on the conquest of Syria by the Romans, B.C. 65 (Stephanus, *Ethnic.*). Eusebius (*Onomast. s.v.*) describes the Decapolis as that part of Peræa 'that lies about Hippos, Pella, and Gadara.' Josephus (*BJ* III. iii. 3) places Gerasa in the district of Peræa, east of Jordan, on the borders of the Arabian desert, and mentions it in connexion with Pella and Philadelphia (*BJ* I. iv. 8). Epiphanius (*Adv. Hær.* i. and ii.) describes Decapolis as around Pella and Basanets, and speaks of the fountain of Gerasa of Arabia. Jamblicus states that it was colonized by veterans of Alexander the Great, which is not improbable from its proximity to Pella, which was probably colonized in this manner.

The early history of Gerasa is unknown; it first appears in history as an important fortified city in the account of its capture (c. 83 B.C.; *BJ* I. iv. 8) by Alexander Jannæus, the Hasmonæan king of the Jews. Having subdued Pella, he directed his march on the city of Gerasa, lured by the treasures of Theodorus, son of Zeno, and, having hemmed in the garrison by a triple wall of circumvallation, carried the place by assault. In *Ant.* XIII. xv. 3 Pella is called Dios, or placed close to it, and Gerasa is called Essa. In A.D. 65 Gerasa, as one of the cities of Decapolis, was probably rebuilt by the Romans. On the revolt of the Jews against the Roman dominion they laid waste the villages of the Syrians and their neighbouring cities, among which were Gerasa and Pella; and 'every city was divided into two armies, encamped one against another'; but the Gerasenes did no harm to those Jews who abode amongst them, and even conducted those who wished it as far as their border (*BJ* II. xv. 1, 5). Shortly after this, Vespasian sent Lucius Annius to Gerasa with an army, who took the city and slew a thousand young men, and plundered and burned the city (*BJ* IV. ix. 1). Nothing further is heard of Gerasa in history; but during the peaceful age of the Antonines (A.D. 138 to 180) it attained a position of the greatest prosperity, and was adorned by monuments, which, still existing, show that it became one of the most important cities of Syria. It subsequently became the seat of a bishopric, and the name of one of its prelates is found amongst those who were present at the Council of Chalcedon. There is no evidence that the city was ever inhabited by the Arabs after the Roman and Byzantine period. In the Talmudic writings and in Jerome, Gerash and Gilead are synonymous. Reland states that coins of Gerasa exist, showing the worship of Artemis in the temple there in 2nd cent. (cf. Schürer, *HJP* II. i. 118). During the Crusades Baldwin (A.D. 1121) besieged a castle constructed of large stones called Jarras, supposed to be Gerasa; but William of Tyre, in speaking of the siege, makes the distance not far from the Jordan; and as Gerasa has no appearance of having been occupied by any settled population since its destruction during the Byzantine period, it was probably some other castle that Baldwin attacked.

It is probable that the fountains and waters of Palestine, where conveniently situated, mark the sites of towns and villages from the earliest times, and that the splendid perennial stream and fountains of *Jerâsh* must have been chosen as a position for a town at a very early date. No identification, however, appears to have been attempted with any success except that by Sir George Grove with reference to Ramoth-gilead. He points out that if Ramoth-gilead and Ramath-mizpah are identical, a more northern position than *es-Salt* would seem inevitable, and that the Arabic version of the Bk. of Joshua gives *Ramat el-Jerash*, thus identifying the Gerasa of the classical geographers with Ramah of Gilead. The Jewish traveller Parchi says that 'Gilead is at present Djerash' (Zunz in Asher's *Benjamin*, 405). See RAMOTH-GILEAD.

Jerâsh is situated in the *Belḳa* of the modern Arabs, near their best pasture ground, which is referred to in the Bible (Dt 3[10] 4[43]; see Driver's note) as plains (*mîshôr*), in RV 'tablelands,' thus having the same signification, to a limited extent, as the Arabic name *Jerâsh*.

There can be no doubt that the very remarkable ruins still existing in good preservation in the highlands of Gilead, called *Jerâsh*, represent the remains of the Roman city of Gerasa of the time of the Antonines; and although these ruins, so far as they have yet been observed, are distinctly attributable to the 2nd to 5th cents., there is no reasonable doubt that they are built on the site of the earlier Greek city of Gerasa. This locality is mentioned by Yakûbi in the 7th cent. as being in his time one of the towns of the Jordan Provinces, and the poet Al Mutanabbi praises the fertility of *Jerâsh*. Yakût in the 13th cent., who had not himself seen the spot, describes it as a 'great city now in ruins' through which runs a stream which turned many mills, and relates that the *Jerâsh* mountains contained many villages.

Jerâsh is beautifully situated in the highlands of Gilead, 20 miles east of the Jordan, the same distance north of 'Ammân (Philadelphia), 22 miles from *Fâhel* (Pella), and 6 miles north of *Wady Zerḳa* (Jabbok). It is 1900 ft. above the level of the Mediterranean, in the midst of hills rising from 500 to 600 ft. higher, until the tablelands (*mîshôr*), called by the Arabs *Belḳa*, are reached, which during part of the year is rich pasture, and for a short period in the autumn appear to be desert. The city occupies a considerable portion of a shallow valley, the ruins stretching some way up the limestone hills; and through the midst runs a delightful perennial stream fringed with oleanders, and falling about 1000 ft. before reaching the *Zerḳa*, 6 miles to south. The city is surrounded by walls, built in the outline of an irregular nine-sided polygon, about 3000 yards in circumference, the stream dividing it into two nearly equal parts: the greater portion to the west, on which side are all the public buildings; the private buildings occupying the east side of the stream and the higher ground to the west. The site of the city is undulating and full of knolls, affording most excellent positions for public buildings. The walls of the city are much decayed, and in some parts have been quite removed—they have been 8 ft. thick, and are built of small squared stones of limestone. There have been at least six gates in the wall— three to west, one to east, and the two principal north and south gates. Between these two gates runs a paved road with a double row of columns on the west side of the stream, close to it on the north and about 100 yards from it on the south;

the public buildings are constructed in connexion with this main thoroughfare. They were all of about the same date, and, taking it all together, this city is the most complete example of the Roman work of the time of the Antonines in Syria. They are constructed on one general plan, and cannot be considered in architectural remains to be inferior to Palmyra, though the ruins of the latter cover a far larger area. Reference to the works of Wood and Dawkins and the photographs taken by *Pal. Explor. Fund* in 1867 will show that each city has a distinct architectural character.

On approaching *Jerâsh* from the south, attention is attracted by a fine arch of triumph of decorated stone in the Corinthian order, with three arched passages and a front of 80 ft., leading to a paved Roman road running for about 300 yards northerly to the southern gate of the city. On the left-hand side is a *naumachia* or theatre for naval contests, about 700 ft. by 300 ft., with its arena below the level of the surrounding ground, in order that it might be filled from an aqueduct which supplied water from the stream. On the left, among the hills, is the Necropolis, and sarcophagi of black basalt with Roman devices are to be seen lying about. The southern gate is in ruins, but it is similar in appearance to the triumphal arch. The main street on entering the city bears to the left, leading to an oval colonnade or hippodrome, 310 ft. by 230 ft., lined with columns 2 ft. 5 in. in diameter, with capitals of the Ionic order, supporting a plain entablature. Immediately to the left on entering the city are a large theatre and a temple. The theatre facing north is open, and is constructed to seat over 2000 people, with a closed stage 110 ft. across; it is lavishly decorated in the Corinthian order. The temple facing nearly east is peripteral, measuring 110 ft. by 85 ft. along the walls outside the cell; the columns are 4 ft. in diameter and spaced at 12 ft. intervals from centre to centre. Near the northern end of the hippodrome the main street, 22 ft. wide, leads in a straight line direct to the north gate, and is adorned with a row of columns on each side with Corinthian capitals supporting an entablature. The columns are about 3 ft. or more in diameter. The road, 22 ft. wide, is paved with hard stone, which has still the marks of chariot wheels, and at the sides are raised pavements for foot passengers. At a distance of about 100 yards is a cross street at right angles, also with a double row of columns, leading up the hill on the left to the west gate, and to the right over the stream by a Roman bridge; four large pedestals, 12 ft. square, at the cross streets still remain, where statues once adorned the city. About 50 yards from the cross streets are some ruined palaces, with columns 4 ft. in diameter, with fragments of Egyptian rose granite and remains of frieze, cornice, and pediment, on which decorations have been lavished with great exuberance, with an inscription apparently containing the name of Marcus Aurelius Antoninus (A.D. 161–180); and at about 100 yards from the cross street, both right and left, are the remains of a series of handsome buildings, one a basilica, grouped in relation to the great temple of the Sun, which stands on a natural eminence nearly in the centre of the city in the western quarter. The temple facing the east measures round the walls of cell 89½ ft. by 44½ ft., the platform is 14 ft. wide on each side. It has at the entrance 12 columns, 5 ft. in diameter, spaced at intervals of 12½ ft. from centre to centre; 11 of these magnificent columns still remain *in situ*, 10 of them surmounted by their Corinthian capitals. All the buildings about the temple have been highly ornamented. From an inscription copied by Burckhardt it would appear that these buildings were erected in the time of Antoninus Pius, A.D.

138–161. Proceeding farther north we come to a second street of intersections, with a handsome rotunda over the intersection; the cross street leads on the left to another theatre, and on the right to an extensive building supposed to have been a bathing establishment. The theatre is not so large as that to the south, and has an open stage or scene. On the east bank of the river to the north is another Corinthian temple facing west, a very unusual aspect for temples of the 2nd and 3rd cents. in Palestine.

There are many other ruins of public buildings not enumerated whose identity has not been established, and a number of inscriptions (more than ten), two of which, near the ruins of a building supposed to have been a church, south of the temple of the Sun, refer to the establishment of Christianity and the discontinuance of pagan worship of about .5th cent., an important piece of evidence in connexion with the subject in Syria (Conder, *Palestine*, p. 180). The stream which runs through *Jerâsh* is principally fed from springs within the city on east side. There are very full accounts of *Jerâsh* in the travels of Buckingham, Burckhardt, Irby, and Mangles, but no recent surveys have been made. *Jerâsh* was visited by the present writer in 1867, and a sketch plan of the city was made and several plans of temples, which have not yet been published. Fifteen photographs of ruins also were taken, which have been published by the *Palestine Exploration Fund*.   C. WARREN.

GERASENES.—The country of the Gerasenes (AV of Mt 8²⁸ **Gergesenes**; Mt 5¹ Lk 8²⁶ **Gadarenes**; RV in Mt Gadarenes, in Mk and Lk Gerasenes) is referred to in NT only in connexion with the casting out of the legion of demons and their entry into the herd of swine. There are three distinct readings of the name of the people in the MSS—Gergesenes, Gadarenes, Gerasenes—as the following table will show:—

	Mt	Mk	Lk
B	Γαδαρηνῶν	Γερασηνῶν	Γερασηνῶν
ℵ	Γαζαρηνῶν (ℵᶜ Γεργεσ.)	Γερασηνῶν	Γεργεσηνῶν
A	(wanting)	Γαδαρηνῶν	Γαδαρηνῶν
C	Γαδαρηνῶν (Cᶟ Γεργεσ.)	Γαδαρηνῶν	Γερασηνῶν (C² Γεργεσ.)
D	(wanting)	Γερασηνῶν	Γερασηνῶν

Thus, as WH (App. p. 11) point out, documentary evidence shows that Γαδαρηνῶν is the true reading in Mt, Γερασηνῶν in Mk and Lk.

The miracle took place 'on the other side' of the Lake of Gennesaret, which is 'over against Galilee' (*i.e.* on the eastern side of the lake) (Lk 8²², ²⁶). And when Jesus 'was come out of the boat, straightway there met him out of the tombs a man with an unclean spirit, who had his dwelling in the tombs' (Mk 5²). This clearly indicates that the tombs were close to the shore of the lake, and from the following passages it appears that the tombs and city were in the proximity: Lk 8²⁷ 'There met him a certain man out of the city who had devils . . . and abode not in any house but in the tombs.' From the following it appears that the hills ran up directly from the coast of the lake: Lk 8³² 'Now there was there a herd of many swine feeding on the mountains . . . and the herd rushed down the steep into the lake, and were choked.'

From this it is certain that 'the country of the Gerasenes' cannot refer to the city of Gerasa in Gilead (*Jerâsh*), as Gerasa is an inland town east of Jordan, near Philadelphia, towards Arabia (*BJ* III. iii. 3, 4), which has certainly been identified with the ruins of *Jerâsh*. It also appears that Gadara cannot be the city spoken of in the incident, as it (now *Umm Ķeis*) is situated about six or more miles south of the Lake of Gennesaret on the summit of a high hill with the deep gorge of the river Hieromax (*Jarmûk*) at its foot, cutting it off from the broad plain shelving down to the lake. There was, however, a district attached to the city of Gadara, and it is possible that a place on the lake called Gerasa (not the Gerasa of the preceding art.) lay within Gadarene territory. Gadara was but 6 miles S.E. of the southern extremity of the lake, and Jos. (*Vita*, 9, 10) mentions Gadarene villages close to the lake side. According to Josephus, however (*BJ* IV. vii. 3), Gadara was the capital of Peræa, which did not extend north of the Hieromax. It is not improbable, however, that during the many vicissitudes of the administration accorded to Gadara its jurisdiction may have extended up the eastern side of the Lake of Gennesaret at the time the miracle occurred.

The problem, then, is to find a site on the east side of the lake which satisfies the biblical description and shows traces of the city and tombs. This has been successfully accomplished by Thomson (*The Land and the Book*, ii. 35), through the identification of the ruins of Kersa or Gersa on the eastern side of the Lake of Gennesaret, nearly half-way down from the northern end, south of the *Wady Samakh* (see further and especially Schumacher, *The Jaulân*, 179). Wilson states (*Recovery of Jerusalem*, p. 368) that about a mile south of this the hills, which everywhere else on the eastern side are recessed from half to three-quarters of a mile from the water's edge, approach within 40 ft. of it. They do not terminate abruptly, but there is a steep even slope, which we would identify with the 'steep place' down which the herd of swine ran violently into the sea. Macgregor (*Rob Roy on the Jordan*, p. 423) states, 'Between *Wady Samakh* and *Wady Fik* there are at least four distinct localities where every feature in the Scripture account of this incident may be found in combination; above them are rocks with caves in them, very suitable for tombs.' Thomson states that there are ancient tombs in the high grounds about the ruins of Kersa. Gergesa and Gerasa may thus be variations of the same name which is now found under the form of *Kersa, Chersa,* or *Gersa,* which now exist close to *Wady Samakh,* subject to the various pronunciations according to whether the people are from the hill country, or the plain, or from the desert. The name Gergesenes appears to be similar to that of a Canaanitish tribe (GIRGASHITES) which, according to Jos 24[11], would appear to have been located west of Jordan, but which Jerome (*Comm. ad Gen.* xv.) locates on the shore of the Sea of Tiberias. Origen also (*Opp.* iv. 140) alludes to the city Gergesa, which stood formerly on the eastern side of the lake, and to the precipitous descent to the water down which the swine rushed. A village, Gergesa, on a hill above the lake, is also mentioned by Eusebius and Jerome (*OS*[2] p. 256, 14; p. 162, 18).

C. WARREN.

GERGESENES.—See GERASENES.

GERIZIM (הַר גְּרִיזִים *har Gĕrizzîm,* the modern *Jebel eṭ-Ṭûr*).—This important mountain faces its northern companion Ebal, having in the narrow pass between them the town of Nâblus (Neapolis), the ancient Shechem. Its height, 2849 ft., makes it lower than the other by 228 ft., but it has far surpassed it in historical and religious associations. The cleft between them (to which possibly the mountain owes its name) presents the only pass from east to west in the mountain range of Ephraim, and, being also on the main road from north to south, its facility of access and central position in the land marked it out as an important place in the kingdom of Israel.

To-day, as the sacred place of the little Samari-

tan community, it is interesting chiefly as a monument to the vitality of religious prejudice. The Samaritan Pentateuch contains a verse giving express commandment that an altar should be built on Mt. Gerizim, making it rather than Ebal or the temple-rock of Jerusalem the first and central shrine of the chosen people and the revealed law. This knowledge of the will of the Almighty is thus confined to a small and dwindling company in a Syrian village, the rest of the world, both Jews and Gentiles, being in darkness and error; and the assumption is to them one of comfort and complacency. The Samaritans and their Mt. Gerizim thus form the world's memorial of sectarianism, after the manner of Natural History showing at once the grub and the leaf it lives upon.

The top of the mountain is broad, bare, and rocky, and among the sacred places scattered over it some refer to the Bible narrative, others to Samaritan events, and others to Christian history. 1. *Patriarchal.*—Abraham entered the Promised Land by the pass of Gerizim, encamping at Shechem by the oak of Moreh, Gn 12[6] (J). Gerizim is also claimed, as against Mt. Moriah at Jerusalem, to have been the mountain to which Abraham was directed when commanded to offer up Isaac, Gn 22[2] (R). Much discussion has taken place over this locality, the evidence bearing chiefly on points of distance, conspicuousness, and the meaning of the words *Moreh* and *Moriah.* The Scripture account scarcely encourages attempted precision, as its reference is merely to 'one of the mountains,' the words 'of Moriah' being an undoubted gloss. On the whole, Gerizim or some neighbouring height accords best with Bible description.

The Samaritans point to a trench on the S.E. end of the Gerizim summit as the spot where Isaac was laid on the altar. The Jews and Moslems agree with the Samaritans in attaching great importance to this trial by sacrifice in the life of Abraham, Jewish tradition stating that Isaac said to his father, 'Bind me fast,' and the Moslems making Ishmael, whom they substitute for Isaac, surpass this zeal by saying, 'Do not bind me.' Samaritan tradition, arguing from the neighbourhood of the village of Salem, makes Gerizim the place where Abraham was met by Melchizedek and the king of distant Sodom (Gn 14[17ff.]). It is also connected with Jacob, who, on his return from Paddan-aram, bought 'the parcel of ground' for his encampment at Shechem, Gn 33[18-20] (E). In addition to this, the Samaritans point to a spot on the summit called *Khurbet Lauzeh,* as the place where Jacob slept, and had the vision of divine protection and promise, Gn 28[11f.] (E).

2. *Israelite.* — Ebal and Gerizim were the mountains on whose sides the tribes assembled under Joshua, according to the command of Moses, to hear the curses and the blessings connected with the observance of the law (Dt 11[29. 32] 27[11. 12], Jos 8[33. 34]). Gerizim was probably selected in preference to Ebal as the mount of blessing, because to one looking eastwards it was *on the right hand,* the side of good fortune (see Driver on Dt 11[29]). The Samaritans point out a piece of flat rocky ground as the site of Joshua's altar and their own temple.

The distance from Ai, taken along with the position of Ebal and Gerizim in the centre of a hostile country, has offered a difficulty to the acceptance of the above narrative in Deuteronomy. A solution was attempted by Eusebius (*Onom. sac.*[2] 253), Epiphanius, and others, by referring Ebal and Gerizim to localities nearer the Jordan Valley. But their connexion with Shechem, to which Josephus (*Ant.* XI. viii. 6), Eusebius, and Jerome themselves refer, has always discountenanced such a theory.

Gerizim comes again into prominence when Jotham delivered his highly figurative parable to the treacherous elders of Shechem (Jg 9⁷⁻²¹).

Tradition has represented these two mountains as brought under the spell of the blessings and curses once pronounced upon them, declaring Gerizim to be beautiful and fertile, while Ebal is bare and barren; but at the present day they show the similarity that might be expected from their proximity, elevation, and composition.

3. *Samaritan.*—It is well known that the Samaritans erected a temple on Gerizim which henceforth became the rival of the temple at Jerusalem in historical claims and sanctity as a religious centre. The occasion that led to its erection, acc. to Josephus (*Ant.* XI. viii. 2, 4), was the marriage between Manasseh of the high-priestly family in Jerusalem and the daughter of Sanballat. This union, and many similar inter-marriages, created the desire for an independent sanctuary, that would be free from the dictation of the Jerusalem authorities. It is practically certain that Josephus' chronology here is incorrect. He places the erection of the schismatic temple in the time of Alexander the Great, who, according to him, authorized its erection; but there can be little doubt that the temple on Gerizim was built a century earlier (*c.* 432 B.C.) by the son-in-law of Sanballat the Horonite referred to in Neh 13²⁸ (cf. *inter alios*, Ryle, *Canon of OT*, 91 f.). This Samaritan temple lasted at least till the time of the Maccabees, when it was probably destroyed (*c.* 110 B.C) by John Hyrcanus (Jos. *Ant.* XIII. ix. 1; *Wars*, I. ii. 6). To what extent this rivalry as to the proper site of worship survived in the time of Christ, is seen in the proverbial hatred between Jews and Samaritans, and in the arguments urged by the Samaritan woman at Jacob's well (Jn 4²⁰·²¹).

4. *Christian.*—The most conspicuous ruins in Gerizim at the present day are those called in Arabic *el-Ḳula'ah*, 'the fortress.' We have here the remains of the church built by the Christians in the reign of Zeno in A.D. 475, which, having been destroyed by the Samaritans, was afterwards enlarged and fortified by Justinian in 530. See SAMARITANS.

The most interesting link with the past is the yearly celebration of the Samaritan Passover on its summit. As the sun sets on the Passover Eve, the seven lambs are slain, ceremonially examined, and roasted in the oven pit. At midnight the covering is removed, and the flesh is eaten by the standing elders with their families in the im-provized tents. Anything left over is scrupulously collected and consumed, so that the letter of the commandment may be kept.

LITERATURE.—Robinson, *BRP* ii. 274 ff.; *SWP* ii. 148 ff.; Stanley, *Sinai and Palestine* (Index); Guérin, *Samarie*, i. 424 ff.; Thomson, *Land and the Book* (Index); Baedeker-Socin, *Pal.* 220, 222; G. A. Smith, *HGHL* 119 f., 384 n. 2; Conder, *Tent-Work*, ch. ii.: Murray, *Guide-book to Syria* (Index); Driver on Dt 11²⁹; Baudissin, *Stud. z. Sem. Rel.-ges.* ii. 252.

                   G. M. MACKIE.

GERON should possibly appear as a proper name in 2 Mac 6¹, according to which Antiochus Epi-phanes sent γέροντα Ἀθηναῖον (AV and RV 'an old man of Athens,' RVm 'Geron an Athenian') 'to compel the Jews to depart from the laws of their fathers.'

GERRENIANS (ἕως τῶν Γερρηνῶν, A Γεννηρῶν, AV Gerrhenians, 2 Mac 13²⁴).— When Lysias, recalled from Pal. by troubles in Syria, made peace with Judas Maccabæus in B.C. 162, he left Hegemonides as commandant 'from Ptolemais to the G.' (AV wrongly, 'made him—*i.e.* Judas—principal governor,' etc.). The true reading and the people intended are both uncertain. The analogy of 1 Mac 11⁵⁹ suggests some place near the border

of Egypt; but Gerrha, between Pelusium and Rhinocolura, was in Egyptian territory. Ewald (*Hist.*, Eng. tr. v. 319) suggested that the word should be understood of the inhabitants of Gerar, an ancient Phil. city S.E. of Gaza; and this view is supported by cod. 55, which reads Γεραρηνῶν (see RVm). On the other hand, Syr. reads Gazar (גזר), *i.e.* Gezer or Gazara, not far from Lydda (cf. 1 Mac 15²⁸·³⁵).   H. A. WHITE.

GERSHOM (גֵּרְשֹׁם or גֵּרְשֹׁם).—1. The firstborn son of Moses and Zipporah (Ex 2²²=18³, both JE, 1 Ch 23¹⁵). In the two former passages the writer ex-plains the name as though it were connected with גֵּר 'a sojourner' and שָׁם 'there,' cf. the LXX form Γηρσάμ (Ex 2²²=18³). Unless Ex 4²⁵ (J) gives us an account of his circumcision we know nothing further of G.'s life, but there are a few scattered notices of his descendants. In the pre-Massoretic text of Jg 18³⁰, supported by some cursive MSS of the LXX, Jonathan, the son of Gershom, the son of Moses, is said to have officiated as priest of the sanctuary of J" at Dan, and it is added that the office was held by members of the family until the Captivity. The MT here reads Manasseh for Moses; so LXX, A, B, L. See Moore, *in loc.* In 1 Ch 23¹⁴ it is stated that the sons of Moses were reckoned amongst the tribe of Levi, *i.e.* in con-tradistinction to the Aaronite branch of the family, who were consecrated for special purposes. Lastly, from 1 Ch 26²⁴ we learn that in the time of David a son of G. named Shebuel was 'ruler over the treasuries,' cf. 23¹⁶ 24²⁰ (Shubael). 2. Gershon, the eldest son of Levi (1 Ch 6¹⁶·¹⁷·²⁰·⁴³·⁶²·⁷¹ 15⁷). See next article. 3. A descendant of Phinehas who journeyed with Ezra from Babylon to Jerus. (Ezr 8²).   W. C. ALLEN.

GERSHON (גֵּרְשׁוֹן, called also **Gershom**, גֵּרְשֹׁם or גֵּרְשֹׁם, 1 Ch 6¹⁶·¹⁷·²⁰·⁴³·⁶²·⁷¹ 15⁷).—All our data about G. and his family come from P and the Chronicler, the latter, however, adding nothing to P's account with regard to G. himself. According to these writers he was the firstborn of the three sons of Levi (Ex 6¹⁶, Nu 3¹⁷, 1 Ch 6¹·¹⁶ 23⁶), born before the migration of Jacob and his family into Egypt (Gn 46¹¹). He had two sons, Libni (for whom we find Ladan in 1 Ch 23²⁶·²¹) and Shimei (Ex 6¹⁷, Nu 3¹⁸, 1 Ch 6¹⁷·²⁰). This is all that we know of G. personally, but of the fortunes of his descend-ants we have fuller particulars. Their history falls into three periods—(1) the wilderness wander-ings; (2) the monarchy; (3) after the Exile.

1. At the time of the census taken by Moses in the wilderness of Sinai, the **Gershonites** were divided into two families, the Libnites and the Shimeites (Nu 3²¹). The whole number of males from a month old was 7500 (3²²), and between 30 and 50 years of age 2630 (4²²⁻³·³⁸⁻⁴¹). Their position in the camp was behind the tabernacle westward (3²³), and their chief at this time was Eliasaph the son of Lael (3²⁴). The office assigned to them by P during the wilderness wandering was the carrying of the curtains, the coverings, the screens, and the hangings of the tabernacle, and of the Tent of Meeting, together with the accompanying cords and instruments (3²⁵⁻²⁷ 4²⁴⁻²⁶ 10¹⁷). In this they were to be at the command of Aaron, and were superintended by Ithamar his son (4²⁷⁻²⁸). Two waggons and four oxen were assigned to them for this service (7⁷). In this respect of office the Gershonites were preceded by the younger family, the Kohathites. The G. are also mentioned at the time of the census taken by Moses and Eleazar in the plains of Moab by the Jordan, when the whole number of the Levites was 23,000 (26⁵⁷). At the allotment of Levitical cities by

Joshua and Eleazar after the entry into Pal., thirteen cities in the territories of eastern Manasseh, Issachar, Asher, and Naphtali were assigned to the Gershonites (Jos 21⁶· ²⁷⁻³³ [P] = 1 Ch 6⁶²· ⁷¹⁻⁷⁶).

2. In the reign of David, as narrated by the Chronicler, we have several references to the Gershonites.* The G. family of Asaph, together with the Kohathite family of Heman and the Merarite family of Ethan or Jeduthun, were, acc. to this writer, specially set apart to administer the temple music (cf. 1 Ch 6³¹⁻⁴⁷ 25¹⁻⁷; and see ASAPH). Consequently, at the bringing of the ark into Jerus., of the 130 Gershonites under the leadership of Joel who are said to have been present (1 Ch 15⁷), Asaph and certain others took part in the music (15¹⁷· ¹⁹ 16⁵· ⁷). Descendants of the two families of Ladan (for Libni) and Shimei are mentioned as 'heads of the fathers' houses' when David divided the Levites into courses (1 Ch 23⁷⁻¹¹), and the sons and grandsons of Ladan are spoken of as superintendents of the treasuries at this time (1 Ch 26²¹⁻² 29⁸). In 1 Ch 26¹ the marginal reading Ebiasaph should be followed. Further, in the reign of Hezekiah G. are mentioned as taking part with the other Levites in the cleansing of the temple (2 Ch 29¹²· ¹³), and in 2 Ch 35¹⁵ the Asaphite singers are recorded as present when the passover was kept in the eighteenth year of Josiah.

3. In the period after the Exile we hear a good deal of the Asaphite branch of the singers. When Zerubbabel returned to Jerusalem, 128 Asaphites (or 148 acc. to Neh 7⁴⁴) were included amongst his followers (Ezr 2⁴¹). At the laying of the foundation of the temple, Asaphites are found leading the music (Ezr 3¹⁰), and special provision appears to have been made for them (Neh 11²²; cf. also 1 Ch 9¹⁵, Neh 11¹⁷ 12³⁵).

The name Gershonites (הַגֵּרְשֻׁנִּי) occurs Nu 3²¹· ²³· ²⁴ 4²⁴· ²⁷· ²⁸ 26⁵⁷, Jos 21³³, 1 Ch 23⁷, 2 Ch 29¹². They are elsewhere called 'the sons of Gershon' (Ex 6¹⁷, Nu 3¹⁸· ²⁵ 4²²· ³⁸· ⁴¹ 7⁷ 10¹⁷), or 'the children of Gershon' (Jos 21⁶· ²⁷), or 'the sons of Gershom' (1 Ch 6¹⁷· ⁶²· ⁷¹ 15⁷). For their history see above. In 1 Ch 26²¹ the word is applied in sing. to Ladan, in 29⁸ to Jehiel.

W. C. ALLEN.

GERSON (A Γηρσών, B Ταρσότομος), 1 Es 8²⁹.— In Ezr 8² GERSHOM.

GERUTH - CHIMHAM (גֵּרוּת כְּמָהָם Kerê, כְּמוֹהָם 'g Kethibh) Jer 41¹⁷.—A khan (?) which possibly derived its name from Chimham, the son of Barzillai the Gileadite, 2 S 19³⁷ᶠ. See CHIMHAM. Instead of גֵּרוּת we should almost certainly read גְּדֵרוֹת 'hurdles,' after Josephus and Aquila (see Graf).

GESHAN (גֵּישָׁן).—A descendant of Caleb, 1 Ch 2⁴⁷. Mod. editions of AV have Gesham, although the correct form of the name appears in ed. of 1611.

GESHEM (גֶּשֶׁם, Γησαμ, Neh 2¹⁹ 6¹· ²; in 6⁶ the form Gashmu occurs).—An Arabian, who is named along with Sanballat the Horonite and Tobiah the Ammonite, as an opponent of Neh. during the rebuilding of the walls of Jerusalem. He may have belonged to an Arab community, which, as we learn from the monuments, was settled by Sargon in Samaria c. B.C. 715 — this would explain his close connexion with the Samaritans; or he may have been the chief of an Arab tribe dwelling in the S. of Judah, in which case his presence would point to a coalition of all the neighbouring peoples against Jerusalem. Since the internal administration of the Persian satraps was not sufficiently firm to prevent petty feuds among subject races in distant parts of the empire, there is nothing unnatural in

the mention of an alliance of Samaritans, Arabians, Ashdodites, and Ammonites against the Jews (Neh 4⁷ᶠ·). Geshem with his confederates mocked Neh.'s intention of repairing the walls (2¹⁹); and when the walls were completed, he joined with Sanballat in inviting Neh. to a conference in the plain of Ono (6¹ᶠᶠ·). His authority was cited in support of the rumour that Neh. intended to rebel against the Persian king (6⁶). H. A. WHITE.

GESHUR, GESHURITE (גְּשׁוּר, הַגְּשׁוּרִי).—A small Aramæan tribe whose territory, together with that of Maacah (wh. see), formed the W. border of Bashan (Dt 3¹⁴, Jos 12⁵ 13¹¹). The Geshurites were not expelled by the half-tribe of Manasseh, to whom their land had been allotted (Jos 13¹³), and were still ruled by an independent king in the reign of David, who married the daughter of Talmai king of Geshur (2 S 3³). After the murder of his half-brother Amnon, Absalom took refuge with his maternal grandfather in 'Geshur of Aram' (2 S 13³⁷ 15⁸). Geshur and Maacah were probably situated in the modern Jaulân (Smith, HGHL p. 548, n. 9), if they are not to be identified with it (Driver, Deut. p. 56 f.). In 1 Ch 2²³ Geshur and Aram are said to have taken the 'tent-villages' of Jair from the Israelites. On the strength of Jos 13² and 1 S 27⁸, it has been maintained that there was another tribe of this name in the neighbourhood of the Philistines. This view has been recently revived by Hommel (AHT p. 237 ff.), who regards Geshur as a contraction for Gê-Ashûr or Gê-Shûr, 'the lowland of Ashûr or Shûr,' and identifies it with the extreme southern portion of Palestine between el-'Arîsh ('the brook of Egypt') and Gaza (or Beersheba). According to Hommel, this tract of country was originally inhabited by the tribe of Asher (Ashûr being treated as the 'broken' or internal plural form of Asher). But even if we could follow him in his view that Shûr (Gn 16⁷ 20¹ 25¹⁸, 1 S 15⁷) was merely a popular abbreviation of Ashûr (see SHUR), and that the latter was so called after the tribe of Asher, his derivation of Geshur must be rejected. Such a contraction as Geshur for Gê-Ashûr or Gê-Shûr (שׁוּר gê-אִיָּא for גֵּיא or אִיָּא שׁוּר), is entirely foreign to the Hebrew language; and, further, the meaning of gê (אִיָּא), constr. st. of אִיָּא) is not 'lowland,' but 'ravine' or 'glen.' It is noteworthy that the B text of the LXX at 1 S 27⁸ gives only one name, omitting Geshur, which is probably an incorrect gloss (see GIRZITE). In the remaining passage (Jos 13²) the context (cf. vv.¹¹· ¹³) renders the present reading very suspicious: possibly we should substitute וְכָל־הַגִּזְרִי ('and all the inhabitants of Gezer') for וְכָל־הַגְּשׁוּרִי ('and all the Geshurites'). In the absence of further proof, therefore, we may conclude that the name Geshur was applied only to the country E. of the Jordan.

In 2 S 2⁹ 'Geshurites' (הַגְּשׁוּרִי) should perhaps be substituted for 'Ashurites' (הָאֲשׁוּרִי). So Vulg., Syr., and Thenius, Ewald, Wellhausen. Others prefer to read הָאָשֵׁרִי ('Asherites,' cf. Jg 1³²). This is adopted by Köhler, Kamphausen, Klostermann, Budde, and others. J. F. STENNING.

GESTURES. — 1. An emotional necessity of Oriental life. Gesture is much resorted to by Orientals in the communication of their thoughts and expression of their feelings. This does not prove them more emotional than Anglo-Saxons, if we use this term of sincerity of feeling and its practical and permanent influence upon conduct, but they have much greater facility and variety in its expression. Where we control our feelings, they are controlled by them, not because the feelings are always stronger, but because the controlling power is less. They are more governed by

---

* It must never be overlooked that it is the habit of the Chronicler to carry back many of the arrangements of his own age to the time of David.

the impression of the moment, and the mood changes with the occasion that produced it. Thus the passage of a funeral procession through an Oriental town makes a reverent hush among the trades and traffic of the street, and the people stand mute and motionless like a guard of honour; among the aged and infirm, lips move in prayer, and eyes are filled with tears; but when the spectacle has passed, the return to other things is rapid, easy, and complete.

In congenial company a jest may cause such merriment that one of the number will call out, 'The Lord cover (forgive) us for this laughter!' In the same way grief is vented to the point of physical reaction and dismissal. In lands that have given freedom to the press, there is an outspoken frankness about the statement of private intention and public affairs, but the feelings of the heart are kept in hallowed reserve; in the East, on the contrary, plans, motives, and expectations are seldom stated simply and sincerely, but the expression of feeling is always profuse and exuberant. The strongest possible terms of devotion to God and attachment to friends are in constant use, but only one of themselves can tell when language is the symbol of feeling and when its substitute. In modern Syria, a mere child detected in theft or falsehood at school boldly calls heaven and earth to witness that he is innocent. In the Arabic grammar, emotional apostrophe is treated as a commonplace of daily speech, and rules are provided for adjuration and imprecation. Conversation is usually conducted in a loud tone of voice; truth, in the interest of truth, is sympathetically exaggerated; the simple 'yes' and 'no' of the European are regarded as cold and deficient in humanity.

The Bible abounds in vivid narrative, and the dramatic form is approached in Job and Canticles, but neither among the Hebrews nor the Arabs has there been any dramatic literature in the European sense of the term. This may be largely due to the fact that their speech is generally so figurative and animated.

Such temperament and surroundings help to explain the fact that the language of Orientals is so rich in figure, and their spoken words to such an unusual degree helped and harmonized by appropriate gesture.

2. *Expressiveness and variety of Oriental gesture.* —To the European, Oriental gesture is lacking in self-command and husbanded energy, and approaches grimace and contortion. The whole body is pressed into the service. Two men engaged in warm dispute appear to be using the deaf and dumb alphabet. The body is one moment bent forward, the next is standing erect; the hands are stretched out in supplication, and then slapped and held on each side of the head in the anguish of distraction and the shock of assumed amazement. The eyes flash, and the voices rise higher, until one yields to the vehemence of the other (2 S 19⁴³), or both are separated by the bystanders (Ex 2¹³). The head is shaken, nodded, jerked, and inclined sideways, forwards, and backwards in a variety of ways reaching in suggested meaning from indifference, impatience, acquiescence, and denial to amazement, sarcasm, denunciation, and disgust. The shrugging of the shoulders is similarly varied to express embarrassment, surprise, ignorance, and irresponsibility. An Oriental reading the Bible naturally supplies this shrug when reading Gn 25³² 37²⁶ 44¹⁶, Ex 3¹³ 15²⁴ 17⁴, 1 S 17²⁹, Ph 1²², the first sentence of Rev 7¹⁴, etc. In salutation the form varies with the relationship. A man greeting his senior or superior brings the hand with a round sweep towards the ground, as if he should be kneeling there, and lifts it to his breast and head,

implying readiness to receive, understand, and obey commands. Relatives or intimate acquaintances meeting each other after an interval kiss each other on both cheeks. A son or daughter kisses the hand of a parent or aged relative, and the same respectful courtesy is shown towards priests as spiritual fathers. Frequently, a man meeting his friend puts out both hands as if to clasp and kiss his hand with the respect of inferior to superior, but the other is expected to defeat this intention, allowing his fingers to be touched, and by withdrawing his hand to claim the equality of a friend. When one enters a room where others are seated, those assembled rise in token of respect and welcome, this being especially observed in the case of the aged.

Many particular gestures and special actions might be noted. The beggar at the door brings his forefinger across his teeth to prove that he has eaten nothing that day (Am 4⁶).

In friendly explanation, as an act of affectionate persuasion, and as a liberty of familiar friendship, the hand is put under the chin, and the face lifted up, or the beard stroked as Joab did to Amasa (2 S 20⁹). The outstretched arm indicates authority and decision, if the hand is also open and extended (Ex 6⁶); but when the fingers and thumb are drawn together to a cone, it implies a respectful request for permission to speak or interfere (Ac 21⁴⁰).

Naturally, the most characteristic gestures are those where the strongest emotions are called forth or appealed to, as in the dance, in bereavement, and the symbolical gestures and attitudes of Oriental prayer. See further such articles as FOOT, HAND, HEAD.   G. M. MACKIE.

GET, GETTING.—1. The verb to 'get' (of which the parts are *get*, *gat* * or *got*, *gotten* or *got*) is frequently used in the sense of 'go,' generally followed immediately by a personal pronoun. Thus 2 S 4⁷ 'they smote him . . . and gat them away through the plain all night' (וַיֵּלְכוּ דֶּרֶךְ הָעֲרָבָה, RV 'went by the way of the Arabah'). Four times in NT ὕπαγε, the imperat. of ὑπάγω, to 'depart,' is so tr⁴, viz. ὕπαγε Σατανᾶ, 'Get thee hence,† Satan,' Mt 4¹⁰ (Rhem. 'Avant Satan'); and ὕπαγε ὀπίσω μου Σατανᾶ, 'Get thee behind me, Satan,' Mt 16²³, Mk 8³³, Lk 4⁸ (the last omitted by RV after edd.). This idiom is still bolder in earlier versions, as in Tind., Mt 27⁶² 'the hye prestes and pharises got them selves to Pilate'; Lk 22⁴¹ 'And he gate him selfe from them, about a stones cast'; Jn 5¹³ 'For Jesus had gotten him selfe awaye, because that ther was preace of people in the place.'

2. The same form of expression (though the idiom is different, the pron. being now the remote object) is often used when the meaning is 'find' or 'gain.' Sometimes the pers. pron. is expressed in the Heb., sometimes not. Thus Gn 34⁴ 'Get me this damsel to wife' (קַח־לִי); Ex 14¹⁸ 'When I have gotten me honour upon Pharaoh' (בְּהִכָּבְדִי); 2 S 20⁶ 'lest he get him fenced cities' (פֶּן־מָצָא לוֹ); Ec 2⁷ 'I got me servants' (קָנִיתִי עֲבָדִים, RV 'I bought men-servants'); 2⁸ 'I gathered me also silver' (כָּנַסְתִּי לִי); Jer 13¹ 'Go and get thee a linen girdle' (קְנֵה לְךָ, RV 'buy thee'). This remote object is expressed otherwise than by a pers. pron. in 1 Mac 3³ 'So he gat his people great honour' (καὶ ἐπλάτυνεν δόξαν τῷ λαῷ αὐτοῦ).

3. Other passages deserving attention are: Gn 4¹ 'I have gotten a man from the LORD' (קָנִיתִי אִישׁ אֶת־,

---

† This passage has given the phrase 'get thee hence' a meaning in mod. Eng. which it did not always carry. Thus Mk 1⁴⁴ Tind. 'Get the hence and shewe thy silfe to the preste'; Jn 5¹¹ Tind. 'Take up thy beed, and get thee hence'; and Zec 6⁹ AV 'Get you hence, walk to and fro through the earth.'

יהוה, RV 'I have gotten a man with the help of the Lord '*); Wis 10⁸ 'they gat not only this hurt, that they knew not the things which were good' (ἐβλάβησαν, RV 'were disabled'); Sir 13¹¹ 'Smiling upon thee [he] will get out thy secrets' (ἐξετάσει, RV 'will search thee out'); 21¹¹ 'getteth the understanding thereof' (κατακρατεῖ τοῦ ἐννοήματος αὐτοῦ, RV 'becometh master of the intent thereof'); 27¹⁹ 'so hast thou let thy neighbour go, and shalt not get him again' (οὐ θηρεύσεις αὐτόν, RV 'thou wilt not catch him again'); 1 Mac 9³² 'when Bacchides gat knowledge thereof' (ἔγνω, RV 'knew it'); 2 Mac 5⁶ 'But Jason slew his own citizens without mercy, not considering that to get the day of them of his own nation would be a most unhappy day for him' (οὐ συννοῶν τὴν εἰς τοὺς συγγενεῖς εὐημερίαν δυσημερίαν εἶναι τὴν μεγίστην, RV 'that good success against kinsmen is the greatest ill success' †).

Getting is used as a verbal subst. in Gn 31¹⁸ 'the cattle of his getting' (מִקְנֵה קִנְיָנוֹ, Dillm. *das Vieh seines Erwerbes*, 'the cattle of his possession'; Kalisch, 'the cattle of his acquisition'); and in Pr 4⁷ 'with all thy getting, get understanding' (בְּכָל־קִנְיָנְךָ, RV 'with all thou hast gotten': the meaning is not 'whatever thou gettest, get understanding,' but 'by means of all thy gains, get understanding'; cf. Mt 13⁴⁶ 'went and sold all that he had, and bought it'). T. Lever (*Sermons*, 1550, Arber's ed. p. 117) translates Is 56¹¹ 'Unshamefaste dogges, knowynge no measure of gredye gettynge.'   J. HASTINGS.

GETHER (גֶּתֶר).—Named in Gn 10²³, along with Uz, Hul, and Mash, as one of the 'sons of Aram' (in 1 Ch 1¹⁷ simply 'sons of Shem'). The clan of which he is the eponymous founder has not been identified. Dillmann considers that Knobel's explanations (*Völkertafel*, 235 f.) from Arabian genealogies, as well as the attempts of Glaser (*Skizze d. Gesch. u. Geog. Arab.* 421 f.), have failed to yield any acceptable results.

GETHSEMANE (Γεθσημανεί).—A 'plot of ground' (χωρίον, Mt 26³⁶, Mk 14³²), which appears to have been on the Mt. of Olives (Lk 22³⁹) and beyond the ravine of the Kidron (Jn 18¹). The 'garden' or enclosure (κῆπος) belonging to it was the scene of our Lord's Agony. The name (from גַּת 'press' and שֶׁמֶן 'oil') means 'oil-press' (on the form of the name see Dalman, *Gram.* 152, 289 n. 3). Leaving Jerusalem by St. Stephen's gate one comes to the traditional site of Gethsemane, at a distance of almost 50 yards beyond the bridge that spans the Kidron. A stone wall encloses a nearly square

* There are two difficulties: (1) קָנִיתִי 'I have gotten' is evidently meant to explain the name קַיִן Cain. See under CAIN. (2) אֶת־יְהוָה is either simply 'the Lord' (אֶת being the sign of the object), or 'with the Lord' (אֶת being the prep.). The prep. is not elsewhere used with יהוה (yet cf. אֶת־חֲמִי || וְשָׁחַתְמִי Job 26⁴). But the direct object gives so difficult a sense that most versions and commentators prefer the prep., as AV and RV. The LXX has Ἐκτησάμην ἄνθρωπον διὰ τοῦ θεοῦ; O.L., Vulg. *possedi* (*acquisivi*, *procreavi*) *hominem per deum*; Luther, 'Ich habe den Mann, den Herrn'; Wyc. 1382, 'I haue had a man bi God,' 1388, 'Y haue gete a man bi God'; Tind. 'I haue gotten a man of the LORDE'; Cov. 'I haue optyened the man of the LORDE'; Rog. 'I haue obteyned a man of the LORD' (gen.); Gen. 'I haue obteined a man by the Lord' [Gen. marg. That is, according to the Lord's promise, as ch. 3¹⁵; some read, To the Lord, as reioycing for the sonne, whom she wolde offer to the Lord as the first frutes of her birth']; Bish. 'I haue gotten a man of the Lord'; Dou. 'I haue gotten a man through God'; Kautzsch, 'Einen Menschen habe ich erhalten mit Hilfe Jahwes.' See Spurrell, *in loc.*, supplemented by König in *Expos.* 5th Ser. vii. 205 f.

† This passage is referred to by Scrivener (*Camb. Bible*, p. 65 n. 1) as one of the colloquial forms which disfigure the AV Apocrypha, though he admits that it keeps up the verbal play of the Greek. It is, however, no colloquial or other English idiom, it is simply a literal tr. of the Greek. The Gen. Bible is more idiomatic, 'not considering that to have the advantage against his kinsmen is greatest disadvantage,' and it preserves the word-play also.

plot of ground, which contains eight very ancient olive trees. Some cling fondly to the idea that these were actual witnesses of the Agony; others hold that this is precluded by the express statement of Josephus (*BJ* VI. i. 1), that during the siege by Titus all the trees in the neighbourhood of Jerusalem were cut down. Robinson, Thomson, and many other recent explorers doubt the accuracy of the tradition which locates Gethsemane, although it is universally admitted that the real site cannot be far from the traditional one. The tradition in question dates only from the 4th cent., and Robinson may be right in his suggestion that the site of Gethsemane, like that of Calvary, was fixed upon during the visit of Helena to Jerusalem, A.D. 326. Eusebius (*OS²* 248, 18) says that Gethsemane was *at*, Jerome (*ib.* 130, 22) that it was *at the foot of*, the Mt. of Olives. The latter adds that a church had been built over it (see the *Peregrinatio Silviæ*, cf. the testimony of Antoninus Martyr at the end of 6th cent.). The traditional site is objected to on the ground that it is too near the city.

LITERATURE.—Robinson, *BRP²* i. 234 f., 270; Porter, *Handbook*, 177; Thomson, *Land and Book*, ii. 483; Stanley, *Sinai and Palestine*, 415; Andrews, *Life of Our Lord*, 413; Keim, *Jesus of Nazara*, vi. 9 ff.; Conder, *Bible Places* (ed. 1897), p. 204; Lees, *Jerusalem Illustrated*, 136; *SWP* vol. iii. sh. xiii. and Jerusalem volume; *PEFSt* (1887), pp. 151, 159; (1889), p. 176.   C. R. CONDER.

GEUEL (גְּאוּאֵל 'majesty of God').—The Gadite sent as one of the twelve spies, Nu 13¹⁵ P.

GEZER (גֶּזֶר, Γάζερ, Γέζερ, Γάζαρα, Γάζης, Vulg. *Gazer*).—Now Tell Jezer, near the village of Abû Shûsheh and 4 miles W.N.W. of 'Amwâs, the ancient Nicopolis (see Euseb. *Onom. Sac.* p. 254, 14), to the right of the road from Jaffa to Jerusalem. The site, which is marked by blocks of unhewn stone and early pottery, would well repay excavation. Here have been found two inscriptions on a rock, one containing the name ΑΛΚΙΟΥ in Gr. letters, the other גור תחם 'the boundary of Gezer' in Heb. characters of the Maccabæan age. M. Clermont-Ganneau, to whom the discovery was due, suggests that Alkios should be identified with a certain Alkios son of Simon, whose sarcophagus has been found at Lydda, and points out that Tell Jezer is the Mount Gisart of the Crusaders. The inscription may define the Sabbatic limit of the city. Josephus (*Ant.* VIII. vi. 1) places the town on the frontier of the territory of the Philistines; and Strabo (XVI. ii. 29), who calls it Gadaris, states that it had been appropriated by the Jews. In 1 Ch 20⁴ Gezer is given in place of the otherwise unknown Gob of 2 S 21¹⁸ (where, however, the Sept. and Syr. read Gath).

When the Egyptians under the Pharaohs of the 18th dynasty conquered Canaan, Gezer was placed under an Egyptian governor. In the time of the Tel el-Amarna tablets (B.C. 1400) the governor was Yapakhi, and we hear of Gezer (*Gazru*) along with Ashkelon and Lachish sending provisions to Jerusalem. Subsequently, however, Gezer was occupied by the Bedâwi sheikh Labai (who had once been governor of Shunem) and his confederate Malchiel, and it joined in an attack on Ebed-tob, the king of Jerusalem. This was the subject of a charge brought against Labai before the Egyptian Pharaoh. When the Israelites entered Canaan, Horam (Ailam in the Sept.) was king of Gezer; he came to the help of Lachish, but was defeated and slain by Joshua (Jos 10³³ 12¹²). The town was included in the southern border of Ephraim, and was assigned to the Kohathite Levites (Jos 16³ 21²¹); the Israelites, however, failed to capture it, and its Canaanite inhabitants paid tribute to the Ephraimites (Jos 16¹⁰, Jg 1²⁹). A recently discovered inscription of Merenptah, the son and successor of Ramses II. (B.C. 1280), in which mention is made of the Israelites, speaks of Gezer having been taken by the Egyptians (or, according to another possible translation, by the people of Ashkelon). In the reign of Solomon it was again taken by an Egyp. Pharaoh, who handed it over to his daughter, Solomon's wife (1 K 9[16]). Solomon thereupon restored it, as well as the neighbouring Beth-horon, and it henceforth remained in Israelitish possession. Under the name of GAZARA (wh. see), Gezer appears repeatedly during the Maccabæan struggles (1 Mac 4[15] 7[45] 9[52] 13[43. 53] 14[7. 34] 15[28] 16[1], 2 Mac 10[32]). It was then an important stronghold, for whose possession both parties contended strenuously. See, further, Clermont - Ganneau, *Arch. Researches in Pal.* (1896), pp. 224 ff.

A. H. SAYCE.

GHOST.—Like 'ghastly' and 'aghast,' 'ghost' has had an *h* inserted in the course of its history—an Italian affectation, says Earle, and for the most part a toy of the Elizabethan period. The Anglo-Saxon form is *gâst*, the connexion of which with Ger. *geist* is obvious. The Middle-Eng. form is 'goost' and sometimes 'gost.' Wyclif's form is 'goost,' Tindale's 'goost' and rarely 'gost,' the Geneva 'gost,' the Rhemish NT and the AV always spell 'ghost.'

The root of the word, according to Skeat, is the Teut. GIS=Aryan GHIS=to terrify, so that the modern use of the word is as close to the primitive meaning as any other. The sense of 'apparition' or 'spectre,' appears, however, to be later in English usage than that of 'breath' or 'spirit,' so that the derivation is a little uncertain. The range of meaning in older English is considerable.

The principal meanings are : (1) *Breath*, as Bp. Andrewes, *Sermons*, ii. 340, ' Ye see then that it is worth the while to confesse this as it should be confessed. In this wise none can do it but by the Holy Ghost. Otherwise, for an *ore tenus* only, our own ghost will serve well enough.'

(2) The soul or spirit of a living person. Thus Chaucer, *Clerke's Tale*, 972—

' ' ' Nat only, lord, that I am glad,' quod she,
" To doon your lust, but I desyre also
Yow for to serue and plese in my degree
With-outen feynting, and shal euermo.
Ne neuer, for no wele ne no wo,
Ne shal the gost with-in myn herte stente
To loue yow best with al my trewe entente ' ' '

So Spenser, *FQ* II. i. 42—

' Whom when the good Sir Guyon did behold,
His hert gan wexe as starke as marble stone,
And his fresh bloud did frieze with fearefull cold,
That all his sences seemd bereft attone :
At last his mightie ghost gan deepe to grone,
As lion, grudging in his great disdaine.'

(3) It is applied especially to the soul or spirit departing from the body. Thus in 'The Forty-two Articles' of 1553 (Gibson, *The XXXIX Articles*, i. 71), Art. III—'For the bodie laie in the Sepulchre, until the resurrection : but his Ghoste departing from him was with the Ghostes that were in prison, or in helle, and didde preache to the same, as the place of S. Peter doeth testify.' Thence arise the phrases 'breathe out, yield up, give up the ghost,' as Chaucer, *Legend of Good Women*, 886—

' When that he herde the name of Tisbe cryen,
On her he caste his hevy deedly yën,
And doun again, and yeldeth up the gost.'

So *Prioresses Tale*, 1862—

' This holy monk, this abbot, him mene I,
His tonge out-caughte, and took a-wey the greyn,
And he gaf up the goost ful softely.'

And Spenser, *FQ* II. viii. 45—

' He tombling downe on ground,
Breathd out his ghost, which to th' infernall shade
Fast flying, there eternall torment found
For all the sinnes wherewith his lewd life did abound.'

(4) The most frequent application of the word is, however, to the spirit of a dead person, a disembodied spirit. Bp. Hall says (*Works*, ii. 114), ' Herod's conscience told him he had offered an unjust and cruell violence to an innocent, and now hee thinkes that John's ghost haunts him.' Cf. also Mk 6[49] Rhem. ' But they seeing him walking upon the sea, thought it was a ghost, and cried out.' The word is found as early as Chaucer quite in the modern sense, as *Prologue*, 8—

' He was nat pale as a for-pyned (=tormented) goost.'

The application to the Holy Spirit is also very early. Thus Malory, *Morte d'Arthur* (Globe ed.), XIII. viii. 7—'In the midst of this blast entered a sun-beam more clearer by seven times than ever they saw day, and all they were alighted of the grace of the Holy Ghost.' Nor is it always accompanied by the adj. Holy : Chaucer (*Seconde Nonnes Tale*, 328) has—

' But ther is better lyf in other place,
That never shal be lost, ne drede thee nought,
Which Goddes sone us tolde thurgh his grace ;
That fadres sone hath alle thinges wrought ;
The gost, that fro the fader gan procede,
Hath sowled hem, withouten any drede.'

(5) Finally, it should be noticed that the word is sometimes applied to a dead body. Spenser, *FQ* II. viii. 26—

' Palmer, (said he) no knight so rude, I weene,
As to doen outrage to a sleeping ghost.'

Shaks. *II Henry VI.* III. ii. 161—

' See how the blood is settled in his face !
Oft have I seen a timely-parted ghost,
Of ashy semblance, meagre, pale, and bloodless.'

This is held to be the meaning of *Hamlet*, I. iv. 85—

' Still am I call'd, unhand me, gentlemen.
By heaven, I'll make a ghost of him that let's me !'

And Dyce quotes from Hooker's *Amanda* (1653), p. 207—

' What stranger who had seen thy shriv'led skin,
Thy thin, pale, ghastly face, would not have been
Conceited he had seen a ghost i' th' bed,
New risen from the grave, not lately dead ?'

In AV 'ghost' is used only in the phrase 'give up' or 'yield up the ghost,' and in the name 'the Holy Ghost.'

1. The poetic and 'Priestly' word גָּוַע *gâwa'*, which means 'to expire,' 'to perish,' is tr[d] 'give up the ghost' in Gn 25[8. 17] 35[29], Job 3[11] 10[18] 13[19] 14[10], La 1[19] ; and 'yield up the ghost' in Gn 49[33]. This tr[n] is partly due to the Geneva Bible (Gn 35[29] 49[33]), but seems in most places original to AV. There is no reason for so special a tr[n] in those passages ; elsewhere *gâwa'* is tr[d] simply 'die,' except Jos 22[20], Job 34[15], 'perish.' The Heb. רוּחַ *rûah*, 'breath,' 'spirit,' is never tr[d] 'ghost.' But נֶפֶשׁ *nephesh*, 'soul,' is twice so tr[d], Job 11[20] 'their hope shall be as the giving up of the ghost' (מַפַּח־נָפֶשׁ ; AVm 'a puff of breath') ; and Jer 15[9] 'she hath given up the ghost' (נָפְחָה נַפְשָׁהּ). In To 14[11] we find ψυχή tr[d] in the same way, 'he gave up the ghost in the bed' (ἐξέλιπεν [B ἐξέλειπεν] αὐτοῦ ἡ ψυχὴ ἐπὶ τῆς κλίνης). In NT we do not find ψυχή so tr[d], but πνεῦμα twice, Mt 27[50] ' Jesus, when he had cried again with a loud voice, yielded up the ghost' (ἀφῆκε τὸ πνεῦμα ; RV 'yielded up his spirit') ; and Jn 19[30] 'he bowed his head and gave up the ghost' (παρέδωκε τὸ πνεῦμα ; RV 'gave up his spirit'). Though ψυχή is not tr[d] 'ghost,' the verb ἐκψύχω, which occurs three times, is twice (Ac 5[5] 12[23]) tr[d] 'give up the ghost,' and once (Ac 5[10]) 'yield up the ghost.' Similarly ἐκπνέω, which also occurs three times (Mk 15[37. 39], Lk 23[46]), is each time tr[d] 'give up the ghost.' Finally, the phrase ἐν ἐσχάτῃ πνοῇ (lit. as RV 'at the last gasp') is rendered in 2 Mac 3[31] 'give up the ghost.'

2. Wherever πνεῦμα is accompanied with ἅγιον it is tr[d] in AV after all the previous versions 'Holy Ghost' (in 1611 always spelt 'holy Ghost,' which is the more surprising that Rhem. NT has almost always 'Holy Ghost'). When πνεῦμα occurs without ἅγιον, and the reference is to the Holy Ghost, it is tr[d] 'spirit' or 'Spirit.' The RV has a few times, Amer. RV always, replaced 'Holy Ghost' by 'Holy Spirit' ; both have generally accepted 'give up' or 'yield up the ghost.' See articles HOLY SPIRIT and SPIRIT.   J. HASTINGS.

GIAH (גִּיחַ).—Named in the account of Joab's pursuit of Abner, 2 S 2[24], 'the hill of Ammah that lieth before Giah by the way of the wilderness of Gibeon.' Ammah is prob. taken correctly as a proper name, although it cannot be identified. Theod., indeed, tr. it by ὑδραγωγός, 'aqueduct' (so Vulg. *aquœductus*), but this would necessitate the article, הָאֵמָה (cf. Wellh. and Driver, *ad loc.*). Wellh. proposes to eliminate Giah from the text, and for 'גּ מֶרְדַּךְ דֶּרֶךְ גַּיִם עַל־פְּנֵי of MT to substitute עַל־פְּנֵי '3, חֲרֵדָהּ, בְּכִרְדָּף, holding that גַּיִם has arisen out of גַ ח 3 (cf. the LXX Γαί, *i.e.* גַּיְא 'ravine'). It was natural to interpolate a *gai* answering to the preceding 'hill,' and the ח of גַּיִם might readily arise from the ח of חֲרֵדָהּ. This emendation is accepted by Budde (in *SBOT*) and Kittel (in Kautzsch's *AT*).

J. A. SELBIE.

GIANT.—Most peoples have traditions in regard to gigantic men existing in earlier times. Not many decades ago these traditions were supposed to be confirmed by discoveries of remains of prehistoric men of enormous size. But a close scrutiny of the evidence indicates that prehistoric men were not larger than the men now living, and that the difference between the largest men that ever lived and men of normal size is less than used to be thought. Moreover, the giants of the traditions, when we come to study the subject closely, are found to be more or less confused with mythological beings or with ghosts, thus becoming, in a measure, unreal.

There was a time when the biblical accounts of giants were interpreted and coloured by the traditions and supposed historic remains. More lately there is a tendency to interpret them in the light of the unreality that is now assigned to the extra-biblical traditions. These facts are a reason for scanning carefully the biblical evidence and confining ourselves very closely to it.

In our EV three different words are translated giant. In Gn 6⁴ and Nu 13³³ is used the word נְפִילִים (in LXX and Gr. *Enoch* οἱ γίγαντες). See NEPHILIM. This word denotes beings analogous to the demigods of the Greek and Latin mythology. When applied to the giant inhabitants of Pal. (Nu 13³³), it should perhaps be regarded as a figure of speech. The word used in Job 16¹⁴ is *gibbor* (גִּבּוֹר), a mighty man (RVm), a hero, an armed assailant, not a giant. The same word is used in the plur. in Gn 6⁴, apparently as an equivalent for Nephilim, and is tr. in the Sept. γίγαντες; but it is evidently the equivalent of the word 'heroes' as used in mythological legends.

The true Heb. word for giant is different from these. In 2 S 21¹⁶. ¹⁸. ²⁰. ²² is the word *raphah* (רָפָה), tr⁴ giant, and in 1 Ch 20⁴. ⁶. ⁸ is the variant *rapha* (רָפָא). From the same stem, in this variant form, comes the plur. *rĕphaim* (רְפָאִים, also used for the 'shades,' see REPHAIM), and this is the proper equivalent of our Eng. word 'giants.'

Raphah means *to become limp*, to be slack, to be loosened. It often describes the physical and moral condition of one who goes to pieces through fear or discouragement, one who is physically and spiritually relaxed through terror or panic (in *Qal*, Jer 6²⁴ 49²⁴ 50⁴³; *Hithp.*, Jos 18³, Pr 18³ 24¹⁰). Many regard the word *rĕphaim* as the plur. of the gentilic adject. *rĕphai*, Rephaite; but its use indicates that it is rather a common noun in the plur., and it will be so treated in this article.

1. GEOGRAPHICAL DISTRIBUTION.—In David's time, the accounts say, there were *rephaim*, that is to say, giant people, living in Gath, and they mention none elsewhere. The Goliath whom David slew was one of these (1 S 17 *et al.*). So were Ishbi-benob, Saph (in 1 Ch 20⁴ Sippai), Goliath the Gittite (in 1 Ch 20⁵ Lahmi, the brother of Goliath the Gittite), and a man of stature with twenty-four fingers and toes (2 S 21¹⁶⁻²², 1 Ch 20⁴⁻⁸). See each of these names, in its place. Some of these men individually, and all four of them collectively, are said to have been born 'to the *raphah* (in 1 Ch 20⁶. ⁸ *rapha*') in Gath.' Certainly *raphah* is here not a proper name. It is to be tr⁴ 'the giant.' It is to be understood either individu-

ally or collectively. If individually, then probably 'the giant' is the Goliath whom David slew, and the four men here mentioned are his sons. If collectively, then the assertion is that the four were of the breed of the giants that lived at Gath.

Some centuries earlier, just before the conquests by Moses and Joshua, the *rephaim* were more widely distributed. At that time, Og, the king of Bashan, was the only remaining representative 'of those that were left of the *rephaim*' E. of the Jordan (Dt 3¹¹). W. of the Jordan the ANAKIM (wh. see) had their principal seat, perhaps, at Hebron and its vicinity (Nu 13²², Jos 14¹²⁻¹⁵ 15¹³. ¹⁴ 11²¹, Jg 1²⁰); but there were Anakim also in the mountain country of Israel as well as in the mountain country of Judah, and among the Phil. cities near the Mediterranean (Jos 11²¹. ²²). Further, there seem to have been *rephaim* in the forest region near Mount Carmel (Jos 17¹⁵). There are traces, too, of giant occupation, either then or earlier, in such geographical names as the valley of Rephaim (Jos 15⁸ 18¹⁶ etc.), near Jerus., and 'the Avvim,' one of the cities of Benjamin (Jos 18²³). And it is presumable that they occupied yet other localities at this date.

Going back to earlier times, two passages are especially important. In Dt 2¹⁰ᶠ Moses is represented as mentioning, for the encouragement of Israel against the Anakim, several giant peoples that had been dispossessed by other peoples. In Gn 14 we have an account of the several peoples that were attacked by the four kings in their march southward, in the days of Abraham. The peoples mentioned in these two passages are mainly the same, and they are so mentioned as to enable us to locate them geographically. The four kings 'smote Rephaim' (Gn 14⁵), and this region must have been so called because there were *rephaim* then living there, E. of the Jordan, well to the N., the region where Og afterwards reigned. Proceeding S. they smote the Zuzim, apparently the same with the Zamzummim, who occupied territory afterwards held by the Ammonites, and who are said to be *rephaim* (Gn 14⁵, Dt 2²⁰). Still marching S., they reached the Emim, who are also said to be *rephaim*, in the territory afterwards held by Moab (Gn 14⁵, Dt 2¹⁰. ¹¹). Yet farther S., in the country of Seir, they attacked the Horim, who were probably *rephaim*, though this is not expressly stated (Gn 14⁶, Dt 2¹². ²²).

W. of the Jordan, the Avvim were near Gaza at a very early period (Dt 2²³). The *rephaim* are mentioned along with the Kenite, the Hittite, the Perizzite, the Amorite, etc. (Gn 15²⁰), as in the land, apparently, in Abraham's time. The Anakim are not mentioned by name in connexion with this early period, but we are told that 'Sarah died in the city of Arba, which is Hebron, in the land of Canaan' (Gn 23²); and that 'Jacob came to Isaac, his father, to Mamre, the city of the Arba, which is Hebron' (Gn 35²⁷). Evidently, the writer of these statements held that the city was called by the name of Arba in the time of Jacob and of Abraham. It follows that he held that the Anakim were already there, for Arba 'was the great man among the Anakim' (Jos 14¹⁵). And from Nu 13²² it is difficult to avoid the conclusion that it was the Anakim who built Hebron 'seven years before Zoan of Egypt.'

2. HISTORY OF THE GIANT PEOPLES.—If what has been said is true, we are to think of them as widely spread in Pal., on both sides of the Jordan, as early as the time of Abraham. They are expressly said to have preceded the Caphtorite Philistines, the Ammonites, the Moabites, the Edomites, the Israelites; it is not said whether they preceded the Can. peoples. Some affirm them

to have been the aborigines of Palestine. This is not in itself improbable, and it is perhaps confirmed by what we know of their characteristics. In particular, the name Horite is supposed to denote a cave-dweller, and if we regard the Horites as *rephaim*, this is an argument of some weight.

Not all scholars accept the opinion stated above, that the Anakim and other *rephaim* were W. of the Jordan in Abraham's time. There is a theory that these were immigrants from the *rephaim* E. of the Jordan, after the invasion by the four kings; but this lacks confirmation. It is said, further, that the Anakim cannot early have had their seats W. of the Jordan, because the country was then in the possession of other peoples. But, as we shall presently see, the *rephaim* lived among other peoples during most of their known history.

As another objection, one might plausibly say that Arba was the father of Anak, and the three chiefs whom Caleb conquered were sons of Anak, and therefore the Anakite possession dated back only to the generation before the Exodus. But this inference is based entirely on the inexactnesses of translations. Arba is not said to have been the father of Anak, but 'the father of the Anak' (Jos 15[13]), 'the father of the Anok' (Jos 21[11]). The article here makes a difference. Arba is not said to be the father of some person named Anak or Anok, but the father of the Anak stock. This is another way of saying that he was 'the great man among the Anakim' (Jos 14[15]). Again, Sheshai and Ahiman and Talmai are not said to have been the children of a person called Anak, but 'the children of the Anak' (Nu 13[22], Jos 15[14]), 'the three sons of the Anak' (Jg 1[20]). In other words, Arba was thought of as the greatest man commemorated in the traditions of the Anakim, and in that sense the father of the Anakim; and the three chiefs were the greatest living leaders of the Anakim. There is nothing here to disprove the antiquity of the Anakim. See further Moore, *Judges*, p. 24.

The *rephaim* seem to have had strong local attachments. Once in a locality, they remained there, unless they were wholly extirpated. After many centuries Moses, and Joshua, and Jair, and Caleb found Og in the old seats of the Rephaim, and the tribesmen of Arba at the city of Arba, and the Horite still living in Seir, though incorporated among the Edomites. Yet more marked seems to have been the persistence of the Avvim in the Phil. country (Dt 2[23]). The Caphtorim had destroyed them, but they were still there in the time of Joshua (Jos 13[3]), and survived his conquests. Presumably, they are to be identified with the Anakim who were left in Gaza, in Gath, and in Ashdod, the name Anakim being here used generically (Jos 11[22]). Presumably, Goliath and the other giants of David's time came of this stock.

3. THE GIANTS IN THEIR RELATIONS TO OTHER PEOPLES.—The diction of OT, when it speaks of the giant peoples, has a marked peculiarity which is not preserved in the EV; the gentilic name is always used in the plur., not in the sing. as in the case of other peoples. For example, we have 'the Gazite and the Ashdodite, the Ashkelonite, the Gittite, and the Ekronite, and the Avvites' (Jos 13[3]); 'the Hittite, and the Perizzite, and the Rephaites (father, *rephaim*), and the Amorite' (Gn 15[20]). Curiously, the names Caphtorim and Pelishtim follow the same usage with those of the giant peoples, 'the Philistine' never occurring in the singular to denote the people, but only to denote some individual. If the Horites were giants, their name is exceptional, 'the Horite' being the designation commonly used.

This use of language is certainly significant.

Apparently, it shows that the writers of OT regard the giants, not as a group of nationalities or peoples, but simply as a breed of men, existing in several varieties. With this agree statements made concerning the giants at all periods. The Davidic giants, though children of the *raphah*, were politically Philistine and Gittite. Og, though of the breed of the *rephaim*, was politically Amorite (Jos 2[10] etc.). In the time of the conquest, the Anakim around Hebron were politically Amorite; in the time of Abraham, it is probably fair to infer that they were politically Hittite. Giants as they were, and formidable, they maintained their existence only where they became associated with some other race, the other race being always dominant. The case of the Horites, maintaining their position as a people among peoples, is probably to be accounted for by some peculiar turn taken in their relations with Esau and his Hivite connexions by marriage.

4. PECULIARITIES OF THE GIANT RACE.—They were of great stature. Probably, no authentic measurements of men exceed those of the Goliath whom David slew. The Israelites seemed as grasshoppers by the side of the Anakim.

There is no ground in the biblical accounts for inferring that they were monstrous in shape. The six-toed man of David's time must be regarded as exceptional and not typical. The name Avvim may be from a stem that denotes crookedness, physical or moral, but it is insufficient as evidence that the Avvim had distorted bodies. The Anakim are verbally 'men of neck,' and this is commonly interpreted to mean that they were long-necked. But it is quite as likely to mean that they were thick-necked. The name Emim, 'formidable ones,' may indicate that fearsomeness was the principal characteristic of the giants, but their terribleness apparently was due to their size and prowess, and not to anything uncanny about them.

The name Horite is supposed to denote cave-dweller; but even if the *rephaim* were originally cave-dwellers, most of them were certainly not so within the time during which we have information concerning them.

They were a numerous stock. 'A people great and many, and tall as the Anakim,' is a phrase used more than once.

Yet the *rephaim*, as a whole, were inferior to the peoples of normal stature who surrounded them. Individuals among them were leaders—for example, Og, or the three chiefs at Hebron; but these were exceptional. We might infer this from the general history of mankind, but it is better to infer it from the fact given in the Bible, that the *rephaim*, coming in contact with other men, became either extinct or subordinate. Doubtless they were more formidable, however, as fighters in the Amorite or Philistine armies than they would have been by themselves.

5. MENTION IN LATER TIMES.—We have no clear facts concerning the giants later than the time of David. In the LXX of Jer 47[5] we read: 'Ashkelon is cast away, the remnant of the Enakim.' Those who prefer this to the Heb. text find in it proof of a survival of men of the giant breed even to that date, but this is precarious.

Later writers confuse the *rephaim* with the *Nephilim*, speak of their foolishness, and of their bones or other relics as on exhibition at Hebron, or Damascus, or elsewhere (Jth 16[7], Wis 14[6], Sir 16[7] 47[4], Bar 3[26]; Jos. *Ant.* v. ii. 3; Benjamin of Tudela, *Itin.* p. 56). Yet others enlarge upon the biblical statements with the most extraordinary assertions, measurements, and legends.

For **Valley of the Giants** (RV, Vale of Rephaim), Jos 15[8] 18[16], see REPHAIM (VALLEY OF).

LITERATURE.—The older literature of this subject is voluminous. See, for example, Grotius, *De Veritate*, i. 16; Pritchard, *Natural History of Man*, v. 489 ff.; Kurtz, *Die Ehen der Söhne Gottes*, Berlin, 1857; Sennert, *Dissert. Hist. Phil. de Gigantibus*, 1663. See also the article 'Riesen' in Herzog's *RE*; Porter, *Giant Cities of Bashan*, 1860; Lenormant, *Les Origines de l'Histoire*, 1880–1882; Schwally, *ZAW*, 1898, p. 127 ff.

W. J. BEECHER.

GIBBAR (גִּבָּר 'hero').—A family which returned with Zerub. (Ezr 2²⁰). The name is probably an error for Gibeon (גִּבְעוֹן) of Neh 7²⁵. See GENEALOGY.

GIBBETHON (גִּבְּתוֹן 'mound,' 'height').—A town which is mentioned, along with Eltekeh and Baalath, as belonging to the tribe of Dan, and as a Levitical city (Jos 19⁴⁴ 21²³). In the time of the early kings of northern Israel G. was in the hands of the Phil., and was a place of importance. Nadab, king of Israel, was besieging it when he was slain by his successor Baasha; and a quarter of a century later Omri was similarly engaged when he was made king by the army, to succeed Zimri (1 K 15²⁷ 16¹⁵⁻¹⁷). In *Onom. Sac.*² (246, 255) a Gabathon is mentioned 17 miles from Cæsarea. But this is nearly W. of Samaria, and much too far to the north to agree with the biblical notices of G. The Pal. Survey maps identify it with *Kibbiah*, well down the western slope of the mountain country, 840 ft. above the sea, in lat. 31°·58 and long. 35°·1, nearly equidistant from Jerusalem, Shechem, and Joppa. W. J. BEECHER.

GIBEA (גִּבְעָא).—A grandson of Caleb (1 Ch 2⁴⁹). It is now generally admitted that the list of the descendants of Judah through Caleb given in 1 Ch 2⁴²ᶠᶠ. is geographical rather than genealogical, and comprises all the towns lying in the *Negeb* of Judah, to the S. of Hebron (Wellh. *Proleg.* p. 217). G. is probably only a variation in spelling of the more common Gibeah (גִּבְעָה). See GIBEAH 1.

J. F. STENNING.

GIBEAH (גִּבְעָה a 'hill,' as distinct from a 'mountain,' or 'mountainous district' [הַר]).—A careful examination of all the passages in which Gibeah occurs as the name of a place, seems to show that the uncertainty and confusion which have hitherto existed with regard to the actual situation of G. are largely due to two causes. In the first place, the older translators failed in many cases to distinguish between the use of the word as an appellative and its use as a proper name, the result being to multiply the number of the places bearing this name. Secondly, the name itself is so closely allied, both in form and meaning, to that of another well-known spot, viz. Geba (גֶּבַע), that the two have frequently been interchanged, and the difficulties of identification considerably increased. A consideration of these two facts makes it probable that the actual number of places mentioned in the OT under this name (excluding those which are further defined by some additional word) is to be reduced to two.

1. A city of Judah (Jos 15⁵⁷), possibly one of two villages called *Gabaa*, *Gabatha* (Lagarde, *Onomast.* 255. 160). The exact site is unknown, but the context clearly shows that it was situated in the neighbourhood of Maon, Carmel, and Ziph, on the fertile plateau which lies to the S.E. of Hebron (*Hist. Geog.* pp. 306 n., 317).

2. A city of Benjamin (Jg 19¹²ᶠ·), described elsewhere as 'of Benjamin' (1 S 13². ¹⁵ 14¹⁶, cf. Jg 19¹⁴ 'which belongeth to Benjamin'), and 'of the children of Benjamin' (2 S 23²⁹); most probably it is to be identified also with 'G. of Saul' (1 S 11⁴, Is 10²⁹, cf. 1 S 10²⁶), and with 'the hill (RVm Gibeah) of God' (1 S 10⁵).

From the somewhat scanty notices supplied by the historical books of the OT, we gather (*a*) that Gibeah was quite distinct from Geba (1 S 14¹·⁵, Is

10²⁹); (*b*) that it lay to the N. of Jerusalem, close to the main N. road, and S. of Ramah (Jg 19¹²⁻¹⁴); (*c*) that just N. of the town, the main road divided into two branches, one of which led to Bethel, and the other diverged to Geba (Jg 20³¹). The situation of *Tell* (or *Tuleil*) *el-Fûl*, with which Gibeah has been identified by Robinson (*BR*² i. 577–579) exactly fulfils all these requirements. It is the name given to a hill situated about four miles to the N. of Jerusalem, and lying a quarter of a mile to the E. of the main road. *Er-Râm* (Ramah) lies farther to the N., while the main road from Jerusalem divides in two just beyond *Tell el-Fûl*, one branch diverging to the right to *Jeba* (Geba), and the other going northwards to *Beitîn* (Bethel). The writings of Josephus furnish additional proof, not only of the correctness of this identification, but also of the identity of Gibeah and G. of Saul. He relates (*BJ* v. ii. 1) that Titus, while advancing to the siege of Jerusalem, halted for a night at Gophna (*Jufna*), and the following night encamped 'at a place called the Vale of Thorns, near a certain village called Gabath-Saul, which signifies "Hill of Saul," distant from Jerusalem about 30 stadia.'* During the night a legion coming from Emmaus ('*Amwâs*, Nicopolis) joined the main army; the reinforcement had doubtless come up by the road which in the present day joins the northern road just above *Tell el-Fûl*. Cf. also Jerome, *Ep.* 108. 8 (*Opp.* ed. Vallarsi, i. 690), and Robinson, *l.c.*

The town of Gibeah is associated with several striking events in the early history of Israel. (1) It occupies an important position in the second of the two supplementary narratives which conclude the Book of Judges (ch. 19–21). A certain Levite from the hill country of Ephraim is forsaken by his concubine, who flees to her father's house in Beth-lehem-judah. Here she is followed by the Levite, who remains several days in Beth-lehem, enjoying the hospitality of his father-in-law. Despite the entreaties of the latter, they start on the return journey late in the afternoon of the fifth day (19⁸· ⁹), and towards nightfall reach Jebus or Jerusalem. Being unwilling to 'turn aside into the city of a stranger,' the Levite presses on in the hope of reaching either Gibeah or Ramah (v.¹³), and finally spends the night at the former place. Here they are hospitably received by an old man, a sojourner in the place; but during the night the Benjamite inhabitants beset the house, and demand that the Levite be given up to them. The latter, in self-defence, surrenders his concubine to them, and in the morning finds her on the threshold dead from their ill-usage. He then returns to his home, cuts up her body into twelve pieces, and sends them throughout the borders of Israel (19¹⁵⁻³⁰). Ch 20 describes how the Benjamites refuse to surrender the men of Gibeah to the assembled tribes, who in consequence attack Gibeah, and destroy the tribe of Benjamin, with the exception of 600 men. The kernel of the story is undoubtedly historical, but it has been worked over and expanded by 'an author of the age and school of the Chronicler' (Moore, *Judges*, p. 402 ff.). Throughout the narrative the name of the place is given as Gibeah simply, except in 19¹⁴ 20⁴ ('that belongeth to Benjamin'), and in 20¹⁰, where the text wrongly gives 'Geba of B.' (לגבע) for 'Gibeah of B.'; the similarity of the two names has caused the same error elsewhere.

In 20³¹, however, another Gibeah seems to be referred to by the narrator. After twice suffering defeat at the hands of the Benjamites, the men of Israel lay an ambush against Gibeah, and then entice the Benjamites into 'the highways, of

---

* πρός τινι κώμῃ Γαβὰθ Σαοὺλ καλουμένῃ· σημαίνει δὲ τοῦτο λόφον Σαούλου, διέχων ἀπὸ τῶν Ἱεροσολύμων ὅσον ἀπὸ τριάκοντα σταδίων.

which one goeth up to Bethel, and the other to Gibeah, in the field.' From this passage it has been concluded that there was another place called Gibeah in the immediate neighbourhood, which was distinguished by the addition of 'in the field.' But this view is opposed by the accentuation, according to which 'in the field' is parallel to 'in the highways' (so RV). It is evident that Gibeah is a mistake for Geba (*Jeba*), the road to which branches off just N. of *Tell el-Fûl*; Moore thinks it probable that the author had 'no clear conception of the topography' (*Judges*, p. 436).

Again in v.[33] it is stated that the Israelite liers-in-wait 'brake out of their place, even out of Maareh-geba.' AV and RVm give 'even out of the meadow of Gibeah,' their translation being based on that of the Targum. The rendering 'meadow' (for מַעֲרֵה), however, is very questionable, and it has been proposed to follow the Pesh., and render, with a change of the vowel points, 'cave.' The correct reading is doubtless that preserved by one large group of Greek MSS and Jerome, viz. 'from the W. of Gª' (מִמַּעֲרַב לְגֶבַע, cf. Jos 8[9. 12]). See Moore, *Judges*, pp. 437, 438.

(2) From 1 S 10[26] * we learn that Gibeah was the native village of Saul, to which he returned after his election as king; from this time onwards it is frequently called 'G. of Saul.' (The identity of the two places is sufficiently clear from the narrative of 1 S 13 and 14). It was here that Saul, while pursuing his ordinary occupations, heard of the grievous plight of Jabesh-gilead in consequence of the attack of Nahash the Ammonite (11[4]). The occasion foreshadowed by Samuel (10[7]) had now arrived, and Saul, following the promptings of the divine spirit, at once took action. He slew a yoke of oxen, and sent portions of them throughout the borders of Israel, bidding the people follow after him. The summons was promptly obeyed, and by means of a forced march Saul effected the release of Jabesh-gilead. From the account of the war with the Philistines (1 S 13. 14), which occupied the greater part of Saul's reign, Gibeah would seem to have been of considerable strategic importance. The exact sequence of events, however, is not quite clear, chiefly owing to the corruptness of the text, and the confusion which clearly prevails with regard to the two places Geba and Gibeah. According to the more probable view, Saul, with 2000 men, took up his position at Michmash (*Mukhmâs*), on the N. side of the *Wâdy Suweinît*, from which he commanded the heights of Bethel, while Jonathan, with 1000 men, remained at Gibeah, some three miles farther south (13[2]). The signal for revolt was given by Jonathan, who destroyed the pillar † of the Philistines at Gibeah (emending v.[3] 'and the Philistines heard saying, The Hebrews have revolted. And Saul blew the trumpet,' etc.; cf. Driver, *Sam. ad loc.*); the Phil. at once mustered in great force, and marched against the Israelites. Unable to withstand the advance of the enemy, Saul retreated down the eastern passes to Gilgal in the Jordan Valley, while the Philistines seized the deserted camp at Michmash (vv.[4. 5]). For a time the cause of Israel seemed hopeless, but Saul, having collected some 600 men, the remnant of his forces, effected a junction with Jonathan at Gibeah (v.[15] following the LXX; in v.[16] Geba must be a mistake for Gibeah). In the meantime the Philistines overran the country in three directions (for 'the border' [הגבול], v.[18], the LXX has הגבע; we should probably

read הגבעה Gibeah, since it would be meaningless to talk of a company of spoilers starting from Michmash in the direction of Geba, situated on the opposite side of the *Wâdy Suweinît*). Hostilities between the opposing forces were again initiated by Jonathan. On this second occasion, accompanied only by his armour-bearer, he apparently proceeded from Gibeah to Geba, and thence (cf. 14[1] 'that is on yonder side') made his desperate effort against the Philistine garrison at Michmash. The latter, believing, no doubt, that the two warriors were supported by a large force, offered but little resistance, and no fewer than twenty were slain at the first onset (14[14]). The panic caused by this sudden attack rapidly spread throughout the Philistine camp, which soon became the scene of the wildest confusion. The news was conveyed to Saul at Gibeah by his scouts or outposts (v.[16]), and a general onslaught on the terrified Philistines, in which the whole country joined, was successfully carried out. It does not seem, however, that the Israelitish victory on this occasion had more than a temporary effect, for we are told later on that 'there was sore war against the Philistines all the days of Saul' (14[52]).

(3) In the appendix to 2 S (21–24) Gibeah is mentioned as the scene of the tragic incident of the hanging of the seven sons of Saul (2 S 21[1-14]). The famine, which had troubled the land for three years, is declared by J″ to be due to the slaughter of the Gibeonites by Saul, though no such act is recorded in the history of Saul's reign. To appease the wrath of J″, seven descendants of Saul were handed over to the Gibeonites, and hanged by them. See RIZPAH.

(4) Lastly, in the imaginative description of the march of Sennacherib against Jerusalem given by Isaiah (10[28-32]), the Assyrians are represented as advancing in a straight line from the North, undeterred by any obstacle. The prophet depicts the last stages of their victorious advance; the passage of the steep defile of the *Wâdy Suweinît* is secured by despatching a troop in advance to Migron, S. of the pass; the main army is thus enabled to cross in safety, and encamps at Geba; while the villagers of Ramah and Gibeah take refuge in flight (cf. Driver, *Isaiah*, pp. 71, 72). The passage is important as establishing the fact that Geba and Gibeah were two distinct places.

3. There are several place-names compounded with Gibeah (or Gibeath, גִּבְעַת the *st. constr.*), which are translated in the RV text by 'hill,' but given as 'Gibeah' in the margin. These are—

(1) *Gibeath hā'ărālôth* (גִּבְעַת הָעֲרָלוֹת), 'the hill of the foreskins' (Jos 5[3]), between the Jordan and Jericho, so called as the scene of the circumcision, after the passage of the Jordan. See GILGAL.

(2) *Gibeath-Phinehas* (גִּבְעַת פִּינְחָס), 'the hill of P.' in Mt. Ephraim (Jos 24[33]). The exact site is unknown. Conder (*PEF Mem.* ii. 218) follows Schwarz (*HL* p. 118) in identifying it with '*Awertah* near *Nablûs* (Shechem); so apparently G. A. Smith. Guérin (*Judée*, iii. pp. 37, 38; *Samarie*, pp. 106–109), chiefly on the authority of Jerome (*Ep.* i. 888), identifies it with *Jibia*, three miles N. of *Kuryet el-Enab* (so Dillmann).

(3) *Gibeath hammōreh* (גִּ"נ הַמֹּרֶה), 'the hill of Moreh,' usually identified with the modern *Jebel Duby*, a slight eminence on the N. side of the valley above Shunem (*Solam*). On this view, which identifies 'the spring of Harod' (which see) with '*Ain Jālūd*, at the foot of Mt. Gilboa, about half an hour to the E. of Jezreel (*Zer'in*), the camps of Gideon and the Midianites (Jg 7[1]) would occupy much the same position as those taken up at a later period by Saul and the Philistines (1 S 28[4], cf. 29[1]). So G. A. Smith, *Hist. Geog.* p. 397 f.; Stanley, *Sinai and Palestine*, 1856, p. 341 f. Moore, however

---

* 1 S 10[25-27] has been clearly shown by Budde (*Richter und Samuel*, p. 174 f.) to be a harmonistic insertion of the editor; but this fact does not affect the point at issue.

† So Driver, Wellh., Th.; RV gives 'garrison.' The נְצִיב was probably a pillar erected in token of Philistine domination. See Driver, *Sam.* p. 61.

(*Judges*, p. 200 f.), objects that this view is based on the notice in 6³³, which is not from the same source as 7¹ (J), and prefers therefore to place *G. hammōreh* near Shechem (Gn 12⁶, Dt 11³⁰). See MOREH.

(4) *Gibeath ha-Elohim* (הָאֱלֹהִים ''נ), 'the hill of God,' probably the same as Gibeah 2. It was the spot at which Saul, on his return from the city of Samuel, was to meet a band of the prophets (1 S 10⁵). In v.¹⁰ it is called Gibeah, or 'the hill' simply; and as it is stated that there was a garrison (or rather 'pillar') of the Philistines there, it may safely be inferred that it is identical with ' G. of Benjamin' (cf. 13². ³ ; in v.³ we must read Gibeah for Geba).

(5) *Gibeath ha-Hachilah* (1 S 23¹⁹ 26¹). See HACHILAH.

(6) *Gibeath Ammah* (1 S 2²⁴). See AMMAH.

(7) *Gibeath Gareb* (Jer 31³⁹). See GAREB.

J. F. STENNING.

GIBEATH (גִּבְעַת), Jos 18²⁸ = GIBEAH No. 2 (which see). **Gibeathite** (גִּבְעָתִי), 1 Ch 12³, gentilic name from Gibeah (of Benjamin?).

GIBEON (גִּבְעוֹן, Γαβαών).— An ancient city of Canaan belonging to the Hivites * (Jos 9³ᶠ·), and apparently the capital of a small independent state (9¹⁷) ; it was 'a great city, as one of the royal cities . . . greater than Ai' (10²). It was later assigned to the tribe of Benjamin (18²⁵), and eventually made over with its suburbs to the descendants of Aaron (21¹⁷).

The identity of G. with the village of *el-Jîb*, which lies some 5 or 6 miles to the N.W. of Jerusalem, is practically beyond dispute. The modern village still preserves the first part of the older name, while its situation agrees in every respect with the requirements of the history of the OT. Just beyond *Tell el-Fûl* (Gibeah), the main N. road from Jerusalem to *Beitîn* (Bethel) is joined by a branch road leading up from the coast. The latter forms the continuation of the most southerly of the three routes which connect the Jordan Valley with the Maritime Plain (Smith, *HGHL* p. 248 f.) After the Israelites had crossed the Jordan at Gilgal and destroyed Jericho, their most direct means of access to the central plateau lay by the *Wâdy Suweinît*. From Michmash at the head of the valley the way ran almost straight across the tableland to the vale of Aijalon. Now, just before this road leaves the higher ground and descends into the Shephelah, it divides into two, the one branch leading down by the *Wâdy Selman*, the other running in a more northerly direction by way of the two Bethhorons (Smith, *HGHL* p. 210 n. 2). Here, on this open fertile plateau, slightly to the S. of the main road, rises the hill on which the modern village of *el-Jîb* is built, right on the frontier line which traverses the central range to the S. of Bethel. It was this natural pass across Palestine which in early times served as the political border between N. and S. Israel, and it was owing to its position on this frontier that G. acquired so much prominence in the reigns of David and Solomon. A short distance to the E. of the village, at the foot of the hill, there is further a stone tank or reservoir of considerable size, supplied by a spring, which rises in a cave higher up. Thus we find that the physical features of the modern *el-Jîb* correspond in every respect with those of the ancient Gibeon as set forth in the historical books of the OT.

1. We learn from the Bk. of Joshua, that after the destruction of Jericho and Ai by the Israelites the inhabitants of G. devised a scheme by which they hoped to avoid the fate that had befallen

their neighbours. They accordingly despatched an embassy to the Israelite camp at Gilgal for the purpose of misleading the enemy by representing that they were not inhabitants of Canaan, but came from a far distant country. In support of this statement the embassy drew attention to the condition of their provisions and garments, which bore apparent traces of having been brought from a long distance. Their request for an alliance was at once granted by Joshua and the princes, and a covenant ratified between the two peoples. Within three days, however, the trick played by the men of G. was fully exposed, but, on account of the covenant oath, Joshua and the princes of the congregation determined to abide by the alliance, while they condemned the Gibeonites to perpetual service as ' hewers of wood and drawers of water' to all the congregation' (Jos 9³⁻²⁷). Meantime the neighbouring Amorite kings under Adoni-zedek of Jerusalem had combined to resist the forces of Joshua, and as a first step to lay siege to G. An urgent summons for help was sent to the Israelites, to which Joshua promptly responded by making a forced night-march from Gilgal with all his troops. The confederate kings were utterly routed by the Israelites, who pursued the flying foe down the valley of Aijalon as far as Makkedah in the Shephelah. It was on this occasion that, at the prayer of Joshua, ' the sun stayed in the midst of heaven, and hasted not to go down about a whole day' (10¹⁻¹⁴; see BETH-HORON). We learn from 2 S 21¹ᶠ· that the Gibeonites were nearly exterminated by Saul, but no details are supplied in the narrative of his reign. Reparation was made by David through the sacrifice of seven of Saul's descendants.

2. We next hear of Gibeon at the beginning of David's reign, when he was as yet king of Judah only, and was still opposed by Ishbosheth the son of Saul. During the struggle for supremacy two bodies of troops, under their respective generals,— Joab the son of Zeruiah and Abner the son of Ner, —met, as if by agreement, on the frontier at Gibeon. The battle went in favour of David's men, and in the subsequent flight of Abner the latter slew Asahel, the younger brother of Joab (2 S 2¹²⁻³²). The story clearly belongs to the older narrative (J¹) of the books of Samuel, and is undoubtedly genuine, though vv.¹⁴⁻¹⁶ seem to interrupt the main narrative. These verses describe the mortal combat that took place between the 12 champions of each party. The name given to the spot, *Helkath-hazzûrim* (חֶלְקַת הַצֻּרִים ' the field of sword-edges'), has probably been more correctly preserved in the LXX (Μερὶς τῶν ἐπιβούλων, *i.e.* הַצֹּדִים ' ח ' the field of the liers in wait' ; cf. Driver, *in loc.*), and should be transliterated *Helkath-hazzôdim*. The ' pool of Gibeon' here mentioned (v.¹³) is doubtless the reservoir referred to above. Similarly, in Jer 41¹¹ᶠ· Johanan the son of Kareah is stated to have delivered the captives of Mizpah from the hands of Ishmael the son of Nethaniah, ' by the great waters that are in Gibeon.' It was at this spring also, according to Josephus (*Ant.* v. i. 17), that Joshua surprised the five kings of the Amorites when they were besieging Gibeon.

3. Owing to the great similarity between the two names (see GEBA, GIBEAH), *Geba* seems to have been substituted for *Gibeon* in 2 S 5²⁵. The parallel passage (1 Ch 14¹⁶) gives *Gibeon*, and this reading is also supported by the LXX and by Is 28²¹, which connects Gibeon with Perazim as in 2 S 5¹⁷⁻²⁵. Further, the Philistines were encamped in the valley of Rephaim to the W. of Jerusalem (Smith, *HGHL* p. 218, by a *lapsus calami* or a printer's error, places the valley S.E. of Jerusalem ; it is correctly placed in the map, Plate IV.), while David was advancing from the S., when com-

---

* According to 2 S 21² the Gibeonites were 'of the remnant of the Amorites.'

manded to 'make a circuit behind them' (v.[23]). His attack therefore *from Gibeon* to the N.W. of Jerusalem suits the requirements of the context ; Geba was too far to the E.

4. The rebellion of Absalom, which culminated in his death, was quickly followed by an outbreak on the part of the men of Israel under one Sheba the son of Bichri (2 S 20[1f.]). The task of suppressing the revolt was at first assigned to Amasa, but owing to his dilatoriness Abishai * was also sent in pursuit. The latter was accompanied by Joab, and the two parties of David's troops met 'at the great stone which is in G.' (20[8]). Not suspecting any evil, Amasa advanced to salute Joab, and was treacherously slain by him. The 'great stone of G.' is not mentioned elsewhere ; it was probably a pillar or cairn of stones such as we frequently find in connexion with the OT sanctuaries, *e.g.* at Mizpah, Bethel, Gilgal (cf. W. R. Smith, *RS* 186 f.).

5. It was, however, as the site of a *bāmāh*, or 'high place,' that G. was especially famous. At this sanctuary, because it was 'the great high place' (הַבָּמָה הַגְּדוֹלָה), Solomon inaugurated his reign by offering a thousand burnt-offerings, and received the divine blessing in a dream by night (1 K 3[1f.]). It is true that, according to 2 Ch 1[3], G. is represented as containing the 'Tent of Meeting of God' as well as the brazen altar ; but this statement would seem to have no other foundation than the desire of the Chronicler to reconcile the action of the young king and its approval by J″ with the enactments of the later priestly legislation (cf. Wellhausen, *Proleg.*[4] p. 182 f.). The earlier history knows nothing of the presence of the Tent of Meeting at G. (according to 1 S 1[9] 3[3] it was already replaced by a temple at Shiloh ; 1 S 2[22b] is omitted in LXX, and is clearly a later addition ; so Driver, Budde, Wellhausen, Klost.), while 1 K 8[1f.] clearly places it, together with the ark of the covenant, 'in the city of David, which is Zion.'

'Men of G.' are mentioned as among those 'which came up at the first,' *i.e.* who returned from Babylon under Zerubbabel (Neh 7[25] ; in the corresponding list of Ezra 2[20] Gibbar is probably a mistake), and also as taking part in the repairing of the wall of Jerusalem under Nehemiah (Neh 3[7]).

Lastly, Gibeon is mentioned by Josephus (*BJ* II. xix. 1) as the place where Cestius Gallus encamped on his march from Antipatris to Jerusalem, after he had fired the town of Lydda (Διὰ Βαιθωρὼν ἀναβὰς στρατοπεδεύεται κατά τινα χῶρον Γαβαὼ καλούμενον, ἀπέχοντα τῶν Ἱεροσολύμων πεντήκοντα σταδίους ; elsewhere he puts the distance at 40 stadia). See Robinson, *BRP*[2] pp. 454–57 ; Guérin, *Judée*, i. pp. 385–91.   J. F. STENNING.

GIDDALTI (גִּדַּלְתִּי 'I magnify [God]').—A son of Heman, 1 Ch 25[4. 29].†

GIDDEL (גִּדֵּל 'very great').—**1.** The eponym of a family of Nethinim, Ezr 2[47] = Neh 7[49], called in 1 Es 5[30] **Cathua**. **2.** The eponym of a family of 'Solomon's servants,' Ezr 2[56] = Neh 7[58], called in 1 Es 5[33] **Isdael**.

GIDEON (גִּדְעוֹן ?=*feller, hewer*), also called Jerubbaal (יְרֻבַּעַל Jg 6[32] etc.) and Jerubbesheth (יְרֻבֶּשֶׁת 2 S 11[21]), son of Joash, of the clan of Abiezer in the tribe of Manasseh, a native of Ophrah ;‡ deliverer of Israel from the Midianites (Jg 6–8). The nomad

---

Arabs of the Syrian and Arabian desert had invaded the central district of Palestine. They must have entered it by the only natural approaches from the Jordan Valley, the Wady Fâr'a, which leads into the neighbourhood of Shechem, and the Nahr Jalûd, which opens on to the plain of Jezreel. The scene of the invasion and conflict lay in this region. Manasseh and Ephraim were the principal sufferers ; accordingly a Manassite is the hero of the deliverance, and Ephraimites take part in completing it (7[24-8][3]).

On one of their marauding expeditions the Midianites had murdered Gideon's brothers at Tabor (8[18]) ;* personal revenge, therefore, was one of the motives which instigated his action (8[4-21]). National interests, however, were superadded. According to one ancient account, Gideon was called by an angel of the Lord to save Israel from the hand of Midian (6[11-24]). The angel of J″, *i.e.* J″ Himself in the form of an angel (vv.[16. 23]), appears under the holy tree of Ophrah. He summons Gideon to the task of deliverance. The meal which is offered to the pilgrim stranger is miraculously consumed, and the angel disappears. Gideon, convinced by the miracle, builds an altar to J″-shalom.†

There follows what seems to be a second version of the call of Gideon (6[25-32]). He is bidden destroy the village altar of Baal, and the sacred post beside it (*ashērah*), erect an altar to J″, and offer a bullock.‡ The people of Ophrah are incensed at the destruction of their holy place, and threaten Gideon with death. His father rescues him by a witty taunt, which secures for Gideon the name Jerubbaal.§

After this Gideon collects the men of his clan Abiezer (v.[34]), and encamps with them by the spring of Harod, on the S.E. edge of the plain of Jezreel, near the Midianite army (7[1]).‖ He pays a night visit to the enemy's camp, and overhears the telling of a dream, which encourages him to act at once (7[9-15]). He skilfully posts his men under cover of night ; the alarm is given ; the camp is thrown into a panic, and the Midianites break up in flight towards the Jordan (vv.[18-22]).¶ There are clearly two accounts of the subsequent course of events. According to one (7[24-8][3]), Gideon summons Ephraim to cut off the flight of the

---

* Mt. Tabor is rather remote from the topography of the narrative. Tabor by Bethel (1 S 10[3]) is nearer Shechem. Moore suggests מִבְּבוֹר (cf. 9[37]), altered to תבור to suit 6[33] : Budde תבן (9[50]).

† In v.[16a] omit יהוה, so Budde. V.[17b] prob. editorial addition, anticipating v.[21f]. V.[20] is perhaps secondary ; the narrative does not imply that G. intended to offer a sacrifice. V.[22a] editorial, anticipates G.'s recognition of the angel. With this § cf. Gn 18[1ff.] J, and Jg 13[2-23]. This § is ascribed by some critics to J.

‡ In v.[25] the words 'bullock, even the second bullock of seven years old,' are corrupt and ungrammatical. פר השׁני and פר השׁור are doublets.

§ The name cannot='one who strives with Baal,' as the text would ingeniously suggest ; but 'Baal strives,' Baal being a name for J″, used without offence in early times ; cf. Eshbaal, Meribaal, etc. But Jerubbaal should prob. be written Jerubaal ='Baal (*i.e.* J″) founds,' cf. Jeruel, Jeremiah (Wellh. *Text d. B. Sam.* p. 31. So Bu., Moore). In v.[31] 'he that will plead . . . morning' interrupts the condition. cl. ; 'because one hath broken down his altar' is repeated from v.[32] ; both should be struck out as insertions. This § is attributed to E.

‖ The account (7[2-8]) of the test by which Gideon's large army was reduced to 300 belongs to some later tradition. It is obviously connected with 6[35] ; but this verse is inconsistent with 7[23], and neither can be original. At end of 7[5] note LXX A+ μετασπάσεις αὐτὸν καθ᾽ αὐτόν. In v.[6] 'putting their hand to their mouth' is a gloss ; it should come at the end of the verse.

¶ This paragraph has been a good deal altered by editors. Two versions of Gideon's stratagem seem to have been combined. In the one version the 300 are armed with pitchers and torches ; in the other, with trumpets only. The text has been greatly confused by harmonizing additions ; see the commentaries. In v.[20] the word 'a sword,' RVm, is prob. a gloss. In v.[22b] the two narratives are combined again in describing the direction of the flight.

---

* In v.[6] *Joab* is read instead of *Abishai* by Then., Wellh., and Driver, but Budde defends the MT. See JOAB.

† On the extraordinary conglomeration of names in this verse and the inferences that have been drawn therefrom, see Ewald, *Lehrbuch*, § 274*b* ; W. R. Smith, *OTJC*[2] 143 n., and notes, *ad loc.*, in Haupt's *Sacred Bks. of OT* (by Kittel), and in Kautzsch's *AT*.

‡ Site not identified. Gideon's home must have been near Shechem (ch. 9), and exposed to the Midianite inroads (6[11]).

Midianites at the Jordan ford. The movement is successful, and the Ephraimites capture and slay the two princes Oreb and Zeeb.* In the pride of their success, the Ephraimites quarrel with Gideon for not having called in their assistance earlier. But Gideon appeases their jealousy by a shrewd speech : 'Is not the gleaning of Ephraim better than the vintage of Abiezer?' This certainly looks as if the victory were won, and the 'vintage' over : the Ephraimites had completed the work of Gideon on the W. side of the Jordan crossing. In the other narrative, however (8⁴⁻²¹), we find Gideon in hard pursuit, with his 300, on the E. of Jordan. So far from having won a victory, the chances of success seem so unlikely that the people of Succoth and Penuel treat the pursuers with mockery, and refuse provisions for the wearied troops. At length, however, Gideon reaches the place where the Midianites are encamped, takes them by surprise, captures the two kings, Zebah and Zalmunna,† and returns in triumph, punishing Succoth and Penuel on the way. He then kills the two kings with his own hand, in revenge for their murder of his brothers. The divergence of the two accounts is apparent. An attempt to combine them can be made, as is done, e.g., by Kittel.‡ He regards the exploit of Ephraim at the ford as merely an episode in the pursuit, which is continued by Gideon and his men on the E. side of the river, and overcomes the difficulty of 8¹⁻³ by supposing these verses to be merely an imitation of 12¹⁻³. It seems, however, much more likely that we have in 8⁴⁻²¹ clearly a very ancient and homogeneous fragment, a narrative of the pursuit and final defeat parallel to 7²⁴⁻8³.§ Whether 8⁴⁻²¹ is a direct continuation of 7⁹⁻²² or not, is difficult to say. It implies some account of a successful rout of the Midianites, but not necessarily that given in 7⁹⁻²². Perhaps we have here an ancient fragment, of which the beginning has been lost.‖ The Midianites triumphantly overthrown, Gideon's grateful countrymen offer to make him king. He declines ; but asks for the golden earrings taken in the spoil. With these he makes an *ephod, i.e.* apparently an image of J", *overlaid* with metal,¶ and sets it up in his house at Ophrah (8²⁴⁻²⁷ᵃˣ in the main). The judgment of a later age condemned the action, and saw in it the cause of subsequent disaster (v.²⁷ᵇ⁄₃ᵇ). The usual formula of the editor brings the story to a close (v.²⁸). The account of Gideon's family, the birth of Abimelech, and Gideon's death and burial (vv.³⁰⁻³²), seems to come from the hand of the final editor, who was familiar with P in Genesis,** and intended these verses to form a connecting link with the story of Abimelech in ch. 9. The remaining vv.³³⁻³⁵ belong to the Deuteronomic framework of the Book of Judges. The story of Gideon is told in an extremely complicated narrative. Two main documents can be traced, but these have been so interwoven both before and after the Deuteron. redaction of Judges, that the analysis in detail must be regarded more as a critical experiment than as possessing any degree of certainty. In this article the two main narratives have been followed, and secondary elements noticed chiefly in footnotes.   G. A. COOKE.

* It is interesting to note that the powerful tribe of Bedawîn, the Beni ʿAdwân, who range over the S.E. side of Jordan, still call their chief by the hereditary title of Dhiab=Zeeb=wolf.
† Apparently intended to mean *Victim* and *Protection withheld.* But the latter name is prob. compounded with צלם, *Ṣalm,* name of a deity, cf. צלמשזב on Aram. inscr., *CIS* cxiii, cxiv.
‡ *Gesch. d. Hebr.* ii. p. 72. The attempt is also made in the text by insertion of the words 'beyond Jordan' at end of 7²⁵.
§ The number 300 is common to both accounts.
‖ So Kautzsch, *Heil. Schr.* p. 263.
¶ Cf. 17⁵, 1 S 21⁹, Hos 3⁴ ; W. R. Smith, *OTJC*² p. 241. See full discussion in art. EPHOD, No. 2, vol. i. p. 725 f.
** V.³⁰ cf. Gn 46²⁶, Ex 1⁵ cf. Gn 35¹¹ P ; v.³² cf. Gn 25⁸ 15¹⁵ P.

GIDEONI (גִּדְעֹנִי 'my cutter down').—Father of Abidan, prince of Benj., Nu 1¹¹ 2²² 7⁶⁰· ⁶⁵ 10²⁴ P.

GIDOM (גִּדְעֹם).—The limit of the pursuit of Benjamin by the other tribes, Jg 20⁴⁵. Possibly the word is not a proper name, but may be read as an infinitive, 'till they cut them off' (Moore, *ad loc.*). No place of the name of Gidom is mentioned elsewhere. LXX B has Γεδάν, A Γαλααδ (Gilead). Another variant is Gibeah or Geba.

GIER EAGLE ('gier' is the same as the German *Geier,* 'vulture,' 'hawk') is trⁿ in AV of רָחָם (*rāḥām*) in Lv 11¹⁸ and Dt 14¹⁷, in both of which passages RV has 'vulture' (Driver more specifically ' carrion vulture'). RV gives 'gier eagle' also as trⁿ of פֶּרֶם (*pereṣ*) in Dt 14¹², where AV has 'ossifrage' (lit. 'bone breaker'). The *pereṣ* is the bearded vulture or *Lämmergeier,* 'the largest and most magnificent of the vulture tribe' (quoted by Driver, *Deut.* p. 162, from Tristram, *Nat. Hist. of Bible,* p. 171). The name of the *rāḥām* is literally preserved in the Arab. *rakham,* the *Pharaoh's Hen, Neophron percnopterus.*

The adult *rakham* has the front of the head and the upper part of the throat and cere naked, and of a bright lemon-yellow. The plumage is of a dirty white, except the quill feathers, which are of a greyish black. Its appearance when soaring is very striking and beautiful. It is the universal scavenger of Egyptian cities. It is found in great abundance also in Palestine and Syria. See EAGLE.   G. E. POST.

GIFT.—This, or the similar term **present**, is used to tr. a variety of Heb. and Gr. words, the principal of which are the following :—

1. מִנְחָה Gn 32¹³ 33¹⁰ (parallel to בְּרָכָה, lit. 'blessing' in 33¹¹ ; cf. 1 S 30²⁶, 2 K 18³¹, Is 36¹⁶), esp. of a gift offered by way of homage, *e.g.* 1 S 10²⁷, Ps 45¹² (cf. the 'gifts' presented by the Magi, Mt 2¹¹), or tribute, Jg 3¹⁵· ¹⁷ᵗ·, 2 S 8²· ⁶, 1 K 4²¹ [Heb. 5¹], 1 Ch 18², 2 Ch 26⁸ 32²³ (cf. אֶשְׁכָּר of Ps 72¹⁰, Ezk 27¹⁵). *Minḥâh* used also of a gift (offering) to God, Gn 4⁴, 1 S 26¹⁹, Mal 3⁴ etc., and in Ezk and P is a technical term for the 'meal-offering,' Lv 2¹ff. and oft., Ezk 46²⁰ etc. The NT equivalent is δῶρον, *e.g.* Mt 2¹¹ 5²³ 8⁴ 23¹⁸, He 5¹ 8³ 9⁹. δῶρον also answers in the LXX to קָרְבָּן (*ḳorbān*), which in Ezk 20²⁸ 40⁴³ and frequently in Lv and Nu (but only by P) is used for an 'oblation.' See art. CORBAN for a full account of the meaning of 'gift' in such passages as Mt 15⁵, Mk 7¹¹.

2. מַשְׂאֵת (pl. מַשְׂאוֹת) is the word used of the 'mess' which Joseph gave to his brethren Gn 43³⁴, which David sent to Uriah 2 S 11⁸, of the 'gifts' which Ahasuerus sent upon the occasion of his feast Est 2¹⁸, and of the ritual offerings referred to in 2 Ch 24⁶· ⁹ and Ezk 20⁴⁰. It is used in Jer 40⁵, along with the similar term אֲרֻחָה of the 'victuals' (RVm 'allowance') and 'present' which Jeremiah received from Nebuzar-adan. An allowance (אֲרֻחָה) of the same kind was given to the captive king Jehoiachin, 2 K 25³⁰=Jer 52³⁴. The 'exactions of wheat' (מַשְׂאַת־בַּר) of Am 5¹¹ are 'the presents which the poor *fellahin* had to offer to the grasping aristocrats out of the hard-won produce of their toil' (Driver, *ad loc.*).

3. מַתָּן (from נָתַן 'give'), מַתָּנָה (in Dn 2⁶· ⁴⁸ 5¹⁷ Aram. מַתְּנָא), מַתַּת (a by-form found only in 1 K 13⁷, Pr 25¹⁴, Ec 3¹³ 5¹⁸, Ezk 46⁵· ¹¹). This is the most general term for 'gift.' It is used in Gn 24⁵³ and 34¹² of the present given to a bride in addition to the 'dowry' (*i.e.* purchase price, מֹהַר) paid to her relatives ; in Gn 25⁶ of the portions settled by Abraham on the children of his concubines (cf. the action of Jehoshaphat, 2 Ch 21³) ; of gifts to the sanctuary or to a deity, Ex 28³⁸, Nu 18¹¹, Dt 16¹⁷, Ezk 20²⁶ (in this last of the sacrifice of children) ;

in Ps 68¹⁸ * of 'gifts' in token of homage; in Pr 15²⁷ Ec 7⁷ of 'gifts' intended by way of bribe; in Dn 2⁶·⁴⁸ 5¹⁷ of the 'gifts' of Nebuchadnezzar and Belshazzar.

4. שֹׁחַד. This always (even in 1 K 15¹⁹, 2 K 16⁸ practically) means a 'bribe.' The taking of bribes by those appointed to dispense justice is forbidden in Ex 23⁸ (repeated in Dt 16¹⁹), and is frequently alluded to in OT, e.g. Dt 10¹⁷ 27²⁵, Is 1²³ 5²³ 33¹⁵, Mic 3¹¹, Ezk 22¹², Ps 15⁵, Pr 17³³. 'It blindeth them that have sight' (פִּקְחִים, Ex 23⁸; or 'the eyes of the wise,' עֵינֵי חֲכָמִים Dt 16¹⁹), and 'perverteth the words of the righteous.'

5. נִדֶּה (Baer נֵדֶה) and נָדָן each occur only in Ezk 16³³ of a 'gift' in the sense of the hire of a harlot. The ordinary term for this is אֶתְנַן, which occurs in the same context, Ezk 16³¹·³⁴ (cf. Dt 23¹⁹, Is 23¹⁷f., Hos 9¹, Mic 1⁷).

In NT, while δῶρον and δόμα have generally a material sense, δωρεά (once in Jn, 4 times in Ac, 5 times in Paul, once in He) appears always to be used of a 'gift' belonging to the spiritual or supernatural order. The 'gifts' (AV 'offerings,' RV ἀναθήματα) to which the attention of Jesus was called (Lk 21⁵) would be such as Josephus (BJ v. v. 4) describes, most of which had been presented to the temple by Herod. The Greek word in the same sense occurs (only) in 2 Mac 9¹⁶ (cf. for the *idea* 3³ and 3 Mac 3¹⁷). For the gifts (χαρίσματα) of the early Church, see CHURCH, pp. 427 f., 434 f.

The above analysis will show the variety of occasions upon which a 'gift' might be offered and the variety of forms it might take amongst Orientals. It had its place in their dealings both with their fellow-men and with their God or gods. One did not come before prophet (1 S 9⁷) or king (1 K 10¹⁰) or God (Ex 23¹⁵) with empty hands. The English words 'gift' and 'present' are apt, indeed, to convey an idea of spontaneity about the transaction which was generally absent. The 'present' of Ehud to Eglon (Jg 3¹⁷ff.) was really tribute, belonging to the same category as that offered by Jehu to Shalmaneser (see Moore on Jg 3¹⁷). It is very important also to remember that while a man might offer a 'present' to his bride-elect, the 'dowry' (מֹהַר) was not a 'gift' but a *price* paid to the family of the bride as compensation for the loss of her services (W. R. Smith, *Kinship and Marriage in Early Arabia*, 78 f.). The *mōhar* might consist of money (Gn 34¹², Ex 22¹⁵, Dt 22²⁹), of personal service (Gn 29²⁰·²⁷), or of military services (Jos 15¹⁶, Jg 1¹³, 1 S 17²⁵ 18²⁴, 2 S 3¹⁴). From Dt 22²⁹ we may probably infer that an average *mōhar* was 50 shekels of silver (see Driver, *ad loc.*)

So firmly established is the custom in the East of giving a present upon certain occasions that the latter is demanded as a right. Lane (*Modern Egyptians*, Gardner's ed. p. 168) mentions that while male servants at Cairo are paid very small wages (from four to eight shillings a month), they receive many presents from their master as well as from his visitors and from the tradespeople with whom he deals. An Oriental servant, on quitting his master's service, always expects not only his wages but a present as well, in token of friendship and satisfaction. This rule holds good from the lowest menials up to the highest officials. (For interesting examples see Trumbull, *Oriental Social Life*, 327 ff.). This practice may throw light upon the asking (not 'borrowing') by the Israelites of

jewels of gold and silver, etc., from the Egyptians (Ex 11² 12³⁵), although it is more than doubtful whether it accounts for the possession by the people of such stores of gold as are said to have been used in the construction of the Tabernacle of the Priestly Code.

Many of the usages connected with 'gifts' cluster round marriage. Abraham's servant gave a present to Rebekah when he went to woo her on behalf of Isaac (Gn 24²²). After the conclusion of a marriage contract, Lane tells us, presents are expected by various functionaries connected with the different families. Presents are sent to the bridegroom's house by his friends and by all who are invited to the wedding. The bride's presents, including her trousseau, are sometimes borne in procession to her home in advance of her going to the house of her husband, or they are borne before her upon that occasion (Trumbull, *op. cit.* 44). At his first interview with his bride after the marriage ceremony, the bridegroom makes her a present of money, which is called 'the price of the uncovering of the face.' A marriage-portion (שִׁלֻּחִים) might be given to the bridegroom by the father of the bride (1 K 9¹⁶ Pharaoh and Solomon, cf. Jg 1¹⁴f. Caleb and Othniel).

In the East friends frequently send presents to one another, but no pretence is ever made that a *quid pro quo* is not expected. David was as little disinterested when he sent a 'present' to the elders of Judah (1 S 30²⁶) as Ephron the Hittite was sincere in his offer to give the cave of Machpelah *gratis* to Abraham (Gn 23¹¹). The 'gift' expected from Nabal (1 S 25⁸) was really a species of blackmail.

The power of a gift to propitiate one has always been recognized. Jacob made sure of appeasing Esau by the present he sent before him (Gn 32²⁰). The same notion was transferred to one's dealings with God, δῶρα θεοὺς πείθει, δῶρ' αἰδοίους βασιλῆας (Hes. *ap.* Plat. *Rep.* 390 E). Gifts were offered in homage to God (Mal 1³), or to procure His favour or support. A prayer would often take the form of a conditional vow, 'If J'' will be with me, I will offer so and so to Him' (*e.g.* Jg 11³⁰ Jephthah, Gn 28²⁰ff. Jacob). The notion of propitiating the Deity by a gift comes out in David's words to Saul, 'If J'' hath stirred thee up against me, let him be gratified by an oblation,' 1 S 26¹⁹. It is true at the same time that the 'gift theory' of sacrifice does not furnish an adequate explanation of all the facts connected with even the ordinary oblations, much less with the holocaust, and least of all with human sacrifice (cf. W. R. Smith, *RS* 375).

The blinding effect of a 'gift' upon the administrators of justice is described in the above citations, Ex 23⁸, Dt 16¹⁹. Bribery of judges has always been common in the East. Lane (*Modern Egyptians*, p. 103 ff.) gives a remarkable instance of its occurrence in the court of the Ḳâḍi at Cairo. Felix expected a bribe from St. Paul, Ac 24²⁶.

A 'gift' in OT times sometimes took the form of sending 'portions' (מָנוֹת) from a feast to friends or to the poor, Est 9¹⁹·²², Neh 8¹⁰·¹² (cf. Rev 11¹⁰). The most honoured of the guests present received the largest and finest portion (Gn 43³⁴, 1 S 1⁴ 9²³; cf. *Iliad*, vii. 321, viii. 162, xii. 310; *Odyssey*, iv. 65 f., xiv. 437; Diod. v. 28).

In the NT we find the Philippians singled out for commendation for the 'gift' (δόμα) which they sent once and again to St. Paul's need (Ph 4¹⁶f.).

---

* In Eph 4⁸, as is well known, St. Paul gives a peculiar turn to this passage, his ἔδωκεν δόματα τοῖς ἀνθρώποις corresponding as little to the LXX ἔλαβες δόματα ἐν ἀνθρώπῳ as to the MT לָקַחְתָּ מַתָּנוֹת בָּאָדָם. This is not the place to examine the legitimacy or the motives of the apostle's procedure. A full discussion of the whole question will be found in Meyer, *ad. loc.* (cf. Driver, *Expositor*, Jan. 1889, p. 20 ff.). See also art. QUOTATIONS.

LITERATURE.—Lane, *Modern Egyptians* (Index, *s.* 'Presents'); W. R. Smith, *RS* 162, 328 ff., 365, 373 ff., 440 f.; Benzinger, *Heb. Arch.* 139, 436 f., 433 f.; Trumbull, *Studies in Oriental Social Life*, 22, 35, 44, 319 ff.; Schürer, *HJP* (Index, *s.* 'Gifts'); cf. also art. on 'Giving' by G. M. Mackie in *Expos. Times*, 1898, ix. 367 ff.

J. A. SELBIE.

GIHON (גִּיחוֹן, Γηών, *Gehon*).—One of the four rivers of Paradise (Gn 2¹³). If Eden is Edin, the 'Plain' of Babylonia, we must look for the Gihon in one of the rivers which in early days flowed into what the Babylonians called 'the salt river,' or Persian Gulf, close to the garden of Eridu, where grew the sacred tree of Bab. tradition. As two of the rivers were the Tigris and the Euphrates, our choice of the other two is limited. The G. compassed 'the whole land of Cush,' the Kassi or Kassites of the cuneiform inscriptions, whose original seat was in W. Elam, from whence they descended into Chaldæa, and there founded a dynasty of kings. The G. would seem, therefore, to have been the Kerkhah of modern maps (see EDEN). In Jer 2¹⁸ the Sept. substitutes Gihon (Γηών) for Sihor, the Nile, in consequence of a belief that had arisen among the Jews that the Cush of Gn 2¹³ was the African Ethiopia (see note *ad loc.* in Streane, *Double Text of Jeremiah*). In Sir 24²⁷ the Gihon is introduced metaphorically into a description of wisdom.

A. H. SAYCE.

GIHON (גִּיחוֹן).—A spring near Jerusalem (1 K 1³³. ³⁸. ⁴⁵). Hezekiah 'stopped the upper spring of the waters of Gihon and brought them straight down on the west side of the city of David' (2 Ch 32³⁰). Manasseh 'built an outer wall to the city of David, on the west side of Gihon, in the [torrent] valley' (2 Ch 33¹⁴). These indications suffice to show that Gihon was in the Kidron ravine. The name ('bursting forth') and the notice of the aqueduct (see SILOAM) show that the spring now called the 'Virgin's Fountain' is intended. See BETHESDA, ENROGEL.

LITERATURE.—Robinson, *BRP²* i. 239, 345 (locates Gihon to the *west* not *east* of Jerusalem); Baedeker-Socin, *Palest.* 101; Guthe, *ZDPV*, 1882, p. 359 ff.; Sayce, *HCM* 381 ff.

C. R. CONDER.

GILALAI (גִּלֲלָי).—A Levitical musician (Neh 12³⁶).

GILBOA (גִּלְבֹּעַ always with article except in 1 Ch 10¹. ⁸; LXX Γελβούε; meaning uncertain. For early explanations see Lagarde's *Onom. Sacra*, pp. 35, 180, 189).—A range of hills, now known locally as *Jebel Fuḳû'a*, forming an arc of a circle to the E. of the plain of Esdraelon, and extending from Zer'in first S.E. and then S. The range consists of limestone, mixed in the northern and western parts with chalk, the wearing away of which has caused rugged channels. The highest and steepest part is on the N. side, just where it begins to bend south. Here it rises to a height of more than 2000 ft. above the valley of the Jordan (*i.e.* about 1700 ft. above sea-level). Towards the S. the sides slope more gradually, and sink to a height of a few hundred feet. As the plain on the W. is 300 ft. *above*, and the Jordan Valley is the same number of feet *below* sea-level, Gilboa is much more imposing on the east than on the west. The W. side is drained by the Kishon, one of the sources of which is on its slopes; the N. side by the Nahr Jalud, which rises near Zer'in and flows to the Jordan; the E. side by small streams running down to the Jordan Valley. Except on the lowest parts of the W. side the range is devoid of vegetation. At the present time there are two or three small villages on the slopes. One of them, *Jelbun*, still preserves a reminiscence of the ancient name of the hill. *Zer'in* is the old Jezreel, while Conder thinks that *Fuḳû'a* is possibly Aphek, and *Mujedd'a* at the eastern foot of the range the probable site of Megiddo.

Gilboa is mentioned in OT only in connexion with the camp of the Philistines and the death of Saul (1 S 28⁴ 31¹. ⁸, 2 S 1⁶. ²¹ 21¹², 1 Ch 10¹. ⁸). Saul and the Israelites went from Gilboa to the fountain which is in Jezreel. Near it they were defeated by the Philistines, and on its slopes they

fell down wounded, and Saul and Jonathan were slain. But though mentioned so seldom, Gilboa, being the eastern boundary of the great battlefield of Palestine (cf. ESDRAELON), has at all times played an important part in the history of the country from the days of Saul to those of Saladin and Napoleon.

LITERATURE.—Robinson, *Physical Geog. of Palestine*, 23–25; Trelawney Saunders, *Introd. to Survey of Western Palestine*, 129, 155 ff., 212 ff.; G. A. Smith, *HGHL* 400 ff.; Baedeker-Socin, *Pal.* 244.

G. W. THATCHER.

GILEAD (גִּלְעָד).—**1.** The 'son' of Machir (son of Manasseh) in Nu 27¹ 36¹, Jos 17³ (all P), 1 Ch 7¹⁷, as conversely Machir is said to have 'begotten' Gilead in Nu 26²⁹, and is called the 'father' of Gilead in 1 Ch 2²¹. ²³ 7¹⁴. The eponymous ancestor of the district called Gilead (which see). An analogous personification no doubt underlies the statement (Jg 11¹) that 'Gilead begat Jephthah' (viz. by an illegitimate wife). 'Gilead is the name of a region or of its population (Jg 5¹⁷), not of a man' (Moore, *ad loc.*), and a piece of tribal history is related (as sometimes happens in the OT) as though it were the domestic history of an individual; Jephthah's relations with the other inhabitants of Gilead being represented (v.²) as his relations with the legitimate sons of his father Gilead. See further MANASSEH. **2.** A Gadite, the son of Michael, 1 Ch 5¹⁴.

S. R. DRIVER.

GILEAD (גִּלְעָד, Γαλαάδ).—This name is applied to persons, to a tribe or family (Nu 36¹), to a particular city (Hos 6⁸),* to a mountain, and to a district east of the Jordan, whose dimensions varied somewhat when spoken of by different writers. It appears first in the account of Jacob (Gn 31²⁵), and thereafter is of frequent occurrence during the entire period of biblical history. As a geographical term it was still in use in the time of Josephus.

The present article is to deal with Gilead as a division of the Holy Land, its physical features, its geographical limits, and its historical associations.

From the mountains of Western Pal. the entire length of G. can be seen, and a large portion of its territory brought under the eye at once. It appears thence like a vast mountain range, varying from 3000 to 4000 ft. in height. To make up this height the depression of the Jordan Valley is reckoned, which is from 700 to 1300 ft. below the level of the Mediterranean. The summit of this range does not rise into peaks, but is pretty uniformly level. Valleys, wooded sections, and bold headlands are noticed, which give the impression that the country is wild and rugged. On the other hand, if from any point in the plain of Bashan, which bounds G. on the east, one looks westward to this range, he sees only a long line of low picturesque hills. The reason is that Bashan is a plateau rising 2000 or more feet above the sea-level. From this point no one would think of describing G. as 'rough and rugged.' Again, when one comes to travel through G. in different directions, he finds himself in the midst of charming natural scenery, where streams, springs, and forests, rich fields, gentle slopes, and quiet valleys attract the eye. Thus, according to the point of view of the observer, three very different descriptions of this region can be given, each having the merit of apparent accuracy.

The etymology of the word as given by Gesenius and Fuerst, viz. 'hard, stony region, rocky mountain,' does not indicate the character of the country; certain limited sections might be thus described, but outside of these G. is in the main a fertile and beautiful country. Josephus (*Wars*, III.

* Possibly also in Jg 10¹⁷. For Gilead of Hos 6⁸ some MSS of the LXX, which belong to the Luc. recension, read Gilgal (Γάλγαλα), which Nowack considers (comparing 4¹⁵ 9¹⁵ 12¹²) worthy of consideration. See further Dillmann on Gn 31⁵⁴.

iii. 3) says that 'it is not favourable for the growth of delicate fruits,' but that does not invalidate the statement just made as to its general character.

In the conquest of the east Jordan country by Moses and Joshua (Nu 21), G. is not mentioned, although the sections as conquered one after another can be pretty clearly defined. Attention to these details will help us in fixing its geographical limits. Occasionally G. was used so as to include the entire country between Hermon on the north and the river Arnon on the south (Jos 22⁹), but generally the region south of Heshbon and the north end of the Dead Sea, *i.e.* the territory of Reuben, was not included, and in the opposite direction the south end of the Sea of Galilee was its northern limit. The Jordan was its western boundary, and the eastern was the point where the hills meet the Bashan plain.

The entire country was called Amorite, with the exception of the district about Rabbath of the children of Ammon (*Amman*), the Upper Jabbok, which was not then conquered. Sihon was crushed at Jahaz, south of Heshbon (Nu 21²³), but the Jazer region, north of Heshbon, held out, and required a special expedition to subdue it (Nu 21³²). The third step was the successful battle with Og at Edrei, far to the N.E. of Jazer (Nu 21³³). The three final steps in the conquest of the northern portion of the country are mentioned in connexion with Machir, Jair, and Nobah (Nu 32⁴⁰⁻⁴²).

In the division of the territory between the two and a half tribes the phrase 'half Gilead' occurs several times. Half belonged to Gad and half to Manasseh (Dt 3¹³, Jos 13³¹). G. had previously been divided in the same way between the two kings Sihon and Og (Jos 12²ˑ⁵). The Hebrews simply retained, it appears, the old distinction. The suggestion has been made that the valley of the Jabbok should be the line dividing the two sections; but the objections to this view are serious, first, because this valley would not divide G. into halves; secondly, it would give to the tribe of Gad a small territory, and to Manasseh a very large one, whereas the number of warriors in these two tribes was about equal, requiring a more equal distribution of land.

The two and a half tribes may have differed in their tastes from their brethren, for they seem to have been exceptionally rich in cattle, and these wide pasture lands appealed to them as desirable for their future home (Nu 32¹). The present writer having lived in that region for months, and travelled through it in many directions, has often been impressed with its attractiveness, in contrast, for instance, with the rocky hills of Judæa. Its natural beauties, of many varieties, form landscape pictures which it is delightful to recall.

It is no wonder that these tribes were eager to call these lands their own. The portion of the Jordan Valley which belonged to G. was of such fertility that it might easily be made one of the gardens of the world. Streams descended from the hills; there were numerous fountains of sweet cool water, and copious sulphur springs existed in the valley at several different points (Merrill, *East of the Jordan*, pp. 143, 178, 183, 430). The great valleys of G. were likewise celebrated. Not to mention that of Heshbon on the south, there was that of the Jabbok, *Zerka*, famous in connexion with the history of Jacob; the *Menadireh*, near the south end of the Sea of Galilee, having a stream nearly equal to the Jordan in size; also *Yabis* and *'Ajlun*, along the latter of which ran the great road between Shechem and Ramoth-gilead.

Among the principal cities of G. were Mahanaim, Succoth, Penuel, Mizpeh, Jazer (which was one of the census stations when David numbered the people—an evidence of its central position and importance), Jabesh-gilead, Ramoth-gilead (which was a city of refuge, Jos 20⁸), and, in later times, Pella, Gerasa, and several others of the cities of the Decapolis. Of the three commissariat officers of Solomon who were assigned to the country east of the Jordan, two were stationed in Gilead proper —one at Ramoth, and the other at Mahanaim (1 K 4¹³ˑ¹⁴). It is noticeable that four of its chief cities had the name Gilead affixed to them, viz. Ramoth, Jabesh, Mizpeh, and Jazer (1 Ch 26³¹).

G. was to Pal. a sort of bulwark on its eastern border against invading armies from the south, east, and north, and it was a wise providence that planted there the most warlike tribes, ever ready to defend the national life (Jos 17¹, 1 Ch 5¹⁸). As if in keeping with this idea, much of the history of G. which has a conspicuous place in the biblical records has to do with wars, partly of conquest and partly of defence against powerful enemies. At one time the Hebrews had conquered all the desert tribes lying to the east of them, and had occupied their lands (1 Ch 5). The Ammonites, who for a long time had resisted the invaders, were at last, under Jephthah, thoroughly subdued, and twenty of their strongest cities taken from them (Jg 11³²ˑ³³). The same hero, partly by bravery and partly by a curious stratagem, gained a great victory over the Ephraimites (Jg 12). It was on the soil of G. that Gideon swept back to their desert home the routed hosts of Midian (Jg 8). Here occurred the fierce battle between the army of David and that of Absalom, in which the latter lost his life (2 S 18). Furthermore, at the national stronghold, Ramoth-gilead, battle after battle was fought for its ownership. The Syrians of Damascus had captured it, and an attempt to regain it cost Ahab his life. A little later Joram succeeded in wresting it from the enemy, and held it against the powerful assaults of Hazael the Syrian king (2 K 9¹⁴). Once, indeed, and probably on several other occasions during their history, the strength of the brave inhabitants was broken by invading armies from Assyria, and, according to custom, Tiglath-pileser carried them away captive (1 Ch 5²⁶). See George Smith, *Assyrian Eponym Canon*, ch. vi. on 'Assyrian Notices of Palestine,' pp. 106–150.

Another phase of interest attaching to G. was that it was a refuge for royalty. It was here that Saul's son Ish-bosheth was made king by Abner (2 S 2⁸ˑ⁹). Thither Absalom fled when he feared the anger of his father, and there he remained three years (2 S 13³⁸). David, in turn, found an asylum among its friendly inhabitants when the rebellion of Absalom was at its height (2 S 17²⁷⁻²⁹).

G., however, was not always a scene of conflict, for some of the pleasantest incidents of sacred history are connected with it. It was the place of reconciliation between Jacob and Laban, when the memorable words were uttered, 'The Lord watch between me and thee when we are absent one from another' (Gn 31⁴⁹). No less characteristic and beautiful, taking all its incidents, was Jacob's reconciliation with Esau (Gn 33). When the brave men of Jabesh-gilead risked their lives to recover the bodies of Saul and his sons from the enemy, and from terrible disgrace, there was displayed in that act the highest type of both loyalty and humanity (1 S 31¹¹⁻¹³). The kindnesses shown by the people of G. to David in the hour of his sore extremity were the expression of true-hearted pity for their humiliated king; and a little later Barzillai's leave-taking of him on the banks of the Jordan was surpassingly tender (2 S 17²⁷⁻²⁹ 19³¹ff.). Again, we see Elijah, the greatest prophet of OT, coming forth from his home in the Gilead hills (1 K 17¹), and taking a foremost place among the spiritual leaders of the world. Still later and brighter we find our Lord making to this region at least two interesting visits; and not long after His death, when the armies of Rome were at the gates of Jerus., we find the Christians of the Holy City, now doomed to destruction, taking refuge in Pella, at that time one of Gilead's most attractive cities (Euseb. *HE* iii. 5).

In the history and struggles of the Maccabæan period G. played an important part; and later, during the Roman occupation, its natural resources were highly developed. These, even in the present degraded condition of the country, are seen to be great, and, under more favourable conditions of government than now exist, a wonderful degree of prosperity might easily be restored to ancient Gilead.   S. MERRILL.

GILEAD, BALM OF.—See BALM.

GILEAD, MOUNT (הַר הַגִּלְעָד).—In Jg 7³, when Gideon, before his conflict with the Midianites, is about to reduce the number of the people with him, there occur the words, 'Whosoever is fearful and trembling, let him return and make a circuit (?) * from *Mount Gilead.*' Gideon's men are encamped (see v.¹) on the N. or N.W. spur of Gilboa; and as Gilead, in the ordinary acceptation of the term, was on the *East* of Jordan, it becomes a question what is here meant. (1) Studer (*Comm. ad loc.*) supposed that as the Midianites lay in the Vale of Jezreel, N. of Gilboa, between the men of Asher, etc. (6³⁵), and their homes, they were bidden to cross the Jordan, and so, by a circuit through Mt. Gilead, evade the enemy. If such were the author's meaning, it would be very obscurely and indirectly expressed. (2) Le Clerc (1708) proposed to read 'from Mount Gilboa' for 'from Mount Gilead'; and this reading is adopted by Hitz., Berth., Keil (alternatively), Grätz, Reuss, and others. The mention of the spot on which the host was encamped has been deemed 'superfluous' (Stud.). Yet the narrator (who, it is to be remembered, really penned the sentence) may have thus specified it for the sake of emphasis. (3) The Vale N. of Gilboa is now called the *Nahr Jalûd*, and there is a spring, *'Ain Jalûd*, issuing forth from the foot of Mt. Gilboa, about 1¾ miles E.S.E. of *Zerin* (Jezreel), and probably the 'Spring of **Harod**' of Jg 7¹; and it is possible that the part of the Gilboa range on which Gideon's men were, may have been called 'Mount Gilead'; there are cases in which the original ע is not preserved in a modern name (cf. Keil [altern.], G. A. Smith, *Geogr.* p. 398 n.). (4) Moore emends וַיִּצְרְפֵם גִּדְעוֹן: 'Let him return. And Gideon tried them; and there returned,' etc. But 'let him return' is rather abrupt (contrast Dt 20⁸); and *try* (test), in spite of v.⁴, is not altogether suitable in v.³. On the whole, (2) seems the most probable.   S. R. DRIVER.

GILEADITES.—By this term a branch of the

---

* The word is a ἅπ. λεγ., and the meaning is far from certain. No root צפר, *to go round*, is known in either Heb. or the cognate languages. צפר in the Mishna, and ضمر in Arab., are

to braid, plait; hence צְפִירָה, Is 28⁵, a *plaited garland* or *chaplet* (Aq. Theod. πλέγμα), and in the Mishna the *plaited rim* of a basket. The only support for a verb צפר *to go round* would be either (1) the assumption that it was the root of צְפִירָה in the obscure passage Ezk 7⁷ (in v.¹⁰ the sense *chaplet* suffices), supposing—what is anything but certain—that it there means *the round* (of fate), or *the turn* (of fortune—καταστροφή); or (2) the supposition that it was a denominative from צְפִירָה *garland*, regarded simply as something *forming a circle*. It is evident how hypothetical either of these etymologies is.

Arab. ضمر means also *to leap in running*, *to bound* or *run quickly*; hence Siegfried-Stade, *to spring away*. It is, no doubt, possible that the root may have been in use in Heb. in this sense. AV *depart early* (denom. from the Aram. צְפְרָא *morning*) is quite out of the question.

---

tribe of Manasseh is first meant, and the order of descent appears to have been: Manasseh the father of Machir, the father of Gilead, 'of whom came the family of Gileadites' (גִּלְעָדִי Nu 26²⁹). Secondly, the inhabitants of the district are likewise thus called, and for this purpose the phrase 'men of Gilead' is also employed (אַנְשֵׁי גּ Jg 12⁴). Jair (Jg 10³), Jephthah (Jg 11¹), and Barzillai, who befriended David (2 S 17²⁷), are specially mentioned as 'Gileadites.' Sometimes the name of the district, גִּלְעָד, is rendered 'Gileadite,' as in Jg 12⁵. In mentioning the cause of the war between Gilead and Ephraim, a peculiar charge is made against the Gileadites which it is difficult to explain (Jg 12⁴). Evidently, bitter reproach or supreme contempt was meant, and the charge or insinuation was resented with great violence and bloodshed.
                                             S. MERRILL.

GILGAL (גִּלְגָּל 'a circle' of stones, 'a cromlech,' always with the article, except Jos 5⁹, where a theory of the origin of the name is given. LXX has generally Γάλγαλα in the plur. (Jos 4¹⁹· ²⁰ 5⁹ 10⁷, 1 S 13¹⁵ etc. etc.), but also in the sing., τὴν Γάλγαλα (1 S 7¹⁶), τῆς Γάλγαλα (1 S 10⁸ A, B has Γαλαάδ); for the sing. indeclinable form Γαλγάλ see Jos 14⁶ (B) 15⁷ (A, B has Τααγάδ), Hos 9¹⁵ etc. These forms are used indifferently in reference to the same Gilgal. Vulg. *Galgala*, always in the plural).

Three distinct Gilgals are indicated by the references. **1.** A place between Jericho and the Jordan (Jos 4¹⁹), בְּקְצֵה מִזְרַח יְרִיחוֹ 'in the extreme east of Jericho, *i.e.* on the eastern border of its territory' (Gesenius). It was the first camp of the Isr. after crossing the Jordan (Jos 4¹⁹). Twelve memorial stones taken from the bed of the river were here erected (v.²⁰). Circumcision of those born in the wilderness (5²⁻⁹), consequently the place called Gilgal in memory of the rolling away (גּלל) of the reproach of Egypt (v.⁹). The passover celebrated (v.¹⁰). The manna ceases (v.¹²). Joshua returns every night to this camp during the siege of Jericho (6¹¹). The Gibeonites make their treaty with Joshua here (9³⁻¹⁵). They ask aid from Joshua at Gilgal against the league of the five kings of the Amorites (10⁶). Joshua ascends with the men of war (v.⁷), and after a successful battle returns to the camp (v.¹⁵). After taking Makkedah (v.²⁸), Libnah (v.²⁹), Lachish (v.³²), Eglon (v.³⁵), Hebron (v.³⁷), and Debir (v.³⁸), and after smiting his enemies from Kadesh-barnea to Gaza, he returns again to Gilgal (v.⁴³). After completing the northern campaign, culminating in the great battle against the allied kings at the waters of Merom, Joshua is again found at Gilgal (14⁶), where he assigns by lot the inheritance of Manasseh, Judah, and Ephraim. The inference is that Gilgal was the central camp for the people, not only during the nearer campaigns, but 'until the land rested from war' (11²³). In 18³ we find the whole congregation assembling at Shiloh, where the other lots were granted.

A Gilgal appears prominently in the history of Saul and Samuel. It was one of the places where Samuel judged the people in his yearly circuit, which included Mizpah and Bethel. These three places are called sacred in the LXX (1 S 7¹⁶ τοῖς ἡγιασμένοις τούτοις). It was clearly one of the central places for sacrifice (10⁸ 13⁹⁻¹⁰ 15²¹); and here Samuel hewed Agag in pieces before the Lord (15³³). Here Saul was crowned (11¹⁴⁻¹⁵), and rejected as king (15²⁶). Though it is not certain that this is the Gilgal of the camp, it is placed here, as the following points favour the identification:—(1) References are made to going *down* to Gilgal from the hill-country (10⁸ and 15¹²), and *up* to Gibeah (13¹⁵). (2) The sacredness of the spot may have been due to the setting up of the twelve stones. We may also notice that while Saul was in Gilgal in fear of the Philistines, many Hebrews crossed the Jordan to Gad and Gilead.

The Gilgal of the camp is plainly mentioned in 2 S 19¹⁵, where the people assemble at Gilgal to conduct David back over Jordan on his return from exile.

The Gilgal of Hos 4¹⁵ 9¹⁵ 12¹¹ and Am 4⁴ 5⁵ (in connexion with Bethel), evidently a place whose sanctity had been violated, seems to be the Gilgal mentioned above as a central place of worship, and is placed under this head for the reasons given. It may be identical with the **Beth-gilgal** of Neh 12²⁹.

The Gilgal of Jos 15⁷ also should be here, as it is placed in Benjamin near the north border of Judah, over-against the going up of Adummim, which has been identified with the peak Ṭala'at ed-Dumm, south of the Wady el-Kelt, about half-way from Jericho to Jerusalem. [Driver thinks this impossible. See GELILOTH.] In the parallel passage, 18¹⁷, it is called **Geliloth** (גְּלִילוֹת). There has been much dispute as to the identity of the Gilgal of Dt 11³⁰, but upon the whole it should most probably be placed here (see the very careful note by Driver, *ad loc.*, also 2nd ed. p. xxi; and G. A. Smith, *HGHL*, App. 675; Buhl, *GAP* 202). This Gilgal is to be looked for between Jericho and the Jordan. In 1865 Zschokke heard the name *Jiljûlieh* applied to a mound or *tell* near the tamarisk, *Sejeret el-Ithleh*, 4½ miles from the Jordan and 1¼ miles from modern Jericho. In 1874 Conder recovered the same name, as applied to a *birket* or pool near the tree. According to Jos. (*Ant.* v. i. 4), Galgala is 10 stadia from Jericho and 50 from the Jordan. The former distance corresponds very well with the position of the *birket*. The distance of 50 stadia is impossible, as the plain is only from 50 to 52 stadia wide at this part, but reading 30 (λ') we get the distance from the Jordan at once, 3½ miles, which corresponds better to the position of *Birket Jiljûlieh*. In the 4th cent. Jerome (see 'Galgala' in the *Onomasticon*) describes it as a deserted spot, 2 miles from Jericho, held in great veneration by the inhabitants of the region. Whether the twelve stones were still pointed out is not clear, as the expression in the *Epitomæ Paulæ* (§ 12), 'Intuita est castra Galgalæ et secundæ circumcisionis mysterium et duodecim lapides,' may mean *considered*, and not *beheld*. Arculf (A.D. 700) saw a *Galgalis*, 5 miles from Jericho, with a large church covering the twelve stones of commemoration. Willibald (c. 730) mentions a moderately-sized church of wood, and places Galgala 5 miles from the Jordan, which he says is 7 miles from Jericho. In the 13th and 14th cent. the stones are mentioned by Thietmar and Ludolf de Suchem respectively. Thus the site of the *Birket Jiljûlieh* corresponds very well to the description of Josephus, Jerome, and Willibald. Hence the early Christian tradition may have been based on an older Jewish identification.

The *birket* measures 100 ft. by 84, outside measurement, with walls 32 in. thick, constructed of roughly-hewn small stones, apparently without cement. North of the pool may be traced lines of similar masonry, covering, according to the present writer's observations, a space 300 yards long, and apparently representing the foundations of three constructions. Conder sees here the ruins of a monastery. South and east of the pool there are 25 mounds, scattered irregularly over an area ⅛ of a mile square.* These are all small, the largest measuring about 50 ft. in diameter and 10 ft. in height. Two of these mounds show superficial traces of ruins, the rest being mere heaps of earth. Ganneau excavated two: the first revealed pottery, tesseræ, and glass, the second merely sand.

* For plan see p. 182, PEFSt, 1894.

Conder recovered from the natives a tradition which connected this site with a City of Brass, taken from the infidels by a great Imâm, who rode around the city and blew at the walls, which fell. Conder thus sums up (*Mem. PEF*, vol. iii. p. 173): Birket Jiljûlieh appears to be the early Christian site; there is nothing against its being the original one.

2. Another Gilgal is mentioned in 2 K 2¹ and 4³⁸ in the history of Elijah and Elisha. From 4³⁸ we cannot assume that it was a seat of a school of prophets, as these may have come from Bethel (cf. 2³). There is a large modern village called *Jiljilie*, on the top of a high hill, about 8 miles N.W. of Bethel, from which it is separated by the great Wady el-Jîb (*Mem. PEF*, vol. ii. p. 290). It is 450 ft. lower than Bethel, but the descent into this valley may account for the statement that Elijah and Elisha went *down* to Bethel. This expression rules out the Gilgal of the Jordan valley.

3. In Jos 12²³ the king of the Nations of (RV Goiim in) Gilgal (לְגִלְגָּל לְגוֹיִם, LXX Γεεὶ τῆς Γαλειλαίας, adopted by Dillm.) is named among the conquered kings, in the part of the enumeration following the maritime plain from north to south. The name occurs immediately after Dor, the modern Tantura. About 30 miles S.S.E. of Tantura there is the modern village of *Jiljûlieh*, which may be on the site of this Gilgal.   F. J. BLISS.

GILOH (גִּלֹה). Driver [*Text of Sam.* p. 241] points out that the gentilic גִּילֹנִי implies that the original form was גִּילֹה, from the root גִּיל or גּוּל, not from גלה.—A city in the southern hills of Judah (Jos 15⁵¹), the birthplace of Ahithophel the **Gilonite**, the famous counsellor of David (2 S 15¹² 23³⁴). Its site is uncertain. There is a ruin called *Jâla* on the hills N.W. of Hebron. See *SWP*, vol. iii. sh. xxi.   C. R. CONDER.

GIMEL (ג).—The third letter of the Heb. alphabet, and as such used in the 119th Psalm to designate the 3rd part, each verse of which begins with this letter. It is transliterated in this Dictionary by *g*.

GIMZO (גִּמְזוֹ; cf. Assyr. proper name *Gamuzanu* [Pinches, *Hebraica*, July 1886, p. 222]).—A town noticed with Aijalon and other places on the border of Philistia (2 Ch 28¹⁸). It is the modern *Jimzu* near Aijalon. See *SWP*, vol. iii. sh. xvii.; Robinson, *BRP*² ii. 249; Baedeker-Socin, *Pal.* 21.   C. R. CONDER.

GIN.—Two Heb. words are so tr⁴ in AV: (1) פַּח *paḥ* in Job 18⁹, Is 8¹⁴, and מוֹקֵשׁ *môkêsh* in Ps 140⁵ 141⁹, Am 3⁵, Job 40²⁴ AVm. The usual trⁿ of both words is 'snare.' As Driver shows, however (*Joel and Amos*, on Am 3⁵), the *paḥ* is the *snare*, the *môkêsh* something without which the snare is useless, perhaps the *bait*. See SNARE.

In the 1611 ed. of AV the word is spelt 'ginne' in Is 8¹⁴, Am 3⁵, Job 40²⁴ᵐ; but in Job 18⁹, Ps 140⁵ 141⁹ the spelling is 'grinne.' 'Grinne' was changed in 1613 to 'grin'; Dr. Paris in his ed. of 1762 cast out the *r*, and the word has been 'gin' ever since. But 'gin' and 'grin' are not the same. 'Grin,' from Anglo-Sax. *grin* or *gryn*, has many forms in Middle-Eng. (Wyclif's Bible, 1382, shows *grene*, *grane*, *gryn*, *grynne*), and does mean a 'trap.' 'Gin' is probably a contraction of 'engine' (Fr. *engin*), which comes from Lat. *ingenium* and is used of any ingenious contrivance. A trap, however, is a contrivance, and so the words got mixed in spelling and in meaning.

In early writers 'gin' is used both abstractly of a contrivance, device, and concretely of an instrument contrived for war, torture, or the like. Thus Piers Plowman, (B) xviii. 250—

'For gygas the geaunt with a gynne engyned,'

that is, 'For Gigas the giant with a contrivance contrived'; Spenser, *FQ* II. iii. 13—

'Which two, through treason and deceiptfull gin, Had slaine Sir Mordant and his lady bright.'

As an instrument of torture, *FQ* I. v. 35—

'Typhoeus joynts were stretched on a gin.'

The word 'grin' by and by went out of use, and 'gin' became restricted to the meaning of trap or snare. T. Fuller, *Holy Warre*, v. 1 (p. 247), says, 'Now Satan, the master-juggler, needeth no wires or ginnes to work with, being all ginnes himself; so transcendent is the activity of a spirit.' It was specially applied to snares for birds, as T. Adams, *Works*, i. 7, 'For hunting, they have nets; for fowling, gins; for fishing, baits'; and iii. 17, 'In the air, the birds fly high above our reach, yet we have gins to fetch them down.'   J. HASTINGS.

GINATH (גִּינַת, Γάωνθ AB, Γωνώθ Luc.).—Father of Tibni, who unsuccessfully laid claim against Omri to the throne of Israel (1 K 16²¹·²²).

GINNETHOI, AV **Ginnetho** (גִּנְּתוֹי).—A priest among the returned exiles (Neh 12⁴). The name appears in Neh 12¹⁶ 10⁶ as **Ginnethon** (גִּנְּתוֹן). See GENEALOGY.

GINNETHON.—See GINNETHOI.

GIRDLE.—See DRESS, vol. i. p. 626ª.

GIRGASHITE (in Heb. always sing. הַגִּרְגָּשִׁי 'the Girgashite,' and rightly so rendered in RV; in LXX and Josephus ὁ Γεργεσαῖος; in AV only twice in sing. Gn 10¹⁶, 1 Ch 1¹⁴; elsewhere plural, 'Girgashites').—Very little is known of this people, whose name, though occurring several times in OT in the list of Can. tribes * (Gn 10¹⁶ 15²¹, Dt 7¹ [and 20¹⁷ in Sam. and LXX], Jos 3¹⁰ 24¹¹, 1 Ch 1¹⁴, Neh 9⁸) affords no indication of their position, or to what branch of the Can. they belonged, except in two instances, namely, Gn 10¹⁶, where the G. is given as the name of the fifth son of Canaan, and Jos 24¹¹, where the G. would seem to have inhabited the tract on the west of Jordan, the Isr. having been obliged to cross over that river in order to fight the men of Jericho, among whom were the Girgashites. It has been suggested that a town (now in ruins), near the mouth of the Wady Samakh, called Kersa, might be identified with Gergesa; the former being pronounced, it is said, nearly the same as the latter by the Bedawin. Gergesa contains, moreover, the same consonants as the Heb. גִּרְגָּשִׁי (*Girgashi*, LXX οἱ Γεργεσαῖοι; see GERASENES, p. 160ª), found in Gn 15²¹, Dt 7¹ etc., and, if the same word, would be the district or chief town of the G., which, according to Jerome and Eusebius (*OS.*² p. 256, 14, p. 162, 18), was situated on a hill sloping steeply to the shore of the Sea of Galilee. There is, then, a probability that Girgashi, Kersa, and Gergesa (where our Lord healed the demoniac and allowed the demons to enter into a herd of swine which ran down the steep into the sea) are one and the same.

A fragment of an Assyr. tablet (K. 261, Brit. Mus.) possibly throws a ray of light on this people. In that text the Kirkisâti, possibly the Girgashites,† are mentioned more than once, in one case accompanied by the adjective *rabbâti*—'numerous.' These Kirkisâti seem to have been one of the nations attacked by an early ruler named

Gazzâni (? father of Tidal). According to Origen (*in Jo* vi. 41), the Girgashites (οἱ Γεργεσαῖοι) were so called from an old town, on the shore of the lake, called Gergesa. This is hardly far enough east to make the Assyr.-Bab. Kirkisâti identical with the Girgashites, unless (as is possible) we suppose them (being a 'numerous' people) to have founded colonies in or near Mesopotamia; or that the Bab. ruler led an army all the way to the 'land of the Amorites,' as, in fact, many of the kings of Babylonia and Assyria are recorded to have done,—indeed, the 14th ch. of Gn not only states that the Bab. kings there mentioned went so far, but that one of their allies was Chedorlaomer, king of Elam, a country situated at a still greater distance. It is noteworthy that the Talmud contains a tradition of the G. appealing to Alexander the Great, during his sojourn in Palestine, complaining of having been banished from Canaan by the Jews, and asking justice. The existence of the G. at such a late period implies that they were, in early times, an important tribe or nationality, thus agreeing with what is stated in OT, and with the Assyr. reference to the Kirkisâti.

I. A. PINCHES.

GIRZITE (Kethibh הַגִּרְזִי, Ķerê הַגִּזְרִי, the Gizrite; B τὸν Γεσειρί, A τὸν Γεσερεὶ καὶ τὸν Γεζραῖον).—Acc. to 1 S 27⁸, David and his men, while living at the court of Achish king of Gath, 'made a raid upon the Geshurites (which see), and the Girzites (RVm Gizrites), and the Amalekites: for those nations were the inhabitants of the land, which were of old, as thou goest to Shur, even unto the land of Egypt.' The LXX (B) is probably correct in reading only one name 'Gizrites' for 'Geshurites and Girzites,' viz. the Canaanite inhabitants of Gezer, a town on the S.W. border of Ephraim (Jos 10³³ 16³·¹⁰, Jg 1²⁹), the modern *Tell Jezer*, between Emmaus ('*Amwâs*, Nicopolis) and Ekron ('*Akir*). The original population, which had not been driven out by the Ephraimites, retained its independence till the days of Solomon, when Pharaoh king of Egypt conquered the city, and gave it with his daughter to Solomon; the latter rebuilt it (1 K 9¹⁵⁻¹⁷). See GEZER; and cf. Moore, *Judges*, p. 47 f.; G. A. Smith, *Hist. Geog.* p. 215 f.

J. F. STENNING.

GISHPA, AV **Gispa** (גִּשְׁפָּא).—An overseer of the Nethinim (Neh 11²¹), but text probably corrupt (cf. Berth.-Ryssel *ad loc.*). See GENEALOGY.

GITTAIM (גִּתַּיִם).—A town of Benjamin (?), 2 S 4³, noticed with Hazor and Ramah, Neh 11³³. The site is unknown.

GITTITES.—See GATH.

GITTITH.—See PSALMS.

GIVE.—1. The verb [אָזַן] *âzan*, which is formed from אֹזֶן the *ear*, is used in the Hiphil, meaning 'to listen,' 41 times, and 32 times it is trᵈ in AV 'give ear,' the other renderings being 'hearken' Gn 4²³, Nu 23¹⁸, Job 9¹⁶ 33¹ 34¹⁶ 37¹⁴, 'hear' Ps 135¹⁷ 140⁶ (RV 'give ear'); 'give good heed' Ec 12⁹ (RV 'ponder,' RVm 'give ear'). Sometimes it is God that gives ear or is entreated to give ear, sometimes it is man. In Apocr. the phrase also occurs, 2 Es 8²⁴ (*auribus percipere*); Wis 6² (ἐνωτίζομαι); Sir 4¹⁵ (ὑπακούω), 6²³ (ἀκούω). It is not found in NT. For the phrase cf. Marlowe, *Faustus*, v. iii. 'The devil threatened to tear me in pieces if I once gave ear to divinity; and now 'tis too late'; and Milton, *PL* ix. 1067—

'O Eve, in evil hour thou didst give ear To that false worm, of whomsoever taught To counterfeit man's voice.'

2. The verb to 'give' is used with various sub-

---

* In the Hex. Girgashite is mentioned only by JE and D.

† See the remark upon the resemblance of the pronunciation of Kersa and Gergesa, above.

stantives to form phrases, some of which are archaic and biblical, others obsolete. 1. *Give attendance*, 1 Ti 4¹³ 'give attendance to reading' (πρόσεχε, RV 'give heed'); He 7¹³ 'no man gave attendance at the altar' (προσέσχηκε). 2. *Give heed*, Wis 6¹⁸ 'the giving heed unto her laws' (προσοχή); 1 Ti 1⁴, He 2¹ (προσέχειν); cf. Ps 39² Wyc. 1388, 'Y abidynge abood the Lord; and he gaf tent to me' (LXX προσέσχεν μοι). 3. *Give diligence*, 2 P 1⁵ 'giving all diligence' (σπουδὴν πᾶσαν παρεισενέγκαντες, RV 'adding all diligence'); 1¹⁰ 'give diligence' (σπουδάσατε); Jude³ 'when I gave all diligence' (πᾶσαν σπουδὴν ποιούμενος). 4. *Give audience*, Ac 15¹² (ἀκούω, RV 'hearken'); 22²² (ἀκούω, RV as AV). 5. *Give reverence*, He 12⁹ (ἐντρέπομαι). 6. *Give occasion*, Dt 22¹⁴ 'if man take a wife . . . and give occasions of speech against her' (וְשָׂם לָהּ עֲלִילֹת דְּבָרִים, RV 'lay shameful things to her charge'; Driver, 'frame against her wanton charges'; the phrase, which is uncertain in meaning, is fully discussed by Driver, *Deut.* p. 254 f.), so 22¹⁷, 2 Co 5¹² (ἀφορμὴν διδόντες). 7. *Give testimony*, Sir 36¹⁵ 'Give testimony unto those that thou hast possessed from the beginning, and raise up prophets that have been in thy name' (δὸς μαρτύριον); Ac 13²² 'he raised up David to be their king; to whom also he gave testimony, and said' (ᾧ καὶ εἶπεν μαρτυρήσας, RV 'bare witness'); so 14³. For 2 K 11¹² 'And he brought forth the king's son, and put the crown upon him, and gave him the testimony' (אֶת־הָעֵדוּת), AV 1611 'the Testimonie'), see TESTIMONY. 8. *Give witness*, Job 29¹¹ 'when the eye saw me, it gave witness to me' (וַתְּעִידֵנִי); Ac 10⁴³ 'To him give all the prophets witness' (μαρτυροῦσιν, RV 'bear . . . witness'). 9. *Give record*, 1 Jn 5¹⁰ 'the record that God gave of his Son' (ἣν μεμαρτύρηκεν ὁ θεός, RV 'the witness that God hath borne concerning his Son'). 10. *Give word*, Ps 68¹¹ 'The Lord gave the word' (אֲדֹנָי יִתֶּן־אֹמֶר, RV 'The Lord giveth the word'). 11. *Give voice*, Ps 18¹³ 'The Lord also thundered in the heavens, and the Highest gave his voice' (עֶלְיוֹן יִתֵּן קֹלוֹ, RV 'the Most High uttered his voice.' Cf. Gn 45² AVm and RVm 'And he gave forth his voice in weeping' for text 'And he wept aloud,' Heb. וַיִּתֵּן אֶת־קֹלוֹ בִּבְכִי; and Jer 25³⁰ Cov. 'He shal geve a greate voyce (like the grape gatherers)'; Ac 26¹⁰ 'when they were put to death, I gave my voice against them' (κατήνεγκα ψῆφον, RV 'gave my vote'). 12. *Give commandment*, Ex 25²² 'I will commune with thee . . . of all things which I will give thee in commandment unto the children of Israel' (אֲצַוֶּה אוֹתְךָ); 1 Ch 14¹² 'And when they had left their gods there, David gave a commandment, and they were burned with fire' (וַיֹּאמֶר דָּוִיד, RV 'gave commandment'); Ezr 4²¹ 'Give ye now commandment to cause these men to cease' (שִׂימוּ טְעֵם, RV 'Make ye now a decree'); Ps 71³ 'thou hast given commandment to save me' (צִוִּיתָ); Jn 14³¹ 'as the Father gave me commandment, so I do' (TR ἐνετείλατό μοι, L Tr WH ἐντολὴν ἔδωκέν μοι); Ac 1² (ἐντειλάμενος); 23³⁰ (παραγγείλας, RV 'charging'); He 11²² (ἐνετείλατο). 13. *Give charge*, 2 S 18⁵ 'when the king gave all the captains charge' (בְּצַוֹּת); Job 34¹³ 'Who hath given him a charge over the earth?' (פָּקַד עָלָיו, RV 'Who gave him a charge?'); Jer 47⁷ (צִוָּה־לֹ); Mt 4⁶ 'He shall give his angels charge concerning thee' (ἐντελεῖται), so Lk 4¹⁰; 1 Ti 5⁷ 'And these things give in charge'* (καὶ ταῦτα παράγγελλε, RV 'These

---

* Twice the phrase 'give in charge' occurs in Shaks. in the same sense of 'command,' but in a context which suggests the mod. meaning 'give charge of,' *I Henry VI.* II. iii. 1—

'Porter, remember what I gave in charge;
And when you have done so, bring the keys to me';

Tempest, v. i. 8—

'How fares the king and 's followers ?
Confin'd together
In the same fashion as you gave in charge,
Just as you left them; all prisoners, sir.'

---

things also command'); 6¹³ 'I give thee charge' (Παραγγέλλω σοι, RV 'I charge thee'). 14. *Give judgment*, 2 K 25⁶ 'and they gave judgment upon him' (וַיְדַבְּרוּ אִתּוֹ מִשְׁפָּט, AVm 'spake judgment with him,' RVm 'spake with him of judgment'); so Jer 39⁵. ⁹. Cf. Sir T. More, *Utopia* (Lumby's ed. p. 15), 'An other sorte sytteth upon their allebencheis, and there amonge their cuppes they geve judgment of the wittes of writers.' 15. *Give sentence*, Jer 4¹² 'now also will I give sentence against them' (אֲדַבֵּר מִשְׁפָּטִים, RV as AVm 'utter judgments'); Lk 23²⁴ 'Pilate gave sentence that it should be as they required' (ἐπέκρινε). 16. *Give counsel*, 2 S 17⁷ 'the counsel that Ahithophel hath given is not good at this time' (הָעֵצָה אֲשֶׁר־יָעַץ), so 1 K 12⁸⁻¹³, 2 Ch 10⁸. 17. *Give assurance*, Ac 17³¹ (πίστιν παρασχών). 18. *Give place*, (a) literally, Is 49²⁰ 'give place to me that I may dwell' (גְּשָׁה־לִּי); Sir 29²⁷ 'Give place, thou stranger, to an honourable man' (ἔξελθε, RV 'go forth'); Mt 9²⁴ 'Give place: for the maid is not dead' ('Αναχωρεῖτε); and (b) figuratively, Gal 2⁵ 'To whom we gave place by subjection, no, not for an hour' (εἴξαμεν). Cf. Ro 12¹⁹, Eph 4²⁷, and *Babees Book* (Early Eng. Text Soc.), p. 103—

> 'Sit thou not in the highest place,
> Where the good man is present,
> But gyue him place : his maners marke
> Thou with graue aduysement.'

Knox in his 'Godly Letter to the Faithful in London' (*Works*, iii. 167), says, 'But, Deir Brethrene, be subject unto God, and gif place to his wraith, that ye may eschape his everlasting vengeance.' Cassius says to Brutus (Shaks. *Jul. Cæs.* IV. iii. 146)—

> 'Of your philosophy you make no use,
> If you give place to accidental evils.'

Tindale uses 'give room' in the same way, *Prologe* to the Pentateuch, 'Isaac, when his welles which he had digged were taken from him, geveth rowme and resisteth not.'

3. To 'give oneself to' is a phrase of occasional occurrence, representing various expressions in the original, but always implying energy or absorption in the pursuit spoken of. It occurs Ec 2³ 'I sought in mine heart to give myself unto wine' (לִמְשׁוֹךְ בַּיַּיִן, lit., as AV, 'to draw my flesh with wine,' RV 'to cheer my flesh with wine'); Ac 6⁴ 'we will give ourselves continually to prayer' (προσκαρτερήσομεν, RV 'we will continue stedfastly in prayer'); 1 Co 7⁵ 'that ye may give yourselves to fasting and prayer' (TR ἵνα σχολάζητε τῇ νηστείᾳ καὶ τῇ προσευχῇ, edd. ἵνα σχολάσητε τῇ προσευχῇ, RV 'that ye may give yourselves unto prayer'); 1 Ti 4¹⁵ 'give thyself wholly to them' (ἐν τούτοις ἴσθι). Sometimes the phrase is restricted to some part of the person, as the *heart*, Ec 1¹³. ¹⁷ 'I gave my heart to know wisdom,' Sir 39⁵; or the *mouth*, Ps 50¹⁹ 'Thou givest thy mouth to evil' (פִּיךָ שָׁלַחְתָּ בְרָעָה). And then we have the frequent phrase *given to*, with the same meaning and used both of good and bad pursuits. The expressions in the original are as a rule much more forcible than the Eng. phrase. They are, Pr 23² 'if thou be a man given to appetite' (אִם־בַּעַל נֶפֶשׁ אָתָּה, lit. 'if the owner of soul [=desire] thou'; so Ec 8⁸ 'given to it [wickedness]'); Pr 24²¹ 'meddle not with them that are given to change' (עִם־שׁוֹנִים 'changelings,' or perhaps, as Del., 'revolutionaries'); Jer 6¹³ 8¹⁰ 'given to covetousness'(בֹּצֵעַ בָּצַע, lit. '[greedy] gainer of [greedy] gain'); 1 Es 2²⁷ 'given to rebellion and war' (συντελοῦντες, lit. 'accomplishing'); Sir 17¹⁶ 'given to evil' (ἐπὶ τὰ πονηρά, RV omits); 19¹ 'given to drunkenness' (μέθυσος, RV 'that is a drunkard'); Ac 17¹⁶ 'wholly given to idolatry' (κατείδωλον οὖσαν, RV 'full of idols'); Ro 12¹³ 'given to hospitality' (τὴν φιλοξενίαν διώκοντες, lit. 'pursuing hospitality,' as RVm); 1 Ti 3² 'given to hospitality'

(φιλόξενος, lit. 'guest-loving'); 3[3] 'given to wine' (πάροινος, RV 'brawler'; so Tit 1[7]); 3[8] 'given to much wine' (οἴνῳ πολλῷ προσέχων); Tit 1[7] 'given to filthy lucre' (αἰσχροκερδής, lit. 'basely greedy,' RV 'greedy of filthy lucre'); 2[3] 'given to much wine' (οἴνῳ πολλῷ δεδουλωμένας, RV 'enslaved to much wine').

4. In the sense of *grant, admit,* 'give' is often found in writers of the date of AV. Thus Shaks. *Winter's Tale,* III. ii. 96—

> 'The crown and comfort of my life, your favour,
> I do give lost; for I do feel it gone';

and Milton, *PL* ii. 14—

> 'Though oppressed and fallen
> I give not heaven for lost.'

This idiom does not occur in AV, but closely associated with it is the sense of *give leave to,* seen in Mt 13[11] 'Unto you it is given to know' (ὑμῖν δέδοται γνῶναι); and 1 Co 12[3] 'I give you to understand' (γνωρίζω ὑμῖν, lit. 'I make known to you'), phrases which are as old as Wyclif, and in common use still. Cf. Milton, *PL* ix. 818—

> 'Shall I to him make known
> As yet my change, and give him to partake
> Full happiness with me, or rather not,
> But keep the odds of knowledge in my power
> Without copartner?'

There is a further extension of this sense in Job 24[23] 'Though it be given him to be in safety,' *i.e.* though he be not merely permitted but enabled.

5. When followed by certain adverbs, 'give' is used in ways that are at least archaic now. (1) *Give again=*give back, restore, Lv 25[51. 52] (שִׁיב), RV 'give back'); Ezk 33[15] 'If the wicked restore (שִׁיב) the pledge; give again (שַׁלֵּם, lit. 'make complete') that he had robbed . . . he shall surely live'; Lk 4[20] 'And he closed the book, and he gave it again to the minister' (ἀποδούς, RV 'gave it back'). See AGAIN. (2) *Give forth,* Nu 20[8] 'Speak ye unto the rock before their eyes'; and it shall give forth his water' (נָתַן); Ac 1[26] 'And they gave forth their lots' (ἔδωκαν). (3) *Give out,* Jos 18[4] 'Give out from among you three men for each tribe' (='choose out,' which is Coverdale's tr[n], 'give out' is the Bishops' tr[n], Heb. הָבוּ לָכֶם, RV 'appoint for you'; in Dt 1[13] the same phrase is tr[d] 'take you' in both AV and RV; it occurs also in Jg 20[7], 2 S 16[20]) Jer 4[16] 'watchers come from a far country, and give out their voice against the cities of Judah' (יִתְּנוּ; cf. Mk 15[37] Wyc. [1388], 'And Jhesus gaf out a greet cry, and diede'); Ac 8[9] 'Giving out that himself was some great one' (λέγων, lit. 'saying,' as all previous Eng. versions, Vulg. *dicens,* but Luther *gab vor*). (4) *Give over,* always with the meaning 'surrender,' modern 'give up,' Ps 118[18] 78[50. 62], Is 19[4], Sir 23[6] 30[21] 33[20], Ro 1[28], Eph 4[19]. Cf. Pr. Bk., Collect for St. Andrew's Day (1559–1604), 'Grant unto us all, that we being called by thy holy word may forthwith give over ourselves obediently to follow thy holy commandments' (changed in 1662 into 'give up ourselves'). (5) *Give up,* 2 S 24[9] 'And Joab gave up the sum of the number of the people unto the king' (וַיִּתֵּן)='delivered,' as most earlier versions (LXX ἔδωκεν, Vulg. *dedit*).   J. HASTINGS.

GIZONITE (הַגִּזוֹנִי).—A gentilic name which occurs in 1 Ch 11[34] in the colloc. הָשֵׁם הַגִּזוֹנִי 'Hashem the Gizonite.' In all probability this should be corrected to יָשֵׁן הַגֻּנִי 'Jashen (cf. the parallel passage 2 S 23[32]) the Gunite' (so Klosterm., Budde, Driver, Kittel). The 'Gunite' (Nu 26[48]) is confirmed by the reading of A and Luc. Γωννί or Γουνί, and even by the meaningless Σομολογεννουνεῖν of B. See JASHEN.

GIZRITE.—See GIRZITE.

GLASS (וְכוּכִית, ὕαλος) is an artificial substance,

fusible, usually more or less transparent or translucent, and composed of a mixture of metallic silicates. One of the metals present is always either potassium or sodium, the other being generally calcium or lead. Thus modern window glass contains the silicates of sodium and calcium, crown glass those of potassium and calcium, and flint glass those of potassium and lead. Other metals such as iron may be present, either accidentally as impurities, or designedly as colouring matters. Although the references to glass in Scripture are few, its manufacture is of high antiquity, and in the progress of civilization it has served many purposes both of use and ornament.

The origin of the art of glass-making is obscure. The account given by Pliny (*Nat. Hist.* xxxvi. 25), of its accidental production through the melting of blocks of 'nitrum' employed by some sailors to support their caldron over a fire which they had made on the sands at the mouth of the river Belus in Syria, is well known but fabulous. The assertion, however, that no fire burning in the open air could possibly give rise to sufficient heat for the formation of glass, is incorrect, as crude glass is known to have been produced during the burning of a stack of wheat. But, even if Pliny's narrative were credible, the glass he describes, consisting of a single alkaline silicate, would have been soluble in water, and of no practical use. It is probable that the process of vitrification was first observed in the course of metallurgical operations. The art was widely known in the ancient world, and, while its origin may be difficult to localize, it is in Egypt that the earliest traces of it have hitherto been found. Glass-blowers are represented on the walls of the Tomb of Ti at Sakkhara, which dates from the 5th dynasty, and on many other tombs of later date, such as those at Beni-Hasan (Usertesen I., 12th dynasty, B.C. 3500). There is similar pictorial evidence that glass vases were used for wine in Egypt at least as early as the Exodus. Glass was also known in very ancient times in Assyria and Babylonia (see vol. i. p. 220a), and even in China.

The earliest glass was opaque or semi-opaque. The art of making it transparent was a later development; and even the first transparent glass was not colourless, but tinted. The oldest *dated* specimen of glass as yet known is a small ornament found at Thebes, in the shape of a lion's head. It is of opaque blue glass, and bears the name of Nu-Antef IV. (11th dynasty). Next to it comes an opaque glass jug of turquoise blue colour with yellow ornaments, having round the neck the name and titles of Tahutmes III. (18th dynasty). The oldest dated *transparent* glass known is a vase found by Layard at Nimroud, and bearing the name of Sargon (B.C. 722–705). (These objects are all in the British Museum. The first is figured in the Introduction to the *Catalogue* of glass objects in the South Kensington Museum, p. ix, the second in Wilkinson's *Anc. Egyp.* ii. 140, and the third in Layard, *Nin. and Bab.* p. 197).

The sands at the mouth of the Belus, the scene of Pliny's legend, were famous for their glass-making excellence, and were largely exported for this purpose to Sidon and elsewhere (Strabo, *Geog.* XVI. ii. 25; Jos. *Wars,* II. x. 12). Pliny refers to Sidon as a famous seat of glass manufacture, and Strabo also mentions the glass-works of Alexandria. Glass has been made in Hebron since very early times, and the glass-works there are said to supply in modern times a large part of the glass-ware used in Southern Syria, Egypt, and Arabia.

The references to glass in OT are few, and only one is direct, viz. that in Job 28[17], where RV so renders וּזְכוּכִית (AV *crystal*), following LXX ὕαλος and Vulg. *vitrum,* the allusion being to a rare and valuable substance, than which wisdom is still more precious. From Pr 23[31] it may be inferred that drinking-cups of transparent glass were used by the Hebrews. The phrase 'treasures hid in the sand,' in the blessing of Zebulun (Dt 33[19]), is interpreted in the Targum of Ps-Jonathan as referring to the sands of the Belus with their glass-making properties. (See Driver, *Deut.* p. 410). It has been supposed that the name מִשְׂרְפוֹת מַיִם 'burnings of waters' (Jos 11[8] 13[6]) may refer to glass-works, but the allusion may only be to the hot springs in the neighbourhood (for the various opinions and authorities see Keil, *in loc.*). There is a legend in the Koran (ch. 27) about a glass pavement in Solomon's palace at Jerus. which the queen of Sheba mistook for water. Recent excavations attest that glass was in use in Palestine at a very early date, and was most common during the Roman period (Warren, *Underground Jerusalem,* p. 518).

The Gr. word ὕαλος or ὕελος was applied by classical writers, not only to glass, but to mineral substances with similar properties (Herod. iii. 24 ; Achilles Tatius, ii. 3). Glass, indeed, was early used for making imitation gems (Pliny, xxxvi. 26), which Herodotus calls λίθινα χυτά (ii. 69). In NT ὕαλος and ὑάλινος are found only in Rev. The adj. is used in 4⁶ 15² of a sea ; the noun occurs in 21¹⁸· ²¹, gold being compared to it. In the former instances there may be an allusion to limpid transparency (in 4⁶ the sea is ὁμοία κρυστάλλῳ, cf. 22¹), but in the latter, notwithstanding the adj. διαυγής in 21²¹, the reference is obviously to brilliant lustre. Probably in all instances the point of the comparison is *smoothness* and *sheen* (in 15² the sea is μεμιγμένη πυρί, and in 22¹ the 'crystal' river is λαμπρός).

All other passages where glass occurs in AV refer to mirrors, and these were almost universally of polished metal. Pliny (*Nat. Hist.* xxxvi. 26) speaks of mirrors in connexion with the glass manufacture of Sidon, but his words seem to describe an unsuccessful experiment (see MIRROR). Windows in Pal. do not appear to have been glazed in ancient times, though glazed windows have been found in the ruins of Pompeii (Smith's *Dict. Antiq. s.v. vitrum*).

LITERATURE.—Dunlop, *Glass in the Old World*, where many authorities are mentioned ; Nesbitt, Introd. to *Catalogues of Slade collection in Brit. Mus.* and of glass articles in S. Kens. Mus. ; Wilkinson, *Anc. Egyp.* ii. 140 ff. ; Perrot and Chipiez, *Hist. of Art in Ancient Egypt*, 375, and in *Chaldæa and Assyria*, 306 ; Erman, *Ancient Egypt*, 458 ; Maspero, *Egyptian Archæology*, 253 ff.   JAMES PATRICK.

GLASS.—The word 'glass,' which is now colloquial Eng. for 'mirror,' occurs with this meaning in AV, both in OT and NT. In Is 3²³ 'the glasses' are part of the 'bravery' of the daughters of Zion (הַגִּלְיֹנִים, RV 'hand mirrors'). The translation is disputed by Ewald, who prefers 'gauzes,' 'transparent garments,' but it is generally accepted. 'Glass' is, however, an unfortunate rendering, as the material of which the *gillâyôn* was made was polished metal. The same word is used in 8¹ of a writing-tablet. In Ex 38⁸ we read of 'the looking-glasses (1611 'looking glasses') of the women assembling' (מַרְאֹת הַצֹּבְאֹת, AVm 'brasen glasses,' RV 'mirrors of the serving women'), which were given to make the laver of brass and its brazen foot in the tabernacle.* And in Job 37¹⁸ the sky is 'as a molten looking-glass' (1611 'looking glasse,' Heb. כִּרְאִי מוּצָק, RV 'as a molten mirror').

In Sir 12¹¹ the metaphor is used of a person wiping the rust off a looking-glass, but never being able to wipe it altogether away. The Gr. word is ἔσοπτρον (RV 'mirror'), which is found once elsewhere in LXX, Wis 7²⁶, where it is trᵈ in AV 'mirror' (the only occurrence of that Eng. word). This is the Gr. word which is trᵈ 'glass'= 'mirror' in NT. It is found only in 1 Co 13¹², Ja 1²³ (RV 'mirror'). In 2 Co 3¹⁸ the verb κατοπτρίζω (which occurs only here and in the middle voice) is trᵈ 'beholding as in a glass' (RV 'reflecting as a mirror,' RVm 'beholding as in a mirror'). Cf. Spenser, *Hymne of Heavenly Beautie*—

'Those unto all he daily doth display
And show himselfe in th' image of his grace,
As in a looking-glasse, through which he may
Be seene of all his creatures vile and base,
That are unable else to see his face,
His glorious face ! which glistereth else so bright,
That th' Angels' selves can not endure his sight.'

T. Adams in like manner speaks of seeing *through* a glass (*Practical Works*, ii. 27), 'He that hath seen heaven with the eye of faith, through the glass of the Scripture, slips off his coat with Joseph, and springs away.' But he also uses 'in a glass' (ii. 2), 'The world is a glass, wherein we may contemplate the eternal power and majesty

* For the religious significance of this passage, see Cobb, *Origines Judaicæ* (1895), p. 233 ff. ; also Schechter, *Studies in Judaism* (1896), p. 381 f., and *Expos. Times* (1896–97), viii. 1.

of God.' So Tindale (*Expositions*, Parker Soc., p. 89) speaks of the law as a glass in which a man sees his own damnation. Bp. Hall, in his 'Contemplations' (*Works*, 1634, ii. 107), uses the word literally : 'How witty wee are to supply all the deficiencies of nature : if wee be low, wee can adde cubits to our stature ; if ill colored, wee can borrow complexion ; if hayreless, periwiggs ; if dim-sighted, glasses ; if lame, croutches.' And again, metaphorically (*Works*, ii. 119), 'There cannot be a better glasse wherein to discerne the face of our hearts then our pleasures.' Knox employs 'mirror' and 'glass' together, 'Epistle to Mrs. Elizabeth Bowes' (*Works*, iii. 338) : 'The expositioun of your trubillis, and acknowledging of your infirmitie, war first unto me a verie mirrour and glass whairin I beheld my self sa rychtlie payntit furth, that nathing culd be mair evident to my awn eis.' See preceding article and MIRROR.   J. HASTINGS.

GLEANING.—The Hebrew law on this subject is contained in Lv 19⁹ᶠ· 23²² (both H) and Dt 24¹⁹⁻²¹. The first of these passages reads, 'When ye reap the harvest of your land, thou shalt not wholly reap the corners (פֵּאָה)* of thy field, neither shalt thou gather (תְּלַקֵּט) the gleaning (לֶקֶט) of thy harvest. And thou shalt not glean (תְעֹלֵל)† thy vineyard, neither shalt thou gather (תְּלַקֵּט) the fallen fruit (פֶּרֶט) of thy vineyard ; thou shalt leave them for the poor and for the stranger (גֵּר).' In Dt 24¹⁹⁻²¹ the law regarding gleanings in the cornfield and the vineyard is stated in substantially the same terms, and a similar provision is extended to the olive garden, 'When thou beatest (תַּחְבֹּט, a technical term ; cf. Is 27¹²) thine olive tree, thou shalt not go over the boughs again, it shall be for the stranger, for the fatherless, and for the widow.' The story of Ruth illustrates the working of the above provisions, which give point also to the question of Gideon, 'Is not the gleaning (עֹלֵלוֹת) of Ephraim better than the vintage of Abiezer ?' (Jg 8²).   J. A. SELBIE.

GLEDE (רָאָה, γύψ, *vultur*, Dt 14¹³).—In the passage (Lv 11¹⁴) the word דָּאָה *dâ'âh*, also trᵈ in the LXX γύψ, occurs in a corresp. position in the verse, and there can be little doubt that the רָאָה of Dt is a textual error for דָּאָה. In that passage AV tr. it 'kite' and RV 'vulture.' *Dâ'âh*, from a root signifying *to dart* or *fly swiftly*, is undoubtedly one of the raptatores, but which it is impossible to say with certaintory. Glede is an old name for the kite, and has been adopted by RV as well as AV for *râ'âh*. Tristram (*Nat. Hist. of Bible*, p. 186) thinks that רָאָה may refer to the *buzzard*, *Buteo vulgaris*, Leach, which is one of the birds known in Arabic as '*aḳâb*, and one of those known as *shâhîn*. See FALCON, KITE, VULTURE.   G. E. POST.

GLISTER.—The three verbs 'glisten,' 'glister,' and 'glitter' come from the same Teutonic base, *gli*, to shine, 'glitter' being traced to the Scandinavian, 'glisten' and 'glister' being apparently English in their earliest form. 'Glister' is simply a frequentative form of 'glisten.'

* This is the technical term which gave its name to the Talmudic tract *Peah*, in which the interpretation of the 'corners' and the whole subject of the rights of the poor to the produce of the land are discussed.

† עֹלֵלוֹת is used of the gleanings of a vineyard (Jg 8², Is 24¹³, Jer 49⁹, Mic 7¹) or of an olive tree (Is 17⁶), not of grain (לֶקֶט). The verb is used figuratively in Jg 20⁴⁵ of the fate of the flying Benjamites, 'And they gleaned of them (וַיְעֹלְלֻהוּ) in the highways five thousand men,' and in Jer 6⁹ 'They shall thoroughly glean (עוֹלֵל יְעוֹלְלוּ) the remnant of Israel as a vine.' The other verb is used in Jg 17 of the seventy kings that gathered (מְלַקְּטִים) their meat under the table of Adoni-bezek ; so frequently of picking up such articles as arrows, wood, etc.

The form 'glisten' is not used in AV :* 'glister' is found five times in AV of 1611 ; 'glitter,' nine times. Both words are used freely by writers of the period, and apparently without difference of meaning, so that the MSS and texts are sometimes uncertain. The tendency of later editions is to change 'glister' into 'glitter,' as has been done (since 1762) in AV with Job 20²⁵, which was 'glister' in 1611 ; and as is constantly done now in quoting the proverb, 'All that glisters is not gold,' a proverb found in Shaks. (*Merchant of Venice*, II. vii. 65), as well as in earlier writers, as T. Lever (*Sermons*, 1550, Arber's ed. p. 22), 'Alas, good brethren, as trulye as al is not golde that glystereth, so is it not vertue and honesty, but very vice and hipocrisie, wherof England at this day dothe most glorye.' As long as this proverb was quoted correctly (*i.e.* as long as 'glister' remained in good English use), it had a tendency to give 'glister' a depreciatory sense. This has been noticed in Milton (see Verity's notes on *Lycidas* in 'Pitt Press Milton,' p. 126). But there is no such distinction in AV. In course of time 'glister' went out of use, and now 'glitter' (perhaps under the influence of the same proverb) is often used with the depreciation of 'glister,' while 'glisten' has taken up the more honourable sense which once belonged to 'glitter.'

The occurrences of 'glister' in AV 1611 are : (1) Job 20²⁵ 'the glistering sword cometh out of his gall' (בָּרָק *bārâk*, a word used either lit. of 'lightning,' and then mostly in the plur. 'lightning flashes,' or fig. of the lightning-flash of a weapon. This fig. use is always applied to a weapon. AV then tr. by 'glitter' in Dt 32⁴¹, Ezk 21¹⁰·²⁸, Nah 3³, Hab 3¹¹ ; but in Ezk 21¹⁵ the feeble trⁿ is found 'it is made bright,' RV 'it is made as lightning,' as in vv.¹⁰·²⁸. In Dt 32⁴¹ the Heb. is particularly bold : 'If I whet the lightning of my sword,' as RVm, EV 'If I whet my glittering sword'). We find 'glister' applied to armour by Spenser, *FQ* I. i. 14—

> 'His glistring armor made
> A little glooming light, much like a shade.'

And by North, *Plutarch*, p. 395, 'For the glistering of their harness, so richly trimmed and set forth with gold and silver, the colours of their arming coats upon their curaces, after the fashion of the Medes and Scythians, mingled with the bright glistering steel and shining copper, gave such a show as they went and removed to and fro, that made a light as clear as if all had been on a very fire, a fearful thing to look upon.' The early Eng. versions apply the word frequently to fire, as Cov. Is 50¹¹ 'Ye walke in the glistringe of youre owne fyre' ; Ezk 1⁴ 'And I loked, and beholde, a stormy wynde came out off the north with a greate cloude full of fyre, which his glistre lightened all rounde aboute' ; and v.¹³ 'and the fyre gaue a glistre,† and out off the fyre there wente lighteninge.'

(2) 1 Ch 29² 'glistering stones' (אַבְנֵי־פוּךְ ; RV 'stones for inlaid work'). RV is rather an interpretation than a translation. The *puk* was an eye-paint made of antimony, much used by Eastern ladies, and not confined to ladies (see Lane, *Mod. Egyptians*, Gardner's ed. p. 53 ; and

Shaw, *Travels in Barbary*², 229). The word occurs also in 2 K 9³⁰, where in AVm the Heb. is trᵈ literally, 'Jezebel . . . put her eyes in painting' ; Is 54¹¹, where 'I will lay thy stones in fair colours' is lit. as RVm 'in antimony' (it is the mortar, says Orelli, with which the new stones of Jerusalem will be set, that they may shine forth like dazzling eyes) ; and Jer 4³⁰ where the eye-paint is directly spoken of. The nearest parallel to our passage is Is 54¹¹, and the 'glistering' of AV is better than the 'inlaid' of RV ; for some kind of coloured, brilliant stone seems meant. The LXX rendering is λίθους πολυτελεῖς ('very costly stones') ; Vulg. *quasi stibinos* (*stibium*, antimony) ; Wyc. 1388 'stonys as of the colour of wymmens oynement' ; Luth. *eingefasste Rubinen* (taking the previous word along with this) ; so Cov. 'set Rubyes' ; Rog. 'set stones,' with marg. 'some read Carbuncle, or ani other precious stone called Stibion' ; Gen. 'carbuncle stones' ; Bish. 'glystering stones' ; Dou. 'as it were stibians,' with marg. 'a kind of finne white stone' ; Ostervald, *pierres d'escarboncle* ; Segond, *pierres brillantes* ; Kautzsch, *Puchsteine*, with marg. '*pukh* bedeutet anderwärts die Augenschminke, bezeichnet also wohl einen schwarzglänzenden Stein' ; Cheyne, 'stones of (*i.e.* edged with) antimony.' For the Eng. word cf. Spenser, *FQ* I. iv. 8—

> 'A mayden Queene that shone, as Titans ray,
> In glistring gold and peerelesse pretious stone.'

(3) 2 Es 10²⁵ 'And it came to pass, while I was talking with her, behold, her face upon a sudden shined exceedingly, and her countenance glistered, so that I was afraid of her and mused what it might be' (*species* [Fritzsche *specie*] *coruscus fiebat visus ejus*, RV 'her countenance glistered like lightning'). The countenance has the epithet 'glister' applied to it in Spenser's *Hymne of Heavenly Beautie*, quoted under GLASS—

> 'His glorious face ! which glistereth else so bright,
> That th' Angels selues can not endure his sight.'

(4) 1 Mac 6³⁹ 'Now when the sun shone upon the shields of gold and brass, the mountains glistered therewith, and shined like lamps of fire' (ὡς δὲ ἔστιλβεν ὁ ἥλιος ἐπὶ τὰς χρυσᾶς καὶ χαλκᾶς [A omits καὶ χαλκᾶς] ἀσπίδας, ἔστιλβεν τὰ ὄρη ἀπ' αὐτῶν, καὶ κατηύγαζεν ὡς λαμπάδες πυρός ; RV 'Now when the sun shone upon the shields of gold and brass, the mountains shone therewith, and blazed like torches of fire'). The verb στίλβειν occurs once in NT, Mk 9³ in the narrative of Christ's transfiguration, τὰ ἱμάτια αὐτοῦ ἐγένετο στίλβοντα, where RV renders 'his garments became glistering,' after Rhem. version.

(5) Lk 9²⁹ 'And as he prayed, the fashion of his countenance was altered, and his raiment was white and glistering' (ὁ ἱματισμὸς αὐτοῦ λευκὸς ἐξαστράπτων ; RV 'became white and dazzling'). This is the only occurrence in NT of the Gr. compound ἐξαστράπτειν. It is found in LXX, Ezk 1⁴ of the flashing of flames of fire, 1⁷ and Dn 10⁶ of the glittering of burnished brass, and Nah 3³ of flashing spears. The simple verb is used twice by St Luke (and by no other NT writer), 17²⁴ of the flashing of lightning, and 24⁴ of the 'shining garments' (RV 'dazzling apparel') of the angels at the tomb.* The meaning of the simple verb, then, is to flash as lightning, and the compound means to flash forth, and may be consciously chosen (as Farrar holds) to suggest that the flashing was from some *inward* radiance. The versions as a rule are feeble and inadequate : Vulg. 'vestitus ejus albus et refulgens' ; Wyc.

---

* Nor in Shaks. or Milton, though it is at least as old as Udall, on Ac 10 : 'And sodainly beholde a certain man, whose countenaunce was full of maiestie, stood visible before me, in a glistening garmente.'

† In the New Ed. of Jamieson's *Scottish Dictionary* (vol. ii. 1886) we find the entry : 'GLISTER, subst. Lustre, glitter, "The glister of the profeit, that was jugeit heirof to have insewit to Scottis men, at the first sicht blindit mony menis eyis"—Knox, *Hist.* p. 110. Su.–G. *glistra*, scintilla, Teut. *glinster*, id. *glinsteren*, *glisteren*, scintillare, fulgere. Although *glister* be used in Eng. as a verb, I have not observed that it occurs as a subst.' But here are two examples from Coverdale, and at v.¹³ the Gen. and Bishops' Bibles have the subst. also.

* Cf. Milton, *Comus*, 219—
> 'I see ye visibly, and now believe
> That he, the Supreme good, t' whom all things ill
> Are but as slavish officers of vengeance,
> Would send a glistering guardian, if need were,
> To keep my life and honour unassail'd.'

'his clothing whit shining'; Luther 'sein Kleid war weiss, und glänzte'; Tind. 'his garment was whyte and shoon'; so Cov. (shyned), Rog., Cran., Gen. 1557; Gen. 1560 'his garment *was* white and glistered'; Bish. 'his garment shining very white'; Rhem. 'his raiment white and glistering'; Ost. 'ses habits *devinrent* blancs *et* resplendissants *comme un éclair*'; Olt. 'ses vêtements devinrent éblouissants de blancheur'; Seg. 'Son vêtement devint d'une éclatante blancheur'; Weizsäcker 'sein Gewand ward strahlend weiss.' The RV word 'dazzling' (introduced also at Lk 24⁴) is new, and involves a new idea which the Gr. word does not suggest, and which transfers the mind from the sight to the spectators.*

By a strange contrast Tindale uses 'glistringe whyte' (Lv 13². ²³) of the 'bright spot' in the skin which had to be examined for leprosy. Bunyan more appropriately (*Holy War*, p. 146) makes Emmanuel command 'that those that waited upon him should go and bring forth out of his Treasury those white and glistering robes *that I*, said he, *have provided and laid up in store for my* Mansoul.' And Rutherford (*Letters*, No. 51) writes to Marion M'Naught, 'I dare in faith say and write (I am not dreaming), Christ is but seeking (what He will have and make) a clean glistering bride out of the fire.'   J. HASTINGS.

GLORIOUS.—The adj. 'glorious' had a wider application formerly than it has now. Thus Sylvester, *Du Bartas's Weeks*, ii.—

> ' Yet will I not this Work of mine give o're.
> The Labour's great : my Courage yet is more ;
>
> Ther's nothing Glorious but is hard to get.'

It is applied in AV not only to the king (2 S 6²⁰), and the king's daughter (Ps 45¹³), but also to the beauty of Ephraim standing above its fertile valley (Is 28¹. ⁴), and the security of Tyre 'in the heart of the seas' (Ezk 27²⁵); Wisdom is glorious (Wis 6¹²), and the 'fruit of good labours' (3¹⁵), and the 'long robe of righteousness' (Sir 27⁸); and (not only figuratively but literally) dress is described as glorious, Esther's (Ad. Est 14² 15¹), the apparel of the young men of Judah in the peaceful days of Simon (1 Mac 14⁹), and even Nicanor's apparel (2 Mac 8³⁵).

But the most evidently obsolete use of the word is when it means *boastful*, or as we still say *vainglorious*, Ad. Est 11¹¹ 16⁴ ('lifted up with the glorious words of lewd persons that were never good,' τοῖς τῶν ἀπειραγάθων κόμποις ἐπαρθέντες, RV 'boastful'). This meaning of 'glorious,' which follows Lat. *gloriosus*, was once common, and is still retained by the French *glorieux*. Thus Bacon (*Essays*, 'Of Followers and Friends,' Gold. Treas. ed. p. 198), 'Likewise Glorious Followers, who make themselves as Trumpets, of the Commendation of those they Follow, are full of Inconvenience'; and 'Of Vaine-glory' (p. 216), 'They that are Glorious must needs be Factious; for all Bravery stands upon Comparisons.' So Chapman, *Homer's Iliads*, xiii. 738—

> 'Vain-spoken man and glorious.'
>   J. HASTINGS.

GLORY (IN OT).—In EV 'glory' most frequently corresponds to the Hebrew כָּבוֹד, which is also, owing to the difference between Hebrew and English idiom, in some cases tr⁴ by 'glorious' (*e.g.* Is 4² 11¹⁰, Neh 9⁵). But several other Heb. words are also sometimes tr⁴ by 'glory' or 'glorious,' viz. אַדִּיר, אַדֶּרֶת, and the Niph. and Hiph. of the vb. [אדר] in Zec 11³ and v.² (RVm), Ex 15⁶. ²¹, Is 42²¹; אוֹר Ps 76⁴; הוֹד

---

e.g. Ps 45⁸ 148¹³ ; הָדָר *e.g.* Is 5¹⁴ (cf. הֲרוּר 63¹), Ps 90¹⁶ ; תִּפְאָרָה *e.g.* Ps 16³¹ 20²⁹ ; צְבִי *e.g.* Is 13¹⁹ 24¹⁶. In Dn 'glory' occurs several times as trⁿ of the Aram. יְקָרָא. The verb 'to glory' in EV generally corresponds to הִתְהַלֵּל 'to make one's boast of,' *e.g.* Jer 9²³f. ; and 'to glorify' or 'be glorified' to various verbal forms of the roots כבד and פאר.

Full details as to the various Heb. words must be sought in the Heb. lexicon or in commentaries on the various passages. Generally speaking, the English term is sufficiently clear from the context in spite of the number of the Heb. words which it renders. But we have to consider here some characteristic or peculiar uses of the term, especially the important ideas expressed by the phrase 'the glory of J''.'

i. 1. The 'glory' of men or of material objects calls for little explanation. A man's 'glory' is sometimes the outward tokens of his prosperity, such as silver and gold, or the splendour of his appearance; sometimes his reputation, the esteem in which he is held. For the first sense we may refer to Is 61⁶, where the term stands in parallelism with 'wealth.' Again in Hag 2⁷ 'glory' is parallel to the 'desirable things of all nations'; we must consider these to, be more explicitly described by the next verse as consisting of silver and gold, and these in their turn (v.⁹) as constituting 'the latter glory' of the temple; cf. also Is 66¹¹f., Ps 49¹⁶. ¹⁷, Nah 2⁹. In the last passage we are near to what was perhaps the original meaning of the Heb. *kābôd*, viz. 'weight'; cf. the use of the vb. *kābēd* in *e.g.* Job 6³, and the noun *kōbed* in Pr 27³. We may notice also the association of the word (*kābôd*) with '*ôsher* 'riches' in Est 5¹¹, where it also stands in parallelism with *rôb*, 'multitude.' So the glory of a king (or a nation) consists in the warriors that betoken his might, Is 8⁷ 17³f. 21¹⁶ ; of Lebanon (Is 60¹³), in the trees with which it is covered; the 'king's daughter' of Ps 45¹³ is 'all glorious' in virtue of her richly adorned clothing; cf. Ex 28², and metaphorically Job 19⁹.

2. For instances of 'glory' in the sense of 'reputation' see Ps 4², Job 29²⁰, 2 S 6²⁰ ('How glorious was the king of Israel,' *i.e.* 'how much reputation did he gain for himself'—ironically). But in most cases where the Heb. word (*kābôd*) has this sense, it is tr⁴ in EV by 'honour,' *e.g.* Ec 10¹, Pr 21²¹.

The usage in Ps 73²⁴, if the text be correct, is isolated; 'glory' here appears to mean the splendour into which men pass, who like Enoch and Elijah are translated by God; so RV text; RVm is hardly so probable a translation. Against the text, see, however, *e.g.* Wellh. in *SBOT*.

3. The 'glory' of a nation may be, as we have seen, its warriors as betokening its might. But it is a favourite prophetic doctrine that Israel's might does not consist in its armies and weapons of war, but in J'' (cf. Is 31¹⁻³, Zec 4⁶, Ps 20⁷). Hence, perhaps, we may derive a noticeable usage whereby J'' is described as Israel's glory. Thus Jeremiah (2¹¹) says, 'Hath a nation changed their gods which yet are no gods? but my people have changed their glory (*i.e.* J'') for that which doth not profit' (*i.e.* for other gods) ; and probably Hos 4⁷ᵇ originally ran 'they have exchanged their glory for infamy' with a like meaning. Cf. also Ps 3³ (cf. 62⁷) 106²⁰.

4. Another noticeable use of the term is to describe the self; thus it forms the parallel to 'my soul,' a frequent Hebrew term for self, in Gn 49⁶ 'O my soul, come not thou into their council; unto their assembly, my glory, be not thou united'; and to 'heart' in Ps 16⁹ 108¹. Cf. also Ps 7⁶ 57⁸ and 30¹² (where read כְּבוֹדִי for כָּבוֹד). This usage is generally explained as a poetical expression for 'self'; and, unlike 'soul,' 'glory' in this sense certainly is confined to poetical passages. For a somewhat parallel usage we might then compare

---

* 'White and dazzling' is Mrs. Lewis's trⁿ of the Sinaitic Palimpsest, but with marg. 'like lightning.' ܟܒܪ ; cf. Delitzsch's Hebrew translation of the Gospels, הָלְכִין וְהַבְרִיק.

'my darling' (יְחִידָתִי) in Ps 22²⁰. But another explanation deserving of attention has been offered (see *e.g.* Dillm. on Gn 49⁶). In Assyrian *kabidtu* (כָּבֵד 'liver') is frequently used as a synonym for *napištu* (= נֶפֶשׁ 'soul'); it has therefore been suggested that in the Hebrew passages above cited we ought to point *kĕbēdî* instead of *kĕbôdî* and tr. literally 'my liver,' *i.e.* 'myself'; the liver, which was thought to be a seat of life, affording as suitable a periphrasis for the self as 'the soul'; cf. La 2¹¹ and (for Assyrian usage) Fried. Delitzsch, *Assyrisches Handwörterbuch*, p. 317a (*s.v. kabidtu*). Some support is given to this view by the fact that the LXX translates the word in Gn 49⁶ by τὰ ἥπατά μου (*i.e.* 'my liver'); on the other hand, in the Psalms (which were translated later) the regular rendering is δόξα (otherwise 15[16]⁹).

ii. **The Glory of J″.**—The glory of J″ (כְּבוֹד יהוה) or of God (כְּבוֹד אֵל, אֱלֹהִים) is, like 'the name of J″' (8²), with which it stands in parallelism in Is 59¹⁹, Ps 102¹⁵,* a summary term for the self-revealed character and being of God. It is also frequently used, especially in certain writings, to denote a particular physical appearance indicating the divine presence. It has been generally assumed that the latter is the original usage; but this, as will be seen, is far from certain, and, in any case, the sharply defined significance of the term in P cannot be traced back to early times. In several cases the meaning of the term is ambiguous, and it has been interpreted by some commentators in the one, by others in the other, of the two senses just indicated. But the cases in which the meaning is quite unambiguous render it possible and convenient to divide our examination of the usage and more detailed significance of the term into two sections, according as the reference is to the self-revealed character or to the physical manifestation of God. In conclusion, we shall have to consider certain ambiguous passages, and the relation between the two meanings.

1. *The glory of J″ as a term for the self-revealed character and being of God.*—Since Ex 33¹⁷⁻²³ belongs, in all probability, to a secondary (7th cent.) stratum of J (see below, § 3), the earliest occurrence of the phrase is in Isaiah, who uses it (6³) quite unambiguously to denote the divine nature as revealed in the world; J″'s glory is the outward manifestation of His holiness. The sense is probably similar in 3⁸, where Judah's sin is represented as culminating in this: that she wilfully opposed herself to a God who had manifested Himself to her in His majesty and might (cf. Am 3²). Although these are the only two passages in Isaiah's writings in which the phrase actually occurs, the underlying idea of J″'s power and might as manifested in nature and history is fundamental with the prophet; cf. especially 2¹⁰· ²¹, where the recurring term is similar, but not as in EV identical, with the one we are discussing—the glory of His majesty (הֲדַר גְּאוֹנוֹ) in vv. ¹⁰· ¹⁹· ²¹. We may therefore reasonably attribute to Isaiah a commanding influence over both the phrase and the idea as they appear in subsequent literature. The direct influence of Is 6³ is seen in Hab 2¹⁴, and also, in all probability, in Nu 14²¹ (cf. *e.g.* Kuenen, *Hexateuch*, p. 247). In Nu 14²² the glory of J″ is specifically the manifestation of His nature in history, in the life of the nation; and this is the case also in Dt 5²⁴ [Heb. 5²¹], although at first sight the context generally might suggest that the phrase signifies here a physical appearance; but the accompanying synonym 'his greatness,' the meaning of which is unambiguous (cf. 3²⁴ 9²⁶ 11²), is decisive against this. The same predominant reference to history marks Ezekiel's use

of the phrase in 39²¹, and underlies his use of the verb (נִכְבַּד = to show oneself glorious, to manifest one's glory) in 28²² 39¹³. The phrase is quite clearly to be taken in the same sense in Is 66¹⁹, where J″'s glory is the counterpart of His 'fame,' and is to be declared among the nations (yet on this and the preceding verse see Dillm.); according to Cheyne (in his *Commentary*) also in Is 40⁵. In the Psalms the particular nuance of the phrase differs in different passages. Judging from the general tenor of the Psalms, it is God's manifestation through His control of the lives of nations or individuals that the respective writers intend mainly to imply by their use of the phrase in 57⁵· ¹¹ 63² (cf. Ps 73¹⁷—in the sanctuary the Psalmist realizes the meaning of J″'s moral government, and so perceives 'his glory'), 72¹⁹ (= Is 6³, Nu 14²¹), 96³ ('his glory' || 'his marvellous works'), 97⁶ (|| 'his righteousness'), 102¹¹ᶠ. (cf. Is 59¹⁹), 138⁵ (|| 'the ways of J″'); cf. also 'the glory of thy kingdom' || 'thy power,' 'the glory of the majesty of his kingdom' || 'his mighty acts,' 45¹¹ᶠ. On the other hand, in 19¹, where it is parallel to 'handy work' (מַעֲשֵׂה יָדָיו), and in 104³¹, the chief emphasis lies on the fact that the natural world is a revelation of God; this is perhaps also the case with 8²,* although in this psalm it is, in particular, man's place in nature that reveals God's nature and purpose. Pr 25² in connexion with the foregoing usages, and in the light of such passages as Job 28, may be interpreted to mean that the very mysteries of nature, the sense that there is much hidden which is not revealed, contributes to man's perception of God's nature. The term 'glory,' especially in a phrase that recurs more than once and deserves particular attention, is also used in the modified sense of the praise which God's character, as revealed in His works and deeds, should call forth; thus 'the glory of his [J″s] name' or 'the glory due unto his name,' where both renderings of the RV represent the same Hebrew phrase (כְּבוֹד שְׁמוֹ), means the praise due to His self-revealed character from those to whom it has been revealed (29² 66² 96⁸), and similarly the glory of J″ (Is 42⁸ 43⁷ 48¹¹; cf. also Ps 79⁹ in connexion with v.¹³). In 113⁴, as the parallel indicates, the phrase is barely more than a periphrasis for J″.

2. *The 'glory of J″' denoting a physical phenomenon indicative of the divine presence.*—With the exception of a single Jahwistic passage (Ex 33¹⁷⁻²³), and, according to a possible interpretation, a single passage in Jeremiah (17¹²) which must be left for discussion in the next section, this usage first appears in Ezekiel, who in any case appears to have exercised as great an influence on this modification of the idea as Isaiah on that discussed in the foregoing section. Ezekiel, as we have seen, does indeed employ the phrase and the cognate verb in the manner already discussed in the preceding section; but generally with him the glory of J″ is a bright or fiery appearance that resembles the rainbow (1²⁸ 10⁴), causing the ground, where it appears, to shine (43²); moves from one place to another (9³ 10⁴· ¹⁸ 43²), or is borne from one place to another on cherubim (10¹⁹ 11²²ᶠ.), each movement being accompanied by a rushing sound (2¹², where read ברום for ברוך, and translate 'a great rushing when the glory of J″ was lifted up from its place'). Again, as in the vision of the coming judgment the 'glory of J″' is seen by Ezekiel to leave Jerusalem (11²³), so in the vision of coming restoration it is seen returning to the city (43²ᶠᶠ.).†

---

* Cf. the combination שֵׁם כְּבֹרֶךָ in Neh 9⁵ (cf. Ps 72¹⁹).

* In the theophany of Hab 3³ the word used for 'his glory' in v.³ is different in the Hebrew (הוֹדוֹ). So also in Ps 148¹³.

† Contrast the early narrative in Samuel of the loss of the ark to the Philistines (1 S 4²¹· ²²). The ark symbolized J″'s presence; with it J″ is felt to be leaving Israel; but the 'glory' which departs is the glory of Israel. The possession of the ark was

In brief, with Ezekiel, 'the glory of J"' has become a term for a theophany; and accordingly when Ezekiel sees it, he worships (44[4]). But it is important to observe that throughout it is a theophany seen *in vision*; Ezekiel no more regards the appearance which he terms the glory of J" as visible to the natural eye, than he regards the whole complex appearance of the chariot in ch. 1 as being so visible. It is further to be observed that in 39[21] the only passage where he refers to the 'glory of J",' except in his visions, he uses the phrase in the sense discussed in § II. 1. Zechariah associates fire and glory when he says, 'For I, saith the LORD, will be unto her a wall of fire round about, and I will be the glory in the midst of her' (2[5]); but he is evidently speaking in metaphor. In P the usage is different; the idea that the glory of J" is the divine nature manifested through the divine activity only finds expression—and that, perhaps, not quite consciously—in the use of the verb (נִכְבַּד), discussed above, in Ex 14[4. 17. 18], Lv 10[3]. The actual phrase 'the glory of J"' is *invariably* used by P of a physical phenomenon manifest to ordinary natural vision. The 'glory of the LORD' first appeared at the time of the giving of the Law on Sinai; it then 'abode upon Mount Sinai,' and its appearance was 'like devouring fire on the top of the mount in the eyes of all the children of Israel' (Ex 24[16-18]). As a consequence of coming into close proximity with 'the glory of J"' (Ex 24[18]), Moses' face shone with a brightness so fierce that he had to veil his face when he came before the people (Ex 34[29-35]). With the exception of this unique occasion, 'the glory of J"' invariably appears at the tabernacle; see Ex 29[43] 40[34. 35] 16[7. 10] [a misplaced narrative which should follow the narrative of the erection of the tabernacle: in v.[10] restore המקדש (towards) the sanctuary, for the senseless redactorial המדבר=(towards) the wilderness; cf. *e.g.* Dillm. *ad loc.*], Lv 9[6. 23], Nu 14[10] 16[19] 16[42] (He 17[7]) 20[6]. The appearance of 'the glory of J"' to the people was either a sign of the divine favour (Lv 9[6. 23]), or, more frequently, a warning of divine anger, *e.g.* Ex 16[7. 10], Nu 14[10]. It is never directly stated of 'the glory of J"' in connexion with the tabernacle that it was a fiery appearance; but this is clearly implied, for there, as on Mt. Sinai, it appears in connexion with cloud (Ex 16[10], Nu 16[42], and in Nu 14[10] [LXX], cf. also Lv 9[23. 24]). The cloud, it must be remembered, according to P, always abode upon or covered the tabernacle, and became fiery in appearance at night (Ex 40[38] 9[16]). We must therefore seek the peculiarity of 'the glory of J"' (as conceived by P) in the fact that it was a sudden fiery appearance in the cloud by *day* (cf. Ex 16[7. 10]—note 'in the morning'), Nu 16[16. 19], cf. Lv 10[2. 3]. Closely related to P's conception is that found in 1 K 8[11]=2 Ch 5[14] 7[1. 3], all of which passages have been influenced by P (on 1 K 8[1-11] see Cornill, *Einleitung*, p. 109).

3. Before attempting to discuss *the relation between the two conceptions* already considered, we must examine certain passages where the phrase either possesses a different meaning or is ambiguous. Most important is the passage in Ex 33[17-23]. This scarcely belongs to the earliest stratum of J. If it is correctly assigned by Kuenen (*Hexateuch*, p. 246 f.) and others (cf. Wellhausen, *Composition*, p. 96; see Driver, *LOT*[6] p. 38) to the 7th cent., the earliest usage of the phrase in the extant literature is by Isaiah. Now, the conception of the author of Ex 33[17-23] is clearly not identical with Isaiah's; but neither is it reasonable to identify his conception with that of Ezekiel or P. In Ex 33[17-23] 'the glory of J"' is

Israel's glory; the loss of it the departure of their glory (cf. § I. 3 above). The passage has not therefore a direct bearing on the conception of 'the glory of J".'

used with reference to a theophany in human shape; in reply to Moses' request that he may see J"'s glory, J" promises that though he cannot see His face, and therefore, while His glory is passing by, Moses' face must be covered, yet, when His glory has passed by, he may look after J" and see His back. The idea is clearly not the same as in 16[10] or 24[17]. In the Jahwistic passage we have a glorious *appearance in human form to Moses only*; in P, *a fiery appearance*, which can hardly have been, and is certainly not implied to have been, in human form *to all the people*. Jer 14[21] (cf. also 17[12], which, however, is perhaps post-Jeremianic—cf. Cornill, *Einleitung*, p. 167; Driver, *LOT*[6] p. 237) might at first appear to presuppose Ezekiel's or P's conception; but we really do more justice to the context, which is entirely concerned with J"'s activity in history and nature, by following the suggestion of the parallel term 'thy name,' and interpreting the phrase 'the throne of thy glory' in accordance with the usage discussed in § II. 1; cf. also Giesebrecht on 17[12]. In certain late * passages of the Bk. of Isaiah it is most natural to interpret the phrase of a physical appearance; but all these passages are of a poetical character; see 35[2] 58[8] 60[1. 2], and perhaps also 40[5] (cf. Dillm. *ad loc.*). The same interpretation should possibly be given to Ps 26[8b]—'the place of the tabernacle of thy glory' (מְקוֹם מִשְׁכַּן כְּבוֹדֶךָ)—where the phraseology at any rate has probably been suggested by P. Perhaps we ought also to compare in the present connexion the (probably non-Isaianic) reference in Is 11[10]; cf. also 60[13].

In the light of the preceding survey of the exegetical and critical data, the most probable conclusion appears to be that 'the glory of J"' was originally used to express the manifestations of J"'s power and might, or more generally of His nature; through Isaiah the phrase became enriched and deepened in meaning, and subsequently continued to express this idea, and became reflected also in the Niphal of the verb. Comparatively early, however, viz. in Ex 33[17-23], we find the phrase also used in connexion with, and perhaps itself expressing, a theophany in human form: possibly, however, 'glory' is here merely a periphrasis for self, just as it is in connexion with a human subject in an early poem (Gn 49[6]), and several psalms (*e.g.* 7[5] 16[9] 57[8] — yet on this usage cf. § I. 4); note the equivalence in Ex 33[22] 'while *my glory* passeth by . . . until *I* have passed by.' The phrase first unmistakably expresses a physical phenomenon in Ezekiel, who uses it to express the form under which *in his visions* he realizes the movements of J", more especially the coming removal of His presence from Jerusalem and His subsequent return after the Exile is ended. But it is not till we come to P in the 5th cent. that the phrase is used of a physical phenomenon actually supposed to have been visible to the natural eye. This writer uses it of a particular fiery appearance, by which the Deity indicated His presence in the tabernacle. The *idea* of such a theophany in fire and cloud is unquestionably ancient, as we may see in the case of the burning bush, or in J's account of the Pillar of Fire and Cloud; the use of the particular phrase 'glory of J",' which originally possessed an entirely different significance, to express that idea, is first suggested by Ezekiel, and first really appropriated by P and his school (1 K 8[11], 2 Ch 7). As understood by P, 'the glory of J"' is closely related to the Shechinah of later Jewish theology (on which cf. Weber, *Die altsynagog. Paläst. Theol.* pp. 179-184). How thoroughly the priestly writer has

* Cf. Cheyne, *Introd. to Book of Isaiah*, pp. 208 ff., 298, 381 (all post-exilic passages).

materialized the earlier conception may be seen by a comparison with Dt. The recurring promise of that book is that God will cause *His name* to dwell at the one sanctuary. P has materialized this into a physical phenomenon. If we have rightly interpreted the phrase in certain post-exilic passages in the Bk. of Isaiah of a physical phenomenon, we may probably account for the use by the combined influence of Ezekiel, and such stories connected with the Exodus as those of the pillar of cloud (cf. Is 4[5]).

LITERATURE.—In addition to *OT Theologies* and *Commentaries*, consult especially Duhm, *Theologie der Propheten*, p. 169 ff. ; Baudissin, *Studien zur sem. Religionsgeschichte*, pp. 104–108 ; Cheyne, *Origin of the Psalter*, p. 331 f. (notes w and x).

G. B. GRAY.

GLORY (NT).—The tr. in NT (AV and RV) once of κλέος 'renown' (1 P 2[20] only), and, in its verbal signification, occasionally representing καυχᾶσθαι 'to boast' and its cognates καύχησις 'boasting' (Ro 15[17]) and καύχημα 'something to boast of' (1 Co 9[16]) ; but almost entirely confined to the rendering of δόξα and its correlatives. Δόξα runs parallel in its significations with its parent δοκέω, though finally going beyond it. The history of this verb, from the oldest Greek downwards, shows that the chronological order of its meanings is (1) intrans. 'I seem,' (2) trans. 'I think'; the extension from δοκεῖ μοι 'it seems to me,' to δοκῶ 'I think,' being due to the same personalization as is the Eng. extension of 'If it please you' to 'If you please.' Its fundamental idea appears to be *subjective judgment*, which may be right or wrong, as opposed to φαίνεσθαι, which is objective and external to the thinker,—the *look* of a thing ; which also, of course, may be either veracious or misleading. But δόξα stands for the classical sense of *opinion* once only in sacred literature, viz. 4 Mac 5[18] ; and as mere *outward appearance* in opposition to *reality* (Plato, Xenophon) it does not occur in NT ; for whereas the LXX version of Is 11[3] allowed itself δόξα there for the 'sight of the eyes' as the false guide to judgment, the NT at Jn 7[24] has 'judge not according to ὄψις.' But while it ignored the precise senses of *appearance* and *opinion*, the NT usage, following that of the LXX, accepted the classical and LXX development of *outward appearance* (rather than *opinion*) into *reputation*, and affords abundant instances of the LXX non-classical expansion of the same idea into *outward splendour* or *manifested excellence*. Both *reputation* and *splendour* (or *manifested excellence*) find their common expression in *glory*. Thus Jn 12[43] 'They loved the glory (honour) from men rather than the glory from God'; Lk 2[9] 'The glory (brightness) of the Lord shone round about them'; and 2 Co 3[9] 'Much rather doth the ministration of righteousness exceed in glory (manifested excellence).' [Cf. OT בָּבוֹד *kābôd*, in its varied senses : *honour* (to God) Jos 7[19], or men Gn 31[1] (Jacob) ; *brightness* (in the cloud), the rabbinical *Shechinah* Ex 16[10] ; or *beauty of appearance* Is 60[13] (Lebanon, cf. 1 Co 15[40. 41]) ; *manifested excellence* Ex 33[22] 'my glory,' cf. v.[19] 'my goodness'].

These senses in NT are common and undisputed, as is also the closely related sense of *majesty or magnificence of king or ruler*, e.g. of God, in doxologies, 1 P 4[11] ; of Christ, Ja 2[1], 2 Th 1[9] ('the glory of his might'), cf. He 1[3] ; and of man as ruling for God, 1 Co 11[7] (the woman making conspicuous the authority of the man). But there are still differences of opinion as to the sense of *brightness* and the extensions of it. When used of God, of Christ, of regenerated and glorified humanity, how far is it literal, symbolical, ethical ? That it is *ethically* used of God is obvious from such passages as Ro 3[23] 'All have sinned and fall short of the glory of God,' *i.e.* the manifested perfection of His char-

acter, or, according to the context (vv.[21. 22]), His *righteousness*. That it is ethically used of Christ is obvious from Jn 1[14] 'We beheld his glory . . . full (as He was) of grace and truth.' That it is ethically used of human nature in the process of glorification, *i.e.* of ethical and spiritual transfiguration, is obvious from 2 Co 3[18] 'We all, with unveiled face, mirroring in ourselves the glory of the Lord, are being transformed into the same image from glory to glory, even as from the Lord *the Spirit.*'

A *literal* element also presents itself. The conception and description in NT of the divine manifestation in heaven and on earth, of the form of heavenly beings, and of the future appearance (according to St. Paul) of the glorified children of God in the heavenly body, are in the line of the OT theophanies and angelophanies with their light and brightness. This fact is clear from the 'glory of the Lord' round the shepherds (Lk 2[9]), from the transfiguration of Christ (Lk 9[32]), from the appearance of Moses and Elias 'in glory' (Lk 9[31]), from St. Paul's vision of the Lord in the way (Ac 9[3] and parallel passages in Ac 22 and 26), and from the 'body of glory' (Ph 3[21]), perhaps suggested by this vision. By this apparent literalism in the conceptions of the divine and the coming 'glory,' Pfleiderer is induced to define the specially Pauline δόξα as 'the brilliant light which is everywhere the manifestation of the πνεῦμα, and forms a special attribute of the majesty of God' (*Paulinism*, Eng. tr. i. 135), the πνεῦμα being 'heavenly, supersensuous matter,' 'originally belonging to God and then to Christ the Son of God, in such wise that it constitutes their divine essence, and is presented in a concrete form in them' (i. 200). And Weiss, while denying that the 'essence of the Spirit is (in St. Paul) conceived as a luminous substance' (*Bib. Theol. of NT*, Eng. tr. i. 397), affirms that 'it is characteristic of the Pauline theology that the apostle has transformed the (earlier and vaguer) idea of the divine δόξα into an altogether concrete notion,—that of a heavenly radiant light proceeding from a supermundane substance of light' (i. 396), 'a luminous light-substance in which God reveals Himself' (ii. 187, n. 7). 'Out of it are formed the bodies of the heavenly beings, and . . . this same δόξα will believers yet bear when they are conformed to His image, to whom, as the Lord of the Spirit, this δόξα belongs.' Weiss, indeed, disclaims materialism in this interpretation ; but it is hard, with this disclaimer, to see what is meant by 'supermundane substance.' Dr. Sanday also (*Romans*, p. 85), quoting from Weber (*Altsyn. Theol.* p. 214) the rabbinical view that 'the glory' (the first among the six things lost by Adam at the fall) was a reflection from the divine glory which, before the fall, brightened Adam's face, goes on to say : 'Clearly, St. Paul conceives of this glory as in process of being recovered : the physical sense is also enriched by its extension to attributes that are moral and spiritual.'

It is proverbially difficult, of course, to distinguish sometimes, in St. Paul's expressions, the literal from the freely symbolical : the discriminating critic will find this difficulty not only with δόξα but also with σάρξ, σῶμα, and πνεῦμα ; and it is a difficulty that must be expected to arise when, in an old vocabulary, verbal expression has to be found for new thought. In this exigency words are often selected which, being in themselves subjective as well as objective, admit of being wholly subjectivized. One of these plastic words appears to be δόξα in the moulding hands of St. Paul : a word elastic and not rigid, a word 'thrown out at an idea' (like the words just mentioned), and not intended mechanically to define it. It seems unjustifiable, therefore, to chain St. Paul to the rigid, concrete conception of a literal light substance (even though it be elevated into the cloudland of the supersensuous or supermundane), whether for the πνεῦμα (in God and Christ), or for the heavenly body of Christ and of the believer to be glorified through Him. In 2 Co 3¹⁸, above quoted, the ethical sense of the glory is so preeminent as to suggest not merely an 'extension of the physical' but even a supplantation of it; and this ethical conception comes out again plainly enough in Ro 5² and 3⁷, where righteousness is the burden of the thought. A non-Pauline, but not an anti-Pauline, illustration is furnished by Jn 1¹⁴, also above quoted: there the bright cloud (δόξα, Ro 9⁴) in the tabernacle (cf. ἐσκήνωσεν) serves St. John for the historical and allegorical foundation of the idea of the Logos in the tabernacle of the flesh, and the incarnate God in the world of men or among the Jewish people.

Prudence may well, therefore, lead us to pause before we go further than this,—that the 'brightness' accompanying Theophany, Christophany, Angelophany, in OT or NT times, and the double meaning *brightness* and *manifested perfection*, contained in δόξα, led St. Paul to avail himself of it as the most significant symbol for the manifestation of perfected human nature; being also for him the most significant inherited symbol of the divine perfection as manifested to the human eye. His root-idea is spiritual : in the new life the Spirit is the vitalizing principle, and the new body 'raised in glory' (1 Co 15⁴³) (σῶμα not necessarily, with St. Paul, connoting the material) will be spiritual (πνευματικόν), the expression and the organ of the spiritual life.   J. MASSIE.

GNAT (κώνωψ).—A term for any insect of the *Culicidæ*, a family of dipterous insects, with bristly stings, included in a flexible proboscis. They penetrate the skin, suck the blood, and at the same time inject a poisonous fluid, which causes swelling, and sometimes ulcerations. The humming noise produced by their wings in flight disturbs the rest of their victims, as they are for the most part nocturnal in their habits. The commonest species of gnat in Bible lands is the *mosquito*. The gnat is mentioned only once (Mt 23²⁴), where 'strain at' of AV is plainly wrong, and 'strain out' of RV right.   G. E. POST.

GNOSTICISM is the comprehensive name used to embrace a large number of widely ramified sects, on the borderland between Christianity and heathen thought, which flourished in the 2nd cent. The name in this sense is modern. There were, indeed, sects who called themselves Gnostic (γνωστικοί), as claiming a deeper knowledge of spiritual things, and Church writers (especially Irenæus) were fond of bringing different false teachers under the condemnation of 1 Ti 6²⁰; but there was no common name for these varying systems, and the limit assigned to the present use of the word must be to a certain extent arbitrary. The following are among the tendencies characteristic of the so-called Gnostic sects :—(1) An attempt to grapple with the problems of creation, and especially the origin of evil; (2) an attempt at its solution by theories which postulate a string of emanations extending between the first God and the visible universe, thus concealing the difficulties of the problem rather than solving it; (3) a tendency towards dualism, resulting either in asceticism or licentiousness; (4) a syncretistic tendency, combining in an artificial manner with some more or less misunderstood Christian doctrines, elements from classical, Oriental, and Jewish sources, or even from common magic; (5) a tendency towards a Docetic Christology, *i.e.* one which looked upon

the earthly life of Christ, or at any rate the sufferings, as unreal; (6) a tendency to represent γνῶσις (knowledge) as something superior to mere faith, and the special possession of the more enlightened. Some of these characteristics are more common in one, some in another of the heresies called Gnostic, nor probably is it possible to find any one idea common to them all.

i. The following is an account of the various places in the NT where reff. to Gnosticism have been found or imagined. These reff. have played a very large part in the critical discussions of the last sixty years, and in some cases touch on problems not yet solved. For a fuller discussion reference is given to the various separate articles.

1. In Ac 8⁹⁻²⁴ we have our earliest account of SIMON MAGUS (wh. see), who has played a large part in the history of Gnosticism, and is regarded by ecclesiastical writers as the father of all false teaching. Many doctrines characteristic of Gnosticism are attributed to him in later writers, and works of his are quoted—how far genuine is very doubtful. From Acts we learn that he practised 'magical arts,' and was called the Great Power of God (οὗτός ἐστιν ἡ δύναμις τοῦ θεοῦ ἡ καλουμένη μεγάλη). Both these were consistent with the tendencies we call Gnostic.

2. In 1 Co we find St. Paul using the word γνῶσις, which generally in NT implies a deep knowledge of spiritual things in a bad sense, and contrasting it with ἀγάπη (1 Co 8¹ 'knowledge puffeth up, but love edifieth'). There was a tendency to lay undue stress on intellectual gifts.

3. In the Ep. to the COLOSSIANS (wh. see) false teachers are attacked who combined asceticism, scrupulousness concerning food, new moons, and sabbaths with angel worship (θρησκεία τῶν ἀγγέλων), and apparently a tendency to depreciate the person of Christ. Their teaching is called 'the philosophy and vain conceit' (διὰ τῆς φιλοσοφίας καὶ κενῆς ἀπάτης), is said to be according to the traditions of men, after the elements of (see ELEMENT) the world (κατὰ τὰ στοιχεῖα τοῦ κόσμου), and a voluntary humility (ταπεινοφροσύνη, Col 2⁸⁻²³). According to Baur (*Ch. Hist.* Eng. tr. i. 127), 'the numerous echoes of Gnosticism and its peculiar doctrines, which are to be found in the three Epp. to the Ephesians, Colossians, and Philippians, are sufficient, had we no other ground to go upon, to fix the position of these works in the post-apostolic age.' But this extreme statement has long ceased to be accepted. It has been pointed out by many that the Colossian heresy was clearly Judaistic, and that 2nd cent. Gnosticism was strongly anti-Jewish. Lightfoot accounted for the 'Gnostic' tendencies by supposing a Judaism modified under influences similar to that of the Essenes. Hort (*Judaistic Christianity*, p. 128) denies that there is any 'tangible evidence for Essenism out of Palestine,' and considers that we are on 'common Jewish ground,' but the Judaism of the Dispersion and not of Palestine.

4. 'Still more directly and indubitably do the Pastoral Epistles carry us to the period of the Gnostic heresy,' writes Baur, while here again his position is almost universally modified or set aside. The false teachers of these Epistles (see PASTORAL EPP., TIMOTHY, TITUS), to dwell only on leading features, taught a different doctrine (ἑτεροδιδασκαλεῖν), consisting of fables and endless genealogies (1 Ti 1⁴), foolish questionings, strifes, and fighting about the law (μάχας νομικάς), Tit 3⁹; they forbade to marry, and commanded to abstain from meats (1 Ti 4³). Their teaching is described as profane babblings and oppositions of the knowledge which is falsely so called (ἀντιθέσεις τῆς ψευδωνύμου γνώσεως). This last phrase seemed to suggest a reference to Marcion, and is so taken

still by Harnack, who regards the verse as a later interpolation ; and the Fathers were accustomed to hold that the expressions concerning 'genealogies' referred to Valentinian and other theories of emanations, while the prohibition of marriage suggested Encratite doctrine. But none of these allusions were really necessary, and the expression 'Jewish fables' (Tit 1¹) shows that we cannot be dealing with the anti-Jewish Gnosticism of the 2nd cent. Lightfoot sees a development of the Colossian heresy ; and Hort, although his explanations are in some cases thoroughly convincing, perhaps goes too far in banishing all of what we should call Gnostic tendencies.

5. The First Epistle of St. John directly, the Gospel indirectly, combat a form of teaching which denied that Jesus Christ had come in the flesh (1 Jn 4¹⁻³). The most common explanation is to see in this a refutation of the peculiar form of Docetism associated with Cerinthus, with whom St. John is connected historically by tradition.

6. In the Apoc. we have reference to certain NICOLAITANS (wh. see), who are classed by Fathers (e.g. Iren. I. xxvi. 3) among heretics, to the teaching of one JEZEBEL (wh. see), and to some who knew the deep things of Satan (τὰ βαθέα τοῦ Σατανᾶ), a phrase which has a Gnostic ring about it (Rev 2⁶. ¹⁵. ²⁰. ²⁴).

7. In the Ep. of JUDE and in 2 PETER (wh. see) there is a violent polemic against certain Antinomian tendencies. It has been the custom to see here a definite allusion to some of the Antinomian sects of the 2nd cent. Harnack (Chronologie der altchristlichen Litteratur, ii. 466), for example, sees a reference to the Antinomian Gnostic sects described by Irenæus. But a careful analysis of the language of both the Epistles shows that it was at any rate primarily practical immorality that was in both cases attacked. They are 'ungodly men,' 'turning the grace of our God into lasciviousness,' they have 'given themselves over to fornication', 'they are blasphemous in their language,' they 'are sensual' (Jude v.⁴. ⁷. ¹⁰. ¹⁹), 'they walk after the flesh in the lust of defilement,' and 'despise dominion' (2 P 2¹⁰) ; to this corresponds the statement that they have fallen back into their old evil ways (2 P 2²¹⁻²²), and a theoretical basis seems to be given in the disbelief in the Parousia which is growing up. Even the expression 'denying their Master,' which occurs in both Epp. (Jude v.⁴, 2 P 2²), may mean only denying Him by lives unworthy of Him. In any case, even if the existence of a theoretical Antinomianism as well as practical immorality cannot be entirely denied, there are certainly no clearly defined traces of later Gnosticism implying the existence of any special 2nd cent. sect, and compelling us to place the two Epp. in the 2nd century.

The above are the references, real or supposed, to Gnosticism in the NT. A theory which flourished for some time referred them all to heresies of the 2nd cent., and signs therefore of the late date of the NT writings. This theory seems now to be given up or much modified, as may be seen by consulting the various modern commentators, and it is really more correct to say that the developed Gnostic heresies of the 2nd cent. presuppose the NT. Many of the names of the Valentinian æons were derived from the prologue to St. John's Gospel. The Gnostics often used NT doctrines which they only half understood, and misapplied biblical texts. But if we cannot find what is now called Gnosticism in the NT, there are signs of the tendencies out of which it grew. Even Hort, who shows how much which was formerly explained as Gnostic is perfectly explicable as Jewish, admits that there are elements for which we cannot account, and that the Judaism

of the Dispersion is different from the Judaism of Palestine. If we put together our data in the NT, we notice that to a very large extent it comes from Asia Minor. The Colossian Epp., those to Timothy, the Apocalypse, Cerinthus, the Ignatian letters, are all alike indications of a clearly defined tendency. To say that the origin of this is Essene influence certainly goes beyond our data, but the illustrations given by Lightfoot derived from the teaching of the Essenes and Therapeutæ are perfectly legitimate as showing that the Judaism of the 1st cent. was capable of being affected by very various and extraneous elements. The Jews in Phrygia (Ramsay, Cities and Bishoprics, ii. p. 674) were, we know, peculiarly lax, and influenced by the surrounding heathen life and thought. The great movements of the 2nd cent., heathen, Jewish, and Christian, which arose from the intense spiritual earnestness with which Christianity had inspired the world, brought into life elements that had been working silently ever since the unification of the Roman Empire had broken down the old national religions, had brought into contact with one another very different faiths, and had turned men's minds from the political interests, which are always impossible under a personal government, to the problems and questions of religion. From this point of view, the embryo Gnosticism of the NT takes its proper place in the history of religious development.

There are other points of view from which the developed Gnosticism of the 2nd cent. affected the Bible, mainly the history of the Canon, of Interpretation, and of the Text. The idea of a CANON (wh. see) as a collection of several books was not created by Gnosticism, but opposition to that movement made the definition of its limit necessary. There were collections of sacred writings before Marcion, but tne work of Marcion and the existence of many apocryphal writings showed the necessity of strict definition. Our first recorded commentary on any book of Scripture is that of Heracleon the Valentinian on St. John. And the belief at any rate that heretics mutilated Scripture caused careful attention to be paid to the transmission of the sacred text. How far any of the various readings still existing may be due to Gnostic influence is at present an open question.

LITERATURE.—On Gnosticism generally, by far the best work for English readers is Mansel's Gnostic Heresies, where there is a very full discussion of the biblical passages. In as far as it is behind modern criticism, it may be supplemented by the articles in Smith's Dict. of Christian Biography, where references are given to the special literature. On Biblical Gnosticism see esp. Lightfoot 'On the Colossian Heresy' in his Epistle to the Colossians, and Hort, Judaistic Christianity. For special literature on the Bible passages see the articles referred to.

ii. On account of his relation, real or supposed, alike to 1 Jn and to developed Gnosticism, it will be worth while to examine in detail the opinions of Cerinthus, so far as these can now be recovered. He taught in the province of Asia at the end of the 1st century.

I. HIS TEACHING.—The only method of acquiring critical information concerning his teaching is to distinguish the different sources from which it comes. (1) Polycarp († 154), acc. to Irenæus (Hær. III. iii. 4 ; Eus. HE III. xxviii. 6, IV. xiv. 6), related a story of the Apostle John. On going into a bath he saw C. there, and immediately rushed out saying, 'Let us flee lest the bath fall on us, for C., the enemy of the truth, is within.' Even if the incident be, as is possible, either exaggerated or a myth, it would not have arisen so early unless there were grounds for bringing the two together ; the story may therefore be taken as sufficient and conclusive evidence for placing C. at the end of the 1st cent. The later date implied in less trustworthy authorities (Pseudo-Tertullian, 3, etc.) seems simply to have arisen from taking the order of Irenæus as chronological.

(2) Irenæus himself (c. 200) tells us that St. John wrote his Gospel to correct the errors of C. (*Hær.* III. xi. 1). He describes them as follows (*Hær.* I. xxvi. 1). C. taught in Asia; he said that the world was not made by the first God, but by a power separate from Him and independent of Him. Jesus was not born from a virgin, but was the son of Joseph and Mary like other men, but distinguished by his superiority in justice and prudence and wisdom. After his baptism the Christ descended on him in the form of a dove, and announced the unknown Father. At the end of his life the Christ left Jesus, Jesus suffered and rose again, the Christ being spiritual remained without suffering.

(3) The common source of the three writers, Pseudo-Tertullian (§ 3), Philaster (§ 36), Epiphanius (*Hær.* xxviii.), is generally supposed to have been an early treatise by Hippolytus (190). The account it contains seems to be much less accurate than that of Irenæus. The God of the Jews was one of the angels who created the world, and who gave the law. Christ was a man, the son of Joseph and Mary, on whom apparently a power came down. C. had Judaistic tendencies. He supported circumcision and the Sabbath, and rejected the Apostle Paul. He was identified with the opponents of the apostles in the Ac, an identification which Epiphanius developed at great length. It may be noticed that there is an element of inconsistency in this account. Cerinthus is a Judaizer, although he puts the God of the Jews in such an inferior position.

(4) In his later treatise (*Ref. Omn. Hær.* vii. 33, x. 21) Hippolytus (220–230) derives his information from Irenæus, adding the statement that C. was educated in Egypt.

(5) The only other information of importance is that of Caius (c. 200), the Rom. presbyter (*ap.* Eus. *HE* III. xxviii.), who ascribes to him a gross Chiliasm. There was to be a kingdom of Christ upon earth; it was to last 1000 years, and to be a time of fleshly indulgence—a perpetual marriage feast. This statement is repeated or corroborated by Dionysius of Alexandria (*ap.* Eus. *HE* III. xxviii. 4, 5, VII. xxv. 2–5).

It is unnecessary to examine later writers, who all seem merely to combine, or exaggerate, or corrupt the above accounts. If we examine these in detail, we shall notice that there are three quite independent traditions. Irenæus has no reference to Judaistic views, and Caius alone describes the Chiliastic opinions. The account in Irenæus is far the clearest and most trustworthy; to that we may add the information of Caius, remembering that the repulsive side may very likely be exaggerated. How far we can accept Hippolytus I., which clearly gives an inaccurate and confused account, may be doubtful.

II. THE CANON.—A special interest attaches to C. in relation to certain books of NT. Caius (*loc. cit.*) makes the following statement concerning him: Κήρινθος ὁ δι᾽ ἀποκαλύψεων ὡς ὑπὸ ἀποστόλου μεγάλου γεγραμμένων, τερατολογίας ἡμῖν, ὡς δι᾽ ἀγγέλων αὐτῷ δεδειγμένας, ψευδόμενος ἐπεισάγει. 'C., the man who makes use of revelations purporting to have been written by a great apostle, lyingly imposes upon us marvellous prodigies which he professes to have been shown him by angels.' Dionysius seems to have had this passage in his mind when he states that some ascribed the Apoc. to Cerinthus. It is doubtful, however, whether the words of Caius will bear this meaning. They may mean that Cerinthus used forged Apocalypses, or interpreted the Apocalypse in his own way, or possibly that he

was the author of it; and we have other grounds for believing that Caius did not accept the book. The opinion that C. was the author of the Apoc. was also held by some heretics mentioned by Philaster (§ 60), and by those whom Epiphanius (*Hær.* li. 3, 4) calls Alogi. This opinion seems to have been one invented by those who disliked the Apoc. for the support it was supposed to give to Chiliastic opinions. Acc. to Epiphanius, these same Alogi ascribed to Cerinthus the Gospel of St. John —a statement which is certainly absurd, and looks as if it were an exaggeration of the statement in Philaster, who says that they reject the Gospel but does not say that they ascribe it to C. We are also told, if we are to believe Hippolytus I., that C. rejected the writings of St. Paul, the Acts of the Apostles, and all the Gospels except that according to St. Matthew, and that he accepted this only in a mutilated form.

III. RELATION TO ST. JOHN.—As we have seen, the most authentic accounts of C. make it quite clear that his teaching was Docetic, and that he was a contemporary of St. John. If we examine the writings traditionally ascribed to the latter, it becomes perfectly clear that he had a false teaching before him of a Docetic character. These two traditions then corroborate one another. The one demands an environment which the other supplies; nor does it seem in the least probable that either was invented to account for the other.

It may be further suggested that the developed Docetism taught by Cerinthus implies a developed theory concerning Christ's divinity from which it was a deviation, and that his heretical teaching concerning the birth of Christ has all the appearance of being developed in opposition to a belief in the Virgin birth.

LITERATURE.—References to ancient authors are given throughout the art.; the most useful modern book is prob. that of Hilgenfeld, *Ketzergeschichte*, pp. 411–421; see also Hort, *Judaistic Christianity*, pp. 188–191; Renan, *Les Évangiles*, p. 417 ff.; Westcott, *On the Canon*, ch. iv. § 1, and most early Church histories. The art. in Smith's *Dict. Chr. Biog.* is uncritical.

A. C. HEADLAM.

GO.—The verb to 'go' is found in the English versions of the Bible in many senses and constructions that have now gone out of use. A careful study of its occurrences will repay the labour it costs.

1. With all its freedom of usage there is a precision in the movement expressed by 'go' which we have now lost. If a person 'runs' or 'rides' we now can say that he 'goes'; but running and riding were formerly contrasted with going, which was therefore used as we now should use 'walk.' Thus Chaucer, *Knightes Tale*, 1351—

'That other wher him list may ryde or go,
But seen his lady shal be never-mo.'

Shaks. *Lear*, I. iv. 134—

'Ride more than thou goest';

and *Tempest*, III. ii. 63, 'As proper a man as ever went on four legs.' So Ascham, *The Scholemaster*, 151, 'I purpose to teach a yong scholer to go, not to daunce.' The use is found as late as Watts, *Come, Holy Spirit*—

'Our souls can neither fly nor go
To reach immortal joys.'

In the earlier versions this meaning is often found. Thus Is 40³¹ Wyc. (1388), 'But thei that hopen in the Lord, schulen chaunge strengthe, thei schulen take fetheris as eglis: thei schulen renne, and schulen not trauele; thei schulen go, and schulen not faile' (Cov. 'When they go, they shal not be weery,' Gen. 'they shal walke and not faint,' so AV); Mk 5⁴² Tind., 'And streyght the mayden arose, and went on her fete' (so Gen. 1557, but 1560 'walked' as AV, Gr. περιεπάτει); Hos 11³ Cov. 'I lerned Ephraim to go.' The last example has been retained by AV and RV, 'I taught Ephraim to go' (תִּרְגַּלְתִּי, lit., as Pusey, 'I set on his feet'). Other examples in AV are Pr 6²⁸ 'Can one go upon hot coals, and his feet not be burned?' (after Wyc. 'go on colis,' אִם־יְהַלֵּךְ אִישׁ, RV 'walk'); Is 59⁸ 'they have made them crooked paths; whosoever goeth therein shall not know peace' (after Cov. 'their wayes are so croked, that who so euer goeth therein, knoweth nothinge of peace,' כֹּל דֹּרֵךְ בָּהּ); Jer 10⁵ 'they must needs be borne, because they cannot go' (Wyc. 'for thei moun not go,' כִּי־לֹא יִצְעָדוּ). See also Jos 18⁴, Pr 4¹⁴ 6²² 9⁶, Mic 2⁸, Mk 12³⁸, where RV has 'walk' for AV 'go.'

2. 'Go' is sometimes superfluous or nearly so, as in Jos 9⁴ 'They did work wilily, and went and made as if they had been ambassadors' (וַיֵּלְכוּ וַיִּצְטַיָּרוּ); Is 37³⁷ 'So Sennacherib king of Assyria departed, and went and returned, and dwelt at Nineveh' (וַיֵּלֶךְ וַיָּשָׁב). Somewhat similar is the very frequent use of 'go' immediately before some other verb, as 2 K 1⁶ 'There came a man up to meet us, and said unto us, Go, turn again unto the king that sent you.' Occasionally a pronoun intervenes between the verbs, as 1 K 20⁸³ 'Then he said, Go ye, bring him.' In AV the usage is almost confined to the imperat., though some other moods occur, as 1 S 29⁸ 'What hast thou found in thy servant . . . that I may not go fight against the enemies of my lord, the king?' (RV 'go and fight'). Cf. Shaks. *Hamlet*, I. v. 132—

'And for my own poor part,
Look you, I'll go pray.'

In these phrases the verb to 'go' has no such independent meaning as we associate with it, implying removal from a place; it expresses no more than the setting about the act contained in the following verb. And this is often all that it contains when 'and' comes between the two verbs, as Dt 31¹ 'And Moses went and spoke these words to all Israel'; Ex 2¹ 'And there went a man of the house of Levi, and took to wife a daughter of Levi'; 2 K 3⁷ 'And he went and sent to Jehoshaphat the king of Judah, saying, The king of Moab hath rebelled against me' (see 'Go to' below). This auxiliary use of 'go' is seen also in expressions like 'go childless' Gn 15² (וְאָנֹכִי הוֹלֵךְ עֲרִירִי), which may mean, however, 'and I am going hence [*i.e.* to die] childless [lit. 'naked '],' as Del., Dillm., Spurrell, and RVm); 'go mourning,' Job 30²⁸ (קֹדֵר הִלַּכְתִּי בְּלֹא חַמָּה, Dav. 'I go blackened, not by the sun,' so RVm); 'go crouching,' Sir 12¹¹ (πορεύεται συγκεκυφώς); 'go gay,' Bar 6⁹ (παρθένῳ φιλοκόσμῳ, EV 'for a virgin that loveth to go gay,' Gifford 'fond of ornament,' the only occurrence of the Gr. word in LXX or NT). Cf. Shaks. *Othello*, II. i. 151—

'She that was ever fair, and never proud;
Had tongue at will, and yet was never loud;
Never lack'd gold, and yet went never gay.'

And Milton, *University Carrier*, ii. 22—

'Ease was his chief disease, and to judge right,
He di'd for heaviness that his cart went light.'

3. To go is often to proceed, advance, make progress, whether literally or figuratively, as Shaks. *I Henry IV.* I. iii. 292—

'No further go in this
Than I by letters shall direct your course.'

In 2 Mac 4⁴⁰ we find the unusual expression (it does not occur in Shaks.) 'a man far gone in years,' which RV retains. The Gr. (προβεβηκὼς τὴν ἡλικίαν) is common enough, the identical phrase occurring again in 6¹⁸, where it is trⁿ 'an aged man,' RV 'well stricken in years.' Cf. Gn 24¹ 'And Abraham was old, and well stricken in age,' AVm 'gone into days.' But the most important use of 'go' in this fig. sense is to express the progress of an undertaking, as in 2 S 1⁴ 'And David said unto him, How went the matter?'

(מֶה־הָיָה הַדָּבָר, lit., as AVm, 'What was the thing?'); and To 10⁸ '1 will send to thy father, and they shall declare unto him how things go with thee' (τὰ κατὰ σέ). Cf. Tind. *Prologe* to the Pent. of 1534, 'Then go to and reade the storyes of the byble for thy lerninge and comforte, and se every thinge practysed before thyne eyes: for accordinge to those ensamples shall it goo with the and all men untill the worldes ende.' Cf. also Job 8¹³ Cov. 'Even so goeth it with all them, that forget God,' and Hos 10¹⁵ Cov. 'Even so shal it go with you (o Bethel) because of youre malicious wickednes.' So Shaks. *Winter's Tale*, III. ii. 218—

'Howe'er the business goes, you have made fault
I' the boldness of your speech.'

The idiom is not obsolete; on the contrary, it has lately received a further and bolder extension, which may be illustrated by the following quotation from *Harper's Magazine*, lxxvi. 808, 'Society has invented no infliction equal to a large dinner that does not go, as the phrase is. Why it does not go when the viands are good and the company is bright, is one of the acknowledged mysteries.' More frequently, however, some adverb accompanies 'go,' to express the manner of progress. In AV we find: (1) *Go well*, Dt 4⁴⁰ 'that it may go well with thee'; Heb. יִיטַב לָךְ, which occurs also 5¹⁶ 12²⁵. ²⁸ (EV 'go well with'), 5²⁹ 6³. ¹⁸ 22⁷ (EV 'be well with'); and the similar phrase וְטוֹב לְ in 5³³ (EV 'that it may be well with '), 19¹³ (EV 'go well with '). The Eng. phrase occurs also in 2 Ch 12¹² 'in Judah things went well' (הָיָה דְּבָרִים טוֹבִים); Pr 11¹⁰ 'When it goeth well with the righteous, the city rejoiceth' (בְּטוֹב צַדִּיקִים); To 12¹⁷ 'it shall go well with you' (εἰρήνη ὑμῖν ἔσται, RV 'ye shall have peace '); 14⁹ 'that it may go well with thee' (ἵνα σοι καλῶς ᾖ, RV 'that it may be well with thee '); Sir 1¹³ 'Whoso feareth the Lord, it shall go well with him at the last' (τῷ φοβουμένῳ τὸν Κύριον εὖ ἔσται ἐπ' ἐσχάτων).* Cf. Shaks. *K. John*, III. iv. 4—

'Courage and comfort! all shall yet go well.
What can go well, when we have run so ill?'

(2) *Go ill*, Job 20²⁶ 'it shall go ill with him that is left in his tabernacle,' so RVm, but RV 'it shall consume that which is left in his tent,' Dav. 'it shall devour him that is left in his tent' (Heb. יֵרַע שָׂרִיד בְּאָהֳלוֹ); Ps 106³² 'they angered him also at the waters of strife, so that it went ill with Moses for their sakes' (וַיֵּרַע לְ). So Shaks. *Cymb.* I. vii. 95—

'Doubting things go ill often hurts more
Than to be sure they do.'

(3) *Go evil*, 1 Ch 7²³ 'it went evil with his house' (בְּרָעָה הָיְתָה). (4) *Go sore*, 1 S 31³ 'And the battle went sore against Saul' (וַתִּכְבַּד אֶל); 1 Ch 10³ (וַתִּכְבַּד עַל). This is Coverdale's trⁿ; Wyc. 1382, 'And al the charge (1388 'weighte ') of the batayl is turned unto Saul,' and Dou. 'And the whole weight of the battel was turned upon Saul,' are after the Vulg. 'Totumque pondus proelii versum est in Saul'; LXX is more literal, καὶ βαρύνεται ὁ πόλεμος ἐπὶ Σαούλ. Cf. Tindale, *Works*, i. 90, 'What shall we then say to those Scriptures which go so sore upon good works?' (5) *Go right*, Sir 49⁹ 'and directed them that went right' (RV 'and to do good to them that directed their ways aright,' reading καὶ ἀγαθῶσαι [for AV καὶ κατώρθωσε] τοὺς εὐθύνοντας ὁδούς).

4. One of the ways by which the verb to 'go' extended its meaning was by accepting 'went' as its past tense. 'Went' was the past tense of the verb to 'wend,' and had originally but little connexion with 'go' in meaning, as it had none in etymology. For 'go' is now the opposite of 'come'; but as a river may 'come winding' as well as 'go winding,' it was possible formerly to say that it 'came and went,' and yet express move-

* 'Go well' occurs in another sense in Pr 30²⁹ 'There be three things which go well' (RV 'are stately in their march ').

ment in only one direction. Hence we find 'went' and even 'go' used of a river, where the meaning is 'took its (winding) course.' Thus Gn 2¹⁰ 'And a river went out of Eden to water the garden' (צֵא), LXX ἐκπορεύεται, Vulg. 'egrediebatur,' Wyc. 1832, 'And a flood gede out of the place of delice to watre paradis'). Cf. Milton, *Lycidas*, 103—

'Next Oamus, reverend sire, went footing slow.'

'Wend' has practically gone out of use, and 'yode' the original past tense of 'go' is obsolete long since, so that 'go' and 'went' serve as present and past with the same meaning throughout. Before passing from this matter of form, it may be well to notice the old-fashioned 'let us be going' (Jg 19²⁸ 'Up and let us be going'; קוּמִי וְנֵלֵכָה, Mt 26⁴⁶ ἄγωμεν), which would now be called a 'Scotticism,' though RV retains it. The identical phrase (ἐγείρεσθε ἄγωμεν) tr⁴ in Mt 'Rise, let us be going,' is found in Mk 14⁴², where AV gives 'Rise up, let us go,' but RV 'Arise, let us be going,' as in Mt 26⁴⁶. Again, in Jn 14³¹ we find ἐγείρεσθε ἄγωμεν ἐντεῦθεν, but 'let us be going hence' proved too much for RV; both versions give 'Arise, let us go hence.' Another grammatical peculiarity is found in Is 15⁵ 'for by the mounting up of Luhith with weeping they shall go it up,' for 'go up it,' the object preceding its preposition. Cf. North's Plutarch, *Pelopidas*, p. 324, 'Notwithstanding, when they came to the hilles, they sought forcibly to clime them up.'

5. The verb to 'go' forms with other words, chiefly adverbs, some noteworthy expressions.

1. *Go about:* This phrase has three clearly distinguishable meanings (see ABOUT). (1) 'Go round,' Jos 6¹¹ 'So the ark of God compassed the city, going about it once' (הַקֵּף); (2) 'Go from place to place,' as Ac 10³⁸ 'who went about doing good'; and (3) 'set oneself to do,' 'attempt,' as Ac 26²¹ 'For these causes the Jews caught me in the temple, and went about to kill me.' The verbs tr⁴ 'go about' with the second meaning are סָבַב sâbhabh, lit. 'turn' (Jos 16⁶, 1 S 15¹², 2 K 3²⁵, 2 Ch 17⁹ 23², Ps 55¹⁰ [Piel], Ec 2²⁰, Ca 3² [Piel], 3³ 5⁷), הָלַךְ hâlak, 'go' (Pr 20¹⁹), שׁוּט shût, 'wander' (Nu 11⁸), סָחַר sâhar, usually 'traffic' (Jer 14¹⁸), חָמַק hâmak, 'turn away' (Jer 31²² Hithp. = 'turn hither and thither'), περιάγω 'lead or go round' (Mt 4²³ 9³⁵, Ac 13¹¹), and διέρχομαι 'go through' or 'throughout' (Ac 10³⁸). Cov. uses the same phrase in Job 27¹² 'Wherfore then do ye go aboute with soch vayne wordes'; Hos 11¹² 'Ephraim goeth aboute me with lies' (EV 'compasseth me'); and Tind. in Jn 7¹ 'After that, Jesus went about in Galile and wolde not go about in Jewry.' Cf. Shaks. *Macbeth*, I. iii. 34—

'The weird sisters, hand in hand,
Posters of the sea and land,
Thus do go about, about.'

But the third meaning is the most archaic now. It occurs only once in OT, Dt 31²¹ 'I know their imagination which they go about' (עֹשֶׂה, AVm 'do,' Driver, 'worketh' [the 'people' being singular], lit. 'maketh'). In Apocr. once also, 1 Mac 11¹ 'the king of Egypt . . . went about through deceit to get Alexander's kingdom' (ἐζήτησε, RV 'sought'). In NT seven times, Jn 7¹⁹. ²⁰, Ac 21³¹, Ro 10³ (ζητέω), Ac 26²¹ (πειράομαι), 24⁶ (πειράζω), 9²⁹ (ἐπιχειρέω). These verbs all mean to 'try,' 'attempt,' and are so tr⁴ elsewhere. Thus in Jn 7¹⁹. ²⁰ ζητέω is tr⁴ 'go about,' but in 7²⁵ 'seek.' The earlier VSS have the phrase 'go about' still oftener. Thus in Tind. we find it Mt 13²⁹ 'whill ye go aboute to wede out the tares'; Mk 12¹² 'they went about to take him, but they feared the people'; Lk 17³³ 'Whosoever will goo about to save his lyfe shall loose it'; Jn 10³⁰ 'Agayne they went aboute to take him: but he escaped out of their hondes.'

So Cov. in Job 32²² 'For yf I wolde go aboute to please men, I knowe not how suone my maker wolde take me awaye'; and Rhem. in Lk 1¹ 'Because many have gone about to compile a narration of the things that have been accomplished among us.' Hooker begins his *Eccles. Polity* with the phrase, 'He that goeth about to persuade a multitude, that they are not so well governed as they ought to be, shall never want attentive and favourable hearers.' And it is common in Shaks., as *Henry V.* IV. i. 212, 'You may as well go about to turn the sun to ice with fanning in his face with a peacock's feather.'

2. *Go abroad:* There are two meanings : (1) 'Go from home,' 'go out of doors'; Dt 23¹⁰ 'then shall he go abroad out of the camp' (וְיָצָא אֶל־מִחוּץ לַמַּחֲנֶה). So Shaks. *II Henry IV.* I. ii. 107, 'I am glad to see your lordship abroad; I heard say, your lordship was sick; I hope, your lordship goes abroad by advice.' (2) 'Go hither and thither'; Ps 77¹⁷ 'Thine arrows also went abroad' (יִתְהַלָּכוּ, 'went hither and thither'—Del., Cheyne; God's arrows being the flashes of lightning); Mt 9²⁶, Jn 21²³ (ἐξέρχομαι); Lk 5¹⁵ 'But so much the more went there a fame abroad of him' (διήρχετο). T. Lever (*Sermons*, Arber's ed. p. 29) uses the phrase more boldly, suppressing the verb 'go': 'loke at the merchauntes of London, and ye shall se . . . their riches muste abrode in the countrey to bie fermes out of the handes of worshypfull gentlemen, honeste yeomen, and pore laborynge husbandes.'

3. *Go after:* (1) 'Walk behind'; Jos 3³ 'When ye see the ark of the covenant of the LORD your God, and the priests the Levites bearing it, then ye shall remove from your place, and go after it' (וַהֲלַכְתֶּם אַחֲרָיו). (2) 'Follow'; 2 S 20¹¹ 'He. that favoured Joab, and he that is for David, let him go after Joab' (אַחֲרֵי, no verb in Heb., RV 'let him follow'). In NT with Gr. ἀπέρχομαι ὀπίσω Mk 1²⁰, Jn 12¹⁹, Jude⁷; without ὀπίσω Lk 17²³, and with πορεύομαι ὀπίσω Lk 21⁸. But especially to follow so as to become a votary of, sometimes of J" in OT (Jer 2²), but most frequently of 'other gods,' the Heb. phrase being הָלַךְ אַחֲרֵי (Dt 6¹⁴ 11²⁸ 13² 28¹⁴—the Heb. phrase occurs also 4³ EV 'follow,' 8¹⁹ EV 'walk after'—Jer 2²³ 11¹⁰ 25⁶ 35¹⁵). The same Heb. is used of following 'strangers' (Jer 2²⁵), 'lovers' (Hos 2¹³), and the 'strange woman' (Pr 7²²); and it has a fig. use in Ezk 33³¹ 'their heart goeth after their covetousness' (RV 'their gain'). In 1 K 11⁶ the same idea is otherwise expressed, 'Solomon . . . went not fully after the LORD' (לֹא מִלֵּא אַחֲרֵי). (3) 'Pursue'; Jos 8¹⁷ 'And there was not a man left in Ai or Bethel, that went not out after Israel' (יָצְא אַחֲרֵי), Ezk 9⁵ 'Go ye after him through the city, and smite' (עִבְרוּ אַחֲרָיו). (4) 'Seek'; Lk 15⁴ 'go after that which is lost' (πορεύεται ἐπὶ τὸ ἀπολωλός).

4. *Go again:* always = 'go back' (see AGAIN), as 1 S 25¹² 'So David's young men turned their way, and went again, and came and told him all those sayings' (וַיָּשֻׁבוּ, RV 'and went back'); 2 K 4³¹ 'Wherefore he went again to meet him' (וַיָּשָׁב, RV 'he returned'). The Heb. is always שׁוּב 'turn,' the Gr. ἐπιστρέφω (Ac 15³⁶).

5. *Go along:* The expression occurs Nu 21²², Dt 2²⁷, Jos 17⁷, Jg 11¹⁸, 1 S 6¹², 2 S 3¹⁶ 16¹³, Jer 41⁶, and always stands for the simple verb הָלַךְ to 'go.' In Jos 17¹⁷ it is the 'border' that is said to 'go along,' a Heb. idiom taken bodily into the Eng.; it is more frequent as 'go out,' see below.

6. *Go aside:* 'to go to one side.' (1) Literally, Heb. סוּר (Jer 15⁵ 'Who shall go aside to ask how thou doest?' RV 'turn aside'); Gr. ἀναχωρέω (Ac 23¹⁹ 26³¹), ὑποχωρέω (Lk 9¹⁰), ἀπέρχομαι (Ac 4¹⁵). (2) Metaphorically, 'to go wrong,' Heb. שָׂטָה sâtâh (Nu 5¹². ¹⁹. ²⁰. ²⁹), סוּר (Dt 28¹⁴, Ps 14³ 'They are all gone aside, they are altogether become filthy'). The same idea is expressed by the verb alone in

Article IX (*XXXIX Articles*, 1571), 'man is very farre gone from originall righteousnes.'

7. *Go astray:* both literally and figuratively, but always the trⁿ of a simple verb, mostly תָּעָה 'to err' (Ex 23⁴, Ps 58³ 119¹⁷⁶, Pr 7²⁵, Is 53⁶, Jer 50⁶ [Hiph. 'cause to go astray'], Ezk 14¹¹ 44¹⁰ *bis.* ¹⁵ 48¹¹ *ter*); also נִדַּח (Dt 22¹ 'Thou shalt not see thy brother's ox or his sheep go astray, and hide thyself from them,' נִדָּחִים 'driven away,' *i.e.* parted forcibly from the herd through some mishap— Driver); שָׁגָג (Ps 119⁶⁷ 'Before I was afflicted I went astray'); שָׁגָה (Pr 5²³ and [Hiph.] 28¹⁰ 'cause to go astray'). In NT always πλανάομαι (Mt 18¹². ¹³, 1 P 2²⁵, 2 P 2¹⁵).

In Gn 6³ RVm gives 'in their going astray they are flesh,' the text being 'for that he also is flesh.' The difficulty is with the word בְּשַׁגָּם [Baer בְּשַׁגַּם]. It has been taken as composed of שֶׁ [=אֲשֶׁר] and גַּם 'also.' So all the Versions, the Jewish interpreters, and most modern expositors. Thus LXX διὰ τὸ εἶναι αὐτοὺς σάρκας, Vulg. 'quia caro est,' Wyc. 'for flehs he is,' Luth. 'denn sie sind Fleisch,' Tind. 'for they are flesh,' Cov. 'for he is but flesh also' (the first version to recognize the גַּם), Gen. 'because he is but flesh,' Bish., Dou. 'because he is flesh,' Olt. 'car aussi ne sont-ils *que* chair,' Segond 'car l'homme n'est que chair.' But שֶׁ is nowhere else found for אֲשֶׁר in Gn, or even in the Pent., and the גַּם 'also' seems superfluous. Hence some modern scholars make the word an inf. of שָׁגַג, and translate somewhat as RVm. Dillmann and Kautzsch consider the word to be corrupt, and refuse to translate; Ball suggests בְּעֲוֹנָם (Lv 26³⁹), and translates 'owing to their guilt they are flesh.'

8. *Go a warfare:* 1 Co 9⁷ 'Who goeth a warfare any time at his own charges?' (τίς στρατεύεται, RV 'What soldier ever serveth at his own charges?'). Elsewhere the Gr. verb is trᵈ 'war' (2 Co 10³, 1 Ti 1¹⁸, 2 Ti 2⁴, Ja 4¹, 1 P 2¹¹), as 1 P 2¹¹ 'abstain from fleshly lusts, which war against the soul'; except Lk 3¹⁴, where the ptcp. (στρατευόμενοι) is trᵈ 'soldiers.' For the Eng. phrase (which comes from Tind. 'Who goeth a warfare eny tyme at his awne cost?') cf. Tindale's *Prologe* to Leviticus, 'For the holy gost is no dome god nor no god that goeth a mumminge'; and Defoe, *Crusoe* (Gold. Treas. ed. p. 555), 'We then went to consulting together what was to be done.'

9. *Go away:* (1) 'Pass away,' 'perish,' Job 4²¹ 'Doth not their excellency which is in them go away?' (יִסַּע, RV 'Is not their tent-cord plucked up within them?' for the word trᵈ 'excellency' means also a 'cord,' and the verb means first of all 'to pull up' a tent-peg or cord, though it thence is extended to the meaning 'break up an encampment,' 'go away.' Davidson translates the whole verse—'If their tent-cord is torn away in them, do they not die, and not in wisdom?' and remarks (*Expos.* III. iv. 279 f.), 'The striking of the tent is a graphic and not uncommon image for the removal which comes in death') ; Jer 6⁴ 'Woe unto us ! for the day goeth away, for the shadows of the evening are stretched out' (פָּנָה, RV 'declineth'). (2) 'Turn aside from,' 'desert,' Ezk 44¹⁰ 'And the Levites that are gone away far from me, when Israel went astray . . . they shall even bear their iniquity' (אֲשֶׁר רָחֲקוּ, RV 'that went far from me'); Mal 3⁷ 'Even from the days of your fathers ye are gone away from mine ordinances' (סַרְתֶּם, RV 'ye have turned aside'); Jn 6⁶⁷ 'Then Jesus said unto the twelve, Will ye also go away?' (μὴ καὶ ὑμεῖς θέλετε ὑπάγειν), 12¹¹ 'many of the Jews went away, and believed on Jesus' (ὑπῆγον). (3) 'Escape,' 1 S 24¹⁹ 'For if a man find his enemy, will he let him go well away' (בְּדֶרֶךְ טוֹבָה, lit. 'will he send him along a prosperous way?').

10. *Go a whoring:* This strong expression, which comes from Tindale (Wyc. has 'do fornicacioun'), is used to tr. the Heb. verb זָנָה *zânâh*, 'to commit fornication,' when followed by אַחֲרֵי 'after' (Ex 34¹⁵. ¹⁶, Lv 17⁷ 20⁵. ⁶, Nu 15³⁹, Dt 31¹⁶, Jg 2¹⁷ 8²⁷. ³³, 1 Ch 5²⁵, Ezk 6⁹ 23³⁰, and once in Ex 34¹⁶,

where the vb. is Hiphil, 'make thy sons go a whoring after their gods') ; also when *zânâh* is followed by מִן 'from' (Ps 73²⁷ 'Thou hast destroyed all them that go a whoring from thee'), בְּ 'with' (Ps 106³⁹ 'went a whoring with their own inventions'), מִתַּחַת 'from under' (Hos 4¹²), and מֵעַל 'from' (Hos 9¹). It is used once without a prep. following, 2 Ch 21¹³ 'And hast made Judah and the inhabitants of Jerusalem to go a whoring' (וַתֶּזֶן). The Heb. phrase is always a figure of speech, and expresses 'the disloyal abandonment of J″ for other gods'—Driver. It suggests, adds Moore, both the sin of unfaithfulness and the sin of prostitution, the giving up of oneself, body and soul, to other gods. But whether it was a figure always, it is hard to say. In view of the fact that actual prostitution was not an uncommon feature in ancient Semitic cults, Driver thinks the original sense not improbably literal. It depends upon the date of the origin of the expression. Moore believes that it originated with Hosea, 'whose own bitter experience with his adulterous wife became for him the type of the relations of J″ and Israel.' Modern translators try to soften the expression : thus Cheyne in Ps 73²⁷ 'every one that wantonly deserts thee.' RV retains, but Amer. RV prefers 'play the harlot.'

11. *Go back:* Besides the literal sense, notice (1) to 'depart from an engagement or course of action,' Jg 11³⁵ 'I have opened my mouth unto the LORD, and I cannot go back' (וְלֹא אוּכַל לָשׁוּב) ; Ezk 24¹⁴ 'I will not go back, neither will I spare, neither will I repent' (לֹא־אֶפְרַע). (2) To 'decline to a worse way,' Jos 23¹², Job 23¹², Ps 53³ 80¹⁸, Jn 6⁶⁶. Cf. Jer 44³ Cov. 'they wente backe to do sacrifice and worshipe unto straunge goddes.'

12. *Go beyond* is used in two senses : (1) to 'go outside of,' 'pass': Nu 22¹⁸ 'I cannot go beyond the word of the LORD my God, to do less or more'; 24¹³ 'I cannot go beyond the commandment (RV 'word') of the LORD, to do either good or bad of mine own mind' (both לַעֲבֹר). Cf. Heywood, *Works*, i. 210, 'Shoomaker, you goe a little beyond your last.' (2) To 'overreach,' 1 Th 4⁶ 'That no man go beyond and defraud his brother' (τὸ μὴ ὑπερβαίνειν, RV 'transgress,' RVm 'overreach'). So *Life of T. Cromwell*, IV. v. 120, 'We must be wary, else he'll go beyond us'; and Shaks. *Henry VIII.* III. ii. 409—

'There was the weight that pull'd me down. O Cromwell,
  The king has gone beyond me.'

13. *Go for, i.e.* 'be accounted,' 1 S 17¹² 'the man went among men for an old man in the days of Saul' (זָקֵן בָּא בַאֲנָשִׁים, RV 'was an old man in the days of Saul, stricken *in years* among men').

The AV trⁿ is a bold and apparently an original attempt to render the Heb. literally. The nearest form in the previous versions is that of the Gen. Bible, 'this man was taken for an olde man in the days of Saul.' But the Heb. will not render so. The only literal rendering that the Heb. will stand is, 'and the man in the days of Saul was aged, entered in among men,'—which, as Driver says, affords no intelligible sense. Two suggestions have been made, the one to omit בָּא, when we get simply 'and the man in the days of Saul was aged among men' ; the other, to change בַאֲנָשִׁים into בַשָּׁנִים, and translate 'and the man in the days of Saul entered into years.' The objection to the second is that the phrase elsewhere is always זָקֵן בָּא בַיָּמִים, and Driver, on the whole, prefers the first. (See *Heb. Text of Samuel*, p. 108 f.; and a severe criticism by Jennings and Lowe of the RV trⁿ, which they consider to be impossible as a rendering of the Massoretic text, in *Expos.* III. ii. 63).

The AV trⁿ, though impossible as a rendering of the Heb., is good idiomatic English. Thus Sidney, *Arcadia*, p. 10, 'But because a pleasant fellow of my acquaintance set forth her praises in verse, I will only repeat them, and spare mine owne tongue, since she goes for a woman'; and Shaks. *Macbeth*, III. i. 92—

'We are men, my liege.
Ay, in the catalogue ye go for men.'

14. *Go forth:* Among other expressions (see FORTH) notice especially 'motion away from a given spot,' in Lk 8[14] 'And that which fell among thorns are they, which, when they have heard, go forth' (πορευόμενοι, RV 'as they go on their way'). Cf. Lk 5[8] Rhem. 'Which when Simon Peter did see, he fel downe at Jesus knees, saying, Goe forth from me, because I am a sinful man, O Lord.'

15. *Go forward*—see under FORWARD.

16. *Go hard* = 'go close,' Jg 9[52], see HARD.

17. *Go in and out:* This phrase is found in Ac 1[21] 'all the time that the Lord Jesus went in and out among us' (εἰσῆλθεν καὶ ἐξῆλθεν ἐφ' ἡμᾶς), and the meaning may be no more than 'passed his time,' though the ἐφ' seems to imply leadership, whence RVm 'over us.' In 9[28] occurs the fuller phrase 'coming in and going out,' 'And he [Saul] was with them coming in and going out at Jerusalem' (εἰσπορευόμενος καὶ ἐκπορευόμενος, RV 'going in and going out'), where, again, some more definite activity is meant than merely 'spending his time,' probably something like what is now called 'aggressive work.' In OT this fuller phrase occurs repeatedly (Nu 27[17. 21], Dt 28[6. 19] 31[2] 33[18], Jos 14[11], 1 S 18[13. 16] 29[6], 2 S 3[25], 1 K 3[7], 2 K 11[8] 19[27], 1 Ch 27[1], 2 Ch 1[10] 15[5] 16[1] 23[7. 8], Ps 121[8], Is 37[28], Jer 37[4], Zec 8[10]). While always recognized as an idiomatic expression for a man's *active* life, it is sometimes clearly used in a more technical sense than that. When Moses says (Dt 31[2]), 'I am an hundred and twenty years old this day; I can no more go out and come in,' he intimates his failing fitness to be Israel's leader. More distinctly Joshua states (Jos 14[11]) that in his 85th year he is still fit to be their leader in war: 'As yet I am as strong this day as I was in the day that Moses sent me: as my strength was then, even so is my strength now, for war, both to go out and to come in.' Of David it is said (1 S 18[13]), 'Saul removed him from him, and made him his captain over a thousand; and he went out and came in before the people,' where the reference must be to military expeditions. Solomon says (1 K 3[7]), 'I am but a little child; I know not how to go out or come in,' and declares his unfitness to be *king.* See *go out* below. The phrase 'go in and out' occurs in Ex 32[27] in the sense of 'go to and fro' (as RV); and in Jn 10[9] 'by me, if any man enter in, he shall be saved, and shall go in and out, and find pasture' (εἰσελεύσεται καὶ ἐξελεύσεται, RV 'shall go in and go out') as in Ac 1[21], but figuratively to express the liberty of the sons of God.

18. *Go on:* (1) Continue a course begun, proceed, as in Shaks. *Othello,* III. iii. 413—

> 'I do not like the office;
> But, sith I am entered in this cause so far,
> Prick'd to 't by foolish honesty and love,
> I will go on.'

Generally of a journey, Gn 29[1] 'Then Jacob went on his journey' (וַיִּשָּׂא רַגְלָיו, lit. 'lifted up his feet,' as AVm, RVm); so Ac 10[9] 'as they went on their journey' (ὁδοιπορούντων ἐκείνων, RV 'as they were on their journey'); Mt 4[21] 'And going on from thence, he saw other two brethren' (προβὰς ἐκεῖθεν, lit. 'going forward thence'). In 1 S 10[3] the simple verb חָלַף 'to pass on,' is tr[d] 'go on forward.' In Gn 19[2] 32[1], 1 S 26[25] 28[22] we find the fuller expression 'go on one's way.' See *Go one's way* below. Sometimes the meaning is simply 'continue,' 'persist,' as 1 S 14[19] 'the noise that was in the host of the Philistines went on and increased' (וַיֵּלֶךְ הָלוֹךְ וָרָב, LXX ἐπορεύετο πορευόμενος καὶ ἐπληθύνεν); Ps 68[21] 'such an one as goeth on still in his trespasses' (מִתְהַלֵּךְ בַּ); in Ezr 5[8] it is to 'advance,' 'make progress,' 'this work goeth fast on and prospereth'; and in He 6[1] the phrase is fig. 'let us go on unto perfection' (φερώμεθα, RV 'press on '). (2) To go to meet an enemy, generally 'go

out,' Job 39[21] 'he goeth on to meet the armed men' (RV 'he goeth out'). (3) To go forward, towards the front, said of the 'border' of a territory, Nu 34[4. 9]. See *Go out*, below.

19. *Go out:* Besides its uses in modern English, this phrase has some peculiarly biblical senses, which are for the most part due to the freedom with which the verb יָצָא is employed in Hebrew. (1) To go from home: Ru 1[21] 'I went out full, and the Lord hath brought me home again empty'; so Adonijah is threatened by Solomon, 'on the day thou goest out, and passest over the brook Kidron, thou shalt know for certain that thou shalt surely die'; and of Abraham it is said in He 11[8] 'when he was called to go out . . . he went out' (ἐξελθεῖν . . . ἐξῆλθεν); while it is one of the rewards of the Christian victor that he will be at home in the Church of which he is to be a pillar, and 'shall go no more out' (Rev 3[12] ἔξω οὐ μὴ ἐξέλθῃ ἔτι, RV 'he shall go out thence no more'). In 2 Ch 18[21] 'I will go out and be a lying spirit in the mouth of all his prophets. And the Lord said . . . go out, and do even so' (in 1 K 22[22] 'go forth,' as here), the reference is the same as in Job 1[12] 2[7] 'So Satan went forth from the presence of the LORD.' Less definitely, Gn 41[45] 'And Joseph went out over all the land of Egypt'; 2 Ch 19[4] 'Jehoshaphat . . . went out again through the people from Beersheba to Mount Ephraim' (a formula during the separation of the kingdoms for the old 'from Dan to Beersheba'); and Ps 81[5] 'This he ordained in Joseph for a testimony when he went through the land of Egypt' (בְּצֵאתוֹ עַל־אֶרֶץ מִצְרַיִם, RV 'when he went out over the land of Egypt,' the ref. being apparently, as in AV, to Joseph's administration (Gn 41[45]), which is surprising, seeing that modern English commentators almost unanimously find the ref. to be to God).

> The passage is difficult; there are three ways of taking it : (*a*) The ancient VSS tr. 'when he (Israel) went out from the land of Egypt,' as LXX ἐν τῷ ἐξελθεῖν αὐτὸν ἐκ τῆς Αἰγύπτου ; Vulg. 'cum exiret de Terra-Ægypti,' after which Wyc. 1388, 'whanne he gede out of the lond of Egipt,' and Dou. 'when he came out of the Land of Aegypt' (with the marg. 'The people of Israel signified by Joseph, as Ps 80[1]'); and so all the Eng. VSS before AV. But the tr[n] is quite impossible, the עַל never meaning *ἐκ* 'out of,' or anything approaching that. (*b*) 'When he (Joseph, in person) went out over the land of Egypt,' a direct ref. to Gn 41[45], which gives no appropriate sense. (*c*) 'When He (J[′′]) went forth against the land of Egypt,' a reference to the death of the firstborn, and especially to Ex 11[4] 'I will go forth through the midst of Egypt.' So Del., Perowne, Burgess, de Witt, Kirkpatrick, and nearly all recent commentators. Kay thinks that, while the ref. is to God, the special language recalls Gn 41[45] : as Joseph once went out over the land of Egypt to benefit them, so now, since they have forgotten their benefactor, Joseph's God will go out over the land in righteous judgment. Cheyne believes the present Heb. text to be corrupt, and that the VSS exhibit the true text; he therefore would render, as (*a*), 'when he (Israel and Joseph) went forth from the land of Egypt.' So Wellh. (in Haupt) who reads מֵעַל for עַל (but is מֵעַל ever used simply of *leaving*?).

(2) To spread abroad : 1 Ch 14[17] 'And the fame of David went out into all lands'; Est 9[4] 'For Mordecai was great in the king's house, and his fame went out throughout all the provinces' (הוֹלֵךְ, RV 'went forth'). (3) In reference to war, the phrase assumes a highly technical sense, so much so that 'to go out' standing alone may be understood to mean 'to go out to make war.' Take the foll. passages in order: Nu 22[32] (the Angel of the LORD to Balaam) 'behold, I went out to withstand thee'; Dt 28[25] 'thou shalt go out one way against them, and flee seven ways before them'; Jg 2[15] 'Whithersoever they went out, the hand of the LORD was against them for evil'; Jg 5[4] 'LORD, when thou wentest out of Seir, when thou marchedst out of the field of Edom, the earth trembled' (see Moore, who holds the ref. to be to the battle just fought); 20[1] 'Then all the children of Israel went out'; 1 S 8[20] 'Nay, but we will have a king over us . . . that our king may judge us,

and go out before us, and fight our battles' ; 18[5] 'And David went out whithersoever Saul sent him' (RVm 'went out ; whithersoever Saul sent him, he behaved himself wisely') ; 1 K 2[46] 'So the king commanded Benaiah the son of Jehoiada ; which went out and fell upon him [Shimei], that he died' ; 1 Ch 20[1] 'at the time that kings go out' (both VSS add 'to battle' in italics) ; Is 52[12] 'For ye shall not go out with haste, nor go by flight' ; and Am 5[3] 'The city that went out by a thousand shall leave an hundred.' (4) Another half-technical sense, which is in danger of being confused with the last, is found when 'go out' means 'go out of bondage,' mostly in reference to the exodus from Egypt or to the jubilee release. The chief references to the exodus are Ex 12[41] 14[8], Nu 33[3], Ps 114[1] ; to the jubilee release, Ex 21[3 bis. 7], Lv 25[28. 30. 31. 33. 54] 27[21], the fuller expression 'go out free' occurring Ex 21[2. 5. 11] ; 2 K 13[5] refers to the deliverance from the Syrian oppression ; and Is 55[12] to the return from the Babylonian Captivity, with no doubt a fuller entrance into Messianic blessing. (5) By a peculiar Heb. idiom the 'border' or 'coast' of a territory is said to 'go out,' that is, 'proceed onward' to such a place. So frequently in Jos 15. 16 and elsewhere, the verb אָצָא being generally rendered 'go out' and עָלָה 'go up.' But notice especially the subst. תּוֹצָאָה denoting the end or extremity of a boundary line, generally used in the plu. and tr[d] 'goings out,' but 'outgoings' in Jos 17[9. 18] 18[19] 19[14. 22. 29. 33], which RV turns into 'goings out.' (6) Go out means 'proceed from' in Lv 10[2] 'And there went out a fire from the LORD' ; Jer 21[12] 'lest my fury go out like fire' (תֵּצֵא) ; Mk 5[30] = Lk 8[46] 'And Jesus, immediately knowing in himself that virtue had gone out of him' (τὴν ἐξ αὐτοῦ δύναμιν ἐξελθοῦσαν) ; Lk 6[19] 'there went virtue out of him and healed them all' (παρ' αὐτοῦ ἐξήρχετο, RV 'came forth from him') ; 2[1] 'And it came to pass in those days, that there went out a decree from Cæsar Augustus' (ἐξῆλθεν). Cf. Jer 44[17] Cov. 'what so ever goeth out of oure owne mouth, that will we do.' (7) 'Go out' implies religious separation in Is 52[11], Jer 51[45], 1 Jn 2[19]. (8) 'Go out of the way' in Ro 3[12] means to 'go astray' (πάντες ἐξέκλιναν, RV 'They have all turned aside'). See go the way, below.

20. Go to : This obsolete expression, which is found 11 times in AV, seems to have been introduced by Tindale, who uses it in other places, as Dt 2[24] 'Goo to and conquere and provoke him to batayle' ; 2[31] 'goo to and conquere, that thou mayest possesse thy londe.' Abbott (Shakespearian Grammar, p. 122) says that the 'to' has an adverbial force, as in 'to and fro' ; and as 'go' in Elizabethan English meant motion generally, not necessarily motion from, 'go to' meant little more than our stimulative 'come.' This is practically how Johnson explains the phrase—'Come, come, take the right course,' spoken sometimes sarcastically, sometimes encouragingly. In Shakespeare it is always an exclamation, expressing either scorn, as Winter's Tale, I. ii. 182—

'Go to, go to ! How she holds up the neb, the bill to him !' ;

or disapproval, as Macbeth, v. i. 51—'Go to, go to : you have known what you should not' ; or merely dismissal, as Merry Wives, I. iv. 165—'But, indeed, she is given too much to allicholly and musing. But for you—well, go to' ; or even encouragement, Merry Wives, II. i. 7—'You are not young, no more am I : go to then, there's sympathy' ; always, however, mixed with impatience. But if 'go to' is a mere exclamation in Shaks. and Elizabethan English generally, it is often more than that in AV, for it must not be forgotten that AV represents a much earlier stage of English than its date of 1611. There it is (except perhaps in Ja) a verb in the imperative, and expresses lively encouragement.

This is clearly seen in 2 K 5[5] 'And the king of Syria said, Go to, go, and I will send a letter unto the king of Israel.' Its occurrences are Gn 11[3. 4. 7] הָבָה voluntative, fr. יָהַב to grant), 38[16] 'go to, I pray thee' (הָבָה־נָּא ; the only remaining example of הָבָה, Ex 1[10], was tr[d] by Tindale 'Come on,' and this was retained in subsequent versions) ; Jg 7[3] 'go to, proclaim' (קְרָא 'cry now !') ; 2 K 5[5] 'go to, go' (לֶךְ בֹּא, lit. 'go, go in,' perhaps as Ball, 'depart thou [thither], enter [the land of Israel]' ; LXX Δεῦρο εἴσελθε) ; Ec 2[1] 'go to now' (לְכָה־נָּא) ; Is 5[5] 'And now, go to ; I will tell you' (וְעַתָּה אוֹדִיעָה־נָּא אֶתְכֶם) ; Jer 18[11] 'go to, speak' (אֱמָר־נָא) ; Ja 4[13] 5[1] 'Go to now' (Ἄγε νῦν). Tindale in his exposition of Mt 5[15-20] (Expos. p. 124) has 'go to and prove it' ; and (p. 128) 'go to, and judge their works' ; and in the Prologe to the Pent. he says, 'Then go to and reade the storyes of the byble for thy lerning and comforte,' where the verbal force of the expression is always manifest. But he even uses 'went to' in Nu 11[4] 'And the children of Ysrael also went to and wepte and sayde : who shall geve us flesh to eate ?'

21. Go one's way : This full phrase sometimes represents an equally full expression in the original : thus, Gn 32[1] 'And Jacob went on his way,' Heb. הָלַךְ לְדַרְכּוֹ, so 19[2], Nu 24[25], Jos 2[16], Jg 18[26], 1 S 1[18] 26[25] 28[22], Jer 28[11]. But generally (always in NT) it is the rendering of a common verb with no adjunct. The verbs are אָזַל (Pr 20[14]) ; נָסַע (Zec 10[2]) ; הָלַךְ (Gn 12[19] 14[11] 18[33] 24[61] 25[34], Ex 18[27], Jg 19[5. 14], Neh 8[10], Ec 9[7], Dn 12[9. 13]) ; βαδίζω (Bar 4[19]) ; πορεύομαι (Lk 4[30] 7[22] 17[19], Jn 4[50], Ac 9[15] 21[5] 24[25]) ; ὑπάγω (Mt 5[24] 8[4. 13] 20[14] 27[65], Mk 1[44] 2[11] 7[29] 10[21. 52] 11[2] 16[7], Lk 10[3], Jn 8[21] 16[5] 18[8], Rev 16[1]) ; and ἀπέρχομαι (Mt 8[33] 13[25] 20[4] 22[5. 22], Mk 11[4] 12[12], Lk 8[39] 19[32] 22[4], Jn 4[28] 11[28. 46], Ac 9[17], Ja 1[24]). Sometimes what appears to be the plu., but may be an old genitive, is used, 'go your ways.' The phrase is good idiomatic Eng., and is still used in Scotland and the north of England, but often it is too cumbrous, sometimes singularly so, as in Ja 1[24] κατενόησεν καὶ ἀπελήλυθεν, which Mayor translates 'just a glance and he is off' (RV 'goeth away'). AV has a few times rejected it when found in earlier versions, as Mk 1[20] Tind. 'And they leeft their father Zebede in the shippe with his hyred servauntes, and went their waye after him' ; Lk 8[14] Rhem. 'And that which fel into thornes, are they that have heard, and going their waies, are choked with cares.' Shaks. has it often, as Hamlet, III. i. 132—'We are arrant knaves all ; believe none of us. Go thy ways to a nunnery.'

22. Go the way : This phrase, which has no connexion with the preceding, is used both literally and figuratively. (1) Ru 1[7] 'and they went on the way to return unto the land of Judah' (וַתֵּלַכְנָה בַדֶּרֶךְ) ; 2 K 25[4] 'and the king went the way toward the plain' (וַיֵּלֶךְ דֶּרֶךְ הָעֲרָבָה, RV 'went by the way of the Arabah'), so Jer 39[4] ; Jer 31[21] 'set thine heart toward the highway, even the way which thou wentest' (דֶּרֶךְ הָלָכְתְּ). (2) Jos 23[14] 'And behold, this day I am going the way of all the earth' (אָנֹכִי הוֹלֵךְ הַיּוֹם בְּדֶרֶךְ כָּל־הָאָרֶץ ; so 1 K 2[2] ; Job 16[22] 'when a few years are come, then I shall go the way whence I shall not return' (וְאֹרַח לֹא־אָשׁוּב אֶהֱלֹךְ).

J. HASTINGS.

GOAD.—1. דָּרְבָן (בּ without daghesh, cf. קָרְבָּן (once) and אֶבֶן ; see Driver, Text of Sam. p. 80, and references there) occurs in a corrupt passage, 1 S 13[21] 'to set the goads.' A fem. form in plur. absolute is found in Ec 12[11], where we read that the words of the wise are as goads (כַּדָּרְבֹנוֹת). 2. מַלְמָד (Siegfried-Stade ; Moore thinks מַלְמָד probably the absolute form) only in Jg 3[31], where Shamgar is said to have killed 600 Philistines with an ox-goad (בְּמַלְמָד הַבָּקָר. The goad was a pole of some 8 ft. in length, 'armed at one end with a spike, at the other with a chisel-shaped blade for cleaning the plough, and on occasion would make a very good substitute for

a spear' (Moore, *Judges*, 105). See further AGRI-
CULTURE in vol. i. p. 49ᵃ, where the ox-goad is
figured, and Schumacher, 'Der arab. Pflug,' in
ZDPV xii. 160 f.

In Apocr. 'goad' occurs in Sir 38²⁵ 'How shall
he become wise that holdeth the plough, that
glorieth in the shaft of the goad (κέντρον)?' In
NT 'goad' (RVm 'goads') is substituted by RV
for 'pricks' of AV in Ac 26¹⁴ 'It is hard for
thee to kick against the goad' (πρὸς κέντρα
λακτίζειν; in Ac 9⁵ these words do not belong to
the true text). The same figure is employed by Greek
and Latin writers (*e.g.* Pindar, *Pyth.* ii. 173;
Aesch. *Agam.* 1633, *Prometh.* 323; Eurip. *Bacch.*
791; Terence, *Phorm.* I. ii. 28).   J. A. SELBIE.

GOAH (נֹּעָה).—An unknown locality near Jerusalem (Jer 31³⁹). LXX gives, instead of a proper
name, ἐξ ἐκλεκτῶν λίθων.

GOAT.—Of the six Heb. words used for the tame
goat, one signifies the *g. generically*, and, where the
context indicates it, the *she goat*. One is used in
the masc. and fem. forms to indicate the *he g.* and
she g. respectively. Three are used for the *he g.*
only. One is used in AV for the *scapegoat*, which
was prob. no goat at all, and is therefore transliterated in RV *azâzél*. Beside these there is one
word which undoubtedly signifies the *wild g.*,
and another which prob. refers to the same.

1. עֵז, αἴξ, ἔριφος, capra, hœdus, Arab. *ma'z*,
fem. *'unz.* The plu. עִזִּים *'izzîm* signifies the g. generically (Ex 12⁵ etc.). In this sense שֵׂה עִזִּים (Dt 14⁴)
signifies a *head* or *individual* of the goats, גְּדִי עִזִּים (Jg
6¹⁹) a *kid* of the goats. It is also used for *she goats*,
the context showing the meaning (Gn 30³⁵ 31³⁸ 32¹⁴
etc.). It is also used elliptically for *goat's hair* (Ex
26⁷ etc.). In the sing. (Lv 17³) it sometimes signifies an *individual g.*, without reference to sex; at
others, where the context points out the meaning, a
she g. (Gn 15⁹). The Aram. plu. עִזִּין (Ezr 6¹⁷) also
refers to *goats generically*, and the construct state
צְפִירֵי עִזִּין signifies 'he goats of the goats' (cf. Dn 8⁵·⁸).

2. שָׂעִיר *sâ'ir*, χίμαρος, hircus. This word occurs
freq. in Lv and Nu as the designation of the g. of
the sin-offering. In its masc. form in construct
state with עִזִּים it signifies the *he g.* (Lv 4²³), and in
its fem. שְׂעִירָה *se'îrah*, χίμαιρα, in construction with
עִזִּים, the *she g.* (Lv 4²⁸). The compound expression
is in AV rendered 'a kid of the goats,' in RV
better, simply 'goat.' *Sâ'ir* comes from the root
שָׂעַר *sa'ar*=*shag* or *rough hair* (cf. Arab. *sha'r*). In
this sense it is used with צָפִיר, one of the words for
he g., to indicate his *shagginess*, Dn 8²¹ (AV 'rough
g.,' RV 'rough he g.,' lit. 'the *he g.* the shaggy').

3. עַתּוּד *'attûd*, used only in plu. עַתּוּדִים *'attûdîm* (the
same as the Arab. *'atûd*, plu. *a'tîdah*), τράγοι, κριοί,
χίμαροι, hirci. It is tr⁴ in LXX of Ps 50⁹ χιμάρους
(AV and RV 'he goats,'), and v.¹³ τράγων (AV and
RV 'goats'). It is rendered (Gn 31¹⁰·¹²) AV
'rams,' AVm and RV 'he goats,' LXX οἱ τράγοι
καὶ οἱ κριοί, as if the translator were uncertain
which was intended, or meant to indicate that
both were included, or else read from a different
text. '*He goats* ('attûdîm, LXX δράκοντες) before
the flocks' (Jer 50⁸) signifies *leaders*. 'Chief ones
('attûdîm, LXX ἄρξαντες) of the earth' (Is 14⁹) is
a metaphorical rendering of *he goats*, AVm
'leaders' or 'great goats,' RVm *he goats*. 'Punished the goats' (RV 'he goats'), LXX ἀμνούς
(Zec 10³) refers to *chiefs*.

4. צָפִיר *zâphir*, τράγος, hircus; צְפִיר הָעִזִּים *zâphir
ha'izzim*, τράγος αἰγῶν (Dn 8⁵·⁸); צְפִירִים *zâphirîm*,
χιμάρους (2 Ch 29²¹, Ezr 8³⁵). Aram. צְפִירֵי עִזִּין, χιμάρους αἰγῶν (Ezr 6¹⁷). This word (Aram. and late
Heb.), from the root צָפַר *zâphar*, signifying *to leap*,
refers to the *he goat* alone. It is combined with
sâ'ir. See (2).

5. תַּיִשׁ *tayish*, τράγος, aries, hircus. The same as
the Arab. *tais*, and means a *he goat* only (Pr 30³¹).
Plu. תְּיָשִׁים *têyâshîm*, τράγοι (Gn 30³⁵ 32¹⁴, 2 Ch 17¹¹,
not in LXX).

6. עֲזָאזֵל *'azâzêl*, ἀποπομπαῖος, caper emissarius, AV
scapegoat, RV *Azazel* (Lv 16⁸·¹⁰·²⁶). See AZAZEL.

Goats have always been a large item in the
wealth of the people of Bible lands. Laban had
large flocks of goats (Gn 30³³·³⁵). Jacob gave two
hundred she goats and twenty he goats to Esau
(Gn 32¹⁴). Nabal had a thousand goats (1 S 25²).
Sheep and goats were kept together in flocks
(Mt 25³²·³³). Kids especially were used as food
(Gn 27⁹, Jg 6¹⁹ 13¹⁵, Lk 15²⁹). The prohibition
against 'seething a kid in his mother's milk'
(Ex 23¹⁹ 34²⁶, Dt 14²¹) may refer to the dish known
to the Arabs as *leben immu*, *i.e.* 'his mother's
milk.' It consists of meat, stewed in clabber, with
onions, mint, and other condiments. It was
probably not intended to prohibit this savoury
dish altogether, but to prevent the unnatural-
ness of stewing a kid in its own mother's milk.
(For other possible explanations see W. R. Smith,
RS p. 204 n., and Driver on Dt 14²¹.) A provision of a similar kind forbade the taking of a
hen bird with her brood, or her eggs (Dt 22⁶). The
Jews, however, interpret the passage as interdict-
ing them from this mode of cooking flesh altogether. Goat's milk was nevertheless much used
then as now (Pr 27²⁷). Goats were readily convert-
ible into money (Pr 27²⁶). The 'bottles' in which
wine was kept (Jos 9⁴, Ps 119⁸³, Mk 2²²) were made of
g. skins. They were made by cutting off the head
and legs, and drawing the carcase out by the neck,
and then tying the neck, legs, and vent, and tan-
ning the skin, with the hairy side out. Goat's
hair was used in the construction of the Tabernacle (Ex 26⁷ 35²⁶ 36¹⁴) and for other purposes
(1 S 19¹³). Its usually black colour is alluded to
(Ca 4¹ 6⁵). The intractable and mischievous nature
of the goat is contrasted with the gentle and
innocent disposition of the sheep (Mt 25³²·³³). The
goat is mentioned in Apocr. (Jth 2¹⁷).

The goats of Bible lands, *Capra mambrica*, L.,
have long pendent ears. These are alluded to by
Am 3¹² 'as the shepherd taketh out of the mouth
of the lion two legs, or a piece of an ear.'
Some Syrian goats are white or mottled, but
most of them are black. They are destructive to
young trees, and are the principal impediment to
the propagation of forests on the bare mountain
tops, where they find their favourite pasture.

The he goat was used as a symbol of the Macedonian empire (Dn 8⁵). The stately gait of the he
goat is alluded to (Pr 30²⁹⁻³¹).

Two words are used for wild goats:—**1.** יְעֵלִים
ye'êlim. This word occurs in three passages, viz.
1 S 24², where LXX has for 'upon the rocks of
the wild goats,' ἐπὶ πρόσωπον Ἐδδαιέμ, Ps 104¹⁸,
where it has ἐλάφοις, and Job 39¹, where for 'wild
goats of the rocks' it has τραγελάφων πέτρας. This
animal is without doubt the *ibex*. The root יָעַל
yâ'al, *to climb*, corresponds well with its habits.
Its Arab. name *wa'l* is evidently the same as the
Hebrew. The animal is also called *beden* by the
Arabs. Its scientific name is *Capra beden*, Wagn.,
or *C. Sinaitica*, Ehrh. It is found in the wilderness on both sides of the Dead Sea, and in Sinai
and the Syrian Desert. There is an *'Ain el-wu'ul,
fountain of the wild goats*, about six hours E. of
Khareitun. The word *wa'l* is used in Pal. for the
roebuck. The name En-gedi (Arab. *'Ain-Jidy*),
fountain of the kid, was doubtless given with reference to this animal. It is about the size of the
domestic goat. The horns are from 2½ to 3 ft. in
length, curved almost to a semicircle, and reinforced
by large rough rings on the front face. Its flesh
is said to be excellent. It may have been the

venison which Isaac asked Esau to bring him (Gn 27³).

יַעֲלַת־חֵן the 'pleasant roe,' RV 'pleasant doe' (Pr 5¹⁹), is the female ibex, but tr^d by LXX πῶλος, *a foal*, Vulg. *hinnulus*.

2. אַקּוֹ *'akkô*. This animal is only once mentioned (Dt 14⁵). Possibly ὄρυξ, in the LXX rendering of the passage, is the equivalent of *'akkô*; but this is uncertain, as the LXX gives only five out of the seven animals mentioned in the Hebrew. Some suppose it to be the *roebuck*; but this animal is mentioned in the same list under the name *yaḥmûr*. Others suppose it to be the *paseng*, *Capra ægagrus*, Cuv., the wild original of the domestic goat. It is, however, most probably another name for the *yâ'êl*, or a kindred species.

For **Goat's Hair** see HAIR; and for **Scapegoat** see AZAZEL.   G. E. POST.

GOB (גֹּב).—A locality mentioned only in 2 S 21¹⁸. ¹⁹, where David fought the second and third of the four battles with the Phil. that are there mentioned. Most copies of the LXX have Γέθ in the first instance (with which agree the Syr. and a few Heb. copies), and Ρόμ in the second; while some Hebrew copies have Nob. The parallel passage (1 Ch 20⁴⁻⁸) locates the first of these two battles at Gezer (cf. Jos 10³³), and omits to mention the place of the second. Certainly they were not at Nob, but in the land of the Philistines. Wellhausen, followed by Driver and Budde, finds Gob also in 2 S 21¹⁶, where he would read וַיֵּשְׁבוּ בְגוֹב, 'and they dwelt in Gob,' instead of וְיִשְׁבּוֹ בְנֹב, 'and Ishbi-benob.' (See Wellhausen's or Driver's *Sam.*, *ad loc.*, and Budde's note in Haupt's *OT*).   W. J. BEECHER.

GOBLET is found only in Ca 7² 'Thy navel is [like] a round goblet.' The Heb. term is אַגָּן (prob. from a root signifying 'circular,' 'round'). It is used in plur. (אַגָּנֹת) in Ex 24⁶ of the 'basins' (Socin, *Opferbecken*) in which Moses collected half of the sacrificial blood. In Is 22²⁴ (the only other occurrence of the Heb. word) it is tr^d both in AV and RV 'vessels of cups,' where 'basin-vessels' (Guthe, *Beckengeschirr*) or 'bowl-shaped vessels' (Cheyne) would be a more accurate rendering. For the Eng. word cf. 'Annotations to Lk 22' in Rhem. NT, 'The new Testament is begonne and dedicated in his blud in the Chalice, no lesse than the old was dedicated, begonne, and ratified in that blud of calves contained in the goblet of Moyses.'   J. A. SELBIE.

GOD (IN OT).—

   i. Existence of God.
   ii. Anthropomorphisms.
   iii. Names of God.
      (1) Names expressing the general notion of Deity, *e.g.* El, Elohim.
      (2) Descriptive Titles, *e.g.* El Shaddai, El Elyon.
      (3) Personal name of the God of Israel, Jehovah (*Yahweh*).
   iv. Idea of God in various periods.
      (1) Pre-Mosaic period.
      (2) From the Exodus to the revolution of Jehu.
      (3) Prophetic period.
      (4) From the destruction of the State onwards.

i. EXISTENCE OF GOD.—The OT belonging to the historical period, many questions now discussed in the history of religion lie behind it. It never occurred to any writer of the OT to prove or argue the existence of God. To do so might well have seemed a superfluity, for all prophets and writers move among ideas that presuppose God's existence. Prophecy itself is the direct product of His influence. The people of Israel in their relations and character are His creation. It is not according to the spirit of the ancient world in general to deny the existence of God, or to use arguments

to prove it. The belief was one natural to the human mind and common to all men. Scripture does indeed speak of those who say in their heart there is no God (Ps 14¹ 53¹); but these are the fools, that is, the practically ungodly, and their denial is not a theoretical or speculative one, but merely what may be held to be the expression of their manner of life. Even the phrase 'there is no God' hardly means that God is not, but that He is not present, does not interfere in life; and, counting on this absence of God from the world and on impunity, men become corrupt and do abominable deeds (Ps 14, Job 22¹²ff.), and for their wickedness they shall be turned into Sheol, the region of separation from God, together with all the nations that forget God (Ps 9¹⁷). Yet even this forgetfulness of God by the nations is something temporary. It is a *forgetting* only, no obliteration of the knowledge of God from the human mind, and these nations shall yet remember and turn unto the Lord (Ps 22²⁷).

Again, as Scripture nowhere contemplates men as ignorant of the existence of God, it nowhere depicts the rise or dawn of the idea of His existence in men's minds. In the historical period the idea of God's existence is one of the primary thoughts of man; he comes possessed of this thought to face and observe the world, and his conception of God already possessed explains the world to him; the world does not suggest to him an idea hitherto strange, that of God's existence. And, of course, the bare idea of God's existence is not the primary thought which Scripture supposes all men to possess; this abstract conception has gathered body about it, namely, a certain circle of ideas as to what God is. And with these ideas the Hebrew took up his position over-against the world. To him God and the world were always distinct. God was not involved in the processes of nature. These processes were caused by God, but He was distinct from them. The Hebrew, however, came down from his thought of God upon the world, he did not rise from the world up to his thought of God. His thought of God explained to him the world, both its existence and the course of events upon it; these did not suggest to him either the existence or the nature of God, these being unknown to him. His contemplation of nature and providence and the life of man was never of the nature of a search after God whom he did not know, but always of the nature of a recognition of God whom he knew. When the singer in Ps 19 says 'the heavens declare the glory of God,' his meaning is that the glory of God, who is and is known and is Creator, may be seen reflected on the heavens. But the psalmist only saw repeated on the heavens what he already carried in his heart. And when in Is 40²⁵ff. J″ asks, 'To whom then will ye liken me? Lift up your eyes on high and behold: Who hath created these things? bringing out their hosts by number'— it is assumed as known that J″ is Creator, and that His omnipotence is revealed in the nightly parade of His hosts on the sky, not one failing to answer the roll call, and the inference is that, with this God for their God, Israel cannot despond or be faint-hearted — 'Why sayest thou, O Jacob, My way is hid from the Lord? An everlasting God is J″, creator of the ends of the earth; He fainteth not, neither is weary. He giveth power to the faint.' The passage teaches nothing new or unknown; it recalls what is known, reburnishing the consciousness of it, in order to sustain the faith and the hopes of the people. There is, however, in one or two passages an approximation to some of the arguments of Natural Theology. In Ps 94⁸ff. it is said, probably of the excesses of the heathen rulers of Israel, 'They break in pieces thy people,

O Lord. Yet they say, The Lord doth not see. Understand, ye brutish among the people : He that planted the ear, shall He not hear ? He that formed the eye, shall He not see ?'

The OT as little thinks of arguing or proving that God may be known as it thinks of arguing that He exists. Its position is here again, so to speak, far in front of such an argument. How should men think of arguing that God could be known when they were persuaded they knew Him, when they felt they were in fellowship with Him, when their whole mind was filled and aglow with the thought of Him, and when His Spirit was within them ? The peculiarity, however, of the OT comes out when the question is raised, *How* is God known ? And here the characteristic conception of the OT is that of Revelation—if men know God, it is because He has made Himself known to them. The idea of man reaching to knowledge or fellowship of God through his own efforts is foreign to the OT. God speaks, He appears : man listens and beholds. God brings Himself near to men, He enters into a covenant with them, He lays commands on them : they receive Him when He approaches, accept His will and obey His behests. Moses and the prophets are nowhere represented as thoughtful minds, reflecting on the Unseen and ascending to elevated conceptions of Godhead : the Unseen manifests itself to them, and they know it. God reveals Himself to the patriarchs in angelic forms, to Moses in the bush and on the mount, to the prophets in the spiritual intuitions of their own minds. The form of manifestation may change, but the reality remains the same. The conviction in the mind of the prophet, that God revealed Himself and His word to him when the truth broke upon his mind, was not less vivid than that of the patriarch who was visited by angelic messengers when sitting at the door of his tent, or that of Moses who saw the God of Israel in the mount. This view of God's self-manifestation, and that He takes the initiative, is the characteristic conception of the OT. The view may not be peculiar to Israel, for increasing knowledge of the Semitic peoples tends to show that on general questions about Deity, such as His relation to the world and to men's actions, they all thought very much alike ; the supremacy of Israel lay, not in these points, but in the ethical nature which they ascribed to their God, and in the redemptive hopes for mankind and the world which flowed from this conception of His nature. Interesting psychological questions are raised by such visions as that of Moses at the bush (Ex 3), that of Jacob at Jabbok (Gn 32²⁴ᶠᶠ.), and that of Isaiah in the temple (Is 6). Such questions may never be answered, but there are two points not to be lost sight of in estimating the OT conception of Revelation. *First*, though it is the OT manner throughout to signalize the divine operation alone, and to pass over in silence any preparation or co-operation in the mind of man, we are entitled and compelled to throw back into these ancient histories something of our knowledge of how men's minds operate now when God is moving them. Isaiah's vision was no doubt preceded by reflection on the nature of J″ and on the state of the nation, and the inevitable issue forecast. And similar reflections must have occupied the mind of Moses, along with aspirations in regard to himself and his people. These revelations of God to men were never mere objective calls to take a certain place or do a certain duty, there was always a personal element in them, they were a crisis in the individual religious life. It was this new personal relation to God, which was as real in the case of Moses as in that of Isaiah, that was the source of the power which such men wielded over the masses of their fellow-men. More

than one commentator has said that Isaiah, in offering a sign to Ahaz in the heavens above or the depth beneath (Is 7¹¹), was playing a dangerous game, and might have been left in the lurch. It is sufficient preliminary answer to say that Isaiah did not think so.¹ But it may be added that there was in Isaiah something of that same consciousness which expressed itself in Christ when He said, 'I know that thou hearest me always.' Therefore, *secondly*, the reality of the divine influence must be upheld also. The idea of Revelation cannot be regarded as a mere Hebrew conception which, translated into modern thought, means nothing but the natural operations of the mind in the sphere of religion. Such a view leaves unexplained the consciousness of the prophets, the contents of their prophecies, and the religious life which they manifested. But, of course, however much the OT reposes on the ground that all knowledge of God comes from His revealing Himself, and that there is such a revelation, it is far from implying that this revelation of God is a full display of Him as He really is. An exhaustive communication of God cannot be made, because the creature cannot take it in (Job 11⁷ᶠᶠ.). At the same time there is no trace in the OT of the idea that God as revealed to men is not God as He really is in Himself, or that His revelation of Himself is meant merely to be regulative of human life, while what He is in truth remains far away in a transcendental background out of which it is impossible for it to advance, or into which it is impossible for men to penetrate. The revelation God gives of Himself is a revelation of Himself as He is in truth, though it may be impossible to reveal Himself fully to men. The OT conception of God is that of a Person with ethical attributes ; it nowhere speculates on His physical essence. God is nowhere called spirit in the OT ; like men, He has a spirit ; but spirit never denotes substance, but always connotes energy and power, especially life-giving power.

ii. ANTHROPOMORPHISMS. — From the earliest period when God is spoken of, He is regarded as a Person. The word J″ is a personal name. From the Exodus downward He is so spoken of in contemporary literature : 'Sing unto the Lord, for he hath triumphed gloriously' (Ex 15²¹) ; He is one whom men may 'love' (Jg 5³¹) ; He is self-conscious, and swears 'by his holiness' (Am 4²), that is, by His Godhead (Gn 22¹⁶). The idea expressed by M. Arnold, that the conception of God in Israel was first that of some power external to themselves which they perceived in the world, a power making for a moral order or identical with it, and which they afterwards endowed with personality, inverts the OT representation, in which God is fully personal from the first, while His moral being becomes clearer and more elevated, or, at least, receives fuller expression. The question rather rises whether the very vividness with which God's personality was realized in Israel did not infringe upon other conceptions necessary to a true idea of God, such as His transcendence ? Was He not conceived as a magnified human person subject to the limitations of personality among men ? Now, of course, all OT statements about God are given in the region of practical religious life. A theology of the schools where the laws of exact thought prevail was unknown in the OT period. There may be observed, indeed, the beginnings of such a theology in the Alexandrian translation, and more clearly in the Aramaic versions and in Jewish writings of this age. These express themselves, in regard to God, in a form that seeks to be more severe and exact, using circumlocutions for the anthropomorphisms of the OT—a fact which indicates that these caused some offence. But in the OT such anthropomorphisms are freely used, as we use them still. And their use is usually justified by the statement that man was made in the image of God. It is possible that by some in Israel, just as by some among ourselves, His personality was so vividly realized as to obscure or repress some other conceptions of Him which also have their rights. But this can hardly be charged against the OT. When it speaks of the hand, arm, mouth, lips, and eyes of God; when He makes bare His holy arm (Is 52[10]), lifts up a signal to the nations (49[22]), is seen at the head of the Medes mustering His hosts, and His military shout is heard (13[4]), all this is but vivid conception of His being, His intelligence, His activity and universal power over the nations whom He directs. The human is transferred to His personality, as it could not but be; it is transferred graphically, as could not but happen when done by the poetical, vivacious, and powerful phantasy of the people of Israel. The language only testifies to the warmth and intensity of the religious feelings of the writers.

Another class of passages deserves attention. God is said to have walked in the garden in the cool of the day (Gn 3[8]); to have come down to see the tower which men did build (11[5]); to have been one of three men who appeared to Abraham, and to have eaten that which was set before Him (18[1. 8]); to have wrestled with Jacob (32[24ff.]), and the like. Such passages, in addition to being a testimony to the vividness with which God's personality was conceived, are evidence also of the religious feeling that God did reveal Himself to men, and enter into the closest fellowship with them. Different minds may estimate these early narratives in different ways. So far as we consider the experiences, say of Jacob at Jabbok, real, we may suppose that with these early men a spiritual impression always reflected itself in an accompanying extraordinary physical condition, just as among the early prophets the ecstasy was usual, while, among the later prophets, though still occasional (Is 8[11]), it became rare. And so far as we may consider the details of the description due to the narrator, it may be evidence that he could not conceive a spiritual experience apart from a corresponding physical accompaniment. And if early men so felt, it would not be judicious to deny that God might use an objective phenomenon, such as the burning bush, as a means of awakening the religious mind, just as our Lord used His miracles as a means of reaching the mind of those for whom He performed them. But these local manifestations of God never suggest that He was locally confined. It has been argued that Sinai was the local seat of J″ before the Exodus, and that it was only later that He was believed to have removed to Canaan. In David's day it was certainly believed that Canaan was His 'inheritance' (1 S 26[19]); and the oldest Pent. narrator speaks of Him 'coming down' upon Mount Sinai (Ex 19[11. 20]). When the Ark, to which His presence was in some way specially attached, was captured by the Philistines, and Shiloh destroyed, the priests continued His worship with all the old ceremonial of shewbread and the like at Nob (1 S 21[6]). The multitude of altars scattered over the country, if they did not suggest the positive idea of His ubiquity, suggested, at least, that there was no place where He might not let Himself be found, and the idea was confirmed by new self-manifestations in fresh places, as to Gideon (Jg 6[20]), to Saul (who seems to have built many altars, 1 S 14[35]), and to David (2 S 24[18]). The idea men had of all these places was that expressed by Solomon in regard to the temple: 'The heaven of heavens cannot contain thee, how much less this house

that I have builded' (1 K 8[27]). But while God was thus present on earth, the tempest or the thunderstorm was at the same time a theophany in the heavens. Two beliefs characterize the Hebrew mind from the beginning: first, the strong belief in causation—every change on the face of nature, or in the life of men or nations, must be due to a cause; and, secondly, the only conceivable causality is a personal agent. The unseen power under all things, which threw up all changes on the face of the world, which gave animation to the creature or withdrew it, which moved the generations of men upon the earth from the beginning (Is 41[4]), bringing Israel out of Egypt, the Philistines from Caphtor and the Syrians from Kir (Am 9[7]), was the living God. Some phenomena or events, such as the thunderstorm or the dividing of the sea, might be more striking instances of His operation than others. They were miracles, that is, wonders, but they did not differ in kind from the ordinary phenomena of nature, from His making the sun to rise and sealing up the stars (Job 9[7]), from His clothing the heavens with blackness (Is 50[3]) and making them clear again with His breath (Job 26[13]). Everything is supernatural, that is, direct divine operation. The regular alternation of day and night is due to J′″s covenant with them (Jer 33[20. 25]).

Another class of passages may be referred to. The first class cited vividly suggested the personality of God. The second class added the idea that He manifested Himself to men in place and circumstance, though with no implication that He was locally confined. This third class brings in the idea of the moral in His personality. Thus He repents that He made man (Gn 6[6]), and also of the evil He intended to do (Ex 32[14]); He is grieved (Gn 6[6]), angry (1 K 11[9]), jealous (Dt 6[15]), gracious (Ps 111[4]); He loves (1 K 10[9]), hates (Pr 6[16]), and much more. All the emotions of which men are conscious, and all the human conduct corresponding to these emotions, are thrown back upon God. Now, it may be true that from another point of view God must be held free of all passion, and not subject to such change as is implied in one emotion succeeding another. Still, this latter conception if carried to its just conclusions would reduce God to a being not only absolutely unmoral, but even impersonal. The religious mind could express its relations to God in no other way but by attributing to Him a nature similar to its own. Scripture is not unaware that this mode of conception may be pushed too far: 'The Lord is not a man that he should repent' (1 S 15[29]). What is of importance, however, in these representations of God is the general conception which they combine to suggest, viz. the moral Being of God.

iii. NAMES OF GOD.—(1) Some names express the general notion of Deity, as ʼEl, ʼElohim, ʽGod'; (2) others are descriptive titles applied to Deity, as ʼEl Shaddai (AV 'God Almighty'), ʼEl ʼElyôn, 'God Most High'; while (3) from the Exodus, J″ is the personal name of the God of Israel. The names El, Elohim, Shaddai, and J″ are probably all prehistoric, and their meaning is very obscure.

(1) The name El (אל) is the most widely distributed of all names for Deity, being used in Babylonian, Aramæan, Phœnician, Hebrew, and Arabic, particularly southern Arabic. It thus belongs to the primitive Shemitic speech before it became modified into dialects, though conceivably one or more of the dialects may have retained in use the root with which it is connected. (a) It has been referred to the Heb. root אל 'to be strong,' of which it would be the ptcp., meaning 'the strong.'* (b) Others have referred it to an

* Gesenius.

Arab. root *'ûl*, meaning 'to be in front' (hence *awwal*, 'first'), 'to govern,' and assigned to it the sense of 'leader.'[*] This meaning would be more in harmony with other Semitic names for God, such as *baal*, *'adôn* 'lord,' *melek* 'king,' etc. It is, however, against such derivations, which should give an unchangeably long *ê* in *el*, that the first vowel is short in Bab. *'ilu* and in Arab., and changeable in Heb., as אֱלֵיכֶם. (c) Some others have suggested a root אלה, either a cognate form to *'ûl*, 'to be strong,' considering the word an abstract = 'power,' 'might';[†] or a word connected with prep. אֶל 'unto,' God being the goal towards which men strive.[‡] This last meaning is too abstract for a primitive name of Deity, and altogether improbable. No plausible derivation of the term has been suggested. In Heb. prose the word is usually connected with an epithet, as 'the living God' (אֵל חַי), 'the eternal God,' 'God Most High'; but in the prophets and poetry it is used alone for 'god' or 'God,' and in a few cases is found in the plur. 'gods.' It has maintained its place all through the language as well as in other dialects in the formation of proper names.

Elohim is a plur. of which the sing. is אֱלֹוהַּ, Aram. *'ĕlâh*, Arab. *'ilâh* (with art. *'al'ilâh*=*'allâh*, 'God'). The sing. is used in poetry (Ps 18, Dt 32), and occasionally in very late prose. It has been contended (a) that the sing. is an artificial form coined from the plur. *Elohim*; and (b) that *Elohim* is really the plur. of *el*, formed by inserting *h*, as occasionally happens. But decidedly against (a) is the existence of the similar sing. form in Aram. and Arab., which there is no reason to suppose late; and against (b) is the fact that it is only in plurals of *fem.* form that there is an insertion of *h* (Syr. plur. *shemohin*, 'names,' cannot be held primary, as the word 'name' has *fem.* plur. in Heb. and western Aram.). *El*, too, has its own proper plur. *'elîm*. The attempt to connect the word with *'elah*, *'elon*, names of trees,[§] may be safely neglected. Whether the term *'ĕlôah* be connected with *'el*, and what its meaning is, remains uncertain. The use of the plur. *Elohim* is also difficult to explain. The plur. had so obtained the upper hand in usage that the more archaic sing. was confined to poetry. The plur. can scarcely be a remnant of polytheism; the Shemites did not use the general expression 'the gods' for Deity, like Lat. *Dii* (the Assyr. 'the Ishtars'='goddesses,' is like Heb. 'the Orions'= 'constellations,' Is 13[10]); and the suggestion that the plur. was first used of the deities of some particular locality[‖] is not without its difficulties, as usually each locality had only one deity. The idea that *Elohim* expressed the fulness of mights or powers contained in God[¶] is too abstract, apart from the uncertainty whether the sing. meant 'might.' After all, perhaps, the plur. may be easiest explained as a plur. of eminence, like *'adônîm*, *bĕ'âlim*, 'lord,' *tĕrâphîm* (1 S 19[13. 16]), and possibly *nôgĕsîm*, 'ruler' (Is 3[12]). The plur. appears also in Ethiopic *'amlâk*, 'God' (unused sing. *malek*), and in the Amarna letters the plur. *ilâni*, 'God,' is used in addressing the Egyptian king.

(2) As is the case with *El* and *Elohim*, the meaning of **El Shaddai** is altogether uncertain. *Shaddai* is probably an epithet, as it qualifies *El*, just as **Elyon**, 'Most High,' does. The name is old (Gn 49[25]), and is said by P to have been the patriarchal name of God (Gn 17[1], Ex 6[3]). The fanciful derivation שַׁדַּי (= אֲשֶׁר שַׁי) 'the sufficient' was perhaps known to LXX (ἱκανός, in this sense twice in Ru, thrice in Job, once in Ezk), and also the sense 'mighty,' 'almighty' (ἰσχυρός, παντοκράτωρ in

* Nöldeke.   † Dillmann.   ‡ De Lagarde.
§ Kayser-Marti, *AT Theologie*, p. 22.
‖ W. R. Smith.   ¶ Dillmann.

Job). If derived from שדד, the name would not mean 'the Almighty,' but 'the destroyer,' signifying presumably the storm-god, or possibly the scorching sun-god; if from Aram. שרא 'to pour,' it would have the similar sense of the rain-giver.[*] Such derivations have little to recommend them. Equally far from probability is the conjecture that the word should be read שַׂדִּי 'my lord' (Arab. *sayyidi*).[†] In Heb. *shēdîm* means 'demons' (Ps 106[37]), and Dt 32[17] when naming them adds 'no god.' Such a topsy-turvy of meaning is a triumph of etymology. More recently reference has been made to the Assyr. *shadu*, 'mountain,' from root 'to be high,'[‡] with the suggestion that *Shaddai* either means 'mountain' (cf. *ẓûr*, 'rock,' as title of God) or has the adjectival sense of 'most high.' The most that can be said is that the meaning 'almighty' has a certain tradition in its favour.

(3) The name **Jehovah** is also probably an ancient name (Gn 4[26]), though at the Exodus it received a special meaning by being connected with the Heb. verb 'to be.' (a) The pronunciation 'Jehovah' has no pretence to be right. The word יהוה acquired such a sacredness that, in reading, the name *'ădônâi*, 'lord,' was substituted for it;[§] hence in MSS and prints the vowels of *'ădônāi* were attached to the letters יהוה, and 'Jehovah' (יְהֹוָה) is a conflate form with the consonants of one word and the vowels of another. It is not older in date than the time of the Reformation (1520). (b) The contracted forms in which the name appears suggest that the original form of the word was יַהְוֶה *yahweh* or *yahve* (a Greek transliteration is Ιαβέ). (c) The occurrence of this name or a similar one in Assyr. cannot be regarded as certain. Hommel believes he has discovered in western Shemitic a divine name *i*, *ai*, or *ya* (*e.g.* I-zebel, Jezebel), which he considers the original form of the name, the Heb. יהוה being a more modern expansion. The last part of his conjecture at any rate cannot be considered probable. (d) The word being prehistoric, its derivation must remain uncertain. It has been connected with Arab. *hawa*, 'to blow' or 'breathe,' J″ being the god who is heard in the tempest—the storm-god; or with the verb *hawa*, 'to fall' (Job 37[6]), in the causative meaning 'the prostrator'—again the lightning-god; or with Heb. *hayah* (old form *hawah*), 'to be' in causative 'make to be'), *i.e.* 'the creator,' or fulfiller of his promises; and so on. (e) In Heb. writing of the historical period the name is connected with Heb. *hayah*, 'to be,' in the imperf. Now with regard to this verb, *first*, it does not mean 'to be' essentially or ontologically, but phenomenally; and *secondly*, the impf. has not the sense of a present ('am') but of a fut. ('will be'). In Ex 3[10ff.], when Moses demurred to go to Egypt, God assured him, saying, כִּי אֶהְיֶה עִמָּךְ ('EHYEH *'immāk*) 'I will be with thee.' When he asked how he should name the God of their fathers to the people, he was told אֶהְיֶה אֲשֶׁר אֶהְיֶה ('EHYEH *'ăsher* EHYEH). Again he was bidden say, 'אֶהְיֶה 'EHYEH hath sent me unto you'; and finally, 'יהוה YAHWEH, the God of your fathers, has sent me unto you.' From all this it seems evident that in the view of the writer *'ehyeh* and *yahweh* are the same: that God is *'ehyeh*, 'I will be,' when speaking of Himself, and *yahweh*, 'he will be,' when spoken of by others. What He will be is left unexpressed—He will be with them, helper, strengthener, deliverer.[‖]

The name J″ can hardly have been altogether

* So W. R. Smith.   † Nöldeke.
‡ Frd. Delitzsch, *Prolegomena*, 95 ; Hommel, *AHT* 110.
§ Lv 24[11] 'blasphemed the name' is already in LXX 'named the name.' But as to Jewish interpretation, cf. Dalman, *Der Gottesname Adonai*, 44 ff.
‖ On the word see Driver, 'The Tetragrammaton' in *Studia Biblica*, Oxf. 1885.

new to Israel before their deliverance. A new name would have been in those days a new God. The name of the mother of Moses, *Yôkebed* (Ex 6[20]), contains the word, and, if not among the tribes generally, the name was probably in use in the tribe of Levi, to which Moses belonged. The view (Tiele, Stade) that Moses became acquainted with the name among the Midianites, into a priestly family of which he had married, has no direct support in Heb. tradition. But the people in Egypt had, no doubt, connexions with the desert tribes on the east of them, as the flight of Moses to Midian suggests. The Kenites, the Midianite relatives of Moses, attached themselves to Israel (Jg 1[16] 4[11]). And the Rechabites, who originally may also have been Kenites (1 Ch 2[55]), were fervent worshippers of J″ (2 K 10[15ff.]), and strenuous upholders of the severer nomadic ideal of religious life as against the corruptions which Israel's acceptance of the Canaanite civilization had introduced. Moses, too, demanded liberty to go 'a three days' journey into the wilderness' to sacrifice to the God of the Hebrews (Ex 3[18] 5[3]). These things at least suggest the question whether the name J″ was not known also in the Sinaitic peninsula (cf. Ex 18[11], Dt 33[2ff.], Jg 5[4ff.]).

iv. IDEA OF GOD IN VARIOUS PERIODS.—(1) *The pre-Mosaic period.*—It has been made a question how much of the narratives regarding the patriarchal ancestors of Israel is history and how much legend. The stories were written down probably between the middle of the 10th and the middle of the 8th centuries, and it has been argued that they reflect in the main the religious ideas of this period. But the historians (J, E) from whom we have them did not invent them, but transcribed them from the national consciousness, and they must in any case reflect the ideas of an age considerably anterior to their own date as literature. The theory that names like Abraham and Sarah are those of extinct deities is perhaps overcome. But how far the wanderings of Abraham, Jacob, and Joseph, and their relations with other peoples, reflect tribal rather than individual movements, is liable to dispute. It is strange that while Edom, Moab, and the like have all one eponymous ancestor, Israel has three, all most unlike one another. Shall we hold them three distinct ideals? Or is Abraham the ideal of what Israel should be, and Jacob the type of that which it was? The story of Jacob and his brother Esau has been read as reflecting the historical relations of the peoples Israel and Edom, and their respective characters. If so, the historian who depicted his own people as crafty, unscrupulous, and godly, and their bitterest enemy as the careless, noble, natural man, was a humorous satirist of the highest rank. Historically, however, his satire must be judged less than just to his own people and more than partial to Edom. Abraham appears a purely personal figure. He may be transfigured by religious idealism, but the name must be traditional.

Apart from the patriarchal histories, sources of information for the condition of prehistoric Israel might be (1) the religious condition of the related peoples, Edom, Moab and Ammon, and Ishmael or the Arabs; and (2) any survivals appearing in post-Mosaic Israel from a lower stage of religion, *e.g.* stone, tree, and fountain worship, or rites connected with the dead, the possible remains of ancestor worship. Unfortunately, our knowledge of the peoples related to Israel belongs to a period long after the Exodus, being derived from the Bible or inscriptions. The assumption that the tribes which united to form Israel stood at the Exodus on the same religious plane as these peoples has its difficulties. When we consider the elevation at which eventually Israel stood above these

nations we hesitate to fix any historical period, particularly so comparatively modern a period as the Exodus, at which they must have stood on a level. However powerful and creative the genius of Moses may have been, he did not create a religion, any more than he did a nation, out of nothing. It is usually assumed that these small peoples, such as Edom and Moab, to which Israel was related, were henotheistic, *i.e.* worshippers of one god to the exclusion of all others. The assumption seems without foundation. Moab had a chief god Chemosh, but a nation so polytheistic as Assyria had also a chief god, Asshur, and so other nations. A composite god, Ashtar-Chemosh, is named on the Moabite Stone; and as it is only in S. Arabia that Ashtar (Athtar) is *masc.*, the deity here allied with Chemosh is probably Astarte. Neither is it certain that the Baal of Peor or of Meon was Chemosh. Mount Nebo may also be named from the god. Various deities also appear among the Edomites, as Ḳaush or Ḳos and Ḳuzaḥ. The personal names Hadad, Baal-ḥanan, Malikram* are all theophorous. And Dusares (Dhu-shShara, 'lord of Shara') was worshipped at Petra, though this may have been later.† And, of course, the Arabs in addition to a number of gods had the three great goddesses (the daughters of 'Allâh), *al Lât* (*al-ilâhat*, 'the goddess' of the sun), *al 'Uzza* ('the powerful,' possibly the Venus star), and *Manât* ('fate,' 'fortune,' τύχη, cf. Meni, Is 65[11]). A monolatrous Shemitic people is not discoverable in the historic period. The territorial position of peoples like Moab and Edom exposed them greatly to influence from neighbouring nations. The name *Hadad* in Edom may suggest Aramæan influence, and *Ashtar* in Moab the influence of the Canaanites; but the occurrence of the latter name in a royal document like the inscription of Mesha implies that the worship of Ashtar was national. If these small peoples be supposed to have been originally monolatrous, their history exhibits a degeneration and movement towards polytheism. While the fundamental ideas of Deity may be presumed to have been similar among all the Shemitic peoples, if they could be ascertained, the complete difference in the divine names current among these small nations and in Israel suggests a prolonged period of separate religious development, and renders any comparison of their religion with that of Israel at the Exodus barren of results.

Certain usages are supposed to point to ancestor worship among the Hebrews. The **teraphim, a** term completely obscure, have usually been considered household gods; though household gods need not necessarily be images of ancestors. In one passage the *teraphim* appear in a house (1 S 19[13. 16]); in others they are represented as placed in temples (Jg 17[5] 18[14], Hos 3[4]). Laban calls them his 'gods' (Gn 31[30]); that they were of human form or size can hardly be inferred from 1 S 19. *Teraphim* are usually coupled with EPHOD (wh. see), and in Israel were certainly used in consulting J″ and gaining oracles from Him (Hos 3[4]), though their use is condemned (1 S 15[23]). Nebuchadnezzar also used them to obtain an oracle from his gods (Ezk 21[21]). That the 'Elohim' to which the servant was to be brought who desired to remain for ever with his master (Ex 21[6]) was a family idol, ‡ is wholly improbable from the context. The practice of cutting off the hair in mourning for the dead was probably a softening of the former more extravagant custom of tearing out the hair. § The practice seemed perfectly

* Baethgen, *Beiträge*, 11 ff.; Buhl, *Gesch. der Edomiter*, 47 ff.
† Wellh., *Reste*[2], 49.
‡ Schwally, *Leben nach dem Tode*, 37.
§ Wellh., *Reste*[2], 182. The passage Jer 41[5] shows that 'cutting' one's flesh (Lv 19[28], Jer 16[6] 47[5]), whatever it originally meant, was then merely a token of excessive grief. Cf. Hos 7[14].

harmless to the prophets (Is 3^{24} 15^2, Mic 1^{16}), though forbidden later (Dt 14^1, Lv 21^5); but the prohibition may repose on the feeling that the rite was characteristic of a religion alien to that of J." If Dt 26^{14} mean that food was offered to the dead, such an offering was not of the nature of a sacrifice, but merely an expression of the feeling which the mourner strove to cherish that the departed were not dead, as appears from a multitude of passages in Arab. poetry. The mourner cried to the dead, 'Be not far'! though he had to answer himself, 'Nay, every one that is beneath the ground is far'! (Ḥamasa, 373). When two friends visited the grave of their comrade, and drinking each his cup of wine poured the third upon the grave, they only gave their friend his share as if he were alive (Ḥam. 398). There is no evidence that the dead were thought dangerous, and requiring to be placated by offerings. The name 'Elohim' bestowed on the spectre of Samuel (1 S 28^{13}) is strange, but the single instance can hardly suffice to prove that the dead in general were regarded as 'Elohim'; all other statements regarding the dead, the name *rephāim* given to them, and the fact that the *'ōbs* twittered and muttered and spoke low out of the ground (Is 8^{19} 29^4), indicate that they were regarded as anything but powerful 'gods.' *

Certain things, such as Jacob's vision at Bethel (Gn 28), and names like the 'Oak of Moreh' ('the oracle,' Gn 12^6), the 'Oak of the soothsayers' (Jg 9^{37}), have been thought remains of the animistic stage of religion still surviving in the historical period. Certainly, the names *Baal* 'lord,' *Melek Milk, Milcom* 'king,' *al Lat* 'the goddess,' all show that the stage of promiscuous or general animism, if it ever existed, had long been overpast by all the Shemitic peoples. But to primitive minds the difficulty of realizing a deity apart from a local abode or some form would be great, and it was natural to localize the god in some fertile spot, grove or evergreen tree, or fountain of living water, where his beneficent operation was most perceptible. Why great or prominent blocks of stone should have been regarded as his dwelling-place is more obscure. At a later period men perhaps invited the presence of the deity by erecting pillars, *mazzēboth*, or artificial trees, *'ashēra*, when the natural objects were not at hand. This difficulty of realizing a deity without abode and apart from some form explains the use of images, particularly when consulting him for an oracle, and it explains also the erection of a 'house' for the god. The difficulty was felt all through the history of Israel: at the Exodus (Ex 32), in the time of the Judges (Jg $8^{24ff.}$ 17^3), and much later (Is 2^8), as it has been felt in large sections of the Christian Church. The Ark, to which the presence of J" was attached, relieved the difficulty without representing J" under any form. When a house was built in which J" was present, the Ark lost its significance and disappeared. The Ephod, whatever it was [EPHOD], was used when an oracle was sought. In David's days its use was held legitimate (1 S 21^9 23^6), afterwards it disappears from the legitimate cultus.

From the Exodus J"'s revelation of Himself was given, and men's thoughts of Him suggested through the national history. He showed what He was in great deeds rather than declared it in words. He was less the God of nature than of human history. Even when He performed wonders in nature it was usually in connexion with the life of the people and for moral ends, but in history His higher ethical attributes and purposes received direct illustration. Further, His operations being on the stage of Israel's

national history, were much more conspicuous and easily read than they would have been if performed in the life of individuals. His deliverance of the nation from Egypt revealed His power and redemptive goodness on a scale that left an impression never effaced from the heart of the people. His destruction of the nation, predicted by the prophets and fulfilled, taught once for all that He was the righteous God and moral Ruler of the nations.

The religious development of Israel is virtually a development in the idea of God. As God was the only force in the world, particularly in human history, when a crisis occurred in history some conception of God had to be called in to explain it; and when mysterious problems arose in the national or individual life, the problem was immediately reflected back upon God, and became one in regard to His nature or action. In Israel the religious progress appears in the form of a conflict. And if a conflict implies lower elements and conceptions, it also implies a higher element which was conscious of the lower, and strove either to eject it or transform it. Such a transmuting force existed in Israel from the beginning, producing the results which mankind now inherit. This force may be identified with the moral in the conception of J". Mere progress in itself does not decide that the progress was natural or supernatural. Our convictions in regard to this point will be formed rather from our contemplation of the results eventually achieved, from contrasting these results with those attained anywhere else, and from the trust we place in the consciousness of the prophets and leaders of Israel who felt that they were inspired. In a general way the religious history of Israel may be divided into three periods, in each of which the conflict resulted in a clearer conception of God, or of J" the God of Israel :—

(*a*) The period from the Exodus to the revolution of Jehu.—The revolution of Jehu put its seal on the life-work of Elijah; it gave national expression to his demand : 'If J" be God, follow him' (1 K 18^{21}). To the mass the struggle probably appeared an external one between two names, two deities; and it issued in the acceptance of the one. The numerical oneness of God was recognized. To Elijah and others the question was not one of numerical unity only, but also of moral nature.

(*b*) The prophetic period.—The conflict resulting in the recognition of J" as God alone, at least in Israel, was followed by one more inward. Though Baal as another than J" was set aside, Baal had incorporated himself in J". Now, the conflict was not between J" and another, it was an internal one between J" and Jehovah-Baal, between two conceptions of Him—the popular and the prophetic. In the popular conception J" was still mainly their national god, the god of the land, giver of its corn and wine, and whose most pleasing service was sacrifice and offering; while to the prophets He was a purely ethical Being, elevated far above the people, the righteous Ruler, to whom material offerings were inappreciable, and whose service could be nothing but a righteous life. What proportion existed between the prophetic party and the more backward popular mass cannot be known. The prophets now broke with the people as a whole, as they believed J" had broken with it and determined to destroy it. In earlier times prophets had broken only with particular dynasties and threatened them with destruction. But there was no difference in principle between the earlier and the canonical prophets; the grounds on which J" rejected a dynasty and the people were alike moral (1 K 22). A hundred years before the time of the canonical prophets, Elijah by his words, 'the children of Israel have forsaken thy covenant,' and by his flight to Horeb,

---

* Against the construction put by Schwally on Jer 16^7, see Giesebrecht, *Jerem.*, and Driver, *Deut.* 292.

expressed his feeling that the breach was now one between J″ and the people. Yet the breach was not absolute or final. Isaiah's conception of the Remnant appears already in Elijah's days: 'I will leave me 7000 men in Israel' (1 K 19[18]). The destruction of the state, foretold by the prophets, verified the prophetic conception of J″: He was the righteous Ruler of the nations. It verified also their judgment upon the past religious life of the people.

(c) From the destruction of the State onward.—The prophetic principles regarding J″ had been conspicuously illustrated in the national history: J″ was God alone; He was righteous; His nature was inscribed in letters of fire across the people's life and experience. But being written on the national history, these principles were as yet, to the individual mind, rather abstract. They were schematic, diagrammatic, seen to be true on the great scale and intellectually, hardly yet felt to be true in the experience of the individual. They had to be assimilated into the personal experience, equated by reflection with the condition of the world, the state of the people, the life of the individual. The process raised great problems, all of which became problems about God. (a) J″ was God alone and righteous, yet He took no pains to assert Himself against the world. He slept; the throne of the universe seemed vacant; the nations knew Him not, and wrought unchecked their cruelties on the earth. (β) So, too, Israel was His people; they possessed the truth; His cause and theirs was one; because the eternal truth was in their hearts they were righteous as against the world, but all appeals to His tribunal were vain; their passionate cries that He would arise and plead their cause, and their passionate hopes, 'he is near that will justify me,' only expired on the air. (γ) And in like manner the individual pined away solitary and deserted: 'Mine eyes fail while I wait for my God' (Ps 69[3]). More daring spirits like Job rose in rebellion: the throne of the world was not vacant, it was filled by an Immorality; the human conscience rose, and, proclaiming itself greater than He, deposed Him from His seat. The OT closed leaving these conflicts still undecided, though not without efforts towards a reconciliation. The people found a peace in hope and the future, and endured as seeing Him who is invisible. The individual spirit, too, caught glimpses of a future beyond the borders of this life, and in the ecstasy of faith could say, 'I know that I shall see God.' A few in their loftiest moments were able to bring the reconciliation into the present and feel it if not think it. Though J″ was seen in the world and in events, He was not exhausted by them, He stood above them and apart. The mind, too, was its own place, it could detach itself from its external conditions. And thus J″ and the soul had fellowship, through no medium, spirit with spirit—'Nevertheless I am continually with thee' (Ps 73[23]).

(2) *The Exodus to the revolution of Jehu.*—From the Exodus onward J″ was the God of Israel. People and prophets were at one in this. Israel never had any other native God but J″; if portions of the people declined to the service of the local Baals, J″ was always the national God, and a conscience within the people constantly recalled them to His service. From Hosea downwards writers are in the habit of stigmatizing the corrupt worship of J″ at the high places as Baal worship, —as no doubt in principle it was,—but probably strict idolatry, in the sense of worship of other gods than J″, was never very widespread either in the north or south, though towards the decline of the Judæan state various Eastern idolatries were practised by some classes of the people. That J″ was God of Israel was the faith of all, though the faith might mean different things to different minds, or among different classes. To some it might mean merely that J″ was Israel's national God as other peoples had also their gods (Mic 4[5]); to others it might mean something higher. A Shemitic mind might rise to general conceptions very slowly; and while practically J″ was the only God to him, the theoretical notion that He was God alone might not have occurred to him. It perhaps needed that internal conflict which arose through the slowness of the popular mind, and that outward collision with idolatrous nations which occurred in the days of the great prophets to bring the unity of God to speculative clearness. Heb. tradition places the Decalogue at the beginning of Israel's national development, and the prophets by their references to the moral *Torah* as known to the people from the first, but 'forgotten' by them, appear to follow the tradition. Moses is everywhere regarded as a prophet, and probably his teaching, like that of the prophets, consisted (apart from his lofty conceptions of God) in the main of social and civil ethics. Though the first commandment does not say that J″ is God alone, the negative element, 'Thou shalt have no gods before me,' is without a parallel in the history of religions. J″ was a jealous God. Why was He jealous? Jealousy is the reaction of one's self-consciousness against a wrong done him. What was the idea held of J″ when it was thought His consciousness of Himself would feel other gods beside Him intolerable? If the Decalogue be Mosaic, there was virtual monotheism in Israel since the Exodus, though it might be only among the higher minds, and more latent than conscious. And that which made J″ unique at least, if not alone, was His moral being. Writers of all schools are agreed that ethical elements entered into the conception of J″ from the beginning. There was at least on His nature a crescent of light, which waxed till it overspread His face, and He was light with no darkness at all. When Moses sat judging the people, dispensing right and justice in the name of their God, it could not but appear to the people that He was a God of righteousness. It has been contended that in subsequent history J″ sometimes displayed 'unaccountable humours,' that is, moods of mind and a kind of action not reducible under the moral idea. The arguments for this are not quite cogent. At all events, Israel entered upon national existence with two articles of faith: that J″ was their God alone, and that in His Being He was moral, the impersonation of Right and Righteousness. And emotional energy was given to these two articles by the consciousness of having been redeemed by their God. Behind the people's national life lay the consciousness of redemption as much as it lies behind the life of the Christian. Israel's self-consciousness as a nation was virtually identical with its consciousness of J″, its God. J″, indeed, was all in all, the people little else than the medium through which He displayed Himself. The old anthology recording Israel's conflicts with the nations is called 'The Book of the Wars of J″' (Nu 21[14]). Meroz is cursed, because it came not 'to the help of J″' (Jg 5[23]). The people's victories are 'the righteous acts of J″, the righteous acts of His rule in Israel' (Jg 5[11]). The furore of enthusiasm for J″ in the song of Deborah reflects back light on the Exodus and the work of Moses. The conceptions regarding J″ found in the oldest literature differ little from those of the prophetic age and subsequent times, except that they are less broadly expressed. (a) The dwelling-place of J″ was often at least conceived as superterrestrial. He 'came down' to see the tower which men did build (Gn 11[5]), and to discover if the wickedness of Sodom corre-

sponded to the cry against it (18²¹), and He rained fire on the cities of the plain from J″ 'out of heaven' (19²⁴). To Moses He said He had come down to save His people (Ex 3⁸). But, though heaven was His throne, He manifested Himself over all the earth,—to Abraham in Ur and Canaan; to Jacob in Mesopotamia, to whom He also said, 'Fear not to go down to Egypt; I will go down with thee' (Gn 46³); to Moses at Sinai and in Egypt; to His people, going before them into Canaan (Ex 33¹⁵). There, though His presence was specially attached to the Ark, He also revealed Himself to Joshua as the captain of the Lord's hosts (Jos 5¹⁴), and by His spirit He ruled the people, raising up judges, inspiring Saul and David. (b) As to His relation to nature, it is said in the oldest Creation narrative that He made heaven and earth, and all the creatures, as well as man (Gn 2). On the highest scale He commands nature, sending a universal flood upon the earth, opening the windows of heaven and breaking up the fountains of the great deep (Gn 7). By some convulsion of nature He 'overthrows' the cities of the plain (Gn 19). Before Joshua He made the sun and moon stand still in the sky (Jos 10¹²); and at His command the stars fight in their courses against Sisera (Jg 5²⁰). All earthly and heavenly forces obey Him. He caused an east wind to blow, and rolled back the sea (Ex 14²¹); He brought locusts on Egypt (10¹³), and turned the river into blood (7¹⁹); He sent hail and fire (9²³) and darkness (10²²). In the days of Ahab He scourged the land three and a half years with a drought (1 K 17¹), and in the time of David devastated the people with a pestilence (2 S 24¹⁵). (c) In the early literature Israel had not yet entered greatly into relation with the nations; the teaching of Scripture regarding J″'s rule of the nations first appears in the prophets when the great Assyrian and Babylonian empires came upon the stage of the world's history. But the same conceptions appear in the earlier literature as in the later. J″ showed His power over Egypt when He brought out the people with a high hand, slew the firstborn, and overwhelmed the army in the sea. He drove out the nations before Israel, and gave David his victories over Aram and the peoples around. In Israel itself He is the Living God and Ruler. His angel leads the hosts of Joshua and Barak. The government of the people is in His hand. When in early times a crisis arises, He raises up a judge to save the people; when the old order changes, He elects Saul to the throne; and when the age of conflict is over and an era of peaceful development is inaugurated, He 'builds an house' for David, making his dynasty perpetual. Human leaders are but the form in which J″ clothes His own efficiency, for it is His spirit animating them that makes them heroes and saviours, such as were the judges and Saul. The spirit of J″ is J″ exercising efficiency. And though this efficiency is most visible in the external rule of the people it operates also in the sphere of thought, raising up prophets and Nazirites. The external and the inward often go hand in hand, as when David made Jerusalem the spiritual as well as political capital of the kingdom, and when prophets of the Lord like Nathan and Gad became his advisers. (d) J″'s rule of the world and of His people is moral. For his sin Adam forfeited Eden; for their wickedness mankind were drowned by a flood, and the cities of the plain overthrown. Ahab's sin was chastised by a drought, and David's by a pestilence. The histories being so greatly public annals, little is said of the relation of J″ to the individual. But such histories as those of Sarah, Rachel, and Hannah indicate how closely connected J″ was

thought to be with family life; and such narratives as the covenants between Jacob and Laban (Gn 31⁴⁴ff.), Abraham and Abimelech (21²²ff.), Joshua and the Gibeonites (Jos 9¹⁵), show how He entered into the common life of men. That J″'s treatment of the individual was considered moral everywhere appears, e.g. the brethren of Joseph (Gn 42²¹ff.), Korah (Nu 16³⁵ff.), Achan (Jos 7¹⁵), Hophni and Phinehas (1 S 3¹³), Ahab (1 K 21²⁰ff.). In Ex 32³³ J″ says, 'Whosoever hath sinned against me, him will I blot out of my book.' And in narrating the death of Abimelech, the very ancient historian says, 'Thus God requited the wickedness of Abimelech which he did unto his father' (Jg 9⁵⁶·⁵⁷). And on reward of righteousness, comp. David's words, 1 S 26²³ 'The LORD render to every man his righteousness.' Cf. 2 S 2⁵, 1 K 18¹²ff.. And, finally, (e) the idea of J″'s foresight and predetermination is illustrated in the protevangelium (Gn 3¹⁴·¹⁵), in the covenant promises to Abraham (Gn 15), in the destinies appointed for Jacob and Esau (25²³ 27³⁷ff.·³⁹ff.·), and in the place and character predicted for the children of Jacob (Gn 49).

The earlier part of the period from the Exodus to the fall of the house of Omri was a time of warfare with external enemies till J″ gave His people rest under David; and it has been thought that the name 'J″ of Hosts,' or fully, 'J″, God of Hosts' (אֱלֹהֵי צְבָאוֹת 'י), may have arisen during this time of conflict—the 'hosts' being those of Israel. It is strange that the name is not found in the Hex., appearing in Samuel, and particularly in the prophets. It is possible that the title had some concrete origin such as is suggested, and that it did not originally refer to the hosts of heaven, whether stars or angels, nor to the general cosmic forces of the universe. In the prophets, however, there is certainly no reference to the hosts of Israel. Between the time of the battle-cry, 'the sword of the Lord and of Gideon' (Jg 7²⁰), and the words of Isaiah, 'In returning and rest shall ye be saved' (Is 30¹⁵), a world had passed away and a new one arisen. The ancient name 'J″ of Hosts' was used as the loftiest name for J″, suggesting His royal majesty and infinite power; but in all likelihood the prophets used the name as a single title without analyzing it, and never asking themselves what the 'hosts' were. J″ of Hosts means God of the universe.*

(3) *The Prophetic period.*—J″ was pre-eminently the God of human history, and it was in their history that the people learned to know Him. The stages through which the history ran led the people's thoughts ever more from the external to the inward in J″. First, the victories He gave them at the Exodus, at the entrance into Canaan, and in David's days, revealed the might of J″. Then, their defeats in after days, and the dissolution of the state, gave them a sight into His inward being. No prophet or writer ever attributed Israel's disasters to the might of the nations or their gods; they were due to J″ their God Himself. They were chastisements, revealing His moral being. And finally, in the depression that lay on them from the Exile, never uplifted, they learned to transcend both history and external conditions, and to know J″ as a spiritual fellowship. They were ever with Him (Ps 73²³). They were satisfied with His likeness (Ps 17¹⁵); J″ was God of the spirits of all flesh (Nu 16²² 27¹⁶). His afflictions had already enabled Jeremiah to reach this stage, in whom we see prophecy transfigured into piety.

Under Solomon, Israel entered into the circle of civilized nations. His father David was a fervent Jehovist; fervour was scarcely characteristic of himself in any direction. As he built houses for

* See Kautzsch, *ZAW*, 1886; *PRE*² *s.* 'Zebaoth'; Borchert, *SK*, 1896.

the gods of the neighbouring peoples among whom he found his wives, he cannot have been a logical monotheist. Neither was Ahab this even a hundred years later, though there is no evidence, but the reverse, that he abandoned the worship of J″. The century after Solomon witnessed the complete absorption of the native population ; but if Israel subdued the Canaanites, it was in turn conquered by them. It inherited their civilization, but the heritage included a legacy of debased moral conceptions and practices. J″ took possession of the native shrines, and so became God of the land ; but as He was worshipped where the Baals had been before, to many He might seem not unlike them. The confusion was increased by the fact that the name *baal, i.e.* 'lord,' was applied to J″.* Processes had been going on for long of which we have no clear account. It was in a way a fortunate thing that Ahab introduced the worship of the Tyrian Baal. It brought matters to a pass, and awoke men to see what was at stake. The persecution of the J″ party was no doubt caused by their opposition, for Ahab was no propagandist. Though Elijah was the spokesman of the party, he had a wide movement behind him. Obadiah, the chamberlain, hid 100 prophets of J″ in caves (1 K 18⁴). The disaffection had invaded the army. When the people 'limped between two opinions' (18²¹), it was a struggle between their own convictions and the influence of the court. Some indeed, like the Rechabites, were more radical, seeing in the Baal worship only a feature of the Canaanite civilization accepted by Israel, which they would have swept away, returning to the ancient ideal of a nomadic life. And Hosea appears to express a similar sentiment when he says that J″ shall allure Israel into the wilderness and give her her vineyards from there (2¹⁴·¹⁵). At last the spirit of revolt embodied itself in Jehu, and swept away the house of Omri and Baal together. J″ stood with no rival. It was a great though only an external victory. The scene of conflict now changes to the nature of J″ Himself, and the conflict is waged by the canonical prophets.

The prophets taught nothing new about J″,† though, with history as their lesson-book, they taught many things more clearly. And to many who had been blind to J″'s operations in the past, what they taught may have seemed strange and even incredible. Each prophet has some special truth about J″ to declare, and the truth is perhaps a reflection of his own kind of mind. But as the separate colours combine to form the pure light, all their separate truths unite to reveal the full nature of J″, for it takes many human minds to make up the divine mind. The prophets, like their predecessors, are, first of all, *seers* ; their function is to foresee and predict ; their teaching about the nature of J″ only sustains their predictions. The simultaneous rise of four men such as Amos, Hosea, Isaiah, and Micah, each independent of all the others, is a mystery. Amos says, 'The Lord God doeth nothing without revealing his counsel to his servants the prophets' (3⁷). But the revelation was probably in some way mediated. Did the prophet's ear catch distant sounds of movements among the nations, unheard by other ears ? or was it their thought of J″, ever becoming more powerful and engrossing, that led them to project the calamitous future ? Probably it was both combined. It is usually argued that the prophets reached their monotheism along the line of the ethical conception

of J″ ; from being the Unique One J″ became the Only One. Possibly their minds moved along several lines. The prophets of the 8th cent. do not formally declare J″ to be God alone, though they silently ignore all other gods ; it is only in the age of Dt and in that of Deutero-Isaiah that J″'s sole Godhead is directly expressed.

It is now a common-place to say that Amos taught that J″ is absolute Righteousness, the impersonation of the moral idea ; that moral evil alone is sin ; and that the only service J″ desires is a righteous life (though Amos also teaches that J″ is good and compassionate, 2⁹ᶠᶠ· 7¹ᶠᶠ·) ; and that Hosea represents J″ as unchanging Love, which no ingratitude of His people can weary or alienate (though Hosea does not forget the righteousness of J″, 2¹⁹) ; and that to Isaiah J″ is the transcendent Sovereign and universal Lord (though he, too, recognizes the fatherly goodness and nurture of J″, 1² 5¹ᶠᶠ·). Isaiah expresses his conception in the term *kădôsh*, of which 'holy' is a very imperfect rendering. 'Holiness' is not primarily a moral quality, it is the expression of Godhead in the absolute sense. 'The Holy One of Israel' is a paradox, meaning that the transcendent God has become God of Israel. Isaiah in one thought goes beyond his predecessors (but see HOSEA) : he insists on religiousness—that the *consciousness* of J″ should be ever present in the mind. The want of this consciousness, insensibility to the Lord the King, failure to recognize Him in the events of history and human life,—this is sin (1³ᶠᶠ·). And it is the cause of all sin, of the levity of human life (5¹²), and the self-exaltation both of men and nations (2¹⁰ᶠᶠ· 9⁹ 10¹²). The prophetic ideas form but half their teaching, the greater half lies in their own life and personal relation to God. Taken as a whole, the prophetic teaching amounts to the full ethicizing of the conception of J″. And the moral is of no nationality ; it transcends nationality, and is human. The righteous God is God universal, over all. The principles of the human economy have at last clearly reflected themselves in the consciousness of the prophets, and human history is seen to be a moral process. And the idea naturally suggested the other idea of the issue of the process, the eschatology, which is the realizing of perfect righteousness in the world of mankind (Is 1²⁶ 9⁷). The movement of the prophetic thought towards universalism was aided by the entrance of the great empires of Assyria and Babylon on the stage of history. This gave them a new idea, that of the world ; it created a new antithesis, J″ and the world ; and it opened a new realm for the rule of the King, all the nations of the earth. Universalism is most broadly taught in Deutero-Isaiah ; but there it is a theological deduction from the unity of God. J″ is God alone, the first and the last, initiating all movements and leading them to their issue ; and His salvation shall be to the ends of the earth (49⁶). The loftiest thoughts of God expressed in Scripture are found in Job and Deut.-Isaiah. In the latter writer all the operations and attributes of J″ are combined to sustain the faith that he is Redeemer of Israel and Saviour of all mankind,—His creation of the earth (45¹⁸ᶠᶠ·) and man (42²⁵ᶠᶠ·), His call of Israel to be His servant and revelation of Himself within it (42¹⁻⁶ 45¹⁹⁻²⁰ 49¹⁻⁶), and its Restoration (49⁷ᶠᶠ· 50⁴ᶠᶠ·),—all these are in order that all the ends of the earth may look unto Him and be saved (45²² 49⁶ 51⁴ᶠᶠ·).

(4) *From the Exile onwards.—Attributes.*—In the last period of Israel's history new conceptions of God hardly emerge. The period was rather one of assimilation of the prophetic teaching into the individual mind and experience. What the prophets had taught of the nature of J″, of His

---

* This may be inferred from the fact that names compounded with Baal occur not only in Saul's but in David's family. Cf. also Hos 2¹⁶.

† See, now, Wellh. *Isr. u. Jüd. Geschichte,* 110.

purpose, and particularly of the eschatological issues of His purpose, formed the subject of reflection, and efforts were made to verify it in experience. The efforts, as has been said, raised problems which, if they baffled solution, led to a more inward knowledge of God (Ps 73[16ff.]). The problems were mainly three : God and the world ; God and Israel His people ; and God and the life and destiny of the individual (see above).

Perhaps in this period fuller and more formal expression is given to the attributes of God. But a detailed account of the divine attributes is of little moment or worth. When the idea is reached that God is a transcendent moral Person, it is but a matter of deduction or analysis to tabulate His attributes, for 'moral' embraces not only righteousness, but goodness, love, and compassion. In earlier times J″ revealed His nature in actions which illustrated some one of His attributes. The very surprising ancient passage Ex 34[5ff.], in which J″ proclaimed His name, that is, His whole being, left little to be added later : 'Jehovah, Jehovah God, merciful and gracious, long-suffering, and abundant in goodness and truth, forgiving iniquity, and transgression, and sin, and that will by no means clear the guilty.' In later times two causes contributed to a more frequent reference to the attributes of God : *first*, the tendency to reflection on His nature and on His historical operations, and their religious meaning. This tendency appears in Ezk, and Deutero-Isaiah, and downwards. The latter prophet is fond of turning God's creative and historical acts (43[16]) into attributes ; and thus His relation to the world as Creator becomes the basis and guarantee of His relation to it as Saviour (45[18ff.]; cf. the cosmic christology of St. Paul's later Epp.). And, *secondly*, when the people wrestled with their God over their adverse destiny and hopes deferred, calling to mind His wonders of old (Ps 77[11], and the historical Pss), and the 'sure mercies' promised to David (Pss 89. 132), and appealing to Him not to be far (Ps 22), to make no tarrying, but shine forth for their salvation and stir up His might, they naturally often dwell on His attributes, for prayer is mostly calling to God's mind that which He is. Yet, however varied the emotions be in these psalms, in contents they hardly go beyond the prayers of Moses (Ex 32[11ff.], Nu 14[13ff.], Dt 9[25ff.]). The ethical being of J″ in combination with His attributes of omniscience and omnipresence is very profoundly realized by the author of Ps 139. (On special points in the various attributes see the separate articles).

The OT can scarcely be used as authority for the existence of distinctions within the Godhead. The use of 'us' by the divine speaker (Gn 1[26] 3[22] 11[7]) is strange, but is perhaps due to His consciousness of being surrounded by other beings of a loftier order than men (Is 6[8]). Some other things are suggestive, if nothing more. The **angel of J″** is at once identical with J″ and yet different from Him. In Ezk and later prophets there is a movement towards hypostatizing the Spirit of God (see ANGEL). The 'word' of God is sometimes spoken of as if it had an objective existence, and possessed a native power of realizing itself. The 'wisdom' of God in some passages is no more an attribute of God, but a personification of His thought. In Pr 8 'wisdom' is God's world-plan or conception, the articulated framework of the universe as a moral organism. Its creation is the first movement of the divine mind outward. Being projected outside of the mind of God, it becomes the subject of His own contemplation ; it is 'with' God. It is also His architect in creation, for creation is only the divine wisdom realizing itself. And as one work of creation arises after another

embodying it, its self-realization is as if it 'played before J″', and this play of self-expression was most joyous in the moral economy of man (cf. Jn 1[1-3], Eph 3[9], Col 1[16. 17]). Whether the 'servant of the LORD' be a true being, or only a conception personified into a being, he may be defined as the word of God incarnated in the seed of Abraham. And if even the loftiest Messianic conceptions of the OT remain short of the idea that God 'became' man, yet in Is 9[1-7] J″ is manifested in the fulness of His being in the Messianic King (cf. chs. 7. 11).

LITERATURE.—The *OT Theologies* ; Vatke, *Religion des Alt. Tests.* 1835 ; Kuenen, *Religion of Israel* (trans.), 1874, *National and World Religions* (Hibbert Lect.), 1882 ; Duhm, *Theologie der Propheten*, 1875 ; Nestle, *Die Isr. Eigennamen* (also divine names), 1876 ; Baudissin, *Studien zur Semit. Religionsgeschichte*, 1876-78 ; König, *Hauptprobleme der altisr. Religionsgesch.* 1884 ; Stade, *GVI*, 1887 ; Kittel, *Hist. of the Hebrews* (trans.) ; Baethgen, *Beiträge zur Semit. Religionsgesch.* 1888 ; Montefiore, *Lectures on Relig. of the Hebrews* (Hibbert Lect.), 1892 ; Smend, *Lehrbuch der AT Religionsgesch.* 1893 ; W. R. Smith, *RS*[2], 1894 ; J. Robertson, *The Early Relig. of Israel*[5], 1896 ; Tiele, *Gesch. der Religion* (Germ. trans.), 1895-96 ; Jevons, *An Introduction to the History of Religion*, 1896 ; Sellin, *Beiträge zur Isr. und Jüd. Religionsgesch.* 1896-97 ; Chantepie de la Saussaye, *Lehrbuch der Religionsgesch.*[2] (p. 242 ff. 'Relig. of Israel,' by Valeton), 1897 ; Wellhausen, *Israel. u. Jüdische Geschichte*[3], 1897, *Reste Arabischen Heidentumes* (Skizzen iii.), 1887, ed. 2, 1897 ; Ottley, *Aspects of the OT* (Bampton Lect.), 1897 ; Hommel, *AHT*, 1897.

A. B. DAVIDSON.

GOD (IN NT).[*]—The main object of this art. must be to draw in broad outline the doctrine of God in the NT, so as to show more particularly what new elements are added, and what old elements are specially developed or emphasized. The details of the subject may be left to the special arts., but it is important to mark distinctly those points in which NT presents an advance upon OT.

With this object in view, our inquiry will naturally follow some such lines as these—

  I. TENDENCIES OF CONTEMPORARY JUDAISM.
    1. Monism.
    2. Transcendence.
    3. Particularist Limitations.
  II. TEACHING OF NT.
    1. Attributes of God.
      (i.) Fatherhood.
      (ii.) Love.
      (iii.) Righteousness.
    2. Revelation of God.
      (i.) Through the Son.
      (ii.) Through the Holy Ghost.
    3. Distinctions in the Godhead.
      (i.) The Father and the Son.
      (ii.) The Holy Ghost.

I. TENDENCIES OF CONTEMPORARY JUDAISM.— It is impossible not to be impressed by the intense and passionate loyalty of Jews to the idea of God as they conceived that it had been handed down to them. The repudiation of idolatry could not have been more complete. It was this uncompromising monotheism which formed at once the largest and the purest element in the antipathy which the Jews felt for the heathen world, and in their impatience of its domination. The well-known instance of Caligula's attempt to set up his statue in the temple shows how the whole nation was stirred to its depths by the threat of such a sacrilege (Philo, *Leg. ad Gaium*, §§ 32–43 ; Jos. *Ant.* XVIII. viii. 2–9, *BJ* II. x. 1–3). And smaller incidents, like the hewing down of the golden eagle from the gate of the temple under Herod (*Ant.* XVII. vi. 2, *BJ* I. xxxiii. 2–4), and that of Pilate and the shields (*Ant.* XVIII. iii. 1, *BJ* II. ix. 2, 3 ; Philo, *ad G.* § 38), illustrate the jealousy with which the slightest approach of heathen profanation was resisted.

Christian apologists have often done scant justice to the intensity of this faith, which was utterly disinterested and capable of magnificent self-

* The writer of this portion of the art. very much regrets that he has not had the advantage of seeing the previous portion before writing.

sacrifice. Those who believe most firmly that the Christian creed is an advance upon it are yet bound to recognize that it formed the base, broad and deep, on which that creed has been built. Judaism with all its faults and with all its corruptions was yet the religion of the Chosen People. However imperfectly it embodies the leading principles of Psalmists and Prophets, it yet had those principles behind it. It made great mistakes in the estimate and in the interpretation of its own past, but these very mistakes would seem to have been honest, and in the first instance at least mistakes of the head rather than of the heart.

A Christian cannot afford to misjudge or undervalue the better elements in Judaism, even in that branch of Judaism which rejected Christianity. At the same time he cannot help seeing certain weak points in it—points in which it demanded improvement, and which it has been one of the great results of the coming of Christ to improve. This holds good even of one of its best features, its doctrine of God. And that in three respects.

1. *MONISM.*—It was of the essence of the Jews' belief that God is One. The Jew repeated solemnly every day the words of Dt 6⁴ 'Hear, O Israel,· J″ our God is one J″.' A stress was laid on 'one' to mark the contrast to the gods of the heathen. And it is said that Rabbi Akiba died his martyr's death with this word 'one' on his lips (Weber, *Jüd. Theol.*² § 31, p. 151). Our Lord, as we know, took the same text as a starting-point of His own teaching (Mk 12²⁹ᶠ·). And yet, after all, it expresses, or was apt to express, in the mouth of a Jew a rigid abstract idea of Oneness. The Jews appealed to it at a later date against the Christian doctrine of the Trinity. And it did for them exclude the deeper truth contained in that doctrine —the truth that God is not a mere Monad, self-centred and self-absorbed, without scope for the exercise of the highest affections within itself, but a Monad so distributed as it were within itself as to admit of a perfect interchange and reciprocity of those affections which can exist only as between persons. On this side the Jewish monotheism could not help being bare and dry and inadequate to the true richness and fulness of Deity.

The passages of OT in which the plural is used in reference to the divine action led the Jews to make some small approach towards the Christian conception by the idea of an 'upper or celestial *familia* or tribunal' (Taylor on *Pirḳe Aboth,* ii. 2). Taylor quotes *Sanhed.* 38b : 'The Holy One, blessed is He, does nothing without consulting the *familia superna,* for it is said (Dn 4¹⁷), "This matter is by the decree of the watchers, and the demand by the word of the holy ones."'

2. *TRANSCENDENCE.*—At the time of which we are speaking there was a marked and widespread tendency in the higher minds to widen the chasm between God and the world. Philosophy was straining after a conception of the Supreme Good or the Supreme Being as transcending the conditions of finite existence (οὐκ οὐσίας ὄντος τοῦ ἀγαθοῦ, ἀλλ' ἔτι ἐπέκεινα τῆς οὐσίας πρεσβείᾳ καὶ δυνάμει ὑπερέχοντος, Plato, *Rep.* 509 B). This was especially characteristic of Platonism, which contributed so much to the thought of Philo. And a like effort might be seen in the Oriental religions which were in contact with Judaism on another side. It may not be easy to say how far the movement in Judaism itself was sympathetic to these influences and how far it was internal and spontaneous; but that there was such a movement is evident.

(a) *Names of God.*—One marked indication of it is the treatment of the divine names. The great covenant name Jehovah (Jahweh) was considered too sacred to be pronounced aloud except in the temple (Schürer, *GJV* ii. 241, 381; Eng. tr. II. i. 296, ii. 82). Besides the common substitution of *Adonai* or *Elohim* in reading, a number of paraphrases were in use, all prompted by the instinct of reverence : 'Heaven,' 'Place,' or 'Space' (ὁ τόπος in Philo), 'the Name,' 'the Holy One, blessed is He' (Taylor on *Pirḳe Aboth,* iv. 7). In Greek the usual substitute was Κύριος. This conveyed, of course, indirectly the full connotation of J″; directly, it gave prominence to the idea of sovereignty. This idea meets us in a great variety of forms : 'God, King, Lord of the world'; 'Lord of all,' 'God, Lord of heaven,' 'Lord of the whole creation of the heaven,' 'Lord of lords, of the mighty, of the rulers,' *dominator dominus* (8 or 9 times in 2 Es) ; 'Great King,' 'King of kings,' 'King on the lofty throne' ; 'Lord of judgment, of righteousness,' *deus, dominus omnipotens.* In close connexion with the sovereignty of God is His majesty : 'the Great One,' 'the Great Glory,' 'the Holy and Great One,' 'the Honoured and Glorious One,' 'the Mighty One,' *fortis, fortissimus* (esp. in 2 Es and Apoc. Bar). Less frequent is the idea of creation as an attribute of God (Enoch 81⁵ 94¹⁰, Assump. Mos. 10¹⁰), and that of eternity (Enoch 25³ 75³, Assump. Mos. 10⁷ ; cf. Cheyne on Is 40²⁸). After the simple titles Θεός and Κύριος, probably the commonest in the literature of this period is 'Most High' (ὕψιστος, *altissimus, excelsus,* ἐν ὑψίστοις κατοικῶν : on this title cf. Cheyne, *Bamp. Lect.* p. 83 f.). We may take this as the most direct expression of the idea which we call 'transcendence.'

On the names of God the reader may consult the excellent indexes in Charles, *Book of Enoch* and *Assump. of Moses,* and Bensly-James, *Fourth Bk. of Ezra.* There is less material in Pss of Sol and Test. of XII. Patriarchs. A list of the divine names in the earlier part of the Talmud is given in an essay by Löw, *Gesamm. Schr.* i. 177-186 (Schürer, *LThZ,* 1891, col. 275).

(b) *Removal of Anthropomorphisms.*—The older forms of Judaism are well represented in the Targums. In these the growing conception of the transcendence of God is clearly marked. The simple anthropomorphisms which are so common in OT are paraphrased away. The ground is cut from under them at the outset, as the creation of man in the likeness of God (Gn 1²⁶) is changed into his creation in the likeness of the ministering angels. God is represented as taking counsel with the angels, and creating man in their image. In pursuance of this tendency, where God is represented as 'coming down,' as seeing and hearing, etc., we find substituted the vaguer expressions, 'God revealed Himself,' 'it was revealed before God.' When we are told in Gn 18⁸ that Abraham's heavenly visitants 'ate' what was set before them, the later (though in this case not the oldest) Targum paraphrases 'it seemed to him as though they ate ' ; and in like manner in the case of Lot (Gn 19³). Even the ascription to God of mental acts, such as 'knowledge' (Gn 3⁵, Ex 3¹⁹) or 'intending' (Gn 50²⁰), is avoided, and that in the older Targum of Onkelos. Other expressions which attribute to God the conditions and even the passions of man are removed (*e.g.* the 'man of war' in Ex 15³), anger (Ex 15⁸, Ps 10⁵), repentance (Ex 32¹²). Along with these changes go a number of others, the object of which is to spiritualize the realistic descriptions of the intercourse between God and man. In this way even Jacob's wrestling and Moses' speaking with God 'face to face' disappear ; and in places where God and man are, as it were, bracketed together a distinction is introduced, *e.g.* Ex 14³¹ '[the people] believed in the LORD and in his servant Moses' becomes 'believed in the LORD and *in the prophecy of Moses*' ; Nu 21⁵· ⁷ '[the people] spake against God and against Moses' becomes 'murmured before J″ and disputed with Moses' (Weber, *Jud. Theol.*² pp. 154-157).

The Greek version of OT (Sept.) is several centuries older than the written Targums as they have come down to us. And there, too, a very similar set of changes may be noted. There, too, we find paraphrases for God's 'repenting,' for the descriptions of God as seen, for 'the LORD is a man of war' (Drummond, *Philo Judæus*, i. 158 f.). The fragments quoted by Clem. Alex. and Euseb. show that one of the earliest Judæo-Alexandrian writers, Aristobulus, whose date is placed at about B.C. 170–150, had already discussed and explained at length the anthropomorphisms in OT (Schürer, *GJV* ii. 763 ; Eng. tr. II. iii. 240). And Philo deliberately rejects all real anthropomorphism or anthropopathism, though he regards the use of anthropomorphic expressions as a necessity, especially for the unlearned (Drummond, *op. cit.* ii. 12–15).

We have thus abundant evidence as to the general set of the current of thought in the century immediately before and immediately after the Christian era. And yet at a later date, and it may be to a certain extent even at this date, other causes were operating to bring back anthropomorphisms of a particular kind. We shall see this when we come to speak presently of the limitations imposed upon Judaism by its excessive self-consciousness of national privilege. However much it might avoid the conceiving of God as made in the likeness of man generally, it had not the same hesitation to conceive of Him as made in the likeness of the ideal Jew (see below, p. 208ᵃ).

(*c*) *Intermediate Beings.*—In proportion as God was removed from direct contact with the world of matter, it became necessary to fill up the gap with intermediate agencies. So Philo : 'God generated all things (out of matter), not touching it Himself, for it was not right for the Wise and Blessed to come in contact with indeterminate and mixed matter ; but He used the incorporeal powers whose real name is ideas, that each genus might receive its fitting form' (*De Sacrificant.* 13 ; *ap.* Drummond, *Philo Judæus*, ii. 113, with a slight difference of translation). Philo thus explains the action of God upon matter by the intervention of certain 'powers,' to which he also gives the Platonic name of 'ideas.' These, again, he sometimes calls 'Logoi,' which, in their turn, are summed up under the comprehensive name of 'Logos,' a quasi-personification of the divine reason. This is familiar ground (see art. LOGOS). Palestinian theology did not go so far as Alexandrian in the use which it makes of intermediate agencies ; but it, too, has and uses them. The most important of these for our purpose are the '*Memra*' or Word of J", the *Shechinah*, and the *Holy Spirit*.

The *Memra* is a personification, almost a hypostatizing, not of the Divine Reason, but of the executive Divine Word, on the model of such passages as Is 55¹⁰·¹¹ 'As the rain cometh down, and the snow from heaven, and returneth not thither . . . so shall my word be that goeth forth out of my mouth ; it shall not return to me void, but it shall accomplish that which I please, and it shall prosper in the thing whereto I sent it.' This executive Word of God is constantly substituted in the Targum, in places where the OT refers the action directly to God Himself. The introduction of the *Memra* is the chief expedient for the removal of anthropomorphisms of which mention has just been made. All bodily appearance or bodily action is ascribed, not to God, but to His *Memra*. It is the medium through which the presence of God among His people is realized. The intervention of God in history is conducted through the *Memra*. The *Memra* covers the whole ground over which God is represented as acting, as manifested, as revealed. It is remarkable that this conception, though extremely frequent in the

Targums, is not found in the Talmud. But we cannot doubt that it existed, though perhaps on a more limited scale, in the period of the NT.

The place of the *Memra* is taken in the later Talmudic literature by the *Shechinah*. In the Targums the two conceptions stand side by side, the *Shechinah* representing the manifested glory of the divine presence. The *Shechinah* differs from the *Memra* as being, at least at this earlier date, impersonal. Prayer and trust are predicated of the one, but not of the other. The *Memra* does, and the *Shechinah* does not, take an active part in the redemption of Israel. The Greek equivalent δόξα is of frequent occurrence in the NT (Weber, §§ 38, 39).

In the OT there are a few allusions to the *Holy Spirit* (see sep. art.). One of the principal is Ps 51¹¹ 'Take not thy Holy Spirit from me,' where its function is clearly indicated as keeping alive religion in the soul, and as the special medium of communication between God and the spirit of man. The 'Spirit of God' is repeatedly spoken of as the source of inspiration and revelation. It is, in particular, the moving cause of the utterances, and, so far as they are divinely prompted, of the actions of the prophets and other organs of the Deity. In one OT writing there is a tendency to go further than this, and to make of the Holy Spirit a distinct hypostasis. This is Deutero-Isaiah, where we have such expressions as, 'The LORD God hath sent me, and his Spirit' (48¹⁶), and 'They rebelled and grieved his Holy Spirit' (63¹⁰ ; cf. Cheyne, *ad loc.*). There is hardly any clear advance upon this until we come to NT. The conception is not one that is largely used : ἐν πνεύματι ἁγίῳ occurs once in Ps.-Sol (17⁴²) and 'immitte in me Spiritum Sanctum' in 2 Es 14²². But in neither case is there any attribution of personality. In Targ. and Talm. there is a fluctuating use, the tendency to personify being sometimes greater than it is at others (רוּחַ is both masc. and fem., but more often the latter, the sense of which is more impersonal, Weber, p. 191). The conception cannot be said to have assumed a fixed form at the time when NT literature begins.

Besides these intermediate agencies there is the *Messiah* ('Son of Man' in Similitudes of Bk. of Enoch), whose function is esp. that of judgment and of the restoration of the chosen people. And there is also the whole celestial hierarchy of *angels*, which, from the Persian domination onwards, had become more and more defined and elaborated.

The Jew had a valuable corrective against the injurious effects of an exaggerated doctrine of the transcendence of God in the OT doctrine of His omnipresence, though this was not one of the doctrines which took the strongest hold on the Jewish mind. 'In the development of the Jewish religion, this conception of God's omnipresence was only reached at a comparatively late period, and it was for long crossed and obscured by other simpler and more childish notions. To the moral attributes of Deity, to His supreme pity and justice, there are endless references in the Psalter and the Prophets ; to the divine omnipresence there are but few. And, indeed, there is an element of philosophy and of mysticism in this conception, to neither of which the native Hebrew mind was pre-eminently prone.' Still, the doctrine finds magnificent and classical expression in Ps 139 ; and it is natural that the modern writer, who seeks for the germs of a belief in the immanence of God as well as in His transcendence, should fall back upon this (see Montefiore in *Aspects of Judaism*, London, 1895, pp. 107–124). On the relation of immanence and transcendence in the theology of Philo, see Herriot, *Philon le Juif*, p. 211 ff.

3. *PARTICULARIST LIMITATIONS.* — Although there was in Judaism this tendency to emphasize the transcendence of God, and although the attitude of mind corresponding to this tendency was one of reverential awe, which is often finely expressed, there was at the same time another set of tendencies which were apt to run counter to this, and to bring back in an unattractive form the

very faults from which Judaism was trying to free itself. These counter-tendencies had their root in the overweening estimate of the Law and the rabbinical study of the Law, and of the privileged position of the Jewish people.

The fundamental mistake of Judaism, fraught with disastrous consequences along the whole line of religious belief and practice, was its neglect of the Prophets in comparison with the Law, and its failure to grasp the principle that the Law was to be interpreted in the spirit of the Prophets and not by the rules of a minute literalism. The Jew believed that his Law came from God, and we must do justice to the strength and tenacity of this belief. It is easy to see how many of his errors of interpretation flowed directly from it. But it must be confessed that his zeal was not according to knowledge (Ro 10²). However well meant in the first instance, it was often strangely devoid of insight (though from time to time flashes of insight may be discerned in it for which we are hardly prepared by the general tenor of the surroundings). But this lack of insight caused the Jew to fall a too ready victim to the warping effect of interested motive. His love of the Law as the gift of God became pride in himself as the exponent of the Law, pride in his race as the recipients of the Law, security in the consciousness of formal obedience as though it dispensed from the prolonged and more difficult task of true spiritual conformity. Not that the rabbinical teachers by any means always lost sight of this, but that through this process of self-deception a standard which, on the face of it, seemed to be extremely high became in practice miserably perverted and low. [We are compelled to use such language, by an impartial study of Judaism in the 1st cent. of the Christian era as it appears not only in Christian writings but in the pages of the Jewish historian. The Christian, however, should remember that, though true, this is not the whole truth; there are exceptions and qualifications].

The Jew's horizon was almost limited by the Law. It absorbed the energies of the strongest minds, and the possession of it created a national self-consciousness which was anything but well adapted 'for reproof, for correction, for instruction in righteousness.' This state of things reacted strongly upon the conception of God. Judaism sought to get rid of anthropomorphisms drawn from common human nature only to substitute for them another set of anthropomorphisms, in some ways less innocent, drawn from rabbinical human nature. It expelled *idola tribus*, only to fall a prey to *idola specus et theatri*.

Thus God Himself was regarded as devoted to the study of His own Law, and not only of the Law, but even of the rabbinical developments of the Law. By day He 'is engaged upon the 24 Books of the Torah, the Prophets, and the Hagiographa, and by night He is engaged upon the 6 divisions of the Mishnah. God is even represented as having companions in the study of the Torah. At least we have, according to *Baba Mezia*, 85ᵇ, even in heaven an assembly, like the high schools on earth, devoted to the investigation of the Torah. Here the great Rabbis sit in the order of their merit and of their knowledge of the Law, studying *Halacha*, and God studies with them. They dispute with one another and lay down Halacha' (Weber, p. 158).

We may make allowance for such extravagances as this, and see in them only a play of fancy growing naturally out of the view that the Law embodied the Wisdom of God. But we see how the idolatry of the Law tended to contract the range of spiritual vision. And still more mischievous results followed when the Law and all the rest of the divine ordinances were regarded as having for their final cause the profit and glory of Israel.

LITERATURE. — Much material may be found in the larger works on the Life of Christ and the history and condition of the Jewish People (Edersheim, Schürer, etc.), or the works of Siegfried and Drummond on Philo (to which may be now added Herriot, *Philon le Juif*, Paris, 1898); in the editions of *Pseudepigrapha*, to which reference has been made above; and in Taylor's *Pirḳe Aboth*. But the most convenient and complete of all the collections bearing directly on Jewish thought and theology is the posthumous work of Ferdinand Weber, formerly called *System d. altsynagogalen palästinischen Theologie* (Leipzig, 1880), and in the new and improved edition brought out under the superintendence of Schnedermann, *Jüdische Theologie auf Grund d. Talmud u. verwandter Schriften* (1897). Weber, though of Jewish origin, wrote from the Christian standpoint; and the reader who desires to see what is to be said from the Jewish side will find it attractively presented in Montefiore's *Hibbert Lectures* (London, 1892), and in artt. in *JQR*.

II. THE TEACHING OF THE NT.—We thus have as the starting-point for the teaching of NT an idea of God very tenaciously held, up to a certain point high and pure, and still bearing at times, though fitfully and uncertainly, the marks of its inspired origin; but as a rule contracted and petrified, with far too much of the life and warmth of the old belief of Psalmists and Prophets dried out of it, and in many minds seriously infected with a cancerous growth of self-love and self-righteousness. How did Christianity vivify, restore, enlarge, and enrich this idea? It did so (1) by asserting with greatly increased breadth and emphasis certain of the attributes of Godhead; (2) by presenting in the person of Jesus Christ a special revelation, brought home in the most palpable of forms, of the nature of God as expressed in these attributes; and (3) by opening the eyes of men to the truth that God is not, as was supposed, a simple Monad, but that within the Oneness of His Being there were included certain distinctions which made possible a constant flow and return of the highest and purest affections, dimly shadowed in the like affections of men, and putting a crown to the divine perfections.

1. *THE ATTRIBUTES OF GOD.* — In respect to the attributes of God the teaching of NT grows directly out of that of OT, but in each case greatly strengthens, deepens, and extends that teaching. The leading particulars in which it does this are as follows:—

(i.) *Fatherhood.*—Perhaps there has been a tendency to minimize too much the part which the conception of God as Father plays in OT (Holtzmann, *Neutestl. Theol.* i. 48 ff.). Not only is the relation of God both to Israel as a whole and to the individual Israelite compared to that of a father (Dt 1³¹ 8⁵, Ps 103¹³), but God is frequently represented as the Father of Israel (Dt 32⁶, Jer 3⁴· ¹⁹ 31⁹) and of Israelites (Is 63¹⁶ 64⁸, Wis 2¹⁶ 14³, Sir 23¹· ⁴, To 13⁴). We have also the correlative expressions: Israel is 'God's son,' Ex 4²²ᶠ· (cf. Wis 18¹³, Sir 37¹²), Hos 11¹, Jer 3¹⁹ 31²⁰, Ps 89²⁷, and individuals in Israel His 'children' (Dt 14¹). Some of these passages are enunciated with full prophetic πληροφορία (Ex 4²²ᶠ·, Hos 11¹, Is 63¹⁶), and must be numbered among the axiomatic utterances of OT religion. We note also, that while the relation of son to father is predicated both of Israel as a whole, and mediately through the nation of individual Israelites, it is also predicated with especial force of the theocratic king whom, with the sequel of the history before us, we regard as a type of the Messiah (Pss 2 and 89).

There were therefore no lack of points of contact and connexion between the teaching of OT and of NT. And yet the doctrine of NT assumes such different proportions as almost to amount to a new revelation. So far as the idea of the Divine Fatherhood really entered into the popular consciousness, it was chiefly as an item in the general sense of privilege. Even that had its good side, and this good side was the saving virtue of Judaism. But the virtue and its corruption lay too near together. Over wide tracts of Judaism the former was very largely swallowed up by the latter. A new impulse was needed if the idea of the Fatherhood of God was to retain its highest qualities of warmth and intimacy, and was at the same time not to be the privilege of a chosen few, but was to be brought home to the common consciousness of mankind.

No one doubts that Christianity has succeeded in doing this. From the beginning of NT to the end the lesson of God's Fatherhood is presented in such mass and volume as to identify it with the very essence of Christianity in a sense which does not apply to any other religion. And this is a clear case in which all subsequent teaching does but reflect the teaching of the Founder. One of the leading features in that teaching is the (inherited) conception of God as King (the kingdom of God as representing His penetrating and pervasive sovereignty); but side by side with this, and in full equality with it, is the conception of God as Father. No name of God was more constantly on the lips of Christ; and no other name so dominated the whole thought of God, as He not only cherished it for Himself, but bequeathed it to His disciples. Fatherhood is no longer one attribute among many, but it is a central attribute which gives a colour to all the rest. It is characteristic of Jesus that He repeatedly argues downwards from this attribute as furnishing a safe basis for deduction (Mt 6[26. 32] 7[9-11] 10[29-31] etc.).

The idea of the Fatherhood of God is presented in the teaching of our Lord upon three planes. (a) God is Father of all mankind. His fatherly attributes are displayed even to 'the unthankful and the evil' (Lk 6[35], cf. Mt 5[45]). (b) He is in a special sense the Father of believers, disciples of Christ. In the uncertainty which attends the exact circumstances of many of His discourses, it may be often doubtful as to how far the phrase ὁ πατὴρ ὑμῶν extends beyond these. Probably, as a rule its application starts from the inner circle. But it is also probably not confined to this. It is certainly impossible in view of such sayings as Mk 9[40] ('he that is not against us is for us') to regard it as bounded by any hard-and-fast line. All those to whom Jesus speaks are potential disciples. The two classes run into each other. To both God stands in the relation of Father; but the fulness of His love is naturally felt by those who have learnt to come to Him as His children. (c) There is, however, yet a third sense in which the Fatherhood of God is unique. Jesus does not speak of 'our Father' as embracing both Himself and His disciples, but of 'My Father' and 'your Father.' In this He takes up the special sense in which (as we have seen) the terms 'Father' and 'Son' were applied to the theocratic King. The ministry of Jesus begins with an announcement from heaven: 'Thou art My beloved Son, in Thee I am well pleased' (Mk 1[11]). And this announcement is repeated on another culminating occasion (Mk 9[7]). It is by virtue of this unique relationship that the revelation of God which Jesus gives is also unique (Mt 11[27]). It contains further implications as to the nature of the Godhead. To both these points we shall return.

All the three planes of Fatherhood and Sonship reappear in the teaching of the apostles. The first is, as with our Lord Himself, the least prominent. Still it is not absent (Ac 17[28]), and it must always be remembered that if the Fatherhood of God is in the first instance and in the fullest sense for Christians (Ro 8[15-17], Gal 4[6], 1 P 1[17]), they hold their privileges in trust for the rest of the world. The fulness of the Gentiles, and after it the fulness of Israel, is some day to be brought in (Ro 11[25ff.]). The peculiar Sonship of Christ is very prominent in the apostolic writings. It is clear that the apostles too, and we may say the whole Church, regarded the relation indicated by it as unique. It is the full recognition of this by virtue of which Christians are Christians (see below, p. 214[b], and art. CHRISTOLOGY).

(ii.) *Love.*—One of the points included under the Fatherhood of God is the extension of a Father's love to all who stand to Him in the relation of children. There had been a school of Prophets and Psalmists, of which Jeremiah seems to have been a leader, who laid especial stress on the 'loving-kindness' of J″, *i.e.* the feeling of kindness and compassion which grows out of the covenant relation, the love of God for Israel as the covenant people. In the NT the horizon widens: God is a Father, not to Israel alone, but to all who claim their sonship. Towards them He turns, not paternal severity, but paternal love. The writers of NT generalize this love, so that one of them says in set terms 'God is love' (1 Jn 4[8]). Here is another salient characteristic of Christianity. As it insists far more than every other known religion that God is Father, so also is it the one religion which lays down in this emphatic way that 'God is love.'

There are two distinguishing features in this proposition that 'God is love.' (a) The argument on which it is mainly based is that supplied by the death of Christ. St. John lays down this in his Gospel: 'God so loved the world, that he gave his only-begotten Son, that whosoever believeth on him should not perish, but have eternal life' (Jn 3[16], an enlargement by the evangelist of the discourse with Nicodemus). In the First Ep. when he returns to the idea he draws the same inference from the same premises a little more widely stated: 'Herein was the love of God manifested in us, that God hath sent his Only-begotten into the world, that we might live through him' (1 Jn 4[9]). And it is a noticeable fact that St. Paul, to whom this attribute of the Godhead is no less prominent, grounds it also upon the stupendous sacrifice of the death of Christ: 'God commendeth his own love towards us, in that, while we were yet sinners, Christ died for us' (Ro 5[8], cf. vv.[5-7] and 8[31-39]).

(b) The unwavering confidence of the biblical writers in the love of God may indeed be set down to revelation. The philosopher who sought to infer the character of the Author of Nature inductively from His works would not be able to adopt this tone. The waste which attends the processes of nature is accompanied by too much suffering. He might on the whole, and upon a balance of 'for' and 'against,' decide that the evidence for a benevolent purpose preponderates, and he might also see reason to think that that purpose became clearer in the progressive evolution of things; but further than this he could not go. He could not speak of benevolence as absolute; he could not say 'God is love.' The belief expressed in these words is not the product of an induction. None the less, when once it is entertained, and entertained on such grounds as those which the NT writers assign for it, the phenomena of the world may then be found compatible with it. The Christian may still cling to his belief, and trust that what is at present dark to him will be made clear in God's good time.

(iii.) *Righteousness.*—There can be no mistake as to the meaning and implications of the Fatherhood and Love of God. The case is different as to His Righteousness. Righteousness is a word of such varied signification that the exact sense in which it is used in any particular passage may really be doubtful; and there are certain places in NT where its meaning, as applied to God (δικαιοσύνη θεοῦ), has been a subject of much discussion.

We may say that there are really four leading senses which the phrase δικ. θεοῦ will bear. It may mean (a) 'rightness' or 'goodness' in general, including all moral excellence; or (b) in a narrower sense 'judicial righteousness,' the strict application of the standard of right by the judge; or (c) an application of that standard which is not strict but leans to the side of mercy towards the offender, and takes especial care of the weak and defenceless. Lastly, (d) there are a number of passages in the writings of St. Paul where it has been thought that δικ. θεοῦ ceases to be strictly an attribute of God at all, and comes to mean rather a state of man in the sight of God. This use we must consider. But it will be best to make our way upwards from the easier senses to the more difficult.

(a) It may be doubted whether there are any passages in NT where δικ. θ. is used precisely in this wide sense (unless we regard the case discussed below as in effect an application of it). But δικ. is frequently used of men in the sense of general uprightness or virtue; and this is brought into relation to God almost as if it were δικ. ἐνώπιον αὐτοῦ, 'righteousness in his sight,' or 'of which he approves.'

In Lk 1⁷⁵ we have λατρεύειν αὐτῷ ἐν ὁσιότητι, κ. δικαιοσύνῃ ἐνώπιον αὐτοῦ, where ἐνώπ. αὐτ. strictly defines λατρεύειν, but in effect gives the wider meaning to δικ. In Mt 6³³ it is a question whether the reading of most critical texts (incl. WH) τὴν βασιλείαν καὶ τὴν δικαιοσύνην αὐτοῦ (sc. τοῦ θεοῦ) can stand, and whether we ought not, with Lachmann, Weiss, and Holtzmann, to prefer the reading of cod. B, τὴν δικ. κ. τ. βασ. αὐτοῦ. In that case τ. δικ. would be absolute; to 'seek God's righteousness' would be an expression without parallel in the Gospels; we should have to connect it with Is 54¹⁷ quoted below. Ja 1²⁰ comes under the next head, and in 2 P 1¹, where righteousness is referred to Christ, the sense is akin to (d).

(b) The simple judicial sense, though deeply rooted in language and always present in the background of thought, is not prominent in NT except in Rev. It naturally has a place in St. Paul's speech at Athens (Ac 17³¹). It occurs also in 2 Ti 4⁸ and in Rev 16⁵·⁷ 19². ¹¹. And the same idea is conveyed by δικαιοκρισία in Ro 2⁵.

(c) The more distinctive senses in which righteousness is predicated of God come under the last two heads, and one of these, as has been said, is still somewhat of a problem. Both these remaining senses are certainly based upon the use of OT, and to understand them we need to recall the conditions of society in OT times. The OT covers a period of transition from comparative barbarism to comparative civilization. In all the earlier and less settled portions of such a period the rallying-point of society was the judge. It was a matter of the greatest moment that he should be strong enough to deal out even-handed justice without fear or favour. He would be beset by turbulent and powerful chieftains, who would make his task an extremely difficult one. By degrees it would be increasingly felt that the judge (or the king as judge) was the one refuge for all the weak and defenceless classes—the poor, the fatherless, the widow, the stranger; and his more characteristic functions would seem to be, not so much the safeguarding of equal rights, as the special protection of those who most needed protection. For king or judge to discharge this function in the face of all the dangers and uncertainties of his own position must often have required no little force and elevation of character. Hence we are not surprised to find either the great importance attached to righteousness as a name for this quality, or that it came often to mean vindicating the rights of the oppressed or dealing gently and leniently with

the weak. We are apt to put righteousness in contrast to mercy, as Marcion opposed the 'just or righteous God' (δίκαιος) to the 'good God' (ἀγαθός); but to the Heb. 'just' or 'righteous' often meant 'merciful.'

These senses can be abundantly illustrated from OT. One conspicuous passage may be given out of many: Job 29¹⁴⁻¹⁷ 'I put on righteousness, and it clothed me: my justice was a robe and a diadem. I was eyes to the blind, and feet was I to the lame. I was a father to the needy; and the cause of him that I knew not I searched out. And I brake the jaws of the unrighteous, and plucked the prey out of his teeth' (cf. vv.⁹⁻¹³).

It was an inevitable process that this use of the word 'righteousness' as applied to men reacted upon its application to God. More and more as time went on, esp. in Deutero-Isaiah and certain psalms, the righteousness of God comes to be, not His strict justice, but His healing, rescuing, justice. He is not 'a just God and yet a Saviour,' but 'a just God and a Saviour' (Is 45²¹; cf. δίκαιος καὶ δικαιῶν, Ro 3²⁶). The two conceptions of 'righteousness' and 'salvation' are very frequently placed in juxtaposition: Ps 24⁵ 'He shall receive a blessing from the LORD, and righteousness from the God of his salvation'; 31¹·² (cf. 71²) 'Deliver me in thy righteousness. . . . Be thou to me . . . an house of defence to save me'; 71¹⁵ 'My mouth shall tell of thy righteousness and of thy salvation all the day'; 98² 'The Lord hath made known his salvation: his righteousness hath he openly showed in the sight of the nations'; 143¹¹ 'In thy righteousness bring my soul out of trouble'; Is 46¹³ 'I bring near my righteousness, it shall not be far off, and my salvation shall not tarry'; 51⁶ (cf. ⁸) 'My salvation shall be for ever, and my righteousness shall not be abolished'; 56¹ 'My salvation is near to come, and my righteousness to be revealed'; 59¹⁷ (cf. 61¹⁰) 'He put on righteousness as a breastplate, and an helmet of salvation upon his head'; 63¹ 'I that speak in righteousness, mighty to save.'

In the *Pseudepigrapha*, speaking generally, the 'righteousness of God' is, as a rule, His judicial righteousness, as seen in the rewarding of the righteous and the punishment of the wicked. But we do also occasionally find its merciful side put forward, as in 4 Ezra (ed. Bensly-James) 8³⁶ : *In hoc enim adnuntiabitur iusticia tua et bonitas tua, domine, cum misertus fueris eis qui non habent substantiam operum bonorum.*

It is to be noticed also that in connexion with the righteousness of God there arises the idea of a righteousness in man ‾derived‾ from God. Thus in Is 54¹⁷ 'This is the heritage of the servants of the Lord, and their righteousness which is of me, saith the LORD.' And a like use is found in Bar 5². ⁹ 'Cast about thee the robe of the righteousness which cometh from God (τῆς παρὰ τοῦ θεοῦ δικαιοσύνης); set a diadem on thy head of the glory of the Everlasting. . . . For God shall lead Israel with joy in the light of his glory with the mercy and righteousness that cometh from him' (δικ. τῇ παρ' αὐτοῦ).

There do not seem to be any instances in NT of a use of the 'righteousness of God' quite on the same footing with that in Deutero-Isaiah and the Psalms. But when we consider the collection of passages just quoted from these and from other books, we seem to be upon the line of antecedents of a very marked and characteristic doctrine, which is associated specially with St. Paul.

(d) The Pauline doctrine. We have spoken of this doctrine as still constituting a problem in the exegesis and theology of NT. It is a problem which has been sharply accentuated in recent years, but, if not yet wholly solved, it would appear to have been at least placed on the road to solution.

In Ro 1[17] St. Paul formulates the thesis of the Epistle. It is an announcement to the world of the righteousness of God revealed in the gospel from faith to faith ($\delta\iota\kappa\alpha\iota o\sigma\acute{\nu}\nu\eta$ $\gamma\grave{\alpha}\rho$ $\theta\epsilon o\hat{\upsilon}$ $\dot{\epsilon}\nu$ $\alpha\dot{\upsilon}\tau\hat{\wp}$ [sc. $\tau\hat{\wp}$ $\epsilon\dot{\upsilon}\alpha\gamma\gamma\epsilon\lambda\acute{\iota}\wp$] $\dot{\alpha}\pi o\kappa\alpha\lambda\acute{\upsilon}\pi\tau\epsilon\tau\alpha\iota$ $\dot{\epsilon}\kappa$ $\pi\acute{\iota}\sigma\tau\epsilon\omega s$ $\epsilon\dot{\iota}s$ $\pi\acute{\iota}\sigma\tau\iota\nu$). Here the key-phrase is evidently $\delta\iota\kappa.$ $\theta\epsilon o\hat{\upsilon}$; but what exactly does it mean?

A few years ago there seemed to be a strong consensus of the best exegetes (Meyer, Weiss, Lipsius, Godet, Oltramare, and in England, Vaughan, Liddon, Beet, Moule, unequivocally, and Gifford with rather more qualification) in favour of taking $\delta\iota\kappa.$ $\theta\epsilon o\hat{\upsilon}$ as a righteousness, which though in some sense or other God's ('a righteousness of which God is the author,' most Comms.), yet denotes more directly a state of man ('of which man is the recipient'). And whatever may be urged against this view, the arguments for it are so strong that it seems impossible to regard it as devoid of a substantial basis of truth. St. Paul appears to make his own meaning more explicit in Ph 3[9], where he substitutes the phrase $\tau\grave{\eta}\nu$ $\dot{\epsilon}\kappa$ $\theta\epsilon o\hat{\upsilon}$ $\delta\iota\kappa\alpha\iota o\sigma\acute{\upsilon}\nu\eta\nu$ $\dot{\epsilon}\pi\grave{\iota}$ $\tau\hat{\eta}$ $\pi\acute{\iota}\sigma\tau\epsilon\iota$. And if it is said that this is the view of a later Epistle, and that it is differentiated from Ro by the insertion of $\dot{\epsilon}\kappa$, the same antithesis of $\dot{\eta}$ $\tau o\hat{\upsilon}$ $\theta\epsilon o\hat{\upsilon}$ $\delta\iota\kappa.$ and $\dot{\eta}$ $\dot{\iota}\delta\acute{\iota}\alpha$ $\delta\iota\kappa.$ occurs in Ro 10[3], where in spite of the absence of $\dot{\epsilon}\kappa$ the former phrase can hardly be ambiguous. And other arguments derived from the transition from $\delta\iota\kappa.$ $\theta.$ to $\dot{o}$ $\delta\acute{\iota}\kappa\alpha\iota os$ in the quotation from Habakkuk in Ro 1[17], and from the evident parallel in 3[21, 22] (where $\delta\iota\kappa.$ $\theta.$ is defined by $\delta\iota\kappa.$ $\theta.$ $\delta\iota\grave{\alpha}$ $\pi\acute{\iota}\sigma\tau\epsilon\omega s$, $\kappa.\tau.\lambda.$), are hardly less cogent.

We must therefore include in the conception a righteousness which, whatever its origin, at least *ends* by denoting a state of man. But, on the other hand, it is no less impossible to explain $\delta\iota\kappa.$ $\theta.$ as *in the first instance* anything else than *the personal righteousness of God*. This is the sense of the phrase in the immense majority of the cases in which the word is used in OT and in other writings outside the Epp. of St. Paul. A phrase so familiar and so deeply rooted in the common language of men could not be violently wrenched from its usual associations and transferred to others without more explicit warning than any that is given.

At the same time those appear to be equally wrong who (like Häring in the treatise mentioned below) insist that the phrase can only have one meaning in such a way as to compel a choice between the two alternatives. When they speak of 'one meaning,' what they have in view is a definite logical tying-down of that meaning which is not necessitated by language. The array of logical possibilities set out by Häring (pp. 14–17) certainly was not present to the mind of St. Paul, nor was he compelled to discriminate everything that may be capable of discrimination. Language has in its earlier stages an elasticity of use which it may by degrees lose.

To understand the real drift of St. Paul, we ought to bear in mind, not so much the distinctions which we can draw, as those which had been actually drawn when he wrote. He really sums up a long previous development. He sums it up, and the language which he uses bears traces throughout of its several phases; but at the same time he puts upon it a new stamp; he focuses, concentrates, and defines it in a new sense of his own.

It may be worth while to note how the previous phases of which we have been speaking enter into his conception. They would do so in some such order as this—

(a) The broad fundamental meaning of $\delta\iota\kappa\alpha\iota o$-$\sigma\acute{\upsilon}\nu\eta$ is *conformity to right*. As applied to God it is the sum of all moral excellence, of which He is the standard to Himself. Even when the word is used in narrower senses, this still remains in the background of the apostle's mind, and from time to time comes more to the front.

(β) In a primitive state of society, the decisions of the chieftain or king acting as judge are the standard of right. And the virtue most highly valued in the judge is that of equal dealing between man and man. There was therefore a tendency for the broad idea of righteousness in the ruler to contract into the narrower idea of justice.

(γ) In such a state of society, however, something more than simple justice was needed. The king or chief was the one efficient champion of the weak against the strong, of the poor against the rich, of the friendless against the powerful. Thus in the opinion of the common people, or of the masses, the form of righteousness for which they looked was even more than justice, *care for the weaker side*.

(δ) In direct dealings with the poor and weak, where the question was rather of what we should call criminal than of civil law, the virtue of the judge would be *mildness* and lenience, not exacting the full penalties for misdoing; in other words, treating an offender as innocent, or not so guilty as he really was.

(ϵ) Such acquittal or remission of punishment would be the act of the judge, of his own free grace pardoning the guilty. When the judge, for whatever reason, dismisses the culprit, pronouncing him 'righteous,' or free from guilt in the eye of the law, it is really the judge himself who, by his verdict, is the author of that righteousness or guiltlessness, and not the person acquitted. And the motive which impels the judge to this is his own personal righteousness of character, manifested under the particular aspect of lenience in judging.

(ζ) This is the process that really takes place when the sinner is indicted before the judgment-seat of God; and that not merely at the final judgment, but whenever his state in God's sight is considered. The motive which prompts the absolution is no righteousness of the sinner's own, but the righteousness of God.

(η) When we attempt to analyze the nature of that righteousness, we might, on a superficial view, identify it with the narrower sort of judicial righteousness which is seen in the mild treatment or forgiveness of the guilty. But the righteousness of God, as St. Paul regards it, is something much more than this. The mildness of a judge may have in it no higher ingredient than a certain easy good nature because it is indifferent to guilt. The forgiving righteousness of God is not of this kind. It embraces nothing less than the whole scheme of salvation, in which the central feature is the atoning death of Christ. The absolution of the sinner is no act of momentary indulgence, but a deliberately contemplated incident in a vast and far-reaching plan which has for its object the restoration of the human race.

(θ) The leading factor in it, then, is the supreme energizing righteousness of God, which in the course of its operation includes several minor kinds of righteousness, and which ends by attributing to the sinner a condition of righteousness which he has very imperfectly realized for himself. So that from his point of view it may well be called a righteousness not his own, but 'of' or 'from God.' We have seen that as far back as Deutero-Isaiah and Baruch there were traces of this conception ($\dot{\eta}$ $\pi\alpha\rho\grave{\alpha}$ $\tau o\hat{\upsilon}$ $\theta\epsilon o\hat{\upsilon}$ $\delta\iota\kappa\alpha\iota o\sigma\acute{\upsilon}\nu\eta$). St. Paul therefore was not the first to introduce it. But it is a mistake to regard it as forming the whole or even the main part of his conception.

LITERATURE.—On this part of the subject the reader may consult the commentators on Romans, and in particular those mentioned above; also Pfleiderer, *Paulinismus*; Holsten, *Evang. d. Paulus*; Ritschl, *Rechtfertigung u. Versöhnung*. The stand which has recently been made for explaining δικ. θεοῦ of the personal righteousness of God is associated in this country esp. with the late Dr. James Barmby, *Pulpit Comm. on Ro.*, and *Expositor*, 1896, ii. 124 ff., and Dr. A. Robertson in *The Thinker*, Nov. 1893; cf. *Exp. Times*, Feb. 1898, p. 217. In Germany an art. by Kölbing to somewhat similar effect appeared in *SK*, 1895, p. 139 ff., followed by a monograph on the subject by Prof. Häring of Tübingen (ΔΙΚΑΙΟΣΥΝΗ ΘΕΟΥ *bei Paulus*, Tübingen, 1896). Further literature is given on p. 5 of this treatise. The German writers were quite independent of the English, who preceded them in time. On the history of the OT conception there is a valuable tract by Dalman, *Die richterliche Gerechtigkeit im AT*, Berlin, 1897, which suggested much of the line of treatment followed above.

2. *THE REVELATION OF GOD.*—The more theological writers of NT clearly lay it down that in Christianity a new revelation is given of the nature and character of God. They connect this new revelation, (i.) with the coming of Christ, and (ii.) with the special outpouring of the Holy Ghost.

(i.) *The Revelation through Christ.* — The new disclosure of truths about God differed from all previous disclosures, inasmuch as it was no longer confined to a divine prompting of the minds of men, but was made through the incarnate presence of the Son of God Himself. After having in time past spoken to the fathers 'in' the prophets, God had at last spoken 'in' One who was not only prophet but Son (He 1[1. 2]). This distinction of the New Covenant is emphasized most by St. John, but it is also expressed unequivocally by St. Paul, and Ep. to Hebrews, and the Synoptic Gospels refer to it sufficiently to confirm the evidence of the Fourth Gospel that the principle underlying it was brought out by our Lord Himself.

We may take two passages of St. John as typical of a great number of others: Jn 1[18] 'No man hath seen God at any time: God only-begotten [reading μονογενὴς θεός with אBCL, etc., Tregelles, Weiss, WH, RVm] who is in the bosom of the Father, he hath declared him'; and 14[7-11] 'If ye had known me, ye would have known my Father also: from henceforth ye know him, and have seen him. Philip saith unto him, Lord, show us the Father, and it sufficeth us. Jesus saith unto him, Have I been so long time with you, and dost thou not know me, Philip? he that hath seen me hath seen the Father: how sayest thou, Show us the Father? Believest thou not that I am in the Father, and the Father in me? the words that I say unto you, I speak not from myself: but the Father, abiding in me, doeth his works. Believe me that I am in the Father, and the Father in me: or else believe me for the very works' sake.'

These passages might be said to be a compendium of a great part of the Gospel, and we may add the Epp. of Jn. This will appear from observing the number of parallels which exist for almost every clause. 'No man hath seen . . . he hath declared,' 'he that hath seen me hath seen'; cf. 3[32] 5[37] 6[46] 13[20] 15[24] 17[26], 1 Jn 1[1·3] 2[23]. 'Who is in the bosom of the Father,' 'I in the Father, and the Father in me'; cf. 8[16] 10[38] 14[20] 16[32] 17[21-23]. 'Not from myself'; cf. 5[19] 7[16] 8[28] 12[49]. 'Doeth his works'; cf. 4[34] 5[19-21. 36] 9[4] 17[4].

St. Paul does not enlarge upon this aspect of the Incarnation of the Son to the same extent as St. John. Still, he expresses it quite unambiguously when he describes Him as εἰκὼν τοῦ θεοῦ τοῦ ἀοράτου (Col 1[15]), a term which he had used in an earlier Epistle (2 Co 4[4]) in such a way as to show that the conception was even at that date fully established. It is also implied in the ἐν μορφῇ θεοῦ ὑπάρχων of Ph 2[6]. The fulness of the revelation made through Christ is the subject of 1 Co 1[30] ὃς ἐγενήθη σοφία ἡμῖν ἀπὸ θεοῦ (cf. 1[24] Χριστὸν θεοῦ δύναμιν καὶ θεοῦ σοφίαν; also 2[6. 7]), Eph 1[8-10], Col 2[3] ἐν ᾧ

εἰσὶν πάντες οἱ θησαυροὶ τῆς σοφίας καὶ γνώσεως ἀπόκρυφοι.

In close agreement with the language of St. Paul is He 1[3] ὢν ἀπαύγασμα τῆς δόξης καὶ χαρακτὴρ τῆς ὑποστάσεως αὐτοῦ. On the exact force of these expressions (which are parallel to if not suggested by Wis 7[25f.]) see Westcott, etc., *ad loc*. The purport of them is that Christ, visible and active, brought home to the sight and minds of men the essential nature of God. This is an expansion in a more 'ontological' or 'metaphysical' sense of the opening words of the Epistle. This sense is too deeply ingrained in the language of NT to be eliminated.

Although, as has been said, it is the more theological writers who lay the greatest stress upon this aspect of the Son as revealing the Father, there is one conspicuous passage in the Synoptics in which it is clearly implied. The verse Mt 11[27], with its very close parallel in Lk 10[22] (both passages should be taken with their full context), is in form so like the characteristic sayings of Christ; it fits into and interprets such a number of other passages (Mt 16[16], Mk 2[10] 4[41] 9[7] etc.), and, while in remarkable agreement with the general verdict of the primitive Church, stands so apart from the particular tendencies of the Synoptic Gospels that it would be wanton to doubt its genuineness. To make the picture of Christ on earth consistent, we need to see in it not merely the beneficent Teacher, but the Son of God, as this name is understood by the writers of deepest insight.

(ii.) *The Revelation through the Holy Ghost.* — If we look at the Fourth Gospel from another point of view, we shall find it dominated by the consciousness of a double revelation. That through the Incarnate Son of which we have just been speaking is one; that through the Holy Ghost is the other. Looking back over the space of time that had elapsed since the Ascension, the writer sees that a great force has been at work in the Church, the effect of which he regards as a direct fulfilment of prophecies by our Lord Himself before His departure. A second 'Advocate' ('Comforter' AV, RV) was to come after He was gone. It was to be a dispensation like His own, and was to be characterized by a like dissemination of truth, not so much wholly new truth as a revival and reinvigorating in the minds of the apostles and others who came within its range of truth already taught by Himself: 'These things have I spoken unto you, while yet abiding with you. But the Comforter, even the Holy Spirit, whom the Father hath sent in my name, he shall teach you all things, and bring to your remembrance all that I said unto you.' . . . 'Howbeit when he, the Spirit of truth, is come, he shall guide you unto all the truth: for he shall not speak from himself; but what things soever he shall hear, these shall he speak: and he shall declare unto you the things that are to come. He shall glorify me: for he shall take of mine, and shall declare it unto you. All things that the Father hath are mine: therefore said I, that he taketh of mine, and shall declare it unto you' (Jn 14[25. 26] 16[13-15]). There is an accent about all the passages in which the writer refers to this subject which is far more like the accent of real experience than a product of pure reflection without concrete experience behind it. The writings of the Fourth Evangelist contain no express reference to the Day of Pentecost and the history recorded in the Acts, but they contain a number of allusions which are well explained by that history. St. Luke in like manner has no express mention of the Paraclete, but both his Gospel and the Acts bear frequent testimony to the work of the Paraclete under His other name, the Holy Spirit. Here as in the Fourth Gospel we have a historical retrospect of facts and impressions recalled after a considerable lapse of time, but in the Epp. of St. Paul we are in the midst of the events, and we are allowed to see into the inner mind of one of the leading actors in them. From the language of St. Paul we may learn what is meant by being 'taught all things and having all things brought to remembrance,' or rather as he had not been an immediate disciple of Christ we are enabled to understand the πληροφορία with which he spoke. He certainly felt that the Gospel which he preached had its source outside himself. Nowhere, perhaps, does this come out more clearly than in the first of all his Epistles. Writing to the Thessalonians he says, ' For this cause we also thank God without ceasing, that when ye received from us the word of the message, even the word of God, ye accepted it *not as the word of men, but, as it is in truth, the word of God,* which also worketh in you that believe' (1 Th 2¹³). This is the central principle of the apostolic preaching. It is the 'demonstration of the Spirit and of power' of which he speaks elsewhere (1 Co 2⁴). And the substance of the preaching is just the new revelation about God and Christ and the Holy Spirit, and their united work for the salvation of men. ' Things which eye saw not and ear heard not . . . unto us God revealed them through the Spirit : for the Spirit searcheth all things, yea, the deep things of God' (1 Co 2⁹·¹⁰).

Thus the method of divine revelation in the NT is very similar to that in OT. It is brought about through the action of the Holy Spirit upon certain selected instruments, with just the difference on which stress is laid in Ep. to Hebrews, that whereas, under the Old Covenant, God had spoken in and through the prophets, under the New He spoke ' in ' and through the Son, and those expressly chosen and trained by the Son.

LITERATURE. — On the training of the apostles to be the vehicles of the new revelation, see Latham, *Pastor Pastorum* (Cambridge, 1890). Reference may also be made to the *Bampton Lectures* for 1893 on ' Inspiration,' and other works on the same subject.

3. *DISTINCTIONS IN THE GODHEAD.* — In the previous sections of this article we have had gradually to discriminate between the operation and functions of what we now call the different ' Persons' in the Godhead. At the time of which we are speaking (the period covered by NT) there was no such conception in the general mind as that of ' personality.' The term ' person' was just coming into use through the defining influence of Roman Law acting upon popular language (the distinction of *persona* and *res* appears to have come in during the 1st cent. B.C., shortly before the time of Cicero). But a long process had to be gone through before the idea of personality acquired an exact connotation ; and that process was to a large extent involved in the theological controversies on the subject of the Trinity, the result of which was the formulated doctrine of Three Persons in One God, as we have it in what is commonly known as the Athanasian Creed.

It would be an anachronism to expect a definition of the doctrine in NT. And yet the doctrine is really a working out of *data* contained in NT. It is a rendering of these data intelligible to the consciousness as part of a reasoned and formulated whole. The Christian theologian is well aware that the only expression possible to him is approximate : he applies to the whole construction the *dictum* of St. Augustine ; he says what he says, *non ut illud diceretur sed ne taceretur* (*De Trin.* v. 9). But he is almost compelled to say something, and the deliberate judgment of the Church has been that he is warranted in saying so much as he does.

In any critical study of that which we call by anticipation the doctrine of the Trinity in the NT, the starting-point must undoubtedly be the benediction in 2 Co 13¹⁴ ' The grace of the Lord Jesus Christ, and the love of God, and the communion of the Holy Ghost, be with you all.' In this verse we have an utterance of the mind of the apostle, which he knows will find an echo in the minds of his readers at a fixed point in time and place, probably about twenty-six and in any case not more than twenty-eight years after the Ascension. We are left to draw our conclusions as to the belief of the Church at this time. It is, of course, true that the object of the passage is not dogmatic. If it had been, its significance would have been less. It is not the expounding of any new doctrine. It is not even the expounding of doctrine at all. It is only an invocation of blessing. But the peculiar form which this invocation takes, points to much previous preparation in thought and teaching ; it points to a settled, and we are obliged to think, uncontested belief, common alike to the writer and his readers.

The peculiarity of the belief consists in the remarkable way in which a group of spiritual blessings, such as man is accustomed to look for directly from God, is not referred to the Godhead conceived singly as a Monad, but distributively as Three, and yet Three so bracketed together as to be at the same time One. · No graduated interpretation of the Three Names is possible. If it were, we should have Beings who were not Man and yet not wholly God. In the Arian Controversy an attempt was made to establish this interpretation ; but it utterly and hopelessly failed.

The other alternative remains, that St. Paul and the Church of his day thought of the Supreme Source of spiritual blessing as not single but threefold—threefold in essence, and not merely in a manner of speech. How did he come to think thus ? How was it that a Church so far from the centre of things and at so early a date was prepared to receive without question an assumption which to us seems to make such large demands upon the intellect ?

It was certainly not a matter of course. We have seen that there was a certain tendency to hypostatize the Word of God, the Wisdom of God, the Spirit of God, even the Glory of God. The Messiah was thought of as more than human if less than in the full sense divine. But all these conceptions were fluid and tentative. Jewish theology had no fixed and settled belief in regard to them. Even if we add to OT the other writings current at this period, *Apocrypha* and *Pseudepigrapha*, the Jewish Apocalypses and the Sayings traditionally handed down of the oldest Rabbis, still we should not find anything to suggest a combination of the three terms handled with the precision with which St. Paul handled them.

One passage there is which would abundantly account for St. Paul's language if we could accept it as historical. That is the command to the apostles at the end of the first Gospel to go and baptize all nations ' into the name of the Father and of the Son and of the Holy Ghost' (Mt 28¹⁹). This belongs to a comparatively late and suspected part of the Gospel. But one tradition may be later than another and more limited in circulation, and yet not be any less authentic. Now, the *Didaché* shows us that we no sooner cross the frontier of the apostolic age than we find baptism into the Threefold Name in full possession of the field (*Did.* vii. 1, 3). The tradition is continuous. It is taken up by Justin (*Apol.* i. 61), and Tertullian expressly tells us that the person baptized was dipped three times in recognition of the Threefold Name (*Prax.* 26). The practice, then, is at least very old. And it is no slight confirmation of the statement in the first Gospel that if it were true it would supply just the explanation that we want at once of the established rite and of St. Paul's language. In any case we seem compelled to assume that there was some foundation for both in the teaching of our Lord Himself. If there was not, at what point in the six-and-twenty years can the usage (doctrinal or liturgical) have been introduced in a manner so authoritative as to impose it upon St. Paul and the Churches of his founding? We may greatly doubt if any satisfactory answer can be given to this question.

On the other hand, the moment we assume that our Lord did really give this alleged command, and that He really did prepare for it by some corresponding teaching, a number of other facts are accounted for. We find the very teaching of which we are in search in many places of the Last Discourse as recorded by St. John (Jn 14[16. 26] 15[26] 16[7. 10. 13. 15]). And with such teaching in the background a variety of phenomena in St. Paul's Epp. fall into their place which would otherwise be very intractable.

(i.) *The Father and the Son.*—The Epistle (2 Co) ends with a triple benediction, and it begins with a double benediction. 'Grace and peace' are invoked upon the Corinthian Christians 'from God our Father, and from the Lord Jesus Christ.' We observe here the same sort of bracketing of the two Divine Names as in the case of the Three. Although there is a distinction of names, and although there may be a certain distinction and special distribution of function, the source of spiritual blessing is in its essence One.

The fact that there is this alternation within the same Epistle of the Two names and the Three, shows that the one expression is in no way inconsistent with the other. A like alternation is found side by side in several other of St. Paul's Epistles. For instance, in 1 Co 12[4-11] we have the Triad : Lord, God, Spirit ; in 1 Co 1[3] and 8[6] we have (in the latter passage very expressly) the Duad : God [the (our) Father] and Lord [Jesus Christ]. In like manner, in Ro 8[14-17. 26-30] we have the Triad, though not formally drawn out, just as clearly presupposed as in vv.[31-39] (cf. 1[7] etc.) we have the Duad ; and a like relation appears in Eph 2[18] 3[2-5. 14-17] 4[4-6] 5[18-20] compared with 1[2. 3. 17] 2[4ff.] 5[5] 6[6. 23].

Nor is this alternation confined to the Pauline Epistles. It is seen again in 1 P 1[2. 3-12] 4[13-19] by the side of 1[17-21] 2[5] 3[15-18. 20-22] etc. ; and it is as conspicuous in 1 Jn 5[4-8] compared with the general tenor of the Ep., which is constantly setting 'the Father' and 'the (His) Son' over-against each other. We may also compare Jude [20. 21] with 1. 4. 24. 25 ; Rev 1[4-6] 2[26-29] 3[5. 6. 12. 13. 21. 22] with 5[6-13] 7[9-17] etc. And we are further reminded that in the *Didaché* baptism in the name of the Father, Son, and Holy Spirit is spoken of almost in the same breath with baptism in the name of Christ (*Did.* vii. 1, 3 and ix. 5).

There is thus an easy transition from the one way of speaking to the other. There is really a threefold usage. The apostles and early Christians generally speak of God, of God the Father, and God the Son, of God the Father, Son, and Holy Spirit, according to the context and the particular purpose with which they are writing ; but the three modes of expression, so far from being mutually exclusive, are, in fact, closely connected and correlated. And it is noticeable, that while there is this free and natural interchange of the three terms, no fourth term is ever added to the three as at all upon the same footing. The mental bracketing of which we have spoken appears to subsist throughout. The usage, although it is in

some respects wide and varied, is yet in others strictly circumscribed, and is regulated by fixed laws. When we look into it more closely we seem to become aware of a gradual development and expansion, if not in the original presentation of the doctrine, yet in the order in which the different parts of it—so to speak—become consciously and definitely realized by the apostles and first disciples. If (as we have seen reason to think) they had received fuller teaching on the subject directly from the Lord Himself than is contained in our extant Gospels, this did not prevent them from grasping the truth only by degrees, and the very gradualness with which it was grasped would account for some of the first statements being lost to us. It is the later teaching of events calling the earlier teaching to remembrance (Jn 14[26]) which has preserved for us so much of this as we have. It is a matter of common experience that there are lessons latent in the mind which only become vividly realized when something occurs to bring them home, or when the logic of thought naturally reaches them.

In the case of the apostles the logic of thought started from Christ, the Incarnate Christ, whom they had seen with their eyes, and their hands had handled in the days of His flesh. If Christ was God, then it was certain that there must be in the Godhead some such distinction as that which we call personal ; the attributes of personality attached to Him as unmistakably as to the apostles themselves. And if beneath these there lay a substratum of unity with the Power which ruled the heavens, that unity must still be such as admitted of personal distinction.

The language which the apostles use is thoroughly accounted for by the evidence of their own senses, taken with the utterances of Jesus Himself. The keyword which is constantly upon His lips is the name 'Father' with its correlative 'Son.' These terms established themselves from the very first in the Christian consciousness as the true expression of the mutual relation. That they must have done so appears from the fundamental place which they had in the theology of St. Paul, in spite of all the independence which he claims for its origin. No better argument exists for the view that at the time when he wrote his extant Epistles he had already some form of evangelic document before him. In any case he must have been familiar with an extremely solid and unanimous tradition. To that tradition it is not too much to say that all Christian speculation on the wider relations of the Godhead goes back. The central point in all subsequent argument is the relation of 'Father' and 'Son.' And the difference which in all ages has marked off a loyal from a disloyal interpretation of the data of Christianity has been this, that the one insisted upon a real Fatherhood and a real Sonship, which the other has attempted to explain away. This was the principle at issue in the Arian Controversy. And there has probably never been a controversy argued out more thoroughly or with a more abundant expenditure of both intellectual and moral force. The outcome of it was the definite and triumphant affirmation of the position that the Father is essentially Father and the Son essentially Son. The most abstruse clauses in the Athanasian Creed are nothing but the emphatic assertion and the systematic safeguarding of this.

(ii.) *The Holy Spirit.*—In framing their doctrine of the Holy Spirit, as in framing their doctrine of the Son, the apostles had before their minds a definite series of facts. There was a certain group of phenomena which they consistently referred to the action of the Spirit. The phenomena of what we call 'inspiration,' the divine influence of which they were conscious in preaching and teaching; the special and remarkable 'gifts' ($\chi\alpha\rho\iota\sigma\mu\alpha\tau\alpha$) which distinguished in an eminent degree the first generations of Christians; and, generally speaking, the felt communion of the human spirit with the divine, were regarded by them as manifestations of the activity of the Holy Ghost. If we read the three chs. 1 Co 12-14 we see that St. Paul felt himself to be in the midst of such activity; and there are many other allusions to it. The Early Church appears to have dated the energies at work within it in a special sense from the first Pentecost after the Ascension. They called this an 'outpouring' of the Holy Ghost, seeing in it a fulfilment of prophecy (Ac 2[17. 18. 33], Tit 3[6]).

But how was it that they came to speak of the work of the Holy Spirit as the work of a *person*? That they did so appears not only from such incidental passages as Ro 8[26], 1 Co 12[11], Eph 4[30], but still more from the great Trinitarian texts 2 Co 13[14] and Mt 28[19], in which the Holy Ghost is placed on precisely the same footing as the Son and the Father. We have seen that this can have been no momentary freak of language, but that it must have had a broad foundation in the consciousness of the apostolic Church. Between the fluid usage of contemporary Judaism and the fixed usage of the apostles and their successors there intervenes the teaching of Jesus. And it seems impossible not to refer to this the impulse which determined the direction of Christian thought upon the subject. The fragments of that teaching which have been preserved for us in the Fourth Gospel (Jn 14[16ff. 28] 15[26] 16[7-14]) seem to imply a yet fuller context which has been lost; but of themselves they are sufficient to warrant the faith which the Church has evidently held from the first, though as the centuries went on it was compelled to define it with increasing distinctness.

There are two classes of passages in NT relating to the Holy Ghost. On the one hand, there are those of which we have been speaking, where the Third Person (of later theology) is clearly distinguished from the First and Second, and represented as confronting them. And, on the other hand, there are passages in which the Third Person is as closely associated with the First and Second. The Spirit is repeatedly spoken of as the 'Spirit of God.' And the relationship indicated by this phrase is explained in 1 Co 2[10t.] as analogous to that of the spirit in man. 'For the Spirit searcheth all things, yea, the deep things of God. For who among men knoweth the things of a man, save the spirit of the man which is in him? even so the things of God none knoweth, save the Spirit of God.' But He who is thus described as the 'Spirit of God' is also described as the 'Spirit of Christ.' So notably in Ro 8[9t.] 'But ye are not in the flesh but in the Spirit, if so be that the Spirit of God dwelleth in you. But if any man hath not the Spirit of Christ, he is none of his. And if Christ is in you,' etc. Here 'Christ' takes up the 'Spirit of Christ,' and that, again, takes up the 'Spirit of God' (defined a little later as the 'Spirit of Him that raised up Jesus from the dead') in such a way as to show that, at least for the purpose of the writer, the three terms are convertible. Nor is this the only place in which we read of the 'Spirit of Christ' (cf. 1 P 1[11]), or 'of Jesus' (Ac 16[7] RV), or 'of Jesus Christ' (Ph 1[19]), or 'of [the] Son' (Gal 4[6]), or 'of the Lord' (=Christ, 2 Co 3[17]).

Again, we have to remember that the conception of the incarnate Christ is referred to the direct operation of the Holy Ghost (Lk 1[35]), and that His endowment with the fulness of divine power for His ministry is also dated from the descent of the Holy Ghost at His baptism. This is the 'anointing with the Holy Ghost' of Ac 10[38] as the sequel to which He is 'full of the Holy Spirit' (Lk 4[1]), and acts through the Holy Spirit (Mt 12[28], Ac 1[2], He 9[14]); He also communicated the Holy Spirit to the apostles (Jn 20[22]).

There is thus another side to the mystery of the Triune God. Although in one sense Three, He is in another no less One. There is such a mutual interaction, such a fundamental unity, as prevents distinction from amounting to separation. The Three Persons are not three individuals. There are not three Gods, but One God.

This is the evident drift of the data which NT has handed down to us; and it is to these data that the later theology has sought to do justice. They find their most complete and ripest interpretation in the balanced clauses of the *Quicumque*. Those clauses are, no doubt, relative to the line of thought which leads up to them. Compared to some aspects of the biblical teaching, they will appear secondary where this is primary. It is more important for the great mass of Christians to have it brought home to them that God is love, that the proof of His love is the incarnation and death of His Son, and that He does impart of His own righteousness to men, than that (*e.g.*) the Son is 'not made nor created, but begotten.' But the significance of this latter proposition is that Christ is truly Son. And the question whether He is truly or only figuratively Son is a vital question, as vital now as it was in the days of Nicæa or Chalcedon. The question was quite sure to be raised, and, being raised, it has to be answered. The phrasing of the answer may vary with the philosophy of the time, but its substance cannot be any other than that which has been so deliberately adopted and ratified.

LITERATURE.—No considerable monograph on the doctrine of God as Triune has appeared since Baur's *Die christliche Lehre von der Dreieinigkeit u. Menschwerdung Gottes*, 3 vols., Tübingen, 1841-1843, and G. A. Meier, *Die Lehre von der Trinität in ihrer historischen Entwickelung*, 2 vols., Hamburg u. Gotha, 1844. A thorough discussion of the beginnings of the doctrine in English is still a *desideratum*. There is an instructive chapter on the Holy Spirit in Milligan, *The Ascension of Our Lord* (1892), pp. 166-226. [The literature on the previous sections of this art. has been given under each section].

W. SANDAY.

GOD, CHILDREN (SONS, DAUGHTERS) OF, are biblical phrases for near and blessed relations to God, but used with various applications and meanings. In NT the words 'children' ($\tau\acute{\epsilon}\kappa\nu\alpha$) and 'sons' ($\upsilon\acute{\iota}o\acute{\iota}$) are distinguishable in meaning: the former, in which the idea of origin is most prominent, is the favourite expression of St. John; while the latter, emphasizing rather the notion of relation and privilege, is the one used by St. Paul. But even in NT the distinction is not an absolute one; and in OT, though both ideas are found, the words are not definitely marked off.

It is therefore advisable to consider both phrases together, while marking their various shades of meaning: and their significance may best be understood by examining the places where they occur, as nearly as possible in their historical order.

A. IN THE OT.—In OT this cannot be done with certainty, because of the doubts and differences of opinion among scholars as to the dates of many of its books. But a pretty sure starting-point can be found in the Bk. of Hosea, the date of which, in the reign of Jeroboam II. of Israel, is universally admitted. In this prophecy the relation of Israel to God is depicted, first, as that of a wife to her husband (chs. 1-3). This describes the nation or land as a whole, and individual Israelites are represented as her children, who as born to God are children of God. The unfaithful wife is repudiated (2[2]); but when led to repentance, as described in that parable (2[6-23]), so wonderfully parallel to our Lord's of the Prodigal Son, she again obtains mercy, and is once more the people of God ($2^{1.\ 23}$). In anticipation of that blessed restoration, it had been declared (1^{10}) that the children of Israel would be called 'sons of the living God.' They are so named as born of her whose husband is J″, *i.e.* who is in covenant with God.

So, when the same figure of the conjugal relation of God to Israel is used by Ezk, the actual children of the nation are called God's children for the same reason (Ezk $16^{20.\ 21}$ 'thy sons and thy daughters whom thou hast borne unto me . . . my children,' 23^{37} 'their sons whom they bare unto me '). In these and similar passages, the notion of birth or origin is evidently the prominent one ; and in Ezk 16^{21}, though the Heb. word is 'sons' as in the preceding verse, the LXX like the EV have rendered it by τέκνα, 'children.' As thus conceived, to be children of God is the same thing as to be born members of the nation or community that is in covenant with God. This notion of being God's children may probably be traced in the words of the Pharisees to Jesus, 'We were not born of fornication ; we have one Father, even God' (Jn 8^{41}), *i.e.* we are members of a people in covenant with God and true to him.

But Hosea also gives another conception of Israel's relation to God in 11^1 'When Israel was a child, then I loved him, and called my son out of Egypt.' With this must be taken Ex $4^{22.\ 23}$, where God says to Pharaoh, 'Isr. is my son, my firstborn : and I have said unto thee, Let my son go that he may serve me ; and thou hast refused to let him go : behold, I will slay thy son, thy firstborn.' Here 'my son'='my people' in God's previous words to Moses, and there is no emphasis on the idea of birth or origin ; for 'firstborn' evidently conveys the notion simply of most precious or beloved, as in Zec 12^{10}. It is the relation of Israel to God, and the value God puts on him, that is indicated : and so appropriately ' son,' not ' child,' is the word employed. The context that follows in Hos $11^{3.\ 4}$ shows that fatherly training and teaching are included in the notion, and in $^{8.\ 9}$ fatherly pity and love. But throughout it is the people as a whole that is here called God's son. The relation that was before depicted as that of a wife to her husband, is now spoken of as that of a son to his father.

These two figures are still more closely connected in the first great discourse of Jer (chs. 2. 3), where the fundamental idea is that Israel has been J‴'s unfaithful wife, while yet on her repentance she is invited to say, ' My father, thou art the guide (or companion) of my youth' (Jer 3^4). The phrase, ' guide, companion, or friend of youth,' is used in Pr 2^{17} for a husband, and prob. that is its significance also in Jer 3^4 ; and the employment of the words 'my father,' as parallel, is not unnatural in a state of society when the head of the house stood almost in the same relation to his wife as to his children. In Jer 3^{14} ' Return, O backsliding children, saith the Lord, for I am a husband unto you : and I will take you one of a city, and two of a family, and I will bring you to Zion,' we have the people as a whole viewed as J‴'s wife, and its members as his children ; and so also in vv. $^{19.\ 20.\ 22}$. But here the Israelites are called children of God, not, as in Hos and Ezk, simply as born of the people which is J‴'s wife, but as taken by him one by one, and returning to him with personal repentance. The idea of physical origin has passed away, and the notions connected with sonship seem to be mainly divine pardon, protection, and inheritance.

This whole passage also shows how the figure of God's marriage to Israel served an important purpose, in elevating the notion of the relationship from a merely physical to a moral and spiritual one. The heathen peoples, esp. in the Semitic race, conceived themselves as children of the deity in a grossly physical sense, as appears even here (Jer 2^{27} ' which say to a stock, Thou art my father ; and to a stone, Thou hast begotten me '). The conjugal relation, as founded, not on nature, but on a covenant of love, involving duties and responsibilities, gave a foundation for the moral appeals of the prophets, and made possible such a transition as we see in Jeremiah's teaching, to a higher view of sonship to God as an individual privilege.

A similar and perhaps more direct transition, from the collective to the individual relation, is made in Dt 14^1 ' Ye are the children of (lit. sons to) the LORD your God . . .,' v. ^{2} ' For thou art an holy people unto the LORD thy God, and the Lord hath chosen thee to be a peculiar people (*i.e.* a people of his own possession), above all peoples that are on the face of the earth.' Here sonship is ascribed to the Israelites individually on the ground that the people as a whole is holy, *i.e.* separated to God by his special choice of them to be his own possession (see Ex $19^{5.\ 6}$). The notion of birth or origin is here entirely absent, and that of privilege and corresponding duty is the one conveyed by the name ' sons of God.'

Dt also contains a passage remarkably rich in ref. to the sonship of Isr. in the song ascribed to Moses in ch. 32. Here God is called the people's Father because he bought, made, and established it (vv. $^{6.\ 15}$), begat, gave birth to (v. ^{18}), led and nourished it (vv. $^{10-14}$). These expressions refer to the divine action in forming Israel into a nation by delivering it from Egypt and training it in the wilderness. On the ground of this, the individual Israelites are called 'his sons and his daughters' (v. ^{19}), 'children' (v. ^{20}) ; and they are blamed for their provocation. But it is indicated that they who deal corruptly with God are not his children (v. ^{5}), and that God will take others to be his people so as to provoke them to jealousy (v. ^{21}), while the nations are called to rejoice with (or as being) his people (v. ^{43}). Here we see distinctly a moral significance attached to the title ' sons' or ' children of God.' Though it belongs properly to Israelites, it is forfeited by them if they are not faithful to God, and it may be given to men of other nations as well. Hence it is sometimes given specially to the godly, as in Ps 73^{15} ' the generation of thy children' ; Pr 14^{26} ' In the fear of the Lord is strong confidence ; and his children shall have a place of refuge.' See also the comparison in Ps 103^{13}. On the other hand, the privilege is ascribed to Gentiles, especially in the prophecies of their calling in the later book of Isaiah. God still calls Israelites ' my sons' (Is 45^{11}), because they are sons of Zion (49^{17}), who has been married to J″ though put away for a time (50^1 and 54). But she is to receive children of whom she shall say, ' Who hath borne me these ? ' (49^{21}), *i.e.* God and his Church are to have people from among the Gentiles sharing the blessings of Israel and enhancing her glory. Or, if those unexpected children are merely the exiled and forgotten Israelites, their sonship is now entirely independent of physical descent. ' For,' they say, ' thou art our Father, though Abraham knoweth us not, and Israel doth not acknowledge us : thou, O Lord, art our Father ; our Redeemer from everlasting is thy name ' (Is 63^{16}, cf. 64^8 65^1 66^{19-21}). Even if sonship is not here directly extended to the Gentiles, the principle is laid down which implies that. But it is not on the ground of nature or creation that this is done, but expressly on that of redemption and grace, only a redemption not merely external and national, like that of Israel from Egypt, but spiritual and therefore universal.

In Mal 1⁶, J″, appealing specially to the priests, calls himself a father and a master, as looking for the honour and fear given to earthly fathers and masters. In ch. 2¹⁰ the prophet asks, ' Have we not all one Father ? hath not one God created us ? ' as a basis for a rebuke to the Jews for marrying heathen wives, v.¹¹ ' Judah hath profaned the holiness of the Lord which he loveth, and hath married the daughter of a strange god.' Here plainly the fatherhood is not conceived as extending to all men, and the creation spoken of is the formation of Israel as a nation, as in Is 43¹ 44² and elsewhere. In the time of Malachi it was necessary to insist on the separation of the restored Jewish community from the surrounding idolaters, and he makes no mention of the calling of the Gentiles. But he indicates (ch. 3¹⁶, ¹⁷) that the true children of God are they that fear him, of whom the Lord says, ' I will spare them as a man spareth his own son that serveth him.'

Thus the OT affords a rich variety of statements about sonship to God as ascribed to men, which seem to exhibit successive stages in a development and elevation of the idea. (1) From the first it appears to be raised above the gross physical notion by the conception of it as origin from the people that is married to J″. Then (2) it is conceived as being members of the people that J″ has created as his son ; (3) as being taught and trained by J″ as a father ; and (4) as not constituted by mere natural descent, but by the fear of the Lord, and so possible for those who are not by birth members of the people of Israel.

Before proceeding to consider how this line of teaching is completed by Christ and his apostles, it will be proper to refer to a few passages in OT where the name 'sons of God' is given apparently to superhuman beings. In Job 38⁷, where J″ challenges Job for ignorance of his wonderful works, he describes the creation of the world as being, 'When the morning stars sang together, and all the sons of God shouted for joy.' The parallel seems to be similar to the usage by which the hosts of God denote sometimes the stars and sometimes the angels : and since in Job 1⁶ and 2¹ Satan, undoubtedly conceived as a superhuman spirit, is described as presenting himself among the sons of God, it is probable that in all these places the name is given to angels, and is used to indicate their nature, as the more common name 'angels' still retained its original reference to their office as messengers of God. It would indicate beings akin to God as being spiritual and superhuman, though derived from and inferior to the Creator. They are also called his 'holy ones' (Dt 33², Ps 89⁵), and his 'hosts' (Ps 103²¹ etc.). In Ps 29¹ and 89⁶ 'sons of the mighty' should prob. be rendered 'sons of God' or 'of gods,' but it is not a usual form of the name when used of the true God. The phrase is sometimes used in the way in which in Heb. 'son of man' is simply 'man,' 'son of oil'=fruitful, 'sons of flame'=sparks ; and as in early times the Israelites did not doubt the existence of the deities of the nations around them, they called them gods (e.g. Ex 15¹¹), which was afterwards softened into 'sons of God,' or 'of gods' (Ps 89⁶), and then into 'angels of God' (as in LXX Ps 97⁷· ⁹).

The passage in Gn 6¹⁻⁴ has been variously understood from very early times, and no interpretation is free from difficulty, but modern scholarship inclines to the view that by 'sons of God' are meant angels.

In Ps 82¹· ⁶ 'sons of the Most High' is synonymous with 'gods,' and is applied to rulers and judges in the congregation of God as invested by him with power, and called to rule in his name.

B. IN THE NT.—As the Bible contains no distinct doctrine about angels, it is impossible to form any definite conception of the relation implied in the name 'sons of God' given to them in OT, esp. as the usage is not followed out in NT, where in the Ep. to Hebrews it is denied that God ever gave the name 'my son' personally to any of the angels, that being the more excellent name obtained by him who is the effulgence of God's glory and the very image of his substance (He 1³⁻⁵).

1. THE TEACHING OF JESUS.—While keeping silence as to the sonship of angels, Jesus and his apostles have much to say as to the truth and blessedness of men being sons or children of God. In the teaching of our Lord himself the fatherhood of God occupies a very large place, and is far more fully exhibited than in OT. Jesus came to reveal

God, and the name in which he summed up his disclosure of his character was 'the Father.' He is the Father by way of eminence as being full of love, pity, and kindness, such as Jesus himself showed in his own person. And this love extended to the most unworthy and sinful, and to Gentiles who were outside the commonwealth of Israel. Thus it is assumed in Christ's teaching that the blessing of being sons of God is not limited to the Jewish nation, though that is nowhere expressly said, and though Jesus declares that such prayers as the Gentiles offer are not to be made by those who know God as their Father in heaven (Mt 6⁷· ⁸). To be called sons of God is one of the blessings of the kingdom of God which he proclaimed, promised to its members, esp. as peace-makers and as loving their enemies (Mt 5⁹· ⁴⁵⁻⁴⁸). As that kingdom is to be open to all nations (Mt 8¹¹), and to men simply as sinners (Mt 9¹²· ¹³), it is free to all or any to be sons of God, and in that aspect his Fatherhood may be called universal ; he has a fatherly heart towards all men, loves and pities all, and freely forgives the most sinful when they return to him. This is the lesson of the Parable of the Prodigal Son (Lk 15), and it is a most gracious and blessed one. In order to be entitled to call God our Father we need no other warrant than that we are sinners, willing to confess our sin and ask his forgiveness.

The blessings of being sons of God acc. to Jesus' teaching are forgiveness and gracious reception when we come to God as penitents ; the assurance that God will hear our prayers, and give us good things when we ask him (Mt 7¹¹) ; that he cares for our welfare, and that we can trust him to provide for all our earthly needs, so that without anxiety about these we may make it our great aim to be like him (Mt 6³¹⁻³⁴) ; the Spirit of our Father to speak in and through us when we are called to speak for Christ (Mt 10¹⁹· ²⁰) ; and, finally, the full enjoyment of the kingdom (Lk 12³², Mt 25³¹).

Jesus always uses the term 'sons,' not 'children,' of God, thus directing our attention to the nature of the relation rather than to the origination of it. His main teaching is that we stand to God in a relationship in which we can trust him as loving us and caring for our soul's welfare, and can speak to him with freedom and confidence. Plainly, too, this is a personal and individual relation. We have such privileges each for ourselves, and not merely as members of any nation or community.

At the same time, Jesus teaches that this relation of sonship to God is connected with his own person, and to be enjoyed through him. He claimed for himself a peculiar sonship, speaking of God as 'my Father' in a way that, according to Jn 5¹⁸, exposed him to a charge of blasphemy for making himself equal with God ; and he made our entering the kingdom of God depend on our not only calling him Lord, but doing the will of his Father in heaven (Mt 7²¹), and that is the same as doing his words (ib. ²⁴). He declared that no one knew the Father but the Son, and he to whomsoever the Son wills to reveal him (Mt 11²⁷) ; and he revealed the Father, not only by his words, but by his whole character and life. Hence he invited the weary and heavy-laden to come to him and learn of him, and this was his call in general to all who would enter the kingdom of God. He desired men to see in his own person and life what real sonship to God was, what childlike trust, what loving obedience, what zeal for his Father's honour and patient submission to his will it involved, and what rest and peace it brought with it. Into this blessedness he desires to bring men, and he recognizes those who will do the will of his Father in heaven as his brethren (Mt 12⁵⁰). They are sons of God through him and with him. Their following him implies a renouncing of earthly goods and even of life itself, such as is impossible to man and possible only to God (Mk 10²⁷). Hence to enter the kingdom of God requires a conversion and becoming as little children, which in Jn 3³˙ ⁵ Jesus calls being begotten anew of the Spirit.

Thus our Lord's teaching about sonship to God, though it is entirely of a practical religious character rather than scientific and theological, yet involves as its basis two ideas that he could not in his earthly life fully develop. One is that true sonship to God is a participation of his own unique relation to the Father, which is the archetype of all filial relationship to God, and the other is that it becomes ours through the impartation of a new life from God, in the strength of which we are enabled to renounce our own self-centred life. The former of these ideas is suggested by the fact that while Jesus habitually calls God his own Father, he as expressly calls those his brethren, whom he teaches to address God as 'our Father.' This shows that though he (e.g. Jn 20¹⁷) makes the distinction between his own relation to God expressed in 'my Father,' and ours expressed by 'your Father,' he does not mean that God is our Father in a quite different sense from that in which he is his, for in that case we would be only nominally and not really his brethren ; but he would intimate that while his Sonship is indeed unique as being original and absolutely perfect, we partake of it through him. But this could not be fully explained as long as the truth about his own person could not be clearly revealed.

The other idea is implied in Jesus' teaching that God's sons are those who trust him and are like him, and that for us this implies a great change of mind and heart, a turning our back on our worldly selves, such as can be effected only under the influence of a power from God. But this, too, could not be made plain till the coming of the Spirit, whom Jesus promised to complete his teaching.

The outcome of that teaching is to be seen in the apostolic Epistles, and in these we find the former idea developed more especially by St. Paul and the latter by St. John.

2. THE TEACHING OF PAUL.—St. Paul views Christianity chiefly in its bearing on the personal relation between man and God. Apart from the salvation of Christ, that relation is that of a transgressor of the eternal moral law to the righteous Lawgiver and Judge, hence it is a state of condemnation and death. From that he is redeemed by the propitiation which consists in the obedience and sacrifice of Christ the Son of God. The truth that our Redeemer is God's own beloved Son is repeatedly emphasized in connexion with his sacrifice as enhancing the love of God and the self-emptying grace of our Lord ; and St. Paul undoubtedly regarded Christ's Sonship as not merely an official or Messianic, but a pre-existent and eternal relation to God. But in his view Jesus' death is our redemption only in virtue of our being one with him in it by faith, so that by it we die to sin and to the law, and are freed from its curse. Since, then, we are redeemed from our natural state of condemnation as sinners by dying in and with the Son of God, who loved us and gave himself for us ; since we live now only in him, our relation to God is henceforth the same as his, we are sons of God in Christ Jesus, because by faith, sealed in baptism, we have put on Christ (Gal 3²⁶˙ ²⁷). It has been questioned whether here and in Ro 6³, where St. Paul uses the limiting (?) pronoun 'as many as' and the phrase 'baptized into Christ,' instead of the usual one 'baptized into the name of Christ,' he refers to the outward rite of water baptism at all, and not rather to the inward washing from sins by real union to the Saviour. Most commentators, however, consider that there is no reasonable doubt that by baptism into Christ he means the sacrament. But if this be so, the apostle certainly assumes that it was received in faith and sealed a real union to Christ, which is the ground of our sonship.

The sonship of believers in Christ, St. Paul connects with the OT view of the Israelites being God's sons in virtue of the covenant and promise to Abraham (Gal 3²⁹), and he proceeds to explain the special privileges brought by Christ by comparing the position of Israel under the law to that of children under age, who, though really sons and heirs, have not practically more liberty than servants, but are under guardians and stewards by whom they are governed and their property is managed. So God's children, before Christ came, being immature, were in subjection to what St. Paul calls ' the rudiments of the world,' i.e. elementary teaching by precepts relating to outward things, such as meats, times, and seasons. But it is remarkable that the apostle speaks of the Gentiles also as in their heathen state having been under such rudiments (Gal 4³˙ ⁹), so that we may infer that he recognized a certain divine training even of them, as elsewhere he speaks of them being a law to themselves (Ro 2¹⁴⁻¹⁶). He views Christ's coming and work both as giving sonship to those who were only servants, and also as giving full filial rights to those who were children under age. But not as if it were the former only to Gentiles and the latter to Jews as such ; but that it was a real gift of sonship to all, whether Jews or Gentiles, who were without God ; and to all who were really seeking him, in whatever nation, though they might be very immature in their spiritual life, it was the bestowal of the full privileges of sons of full age having free and direct access to God as their Father. This view is in accordance with the highest conception attained in the OT, that in Deutero-Isaiah from which and other prophetic Scriptures St. Paul quotes in his discussion of the relations between Israel and the Gentiles in Ro 9–11.

In order to bring out the privilege of being made sons of God, St. Paul employs the notion of adoption as recognized in the Roman law. See ADOPTION.

Among the privileges flowing from sonship in Christ he mentions the bestowal of the Spirit, as the Spirit of God's Son, or of adoption, who cries in us, i.e. moves us to cry, 'Abba, Father' (Gal 4⁶, Ro 8¹⁵), and with this is connected the access we have with boldness to God as our Father (Eph 2¹⁸ 3¹²). Another benefit flowing from sonship is the inheritance which we have in and with Christ (Gal 3²⁶˙ ²⁹ 4⁷, Ro 8¹⁷). This means that the glory that is to be revealed is as sure to us as if we had a right to it in strict law, and at the same time is the free gift of the Father's love. In connexion with this St. Paul develops the idea that believers in Christ, though poor, afflicted, and persecuted in this world, yet really have the Messianic blessings promised in the OT as those of the kingdom of God, because they can rejoice in their tribulations, since these are means of their perfection, and are inconsiderable in view of the promised glory (Ro 5³⁻¹¹ 8¹⁸⁻³⁶, 2 Co 4¹⁶⁻⁵⁹). The further notion that afflictions are chastisements sent by God in love, and for our real and truest good, is expressed in the Ep. to Hebrews (12⁵⁻¹¹) as a special blessing of God's children more distinctly than in the Pauline Epistles. For St. Paul does not conceive our relation to God as that of young children needing discipline, but rather as that of sons of full age in a relation of freedom and love to our heavenly Father. Hence he is not fond of the expression *children* (τέκνα) unless when the form of his argument from OT leads him to use it, as in Ro 9⁷·⁸. So, too, he does not use the idea of our being begotten anew of the Spirit to describe the beginning of Christian life; he conceives it rather as a new creation or a raising from death. In Tit 3⁵ the word 'regeneration' is not the common expression for what is generally so called, and it is not certain that it refers to the new birth of individuals.

3. THE TEACHING IN HEBREWS. — Here again the notion of children is more prominent than that of sons, and the idea in ch. 12 is the position of young children needing education and chastisement. This writer also has in view the beginning of the relation in a birth rather than in adoption, for he calls God the Father of spirits in contrast with the fathers of our flesh (12⁹). It is unnatural to suppose that he meant by these words to teach the philosophical doctrine that men derive from their earthly parents only their bodies, and their spirits directly from God. Whether this be true or not, the idea of the writer was manifestly the religious one, that while our relation to our earthly parents is physical, our relation as children to God is spiritual. But that he does not conceive this relation as a universal one, is plain from the fact that he speaks of the possibility of being without chastisement, and so being bastards and not sons (v.⁸), here using the Pauline term for the relation.

There is one utterance of St. Paul, in his speech at Athens (Ac 17²⁸·²⁹), where he says of all men as such that they are the offspring (γένος) of God, because he has made us with the purpose that we shall know him; he is not far from any one of us, since in him we live and move and have our being. This relation is clearly not the same as that which the apostle in his Epistles ascribes to Christians when he says they are sons of God through faith in Jesus Christ. It does not include the blessings of freedom, of the spirit of adoption, or of being heirs of God. Hence, if this universal relation is to be called sonship, it must be clearly distinguished from that Christian sonship of which he speaks most frequently and most fully. But if it be considered that St. Paul does not use the word 'sons' (υἱοί), but the more indefinite one 'offspring' (γένος), that he borrows this from a Greek poet, and that the only use that he makes of the statement is to show that since we are so like God it is foolish to think that the Deity can be represented by material images, it cannot but appear very precarious to infer from this expression that St. Paul would say that all men are sons of God, or that the relation that is formed by our creation in God's image deserves to be called sonship. He does indeed teach that all things were created through and in the Son of God, who appeared on earth as Jesus Christ (Col 1¹⁵⁻¹⁷); and he declares in the warmest and most glowing language the love and kindness, goodness and patience of God towards all men, seeking to lead them to repentance. If we think that these truths are fairly expressed by saying that God is the Father of all men, and they his sons, we may, on our own responsibility, use these phrases; but we should remember that St. Paul does not use them in such a sense, but means by being sons of God something far more blessed.

The Palestinian apostles do not use the Pauline term 'adoption'; but they describe in different ways how men are made 'children' of God, employing that word rather than 'sons,' because they emphasize the spiritual birth by which we are renewed.

4. THE TEACHING OF JAMES. — In the Ep. of James (1¹⁷) God is called the Father of lights, from whom cometh down every good giving and every perfect boon, and to whom must not be attributed any temptation to sin, because he is unchangeable in goodness. Then it is added: 'Of his own will he brought us forth by the word of truth, that we should be a kind of first-fruits of his creatures' (1¹⁸). The 'we' here are clearly those who, as afterwards said, have 'the implanted word,' which is able to save their souls (1²¹). This reminds us of Jesus' Parable of the Sower and the Seed, where the word of the kingdom is compared to seed having a living power of germination and producing new life, and the fruit of the good seed is said to be the sons of the kingdom (Mt 13³⁸), in opposition to the sons of the evil one. In Ja 1²⁷ God is called the Father absolutely, to show that he is truly and purely worshipped by visiting the widows and fatherless in their affliction; and in 3⁹, where is exposed the inconsistency of blessing God while we curse men, God is called the Lord and Father; but, as if to leave no doubt that all men are included, they are described, not as children of God, but as made after the similitude of God. It is maintained by many that since all men are made in God's image, and cared for by him with infinite goodness and love, they are all his children; and if they think it best to use the phrase in that sense, no one can object to their doing so, and the thing meant is most certainly taught in Scripture; but it does not appear that the apostles called it by the name of sonship, and it does appear that they described believers as sons of God in a higher sense because born again by his word and Spirit.

5. THE TEACHING OF PETER. — In 1 P 1³ it is said that 'the God and Father of our Lord Jesus Christ, according to his great mercy, begat us again to a living hope by the resurrection of Jesus Christ from the dead, into an inheritance incorruptible, undefiled, and unfading, reserved in the heavens for us.' This by itself might be merely a rhetorical way of saying that the historical fact of Jesus being raised to life after his death and burial awakened in the souls of his followers a hope of immortal blessedness that made them practically new men, animating them with new life. But when we read further on in the same chapter (1 P 1²³), 'having been begotten again, not of corruptible seed, but of incorruptible, through the word of God which liveth and abideth for ever,' we can hardly doubt that the apostle means to describe a change that is wrought, not merely by the impression made by an event even as great and important as the resurrection of Christ, but by an influence working directly on our souls, and making us, as afterwards described (2²), as newborn babes in our religious life and relation to God. This corresponds to what Jesus taught of the need of being turned, so as to become as little children (Mt 18³), as well as of being begotten of the Spirit (Jn 3³⁻⁸). It seems, therefore, to be in ref. to this new birth that St. Peter speaks of Christians calling God, the impartial Judge, Father (1 P 1¹⁷), not as in the AV, 'if ye call on the Father,' but 'if ye call him Father who without respect of persons judgeth according to every man's work.' It is plainly not all men by whom God is to be addressed as Father, but believers in virtue of their having been begotten again. So, too, they are called to show themselves obedient children (1¹⁴), or children of obedience. Throughout, the idea of birth is the prominent one, rather than that of the relation and privileges of sons. These are not developed as they are by St. Paul and by the writer to the Heb., the only one specially mentioned being the inheritance (1 P 1⁴). It is in harmony with this conception of believers being children of God be-

cause born or begotten of him, that in 2 P 1⁴ they are said to become partakers of the divine nature. Also we may observe that in 1 P God is distinctively called the God and Father of our Lord Jesus Christ (1³), and the notion of our being in Christ and dying with him to sin is also in the writer's mind (2²⁴ 4¹). The opening sentence is formed after the pattern of that of the Ep. to the Eph.; but while St. Paul blesses God because he has foreordained us to adoption (Eph 1⁴), St. Peter seems to have expressed the same idea of sonship by divine gift, in the more concrete form of a begetting.

6. THE TEACHING OF JOHN.—The teaching of St. John on this subject combines the elements of the Pauline and Petrine, though it is more akin to the latter, and uses the term 'children' rather than sons of God. The keynote to it may be found in the Prologue to the Gospel (1¹². ¹³), 'to as many as received him (the Logos) he gave the right to become children of God, even to them that believe on his name : which were begotten, not of blood nor of the will of the flesh, nor of the will of man, but of God.' Here we have the right to become children of God bestowed by Christ, which answers to St. Paul's statement, 'God sent forth his Son . . . that we might receive the adoption of sons.' The word 'adoption' is not employed; but the right to become children expresses the same thing in less technical language. Further, this is said to be given to those who receive Christ by believing on his name. St. Paul had also written, 'Ye are all sons of God by faith in Jesus Christ ; for as many of you as have been baptized into Christ have put on Christ' (Gal 3²⁶ᶠ.). Thus for St. John, as well as for St. Paul, our sonship to God is through union to Christ the only-begotten Son, and that union is effected by faith.

But St. John adds to this the conception found in St. James and St. Peter of a birth or begetting of God, which he emphatically distinguishes from the natural birth in every aspect of it. Those who believe in Christ's name are they who were begotten of God ; and that this is not done by the process of natural generation is shown by a threefold contrast : not of blood, i.e. they did not become sons of God through or in virtue of their being of the one blood of which God has made all mankind. Neither was it by any movement or impulse of their own nature, whether the spontaneous tendencies of its animal faculties ('the will of the flesh'), or even the voluntary acts of personality ('the will of man'). The contrast is more briefly and pointedly expressed in our Lord's discourse with Nicodemus as between being begotten of the flesh and of the Spirit (Jn 3⁶). St. John seems to conceive the Divine Spirit as a principle or power of life and holiness proceeding from God, given to Jesus Christ in all its fulness and by him communicated to his disciples. It is not unworthy of notice that Iren. and Tertull. apply Jn 1¹³ to Christ, apparently reading the verb in the singular ('who was born'); and though that reading is only found in some Lat. MSS and cannot be received, yet in 1 Jn 5¹⁸ our Lord, according to the most natural interpretation, is called 'he that was begotten of God.'

St. John seems chiefly anxious to show that the believer's being a child of God necessarily involves likeness to God in character and life ; and hence, while he ascribes this privilege to the wonderful love of the Father (1 Jn 3¹), and to our being united to Christ by faith (Jn 1¹²), he dwells most fully on the truth that our sonship is due, not merely to the gracious act of adoption by the Father and our being made one with the Son through faith, but also to our receiving a new life from the Spirit of God, which communicates to us that very principle of love which is the

essence of God. In 1 Jn 2²⁹ he says, 'every one that doeth righteousness is begotten of him,' and the uniform usage of the apostle seems to show that he means of God, though it is of Christ that he has been speaking just before. Wherever there is real righteousness in any man it is derived from him who is the archetype and source of all righteousness. Then, after expressing his joyful sense of the greatness of the Father's love and the reality of the sonship that it bestows, he returns to the subject of the inconsistency of that sonship with sin and its inseparable connexion with righteousness, and at 3⁹ he says, 'Whosoever is begotten of God doeth no sin, because his seed abideth in him, and he cannot sin because he is begotten of God.' The statement is evidently an ideal one, describing the Christian life in its ultimate perfection when we shall be like him, for we shall see him as he is (v.²). But it is put in the present, because that perfection is really given in principle and germ to all who are begotten of God even now. The impossibility of their sinning is not to be achieved by any further or additional gift or power, but by the life from God that is given at the first, when it comes to its full maturity. That principle of sinlessness is called the seed of God which abides in his children. This seems to denote a spiritual life derived from God, whereby, as it is put in 2 P 1⁴, we become 'partakers of the divine nature'; it is what Jesus indicates when he says, 'That which is born of the Spirit is spirit' (Jn 3⁶). The divine nature acc. to St. John is love (1 Jn 4⁸. ¹⁶), and this love is implanted in us when God gives us of his Spirit. So in a spiritual sense our being begotten of God is not a mere metaphor, but a proper statement of what is a real communication of the most essential life of God. But, while giving this high transcendent view of the nature of believers' sonship to God, St. John is careful to insist that its reality must be proved by the practical test of conformity to the moral law in the common affairs of daily life. He does not allow the mystical union with Christ and God to obscure the distinct personal relations between us and God. There is to be a day of judgment, and one of the blessings of the children of God is to have confidence in that day, and not to be ashamed before Christ at his coming. In the present life the relation of the children of God to him as their Father, implies confession of sin and prayer for others as well as themselves, and requires perfect truth and frankness. The blessings of sonship to God are summed up by St. John in the one great idea of eternal life.

The world outside of Christ is described as lying in the evil one (1 Jn 5¹⁹), of the evil one, children of the devil (3¹⁰) ; but Christ is the propitiation for the whole world (2²) ; and as the love of God is manifested in sending his Son to be a propitiation for our sins (4¹⁰), it is implied that God's fatherly love has a universal aspect, though all men are not really, in St. John's view, God's children.

LITERATURE.—The subject of our sonship to God has not been much discussed until recent times, though it came incidentally into consideration in connexion with the Sonship of Christ, as in Athanasius' *Orat. agst. Arians* (esp. *Or.* ii.), and in the systems of theology, as in Calvin's *Inst.* (I. xiv. 18, II. xiii. 1, III. ii. 23), and practical treatises, as Thomas Goodwin's *On the Work of the Holy Ghost.* In modern times such writers as F. D. Maurice, F. W. Robertson, etc., have made great use of the idea that all men are children of God, to exclude the doctrine of God's judicial dealings. R. S. Candlish discussed the subject in his Cunningham Lectures on the *Fatherhood of God,* maintaining that sonship belongs to believers, and is founded on that of Christ. T. J. Crawford in his *Fatherhood of God* criticised these positions, and maintained a twofold sonship—one universal, founded on Creation, and another special, bestowed on believers in Christ. Another work that appeared at the same time is *The Divine Fatherhood,* by C. H. H. Wright, taking mainly Dr. Candlish's view. The other side is strongly maintained in A. M. Fairbairn's *Christ in Modern Theology.*

In these discussions the subject was connected more or less with far-reaching questions of systematic theology, and the notion of sonship to God plays an important part in the *Dogmatik* of R. A. Lipsius. Its exegetical discussion belongs properly to the Bib. Theol. of the NT, and reference may be made to the works, on that subject, of Schmid, Weiss, Beyschlag, also to Wendt's *Teaching of Jesus*, and to Bruce's *The Kingdom of God* and *St. Paul's Conception of Christianity*. There is a very interesting special study of St. Paul's conception of adoption in relation to Rom. law by W. E. Ball in the *Contemp. Rev.* Aug. 1891.

J. S. CANDLISH.

GOD FORBID.—See FORBID.

GODHEAD.—This word occurs three times in AV. Ac 17²⁹ ' We ought not to think that the Godhead is like unto gold, or silver, or stone, graven by art and man's device' (Gr. τὸ θεῖον); Ro 1²⁰ ' For the invisible things of him from the creation of the world are clearly seen, being understood by the things that are made, even his eternal power and Godhead' (Gr. θειότης); Col 2⁹ ' For in him dwelleth all the fulness of the Godhead bodily' (Gr. θεότης). In each case the Gr. word is appropriately employed, and the one could not have been used for the other, so that to give 'Godhead' as the tr^n of them all is most unhappy.

In Ac 17²⁹ τὸ θεῖον, 'the Divine,' is chosen by St. Paul in his speech to the Athenians as a familiar philosophical expression which enables him to carry their thoughts easily with him. Even they, with scarcely a personal conception of God, ought not to debase their conception to the level of men's handiwork. Hence RVm 'that which is divine' is better than text 'the Godhead,' though 'the Divine' would have been better. Wyc. errs on the other side when he offers 'godly thing' (after Vulg. *Divinum*). Tindale gave 'godhed,' and was followed by all the Versions except the Rhemish, which has 'the Divinitie,' though 'Godhead' is given as an alternative in the Annotation to the verse. The Gr. expression occurs nowhere else in biblical Greek, though the adj. θεῖος is common in LXX and occurs in 2 P 1³·⁴ (EV 'divine').

Lightfoot (on Col 2⁹) expresses the difference between θειότης and θεότης thus: θειότης is the quality, θεότης the essence of God. The distinction is best seen by observing that θεότης comes from θεός 'God,' while θειότης comes from θεῖος 'Divine.' Therefore Sanday - Headlam (on Ro 1²⁰) more happily: θεότης = Divine Personality, θειότης = Divine nature and properties (cf. Bengel [on Col 2⁹]: ' Non modo divinæ virtutes, sed ipsa divina natura,' and see Trench, *NT Synonyms*, p. 6 ff.). It is at once seen how appropriately St. Paul uses θειότης in Ro 1²⁰ where he speaks of such attributes of God as can be read in the book of Nature; and how appropriately θεότης in Col 2⁹ where he asserts of the Son that in Him dwells the fulness of the entire (revealed and unrevealed) Personality of God. The Latin Versions were forced to use *divinitas* for both words. But its insufficiency to represent θεότης was early felt, and Augustine says (*De Civ. Dei*, vii. 1): ' Hanc divinitatem vel, ut sic dixerim, deitatem: nam et hoc verbo uti jam nostros non piget, ut de Græco expressius transferant id quod illi θεότητα appellant.' The same feeling is now finding expression in English, and theologians prefer to speak of the Deity rather than of the Divinity of Christ, since the former word alone gives Him the full Personality of God. The Eng. Versions from Wyclif to AV make no distinction, but use 'Godhead' at both places, except that the Rhem. NT has 'Divinitie' at Ro 1²⁰. Yet Beza (on Col 2⁹) had shown the distinction: ' Non dicit, τὴν θειότητα, id est divinitatem, sed τὴν θεότητα, id est deitatem.' Luther also was content with 'Gottheit' for both words; but De Wette gives 'Göttlichkeit' for θειότης; while Weizsäcker

gives 'Gottesgüte.' RV has 'divinity,' retaining 'Godhead' for θεότης.

Each word occurs once only in NT. Nor is θιότης found in LXX, and θειότης only once, Wis 18⁹ (καὶ τὸν τῆς θειότητος νόμου ἐν ὁμονοίᾳ διέθεντο, AV 'and with one consent made a holy law,' AVm 'or a covenant of God or league,' RV 'and with one consent they took upon themselves the covenant of the divine law,' RVm 'Gr. *law of divineness*'). On this Westcott (*Lessons of the RV of NT*, p. 111 f.) draws attention to 'the care taken by the Revisers to represent words of a single occurrence in the original by words of single occurrence in the Eng. version.' Besides 'divinity' in Ro 1²⁰ for θειότης and 'Godhead' (for which he seems to prefer 'deity') in Col 2⁹ for θεότης, he mentions 'apparition' for φάντασμα Mt 14²⁶, Mk 6⁴⁹; 'awe' for δέος He 12²⁸; 'billows' for σάλος Lk 21²⁵; 'concealed' for παρακαλύπτεσθαι Lk 9⁴⁵; 'conduct' for ἀπαγωγή 2 Ti 3¹⁰; 'confute' for διακατελέγχεσθαι Ac 18²⁸; 'demeanour' for κατάστημα Tit 2³; 'discipline' for σωφρονισμός 2 Ti 1⁷; 'disrepute' for ἀτιμαγμός Ac 19²⁷; 'effulgence' for ἀπαύγασμα He 1³; 'goal' for σκοπός Ph 3¹⁴; 'impostor' for γόης 2 Ti 3¹³; 'to interpose' for μεσιτεύειν He 6¹⁷; 'justice' for ἡ Δίκη Ac 28⁴; 'to moor' for προσορμίζεσθαι Mk 6⁵³; 'sacred' for ἱερός 1 Co 9¹³, 2 Ti 3¹⁵; 'to shudder' for φρίσσειν Ja 2¹⁹; 'stupor' for κατάνυξις Ro 11⁸; 'to train' for σωφρονίζειν Tit 2⁴; 'tranquil' for ἤρεμος 1 Ti 2²; 'undressed' for ἄγναφος Mt 9¹⁶, Mk 2²¹; and 'without self-control' for ἀκρατής 2 Ti 3³.

In modern English the word 'Godhead' is mostly confined to a neuter sense, as if it were the proper tr^n of τὸ θεῖον, and of that alone. In older English it was a synonym for 'divinity,' which, as we have seen, was not distinguished, as it is scarcely distinguished yet, from 'deity.' The Rhem. NT has the marg. note to Jn 6⁶⁶ ' Heretikes beleeve not the real presence because they see bread and wine, as the Jewes believed not his Godhead because of the shape of a poore man.' Tindale (*Works*, i. 200) speaks ironically of 'the Pope's godhead.' And Chaucer (*Knightes Tale*, 1523) uses the word as a syn. for 'deity'—

> ' If so be that my youthe may deserve,
> And that my might be worthy for to serve
> Thy godhede, that I may been oon of thyne,
> Than preye I thee to rewe upon my pyne.'

J. HASTINGS.

GODLESS.—This word is found but once in AV, 2 Mac 7³⁴ ' O godless man'; Gr. ὦ ἀνόσιε; RV ' O unholy man,' as EV translate the same adj. in 1 Ti 1⁹, 2 Ti 3², its only occurrences in NT.

But RV has given 'godless' as the tr^n of חָנֵף *hâneph*, in preference to AV 'hypocrite' in Job 8¹³ 13¹⁶ 15³⁴ 17⁸ 20⁵ 27⁸ 34³⁰ 36¹³, Pr 11⁹, Is 33¹⁴; and the same translation might have been given in the three remaining passages : Is 9¹⁷ (AV 'hypocrite'); 10⁶, Ps 35¹⁶ (AV 'hypocritical'), where, however, RV gives 'profane.' For there is no doubt that 'hypocrite,' though it is the tr^n of all the versions since Wyclif, misses the meaning. The verb is used in the Qal in the sense of ' be polluted,' whether of land (Is 24⁵, Jer 3¹, Ps 106³⁸ so tr^d in EV, except Is 24⁵ AV 'defile,' but Mic 4¹¹ of Zion, EV 'defile') or of persons (Jer 23¹¹, EV 'be profane'); and in the Hiphil 'to pollute' of land (Nu 35³³ *bis* AV 'pollute'—'defile,' Jer 3² AV 'pollute,' 3⁹ AV 'defile,' RV always 'pollute'), and of persons (Dn 11³² AV 'corrupt,' RV 'pervert,' RVm 'make profane'). Hence the idea of the adj. is separated from God so as to be openly hostile; not 'hypocritical,' but 'profane,' 'godless.' There are two substantives, each of which occurs once, חָנֵף Is 32⁶ (AV 'hypocrisy,' RV 'profaneness'), and חֲנֻפָּה Jer 23¹⁵ (AV 'profaneness,' AVm 'hypocrisy,' RV 'profaneness').   J. HASTINGS.

GODLINESS is in NT the equivalent of the Gr. term εὐσέβεια (1 Ti 2² 3¹⁶ 4⁷·⁸ 6³·⁵·⁶·¹¹, 2 Ti 3⁵, Tit 1¹, also Ac 3¹² [RV], 2 P 1³·⁶·⁷ 3¹¹), except in one passage (1 Ti 2¹⁰), where θεοσέβεια is used. ' It properly denotes,' says Ellicott, ' only "well - directed reverences" (Trench, *Synon.* § 48), but in the NT is practically the same as θεοσέβεια, and is well defined by Tittmann (*Synon.* i. p. 146) as "vis pietatis in ipsâ vitâ vel externâ vel internâ" (cf.

Eusebius, *Præp. Evang.* i. p. 3). Thus, then, εὐσέβεια conveys the idea, not of an "inward, inherent holiness," but, as Alford (on Ac 3¹²) correctly observes, of an "operative cultive piety" (*Pastoral Epistles*, p. 27). The substantive is used by St. Paul only in the Pastoral Epistles ; and Pfleiderer (*Paulinism*, Eng. tr. ii. 210) maintains that in these writings, the Pauline authorship of which he denies, εὐσέβεια takes the place of the Pauline πίστις as 'the fundamental idea of the Christian holy life.' Weiss, however, denies this, and holds that 'as εὐσέβεια occurs along with πίστις (1 Ti 6¹¹), it is clear that it must rather be the basis of life from which true faith springs' (*Bib. Theol. of NT*, Eng. tr. ii. 129). St. Paul's use of the term 'ungodly' (ἀσεβής), in Ro 4⁵ 5⁶, as descriptive of all mankind apart from Christ, would suggest that the more distinctively Christian sense of the term 'godly' is to be preferred in St. Paul's letters, as equivalent, not to reverence for God generally, but to the Christian feeling towards God as the Father of our Lord Jesus Christ. On the other hand, in Ac 10²·⁷ the adjective εὐσεβής, translated 'devout,' is used to describe a man who, though a worshipper of God, was not even a Jewish proselyte. In the Sept. εὐσέβεια is used in some passages (Pr 1⁷, Is 11²) as the equivalent of the phrase 'the fear of the Lord,' but in others θεοσέβεια (Gn 20¹¹, Job 28²⁸). Thoughout the OT man's duty towards God is defined as *fearing God* (Schultz, *OT Theol.* Eng. tr. ii. p. 55) ; and in the 'Wisdom' literature the fear of the Lord (יִרְאַת יְהֹוָה) is assumed as the fundamental principle of piety and morality (Job 28²⁸, Ps 111¹⁰, Pr 1⁷ 8¹³, Ec 12¹³. See Oehler's *OT Theol.* Eng. tr. ii. p. 446). For the use of the adjective or adverb 'godly' in 2 Ti 3¹², Tit 2¹², 2 P 2⁹ see the following article. Elsewhere in St. Paul's letters the same word is used in AV to render either the genitive θεοῦ (2 Co 1¹² 11², 1 Ti 1⁴) or the phrase κατὰ θεὸν (2 Co 7⁹·¹⁰·¹¹) ; while in 3 Jn ⁶ 'godly sort'=ἀξίως τοῦ θεοῦ, a use of the adjective which the meaning of the substantive does not warrant ; and it is to be regretted that the RV retains this rendering in some passages. It must be added that in some OT passages (Ps 4³ 12¹ 32⁶) the adjective 'godly' is used to render the Heb. word חָסִיד, which not only describes God's relation to man, but also describes the mutual relations of men (see Cheyne, *Hosea*, 62 n.) ; and the use of this word shows that the OT phrase 'the fear of the Lord' does not mean any slavish dread of God, but a reverence which does not exclude love. The NT godliness also means a reverence that includes all the emotions which the revelation of God in Christ inspires.   A. E. GARVIE.

GODLY is used both as an adj. and as an adverb. The adj. occurs only four times in OT : (1) thrice as trⁿ of חָסִיד, which is properly 'kind,' but from the prominence of this quality in God, and in them that are like Him, comes to mean 'pious,' 'godly' ; so Ps 4³ 32⁶, and as subst. 'the godly man' Ps 12¹ ; and (2) once as trⁿ of אֱלֹהִים 'God,' Mal 2¹⁵ 'a godly seed,' lit., as AVm 'a seed of God.' The proper equivalent of 'godly' in Gr. is εὐσεβής, which in Sirach is one of the characteristics of the 'wise man' (ὁ σοφός), as distinguished from the 'fool' (ὁ μωρός) who is ἀσεβής 'godless' ; and in the plur. this practically becomes a subst. equivalent to 'the Wise.' Thus Sir 39²⁶·²⁷ 'The principal things for the whole use of man's life are water, fire, iron, and salt, flour of wheat, honey, milk, and the blood of the grape, and oil, and clothing. All these things are for good to the godly (τοῖς εὐσεβέσιν) ; so to the sinners (τοῖς ἁμαρτωλοῖς) they are turned into evil.' This word, which occurs thrice in NT, is only once trᵈ 'godly,' 2 P 2⁹ 'The Lord knoweth how to deliver

the godly out of temptation' (εὐσεβεῖς) ; in Ac 10²·⁷ it is trᵈ 'devout' by both AV and RV, the word being applied to Cornelius and to one of his soldiers. The TR gives εὐσεβής in Ac 22¹² in reference to Ananias, but edd. after the best MSS prefer εὐλαβής, which elsewhere (Lk 2²⁵, Ac 2⁵ 8²) is trᵈ by EV 'devout,' as here. In He 12²⁸ the subst. εὐλάβεια is trᵈ 'godly fear,' for which RV gives 'reverence,' RVm 'godly fear.' But in 5⁷ (the only other occurrence of the Greek word) RV tr. ἀπὸ τῆς εὐλαβείας, 'for his godly fear,' AV 'in that he feared.' (See this passage discussed in *Expos. Times*, vi. 434, 522 ; vii. 4, 118, 502). In 2 Co 1¹² 11², 1 Ti 1⁴ ' godly' is the trⁿ of θεός 'God' (cf. Mal 2¹⁵ above) ; thus 2 Co 1¹² 'in simplicity and godly sincerity' (ἐν ἁπλότητι [edd. ἁγιότητι] καὶ εἰλικρινείᾳ [T WH -ίᾳ] θεοῦ [edd. τοῦ θεοῦ], RV 'in holiness and sincerity of God') ; 11² 'I am jealous over you with godly jealousy' (θεοῦ ζήλῳ, RV 'with a godly jealousy,' RVm 'Gr. a jealousy of God') ; 1 Ti 1⁴ 'Neither give heed to fables and endless genealogies, which minister questions rather than godly edifying (οἰκοδομίαν) which is in faith' (RV 'a dispensation of God,' οἰκονομίαν θεοῦ, RVm 'a stewardship of God'). The AV of 1611 omits 'godly' from the last passage (evidently by an oversight, for it is found in all the versions from Tindale to the Bishops), and it was not inserted till 1638. Wyc. has 'edificacioun of god,' and Rhem. 'the edifying of God,' after Vulg. 'ædificationem Dei.'* Elsewhere 'godly' as an adj. is the trⁿ of some attributive phrase in the original. In 2 Co 7⁹ 'after a godly manner,' 7¹⁰ 'godly,' and 7¹¹ 'after a godly sort,' all represent κατὰ θεόν 'according to God' as AVm (RV changes 7⁹ into 'after a godly sort') ; and in 3 Jn ⁶ 'after a godly sort' stands for ἀξίως τοῦ θεοῦ, lit. 'worthily of God,' as RV.

As an adverb 'godly' was once in common use, as Tindale, *Pent.* 'A prologe' (Mombert's ed. p. 12), 'Every man must worke godly and truly to the uttermoste of the power that god hath geven him : and yet not truste therein' ; and *Preface to AV*, 1611, p. 5, 'The godly-learned were not content to have the Scriptures in the Language which themselves understood.' 'Ungodly' was used in the same way, as Mt 22⁶ Tind. 'The remnaunt toke his servantes and intreated them ungodly and slewe them' ; and T. Lever, *Sermons* (Arber's ed. p. 118), 'Do ye not se how that prebendes whiche were godly founded as moste convenient and necessarye lyvyngs for preachers to healp the byshoppes and the persons too enstructe the people, be now ungodly abused to corrupte the byshoppes ?' But there was a feeling against using the same form as adj. and adverb. Hence 'godlily' was sometimes used, as Knox, *Hist.* 136, 'That by his grave counsell, and godly exhortation, he would animate her Majestie constantly to follow that which godlily she had begun' ; and sometimes the word was avoided. In Pr. Bk., Collect for Good Friday, 'That every member . . . may truly and godly serve thee' is found in all edd. from 1549 to 1662, but in the Scotch Liturgy 'godly' was changed into 'worthily.' 'Godly' is used as an adv. thrice in AV, 2 Mac 12⁴⁵ 'there was great favour laid up for those that died godly' (μετ' εὐσεβίας, RV 'in godliness,' RVm 'on the side of godliness') ; 2 Ti 3¹², Tit 2¹² (εὐσεβῶς).   J. HASTINGS.

GOD, SON OF.—See SON OF GOD.

GOD, SONS OF.—See GOD, CHILDREN OF.

GOEL (AVENGER OF BLOOD).—'Goel' (Heb. גֹּאֵל gō'ēl) is an important technical term of Hebrew jurisprudence. The primary meaning of the root

---

* For examples of the way in which RV has endeavoured to express this idiom (originally Hebrew) in English, see Westcott, *Lessons of RV of NT*, p. 32 ff.

גָּאַל is 'to make a claim,' *vindicare*, in the sense of claiming something that has been lost or forfeited, 'to resume a claim or right which has lapsed' (Driver); hence the *goel* is etymologically 'the claimant,' *vindex*, in practice 'the next of kin.' We shall consider the rights and privileges of the *goel*, (i.) in civil and (ii.) in criminal law.

i. In civil law the following were the chief rights and responsibilities of the *goel*. (*a*) When, through stress of circumstances, a Hebrew was compelled to sell part of his patrimony, it was the duty of 'his kinsman that is next to him' (RV)—in ordinary language his next of kin—'to redeem (גָּאַל) that which his brother had sold' (Lv 25²⁵). This duty is in accordance with one of the fundamental ideas at the basis of the Hebrew law of real estate, by which land was the inalienable property of the clan (מִשְׁפָּחָה). According to the priestly legislation, indeed, the clan or tribe in its turn the feudatory of J″, from whom, as the real owner of the soil, the land was held in fee (Lv 25²³). In the particular case under consideration, the various degrees of kinship are not stated, but they were no doubt identical with those laid down for the analogous case next to be considered (under *b*); that is, the right of redemption (מִשְׁפַּט גְּאֻלָּה Jer 32⁷) appertained first to full brothers of the vendor; whom failing or who renouncing, it passed to his uncles on the father's side; whom failing, to their sons, *i.e.* the vendor's cousins on the father's side; whom failing, to 'any that is nigh of kin unto him of his family' (מִשְׁפָּחָה Lv 25⁴⁹). From the historical instance of the purchase by Jeremiah of his cousin Hanamel's property in Anathoth (Jer 32⁸⁻¹²), it appears that the *goel*, or next of kin, had the right of pre-emption, or the right to the refusal of the property before it was exposed in the open market, as well as the right of redemption after it had been sold. In either case the prophet was his cousin's *goel*. Under this head, as it seems to us, must be placed the much-disputed case of Ruth the Moabitess (which many authorities regard as a case of levirate marriage), for the first and chief part of the transaction before the elders of the city (Ru 4¹ff.) is clearly the redemption of the 'parcel of land which was our brother Elimelech's' (4³⁻⁶). To this, the primary duty of the *goel*, the taking of Ruth in marriage is to be regarded as subordinate. Nothing is said of the precise relationship subsisting between Naomi—who here, contrary to the Pentateuchal laws, appears as her husband's heir—and the true *goel*, nor between him and Boaz, to whom, on the former renouncing, the right of redemption fell. Throughout the Bk. of Ruth our translators have rendered the Hebrew *gô'ēl* by 'kinsman.'

(*b*) A second duty of the *goel* in civil law was to redeem, not the property, but the person, of his kinsman, in the event of the latter being compelled by poverty to sell himself as a slave to a stranger or a sojourner (Lv 25⁴⁷⁻⁴⁹). The order in which kinship was to be reckoned has already been given. For the details of the transactions under this and the foregoing head, see the art. JUBILEE. From this function of the *goel* as a 'redeemer' there has proceeded an extensive use of the verb *ga'al* in the sense of 'redeem,' with God Himself for the subject. Thus God is said to redeem Israel from the bondage of Egypt (Ex 6⁶ 15¹³, Ps 74² etc.) and from exile in Babylonia. The idea of J″ as His people's *goel* is a special characteristic of Deutero-Isaiah (41¹⁴ 43¹⁴ 44⁶·²⁴ and oft.), as is the correlated idea of His people as the redeemed (גְּאוּלִים) of J″ (51¹⁰ 62¹² 63⁴, cf. 35⁹).

(*c*) A third duty of the *goel* is mentioned incidentally in the course of an ordinance supplementing a previous law regarding certain cases of restitution (Lv 6¹⁻⁷, MT 5²¹⁻²⁶). The new law provides for a case where the injured person may have died before payment of the conscience-money; in which case the money, it is assumed, is to be paid to the *goel* of the deceased (Nu 5⁸), whom failing, to the priest.

ii. In criminal law the next of kin had laid upon him the duty of enforcing the claim for satisfaction for the blood of a murdered kinsman; in this capacity he received the special name of the *gô'ēl had-dām*, 'the **avenger** (AV also 're-venger') of blood.' The custom of blood-revenge, as it is called, is almost world-wide in its range, and is especially characteristic of society in a certain stage of its development (see esp. the work of A. H. Post, *Entwickelungsgeschichte des Familienrechts*, §§ 15–18 'Die Blutrache,' with the modern literature on p. 113). It rests ultimately on the two fundamental principles of the sacredness of human life (cf. Gn 9⁵·⁶ 'whoso sheddeth man's blood, by man shall his blood be shed'), and the solidarity of the clan or tribe in primitive societies. When, with the advance of civilization and the gradual evolution of the state, the duty of safeguarding the rights of the community passes to the state, blood-revenge is obsolescent or obsolete. Hence blood-revenge as practised by imperfectly organized communities has often been compared to war waged by modern states for the vindication of their rights. The Semitic peoples have practised this custom from prehistoric times, and the earliest Hebrew legislation, that of the Book of the Covenant (see below), found it in full operation. Indeed it is not too much to say that the aim of the Hebrew legislators, from first to last, was so to regulate the practice that the shedder of blood should be, as far as possible, protected from the hasty and unconsidered vengeance of the next of kin, by providing for the judicial investigation of each particular case, and the safe-keeping of the accused until such investigation was completed.

Among the Hebrews, then, in primitive times, the murdered man's next of kin, *i.e.* his *goel*, was bound by tribal custom to avenge his blood by compassing the death, not merely of the murderer himself, but of all his family; for the family was in these early times the unit of society, and so the murderer's guilt was shared by all his family (cf. Jos 7²⁴, 2 K 9²⁶). Such, at least, is the Arab custom, and the law of Dt 24¹⁶ seems first to have limited the responsibility for a crime to the criminal alone (2 K 14⁶). The Book of the Covenant deals with crimes of violence by formulating, first of all, the general principle of a life for a life (Ex 21¹²; cf. Gn 9⁶); it then proceeds to impose an all-important restriction on the exercise of indiscriminate blood-revenge, by emphasizing the distinction between accidental (v.¹³) and deliberate manslaughter (v.¹⁴). In both cases the manslayer is presumed to flee to the altar of the local sanctuary from the vengeance of the *goel* (cf. 1 K 1⁵⁰ 2²⁸); but when deliberate murder has been done, the criminal must forthwith be handed to the *goel* (so we must infer), as the representative, not merely of the kin of the murdered man, but even of God Himself, the Supreme Avenger (Ps 9¹², MT ¹³). This natural distinction between wilful murder and accidental homicide is elaborated in both the later codes (for the legal distinction see **Homicide** and **Murder** under CRIMES AND PUNISHMENTS), which are chiefly distinguished from the older and simpler code above referred to by the provision of the cities of refuge (for which see REFUGE, CITIES OF), where the manslayer was to find protection from the hasty vengeance of the *goel* ('lest the avenger of blood pursue the manslayer *while his heart is hot*,' Dt 19⁶), until it should be decided whether he was guilty of murder or of accidental homicide (Nu 35⁹⁻³⁴, Dt 19¹⁻¹³, Jos 20). Another important restriction consisted in the new proviso that two witnesses, at least, should be required to establish the crime of murder (cf. Nu 35³⁰ with Dt 19¹⁵). The right of pronouncing whether a particular case was one of accidental or intentional homicide seems to have been vested in the elders (Dt 19¹²), as the official representatives of the community (עֵדָה Nu 35¹². ²⁴. ²⁵) to which the accused belonged. The elders of the city of refuge to which he had fled must have formed, according to Jos 20⁴,* a court of first instance. On the accused being, after trial, found guilty of wilful murder, he is handed over to the goel, whose function, as restricted by successive legislation, has now become little more than that of a public executioner. If the verdict, on the other hand, is that of accidental homicide, the congregation (עֵדָה) was authorized 'to deliver the manslayer out of the hand of the avenger of blood,' and to 'restore him to his city of refuge,' where he was obliged to remain till the death of the then high priest (Nu 35²⁵). Until this event the accused was in so far still at the mercy of the goel, that, if he were found by the latter 'beyond the border of his city of refuge,' he might be put to death with impunity (Nu 35²⁶. ²⁷).

A characteristic feature of blood-revenge, as thus regulated by Hebrew legislation, is the very limited extent to which compensation for blood (even when accidentally shed) by a money payment was admitted. Among many widely different peoples, money-compensation—the Greek ποινή, the Saxon wergeld — was legally admitted, but among the Hebrews such compensation or ransom (כֹּפֶר) was expressly forbidden for the case of wilful murder (Nu 35³¹), and was admitted only in the case of a man or woman gored to death by an ox (Ex 21³⁰).

It is impossible to say how long the custom of blood-revenge by means of the goel remained in force among the Hebrews. The case stated by the woman of Tekoa in 2 S 14⁶⁻¹¹ reveals its prevalence in the reign of David, and, at the same time, is instructive as showing how the growing power of the central authority had already begun to exercise a salutary control over this ancient practice. According to the Chronicler, Jehoshaphat required all cases of bloodshed to be brought before the new high court of justice in the capital (2 Ch 19¹⁰); but, unfortunately, we cannot be sure how much of this narrative is historical and how much a reflection of the practice prevailing in the Chronicler's own time (cf. Kittel, Hist. ii. p. 284).

From the technical sense of one enforcing the claims of justice in the special case of bloodshed, as explained above, the term goel in later Hebrew acquired the more general signification of 'advocate,' one who enforces the claim of the oppressed (Ps 119¹⁵⁴) and the orphans (Pr 23¹¹). In this more general sense the word is perhaps to be understood in the difficult passage Job 19²⁵ 'I know that my goel liveth' (see Budde, in loc.).

LITERATURE.—For a modern systematic presentation of the topic discussed under this art. see Nowack's Heb. Archæol. i. Kap. 2, 'Rechtsverhältnisse,' esp. §§ 61 and 64 on Criminal Procedure and Law of Inheritance. For the latter see also Erbrecht in Riehm, HBA², and HEIR in this Dictionary. For inheritance among the Arabs see W. R. Smith, Kinship and Marriage in Early Arabia, Index s. 'Inheritance, Laws of.' On the general subject of Blood-revenge see Kohler, Zur Lehre von der Blutrache, 1885; A. H. Post, Studien zur Entwickelungsgeschichte des Familienrechts, 1890, 6th section, 'Die Blutrache,' pp. 113–136; among the Arabs in particular, Burckhardt, Notes on the Bedouin, etc. i. p. 148 ff.; W. R. Smith, RS p. 33 f., cf. Index, s. 'Blood-revenge'; for the blood feuds of the modern Syrian

* On the composite character of this chapter see the Commentaries of Dillmann and Oettli; and for the difficulties in harmonizing the different provisions with regard to the CITIES OF REFUGE see that article.

fellahin see Baldensperger's notes in PEFSt, 1897, p. 128 ff. On blood-revenge among the Hebrews see the articles 'Blutrache' in Riehm, HBA², and in PRE² (in 3rd edition now being issued the subject is to be treated under 'Gericht'); Bissell, The Law of Asylum in Israel, 1884, and the articles on MURDER and REFUGE (CITIES OF) in this Dictionary, along with the modern commentaries on the relative passages.

A. R. S. KENNEDY.

GOG (גּוֹג).—**1.** The eponymous head of a Reubenite family, 1 Ch 5⁴. **2.** See following article.

GOG (גּוֹג, Γώγ).—The 'prince of Rosh, Meshech, and Tubal,' from 'the land of Magog,' and representative of the northern hordes who were to invade W. Asia in the day 'when Israel dwelleth securely' (Ezk 38. 39, cf. Rev 20⁸). George Smith proposed to see in him Gagi, the ruler of the land of Sakhi, who is mentioned in the annals of the Assyr. king Assurbanipal. But the situation of Sakhi is unknown, and the Heb. name corresponds with that of the Lydian king who is called Gyges by the Greeks, and Gugu in the cuneiform inscriptions. Gyges was the first king of W. Asia Minor who became known to the Assyrians, and consequently his name may perhaps have become a title applied by them to the subsequent kings of that part of the world. The Cimmerians (Gomer) are included in the army of Gog; and as the invasion of Asia Minor by them brought about a great displacement of population, one result being the retreat of the Moschi and Tibareni (Meshech and Tubal) from Cappadocia to the shores of the Black Sea, it is possible that the irruption of the northern barbarians into Syria was connected with that event. (See MAGOG, and cf. Schrader, KAT², and the Comm. of Davidson and Bertholet, ad loc.).

A. H. SAYCE.

GOIIM (גּוֹיִם) is the Heb. word which in EV is variously rendered 'Gentiles,' 'nations,' 'heathen' (see Preface to RV of OT). In the obscure expression in Gn 14¹, where AV has 'king of nations,' RV retains Goiim (possibly a corruption from Guti) as a proper name, although RVm offers the alternative rendering 'nations.' The same difference in rendering between AV and RV is found also in Jos 12²³. See, further, GENTILES, and next article.

GOIIM (גּוֹיִם), 'Nations,' the name of the kingdom of Tidal (Gn 14¹). The name of Tidal has been found by Pinches in a mutilated cuneiform tablet, where it is written Tudghula; and as in another broken tablet of the same series it is said that Kudur-Laghamar or Chedorlaomer, 'the king of Elam,' had 'collected the Umman Manda' or 'barbarian nations' in order to attack Babylon, it seems probable that it was of these Umman Manda that Tudghula was king. They represented the Kurdish tribes on the northern frontier of Elam. (See the paper of Mr. Pinches on Certain Inscriptions and Records referring to Babylonia and Elam, in the Transactions of the Victoria Institute, xxix. 45–81). A. H. SAYCE.

GOLAN (גּוֹלָן).—This appears to have been always a prominent place, and many historical facts about it are known, still its site has never been recovered. It was in Bashan, and belonged to the territory of Manasseh (Dt 4⁴³, cf. Driver, ad loc.). It was a Levitical city and likewise a city of refuge (Jos 20⁸ 21²⁷). About the beginning of our era it is mentioned in connexion with certain battles or sieges, and at that time, if not earlier, it had given its name to a district of such size that the territory was divided into Upper and Lower Gaulanitis, which together formed the E. boundary of Galilee (Jos. Wars, I. iv. 4, 8; III. iii. 1, 5; IV. i. 1; Schürer, HJP I. i. 304 n). The terms 'Upper' and 'Lower' no doubt divided the region from N. to S.; still the upper region is not distinguished by highlands, as might be supposed ; for the entire country, while rolling, maintains a pretty uniform level.

One division of the region E. of the Sea of Galilee is known at present as Jaulân (see Schumacher, *Survey of the Jaulân*, 1888), and this name represents the Gaulanitis of NT times and the Golan of Heb. history. With these indications it might be supposed that the task of recovering the place itself would be an easy one ; but this is a case where modern research does not afford us much help. Nor does any light come from the meaning of the word, something *surrounded*, hence *a district*. Possibly, the political disturbances which visited that country from time to time, and the introduction of other settlers in place of the Jewish inhabitants, have obliterated all traces of the exact locality.

We have an indication in the Talm. (*Makkôth*, 9b), to which prob. some weight should be given, that Golan was due E. of Kedesh-naphtali, or rather that the cities of refuge were situated in pairs over-against each other, E. and W. of the Jordan. As this indication is true in the case of Shechem and Ramoth-gilead, there is no reason why it should not be true also in the other two cases.

The present writer has searched the region pretty thoroughly for the site of this ancient city, but has been unable to decide the question beyond dispute. *Nawâ* has been suggested ; and the objection raised to it, that 'it is much too far to the east,' has no weight, since it is about the same distance to the E. as Ramoth-gilead. It might be a valid objection to say that it is too far south.

It must be remembered that the country just E. of Ramoth-gilead was not thickly settled, and hence was not very wide at that point, while E. of the Sea of Galilee it broadened out to nearly three times that width ; and this would be an imperative reason for appointing, as the N. city of refuge, a place much farther to the E. than either of the others on that side of the river. This fact, together with the indication from the Talmud, would point to *es-Sanamein* as a possible site for Golan. The question of the actual site of this city of refuge is one, however, that is yet to be determined. S. MERRILL.

GOLD.—The essential word for gold in Heb. is *zāhābh* (in Aram. parts of Ezr and Dn *dĕhabh*, Arab. *dhahab*). Four other words occurring in Job are tr⁴ 'gold' in AV, viz. *bezer*, Job 22²⁴, RVm 'ore' (the same word occurs in v.²⁵ ‖ *keseph* 'silver') ; *şĕgôr*, 28¹⁵ ; *pāz*, 28¹⁷ ; and *kethem*, 28¹⁹ (the last two often used elsewhere ; cf. פֶּ֫תֶם אוֹפִ֑יר Job 28¹⁶, Ps 45¹⁰, Is 13¹⁷ ; זָהָב א 1 Ch 29⁴, and אוֹפִיר alone, Job 22²⁴ᵇ). Another word for gold is *hârûz*, the usual Phœn. word, but in Heb. confined to poetry, Ps 68¹³, Pr 3¹⁴ 8¹⁰·¹⁹ 16¹⁶ (Driver, *Text of Samuel*, p. xxviii). It probably comes from a root meaning 'to be yellow.' By some the Phœnician word is thought to be the source of the Gr. χρυσός.

That Syrians early had command of sources of gold is evident from the wealth of gold vessels and ornaments taken by the Egyptians in their depletion of Syria under the 18th dynasty. The gold of Egypt came at first from Nubia, and later from the eastern desert ; but that of Syria probably came from Midian. At the first Midianite war the Israelites are said to have given as an offering about half as many shekels of gold as the girls of the captives taken (Nu 31⁵²). This would imply an offering of about three shekels from each family destroyed, and therefore a much greater wealth as a total. Again, Gideon personally gets 1700 shekels of gold ear-rings from the slaughtered Midianites

(Jg 8²⁶), besides the rich spoil of gold from the royal trappings. That great wealth and ability should have existed there, is very likely, considering the civilization of the Amu on the Egypt. monuments, who probably came thence ; and the conquest of Egypt by foreigners (Khyan, Yakub-el, and others) most likely from the same land. The absence of gold in the looting of Palestine under Joshua (the only piece named being an ingot of fifty shekels at Jericho, Jos 7²¹) is probably due to the thorough exhaustion of the country by repeated pillaging under Ramses III. The quantities of gold mentioned are not at all improbable, looking to the wealth otherwise recorded. Putting amounts roughly into monetary value, we see

Tahutmes III. First year, plunder of Syria	£20,000
Later years, perhaps	30,000
One year from Nubia	28,000
Other years, perhaps	22,000 ?
In one reign received	£100,000 ?
Ramses III. offered to Amen, mainly from Syria, £120,000 ; probably total plunder	1,000,000 ?
Total amount stated for Tabernacle	90,000
Spoil of Midian, offered £16,000 ; total at least	100,000 ?
Gideon (Jg 8²⁶) gets £2000 ; total at least	10,000 ?
Hezekiah gives Sennacherib	90,000

These values will give a general idea of the amounts of gold dealt with in OT accounts, and their relation to the plunder which the Egyptians got in powerful reigns.

There does not appear to be any common word for alloys of gold in Heb.; and probably, therefore, the electrum or gold-silver alloy, so usual in Egypt, was not frequent in Palestine. See also MINING. W. M. FLINDERS PETRIE.

GOLDSMITH is the tr. of צֹרֵף in both AV and RV of Neh 3⁸·³¹·³², Is 40¹⁹ 41⁷ 46⁶, and of RV in Jer 10⁹·¹⁴ 51¹⁷, where AV has 'founder.' From early times elaborate gold work was made in Egypt ; and the exquisite delicacy and finish of the jewellery found at Dahshur, of about B.C. 2500, shows that nothing has been gained in technical ability since that date. The special feature of this jewellery is the *cloisonnée* work of hundreds of minute pieces of coloured stones, each cut to a precise shape, and each inserted in a perfectly fitting socket, made by invisible delicate soldering of thin strips of gold. The preparation of the base, and the cutting of the inserted pieces, are alike beyond anything done in later ages. The same system was employed throughout Egyptian history in varying degrees of delicacy ; and such work must have been the starting-point for Hebrew and Phœnician gold work.

In the account of the tabernacle both cast and beaten gold are mentioned. The hammering out of the lampstand, lamps, and trimmers from one talent of gold is specified particularly (Ex 25³¹ᶠᶠ·). The talent was probably 135 lb. troy, about 160 cubic in. of gold ; allowing 20 cubic in. for the lamps and fittings, and as much for the foot, this would imply (if the whole were about 3 ft. high) that the stem and branches of the lampstand were about ¾ in. thick, including the ornaments. Such a weight, therefore, is quite consistent with this strength required, and the conditions of working such a mass. The form of the lampstand is so familiar from the Arch of Titus that we need not refer to it here. The hammer-work of the two cherubim (Ex 25¹⁸) does not involve any special difficulties, as they were doubtless joined ; and Egyptians were long before this adepts at soldering gold. But there is a question involved in the gold plating of the tabernacle boards (Ex 26²⁹). The total gold used was 29 talents, of which 1 was used for the lampstand, and we must allow at least 2 for the cherubim and mercy-seat. This leaves 26 talents for plating. The area of the boards and bars is about 1860 square cubits, that of the furniture only 54 cubits. This implies that the gold-plating was only $\frac{1}{300}$th of an in. thick. Such would be quite impossibly tender for a skin on heavy weights, such as the boards (which weighed at least 4 cwt. each), unless it were very firmly attached; otherwise, if a nailed sheathing, it would be soon torn by moving. The gilding, therefore, on such a scale as is stated, would need to be by the usual Egyptian method of sticking rather thick gold-foil firmly on to the wooden basis. The ark and altars may have been more thickly plated, as their area was but a small portion of the whole.

The very practical nature of these statements of quantities has an important bearing on the historical character of the account, which we do not enter on here.

The making of wire is expressly described as done by cutting sheet gold into narrow threads (Ex 39[3]); and such wire for embroidery must have drawn somewhat more from the amount of the gold stated above.

One mention in Kings deserves notice. The shields of gold which were carried by the royal bodyguard (1 K 14[26. 27]) weighed 3 manehs each (1 K 10[17]). This is about 16 cubic in., and if the shields were about 2 ft. in diameter they would be but $\frac{1}{10}$th of an in. thick; they were therefore not entirely of gold, but had a back of bronze or wood. Such work is rather implied by the expression 'gold fitted upon the carved work' of the temple doors (1 K 6[35]). It appears to have been *repoussé* work of gold, with a wooden backing to support it and maintain the shape, helped by an intermediate coat of stucco or plaster as in Egyptian work.   W. M. FLINDERS PETRIE.

GOLGOTHA (Γολγοθά, from Heb. גֻּלְגֹּלֶת 'skull,' Aram. גֻּלְגָּלְתָּא).—The Hebrew name of the place where the crucifixion took place, Κρανίον and *Calvaria* being the Greek and Latin equivalents. Calvary is mentioned only in AV of Lk 23[33], being replaced by 'the skull' in the RV.

Mt 27[33] AV 'A place called Golgotha, that is to say, a place of a skull.'
  ,,   RV 'A place called Golgotha, that is to say, the place of a skull.'
Mk 15[22] AV, RV 'The place Golgotha, which is, being interpreted, The place of a skull.'
Lk 23[33] AV 'The place which is called Calvary.'
  ,,   RV 'The place which is called The skull.'
Jn 19[17] AV 'A place called the place of a skull, which is called in the Hebrew, Golgotha.'
  ,,   RV 'The place called the place of a skull, which is called in the Hebrew, Golgotha.'

Three evangelists agree in calling the spot the place 'of a skull,' while St. Luke calls the place 'The skull.' This difference may appear to allow of two explanations as to the name of the locality.

(1) It may have been the place of public execution, where bodies were allowed to be devoured by birds and beasts, etc. (Gn 40[19], 2 K 9[35], Herod. iii. 12), and thus have acquired this name. It was probably distinct from the place of stoning, because at this time the Jewish Sanhedrin, though it could condemn, could not put to death (*Ant.* IX. i. 1), without the intervention of the Roman governor (Jn 18[31] 'The Jews therefore said unto him, It is not lawful for us to put any man to death'). Our Lord was crucified under Pilate for sedition against Cæsar, owing to the clamour of the Jews, in order to avoid a tumult (Mt 27[23]). This method of punishment for this offence among the Jews was common at this time (*Ant.* XVII. x. 10, *BJ* II. xiv. 9). On account of the Jewish law (Dt 21[23]), the corpses of Jewish criminals executed by crucifixion were allowed burial (Mt 27[58], Jn 19[38]); and this was omitted only under very exceptional circumstances, as when the Idumæans, called in

by the Zealots during the civil war at Jerusalem previous to the destruction of the city by the Romans, 'cast away their dead bodies without burial, although the Jews used to take so much care of the burial of men, that they took down those that were condemned and crucified, and buried them before the going down of the sun' (*BJ* IV. v. 2).

(2) The name may have been derived from the appearance of the place itself, from its round and skull-like contour, the Hebrew word Golgotha being applied to the skull from its rounded form. There is no indication, however, in the Bible that Golgotha was a knoll or hillock, and the expression 'Mount Calvary' appears to have come into use after the 5th cent. The *Itiner. Hieros.* speaks of it as 'Monticulus Golgatha.' Rufinus has the expression 'Golgothana rupes' (*Hist. Ecc.* ix. 6), and Bernhard again has 'Mons Calvariæ.' At that time the usage appears to have become fixed, and is found in works of all later pilgrims and writers (Robinson, *BRP*[2] i. p. 376).

The place of execution, both with the Romans and the Jews, was without the city or camp (Plaut. *Mil. Glor.* ii. 4. 6; Dt 17[5], 1 K 21[13], Ac 7[58], He 13[12], Lv 24[14], Nu 15[36]), and accordingly 'the place where Jesus was crucified was nigh to the city' (Jn 19[20]). The use of the definite article '*the* place of a skull,' '*the* place which is called The skull,' indicates that it was a known spot, probably the ordinary place for crucifixion of malefactors. Golgotha was in a conspicuous position, as it is related that multitudes 'came together to this sight,' and it could be seen by those 'who stood afar off' (Mk 15[40], Lk 23[49]); and it was near a highway leading from the country, where people were passing to and fro (Mt 27[39], Mk 15[21. 29], Lk 23[35]). It was also near a garden and tombs (?) : 'Now in the place where he was crucified there was a garden; and in the garden a new tomb, wherein was never man yet laid'; and the tomb was 'nigh at hand' (Jn 19[41]); it was Joseph's 'own new tomb,' the tomb of a rich man of Arimathæa (Mt 27[60]).

The traditions which relate to Golgotha are very numerous, but there are none recorded earlier than the 4th cent. There can be no doubt that the present traditional site of Golgotha is that which was recovered by Constantine, but beyond this there can be no certainty. Eusebius alone of the writers of the 4th cent. describes this circumstance (Euseb. *Life of Constantine*, iii. 25) connected with the finding of the Holy Sepulchre; he was living in Palestine at the time, and was present at the dedication of the Church of the Resurrection, A.D. 335. This is summarized by Besant and Palmer (*Jerusalem*, p. 58) in the following words: 'In the time of Constantine a report existed that the spot then occupied by a temple of Venus was the site of our Lord's burial-place. Constantine took down the temple, meaning to build the church upon it; but, in removing the earth, supposed to be defiled by the idol-worship that had taken place upon it, they found to their extreme astonishment the cave or tomb which is shown to this day. Then came the building of the Basilica.' Most of the historians in the 5th cent. relate the discovery of the Holy Sepulchre with that also of Calvary, and attribute it to the aged empress Helena, the mother of Constantine. 'There is a tradition that Adam was buried under Mount Calvary. This tradition is mentioned and condemned by Jerome (*Comm. in Matth.* lib. iv. c. 27) and other early ecclesiastical writers. But the pilgrims, Breydenbach, Zuallardo, and Cotovicus, not only say that the head of Adam was found here, but some (as Bernardino) would have us believe that it is still to be seen in the fissure of the Apse'

(*The Holy City*, pt. II. ch. iii.). The tradition further went, that at the crucifixion drops of Christ's blood fell on the *skull* of Adam and restored him to life (Mt 27[52, 53], Eph 5[14]; Epiphanius, *Adv. Hær.* xlvi. 5; Sæwulf, *Early Travels in Palestine*, pp. 39, 66; *W. Tyr.* lib. 13, p. 851).

There are many arguments in favour of the traditional site of Golgotha in addition to the tradition already referred to, but, until it can be ascertained whether it is within or without the city wall of the time of Christ, the whole question must still remain in doubt. The road from the tower of Antonia leading into the old road from the city to Jaffa would probably have passed close to the site, and on this road, outside the Jaffa gate, public executions have taken place in quite recent years, up to 1868. There are rock-cut tombs in the immediate neighbourhood, including that of the Holy Sepulchre.

During recent years several sites to the north of the city have been suggested as the site of Golgotha, in order, apparently, to comply with the view that the place of execution should be situated on the north side of the city (Lv 1[10, 11]); but, though this may have been necessary for the Jewish place of stoning, there is nothing to indicate that the place of crucifixion during the Roman occupation was located according to Jewish ritual, or that it was identical with the place of stoning.

A knoll above 'Jeremiah's grotto' has been suggested by Otto Thenius in 1849 (followed by General Gordon, Colonel Conder, and others) as the genuine Calvary, on the ground principally that it is the place of stoning according to modern Jewish tradition.   C. WARREN.

GOLIATH. — The giant whom David slew at Ephes-dammim (1 S 17). In the account of the fight he is spoken of as a Phil. from Gath. He was so politically, but it does not follow that he was of the ordinary Phil. blood. Presumably, he was of the *rephaite* or giant breed, elsewhere spoken of as living at Gath (2 S 21[15-22], 1 Ch 20[4-8]), and was descended from the ancient Avvim or Anakim (see ANAKIM, AVVIM, GIANT, RAPHA, REPHAIM). The Heb. text makes him 6 cubits and a span in height. Josephus and some MSS of the Sept. reduce this to 4 cubits and a span. On general principles the Heb. reading is the more authoritative, and it fits best the figures given for the tremendous weight of his armour and weapons. Counting the cubit at 21 in., this would make him over 11 ft. high, and over 9 ft. high if we count the cubit a handbreadth shorter. If he was measured in his armour, from the ground to the top of his helmet-crest, this is not incredible, though he is probably the largest man of whom we have any authentic record.

The details of the fight are familiar, and need not be repeated here. It is often said that the account is quite Homeric. It is especially so in the boastful speeches the two champions make before the combat begins. The proposed condition of the fight was that the side whose champion was overcome should submit to the other. This was not done, for some reason. Instead, Israel fell upon the Philistines and defeated them with great slaughter. The incident in 2 S 23[9-12], 1 Ch 11[12-14], belongs to this battle, for Pas-dammim (1 Ch 11[13]) is Ephes-dammim; and it shows that the Israelites had hard fighting, and not merely an unresisted pursuit. It also shows that David in later years remembered his first comrades in battle.

The story of David and Goliath is a favourite theme in the Rabbinical and the Arabian literature, where it is illuminated with no end of grotesque and extravagant additions.

The Goliath of 2 S 21[19] is a different person; but see DAVID, vol. i. p. 562[b], ELHANAN, LAHMI.
W. J. BEECHER.

GOMER (גֹּמֶר, Γάμερ, Γόμερ).—**1.** Gomer, the son of Japheth and father of Ashkenaz, Riphath, and Togarmah (Gn 10[2, 3]), is the Gimirrâ of the Assyr. inscriptions, the Cimmerians of the Greeks. The Cimmerians were an Aryan people who inhabited the Crimea and the adjoining districts of southern Russia, and in the 7th cent. B.C. poured through the Caucasus into W. Asia (Herod. iv. 12). They attacked the northern frontier of the Assyr. empire in concert with the Minni, the Medes, the people of Sepharad (Sapardâ), and other populations whose territories they had already overrun; but in B.C. 677 their leader, Teuspa (Teispes), was defeated by Esarhaddon, and they were driven partly eastward, where they overthrew the old kingdom of Ellipi and built Ecbatana, partly westwards into Asia Minor. Here they sacked Sinôpê and Antandros, which they held for 100 years, and finally invaded Lydia. Gyges or Gugu, the Lydian king, sent an embassy to Nineveh for help; in the end, however, he was slain in battle, and his capital, Sardis, captured by the invading hordes. His successor, Ardys, succeeded in exterminating or driving them out of the country. Meanwhile Phrygia had been occupied by them, and the temple of Artemis at Ephesus burned by their leader, Lygdamis (who seems to be the Tugdamme of the inscriptions of the Assyr. king Assurbanipal). Lygdamis was subsequently slain in Cilicia (Strabo, i. 3, 16), but Cappadocia had been so completely conquered by them as to bear henceforward among the Armenians the name of Gamir. In Ezk 38[6] Gomer is included in the army of Gog.

2. The daughter of Diblaim and wife of Hosea (1[3]). See HOSEA.   A. H. SAYCE.

GOMORRAH (עֲמֹרָה, LXX and NT Γομόρρα or Γόμορρα; see Winer-Schmiedel, § 6, 8[b]; Arab. *ghamara*, 'to overwhelm with water').—One of 'the cities of the Plain'; its position along with that of Sodom and the other three is now pretty generally admitted to have been in the Arabah, or plain, which lies to the north of the Dead Sea. Of the five original cities, all but Zoar (or Bela) were destroyed by fire from heaven (Gn 19[23-29]). The situation has been verified by Tristram, who, on placing himself in the required positions, was able to recognize the view described as it was regarded by Lot on selecting his future residence (Gn 13[10]), and by Abraham during the destruction of the doomed cities (19[27]).* According to Josephus the vale became Lake Asphaltitis on the destruction of Sodom (*Ant.* I. ix.), but in another place he indicates that the country of Sodom borders upon it (*Wars*, IV. viii. 4). It has elsewhere been shown that the Dead Sea does not owe its existence to miraculous interposition (see DEAD SEA); and the view that the waters cover the sites of the cities of the Plain is now generally discarded. Certain ruins about a mile from the shore of the Dead Sea north of Râs el-Feshkhah, marked Khumrân (or Gumrân) on the Survey Map of Palestine, have been supposed by de Saulcy to mark the site of Gomorrah, and the position as well as the name lend probability to the view.

Throughout Scripture the cities of the Plain are used as examples of the judgments which fall on nations and cities in consequence of crime, and as warnings to mankind. In the time of Abraham and Lot the wickedness of these cities appears to have reached its climax (Gn 18[20]), and in several

---

* *Land of Israel*[2], pp. 363–366. The arguments of Tristram on this subject appear quite conclusive, and should be studied by those who have not had the opportunities of this writer of personal inspection of the localities.

passages is referred to as an example to be shunned (Jer 23[14], 2 P 2[6], Jude [7]), and a warning for the future (Dt 29[23], Is 1[9] 13[19], Jer 49[18] 50[40], Am 4[11], Ro 9[29]).　But our Lord warns us that the rejection of the gospel message carries with it a greater degree of guilt than that of the cities of the Plain (Mt 10[15]).　　　　　　　　　　　　　E. HULL.

GOOD, GOODS.—The word 'good' is chiefly the rendering in OT of טוֹב, which is a verb, an adj., and a subst.; and in Apocr. and NT chiefly of ἀγαθός and καλός; and its meanings are determined far more by the meanings of those terms than by the native genius of the Eng. language.　In other words, we have to deal with *biblical* English, some of whose peculiarities have been adopted into the common speech, through the influence of AV (though not always in their proper sense), and some have not.

1. As an adj. 'good' is used to express the following ideas :—

1. *Agreeable, pleasant:* Gn 3[6] 'And when the woman saw that the tree was good for food'; 31[24, 29] 'Take heed that thou speak not to Jacob either good or bad'; 49[15] 'And he saw that rest was good'; 1 S 25[8] 'We come in a good day'; 29[9] 'And Achish answered and said to David, I know that thou art good in my sight, as an angel of God'; Job 13[9] 'Is it good that he should search you out?'; Ps 45[1] 'My heart is inditing a good matter'; 133[1] 'Behold, how good and how pleasant it is for brethren to dwell together in unity'; Pr 15[23] 'A word spoken in due season, how good is it!'; 24[13] 'My son, eat thou honey, because it is good'; Ro 16[18] 'By good words and fair speeches [they] deceive the hearts of the simple' (χρηστολογίας καὶ εὐλογίας, RV 'smooth and fair speech,' Sanday-Headlam 'fair and flattering speech'; it is the only occurrence of χρηστολογία in bibl. Greek). In this sense we find 'good tidings' 2 S 18[27], Lk 2[10], 1 Th 3[6]; 'good news' Pr 15[25]; 'good report' Pr 15[30], Ph 4[8] (εὔφημος, Lightfoot, 'winning,' 'attractive').

2. *Of good quality* (as compared with others of its kind), *highly esteemed:* Gn 1[4] 'And God saw the light that it was good'; 2[12] 'And the gold of that land is good'; 43[11] 'Take of the best fruits in the land' (RV 'choice'); 1 K 2[32] 'Who fell upon two men more righteous and better than he, and slew them with the sword'; 10[18] 'Moreover the king made a great throne of ivory, and overlaid it with the best gold' (RV 'finest'); Ps 111[10] 'A good understanding have all they that do his commandments'; Ec 7[1] 'A good name is better than precious ointment' (Heb. 'a name'); Sir 26[21] 'Having the confidence of their good descent'; Mt 7[17] 'Every good tree bringeth forth good fruit'; 12[12] 'How much then is a man better than a sheep?' (RV 'of more value,' Gr. πόσῳ διαφέρει); Lk 5[39] 'No man also having drunk old wine straightway desireth new; for he saith, The old is better' (TR χρηστότερος, most edd. χρηστός whence RV 'good'); Ac 10[22] 'of good report' (Gr. μαρτυρούμενος, RV 'well reported of'); 23[1] 'I have lived in all good conscience' (πάσῃ συνειδήσει ἀγαθῇ); 1 Co 12[31] 'Covet earnestly the best gifts' (TR κρείττονα; edd. μείζονα, RV 'greater'); Ph 2[3] 'Let each esteem others better than themselves'; 1 Ti 3[7] 'To have a good report'; Ja 2[3] 'Sit thou here in a good place' (κάθου ὧδε καλῶς).

3. *Profitable, advantageous:* Pr 31[18] 'She perceiveth that her merchandise is good' (RV 'profitable'); Ec 9[4] 'A living dog is better than a dead lion'; 10[11] 'and a babbler is no better' (RV 'then is there no advantage in the charmer'); Mt 18[6] 'It were better for him that a millstone were hanged about his neck' (RV 'it is profitable'); Lk 14[34] 'Salt is good.'　And the phrase 'good for nothing' Jer 13[10], Wis 13[10], Mt 5[13].

4. *Befitting, appropriate:* Gn 40[16] 'When the chief baker saw that the interpretation was good'; Ru 2[22] 'It is good, my daughter, that thou go out with his maidens'; 2 S 17[7] 'The counsel that Ahithophel hath given is not good at this time'; Pr 19[2] 'That the soul be without knowledge, it is not good'; Ec 7[11] 'Wisdom is good with an inheritance'; Mt 17[4] 'It is good for us to be here'; Mk 14[21] 'Good were it for that man if he had never been born'; 1 Co 5[6] 'Your glorying is not good.'

5. *Happy, prosperous:* Ps 112[5] 'A good man showeth favour' (טוֹב־אִישׁ חוֹנֵן, RV 'Well is it with the man that dealeth graciously'; Perowne, 'Happy is the man'; but AV may have understood the word in the moral sense).　In OT טוֹב is an epithet of the heart, but EV tr. otherwise : 1 K 12[7] ‖ 2 Ch 10[7] 'glad'; Est 5[9] 'glad'; Pr 5[15] AV 'merry,' RV 'cheerful'; Ec 9[7] 'merry.' But we find in Apocr., Sir 30[25] 'A cheerful and good heart will have a care of his meat and diet'; and Bar 4[30] 'Take a good heart, O Jerusalem.' Cf. the phrase 'of good cheer' (= in old Eng. 'of happy countenance,' since the 'cheer' was the 'face'), generally as an imperative, 'Be of good cheer!' Est 15[9], Wis 18[6], Bar 4[5], Mt 9[2] 14[27], Mk 6[50], Jn 16[33], Ac 23[11] 27[25]; but also Ac 27[22] 'I exhort you to be of good cheer'; 27[36] 'Then were they all of good cheer'; and, in a somewhat different sense, Sir 18[32] 'Take not pleasure in much good cheer.' So Herbert, *Temple*, 'Employment,' 16—

　'Life is a businesse, not good-cheer.'

6. *Kind, gracious:* 1 S 25[15] 'But the men were very good unto us, and we were not hurt'; 2 Ch 30[18] 'The good LORD pardon every one'; Ps 86[5] 'For thou, Lord, art good, and ready to forgive'; Nah 1[7] 'The LORD is good, a stronghold in the day of trouble'; Sir 35[8] 'Give the Lord his honour with a good eye' (ἐν ἀγαθῷ ὀφθαλμῷ); 2 Mac 11[6] 'They and all the people with lamentation and tears besought the Lord that he would send a good angel to deliver Israel'; Tit 2[5] 'Keepers at home, good, obedient to their own husbands' (RV 'kind'). Cf. Milton, *Lycidas*, 184—

　'Henceforth thou art the genius of the shore, In thy large recompense, and shalt be good To all that wander in that perilous flood.'

And *PL* viii. 651—

　'Thou to Mankind
　Be good and friendly still, and oft return!'

7. *Upright, righteous,* morally and religiously good: 1 S 12[23] 'I will teach you the good and the right way'; Mic 6[8] 'He hath showed thee, O man, what is good'; 7[2] 'The good man is perished out of the earth'; Mt 5[45] 'He maketh his sun to rise on the evil and on the good.'

8. Of quantity, *considerable:* 'A good way off,' Gn 21[16], Mt 8[30]; 'a good way from,' Jg 18[22]; 'for a good space,' 2 Mac 7[5]; 'a good while,' Gn 46[29], Ac 18[18].　But 'good measure' (Lk 6[38]) is 'abundant measure'; and to 'give good ear' (Wis 8[12]) is to be very attentive.　In 2 Es 16[21] occurs the phrase 'good cheap,' 'Behold, victuals shall be so good cheap upon earth, that they shall think themselves to be in good case' (so RV; Lat. *erit annonæ vilitas*).　'Cheap' is from the Anglo-Saxon *céap*, a market, a price; and Abbott (*Shaks. Grammar*, 132) thinks the phrase may arise from the omission of the prep. : 'good cheap'='at a good price' (for the buyer), 'at a bargain,' as in Shaks. *III Henry VI.* v. iii. 14—

　'The queen is valued thirty thousand strong';

Merch. of Venice, III. i. 57—'He hath disgraced me and hindered me half a million.' But the oldest explanation is to refer the phrase to the French *bon marché*. So Palsgrave (1530), Introd. 49,

'*Marché*, a bargene or a marketstede or cheepe, as good cheepe, *bon marchie*.' And this is the explanation accepted by Murray (*Oxf. Eng. Dict. s.v.* 'cheap'). That the prep. may go with it, however, is shown by Caxton, *Chron. Eng.* ccxvii. 205, 'They toke the kynges prises for hir peny worthes at good chepe.' The meaning is simply 'che, ᵽ' (that word being now an adj., which was forme, ᵗly a subst., a somewhat rare change in English). Thus Sir D. Lindsay, ii. 197—

> 'To sell richt deir, and by gude-chaip,
> And mix ry-meill amang the saip,
> And saiffrone with oyl-dolie.'

The phrase is not uncommon in early authors: Lever, *Sermons*, 1550 (Arber's ed. p. 130), 'For they that be true merchauntemen to by and sell in dede, shoulde and doo provide great plentye and good chepe by honest byenge and sellynge of theyr wares'; Rutherford, *Letters* (cxvi.), 'Law and justice are to be had by any, especially for money and moyen; but Christ can get no law, good cheap or dear'; and Herbert, *Temple*, 'Providence,' 97—

> 'Hard things are glorious, easie things good cheap.'

'Better cheap' was also used, as Lever in the same sermon as above (p. 130), 'Take awaye leasmongers, regrators and all suche as by byinge and sellynge make thyngs more dere, and when they be gone, all thyngs wylbe more plentye and better chepe.' So Rutherford, *Letters* (ccxv.), 'I trow that (if I were as I have been since I was his prisoner) I would beg lodging for God's sake in Hell's hottest furnace, that I might rub souls with Christ. But God be thanked, I shall find him in a better lodging. We get Christ better cheap than so.'

In He 11¹² occurs 'as good as dead,' another phrase in which 'good' is used to express extent, quantity rather than quality. The Gr. is simply the perf. ptcp. of the verb (νενηκρωμένος), which in Ro 4¹⁹, in a precisely parallel passage and construction, is trᵈ in AV simply 'dead,' but RV gives 'as good as dead' there also. The phrase is from Tindale, whom most versions follow; but Wyc. has 'nygh deed,' Gen. 'dead,' Rhem. 'quite dead.' It is good idiomatic Eng., though Moon (*Revisers' English*, p. 126) speaks of 'the strange contradiction in the use of the word *good* for *bad*'; but it probably expresses less emphasis now than formerly. Cf. Tindale's use of 'a good' for 'in good earnest,' 'thoroughly,' Dt 9²¹ 'And I toke youre synne, the calfe which ye had made, and burnt him with fire and stampe him and grounde him a good, even unto smal dust.'

2. The uses of 'good' as a subst. may be given under three heads:

1. Material Possessions, *goods*: Gn 45²⁰ 'The good of all the land of Egypt is yours'; 1 Ch 29³ 'I have of mine own proper good, of gold and silver' (RV 'I have a treasure of mine own of gold and silver'); 1 Jn 3¹⁷ 'Whoso hath this world's good' (τὸν βίον τοῦ κόσμου, RV 'this world's goods'). Cf. Chaucer, *Parlement of Foules*, 462—

> 'And but I bere me in hir servyse
> As wel as that my wit can me suffyse,
> Fro poynt to poynt, hir honour for to save,
> Tak she my lyf, and all the good I have.'

So Ex 22⁸ Tind. 'Yf the thefe be not founde, then the goodman of the housse shalbe brought unto the goddes and swere, whether he have put his hande unto his neighbours good'; Dn 11¹³ Cov. 'For the kinge of the north shal . . . come forth . . . with a mighty hoost and exceadinge greate good' (רְכוּשׁ, AV 'riches,' RV 'substance'); and Adams, *Practical Works*, i. 52, 'His heart is proportionably enlarged with his house: his good and his blood riseth together.' But in this sense the

expression is more frequently 'goods' or 'good things,' as Ec 5¹¹ 'When goods increase, they are increased that eat them'; Gn 45²³ 'Ten asses laden with the good things of Egypt.'

2. Material and moral blessing, *benefit*: Ps 119¹²² 'Be surety for thy servant for good'; Ec 5¹¹ 'What good is there to the owners thereof?' Ad. Est 15¹⁰ 'Who saved our life and continually procured our good'; Wis 5⁸ 'What good hath riches with our vaunting brought us?' Sir 2⁹ 'Ye that fear the Lord, hope for good'; 2 Mac 11¹⁵ 'Then Maccabeus consented to all that Lysias desired, being careful of the common good' (τοῦ συμφέροντος φροντίζων); Ro 15² 'Let every one of us please his neighbour for his good to edification' (RV 'for that which is good.' Cf. Shaks. *As You Like It*, II. i. 17—

> 'And this our life, exempt from public haunt,
> Finds tongues in trees, books in the running brooks,
> Sermons in stones, and good in everything.'

In this sense we find 'good things' in Sir 39²⁵ 'For the good are good things created.' And the phrase 'to come of good' occurs 2 Mac 14³⁰ 'Perceiving that such sour behaviour came not of good, he gathered together not a few of his men, and withdrew himself from Nicanor' (ἀπὸ τοῦ βελτίστου). Cf. Shaks. *Henry V.* IV. viii. 4—'Captain, I beseech you now, come apace to the king; there is more good toward you, peradventure, than is in your knowledge to dream of.'

3. Moral or spiritual good, *goodness*: Gn 2⁹ 'the tree of [RV adds 'the'] knowledge of good and evil'; Ps 14¹·³ 'There is none that doeth good'; Is 7¹⁵·¹⁶ 'to refuse the evil, and choose the good'; 2 Es 2¹⁴ 'I have broken the evil in pieces, and created the good'; Sir 33¹⁴ 'Good is set against evil, and life against death'; Ro 3⁸ 'Let us do evil, that good may come'; He 5¹⁴ 'those who by reason of use have their senses exercised to discern good and evil.' In this sense 'the good' sometimes is plu., 'good persons,' as Pr 14¹⁹ 'The evil bow before the good' (טֹבִים); sometimes, however, sing., as Sir 12⁷ 'Give unto the good (τῷ ἀγαθῷ), and help not the sinner.'

These different meanings of 'good' are all illustrated in the history of the interpretation of Ps 16². The Mass. Heb. is טוֹבָתִי בַּל־עָלֶיךָ; its translations may be ranged in three classes according as טוֹב 'good' is understood.

1. *Goods*: LXX ὅτι τῶν ἀγαθῶν μου οὐ χρείαν ἔχεις [B omits whole clause]; Arab. 'And indeed thou needest not my goods'; Vulg. 'Quoniam bonorum meorum non eges'; Wyc. [1380] 'For of my goodis thou nedist not'; [1388] 'For thou hast no need of my goodis'; Cov. 'My goodes are nothinge unto me,' followed by Rog., Cran., Bish.; Dou. 'Because thou needest not my goodes,' with marg. note, 'Christ's passion was not needful nor profitable to God but to man'; Burgess, 'My goods are at thy disposal' (reading בַּעְלְךָ 'lorded over [owned] by thee' for בַּל־עָלֶיךָ 'not over thee').

2. *Good*: Syr. 'My good is from thee'; Symm. ἀγαθόν μου οὐκ ἔστιν ἄνευ σοῦ; Jerome, 'Bene mihi non est sine te'; D. Kimchi, 'My good is not (obligatory) upon thee'; Ewald, 'Thou art my highest good!'; J. A. Alexander, 'My happiness is not independent of thee'; Del. 'Besides thee there is for me no weal'; Perowne, 'I have no good beyond thee,' who is followed by RV, Jennings, and Kirkpatrick; Kay, 'My prosperity has no claims on thee'; Thrupp, 'My happiness! there is naught in comparison of thee'; Cheyne, 'Without thee my welfare is naught'; or (Parchment ed.) 'Welfare have I none without thee'; De Witt, 'I have naught that is good beside thee'; Segond, 'Tu es mon souverain bien!' Kautzsch, 'Es giebt für mich kein Gut ausser dir!' Wildeboer (in *Feestbundel aan Prof. M. J. de Goeje*, Leiden, 1891 : see Cheyne in *Expos. Times*, iii. 164, and in *Expos.* III. Ser. v. 78), 'Thou art the good of [the people which thy prophet called] thy wedded one' (reading בְּעֻלָתְךָ); but later (in *Theol. Tijdschrift*, Nov. 1893 : see Taylor in *Expos. Times*, v. 384), 'Thou art my Lord, the treasure of her whom thou hast married' (reading בְּעַלָתֶךָ); King, 'My good, beyond which there is none.'

3. *Goodness*: Aq. ἀγαθωσύνη μου οὐ μὴ ἐπὶ σέ; Gen. (after Calvin), 'My welldoing extendeth not to thee' (with marg. note, 'Thogh we can not enriche God, yet we must bestowe God's gifts to the use of his children'); J. Kimchi, 'The good which I am doing does not extend so far as thee'; AV, 'My goodness *extendeth* not to thee'; Ost. 'Le bien que je fais ne *vient* point jusqu' à toi'; Sharpe (p. 8), 'My goodness! nothing beside thee' [is good], but (p. 151), 'Adonai art thou, O my goodness,

there is nothing beside thee to the holy who are in the land'
(p. 387, 'to the saints who are in the earth').

The word **goods** had formerly a wider application than it has now. Thus Dt 28[11] 'And the LORD shall make thee plenteous in goods'; 2 Ch 21[14] 'Behold with a great plague will the LORD smite thy people, and thy children, and thy wives, and all thy goods.' RV changes 'goods' of AV into some other word in the foll. places: Gn 24[10] 'all the goods of his master were in his hand' (כָּל־טוֹב, RV 'all goodly things,' RVm as AV); 31[18] 'And he carried away all his cattle, and all his goods which he had gotten' (רְכֻשׁוֹ אֲשֶׁר רָכָשׁ, RV 'all his substance which he had gathered'); Nu 35[3] 'the suburbs of them shall be for their cattle, and for their goods' (לִרְכֻשָׁם, RV 'for their substance'); Dt 28[11] 'plenteous in goods' (לְטוֹבָה, RV 'for good'); 2 Ch 21[14] 'all thy goods' (רְכוּשֶׁךָ כָּל, RV 'all thy substance'); Neh 9[25] 'houses full of all goods' (כָל־טוּב מְלֵאִים, RV 'full of all good things'); Job 20[10] 'his hands shall restore their goods' (אוֹנוֹ, RV 'his wealth'); 20[21] 'therefore shall no man look for his goods' (טוּבוֹ לֹא־יָחִיל אֵין־שָׂרִיד, RV 'Therefore his prosperity shall not endure'); Zeph 1[13] 'their goods shall become a booty' (חֵילָם, RV 'their wealth'); Sir 14[5] 'he shall not take pleasure in his goods' (ἐν τοῖς χρήμασιν αὐτοῦ, RV 'in his possessions'); Mt 24[47] 'Verily I say unto you, That he shall make him ruler over all his goods' (ἐπὶ πᾶσι τοῖς ὑπάρχουσιν αὐτοῦ, RV 'over all that he hath'); Lk 15[12] 'the portion of goods that falleth to me' (τὸ ἐπιβάλλον μέρος τῆς οὐσίας, RV 'the portion of *thy* [RVm 'the'] substance'); He 10[34] 'took joyfully the spoiling of your goods' (τῶν ὑπαρχόντων ὑμῶν, RV 'your possessions'); Rev 3[17] 'I am rich, and increased with goods' (πεπλούτηκα, RV 'have gotten riches').   J. HASTINGS.

GOOD, CHIEF.—According to Scripture, the chief good for man is of a moral and spiritual nature. The fact that man was made in the image of God (Gn 1[27]) is determinative. God is the highest and best of beings; and man, His image, while recognizing the relative goodness which is conveyed through material blessings, *e.g.*, discerns the chief good, that which answers to our deepest needs, and leads us to the goal which our own nature establishes for us, in the region of the unseen, the spiritual and divine. God is revealed in the OT as holy, and Israel is chosen to be a holy people to Himself. The chief good is thus secured to the nation as a nation, by faithfulness in worshipping the God of Israel and in keeping His law. It consists in God's favour and friendship, and victorious aid against the nation's enemies; it appears in the acquisition of blessings which, in the absence of a clearly conceived doctrine of immortality, can only take the form of worldly prosperity (Dt 28[1ff.]). The enigmas with which faith is often confronted, if it remains at any such low stage of development, are exemplified in the Bk. of Job; but there too, as we see, the struggle for light and peace goes on, not without success.

At all times the individual must have had his personal religious needs, and God must have had a regard for him, simultaneously with the favour which He showed to Israel. Accordingly, in many parts of OT a supreme good is represented as brought near to the soul of the godly person. It is obtained by worshipping the true God, and turning from sin to the righteousness of the law; and so healthful and comforting is it in the experience of its possessor that it is described by a special term, *blessedness*, a mode of designation which is still preserved. Other good things procure for men a measure of happiness, but only the chief good of religion confers blessedness (Ps 1. 23. 32[1, 2], Pr 3, Is 55, etc.). The overthrow of the

Jewish nation at the period of the Captivity taught the members that if a true blessing was thereafter to be looked for at all, it must be sought by pious individuals in the privacy of their own souls, and in the pursuit of righteous purposes such as God could approve (Jer 31[31ff.], Ezk 18).

Christ came preaching the kingdom of God. Men were invited to seek first the kingdom of God and His righteousness. In that case they might have nothing, but yet they would have all; they should trust their Father in heaven, and suppress anxiety (Mt 6[31ff.]). But, again, the Infinite Spirit is not sufficiently known even to the heart that turns to Him as Father. Christ has declared Him. Jesus was perfectly righteous in His human circumstances, and presented in Himself a copy of the divine nature which is level to our apprehension. In seeking the perfect blessing, men have thus to learn of Christ (Mt 11[29]), to acknowledge Him as the Light of the world (Jn 8[12]), to receive Him as the Bread that came down from heaven (Jn 6[27ff.]), etc. Further, the righteousness and love of Christ were proved to be invincible and infinite by His voluntary endurance of death. The fullest revelation of divine goodness is seen in the cross of Christ, and through it man obtains the chief good, viz. full forgiveness, and power to live a life which approaches the perfect standard (1 Co 1[18ff.], Gal 6[14], Eph 2[18ff.], Col 1[9ff.], He 12[1ff.], 1 P 2[19ff.]).

It is implied in Scripture that material possessions and intellectual advancement are good, and are legitimate objects of desire and pursuit. It is even an imperative duty to seek them, the obligation of the Christian being to do the most good he can, and therefore to call into requisition the best means attainable. People should use the world (1 Th 4[11]), and if any will not work, neither ought he to eat (2 Th 3[10]). Men require to be not slothful in business (Ro 12[11]). It follows that the intellect, which enables us to subdue the world, ought to be cultivated. But then all powers and possessions have to be subordinate to the paramount aims of Christian love and righteousness. The chief end and privilege of man is to glorify God (Col 3[17], 1 P 4[10, 11]).

The chief good which is attainable by man in this world is only relatively to be so described. A Christian spirit is indeed better than all riches; it knows a peace which the world cannot give or take away (Jn 14[27]); its faith overcomes the world (1 Jn 5[4]); and through Christ, its Light, it derives instruction and blessing from everything that affects it, and often, as it were, sees heaven opened (2 Co 3[18]). Hence it finds all gloomy pessimistic views of life unwarrantable. But sin and pain survive till death, even in all believers. A good which is absolute and unqualified is not to be tasted therefore on earth. The Christian, however, has the comfort and stimulus of the highest hope. A good which is perfect is anticipated as the reward of the glorified saints. It consists in their everlasting service of God (Rev 7[15ff.] 21[3, 4]).   G. FERRIES.

GOODLY, GOODLINESS.—Though 'goodly' was at one time used adverbially also, it is employed in AV as an adj. only. There is it found with two different meanings (and the mod. meaning, *considerable, pretty large*, 'a goodly number,' is not one of them).

1. Fair to look upon, fine, handsome. In this sense it is applied to *persons*, as Gn 39[6] 'Joseph was *a goodly person*, and well favoured';* of

* Tindale's trn; Heb. יְפֵה תֹאַר, lit. 'fair of form'; LXX καλὸς τῷ εἴδει; Vulg. 'pulchra facie,' and Wyc. 'fayr in face,' which limit the meaning, the same epithet being used of fruit (Jer 11[16]); RV 'comely.' The Heb. epithet is often used of women, as of Rachel (Gn 29[17], where the whole phrase is exactly the same as is used here of Joseph, EV 'Rachel was beautiful and well favoured'), of Abigail (1 S 25[3], where EV give 'of a beautiful

garments, as Ex 39²⁸ 'goodly bonnets of fine linen'; of trees, as Ps 80¹⁰ 'the boughs thereof were like the goodly cedars' (אַרְזֵי־אֵל, lit. as AVm and RV 'cedars of God'); of cities (Dt 6¹⁰), mountains (Dt 3²⁵), horses (Zec 10³); and not only of majestic things, but of vessels (2 Ch 36¹⁰·¹⁹), precious stones (Mt 13⁴⁵, Lk 21⁵), and even 'heritages' (Ps 16⁶, Jer 3¹⁹). It is also used of a price (Zec 11¹³) paid for a slave, 'a handsome price!' spoken ironically there. In illustration we have Cov. using the word of Jerusalem, Ezk 16¹³ 'marvelous goodly wast thou and beutifull, yee even a very Queene wast thou'; and of Tyre, 27⁴ 'thy builders have made the marvelous goodly.' The Douay describes a cup so, Ps 23⁵ 'Thou hast fatted my head with oyle: and my chalice inebriating how goodlie is it!' and Bacon horse-trappings (Essays, 'Of Masques,' p. 158), 'For Justs and Tourneys and Barriers, the glories of them are chiefly . . . in the Goodly Furniture of their Horses and Armour.' Fuller illustrates 2 S 23²¹ 'he slew an Egyptian, a goodly man' (lit., says Kirkpatrick, 'a man of appearance,' a notable man, which is explained in 1 Ch 11²³ to mean 'a man of great stature,' with the addition 'five cubits high'), when he says (Holy Warre, II. vii. p. 51), 'And though the Goths had a law, alwayes to choose a short thick man for their King; yet surely a goodly stature is most majesticall.'

2. Fair in speech, agreeable : Gn 49²¹ 'Naphtali is a hind let loose: he giveth goodly words' (אִמְרֵי־שָׁפֶר, a difficult passage, see Spurrell: the EV comes from Tindale, and is a good trⁿ of the MT).* Cf. T. Lever, Sermons (Arber's ed. p. 73), 'Iudas pretence was wondrous goodly, to sell the oyntment for a great summe of money, to relieve the poore with.'

The compar. and superl. of the adj. are also used in AV, 1 S 9² 'And he had a son whose name was Saul, a choice young man and a goodly: and there was not among the children of Israel a goodlier person than he'; 1 S 8¹⁶ 'your goodliest young men'; 1 K 20³ 'thy wives also and thy children, even the goodliest, are mine'; 1 Mac 8⁸ 'the goodliest countries.' So Shaks. Tempest, I. ii. 483—

'I have no ambition
To see a goodlier man.'

Chaucer, Troilus, ii. 880—

'Ma dame, y-wis, the goodlieste mayde
Of greet estat in al the toun of Troye.'

The subst. **goodliness** occurs but once, in a beautiful passage where it is a most appropriate translation, Is 40⁶ 'All flesh is grass, and all the goodliness thereof is as the flower of the field.' The meaning of the Eng. word (which comes from the Bishops' Bible) is evidently 'that which makes it fair to look upon,' beauty, charm, as in Hooker, Eccles. Polity, v. 15, 'What travail and cost was bestowed that the goodliness of the temple might be a spectacle of admiration to all the world!' The RV retains the word. But the Heb. is חֶסֶד ḥesed, which everywhere else (and it is very common) means kindness. Nearly all mod. commentators (Ges., Hitzig, Del., Nägels., Cheyne, Dillm., Orelli, and Oxf. Heb. Lex.) accept this solitary instance as sufficient, supporting it by saying, as Cheyne, that its synonym ḥēn has the double sense of favour and gracefulness. So Cov. 'bewtie'; Gen. 'grace'; and apparently Ja 1¹¹ εὐπρέπεια. On the other hand, LXX gives δόξα; Vulg. 'gloria,' after which Wyc. and Dou. 'glorie,' and so the verse is quoted in 1 P 1²⁴: hence Lowth emends countenance,' Gen. simply 'beautiful,' LXX again ἀγαθῷ τῷ εἴδει σφόδρα), and of Esther (Est 27 יְפַת־תֹּאַר וְטוֹבַת מַרְאֶה, EV 'fair and beautiful,' AVm 'fair of form and good of countenance').

* The reading of most VSS and edd. is, 'Naphtali is a slender terebinth giving forth goodly boughs'; but G. A. Smith, in Expos. IV. Ser. vii. 166, prefers the MT, saying that it is 'beautifully expressive of a people in the position of Naphtali.'

the Heb. to הוֹרוּ, and Ewald to כְּבֹרוּ (whom Briggs follows), getting 'the glory thereof,' which does not seriously alter the translation or the meaning. Salmond (on 1 P 1²⁴) happily illustrates the thought from Landor: 'There are no fields of amaranth on this side the grave; there are no voices, O Rhodopè, that are not soon mute, however tuneful; there is no name, with whatever emphasis of passionate love repeated, of which the echo is not faint at last.'   J. HASTINGS.

GOODMAN.—The ordinary word for a 'man' in Heb. (אִישׁ) is once trᵈ 'goodman' in AV, Pr 7¹⁹ 'the goodman is not at home.' This has passed from Cov. through the Bishops' to AV, and it is accepted by RV. The Gen. and Dou. have 'my husband is not at home'; and so Wyc. 1388, 'myn hosebonde is not in his hows'; but 1382, 'Thir is not a man in hir house,' after Vulg. 'Non est enim vir in domo sua.' This is exactly how the word 'goodman' has been used in Scotland from the beginning of written speech at least, and how it is in constant use still. Jamieson quotes from Douglas, Virgil, 255, 14—

'To Vulcanis hir husband and gudeman,
Within his goldin chalmer scho began
Thus for to speik.'

Once Shaks. uses the word in the same sense, putting it into the mouth of the low-born Christopher Sly, Taming of the Shrew, Ind. ii. 107—

'Sly. Where is my wife?
Page. Here, noble lord: what is thy will with her?
Sly. Are you my wife, and will not call me husband?
My men should call me lord: I am your goodman.'

The word is found also in NT as trⁿ of οἰκοδεσπότης, 'master of the house.' This Gr. word occurs 12 times in the Synoptics and nowhere else (Mt 10²⁵ 13²⁷·¹¹ 20¹·¹¹ 21³³ 24⁴³, Mk 14¹⁴, Lk 12³⁹ 13²⁵ 14²¹ 22¹¹: in the last passage τῆς οἰκίας is added). The Vulg. rendered by 'paterfamilias' everywhere except Mk 14¹⁴ 'dominus domus,' and so Wyc. gave 'housbond man' everywhere except Mk 14¹⁴ 'lord of the hous.' Tindale introduced the phrase 'goodman of the house,' using it everywhere except Mt 10²⁵ 'lorde of the housse,' 13²⁷·⁵² 20¹ 21³³ 'householder.' Cov. preferred 'good man of the house' in Mt 10²⁵, and 'householder' in 20¹¹; otherwise he followed Tind., whom the rest of the versions before the Rhemish copied exactly. The Rhem. gives 'householder' in Mt 13⁵² 20¹ 21³³, Lk 12³⁹; 'master of the house' in Mk 14¹⁴, Lk 14²¹; elsewhere 'goodman of the house.' AV follows Tind. except in Mt 10²⁵, Lk 13²⁵ 'master of the house.' The result is sometimes curious. Thus, as Trench points out, in the parable of the Labourers in the Vineyard, the 'householder' of Lk 20¹ becomes the 'goodman of the house' in 20¹¹. RV has redressed this anomaly, but still presents three different translations of the word, 'master of the house' in Mt 10²⁵ 24⁴³, Lk 12³⁹ 13²⁵ 14²¹; 'householder' in Mt 13²⁷·⁵² 20¹·¹¹ 21³³; and 'goodman of the house' in Mk 14¹⁴, Lk 22¹¹.

The word is a combination of 'good' and 'man' (not, says Skeat, a corruption of Anglo-Sax. gumman as suggested by Aldis Wright); and it is probable that the meaning 'master' arose from the meaning 'husband,' in which, it must be remembered, it is one of many similar combinations, as good-father, good-sister, etc.; in fact, all relatives by marriage were once so designated in England, and are still so designated in Scotland. How completely the adj. portion was swallowed up in the complete word * is illustrated by Trench

* Being now one word, 'goodman' should be accented, as Earle remarks (Philology, p. 616), on the first syllable, like chapman, and so distinguished from the two separate words 'good man.' In AV of 1611, however, it is given as 'good man' everywhere except Pr 7¹⁹ and Lk 22¹¹ where it is 'good-man.'

(*On the AV of the NT*, p. 96) in the line from Golding's *Ovid*, i.—

> 'The goodman seeks the goodwife's death.'

But it often furnished a word-play : Thus Cotgrave, *Dict. s.v.* ' Maistre '—' Also a title of honour (such as it is) belonging to all artificers, and tradesmen ; whence Maistre Pierre, Maistre Jehan, etc. ; which we give not so generally but qualify the meaner sort of them (especially in countrey townes) with the title of goodman (too good for many).' So Shaks. *Twelfth Night*, IV. ii. 141—

> 'Like a mad lad,
> Pare thy nails, dad ;
> Adieu, goodman devil.'

And Fuller, *Holy State*, ' as he is called goodman, he desires to answer to the name, and to be so indeed.' Tindale uses the word once in the Pent., Ex 22⁸ ' the goodman of the housse shal be brought unto the goddes ' (בַּעַל־הַבַּיִת, EV ' the master of the house '). Rutherford more than once describes Christ as ' the goodman of this house, His dear Kirk.'   J. HASTINGS.

GOODNESS.—See GOOD and RIGHTEOUSNESS.

GOPHER WOOD (עֲצֵי־גֹפֶר *'ăẓê-ḡôpher*, ξύλα τετράγωνα, *ligna lævigata*, Gn 6¹⁴).—We have no clue for the etymology of the cognate dialects as to the kind of tree referred to. Celsius (*Hierob.* i. 328) argues that it is the *cypress*, from the similarity of sound between *gopher* and κυπάρισσος. Vossius argues that it was a *resinous tree*, from the similarity of sound between גֹפֶר and כֹּפֶר ' resin.' Dillmann opposes Lagarde's view that גֹפֶר is a contraction or clerical error for גָּפְרִית *gophrith* = ' pitch.' In any case it was a wood suitable for shipbuilding, and the ark was constructed of it. In *ZATW*, 1898, Heft i. p. 163, Cheyne suggests that the cuneiform phrase which underlies Gn 6¹⁴ was misunderstood, but that some variety of cedar is intended.   G. E. POST.

GORGET.—In 1 S 17⁶ Goliath is described as having ' a target of brass between his shoulders '; in the marg. it is a ' gorget.' The ' gorget ' was a piece of armour for protecting the gorge or throat. Spenser has the word in *FQ* IV. iii. 12—

> 'His weasand-pipe is through his gorget cleft.'

And Jonson, *Catiline*, iv. 2 (Cæsar pointing to Cicero)—

> 'See how his gorget peers above his gown,
> To tell the people in what danger he was.'

Sir Walter Scott has it in *Woodstock* (Ch. I.), and in the *Lay*, v. 22—

> 'Undo the visor's barred band,
> Unfix the gorget's iron clasp,
> And give him room for life to gasp.'
                                            J. HASTINGS.

GORGIAS (Γοργίας).—A general of Antiochus Epiphanes, who is described as ' a mighty man of the king's Friends ' (1 Mac 3³⁸), and a captain who ' had experience in matters of war ' (2 Mac 8⁹). When Antiochus set out on his Parthian campaign (B.C. 166 or 165), his chancellor, Lysias, who was charged with the suppression of the revolt in Pal., despatched a large army to Judæa under the command of Ptolemy, Nicanor, and Gorgias. The Syrians met the Jews under Judas Maccabæus at the entrance to the hill-country of Judæa, and encamped at Emmaus. From this point G., with a body of 6000 men, attempted to make a night attack upon the Jews ; but Judas, hearing of his advance, hastily quitted his camp, and, falling suddenly on the camp of the Syrians in the early morning, defeated them with great loss. When G. returned from a vain pursuit among the mountains, he found the Syrian camp on fire, and

the Jews drawn up ready for battle ; and, without risking an encounter, he fled to the Phil. country (1 Mac 3⁴⁰–4²⁵ ; Jos. *Ant.* XII. vii. 4 ; 2 Mac 8¹²⁻²⁹). From 2 Mac 10¹⁴ff. it appears that G., who is described as commandant of the district (στρατηγὸς τῶν τόπων), remained in that country after his defeat, and continually harassed the Jews by means of his mercenary troops, assisted by the Idumæans. Two or three years later Judas led an expedition against Gilead, and, in the absence of his brothers, entrusted the command of the Jews to two officers, Joseph the son of Zacharias, and Azarias. Contrary to Judas' orders, they attacked the Syrians in Jamnia, but were repulsed by G. with heavy loss (1 Mac 5¹⁶ff. ⁵⁵⁻⁶⁴ ; Jos. *Ant.* XII. viii. 6). In 2 Mac 12³²⁻³⁷ this defeat is barely mentioned, but we are told how Judas defeated G., and how the accursed (τὸν κατάρατον) G. himself was nearly taken prisoner by a Jewish horseman named Dositheus. The description of G. in 2 Mac 12³² as ' governor of Idumæa ' is perhaps an error for ' governor of Jamnia ' (so Grotius, and cf. Jos. *Ant.* XII. vi. 8).   H. A. WHITE.

GORTYNA (<εἰς> Γόρτυναν A, Γορτῦναν אV, 1 Mac 15²³).—The most important city in Crete, after Gnossus, situated about midway between the two ends of the island. After the successful embassy sent by Simon Maccabæus to Rome (B.C. 139), the Roman Senate drew up a decree in favour of the Jews, guaranteeing the independence of their territory. Among a number of small autonomous states and communes to which copies of the decree were sent, G. is mentioned. From this we may infer that Jewish residents were then to be found in Crete. For the evidence that G. was at that time an independent community, see Marquardt, *Röm. Staatsver.* i. 333 f.   H. A. WHITE.

GOSHEN.—**1.** Named in connexion with the conquests of Joshua in the *south* of Judah (Jos 10⁴¹ 11¹⁶, both D²). Its exact situation has not been discovered. It was a district (אֶרֶץ), not a city. **2.** A *town* in the *hill-country* of Judah (Jos 15⁵¹, P). Its site is unknown. **3.** See next article.

GOSHEN (גֹּשֶׁן city ?, Gn 46²⁸. ²⁹, the point at which Jacob aimed in going down into Egypt ; and land of G., Gn 45¹⁰ 46²⁸⁻³⁴ 47¹. ⁴. ⁶. ²⁷ 50⁸).—The country in Egypt in which Joseph proposed that his father and brethren should dwell during the famine, that they might profit by the wealth of Egypt, and be near to him (Gn 45¹⁰), which Pharaoh accordingly granted to them (47⁶), and in which the children of Israel remained, with their flocks and herds, through the oppression, until the Exodus (Ex 9²⁶, cf. 12³²). It was suitable for a pastoral tribe, which would be, as such, an abomination to the Egyptians (Gn 46³⁴). It evidently lay on the Syr. frontier (Gn 46²⁸), and was considered appropriate for the temporary settlement of foreigners. When it is described as ' the best of the land ' (Gn 47⁶), that was no doubt from a shepherd's point of view, and it is generally considered that the Pharaoh who welcomed Jacob to Egypt belonged to one of the foreign dynasties, known as the Hyksos or Shepherd dynasties, and who were themselves hated by the Egyptians. The LXX, made, it must be remembered, in Egypt, has important readings. ' In the land of G.' (Gn 45¹⁰) is ἐν γῇ Γέσεμ 'Αραβίας, so also 46³⁴ ; in the later passages the defining word 'Αραβίας is dropped. In the Apocr. book of Judith (1⁹. ¹⁰) γῆ Γέσεμ appears to be roughly all the borderland of Egypt E. of a line drawn from Tanis to Memphis, *i.e.* all the E. borderland of the Delta, with perhaps a good slice of the Delta itself, within the Pelusiac arm of the Nile. Acc. to the LXX the city of G. should be

Heroopolis; Gn 46²⁸ 'and he sent Judah before him unto Joseph, to show the way before him unto G.; and they came into the land of G.,' is simply συναντῆσαι αὐτῷ καθ' Ἡρώων πόλιν, εἰς γῆν 'Ραμεσσή, 'to meet him (Joseph) at Heroopolis, into the land of Ramesse'; and in the next verse '(Joseph went up to meet his father) to G.' καθ' Ἡρώων πόλιν, at Heroopolis. Hence we see that the Jewish view and tradition in the last centuries before Christ made the city of Heroopolis, near what was then the head of the Red Sea, the point at which Joseph met Jacob. Heroopolis is now fixed by Rom. milestones at Tell el-Mashkûta in the Wady Tumîlât, and is probably identical with Pithom. It was the first important station in Egypt on the S. road from Syria, and therefore a very likely place for such a meeting. But the city of G. can hardly have been identical with Heroopolis, even to the Jews; this mention of Heroopolis must rather perhaps be considered as the translators' improvement on the original.

The land of G. is to them the land of Gesem of Arabia. Now, from Ptolemy we know that Arabia was the name of a nome on the E. border of the Delta, with the capital Phacussa; and acc. to Strabo, Phacussa was the point at which the canal to the Red Sea branched from the Nile. At the spot which best answers to this description, viz. Saft el-Henneh, monuments have been found naming Per-Sopd and Ķes, or Ķesem. In the nome-lists of Ptolemaic times the xxᵗʰ nome has the capital Per-Sopd, or Ķesem, and is itself called Sopd. There can be no doubt that this is the nome of Arabia, and that Ķesem is the equivalent of the LXX Gesem. In some cases the name of the city seems to be written Ķes, which then can be at once identified with the principal element in the Gr. Phacussa. It would thus appear that Saft el-Henneh is the ancient Per-Sopd, Phacussa, Ķes, and Ķesem. There is, however, evidence of another kind that partly contradicts this. Farther N.E., beyond the entrance of the Wady Tumîlât, there is an important village called Fậûs, once capital of a large district corresponding to the Arab. nome, and identified by the later Copts with Phacussa. It is difficult to avoid the conclusion that the Arab. nome had two capitals—one Per-Sopd = Saft (el-Henneh), the other Ķes or Ķesem = Faḳûs. Strabo would then have confused the two capitals in making Phacussa instead of Per-Sopd the point at which the canal branched off. If Jacob aimed at reaching Faḳûs, he would probably have followed the N. route, close to the sea, since the S. route, to Heroopolis, would have taken him considerably out of his way. Why, then, does the LXX introduce Heroopolis for G.? It will be seen that the subject is still surrounded with almost incredible difficulties. When we know what ancient site was occupied by the modern Faḳûs, where considerable mounds still exist, it will be possible to speak with greater certainty.

With regard to the extent of the land of G., if Judith is to be taken as authoritative, it included at least four Egyptian nomes outside the Delta, viz. the Sethroite on the N.E. frontier, the Arab. and the Heliopolitan, and that of Heroopolis in the Wady Tumîlât. Possibly, however, it should be restricted to the Arab. nome, perhaps from about Belbeis to Faḳûs, although the Wady Tumîlât ought also to be included. By comparing Gn 47⁴·⁶· with ¹¹ we find that the land of Ramesse and the land of G. are almost or quite identical.

It is, of course, possible that G. is an entirely foreign name, unknown to the ancient Egyptians, and that the LXX translators were only making conjectures as to its identification. Of two things we may be certain, that it lay on the E. border of the Delta, and furnished excellent pasture; and if it did not produce luxuriant harvests of corn and vegetables, like the ancient Arab. nome, we find that the Israelites dwelling there were at least plentifully supplied with 'leeks, onions, and garlic' (Nu 11⁵).   F. LL. GRIFFITH.

GOSPEL.—Anglo-Sax. *Godspell* = 'God story' (not 'good story'),—the tr., from Anglo-Sax. times, of εὐαγγέλιον in NT. In Homer, in the sing., and in Attic Gr., in the pl., it signified a *reward* or a *thank-offering for good tidings.* In later Gr. (Plutarch, in the pl., Lucian, in the sing.) it signified also the *good tidings* itself. In LXX, 2 S 4¹⁰, the Attic meaning and the plural occur : in the two remaining instances (sometimes quoted for the sense *good news*), 2 K 18²²·²⁵, it is probable that the non-classical fem. sing. εὐαγγελία ought to be read (cf. vv. ²⁰·²⁷, where this form is certain). In NT the neut. sing. alone is found (in Lk never ; in Ac twice ; in Rev once ; in Jn—Gosp. and Epp. —never, whether subst. or vb.), and in the sense of *good news* only ; a sense, moreover, always specialized, in accordance apparently with the Deutero-Isaian εὐαγγελίζομαι, as may be gathered from the quotation and comment in Ro 10¹⁵·¹⁶, 'How beautiful are the feet τῶν εὐαγγελιζομένων ἀγαθά ! But they did not all obey τῷ εὐαγγελίῳ.'

The content of this NT gospel had two stages. (1) In the mouth of Christ and of those whom, while He was on earth, He sent forth to proclaim it (Mt 10⁷, Lk 9² 10⁹ [Mk 16¹⁵]), it was the good tidings of the kingdom of God (Mk 1¹⁴·¹⁵, Mt 4²³ 9³⁵) which He had come to establish ; and this is called in Mk 1¹⁴ 'the good tidings of God,' *i.e.* coming from God (cf. 1 P 4¹⁷) ; in Ac 20²⁴ 'the good tidings of the free favour of God' ; in 1 Ti 1¹¹ 'the good tidings of (*i.e.* about) the glory (*i.e.* the manifested perfection) of the blessed God.' This good tidings about the kingdom Christ had also associated inseparably with His own person : Mk 8³⁵ 10²⁹ 'For my sake and the gospel's' : hence it is likewise called in Mk 1¹ 'the gospel of (*i.e.* about) Jesus Christ' ; and thus it enters upon the second stage in its meaning.

(2) After Christ's death and resurrection it became the *good tidings* (not so much brought by, and proclaimed by, as) *about Christ* (cf. Ro 1¹ 'The good tidings from God about [περὶ] His Son') ; see 1 Co 9¹² ; also 'the good tidings of (about) the glory (the manifested perfection) of Christ,' 2 Co 4⁴ ; or, simply, 'the good tidings,' 1 Co 9¹⁸. So the apostolic (chiefly Pauline) use may be defined as *the good tidings, coming from God, of salvation by His free favour through Christ.* See Eph 1¹³ ('of our salvation'), Eph 6¹⁵ ('of peace'). Probably, though not so certainly as Weiss seems to think, the word (like our word *preaching*) sometimes expresses not so much the content itself as the act of proclaiming it : in this way we may perhaps explain the genitives of those who preach and those who hear in such passages as 2 Co 10¹⁴ 'We came as far as unto you in the gospel *of Christ*,' 2 Co 4³ 'our gospel,' Ro 2¹⁶ 16²⁵ 'my gospel,' *i.e.* our, my, exposition of the gospel ; and Gal 2⁷ 'I have been intrusted with the gospel (the preaching of the gospel) *to the uncircumcision*, even as Peter with the gospel *to the circumcision*' ; not the content being different, but the sphere and the emphasis (cf. 1 Co 15¹¹ 'Whether it be I or they, so we preach, and so ye believed'). In each of the passages where 'my gospel' or 'my preaching of the gospel' occurs, the writer appears, according to the context, to be laying stress on some particular point which it has been his way to expound with special fulness as having been emphatically borne in upon him at the time of his preaching, or as closely affecting the case of the people to whom he is writing. Thus *Christ*

the Judge, the characteristic of the early missionary preaching (Ac 17³¹), is the element on which he lays stress in the 'our gospel' of 1 Th 1⁵ (cf. vv.⁷⁻¹⁰ and 2 Th 1⁶⁻¹⁰). Again, in Ro 2¹⁶, after his theme has been the equal responsibility of Jew and Gentile as doers of law, he recalls his proclamation of the fact that God will judge by Jesus Christ all men alike, not by their outward situations but by their inward attitudes (τὰ κρυπτά). Once more, in 2 Ti 2⁸, in order to encourage Timothy in the midst of suffering, the writer shows how, in 'his Gospel,' he lays stress upon the glorified state of Jesus the man and Christ the king,—king by royal descent and fulfilling prophetic anticipation. (Cf. 2 Co 4³ τὸ εὐαγγέλιον ἡμῶν, and v.⁵ Χριστὸν Ἰησοῦν Κύριον, the *Lordship* of the raised Christ being, in fact, the sum of the Pauline preaching, Ph 2¹⁰). In none of these passages is there a single sign that he is hinting at a specific difference in the content of the gospel preached by himself and by the Twelve.

The later sense of εὐαγγέλιον, a *gospel in writing*, and then *one of the Four Gospels*, does not appear in NT, though the way may be prepared for it by the usage in Mk 1¹ (see above). A second stage may be noted in the *Didaché*, c. xv. : 'Reprove one another, not in anger, but in peace, as ye have it in the gospel.' Here it seems to stand for a written body of Christian truth. Immediately afterwards we read : 'Your prayers and your alms and all your deeds so do ye as ye have it in the gospel of our Lord.' This might be a written collection of the teachings of Christ. Harnack—taking into account the text of the Lord's prayer (viii. 2), also said to be 'as the Lord commanded in his gospel,' and xi. 3, 'Touching the apostles and prophets, according to the ordinance (δόγμα) of the gospel so do ye'—suggests the *Gospel of the Egyptians* as the source (*Texte* ii. Proleg. 69 ff. and 79). The plural εὐαγγέλια, of the Four Gospels, does not occur till Justin Martyr (*Apol.* i. 66).

J. MASSIE.

GOSPELS.—

This article will be taken up mainly with the subject of the Origin and Composition of the **Four** Canonical Gospels and their credibility as historical witnesses. These are points which can best be discussed for the four together, owing to the nature of the evidence, which is in part the same, or of similar character for all, in part arises directly from comparing them. Such an assignment of the space at command will, nevertheless, be felt to be disproportionate when the manifold interest of the Gospels, their exquisite beauty, the richness of the moral and spiritual instruction which they convey, and their preciousness to the Church, are considered. Yet it is rendered inevitable by the recent course and present position of critical inquiry, and the intrinsic importance of the questions as to the authorship of the Gospels, their relations to one another, or the sources used in them. The amount of controversy which there has been on these subjects during the last 100 years has been enormous, and the evidence bearing on them is exceedingly complex. The attempt to discuss them, even with that degree of fulness which seems to be required in an article such as this, will render it impossible here to treat the Gospels from other points of view. At the same time, it ought to be remembered that there is hardly any aspect under which the Gospels may be regarded, which may not contribute some element that ought to be taken into account in a full appreciation of their character even as historical documents. In particular, it is necessary for this purpose that there should be a sympathetic and discerning study of their doctrinal teaching and of its relation to the faith of the early Church generally, as it may be gathered from other sources.

I. TRADITION AS TO AUTHORSHIP. — The first three Gospels do not within their actual compass (*i.e.* apart from the titles) give any precise indication of their authorship. As to the fourth, in a concluding passage which appears to be an addition to the original work, it is alleged to have been written by the disciple 'whom Jesus loved, which also leaned back on his breast at the supper' (cf. Jn 21²⁴ with v.²⁰), and to whom other allusions of the same kind in the course of the work doubtless also refer.

It cannot be asserted that the titles κατὰ Ματθαῖον, etc., proceeded from the authors themselves. The names rest, indeed, on as good MS evidence as any part of the text. But, from the nature of the case, they might have been prefixed at some time subsequent to the issue of the first copies. They unquestionably represent, however, the belief of the most important Churches before the time when Irenæus wrote the first three books of his great work on *Heresies*, which he composed during the episcopate of Eleutherus (*circ.* A.D. 175–190). For a general consideration of the evidence up to this time we must refer to the art. NT CANON. It must suffice here to say, (1) that although our four Gospels did not at once attain that position of unique authority which they held not long after the middle of the 2nd cent., yet it is easiest to explain the history of their reception in the Church on the supposition that they were authentic records of the apostolic age concerning the life and work of Jesus Christ, and that they were this to a degree of fidelity and fulness, in which no other documents even then existing could compare with them ; and (2) that the testimony of tradition raises a strong presumption in favour of the belief that they had severally some real connexion with the men whose names they bear. The formulas themselves, κατὰ Ματθαῖον, etc., or εὐαγγέλιον κατὰ Ματθαῖον, etc., need not as first used have implied more than this. They would be compatible with the belief that the work in question contained virtually the teaching of the man specified, though he had not himself written it down.

Further than this the external evidence by itself will not take us ; nevertheless, it furnishes an important element for the solution of the problem.

There are two or three more circumstantial traditions in regard to the composition of the Gospels which need to be mentioned, because they have, as we shall presently see, served to suggest or been used to confirm some of the chief theories designed to explain the internal phenomena of the Gospels. The most important are contained in two fragments, preserved in Eusebius' *HE* (iii. 39), of a work of Papias which may probably have been written about A.D. 140. Often as they have been quoted, it may be well to give them here. The first relates to a writing by Mark—

'This also the presbyter used to say : Mark having become the interpreter (ἑρμηνευτὴς γινόμενος) of Peter, wrote down accurately—not, however, in order (τάξει)—as many as he remembered of the things either spoken or done by Christ. For he neither heard the Lord nor attended on Him, but afterwards, as I said, (attended on) Peter, who used to give his instructions according to what was required, but not as giving an orderly exposition (σύνταξιν) of the Lord's words. So that Mark made no mistake in writing down some things as he recalled them. For he paid heed to one point, namely, not to leave out any of the things he had heard, or to say anything false in regard to them.'

The second fragment is as follows—

'Matthew, however, wrote the Oracles in the Hebrew tongue, and every man interpreted them as he was able.'

The presbyter, on whose authority the former of these statements is made, was named John ; and though he is to be distinguished from the apostle of that name, he was a companion of apostles and a personal follower of the Lord. Papias himself had conversed with this man, as we learn from another fragment (*ib.*). And from what we are told in that fragment as to the means by which Papias gathered information, it is reasonable to suppose that his statement as to Matthew's record was derived from the same or a similar source.

The more extreme critics of the earlier part of the present century used to argue that these accounts could not refer to our second and first Gospels. It is, however, coming to be admitted very widely among students of early Christian history that the statements in question would, at least at the time when Papias was writing, be connected with our Mt and Mk ; for it is hard to imagine that these could in the interval between that time and the third quarter of the 2nd cent. have been substituted for other works bearing the same names, and could have completely expelled such predecessors. This, however, does not preclude the possibility that there may have been differences greater or less between the writings to which Papias referred the traditions preserved by him and the works concerning which the statements under consideration had been originally made. There was more particularly room for difference between the Greek Gospel according to Mt and the Hebrew work spoken of, which would not be readily detected owing to the general ignorance of Hebrew among Greek-speaking Christians. The description given of the work seems to point to a record in which discourses and sayings of Jesus decidedly predominated over mere narrative. The word λόγια, indeed, means ' oracles ' and not ' discourses.' But while the term ' the oracles ' might well have been applied from the first have been applied to our Lord's words, it is hardly likely that it should so early have been applied to a writing of the NT as such. Moreover, even when the inspiration of the NT had come to be as clearly recognized as that of the OT, the term ' *the* oracles ' would not have been a fitting one for a single work, simply on the ground that it formed part of the collection.

Passing by Lk, concerning the composition of which tradition has nothing very significant to tell us, we subjoin an interesting statement regarding Jn. Clement of Alexandria relates (*ap.* Euseb. *HE* vi. 14), as a tradition handed down from the elders of former times, ' that John last of all, perceiving that the outward facts had been set forth in the Gospels, being urged on by his friends and inspired by the Spirit, composed a spiritual gospel.'

II. INTERNAL PHENOMENA.—Thus far we have spoken of the evidence supplied by tradition. It remains to be seen to what extent this confirms or is confirmed by the characteristics of the Gospels themselves. We proceed, therefore, in the first place, to consider the signs of relationship between the first three Gospels and the manner in which these are to be accounted for, or in other words the Synoptic Problem.

i. **The Synoptic Problem.**—(1) *The facts to be explained.* On comparing the first three Gospels, we observe in them a remarkable amount of similarity, both in the substance, the general arrangement and the precise order of their narratives, and the actual words and phrases employed. The general view of the course of events given in these Gospels is almost exactly the same, from the ministry of the Baptist onwards, the subject with which Mk opens. Not only so, but to a great extent they omit the same and record the same deeds and discourses and incidents. This common character becomes specially noticeable when we compare them with Jn, the contents of which are widely different ; and the suitability of the name Synoptic, which has been given to the first three, comes home to us with special force when that contrast with the Fourth is borne in mind. Nevertheless, even had we possessed the first three only, the amount of agreement between them would have called for explanation. For they are very brief accounts of a very full though comparatively short life. Moreover, they all make summary references to journeyings, periods of preaching and teaching, the working of many miracles of which they relate no details. The fact that out of all this possible material they preserve so largely the same selection, and that they deliver it so nearly in the same form, must be due to some cause or causes.

So far we have spoken in general terms of the resemblances between the first three Gospels. But, in the closer study of the fact, resemblances between pairs of them have also to be taken into account. The two most important groups of phenomena are in fact (*a*) the resemblances of Mk with Mt and Lk, either together *or* separately, and (*b*) the wholly additional matter common to Mt and Lk, but not contained in Mk.

(*a*) With regard to the former, it is to be observed that by far the larger number of the narratives and pieces of discourse contained in Mk are given also in both Mt and Lk, and nearly all in either one or the other. Also that for the most part the order of narrative is the same in all three ; so that we may speak of a Synoptic outline. The exceptions are somewhat more considerable in Lk than in Mt ; but it is noteworthy that they are almost entirely different in the two. Further, the same mode of relating incidents, conversations, and sayings is frequently to be observed in all three, to the extent even of the same sequence of clauses, the same words and phrases being adopted ; but, even where this is not the case, there is very frequently similar close parallelism between Mk and one of the others ; and, as before, this holds most often between Mt and Mk.

(*b*) The additional matter, referred to above, which is common to Mt and Lk, consists for the most part of discourses and sayings. In a considerable portion of it the resemblance even in language is very great ; in other parts of larger total extent the similarity of form is noticeably less, though the substance is the same. In place, however, of that similarity of order which we remarked upon in the case of the relations of Mt and Lk with Mk, we find in that of the matter now under consideration a great diversity of arrangement. In Mt we seem to see a disposition to mass it in discourses of some length, while in Lk various portions of it are given as belonging to various occasions. Again, they combine it very differently with the Synoptic outline.

Besides the features which have been mentioned, there are some others that are less strongly marked, of which it will be most convenient to defer the notice till we have occasion to speak of the attempts which have been made to explain them, and which have served to fix attention on them. It is, indeed, true of those broader characteristics also, which have been described, that the clear and accurate observation of them has progressed hand in hand with the discussion of their causes. And it is one of the most certain gains to be expected from the study of the problem before us, that (whether we succeed in solving it or not) we cannot fail, through framing and testing our hypotheses, to become better acquainted with the actual contents of the Gospels, and to have both their common substance and their individual traits imprinted more deeply upon our minds.

We will proceed to take a rapid survey of the theories that have been devised to account for the phenomena.

(2) *The theories that have been propounded.*— Explanations of three kinds may be employed, while the principles involved in each may also be in various ways combined. The three chief kinds were all in one way or another tried within the first 30 years, from the time when, rather more than a century ago, active speculation on the subject began.

(*a*) Direct dependence of one or of two of our present Gospels on the third, or of one on both the other two, might be assumed. This was the simplest kind of explanation of resemblances between them that could be given, and that which therefore lay most ready to hand. It had been employed by Augustine long before in one of the earliest examples of an interest, which was but momentary, in the literary criticism of the Gospels (*De Consensu Evangelistarum*, i. 2). He speaks of Mark as the 'pedisequus et breviator' of Matthew. When, however, towards the latter part of the 18th cent. the critical study of the relations of the Gospels to one another began in earnest, the theory was also put forward that Mk's was the original Gospel, which the others had expanded, while some even claimed this position for Lk. But the most celebrated theory of this period was Griesbach's, according to which Mk was regarded as a compilation from both Mt and Lk (*Commentatio quâ Marci evangelium totum e Matthæi et Lucæ commentariis descriptum esse monstratur*, A.D. 1789–90).

(*b*) Resemblances might be traced to the use of common documents, and more room was left in this way than by the last kind of explanation for the differences between the Gospels to have arisen, which are remarkably intermingled with their resemblances. Eichhorn, whose twofold hypothesis was for a long time the most notable one of the type which we are now considering, made special efforts to account for the differences. He supposed that there was one chief document, an *Urevangelium*, or primitive Gospel, to which various additions, derived from oral teaching, were made as time went on. The sections common only to two Gospels were explained by two evangelists having used the same copy. These were the governing ideas of his theory, both in its earlier

and later form. At first (A.D. 1794) he attributed the differences between the Synoptic Gospels to the translation of the primitive Gospel by different persons (the evangelists themselves and others), and the verbal similarities to the use in part of the same translations by the evangelists, along with different ones and with the original. But the process here imagined of translation and of the cross use of other translations was felt to be too complicated. It was difficult, also, in this way to account for the large amount of the same or closely similar language. This pointed to a common Greek basis. Accordingly Eichhorn, in a revised form of his theory, assumed a single translation of the primitive Aramaic Gospel into Greek, and supposed *this* Greek document to have received additions and modifications, extending in his imagination the operation of this cause of variations, to make up for that of a multiplicity of translations which he had abandoned.

(*c*) The common source was supposed to be an oral tradition to which a high degree of fixity had been given. Oral tradition could readily account for differences. But could it account for the strange resemblances? A theory based on it could claim to be scientific only in so far as it could suggest and render probable the existence of special historical conditions in the case in question, which would make it natural that the tradition should be characterized by a fixity of form approximating to that of a written document, though still possessing somewhat greater pliability. Such a theory seems to have been first conceived, and was certainly first clearly set forth, by J. C. L. Gieseler, the celebrated Church historian, in his *Historisch-kritischer Versuch über die Entstehung und die fruehesten Schicksale der schriftlichen Evangelien* (A.D. 1818). Most of those who have found in oral tradition the key to explain the characteristics of the Synoptic Gospels, have, if they have shown any just appreciation of the nature of the problem to be solved, reproduced in the main very closely the features of Gieseler's conception and his arguments. There was not room in this case for the same diversity as in the forms which could be given to the hypotheses of direct dependence and of common documents. At the same time, even the oral theory has been to some extent elaborated since Gieseler's time to meet a fuller analysis of the phenomena.

The name which must be mentioned next, in order that the course which investigation into the origin of the Gospels has actually followed may be rightly apprehended, is that of the great Schleiermacher. Instead of Eichhorn's single parent document, he assumed a number of more or less extensive compilations of narratives, the idea of which, and his name for them (διηγήσεις), he took from Lk 1[1]. This theory, which has been called *Diegesentheorie*, he put forth in his work on Lk (1817). The view, however, of his which has exercised a determining influence on subsequent criticism is not this, but his interpretation of the fragment of Papias concerning Mt, published in *SK* (1832). It was to the effect that Matthew put together only a collection of discourses and sayings which was afterwards embodied in our Mt. Next very naturally came the suggestion that this document was the source also of the matter in the third Gospel which it has in common with the first, and which is not in the second. And we find this view more or less clearly indicated by Credner (1836) in his *Einleitung* (§§ 87–89 and 91, pp. 201–206). He supposes also that the reminiscences of Peter's teaching alluded to in the other fragments of Papias were worked up by another writer into our Mk (*ib.* § 90).

The step most needed, however, in order that any decided progress should be made in solving the

Synoptic problem was, that a clearer and juster view than had so far prevailed of the relations between Mk and the other two Synoptics should be attained. And the way to this had already been opened by C. Lachmann in his article, 'De Ordine Narrationum in Evangeliis Synopticis,' in *SK* p. 570 ff., 1835. He contended for the 'priority' of Mk, though he left open the question whether it was prior in the sense of representing an earlier form of the oral Gospel than the two others, or as having more simply and fully embodied a document used by the other two. C. H. Weisse, in his *Die Evangelische Geschichte* (1838), adopted the latter alternative, and combined with it the view that, along with this document, Matthew's 'Logia' was also used both in our first and our third Gospel. Here for the first time was that 'two-document hypothesis' which has since, and especially during the last 40 years or so, found so much favour. In the same year as that in which the above-named epoch-making book of Weisse's appeared, C. G. Wilke published a work on the theme, *Matthäus oder Marcus*, in which he did good service on behalf of Mk's priority, and of the documentary as against the oral hypothesis.

Nevertheless, the Tübingen School, which was just then rising into importance, and which for a considerable period held the most prominent place in the world of criticism, so far as Christian *Origines* were concerned, had committed themselves to the position that Mt was the first and Mk the last of the Synoptics. Later members of the school gave up the priority of Lk, but not of Mt. In the method of this school, the examination of the simple literary phenomena of the Gospels played only a very subordinate part. So far as these critics discussed the Gospels themselves and compared them, their object was chiefly to show how the several Gospels, by virtue of their individual characteristics, fitted in with and illustrated their own more general theories as to parties among the early Christians, and their tendencies. They endeavoured to distinguish the bias of each writer which had led him to mould the narrative in a particular way; and on the ground thereof they assigned to each document its age and the measure of historical importance which they were willing to accord it. They insisted in an exaggerated way on the peculiarities of the several Gospels, and drew unwarranted inferences therefrom; nevertheless, their work may be of use in preventing us from overlooking the individuality of the several Gospels, which in some other speculations is too much ignored.

The disposition of this school was to proceed to broad generalizations which had neither been reached nor verified by a careful and impartial examination of all the facts. In spite of the great ability of the chief men among them, and the permanent mark which they have left upon the study of early Christian history, their theories have in the main been overthrown, and that largely by men almost as 'free' as themselves from orthodox prepossessions. And in no respect has this been more signally the case than in regard to their criticism of the Synoptic Gospels.

The chief critical work of the last 40 years or so has been the lineal continuation and development of that of Weisse and Wilke. That is, the general tendency of it has been to establish more firmly the position that either the three Synoptic Gospels all made large use of a document which is to be seen with fewest additions, omissions, or changes of any kind in Mk; or that Mk itself is virtually that document; and further, that there existed another very early 'source,' a collection mainly of discourses and sayings, to which the matter common to Mt and Lk is to be traced.

Among the large number of critics, however, who would agree in these propositions when stated thus in general terms, there are not unimportant differences. The most considerable, perhaps, is that while (a) many, agreeing with Weisse, suppose that both the first and third evangelist had and used this collection in the same, or substantially the same form, and that the diversity in the mode of the presentation of the common matter in the Gospels is due to the different treatment of the same document by the two evangelists, (β) there are others who suppose that the collection must have come into the hands of the third in a markedly different form from that in which the first had it. The former view is that which has been most before the world: it is held by H. J. Holtzmann (*Die Synoptischen Evangelien*, 1863; *Einleitung in NT*, 1886), B. Weiss (*Marcus-Evang.* 1872; *Matthäus-Evang.* 1876; *Leben Jesu*, 1882; *Einleitung*, 1886), H. Wendt (*Lehre Jesu*, 1886), and others. But some eminent names may be cited on the side of the second view,—Reuss (*Hist. of NT*, p. 190 ff.), Lipsius (his views on the Synoptic problem are described by his pupil Feine, *JB für Protest. Theol.* 1885, pp. 1, 2). Weizsäcker may be said to hold an intermediate position (*Untersuch.* pp. 129–220).

Differences there are, also, among critics of the former of these two groups. One of the chief of these relates to the question whether the 'Logia' is most faithfully reproduced, especially as to order and arrangement, in Mt or Lk. Holtzmann and Wendt are on the side of Lk, B. Weiss of Mt. There are differences, again, as to the character and contents of the 'Logia.' Thus Holtzmann traces to it some portions of Lk which are peculiar to that Gospel as well as those common to Lk and Mt; while Weiss insists that historical circumstances must have been narrated in it as well as discourses.

Another important subject of controversy relates to the part of Mark, the disciple of Peter, in the composition of our second Gospel. In B. Weiss' view, Mark's Gospel, derived chiefly from his reminiscences of Peter's teaching, was itself the document used (along with the 'Logia') by our first and third evangelists. On the other hand, the matter common to the three Synoptics may be supposed to be derived from a document older than any one of them. This only leaves room for Mark to have introduced touches here and there. Again, B. Weiss supposes that Mark himself (as well as the first and third evangelists) made use of the 'Logia,' though to a much more limited extent, and that thus the first and third used the 'Logia' both directly and also in a measure mediately through Mk. But for this complicated theory he has found few adherents. [Resch (*Agrapha*, p. 27 f.) and Titius (*Theol. Studien* in honour of Weiss, Göttingen, 1897) may be mentioned as adopting it.]

Other critics, again, hold that the third evangelist must have known and to some degree made use of our Mt as well as his principal and older sources. Such arguments as may be adduced for this view have been most fully set forth by E. Simons in his monograph, *Hat der dritte Evangelist den kanonischen Matthäus benützt?* 1880.

The endeavour has also been made in recent times to supplement the theories as to the relations of the Synoptic Gospels by tracing back varieties of form to different translations of the oldest Hebrew document. This attempt has especially been carried out by A. Resch in his laborious investigations, in the course of which he examines the citations of our Lord's teaching in the whole range of early Christian literature, and compares them with parallels in the Gospels. See his

'Agrapha' in *Texte u. Untersuch*, v. Heft 4, 1889; and *Aussercanon. Paralleltexte*, x. Heft 1 and 3, 1893–95.

In England the oral theory has been far more widely accepted than it seems ever to have been in Germany, though among ourselves also it has, to a considerable degree, lost its hold in recent years. English readers will, however, rightly require that it should be kept in view in any discussion of the problem. The most recent advocate of it is the Rev. A. Wright (see his *Composition of the Four Gospels*, 1890; *Synopsis of the Gospels*, 1896; and *Problems in NT*, 1898). He has given to the theory a new development by supposing that the catechetical instruction of Christians in the facts of the Gospel history was carried out in a very systematic manner, and that there existed different schools of catechists. To the present writer it seems that no form of the oral hypothesis can furnish an adequate explanation of the phenomena of the Gospels; yet he believes that the influence of the period of oral teaching needs to be taken into account, in dealing with the whole problem of the origin of the four Gospels, far more than it commonly is by the adherents of the various documentary hypotheses.

The decision of most of the questions included in the subject before us must depend on the patient examination of a mass of particulars which cannot be set forth here. But it may be well to indicate in general terms the nature and bearing of the evidence on some of the chief points at issue. We pass on, therefore, to consider—

(3) *The Source or Sources of the matter and order common to the three Synoptic Gospels.*—It will not be profitless, in the first place, briefly to give the reasons for which Griesbach's theory has been generally abandoned. That theory is at first sight tempting. It seems to account readily for the fact that not only do we find in Mk so much that is common also to Mt and Lk, but that traits and words and expressions which occur, some in Mt, some in Lk, in narratives that are parallel, are frequently found in combination in Mk; so that this Gospel, while it is on the whole shorter, is generally fuller in the narratives it does contain. It is not impossible that in some, and even a good many cases, words, etc., from Mt or Lk may have been introduced, *e.g.* by the hand of an editor, into the second Gospel as we have it. But the theory of compilation cannot explain the phenomena as a whole. For (*a*) to carry out the process of analysis and combination to the extent required by this hypothesis would be a very complicated and difficult task, such as no one, especially in that age, would be likely to undertake. The supposition that Mt and Lk reproduced Mk, or the document embodied therein, with some abbreviations and alterations which are largely different because they acted independently, is a far simpler one. Moreover, it accounts for a large part of the similarity between Mt and Lk themselves, which, on Griesbach's theory, is left wholly unexplained. (*b*) The reasons that can be alleged on Griesbach's theory, for Mk's relinquishing the order of narratives in Mt to follow Lk, and *vice versâ*, and for his omission of so much which those Gospels contain, though he is supposed in other cases to have combined them, appear to be very arbitrary. (*c*) A mere compiler could hardly have been able to give to his work the force and freshness and vividness which peculiarly characterize Mk.

We turn to the question whether the chief source common to the three was a certain tradition of oral teaching or a document. In judging of the adequacy of the former to account for the facts, it seems important, first of all, to distinguish between the effect which oral teaching might have, on the one hand, in determining the general character of the selection and presentation of the matter recorded, and, on the other hand, in securing a fixed order of sequence in the relation of particular incidents and pieces of discourse. Now, the contents and general form of the Synoptic outline, as we see it most simply in Mk, is such as might naturally arise from the circumstances and needs of the preaching of the gospel, as soon as its message was delivered to those who had not themselves known Jesus. In the earliest days after Pentecost, among the people of Jerusalem and the crowds from Galilee to whom the great Prophet of Nazareth had been a familiar figure, it was enough for the apostles to testify that He had risen from the dead. Even to a man like Cornelius, whom the fame of His deeds could not but have reached in a more or less distinct and accurate form, it might be enough to say, 'The word which he sent unto the children of Israel, preaching good tidings of peace by Jesus Christ (he is Lord of all)—that saying, ye yourselves know, which was published throughout all Judæa, beginning from Galilee, after the baptism which John preached; even Jesus of Nazareth, how that God anointed him with the Holy Ghost and with power; who went about doing good, and healing all that were oppressed with the devil; for God was with him. And we are witnesses of all things which he did, both in the country of the Jews and in Jerusalem; whom also they slew, hanging him on a tree' (Ac 10$^{36-39}$). But more and more, as years passed, and as the gospel was carried to fresh circles, men would wish to have particulars about the life and work of Jesus; and it would be necessary that a right impression of Him and His ministry should be imparted, in order that the meaning of His cross and resurrection should be in any measure understood. For this purpose an expansion would be needed of that brief summary which has just been quoted. The preachers would seek to set before their hearers in a comprehensive manner, and within such limits as oral teaching imposed, a view of the person of Jesus in its attractive grace and holiness and goodness, as He had been known to themselves and to the multitudes who followed Him, to enable them to realize His supernatural character, as it was evidenced by His wonder-working power, and the authority with which He spake. A detailed chronicle was not what was wanted; they wished simply to impart a clear conception of His mission and His credentials. The desired end could be best attained by a sketch which should give prominence to the salient features of His work, and which, while it contained some comprehensive descriptions of His occupations at different periods, and of the impression produced by His teaching and miracles, and marked a few chief epochs in His ministry, should be confined, for the rest, to an account of some important incidents and sayings, selected as examples out of a mass of others that might have been told. When they passed to the last days of His life, and His death, the mode of treatment would naturally be different. Here it would be no longer a question merely of illustrations. Besides all other reasons for giving a fuller narrative, such as the natural interest of the closing scenes, and the deep impression which all their details had made on the minds and hearts of the preachers themselves, it was necessary to press home and to justify the idea of a suffering Messiah. In addition to these aims, which tended to impart a particular form to the accounts orally delivered, the close intercourse maintained among the original group of Christian missionaries, even after they had begun to move about, and the similarity of the conditions under which this group at least was doing its work, and the influence which a few of the stronger characters would exert, together with the simplicity of mind and want of general education of the early disciples, would tend to establish and confirm a habit of telling the story in a particular way common to them all.

Now, the general mode of presenting the life and work of Jesus Christ in the Synoptic Gospels corresponds to that which has just been described. In other words, it is such as we might have expected, if the characteristics of the oral method of communicating the facts most needful to be known came to be imprinted on the written narrative. The form of the common record is not that which would have been naturally adopted by a writer who approached his subject and made use of his materials in the spirit and manner of a chronicler or biographer.

The range of the parallelism between the Synoptics must be considered in this connexion. The fact that it begins with the ministry of the Baptist may well be accounted for by all three having used a document which began thus. But even so, the cause of this being made the starting-point in such a document seems worthy of consideration, especially when we observe how that of the apostolic preaching as described in Acts was wont to be the same (cf. Ac 1^{22} $13^{24. 25}$). We can understand that it was a natural one for those who had such an aim as has been above suggested. The mystery of Christ's birth could not be freely spoken of at first to the unconvinced. On the other hand, the testimony of His great predecessor, whose work had made such a wide impression, afforded a fitting point of departure for commending Jesus to the faith of men. In this respect also, then, the habits of the period of oral teaching seem to have left their mark.

Considerations which are in part analogous may help also to explain why the parallelism between the Synoptics terminates where it does in the midst of the evidences of the resurrection. All three describe in a very similar manner the visit of the women to the tomb, and the appearance of the angel (Lk two angels) to them. After this point they differ widely. The assumption that they used a common document, which ended abruptly here, will go far to account for this. Still it is remarkable that it should have terminated in this fashion, and also that the difference in the concluding narratives should be so wide as it is. The early history of the preaching of the gospel may possibly again furnish a clue to the right explanation. At first the apostles were mainly occupied with bearing testimony to the resurrection of Jesus. They were themselves profoundly convinced of this great fact, and they called upon men to believe it on their word. They did not care to enter upon an elaborate tabulation of all His appearances; such would not be demanded of them. They would speak now of one, now of another. Subsequently, as we have said, the need for some account of the life and teaching and death of Jesus arose. The two things were in a measure distinct, and might for a time be kept so. Moreover, a certain method of narration might, under the conditions which we have indicated, have been commonly observed in the latter case, such as may never have existed in regard to the testimony to His resurrection.

The correspondences between the Synoptics in words and phrases show that they are connected by derivation from common sources of information, which were in Greek. This, however, does not of itself put the oral theory out of court, though it has sometimes been supposed to do so. For when we remember that the Aramaic-speaking territory in Palestine was surrounded by a belt of Greek-speaking districts, and also that many Hellenists yearly visited Jerusalem, we can see that from very early days—from the moment, indeed, that the Church began to expand—an oral tradition in Greek must have arisen, corresponding to that in Aramaic.

The resemblance, however, between the three Synoptic Gospels extends far beyond those broad features of which above we have so far been speaking. If the additional matter in Mt and Lk be omitted, there will be found remaining in each of them, with, comparatively speaking, very few exceptions, the contents of Mk given in exactly the same order,—the same sequence being maintained not merely in respect to events which stood in close historical connexion, but also in respect to sections which do not appear to have been so united. This seems clearly to point to the use of a common document. It is specially difficult to understand how, after insertions, sometimes of considerable length, the common thread could again and again have been taken up in the first and third Gospels exactly where it had been dropped, solely under the operation of tradition. But it is exactly what would happen if the writers had a document before them.

A comparison of the language, the words, the succession of clauses, the structure of sentences and paragraphs in the Synoptic Gospels, leads to the same conclusion. The extent of the element common to all three is remarkable. But, in order that the evidence bearing on the question at issue may be appreciated, it is necessary that attention should be fixed, not so much on this, as on the resemblance of Mt and Lk separately to Mk. Between these pairs, and especially between Mt and Mk, there will be found to be close similarity, amounting frequently to identity, saving a few words here and there, in sentence after sentence and passage after passage. Moreover, the character of the resemblances should be noted. We can understand that even in oral tradition striking sayings should have been preserved in a fixed form; and there would be special reason for fidelity in repeating all the teaching of the Lord. But there is also in the Synoptic Gospels an amount of close agreement in ordinary narration which is very difficult to explain by oral transmission, because there could be no sufficient motive for the care necessary to secure it.

Advocates of the oral theory allege the retentiveness of Eastern memories, and the habit of preserving orally the Rabbinic traditions, or the instances, common among Mohammedans, of being able to repeat the whole or large portions of the Koran. But it should be remembered that what has to be explained in the present case is, not the preservation of a record after its very words had come to be regarded as sacred, but the process itself of forming the fixed tradition. Could it have been fixed down to so many mere turns of expression as the result of the work of the apostles' teaching and preaching freely? And would either they or their immediate fellow-workers in instructing others have had any reason to insist on the reproduction of what they taught with that sort of uniformity?

Again, it is said that the oral theory alone will account for the differences between the Gospels. But the force of this argument seems to depend on adopting a point of view which is too much that of our own time. The writers of our Gospels would feel themselves to be far more nearly on a level with those of the documents (assuming that they had such before them) which they used, than men of later generations could. And it is the natural tendency of historians who embody matter from other writings in their own works to abbreviate parts of it, to improve the style, or at least to alter it in accordance with their own habits of expression, and at times, after picturing to themselves the scenes described, to represent them in their own way. Many of the differences between Mk and the two other Synoptic Gospels are of this character. This is especially the case in regard to Lk, the differences between which and Mk are, as has been said, the greatest. Moreover, even in the case of intentional quotation, there was in ancient times less desire for scrupulous accuracy in regard to the exact words used than there is at the present day.

(4) *The Source or Sources of the matter common to Mt and Lk.*—The phenomena here are in various respects different from those examined under the last head, and other considerations have to be applied to them. The material in question forms such a distinct mass that even on the oral hypothesis it must be supposed to have been collected and shaped separately from that account of the life and work of Christ upon which our attention has so far been fixed, and to have been subsequently in the first and third Gospels combined therewith. And indeed we may, with at least as good reason as before, attribute an important share to the influences of the period of oral teaching in forming the body of tradition now in question, though the needs to be met were different from those which called forth a general presentation of our Lord's work. Disciples who were familiar with the main facts of His life would be impelled to recur again and again to His precepts, which were to be the guide and support of their lives. Those sayings especially would be called to mind and repeated which set forth the character that was to distinguish the true followers of Christ, or which gave an authoritative decision in matters of ordinary conduct, or which inculcated the spirit that was to govern the members of the infant Christian communities in their relations with one another, or prescribed the rules that were to guide the missionaries of the gospel, or which afforded a solace and stay under persecution and sorrow, or, lastly, which spoke of that great consummation, that coming of the Lord and judgment upon an evil world, for which their hearts yearned so eagerly. In view of these wants, it would be exceedingly probable that sayings, parables, and discourses upon these themes should soon come to be put together and handed on in the shape of larger or smaller collections even before they were written down (cf. Weizsäcker, *Apost. Zeitalter*, pp. 369–401). They would form, as it were, a body of divine law, treasured in the communities of Christians. The form and contents of the discourses in Mt specially suggest this origin. Other traits appear in Lk which would also be natural after such a history of the preservation of the material.

But can the resemblances between these two Gospels be explained solely on the oral theory? Those who think so have a stronger case here than in regard to the resemblances between the same Gospels and Mk. There the close parallelism between the sequence of sections furnished a strong argument against that theory; here the great dissimilarity of arrangement is a serious difficulty in the way of the hypothesis that the same document was used by both evangelists. There, again, the similarity is found in ordinary narrative; here the matter in question consists almost entirely of Christ's own teaching, which would be likely to be preserved with special accuracy even in oral repetition. Nevertheless, there is in a considerable portion of the passages under consideration an amount of verbal agreement which it is hard to account for without supposing some intervention of writing.

By those who suppose that the use of a single documentary source, which contained all this matter, will explain the phenomena, efforts are made to reconstruct that document through a critical comparison of Mt and Lk. In each it may certainly have been altered in different ways and at different points; and it will be fair to remember that the divergence between the two Gospels, as they now lie before us, would in all probability be greater than that between either of them and the common source. Further, many pieces of teaching in it may have been introduced by formulas such as 'Jesus said,' which specified no particular occasion. The recently discovered Oxyrhynchus fragment affords an illustration of sayings so compiled. The very different positions which the same sayings occupy in the first and third Gospels may thus be less inconsistent with their derivation from a common document than we at first fancy. Possibly, it would not have been necessary for either of the evangelists to do such violence to the source as we may be inclined at first to fancy, in pursuing different plans in the arrangement of their material. That the first was inclined to mass together similar material, seems to be rendered probable by the fact that there are one or two cases in which pieces of teaching from Mk and from another source seem to have been woven together in Mt, which in Lk remain separate. Thus Lk has an account of a charge to the Twelve (9^{3-6}) which is closely parallel to Mk 6^{8-13}. He has also an address to the Seventy in ch. 10. Now, the substance of vv.$^{3-12}$ of the latter is found woven with the substance of Mk 6^{8-13} in Mt 10^{7-16}. Something of the same kind may perhaps be observed in comparing Mt 24. 25, Mk 13^{1-37}, Lk 21^{5-36} 17^{22-37} 12^{39-46} 19^{12-28}. Yet, to show how cautious we must be in drawing inferences, it may be worth while to observe that in Lk 10^{12-15} compared with Mt 10^{15} and 11^{20-24}, the usual parts, so to speak, of the two evangelists are reversed.

In connexion with the question before us, the greater or less clearness and naturalness of the contexts in which the same sayings occur in Mt and Lk respectively must also be taken into account. But this is a subject on which there is wide diversity of view. To the present writer it seems that the connexions are far more often obscure and difficult in Lk than in Mt. But however this may be, and when every allowance has been made which our ignorance of the actual form of the common document may suggest, it remains very difficult to believe either, on the one hand, that any one in the circle in which the first Gospel must have been composed should have employed the amount of literary art and labour necessary to construct the discourses found in that Gospel out of fragments; or that, on the other hand, the third evangelist, if he had those wholes before him, should have felt it to be his duty to break them up.

Moreover, the hypothesis that the two evangelists derived all this matter from the same document, is as incapable as the oral theory of explaining the singular phenomenon referred to above as to the degree of agreement in different parts (see i. (1) (*b*)). For the character of the subject-matter in the two classes of parallel passages affords no reason for either evangelist having preserved it with so much less fidelity in the one case than in the other. It would seem to be more possible to account for the facts by supposing that two compilations which had in the main an independent history, though copies of some of the same written fragments have passed into each, have been embodied in the first and third Gospels respectively.

(5) *Some subsidiary features of relationship.*— There are no groups of facts indicative of connexion between the Synoptic Gospels, or between pairs of them, which are at all comparable in extent and prominence with those discussed under the two last headings. A few others, however, which need investigation must be briefly noticed.

(*a*) In spite of the signs of 'priority' in Mk on the whole, there are cases in which Mt or Lk or both of them have a stronger appearance of originality in particular words, or turns of expression, and even in the character of a whole section. Mk 1^{40-45} 2^{1-12} 3^{1-6}, compared with their parallels, may be taken as examples. Similarly, there are instances in which Mk has words or phrases not like his usual style, and which occur more frequently in one or both the others (*e.g.* ὁ πατὴρ ὁ ἐν τοῖς οὐρανοῖς in Mk 11^{25} = Mt 6^{14}. It appears only here in Mk, but is common in Mt).

(*b*) Again, although the records of Christ's *teaching* are so much more limited in Mk than in Mt and Lk, that Gospel has, in certain cases, accounts of discourses which, so far as they extend, are closely parallel with Mt and Lk; at the same time, the accounts of these two are longer and, to a greater or less degree, parallel with one another. Here, plainly, Mk is not the source, and does not in all respects most fully represent it (*e.g.* cf. Mk $1^{7.8}$ with Mt 3^{7-12} and Lk 3^{7-17}; Mk 3^{22-30} with Mt 12^{24-37} and Lk 11^{15-26} and 12^{10}).

(*c*) In narratives in which Mt and Lk are on the whole closely parallel with Mk, they yet have little touches, phrases, etc., in common, which are not in Mk (*e.g.* cf. Mk 2^3 with Mt 9^2 and Lk 5^{18}; Mk 2^9 with Mt 9^5 and Lk 5^{23}; Mk 2^{22} with Mt 9^{17} and Lk 5^{37}).

Holtzmann's assumption, in his *Synopt. Evang.*, that although the source common to the three Synoptic Gospels is on the whole most nearly reproduced in Mk, yet there are cases in which it has been more exactly preserved in the other two, seems capable of explaining many at least of these phenomena in a simple manner. It should, further, be remembered that some discourses or incidents of which that document may have contained accounts, may also have been elsewhere recorded in a fuller or slightly different form, and that Mt and Lk may have known of these other records, and have adopted them, or at least been influenced by their recollection of them, in particular instances.

These considerations render it unnecessary to suppose, with B. Weiss, that Matthew's 'Logia' (if we may for convenience so speak) was used in the composition of Mk, as well as in Mt and Lk, though in Mk only to a very much smaller extent. They also go far to destroy the force of such evidence as is alleged in support of the view that our *first* Gospel was known and made use of by our third evangelist. The wide differences between the two render it very difficult to suppose this to have been the case. Ways of accounting for coincidences between them which do not assume knowledge of one Gospel by the writer of the other are therefore to be preferred. In addition to those already suggested, it may be observed that accidental agreement, revision by later hands, and unintentional assimilation of the texts of the two by copyists, may well in conjunction be responsible for a considerable number of the instances. Others explain the class of phenomena to which we are referring, by the supposition (alluded to above, p. 237) that the third evangelist knew the first. Holtzmann himself has adopted this view, thus rendering his earlier hypothesis, that the original common document differed in certain respects from Mk, and is at times more exactly

reproduced in the first and third Gospels, to a great extent unnecessary, as he has explained in his *Einleitung*, pp. 363, 364. It is only suggested, however, that the third evangelist was influenced by 'reminiscences' of Mt, which is in itself a confession that the evidences of dependence are somewhat vague and scanty. We believe that we shall have the majority of critics on our side in asserting that they are altogether too slight to withstand the case that may be made out, on pure grounds of general probability and apart from any theory of inspiration, against any knowledge of the first Gospel by the writer of the third, from the wide divergences between them.

(6) *Features peculiar to the Synoptic Gospels severally, and summary with regard to the composition of each.*

As the question of the composition of Mt is the most complex and difficult, we will reserve it till the last, and begin—

(*a*) With *Mark*. It will, I believe, be very generally allowed by critics at the present day that the Mark who is referred to in NT had a part of some kind in the composition of our second Gospel ; for the tradition to that effect is too strong to be altogether set aside. But what was that part? It is well known that this Gospel is distinguished by many touches which it is specially natural to attribute to recollection of St. Peter's teaching. But did these form part of the work which was used in the composition of Mt and Lk, and were they eliminated by the writers of these Gospels? In other words, was our Mk itself, as we have it, one of the original documents into which the Synoptic Gospels are to be analyzed ? Or, on the other hand, did Mark himself take a document—the same which was used in Mt and Lk—and revise it, though much more slightly, only adding to it traits here and there which he had derived from his close intercourse with St. Peter? It cannot be said that criticism has as yet even approximated to a decision on this point. If a well-assured position in regard to it is ever reached, it must be mainly through a careful examination and weighing of all those individual points in which Mk differs from the other two Synoptic Gospels in parallel contexts, in order to ascertain whether they can best be explained as the result of alteration in Mk, or revision in the two others. But, in regard to point after point, several considerations have to be borne in mind ; there is also a possibility sometimes of other explanations of the facts ; and throughout, the bias of each critic is apt to tell in favour of one theory or another, so that it is an exceedingly difficult matter to form a sound general impression.

(*b*) The question of the authorship and composition of the *third Gospel* cannot be separated from that of the Acts of the Apostles. It is generally admitted, on the ground of remarkably plentiful indications of style and other characteristics, that the composition of these two books was the work of the same hand ; and further, that the second of them includes accounts of some of St. Paul's missionary journeys by one who was himself a companion of his at the time. But the question of the authorship is at first sight rendered complex by evident signs that other sources have been used as well in certain parts of both works. It will, however, I believe, be found to be much simpler than is generally supposed. For those portions of the Acts, or certain of them, which are allowed to be by a companion of St. Paul are, if I mistake not, marked to an eminent degree by those special words and expressions which are found throughout the two works, though in many parts they are scattered sparsely. That is to say, the man who wrote those memorials of journeys in which he himself accompanied the apostle, was the same who put together accounts, written and oral, which he obtained from others, of the life and teaching of Christ and the early history of the Church, and in reproducing them left upon them some marks of his own literary habits. (See *Expositor*, 1893, pt. i. p. 336 f.) If, then, the author of the Gospel and the Acts was a companion of St. Paul, it will be readily allowed that he was none other than Luke, who is singled out by tradition.

St. Luke has placed a short introduction at the beginning of his Gospel (1¹⁻⁴) which is full of significance both as to the method in which the knowledge of the life and teaching of Christ was preserved generally, and as to the purpose of his own book. He distinguishes virtually two periods in the history of the transmission of the facts up to the time at which he was writing. First they were delivered orally by those who 'from the beginning were eye-witnesses and ministers of the word'; then after a time attempts began to be made to write down what had been thus learned, or portions of it. Individual members of the Church were also more or less fully and carefully instructed in the facts.

Advocates of the oral theory have asserted that St. Luke treats the written accounts to which he refers as no longer possessing importance. They find this meaning in the aorist ἐπε-χείρησαν. But the force of the aorist will be fully recognized if we regard it as emphasizing the difficulty of the task and the tentative character of the efforts to perform it. Unquestionably, his aim was to supply something more adequate. But there is nothing in his language inconsistent with the supposition that he was prepared to make use of any suitable written material that came to his hand, as well as of traditions orally delivered. And it is in every way most natural to suppose that he would do this.

If the arguments described above (i. (3)) be sound, the record which is most nearly represented in Mk, or that Gospel itself, was one of the chief documents that he used. He may besides this have had another document, whence mainly he derived that subject-matter which is common to him with Mt—a document where it was arranged to a great extent in a manner different from that in which we find it in the first Gospel. Or, again, he may have obtained it by an independent labour of collection, by himself transcribing short pieces which had been early committed to writing, or by making extracts from longer accounts, such as those to which he seems to refer in his preface, and also by writing down some things immediately from oral tradition. In one or other of these ways, also, he acquired those additional parables, pieces of teaching, and incidents, special to his Gospel which he introduces into the Synoptic outline, including them more particularly in the long insertion between Christ's departure from Galilee (9⁵¹) and His final ascent to Jerusalem (19³¹), the point at which Lk again begins to run parallel to the other two Synoptic Gospels. His account of the birth of John the Baptist, and the birth and early years of our Lord, may very probably have been taken from some special written narrative. It has a peculiarly Aramaic colouring and other features of its own. It would have been a very congenial occupation to a man such as from his two works we know the author of the third Gospel to have been, to make notes of information that he received concerning the life and work of Jesus, to copy out and keep precious pieces of His teaching. He may have begun to do this long before he set forth the material he had amassed in his Gospel, or even thought of doing so; and visits to Pales-

tine, as on the occasion when St. Paul was seized at Jerusalem and imprisoned at Cæsarea, would give him very favourable opportunities for going on with this work.

(c) The question as to the composition and authorship of the *first Gospel* is rendered specially complicated by the fact that there is a strong and unwavering early tradition that the Apostle Matthew wrote in Hebrew, while the relations of our Mt with the other Synoptics, and especially with Mk, which are evidently through the Greek, are of a kind to preclude the idea that, as it stands, it is a mere translation. The manner in which these facts are recognized and dealt with by such an eminent advocate of the oral theory as Westcott is very instructive. 'The parts,' he writes, 'of the Aramaic oral Gospel which were adopted by St. Matthew already existed in the Greek counterpart. The change was not so much a version as a substitution; and frequent coincidence with common parts of St. Mark and St. Luke, which were derived from the same oral Greek Gospel, was a necessary consequence' (*Introd.* p. 228 n.). It is, however, very difficult to conceive how the process suggested could have been carried out in such a way as to produce the actual phenomena. It is much simpler to suppose that, with the view of supplementing a Greek document which existed already (viz. Mk or the document most nearly represented by it), he translated from a Hebrew (or Aramaic) Gospel, which may well have been composed by, or may at least in some way have been connected with the teaching of, the Apostle Matthew. But we seem to have no means of deciding whether such a work contained other portions corresponding to the matter in Mk. It may have done so, and the touches peculiar to Mt and that Hebraic tone and disposition to emphasize the connexion between the new dispensation and the old, which are more or less noticeable in it as a whole, may be thence derived. The manner also in which the subject-matter taken from the different sources has been combined in the Greek Mt may have been influenced by the order in the Hebrew work. For although Papias' description of St. Matthew's work as 'The Oracles,' as well as the nature of the matter which there is most reason to suppose taken from it, make it highly probable that it was specially characterized by the records it gave of Christ's *teaching*, its contents need not have been strictly confined to this. Some light might be thrown on these points if we knew more of the *Gospel according to the Hebrews*; for it is not unnatural to surmise that this heretical Gospel may have been based upon, or have borne some similarity to, the Hebrew Mt. Unfortunately, our knowledge of this work also is so scanty that no conclusions can be safely drawn from it. (All that is known respecting the Gospel according to the Hebrews has been recently put together and reviewed by Harnack, *Chron.* i. p. 625 ff.).

Once more, however, it is difficult to conceive in a simple manner how the Greek Mt could have been translated from a Hebrew original, even in those parts where it is not parallel with Mk; for its observed relations with Lk have also to be taken into account. How does there come to be in these two Gospels that singular combination of parallel passages whose verbal similarity is such that they could not have been obtained through independent translation, with others sufficiently different to be so accounted for? We may, perhaps, get a hint of the circumstances under which this resulted from Papias' reference to a time when there was no received representative of Matthew's Hebrew work, but each translated it as he could. Such a state of things may well have led to the translation of different portions having been written down at different times. Some of these translated fragments may have become current before others, and so have been embodied in both Mt and Lk.

Finally, it is to be observed that, in spite of the difficulties which we have discussed in regard to the connexion between our Greek Mt and a Hebrew source, it is marked by features which fully justify us in regarding it as that setting forth of the Gospel history in Greek which kept closest both in spirit and in form to the mode of presenting the Gospel in the Aramaic-speaking Church.

ii. **The Fourth Gospel, especially in its relation to the Synoptic Gospels.**—It is impossible to review here the whole subject of the authorship and historical character of the Fourth Gospel, and many points connected therewith may be more naturally treated in the article specially devoted to this Gospel. In a general article on the Gospels, however, it will be suitable, and even necessary, that we should compare the first three Gospels as a class with the fourth, and consider some of the questions raised by the contrast which they present. Some of the chief difficulties felt in regard to the genuineness and authenticity of Jn are in point of fact due to, while others have been mainly suggested and are emphasized by, its differences from the Synoptics. It is also not less true, though it has been less commonly noticed, that there are features in the Synoptic Gospels which are not easily understood when they are viewed in the light of Jn; for the superior credibility of the respective accounts is by no means always on one side.

We will therefore touch on the main respects in which the representations of the life and work and person of Christ in Jn and the Synoptic Gospels need to be examined in relation to one another, and then discuss briefly the problem how the subject as a whole should have come to be presented in these two ways, and whether it is consistent with the truth of each, and with the traditional authorship of the Fourth Gospel.

(1) *The march of events, manner in which Christ's person and office were manifested, and method and effects of His ministry.*—That Synoptic outline, to which allusion has already been made, is of a simple character. Immediately after the baptism of Jesus and His temptation in the wilderness have been recorded, it proceeds to the opening of His ministry in Galilee, and is entirely occupied with His works and teaching in that district and the neighbouring parts to the east and north, till His final departure therefrom. It seems then to conduct Him continuously to Jerusalem for that Passover at which He suffered, though it does so by more or less protracted and circuitous journeyings, in the course of which He is still seen engaged in His work of teaching and healing. For anything the Synoptic Gospels say, we might suppose that Jesus paid no visit to Jerusalem during His ministry till that time when He was crucified. Further, we note that between the two limits, the first proclamation of the gospel in Galilee and His crucifixion, not one of them gives chronological marks properly so called. They scarcely even note the passing of the seasons. (There is an indication of the occurrence of a spring-time, Mt 12^1 = Mk 2^{23} = Lk 6^1, and there are one or two allusions to observances which were connected with particular times of year). It is true that the more carefully we study the Synoptic Gospels, the more clearly do we perceive in our Lord's work as they represent it certain stages and turning-points which follow one another according to a very natural order of development. And we may conclude that their arrangement of His words and deeds corresponds in the main to successive periods in His life. But these periods can be ascertained only by a study of the internal character of the narrative.

In the Fourth Gospel, on the other hand, the flight of time during Christ's ministry is marked, not indeed by ordinary chronology or references to events of external history, but by the mention of several Jewish feasts. This Gospel is in fact chiefly taken up with records of what happened during the visits of Jesus to Jerusalem on the occasion of these feasts. In a word, the centre of interest in the Synoptic Gospels is Galilee, in the Fourth it is Jerusalem and Judæa.

When the two plans of narration are compared, it is found possible to fit them together, without forcing, to an extent which is remarkable, considering the difference between their plans, and the absence of any indication on the part of the fourth evangelist as to how the contents of his Gospel are to be combined with the Synoptic record. He represents Jesus as in the neighbourhood of John the Baptist subsequently to His baptism, and as then returning to Galilee. The first visit to Jerusalem which he describes is for a Passover that happened soon after this, and before (as it would seem) the commencement of His regular ministry in Galilee (Jn 1^{29}–2^{12}). In the holy city itself and in Judæa, at the time of this feast, Christ's public work began, according to Jn (2^{13}–4^3). He returns to Galilee by the most direct route, through Samaria, and preaches there during His brief stay ($4^{4\text{-}42}$). So we are brought to a point ($4^{43\text{-}54}$) corresponding with the beginning and early days of the ministry in Galilee described in the Synoptic Gospels. The fourth evangelist then proceeds to give an account of a visit to Jerusalem for a Jewish feast. It is the only one occurring during the period of the Galilæan ministry, and curiously in this single instance he does not specify what feast it was (ch. 5). In 6–7^9 we have narratives connected with Galilee, some of the main incidents of which are given also in the Synoptics, and which belong, according to all the evangelists, to the latter part of His ministry there. Jn gives notes of time; this section in his Gospel relates to the interval between the approach of a Passover (March), for which Jesus did not go up to Jerusalem, and the following Feast of Tabernacles (September), when He finally left Galilee. In contrast with the impression given us by the Synoptic Gospels, Jesus, according to Jn, went straight to Jerusalem for this feast, and His journey thither must have been swift (Jn $7^{2\text{-}14}$). There followed at the beginning of winter the Feast of Dedication, for which Jesus was also there. It is not easy to decide how much of Jn 7^{14}–10^{39} is connected with the former, how much with the latter, of these feasts; how much, again, belongs to the intervening weeks, or whether Jesus spent the whole of this time in Jerusalem and its immediate neighbourhood, or retired for any part of it to a greater distance. The interval between the Feast of Dedication and His last Passover He spent in Peræa, where He still taught and won disciples ($10^{40\text{-}42}$), and in the north-east corner of Judæa (11^{54}), saving His visit to the neighbourhood of Jerusalem for the great miracle at Bethany ($11^{1\text{-}44}$). The Synoptic Gospels are so far in agreement with Jn that they indicate a ministry in this same region before the final going up to Jerusalem (Mt $19^{1\cdot 2}$ = Mk 10^1, Lk less definitely). The Synoptic and Johannine narratives begin to correspond more closely at the approach to the city on this last visit, though there are still many divergences in detail.

As regards the main and most characteristic difference thus far noticed between the first three Gospels and Jn, it is fair to say that all considerations of historical probability are in favour of Christ's having made frequent visits to Jerusalem, such as are related by the latter. As a religious Jew, and especially one who would not be detained by any of the occupations of a secular calling, He would naturally attend many of the feasts. It is, moreover, inconceivable that, having His great prophetic mission to discharge, He would confine His teaching till the last few days of His life to the north and east of Palestine, and never seek to declare His message in the great centre of the religious life of the chosen people, where the effects of doing so would be so much farther-reaching, and all the local associations would add to the significance of His words and deeds. Again, the catastrophe described by the Synoptic Gospels themselves, and the manner in which it was brought about,—the enmity of the ruling priests, lawyers, and Pharisees in Jerusalem,—must have been prepared for. The work of Jesus in the country districts could hardly of itself have threatened their authority in such a way as to inspire their determination to destroy Him. The two or three days of teaching in Jerusalem which preceded their formal conspiracy against Him would have been altogether insufficient to bring their hostility to a head, if there had not been already deep-seated hatred. Various slight indications in the Synoptic Gospels, such as instances of His having disciples and friends in Judæa, may be also more easily explained if He had actually taught there during the earlier part of His ministry.

We pass on to consider the representation of the history, viewed not so much as a series of events as in its moral and spiritual aspects. From the Synoptic Gospels it appears that Jesus made the formation of a little band of devoted disciples and their instruction and training a primary aim of His earthly ministry. (See esp. Mk $3^{13, 14}$, Mt $13^{10-17, 51, 52}$, Mk 4^{34}, Mt 10). In Jn this work is more minutely and fully related. We see the first gathering of a few around Him (1^{35-51}), which would naturally precede any formal call to definite service, such as that which is referred to Mt 4^{18-22} = Mk 1^{16-20}. From the beginning almost of His public ministry He moves about surrounded by a few who have attached themselves to Him (Jn $2^{2, 12}$ 3^{22} $4^{2, 8, 27}$). The impression made on them by His deeds and words is specially recorded (Jn $2^{11, 17}$ 4^{27}). The conditions necessary for the slow growth and due probation of their faith were not interfered with by the singularly full and exalted declarations concerning His person and work made even by the Baptist ($1^{29, 36}$), and throughout by Himself to disciples (1^{51} 3^{13-15}), and also in the hearing of a wider circle as early as the second recorded visit to Jerusalem (5^{17-47}). For, distinct though these claims might be, their nature and the language in which they were expressed were so new, and His course of conduct as a whole corresponded so little with common expectation, that to apprehend His meaning rightly was a matter of great difficulty, and the faith even of those most favourably disposed to receive Him, or who had already given Him their allegiance, was put to a severe test thereby. The reality of the trial appears alike in Jn and the other three (comp. Jn 6^{66-71} with Mt 16^{13-19} = Mk 8^{27-30} = Lk 9^{18-20}). In each account the faith of the Twelve is recognized as a great victory, and they are contrasted with others. A class of persons who had for a time taken up the position of disciples, but who afterwards fell away through the perplexity which He caused them,—through becoming disappointed in Him,—is clearly portrayed in Jn (6^{60-65}; and cf. 7^3 $8^{31ff.}$ $11^{45, 46}$ 12^{11}), though in the Synoptic Gospels they hardly come before us.

Jesus Himself saw that some of those who professed to be disciples were of this unreliable character, before either they themselves or others knew it (2^{23-25}). That there should have been this class is in every way probable, under the conditions of the case, and in view of facts like the wide popularity for a time of the Prophet of Nazareth, which the Synoptic Gospels, too, relate. But it is almost inconceivable that any one writing at the end of the 1st or beginning of the 2nd cent. should have described them in a manner so true to historical circumstances, except from actual recollection of instances. There was no motive or guidance for doing so in the trials of the Church at that time. Those who fell away then did so under the influence of the love of the world, or of philosophy, or the fear of persecution. A moral in regard to the last-named cause of defection might be pointed from examples of secret believers who were afraid to confess Christ, and such are spoken of in Jn (12^{42} 19^{38}; cf. also 7^{13}), but they are a distinct class from those mentioned above, whose conduct was such as would have occurred among those who were compelled to judge of the claims of Jesus during His lifetime, but not afterwards.

The chief points on which the conflicts of Jesus with the Jews turn in the Synoptic Gospels, appear also in Jn (cf. Mt 12^{38-45}; Mt 16^{1-4} = Mk 8^{11-13}; Lk $11^{16, 29-32}$ with Jn 2^{18}). They make charges of demoniacal possession (cf. Mt 9^{34}, Mt $12^{24ff.}$ = Mk $3^{22ff.}$ = Lk $11^{15ff.}$ with Jn $8^{48, 49, 52}$ $10^{19, 20, 21}$). They charge Him with disregarding the Sabbath (cf. Mt $12^{1ff.}$ = Mk $2^{23ff.}$ = Lk $6^{1ff.}$, Mt $12^{9ff.}$ = Mk $3^{1ff.}$ = Lk $13^{10ff.}$ $14^{1ff.}$ with Jn $5^{10, 16, 18}$ $7^{22, 23}$ $9^{14, 16}$). At the same time the difference in the illustration which Christ uses as an *argumentum ad hominem* in Mt 12^{11} and in Jn 7^{22} should be noticed, and the exquisite suitability of each to the particular scene of controversy. The one would come home to the country-folk of Galilee, to whom such a case of conscience may even have been already familiar; the force of the other would be felt by the Jews of Jerusalem, with their high sense of the importance of such points of ceremonial law.

As regards the character of the miracles in Jn, it is curious that he does not relate any example of the cure of one possessed with a devil—which, according to the Synoptic Gospels, was one of the commonest kinds of our Lord's miracles. This is the more singular because teaching as to an important aspect of Christ's mission could be deduced from such miracles, and was so by Christ Himself, according to the Synoptic narrative (Mt 12^{25-30} = Mk 3^{23-27} = Lk 11^{17-26}). On the other hand, the first miracle recorded in Jn (2^{1-11}) is of a different type from any in the Synoptics. The other miracles in Jn are either the same as, or similar in kind to, those which they relate. The miracle of raising Lazarus, however, seems to surpass in wonder the raising of Jairus' daughter and of the widow's son, though on consideration it may well be questioned whether it does so to an appreciable extent. But it is in any case remarkable that so great a miracle, and one which, according to Jn, served to precipitate the action of the Jewish Sanhedrin, should be omitted in the Synoptic account. While recognizing this, it may be well to notice that the miracle of Christ which must seem the most stupendous of all from the point of view of naturalism,—'that of feeding the multitude,'—is related by all four evangelists.

Speaking generally, although Jn gives us a profounder view of the meaning of our Lord's work, and unfolds the great drama of the belief and unbelief which He provoked, with a more awful sense of its import than the Synoptic Gospels do, yet, in respect to the broad features of the history, they are either in essential agreement, or are not necessarily inconsistent with one another.

(2) *Comparison in detail of passages in which the first three and the fourth Gospels are parallel or approximate to one another, or are in conflict.*—We must be content with touching on a few points of special interest.

(*a*) The work of the Baptist (cf. Jn 1^{19-36} with Mt 3^{1-17} = Mk 1^{2-8} = Lk 3^{1-17}). Alike in the Synoptic outline and in Jn, the work of the Baptist is the starting-point of the history. But on comparing their accounts it is to be noticed, that while we have in the former a general description of the Baptist's preaching before the baptism of Jesus and of that event itself, the latter takes up the history at a time a little (probably a few weeks) later, when the Baptist had reflected on the signs which accompanied the baptism of Jesus, and when he could not only speak of 'the Coming One,' but point Him out. It does not appear from the Synoptic account who saw the signs and heard the voice. The words spoken from heaven have in Mk and Lk the form of an address to Jesus; nevertheless, it cannot be supposed that these evangelists, any more than Mt, imagined them to have been spoken simply for the assurance of Jesus. All three, we cannot doubt, record them as a proof of His Messiahship. From Jn it may be inferred that the knowledge of these signs rested on the evidence of the Baptist, who declared what he had seen and heard. To him the revelation was granted, as to one fitted by his exceptional spiritual enlightenment to receive it, not to all the bystanders, or, at all events, not to them with the same clearness. And this assuredly was in accord with the laws of God's spiritual kingdom. The views of the person and work of Christ taught or implied in the Baptist's language will be referred to below.

(*b*) The cleansing of the temple (Jn 2^{13-22} cf. with Mt $21^{12. 13. 23}$ = Mk $11^{15-17. 28}$ = Lk 19^{45-48} 20^2). It is a well-known difference between the Synoptic Gospels and Jn, that while he records a cleansing of the temple at the very beginning of the public work of Jesus, they place their corresponding narrative among the events of the last week of His life. There is nothing inherently difficult in the supposition that such an act should have been performed by Jesus at each of these epochs in His ministry. If on an early visit to Jerusalem He saw the traffic desecrating the temple courts, as He must in all probability have done, it would be natural that He should be moved to righteous indignation against it. Nor need He have felt restrained by the fear of too soon proclaiming His Messiahship. By such an act He did not obviously do this; it was one which any prophet might have performed. The consciousness of a character higher even than that of a prophet is revealed only in words of mysterious import. It is likely enough also that the abuse would again in a short time appear, in spite of His rebuke. If, however, we assume that the difference between Jn and the other Gospels as to the time of the cleansing arose through reminiscences, which were fundamentally the same, having been combined and connected in diverse ways, the account of the fourth evangelist is certainly not the less reliable of the two. For he must have known that given by the first three, since, even if he were not acquainted with their Gospels, the fact of their all recording this tradition implies its being widely spread; and he would not have departed from it, whether in order to correct or to supplement their narrative, except on the ground of possessing good information. It is to be added that in respect of vividness, and of the appropriateness with which the scene and the several parts of the action are represented, the superiority is on the side of Jn. One or two differences in the two accounts appear to accord with the difference of time.

(*c*) The feeding of the five thousand and crossing of the lake (Jn $6^{1-14. 15-21}$ cf. with Mt $14^{13-21. 22-33}$ = Mk $6^{30-44. 45-52}$ = Lk 9^{10-17}). This is the narrative in which Jn and the Synoptic Gospels are most closely parallel. As is commonly the case in Jn, the relation of the miracle is followed by teaching concerning spiritual mysteries, which appear to be suggested by the miracle, so that we are led almost to regard it as an acted parable. But the fact that the Synoptic Gospels record the miracle, without giving any corresponding discourse, shows that the fourth evangelist cannot be rightly accused of inventing the miracle as a basis for the discourse, and if he did not in this case, there is the less reason to suppose that he did so in others. Jn agrees in many points of detail and in some phrases with the Synoptic Gospels, esp. with Mk and Mt. It is possible that these may be due in part to acquaintance with these Gospels, or with the document embodied in them. But a common tradition would equally well account for such correspondences as may be observed. Indeed, this is the most probable explanation of the relation between Jn $6^{12. 13}$, Mt 6^{20}, Lk 9^{17}. He would seem to give here in a fuller form the incident of which they have preserved a partial reminiscence.

Even in this narrative, where the resemblance between the four evangelists is greatest, Jn is still very independent. And many of the touches peculiar to him are such as would be imparted by an eye-witness. There is greater particularity in his account, *e.g.* words which, according to the Synoptic Gospels, were spoken to or by the disciples generally, were, according to Jn, addressed to or spoken by individuals amongst them. The more lifelike character of his account of the conclusion of the incident of the miracle should also be noticed. There was a scene of excitement and enthusiasm, and Jesus, after His wont, quietly withdrew (Jn vv.$^{14. 15}$). This we can understand far better than that the multitudes should have been willing to disperse, simply on being bidden to go, after witnessing such a work (Mt v.^{23} = Mk vv.$^{45. 46}$).

(*d*) The closing scenes. It will be impossible to do more than allude to a few of the divergences from and additions to the Synoptic Gospels which we find in Jn. As regards the much discussed subject of the Day of the Crucifixion, it must suffice to say that, whatever may be the difficulties arising from the Synoptic language concerning the Last Supper, the view that Jesus was crucified on the 14th of Nisan, which is the natural inference from Jn's language, must be accepted as the most probable. On this assumption, his statements throughout are clear and self-consistent, while they are supported also by some indications in the other Gospels. To pass on, there are many signs of accurate knowledge in Jn's whole account of the last evening with the disciples, the arrest, and condemnation of Jesus. For instance, the preliminary investigation before Annas, and the fact mentioned in Jn and nowhere else that he was the father-in-law of Caiaphas, fit well with all the statements contained in Josephus regarding the succession of members of the family of Annas to the office of high priest during Annas' own lifetime. Again, when Jesus is brought to Pilate, we obtain from Jn a clear and thoroughly probable view of the scene and of the successive acts of the drama. The prisoner, as was natural, is conducted at once within the governor's house, while the Jewish rulers remain outside for a ceremonial reason (18^{28}). Pilate passes to and fro. In vv.$^{29-32}$ he is outside parleying with the Jews; in vv.$^{33-37}$ he proceeds with the examination of the prisoner; vv.[38-40] Pilate again parleys with the Jews. 19[1-5] Jesus is mocked and led out to them; vv.[6-16] they succeed by their clamour in securing His condemnation. In Mt 27[11-26] = Mk 15[1-15] the positions and the parts of the several actors are not nearly so distinctly indicated.

(3) *The peculiar doctrinal character of Jn.*—It is necessary to inquire whether the representation given us in the Fourth Gospel of the teaching of Christ, or the belief of others, has been affected by the special doctrinal point of view of the writer in a way to destroy its substantial truth.

We may first notice some signs that he was, to say the least, not wholly unconscious of the importance of preserving faithfully the language and thought of the time concerning which he was writing. The most striking is the fact that the term 'the Logos,' which, as he uses it in the Prologue, gives the very keynote of the Gospel, is nevertheless nowhere put by him into the mouth either of Jesus or any other speaker. But, again, he distinguishes more than once between the manner in which the disciples viewed acts and words of Christ at the time, and afterwards in looking back upon them (2[22] 12[16], cf. also the Lord's words to Peter, 13[7]). He does not read the full belief of a later time into the earliest days of discipleship. It should be noticed also that the evangelist need not be supposed to give 3[16-21] and [31-36] as parts of the words spoken respectively by Christ and by the Baptist. On the contrary, they seem rather to be comments by the evangelist himself, which are not intended by him to be viewed in any other light.

At the same time, the way in which the record almost insensibly passes into exposition in these cases, suggests that the two may sometimes be even more closely conjoined. It is natural, and often almost necessary, under the limits of space to which all are subject, for any writer or speaker, in giving the substance of what has been spoken by others, so to report them as to bring out that which he conceives to have been the significance of their words. There might, no doubt, be a special tendency to do this on the part of one who, like the writer of the Fourth Gospel, had the definite object of impressing truth in which he profoundly believed. That which he had even quite soundly inferred as the conclusion from all that he had experienced and learned, might thus have unduly influenced him in his account of what was said on some particular occasions. Two instances in which it seems specially likely that his own perception of the meaning of Christ's work may be affecting his record, are the words which he assigns to the Baptist (1[29]), and to the Samaritans (4[42]). It is difficult to suppose that even the former, much less the latter, could already at that time have attained to a belief in Jesus as the Saviour '*of the world.*' We will go on to compare Jn 1[30] with the somewhat similar saying in the Synoptic Gospels (Mt 3[11] = Mk 1[7] = Lk 3[16]). In view of the stress laid in other passages in Jn on the pre-existence of Christ, it seems most probable that the evangelist himself would have held that this truth was conveyed in the words ὅτι πρῶτός μου ἦν. Yet this phrase is an enigmatical one; it does not strictly express any idea but that of essential priority, which might be in point of rank as well as of time. So regarded, it does not differ widely from the phrase in the Synoptic Gospels, ἰσχυρότερός μου, which also is enigmatical. Each brings out a somewhat different view of Christ's superiority. It would have been easy for the fourth evangelist to have made the assertion by the Baptist of the doctrine of Christ's preexistence more distinct. Thus, although he may have been in a measure influenced in the form

which he gives to the Baptist's words by the desire to teach through them an important article of faith, he has in doing so evidently been kept under control by his sense of historical truth.

We proceed to consider briefly the contents of Christ's own teaching as it is recorded in Jn.

(*a*) His unique relation to the Father—the unfolding of all that was comprised in the words '*My* Father.' In the matter common to Mt and Lk one passage is included (Mt 11[25-30] = Lk 10[21, 22]) which is characterized by the thoughts and many of the expressions on this subject that we are accustomed to regard as most distinctly 'Johannine.' Mt 24[36] = Mk 13[32] supplies another instance of the use of ὁ υἱός and ὁ πατήρ as absolute terms. The preservation of this teaching, even though to such a limited extent, in the Synoptic Gospels, goes far to establish the credibility of the fuller record in Jn. If Christ dwelt on this theme at all, there is every reason to think that He must have done so more often and largely than they indicate. That He did so is also rendered probable by a striking, even though indirect, piece of evidence in St. Paul's Epistles. St. Paul more than once uses the phrase 'the Father of our Lord Jesus Christ' (Ro 15[6], 2 Co 1[3] 11[31], Eph 1[3], Col 1[3]). This remarkable expression may most naturally have had its origin in the historical fact that Jesus was accustomed to dwell upon the theme that God was, in an altogether unique sense, His Father.

(*b*) Christ's attitude to the Mosaic Law. It is certain that we derive in part a different impression on this subject from the Synoptic Gospels and Jn. There is nothing in the former corresponding to the phrases '*your* law' (Jn 8[17] 10[34]) and '*their* law' (15[25]). In their record of our Lord's condemnation of the legalism of the scribes and Pharisees, the distinction between the law of Moses itself and the additions made to it in tradition appears more clearly (Mt 15[2-9] = Mk 7[1-13]). In one saying recorded in Mt (23[2, 3]), Christ even maintains the authority of the scribes on the ground that they are the representatives of Moses. There seems, at first sight, to be nothing in the Fourth Gospel equivalent to the assertion in Mt 5[17-19] (= Lk 16[17]) concerning the permanent validity of every point of the law; while in it the spiritual meaning of the OT, and the superiority of Christ to Moses (*e.g.* 7[19-23]), are far more fully brought out.

Nevertheless, on a close examination, there appears to be fundamental similarity between their respective representations. The saying concerning the permanent validity of the law in Mt is immediately followed by the great passage which shows what Christ meant by its true fulfilment; while the words in Jn 10[35] 'the scripture cannot be broken'—where 'the scripture' referred to is one occurring in what has just before been described as '*your* law'—appear to involve a principle equivalent to that laid down in the saying in Mt 5[17-19]. Further, the remarkable correspondence in the thought of Mt 19[8] = Mk 10[5-9] and of Jn 7[22] should be noted. In both a distinction is drawn between the law of Moses and a more primitive law.

(*c*) Eschatology. The Jewish form of eschatological expectation is more marked in Christ's teaching given in the Synoptic Gospels than in Jn. In the latter we are especially taught that spiritual and eternal laws and principles are great facts of the present, and that judgment is ever being executed through their continuous and mysterious operation. So far as our thoughts are turned to the future consummation, they are especially fixed on the blessedness of completed union with Christ, and the circumstances attendant upon His coming drop out of sight. The Synoptic Gospels may be taken as witnesses to the fact that Jesus did make use of the current imagery in speaking of the things to come. But the view can hardly seem improbable to any one, that, on this subject at all events, the mind of the Master is more fully reflected in Jn.

(d) The maxims in regard to conduct which the Synoptic Gospels—more especially Mt and Lk—contain, are among the most precious portions of these Gospels. In the earlier part of Jn this element is absent, but it receives a large amount of recognition in the discourses at the Last Supper. Here the law of Christian love, and the duty of humbly ministering to others ($13^{1-15. 34. 35}$, $15^{12. 17}$), and generally of keeping Christ's commandments (14^{15} 15^{10}), are insisted on. Here, also, sayings on the conditions and privileges of discipleship occur, identical with, or closely parallel to, some of those which are found in other contexts in the first three Gospels. (Cf. Jn 12^{25} with Mt $16^{25. 26}$ =Mk $8^{35. 36}$=Lk $9^{24. 25}$, and cf. also Mt $10^{37. 39}$= Lk 17^{33} and Lk 14^{26}. Again, cf. Jn $13^{13. 14}$ with Mt 10^{24a}, Lk 6^{40}; and Jn 13^{16} and 15^{20} with Mt 10^{24b}. Again, cf. Jn 13^{20} with Mt 10^{40}=Lk 10^{16}). The encouragements to pray in these chapters of Jn should also be compared with sayings on prayer in the Synoptic Gospels.

(4) *The style of Christ's teaching.*—The difference between Jn and the Synoptic Gospels in this respect seems not to be so great in reality as is often imagined. Justin Martyr's description of our Lord's teaching as consisting in 'short, pithy, and abrupt sayings,' applies, no doubt, with special truth to the Synoptic records of it. But in Jn, too, its style is essentially proverbial or 'gnomic.' The sentences are short and oracular. The discourses consist of a series of separate propositions, and the development of the thought is effected, not through a ratiocinative argument of an ordinary kind, but by slightly altering the form of a proposition, or by placing it in a different connexion.

Again, the use of parables appears from the first three evangelists to have been specially characteristic of Christ. He employed them, however, more particularly in addressing the multitudes; and this part of His teaching is hardly at all recorded in Jn. Moreover, we have in Jn one genuine parable (10^{1-6}), followed in vv.$^{7-10}$ by its interpretation. Jn 10^{11-18} appears to be the interpretation of another parable, the parable itself being omitted by the evangelist (see Weizsäcker, *Untersuch.* pp. 252, 253). Or perhaps it may be truer to say that parable and interpretation are here merged in one. Although He was wont to teach His disciples by expounding to them the parables which they heard Him address to the people (Mt $13^{10ff.}$=Mk $4^{10ff.}$=Lk $8^{9ff.}$, Mk 4^{34}), it would be natural that He should vary His method in some such way as we have suggested, when His instruction of the Twelve did not take the form of a supplement to what He had spoken to others.

It has further to be remarked that Christ's own office is the theme of the figures in Jn. The parables related in the Synoptists are concerned most frequently with other subjects, especially the kingdom of God and its laws. Yet this one also is not absent from His thoughts there (cf. the physician, Mt 9^{12}=Mk 2^{17}=Lk 5^{31} and Lk 4^{23}; the servant of J", Lk $14^{16ff.}$; the king's son, Mt $21^{37ff.}$, Mk $12^{6ff.}$, Mt $22^{2ff.}$; the judge, Mt $25^{31ff.}$).

The different aspects under which the life and work and person of Christ are presented in the Synoptic Gospels and Jn may be reconcilable. We have given some reasons for thinking that they are so in great measure. But the question remains, how the existence of such differences in the records can be explained. And it may be

observed that it is one for which even those need to seek an answer who admit only, as the majority of modern critics do, that the Fourth Gospel contains considerable historical elements.

Now, the Fourth Gospel has a clearly defined aim ($20^{30. 31}$, and cf. 1^{1-14}), which goes far to explain the selective method on which the writer has proceeded in constructing his Gospel. When in addition to this we take into account the fact that he must almost certainly have been acquainted with the contents of the Synoptic Gospels, and that he would at least feel under no obligation to recount what was already recorded, and that he may even have avoided the repetition of it when it did not fall in conveniently with the plan of his own work, and that in point of fact he is in the habit of assuming in his readers the knowledge of things that he does not narrate, little difficulty can be created by his omissions.

The difficulty is rather to understand how the first three evangelists should omit so much that we find in Jn. The same reasons did not exist in their case for passing over facts as in that of Jn. To some small extent, indeed, they were influenced in what they relate by the bent of their own minds and the special needs of those whom they addressed. But the very fact that the matter and arrangement of all three are so largely the same, shows that their contents and form must have been in the main determined by some other cause than individual purpose or bias. Their fragmentariness must be due to the limited character of the material that had come to their hand. We have seen that the historical circumstances under which the documentary sources of the Synoptic narrative were shaped, were of a kind to circumscribe their range. But in order to explain the phenomenon now before us—the contrast between the Synoptic and Johannine accounts — it seems necessary to suppose further that the knowledge embodied in the latter had, at the time the first three Gospels were composed, been delivered only within a comparatively limited circle. It is difficult to imagine that even Mark and the editor of the Greek Mt would have remained unaffected by it if it had been widely spread through a considerable part of the Church. And it is impossible to believe that Luke would, seeing that he evidently had sought for information in different directions, and desired to give a certain completeness, so far as he could, to his narrative. There appears to be nothing unnatural in this supposition. The needs of simple Christians, and of the mass of the unconverted, which had led originally to the shaping of the oral instruction in a certain way, and which through it had influenced the character of the earliest documents, would continue to be most generally felt. The number of those able to appreciate the deeper teaching would be small.

III. THE DATE OF OUR GOSPELS AND OF THE SOURCES EMBODIED IN THEM.—In endeavouring to arrive approximately at the date of the Gospels, it is necessary to consider both the testimony of tradition and internal indications.

1. *The Synoptic Gospels.*—If, as is probable, the fragment of Papias about *Mt* is a report of what he had heard many years before from John the Presbyter, and preserves for us the recollections of the latter concerning a period already past when Papias met him, the composition of our Greek Mt would seem to fall within the 1st cent. General considerations respecting the history of the position of this Gospel in the Church point to its belonging at least to the 1st cent. It has often been argued, on the ground of Mt 24^{29}, that the Gospel was composed before the destruction of Jerusalem in A.D. 70; but the words in question may be explained by the fidelity with which the original source has

been preserved. Nor do there seem to be other indications in the Gospel which enable us to assign it with confidence to a time either before or after that or any other date.

On the ground of the strongly supported tradition which connects the *Second Gospel* with Mark, we may somewhat more nearly determine the time of the composition of this Gospel. It would seem, according to the oldest form of the tradition, to have been after St. Peter's death that Mark wrote it, and consequently we cannot place its composition much before A.D. 70. The lower limit will be that of the period after this for which Mark, who must have been in middle life at the date just named, is likely to have lived. Internal indications do not help us in this case any more than in the last.

The lower limit for the composition of the *Third Gospel* is fixed by a consideration similar to that in the last case. Its author was a companion of St. Paul for some years, and there is in point of fact no reason to doubt the tradition which identifies him with Luke, named in St. Paul's Epistles. This Gospel consequently cannot have been written much later than A.D. 80. On the other hand, the greater precision with which the siege of Jerusalem is referred to than it is in Mt and Mk (see Lk 19[43] 21[20]), seems to show that in this Gospel the original form of the prophecy has been somewhat lost, owing to knowledge of the particular circumstances of the event.

But we have seen that sources, documentary and other, are embodied in the Synoptic Gospels. In order, then, to judge how near we are in reality brought to the events related, we have to inquire into the historical character of the matter which the evangelists used, and the faithfulness with which they have reproduced it. This is a fruitful field for study. It is only possible here to say that the subject-matter of the Synoptic Gospels is marked by traits which show that the information proceeds direct from those who have lived amid the surroundings described. The characteristics of Jewish life and thought in Palestine in the first half of the 1st cent. of our era are reflected in the narrative with a truth which could not have been otherwise imparted.

The fact that our Gospels were put forth far from Palestine, in the midst of the Græco-Roman world, and subsequently to, or at the earliest only a short while before, the destruction of Jerusalem, —that great catastrophe which profoundly affected the Jews everywhere, and above all in Palestine, and the Christian Church itself,—becomes (strange to say) a guarantee of their truth. Placed as the evangelists were when they wrote, they could not have accurately reproduced the features of an age which had passed away, as they are found to have done, except from immediate knowledge of their own, the reports of those who possessed it, or the use of documents based on it. Attention may be directed to the following points:— (a) The distribution in Pal. of the Jewish population on the one hand, and of the Grecized cities and regions on the other. It will be found that our Lord's work is confined, saving in a very few cases, which are of the kind that may be truly said to be exceptions that prove the rule, to the pre-eminently Jewish districts. In Galilee itself the incidents of His ministry are connected with Jewish villages and village-towns, not with the places known in the outside world. We may infer what Christ's own plan was for the work of His brief ministry on earth. Only the first evangelist lays stress on it; the records of the second and third, and we may add of the fourth, equally reveal it, but they do so, to all appearance, unconsciously. And although we can on reflection see clearly the reason for such a course of action, it is not one which

would have naturally suggested itself to men who, like the third and fourth evangelists at least, were deeply impressed with the universality of the gospel. (β) The political and social circumstances, the strangely mingled Jewish and Roman institutions and remaining effects of the period of Grecian rule, the relations of the jurisdictions of Herod and the Roman governor and the Jewish priests and elders, and the influence of the Pharisees and scribes. (γ) The popular Messianic expectation, and the temper of different classes in respect to it, its various forms and the beliefs connected therewith. (δ) The subtle correspondences in form between the teaching of Jesus and that of Jewish Rabbis, combined with the vital differences in spirit.

The teaching, again, of our Lord is much of it such as could have been given only by Himself in His own lifetime, or is marked by the prominence of terms and ideas which speedily ceased to be much in vogue in the Church. This serves to show that the character of the record generally can have been comparatively little affected by the thought and language of the Church in a subsequent generation.

The following may be taken as illustrations :— (α) The use of the term and idea 'the kingdom of God' in the Gospels (see *The Jewish and the Christian Messiah*, by the present writer, pp. 226, 227). (β) The use in the Gospels of the title 'the Son of Man' (see *ib.* pp. 243, 244). (γ) The use of the term μαθηταί (see Weizsäcker, *Apost. Zeitalter*, p. 36).

In order that the Gospels may be tested in the respects indicated with the greater precision, those portions of them which appear to be derived from common sources, or from a source peculiar to one or other evangelist, or which are the setting or the remarks furnished by the several evangelists individually, should be separately examined.

2. *The Fourth Gospel.*—The history is contemplated in this Gospel from a point of view acquired through long reflection and experience, and through sharing in the ever-widening work and conflicts of the Church. And yet familiarity with Palestine and with the thought and feeling of its population at the time to which the record refers, is manifested in it not less markedly than in the others. If these two characteristics—the immediate knowledge of the facts, and a wide and large conception of their significance—belong, as appears to be the case, to one and the same person, we must suppose that he was one of the immediate disciples of Jesus whose mind underwent a remarkable growth during his subsequent life. There is next to nothing in the character of John the son of Zebedee, as we see it in the Gospels and the early chapters of the Acts, which marks him out as fitted to be the writer. And the allusion to him in Gal 2[9], as one of the apostles of the circumcision, may seem unfavourable to the belief that he was so. But tradition, which assigns to him the authorship, also represents him as having lived to a great age, and having passed his later years amid the influences of Ephesus. This leaves room for a change in his apprehension of the truth. And, strange as this change from the mode of thought of the Twelve in the early days of the Church at Jerusalem to that of the writer of the Fourth Gospel may seem to us, it is one well within the bounds of possibility, and hardly to be reckoned greater than some of those of which there have been instances among religious thinkers in our own century. It is to be added, that if the characteristics of this Gospel have been correctly described above, the difficulty as to the authorship would be in no way lightened by supposing that the writer was not the son of Zebedee. For there is no other of the earliest Palestinian disciples who, so far as we know, could more easily have become prepared to write the Fourth Gospel.

[The trustworthiness of the traditions as to the old age of John the son of Zebedee has been called in question, more especially of late by Harnack in his *Chron. d. Altchrist. Lit.* i. pp. 320 ff. and 656 ff. For a discussion of this question see NT CANON.]

IV. THE HARMONY OF THE GOSPELS.—A comparison of the Gospels, very different for the most part in its method and object from that which we have been reviewing, has been associated with the name of the Harmonists. Starting from the assumption that the inspiration of Holy Scripture involves its complete immunity from error even in the most unimportant historical details, they endeavoured to reconcile all inconsistencies in parallel accounts in the Gospels, and, when this was found to be impossible, they inferred that different incidents or occasions were referred to. For many years past, however, even those thoughtful students of the Gospels who have believed in the absolute infallibility of every part of Scripture, as well as others who had no wish to deny this thesis, have felt dissatisfied with the expedients resorted to by the Harmonists; and have been more inclined to say that our knowledge is not full enough to admit of such a process being soundly applied, and to suggest that if we were acquainted with all the circumstances the apparent discrepancies would vanish.

Recent criticism is seldom ready to admit that variations in two narratives which have a general resemblance, or in the form and setting of sayings which in substance are the same, point to two similar but distinct events, or to the repetition at different times of the same teaching. It is in the habit of attributing such variations to the natural action of tradition, where they were not due to one or other of the evangelists themselves. It would even account thus for the recurrence of similar sayings (or incidents) in the same Gospel. A tradition, it says, came to be embodied with greater or less differences of form in each of two documents which have been used by the evangelist; he has given the two reports of the same fact as if they were reports of distinct facts. And its chief interest in these 'doublets,' as they are termed, is that they may be a means of discovering more about the original documents. There are cases in which such an explanation appears probable. On the other hand, modern critics overlook far too much the consideration that history does sometimes repeat itself, and in particular that all men who feel that they have a message for mankind necessarily insist often on the truths which they are most anxious to inculcate, and in doing so use again and again the same language. Thus Christ must in all probability have spoken some of His most striking sayings many times. And this may well have been the cause of some at least of the variations and repetitions in our records. We are not, however, entitled to reject any of the above explanations on the ground of an *à priori* theory as to the nature of inspiration. The truth, so far as it is possible for us to ascertain it, can be reached only through the careful weighing of probabilities.

[The following may be taken as instances in connexion with which the various methods of explanation described above may be considered :— Mt 8⁵⁻¹³ cf. with Lk 7¹⁻¹⁰ and with Jn 4⁴⁶⁻⁵⁴ ; Mk 4²¹˙²² with Mt 5¹⁴⁻¹⁶ 10²⁶ and with Lk 8¹⁶˙¹⁷ 11³³ 12² ; Mk 4²⁵ with Mt 13¹² 25²⁹ and with Lk 8¹⁸ 19²⁶.]

A truer kind of harmony may be sought for in the Gospels than that which, in the supposed interests of the Faith, men have too often mistakenly attempted to establish. We may inquire whether there is, or is not, amid all differences an essential inner agreement, or at least compatibility ; whether the several representations of our Lord's Person and Life in them do not give in combination an image marked by unity and completeness. If we can trace in the Gospels such a harmony, we shall have herein the best guarantee that we could desire of their historical truth, and shall derive therefrom the noblest conception that could be formed of the common inspiration of their fourfold testimony.

LITERATURE.—In the following list an attempt is made to enumerate the works which are most important for the study of the problem of the Origin and Composition of the Gospels, in the form which it has now assumed. Works of which the interest is due mainly to their place in the history of past controversy are not here mentioned ; some of them have been named in the preceding article. In addition to books which aim at thoroughness of treatment, a few of a more popular kind have been given. Foreign works which have been translated into English are referred to by English titles, but the dates are those of the originals. It must not be supposed that the books enumerated are in all cases devoted exclusively to the maintenance of the particular views under which they are classed ; *e.g.* 'Introductions' contain reviews of the history of opinion. But it has not been thought worth while in most cases to mention the same work more than once.

For works which discuss the external evidence relating to the Gospels, see NEW TESTAMENT CANON.

SPECIAL AIDS FOR STUDYING THE FACTS.—Rushbrooke, *Synopticon*, 1880 ; A. Wright, *A Synopsis of the Gospels in Greek*, 1896.

REPRESENTATIVES OF THE TÜBINGEN SCHOOL.—It will suffice to refer to F. C. Baur, *Kritische Untersuchungen über die kanonischen Evangelien*, 1847, and for somewhat more moderate views of the same type to Hilgenfeld, *Einleitung in das Neue Testament*, 1875 ; Keim, *Jesus of Nazara* : I. Survey of Sources, 1867 ; S. Davidson, *Introduction to the Study of the New Testament*, 2nd ed. 1882, 3rd ed. revised and improved, 1894.

REPRESENTATIVES OF THE ORAL THEORY.—Westcott, *Introduction to the Study of the Gospels*, 2nd ed. revised and enlarged, 1860, 8th ed. 1895 ; A. Wright, *Composition of the Four Gospels*, 1890 ; Preface to *Synopsis*, 1896 ; and *Some NT Problems*, 1898. (C. Weizsäcker, *Apost. Age*, bk. iv. ch. 2, may be studied with great advantage in regard to the influence of the period of Oral transmission in shaping the records, though he is not an adherent of the Oral Theory).

REPRESENTATIVES OF THE TWO-DOCUMENT THEORY UNDER VARIOUS FORMS.—Holtzmann, *Die Synoptischen Evangelien*, 1863, *Einleitung in d. Neue Testament*², 1886 ; B. Weiss, *The Life of Christ*, bk. i. The Sources, 1882, *A Manual of Introduction to the New Testament*, div. iv., 1886. [Those only who desire to study the subject very fully need examine B. Weiss' *Marcus-Evangelium*, 1872, and *Matthäus-Evangelium*, 1876]; C. Weizsäcker, *Untersuchungen über die evangelische Geschichte, ihre Quellen und den Gang ihrer Entwickelung*, 1864 ; Wendt, *Lehre Jesu*, 1886 ; P. Ewald, *Das Hauptproblem d. Evangelienfrage*, 1890. (The 'main problem' referred to is the question how the Synoptic account came to be limited in the way that it is seen to be when the Johannine is recognized as possessing at least a considerable element of historical truth); Sanday, 'A Survey of the Synoptic Question,' arts. in the *Expositor*, 1891, *Inspiration*, Lect. vi. 1893 ; 'Introductions to the Synoptic Gospels in *Book by Book* ; A. J. Jolley, *The Synoptic Problem for English Readers*, 1893.

ADDITIONAL BOOKS AND ARTS. ON THE FOURTH GOSPEL.—Westcott, Prolegomena in *Commentary on St. John*, 1881 ; Sanday, *The Authorship and Historical Character of the Fourth Gospel*, 1872 ; Watkins, *Modern Criticism considered in its relation to the Fourth Gospel*, 1890 ; Delff, *Das vierte Evangelium* and *Neue Beiträge zur Kritik und Erklärung d. vierten Evangeliums*, 1890 ; arts. in *Contemporary Review* for Sept. and Oct. 1891, by Schürer and Sanday ; also Sanday, 'The Present Position of the Johannean Question,' arts. in *Expositor*, 1891, 1892 ; Harnack in *Zeitschr. f. Theol. u. Kirche*, 2 Jahrg. Heft 3.

WORKS USEFUL IN THE STUDY OF THE LOCAL COLOURING IN THE GOSPELS.—Schürer, *HJP*, 1885, 1890 ; J. Langen, *Das Judenthum in Palästina zur zeit Christi*, 1866 ; Stapfer, *Palestine in the Time of Christ*, 1885 ; F. Weber, *System d. altsynagogalen Palästinischen Theologie*, 1880 ; Wünsche, *Neue Beiträge zur Erläuterung d. Evangelien aus Talmud und Midrasch*, 1878 ; G. A. Smith, *HGHL*, 1894.

V. H. STANTON.

GOTHIC VERSION.—See VERSION.

GOTHOLIAS (Γοθολίας), 1 Es 8³³.—Jesias son of Gotholias returned with Ezra. His name in Ezr 8⁷ is ATHALIAH, which was thus both a male and female name (2 K 11¹). The form is derived from the Heb., the Γ taking the place of the initial Ayin, and not through the Greek of Ezr ('Αθελεί, 'Αθλιά).

H. ST. J. THACKERAY.

GOTHONIEL (Γοθονιήλ).—The father of Chabris, one of the rulers of Bethulia (Jth 6¹⁵).

GOURD (קיקיון *ḳîḳâyôn*, κολοκύνθη, *hedera*).—There are three opinions in regard to the plant intended in Jon 4⁶⁻¹⁰.

(*a*) That of Jerome, expressed in the Vulg. rendering *hedera* (ivy),—an opinion with no support, etymological or botanical, and denounced by Augustine as heresy.

(*b*) That of Celsius (*Hierob.* ii. 273), that it was the *kharwa'*, *Ricinus communis*, L., the *castor-oil tree*. The grounds for this opinion are philological. Dioscorides (iv. 164) describes the κρότων, *i.e.* the *castor-oil tree*, under the name of κίκι, and the Talm. calls castor-oil שׁמן קיק *shemen ḳîḳ*. The plant which God provided to overshadow Jonah, however, was a *vine*, which seems from the context to have trailed over his arbour, and not a small tree like the castor-oil plant, which could not, by any stretch of the imagination, be regarded as a vine.

(*c*) That of the LXX, κολόκυνθα (see **Wild Gourds** below), the *bottle-gourd*, *Cucurbita lagenaria*, L., the *ḳar'ah* of the Arabs. This has the advantage of answering the botanical conditions perfectly. Jonah had constructed a booth, such as the 'lodge in a garden of cucumbers' (see CUCUMBER), of poles and leaves. He sat in the shade of this booth. But the leaves soon withered, and he was exposed again to the blazing sun of Mesopotamia. It is quite customary to plant the bottle-gourd by such booths, or by the trellises near houses. It grows very rapidly, and its broad leaves form an excellent shade. Such a vine, growing over Jonah's booth, suits well the narrative. The rapidity with which the leaves of these gourd-vines die and wither and curl up is also eminently appropriate.

Wild Gourds (פקעות *paḳḳu'ôth*, τολύπη, *colocynthides*). These are the fruits of a vine growing in the fields (2 K 4³⁹). The root of this word signifies to burst open. This etym. would suit the squirting cucumber, *Ecballium Elaterium*, L., in Arab. *ḳithâ el-ḥimâr*. This plant is very common, and its juice is a drastic cathartic, and in large quantities an irritant poison. But it could not, with any propriety, be called a *vine*. It is a perennial erect herb, with a brittle stiff stem and branches, and is quite destitute of tendrils. This would make the term גפן, *qephen*, wholly inappropriate to it. *Cucumis prophetarum*, L., which grows in the deserts around the Dead Sea, and southward to Sinai, has been suggested. But the small size of its ovoid fruit, only an inch long, does not correspond to the *colocynthides* of the Vulgate.

The authority of the LXX and the Vulg. is in favour of the *colocynth*, *Citrullus Colocynthis*, L., the *ḥondol* of the Arabs. This plant is a cucurbitaceous *vine*, growing prostrate on the ground, or trailing by its spiral tendrils over shrubs and herbs. It has a lobed leaf, and a melon 3 to 3½ in. in diameter, which dries when ripe, and when opened discloses a fungous, intensely bitter pulp, containing smooth shining seeds. This pulp is also a drastic cathartic, and, in quantities, an irritant poison. The colocynth corresponds well to the requisites of the passage, that it should be a *vine*, bearing *gourds* (*colocynthides*) of a noxious quality. This plant, which is called in Greek κολοκυνθίς, must not be confounded with κολοκύνθη, which is the cultivated gourd. The *knops* (1 K 6¹⁸ marg. *gourds*, 7²⁴ פקעים *peḳâ'îm*) may have been imitations of this fruit.　　G. E. POST.

GOVERNANCE.—This old form of 'government' occurs occasionally in the versions before AV, as Jer 23¹⁰ Cov. 'Yee the waye that men take, is wicked, and their governaunce is nothinge like the holy worde of the Lorde'; and it has been retained in AV and RV (from Cov.) in 2 Es 11³² 'it had the governance of the world' (*potentatum habuit*);

and 1 Mac 9³¹ 'Jonathan took the governance upon him at that time' (ἐπεδέξατο τὴν ἥγησιν). The word occurs also in the Pr. Bk., as in Morn. Prayer, Third Collect, for Grace, 'That all our doings may be ordered by thy governance,' retained from 1549 in all editions. Sir T. Elyot in *The Governour*, ii. 109, says, 'Finally the Atheniensis, . . . toke to them a desperate corage, and in conclusion expelled out of the citie all the said tyrantes, and reduced it unto his pristinate governance.' And Chaucer, *Hous of Fame*, 958—

> 'Lo, is it not a greet mischaunce, '
> To lete a fole han governaunce
> Of thing that he can not demeine?'

　　　　　　　　　　　　　J. HASTINGS.

GOVERNMENT. — The forms of government among the Hebrews, though they developed with the course of their history, never became as strict or constitutional as among Western nations. It should therefore be kept in mind that the technical terms used in this article must be allowed some elasticity of meaning to suit Semitic institutions. These forms may be treated in the following order :—1. Those of the nomad period, extending from the Exodus out of Egypt to the settlement in Palestine. 2. The new organization due to the change from a nomad to a settled and agricultural life. 3. The institution and nature of the monarchy. 4. The semi-political independence of the Jewish communities among foreign nations. 5. The religious community of Judæa in post-exilic times.

1. When first the Hebrews appear in historical records as an organized body, their government is simple and in accordance with that of other Semitic nomads. During their wanderings in the peninsula of Sinai and East of the Jordan, there are two units of organization—the family and the tribe. A third factor is due to the temporary needs of their circumstances ; it is the leadership of Moses. This chieftainship, however, was only for a special purpose, its power was personal rather than constitutional, and was controlled and modified by the claims of kinship in family and tribe. The suspicion of any attempt to make it more aroused rebellion at once (cf. the JE account of the revolt of Dathan and Abiram in Nu 16, especially v.¹⁶). The officials appointed by Moses at the suggestion of his father-in-law were doubtless selected with due regard to tribal feelings (Ex 18²¹ff·). A thorough study of these two units of society is necessary for the understanding both of this and the succeeding periods of Hebrew history (cf. FAMILY, especially ii. *c*, TRIBE, and the literature given at the end of this article). The father as head (אישׁ) of the *family* had full power of life and death over all its members (cf. Gn 22, Jg 11³⁴ff·). The ruler of the *tribe* was probably, as among the Bedawîn of to-day, one of the heads of families who was distinguished for his courage or his hospitality. His authority, both in legal and in military matters, was personal, and his judgments were observed just in so far as his influence was powerful. This position of authority might continue in the same family for generations, but might be lost at any time, and pass to others owing to loss of prestige. The laws observed were those of custom only, and did not exist in a written form. Matters of strife between different families were referred to the tribal chief ; and if his decisions were in accordance with the customs of the tribe, or otherwise commended themselves to the people, the person condemned submitted, or became an outcast from his own people. If there were no custom to guide the judge, or the case were very difficult, an appeal might be made to the god by means of the sacred lot or oracle. The leadership in time of war naturally fell to the head of the tribe ; and a special

duty of hospitality was laid upon him, but otherwise he lived like any other head of a family. There is no mention of any revenue being assigned to him as an official.

2. The second period extends from the entrance into Palestine to the institution of the monarchy, and includes the history related in the Books of Joshua, Judges, and the first part of the Book of Samuel. It was a time of unrest, change, and adjustment. It is marked by the decay of the tribal feeling as such, and the transference of its traditions to *local* organizations and forms of government. This was due to the fact that a man's neighbours became of much more interest to him than his fellow - tribesmen in his new settled life. The most important person at this time was the 'judge' (שֹׁפֵט). The Hebrew word denotes 'deliverer' or 'ruler' (on the different uses of the word שפט see *Journal of Biblical Literature*, viii. 130–136). The former meaning does not concern us here. With the latter compare the title *sufetes* used in Carthage (Livy, xxviii. 37, xxx. 7) and other cities of North Africa (*CIL* viii. Nos. 7, 765, 10,525). The 'judges' were thus men who by their prowess became influential, and so ruled over their tribes (cf. Moore, *Judges*, pp. xi–xiii). An attempt to continue this office in the same family failed (Gideon and Abimelech). With this attempt we are introduced to a new word for ruler, מֶלֶךְ 'king.' What the original sense of the word was (cf. McCurdy, *HPM* i. § 36) does not concern us, as it had probably lost its original force when it was adopted by the Hebrews. The chief difference between a local or tribal king (מֶלֶךְ) and a 'judge' (שֹׁפֵט) seems to have consisted in the idea of hereditary transmission of office involved in the former (Jg 8²²). This idea of continuity of office may have been derived from an application of the title 'king' to the god. This was a common practice among the Semitic peoples (cf. for Phœnicians and others, W. R. Smith, *RS*, 1st ed. p. 67 ff., 2nd ed. p. 66 ff. ; for the Hebrews, G. B. Gray, *Studies in Hebrew Proper Names*, p. 115 ff.). Among the changes due to the new settled life, it may be noticed that the 'elders' (זְקֵנִים), who in the older tribal organization were the heads of the families, now became an upper class, corresponding to the 'elders' (זְקֵנִים) or 'princes' (שָׂרִים) of the Canaanitish communities (Jg 8¹⁴ 9, cf. Nowack, *Heb. Archæol.* i. 304). It was also probably in imitation of a Canaanitish custom that a city and its 'towns' (literally 'daughters' בָּנוֹת, *i.e.* suburbs) were sometimes united for purposes of common protection and government (Nu 21²⁵·³², Jos 17¹¹, cf. 2 S 20¹⁹). Another prominent figure in the almost formless government of this time was the 'seer' (רֹאֶה), whose intimate relation to the deity was supposed to bestow on him a kind of second sight (cf. Saul's first visit to Samuel in 1 S 9⁶ff·), and led men to appeal to him for decisions in matters of dispute. Samuel may be looked upon as both 'seer' and 'judge.'

3. The institution of the monarchy is generally regarded as marking a crisis in Hebrew history ; and in the historical writings of OT it is looked at and judged from the standpoint of the later religious beliefs. But it did not mean a breaking from the earlier family and tribal customs—now transferred to local organization—which persisted to the end, and prevented the monarchy from ever corresponding exactly to the familiar Western type. As W. R. Smith says, 'With us the king or his government is armed with the fullest authority to enforce law and justice, and the limitations of his power lie in the independence of the legislature and the judicial courts. The old Semitic king, on the contrary, was supreme judge, and his decrees were laws ; but neither his

sentences nor his decrees could take effect unless they were supported by forces over which he had very imperfect control. He simply threw his weight into the scale,—a weight which was partly due to the moral effect of his sentence, and partly to the material resources which he commanded, not so much as king as in the character of a great noble, and the head of a powerful circle of kinsfolk and clients. An energetic sovereign, who had gained wealth and prestige by successful wars, or inherited the resources accumulated by a line of kingly ancestors, might wield almost despotic power ; and in a stable dynasty the tendency was towards the gradual establishment of absolute monarchy, especially if the royal house was able to maintain a standing army devoted to its interests' (*RS*, 1st ed. p. 63, 2nd ed. p. 62). The chief object in the introduction of the monarchy among the Hebrews was 'to have a strong reliable chieftain perpetually guaranteed' (McCurdy, *HPM* i. p. 56).

(*a*) *Mode of succession.*—In the case of Saul the circumstances were extraordinary, therefore the form of his appointment was not regarded as creating a precedent for later times. The growing tendency towards unity had led to the desire among the people, and they turned naturally to the most influential man among them for advice. It was therefore on the nomination of Samuel, supported by the personal valour of his nominee, that Saul was chosen and confirmed in his office at some kind of popular gathering. In the ordinary course of events one of Saul's sons would have succeeded his father. But the fittest among them had perished on the battle-field. Ishbosheth did indeed succeed, thanks to the help of his friends, in securing for a short time the throne of the house of Joseph, but was soon eclipsed by the personal prowess of the king of Judah. The religious influence of the prophets was against him, and treason came to the help of his rival. David became king over all Israel. In the accession of Solomon the principle of hereditary succession takes its natural course, for the king had the right as the father and head of his family to appoint as his successor whichever son he pleased. The heads of the religious and military parties in the state assisted David in carrying his wishes into effect. After this time the succession was regularly observed in Judah, for the Southern kingdom consisted practically of one tribe only, and so was free from intertribal jealousies and feuds. In the Northern kingdom it was very different. Dynasty succeeded dynasty, and in the last twenty years of their existence no fewer than seven kings sat on the throne of Israel. In the rare times of internal quiet, however, the principle of hereditary succession seems to have been recognized as in Judah.

(*b*) *The power of the king and constitution of his household.*—The rule of Saul was characterized by its simplicity. 'The son of Kish ruled in peace at Gibea in the house of his father, leading the very simple life of the last of the judges. On leaving the harem in the morning he seated himself before the gate of the palace. There, surrounded by some attendants, under the protection of a small Benjaminite guard, he gave audience to every comer, inquired as to the news, questioned travellers, received the oral reports of his officers, appeased quarrels, administered justice (2 S 15², cf. 1 S 22¹⁷). Then, when the sun went down, he withdrew into the apartments of the women. At the beginning of each month he gave a feast at which his officers had their assigned places, while he himself presided, his back prudently placed to the wall for fear of assassins (1 S 20²⁵). Finally, when he went out, he was preceded by runners

(1 S 22¹⁷). Such alone were his privileges and his duties in time of peace' (Marcel Dieulafoy, *Le Roi David*, p. 72 f.). All this was changed with the ever-increasing prosperity of David. The king remained leader and father of his people only so long as they had no friendly intercourse with other nations. As soon as the Hebrew nation was recognized, and its friendship sought by other states, the Hebrew king began to imitate the luxury of his peers. A court was formed of the officials, whose common interests grouped them round the king and made access to him ever more and more difficult for the mass of the people. The officials of David's court were—(1) military ; (2) household ; (3) religious. The following are mentioned in his time—(1) The commander of ' the host' (2 S 8¹⁶) ; the commander of the king's bodyguard of Cherethites and Pelethites (2 S 20²³, cf. 8¹⁸). (2) The recorder or remembrancer (מַזְכִּיר 2 S 8¹⁶) ; the scribe or secretary (סֹפֵר 8¹⁷) ; the counsellor (יוֹעֵץ 2 S 15¹²) ; the king's friend (רֵעֶה 2 S 15³⁷ 16¹⁶) ; the keeper of the king's audience (2 S 23²³, cf. 1 S 22¹⁴ LXX) ; the overseer of forced labour (2 S 20²⁴). (3) The priests (2 S 8¹⁷). Prophets do not seem to have been attached to the court, but had free access to the king (cf. 2 S 7. 12).

Under Solomon the pomp and luxury of the court was greatly increased. New buildings and fortified cities (1 K 6. 7. 9) proclaimed the growing power of the monarch, and the separation of the court from the people is indicated by the tolerance of foreign religions and the personal nature of the treaties with foreign powers. Two new officials make their appearance — a chamberlain (עַל־הַבָּיִת 1 K 4⁶) and a superintendent of taxes (1 K 4⁵, and see below under ' Revenue'). After Solomon there was little change in the constitution of the court (but cf. EUNUCH).

(*c*) *Revenue*.—Even in Saul's reign there seems to have been a regular system of taxation of families (1 S 17²⁵, cf. 8¹⁷, and Nowack, *Heb. Archæol.* p. 313). In addition to this the king received gifts (1 S 10²⁷ 16²⁰), and doubtless his share of the booty in war. This last is specially mentioned in the time of David (2 S 8¹¹ 12³⁰). Solomon's revenues were derived (in addition to the above mentioned) from the tribute of subject peoples (1 K 4²¹) ; taxes on merchants (1 K 10¹⁵) ; his sea-trade with Hiram (1 K 10¹¹) ; and a royal regulation of the horse-trade with Egypt (v.¹¹). But the king taxed his own subjects much more rigorously than his predecessors. He divided the kingdom into twelve parts, each being represented by an officer, who was compelled to provide for the king's household for one month in the year (1 K 4). Judah is not mentioned in this division of the land, and was probably exempted from this form of taxation by favour of the king. Nowack, however, thinks there were originally thirteen divisions, and that the number was reduced to twelve by a later writer to agree with the number of the tribes (*Heb. Archæol.* i. 313 note). Later, it seems that the goods of a condemned person might be forfeit to the king (1 K 21). But this may be merely an act of despotism. When reduced to great straits, the king took possession of the treasures, not only of his own treasury but also of the temple, in order to keep off an invading power (2 K 18¹⁵).

(*d*) *Administration of justice*.—There seems to have been little development here during this period. The system mentioned above persisted, modified only by the personal authority of the king and the members of his court (see quotation from W. R. Smith, above). Until B.C. 621 there was no written law except the short religious code contained in the ' Book of the Covenant' (Ex 20–23) ; nor were there any special courts or officials for the ad-

ministration of justice. The method for settling disputes was rather by arbitration than by law in the Western sense. At the same time, the king himself in his capital and its neighbourhood, and his officials in the chief towns, being the most important persons, were naturally appealed to for decisions, though there was no law necessitating appeal to them rather than to any other person. Even such acts in later times as the imprisonments of Jeremiah (Jer 37. 38) and the putting to death of Uriah (Jer 26), were acts of personal violence on the part of the king, and not due to the regular sentence of a court (cf. also the account of the charge against Naboth, and the way in which he was put to death (1 K 22¹³ff.)). After the destruction of the Northern kingdom, an attempt was made in Judah (in 621) to regulate the legal as well as the religious procedure on the lines of the teaching of the prophets by the proclamation of the Book of Deuteronomy (cf. DEUTERONOMY). But the realization of this scheme was prevented by the untimely death of Josiah at the battle of Megiddo, nor was it fully adopted in Judæa until nearly two centuries later.

4. A remarkable feature in Jewish life is the persistence of the religious and semi-political self-government of their communities in the different empires in which they were dispersed. Everywhere we find them submitting their disputes to the judgment of their own officials rather than to those of the state in which they live ; everywhere they claim and are granted special exemption from certain civil laws (as those regarding military conscription) on the ground of religious scruple. Many examples of their peculiar privileges in Palestine are found in the NT (cf. Ac 9² 18¹²⁻¹⁶ 22¹⁹ 26¹¹). But in Alexandria this is even more striking. Thanks to the favour of Alexander the Great, they early established themselves in the position of a favoured people in the new city. That favour was continued to them by the Ptolemies, and they had in addition equal rights with others as citizens (ἰσοτιμία). Their own governor (ἐθνάρχης) is mentioned by Strabo (cf. Jos. *Ant.* XIV. vii. 2). Some of the Roman decrees conferring privileges upon them are preserved by Josephus (*Ant.* x., xvi. vi.). Philo tells us that on the death of a γενάρχης Augustus appointed a γερουσία for the conduct of Jewish affairs (*in Flaccum*, sec. 10). In Rome there was not the same political organization as in Alexandria, but the different synagogues were organized separately, each with its own *gerousia* and officials. (See further Schürer, *HJP* II. ii. 244 ff.).

5. After the fall of Jerusalem in B.C. 586, the Jews became subject to foreign governments, and have remained so since, except for the short interval when the Maccabæan princes ruled, or more exactly from B.C. 142 when Simon ceased to pay tribute, or 139 when the right of coining money proclaimed the independence of Judæa. The civil constitution of this time is, however, no longer distinctively Jewish, but a mere modification of Western forms to suit the religious laws of the people. These laws had come into force at the time when Ezra had brought back from Babylon many of the devoutest Jewish exiles. At a solemn assembly a new community had been formed, which was to realize the idea of the ' remnant' of Isaiah and his successors, a spiritual Judah, subject to the civil government of the suzerain power, but in all matters pertaining to religion following as far as possible the precepts of Deuteronomy and the new law book (P) compiled and edited about this time (cf. Neh 9. 10). Since then the Jews have ever remained subject to this double form of government. The conflict of the two led to their perpetual strife with their civil rulers, and to the

final fall of Jerusalem in A.D. 70. According to Jewish authorities, the chief representative of the religious governing power during this period was the 'Great Synagogue' (כְּנֶסֶת הַגְּדוֹלָה), which existed from Ezra to Simon the Just. Some such body *may* have existed, but much of the literature concerning it contains legendary material (cf. SYNAGOGUE, THE GREAT). At the time of Christ the Sanhedrin had taken its place (cf. SANHEDRIN). For the more strictly civil government of the time of Christ, see art. ROMAN EMPIRE. See also CHURCH GOVERNMENT and HELPS.

LITERATURE.—In addition to the articles in this Dictionary on the separate judges, kings, and other officials mentioned above, see McCurdy, *HPM* i. ch. iii. ; Nowack, *Heb. Archœol.* i. 300–387 ; W. R. Smith, *RS* 70 ff., *Kinship and Marriage in Early Arabia* (*passim*) ; Nallino, 'Sulla costituzióne delle tribù Arabe' in *Nuova Antologia*, terza serie, xlvii. 614 ff. ; Marcel Dieulafoy, *Le Roi David* ; Mommsen, *Provinces of the Roman Empire*, chs. viii.–xi. ; the works on the times of Christ by Schürer, Hausrath, and Holtzmann.

G. W. THATCHER.

GOVERNOR.—This word occurs as the rendering of several Heb. and Gr. terms. In OT it is used most frequently for the *Peḥah* (פֶּחָה), a district ruler administering under a sovereign. The title is employed both for Persian satraps and for their subordinate magistrates. Thus it appears as a designation of Tattenai (Ezr 5³· ⁶ 6⁶), who seems to have been the satrap of a large province which extended from Posideium on the frontiers of Cilicia and Syria to Egypt, and which included Phœnicia, Palestine, and Cyprus (Herod. vi. 91). It is also applied to Zerubbabel, who was appointed under this satrap to the district of Judah (Ezr 6⁷). The subordinate *Peḥah*, as well as his superior, was directly commissioned by the king (Ezr 5¹⁴). The other Heb. words rendered 'governor' are of a less technical character, signifying *leadership*, אַלּוּף Zec 9⁷ 12⁵· ⁶, and נָגִיד 2 Ch 1²; *judicial* and *legislative functions*, חֹקֵק Jg 5⁹; *ruling authority*, מֹשֵׁל Gn 45²⁶, שַׁלִּיט Gn 42⁶, שַׂר 1 K 22²⁶; *administrative oversight*, פָּקִיד Jer 20¹; and *social rank*, נָשִׂיא 2 Ch 1².

In NT the word 'governor' most frequently occurs as a rendering of the Gr. ἡγεμών (Vulg. *præses*, Luth. *Landpfleger*), a term which is used in the plur. for rulers generally (*e.g.* Mk 13⁹, 1 P 2¹⁴), but which more often has a definite application to the Roman *Procurators*, referring in the Gospels to Pontius Pilate (*e.g.* Mt 27², Lk 20²⁰), who is designated *Procurator* by Tacitus—'Christus Tiberio imperante per *procuratorem* Pontium Pilatum supplicio adfectus erat' (*Ann.* xv. 44), and in Ac to Felix (Ac 23²⁶) and Festus (Ac 26³⁰). Judæa was not entirely incorporated in the province of Syria, but the *Procurator* was to a certain extent dependent on the Legate of Syria, the latter having a right to interfere when difficulties arose (Jos. *Ant.* XVIII. i. 1, iv. 2 ; *Bell. Jud.* II. viii. 1). Thus Judæa belonged to the third class of provinces in Strabo's classification (*Geog.* xvii. 3. 25), one containing only a few provinces regarded either as semi-barbarous or as exceptionally insubordinate, *e.g.* Egypt. Augustus preferred the title *Præfectus* (ἔπαρχος) for the governors of such provinces, but by the time of Claudius *Procurator* (ἐπίτροπος) was the recognized name. Josephus employs both ἐπίτροπος and ἔπαρχος, and also the word used in NT, ἡγεμών, for the governor of Judæa. That *Procurator* is the correct title of this official is suggested by the passage from Tacitus quoted above, and by the use of the word ἐπίτροπος in a decree of Claudius as rendered by Josephus (*Ant.* xx. i. 2). Technically, the *Procurator* was a financial officer attached either to a proconsul or to a proprætor for the purpose of collecting the Imperial revenues. But he was always entrusted with magisterial powers for the decision

of questions touching the revenues. In the provinces of the third class he was the general administrator and the supreme judge, with sole power of life and death (Dion Cass. liii. 15), an appeal to Cæsar being allowed in the case of Roman citizens (see CÆSAR). Although it was not necessary that the *Procurator* should be a person of high station where he was only appointed to financial duties, he was required to be a knight where the charge of government was committed to him. Therefore the appointment of Felix, who was a freedman, must have struck the Jews as an insulting innovation. The headquarters of the *Procurator* of Judæa was Cæsarea, which was made a garrison town.

In 2 Co 11³² (AV and RV) the word governor appears as trⁿ of ἐθνάρχης for the *ethnarch* (RVm) of Damascus. See ARETAS, ETHNARCH. The word rendered 'governor' in Gal 4² AV (οἰκονόμος) is trd. 'steward' in RV, as it is elsewhere in NT, *e.g.* Lk 12⁴² 1 Co 4². It indicates a superior servant entrusted with the housekeeping of a family, the direction of the other domestics, and the care of children under age. The 'governor of the feast' (ἀρχιτρίκλινος, Jn 2⁸ AV, RV 'ruler of the feast') was a man appointed to see that the couches and tables were in order, to arrange the courses, to taste the food and wine, etc. (Heliodorus, *Aeth.* vii. 27). In early times, if not later, he was a different person from the 'toast maker' (συμποσιάρχης, Sir 32¹), who was one of the guests chosen by lot to direct the drinking (Grimm-Thayer). 'Governor' in Ja 3⁴ AV (a participle of εὐθύνω, straighten) means 'steersman' (RV).

LITERATURE. — Schürer, *HJP* I. ii. 43–48 ; Marquardt, *Röm. Staatsverwalt.* i. 412 ; Liebenam, *Beiträge zur Verwaltungsgesch. d. Röm. Kaiserreiches*, i. 1–18, 23, 24, 30 ; Hausrath, *NT Times, Time of Jesus*, ii. 83–93.   W. F. ADENEY.

GOZAN, גּוֹזָן, Γωζάν (B Γωζάρ 2 K 17⁶, Χωζάρ 1 Ch 5²⁶).—The country on the river(s ?) of which the Israelites, deported from Samaria by the king of Assyria, had to settle, was identified correctly by Bochart (*Phaleg*, iii. 14) as the Gauzanitis of Ptolemy, v. 18 (Γαυζανῖτις). This region is described as situated between the Chaboras (see HABOR) and Saocoras. The latter river, flowing into the Euphrates from the Masius mountains, cannot be identified ; it must have changed its course or have been dried up. At any rate, we can identify Gauzanitis as the eastern part of Osroëne of the classic writers west of Nisibis and the (later) country of Mygdonia (this name hardly = Gozan, but it is probably connected with the Mitanni of the Amarna tablets), almost in the centre of Northern Mesopotamia. This agrees too closely with the description in the Bible (2 K 17⁶ 18¹¹ 19¹²=Is 37¹², 1 Ch 5²⁶) to admit of any doubt. The modern name Kaushan seems to correspond, but not Zauzân (which means the mountains near the source of the Chaboras). Assyrian lists of provinces mentioning *Guzana* seem to show that the name referred originally to a city, the capital of the province of Guzan. Nisibis, being mentioned parallel to G. as *Naṣibina*, did not belong to this province. See on the Assyrian passages Schrader, *KAT²* 275 ; Delitzsch, *Paradies*, 184. On the question whether the biblical passages speak of several 'rivers of Gozan,' see HALAH. (The view of some scholars, which makes G. a river, was refuted even before the cuneiform texts were found). If the singular 'river' (Massoretic text) is to be kept, this 'river of G.' is the Habor. The plural (LXX) would point to the several brooks from the Masius which form the Habor, possibly also the Baliḥ. 2 K 2¹⁹=Is 37¹² seems to show that Gozan became an Assyrian province only in the 8th century.   W. MAX MÜLLER.

GRACE.—The words most commonly rendered 'grace,' 'be gracious,' etc., in AV are חֵן (verb חָנַן) in OT, and χάρις with its cognate forms in NT. The former appears in such proper names as Hannah, Hanan, Hanun, Hanani, Hananeel ('El is gracious'), Hananiah ('J" hath been gracious'). Its force is 'to be favourable or kindly,' or 'to act in a favourable or kindly way.' Probably, however, חֶסֶד, LXX ἔλεος, corresponds more nearly with the distinctive idea of grace in its NT and general Christian use.* חֵן, for example, has no special connexion with *redemptive* grace, and the LXX use of χάρις, by which חֵן is usually rendered, must be to this extent distinguished from the NT use of the same word. On the other hand, ἔλεος in NT is rather *pity* than *favour*, and denotes God's relation to human misery rather than to human sin.

It is in the various applications of χάρις that the roots of the idea of grace and its specially Christian significance may in the first place be most usefully studied. Χάρις is that which bestows or occasions pleasure. It is applied to *beauty, gracefulness*, whether of person, act, or speech, cf. in LXX Ec 10¹², Sir 21¹⁶ 37²¹, in NT Lk 4²², Eph 4²⁹, Col 4⁶. It thus denotes the favourable, friendly disposition or nature out of which the gracious act proceeds, or that which it creates in the recipient; it is the favour manifested, or the gratitude felt or acknowledged. It is *loving-kindness, goodwill*, in a wide acceptation, and is thus used of the kindness of a master towards his servants, and, by analogy, of the goodness of God to men; cf. Lk 1³⁰, Ac 7⁴⁶, 1 P 2¹⁹. ²⁰. *To be in favour with one* is εὑρεῖν χάριν παρά τινι, ἔχειν χάριν πρός τινα, Lk 1³⁰, Ac 2⁴⁷, cf. Lk 2⁵². An interesting instance of this general sense is at the beginning and end of the Apostolical Epistles, where the writers desire for their readers the grace of God or of Christ, to which grace or favour they recognize that all blessings are to be ascribed — Ro 1⁷ 16²⁰, 1 Co 1³ 16²³, 2 Co 1² 13¹⁴, Gal 1³ 6¹⁸, Eph 1² 6²⁴, Ph 1² 4²³, Col 1² 4¹⁸, 1 Th 1¹ 5²⁸, 2 Th 1² 3¹⁸, 1 Ti 1² 6²¹, 2 Ti 1² 4²², Tit 1⁴ 3¹⁵, Philem 3. ²⁵, He 13²⁵, 1 P 1², 2 P 1² 3¹⁸, 2 Jn ³, also Rev 1⁴ 22²¹.

The special use, however, of χάρις in NT is in reference to the mind of God as manifested towards sinners, His redemptive mercy, whereby He grants pardon to offences, and bids those who have gone astray return and accept His gift of salvation and everlasting life. It is χάρις τοῦ θεοῦ, Ro 5¹⁵, 1 Co 15¹⁰, 2 Co 6¹ 8¹, and other passages, in Tit 2¹¹ the phrase is expanded into ἡ χάρις τοῦ θεοῦ ἡ σωτήριος; in 2 Ti 2¹ into ἡ χάρις ἡ ἐν Χριστῷ as manifested in and through Christ, whence, by a natural transference, it becomes ἡ χάρις τοῦ κυρίου ἡμῶν Χριστοῦ, as in the above-mentioned salutations, and finally establishes itself as a well-understood expression, able to stand alone without further explanation, as in the ἡ χάρις of Ro 5¹⁷. ²⁰. It is in this connexion that the full meaning of χάρις is brought out as involving *spontaneous* favour. Its fundamental thought is that the benefit conferred is recognized by giver and receiver alike as not *due*; it is that to which the receiver has no *right*, which has not been earned, or perhaps deserved, but which the giver freely, out of pure goodness, bestows. This spontaneous character, along with the more or less direct reference to the *pleasure* or *joy* either designed or experienced,—which is indeed suggested by the connexion of the word with χαίρειν, 'to rejoice,'—is always implied, and, singularly enough, comes out more clearly in the scriptural than in the classical use of the term. It has been justly remarked that 'it depended upon Christianity to realize its full import, and to elevate it to its rightful sphere' (Cremer). Thus κατὰ

On the distinctive meaning of חֶסֶד, cf. W. R. Smith, *Prophets* ¹, 160 f., 460 f.

χάριν is contrasted with κατὰ ὀφείλημα, Ro 4⁴, while χάρις is contrasted with ἔργα, Ro 11⁶, and with νόμος Jn 1¹⁷, Ro 4¹⁶ 6¹⁴. ¹⁵, Gal 5³. ⁴.

From signifying the disposition and design to bring about the salvation of men, χάρις comes to be used of the *power* or influence by which this purpose is executed, Ac 18²⁷, 2 Co 4¹⁵ 6¹, 2 Th 1¹², and then further of the *results*, general and specific, of that action. Thus it stands for the spiritual state of those who have come under the power of divine grace, Ro 5², 2 Ti 2¹, 1 P 5¹², 2 P 3¹⁸; and for the evidences or tokens of such experience, as when the alms contributed by the Christian Churches are so designated, 1 Co 16³, 2 Co 8⁶. ¹⁹, or the sum of earthly blessings (πᾶσα χάρις, 2 Co 9⁸), or the various powers and gifts manifested by Christians (in the striking phrase ποικίλη χάρις, 1 P 4¹⁰), or the power and equipment for the exercise of the apostolic office, Ro 1⁵ 12⁵. ⁶ 15¹⁵, 1 Co 3¹⁰, Gal 2⁹, Eph 3². ⁷. At the same time χάρις does not appear to be employed in NT for the act or gift apart from that reference to the pleasure or benefit conveyed by it, which we have already noted. The word for gift in itself is δῶρον or δωρεά. Hence it has been pointed out that 'διδόναι χάριν in Scripture must not be confounded with the same expression in profane Greek, where it means *to perform an act of kindness*; in Scripture it signifies "to give grace," "to cause grace to be experienced"; see Eph 4⁷, 1 P 5⁵, Ja 4⁶, Ro 12⁶, 1 Co 1⁴, 2 Co 6¹ 8¹ (cf. Ac 11²³)'—Cremer. The gift which enables the recipient to be in his turn a source of pleasure or profit to others is more frequently χάρισμα; where χάρις and χάρισμα approximate in signification, it will usually be found that the former is more general,—as, *e.g.*, when χάρις τοῦ θεοῦ is used by St. Paul in reference to his office, it applies to the whole of his ministry, rather than to specific equipments for it. Finally, the use of χάρις for 'thanks,' the correlative of *favour*,—the 'return favour,' as it were,—illustrates the process of growth and transference in the use of the word which we have so far traced.

The teaching of the Bible as to grace cannot, however, be exhausted by the analysis, however minute, of any one word or expression. Its fundamental implication of a kind and merciful disposition, manifesting itself in acts of unmerited goodness, especially towards the sinful and erring, brings grace as one of the divine attributes into close relation with others, and the revelation of it may, it is obvious, be even more frequent in act than in word, conveyed therefore rather by description than direct expression. Not in declarations merely, but in the whole series of the divine dealings with mankind, grace is exhibited. The whole biblical history might be claimed as a record of its manifestation. It thus takes different forms, and includes a wide area of operation. It is allied to the *goodness* which God shows to all His creatures, and which the Psalms so frequently celebrate —33⁵ 119⁶⁴ 145, etc.; to the *compassion* which has as its objects the needy and unfortunate, Ps 25⁶ 103⁸, Lk 1⁷², 2 Co 1³; to the *long-suffering* which bears with the unthankful and the evil, Ex 34⁶, Ro 9²²; to the *patience* which defers as long as possible the punishment of sin, Ps 145⁸, Ro 2⁴. It belongs therefore to the circle of divine attributes, the keynote of which is Love. In all the phases of what we have already seen to be its highly complex significance,—whether as mercy and favour in general, or as the manifestations of God's goodwill in the form of temporal or spiritual advantages, or as His disposition to pardon the sinner, or His redemptive scheme as a whole, or the influences by which souls are turned to Christ, kept, strengthened, and increased in faith and love, and impelled to the exercise of Christian virtues,— in all of these, grace implies that God overcomes, not by necessity or force, but by the freeness of His love, Ro 5[20. 21]. This is the reason why grace is not only one of the perfections of God, but one of the distinctive features of the Christian revelation. Revelation is marked by progress. The God who is at first hidden from men, so that they seek Him, if haply they may feel after Him and find Him, is at length made known, but first as a *jealous* God (ὀργὴ θεοῦ), only afterwards as a *gracious* God. And the revelation is completed when 'the LORD, the LORD, a God full of compassion and gracious, slow to anger and plenteous in mercy and truth; keeping mercy for thousands, forgiving iniquity and transgression and sin, and that will by no means clear the guilty' (Ex 34[6. 7] RV), which is the loftiest OT conception of God, becomes in the NT 'the God and Father of our Lord Jesus Christ.' We proceed, therefore, to consider somewhat more minutely the elements which enter into the conception of grace and the forms which it assumes in OT and NT respectively.

i. OLD TESTAMENT.—'The law was given by Moses,' says St. John (1[17]); 'grace and truth came by Jesus Christ.' Yet the relation of OT to NT is misconceived when it is apprehended as one of antithesis rather than development. There is no doubt that the religion of OT is ordinarily represented as founded upon law, and that the very considerable element of grace which enters into it is ignored. But OT piety recognizes that what righteousness it has is founded in divine grace and imparted through divine revelation. It is grace which gives the law itself (cf. Gal 3[19-24]), and faith, which is that by which grace is received and made effective, is not overlooked—Gn 15[6], Ex 14[31], Nu 20[12], Dt 1[32] 9[23], 2 Ch 20[20], Ps 106[12. 24], Is 7[9] 28[16], Hab 2[4]. It is true that as grace gives the law, so through the law it seems to give men a *right* or *claim* in virtue of their compliance with the law, which is inconsistent with the later revelation of faith as the principle of the new life. The favour (in the Psalmist and Prophets, the righteousness) of God gives to the obedient (or the repentant, cf. Ps 17 and 26, also Ps 7) a claim, as it were, against God, Ps 119[132] etc. At the same time OT fully recognizes that it is the divine grace which forgives sin (Ps 32. 51. 130. 143). Grace, as an attribute of God, appears in OT in conjunction with *truth*, or *faithfulness* (Ps 85[10] 89[14] 98[3] etc.), but also with *righteousness* and *judgment* (Hos 2[19]). God is gracious as hearing prayer (Ex 22[27]), as departing from His anger (Ex 32[12]), and as exercising freely His choice of love (Ex 33[19]); He lifts upon the pious the light of His countenance (Nu 6[25]). It is by the divine *acts* that this attitude of forbearance and conciliation is more particularly manifested. Even in the midst of the ruin occasioned by the Fall, the purpose of mercy is represented as being declared and its work begun, words of promise mingle with words of condemnation, the divine solicitude shines amidst the clouds of divine anger (Gn 3[15. 21]). Through the same tenderness Abel and Enoch find favour in the sight of God, Noah is warned and escapes the general doom (Gn 6[8]), Abraham is selected to be the bearer of the new revelation (Gn 12. 15), and the promises made to him are repeated to his descendants (Gn 26. 28). Through it Moses is chosen and fitted for his work (Ex 33[17]). In all that concerns Israel as a people the same free choice is exhibited and exercised. The promises freely made to the fathers are fulfilled when, through Moses, Israel is chosen from among all nations (Ex 19[5], cf. Dt 10[14]) to be the people of God, and that from no merit of its own (Nu 11. 12. 14. 21, etc.; cf. Dt 9[7] etc.). This choice is evidenced by the deliverance from Egypt (Ex 15[13. 16]), and is a pure act of grace (Dt 7[7] 8[14-18] 9[4-6]). In the

Prophets we have a further development of this point of view. Their whole religious attitude is determined by it. That God had chosen Israel to be His people is their most sincere conviction, and the problems which perplexed them, and gave birth to some of their most profound and spiritual suggestions, arose out of the relation of the sins of the people and the consequent divine chastisements, to this firmly held conviction (cf. Is 55[6] 63[9] 65[1], Jon 4[11], Mic 7[18. 19]). It is true that as, on the one hand, the unworthiness of the mass of the people led them to distinguish from the nation at large the true Israel, the faithful remnant; so, on the other hand, they were led to conceive the possibility of God's gracious purpose as embracing those who were not of Israel, and of the heathen being brought through Israel into the enjoyment of some of Israel's privileges. At the same time, all their wealth of metaphor is employed to depict God's loving care and guidance, His deliverances and compassions as illustrated in the history of the people, and to emphasize His continued patience, His touching appeals and generous offers, and the glory of His declared purposes. Even in His anger God remembers mercy (La 3[31], Jl 2[13], Hab 3[2]), and yet all that He does is on behalf of those who are too often ungrateful and rebellious (Is 43[21-25] 44[1-5] 48[8-11], Jer 18[8-11], Ezk 16[1ff.], cf. Ps 78). In the relation of the individual to the nation we find an important modification of the idea of grace. Grace is mediated to the individual through the nation. His imperfections are forgiven because he is a member of a chosen people; as belonging to an elect nation he is himself elect. The Pss express this assurance of the believer, which finds utterance in his prayers when afflicted and his thanksgivings after deliverance (Ps 3[4. 7] 4[8] 7[10] 11[7] 16. 17[7-9] 18. 32. 51. 103, etc.). If thus in the view of the Psalmists and Prophets there is no limit to God's willingness to be reconciled, if even His judgment has a core of mercy, and His love always proves itself stronger than human sin, the other side of OT religion is, in turn, not to be minimized. If God has a special love to Israel, it is through a *covenant* that this love finds expression, and the covenant takes the form of law. The people are bound to obedience, and the blessings of the covenant can be enjoyed only on this condition. So far from grace being ignored in OT, it permeates it, as we have seen, throughout. But grace is not yet fully revealed; it is still dominated by the ideas of righteousness and retribution. It speaks the language of law, and the law is, as already noted, its own greatest gift. Israel has reason to boast itself of its law; the possession of it is an honour and a privilege distinguishing Israel from other nations (Ex 19[4. 5], Dt 33[2-5]). Thus, though by no means the sole element, law remains the distinctive element in OT. Obedience is pre-eminently the condition of blessing. God in giving the law is emphatically the God of Israel (Ex 20[2]). In OT His anger against sin is declared, His mercy and long-suffering are proclaimed; but these rest side by side, an unsolved antinomy, waiting the fuller revelation.

ii. NEW TESTAMENT.—The new 'covenant' is the fulfilment of the old; the plan of grace which lay at the root of the former dispensation comes into full expression in the life and work of Christ (Ti 2[11] 3[4]), and in the declarations of the apostles—Ro 3[24. 25] RV, 'Being justified freely by his grace through the redemption that is in Christ Jesus, whom God set forth to be a propitiation (ἱλαστήριον, Heb. כַּפֹּרֶת, *the place of expiation*, "the central seat of the saving presence and gracious revelations of God," see Cremer, *s.v.*, and, for another view, Sanday-Headlam, *ad. loc.*), through faith, by his blood, to show his righteousness, because of the passing over of the sins done aforetime, in the forbearance of God.' Thus the great work of grace is redemption, which has its origin in God (1 Jn 4[10. 19]), in His eternal good pleasure (εὐδοκία), Eph 1[3-6], and is carried out by His will and power. Therefore, as we have seen, the Christian revelation is called 'the grace of God,' 'the grace of God our Saviour,' 'the grace of our Lord Jesus Christ,' or simply 'grace.' The love which it manifests is expressed, not only by word, but by the most unchallengeable of deeds, when God sends forth His Son and gives Him up as a sacrifice for the sins of men (Jn 3[16], Eph 1[7], Ro 5[6-8] etc.). This love is not called forth by any merit or worthiness on the part of man (2 Ti 1[9], Tit 3[5]), but is the free spontaneous outflowing of divine compassion—'it is the gift of God' (Eph 2[4-9], Ro 3[24] 11[6], cf. 4[4] 5[8]). We may compare the representations contained in the parables of Jesus generally, especially those of Lk 15, and note how He seeks the lost, would shelter Jerusalem as a hen gathereth her chickens together, and calls the weary and heavy laden to Himself. But it is not only this great central act of love, upon which the whole plan of redemption is built up and without which it would be impossible, which is ascribed to divine grace and is its outcome; every step in the subsequent process, all that is embraced in the work of the Holy Spirit, is regarded as due to grace. It is through it that the call comes to men (Gal 1[15], 1 Th 2[13]), and that men are made willing to answer to it (Jn 6[44. 45]). It is the grace of God which opens the heart (Ac 16[14]), which gives repentance (Ac 5[31] 11[18], 2 Ti 2[25], He 6[6]), by which faith is imparted (Eph 1[19], Ph 1[29], cf. Lk 17[5]), also assurance of God's love (Ro 5[5] 8[15. 16]), hope (2 Th 2[16], 1 P 1[3-5]), love towards God (2 Th 3[5]) and towards the brethren (1 Th 4[9]). By means of it we become God's children, righteous and holy (Ac 15[11], Ro 3[24] 4[16], Tit 3[7]), and receive strength to do good and to avoid evil (2 Th 2[17] 3[3]). The position of the redeemed is one of grace (Ro 5[2], 1 P 2[10]), and by it sanctification is completed (1 Th 5[23. 24]). On the one hand, grace may be received in vain (2 Co 6[1]); on the other, men may grow in grace (2 P 3[18]). This grace of the Holy Spirit was promised by Christ Himself (Jn 7[39] 14[26] 15[26] 16[7], Ac 1[5]), is exercised in His service (Jn 14[26] 16[13-15]), and becomes the principle of the new life. The grace of God, in fact, bestows joy and peace and every good work (Ro 15[13], 2 Co 9[8]). It has been remarked that as one cannot be the cause of one's own birth or resurrection, as in such events man must be purely passive, the employment of metaphors like the 'new birth' (Jn 3[3-7]), or the 'new creature' (2 Co 5[17], Eph 2[10]), or the new, the 'resurrection' life (Eph 2[5], Col 2[13] 3[1]), emphasizes the fact that renewal of heart and life is accomplished only by the power, the grace of God. Thus the Christian is what he is by divine grace (1 Co 4[7] 15[10]); and as he ought at all times to pray (1 Th 5[17], cf. 1 Ti 2[8], Mt 7[7-11], Lk 18[1]) to the Source of all good for that of which he feels the need, so, for every benefit which he receives, he ought to give thanks and praise to God (Ro 6[17], 1 Co 1[4], 1 Th 1[2] 2[13] 3[9]).

This positive and direct statement of the teaching of OT and NT with reference to the necessity and value of grace and its range of action might be supplemented and confirmed by a corresponding statement of the corruption and powerlessness of man due to sin as set forth in the same sacred pages. The more helpless man is seen to be, the greater is the need for the intervention of a Power above him and independent of him. This consideration brings us within sight of a problem which has much divided the Church in all ages, but which it does not fall within the province of this article to discuss in these its later developments. The prob-

lem is the relation of the divine to the human in the work of redemption, how far the initiative lies with God and man respectively, or how far they co-operate, and what, indeed, is meant by co-operation in such a case. It has driven Augustine and Pelagius, Calvin and Arminius, into opposite camps. All that can be done here is to inquire how far the roots of the doctrinal views identified with the names of these great teachers can be traced in the Bible. The passages which have been already cited tend on the whole to illustrate one side of this great controversy—that, namely, which grounds salvation on the free loving will and purpose of God. But, no doubt, many others may be, and have been, adduced which set forth no less distinctly the human side of salvation with its responsibilities and activities. This is especially the case with those which contain exhortations to repentance and faith. From the time of the Prophets μετάνοια was a condition of being saved. If men were commanded to repent, the implication was that it is in their power to do so. In some cases, it is true, we cannot argue from an injunction to the possibility of fulfilling it, but in this we cannot dispute that it is, in some sense, possible for man to repent, without taking away all meaning and reality from God's design of saving them. Such references to repentance are found in Ps 95[7f.] (cf. He 4[7ff.]), Ac 2[38] 8[22], Rev 2[5. 16. 21] 3[3] etc., cf. Mt 21[32]. Similarly with faith: μετανοεῖτε and πιστεύετε are usually conjoined, and belief must be as personal as repentance. It is intended to be, not the result of momentary impression, but a spontaneous moral act. In Ro 1[5] faith is spoken of as 'obedience,' a moral attitude which men are expected to assume. Exhortations to faith are found in Mk 1[15] 5[36], Jn 6[29] 10[38] 12[36] 14[1. 11] 20[27], Ac 16[31]. Repentance and faith are the chief elements in conversion. In Jer 31[18] Ephraim cries, 'Turn thou me, and I shall be turned,' where the latter clause ought to be 'I shall return,' or 'that I may turn,' implying the element of personal activity (see art. CONVERSION, vol. i. p. 478[a], footnote); and the image of the closed door in Rev 3[20] indicates that it must be opened from within to Him that knocketh. Allusions to conversion are found in Ac 3[19] 14[15] 26[20], cf. 2 Co 3[16]. While, on the one hand, the work of God begins with the calling, κλῆσις, Ro 8[30], whence Christians are known as κλητοί, Ro 1[7], the hearing must be a willing hearing, not like that of Jerusalem (Mt 23[37]) or of the Jews (Jn 5[40]), but like that of the disciples (Jn 17[6. 8]). The same element of human activity is implied in exhortations to perseverance (Ac 14[22], 1 Co 16[13], 1 Th 3[2]), to watchfulness (Mt 24[42], Mk 13[35], 1 Co 16[13], 1 P 5[8], Rev 3[3] 16[15]), to struggle and endeavour (1 Co 9[24-27], 2 Ti 2[5] 4[7]), to labours on behalf of the brethren (Ro 14[19] 15[2. 14], Gal 6[1]), and, in general, to the exercise of all the virtues, as well as to the performance of all the duties, of the Christian life. In every case language is used which, if it stood alone, would be taken as indicating that these things lie fully within the power of men to observe and do. Repentance, faith, etc., are regarded as works of men as well as gifts of God. Victory in that new life to which they are summoned can be achieved only by the zealous application of every energy of the soul. The promises which are held out to the faithful, and the threatenings which are denounced against the disobedient, all show the responsibility under which we act, the momentous results of choice.

But though later analysis, and the theories which figure in doctrinal history, have brought to light and emphasized this duality in the scriptural representations of human experience in salvation, though some thinkers and teachers have been willing to sacrifice the one side to the other, abolishing human liberty in order to exalt divine grace, or ignoring divine grace in order to safeguard human liberty,—it is noteworthy that the biblical writers betray little consciousness of the antagonism. St. Paul is clear and emphatic in his declarations as to grace—it is absolute, gratuitous—'by grace ye are saved'; but he is no less ready and willing to make his appeal to human liberty (Ro 2³⁻¹⁰, Ph 3¹⁵⁻¹⁷): 'Work out your own salvation,' he cries, 'with fear and trembling, for it is God which worketh in you both to will and to work for his good pleasure' (Ph 2¹². ¹³ RV), where both elements appear together as indefeasible portions of the same Christian experience. If OT closed with an antinomy of wrath and mercy, law and grace, side by side, equally real, but so far from being mutually destructive that in the experience of the devout they were equally necessary and illustrated one another, so NT closes with its own unsolved antinomy,—human individuality, free, responsible, but sinful and degraded, owing its salvation to the love of Him who is rich in mercy, who first loved us, who despite human weakness and wickedness makes that mercy effectual, and the evil that is overcome redound to the praise of the glory of His grace.

LITERATURE.—Among sources of suggestion and material for an exhibition of the biblical doctrine of grace, special mention should be made, in regard to the word χάρις, of Cremer's *Bib. Theol. Lex. of NT²*, and Grimm's *Greek-English Lex. of NT*, J. H. Thayer's edition; and in regard to the classification of passages, of C. Bois's article 'Grace Divine' in Lichtenberger's *Encyclopédie des Sciences Religieuses*; see also the *Biblical Theologies* of Oehler, Schultz, Weiss, Schmid, and the *Historical Theology* (Index, *s.v.*) of Cunningham.   A. STEWART.

GRACIOUS.—This adj. is found with three distinct meanings. **1.** *Favourable, merciful,* the most frequent use of the word, as Ex 33¹⁹ 'And [I] will be gracious to whom I will be gracious, and will show mercy on whom I will show mercy' (וְחַנֹּתִי אֶת־אֲשֶׁר אָחֹן, LXX καὶ ἐλεήσω ὃν ἂν ἐλεῶ, quoted in Ro 9¹⁵). **2.** *Favoured, accepted* (for the word 'gracious' has the distinction of being used actively of the person bestowing, and passively of the person receiving favour). There are two examples in AV, 1 Es 8⁸⁰ 'Yea, when we were in bondage, we were not forsaken of our Lord; but he made us gracious before (ἐποίησεν ἡμᾶς ἐν χάριτι ἐνώπιον) the kings of Persia, so that they gave us food'; Sir 18¹⁷ 'Lo, is not a word better than a gift? But both are with a gracious man'; Gr. παρὰ ἀνδρὶ κεχαριτωμένῳ; Vulg. 'cum homine iustificato,' whence Wyc. and Dou. 'with a iustefied man'; Cov. 'but a gracious man geveth them both,' so Gen. and Bishops. The same form (perf. ptcp. pass. of χαριτόω 'to bestow favour on,' 'bless') is found in Lk 1²⁸ Χαῖρε, κεχαριτωμένη; EV 'Hail, thou that art highly favoured,' AVm 'graciously accepted' or 'much graced'; the previous VSS follow the Vulg. ('Ave gratiæ plena') 'Hail full of grace,' except Gen. 'Hayle thou that art freely beloved,' and Bish. 'in high favour.' Shaks. has this meaning of 'gracious' in *As You Like It*, I. ii. 200—'If I be foiled, there is but one shamed that was never gracious'; and *III Henry VI.* III. iii. 117—

'But is he gracious in the people's eye?'

3. *Attractive, winning.*—There are four examples: (1) Pr 11¹⁶ 'a gracious woman retaineth honour' (אֵשֶׁת־חֵן), lit. 'a woman of grace'; LXX γυνὴ εὐχάριστος; Vulg. 'mulier gratiosa': 'a gracious woman' is Wyclif's trⁿ, and all the versions agree with him. The meaning is 'a woman of grace of appearance.' (2) Ec 10¹² 'The words of a wise man's mouth are gracious' (חֵן, lit. 'are grace, as AVm; cf. Lk 4²² below). (3) Jer 22²³ 'how gracious shalt thou be when pangs come upon

thee.' The Mass. text gives כָּה־נֵּחַנְתְּ (Kethîbh נחנתי), which can only be Niph. of חָנַן to be gracious. Luther understood it in the sense of 'be beautiful,' 'winning,' and trᵈ 'wie schön wirst du sehen'; after whom the Gen. gave 'how beautiful shalt thou be,' and AV 'how gracious shalt thou be.' The passive meaning 'favoured' or 'pitied' gives a better sense, however, and hence RV 'How greatly to be pitied shalt thou be,' and the Bishops, 'O howe litle shalt thou be regarded.' But the versions imply another reading, חַנַּנְתְּ from [אנח], found only in Niph. 'to groan.' Thus LXX καταστενάξεις; Vulg. 'quomodo congemuisti.' This meaning is clearly most suitable, and is adopted by nearly all mod. editors. Wyc. follows Vulg. 'Hou togidere weiledist thou,' and so Dou. 'how hast thou mourned together.' Similarly, Cov. 'O how greate shall thy mourning be.' Rothstein (in Kautzsch) 'wie wirst du ächzen.' (4) Lk 4²² 'And all bare him witness and wondered at the gracious words which proceeded out of his mouth' (ἐπὶ τοῖς λόγοις τῆς χάριτος, RV 'words of grace'). The meaning here, says Plummer, is 'winning words.' He adds, 'The very first meaning of χάρις (χαίρω) is "comeliness," "winsomeness"'—Hom. *Od.* viii. 175; Ec 10¹², Ps 44³, Sir 21¹⁶ 37²¹, Col 4⁶— 'and in all these passages it is the winsomeness of *language* that is specially signified.' Vulg. translates 'mirabantur in verbis gratiæ,' whence Wyc. 'wondriden in the wordis of grace,' and Rhem. 'they marveled in the wordes of grace.' All the rest of the versions, beginning with Tindale, have 'wondered at the gracious words'; and it is doubtful if RV should have returned to 'words of grace'; to have changed the adj. to 'winning' would have prevented misunderstanding and been more in accordance with the Eng. idiom. In illustration of this use of the word we find Bacon, *Essays* ('Of Beauty,' p. 176), 'In Beauty, that of Favour is more then that of Colour, and that of Decent and Gratious Motion, more then that of Favour.' So Shaks. *Twelfth Night*, I. v. 281—

'And in dimension and the shape of nature
A gracious person: but yet I cannot love him.'

And Chapman, *Homer's Iliads*, xviii. 23—

'Himself he threw upon the shore,
Lay, as laid out for funeral, then tumbled round, and tore
His gracious curls.'

                    J. HASTINGS.

GRAFF.—From γράφειν, to write, was formed γραφεῖον, a style or pencil for writing with: this was adopted into Lat. *graphium*; and passed into old Fr. *graffe*, which gave Eng. 'graff,' a slip of a cultivated tree inserted into a wild one, so named because it resembled a pencil in shape. From this substantive was formed the verb 'to graff,' which then yielded another substantive 'graft' (like 'weight' from 'weigh'); and by and by this subst. 'graft' attracted the verb to its own form. So that, whereas both subst. and vb. were once 'graff,' now both are 'graft.' The change from 'graff' to 'graft' was in process in Shakespeare's day. As subst. he uses only 'graff,' *Pericles*, v. i. 60—

'The most just gods
For every graff would send a caterpillar.'

But as vb. he has both 'graff' (with past ptcp. 'graft') and 'graft' (with past ptcp. 'grafted'). Thus *II Henry IV.* v. iii. 3, 'Nay you shall see mine orchard, where, in an arbour, we will eat a last year's pippin of my own grafting'; *Rich. II.* III. iv. 101—

'Pray God the plants thou graft'st may never grow.'

In the Pr. Bk. of 1549 (Collect for 7th Sun. after Trinity, Keiling, p. 129) is the prayer 'Graff in our hearts the love of thy name': this runs through the edd. of 1552 and 1559, but in ed. 1604 is changed into 'graft.' Again in the Com. Service (Keiling, p. 228), 'Grant . . . that the words which we have heard this day with our outward ears, may through thy grace be so graffed inwardly in our hearts,' continues through all the edd. till that of 1662, when it becomes 'grafted.' The word is rare in the Eng. versions. It occurs as a var. reading in Wyclif's NT of 1380 at 1 Ti 6[10]. Then in Ro 11[17] Wyc. (1388) has 'art graffid among them' as tr[n] of ἐνεκεντρίσθης ἐν αὐτοῖς (or rather of the Vulg. 'insertus es in illis'), and at v.[19] 'the braunchis ben brokun, that y be graffid in.' Tindale, however, tr[d] ἐνκεντρίζω by 'graff' in all its occurrences (Ro 11[17. 19. 23 bis. 24 bis.]),* and he was followed by all the versions except Coverdale. Tind. used 'grafte' and 'graffed' as the past tense or past ptcp., and in this also he was strictly followed, except that Rhem. (which tr[d] independently from the Vulg.) used 'graffed' always, and was followed by AV. Cov. has 'grafte' in v.[17], which must be the ptcp. of 'graff,' but in all the remaining occurrences he uses the form 'graft' for the pres. tense and 'grafted' for the past. RV uses 'graft' and 'grafted' throughout.

The subject of grafting will be spoken of under OLIVE. We may illustrate it and the word here by quoting Gosson, *Schoole of Abuse* (Arber's ed. p. 63), 'Though the Mariner have skill to governe his vessel, it lieth not in his cunning to calme the seas: though the countriman know how to graffe an ympe [ἔμφυτος, shoot, scion], his toile will not alter the taste of the Crab.' Holland, *Plinie*, xvii. 14, 'The first is to set the graffe or sion betweene the barke and the wood: for in old time truly, men were afraid at first to cleave the stocke, but soon after they ventured to bore a hole into the very heart of the wood: and then they set fast into the pith just in the mids thereof, but one sion or graffe, for by this kind of graffing, impossible it was that the said pith should receive or bear any more.' Evelyn, *Pomona*, iii.—'Make choice of your graffs from a constant and well-bearing branch. As to the success of graffing, the main skill is, to joyn the inward part of the cion to the sappy part of the stock, closely, but not too forceably; that being the best and most infallible way, by which most of the quick and juicy parts are mutually united, especially toward the bottom.' Bp. Hall (*Works*, ii. 1) uses the form 'griffe': 'Elizabeth was just, as well as Zachary, that the fore-runner of a Saviour might be holy on both sides: if the stock and the griffe be not both good, there is much danger of the fruit.'   **J. HASTINGS.**

GRANARY.—See GARNER.

GRAPES. — See VINE.   **Wild Grapes.** — See COCKLE.

GRASS.—Four words are tr[d] grass in OT:—**1.** יֶרֶק *yerek*, χλωρός. This word signifies *green* or *greenness*. Once it is tr[d] 'grass' (Nu 22[4]); twice 'green thing' (Ex 10[15], Is 15[6]); thrice it is followed by other words, דֶּשֶׁא (Ps 37[2], Is 37[27]) and עֵשֶׂב (Gn 1[30]), and in these cases it is used as an adj. signifying 'green.'

2. חָצִיר *hâzîr*.—This word is from a root (unused in Heb.) signifying *to be green* (Arab. *khadira*), from which is derived the noun *khadrah*, signifying primarily *greenness*, secondarily *purslain*, *cucumbers*, *melons*, and the like. It is now used for *vegetables* or *herbage* in general. In OT *hâzîr* is used once for *leeks*, LXX πράσα (Nu 11[5]). Twice it is tr[d] 'hay' (Pr 27[25] RVm 'grass,' LXX χλωρός; Is 15[6] RV 'grass,' LXX χόρτος). In all the remaining passages in which it is used in both AV and RV it is tr[d] 'grass.' LXX, however, renders it once (Is 35[7]) by ἐπαύλεις, AV and RVm 'a court'; twice (2 K 19[26], Ps 90[5]) by χλόη; twice (1 K 18[5], Job 8[12]) by βοτάνη; once (Is 37[27]) by χόρτος ξηρός; and in the ten other places where it occurs (Job 40[15], Ps 37[2] 103[15] 104[14] 129[6] 147[8], Is 40[6. 7] 44[4] 51[12]) by χόρτος.

3. דֶּשֶׁא *deshe'* (root uncertain; the vb. דשא, Jl 2[22], Gn 1[11], is probably a denominative. Like *hâzîr*, it is variously rendered in both EV and LXX. It is tr[d]

four times 'herb' (2 K 19[26], Is 66[14] LXX βοτάνη; Ps 37[2] LXX χλόη, Is 37[27] where it is dropped out of the LXX); twice 'tender herb' (Dt 32[2] LXX ἄγρωστις, Job 38[27] RV 'tender grass,' marg. 'greensward,' LXX χλόη); once 'green' as an adj. to *pastures* (Ps 23[2] LXX τόπου χλόης); twice 'tender grass' (2 S 23[4] LXX χλόη, Pr 27[25] LXX πόα); and four times 'grass' (Gn 1[11], Jer 14[5] LXX βοτάνη, Job 6[5] LXX σῖτα, Is 15[6] RV 'tender grass,' LXX χόρτος).

4. עֵשֶׂב *'ésebh*. This word (of uncertain root) is tr[d] in ten places 'herb' or 'herbs' (Gn 1[11. 30] 3[18], Pr 27[25], Is 42[15] LXX χόρτος, Gn 2[5] LXX χλωρός, Ex 9[22] 10[12. 15] LXX βοτάνη, Ps 104[14] LXX χλόη); and in eleven 'grass' (Dt 11[15] LXX χορτάσματα, Dt 32[2] RV *herb*, 2 K 19[26], Ps 72[16] 102[4. 11] 106[20], Jer 14[6] RV *herbage*, Am 7[2] LXX χόρτος; Job 5[25] LXX παμβότανον; Is 37[27] left out by LXX altogether).

It will appear from the above analysis—
(a) That all the above terms are indefinite, applying to *herbage* in general.
(b) It is improbable that the Hebrews discriminated rigidly between the true grasses, *i.e.* the modern botanical order *Gramineæ* (or even the group of grass-like plants, including sedges and rushes), and other herbage. If they did, it does not appear from their nomenclature. The Arabic does not contain any such distinction. With all the general culture and knowledge of natural history of our age, grasses, in popular language, include some plants other than those of the order *Gramineæ*, as *pepper-grass, Lepidium sativum*, L.; *orange-grass, Hypericum Sarothra*, L., etc.
(c) It is quite plain that neither the LXX nor our own translators have been at any pains to render these words always by the same Gr. or Eng. equivalent. Thus in Is 15[6] both חָצִיר and דֶּשֶׁא are rendered χόρτος, the first being tr[d] AV *hay*, RV *grass*, and the second AV *grass*, RV *tender grass*. In Is 37[27] חָצִיר is rendered χόρτος ξηρός, AV and RV *grass*, while עֵשֶׂב and דֶּשֶׁא are left out in the LXX, and rendered in AV and RV respectively *grass* and *herb*. In Gn 1[11] דֶּשֶׁא עֵשֶׂב is rendered βοτάνην χόρτου. The reader will detect numerous other illustrations of this point. Much as it is to be regretted that the translators, ancient and modern, have not rendered these words uniformly, we must accept the fact. The nearest we can approach to a specialization of the term is to regard עֵשֶׂב as referring to *herbage* in general, including vegetables suitable for human food; חָצִיר to *grasses*; דֶּשֶׁא to *forage plants*; and יֶרֶק to *verdure*. They might be then rendered as follows: *'ésebh*=herbs, *hâzîr* =grass, *deshe'*=pasture grass or tender grass, and *yerek*=green thing.

Grasses are very numerous in Bible lands. In Pal. and Syria they are represented by 90 genera and 243 species. Few of them grow in masses. Turf is almost unknown. With the exception of the cereals, none of the grasses are cultivated in this land. See HAY.

In NT grass is always the tr[n] of χόρτος. But χόρτος is also tr[d] by *blade* (Mt 13[26], Mk 4[28]) and *hay* (1 Co 3[12]). In Mk, *l.c.*, the χλωρὸς χόρτος is the first evidence of early spring (cf. Jn 6[4. 10]).

                   G. E. POST.

GRASSHOPPER.—See LOCUST.

GRATE, GRATING (מִכְבָּר).—Half-way up the altar of burnt-offering was attached a projecting ledge—such, at least, is the now generally accepted interpretation of the obscure word כַּרְכֹּב (Ex 27[5] 38[4]), regarding which the author of the Priests' Code gives us no further information—which appears to have run right round the altar. Underneath this projection was attached 'a grating (AV grate) of network of brass' (Ex 27[4] RV, 35[16] 38[4. 30] 39[39]),

---

* Besides this passage in Ro, the verb occurs in biblical Gr. only Wis 16[11] in the sense of 'prick' (so AVm and RVm, but RV 'bite'). It comes from κέντρον, a goad.

which completely covered the lower half of the altar. It was probably, as the etymology suggests (see *Oxf. Heb. Lex. sub* כבר), a strong netting made of bronze (נְחֹשֶׁת) wire, with meshes sufficiently open to allow the sacrificial blood to be dashed against the lower part of the altar. For other conjectures regarding the nature and purpose of the *mikbār*, see the art. TABERNACLE (section dealing with the Altar of Burnt-offering).

A. R. S. KENNEDY.

GRATITUDE.—See THANKFULNESS.

GRAVE.—The usual OT word tr⁴ 'grave' is קֶבֶר *ḳeber* (also fem. form קְבוּרָה); and the usual NT word is μνημεῖον (with the occasional μνῆμα). See BURIAL, SEPULCHRE. But in AV שְׁאוֹל *she'ôl* is often so tr⁴, and ᾅδης once (1 Co 15⁵⁵). See HADES and SHEOL.

GRAVE.—In Sir 39³ (and in the 1st Prologue) occurs the expression 'grave sentences' as tr⁴ of παροιμίαι, RV 'proverbs.' The meaning of the adj. is 'weighty,' as in Knox, *Hist.* 406, 'Thus the Queen's Majesty being informed of the truth by her said Advocate, sent again and stayed the said meeting, and sent to the Town a grave Letter'; and Shaks. *Macbeth*, III. i. 21—

'We should have else deserved your good advice,
Which still hath been both grave and prosperous.'

In this use 'grave' is but one step removed from the lit. sense of 'heavy' (as Lat. *gravis*), which we find in Chapman, *Homer's Odysseys*, viii. 257—

'This said, with robe and all, he grasp'd a stone,
A little graver than was ever thrown
By these Phæacians in their wrastling rout.'

One step farther removed is the use of the word in NT as tr⁴ of σεμνός, 1 Ti 3⁸. ¹¹, Tit 2², applied to deacons, their wives, and aged men, in the sense of 'serious.' Cf. T. Fuller, *Holy and Profane State*, iii. 19 (p. 202), 'He is a good Time-server that complyes his manners to the severall ages of this life: pleasant in youth, without wantonnesse; grave in old age, without frowardnesse. Frost is as proper for winter, as flowers for spring. Gravity becomes the ancient; and a green Christmas is neither handsome nor healthfull.' J. HASTINGS.

GRAVE.—The verb to 'grave' is used in earlier versions in the sense of 'dig,' as Is 37²⁵ Cov. 'Yf there be no water, I wil grave and drynke' (EV 'I have digged, and drunk water'). But the only meaning in EV is 'carve,' modern 'engrave.' So Tindale has the word in Gn 4²² 'Tubalcain a worker in metall and a father of all that grave in brasse and yeron'; and in Ex 39⁶ 'And they wrought onix stones cloosed in ouches of golde and graved as sygnettes are graven with the names of the children of Israel.' He also has 'stonegraver' Ex 28¹¹ (EV 'engraver in stone'), and 'graver' as the tool, 32⁴ (EV 'graving tool'). For **Graven Image** see IDOLATRY, IMAGE. J. HASTINGS.

GRAVEL.—Wyclif used 'gravel' as a synonym for 'sand.' Thus Gn 22¹⁷ 'I shal multiplie thi seed as sterris of hevene, and as gravel that is in the brenk of the see'; Mt 7²⁶ 'And every man that herith these my wordis, and doth hem nat, is liche to a man fool, that hath bildid his hous on gravel, or soond'; Ac 27⁴¹ 'And whanne we felden into a place of gravel gon al aboute with the see, thei hurtliden the schipp.'*

In the last passage Rhem. has 'And when we were fallen into a place betwene two seas, they graveled the ship.' This use of 'gravel' as a verb led to the fig. phrase 'to gravel one,' that is, 'bring one to a standstill in argument,' a phrase used by Thomas Fuller in *Holy and Profane State*, ii. 4 (p. 63), 'When Eunomius the Heretick vaunted that he knew God and

his divinity, S. Basil gravells him in 21 questions about the body of an ant or pismire: so dark is man's understanding.'

In AV also there is practically no distinction between 'gravel' and 'sand,' unless it is made by the addition of 'stones.' The word occurs (1) Is 48¹⁹ 'Thy seed also had been as the sand, and the offspring of thy bowels like the gravel thereof' (כִּמְעֹתָיו, RV 'like the grains thereof,' after LXX, Jerome, Targ., Ewald, Del., Orelli, and others; but RVm 'like that of the bowels thereof' [referring to the fish], after Ges., Hitzig, Knobel, Keil, Nägelsbach, and others [Cheyne, 'as the entrails thereof']. The word, which occurs only here, is of uncertain derivation and meaning); (2) Pr 20¹⁷ 'Bread of deceit is sweet to a man; but afterwards his mouth shall be filled with gravel,' and (3) La 3¹⁶ 'He hath also broken my teeth with gravel stones' (both חָצָץ, from [חָצַץ] to divide, therefore 'broken small'); (4) Sir 18¹⁰ 'As a drop of water unto the sea, and a gravelstone in comparison of the sand' (ψῆφος, RV 'a pebble'). J. HASTINGS.

GRAY.—The epithet 'gray' occurs only in reference to hair, and is the tr⁴ either of שִׂיב *sîbh*, to be gray-headed (1 S 12², Job 15¹⁰), or of שֵׂיבָה *sêbhâh*, hoariness, old age (Gn 42³⁸ 44²⁹. ³¹, Dt 32²⁵, Ps 71¹⁸, Pr 20²⁹, Hos 7⁹). RV prefers 'hoary' in Pr 20²⁹.

The word has been spelt both 'gray' and 'grey' from earliest times. Shaks. has in *Hamlet* (II. ii. 199), 'The satirical rogue says here that old men have grey beards,' but in *Lear* (II. ii. 72), 'Spare my gray beard, you wagtail?' In AV 1611 the spelling is uniformly 'gray,' but in Ps 71¹⁸, Pr 20²⁹ the word is usually spelt 'grey' in modern editions.

GREAT SEA (הַיָּם הַגָּדוֹל) Nu 34⁶. ⁷, Jos 15¹². ⁴⁷, Ezk 47¹⁹. ²⁰ 48²⁸), called also הַיָּם הָאַחֲרוֹן the hinder, *i.e.* western sea, Dt 11²⁴ 34², Zec 14⁸, Jl 2²⁰; יָם פְּלִשְׁתִּים *Sea of the Philistines*, Ex 23³¹; הַיָּם *The Sea*, Gn 49¹³, Nu 13²⁹ 34⁵, Dt 1⁷ etc. Lat. *Mare Internum.**

The Mediterranean was essentially the 'Great Sea' and 'Hinder Sea' to the writers of the Bible; being the western boundary of the Holy Land, beyond which their geographical knowledge did not far extend. Maritime adventure and commerce was not the direction in which Israelitish ambition extended, except perhaps for a short period during the reign of Solomon; and although the lands allotted to the tribes of Judah, Dan, Ephraim, Manasseh, Zebulun, and Asher touched the coast of the Mediterranean at various points, the waters of the Great Sea were seldom traversed by their ships. This was due to several causes: first, the history of the Israelites previous to the Exodus was essentially of an inland character; secondly, during and after the invasion of Palestine their efforts were too much directed towards dispossessing the inhabitants and retaining their hold on the countries they had conquered, to give them time and opportunity for extending their sway beyond the coast; thirdly, the absence of natural commodious harbours on the Mediterranean seaboard; and lastly, the presence of the Phœnicians on the north, and of the Philistines on the south, along the coast-line. These nations, especially the former, had command of the sea, and rendered adventure in that direction either useless or impracticable to the children of Israel. From a period as far back as the Exodus the Phœnician settlers had established themselves at various points along the coast, and in course of time formed a confederation, essentially maritime, extending from beyond the Orontes on the north to Joppa (*Japho*) on the south, a length of 300 English miles.† To the south of Joppa the country of the Philistines commenced and extended to 'the River

---

* Wyc. even uses 'gravel' in the plu., Dt 33¹⁹ (1380) 'hid tresours of graveilis' (after Vulg. 'thesauros absconditos arenarum'), Dou. 'sandes.'

* It is intended to treat this subject only in so far as it is connected with biblical history.
† Rawlinson, *History of Phœnicia*, 1889, p 84.

of Egypt,'* thus effectually excluding the Israelites from the command of the sea. The only port, in fact, to which in the time of the monarchy this nation had full access seems to have been Joppa, which, from its position as the nearest to Jerusalem, became the chief centre of the import and export trade. Thither in the time of Solomon the timber required for the construction of the temple and the royal palace, which had been cut in the Lebanon, was transported ; and thither, doubtless, were conveyed the wheat, the barley, the oil, and the wine, which the Phœnicians received in exchange for their firs and cedars (2 Ch 2[10. 15]). In the time of the Maccabees, however, this port became the property of the Jews (1 Mac 10[76]). Another port, Acco,—now known as Acre,—situated on the northern shore of the bay of that name, was assigned to Zebulun ('a haven of ships,' Gn 49[13]), but it is doubtful if it was ever occupied by that tribe for any considerable time. It is the best natural roadstead on the Syrian coast, and was conquered and retained by the Assyrians in their wars with Palestine and Egypt. In later times it played an important part in the wars of the Crusades, and has become celebrated in recent times for its successful resistance to Napoleon, when held by a Turkish garrison and supported by a British fleet under the command of Admiral Sir Sidney Smith (1799). The port under the name of Ptolemais is mentioned as having been visited by St. Paul on his third missionary journey (Ac 21[7]).

Mediterranean Coast.—From the Bay of Iskenderun on the north to el-'Arîsh on the south, a distance of 450 miles, the coast of the Levant (the eastern part of the Mediterranean) is remarkably straight, with few deep bays or prominent headlands. All along the Syrian coast as far as Beirût, the land rises with a rocky and bold front from the waters. At Acre the coast recedes and the land gently slopes upwards along the banks of the Kishon, forming the plain of Esdraelon. South of this valley, the long ridge of Mount Carmel protrudes into the waters and terminates in a bold headland ; and from its southern slopes the Vale of Sharon gradually expands in breadth and ultimately merges into that of Philistia ; and the coast-line follows an almost unbroken semicircular curve towards the Delta of the Nile.

Sandhills.—When the early settlers, coming from the head of the Persian Gulf to the shores of the Mediterranean (about B.C. 1500), first surveyed its blue waters they beheld groves of palms lining the coast, in consequence of which the Greeks called the land 'Phœnicia.'† These palms have long since disappeared, and their place is generally occupied by enormous banks of sand gradually moving inwards from the coast as they are impelled by the westerly winds. Most of the ancient coast towns, both of Phœnicia and Philistia, are buried to a greater or less extent beneath these sandhills, which, when not prevented by artificial means, are still moving inland, and have become a source of danger and loss to the inhabitants. These sandhills, according to Sir H. Kitchener, cover a large tract of country between southern Philistia and Ismailia.

New Testament Notices.—Once in the history of our Lord did He with His disciples visit the coast of the Great Sea ; this was on the memorable occasion when, endeavouring to obtain a brief period of repose, He visited the borders of Tyre and passed through (ἦλθεν διὰ Σιδῶνος) Sidon,‡ and performed a miracle of healing on a Gentile, the daughter of a Syro-phœnician woman. But in

---

* Wady el-'Arîsh ; for an account of this valley, see Hull, *Mount Seir, Sinai, and W. Palestine.* Appendix by Kitchener, 220 (1889).
† *Phœnix dactylifera,* the date palm.
‡ Mt 15[21], Mk 7[24]. On this visit see Farrar, *Life of Christ,* i. 478.

the missionary journeys of St. Paul, and especially in the incidents connected with his final voyage to Rome (Ac 27. 28), we are brought into contact with numerous seaports, headlands, islands, and bays, commencing with Cæsarea on the coast of Phœnicia and terminating with the port of Puteoli (*Puzzuoli*) on the western coast of Italy. In following the narrative of this voyage we can trace its course from point to point on the map, and we gain some insight into the dangers of navigation at a time when the mariner's compass was unknown, when nautical charts were rude, or were perhaps unused by the commanders of ships, and when the heavenly bodies alone were guides to the ship's course when out of sight of land. [For the description of St. Paul's voyages in the Mediterranean, consult Smith, *Voyage and Shipwreck of St. Paul*[2], 1856 ; the works on St. Paul's Life, as Conybeare and Howson, Lewin, Farrar, Stalker, Iverach ; the Commentaries on the Acts ; Ramsay, *St. Paul the Traveller* ; and the various Bible Appendixes, 'Aids' (Queen's Printers), 'Helps' (Oxford), 'Companion' (Cambridge), 'Manual' (Collins)].
                        E. HULL.

GREAT SYNAGOGUE.—See SYNAGOGUE (THE GREAT).

GREAVES (1 S 17[6]) in the phrase מִצְחַת נְחֹשֶׁת *miẓḥath nĕḥôsheth,* 'greave of bronze.' The singular rendering is perhaps to be preferred (not so Wellh. and Driver, *in loco*). The Roman legionary in later times wore *one* greave, and that on his *right* leg. Cf. passage quoted from Polybius (*e*) under ARMOUR.
                        W. E. BARNES.

GRECIANS, GREEKS.—Both these terms are used indifferently in AV of OT Apocr. to designate persons of Gr. extraction (1 Mac 1[10] 6[2] 8[9], 2 Mac 4[36] etc.). In Jl 3[6] AV has 'Grecians,' RV and AVm 'sons of the Grecians,' as the tr. of בְּנֵי הַיְּוָנִים. This is the only passage in OT where either Grecians or Greeks are named, although Greece (under the name JAVAN, which see) is several times mentioned (Dn 8[21] 10[20] 11[2], Zec 9[13]). In NT the linguistic usage of EV makes a distinction between the terms Greeks and Grecians. *Greeks* uniformly represents the word Ἕλληνες, which may denote persons of Gr. descent in the narrowest sense (Ac 16[1] 18[4], Ro 1[14]), or may be a general designation for all who are not of Jewish extraction (Jn 12[20], Ro 1[16] 10[12], Gal 3[28]. See GENTILES). It is remarkable that in Is 9[12] even פְּלִשְׁתִּים (Philistines) is reproduced in LXX by Ἕλληνες. *Grecians,* on the other hand (Ac 6[1] 9[29]), is AV tr. of Ἑλληνισταί (see following art.), which means Gr.-speaking *Jews* (RV *Grecian Jews*). An interesting question is that of the correct reading of Ac 11[20]. Were those to whom the men of Cyprus and Cyrene preached, Grecians or Greeks ? in other words, were they Jews or Gentiles ? The weight of MS authority is in favour of Ἑλληνιστάς (the reading in TR, and adopted in AV and RVm), which has the support of B and indirectly of א* (εὐαγγελιστάς) D[2] L and almost all cursives. It is retained in the text of WH. Internal evidence, on the other hand (see, however, WH's *Introd. to Gr. NT,* App. 93 f.), is generally supposed to necessitate the reading Ἕλληνας which is found in א[3] A D, and is accepted by Scrivener, Lachm. Tisch. Treg. and text of RV (see Scrivener's *Introd. to Crit. of NT*[4], ii. 370 f.).
                        J. A. SELBIE.

GREECE, HELLENISM.—The names *Greek* and *Greece* do not occur in the Gr. or Heb. Bible, being designations under which the *Italian* races came to know Hellas and its inhabitants. In Gn 10[2] *Javan* (Ἰωυάν) is correctly used to denote the Gr. stock in general. So in Æsch. *Pers.* 178, 563 the Persian interlocutors speak of Greeks as the Iâones.

The old Armenians used the same word; and at a very remote date the Yevana are mentioned in the ancient Egyptian epic of Ramses II. among the allies of the Hittites.

As early as the 7th cent. B.C. the names Hellas and Hellenes were used by the Greeks to distinguish themselves from the *Barbari*. And the same are used in the LXX (Jl 3[6], Is 66[19], Ezk 27[13], Zec 9[13]) and in NT.

It has been lately conjectured on archæological grounds that the Philistines were the same race with the Pelasgians, who built the pre-historic city of Mycenæ, and used the primitive alphabet discovered recently by Mr. Arthur Evans in Crete and the Peloponnese. If this be so, the Jews from their first entry into Canaan were in conflict with the forerunners of the historical Greeks. 'That among the various elements,' says Mr. Evans, 'from the Ægean coastlands, who took part in the Philistine confederation, men of Greek stock may already have found a place as early as the 12th or 11th cent. B.C. can at least no longer be regarded as an improbable hypothesis. It is, perhaps, not without some actual warrant in fact that in the LXX of Is 9[12] the Philistines themselves are translated by Ἕλληνες.'[*] Renan (*Hist. of People of Israel*, Eng. tr. ii. 15) adopts the same view.

However this may be, the hist. relations of Jews with Greeks begin mainly about the age of Alexander of Macedon, and as the result of his conquests. He, and the Diadochi kings who succeeded him, deliberately set about the Hellenization of Asia, Syria, and Egypt. If Alexander did not found all the 70 new cities in Asia ascribed to him by Plutarch, he was at least the founder of Alexandria.

But the bloom of Gr. civilization could not be transferred to Asia and Egypt, for it had passed away. The old independent city life was crushed, partly by the previous internecine conflicts of the Greeks, partly by the all-engulfing conquests of Philip and Alexander. Under the Diadochi, who became despots of an Oriental type, there was none of the old Gr. freedom. The new Gr. settlers themselves, brought into close contact with Asiatics, became half orientalized. Something of the old subtlety in speculation remained, something of the plastic skill of the older art. But the combined strength, simplicity, and lovely symmetry of Gr. genius was lost. Moral philosophy alone, in the hands of the Stoics, remained a vigorous activity; but now that the free state was a thing of the past, it was rather the life and duties of the individual than the collective life and needs of the organized community that formed the matter for criticism and theory.

Alexander and his successors invited the Jews to join in this work of colonization, and they responded freely. In Egypt, indeed, there were already Jews serving in the army of Psammitichus I. as early as B.C. 650; and under Jeremiah went many others. But of these was left a mere remnant, when, on the occasion of the foundation of Alexandria, a fresh mass of Jewish colonists was introduced. Here they had an ethnarch of their own, and privileges from the first; and they increased so much that Philo (*in Flac.* ii. 523) before A.D. 40 estimated their number at a million. From Egypt they spread westward, and already, in Sulla's time, were an important class in Cyrene. In the East the bulk of the Jewish race still remained, of course, in the old lands of the Captivity, beyond the Euphrates, there contracting Persian and Assyrian beliefs and culture rather than Greek. But in the Gr. cities of Syria they were, from the

time of the Diadochi, very numerous. In Damascus Jos. (*BJ* VII. viii. 7) says there were 18,000 slain in the war of A.D. 66–70 alone. Antioch was full of them, as were all the coast cities, from Sidon southwards. In Asia Minor, as early as the middle of the 4th cent. B.C., Aristotle met an educated Jew who was Greek not only in speech, but in spirit (Jos. *c. Ap.* i. 22). In Phrygia and Lydia, Antiochus the Great planted 2000 families of Mesopotamian Jews (Jos. *Ant.* XII. iii. 4)—a proof that it was not from the small district of Judæa alone and from the remnant restored by Cyrus that the new Jewish colonists were drawn by the Seleucid kings. However, since Ptol. Lagos transferred 100,000 from Judæa to Egypt (Aristeæ *Epist.*), there must have been a great surplus of population in the Holy Land itself at the beginning of the 3rd cent. B.C. Philo (*de Legat.* ii. 587) has preserved a letter of Herod Agrippa to Caligula, testifying to the extent of the Greek diaspora in the year A.D. 38. 'Jerusalem,' wrote Agrippa, 'is the capital city, not of a single country, but of most, because of its colonies in Egypt, Phœnicia, Syria in general, and Hollow Syria, as also in Pamphylia, Cilicia, most districts of Asia (Minor), as far as Bithynia and the extreme parts of Pontus.' In the same way, he continues, Europe was full of Jews: Thessaly, Bœotia, Macedonia, Ætolia, Attica, Argos, Corinth, the best and larger part of Peloponnese. And not the mainland only. For Eubœa, Cyprus, Crete, and the islands generally, were full of Jews.

Many of these Jewish colonists adopted Gr. speech, habits, and culture. They wrote and thought in Greek. They read the Gr. poets and orators; admired and were spectators of Gr. plays; joined Gr. philosophic sects, Pythagorean, Peripatetic, Stoic or Epicurean. On the other hand, distinctively Jewish sects, like that of the Alexandrian Therapeutæ, ramified, according to Philo (ii. 474), in many parts of the inhabited world, esp. in Greece. Of the interpenetration of the Jewish by the Hellenic genius which resulted, we have left in religious literature three great monuments, the LXX, the NT, and the works of Philo; not to mention numerous extra-canonical apocrypha, some originally written in Aram. or Heb., but mostly surviving in a Gr. form alone. Foremost among the latter in religious interest are the surviving fragments of *Enoch* and the Jewish Sibylline poems. The copious works of Philo have probably survived by mere accident; but that they are a mere remnant of a larger Jewish-Gr. literature is evident from the anonymous references to other writers with which his pages abound. Christian writers, especially Eusebius, have preserved the names of, as well as extracts from, several Hellenistic writers of early date: *e.g.* of a Philo who wrote an epic on Jerus., of a poet Theodotus, and of Ezekiel who wrote a drama about Moses. Among the philosophic writers Aristobulus is remarkable as the first to use, so far as we know, the allegorical method of expounding the Mosaic law, about B.C. 170–150.

These writers were Alexandrine, but there are many more Gr. authors who were probably Pal. Jews or even Samaritans. Among these, Alex. Polyhistor (B.C. 80–40) has preserved to us in his works, as cited by Eusebius, fragments of the chronicler Demetrius (B.C. 222–205), of Eupolemus (B.C. 158–157), and Artapanus, Aristeas, and Cleodemus, all four Jewish historians. Jason of Cyrene (*c.* B.C. 160) wrote a history of the Maccabæan wars, of which 2 Mac is an abridgment made before Philo's age. The Wisdom of Sol. was probably written in Alexandria before Philo's day. Numenius and Longinus, in the 2nd and 3rd cents. A.D., wrote to some extent under Jewish influence, but were not Jews.

---

[*] See art. on 'Primitive Pictographs and Script from Crete and the Peloponnese' in *Journ. of Hellenic Studies*, vol. xiv. pt. 2, 1894, p. 369.

It is of peculiar interest to know how far **Hellenism** had, in the 300 years preceding Jesus of Nazareth, invaded Judæa itself. The circumstance that the strictly Jewish territory of Judæa, Galilee, and Peræa was wedged in between large and affluent Gr. cities on the E. and W., would in itself suggest considerable inroads of Hellenism. Nor must it be forgotten that at least at every passover thousands of Gr.-speaking Jews were present in Jerus., and that many of them were domiciled there, as is clear from their having synagogues.

In Ac 2⁹ we read that on the day of Pentecost there were present in Jerus. Jews not merely from Parthia, Media, Elam, and Mesopotamia, but from Cappadocia, Pontus, Asia, Phrygia, Pamphylia, Egypt, Libya about Cyrene; also sojourners from Rome, Cretans, and Arabians. Not all of these would speak Gr., but many the vernaculars of their districts. But the enumeration shows how polyglot a multitude was to be met with in Jerus. on any feast day. There is no reason to doubt the tradition that the bilingual Jewish doctors who, perhaps, by order of Ptolemy Philadelphus, translated the Law and the Prophets some time early in the 3rd cent. B.C., were sent from Jerus. itself by the high priest Eleasar. For the Jews of Jerus. made, as early as B.C. 300, alliance with Sparta, which was renewed a century and a half later (1 Mac 12⁷·⁸·¹⁹⁻²², cf. 14¹⁸ff·). They also made treaties with Gr. cities in Asia; and under the Seleucids, prior to the Maccab. revolt, rapid strides had been made towards their Hellenization. Nor was this revolt directed against the Gr. language, philosophy, and architecture; but was rather excited by the despotic attempt of Antiochus to enforce idolatry. Still it is probable that the success of the revolt was a check to Hellenizing influences, and stimulated the use, not, indeed, of Hebrew, which was already a dead language, and unintelligible to the masses, but of the local Aramaic. If the returned Jews of an earlier generation had not been so gratuitously intolerant of their old Samaritan coreligionists, there would have been a more compact mass of Sem.-speaking people to oppose the inroads of Gr. language and habits. As it was, the very metropolis of Galilee was a Gr. city.

Whatever reaction against Hellenism the Maccab. uprising may have called into being, it is yet certain that Judæa contained during the 1st cent. B.C. a powerful minority of Gr. Jews. The rulers, even of the patriotic Hasmonæan house, bore Gr. names, and the entire influence of the Idumæan usurpers, Herod and Archelaus, who succeeded, was cast on the side of Hellenism. The temple of Herod was a Gr. building; so were all the other monuments and tombs of that epoch. There was a Gr. circus and hippodrome in Jerus., and Herod was surrounded by Gr. philosophers and writers.

The NT itself bears witness to the strength of the Gr. element in the very cradle of the new religion. Of the apostolic writings there is not a single one—with the dubious exception of the Heb. Matthew—which was not from the first written in Gr.; and the Gr. style of Paul, of Peter, of Jude, of James, and of the authors of the two Gospels which claim apost. authorship, is not the style of writers who were tyros or late learners, but of men who had read and spoken Greek from childhood. They were certainly bilingual Jews; and if it is probable that Jesus habitually taught in Aram., it is not less probable that He, like most of His disciples, knew Greek. Philip, who certainly spoke Gr. (Jn 12²¹, Ac 8³⁵), besides having a Gr. name, came from Bethsaida Julias, a grecized town; whence also came another apostle with a Gr. name, Andrew, and Peter himself (Jn 1⁴⁴). We hear of believing Greeks (not Gr. Jews) in the *entourage* of Jesus (Jn 12²¹); and the cry of anguish,

Eli, Eli, lama sabachthani, could only have been misunderstood by a Gr.-speaking crowd. How strong was the Hellenistic party in the Church from the first, is clear from the fact that it was their grievances which led to the appointment of the seven, all of whom bore Gr. names, while one, at least, was a proselyte of Antioch (Ac 6⁵). The mention of the *widows* of the Hellenists proves that this party in the earliest Church was composed of settled residents in Jerus., and not of mere birds of passage, like the Libyan, Cyrenian, Alexandrine, Cilician, and Asiatic Jews mentioned in the same context. Stephen, who argued with all these, and was also one of the new deacons, must have talked Greek to them; and his speech, which is full of LXX citations, was no doubt delivered in Greek. Later on, in Ac 21⁴⁰, St. Paul, indeed, addresses the mob in Jerus. *in the Heb. dialect,* that is, in Aramaic. But that is far from warranting Schürer's inference (*HJP* II. i. 48), that this mob knew no Greek. For the context (Ac 22²) proves that St. Paul did so only to conciliate them, and therefore as an exception. It is clear that they did not expect it, and were surprised to hear him whom they had just accused of introducing a Gr. into the temple, address them freely in Aramaic. They expected him to speak to them in the same Gr. tongue in which he had been conversing with the chief captain. And it is noticeable that on this occasion, as at Stephen's martyrdom, it was Gr.-speaking Jews (of Asia, Ac 21²⁷) who had stirred up ill-feeling against the followers of the new Messiah.

Many other facts point to the diffusion of a knowledge of Greek in Judæa. The coins of the Hasmonæan epoch bore Greek as well as Aram. legends; those of the Herodean dynasty and of the Romans, Greek alone. The Mishna, which represents the Judæa of that age, is full of Gr. loanwords, even for the commonest objects of life.[*] In the temple the notices warning Gentiles off from the inner precincts were in Gr. and Latin. It is probable even that the poor and despised in the cities of Judæa were more familiar with Gr. than were the rich Sadducees or the legalistic Pharisees. Thus Jos. at the end of his work (*Ant.* XX. xi. 2) writes as follows: 'With Gr. letters I was careful to acquire an adequate grammatical acquaintance; though my country's custom was an obstacle to my *talking* Gr. accurately. For with us they do not approve of those who learn *thoroughly* the language of many races, because they esteem this accomplishment as one common, not only to the inferior class of free men, but to such servants as care to learn. They allow real wisdom to belong only to those who clearly understand the law and can interpret the meaning of the Holy Scripture.' From the above it is clear that though the Jewish aristocracy disdained to *talk* Gr., they did not equally disdain to read and write it; and that a command of the spoken idiom looked at askance by Pharisees, scribes, and Sadducees, was yet diffused among the humbler classes. It was just of these humbler people, the *'am-hāārez,* who knew not the law (Jn 7⁴⁹), but who could often talk Gr., that the teaching of Jesus took hold. They composed the earliest Church, and were the lost sheep of the House of Israel.

The crushing reverses which the Jews experienced at the hands of the Rom. power from 70 till 150 A.D., first in Judæa and later in Cyprus, Alexandria, Cyrene, and elsewhere, drove the race in upon itself and soon established a prejudice against any Jewish books not written in Hebrew. A little before A.D. 70, when the final agony was at hand, it was forbidden by the Rabbis to Jewish fathers to have their sons any more instructed in

Greek,* which proves that till then it had been a common practice. The writing of divorcement might, according to the Mishna, be in Greek (*Gittin*, ix. 8); and the LXX was recognized by official Judaism (*Megilla*, i. 8). In spite of the prejudice aroused against Gr. by the events of A.D. 70, two or three new Gr. translations of OT were made for the use of Gr. Jews in the hundred years which ensued. But the prejudice continued to grow, and the cruelties perpetrated upon Jews by the Christians, so soon as they got the upper hand, must have intensified it. And the result is seen to-day in the circumstance that of all the voluminous Jewish-Greek literature which once existed, nothing survives except what the Christian Church has kept. No doubt the vigilant censorship of the Cath. Church is, in part, responsible for this deprivation, which we of to-day feel so keenly. For the fanaticism which destroyed all heretical works so-called was not likely to spare Jewish books. Still, the prejudices of the Jews themselves must be largely to blame.

The tendencies and characteristics of Greek Judaism will be further dealt with under the articles ISRAEL and RELIGION.

It is enough here to point out that the Gr. Jews were not alien, as is often supposed, from the Messianic hope. The Jewish Sibylline poems know of it; and Philo, in spite of all his Hel. training, held it with intense fervour, as is clear to any one who will read his two tracts *de Præmiis et Poenis* and *de Exsecrationibus*.

The relations of the Jews to their Gr. fellow-townsmen were invariably hostile on both sides. They were constantly ready to massacre each other. This hatred was due to the fact that in each city the Jews formed a community apart, often under archons or ethnarchs, or an assembly of their own. They could join in no heathen festivals, nor eat any meats, nor even use oil for anointing which they had not themselves prepared. How much the Gentiles resented this Jewish exclusiveness is clear from hints in Juvenal, Tacitus, and other ancient writers. The Jews, in fact, held the same position in a pagan community as do the Mohammedans of India among the Hindoos who surround them. Add to this that the Gr. Jews lost no opportunity of making converts among the pagans, and were especially successful in winning over the women. These converts were, of course, obliged to cut themselves adrift from their old friends and families—a circumstance which intensified the hatred of the Greeks for a religion and race at once exclusive and usurping. The propagandism of the Christians had from the first the same result. The new religion, like the old, spread among Gentiles at the expense of family ties and affections; and on their ruin ultimately consecrated the principles and edifice of monasticism. In the Jewish sects of Essenes and Therapeutæ, esp. of the latter, we may trace similar results arising out of similar conditions within Gr. Judaism itself. The Rom. Government, however, always recognized Judaism as the religion of a race, and therefore as something respectable and deserving of protection from Gentile assaults. For Christianity, which was not a national cult, and for that reason a more rapid solvent of family and citizen ties, the Government had less solicitude; and was less anxious, as a rule, to protect it from the storms of popular hatred which it everywhere excited. For further information on such points, see art. on PROSELYTE; and on the whole subject of Greek Judaism, see Schürer, *HJP* (esp. II. i. 11–51, and II. iii. 156–381), before each chapter of which is given an array of the chief authorities on every part of the subject.　　　F. C. CONYBEARE.

*Talmud, *Sota*, ix. 14.

GREEK LANGUAGE.—See LANGUAGE.

GREEK VERSIONS. — See SEPTUAGINT and VERSIONS.

GREEN.—See COLOURS (vol. i. p. 457a).

GREET, GREETING.—In OT 'greet' occurs only once, 1 S 25⁵ 'Go to Nabal, and greet him in my name' (לְשָׁלוֹם בִשְׁמִי לוֹ־וּשְׁאֶלְתֶּם, lit., as AVm, 'and ask him in my name of peace'). The AV is from Wyc. 1388 (through Bish.); the 1382 ed. has 'salute,' which is the word in Cov. and Dou.; Gen. 'aske him in my name how he doeth.'

In Apocr. the usual Gr. formula of salutation, χαίρειν, is tr⁴ 'greeting' in 1 Es 6⁷, Ad. Est 16¹, 1 Mac 12²⁰ 15². ¹⁶; and 'sendeth' or 'send greeting' in 1 Es 8⁹, 1 Mac 10¹⁸. ²⁵ 11³² 13³⁶ 14²⁰, 2 Mac 11¹⁶. ²². ²⁷. ³⁴. RV omits 'sendeth' or 'send.' In 2 Mac 1¹⁰ χαίρειν καὶ ὑγιαίνειν is tr⁴ 'sent (RV send) greeting, and health.' In Sir 6⁵ we have 'a fair-speaking tongue will increase kind greetings' (εὐπροσήγορα, RV 'courtesies').

As a simple formula of salutation χαίρειν occurs but thrice in NT, Ac 15²³ AV 'The apostles and elders and brethren *send* greeting unto the brethren which are of the Gentiles,' RV omits 'send'; 23²⁶ AV 'Claudias Lysias unto the most excellent governor Felix *sendeth* greeting,' RV omits 'sendeth'; Ja 1¹ AV 'James . . . to the twelve tribes which are scattered abroad, greeting,' RVm 'wisheth joy.' And in 2 Jn ¹⁰. ¹¹ λέγειν χαίρειν, which in AV is tr⁴ 'bid one God speed,' is in RV rendered 'give one greeting.' But the most frequent use of 'greet' in AV is as a variation for 'salute' in the rendering of ἀσπάζομαι (Ro 16³. ⁵. ⁶. ⁸. ¹¹, 1 Co 16²⁰, 2 Co 13¹², Ph 4²¹, Col 4¹⁴, 1 Th 5²⁶, 2 Ti 4²¹, Tit 3¹⁵, 1 P 5¹⁴, 2 Jn ¹³, 3 Jn ¹⁴). Elsewhere, with two exceptions, this verb is tr⁴ 'salute'; and there is little doubt that the Revisers have done wisely in giving 'salute' also in the passages where AV has 'greet.' For the unwary reader is sure to imagine a difference of Greek and of meaning when he finds, e.g. in Ph 4²¹ 'Salute every saint in Christ Jesus. The brethren which are with me greet you'; or in 3 Jn ¹⁴ 'Our friends salute thee. Greet the friends by name.'

The two exceptions are (1) Ac 20¹ ἀσπασάμενος ἐξῆλθε πορευθῆναι [edd. πορεύεσθαι] εἰς τὴν Μακεδονίαν, AV 'embraced *them* and departed for to go into Macedonia,' RV 'took leave of them and departed,' Ramsay 'bade them farewell'; (2) He 11¹³ ἀλλὰ πόρρωθεν αὐτὰς ἰδόντες, καὶ πεισθέντες [edd. omit κ. π.], καὶ ἀσπασάμενοι; AV 'but having seen them [the promises] afar off, and were persuaded of *them*, and embraced *them*'; RV 'but having seen them and greeted them from afar,' which Schaff (*Companion to Gr. Test. and Eng. Version*, 1883, p. 454) quotes in his 'Select List of Improved Readings.'

In like manner the subst. ἀσπασμός is tr⁴ 'greeting' in Mt 23⁷, Lk 11¹³ 20⁴⁶, and elsewhere (Mk 12³⁸, Lk 1²⁹. ⁴¹. ⁴⁴, 1 Co 16²¹, Col 4¹⁸, 2 Th 3¹⁷) 'salutation.' RV gives 'salutation' everywhere.
　　　　　　　　　　　　　J. HASTINGS.

GREYHOUND (מָתְנָיִם זַרְזִיר *zarzir mothnayim*, Pr 30³¹).—These Heb. words signify 'one girt in the loins' (AV and RV 'greyhound,' AVm 'horse,' RVm 'war-horse'). Some have supposed that the intention is to describe a wrestler, owing to his commanding figure. The LXX has 'a cock walking proudly among the hens' (see *Oxf. Heb. Lex. s.v.*).
　　　　　　　　　　　　　G. E. POST.

GRIEF.—Grief comes from Lat. *gravis*, heavy, sad, through Fr. *grief* or *gref*. And although it is now used to denote mental anguish only, it formerly covered bodily pain as well. In its use (as in some of the Heb. or Gr. words of which it is the trⁿ in AV) the distinction between bodily and mental pain is not very sharp. Still, its application may be expressed as follows :—

1. *Bodily pain or disease.* (1) Heb. כְּאֵב *kĕ'ēb*, Job 2¹³ 'they saw that his grief was very great' (RVm 'his pain'); so 16⁵·⁶. (2) מַכְאֹב *mak'ôb*, 2 Ch 6²⁹ 'when every one shall know his own sore and his own grief' (RV 'sorrow,' *Oxf. Heb. Lex.* 'pain'—clearly the meaning here); Ps 69²⁶ 'they talk to the grief of those whom thou hast wounded' (RV 'they tell of the sorrow'; RVm 'pain'—so Perowne, Del., Cheyne, de Witt, and others; LXX τὸ ἄλγος). (3) חָלָה *hālâh*, to be sick, used in the Niph. ptcp. as an adj. (qualifying מַכָּה 'wound'), and tr⁴ in EV 'grievous,' Jer 10¹⁹ 14¹⁷ 30¹², Nah 3¹⁹, but as a subst. in Is 17¹¹ and tr⁴ 'grief.' The Hiphil of the same vb. is tr⁴ in Is 53¹⁰ 'Yet it pleased the Lord to bruise him; he hath put him to grief' (RVm 'made him sick,' *i.e.* by bruising him so sorely [see Dillm. *in loc.*], LXX καθαρίσαι αὐτὸν τῆς πληγῆς, Vulg. 'conterere eum in infirmitate,' Orelli 'to crush him by heavy sickness'). (4) חֳלִי *hŏlî*, Is 53³·⁴ (RVm 'sickness'); Jer 6⁷ (RV 'sickness'; the parallel is מַכָּה 'wound'), 10¹⁹ (RVm 'sickness'). (5) ὀδύνη, Sus ¹⁰ 'And albeit they were both wounded with her love, yet durst not one show another his grief.' This meaning of 'grief' is clearly seen in Shaks. *I Henry IV.* v. i. 134—'Can honour set to a leg? No. Or an arm? No. Or take away the grief of a wound? No. Honour hath no skill in surgery then?'; or in Parkinson, *Theatre of Plants* (1640), p. 1489—'The oyle which is made of the berries [of the bay] is very comfortable in all cold griefes of the joynts.'

2. *Mental affliction.* (1) יָגָה *yâgâh*, in Hiph. to cause sorrow, La 3³², and the subst. יָגוֹן *yâgôn*, sorrow, Ps 31¹⁰, Jer 45³ (RV 'sorrow' in both places). (2) כַּעַס *ka'aṣ*, vexation, 1 S 1¹⁶, Ps 6⁷ 31⁹, Pr 17²⁵, Ec 1¹⁸ 2²³; and its dialectic variety כַּעַשׂ *ka'as*, Job 6². (3) λυπέω, to cause grief, 2 Co 2⁵ 'If any have caused grief, he hath not grieved me' (RV 'have caused sorrow'); and the subst. λύπη, Wis 8⁹ 11¹², Sir 37², 1 Mac 6⁸·⁹·¹³. (4) ἀκηδία, Sir 29⁵ 'But when he should repay, he will prolong the time, and return words of grief' (λόγους ἀκηδίας, RV 'words of heaviness,' so the word is tr⁴ by EV in its two remaining occurrences in LXX, Ps 119²⁸, Is 61³). (5) Once the vb. στενάζω, to groan, He 13¹⁷ 'they watch for your souls, as they that must give account, that they may do it with joy, and not with grief' (καὶ μὴ στενάζοντες, RVm 'and not with groaning,' Vaughan 'with lamentations *over lost souls*'). Shaks. uses the word in both the foregoing senses in one line, *II Henry IV.* I. i. 144—

'Even so my limbs,
Weakened with grief, being now enrag'd with grief,
Are thrice themselves. Hence, therefore, thou nice crutch!'

3. In one of the passages referred to above, Pr 17²⁵, the word has evidently an active meaning, though the Hebrew is כַּעַס *ka'aṣ*, which expresses usually the *feeling* of vexation: 'A foolish son is a grief to his father.' This meaning is seen also in Gn 26³⁵ 'Which were a grief of mind unto Isaac and to Rebekah' (מֹרַת רוּחַ, RVm 'bitterness of spirit'); 1 S 25³¹ 'And it shall come to pass . . . that this shall be no grief unto thee, nor offence of heart unto my lord, . . . that thou hast shed blood causeless' (לְפוּקָה, RVm '*cause of* staggering'; LXX βδελυγμός [possibly, says Driver, a corruption of the unusual λυγμός, the word in Aq. and Symm.] καὶ σκάνδαλον = Vulg. 'in singultum et scrupulum cordis'; Dou. 'an occasion of sobbing to thee, and a scruple of heart to my lord'); Jon 4⁶ 'And the Lord God prepared a gourd, and made it to come up over Jonah, that it might be a shadow over his head, to deliver him from his grief' (מֵרָעָתוֹ, RV 'from his evil case'); Sir 26⁶ 'But a grief of heart and sorrow is a woman that is jealous over another woman' (ἄλγος); 1 P 2¹⁹ 'For this is thankworthy,

if a man for conscience toward God endure grief, suffering wrongfully' (λύπας, RV 'griefs'; Vulg. 'tristitias,' hence Wyc. 'sorews *or* hevynesses,' and Rhem. 'sorowes.' But the meaning is clearly 'things that cause sorrow,' 'grievances,' and no doubt this was Tindale's meaning in introducing 'grief,' followed by all the rest of the versions). For 'grief' was frequently used in the sense of 'grievance,' as Shaks. *Pericles*, I. ii. 66—

'Bear with patience
Such griefs as you yourself do lay upon yourself.'

Grievance occurs but once, Hab 1³ 'Why dost thou show me iniquity, and cause me to behold grievance?' (עָמָל, RV 'perverseness' as the word is tr⁴ by AV in Nu 23²¹). The Heb. is a common word for 'toil,' but also has the double sense of misery and mischief—see Davidson, *in loc.* Wyclif's word is 'traveile' after Vulg. 'laborem,' Dou. 'labour'; other VSS 'sorrow.' 'Grievance' seems to be original to AV, and it is used in the sense of affliction, grief, as Shaks. *Two Gent. of Verona*, IV. iii. 37—

'Madam, I pity much your grievances.'

Grieve. The verb to grieve, now almost entirely intrans., is so in AV only once, Jer 5³ 'thou hast stricken them, but they have not grieved' (וְלֹא־חָלוּ, either from חוּל to writhe in pain, or [with most edd.] from חָלָה to be sick [wrongly accented] RV 'they were not grieved'). The trans. vb. occurs often, and with the following meanings :—

1. To make sorry, Dt 15¹⁰ 'Thine heart shall not be grieved when thou givest unto him;' (יֵרַע, lit. 'be evil,' that is 'sad,' the opposite of the 'good' [טוֹב] or 'cheerful heart' of Jg 19⁶·⁹ etc. So 1 S 1⁸, Neh 2¹⁰ 13⁸); 1 S 2³³ 'and to grieve thine heart' (לְאַדִיב, prob. a corrupt reading for וּלְהָדִיב, from דּוּב to pine away—Driver); 15¹¹ 'And it grieved Samuel' (וַיֵּחַר לִשְׁמוּאֵל, which must mean 'was wroth,' as RV. But LXX [ἠθύμησε, 'was despondent'] must have read וַיֵּקַר. Weir suggests וַיֵּצֶר, which is accepted by Driver. Vulg. gives 'conturbatus est,' Wyc. 'was sory,' Dou. 'was strooken sadde,' Gen. 'was moved': but Cov. 'Therefore was Samuel angrye,' which Rog. changed to 'was evell apayd' [= was ill content], and he was followed by the Bishops); Job 30²⁵ 'was not my soul grieved for the poor?' (עָגְמָה); Ps 73²¹ 'Thus my heart was grieved, and I was pricked in my reins' (יִתְחַמֵּץ; RVm 'was in a ferment,' a change for which, says Cheyne [*Expos.* 3rd ser. vi. 44], we may be thankful, adding, 'Fancy a sufferer, of the school of the author of *Job*, saying that "his heart was grieved"'; he also refers to Segond's bold and happy rendering, 'Lorsque mon cœur s'aigrissait, et que je me sentais percé dans les entrailles.' *Oxf. Heb. Lex.* tr. 'my heart was soured or embittered'); Is 54⁶ 'as a woman forsaken and grieved in spirit' (עֲצוּבָה וַעֲצוּבַת רוּחַ; Cheyne, 'as an outcast and downcast woman'; La 3³³ 'For he doth not afflict willingly nor grieve the children of men' (וַיַּגֶּה); Dn 7¹⁵ 'I Daniel was grieved in my spirit in the midst of my body' (אֶתְכְּרִיַּת רוּחִי); 2 Es 10⁸ 'seeing we all mourn and are sad . . . art thou grieved for one son?' ('tu autem contristaris in uno filio'); Mk 3⁵ 'being grieved for the hardness of their hearts' (συνλυπούμενος, the prep., says Gould, probably denoting the sympathetic character of the grief; He was grieved because they hurt themselves).

2. To be heavy on, weary, harass: Gn 49²³ 'The archers have sorely grieved him, and shot at him' (יְמָרֲרֻהוּ; Dillm. 'became bitter against him' [lit. 'treated him bitterly']; Spurrell, 'harassed him'; Job 4² 'If we assay to commune with thee, wilt thou be grieved?' (תִּלְאֶה, lit. 'wilt thou be wearied?') So Pr 26¹⁵ 'The slothful man hideth his hand in his bosom; it grieveth him to bring it again to his mouth' (AVm 'he is weary'); Ps 78⁴⁰ 'How oft did they . . . grieve him in the desert' (וַיַּעֲצִיבוּהוּ); 112¹⁰

'The wicked shall see it and be grieved' (וְכָעָס, *Oxf. Lex.* 'be vexed or indignant,' as in Neh 3³³, Ec 5¹⁶); Ac 4² 16¹⁸ (both διαπονέω). For this meaning of 'grieve' cf. 2 S 3³⁴ Wyc. 'Thin hondis ben not boundun, and thi feet ben not greved with fettris'; Is 7¹³ Cov. 'Is it not ynough for you, that ye be grevous unto men, but ye must greve my God also?'; and Child, *Ballads*, iv. 150—

> 'Yet in suche fere yf that ye were,
>   Amonge enemys day and nyght ;
> I wolde withstonde, with bowe in hande,
>   To greeve them as I myght.'

3. *To cause loathing, to disgust :* Ex 1¹² 'They were grieved because of the children of Israel' (יָקֻצוּ, RVm 'abhorred'); Ps 95¹⁰ 'Forty years long was I grieved with this generation' (קוּט ; LXX προσώχθισα ; Vulg. 'offensus fui,' Wyc. 'offended i was'; Del. 'had I a loathing at'; Kay 'loathed' or 'rejected with abhorrence'). The same vb. (in Hithp.) is tr⁴ 'grieve' in Ps 119¹⁵⁸ 139²¹, where RVm gives 'loathe'; He 3¹⁰·¹⁷ (quotⁿ of Ps 95¹⁰, and the only occurrences in NT of προσοχθίζω, which is the trⁿ in LXX of גָּעַל to loathe, קוּא to spue out, קוּט to be disgusted with, etc.: see Thayer, *s.v.*). Cf. Ex 17¹⁸ Tind. 'And the fishe that is in the river shall dye, and the river shall stinke ; so that it shall greve the Egyptians to drinke of the water of the ryver.'

4. *To give pain, to hurt :* Est 4⁴ 'Then was the queen exceedingly grieved' (וַתִּתְחַלְחַל, *Oxf. Heb. Lex.* 'and she writhed [in anxiety]'); Is 57¹⁰, Am 6⁶ (both חָלָה to be sick, one in Piel 'to become sick,' other in Niph. 'to be made sick'); Ro 14¹⁵ 'If thy brother be grieved with thy meat' (λυπεῖται). This meaning, being always fig. in AV, is scarcely distinguishable from (2) above, but it was once quite distinct, and is used literally by Spenser, *FQ* I. viii. 17—

> 'Threat he rored for exceeding paine,
> That to have heard great horror would have bred ;
> And scourging th' emptie ayre with his long trayne,
> Through great impatience of his grieved head.'

Grievous follows grieve pretty closely in meaning. **1.** *Burdensome,* as Gn 12¹⁰ 'the famine was grievous in the land'; 1 K 12⁴ 'Thy father made our yoke grievous'; Is 15⁴ 'His life shall be grievous unto him'; Ph 3¹ 'To write the same things unto you, to me, indeed, is not grievous'; 1 Jn 5³ 'His commandments are not grievous.' Cf. Ex 18¹⁸ Tind. 'The thinge is too grevous for the, and thou art not able to do it thi selfe alone.' **2.** *Distressing, irritating,* Ex 8²⁴ 'a grievous swarm of flies'; Ps 10⁵ 'His ways are always grievous'; Pr 15¹ 'grievous words stir up anger'; 15¹⁰ 'Correction is grievous unto him that forsaketh the way'; Ac 20²⁹ 'after my departing shall grievous wolves enter in among you.' So Is 19⁴ Cov. 'I wil delyver Egipte also in to the hondes of grievous rulers, and a cruel king shal have the rule of them.' **3.** *Threatening, alarming :* Ps 31¹⁸ 'Let the lying lips be put to silence which speak grievous things.' Cf. Elyot, *The Governour,* ii. 150, 'At these wordes all they that were present began to murmure, and to cast a disdaynous and grevous loke upon Gysippus'; and Bunyan, *PP* (Clar. Press ed. p. 105), 'So when he arose, he getteth him a grievous Crab-tree Cudgel, and goes down into the Dungeon to them.' **4.** *Heinous, severe :* Gn 18²⁰ 'their sin is very grievous'; Jer 16⁴ 'They shall die of grievous deaths.' So Shaks. *Jul. Cæs.* III. ii. 84—

> 'If it were so, it was a grievous fault,
> And grievously hath Cæsar answered it.'

5. *Sorrowful :* Gn 50¹¹ 'This is a grievous mourning to the Egyptians.' Cf. Hakluyt, *Voyages,* i. 159, 'The grievous complaynts of our liege subjects concerning traffique.'

Grievously is either *severely,* Is 9¹, Jer 23¹⁹, Wis 19¹⁶, 2 Mac 9²⁸, Mt 8⁶ 15²²; *heinously,* La 1⁸·²⁰ Ezk 14³; or *painfully,* 2 Mac 7³⁹ 14²⁸. Cf. Taverner's Bible, 3 Mac 4 Heading 'The people had pyty to se them so grevouslye handled'; Udal, *Erasmus' Paraphrase* on Mk 5 'The common sort are wont to take the deathe of yong folkes much grievouslyer then of old.'

Grievousness occurs but twice, Is 10¹ 'Woe unto them that decree unrighteous decrees, and that write grievousness which they have prescribed' (עָמָל, *i.e.* burdensomeness, oppression ; RV 'perverseness' as the same word is tr⁴ by EV in Nu 23²¹. In Hab 1³ it is 'grievance' in AV [as above]); Is 21¹⁵ 'They fled . . . from the grievousness of war' (מִפְּנֵי כֹּבֶד מִלְחָמָה, lit. 'from the face of the weight of war,' Vulg. 'a facie gravis prœlii,' Wyc. 'fro the face of the grevous bataile'). Udal uses the word in the sense of heinousness (*Erasmus' Paraphrase* on Mk 5), 'Consider not the multitude and grievousnes of thyne offences ; onelye regarde that Jesus is he that came to save all men, and is able to doe all thinges with a beck.'

J. HASTINGS.

GRINDER.—The 'grinders' of Ec 12³ are the grinding women at the mill (see MILL). But in the margin of Job 29¹⁷ the 'grinders' are the molar teeth. Cf. Holland, *Pliny,* xi. 37, 'The great grinders which stand beyond the eye-teeth, in no creature whatsoever do fall out of themselves,' and Fuller, *Worthies* (Ches-shire), 'How necessary these are for man's sustenance, is proved by the painfull experience of such aged persons, who wanting their molare teeth, must make use of their gums for grinders.'

GRISLED (modern 'grizzled') is the trⁿ of [בָּרֹד] *bârôd,* 'spotted' (perhaps as with בָּרָד 'hail') in Gn 31¹⁰·¹² of rams, and in Zec 6³·⁶ of horses. Shaks. uses both spellings, *Pericles,* iii., Gower—

> 'The grisled north
> Disgorges such a tempest forth.'

Hamlet, I. ii. 240—

> '*Ham.* His beard was grizzled? No?
> *Hor.* It was, as I have seen it in his life,
>   A sable silvered.'

The word means 'grey,' and in middle Eng. a 'grisel' was a grey-haired man, as Gower, *Conf. Amantis,* iii. 356, 'That olde grisel is no fole.' It has no connexion with grisly=hideous. See COLOURS.

GROSS is used in AV of darkness (Is 60², Jer 13¹⁶), and of man's heart (Mt 13¹⁵, Ac 28²⁷). In the first case 'gross darkness' is trⁿ of עֲרָפֶל, which is tr⁴ simply 'darkness' everywhere except in those two places and in Job 22¹³ (AV 'dark cloud,' RV 'thick darkness'), Dt 5²² (EV 'thick darkness'), Ezk 34¹² (יוֹם עֲ EV 'dark day,' RVm 'day of thick darkness'). The meaning of 'gross' is thus simply 'thick,' 'impenetrable.' In the second case 'make gross' is trⁿ of παχύνω, which means lit. 'make thick or fat,' and fig. 'make stupid,' and occurs in NT only in those two places, where it is an exact quotation from LXX of Is 6¹⁰ (EV 'Make the heart of this people fat'). Gross has thus the metaphorical sense of dull, stupid, crass.

Gross means properly 'large,' 'bulky,' as Shaks. *Lear,* IV. vi. 14—

> 'The crows and choughs that wing the midway air
> Show scarce so gross as beetles.'

Then it expresses that which is big and plain, as Tindale, *Works,* i. 97, 'Scripture speaketh after the most gross manner'; and Udal, *Erasmus' Paraphrase* on 1 Jn 1 (fol. 271), 'In dede the unbelief of mans heart required, that the trueth should be credited by grosse outward experimentes.' And, yet more figuratively, it was used to express density of mind, as Knox, *Hist.* 424, 'The Earle of Athole, who was thought to be a man of grosse judgement.' In NT it expresses more than mental dulness, which involves moral culpability only as it is the result of wilful rejection of light.

J. HASTINGS.

GROUND (אֶרֶץ, אֲדָמָה, γῆ) is used in AV indifferently with 'earth' as the tr. of the Heb. and Gr. words enumerated under EARTH. In RV, on the contrary, there appears to be an attempt (although it has not been carried out with uniformity) to retain 'ground' as the tr. of אֲדָמָה, and 'earth' as that of אֶרֶץ. The following examples of the word deserve notice—

1. In older English 'ground' was used where we should now prefer either 'earth' or 'land,' as Jer 27⁵ 'I have made the earth, the man and the beast that are upon the ground' (עַל־פְּנֵי הָאָרֶץ, RV 'upon the face of the earth'); Ezk 19¹³ 'in a dry and thirsty ground' (אֶרֶץ, RV 'land'). Cf. Is 53⁸ Cov. 'Whose generacion yet no man maye nombre, when he shalbe cut of from the grounde of the lyvinge.' **2.** In Sir 18⁶ 'ground' is used figuratively for the bottom of a thing, 'As for the wondrous works of the Lord, there may nothing be taken from them, neither may anything be put to them, neither can the ground of them be found out.' This is Coverdale's trⁿ, and it has been adopted by all the VSS after him, except the Douay, though the Gr. is merely οὐκ ἔστιν ἐξιχνιάσαι. The Vulg. has simply 'nec est invenire,' whence Wyc. 'nethir it is to fynde,' and Dou. 'neither is it possible to finde.' RV gives 'Neither is it possible to track them out.' Ground is used in the Preface to AV 1611, with the same meaning, 'Therefore let no mans eye be evill, because his Maiesties is good . . . but let us rather blesse God from the ground of our heart, for working this religious care in him, to have the translations of the Bible maturely considered of and examined.' **3.** In 1 Ti 3¹⁵ 'ground' means basis or 'foundation,' 'the church of the living God, the pillar and ground of the truth'; Gr. ἑδραίωμα, AVm and RVm 'stay.' This is the only occurrence of the word in classical or biblical Greek. The Vulg. renders by 'firmamentum,' whence Wyc. 'sadnesse' [=strength], all other VSS having 'ground.' So in Preface to AV, 1611, 'The Edition of the *Seventy* . . . was used by the *Greek* Fathers for the ground and Foundation of their Commentaries.' Cf. T. Fuller, *Holy Warre*, iii. 2, p. 112, 'But well did one in the Council of Trent give these titular Bishops the title of *figmenta humana*, mans devices ; because they have as little ground in Gods word and the ancient Canons for their making, as ground in Palestine for their maintenance.' The same meaning is expressed by the verb 'to ground,' which is found in AV as a ptcp. only, Is 30³² 'And in every place where the grounded staff shall pass, which the LORD shall lay upon him, it shall be with tabrets and harps' (וְהָיָה כֹּל מַעֲבַר מַטֵּה מוּסָדָה, AVm 'every passing of the rod founded' ; RV 'every stroke of the appointed staff,' RVm 'every passing of the staff of doom' *); Eph 3¹⁷ 'being rooted and grounded in love'; Col 1²³ 'If ye continue in the faith grounded and settled' (both τεθεμελιωμένοι). Cf. Mt 7²⁵ ‖ Lk 6⁴⁸, Tind. 'the wyndes blewe and bet upon that same housse, and it fell not, because it was grounded on the rocke.' In Ex 9¹⁸ Tind. uses the word in the slightly different sense of *established*, 'Tomorow this tyme I will send doune a mightie great hayle ; even soch one as was not in Egipte sence it was grounded.' J. HASTINGS.

* The passage is difficult. Most of the Eng. VSS, like the LXX, paraphrase rather than translate. The rendering of AV, which is nearly that of Vulg. ('Et erit transitus virgæ fundatus') is barely intelligible, even after it is improved by Kay, 'And every passing of the staff of sure foundation.' An easy emendation of the Heb. is שֵׁבֶט מוּסָר 'rod of correction,' of Pr 22¹⁵, but Skinner thinks it too easy to be worth much, besides that it only replaces one singular expression by another. Modern edd. as a rule prefer something like RVm. Thus Del. 'every stroke of the rod of destiny'; Plumptre, 'wherever shall pass the destined rod'; Cheyne, 'whenever the destined staff passeth over,' referring to Hab 1¹² 'O Jehovah, thou hast appointed them [same verb] for judgment.'

GROVE.—1. אֲשֵׁרָה, אֲשֵׁירָה *'ăshērâh*, ἄλσος, *lucus*. Wherever the word *grove* occurs as the trⁿ of *'ăshērâh* it should be transliterated as in RV. See ASHERAH.

2. אֵשֶׁל *'eshel*, ἄρουρα. Abraham is said to have planted a 'grove' (AV Gn 21³³ marg. 'tree'). Saul abode 'under a tree' (AV 1 S 22⁶ marg. 'grove in a high place'). The bodies of Saul and his sons were buried 'under a tree' (1 S 31¹³ AV). In all these passages RV correctly renders *'eshel*, which is the same as the Arab. *'athl*, by 'tamarisk tree.' See TAMARISK. G. E. POST.

GRUDGE.—Skeat (*Etymol. Dict.*² *s.v.*) derives 'grudge' originally from the imitative sound *kru* or *gru*, seen in Gr. γρῦ, the grunt of a pig; 'grunt' and 'growl' coming from the same root. Hence its primary meaning is to express audible discontent, murmur, as *Paston Letters*, 138, 'I here a gruggyng.' In this sense 'grudge' is of frequent occurrence in the earlier versions. Thus Lk 15² Wyc. (1380), 'And Farisees and Scribis grucchiden, seyinge, For this man receyveth synful men, and etith with hem' (Tind. and all others 'murmured'); 19⁷ Wyc. (1380), 'And whanne alle men sayen, thei grucchiden, seyinge, For he hadde turned to a synful man' (Tind. 'And when they sawe that, they all groudged'; Rhem. 'they murmured,' and so AV); Ac 6¹ Wyc. (1388), 'the Grekis grutchiden [1380, 'grucchinge'] agens the Ebrews' (Tind. 'ther arose a grudge amonge the Grekes agaynste the Ebrues,' Rhem. and AV 'a murmuring'); 1 Co 10¹⁰ Wyc. (1380), 'Neither grucche [1388, 'grutche'] ye, as summe of hem grucchiden [1388, 'grutchiden'], and thei perisheden of a wastour, *or destrier*' (Tind. 'Nether murmur ye as some of them murmured, and were destroyed of the destroyer'); Mk 14⁵ Tind. 'And they grudged agaynste hir' (Wyc. [both VSS] 'thei groyneden in to hir'; Rhem. and AV 'they murmured against her'); Ps 2¹ Pr. Bk. 'Why do the heathen grudge together?' (changed in 1662 into 'so furiously rage together'). About 1611, says Trench (*On AV of NT*, p. 48), 'to grudge' was ceasing to have the sense of 'murmur openly,' and was already signifying 'to repine inwardly'; and a 'grudge' was no longer an open utterance of discontent and displeasure at the dealings of another, but a secret resentment thereupon entertained. Accordingly 'grudge' of the earlier VSS was sometimes displaced in AV by 'murmur' (a change, however, which had in every such case except Nu 17⁵ been made already by Dou.-Rhem.); but it was retained in a few places, —'by an oversight,' says Trench. These places are : Ps 59¹⁵ 'Let them ['the pack of hounds with which Saul is hunting David'—Del.] wander up and down for meat, and grudge if they be not satisfied' (וַיָּלִינוּ; AVm 'If they be not satisfied then will they stay all night,' so RV 'and tarry all night if they be not satisfied') ;* Wis 12²⁷ 'For look for what things they grudged, when they were punished' (ἠγανάκτουν, Vulg. 'indignabantur,' RV 'whereat they were indignant'); Sir 10²⁵ 'And he that hath knowledge will not grudge when he is reformed' (οὐ γογγύσει ; Vulg. 'non murmurabit,' RV 'will not murmur *thereat*'); Ja 5⁹ 'Grudge not one against another, brethren, lest ye be condemned' (μὴ στενάζετε, Vulg. 'Nolite ingemiscere,' RV 'murmur not').

* AVm and RV give the only possible trⁿ of the Mass. text, and they are in agreement with most mod. edd. (Del., Per., de Witt, Kirkp. etc.), as well as with the Gen. version 'and surely they shal not be satisfied, thogh thei tarie all night.' The AV is the rendering of וַיָּלִינוּ or וְיָלִינוּ, and is after LXX (γογγύσουσιν), Aq., Vulg. ('murmurabunt'), Jer., Wyc. 'thei shal grucche' (1388, 'grutche'), Luth., Cov. ('grudge,' so Rog., Cran., Bish.), Dou. ('murmur'); and it is preferred by Burgess and Cheyne. Wellh. (*PB*) gives 'They shall be sated, forsooth, and be quieted.'

This meaning of the word may be illustrated by Elyot, *The Governour*, ii. 183, 'Semblably there be some that by dissimulation can ostent or shewe a highe gravitie, mixte with a sturdy entretaynement and facion, exilinge them selves from all pleasure and recreation, frowninge and grutchinge at every thinge wherein is any myrthe or solace, all though it be honeste'; so Sir John Maundevile, *Voiage*, p. 69 (ed. 1727), 'Thanne passe men be the welle that Moyses made with his honde in the Desertes, whan the people grucched, for thei found no thinge to drynke.'

In the same sense the subst. 'grudging' has been retained in AV in 1 P 4⁹ 'Use hospitality one to another without grudging' (TR ἄνευ γογγυσμῶν, edd. γογγυσμοῦ, RV 'without murmuring'). Cf. Ex 16⁷ Wyc. 'I have herd forsothe youre grucchynge agens the Lord; what forsoth ben we, that ye grucchen agens us?' (Tind. 'because he hath herde youre grudgynges agaynst the Lorde: for what are we that ye should murmure against us?'); Nu 17⁵ Tind. 'So I wyll make cease from me the grudgynges of the children of Israel which they grudge agenst you.' So Sir T. Elyot, *The Governour*, ii. 150, 'Leave youre grudgynges and menasinge countenaunce towarde Gysippus'; and Chaucer, *Persones Tale*, 499, 'After bakbyting cometh grucching or murmuracion; and somtyme it springeth of impacience agayns God, and somtyme agayns man.'

The modern meaning of the word is found twice in AV, in the phrase 'bear a grudge against,' and in the adv. 'grudgingly': Lv 19¹⁸ 'Thou shalt not avenge, nor bear any grudge against the children of thy people'; 2 Co 9⁷ 'Every man according as he purposeth in his heart, *so let him give*; not grudgingly, or of necessity: for God loveth a cheerful giver' (ἐκ λύπης, lit. 'out of sorrow,' as RVm).

                       J. HASTINGS.

GUARD.—1. The guards of a foreign ruler (king of Egypt, Gn 37³⁶ *al.*; king of Babylon, 2 K 25⁸ *al.*, Jer 39¹⁰ *al.*, Dn 2¹⁴) are called הַטַּבָּחִים *haṭṭabbâhîm* (Aram. טַבָּחַיָּא *tabbâhayyâ*), 'the slayers.' The singular טַבָּח *ṭabbâh* (1 S 9²³. ²⁴) is translated 'cook,' but the literal meaning is 'slayer [of animals],' for in the East the cook has a double duty ('slay and make ready,' Gn 43¹⁶). In RVm (Gn 37³⁶ *al.*) *ṭabbâhîm* is translated 'executioners'; but though the guards carried out executions, it may be doubted if this work gave them their name. In the Apocrypha the guards of a Persian king (1 Es 3⁴) and of Holofernes (Jth 12⁷) are called οἱ σωματοφύλακες.

2. An Israelite king had רָצִים *râzîm*, lit. 'runners' (1 S 22¹⁷ RV [also in 21⁷, if we adopt, with Driver, Grätz's doubtful conjecture רָצִים 'runners,' instead of MT רֹעִים 'herdsmen'], 2 K 11⁶) who ran before his chariot (1 K 1⁵), and kept watch at his door (1 K 14²⁷. ²⁸ = 2 Ch 12¹⁰. ¹¹). In 1 S 31⁶ they are called his 'men' (his 'house,' 1Ch 10⁶). David had also foreign guards, CHERETHITES AND PELETHITES (which see). At a later time the *Carites*, הַכָּרִי *hakkâri* (2 K 11⁴ RV), were probably foreign guards. On the other hand, מִשְׁמַעַת *mishma'ath*, 'guard' (2 S 23²³ =1 Ch 11²⁵) probably means 'council' (as 1 S 22¹⁴ RV), the body which heard (fr. שָׁמַע *shâma'*, 'to hear') the king's affairs (but see Driver, *ad loc.*). The guard had an armoury or guardroom, בֵּא הָרָצִים *tâ' hârâzim* (1 K 14²⁸), perhaps in the house of the forest of Lebanon (1 K 10¹⁷). In the fallen state of Judah after the Return, Nehemiah's guards (if regular guards there were) are called not *râzîm*, 'runners,' for the word suggests 'pomp,' but) אַנְשֵׁי הַמִּשְׁמָר *'anshê hammishmâr*, 'men of the watch' (Neh 4²³).

3. The well-known **Prætorian Guard** is mentioned in two places of the NT, in Ac 28¹⁶ (a passage absent from WH and from RV text) τῷ στρατοπεδάρχῃ (-χῳ), 'the captain of the guard' ('of the prætorian guard,' RVm), and in Ph 1¹³ ἐν ὅλῳ τῷ πραιτωρίῳ, 'throughout the whole prætorian guard,' RV.

4. There is mention in Mt 27⁶⁵. ⁶⁶ (ἔχετε κουστωδίαν, 'ye have a guard,' RV) of the Temple Guard, which, under a Roman officer, was stationed in the Tower of Antonia, and had charge of the high-priestly vestments (Jos. *Ant.* XV. xi. 4).

5. In Mk 6²⁷ σπεκουλάτωρ (Lat. *speculator*, 'a soldier of his guard,' RV) properly means 'a look-out officer.' Ten such officers were attached to each legion. They were used for bearing despatches (Suet. *Calig.* 44), and for executions (Senec. *De Ira*, i. 16). See Wordsworth on Mk 6²⁷, and Benson, *Cyprian*, p. 505 note.

                   W. E. BARNES.

GUDGODAH (הַגֻּדְגֹּדָה).—A station in the journeyings of the Israelites, mentioned only in Dt 10⁷, whence they proceeded to Jotbathah. There can be little doubt that **Hor-haggidgad** in the itinerary of Nu 33³³ indicates the same place. The general considerations which suggest a site for it in or near the Arabah are given in § iv. of the art. EXODUS, and the position of Wady Ghudaghid (which runs into the Wady Jerafeh, see maps of Robinson and Palmer) is suitable, but the identity of name is exceedingly doubtful (see Driver on Dt 10⁷). It should be noted that Gudgodah has the def. art. in Heb., and that the LXX translates Γαδγάδ, as it does in the case of Horhaggidgad (wh. see).

                   A. T. CHAPMAN.

GUESS is used intrans. (followed by 'at') in the sense of 'divine,' 'find out,' Wis 9¹⁶ 'Hardly do we guess aright at things that are upon earth' (μόλις εἰκάζομεν, Vulg. 'difficile æstimamus,' RV 'divine,' RVm 'conjecture'); Sir 9¹⁴ 'As near as thou canst, guess at thy neighbour, and consult with the wise' (στόχασαι τοὺς πλησίον; Vulg. 'cave te a proximo tuo'; RV 'guess at thy neighbours'; Edersheim, 'seek to make out,' or 'search out'). Shaks., who uses the word chiefly transitively, has it in this sense also, as *Ant. and Cleop.* III. iii. 29—

    'Guess at her years, I pr'ythee';

and *Lucrece*, 1238—

    'Their gentle sex to weep are often willing;
     Grieving themselves to guess at others' smarts.'

GUEST occurs three times in EV of OT, and in every instance it is the trⁿ of a Heb. term (קְרֻאִים) which means simply 'called.' A similar term is used in Arabic. Thus we have the 'guests' at Adonijah's feast, 1 K 1⁴¹. ⁴⁹; the 'guests' of the 'foolish woman,' Pr 9¹⁸; the 'guests' whom J″ consecrates to partake of the sacrifice consisting of Israel, Zeph 1⁷ (see Davidson and Nowack, *ad loc.*). In NT we read of the 'guests' (ἀνακείμενοι, lit. 'those reclining') at the wedding feast. In Lk 19⁷ RV more exactly substitutes 'gone in to lodge' for AV 'gone to be guest.' The Gr. is καταλῦσαι, which occurs in the same sense in Gn 19² 24²³. ²⁵ (both לין), Sir 14²⁵. ²⁷ 36³¹ [Eng.²⁶].

Guest-chamber (κατάλυμα) occurs in Mk 14¹⁴, Lk 22¹¹, and in RV is substituted for 'parlour' of AV in 1 S 9²². The Heb. is לִשְׁכָּה, which here means 'sacrificial dining-room.' See INN.

The Heb. term (קָרוּא) may suggest a wayfarer who is hailed and urged to come in, and is suggestive at once of the infrequency of travel and the simplicity of the ancient life. It is still the universal custom for those who are sitting at meat in the open air to invite any passers-by to join them. Masons sitting at their mid-day meal by the roadside invite any passer-by who happens to look at them. In the house, the master or mistress passing through the kitchen where the servants are taking food, will be courteously invited to partake. Usually such invitations are a mere expression of courtesy, and it is not expected that they will be acted upon; but the custom, now largely artificial, explains what the reality must have been.

Job mentions, as an item in his self-defence, that he did not eat his morsel alone (Job 31[17]).

In the East, no figure is more invested with chivalry than the guest. In his own right he cannot cross the threshold, but, when once he is invited within, all do him honour and unite in rendering service (Gn 18. 19, Jg 19; cf. Trumbull, *Oriental Social Life*, 73 ff.). For this relationship of host and guest, see further under HOSPITALITY.

G. M. MACKIE.

GUILT. — See SIN. **GUILT-OFFERING.** — See SACRIFICE.

GUILTY. — The adj. ἔνοχος (= ἐνεχόμενος, 'held in,' 'in the grip of') is tr[d] 'in danger of' in Mt 5[21. 22 *ter*], Mk 3[29] (RV 'guilty of'); and in He 2[15] 'subject to'; but in its remaining occurrences it is rendered in AV 'guilty of,' Mt 26[66] 'He is guilty of death,' RV 'worthy of,' RVm 'liable to'; Mk 14[64]; 1 Co 11[27] 'guilty of the body and blood of the Lord,' so RV; Ja 2[10] 'For whosoever shall keep the whole law, and yet offend in one *point*, he is guilty of all,' RV 'is become guilty of all.' The phrase is quite un-English, and, although it is found elsewhere, as in the translation of the First Article of the *Judgement of the Synode of Dort* (1619), 'Forasmuchas all men have sinned in Adam, and are become guiltie of the curse, and eternall death,' it is used, no doubt, in imitation of the Eng. versions.* The expression is introduced by Wyclif after the Vulg. 'reus est mortis'; Tind. in Mt 26[66], Mk 14[64] used 'worthy of,' and was followed by all the versions, except the Rhem., which again tr[d] the Vulg. 'guilty of,' and the Rhem. tr[n] was accepted by AV; in 1 Co 11[27], Ja 2[10] all the VSS have 'guilty of.' J. HASTINGS.

GULF. — Aldis Wright (in Shaks. *Macbeth*, on IV. i. 23), following Wedgwood, says that 'gulf' in the sense of arm of the sea is derived from Fr. *golfe*, It. *golfo*, and connected with Gr. κόλπος; but in the sense of whirlpool or swallowing eddy it is connected with Dutch *gulpen*, our 'gulp,' to swallow, and with the old Dutch *golpe*, a whirlpool. There are certainly the two distinct meanings, at any rate. Thus Hakluyt, *Voyages*, iii. 206, 'among which high and low lands there is a gulfe or breach in some places about 55 fadome deepe, and 15 leagues in bredth'; and Shaks. *Henry V.* II. iv. 10—

'England his approaches makes as fierce
As waters to the sucking of a gulf.'

In the latter sense the word is used figuratively, as

* Is this T. Fuller's meaning in *Profane State*, v. 5—'Putting her [Joan of Arc] to death would render all English men guilty which should hereafter be taken prisoners by the French'?

T. Fuller, *Holy and Profane State*, ii. 16—'Nor do I honour the memory of Mulcaster for anything so much, as for his Scholar, that gulf of learning, Bishop Andrews.' But it is in the former sense that the word is used in AV. It is found only in Lk 16[26] 'Between us and you there is a great gulf fixed.' The Gr. is χάσμα, which occurs only here in NT, and in LXX only 2 S 18[17] where it translates חַפֵץ the great 'pit' (EV) in the forest into which they cast the body of Absalom. The Gr. χάσμα gives our word 'chasm,' but that word was scarcely in use * before 1611, and is not found in any of the versions. Wyc. (after Vulg. 'chaos † magnum') has 'a greet derke place,' and Rhem. more literally 'a great chaos'; Tind. chose 'a great space,' and was followed by Cov., Rog., Cran.; the Gen. introduced 'a great gulfe' (with 'swallowing pit' in the margin), and the Bishops, AV, RV have accepted that rendering.

The Rabbinical conception of the separation between the two parts of Hades was a thin wall, a mere hand- or finger-breadth (Weber, *Lehre des Talmud*, 326 f.). J. HASTINGS.

GUNI (גּוּנִי). — **1.** The eponym of a Naphtalite family, Gn 46[24] = 1 Ch 7[13] (cf. Nu 26[48] where the gentilic **Gunites** occurs). **2.** A Gadite chief, 1 Ch 5[15]. See GENEALOGY. According to Klostermann, Driver, and Budde, we should also read 'the Gunite' (הַגּוּנִי) for 'Jonathan' in 2 S 23[32]; and for 'the Gizonite' in 1 Ch 11[34]. Luc. has in the first passage ὁ Γουνύ and in the second ὁ Γουνί.

GUR (גּוּר 'dwelling,' 'sojourning'). — An 'ascent' by Ibleam and Beth-haggan, 2 K 9[27]. Possibly, these two are the modern *Yebla* and *Beit Jenn*. But see IBLEAM.

GUR-BAAL (גּוּר־בָּעַל, 'dwelling of Baal'). — An unknown locality named in 2 Ch 26[7]. The LXX has οἱ κατοικοῦντες ἐπὶ τῆς Πέτρας, as though Petra were intended, which is possible, as the inhabitants were Arabs.

GUTTER (צִנּוֹר; RV 'watercourse'). — The meaning of this word, and indeed of the whole passage (2 S 5[8]), is very uncertain (cf. Driver, *in loc.*), but the rendering of the RV is supported by its use in later Hebrew. The same word occurs in the plural at Ps 42[7], where it is usually rendered 'cataracts.'

J. F. STENNING.

* The *Oxf. Eng. Dict.* has found only two occurrences before 1611, Fitz-geffray, *Sir F. Drake* (1596), 31, 'Earth-gaping Chasma's, that mishap aboades'; and Holland, *Pliny*, i. 17, 'The firmament also is seene to chinke and open, and this they name Chasma.'

† For the various readings of the Vulg. see Plummer, *in loc.*

H

HA.—The Heb. interjection הֶאָח *he'âh* is once tr^d 'ha, ha,' Job 39^25 'He saith among the trumpets, Ha, ha,' of the neighing of the war-horse. The Revisers have changed this into 'Aha!' and have been taken to task for giving the horse a human cry. The older versions were still more 'human,' as Wyc. (1382) 'Fy!' or (1388) 'Joie!' Cov. 'tush,' Dou. 'Vah.' 'Ha, ha' comes from the Gen. Bible. See AH, AHA.

HAAHASHTARI (הָאֲחַשְׁתָּרִי, perhaps 'royal,' from Pers. *khshâtra*, 'lordship' or 'realm'; cf. the similar adjective in Est 8^10. 14).—A descendant of Judah, 1 Ch 4^6. See GENEALOGY.

HABAIAH (חֲבָיָה 'J'' hath hidden').—The head of a priestly family which returned with Zerubbabel. On account of their being unable to trace their genealogy they were not allowed to serve (Ezr 2^61). In the parallel passage Neh 7^63 the name is written **Hobaiah** (חֳבָיָה, cf. Baer on Ezr 2^61). In 1 Es 5^38 he is called Obdia. See GENEALOGY.

H. A. WHITE.

HABAKKUK (חֲבַקּוּק, Ἀμβακούμ, *Habacuc*).*—The eighth of the minor prophets. Of Habakkuk's personal life nothing is known with certainty, though it has been inferred, from the fact that he is termed specifically (1^1 3^1) 'the prophet,' that he held a recognized position as prophet, and, from the expression 'on *my* stringed instruments' in 3^19, that he was a member of the temple choir, and belonged, consequently, to the tribe of Levi. The first of these inferences is a possible one,† though it does not add much to our knowledge of Habakkuk. The second is doubtful, both on account of the uncertainty attaching to the pron. *my*, which is against the analogy of other similar notices (Ps 4, etc.), and also on account of the doubt (supposing the pron. to be correct) whether at this time the 'singers' were necessarily Levites.

CONTENTS OF H.'S BOOK.—The book opens with a dialogue between the prophet and his God. He contemplates with dismay the reign of lawlessness and violence in Judah,—'The wicked doth compass about the righteous; therefore judgment goeth forth perverted,'—and expostulates with God for permitting it to continue unchecked (1^2-4). 1^5-11 J'' answers that the instrument of punishment is near at hand—the Chaldæans, that bitter and hasty nation, which march through the breadth of the earth to possess dwelling-places that are not theirs, whose advance is swift and terrible, whose sole law is their own imperious will (v.^7b), who mock at the strongest barriers set to oppose their march, and who, as their victorious arms subjugate one country after another, impiously deify their own might—'this his power becometh

* The form of the name is peculiar. It is, in appearance, an irregular reduplicated form for what would more normally be חֲבַקּוּק (cf. פְּתַלְתֹּל, אֲדַמְדָּם, אֲסַפְסֻף, חֲבַרְבֻּרוֹת), from חָבַק *to embrace* (Gn 29^13 etc.; of a child, 2 K 4^16), whence Jerome, in the Pref. to his Commentary on the prophet, explains it as περίλημψις, or *amplexatio*. Frd. Delitzsch (*Proleg.* 84; *Assyr. Handwörterb.* 281) derives it from the Assyr. *ḥambakûku*, the name of some garden plant. The LXX form Ἀμβακούμ presupposes the pronunciation חֲבַקֻּק, or חַבְקֻק, with the double *b* resolved into *mb* (cf. König, *Lehrgeb.* ii. 473), and the final *k* of the last syllable assimilated to the final *m* of the first syllable (cf. Βαλχιβουλ).

† The title, 'the prophet,' is applied in the superscriptions of their books to none of the other canonical prophets except Haggai and Zechariah. It is, however, very common in the historical books when a prophet is mentioned (as 2 K 14^25 19^2); and it is also appended very often to Jeremiah's name in certain sections of his book (20^2 28^5. 15 etc.).

his god.' But the answer raises only a fresh difficulty in the prophet's mind; as he contemplates the Chaldæans, and thinks of their rapacity, their inhumanity, their savage and contemptuous treatment of the nations falling into their hands, the thought forces itself upon him, Can this be God's method of rectifying injustice? if He has 'ordained' the power of the Chaldæans 'for judgment,' can it be part of His pure and holy purpose that they should to such a degree exceed the terms of their commission, and trample recklessly and indiscriminately upon all the nations of the known world? Is not this the prevalence of wrong upon a larger scale? In 2^1-4 Habakkuk places himself in imagination upon his prophetic watch-tower (cf. Is 21^6), and 'looks out' to see what answer the Almighty will vouchsafe to his 'complaint,' or impeachment of the justice of God's government of the world. J'''s answer, the significance of which is betokened by the terms in which it is introduced—it is to be written, namely, on tablets, that all may read it easily—is this: *The soul of the Chaldæan is elated with pride: but the righteous shall live by his faithfulness.** The answer expresses a moral distinction; and the distinction carries with it the different destinies of the Chaldæan and of the righteous, — destruction (it is implied), sooner or later, for the one, and life for the other. After dwelling for a moment more particularly—in a verse (v.^5), of which the first words are desperately corrupt—upon the ambitious aims of the Chaldæans, the prophet develops at length the ruin destined in the end to overtake him, in the form of a taunting poem (מָשָׁל), which he imagines, with dramatic vividness and propriety, to be pronounced against him by the nations whom he has outraged. The מָשָׁל consists of five 'woes' (cf. Is 5^8ff.), denouncing in succession the insatiable lust of conquest displayed by the Chaldæans, the suicidal policy pursued by them in establishing their dominion, the dishonesty and cruelty by which the magnificence of their cities was maintained, their wild and barbarous triumph over the nations which fell under their sway, their irrational idolatry (vv.^6-19). At the close of the last 'woe,' the prophet passes by contrast from the contemplation of the dumb and helpless idol to the thought of the living God, enthroned in His heavenly palace, before whom the earth must hold reverential silence (v.^20).

Ch. 3 is very different in character from chs. 1. 2. Though called in the title a 'prayer,' the prayer, strictly so called, is limited to v.^2, the main part of the chapter consisting of a lyric ode, of remarkable sublimity and poetic force, in which the prophet develops the thought of J'' coming to judgment, and executing vengeance on His people's foes. The prayer is that J'' would 'revive' His 'work in the midst of years,' *i.e.* renew or repeat, in the midst of the centuries that have passed since the exodus, the great 'work' (Ps 44^1) of deliverance wrought by Him of old. The ode which follows is the amplification of the thought thus expressed. The prophet pictures a theophany (vv.^3-15) in which J'' appears for the deliverance of His people and the discomfiture of His foes. The theophany is manifestly delineated in colours suggested by the thought of the exodus, and in part (as v.^3) even borrowed from old poetic descriptions of it. The tenses (as sometimes is the case in

* Not *faith*: but moral steadfastness and integrity; see the use of אֱמוּנָה in 2 K 12^16 (15) 227, Jer 51 9^3 (2), Pr 12^22 28^20.

Hebrew poetry) are ambiguous; and it may be doubtful whether in vv.$^{3-15}$ the poet is describing, in ideal colours, the past which he desires to see renewed, or the renewed work itself, which his imagination pictures as resembling the past. In either case, he describes (vv.$^{5-7}$) J″ as approaching from His ancient seat in Edom (Paran, cf. Dt 33^2; Teman [in N.W. Edom], cf. Seir and Edom, Jg 5^4); the light of His appearing illumines the heavens; the earth quakes, and nations flee in consternation. In vv.$^{8-11}$ the poet asks, What is the purpose of J″s manifestation? Is He wroth with seas or rivers that He thus comes forth, causing the mountains to tremble, the sea to toss and roar, the sun and moon to hide themselves in terror? No; He comes forth for the salvation of His people, to annihilate those who sought to scatter it, and who delighted in the prospect of being able to ruin the people of God (vv.$^{12-15}$). The description of the theophany ended, the poet, speaking in the people's name, reverts to the thought of v.^{2a}. The prospect of J″s manifestation cannot be contemplated without alarm, even by Israel; the poet's heart palpitates with fear (v.$^{16d. e}$ is very obscure, and in parts evidently corrupt); on the other hand, even when scarcity and barrenness prevail in the land, he still cherishes a calm and joyous confidence in his God, who, he is persuaded, will yet ensure His people's salvation, and equip them (v.^{19}) with fresh life and strength.

DATE OF THE BOOK.—It is clear from internal evidence that H. prophesied towards the beginning of the Chaldæan supremacy; but the precise date of his prophecy is difficult to fix. It depends in fact, at least in part, upon the answer given to a difficult question connected with ch. 1, which must therefore be considered first. The explanation of this chapter adopted above is the usual one; but it must be admitted that there are difficulties connected with it, and that it has failed to satisfy many recent scholars. In the first place, whereas the establishment of the power of the Chaldæans appears, in 1^5 (where it is represented as incredible to those who hear of it) and in 1^6 (where the phrase used is 'Behold, *I am raising up*'), to lie in the future; elsewhere, and especially in 1$^{13-16}$ 2$^{8a. 10. 17}$, the prophet describes their treatment of conquered nations, and reflects upon the moral problems to which this gave rise, in a manner which seems to imply that he and his countrymen were perfectly familiar with it. Secondly, if 1$^{2-4}$ be the prophet's complaint respecting the injustice prevalent in Israel itself, which (1$^{5-11}$) is to be avenged by the Chaldæans, how can he consistently complain of the Chaldæans' treatment of his people, and pronounce judgment upon them on account of it? Thirdly, the subject of the complaint in 2^1 is naturally, it is urged, the same as that of 1$^{2-4}$; whereas, in the explanation adopted above, it is different. Fourthly, the 'wicked' and the 'righteous' in 1^{13} are naturally the same, respectively, as the 'wicked' and the 'righteous' in 1^4; whereas, upon the same explanation, they are different (the wicked and the righteous in Israel itself in 1^4, the Chaldæans and Israel in 1^{13}). Upon these grounds it was argued by Giesebrecht (*Beiträge zur Jesaiakritik*, 1890, p. 197 f.) that the true sequel to 1^4 was 1^{12}; that 1$^{5-11}$ (announcing the *advent* of the Chaldæans) was a complete, independent prophecy, written *before* the rest of chs. 1–2, and not now in its original place, and that 1$^{2-4}$ describes the tyranny of the *Chaldæans* (v.^{3b}), and its consequences as shown in the relaxation of law and religion (vv.$^{3c. 4a}$) in Judah. Wellhausen and Nowack (in their Commentaries) agree. It is true, 1$^{5-11}$ does seem to presuppose a different historical situation from 1$^{12-17}$, and, with 1$^{2-4}$ (as ordinarily understood), may well have been written

down by H. at an earlier date: the book as a whole, as Kirkpatrick observes (*Doctrine of the Prophets*^{1}, 268), 'is the fruit of religious reflection; it exhibits the communing and questioning of the prophet's soul with God,' which doubtless was 'spread over some considerable time,' and presents conclusions which were no doubt reached only after 'a prolonged mental struggle.' Hence there is nothing unreasonable in the supposition that 1$^{2-11}$ reflects the impression left upon the prophet's mind when he first thought of the Chaldæans as the instrument appointed for the punishment of Judah's sin, and that 1$^{12ff.}$ expresses the perplexity which he became conscious of afterwards, when the character of the Chaldæans had become more fully known to him. For the other inferences mentioned above there does not seem to be a sufficient foundation. The explanation which refers 1$^{2-4}$ to the tyranny of the Chaldæans, and its effects in Judah, is unnatural and forced. Nor is there any intrinsic reason why 'righteous' and 'wicked' should refer to the same persons, respectively, in 1^4 and 1^{13}; that would be necessary only if it were the case that the prophet had the same individuals in view in the two passages—which is just what has to be shown, even if the terms of 1$^{2-4}$ are not opposed to it.

A very original view of chs. 1–2 has been propounded by Budde (*Stud. u. Krit.* 1893, p. 383ff.; *Expositor*, May 1895, p. 372ff.). According to this scholar 1$^{2-4. 12-17}$ refers not to the Chaldæans but to the *Assyrians*; 1$^{6-11}$ stood originally after 2^4 as a description of the power (the Chaldæans) which would shortly bring the rule of the Assyrians to an end, and 2$^{6-20}$ gives expression to the joy with which the nations would greet their fall. In the original prophecy the Chaldæans thus appeared as the liberators of Israel from the yoke of Assyria; but events so cruelly belied the *rôle* thus given to them, that it was believed incredible that a prophet could ever have ascribed it to them; accordingly a later editor transferred 1$^{6-11}$ to its present place, adding 1^5 as an introductory verse, and by the transposition so altering the original sense of the prophecy that 1$^{12-17}$ 2$^{4ff.}$ could now be read only as referring to the *Chaldæans*, who thus, from being the power destroying the Assyrians, became the power to be destroyed. The explanation is ingenious; but of a kind that could be deemed probable only if it rested upon exceptionally strong grounds, which, however, in the present instance, cannot be said to be the case; cf. more fully Davidson, pp. 50–55.

The most probable date for the prophecy of H. is shortly before B.C. 600—1$^{2-11}$, if the view adopted above be correct, being written somewhat earlier than the rest of the prophecy. Nabopolassar had made Babylon the seat of an independent monarchy in 625; in 607, with the help (as recently discovered inscriptions inform us *) of the Ummanmanda, Nineveh had been destroyed; in 604, Nabopolassar's son, Nebuchadrezzar, had inflicted a defeat upon Pharaoh-necho at Carchemish (Jer 46^2), the natural result of which, as Jeremiah at once saw (ch. 25, etc.), could only be that the whole of Western Asia would fall into the hands of the Chaldæans. The Chaldæans invaded Judah for the first time in 601 or 600 (2 K 24^1). Our knowledge of the progress of the Chaldæan arms, and of the effects which the news of it produced in Judah, is not minute enough to enable us to fix dates with precision; but while 1$^{2-11}$ may belong to the earlier or middle part of the period which has been here referred to, when (v.^{6}) the power of the Chaldæans was being consolidated, but (v.^{5}) the formidable character which it would ere long ('in your days') attain was still not realized in Judah, the familiarity shown in such passages as 1$^{14-17}$ 2$^{5b. 8. 17}$ etc. with their treatment of subject nations, and the reflections which their threatened interference in Judah arouses in the prophet's mind, point to the close of the same period as that to which the main part of the prophecy belongs.

CRITICAL QUESTIONS CONNECTED WITH THE BOOK.—Those connected with ch. 1 have been sufficiently discussed above; it remains to consider

* See Davidson, p. 137 f., with the references.

those arising in connexion with ch. 2 and ch. 3. As regards ch. 2, Stade (*ZATW*, 1884, p. 154 ff.) and Kuenen (*Einl.* § 76. 4–7 ; 77. 9) argue that the 'Woes' in vv.[9-20] are partly unsuitable if supposed to be addressed to the Chaldæan king, and partly, especially in vv.[12-14], that they consist largely of citations and reminiscences of other passages, including some late ones (*e.g.* v.[12] from Mic 3[10] ; v.[13] from Jer 51[58] ; v.[14] from Is 11[9] ; cf. also v.[16b] with Jer 25[15f.], and vv.[18-20] with Is 44[9ff.] 46[6f.], Jer 10[1-16]), and hence they infer that the original close of H.'s prophecy, 2[6b-8], was expanded in the post-exilic age by the addition of a series of Woes, directed against 'some heathen or heathenly-disposed enemy of the congregation,' or (vv.[13f. 18-20] Kuenen) the heathen generally. It is difficult to think that the grounds for this conclusion are sufficient. Though some of the passages referred to may not suit the Chaldæan *king*, there is no adequate reason for holding them inapplicable to the personified Chaldæan nation ; while as regards vv.[12-14], H. may naturally himself have quoted Isaiah and Micah : v.[13] may well be the original of Jer 51[58] (especially when the very dependent character of the prophecy in Jer 50[2]-51[58] is borne in mind), and there is nothing to prevent 2[18-20] being a satire on the vanities of idolatry, quite independent of II Is or Jer 10. Budde (*l.c.* p. 391 f.) sees no ground for questioning vv.[12]. 9-11. 15-17 ; Wellhausen (p. 164) considers it indubitable that the whole of vv.[9-20] is directed against the Chaldæan (though he thinks that vv.[8b. 17b], where they stand, are unsuitable, and that vv.[12-14. 15-17] contain indications of belonging to a later age than that of H.) ; Nowack questions only vv.[8b. 12-14. 17b-20]. See, further, Davidson, pp. 56–58.

Whether the ode in ch. 3 is really the work of H. may be more doubtful. The title and the musical notes (vv.[3. 9. 13. 19]), both resembling closely those in the Psalter, suggest the inference that it was excerpted from a liturgical collection, and placed here by a compiler (Kuenen, § 76. 8 ; Cheyne, *Origin of the Psalter*, p. 157 ; Wellh. ; Nowack ; and others). The same scholars (following Stade, *l.c.* p. 157 f.) argue further that the ode was originally an independent poem, unconnected with the prophecy of H. : to the circumstances of H.'s age, so clearly reflected in chs. 1–2, there are here no allusions ; the community is the speaker (vv.[14. 18. 19], and no doubt also in vv.[2. 16]) ; it trusts that J″ will interfere in its behalf ; but the description of the foe (vv.[13. 14]) is quite general, there are no features pointing specifically to the Chaldæans ; and the comparison to a murderer delighting 'to devour the afflicted in a secret place' (cf. Ps 10[8. 9]) suggests attacks made insidiously against the theocracy, rather than the open warfare of the Chaldæans ; while, at least in v.[17], the calamities referred to (failure of crops and flocks) are altogether different from those which were the burden of Hab 1–2. Conversely, the promise in 2[4], which is the prophet's consolation, does not at all suggest a theophany as its complement ; and whereas in 2[7ff.] the Chaldæans are overthrown by the natural retribution which overtakes a despot, when his power has become effete, the foe, in ch. 3, is overthrown by the direct interposition of J″. It is true the calamities mentioned in 3[17] might, in the abstract, be regarded as results of the Chaldæan invasion of Judah ; but, as Davidson remarks, 'the verse does not suggest a condition of scarcity and barrenness arising from' such a cause, 'but rather one due to the incidence of severe natural calamities' ; and had the poet been writing under the pressure of a hostile invasion, the invasion itself would naturally have been expected to form the prominent feature in this picture, rather than the misfortunes following in its train. So, again, it is no doubt true that the downfall of the Chaldæan,

though brought about (ch. 2) by natural causes, might in ch. 3 be represented as the result of J″'s interposition (cf. Is 13) ; but even after making every allowance for the fact that chs. 1–2 are only elevated prose, while ch. 3 is written in a lyric strain, it remains that the thoughts most characteristic of chs. 1–2 are not developed further in ch. 3, but replaced by different ones. Kirkpatrick (Smith's *DB*[2] *s.v.*, *Doctrine of the Prophets*, p. 276–283) seeks to show that the ode in ch. 3 forms an integral element in the prophet's book ; but his arguments show, not so much that it is natural or necessary, as that it is *possible* so to explain it ; the destined fall of the Chaldæan tyrant is sufficiently declared in 2[5-20], and ch. 3 is not *needed* to render the announcement more explicit. Nor again, though 2[20] would lead on naturally to the theophany in ch. 3, can it be said, in view of the contrast to vv.[18. 19] which the verse expresses, to require it, or to be incomplete without it. Wellh. (p. 166) insists strongly that vv.[17-19] is not the original close of the poem, and that it cannot be used for determining the real aim of vv.[2-16]. If vv.[17-19] might be regarded as an appendix attached to vv.[2-16] by a later hand, one ground for doubting H.'s authorship of the latter would be certainly removed. There would remain the other differences between 3[2-16] and chs. 1–2, alluded to above ; it is also felt by many to be doubtful whether the *nation* — which seems to be what is intended by the term—would, in the age of H., be described as J″'s 'anointed' (3[13]), and whether this usage does not presuppose a period in which the attributes and position belonging originally to David and his descendants were transferred to the people (cf. Davidson's note). On the whole, while reluctant to conclude that the ode of ch. 3 is not the work of H., and while readily allowing that the reasons adduced do not *demonstrate* that it is not his, the present writer must own that it contains features which seem to him to make it difficult to affirm his authorship confidently.

TEACHING OF THE BOOK. — Theologically, the different point of view of H. as compared with Jeremiah is observable. Jeremiah is so deeply impressed by the spectacle of his people's sin, that he regards the Chaldæans almost exclusively as the instruments of judgment ; their destruction is seen by him only in the distant future, and is viewed rather as involved in God's purpose to restore His people, than as a retribution for their own tyranny and excesses. H., on the other hand, though not unmindful of Judah's faults (1[2-4]), is engrossed chiefly by the thought of the cruelties and inhumanities of the oppressor ; it is these which, in his eyes, call for judgment, and the outraged nations of the earth execute it upon their tyrant. Further, H. is conscious of a problem, a moral difficulty, which is not the case with Jeremiah.[*] The wrong-doing of the Chaldæans is more unbearable than the evil it was meant to punish ; hence their continued successes seem to the prophet to be inconsistent with J″'s righteousness, and it is the existence of this inconsistency which forms the motive of his book. Thus while Jeremiah bewailed the sins and coming misfortunes of his people, for their own sake, H. brooded over the moral problems which the contemplation of them raised in his mind. The age, we may be sure, was to all the faithful servants of God one of trial and perplexity ; but, in virtue of their different temperaments and mental habits, the two contemporary prophets were impressed by different aspects of it.

The central and distinctive teaching of the book

* Jeremiah, it is true, is vexed by the problem of the prosperity of the wicked (12[1-6]), but only in so far as it is exemplified by his own personal opponents.

lies in the declaration of 2^4; and, as indicated above, the true sense of this is, that while the wild excesses of the tyrant carry in them the germ of certain ruin, the 'faithfulness' of the righteous (not his *faith*) will be to him a principle of life. It is evident that this declaration is no *solution* of the moral anomaly which the prophet discerns. The Chaldæan might indeed, in virtue of his very nature, be doomed ultimately to perish, but his empire survived for 70 years; and meanwhile H.'s compatriots, so far from abiding in peace and security, experienced the indescribable hardships of siege and exile. But 'live' is here used in the full and pregnant sense which it sometimes has in the OT (*e.g.* Ezk 18), of living in the light and consciousness of the divine favour; and what H. thus promises is not *mere* material prosperity, but the moral security—of course often not unaccompanied by material benefits—which righteousness brings with it even in the midst of external calamities (cf. Is 33^{14-16}), and the sense of divine approval which even then does not desert it. It is enough for the prophet if he can mitigate the difficulty which pressed upon him, as it pressed no doubt upon many of his contemporaries, by recalling to them these two truths of God's providence, the doom which, at least ultimately, overtakes the tyrant, and the moral security enjoyed by the righteous.

With regard to the use made of 2^4 in the NT, 'another man,' writes Wellhausen quaintly, 'has made the antithesis in this verse famous, by breathing into it another spirit.' Its second clause is quoted, namely, twice by St. Paul (Ro 1^{17}, Gal 3^{11}; cf. also He 10^{38}), in the sense, 'The just shall live by *faith*,' in support of his doctrine of justification by faith. This sense, whether it was intended or not by the LXX translators, whose version the apostle used, was at any rate one which the Greek word used by them permitted; and it was accordingly adopted by St. Paul in his argument. But it is not the sense belonging to the Heb. הָנוּמֱא.* The NT gives us here what is in reality a *development* of the prophet's thought. The apostle, familiar with the verse as it read in the LXX version, amplifies and spiritualizes the words of H., interpreting them in a sense which does not properly belong to them, but which, as it was suggested, or permitted, by the Greek, fitted them in that form for use in his argument.†

LITERARY AND TEXTUAL CHARACTERISTICS.— The *literary power* of H. is considerable. Though his book is a brief one, it is full of force; his descriptions are graphic and powerful; thought and expression are alike poetic; he is still a master of the old classical style, terse, parallelistic, and pregnant; there is no trace of the often prosaic diffuseness which manifests itself in the writings of Jeremiah and Ezekiel. And if ch. 3 be his, he is, moreover, a lyric poet of high order; the grand imagery and rhythmic flow of this ode will bear comparison with some of the finest productions of the Hebrew muse.

The *text* of H. is manifestly, in many places, more or less corrupt,—in some places, unfortunately, even beyond hope of restoration.

LEGENDS RELATING TO HABAKKUK.—Although, as said above, the prophet's personal life is in the OT a blank, Jewish *haggādāh* found much to tell of him,—often, indeed, in defiance of chronology and historical probability. Thus, according to

one legend,—based, no doubt, upon a connexion fancifully established between the command, 'Go, set a watchman,' in Is 21^6 and the words of Hab 2^1 'I will stand upon my watch,'—H. was supposed to have been the sentinel set by Isaiah to watch for the fall of Babylon! Some of the later Rabbis, connecting his name with the words in 2 K 4^{16} 'Thou shalt *embrace* a son,' imagined him even to be the son of the Shunammite woman, whom Elisha restored to life. In the LXX text of Bel and the Dragon, as given in the Cod. Chisianus (Swete, vol. iii. pp. xii, 586), this story is prefaced by the words ἐκ προφητείας Ἀμβακοὺμ υἱοῦ Ἰησοῦ, ἐκ τῆς φυλῆς Λευί, showing both that this story was taken from an apocryphal work attributed to Habakkuk, and also that the prophet was described in it as the son of Jesus (Joshua, or Jeshua), and of the tribe of Levi. What authority there may have been for the statement that his father was Ἰησοῦς, we do not know: the description of him as belonging to the tribe of Levi may be merely an inference from the expression in 3^{19}, quoted above.* According to the 'Lives' of the prophets, which, in two recensions, are attributed respectively to Dorotheus (in the *Chron. Pasch.*, under Ol. 70, ed. Dind. 1832, i. 282) and Epiphanius (*Opp.* 1622 or 1682, ii. 247 f.), he was of the tribe of Simeon, ἐξ ἀγροῦ Βῆθι τοῦ Χάρ (Epiph. ἐξ ἀγροῦ Βηθζοχήρ), which Delitzsch thinks may be the Βαιθζαχαρία where Antiochus Eupator defeated Judas Maccabæus (1 Mac $6^{32.33}$),—though this was not in Simeon, but in Judah, 70 stadia from Bethzur (Jos. *Ant.* XII. ix. 4), and the modern Beit-Sakariyeh, about 10 miles S.W. of Jerusalem (Rob. *BRP* iii. 284). The same writers relate further, that when Nebuchadrezzar advanced against Jerusalem H. fled to Ostrakine (now Straki), a city on the Egyptian coast, 26 miles from the Rhinocorura, but that, after the Chaldæans had withdrawn, he returned to his own lands, where he died and was buried, two years before the return of the Jews from Babylon (B.C. 538). Eusebius states in one place (*Onom.* 246, 68) that his tomb was shown at Gabatha (Gibeah), elsewhere (256, 3; 270, 35), that it was shown at Echelah or Keeila (Keilah),—12 and 18 miles, respectively, S.W. of Jerusalem; and, according to Sozomen (*HE* vii. 29), the site of his grave, at or near Keilah, was revealed in a dream to Zebennus, bishop of Eleutheropolis. In the Middle Ages, however, it was said by Jewish writers that H. was buried at Ḥukkok (Jos 19^{34}), in the tribe of Naphtali, a little N.E. of Tabor. The most widely diffused tradition about H. is that found in Bel and the Dragon $^{33ff.}$, according to which H., while carrying pottage to his reapers, was suddenly directed by an angel to carry it to Daniel, who had been cast a second time, by *Cyrus*, into the lions' den in Babylon: upon protesting that he had never seen Babylon, and did not know where the den was, he was lifted up miraculously by a lock of his hair (cf. Ezk 8^3) and carried through the air to Babylon; having there provided Daniel with his repast, he was immediately taken back by the angel to his own place. Later Jewish writers, and many of the Fathers, allude to the same legend.†

* Though, as Keil observes, it could, at least, not be derived from the LXX; for that does not express the pron. *my*.

† See further, on the legends referred to above, the references and discussion in Delitzsch, *De Hab. Proph. vita atque œtate* (Grimae, 1844), pp. 12–52. The story of Bel and the Dragon quoted (*ib.* p. 32 f.) by Raymundus Martini (*c.* 1250) in a form agreeing substantially with that of the Syriac version, from a Midrash called by him the *Bereshith Rabbah* (not the Midrash generally known by that name), the authenticity of which has been doubted (see *ib.* p. 34), has been found recently in nearly the same form in a MS published by Neubauer, in which it is stated to be excerpted from the Midrash *Rabbah de Rabbah* (*The Book of Tobit*, 1878, pp. viii, xiv, xci–ii, 39–43; cf. the *Speaker's Comm. to the Apocr.* ii. 344 f.).

---

* A word expressing the idea of *steadfastness* or *faithfulness*, might, no doubt, if limited to a relation towards a particular person, pass readily into that of *fidelity*, or *loyalty*, towards him; and this, again, might pass on into that of *belief*, or *faith*, in him; but there is no evidence that this Heb. word passed actually through these possible changes of meaning.

† Comp. similar instances of enlarged meanings in Ro $9^{25f. 29}$ $10^{18. 20}$, Eph 4^8 etc.

LITERATURE. — Delitzsch, *Der Proph. Hab. ausgelegt*, 1843 (very full); Ewald, *Propheten* (iii. 27 ff. in the tr.); Hitzig, Keil, Pusey, Orelli, Wellhausen, Nowack, and G. A. Smith in their Comm. on the *Minor Prophets*; A. B. Davidson (in the *Camb. Bible for Schools*); F. W. Farrar in the *Minor Prophets* ('Men of the Bible'); A. F. Kirkpatrick, *Doctrine of the Prophets*; and the arts. quoted above.   S. R. DRIVER.

HABAZZINIAH (חֲבַצִּנְיָה). — The grandfather of Jaazaniah, one of the Rechabites who were put to the proof by the prophet Jeremiah (Jer 35³).

HABERGEON (שִׁרְיָה *shiryah*), Job 41²⁶.—Obsolete expression (dim. of 'hauberk,' which is formed from Old Norse *hals* neck, and *bergan* to cover) for 'coat of mail' (*shiryan*). In Ex 28³² 39²³ the high priest's robe is compared to a habergeon (Heb. תַּחְרָא *tahrâ*) in that it was strengthened round the collar, 'that it should not rend.'
            W. E. BARNES.

HABOR (חָבוֹר; A Ἀβώρ, B Ἀβώρ and Ἀβιώρ, *Habor*), still called *Khabour*. Strabo (xvii. § 27) and Procopius (*Bell. Pers.* ii. 5) call it *Aborrhas* (Ἀβόῤῥας), Isidore of Charax (p. 248) *Aburas* (Ἀβούρας), Zosimus (iii. 12) *Aboras* (Ἀβώρας), Pliny *Chaboras*, Ptolemy (v. 18) *Chaboras* (Χαβώρας). According to the Bible (2 K 17⁶ 18¹¹, 1 Ch 5²⁶), it flows through Gozan. The Habor is an important tributary of the Euphrates, rising in Mons Masius (now called *Karej Dagh*), to the N. of the celebrated city *Râs el-'Ain* (Resaina), and flowing S.S.W., through a circuitous channel with fertile banks, into the Euphrates at Karkeseea = Abou-psera (Layard), after a course, to a great extent navigable, of nearly 200 miles. Sir H. Layard, standing on the conical hill of Koukab (about lat. 36° 20' long. 41°), saw the main stream running from the N.W. and receiving (on the N.) the waters of the Mygdonius (Jerujer), which entered it after passing Nisibis and other cities. Both banks are covered with mounds, doubtless remains of Assyrian cities. The name of the Habor is found in the Assyrian inscriptions. Tiglath-pileser I. (about B.C. 1120) boasts of having killed ten mighty elephants in the land of Haran and 'on the banks of the Habor.' Assurnazir-apli (B.C. 885–860) crossed the Tigris, conquered the district of the Ḥarmiš (or Ḥar-rit or Ḥaršit), then marched to the Euphrates after subjugating the district around the mouth of the Habor (*piâte ša nâr Ḥabur*, 'the mouths of the river Habor,' from which it would seem that the river flowed into the Euphrates through several outlets). According to 2 K 17⁶ 18¹¹ and 1 Ch 5²⁶ it was to the banks of this river that Shalmaneser and Sargon transported the exiled Israelites. It is now well known that this river has nothing to do with the 'Chebar' of Ezekiel (1³ etc.). The name *Habor* is perhaps of non-Semitic origin, and may mean 'fish-river' (*g'a* 'fish' + *bur* 'river,' Frd. Delitzsch).   I. A. PINCHES.

HACALIAH (חֲכַלְיָה, Χελκ(ε)ιά, Χελκιάς (Luc.), Ἀχαλιά AN, Ἀχελιά (10¹), Neh 1¹ 10¹, AV **Hachaliah**).—The father of Nehemiah. The meaning of the name is doubtful; Wellhausen would read it as Hakkêlejah (חִפֶּלְיָה), *i.e.* 'wait for J'' '; cf. Is 8¹⁷ 64³.
            H. A. WHITE.

HACHILAH (חֲכִילָה 'dark'). — A hiding-place of David which was discovered to Saul by the Ziphites, 1 S 23¹⁹ 26¹⁻³. It was a hill (גִּבְעָה) in S. Judah, on the edge of the wilderness of Ziph; lying on the 'right' (*i.e.* to the south) of the desert (*yeshimôn*), according to the first of the above passages, or, according to the second, 'before' (עַל־פְּנֵי) the desert. It may be the hill *Dahr el-kôlâ*, N. of Wady el-W'ar (*PEF Mem.* ii. 313; Buhl, *GAP* 97). Glaser (*Skizze*, ii. 326) would read Hachilah also in 1 S 15⁷ instead of Havilah (חֲוִילָה).
            C. R. CONDER.

HACHMONI, HACHMONITE. — Both represent one and the same Heb. word חַכְמוֹנִי, but in 1 Ch 27³² the latter is translated as a pr. name, 'Jehiel the son of Hachmoni,' whereas in 1 Ch 11¹¹ Jashobeam is called 'a Hachmonite.' We should probably render it in both cases as a gentilic name. In 2 S 23⁸, which is parallel to 1 Ch 11¹¹, we have 'the **Tahchemonite**' הַתַּחְכְּמֹנִי, which is probably a textual error for הַחַכְמוֹנִי. (Cf. Klosterm., Driver, Wellhausen, Budde, Kittel, *ad ll. cit.*, and see ADINO, JASHOBEAM).   J. A. SELBIE.

HADAD (הֲדַד, הָדָד, Ἀδάδ, Ἀδάρ).—1. Hadad was the supreme Baal or god of Syria (Macrob. *Saturn.* i. 23. 18). The Assyr. inscriptions, however, identify him with the air-god Ramman or Rimmon, and accordingly in Zec 12¹¹ we find Hadad-Rimmon, 'Hadad is Rimmon.' But it is probable that Rimmon in certain parts of Syria represented the sun-god, and not, as in Assyria, the god of the atmosphere. Besides Adad or Hadad, the cuneiform texts give the abbreviated Dadu and Dadda as in use among the Syrians, and from certain Bab. contract-tablets it would appear that Ben-Hadad, 'the son of Hadad,' was another Syrian deity, who, with his father Hadad and mother Atargatis (Athtar-'Athi), made up the usual Semitic trinity. In the religions of Asia Minor the place of Ben-Hadad is taken by Attys, a name which may perhaps be the same as Hadad.
2. (הֲדַד) A son of Ishmael (Gn 25¹⁵ = 1 Ch 1³⁰, AV Hadar. The MT is supported by the LXX (Χοδδάν, Χαλδά, Χοδδάδ, Χονδάν). The Samar. Pent. has הרד, some MSS and the Pesh. have הרד, Targ. Onk. has הרד.
3. A king of Edom, son of Bedad (perhaps for Ben-Dadi; Bu-Dadi is the name of the Can. governor of Yurza [now Yerzeh], S.W. of Taanach in the Tel el-Amarna tablets). He came from the city of Avith, and 'smote Midian in the field of Moab' (Gn 36³⁵ = 1 Ch 1⁴⁶). See further, Hommel, *AHT*, 221 f.
4. Another king of Edom (1 Ch 1⁵⁰), whose name is miswritten **Hadar** in Gn 36³⁹. His capital city was Pau. See *AHT* 264.
5. A member of the royal house of Edom (1 K 11¹⁴ᶠᶠ.) who escaped while 'yet a little child' from the massacre of his family by Joab after David's conquest of Edom. He was carried first to Paran and then to Egypt, where the Pharaoh received him hospitably, and assigned him lands and food. He married the Pharaoh's sister-in-law, and his son Genubath was brought up as an Egyptian prince. After the death of David and Joab, Hadad returned to Edom, and there worked 'mischief' to Solomon. Edom, however, continued to be dependent on Judah, as we learn from 1 K 9²⁶, 2 K 3⁹ 8²⁰.   A. H. SAYCE.

HADADEZER (הֲדַדְעֶזֶר), 'Hadad is a help' (2 S 8³·¹², 1 K 11²³), wrongly written **Hadarezer** in 2 S 10¹⁶·¹⁹, 1 Ch 18³·⁵·⁷·⁸ 19¹⁶·¹⁹. The name is the Heb. equivalent of the Aram. *Hadadidri*, which is given in the Assyr. inscriptions as the name of the king of Damascus, who is called Ben-Hadad II. in the OT. Bricks have been found in Babylonia stamped with the name of Hadad-nadinakh[ês] (Hadad-nadin-akhi) in Gr. and Aram. letters, which makes the reading of the divine name quite certain.
Hadadezer was son of Rehob and king of Zobah (Assyr. Zubitê), on the eastern frontier of Hamath. His dominions included Damascus in the south, and extended to the Euphrates in the north. He was defeated by David 'as he went to recover his border (or rather the pillar which marked the limits of conquest) at the river Euphrates.' The Syrians of Damascus who thereupon came to his assistance were also defeated, and Damascus itself

was occupied by the Israelites. The gilded shields of H. were sent to Jerusalem, and large quantities of bronze were obtained by David in the cities of Berothai and Tibhath (the Tubikhi of the Tel el-Amarna tablets and the Egyp. geographical lists). Toi king of Hamath, who had been at war with H., now sent an embassy to congratulate the Isr. monarch on his victories. At a later date, when war had broken out between David and the Ammonites, H. despatched 20,000 footmen from Zobah and Beth-rehob to the help of the Ammonites, other troops being also furnished by the Syrian princes of Maacah and Tob. The combined host, however, was annihilated by Joab, who proceeded to overrun Ammon. H. now obtained the help of the Aramæans on the eastern side of the Euphrates; but the Syrian army, under the command of Shobach (called Shophach 1 Ch 19¹⁶), was utterly defeated by David at Helam, which is probably the Khalman of the Assyr. inscriptions, usually identified with Aleppo. Josephus (*Ant.* VII. vi. 3) transforms Helam into a Syrian general, Khalaman, and tells us that Hadadezer, under the name of Hadad, was mentioned by Nicolaus Damascenus in his history of Damascus. The battle of Helam completely broke the power of Zobah.

A. H. SAYCE.

HADADRIMMON (חֲדַדְרִמּוֹן), mentioned in Zec 12¹¹ along with the valley of Megiddon. It is commonly supposed to have been the place of national lamentation over the slaughter, by Necoh of Egypt (2 K 23²⁹, 2 Ch 35²²⁻²⁴), of Josiah, the last promising king of Judah. Hitzig suggested (*Commentar über den Jesaja*, 1833, on 17⁸) that the mourning was for Adonis, as in Phœnicia; and he was followed by Movers, Kneucker, Leyrer, W. R. Smith, and Merx. Baudissin (in *Studien zur Sem. Relig.-geschichte*), however, concludes to stand by the former position. LXX reads κοπετὸς ῥοῶνος, and the Vulg. *Adadremmon*. The usual identification is with *Rummaneh*, a small village S. of Megiddo, and N.W. of *Jenin* (cf. G. A. Smith, *Hist. Geog.* 389, n. 2).

LITERATURE.—Baudissin, *Studien*, etc. 295 ff.; Baethgen, *Beiträge z. sem. Relig.-geschichte*, 75, 84, 255 (both these authors discuss fully the component elements of the word); Wellhausen, *Klein. Proph.* 192; W. R. Smith, *RS* 392 n.; Schrader, *COT* on Zec 12¹¹; Bredenkamp, Steiner, Orelli, and Nowack in their *Comm.* on Zec, *ad loc.* See also the separate articles, HADAD and RIMMON.   IRA M. PRICE.

HADAR, Gn 36³⁹.—See HADAD 4.

HADAREZER.—See HADADEZER.

HADASHAH (חֲדָשָׁה).—A town in the Shephelah of Judah, Jos 15³⁷. Its site is unknown.

HADASSAH (הֲדַסָּה 'myrtle').—The Jewish name of Esther (*i.e.* Pers. *stâra*, 'star'). It occurs only in Est 2⁷.

HADES (Ἅιδης, ᾅδης).—The term used in the LXX and NT for the abode of the departed, the unseen world into which men pass at death. It is a word of very frequent occurrence in the OT, of very rare occurrence in the NT. In the AV of the OT it is unhappily rendered by 'hell' (Dt 32²², 2 S 22⁶, Ps 16¹⁰ 18⁵ 116³ 139⁸, and often), 'the pit' (Nu 16³⁰·³³), and 'the grave' (Gn 37³⁵, 1 S 2⁶, Job 7⁹ 14¹³, Ps 30³ 49¹⁴·¹⁵ etc.). The original sense of the English word 'hell' appears to have been simply that of the *hidden*, *unseen* place, and in the general sense 'realm of the dead' it occurs in the statements of the Creeds on the article of Christ's *Descent to Hell*, as well as in old English ('The Harrowing of Hell' in the Exeter Book; Chaucer, *The Milleres Tale*, v. 3572; Spenser, *Son.* 68). Its use in the AV, therefore, has been defended, *e.g.*

by Bp. Horsley, on the ground that 'in its primary and natural sense it signifies nothing more than the unseen and covered place' (*Sermons*, ii. 20). But the English Revisers, recognizing the difficulty of disconnecting the word from its usual associations, have displaced 'hell' by 'Hades' in the NT. In the OT they have adopted a less uniform practice. In the historical books they have left the rendering 'the grave' or 'the pit' in the text, and have placed on the margin the note 'Heb. *Sheol*,' to indicate that it does not signify the place of burial,' as they explain in their Preface. In the poetical books they usually give *Sheol* in the text, and put 'the grave' in the margin. In Is 14 they retain 'hell' in the text and give '*Sheol*' in the margin, on the ground that in that paragraph the word 'hell' has 'more of its usual sense, and is less liable to be misunderstood,' while 'any change in so familiar a passage which was not distinctly an improvement would be a decided loss.' The American Revisers, however, have followed the more consistent course of giving 'Sheol' in the text of the OT, and dispensing with the variant renderings 'the grave,' 'the pit,' 'hell'; as 'Hades' is given by both English and American Revisers in the text of the NT. (See also the article on HELL.)

The word *Hades* is a familiar term in classical Greek. It is usually supposed to be derived from α privative and ἰδεῖν, *videre*, 'see,' and hence it is rendered *Nelucus* by Hermann. This etymology is thought to be rendered extremely doubtful by the presence of the aspiration, and so Voss (*Hymn Dem.* 348) would derive the word from ἅδω, χάδω, in the sense of πολυδέκτης, *der Umfasser*, the 'all-receiving,' 'all-devouring.' Though the Attic form, however, was Ἅιδης, ᾅδης, the more ancient form, as generally in Homer, was Ἀΐδης, -αο and -εω, which form, except in the Epic genitive Ἀΐδεω, occurs also in the Tragic poets. So in Milton (*PL* ii. 963, 964)—

'and by them stood
Orcus and Ades, and the dreaded name
Of Demogorgon.'

In Homer, the word (also in the form Ἀϊδωνεύς there, in Hesiod, and, though rarely, in the Tragedians) occurs only as a proper name, the name of the god of the nether world, Pluto; in Hesiod (*Th.* 455), the son of Kronos and Rheia, and older brother of Zeus. Hence, in Homer, the forms εἰς Ἀΐδαο, εἰν Ἀΐδαο with or without δόμους, δόμοις, in the sense of 'into' or 'in the lower world'; in Attic the forms ἐν and εἰς Ἅιδου; and in the NT the ἐν ᾅδου of the TR, and the later MSS in Ac 2²⁷·³¹ displaced by the εἰς ᾅδην of the RV and the older MSS. Later the word became an appellative, denoting the underworld itself, the habitation of the dead, corresponding to the Latin *Orcus, Inferi, Infernum, Inferna.*

In the LXX and the OT Apocr. the word represents the Heb. שְׁאוֹל, and sometimes other Heb. terms, as בּוֹר (Is 14¹⁹ 38¹⁸), דּוּמָה (Ps 93 [94]¹⁷ 113¹⁵ [115¹⁷]), קֶבֶר (Pr 14¹² 16²⁵, Is 28¹⁵), מוֹת (Job 33²²), צַלְמָוֶת (Job 38¹⁷). These latter, however, are only occasional occurrences. In the vast majority of cases (some 59 in the canonical books alone, and often in the Apocr.) 'Hades' is the equivalent of שְׁאוֹל, and it carries with it the sense which that term has as a designation of the world beyond the grave.

The conceptions formed of that world by different peoples have been very various. They have been largely affected by racial, geographical, and climatic circumstances, and have not been altogether constant in the history of the beliefs of the progressive peoples. By far the more prevalent, however, has been the idea that would most naturally occur to men as they looked down into the grave which hid their departed kinsfolk from their gaze—that of an underworld, the opposite in all respects of the open, visible, sunlit world of activity. In various forms this general conception has held the mind of races as different as the lusty Teutonic tribes, the Zulus of Africa, the savages of North and South America, the Samoan islanders, the Asiatic Karens, the Italmen of Kamschatka, the Egyptians, the Babylonians and Assyrians, the Greeks and Romans. It was also the popular conception of the ancient Hebrews, and the Hebrew form of the idea had special affinity with that of the Babylonians and Greeks. In the OT, therefore, *Hades* expresses the general view of the world of the departed as a dark, deep underworld, in which the deceased continue to exist, but in a state of being devoid of the joy, the activity, the fulness, and the substantiality of real life. For the most part, too, in the OT it is an abode from which there is no return, and in which there are no moral distinctions; a condition involving separation at once from living men and from the living God; one in which rich and poor, king and slave, good and evil, subsist together in the same inane, shadowy, cheerless condition, without positive reward for the righteous or penalty for the wicked. Though not without occasional hints and suggestions of better things, the OT, reflecting the popular Hebrew modes of thought on the subject, presents *Hades* neither as a distinct stadium between death and a larger future, nor as a scene of moral issues, but as the common gathering-place for the departed, into which all alike go down, beyond which there is nothing to be clearly seen or certainly looked for, and from which there is no open way of restoration to the old strength of life, far less any elevation to a new and higher life, near or afar.

The idea of *Hades* and the existence after death, however, did not continue to stand at this level. In course of time, by the experience of faith, the teaching of the prophets, and the operation of other influences which we less clearly understand, it changed in more than one direction. The process is seen in the OT itself, especially in the poetical books and in the writings of the prophets, yet in different ways. In the former, faith is seen overleaping the dark domain of *Hades*, negativing the thought of a perpetual existence in its dreary and futile depths, having visions and forecasts of a more satisfying future (*e.g.* Ps 16. 17. 49. 73, Job 14[13-17] 16[18]-17[9] 19[23-27] etc.). In the latter we find not merely surmises and anticipations, but definite teaching, which grows from less to more till it declares the hope of a resurrection of Israel's dead, and an awakening from the sleep of death to everlasting life or to everlasting contempt (Is 26[19], Dn 12[2. 3]). But that is the most that the OT books give.

The process of change, however, went farther. It is reflected in the apocryphal, the rabbinical, and especially the apocalyptic literature. New ideas became connected with *Hades* and the future, yet without settling into a uniform faith or obtaining general acceptance in any one mode. In some of the books the old conception of *Hades* is continued with little or no change (Sir 17[27. 28] 41[4], Bar 2[17], To 3[6. 10] 13[2], 1 Mac 2[69] 14[30]). In these there is little or nothing beyond a simple acquiescence in the fact of man's mortality (Sir 41[1-4]). In others there is the hope of an immortality for the soul, but no certain hope of a resurrection of the body (Wis 2[23] 3[1-4] 4[13. 14] 15[3]). In others there is the definite statement of the completer belief in a future life with moral issues, the doctrine of the bodily resurrection being in some cases less prominent and less distinct than that of a general continuance of life or return to life (Enoch 22[12. 13] 51[1-5] 61[5] 91[10] 92[3], Ps-Sol 3[16] 13[9] etc.), in others more so (2 Mac 7[9. 14. 23] 12[43. 44]; cf. Sibyll. 1[440] 2[274. 275] 4[228. 229], Apoc. Bar 30[1-5] 50[1] 51[6], 2 Es 7[32]). In others the idea that *Hades* is a place of relative

moral awards appears, though in no very definite or pronounced form (Wis 3[1-10] 5[1-14] 6[18-20] 17[14] etc. as compared with 3[17. 18] etc., 2 Mac 7[9. 11. 14. 29] 12[43-45] 14[46] etc.); while in the apocalyptic books the prevailing conception has come to be that of an intermediate state, with relative rewards for the good and penalties for the evil (Enoch 10[12] 22. 100[5] 103[7] etc., Book of Jub. 5[243] 7[243] 22[21] 24[27] 36; cf. 2 Es 7[31-35. 36*-38.* 61.* 75*-101*] etc. (James, *T. and S.* iii. 2); Apoc. Bar 52[1-3] etc.). In the rabbinical literature further developments of opinion are seen, especially in the direction of regarding *Hades* as an intermediate state with purgatorial processes for those of Israel and (at a later stage) with two distinct compartments or divisions within it—one of preliminary blessedness, and another of preliminary woe. Our Lord and His apostles spoke to the ideas which the Jews of their time had on these subjects as on others. Regard must be had to this in interpreting the occurrences of the word *Hades* in NT. The question is, how far these modifications of the prevalent OT idea of *Hades* are reflected in the NT; what precise sense is to be attached to the term there; and to what extent it has a doctrinal significance or suggests doctrinal conclusions.

The small place which is given to the term itself, or to any equivalent for it, in the NT is the first thing that calls for attention. The word occurs only ten times in all, including parallels, according to the best text. It is found nowhere in John's Gospel, the Epistles of Paul, the Epistle to the Hebrews, or the Catholic Epistles. Three of its occurrences are on Christ's lips, viz. Mt 11[23] (with its parallel Lk 10[15]) 16[18], Lk 16[23]. In two of these the word is obviously used in a figurative sense: in the one to express, in the case of Capernaum, an absolute overthrow, a humiliation as deep as the former loftiness and pride had been great; in the other, to express, in the case of the Church, a security which shall be proof against death and destruction. The third occurrence, in the parable of the rich man and Lazarus, is of a different kind, and has even been taken to put our Lord's *imprimatur* on the Jewish idea of two compartments in *Hades*, distinct from, yet near, one another. The point of the parable, however, is the broad moral lesson of the penalty of a selfish life. Everything else is secondary and ancillary to this. That being so, the use of the word here is ethical rather than doctrinal. It does not take us beyond the broad fact that there is a state of being into which men pass at death, and that the divine righteousness follows them thither with moral decisions affecting their conditions there and reversing antecedent estimates and circumstances. In the second chapter of Acts the word occurs in a quotation from the 16th Psalm, and with an application of that utterance of OT faith to the case of Christ, His death and His resurrection; in which, therefore, it has again the broad sense of the world of the departed into which Christ passed like other men, though only to be raised from it. Neither do the passages in the Apocalypse of St. John carry us beyond this. In the first (1[18]), where Christ claims to have 'the keys of death and Hades,' we have simply the declaration of His power over death and the habitation that receives the dead, His ability to deliver or bring up from these. In the second (6[8]) we have a personification of *Hades* as a demon following *Death*, the rider on the pale horse, to devour those slain by him. In the third and fourth (20[13. 14]) *Death* and *Hades* appear again as demon figures, striking down and swallowing men, but compelled at last to render up their victims, and doomed themselves to be destroyed by Christ. In the passage in 1 Co (15[55]) the reading ᾅδη in the second clause must give place to θάνατε.

We gather, in the second place, that in all the NT passages (except Mt 11²³, Lk 10¹⁵) *Hades* is associated with death; that it expresses the general conception of the invisible world or abode into which death ushers men; and that it presents this habitation of the future, not as a final state, but as an intermediate scene of existence with relative moral distinctions. It appears, further, that the prevalent ideas connected with it, in its association with death, are those of privation, detention, and righteous recompense, the thought of the relative reward of good being subordinate, if expressed at all, to that of the retribution of evil and to that of the penal character pertaining to *Hades* as the minister of death. Otherwise the NT *Hades* shows little or nothing of the change which had come upon the old conception of Sheol, or the world of the dead, in the course of the history of Jewish thought and belief. In none of the passages in which the word itself occurs have we any disclosures or even hints of purgatorial fires, purifying processes, or extended operations of grace. In none of them have we anything approaching the Virgilian picture of the underworld, with its schooling in punishment, its washing out or burning out of guilt, its boon of forgetfulness (*Æn.* vi. 723–731, Mackail's trans.; cf. Conington's *Virgil*, ii. 418, 419). They are silent as regards all such things as the *Limbus Patrum*, the *Limbus Infantum*, etc., of the Roman Catholic theology, the division of Hades into distinct sections for different classes of the dead, the topographical definitions of the underworld in which both poetry and theology have indulged. Nor is there anything in them like the precise and developed doctrine of later times on the condition of men in the space between death and resurrection, or like those theories of a sleep of the soul, a ministry of Christ in *Hades*, a continuance of disciplinary processes, an extension of converting and restoring agencies, and other similar ideas, which have been connected with the general idea of a *Status Medius* in the theologies of various Churches and in the systems of divines of different schools, Roman Catholic, Greek Catholic, and Protestant. In its ideas and in its definite teaching the NT turns for the most part on the present life, with its moral choices and spiritual responsibilities, and on the state of being that follows the judgment, with its final decisions. It makes little of the mysterious space that comes between the two.

LITERATURE.—The books given under the article ESCHATOLOGY, especially Böttcher, *De Inferis*; Güder, *Die Lehre der Erscheinung Jesu Christi unter den Todten*; Weber, *Jüdische Theologie*; Hamburger, *Real - Encyclopädie für Bibel und Talmud*; also Greswell, *Exposition of the Parables*, vol. v. pt. ii.; Rinck, *Zustand nach dem Tode*; Oertel, *Hades*; Craven, Excursus in Lange's *Com. on Revelation*; Schenkel, *Bibellexicon*; Riehm, *Handwörterbuch des biblischen Altertums*; Cremer, *Biblisch-theologisches Wörterbuch*.   S. D. F. SALMOND.

HADID (חָדִיד).—Named along with Lod and Ono, Ezr 2³³ = Neh 7³⁷, peopled by Benjamites after the Captivity, Neh 11³⁴, probably to be identified also with **Adida** of 1 Mac 12³⁸ 13¹³. It is the modern *Haditheh* in the low hills, about 3¼ miles N.E. of Lydda. See *SWP* vol. ii. sh. xiv.; Robinson, *BRP* iii. 143; Guérin, *Judée*, i. 320; Buhl, *GAP* 197.
C. R. CONDER.

HADLAI (חַדְלָי).—An Ephraimite, 2 Ch 28¹². See GENEALOGY.

HADORAM (חֲדֹרָם).—**1.** The fifth son of Joktan (Gn 10²⁷ B 'Οδορρά, 1 Ch 1²¹ A Κεδουράν), and so presumably the name of a Yemenite district or tribe not otherwise known. It has been conjectured that the 'Αδραμῖται (Ptol. vi. 7. 10) or the Atramitæ (Plin. vi. 32, xii. 30) are here referred to, but the latter are probably to be identified with the people

of *Ḥaḍramaut* (see Dillm. *ad loc.*, and art. HAZAR-MAVETH).

2. The son of Tou king of Hamath, who was sent by his father on an embassy to David after the latter's victory over Hadadezer king of Zobah (1 Ch 18¹⁰). In the parallel passage 2 S 8⁹ᵗ· Tou is less correctly given as Toi (תֹּעִי for תֹּעוּ), while Hadoram wrongly appears as Joram (יוֹרָם): the LXX, however, gives Ἰεδδουράν, and in 1 Ch 18¹⁰ Ἰδουράμ.

3. In 2 Ch 10¹⁸ Hadoram (הֲדֹרָם) is given as the name of the superintendent of the levies in the reign of Rehoboam. The parallel passage 1 K 12¹⁸ has preserved the more correct form Adoram (אֲדֹרָם), while the LXX (to 1 Ch) has the fuller form Adoniram ('Αδωνειράμ). See ADONIRAM, and cf. Driver, *Text of Sam.* 267.   J. F. STENNING.

HADRACH (חַדְרָךְ, Assyr. *Ḥatarikka*). — The capital of a region in Syria, and a place of importance in the times of Uzziah and his successors. The name occurs but once in the Bible, namely, in Zec 9¹; but in that one place it is made emphatic. The 'land of Hadrach' is there mentioned as having the same interest with Damascus, and as in relations with 'all the tribes of Israel,' and with Hamath, Tyre, Zidon, the several Philistine peoples, the sons of Javan, Egypt, and especially Assyria.

The Assyr. records for a certain period prominently mention Hadrach in connexion with Damascus, Arpad, Hamath, Samaria, Judah, though they give no details. Assur-dan III. made an expedition thither in his first year, B.C. 772, another in his eighth, and another in his eighteenth year. Hadrach is mentioned in inscriptions that bear the name of Tiglath-pileser (B.C. 745–727), and in others which Assyriologists attribute to Tiglath-pileser, though the fragments of them now known do not bear his name. The period is that in which the 'shepherds' of Israel were Zechariah, Shallum, Menahem, Pekahiah, Pekah, and Hoshea; when the realm of Jeroboam II., including the peoples from the Mediter. to the Euphrates, was falling to pieces before the Assyrian. The Assyr. kings speak of themselves as overthrowing a confederacy, headed by Uzziah of Judah, and extending as far as Hamath. At different times in this period they deported Israelites from the northern tribes, and from east of Jordan (1 Ch 5⁶· ²⁶, 2 K 15²⁹).

Apparently, the identification of Hadrach with Ḥatarikka is beyond doubt, and the writer of this prophecy had this period in mind, whatever bearing these facts may have on the various critical and historical questions that arise (see Schrader, *KAT²* 453, and Del. *Paradies*, 279).
W. J. BEECHER.

HAFT.—'The *haft* of a knife, that whereby you have or hold it,' says Trench (*Study of Words*, 303); and the two words are no doubt etymol. connected, but the connexion is not quite so immediate. Haft occurs once in AV, Jg 3²² 'And the haft also went in after the blade' (הַנִּצָּב, the hilt of a sword, or handle of a knife). Wyc. (who has 'pommel' here, [1388, *ether hilte*]) uses 'haft' in Dt 19⁵ 'the yren, slipt of fro the haft, smytith his freend, and sleeth' (1388, 'helve'). Cf. also Gower, *Confessio Amantis*, iv.—

'But yet ne fond I nought the haft,
Which might unto the blade accorde.'
J. HASTINGS.

HAGAB (חָגָב, 'Αγάβ, Ezr 2⁴⁶).—His descendants were among the Nethinim who returned from Babylon with Zerubbabel. The name, with that preceding it in Ezr, is absent from the parallel list in Neh 7, the loss being apparently due to the similarity between the names Hagabah and Hagab. It appears in 1 Es 5³⁰ as Accaba.
H. ST. J. THACKERAY.

HAGABA (חֲגָבָא, Ἀγαβά B, Ἀγγαβά A), Neh 7[48].—The head of another family of Nethinim who returned from Babylon with Zerubbabel.

HAGABAH (חֲגָבָה, Ἀγαβά).—The slightly different form in which the last-mentioned name appears in the parallel list in Ezr 2[45]. In 1 Es 5[29] it becomes Aggaba (AV Graba, B* om., A Ἀγγαβά).

HAGAR (הָגָר 'flight,' 'emigration').— i. THE NARRATIVES.—Hagar was the name of an Egyptian woman (Gn 16[1] 21[9]) in the service of Sarai. The fact that she is expressly called an Egyptian has given rise to the conjecture that she was one of the 'maidservants' who were presented by Pharaoh at the time when the Egyptian king 'entreated Abraham well' for Sarai's sake (12[16]). It would appear that Hagar stood in that intimate relation with Sarai which we find occupied by the maid-servants of Rebekah (24[59]) and of Leah and Rachel (29[24-29]). She was the property of her mistress, not of her master; and Sarai finding that in the course of nature she could herself have no hope of having children, proposed that Abraham should take Hagar as his concubine. Hagar being Sarai's property, Sarai would claim Hagar's children as her own (cf. Rachel and Leah in 30[3. 9]). Accordingly, Hagar became Abraham's concubine; and, finding herself with child, appears to have suffered herself to indulge in expressions of exultation, as if of triumph over a defeated rival. The true wife and the servant concubine, in their jealousy and hatred, present a picture of Bedawîn tent-life, true enough to facts, however repugnant to Western ideas. Sarai bitterly resented the insult, and complained to Abraham. The patriarch resigned all claim over his concubine; he refused to interfere himself, and handed Hagar over to the tender mercies of Sarai. Sarai's harshness enraged Hagar; and the latter, goaded to desperation, fled from her mistress into the wilderness. The wilderness of Shur 'before (*i.e.* E. of) Egypt' represents probably the desert region of *Jîfar* between Philistia and the E. borders of Egypt proper (cf. Ex 15[22]). Presumably, Hagar bethought herself of fleeing to her native country; for through this desert passed the usual caravan route to Egypt. While she was resting by a spring in the desert the Angel of J" appeared to her (v.[7]); bade her return to her mistress and be submissive to her; he also encouraged her by telling her of the son that should be born to her; his name was to be Ishmael; he would be as untameable as a wild ass; he would be at war with all men; 'in the sight of all his brethren' should he live (not merely, 'to the E. of them,' עַל־פְּנֵי) his wild, independent, defiant life. Hagar, according to the Hebrew tradition, gave the name *Beer-lahai-ro'i* to the spring, because as the angel departed she realized who he was; and she looked after him who had seen her in her affliction and had comforted her. 'The well of the living one who sees me'; this was the popular interpretation of the name of the well in after-times associated with the vision granted to Hagar [see BEER-LAHAI-ROI]. 'The Bedawîn even yet associate with Hagar's name a well a considerable distance south of Beersheba in Muweilih, one of the principal stations on the caravan road, and also a rock dwelling, Bait Hagar, in the neighbourhood' (Dillmann, *in loc.*). Hagar was obedient to the vision, and returned to her mistress. The birth of Ishmael is recorded in the brief extract from P (16[15]), which also mentions that Abram was then eighty-six years old. Eleven years had passed since the call of Abram.

Nothing more is related of Hagar until the 21st chapter, where we are told of the birth of Isaac (vv.[1-7]). On the occasion of the festival which was held perhaps two or three years later (see Delitzsch and Dillmann, *in loc.*), Sarah saw Hagar's son 'playing' (מְצַחֵק, not 'mocking' or 'persecuting,' as no object is expressed); and her maternal jealousy took fire. She was seized probably with a dread lest the inheritance should pass to the son of the concubine. She demanded from Abraham the expulsion of Hagar and her boy. The demand, to Abraham's credit, displeased him sorely. But God spake to him, apparently at night; bade him sacrifice his fatherly feelings, and obey Sarah's word. Abraham the next morning took bread and a skin of water, and gave them over, with the lad, to Hagar, who was thus sent forth a homeless wanderer into the wilderness of Beersheba, in the neighbourhood of which Abraham presumably was encamped (21[14. 32] 22[19]). According to this tradition Ishmael was still a child, and was soon worn out. The water-skin was quickly emptied; Hagar laid the child down under a bush (v.[15]); she saw there was no hope for his life unless she could find water ; in despair, and so that she might not witness his dying agonies, she retired a bowshot's distance. It was then that God heard the voice of the lad (not of his mother); and the angel of God called to Hagar, and encouraged her. The boy was not to die, but to live. 'Arise, lift up the boy, take fast hold of him by thy hand; for I will make of him a great nation.' Then God opened her eyes; she saw, what before she had not perceived, a well of water close at hand; she filled the empty skin with water, and gave her boy to drink. He revived, and grew to be a strong man, a famous archer. He dwelt in the desert of Paran; and his mother, herself an Egyptian, took for him an Egyptian wife (v.[21]).

The purpose which was served by the preservation of these two narratives was probably a different one in each case. In ch. 16 we have a tradition the preservation of which in the Book of Genesis seems to be due to the fact that (1) it illustrated the varied trials to which Abraham's faith and patience were subjected before the fulfilment of the divine promise was granted; (2) it proclaimed the futility of the human endeavours to compass by human means that which could only be accomplished in accordance with the divine purpose. To every Israelite it also emphasized the fact that the chosen family had been providentially watched over from its very beginnings; the humblest members of the household received the blessing of the divine Vision. In ch. 21 we have a similar thought; but here the separation of Hagar from the tent of Abraham is due, not to a voluntary flight, but to an express divine oracle. Undoubtedly, too, this story reflects the pride of the people in the purity of their descent. The nations around Palestine were, according to the popular Hebrew belief, all of them offshoots from the family of Abraham; but the stock of typical patriarchal Israel had no contamination from Canaan or from Egypt.

There was, however, another side to the narratives. It cannot but have struck the Israelite reader that the first mention of 'the Angel of J"' (16[7]) is in connexion with the manifestation to Hagar, this despised Egyptian concubine. The light '*ad revelationem gentium*' had begun to shine; and the story of Hagar is the first of a remarkable series in which appear Tamar, Rahab, Ruth, and Naaman. Thus the story of Hagar is a striking instance, on the very threshold of the history of the Covenant People, of that wider and more generous view of divine mercy which was ordinarily ignored by popular Hebrew particularism.

The name *Hagar* in Arabic denotes a 'fugitive.' The word is familiar to us in *Hegira*, the 'epoch-making' flight of Mohammed. Some have thought that the biblical narratives of Hagar ('flight') and Ishmael ('God heareth') have been expanded out of a mere play upon the words; others have thought that the original names may have been adapted so as to correspond with the distinctive incidents of well-known primitive narratives, and that thus the tradition of actual facts has been made to serve the additional purpose of accounting for the origin of neighbouring tribes. It cannot be doubted that the narratives represent an early Israelite belief that the mountain tribes and clans on the south and south-east frontier of Palestine were descended from the same Hebrew stock, from the same Semitic group, as Israel. The Ishmaelite Bedawîn were regarded as sons of Abraham, but as of inferior caste; and Hagar supplied the recollection of a tradition that they were also connected with Egypt. Renan (*Hist. of Isr.* i. 81 n., Eng. tr.) would derive the name *Hagar* from the Arabic *hagar* (= a rock), 'by the primitive equivalence of ה and ח'; he regards Hagar as the personification of the tribes of Arabia Petræa, and apparently derives the story of Hagar from the resemblance of the two words meaning 'rock' and 'fugitive.'

ii. SOURCES OF THE NARRATIVES.—The story of Hagar is to be found in two passages in Genesis, the one ch. 16, the other ch. 21⁸⁻²¹. The former passage is almost entirely derived from J (the Jahwist narrative), the only exceptions being vv.¹ᵃ·³·¹⁵·¹⁶, which are from P (the Priestly Narrative, so also 25¹²), and vv.⁹·¹⁰, which are probably from the Redactor. The latter passage is entirely from E (the Elohist narrative). The two passages furnish material for instructive comparison. In both cases we have a tradition respecting Hagar, a concubine of Abraham. In the earlier chapter she flies from her mistress; in the later she is expelled by Abraham at Sarah's demand. In both traditions a divine manifestation is granted to her in the wilderness. In ch. 16 (J) it is 'the Angel of JHVH' who appears to her 'in the wilderness, by the fountain (עין) in the way to Shur' (16⁷). In ch. 21 (E) it is God (*Elohim*) who hears her child weeping, and 'the Angel of God' (*Elohim*) who speaks to her, and she sees 'a well of water' (בְּאֵר מַיִם). In ch. 16 (J) Hagar is the 'handmaid' (שִׁפְחָה) of Sarai; in ch. 21 (E) she is the 'bondwoman' (אָמָה). In ch. 16¹¹ (J) Hagar's son is to be called Ishmael because J'' had heard *her* 'affliction'; in ch. 21¹⁷ (E) 'God heard the voice of the lad.'

It is possible, if 16⁹·¹⁰ be an addition by R, that the J tradition regarded Ishmael 'as born and bred in the desert,' and did not record the return of Hagar to the tent of Abraham (Kittel). It was, however, necessary to introduce the mention of her return in order to account for the E tradition of ch. 21.

It will be observed that, according to P, Ishmael was fourteen years old when Isaac was born (Gn 16¹·³·¹⁵·¹⁶ 21¹·²⁻⁵); but in E the language used of Hagar (21⁹⁻²¹) would imply that Ishmael was still a child.

iii. REFERENCES TO HAGAR BY ST. PAUL AND PHILO.—St. Paul, in his Epistle to the Galatians (4²⁵), makes an allegorical use of the story of Hagar. 'Hagar, the bondwoman,' is set over-against 'Sarah, the freewoman'; 'Ishmael, the child after the flesh,' against 'Isaac, the child of the promise.' St. Paul is presenting the antithesis of 'the old covenant' and 'the new,' 'the earthly Jerusalem' and 'the heavenly.' Sinai, the mountain of the law, which was in Arabia, the dwelling-place of 'the son of Hagar' (Bar 3²·³), is set over-against Mount Sion, the mountain of gracious promise, the home of the true Israel (see Lightfoot on Gal 4²⁵).

This allegorical treatment of the story of Hagar corresponded to the rabbinic method of teaching in the apostle's time. St. Paul's expansion of the story (ἐδίωκεν τὸν κατὰ πνεῦμα) reproduced the traditional Jewish feeling (cf. *Bereshith Rabba*, 53. 15) of hostility towards the Arab tribes, whose constant inroads upon the southern frontier of Judæa seemed to repeat the conduct of Ishmael towards Isaac. The **Hagarenes** mentioned in Ps 83⁶, 1 Ch 5¹⁰·¹⁹·²⁰, were regarded as typical members of this group of hostile clans. (These tribes were possibly the same as the Ἀγραῖοι, who are mentioned by Eratosthenes in Strabo, XVI. iv. 2, p. 767, as dwelling in the northern part of Arabia). St. Paul, in his reference to the Hagar narrative, frankly uses it as an allegory (Gal 4²⁴); and, as in at least one other instance (1 Co 10⁴), he does not shrink from employing for his purpose the 'Haggadic' expansion of the original version.

Philo allegorizes the narrative in various passages, notably in *De Cherubim*, I. i. 139 ; *De Congr. Erud. grat.* II. i. 500. Abraham represents the human soul searching after true wisdom and divine knowledge. He is united first to Sarai, the sovereign virtue (ἡ ἄρχουσα ἀρετή), but from her he has no offspring; he has not progressed sufficiently to win spiritual advantage. At her bidding he next unites himself to Hagar the Egyptian—who represents secular learning, the necessary training of the intellect (τὰ ἐπώνυμα τῆς Ἄγαρ προπαιδεύματα). This union is at once fruitful; and its issue is Ishmael, who represents sophistry—Hagar (ἡ μέσος καὶ ἐγκύκλιος παιδεία) and Ishmael (ὁ σοφιστής) must both be driven forth to make way for the reunion with the true virtue which abides forever in the home of the human soul. The name *Hagar* he interprets by παροίκησις (= 'sojourning'), as if it were connected with *gêr* (*De Congr. Erud. grat.* i. 520), 'a sojourner'; cf. παροικεῖ σοφία οὐ κατοικεῖ (*De sacrific. Abelis et Caini*, § 10. i. 170).

iv. LATER TRADITIONS.—Jewish tradition expanded and embellished the story in a variety of ways. In ch. 16 'the desert of Shur' appears as 'the desert of Ḥagra' in the Targum of Onkelos and Jerusalem. In ch. 21 the Targum of Jerusalem adds that Abraham dismissed Hagar 'with a letter of divorce.' The Targums of Jonathan and Jerus. in 25¹ identify Keturah with Hagar, 'who had been bound (rt. *ktr*, קְטוּרָה) to him from the beginning'; so also Rashi. Rashi, in his commentary on 6¹, records the belief that Hagar was a daughter of Pharaoh, who, after seeing the wonders that had been done for Sarah, declared that it was better for his daughter to be a bondservant in the house of Abraham than a mistress in the palace of another. Commenting on 21⁹, he records the Jewish interpretation mentioned by Jerome in his *Quæst. ad Genesim*, according to which Ishmael's 'playing' was a form of 'idolatry' (cf. Ex 32⁶). Again, on v.¹⁴, he says, 'Abraham put Ishmael on Hagar's shoulder; for Sarah had overlooked him with an evil eye, and he had been seized with fever so that he could not walk.'

One of the Jewish derivations of Hagar's name is based upon a play on the words הא אגרך 'here is thy wage.'

'The Moslems naturally modify the biblical account in favour of their own nation; they contend that Hagar was Abraham's lawful wife, and that Ishmael obtained, therefore, as his eldest son, the extensive tracts of Arabia, whilst the younger son, Isaac, received only the limited territory of Canaan; that Hagar was born at Farma, then the capital of Egypt and the residence of the Pharaohs, but that she died at Mecca, and was buried in the precincts of the temple of the Caaba' (Kalisch on Gn 16¹⁻³, quoting D'Herbelot, *Bibl. Orient.* p. 420).

Buxtorf (in his *Lexicon Chald. Talmud. et*

Rabbin., Basle, 1639, *s.v.* חַגְרִי) says, 'Judæi hodie Ungaros sic vocant, quasi Hagrios vel Hagarios Turcas autem Ismælitas vocant. Hinc Psal. 83 pro הַגְרִים in Targum est הוּנְגְרָאֵי Ungari.'

H. E. RYLE.

HAGARENES.—See HAGRITES.

HAGGADA.—See TALMUD.

HAGGAI (חַגַּי 'festal,' LXX 'Aγγαῖος, cf. חַגִּית 2 S 3⁴; Phœn. חגי, חגת, *CIS* lxvii. 1; Palmyr. חגגו, Vogüé, 61*a*).—The prophet whose prophecies are contained in the book which bears his name. His first prophecy is dated the 2nd year of Darius, *i.e.* B.C. 520; his main purpose was to rouse the community of the returned exiles to rebuild the temple at Jerusalem.

A. HISTORICAL INTRODUCTION.—The high hopes with which the Jewish exiles started home from Babylon in 536 were not destined to be fulfilled in the early years of the Return. Instead of proceeding at once to restore the ruined temple to its former glory, the Benê hag-Golah ('sons of the Captivity') were obliged to content themselves with setting up the altar of burnt-offering (Ezr 3²f·, confirmed by Hag 2¹⁴). It is possible that the foundations of the temple were formally laid; * but the great work of restoration remained unaccomplished for the next sixteen years. Various causes contributed to this state of inaction. During the fifty years of the Captivity the Judæan exiles had lived without temple and altar, and no doubt many felt that delay in restoring them need not involve serious damage to religion. The more enthusiastic party would probably have made some effort but for the series of disasters which fell upon the Jewish community. There was, first of all, the active hostility of the neighbouring Samaritans; the firm refusal of whose plausible offer to assist in the building turned them into the implacable foes of Jerusalem (Ezr 4¹⁻⁵). Then the invasion of Egypt by Cambyses in 527 must have brought with it great suffering for the Jewish colonists; no peace or security was possible while Palestine was being overrun by the vast hordes of the Persian army on their way to Egypt (see Zec 8¹⁰, Hag 1⁶). A succession of bad seasons followed; the land suffered from prolonged drought; harvest and vintage failed; the fortunes of the colony sank to their lowest ebb (Hag 1⁶· ⁹⁻¹¹ 2¹⁶· ¹⁷). In Jerusalem itself some of the old social abuses made their appearance; luxury and self-seeking among the wealthier classes took the place of zeal for the cause of religion (Hag 1⁴· ⁹). The leaders of the community did nothing, the first enthusiasm had cooled down, and the great object of the Return remained unaccomplished. Meanwhile important events were taking place in the Persian empire. During the early years of his reign (521–515) Darius was engaged in a desperate struggle to secure the kingdom he had won. Province after province revolted; rebellions broke out everywhere, now in the very heart of the empire, now in its farthest extremities. While Darius was suppressing the Babylonian usurper Nidintubel, Elam and the neighbouring countries attempted to throw off the Persian yoke. At the beginning of 520 Darius subdued Babylon, and then marched against the Median pretender Phraortes; but before this campaign was over, Babylon revolted

---

* All contemporary authorities give the 2nd year of Darius, the 16th of the Return, 520, as the date of the foundation of the temple, Hag 2¹⁵· ¹⁸, Zec 8⁹, Ezr 5². ¹⁶. The account of the laying of the foundations in the 2nd year of the Return, 535, contained in Ezr 3⁸⁻¹³, belongs to a later document, written about 200 years after the events narrated. It is possible that this later account may have some historical basis; there may have been a purely *formal* foundation, such as Haggai and Zechariah could entirely disregard. See Driver, *LOT*⁶ 547.

---

a second time.* It seemed like a vast upheaval of the heathen world, a shaking of the heavens and earth. There were still prophets in Jerusalem who could read the signs of the times, and they were not slow to grasp the bearing of these vast movements upon the interests which they had at heart. The central authority was weakened, the original permit of Cyrus had not been repealed: now was the opportunity for a religious and patriotic enterprise. Haggai came forward in 520 —and Zechariah was soon by his side—with the divine command to start at once upon the rebuilding of the temple. The neglect of this first duty, so the prophet insists, has been the cause of all the recent misfortunes; but when once it has been discharged the divine blessing will descend, and the glorious promises of the great prophet of the Restoration (*e.g.* Is 60) will be fulfilled at last. There will be a shaking of heaven and earth; the powers of the heathen kingdoms will be overthrown; and Zerubbabel, the treasured and chosen of J″, will be preserved for the great hereafter. The prophet's appeal was addressed primarily to Zerubbabel and Joshua, the civil and religious leaders of the community, and it produced the desired effect. The work of rebuilding was taken vigorously in hand; and four years later (516) the temple was solemnly dedicated (Hag 1¹⁴f· 2³· ¹⁸, Zec 4⁶⁻¹⁰ 6¹²⁻¹⁵ 8⁹, Ezr 5¹f· 6¹⁴⁻¹⁸, 1 Es 6¹ 7³).

B. THE PROPHECIES. — The prophecies of Haggai are arranged in four groups, each one headed by the date on which it was delivered. They cover a period of four months, from September to December of the year 520.†

i. *First prophecy:* September; 1¹⁻¹⁵, Haggai comes forward on the 1st of the month, perhaps because there would then be a gathering of the people to celebrate the festival of the new moon. He addresses Zerubbabel by his Babylonian title of *Peḥah* ('governor'), and Joshua by his new title of High Priest (lit. 'great priest'; before the Exile it was 'chief,' lit. 'head priest,' or 'the priest'), because as official leaders of the community they were principally to blame for the neglect of religious and patriotic duty. He denounces the popular excuse that the time had not yet come ‡ for the temple to be built. 'The fact is, you have thought more of your own comfort than of God's glory, and built your own houses in a fashion which recalls the luxury of your forefathers (1 K 6⁹ 7³, Jer 22¹⁴), while you have allowed the temple to lie in ruins. Consider your ways! look back at the experiences of the past sixteen years, and learn the lesson of the disappointment, misery, and insecurity you have suffered. Consider your ways! think of your present state of inaction. If you would regain the favour of God,§ go up to the mountains and fetch timber, and begin at once to build the House. The drought, the bad harvests, the dis-

---

* See the great Behistun inscription of Darius, *Records of the Past*, i. 107-130.

† In the pre-exilic period the year was reckoned from autumn to autumn; but during the Exile a change of reckoning occurred, prob. due to Babylonian influence, and the year ran from spring to spring (see Kз 12²), *i.e.* April-April. The old Heb. names of the months were dropped, and at first the months were known by numbers, as in Hag, Zec; then the Bab. names of the months were gradually introduced as in Zec, Ezr, Neh. See Wellh. *Proleg.*³ 110; Benzinger, *Hebr. Arch.* 201; Nowack, *Lehrb. Hebr. Arch.* i. 218 f.; and art. TIME.

‡ In 1² the text must be corrected to make sense; see VSS and RVm. The first עֵת 'time,' is not given by VSS; it must either be struck out, or pointed עַתָּה 'now,' or corrected to עֹד 'yet.'

§ In commenting on the form of the word 'and I will be glorified,' v.⁸ אכבד for אכבדה (אכברה), the Talm. says, 'There are five points in which the first temple differed from the second; they are the ark and the mercy-seat and the cherubim, the fire, and the Shechinah, and the Holy Spirit, and the Urim and Tummim.' Talm. B. *Yoma* 21b.

eases of the past seasons, are nothing but a punishment * for the selfish neglect of your foremost duty.' The prophet's earnest and direct appeal stirred the slumbering energies of both leaders and people, and they proceeded to do work in the House of J".† This was on the 24th day of the sixth month, i.e. little more than three weeks after Haggai first came forward.

ii. Second prophecy: October; 2¹⁻⁹. In spite of the enthusiasm aroused by the prophet's first address, and before the work could have advanced much beyond the repairing of the foundations, a feeling of despair began to damp the ardour of the workers, both leaders and people. Those who were old enough to recollect the former temple circulated depressing comparisons : ' This new temple will never be like the old one.' ‡ To arrest the spread of this despondent spirit Haggai promptly brought a message, this time of strong encouragement. It was useless to spend vain regrets upon the past, when all their energies were needed for the present. J" was still present with His people ; § and the time was fast approaching for Israel to enter upon its glorious career. The completion of the temple was to be the signal for a convulsion of the universe and a revolution in the Gentile world. Then this very temple, which now appeared too great for their resources and too mean for their desire, would be filled with the treasures of the Gentiles. ‖ That day would see the long-delayed fulfilment of the great promises ; ¶ and then there would be no comparison between the first temple and the second, for the glory of the latter House would far excel the glory of the former.

iii. Third prophecy: December; 2¹⁰⁻¹⁹. On this occasion Haggai came before the people with a parable, a warning, and a promise. There was much still to depress the spirit of the builders

besides the discouraging comparisons of those who could not look beyond the glories of the past. Nothing as yet had taken place to correspond with the inspiring hopes of the prophet. The general state was one of misery, not far from famine. The drought lasted so long that it seemed hopeless to expect any produce from the land. The seed lay useless in the barns ; it was impossible to sow it in the sun-parched earth ; the vines and fig-trees had borne no fruit (v.¹⁹). And yet, said the people, is not the land holy, the favoured soil of J"? Has He not pledged His promise to it ? Is not His altar here ?

To show the falseness of this reasoning, which argued that because the land was holy therefore it must be fruitful, Haggai asks the priests for instruction (torah) on a ceremonial point ; their reply suggests the true principle. The contagion of holiness is transmitted only slightly, if at all (Lv 6²⁷), while uncleanness has a far-reaching effect (Lv 7²¹, Nu 19²²). Altar * and sacrifices avail nothing while the people neglect their first duty. To allow the temple to lie in ruins is the guilt which taints everything ; the blight which rests upon the land is a proof and punishment of their uncleanness.† But now that they have set to work in earnest, and laid the foundation of the temple (v.¹⁸),‡ better days will follow. The seed is in the barns—it shall yield a harvest ; the vines and the fig-trees, as yet unfruitful, shall yield their wine and oil ; and God's blessing shall descend upon His land (v.¹⁹).

iv. Fourth prophecy: same date as iii. The prophet turns from the people to the prince, and addresses Zerubbabel alone. In the vast upheaval which is to accompany the approaching judgement,§ Zerubbabel will remain unshaken. As the representative of the Davidic dynasty, and therefore the object of patriotic hopes,‖ he receives an assurance of the divine protection and the perpetuity of his race.¶ Under Persian domination the prophet dare not promise more.

There can be little doubt that the prophecies of Haggai have come down to us in a very abbreviated form. It is the main heads of his discourses, rather than the discourses themselves, that have been preserved. Compared with Amos and Hosea, the style of Haggai is monotonous and prosaic. He is fond of repetitions, e.g. the reiterated 'Con-

---

* In v.¹⁰ the second word עֲלֵיכֶם ' for your sake,' is prob. an erroneous repetition of the first עַל. In v.¹² the second אֱלֹהֵיהֶם ' their God,' is rendered by LXX, Syr. Vulg. ' unto them,' אֲלֵיהֶם, which is to be preferred.

† V.¹³ is suspicious ; it interrupts the connexion between v.¹² and v.¹⁴ ; and it is not in Haggai's style, e.g. for ' מַלְאַךְ H. writes הַנָּבִיא, for ' בְּמַלְאֲכוּת he writes כַּאֲשֶׁר שָׁלְחוֹ v.¹². See Böhme, ZATW vii. 215 ; Stade, GVI ii. 114 n.; Wellh. Skiz. u. Vorarb.-v. 169 ; Nowack, Kl. Proph. 305. The last part of the verse may have been taken from 2⁴. On this verse was based the curious tradition that Haggai, like John the Baptist and Malachi, was really an angel in human form. See Jerome, Opera, ed. Bened. 1704, tom. iii. p. 1691, and Cyril Alex. Opera, ed. 1638, tom. iii. p. 637, commenting on this verse.

‡ The parallel account in Ezr 3¹² refers to the second year of the Return. But as Ezr 3⁸⁻¹³ was written long after the events recorded (see above), it is not impossible that the ' weeping of the old men ' really belongs to this occasion (so the contemporary authorities, Hag 2³, Zec 4¹⁰), and has been transferred to the earlier date under a misapprehension.

§ The first part of v.⁵ down to ' Egypt' scarcely makes grammar (RVm has to insert ' Remember'), and interrupts the context. LXX omits. Prob. a marginal gloss, which has crept into the text. ' My spirit abideth in the midst of you' (Zec 4⁶) will thus follow ' I am with you.'

‖ In v.⁷ translate ' and the desirable things of all the nations shall come.' The word חֶמְדַּת is sing., but collective in meaning, and so construed with a plur. vb.; cf. Is 60⁵. The construction is rightly understood by LXX καὶ ἥξει τὰ ἐκλεκτά, Pesh. Targ. Ital. Old interpreters referred the verse directly to the Messiah, e.g. Vulg. et veniet desideratus cunctis gentibus, and Jerome, Comment. in loc. This trⁿ is not correct, but the verse is Messianic, in the same sense as Is 60.

¶ Such as Mic 4¹·², Is 22·3 60⁵⁻⁷·¹¹·¹³·¹⁷ 61⁶, Jer 31⁷; cf. Zec 2¹¹ 8²², To 14⁵. Apparently, Haggai's idea is that the Messianic era will begin immediately after the great upheaval which is to follow the completion of the temple. In v.⁹ LXX begins a new sentence with ' And in this place . . .,' adding καὶ εἰρήνην ψυχῆς εἰς περιποίησιν παντὶ τῷ κτίζοντι τοῦ ἀναστῆσαι τὸν ναὸν τοῦτον, which Wellh. (Sk. u. Vorarb. v. 169) ingeniously reproduces by וְשֶׁלְוַת נֶפֶשׁ לְחַיּוֹת כָּל הַיּוֹסֵד לְקוֹמֵם הַהֵיכָל הַזֶּה (cf. 1 Ch 11⁸, Ex 9¹⁸, Ps 12²⁷), ' and rest of soul, to repair all the foundation, to raise up this temple.' The sentence is so peculiar that it is difficult to regard it as a mere addition of LXX ; at the same time it is not easy to see why it should have dropped out of the MT. It is not required to complete the sense of the passage.

* In v.¹⁴ ' there' points to the altar erected immediately after the Return (Ezr 3³). LXX adds at the end of the verse ἕνεκεν τῶν λημμάτων αὐτῶν τῶν ὀρθρινῶν, ὀδυνηθήσονται ἀπὸ προσώπου πόνων αὐτῶν, καὶ ἐμισεῖτε ἐν πύλαις ἐλέγχοντας. So Ital. But first clause is a corrupt reading of שַׁחַר לְקַחְתָּם יַעַן as שַׁחַר לְקַחְתָּם יַעַן, and does not belong to this place ; the second clause is a gloss adapted to the context ; the third is taken from Am 5¹⁰ (Wellh. in loc.).

† V.¹⁵ ' From this day and upwards ' ; the latter word points to the future (cf. 1 S 16¹³ etc.) ; but before giving a promise for the future (v.¹⁹) the prophet recalls, in a parenthesis, the sufferings of the past 16 years (vv.¹⁶·¹⁷) as a warning. In v.¹⁷ the words אֵלַי אֶתְכֶם אֵין are untranslatable and corrupt. Read אֵלָי שַׁבְתֶּם וְלֹא ' and ye did not turn unto me' (Am 4⁹, from which other expressions in this verse are taken).

‡ V.¹⁸ the meaning is, ' Consider, from this day and onwards, nay, start from the day when the foundations were laid four months ago ; J"'s blessing will date from the time when the work began.' The date in v.¹⁸ is awkward and unnecessary ; perhaps inserted by a reader from v.¹⁰.

§ Some verb seems to have fallen out at the end of v.²² ; Wellh. suggests יִפֹּל ' shall fall.'

‖ What Haggai hints, Zechariah makes more explicit ; Zerubbabel is to be the Messianic king of the future (Zec 3⁸ 6⁹ff.).

¶ ' For the signet,' cf. Jer 22²⁹, Ca 8⁶, Sir 49¹¹. The authenticity of vv.²⁰⁻²³ has been questioned by Böhme (ZATW vii. 215 ff.) on the ground of (α) certain differences of style, e.g. v.²⁰ ' the word of J" came unto H.' instead of the usual ' the word of J" came by the hand of H. the prophet,' and (β) the repetition of the prophecy in 26ᵇ 7ᵃ. With regard to (α) cf. v.¹⁰ and Jer 46¹³, MT and LXX ; no great weight can be laid upon the form in which such sentences have been handed down. With regard to (β), the prophecy does not go beyond prophetic thought in Haggai's time ; and as it is addressed to Zerub. alone (hence שֵׁנִית v.²⁰) the repetition is natural, and forms a fitting conclusion to the book.

sider your ways,' 'saith J″ of hosts' (2[7-9. 23]), and the repeated address to Zerubbabel and Joshua by their full titles. At the same time he is capable of finer writing, e.g. 1[6. 11] 2[6. 7. 21. 22]. Compared with his colleague Zechariah, Haggai shows less freedom and variety in his description of the Messianic age. Both prophets belong to the period of the decline of prophecy. They seem to be conscious that their prophetic gift does not possess the direct and copious inspiration of the earlier prophets; for they are careful to assert repeatedly that their word is the word of J″. In one respect they belong to the pre-exilic type, inasmuch as, like Jeremiah and Ezekiel, their names and personalities, and the historical circumstances of their ministry, are well known. Otherwise, they belong to the new school of religious thought which was the product of the Exile. Before the Exile, prophecy was mainly concerned with denunciation of national sins and threats of impending judgment, with summons to repentance and moral reformation ; the prophets had to resist the semi-idolatrous worship of a corrupt society. But after the Exile the conditions were altered ; tendencies towards apostasy and idolatry had disappeared ; and we find that the main interest of Haggai is centred in the temple, and his prophetic gift is exercised in urging the restoration of a material fabric. This change in the subject-matter of prophecy 'is not to be attributed to the inferior religious capacity of the post-exilic period.' * Different circumstances called for a different form of religious expression. New problems had arisen ; it was the work of Haggai, and of the religious teachers who followed him, to meet these problems, and to interpret the religion of Israel in accordance with the needs of a new age.

According to Jewish tradition, Haggai (with Zechariah, Malachi, etc.) was a member of the Great Synagogue : see Talm. *Baba Bathra*, fol. 15a, with Rashi's comment. In *Aboth R. Nathan*, fol. 23b, Haggai, Zech., and Mal. are said to have received the tradition from the prophets who were before them, and to have handed it on to the men of the Great Synagogue.

The versions mention Haggai (and Zechariah) in the headings of the following psalms :—LXX Ps 137. (Tischend.) 145. 146. 147. 148. Vulg. Ps 111 '*Alleluia, reversionis, Aggæi et Zachariæ*,' 145. Itala (Jerome) Ps 6 '*canticum Hieremiæ et Aggæi de verbo peregrinationis, quando incipiebant proficisci*,' 111 (Nestle). Pesh. Ps 125. 126. 145. 146. 147. 148 (Lee). With these cf. Epiphanius (*De vitis prophetarum*, ed. 1682, tom. ii. p. 248), who says of Haggai, καὶ αὐτὸς ἔψαλλε ἐκεῖ (ἐν Ἰερουσαλήμ) πρῶτος ἀλληλουιά. Epiphan. also tells us that Haggai the prophet, while still young, went up from Babylon, and prophesied openly about the return (ἐπιστροφῆς) of the people, and saw the building of the temple of Jerusalem, where he died and was buried honourably near the priests. This tradition of Epiphan. is copied by Dorotheus (*Synopsis de vita et morte prophetarum*, Max. biblioth. vet. patr., Lugd., tom. iii. p. 422), and by Hesychius of Jerus. (ed. Migne, 1865, p. 1362), who says that Haggai was born in Babylon and was of the tribe of Levi, and was buried near the priests because he was of priestly race.

LITERATURE.—A. Köhler, *Die nachexilischen Propheten erklärt* i. Haggai, 1860 ; T. T. Perowne, *Haggai and Zechariah* in the *Camb. Bible*, 1886 ; J. Wellhausen, *Skizzen u. Vorarbeiten*, v. 1892 ; André, *Le Prophète Aggée*, 1895 ; Nowack, *Kl. Proph.* 1897 ; G. A. Smith, *Twelve Proph.* ii. 1898 ; Böhme, *ZATW*, 1887, p. 215 ff. ; Stade, *GVI* ii. 2, 1888 ; Hunter, *After the Exile*, i. ch. vii. 1890 ; Ed. Meyer, *Entstehung des Judenthums*, 1896, etc. See also the literature at end of art. EZRA-NEHEMIAH.

G. A. COOKE.

HAGGI (חַגִּי 'born on a festival').—Son of Gad,

Gn 46[16], Nu 26[15] P. Patronymic, **Haggites**, Nu 26[15].

HAGGIAH (חֲגִיָּה 'feast of J″').—A Levite, descended from Merari, 1 Ch 6[30]. See GENEALOGY.

HAGGITES.—See HAGGI.

HAGGITH (חַגִּית 'festal').—One of David's wives, known to us only as the mother of Adonijah, David's fourth son, whom she bare to him at Hebron, *i.e.* before he became king over all Israel (2 S 3[4], 1 Ch 3[2]). Adonijah is usually introduced as 'the son of Haggith' (1 K 1[5. 11] 2[13]).

HAGIOGRAPHA.—See BIBLE, OLD TESTAMENT.

HAGRI (הַגְרִי, AV Haggeri).—Father of Mibhar, one of David's heroes, 1 Ch 11[38]. Instead of מִבְחָר בֶּן־הַגְרִי, the parallel passage 2 S 23[36] reads מִצֹּבָה בָּנִי הַגָּדִי 'of Zobah, Bani the Gadite,' which is probably the correct text. (Cf. Driver, *Heb. Text of Sam. ad loc.*, and Kittel on 1 Ch 11[38]).

HAGRITE (הַגְרִי).—Jaziz the Hagrite (AV **Hagerite**) was 'over the flocks' of king David, 1 Ch 27[31]. See next article.

HAGRITES (1 Ch 5[10. 19. 20], AV Hagarites).—Hagarenes (AV and RV Ps 83[6], but RVm has Hagrites), הַגְרִים, הַגְרִיאִים, הַגַּרְאִים (LXX Ἀγαρηνοί, Ἀγγαρηνοί, Ἀγαραῖοι, Ἀγεραῖοι). Whether the tribe was of Aramæan or Arabian origin is uncertain. The name first appears in history in 1 Ch 5[10] in the story of the campaign of the Reubenites in the days of Saul, in which the H. are described as driven out of the district lying to the east of Gilead. They are also named along with the two Ishmaelitish tribes, Jetur and Naphish (1 Ch 1[31], Gn 25[15]), and an otherwise unknown tribe, Nodab, as the chief object of attack on the part of the three Israelitish tribes east of the Jordan, on which occasion, according to our present text, the H. and their allies lost 100,000 men (1 Ch 5[19-22]). That their wealth consisted in cattle is indicated in the same passage by the statement that no less than 50,000 camels, 250,000 sheep, and 2000 asses fell into the hands of the conquerors. The question has been often raised as to whether the name H. designates a particular tribe. Bertheau on 1 Ch 5[10] assumes that the name is a late designation of the Bedawîn tribes of Arabia generally current in the times of the Chronicler. It does indeed so happen that the name occurs only in very late writings, only in Ch and in Ps 83. Yet even there, at least in the psalm just referred to, it occurs alongside of the names of other Arabian and even Ishmaelitish tribes, which would have been included under it had it been used in this general sense. Many of the Jewish writers assumed that the H. were simply the descendants of Hagar. Dillmann and others think it extremely doubtful whether the name has any connexion with that of Ishmael's mother. It is not even quite certain that they were Ishmaelites. It is, however, quite evidently the intention of the Chronicler to represent the H. as including several other Ishmaelite tribes, without perhaps regarding them as coextensive with the Ishmaelites. That he associated their name with that of Hagar is also highly probable. Their name occurs in the midst of a group of Aramæan tribes (Schrader, *COT*, ii. 32) in the list of Tiglath-pileser III. (c. B.C. 727). In all probability they are the same as the Ἀγραῖοι of the Greek geographers, described as neighbours of the Nabatæans in Northern Arabia (Strabo, XVI. iv. 2 ; Pliny, vi. 32 ; Ptolem. v. xix. 2). They are certainly not to be identified with the Gerrhæans, a rich commercial people on the Persian

Gulf, of peaceable habits, quite unlike the restless combative Hagrites. Whether or not the οἱ υἱοὶ Ἄγαρ of Bar 3²³ are to be identified with the H. is a matter of little consequence. Perhaps this late writer, belonging to the later years of the apostolic age, intended only a vague reference to children of the East famous for their wisdom. The strange fancy that reads a reference to this people in St. Paul's allegory of Hagar and Sinai (Gal 4²⁴) need only be mentioned as a curiosity in exegesis. On the use and probable meaning of the word Hagar in that passage, see an admirable and extremely interesting note in Lightfoot's *Galatians*¹⁰ (1890), pp. 192–200. If, as some believe, we have a reminiscence of the H. in the name Hedjâz, applied to the northern part of the strip of land to the east of the Red Sea, we must suppose them to have been driven gradually southward from their earlier home. Individual Hagrites appear in the history of David— one, named Jaziz, as the king's chief shepherd (1 Ch 27³¹), another, named Mibhar, as one of the heroes about the king (1 Ch 11³⁸). But see preceding two articles.

LITERATURE.—Ewald, *History of Israel*, i. p. 315; Steiner in Schenkel, *Bibellexikon*, ii. 572 f.; Kautzsch in Riehm, *Handwörterbuch*, 551 f. See also Cheyne, *Book of Psalms*, London, 1888, p. 233, and *Origin of the Psalter*, 1891, p. 97; Glaser, *Skizze*, ii. 407.   J. MACPHERSON.

HAHIROTH.—See PIHAHIROTH.

HAIL.—The interjection Hail! was originally an adj. meaning 'healthy,' 'in good health,' and came from the Scand. *heill*, 'hale,' 'whole.' It appears as a salutation in the oldest English, but always joined to the verb 'to be' in the imperat. and retaining its adj. force. Thus in Anglo-Sax. Gospels, Lk 1²⁸ 'Hâl wes thu'='Hale be thou!' Mt 28⁹ 'Hâle wese ge'='Hale be ye.' So 'All hail' meant originally 'altogether whole,' hail being still an adj. But the verb being omitted, 'hail' and 'all hail' came to be used purely as an interjection. And so Shaks. is able to use 'all hail!' apart from the construction of the sentence, *Rich. II.* IV. i. 169—

> 'Did they not sometime cry "all hail" to me?
> So Judas did to Christ.'

And in *Macbeth*, I. v. 6, he turns 'all hail' into a verb, 'Whiles I stood rapt in the wonder of it, came missives from the king, who all-hailed me, "Thane of Cawdor."'

Hail! is found in the Gospels only, and always as tr. of Χαῖρε (the imperat. of χαίρειν, to rejoice), a common salutation in Greek writers, and represented in Lat. by Ave! or Salve! The Vulg. uses 'Ave!' in all the passages, Mt 26⁴⁹ 27²⁹, Mk 15¹⁸, Lk 1²⁸, Jn 19³. The Eng. 'hail' is as old as Wyc.; it was introduced again by Tind. and accepted by all the VSS except Gen. in Mt 26⁴⁹ 27²⁹ 'God save thee.' In Mt 28⁹ the plu. χαίρετε occurs, where Wyc. gave 'Heil ye'; but Tind. 'All hayle,' whom the rest of the VSS followed, except Gen. 'God save you.'   J. HASTINGS.

HAIL (בָּרָד *bārād*, ἡ χάλαζα) is mentioned in Scripture 31 times, and always as an instrument of divine judgment. A grievous hail was the seventh plague in Egypt (Ex 9¹⁸ᶠᶠ·); and as in that country hail, like rain, falls rarely, and when it occurs is generally slight (the annual rainfall in Cairo being under an inch), the catastrophe was the more remarkable, and was the first of the plagues which were directly fatal to men (vv.¹⁹· ²⁵). Hail is, however, not unknown in Egypt. On Aug. 13, 1832, a brief and local but severe hailshower fell, and some of the stones are said to have weighed several ounces.

The ancient Egyptian word for hail, *ār*, is also applied to a driving shower of sand and stones: in the contest between Horus and Set, Isis is described as sending upon the latter *ār n šā*, 'a hail of sand.' In Coptic hail is named ⲁⲗ ⲛⲧⲉ ⲧⲫⲉ, 'stones from heaven.'

Lightning being also comparatively infrequent, this feature of the plague is emphasized in the narrative, 'flashing continually amidst the hail' (RVm v.²⁴; see also Wis 16¹⁶ᶠᶠ·, Sir 46⁶, Ps 18¹²· ¹³ 78⁴⁸ 105³²).

Hail accompanies electrical disturbances, and is commonest at the earlier part of the day, before the ascending current from the heated land is established, and when there is the greatest variation of temperature and amount of vapour in successive strata of the atmosphere. The vapour, carried aloft by whirling currents, condenses as it ascends through colder strata into waterdrops which at higher levels become frozen, and, when carried laterally out of the ascending current, fall as hail. Often in their descent they are again caught by the ascending vortices and become nuclei of additional condensation, becoming coated with fresh lamellæ of ice. (For forms of hailstones see Buchan's *Meteorology*, 2nd ed. p. 106). In the act of falling, hailstones often cohere, forming by the process of regelation solid masses, which do immense damage to vegetation, and notably to vines (Ps 78⁴⁸). Prof. Joannis of Bordeaux records the fall of stones of 200 grammes weight.

The localization of the plague (Ex 9²⁶) is in accord with common experience. The great hailstorm of 13th July 1788, which destroyed property valued at £1,000,000, crossed Europe in two belts about 12 miles apart, each belt being from 7 to 10 miles wide and about 400 miles long. The hailshower of 18th April 1850, which destroyed £27,000 worth of property in Dublin, left a whole district of the city untouched.

The season of the plague was probably the end of Jan., when the flax was in bloom and the barley (which ripens 6 months after sowing, and is harvested about the end of Feb.) was in the ear (v.³¹). Wheat, which does not come into ear until about a month later, escaped (v.³²), to become afterwards the prey of the locusts (10¹⁵). At this season hailstorms are most frequent in Levantine lands. The storm in the Haurân, recorded by Mohammed el-Chateb el-Bosrawi, which destroyed many men and an immense number of cattle, occurred in Feb. 1860.

Hail falls most commonly by day, at the time when men are at their work (Ex 9¹⁹· ²⁰). Out of 440 consecutive hailstorms registered, only 18 occurred at night. This was noticed long ago by Venerable Bede, 'interdiu sæpius quam noctu decidunt' (*De Nat. Rer.* xxxiv.).

In Ps 78⁴⁸ חֲנָמֵל is used as a parallel with *bārād*. This is a *hapax legomenon*, and is tr. 'frost' (AV and RV), but Kimchi and Ibn Ezra regard it as meaning 'hail.' It is rendered in AVm and RVm 'great hailstones,' which is probably correct. Rashi and the Targumists suppose that the word refers to locusts (see also Lee's *Lexicon*, p. 211). LXX has πάχνη, hoar frost. Michaelis and Ges. conjecture 'ants,' but these guesses are groundless.

By hailstones were the Amorites smitten at Bethhoron, Jos 10¹¹, and the size of the stones is here emphasized, as in Sir 46⁶. There are many authentic records of large stones formed by regelation. In a storm at Kazorla in Spain, 15th June 1829, stones fell which weighed 2 kilos., and in the great storm of 24th July 1818 in Orkney the stones were as large as goose eggs, and in 9 minutes 9 inches of ice had fallen. In a similar shower on 7th May 1865 at Câtalet the hailstorms are said in the official report to have made heaps 16 feet high. One great concreted mass of stones which fell in Hungary, 8th May 1832, was 3 feet in diameter, and another was measured in Ross-shire in Aug. 1849 which was 20 feet in circumference. Such stones do immense damage. In the Indian and Colonial Exhibition there was a corrugated iron roof exhibited which was pierced in several places by hailstones, and a similar occurrence is reported by an eye-witness in *Notes and Queries*, Nov. 19, 1887. (For other examples of destructive hailstorms see Thomson's *Meteorology*, 1849). Hailstorms of great severity are recorded from Bible lands by Kitto and Thomson (*Land and Book*, i. 86). The discomfiture of armies by hail is not confined to this instance. Sennacherib's advance in his 7th campaign, as recorded on the Taylor Cylinder, was stopped by hail, and Esarhaddon's army encountered another storm in the land of Khani Rabbi (*WAI* iii. 15). In 1339 the army of Edward III. was stopped in its march to Chartres by hail (Holinshed); and, later, a violent hailshower completed the defeat of the Austrian army at Solferino (1859).

In Job 38²² God speaks of the treasuries of hail reserved against the day of battle and war, and in Rev 8⁷ 11¹⁹ 16²¹ hail is the type of God's judgment on sin. In the latter passage stones of the weight of a talent, *i.e.* about 2 cubic feet in bulk, are mentioned. In Is 28²⁻¹⁷ the Assyrian invasion is figuratively described as זֶרֶם בָּרָד *zerem bārād*, a flowing of hail, called in v.¹⁵ the overflowing scourge, which is to sweep away the Egyptian alliance, called in the passage 'the refuge of lies.' In Is 30³⁰ it is the power which, in turn, is to overthrow the Assyrian. The 'hail in the downfall of the forest' of Is 32¹⁹ may be an interjected allusion to the Assyrian invasion, but the passage with its shifting figures and assonances is peculiarly obscure. Kimchi conjectures that it may mean that it will only hail in the forest, not on the cultivated land. In Hag 2¹⁷ hail also means divine chastisement. In Ezk 13¹¹⁻¹³ hail represents the judgment of God defeating the hypocrisy which would conceal corruption; 'comminatio Dei qua contumaces verberat' (Rabanus, *de Universo*, xxii. 18). The word used here and in Ezk 38²² אֶלְגָּבִישׁ *'elgâbish* is peculiar, and possibly connected with the *gâbish* of Job 28¹⁸, rendered 'pearls' in AV, 'crystal' in RV. In the rabbinical comment on *Berachoth* (54b) the stones of *'elgâbish* are, by a false etymology, explained as hail which was sent at the prayer of a man (Jos 10¹¹), and stopped by the prayer of a man (Ex 9²⁹). St. Agobard, Bp. of Lyons, wrote a treatise, *de Grandine*, etc., to disprove the notion of human instrumentality in the procuring of hail (A.D. 835).

Literature.—Besides the literature above referred to, see Hengstenberg, *die Bücher Mose's u. Ägypten*, 1841.

A. MACALISTER.

HAIR (שֵׂעָר, once שַׂעַר Is 7²⁰; שַׂעֲרָה; θρίξ, κόμη).—A luxuriant growth of hair on head and chin was regarded by the Hebrews and other Semitic peoples as an important constituent of manly grace. Absalom's long hair is noted as an element in his much prized beauty (2 S 14²⁶). Solomon's youthful horsemen, 'in the most delightful flower of their age . . . had long heads of hair' (Jos. *Ant.* VIII. vii. 3). It was an admired distinction to have bushy (RVm 'curled') locks, 'black as a raven' (Ca 5¹¹). The phrase גָּלָה אֹזֶן 'he uncovereth the ear' (1 S 20². ¹² 22⁸), may possibly refer to long locks, covering the ear, pushed aside to whisper a secret. Among women, long dark tresses were held most captivating (Ca 7⁵), and they have always worn the hair long (Jn 11² 1 Co 11⁵. ⁶); but in NT times long hair was a dishonour to a man (1 Co 11¹⁴). Men dreaded baldness, as suggesting a suspicion of leprosy (Lv 13⁴⁰), and this possibly explains the youths' disrespectful conduct to Elisha (2 K 2²³).

Other Asiatics, and the Greeks, observed similar customs. The Babylonians wore their hair long, 'binding their heads with turbans' (Herod. i. 195). The Greeks loved rich waving hair; the youthful gods, Bacchus and Apollo, were figured with plenteous locks. The Egyptians, on the other hand, shaved both head and face. To be unshaven marked the sloven; if, however, this was due to hardships of war, it was honourable (Wilkinson, *Ancient Egyptians*, ii. 330). Enslaved foreigners were forced to shave (Gn 41¹⁴). The long-haired Asiatics and Greeks excited among the Egyptians both ridicule and disgust (Herod. ii. 37, 49, 91). Boys' heads were shaven very early. Herodotus accounts for the strength of Egyptian skulls by their exposure, clean-shaven, to the full glare of the sun (Herod. iii. 12). The locks in front of the ears were preserved, as the sign of immaturity, and removed when manhood was reached. These locks are represented on the statues of Harpocrates and other younger deities (Wilk. iii. 130). Adult princes wore a badge at the side of the head, which perhaps contained the youthful lock in earlier days, and continued to indicate that while the father lived they had not attained the dignity of kinghood (*ib.* iii. 326). Large use was made of false hair, in wigs (*ib.* ii. 229) and in beards, to the forms of which special significance attached (see BEARD). Women wore their own hair, plentiful growth being highly esteemed. A woman's head was never shaved; but the locks, when long and beautiful, were sometimes cut off and preserved, to be laid in her tomb after death (*ib.* ii. 21 n.). The slavewoman's hair was differently dressed from that of her mistress (*ib.* ii. 338, 339). Moslem influence has modified Egyptian customs. In shaving the heads of men and boys a tuft is left on the crown; the cheek above the under jaw is shaven, and the part under the chin. The moustache is left unshaven. Female infants are never shaved; and women wear their hair long, usually in plaits and ringlets.

Of the terms used for dressing the hair, and the fashions of wearing it among the Hebrews, we may note the following:—מַחְלָפוֹת, LXX σειραί (Jg 16¹³. ¹⁹), of Samson's 'seven locks,' which probably resembled the long 'plaits' affected now by the young Arab warriors. Jezebel 'tired her head,' וַתֵּיטֶב (2 K 9³⁰), which means simply that she set her hair in order. צַמָּה 'locks' (Ca 4¹. ³ 6⁷, Is 47² AV, following Kimchi; RV, following LXX [in Ca σιώπησις, in Is κατακάλυμμα], tr. 'veil'). עֲנָק (Ca 4⁹), literally 'collar' or 'necklace,' *may* have been a lock falling round the neck—Vulg. *in uno crine colli tui.* תַּלְתַּלִּים (Ca 5¹¹), LXX ἐλάται, Vulg. *elathæ palmarum*, tresses hanging gracefully like the pendulous palm branches. דַּלָּה (Ca 7⁵; compare Is 38¹²), is a figure supplied by the thrum, or slender threads binding the web to the weaver's beam. רְהָטִים (Ca 7⁵; compare Gn 30³⁸. ⁴¹), probably 'gutters,' or channels conveying water to the flocks, their orderly arrangement suggesting flowing tresses. מַעֲשֶׂה מִקְשָׁה (Is 3²⁴), literally 'turned work,' applied to curls, or artificially twisted hair. צִיצָה 'a lock,' probably the forelock, from the curve resembling that of a flower or wing. Judith 'braided,' διέταξε, 'the hairs of her head' (10³). For other references to modes of wearing the hair, see 1 Ti 2⁹, 1 P 3³, Jos. *Ant.* XIV. ix. 4, and *BJ* IV. ix. 10.

That the barber's trade was practised we know from Ezk 5¹. The hairdresser and the instruments of his art figure in the Mishna (*Shabbath*, § 6). The Egyptians used wooden combs, with large teeth on one side and small on the other, ornamented as if for wearing in the hair (Wilk. ii. 349). Ointment was commonly used by the

Hebrews in dressing the hair (Ru 3³, 2 S 14², Ps 92¹⁰ 133², Ec 9⁸, Mt 6¹⁷, Jos. *Ant.* XIX. iv. 1). Anointing the hair was a sign of festivity (Ps 45⁷) and a mark of hospitality (Ps 23⁵, Lk 7⁴⁶). Solomon's young horsemen produced striking effects by sprinkling their heads with gold dust every day (Jos. *Ant.* VIII. vii. 3). Herod the Great dyed his hair to conceal his great age (*Ant.* XVI. viii. 1); but the practice was unusual (Mt 5³⁶). Wigs were not unknown (Jos. *Vita*, 11). Orientals have from of old worn ornaments in the hair. It is doubtful if שְׁבִיסִים (Is 3¹⁸), LXX ἐμπλόκια, were 'networks' (RVm) or sun-shaped ornaments, distinguished from the crescent or moon-shaped, mentioned in the same verse (Schrœder, *De Vest. Mul. Heb.* cap. 2). To-day coins are most used by women: the long plaits often worn have frequently one or more gold pieces dangling at the end. A blue bead knotted into the hair of children is a potent charm against the evil eye.

The Hebrews were forbidden to cut off the corners of their hair (Lv 19²⁷). They may have adopted the Egyptian practice of wearing the front locks in youth, removing them on the threshold of manhood. But neighbouring peoples attached a religious significance to this act. The Arabians cut their hair in imitation of Orotal—the Arabian Bacchus—'in a circular form, shaving it round the temples' (Herod. iii. 8). This usage is referred to in Jer 9²⁶ 25²³ 49³². The young man wore his front locks untouched; their removal marked his entrance into man's estate, and his initiation into the worship of Orotal. Among the Bedawîn to-day the front locks are found only on growing lads. The Greek *ephebi* offered the long hair of their childhood at Delphi; the cut adopted was called θησηλς, as the god was said to have cut only his front locks here. The Hebrews were thus distinguished from the idolatrous peoples around them. A curious evidence of this ancient prohibition is seen among the Palestinian Jews, who closely crop the whole head, leaving only the two locks in front of the ears, which hang down in long ringlets by either cheek.

The first hair has often been held sacred. In Arabia, in Mohammed's time, when a child was born its head was shaved, and the scalp daubed with the blood of a slaughtered sheep. Lane noted that at the first shaving of a boy's head the Egyptian peasants slew a goat, and all who cared partook of the feast provided. These were 'the more recent settlers, whose pagan Arabian ancestors . . . gave as alms to the poor the weight of the hair in silver or gold' (Lane, *Mod. Egyp.*). Burckhardt observes that 'among the Maazy Arabs . . . it is a festival in the family when the son's head is shaved for the first time.' Lucian says the Syrian boys and girls of his time, on growing up, cut off and dedicated their first hair at some sanctuary. Phœnician maidens, as a preliminary to marriage, had to sacrifice either their hair or their chastity at the feast of Byblus. Lv 19²⁷ is rendered in the Syriac 'ye shall not let your hair grow long,' and it is explained that the custom of the heathen was 'to let the hair grow for a certain time, and on a fixed date to shave the head in a temple or beside a fountain.'

Herodotus mentions the Egyptian custom of dedicating the weight in silver of the hair taken from a child's head (ii. 65). A similar custom among the Arabs is traced to the example of Fâtima. Absalom's abundant tresses, cut, collected, and weighed 'at every year's end,' the sacred season of pilgrimage, may suggest some similar religious observance. The one clear biblical instance of hair in an offering is in connexion with the Nazirite vow. The hair must grow and

be kept from all pollution during the period of consecration: the bushy locks were the visible sign of the Nazirite's condition. Contact with impurity necessitated the shaving and sanctifying of the head, and the period of consecration began afresh. When the vow was accomplished, the head was shaved at the door of the Tent of Meeting, and the hair burned in the fire under the sacrifice of peace-offerings (Nu 6¹⁻²¹). In Mohammedan law, the resolve to visit a distant shrine is reckoned a vow; and the hair must be neither cut nor even washed, until the purpose is accomplished. Then by cutting the hair the pilgrim passes back from the consecrated to the common condition (Wellhausen, *Skizzen*, iii. 117). Examples are found in St. Paul's vow (Ac 18¹⁸), and that of Bernice (Jos. *BJ* II. xv. 1). A parallel may be traced between this latter and the Greek custom of vowing to offer the hair to the gods in return for help or protection. Achilles dedicated his hair to the river-god Spercheus, on condition of his safe return from Troy. At the great feasts of Byblus and Bambyce offerings of hair were made (*Dea Syria*, VI. lv.). The painted inscription at Citium (*CIS* 86) mentions גלבים 'barbers' among the regular ministers of the sanctuary. The idea more or less consciously underlying these practices probably was, that by means of his hair, part of himself, instinct with his life, the devotee formed a stable link of connexion with the sanctuary and the deity there worshipped.

If an important part of life was conceived as residing in the hair, we can see why that of consecrated persons was so cared for. From Ezk 44²⁰ we gather that certain priesthoods, like those of Egypt, shaved their heads; others, like Samuel, let the hair grow long. Profanation was avoided on the one hand by preventing its growth, on the other by keeping it untouched. Princes were also consecrated persons. נֵזֶר 'a crown' (Jer 7²⁹ RVm) is in origin simply the fillet binding the prince's long hair.

Among the Hebrews, Arabs, and other peoples, cutting the flesh was often associated with shaving the head in mourning, or taking part of the hair to lay in the tomb, or on the funeral pyre. Both practices are prohibited in Lv 19²⁷⁻²⁸ (see also Dt 14¹, Lv 21⁵·¹⁰, Am 8¹⁰ etc.). See CUTTINGS IN THE FLESH, and W. R. Smith, *RS* 305 ff. Arab women, in accordance with immemorial customs, sometimes shave their heads and wrap the hair in cloths stained with their own blood. The habit of tearing the hair in mourning, which still persists among the Jews and other Oriental peoples, may probably be traced to this ancient custom. It was also a sign of mourning to let the hair fall untended and dishevelled (Ezk 24¹⁷, Jth 10³). The Egyptians in mourning let all their hair grow (Herod. ii. 36). The hair of an attached relative was sometimes buried with the mummy (Wilk. ii. 339). Cutting or tearing the hair was common as an expression of violent emotion, as of fear and distress (Est 14²), of sorrow for national sin (Ezr 9³, 1 Es 8⁷¹, 2 Es 1⁸), and of grief over national calamities (Is 3²⁴ 15², Jer 7²⁹ 48³⁷, Ezk 7¹⁸ etc.).

The hair and nails of the dead have often been regarded as charms, making it possible to maintain connexion with the departed. Possession of a man's hair in primitive magic was esteemed a potent means of getting and retaining a hold upon him. Mohammed's hair was preserved, and worn on their persons by his followers. The Arab was accustomed to cut off the hair of his prisoner before setting him free. Perhaps more than insult was intended by shaving David's messengers (2 S 10⁴).

The almond blossom turning white before it falls is the symbol of the hoary hair (Ec 12⁵). The sprinkling of grey hairs unknown to a man indicates the stealthy approach of life's winter (Hos 7⁹). Grey hairs have always been revered in the East. Irreverence to grey hairs marks the ungodly (Wis 2¹⁰). Evil was accentuated if it brought harm on grey hairs (Gn 42³⁸). Wisdom was reckoned as the grey hair to a man (Wis 4¹⁰), and the hoary head as a crown of glory, the reward of a life of righteousness (Pr 16³¹ 20²⁹). For grey hairs to come down to the grave in peace was a token of God's favour (1 K 2⁶˙⁹). Grey hairs laid on men obligations of honourable and chivalrous conduct (2 Mac 6²³). White hair was an element in a glorious appearance (2 Mac 15¹³), especially that of divine majesty (Dt 7⁸, Rev 1¹⁴).

The hair of Samson was regarded as the seat of his strength (Jg 16²²). The hairs of the head are taken as representing the extremely numerous (Ps 40¹² 69⁴), and the exceedingly minute (1 S 14⁴⁵, 2 S 14¹¹, 1 K 1⁵², Mt 10³⁰, Lk 21¹⁸, Ac 27³⁴). Fineness of aim is described as slinging stones at an hairbreadth (Jg 20¹⁶). The Jews swore by the hair (Mt 5³⁶). One of the most binding oaths in the East now is by the beard. The colour of the hair assisted the priest to discriminate leprosy from other ailments (Lv 13). Pollution clung strongly to hair (Lv 14⁸˙⁹). On the meaning of the regulation in Dt 21¹², see Driver's note.

Goats' hair (עִזִּים) is named among acceptable offerings for the sanctuary (Ex 25⁴ 35⁶); it was not used for the interior work, but only for the outer covering of the tabernacle (Ex 26⁷ 36¹⁴). The preparation of the cloth required special skill and dexterity (Ex 35²⁶). Work of goats' hair is directed to be purified after ceremonial pollution (Nu 31²⁰). From the connexion here, it seems to have been employed then, as now, for articles of clothing. The large overall, or 'abâ', commonly worn, is almost invariably of goats' hair. It serves, among other purposes, as waterproof in rain, as great-coat in cold, and as blanket at night: it possibly corresponds to the 'garment' of Ex 22²⁷ (RV). Pillows or cushions are sometimes stuffed with goats' hair (1 S 19¹³). Goats' hair formed the material with which St. Paul was occupied as a tent-maker (Ac 18³), the haircloth for which his native province of Cilicia was noted being known to commerce as *cilicium*. Of this dark-brown stuff the tents of the nomads have been made from of old (Ca 1⁵), and employment is still found for great numbers in preparing materials for the 'hair houses' of the Bedawîn.

Camels' hair (θρὶξ καμήλου) is mentioned only as forming the raiment of John the Baptist (Mt 3⁴, Mk 1⁶). This was possibly the softer wool of the camel, the Arab. *wabr*, of which a more closely fitting garment is made, with sleeves, worn under the '*abâ*' described above (but cf. Jerome, 'non de lana cameli, sed de asperioribus setis').

W. EWING.

HAJEHUDIJAH occurs in RVm of 1 Ch 4¹⁸ in an obscure genealogical list. It is the transliteration of the Heb. הַיְהֻדִיָּה, which, however, probably is not a proper name, but means 'the Jewess' (so RV and RVm). AV reads **Jehudijah**. LXX has αὕτη Ἀδειά. See GENEALOGY.

HAKKATAN (הַקָּטָן 'the smallest').—The head of a family of returning exiles (Ezr 8¹²), called in 1 Es 8³⁸ Akatan. See GENEALOGY.

HAKKOZ (הַקּוֹץ).—**1.** A Judahite, 1 Ch 4⁸; AV **Coz.** **2.** The eponym of a priestly family, 1 Ch 24¹⁰, Ezr 2⁶¹ 7⁶³, Neh 3⁴˙²¹. In Ezr and Neh the first part of the word is taken to be the definite art. by AV, which reads **Koz.** In 1 Es 5³⁸ the name appears as **Akkos.** See GENEALOGY.

HAKUPHA (חֲקוּפָא).—Eponym of a family of

Nethinim (Ezr 2⁵¹, Neh 7⁵³), called in 1 Es 5³⁰ Achipha. See GENEALOGY.

HALACHA.—See TALMUD.

HALAH (חֲלַח) is mentioned 2 K 17⁶ 18¹¹, 1 Ch 5²⁶ as one of the places whither the king of Assyria deported the captives from Samaria. LXX Ἀλάε B (once Ἀλλάε A), in Ch Χαάχ (! for Χαλά), A Χαλά, Vulg. *Hala*, in Ch *Lahela* (!). The description indicates plainly that it is to be sought in Northern Mesopotamia, not far from Nineveh; but the location of the name has always been disputed. The various views are: 1. That Halah is a large city of Assyria, the Calah (כֶּלַח) of Gn 10¹¹, *Kalkhu* of the cuneiform texts, modern Nimrûd between the Tigris and the Upper Zâb, S. of Nineveh (see CALAH). This identification is quite inadmissible on phonetic grounds, as is likewise 2., Halévy's comparison with Cilicia, חלך *Khilakku*. The latter has also the context against it. 3. The region Chalkitis (Χαλκῖτις) in Mesopotamia (Ptol. v. 18. 4), bordering upon Gauzanitis (Gozan) and the country Anthemusia, near the rivers Chabôras (Habor) and Saokoras (or Mygdonius), would suit (so Schrader in Riehm, *Handwörterbuch*), if we were sure that the Greek form represents the same consonants as Halah. Of course, the modern village *Gla*, on the Upper Chaboras (Smith, *Bible Dict.*), cannot represent the name nor the modern Ḥolwan (see below). 4. Bochart (*Phaleg* iii. 4) compared the Calachene (Καλαχήνη) of Strabo (736, comp. Καλακινή, Ptol. vi. 1), a plain of Northern Assyria at the side of Adiabene and Armenia, E. of the Tigris. 5. This name is not to be confounded with the Chalonitis S.E. of Assyria on the Zagrus mountain (Strabo, 529, 736; Plin. vi. 30, i. 27, 31, etc.; Dion. Perieg. 1015; Polyb. v. 54). Isidorus of Charax describes the Parthian province of Χαλωνί-τις, called thus from 'the Greek city Χάλα.' This is evidently the same as Κελῶναι, Diod. xvii. 110, *Albania*, Tab. Pent., the modern Ḥolwan

حلوان. It is claimed that this city appears in Syriac literature as Ḥalah (=חלח, *Assem. Bibl. Or.* iii. 418), and the Καλχάς, *Chron. Pasc.* i. 730, would confirm this. But there are various difficulties attached to this complicated identification, and the Assyrians seem to call Holwan *Ḥalwan*; see Delitzsch, *Paradies*, 205. 6. More probability is attached to the view of Winckler (*Alttestamentliche Untersuchungen*, 108). The LXX understood Halah as a river, ἐν Ἀλάε καὶ ἐν Ἀβώρ, ποταμοῖς (!) Γωζάν, so that the original text may have had the plural 'rivers of Gozan.' Consequently, Winckler proposed the easy emendation בלח for חלח, i.e. the modern Balîkh river (already called *Balikhi* in Assyrian times, Βάλιχα, Βήλιχος, Βίληχα, Belias of the classical writers), flowing into the Euphrates not far from Rakka. This view has been accepted by most modern scholars. 7. Lately, however, Winckler himself has retracted it (*Altorientalische Forschungen*, 292). Two cuneiform documents mention a country *Khalakhkha*, *Ḥalaḥḥa*, i.e. חלח near Haran, in the very same region where the biblical description would place Halah. The exact position cannot yet be determined, owing to the fragmentary state of those documents; but it seems that this last explanation is the best solution of the problem. Possibly, also, the 6th explanation still deserves some attention.

W. MAX MÜLLER.

HALAK (הָהָר הֶחָלָק, Ἀλάκ A, Ἀχέλ B), or 'the smooth mountain,' Jos 11¹⁷ 12⁷ (only). — This eminence has not been identified, but its approximate locality is indicated by the words 'that goeth up to Seir': and it formed the southern limit of Joshua's conquests. We may infer, therefore, that it was the summit of a smooth ascent in the valley of the Arabah to the south of the Ghôr, or Dead Sea basin; and some have supposed that it was the line of cliffs which form the margin of the Ghôr itself, about 6 miles S. of the shore of that lake. This view is, however, probably erroneous, as the expression 'smooth mountain' would not apply to an abrupt range of cliffs formed of alluvial materials, which we have elsewhere (see DEAD SEA, vol. i. p. 575a) identified as 'the ascent of Akrabbim' (Nu 34⁴). But from the margin of the Ghôr the Arabah Valley gradually rises towards the summit level, which it reaches immediately in front of Mount Hor on the borders of Seir; and to this line of elevation the term 'smooth' would not be inapplicable, while at the same time it would be on the line of communication between southern Palestine and Petra, the capital of Seir.

E. HULL.

HALE.—The verbs 'hale' and 'haul,' meaning to drag, are, says Skeat, dialectical varieties of the same word. They are found in all the Teut. languages (as Dutch *halen*, Dan. *hale*), and are etymol. connected with Gr. καλεῖν and Lat. *calare*, to summon. Hale is the older form, and it alone occurs in AV and in Shaks.,* though 'haul' was already in use. The passages are Ac 8³ 'As for Saul, he made havoc of the church, entering into every house, and haling men and women committed them to prison' (σύρων, Amer. RV 'dragging'); Lk 12⁵⁸ 'lest he hale thee to the judge' (μήποτε κατασύρῃ, Amer. RV 'drag'). In both places 'hale' is original to AV, the earlier VSS having 'draw.' For the word cf. T. Lever, *Sermons* (Arber's ed. p. 23), 'This Realme is devyded in it selfe . . . by covetouse ambicion, euerye manne pullynge and halynge towardes them selves, one from another'; T. Fuller, *Holy State*, ii. 7, 'It [the Greek language] is full and stately in sound : onely it pities our Artist to see the vowels therein rackt in pronouncing them, hanging oftentimes one way by their native force, and haled another by their accents which countermand them'; and Milton, *PL* ii. 596—

> 'Thither by harpy-footed furies hal'd,
> At certain revolutions all the damn'd
> Are brought.'

J. HASTINGS.

HALHUL (חַלְחוּל).—A city of Judah mentioned (Jos 15⁵⁸) in the list of the inheritance of the tribe of Judah along with five others, all of which have been identified except Eltekon. Jerome places it near to Hebron (*Onomast. s.* 'Elul'). It is the modern *Ḥalhul*, a large village 4 miles north of Hebron, which lies in the mountains of Judah, on a hill about a mile to the east of the road to Jerusalem. On the opposite side of the road is *Beit-sur* (Beth-zûr), a rocky fastness built by Rehoboam for the defence of his kingdom (2 Ch 11⁷), and used in the wars of the Maccabees as a defence against Idumæa (1 Mac 4⁶¹). Between these two places, lower down, is the fountain *Dhirweh*, the traditional site of the baptism of the eunuch by Philip. Not far to the north is the head of Pilate's great aqueduct leading to Jerusalem, 41½ miles by the aqueduct (13 miles as the crow flies), the fall being 365 ft. in that distance (*Tent Work in Palestine*, 'Halhul'). A mile to the east of *Ḥalhul* is *Beit 'Ainûn*, identified by Robinson as Beth-anoth, where are extensive ruins and large drafted stones. Farther to the north is *Jedûr* (Gedor), a small ruin. About the site of *Ḥalhul* are ruins and rock-cut tombs, including a Byzantine ruin and an ancient church (ruined). The mosque *Neby Yunâs* (Jonah)

is a modern building on a platform of rock, which appears to have been artificially levelled (*BRP* i. 216, iii. 282; *SWP* iii. 329). Ishak Chelo in 1334 (Carmoly, p. 242) speaks of *Ḥalhul* as containing the sepulchre of Gad, David's seer (1 S 22⁵, 2 S 24¹¹; *Benj. of Tud.* by Asher, ii. 437). See, further, Dillm. on Jos 15⁵⁸, and Guérin, *Judée*, iii. 284 ff.

C. WARREN.

HALI (חֲלִי).—A city belonging to the tribe of Asher, Jos 19²⁵. The site is doubtful. It may be the ruin *'Alia* on the hills N.E. of Achzib, about 13 miles N.E. of Acre. See *SWP* vol. i. sh. iii., and Guérin, *Galilée*, ii. 62. Buhl (*GAP* 231) doubts this identification.

C. R. CONDER.

HALICARNASSUS (Ἁλικαρνασσός) was one of the six Dorian colonies on the coast of Caria (see COS). Trœzen was its mother city. Though excluded from the Dorian confederacy (Hexapolis) on account of some ancient dispute (Herod. i. 144), it was a very important city in respect of politics, commerce, literature, and art. During the Persian domination it prospered greatly under a dynasty of *tyrannoi* established by Lygdamis. His widow, Artemisia, dynast in 480, possessed great influence with Xerxes. Maussollos (377–353) made the city supreme over most of Caria and part of Lycia, under the suzerainty of the Persian king. The monument built in his honour by Artemisia, his sister-wife, who survived him, was reckoned one of the seven wonders of the world : scanty remains of it are now in the British Museum. Halicarnassus, having faithfully adhered to the Persian cause, endured a long siege by Alexander the Great, B.C. 334, and was burned by the conqueror. A number of the inhabitants were safe in the acropolis (called Salmakis), which Alexander did not succeed in capturing. They rebuilt the city ; but it never again became a great city, though always* an important one till it was ruined by the Turks. Its prosperity benefited much from the measures of Q. Cicero when he was governor of Asia in B.C. 61. Its silver coinage ceased after B.C. 168 ; but it continued to coin in bronze as late as the 3rd cent. after Christ, and appears in all the lists of bishoprics. In literature its greatness is shown by Herodotus, Dionysius the historian, Dionysius the writer on music, Pigres, Panyasis, etc.

Halicarnassus was one of the states to which the Roman Senate sent letters in favour of the Jews in B.C. 139, 1 Mac 15²³ (see CARIA). It must therefore have been a free and self-governing city at that time. The decree of the city passed in the 1st cent. B.C., granting to the Jews religious liberty and the right to build their *Proseuchai* beside the sea (Jos. *Ant.* XIV. x. 23), attests the existence of an early Jewish colony in the city ; and this was natural, as H. was a considerable centre of trade, owing to its favourable position on a bay opposite Cos, on the north-west side of the Ceramic Gulf. The city extended round the bay from promontory to promontory, and contained, among other buildings, a famous temple of Aphrodite.

The site of Halicarnassus is now called *Bodrum* (*i.e.* 'fortress'), from the Castle of St. Peter which was built by the Knights of St. John (whose headquarters were in Rhodes) under their Grand Master de Naillac, A.D. 1404. The castle stands on the point of a lofty rocky promontory, which projects southwards, and divides the bay of Halicarnassus into two harbours ; in ancient times it was probably an island (Zephyria). A Turkish village occupies part of the site of the city. In

---

* Pope gives 'hauld' in his Shaks. at *II Henry IV.* v. v. 37, and it is approved by some editors. In Ac 8³ AV of 1611 spells the word 'hail.'

* The language of Cicero, *ad Quint. Fr.* I. i, 25 (*pœne desertam urbem*), must not be pressed ; he is exaggerating his brother's services.

the castle were found many remains of the Mausoleum, which were sent to London in 1846 by Lord Stratford de Redcliffe. A very full account of the city, with plans, etc., is to be found in the works of Sir C. Newton, who excavated there in 1857. (*History of Discoveries at Halicarnassus, Cnidus, and Branchidæ,* and *Travels and Discoveries in the Levant.* See also Ross, *Reisen durch d. Inseln Griech.* ; Hamilton's *Researches in Asia Minor*).   W. M. RAMSAY.

HALL.—In Mk 15¹⁶ AV renders ἔσω τῆς αὐλῆς ὅ ἐστιν πραιτώριον, 'into the hall called Prætorium'; and in Lk 22⁵⁵ ἐν μέσῳ τῆς αὐλῆς, 'in the midst of the hall.' Elsewhere AV renders αὐλή either 'palace' (Mt 26³·⁵⁸·⁶⁹, Mk 14⁵⁴·⁶⁶, Lk 11²¹, Jn 18¹⁵), when the reference is to the place where a governor dispensed justice; or 'fold' (Jn 10¹·¹⁶), referring to the place where the flocks were kept all night; or 'court' (Rev 11²), in reference to the court of the temple. RV gives 'court' everywhere except in Jn 10¹·¹⁶ (10¹ ἡ αὐλὴ τῶν προβάτων, AV 'the sheepfold,' RV 'the fold of the sheep,' 10¹⁶ ἡ αὐλή, AV and RV 'the fold'). See PALACE.

The word πραιτώριον is once in AV trᵈ 'Prætorium' (Mk 15¹⁶ as above), and once 'palace' (Ph 1¹³ ἐν ὅλῳ τῷ πραιτωρίῳ, AV 'in all the palace,' AVm 'Cæsar's court,' RV 'throughout the whole Prætorian guard,' RVm 'in the whole Prætorium'). Elsewhere it is rendered either 'common hall' (Mt 27²⁷, AVm 'governor's house'), or 'hall of judgment' (Jn 18²⁸ᵃ, AVm 'Pilate's house'), or 'judgment hall' (Jn 18²⁸ᵇ·³³ 19⁹, Ac 23³⁵). RV gives 'palace' in the text of all those places, with 'Prætorium' in the marg., which Amer. RV prefers in the text. See PRÆTORIUM.

The RV word 'palace' for *prætorium* comes from the Rhem. NT, which has 'Palace' everywhere, except Ph 1¹³ 'court.' Wyclif's word is always 'moot (or mote) halle.' Tind. introduced 'judgement hall.'   J. HASTINGS.

HALLEL (הַלֵּל).—A name given to the group of psalms 113–118 inclusive, which the Jews from an early date have been in the habit of reciting at the three great feasts, at the feast of Dedication and at the new moons. The name 'great Hallel' is sometimes given to this group as a whole, but is usually applied to Ps 136 (or Pss 120–136) with its twenty-six times repeated refrain of praise. Pss 113–118, or 115–118, are called the 'Egyptian' or the 'common' Hallel. During the continuance of the temple the Hallel was recited on eighteen days in the year, but on one night alone, that of the passover. On that occasion it was taken in parts, Pss 113 and 114 being sung before the meal, just before the drinking of the second cup, and Pss 115–118 after the filling of the fourth cup. It is to this sacred song that reference is made in the phrase ὑμνήσαντες, 'when they had sung a hymn,' used of our Saviour and His disciples in Mt 26³⁰ and Mk 14²⁶. See Delitzsch on Ps 113; Talmud, *Sopherim* 18, §2; and compare Edersheim, *The Temple and its Services.*   W. T. DAVISON.

HALLELUJAH (הַלְלוּיָהּ 'praise ye Jʺ,' Ἀλληλουϊά). —The word occurs as a short doxology in the Psalms, usually at the beginning, as Ps 111. 112, or the end, as 104. 105, or both, as 135. 146–150; in 135³ use is different. Except 135, the H. psalms occur in three groups, 104–106; 111–113, 115, 117; 146–150; the 2nd being interrupted by Ps 114. 116. The consecutive occurrence of these psalms may be explained in two ways. (i.) H. was usually added to psalms only of a joyful character, and these might naturally be put together by the compiler, just as hymns of thanksgiving are often put together in our modern hymn-

books. But we see very little evidence in the Psalter of arrangement according to subject. It seems, therefore, more probable that they were taken as they stand from some previous collection or collections in which all the psalms were so marked; just as in a modern hymnary all the hymns taken from *Hymns Ancient and Modern* might be distinguished by Amen at the end. We have an even more complete example of taking the psalms *en bloc* from some other source without rearrangement in 'Songs of Ascents' (Ps 120–134). The occurrence of H. in Ps 106, after the doxology which closes Book iv., may be the insertion of a reviser, to make it agree with Ps 104. 105, which have the H. at the end, when the doxology had come to be regarded as part of the psalm. The H. psalms vary considerably in character. We find such different themes as the praises of the God of Nature (104), the God of Israel (105. 106), God who hears the prayer of the poor (113) and of the sufferer (116), the superiority of God to idols (115). That these psalms are late may be proved from (1) the fact that *Jah* is a contracted and later * form of *Jahu,* which occurs in the early forms *Jesayahu, Jirmeyahu,* as contrasted with the later forms which we know as *Isaiah* and *Jeremiah*; (2) the use of (generally) late grammatical forms as ' for constr. state, as in 113⁵·⁷·⁹, שׁ for אֲשֶׁר, as a prefix in 135² 146³·⁵; (3) the didactic character of 111¹⁰ 112, in the spirit of Ps 1, the Book of Job, and later parts of Proverbs; (4) the subject-matter of such a psalm as 147, which points back to the Restoration (147²); (5) the fact that the historical psalms, 105. 106, presuppose PJE, and were therefore composed after the first compilation of the Hex. (see HEXATEUCH). Notice in 105³¹ the lice of P, as well as, in 105³⁴, the locusts of JE; in 106¹⁷ Dathan and Abiram of JE, as well as, in 106³⁰·³¹, Phinehas, God's avenger of P.

The word passed from OT to NT. In Rev 19¹⁻⁷ it is the keynote of the song sung by the great multitude in heaven, and from the Jewish it found its way into the Christian Church.   F. H. WOODS.

HALLOHESH (הַלּוֹחֵשׁ 'the speaker of charms').— An individual or a family mentioned in connexion with the repairing of the wall (Neh 3¹², AV Halohesh) and the sealing of the covenant (Neh 10²⁴). See GENEALOGY.

HALLOW.—'Who,' says Trench, 'would now affirm of the verb "to hallow" that it is even obsolescent? yet Wallis two hundred years ago observed—"it has almost gone out of use" (fere desuevit).' He is condemning (in *English Past and Present,* p. 139 f.) the American Bible Union for dismissing from their new version words that have a suspicion of age upon them. And it is still quite true that 'hallow' *as a biblical word* is in active use, so that the Revisers felt no necessity for excluding it from either the NT of 1881 or the OT of 1885. In AV and RV it is used as a synonym for 'sanctify,' translating in OT some part of קָדַשׁ *kâdash,* and in NT twice rendering the verb ἁγιάζω (Mt 6⁹, Lk 11², both in the Lord's Prayer). In the Apocr. the same Gr. verb is rendered 'hallow' in 1 Es 1³, Jth 9¹³, Sir 33⁹, 1 Mac 4⁴⁸; and the Lat. verb *sanctificare* in 2 Es 2⁴¹ 5²⁵.

In the older versions it is more common. It is Wyclif's only word; thus Jn 17¹⁹ 'And I halwe my silf for hem, that and [1388 also] thei be halwid in treuthe'; He 2¹¹ 'Sothely he that halowith, and thei that ben halowid, of oon alle.' So Tind. in

---
* See Gray, *Heb. Prop. Names,* 149 ff., and Jastrow in *Journal of Soc. of Bib. Lit.* xiii. (1894), 101–127, and in *ZAW,* 1896, pp. 1–16. In these papers Jastrow further contends that the final יה in many Heb. proper names is not a form of the Divine name at all, but simply *an emphatic afformative.*

Lv 27¹⁶ ' If a man halowe a pece of his enhereted londe unto the Lorde, it shalbe set accordynge to that it beareth'; and in a marg. note on Dt 20⁵ (where his text is, ' Yf any man have bylt a new housse and have not dedicate it'), he says, ' Dedicat: the levites, I suppose, halowed them as we doo oure shippes.' In a note to Lv 8² he spells the word ' holow '—' Hence the pope fett holowenge of chirches, alters, font, belles, and so forth.' Cov. has ' unhallow' in Ezk 44¹⁹ ' they shal put of the clothes, wherein they have ministred . . . lest they onhalowe the people with their clothes.' In his *Expositions* (Parker Soc. p. 180) on 1 Jn 2¹⁸⁻²¹ Tind. uses ' sanctify' and ' hallow' together as quite synonymous : ' Christ in the Scripture is called The Holy, because He only sanctifieth and halloweth us.' This quotation shows the origin of the word also : from A.S. *hálig*, holy, came *hálgian*, to make holy, middle-Eng. *halyien*, later *halwe*.

The words of Mt 6⁹, Lk 11² are as old as Wyc. ' halowid be thi name,' and are found in all the versions except the Rhemish (1582), which has ' sanctified be thy name'; but the mod. editions of Rhem. (as 1898) have changed to ' hallowed be thy name.'   J. HASTINGS.

HALT.—1. *To be lame, to limp* : Gn 32³¹ ' He halted upon his thigh' (עַל־יְרֵכוֹ צֹלֵעַ, Amer. RV ' went halting'). The same vb. is tr⁴ ' halt' in Mic 4⁶· ⁷, Zeph 3¹⁹ (Amer. RV always ' is lame'). T. Fuller (*Holy State*, iii. 15) says, ' Wounds in warre are most honourable : Halting is the stateliest march of a Souldier ; and 'tis a brave sight to see the flesh of an Ancient as torn as his Colours.' And Rutherford, with a reference to Mic 4⁶· ⁷, speaks of ' God's kirk' (*Letters*, No. xli.) : ' He will have her going through a thousand deaths, and through hell, as a cripple woman, halting, and wanting the power of her one side, that God may be her staff.' The adj. ' halt' is given as the tr. of χωλός in Mt 18⁸, Mk 9⁴⁵, Lk 14²¹, Jn 5³, though everywhere else (except Ac 14⁸ ' a cripple' in AV and RV) the same adj. is rendered ' lame' (Mt 11⁵ 15³⁰· ³¹ 21¹⁴, Lk 7²² 14¹³, Ac 3² 8⁷, He 12¹³). In Lk 14²¹ RV gives ' lame,' but keeps ' halt' in the other three places. Tind. has ' halt' in Mt 11⁵ ' The blynd se, the halt goo, the lepers are clensed.'

2. *To stumble, to fail*, Ps 38¹⁷ ' For I am ready to halt,* and my sorrow is continually before me' (לְצֶלַע נָכוֹן), AVm ' ready for halting,' Del. [so Amer. RV] ' ready to fall,' with note, ' if God does not graciously interpose, he will certainly fall headlong'; Wellh.-Furness [in *PB*] ' on the verge of falling'); Jer 20¹⁰ ' All my familiars watched for my halting' (צַלְעִי שֹׁמְרֵי, Streane, ' those who watch my side,' implying a reading צֵלָע, ' ribs,' ' side'; RV ' they that watch for my halting'; Cheyne, ' either laid traps for me, or waited for me to commit some error for them to take advantage of,' who points out that the phrase ' my halting' is taken[?] from Ps 35¹⁵ 38¹⁷). To those two passages in AV the Eng. (not Amer.) RV adds Job 18¹² ' Calamity shall be ready for his halting' (לְצַלְעוֹ, AV and RVm ' at his side'), and Ps 35¹⁵ ' But when I halted they rejoiced' (וּבְצַלְעִי, AV ' But in mine adversity'). Tindal in his exposition of Mt 5¹⁷⁻¹⁹ (*Expositions*, Parker Soc. p. 38) shows us this meaning of ' halt' arising from the meaning already illustrated, ' I come not to destroy the law, but to repair it only, and to make it go upright where it halteth.' Then cf. Glanvill (*Ser.* 5), ' We have many observers, whose malice makes them critical and curious; they lay in wait for our haltings, and are glad at heart when they have caught an opportunity to revile us.' In Preface to AV 1611 the translators

* In this passage in AV Bunyan found the name of Mr. Ready-to-halt.

say of Roman Catholic scholars that they ' doe either make new Translations themselves, or follow new ones of other mens making, or note the vulgar Interpretor for halting.'

3. *To waver*, 1 K 18²¹ ' How long halt ye between two opinions?' (אֶתַּם פֹּסְחִים ; Amer. RV ' go ye halting'). The figure is the uncertain gait of one who is divided in mind between J" and Baal. The same verb is used in v.²⁶ of the irregular dance round the altar of Baal. Cf. Purchas, *Pilgrimage*, 343, ' Their religion halteth betwixt divers religions of the Turkes, Persians, and Christians of the Iacobite and Nestorian Sects.'

4. The mod. sense of *come to a standstill, stop*, does not occur in AV, but is introduced by RV into Is 10³² ' This very day shall he halt at Nob' (לַעֲמֹד, AV ' remain').   J. HASTINGS.

HAM (חָם, Χάμ).—The name of one of Noah's three sons (Gn 10¹ etc.), and founder of one of the three great families into which the biblical ethnologists divide the world. There seems little doubt that this word is the Egyptian name of Egypt (Hier. *Kem*, sometimes *p t' o-n-Kem*, ' land of Egypt,' Demot. *Kemi*, Theb. *Kême*, Bashm. *Kême*, Memph. *Khême*), and indeed in the poetical language of the Psalms the ' land of Ham' is a synonym for Miẓraim (105²³· ²⁷ 106²², cf. 78⁵¹ ; Brugsch, *Geogr. Inschr.* 73). The meaning of the word is ' black,' which appears in the Arab. *aḥamm*, fem. *ḥammā*, as well as in many Coptic derivatives (Peyron, *Lex. Copt.* 66). The origin of the appellation is to be found in the blackness of the soil of the Delta (Plutarch, *de Is. et Osir.* 33), since the Egyptians do not call themselves by this name, which corresponds with an epithet applied to rich soils generally (Ebers, *Ægypten u. die Bücher Mose's*, 55).

2. The narrative of Gn 9²¹⁻²⁴ has been analyzed with great ingenuity by Budde (*Urgeschichte*, 290 ff.), partly after the suggestions of Wellhausen, whose results are in the main as follows. The narrative is based on a document in which the place of Ham was occupied by Canaan; this is rendered practically certain by vv.²⁴· ²⁵, in which Noah, perceiving what his youngest son had done unto him, proceeds to curse Canaan, who is mentioned no less than three times in Noah's speech (vv.²⁵⁻²⁷). It is therefore probable that in v.²² ' Ham, the father of Canaan,' is a correction for ' Canaan' (cf. for the method 1 Ch 20⁵), and indeed these words show very clear signs of alteration. The family of Noah, then, according to the earlier account, consisted of Shem, Japheth, Canaan ; and the legend accounts for the subjugation of the third to the two others, implying a state of things in which the word ' Canaanite' was synonymous with ' slave.' The act imputed to Canaan is that of a little boy, and hence chronological difficulties arise if the Noah of the story be identified with the Noah of the Flood. The three sons, moreover, represent nations occupying the same country (probably Canaan), whose mutual relation is accounted for by the story, but who do not appear to have been intended to represent the progenitors of the nations of the earth. While the name ' Shem' lends itself readily to interpretation, if a caste be signified (' men ot name' or ' note,' whence ' name' or ' note' became personified), only vague conjectures can be made about the original import of ' Japheth'; but l. 16 of the Marseilles inscription shows us that we possess only an imperfect tradition of the caste-system in Semitic peoples.

3. The same ethnologist who made Noah the second founder of the human race had to divide the nations of the earth among his sons ; the names Shem and Japheth being unknown except in this tradition, could be employed without difficulty ; but the name ' Canaan' had very distinct import, and yet was too insignificant to count as one of the three world-races. For this name, therefore, in the ethnological table another known name was substituted, and the native name of Egypt lent itself well to this purpose. That Cush and Miẓraim should be included under the name of Kemi need occasion no surprise, as these two nations were known conjointly; that Cush is made the eldest son (Gn 10⁶) is perhaps due to Ethiopia being farthest from Palestine, but it may have political significance. That Canaan should be reckoned as Hamite has been thought strange, some accounting for it on the ground of national antipathy on the part of the Israelites, while others (*e.g.* Dillmann, *ad loc.*) thought it due to a tradition current in antiquity which made the Canaanites immigrants from the South. The above account of the introduction of the name Ham really gets rid of the difficulty; for Canaan's place having been taken by Ham, a place had to be found for Canaan, and this could only be in Ham's family. Ham's name was not substituted for Canaan's in the speech of Noah, partly perhaps owing to its repeated recurrence, partly perhaps because the curse of slavery could not be made to fall on the powerful nations represented by Ham's elder children. The recension of Gn which we have, where the father is made to sin, and one of the sons to receive the curse, shows us the difficulty solved as far as it was capable of solution.

4. The classification of Canaan under Ham led to a serious result for the ethnological table: whereas Canaan in the older scheme represented a subject caste, the name now had to include all the non-Israelitic inhabitants of Palestine, among whom were many races decidedly 'Semitic' in character, such as the Phœnicians. Some further difficulty was introduced by confusion between the Cush and the Cossaei, but the ground for making all the tribes mentioned in v.⁷ etc. Cushites will probably remain hidden long. The Put (which see) are probably included with the Egyptians and Nubians as being in any case a southern race. The Egyptian classification of mankind compared by M. Lefébure (*PSBA*, 1887, p. 167 ff.), while it offers some slight analogy to that with which we are dealing, does not seem to explain the name 'Ham,' or throw any real light on the problems.

5. The name 'Ham' occurs in 1 Ch 4⁴⁰, where certain settlers at Gerar found the land quiet and well cultivated, because the previous inhabitants were 'from Ham.' Some of the Rabbis compared the statement in Jg 18⁷·²⁷, where very similar language is used about people who lived 'after the fashion of the Sidonians' (also, according to the tables, Hamites, through Canaan), and indeed the passage of Ch would seem to be modelled on that of Jg. It is not, however, easy to render the words in Ch satisfactorily, since 'from Ham' should mean from the country called Ham, which is not here very intelligible, and 'of the children of Ham,' or 'from the days of Ham,' would not naturally be thus abbreviated. There is therefore ground for supposing the text corrupt, and indeed the Pesh. substituted מֵהֶם 'of them' for the חָם מִן of the text. An easier alteration is מנחם, supposing that word to have the sense of the analogous Syriac form מניח 'peaceful, easy-going,' of which examples are given in *Thes. Syr.* col. 2314.

D. S. MARGOLIOUTH.

HAM.—According to Gn 14⁵ Chedorlaomer and his allies smote the Zuzim (who may be the same as the Zamzummim of Dt 2²⁰). This last is vocalized in MT בְּהָם, which is represented by AV, RV 'in Ham.' Jerome (*Quaest. in libr. Gen.*) reads בָּהֶם. Most of the VSS vocalize בָּהֶם, hence LXX ἅμα

αὐτοῖς, 'with them.' Olshausen conjectures בְּחַמָּה 'in Hamath.' It is most probable that a proper name is intended. If 'Ham' be the correct reading, it is the name of a place that is otherwise unknown. Dillmann, following Tuch, suggests that it may have been the ancient name of the Ammonite capital Rabbath Ammon. The strange argument of Sayce (*HCM* 160 f.), that the form חָם points to a direct transcription of Gn 14 from a cuneiform document, is dealt with by Ball (*SBOT, ad loc.*).

J. A. SELBIE.

HAM (חָם), *Land of.*—A poetical designation of Egypt, used in the Psalms in reference to the sojourn there of the children of Isr. (Ps 105²³·²⁷ 106²²); so also 'the tabernacles (RV 'tents') of H.' (Ps 78⁵¹) stands for 'the dwellings of the Egyptians.' Probably in Heb. thought H. was here used as the name of the son of Noah rather than as a name for Egypt. Two derivations have been proposed for it: (1) The native name for Egypt itself was *Kmt*, in Coptic times pronounced Kêmi (hardly Khêmi), and strictly signifying the 'black land' or alluvial soil of the cultivable part, as opposed to the *Deshert* or 'red land,' *i.e.* the sandy deserts which enclosed Kêmi on all sides except the N. (2) The chief Priapic god of the Egyptians was sometimes called Menu (in Greek Min), but at other times probably Khem. If the latter reading is correct, it is almost identical with the name of the progenitor of the Hamitic peoples, and it is very remarkable that the most primitive sculptures hitherto found in Egypt represent this god (see Petrie's *Koptos*). Menu was especially worshipped on the important route from the coast of the Red Sea to Koptos, and this would impress the fact of his worship on the E. neighbours of Egypt. The characteristics of Menu are in accord with the shamelessness recorded of H. in Gn 9²⁰ff·. The derivation from *Kmt* is improbable, for phonetic reasons.

F. LL. GRIFFITH.

HAMAN (הָמָן, Ἀμάν), the son of Hammedatha, appears in the Bk of Est as the enemy of the Jews, and the chief minister of Ahasuerus. He is described as the Agagite (Est 3¹·¹⁰ etc.), but in the LXX as a **Bugean** (Βουγαῖος, 3¹ 12⁶), or a Macedonian (9²⁴ 16¹⁰). The Heb. term we should probably understand of a descent from the Amalekite king Agag (so Jos. *Ant.* XI. vi. 5, and Targ.), in which case the author of the book perhaps meant to contrast the descendant of Israel's ancient enemy with Mordecai, the descendant of Kish, the Benjamite. Provoked by Mordecai's refusal to bow before him, H. procured from the king a decree authorizing the massacre of all the Jews in the Persian dominions on the 13th Adar. He also prepared a gallows 50 cubits high for Mordecai. But queen Esther, having heard of the plot, invited H. and the king to a banquet, and there denounced H., who was forthwith hanged on his own gallows. The queen also obtained permission for her countrymen to defend themselves, and among other victims of the Jews' vengeance the ten sons of H. were slain and their bodies gibbeted.

In later times, at the Feast of Purim, it seems to have been customary to hang an effigy of H.; but as the gibbet was sometimes made in the form of a cross, riots between Jews and Christians were the result, and a warning against insults to the Christian faith was issued by the emperor Theodosius II. (*Cod. Theod.* XVI. viii. 18; cf. 21). The origin of the name H. is uncertain; Jensen connects it with the name of an Elamite divinity, *Humman* or *Humban* (cf. *Oxf. Heb. Lex.* s.v.).

H. A. WHITE.

HAMATH (חֲמָת 'fortress,' 'citadel,' or perhaps 'sacred enclosure,' see W. R. Smith, *RS*¹ 140 [ed.²

p. 150]; 'Ημάθ, 'Εμάθ, Αἰμάθ, Emath).—At the time of Amos, this was the chief city of a kingdom of the same name which surrounded the capital, extending to the S. of Riblah and even including that place (2 K 23³³ etc.). Situated on the banks of the Orontes (now called el-'Âṣi), in a narrow valley with Jebel-el-A'la on its north and south-east, and the Nusairîyeh mountains (the Mons Bargylus of the ancients) to the west, it lay on a very frequented and convenient trade-route. The opening between the Nusairîyeh mountains above Tripoli and the north point of the Lebanon chains is called in the OT 'the entrance of Hamath' (Nu 34⁸, Jos 13⁵, Ezk 47¹³⁻²¹). N. of Homs the Orontes pass leads to Hamath, S. toward Baal-gad in Cœle-Syria, E. to the great plain of the Syrian desert, and W. to the Kal'at al-Hosn and the Mediterranean.

'The entrance' or 'the approach' to Hamath is often mentioned as a territorial limit (Nu 34⁸, Jg 3³ etc.), and usually denotes the accepted northern boundary of Israelitish dominion (Jos 13⁵). The province is called 'Great Hamath' (Am 6²), and is mentioned with Damascus, Tyre, and Zidon (Zec 9²), as well as with Arpad (Jer 49²³) in the prophecies against Hadrach.

Originally a Hamite colony (Gn 10¹⁸), it flourished at the time of David (2 S 8¹⁰) under a king named Toi (or Tou), who had friendly intercourse with the Israelitish ruler. Hamath (possibly identical with Hamath-Zobah [which see] of 2 Ch 8³) came, however, afterwards under the dominion of Solomon (compare 1 K 9²¹·²⁴ with 2 Ch 8⁴), and its king was no doubt among the many princes who 'brought presents and served Solomon all the days of his life.' Hamath was regarded as the granary of N. Syria, and there Solomon built store-cities (2 Ch 8⁴). But, on the death of that king, Hamath seems to have regained her inde-pendence, as is shown by the inscriptions of Shal-maneser II. (B.C. 860), where we see that her king, Irḫulēni, made an alliance with the Hittites, Damascus (under Addu-idri=Ben-Hadad=Ben-Hadad-hidri), Ahab of Israel, and several other states. Jeroboam II. of Israel, about the year B.C. 810, 'recovered Hamath' (2 K 14²⁸) from Judah, and partly destroyed it, as well as Gath, which, in the prophecies of Amos, is spoken of along with it (Am 6²). In the Assyrian inscriptions Eni-ilu (Eniel), king of Hamath, brings tribute to Tiglath-pileser III. (730), who had parcelled out the land of Hamath among his generals, annexing 19 districts to Assyria, and transported 1223 people of Hamath to the sources of the Tigris. Sargon boasts of having rooted out the land of Hamath and dyed the skin of the foolish (?) Ilu-bi'di (variant Yau-bi'di) like wool, colonizing Hamath with 4300 Assyrians. One of those exiled thither by this king was the Mede Deioces. After what seems to have been the capture of the place by Sennacherib's Rabshakeh, or 'chief of the captains,' Hamath lost much of its importance. It is spoken of in Is 11¹¹ as one of the places containing Israelitish exiles, and is mentioned in 1 Mac 12²⁵ in connexion with the movements of Jonathan and Demetrius.

The Greeks and Romans knew it under the name of Epiphaneia, which had been given to it by Antiochus Epiphanes (Jos. Ant. I. vi. 2), though the inhabitants still called it Hamath, and its present name, Ḥamāh, is but slightly changed from its old form. In 1310 Abulfeda, the eminent Arabian scholar, a descendant of the family of Saladin, was appointed governor of the district, which had been under the Moslem power since A.D. 639, and with his death (1331) Hamath's prosperity declined.

In 1812 Burckhardt visited Hamath, saw the 'Hamath-stones' (so-called Hittite inscriptions in relief on black close-grained basalt); and the enormous water-wheels, used for bringing the waters of the Orontes to the houses and gardens situated on the hill above the river. He does not, however, mention the catacombs, said to have ex-isted high up on the right bank. The town, which is divided into four quarters, Hadher, el-Jisr, el-Aleyat, and el-Medine (the quarter of the Chris-tians), contained at Burckhardt's visit about 4446 houses and nearly 11,000 male inhabitants.

LITERATURE.—Pococke, Description of the East, II. i. 143 ff.; Burckhardt, Travels in Syria and the Holy Land (1822), pp. 145 ff.; Robinson, BRP² iii. 551; Baedeker-Socin, Pal.³ 398 f.; Delitzsch, Paradies, 275 ff.; Sayce, HCM (Index); Hommel, Semit. Völker, i. 189; Driver on Am 6²; E. Meyer, Geschichte, § 197.   I. A. PINCHES.

HAMATHITE (הַחֲמָתִי).—The gentilic name from HAMATH (which see), Gn 10¹⁸=1 Ch 1¹⁶.

HAMATH-ZOBAH (חֲמַת־צוֹבָה, B Βαισωβά, A Αἰμάθ Σωβά, Luc. 'Εμαθσουβά).—The identity of this city is still doubtful. By some scholars it is even re-garded as the same as Hamath, but the Greek form Βαισωβά would seem to indicate that it was distinct from that place. It is mentioned only once in the Scriptures (2 Ch 8³), when Solomon is said to have 'prevailed against it,' and, being spoken of in connexion with Tadmor and Hamath, we may conclude that it was in the same neighbour-hood. That it was another Hamath to which Zobah was added to distinguish it from the better-known city of Hamath is possible, but at present unprovable. It has not yet been found in the cuneiform inscriptions, consequently no light is thrown on it from that source.   I. A. PINCHES.

HAMMATH (חַמַּת 'hot spring').—'Father of the house of Rechab,' 1 Ch 2⁵⁵. See GENEALOGY.

HAMMATH (חַמַּת 'hot spring'). — One of the 'fenced' cities of Naphtali, Jos 19³⁵, probably the same as Hammon of 1 Ch 6⁷⁶ [Heb. ⁶¹] and Ham-moth-dor of Jos 21³². It is doubtless the Ḥamata of the Talmud (Erubin, v. 5; Megillah, 2b), the Emmaus or Ammàthus of Jos. (Ant. XVIII. ii. 3) and the modern Hammâm, 35 minutes' walk S. of Tiberias, so famous for its hot baths. There are four springs, the water of which reaches a tempera-ture of 144° Fahr. The taste is described by Robinson as excessively salt and bitter, like that of heated sea-water; there is also a strong smell of sulphur, but no taste of it. The neighbourhood is crowded, especially in the month of July, with patients from all parts of Syria. The baths are considered to be very efficacious in rheumatic com-plaints.

LITERATURE. — Neubauer, Géog. du Talm. 207; Robinson, BRP² ii. 383 ff.; G. A. Smith, HGHL 450 f.; Guérin, Galilée, i. 270 ff.; Buhl, GAP 115, 226; Guthe, ZDPV xiii. (1891) 284; Wilson, Recovery of Jerus. 362.   J. A. SELBIE.

HAMMEAH, THE TOWER OF, AV The tower of Meah (מִגְדַּל הַמֵּאָה, πύργος τῶν ἑκατόν, turris centum cubitorum, turris Emath), Neh 3¹ 12³⁹.—A tower on the walls of Jerus. which stood near the tower of Hananel (which see), between the Sheep gate on the east and the Fish gate on the west. These two towers, which apparently had not been pulled down when the walls were dismantled in the time of Ezra, were probably situated near the north-eastern corner of the city (cf. Jer 31³⁸, Zec 14¹⁰). Perhaps they were both defences of the fortress (birah) which commanded the temple area. The origin of the name 'tower of Hammeah,' or 'tower of the hundred' (RVm), is obscure. It has been suggested in explanation that the tower was 100 cubits high, or that it was approached by 100 steps, or that it required a garrison of 100 men (see Ryssel, *ad loc.*, pp. 153, 201 f.).   H. A. WHITE.

HAMMEDATHA (הַמְּדָתָא, 'Αμάδαθος [?, -ης]), Est 3[1. 10] 8[5] 9[10. 24]).—The father of Haman. The name is probably Persian; for the termination compare Aridatha; possibly the etymology is *mâh* = moon + *data* = given (*Oxf. Heb. Lex.*).

HAMMELECH (הַמֶּלֶךְ) occurs as a proper name in AV and RVm of Jer 36[26] 38[6], but there is little doubt that the rendering ought to be 'the king,' as in RV and AVm (LXX τοῦ βασιλέως).

HAMMER.—The Heb. word מַקָּבָה *makkâbâh* (in Jg 4[21] מַקֶּבֶת) is tr. in Arab. by two words, *mîtadat*, a wooden mallet, and *matrakat*, the ordinary Arabic word for a hammer. It was a *mîtadat*, a mallet used by the Bedawîn and others for driving tent pegs into the ground, which Jael used to kill Sisera, Jg 4[21]. By many, *makkâbâh* is considered to be the source of the name *Maccabæus*, which would thus mean 'the hammerer.' פַּטִּישׁ *pattîsh* (Is 41[7], used fig. in Jer 23[29] of the word of the LORD, and in 50[23] of Babylon, 'the hammer of the whole earth') is evidently the same as the Arab. *fatîs*, a large heavy hammer.

The hammer is probably the most ancient of all tools. In its original form, a stone held in the hand, it is often used at the present day. The form soon changed; a stick fastened to the stone gave the blow more precision and greater force. Metals superseded stones, and great variety was given to the shape of the hammer head, so as to produce a more exact effect. The hammer is a most important and valuable tool; the permanent effect produced by a blow of the lightest hammer is greater than that obtained by the steady pressure of a mass of iron many hundred times its weight.

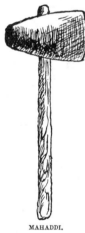

MAHADDI.

Different handicrafts require hammers of different shapes and weights, and, in Syria, each kind has a distinctive name. The hammers used in carpentry and smith work are much the same as those used in the same occupations in Europe. But in masonry the variety of hammers is great. In the quarry the rock is split by a large hammer, weighing from 18 to 22 lb., called the *mahaddi*. The head of this hammer is round at one end, being used for driving wedges into the rock. The other end is flattened from side to side, so as to confine the impact to a narrow line. This end of the hammer is used to strike the rock between the wedges, and the constant beating causes a vibration in the rock, which increases till it splits in the line of the wedges.

When the stone comes from the quarry, it is roughly shaped by the *mahaddi*, and the mason takes another kind of hammer to square it and give it a shape to fit it for building.

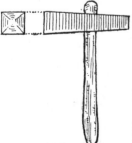

SHAKÛF.

This hammer is called the *shakûf*. Both ends of the head of this hammer are square, but the one is 1 in. square and flat, the other is nearly 2 in. square, but sunk in the centre to the depth of half an inch, so that the edges are sharp. The flat end is used for striking off projections, while the end with sharpened edges is used for squaring and trimming the stone. The stone is often used for building after being trimmed by the *shakûf*, but sometimes a border is made round the face of the stone, leaving the middle rough.

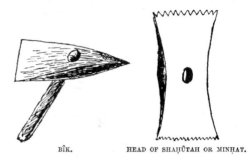

BÎK.   HEAD OF SHAHÛTAH OR MINHAT.

This is done by the *bîk*, which is a hammer with one end pointed, and the other flat and chisel-shaped.

When the stone is to be made smooth it is first made quite flat with the pointed end of the *bîk*, and is then worked over with a hammer called the *shahûtah* or *minhat*.

The *shahûtah* has two very broad chisel-shaped ends, about 4 in. broad, cut into a number of teeth like a saw. The teeth at one end are coarse and about 12 in number, and at the other end smaller and about 24 in number.

When the stone has been carefully gone over with the *shahûtah* it is sometimes polished. This is done by rubbing it with another stone, sand and water being put between.

All these tools are of very ancient date. In the oldest part of the temple of Baalbek marks of all of these tools are found. Even the three immense stones in the west wall have their upper and under surfaces smoothed with the *shahûtah*, only the tool seems to have been much smaller than the one used in Lebanon at the present time, being only about 2 or 2½ in. broad.

The hammer and chisel are used for very fine work, such as carving, or when a very sharp fine edge is to be given to a stone, seldom for any other purpose. The chisel is made of file steel. The hammer, called a *matrakat*, is so shaped that lines drawn along the faces of the hammer would meet nearly at the end of the handle. Wooden mallets are never used.

MASON'S MATRAKAT.

The stone of Lebanon is very hard limestone, which explains why hammers are preferred to chisels in hewing it.   W. CARSLAW.

HAMMOLECHETH (הַמֹּלֶכֶת 'the queen'?).—Acc. to the genealogy in 1 Ch 7[17. 18] H. was the daughter of Machir and sister of Gilead. The correctness of the text is not beyond suspicion. LXX reads Μαλέχεθ. See GENEALOGY.

HAMMON (חַמּוֹן 'hot spring').—**1.** A town in Naphtali, 1 Ch 6[76] [Heb. [61]], prob. identical with HAMMATH (which see). **2.** A town in Asher, Jos 19[28]. Its site is uncertain. Schultz suggested '*Ain Hamûl*, some 10 miles south of Tyre, but Robinson

(*BRP*² iii. 66 note) lays no great stress upon this identification. Renan (*Mission de Phénicie*, 708 ff.) found at *Khurbet Umm el-'Amud*, near the coast immediately N. of the Ladder of Tyre, two Phœnician inscriptions (*CIS* vol. i. pt. i.) in honour of Baal Hammon. In the valley to the E. is '*Ain Hamûl. Umm el-'Amûd*, 'mother of the pillar,' includes the ruins of a building which is probably a temple of Baal. On the hill side lies a great sarcophagus with a rudely carved eagle. The texts belong to the Ptolemaic period (3rd cent. B.C.). The name may be that of the Egyptian God *Amanu* or *Amen*. See *SWP* vol. i. sh. iii., and vol. iii. Appendix. The identification of Hammon with *Umm el-'Amûd* is also considered by Guérin (*Galilée*, ii. 141) and Buhl (*GAP* 229) to be the most probable.

C. R. CONDER.

HAMMOTH-DOR (חַמֹּת דֹּאר).—A Levitical city in Naphtali, Jos 21³², probably identical with HAMMATH (which see).

HAMMUEL (חַמּוּאֵל, AV Hamuel).—A Simeonite of the family of Shaul, 1 Ch 4²⁶. See GENEALOGY.

HAMONAH (הֲמוֹנָה 'multitude,' LXX Πολυάνδριον). —The name of a city to be built in commemoration of the defeat (?) of Gog (Ezk 39¹⁶). The passage is obscure, and the originality as well as the precise reading of the MT doubtful. Instead of וְגַם שְׁמ-עֵיר הֲמוֹנָה, Cornill would read וְנָבַר הֲמוֹנָה 'and it is all over with this multitude.' If the words are an interpolation, the allusion may be to the city of Bethshean, which may have derived its name Scythopolis from the Scythian invasion in the 7th cent. B.C. (See Bertholet, *Das Buch Hesekiel*, 193).

J. A. SELBIE.

HAMON-GOG (הֲמוֹן גּוֹג 'Gog's multitude,' LXX τὸ πολυάνδριον τοῦ Γώγ).—The name to be given to the valley (outside the Holy Land) where Gog and all his multitude are to be buried (Ezk 39¹¹· ¹⁵). This valley, according to the MT, was the 'Valley of the Travellers' (הָעֹבְרִים), a designation which is not found elsewhere. Hence J. D. Michaelis, followed by Bertholet and many others, reads עֲבָרִים (Abarim, Nu 27¹² 33⁴⁷). From the mountain of this name a valley may well have been called Abarim, and the locality suits the context. See further the *Comm.* of Hitzig, Smend, Cornill, Davidson, and Bertholet.

J. A. SELBIE.

HAMOR (חֲמוֹר 'he-ass') appears in Gn 33¹⁹ 34, Jos 24³², Jg 9²⁸ as 'the father of Shechem,' a Hivite by race, and 'the prince (נָשִׂיא) of the land' (Gn 34²). Jacob bought 'the parcel of ground, where he had spread his tent,' from the Hamorites, the Benê Hamor (Gn 33¹⁹ (J), cf. Jos 24³²). A different tradition is preserved in Gn 48²² (E), where Jacob gives Shechem to Joseph, and speaks of having won it by force of arms from the Amorite.

Dinah, Jacob's daughter, having been wronged by Shechem, Shechem makes an offer to take her as his wife; and is supported in his claim by his father, Hamor, who proposes also that there should be freedom of marriage between the families of Jacob and Hamor (34¹⁴⁻¹⁷). To this the sons of Jacob give their consent on condition that the Shechemites accept the rite of circumcision. The Shechemites agree to the terms, and are circumcised (v.²⁴). On the third day, when the Shechemites were unable through illness to defend themselves, Simeon and Levi and their followers fell upon them, murdered Hamor and Shechem, and carried away Dinah to their own home.

In this narrative the narrator has combined two variant traditions. 'In the one, Hamor conducts the negotiations with Jacob regarding Dinah for his son (vv.⁴· ⁶· ⁸⁻¹⁰); he receives a reply (vv.¹⁵⁻¹⁷), and in due course lays it before the assembled citizens of the town for their approval (vv.²⁰⁻²⁴). In the other, Shechem himself asks Dinah from her father and brothers, and after their reply (v.¹¹ᶠ·) immediately submits to the conditions they require (v.¹⁹).' The former is probably the narrative of P, the latter that of J.

That, under the imagery of events occurring in the history of a single family, the story preserves the recollection of important episodes in an early phase of the Israelite community, is a view which has been maintained, in recent years, by many scholars, and most ably, perhaps, by Wellhausen in his *Composition des Hexateuchs* (see especially pp. 312–319, 353–355). According to this view, Hamor and Shechem personify Canaanite clans in central Palestine; and Dinah a branch of the Israelite race, which settling in that region became rapidly merged with the native population. The attack by Simeon and Levi would then represent the recollection of some treacherous violation by these tribes of the terms upon which the new settlers had been welcomed and acknowledged.

The fact that Hamor means 'an ass,' and Shechem 'a shoulder' or 'a mountain-ridge,' makes it probable that we have in these names the appellatives of clans and families rather than of individuals. Mr. G. Buchanan Gray (*Studies in Hebrew Proper Names*, pp. 90, 99–115) has shown, as the result of investigating animal names, that 'before the amalgamation of the Hebrew tribes into a nation, totem worship and totem organization existed among some of the peoples of Canaan' (p. 115); and it is not unreasonable to connect such names as 'ass' (*Hamor*), 'wild ass' (*Piram* Jos 10³, *Anah* Gn 36², *Arad* Jg 1¹⁶), 'mouse' (*Achbor* Gn 36³⁸), with the 'totem-clans' among the early inhabitants of Canaan (cf. Jacobs, *Biblical Archæology*, pp. 64–103, on 'Totem-Clans in the Bible').

H. E. RYLE.

HAMRAN (חַמְרָן), 1 Ch 1⁴¹ (AV Amram).— An Edomite. In Gn 36²⁶ the name is more correctly given as **Hemdan** (cf. Kittel in Haupt's *SBOT* on 1 Ch 1⁴¹).

HAMUL (חָמוּל 'spared'; on the form see Wellh. *Sam.* 19).—A son of Perez and grandson of Judah, Gn 46¹²=1 Ch 2⁵, Nu 26¹. The gentilic **Hamulites** (הֲחָמוּלִי) occurs in Nu 26¹¹.

HAMUTAL (חֲמוּטַל 2 K 23³¹ and 24¹⁸, Jer 52¹ according to MT vocalization. In these last two occurrences the consonants give the form *Hamital* חמיטל, and this is supported by LXX in all three cases: Ἀμειταί, Μιτάτ, Ἀμειταάλ B, Ἀμιτάλ, Ἀμιτάθ, Ἀμιτάλ A, Ἀμιτάλ Luc., meaning possibly 'kin to the dew' *or* 'my kinsman (lit. husband's father) is the dew').—Mother of the kings Jehoahaz and Zedekiah, sons of Josiah. (See on the meaning of the name, Gray, *Heb. Proper Names*, 63; Hommel, *Anc. Heb. Trad.* 322).

C. F. BURNEY.

HANAMEL (חֲנַמְאֵל, perhaps for חֲנַנְאֵל 'El is gracious'; but see Gray, *Heb. Prop. Names*, 307, n. 2).—Jeremiah's cousin, the son of his uncle Shallum. It was from H. that Jeremiah, having the right of redemption, bought a field at Anathoth. Although Jerus. was besieged at the time, the purchase was readily made by the prophet because of his assurance that the time would come when property would once more be secure (Jer 32⁷· ⁸· ⁹· ¹²· ⁴⁴).

J. A. SELBIE.

HANAN (חָנָן, Ἀνάν).—**1.** One of the Levites who assisted Ezra in reading and explaining the Law to the people (Neh 8⁷). He is probably the same as the Levite Hanan who signed the covenant (Neh

10¹⁰ [Heb.¹¹]), as several of the Levit. names in this passage are found also in 8⁷. The name is wanting in the LXX of 8⁷ and of 10¹⁰ (Bא*); but in 1 Es 9⁴⁸ we find Ananias ('Aνανίας A, "Aνvas B). **2.** The son of Zaccur the son of Mattaniah, one of the four treasurers appointed by Neh. over the storehouses in which the tithes were kept (Neh 13¹³). He was probably a Levite, and perhaps represented the singers and porters; for in 11¹⁷ 12⁸· ²⁵· ³⁵ Mattaniah is named as a Levit. house representing the sons of Asaph. Others, however, regard H. as a layman. **3.** A Benjamite chief (1 Ch 8²³). **4.** The youngest son of Azel, a descendant of Saul (1 Ch 8³⁸=9⁴⁴). **5.** One of David's mighty men (1 Ch 11⁴³). **6.** The son of Igdaliah. The sons of H. had a chamber in the temple (Jer 35⁴). **7.** The head of a family of Nethinim who returned with Zerubbabel (Ezr 2⁴⁶, Neh 7⁴⁹). Called **Anan** in 1 Es 5³⁰. **8. 9.** Two of 'the chiefs of the people' who sealed the covenant bore this name (Neh 10²²· ²⁶). See GENEALOGY.   H. A. WHITE.

HANANEL (חֲנַנְאֵל 'El is gracious'). — The name of a tower on the wall of Jerusalem. It is four times mentioned in OT: in Neh 3¹ in connexion with the repairing, and in 12³⁹ in connexion with the dedication of the walls; in Jer 31³⁸ and Zec 14¹⁰ as a boundary of the restored and glorified Jerusalem. In both the passages in Neh it is coupled with the tower of **Hammeah** (which see), and some have supposed it to be identical with the latter. From Neh 12³⁹ we gather that these two (?) towers lay between the Sheep gate and the Fish gate, and from Jer and Zec that the tower of Hananel was at the N.E. corner of the city. Conder thinks that Hananel and Hammeah belonged to the 'castle' or 'fortress' (birah Neh 2⁸, in Gr. βάρις, Jos. Ant. XVIII. iv. 3; BJ I. iii. 3, v. 4) of the temple. See JERUSALEM. Ryle (Ezr. and Neh. 173) also suggests that Hananel may be an 'outwork of the great fortress at the point where the city wall ran into it.' A similar opinion is expressed by Buhl (GAP 141).
     J. A. SELBIE.

HANANI (חֲנָנִי, 'Aνανί, 'Aνανίας Neh 7²).—**1.** A brother, or more prob. near kinsman, of Neh., who brought tidings to Susa of the distressed condition of the Jews in Pal. (Neh 1²). Under Neh. he was made one of the governors of Jerus. (7²). The name is perhaps a shortened form of Hananiah. **2.** A son of Heman (1 Ch 25⁴). **3.** The father of Jehu the seer (1 K 16¹). It was H. who, according to the Chronicler, reproved Asa for entering into alliance with Syria, and whom the angry king cast into prison (2 Ch 16⁷). **4.** A priest of the sons of Immer who had married a foreign wife (Ezr 10²⁰). Called **Ananias** in 1 Es 9²¹. **5.** A chief musician mentioned in connexion with the dedication of the walls of Jerus. (Neh 12³⁶).   H. A. WHITE.

HANANIAH (חֲנַנְיָהוּ 'J" hath been gracious'). —**1.** One of the prophets of the anti-Chaldæan party (LXX calls him ψευδοπροφήτης) in the reign of Zedekiah. His encounter with Jeremiah is related in Jer 28. A native of Gibeon, he was probably a priest (Jos 21¹⁷), like Jeremiah himself, whose characteristic style he seems to imitate in his attack. He, too, stands in the temple (cf. 26²), and, using Jeremiah's constant title for God, he prophesies the return from Babylon within two years (contrast Jeremiah's seventy, 25¹²) of the temple vessels, Jeconiah, and the captives (contrast 22²⁷ 27²), and then, pointing to the yoke on Jeremiah's neck (27²), he concludes as he had begun: 'I will break the yoke of the king of Babylon.' With sad irony Jeremiah replied: 'Amen; the Lord do so,' and then pointed out that, as the general tone of former true prophecy

had been minatory, a prophecy of peace would need an accurate fulfilment to vindicate its divine origin. H. then repeated his oracle in symbolic form (cf. 19¹⁰), breaking Jeremiah's yoke. Jeremiah retired in silence, but soon returned to tell H. that his breaking the wooden bar merely signified that Nebuchadnezzar's yoke would be of iron, and to announce H.'s death—the punishment of a lying prophet (Dt 18²⁰), who had spoken also rebellion against the Lord (Dt 13⁶). Within two months H. died (Jer 28¹⁷).
2. The first of Daniel's three companions (Dn 1⁶). He received the name of Shadrach (whose meaning is much disputed; see Bevan, Comm. on Dan., p. 61). They joined Daniel in his ascetic resolve, and shared his triumph (1¹⁹) and subsequent peril (2¹³). Through their prayers (2¹⁷⁻¹⁹) the king's dream was revealed to Daniel, and at his request (2⁴⁹) they were appointed 'over the affairs of the province of Babylon,' and still further promoted (3³⁰) after their miraculous deliverance from the fiery furnace. In the Gr. interpolation after Dn 3²³ Azariah is most prominent (Song of the three Children vv.²· ²⁶, contrast ⁶⁶). Their deliverance is alluded to 1 Mac 2⁵⁹, He 11³³· ³⁴. **3.** See No. 2 in next article. **4.** 1 Ch 3¹⁹· ²¹ a son of Zerub., identified by Lord A. Hervey with Joanan (Lk 3²⁷), Rhesa being a title of Zerub. which has crept into the text (Smith, DB s. GENEALOGY OF CHRIST). Bertheau conjectures that the six names in 1 Ch 3²¹ are all sons of H. **5.** 1 Ch 8²⁴ a Benjamite. **6.** 1 Ch 25⁴· ²³ a 'son' of Heman, leader of the 16th course of temple musicians. **7.** 2 Ch 26¹¹ one of Uzziah's captains who superintended the organization of the army. **8.** Ezr 10²⁸, 1 Es 9²⁹ Ananias, one of those 'that had married strange women.' **9.** See No. 1 in next article. **10.** Neh 3³⁰ son of Shelemiah; one of those who repaired the wall, possibly = No. 9, and descendant of No. 13. **11.** Neh 12¹² a priest, chief of the course of Jeremiah, when Joiakim was high priest, possibly mentioned 12⁴¹ as present at the dedication of the walls. **12.** Jer 36¹² father of Zedekiah, who was one of the princes of Judah in the reign of Jehoiakim. **13.** Jer 37¹³ grandfather of Irijah, 'a captain of the ward,' who apprehended Jeremiah on the charge of desertion to the Chaldæans.   N. J. D. WHITE.

HANANIAH (חֲנַנְיָה, 'Aνανιά, 'Aνανίας, 'J" has been gracious').—**1.** One of the guild of perfumers (AV apothecaries) who in the days of Neh. repaired a portion of the wall of Jerus., near the 'broad wall' (Neh 3⁸). He is perhaps the same as H. the son of Shelemiah, who is mentioned as repairing another portion of the wall, near the E. gate (3³⁰). **2.** The governor of the castle, i.e. of the birah, or fortress on the N. side of the temple. Neh., who describes him as 'a faithful man, and one that feared God above many,' appointed him one of the two officers in command of Jerus. (Neh 7²).
     H. A. WHITE.

HAND.—The word 'hand' is used in the Eng. versions of the Bible with a variety of meaning which can be but partially illustrated from other literature. This is due to the remarkable freedom with which the Heb. word יָד yâd is employed—a freedom which does not belong to χείρ to the same extent (though even in NT, chiefly through the influence of LXX, χείρ is found in some specially biblical meanings), so that the variety of usage is chiefly characteristic of OT.

It will conduce to clearness if, first of all, a résumé is given of the use of yâd in Heb., following Oxf. Heb. Lex.
1. The hand of man (Gn 3²² etc.), or anthropopathically of God (Ezk 8³); including the wrist (Gn 24²²· ³⁰· ⁴⁷ 38²⁸ bis· ²⁹· ³⁰, Jg 15¹⁴); standing for the finger alone (Gn 41⁴², Est 3¹⁰).
2. The hand as in use, as Gn 49²⁴ 'arms of his hands,' i.e. arms which make his hands serviceable; 2 K 9²⁴ 'he filled his hand with the bow,' i.e. seized it; and 'fill the hand' of the priest

=consecrate, install (perhaps from the idea of giving him the selected portions of the sacrifice : see FILL) ; a 'hand weapon' (lit. 'weapon of the hand') Nu 35[18] ; and idols the work of man's hand (Is 2[8]), as man is the work of God's hand (Job 14[15]). Special ways in which the hand is used are (1) to kiss the mouth (Job 31[27]) ; (2) to be laid on the mouth to express silence (Job 40[4], Mic 7[16]) ; (3) the debt is 'the lending of the hand' (Neh 10[31]), and the creditor 'the master of the lending of the hand' (Dt 15[2]) ; (4) the lifting of the hand (to heaven) is the taking of an oath (Dt 32[40]) or the sign of prayer (Ps 28[2]) ; (5) to shake (lit. 'brandish') the hand is to defy (Is 10[32]) ; (6) to give the hand is to pledge (Ezr 10[19]) or to submit (1 Ch 29[24]).

3. *The hand is strong, helpful*, (*a*) of man : Israel went out of Egypt 'with an high hand' (Ex 14[8]), *i.e.* boldly, defiantly ; and to act 'with an high hand' against *J"*, is to act presumptuously (Nu 15[30]) ; so, to be 'short of hand' (2 K 19[26]) is to be of small power ; to strengthen one's hands is to help (Jg 9[24]), and the dropping down of the hands is the failure of strength (2 S 4[1]). (*b*) Of God : His hands are stretched forth to smite (Ex 9[15]) ; or to deliver (Ex 13[3. 4. 16], Dt 4[24]), the opposite being the 'shortened' hand (Is 50[2] 59[1]) ; it is a 'good' hand when it blesses (Ezr 7[9] 8[18], Neh 2[8. 18]), as protection is in the shadow of the hand of *J"* (Is 49[2]) ; and under inspiration the prophet is in the grasp of God's hand (2 K 3[15], Is 8[11], Ezk 13[3] 3[14. 22] 37[1] 40[1]).

4. The hand is used figuratively to express *strength* or *power* (cf. Assyr. *idu* 'strength') : Jos 8[20] 'there was not in them strength (lit. 'hands') to flee' ; Ps 76[5] 'None of the men of might have found their hands,' *i.e.* their powers are paralyzed in death. Of him who cannot bring a lamb or two turtle doves for sacrifice it is said, 'his hand cannot reach to' (Lv 5[7-11] 14[21]). A display of power is 'a mighty hand' (Dt 34[12] ; cf. Job 27[11], Ps 78[42]) ; and a grand achievement 'a great hand' (Ex 14[31]).

5. (1) The 'hand' is used for the *side*, 1 S 4[13] 'the wayside,' lit. 'the hand of the way' (but see Driver, *ad loc.*) ; Dt 23[7] 'all the side of the river Jabbok' (RV), lit. 'all the hand' ; Gn 34[21] 'the land is wide of both hands,' *i.e.* in all directions ; Jer 6[3] 'every one in his place,' lit. 'in his hand.' (2) Other technical senses are : a *sign* (1 S 15[12], 2 S 18[18]) ; a *part* or *share* (Gn 47[24], 2 S 19[43], 2 K 11[7], Neh 11[1]) ; *time, repetition* (Gn 43[34], Dn 1[20]). And in the pl.: *supports* (1 K 7[35. 36] 10[19 *bis*] ‖ 2 Ch 9[18 *bis*]), *tenons* (Ex 26[17. 19 *bis* 36[22. 24 *bis*]).

6. There are also many peculiar prepositional phrases, but these will be best understood in their Eng. equivalents.

1. The hand is a figure for the *action, influence*, or *power* of God or man : Jg 1[35] 'the hand of the house of Joseph prevailed' ; 1 S 22[17] 'Turn, and slay the priests of the Lord ; because their hand also is with David' ; 2 K 3[15] 'And it came to pass, as the minstrel played, that the hand of the LORD came upon him' ; Ezr 7[6] 'according to the hand of the LORD his God upon him' (so 7[9] 8[18], Neh 2[8. 18], sometimes with 'good' as epithet of 'hand,' the meaning being always the favour of God actively bestowed and proved by its results) ; Job 6[9] 'Even that it would please God to destroy me ; that he would let loose his hand, and cut me off !' Ps 78[42] 'They remembered not his hand, nor the day when he delivered them from the enemy' ; 89[48] 'Shall he deliver his soul from the hand of the grave ?' (RV 'power of Sheol') ; 109[27] 'That they may know that this is thy hand, that thou, LORD, hast done it' ; Pr 21[1] 'The king's heart is in the hand of the LORD, as the rivers of water ; he turneth it whithersoever he will' ; Ec 9[10] 'Whatsoever thy hand findeth to do, do it with thy might' ; Jer 15[17] 'I sat alone because of thy hand' ('The Hand of J" is a fig. expression for the self-revealing and irresistible power of J" ; it is therefore equivalent to the Arm of J" [Is 53[1]], but is used in preference with regard to the divinely-ordained actions and words of the prophets'—Cheyne).

In this connexion the foll. passages deserve attention : 1. Dt 33[8] 'Let his hands be sufficient for him' ; Heb. יָדָיו רָב לֹו ; RV 'With his hands he contended for himself,' RVm 'Let his hands be sufficient for him,' or 'for them.' Driver mentions Stade's 'plausible conjecture' יָרֵב רִיב לֹו (addressed to God) 'with thy hands contend for it' ; but his own tr. is 'with his hands he hath contended for it.' The verse contains Moses' blessing on Judah ; and as Judah's desire for the reunion of the people is given in the previous clause, these words are understood by Driver as expressing Judah's services for the common weal ; LXX καὶ αἱ χεῖρες αὐτοῦ διακρινοῦσιν αὐτῷ ; Vulg. 'manus ejus pugnabunt pro eo' ; Wyc. 1382 'his hoondis shulen fight for it,' 1388 'hise hondis schulen fighte for hym' ; Tind. 'let his handes fyght for him' ; Cov. 'Let his handes multiplye him' (taking רָב from רָבַב 'to increase,' not from רִיב 'to strive') ; similarly Calvin (*Sermons upon Deut.*), Golding's trans. 'Let his handes suffise him, because thou wilt bee his helpe against his enemies' ; whence Gen. 'His hands shalbe sufficient for him, if thou help him against his enemies' ; Bish. 'His hands shalbe good ynough

for him,' whence AV ; but Dou. (after Vulg.) 'his handes shal fight for him.'

2. Ps 17[14] 'Deliver my soul from the wicked, which is thy sword : from men which are thy hand, O LORD' (מְמִתִים־יָדְךָ יהוה) ; RV 'From men, by thy hand,' RVm as AV. Nearly all mod. expositors * take the 'sword' and the 'hand' as the instruments by which *J"* is to rescue the soul of His servant, as RV. But King still accepts the AV tr., which makes wicked men God's sword, and worldly men His 'hand' or instrument (cf. Is 10[5] 'Ho Assyrian, the rod of mine anger !'). The passage is, however, suspected, and its opening words rejected as a gloss by Cheyne, Kautzsch, Wellhausen, *et al.* See *Expos. Times,* v. 431.

3. Ps 80[17] 'Let thy hand be upon the man of thy right hand' (תְּהִי־יָדְךָ עַל־אִישׁ יְמִינֶךָ), *i.e.* 'put forth thy power to protect the people which thy right hand made into a nation and delivered from Egypt'—Kirkpatrick. Wellh.-Furness tr. יָדֶךָ 'thine arm.'

4. Ps 89[25] 'I will set his hand also in the sea, and his right hand in the rivers,' RV ' on the sea . . . on the rivers.' The ref. is to the extent of the King's dominion—from the Mediterranean to the Euphrates.

2. It follows that the hand is often a figure for the person, especially the person acting :† Lv 14[32] 'This is the law of him in whom is the plague of leprosy, whose hand is not able to get that which pertaineth to his cleansing' (RV 'who is not able') ; so Nu 6[21] ; 1 S 23[16] 'And Jonathan, Saul's son, arose, and went to David into the wood, and strengthened his hand in God' (cf. Is 35[3] 'strengthen ye the weak hands, and confirm the feeble knees'). Shaks. occasionally uses 'hand' in the same way, as *Meas. for Meas.* v. i. 491—

> 'Friar, advise him :
> I leave him to your hand.'

3. The above and other idioms are found in the foll. phrases :—

1. *At hand.* To be at hand is to be near, whether of time or of place. When the ref. is to an event, as 'the day of the LORD' (Is 13[6], Jl 1[15], Zeph 1[7]), there is no ambiguity ; but when a person is referred to, it is sometimes a question whether place or time is spoken of. In OT 'at hand' is the tr. of קָרַב to be near (Gn 27[41], Dt 15[9], Ezk 12[23], and [in Piel] Ezk 36[8] 'for they are at hand to come' (קֵרְבוּ לָבוֹא), or the adj. קָרוֹב 'near' (Dt 32[35], Is 13[6], Jer 23[23], Jl 1[15], Zeph 1[7]), of which the most luminous passage is Jer 23[23] 'Am I a God at hand, saith the LORD, and not a God afar off ?' In NT 'at hand' is mostly the tr. of the vb. ἐγγίζω, to come near (Mt 3[2] 4[17] 10[7] 26[45. 46], Mk 1[15] 14[42], Ro 13[12] 1 P 4[7]), or of the adj. ἐγγύς, 'near' (Mt 26[18], Jn 2[13] 7[2], Ph 4[5], Rev 1[3] 22[10]), both of which are used of place and of time ; once also of ἐνίστημι (2 Th 2[2] 'Be not . . . troubled . . . by letter as from us, as that the day of Christ is at hand,' ὡς ὅτι ἐνέστηκεν ἡ ἡμέρα τοῦ Χριστοῦ, edd. Κυρίου for Χριστοῦ, RV 'as that the day of the Lord is now present' ; ‡ Ellicott, 'to the effect that the day of the Lord is now come') ; and once of ἐφίσταμαι (2 Ti 4[6] 'the time of my departure is at hand,' ἐφέστηκε, RV 'is come').

The only doubtful passage is Ph 4[5] 'The Lord is at hand,' ὁ Κύριος ἐγγύς. Most ancient and nearly all mod. expositors understand the reference to be to the Second Advent, the words being a translation of the Aram. Μαράν ἀθά of 1 Co 16[22], which some think may have been a set form of warning in the apostolic Church. But a few take the ἐγγύς to be local, 'The Lord is near us,' either referring to the perpetual presence of Christ (cf. Mt 28[20]), or (taking Κύριος as God) to God's helpful providence in time of need. See Vincent, *ad loc.* (who accepts the ref. to the Second Coming) ; Manning, *Sermons,* iii. 241 ; Harden, *Ch. of Eng. Eccles. Rev.,* Aug. 30, 1890 ; Moule, *Thoughts on the Spiritual Life* (who refer to Christ's constant presence : Moule compares Ps 119[151] 'Thou art near [ἐγγύς], O Lord') ; and *Expos. Times,* ii. 2 f. The chief argument for the Second Coming is the apostle's use of Κύριος, on which see Winer, *Gram.* p. 154.

2. *At no hand.* This phrase occurs only in Preface to AV 1611. Its meaning is 'by no means.'

---

* Including Davidson, *Syntax*, § 109. 3, p. 154.

† This does not spoil Trench's contrast between the mod. custom of describing working men as so many 'hands' and the biblical idiom 'souls' (Ac 24[1]). See *Study of Words*, 95 f.

‡ The AV tr. of this passage brings it into conflict with Ro 13[12] 'The night is far spent, the day is at hand,' making the apostle deny here what he there affirms. RV removes the discrepancy.

Cf. T. Fuller, *Holy Warre*, ii. 36 (p. 92), 'The Caliph demurred hereat, as counting such a gesture a diminution to his State ; and at no hand would give him his hand bare, but gave it in his glove.' Cf. Sir John Harington's version of Ps 137³—

> 'Come, sing us now a song, say they,
> As once you song at anie hand.'

3. *At the hand of*=from : Gn 9⁵ 'And surely your blood of your lives will I require ; at the hand of every beast will I require it, and at the hand of man ; at the hand of every man's brother will I require the life of man' (מִיַּד, lit. 'from the hand of' ; LXX ἐκ χειρός,* Vulg. 'de manu,' Wyc. 'of the hoond') ; 33¹⁰ 'Receive my present at my hand' ; 2 S 13⁵· ⁶· ¹⁰, 2 K 9⁷ 'And thou shalt smite the house of Ahab thy master, that I may avenge the blood of my servants the prophets, and the blood of all the servants of the Lord, at the hand of Jezebel' ; Is 1¹² 'When ye come to appear before me, who hath required this at your hand, to tread my courts?' ; Rev 19² 'He hath judged the great whore . . . and hath avenged the blood of his servants at her hand' (ἐκ τῆς [edd. omit τῆς] χειρὸς αὐτῆς, Vulg. 'de manibus ejus' : the meaning, which is 'from her' or 'upon her,' as 'upon Jezebel' in 2 K 9⁷, is missed by Gen. NT, 'and hath advenged the blood of his servants shed by her hand.' The phrase is frequently used by Shaks., as *Merry Wives*, II. ii. 218, 'Have you received no promise of satisfaction at her hands?' In Neh 11²⁴ occurs the phrase 'at the king's hand,' —'And Pethahiah . . . was at the king's hand in all matters concerning the people' (לְיַד הַמֶּלֶךְ). The meaning of the phrase is clear, but the scope of Pethahiah's office is not so clear. See Ryle (*Ezra and Neh.* in Camb. Bible), and art. PETHAHIAH.

4. *By the hand of*='by,' or 'by means of' : Ex 4¹³ 'And he said, O my Lord, send, I pray thee, by the hand of him whom thou wilt send' (בְּיַד) ; Lv 8³⁶ 'So Aaron and his sons did all things which the LORD commanded by the hand of Moses.'

5. *By strength of hand* : Ex 13⁴· ¹⁴· ¹⁶, as 13¹⁴ 'By strength of hand the LORD brought us out from Egypt.' See 'With a strong hand' below.

6. *To come to one's hand* : Gn 32¹³ 'And he lodged there that same night ; and took of that which came to his hand a present for Esau his brother' (וַיִּקַּח מִן־הַבָּא בְיָדוֹ, LXX καὶ ἔλαβεν ὧν ἔφερεν δῶρα, Vulg. 'separavit de his quæ habebat,' RV 'took of that which he had with him') ; Jg 20⁴⁸ 'And the men of Israel turned again upon the children of Benjamin, and smote them with the edge of the sword, as well the men of every city, as the beast, and all that came to hand' (עַד כָּל־הַנִּמְצָא, AVm 'all that was found,' RV 'all that they found') ; 1 S 25⁸ 'Give, I pray thee, whatsoever cometh to thine hand unto thy servants' (אֵת אֲשֶׁר תִּמְצָא יָדֶךָ, LXX ὃ ἐὰν εὕρῃ ἡ χείρ σου).

7. *Fall in hand with* : Only in Preface to AV, 'For not long after *Christ, Aquila* fell in hand with a new Translation, and after him *Theodotion*, and after him *Symmachus*' ; and 'Neither, to be short, were we the first that fell in hand with translating the Scripture into English.' The meaning is 'set about,' 'undertake,' mod. 'take in hand to.'

8. *From one's hand*=from oneself : Gn 4¹¹ 'And now art thou cursed from the earth, which hath opened her mouth to receive thy brother's blood from thy hand' ; 38²⁰, cf. Ps 71⁴ Wyc. 'My God, tac me awey fro the hond of the synnere ; and fro the hond of the doere agen the lawe.'

9. *In hand.* This phrase has different meanings : (1) 'In progress,' 1 S 20¹⁹ 'when the business was in hand' (בְּיוֹם הַמַּעֲשֶׂה, AVm 'in the day of the business,' LXX ἐν τῇ ἡμέρᾳ τῇ ἐργασίμῃ, Vulg.

'in die quando operari licet'). Cf. Shaks. *Venus*, 912—

> 'Full of respects, yet nought at all respecting,
> In hand with all things, nought at all effecting.'

(2) *In one's hand*='with one,' or 'in one's possession,' Gn 35⁴ 'And they gave unto Jacob all the strange gods that were in their hand' ; 39³ 'And his master saw . . . that the LORD made all that he did to prosper in his hand' ; Dt 24¹ 'let him write a bill of divorcement and give in her hand' ; 1 S 17²² 'And David left his carriage [RV 'baggage'] in the hand (עַל־יַד) of the keeper of the carriage' ; Is 44²⁰ 'Is there not a lie in my right hand?' ; 1 Ch 29¹² 'In thine hand is power and might ; and in thine hand it is to make great, and to give strength unto all.' Sometimes, as in the last passage, the meaning is rather 'in one's power,' or 'under one's control.' So Gn 24¹⁰ 'all the goods of his master were in his hand' ; Job 12¹⁰ 'In whose hand is the soul of every living thing' ; Jer 26¹⁴ 'As for me, behold I am in your hand : do with me as seemeth good and meet unto you' ; Sir 15¹⁴ 'He himself made man from the beginning, and left him in the hand of his counsel' (ἐν χειρὶ διαβουλίου αὐτοῦ, RV 'in the hand of his own counsel').

(3) To 'put one's life in one's hand' is to expose it, risk it, in making a venture. The phrase occurs in Jg 12³, 1 S 19⁵ 28²¹, Job 13¹⁴ ; and in a slightly different form in Ps 119¹⁰⁹ 'My soul is continually in my hand' ; cf. also Ad. Est 14⁴ 'For my danger is in mine hand' (ὅτι κίνδυνός μου ἐν χειρί μου).

(4) In Gal 3¹⁹ occurs the expression 'in the hand of,' meaning 'by means of' : 'the law . . . was ordained by angels in the hand of a mediator,' Gr. ἐν χειρί, a frequent trⁿ in LXX of Heb. בְּיַד. Both the Gr. and the Eng. have accepted the Heb. phrase, regardless of their own proper idiom, and that not only in the use of 'hand,' but also by using 'in'. RV prefers 'by the hand of.'

10. *Lay hand on.* See LAY.

11. *Of one's hand*='from one,' as Gn 21³⁰ 'these seven ewe lambs shalt thou take of my hand' ; 39¹ 'And Joseph was brought down to Egypt ; and Potiphar . . . bought him of the hands [ed. 1611 'hand,' so RV] of the Ishmaelites' ; or=simply 'my,' as Gn 31²⁹ 'It is in the power of my hand [=it is in my power] to do you hurt.'

12. *On this, that hand.* The phrase 'on this (that, etc.) hand' for 'on this side' is now biblical and archaic. Wright (*Bible Word-Book*², 303) quotes Holland, *Pliny*, xxxvi. 5 (ed. 1637), 'The fierie goddesse Vesta, sitting in a chaire, accompanied with two hand-maidens set upon the ground of each hand of her.' Shaks., however, uses the expression quite freely, as *Merry Wives*, II. ii. 24— 'I, I, I myself sometimes, leaving the fear of Heaven on the left hand, and hiding mine honour in my necessity, am fain to shuffle, to hedge, and to lurch.' In AV we find Gn 14¹⁵ 'Hobah, which is on the left hand of Damascus' ; Ex 38¹⁵ 'and for the other side (פֵּאָה) of the court gate, on this hand and that hand (מִזֶּה וּמִזֶּה) were hangings' ; 2 K 23¹³ 'And the high places that were before Jerusalem, which were on the right hand of the mount of corruption' (מִימִין לְ).

13. *Out of hand.* The phrase 'out of the hand of' for 'out of the power of,' especially after the verb to deliver, occurs frequently. But twice we find 'out of hand,' meaning 'at once,' Nu 11¹⁵ 'Kill me, I pray thee, out of hand' (הָרְגֵנִי נָא הָרֹג, LXX ἀπόκτεινόν με ἀναιρέσει) ; To 4¹⁴ 'Give him it out of hand' (παραυτίκα). So North, *Plutarch* (Demosthenes, p. 853), 'Thereupon he went with a chearefull countenance into the assembly of the councell, and told them there, that he had a certaine dreame that promised great good hap,

and that out of hand, unto the Athenians'; Golding, *Calvin's Sermons upon Deuteronomie* (No. 192, on Dt 33[3-7]), 'Wee see then that things shall not [alwayes] come to passe out of hande, immediatly after that God hath promised them'; Golding, *Calvin's Sermons upon Job* (No. 119, on Job 32[1-3]), 'We knowe that the world did out of hand fall away from God'; and (in same sermon) 'Why doth he not kill me out of hande?'

14. *Put one's hand.* Ex 23[1] 'Put not thine hand with the wicked to be an unrighteous witness'—a lit. tr. of the Heb., which means to 'go hand in hand with.'

15. *Under the hand of:* Gn 41[35] 'And let them . . . lay up corn under the hand of Pharaoh' (תַּחַת יַד־פַּרְעֹה); Ex 21[20] 'And if a man smite his servant . . . and he die under his hand'; Nu 4[28] 'their charge shall be under the hand of Ithamar'; Jg 9[29] 'And would to God this people were under my hand!'; 1 S 21[3] 'Now therefore what is under thine hand? Give me five loaves of bread in mine hand.'

16. *With a strong* (*high*, etc.) *hand* is a phrase which is very often used of God's deliverances, Ex 6[1] 13[9] 14[8] 32[11], Dt 5[15] 7[19] etc.

For the theological significance of the word see next article.   J. HASTINGS.

HAND.—The appearance of this word in the Bible is in some cases due to Eng. idiom. Thus the expressions 'at hand' (though Heb. had a corresponding idiom, Job 15[23]), and 'handful' are used where the original idea was simply that of 'nearness' or 'fulness.' So, too, in the term of measurement, 'a palm' or 'handbreadth' טֶפַח, the root idea seems to be that of *extension* only.

For the *hand* proper two words are employed—one of them יָד *yâdh*, denoting it *open* or *flat*, the other כַּף *kaph*, *closed* or *curved*. A third word, חָפְנַיִם *ḥophnaim*, was sometimes used of the *two hands clenched* or *grasping* an object. To these must be added יָמִין *yâmîn*, and שְׂמֹאל *sĕmô'l*, *right* and *left*, which, as in other languages, came to stand by themselves for right and left *hand*.

It is only idiomatic phrases derived from the various functions of the hand that call for notice here. These functions are to mark position, exert power, and express emotion, and the idioms may be conveniently arranged in three corresponding classes.

1. So usual was it to employ the hand to describe situation, that יָד from its sense of *side*, which is 11 times used to tr. it, came to carry that of *place*, and is so rendered 8 times. Cf. *coast* 6 times, *border* twice.

In three of these instances (1 S 15[12], 2 S 18[18], Is 56[5]) *place* evidently stands for a *monument* of some kind, possibly a pillar with a hand sculptured on it as an emblem of power or success. Such monuments appear to have been common in Phœnicia, and the hand has in many countries served as an emblem of good fortune.

'On the right hand,' 'on the left hand,' are, of course, common phrases, while the custom of facing the E. when denoting geographical position made these phrases in Pal. equivalent to S. and N. respectively.

The right hand was the place of an accuser in a court of justice (Ps 109[6], Zec 3[1]); but, from the sense of security given by the presence of a comrade in battle on the unshielded side, the right came to be the place of a protector (Ps 16[8] 109[31], Ac 2[25]).

Religion had also its use for these phrases. To turn from the law of God neither to the right hand nor the left is a frequent scriptural expression for loyalty to the divine King. To sit down at His right hand was the glory reserved for the exalted Son (Ps 110[1], Mk 14[62]).

2. As used to work with or to fight with, the hand became a synonym for *strength* (Jos 8[20]), and supplied innumerable metaphorical expressions, many of which, from their religious use, have become as universal as they are sacred. When he wished to denote God's power, the Israelite spoke of God's *hand*. See ARM. He saw it outstretched to perform wonders of mercy for himself, or wonders of judgment for his enemies. It was a *good* hand and a *mighty* hand, and it was watched 'as the eyes of servants look unto the hand of their masters, and as the eyes of a maiden unto the hand of her mistress' (Ps 123[2]). It became, indeed, an emblem not only of might, exerted to defend or destroy, not only of help and guidance, but of Providence (Ps 77[10]). Prophetic inspiration, too, was often indicated by the phrase 'the hand of the Lord was upon' (1 K 18[46]), while God was said to speak 'by the hand of,' *i.e.* by means of, a prophet.

It is not always easy to determine whether the mention of the hand has passed out of the region of anthropomorphic representation into that of pure metaphor. At all events the imagery is fearlessly bold in expressions like those of Ps 74[11], Is 49[16].

3. The use of the hands to express emotion gave rise to many familiar biblical expressions. They were lifted in prayer (Ps 134[2]), extended in expostulation (Is 65[2]), clasped in a bargain (Pr 6[1]), folded in sleep (Pr 6[10]). By their movement a blessing was conveyed (Lv 9[22]), an oath was registered (Dt 32[40]), or a defiance offered (2 S 20[21]). As a religious symbol, the *imposition of hands* in ordination to a sacred office grew out of the natural gesture that accompanied the patriarchal blessing. See LAYING ON OF HANDS.

The act of cleansing the hands was fruitful in phrases. To wash one's own hands was a protestation of innocence (Dt 21[6.7], Mt 27[24]); to pour water on the hands of another, of dependence or discipleship (2 K 3[11]). The idea of ceremonial purity or impurity enters into the expressions 'clean hands' of the Psalms and 'unwashen hands' of the Gospels.

There is one phrase which, from the obscurity of its origin, causes a little difficulty. 'To fill the hand' (AVm where the text has 'consecrate,' Ex 28[41] etc.) was a regular term for the investiture of a priest. Some explain by the supposition that part of the sacrifice was placed in the neophyte's hand as a symbol of his office. Others think of the presentation of the priestly tithe. Another, and perhaps better explanation, makes the expression entirely metaphorical for the bestowal of office, as we might say 'the priesthood was put into his hands' (cf. Moore's *Judges*, p. 380, and see art. FILL).   A. S. AGLEN.

HANDBREADTH.—See WEIGHTS AND MEASURES.

HANDKERCHIEF.—See NAPKIN.

HANDLE.—The 'handles of the lock' (properly, as RV, 'the handles of the bolt') of the door are referred to in Ca 5[5], the word being כַּף *kaph*, usually the palm of the hand or sole of the foot. See KEY, and Lock under art. HOUSE.

The verb to 'handle' occurs frequently. Its primary meaning, to seize or use with the hand, is seen in Ps 115[7] 'They have hands, but they handle not'; and Wis 15[15] 'gods, which neither have the use of eyes to see . . . nor fingers of hands to handle' (εἰς ψηλάφησιν). So we handle the sword (Ezk 38[4]), the oar (27[29]), the pen (Jg 5[14]), the harp (Gn 4[21]), etc. In NT the meaning is *touch*, or *feel with the hand*. There are two Gr. verbs:

(1) θιγγάνω, Col 2²¹ 'Touch not; taste not; handle not' (Μὴ ἅψῃ μηδὲ γεύσῃ μηδὲ θίγῃς). RV, after Lightfoot, renders 'Handle not, nor taste, nor touch,' for ἅπτεσθαι is stronger than θιγεῖν, and is best tr⁴ by handle if that word is to be used at all, which is somewhat strong for both. (2) ψηλαφάω, Lk 24³⁹ 'Behold my hands and my feet, that it is I myself: handle me, and see'; 1 Jn 1¹ 'That which was from the beginning, which we have heard . . . and our hands have handled, of the Word of life.' If 'handle' was too strong for θιγγάνω, it is scarcely strong enough for ψηλαφάω, which expresses the movement of the hands over a surface, so as to feel it and fix it, or mentally the groping after something, as the Athenians 'felt after' God (Ac 17²⁷, same verb). In He 12¹⁸ (only remaining occurrence in NT) it is used of the 'mount that might be *touched*,' i.e. as Davidson 'palpable and materially sensible.'

But the verb to 'handle' is found in other senses that are less familiar, as: *Be conversant with, have to do with*, Jer 2⁸ 'The priests said not, Where is the Lord? and they that handle the law (תֹּפְשֵׂי הַתּוֹרָה) knew me not'. Almost in the sense intended by Jeremiah, but somewhat more narrowly, this word 'handle' was used about 1611 of the expounding of Scripture, as in James Melvill's *Diary* (Wodrow, p. 182) in reference to the order of worship at Newcastle under Melvill's ministry : 'Ther salbe daylie Comoun Prayers twyse everie day, befor noone at ten houres, and efter at foure, at quhilk tyme a Psalme salbe read and handlit, sa that the soum thairof be schortlie gathered, the partes sett doun in ordour, and some schort notes of doctrine, with exhortation ; bot in sic schortnes that the haill tyme occupied exceid nocht the space of ane halff houre.' And so Wodrow, *Select Biog.* i. 312, 'I have heard him [Mr. John Dykes of Kilrinnie] goe through a long chapter in less than an hour, and pertinently handle every purpose thereof.' This is the very meaning, however, of 2 Mac 2²⁸ 'Leaving to the author the exact handling of every particular' (τὸ μὲν διακριβοῦν). In 2 Co 4² we find the expression, 'handling the word of God deceitfully,' where the meaning is different. The Gr., tr⁴ 'handle deceitfully,' is the simple verb δολόω, to ensnare, corrupt; Vulg. 'adulterantes,' which Wyc. translates 'avoutrynge the word of God,' (1388) 'doynge avoutrye bi'; Rhem. 'adulterating': Tind. has 'corrupte'; Cran. introduced 'handle deceitfully,' which was adopted by Gen., Bish., AV, RV. Tindale's 'corrupt' is probably as near the meaning as one can go. But in the AV trⁿ 'handle' means to *deal with, treat*. So Pr 16²⁰ 'He that handleth a matter wisely shall find good' (מַשְׂכִּיל עַל־דָּבָר), AVm 'he that understandeth a matter,' RV 'he that giveth heed unto the word,' RVm as AV). In this sense the word is used also in 2 Mac 7³⁹ 'Then the king, being in a rage, handled him worse than all the rest' (ἀπήνησεν); 8¹⁷ 'the cruel handling of the city' (αἰκισμός, RV 'shameful handling'); and Mk 12⁴ 'sent him away shamefully handled' (ἀπέστειλαν ἠτιμωμένον, WH ἠτίμησαν, RV 'him they . . . handled shamefully,' Gould 'insulted'; the verb is lit. 'dishonoured.' Cf. Ezk 18⁸ Cov. 'he handleth faithfully betwixte man and man'; Golding, *Calvin's Job* (Ser. cxix. on 32¹⁻³), 'The opinion and imaginacion of Jobs three freends, was that Job was a castaway before God, bycause he was handled so roughly.'   J. HASTINGS.

HANDSOMELY.—In Wis 13¹¹ the adv. εὐπρεπῶς is translated in AV 'handsomely,' which seems a very appropriate translation. The Bishops' Bible has 'comely' (as adv.), and RV 'in comely form.' But it is very doubtful if that can be the meaning of 'handsomely' in AV. Coming from 'hand' it

is equivalent in all early examples to 'handy,' i.e. dexterously, cleverly. Bishop Keith says of Hamilton's *Catechism*, 'It is a judicious commentary upon the Commands, the Belief, Lord's Prayer, Magnificat, Ave Maria ; and the author shows both his wisdom and moderation in handsomely eviting to enter upon the controverted topics,' and the latest edition of the *Catechism* (Mitchell, ed. 1882) is right in saying that '*handsomely eviting* must mean *artfully eluding*.' Bp. Davenant in 1640 writes regarding his *Animadversions* to Dr. Ward, and says, 'For this uce I would have a doozen at the least sent bound : some fairly for the Bishops, all handsomely' (Fuller's *Life of Bp. Davenant*, 1897, p. 447), where 'fairly' means what we now express by 'handsomely,' while 'handsomely' refers to the workmanship, deftly. This is no doubt the meaning of 'handsomely' in AV. The Vulg. gives 'diligenter,' after which Wyc. and Dou. 'diligently,' and it is to be observed that the reading in א is not εὐπρεπῶς, but εὐτρεπῶς. Rutherford (*Letters*, No. lxv.) says, 'Christ hath so handsomely [i.e. dexterously] fitted for my shoulders this rough tree of the cross, as that it hurteth me no ways.' The adj. 'handsome' is in constant use in the same sense, as Tind. *Pent.* (Prol. to Lv), 'Fynallye beware of allegoryes, for there is not a moare handsome or apte a thinge to be gile withall then an allegorye, nor a more sotle and pestilent thinge in the world to persuade a false matter then an allegorye.'   J. HASTINGS.

HANDSTAVES (*makkel yād* ; מַקֵּל יָד Ezk 39⁹).—A kind of club carried by shepherds chiefly for de-

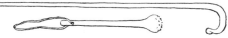

SHEPHERD'S CLUB AND CROOK.

fence against wild beasts. Goliath (1 S 17⁴³) asks David, 'Am I a dog that thou comest to me with staves?' (מַקְלוֹת *maḳlôth*). Cf. *shebhet* under DART.   W. E. BARNES.

HANDWEAPON.—See HAND.

HANDWRITING.—See WRITING.

HANES (חָנֵס).—Is 30⁴ in a difficult context : 'Woe to the rebellious children . . . that walk to go down into Egypt and have not asked at my mouth, to strengthen themselves in the strength of Pharaoh, and to trust in the shadow of Egypt ! Therefore shall the strength of Pharaoh be your shame, and the trust in the shadow of Egypt your confusion. For his princes are at Zoan, and his ambassadors are come to Hanes.' There seems to be no antecedent to 'his' but Pharaoh, so some have thought that the last sentence refers to the movements of Pharaoh's advanced guard towards the frontier ; but it is usually considered that the princes and ambassadors were those of the king of Judah. Zoan is well known to be Tanis. Hanes might well represent the ancient Hunenseten in its passage to the much abbreviated Coptic form Hnês. This was the name of the great city of Heracleopolis Magna in Middle Egypt. About this time, corresponding to that of the 23rd to 25th dynasty in Egypt, that country was in a feeble state, there being seldom if ever a central authority of sufficient power to keep local princes in check. Two invaders, the Eth. Piankhi and the Assyr. Esarhaddon, have given us lists of numerous independent princelings in different cities of Egypt. In the inscription of Piankhi one of these petty rulers is named as of Heracleopolis Magna, but there is no mention of one at Tanis. In Esarhaddon's list of petty states Tanis appears to be one, and another is called Hininshi; but the latter is grouped with the cities of Lower Egypt, and was apparently situated in the central part of the Delta, so that it is difficult to identify it with Hunenseten-Hnês, although there are excellent etymol. and hist. reasons for so doing. There is indeed no sign of divisions in the country in the passage quoted from Is; Pharaoh is named in the sing. as at other times. But the two cities are evidently mentioned as leading ones, and it would be satisfactory to find them in the lists above referred to. If, as Esarhaddon's list would seem to indicate, Hininshi is not Hnês, it may still, perhaps, represent the biblical H., otherwise the latter is prob. Heracleopolis Magna in Middle Egypt. Naville has compared H. with Anysis, a city of Lower Egypt mentioned by Herodotus; again, *Khens* seems to be the Egyp. name of a district in the N.E. delta. The LXX had lost the clue to the meaning of v.[4], and substituted, 'For there are in Tanis princes, wicked messengers' (ὅτι εἰσὶν ἐν Τάνει ἀρχηγοὶ ἄγγελοι πονηροί). An Aram. version gives for Hanes, Tahpanhes, on the N.E. frontier of Egypt. There is at least some similarity in the names.   F. LL. GRIFFITH.

HANGING is frequently mentioned in the OT, but it is very doubtful whether the word, in connexion with capital punishment, has ever the sense which it suggests to modern ears. As the analysis below will show, in most instances where the hanging (or hanging up) of a criminal is referred to, the meaning is that, *after* execution in some other form, his *dead* body was hung up. Again, even if 'hanging' sometimes designates a mode of *execution*, the probability is that it is impaling that is really meant. The scriptural terms and references are as follows :—

1. הָּלָה (in 2 S 21[12] (Ḳerê), Dt 28[66], Hos 11[7] (?) תָּלָא), 'to hang up' anything, *e.g.* the earth Job 26[7], the shields on the tower of David Ca 4[4], the harps of the exiles in Babylon Ps 137[2]; especially of the hanging up of a *dead* body, in Gn 40[19. 22] 41[13] of the chief baker, who was probably first beheaded and then had his body impaled as an aggravation of the punishment, see Dillm. *ad loc.*; in 2 S 4[12] of the murderers of Ishbosheth, whose bodies, after their hands and feet had been cut off, were hung up by David beside the pool in Hebron; in 2 S 21[12] of the bodies of Saul and Jonathan, which were hung up by the Philistines at Beth-shan. The fuller expression '(hang) upon a tree' (עַל־עֵץ) occurs in Gn 40[19], Dt 21[22], Jos 8[29] 10[26 bis], Est 2[23] (in which last passage it is possible that impaling of the *dead* bodies is meant; cf. Herod. iii. 125, ix. 78; Plutarch, *Artax.* 17, *Timol.* 22; Justin, xxi. 4). The Deuteronomic code regulated the Jewish practice (cf. Philo, *de Spec. Leg.* § 28) as follows :— 'If a man have committed a sin worthy of death and he be put to death, and [after his death] thou hang him on a tree, his body shall not remain all night upon the tree, but thou shalt surely bury him the same day, for he that is hanged is accursed of God (קִלְלַת אֱלֹהִים, LXX κεκατηραμένος ὑπὸ θεοῦ, Aq. Theod. κατάρα θεοῦ, *not* 'a curse, *i.e.* reproach, insult *to* God,' as one school of Jewish interpreters understood it), that thou defile not thy land which the LORD thy God giveth thee for an inheritance' (Dt 21[22f.], where see Driver's note). This prescription is noted as having been carried out in the case even of the kings executed by Joshua (Jos 8[29] 10[27]). The requisite publicity has been attained by sunset and the land has been cleansed from the defilement affecting it. (On 'exposure' of this kind and its religious meaning see W. R. Smith, *RS*[1] 351 n.). The exposure of the bodies of Saul's sons (2 S 21[9ff.]) day after day was either ex-

ceptional, or reflects the practice of an age that was a stranger to the mildness of the Deuteronomic code (cf Benzinger, *Heb. Arch.* 333).

The LXX equivalent of הָּלָה is κρεμάννυμι, which appears also in the NT in Lk 23[39], Ac 5[30] 10[39], Gal 3[13], the only difference from OT usage being that it is used in all these passages of the hanging of a *living* body upon a cross. The language of Dt 21[23], although it had of course no direct reference to crucifixion, could readily be transferred to it, and evidently was so transferred by the Jews, as we can gather from Gal 3[13]. It was the hanging up, not the death, that brought disgrace upon the sufferer, and the epithet *Tâlûi* (תָּלוּי 'the hung'), derived from Dt 21[23], is frequently applied in contempt to Jesus by the later Jews. See the very instructive note of Lightfoot, *Galatians*[6], 152[ff.].

The word תָּלָה is almost certainly used of 'hanging' as a mode of execution in Est 5[14] 6[4] 7[9f.] 8[7] 9[13. 14. 25] (possibly also in 2[23]). The EV evidently understands it in the modern sense, for both AV and RV give for עֵץ **gallows** (in the text, although they have 'tree' in the margin). The 'gallows' which was destined for Haman for Mordecai, but was used for his own execution and that of his sons, is said to have been fifty cubits high. It seems most probable that impaling was the form of execution adopted, and that the 'tree' was a stake for the purpose (cf. Haley, *Esther*, 122 ff.). It could be lowered to receive its victim, who would then be raised upon it to that lofty height, that his doom and sufferings might arrest the public gaze.

The same word (תָּלָה) is used in 2 S 18[10] of Absalom, who was 'hanged in an oak,' *i.e.* caught by the neck in the fork of a branch. In La 5[12] we read of princes being 'hanged up by their hand' (בְּיָדָם נִתְלוּ). Löhr would refer *their* to the enemy, that is to say, the princes were hanged up by the hand of the Chaldæans. Others, taking *their* as =*their own*, suggest that there may be a reference to crucifixion.

2. In Ezr. 6[11] the Aram. יִתְמְחָא appears to refer to being fastened on the impaling stake, although the LXX understands it more mildly, πληγήσεται, 'he shall be beaten.'

3. The only clear instances in the Bible of death by hanging, *i.e.* strangulation, are those of Ahithophel and Judas (2 S 17[23], Mt 27[5]), and both these were cases not of execution but of suicide. As a mode of execution it seems to have been only by the later Jews that strangling was adopted (see W. R. Smith, *RS*[2] 419, and art. CRIMES AND PUNISHMENTS, p. 527[a]). In 2 S 17[23] the Heb. term employed is יֵּחָנַק (imperf. Niph. of חנק), the only other occurrences of this root being the Piel ptcp. מְחַנֵּק used in Nah 2[12] of the lion strangling prey for his lionesses, and the noun מַחֲנָק in Job 7[15] 'My soul chooseth strangling'). The LXX has in 2 S ἀπέπνιξεν, in Nah ἀπήγξατο, which is the word used also in Mt 27[5].

4. הוֹקִיעַ, Hiph. of יָקַע which in Qal means 'to be dislocated' (Gn 32[25] of Jacob's thigh) or fig. 'to be alienated' (joined with נֶפֶשׁ and followed by מִן or מֵעַל Jer 6[8], Ezk 23[17. 18]), is used in 2 S 21[6. 9] of the 'hanging up' of Saul's sons by the Gibeonites (cf. v.[13] Hoph. ptcp. הַמּוּקָעִים). Its only other occurrence is Nu 25[4] 'Take all the chiefs of the people and hang (הוֹקַע) them up unto the LORD.' The *Oxf. Heb. Lex.* remarks, 'some solemn form of execution, but meaning uncertain.' Dillmann, Kautzsch, and Kittel tr. simply 'aussetzen' = *expose.* This follows the LXX, which has in 2 S ἐξηλιάζειν and in Nu παραδειγματίζειν. By others it is taken to mean *impale* (Ges., following Aq., ἀναπηγνύναι) or *crucify* (Targ. צלב, Vulg. *crucifigere*, *affigere*). Symm. has κρεμάζειν = *hang*, Vulg. in Nu *suspendere*, but it is probable that the word expressed something more than the ordinary הָּלָה (Driver,

Text of Sam. p. 269). In all probability we should read the same word (הִקְעֻ for חָּקְעֻ of MT) in 1 S 31[10], of the fastening up of Saul's body by the Philistines (so Lagarde, followed by Wellhausen, Driver, Budde, Grätz, Klostermann).

W. R. Smith (*RS*[2] 419) suggests that in the above passages in Nu and 2 S *precipitation from a rock* may be intended. 'They *fell* all seven together' (2 S 21[9]), and for this form of execution reference may be made to 2 K 8[12], 2 Ch 25[12], Hos 10[14]. This explanation, however, seems to lack probability, particularly if we adopt the above textual emendation of Lagarde in 1 S 31[10].   J. A. SELBIE.

HANGING, HANGINGS.—1. The former is the AV rendering of the Heb. term מָסָךְ, the name given in the Priests' Code (1) to the curtain or *portière* closing the entrance to the Tabernacle from the surrounding court (Ex 26[36. 37] 35[15] 'the h. for the door at the entering in of the tabernacle,' 39[38] 40[5] etc.); (2) to a similar *portière* closing the entrance to the court itself (Ex 35[17] 'the h. for the door of the court,' 38[18] etc.); and (3) once, Nu 3[31], for the 'veil' screening off the Holy of Holies from the rest of the Tabernacle, the usual name for which is פָּרֹכֶת (Ex 26[31] and oft.), or more fully פָּרֹכֶת הַמָּסָךְ (Ex 35[12] 39[34] 40[21], Nu 4[5]). In all three cases, as we have said, the AV renders by 'hanging,' with the single exception of Nu 3[26], where we find 'curtain' (see CURTAIN, 2). The Revisers, however, have consistently rendered מָסָךְ by 'screen' throughout.

2. The plur. form 'hangings,' on the other hand, is the equivalent of another technical term of the Priests' Code, קְלָעִים (LXX ἱστία), the hangings which, suspended from pillars, fenced off the court of the Tabernacle from the outer world (Ex 27[9. 11] etc.), hence the fuller designation קַלְעֵי הֶחָצֵר 'the hangings of the court' (Ex 35[17] 38[9] etc.).

For the material, workmanship, and other details of these screens and hangings, see the general article TABERNACLE in this Dictionary.

3. In 2 K 23[7] we read of 'hangings for the Asherah' (RV), which the women *wove* even 'in the house of the LORD' itself. The original, as the margin informs us, has 'houses (בָּתִּים),' by which Jewish tradition understands 'tents' (so RVm) to shelter the image of the goddess. It is extremely doubtful, however, if *bâtim* (or *bottîm*) is correct in this connexion. The LXX here have a transliteration of some different reading (A χεττιείμ, B χεττιείν). Klostermann supposes that the Greek translators read בתיים, a copyist's error for בתים = כֻּתֳנוֹת (cf. Luc. στολάς). See further *Oxf. Heb. Lex.* i. 109a, *s.v.* בַּיִת.   A. R. S. KENNEDY.

HANNAH (חַנָּה, Ἅννα, that is, *grace*).—One of the wives of an Ephraimite named Elkanah, who lived at Ramathaim-zophim (1 S 1[2ff.]). To her great distress H. had no children, and on the occasion of one of the yearly visits which she made with her husband to sacrifice to J″ at Shiloh, where the ark then was, she vowed that, if the Lord would give her a son, she would devote him to Him under the vow of a Nazirite. Her prayer was heard, and a child was born, whom she named Samuel. As soon as he was weaned, which according to Jewish custom might not be until he was about three years old, she took him up to Eli, the priest of the Lord, at Shiloh. On the same occasion she is reported to have given vent to her feelings in the beautiful song of 1 S 2[1-10]. It is necessary to note, however, that this song is pronounced by modern criticism to be wholly unsuited to H.'s position and circumstances, and is thought to have been composed later in celebration of some national success. If so, v.[5b] may have led to its association with H. (see Driver, *LOT*[6] 174). Of H.'s subsequent history we are told only that she was in

the habit of bringing Samuel a little robe (*mĕʽîl*) from year to year when she came up to the yearly sacrifice; and that she became the mother of other three sons and two daughters (1 S 2[21]).   G. MILLIGAN.

HANNATHON (חַנָּתֹן).—A place on the N. border of Zebulun, Jos 19[14]. The site is uncertain, but the name is probably to be identified with the Talmudic *Caphar Hananiah*, which according to the Mishnah (see Neubauer, *Géog. du Talm.* 179, 226) marked the limit of Upper Galilee. This is now *Kefr 'Anân*, at the foot of the mountains of Upper Galilee and N.E. of Rimmon. See *SWP* i. 205, 207.   C. R. CONDER.

HANNIEL (חַנִּיאֵל 'grace of God').—1. Son of Ephod, and Manasseh's representative for dividing the land, Nu 34[23] P. 2. A hero of the tribe of Asher (AV Haniel), 1 Ch 7[39].

HANOCH (חֲנוֹךְ 'dedication' (?)).—1. A grandson of Abraham by Keturah, and third of the sons of Midian (Gn 25[4]). In the parallel list of 1 Ch 1[33] AV gives the form Henoch. 2. The eldest son of Reuben, and head of the family of the **Hanochites** (Gn 46[9], Ex 6[14], Nu 26[5], 1 Ch 5[3]).

HANUN (חָנוּן 'favoured,' cf. Assyr. *Ḫanunu*, king of Gaza).—1. The son of Nahash, king of the Ammonites. Upon the death of the latter, David sent a message of condolence to Hanun, who, however, resented this action, and grossly insulted the messengers. The consequence was a war, which proved most disastrous to the Ammonites, 2 S 10[1ff.], 1 Ch 19[1ff.]. 2. 3. H. occurs in the list of those who repaired the wall and the gates of Jerus., Neh 3[13. 30].

HAP, HAPLY.—Hap, a Saxon word meaning 'luck,' 'chance,' is used once in AV, Ru 2[3] 'And her hap was to light on a part of the field belonging unto Boaz,' where the Heb. is וַיִּקֶר מִקְרֶהָ, LXX καὶ περιέπεσεν περιπτώματι; AVm 'her hap happened'; Cox, 'her lot met her.' T. Fuller (*Holy State*, iii. 12, p. 181) says, 'Many have been the wise speeches of fools, though not so many as the foolish speeches of wise men . . . because talking much, and shooting often, they must needs hit the mark sometimes, though not by aim, by hap'; and imitates the passage in Ru when he says (*Holy Warre*, p. 200), 'his hap was to fall in just among the three captains.'

Haply is 'by hap.' 'Happily' is the same word under a different spelling, and had formerly the same meaning, though it has now come to mean 'by *good* hap.' Happily meaning simply 'by hap,' 'perchance,' is common in Shaks., though mod. edd. usually spell 'haply.' Thus *Hamlet*, II. ii. 402—

    '*Ham.* That great baby you see there is not yet out of his swaddling-clouts.
    Ros. Happily he's the second time come to them.'

In AV 1611 the spelling is 'haply' in 1 S 14[30], Mk 11[13], Lk 14[29], Ac 5[39] 17[27]; but in 2 Co 9[4] 'happily,' which mod. edd. have changed to 'haply' also. Sometimes the word is spelt 'happily,' as in Daye's ed. of Tindale's *Pent.* (1573), '*Enacke*, a kinde of Giauntes so called happily, because they ware chaynes about their neckes.' The word occurs in AV only in the phrases 'if haply' and 'lest haply.'

RV has trd μήποτε by 'lest haply' in all its occurrences, except Mt 25[9] 'peradventure—not,' Jn 7[26] 'Can it be that,' and 2 Ti 2[25] 'if peradventure.' Also μή που (TR μήπως) is so trd in Ac 27[29].   J. HASTINGS.

HAPHRAIM (חֲפָרַיִם).—A town of Issachar, noticed with Shunem and Anaharath, Jos 19[19]. These were to the east of the tribal territory. In the *Onomasticon*, however (*s.* 'Aphraim'), it is stated to be ' now Affarea, six miles from Legio (*Lejjûn*) to the north.' The site in question is now called *el-Ferrîyeh*, on the low hills south of Carmel. It is the site of an ancient town with remarkable tombs. See *SWP* vol. i. sh. viii. In Baedeker-Socin's *Pal.*[2] 238, Haphraim is identified with *el-'Afûleh*, 2 miles W. of *Solam* (Shunem).

C. R. CONDER.

HAPPEN.—**1.** Ro 11[25] 'Blindness in part is happened to Israel,' *i.e.* is fallen upon, has come to (γέγονεν), without the idea of ' hap ' or chance ; RV ' hath befallen.' Cf. Jer 43[8] Cov. ' And in Taphnis the worde off the LORDE happened unto Ieremy.' **2.** 2 S 1[6] ' As I happened by chance upon Mount Gilboa' נִקְרֹא נִקְרֵיתִי, LXX Περιπτώματι περιεπέσαν), *i.e.* ' I chanced to light upon.' Bunyan begins his *Holy War* thus : ' In my Travels, as I walked through many Regions and Countries, it was my chance to happen into that famous Continent of Universe.' Cf. Gn 44[29] Tind. ' Yf ye shall take this also awaye from me and some mysfortune happen apon him, then shall ye brynge my gray heed with sorow unto the grave ' ; and esp. Rutherford, *Letters* (No. xli.), ' I happened upon a convenient trusty bearer by God's wonderful providence.' **3.** 2 Mac 13[7] ' Such a death it happened that wicked man to die,' the usual prep. being omitted. So Pr. Bk., ' Ordering of Priests,' ' And if it shall happen the same Church, or any member thereof, to take any hurt or hindrance by reason of your negligence, ye know the greatness of the fault, and also the horrible punishment that will ensue ' : in 1549 and 1552 the word is ' chance.' **4.** The auxiliary *to be* (as well as *to have*) was formerly used with the verb to ' happen' : so Jer 44[23] ' this evil is happened unto you ' ; Ro 11[25] (as above) ; and 2 P 2[22] ' But it is happened unto them according to the true proverb ' (RV ' It has happened '). Cf. Mt 28[11] Tind. ' When they were gone, beholde, some of the kepers came in to the cyte, and shewed unto the hie prestes all the thinges that were happened.'

J. HASTINGS.

HAPPINESS.—This word, in its subst. shape, does not appear in the Eng. Bible, either in AV or in RV, and its synonym *blessedness* (occurring thrice in AV of NT) has now (see BLESSEDNESS) been changed by the Revisers (in accordance with the form μακαρισμός) into ' blessing ' (Ro 4[6. 9]) and ' gratulation ' (Gal 4[15]). The adj. μακάριος (almost invariably in OT representing Heb. אֶשֶׁר *'ashrê*, lit. *happinesses of*) is common enough in both Testaments. But while, in NT, the Revisers have reduced (cf. Jn 13[17]) the renderings by ' happy' to three (Ac 26[2], Ro 14[22], 1 Co 7[40]), and might consistently have reduced them to one (Ac 26[2]—the external happiness of St. Paul in pleading before Agrippa), the OT Revisers have left *happy* and *blessed* just where they were, except Jer 12[1], where the Heb. word (here alone in AV of OT rendered *happy*) is changed to *at rest*, its proper meaning. Even in Ps 128[1. 2] *happy* and *blessed* are left side by side to represent the same word ; cf. also Pr 16[20] with Ps 34[8]. If Carlyle's dictum (*Sartor Resartus*) has any force, ' There is something higher than happiness, and that is blessedness,' *blessed* is the word for the spiritual region ; and the retention of *happy* so often in RV of OT tends to merge this distinction in a way defensible only on the ground that outward prosperity entered largely into the OT conception of bliss.

The more usual word for *happy* in profane Greek, εὐδαίμων, does not occur in LXX or NT. Probably, the δαίμων component was a stumbling-block to Greek-speaking Jew and Christian ; but the preference for μακάριος is altogether suitable to the atmosphere, since μακάριος, and not εὐδαίμων, represented to the Greeks the happiness of the divine life.

In the course of the gradual elevation of the word μακάριος, and the idea of happiness from the pagan to the Christian level, from Greek tragedy to the Sermon on the Mount, more than one point is worthy of note. While the ordinary pagan notion was purely external, and the tragedians, among the exponents of Gr. thought, will call no man happy till a happy death has set its seal upon a happy life (Soph. *Trach.* 1 ff., cf. Hdt. i. 32) ; yet, in their view, continued prosperity was conditioned by natural piety and reverence (Soph. *Œd. R. passim*, and Hdt. iii. 40) ; and hence their preference for εὐδαίμων, ' with a good genius attending.' The Gr. philosophical schools, on the other hand, looking for a happiness secure from ' the slings and arrows of outrageous fortune,' discerned its possibility, some mainly in the moral, as Socrates, who defined happiness as εὐπραξία, *well-doing*, rather than εὐτυχία, *good luck* (Xen. *Mem.* iii. 9. 14) ; others, more strictly in the intellectual, as Plato, whose notion of happiness reached its climax in the wisdom consisting in the cognition of the Ideal Good (*Rep.* 519), this cognition being the crowning point of the ' resemblance to God as far as possible ' (*Theæt.* 176b) ; others, as Aristotle, in the intellectually practical, ' the life in obedience to the intellect,' ' the rational virtuous activity of the soul in a life fully provided,' ' the performance by man of the peculiar work which belongs to him as man ' (*Eth. Nic.* i. 6, ii. 5, x. 4) ; while the Stoics looked for happiness in a life ' conformed to nature,' and combined with ἀταραξία, *absence of all emotion*.

The difference between such philosophical notions of happiness and the biblical, lies not so much in inwardness, as in the fundamental conditions of that inwardness, its relations, its developments, its possibilities. The *blessedness* even of some of the noblest conceptions of the OT is linked to the external (Ps 34[8. 12. 13. 14]), though sometimes the external seems to be transcended (Ps 84[5. 7] 47 119[1. 111]), and, even when the external is foremost, it always connotes righteousness and the consequent favour of God towards individual, family, or race, in the present or in the Messianic age (see BLESSEDNESS). But the element in biblical happiness which had been lacking to all previous thought was the *personal relation*, and that not only as faith in God, personal and ever-present (Ps 33[12. 20. 21]), but as love for Him, this being the highest requisite (Dt 6[4. 5], Jg 5[3], Ps 4[6. 7]) ; and the most satisfying blessedness is to be in His presence and to behold His face (Pss 16. 17. 49). In NT we reach the ' roof and crown.' The happiness is now clearly inward, spiritual and present (Mt 5[2ff.]) ; and now the way to the personal relation is opened up through Jesus Christ, personal, loving (Jn 15[9]), ever-living (Jn 14[6], He 10[20]). Whatever the outward may be (Ro 8[33f.]), He is *God with us* (Mt 1[23] 18[20]) ; nay, veritable evils endured for Him and with Him actually make us blessed now (Mt 5[10f.], 1 P 4[14]). More than this, He is *Christ in us*, the hope of glory (Col 1[27]) ; for the time shall come when, all hindrances being taken away, and the internal embodying itself in external realization,[*] ' we shall be like him ' (1 Jn 3[1. 2], cf. Plato above cited) in the full enjoyment of the eternal life (1 Jn 5[11], Mt 25[46], Mk 10[30], Jn 17[22-24]). (See articles by the present writer, *Expositor*, 1st series, vols. ix. x. ' A Word Study in the NT, μακάριος ').

J. MASSIE.

HAPPIZZEZ (הַפִּצֵץ, AV **Aphses**).—The head of the 18th course of priests, 1 Ch 24[15]. See GENEALOGY.

[*] Compare the μακαριστάτη εὐδαιμονία, *the most blessed happiness*, offered by Virtue to Hercules, as the sure reward of following her (Xen. *Mem.* ii. 1. 21).

HARA (הָרָא, Vulg. *Ara*) occurs 1 Ch 5²⁶ as one of the cities or regions to which the Israelitish captives from Samaria were deported by the Assyrians. Modern scholars have often tried the hazardous etymology from הַר 'mountain' (presupposing a bad orthography instead of הרה !). From this etymology and the corresponding words of Kings, they concluded that the Western part of Media was meant, called Media Magna by classic writers, '*Irāk̲ al-ajamî* 'the Persian I.,' by the Arabs, or *al-Jibāl*, *i.e.* 'the mountainous region,' *Kohistan* by the Persians. But the name is wanting in the LXX (only Lucian's recension, ed. de Lagarde, has Ἀρραν, which looks like an emendation to the name חרן Haran). The corresponding passages 2 K 17⁶ 18¹¹ have the expression עָרֵי מָדַי 'the Median cities,' but LXX ὄρη Μήδων 'the Median mountains.' This latter reading (which seems to be the more original text) furnishes the key to the name *Hara*. It is evidently due to a misreading of that original text הרי מדי, and represented originally *hārê* 'mountains of.' This misunderstanding is usually attributed to the Chronicler; but after the LXX, it would be rather an awkward addition by a later reader who missed the expression added in Kings. Of earlier comparisons hardly any deserve to be mentioned. Bochart (*Phaleg*) thought of Aria in Persia (Herod. iii. 93, vii. 62, 66). The name begins with an *h* according to the Persian inscriptions, but the country is too remote. No Assyrian king ever possessed Aria (Herod. vii. 62 is mistaken, and contradicts himself, identifying Arians and Medians). W. MAX MÜLLER.

HARADAH (חֲרָדָה, Χαραδάθ).—A station in the journeyings of the Israelites, mentioned only Nu 33²⁴·²⁵. It has not been identified.

HARAN (הָרָן, 'mountaineer' (?)).—**1.** Son of Terah, younger brother of Abram, and father of Lot, Gn 11²⁶ (P), also father of Milcah and Iscah, v.²⁹ (J). Dillmann rejects the view of Wellh. (*Prol.* 330) and Budde (*Urgesch.* 443) that הרן is a mere variation of חרן. **2.** A Gershonite Levite, 1 Ch 23⁹.

HARAN (חָרָן, Χαρρά, Χαρράν; *Haran*) is situated in the N.W. of Mesopotamia on the Belias, a tributary of the Euphrates, S.E. of Edessa (*Oorfa*), in a country rendered very fertile by watercourses from the Belias, which rises, at a distance of several miles, from the hills S. of the Euphrates. The origin of Haran is lost in antiquity, but it must have been early inhabited by Semites, perhaps Babylonians, the name of the city being expressed in cuneiform by an ideograph (*Ḫarranu*, 'road'), which was probably given it on account of its being a crossing point of the Syrian, Assyrian, and Babylonian trade-routes. The merchants of this city are mentioned in Ezk 27²³.

Nothing remains of the ancient city but a long range of mounds on both sides of the river and the ruins of a castle or fortress of a very ancient date, built of large blocks of basaltic rock; it has square columns 8 ft. thick supporting an arched roof 30 ft. high. The town is now represented only by a village on the slope of the hill. The small houses or huts are built (perhaps for want of timber) in the peculiar fashion depicted on the Assyrian bas-reliefs, *i.e.* with domed roofs. According to tradition, the well where Rebekah was met by Abraham's messenger (Gn 24¹⁵) is near the city.

Haran is first mentioned when Abram and his family dwelt there after leaving Ur of the Chaldees on his way to Canaan (Gn 11³¹), and there the descendants of his brother settled, hence the name of 'the city of Nahor,' which it also bears (cf. Gn 24¹⁰ with 27⁴³). Haran is frequently mentioned in the cuneiform writings. Tiglath-pileser I. (B.C.

1120) in his great cylinder-inscription says that he killed ten elephants in 'the land of Haran,' and four he captured alive and took to his capital Asshur. Sargon says that he 'spread out his shadow over the city Haran, and as a soldier of Anu and Dagon wrote its laws'; and Sennacherib speaks of Gozan, Haran, and Rezeph as having been destroyed by one or more of his predecessors (2 K 19¹²). The name of the eponymy for the years B.C. 742 and 728, Bel-Ḫarrani-bêli-uṣur, 'Lord of Haran, protect (my) lord,' would seem to indicate that Haran was then a very important city.

The great tutelary deity of Haran was the moon-god, Sin in Assyrian, known among the Semitic nations as Baal-Kharran or Lord of Haran, though other deities must have been worshipped there. An inscribed seal in the British Museum represents a priest in adoration before an altar, a small figure in the distance, and above the altar a star with the words 'The God of Haran.' Assur-bani-apli speaks of the god Sin as dwelling in Haran. The tablet K. 2701*a*, which is a letter apparently sent to Assur-bani-apli, seems to refer to the crowning of his father Esarhaddon when on his way to Egypt. Reference is made therein to the '*bethel*' or temple at Haran, where the ceremony took place, and on this occasion the god Sin is said to have appeared to those present: 'When the father of the king my lord went to Egypt, he was crowned (?) in the *kanni* of Ḫarran, the temple * of cedar. The god Sin stood over the standard (?), two crowns upon his head, [and] the god Nusku stood before him. The father of the king my lord entered—[the crown] was placed upon his head,' etc. Later on, Nabonidus relates that Sin was angry with Haran and with his temple E-hul-hul (the house of joy) within it, and therefore allowed the Umman-manda (wandering hordes of Medes) to come and destroy it. Nabonidus then received from the gods Merodach and Sin, in a dream, instructions to rebuild the temple at Haran, and, when he pointed out that the Medes still surrounded the city, he was told by those gods that they would be destroyed, which destruction took place three years later under Cyrus. The city being relieved of the presence of the enemy, Nabonidus was able to finish the work of Shalmaneser and Assur-bani-apli, and, at the same time, to embellish the city. In the 5th cent. A.D. the Sabæans of Haran seem to have worshipped the sun as 'Bel-shamin,' the lord of heaven, later on using the Greek name of Ἥλιος. Gula (under the name of 'Gadlat') and Tar'ata (Atargatis or Derceto) are given by St. James of Seruj as the favourite goddesses of Haran. There was also a chapel dedicated to Abraham. The Roman general Crassus was defeated near Haran, but subsequently the province of Edessa fell into the power of the Romans, and Haran appears as a Roman city in the wars of Caracalla and Julian. It is worthy of notice that Haran retained until a late date the Chaldæan language and the worship of Chaldæan deities.

LITERATURE.—Del. *Paradies*, 185; Schrader, *COT*, *Keilinschriften und Geschichtsforschung*, 355-536; Ainsworth, *Euphrates Expedition*, i. 203; Sachau, *Berlin Acad.*, Feb. 14, 1895; Rawlinson, *Herod.* i. 503 n.; Hommel, *AHT* (Index, *s.* 'Haran'); Sayce, *HCM* and *EHH* (both Index). I. A. PINCHES.

HARARITE, THE (הַהֲרָרִי), according to Ges. (*Thes.* 392) = 'a mountain-dweller,' but more probably it should be taken as a gentilic adjective = 'a native of Harar.' No such place is mentioned in the OT, but we may infer from 2 S 23¹¹ᶠ· that it was situated somewhere near the Philistine frontier, probably in the Shephelah. Two (not three) of David's heroes are distinguished by this title.

* Lit. bethel (bêt-ili).

1. Shammah the son of Agee, 'one of the thirty' (2 S 23³³ ὁ Ἀρωδείτης). In the parallel 1 Ch 11³⁴ Shammah is probably to be read for Shagee (see Driver, *Sam. l.c.*). Further, in 2 S 23¹¹ (where we must read '*the* Hararite' [הַהֲרָרִי for הָרָרִי]) it is probably Shammah and not Agee (wh. see) who is thus designated. The LXX to 2 S 23¹¹ (ὁ Ἀρουχαῖος) points to a reading 'the Archite' (הָאַרְכִּי), which is partly supported by its rendering of 1 Ch 11³⁴ (B ὁ Ἀραχεί and ὁ Ἀραρεί; A ὁ Ἀραρί). See AGEE, SHAMMAH.

2. Ahiam the son of Sharar (2 S 23³³; read הַהֲרָרִי for הָאֲרָרִי; B Σαραουρείτης, A Ἀραρείτης). In the parallel 1 Ch 11³⁵ Sharar appears as Sacar (אֶחָיאָם שָׂכָר הַהֲרָרִי; בֶּן שָׂכָר הַהֲרָרִי; B ὁ Ἀραρεί, A ὁ Ἀραρί). See AHIAM, SHARAR.   J. F. STENNING.

HARBONA (חַרְבוֹנָא Est 1¹⁰) or **HARBONAH** (חַרְבוֹנָה 7⁹). LXX has Θαρρά in 1¹⁰ (B), Βουγαθάν in 7⁹.—The third of the seven eunuchs or chamberlains who waited upon king Ahasuerus. It was he who suggested that Haman should be hanged upon the gallows which he had prepared for Mordecai. The name seems to be Persian: *harban=donkey-driver.*   H. A. WHITE.

HARBOUR.—See HAVEN.

HARD.—The various meanings of 'hard,' whether as adj. or adv., may be given as follows: 1. Literally, *not soft*, only Job 41²⁴, Ezk 3⁹, Wis 11⁴, Sir 40¹⁵ 48¹⁷. 2. *Unfeeling, cruel:* Ps 94⁴ 'How long shall they utter and speak hard things?' (RV 'They prate, they speak arrogantly'); Wis 19¹³ 'they used a more hard and hateful behaviour toward strangers' (RV 'grievous indeed was the hatred which they practised toward guests'). Cf. Wyclif, *Works,* iii. 115, 'The vi tyme we schul trowe, that aftyr xxxij yer he suffrid hard passioun, undir Pounce Pilate.' 3. *Trying, exacting:* Ex 1¹⁴ 'hard bondage' (RV 'hard service'); 2 S 3³⁹ 'The sons of Zeruiah be too hard for me'; Ps 88⁷ 'Thy wrath lieth hard upon me'; Pr 13¹⁵ 'The way of transgressors is hard' (RV 'The way of the treacherous is rugged'); Mt 25²⁴ 'Lord, I knew thee that thou art an hard man'; Jn 6⁶⁰ 'This is an hard saying; who can hear it?'; Ac 9⁵ 'It is hard for thee to kick against the pricks'). 4. *Obdurate:* Jer 5³ 'They have made their faces harder than a rock'; Ezk 3⁹ 'As an adamant harder than flint have I made thy forehead.' Cf. Shaks. *Ant. and Cleop.* III. xi. 111—

> 'But when we in our viciousness grow hard,
> (O misery on't) the wise gods seel our eyes.'

5. *Strenuous:* only Jon 1¹³ 'the men rowed hard.' 6. *Difficult:* as Gn 18¹⁴ 'Is anything too hard for the Lord?' (RVm 'wonderful'); 1 K 10¹ 'She came to prove him with hard questions'; Mk 10²⁴ 'How hard is it for them that trust in riches to enter into the kingdom of God!' Cf. Rhem. NT, Preface, 'Moreover, we presume not in hard places to mollify the speaches or phrases, but religiously keepe them word for word, and point for point.' 7. *Close,* as Jg 9⁵² 'And Abimelech . . . went hard unto the door of the tower to burn it with fire'; Ps 63⁸ 'My soul followeth hard after thee'; Ac 18⁷ 'Justus . . . whose house joined hard to the synagogue.' This meaning of the word is common in early writers: cf. Lk 2⁹ Tind. 'And loo, the angell of the lorde stode harde by them'; Job 17¹ Cov. 'I am harde at deathes dore.' It is sometimes used of time, as in Rhem. NT, note to Jn 20²¹ 'Though he gave them his peace hard before, yet now entering to a new divine action, to prepare their hartes to grace and attention, he blesseth them againe.'

For **Harden, Hardening,** see next article.

Hardiness.—This subst. occurs only in Jth 16¹⁰

'The Persians quaked at her boldness, and the Medes were daunted at her hardiness' (θράσος, RV 'boldness'). Cf. Sir T. Elyot, *Governour,* ii. 47, 'What avayled fortune incomparable to the great kynge Alexander, his wonderfull puissance and hardynes, or his singular doctrine in philosophy, taught hym by Aristotle, in deliverynge hym from the deth in his yonge and flourishing age?' So Cov. uses 'hardy' for 'bold' in Dn 11¹⁶ 'no man shalbe so hardy as to stonde agaynst him'; and Barlowe, 'hardily' for 'boldly' (*Dialoge,* p. 68), 'Use they such crafty conveyaunce in promotyng theyr Gospell? Ye hardely, and that without any shame when they be detected of it.'

Hardly does not occur in AV in the mod. sense of 'scarcely.' Its meanings there are two: 1. *Harshly, grievously,* Gn 16⁶ 'And when Sarai dealt hardly with her, she fled from her face' (וַתְּעַנֶּהָ, AVm 'afflicted her'); and Is 8²¹ 'hardly bestead and hungry' (Amer. RV 'sore'; see BESTEAD). RV introduces 'hardly' in this sense into Job 19³. 2. *With difficulty,* Ex 13¹⁵ 'And it came to pass, when Pharaoh would hardly let us go, that the LORD slew all the firstborn in the land of Egypt' (כִּי־הִקְשָׁה פַרְעֹה לְשַׁלְּחֵנוּ, RVm 'hardened himself against letting us go'); Mt 19²³ 'Verily I say unto you, That a rich man shall hardly enter into the kingdom of heaven' (δυσκόλως; RV 'It is hard for a rich man to enter,' a change that is commended by Beckett [*Should RV be Authorised?* p. 100] as much better, though less literal than AV, since the latter suggests, according to our mod. idiom, that a rich man can scarcely enter the kingdom of heaven. The same Gr. adv. occurs in Mk 10²³, Lk 18²⁴, and is trᵈ in the same way in AV, a trⁿ which RV accepts in these places); Lk 9³⁹ 'and bruising him hardly departeth from him' (μόγις, WH μόλις); Ac 27⁸ 'And, hardly passing it, came unto a place which is called The fair havens' (μόλις, RV 'with difficulty'). This meaning of 'hardly' may be seen in North's *Plutarch,* p. 889, 'Demetrius was so scared, that he had no further leysure, but to cast an ill-favoured cloke about him, the first that came to hand, and disguising himselfe to flie for life, and scaped very hardly, that he was not shamefully taken of his enemies for his incontinencie'; and T. Adams, *II Peter* (on 1⁴), 'He that hath done evil once, shall more hardly resist it at the next assault.'

Hardness.—2 Ti 2³ 'Thou therefore endure hardness, as a good soldier of Jesus Christ' (σὺ οὖν κακοπάθησον, edd. συνκακοπάθησον, RV 'Suffer hardship with me,' RVm 'Take thy part in suffering hardship'). Hardness for mod. 'hardship' is found in Shaks., as *Cymb.* III. vi. 21—

> 'Plenty, and peace, breeds cowards; hardness ever
> Of hardness is mother.'

Elsewhere 'hardness' is either lit. of the clods (Job 38³⁸), or fig. of the heart (Mt 19⁸, Mk 3⁵ 10⁵ 16¹⁴, Ro 2⁵).   J. HASTINGS.

HARDENING.—The moral difficulty of this subject is the ascription in OT of the hardening of men's hearts to God. Pharaoh's is the typical case; and his story is so vivid in its dramatic unity and details that we cannot wonder that practically his case is regarded as if it were unique. But it is not so; it is only a striking example of a class. Pharaoh's history sets before us the picture of a conflict between the proud head of a great empire and the Almighty, a conflict in ten onsets, or a drama in ten acts, in the last of which the human tyrant comes to the ground. As his case is a typical one, it is important to note the salient features. First of all, the result is twice foretold. The Lord says, 'I will harden his heart' (Ex 4²¹ 7³). In the case of the first five plagues and the seventh (river turned into blood, frogs, lice, flies, murrain, and hail) the phrase is ' Pharaoh hardened his heart' or 'his heart was hardened' (Ex 7[14. 22] 8[15. 19. 32] 9[7. 34. 35]). In the sixth, eighth, and ninth (boils, locusts, darkness) the phrase is 'the Lord hardened his heart' (9[12] 10[20. 27]). Thus the result is not ascribed to God only; both the divine and the human agencies are recognized. Whatever God had to do with the result, Pharaoh's freedom of action was not interfered with. Again, it is significant that 'the Lord hardened his heart' *follows* 'Pharaoh hardened.' It is the phrase used, with one exception, in the second severer series of divine judgments. When the lighter ones failed, heavier ones were sent. And even in the second series the result in one case is ascribed solely to Pharaoh (hail, 9[34. 35]). Is it not evident that the divine action described in 'the Lord hardened' was a punishment for the previous disobedience of the king? Is it not equally certain that each judgment, up to the last one, while a punishment, was also a merciful warning and call to repentance? At each stage Pharaoh might have yielded instead of refusing. It should be noted that the phrase 'the Lord hardened' is peculiar to the OT; in the NT it occurs only in quotations from the Old.

The two modes of speech, however, are not confined to Pharaoh's case, but are common in OT. We find 'the Lord hardened' in Jos 11[20], Dt 2[30], Is 63[17], etc., the other phrase in passages like 1 S 6[6], 2 Ch 36[13], Ps 95[8]. The language in such passages as Jg 9[23], 2 S 24[1] may seem even more startling. But if we look into the context we shall find that, as in Pharaoh's case, the divine action is a punishment of sin. This language, which before reflection seems to shock our moral sense, is partly to be explained by the OT habit of recognizing the divine action everywhere in nature and history. The thunder is God's voice; storm and tempest do His will; heathen monarchs and empires are His instruments. Men at that early stage of revelation did not discriminate as we do between the different causes at work in events. If they did reflect, they would no doubt see that the two forms of language applied to the same events under different aspects. Very little observation would show them, as it shows us, that divine appeals and commands never leave men as they find them. If not yielded to, they increase insensibility, benumb and gradually deaden moral feeling. This effect is contrary to the divine purpose, and is entirely man's fault; but it is natural and inevitable. The more powerful the appeals, the more rapid the hardening process, until God's Spirit withdraws, and leaves man to his own ways (Ro 1[28]). Looked at from the human side, Pharaoh, like every smaller transgressor, is seen acting with perfect freedom, consciously pitting his own will against God's, despising louder and louder warnings of ruin, self-punished and self-destroyed. Looked at from the divine side, God is seen commanding, forewarning, repeating rejected opportunities, doing everything to ensure submission and safety but coerce,—and at last leaving to destruction. It is evident that we have here again the old problem of reconciling the divine foreknowledge and government with human freedom and responsibility. Each element is attested by its own evidence. Both are necessary to a complete explanation. The two regions meet at some point invisible to human eye and undefinable in human speech and thought. 'To the Hebrew mind what we call secondary causes scarcely exist, at least in the sphere of religion. That which, in given circumstances, is the inevitable result of God's providential dispensations is viewed absolutely, apart from its conditions, as a distinct divine purpose' (Skinner on Is 6[10]).   J. S. BANKS.

HARE (אַרְנֶבֶת *'arnebheth*, δασύπους, *lepus*).—Four species of hare are found in Bible lands. They are all called by the Arabs *'arnabeh*, which is the same as the Heb. **1.** *Lepus Syriacus*, Hempr. et Ehr. It is a little smaller than the Eng. hare, and of a dark grey colour. It is common along the coast, and in the wooded and hilly districts of Pal. and Syria. **2.** *L. Sinaiticus*, Hempr. et Ehr. This species is much smaller, with a longer and narrower head, and longer ears, and is of a lighter grey. It is found in the valleys about the Dead Sea, and southward to Sinai. **3.** *L. Ægyptius*, Geoffr. This animal is not more than 18 in. long from the tip of the nose to the root of the tail. The ears are long, and fringed inside with white hairs. It is of a light sand colour above, and nearly white beneath. It is abundant in the Jordan Valley, and in S. Judæa and the N. part of et-Tîh. **4.** *L. Isabellinus*, Rüpp. The *Nubian hare*. This species is even smaller than the last, and is of a rich fawn colour. It is found only in the S.E. deserts of Palestine.

The hare is a *rodent*, and not a *ruminant*. The statement (Lv 11[6], Dt 14[7]) that it 'cheweth the cud' is to be taken phenomenally, not scientifically. The Arab of the present day regards it as a ruminant, and for that reason eats its flesh. As Tristram well says, 'Moses speaks of animals according to appearances, and not with the precision of a comparative anatomist, and his object was to show why the hare should be interdicted, though to all appearance it chewed the cud, viz. because it did not divide the hoof. To have spoken otherwise would have been as unreasonable as to have spoken of the earth's motion, instead of sunset and sunrise.'   G. E. POST.

HAREPH (חָרֵף).—A Judahite chief, 1 Ch 2[51]. See GENEALOGY.

HARHAIAH (חַרְהֲיָה, Ἀραχίας, but ABℵ omit the clause, Neh 3[8]).—Some Heb. texts read חַרְהָיָה, or even חַרְהֲיָה. Uzziah the son of H., a goldsmith, repaired a portion of the wall of Jerus. in the days of Nehemiah.

HARHAS (חַרְחַס, Ἀραάς B, Ἀρόάς B[b], Ἀράς A, Ἀδρά Luc.).—Ancestor of Shallum, the husband of Huldah the prophetess (2 K 22[14]). Called **Hasrah** חַסְרָה 2 Ch 34[22].

HARHUR (חַרְחוּר 'fever'? or 'freeborn').—Eponym of a family of Nethinim (Ezr 2[51], Neh 7[53]), called in 1 Es 5[31] Asur. See GENEALOGY.

HARIM (חָרִם, חָרֵם 'consecrated,' cf. Sabæan pr. name חרם).—**1.** A lay family which appears in the list of the returning exiles, Ezr 2[32]=Neh 7[35]; of those who had married foreign wives, Ezr 10[31]; and of those who signed the covenant, Neh 10[27] [Heb.[28]].

2. A priestly family which appears in the same lists, Ezr 2[39]=Neh 7[42], Ezr 10[21], Neh 10[5] [Heb.[6]]. The name is found also among 'the priests and Levites that went up with Zerubbabel,' Neh 12[3], where it is miswritten **Rehum** (רְחוּם); among the heads of priestly families in the days of Joiakim, Neh 12[15]; and as the third of the 24 courses, 1 Ch 24[8]. To which family Malchijah the son of Harim, one of the builders of the wall (Neh 3[11]), belonged cannot be determined. See GENEALOGY.

                    H. A. WHITE.

HARIPH (חָרִיף, חָרֵף, cf. חֹרֶף 'autumn').—A family which returned from exile with Zerubbabel (Neh 7[24]), and signed the covenant, Neh 10[19] [Heb.[20]]. In Ezr 2[18] the name appears as JORAH; so Lucian in Neh 7[24] Ἰωρήε. Hareph (חָרֵף) is named as a Calebite in 1 Ch 2[51], and one of David's companions in 1 Ch 12⁵ is termed a **Haruphite** (חֲרוּפִי, *Kethibh*), or Hariphite (חֲרִיפִי *Kerê*). The latter reading, if correct, perhaps points to a connexion with Hariph. See GENEALOGY.

H. A. WHITE.

HARLOT (זוֹנָה, אִשָּׁה נָכְרִיָּה, קְדֵשָׁה, LXX and NT πόρνη) is the name used in our English versions to describe different classes of women who come under the ban of morality. It is sometimes applied generally to women, including married women, of profligate life (Pr), but specially it denotes those who systematically gave themselves up to such a course of life, either for gain, or as a form of religious service. The existence of a class roughly corresponding to that which the name suggests to us may be traced throughout the history of Israel, originating as it did out of universally working conditions, and after the Solomonic period developing to the full its shamelessness, its seductive arts, and its blighting influence (Is 23¹⁶, Jer 3³ 5⁷, Ezk 16²⁵, Pr 7¹⁰ 29³). But in OT times the harlot represented more than a moral problem and a moral danger of the utmost gravity. It is not too much to say that she was the concrete embodiment of the most powerful and insidious force menacing the purity and permanence of Mosaism. Like their kindred who took possession of the valley of the Euphrates, like the Greeks who were invaded by Phœnician commerce and culture, the Hebrews in Canaan found themselves in contact with a type of religion which deified the reproductive forces of nature, and paid them homage in the form of licentious rites and orgies. The harlot was thus invested with sanctity as a member of the religious caste, and the question was whether a licentious cult was to establish itself in the soil of Jahwism even as it naturalized itself in Babylon (cf. Herod. i. 199), and in Cythera and Corinth (Strabo, viii. 6). And undoubtedly the Canaanitish leaven deeply infected the popular Hebrew religion. In the story of Tamar's intrigue to secure her rights from the house of her deceased husband (Gn 38), she is spoken of as a קְדֵשָׁה—one of the consecrated class—when she sits at the entrance of a village in the guise of a harlot. Especially does Hosea (4¹⁴) give us a vivid picture of the extent to which the local sanctuaries, where the worship of Baal and Astarte had been syncretized with that of J″, were coloured by the legitimated prostitution of servants of the divinities. In some sanctuaries a still lower depth was reached, and emasculated enthusiasts (קְדֵשִׁים) earned for the shrine 'the wages of a dog' by giving themselves up to that 'which is against nature.' These practices the prophets of the 8th cent. denounced as the height of impiety and the sure provocation of national judgments (Am 2⁷, Hos 4¹³ff.). By Asa and Jehoshaphat steps were taken to purge the land of the viler abomination (1 K 15¹² 22⁴⁶, cf. 14²⁴); and the Deuteronomic code explicitly banished both classes of 'paramours' from Israel, and prohibited the acceptance of their unholy gains as temple-revenue (Dt 23¹⁷·¹⁸, where see Driver's note *in loc.* with reff.). With idolatry prostitution was made an end of by the Exile. The Levitical legislation recalls the abominations of the Canaanites as the special ground of their rejection and destruction (Lv 20²³), and appears to have the class of harlots solely in view as created and sustained by moral depravity. The more important of its enactments are that which forbids a priest to take a harlot to wife (Lv 21⁷), and the injunction that the daughter of a priest playing the harlot shall be burnt with fire (v.⁹).

Upon the OT treatment of the subject it may be remarked as startling that there is no express condemnation of sexual immorality which does not involve violation of the marriage-bond. At the

most, fornication seems to be condemned in Pr as health- and wealth-destroying folly, while the general tenor of the OT morality is content to proscribe adultery and religious prostitution. In explanation of this, it may be observed that the true ethical attitude towards prostitution was impossible so long as marriage was in the transitional stage mirrored in OT, and that the OT at least unfolded a conception of the divine holiness and its relation to sexual purity which was destined to mature into the higher sexual morality.

In NT the harlot, again, is associated with an important element of teaching. While it was part of the mission of the prophets to refute the horrible idea of the sacredness of her calling, it was a characteristic part of the work of Jesus to rescue her from the Pharisaic tribunal, and bring her within the pale of mercy and redemption (Mt 21³¹·³²). She illustrates at once the compassion of Jesus, His insight into the unexpressed longings and possibilities of degraded human nature, and the regenerative power of sympathy. In the apostolic writings we see some repetition of the conflict between the genius of revealed religion and the lax and antagonistic sexual morality of heathenism. In the Epistles to the Corinthians especially, St. Paul was addressing a community whose licentiousness had become a byword even in the putrefying cities of the classical world; and it is necessary for him to enlighten the Christian conscience as to the incompatibility of union with Christ with its hideous contrast in filthy 'conversation' (1 Co 6¹⁵·¹⁶). And in various apostolic passages the prohibition of the Decalogue is explicated or extended so as expressly to exclude the sin in question (Gal 6¹⁹ff.).

From the prophetic period the harlot was not only involved in, but was the symbol of, idolatry. The experience of Hosea seems to have suggested her faithlessness and fickleness as a fit emblem of the dealings of Israel with her true Lord and with other gods (see IDOLATRY).

LITERATURE.—On Prostitution as a religious institution in the ancient world, see Lucian, 'De Dea Syria'; Pausanias, 'Descriptio Græciæ'; Movers, *Die Phönizier*. On the special subject Selden, 'De uxore Hebraica'; Hamburger's *Lexicon*; Benzinger, *Hebräische Archæologie*.

W. P. PATERSON.

HAR-MAGEDON.—Rev 16¹⁶ ' And he (AV; who? the sixth angel or the Almighty? RV 'they,' the three unclean spirits of v.¹⁷) gathered them (the kings of the whole world, not 'the spirits of the Demons,' as Hommel explains in the passage to be quoted below) together into the place, which is called in Hebrew Armageddon' (AV, 'Har-Magedon' RV). The reading, as well as the meaning and even the context, of this *hapax-legomenon* is very uncertain.

(1) The TR spells Ἁρμαγεδδών; Lachmann, Tregelles, Tischendorf, Alford, Ἁρμαγεδών; WH Ἁρ Μαγεδών (the second word spaced out and in quotation type, referring to Zec 12¹¹ [Heb.]). Several Greek MSS have but Μαγεδών or Μαγεδδών (thus Q). The shorter reading is supported by Tyconius and, now, by the (older) Syriac translation discovered and edited by Gwynn (Dublin, 1897): ܡܓܕܘ. The later Syriac translation (commonly printed with the Peshiṭta) has ܐܘܡܓܕܘ (not quoted in the *Thesaurus Syriacus*, col. 390). The shorter form must have arisen at a time when the whole word was considered to be a compound.

(2) The oldest explanation put forward in the Church seems to be that of Hippolytus, unhappily preserved only in Arabic (P. Lagardii, *ad Analecta sua Syriaca Appendix*, Lipsiæ, 1858, p. 27 n. 18): ' the meaning of this expression is *the smooth* (soft,

trodden) *place* الموضع الوطي.' Is this = πεδίον ἐκκοπτομένου, the Septuagint rendering of בִּקְעַת מְגִדּוֹן in Zec 12[11]? (For the Arabic expression comp. وطية قدم = βῆμα ποδός, Ac 7[5]). It is added that Hippolytus understood it of the valley of Jehoshaphat, Jl 4[2] [Eng. 3[11]][12] (Hippolytus ed. [Bonwetsch-] Achelis, I. ii. 236).

Origen-Eusebius excluded the Apocalypse from their Bible Dictionary, but in the *Onomastica Vaticana* Ἀρμαγεδδών is explained: εἰς τὰ ἔμπροσθεν ἐξέγερσις (*Onomastica sacra*, ed. de Lagarde, p. 187, l. 45), *i.e.* עֵר מְקָרֵם, and Jerome, who saw in it Mt. Tabor, explained likewise (*ib.* 80, 11): 'Armageddon (cod. H -gedon): *consurrectio tecti* (? עֵר קִנֵּן) *sive consurrectio in priora*, sed melius *mons a latrunculis* (cod. H om. *mons*; הַר מְרִירוּד) vel *mons globosus*' (נַר מְּנִד; ה'; נַר = coriandrum).

(3) For a long time the explanation (הַר מְגִדּוֹן) 'the mount (of) Megiddo,' was considered pretty certain; see Westcott-Hort, ii. p. 313, who compare Ἀρ Γαριζείν, Ἄρ Σαφάρ, to which may be added, from the Hexapla, Ἄρ Σιών, Ps 47 (48)[3]. Older scholars had also compared Ἀρσαμόσατα of the Classics, while Westcott-Hort prefer to see in the latter name another example of Ἀρ = עֵר (עִיר) 'town,' as in עֵר מוֹאָב (Nu 21[28], Is 15[1]; transliterated in the latter place Ἀρ Μωάβ by Theodotion). The latter explanation was put forward long ago by Hiller and adopted by Hitzig, Hilgenfeld, Völter, and others. A third explanation started from the root חרם (comp. חָרְמָה Nu 21[28]; חָרְמוֹן); thus Luther in his marginal gloss 'verdammte Krieger, verfluchte Rüstung . . . ab *Herem* et *gad*.' Older explanations need not be quoted here; see Poole, *Synopsis Criticorum*, ed. Franc. (1712) vol. v. 1829. Makkedah (מַקֵּדָה, LXX Μακηδά), where 'the five kings' were slain (Jos 10[16. 26]), lies too far away to be thought of.

(4) Upon the whole, to find an allusion here to MEGIDDO (see article) is still the most probable explanation. Megiddo was famous for the defeat and death of Josiah (2 K 23[29], 2 Ch 35[22]; alluded to Zec 12[11]) but it is not on account of this unhappy event that the place seems to be mentioned, but because of the victory over 'the kings of Canaan' (Jg 5[19]). It has been objected that Megiddo lies in the plain (ἐν τῷ πεδίῳ M., 2 Ch 35[22]; ἐπὶ ὕδατι M., Jg 5[19]; עַל מֵי מְגִדּוֹ), and that a mountain was not a fit battleplace (Bousset, *ad loc.*). But in the very context of Jg 5 'Mt. Tabor' and 'the high places of the field' are mentioned (Jg 4[6. 8. 12] 5[18]).

(5) Hommel ('Inschriftliche Glossen u. Exkurse zur Genesis u. zu den Propheten,' *Neue Kirchliche Zeitschrift*, 1890, vi. pp. 407, 408) seems to have been the first who saw in Har-Magedon the הַר מוֹעֵד of Is 14[13] (the mount in the north where the gods meet), supposing that a redactor corrected an original μαυέδ or μωέδ into μαγεδδω. He might have recalled the fact that in certain cases ע is transliterated by γ. This view was carried out by Gunkel (*Schöpfung und Chaos*, 1894), who finds here the remnant of an ancient tradition about the battle of the gods on a mountain, and reminds us of the gathering of the fallen angels on Mt. Hermon, Enoch 6[6]. (To the literature quoted by Bousset also: *The Book of the Secrets of Enoch*, edited by R. H. Charles, Oxf. 1896, ch. xviii. p. 22). Siegfried (*Theol. Lit.-zeitung*, 1895, col. 304) also thinks that in Harmagedon the הַר מוֹעֵד of Is 14[13] and Μεγιδδώ seem to have coalesced. Ewald (*Die Johanneischen Schriften*, ii. 1862, 294) found by calculation that ארמדין and רומה הגדולה 'the great Rome,' have the same numerical value—304. The question whether there is in the passage an allusion to Nero and the Parthians must be left to the commentators on the Apocalypse. The solution of the riddle is to be sought for in the apocalyptic literature of the Jews.

EB. NESTLE.

HARNEPHER (חֶרְנָפֶר).—An Asherite, 1 Ch 7[36]. See GENEALOGY.

HARNESS.—In AV harness always means armour, and to harness means to put on armour, RV gives 'armour' in 1 K 20[11], 2 Ch 9[24], and 'armed' in Ex 13[18]; while Amer. RV prefers 'armour' also in 1 K 22[34], 2 Ch 18[33]; both have left Jer 46[4] untouched: 'Harness the horses.' The meaning is not (as Cheyne and most edd.) yoke the horses to the chariots, but put on their accoutrements. These being chiefly of armour, 'harness' was once a good tr[n], but now it is misleading. Cf. 1 Mac 6[43] 'One of the beasts, armed with royal harness, was higher than all the rest' (RV 'breastplates'). In Apocr. 'harness' occurs also, 1 Mac 3[3] (RV retains), 6[41] (RV 'arms'), 2 Mac 3[25] 5[3] 15[28] (RV all 'armour'); and the verb in 1 Mac 4[7] (RV 'fortified'), 6[38] (RV 'protected'). Examples of the word are, Nu 32[20] Tind. 'And Moses sayed unto them, Yf ye will do this thinge, that ye will go all harnessed before the Lorde to warre, and will go all of you in harnesse over Iordane before the Lorde . . . then ye shall returne and be without sinne agenst the Lorde and agenst Israel'; Is 22[6] Cov. 'I sawe the Elamites take the quyvers to carte and to horse, and that the walles were bare from harnesse'; Knox on Ps 6 (*Works*, iii. 141) represents David as saying, 'Didest not thou anis inflame my heart with the zeale of thy halie name, that when all Israell wer so effrayit that none durst encounter with that monster Goliath, yit thy Majesties spreit maid me so bold and valiaunt, that without harnes or weaponis (except my sling, staf, and stonis) I durst intrpryes singular battell aganis him?' And Tindale on 1 Jn 5[18] says, 'And as men of war they ever keep watch and prepare themselves unto war, and put on the armour of God, the which is God's word, the shield of faith, the helmet of hope, and harness themselves with the meditation of those things which Christ suffered for us.'

J. HASTINGS.

HARNESS.—(1) For *shiryan* (שִׁרְיָן) 1 K 22[34] ‖ 2 Ch 18[33]), 'shirt of mail.' RV (Amer.) 'coat.' See BREASTPLATE. (2) For *neshek* (נֶשֶׁק 2 Ch 9[24]), 'arms' (defensive or offensive), RV 'armour.' (3) For πανοπλία (2 Mac 15[28]), 'the complete offensive and defensive equipment of a soldier'; RV 'full armour.'

Harnessed for *ḥămushim* (חֲמֻשִׁים Ex 13[18]), RV 'armed.' See ARMS, ARMOUR.

W. E. BARNES.

HAROD (חֲרֹד).—A spring (עַיִן, not 'well' AV) beside which Gideon and his army encamped prior to their attack upon the Midianites (Jg 7[1]). It was here that the famous test by the mode of drinking took place. In v.[3] there is probably a characteristic play upon the word חֲרֹד, 'whosoever is fearful and *trembling*' (חָרֵד). The site of Harod is not quite certain, although it is extremely probable that it should be identified with 'Ain Jalûd [Gilead (?); see GILEAD (MOUNT)], about 1¾ miles E.S.E. of *Zerin* (Jezreel). Robinson describes this as a spring of excellent water, spreading out into a fine limpid pool of 40 to 50 ft. in diameter, which abounds in fish. A stream sufficient to turn a mill issues from it. 'Ain Jalûd was probably also the spring beside which Saul encamped before the battle of Gilboa (1 S 29[1]). It 'flows out from under a sort of cavern in the wall of conglomerate rock, which here forms the base of Mt. Gilboa' (Robinson). 'Ain Jalûd is mentioned in the days of the Crusades as *Tubania* (Will. Tyr. xxii. 26). Bohaeddin (*Vit. Salad.* p. 53) gives the name as 'Ain el-Jalût ('spring of Goliath'). This is no doubt a reminiscence of a Jewish legend (Asher, *Benj. of Tudela*, ii. 429 f.) that it was here that David slew Goliath.

LITERATURE.—Robinson, *BRP* 2 ii. 323 f. ; Buhl, *GAP* 106 ; G. A. Smith, *HGHL* 397 f. ; Guérin, *Samariée*, i. 308 f.

J. A. SELBIE.

HARODITE (הַחֲרֹדִי).—A designation applied in 2 S 23²⁵ to two of David's heroes, Shammah and Elika. The second is wanting in LXX and in the parallel list in 1 Ch 11²⁷. In the latter passage, by a common scribal error (ר for ד and ה for ח) the Harodite (הַחֲרוֹדִי) has been transformed into the **Harorite** (הַחֲרוֹרִי). So *Oxf. Heb. Lex.*, Siegfried-Stade, Driver, Kittel ; cf. GENEALOGY, vol. ii. p. 132. 'The Harodite' was probably a native of *'Ain-ḥarod*, Jg 7¹. See preceding article.

HAROEH (הָרֹאֶה 'the seer').—A Judahite, 1 Ch 2⁵². Perhaps the name should be corrected to Reaiah (רְאָיָה). Cf. 1 Ch 4², and see GENEALOGY.

HARORITE.—See HARODITE.

HAROSHETH of the Gentiles (חֲרֹשֶׁת הַגּוֹיִם) was the dwelling place of Sisera (Jg 4²), from which he advanced against Barak (v.¹³) and to which he fled after his defeat (v.¹⁶). The descriptive epithet 'of the Gentiles' is obscure ; it *may* have been given to distinguish this place from a neighbouring *Israelite* Harosheth. H. is generally identified (by Moore rather doubtfully) with *el-Ḥarathîyeh*, on the right bank of the lower Kishon, at a point which commands the entrance to the Great Plain from the Plain of Acre and the commercial roads that led through it. Buhl objects that Harosheth cannot have been near the Kishon, and that a long distance must have separated it from the battlefield (cf. Jg 4¹³. ¹⁶). This objection would have much more force if we could be sure that the story is a unity, but, upon the theory of a Jabin and a Sisera narrative having been combined, the situation of *el-Ḥarathîyeh* suits the Harosheth, which is uniformly connected with Sisera as Hazor is with Jabin. See further, JABIN, JAEL, SISERA.

LITERATURE.—Thomson (the first to identify with *el-Harathîyeh*), *Land and Book* 2, ii. 215 ff. ; G. A. Smith, *HGHL* 393 f. ; Baedeker-Socin, *Pal.* 2 241 ; Buhl, *GAP* 214 ; *SWP* vol. i. sh. v. ; Conder, *Tent-Work*, i. 132 ; Moore, *Judges*, 107 f., 119, 122.

J. A. SELBIE.

HARP.—See MUSIC.

HARROW.—**1.** In modern agriculture the harrow is used both for breaking stiff soil and preparing it for the seed, and for covering in the seed when sown. For the latter purpose the harrow was certainly not used either in Bible times or later by the Jews, who ploughed in the seed (the technical word for which was חָפָה, see Vogelstein, *Die Landwirthschaft in Palästina zur Zeit der Mishnah*, 1 Theil, 'Der Getreidebau,' 1894, p. 36) as their successors the Syrian fellahin do to this day (*PEFSt*, 1891, p. 116, *ZDPV* xii. p. 29).* As to the use of the harrow in preparing the ground for seed, the case is not so clear. On the one hand, we find in three passages of the OT unmistakable reference to some method, in addition to ordinary ploughing, for breaking up the soil preparatory to sowing. 'Doth the ploughman plough continually?' it is asked, 'doth he continually open and break the clods of his ground?' (Is 28²⁴ RV). The last of these operations (Heb. יְשַׂדֵּד) is usually understood as, and often rendered by, harrowing (*e.g.* by Cheyne, Delitzsch, etc.). The same word is found in two other passages (Hos 10¹¹, Job 39¹⁰), where it certainly denotes some agricultural operation by

* Roman writers regard harrowing *after* sowing as bad husbandry (see 'Agriculture' in Smith's *Dict. of Antiquities*).

means of an implement to which an ox or other animal might be harnessed, as in the question, ' Canst thou bind the wild ox with his band in the furrow, or will he harrow (יְשַׂדֵּד) the valleys after thee ?' (Job 39¹⁰ RV—the only passage where the verb is so rendered in our EV). On the strength of these passages it has been the custom to regard harrowing as the operation intended, and the harrow as in ordinary use among the Hebrews for the purpose stated. (See AGRICULTURE, vol. i. p. 49ᵃ).

On the other hand, we must reckon with the following facts :—(*a*) the harrow is an implement unknown to the ancient Egyptians (Wilkinson, *Manners and Customs*, etc., ed. Birch, ii. 395) and the early Greeks (Büchsenschütz, *Besitz. und Erwerb*, etc. 304) ; (*b*) the harrow itself is not named either in the OT—see 2 below—or in the Mishna, which is so rich in the technical vocabulary of agriculture (see esp. Vogelstein's exhaustive study above cited, p. 42, n. 33) ; (*c*) it is not in ordinary use among the Syrian peasantry to-day (*ZDPV* xii. 31, and cf. list of modern agricultural implements by Post, *PEFSt*, 1891, p. 110). In the face of these facts, the use of the harrow by the Hebrews must at least be left an open question. It is not improbable that שָׂדַד may be a technical term for one of the various ploughings which were customary, in later times at least, before the soil was ready to receive the seed (cf. Vogelstein, *op. cit.* p. 36, n. 68), and may possibly correspond to our cross-ploughing. The Greek translators of Job, it may be noted, understood it of ploughing (ἑλκύσει σου αὔλακας ἐν πεδίῳ, 39¹⁰), and we know that the Roman authorities much preferred ploughing to harrowing as a means of breaking up the stiff surface (Pliny, *Nat. Hist.* XVIII. ch. xlix. ; Columella, II. iv. 2).

2. Throughout this discussion we have avoided any reference to the two passages in our EV where harrows are expressly mentioned. The captive population of Rabbah 'of the children of Ammon,' David, we read, 'put under saws, and under harrows of iron (חֲרִצֵי הַבַּרְזֶל), and under axes of iron,' etc. (2 S 12³¹, and with slight variations 1 Ch 20³). By 'harrows of iron' it has been usual to understand — following the LXX ἐν τοῖς τριβόλοις τοῖς σιδηροῖς—the threshing-board or drag (חָרוּץ Am 1³, Job 41²² [Eng.³⁰]) of the husbandman, with its under side set with nails and sharp flints (see AGRICULTURE, vol. i. p. 50ᵇ). It is extremely doubtful, however, if this cruelty can be laid to David's charge. Almost all modern scholars are in favour of a rendering resembling that suggested in the margin of our RV. In this case the word rendered ' harrows,' which etymologically denotes a sharp instrument, may be the 'pick,' and the whole would read : 'he put them (to forced labour) with saws, and with picks, and axes of iron, and made them labour (reading הֶעֱבִיד for הֶעֱבִיר) at the brick-mould.' (See Driver, *Text of Sam.* 226 ff. ; Condamin, *Rev. Bibl.*, April 1898, p. 253 ff.).

A. R. S. KENNEDY.

HARSHA (חַרְשָׁא).—Eponym of a family of Nethinim (Ezr 2⁵², Neh 7⁵⁴), called in 1 Es 5³² Charea. See GENEALOGY.

HARSITH (חַרְסִית Kerê, חַרְסוּת Kethîbh).—The name of a gate in Jerusalem (Jer 19² RV). RVm has 'the gate of potsherds,' *i.e.* where they were thrown out (*Oxf. Heb. Lex.*). AV deriving the word from חֶרֶס 'sun,' has 'the east gate,' AVm 'the sun gate.' LXX has B Θαρσείς, אᶜ·ᵃ Χαροίθ, AQ Χαρσείθ. This gate led into the Valley of Hinnom. See JERUSALEM.

HART (אַיָּל *'ayyâl*, ἔλαφος, *cervus*).—The Arab. *'iyyal* undoubtedly refers to the same animal. It is probably *Cervus Dama*, L., the true *fallow deer*, but not that of AV Dt 14[5], 1 K 4[23], which is a mistr[n] of *yaḥmûr*, and should read *roebuck*. The fallow deer is found in Amanus, and is said by Tristram to exist also in the wooded region N.W. of Tabor, and by the Litany River. The present writer has not, however, been able to verify this statement. Hasselquist met with it on Mt. Tabor. It may have become extinct there only in recent times. It seems clear from the fact that it appeared daily upon Solomon's table (1 K 4[23]), and from the freq. allusions to it in OT, that it was once abundant in Pal. and Syria. It is expressly mentioned as allowed for food (Dt 12[15. 22] 15[22] 14[5]). Its power of leaping is noted (Is 35[6]), esp. that of its fawn (Ca 2[9. 17] 8[14]). Its weakness when hungry is spoken of (La 1[6]), as also its longing for water (Ps 42[1]). The former passage certainly, and the latter prob., alludes to the chase.

The **Hind** (אַיָּלָה *'ayyâlâh*) is also freq. mentioned. Naphtali is compared to a 'hind let loose' (Gn 49[21], where, however, the text appears to be corrupt, see Ball's note in Haupt's *OT*). Her calving is alluded to (Job 39[1], Ps 29[9]), and she is spoken of as deserting her young for lack of pasture (Jer 14[5]). She is sure-footed (2 S 22[34], Ps 18[33], Hab 3[19]). The tune **Hind of the Morning** (marg. title Ps 22 for *Aijeleth hash-Shahar*) may illustrate the early habits of the deer tribe in search of water and food. The writer has often seen gazelles, at break of day, feeding in the desert.   G. E. POST.

HARUM (הָרֻם, but the vocalization is doubtful). —A Judahite, 1 Ch 4[8]. See GENEALOGY.

HARUMAPH (חֲרוּמַף, Ἐρωμάφ, Ἐρωμάθ B, Neh 3[10]). —Jedaiah, the son of H., assisted in repairing the walls of Jerus. under Nehemiah.

HARUPHITE.—1 Ch 12[5]. See HARIPH.

HARUZ (חָרוּץ, perhaps 'keen' or 'diligent'; Ἀρούς BA Luc.)—Father of Meshullemeth, mother of Amon king of Judah (2 K 21[19]).

HARVEST.—See AGRICULTURE and VINTAGE.

HASADIAH (חֲסַדְיָה 'J″ is kind').—A son of Zerubbabel, 1 Ch 3[20]. The Gr. form **Asadias** occurs in Bar 1[1]. See GENEALOGY.

HASHABIAH (חֲשַׁבְיָה).—**1. 2.** Two Levites of the sons of Merari, 1 Ch 6[45] 9[14], Neh 11[15]. **3.** One of the sons of Jeduthun, 1 Ch 25[3]. **4.** A Hebronite, 1 Ch 26[30]. **5.** The 'ruler' of the Levites, 1 Ch 27[17]. **6.** A chief of the Levites in the time of Josiah, 2 Ch 35[9], called in 1 Es 1[9] Sabias. **7.** One of the Levites who were induced to return under Ezra, Ezr 8[19], called in 1 Es 8[48] Asebias. **8.** One of the twelve priests entrusted with the holy vessels, Ezr 8[24], called in 1 Es 8[54] Assamias. **9.** The 'ruler of half the district of Keilah,' who helped to repair the wall, Neh 3[17], and sealed the covenant, Neh 10[11] 12[24. 26]. **10.** A Levite, Neh 11[22]. **11.** A priest, Neh 12[21]. In all probability these eleven are not all distinct, but we have not sufficient data to enable us to effect the necessary reduction of the list. See GENEALOGY.

HASHABNAH (חֲשַׁבְנָה for חֲשַׁבְיָה ?).—One of those who sealed the covenant (Neh 10[25] [Heb. 26]).

HASHABNEIAH (חֲשַׁבְנְיָה for חֲשַׁבְיָה ?).—**1.** Father of a builder of the wall (Neh 3[10]). **2.** A Levite, Neh 9[5] = Hashabiah of Ezr 8[19. 24], Neh 10[11] 11[22] 12[24]. See GENEALOGY.

HASHBADDANAH (חַשְׁבַּדָּנָה). — One of the men,

probably Levites, who stood on the left hand of Ezra at the reading of the law (Neh 8[4]). In 1 Es 9[44] Nabarias.

HASHEM.—See GIZONITE, JASHEN.

HASHMANNIM.—See PSALMS.

HASHMONAH (חַשְׁמֹנָה).—A station in the journeyings of the Israelites, mentioned only Nu 33[29. 30]. The LXX reading (Σελμωνά, Ἀσελμωνά, AF) appears to confuse this station with the Zalmonah of v.[41].

HASHUBAH (חֲשֻׁבָה 'consideration').—A son of Zerubbabel, 1 Ch 3[20]. See GENEALOGY.

HASHUM (חָשֻׁם).—**1.** The eponym of a family of returning exiles (Ezr 2[19] 10[33], Neh 7[22] 10[18]), called in 1 Es 9[33] Asom. **2.** One of those who stood on Ezra's left hand at the reading of the law (Neh 8[4]). In 1 Es 9[44] Lothasubus. See GENEALOGY.

HASIDÆANS (Ἀσιδαῖοι from חָסִיד 'pious,' in the sense of active love to God [Cheyne, *Ps.* 378], or because piety is supposed to be implied by kindness [*Oxf. Heb. Lex. s.v.*]; grecized into Ἀσιδαῖοι) occurs in three passages in the Apocr. 1 Mac 2[42] (A) speaks of a company Ἀσιδαίων (some important MSS read Ἰουδαίων), and describes them as devoted to the law. 1 Mac 7[12. 13] associates them with 'a company of scribes,' who were satisfied that Alcimus should be high priest because of his Aaronic descent. 2 Mac 14[6] confounds them with the Hasmonæans (which see), whom, however, they did not always support (see 1 Mac 7[10-14]). But, though not mentioned elsewhere by name, their beliefs and practice are shown in such passages as 1 Mac 1[63] 2[34], 2 Mac 6[18ff.] 7[10-12], Jth 12[2]; Jos. *Ant.* XIV. iv. 3. They were not a political but a religious party, composing the inner circle of the strictest legalists, and indisposed to interfere in civil government except in defence of Mosaism. They were not the progenitors of the Essenes, from whom they differed on the crucial question of sacrifice, but of the Pharisees, with whose rise their name as that of a party disappears (Wellhausen, *Phar. und Sadd.* 76 ff.; less correctly, Hamburger, *RE* ii. 132–137, 1038–1059). The name occurs in OT frequently, but is not yet proved that it is used in a technical sense, even in Ps 116[15] 149[5. 9]. In later Jewish literature the word denotes a rigid observer of the law (*Berachoth* v. 1; *Chagigah* ii. 7; *Sotah* iii. 4; *Aboth* ii. 10; *Niddah* 17α); but it was not until more recent times that its use strictly as the name of a special sect, rather than as descriptive of the habits of the extreme members of a larger party, was revived.   R. W. MOSS.

HASMONÆAN, the family name of the Maccabees. It occurs in Jos. [who claimed (*Ant.* XVI. vii. 1) alliance with the family], under the forms of Ἀσαμωναῖοι and Ἀσσαμωναῖοι, and is derived from the name of an ancestor Ἀσαμωναῖος, who is represented as the great-grandfather of Mattathias (*ib.* XII. vi. 1). In the Talm. the family appears as בְּנֵי חַשְׁמוֹנַאי (*Middoth*, i. 6), and as חשמ׳ בית (*Sabb.* 21[b]; also Targ. Jonathan to 1 S 2[4]). The original ancestor חַשְׁמֹן is not otherwise known; but his name is connected with חַשְׁמֹן 'fruitfulness' by Fuerst, with חשם in the sense of 'to temper steel' by Herzfeld, and with חַשְׁמַנִּים 'opulent' (Ps 68[32] [Eng. 31]) by Ewald and others. The last suggestion is most probable, but is not unlikely to give way before Wellhausen's conjecture (*Pharisäer* etc. 94) that τοῦ Συμεών of 1 Mac 2[1] is a misrendering of חַשְׁמֹן בֶּן. That would explain the apparent absence of allusion to Ḥashmon in 1 Mac, and make him the grandfather of Mattathias. The exploits of Judas caused the family to be afterwards generally known as the Maccabees; but this designation does not once occur in old Heb. literature. Hasmonæan or Hasmunæan is found in its stead, and can hardly have been entirely excluded from the Heb. or Aram. original of 1 Mac.   R. W. MOSS.

HASRAH.—See HARHAS.

HASSENAAH (הַסְּנָאָה).—The sons of H. built the fish-gate (Neh 3³). Their name, which is prob. the same as HASSENUAH (wh. see), seems to be derived from some place Senaah (cf. Ezr 2³⁵, Neh 7³⁸, and Berth.-Ryssel, ad loc.).

HASSENUAH (הַסְּנֻאָה).—A family name found in two different connexions in the two lists of Benjamite inhabitants of Jerus., 1 Ch 9⁷, Neh 11⁹.

HASSHUB (חַשּׁוּב 'considerate').—**1. 2.** Two builders of the wall, Neh 3¹¹· ²³. **3.** One of those who signed the covenant, Neh 10²³ [Heb.²⁴]. **4.** A Levite of the sons of Merari, 1 Ch 9¹⁴, Neh 11¹⁵.

HASTE.—The verb 'to haste' is used transitively in Ex 5¹³ 'And the taskmasters hasted them, saying, Fulfil your works' (RV 'were urgent'); Is 16⁵ 'And in mercy shall the throne be established; and he shall sit upon it in truth in the tabernacle of David, judging, and seeking judgment, and hasting righteousness' (RV 'swift to do righteousness'); 1 Es 1²⁷ 'the Lord is with me hasting me forward'; and 2 Mac 9⁷ 'commanding to haste the journey.' So in Wyc., as Pr 13¹² 'Substaunce hastid shal be lassid [=lessened]'; and in Shaks., as *I Henry IV.* III. i. 143, 'I'll haste the writer'; and *Romeo,* IV. i. 11—

> 'Now, sir, her father counts it dangerous,
> That she doth give her sorrow so much sway,
> And in his wisdom hastes our marriage,
> To stop the inundation of her tears.'

The intrans. sense is more common, as 1 S 20³⁸ 'And Jonathan cried after the lad, Make speed, haste, stay not.' Cf. Is 26⁹ Cov. 'My soule lusteth after the all the night longe, and my mynde haisteth frely to the.' And the reflexive use is not infrequent, as Gn 19²² 'Haste thee, escape thither.'   J. HASTINGS.

HASUPHA (חֲשׂוּפָא Ezr 2⁴³, חֲשֻׂפָא Neh 7⁴⁶, where AV inaccurately gives **Hashupha**).—The head of a family of Nethinim who returned with Zerub., called in 1 Es 5²⁹ Asipha. See GENEALOGY.

HAT.—Hats are mentioned once in AV, but it is quite certain that this is a mistranslation. When Shadrach, Meshech, and Abed-nego were about to be cast into the fiery furnace, they were 'bound in their coats, their hosen, and their hats' (RV 'their hosen, their tunics, and their mantles'). The Aram. is כַּרְבְּלָתְהוֹן, from which comes the denom. vb. כְּרְבֵּל (Pual ptcp. מְכֻרְבָּל), which coupled with מְעִיל is used of David in 1 Ch 15²⁷ as 'clothed with a robe of fine linen.' The RV 'mantle' in Dn 3²¹ is probably as nearly accurate a trⁿ of כַּרְבְּלָא as one could suggest, although Marti favours the meaning 'cap' = Assyr. *karballattu*, a word which, however, Zehnpfund (*Beiträge z. Assyriologie,* ii. 535) contends itself means 'Kriegs[?]-mantel,' 'war-cloak.' See *Oxf. Heb. Lex. s.* [כרבל].   J. A. SELBIE.

HATHACH (הֲתָךְ, Ἀχραθαῖος, Est 4⁵· ⁶· ⁹· ¹⁰, AV Hatach).—A eunuch appointed by the king to attend on queen Esther. By his means Esther learnt from Mordecai the details of Haman's plot against the Jews.

HATHATH (חֲתַת 'terror').—A son of Othniel, 1 Ch 4¹³. See GENEALOGY.

HATIPHA (חֲטִיפָא).—Eponym of a family of Nethinim (Ezr 2⁵⁴, Neh 7⁵⁶), called in 1 Es 5³² Atipha. See GENEALOGY.

HATITA (חֲטִיטָא, cf. Aram. חֲטַט 'to dig').—Eponym of a guild of porters (Ezr 2⁴², Neh 7⁴⁵), called in 1 Es 5²⁸ Ateta.

HATRED.—The actual word 'hatred' is seldom found in the Bible. In the OT it represents three different words, two of which (אֵיבָה and מַשְׂטֵמָה occurring four times) mean more precisely 'enmity' (as of one nation towards another), and are so rendered by RV (Ezk 25¹⁵ 35⁵, Hos 9⁷· ⁸), while the other (שִׂנְאָה) which occurs thirteen times) denotes the opposite of love (with which it is explicitly contrasted, Ps 109⁵, Pr 10¹² 15⁷, cf. Ps 97¹⁰). In all the cases in which they occur, the words have a personal significance, and express human feelings—the absence of sympathy and love and kindly sentiments, or the state of active ill-will, on the part of men towards men. In NT the word is found once only (ἔχθραι, lit. 'enmities,' so RV) in one of the lists of vices given by St. Paul (Gal 5²⁰).

The verbs, however, which have the meaning 'hate' are frequent both in OT and NT in various connexions. In OT שָׂטַן 'oppose,' corresponding to 'enmity,' occurs five times (in three of wh. instances RV renders 'persecute,' Gn 49²³, Job 16⁹, Ps 55³), always of personal animosity against a person. Far more frequent is שָׂנֵא, of which the Eng. 'hate' is the closest equivalent. It may be said to be used both in a good sense and in a bad sense, when the feeling denoted is praiseworthy and when it is not. It occurs about 125 times, and in three cases out of four it is used in a bad sense. In about half the full number of instances the objects of hatred are persons, men or women; twelve times it is God himself who is 'hated' (e.g. Ex 20⁵ ‖ Dt 5⁹); only some ten times when the word is used in a bad sense is the object not a person but a principle (e.g. Job 34¹⁷, Ps 50¹⁷, Pr 1²²· ²⁹). Of the comparatively few cases in which the word is used in a good sense the allusion is in half the number to the divine hatred of evil and sin, God being represented as personally hating evil persons or things, either directly or through his chosen spokesman (Dt 12³¹ 16²², Ps 5⁵ 11⁵, Pr 6¹⁶, Is 1¹⁴ 61⁸, Jer 12⁸ 44⁴, Am 5²¹ 6⁸, Hos 9¹⁵, Zec 8¹⁷, Mal 1³ 2¹⁶). In the remaining cases it is used of men's dislike and aversion from things (e.g. Ex 18²¹, Ps 45⁷ 119¹⁰⁴) or persons (Ps 26⁵ 31⁶) which have an evil character. In a few passages in the later books of the OT there is a special usage similar to that which is found in some cases in the NT (e.g. Lk 14²⁶, Mt 6²⁴) to express as forcibly as possible aversion from or disregard of the interests or claims of one thing relatively to those of another (Pr 13²⁴ 29²⁴, Ec 2¹⁷· ¹⁸).

In NT the reference (the Gr. is μισέω) is in a large majority of instances to malicious and unjustifiable feelings on the part of the wicked towards persons who have not deserved evil. In half the remaining instances the word is used of a right feeling of aversion from that which is evil (Ro 7¹⁵, He 1⁹, Jude ²³, Rev 2⁶· ¹⁵, 17¹⁶); in the others the expression is somewhat hyperbolical, the context denoting relative preference of one thing over another (Mt 6²⁴ ‖ Lk 16¹³, Lk 14²⁶, Jn 3²⁰ 12²⁵, Eph 5²⁹).

These passages taken together reveal a clear difference in ethical standpoint between OT and NT, such indeed as is suggested by the saying of Jesus, 'Ye have heard that it hath been said, Thou shalt love thy neighbour, and hate thine enemy. But I say unto you, Love your enemies . . .' (Mt 5⁴³ᶠ·). The 'imprecatory' psalms show plainly that there was under the old covenant no sense of incongruity in appealing to God for aid in carrying out the fiercest hatred, in executing vengeance on an enemy. There are cases, no doubt, where the psalmist rises above mere personal animosity, and has in view the enemies of Israel and therefore of Israel's God; but the standard is not always at the height it reaches in the cry, 'Do not I hate them, O Lord, that hate thee?' (Ps 139²¹), and 'There is no peace, saith my God, to the wicked' (Is 57²¹). See PSALMS.

The teaching of Christ leaves hatred of evil alone admissible. St. John's strong assertion, 'Whosoever hateth his brother is a murderer' (1 Jn 3¹⁵), is a true comment on the spirit of Christian ethics. The dominant principle of brotherly love, the brotherhood of mankind, is to control all the relations of life. Every thought of self, every personal consideration, all sense of personal injury, must be eliminated. 'Love your enemies . . . and pray for them which despitefully use you,' excludes the possibility of personal hatred; sin must never be resented as a personal wrong, with a personal feeling against the offender. To bear malice, to wish for evil towards a fellow-creature, to close our sympathies against him,—this in the teaching of Christ (and the interpretation of St. John) is to be guilty of spiritual murder. The real sin is the inward disposition, the wish, the purpose of evil; the act is only the outward show of it (cf. Mt 15¹¹. ¹⁷⁻²⁰ 10²⁸). On the other hand, hatred of sin and evil in all its forms—evil, because it is evil and is opposed to the purpose of God—is a necessary corollary of all the great principles of the Gospel of Love.

J. F. BETHUNE-BAKER.

HATTIL (חַטִּיל, cf. Arab. *hatila* 'to be quivering').—Eponym of a family of 'the children of Solomon's servants' (Ezr 2⁵⁷, Neh 7⁵⁹), called in 1 Es 5³⁴ Agia. See GENEALOGY.

HATTUSH (חַטּוּשׁ).—1. A priestly family, which appears among those 'that went up with Zerubbabel,' Neh 12²; and at the signing of the covenant, Neh 10⁴ [Heb.⁵]. 2. A descendant of David, who returned with Ezra from Babylon, Ezr 8² (read in 1 Es 8²⁹ 'of the sons of David, Hattush the son of Shecaniah'); see also 1 Ch 3²² (but if we accept the LXX reading here, a younger Hattush must be meant). 3. A builder at the wall of Jerus., Neh 3¹⁰. See GENEALOGY. H. A. WHITE.

HAUNT.—To haunt is in older English simply to frequent, to make one's stay, be familiar with, and conveys no reproach. Thus Jn 3²² Tind. 'After these thinges cam Jesus and his disciples into the Jewes londe, and ther he haunted with them and baptised' (διέτριβε, AV 'tarried'); 11⁵⁴ Tind. 'Jesus therfore . . . went his waye . . . into a cite called Ephraim, and there haunted with his disciples' (διέτριβε, AV 'continued'); Rutherford, *Letters* (No. 1), 'I trust you will acquaint her with good company, and be diligent to know with whom she loveth to haunt.' So in AV, 1 S 30³¹ 'to all the places where David himself and his men were wont to haunt' (אֲשֶׁר־הִתְהַלֶּךְ־שָׁם); Ezk 26¹⁷ 'the renowned city, which wast strong in the sea, she and her inhabitants, which cause their terror to be on all that haunt it!' (לְכָל־יוֹשְׁבֶיהָ, RVm 'on all that inhabited her'); and the subst. in 1 S 23²² 'Go, I pray you, prepare yet, and know and see his place where his haunt is' (רַגְלוֹ, lit. 'his foot' as AVm and RVm). J. HASTINGS.

HAURAN (Αὐράνος, 2 Mac 4⁴⁰), described as a man 'far gone in years and no less also in madness.' At the head of a large body of armed men he endeavoured to suppress a tumult in Jerusalem provoked by the continued sacrileges of Lysimachus, brother of the apostate high priest Menelaus. Some MSS and the Vulg. support the reading *Tyrannus*, but the more familiar name is less likely to have been altered by copyists.

H. A. WHITE.

HAURAN (חַוְרָן; for various conjectures as to meaning, see *Oxf. Heb. Lex.*; Αὐρανῖτις; Arab. حَوْرَان, or in common speech *el-Ḥaurân*.—This was the name given, with varying definition of boundaries, to a tract of land E. of the Jordan, N. of Gilead, extending E. to the desert. In Ezk 47¹⁶. ¹⁸ the Jordan is made the border-line between Haurân, Damascus, and Gilead on the one hand, and the Land of Israel on the other. Haurân is there the whole district between Damascus and Gilead, from the lip of the Jordan Valley eastward. This practically corresponds with the province under the Turkish governor of Haurân to-day, whose seat is in el-Merkez, and whose jurisdiction includes Jedûr, Jaulân, and part of the hill-country south of the Jarmuk, as well as the region now specially called Haurân.

A series of beautiful cone-like hills, extinct volcanoes all, runs southward from the roots of Gt. Hermon, through Jedûr and Jaulân. Almost parallel with these, along the edge of the desert eastward, stands the great basaltic dyke, known at different times as Mons Asaldamus, Jebel Haurân, and Jebel ed-Druze. Between these two ranges lies a vast hollow, about 45 miles in breadth. In length, from Jebel el-Aswad in the N. to the bank of the Jarmuk in the S., it is nearly 50 miles; while away to the S.E. it runs out into the open desert. If we derive the name from *hawr*, a 'hollow,' with the place-ending *ân*, it may very well have applied to this gigantic vale.

The natives now say that Haurân consists of three parts, viz. en-Nukrah, el-Lejâ, and el-Jebel. These are clearly defined districts. (1) En-Nukrah, 'the cavity,' lies between the range of ez-Zumleh on the S.W., the slopes of Jaulân to westward, the volcanic fields of el-Lejâ on the N., and Jebel ed-Druze on the E. The wide reaches forming the floor of the hollow are rich, and fairly cultivated. This is the great grain-growing tract E. of Jordan. The elevation of the plain is from 1500 to 2000 ft. above sea-level. (2) El-Lejâ may be roughly described as a triangle, about 24 miles in length, with a base line of about 20 miles in the S., the apex being at Burak in the N. It is composed entirely of cooled lava, which is thrown about in the most grotesque and fantastic forms. The general aspect is dark, stern, forbidding. Soil is scanty, and but indifferently tilled. There are a few springs, but for the most part the inhabitants depend upon rain water, collected in cisterns or natural cavities in the rock. Great tracts to the N.E., owing to lack of water, are left absolutely tenantless during the summer months. The borders, where the lava waves drop to meet the emerald of the surrounding plain, are so distinctly marked that many have supposed this must be the *hebel 'Argob*—the measured lot of Argob¹ of Dt 3⁴. ¹³. ¹⁴, 1 K 4¹³ (but see ARGOB). The handful of peasants in the western parts are completely at the mercy of the Arabs of el-Lejâ, of whom a local proverb asserts that 'greater rascals do not exist.' The Druzes hold the district to the S.E. The name el-Lejâ, 'the asylum,' or 'refuge,' signifies the use to which the place is often put. The present writer has met, in the heart of el-Lejâ, men who had been charged with various offences in Mt. Lebanon and elsewhere, who, as soon as they passed the rocky ramparts round the borders, felt perfectly safe from the officers of the law. (3) El-Jebel is, of course, the great range which bounds the eastward view, of which el-Kuleib, 5730 ft. high, and

Salchad, with its mighty fortress crowning the southern heights, are the most outstanding features. The range effectually guards the fertile reaches to westward against the encroachment of the desert sands. The mountain is referred to in the Mishna as 'Mount Haurân,' one of the stations whence flashed the fire-signals announcing the advent of the new year (*Rosh hash-Shanah*, ii. 4). The name Jebel Haurân is now interchangeable with Jebel ed-Druze. After the terrible massacres of 1860, many Druze families moved eastward, occupied the S.E. district of el-Lejâ', and became masters of the greater part of the mountain. The inaccessible nature of the country gives them a great advantage over any attacking force. Until recent years their submission to the Turkish Government has been hardly more than nominal. With the exception of the clumps of trees around Sheikh Sa'ad, the reputed home of Job, and el-Merkez, the plain is treeless. In el-Lejâ, here and there, are a few stunted shrubs. The mountain is well wooded, and fruitful vineyards cling to many of the slopes.

Materials for the history of Haurân are very scanty, and do not go beyond the 1st cent. B.C. Towards the end of his reign Alexander Jannæus brought the western part of Haurân under his dominion; but eastward, Aretas the Arabian, or rather Nabatæan, held sway. The Nabatæans were driven southward by the Romans B.C. 64, but continued to hold Bozrah and Salchad. Herod the Great, succeeding to the government, did much to hold in check the lawless bands who infested the province, and indulged his taste for temple building. The oldest Greek inscription in these parts was found in a ruined temple at Sî'a, near Kanawât, on the pedestal of a statue erected to him during his lifetime. Under his son Philip a period of great prosperity seems to have been enjoyed. On Philip's death, after an interval of 3 years, Herod Agrippa received the province from Caligula. In an inscription found at Kanawât, he speaks of the inhabitants 'dwelling in caves like wild beasts' (Waddington, 2329a). Agrippa died in A.D. 44, and for 9 years the province was administered by the Romans. Then Claudius gave it to Agrippa II., who died A.D. 100, when the region was finally associated with the Roman province of Syria. In A.D. 106 the Nabatæans were at last reduced, and the province of Arabia constituted. The capital of the new province was Bozrah, which city is so closely identified with Haurân that an ancient proverb says, 'the prosperity of Bozrah is the prosperity of Haurân.'

Under the Romans civilization advanced, and, as evidenced by the remains of churches and inscriptions, Christianity made rapid progress. In A.D. 632 the Moslem hordes from Arabia burst over the province like a tornado, and the blight swiftly fell, which lies heavy on the land to-day. The latest notice of a Christian building is an inscription found by the present writer at el-Kufr, which records the foundation of a church in A.D. 720 (see *PEFSt*, July 1895, Inscrip. No. 150). Of the cities whose dark ruins are so numerous throughout the region, none can be said with certainty to date beyond the Roman period; although several, such as Kanawât and Bozrah, evidently occupy ancient sites. Many houses, built entirely—both walls and roof—of basalt, the heavy doors and window shutters of the same durable material, still easily swinging on their stone hinges, stand to-day almost as complete as when, centuries ago, their last tenants departed. The underground dwellings for which the district is noted doubtless belong to a much more remote antiquity. The crumbling villages that dot the plain and stud the mountain slopes are nearly all built of materials taken from neighbouring ruins. They have yielded a fine harvest of inscriptions, relating chiefly to the earlier centuries of our era. The rude builders, ignorant of the value attaching to these remains, have destroyed much. Thus it comes that 'written stones,' carved capitals, and bits of sculpture, memorials of a great and splendid past, may now so often be found amid surroundings of squalor and decay.

LITERATURE. — Wetzstein, *Reisebericht über den Haurân* (1860); Delitzsch, *Hiob*[2] 597 ff.; Baedeker-Socin, *Pal.* 195 ff.; Schumacher, *Across the Jordan*; G. A. Smith, *HGHL* 552 f., 609 ff.; Buhl, *GAP* (Index); Schürer, *HJP* (Index, *s.* 'Auranitis').
                          W. EWING.

HAVE.—Although 'have,' both as auxiliary and as finite verb, is used in many archaic expressions in AV, its meaning is nearly always obvious, and its obsolete uses are few. The foll. examples may be given:—

1. To have, as a finite verb, is to possess, as Lk 8[27] 'there met him out of the city a certain man, which had devils long time' (ὃς εἶχε, edd. ἔχων); 2 Co 1[9] 'But we had the sentence of death in ourselves' (ἐσχήκαμεν, RV 'yea, we ourselves have had the answer of death within ourselves').

2. Have, followed by some subst., has the force of the verb corresponding to the subst., as 'have indignation,' Mt 26[8], Mk 14[4] (cf. Lk 15[28] Rhem. 'But he had indignation and would not go in'); 'have compassion,' Lk 15[20], He 10[34]; 'have understanding,' Lk 1[3]; 'have regard,' Ac 8[11]; 'have knowledge,' Ac 17[13]; 'have rejoicing,' Gal 6[4]; 'have trial,' He 11[36]. Cf. Ac 20[3] Rhem. 'he had councel to returne through Macedonia.'

3. Have is sometimes equivalent to 'hold,' as Ja 2[1] 'My brethren, have not the faith of our Lord Jesus Christ, the Lord of glory, with respect of persons' (μὴ ἔχετε, RV 'hold not'); Ac 25[26] 'Wherefore I have brought him forth before you . . . that, after examination, I might have somewhat to write' (τῆς ἀνακρίσεως γενομένης). So 'have in abomination,' Lv 11[11], 1 S 13[4]; 'have in derision,' Ps 119[51], Ezk 23[32], 1 Es 1[51], Wis 5[3]; 'have in honour,' 2 S 6[22]; 'have in remembrance,' Ac 10[31]; 'have in reputation,' Ac 5[34]; 'have in reverence,' Ps 89[7]. Cf. He 13[4] Tind. 'Let wedlocke be had in pryce in all poyntes'; North's *Plutarch*, p. 876, '[Cicero] scorned and disdained all Pompeys preparations and counsels, the which indeed made him to be had in iealousie and suspition'; Ridley, *Brefe Declaration* (Moule's ed. p. 163), 'For all the churche of Christ bothe hathe and ever hathe hadde hym [Augustine] for a man of most singular learnyng, witte, and diligence.'

4. Have has sometimes the meaning of 'carry' or 'take,' as 2 Ch 35[23] 'And the king said to his servants, Have me away; for I am sore wounded' (הַעֲבִירוּנִי); 2 K 11[15], 2 Ch 23[14] 'Have her forth without the ranges' (הוֹצִיאוּ אֹתָהּ); 2 S 13[9] 'Have out all men from me' (הוֹצִיאוּ). Cf. Is 53[8] 'He shal be had awaye, his cause not herde, and without eny judgment'; Jn 2[16] Tind. 'Have these thinges hence, and make not my fathers housse an housse of marchaundyse.' So Knox, *Hist.* 151, 'who being slain, was had to the Queen's presence'; Adams, *Works*, i. 65, 'Herefore they bequeath so great sums for masses and dirges and trentals to be sung or said for them after they are dead, that their souls may at the last be had to heaven, though first for a while they be reezed in purgatory.'

5. Such phrases may be noticed as, 'Have in one's heart to,' 1 Ch 28[2] (cf. Ph 1[7] 'I have you in my heart'); 'I would have you without carefulness,' 1 Co 7[32]; 'I would not have you ignorant,' 2 Co 1[8]; 'Who will have all men to be saved,' 1 Ti 2[4] (ὃς θέλει, RV 'Who willeth that all men should be saved'). Cf. Jn 21[22] Tind. 'Yf I will

have him to tary tyll I come, what is that to the?'

6. As a grammatical point observe 'had' not only for 'would have' (as Gn 43¹⁰, Lk 24²¹), but for 'would' alone, Ps 84¹⁰ 'I had rather be a doorkeeper in the house of my God, than to dwell in the tents of wickedness.' The Revisers have been taken to task (Moon, *Revisers' English*, p. 135; *Eccles. English*, p. 190) for accepting this construction from AV. No doubt 'I would rather' is more grammatical, but 'I had rather' has the best authority and is still in use. Cf. T. Fuller, *Holy State*, ii. 16, p. 109, 'Some men had as lieve be schoolboyes as Schoolmasters, to be tyed to the school as Cooper's Dictionary and Scapula's Lexicon are chained to the desk therein.' Again, such a form as we find in He 11¹⁵ 'They might have had opportunity to have returned' is now reckoned ungrammatical. It is common in Shaks., as *Hamlet*, v. i. 268—

> 'I hoped thou shouldst have been my Hamlet's wife;
> I thought thy bride-bed to have deck'd, sweet maid.'

So *Merry Wives*, IV. v. 41—

> 'I had other things to have spoken with her.'

See Abbott, *Shaks. Gram.* § 360. RV has the modern form, 'they would have had opportunity to return.'   J. HASTINGS.

HAVEN.—**1.** חוֹף, properly 'coast,' 'strand,' from [חפף] 'enclose,' 'surround.' This word is rendered 'haven' by AV and RV in Gn 49¹³ *bis*, and by RV in Jg 5¹⁷ (AV 'shore'). Its only other occurrences are Dt 1⁷ [AV '(sea)side,' RV '(sea)shore'], Jos 9¹ [AV 'coasts (of the sea'), RV 'shore (of the sea')], Jer 47⁷, Ezk 25¹⁶ [AV and RV '(sea)shore']. **2.** מָחוֹז Ps 107³⁰ (only). **3.** λιμήν, Ac 27⁸·¹².

Havens are seldom mentioned in the Bible, probably for the reason that Palestine proper scarcely possesses any **harbours,** and the Israelites were not a maritime nation. The harbours in OT times on the Mediterranean coast were in possession of the Phœnicians and the Philistines (see GREAT SEA); and as regards that of Ezion-geber, at the head of the Gulf of 'Aḳabah (or Ælanitic Gulf), it was only for a short period in possession of the kings of Israel, notably in the reign of Solomon (1 K 9²⁶). The earliest mention of the word 'haven' (Gn 49¹³) is in connexion with the blessings pronounced by Jacob on the future tribes, where it is said of Zebulun that he 'should dwell at the haven of the sea, and that he should be for an haven of ships, and his border (should reach) unto Zidon.' It is doubtful if, in the distribution of the Promised Land, the tribe of Zebulun actually touched the coast, though it reached as far west as Mount Carmel. From the port of Accho (Acre) the tribe was debarred by the predominating power of the Phœnician Sidonians, who in the time of the Judges 'oppressed Israel' (Jg 10¹²); but it is a fair supposition that the terms of Jacob's Blessing point to the importance of the Bay of Acre as the future 'Key of Syria,'* and express the desire that it should come into the possession of Zebulun.

Next in importance and sequence of time to Sidon was the seaport of Tyre, situated about 20 miles S. of Sidon, and, like it, having a double harbour to the N. and S. of the promontory, which jutted out from the coast and terminated in a ridge of coralline rock. It was one of several islets lying at some distance from the shore. Only the events connected with the biblical history of Tyre and Sidon can here be referred to.† In the time

of Solomon, Tyre had reached a high state of eminence under Hiram, who rendered assistance to Solomon in the building of the temple (1 K 5) and in supplying sailors for the fleet built at Ezion-geber, which traded to Ophir for gold (1 K 9²⁶). (See RED SEA). In NT history these cities are memorable for the visit of our Lord to their neighbourhood (Mt 15²¹), and the miracle of healing in the case of the daughter of the Syrophœnician woman (Mk 7²⁵). But the glories of Tyre and Sidon have long since departed. In the height of their prosperity these Phœnician cities were centres of cruelty, licentiousness, and idolatry, which sealed their doom. When Alexander captured Tyre, the population of the city appears to have been about 40,000 souls; it is now a miserable fishing village with about a tenth of that number of inhabitants. The prophecies of Ezekiel have been literally fulfilled in the present state of these once flourishing cities (Ezk 26¹² 27³²).

The **Fair Havens** (wh. see) are of interest in connexion with the voyage of St. Paul to Italy (Ac 27¹²), and their position has been clearly determined; the name being preserved in the present *Kaloi Limenes.** They consist of two contiguous roadsteads on the S. side of the island of Crete (Kandia), about 5 m. E. of Cape Matala (Theodia), and not far from the city of Lasea, of which they were the ports. In this position ships were secure against winds from the N.E., such as 'Euraquilo,' which burst upon the ship carrying the apostle at a later period of his voyage after leaving the island.†   E. HULL.

HAVILAH (חֲוִילָה, Εὐειλάτ, Εὐειλδ, *Hevila*).—A son of Cush according to Gn 10⁷, 1 Ch 1⁹, of Joktan according to Gn 10²⁹, 1 Ch 1²³. In Gn 2¹¹·¹² the Pison is said to compass the land of H., where there was gold, bdellium, and 'the *shōham*-stone,' while in Gn 25¹⁸ the Ishmaelite tribes are described as extending 'from Havilah unto Shur,' the eastern frontier of Egypt, and in 1 S 15⁷ Saul is stated to have smitten the Amalekites or Bedawîn from Havilah (but here Glaser, *Skizze*, ii. 326, would read *Hachilah*) to Shur. H. will thus be the 'sandy' desert of N. Arabia extending from the Joktanite district of Ophir on the Persian Gulf to the neighbourhood of Edom. Glaser identifies it with Jemâma in N.E. Arabia, but its western boundary will have been nearer the Shur or 'Fortified Lines' of Egypt. The *shōham*-stone which came from it was perhaps the Assyrian *samtu*, which seems to have been the malachite or turquoise. At an early period the Arabian tribes made their way across the Red Sea to the opposite coast of Africa; hence H. is included among the descendants of Cush. The name of the Cushite Havilah is possibly preserved in the classical Aualis, now Zeila' in Somâli-land. A district of Khaulân (Ḥaulân) is mentioned in the inscriptions of S. Arabia; this is either Khaulân in Tihâmah, between Mecca and San'a, or another Khaulân S.E. of San'a. Niebuhr further found a Ḥuwailah on the Persian Gulf. The name, in fact, was widely spread in Arabia, and Yakut states that Ḥawîl was the name of a dialect spoken by the people of Mehri in the east of Hadramaut. The Mehri is the modern representative of the language of the Sabæan inscriptions.

LITERATURE.—Dillmann, *Genesis*, Eng. tr. i. 129 f.; Glaser, *Skizze*, ii. 323 ff.; E. Meyer, *Gesch. d. Alterthums*, i. 224; Sayce, *HCM* 98 ff.; papers in the *Expos. Times*, viii. (1897), 378, 431 f., 473, 525, by Hommel, Cheyne, and Nestle.
           A. H. SAYCE.

---

* Rawlinson, *Hist. Phœn.* 83, 407; Conder, *Tent-Work in Pal.* 95.

† For charts of Tyre and Sidon, see Rawlinson, *Phœnicia*, pp. 66, 71.

* Smith of Jordanhill, *Voyage and Shipwreck of St. Paul²*, 1856; Ramsay, *St. Paul the Traveller*, ch. xiv.

† The storm was probably an anticyclone, which at first drove the ship in the direction of the Syrtes, but afterwards carried it, by its rotatory motion, northwards into that part of the Mediterranean called 'Adria,' now known as the Ionian Sea.

HAVVOTH-JAIR (חַוֹּת יָאִיר, *i.e.* ' the tent-villages * of Jair ').—A group of towns in Gilead, in the territory that was reckoned to the half-tribe of Manasseh. In Dt 3¹⁴ and Jos 13³⁰ (both D²) the Havvoth-Jair are improperly located in *Bashan*, and in the latter passage they appear also to be confounded with the sixty fortresses of the Argob from which they are expressly distinguished in 1 K 4¹³. Unsuccessful attempts have been made by Keil and others to harmonize the statements of D² with the testimony of JE (Nu 32³⁹⁻⁴¹, corroborated by Jg 10⁴, 1 K 4¹³, 1 Ch 2²²) that the Havvoth-Jair were situated in *Gilead*. Varying explanations of the origin of the name are offered in OT. While in Nu 32⁴¹ and Dt 3¹⁴ Jair is a contemporary of Moses, in Jg 10⁴ he is one of the judges. This variety of statement corresponds to the different OT traditions as to the settlement of the territory E. of the Jordan. The oldest narratives of the Hex. know of only *two* trans-Jordanic tribes, Reuben and Gad. (Compare Nu 32¹⁻³² with vv.³³˙ ³⁹⁻⁴²). Even in the Song of Deborah (Jg 5¹⁴) Machir is still one of the W. tribes, and only at a much later date became the designation of the Manassites in Gilead. This latter district, there is reason to believe, was really conquered from the *west*, after the occupation of Canaan proper. Hence in Jg 10⁴ (which, however, is ethnographical rather than historical) there may be preserved the memory of an expedition led across the Jordan by Jair after the territory originally occupied by Manasseh had proved too small for that tribe. See further, JAIR.

LITERATURE.—Budde, *Richt. u. Sam.* 34, 38f., 87, 97 ; Kuenen, *Hex.* (Macmillan), 47, 101, 254 ; Wellhausen, *Comp.* 117, 218 n., *Hist. of Isr. and Jud.* 33 n. ; Driver, *Deut.* 55 f. ; Graf, *Der Stamm Simeon*, 4 f. ; Moore, *Judges*, 274 f. ; W. R. Smith, *RS*, 256 n.   J. A. SELBIE.

HAWK (נֵץ *nêz*, ἱέραξ, *accipiter*).—A generic word for birds of the hawk tribe. It probably includes all the species of the genera *Accipiter*, *Falco*, *Circus*, and *Pernis*, and perhaps *Buteo*, and excludes those of *Milvus* and *Elanus*, which have special names in Hebrew, *da'âh*, *dayyah*, and *'ayyâh* (see GLEDE, KITE). The following is a list of the hawks found in Palestine and Syria :—

1. *Accipiter nisus*, L., the *Sparrow Hawk* (Arabic *bâshik*). It is common over the whole country. 2. *A. brevipes*, Sev., the *Levant Sparrow Hawk*. It is much rarer than the last. It is recognized by its short thick tarsi. 3. *Pernis apivorus*, L., the *Honey Buzzard*. It is one of the resident species, but is rather rare. 4. *Falco peregrinus*, Tunst., the *Peregrine Falcon* (Arabic *Tair-el-hurr*). It is confined to the coast and western watershed of the mountains. 5. *F. lanarius*, Schl., the *Lanner* (Arabic *shâhin* and *sokr*). This is the most common of the large falcons, and is a permanent resident. It resorts more esp. to the deserts. It is trained by the natives for falconry. 6. *F. Sacer*, Gmel., the *Saker Falcon* (Arabic *sokr*). It is confined to the upland forests E. of the Jordan. It is esteemed by the Arabs the finest of all the falcons, and the name of *Beni-Sokr*, one of the tribes E. of the Dead Sea, is derived from this species. 7. *F. subbuteo*, L., the *Hobby*, is a summer visitor to Pal. 8. *F. eleonoræ*, Gene., the *Eleonora Falcon*, is also a summer visitor only. Tristram found it only in the Buka' (Cœlesyria). 9. *F. æsalon*, Tunst., the *Merlin*, is a winter visitor to Palestine. 10. *F. vespertinus*, L., the *Red-legged Hobby*, is a rare summer

visitor. 11. *F. tinnunculus*, L., the *Kestrel* (Arabic *bâshik*), is the commonest of all the hawks, and is universal throughout Pal. and Syria. 12. *F. cenchris*, Cuv., the *Lesser Kestrel*, is a spring and summer visitor, but, on its arrival, consorts with the last. 13. *Circus æruginosus*, L., the *Marsh Harrier* (Arab. *dari'ah*), is common over the marshes and plains. 14. *C. cineraceus*, Mont., the *Ash-coloured Harrier*, is rare, but resident. 15. *C. cyaneus*, L., the *Hen Harrier*, is also common. 16. *C. Swainsonii*, Smith, the *Pallid Harrier*, is especially found along the coast. The plumage is almost white. 17. *Buteo vulgaris*, Leach, the *Common Buzzard* (Arabic *'akâb*), may be the *Glede*. 18. *B. ferox*, Gmel., the *Long-legged Buzzard* (Arab. *shâhin*), is the largest of the hawk tribe, equalling in size some of the smaller eagles.

The above list amply justifies the expression ' after his kind ' (Lv 11¹⁶, Dt 14¹⁵). It also justifies the expression in Job 39²⁶, where it is asked, ' Doth the hawk fly by thy wisdom, and stretch her wings toward the south?' if by this, as is generally thought, an allusion is intended to the migratory habits of some of the species. Some think, however, that the allusion is simply to the power of flight of all the hawks. No allusion to hunting with falcons is found in the Scriptures. All the birds of this tribe were unclean to the Hebrews.
                                        G. E. POST.

HAY.—The word occurs three times in AV (Pr 27²⁵ RV ' hay,' m. ' grass,' Is 15⁶ RV ' grass,' 1 Co 3¹²). In both the OT passages the Heb. is חָצִיר *hazir*, which is rendered by the LXX in the first passage χλωρός, and in the second χόρτος. In 1 Co the orig. is χόρτος. There does not seem to be any good reason for the trⁿ *hay* in any of the above passages. The meaning is equally clear if the word be rendered *grass* (see GRASS). חֲשַׁשׁ *hashash* has been thought by some to refer to *hay*. It corresponds to the Arabic *hashîsh*, which signifies *weeds*, or *green fodder*. In Is 33¹¹ it is rendered AV, RV ' chaff,' and in Is 5²⁴ AV ' chaff,' but RV ' dry grass.' It is customary in Bible lands to cut or pull grass and other fodder plants, and give them to live stock. Women, with large back loads or donkey loads of such fodder, may be seen any morning at the gates, or in the market places of the cities, where they offer it for sale. Large areas are sown in barley, vetch, clover, medick, and other forage plants, to be cut and given to domestic animals in the spring and early summer. It is clear that it was also the custom in Bible days to cut grass for this purpose (Ps 37² 72⁶ 129⁶˙ ⁷, Am 7¹). But it is not customary to *dry* such cut-grass as we do in making hay, to be stored up as winter fodder, and there is no evidence that the Hebrews had such a custom. In fact it would be out of place, as the winter is the season of green grass here, and the flocks continue to crop the stubble to the end of the harvest season in midsummer, and after that find a scanty but sufficient pasturage until the early rains cause the ' tender grass ' to sprout up with marvellous rapidity. Stall-fed animals have cut-straw mixed with their barley, and this seems to contain a considerable amount of nourishment, and to answer the purpose of hay. Stall-fed milch cows are fed mainly on this fodder, and continue fat, and give milk on it. It would therefore be better to render *hashash* by *cut-grass* rather than by *dry grass* or *hay*.   G. E. POST.

HAZAEL (חֲזָאֵל, חֲזָהאֵל ' whom God beholds.' Ἀζαήλ BA Luc. Assyr. *Haza'ilu*.)—A powerful king of Syria who reigned contemporaneously with Jehoram (last 3 or 4 years), Jehu, and Jehoahaz kings of Israel, and Jehoram, Ahaziah, Athaliah, and Joash of Judah. Hazael is first mentioned 1 K 19¹⁵˙ ¹⁷, where Elijah at Horeb re-

---

* *Havvôth* is probably connected with the Arab. *hiwâ*, ' a collection of tents.' ' It may have originally denoted a group of Bedawîn tents, but with the transition to pastoral life it would naturally be applied to more permanent settlements ' (Moore, *Judges*, p. 274).

ceives commission to anoint him king over Syria, that he may execute J'''s vengeance against the Baal worshippers of Israel. At this time he must have been an official at the court of the Syrian king Ben-hadad II., for some time later he was sent to Elisha at Damascus to inquire the issue of his master's sickness. The prophet marked him out as the future king of Syria and oppressor of Israel, and accordingly Hazael seized the earliest opportunity to murder Ben-hadad and usurp the throne (2 K 8⁷⁻¹⁵). He seems to have been soon engaged in hostilities with the neighbouring kingdom of Israel, meeting the allied forces of Jehoram and Ahaziah of Judah at Ramoth-gilead (2 K 8²⁸·²⁹ 9¹⁴·¹⁵). Hazael gained a series of successes against Jehu, devastating all his country E. of Jordan, from the Arnon in the S. to the land of Bashan in the N. (2 K 10³²·³³); and throughout the reign of Jehoahaz, Jehu's successor, he made constant encroachment upon the territory of Israel (2 K 13²²). It was not till after Hazael's death that Joash son of Jehoahaz was able successfully to repel the aggressions of Syria under Ben-hadad III. son of Hazael (2 K 13²⁴·²⁵). A century later the remembrance of Hazael was still fresh in the minds of the men of Israel, and Amos uses the expression 'the house of Hazael' as a parallel to 'the palaces of Ben-hadad' (Am 1⁴). Hazael further directed his arms against the S. of Palestine, besieging and taking Gath, and then marching against Jerusalem, from which he was only bought off by tribute sent by Joash king of Judah out of the temple treasures (2 K 12¹⁷·¹⁸). According to 2 Ch 24²³·²⁴ a battle took place, in which the Syrians with a small army defeated the larger forces of the king of Judah.

Hazael figures more than once in the cuneiform inscriptions. Shalmaneser II., who in the early part of his reign had defeated an alliance formed by *Dadidri* (Ben-hadad II.), Ahab of Israel, and other kings, and again in the 14th year of his reign had a second time worsted *Dadidri* (*COT* i. 191 ff.), states that in his 18th year (B.C. 842) he joined battle with Hazael of Damascus, who had assembled a large army and entrenched himself upon the mountain of Sanir in the Anti-Lebanon. The Syrian king was defeated, and lost 16,000 warriors, 1121 chariots, and 470 horsemen, together with his stores. Barely escaping with his life, he shut himself up in Damascus, which was besieged by the enemy, but, apparently, not captured, since Shalmaneser merely states 'his plantations I destroyed.' The same inscription speaks of Jehu as paying tribute to Shalmaneser 'at that time'; and it may thus be plausibly inferred that the aid of Assyria against the Syrians had been solicited by Jehu, as was done by Ahaz of Judah in later times (2 K 16⁷ᶠᶠ·). Three years later, in the 21st year of his reign, Shalmaneser again marched against Hazael and took possession of his cities (*COT* i. 197 f., 200 f.).

C. F. BURNEY.

HAZAIAH (חֲזָיָה 'J'' hath seen').—A descendant of Judah (Neh 11⁵). See GENEALOGY.

HAZAR-ADDAR (חֲצַר־אַדָּר, ἔπαυλις Ἀράδ).—A place on the southern border of Canaan, west of Kadesh-barnea, Nu 34⁴. It appears to be the same as **Hezron** (which see) of Jos 15³, which in the latter passage is connected with but separated from **Addar** (which see).

HAZAR-ENAN (חֲצַר עֵינָן, once Ezk 47¹⁷ **Hazar-enon** עֵינוֹן).—A place mentioned in Nu 34⁹·¹⁰ as the northern boundary of Israel, and in Ezk 47¹⁷ 48¹ as one of the ideal boundaries. It was perhaps at the sources of the Orontes. Buhl (*GAP* 67, 111, 240) and Bertholet (*Hesekiel*, 244) suggest that it is

identical with the well-known Banias, while v. Kasteren would locate it at *el-Ḥaḍr* farther to the east, on the way from Banias to Damascus, but these sites appear to be too far south.

C. R. CONDER.

HAZAR-GADDAH (חֲצַר־גַּדָּה).—An unknown town in the extreme south of Judah (Jos 15²⁷).

HAZARMAVETH (חֲצַרְמָוֶת). — The eponym of a Joktanite clan, Gn 10²⁶ = 1 Ch 1²⁰, described as a 'son' of Joktan, fifth in order from Shem. The name occurs in Sabæan inscriptions as חצרמות and חצרמת (*ZDMG* xix. (1865) 239 ff., xxxi. 74 ff.). Its identity with the modern *Ḥaḍramaut* is certain, and Hazarmaveth is probably also the same as the land of the Χατραμωτῖται, one of the four chief tribes of S. Arabia as described by Strabo (XVI. iv. 2). They were celebrated for their traffic in frankincense. For their history see ARABIA, p. 133ᵇ. The modern *Ḥaḍramaut* is not so extensive as the ancient.

LITERATURE.—Dillmann and Spurrell on Gn 10²⁶; in addition to above references to *ZDMG* see also xxii. 658, xxx. 323, xliv. 186; Glaser, *Skizze*, ii. 20, 423 ff.; especially for account of inscriptions, Hommel, *AHT* 77 ff., 270, 274, 318 f., 321 n., and Sayce, *HCM* 39 f.

J. A. SELBIE.

HAZAR-SHUAL (חֲצַר שׁוּעָל).—A place in S. Judah (Jos 15²⁸ = 1 Ch 4²⁸) or Simeon (Jos 19³), repeopled by Jews after the Captivity, Neh 11²⁷. It may be the ruin *S'awi* on a hill E. of Beersheba. See *SWP* vol. iii. sh. xxiv.

HAZAR-SUSAH (חֲצַר־סוּסָה, in 1 Ch 4³¹ **Hazar-susim** חֲצַר־סוּסִים).—A city in Simeon, Jos 19⁵ = 1 Ch 4³¹. The name means 'horse-village,' and is noticed along with Beth-marcaboth, 'place of chariots.' These places were apparently in the southern plain, and were no doubt stations of a cavalry force, probably Egyptian. The sites are unknown. There is a ruin *Susin*, W. of Beersheba. See *SWP* vol. iii. sh. xxiv.

C. R. CONDER.

HAZAR-SUSIM.—See HAZAR-SUSAH.

HAZAZON TAMAR (חַצְצֹן תָּמָר. 'Hazazon of the palm-tree') is mentioned in Gn 14⁷ as inhabited by Amorites, and as destroyed, along with En-mishpat (Kadesh) and the Amalekite country, by Chedorlaomer. In 2 Ch 20² it is identified with En-gedi as the basis for an invading army from Edom (so read instead of Syria). Josephus (*Ant.* IX. i. 2), speaking of this campaign, says the invaders pitched at En-gedi, where grow the best kind of palm-tree and the opobalsamum.

Most probably the words preserve the older name of En-gedi (which see), and may still survive in the *Wady Husaseh*, N.W. from '*Ain Jidy* (Engedi). See Rob. i. 506; G. A. Smith, *Hist. Geogr.* 271. Jerome (*Quæst. in Gen.*) translates the name *urbs palmarum*, which (cf. Jos. *supra*) suggests a comparison with that 'city of palm-trees' out of which (Jg 1¹⁶) the Kenite clan went up with Judah. In that case it may have been this Kenite settlement on the rocky nest of En-gedi which Balaam saw from the heights of Moab, and to which he referred (Nu 24²¹). G. A. Smith suggests (*Hist. Geogr.* p. 269 ff.) that here we must look for the Tamar of 1 K 9¹⁸ (*Kethibh*) and Ezk 47¹⁹ 48²⁸.

It is, however, possible that Hazazon-tamar may be, not En-gedi, but the Tamar of Ezekiel, and that the latter lay S.W. of the Dead Sea. In that case Jg 1¹⁶ may mean that the Kenites, entering Palestine by the south, joined the invading Judahites on the south of Arad. A. C. WELCH.

HAZEL (לוּז *lûz*, καρύον, *amygdalus*).—This word, trᵈ in AV *hazel* (Gn 30³⁷), is better rendered RV *almond,* for (1) the word לוז is the same in form as the Arab. *lauz,* which signifies *almond* ; (2) the *hazel* does not grow in Mesopotamia, where Laban lived, while the *almond* is universal.   The objection that there is another name שָׁקֵד *shâkêd* for almond is not decisive, as many plants and animals have two or more names.   G. E. Post.

HAZER = HATTICON (חֲצַר הַתִּיכוֹן, 'the middle Hazer').—A place named amongst the boundaries of (ideal) Israel, Ezk 47[16]. It is described as ' by the border of Hauran.' If the MT be correct, Hazer-hatticon is quite unknown ; but there can be no reasonable doubt that we ought, with Smend, Cornill, Bertholet, etc., to emend to **Hazar-enon** as in vv.[17, 18] and 48[1]. Wetzstein, indeed, proposes [*ZKW* (1884) v. 114] to identify Hazer-hatticon with *Ḥaḍar* to the north of *Jebel Druze,* 'at the foot of the eastern corner of Hermon.' See further, Davidson, *Ezekiel,* p. 352.

HAZERIM (חֲצֵרִים; Ασηδώθ, AF Ασηρώθ).—Mentioned in AV of Dt 2[23] as the locality in which the Avvim (wh. see) dwelt ' as far as Gaza.' There is no doubt that the word is not really a proper name, but that it should be rendered (as it is in RV) by *villages.* The clause describes how the Avvim dwelt, until they were expelled by the immigrant Caphtorim (or Philistines) ; they did not dwell in fortified cities, but in *villages,* or unwalled settlements (Lv 25[31]), consisting, probably, of rudely-built huts of mud or stone, roofed with leaves or grass. Villages are usually mentioned as the dependencies of towns (*e.g.* Jos 13[23]) ; but sometimes a particular tribe is characterized as inhabiting them, as Gn 25[16] (Ishmaelites), Is 42[11] (Kedar) ; and according to this archæological notice, the Avvim, or original occupants of a part of S.W. Palestine, dwelt in them similarly.
                                    S. R. Driver.

HAZEROTH (חֲצֵרוֹת ; Ασηρώθ).—A station of the Israelites in the wilderness, mentioned both in Nu 11[35] 12[16] (JE) and in the itinerary 33[17] (P),—in the latter as the second station after leaving Sinai (the first being Ḳibroth-hatta'avah). Burckhardt (*Syria,* 1822, p. 495) suggested tentatively (' perhaps ') that it might be 'Ain el-Ḥuḍerah, about 40 miles N.E. of Jebel Mûsa, and not quite half-way between Jebel Mûsa and 'Aḳabah ; and this identification has been accepted by many subsequent writers, as Robinson, *BR*[2] i. 151 ; Ewald, *Hist.* ii. 191 ; Stanley, *Sin. and Pal.* 81 f. (though not very confidently) ; Palmer, *Desert of the Wanderings,* 260–262 (cf. 313 f.), etc. ; Dillm., however (on Nu 11[35]), hesitates. All things considered, the identification seems fairly probable. The site is most fully described by Palmer (with an illustration).* It lies a little to the left of the main route from Jebel Mûsa to 'Aḳabah, which here, after leaving the Wâdy Sa'al, passes through a sandy plain (in the midst of which is a conspicuous eminence, called Huḍeibat el-Ḥajjâj, or the Pilgrims' Hill), prior to entering the Wâdy Ghuzâleh. Ascending for about 10 minutes from the camel track in this plain, the traveller reaches a cleft or gorge in the limestone rock, through which he looks down (towards the N.W.) upon the Wâdy Ḥuḍerah, winding along between fantastic, brilliantly-coloured sandstone cliffs, with a ' forest of mountain peaks and chains ' beyond, and ' on their left a broad white wâdy leading up towards the distant mountains of the Tîh.' In the middle of the Wâdy Ḥuḍerah, beneath a lofty cliff, lies the dark green palm-grove of 'Ain Ḥuḍerah, with the fountain rising in the rock behind. The water from the

* A clearer view of the topography of the district may, however, be obtained from the *Ordnance Survey of Sinai* (1869), i. 122 f., with the accompanying map of the peninsula.

fountain, which is still used as a watering-place for camels, ' is conducted by an aqueduct, cut in the solid granite, into a reservoir or pool, from which it is let out by a rude sluice to irrigate the gardens which the Arabs still cultivate here. The remains of several well-constructed walls point to a former and perhaps Christian occupation of the place.' A few miles to the N. of 'Ain Ḥuḍerah there circles round the Wâdy el-'Ain, containing a stream of clear, fresh water, which joins ultimately the Wâdy Ghuzâleh, to the N.E.

Keil objects that el-Ḥuḍerah, being only ' 18 hours' from Jebel Mûsa, is too near for Hazeroth, as the Israelites were 3 days (Nu 11[33]) in reaching Ḳibroth-hatta'avah, the station before Hazeroth (11[35]) ; and thinks that Hazeroth must have been some place on the more direct route to Kadesh (13[26]), such as the station Bir eth-Themed, on the Tîh-plateau (cf. Trumbull, *Kadesh-barnea,* 78, 314 f.). It would no doubt be a mistake to regard the identification as certain ; still it may be questioned whether, under the circumstances, Keil's objections are cogent ; and although the more usual route from Sinai to Kadesh may be through the Wâdy Zulaka, on to el-'Ain and Bir eth-Themed (Robinson, i. 148, 198, with the map), yet a route past 'Ain el-Ḥuḍerah, through the Wâdy Ghuzâleh, and up the Wâdy Wetîr (p. 153, with the map,—apparently the E. half of the Wâdy el-'Ain of the Ordnance Survey map), does not seem to be so greatly more circuitous as to be pronounced out of the question. Dillm. thinks the evidence insufficient to show where Hazeroth was.

Whether the Hazeroth of Dt 1[2] (LXX Αὐλῶν) be the same place depends upon the answer given to the difficult question, what the topographical notes contained in that verse are intended to mark (see Dizahab). If this verse defines a locality in the Steppes of Moab, Hazeroth will be some place there, otherwise unknown ; if it describes—or in its original form described—places passed by the Israelites previously, it may be the Hazeroth of Nu 11[35] etc. Sayce's location of Hazeroth (*Early Hist. of Hebrews,* 214) as ' near Paran on the borders of Moab' has nothing to recommend it, being inconsistent with the situation presupposed in either Nu or Dt.   S. R. Driver.

HAZIEL (חֲזִיאֵל ' vision of El ').—A Gershonite Levite in time of Solomon, 1 Ch 23[9]. See Genealogy.

HAZO (חֲזוֹ, Ἀζαῦ).—The eponym of a Nahorite clan, Gn 22[22]. It is no doubt identical with *Ḥazû,* which along with *Bazû* (Buz of v.[21]) is mentioned in an inscription of Esarhaddon (see Delitzsch, *Paradies,* 306 f., also in *Zeitsch. f. Keilschriftforsch.* (1885) 93 ff. ; Schrader, *KAT*[2] 141, 221 [*COT*[2] i. 127, 212], and *Keilinschriften u. Geschichtsforsch.* 399 ; Tiele, *Geschichte,* 337 ; Dillmann on Gn 22[21f.]).

HAZOR (חָצוֹר, חָצֹר).—**1.** A Canaanite city of Galilee, the chief place of that region, ruled by a dynasty which seems to have had the dynastic name of Jabin, Jos 11[1] 12[19], Jg 4[2, 17]. The great battle with the king of Hazor took place at the Waters of Merom, Jos 11[5ff.] (see art. Jabin). Hazor was fortified by Solomon (1 K 9[15]), and captured by Tiglath-pileser (2 K 15[29]) in B.C. 734. Jonathan the Hasmonæan, after encamping ' at the water of Gennesareth, early in the morning gat him to the plain of Hazor,' 1 Mac 11[67]. Josephus (*Ant.* v. v. 1) places Hazor near Kedesh, on the plateau looking down on the *Hûleh* lake, which he regards as being the Waters of Merom. This leads to the supposition that *Tell el-Hurrawiyeh,* a large ruined site in the required position, is intended. The mountain to the west still bears the name *Jebel Ḥadhireh.* This is the only known indication, and, as far as the biblical notices are concerned, it would be equally possible to place Hazor farther south, where, at the foot of the chain of Upper Galilee, is found an important ruined site called *Ḥazzur,* in a position more appropriate to the use of the chariots which belonged to the king of Hazor. This latter would also suit well the Hazor of 1 Mac 11[67] and Jos. *Ant.* XIII. v. 7. From Hazor two letters of the Tel el-Amarna collection were written in the 15th cent. B.C. to the king of Egypt. They are much damaged, but they speak of an attack on the place, and ask for aid. In one of them the king's name is given; and though the first syllable is damaged, it may be read *I-eba-enu*, *i.e.* 'Jabin.' Hazor is also noticed, with places in Upper and Lower Galilee, by the *Mohar* (an Egyptian traveller of the 14th cent. B.C.) on his way from the seacoast to the Lake of Tiberias. See *SWP* vol. i. sh. iv.

LITERATURE.—*SWP* vol. i. sh. iv.; Robinson, *BRP*[2] iii. 63, 81, 365, 401 f.; Buhl, *GAP* 113, 182, 236; Guérin, *Galilée*, ii. 363 ff.; Baedeker-Socin, *Pal.*[3] 264; Schürer, *HJP* I. i. 249; Dillmann on Jos 11[1]; Sayce, *HCM* 309, 336.

2. A town of Benjamin, Neh 11[33], now the ruin *Hazzur* close to Gibeon on the south. See *SWP* vol. iii. sh. xvii.; *Oxf. Heb. Lex.*, Siegfried-Stade, and Buhl (*GAP* 177) suggest that it may be identical with Baal-hazor of 2 S 13[23]; but see BAAL-HAZOR. **3.** In Jos 15[23] a Hazor in the Negeb of Judah is noticed. **4.** In Jos 15[25] another Hazor appears to be mentioned, which is identical with *Kerioth-hezron* (wh. see). **5.** An unknown Arabian locality (Jer 49[28]) mentioned along with Kedar as smitten by Nebuchadrezzar.   C. R. CONDER.

HAZOR-HADATTAH (חָצוֹר חֲדַתָּה).—The text (Jos 15[25]) is not beyond suspicion. If it is correct, the name may mean 'new Hazor,' with Aram. ח in חֲדַתָּה (*Oxf. Heb. Lex.*). LXX omits. The place was in the Negeb of Judah, but the site is unknown. It appears to be connected with 'Kerioth-hezron, which is Hazor.' See HEZRON.

    C. R. CONDER.

HAZZELELPONI (הַצְלֶלְפּוֹנִי, AV **Hazelelponi**).—A female name in the genealogy of Judah, 1 Ch 4[3]. See GENEALOGY.

HE (ה).—The fifth letter of the Hebrew alphabet, and as such used in the 119th Psalm to designate the 5th part, each verse of which begins with this letter. It is transliterated in this Dictionary by *h*.

HE.—After the Heb. idiom (see Davidson, *Syntax*, § 106) a personal pronoun is sometimes inserted superfluously as the subject of the verb. Gn 4[4] 'And Abel, he also brought of the firstlings of his flock' (וְהֶבֶל הֵבִיא גַם־הוּא); Dt 1[30] 'The LORD your God which goeth before you, he shall fight for you'; Jos 22[22] 'The LORD God of gods, the LORD God of gods, he knoweth'; Is 9[15] 'The ancient and honourable, he is the head; and the prophet that teacheth lies, he is the tail.' In such cases there is a certain emphasis placed upon the subject, but, as Davidson points out, it is slight, and to translate 'as for the ancient and honourable' is to exaggerate it, though that construction may be permitted in a long sentence like 2 Ch 34[26], 'And as for the king of Judah, who sent you to enquire of the LORD, so shall ye say unto him' (. . . וְאֶל־מֶלֶךְ יְהוּדָה תֹאמְרוּ אֵלָיו; RV 'But unto the king of Judah . . . thus shall ye say to him'). The same idiom is found in Apocr. and NT, as 2 Mac 4[4. 5] 'Onias seeing the danger of this contention . . . he went to the king' (RV omits 'he'); Jn 1[18] 'No man hath seen God at any time; the only-begotten Son which is in the bosom of the Father, he hath declared him' (ὁ ὢν εἰς . . . ἐκεῖνος). There are many examples of this construction in Heb. that are not transferred into English. On the other hand, the example quoted from 2 Mac * is peculiar to the Eng. version, for this method of emphasizing a subject, or of catch-

* So also He 9[11. 12].

ing it up again after a long parenthesis, belongs to all composition. An example of each kind may be quoted from Shaks. *Com. of Errors*, V. i. 229—

  'There did this perjured goldsmith swear me down,
    That I this day of him received the chain,
    Which, God he knows, I saw not';

Hamlet, I. ii. 22—

  'Now follows, that you know, young Fortinbras,
    Holding a weak supposal of our worth,
    Or thinking by our late dear brother's death
    Our state to be disjoint and out of frame,
    Colleagued with the dream of his advantage,
    He hath not failed to pester us.'

See also under IT, WHICH.

In Bel [3. 4] there is an interchange between *him* and *it*, 'Now the Babylonians had an idol, called Bel, and there were spent upon him every day twelve great measures of fine flour. . . . And the king worshipped it, and went daily to adore it' (Gr. εἴδωλον . . . αὐτὸν . . . αὐτὸν . . . αὐτῷ). Cf. Tindale, *Expositions*, p. 96 (on Mt 6[16-18]), 'If thou wouldest kill thy body, or when it is tame enough, pain him.' Similar occurrences of a masc. pronoun for a neut., or a neut. for a masc., are found in the earlier versions, and are due usually to a literal regard for the gender of the Greek word. Thus Jn 1[3] Tind. 'All thinges were made by it, and with out it was made nothinge that was made' (so all the VSS before AV except Wyc. and Rhem.); but 15[18] 'Yf the worlde hate you ye knowe that he hated me before he hated you' (so Cran., but Gen. changed to 'it' and was followed by the rest). Cf. Mt 18[9] Rhem. 'And if thine eye scandalize thee, plucke him out, and cast him from thee'; and Wyc. *Works*, iii. 150, 'Ffor loued thing drawes men to hit, as tho stoon of a damaunt drawes irne unto hym.' In 2 S 12[15. 21] 'it' is applied to Bathsheba's child, but 'he' and 'him' in vv.[19. 23]. RV retains this as well as the more glaring discrepancy in Bel [3. 4], and adds at least one instance of its own, Mt 14[12] 'And his disciples came and took up the corpse and buried him' (reading αὐτὸν for αὐτό, AV 'it'), Mk 6[29] 'And when his disciples heard thereof, they came and took up his corpse, and laid it in a tomb' (retaining αὐτό here).

A clear example of the ancient dative *him* (='for him') remains in 1 K 13[13] 'And he said unto his sons, Saddle me the ass. So they saddled him the ass.' Other instances are 2 K 10[7] 'they . . . sent him them to Jezreel'; Sir 8[12] 'Lend not unto him that is mightier than thyself; for if thou lendest him, count it but lost'; and with *me*, 1 K 13[6] 'pray for me, that my hand may be restored me again.' But these instances are scarcely obsolete. In Ps 7[13] we read, 'He hath prepared for him the instruments of death.' Coverdale's tr[n] was 'He hath prepared him the weapons of death.' This became in Psalter of 1539 'He hath prepared hym the instruments of death,' and it remained in 1640, but in 1662 it was changed to 'for him,' because (as Earle shows) 'prepared him' must be 'prepared for himself' (*sibi*), which is clearly wrong.

Him is occasionally used reflexively: 2 K 13[15] 'And Elisha said unto him, Take bow and arrows. And he took unto him bow and arrows'; Mt 9[22] 'But Jesus turned him about, and when he saw her, he said, Daughter, be of good comfort' (ἐπιστραφείς, edd. στραφείς, RV 'turning'): so with *you*, Hag 1[6] 'Ye clothe you, but there is none warm'; and with 'them,' 2 K 17[9. 10] 'they built them high places in all their cities.' Examples are frequent in Shaks., as *Macbeth*, V. iv. 4—

  'Let every soldier hew him down a bough.'

And *himself* for *he himself*, which occurs in Mt 8[17] 'Himself took our infirmities and bare our sicknesses,' may be illustrated by *Two Gent. of Verona*, III. i. 143—

    ' Himself would lodge where senseless they are lying.'

On **his** as the sign of the poss. case see HIS ; and on *his* for *its* see ITS.   J. HASTINGS.

HEAD is the translation in OT of רֹאשׁ (in 1 Ch 10^10 גֻּלְגֹּלֶת 'skull'; in 1 S 19^16 26^7. 11. 16, 1 K 19^6 מְרַאֲשֹׁת the place where or the object on which the head is laid; in Aram. portions of Dn רֵאשׁ) and in NT of κεφαλή. The word is used very frequently both in a literal and a metaphorical sense.

(*a*) *Of men* (Gn 40^16, Lv 8^12, Ca 8^3, Mt 5^36, Mk 6^24, Lk 7^38 etc. etc.); opposed to 'foot' or used along with it in such expressions as 'from head to foot' (Lv 13^12, cf. Is 1^6); the son of the Shunammite cries, from the effects of sun-stroke, ' My head, my head ' (2 K 4^19).

(*b*) *Of animals* (Gn 3^15), the serpent's head to be bruised [? see Dillm. *ad loc.*] by the seed of the woman, Ex 12^9 the head of the paschal lamb, Job 40^31 [Eng. 41^7] of the crocodile. A 'dog's head' is an expression of contumely, 2 S 3^8.

(*c*) In a transferred sense, of *inanimate objects*, *e.g.* the tower of Babel whose top (רֹאשׁ) was to reach to heaven Gn 11^4, Jacob's ladder 28^12, and frequently of mountains Ex 17^9f. 19^20 etc. We read of the head of Jacob's bed Gn 47^31 (cf. He 11^22 where ἐπὶ τὸ ἄκρον τῆς ῥάβδου αὐτοῦ is borrowed from the LXX, which must have read מַטֶּה 'staff' instead of מִטָּה 'bed.')

Similar to this is the usage of 'head' to denote the *beginning* or *source* of something, *e.g.* in Gn 2^10 the river which issued from the Garden of Eden was parted into four 'heads,' *i.e.* stream-beginnings (Dillm.), each of which became a river with a separate course (cf. the use of רֹאשׁ in Is 51^20, Ezk 16^25 21^21, where it means the beginning of roads and streets).

(*d*) Another very common metaphorical sense of 'head' or 'heads' is to denote *the principal person* or *persons* in a community (*e.g.* Ex 6^14. 25 18^25, Nu 1^4. 16 7^2 10^4 13^3 17^3 25^4. 15 30^1, Dt 1^15 5^23 28^13. 44, Jos 22^21, 1 Ch 5^24, Is 9^14. 15 (where 'head' and 'tail' are opposed). Allied to this is the NT reference to the man as head of the woman Eph 5^23, and to Christ as head of the Church Eph 4^15 5^23, Col 1^18 2^19 (where also the idea of the head as a vital part is probably included), and as head over all principalities and powers Col 2^10.

'Heads' are used in apocalyptic literature to denote kings or empires (cf. the golden head of the image seen in Nebuchadrezzar's dream, Dn 2^32, which represented that king and his dynasty; the four-headed beast of 7^6; the beast with seven heads and ten horns of Rev 13^1, with one of the heads wounded to death, v.^3, on all of which see DANIEL, REVELATION, and Bruston, *Études sur Daniel et l'Apocalypse*).

The circumstance that the head is a principal seat of life explains the words of Achish to David, ' I will make thee keeper of mine head ' (1 S 28^2), *i.e.* body-guardsman; cf. Ps 140^7 'Thou hast covered (סַכֹּתָה) my head in the day of battle'; Dn 1^10 'endanger my head.' The head of an enemy might be cut off and exhibited as a trophy, or as a proof of death, Jg 7^25, 1 S 17^54. 57 31^9, 2 S 4^7 20^21f., 2 K 10^6ff. *Swearing by the head* is mentioned as a Jewish practice in Mt 5^36. The character of the head as a vital part accounts also for certain superstitions connected with the head of a sacrificial victim. While in Ex 12^9 it is expressly enjoined that the head and viscera of the paschal lamb are to be eaten, a different practice was widely followed amongst Orientals. The same taboo attached to the head as to the blood. Among the Egyptians the head * of the victim was thrown into the Nile,

    * Which was regarded as a special seat of the soul.

while by the Iranians it was dedicated to Haoma, that the immortal part of the animal might return to him. A dried human head or the head of an animal was frequently used by the Semites as a charm (W. R. Smith, *RS* 359, 362, 449, 456).

Jacob placed his hands upon the heads of Ephraim and Manasseh as a symbol of conveying the blessing to them (Gn 48^14ff. ; cf. Gn 49^26, Pr 10^6 11^26). In like manner, evil is spoken of as being requited or returning on one's head (Jg 9^57, 2 Ch 6^23 etc.). The *laying of one's hands on the head of a sacrificial victim* (Ex 29^15, Lv 1^4 4^29. 33 etc.) is very frequently interpreted as a symbolical transference of sin to the animal; but while this is distinctly recognized in the case of the scape-goat (Lv 16^21), it is not so certainly implied for the ordinary burnt-offering (see W. R. Smith, *RS* 401 f.).

The *hoary head* is a symbol of old age (Lv 19^32, 1 K 2^6. 9, Pr 16^31, Is 46^4, cf. Job 41^32); it is to be honoured, Lv 19^32; it is pronounced a crown of glory, the reward of uprightness, Pr 16^31.

While the general sense of the expression, 'heap coals of fire upon the head' (Pr 25^22, Ro 12^20) is clear enough (St. Paul paraphrases, 'Overcome evil with good'), its origin is somewhat uncertain (see Wildeboer, Reuss, etc., on Pr ; and Meyer, Godet, Sanday-Headlam, etc., on Ro, *ad loc.*). A good illustration of the working of the principle is supplied by the words of Saul to David, 1 S 24^17 26^21.

To lift up the head, when spoken of oneself, may mean to recover from disaster (Jg 8^28, Zec 1^21), or, generally, to succeed or to carry oneself proudly Ps 83^3 110^7 (cf. its use in 24^7 of gates and see Wellh. *ad loc.* in Haupt's *PB*). To 'lift up the head' of another is used of raising to honour (Gn 40^13 of Pharaoh's chief butler, 2 K 25^27 of the captive king Jehoiachin, who was taken out of prison by Evil-Merodach). In Gn 40^19, with a designed contrast to the treatment of the butler, it is said that Pharaoh will 'lift up the head of the chief baker from off (מֵעַל) him,' the reference being to beheading.

When Elisha was told that 'the LORD will take away thy master from thy head' (2 K 2^3. 5), the reference is probably to the custom of pupils sitting at the feet of their teacher (so Siegfried-Stade ; cf. Ac 22^3).

To wag or *shake the head* was a sign of contempt or of malicious enjoyment, Ps 64^8 (RV), Jer 18^16 (both נוד), La 2^15 (נוע) ; cf. Ps 44^14, Jer 48^27 (both מָנוֹד רֹאשׁ 'a shaking of the head'); Mt 27^39, Mk 15^29 (κινοῦντες τὰς κεφαλάς, of the men who derided the suffering Saviour).

The *head of one under a vow* was not shaven till its completion (Nu 6^18ff., Ac 18^18 21^24). See further under NAZIRITE. The Israelites were forbidden to 'round the corners of their heads' (Lv 19^27) in token of mourning (cf. Dt 14^1, where 'making baldness between the eyes' refers to the custom of shaving the front part of the head ; see Driver, *ad loc.*, and on Am 8^10, and W. R. Smith, *RS* 306 f.).

Anointing the head was a common practice amongst the Jews (Ps 23^5, Mt 6^17 26^7, Mk 14^3, Lk 7^46). See further under ANOINTING.

To cover (חָפָה) *the head* was a token of mourning [2 S 15^30 David and his men when fleeing from Absalom, Jer 14^3, Est 6^12 (‖ אָבֵל)]. The same was expressed by *putting the hand upon the head* (2 S 13^19 Tamar after Amnon's outrage) or putting *ashes* (אֵפֶר) or *earth* (אֲדָמָה) upon it (Jos 7^6, 1 S 4^12, 2 S 1^2 13^19, La 2^10). It is possible that this custom is alluded to in Am 2^7 ' that pant after the dust of the earth on the head of the poor,' *i.e.* who are so avaricious that they are eager to secure even the dust strewn upon their heads by the poor in token of their distress (see full discussion in Driver, *ad loc.*).

To have the head covered (κατακαλύπτεσθαι) in the Christian assemblies is enjoined upon women by St.

Paul (1 Co 11[5]). The contrary rule applies to men (v.[4]). Much obscurity attaches to v.[10] 'For this cause ought the woman to have power (ἐξουσίαν, RV '[a sign of] authority,' AVm *i.e.* 'a covering, in sign that she is under the power of her husband,' RVm 'authority over') on her head because of the angels' (διὰ τοὺς ἀγγέλους). This passage will be fully discussed in art. POWER (see also WH's remarks on the text). It may be noted, meanwhile, that what is emphasized is the presence of angels *in the sanctuary*, and not the ordinary Jewish notion (Taylor, *Sayings of the Fathers*[2], p. 156) about guardian angels, two of whom were supposed to be *always* in attendance on every human being.

It is generally supposed that in Est 7[8] there is an allusion to a Persian custom of covering the head or face *in token of sentence of death* (so *Oxf. Heb. Lex.*, V. Ryssel in Kautzsch's *AT*, etc.). In support of this interpretation appeal is made to a similar custom among the Romans ('Caput obnubito, infelici arbori suspendito,' Cic. *pro Rabirio*, iv. 13) and the Macedonians ('Capite velato in regiam adducunt,' Quint. Curt. vi. 8. 22). But in the *Rev. Biblique Internat.* (April 1898, p. 258 ff.) A. Condamin gives reasons for doubting whether either of these passages is relevant. Some evidence from such a quarter as Herodotus would be much more to the point. Moreover, the LXX have evidently followed a different text, or at least have interpreted differently from the MT (וּפְנֵי הָמָן) and the Vulg. (*operuerunt faciem eius*). They give Ἀμὰν δὲ ἀκούσας διετράπη τῷ προσώπῳ (cf. Jos. *Ant.* XI. vi. 11, Ἀμάνου δὲ πρὸς τοῦτο καταπλαγέντος καὶ μηδὲν ἔτι φθέγξασθαι δυνηθέντος). Condamin maintains that the order of the words in MT and the absence of אֶת with פְּנֵי plead in favour of this tr[n], 'the face of Haman became troubled' (so Siegfried-Stade, *Hamans Gesicht verschleierte = verdüsterte sich*). The context also he uses in support of his interpretation. If the MT חפו (either Qal or Pual) is considered insufficient to support the LXX rendering, it would be easy, he points out, to emend to חפרו. It may be added that חָפָה is never used elsewhere of covering the *face* but always the *head* (cf. Est 6[12], 2 S 15[30], Jer 14[3]). When the face is spoken of, the verbs employed are כָּפָה (Job 9[24] 23[17] 24[15] etc.) or הִסְתִּיר (Ex 3[6], Job 13[24] etc.).

With the Hebrews not the head but the heart was the seat of intellect. See HEART.

J. A. SELBIE.

HEADBAND.—See BAND and DRESS.

HEADSTONE is erroneously printed in mod. edd. of AV as one word; in 1611 it is 'head stone' (as RV), and means simply the topmost stone of the building.

HEADTIRE.—See DRESS and TIRE.

HEADY.—This is the tr[n] in 2 Ti 3[4] AV of προπετής, which in Ac 19[36], its only remaining occurrence in NT, is tr[d] 'rashly' (RV 'rash'). Heady is from Tindale; and has been adopted by all the VSS thereafter, except Rhem. 'stubburne,' and RV which uses its mod. equivalent in this sense, 'headstrong.'* In enumerating 'the heap of inconveniences that spring by intemperate and superfluous eating and drinking,' Tindale says (*Expositions*, p. 93, on Mt 6[16-18]), 'Our fashions of eating make us slothful, and unlusty to labour and study; unstable, inconstant, and light-mannered; full of wits, after-witted (as we call it), incircumspect, inconsiderate, heady, rash, and hasty to begin unadvisedly, and without casting of perils.' Calvin (in Golding's tr[n]) uses the word of Job's passions (on Job 32[1-3]), 'Seeing then that

* Headstrong occurs in AV, Sir 30[8], of a horse, as tr[n] of ἐκληρός.

Job had so heady passions, no doubt but in so dooing hee made himselfe more rightuous than God.' *High-mind* and *Heady* are the names of the guns which the inhabitants of Mansoul placed at Ear-gate to keep the King's forces out (Bunyan, *Holy War*, p. 50). Bp. Hall uses the word as equivalent to hasty (*Works*, ii. 109, on 'Zacheus'), 'There must be no more hast than good speed in our performances; we may offend as well in our heddye acceleration, as in our delay; Moses ran so fast downe the hill that he stumbled spiritually, and brake the Tables of God.'   J. HASTINGS.

HEALTH.—This word has become greatly narrowed in meaning since 1611. Now restricted to the state of the body, it then expressed also the condition of the soul, the relation to God of the whole person. Hence in 'Morning Prayer,' 'We have left undone those things which we ought to have done, and we have done those things which we ought not to have done, and there is no health in us,' which has retained its place since the Pr. Bk. of 1552. But in the Communion Service, 'health' of 1604, 'And as the Son of God did vouchsafe to yield up his soul by death upon the cross for our health,' is found as 'salvation' in 1662. So we find in Wyc., Ac 28[28] 'Therfore be it knowen to you, for to hethen men this helthe of God is sent'; and in Tind. (as well as in Wyc.), Lk 19[9] 'This day is healthe come unto this housse.' Cf. also Erasmus, *On the Creed*, p. 40, 'The first degre [=step] than unto helthe is *Credere deum esse* (*id est*) to believe that there is God.' This is the meaning of 'health' in Ps 42[11] 43[5] 'Who is the health of my countenance' (Wyc. 'the helthe of my chere'). The Heb. is יְשׁוּעָה, which is tr[d] 'salvation' in Ps 62[1], Is 56[1] (Wyc. as usual 'helthe,' Cov. 'savynge health'), and elsewhere. In Ps 62[2] the word is used of the *person*, 'He only is my rock and my salvation' (='saviour,' which is Cheyne's tr[n] in Ps 42[11] 43[5]; RVm gives 'help,' which is Coverdale's word). Again in Ps 67[2] 'That thy way may be known upon earth, thy saving health among all nations'; 'saving health' stands for the same Heb. word (Wyc. 'helthe'; 'savynge health' being from Coverdale, who uses the phrase in other places, as Is 51[8] 'But my rightuousness shal endure for ever, and my savynge health from generacion to generacion').

But 'health' was often used in a still wider sense, denoting the prosperity or safety of a person or a place. As expressing 'safety' it occurs in Ac 27[34] 'Wherefore I pray you to take some meat: for this is for your health' (σωτηρία, RV 'safety'). Cf. Ac 27[20] Wyc. 'Sothely nether sunne nether sterris apperinge bi mo dayes, and tempest not litil schewinge nygh, now al the hope of oure heelthe was don awey.' See MEDICINE.

J. HASTINGS.

HEART, לֵב or לֵבָב, καρδία.—In the AV of the OT other Hebrew expressions for the inward parts of the body are also rendered by 'heart': *e.g.* קֶרֶב in Ps 39[3], מֵעֶה Ps 40[8]. 'Heart' has thus the general sense of *the midst, the innermost or hidden part of anything*, in such instances as the 'heart of the sea,' Ex 15[8]; of heaven, Dt 4[11] (RV and AVm); of a tree, 2 S 18[14ff.]; of the earth, Mt 12[40].

But its ruling use is (1) for *the bodily organ*, of the centrality of which as the seat of life the ancients had on the whole a correct view. Since in Bible phrase 'the life is in the blood' (Lv 17[14]), that organ which forms the centre of its distribution must have the most important place in the whole system. So by an easy transition 'heart' came (2) to signify *the seat of man's collective energies*, the focus of the personal life.

This secondary or psychical meaning it holds unchanged and undisputed through the whole of the biblical writings. Its prominence as a psychological term in the Scriptures and in other ancient books is no doubt due partly to the fact that the physical heart bulked so much more largely in the view of those times than the head or brain. How rarely are any functions of thought attributed to the latter in the OT (see only Dn 2²⁸ 4². ⁷. ¹⁰ 7¹. ¹⁵ as exceptions). This fact introduces the only difference in the Bible use of 'heart' metaphorically from that of everyday modern speech. As from the fleshly heart goes forth the blood in which is the animal life, so from the heart of the human soul goes forth the entire mental and moral activity. To it also all the actions of the human soul return. '*In corde actiones animæ humanæ ad ipsum redeunt*' (Roos). There the soul is at home with itself, becomes conscious of doing and suffering as its own. 'The heart knoweth the bitterness of the soul,' or 'of itself' (Pr 14¹⁰).

Heart is therefore the organ of conscience, of self-knowledge, and indeed of all knowledge. For though the reflective function is prominent, we must note that all inner human movements are denoted by this word in Scripture; the rational and intellectual as well as other. This is the main distinction between the biblical and the modern usage of the word. In the OT it by no means signifies mainly or only the emotional or volitional elements in human nature, but pre-eminently the intellectual (hence בֵּל אֵין = 'without understanding'). It is only in the later Scriptures that the Greek habit of distinguishing the rational from the emotional finds place.

The following analysis of the OT uses of לֵב and לֵבָב is abridged from that of *Oxf. Heb. Lexicon* :—
1. Of the *inner man in contrast with the outer*; opposed to flesh Ps 73²⁶, garments Jl 2¹³, hands Ps 73¹³, La 3⁴¹ (?), eyes Nu 15³⁹, 1 S 16⁷, ears Ezk 3¹⁰, mouth Dt 30¹⁴, speech Ps 28³ 78¹⁸.
2. The inner man, *comprehending mind, affections, will*; note *e.g.* the frequent 'with all the heart and with all the soul' (בְּכָל־לֵבָב וּבְכָל־נֶפֶשׁ) Dt 4²⁹ 6⁵ and oft.; cf. 'what is in the heart' (אֲשֶׁר בִּלְבָב) Dt 8², 'with the heart' (עִם לְבָב) Dt 8⁵.
3. With specific reference to *mind, e.g.* אַנְשֵׁי לֵב 'men of mind' Job 34¹⁰. ³⁴, knowledge Dt 8⁵, 1 K 2⁴⁴, thinking, reflection, Is 10⁷, memory 1 S 21¹².
4. With specific reference to *inclinations, resolutions, determinations of the will, e.g.* 'set the mind to' (אֶל) 1 S 7³, 1 Ch 29¹⁸, 'Pharaoh's mind was changed' (לֵב הֵפֵּךְ) Ex 14⁵.
5. With specific reference to *conscience*, 'my heart (*i.e.* conscience) shall not reproach me' Job 27⁶.
6. With specific reference to *moral character*: God tries the heart 1 Ch 29¹⁷; 'uprightness of heart' Dt 9⁵, heart perfect with (עִם) 1 K 8⁶¹; heart as seat of naughtiness 1 S 17²⁸ (?), pride Ps 101⁵; heart circumcised or uncircumcised Dt 10¹⁶, Lv 26⁴¹, hardened Dt 2³⁰.
7. Heart=*the man himself*, Ps 73¹⁷ 81⁷ 9⁴, Is 14¹³.
8. As seat of the *appetites*, Ps 104¹⁵.
9. As seat of *emotions and passions, e.g.* joy Is 30²⁹, trouble 1 K 8³⁸, anger Dt 19⁶, hate Lv 19¹⁷.
10. As seat of *courage* (for which usually רוּחַ) Dn 11²⁵.

Because it is the focus of the personal life, the workplace for the appropriation and assimilation of every influence, in 'heart,' according to Scripture, lies the moral and religious condition of the man. Only what enters the heart forms a possession of moral worth, only what comes from the heart is a moral production. The Bible places human depravity in the 'heart' because sin is a principle which has its seat in the centre of man's inward life, and thence 'defiles' the whole circuit of his action (Mt 15¹⁹. ²⁰). On the other hand, it regards the 'heart' as the sphere of divine influence, the starting-point of all moral renovation: 'The work of the law written in their hearts' (Ro 2¹⁵); 'A new heart will I give you' (Ezk 36²⁶); 'Purifying their hearts by faith' (Ac 15⁹). Once more, the 'heart' as lying deep within contains 'the hidden man' (1 P 3⁴), the real man. It represents the true character, but conceals it; hence it is contrasted with the 'outward appearance,' and is declared to be the index of character only for Him who 'searches the heart and tries the reins of the children of men' (1 S 16⁷; Jer 17¹⁰ 20¹²).

This scriptural usage—making the heart the source of the moral life—lends firmness and simplicity to its teachings about sin and grace. That man's moral corruption is seated in his heart means that not the substance of human nature or the personality of man is perverted, but his principles of action. That the saving process begins with 'a new heart' means that not another self or personality is substituted, but that new principles of action are introduced. Hence the whole doctrine of sin and grace is biblically grounded in a way to free it from mistake or exaggeration.

On the relation of the term Heart to Soul, Spirit, Reins, Conscience, see under these words.

LITERATURE.—*Oxf. Heb. Lex. s.* לֵבָב and לֵב ; Cremer, *Bib.-Theol. Lex.*, and Thayer-Grimm, *s.* καρδία ; Oehler, *Theol. of OT*, i. 221 ff., ii. 449; Schultz, *OT Theol.* ii. 248; Weiss, *Bib. Theol. of NT* (' Heart' in Index). J. LAIDLAW.

HEARTH.—The word ' hearth' is found in seven passages of our AV, in all of which, with one exception (Is 30¹⁴), it has been discarded by the Revisers. On the other hand, it has been introduced three times into their text (Lv 6⁹ [Heb.²], Ezk 43¹⁵. ¹⁶), and once besides in an explanatory note in the margin (Is 29¹; for all of these see No. 4 below).

1. The primitive domestic hearth was a mere depression in the earthen floor of the living-room, where the family meal was cooked, and around which, in the cold season, the family gathered for warmth. The Hebrew name for the hearth was perhaps מוֹקֵד *môkêd* (Ps 102³ [Heb.⁴] ' my bones are burned as an hearth' AV; but RV has ' as a firebrand,' cf. LXX φρύγιον, with the former rendering in the margin). This word would thus be identical in meaning as well as in form with the Arabic *mauḳid*.* The nearly allied יָקֻד (Is 30¹⁴), by AV and RV rendered ' hearth,' is more strictly *the burning mass,* a meaning which many would give to *moḳed* (see both words in *Oxf. Heb. Lex.*). The same uncertainty attaches to the form מוֹקְדָה *môkĕdah* (Lv 6⁹ [Heb.²] ' the burnt-offering shall be on the hearth' RV ; ' on its firewood' RVm), which is probably not an independent word, but the masc. form (*môkêd*) with suffix (so Dillm., Strack, etc.). A detailed description of the modern Syrian hearth (*mauḳdi*) is given by Landberg (*Proverbes et Dictons,* pp. 73, 74), with illustration (p. 455). The smoke from the hearth, on which various kinds of fuel, wood, charcoal, dung, etc. (see COAL, FUEL) were burned, escaped as best it might through door or latticed window (אֲרֻבָּה, Hos 13³ AV, RV ' chimney '), since chimneys were unknown (see CHIMNEY).

2. In the houses of the wealthier classes, at least, braziers or chafing dishes were in common use. Thus Jehoiakim on a memorable occasion had Jeremiah's roll 'consumed in the fire that was in the brazier' (הָאָח Jer 36²². ²³ RV ; AV in each case ' on the hearth'; LXX ἐπὶ τῆς ἐσχάρας, which is ambiguous) in his ' winter house.' A similar firepan is referred to in Zec 12⁶ (' like a pan of fire' כִּיּוֹר אֵשׁ ; so RV, but AV ' like a hearth of fire'). Cf. for NT times Jn 18¹⁸ 21⁹.

3. In Gn 18⁶ Sarah is requested to ' make cakes upon the hearth' (AV), for which RV has, more literally, ' make cakes.' The cakes in question, termed '*ugôth* (עֻגוֹת), were really baked ' upon the hearth' by being covered with the hot ashes, and are therefore accurately rendered by the Vulgate

* So Del. *in loc.*, and Siegfried-Stade's *Lex.* For other possible significations of מוֹקֵד see Bæthgen's note in his *Handkommentar, in loc.*

subcinericios panes (LXX ἐγκρυφίας). See BREAD, vol. i. p. 318.

4. We have seen (under No. 1 above) that, according to a possible interpretation, the top of the altar of burnt-offering was known as its 'hearth' (Lv 6⁹ [Heb.²] in RV). This is confirmed by the description in Sirach of Simon the high priest standing 'by the hearth of the altar' (ἑστὼς παρ' ἐσχάρᾳ βωμοῦ, Sir 50¹²). The upper portion of the altar also receives a special name from Ezekiel, viz. 'Arî'ēl (הָאֲרִיאֵל, so Kerê 43¹⁵·¹⁶), the origin and precise significance of which are uncertain. Most recent scholars are in favour of the meaning adopted by the Revisers, 'altar hearth' (AV wrongly 'altar.'*).

The enigmatical term *Ariel* (אֲרִיאֵל), by which Isaiah (29¹ff.) designates Jerusalem, is also, by various modern writers, understood in this sense of 'altar hearth' (cf. RVm 'hearth of God.' See comm. of Duhm and Skinner, *in loc.*; also ARIEL in vol. i. with reff. there, to which add Cheyne, *Isaiah*, in Haupt's ' Polychrome Bible').

A. R. S. KENNEDY.

HEATH (עַרְעָר *'ar'ar*, עֲרוֹעֵר *'ărō'ēr*, ἀγριομυρίκη, ὄνος ἄγριος, *myrica*). — This is AV translation of the Hebrew name of a plant growing in the desert, doubtless identical with the *'ar'ar* of the Arabs, *Juniperus Phœnicea*, L., which grows on the W. face of the range of the mountains of Edom, overlooking the 'Arabah. Its branches, clothed with minute scale-like leaves, may well entitle it to the name 'naked tree' (AVm Jer 48⁶). In this and the only other passage where the word occurs (Jer 17⁶), RVm has ' a tamarisk tree.' There is another species of *Juniper*, called by the Arabs *'ar'ar*. It is *J. oxycedrus*, L. This species is not, however, a desert plant. It grows in the middle and subalpine regions of Syria. It is unlikely that this is the plant referred to. One species of heath, *Erica verticillata*, Forsk., grows on sandstone and chalky rocks, at an altitude of from 300 to 3500 ft., on the W. face of Lebanon and the chains to the northward. This cannot be the plant intended. There are no heaths in the desert. G. E. POST.

HEATHEN.—The title 'Nations' in Scripture (Heb. *Goïim*, Gr. *Ethnē*), originally covering the nations of the world as a whole, soon comes to designate exclusively the non-Jews, the uncircumcised. Scripture casts its view, and it is a sympathetic view, over the whole human race, before it treats of the forefathers of the Israelites in particular. Though many of the Jews of later times became proudly exclusive in their treatment of those who did not belong to the privileged people, the religion of Scripture gives no warrant for such an attitude on their part; it is fundamentally characterized by the spirit of humanity. The synopsis of the peoples of the earth given in Gn 10, by connecting them all with Noah, presents them as related to each other like kinsmen. Dillmann (*Genesis*, p. 176) points out how other races too, Egyptians and Phœnicians, Assyrians and Babylonians, even Indians and Persians, had a certain knowledge of the earth and its inhabitants, but usually paid little attention to foreigners, except when influenced by political or commercial reasons, and often despised them as mere barbarians. ' Here in Genesis, on the other hand, all the peoples that were known by repute, most of whom could not have stood in any intimate relation to the countrymen of the writer, are included in his survey. All the divisions of mankind are collected in a genealogical tree, and Israel is held to be only an ordinary branch on the stock of

---

* For הָהַרְאֵל *har'ēl*, Ezk 43¹⁵ᵃ (RV 'upper altar'), we should read as above הָאֲרִיאֵל, or perhaps throughout הָאֲרִאֵל, as on the Moabite Stone (Smend and Socin, lines 12, 17).

universal humanity.' The same breadth of outlook is indicated in the announcements that God created *man* in His own image (Gn 1²⁷), that He blessed *Noah and his sons*, and assigned a penalty for the shedding of *man's* blood (Gn 9¹·⁶). Even in giving the promise of special favour to Abraham and his seed, God showed Himself gracious to the other inhabitants of the world as well. One race was chosen and disciplined for the ultimate good of the whole. In Abraham all the families of the earth were to be blessed (Gn 12³).

At the same time, we see the severest treatment of the heathen approved of in the OT. Efforts were made to extirpate the Canaanites after the land of Pal. was entered, and the OT represents that it was a great sin to spare them (Ex 23²⁷ff., Nu 33⁵²ff., Dt 20¹⁶ff.). The disaster that befell the Canaanites is viewed, however, as the consequence of their utter moral corruption, their grievous sin against the light of nature; the reflection stirred by their ruin is comparable to that which is now occasioned by the action of inexorable laws of Providence on demoralized nations of modern times. Israel was commanded to make no marriages with the inhabitants of the land that remained (Dt 23¹²), and to make no league with them (Jg 2²). The prophets had an arduous struggle to keep Israel's worship of J" separate from that which was contaminated by the idolatrous heathen rites as practised on the high places. Heathenism, with its distinguishing feature of idolatry, remained a congenial faith, even to the people of God, and spiritual monotheism was a new thing which was, for obvious reasons, repugnant to them. The centralization of Jewish worship at the temple, as enjoined in Dt, was mainly due to the purpose of the prophets to isolate the chosen people from all their heathen neighbours. The natural, racial, inherited proclivities of the Israelites could not be extinguished, and the nation could not advance in the knowledge and service of the true God otherwise than by the method of seclusion from the surrounding tribes.

The prophets, however, far from cherishing a spirit of blind hostility towards the heathen, foresee the day when the nations will be gathered into the one family of God's people, having rest and comfort, and enjoying the blessings of the law that goes forth from Jerusalem. The golden age of the world, according to the OT, is in the future, and the heathen will participate in its glory (Is 40–66). The Bk. of Jonah sets forth God's tender regard for the heathen.

Jewish exclusiveness as towards the heathen culminates in the post-exilic age. The Jews being shorn of political influence, became the more confirmed in their devotion to their faith, and hedged it round with an elaborate system of ritual (the Levitical law). The barrier between them and the heathen thus became more impassable than ever.

As the Greeks spread along the shores of the Mediter., and their speech and customs became more prevalent (2 Mac 4¹⁰ff.), they, as the principal representatives, stood for the heathen generally (Ro 10¹², 1 Co 10³² 12¹³, Gal 3²⁸; cf. Jn 7³⁵). The Jewish view of the heathen is marked by conflicting elements, and needs to be superseded. The heathen are at once held in repugnance, and called to the highest honour.

Christianity was, in the first instance, a development and modification of Judaism. As the world had needed preparation for the coming of Christ, so He took up the work which was begun among the Jews and completed it. But the principle of universalism is involved in His doctrine of the kingdom of God as a kingdom of righteousness and love; in His doctrine of God as the Father of individual spirits, who welcomes the returning prodigal on the sole condition that he repents and has faith (Lk 15); or, again, in His announcement that God is a spirit, who must be worshipped in spirit and in truth (Jn 4²³). God is the Father of all, and the conditions of acceptance with God are such as all men can and ought to fulfil.

What was implicit in the doctrine of Christ on this matter was made explicit, after a period of conflict with the other apostles, by St. Paul. To the latter there is no distinction between Jews and Gentiles, except that the Jews, as being the better prepared, through the oracles of God entrusted to them, have the privilege of hearing the gospel first (Ro 3²). But the Gentiles, too, have had a measure of training by the law, that which is known through nature and conscience; and if they turn to God and keep the law, their uncircumcision will be counted to them for circumcision (Ro 2¹⁴·²⁶). In all this a continuous plan is seen to be worked out by God, for those who sincerely believe are the true descendants of Abraham, having his faith; and they are the truly circumcised, for true circumcision is of the heart (Ro 2 ff.).

According to the gospel, heathenism proves to be, not a matter of nationality, but of spirit and character. So in the OT the moral aspect of it is frequently emphasized, especially in the Psalms, where heathenism is often synonymous with wickedness. Its essence is set forth by Christ in Mt 6³¹·³². To the heathen mind God is a power that needs to be appeased or conciliated for *worldly* purposes. The world only is sought with desire—protection from disease or misfortune, material prosperity, enjoyment bodily or mental. By the faithful spirit, on the other hand, religion is made the first choice, and the God who is worshipped is seen in His true character, is recognized as the true God; He is reverenced as a righteous Spirit, and loved more than aught else for His fatherly goodness. In this way distinctions of race, name, or profession pass over into such as are moral and spiritual. See FOREIGNER, GENTILE, GER.

G. FERRIES.

HEAVEN.—The word 'heaven' is used in a variety of senses in the OT and NT, but especially in that of the dwelling-place of God, the abode from which Christ came and to which He has returned, and the destination of the perfected saints. The etymological associations of the term are extensive. It is of uncertain root, though it may be connected with the Lat. *capere*, and the Eng. *have* and *heave*. It appears in different forms in many European languages, Sw. *hefva*, Da. *haeve*, Go. *haffan*, Ic. *hefja*, *hifinn*, Ger. *heben*, OHG *heffan*, AS *hebban*, ME *heuen*; in Chaucer, *CT*, 552; in Robert of Gloucester, however, *hebben*. (See Skeat, *Etymol. Dict.²*).

In the OT it usually represents שָׁמַיִם, Aram. שְׁמַיָּא, which expresses 'heaven' in respect of its height; and in the NT οὐρανός, οὐρανοί, which may be connected with ὄρνυμι = *lift*, *heave* (cf. Ger. *Luft*, Scot. 'the lift'), and the Vedic *varuna*, from *var = tegere* (see M. Müller, *Oxford Essays*, p. 41). In the LXX οὐρανός stands not only for שָׁמַיִם, שְׁמַיָּא, but also for אֵל, אֱלוֹהַּ, שַׁחַק, מָרוֹם, תְּהוֹם, חֶבֶל, הוֹצֵאת, רָקִיעַ. In our AV the word 'heaven' represents in addition to שָׁמַיִם mainly three words of different significations, רָקִיעַ, מָרוֹם, שְׁחָקִים, שֶׁחַק. But there are also certain words of which it is erroneously made the equivalent. One of these is the term גַּלְגַּל, which expresses the idea of roundness, and is rendered 'heaven' in Ps 77¹⁸ (AV), as if it meant the 'round orb of the sky,' but which conveys rather the notion of a 'whirl,' and may be best rendered 'whirlwind' (so RV). Another is עֲרָבוֹת, in Ps 68⁴, in the description of J" riding

'on the heavens.' But while the term might be taken, as it is by some, in the sense of the large expanse of the sky, it is more accordant with its usual meaning to take it in the sense of 'deserts.' Another is the term עֲרִיפִים, which is rendered 'darkness' by the Syr. and the Vulg., and 'heavens' in the AV in Is 5³⁰; but it means properly 'droppings,' 'clouds,' and expresses probably the idea of the clouds ready to discharge their rains. In Ps 89⁶·³⁷, too, the word שַׁחַק is rendered 'heaven,' which properly denotes 'dust,' and may best be rendered the 'clouds' or the 'skies.'

The chief ideas attached to the word 'heaven' in the OT, therefore, are the following. It is used (1) in the largest sense, to signify the one half of the whole system of things, the upper division of the created world, the phrase 'the heavens and the earth' expressing the universe as a whole (Gn 1¹). More specifically it is used (2) to denote the *firmament* (στερέωμα), the sky, the expanse which God made on the second day of His creative work, after the formation of the 'earth' and the institution of 'day' and 'night' (Gn 1⁶·⁸). This 'expanse' is represented as dividing the waters above from the waters beneath. In speaking of it in its different aspects, the OT writers employ a great variety of terms, both literal and boldly metaphorical, which naturally move within the limits of the popular conceptions that prevailed among the Semitic and other ancient peoples on the subject of the system of things, and the place which the earth held in it as its centre and the proper object of God's creative action. The simple ideas which meet us in ancient Greek poetry (cf. Homer, *Il.* xvii. 425, *Od.* iii. 2; Pindar, *Ol. Od.* 10, *Nem.* vi. 3) and in the oldest literature of the East (*e.g.* the Vedic hymns, the Babylonian tablets, etc.), are also expressed in the OT. The 'firmament,' or vault of heaven, is described in terms of a strong cover, curtain, or roof provided for the earth (Is 40²², Ps 104²), resting on pillars, on the mountains and the waters of the earth (2 S 22⁸, Job 26¹¹, Pr 8²⁷·²⁹). Its beauty is described as that of crystal or sapphire (Ex 24¹⁰, Job 37¹⁸, Ezk 1²⁶·²⁸). It is represented as the region of the fowls, the winds, the clouds (Dn 4¹² 7²·¹³). In it the ancient Hebrews, like the Greeks and Romans (cf. Plutarch, *De plac. phil.* 2¹⁴, Pliny, 2³⁹), conceived God to have placed the fixed stars and the planets (Gn 1¹⁷, Is 14¹² 34⁴).

It is used also (3) to denote the peculiar abode of Deity, with which the ideas of elevation, majesty, glory, power, holiness, unchangeableness are associated. It is the place to which prayer ascends (2 Ch 30²⁷), which makes J"s throne (Is 6¹ 66¹), which is His peculiar possession in contrast with the earth which He has given to the sons of men (Ps 115¹⁶). It is the 'height' or 'heights' (Job 22¹², Ps 148¹), supramundane, above the firmament and all created things (Ps 29³·¹⁰ 104²·³). As the dwelling-place of God it is described in terms of a temple, a sanctuary, a palace, a throne (Ps 11⁴, Mic 1², Hab 2²⁰ etc.). The ideas of the supramundane abode are taken so naturally from the visible things of the mundane holy place, which was the centre of the Jewish worship of God and the place where He was specially to be found, that it is sometimes difficult to say which of the two was immediately in the writer's thought (*e.g.* in Is 6; see Riehm, *HW*, under the word *Himmel*). It is the place, too, in which God has His court of angels (Job 1⁶ 2¹, implicitly). But while it is often thus spoken of as the peculiar habitation of God, it is also described as incapable of containing Him, and the prophets declare His greatness to be such as to surpass all the bounds of space and all idea of residence within the limits even of the heaven of heavens (Is 40¹² 66¹; cf. 1 K 8²⁷).

But it is also used, (4), in the eschatological sense, to express the new constitution of things which shall in the end take the place of the present imperfect order. In many passages the quality of the changeless and enduring is ascribed to 'heaven,' especially in contrast with the mutable earth and the perishable life of man (Jos 11[21], Ps 72[5. 7. 17] 89[29], Jer 31[35. 36] 33[25. 26]). But it is also exhibited as an aspect of the changeful and transitory, as contrasted with the changeless being and eternal years of God Himself (Ps 102[25-27], Is 51[6]). And the OT looks forward to a day of divine judgment, the issue of which shall be the dissolution of the present order, the renewal of the system of things, and the creation of a glorious condition of which a restored heaven shall form part (Is 65[17] 66[22]).

The NT takes over the general OT idea of 'heaven,' but with certain differences and enlargements. It has the same general conception of 'heaven' as a region above earth. As the OT speaks of a ladder reaching to heaven (Gn 28[12]), of Elijah as going 'up' in a whirlwind to heaven (2 K 2[11]), of the 'heights' of heaven (Job 11[8]), etc., so the NT speaks of the angels of God ascending and descending in relation to heaven (Jn 1[51]), of St. Paul as 'caught up' to the third heaven (2 Co 12[2]), of St. John as seeing a door opened in heaven and hearing a voice saying, 'Come up hither' (Rev 4[1]), of the holy city as descending from God out of heaven (Rev 21[2]), etc. In the NT it is also the name given to the peculiar dwelling-place of God, and Christ's doctrine of God as our 'Father in heaven' adds to the OT conception of its majesty and remoteness and holiness the new ideas of security, grace, and love. The whole conception of heaven as the habitation of Deity is made more definite by its being presented as the scene of the present life and activity of Christ. It is the place from which He came to earth and to which He re-ascended (Mk 16[19], Lk 24[51], Ac 1[11]); the habitation which 'must receive' Him 'until the times of the restitution of all things' (Ac 3[21]); the scene of His present reign and His present work. In heaven He is in 'the presence of God' (He 9[24]), and there His glory can be seen (Jn 17[24]). The scene of Christ's risen life and the work of intercession which He carries on in it are described with special fulness in the Ep. to the Heb., and in terms of the ancient Jewish sanctuary, its conditions, its sanctities, and its services (He 8[1 etc.] 9[24]). Heaven is also the abode of the angels (Mt 18[10] 22[30], Rev 3[5]), and the place from which the Holy Ghost is sent down (1 P 1[12]).

It is chiefly in its eschatological applications that the word 'heaven' is used in the NT. The idea of a renewal of heaven as well as earth that is associated in the OT with the judgment of the end, is given more distinctly in the NT. In certain large and significant passages the NT speaks of a redemption of the whole creation from the bondage of corruption (Ro 8[21]), of a gathering together and a reconciliation of things in heaven as well as things on earth (Eph 1[10], Col 1[20]), of a time of the restitution of all things (Ac 3[21]), of a day when all things shall be made new (Rev 21[5]), of the formation of a 'new heaven' as well as 'a new earth, wherein dwelleth righteousness' (2 P 3[12. 13], Rev 21[1]). The NT associates this renewal of the heavens with Christ's Second Coming and the Final Judgment, and connects the hope of a new scene and order for man's life with that of the final perfection of his life. Further, in the NT 'heaven' is in particular the final home of the righteous. It is the place which Christ has gone to prepare for them (Jn 14[2]), the place from which He is to come with His holy angels (Mt 24[30], Mk 13[26], Lk 21[27], Rev 1[7]) for the final arbitrament of things, and into which His own shall be received that they may be with Him and see His glory

(Mt 5[12], Lk 6[23], 2 Cor 5[1], Eph 6[9], He 10[34] etc.). So it is the sum of all good, and the goal of man's hope (Mt 6[19], Lk 6[23] 10[20], Ph 3[20], 1 P 1[4], He 12[23]).

There are other questions regarding the 'heaven' of the Bible which are of interest and require consideration. Some relate to the use of the term, others to the ideas of heaven which find expression in the Scriptures. Among these is the question whether the word 'heaven' or 'heavens' occurs either in the OT or in the NT as a metonymy for *God*. The Jew of later times had so exaggerated a sense of the sanctity of the divine name, that he did not allow himself to utter the most proper designation of God, but had recourse to equivalents. There is abundant evidence to show that by our Lord's time the word 'heaven' or 'heavens' was in frequent use in this way; and it is held by not a few competent scholars that the Jewish formula מַלְכוּת שָׁמַיִם is an instance of this, and that St. Matthew's phrase, 'the kingdom of heaven,' is literally the same as 'the kingdom of God,' which is the expression of the other evangelists and of St. Paul (see Cremer, *Bib.- theol. Lex.*, *sub voce* βασιλεία; Thayer's *Lex.*, *sub voce* οὐρανός; Edersheim's *Life and Times of Jesus the Messiah*, i. 265; *Jhrb. f. prot. Theol.* 1876, p. 166, etc.; Schürer, *HJP*, Eng. tr. div. II. vol. ii. p. 171). The instances of this use furnished by the Bible are at the best very scanty, and even the most probable cases are negatived by many. There seems, however, to be at least one sufficiently clear instance in the OT (Dn 4[26]), and another, though more disputable, in the NT (Lk 15[18]), where, however, it may be (as it is taken, *e.g.*, by Meyer and others) a personification of the heavenly world 'as injured and offended.'

Another question is whether the conception of a *series* of heavens is found in the Scriptures. This has been answered in the negative, and the terms which seem to imply the influence of such a conception have been taken for plurals of majesty, or large, rhetorical expressions of the idea of infinity. But the evidence is all in favour of the affirmative answer. The plural form of the Hebrew word points in that direction. Much more decidedly is this the case with such forms as 'the heaven of heavens' (Dt 10[14], 1 K 8[27], Ps 148[4]), 'all the heavens' (Eph 4[10] RV), 'the third heaven' (2 Co 12[2]). The same may be said of the peculiar phrase 'in the heavenly places,' or 'in the heavenlies' (ἐν τοῖς ἐπουρανίοις), which occurs five times in the Ep. to the Eph. (1[3. 20] 2[6] 3[10] 6[12]), and has in each a local sense. To which must be added the idea of Christ as the great High Priest who has 'passed through the heavens' (He 4[14]), and is 'made higher than the heavens' (He 7[26]). The affirmative reply is also in harmony with the fact that the idea of a plurality of heavens prevailed among other ancient peoples, and in particular among those that were in contact with the Jewish nation at different periods of its history, such as the Babylonians and the Persians. This conclusion is further confirmed by the large place which is given to this idea in the Rabbinical literature, and in the apocalyptic and other pseudepigraphic books, both Jewish and Christian,—especially the Slavonic Enoch, the apocalyptic parts of the Testaments of the Twelve Patriarchs, 4 Ezra, the Ascension of Isaiah, the Apocalypses of Moses, Ezra, John, Isaac, Jacob.

With this is connected the further question whether the plurality that is recognized is one of three heavens or of seven. It has been thought by some that only the idea of a series of three heavens is found in Scripture. It has been pronounced by some (Estius, Le Clerc, Bengel) to be the *doctrine* of the Bible that there are only three heavens. Origen (*Con. Cels.* vi. p. 289) denied that St. Paul had the idea of seven heavens, and the idea of a threefold heaven obtained a considerable place in the Church (Suicer, *Thes.* ii. p. 520, etc.). But the evidence which bears out the existence of the idea of a plurality of heavens also favours the idea of a sevenfold series of heavens. Among the Babylonians a sevenfold division of heavens seems to have prevailed. They had the conception of seven world-zones; they surrounded their cities, Erech and Ecbatana, with seven walls; they thought of hell as divided into seven parts by seven walls. And though no explicit reference to it appears to have been discovered as yet among the inscriptions, it is reasonable to suppose that their heaven was also divided into seven sections (Jensen, *Kosm. der Babyl.* pp. 232–252; Sayce, *Hib. Lect.* pp. 221–227). In the Zoroastrian books, but not in the earliest, we find the idea of a succession of seven heavens, which were traversed by Sosioch in seven days, Zarathrustra himself occupying a golden throne in the seventh. The Jews were familiar, too, with the planets, of which four are mentioned by name in the OT (2 K 17^{30}, Am 5^{26}, Is 14^{12} 46^{1} 65^{11}). The same conception of seven heavens appears to have been almost universal among the Rabbis, only R. Juda being mentioned as diverging from the general doctrine, and teaching the existence of but two heavens. The pseudepigraphic writings, and very definitely the Slavonic Enoch and the Testaments of the Twelve Patriarchs, give the same enumeration of the heavens, and describe them at length. It is hazardous to infer, as Meyer does, from the notice of *Paradise* in 2 Co 12^{4} that St. Paul thought of it as higher than the third heaven and belonging to a fourth heaven; for in the pseudepigraphic literature *Paradise* is repeatedly represented as being in the third heaven. But, in view of the evidence, the most reasonable conclusion is that the conception of the heavens which pervades the OT and the NT (not excepting the Pauline writings, though St. Paul mentions only the *third* heaven and *Paradise*) is that of a series of seven heavens.

This idea of a plurality of heavens as it appears in the Biblical writings, however, is free from the extravagances and puerilities which we find associated with it in the extra-canonical literature. In the Testaments of the Twelve Patriarchs, *e.g.*, curious details are given of each of the several heavens. The first is full of darkness and gloom; the second, of fire, ice, and snow. The third contains the hosts that are to execute judgment on the spirits of deceit and of Beliar. In the fourth are thrones and authorities; in the fifth and the sixth are angels with different offices. In the seventh dwells the Great Glory. In the Slavonic Enoch there is a still more elaborate description. In the first heaven, it is there said, are 'a very great sea,' and 'the elders and the rulers of the stars,' and treasuries of snow, ice, clouds, and dew. In the second are the prisoners reserved for eternal judgment. In the third are found the Garden of Eden, and the tree of life and an olive tree ever distilling oil. In the fourth are seen the course of the sun and moon, the angels, and the phœnixes and the chalkidri that wait upon the sun. In the fifth are the watchers, troubled and silent, on account of their fallen brethren. In the sixth are seven bands of angels, very bright and glorious, students of the courses of sun, moon, and stars, also the angels over the souls of men, with seven phœnixes, seven cherubim, and seven six-winged creatures. In the seventh are the heavenly hosts, the ten great orders of angels, and the Lord Himself on His lofty throne. In the Rabbinical books we find similar trivialities. In the *Beresh. rabba*, c. 6, the *Bammidbar rabba*, c. 17, and the *Chagiga*, xii. 6, *e.g.*, the differences between the

several heavens are given in extreme and fanciful detail. The first or lowest heaven is called *Vilon* (וילון, Lat. *velum*), and is empty. The second is called *Rakia*, and contains the sun, moon, and stars. The third is called *Shechakim*, and contains the mills that grind the manna for the righteous. The fourth is called *Zebul*, and in it are the heavenly Jerusalem, the temple, the altar, and Michael. The fifth is named *Maon*, in which are the 'hosts of angels, praising God by night, but keeping silent by day that God may hear the praises of Israel.' The sixth is named *Machon*, and it holds the treasuries of the snow, hail, rain, and dew. The seventh is known as *Aravoth*, the seat of judgment and righteousness, with the treasuries of life, peace, and blessing. In it, too, are the souls of the righteous dead, the spirits and souls of men yet to be born, and the dew with which the dead shall be awaked. And in it are the Seraphim, Ophannim, Chayyoth, and other orders of angels (cf. Dante, *Par.* c. 27), and God Himself on His eternal throne. The Ascension of Isaiah gives another incongruous description of the series of heavens.

Similar speculations, and, if possible, even more tasteless and absurd, appear to have been indulged in by certain heretical leaders and their sects. Irenæus (*Cont. Hær.* bk. i. c. v. 2) and Tertullian (*Adv. Valent.* 20) speak of the fancies of the Valentinians on the subject. From Irenæus (*Adv. Hær.* bk. i. c. xxx. 4, 5), Origen (*Con. Cels.* vi. 31), and Epiph. (*Hær.* xxvi. 10), we learn also that the Ophites held the doctrine of a Hebdomad of heavens ruled by seven potentates. Others, *e.g.* the Gnostic Marcus (Iren. *Adv. Hær.* bk. i. c. xvii. 1), reckoned eight heavens, and Basilides (August. *De Hær.* i. 4) held there were 365. Nor are the Christian apocalypses, such as the Apoc. Mosis, the Apoc. Esdræ, the Apoc. Johannis, less given to such speculations. The belief in a series of seven heavens, with some of the curious theories which prevailed so extensively on the subject, penetrated indeed into the Christian Church, and was more or less favoured by some of the leading Fathers. Clement of Alexandria, *e.g.*, mentions it in terms which suggest that he did not question its validity (*Strom.* iv. 25). Origen refers to it in much the same way, explaining, however, that there was no authoritative doctrine on the subject (*De princ.* ii. 11). Augustine has an uncertain theory of his own, implying three heavens (*De Gen. ad lit.* xii. 5, 27). Even near the end of the 4th cent. these notions held such a place in Christian thought, that Philastrius pronounced it a heresy to deny the plurality of the heavens, though the question of the particular number, whether two, three, or seven, was left open (*De Hær.* bk. 94). At last, however, the reaction came, and Chrysostom declared the whole conception of a series of heavens to be a human fancy, and contrary to Scripture. Repudiated by the Church, it was adopted by Mohammedanism. It is affirmed in the Koran (*e.g.* c. 22, 41), and in later Mohammedan writings it appears in the crudest possible forms.

The ideas of 'heaven' and the 'heavens' which are expressed in Scripture are of a different order. Neither in the OT nor in the NT have we anything like those far-fetched ineptitudes. It is the more remarkable that it should be so, in view of the fact that these things prevailed so long and so widely, and had so great a hold, not only of ethnic faith, but also of Jewish and Christian thought. Later Christian theology has relapsed from time to time into such theorizings, distinguishing between the heaven of clouds, the heaven of stars, and the empyrean; between the *visible* heaven or firmament, the *spiritual* heaven, the abode of saints and angels, and the *intellectual* heaven, which is the scene of the immediate vision of God (*Elucidar.* c. 3) ; between the *cœlum sidereum*, the *cœlum crystallinum*, and the *cœlum empyreum* (John of Dam., Thomas Aquin., etc.) ; or between the *regio nubifera*, the *regio astrifera*, and the *regio angelifera* (Grotius). But such strained refinements have no place in the Hebrew and Christian Scriptures. In all their statements the Biblical books have the notes of simplicity and restraint. In many things they practise a reverent reserve.

There is at the same time a progress in the ideas of heaven which appear in them. These become more definite, more spiritual, and more sharply contrasted both in purity and in elevation with the conceptions found elsewhere. It was not alien to the common Jewish understanding, as it is seen in the curious literature of Judaism, to associate the presence of evil and trouble with one or other of the divisions of heaven. In the Testaments of the Twelve Patriarchs the second heaven is the habitation of the spirits of the lawless who are in confinement and punishment. In the Slavonic Enoch the second heaven contains the apostate angels who had transgressed with their prince, and were in reserve there against the judgment. In the third heaven, according to the same book, Enoch saw not only the Garden of Eden, but in its northern region a place of punishment, which had 'fire on all sides and on all cold and ice,' prepared for those who dishonoured God on earth and committed deeds of evil. And in the fifth heaven he saw the many hosts of the Watchers (ἐγρήγοροι), with their countenances withered and melancholy and their lips always silent, by reason of their sadness for their brethren, who rebelled in lust of empire and were imprisoned in the darkness of the second heaven. Such ideas were not altogether strange to the dramatic imagination of the OT, as is seen in the representation of the lying spirit that stood before the Lord (1 K 22²¹), and in the appearance of Satan along with the angels in the presence of God (Job 1⁶·⁷ 2¹·²·⁷). In the NT the nearest approach to such conceptions is the Pauline designation of the 'heavenly places,' the superterrestrial regions, as the sphere in which 'the spiritual hosts of wickedness' dwell and work (Eph 6¹²). But in all its positive elements the Bible view of heaven is far removed from these things ; and the vision which the NT Apocalypse gives of war in heaven between Michael with his angels and the dragon with his, ends in the overthrow of the latter, and the casting of the conquered ones 'out into the earth.'

Moreover, the ideas of heaven as the dwelling-place of God and the final abode and recompense of the righteous, move on in the course of the revelation of truth which is made in the Scriptures to larger and loftier things. In the OT heaven as the dwelling-place of God is presented chiefly in relation to the divine majesty and remoteness. In the NT it appears in the new and higher aspect of the Father's house, the place that has received the risen Christ, the scene of the activity of the great High Priest and the Advocate with the Father (He 4¹⁴, 1 Jn 2¹). In the OT it is scarcely known as the future inheritance of the righteous. The eye of the OT looked mainly on the present, and the consummation which it expected was one that was to take place on earth. It had glimpses of things beyond, and at last rose to a clearer and more definite vision of an after life. But the completion of life which it looked to was something to be realized in this world, and the heaven which made its hope was a heaven to be found mainly in the joy of a near fellowship with God here and now. In the NT the heaven which is to be our final home and the goal of our hope is a heaven that is above this world and beyond

time, not only superterrestrial, but supramundane, the transcendent heaven which is brought to light in the gospel.

The nature of this heaven, its conditions, and the things in which its blessedness consists, are nowhere given in definite or dogmatic statement. They are presented to faith and to the spiritual imagination by many suggestive expressions and by a great variety of figurative phrases. Heaven itself is described as a *kingdom*, one 'prepared from the foundation of the world,' the 'Father's kingdom,' the 'kingdom of God,' an 'eternal' or 'everlasting kingdom' (Mt 25³⁴ 26²⁹, Lk 22¹⁶, 2 P 1¹¹, Jude ²¹) ; an *inheritance*, one of which we have the 'earnest' here, the 'inheritance of the saints in light,' an 'eternal inheritance,' an 'inheritance incorruptible, and undefiled, and that fadeth not away' (Eph 1¹⁴, Col 1¹², He 9¹⁵, 1 P 1⁴) ; a 'house of many mansions' (Jn 14¹) ; a place prepared by Christ (Jn 14²·³) ; a 'better country,' a 'city prepared' (He 11¹⁶). Once at least it is described as *Paradise* (Lk 23⁴³)—a term probably of Median origin, selected by the LXX as the rendering for the Garden of Eden, and used in Jewish literature to express the idea of a home of innocence and peace, with reference sometimes to the Eden of the past, sometimes to an Eden of the future, sometimes to an earthly Eden, sometimes to a heavenly (see article on PARADISE). Its life is set forth as an existence like that of the angels (Mk 12²⁵, Lk 20³⁶), an 'eternal life' (Jude ²¹), a 'life that is life indeed' (1 Ti 6¹⁹), a 'rest' (He 4¹ etc., Rev 14¹³), a life of worship, praise, service (Rev 5⁹ etc., 22⁴). Its happiness is expressed by a rich and varied imagery, as reward, a 'great reward,' a 'full reward,' royalty, an everlasting reign, an everlasting existence, a partaking of the tree of life and the hidden manna, a new name, the dignity of a pillar in the temple of God, a place on the throne, praise, honour, glory, that which is within the veil, the presence of God's glory, a prize, a crown, the 'crown of life,' a 'crown of righteousness,' the promise, a manifestation, a salvation from wrath, the adoption, the vision of God, the being like Christ, the seeing of Him as He is, joy, 'exceeding joy,' 'the joy of the Lord' (Mt 5¹², 1 Co 3⁸·¹⁴, Col 3²⁴, 2 Jn ⁸, Rev 22¹², 2 Ti 2¹², Rev 22⁵, He 10³⁴, Rev 2⁷·¹⁷ 3¹²·²¹, 1 P 1⁷, He 6¹⁹, Jude ²⁴, Ph 3¹⁴, 2 Ti 4⁷, 1 Co 9²⁵, 2 Ti 4¹⁸, Ja 1¹², 1 P 5⁴, Rev 2¹⁰, He 9¹⁵, Ro 8¹⁹ 5⁹, 2 Ti 2¹⁰, Ro 8²³, Rev 22⁴, 1 Jn 3², Jude ²⁴, Mt 25²¹).

Theology has sought to answer many questions relating to heaven which Scripture suggests, but which it does not itself follow to their conclusions. It has occupied itself with the question as to how the spirituality and omnipresence of the Divine Being can be reconciled with the predication of heaven as His peculiar dwelling-place. It has also discussed the question whether heaven is to be regarded as a place or only as a condition. These are questions which are beyond the range of our present faculties and experience. Scripture freely speaks, on the one hand, of God as everywhere present and as manifesting Himself in different ways in all parts of His creation, and, on the other hand, as specially present in heaven and manifesting His glory in a peculiar sense there. And we can only say that it is with Him, though in a higher sense, as it is with the sun 'which shines everywhere, yet especially displays its full splendour in the firmament' (Oosterzee, *Chr. Dog.* p. 258). Neither can we disconnect the idea of locality absolutely from our conception of heaven. It belongs to the condition of our present mental life and experience to think of heaven more or less in terms of locality, even when we think of God who is spirit, much more when we think of the future home of beings like ourselves.

Theology also has engaged itself greatly (in some eras, however, much more than in others) with the question of the nature of the existence in heaven, the heavenly activities, the felicities of heaven. Sometimes it has committed itself to rude, material, sensuous conceptions; sometimes it has defined heaven as essentially a condition of passivity, contemplation, or quiescence. But for the most part, and in the case of its greatest names, it has avoided these extremes. Even Justin Martyr (*Adv. Hær.* 57), Irenæus (*Apol.* i. 8), and the Fathers who accepted the millenarian doctrine, thought of the immediate communion with God as the essence of the blessedness of heaven. Origen affirmed the progress of life in heaven, and dwelt largely on the intellectual conditions of heaven, regarding its chief joy as found in the satisfaction of the desire of knowledge (*De prin.* II. xi. 2). Greg. Naz. (*Orat.* xvi. 9), Greg. Nyss. (*Orat. Cat.* c. 40) and others, placed its felicity chiefly in the increase of knowledge and in intercourse with all the saints. Augustine (*De Civ. Dei*, xxi. 29, 30), agreeing with all others that the enjoyment of God is the substance of the bliss of heaven, added specially to that the recovery of man's true liberty. While the mystics of all ages have inclined to reduce the various Scriptural representations of heaven to metaphors of subjective states, the schoolmen generally construed them as implying locality, and speculated on the region, its divisions, and its employments. Extreme realistic views of heaven have been advocated by theosophic theologians in all times. And in the system of Emmanuel Swedenborg, with its principle of correspondence, in virtue of which the spiritual world is the outbirth of the invisible mental world and the natural world that of the spiritual world, we have a curious doctrine of the constitution of heaven as the subject of a revelation, and find the existence of three distinct heavens, consisting of three orders of angels, affirmed.

The Scriptures themselves are silent on many things on which theology has dilated. They give us a large, general view of heaven as the final home of God's servants; of its rewards as having degrees corresponding to the character and the service; of its blessedness as found in freedom from all sin, pain, sorrow, in the manifestation of the eternal love and glory, in the realization of hope, the possession of all good, the presence of Christ, the immediate vision and fellowship of God. It leaves much to the sanctified imagination, and makes its final teaching this—'Eye hath not seen, nor ear heard, neither have entered into the heart of man, the things which God hath prepared for them that love him' (1 Co 2⁹).

LITERATURE.—The books on *Biblical Theology*, especially those by Oehler, Schultz, Dillmann for the OT, and Schmid, Weiss, Beyschlag, Baur, Hahn for the NT; the systems of Dogmatics and Eschatology, especially those by Plitt, Rothe, Schleiermacher, Dorner, Schweitzer, Kliefoth, Atzberger; the Lexicons of Cremer and Thayer; Edersheim's *The Life and Times of Jesus the Messiah*; Hamburger's *Real-encyclopädie*; Eisenmenger's *Entdecktes Judenthum*; Schöttgen's *Horæ Hebraicæ*; Gfrörer's *Jahrhundert des Heils*; Schürer's *The Jewish People in the Time of Jesus Christ*; Weber's *Jüdische Theologie*; Wetstein on 2 Co 12; Morfill and Charles's *Book of the Secrets of Enoch*; Jeremias, *Die Babyl.-assyr. Vorstellungen vom Leben nach dem Tode*; Kohut, *ZDMG* xxi.; Feuchtwang, *Ztschr. f. Assyr.* iv.; Weber, *Die Lehren des Talmud*.

S. D. F. SALMOND.

HEAVE-OFFERING.—See SACRIFICE.

HEAVINESS.—Besides the literal sense of ponderous, **heavy** is used in two fig. meanings: **1.** *Burdensome*, as Nu 11¹⁴ 'I am not able to bear all this people alone, because it is too heavy for me'; 1 Es 5⁷² 'But the heathen of the land lying heavy upon the inhabitants of Judea, . . . hindered their building' (ἐπικοιμώμενα [Fritzsche conjec. ἐπικείμενα] τοῖς ἐν τῇ Ἰουδαίᾳ; Wis 17²¹ 'Over them only was

spread an heavy night' (βαρεῖα); 2 Mac 5²³ 'Menelaus, who worse than all the rest bare an heavy hand over the citizens' (ὑπερήρετο τοῖς πολίταις, RV 'exalted himself against his fellow-citizens'). Cf. T. Lever, *Sermons* (Arber, p. 64), 'And their landlords which shuld defend them, be most heavye maisters unto them.' **2.** *Sorrowful*, as 1 K 20⁴³ 'And the king of Israel went to his house heavy and displeased' (סַר); 1 Es 8⁷¹ 'And as soon as I had heard these things, I rent my clothes, and the holy garment, and pulled off the hair from off my head and beard, and sat me down sad and very heavy' (σύννους καὶ περίλυπος, RV 'sad and full of heaviness'); 2 Es 12⁴⁶ 'Be of good comfort, O Israel; and be not heavy, thou house of Jacob' (*noli tristari*; RV 'be not sorrowful'); Mk 14³³ 'And he taketh with him Peter and James and John, and began to be sore amazed, and to be very heavy' (ἀδημονεῖν, RV 'sore troubled'). So Lk 18²³ Tind. 'When he heard that, he was hevy; for he was very ryche'; Is 1⁵ Cov. 'The whole heade is sick, and the herte is very hevy'; Hall, *Works*, ii. 144 (on 'Jairus and his daughter'), 'What a confusion there is in worldly sorrow? The mother shreekes, the servants cry out; the people make lamentation, the minstrelles howle, and strike dolefully; so as the eare might question whether the ditty or the instrument were more heavie'; Erasmus, *The Commune Crede*, Eng. tr., fol. 73*b*, 'And that Christ suffered in soule also, even his owne selfe doth witnesse, sayenge, My soule is hevy even unto the deathe.'

The adv. **heavily** means 'with difficulty' in Ex 14²⁵ 'And took off their chariot wheels that they drave them heavily' (בִּכְבֵדֻת, lit. 'with heaviness,' the only example of the Heb. word). The meaning is rare in Eng.; cf. Mt 13¹⁵ Rhem. 'For the hart of this people is waxed grosse, and with their eares they have heavily heard, and their eies they have shut.' Heavily occurs also once in the sense of grievously, oppressively, Is 47⁶ 'upon the ancient hast thou very heavily laid thy yoke'; and once as sorrowfully, Ps 35¹⁴ 'I bowed down heavily, as one that mourneth for his mother' (RV 'I bowed down mourning'; see Abbott, *Original Texts*, 1891, p. 214).

Heaviness occurs often, but always with the meaning of grief. Thus Pr 10¹ 'A wise son maketh a glad father: but a foolish son is the heaviness of his mother'; 12²⁵ 'Heaviness in the heart of man maketh it stoop: but a good word maketh it glad'; Is 61³ 'To appoint unto them that mourn in Zion, to give unto them beauty for ashes, the oil of joy for mourning, the garment of praise for the spirit of heaviness'; 1 Es 8⁷¹ 'I sat still full of heaviness until the evening sacrifice' (περίλυπος); 2 Es 10⁸ 'And now, seeing we all mourn and are sad, for we are all in heaviness, art thou grieved for one son?' ('quoniam omnes contristati sumus,' RV 'seeing we are all in sorrow'); Sir 22⁴ 'She that liveth dishonestly is her father's heaviness' (εἰς λύπην γεννήσαντος, RV 'the grief of him that begat her'); 38¹⁸ 'of heaviness cometh death, and the heaviness of the heart breaketh strength' (both λύπη, RV both 'sorrow'); Ro 9² and 2 Co 2¹ (both λύπη, RV both 'sorrow'); 1 P 1⁶ 'Ye are in heaviness' (λυπηθέντες, RV 'Ye have been put to grief'); Ph 2²⁶ 'For he longed after you all, and was full of heaviness' (ἀδημονῶν, RV 'was sore troubled'). In their Preface the AV translators say of the Scriptures, 'If we be ignorant, they will instruct us; if out of the way, they will bring us home; if out of order, they will reforme us; if in heaviness, comfort us; if dull, quicken us; if colde, inflame us.' The older versions have the word very often, as Jn 16⁶ Wyc. 'sorwe, *or heuynesse*, hath fulfillid youre herte'; Ps 30⁵ Cov. 'hevynesse maye well endure for a night, but joye commeth in the

mornynge' (Cran. 'hevynesse maye endure for a night,' and so Pr. Bk.). Cf. Erasmus, *The Commune Crede*, fol. 31*b*, 'Agayn of the defaulte and wante of fayth springeth superstition, sorcerie, idolatry, and covetousness cosen to it, ambition, blasphemy, hevynes, desperation, pride, fear of death, desyre of vengeaunce, fynally what so ever vices or synnes do raygne in the whole worlde.'
J. HASTINGS.

HEBER (חֶבֶר 'association' or 'spell,' from חבר to 'unite,' especially by spells : possibly connected with Ḥabiri, *Journal of Bibl. Lit.* xi. 118, xii. 61).—**1.** A man of Asher and son of Beriah (Gn 46[17], Nu 26[45], 1 Ch 7[31. 32]). He founded what appears from the last passage to have been the principal clan in his tribe. The gentilic name **Heberites** occurs in Nu 26[45]. **2.** The Kenite, according to Jg 4[17] 5[24], husband of Jael. He separated himself (Jg 4[11]) from his Bedâwin caste of Kenites or nomad smiths, whose wanderings were confined chiefly to the south of Judah, and settled for a time near Kedesh, on the plain to the west of the Sea of Galilee (Conder, *Tent-Work*, ii. 132; G. A. Smith, *Hist. Geog.* 369, note l). According to the narrative of Jg, Sisera in his flight after defeat by Barak was invited by Jael to take refuge in her husband's encampment, and was there killed by her in his sleep. But Jg 5[24b] is shown by the metre to be probably a gloss from 4[17], which again appears to relate to a different locality from that of 4[11]. On the whole it is not unlikely that two traditions are blended, and that in the original stories the unnamed wife of Heber dealt with Jabin in a similar way to that of Jael with Sisera. **3.** A man of Judah, son (1 Ch 4[18]) of Mered by his Jewish, as distinguished from his Egyp., wife. Beyond his genealogy, nothing is recorded of him except that he was the 'father' or founder of Soco. **4.** A Benjamite and member of the family of Elpaal (1 Ch 8[17]), which appears to have been of pure Heb. blood on both sides, as contrasted with its kindred of partially Moabite descent (1 Ch 8[8. 11]).
R. W. MOSS.

HEBREW, '*ibri*, עִבְרִי, עִבְרִים, עֶבְרִים).—Ebrew (Shaks. *I Hen. IV.* II. iv. 198 ; AV 1611 Dt 15 heading): Ebreus (Wycl. 2 Co 11[22]) : through Norm. *Hebreu, Hebræus,* Ἑβραῖος, Aram. '*ibrai,* det. forms, '*ibrā'ah*,'*ibrāyah* (עֶבְרָי, עֶבְרָאָה, עֶבְרְיָה, Dalm. *Jüd.-Pal. Aram. Gramm.* p. 155). The Greeks were thus evidently first acquainted with the word through Aramaic-speaking peoples. If, as may be presumed, this was by way of N. Syria and Asia Minor, it throws no light on the date at which they came personally in touch with the Hebrews. As, however, Ἑβραῖος occurs only in later Greek (LXX, Pausanias ; *v. infra*), it is possible that it was formed at a time when Aramaic was becoming the prevailing language of the Hebrews themselves, *i.e. c.* 300 B.C.

I. USAGE OF THE WORD.—(A) *Old Test.*—Not in P nor, save in Jer 34[9. 14] (quot. from Dt 15[12]), in documents certainly later than 7th cent. B.C., presumably because it has no theological or theocratic connotation but is purely secular, and 'Jew' (wh. see) took its place from the 7th cent. onwards. It is apparently the oldest designation of the chosen people (whether in its primitive use confined to them or not, see II. ii.) in contrast to those of another race. We thus find it used : i. by others—Gn 39[14. 17] [J²] 41[12] [E], Ex 2[6] [E], Egyptians ; 1 S 4[6. 9] [E¹] 13[19] [J²] 14[11] [J¹] * 29[3] [J¹], Philistines. ii. By Jews in addressing others—Gn 40[15] [E], Egyptians ; Ex 3[18] 7[16] 9[1] [all J], words that Moses was commanded by God to use to Pharaoh ; 5[3] [J], words so used by him ; Jon 1[9], by Jonah to the

sailors who were presumably Phœnicians. iii. With a contrast to others expressed or clearly implied—Gn 14[13] [' Exilic Midrash'??], Canaanites and Chedorlaomer's army ; 43[32] [J²], Ex 1[15. 16. 19] [E] 2[7. 11. 13] [E], Egyptians ; 1 S 13[3. 7] * [J¹], Philistines ; 14[21] [J¹], Philistines and, apparently, the bulk of Israel that were already with Saul ; Ex 21[2] [' Bk. of the Covenant'], Dt 15[12], Jer 34[9. 14] 'a Hebrew slave' is contrasted with one of any other nationality.

(B) *Apocrypha.*—The word does not occur often, but the usage is similar, as far as it goes. i. Used by others, Jth 12[11] (Holofernes, an 'Assyrian'), 14[18] (Bagoas, an 'Assyrian').[†] ii. By Jews in addressing others, Jth 10[12] ('Assyrians'), 2 Mac 7[31] (Syrians). iii. With a contrast to others expressed or clearly implied, 2 Mac 11[13] (Syrians) [‡] 15[37] (Syrians). iv. The Prologue of Sir is slightly different, for it is there used distinctly of the Hebrew language in contrast to Greek, the discovery of the original of Sir showing that Hebrew, not Aramaic, was intended.

(C) *New Testament.*—The phenomena here are more difficult. 'Hebrews' are contrasted with 'Hellenists' (Ac 6[1]),[§] *i.e.* those Jews who favoured Hellenism and practised Greek customs, and therefore, either by preference or by residence abroad, usually spoke the Greek language. Hebrews would therefore be those who more truly answered to the old idea of the people, the more conservative members who prided themselves on maintaining the old customs, and rejected as far as possible the insidious influence of Hellenism (2 Co 11[22], Ph 3[5], though St. Paul was a Jew of the Dispersion). In this way it is intelligible how 'Hebrew,' when used of language, may mean either Aramaic (Jn 5[2] 19[13. 17. 20] 20[16] Ἑβραϊστί, and probably Ac 21[40] 22[2] 26[14] τῇ Ἑβραῖδι διαλέκτῳ) or Hebrew proper (Rev 9[11] 16[16] Ἑβραϊστί).[||] In other words, the evidence now available tends to show that the use of 'Hebrew' does not refer fundamentally to the language,[¶] but rather to the historic position and worth of the nation. It is not a linguistic but a national word. Hence Josephus[**] can remark that the Heb. say for 'red' ἄδωμα (*Ant.* II. i. 1) and for Pentecost ἀσαρθά (*Ant.* III. x. 6), *i.e.* pure Aram. (עֲצַרְתָּא, אֲדוֹמָא).[††]

II. ORIGINAL MEANING OF THE WORD.—*Quot homines tot sententiæ,* for a word that goes back to such primitive times readily lends itself to guesses on the part of those unacquainted with Hebrew, or acquainted with it only in its biblical form.

i. The derivation from *Abram* (אַבְרָם) [‡‡] is of course impossible, for א and *y* do not readily interchange,[§§] and the loss of the final ם would be inexplicable. At most, the similarity of sound between the

<hr>

* Klostermann and Budde read 'a great multitude' (עַם רָב).

† Contrast the use of 'Israel' in Jth, when God's mercies are spoken of, or when there is no thought of members of another nation, *e.g.* 158ff. 'Jews' is apparently not found in Jth.

‡ Notice the allusion to victories of the Hebrews of old.

§ Cf. the συναγωγή Αἰβρίων at Rome mentioned on one, and apparently a second, inscription (see Schürer, *HJP* II. ii. 248, and Berliner, *Gesch. d. Juden in Rom* i. 64. Berliner, referring to Derenbourg, thinks Αἰβρίων here means Samaritans, but surely wrongly).

|| Cf. Prologue to Sirach, *supra.*

¶ As Trench, *NT Synonyms,* § xxxix.

** Cf. A. Meyer, *Jesu Muttersprache,* 1896, p. 40.

†† In the time of Eusebius, when the distinction between 'Hebrew' and 'Hellenist' was hardly regarded by a Gentile Christian, even Philo can be called a Hebrew by birth (τὸ γένος ἀνέκαθεν Ἑβραῖος ἦν, *HE* II. iv. 3). For other examples of Ἑβραῖος, *Hebræus,* being used in the widest national sense, see Plut. *Sympos.* iv. qu. 6. 1 ; Pausanias, i. 5, § 5, v. 5, § 2, and 7, § 4, vi. 24, § 8, x. 12, § 9 ; Appian, civ. 2. 71 ; Porphyry, *vit. Pyth.,* Leipzig, 1816, p. 22 (if the reading is genuine) ; Tac. *Hist.* v. 2.

‡‡ Quid ergo probabilius sit Hebræos tanquam Heberæos dictos, an tanquam Abrahæos, merito quæritur, Aug. *Quæst. in Gen.* § 24 ; cf. Euseb. *Præp. Evang.* x. 14.

§§ עבר is represented by אבר in recent Assyrian lexicons, but this is because there is no differential sign for either א or y at the beginning of a syllable.

'Hebrews' and their most famous ancestor may have assisted in limiting the term to them.

ii. *Eber* (עֵבֶר Gn 10²¹. ²⁴. ²⁵ 11¹⁴⁻¹⁷, 1 Ch 1¹⁸. ¹⁹. ²⁵) * is a much more plausible explanation. Assuming him to be a real person, it would be a patronymic, used in two forms, (*a*) Hebrew (עִבְרִי), (*b*) *bĕnē 'Eber* (Gn 10²¹) ;† cf. *bĕnē Lot* (Ps 83⁹), and *bĕnē Israel*.‡

iii. From עבר as verb or preposition, designating the Hebrews as those who have come across, or who belong properly to the land across, some well-known boundary. Euseb.(*Præp. Evang.* vii. 8, xi. 6) prefers to any other a spiritual interpretation, that the Hebrews were those who had passed over from the worship of false gods and the pleasures of the flesh to the service of the God of all and the life of true wisdom and piety. But this is homiletical, not scientific. Three natural boundaries have been suggested.

(*a*) The Red Sea. 'Why was Moses to say to Pharaoh, The LORD God of the *Hebrews* hath met with us? Because they had crossed over the Red Sea' (*Exod. R.* § 3 middle, by a Rabbin. conceit).

(*b*) The Jordan. So Wellhausen (*Isr. u. Jüd. Gesch.* p. 7, 1894), who thinks it was given to them by their neighbours in Western Palestine after they had crossed over. He thinks, however, that in old usage the term was so extended as to include the Edomites, with whom the Hebrews were originally united. Thus 'Hebrews' would mean those who dwelt עֵבֶר הַיַּרְדֵּן, cf. Gn 50¹⁰ and often (so Stade, *Lehrb.* § 1*b*; Kautzsch [doubtfully], *Heb. Gram.* § 2*b*).

(*c*) Euphrates. (1) In the sense that the Hebrews came from the east of Euphrates to the west, *i.e.* when Abraham crossed it from Haran on the way to Canaan. So Origen (in Field's *Hex.* on Gn. xiv. 13) περάτης (LXX) καλεῖται ὁ Ἀβραάμ, ἐπειδὴ ἀπὸ τῆς Χαλδαίων χώρας διαπεράσας τὴν Μεσοποταμίαν, ἦλθεν εἰς τὰ μέρη τῶν Χαναναίων. This was also the reference of Augustine's word, *transfluvialis* (*Quæst. Gen.* § 29), and presumably of Aquila's περαΐτης, which Field thinks was formed by him from πέραν rather than περάω (περάτης) [to definitely correspond to the Hebrew (הָעִבְרִי not עִבְרִי)].§ 'Hebrew' will thus, according to this derivation, be from עֵבֶר in the same meaning that it has in *mē'ēber* (1 K 14¹⁵), and perhaps in the phrase '*ebrē nāhār* (Is 7²⁰)‖ (so Dillm. on Gn 11¹²).

(2) In the sense that the Hebrews went from west to east, the standpoint of the speaker being, that is to say, east of Euphrates. So Hommel in the Appendix to his *Ancient Hebrew Tradition: illustrated by the Monuments*, 1897 (contrast his earlier opinion, p. 258), after comparing Glaser's investigations of Minæan inscriptions with cuneiform documents. He supposes that *Ebir nâri* (= *Eber hannā-hār* of the Bible, '*Ibr naharân* Minæan) was originally the region between Borsippa and Ur, *i.e.* on the west of the lower Euphrates, including the adjoining Country of the Sea to the southward. This is the region, therefore, indicated in Jos 24² as the home of Abraham and the Western Semitic tribes who trace their origin to him. It was

'across the River' to the Babylonians among whom Abraham or his forefathers came, and he was called '*Ibri*, as belonging to that land '*Eber*, the term travelling with him and his descendants. In this way we can understand that (*a*) *Ebîr nâri* is used of the country west of Euphrates (and even of Palestine in an inscription of *c.* 1100 B.C.) ; (β) the biblical *Eber han-nāhār* in, perhaps, all other places than 1 K 14¹⁵ means the same : (γ) '*Eber* in Nu 24²⁴ need not mean either the Hebrews (so most commentators) or those non-Assyrian peoples who lived east of Euphrates (Dillm.), but a district in the north-west of Arabia.*

Upon the evidence before us this explanation appears to some the most satisfactory.† [See, however, Margoliouth's criticism of Hommel in *Expos. Times*, Aug. 1897, p. 500*b*. Even Sayce (*EHH* p. 8), after mentioning Hommel's theory, says, 'The origin and first use of the name (Hebrew) are still a matter of doubt']. But we should like further evidence of the use of such a word as '*Ibri* in the inscriptions. Have we this?

III. EVIDENCE OF THE MONUMENTS AND INSCRIPTIONS.—Have we any mention in these of the Hebrews by name? Two identifications have been proposed.

i. '*Apri* or '*Epri* of the Egyptian monuments has been said to be merely an Egyptian transliteration of 'Ibri. This identification has been almost given up, but Hommel (*loc. cit.* p. 259) is disposed to regard it not unfavourably, comparing for the change of labial the Egyptian *hurp* taken from the Canaanite *hereb*, 'sword,' and pointing out that, although 800 'Epriu (Egypt. plur. of 'Epri) drawn from the foreign residents of 'An in the east of Goshen were employed under Ramses IV. long after the Exodus, yet it is possible that some of the Israelites remained behind and mingled with other foreigners. But the identification is, to say the least, very precarious.

ii. The Khabiri, or Abiri (for Assyriologists transliterate the word in both ways) of the Tel el-Amarna tablets. They are described in the letters of the king of Jerusalem to his suzerain, the Pharaoh, *c.* 1400 B.C. (Hommel), as attacking districts and towns in what we now know as the Negeb, the Maritime Plain, and Judah, and, perhaps, as even laying siege to Jerusalem itself. The king urgently applies for reinforcements, saying, 'If troops can be sent before the end of the year, then the territory of my lord the king may yet be retained ; but if no troops arrive it will assuredly be lost.' The difference in the form of the word (*Khabiri* or *Abiri* and '*Ibri*) matters little, for 'the

---

* Augustine (see note ‡‡ p. 325) prefers it in *Retract.* ii. § 16, *De Civ.* xvi. § 3 ; cf. Euseb. *Præp. Evang.* vii. 6.

† Shem is here called אֲבִי כָּל־בְּנֵי עֵבֶר J², unless with Ball (Haupt's *OT*) כָּל־בְּנֵי is to be considered as an interpolation by P.

‡ Sayce (*Expos. Times*, Mar. 1897, p. 258) suggests that '*Eber* = Bab. *Ebar*, 'a priest.' If so, and if 'Hebrews' be derived from it, the paronomasia in 1 S 13⁷ (common text) is due to a faulty philology.

§ Fürst (*Lex. s.v.* עִבְרִי) thinks that 'Hebrew' was *limited* to the Israelites by '*eber hannāhār* gradually changing into '*eber hayyardên* (Jordan). So to Jews עֵבֶר was naturally Eastern Palestine (Jos. often, *e.g. Ant.* XIII. ii. 3, cf. πέραν τοῦ Ἰορδάνου, Mk 10¹) and περαΐτης an inhabitant of that province (Jos. *BJ* II. xx. 4).

‖ Nisibis in Mesopotamia is described as being ἐν τῇ περαίᾳ τῇ πρὸς τῷ Τίγρητι ποταμῷ (Steph. Byz. *s.v.* Νίσιβις).

* So also the Asshur of this verse may represent the Minæan A'shûr, which seems to be a district to the S.E. of Gaza. It would then appear to be an earlier form of Shur (Gn 20¹). It should also be noticed that this wide use of '*Eber* explains how among the *bĕnē 'Eber* are found both a western branch in S. Arabia of Joktan and other tribes (Gn 10²⁵⁻³⁰) (J), as well as an eastern branch round the lower Euphrates in Peleg, the direct ancestor of Nahor and Abraham, with subdivisions arising in Isaac and Ishmael. 'Hebrews' is not, apparently, so used. We may suppose that, even if present in the original documents, the Hebrew editors and copyists preferred some less ambiguous term.

† Akin to this explanation is that which derives 'Hebrews' from the Arabic '*eber* in the sense of a 'tract along the banks of a river (as the place for passing over), and κατ᾿ ἐξοχήν, that of the Euphrates, the whole tract of land stretching from the east bank of the Euphrates to the Tigris, and *from the west bank to the Arabian Desert* (*berrîjet el-'arab*), from which, according to the Turkish Kâmûs and *Lex. Geographicum*, ii. 232, 233, is derived '*Ibri* or '*Ibrâni*, the name of the Jewish people, as having come from the land stretching from the bank of the Euphrates to the Tigris' (Delitzsch on Is 7²⁰). W. R. Smith (*Enc. Brit.*⁹ *s.v.* 'Hebrews') mentions this conjecture, which makes Hebrews to be 'dwellers in a land of rivers,' adding, 'this goes well with Peleg (watercourse), as in Arabia we have the district Falag, so named because it is furrowed by waters' (Sprenger, *Geogr. Arab.* p. 234). In Doughty (*Arabia Deserta,* ii. 38) Fálaj is rendered 'the splitting of the mountain'; but the two derivations are not contradictory if, as it seems, Fálaj is a mountainous district with many torrents.

Canaanite 'Ayin, with which guttural the word 'Ibri commences, is elsewhere in the texts represented by the cuneiform *Kh*, and there are analogous instances of the abbreviation of an earlier form like 'Abiri into a later form such as 'Ibri.' * But the identification is at present quite uncertain: (*a*) the king appears to be describing an attack from the west side of Jordan, whereas the Hebrews came from the east side; (*b*) the names of persons do not agree with those mentioned in Joshua; (*c*) the date is much earlier than that which is now usually given to the Exodus, 1322 (Lepsius), or even 1200 (Petrie). But (*a*) the first difficulty may be fairly met by saying that the letters do not necessitate an attack from the west only, that the OT account is very brief, the conquest of even southern Palestine possibly extending over many years, and that much of the south-west country may have been taken before the king of Jerusalem felt in much danger.† (*b*) The second difficulty is not conclusive, as persons appear to have been known under different names. (*c*) The third depends wholly on the accuracy of the date given to the Exodus. If this is accepted, the *Khabiri* can be identical with the Hebrews only by some of the Hebrews having returned to Palestine before the Exodus; but though this may be consistent with raids having been made, or small detachments having separated themselves, the letters imply the approach of a large body. Hence, either *Khabiri* has a purely accidental resemblance to 'Ibri,‡ or the date of the Exodus must be placed much earlier. § We cannot as yet say which is right.

Hebrewess, Hebrew Woman (עִבְרִיָּה), Jer 34⁹, Dt 15¹², in contrast to slaves of other nationalities. Ex 1¹⁵· ¹⁶· ¹⁹ 2⁷ [E], in contrast to Egyptians.

A. LUKYN WILLIAMS.

HEBREW LANGUAGE.—See LANGUAGE.

HEBREWESS.—See HEBREW.

HEBREWS, EPISTLE TO.—

i. AIM AND CENTRAL IDEA.—This Epistle is one of the most important writings in the NT. It contains a distinct type of Christian thought, and in that respect may be classed with the Synoptic Gospels, the Pauline Epistles, and the Gospel of John, which also contain, each, a distinctive conception of the good that came to the world through Jesus Christ. It is in aim

* Hommel, *loc. cit.* pp. 156, 231.
† Or may there have been a temporary and partial attack from the south early in the wanderings, such as Nu 21¹·³ perhaps indicates? Jg 1¹⁶·²¹ may possibly refer to the same time.
‡ So Hommel, who identifies the *Khabiri* with those after whom Hebron was called (Jg 1¹⁰). He thinks it is properly identical with Kheber in Gn 46¹⁷, and represents part of the tribe of Asher who came into Palestine before the other Hebrews (*loc. cit.* p. 236).
§ Professor Orr (*Expositor*, March 1897) argues strenuously for the first years of Amenhotep II., B.C. 1449–1423.

and method an apologetic writing, intended to help certain Christians, who had no true insight into the nature and worth of the Christian religion, to reach a better understanding of its excellence, and so to fortify them against temptations to apostasy. But the apologetic argument rests on a very definite theological position. The author has a very clear idea of the nature, and a very high estimate of the value, of Christianity. He attaches to it the value of the perfect and therefore the final religion, and he assigns to it this value because he regards it as the religion of *free, unrestricted access to God*. This is the central dogmatic thought of the Epistle, as indicated in 7¹⁹, where Christianity is by implication set forth as the religion of the better hope *through which we draw nigh unto God*. No religion, in the writer's judgment, can be satisfactory which does not establish intimate relations between God and man. Herein, for him, lies the great inferiority of Leviticalism in comparison with Christianity. He conceives of Leviticalism as a religion which kept men at an awful distance, and the veil between the holy and the most holy place is in his view the symbol of that radical defect. It is self-evident to him that a religious system which shuts God up in a dark inaccessible shrine cannot be the perfect form of religion. It must eventually give way to a better. Christianity is that better religion. It knows of no veil, and no inaccessible holy place. Christ is not only a High Priest, but a *forerunner*, πρόδρομος: where He goes, though it be into the very presence of God, all believers in Him may follow.

ii. METHOD.—This is the radical contrast between Christianity and Leviticalism. This central contrast, however, is suggestive of many others, and the method adopted by the writer in the prosecution of his apologetic aim is to exhibit in detail the points in which the religion of the NT is superior to that described in the books of Moses. His idea of Christianity is that it is the best possible religion; but what he sets himself to prove is that it is *better* than the Levitical religion. It is not difficult, however, to read between the lines, and to see behind the apologetic *better* the dogmatic *best*.

The comparison of the two religions runs through the whole theoretic part of the Epistle from 1¹ to 10¹⁸. It begins at the circumference and ends at the centre. The central truth is the priestly performance of Christ by which we are brought into filial relations with God. But the comparison begins with the agents of *revelation*, and proceeds from that starting-point to compare the agents of *redemption*. Under each of these two categories two sets of agents are ascribed to the old religion: prophets and angels under the head of revelation, and Moses and Aaron under the head of redemption. Thus there are four separate comparisons to be made—(1) between Christ and prophets, (2) between Christ and angels, (3) between Christ and Moses, (4) between Christ and Aaron. The first is made in 1¹·³, the second in 1⁴·¹⁴, the third in 3¹·⁶, and the fourth in 8¹–9²⁸.

(1) *Christ and Prophets.*—The contrast is least emphatic in reference to the prophets, as they might be looked on as belonging in spirit to the new dispensation rather than to the old Levitical one. But there is a latent antithesis here also, traceable in the words carefully selected to describe prophetic revelation,—πολυμερῶς, πολυτρόπως. These adverbs convey the idea that the ancient revelation was fragmentary (in many parts) and tropical (in many modes); and it is implied, though not expressly stated, that the revelation made by Christ was free from both defects—complete and real, and therefore final. All this is in effect said by

the phrase ἐν υἱῷ, used to describe the agent of the Christian revelation. In the end of the days God spake to men by one having the standing of a son. A son knows all that is in a Father's mind; when He has spoken there is nothing more to be said.

(2) *Christ and Angels.*—We are apt to think that the second comparison, that between Christ and angels, might have been dispensed with. But the author was writing for the benefit of *Jews* (this, in the meantime, may be assumed; it is the impression one naturally first takes from the book), and angels held a prominent place in contemporary Jewish religious thought. To them was assigned the function of executors of God's will in the natural world, and also that of intermediaries between J″ and Israel in the lawgiving. The law was a word spoken by angels (2^2, cf. Ac 7^{53}, Gal 3^{19}). Therefore, whatever the writer's own thoughts might be as to the position of angels in the universe and in the history of revelation, he was under the necessity of deferring to current opinion and speaking of them as rivals to Christ. Therefore his second thesis is: Christ better than angels, his proof consisting of a mosaic of OT texts which bring out a threefold contrast: Christ to angels as son to servants, as king to subjects, as creator to creatures. The conclusion is that the essential function of angels is to *serve*. They are ministering spirits—all of them, even the highest archangel—to God, to Christ, even to *Christians*—'sent forth for service to those who are about to inherit salvation' (1^{14}).

(3) *Christ and Moses.*—For Moses the writer had a much deeper respect than for angels, whose rôle he probably conceived to be greatly inflated in Jewish theology. Moses was a great historic reality, whose functions in behalf of Israel at the creative epoch of her history he was not tempted to disparage. But even Moses occupied a place of subordination compared to Jesus, and he does not hesitate to point the fact out, contriving, however, to do so in a manner that could not wound Jewish susceptibilities. He knows how to praise Moses while yet giving him the second place. *Faithful* in all God's house, on God's own testimony, yet faithful only as a *servant*. But Christ was faithful as a *son*.

(4) *Christ and Aaron.*—While the comparison between Christ and Moses is despatched in a few sentences, that between Christ and Aaron runs through two chapters. This is not due to the writer having a higher esteem for Aaron than for Moses. The reverse was the fact. While for his mind Moses was probably one of the world's greatest men, and the Exodus one of the great heroic achievements of human history, the character and functions of the first high priest of Israel seem to have inspired him with only moderate respect. All that elaborate ritual on the great Day of Atonement, in which the high priest played the principal part, seemed to him much ado about nothing. For the blood of bulls and of goats could not take away sin. How poor that Levitical sacrificial system compared with the one sacrifice of Christ, who by an eternal spirit offered *Himself* to God! But why, then, make the comparison, and at such length? Because he is writing for people who think Aaron a very august figure, and his sacerdotal service one of very great importance; and because his apologetic method requires him to use Aaron as a type whereby to convey to ill-instructed Hebrew Christians some rudimentary ideas as to the nature of Christ's sacerdotal functions.

(5) *Christ and Melchizedek.*—One other OT personage is brought upon the stage in the course of the argument—*Melchizedek.* He is introduced, however, not for the purpose of contrast, but to aid in the embodiment of the writer's lofty conception of Christ's priestly function. His thesis here is not, Christ *greater* than Melchizedek, but, Christ *like* Melchizedek. His use of this historic figure also serves an apologetic purpose, but in a different way. He had a difficulty to meet in connexion with the doctrine that Christ was a priest. Jesus did not belong to the tribe of Levi. That was an insurmountable obstacle to the recognition of Him as a priest for law-ridden minds. How, then, does the writer deal with it? In effect thus: 'I know quite well that Jesus could not be a priest on earth, *i.e.* one of the only class of priests you Jews are acquainted with, because He did not belong to the tribe whence the priests are taken. But the Heb. oracles know of another priesthood besides the Levitical, whereof they make honourable mention—that of Melchizedek, priest of the Most High God. It was a more ancient priesthood than that of Aaron. Do you reply: yes, ancient enough, but rude, suitable only for primitive times, and, of course, superseded by a regularly established sacerdotal class, like that of Aaron and his family? I say, not so, for in a psalm later than the institution of the Levitical priesthood, and recognized by you all as Messianic, the Melchizedek priesthood is referred to as if it were the ideally perfect type. "A priest for ever after the order of Melchisedek." The Christ is to be a priest after this ideal type. And He is appointed by an oath of God which implies that it is an appointment of unique importance. And God declares that He will not repent of the appointment, which teaches by implication that God has repented of another kind of priesthood, and that it will pass away, and that the new priesthood will be of such excellence that it will never need to pass away.' We have here an apologetic use of the ancient priesthood of the king of Salem, analogous to that made by the Apostle Paul of the promise given to Abraham long before the era of the lawgiving.

iii. THEOLOGICAL IMPORT.—This rapid sketch may suffice to give some idea of the drift of this Epistle on its apologetic side. But our main concern is with its positive theological significance, to which we now turn.

It is important for a true appreciation of the theological ideas of the Epistle to keep steadily before us its central conception of Christianity as the perfect and final religion, both perfect and final because it brings men really nigh to God. All religions aim at this, Leviticalism included. Nevertheless, it had a veil dividing the tabernacle into two compartments, and a most holy place into which no man might go save the high priest, and he only once a year, and then only with due precautions. Christianity is the one religion that has really solved the problem. In the language of the Epistle it perfects the worshipper as pertaining to the conscience (9^9), or purges his conscience from dead works to serve the living God. It really takes away sin (10^4), so that believers in Jesus can draw near with true heart and full assurance of faith to the very presence of God (10^{22}). There can never be any reason for superseding such a religion. Therefore Christianity is eternal. The epithet 'eternal' is applied many times to the Christian religion and all that belongs to it. We read of an 'eternal salvation' (5^9), an 'eternal redemption' (9^{12}), an 'eternal spirit' (9^{14}), an 'eternal inheritance' (9^{15}), and an 'eternal covenant' (13^{20}). It is clear from such iteration that the thought of the perennial, because perfect, absolute character of Christianity is not incidental and subordinate, but fundamental in the author's system. It dominates his mind and affects his manner of viewing everything belonging to the Christian faith. As it is absolute, perfect, the ideal realized, so are all the personalities and functions connected with it. The Christian revelation is the ideal realized in that department. It is God's final, because full, complete word to men, to which nothing needs to be added. The Person by whom God spoke that last word is perfect in Himself, and in His functions as Revealer and Redeemer. His sacrifice is perfect, and possesses eternal validity and value.

(1) *CHRISTOLOGY.*—This general statement prepares us to find in the Epistle a very exalted conception of *Christ.* The first thought about Him to which we are introduced, in the very first sentence, is that He stands to God in the relation of Son (ἐν υἱῷ). It is observable that, in all the four comparisons already referred to, the superiority of Jesus Christ is made to rest on the foundation of *His Sonship.* That is why He is greater than the prophets as the agent of revelation. The Sonship of itself guarantees a perfect, therefore final, revelation. The reason is that Sonship involves likeness and intimacy. To know the Son is to know the Father, and the Son knows all that is in the Father's mind. In like manner the superiority of Christ to angels is made to rest on His Sonship. The Son is begotten; angels, with all other creatures, are made; the Son as the heir of His Father is destined to sit on a throne and be an object of homage to the universe, angels not excepted. Therefore His word, as the Revealer, claims more attention than that spoken by angels, with whatever solemn accompaniments, on Sinai. So also Sonship raises Christ above Moses, however great his character, and however epoch-making his function as the Leader of the Exodus and the organizer of a horde of slaves into a nation. Moses was the greatest in God's house, yet only greatest among servants; Christ is not only greater, but belongs to another category, that of Son. Finally, Sonship is the ground of Christ's incomparable superiority to Aaron. Aaron, though an important personage within the Levitical system, was after all but a sacerdotal drudge, ever performing ceremonies which had no real value: 'daily ministering and offering oftentime the same sacrifices which can never take away sin' (10[11]). But our great High Priest is Jesus the *Son of God* (4[14]), who, as a Son, learned obedience through suffering (5[8]), and who after His Passion, voluntarily endured, was, as the Son, 'consecrated for evermore' (7[28]).

These contrasts compel a lofty conception of Christ's Person as the Son of God. Sonship taken in a diluted sense will not bear the argumentative stress laid on it. Sonship must be taken in a unique sense, not in a sense common to Christ with men and angels, or even in a sense applicable only to the great epoch-making characters of history, the heroes of the human race. Why should Sonship make Christ greater than the prophets as agents of revelation, unless it be of such a character as to involve absolute likeness of nature and perfectly intimate fellowship? We know what the author of the Fourth Gospel means when he says, 'No man hath seen God at any time: the only-begotten Son who is in the bosom of the Father, he hath declared him.' The author of our Epistle must mean something similar when he makes Sonship the ground of Christ's ability to speak the final satisfying word of God to men. And he shows that he does, and that he desires his readers to put the greatest fulness of meaning into the expression ἐν υἱῷ by the comment he immediately goes on to make, wherein he gives, at the outset, a statement of his Christological position. In this statement he represents the Son as made by God the heir of all things, an attribute arising naturally out of the relation of Sonship,

especially as the Son is the first-begotten (πρωτό-τοκος, 1[6]). Further, the Heir of all is represented as the Maker of all—by Him God made the ages (τοὺς αἰῶνας) or worlds. This implies pre-existence, or rather, seeing no reference has yet been made to an earthly state, ancient existence. It takes us back to the 'beginning' spoken of in Gn 1[1] and in Jn 1[1], to the primitive era of world-making. It gives to the Son the position assigned to the Logos in the system of Philo, that of God's agent in the universe, the statement being supplemented and completed by the added clause in 1[3]: 'bearing all things by the word of his power.' The Son thus appears acting for God in the creation and preservation of the world. To all intents and purposes this means that the Son is a Divine Being, the active Deity of the universe. The presumption is that He is an Eternal Being, *a parte ante* as He is *a parte post*, a Son from eternity as well as for evermore (7[28]), though the function of world-making implies strictly only antecedence to the things made.[*]

The eternal being of the Son is more clearly implied in the phrase following, wherein the Son is called the radiance of the glory and the exact image of the essence of God (ἀπαύγασμα τῆς δόξης καὶ χαρακτὴρ τῆς ὑποστάσεως αὐτοῦ). There might be a time when God was without a world, but there never was a time when God was without glory. It is the nature of that glory to manifest itself; like the sun it must shine, and the shining is eternal as the glory. The Son of God is the shining of His glory, and therefore eternal as the glory. Probably, however, the aim of the writer in using these remarkable expressions is not so much to declare the eternal being of the Son, as to indicate His supreme qualification for the function of fully revealing God. Who so fit to make God known as one who is related to Him as the sun's rays to the sun, and who resembles Him as the image impressed on wax resembles the seal? His word will be as the bright light of day, than which nothing can be brighter, and He may say of Himself, 'He that hath seen me hath seen the Father.' The precise theological significance of these phrases cannot easily be determined; or rather, one should say, it is doubtful if they possess any such significance. They do not absolutely exclude Sabellianism or Arianism. The Sabellians laid stress on the term ἀπαύγασμα, as suggesting the idea of a model manifestation rather than of a distinct personality. The Arians, on the other hand, emphasized the term χαρακτήρ, as implying a position of subordination and dependence for the Son in relation to the Father. The orthodox, on their side, maintained that, by the combination of the two, both errors were excluded—the former phrase implying identity of nature, so excluding Arianism; the latter implying independent personality, so excluding Sabellianism.

The final clause of the Christological statement represents the Son as taking His seat 'on the right hand of the Majesty on high.' It is the place which befits one whose position and functions in the universe are such as previously described. The dignity answers to His nature as the Son, and to His vocation as the maker and sustainer of worlds. The language is grand and solemn, and is intended to convey the impression that the Son's place is the highest possible beside that of God. It may indeed be said that to place the Son *beside* God is not to make Him God.[†] Formally the distinction may be valid, but it cannot prevent the inference to Deity being drawn. He who

---

[*] Ménégoz, *La Théologie de L'Épître aux Hébreux,* finds in the Epistle only an Arian Christology, *vide* ch. i. on *Le Christ.*
[†] So, in effect, Ménégoz, p. 87.

sitteth at the right hand of God is God for all who believe in His exaltation. This exaltation, though only what corresponds to the nature of the exalted One, is a new event in His history. It takes place after He has performed a signal service for men, referred to in the words 'when he had purged our sins.' It is from this phrase only, so far as the person is concerned, that we learn that the 'Son' ever had a place in the history of this earth. He might have done all that is ascribed to Him, even spoken the final word of God, without being man. His word, like the law, might be that of an angel, spoken from heaven. But purging sin is a sacerdotal act, a function nowhere ascribed to angels, but only to men. That the purification was performed by one in the likeness of men would be very evident if the words 'by himself' ($\delta\iota'$ $\dot{\epsilon}\alpha\upsilon\tau\circ\hat{\upsilon}$) were part of the text. But that great thought, unfamiliar to the first readers though commonplace to us, would not be introduced by so skilful a writer till it had been carefully prepared for. The 'Son,' then, was man when He performed for us men a priest's part, how, remains to be seen, and it was after He had done this that He took His place at the right hand of Divine Majesty.

(a) *Incarnation.*—The 'Son' *became* man. This momentous event is alluded to in various places and in diverse forms of language; now in terms borrowed from the Psalter as being made a little lower than the angels (2^9), now as becoming partaker of blood and flesh (2^{14}), and at another time by the very general expression 'in the days of his flesh' (5^7). Under what precise conditions the Son entered humanity, whether, *e.g.*, by ordinary generation or otherwise, is nowhere indicated. The term 'children' applied to men in 2^{14}, and the expression 'likewise' ($\pi\alpha\rho\alpha\pi\lambda\eta\sigma\iota\omega\varsigma$) applied to the Son's becoming a participant in human nature, may justify the inference that the author conceives of Him as being born, and passing from childhood to manhood. This would scarcely be worth remarking, were it not that in the prologue of the Fourth Gospel these details are left doubtful. There the Logos simply becomes flesh, and dwells for a season among men.

(b) *Earthly Life of Jesus.*—What knowledge our author had of the earthly history of the Son, whether, *e.g.*, he was acquainted with the evangelic tradition as embodied, say, in the Gospel of St. Mark, does not clearly appear. He certainly knew more than, after a cursory perusal of the Epistle, we might think. He knew of the temptations of Jesus (2^{18} 4^{15}), of the scope that His earthly experience afforded for the exercise of faith (12^2), of His agony in the garden (5^7), of the opposition He endured at the hands of evil, or ignorant, prejudiced men (12^3), of His gentle bearing towards the erring (5^2), of His work as a preacher of the good tidings (2^3), of His being surrounded by a band of companions who afterwards became a source of valuable and trustworthy information concerning the words of the Master (2^3). Of course, one who knew so much had the means of knowing more. In his description of the agony he seems to indicate knowledge of particulars not reported in the Gospels, when he represents Jesus as offering up prayers 'with strong crying and tears,' though it has been suggested that he borrowed this part of the picture from Ps $22^{14.\ 24}$.*

(c) *The State of Humiliation.*—Be this as it may, one thing is certain, the writer has a magnificent conception of the moral significance of the earthly life of the Son as a whole; of the historic career of Him whose human name 'Jesus' he for

the first time introduces in 2^9. He perceives clearly the pathos of that life, the humiliation and the glory in the humiliation. It may be, as has been said, that it is the exalted Jesus he has constantly in his eye, but he never forgets that the exalted One passed heroically through a severe curriculum of temptation and suffering, which awakens in his mind, as he contemplates it, admiration and love. There is no trace in his pages of the tendency, very perceptible in the Gospel of St. Luke, to tone down those elements in Christ's experience which might be thought out of keeping with the image of the exalted Lord as it presented itself to the eye of faith. [Compare St. Luke's report of the agony in the garden (leaving out the unauthentic verses, $22^{43.\ 44}$) with the brief but strong statement on the same subject in this Epistle]. He was not without temptation to follow this policy, arising out of the state of feeling prevailing in the community of believers for whose benefit he wrote. Their conceptions of the Christian religion seem to have been crude, ignorant, and superficial all along the line. They did not yet understand even the first principles of Christian belief (5^{12}). The best clue to the nature of their deficiencies in Christian knowledge is to note the things emphasized and reiterated by their instructor. One of these things is the *humiliation of Christ.* That, therefore, was one of their stumbling-blocks. If the Son was so great as you say, how could He be tempted, and suffer death, and death in such an ignominious form? Such was one of their perplexities. One writing to a community in this state of mind was tempted to throw a veil over the indignities of the Saviour's life; to pass over in silence this, to understate that. But there is neither silence nor understatement. 'In all points tempted like as we are' (4^{15}); 'prayers and supplications, with strong crying and tears' (5^7); 'though he were a Son, yet learned he obedience by the things which he suffered' (5^8); 'endured the cross, despising the shame' (12^2); 'endured such contradiction of sinners against himself' (12^3). This depicting in dark colours of the tragic humiliating side of Christ's earthly experience means much. It means, for one thing, that the writer sees in that aspect nothing to hide or be ashamed of; rather something to rejoice in and to be thankful for. He beholds glory *in* the humiliation, honour *in* the shame, *contemporary* honour, not merely honour following and compensating, in a state of exaltation. It means, further, that he does not despair of getting his readers to see this also. At least he is determined to try, because he knows that, until they see it, their faith is unintelligent, and their Christian standing very insecure.

Its Rationale.—The main contribution towards this object is to be found in ch. 2^{5-18}. The leading purpose of this very important section, crammed full with deep weighty thoughts, is to set forth the rationale of the earthly humiliation of Christ. And the drift of it is: *a glory in the humiliation.* On this theme three possible positions may be taken up — (1) the glory of the Son and the humiliation of Jesus incompatible, the position of unbelief; (2) the humiliation a temporary veiling of the glory compensated for by subsequent resumption of glory, the common position of average Christian belief; (3) the humiliation itself glorious when seen in the light of its aim and result, the position of enlightened faith. The writer of our Epistle occupies this highest position, his readers not being far from the lowest. He holds the humiliation itself to be glorious, and worthy of God the first cause and last end of all, profitable to Christ Himself, and full of benefit to us. It *became* God, he teaches, to subject His Son Jesus to suffering (2^{10}). It profited Jesus by perfecting Him for His office as Captain of Salvation, developing in His character the virtues of patience and sympathy, which are necessary to efficient captaincy ($2^{10.\ 17.\ 18}$). It is beneficial to us, for we have in Jesus one of whose interest we can be assured, and to whom we can always come with confidence that He will grant us seasonable succour (4^{16}). Such, in brief, is our author's splendid theodicy, his demonstration of the moral fitness of Christ's tragic experience. In the light of it we can have no doubt as to what he means when in ch. 2^9 he speaks of Jesus as 'crowned with glory and honour, that he, by the grace of God, should taste death for every man.' He means just what he plainly says, that God showed His favour to His Son in appointing Him to an office in connexion with which He should have to taste death for men, and that, in the very act of tasting death as Captain of Salvation, the Son was crowned with glory and honour. These things are *true*; they are also *relevant* to the situation. No one has really mastered the problem presented in the antinomy between glory and humiliation till he has got insight into their truth, and thorough mastery was what the writer possessed and aimed at for his readers. There is no difficulty in understanding his words. The difficulty felt by most interpreters arises from their unwillingness to credit him with clear insight into the moral order of the world. Such insight they appear to think beyond the reach of any writer in the first Christian century, even though inspired.

(*d*) *Christ's Priesthood.*—Passing from the subject of Christ's person to His priestly function, the subject may be introduced with the remark that the writer takes advantage of any means that offers itself of making intelligible to his readers the suffering experience of Christ. He is glad to be able to show them *from any point of view* that it behoved Jesus to die. Sometimes his lines of thought are remote enough from any recognized theories of atonement, as when he bases the thesis that Jesus had to die once *only* on the analogy of general human experience ($9^{27.\ 28}$). The reason which he assigns in the same context for Christ's dying *once*, viz. that a testator must die before his will can come into effect, is also peculiar, inasmuch, as it is enough that a testator die anyhow, it is nowise necessary that his death should be of a sacrificial character. One wonders at the introduction of so elementary and inferior a view close upon the grand conception contained in 9^{14}; and all the more when it is observed that in order to get a chance of introducing it he has to take advantage of the double meaning of $\delta\iota\alpha\theta\acute{\eta}\kappa\eta$, as signifying at once an alliance or covenant and a testament. In the case of a covenant there is no necessity for the death of either party, therefore after the word has been used in the sense of a covenant in 9^{15} it is employed in the other sense without any apology. The reason for this must be found in the ignorance of the first readers. They had, it must be supposed, no understanding of the rationale of Christ's death from any point of view, and therefore their instructor felt that it was a point gained if he could assign any reason for that death level to their understanding. It is essential to our understanding of the Epistle that this state of ignorance in the first readers be constantly borne in mind. If we come to it, as some interpreters do, with the assumption that the whole doctrine of the atonement was familiar to the persons addressed, and that in all that the writer says on the subject of Christ's priestly work he is simply repeating commonplaces, we incapacitate ourselves for attaining any true insight into its meaning. The truth is, he is writing to persons who do not know the alphabet of the subject, and the problem for him is to get into their dull minds by any means the idea : Jesus, though the Christ, the Son of God, must die. For this purpose several lines of thought are pressed into the service : Jesus must die, as all men die, *once*; He must die, as a testator dies before his heirs enter into possession of his inheritance; He must die for His own advantage as the Captain of Salvation, because He could not be a good fit captain unless He were perfected by suffering; He must die as a priest, not indeed as a priest after the type of Aaron, who offered animals as sacrificial victims, but as a priest of a higher order, that of *Melchizedek*.

(*a*) *The Melchizedek Type.*—The excursus about Melchizedek in ch. 7 is of essential importance to the author's doctrine of Christ's priesthood. It were an entire mistake to regard it as a discussion on a curious topic in theology on which the writer happened to have some pet ideas. In that case the complaint he makes of the dulness of those to whom he writes is altogether unjustifiable. A man may be a good Christian, and yet remain ignorant, or even incapable of understanding an abstruse theologoumenon on the Melchizedek priesthood. The question at issue is really the fundamental one : was Christ in any sense a priest? The writer's conviction is that the priesthood of Christ is not understood in its reality and worth, unless it be seen to be of the Melchizedek type.

In ch. 5^{10} the author indicates the programme of his discussion on the priesthood of Christ in these words : an *High Priest*, after the *order* of *Melchizedek*. His plan is to employ two types of priesthood to indicate its nature—the order of Aaron, and the order of Melchizedek. His purpose is not, as some have imagined, to teach that Christ occupied in succession two priestly offices, one like that of Aaron, another like that of Melchizedek, the former on earth, the latter in heaven. His intention is rather to utilize the Aaronic priesthood to set forth the *nature* of Christ's priestly functions, and the Melchizedek priesthood to set forth their *ideal worth* and *eternal validity*. The two aspects are taken up in the inverse order to that in which they are named in the programme : first, a priest after the order of Melchizedek (ch. 7); second, a high priest after the order of Aaron (chs. 8. 9).

Every order or species has its characteristic notes or marks; therefore the first thing to be done is to determine the marks of the Melchizedek 'order.' To this task the writer addresses himself in ch. 7^{1-3}, which contains a summary of the facts about Melchizedek as stated in Gn 14^{18-20}, with a commentary pointing out their religious significance, and extracting from the facts the desired marks of the type. To make the facts serve his purpose the writer finds it necessary to attach importance, not merely to what is said of Melchizedek, but to what is not said,—to the silences as well as to the utterances of history; also to give ideal meaning to the names occurring in the story. This method of interpretation may seem vicious. We may call it allegorical, or allege that it is borrowed from Philo; the important thing to note is that it *is* his method. By this way he reaches what he is in quest of—the notes of the type. These are, in all, five. Taking them in the order in which they are referred to in the commentary, they are these : the Melchizedek type of priesthood is, first, a *royal* priesthood (*king* of righteousness); second, a *righteous* priesthood (king of *righteousness*); third, a priesthood promotive of *peace*, or exercised in the country of peace (king of Salem=king of *peace*); fourth, a *personal*, not an inherited dignity (without father, without mother, *i.e.* so far as the record is concerned); fifth, it is an *eternal* priesthood (without beginning of days or end of life—so far as the record is concerned). The first four may be conceived as standing to the fifth in the relation of cause to effect. Because the priesthood in question possesses these characteristics, it is eternal.

Observe, now, what the writer is really doing in making this ingenious commentary on the brief narrative in Genesis. He is trying to fix the characters of an *ideal* priesthood. He is solving the problem, What is the highest conceivable type or kind of priesthood? He might have adopted the method of philosophic speculation for the purpose, instead of the method of interpreting an OT text. The question may be asked, Does the latter method fully serve the purpose—give us all the essential features of the ideal? To answer it, one must have in one's mind a conception of the ideal. Now, without hesitation one would say that these things at least must enter into the idea of a priesthood of the highest order. The priest must be *really*, not ritually, holy; he must not be a mere sacerdotal drudge, but one whose priestly ministry is a course of *gracious condescension*—a *royal* priest; he must be one who, by his personal worth and official acts, can establish a reign of righteousness, peace, and perfect fellowship between man and God; finally, he must be one who ever liveth, whose priesthood does not pass from him to another, as a guarantee for the maintenance of peace.

But what about sacrifice, the most essential feature, one would say, in the vocation of a priest? We observe that in the close of the Melchizedek excursus, in a description of the ideal priest, which seems intended to supplement and complete the definition of the Melchizedek type, it is said that the ideal priest does not need to repeat sacrifice (7²⁷). But there is a previous question: does he offer sacrifice at all, and what is his sacrifice? By the method of laying stress on the silences, one would say that in the Melchizedek type there is no sacrifice at all, no mention being made of such in the history. If this were so, then it would seem to follow that precisely the most vital feature in the priestly office of Christ—the sacrificial offering of *Himself*—lay outside the type, as something *sui generis*, having nothing analogous to it either in the priesthood of Melchizedek or in that of Aaron. That would be a serious flaw in the writer's apologetic argument, too serious for him to have overlooked it. We must look more closely to see whether self-sacrifice be not immanent in the other characteristics of the ideal priest. We start from the statement that the ideal priest needs not to *repeat* sacrifice, like the high priests of Israel (7²⁷). Why so? Because of the other characteristics, especially that pointed at by the epithets holy, harmless, undefiled, which unfold the contents of the idea of righteousness. Because the ideal priest is holy (ὅσιος) in relation to God, benevolent (ἄκακος) towards men, and free from any fault that might disqualify for priestly functions (ἀμίαντος), therefore he needs not to repeat sacrifice. But for the same reason he must offer one sacrifice, himself. One who answers to the description king of *righteousness*, one who realizes in his character the ethical ideal, cannot escape the sacrifice of himself in this world. That is not said, but surely it must have been in the writer's mind. It was self-evident to him that one who had all the other characteristics of the Melchizedek type must have this one also, that he was ready to lay down his life for righteousness, equally so that he would be called on to do this, living as a holy one in an unholy world.

The self-sacrifice of the ideal priest, the priest after the Melchizedek type, can be reached by another line of deduction, viz. from the *royal* character of the type. The ideal priest is not a legal drudge, but a king who graciously condescends. Carry out the idea of condescension to its utmost limit and it will yield the result of a life laid down for others: this is the *ne plus ultra* of condescension and voluntary sacerdotal service, and the requirements of the ideal cannot be satisfied with anything short of it. 'The Son of Man came not to be ministered unto, but to minister, and to give his life a ransom for the many.' 'Who loved me, and gave himself for me.'

It is obvious that in these thoughts we pass out of the region of the ritual into the ethical, and are dealing with a kind of sacrifice of entirely different character and of incomparably greater value than those pertaining to sacrifices of Levitical victims. But to this there will be occasion to refer at a later stage. Meantime it remains to indicate the use made of the Aaronic priesthood in the exposition of the priestly office of Christ.

(β) *The Aaronic Type.*—The chief use is that of a foil. The burden of the section, chs. 8¹–9²⁸, is: the priestly ministry of Christ immeasurably superior to that of Aaron. The rubric of the whole passage is: *the more excellent ministry.* But as comparison can be made only between things having a certain resemblance, eulogy runs along the line of parallelism. Superiority is established on a basis of similitude. The points of resemblance are very general. Common to both is *sacrifice*, a *sanctuary* where sacrifice is offered, and a grand representative *ceremonial* in which the two systems culminate. The first point is briefly noticed in 8³. Every high priest is appointed to offer sacrifice, therefore this man (Jesus) must also have something to offer. The vague statement is meant to provoke thought in dull Heb. readers. 'This man, if He be a priest, must have something to offer. What can it be? He has indicated what it is already—HIMSELF' (7²⁷), but he knows they have not grasped it, and he provokes them to reflection: 'What can it be? Not bulls and goats, of course; what then?' The second topic, the two sanctuaries, is handled at greater length (9¹⁻⁵·¹¹). The construction and furniture of the Levitical tabernacle are minutely described, not, however, in an antiquarian spirit, but with a definite apologetic aim. The salient points in the description are the division of the sanctuary into two compartments separated by a *veil*, and the peculiar manner in which the location of the altar of incense (θυμιατήριον) is indicated. Of course it is the altar of incense that is meant; there should never have been any doubt about that. And it is represented as *belonging to* (not physically within) the Holy of Holies. The phrase is: the Holy of Holies *having* the golden altar of incense. The meaning is: that altar, though standing without the veil, being required for daily service, belonged of right, in spirit and function, to the inner shrine. And this antinomy—without in fact, within by right—is meant to startle into thought the sluggish minds of Hebrew Christians. 'Whence this puzzle as to the whereabouts and relations of the altar of incense? See ye not, it is all due to the *existence* of that *veil*, the emblem of a rude, imperfect, transient religion?' In comparison with the earthly tabernacle, the one in which Christ officiates is described as 'the greater and more perfect tabernacle, not made with hands' (9¹¹), and not belonging to the visible creation, not constructed out of material things, like the precious cloths, woods, and metals of the old tabernacle, which, however precious, were, like all material things, destined to wax old and vanish away.

The ceremonial selected for comparison is that of the great Day of Atonement. In that stately ceremonial the Levitical ritual culminated and was seen at its best. In it also, and in it alone, the Holy of Holies came into use. It was the one service in the year in which Israel's representative man came into the immediate presence of God. It also lent itself to comparison at this vital point, the high priest's entrance into the inner shrine being comparable to the entrance of Jesus into heaven. The latter event is therefore naturally expressed in terms of the former, giving rise at points in the description to obscurities, such as the representation of Christ entering *through His own blood* into the holy place (9^{12}).

All through, the unexpressed refrain 'more excellent' is audible, but it arrests the ear specially in connexion with the closing comparison between the effects of the two priestly functions—that of Aaron on the great Day of Atonement, and that of Christ when after His death on the Cross He entered into heaven. The effect of the one was to cancel the errors, or ignorances (ἀγνοημάτων, 9^7), of the people throughout the bygone year, to wipe out all the offences against Levitical law committed in a twelvemonth, so that they might make a fresh start. The effect of the other was to obtain an 'eternal redemption' (αἰωνίαν λύτρωσιν). Comparison here becomes futile: it is a comparison of the finite to the infinite.

(*e*) *Theory of Redemption.*—For modern readers the great thoughts of the Epistle to the Hebrews are obscured by being expressed so largely in terms of Levitical ritual. The apologetic, which was meant to elucidate, now serves to some extent as a veil to hide the true meaning. It is therefore desirable to make the most of those passages in which the writer, so to speak, shakes himself clear of his apologetic trammels, and expresses his ideas in terms of universal validity. There are two sentences in which he does this in reference to the significance of Christ's death. These are 2^{11} 9^{14}, the former containing the great axiom: the sanctifier and the sanctified are all of one; the latter, the sublime thesis that Jesus offered Himself a sacrifice through an *eternal spirit*. The earlier text enunciates the *principle* of redemption, the later explains the infinite efficacy of redemption achieved. The principle is: solidarity between sanctifier and sanctified; the two one in all possible respects, the more respects the better, the one radical difference of holy and unholy always excepted; the more points of contact the greater the sanctifying power. The rationale of infinite value is 'through an eternal spirit.' In the interpretation of this profoundly suggestive expression, theologians are unhappily not at one. To the present writer it has ever been associated with certain broad thoughts that help him to understand the value of Christ's self-offering as compared with Levitical victims. In the first place it suggests that Christ's offering was an affair of *spirit*, not merely of blood-shedding. It expressed a *mind* on the part of the victim. Of course that mind had certain ethical characteristics. Jesus offered *Himself*. So the mind embodied in His sacrifice was *free, loving, holy*; a mind of supreme moral value in the sight both of God and of enlightened men. None of these epithets, however, is used to qualify the spirit in which Jesus offered Himself to God. The epithet chosen is 'eternal.' It is selected because it serves to raise the sacrifice of Christ above the limits of time. Spirit is in its nature eternal, and the sacrifice of Christ as a spiritual transaction has an efficacy and value for all time, for the time that went before the Christian era, as well as for the time coming after. It is not a mere historical event which had no

influence before it took place, and whose influence, after it happened, was destined to wane with the lapse of ages. It is an eternal fact having absolute value with God from everlasting to everlasting. But the ethical and the eternal aspects go together, the one conditioning the other. It is because the spirit in which Christ offered Himself was ethically perfect—free, loving, holy—that it has eternal value. In this remarkable phrase, combining these two aspects, the spiritual insight of the writer reaches its highest water-mark. Nothing better, more penetrating, more felicitous, on the subject of our Lord's death and its significance is to be found in Scripture.

(*f*) *Christ's Priesthood in Heaven.*—Before leaving the theme of the priesthood, we may notice briefly a question that has troubled interpreters. The priestly ministry of Christ is located in heaven, yet the sacrifice the Priest presents there appears to be none other than that offering of Himself which He made once for all; an event, so far at least as the initial stage of it, the blood-shedding, is concerned, happening on earth and within this visible world. The key to the solution lies in this, that for the writer heaven is the locus of *realities*, while earth is the locus of *shadows*. In heaven is the *true* tabernacle, the tabernacle which realizes the ideal of a sanctuary (8^2 τῆς σκηνῆς τῆς ἀληθινῆς); there are the 'patterns' or types of which the vulgar realities of earth are but imperfect copies. For our author the 'true' and the 'heavenly' are synonyms. Whatever is true is heavenly, belongs to the upper world of realities, and whatever belongs to this upper world is true and real. If, therefore, Christ's self-sacrifice be a true sacrifice, it belongs to the heavenly world, no matter where or when it takes place. And Christ's sacrifice is, for the author, a true sacrifice, because it is an affair of spirit. Flesh and blood, whether of man or beast, are of the earth earthy, and belong to the realm of shadows. Even the blood of Christ viewed materially can find no place in heaven. Hence it is vain to attempt solving the above-stated problem by distinguishing between the first stage of the sacrifice —the death, or blood-shedding—and the second, the sprinkling of the shed blood on the mercy-seat within the sanctuary, relegating the former to earth as something lying outside the sphere of Christ's proper priestly activity, and to locate the latter in heaven as the point at which the priestly ministry begins. Christ's sacrifice finds entrance into heaven when blood is transmuted into *spirit*. In other words, the shedding of Christ's blood is a *true* sacrifice, as distinct from the shedding of the blood of bulls and goats, which was only a *shadow* of sacrifice, because it is the manifestation of a mind or spirit. And because it is that it belongs to heaven, though it takes place on earth. The magic phrase 'through an eternal spirit' lifts us above distinctions of time and place, and makes it possible for us to regard Christ's offering of Himself, in all its stages, as a transaction within the celestial sanctuary.

This conception of heaven as the place of realities, as distinct from earth as the place of shadows, is the philosophic presupposition of the system of positive Christian thought contained in our Epistle. It reminds us of Plato and of Philo. Whether our author was acquainted with the writings of either the Gentile or the Jewish philosopher is a question on which opinion differs, and on which a few remarks will be offered at a later stage. The important matter is, not to ascertain where he got this speculative conception, but to note carefully the fact that it was in his mind, and to keep it before our own minds in interpreting his words. At no point in the Epistle is it more necessary to do so than at that remarkable sentence in which the writer expresses his final deepest thought concerning the nature and worth of Christ's sacrifice.

(g) *Salvation.*—From the doctrine of Christ's priestly office to the conception of *salvation* contained in our Epistle, the transition is easy. The author describes the 'great salvation' variously, but always in terms suggested by the primitive history of man as contained in the early chapters of Genesis. He first represents it as consisting in lordship in the world to come, founding on a quotation from the 8th Psalm, which is a poetic echo of the statement regarding man's place in the world in Gn 1^{26} (ch. 2^{5-8}). Next he conceives it as deliverance from the power of death exercised by the devil, with obvious allusion to the history of the Fall in Gn 3, wherein death is set forth as the penalty of sin (ch. $2^{14.\ 15}$). Finally, he exhibits it as the full final realization of the divine idea and promise of *rest*, to which he applies the felicitous thought-suggesting name *Sabbatism* ($\sigma\alpha\beta\beta\alpha\tau\iota\sigma\mu\acute{o}s$), so making the final bliss of redeemed man consist in entering into the rest which God Himself enjoyed when He had finished the work of creation (ch. 4^9, cf. Gn 2^2). Taken together, the three conceptions suggest the thought of Paradise restored, the divine ideal of man and the world and their mutual relations realized in perpetuity, man made veritably the lord of creation, delivered from the fear of death, no longer subject to servile tasks, but occupied only in work compatible with perfect repose. From all the three points of view, salvation is a thing in the future. It is an apocalyptic vision. Fruition lies in the Beyond. Dominion, deathlessness, and Sabbatism belong to the world to come, and are objects of hope for those who bear the Christian name.

But salvation is not altogether in the future; it is a present good as well. Christians, as such, are conceived of as 'sanctified' ($\dot{\alpha}\gamma\iota\alpha\zeta\acute{o}\mu\epsilon\nu o\iota$) and even 'perfected.' These words, however, do not bear quite the same meaning as that which we, familiar with the Pauline theology, are apt to attach to them. In the Epistles of St. Paul sanctification is *ethical*, and means making the Christian holy in heart and life. In the Epistle to the Hebrews this ethical sense appears (though the point has been disputed) occasionally to be traced, as in ch. $12^{10.\ 14}$, but more commonly the term is used in a theocratic sense, to express the idea of being put in right covenant relations with God, as in the text: 'By one offering he hath perfected for ever them that are sanctified' (10^{14}). The sanctified in this theocratic sense are equivalent to St. Paul's 'justified.' In ch. 2^{11} the word $\dot{\alpha}\gamma\iota\alpha\zeta\acute{o}\mu\epsilon\nu o\iota$ should probably be taken in both senses. The statement the verse contains is of the nature of an axiom, to the effect that whatever parties stand to each other in the relation of sanctifier to sanctified are *ipso facto* 'of one,' have one interest, form a brotherhood bound together by community of nature, experience, and privilege. The principle holds good, whether we understand the sanctifying function theocratically or ethically. If the function of the sanctifier be to place the sanctified, *i.e.* those to be sanctified, in right relations with God, then the more points of contact the better. There must be unity in God's sight, so that what He does is done in the name of those He seeks to sanctify, and avails for their benefit. He must be one with them in death, as it is by His death that He makes propitiation for their sins. He must possess, in common with them, humanity, for otherwise He could not die. Finally, He must be one with them in experience of trial and temptation, because thereby is evinced the sympathy that wins trust, and unless the priest is trusted

it is in vain that He transacts. On the other hand, if the sanctifier's function be to make his clients ethically holy, then, again, the more points of contact between Him and them the better. In that case, the sanctifying power lies in the example of the sanctifier: in His character, His history as a man. He makes men holy by reproducing in His own life the ideal of human character, and bringing that ideal to bear on their minds by living a truly godly life under conditions similar to those under which they are placed. In short, His power to sanctify ethically depends on likeness in nature, position, and experience.

The word $\tau\epsilon\lambda\epsilon\iota\acute{o}\omega$ is sometimes also used in our Epistle to denote the establishment of right relations between man and God, that is to say, as equivalent to 'justify' in the Pauline vocabulary. So in the text: 'By one offering he hath perfected for ever them that are sanctified.' Perfecting here means giving the worshipper a satisfactory assurance that his sins are forgiven. What the word means in any given case depends entirely on the connexion of thought. In general, it signifies to reach the end, and the specific sense depends on the nature of the end in view. Thus perfecting as applied to Christ in 2^{10} signifies to make Him a fully-equipped Captain of salvation. Applied to the fathers, who died in faith, not having received the promises in 11^{40}, it means getting at length what they had lived and longed for when the company of the saved is complete.

Condition of Salvation.—What is the condition of salvation in our Epistle? We know what it is in St. Paul's theology. We are justified by *faith*. Faith is a great word in the Epistle to the Hebrews also, but its use there is not quite the same as in the Pauline letters. In the apostle's system faith has two functions. It accepts as a gift the 'righteousness of God,' and it works through love as a sanctifying power. Of the former function there is no clear trace in Hebrews. Instead of faith we find obedience in the text: 'He became the author of eternal salvation to all them that *obey* him' (5^9). We come nearer to the Pauline conception of justifying faith in 10^{22}, where the writer exhorts his readers to draw near with a true heart in full assurance of faith, where faith means confident expectation of welcome for Christ's sake. The function of faith as a force making for personal righteousness or noble conduct is very prominently set forth in ch. 11, where, in a series of well-chosen instances, it is exhibited as a power helping men to make their lives sublime. But the secret of its power is peculiarly conceived in Hebrews. In St. Paul's system faith derives its power from its personal object, the Lord Jesus Christ. It unites us to Him, and from Him flows a transforming influence. In Hebrews the secret of faith's power is its psychological character as a faculty of the human mind, whereby it can make the future as if it were present, and the unseen as if it were visible. So viewed, faith as a principle making for heroism is not confined to the Christian world. It is as wide as humanity, and can turn out heroes and heroines in every land. Hence even a Rahab finds a place in the roll of those who obtained a good report through faith.

(2) *FATHERHOOD OF GOD.*—The doctrine of the Fatherhood of God and the sonship of men, central in our Lord's teaching, and prominent also in the Pauline letters, is not very conspicuously taught in our Epistle. It makes a formal appearance chiefly in the hortatory section. There God is called 'the Father of spirits' (12^9), and it is taught that His supreme aim in all His dealings with His children is to make them partakers of His holiness (12^{10}). The phrase 'Father of spirits'

seems to imply a paternal relation of God to men as such, coextensive with the human family, or, rather, inclusive of the human family, embracing it in a larger category, the world of spirits, including men living in the flesh but having a spirit, the spirits of just men made perfect, and angels. In the theoretical part of the Epistle the Fatherhood of God is referred to, or implied, mainly in reference to the Sonship of Christ. But while this is so, it must be ascribed to the exigencies of the apologetic argument controlling the train of thought rather than to the peculiarity of the writer's theological system, that the doctrine of the Fatherhood is so comparatively in the background. No man could be insensible to the importance of that doctrine who had such a vivid sense of the distinction and glory of Christianity as the religion of free access to and intimate fellowship with God. This central conception covers the whole ground. A religion of unrestricted access is a religion of sonship. Its spirit is *filial*, not *legal*; its watchword *trust*, not *fear*. It brings its votaries to Mount Zion, not to Mount Sinai. At another point the doctrine of sonship is immanent in the Epistle, though not formally named. This is where faithful Christians are called the comrades of Christ. 'We have become fellows of Christ if we hold fast the beginning of our confidence stedfast unto the end' (3[14]). So we render the passage, taking μέτοχοι in the sense it bears in 1[9]. The faithful the fellows of Christ, God's Son—such is the writer's idea, implying also, of course, that they are sons in the same house and family of God. This is just what was to be looked for from one who grasped the significance of the great principle, Sanctifier and sanctified all of one. It is but the other side of that great truth. The one side is Christ's oneness with those He undertakes to sanctify, and His readiness to accept all the conditions necessary to His complete identification with them. The other side is the unity of the sanctified with Christ, complete equality with Him in privilege. They are *sons*, therefore, as indeed they are called in 2[10], and therefore Christ's brethren. He was not ashamed to call them brethren even when they were in an unsanctified state (2[11]); how much less will He be ashamed to call them brethren when they have experienced His sanctifying power! Therefore we need have no hesitation in taking μέτοχοι in the fullest sense of comradeship. In doing so we only assume that the author understands his own system of thought, and it may be added that he is in sympathy with the teaching of our Lord and with the conception of the relation between Christ and His people that pervades the entire NT. For the religion of the NT is throughout filial, and God, whether often or seldom so named, is always Father. The dialects for the purposes of theological reflection are various, but the central religious intuition is one.

iv. RELATION TO PHILO.—Such in brief outline is the theological import of the Epistle. We have avoided preliminary discussion of the questions belonging to the head of Introduction, because we did not wish to give any countenance to the idea that a right understanding of the Epistle depends on the previous settlement of doubtful questions respecting its author, its first readers, its date, its theological affinities, etc. We do not believe anything of the kind. It has been said, *e.g.*, that no one can understand the Epistle who does not regard it as the writing of one belonging to the *School of Philo* and thoroughly conversant with his philosophy. We are inclined to think, on the contrary, that to be too sure of this, and to lay great stress on the supposed fact, is the direct way to misunderstanding. It is possible to understand the main drift of the Epistle while remaining in suspense as to the connexion with Philo. It is best to commence the study of the work tolerably uncommitted on the point. It is quite proper, as we go along, to keep our eyes open to all traces of affinity with Philo, so that on arriving at the end of the book we may have, not only a distinct idea of its theological drift, but also a more or less probable opinion on the subordinate question as to the connexion of its author with the Alexandrine school of religious philosophy. But that question, however interesting, is not vital.

That there are affinities of thought and style is not to be questioned, and, indeed, has already been indicated in a passing way. The author's mode of conceiving heaven as the place of realities and the earth as the place of shadows is an instance in point. That peculiarity is a fact patent to any attentive reader altogether apart from the question to what source it is to be traced. We might notice it though we had never heard of Plato or Philo. The only effect of the hypothesis that the writer was a disciple of the Jewish philosopher is somewhat to sharpen our attention and lead us to attach more importance to it than we otherwise would, perhaps more than it deserves. But there need be no jealousy as to having our attention directed to phenomena of this kind. No question of religious importance is involved, and the multiplication of instances of affinity in word and thought between *Hebrews* and the writings of Philo serves the purpose, at least, of increasing our acquaintance with the literary characteristics of our Epistle.

Among the verbal affinities with Philo the following may be specified. Philo, like our author, uses the *prophets* for the OT. 'Απαύγασμα and χαρακτήρ find a place in his vocabulary, θυμιατήριον is used by him (not in LXX) for the altar of incense. Among the functions he ascribes to the Logos is that of cutter (τομεύς), even as our author describes the word of God as more cutting (τομώτερος) than any two-edged sword. The unusual words τραχηλίζω (4[13]) and μετριοπαθέω (5[2]) both occur in Philo. Less remarkable is the coincident use by the two writers of the epithets τεχνίτης and δημιουργός in reference to God (11[10]). Among the thought affinities may be reckoned the distinction between τὰ φαινόμενα (11[3])=Philo's ὁ ὁρατὸς κόσμος, the visible world, and the non-visible things (μὴ ἐκ φαινομένων, 11[3])=Philo's κόσμος νοητός, the world of ideas; the conception of heaven as the country or home (πατρίς, 11[14]) of the soul; the application to Christ of attributes ascribed in Philo to the Logos, such as πρωτότοκος (1[6]) answering to πρεσβύτερος υἱός or πρωτόγονος in Philo; θεός (1[9]), ἀρχιερεύς. To these instances thoroughgoing advocates of dependence on Philo would add the whole Melchizedek excursus, but without good reason. At this point our author drew his inspiration, not from Philo, but from the Heb. prophet who wrote the 110th Psalm. Philo does not quote or refer to the text about Melchizedek in that psalm, and there is nothing in all his writings to show that he followed the psalmist, or set the example to our author, in ascribing to the priest of Salem an ideal significance. Bleek states, with strict truth, that in Philo the significance of Melchizedek is always treated in an incidental manner.* As to the attribute of cutting, ascribed to the word of God in *Hebrews*, and to the Logos in Philo, the resemblance is in word rather than in thought. Our author is not thinking of the personal Logos in the passage in question, and the function he ascribes to the Word is *ethical*, exercised in the spirit of man, whereas the function Philo had in view was that of dividing the material of which the world is made into genera and species. On the whole, if, as is not improbable, the writer was more or less familiar with the ideas and philosophic dialect to which the Alexandrian school of Jewish philosophy gave wide currency in the first Christian century, there is no evidence in his work of abject discipleship, but at most of a very free independent use of words and ideas hailing from that quarter, just so far as they would serve his purpose.

v. RELATION TO ST. PAUL.—A similar relation of independence towards the *Apostle Paul* must be claimed for the Epistle. That the apostle was not the author of it is now so generally admitted that it is hardly worth while discussing the question. The diversity in the use of important theological terms such as ἀγιάζω and πίστις, the broad contrast in style, the marked individuality of the

* *Hebräerbrief*, ii. p. 323, note *a*.

two authors in respect of religious temperament, all shut one up to this conclusion. As to the difference of style, it is a matter of detail, with reference to which a decided impression can be made only by a large accumulation of instances, but the following statement gives a sufficient idea of it. 'St. Paul was not free from Hebraism, and derives force from the simplicity of his language; the author (of Hebrews) expresses himself in idiomatic and polished Greek, and delights in the pomp of stately phrases and full-sounding derivatives. They differ in the elementary framework of their sentences by employment of different constructions and different connecting particles. Dialectical subtlety, impetuous bursts of natural eloquence, mighty thoughts struggling for expression in disjointed sentences, are the characteristic features of St. Paul's style. Rhetorical skill, studied antithesis, even flow of faultless grammar, and measured march of rhythmical periods, combine to stamp upon the Epistle a distinct and unique character of its own.'* Behind this difference of style lies an even more marked difference in religious temperament and experience. St. Paul is a man of great moral intensity; the author of Hebrews has about him an air of philosophic repose. We feel in every page of the Pauline Epistles that the man who wrote them has passed through a great religious crisis In reading *Hebrews* we have no such feeling. Instead of a tragic experience there has been a smooth quiet studious life, whose passage into Christian faith has resembled the dawn of day rather than the sudden flash of light from heaven which smote Saul of Tarsus to the earth on the way to Damascus. A significant index of this equable flow is the entire absence from our Epistle of the well-known Pauline antitheses: law and grace, faith and works, flesh and spirit. There are antitheses here also, but they are less pronounced, — shadow and substance, type and antitype,—pointing at, not radical contrariety, but different stages in the religious development of mankind.

The writer of *Hebrews* was not only not St. Paul, but not even a disciple of St. Paul. To a great extent the proof of the one thesis is at the same time the proof of the other. That he was acquainted with the Pauline literature has been confidently asserted, but cannot be clearly shown.† There are doubtless things that remind us of Pauline texts, *e.g.* the description of the law as 'the word spoken by angels' (2^2), which recalls a similar thought in Gal 3^{19}, and the idea of the heavenly Jerusalem (12^{22} 13^{14}) found in the same Epistle (4^{25}). But these may be mere coincidences in the use of conceptions belonging to the common stock of contemporary religious thought. Acquaintance with Philo's writings can be alleged with much greater show of reason.

But while not a follower of St. Paul, our author is in thorough sympathy with all the leading positions of Paulinism. Without doubt he stands on the ground of universalism. No express text, indeed, can be cited in support of this assertion. From beginning to end there is not a single allusion to Gentile Christians, or the slightest indication that the writer is aware of the existence of such people. He seems to have in view throughout, God's ancient people, and to have for his sole aim to enable Hebrew Christians to remain steadfast in the faith amid circumstances of trial. He takes no advantage of opportunities for indicating the universal destination of the gospel; not even in 2^{16}, where it would have

been so natural to have said, He (Jesus) took not hold of (in order to save) angels, but He took hold of *mankind*; instead of which he says, He took hold of the seed of Abraham. Nevertheless, the Epistle breathes throughout the spirit of universalism. The whole scheme of thought, though excogitated for the benefit of Hebrews, is capable of universal application, and implies that Christianity is the concern of all mankind. The remark holds true especially of the Christology. The cosmic relations in which the Son is set in the proem indicate that the word spoken by God through Him is a revelation for the whole world. It is only in universalist writings, such as the Epistles of St. Paul and the Gospel of St. John, that a cosmic Christology is to be looked for. Not less universalist in tendency is the view of the sacrifice of Christ presented in ch. 9^{14}. The doctrine takes its colour from Levitical institutions, but in its core it is not Jewish but human. The phrase *by an eternal spirit* lifts the whole subject above the distinctions, not only of time and space, as already pointed out, but also of race and nationality. It has the same ring as the great epoch-making text in St. John's Gospel: 'The hour cometh, when ye shall neither in this mountain, nor yet at Jerusalem, worship the Father. . . . The hour cometh, and now is, when the true worshippers shall worship the Father in spirit and in truth' ($4^{21.\ 23}$).

Our author is in thorough sympathy with St. Paul's conception of Christianity as a *spiritual religion*. He sees not less clearly than the apostle the utter worthlessness of rites and ceremonies, except as a shadow of good things to come. He makes no allusion to circumcision, but doubtless he would have been in full sympathy with the Pauline polemic against those who attached religious value to that rite. His own controversy is with those who attach overweening importance to Levitical ceremonial; but it is not less thoroughgoing than the apostle's, and it rests upon the same principles and postulates.

Once more, our author is at one with St. Paul in his conception of Christianity as a religion of free grace. His own conception of it as the religion of unrestricted access to God is an exact equivalent. It is the same truth set in a different antithesis. St. Paul opposed grace to legal works, our author opposes the privilege of free access to the distance at which Levitical regulations kept worshippers from God. The counsel 'Draw near' presupposes a gracious Father to be approached, from whom all spiritual good may be confidently expected: pardon of sin, seasonable succour in all times of temptation. In Hebrews as in Rom. and Gal. salvation is a free gift.

vi. WAS THE AUTHOR JEW OR GENTILE?— Whether the author of our Epistle was a born Jew or a Gentile cannot be decided. The style and the rhetorical structure of the writing make for the latter alternative, the familiarity with Jewish institutions for the former. Both might be combined in a Jew of Alexandrian Hellenistic culture like Apollos, with whom, since Luther threw out the suggestion, there has been a disposition to identify the author, though the hypothesis has no support in ancient tradition. The question of nationality is of subordinate importance. The only question of vital interest in connexion with the theological import of the Epistle is whether the author represented the standpoint of Jewish Christianity with its limited sympathies and its contracted religious ideas. A tendency to take this view of his position has been more or less apparent in some recent contributions to the exegetical literature of the subject. In so far as it is adopted, it makes the understanding of the book hopeless. We cannot too firmly grasp the fact that in his

---

* *The Epistle to the Hebrews*, by F. Rendall, *vide* the *Appendix*, pp. 26, 27.
† *Vide* von Soden in *Handkommentar*, Einleitung, p. 2.

essential ideas the writer soars high above all Jewish-Christian narrowness. In his method of interpreting Scripture, in his modes of argument, and even in some of his subordinate conceptions, he may be a man of his time and people ; but in his great central thought of Christianity as the religion of free access and of spiritual reality, he belongs to all time and to all peoples. Whether he came before St. Paul or after him in point of time, he is of the same spiritual brotherhood. He has seen with open face the true nature and the grandeur of the Christian faith.

vii. JEW OR GENTILE READERS ?—In asserting the universal outlook of our author, we were obliged to admit that on the face of his work he seems to concern himself only with Jewish readers. Till recent times no doubt has been entertained that the inscription *To the Hebrews*, though not original, correctly indicated its destination. But of late there has been a tendency, supported by weighty names, to set this tradition aside, and to hold that the first readers must have been *Gentiles*, not Jews. Among those who share this opinion are Schürer, Weizsäcker, Pfleiderer, and, above all, von Soden. Among the grounds on which this hypothesis is made to rest are such as these : the fundamentals enumerated in $6^{1,2}$ are such as were suitable for catechumens of pagan antecedents ; the expression ' the living God ' (9^{14}) suggests an antithesis between the true God and pagan idols, and the moral exhortations, addressed to the readers, possess special appropriateness only when conceived as meant for Gentile Christians. The numerous phrases which seem to imply readers of Heb. extraction are explained so as to harmonize with the hypothesis, by the assumption that, at the time when the Epistle was written, the Gentile Church had served itself heir to the title and privileges of the elect people. To the question, what need for so elaborate a plea for Christianity *versus* Leviticalism in an Epistle written for Gentile Christians ? the answer given is : The type of Gentile Christianity the author had to deal with was an eclectic syncretistic system, into which an amateur attachment to Levitical institutions entered as an element, and became so strong as to endanger the Christian faith with which it was associated, especially in a time of persecution.[*]

That an amount of ingenuity has been expended in support of this hypothesis, sufficient to make it appear plausible, is frankly admitted. But that the case has been proved we are far from thinking. We sympathize with Ménégoz when he says : ' What strikes us, in this Epistle throughout, is a Jewish " flavour of the soil," and an absence of all allusion to pagan worship so complete that we have difficulty in comprehending how anyone can discover in t the least indication of its being meant for readers of pagan antecedents. We do not say there were no pagan Christians in the community, there may have been for aught we know, but in the texts we see no trace of them.' [†] Ostensibly the first readers are Hebrews, and Hebrews alone ; that is generally acknowledged. The *onus probandi* lies on those who affirm that they were not really such, and it requires a very elaborate display of exegetical ingenuity to explain away the apparent Jewish costume and physiognomy. If the readers were indeed Gentiles, they were Gentiles so completely disguised in Jewish dress, and wearing a mask with so prolonged Jewish features, that the true nationality has been successfully hidden for nineteen centuries, and even now, after learned critics have done their best to show us the Gentile behind the Jew, we shake our heads in honest insurmountable doubt, and feel constrained to agree with Westcott when he pronounces the argument of von Soden ' an ingenious paradox.' [‡]

viii. LOCATION OF FIRST READERS.—Where the Heb. community, to which the Epistle was addressed, was located, is a much debated question of inferior moment to that just disposed of. Palestine, Alexandria, Rome are the rival hypotheses, and weighty authorities can be cited for each of them.[§]

[*] So in effect Pfleiderer in *Urchristenthum*, p. 620.
[†] *La Théologie de L'Épître aux Hébreux*, pp. 26, 27.
[‡] *The Epistle to the Hebrews*, Introduction, p. xxxv.
[§] One of the most recent and able contributions in support of the Rome hypothesis may be found in Réville's *Origines de l'Épiscopat*, 1894.

It is not necessary here to go into details on the subject, as the topic has no vital bearing on the theology of the Epistle. If we attach weight to the inscription *To the Hebrews* as indicating, not merely Jewish nationality, but a section of the Jewish people distinguished by the epithet ' Hebrew,' it points to Palestine or Syria as the locality of the first readers. ' Hebrews ' means Jews speaking Hebrew. But as the Epistle was written in Greek, these ' Hebrews ' must have been bilinguals acquainted with Greek as well as their mother-tongue. Such bilingual Jews would be found more readily in a Syrian city like Antioch than in Jerusalem. Other things point in the same direction, *e.g.* the statement in 2^3 that the persons addressed had heard the gospel, not from the lips of the apostles, but at second hand. This would apply to the Syrian Churches, which were founded by the scattered members of the Jerusalem Church after the death of Stephen.[*]

ix. DATE.—The *date* of the Epistle has more than curious interest. The solemn earnest tone of the hortatory parts speaks to a great crisis, such as that of the destruction of Jerus. and of the Jewish state, *impending*. All seems to say : a judgment-day is approaching (10^{25}). The Epistle is a supreme effort to avert apostasy at a time of extreme peril. A general overturn is at hand, when all things that can be shaken—cities, walls, temples, hoary religions—will be shaken to make room for the kingdom that cannot be shaken ($12^{26,27}$). There is therefore a high degree of probability in the suggestion that the Epistle was written when the war, which issued so disastrously for the Jewish people, was raging and drawing near to its awful crisis. ' The fatal year A.D. 70 had arrived, and the Roman armies had gathered round Jerus. ; if the daily sacrifice had not already ceased, the siege had at all events begun ; for until Jerus. was " compassed with armies " no Hebrew Christian would have ventured to address to his Heb. brethren so unsparing a condemnation of the national religion.' [†] The last statement in this quotation may be doubtful, for the prophetic men of Scripture always had the courage to utter their convictions at the proper time, but the selection of the period most suitable to the message delivered is otherwise appropriate. And the date called for by the solemnity of the message is borne out by minute hints occasionally dropped, *e.g.* by the allusion to the 40 years during which the people of Israel saw God's works (3^9). The mere circumstance that the writer connects the 40 years with the seeing of God's works, rather than with the trying of God's patience, as in the psalm quoted from, is significant. He does it intentionally, and as one aware of the original connexion, as is evident from 3^{17}, where he returns to the original connexion. What is his intention? To suggest a parallel between the case of Israel in the wilderness and the Heb. Church to this effect : ' Your fathers saw God's wonderful works, which ought to have kept them true to Him, for 40 years, yet they perished through unbelief. You have seen the wonders of God's grace in the Christian Church for the same period of time ; see that ye perish not likewise on Israel's judgment-day.' Reckoning the 40 years from the beginning of the Church, corresponding to the Exodus, the period would take us down to the fateful year 70 or thereby.

That the Epistle was not written at a later date has been argued from the fact that throughout the writer seems to speak of the Levitical ritual as if it were still in force. This, however, it is

[*] See on this Rendall, *Epistle to the Hebrews*, Appendix, p. 65.
[†] Rendall, *Appendix*, p. 74.

now generally admitted, is not conclusive, as the author appears to write of that ritual from an ideal point of view. It may have been a thing of the past as an actual fact, yet present for his mind as an object of thought. The possibility of this must be admitted in view of the fact that it is not the temple but the old tabernacle the writer has in view as the scene of Levitical worship (see 9². ⁶. ⁷).

x. AUTHOR.—The Epistle is anonymous, and the author has remained unknown. Apollos, as described in Ac 18²⁴⁻²⁸, is the *kind* of man wanted —a Hellenistic Jew of Alexandrian culture, acquainted both with the OT Scriptures (in the Gr. version) and with contemporary philosophy. With this we must be content. Other conjectures thrown out from time to time have comparatively little to commend them. The most interesting, and one of the most ancient, is that which ascribed to Luke the Evangelist a share in the production of the work, at least to the extent of translating into good Greek a supposed Heb. original from the hand of the Apostle Paul. Clement of Alexandria entertained this opinion, and through Eusebius (*HE* iii. 38) it became the prevailing view that the Epistle was, in thought, the work of St. Paul, and in a Gr. version the literary work of St. Luke or Clement of Rome. A number of resemblances between the style of St. Luke in the Gospel and in Ac and that of our Epistle have been pointed out, so as to lend at least plausibility to the hypothesis that the evangelist is responsible for the Epistle in its Gr. dress. But if Luke might have been the translator (on the improbable hypothesis of a Heb. original), he certainly could not have been the author. The striking contrast between his account of the agony in the garden and that given in the Epistle is sufficient to settle that question.

We must be content to remain in ignorance as to the writer of this remarkable work. Nor should we find this difficult. Some of the greatest books of the Bible, such as *Job* and the second part of *Isaiah*, are anonymous writings. It is meet that this one should belong to the number, for it bears witness in its opening sentence to One who speaks God's final word to men. In presence of the Son, what does it matter who points the way to Him? The witness-bearer does not desire to be known. He bids us listen to Jesus and then retires into the background. We need have no anxiety about finding for his work an apostolic author who shall guarantee its inspiration and canonicity. The book speaks for itself. It is worthy to be in the NT. It rendered an indispensable service as an aid to faith in a transition time when an old world was passing away and a new world was coming into being.

LITERATURE. — Bleek, *Der Brief an die Hebräer.* 2 vols.; Kuinoel, *Commentarius in Ep. ad Hebræos*; Delitzsch, *Com. on the Ep. to the Hebrews*, 2 vols. (T. & T. Clark); Hofmann, *Die heilige Schrift d. NT*, vol. v.; Lünemann, *Kritisch-exegetisches Handbuch*; Riehm, *Der Lehrbegriff des Hebräerbriefs*; Westcott, *The Epistle to the Hebrews*; Rendall, ditto; Vaughan, ditto; Davidson in *Handbooks for Bible Classes*; Edwards in *Expositor's Bible*; von Soden in *Handkommentar*; Ménégoz, *La Théologie de L'Épître aux Hébreux.*

A. B. BRUCE.

HEBRON (חֶבְרוֹן 'association').—**1.** The third son of Kohath, known to us only from P (Ex 6¹⁸, Nu 3¹⁹) and the Chronicler (1 Ch 6². ¹⁸ 15⁹ 23¹². ¹⁹). Nothing further is known of him personally, but there are a few scattered notices of his descendants. The **Hebronites** are mentioned with the three other Kohathite families at the census taken in the wilderness of Sinai (Nu 3²⁷), and appear again at the later census in the plains of Moab (26⁵⁸). In 1 Ch 15⁹ it is said that 'of the sons of H., Eliel the chief, and his brethren fourscore,' were amongst the Levites assembled by David when he brought the ark from the house of Obed-edom into Jerus., and in 1 Ch 23¹⁹ that when David numbered the Levites there were reckoned four sons of H., Jeriah, Amariah, Jahaziel, and Jekameam (cf. 24²³), while 1 Ch 26 mentions some members of the Hebronite family as holding certain offices under David (26²³. ³⁰. ³¹). **2.** A son of Mareshah and father of Korah, and Tappuah, and Rekem, and Shema (1 Ch 2⁴²⁻³). It is possible that in these vv. the names are those of localities rather than individuals.   W. C. ALLEN.

HEBRON (חֶבְרוֹן 'association,' Χεβρών, Arab. *el-Khalîl*).—A very ancient city in the southern part of Canaan, built 'seven years before Zoan in Egypt,' Nu 13²² (JE). Josephus (*Ant.* I. viii. 3) also states that it was seven years older than Tanis (Zoan) in Egypt, and also (*BJ* IV. ix. 7) that it was the oldest city in Palestine, older even than Memphis in Egypt, and that its age in his time was 2300 years; thus making it a rival of Damascus, which he states (*Ant.* I. vi. 4) was founded by Uz, the grandson of Shem.

Hebron included Mamre, Gn 13¹⁸ (J). Abram, when he moved his tents after separating from Lot, 'came and dwelt by the terebinths of Mamre, which are in Hebron': these trees were in possession of Mamre the Amorite, brother of Eshcol and Aner, with whom Abraham was confederate (Gn 14¹³). When Sarah 'died in Kiriath-arba' ('the same is Hebron,' Gn 23²), Abraham entreated the children of Heth for a burying-place for her, and bought the field of Ephron containing the cave 'which was in Machpelah which was before Mamre' ('the same is Hebron in the land of Canaan'), Gn 23¹⁷. 'Now the name of Hebron beforetime was Kiriath-arba ('the city of Arba'), the greatest man among the Anakim,' 'the father of Anak' (Jos 14¹⁵ 15¹³, Jg 1¹⁰). As Machpelah was before or over-against Hebron (Mamre), it would appear that though close together they were distinct places.

The first mention of the giants who occupied Hebron is made in the account of the spies (Nu 13²²) sent by Moses into the land of Canaan, when the sons (Ahiman, Sheshai, and Talmai) of Anak were at Hebron. It would thus appear that at the time of Abraham there were both Amorites and children of Heth at Hebron, and also that the children of Anak were connected with the place, as they were there in the time of Moses, and the city itself was originally called after Arba the father of Anak (but see Moore, *Judges*, p. 23; and Hommel, *Anc. Heb. Trad.* p. 234, who make Kiriath-arba = *Tetrapolis*). There is no record as to whether the Anakim were Canaanites in common with the Amorites and children of Heth; but it would appear that they were not Rephaim, Zuzim, or Emim who dwelt east of the Jordan, and who are mentioned as being as tall and powerful as the Anakim, and not as the same tribe (Gn 14⁵ 15²⁰, Dt 2¹¹. ²¹). It has been pointed out [cf. Wellhausen, *Comp. d. Hexat.* p. 341 (1889)] that Amorite is the *general* name of the primitive population of Canaan, and that these names are descriptive titles, and not the names of distinct tribes (Gn 14¹³ 23⁵, Jg 1¹⁰), but they were probably *originally* distinct (see Driver, *Deut.* 11 f.).

The Jewish writers take Kiriath-arba to mean the city of *four*, which they refer to four saints,— Abraham, Isaac, Jacob, and Adam,—in which Jerome also concurs. Sir John Maundeville (in A.D. 1322) states that at the time of his visit the Saracens called Hebron *Karicarba*, while the Jews called it Arbothe; and he also refers to Adam being buried there.

Hebron became after the entry into the Promised Land a city of Judah, situated (Jos 15⁵⁴) in the hill-country (Jos 20⁷ 21¹¹), and is stated by Eusebius

(*Onom. s.v.* Αρκώ) to be 22 miles south of Jerusalem and 20 miles north of Beersheba. It is now called *el-Khalîl* ('The Friend') by the Mohammedans.

Hebron played an important part in the early history of the Hebrews until Jerusalem became the capital of Palestine. Abraham, after waxing rich and separating from Lot, came and dwelt by the terebinths of Mamre, which are in Hebron, and built an altar there unto the Lord (Gn 13[18]). From here he went to the rescue of Lot, and brought him back after defeating Chedorlaomer and the kings that were with him; here his name was changed from Abram to Abraham, and it was here that he entertained the angels unawares (Gn 14[13ff.] 17[5] 18[2]). Here Isaac was born, and Sarah died and was buried in the cave of the field of Machpelah, bought by Abraham as a burial-place. Here also Isaac and Jacob lived part of their lives (Gn 35[27] 37[14]); from here Jacob sent Joseph to seek his brethren, when he was taken into Egypt, and from here Jacob and his sons followed after (Gn 35[14] 46[1]). Here the three patriarchs and their wives, except Rachel, were buried (Gn 49[30. 31] 50[13]). Here the spies sent by Moses saw the Nephilim or giants, the sons of Anak (Nu 13[22]).

Hebron was taken by Joshua and given as an inheritance to Caleb, who drove out the three sons of Anak (Jos 14[12] 15[14]). It was made one of the six cities of refuge (Jos 20[7], Jos. *Ant.* v. i. 24, ii. 3), and given with its suburbs to Kohathite Levites; but the fields of the city and the villages thereof were given to Caleb (Jos 21[11]). One of the exploits of Samson was to bring the gates of the city of Gaza and place them on the top of the mountain that is before Hebron (Jg 16[3]). Hebron was one of the cities to which David sent a portion of the spoils after smiting the Amalekites; here he was anointed king over the house of Judah; and here he remained king of Judah seven and a half years, and six sons were born to him (2 S 2. 3).

Here Abner was treacherously slain by Joab at the gate, and was buried; and here the sons of Rimmon the Beerothite, after their hands and their feet had been cut off, were hanged 'beside the pool' (2 S 3[27] 4[12]). Here came all the elders of Israel, and anointed David king over Israel (2 S 5[3]). Here it was that Absalom came to be declared king (2 S 15[7ff.]). At this time there was a spot here for worshipping the Lord, probably the altar said to have been erected by Abraham to the Lord by the terebinths of Mamre (Gn 13[18] 15[17]). (But see Jerome, *Quæst. Hebr.* on 2 S 15[17]).

According to Josephus (*Ant.* VIII. ii. 1), king Solomon went to Hebron to sacrifice to the Lord 'upon the brazen altar that was built by Moses'; and here the Lord appeared to Solomon, who prayed for a sound mind and good judgment; but it is stated in the Bible (1 K 3[4]) that this took place at the great high place at Gibeon.

Rehoboam fortified Hebron (2 Ch 11[10]), and it was occupied after the Captivity, when it was called by its old name Kiriath-arba (Neh 11[25]). Judas Maccabæus captured it from the Edomites, and 'pulled down the strongholds thereof, and burned the towers thereof.' It had thus at that time ceased to be a city of Judah (1 Mac 5[65]; *Ant.* XII. viii. 6).

At the time that Vespasian was making preparations for the final siege of Jerusalem, Simeon bar-Gioras made a sudden raid into Edom and took Hebron without bloodshed; but it was shortly afterwards recaptured by Cerealis, one of the commanders of Vespasian's army, and was burnt down (*BJ* IV. ix. 7, 9). Josephus states that at this time the monuments of the posterity of Abraham were to be seen at Hebron, 'the fabric of which monuments is of the most excellent marble, and wrought after the most elegant manner. There

is also shown at a distance of six furlongs from the city a very large turpentine tree, which has continued since the creation of the world.'

In the 4th cent. the sepulchres of the patriarchs were still shown at Hebron, built of marble and of elegant workmanship. The church described by Eusebius at the terebinths appears to have been the Great Basilica of Constantine, remains of which are still to be seen (*Onomast.* art. 'Arboch') to the north of Hebron. The Bordeaux Pilgrim (A.D. 333) describes the monument of Abraham as a quadrangle built of stones of admirable beauty. Antoninus Martyr (*Itin.* 30) describes a quadrangle with an interior court, open to the sky, into which Jews and Christians entered from different sides, burning incense as they advanced. In the 6th cent. Arculf visited Hebron when it was occupied by the Saracens, and he describes the sepulchre as small and mean, situated about a stadium from Mamre on the east, and surrounded by a low wall. Willibald in the 8th cent. passed here, and mentions the sepulchres in the castle *Aframia*; and Sæwulf, 1103, speaks of the monuments to the patriarchs being surrounded by a very strong castle. In 1167 Hebron was erected into a bishopric under the Latins. William of Tyre says that there never was a Greek bishop before this, but only a prior. Benjamin of Tudela, who visited Hebron in 1163, states that the ancient city was standing on a hill in ruins; while the modern city stood in the valley in the field of Machpelah. He also describes the iron door leading to the caves.

Hebron (*el-Khalîl*, 'the friend') is one of the four sacred cities of the Moslems, and the shrines of the patriarchs are very jealously guarded by them. The town is built without walls, and contains about 18,000 Moslems and 1200 to 1500 Jews. It is situated in a shallow valley surrounded by rocky hills, from which spring no fewer than 25 sources of water. Luxuriant vineyards still clothe the hills and vales, and produce some of the best grapes in Palestine, and groves of olive and fruit trees abound. The town is divided into four quarters; the houses are built of stone, with partially flat and partially domed roofs, on account of the scarcity of large timber for rafters. The valley in which the town is built runs from north to south; the main quarter lies on the eastern slope, with the *Harâm* or sacred area conspicuously rising above it. Two other quarters are to be seen in the north and west slopes, and one to the south. The streets opening on to the main roads have gates. At the northern end of the main quarter is a pool of ancient construction, 85 ft. by 55 ft., and low down in the valley southward is a larger one, also of high antiquity, over 130 ft. square and 28 ft. deep, the traditional spot where the murderers of Ishbosheth were hanged.

There are a large number of traditional sites about Hebron. In '*Ain Keshkaleh* may be found the name Eshcol, although this identification is philologically difficult. At '*Ain Judeideh*, west of the *Harâm*, is a vault where Adam and Eve are said to have mourned for Abel; and above are the *Deir el-Arabîn*, said to be the tombs of Jesse and Ruth; and the *Kabr Hebrûn*, said by the Hebron Jews to be the tomb of Abner. At the foot of this hill is the *Ager Damascenus*, from which was obtained the red earth of which Adam was made.

About two miles to the west of the *Harâm* is a venerable oak (Sindiân), one of the finest in Palestine. It measures 22½ ft. around the lower part. It is probably the tree described as a terebinth by Sir John Maundeville, Belon, and others. Since the 12th cent. it has been pointed out to Christians as 'Abraham's Oak,' under which Abraham pitched his tent. About two miles to the north, near the road to Jerusalem, is the *Râmat el-Khalîl*, called by the Jews of Hebron the house of Abraham. Here are the foundations of an immense building—200 ft. by 165 ft.—of large squared stones, of which two courses only remain, regarded by the Jews as the place of Abraham's tent and the terebinth at Mamre. Guérin (*Judée*, iii. 214) suggests that this enclosure was built round the tree under which the patriarch was supposed to have pitched his tent. Jerome speaks of a fair having been held annually on this spot. It seems probable that from 1st to 12th cent. this was the traditional site of Mamre. It is suggested (*SWP* iii. 323) that this building may have been the market mentioned by Sozomen (*Hist.* ii. 4) as the place where Hadrian sold Jewish captives for slaves (A.D. 165), close to which Constantine afterwards built his basilica at the terebinth of Mamre, the foundations of which are still to be distinguished (Conder, *Palestine*, 85).

It is quite clear that, if the present traditional sepulchres of the patriarchs are genuine, the present site of the city which stands around the *Harâm* cannot coincide with the site of the ancient city of Abraham's time, which was over-against the sepulchre; and this idea appears to have been present to the minds of the early Christian writers, who mention a site on the north-west of the modern city as the original Hebron.

The *Harâm* or 'sacred area' is a quadrangle 197 ft. by 110 ft. externally. The masonry of the wall is identical with that of the Wailing Place at Jerusalem, and is therefore probably not later than Herodian. The height of the ancient wall still standing is about 40 ft., and above this rise walls of modern construction, with lofty minarets at N.W. and S.E. corners. Within the enclosure is a mosque, probably the remains of the church built in the 11th cent. when the bishopric was established, and the monuments to the patriarchs are within. The tombs themselves are, however, below in the rocky cavern, and the iron door which is said to lead to them was shown to the present writer at the bottom of the flight of steps on the outside wall in 1867 (see account by Benjamin of Tudela, *Early Travels in Palestine*, p. 86; *PEF Mem.* iii. 333; Cte. Riant, *Archives de l'Orient Latin*, ii. 411, and art. MACHPELAH; *Onomast.* arts. 'Arboch' and 'Drys'; Antonini Mart. *Itin.* 30, *Early Travels*). 　C. WARREN.

HEDGE is used in AV to translate words of two different Heb. stems. One of these (*gâdar*, גָּדַר) refers to stone walls, though, perhaps, in some instances, to a stone wall crowned with thorns. In AV its derivatives are often tr. by the word 'wall.' In RV they are prevailingly, though not always, tr. by the word 'fence.' The other stem (*sûk* or *sâkak*, שׂוּךְ or שָׂכַךְ) refers to a thorn hedge. The Gr. φραγμός, tr. 'hedge' in Mt 21³³, Mk 12¹, Lk 14²³, denotes a fence of any kind, whether hedge, or wall, or palings. The purpose of the hedge, as the term is used in the Bible, is either to protect that which is enclosed in it (*e.g.* Job 1¹⁰), or to restrain and hinder (*e.g.* Job 3²³, Hos 2⁶). See FENCE. 　W. J. BEECHER.

HEED.—Heed is either 'carefulness,' as Is 21⁷ 'And he hearkened diligently with much heed' (וְהִקְשִׁיב קֶשֶׁב רַב־קָשֶׁב); LXX ἀκρόασαι ἀκρόασιν πολλήν; Vulg. 'et contemplatus est diligenter multo intuitu,' whence AV through Gen. 'And he hearkened and toke diligent hede'; Orelli, 'And has listened with most eager listening '); or simply *attention*, as Ac 3⁵ 'And he gave heed unto them, expecting to receive something of them' (ἐπεῖχεν αὐτοῖς). The phrase is always (except Is 21⁷ above) 'take heed' or (less often) 'give heed,' and the only noticeable occurrence is Sir 6¹³ 'Separate thyself from thine enemies, and take heed of thy friends' (πρόσεχε) This trⁿ is from Wyc. and Dou. after Vulg. ' ab amicis tuis attende,' the other VSS having ' beware of,' which RV adopts. The meaning of AV is probably ' pay attention to' suspiciously, as in North's *Plutarch* (Cicero, p. 879), 'After that time, Cicero and he were alwaies at iarre, but yet coldly enough, one of them taking heed of another.' But Shaks. uses the phrase in the sense of ' pay attention to' without suspicion, as *Jul. Cœs.* I. ii. 276, 'Three or four wenches, where I stood, cried "Alas, good soul!"—and forgave him with all their hearts; but there's no heed to be taken of them : if Cæsar had stabbed their mothers they would have done no less'; and Coverdale uses it in the sense of 'take care of,' Hos 13⁵ 'I toke diligent hede of the in the wildernesse that drye londe.'
　　　　　　　　　　　　　　　　J. HASTINGS.

HEGAI or **HEGE** (הֵגַי Est 2⁸. ¹⁵, הֵגֵא 2³, Γαί).—A eunuch of Ahasuerus, and keeper of the women, to whom the maidens were entrusted before they were brought in to the king. The name is probably Persian ; cf. Ἡγίας, who is named in Ctesias (*Pers.* c. 24) as a courtier of Xerxes (so Roediger, *Thes.* Add.). 　　　　　　　　　　H. A. WHITE.

HEGEMONIDES (Ἡγεμονίδης, 2 Mac 13²⁴).—An officer left in command (στρατηγός) of the district from Ptolemais to the Gerrenians (which see), by Lysias, when he was forced to return to Syria to oppose the chancellor Philip (B.C. 162). AV translates 'made him (Maccabæus) principal governor,' but no parallel for such a use of ἡγεμονίδης is to be found. Syr. recognizes the proper name, but Vulg. reads *Ducem et principem*. 　　H. A. WHITE.

HEIFER (in all the passages cited below, the Heb. term. is עֶגְלָה except Nu 19²ᶠᶠ·, Am 4¹, Hos 4¹⁶, where it is פָּרָה. In the only NT occurrence, He 9¹³, the Greek is δάμαλις).—The heifer is repeatedly mentioned in the Bible, in connexion both with agriculture and with ritual services.

That it was customary to use heifers for ploughing is evident from the saying of Samson, 'If ye had not plowed with my heifer, ye had not found out my riddle,' Jg 14¹⁸. Ploughing and harrowing are both specified in Hos 10¹¹, and from this passage as well as from Jer 50¹¹ we gather that heifers were employed to tread out the corn.

A heifer of three years old was one of the animals divided by Abraham upon the occasion of his solemn covenant with J″, Gn 15⁹ (J). A heifer was the animal offered by Samuel at Bethlehem, 1 S 16². When a murder had been committed, the author of which could not be traced, a special atoning ceremony was prescribed, Dt 21³ᶠ·. The elders of the nearest city had to take a heifer which had never been used for work away to a barren spot where there was a wady with running water, and there break its neck. Thereafter they washed their hands over the carcase, solemnly testified their innocence of the murder, and prayed that J″ would forgive His people for the crime that had been committed in their midst (see notes of Driver and Dillm. *ad loc.*, also W. R. Smith, *RS*¹ 351). For the ritual prescribed in Nu 19²ᶠᶠ· and referred to in He 9¹³, see RED HEIFER. In Nu 19¹⁷ AV reads, 'They shall take of the ashes of the burnt heifer of purification for sin,' which gives the *sense* (if not the exact trⁿ) of מֵעֲפַר שְׂרֵפַת הַחַטָּאת better than RV, 'They shall take of the ashes of the burning of the sin-offering' (cf. *Oxf. Heb. Lex. s.* חַטָּאת). The reference is to v.⁹.

The word 'heifer' is several times used in similes. Egypt is compared to a heifer in Jer 46²⁰, so is Chaldæa in 50¹¹, the points of resemblance being probably beauty, strength, and wantonness (cf. Am 4[1] 'kine of Bashan' applied to the ladies of Samaria). Israel is compared in Hos 4[16] to a stubborn heifer that will not accustom itself to the yoke (Nowack), and in Hos 10[11] to a heifer which has hitherto had the easy task of treading out corn, but is now to have the harder work of ploughing and harrowing.

For 'heifer of three years old' of Is 15[5], Jer 48[34] (AV and RVm) see EGLATH-SHELISHIYAH.

J. A. SELBIE.

HEIR.—i. TERMS. יָרַשׁ *yārash*, and נָחַל *nāḥal*, LXX κληρονομέω, κατακληρονομέω, etc., Vulg. *heres sum*, etc., 'inherit'; ptcp. יוֹרֵשׁ *yōrēsh*, LXX κληρονόμος, etc., Vulg. *heres*, etc., 'heir'; יְרֻשָּׁה *yĕrushshāh*, יְרֵשָׁה *yĕrēshāh*, מוֹרָשָׁה *mōrāshāh*, נַחֲלָה *naḥălāh*, LXX κληρονομία, κλῆρος, etc., Vulg. *hereditas*, etc., 'inheritance'; יָרַשׁ, נָחַל, and their derivatives are also commonly used in the more general sense of 'possess,' 'acquire'; and figuratively of the relation between God and His people, *e.g.* J" is the *naḥălāh* of Levi, Dt 10[9], and Jacob is the *naḥălāh* of J", Dt 32[9]; בְּכוֹר *bĕkhōr*, LXX πρωτότοκος, Vulg. *primogenitus*, 'firstborn'; בְּכוֹרָה *bĕkhōrāh*, LXX τὰ πρωτοτόκια, πρωτοτοκεῖα, Vulg. *primogenita* (neut. pl.), 'birthright,' 'right of the firstborn'; גֹּאֵל *gōʾēl*, LXX ἀγχιστεύς, ἀγχιστεύων, λυτρωτής, συγγενής, Vulg. *cognatus, propinquus, ultor*, 'next-of-kin'; גָּאַל *gāʾal*, LXX ἀγχιστεύω, λυτρόω, etc., Vulg. *propinquitatis jure retinere, eruere, redimere*, etc., 'act as next-of-kin'; גְּאֻלָּה *gĕʾullāh*, LXX ἀγχιστεία, λύτρον, λύτρωσις, etc., Vulg. *propinquitas*, etc. On *bĕkhōr*, *gōʾēl*, and derivatives, see further below.

ii. INHERITANCE. The fact that the terms for *heir*, etc., for the most part meant originally, and continued to mean, *possess*, etc., indicates a certain lack of emphasis on the difference between inheritance and other ways of acquiring and holding property. Land, the most important kind of property, belonged to the family and the clan rather than to individuals, as is shown by the Jubilee and other land laws. All land was, as it were, entailed. Other property too—cattle, slaves, and, in some instances, wives—was inherited. The heir succeeded to the headship of the family, which included the control of the family property. Moreover, the heir succeeded as a right, according to law and custom; he took possession of what had become his. Wills were unknown in ancient Israel, though sometimes (cf. below) a father would interfere with the natural course of things to benefit a favourite son. The phrase 'set thy house in order,' צַו לְבֵיתֶךָ, shows that a dying man would sometimes arrange the disposition of his property, and the future status of the members of his family; but probably in accordance with recognized custom, if not with binding law. The blessing of the dying father would usually confirm the firstborn in his right, but might also, as in the blessings of Isaac and Jacob, transfer it to someone else.

iii. RIGHT OF THE FIRSTBORN, BIRTHRIGHT. The prevailing custom, which is everywhere taken for granted, was that the eldest son succeeded his father as head of the family, and took the largest share of the property. Thus we have the special terms *bĕkhōr, bĕkhōrāh*, for 'firstborn,' 'right of the firstborn.' The genealogies of Gn 5, etc., mention the firstborn, and him only. 1 Ch 5[1] speaks of Reuben having an original right of pre-eminence, which he lost by misconduct. In 2 Ch 21[3] Jehoram succeeds Jehoshaphat, 'because he was the *bĕkhōr*.' Probably the eldest son, if an adult, succeeded to the high priesthood; but the exceptions were numerous, both in the royal and sacerdotal dynasties. According to Ex 13[2], JE, the firstborn of every mother was sacred to J". In Dt 21[17] the *bĕkhōrāh* is a 'double portion,' פִּי שְׁנַיִם. The difference of status between the mothers of a man's children, often only loosely defined, was a fruitful

source of discord as to the *bĕkhōrāh*. Reuben, the son of an inferior wife, is reckoned as Jacob's *bĕkhōr*; he is deposed for misconduct, not on account of his mother's status. On the other hand, Sarah claims that, because Ishmael is the son of a concubine, he shall not even share the inheritance with Isaac, Gn 21[10]. Evidently, the prior right of the son of the wife over that of the concubine depended upon the feeling of the father towards mother and son, and probably also on the influence of the mother's family.

iv. CASES WHERE THE FIRSTBORN WAS PASSED OVER FOR OTHERS—JUNIOR RIGHT. The exceptions to the rule of the succession of the eldest son are numerous and striking. The line of divine election among the patriarchs usually passes through younger sons, Abraham apparently, Isaac, Jacob. According to 1 Ch 5[1. 2], the *bĕkhōrāh* was transferred from Reuben to Joseph. In Gn 49 Jacob puts Ephraim before his elder brother Manasseh. According to Ex 7[7] (P), Moses was the junior of Aaron. David was the youngest son of Jesse; and Solomon, one of the youngest, at any rate, among the many sons of David. We may take the circumstances of the succession of Solomon as typical. The father would often secure the succession for a favourite son by appointing him his successor, or even by associating him with himself in his lifetime. Such arrangements have always been common, especially in the East. The favourite wife would often be the one last married, and the favourite son the youngest. Apart from 2 Ch 21[3], it is never stated that the eldest son succeeded his father as a right. Great men with large harems and numerous families would follow the example of the kings. The transference of the *bĕkhōrāh* from Reuben to Joseph, and from Esau to Jacob, shows that such a change might be made for sufficient cause, and therefore, of course, on any plausible pretext: a case is mentioned in 1 Ch 26[10]. A further proof of the occasional transference of the *bĕkhōrāh* at the will of the father is the prohibition of the practice in Dt 21[15-17].

The frequent succession of youngest sons suggests that the very widespread custom of 'Junior Right' or succession by the youngest existed in pre-monarchical Israel, and survived in some measure in later times. J. Jacobs (*Studies in Biblical Archæology*, p. 47), partly following Sir H. Maine, says: 'The custom would naturally arise during the later stages of the pastoral period, when the elder sons would in the ordinary course of events have set up for themselves by the time of the father's death. The youngest would in these circumstances naturally step into the father's shoes, and acquire the *patria potestas*, and with it the right of sacrificing to the family gods by the paternal hearth.' On the other hand, when the heir was a minor, the inheritance was probably often seized by adult kinsmen. Witness the constant complaints of the wrongs done to orphans.

v. WHO INHERITED WHEN THERE WERE NO SONS. In Nu 27[5-10] (P), in connexion with the daughters of Zelophehad, the following provision is made for this and similar cases: 'If a man die and have no son, ye shall cause his inheritance to pass unto his daughter. If he have no daughter, ye shall give his inheritance unto his brethren. If he have no brethren, ye shall give his inheritance unto his father's brethren. If his father have no brethren, ye shall give his inheritance unto his kinsman, שְׁאֵר, who is next to him in his clan, מִשְׁפָּחָה.' In Nu 36[6] it is further provided that heiresses must marry in their own clan. Though the law itself is late, the provisions are obvious and probably ancient, except perhaps the preference given to daughters. A member of another clan marrying an heiress joined her clan, Ezr 2[61], Neh 7[63], cf. BERIAH. Jeremiah's acquisition of his uncle's field, Jer 32[7], is an example of the rights of a kinsman in the family property.

Jacob's action in reckoning Ephraim and Manasseh as his sons is doubtless typical of cases of adoption. Similarly, women would sometimes, as in the case of Sarah, Rachel, and Leah, reckon children born to their husbands by their slaves as their own; but, as we have seen, the rights of such children were uncertain. In 1 Ch 2[34. 35] a genealogy is traced through the issue of a Jewess and an Egyptian. Abraham, Gn 15[3], expects that his slave will be his heir, cf. Pr 30[23], where, however, the translation is not certain. The last two cases would also be typical.

The succession is as a rule confined to the father's kin on account of the family *sacra*. W. R. Smith (*Kinship and Marriage in Early Arabia*, p. 95) points out that women could not inherit in early Arabia (cf. Benzinger, p. 355), and that there could be no question of a widow inheriting because she was a part of a man's property, and went with the rest of the estate to the heir. This principle is illustrated in Israel by the law of the levirate marriage, the case of Ruth, the incident in 2 S 16[15-23], and the incident of Adonijah and Abishag —to succeed to the king's widow implied succeeding to the throne. By the law of the levirate marriage (Dt 25[5-10]; cf. Gn 38, Ru 4) the firstborn son of a man's widow by his brother, or *gō'ēl*, became his heir; (cf. GOEL, MARRIAGE, and see Driver on Dt 25[5ff.]).

vi. PROVISION FOR CHILDREN OTHER THAN THE CHIEF HEIR. The principle that the land belongs to the family, involves the providing for the rest of the family by the head who controls the family property. Probably, in early times the maintenance of younger children was provided for according to this principle by customs no longer traceable. Abraham, however, sends his younger children away with gifts (Gn 25[6] [JE]); according to 2 Ch 11[23] Rehoboam dispersed his sons among the walled towns of Judah and Benjamin, made ample provision for them, and gave them wives, in order to secure the throne for a favourite son, Abijah. Sons would often be got rid of in this fashion to secure an undisputed succession for a favourite. Other typical cases are those of Ishmael and Jephthah, who were sent away without any share of the inheritance. Daughters would almost always be married; unmarried daughters would be kept and have husbands found for them by their brothers, and where there were sons there would be no question of their sharing the inheritance. Job 42[15] specially mentions that Job's daughters shared with their brothers, doubtless because this was exceptional.

Dt 21[16] speaks of the father 'causing the son to inherit that which he hath,' which seems to imply some power on the part of the father to determine the inheritance of his property (Dillm., Driver, *i.l.*; cf. ii.). But this is strictly limited by the context, and it must have been similarly limited by ancient custom. The law, probably, is partly a protest against the violation of such, and partly a provision for new conditions. There is nothing in the history to suggest the subdivision of the family land at each successive generation. Benzinger (p. 354) is doubtful whether any such subdivision took place. It seems very unlikely. Unless, therefore, the above Deut. laws are confined to personal property they are probably late, perhaps were never effective.

The New Testament. No question of the laws or customs of inheritance arises in connexion with the NT. Christ is the (firstborn) son and heir in the parable of the Wicked Husbandmen (Mk 12[7] etc., and in He 1[2]); Christians are heirs of God's promises, etc. (Ro 8[17], Gal 3[29] 4[1. 7], He 6[17],

Ja 2[5] etc.). The figure of inheritance is also used in reference to Abraham, and to the Israelites, etc. Διαθήκη is often translated 'testament' by AV, especially in reference to the institution of the Lord's Supper (Lk 22[20] etc., 1 Co 11[25]), but it should be 'covenant,' except perhaps in He 9[16. 17], where the rendering 'testament' is defended by many scholars (see commentaries, *i.l.*). RV has 'covenant' throughout, often with 'testament' in the margin, except that in He 9[16. 17] 'testament' is placed in the text, and the margin states that the Greek word means either 'covenant' or 'testament.' In Lk 12[13] we read that 'one said unto him, Master, bid my brother divide the inheritance with me.' See also INHERITANCE.

LITERATURE.—Benzinger, *Heb. Arch.* p. 354 ff.; Nowack, *Lehrbuch der Heb. Arch.* p. 348 ff.; Jacobs, *Studies in Biblical Archæology*, p. 48 ff. See also Sanday-Headlam on Ro 8[12-17]; Beyschlag, *NT Theol.* i. 385 f., ii. 346; Weiss, *Bibl. Theol. of NT*, Index; Westcott, *Hebrews*, 167-169.   W. H. BENNETT.

HELAH (חֶלְאָה 'rust'?).—One of the wives of Ashhur the 'father' of Tekoa, 1 Ch 4[5. 7]. See GENEALOGY.

HELAM (חֵילָם, in 2 S 10[17] with ה *locale* חֵלָאמָה and the Massoretic note א *יתיר*. Budde, however, maintains that חֵלָאם is the correct form).—The Aramæans from beyond the river,* whom Hadarezer summoned to his aid, came to Helam (2 S 10[16]) and were there met and defeated by David (v.[17f.]). As far as the *form* of the word is concerned, חֵילָם in v.[16] might mean 'their army' (so Aq. ἐν δυνάμει αὐτῶν, followed by Thenius). There can, however, be little doubt that the LXX (Αἱλάμ), Pesh. and Targ. are right in taking it as a proper name (so Ewald, *Hist.* iii. 155 n. 2; Bertheau, Wellh., Driver, Budde, Kittel). Cornill, upon the ground of the LXX Ἡλιάμ, introduces Helam also in Ezk 47[16] (cf. also Bertholet, *ad loc.*). In this case it must have lain on the border between Damascus and Hamath.   J. A. SELBIE.

HELBAH (חֶלְבָּה).—A town of Asher, Jg 1[31]. Its identity is quite uncertain. (For various attempts to fix its site, see Moore, *ad loc.*).

HELBON (חֶלְבּוֹן).—A place from which wine was brought to Tyre, Ezk 27[18]. It is the modern *Ḥalbûn* on the east slope of Antilebanon, about 13 miles N. of Damascus. The region around, on Hermon and the Antilebanon, is remarkable for its vineyards to the present day. The wine of Helbon is mentioned also in the cuneiform texts, and the Persian kings are said to have preferred it to any other. It has sometimes been wrongly supposed that Helbon is to be identified with Aleppo.

LITERATURE.—Robinson, *BRP*[2] iii. 471 f.; Del. *Paradies*, 281; Wetzstein, *ZDMG* xi. (1857) 490 ff.; Baedeker-Socin, *Pal.* 341; Schrader, *COT*[2] ii. 121; Bertholet on Ezk 27[18].   C. R. CONDER.

HELDAI (חֶלְדַּי; B Χολδειά, A Χολδαί).—1. The captain of the military guard appointed for the twelfth monthly course of the temple service (1 Ch 27[15]). He is probably to be identified with 'Heleb the son of Baanah the Netophathite,' one of David's thirty heroes (2 S 23[29]; A 'Αλάφ, B omits). In the parallel list (1 Ch 11[30]; B Χθάοδ, A Χοδδδ and 'Ελάδ) the name is more correctly given as **Heled.** The form *Heldai* is supported by Zec 6[10] (see below), and should probably be restored in the other two passages.

2. According to Zec 6[10], one of a small band who brought gifts of gold and silver from Babylon to those of the exiles who had returned under

* The Euphrates, *not* the Orontes as Hitzig maintains. See Wellh. *Sam.* 179 f.

Zerubbabel. From these gifts Zechariah was bidden to make a crown for Joshua the high priest, which was to be placed in the temple as a memorial of Heldai and his companions. In v.[14] Helem (חֵלֶם) is clearly an error for Heldai; the Peshiṭta in both places reads Holdai or Huldai (ܚܘܠܕܝ).

J. F. STENNING.

HELEB (חֵלֶב 2 S 23[29]).—See HELDAI 1.

HELED (חֵלֶד 1 Ch 11[30]).—See HELDAI 1.

HELEK (חֵלֶק 'portion'). — Son of Gilead the Manassite, Nu 26[30], Jos 17[2] P. Patronymic, **Helekites**, Nu 26[30].

HELEM.—**1.** (חֵלֶם) A man of Asher, 1 Ch 7[35]. 'The name must be altered to חוֹתָם (v.[32]) to fit the context; otherwise we should have חֵלֶם in v.[32] instead of חוֹתָם' (Kittel in *SBOT*). **2.** (חֵלֶם) An exile who was sent from Babylon with gifts of gold and silver for the sanctuary at Jerusalem, Zec 6[14]. He is called in v.[10] **Heldai** (חֶלְדָּי). LXX has τοῖς ὑπομένουσιν, not treating this and other nouns in the same passage as proper names.

HELEPH (חֵלֶף). — A town on the border of Naphtali, Jos 19[33]. Although mentioned in the Talmud (*Megillah* i. 1, see Neubauer, *Géog. d. Talm.* 224), Heleph has not been identified.

HELEZ (חֵלֶץ 'vigour'; B Σέλλης, A Ἕλλης, Luc. Χάλλης).—**1.** One of David's thirty heroes (2 S 23[26]). He is described as 'the Paltite,' *i.e.* a native of Beth-pelet in the Negeb of Judah (cf. Jos 15[27], Neh 11[26]). But in the two parallel lists (1 Ch 11[27] and 27[10]) both the Hebrew text and the LXX (ὁ Φελωνεί; ὁ ἐκ Φαλλούς) read 'the Pelonite,' a variant which is supported by cod. A at 2 S 23[26] (ὁ Φελλωνεί; B reads ὁ Κελωθεί; the former reading is further inconsistent with 1 Ch 27[10], where Helez is expressly designated as 'of the children of Ephraim.' From the latter passage we learn that he was in command of the military guard appointed for the seventh monthly course of the temple service. See PELONITE.
2. A Judahite, 1 Ch 2[39]. J. F. STENNING.

HELI ('Ηλεί = Heb. עֵלִי). — **1.** The father of Joseph, in the genealogy of Jesus, Lk 3[23]. **2.** An ancestor of Ezra, 2 Es 1[2]. Omitted in parallel passages, 1 Es 8[2], Ezr 7[2. 3]. See GENEALOGY.

HELIODORUS ('Ηλιόδωρος).—The chancellor (ὁ ἐπὶ τῶν πραγμάτων) of Seleucus IV. Philopator. At the instigation of APOLLONIUS (which see), he was sent by the king to plunder the private treasures kept in the temple at Jerus.; but he was prevented from carrying out his design by a great apparition (ἐπιφανία),—a horse with a terrible rider struck him to the ground, while two young men scourged him severely. H. was carried out of the temple by his guards speechless and prostrate, but was restored at the intercession of the high priest Onias (2 Mac 3[7ff.]). Some have supposed that the discomfiture of H. was due to a device of Onias (cf. v.[32], so Rawlinson in *Speaker's Comm.*). Jos., who seems to have been unacquainted with 2 Mac, makes no mention of the mission of H.; but in 4 Mac 4 a similar story is related of Apollonius. In B.C. 175 H. murdered Seleucus, and attempted to seize the Syrian crown; but he was driven out by Eumenes of Pergamus and his brother Attalus, and Antiochus Epiphanes, brother of Seleucus, ascended the throne (App. *Syr.* 45; Liv. xli. 24). There is commonly supposed to be a reference to H. in Dn 11[20], but the interpretation of the passage

is doubtful (cf. Bevan *in loc.*). Further, H. is frequently reckoned as one of the *ten* or the *three* kings of Dn 7[7t.].   H. A. WHITE.

HELKAI (חֶלְקָי, perh. shortened for חֶלְקִיָּה).—A priest (Neh 12[15]). See GENEALOGY.

HELKATH (חֶלְקָת and חֶלְקַת 'portion,' 'possession').—A Levitical city belonging to the tribe of Asher, Jos 19[25] 21[31]. The site is uncertain. The same place, owing perhaps to a textual error, appears in 1 Ch 6[75] [Heb. 60] as Hukok.

HELKATH-HAZZURIM.—The name given to the spot at Gibeon where the fatal combat took place between the twelve champions chosen on either side from the men of Abner and Joab, 2 S 2[16]. The name חֶלְקַת הַצֻּרִים means 'the field of sword edges.' This is accepted by Driver (*Text of Sam. ad loc.*), who compares Ps 89[44] [Eng. [43]] צֻר חַרְבּוֹ 'the edge of his sword.' Others prefer to follow the LXX μερὶς τῶν ἐπιβούλων and read הַצֹּדִים 'ח 'the field of the liers in wait' (so Ewald, *Hist.* iii. 114; Wellh. *Sam. ad loc.*; Budde, *SBOT, ad loc.*). Thenius reads הַצָּרִים 'ח 'the field of the adversaries.'   J. A. SELBIE.

HELKIAS (Χελκίας, Gr. form of Heb. חִלְקִיָּה, Hilkiah; in AV of Apocr. reproduced as Chelcias, Helkias, and Helchiah; RV uniformly Helkias). —**1.** The high priest Hilkiah in Josiah's reign. He is mentioned in 1 Es 1[8] = 2 Ch 35[8] as a governor of the temple, subscribing handsomely to Josiah's great Passover; in 1 Es 8[1] (cf. Ezr 7[1]) as the great-grandfather of Ezra; and in Bar 1[7] as father of Joakim, who was governor of the temple in the reign of Zedekiah. **2.** A distant ancestor of Baruch (Bar 1[1]). **3.** The father of Susanna (Sus vv. [2-29]). J. T. MARSHALL.

HELL.—The term used in Old English to designate the world of the dead generally, with all the sad and painful associations of the dark region into which the living disappear. In modern English it has the specific sense of the place and condition of penalty destined for the finally impenitent among the dead. With this it expresses also the abode of evil spirits. It is cognate or connected with the German *hehlen* = *hide*, *hüllen* = *cover*, A.S. *helan*, Lat. *celare*, etc. It appears in much the same form in many of the European languages : Ger. *hölle*, Sw. *helvete*, Go. *halja*, Da. *helvede*, Du. *hel*, Ice. *hel*, O.H.G. *hella*, A.S. *hel*, *helle*, M.E. *helle* (cf. Chaucer, *CT* 1202). The Teutonic base, *hal* = *hide*, akin to *kal*, *kar* (in the older form), is supposed by Skeat to be a 'development from a root *skar*, of which the meaning was 'to *cover*.' Etymologically, therefore, the term denotes the *covered, hidden, unseen* place.

In our AV the word 'hell' is unfortunately used as the rendering of three distinct words with different ideas. It represents (1) the שְׁאוֹל of the Heb. OT, and the ᾅδης of the LXX and the NT, which have the general sense of the 'realm of the dead.' In this employment of the word the AV translators were justified so far by the sense which it had in their day, and by the fact that it was applied to the world of the departed generally in the Creeds, in Spenser, in Chaucer, in mediæval miracle and mystery plays, and in Old English religious poetry. It is not the only word which the translators of 1611 used as an equivalent for שְׁאוֹל and ᾅδης. At times they used 'the pit' (Nu 16[30. 33]), and in a number of cases 'the grave' (Gn 37[35], 1 S 2[6], Job 7[9] 14[13], Ps 30[3] 49[14. 15] etc.). But 'hell' is their most usual rendering in the OT (Dt 32[22], 2 S 22[6], Ps 16[10] 18[5] 116[3] 139[8], Pr 5[5] 7[27] 9[18] etc.), and the rendering to which they adhered in all the NT passages, however different in their shades of meaning, in which they found some form of ᾅδης (Mt 11²³ 16¹⁸, Lk 12⁵ 16²³, Ac 2²⁷· ³¹, 1 Co 15⁵⁵, Rev 1¹⁸ 6⁸ 20¹³· ¹⁴). It is now an entirely misleading rendering, especially in the NT passages. The English Revisers, therefore, have substituted 'Hades' for 'hell' in the NT. In the OT they allow the word 'hell' to remain in the text of Is 14, and give *Sheol* in the margin. In the poetical books they usually give *Sheol* in the text; while in the historical books they place *Sheol* in the margin, and allow the renderings 'the grave' and 'the pit' to stand in the text. In the American Revision the word 'hell' is entirely discarded in this connexion (as are also the terms 'the grave,' 'the pit'), and with a wise consistency *Sheol* is substituted all through the text of the OT, as *Hades* is in the text of the NT. (See also article on HADES.

The word 'hell' is used (2) as equivalent to τάρταρος in the verbal form ταρταρώσας in 2 P 2⁴ (cf. Jude⁶). In that passage it is retained by the RV, though it might be better rendered 'cast them down to Tartarus.' The particular case in view there is that of the punishment of fallen angels, and the word is applied to the intermediate scene and condition of penalty in which those offenders are detained, held in chains of darkness, in reserve for the final judgment. In this one instance the NT adopts the heathen term for 'hell'—the word which in Plato (*Phæd.* 113 E) designates the place into which the incurably corrupt are hurled with a view to their endless imprisonment; and which in Homer (*Iliad,* viii. 13, etc.) is the name given to the murky abyss, lying as deep beneath Hades as earth is beneath the sun, in which the sins of insurgent and defeated immortals, Kronos, Iapetos, and the Titans, are punished.

In this the paragraph in question, together with the corresponding passage in the Ep. of Jude (v.⁶), attaches itself to ideas on the subject of the punishment of angels, which have a considerable place in the literature of Judaism, especially the apocalyptic writings. These ideas assumed strange and amorphous forms, unlike anything in the NT, as regards both the place and the nature of the penalty. The Book of Jubilees and the Apocalypse of Baruch, *e.g.,* both speak of the fallen angels as 'tormented in chains,' and the former represents them as bound in the depths of the earth until the day of the great judgment (Bk. of Jub 5²⁴³ 7²⁴⁸ 22²¹ 24²⁷ etc., Apoc. of Bar 56¹⁰⁻¹³). The Book of Enoch dilates at greatest length on these things. Enoch is described as receiving a commission to announce the impending judgment of the fallen angels. Their leader, Azâzel, is doomed to be covered with darkness until the great day of judgment. The prison in which they are confined until the day of decision consigns them to the final retribution, is seen by Enoch. It is described as different from the abyss of fire, in the extremest depth of earth, into which they are in the end to be cast, and in certain parts of the book this preliminary place of punishment is represented, as was the case also with the *Tartaros* of the Greeks, as in the void at the end of heaven and earth (Bk. of Enoch 10⁶ 13²¹ 18¹¹ 21⁷ 54⁶ 90²⁴).

The word 'hell' is used (3), and more properly, as the equivalent of γεέννα, the designation of the place and state of the just retribution reserved for the finally impenitent after the judgment. This word γεέννα (less correctly, in view of its derivation from the Aramaic, γέεννα), *Gehenna,* occurs twelve times in the NT, and for the most part only in the Synoptists. It is not found in the Johannine writings, nor in the Bk. of Acts, nor in any of the Epistles except once in one of the Catholic Epp. (Ja 3⁶). But in the Synoptical Gospels it is found eleven times, and in a variety

of phrases—'in danger of the Gehenna of fire' (Mt 5²²), 'to be cast into Gehenna' (Mt 5²⁹· ³⁰ 18⁹, Mk 9⁴⁵· ⁴⁷), to 'destroy . . . in Gehenna' (Mt 10²³), 'the child of Gehenna' (Mt 23¹⁵), the 'damnation' or 'judgment of Gehenna' (Mt 23³³), to 'go into Gehenna' (Mk 9⁴³), to 'cast into Gehenna' (Lk 12⁵). It is found, therefore, in each of the three Synoptists. In all the instances of its use in the Gospels it is given as a word from Christ's own lips, and in one case we have the parallel narrative of Mt and Mk (Mt 18⁹, Mk 9⁴⁵). It belongs to the tradition common to the first two evangelists, and there is every reason to believe that it forms part of the primitive report of Christ's words. Hence the importance of defining with all due care its precise sense, point, and connotation.

This term *Gehenna,* γεέννα, which is the solemn NT designation of *hell,* represents the Aram. םַנֵּיהִג and the Heb. םֹנִּה יֵּג 'the valley of Hinnom' (Neh 11³⁰), more fully םֹנִּהֶ ־נֶב יֵּג 'the valley of the son of Hinnom' (Jos 15⁸ 18¹⁶, 2 Ch 28³, Jer 7³²), and יֵנְב יֵּג םֹנִּה 'the valley of the children of Hinnom' (2 K 23¹⁰, acc. to the *Kethîb*). It is taken by some to mean the 'valley of howling' or 'the valley of lamentation,' םָנִּהֶ being supposed to come from an obsolete ןַנָה (Arab. *hanna,* 'cry' or 'wail'). But far more probably the *Hinnom* is a personal name. The place so named after one unknown was a deep narrow gorge in the vicinity of Jerusalem, understood to be on the south side, forming a continuation of the valley of Gihon and separating the hill of Zion from the 'hill of Evil Counsel.' It is usually identified with the modern *Wady er-Rebâbi,* though this is contested by some (see Conder in *Encyc. Brit.* xiii. 640). It is repeatedly mentioned in the OT. The border of Judah is described as going up 'by the valley of the son of Hinnom unto the south side of the Jebusite . . . and to the top of the mountain that lieth before the valley of Hinnom westward'; while the border of Benjamin is said to have 'come down to the end of the mountain that lieth before the valley of the son of Hinnom' and to have 'descended to the valley of Hinnom to the side of Jebusi on the south' (Jos 15⁸ 18¹⁶; cf. Neh 11³⁰). It is described as 'by the entry of the East gate' (Jer 19²), and as having the valley of Tophet or Topheth in it (2 K 23¹⁰, Jer 7³¹ 19⁶). Jerome speaks of it as having been of old a pleasant place, and as having again in his own time the attraction of gardens. But under Ahaz, Manasseh, and Amon it was made the scene of the gross and cruel rites of heathen worship, idolatrous Jews passing their children through the fire there to Molech (2 Ch 28³ 33⁶, Jer 7³¹). Hence king Josiah, when he put down the idolatrous priests who had burned incense to Baal under the apostate kings of Judah, also 'defiled Topheth, which is in the valley of the children of Hinnom, that no man might make his son or his daughter to pass through the fire to Molech' (2 K 23⁵· ¹⁰). It was also declared by Jeremiah that the place should be 'no more called Tophet, nor The valley of the son of Hinnom, but The valley of Slaughter' (Jer 19⁶). After its pollution by the pious son of Amon it became an object of horror to the Jews, and is said to have been made a receptacle for bones, the bodies of beasts and criminals, refuse and all unclean things (so Kimchi). The terrible associations of the place, the recollections of the horrors perpetrated in it and the defilement inflicted on it, the fires said to have been kept burning in it in order to consume the foul and corrupt objects that were thrown into it, made it a natural and unmistakable symbol of dire evil, torment, wasting penalty, absolute ruin. So it came to designate the place of future punishment, and the Talmudic theology spoke of the door of hell as being in the valley of Hinnom (Barclay, *City of the Great King*, p. 90).

It has not this sense in the OT. The nearest approach to it is in such a passage as that in which the prophet makes the demand, 'Who among us shall dwell with the devouring fire? Who among us shall dwell with everlasting burnings?' (Is 33¹⁴). But the place is not mentioned there, and the fires in question are not those of a retribution after death, but those of the divine wrath and righteousness which now and on earth search all sinners, those in Sion no less than those in Assyria. The terrible description of judgment with which the Second Isaiah closes his great prophecy of grace might seem even more in point (Is 66²⁴). It is possible that the horrors of the valley of Hinnom suggested the awful figures in which the prophet there declares of the returning Israelites, that they shall 'look upon the carcases of the men that have transgressed' against Jehovah, 'for their worm shall not die, neither shall their fire be quenched; and they shall be an abhorring unto all flesh' (RV). But apart from the fact that here again the place is not named, and from the question whether the passage may not be of too early a date (as Dillmann supposes) for such a colouring, the vengeance which is intimated is not one that is to be looked for in the other world, but one which overtakes the transgressors in this world in the form of miserable overthrow and uttermost dishonour. It assumed this sense, however, in the period between the close of OT prophecy and the Christian era. By the time when Christ taught and the apostles preached, the word *Gehenna* had a well-understood meaning. We can follow the history of the term, and see how it came to have that sense. The history shows us also the variations in the application of the word, and the different ideas which were connected with it.

The OT itself offered the point of issue for the process of development. As its view of the future became enlarged, and the old notion of a *Sheol* which was without moral distinctions, and dealt out to all the dead the same joyless inane existence, began to give place to the loftier and more definite conception of a future embracing a resurrection, the foundations of the doctrine of a heaven and a hell were laid. The idea of a final judgment, which went with that of a resurrection (Dn 12²), led naturally to the twofold expectation of a special place of reward for the righteous, and a special place of punishment for the unrighteous in a world beyond the grave. The Jewish literature shows us how this belief shaped itself. It makes it plain, too, that *Gehenna*, as the definite place of future retribution, was originally understood to be something distinct from Sheol or Hades, though other ideas were attached to it now and again or in particular schools. The apocalyptic writings are of special importance in this matter, and the Bk. of Enoch above all others. It is perhaps in it that we have the first definite occurrence of the word as the designation of the place of just retribution destined for the wicked after the final judgment. In *Enoch*, however, as in the apocalyptic writings in general, there is much that is fantastic, and the statements which meet us in different parts of the book are by no means uniform. In certain sections, which are probably more deeply affected by Hellenic ways of thinking, *Hades* appears as a preliminary scene of reward and punishment, and is represented as lying in the remotest tract beyond the ocean. In it the souls of dead men wait the final condition, and have a foretaste of that condition. This moralised Hades is described as having in it intermediate abodes of four distinct kinds for four different orders of men: one for the righteous who died of oppression, and another for the rest of the

righteous dead; one for sinners who were not judged by injustice or persecution on earth, and another for those who paid part of the penalty of their offences in their lifetime here (Bk. of Enoch 5. 22. 103⁷ etc.). More usually these preliminary scenes of weal and woe were spoken of as only two —one for the good, called also *Paradise* and the *Garden of Eden*; and one for the evil, separated from the other by a wall or gulf, and called, at least in the later Jewish books, by the name *Gehinnom, Gehenna*. In the *Slavonic Enoch*, again, or *The Book of the Secrets of Enoch*, the second of the seven heavens is the prison - house of the apostate angels who wait the eternal judgment, and the northern region of the third heaven is the place of punishment prepared for those who did not honour God (chs. 7 and 10). In the *Testaments of the Twelve Patriarchs* the place in which the spirits of the lawless are confined with a view to their punishment is the second heaven (*Test. of Levi*, ch. 3). In the literature of Alexandrian Judaism, on the other hand, in which we have the doctrine of an incorporeal immortality, and the idea that the souls of the pious dead are received at once by God into heaven, *Hades* is the place of punishment for the wicked dead, and is again practically identified with *Gehenna* (Wis 3¹⁰⁻¹⁴ 4¹⁰⁻¹⁹ 5¹ etc.; cf. Joseph. *De Bell. Jud.* II. viii. 11, 14). There is evidence enough, therefore, that opinion varied at different periods and in different sections of Judaism. In the theology of the Talmud and Midrash, *Gehinnom, Gehenna* meant the scene of penalty, while in certain phases of Jewish belief it appears to have been regarded at once as a place of punishment for the heathen and as a place of purgatorial detention for imperfect Israelites. But with all this there is reason to say that its original sense was that of the final place of retribution, that it was distinguished from *Hades* and from every form of an intermediate state, and that it had this meaning with the Jewish people generally (however it might be with the speculations of the schools) in Christ's time. The apocalyptic writings, which speak of a separation of the just from the unjust between death and the resurrection, also speak of a final punishment after the judgment, and describe the place of that retribution in terms which point to Gehenna. Enoch seems to identify it with the local *Ge-Hinnom*. He comes to the middle of earth, and sees a happy region of hills and valleys. But between the holy hills he sees an accursed valley where 'shall be gathered together all those who speak with their mouths unseemly words against God, and speak impudently of his majesty' (Bk. of Enoch 27². ³). Elsewhere in the same apocalypse this place of final retribution is described as 'in the midst of the earth' and 'full of fire' (90²⁴⁻²⁶). And in express terms the Fourth Book of Ezra speaks of the 'gulf of torments' and the 'furnace of Gehenna' that shall be revealed (6¹⁻¹⁴ 7³⁶, Churton). 'Hell,' therefore, as expressed by γέεννα in the NT, is not the penal side of Hades (so, *e.g.*, Grimm's *Wilkii Clavis*, etc.), but the final retributive scene and condition (see Meyer on Mt 5²²).

It has further to be asked whether the term 'hell,' *Gehenna*, in the NT expresses the idea of a penal condition that is *permanent*. What the common belief of the Jews was on the subject of the nature and the duration of the final retribution at the time to which the NT writings belong, is a disputed question, and one by no means easy to answer. The literature, however, that is most pertinent to the question does not favour the idea that the doctrine of an ultimate restoration of all souls was the prevalent doctrine among the Jews of that period. It leaves us a choice between two views, annihilation and everlasting punishment, and the conclusion to which it points is that the latter was the belief of the great mass of the people. The apocryphal books speak in the most unambiguous terms of the lot of the wicked dead as final and enduring. In the Bk. of Judith, for example, the vengeance of the day of judgment is described as 'fire and worms' in the flesh of those who rise up against Israel, which 'they shall feel and weep for ever' (16[17]). In one of the Bks. of Maccabees the lot of the tyrant is declared to be 'eternal torture by fire,' and 'interminable torments' (4 Mac 9[5. 9] 10[10]). Another of these books speaks of the 'furnace of hell,' and of the despisers of the Most High as doomed to be 'henceforth in torments, always in pain and anguish of seven kinds' (4 Ezr 7[36. 79. 80]). As a general rule, the pseudepigraphic writings are equally explicit. They speak of the penalty of the wicked as an 'everlasting curse'; of the last day as a 'day of judgment and punishment and affliction upon the revilers to eternity'; of the 'abyss of fire' in which the impious shall be 'locked up for all eternity'; of a 'just judgment, in eternity for ever' (Bk. of Enoch 5[5. 6] 22[4-11] 10[11-14] 27[2. 3]; cf. Apoc. Bar 44[15] etc.). The testimony of Josephus, too, with all necessary abatements, is to the effect that both Pharisees and Essenes believed in everlasting punishment (BJ II. viii. 11, 14; Ant. XVIII. i. 3). On the other hand, the final retribution of the impenitent is in not a few cases expressed in terms of a *destruction*, a *perdition*, and the like (Ps. Sol 3[13] 9[9] 12[8] 13[10] 15[13], Bk. En 99[11] etc.); from which it is inferred that the penalty in question was regarded as an ultimate extinction of being. Such expressions have to be read, however, in the light of the general Jewish conception of *Sheol*. So read they may convey the idea that there is no deliverance for the wicked from Sheol, but do not necessarily mean that the doom in question was absolute extinction of existence. They are also to be measured by other statements of a more definite and unmistakable kind, with which they are accompanied, and by the contrasts in which they are placed with descriptions of the lot of the righteous as an enduring one. In the Rabbinical books there is a wider variety of opinion. Gehenna appears there at times as a purgatory, and statements are found which indicate that at least at certain periods there were those who favoured the doctrine of annihilation, and those who inclined to the hope of a final universal restoration. But these were rather the dogmas or speculations of the schools than the belief of the people, and they belong to a later period. Even in the case of the great Rabbis who spoke of a limited punishment, exception was made of certain classes of sinners. The school of Hillel, e.g., taught that sinners of the heathen and others were punished in Gehinnom for a space of twelve months, and afterwards were consumed. But the Minim (the Christians), the Epicureans, those who deny the divine origin of the Torah and the truth of the resurrection, and those who sin like Jeroboam, the son of Nebat, were said to 'go down to Gehinnom,' and to be 'punished there to ages of ages.' The same is the statement made, but at greater length and in still more explicit terms, in the *Rosh Hashshanah*, in a passage which is described as the 'classical passage of the Talmud' on the subject (Plumptre, *The Spirits in Prison*, p. 52). The most probable conclusion appears to be this—that, while there were variations in belief from time to time, especially in the direction of annihilation, and divergent speculations in the Rabbinical schools, the idea generally connected with the term *Gehenna*, 'hell,' in our Lord's time was that of an irreversible doom for the wholly wicked, and that in His teaching as well as in that of His apostles the word was used

in its popular and prevalent sense (see Schürer, *HJP* II. ii. 183; Edersheim's *Jesus the Messiah*, ii. pp. 440, 791; Meyer, *Comm.* on Mt 5[22]; Holtzmann, *Hand-Com.* on Mt 5[22], Mk 3[29] 9[48]).

Other terms are also used in the NT to express the penalty and the condition indicated by the word *Gehenna*, 'hell.' In the evangelical records of Christ's own discourses such terms are found employed as 'eternal fire'; 'unquenchable fire'; the place where 'their worm dieth not, and their fire is not quenched'; the 'prison' from which there is no coming out until 'the last farthing' is paid; 'eternal punishment' as contrasted with 'eternal life'; exclusion from the kingdom; banishment from Christ; 'weeping and wailing, and gnashing of teeth'; the 'outer darkness,' etc. (Mt 18[8. 9], Mk 9[43-49], Mt 5[25. 26], Lk 12[58. 59], Mt 25[46] 7[21-23] 13[42] 25[30]). Elsewhere the final destiny of the unrighteous is described as 'the mist of darkness for ever' (2 P 2[17]); the 'blackness of darkness for ever' (Jude [13]); the 'fierceness of fire' and 'perdition' (He 10[27. 39]); 'great tribulation,' 'burning with fire,' being 'without,' the 'second death,' being cast into the 'lake of fire,' the 'lake that burneth with brimstone and fire' (Rev 2[22. 23] 18[8. 9] 22[15] 21[1] 20[6. 14] 21[8] 20[10] 19[20]); the 'wrath to come,' 'wrath and indignation, tribulation and anguish,' 'death,' 'punishment,' 'destruction,' 'eternal destruction from the face of the Lord' (Ro 2[5], 2 Th 1[9], Ro 2[8] 6[21], Ph 3[19], 2 Th 1[9]). Beyond these terms of large suggestion, which are as remarkable for their variety as for their figurative force, the NT does not carry us. Theologians have gone further, and have ventured on many definitions of things left undefined in the Scriptures. They have distinguished between two forms of the future penalty, the *pœna sensus* and the *pœna damni*. They have spoken sometimes of the 'fire' of Gehenna as a material fire (cf. Petavius, *De Angel.* iii. 5), and sometimes as a figurative (Origen, *De Prin.* ii. 4). They have indulged in fruitless questions regarding the locality of hell, the *Limbus* or 'fringe' of hell, and much else. The NT is silent on many things on which imagination and speculation have both spent themselves largely and to little profit. It speaks much less of the retribution of the impenitent than of the reward of the righteous. In what it does say of the former it gives no satisfaction to curious inquiry. It limits itself to intimations which address themselves to character and conduct, and which convey the impression of the untold moral issues that depend upon the present life.

LITERATURE.—The great Commentaries, especially Meyer; the great NT Dictionaries, especially Thayer and Cremer; the systems of Biblical Theology and Dogmatics, especially Oehler, Riehm, Schultz, Weiss, Beyschlag, Dorner, Rothe, Martensen, Plitt, Philippi, Kuhn, Schweitzer; Alger, *Critical History of the Doctrine of a Future Life*; Atzberger, *Eschatologie*; Kliefoth, *Eschatologie*; Pusey, *What is of Faith as to Everlasting Punishment?*; Gfrörer, *Jahrhundert des Heils*; Drummond, *Jewish Messiah*; Stanton, *Jewish and the Christian Messiah*; Hamburger, *RE*; Weber, *Jüdische Theologie*; Böttcher, *De Inferis*; Dillmann, *Das Buch Henoch*; Charles, *Book of Enoch*; Driver, *Sermons on OT*, Sermon iv.; Edersheim, *Jesus the Messiah*; Delitzsch, *Bib. Psychol.*; Kabisch, *Die Eschatol. d. Paulus.*

S. D. F. SALMOND.

HELLENISM.—See GREECE.

HELM.—The helm is now the handle which moves the rudder, but it was formerly used loosely for the whole steering apparatus. Hence in Ja 3[4] it is given as tr[n] of πηδάλιον, a rudder. It was Tind. who introduced 'helm' here, and he was followed by all the VSS except Gen., which has 'rudder,' and Rhem., which has 'sterne.' RV follows Geneva. The only other occurrence of π. in NT is in Ac 27[40], where Tind. and all after him give 'rudder.' Wyclif's word in both passages is 'governayle.' See SHIP.

HELMET (קוֹבַע *ḳôbhaʽ* or כּוֹבַע *ḳôbhaʽ*'—Greek περι-κεφαλαία) was probably made of skin as a rule, since helmets of bronze (Goliath's 1 S 17⁵, and Saul's *ib.* v.³⁸) are mentioned as something special. The form of an ancient helmet is shown in the illustration of Assyrian soldiers given under BATTERING-RAM. The helmets worn by the Romans were made either of leather (the *galea*) or of metal (the *cassis*). The helmet included plates to protect the cheeks, a band for the forehead, and a collar-like projection to protect the back of the neck. Such a helmet, when closed, showed little besides the eyes, nose, and mouth. (See illustrations in *Lindenschmit*, Tables ix. x. and xxii.).

Isaiah (59¹⁷) describes the Lord as arming Himself for His people with righteousness as a coat of mail, and with salvation as a helmet. It is clear from the parallelism existing between the two halves of the verse (righteousness = vengeance, salvation = zeal) that the passage means that God arises with punishment for the enemy and with deliverance for His people. The 'helmet of salvation' is the helmet of the Lord's deliverance. St. Paul applies the phrase (Eph 6¹⁷) differently; on the Christian's head rests (1 Th 5⁸) a helmet *of the hope* of salvation.   W. E. BARNES.

HELON (חֵלֹן 'valorous').—Father of Eliab, the prince of Zebulun at the first census, Nu 1⁹ 2⁷ 7²⁴. ²⁹ 10¹⁶ (P).

HELP.—As a verb 'help' is used in AV in some archaic phrases: (1) *Help forward*, Zec 1¹⁵ 'I was but a little displeased and they helped forward the affliction,' *i.e.* aggravated. Golding uses the phrase in a good sense in *Calvin's Isaiah* (on 40³), 'what an excellent consolation is this, to heare that God useth the service of Infidels, yea and when his Church hath need, to make all creatures put to their hands for the helping forward of our salvation.' Milton uses the verb without 'forward' in the same sense as in Zec, *PL* vi. 656—

'Their armour helped their harm, crush'd in and bruised
    Into their substance pent.'

(2) *Help to* = furnish with, 1 Mac 8¹³ 'Whom they would help to a kingdom, those reign' (οἷς δ' ἂν βούλωνται βοηθεῖν καὶ βασιλεύειν, βασιλεύσουσιν [κ βασιλεύουσιν], RV 'Whomsoever they will to succour and to make kings, these do they make kings'). Cf. *Piers Plowman*, p. 27—

'Trywe charite
That most helpe the men to hevene.'

(3) *Help up*, Ec 4¹⁰ 'Woe to him that is alone when he falleth : for he hath not another to help him up' (RV 'lift him up'). So Is 49⁸ Cov. 'I wil make the a pledge for the people, so that thou shalt helpe up the earth agayne'; and Shaks. *Timon*, I. i. 107—

'Tis not enough to help the feeble up,
But to support him after.'

Help, both as vb. and subst., has often a fuller meaning than 'assistance,' it often means 'deliverance,' almost as much as 'salvation.' See esp. Ps 60¹¹ = 108¹² 'Give us help from trouble : for vain is the help of man' (עֶזְרָה . . . תְּשׁוּעָה, where the second word is usually tr⁴ 'salvation,' as AVm, RVm; LXX βοήθεια . . . σωτηρία; Vulg. 'auxilium . . . salus'). Cf. Jer 8²⁰ Tav. 'The harvest is gone, the sommer hath an ende, and we are not healped'; Ps 22⁵ Cov. 'They called upon the, and were healped : they put their trust in the, and were not confounded' (so Pr. Bk. 'They called upon thee, and were holpen').

In Gn 2¹⁸. ²⁰ Eve is described as 'an help meet for' Adam. The Heb. is the usual word for 'help' (עֵזֶר), but the meaning is not, as vulgarly supposed 'a help to Adam,' one that will give herself to serve Adam. This mistake has caused the word 'helpmate' to be used of the wife (sometimes evidently under

the impression that that is the term in Gn), as even Abp. Sharp, *Works*, IV. Ser. xii. 'God made man first, and out of him created woman ; and declared withal, that he therefore created her that she might be a help-mate for the man.' The meaning is a helper (the word is of course concrete as in Ps 70⁵) that will assist him in the work given him to do, carrying it on in the same spirit, as Vulg. 'adjutorium similem sibi.' The meaning is well illustrated by Southey, *Wesley*, ii. 188, 'It had therefore been much impressed upon his [Whitefield's] heart that he should marry, in order to have a help meet for him in the work whereunto he was called.' Tindale's trⁿ is (2¹⁸) 'I will make hym an helper to beare him company.' Cf. To 8⁶ 'Let us make unto him an aid like unto himself' (βοηθὸν ὅμοιον αὐτῷ, exactly as LXX of Gn 2³⁰, RV 'a helper like unto him'). Pennant, however (*Brit. Zool.* 'The Hog'), uses the word 'helpmate' in this sense : 'In Minorca the ass and the hog are common helpmates, and are yoked together in order to turn up the land.'

The plu. form 'helps' occurs thrice : (1) 2 Mac 8¹⁹ 'Moreover he recounted unto them what helps their forefathers had found' (ἀντιλήμψεις, RV 'the help given from time to time in the days of their ancestors'). (2) Ac 27¹⁷ 'they used helps, undergirding the ship' (βοηθείαις ἐχρῶντο). Page and Walpole's note is good : 'Cables passed round the hull and tightly secured on deck to prevent the timbers from starting, especially amidships, where in ancient ships with one large mast the strain was very great. The technical English word is *frapping*, but the process is rarely employed now.' See Smith, *Voyage and Shipwreck of St. Paul*², 105, and art. SHIP. (3) 1 Co 12²⁸ 'And God hath set some in the church, first apostles . . . helps, governments, diversities of tongues' (TR ἀντιλήψεις, edd. ἀντιλήμψεις, AV 1611, 'helpes in governments'). See next article.

In AV 1611 and in most edd. still, the past ptcp. is 'holpen' in Ps 83⁸ 86¹⁷, Is 31³, Dn 11³⁴, Lk 1⁵⁴ ; RV retains the form, but Amer. RV prefers 'helped' in all but the last. The past tense is always 'helped'; and 'helped' occurs as past ptcp. in 1 Ch 5²⁰, 2 Ch 26¹⁵, Ps 28⁷, Is 49⁸.   J. HASTINGS.

HELPS (ἀντιλήμψεις, *opitulationes*).—In LXX (in Pss [for several Heb. words], 1 Es, Sir, 2, 3 Mac) ἀντίλημψις implies 'succour,' as of stronger to weaker, not the 'help' of an assistant to superior, *e.g.* Sir 11¹² προσδεόμενος ἀ., 3 Mac ἀ. ἐξ οὐράνου, cf. Jos. *BJ* IV. v. 1. Similarly in papyri of the age of the Ptolemies ἀ. = βοήθεια, as in the phrase τυχεῖν ἀντιλήμψεως (cf. 2 Mac 15⁷, 3 Mac 2³³); while ἀντιλήμπτωρ is a style of the king with whom is asylum (καταφυγή, cf. 2 S 22³). In NT it occurs only in 1 Co 12²⁸, along with κυβερνήσεις, to which LXX usage attaches the meaning 'wise counsels' (תַּחְבֻּלוֹת Pr 1⁵ 11¹⁴ 24⁶ [Job 37¹² Symm., Pr 20¹⁸ Theod.]: so κυβερνᾶν, Pr 12⁵, Wis 10⁴ 14⁶, Sus 1⁶ ; Hesych. paraphrases by προνοητικαὶ ἐπιστῆμαι καὶ φρονήσεις. Gloss. on Pr 1⁵ ἐπιστήμη τῶν πρακτομένων). The list of God-given gifts to the Church enumerates 'first apostles, second prophets, third teachers, next powers, next *charisms* of healings, succours, counsels, kinds of tongues'; while in the interrogative recapitulation, which follows in vv.²⁹. ³⁰, 'succours' and 'counsels' fall out, probably as being less charismatic than the rest and more widely diffused among the brethren. This is confirmed by the analogous list of *charismata* in Ro 12⁶⁻⁸, where the moral also is the same, viz. the duty of the many members to use their functional gifts for the common organic well-being. It is indeed hard to find in the latter list any single synonyms for 'succours' and 'counsels': rather they may well cover several things—the one, personal service (διακονία, cf. Phœbe as διάκονος, 16¹), charity (ὁ μεταδιδούς) or acts of mercy (ὁ ἐλεῶν); the other, instruction (διδασκαλία) and exhortation *

* ὁ προϊστάμενος is ambiguous, as (1) Phœbe is called προστάτις πολλῶν, *i.e.* patroness (a *patrona* in relation to *clientes*, as it were), which probably has reference to beneficence rather than rule ; (2) προστασίαι (κατὰ πονουμένων) is a recognized equivalent for ἀ. (see Suicer, *s.v.*). This must be remembered even in 1 Th 5¹².

(παράκλησις). But in any case the various activities are so intermingled as to exclude special reference to any officials. We are still at the stage when functions in the *ecclesia*, not functionaries, are everything (cf. 1 P 4[10. 11]). In a somewhat later list (Eph 4[11]) it is otherwise ; and we get 'shepherds and teachers' in place of 'succours and counsels.' But meantime these gifts explain and are explained by Gal 6[1. 2], where 'the spiritual' help their weaker brethren to recover their footing, 'bearing one another's burdens'; and by 1 Th 5[14], where the brethren in general are to 'put in mind the unruly, comfort the faint-hearted, uphold the weak' (ἀντέχεσθαι τῶν ἀσθενῶν, the very words by which Theophyl. defines ἀντίλημψις). From this passage we further learn that it is unsafe to refer ἀ. and κυβ. to distinct offices, even when more or less regular officials are in question. In 1 Co itself we find only one class of regular workers (16[15-18]), members of the household of Stephanas, who have 'devoted themselves unto ministry to the saints,' and to whose wise counsels the brethren are exhorted to yield subordination. In them, we can hardly doubt, the gifts of 'succour' and 'counsel' dwelt in eminent degree ; and we may infer the like of those named in 1 Th 5[12], where κοπιᾶν, προϊστάναι, νουθετεῖν may be coextensive with ἀ. and κυβ. Finally, Ac 20[35] comes in to clinch these conclusions. Speaking to Ephesian elders, whom he describes as guardians of the flock (28), St. Paul bids them toil (κοπιᾶν) to succour the weak (ἀντιλαμβάνεσθαι, cf. Lk 1[54], also σύναντ. Ro 8[26]), being mindful of their Lord's golden word. Just above he has spoken of the need of wise counsel on their part. So that, once again, we get ἀ. and κυβ. combined in an undifferentiated official class, here called 'elders.' The 'succour' in question, in keeping with linguistic usage, is that later on rendered by 'bishops' rather than 'deacons.' But so far there is no evidence of any such formal distinction, which meets us first in Ph 1[1]—where indeed there is as yet no trace of subordination of the one class to the other (cf. their parallel position in 1 Ti 3[1-13], *Teaching* 15[1]). In 1 Co 12[28], on the other hand, the 'succours' and 'counsels' not only occur on the same level, as it were, but what was later thought the humbler function actually comes first (there is nothing to suggest Meyer's 'climactic juxtaposition'). This makes the two terms most significant for primitive Christianity and its ministerial conceptions. Ἀντ., then, means 'anything that could be done for poor or weak or outcast brethren, either by rich or powerful or influential brethren or by the devotion of those who stood on no such eminence'; while κυβ. denotes guidance by 'men who by wise counsels did for the community what the steersman or pilot does for the ship' (Hort).

LITERATURE.—For the word, Schleusner, *Lex. NT*; Deissmann, *Bibelstudien* (1895), p. 87 (for the papyri); for the sense, Weizsäcker, *Ap. Age*, ii. 318 ff., Hort, *Chr. Eccl.* p. 157 ff., commentaries on 1 Co.   J. V. BARTLET.

HELVE.—Dt 19[5] 'As when a man goeth into the wood with his neighbour to hew wood, and his hand fetcheth a stroke with the axe to cut down the tree, and the head slippeth from the helve, and lighteth upon his neighbour, that he die ; he shall flee unto one of those cities, and live.' This idiomatic tr[n] is almost word for word from Tindale, including the word 'helve' for the handle of the axe. But that word is as old as the Wyclifite version of 1388, 'and the yrun slidith fro the helve' (the 1382 ed. has 'haft'). The word, though still in use locally, does not seem to occur in the Eng. VSS except in this place (where Dou. has 'handle,' translating directly the Vulg. *manubrium*), nor is it found in Shaks. or Milton. It is preserved in the proverb 'to throw the helve after

the hatchet,' *i.e.* give up everything, as Howell, *Forreine Travell*, § 9, 'If shee should reduce the Spaniard to that desperate passe in the Netherlands, as to make him throw the helve after the hatchet, it would much alter the case.'

The Heb. is עֵץ 'wood' or 'tree,' the same word as has been tr[d] 'wood' and 'tree' already in the same verse; hence RVm suggests that the axe is supposed to glance off the tree it is working on, which is probably correct. The LXX is τὸ ξύλον, 'the tree'; and the words tr[d] 'haft' (Jg 3[22]) and 'handle' (Ca 5[5]) differ from this word.   J. HASTINGS.

HEM.—See DRESS, FRINGES.

HEMAM (הֵימָם).—The eponym of a Horite clan, Gn 36[22], called in 1 Ch 1[39] **Homam** (הוֹמָם). LXX has in both passages Αἱμάν. Kittel (in *SBOT*, 1 Ch 1[39]) declares in favour of the reading Hemam, which answers to the Lucianic Ἡμάν. Dillmann (on Gn 36[22]) points out that Knobel's comparison of *Hemam* with *Ḥumaimeh*, a town south of Petra, is against the phonology.

HEMAN (הֵימָן 'faithful'). This name occurs in three connexions. One man is probably referred to. **1.** 1 K 4[31] one of the four sages whom Solomon excelled in wisdom. Ethan, being specially termed the Ezrahite, appears to be by that distinguished from the other three, sons of Mahol. **2.** However, one of the titles of Ps 88 ascribes its authorship to Heman the Ezrahite. If this be reliable, he might be Ethan's brother, and Mahol father only of Calcol and Darda (Keil). It can scarcely be doubted that the Chronicler (1 Ch 2[6]) interprets Ezrahite as Zerahite, when he makes all four sages sons of Zerah, son of Judah (so Grotius). Delitzsch maintains the identity of the Heman of 1 K 4[31] with the author of Ps 88. He also conjectures that this Heman has dramatized his own experiences in the Book of Job, 'a Chokma-work of the Solomonic age.' **3.** 1 Ch 6[33] 15[17. 19] 16[41. 42] 25[1-6], 2 Ch 5[12] 35[15] (1 Es 1[15] Zacharias). A Kohathite Levite, one of the three precentors of David's temple choir. There are two suspicious features in the Chronicler's account of his family : (*a*) He is made the grandson of the prophet Samuel (1 Ch 6[33]). But Samuel was an Ephraimite (1 S 1[1]). Is not this the Chronicler's characteristic explanation of Samuel's constant offering of sacrifice? (*b*) In 1 Ch 25[4] Ewald and Wellhausen (W. R. Smith, *OTJC*[2] p. 143, n.[1]) have shown that the last six names of Heman's 'sons' are merely the words of an anthem : '(1) I have given great (2) and lofty help (3) to him that sat in distress; (4) I have spoken (5) a superabundance of (6) prophecies.' W. R. Smith (*OTJC*[2] p. 204) maintains, moreover, that the three guilds of singers did not exist until the time of Alexander the Great (Neh 11[17] 12[24]). If this be true, the notices of Heman in Chronicles are unhistorical. Ewald (*HI* iii. p. 278 n.[2]) conjectures that the Levitical schools of music adopted the Judahites Ethan and Heman into their family. Keil, on the other hand, says that the Levites Ethan and Heman are called Ezrahites because incorporated into the Judæan family of Zerah (cf. Jg 17[7], 1 S 1[1]). The title 'seer' (*ḥôzeh*), applied to Heman (1 Ch 25[5]), as also to Asaph and Jeduthun, may refer merely to musical skill. Cf. the use of 'prophecy,' 1 Ch 25[1-3].   N. J. D. WHITE.

HEMDAN.—See HAMRAN.

HEMLOCK.—A word occurring in AV in two places (Hos 10[4], Am 6[12]). In the former RVm has *rôsh* (see GALL (2) רֹאשׁ). The Heb. equivalent of the latter is לַעֲנָה *la'ănâh*, which is everywhere else rendered by AV *wormwood*. RV so renders it in this passage. Neither word refers to the poison hemlock, *Conium maculatum*, **L.**, much less to the hemlock tree, *Abies*.   G. E. POST.

HEN.—See COCK.

HEN (חֵן).—In Zec 6¹⁴ ' Hen the son of Zephaniah ' is mentioned amongst those whose memory was to be perpetuated by the crowns laid up in the temple (so AV, RV). Wellhausen (*Kl. Proph., ad loc.*) substitutes for Hen the name Joshua [Josiah] found in v.¹⁰, and in like manner corrects Helem of v.¹⁴ into Heldai of v.¹⁰. The LXX does not treat the word as a proper name, reading εἰς χάριτα υἱοῦ Σοφονίου. This is followed by Ewald, Hitzig, Keil, Orelli, Marti (in Kautzsch's *AT*), who gives ' Freundlichkeit,' and RVm ' for the kindness of the son of Zephaniah.'   J. A. SELBIE.

HENA (הֵנַע) 2 K 18³⁴ [wanting in the parallel passage, Is 36¹⁹], 19¹³=Is 37¹³).—According to some a city in Syria, but probably to be taken rather as a divine name. In that case it should be identified with the Arabic star name *al-han'a*; and *'Iwwâ* (better *'Awwâ*), coupled with it, will be identical with the star name *al-'awwâ'u* (cf. Hommel, ' Hena' and 'Awwa' in *Expos. Times*, April 1898).   F. HOMMEL.

HENADAD (חֵנָדָד ' favour of Hadad ').—A Levite chief (Ezr 3⁹, Neh 3¹⁸· ²⁴ 10⁹). See GENEALOGY.

HENNA.—See CAMPHIRE.

HEPHER (חֵפֶר, ' digging ').—**1.** Son of Gilead the Manassite, and father of Zelophehad, Nu 26³² 27¹, Jos 17²ᵗ· P. Patronymic, **Hepherites**, Nu 26³². **2.** One of the tribe of Judah, 1 Ch 4⁶. **3.** A Mecherathite, one of David's heroes, 1 Ch 11³⁶.

HEPHER (חֵפֶר).—A Canaanite royal city, named immediately before Aphek, Jos 12¹⁷. The site is uncertain. The land of Hepher ('ח אֶרֶץ) is mentioned in 1 K 4¹⁰ along with Socoh.

HEPHZI-BAH (חֶפְצִי־בָהּ ' she in whom is my delight.' So in Phœnician חפצבעל ' the delight of Baal ').—**1.** The mother of Manasseh, king of Judah (2 K 21¹). **2.** Symbolic name of the Zion of Messianic times (Is 62⁴).

HERALD (Aram. כָּרוֹז, emphat. כָּרוֹזָא; see Kautzsch, *Gram.* § 64, 4).—The word so translated occurs only once, in Dn 3⁴. If=Gr. κήρυξ (but see Bevan, 107 n.) it will be one of those words in the Bk. of Daniel that prove its author to have lived ' after the dissemination of Greek influences in Asia ' (Driver, *LOT*⁶ 502); such words are קִיתָרֹס (κίθαρις), and the names of other musical instruments, mentioned in connexion with the herald's proclamation on this occasion. No distinct mention is made in the annals of Hebrew warfare of the herald in his function of summoning conflicting parties to conference, or of demanding the submission of beleaguered places. Goliath utters his own challenge (1 S 17⁸ᶠ·). When Sennacherib invaded Judah, his demands were made known by the Tartan, the Rab-saris, and the Rab-shakeh, apparently prominent military and civil personages (2 K 18¹ᶠᶠ·). The official referred to in Daniel may, however, have performed such duties in Babylonian military operations, as on this occasion he is employed to make known the monarch's will at a high religious observance. Κῆρυξ is applied by St. Paul to himself (1 Ti 2⁷, 2 Ti 1¹¹) as a preacher of the divine revelation in Jesus Christ, on both occasions in conjunction with ἀπόστολος. Noah is called (2 P 2⁵) ' a herald of righteousness.' See PREACHING.   G. WALKER.

HERB.—See GRASS.

HERCULES ('Ηρακλῆς) is mentioned by this name only in 2 Mac 4¹⁹· ²⁰, where Jason, the brother of the high priest Onias III., who had secured by bribery his own appointment in the latter's place, and the head of the Hellenizing party in Jerus. (B.C. 174), sent 300 silver drachmas (about £12, 10s.) to Tyre as an offering in honour of H., the tutelary deity of that city. We know from the precedent of Alexander the Great (Quint. Curt. iv. 7) that it was customary for kings to send offerings to H. at Tyre (' quem praecipue Tyrii colerent '). The same deity is mentioned by Silius Italicus (iii. 14 ff.) as being worshipped at Gades, an old Phœn. colony. He was otherwise known as Mel-Carthus or Melek-Kartha=' Lord of the city.' In a Phœn. inscription (*CIS* I. i. 122) he is called Adonēnu Melkarth Ba'al Tzure=' Our Lord Melkarth, Baal of Tyre.' Jos. (*Ant.* VIII. v. 3; *c. Ap.* I. i. 18) also mentions H. and Astarte together, as Baal and Ashtoreth are often joined. The worship of the Tyrian Baal became widely prevalent in Israel on the marriage of Ahab with the Phœn. princess Jezebel (1 K 16³¹· ³³), and in Judah during the reign of Ahaziah and the usurpation of his mother Athaliah, the daughter of Ahab (2 K 8²⁷ 11¹⁸).

H. was worshipped at Tyre from very early times, and his temple in that place was, according to Herod. ii. 44, as old as the city itself, 230C years before his own time. As a personification of the sun he afforded an example of nature-worship so common among the Phœn., Egyp., and other nations of antiquity. The Greeks may have borrowed their deities from strangers, and, substituting individuals for abstract qualities or for the forces of nature, claimed for them an indigenous origin. Hercules ('Ηρακλῆς=' renown of Hera ') was with them the heroic embodiment of strength, a demigod powerful enough to restore even the dead to life (Eur. *Alcestis*, 1136). The connexion between the sun and strength can be easily traced.   C. H. PRICHARD.

HERD.—Three words in Heb. are trᵈ ' herd.' **1.** בָּקָר *bâkâr*, βοῦς. This word is generic for *oxen*. It is not like *ẓôn*, applicable to two or more species. Wherever it is used, therefore, it might without loss, and with sensible advantage, be translated *oxen*. **2.** עֵדֶר *'êdher*, βουκόλια. This word occurs once (Jl 1¹⁸) in the construct state with *bâkâr*, and the expression is trᵈ ' herds of cattle.' It would have been better to translate *herds of oxen*. In the same verse *'êdher ẓôn* is trᵈ ' flocks of sheep,' being prob. intended to include *goats* as well. See FLOCK, SHEEP. **3.** מִקְנֶה *mikneh*. This word is usually rendered ' cattle.' See CATTLE. In construction with *bâkâr* (Gn 47¹⁷) it is trᵈ ' cattle of the herds,' AV, RVm; while RV text renders the two words by one, ' herds.' The construct expression מִקְנֵה הַבָּקָר (v.¹⁸) is rendered ' herds of cattle,' AV, RV.

The NT word for herd is ἀγέλη, but it is used only for *swine* (Mt 8³⁰ etc.).   G. E. POST.

HEREDITY.—The law that like begets like, and that therefore children inherit the qualities and the responsibilities of their ancestors, is not scientifically stated in the Bible, but, in so far as it is matter of common experience, it is implied.

The simplest form in which it presents itself to observation is in the case of similarity of physical and moral features. Thus it is remarked by Raguel (To 7²) ' how like ' Tobias is to his father Tobit. And, again, it is said of a good son, ' His father dieth, and is as though he had not died ; for he hath left one behind him like himself ' (Sir 30⁴). That the father's character is often repeated in his son is too common a phenomenon to escape notice. It is said, *e.g.*, of Abijam (1 K 15³), of Nadab (1 K 15²⁶), and of Ahaziah (1 K 22⁵²), that they walked in the evil ways of their fathers; and of Jehoshaphat (1 K 22[43]) and Amaziah (2 K 14[3]), that they followed their fathers' good example. This does not, indeed, constitute a universal rule. Good fathers often have bad sons, as we see in the case of Eli, and bad fathers have good sons; and even where the evil taint is reproduced, it is apparent in different individuals in different degrees. But with a people so quick to discern the ties of kindred, so imbued with a sense of national solidarity as were the Hebrews, the law of heredity was expected to fulfil itself. 'Who can bring a clean thing out of an unclean?' (Job 14[4]) was a question with the answer, 'Not one.' They were accustomed to trace the characteristics of a tribe or a family in the person and career of its founder. Thus Esau is the true ancestor of the wild Edomite peoples, as Jacob is of the chosen race; and the enmity between the brothers Esau and Jacob reproduces itself in the thought of Obadiah in the jealous hate of Edom for Israel.

But not only do children inherit qualities of body and mind from their fathers; they inherit, as well, responsibility. This is the perpetual burden of the Pentateuch. The sins of the fathers are visited upon the children unto the third and fourth generation (Ex 20[5], cf. Is 14[21]); the divine punishments follow the family of the sinner (Lv 20[5]). And as with sin, so with righteousness; its consequences are equally inherited, and the inheritance is more permanent than that of evil, for the LORD shows mercy unto them that fear Him 'unto a thousand generations.' Israel is beloved 'for the fathers' sake'; and the tenure of the inheritance of blessing is more lasting than the curse which follows sin.

The sense of responsibility seems, indeed, in the OT to attach itself to the family and the nation quite as much as to the individual. The sense of individuality was less felt in early ages than it is in modern life, where it has been strongly emphasized. But at the same time the ultimate responsibility of the individual to God is not overlooked in the OT. The Hebrews of the Captivity put forward as excuse for their miserable condition the sad proverb, 'The fathers have eaten sour grapes, and the children's teeth are set on edge'; but Ezekiel (ch. 18) warns them against its misinterpretation. Men do, indeed, suffer through their fathers' sins, but the soul is ultimately responsible to God for its own sin alone. 'The soul that sinneth, it shall die' (Ezk 18[20]). See FALL.

We here come upon the great moral difficulty, felt by the Hebrews as by us, though not so keenly, as to the reconciliation of the two principles of the transmission of qualities from father to son, and of personal responsibility. On the one hand, it may be said that 'the dead rule the living'; each man is not only an individual, but a member of a series, or rather of an organism, in which each part is dependent on and affects every other. This, if pressed without qualification, results in the doctrine of traducianism, according to which a man's soul is the product of that of his parents—a doctrine which it is difficult to state so as to save the freedom of the will. On the other hand, we must conceive of each individual as in direct personal relations of responsibility with God; he is therefore not merely the product of the past history of his race, and a factor in the evolution of its future, but a fresh beginning with a soul which is, in part, a new creation (creationism).   J. H. BERNARD.

HEREAFTER.—Where the witches (in Shaks. *Macbeth*, I. iii. 50) cry

' All hail, Macbeth, that shall be king hereafter,'

they clearly mean 'at some time to come.' This is the present meaning of the word, and it is found a few times in AV, esp. Jn 13[7], Rev 1[19] 4[1] 9[12], where the Gr. is μετὰ ταῦτα, 'after these things.' But where (in the same play, I. iv. 38) Duncan says,

' We will establish our estate upon
Our eldest, Malcolm; whom we name hereafter
The prince of Cumberland,'

he as clearly means 'from this time forward,' 'henceforth.' This is the most frequent meaning of the word in AV, and it demands attention because the mod. meaning of the word is apt to make one miss the sense of the passage. In Mk 11[14] 'No man eat fruit of thee hereafter for ever' (μηκέτι, RV 'henceforth') there is no danger of mistake; but in Mk 26[64] 'Hereafter shall ye see the Son of man sitting on the right hand of power, and coming in the clouds of heaven,' it is not evident from the English version that the meaning is 'from now,' 'henceforth' (ἀπ' ἄρτι, RV 'Henceforth'). But that is the meaning also in Jn 1[51] 'Hereafter ye shall see the heaven open, and the angels of God ascending and descending on the Son of man' (where, however, edd. omit ἀπ' ἄρτι of TR, whence RV 'Ye shall see,' etc.); and in Lk 22[69] 'Hereafter shall the Son of man sit on the right hand of the power of God' (ἀπὸ τοῦ νῦν, RV 'henceforth'), and even in Jn 14[30] 'Hereafter I will not talk much with you' (οὐκ ἔτι, edd. οὐκέτι, RV 'no more'). In 1 Ti 1[16] 'for a pattern to them which should hereafter believe on him to life everlasting' (πρὸς ὑποτύπωσιν τῶν μελλόντων πιστεύειν), and in the OT passages (Is 41[23], Ezk 20[39], Dn 2[29. 45]), the meaning is more indefinite, 'at any time after this' (observe that the אֲשֶׁר־יֹחַל of Is 41[23] is in 42[23] tr[d] 'for the time to come'). In Gal 6[17] the Wyclifite version of 1388 is 'And heraftir no man be hevy to me,' while the version of 1380 gives 'Fro hennis forth no man be hevy to me.'

Hereafter is one of a number of so-called pronoun-adverbs, of which 'here' is the first part, always with the meaning of 'this.' The others found in AV are—

Hereby. In the Eng. language even of the beginning of the 17th cent. 'hereby' had sometimes a local meaning, as in Shaks. *As You Like It*, IV. i. 9—

' Where is the bush
That we must stand and play the murderer in?
Hereby, upon the edge of yonder coppice.'

But in AV it is always instrumental, 'by this means,' as 1 Jn 2[3] 'And hereby do we know that we do know him, if we keep his commandments' (ἐν τούτῳ, a very common expression in this Epistle, and generally tr[d] 'hereby').

Herein, lit. 'in this'; in NT always instrumental and always the tr[n] of ἐν τούτῳ; in OT it occurs Gn 34[22] 'Only herein will the men consent unto us for to dwell with us . . . if every male among us be circumcised' (בְּזֹאת, RV 'on this condition'); and 2 Ch 16[9] 'Herein thou hast done foolishly' (עַל־זֹאת).

Hereof. Observe 1 Mac 16[22] 'Hereof when he heard, he was sore astonished' (καὶ ἀκούσας, RV 'And when he heard'); Mt 9[26] 'And the fame hereof went abroad into all that land' (ἡ φήμη αὕτη, AVm and RVm 'this fame'); He 5[3] 'And by reason hereof he ought, as for the people, so also for himself, to offer for sins' (TR διὰ ταύτην, edd. δι' αὐτήν, RV 'by reason thereof'). Cf. T. Fuller, *Holy Warre*, iii. 5, p. 117, 'But hereof hereafter.'

Heretofore = hitherto, as tr[n] of תְּמוֹל שִׁלְשֹׁם (Ex 4[10] 5[7. 8. 14], Jos 3[4], Ru 2[11]), or שִׁלְשֹׁם אֶתְמוֹל (1 S 4[7]), lit. 'yesterday three days,' a primitive method of referring to past time. See TIME. In NT, 2 Co 13[2] 'I write to them which heretofore have sinned' (τοῖς προημαρτηκόσιν).

Hereunto: Ec 2²⁵ ' For who else can eat, or who else can hasten hereunto, more than I ?' (חוּץ, RV ' have enjoyment,' RVm ' hasten thereto '; LXX πίεται ; Vulg. ' deliciis affluet '; Gen. ' colde haste to outward things' (taking חוּץ so), with marg. note to ' outward things,' *meaning to pleasures*) ; 1 P 2²¹ ' For even hereunto were ye called ' (εἰς τοῦτο).

Herewith, only Ezk 16²⁹, Mal 3¹⁰, both as trⁿ of בְּזֹאת ' with this.' RV adds Lv 16³ (same Heb., AV ' thus ').

                   J. HASTINGS.

HERES (חַר־חֶרֶם).—**1.** A mountain named along with Aijalon and Shaalbim as one of the localities from which the Danites failed to expel the Amorites, Jg 1³⁴f. As the word ḥereṣ=shemesh, ' the sun,' it is very probable * that the Heres here referred to may be Beth-shemesh (1 K 4⁹, 2 Ch 28¹⁸) or Ir-shemesh (Jos 19⁴¹), on the boundary between Judah and Dan. This is the modern 'Ain Shems to the S. of Wady Ẕurar, opposite Ẕur'ah (Zoar). The LXX (A) has ἐν τῷ ὄρει τοῦ Μυρσινῶνος, which implies a reading, תַר־חֶרֶם=' mountain of the myrtle grove.'

LITERATURE.—Robinson, *BRP* ii. 224 f. ; Guérin, *Judée*, ii. 18–22 ; Moore on Jg 1³⁵ ; *Oxf. Heb. Lex.* and Siegfried-Stade, s. חֶרֶם.

2. In Jg 8¹³ (RV) ' the ascent of Heres' (מַעֲלֵה הֶחָרֶם) is mentioned as the spot from which Gideon returned after the defeat of Zebah and Zalmunna. Both the topography and the text of the narrative are doubtful. RV has the support of LXX A, ἀπὸ ἀναβάσεως Ἀρες. B reads ἀπὸ ἐπάνωθεν [τῆς παρατάξεως] † Ἀρες. Aq. and Symm. read הֶהָרִים ' the mountains,' and this is adopted by Siegfried-Stade. AV takes ḥereṣ as an appellative and tr. ' before the sun was up '; Targ. Rashi ' before the sun set.' Both these last renderings are pronounced by Moore to be impossible (see his note).

The same word ḥereṣ appears in the proper name **Timnath-heres** (wh. see), Jg 2⁹ ; but by an intentional metathesis, to avoid anything that savoured of idolatry, *Timnath-heres*=' portion of the sun,' appears to have been changed into **Timnath-ṣerah,** Jos 19⁵⁰ 24³⁰.

For עִיר הַחֶרֶם of Is 19¹⁸ see IR-HA-HERES.

                   J. A. SELBIE.

HERESH (חֶרֶשׁ).—A Levite, 1 Ch 9¹⁵. See GENE-ALOGY.

HERESY (αἵρεσις, *hæresis, secta* ; in LXX only for ' free choice,' cf. βούλησις, Hesych.).—Αἵρ. in the common sense of ' heresy ' never occurs in NT. Here its dominant meaning is ' sect ' or ' party ' (τὸ αἱρεῖσθαι τὸ ἴδιον καὶ τούτῳ ἐξακολουθεῖν, Ath. Quæst. 38 de Parab.). In later classical usage it is the usual word for a philosophic school or sect, as selected by its adherents (see Diog. Laert. i. 19 f., etc., *e.g.* αἵρ. λέγομεν τὴν λόγῳ τινι ἀκολουθοῦσαν) ; in Philo it often stands for προαίρεσις=*religio* ; and in NT its use is of *a religious party* (as in Jos.), with a more or less deprecatory suggestion, as of the self-willed or sectarian spirit. So always in Ac, whether of the Sad. (5¹⁷), the Phar. (15⁵ 26⁵ Φ.), or the Christians, as seen from outside (24⁵ πρωτοστάτην τῆς τῶν Ναζωραίων αἵρ. ; 24¹⁴ κατὰ τὴν ὁδὸν ἣν λέγουσιν αἵρ.—an excellent instance ; 28²², the Christian sect πανταχοῦ ἀντιλέγεται). In the Pauline Epistles the like clearly prevails. In Gal 5²⁰ it occurs in a list of ἔργα τῆς σαρκός, a manifestation of the unchastened self-assertive or egoistic principle (cf. 1 Co 3³·⁴) ; its immediate neighbours bring ' caballings' (ἐριθεῖαι) and divisions (διχοστασίαι), while itself denotes partisanship (cf. Ro 16¹⁷). This was a special vice of the

* So Studer, Bertheau, Keil, Budde, and others.
† The words in brackets are evidently an accidental repetition from the previous clause (see Moore's note).

Greek temper; so that we are not surprised to find St. Paul saying in 1 Co 11¹⁹ that αἵρ. are part of God's providential discipline whereby sterling characters may be brought to light. This principle is given as the ground of his own attitude to the news that dissensions or ' schisms' (σχίσματα) exist in the Christian body at Corinth. It is probable, then, that αἵρ. are here practically synonymous with σχ., the latter term being fixed by the context to practical negations of sympathy and fellowship, especially as between rich and poor (taking outward effect at the Feast of Love itself). Coteries were formed, and the corporate unity vanished (αἵρ. ἐνταῦθα οὐ ταύτας λέγει τὰς δογμάτων ἀλλὰ τὰς τῶν σχ., Chrys. *Hom. ad loc.* ; so Theodoret, Theophyl. etc., *ap.* Suicer. To a later mode of thought belongs Aug.'s definition, *hæresis autem schisma inveteratum*). So far we have no reason to connect αἵρ. (or even σχίσματα, *pace* 1 Co 1¹⁰), where alienation in sentiment, arising out of intellectual contentions (ἔριδες) of secondary import, is in question, cf. 12²⁵, Jn 7⁴³ 9¹⁶ 10¹⁹) with serious doctrinal divergences in the Church, but rather with breaches in the harmony of love. It means a factious division, or the spirit that underlies it. And this is probably the shade of meaning attaching to the adjective αἱρετικός, ' factious,' or self-willed, in Tit 3¹⁰ (cf. Ro 16¹⁷). A twofold development, however, is found in the use in 2 P 2¹, where αἵρ. ἀπωλείας are spoken of as being illicitly introduced. Here the qualifying gen. (=' leading to ruin,' cf. Ph 3¹⁹) and the verb alike suggest the new sense of *falsely chosen* or erroneous *tenets*. Already the emphasis is moving from persons and their temper to mental products, —from the sphere of sympathetic love to that of objective truth. But one change more remains to be made ere the biblical use passes wholly into the patristic and ecclesiastical. For the nature of the erroneous doctrine is here directly immoral (cf. Jude ⁴) ; and so αἵρ. preserves part of the ethical connotation which is essential to its NT usage. The earliest case of its meaning pure theological error is also its earliest occurrence outside the NT, viz. Ign. *ad Trall.* 6, ἀλλοτρίας δὲ βοτάνης (=Docetism) ἀπέχεσθε, ἥτις ἐστιν αἵρεσις, cf. *ad Eph.* 6. And in proportion as the conception of ' faith,' and the standard for testing it, became intellectual, the original sense of αἵρ., as a light and irresponsible exercise of native egoism in defiance of the claims of love, receded into the background (cf. Tert. *De præsc. hær.* 6, ' Quarum opera sunt adulteræ doctrinæ, hæreses dictæ Græca voce *ex interpretatione electionis*, qua quis sive ad instituendas sive ad suscipiendas usitur '). Finally, neither σχ. nor αἵρ. in the NT ever denotes a party that has withdrawn from the religious communion amid which it arose. In Judaism the co-existence of the Pharisees, Sadducees, and Essenes was not deprecated. In the more intimate unity of each Christian *ecclesia* ' rents' or ' factions' were felt to impair directly the vital functions of the local body in its κοινωνία of love, and so assumed a moral significance. Separate Christian communions, and the applicability to them of the terms σχ. and αἵρ., were problems of the future.

LITERATURE.—Schleusner, *Lex. NT* ; Suicer, *Thes. Eccl.* Comm. *ad loc.* ; Burton, *Bamp. Lect.* 1829, and esp. Campbell, *The Four Gospels*, vol. i. Diss. ix. § iv.

                   J. V. BARTLET.

HERETH (חֶרֶת).—A forest (יַעַר) which was one of the hiding-places of David, 1 S 22⁵. The LXX, reading עִיר instead of יַעַר, has ἐν πόλει Σαρείκ (B) . . . Ἀριαθ (A). The reference may be to the wooded mountain E. of Adullam, where the village of *Kharâs* now stands. See *SWP* vol. iii. sh. xxi.

                   C. R. CONDER.

HERITAGE is used in AV (and retained in RV

except in 1 P 5³ 'the charge allotted to you' for AV 'God's heritage,'* Gr. οἱ κλῆροι) as a synonym for 'inheritance,' which has now displaced it except in biblical language and Scots law. See HEIR, INHERITANCE.

HERMAS ('Ερμᾶς), one of those saluted by St. Paul in Ro 16¹⁴. The name is common amongst slaves (although not quite so much as Hermes). It was in its origin an abbreviated form of various names such as Hermagoras, Hermodorus, Hermogenes. He is commemorated in the Roman Calendar on May 9. According to the *Menologium Basilianum*, Nov. 4, he became Bishop of Philippopolis in Thrace.

The name Hermas is also well known as that of the author, or at any rate the professed author, of the Pastor or Shepherd, a well-known allegorical work, belonging to an early period of Christian literature, which for a time made some claims to be inserted in the NEW TESTAMENT CANON (which see). This book need only be referred to here, because from time to time its author has been identified with the Hermes mentioned in Ro 16¹⁴. Origen, in his commentary on this passage, writes : 'I think that this Hermas is the author of the book called the Pastor, which appears to me a very useful writing (*scriptum* is not technical), and, I think, divinely inspired.' Origen's statement is a pure conjecture, based apparently only on the identity of name. His opinion was followed by others, but was never widespread, as the book became less and less popular ; in later times it has been held by Cotelier, Cave, Pearson, and others. There is little to be said for it. The name was about as common as John is with us, and gives no clue at all ; the date of the book may be doubtful, but its tone is certainly not that of the 1st cent. ; the author never claims in any way to be a contemporary of the apostles, and very definite historical evidence places him a little before the middle of the 2nd cent. This is not the place to pursue the subject further, but for the benefit of those unacquainted with the book it may be stated that it consists of a series of Visions, Parables or Similitudes, and Mandates or Commands, conveying for the most part moral teaching, and has been called —not perhaps very happily—the Pilgrim's Progress of the Early Church. A further account may be found in *Dict. Chr. Biog.*, and a text and translation in Lightfoot's *Apostolic Fathers*.

A. C. HEADLAM.

HERMES ('Ερμῆς).—The name of a Christian, quoted with some others in Ro 16¹⁴. It is one of the commonest of all slave names. The Greek *Menaea* and *Menologium* make him Bishop of Salona in Dalmatia, and one of the Seventy disciples. He was commemorated April 8.

A. C. HEADLAM.

HERMOGENES ('Ερμογένης) is mentioned by St. Paul (2 Ti 1¹⁵) as having, along with Phygelus and others in Asia, and in contrast to Onesiphorus, been ashamed of his chain. It is impossible now to say what form the denial took, or what led to it. Most likely it was caused by fear lest friendship with the imprisoned apostle might involve him in the same fate. Early traditions, of no historical value, however, associated him with magicians. Nothing is known of H. except what is stated by St. Paul, that he was of those in Asia who turned away. It is not easy to decide what is meant by those 'in Asia.' It has been variously held to mean, all Asiatics then in Rome, the Ephesians who had accompanied St. Paul to Rome,

public opinion in Asia Minor, and the Asiatic sentiment in Rome. See PHYGELUS.

W. MUIR.

HERMON (חֶרְמוֹן, 'sacred [mountain]' ; cf. Sab. מחרם 'temple,' Arab. *ḥaram*, 'sacred enclosure,' and *ḥormah*, 'asylum').—The great outlier of Antilebanon, at the springs of Jordan. See PALESTINE. It was called *Sirion* by the Zidonians, and *Senir* by the Amorites (Dt 3⁹). The first of these names is used poetically in Ps 29⁶. *Senir* occurs also in Ezk 27⁵, Ca 4⁸, 1 Ch 5²³. Perhaps it may be inferred from the latter two passages (where it is used along with Hermon) that *Senir* originally denoted a particular part of the mountain-range (so Driver, Buhl, etc.). The name appears in the cuneiform texts as *Saniru* (Schrader, *KAT*² 159 [*COT*² 146]), and the Anti-lebanon N. of Damascus between Baalbek and Emesa is still called *Sanir* by the Arabs. Sayce (*RP*² vi. 41, *HCM* 341) traces a knowledge of the name *Senir* also to the Egyptians. In Dt 4⁴⁸ another name, *Sion* (שִׂיאֹן), is given to Hermon. It is held by some that *Sion* is here a textual error for *Sirion* (שִׂרְיֹן, the reading of Syr.), but this is doubtful (see Driver, *ad loc.*). 'Mount Hermon' (הַר חֶרְמוֹן) is used in Dt 3⁸, Jos 11¹⁷ 12¹·⁵ 13⁵·¹¹, 1 Ch 5²³, 'Hermon' alone in Jos 11³, Ps 89¹² 133³, Ca 4⁸. The circumstance that the mountain has three peaks accounts for the plur. form חֶרְמוֹנִים 'the Hermons' (RV ; not 'the **Hermonites**,' AV) in Ps 42⁶.

Hermon was held by Hivites (Jos 11³); it was the northern limit of conquest (12¹·⁵ 13⁵·¹¹). Its sacred character appears from Ps 89¹² (where it is coupled with Tabor), and from the name Mount **Baal-hermon** (Jg 3³), 'the mountain of the Baal of Hermon.' Cf. 1 Ch 5²³. The dew of Hermon is noted as falling on Zion (Ps 133³), and its wild character is noticed in Ca 4⁸. The fir trees of Senir are mentioned in Ezk 27⁵.

Mount Hermon is the most conspicuous feature in the scenery of Palestine, rising 9200 ft. above the Mediterranean in a dome-like summit, usually covered with snow till late in summer. There are three low peaks on the top, with a connecting plateau. Lower down, the sides are covered with vineyards round the Druze villages. On the sandstones to the west there are still pines and firs, but the upper part is quite barren, and covered with snow-worn gravel between the cliffs. This mountain is the only place where the Syrian bear is known to exist. The view from the top is magnificent, including the Lebanon and the plain round Damascus. Towards the west Tyre and Carmel are seen, on the south the mountains of Upper Galilee and the plains of Lower Galilee. The Hûleh lake and the Sea of Galilee lie beneath as on a map. This view is, however, obscured in summer by the sudden formation of clouds on the summit.

Hermon was perhaps the 'high mountain' of Mt 17¹, Mk 9² ('the mountain' of Lk 9²⁸) near Cæsarea Philippi, which was the scene of the Transfiguration and of the cloud which covered the disciples. In the Roman period it was a sacred centre, and small temples were built on the slopes on every side, while the highest point was encircled with a masonry wall, and seems to have supported an altar. Close by is a rock-cut chamber on the plateau. In the 4th cent. A.D. (see *Onomast. s.* 'Aermon') there was still a temple at which the people of Paneas and Lebanon worshipped, on the summit of Hermon. In the 10th cent. it became the centre of the Druze religion, and to it Sheikh ed-Derâzi, the founder of the latter creed, retired from Egypt. At Hasbeya, on its western slopes, the sacred books of the sect were found by the French in 1860. Hermon is called *Jebel esh-Sheikh*, or 'mountain of the chief,' for this reason,

---

* In Job 31² on the other hand, 'heritage' of RV takes the place of 'inheritance' in AV ; the Heb. is the usual word חֵלֶק.

being the residence of the religious Sheikh of the Druzes. The translation sometimes suggested, ' chief of mountains,' is grammatically impossible. Hermon was visited by the present writer in 1873 (when the height and geographical position were determined) and in 1882.

LITERATURE.—*SWP* (Jerusalem volume, Appendix, and Volume of Special Papers); Robinson, *BRP* iii. 357; Baedeker-Socin, *Pal²* 301; Conder, *Tent - Work*, ch. viii.; Buhl, *GAP* 110; Neubauer, *Géog. du Talm.* 10, 39; Delitzsch, *Paradies*, 104; Wetzstein, *ZKW* v. (1884) 115; W. R. Smith, *RS¹* 93, 145; Merrill, *East of Jordan*, 431; Halévy, *REJ* xx. 206; *ZDPV* iv. 87, vi. 6; *ZDMG* xix. 176, 252; Driver on Dt 3⁹ and 4⁴⁸; Moore on Jg 3³.   C. R. CONDER.

HERMONITES (Ps 42⁶, AV).—See HERMON.

HEROD (DYNASTY OF).—
    i. Index to Names of Family.
    ii. Genealogical Table.
    iii. Chronological Table.
    iv. Origin of Dynasty.
    v. Herod the Great.
    vi. Successors of Herod.
      (1) Archelaus.
      (2) Herod Antipas.
      (3) Philip.
      (4) Herod, called Philip.
      (5) Agrippa I.
      (6) Agrippa II.
    vii. Women of the Family.
      (1) Herodias.
      (2) Salome.
      (3) Bernice.
      (4) Drusila.
    viii. Character of Dynasty.
      Literature.

i. INDEX OF HEROD FAMILY. — In this index every member of the family mentioned in Josephus is recorded. The numbers refer to the genealogical table. The names that occur in NT are printed in clarendon capitals.

AGRIPPA I. (49), son of Aristobulus, grandson of Herod, king of Judæa; m. Cypros, dtr. of Phasael. *Ant.* XVIII. v. 4, XIX. ix. 1; *BJ* II. xi. 6; Ac 12

AGRIPPA II. (66), son of Agrippa I. *Ant.* XVIII. v. 4, XIX. ix. 1; *BJ* II. xi. 6; Ac 25. 26.

Agrippa (64), son of Aristobulus and Salome. *Ant.* XVIII. v. 4.

Agrippa (73), son of Felix and Drusilla. *Ant.* XX. vii. 2.

Agrippinos (78), dtr. of Mariamne, dtr. of Agrippa I. and Demetrius. *Ant.* XX. vii. 3.

Alexander (23), son of Herod by Mariamne I.; m. Glaphyra, dtr. of Archelaus, king of Cappadocia; put to death by his father in B.C. 7. *Ant.* XVIII. v. 4, XVI. i. 2, XVI. vi. 6.

Alexander (42), son of Phasael and Salampsio. *Ant.* XVIII. v. 4.

Alexander (51), son of Alexander, grandson of Herod. *Ant.* XVIII. v. 4.

Alexander (80), son of Tigranes (61). *Ant.* XVIII. v. 4.

Alexandra (43), dtr. of Phasael and Salampsio. *Ant.* XVIII. v. 4.

Alexas (19), 3rd husband of Salome, Herod's sister. *Ant.* XVII. i. 1.

Alexis Selcias (54), son of Alexas (19); it is not stated whether by Salome or not. *Ant.* XVIII. v. 4.

Antipas or Antipater (1), governor of Idumæa, grandfather of Herod. *Ant.* XIV. i. 3.

ANTIPAS (27), son of Herod and Malthace; tetrarch of Galilee, m. (1) dtr. of Aretas, (2) Herodias. *BJ* I. xxviii. 4; *Ant.* XVII. i. 3, XVIII. v. 4; Mt 14¹⁻⁶, Mk 6¹⁴ 13²¹ 237-15, Lk3¹· 19 87. 9.

Antipater (2), minister of Hyrcanus, father of Herod. *Ant.* XIV. i. 3, XIV. vii. 3.

Antipater (21), eldest son of Herod by Doris; m. a daughter of Antigonus, the last of the Hasmonæans; put to death by his father B.C. 4. *BJ* I. xxviii. 4; *Ant.* XIV. xii. 1, XVII. v. 2.

Antipater (36), son of Salome, Herod's sister; m. Cypros, dtr. of Herod and Mariamne. His father's name is not mentioned. *Ant.* XVII. ix. 5, XVIII. v. 4.

Antipater (40), son of Phasael and Salampsio. There seems to be some confusion between this Antipater and the son of Salome (36). *Ant.* XVIII. v. 4.

ARCHELAUS (28), son of Herod by Malthace, ethnarch of Judæa; m. (1) Mariamne, (2) Glaphyra, his brother Alexander's widow. *Ant.* XVII. i. 3; Mt 2²².

Archelaus (76), son of Chelcias, 1st husband of Mariamne, dtr. of Agrippa. *Ant.* XIX. ix. 1.

Aristobulus (22), son of Herod by Mariamne I.; m. Bernice, dtr. of Salome and Costobar; put to death by Herod B.C. 7. *Ant.* XVI. i. 2, XVII. i. 2, XVIII. v. 4.

ARISTOBULUS (47), son of Aristobulus (22), grandson of Herod; m. Jotape, dtr. of Sampsigeramus, king of Emesa. *Ant.* XVIII. v. 4. See under ARISTOBULUS for the supposed ref. to him Ro 16¹⁰.

Aristobulus (57), son of Herod of Chalcis, great-grandson of Herod, king of Armenia Minor; m. Salome, dtr. of Herodias. *Ant.* XVIII. v. 4.

Aristobulus (65), son of Aristobulus (57) and Salome. *Ant.* XVIII. v. 4.

Azizus (71), king of Emesa, husband of Drusilla. *Ant.* XX. vii. 1.

Bernice (37), dtr. of Salome and Costobar; m. Aristobulus, son of Mariamne I., mother of Agrippa I. *Ant.* XVIII. v. 4.

BERNICE (68), dtr. of Agrippa I.; m. (1) Herod of Chalcis, (2) Polemon of Cilicia; favourite of Titus. *Ant.* XVIII. v. 4, XIX. ix. 1; *BJ* II. xi. 6; *Ant.* XX. vii. 3; Ac 25¹³. ²³ 26³⁰.

Bernice (79), dtr. of Mariamne (69) and Archelaus (76). *Ant.* XX. vii. 1.

Bernicianus (58), son of Herod of Chalcis and Bernice. *Ant.* XX.v.2.

Cleopatra (14), a woman of Jerusalem, wife of Herod, mother of Philip the tetrarch. *BJ* I. xxviii. 4; *Ant.* XVII. i. 3.

Costobar (18), governor of Idumæa, 2nd husband of Salome, Herod's sister, whom she divorced. *Ant.* XV. vii. 9.

Cypros (3), an Arabian of noble family, wife of Antipater, mother of Herod. *Ant.* XIV. vii. 3.

Cypros (25), dtr. of Herod by Mariamne I.; m. Antipater (36), son of Salome. *Ant.* XVIII. v. 4.

Cypros (45), dtr. of Phasael, wife of Agrippa I., mother of Agrippa II. *Ant.* XVIII. v. 4.

Cypros (53), dtr. of Cypros (25) and Antipater (36), granddaughter of Herod; m. Alexas Selcias. *Ant.* XVIII. v. 4.

Cypros (62), dtr. of Cypros (53) and Alexas. *Ant.* XVIII. v. 4.

Demetrius (77), Alabarch of Alexandria, 2nd husband of Mariamne, dtr. of Agrippa. *Ant.* XX. vii. 3.

Doris (10), 1st wife of Herod, a woman of the people, mother of Antipater. *BJ* I. xxviii. 4; *Ant.* XIV. xii. 1.

DRUSILLA (70), dtr. of Agrippa I.; m. (1) Azizus, king of Emesa, (2) Felix, the Roman procurator. *Ant.* XVIII. v. 4, XIX. ix. 1, XX. vii. 1, 2; *BJ* II. xi. 6; Ac 24²⁴.

Drusus (67), second son of Agrippa I. and Cypros, died in youth. *Ant.* XVIII. v. 4.

Elpis (17), 8th wife of Herod. *BJ* I. xxviii. 4; *Ant.* XVII. i. 3.

FELIX (72), Roman procurator, husband of Drusilla. *Ant.* XX. vii. 1–2; Ac 23, 25.

Glaphyra (38), dtr. of Archelaus of Cappadocia; m. (1) Alexander, son of Mariamne I., by whom she had children; (2) Juba, king of Mauritania; (3) Archelaus. *Ant.* XVI. i. 2, XVII. xiii. 1, 4.

HEROD (6), called THE GREAT, son of Antipater; 8 wives of his are enumerated, and he had 2 others; he had 8 sons and 6 daughters. He died B.C. 4. *Ant.* XIV. vii. 3, XVII. i. 3; *BJ* I. viii. 9, I. xxviii. 4; Mt 2¹⁻²², Lk 1⁵.

HEROD (26), perhaps called PHILIP, son of Herod and Mariamne II.; m. Herodias; father of Salome. *BJ* I. xxviii. 5; *Ant.* XV. ix. 3 XVII. i. 2, XVIII. v. 4; Mt 14³, Mk 6¹⁷, Lk 3¹⁹.

HEROD ANTIPAS. See ANTIPAS (27).

Herod (30), son of Herod and Cleopatra (14). *Ant.* XVII. i. 3.

Herod (41), son of Phasael and Salampsio. *Ant.* XVIII. v. 4.

Herod (46), son of Aristobulus, grandson of Herod, king of Chalcis; m. (1) Mariamne, dtr. of Olympias; (2) Bernice. *Ant.* XVIII. v. 4, XX. v. 2; *BJ* II. xi. 6

Herod (63), son of Aristobulus (57) and Salome. *Ant.* XVIII. v. 4.

HERODIAS (50), dtr. of Aristobulus, granddaughter of Herod; m. (1) her uncle Herod, called Philip; (2) Herod Antipas. *Ant.* XVIII. v. 4; Mt 14³, Mk 6¹⁷, Lk 3¹⁹.

Hyrcanus (59), son of Herod of Chalcis and Bernice. *Ant.* XX. v. 2.

Joseph (4), uncle of Herod, and also, by marriage with Salome, brother-in-law. Appointed ruler during his visit to Antony, and put to death B.C. 34. *Ant.* XV. iii. 5–9.

Joseph (7), brother of Herod, slain in battle by Antigonus. *Ant.* XVII. vii. 3, XV. 10.

Joseph (35), nephew of Herod, son of Joseph (7); m. Olympias, dtr. of Herod and Malthace. *Ant.* XVII. i. 3, XVIII. v. 4.

Jotape (48), dtr. of Sampsigeramus, king of Emesa, wife of Aristobulus, Herod's grandson. *Ant.* XVIII. v. 4.

Jotape (60), dtr. of Aristobulus and Jotape. *BJ* II. xi. 6; *Ant.* XVIII. v. 4.

Jotape (74), dtr. of Aristobulus, king of Commagene; m. Alexander (71), son of Tigranes. *Ant.* XVIII. v. 4.

Malthace (13), a Samaritan woman, wife of Herod, mother of Archelaus. *BJ* I. xxviii. 4; *Ant.* XVII. i. 3.

Mariamne I. (11), granddaughter of Hyrcanus, wife of Herod; put to death by him B.C. 29. *Ant.* XVIII. v. 4; *BJ* I. xii. 3.

Mariamne II. (12), dtr. of Simon the high priest, mother of Herod called perhaps Philip. *BJ* I. xxviii. 4; *Ant.* XV. ix. 3.

Mariamne (39), 1st wife of Archelaus; divorced by him. *Ant.* XVII. xiii. 4.

Mariamne (56), dtr. of Joseph and Olympias; m. Herod, king of Chalcis. *Ant.* XVIII. v. 4.

Mariamne (69), dtr. of Agrippa I. and Cypros; m. (1) Archelaus, (2) Demetrius. *Ant.* XVIII. v. 4.

Olympias (29), dtr. of Herod and Malthace; m. Joseph, Herod's nephew. *Ant.* XVII. i. 3.

Pallas (15), 6th wife of Herod. *BJ* I. xviii. 4; *Ant.* XVII. i. 3.

Phaedra (16), 7th wife of Herod. *BJ* I. xxviii. 4; *Ant.* XVII. i. 3.

Phasael (5), eldest brother of Herod. *Ant.* XIV. vii. 3, XIII. 10.

Phasael (20), son of Phasael (5), nephew of Herod; m. Salampsio, dtr. of Herod and Mariamne. *Ant.* XVIII. v. 4.

ii. GENEALOGY OF THE HEROD DYNASTY.

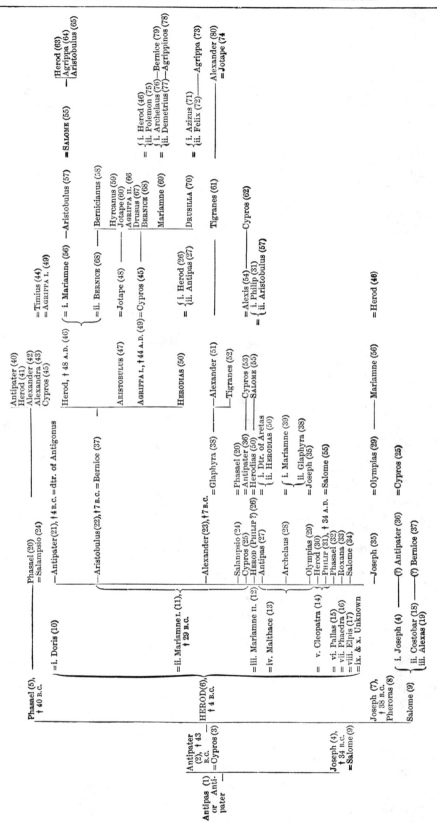

NOTE.—1. Each generation is confined to a single column.
2. The numbers as far as possible go consecutively down the columns.

Phasael (32), son of Herod and Pallas. *Ant.* XVII. i. 3.

Pheroras (8), brother of Herod. *Ant.* XVII. i. 3.

PHILIP. See HEROD (26).

PHILIP (31), son of Herod by Cleopatra; tetrarch of Trachonitis, etc.; m Salome, dtr. of Herodias. *Ant.* XVII. i. 3, XVIII. v. 4; Lk 3¹.

Polemon (75), king of Cilicia, 2nd husband of Bernice. *Ant.* XX. vii. 3.

Roxana (33), dtr. of Herod by Phaedra. *Ant.* XVII. i. 3.

Salampsio (24), dtr. of Herod by Mariamne I.; m. Phasael, Herod's nephew. *Ant.* XVIII. v. 4.

Salome (9), sister of Herod. *Ant.* XIV. vii. 3; *BJ* I. viii. 9.

Salome (34), dtr. of Herod by Elpis. *Ant.* XVII. i. 3.

SALOME (55), dtr. of Herodias by her first husband Herod (Philip); m. (1) Philip the tetrarch, (2) Aristobulus, son of Herod of Chalcis. *Ant.* XVIII. v. 4; Mt 14⁶, Mk 6²².

Tigranes (52), son of Alexander and Glaphyra, grandson of Herod; sent as king to Armenia. *Ant.* XVIII. v. 4; Tac. *Ann.* vi. 10.

Tigranes (61), son of Alexander (51), great-grandson of Herod; sent as king to Armenia. *Ant.* XVIII. v. 4; Tac. *Ann.* xiv. 26, xv. 1.

Timius (44) of Cypros; m. Alexandra (43), dtr. of Phasael, and had no children. *Ant.* XVIII. v. 4.

iii. CHRONOLOGY OF THE HEROD DYNASTY.—

B.C.

69. Death of Alexandra. Accession of Aristobulus II. ANTIPATER, father of Herod, first becomes of importance.

63. Capture of Jerusalem by Pompey. Aristobulus deposed. Hyrcanus II., high priest, without the title of king.

54. Crassus robs the temple.

47. Cæsar arranges Syria.
Hyrcanus receives the title of ethnarch.
HEROD governor of Galilee.
PHASAEL governor of Jerusalem.

44–42. Cassius in Syria.

43. Death of ANTIPATER.

41. Antony in Syria. HEROD and PHASAEL named tetrarchs.

40. Parthian invasion. Death of PHASAEL. Mutilation of Hyrcanus. Flight of HEROD. Antigonus assumes the title of king and high priest.
HEROD given the title of king of Judæa by Antony and Octavius.

37. Marriage of HEROD and Mariamne.
Capture of Jerusalem. Death of Antigonus.

35. Death of Aristobulus III.

34. Death of Joseph, Salome's husband.
Visit of Cleopatra.

31. Battle of Actium. Herod joins the party of Augustus.

30. Death of Hyrcanus II. Augustus in Syria. Extension of Herod's power.

29. Death of Mariamne.

28. Death of Alexandra.

25. Death of Costobar. Also of the sons of Babas.
Institution of games. Building of a theatre and amphitheatre in Jerusalem.

20. The building of the temple begun.

15. Visit of Agrippa to Jerusalem.

14. Beginning of dissensions at court concerning Alexander and Aristobulus.

12. Visit of Herod to Rome with his two sons.

7. Death of Alexander and Aristobulus.

6. Antipater goes to Rome. Herod's first will.

5. Imprisonment of Antipater. Herod's second will.

4. Outbreak under the Rabbis Judas and Matthias.
Antipater executed.
Herod's third will.
DEATH OF HEROD THE GREAT.
ARCHELAUS becomes ethnarch of Judæa,
ANTIPAS tetrarch of Galilee, and
PHILIP of Trachonitis.

A.D.

6. ARCHELAUS deposed. Judæa under Roman procurators.

34. Death of PHILIP.

37. AGRIPPA becomes tetrarch of Trachonitis.

39. Banishment of ANTIPAS.
AGRIPPA receives his tetrarchy.

41. AGRIPPA becomes king of Judæa.

44. DEATH OF AGRIPPA I. Judæa again under Roman procurators.

50. AGRIPPA II. becomes tetrarch of Chalcis.

53. He receives in addition the tetrarchies of Philip and Lysander (Abila), and, a little later, part of Galilee.

70. Destruction of Jerusalem.

100. Death of AGRIPPA II.

iv. ORIGIN OF THE DYNASTY OF THE HERODS.

—The dynasty of the Herods rose into prominence during the confusion which resulted from the decay of the Hasmonæan dynasty, the transference of Syria and Palestine to the sway of the Romans, and the civil wars which marked the decay of the Republic. Their ancestor was Antipater or Antipas, a man of wealth and capacity whom Alexander Jannæus had made governor of Idumæa. So much is clear, but of the origin of the family there are very contradictory accounts. Nicolaus of Damascus said, according to Josephus (*Ant.* XIV. i. 3), that he was of the stock of the Jews who first came back from Babylon. This appears to have been a fiction invented for the benefit of Herod. Josephus evidently looked upon him as an Idumæan; as such he was considered half a Jew. But Pharisaic and perhaps Christian hatred was not satisfied with this. He is stated by Justin to have been a native of Ashkelon (*Dial.* c. 52), and therefore of the hated Philistine race; while Julius Africanus (*ap.* Eus. *HE* I. vii. 11) improves the story by telling us that some Idumæan robbers had attacked Ashkelon and carried away the father of Antipater, who was the son of one of the temple slaves; the priest of the temple was not able to ransom him, and so he was brought up as an Idumæan; this story Africanus had from the kinsmen of the Saviour. Whatever was the origin of the family, its ability is undoubted. Antipater's son, who bore the same name as himself, first appears in history on the death of Alexandra, the Maccabæan queen, in 69. Her eldest son, Hyrcanus II., a man of a peaceful and quiet disposition, allowed himself to be set aside by his younger brother, Aristobulus II., a man of very different character. Antipater, who had been building up for himself a strong position in Idumæa by allying himself with the Arabs at Petra and the Philistine cities, saw his opportunity; under Aristobulus he would be nobody, under Hyrcanus he would rule the country. He attached himself to Hyrcanus, persuaded him not to submit to his younger brother, and, so far as we know, remained absolutely faithful to him the whole of his life, quite content to have the reality of power, and too wise or too loyal to endanger his position by arousing dynastic hatred. At first he attempted to restore Hyrcanus with the assistance of Aretas, king of the Nabatæan Arabs, —(his wife Cypros belonged to one of the noblest families of that country),—but before the war was concluded a new power appeared on the scene. In 66 Pompey had defeated Mithridates, and was now pursuing his first march through Asia. On his approach all the rival parties of every state and country attempted to gain him to their side. Aristobulus, Antipater on behalf of Hyrcanus, and the Pharisaic party who wished to restore the theocracy, rivalled one another in bribes, complaints, and promises. Pompey was, as always, deliberate, and it soon became apparent that Aristobulus was too proud to submit, too faithless to be an ally, and too powerless to restrain the people from rebellion. When the Romans approached Jerusalem, the party of Hyrcanus delivered the city over without a blow; the war party with Aristobulus retired to the temple fortress. A siege followed, in which the defenders exhibited the fanatical courage which the Jews always have shown when their cause is hopeless, and observed the law so strictly that they refused to destroy their enemies' works on the Sabbath day. The city was taken by assault in the autumn of 63, about the fast of the Atonement, and the priests continued to offer the sacrifices in the midst of the battle and were cut down at the altar. Pompey violated the Holy of Holies, but did not plunder the wealth of the temple. Aristobulus and his family were carried captive, and the priest-king of the Jews had to adorn a Roman triumph. The kingdom was reduced in size, the Greek towns were freed, but the hierarchy was untouched. Hyrcanus was made high priest without the title of king, and Antipater became the most important person in the country. This was the first instance in which Antipater showed the marvellous power his family possessed of securing the support of every successive Roman of distinction. Historians generally ascribe it to their capacity for bribing, and this they undoubtedly possessed. Moreover, they had the wisdom to know that bribes must be large. But that was not enough. They were distinguished by being always faithful to the Romans, always competent, and always agreeable. To attach themselves to each successive Roman who became powerful, to spare nothing in his support, and to add to the services they had rendered an agreeable private friendship, was the secret of their success.

The next twenty years gave many proofs of this. Antipater helped Scaurus in an expedition against Aretas, and persuaded Aretas to submit. He made the acquaintance and even the friendship of Mark Antony. He assisted Gabinius in a war with Archelaus with corn and weapons and money, and Gabinius settled the affairs of Jerusalem as Antipater wished (*Ant.* XIV. vi. 4). When Cæsar was in Egypt after the battle of Pharsalia, Antipater saved him when he was in great danger. Cæsar, in return for this and many other services, confirmed Hyrcanus in the high priesthood, and made Antipater a Roman citizen. Afterwards he made Hyrcanus ethnarch, Antipater procurator, and allowed the walls of Jerusalem to be rebuilt, while he conferred privileges on the Jewish race everywhere. When Cassius, after the death of Cæsar, came to Syria to collect money and show how hateful the cause of the Republic could be, Antipater and his sons had the wisdom to provide him with all he required, thus saving their cities from slavery. Antipater was murdered in the year B.C. 43 by a certain Malichos. 'He was distinguished,' says Josephus, 'for piety and justice and love of his country.' His eldest son Phasael had been made governor of Jerusalem, his second son Herod governor of Galilee. The latter had already shown the energy and the brilliant military capacity for which he was afterwards distinguished. When Antony came to Syria after the battle of Philippi, Herod exhibited all the address of his father by securing his friendship; he and his brother were made tetrarchs, and many members of the Pharisaic party, who persisted in bringing accusations against them, were put to death.

During all these twenty years of Antipater's rule, the younger branch of the Hasmonæan family, Aristobulus and his sons, had persisted in disturbing the country. They had clearly a considerable body of supporters, and it seems almost as if the Romans had allowed them to exist in order to prevent the country from becoming too strong. In the year 40 a Parthian invasion gave Antigonus, the last survivor of the family, his opportunity. He succeeded in getting possession of the persons of Hyrcanus and Phasael; the former he mutilated, the latter put himself to death; Herod only just escaped with his female relations to the fortress of Masada, and Antigonus had a troubled reign of three years. But Herod was not to be daunted; he fled to Rome, explained how Antigonus had allied himself with the Parthians, and much to his own surprise—for he had only hoped that the younger Aristobulus, his own brother-in-law, might become ruler—was made king of Judæa by Antony, Octavius, and the senate. It took him, however, three years to win the kingdom that had been given him, and it was only in the autumn of 37 that he succeeded in taking Jerusalem, and brought the Hasmonæan dynasty to an end.

v. REIGN OF HEROD THE GREAT, B.C. 37-4.— 'C'était, en somme, une fort belle bête, un lion à qui on ne tient compte que de sa large encolure, et de son épaisse crinière, sans lui demander le sens moral.' So writes Renan; yet the character of Herod is not so easy to sum up, for to be a successful tyrant a certain minimum of morality is required, and that Herod, at any rate until the end of his life, possessed. Nor can we be certain of our information. His reign was a deliberate violation of all the religious instincts of the people, and the friends of the Hasmonæans and the Pharisees were equally interested in putting the worst construction on his acts. Josephus himself prided himself on his priestly family and connexions, yet he is not altogether unfair; much of his information came from Nicolaus of Damascus, who had written an apologetic account of his royal patron, and he suggests that many of the crimes of Herod were the necessity of his position. Physically, Herod was magnificent in his beauty and strength, and these qualities were not more conspicuous than his skill in war. He was clever, able, but unscrupulous and ambitious. He was munificent to his friends, capable of being magnanimous even to his enemies, *e.g.* to Shemaia, but absolutely unscrupulous when necessity seemed to demand it. How far he attempted to gain the kingdom we cannot say: when he received it he accepted the position without hesitation, and allowed nothing to check his ambition. Yet he was a good ruler up to a certain point, and knew well how to manage the Jews. He suppressed insurrection with absolute severity, yet he never indulged in religious persecution. He was munificent to the people: when famine came, he stripped his palace of gold and silver to buy corn. Whatever his feelings towards the Jews, he was always a good friend to them, and used his influence with Augustus to obtain privileges for them in various parts of the world. Although he was probably absolutely irreligious, he respected the Jewish religion so far as to demand that Sylläus, the Arabian, who wished to marry Herod's sister, Salome, should adopt the Jewish customs (*Ant.* XVI. vii. 6), refrain from any images or statues in the buildings he put up within Jewish territory, and put no effigy on his coins. He had the strong lusts and passions of an Oriental; the position of a tyrant and usurper surrounded him with plots, suspicions, and intrigues. As he grew older his cruelty and suspiciousness increased, and the misery of his old age seemed to be a judgment on the crimes of his life. There has been some discussion whether he deserved the title of Great. The fact that his life and works left no permanent results, that his house was built on the sand, may make us hesitate to give it him. But, taken in his person and in his career, he was one of the most conspicuous and interesting figures of his time. If he was not great, he had almost all the qualities which might have made him so.

The reign of Herod is divided by most historians into three periods. The first from 37-25, the period during which he consolidated his power. The second from 25-13, the period of his greatest prosperity. The third from 13 to his death B.C. 4, the period of family feuds.

(1) *Consolidation of Herod's power*, 37-25.—When Herod and the Romans captured the city, he did his best to restrain the butchery of the people and the plunder of the temple, and his vengeance on his enemies was possibly not greater than the necessities of the position demanded. He obtained from Antony the death of Antigonus, put to death forty-five of the principal men of his party, and replenished his coffers from their property; but Pollio and Sameas (Abtalion and Shemaia), the two leading Pharisees, he treated with great respect, and seems to have succeeded in making all but the most extreme section of the party acquiesce in his rule, as a judgment of God which had to be borne.

Shortly before the siege of Jerusalem, Herod had married Mariamne, granddaughter of Hyrcanus, to whom he was violently attached. He had hoped by this alliance with the old dynasty to strengthen his position, but he only succeeded in introducing dissension into his own family. Mariamne and her mother, Alexandra, who seems to have been a violent and unscrupulous woman, treated Herod's sister, Salome, and his mother, Cypros, with the most absolute contempt as low-born foreigners. Salome retaliated by raising Herod's jealousy, and accusing Alexandra and her family of disloyalty and conspiracy. As far as Alexandra is concerned the accusations were un-doubtedly true, in other cases they were more doubt-ful. At any rate, first Aristobulus, the younger brother of Mariamne, who had been made high priest, and whose only crime was that he was too popular, was put to death; then the aged Hyrcanus, who had returned from Babylon at Herod's invita-tion, and had always been absolutely subservient to his Idumæan subjects; then Mariamne, his wife, of whom he was passionately fond, and whose death caused him infinite misery; last of all, Alexandra herself, the cause of all the misery, who during Herod's illness began secretly to rebel against him, and during all this time had been engaged in con-stant intrigues. The last victims to Herod's sus-picions and severity were Costobar, governor of Idumæa, for a time Salome's husband, and some other mysterious persons, the sons of Babas, who seem to have been adherents of the Hasmonæan party. By the year 25 every possible rival had been removed; Salome's spite had been gratified; and Herod's position had been secured by the sacrifice of his passion or affection.

During the same time he was employed in consolidating his position with the Romans. He retained the friendship of Antony in spite of the opposition of Cleopatra, who wished to be queen of Jerusalem. Like Augustus, he had the wisdom to resist the temptation of her charms, and he also refrained from putting her to death. He fitted up a force in order to assist Antony at Actium, but had the good fortune to be employed at the time in an expedition against the Arabs. As soon as the victory of Augustus was certain, he went at once to him in accordance with the traditions of his family; he said frankly that he had been a good friend to Antony, and had done every-thing to help him, and he promised to be an equally good friend to him. Augustus accepted his friendship, and confirmed him in his kingdom. Herod on every opportunity was as good as his word. He rendered Augustus very material assist-ance, received various extensions to his kingdom, and the friendship of Augustus, Agrippa, and Herod became proverbial. From this time Herod's position was assured.

(2) *Period of Herod's prosperity*, B.C. 25–13.— Herod was now able to govern as he wished. He was rich, prosperous, and secure, and he devoted him-self to the Hellenizing of his countrymen and the gratification of his taste for magnificence in build-ing. In B.C. 25 he celebrated at Jerusalem the quin-quennial games in honour of Augustus, and built there a theatre, amphitheatre, and a hippodrome. Throughout Palestine a number of new cities were founded, the most important of which was Cæsarea on the seacoast. Here and in other Greek cities he built temples to Augustus. He turned Samaria, which he renamed Sebaste, into a magnificent city; nor did he confine his buildings to his own dominions, his benefits reached as far as Rhodes and Athens. But his greatest work was the reconstruction of the temple. This he began in the year B.C. 20. The more sacred portions were completed in eight years; the building was not

finished until the year A.D. 63, a few years before its final destruction. It was only a partially completed building in the time of our Lord, and existed only eight years after it was finally fin-ished. To the other works must be added palaces, fortresses, parks, and pleasure grounds; and to the other signs of Hellenizing tendency, the Greek writers and teachers whom Herod attracted to his court, the principal of whom was Nicolaus of Damascus, his secretary and biographer.

(3) *Period of domestic troubles*, B.C. 13–4.—It is probable that we are inclined to exaggerate the troubles of Herod's last years, or rather to look at them from the point of view of the last three or four years of his life. Herod was considered a second Solomon, as the great Jewish king, and the rebuilder of the temple; he was, like him, also as a polygamist. The Jews were allowed more than one wife, but it was hardly the fashion at this time to take advantage of the licence to any great extent. Herod had ten altogether—nine at one time. He had eight sons and six daughters. The family troubles arose through the dissensions between the sons of Mariamne, the Hasmonæan, on the one side, Salome his sister and Antipater his eldest son on the other. Alexander and Aristo-bulus had been brought up at Rome; when they returned, their beauty, their popular qualities, and their legitimate descent attracted the atten-tion of the people, and they became the centre for numerous intrigues and an object which fanati-cism could put before itself. We need not follow the course of the intrigues. They nearly involved Herod in difficulties with the Roman government. They led Augustus to say that it was better to be Herod's pig than his son. Eventually, the two sons of Mariamne were strangled at Samaria (B.C. 7), and Antipater, after being imprisoned for some time, was executed, as the last act of his father's life, for a too premature act of self-asser-tion. Meanwhile, Herod was afflicted with a painful and loathsome disease. Fanaticism began to break out. The pupils of the Rabbis, Judas son of Sariphæus and Matthias son of Margaloth, were incited to destroy the symbol of idolatry, the golden eagle which adorned the gable of the temple, and the leaders were burnt alive. Herod's cruelty increased with his sufferings. He is said to have assembled all the leading people of Jeru-salem in the hippodrome, that on his death they might be put to death, and there might be real grief at his funeral. He died five days after he had caused Antipater to be put to death, after great sufferings.

(4) *Herod and the murder of the Innocents.*— Herod comes into connexion with the gospel narra-tive, in two ways. Both St. Matthew (2[1]) and St. Luke (2[1]) agree in stating that it was during his reign our Lord was born. There is no reason to doubt that statement, only it has become quite clear that it could not also be during a taxing under Quirinius (see CHRONOLOGY OF NT, i. 404 f.). St. Matthew also gives us an account of the visit of the wise men, of their interview with Herod, and of the subsequent murder of the infants under two years old at Bethlehem. We have no other account of the event, which could not have been conspicuous in Herod's life; and all that it is necessary to say is that it was exactly consistent with his character, especially during the later years of his life. Reference is especially made to *Ant.* XVI. xi. 7, XVII. ii. 4—events which can have nothing to do with the massacre at Bethlehem, but show conclusively the temper of the king. Macrobius (5th cent.) says, *Augustus, cum audisset inter pueros quos in Syria Herodes, rex Judæorum, intra bimatum jussit interfici filium quoque eius occisum, ait: Melius est Herodis porcum esse quam*

filium (Macrob. *Saturn.* ii. 4), a statement which is so confused as to be quite valueless.

vi. The SUCCESSORS OF HEROD.—Herod had made three wills. By the first he nominated Antipater his successor; if he died before his father, Herod, son of the second Mariamne (see HEROD, below), was to succeed; by the second, Antipas was declared his successor; by the third, Archelaus was to be king, and Antipas and Philip were to have tetrarchies. After suppressing some disturbances on his father's death, Archelaus went to Rome to claim his inheritance, to the same place went Antipas to attempt to obtain what had been left him under the second will, and a little later came Philip, not for his own sake, but to support the claims of Archelaus. Other deputations came asking to be freed from the rule of the Herods altogether. While Augustus delayed to give his decision, disturbances broke out throughout all Palestine, which were with difficulty suppressed. Ultimately, Augustus practically confirmed Herod's will. Archelaus was to govern Judæa, Samaria, and Idumæa, but only with the title of ethnarch, not of king; Antipas, Galilee and Peræa; Philip, Trachonitis and Ituræa. When Archelaus came home he removed the high priest Joazar, son of Boethius, who had taken part in the rebellion. There can be little doubt that this expedition of Archelaus to obtain the kingdom suggested the parable in Lk 19¹¹ etc. of the nobleman who went to a far country to receive a kingdom.

(1) ARCHELAUS ('Αρχέλαος) was the elder of the two sons of Herod by Malthace, a Samaritan woman (*Ant.* XVII. i. 3). He was brought up at Rome with his own brother Antipas, at a private house. He had been accused by Antipater of disloyalty, and so had been at first kept out of any inheritance. His visit to Rome has been narrated above. After he had acquired the kingdom, there is little related of him. He outraged Jewish sentiment by marrying Glaphyra, widow of his brother Alexander, although she had had children by him, and had another husband (Juba of Mauritania) living, and his own wife was alive. He built a palace at Jericho, and a village in his own honour of the name of Archelais. He was the worst of all Herod's sons that survived, and, after nine years of his rule, the people of Judæa and Samaria could no longer endure his cruelty and tyranny. They complained to Augustus, who summoned Archelaus to Rome, and, after hearing the case, banished him to Vienne. From this time to the year A.D. 41 Palestine was under Roman procurators.

Archelaus is mentioned once in the NT, in Mt 2²².

(2) ANTIPAS or HEROD ANTIPAS ('Αντίπας), called in NT 'Herod the tetrarch.' He was the son of Herod by Malthace, and in the second of his father's wills had been designated sole heir. Ultimately, he received only Galilee and Peræa, a district which brought him in a yearly revenue of 200 talents. The two portions were divided from one another by the confederation of Greek cities called Decapolis. He seems to have had the ability to govern his country, a decidedly difficult one, and, like his father, he was distinguished for his love of building. He built as his capital Tiberias on the Sea of Galilee.

His first wife was a daughter of Aretas, king of the Nabatæans, but once on a visit to Rome he visited the house of his brother Herod (Philip), son of the younger Mariamne. This Herod had married Herodias, his niece, daughter of Aristobulus, and had by her a daughter, Salome. With Herodias Antipas fell violently in love, and determined to divorce his wife and marry her. This the daughter

of Aretas became aware of, and fled to her father for protection.

About this time the territory of Antipas was the scene of the preaching of John the Baptist and of our Lord. It is needless to repeat the story which is told us in the Gospels of John the Baptist, of Herodias, of John's rebuke, imprisonment, and ultimate death (Mt 14¹ff·, Mk 6¹⁴ff·, Lk 3¹⁹). According to Josephus, the reason Herod gave for imprisoning him was the fear that he might create a revolt or disturbance among the people. The execution took place at the fortress of Machærus, beyond the Jordan (*Ant.* XVIII. v. 2).

We have more than one reference to Antipas during our Lord's ministry, apart from his relations to John the Baptist. When he heard of the fame of Jesus, his conscience smote him, and he was frightened, thinking that John the Baptist had risen from the dead (Mt 14¹, Mk 6¹⁴, Lk 9⁷). Jesus therefore went to Bethsaida Julias in the territory of Philip. Later, apparently when going through Peræa (Lk 13³¹), a rumour is spread that Antipas desires to kill Him, and Jesus speaks of him as 'that fox,' alluding to his well-known character for craft. He wanted to drive out of his country a teacher who might cause some disturbance, and yet to be free from the guilt of condemning a second prophet (Lk 13³¹). At that time, according to St. Mark (8¹⁵), He had condemned the leaven of Herod. St. Luke (23⁷⁻¹⁵) relates also an examination of our Lord before Antipas (who had wished to see Him for some time); the result of this was the reconciliation of Pilate and Herod. This was presumably only an informal examination, and not part of the regular trial. It is referred to again in Ac 4²⁷, and is prominent in the Gospel of Peter. It may be noticed that St. Luke appears to have had special means of information about the Herod dynasty, and that his information is apparently accurate. He does not, like St. Mark, incorrectly call Antipas king (Lk 8³, Ac 13¹).

The marriage with Herodias was the cause of Antipas' fall. First a war broke out between him and Aretas (A.D. 36), although nine years later apparently than the flight of Herod's first wife. Antipas suffered a severe defeat, which some considered, according to Josephus, to be a punishment for what he had done to John the Baptist (*Ant.* XVIII. v. 2). Again later, Herodias persuaded her husband to go to Jerusalem and demand the title of king from Caius, being jealous of what the latter had done for Agrippa. The result of the application was that Agrippa brought charges against him which caused his banishment (*Ant.* VIII. vii. 2). His place of banishment was Lugdunum in Gaul (*Ant.* XVIII. vii. 2), but Spain, according to *BJ* II. ix. 6, was the place where Antipas died. It has been suggested that this was *Lugdunum Convenarum* at the foot of the Pyrenees, and not the better-known place of that name. (See Smith's *DB*² I. ii. 1347).

(3) PHILIP (Φίλιππος) was the son of Herod the Great by Cleopatra, a woman of Jerusalem (*Ant.* XVII. i. 3). He had been educated at Rome, like the remainder of Herod's sons. The territory to which he succeeded on the death of his father and by the decision of Augustus (see above), consisted, according to Josephus, of Batanea, Trachonitis, Auranitis, Gaulanitis, and Paneas (*Ant.* XVII. viii. 1, xi. 4, XVIII. iv. 6; *BJ* II. vi. 3), according to St. Luke (3¹) the country of Ituræa and Trachonitis, Φιλίππου δὲ . . . τετραρχοῦντος τῆς Ἰτουραίας καὶ Τραχωνίτιδος χώρας. (On the meaning of this passage see ITURÆA). Speaking generally, it implied the district to the N. and E. of the Sea of Galilee. Its revenues were computed at 100 talents, and his title was that of tetrarch. He ruled for 38 years from his accession in B.C. 4

until his death in A.D. 34, without any startling event and without reproach. He was distinguished from the other sons of Herod by the absence of ambition, of cruelty, and of lust. He was only once married, to Salome the daughter of Herodias, and had no children. His character is summed up by Jos. *Ant.* XVIII. iv. 6. ' He was moderate and peaceful in his rule, and spent his whole life in his country. He went out with only a small retinue, always taking with him the throne on which he might sit and judge. Whenever he met any one who had need of him, he made no delay, but set down the throne wherever he might be and heard the case.'

His name is chiefly remembered by the city of CÆSAREA PHILIPPI, which he founded on the site of Paneas at the head waters of the Jordan. It was called Cæsarea in honour of the emperor, and received the name of Philippi to distinguish it from the more important city on the seacoast. He also rebuilt BETHSAIDA, situated on the left bank of the Jordan where it flows into the Lake of Gennesareth, and called it Julias. It was to this city, in all probability, that our Lord retired to escape the attention of Herod Antipas (Lk 9[10]). He also showed his loyalty to the emperors by placing the busts of Augustus and Tiberius on his coins, a course which was possible mainly owing to the non-Jewish character of the population.

On his death his territory was joined to the province of Syria, but its taxes were collected separately. Caligula immediately on his accession gave it to Agrippa.

(4) HEROD, called PHILIP, was the son of Herod by Mariamne, daughter of Simon the high priest. Her father was a priest, of too low class to be allied with him, but too important to be despised. Herod was wise enough not to use his authority to her detriment, but did not scruple to make her father high priest (*Ant.* XV. ix. 3). Herod had been named in his father's first will, but, owing to the treachery of his mother, was left out in subsequent wills (*BJ* I. xxx. 7), and lived and died a private person, apparently in Rome (*Ant.* XVIII. v. 1). His claim to distinction is that he was the first husband of Herodias. Apparently, he also bore the name of *Philip* (Mt 14[3], Mk 6[17]).

In Mk 6[17] all MSS read τὴν γυναῖκα Φιλίππου τοῦ ἀδελφοῦ αὐτοῦ. In Mt 14[3] Φιλίππου is omitted by D, the Vulgate, and some Old Latin MSS. In Lk 3[19] it is omitted by א B D, the Vulg., Old Latin, and was probably not part of the original text.

The discrepancy may be explained either (1) by assuming that Philip was the other name of Herod. This is all the more probable, as in the passage of Josephus (*Ant.* XVIII. v. 4) Herod Antipas is also called simply Herod. Against this is the fact that St. Luke, who generally has by far the most accurate information concerning the Herods, does not give the name; (2) by supposing that there is a confusion between the first husband and the son-in-law of Herodias, for her daughter Salome married Philip the tetrarch.

(5) AGRIPPA I. was born about the year 10 B.C., being 54 years old at the time of his death in A.D. 44 (*Ant.* XIX. viii. 2). He was the son of Aristobulus, son of Herod the Great by Mariamne, granddaughter of Hyrcanus. His mother was Bernice, daughter of Salome, Herod's sister, and of Costobar (*Ant.* XVIII. v. 4). Not long after his birth his father was put to death by Herod, and he himself with his mother sent to Rome, where he was brought up. His mother was a friend of Antonia, widow of the elder Drusus, and he himself enjoyed the friendship of the younger Drusus. This imperial friendship appears to have been of doubtful advantage. He was magnanimous, reckless, and extravagant, spent large sums in bribing the imperial freedmen, got hopelessly into debt, and, on the death of Drusus, lost the imperial favour. He had to leave Rome, and during the next fourteen years of his life was subject to many strange vicissitudes. At one time he had even meditated

suicide. When Tiberius died (March 16, A.D. 37) he was in prison, but the accession of Caligula, which he had looked forward to so indiscreetly as to lose his liberty, at length brought the change of his fortunes. The new emperor immediately gave him the tetrarchies of Philip and Lysanias, the title of king, and a golden chain equal in weight to the iron chain with which he had been bound (*Ant.* XVIII. vi. 10), while the senate added the honorary title of prefect. In 38 he visited his new possessions, but in 39 he was back in Rome. He was responsible for the banishment of Herod Antipas in 39, and received his tetrarchy in addition to the other two. More creditable to him was the wisdom and boldness with which he persuaded Caius not to erect a statue of himself in the temple at Jerusalem. The death of Caligula (41) and the accession of Claudius gave him an opportunity of winning the goodwill of the latter ; and he received Judæa and Samaria in addition to his other possessions, and ruled therefore over all the territory of his grandfather.

It is from this date that his three years of actual rule began. Its leading feature, and one which harmonizes with the narrative in the Acts, was his friendliness to the Jews and his regard for Jewish customs. He began his reign by offering all the fitting sacrifices in the temple, omitting nothing that the law enjoined ; by paying the cost of many who wished to fulfil their Nazirite vows ; and by dedicating in the temple the golden chain which he had received from Caius. His determination to uphold the privileges of his people was speedily shown. Some young men in the town of Dora had erected a statue of the emperor in the Jewish synagogue in that place. This angered Agrippa, for it meant the overthrow of the laws of the country, and he used his influence to persuade Petronius the governor of Syria to interfere, which he did, not only ordering the removal of the statue, but punishing those who had erected it. For his loyalty to Judaism both Josephus (*Ant.* XIX. vii. 3) and the Pharisees (Schürer, I. i. p. 444) are loud in his praise. His conduct is contrasted with that of Herod the Great, who showed all his benevolence towards the Gentile cities. He constantly lived in Jerusalem, and preferred it. He kept the laws of his country in purity. He lived a life of the strictest holiness, and allowed no day to pass without offering the sacrifice. So the Mishna tells us how he in person used to offer the first-fruits ; and a story is told that at the Feast of Tabernacles, as he read the words, Dt 17[15] ' Thou mayest not set a stranger over thee which is not thy brother,' he burst into tears. And the people cried out, ' Be not disturbed — thou art our brother ! thou art our brother !' He also used his political influence—which was considerable—to spread Judaism. When he betrothed his daughter Drusilla to Epiphanes, son of Antiochus, king of Commagene, he made him undertake to be circumcised.

Quite in accordance with this character is the narrative in Ac 12. He began a persecution of the Church. He slew James the brother of John with the sword, and, finding that this was pleasing to the Jews, proceeded to take Peter also. These events happened during the Passover. Another side of his Judaizing policy is shown by the attempts which he made—both frustrated by the interference of the governor of Syria, Marsus—to strengthen his kingdom. He enlarged the walls of Jerusalem, and while at Tiberias received no less than five vassal princes — Antiochus of Commagene, Sampsigeramus of Emesa, Cotys of Armenia Minor, Polemon of Pontus, and Herod of Chalcis, his own brother. That he was foolish enough to meditate any treason is improbable ; he was too fond of peace, and knew too well what was the power of Rome; if he had any object beyond that of increasing his own magnificence, it was probably the extension of Jewish influence among them.

Of his death, which happened in A.D. 44, after the beginning of the month Nisan (see CHRONOLOGY, vol. i. p. 416), we have two independent accounts. According to Josephus (*Ant.* XIX. viii. 2), during the third year of his reign over all Judæa he came to Cæsarea. There he presided at games in honour of Cæsar, surrounded by all the leading men of the province. On the second day he put on a robe of silver of wonderful make. When the first rays of the sun struck it, it produced a wonderful effect. Immediately there were cries addressing him as a god, 'Be propitious; if up to now we feared thee as a man, henceforth we confess that thou art more than mortal.' The king did not rebuke them. Shortly afterwards, looking up, he saw an owl sitting over his head on a cord. He knew that the bird, which had formerly been a messenger of good, was now a messenger of evil, ἄγγελόν τε τοῦτον εὐθὺς ἐνόησεν κακῶν εἶναι, τὸν καί ποτε τῶν ἀγαθῶν γενόμενον. He was immediately seized with severe pains, and died after five days. The allusion to the owl is to an omen which had portended his good fortune when he was a prisoner in Rome (*Ant.* XVIII. vi. 7).

According to the Acts, Herod, after the release of Peter, *i.e.* after the Passover, went down to Cæsarea. He was angry with the people of Tyre and Sidon, and a deputation from them came before him asking for peace. Herod, on a day arranged, put on his royal robe, and sitting on his throne made an address to them. The people cried, It is the voice of a god, and not of a man. And immediately an angel of the Lord struck him, because he gave not God the glory; and he was eaten of worms, and died.

It is quite clear that there is a substantial agreement between these passages as to the main incident, but a difference which is quite incompatible with any literary obligation on the part of the author of the Acts.

Agrippa had married Cypros, daughter of Phasael, who was son of Phasael, Herod's brother. Her mother was Salampsio, daughter of Herod by Mariamne, granddaughter of Hyrcanus. He had two sons, AGRIPPA (see below) and Drusus, who died young, and three daughters, BERNICE, Mariamne, and DRUSILLA.

(6) AGRIPPA II., or, as he describes himself on coins, Marcus Julius Agrippa, was the son of Agrippa I. and Cypros. He was only 17 years old at the death of his father in 44, and Claudius was persuaded not to give him his father's kingdom owing to his youth. Agrippa then arrived at Rome, and used his influence on behalf of the Jews (*Ant.* XX. vi. 3). On the death of his uncle, Herod of Chalcis, he received the tetrarchy of the latter and the oversight of the temple (*Ant.* XX. v. 2; *BJ* II. xii.). In the year 53 he gave up Chalcis and received the tetrarchies of Philip and Lysanias. Later, Nero added various cities in Galilee and Peræa (*Ant.* XX. vii. 1, viii. 4). Of his relations to his sister Bernice the worst reports were current. Like all the Herods, he tried to combine Judaism and Hellenism. He improved his capital city, Cæsarea Philippi, and called it Neronias; he adorned Berytus with many statues and buildings; his coins bore effigies of the emperors. But Rabbinical tradition records his interest in Jewish questions; he attempted to extend Judaism among the surrounding kings, and under him the temple was finished (*Ant.* XX. ix. 6).

In Ac 25. 26 we have an account of the speech of St. Paul before Agrippa, Bernice, and Festus. St. Paul's compliment, that Agrippa was 'expert in all customs and questions which are among the Jews,' was well deserved, and the somewhat enigmatic 'Almost thou persuadest me to be a Christian' may be interpreted according to our conception of Agrippa's character.

Agrippa did what he could to check the growing storm (*BJ* II. xv. 1), and during all the war was on the side of the Romans. He took part in the festivities which succeeded the victory (*BJ* VII. ii. 1), and received a considerable increase of territory. Of his later life we only know that Josephus corresponded with him and received from him information for his history (Jos. *Vita*, 65). He died about the year 100 A.D., the last of the Herods.

vii. WOMEN OF THE FAMILY.—(1) HERODIAS (Ἡρωδιάς, WH Ἡρῳδιάς) was daughter of Aristobulus, son of Herod by Mariamne, daughter of Hyrcanus. Her mother was Bernice, daughter of Salome, Herod's sister. She was thus sister of Herod of Chalcis, of Agrippa I., and of the younger Aristobulus (*Ant.* XVIII. v. 4). According to Josephus, she married first of all Herod, son of Herod the Great by Mariamne, daughter of Simon the high priest, and by him had a daughter of the name of SALOME. According to Ac 6[17], and probably Mt 14[3], her first husband's name was PHILIP (wh. see). Prompted apparently by ambition, she left him and married his brother Antipas. It was this marriage that drew upon them the rebuke of John the Baptist, and caused the tragedy that followed (Mt 14[8-11], Mk 6[14-18]); and it was Herodias' ambition which caused Antipas his final ruin. 'She said life was unbearable for them if Agrippa, who came to her husband in such extreme poverty, now returned a king, while he himself, the son of a king, was contented with a private life' (*Ant.* XVIII. vii. 1). Her pride made her faithful to her husband in misfortune. Josephus represents her as saying to Caius, when he told her that it was only her brother who prevented her from sharing the calamity of her husband, 'You indeed, O emperor! say this in a magnificent manner, and as becomes you; but the love which I have for my husband hinders me from partaking of the favour of your gift; for it is not right that I, who have been a partner in his prosperity, should forsake him in his misfortunes.'

(2) SALOME was the name of the daughter of Herod (Philip) and Herodias who danced before Herod Antipas as mentioned Mt 14[3-6] and Mk 6[17-22] (but cf. reading of WH in v.[22]). She married (1) Herod Philip, tetrarch of Trachonitis, by whom she had no children, and (2) Aristobulus, son of Herod of Chalcis, by whom she had three children—Herod, Agrippa, and Aristobulus (*Ant.* XVIII. V. 4).

(3) BERNICE or BERENICE (Βερνίκη) was the eldest daughter of Agrippa I. She was born about the year 28, being 16 years old at the time of her father's death in 44 (*Ant.* XIX. ix. 1). She was betrothed first to Marcus, son of Alexander the alabarch, but seems never to have been married to him (*Ant.* XIX. v. 1, but there is some doubt as to the reading); then about the year 41, being then 13 years old, she was married by her father to her uncle Herod, for whom he obtained from Claudius the kingdom of Chalcis. By him she had two sons, Bernicianus and Hyrcanus (*BJ* II. xi. 6). Herod of Chalcis died in 48. Bernice then lived at her brother's house, and the worst rumours were afloat concerning their relationship—rumours which reached as far as Rome (cf. Juv. *Sat.* vi. 156–160: '. . . adamas notissimus et Beronices in digito factus pretiosior; hunc dedit olim Barbarus incestæ, dedit hunc Agrippa sorori, observant ubi festa mero pede sabbata reges, et vetus indulget senibus clementia porcis. . . .'). In order to allay these suspicions she induced Polemon, king of Cilicia, who was

attracted by her wealth, to be circumcised and to marry her. But she soon left him, δι' ἀκολασίαν Josephus tells us, and returned to her brother (*Ant.* xx. vii. 3). About the year 58 we find her with Agrippa visiting Festus to greet him on his appointment, and so, like her younger and equally notorious sister, Drusilla, listening to St. Paul. It may be noticed that great emphasis is laid on her presence. She was one who could always attract attention to herself (Ac 25[13. 23] 26[30]). The next that we hear of her is in the spring of 66. She was in Jerusalem performing a Nazirite vow. Horrified by the massacre which Florus had ordered, she attempted to stop it, first sending her attendants to Florus, ultimately appearing herself (so it was said) barefooted before him. The only result seems to have been that the soldiers murdered their victims before her face and attempted to kill her. But, after her palace was burnt by the Jewish populace, she became an ardent supporter of the Roman cause and the Flavian dynasty (*BJ* II. xv. 1, xvii. 6). Already in 68 there seem to have been intimate relations between her and Titus (Tac. *Hist.* ii. 2); in 75 she came to Rome with her brother, and the intimacy was renewed. She lived in the Palatine with him, behaved as his wife (πάντα ἤδη ὡς καὶ γυνὴ αὐτοῦ οὖσα ἐποίει, Dio Cass. lxvi. 15), and was said to have been promised marriage (*insignem reginæ Bernices amorem cui etiam nuptias pollicitus ferebatur*, Suet. *Tit.* 7). But the unpopularity of the connexion persuaded Titus that he must give her up, and when she returned to Rome after the death of Vespasian he took no notice of her ('Berenicen statim ab urbe dimisit invitus invitam,' Suet. *loc. cit.*; Dio Cass. lxvi. 18; and Au. Vict. *Epit.* 10); but even her fidelity to her royal lover was not free from suspicion, and a reputed paramour was murdered by the orders of Titus. After this period she vanishes from history. The only other memorial of her is an inscription found at Athens (*CIG* 361; *C. I. Att.* III. i. 556)—

Ἡ βουλὴ ἡ ἐξ Ἀρείου πάγου καὶ ἡ βουλὴ τῶν χ΄ καὶ ὁ δῆμος Ἰουλίαν Βερενείκην βασίλισσαν μεγάλην, Ἰουλίου Ἀγρίππα βασιλέως θυγατέρα καὶ μεγάλων βασιλέων εὐεργετῶν τῆς πόλεως ἔκγονον. . . .

A simple narrative of Bernice's life is really more eloquent than any comment. She was the last member of the family who played any prominent part in history.

(4) DRUSILLA (Δρουσίλλα) was the youngest of the three daughters of Agrippa I. She was born about the year 38, being 6 years old at the time of her father's death, in 44 (*Ant.* XIX. ix. 1); but she had already been betrothed by her father to Epiphanes, son of Antiochus, king of Commagene. He, however, refused to fulfil his promise to be circumcised, and the marriage never took place. Her brother at the completion of the 12th year of Claudius (53) received from the emperor the northern part of Palestine, and then gave Drusilla, now about 14 years old, in marriage to Azizus, king of Emesa, who was willing to be circumcised. The marriage was neither happy nor of long continuance. Felix, procurator of Palestine, a freedman who had the distinction of being the husband of three queens (Suet. *Claudius*, 28), was so overcome by her beauty that he attempted to gain her for his wife. He sent, to effect this purpose, a man of the name of Simon, a Cyprian by birth, who had the reputation of being a 'magician.' She, unhappy in her marriage and wishing to escape her sister Bernice's jealousy, deserted her husband and transgressed the Jewish law so far as to consent to marry a Gentile. This marriage cannot have taken place earlier than 53 or later than 54, for in the first year of Nero (54–55) Azizus died, and we are particularly told that she left her husband. Drusilla had one son by Felix, called Agrippa, who perished in an eruption of Mt. Vesuvius in the reign of Titus, it is added σὺν τῇ γυναικί, which is interpreted by some to refer to his mother, by others to a wife of his own.

In Ac 24[24] we are told how Felix with Drusilla his own wife (τῇ ἰδίᾳ γυναικί, RV), a Jewess, heard St. Paul speak of faith in Christ, and how, when he spake of righteousness, and self-restraint, and judgment to come, Felix trembled.

viii. CHARACTER OF THE HEROD DYNASTY.—In conclusion, it will be convenient to sum up some characteristics of the dynasty of the Herods.

(1) In the first place, we may take them as typical representatives of the *Reges Socii* under the empire. Of no other of the provinces have we the same detailed information as of the Jews in Josephus, and we are able to see the system of what we should call 'Protected states' at work. The kings and other rulers were absolutely dependent on the imperial power; they had no right of making war, their wills were only valid when confirmed by the emperor; they were expected to provide auxiliary troops when necessary. How clearly the Herods realized the limitations of their power is shown by the skilful manner in which they conciliated the Romans. Within their own territory they were supreme, but even here they were liable to accusations from their subjects. The value of the system in governing Orientals, whose character was so difficult for Romans to understand, may be realized by the contrast afforded to the government of the procurators. If Agrippa had lived there would perhaps have been no Jewish war.

(2) In relation to Judaism the first and most obvious characteristic of their rule is the Hellenizing influence that it represented. However distasteful to a large number of the people, however alien to their religious spirit, there is no doubt that the influence was considerable. It produced the inevitable reaction which was one of the causes of the final war, but it modified the ideas of those even who resented it. For Judaism to play its part in the world, it was necessary for it to have some contact with the spirit of Hellenism; and that the Herods gave it.

(3) The peculiar character and influence of Antipater and his descendants undoubtedly made Judaism a much more conspicuous factor in the Græco-Roman world than it would have been otherwise. We know how Cæsar recognized the Jews as one of the three divisions of people; we know how from him they obtained recognition of their privileges in a marked way, and this was to a considerable extent due to the Herods. Moreover, the social influence of the Herods seems to have been a considerable factor in extending Judaism among the other kings of the East.

(4) And how far were the Herodian monarchy and aspirations a natural product of Judaism? They were not absolutely inconsistent with its history, they were in keeping with its higher aspirations. From the days of Solomon temporal sovereignty had always been a dream of many of the people. It achieved its most prominent success in Herod, and the very success made the religious conscience of the people reject it. Ultimately, Christianity and Rabbinism became the two real products of Jewish history. 'The leaven of Herod' was felt to be unsound.

LITERATURE.—Our authorities may practically be reduced to two. Josephus has narrated to us the history of the whole Herod family with great fulness, and to supplement him we have only isolated references in other writings. A history from Rabbinical sources is given by Derenbourg, *Essai sur l'histoire et la géographie de la Palestine*. Modern authorities may practically be confined to Schürer, *Geschichte des Jüdischen*

Volkes im Zeitalter Jesu Christ (there is an English translation), who gives full references to all authorities ancient and modern. The best monographs are by Keim, in *Schenkel's Bibel-lexicon*. Accounts of the Herods are given by Stanley and Milman, and there is a popular work by Farrar. The articles in Smith's *DB* by Westcott are good.

A. C. HEADLAM.

HERODIANS ('Ηρωδιανοί, WH -ρῳδ-).—The Herodians are mentioned twice in the Gospels (Mk 3⁶ in Galilee; Mt 22¹⁶ = Mk 12¹³ in Jerus.), along with the Pharisees, as adversaries of Jesus. Some of the later Church Fathers (*e.g.* Tertullian) regarded them as a religious party, who held Herod to be the Messiah; but this is altogether improbable. They were apparently a political party, most probably the adherents of the dynasty of Herod. At the death of Herod (B.C. 4), his kingdom was divided among his sons, Idumæa, Judæa, and Samaritis being allotted to Archelaus. When Archelaus was deposed (A.D. 6 or 7), a Roman procurator was put in his place, and thenceforward Judæa continued under procurators, with the exception of a brief interval, during which Herod Agrippa I. united under his sway all the dominions of his grandfather. It was doubtless the constant desire of the family of Herod to restore the kingdom of their father; and the Herodians would seem to have been the party of those who favoured their pretensions. They were neither the adherents, in particular, of Herod Antipas, tetrarch of Galilee, nor exactly the friends of Rome; but those among the Jews who, in more or less veiled opposition to the Roman procuratorship, as well as to the idea of a pure theocracy, desired the restoration of the national kingdom under one or other of the sons of Herod. Their alliance with the Pharisees in opposition to our Lord was not due to religious or political sympathy, but to the recognition by both parties that Jesus was their greatest common foe. The question regarding the tribute paid to Cæsar (Mt 22¹⁷, Mk 12¹⁴) was skilfully calculated to draw from Him an answer that would either lead to His being accused of sedition against Rome (Lk 20²⁰), or discredit Him among the people. In order to get rid of Jesus, the Pharisees, who combined even with the Sadducees, would not scruple to enter into a temporary alliance with the Herodians, however much they were opposed to their religious and political sentiments. (See Keim, *Jesus of Nazara*, iii. 157 ff., and in Schenkel's *Bibellex.* iii. 65 ff.)   D. EATON.

HERODIAS.—See HEROD, pp. 353, 360ᵇ.

HERODION ('Ηρωδίων, WH -ρῳδ-).—A Christian mentioned Ro 16¹¹, apparently a Jew (συγγενής), and perhaps a freedman of the Herods. See ARISTOBULUS, vol. i. p. 148ᵃ.

HERON (אֲנָפָה *'ănâphâh*, χαραδριός, *charadrion*).— This word designates an unclean bird (Lv 11¹⁹, Dt 14¹⁸), not otherwise mentioned in the Bible, but sufficiently well known to be taken as a type of a class. The LXX rendering simply means a *swamp bird*. The fact of the occurrence of this name immediately after חֲסִידָה *stork*, and followed by the expression 'after her kind,' gives the only clue we have to the bird intended. Of the birds suggested by various authorities, as the *eagle*, *parrot*, and *swallow*, none would go in a group with the *stork*. The *heron*, on the other hand, belongs to the same group, and, unlike the stork, of which only one species is found in the Holy Land, has no fewer than six species of the genus *Ardea* alone. The most common of these is *A. cinerea*, L., the Grey Heron (Arab. *dŭnkeleh* and *ghŭrnûk*). Less common is *A. purpurea*, L., the Purple Heron; *A. alba*, L., the White Egret; *A. garzetta*, L., the Lesser Egret; *A. bubulcus*, Audouin, the Buff-backed Heron or

White Ibis (Arab. *Abu-Bekr*); *A. ralloides*, Scop., the Squacco Heron. There are also three other genera 'after their kind,' *Ardetta minuta*, L., the Little Bittern; *Nycticorax griseus*, L., the Night Heron; and *Botaurus stellaris*, L., the Bittern. In the absence of a better we may retain the rendering of EV 'heron.' RVm (Lv 11¹⁹) gives 'ibis.'

G. E. POST.

HESHBON (חֶשְׁבּוֹן, LXX 'Εσεβών, 'Εσβών, Jos 21³⁹ B) ('device' or 'reckoning'; note play on the word in Jer 48² 'in H. they have *devised* . . .').—The chief city of Sihon king of the Amorites, captured by the Israelites on their way to the Jordan. The defeat of Sihon is related Nu 21²¹⁻²⁶ (E), Dt 2²⁴⁻³⁷, referred to briefly Dt 1⁴ 3⁶ 4⁴⁶ 29⁷, Jos 9¹⁰ 12². ⁵ 13²¹. ²⁷, Neh 9²², more fully in Jephthah's message to the king of the Ammonites, Jg 11¹⁹⁻²². In these passages Sihon is spoken of as 'king of' or 'dwelling in' Heshbon. In the distribution of the land H. is assigned to Reuben by Moses, Nu 32³. ²⁷ (E), and Joshua, Jos 13¹⁰. ¹⁷. ²¹. The inheritance of Gad extended from H. to Ramath-mizpeh, Jos 13²⁶ (P); and in the list of Levitical cities (Jos 21³⁹ (P), 1 Ch 6⁸¹] H. is reckoned as belonging to Gad.

In the prophecies of Isaiah and Jeremiah (Is 15⁴ 16⁸. ⁹, Jer 48². ³⁴. ⁴⁵ 49³) H. and cities in its neighbourhood are mentioned as cities of Moab. For these passages, and the reference to H. in the song quoted Nu 21²⁷ᶠ·, see MOAB and SIHON. The Jews are again in possession of H. in the time of Alexander Jannæus (Jos. *Ant.* XIII. xv. 4, where H. is described as in the country of Moab), and the surrounding district is called in Herod's time Essebonitis (*Ant.* XV. viii. 5) and Sebonitis (*BJ* II. xviii. 1). Whether in the account of places taken by Judas Maccabæus (1 Mac 5²⁶. ³⁶, Jos. *Ant.* XII. viii. 3) H. is mentioned, is doubtful [see notes on passage in 1 Mac (*Camb. Bible for Schools*) and the various readings in Niese's *Josephus*].

In the *Onomasticon* H. ('Εσβοῦς) is described as 'urbs insignis' in the mountains, 20 miles (Roman) from the Jordan. The name occurs as the seat of a bishopric in the acts of the Council of Chalcedon. St. Sylvia of Aquitania describes *Esebon* as visible from Mt. Nebo, which is confirmed by modern travellers, and adds that it is now called *Exebon* —an interesting piece of evidence as to the pronunciation of the name in her time (*Palestine Pilgrims Text Society*, vol. i. 28). In the life of Saladin in the same series (vol. xiii. p. 97) occurs the modern name *Hesbân*, and Abulfeda mentions it as inhabited (*Geography*, Arabic text, edited by Schiers, p. 129, and translated by Lestrange, *Pal. under the Moslems*, p. 456). The site is now covered with extensive ruins, chiefly Roman, and by the side of the plateau on which these are situated runs a stream issuing from a cave, at which the tribes in the neighbourhood obtain water for themselves and their cattle. From the stream a steep winding mountain-path leads upwards to the city, and at the top of the ascent passes through a sort of passage cut through the rocks, about 3 or 4 yards wide. Buhl (*Palästina*, p. 123) remarks that in a branch of Wâdy Hesbân, N.W. of the city, are traces of ancient pools and conduits. It requires some imagination on the part of travellers to identify the *one* large ruined reservoir noted by them with 'the **pools of Heshbon**' by the gate of Bath-rabbim' (Ca 7⁴); but the position of the stream outside the present ruins, and the descriptions given above, fully illustrate the passage. Further information may be obtained from Reland's *Palestina*, containing reff. to Talmud, Ptolemy, Pliny, etc.; Conder, *Heth and Moab*, p. 125 ff.; *PEFSt*, 1882, 1888.

A. T. CHAPMAN.

HESHMON (חֶשְׁמוֹן).—An unknown town in the extreme south of Judah, Jos 15²⁷.

ḤETH (letter).—See CHETH.

HETH (חֵת, etym. and meaning unknown).—
According to J (Gn 10[15] = 1 Ch 1[13]), a son of Canaan.
P (mistakenly, as Budde, Stade, Ed. Meyer, etc.,
think) locates Bĕnê-Heth at Mamre in the time
of Abraham, who purchased from Ephron the
Hittite the cave of Machpelah, Gn 23[3ff.] 25[10] 49[32].
The wives of Esau are described in Gn 27[46] as
'daughters of Heth,' a designation which is
identified in the same verse with 'daughters of the
land' and in 28[1, 8] with 'daughters of Canaan.'
'It appears that חֵת (ם) had their proper seat in
the north (where also they were encountered by
Assyrians from time of Tiglath-pileser I. and by
Egyptians from time of Tahutmes III., cf. also
Jg 3[3], Jos 11[3]), but that individual Hittites were
known in Israel (cf. besides 1 S 26[6], 2 S 11[3] etc., 1 K
9[20]); that the Hittites were regarded (by J E D) as
one of the peoples of Canaan, and that the name
even came to be used in a more general sense for
Canaanites. Only in P do they appear as having
a definite settlement in the south' (*Oxf. Heb. Lex.*).
Sayce's argument for the presence of Hittites in
Hebron is disproved by Gray (see *Expositor*, May
1898, p. 340 f.). J. A. SELBIE.

HETHLON (חֶתְלֹן).—An otherwise unknown city,
named in Ezk 47[15] 48[1] as situated on the ideal
northern boundary of Israel, in the neighbourhood
of Hamath and Zedad (cf. Nu 34[8]). Provided the
text is not corrupt, Hethlon is probably (so Furrer,
ZDPV viii. 27) the modern Ḥeitela N.E. of Tripoli.
The LXX has in Ezk 47[15] περισχιζούσης and in 48[1]
περισχίζοντος. It may be mentioned that v. Kasteren
proposes to identify Hethlon with the modern
ʿAdlûn N. of the mouth of the Ḳasimiyeh, which
he takes to have been the ideal northern boundary
of Israel. Bertholet (*Hesekiel, ad loc.*) and Buhl
(*GAP* 66 f.) are inclined to favour v. Kasteren's
identification. F. HOMMEL.

HEWER OF WOOD.—The Gibeonites, for their
fraud practised upon Joshua, were condemned to
become 'hewers of wood (חֹטְבֵי עֵצִים) and drawers of
water' for the congregation (Jos 9[21, 27]) and for the
house of God (9[23]) or altar of J″ (9[27]). The phrase
occurs also in Dt 29[11], where it is applied to
strangers serving individual Israelites. Perhaps a
more accurate translation, and one that better
brings out the menial nature of the occupation, is
'gatherers of firewood' (see Driver on Dt 29[11]);
though the word for 'hewers' is used alone in
2 Ch 2[10] of those that hew timber for building.
See DRAWER OF WATER.

HEXATEUCH.[*]—The name Hexateuch is now
generally given by critics to the first 6 books of
OT on the analogy of the Pentateuch, the name
long given to the first 5. The object of the change
of name is to show that the 6 rather than the 5 form
a complete literary whole, and may be looked upon
as one book in 6 parts. It is not intended by the
title either to exclude the possibility that the
Hexateuch, like the rest of OT, was subject to constant revision, or to imply that the sources out of
which it was compiled are necessarily to be found
only in these books. A century ago it was a
matter of common belief that the Pentateuch was
written by Moses ; but this belief never rested on
anything but tradition, and will not bear examination. It will be shown that, in fact, these books are
the result of complicated literary processes ex-

---

[*] In this article the following abbreviations are used :—J =
Jahwistic document, E = Elohistic document, JE = J and E
combined, D = Deuteronomic Code, JED = JE and D combined,
P = Priestly document, Pʰ = the Code of Holiness, Pg = the main
work of P, J², E², etc. = the schools of J, E, etc., R = Reviser, at
whatever period.

---

tending over a long period. As the Mosaic authorship will be thus disproved at the very outset, it
requires no separate discussion.

i. THE COMPOSITE CHARACTER OF THE HEXA-
TEUCH.—This is proved by (*a*) *the many unnecessary
repetitions.* Thus the creation of beasts and birds
is related in Gn 1[21-25] and again in 2[19], of man in
1[27] and in 2[7]. The corruption of man and his
threatened punishment are described in 6[1-7], and
repeated almost immediately afterwards in 6[11-13]
[see FLOOD]. Abraham's departure from his native
land is told in 11[31] and in 12[1-4a]. The latter cannot
have originally referred to his departure from
Haran, which was not his native land (see 12[1]).
The statement of the destruction of the 'cities of
the Plain' and Lot's escape in 19[29] is clearly unnecessary after the detailed account of the events
just given. The charge given to Jacob to flee to
his uncle Laban is twice related, in 27[42-45] and in
28[1-7]. So in Joseph's early history is the passing
of the trading caravans, and his being taken down
into Egypt, cf. 37[25-27] 39[1] with 37[28a, 36]. The
giving of names to certain sacred spots is in
many cases twice recorded, *e.g.* Beersheba 21[22-34]
26[26-33], Bethel 28[10-22] 35[9-15]. We have even three
accounts of the laughter which occasioned the
naming of Isaac 17[17] 18[12] 21[6, 7]. In the other books
we find similar, though less frequent, repetitions.
The name J″ is twice revealed to Moses Ex 3[13-15]
6[2-9]. The naming of Meribah and the events which
gave rise to it are twice related Ex 17[1-7], Nu 20[1-13].
Of the incidents of the manna and the quails, each
occurs twice Ex 16, Nu 11. The frequent repetition
of similar laws throughout the legislative portion
of Hex. is obvious to the most casual reader. We
have striking examples in the laws for the burnt-
offering Lv 1. 22[17-33], the thank-offerings Lv 3. 7[11-21].
In Joshua we find in 12[1-6] 13[8-12] two descriptions of
the territory given to the trans-Jordanic tribes,
quite distinct from the more detailed account of
the portions assigned to the separate tribes in
13[15-31]. The way in which Caleb obtained his
portion is fully narrated in 14[6-15], and stated again
as though a fresh fact in 15[13], and enlarged upon
in 15[14-19]. The lot for the children of Joseph is
shortly described in 16[1-3], and then given again in
rather greater detail, but with some repetitions, in
vv.[4-9]. It should be also borne in mind that the
number of repetitions, of which in any case this is
by no means a complete list, is largely increased if
we regard as such what in their present form
appear as similar incidents occurring on different
occasions. Thus there can be little doubt that the
three deceptions on the part of a patriarch's wife
narrated in Gn 12[10-20] 20[1-18] 26[1-11] are mere variants
of the same story. The same is true of the ex-
pulsions of Hagar in Gn 16. 21[9-21].

(*b*) *Frequent discrepancies and inconsistencies.*—
The Creation story beginning with Gn 2[4b] differs
from that of 1[1]-2[4a] in almost every particular, but
most notably in the order of creation, the manner
in which man is created, and in the creation of one
single woman after that of a single man. The
Flood according to 7[12, 17] 8[6, 10, 12] lasted 54 days,
according to 7[24] 8[3] at least 150. [For other discrepancies see FLOOD]. Abraham's incredulity with
reference to the possibility of Isaac's birth is mentioned in 17[17] without comment, as though quite a
natural thing. Precisely the same incredulity on
Sarah's part is severely reprimanded in 18[12-15], and
a different occasion and explanation of Sarah's
laughter is given in 21[6, 7]. The youth of Sarah
implied in 12[10-20] 20[1-8] is inconsistent with Sarah's
age as stated in 17[17]; and it is strange that
Abraham, so old that his begetting of Isaac is
regarded as an unheard of miracle in 17[17] 18[11],
should after Sarah's death have married a second
wife, and had several children 25[1-6]. The caravan

which bought Joseph consisted according to 37$^{25-27}$ 39^1 of Ishmaelites, according to 37$^{28. 36}$ of Midianites. Often totally different explanations are given of the same name, as of Issachar, which in 30$^{15. 16}$ is connected with the *hire* for the love-apples given by Leah to Rachel, in 30^{18} with the *hire* given by God to Leah for giving her handmaid to her husband. In 30^{20a} Zebulun is so named because God had given Leah a good dowry (זבד), in v.^{20b} to express the hope that Jacob would dwell (זבל) with her. Joseph is so called in 30^{23} because God had taken away (אסף) Rachel's reproach, in ver.^{24} in the hope that J'' would add (יסף) another son. In 32^2 Mahanaim is so called because of the *companies* of angels which Jacob met there, in 32$^{7-10}$ there is a significant mention of the *two companies* of people, flocks, etc., that were with Jacob. In the early history of Exodus we find a certain number of incidents which imply that the Israelites were living among the Egyptians, as the story of the midwives 1$^{15-22}$, and especially the events of the Passover night, when the houses of the Israelites had to be marked 12$^{7. 13}$, and the Israelitish women were able to ask for jewels of their Egyptian neighbours 12$^{35. 36}$. In many other passages the Israelites are described as living in Goshen, a country quite separate from the rest of Egypt, and distinguished by immunity from plagues (see esp. Gn 46^{34}, Ex 8^{22} 9^{26}). The law requiring that altars should be made of earth or unhewn stones, Ex 20^{24}, is inconsistent with the directions given so soon after for the altar of acacia wood overlaid with brass in 27$^{1-8}$; and the permission to erect such altars as the first in every place where J'' should record His name, implying a large number of sanctuaries, does not accord with the frequent directions in Dt that offerings should be made only in the place which J'' should choose, Dt 12$^{4-11}$ etc. Many other inconsistencies of the same kind will be noticed in the course of this article. [See EXODUS, LEVITICUS].

(c) *Want of continuity and order in the narrative.*—A history of Noah should have begun, not at Gn 6^9, but certainly before 6^8, and most probably before 5^{29}. A history of Noah's sons Gn 10^1 should have included 9$^{18-27}$. In Gn 20^1 'Abraham journeyed *from thence*,' should naturally have followed some statement mentioning the place where he was, instead of a chapter dealing with the history of Lot. Ch. 35^9 implies that Jacob had just returned from Paddan-aram, and precludes the events of ch. 34. At any rate, it is out of place after the revelation in 35^1. In 37^{2b} 'Joseph being seventeen years,' etc., in the present text follows what is evidently the beginning of a history, or more probably a genealogy, of Jacob. Ex 7$^{8-13}$ follows awkwardly after 7$^{1-7}$. It would be naturally at the first interview that Pharaoh would demand a wonder. Ch. 11^4, in which Moses speaks as a matter of course to Pharaoh, comes strangely after 10^{29}, in which he agrees never to see Pharaoh's face again. In the Sinaitic narrative as it now stands, it is almost impossible to get any intelligent idea of the order of events. In Ex 19 alone, Moses, the old man of 80, ascends and descends the mount no fewer than 4 times 19$^{3. 7. 8b. 9b. 14. 20. 25}$. Ch. 20 follows very abruptly upon 19^{25}. Moses ascends again apparently in 20^{21}, and no fewer than 3 times in ch. 24, without any descent being mentioned between 24$^{9. 13. 18}$. In ch. 33 there is obviously no connexion between vv.^{12} and ^{11}, and it is difficult to see the connexion between vv.$^{7-11}$ and the rest of the chapter, and throughout there is a want of any definite order in the various pleadings of Moses with God. Lv 26^{46} marks the conclusion of the Sinaitic legislation, and yet other cases follow in ch. 27, and a second similar conclusion is given at the close, 27^{34}. Nu 7$^{1-9}$ seems to imply that prepara-

tions for the journey from Sinai were made directly after the completion and consecration of the tabernacle, and it is difficult to see what room is left for the legislation contained in the whole of Leviticus. The account of the spies in ch. 13 and the rebellion of Korah, Dathan, and Abiram in ch. 16 involve numerous petty difficulties if read as continuous narratives (see below, iii. 2. *C*). The writing of Moses' song in Dt 31^{22} and of the law in 31^{24} are clearly out of place, the former referring to the following chapter, the latter to the laws given in previous chapters. The breaks in Joshua are not so obvious at first sight, but a careful reader will see that the book represents two different conceptions of the conquest of Canaan— one a rapid and complete conquest of almost the whole land under Joshua, and a *subsequent* allotment of the conquered portions; the other a gradual settlement carried out by the independent action of several tribes, an allotment having taken place *before the conquest*. The latter conception is more in agreement with Jg 1. But the accounts in Joshua which embody these two ideas have been so carefully interwoven that if that book stood alone it would be difficult to found an argument upon them.

(d) *Differences of style and conception.*—These, especially so far as they are connected with special phraseology, will be treated more fully at a later stage of the inquiry. It will be sufficient for the present, in addition to what has been already said of the Bk. of Joshua, to point out two very striking examples. (1) Notice the very remarkable difference in the whole tone and character of the two Creation stories, Gn 1-2^{4a} and 2^{4b} etc. The first describes creation as taking place in a systematic order, reaching its climax in man created *male and female*, everything being made out of nothing by a separate *fiat* of almighty God. In the second, all other things belonging to the earth (the heavenly bodies are not mentioned) are made, after the existence of the first man, in the order best suited for his wants, ending in the creation of woman. Men at least are moulded out of another material, the first man out of the dust of the ground, the first woman out of a rib taken from her husband. J'' walks and talks almost as a man with men. The first account is in form artificial and rhythmical, the second graphic and picturesque. (2) We may observe the same kind of difference in the conception of Moses. According to Ex 15^{22} 4$^{10-17}$ he is indeed an able and practical leader, but a weak and timid speaker, who is allowed to engage Aaron as his spokesman. In Dt he appears as the most fluent and eloquent speaker of the Bible.

It can hardly be denied that these facts taken together form an irresistible argument for the belief that the Hex. was compiled from a variety of sources. It has been sometimes suggested that Moses *compiled* Genesis, but actually *wrote* the last four books of the Pentateuch. This does not meet the facts of the case, because, as already seen, the same phenomena which prove Genesis to be a compilation and not an original work appear abundantly in Exodus, and evidently enough in the other books of the Hexateuch. The compilation must therefore have taken place considerably after the time of Moses.

ii. METHOD OF COMPOSITION.—*A*. Three views at least are possible, which we may call (1) conglomeration or crystallization, (2) expansion, (3) stratification.

(1) The first would imply that a number of fragments, handed down either in writing or by oral tradition, were collected together so as to form a literary whole. If the fragments were collected at one single time the process might aptly be called conglomeration. Crystallization

becomes the more appropriate term if we suppose that the fragments were gathered by degrees round some earlier nucleus. In fact it approaches more or less closely to (2).

(2) The second hypothesis is that a small original document, or a very definite oral tradition, was expanded by frequent revision at subsequent periods.

(3) Stratification is intended to imply that certain more or less independent documents, dealing largely with the same series of events, were composed at different periods, or, at any rate, under different auspices, and were afterwards combined, so that our present Hex. contains these several different literary strata.

There is probably some degree of truth in all these hypotheses, but there are strong reasons for believing that the last most nearly expresses the truth, and with some modifications it is the accepted theory of the great body of modern critics. The necessary modifications are : (a) that each stratum, before its incorporation into the united work, was subject to more or less revision, and in some cases considerable expansion from time to time ; (b) that the combination of the several strata was itself a gradual process, some being already combined before others had been produced ; (c) that the whole when combined was subject to editorial revision ; (d) that certain fragments remain which probably did not originally belong to any of these larger strata, but have been connected with them either by the original writers or by later revisers.

B. The main grounds for accepting this third hypothesis (stratification) are : (1) that the various literary pieces, with very few exceptions, will be found on examination to arrange themselves by common characteristics into comparatively few groups ; (2) that an original consecution of narrative may be frequently traced between what in their present form are isolated fragments. This will be better understood by the following illustration. Let us suppose a problem of this kind : Given a patchwork quilt, explain the character of the original pieces out of which the bits of stuff composing the quilt were cut. First, we notice that, however well the colours may blend, however nice and complete the whole may look, many of the adjoining pieces do not actually agree in material, texture, pattern, colour, or the like. Ergo, they have been made up out of very different pieces of stuff. So far, we have only proved what may turn out to be the first hypothesis of those given above, a conglomeration of fragments. But suppose that we further discover that many of the bits, though now separated, are like one another in material, texture, etc., we may conjecture that these may have been cut out of one piece. But we shall prove this beyond reasonable doubt if we find that several bits when unpicked fit together, so that the pattern of one is continued in the other ; and, moreover, that if all of like character are sorted out they form, say, four groups, each of which was evidently once a single piece of stuff, though parts of each are found missing because, no doubt, they have not been required to make the whole. But we make the analogy with the Hexateuch even closer, if we further suppose that in certain parts of the quilt the bits belonging to, say, two of these groups are so combined as to form a subsidiary pattern within the larger pattern of the whole quilt, and had evidently been sewn together before being connected with other parts of the quilt ; and we may make it even closer still, if we suppose that, besides the more important bits of stuff, smaller embellishments, borderings, and the like, had been added so as to improve the general effect of the whole.

C. It will now be shown that this view of the composition of the Hexateuch is borne out by an examination of the books. To do so we will first call attention to a few isolated facts, the bearing of which on the general question will afterwards appear. (1) It is obvious to the most casual reader that the Bk. of Dt, speaking generally, differs strikingly in style and character from the other books of the Hexateuch. It produces when read a different impression, just as St. John produces a different impression from the other Gospels. On examination we discover that this difference of impression is chiefly due to its highly spiritual tone and its constant appeal to the emotions. (2) In Ex 20²²–23. 24³⁻⁸ we find a definite body of laws, religious and civil, both marked by their singularly primitive character, described as written in a b ok, and marking the basis of a special covenant between God and man. (3) Throughout a large part of Exodus, the whole of Leviticus, and the greater part of Numbers, we meet with a large number of laws, mainly ritual, but partly civil, marked, however, throughout by a sameness of tone and spirit, the stress being always laid on ceremonial observances. Thus we find three distinct codes—the Covenant code (C), the Deuteronomic (D), the Levitical or Priestly (P). These will be found on comparison to differ, not only in general tone and spirit, but also in several definite details, both in their religious and civil portions. For instance, compare C's altar of earth or rough stone (Ex 20²⁴⁻²⁶) with P's elaborate altar of acacia wood overlaid with brass (27¹⁻⁸), the offerer apparently himself the priest in C (Ex 20²⁴) with the Levites all priests in D (Dt 18¹ etc.), and the elaboration of High Priest, Priests and Levites of P, as frequently throughout Leviticus, etc. Notice the differences in the feasts both in number and character : in C three, entirely agricultural, depending in time on the season, namely, Unleavened Bread, Harvest, Ingathering, Ex 23¹⁴⁻¹⁶ (15ᵇ appears to be a later interpolation, cf. 34²²) ; in D also three : Passover and Unleavened Bread, Weeks, Booths, Dt 16, mainly agricultural, but the first in part historical as a memorial of the departure from Egypt in haste, the last two still dependent on the seasons, vv.⁹· ¹³, or the second only relatively fixed if the Passover is to be identified with the beginning of harvest ; in P six holy seasons, besides the Sabbath, mentioned in the same category : Passover, Wavesheaf, Weeks, Trumpets, Day of Atonement, Booths, Lv 23. Two of these only, Wave-sheaf and Weeks, are solely agricultural, the last partly agricultural and partly historical. The meaning of Trumpets is not explained ; the Passover is historical, the Day of Atonement purely religious. The law of the manumission of slaves presents similar contrasts. In C (Ex 21²⁻⁶) the Hebrew slave, bought as a matter of course, after six years' servitude is allowed to go free, but without the wife procured for him by his master and the children born in servitude. If *from love of these or his master* he elects to stay, his ear is bored, and he becomes his master's slave for ever. In D (Dt 15¹²⁻¹⁸) the Hebrew slave who, in spite of his slavery, is, being a Hebrew, his master's brother, after six years' servitude (or possibly such of them as remained till the Sabbatical year, cf. 15¹⁻¹¹) is to be manumitted with liberal presents in gratitude for his great service. Nothing is said of his wife and children, but it seems probable that they were to be manumitted too. If from *love for his master and his master's family* he elects to stay, he is treated as in C. In P (Lv 25³⁹⁻⁵⁵) if a Hebrew, here called a brother, is sold into slavery through poverty (it is not conceived possible under any other circumstances), he is not to be treated as a slave at all, but as a hired servant. He is to be manumitted *with his wife and children* in the year of jubile, when he returns to his family and family possessions, which are then restored to him. But, even before this, any relative had the power to redeem him, or he might redeem himself. Slaves proper were to be only from the heathen around, or from the stranger that sojourned with them, and these were an absolute possession and heirloom.

That these three laws here contrasted belong to different dates is obvious. The similarity of form makes it equally clear that they are different versions, by revision, of the same law. The order of dates, both with respect to these and the religious laws before compared, is easily determined. The natural order is from the simpler to the more elaborate ritual, from the more barbarous to the kindlier treatment of fellow-countrymen. We should expect that in course of time feasts would be added, and for the sake of general convenience their dates more definitely fixed, and the priesthood become more ordered and defined. We know, too, that, as the danger of foreign invasion increased, the idea of a nation and of a religion both absolutely different from all others became more and more prominent, and hence a marked distinction between the treatment of the foreigner and the Israelite is a characteristic of late date (cf. Neh 13[23-31]). We gather, then, that C, D, P is the historical order of these codes. It will be seen on examination how, in almost every particular, D marks a transition between C and P in the law of manumission. In C the treatment of slaves is harsh. They are regarded as little better than the absolute property of their masters. They have only the one chance of freedom, which, if they have married in slavery, can only be accepted at the cost of breaking the sacred ties of family. In D this harshness almost, if not entirely, disappears. It is suggested that the master might treat his slave so kindly that the latter would, apart from all other considerations, prefer his service to liberty, and if he did not the master was to reward him liberally. But if the slave elected to remain he had no second chance of liberty. In P the kindness hinted at in D becomes a legal requirement. The Hebrew slave had always through redemption a chance of liberty, and could not legally remain, even nominally, a slave after the year of jubile. The perpetual servitude of a Hebrew was in no case permissible.

D. How are these three codes related to the narrative portions of the Hexateuch? We may begin by examining Genesis. We find that the greater part of the book is divided into groups of longer or shorter pieces, generally paragraphs or chapters, distinguished respectively by the almost exclusive use of Elohim or J″ as the name of God. As the latter is the ordinary word throughout the other books of the Bible, it suggests at once that Elohim is purposely used in those sections where it occurs, because, according to Ex 3[13-15] 6[2-8], the name J″ was first revealed to Moses in Midian, and it seemed improper to anticipate the name, even in the narrative portions of an earlier period. Further, it shows that this scruple was felt by one or more writers, but not by all. The theory advocated by some opponents of biblical criticism, that the names are used by the same writer with special reference to the subject in hand, Elohim representing the God of power, J″ the God of love, or other such distinctions, does not tally with the facts. Why in two narratives both dealing with Creation, and in two narratives both dealing with Abraham and Sarah's deceit, should Elohim be used in one of them and J″ in the other? But in other sections the name of God either seldom occurs, or Elohim is used by or to strangers, in which case J″ is on other grounds inappropriate; or again, in certain sections the two names seem to be used indifferently.

Again, beyond Ex 6, the name of God is of less use as a criterion, because Elohim occurs seldom. We will provisionally designate the group of passages in which J″ is used as J, those in which Elohim is used as E. On further examination we discover that while J is, generally speaking, consistent in style and character, E, on the other hand, falls into two very distinct groups. One of them, which we will call provisionally E[1], is very much like J in general character and in the subjects with which it deals, and, moreover, has in many parts been combined presumably with J. The other, E[2], is entirely unlike either of these in style, but will be found on further examination to bear in point of language and character a close affinity to the P code. This is shown partly by the love for ceremonial law, as the Sabbath (Gn 2[2. 3]), the provision against eating blood (Gn 9[4]), the rite of circumcision (17, etc.); but even more remarkably by the use of the characteristic vocabulary and style of P. For example, in Gn 1–2[3a] 'after his (her or their) kind' occurs very frequently as well as in 6[20] 7[14]. It also occurs in Lv 11[14-29] (9 times), and far less frequently in the parallel passage of D (Dt 14[11-18]); 'be fruitful and multiply' occurs in Gn 1[22. 28] 8[17] 9[7] 35[11], Lv 26[9]. 'Everything that creepeth upon the earth (or ground),' Gn 1[25. 26. 30] 6[20] 7[8. 14. 21] [contrast 7[23] of J], Lv 11[41-46]. We see, then, that the most characteristic phrases of Gn 1–2[3a] occur not only in similarly characterized (*i.e.* E[2]) passages of Genesis, but also in the code of P. We are thus justified in regarding P and E[2] as parts of a single source, and in future we shall understand P as including both. If we examine the narrative portions of Exodus and Numbers, we find the same phenomena, except that as here J″ is most frequently used as the name of God after Ex 3, it becomes more difficult to distinguish J and E. P can usually be separated with little difficulty because of its very marked character. Now, if we compare C with J and E, we find that it bears close affinities in point of language to both, so that we may call it JE, meaning thereby that in its final form it is probably a combination of both, and we shall further find it convenient to use this expression for the present for the J and E elements generally, without at this stage making any attempt to distinguish them. We shall find that by far the larger part of the narratives, as distinct from the laws, of Exodus and Numbers belong to JE, whereas, with special exceptions, the legal portions belong to P. In the last chapters of Dt and in the whole of Joshua we find elements of JE. In the latter book we also find elements which connect it with D (see below iii. 1. *C*). It should be observed that not only do we find here and there different *separate pieces* in the Hexateuch, shown by their characters to belong to these three sources, P, D, JE, but the pieces will often be found connected together by an obvious continuity of subject when pieced together, like the bits of patchwork in the illustration with which we started. For example, if we read continuously Gn 11[27-32] 12[4b. 5] 13[6a. 11b. 12a] 16[1a. 3. 15-16] 17. 19[29] 21[1a. 2b-5] 23. 25[7-11a], passages mainly, on other grounds, attributed to P, we get an almost continuous and complete, though very concise, account of Abraham's life. When we consider the number of revisions which the books of OT must have passed through, this is remarkable, and shows what a strong inclination the composers and editors must have had to preserve everything which they found.

iii. CHARACTERISTICS OF THE DIFFERENT SOURCES.—What has hitherto been said is little more than a statement of what has been proved by the critical investigation of some three-quarters of a century. A really satisfactory proof can only be obtained by one who has the patience to work out the problem step by step for himself. But to do this adequately a fuller account of these sources is necessary. For the convenience of the critical student these will now be taken in their order of difficulty, the first being that which can be most easily distinguished, and so with the rest.

1. D.—*A. Characteristics of D.*—As already observed, (*a*) *the larger traits of D* are very easily recognized. A serious student cannot fail to notice the hortatory character of Dt, its tone of gentle pleading, its spirituality as regards both God and man. God has no outward and visible form (Dt 4^{12}) ; God is near man, and His law is within man's heart (30^{11-14}); man's relation to God is by nothing more truly expressed than by love (6^5 10^{12}). The heart needs circumcision (10^{16} 30^6). Dt may be called the Gospel of the Hexateuch. Comparatively little importance is attached to religious ceremony. Though opposed to anthropomorphism, the writer expresses, in a very marked way, the personality of God in language which implies anthropopathic views; notice esp. 5^9 6^{15}. (*b*) *The aims and contents of Dt* are equally characteristic. It seeks emphatically to establish the worship of one God (6^4), and enjoins the absolute destruction of all visible representations of J″ as well as of heathen gods, the first by implication (4^{15}), the second by reiterated statement (7^{25} etc. $12^{2.\ 3}$ etc.), the abolition of all places of worship except the one sanctuary chosen by God ($12^{5-7.\ 11.\ 14.\ 18.\ 21}$ $16^{2.\ 6}$ etc.). Here, and here alone, they were to offer their sacrifices and keep their feasts. (*c*) Among *the institutions contemplated*, or perhaps we should rather say *described*, *by Dt* are a monarchy (17^{14-20}), a prophetic order (18^{15-22}), a priesthood of Levites ; that is to say, every Levite is a priest without distinction ; the phrase 'the priests the Levites' occurs frequently (17^9 18^1 etc.). (*d*) *The style of Dt* is smooth and flowing, tending to redundancy, generally pleasing to the ear, but at times perhaps a little tedious. Notice especially the accumulation of synonyms, or of words of the same class. Such phrases as 'with all thy *heart*, with all thy *soul*,' etc. ; 'the *ordinances*, the *statutes*, and the *judgments*' ; 'the *stranger*, the *widow*, and the *fatherless*,' are frequent. There is, too, a constant repetition of favourite phrases (see below, *B* (2)).

B. Language of D.—We shall find it convenient to distinguish (1) *favourite words*, especially where one synonym is used in preference to another ; (2) characteristic *phrases and expressions*. Under (1) notice especially Horeb (for Sinai), אָמָה 'a maidservant' (שִׁפְחָה only in 28^{68}) ; חֵטְא, the unusual word for 'sin' (the common form חַטָּאת occurs thrice only), אֲדָמָה 'earth' or 'ground,' very frequently in former sense (for common אֶרֶץ) ; לֵבָב 'heart,' very frequent (לֵב only 4 times) ; לִמֵּד 'to teach,' very frequent, marking the didactic character of the book ; קְלָלָה 'a curse,' frequent (אָלָה occurs 6 times, 5 of them in Dt 29) ; קֶרֶב with בְּ or מִן 'in' or 'from the midst of' (for תּוֹךְ) ; שָׁמַר 'to keep, observe,' very frequent, esp. of keeping God's laws, etc. ; also in Niphal in such phrases as 'take heed to thyself.' Under (2) the phrases ' J″ thy (your, etc.) God,' 'hear, O Israel,' 'prolong thy (your) days,' 'cleave to J″ thy God,' 'serve other gods, which neither you nor your fathers have known,' 'that it may be well with thee,' 'that thou mayest possess the land,' 'at that time,' are sufficiently familiar. Under both (1) and (2) we have given only a few of the most striking examples out of many. To show the full force of the argument we should have to point out the *relative frequency* of a very much larger number of words and phrases. But those given are so thoroughly characteristic that they will be at once recognized as specially belonging to Deut. by any one at all familiar with that book. Turn for example to Dt 6^{1-3}. In these 3 verses, taken

almost at random, at least 8 examples occur of the words and phrases mentioned above ; indeed there is hardly a single phrase in them, excepting 'a land flowing with milk and honey,' which does not illustrate the peculiar style of the book. It should be realized, too, that such differences of style as we can feel and appreciate go far beyond what can be expressed categorically, just as we may recognize a friend's face, or even his step or his handwriting, from a thousand, although we could but very imperfectly describe the manifold peculiarities which make up its individuality of character. These remarks are also true, more or less, of the characteristics of the other sources of the Hexateuch.

C. Extent of D.—Hitherto we have spoken of D as though it coincided exactly with Dt ; but, as a fact, we find on examination (*a*) that the peculiar characteristics which mark D are not found in some few sections of Dt at all. (*b*) In other parts of Dt they are found less constantly, and these have also some peculiarities of their own. (*c*) The characteristics of D, or some of them, are found also in some other parts of the Hexateuch. In other words, D may be used in a narrower and a wider sense. In the narrower sense it includes only Dt 5–34 (or perhaps 12–34), except at least 31^{14-23} 32^{48-52} 34^{7-9} (see below, iii. 2 *C*). The portions of Hex. outside of Dt belonging to D in the wider sense are not so easily determined, though the fact that some do so belong may be regarded as certain. The reason is that in other parts of the Hex. we find very few passages which appear to have been originally written by D, but several which seem to have been revised by one or more writers in the spirit and style of D, because we find in them traces also of the characters which distinguish the earlier documents. Such revisions give rise to some of the greatest difficulties of biblical criticism, and it requires very nice handling to disentangle the various literary elements, but their extent is not large enough to throw the least serious doubt on the larger results of criticism, nor can there be any serious doubt of the fact of such revisions having taken place. As far as D is concerned, the revision seems to have varied very much in different cases. Sometimes a mere characteristic touch is added. Sometimes D must have rewritten passages altogether. Sometimes again D appears to have expanded the narratives, etc., by considerable insertions. This being the case, we can hardly be surprised at a considerable difference of opinion among critics. Thus Dillmann finds in Genesis a large number of passages belonging to D, whereas several critics find none at all. The most characteristic D passage of Genesis is 18^{19}. The suggestion that Abraham would or should command his children reminds us of Dt 4^{10} 6^7 11^{19} etc. 'Keeping' (of God's commandments) and 'doing judgment,' etc., are characteristically Deuteronomic ; for the latter cf. Dt 6^1. Notice also the use of the synonyms 'justice' and 'judgment.' Ex 13^{3-16} is believed by many critics to have been revised by D. The solemn injunction to remember a great event in v.³, the emphatic use of ' this day' in vv.³· ⁴, the direction to instruct the children in v.¹⁴, the striking metaphors of vv.⁹ and ¹⁶, are all familiar characters of D (see Dt 16^3 6^{20} 6^8 11^{18}), though it is, of course, possible, on the other hand, that Dt $6^{8.\ 20-25}$ are in reality expansions of this very passage. There are also characteristic D touches in Ex 15^{25b-26}, 'a statute and an ordinance,' 'diligently hearken,' ' J″ thy God,' 'commandments and statutes.' When several touches of this sort occur together, it is extremely improbable that they are the result of a mere coincidence. Perhaps the most instructive example of a D revision is in the Decalogue in Ex 20. The expansion of the Decalogue, as distinct from the short commandments, which probably were the original 'ten words,' is full of D phrases: for example, 'J″ thy God' (vv.[2. 7. 10. 12]), 'jealous God' (v.[5]), 'love me and keep my commandments' (v.[6]), and especially 'that thy days may be long' (v.[12]). There appear to be traces of a similar revision in Ex 34[10b-15]; and Nu 21[33-35] is by several critics regarded as interpolated from Dt 3[1-3]. When we come to Joshua we find that passages so characterized, instead of being as it were sporadic, become frequent; but except in 23, which is throughout Deuteronomic in style, they are mostly confined to the first 13 chapters. This seems to show that previous accounts of the conquest of Canaan were rewritten by D, who also added supplementary passages, such as 18[7] 21[43]-22[8] 23 and parts of 24, while in the earlier books, as in some of the Exodus passages already cited, the D elements are so fused as to make an exact analysis very difficult and uncertain.

D. Date and Origin of D.—D, or part of D, has long been recognized as the book found in the temple in Josiah's reign, the account of which is given in 2 K 22, chiefly on the following grounds. (1) The whole of the Pentateuch, or even of the legal portions of it, could not have been read *twice in one day*, as was apparently the case with this book (2 K 22[11] 23[2]). (2) Josiah's reforms, confessedly based upon this discovered book, were, in fact, carried out in the spirit of Dt (*a*) by the destruction of the high places, not only idolatrous, but those in which J″ had been worshipped (2 K 23[8. 9]), so that the one single sanctuary, so emphatically ordered in Dt, then first became an established fact (it is clear that the attempt of Hezekiah, 2 K 18[4], to put down the high places was only partial or tentative); and (*b*) in connexion with this by the keeping of the passover at Jerusalem, cf. 2 K 23[21-23] with Dt 16[5. 6]; (*c*) by the abolition of the Asherim and of all idolatrous images and symbols of worship. (3) The stress laid upon the prophetic order is specially suitable to this period, when the prophets exercised so great and wide an influence. That Jeremiah should have been permitted to utter such prophecies as those contained in chs. 7 and 22 with reference to the temple worship and the royal house without molestation, shows the awe which the prophet's office inspired. (4) The peculiar ideas and thoughts, and to a certain extent the phraseology, of D penetrate Jeremiah's prophecies, and in a less degree those of Ezekiel, as we should expect from a newly-written, epoch-making book. Take, for example, such remarkable thoughts as the spiritual circumcision, cf. Dt 10[16] 30[6] with Jer 6[10] 9[25. 26], Ezk 44[7], and the law written in the heart, cf. Dt 30[11-14] with Jer 31[31-34] and Ezk 36[27]. But in both cases, the latter especially, the peculiarities in the *style*, etc., of these prophetic writers forbid our ascribing Dt to either prophet. And yet some of the ideas of Dt are to be found in a less complete form in Isaiah, and in this connexion we may bear in mind the first attempts by Hezekiah to put down the worship of the high places. From these facts we may conclude that Dt, or the essential part of it, was written either in the reign of Manasseh, or very early in that of Josiah. (1) If the former, it may have been the work of some priest or priests, who employed the time spent in forced seclusion in committing to writing their view of the law, derived partly from earlier documents, partly from the traditional teaching of the priests, and coloured largely, no doubt, by the religious ideas and feelings of their own time. In this way round an earlier nucleus a new body of laws might have gathered, which would naturally have developed all the more rapidly, as the priests, unable during the long reign of Manasseh to perform their ordinary functions, had more leisure for spiritual meditation, just as afterwards the Mishna resulted from the expulsion of the Jews under Hadrian. If so, this law-book was probably hidden by some priest for safety in the temple, in the hope that it might survive those troublous times as the written record of God's law, and the discovery of it may have been perfectly genuine. Even supposing that its existence and whereabouts were secrets known to the priests, this would not present a very serious moral difficulty. Just as the writer or writers of Dt in describing the customs and laws of their own times genuinely believed that they were giving the laws dictated by Moses by express revelation, their successors would have held the same belief, even though they may have known that they had been secretly written down, just as late Jews firmly believed that besides the Pentateuch a very large number of laws had been handed down from Moses by oral tradition. To understand the views of such an age we must first realize the entire absence of anything approaching to literary criticism. (2) Although not a *necessary* result of accepting the later date, the majority of critics believe this book of the law to have been the result of a pious fraud promulgated by Hilkiah and Shaphan with the intention of deceiving Josiah into the belief that the reforms which they desired were the express command of God revealed to Moses. We must reserve for a later stage some remarks about the various extensions and modifications of D. It will be enough at present to say that according to either view the book discovered can hardly be the whole of Dt, but rather the law which it contains, *i.e.* in the main, 12-29[1] or 12-31[13], with possibly the addition of 5-11.

2. P. The Priestly Book.—*A.* The most striking *general characteristics* of P are: (1) first and foremost, *the love of ceremonial law*, most obvious, of course, in the legal sections, as in Leviticus and the Priestly laws of Exodus and Numbers, but very noticeable also in the narrative sections, as shown, for example, in the institution and reference to the Sabbath in Gn 2[2. 3], Ex 16[21-30]; the prohibition against eating blood, Gn 9[4]; the rite of circumcision, Gn 17. 21[3-5]; the Passover, Ex 12[1-20], Jos 5[10-12]. (2) *Fondness for statistical details*, esp. those connected with persons and dates. The exact lengths of the lives of the patriarchs are always given, Gn 5. 9[29] 11[10-32] etc. By the age of a patriarch are marked the exact dates of important events, such as the beginning and end of the Flood, Gn 7[11] 8[13], in which last the very day of the month is given; the institution of circumcision, 17[24]; the age of the father at the birth of the firstborn (or covenant?) son, Gn 5. 11[10-26]. The exact details and dimensions of the ark are given, 6[14-17], as well as of every part of the tabernacle and its contents, Ex 25-31[17] 35-40. Notice also the frequent insertion of genealogies, for the most part little more than lists of names, Gn 5. 11[10-26] 25[12-18] 36. (3) *A tendency to symmetry and similarity of phraseology* in describing similar events. Notice, for example, in Gn 1 the regular repetition of such phrases as 'and God said' and 'God saw that it was good,' 'and the evening and the morning were the first (second, etc.) day.' The genealogies of Gn 5 and 11 are like recurring patterns, the verses scarcely varying except in the name and the number of years. In the five wonders of P in Ex 7-9 (see below iii. 2. *C*) there is a similar framework of phraseology into which the varying details are inserted. 'J″ spake unto Aaron (or unto Moses and Aaron)'—direction how to perform the wonders, beginning in the first four with 'take thy rod,' or an equivalent phrase—statement that the plague was done accordingly—that the magicians could (or could not in the last two) do so with their enchantments—and that Pharaoh's heart was hardened (with some variation of phrase), 'and he hearkened not unto them as J″ had spoken.' (4) We see also the same tendency to symmetry in the insertion of *the same or similar headings* in introducing subjects of a like kind, as 'these are the generations of,' Gn 2⁴ (transposed probably from before Gn 1¹) 5¹ 6⁹ 10¹ 11¹⁰· ²⁷ 25¹²· ¹⁹ 36¹ 37²ᵃ, 'and Moses gave unto the tribe of,' Jos 13¹⁵· ²⁴· ²⁹; 'and of *similar conclusions* at the end of a subject or part of a subject, as, for example, in Gn 10⁵· ²⁰· ³², Ex 25⁹· ⁴⁰ 26³⁰, Jos 13²³· ²⁸. (5) *In form* P is in its narrative portions little more than *a collection of dry annals*. Stories are seldom inserted, and when they are it is for the sake of some ceremonial provision, as the Creation story of Gn 1 for the Sabbath, the Flood story as an introduction to the prohibition against eating blood. Both lack the picturesqueness of the corresponding J stories, and all that P has to say of the destruction of Sodom and Gomorrah is the bare statement of 19²⁹. There is nothing thought worth preserving of P's history of Joseph except the short statistics of Gn 37¹⁻²ᵃ 41⁴⁶ᵃ 46⁶· ⁷, and possibly 47⁶ᵃ· ⁷⁻¹¹ ²⁷ᵇ· ²⁸. (6) P's *style is stiff and formal*, and seldom marked by delicate poetic feeling or grace of treatment, though occasionally stately and dignified, as in the Creation narrative, where the symmetry is certainly melodious, and adds grandeur to the conception. The repetitions help us to realize the almighty power of God. So, too, in the description of the five wonders in Egypt, Ex 7–9, the repetitions serve to intensify the stubborn obstinacy of Pharaoh in resisting the divine power. Again, Gn 23, though introduced by P with the obvious purpose of accounting for the burying-place of the patriarchs, is distinctly interesting because of its archæological quaintness, and is probably based upon some ancient document. The same is true of Gn 14, if, as some critics maintain, in its present form it belongs to P.

B. Vocabulary and Language of P.—In Genesis and Ex 1–5, prior that is to the revelation of the name J″, P always uses as the name of God 'Elohim' or שַׁדַּי אֵל 'God Almighty,' the latter esp. of His revelation of Himself to the patriarchs, cf. Ex 6² with Gn 17¹ 35¹¹ 48³; P uses בְּנֵי יִשְׂרָאֵל 'the sons of Israel,' not 'Israel,' so also 'the children of Heth' ('Hittite' only in sing.); אֲנִי (130 times) for the more archaic אָנֹכִי (once only in P); נֶאֱסַף in the phrase '*gathered* to his people,' of burial; 'according to their generations'; זָכָר וּנְקֵבָה 'male and female,' Gn 1²⁷ 6¹⁹ (in 7² J has אִישׁ וְאִשְׁתּוֹ 'man and his wife'), Lv 3¹· ⁶ etc.; 'thou (you, etc.) and thy seed after thee,' Gn 9⁹, Ex 28⁴³; בְּיַד 'by the hand of,' with words of command; 'that soul shall be cut off from his people,' and similar phrases, Gn 17¹⁴ (contrast 'shall surely be put to death' in the Book of the Covenant, Ex 21 (E)); לִין 'to murmur' (only in P); מִין 'kind,' Gn 1 (throughout), Lv 11¹⁴· ¹⁵; מִּשְׁכָּן 'the dwelling,' of the tabernacle (about 100 times); עֵדָה 'testimony,' as in the phrase 'the ark of the testimony' (only thrice in JE, and that in disputed passages); בְּעֶצֶם הַיּוֹם הַזֶּה 'in the bone of this day,' *i.e.* 'in this very day,' 14 times; 'be fruitful and multiply,' very frequent; 'Paddan-aram,' never 'Naharaim' (the abode of Laban is called 'Haran' in JE, cf. Gn 28¹⁰ 29⁴ with 28² 33¹⁸ 35⁹, 'the children of the East' in 29¹); 'Sinai' (never 'Horeb'). There is also an avoidance of several otherwise common words and phrases, such as אָנָּא with imperatives, גָּרַשׁ 'drive out,' עָשָׂה חֶסֶד 'do mercy,' וַיּוֹסֶף 'and he added' to do something, *i.e.* did it again, לְפִי חָרֶב 'by the mouth, *i.e.* the edge, of the sword,' though these last two are so common as in a literal Greek translation to have found their way into the language of NT (Lk 20¹¹· ¹² 21²⁴, He 11²⁴), 'a land flowing with milk and honey' (except in Lv 20²⁴). In this list, which is only a small selection out of many, all sacrificial terms and words of a like

nature, which might be accounted for simply by the peculiar subject-matter of P, have been studiously avoided. In P the argument from language is quite as strong as that derived from the general character of that document. In most passages either taken alone would form conclusive evidence.

C. Extent of P.—In Genesis P can be at once distinguished from J by the use of *Elohim*, from E by its general characteristics, style, and vocabulary. All the Elohistic passages of 1–11 belong to P, and create little or no difficulty. In the rest of Genesis we find belonging to P: (1) *Short historical notices* dealing with (a) leading events, such as the rescue of Lot from the cities of the Plain, 19²¹; Jacob's return from Paddan-aram, 31¹⁸ 33¹⁸; his descent into Egypt with a characteristic statement of date, 46⁶; the settlement of Esau in Seir, 36⁶⁻⁸; (b) *statistics of births, deaths, and marriages*, 16³· ¹⁵ 21³ 25²⁶ᵇ etc.; (c) *chronological details*, 12⁴ᵇ 41⁴⁶. (2) *Genealogies*, 25¹²⁻¹³ 35²³⁻²⁹ (ch. 36 as a whole is probably a still later insertion). (3) *The blessings* of Abram, Sarai, and Ishmael, connected with the rite of circumcision, and in the case of the first two the change of name, ch. 17; of Jacob by his father in connexion with his dismissal and projected marriage with one of his own family in contrast to the heathen marriage of Esau, 27⁴⁶–28⁹; and again directly by God, with change of name, 35⁹⁻¹⁵. (4) The purchase of Machpelah, explaining the origin of the burial-place of the patriarchs, ch. 23, who, according to P, were all buried there, as well as their wives, 23¹⁹ 25⁹ 49³¹ 50¹³.

In the Sinaitic portion of Exodus the P sections are obvious. We may, without hesitation, ascribe to P 24¹⁵ᵇ⁻¹⁸ (or ¹⁸ᵃ) 25¹–31¹⁷ (or possibly ¹⁸) 35–40. In the earlier parts of Ex, P is more fragmentary, but it will be readily recognized that the following passages contain several of its characteristics and are evidently connected together. In 1¹⁻⁷ we have a genealogical notice, with the statement in v.⁷ that the Israelites were 'fruitful and multiplied.' 2²³ᵇ⁻²⁵ is a passage with *Elohim* as the name of God, and refers back to the patriarchal covenant of Gn 17, etc., and therefore must also be assigned to P. We find the connexion between these two sections in 1¹⁴ a *concise* doublet of vv.⁸⁻¹³, which latter has not the characters of P, and belongs therefore to another source (JE). In 6²⁻⁹ we have P's version of the revelation of the sacred name J″ (contrast 3) marked as P's by שַׁדַּי אֵל (see above, iii. 2. B). 7¹⁻⁷ is clearly P's introduction to its five wonders (vv.⁶ and ⁷ are very characteristic of P). P's five wonders follow in 7⁸⁻¹³ *rod into serpent*, 7¹⁹⁻²⁰ᵃ· ²¹ᵇ⁻²² *water into blood*, 8⁵⁻⁷· ¹⁵ᵇ· [Heb. 8¹⁻³· ¹¹ᵇ] *frogs*, 8¹⁶⁻¹⁹ [Heb. 8¹²⁻¹⁵] *lice*, 9⁸⁻¹² *boils*, and 11⁹· ¹⁰ (by some ascribed to R) appears to mark the conclusion. In 12¹⁻²⁰· ²⁸ we have the ordinances of the passover, marked as P's both by its language and ceremonial character. Ch. 16, *in its present form*, appears largely to belong to P (special points of interest for P being the stringency of the Sabbath requirements, vv.²⁶⁻³⁰, and the preservation of the pot of manna), though parts of the chapter are regarded by many critics as later. The rest of P in this part of Exodus consists merely of short statements giving an itinerary of the journey from Egypt to Sinai.

The whole of Leviticus evidently belongs to P in the wider sense of the word, and almost the whole of Numbers. The exceptions are : (a) Nu 10²⁹⁻¹² ; (b) 13. 14; (c) 16; (d) 20–21; (e) 22²–25⁵ ; (f) 32. Of these (a) and (e) belong entirely to JE (see BALAAM). In (d) and (f), if we except perhaps 20¹⁻¹³, only unimportant fragments of P have been introduced. In (b) (the account of the spies) and (c) (the rebellion of Korah, Dathan and Abiram), P's narrative has been combined with JE, but in both it can generally be separated without much difficulty. In 13¹⁻¹⁷ we have the list of the spies, their fathers and their tribes, symmetrically arranged with a characteristic heading and conclusion, 'these are the (their) names,' etc., vv.[4] and [16], a descriptive summary of the geographical range of their search (omitting the picturesque details of JE, such as the huge bunch of grapes, and the terrific giants), and the *date* of their return, vv.[25. 26a]. In their report no mixture of character is displayed, but there is a sharp contrast between the bad report of the ten spies, v.[32a], and the good report of Joshua and Caleb, 14[6. 7], of whom the latter only appears in JE. The effects on the congregation, as told in the P narrative, are probably to be found in 14[1. 2] (in part) [5] and [10]. This last verse has P's characteristic 'tent of meeting.' P's narrative seems to be continued in v.[26], but in this section the analysis is far more difficult and uncertain. In ch. 16 we can separate with little trouble P's rebellion of the *Levitical* Korah from JE's *popular* rebellion of Dathan and Abiram, the one against the high priesthood of Aaron, the other against the secular authority of Moses. Quite apart from the critical characters which mark the various sections of the chapter, it is evident that we have not here a single consistent account of a double rebellion, against Church and State, so to speak. For example, in v.[22] there is an allusion to the sin of 'one man,' evidently Korah, the 250 of v.[35] being merely his satellites; but almost immediately after, in v.[24], Dathan and Abiram are connected with Korah, as though acting in concert. In v.[25] the first two appear alone, and in v.[26] the warning to depart out of their tents, which as given by God in v.[24] refers to all three, is given by Moses only with reference to Dathan and Abiram. The test by which the claim of these two is to be tried, vv.[29. 30], is different from that threatened to Korah and his men in v.[7]. The latter, which is to take place while they are engaged in offering incense, is evidently connected with the punishment of v.[35]. There can be little doubt that in P's original account Korah was consumed by fire with the 250. It is probable that when the accounts were welded together his name was added in v.[32], and those of Dathan and Abiram in vv.[24] and [27a]. Except for some such modifications we can recognize P's narrative in vv.[1-11. 16-24. 27a. 35-50]. The portions of Dt commonly assigned to P are 4[41-43], the appointment of the cities of refuge, a necessity which arose in course of time out of the abolition of the high places where sanctuary was originally permitted, 32[48-52] 34[1a. 7-9]. P's account of the last days of Moses contains, among other characteristics of P, Moses' exact age, 34[7], and the statement that 'the children . . . did as J″ commanded Moses,' 34[9].

In Joshua the P portions are somewhat curiously distributed. P must certainly have contained some account of the conquest of the country, but it is probable that this was told in a dry and summary manner, and that the compilers preferred the more detailed and interesting account of the older sources. Certain it is that in chs. 1–12, containing the account of the conquest of the country, the only fragments which can be definitely recognized as derived from P are the accounts of the passover and other events in Gilgal told in 4[19] 5[10-12], and of the covenant made with the Gibeonites by the princes of the congregation, 9[15b. 17-21. 27a]. There are also suspicions of P in such details as those given in 3[4a] 4[13] 7[18b], but we certainly cannot prove from them what the range of P's narrative really was. Beyond ch. 12 there is some difficulty, as there is evidence of mixture with other sources, but the following passages *in their present form* with little doubt belong to P, 13[15-33] 14[1-5] 15[1-12. 20-62] 16[4-9] 17[1a. 3-6] (notice, among other things, the characteristic headings). With ch. 18 we get on clearer ground. With the exception of 18[2-10] and

19[40b-47. 49-50], 18–21[42] and 22[9-34] belong almost entirely to P. It should be observed, however, that in this general analysis of P we have not, as a rule, attempted to distinguish between the work of P proper and later revisers.

D. Date and Origin of P.—(1) The date *cannot be earlier than Solomon's Temple.* The condition of religious worship evidenced by the Books of Judges and Samuel, for example the social character of the sacrificial feasts, Jg 21[19], 1 S 9[12-24] 20[18-24] etc.; the performance of sacrificial rites by other than Levites, as by Samuel, 1 S 7[9] 10[8] etc. (though an Ephraimite, 1 S 1[1]), David, 2 S 6[17], and David's sons, 2 S 8[18]; the illegality of the priestly portions, 1 S 2[12-17], which though *enjoined* by the Levitical law are here regarded as so sinful as to warrant the downfall of the house of Eli (2[22b.] is a very late gloss, not found even in the best MSS of the LXX),—all show that the laws of P were either unknown, or absolutely ignored during this early period. (2) Even after Solomon's reign, even if we could suppose that 1 and 2 K always give us an accurate account of the matter, and were not themselves influenced by P or kindred elements, the Levitical law would appear to have been only very partially observed. There are few references to it beyond the elaborate descriptions of the temple in 1 K 5–7. It is still disregarded by such great lights as Elijah and Elisha, who as prophets themselves sacrificed just as Samuel had done, and that without any regard for the one sanctuary which P throughout supposes, for example Lv 17[3. 4]. (3) This argument from silence is strengthened by the remarkable fact that in Chronicles we have in many respects a Levitical version of the same facts as those differently related in Samuel and Kings; as, for example, of the bringing up of the ark from Kiriath-jearim (contrast 2 S 6 with 1 Ch 15–16[6]), and the conspiracy against Athaliah (contrast 2 K 11 with 2 Ch 22[10]–23), making it almost certain that the Books of Samuel and Kings were in the main written before, those of Chronicles after, the institutions of P were formulated. (4) A further *terminus a quo* is furnished by a comparison between the codes of D and P. We have already shown at some length reasons for believing that *the code of P was subsequent to that of D* (see above, ii. *C*), showing in every respect signs of greater elaboration and development. (5) The style of P shows, by its stiffness, artificiality, and conciseness of treatment, that it is dealing with a dead past—a mere summary composed out of old written records, not the perpetuation in literary form of a still living tradition. All these facts point in the same direction, that P was far later than JE, and probably considerably later than D. Indeed, a considerable distance of time is required to account for the difference of vocabulary. (6) *There is no historical event likely to account for P previous to the Exile.* Such a document as compared with D marks a reformation, one might almost say a revolution, in religious worship. But it may easily be accounted for by the Exile itself. Outside of P there was no complete system of ritual laws. In all probability, they were largely traditional and of gradual growth. Some of them were codified in Dt, but a great many points are not mentioned, for precisely the same reason that many points of ritual are left untouched in the rubrics of the English Prayer-Book, because they are matters of common knowledge settled by prevailing custom. If a stranger could be supposed to have to conduct a service in an English Church, he would not know what he was expected to say, or whether he was expected to say anything, before and after the sermon, in what part of the Church he was to read the lessons, the Litany, or preach the sermon, and many other things of the kind. How many more serious questions must naturally have arisen concerning the ritual of sacrifice, involving, as it did, so much manual work! These things were originally decided, it is probable, by local custom. When religious worship had become centralized at Jerusalem they would probably be settled authoritatively by the body of priests, who are likely to have followed in the main the traditions of the old sanctuary of Jerusalem. (7) But when the line of tradition was broken by the Exile the need would have arisen for more elaborate directions, and we do actually find the prophet Ezekiel framing a sort of manual of ritual, though in some respects ideal and visionary (chs. 40–48). (8) But the troubles and disturbances which followed upon the Restoration must have made it difficult to establish any complete system of worship, and we do not hear of any complete religious organization till the time of Ezra. It would probably then be near the truth to say that P is *the result of the religious movement which began with Ezekiel in Babylon, and found its completion with Ezra.* Just as the book of the Law found in the house of J'' in Josiah's reign was D, or the nucleus of D, so it is likely that the law-book read by Ezra, Neh 8, was P, or the essential part of P. It is important to observe that the legal ordinances referred to in Neh are to be found in P rather than in D; for example, the custom of dwelling in booths, 8^{13-18}.

3. JE. The Jahwistic and Elohistic Sources.—
A. When we have taken away from the Hexateuch all the passages which can with a fair degree of probability be assigned to D or P, we find that the remainder forms a fairly complete and homogeneous whole, giving us, by a succession of narratives more or less connected, an outline of Jewish history from the Creation to the Settlement in Palestine, in fact covering, speaking generally, the same ground as P. This remainder we might have regarded as one literary source, were it not that a difference of authorship is discovered by the use of *Elohim* and J'' in Gn–Ex (see above, ii. *D*), which enables us to distinguish at once a certain number of sections as belonging to J and E respectively. Thus to J belong 2^{4b}–4^{26} 5^{29} 6^{1-4} 7–8 (ptly.) 9^{20-27} $10^{8-19. 21}$ 11^{1-9} $12^{1-4a. 6-20}$ $13^{1-5. 6b-11a. 12b-18}$ 15 (with some mixture perhaps of E), $16^{1b-2. 4-14}$ 18. 19^{1-28} 22^{20-24} (unless the insertion of a reviser) 24. 28^{13-16} 38. 39. To E we may with equal certainty assign 20^{1-17} 21^{6-32} 22^{1-13} $28^{10-12. 17-22}$ $31^{4-17a. 19-44}$ 31^{51}–32^2 35^{1-5} 40–42. 45 (almost entirely) 46^{1-5} $48^{1. 2. 8-22}$ 50^{15-26}. But in other sections either the name of God seldom occurs, or the names at first sight seem used indifferently, the sections being in the latter case generally compounded, as a close examination shows, of both sources. After Exodus, though we can readily see that both sources still continue, the distinction becomes more difficult, because though E, unlike P, still uses the name *Elohim* sometimes, J'' is more generally used; but even here this occasional use of *Elohim* is often helpful in discovering E sections. The mixture of divine names in Gn–Ex 3 sometimes arises from the fact that E *purposely* uses the name J'' and *vice versâ*. Thus E of necessity used the name J'' in Ex 3^{14} itself, but also in Gn 28^{22}, where the name has a peculiar emphasis, the point being that Jacob promises to worship his country's God even in a strange land; the name is, however, sometimes assigned to a reviser. This is probably the case also with Gn 22^{14}, unless it be actually a Jahwistic passage inserted in the E story. On the other hand, *Elohim* is sometimes used by J: (1) When God is spoken of by those not in covenant with J'', as by Adam and Eve before the time of

Seth, when men began to call on the name of J'' (Gn 4^{26}), and by the Serpent (Gn 3^{1-5} 4^{25} etc.). (2) When emphasis is laid on God's abstract nature, especially in contrast to man, Gn 16^{13} 32^{30} (see below, iii. 3. *B*). (3) In the construct state, when with a following word it is used descriptively of God, as 'God of Abraham,' 'of heaven and earth,' etc., Gn $24^{3. 7. 27}$ 26^{24} etc.

B. The separation of J and E in mixed passages, and those especially in which the name of God is for any of the reasons given not a sufficient criterion, as in the later books of the Hexateuch, is a matter of considerable difficulty, there being no characters of J or E so marked as to enable us (as we could with D and P) at once to assign the sections in which they occur to either source; but it can in most cases be decided with a fair degree of certainty. Moreover, the more the passages which can be definitely assigned to one source or the other, the easier the task becomes, because we obtain a larger number of criteria by which to recognize either source. But in spite of the labours of critics there still remains a considerable number of passages in which the division of sources is very uncertain. There is, too, always a certain danger of using as criteria comparatively rare words or phrases, which possibly by accident happen to occur once or twice in one source or the other. The reasonings by which the critical results are obtained are very complicated. They are chiefly those suggested by breaks in the narrative, points of contact, whether by continuity of language or connexion of subject, with known E or J fragments, and the like. Such arguments are often more trustworthy than those derived from vocabulary. We can make this clearer by analyzing Gn 32 as an example. Here there is no P passage, and the whole certainly belongs to JE. Vv.[1] and [2] (Heb.[2. 3], and so on with the other verses) are obviously the conclusion of an E section (31^{51}–32^2), the name *Elohim* being used throughout and constantly, though the section has no P characteristics. It will be seen on examination that vv.[3-13a] belong to J. For (1) there is no apparent continuity between vv.[2] and [3]. (2) On the other hand, vv.[3-13a] form a narrative continuous in itself without any obvious breaks, and the same is true of vv.[13b-21]. (3) Vv.[3-13a] contain parallels, differing in detail, both with the preceding and the following paragraphs, and therefore belong to a different source from either. Thus v.[10c] gives a different explanation of Mahanaim from that given in v.[2], and in vv.[13b-21] Jacob is (*a*) *again described* as dividing his property in view of the coming of Esau, but (*b*) *differently*, each drove by itself, vv.[16. 17], instead of the whole into two, v.[7], and (*c*) *with a different purpose*, in order to propitiate his brother by degrees with an accumulation of peace-offerings, vv.[17-20], not that one might escape if Esau attacked the other, as in v.[8]; (*d*) *the property is differently described*, goats being added, slaves—male and female—omitted, or rather male slaves mentioned, not as part of the proposed present, but as having charge of it, cf. vv.[14-16] with [5. 7]. Again, v.[21b] is a repetition of v.[18a]. (4) Again, both vv.[3-13a] and [13b-21] have points of contact with other known J and E sections respectively. Thus the possessions of $32^{5. 7}$ correspond very closely with 30^{43}, which belongs to J's account of the manner in which Jacob obtained his wealth *by trickery*, 30^{35-43}, and stands in contrast to E's account, which describes it as *a miracle* revealed by God in a dream, 31^{4-17}, or, at any rate, as so explained by Jacob. The latter passage is marked as E's by the constant use of *Elohim*. Again, 32^9 refers to 31^3, an evidently J passage. So far all is clear, but in vv.[22-32], which has the appearance of a complete and unmixed passage, there is some difficulty. At first sight we should naturally think that it belongs to E, because of *Elohim* in vv.[28] and [30], and it is so referred by Dillmann ; but the word, which is after all only one out of many criteria, may have been used purposely to express the abstract idea of God. The divine nature was such that even to see God, far more to wrestle with Him, meant death. And there are, in fact, many reasons for ascribing the passage to J. (1) The crude anthropomorphism is more in accordance with J's conception of God, see Gn 3[8] 8[21] 11[5] 18[1. 2], Ex 4[24] etc. E, indeed, is fond of dreams described as dreams (Gn 20[3] 28[10-12] 40. 41), but with J even these are described realistically (see Gn 15[17], and cf. 28[13-16] (J) with 28[12. 17 etc.] (E)). (2) Stories explanatory of place-names are far more characteristic of J than of E. (3) V.[23b] is a doublet of v.[21], which speaks of the present as having already gone over. We may confidently then assign to E 32[1. 2. 13b-21], to J 32[23-13a. 22-32]. The examination of this chapter will give some idea of the methods by which J and E may be often separated, but it must be admitted that in many cases, as in Gn 27[1-45], the analysis is much more difficult and uncertain.

C. For a complete analysis of JE throughout the Hexateuch the reader is referred to the critical works enumerated at the end of this article, especially the Tables prefixed to Holzinger's work, and artt. EXODUS, NUMBERS, etc. Sometimes the subject-matter forms indirectly a sufficient criterion for E or J. In the last chapters of Genesis and the early chapters of Exodus we find, as already noticed, two distinct traditions with regard to the locality occupied by the Israelites—one representing them as being in Goshen, apart from Egypt ; the other as being among the Egyptians, employing the same midwives, able in the hurried departure of the night-journey to borrow jewels of their Egyptian neighbours, their houses so close together that the difference put by J" between the Egyptians and Israel in the plague of the firstborn was a miracle of Divine Providence. The second view is certainly that of P (see Gn 47[6a. 7-11]), but we find it also running through several JE sections. Now there are several reasons for ascribing Gn 46[28]-47[5] to J, among them being the prominence given to Judah, as in what we have reason to believe to be the J fractions of 37. 38. and 43, and the use of the word 'Israel' for 'Jacob,' the latter being generally found in E. It will therefore follow that in the JE portions all the sections in which Goshen is spoken of as the home of the Israelites belong to J, the rest to E.

D. The general characteristics of JE stand in marked contrast to P. The narratives are full of life and movement, and have a genuine local colour. The characters are men and women with flesh and blood, engaged in all the real and varied occupations of a simple and natural life. The stories are never so subordinated to a religious or historical purpose as to lose their individual interest. They give the impression that, from whatever sources the writers may have derived the thread of their stories, the colouring is that of a life with which they were familiar in all its aspects. But beyond this it will be found that J and E have each sufficiently marked characters of their own. The God of E is a God separate from man, who reveals Himself usually by a voice from heaven, often that of an angel, as in Gn 21[17] 22[11] (where *Elohim* seems to have been altered into J" to agree with 22[14]) ; so in Gn 28[12] the angels need a ladder to ascend and descend to and from God (contrast J's account in ver.[13] 'and behold J" *stood beside him* '). Or God reveals Himself by a dream, as in Gn 20[3] 31[11]. Even when anthropomorphic expressions are used, as 'God came,' Nu 22[20],

' the finger of God,' Ex 31[18b], 'spake unto Moses face to face,' Ex 33[11] (cf. Nu 12[8]), they do not seem, as in J, to convey any definite anthropomorphic idea. But the J" of J is much more human. Though recognized as 'the God of heaven' and the 'God of earth,' Gn 24[3] etc., He was yet believed on occasions to have in His own person walked and talked with men, Gn 3[8] 18[1 etc.]. 28[13], Ex 4[24], so that Abraham actually mistook Him for a man, and Jacob wrestled with Him by night, Gn 32[24]. He needed to go down in order to see the city and the tower, which the children of men builded, and again to see whether the Sodomites had done altogether according to the cry which had reached Him in heaven, Gn 11[5] 18[21]. E has a good deal more to say of religious worship, especially in connexion with different localities, such as Bethel and Shechem, so much so that God is once actually called 'the God of Bethel,' Gn 35[7]. To E belong the earliest sacrificial laws, Ex 20[22-26]. E mentions the construction of the holy Tent of Meeting, 33[7-11], and the ark, which is spoken of almost as though it were itself an object of religious worship, Nu 10[33-36]. E also speaks of other primitive symbols of worship, as, notably, pillars, Gn 28[18. 22] 31[45] 35[14] (probably taken from E though in a P section), Ex 24[4] ; teraphim, Gn 31[19. 30] ; the brazen serpent, Nu 21[4-9] (cf. 2 K 18[4]). But such symbols do not always meet with approval. Jacob as an act of exceptional piety makes his family put away their strange gods (*teraphim*) and ear-rings (a religious charm ?), Gn 35[2-4] ; the calf-worship is condemned, Ex 32. E also has a reference to tithe in Gn 28[22]. In J the feasts of the sacrificial laws, in their earliest form at any rate, have less of a ritual element, Ex 34[10-28a], cf. 23[10-33]. As compared with E, J's narratives are, on the whole, more graphic and picturesque, and appeal more powerfully to the imagination, as especially Gn 2[4b]–3. 24, Ex 2 ; but this is partly due to the subjects treated of. J's style is remarkably easy and simple, that of E is somewhat more stiff and formal, and the treatment more dignified, as in Gn 22. We have a good illustration of their difference of character in their treatment of the marvellous. In J the most wonderful phenomena appear quite natural. The writer feels himself in an ideal fairy land in which no wonders are surprising. When we are told that J" brings the animals to the man to see what he would call them, we do not think of asking how this was possible, or even how it was done. But in other cases what in E are insisted upon as miracles, are in J ascribed to natural means. In J Jacob obtains his flocks and herds by a cunning trick thoroughly in keeping with his character, Gn 30[35-43]. In E it is by a special act of God's providence, 31[4-13]. In J the wonders of Egypt are performed by natural agency. It is an east wind that brings the locusts, Ex 10[13], that drives back the waters of the Red Sea, 14[21]. In E these are performed by the, so to speak, magic power of Moses' rod. Similarly, Amalek is defeated by the virtue of Moses' uplifted hand. The story of Jacob and Laban illustrates also another tendency of E, to soften moral difficulties. The deception of his old father had been largely the fault of his mother, and also took place before the covenant with God at Bethel, and therefore might be passed over, but Jacob's dishonesty in dealing with Laban seemed inconsistent with the character of a patriarch. Notice again how E justifies the expulsion of Hagar, which in J is merely the result of jealousy (Gn 16[4-6]), by representing it as the express command of God (21[12]). There are also some important differences in the subject-matter of these two. In J Moses acts by and for himself. In E much importance is attached to subordinates. Aaron assists him in his miracles, and Jethro gives him practical advice, and leads him in the wilderness, Ex 18. Joshua acts as his minister, 24¹³. In J the patriarchs are connected with Hebron, Gn 13¹⁸ 18¹, in E with Beersheba, 22¹⁹ 28¹⁰ 46⁵, and Shechem, 33¹⁹ 48²². In J Judah takes the leading part among Joseph's brethren, Gn 37²⁶ 43¹⁻¹⁴ 44¹⁴. ¹⁶. ¹⁸ 46²⁸, in E Reuben, 37²¹. ²². ²⁹ 42²². ³⁷. In E the prophetic element is more prominent than in J. Abraham, Gn 20⁷· ¹⁷, and Moses, Ex 33¹¹ (E?), Nu 12⁸, Jos 14⁶ (cf. also Ex 20¹⁸⁻²¹, Nu 11² 21⁷), are described as prophets, Miriam as a prophetess, Ex 15²⁰. Joshua is the prophetic successor of Moses, both in wonder-working, Jos 8, and in his final exhortation and the promulgation of his law-book, 24.

E. Besides the use of *Elohim* and *J‴* respectively, we find the following words and phrases characteristic of these two documents :—

E.—'Amorites' (used as name of aborigines of Palestine) for 'Canaanites.' 'Horeb' for 'Sinai.' 'Jacob' for 'Israel' (yet latter occurs in several E passages, esp. Gn 48–50, perhaps introduced by R). 'Jethro' for 'Raguel' of J. 'The man Moses,' three times. אָמָה 'handmaid,' for שִׁפְחָה (J) *invariably*, as in Ex 21. בְּעִיר 'beast' (only in E). בַּעַל 'lord' in its several uses as 'husband' (J and P have אִישׁ in this sense, E never). חִזֵּק לֵב 'harden heart,' Ex 1–12, for הִכְבִּיד, כִּבֵּד לֵב (J). כֹּה of place (J applies it to time). לֵבָב for לֵב (J). נִסָּה 'try,' 'prove,' esp. of God, as in Gn 22¹, Ex 15²⁵ 20²⁰ (?Ex 16⁴ 17²· ⁷). הֶעֱלָה 'bring up,' of bringing up the Israelites out of Egypt. פָּגַע בְּ 'to light upon,' as in Gn 28¹¹. רַגְלַיִם, lit. 'feet,' in sense of 'times,' Ex 23¹⁴. רָפָא 'heal,' with God as subject, Gn 20¹⁷, Nu 12¹³ (so a ground for ascribing Ex 15²⁶ in its original form [see above, iii. 1. *C*] to E). שִׂים לְגוֹי, lit. 'put for a nation,' for לְגוֹי לְגוֹי עָשָׂה, lit. 'make for a nation' (J). תְּמוֹל שִׁלְשֹׁם 'the day before yesterday,' with בְּ or כְּ, certainly characteristic of E, though in some of the Ex passages all critics do not agree. פָּתַר 'interpret' of dreams.

J.—אֲרַם נַהֲרַיִם 'Aram Naharaim' for 'Paddan-aram' (P). 'Israel' for 'Jacob.' 'Sinai,' as in P, for 'Horeb' (D, E). 'Canaanites,' but 'Perizzite,' Gn 13⁷ 34³⁰, Jg 1⁴· ⁵ (according to Meyer an interpolation). 'To find grace in the eyes of,' very frequent in J, also in some JE passages. 'To call on the name of *J‴ frequent.* 'To run to meet' *frequent.* Israelites called 'Israel,' not 'sons of Israel' (P), so 'Egypt' for 'Egyptian,' 'Reuben,' 'Gad,' etc., of the separate tribes. 'His brother,' in genealogies. אֲדָמָה 'land,' where אֶרֶץ would be used by E and P. אָנֹכִי for אֲנִי, usually. לָקַח לוֹ אִשָּׁה 'took him a wife,' regular formula in J, but once in E. בֹּאֲכָה 'as thou goest.' בִּי אֲדֹנִי 'I pray thee, my lord,' frequent but not exclusively in J. חָיָה 'to preserve seed alive.' חָרֵב 'to be dry,' as of the Flood, for יָבֵשׁ (P). טֶרֶם for בְּטֶרֶם (E, only once in J). יָלַד Qal, 'to beget.' יָשַׁב בְּקֶרֶב 'dwell in the midst.' כָּבֵד in sense of 'to be great, important.' לֵב for 'self,' as Gn 6⁶ 8²¹. מִסְפּוֹא 'fodder,' Gn 24²⁵· ³² (E has מָזוֹן, Gn 45²³). נָא with imperatives, etc. (in Gn 40 times in J, 6 in E). נִשְׁמַת חַיִּים 'breath of life,' Gn 2⁷ 7²² (רוּחַ inserted), for רוּחַ חַיִּים (P), הָפַּעַם הָזֹּאת, etc., frequent. צָעִיר, צְעִירָה of younger brothers and sisters (E קְטַנָּה). קָרָא עָלֵי *frequently*, but once in E, Gn 21³¹. שִׁפְחָה with P, etc., for אָמָה (E). Notice also a preference for the verbal suffix אֶת.

F. Date and Origin of JE.—The fact that most of the contents of JE are referred to by Amos and Hosea makes it *probable* that JE was prior to these prophets, but not absolutely certain, because, when these books were written, the stories may still have been current only in the form of oral tradition, and the absence of any mention of the story of Joseph, so full of religious and moral suggestions, is remarkable, though in such short

books it is far from conclusive. But the priority to these prophets is made still more likely by the attitude of E towards religious symbols (see above, iii. 3. *D*). Hosea and Amos, while they show that such symbols still existed as a matter of course, evidently regarded them with disfavour. It is significant also that E, though disapproving of human sacrifice, exhibits no horror at the thought of it. To accept the blood of victims instead was a gracious act of God, who was willing in mercy to waive His just rights (Gn 22). Again, the fact that E speaks of Abraham, Moses, etc., as prophets (see iii. 3. *D*), points to a time when the prophet occupied an influential position. Add to this that the highest teaching of JE resembles that of the prophets. We can hardly then be far wrong in regarding the times of Hosea and Amos as the *terminus ad quem* for JE. But the differences of character between J and E, especially in their theological conceptions, tend to show that J is the older of the two documents. Moreover, the differences that we find within each of these documents, but most especially in J (see below, iii. 4. *A*), make it likely that both J and E were originally collections of stories varying in date, and probably handed down for the most part, if not entirely, by oral tradition, some of them, it may be, centuries before they were committed to writing. Probably, as among other nations, the oldest which acquired a fixed form were popular songs describing some great national events, such as the Song of Miriam (Ex 15) and those preserved in Nu 21 (cf. also the Song of Deborah, Jg 5). In Gn 4²³· ²⁴ we have evidently a fragment of a song far older than the text with which it is incorporated. The chief allusion in the poem was apparently not understood, or at any rate is left unexplained by J. The attempt to fix the date of JE by comparing the patriarchal stories with the relations between the Israelites and the surrounding tribes is not very satisfactory. It may be true that the origin attributed to the Moabites and Ammonites is due to the animosity felt against these related peoples, but the animosity was so constant, at least from the time of the Judges, that we get little help in fixing the date of the story. Again, to refer the whole story of Joseph to the ascendency of the Northern kingdom in the time of Jeroboam II., and date its origin at this period, is to suppose it a deliberate invention, not, as the analogy of other such stories renders far more probable, a legend which had gradually grown up by oral tradition. From the importance attached to the local sanctuaries of Bethel, Shechem, and Beersheba (which last belonged to Simeon, one of the ten tribes), and the great prominence of Joseph, the father of Ephraim and Manasseh, it has generally been supposed that E at any rate was the product of the kingdom of Israel. Add to this that the North, the mission field of Elijah and Elisha, was in early times the chief scene of literary and prophetic activity. These arguments apply also, but with less force, to J, where Hebron takes the place of Beersheba as the abode of Abraham and Jacob; and Judah, instead of Reuben, holds a prominent place in the history of Joseph. From these facts it has been argued that J, though its material was originally derived from the same source as E, either in oral or written form, is *in its present form* the work of a Jewish composer or editor.

G. It is probable that J and E were blended into one whole before D's law-book was composed, as Dt 5–11 suppose it. Even if these chapters are not the work of D proper, they must have been added very shortly after.

4. Distinctions within the various sources.— We have hitherto regarded the different sources of the Hexateuch, for the most part, as though they were each homogeneous in character. In a certain sense they are, in that they possess individual characters which distinguish each from the rest; but within these are found considerable variations, just as we find among plants or animals several distinctly characterized species under one genus, or, to use a still better simile, varieties under one species. It is, in fact, probable that each of these larger sources represents in itself the result of a literary process extending in some cases over centuries.

A. For example, in the J sections of Gn the Flood story, with the beginnings of civilization and the dispersion of races following upon it (11[1-9]), seems hardly consistent with the growth of civilization described in 4[16-24]. It has also been suggested that Noah the inventor of wine (9[20-27]) belongs to a distinct cycle of legends from Noah the hero of the Flood, and that 6[1-4] gives a different explanation of the origin of sin from 3. Finally, it seems probable that the story of Nimrod, etc. (10[8-15]), came from the same cycle of stories as the Flood story, and is also of Accadian origin. Hence some critics have drawn a definite distinction between two series of stories, which they have denoted as J[1] and J[2] respectively. To the latter Wellhausen ascribes J's Flood, together with 10[8-15. 18b. 19. 21. 25-30] 11[1-9]. Some critics, however, have ascribed 6[1-4] as well as 10[16-18] to revisers of JE (JE[s]). Attention has been called to the fact that whereas in J[2] the three sons of Noah are Japheth, Ham, Shem (Gn 10), the sons of Noah in J[1] (9[20-27]) were originally, as vv.[26. 27] apparently show, Shem, Canaan, Japheth. In Gn 12 and later chapters J[2] has been found by some critics a convenient peg on which to hang unknown fragments, interpolations, etc., such as 12[10-20] 18[17-19. 22-33a], and even 20[18], passages usually referred to JE[s] or R.

B. Distinctions in E are not so frequently insisted on, but some critics have referred to an earlier source, E[1], such passages as show traces of archaic ideas or expressions, such as the anthropomorphic expressions of Gn 20[3-7] (cf. Nu 22[20], etc.), the ancient custom referred to in Gn 20[16], the word קְשִׂיטָה in Gn 33[19], Jos 24[32].

C. In D we can trace several different stages. It is now generally admitted that the Deuteronomic Code begins either with Dt 5 or with Dt 12. Dt 1-4, and perhaps also 5-11, were afterwards written as an introduction, and still later the history was continued with the Deuteronomic recension of Joshua. It seems likely that these were the gradual work of the Deuteronomic school, extending well on into the period of the Jewish captivity. The D elements of the earlier books of the Hexateuch are sometimes ascribed, not to this school, but to the compilers of JE. At any rate, they probably belong to a comparatively early period.

D. In P the fact of constant revision and gradual compilation is easy to prove, but it is not so easy to say how many distinct stages there were in its history, still less to assign the exact dates to which they belong. The following facts are, however, capable of easy demonstration.

(1) The nucleus of P lies in what is known as the Code of Holiness (P[h]) contained in Lv 17-26, though these chapters now contain many interpolations (esp. 22[17-25. 29. 30] 23[1-8. 23-38] 24[1-14]). This section is marked off from the rest of the P legislation (a) by its highly spiritual character and intense feeling of reverence for the holiness of God and everything connected with His service. P[h] is the centre and kernel of the new religious movement; (b) by its intimate relation to the ideal of ritual, etc., sketched out by Ezekiel, chs. 40-48; (c) by its use of a special terminology, words and phrases being found which occur nowhere else. It will be sufficient here to call attention to such phrases as 'I am J″,' 'I J″ am your God,' 'I your God am holy,' and the like; 'walk in my (etc.) ordinances,' 'do and keep my statutes and my judgments,' אֲנִי יְהוָה, 'I will set my face,' 'that man shall be cut off from his people,' 'my (J″'s, etc.) Sabbaths.' For a more complete list see Driver, LOT[6], 49. (d) By discrepancies between P[h] and the general body of Levitical law. Thus in P[h] the later distinction between the high priest and the ordinary priests is still in the making. The chief priest is but primus inter pares (the priest who is greater than his brethren, Lv 21[10]). Notice that the injunction which in Lv 21[10] is laid upon the chief priest only, not to let the hair of his head go loose, or rend his clothes, is in Lv 10[6. 7] laid upon all the priests. The Feast of Booths lasted, according to the original text of Lv 23[39-44], 7 days instead of 8, and is still determined by the season, 'when ye have gathered in the fruits of the land'; the addition of the 8th day and the words 'on the 15th day of the 7th month' in v.[39], evidently are interpolations (inconsistent with vv.[40-42]) added when the laws were incorporated into the larger code. On the other hand, it is possible that P[h] included passages now outside Lv. 17-26, as esp. Ex 6[6. 7], Lv 11[1-23. 41-47] in their original form. With reference to the relation of P[h] to Ezekiel, it should be noticed that the resemblance extends not only to the general tenor of the subject, a thing in itself striking enough, but even to the style and phraseology; and in this respect it is not confined to these chapters of Ezekiel, but several expressions of P[h] are found scattered in various parts of the prophet [see Kuenen, § 15, note 10]. That P[h], therefore, was written either by Ezekiel himself or by one imbued with his spirit, and in all probability a contemporary, does not admit of reasonable doubt, and we cannot be far wrong in assigning it to the latter half of the Exile.

(2) The next in order of time, and the most important of the Priestly documents, is the historical and legislative work known frequently as P[g], which contains all of P excepting P[h] on the one hand, and certain later accretions in the legislative portions on the other. The central feature of P[g] is the promulgation of the laws, which are all represented as revealed to Moses on Mt. Sinai. P[g] was probably, as already suggested, the law promulgated by Ezra, Neh 8. 9[3]. Notice that the Feast of Booths is kept eight days according to P[g], see Nu 29[35].

(3) A third stage is reached in the union of P[g] and P[h], but whether it took place before or after the promulgation of P by Ezra cannot be determined. All that can be said with certainty is that Ezra was the head, perhaps the founder, of a school of scribes specially suited for carrying out a work of this kind.

(4) Lastly, there is evidence of various additions and revisions of the Priestly Code made from time to time (P[s]). The most important of the former in Ex–Nu are Ex 30. 31[1-17] 34[29-35] 35-40, Lv 1-7. 8. 11[24-40] 12-15. 16 (in part), most of Nu 1-10[28] 15. 19, the whole of 28-31. To these we should add the additions to P[h], esp. in Lv 23, to make it agree with P[g]. The necessity of supposing such additions to P[g] cannot be here proved at length. It is enough to say generally that the proof lies in certain repetitions, inconsistencies, and want of sequence. For example, Ex 35-40 Lv 8 taken together are a repetition of Ex 25-29. Ex 30[1-10] describes a special altar of incense of which there is no mention in the list of holy things in 26[31-37]. Cf. Lv 16[12], which seems to imply that the one altar was used both for incense and sacrifice. Ex 30 (or at any rate 35) –Lv 8 breaks the sequence between Ex 29 and Lv 9, and Lv 1-7 is itself a

collection of laws with several slight inconsistencies. Finally, Lv 11-15 breaks the connexion between 10 and 16.

(5) To these we should also add the incorporation of the already united JED into P; but to what date either this or the various supplements spoken of under (4) belong, cannot be determined. Probably, the latter represent a long and very gradual process. Kuenen argues from the difference of arrangement found in the LXX translation of Ex 35-40, belonging to 3rd cent. B.C., that the final redaction of these chapters was even then hardly completed.

5. Editorial Revisers.—It has not been found practicable within the limits of this article to give a complete estimate of the work of the various editorial revisers. That several alterations were made as the different sources were welded together is practically certain. A few examples of editorial emendations must suffice. In Gn 22² 'the land of Moriah' is very suspicious (esp. if, according to Gn 14, Jerusalem was already in existence), inasmuch as (1) the name Moriah does not appear again until the very late Book of Chronicles, (2) E otherwise shows no partiality towards Judah, (3) it could not have taken 3 days to get from Beersheba to Jerusalem, see v.⁴. It is probable, therefore, that an original 'Amorite' or name of some Ephraimitish mountain, which had perhaps become illegible, was altered by a reviser with Southern propensities, possibly JE, but more probably Pˢ. 22¹⁴⁻¹⁹ is certainly not part of the E narrative, but is possibly some fragment of J worked in to suit the story. It is, however, to be observed that in v.¹⁸ 'be blessed' is הִתְבָּרְכוּ, not וְנִבְרְכוּ as elsewhere in J; so some have regarded it as the work of a reviser. In 35¹⁴, ¹⁵ we have probably the working in of an E fragment in a section of P (see above, iii. 3. D). Ex 34¹¹⁻²⁶ has been revised by JE or D to agree with other passages, and in vv.²⁹⁻³⁵ it is followed by a story embodying perhaps an old tradition, but written in the spirit and style of P.

iv. SUMMARY.—We may now summarize in this way the probable history of the Hexateuch. For many centuries probably the only records of the past were those contained in song and saga. It is very possible that, as with the ancient Icelanders, these were recited at religious festivals (Ex 15¹, ²⁰, ²¹, cf. Jg 11⁴⁰). The first attempts to collect these, so as to form a *connected written history*, probably date from the 8th or 9th cent. B.C., and originated presumably in the schools of the prophets. There are sufficient evidences of two distinct versions of this ancient history, J and E; but though they deal for the most part with the same cycle of subjects, and E is probably the later of the two, there is no proof that there is any *literary* connexion between them. Later on, towards the close of the 7th cent., these two documents were combined together, but so skilfully that it is often very difficult to separate them (JE). About the same time in Jerusalem a code of ritual regulations and customs, commonly believed to have been revealed by God to Moses, was set forth in writing and afterwards published in the reign of Josiah (D). This code was shortly afterwards provided with a historic setting and combined with the earlier history, and the whole, especially the conquest of Canaan, revised by the same school (JED). It has been conjectured by Kuenen, who has been followed by several other critics, that E's Book of the Covenant, Ex 20²²-23, was originally represented as drawn up on the plains of Moab, and that, when the code of D was substituted for it, the former was put back so as to form part of the Sinaitic legislation. This will account both for the present difficulty in connecting Ex 20²²-24¹¹ with its context, and also for the fact that, while in the historical summary of Dt 1-4

there is no reference to the Bk of the Covenant, several of its provisions in a revised form appear in the main body of D. During the Exile, possibly before the work of Dˢ was complete, a new body of ritual law, more priestly in its character, was drawn up, probably by some disciple of Ezekiel, and very possibly under his direction (Pʰ). This was followed by a new version of the whole history, and especially the legislation, conceived in a still more sacerdotal spirit, which was probably completed about a century later, and promulgated by Ezra and Nehemiah (Neh 8. 9) (Pᵍ). Finally, by the union of this with Pʰ, and the additions of new laws and regulations from time to time, and various editorial revisions extending down to it may be the 3rd cent. (Pˢ), we get our present Hexateuch.

v. THE HISTORICAL VALUE OF THE HEXATEUCH. —It is, of course, obvious that the Hexateuch as it stands is not strictly a historical work. It did not need criticism to discover this, but criticism makes it absolutely certain. It shows that the most definite and statistical details, those given namely in P, are the least to be depended upon, being unknown to the earliest writers, and apparently the calculations of a writer very far removed from the events described. There is also observable throughout a tendency in the various writers to throw back into their composition the customs, etc., of their own times. Thus the whole body of laws, originating in local custom, or handed down as common law and promulgated from time to time, would come to be fathered on Moses; just in the same way as the Chronicler read into the old documents the ritual of his own day. Similarly, it is probable that the contemporary religious and social customs of Northern Israel are in JE described as those of their ancestors who lived in a distant past. Regarded as a history of the ancient migrations of the Israelites, their establishment as a religious and political community, and their settlement in Canaan, the Hexateuch contains little more than a general outline on which to depend. We may gather that the Israelites were one among a number of Semitic peoples, who after long migration settled in or near Egypt, from which after a period of serfdom they finally escaped, and after further migrations gradually gained a footing in the trans-Jordanic territory, and afterwards made various incursions across the Jordan; until, finally, the larger part of the territory, especially on the hills where the Canaanitish chariots were useless, fell into their hands. That so many traditions and stories should have attached themselves to Abraham and Moses, even though many of them may be inapplicable or exaggerated, shows what a deep impression their personality and work made upon their generation, and it is hardly too much to say that probably all that was noblest and best in the nation must be attributed to such men as these who first sowed the seed, of which the prophetic teaching was the fruit. But if the Hex. has little to tell us of the early history of Israel, it has much to tell us of the times in which the authors lived. The habits and customs, the ideas, above all those connected with morality and religion, are faithfully represented. And thus we are enabled to trace something more than an outline of that history of religion which was the needful preparation for the teaching of Christ.

LITERATURE.—J. W. Colenso, *The Pentateuch and Book of Joshua critically examined*, 7 parts, London, 1862-1879; W. R. Smith, *OTJC*², Edinburgh, 1892; Driver, *LOT*¹, Edinburgh, 1891, ⁶, 1897; B. W. Bacon, *The Genesis of Genesis*, Hartford, 1892; Bissell, *Genesis Printed in Colours*, Hartford, *The Pentateuch, its origin and structure, an examination of recent theories*, New York; Fripp, *The Composition of the Book of Genesis, with English Text and Analyses*, London, 1892; Kuenen, *An Historico-critical Inquiry into the Origin of the*

Hexateuch, translated from the Dutch by P. H. Wicksteed, London, 1886 ; Addis, *The Documents of the Hexateuch*, pt. i. London, 1892, pt. ii. 1898 ; Wellhausen, *Die Comp. d. Hexateuchs und der historischen Bücher des AT*, Berlin, 1889 ; Baentsch, *Das Bundesbuch*, Halle, 1892 ; Cornill, *Einleitung in das AT*, Freiburg in B. 1892 ; Kautzsch and Socin, *Die Genesis mit äusserer Unterscheidung der Quellenschriften übersetzt*[2], Freiburg in B. 1891 ; Kautzsch and others, *Die H. Schrift des AT übersetzt*, Freiburg in B. 1894 ; Aug. Dillmann, *Kurzes Exegetisches Handbuch. Gn.*[6] 1892, *Ex-Lv*[2], 1897, *Nu, Dt, Jos*, 1886. A systematic statement of Dillm.'s views is given in the *Schlussabhandlung* at the end of the last [Eng. tr. of *Genesis*, T. & T. Clark, Edinburgh, 1897] ; Budde, *Die Biblische Urgeschichte*, Giessen, 1883 ; Holzinger, *Einleitung in den Hex. mit Tabellen über die Quellenscheidung*, Freiburg in B. 1893. These are only a selected few out of a very large number of works dealing with different aspects, or parts, of the great critical problem. A great deal of useful information will be found in the commentaries on the separate books.　　　　F. H. WOODS.

HEZEKIAH (on forms and meaning of the Heb. name see next article).—**1.** A king of Judah (see next art.). **2.** An ancestor of the prophet Zephaniah (Zeph 1[1]), possibly to be identified with the king of the same name. **3.** Head of a family of exiles who returned, Ezr 2[16] = Neh 7[21] (cf. 10[17]).

HEZEKIAH חִזְקִיָּהוּ or יְחִזְקִיָּהוּ, also חִזְקִיָּה or יְחִזְקִיָּה ' J″ hath strengthened ' or ' J″ strengtheneth,' LXX Ἐζεκίας, Assyr. *Ḥazaki(i)au*.—A king of Judah, son and successor of the feeble and superstitious Ahaz, with whom he contrasts as favourably as with his own son and successor Manasseh. He is conspicuous in Jewish history as the first king who is said to have attempted a reformation of religion on the principles which we find formally laid down in the Bk. of Deuteronomy (2 K 18, 2 Ch 29 ff. ; see HIGH PLACE, ii. p. 382[b]) Special interest also attaches to his reign on account of his close personal connexion with the prophet Isaiah, who occasionally exerted a great influence over him (especially in the memorable crisis which issued in the deliverance of Jerusalem from Sennacherib), and also because of the strong light thrown upon his times by the cuneiform inscriptions as well as by extant prophecies. H.'s history is recorded in 2 K 18[13]–20[19], Is 36–39, and 2 Ch 29–32. The two former are very much alike, K being on the whole more full and exact, and IS having been borrowed from it by the compiler, who added the Song of H. (Is 38[9-20]), but omitted the annalistic fragment in 2 K 18[14-16] as not suiting his purpose, which was to trace the fulfilment of the prophecies of Isaiah in connexion with the siege of Jerusalem. Kings is evidently based not only on State annals, but also on prophetic narrative (derived partly from authentic documents, partly from tradition), which bears traces of the style of D in 37[4. 34. 35] 38[1. 3. 5] 39[1], and cannot be assigned to Isaiah (as suggested by 2 Ch 26[22] 32[32]) nor yet to a contemporary, in view of (*a*) the nature of the statements in 37[7. (38). 36] 38[5], (*b*) such late words as יְהֻדִית (36[11. 13]), (*c*) the apparent anachronisms in 36[19] 37[38], and (*d*) the want of order and coherence in the narrative when carefully examined and compared with the Assyr. records.

The chronology of Hezekiah's reign is beset with special difficulty. According to 2 K 18[10] the Fall of Samaria (722 as determined by Assyriologists) took place in the 6th year of H., which would give 728-7 as the date of his accession (Ewald, Bredenkamp, Delitzsch, Orelli, Strack, Driver, Kirkpatrick, Duhm, Skinner. Ussher, Winer, W. R. Smith make it 725). In 2 K 18[13], on the other hand, the invasion of Jerus. by Sennacherib (701) is said to have taken place in the 14th year of H., who must thus have commenced to reign in 715-4 (Kamphausen, Wellhausen, Ed. Meyer, Kittel, Guthe, Stade, Cornill, Hommel, Cheyne).

An attempt has been made to reconcile the earlier date with 2 K 18[13] by supposing 14th to be a mistake for 24th (Bredenkamp), 27th (Rawlin-

son), 29th (Oppert), also by taking vv.[13-16] to refer to a campaign of Sargon in 711 (the name ' Sennacherib ' being considered a late and erroneous insertion), a theory first advanced by E. Hincks (who confined the reference to Sargon to v.[13]) ; but for reasons stated by Kuenen, W. R. Smith, and others, the theory of such an invasion by Sargon is now generally abandoned, and the best solution is probably to be found in a rearrangement of the narrative. We have a clue to such rearrangement in 2 K 20 (Is 38), which records a sickness of H. that must have taken place in the 14th year of his reign if the latter extended to 29 years, and if H. lived 15 years after his recovery (2 K 18[2] 20[6], Is 38[5]). This sickness the compiler seems to have connected with the invasion by Sennacherib (2 K 20[6b], Is 38[6]), applying to the invasion the note of time (14th year), which properly belonged to the sickness, and introducing the latter with the words ' In those days,' which may have originally belonged to the invasion. This view is supported by the fact that the account of Merodach-baladan's embassy, which took place after the sickness (2 K 20[12], Is 39[1]), ought certainly to have come before the invasion, as after that event Merodach-baladan was not in a position to send ambassadors, his downfall having taken place the year before (702) ; nor was H., after being impoverished by the war (2 K 18[13-16]), possessed of such treasures as would be likely to excite the admiration of his visitors (2 K 20[13], Is 39[2]). A middle date is suggested by Winckler (followed by McCurdy), who takes 2 K 16[2] as his guide, setting aside both 18[10] and 18[13], and fixes H.'s accession at 720–19. The earlier date, however, besides having 18[10] to rest on, fits in with the subsequent chronology of the kings of Judah, and agrees with Jer 26[18f.], which represents H. as under the influence of the prophet Micah, who is known to have prophesied before the Fall of Samaria (Mic 1[6]). On the other hand, it aggravates the discrepancy between the age of Ahaz at his death (by reducing his reign from 16 to 8 years, while the 715 date gives him 20 years of a reign) and the age of H. at his accession, which is stated in 2 K 18[2] to be 25 years (but in LXX 20),—a difficulty which Whitehouse meets by supposing that H. was co-regent with his father from 727 to 715, and that his 14th year is to be reckoned from the latter date, when he was in a position to initiate a new policy following the counsels of Isaiah.

This uncertainty as to the chronology is of less importance, as the interest of H.'s reign, in the light both of prophecy and the Assyr. records, practically closes with the invasion in 701. Even if we suppose him to have lived till 686 (as the later date for his accession would imply), we gain little or no additional information regarding the events of his reign. Assuming that H. came to the throne in 727, it was as a young and inexperienced prince in the midst of faithless and time-serving politicians, who scorned the teaching of the prophets, and a like-minded priesthood. The deplorable state of morality and religion is evident from Mic 1 ff. (cf. Is 28) delivered on the eve of the siege of Samaria, *i.e.* about 725. These testimonies, as well as the fact that the anti-prophetic party continued in the ascendant till 701, oblige us to receive with caution the circumstantial account given by the Chronicler (2 Ch 29[3ff.]) of the reforms effected by H. in the very first year of his reign. He is said to have purified and refurnished the temple, which had been shut up by Ahaz after being despoiled of its treasures, to have renewed the ancient sacrifices with great magnificence and pomp, to have ordained a joyful celebration of the long-neglected Passover, after purging Jerus. of its idolatrous altars and sending out invitations to the Israelites in the north, 'the remnant that had escaped out of the hands of the king of Assyria.' So great was the enthusiasm said to have been evoked that it led to a general crusade against the images and altars and high places in the cities of Judah and Benjamin, Ephraim and Manasseh, both king and people at the same time giving evidence of their devotion by their munificent provision of tithes and offerings for the support of the priests and Levites, who were now carefully registered and organized. The only part of these reforms that is recognized in K is the removal of 'high places' and destruction of 'pillars' and 'Asherah' (2 K 18[4, 22]), but a remarkable instance of H.'s zeal for purity of worship is also given (v.[4]) in his destruction of 'the brazen serpent that Moses had made' which had become an object of worship in Jerusalem (see NEHUSTAN).

While it is generally admitted that H. paved the way for the reformation carried out by Josiah in the next century, not only prohibiting idolatry, but seeking to centralize the national worship by destroying the local sanctuaries in the provincial cities of Judah, around which heathen practices were apt to gather (cf. Mic 1[5] 5[12-14], Is 30[29] 31[9] 1[29] 2[20]), it is held by Wellhausen, W. R. Smith, Nowack, Stade, and others, that the reforms could only have taken place after the Assyrian invasion, which brought dishonour on the provinces, but was the means of exalting Jerus. and glorifying its protecting deity, thus counteracting the idolatrous tendencies inherited from the previous reign. In proof that the reformation could not have been earlier, they cite the allusions to prevalent idolatry in such late prophecies of Isaiah as 30[22] 31[7] (c. 702). These indeed show that the reformation had been far from perfect (cf. 2 K 23[13] and revulsion under Manasseh), being largely due to royal command; but the whole traditional account of H.'s reign points to an earlier date for his turning to J". Cf. Jer 26[18f.] already referred to, the eulogistic summary in 2 K 18[3-7], H.'s plea for divine favour in 20[3], and the demolition of high places, etc., ascribed to him by the Rabshakeh in 18[22], which, even if an interpolation (Cheyne), was not likely to be introduced unless it had some basis of tradition to rest on.

In addition to his work as a religious reformer, H. revived in some measure the glories of his great-grandfather Uzziah by successful inroads upon the Philistines, over one of whose cities (Ekron) we find him in 701 holding a position of suzerainty; by his care for the interests of national defence, repairing the walls and fortifications of Jerus., fitting up arsenals, constructing aqueducts and reservoirs for securing to Jerus., and cutting off from besiegers, a permanent supply of water; by building cities, and encouraging trade and agriculture through the erection of shelters for sheep and cattle and of store-houses for produce. Whether the underground tunnel leading from Gihon (the modern 'Fountain of the Virgin') to the upper pool of Siloam (1708 ft. long, and a work of great engineering skill) is to be identified with 'the conduit' mentioned in 2 K 20[20] as the work of H., and apparently referred to in 2 Ch 32[30] (cf. 32[4] 22[9-11] and Sir 48[17]), is still a moot point, different opinions being held by experts as to the age of the inscription (discovered in 1880) at the mouth of the tunnel, which is in round characters and in old Hebrew but bears no date,* the question being also complicated by the mention of an already existing Shiloah in Is 8[6], on which see Dillmann's note, and Stade, GVI 593 f.

Among the merits which tradition assigned to H. was a taste for music and literature. In his

* See PSBA, May, July, 1897, Feb. 1898 (papers by Pilcher, Conder, Davis), and Expos. Times, Apr. 1898, p. 292 f., and May 1898, p. 384 (the latter by A. B. Davidson).

restoration of the temple service, music, both vocal and instrumental, has a prominent place (2 Ch 29[25-30]). In Pr 25[1] we read of 'the men of Hezekiah' who copied out the proverbs of Solomon, and in the Talm. (Baba bathra, f. 15a) 'H. and his associates' are credited with the 'writing' of certain books of the OT. Is 38[9-20] even contains a song which bears in its superscription to have been written by H. at the time of his sickness and recovery. But it is absent from 2 K, and its late insertion in Is appears to have disturbed the text, displacing v.[21f.]. Moreover, it has no distinct marks of its alleged royal authorship, and bears a strong resemblance to Job and the later Psalms. For these reasons it is considered post-exilic by most recent critics, and is even supposed by Cheyne to refer (like Ps 88 and La 3) to the experience, not of an individual, but of the church-nation. In all probability, it was introduced into Is from a collection of liturgical songs (v.[20]). The sickness referred to appears to have been of the nature of a boil or an abscess, being described by the same name (שְׁחִין) as is applied to one of the plagues of Egypt (Ex 9[9]) and to the disease of Job (2[7]). Its connexion with leprosy (Lv 13[18]) explains the promise given to H. that on the third day he would 'go up unto the house of J".' The effect produced on H. by the prophetic announcement that his illness was to prove fatal, illustrates his tender and emotional nature, and enables us to understand the influence exerted over him by the wise and fearless counsellor who on this as on other occasions interpreted to him the will of J". With regard to the sign given to H. by the prophet in token of his recovery, if the fuller text in K be accepted as the original, the narrative must be held to imply a claim on the part of Isaiah to a miraculous control of the forces of nature (20[9]); but if K be regarded as an expansion and Is be held to be the original (Stade, Duhm, Dillmann), it is possible to explain the deflection of the shadow as the result of a partial eclipse of the sun or of refraction of light by the atmosphere, the mode of expression in Is 38[8b] being similar to that in Jos 10[13], and capable of similar interpretation (see DIAL).

Probably, it was shortly after this sickness (c. 714) that the messengers arrived from Babylon (2 K 20[12-19], Is 39). Even if we must regard the promise of deliverance from the king of Assyria in 2 K 20[6b] Is 38[6] as an interpolation, it is certain that about this time H. had reason to apprehend danger from that quarter. Almost from the commencement of his reign (cf. Is 28) there had been a growing feeling at Jerus. in favour of an alliance with Egypt. The feeling was shared by most of the Phœn. and Philistine powers, and in 720 a bold attempt was made by Gaza, with the support of Egypt, to throw off the supremacy. The defeat of the allied forces at Raphia crushed the movement before it broke into a general revolt; but Judah was no doubt more or less implicated, and it may have been to what took place at this time that Sargon refers in his Nimrod inscription (c. 717) when he speaks of himself as the 'conqueror of the remote land of Judah'—unless we suppose (with Winckler and Delitzsch) that Judah is here used by mistake for Israel. For the next seven or eight years Sargon was fully occupied in the consolidation of his empire in the east, and during that time the impression made on Judah and its neighbours by the fate of Samaria and Damascus had almost worn off, and a widespread conspiracy was forming against the domination of 'the great king.' With this we may connect the embassy from Merodach-baladan, Sargon's chief rival, who held the throne of Babylon from 721 till 710 when he was overthrown, only to regain his independence after Sargon's death, when he again wore the crown for about nine months, in 704–3; and to the latter period a few critics would assign his embassy to Jerus. (Wellhausen, W. R. Smith, Cheyne, McCurdy). The ostensible object of the visit was to congratulate H. on his recovery (cf. 2 Ch 32³¹), but the real purpose (of which the accompanying gifts were a well-understood sign) was to court an alliance against the Assyr. power. The welcome which H. gave to the messengers, and the pride with which he showed them his sacred treasures and military stores, brought upon him, as might have been expected, the severest censure of the prophet; but the prediction of a Babylonian captivity for his family and possessions wears the appearance of a 'vaticinium ex eventu,' having nothing in common with the general tone of Isaiah's teaching at this time, which represents everything as culminating in the great struggle with Assyria. Notwithstanding the prophet's inflexible opposition to any alliance either with Babylon or Egypt, the danger of Judah's being involved in hostilities only became more threatening during the next few years (713–10), as we may judge from the intense earnestness of the prophet's utterances in connexion with the siege of Ashdod (Is 20), when he felt called of God to go about for three years 'naked and barefoot' in token of the fate which would overtake the Egyptians and their allies, as well as from Sargon's Ashdod inscription, which mentions the king of Judah among other tributaries who were at this time 'plotters of sedition,' stirring up rebellion against him and bringing gifts of friendship to Pharaoh, king of Egypt.

The death of Sargon in 705, and the accession of a new and untried king, was the signal for a fresh attempt on the part of many vassals to regain their independence. In the first instance Sennacherib directed his attention to his rebellious subjects in the east, and it was not till 701 that he turned his arms against Palestine in his third campaign, of which we have several monumental records, the fullest being that on the Taylor cylinder. But the rebels were slow in arriving at concerted action, owing to their dependence on Egypt; and in several of Isaiah's discourses about this time (chs. 29–32, cf. 18) we can trace the secret negotiations with Egypt, against which the prophet inveighs vehemently, predicting the utter failure of the hopes his countrymen were setting on 'Rahab that sitteth still' (30⁷ RV), and the shame and ruin they would bring upon themselves by their faithless and short-sighted policy—which was destined, however, to issue in a marvellous deliverance which would prove the regeneration of the national life. By this time H. had openly thrown off his allegiance under the influence of his premier, Shebna, apparently of foreign extraction, whose downfall is predicted by Isaiah a little later in 22¹⁵ff·, and who afterwards appears in an inferior office in 36³. That H. took a leading part in the revolt is evident from the fact recorded by Sennacherib in the cylinder referred to (col. ii. ll. 70 ff.), that H. had imprisoned at Jerus. Padi, king of Ekron, whose subjects had dethroned him on account of his loyalty to Assyria.

After reducing or receiving the submission of a number of powers on the east and north of Palestine, Sennacherib proceeded southward along the Maritime Plain, to punish the ringleaders in the revolt. In doing so, it is possible that he may have despatched a portion of his army to invade Judah from the north, and of this some writers find evidence in the description of the Assyr. advance in Is 10²⁸⁻³². But probably this is only an ideal picture, and the great prophecy of which it forms part (10⁵–11¹⁶), proclaiming both the mission and the doom of Assyria, admits of other dates, e.g. 711 (Cheyne [who, however, connects

vv.²⁷ᵇ⁻³² with the siege of Samaria in 722], Guthe, Dillmann, Giesebrecht) and even earlier (W. R. Smith, G. A. Smith). The Assyr. record goes on to tell that Sennacherib took Ashkelon, and that his approach had struck terror into the hearts of the men of Ekron when he was confronted by a great army of Egyptians and Sinaitic Arabians under several of their kings, who had come to the relief of Ekron. These he defeated at Eltekeh (Altaku), and afterwards took Ekron. It was only then apparently that he sent his troops into Judah, where (he says) they took 46 fenced cities and small towns without number, carrying off 200,150 captives (probably an exaggeration) and obliging H. to sue for peace, which was granted him on payment of heavy exactions, including 30 talents of gold and 800 talents of silver, a narrative which is in substantial agreement with 2 K 18¹³⁻¹⁶, even the discrepancy between the 300 and the 800 talents of silver being perhaps accounted for by the different standards of the two countries (Brandis, Münz-system, p. 98).

Such crushing calamities (Is 1⁵ff·) could not fail to be regarded as a vindication of the prophet's counsel, and a condemnation of the policy to which he had been so strongly opposed. H.'s eyes were now opened to see where the true interests of his kingdom lay; and from this time we find Isaiah enjoying his fullest confidence, and guiding the national policy. But there were some on whom the lesson was lost, painful though it had been—citizens who gave themselves up to shameless mirth and revelry as soon as they saw the beleaguering force preparing to withdraw (Is 22). They thought the crisis was over, but it was not so. For Sennacherib soon realized the danger to which his army would be exposed if he advanced into Egypt, leaving such a strong fortress as Jerus. in the hands of a doubtful vassal like H.; and even at the expense of a breach of faith with H. (Is 33¹·⁸, Jos. Ant. x. i. 1) he resolved to make a fresh demand for its surrender. Recent critics (Stade and his followers) have detected in the long narrative (2 K 18¹⁷–19³⁷) a somewhat confused combination of two different accounts, which, if referring to two different occasions, ought to be transposed; and Tiele would even place last of all the events related in 2 K 18¹⁴⁻¹⁶. The problem is too intricate to be dealt with here. But there is no reason to doubt that Sennacherib made a renewed attempt from Lachish (with which his military achievements are associated in recently-discovered monuments, although he himself does not mention it even by name), and perhaps also from Libnah, to which he may have retreated on hearing that Tirhaka was coming out to meet him (2 K 19⁸). That he failed to take Jerus. is almost implied in his own vague statement that he shut up H. like a bird in a cage; and his concluding boast about the tribute and other gifts being sent to him at Nineveh (instead of to Lachish, as related in Scripture) is evidently introduced to save any necessity for recording his subsequent disasters. These disasters are involved in mystery. But the biblical account finds an echo in the story told by Herod. (ii. 141), the destruction of his army being probably due to a plague (2 K 19³⁵, Is 37³⁶, cf. 2 S 24¹⁵ᶠ·, 1 Ch 21¹²ff· and Is 6⁴ᶠ·) in the pestiferous region on the borders of Egypt where the Crusaders and others have had a similar experience (cf. 2 K 19²⁴ RV). The impression made on Sennacherib was such that though he lived for twenty years longer he never again entered Pal. or besieged Jerusalem. On the other hand, the dramatic account of the conference between his three emissaries (all whose names have now been identified with the titles of Assyr. officers) and the three Jewish deputies, on a famous spot under the walls of Jerus. (cf. Is 7³), bears the stamp of historical reality, as does also the letter which H. is said to have afterwards received from him. In the prophetic words which are embodied in the narrative we have for the most part the genuine utterances of Isaiah, harmonizing with that 'most beautiful of all his discourses' (ch. 33) which marks the peaceful and triumphant close of his ministry, and which finds an echo in the 46th, perhaps also in the 48th, 75th, and 76th Psalms.

The event which was thus commemorated was one of the most impressive and glorious in Heb. history, and has taken rank in the estimation of the Jews with the Exodus from Egypt and the Return from Babylon. It was a most fateful moment, not only for Israel but for its religion; and while the victory of faith was mainly due to the influence of the one inspired man who held fast the conviction that in the Lord J" was everlasting strength, and that amid all wreck and ruin He would preserve Mt. Zion inviolate as His holy habitation, the glory of the time falls also on the sovereign who shared his lofty spirit and fulfilled in some degree his Messianic hopes, when he made such a heroic stand against the dreaded invader before whom all the other kings of Palestine and Philistia had succumbed. Not unfitly, therefore, it stands written that 'after him was none like him among all the kings of Judah, nor any that were before him' (2 K 18⁵).

LITERATURE. — Driver, *Isaiah* ² ('Men of the Bible' series), *LOT*⁶, esp. 226 f.; Cheyne, *Book of Isaiah*, 1870, *Prophecies of Isaiah*, 1880, 1884, *Introd. to Bk. of Isaiah*, 1895, Haupt's *PB*; G. A. Smith, *Isaiah*, vol. i. ('Expositor's Bible'); Skinner, *Isaiah* (Camb. Bible); Delitzsch, Dillmann-Kittel, Duhm, Orelli, in their Comm. on *Isaiah*; Stade, *GVI* i.; Kittel, *Hist. of Heb.* (Index); W. R. Smith, *Prophets of Israel* (Index); Schrader, *COT*²; McCurdy, *HPM*; Tiele, *Assyr.-Bab. Gesch.*; Sayce, *HCM* (Index); Wellhausen, *Jahrb. f. deutsche Theol.* 1875, p. 607 ff.; Kamphausen, *Die Chronol. d. Heb. Könige*, 1883.

J. A. M'CLYMONT.

HEZION (חֶזְיוֹן 'vision'; Ἀζείν B, Ἀζαήλ A, Luc.). —Father of Tabrimmon and grandfather of Benhadad, the Syrian king whose alliance was sought by Asa, king of Judah, against Baasha, king of Israel (1 K 15¹⁸). It has been plausibly suggested (Ewald, Thenius, Klostermann, etc.) that Hezion is identical with Rezon of 1 K 11²³, the founder of the kingdom of Damascus, and an adversary to Solomon. The three generations of Syrian kings may very well correspond with the four generations of the kings of Judah, since Abijam, Asa's predecessor, reigned for three years only. The place of Rezon in 1 K 11¹⁴ [Heb.²³] B reads Ἐσρώμ, Luc.

Ἐσρών, Pesh. רכיזא; and Klostermann regards חֶזְרוֹן Hezron as the original form of the name in both passages 11²³ 15¹⁸. C. F. BURNEY.

HEZIR (חֵזִיר, either for חֲזִיר 'boar,' or cf. New Heb. חִזּוּר 'apple').—**1.** The 17th of the priestly courses (1 Ch 24¹⁵). **2.** A lay family, which signed the covenant (Neh 10²⁰ [Heb.²¹]). For the name cf. the inscription on the grave of the 'sons of Hezir,' dating from the 1st cent. B.C. (see Driver, *Text of Sam.* p. xxiii). See GENEALOGY, III. 15.
H. A. WHITE.

HEZRO, HEZRAI (*Kethibh* חֶזְרַי, *Kerê* חֶזְרוֹ; Ἀσαραί). —One of David's thirty heroes (2 S 23³⁵). He was a Carmelite, *i.e.* a native of Carmel, the modern *Kurmul*, in the hill-country of Judah (see CARMELITE). In the parallel list (1 Ch 11³⁷) the reading of the *Kethibh* (Hezro) is retained, but the LXX supports the form Hezrai (B Ἡσερέ; א Ἡσεραί; A Ἀσαραί). J. F. STENNING.

HEZRON (חֶצְרֹן and חֶצְרוֹן).—**1.** A son of Reuben, *i.e.* the eponymous head of a Reubenite family, Gn 46⁹, Ex 6¹⁴, Nu 26⁶ = 1 Ch 5³. **2.** A son of Perez and grandson of Judah, *i.e.* the eponymous head of

a Judahite family, Gn 46¹², Nu 26²¹ = Ru 4¹⁸. ¹⁹, 1 Ch 2⁵. ⁹. ¹⁸. ²¹. ²⁴. ²⁵ 4¹. This Hezron appears also in the NT in the genealogy of our Lord, Mt 1³, Lk 3³³ (in both of which passages AV following TR Ἐσρώμ has *Esrom*. WH has in Mt Ἑσρώμ, in Lk Ἑσρών). The gentilic name **Hezronites** (חֶצְרֹנִי) occurs in Nu 26⁶ referring to the descendants of No. 1 above, and in v.²¹ referring to those of No. 2.
J. A. SELBIE.

HEZRON (חֶצְרֹן).—**1.** A town in the south of Judah (Jos 15³) = Hazar-addar of Nu 34⁴. It appears to be different from **2.** Kerioth-hezron (קְרִיּוֹת חֶצְרוֹן), Jos 15²⁵, which is prob. identical with Hazor, No. **4.** The name Hezron probably survives at *Jebel Hadhireh*, a mountain in the Tîh desert N.W. of Petra. C. R. CONDER.

HIDDAI (הִדַּי; B Ἀδαοί and Ἀδροί;* A Ἀθθαί). — One of David's thirty heroes (2 S 23³⁰). He is described as 'of the brooks [נַחֲלִים, 'torrent-valleys'] of Gaash,' and probably lived in the neighbourhood of Mt. Gaash (cf. Jos 19⁵⁰ 24³⁰, Jg 2⁹) in the hill-country of Ephraim. Thenius and Wellh. prefer the alternative form **Hurai** (חוּרַי; B Οὑρεί; A Οὑρί), which is given in the parallel list 1 Ch 11³².
J. F. STENNING.

HIDDEKEL (חִדֶּקֶל).—The name given to the Tigris in Gn 2¹⁴, Dn 10⁴. In the Sumerian or pre-Semitic language of Babylonia, the river was called Idikla and Idikna, which the Semitic Babylonians modified into Diklat by dropping the initial vowel and affixing the Semitic feminine suffix. Diklat is the Diglit of Pliny (*HN* vi. 27) and the Dijlah of to-day. The Persians assimilated the name to their own word *tigra* 'an arrow' (see Strabo, xi. p. 529; Q. Curt. iv. 9. 16; Eust. *ad Dionys. Perieg.* v. 984), from which was derived the Gr. *Tigris*. It is possible that in the first syllable of Idikla we have the Sumerian *id*, 'river.' See further Del., *Paradies*, 110 f., 170 ff. A. H. SAYCE.

HIEL (חִיאֵל 'brother of God' or 'he whose brother is God.' The name is a contraction of אֲחִיאֵל *Ahiel*, and this form appears in LXX [Ἀχειήλ B, Ἀχιήλ A]. Cf. חִירָם for אֲחִירָם, and Phœn. מלכת for אחמלכת).—A Bethelite, famed as the rebuilder of Jericho, in the reign of Ahab (1 K 16³⁴). He is said to have laid the foundations of the city at the cost of the life of Abiram his firstborn son, and to have set up the gates with the loss of his youngest son Segub; in fulfilment of Joshua's curse pronounced against the rebuilder of Jericho (Jos 6²⁶). The meaning of this statement possibly is that the builder *sacrificed* his sons, perhaps by enclosing them alive in the foundation and wall, in order to secure the prosperity of the city by this costly blood-offering. See FOUNDATION. Or, the tradition may have been that, through failure to perform such a rite, his eldest and youngest born sons were claimed by the offended deity at the initiatory and final stages of the building operations. For instances, from various sources, of the widespread primitive custom of human sacrifice 'in order to furnish blood at the foundations of a house or of a public structure,' cf. H. C. Trumbull, *The Threshold Covenant*, p. 46 ff. It may be urged, however, that the language of 1 K 16³⁴ implies not a usual practice, but the occurrence of something *involuntary* on the part of Hiel; *e.g.* that the death of his sons was the result of accidents during the building operations. C. F. BURNEY.

HIERAPOLIS (Ἱεράπολις, in more classical form Ἱερὰ Πόλις, and in ruder native Greek Ἱερόπολις), a city on the north edge of the Lycus valley,

* The rendering of B is not found at v.³⁰ but after v.³⁹, where it is out of place. Its omission in the first instance would appear to be accidental.

probably originally Lydian, but in the Roman period always reckoned to Phrygia, played a highly important part in the early history of Christianity. In the Bible it is mentioned only in Col 4[13] in association with Laodicea. Standing on the site on the north edge of the Lycus valley, one looks due south across the hollow valley about 6 miles to Laodicea on a slight rising ground, while Colossæ, about 12 miles distant to the south-east, is concealed by the low hills that separate the upper or Colossian glen from the lower or Laodicean glen of the Lycus. Hierapolis, probably, was originally the 'Holy City' of the tribe Hydrelitai, which possessed the north bank of the Lycus; and Kydrâra (*i.e.* Kydrêla, Hydrêla) in Herod. vii. 31 is probably another name for it. It was marked out to the inhabitants by its marvellous medicinal hot springs as the place where divine power was plainly present. The water of these springs is strongly impregnated with alum (being on that account very useful for dyeing purposes), as Hamilton mentions, and it forms a calcareous deposit with extraordinary rapidity, so that the site is almost entirely covered with encrustation formed since the city was ruined, while the precipitous rocks on the south side of the city, over which the water tumbles in many rivulets, have been transformed into the appearance of 'an immense frozen cascade' (Chandler).* Even more remarkable was the Ploutonion or Charonion, a hole just large enough to admit a man, reaching deep into the earth, from which issued a poisonous vapour, the breath of the realm of death. Strabo had with his own eyes seen sparrows stifled by this vapour. The city, though devoid of political importance, derived high social consequence and prosperity in the peaceful Roman period from its religious character; and here, as the special stronghold of Satan, Christianity fixed itself from the first. The filling up of the Charonion, the dwelling place of the hostile power, may be plausibly attributed to Christian action in the 4th cent.

From the NT narrative (Ac 19[10] and Col) it is clear that the Church in Hierapolis was founded through the influence diffused over Asia from St. Paul's residence in Ephesus (perhaps by Timothy, Col 1[1]). But later legends† describe the Apostle Philip as the evangelist both of Tripolis (about 10 miles to the north-west, and also in view) and of Hierapolis, in which the Apostle John also preached; and the Hierapolitan Echidna (*i.e.* the serpent-form in which the Phrygian god Sabazios was there and everywhere represented) is described as their special enemy. It appears well attested that Philip preached and resided in Hierapolis, and that he was buried there with his two daughters, who were virgins, while a third daughter of his was married and buried in Ephesus (Eusebius, *HE* iii. 31, quoting Polycrates, bishop of Ephesus about A.D. 190). Owing to mere confusion of name, Philip the deacon (who had four prophetic daughters, Ac 21[8]) is connected by some authorities with Hierapolis; but legend and an inscription‡ found in the city agree with the earliest historical authority, Polycrates. The city, apparently, assumed for a time the name Philippopolis, for Tatianus, bishop of Philippopolis in Phrygia, at the Council of Chalcedon, A.D. 451, was in all probability bishop of Hierapolis,§ and so also Andreas of Philippopolis in Phrygia in A.D. 692. Ten Christian inscriptions of Hierapolis are published;‖ two of them may perhaps be Jewish, if not Jewish-Christian.

Probably, nowhere in Asia Minor was the opposition between the native superstition and the

Christian religion so strongly accentuated as in Hierapolis. In greater cities, like Ephesus, political considerations came in to complicate the antagonism. But Hierapolis was important only as the home of religion; the native superstition is there revealed to us in its sharpest and most aggressive form, as the worship of the mother goddess Leto (see DIANA) and her son Lairbenos (a form of Sabazios).

The early coins of the city, until about the time of Christ, bear the ruder native name *Hieropolis*, while those of Augustus' later period and all subsequent emperors have the more correct form *Hierapolis*; the change of spelling shows that a step in the Hellenization of the city was made about that time (though private persons seem to have occasionally used the form *Hieropolis* much later).* The Christians preferred the form *Hierapolis.*†

In the apostolic period H. was a flourishing city, to whose medicinal springs numerous visitors flocked; its prosperity lasted through the Roman period (as is shown by its rich coinage); and it easily recovered from such losses as that of the earthquake which probably injured it in A.D. 60 (Tacitus, *Ann.* xiv. 27). Epictetus is the only important figure in literature connected with Hierapolis. It was made by Justinian, if not earlier, a metropolis; and the north-west part of the great province of Phrygia Pacatiana was placed under it.‡ The fact that several Christian martyrs were executed at Hierapolis § shows that it was a leading city under the Empire, where the proconsul held trials. The Neokorate in the Imperial religion was conferred on it by Caracalla about A.D. 215 (*Athen. Mittheil.* xix. p. 118).

LITERATURE.—On the topography and history, see Hamilton and older travellers: a plan of the city is given by Tremaux, *Voyage Archéol. en Asie Mineure*; fullest discussion in Ramsay, *Cities and Bishoprics of Phrygia*, vol. i. pt. i. pp. 84–120, 124 f., and 172–175; on the Christian Antiquities, pt. ii. pp. 500 f., 545 ff.; and on the pagan religion in Hierapolis, pt. i. pp. 86–105, 133–140. See also J. G. C. Anderson in *Journal of Hellenic Studies*, pp. 17, 411. The elaborate work on Hierapolis by Judeich, etc., announced for some years as in the press, has not yet appeared.

W. M. RAMSAY.

HIEREEL ('Ιερεήλ), 1 Es 9[21].—The corresponding name in Ezr 10[21] is JEHIEL.

HIEREMOTH ('Ιερεμώθ).—**1.** 1 Es 9[27]. In Ezr 10[26] JEREMOTH. **2.** 1 Es 9[30]. In Ezr 10[29] JEREMOTH (RVm 'and Ramoth').

HIERMAS (A 'Ιερμάς, B 'Ιερμά), 1 Es 9[26].—In Ezr 10[25] RAMIAH.

HIERONYMUS ('Ιερώνυμος).—A Syrian officer in command of a district of Pal. under Antiochus V. Eupator, who harassed the Jews after the withdrawal of Lysias in B.C. 165 (2 Mac 12[2]).

HIGGAION.—See PSALMS (Titles).

HIGH, HIGHMINDED. — High is occasionally used in the sense of 'tall,' as 1 S 9[2] 'From his shoulders and upward he was higher than any of the people' (נָּבֹהַּ); Jth 16[7] 'For the mighty one did not fall by the young men, neither did the sons of the Titans smite him, nor high giants set upon him' (ὑψηλοὶ γίγαντες). So occasionally in Shaks., as *Merch. of Venice*, v. i. 163—

> 'A kind of boy, a little scrubbed boy,
> No higher than thyself.'

From the literal sense, 'high' passes readily into certain figurative applications, but that which we

---

* Whence the modern name Pambuk-Kalessi, 'Cotton Castle.'
† See Bonnet, *Narratio de miraculo Chonis patrato*.
‡ See Ramsay, *Cities and Bishoprics*, i. pt. ii. p. 552.
§ *Ib.* i. pt. i. p. 344 f.   ‖ *Ib.* i. pt. ii. pp. 543–553.

* *Corpus Inscr. Attic.* iii. 129, l. 29, and perhaps *Acta Concil. Constantinop.* A.D. 347, refer to this city, not Hieropolis near Sandykli. See *Cities and Bishoprics*, i. pt. i. pp. 87 f., 107, pt. ii. p. 681.
† *Cities and Bishoprics*, i. pt. ii. p. 682.
‡ *Ib.* pt. i. pp. 108 f., 121.
§ *Ib.* pt. ii. p. 494.

take as fig. would often to the religious consciousness of Israel be quite literal. See GOD, RELIGION, and compare the following passages : Ps 71[19] 'Thy righteousness also, O God, is very high'; 92[8] 'But thou, LORD, art most high (RV 'art on high') for evermore'; Is 6[1] 'I saw also the LORD sitting upon a throne, high and lifted up'; 57[15] 'For thus saith the high and lofty One that inhabiteth eternity'; 2 Co 10[5] 'Casting down imaginations and every high thing that exalteth itself against the knowledge of God' (πᾶν ὕψωμα); with many more. But in the foll. the fig. sense is complete, Dt 26[19] 'And the LORD hath avouched thee this day to be his peculiar people . . . and to make thee high above all nations which he hath made, in praise, and in name, and in honour'; 32[27] 'Our hand is high (RV 'exalted'), and the LORD hath not done all this'; 'a man of high degree' 1 Ch 17[17] הָאָדָם הַמַּעֲלָה, text certainly corrupt), or 'men of high degree' Ps 62[9] (בְּנֵי־אִישׁ). Cf. Lk 16[15] Wyc. 'that that is high to men, is abhomynacioun bifor god.' So frequently in Shaks., as *Two Gent. of Verona*, II. iv. 106—

> 'Too low a mistress for so high a servant.'

In this way 'high' takes on an offensive meaning, *haughty*, as Ps 101[5] 'Him that hath an high look and a proud heart will not I suffer'; Pr 21[4] 'An high look, and a proud heart, and the plowing of the wicked is sin' (רוּם עֵינַיִם, lit. as AVm, 'haughtiness of eyes'); which can also be illustrated from Shaks., as *I Henry VI.* IV. vii. 39—

> 'Once I encountered him, and thus I said :
> "Thou maiden youth, be vanquished by a maid" ;
> But with a proud majestical high scorn,
> He answered thus : " Young Talbot was not born
> To be the pillage of a giglot wench." '

Notice in this connexion the phrase 'high calling,' Ph 3[14], lit. 'calling upward' (ἄνω κλῆσις) as RV, which is better than the 'heavenly calling' of Lightfoot and others, though that is the ultimate destination.

In the phrase 'high day' we find two different meanings—(1) 'great,' practically equivalent to 'holy' in Ad. Est 16[22], Sir 33[9], Jn 19[31]; and (2) the same as modern 'broad,' referring to the full light of day, in Gn 29[7].

For **Most High** see GOD ; for **High Place** see the following art.; for **High Priest** see PRIESTS AND LEVITES ; and for **Highest Room** (Lk 14[8] πρωτοκλισία) see HOSPITALITY, HOUSE, ROOM.

In Ro 11[20] [WH μὴ ὑψηλὰ φρονεῖν] and in 1 Ti 6[17] the verb ὑψηλοφρονεῖν is tr[d] 'to be highminded'; and in 2 Ti 3[4] the ptcp. τετυφωμένος is tr[d] 'highminded' (RV ' puffed up '). Thus in all its occurrences in AV **highminded** has the bad sense of 'haughty,' 'overweening,' its almost invariable meaning at the time. As Davies points out (*Bible English*, p. 207), Andrewes uses the word in a good (though not in the modern) sense when he says (*Sermons*, v. 50), 'O that you would mind once these high things, that you would be in this sense high-minded,' but it is plain that he is accommodating the word to his purpose; elsewhere he uses it in the same sense as AV. Cf. *Babees Book* (E.E.T.S.), p. 93, 'A hye mynded man thinketh no wight worthy to match with him.'

Highness, which, except in reference to persons of rank, is now displaced by 'height,' is found twice in AV, Job 31[23] 'For destruction from God was a terror to me, and by reason of his highness I could not endure' (שְׂאֵת; RV 'excellency'; Amer. RV 'majesty,' which is Davidson's word); and Is 13[3] 'I have commanded my sanctified ones, I have also called my mighty ones for mine anger, even them that rejoice in my highness' (עַלִּיזֵי גַּאֲוָתִי; RV 'my proudly exulting ones,' RVm 'them that exult in my majesty'). Cf. 2 Co 10[5] Wyc. (1388)

'And we distrien counsels, and alle highnesse that higheth it silf aghens the science of God.' Fisher (on Ps 143) shows the word passing to its mod. sense : 'Blessed Lorde vouchsafe give us leve to speake unto thy hyghnes in this matter.'

Highway.—See WAY.   J. HASTINGS.

HIGH PLACE, בָּמָה pl. בָּמוֹת. LXX τὸ ὑψηλόν, about 56 t.; ἀβαμά, ἀββαμμά (ἀβανά B, ἀββανά A), Ezk 20[29]; τὰ ἀγαθά, Is 58[14]; ἄλσος, Jer 26[18], Mic 3[12]; ἁμαρτία=חֲטָאת, Mic 1[5]; βαιμών, Jos 13[17]; Βαμά, 1 S 9[12. 13. 14. 19. 25 10[5], 1 Ch 16[39] (21[29] Lag.), 2 Ch 1[13], A. Lag.; Βαμώθ, Jos 13[17] Lag., 1 Ch 21[29]; βουνός, 1 S 10[13], Ps 78[58] (Jer 26[18], Symm., Mic 3[12], Theod.); βωμός, Is 15[2] 16[12], Jer 7[31] 32[35] 48[35], Am 7[9], Hos 10[8]; ἔδαφος, Job 9[8]; εἴδωλον, Ezk 16[16]; ἔρημος, Ezk 36[2]; θυσιαστήριον, 2 Ch 14[3]; ἰσχύς, Dt 32[13]; λίθος, 2 K 23[15]; μετέωρος, 2 K 12[3] 15[4] Lag.; οἶκος=בַּיִת, 2 K 23[8. 13]; στήλη, Lv 26[30], Nu 21[28] 22[41] 33[52]; ὑψηλός, Ps 18[34]; ὑψηλότατος, 1 K 3[4]; ὕψος, 2 S 1[19. 25] 22[34], Am 4[13], Mic 1[3]=עַל־בָּמֳתֵי, Is 14[14]=ἐπάνω]. In some other passages the LXX renderings prob. rest on a different text from MT.

I. The original signification of the word cannot now be exactly determined, but that it denoted 'high, rising ground' is probable for the following reasons :—(a) The corresponding word in Assyr. (*bamâtu*, pl. *bamâti*) is said to mean 'height.' Del. (*Assyr. Hwb.*) renders 'Höhe (opp. Thal), și-i-ru ba-ma-a-ti Feld und Höhen.' (b) We read of people 'going up' to (1 S 9[13. 19], Is 15[2]) and 'coming down' from (1 S 10[5] 9[25]) a high place. (c) בָּמָה is used to explain רָמָה 'high hill' גִּבְעָה (Ezk 20[29]).

II. In poetical language the word is used quite generally to denote the mountain fastnesses of the land, which ensure dominion to their holder (Ezk 36[2]). In this sense it is used of Israel (Dt 32[13] 33[29], Is 58[14]; cf. 2 S 22[34]=Ps 18[33], Hab 3[19]); of God (Am 4[13], Mic 1[3]; cf. Job 9[8] 'the waves,' marg. 'heights,' RVm 'high places,' 'of the sea'; cf. also Is 14[14] 'heights,' lit. 'high places,' 'of the clouds,' 'of the king of Babylon.' But much more frequently it signifies 'high places' as places of religious worship. That these were the customary and legitimate places of worship for the Isr. until the 7th cent. there is abundant evidence. Samuel was accustomed to sanction such worship by his presence and blessing (1 S 9[12. 13. 14. 19]). They were situated on the outskirts of the city (1 S 9[25] 10[5. 13]). In the days of Solomon 'the people sacrificed in the high places' (1 K 3[2]). Solomon himself, we are told, 'sacrificed and burnt incense in the high places' (1 K 3[3]), and, in particular, at Gibeon 'the great high place' (1 K 3[4]). The same is true of the reigns of Rehoboam (1 K 14[23]), Jeroboam (1 K 12[31. 32] 13[2. 32. 33]), Asa (1 K 15[14]), Jehoshaphat (1 K 22[43]), Jehoash (2 K 12[3]), Amaziah (2 K 14[4]), Azariah (2 K 15[4]), Jotham (2 K 15[35]), Ahaz (2 K 16[4]), and Elijah laments bitterly that the local sanctuaries of J" had been destroyed (1 K 19[10. 14]). True, the compiler of the Bks. of Kings looks upon the worship at high places as a stain upon the government of these rulers, and sees in it additional ground for condemnation of the apostate kings (*e.g.* Manasseh, 2 K 21[3]), and one cause of the captivity of the northern tribes (2 K 17[9. 11]); but this is due to his inability to recognize that a custom which in his own day was under the ban of the ceremonial law, had ever been legitimate in monarchical times. It may seem strange perhaps that in the Bks. of Kings this worship should meet with such condemnation, whilst in Samuel the many allusions to it are passed over unnoticed ; but this is explained by the fact that the editors of these books were influenced by the theory that such worship at high places was lawful before the erection of Solomon's Temple, but was inexcusable afterwards ; cf. 1 K 3[2] 'Only the people sacrificed in the high places, because there was no house built for the name of the Lord until those days.' In the passages already cited, high places are expressly mentioned, but in very many other cases the existence of sanctuaries of J″ all over the country in the period before the establishment of the monarchy is presupposed, *e.g.* at Bochim (Bethel?) (Jg 2⁵), Ophrah (6²⁴ 8²⁷), Zorah (13¹⁶⁻¹⁹), Shiloh (18³¹), Bethel (20¹⁸·²³·²⁶ 21²·⁴), Mizpah (Jg 20¹, 1 S 7⁹), Ramah (7¹⁷ 9¹²), Gibeah (10⁵ 14³⁵), Gilgal (10⁸ 11¹⁵ 13⁹ 15²¹), Bethlehem (16² 20⁶·²⁹), Nob (21¹), Hebron (2 S 15⁷), Giloh (15¹²), and the threshing-floor of Araunah (2 S 24²⁵). For a sanctuary that was purely Israelite in origin, cf. that at Dan (Jg 18³⁰).

But, widespread as was the worship at the local high places, there were gradually developed tendencies towards a centralization of the worship of J″. It was very natural, for instance, that the sanctuary at which the ark was stationed should enjoy a certain pre-eminence over the surrounding high places. Thus Shiloh (1 S 1³) and, at a later period, Jerus. no doubt overshadowed the neighbouring sanctuaries and attracted worshippers from a wide area. Again, the establishment of the monarchy indirectly favoured religious, as directly it brought about political, unity. And, lastly, in the worship at high places itself there lurked a danger which eventually brought about their overthrow. This danger was twofold. Many of the more important of the high places had been the sites of Can. shrines (Dt 12²·³⁰, Nu 33⁵²). With the place of worship the Isr. had taken over also the symbols of worship, the *Mazzébahs* (see PILLAR) and the *Ashérahs* (wh. see). What was more likely than that the lascivious tendencies which had characterized the older forms of worship should lie hidden beneath these external symbols, and, defying expulsion, should burst forth from time to time into fresh vigour? Or, again, what was more probable than that J″ should seem to be brought down to the level of the Can. gods, of whose shrines He had taken possession, and whose name He sometimes assumed, and so become confounded with them alike in outward worship and in moral characteristics? [For such confusion of J″ with the Can. Baalim, cf. Hos 2¹⁶·¹⁷, and the proper names Jerubbaal (Jg 6³²), Meribbaal (1 Ch 8³⁴), Beeliada (1 Ch 14⁷); and see Moore on Jg 6³², with the references there given].

How real these dangers were may be learned from the vigorous way in which the prophets of the 8th cent. denounce the worship at high places as it existed in their own day. Cf., for the northern kingdom, Hos 10⁸ ‘The high places of Aven, the sin of Israel shall be destroyed; the thorn and the thistle shall come up upon their altars’ (2. 4¹³·¹⁵·¹⁷ 5¹ 8⁵·¹¹ 10¹·² ⁵ 12¹¹ 13²); Am 7⁹ ‘The high places of Isaac shall be desolate, and the sanctuaries of Israel shall be laid waste’ (4⁴ 5⁵ 7¹³ 8¹⁴); and for Judah see Mic 1⁵ ‘What are the high places of Judah? are they not Jerusalem?’ (where, however, we should probably read, with the LXX, ‘sin’ for ‘high places’) (5¹³ 6⁷). Micah, writing probably after the fall of the northern kingdom, declares that the sanctuary at Jerus. is destined to the same fate that has fallen upon the high places of the sister kingdom. ‘Jerus. shall become heaps, and the mountain of the house as the high places of a forest,’ *i.e.* as the high places that have been converted into waste forest-land by the invading army (3¹²=Jer 26¹⁸; cf. Ezk 36²).

It should be noticed that what these writers denounce is, not the worship at high places in itself, but the corruption that has contaminated the worship of J″ at the local high places, and that they regard the approaching destruction of the high places, which they foretell, as part of a temporary loss of a national existence. Cf. Hos 3⁴ ‘Without king, and without prince, and without sacrifice, and without ephod or teraphim.’ The growing feeling against the corrupted local sanctuary worship was no doubt fostered by the introduction of foreign cults by some of the kings. Thus Solomon, we read, built high places for Chemosh and for Molech (1 K 11⁷), for Ashtoreth (2 K 23¹³); Ahab built an altar for Baal (1 K 16³¹·³²); Manasseh did the same (2 K 21³; cf. Jer 7³¹ 19⁵).

For this corrupt state of things there were two possible solutions. There might be reformation, or there might be abolition combined with the centralization of the worship of J″ at Jerusalem. The latter was the course actually taken when the unifying tendencies of which we have spoken ripened into maturity. The compiler of the Bks. of Kings ascribes it to Hezekiah (2 K 18⁴·²² 21³), but there are reasons for doubting the accuracy of his statement. 2 K 18⁴ᵃ seems to be a later addition to the original passage; v.²² occurs in a section that is certainly of a late date; 21³ is due to the compiler; Hezekiah's reform, if historical, must have been singularly ineffective, for in the accounts of Josiah's reformation we have no hint of earlier steps in the same direction; lastly, Isaiah betrays no hostility to the high places as such (cf. Wellh. *Proleg.* p. 46; Nowack, *Heb. Arch.* ii. 14; Montefiore, *Hib. Lects.* p. 164; and, for a conservative view, Kittel, *Hist. of the Heb.* ii. 356). But, whatever may have been the action of Hezekiah with regard to the high places, the legislation of Josiah (B.C. 639–608) against them was carried through systematically and with thoroughness. Inspired by the then lately promulgated (B.C. 621) law of Deuteronomy (ch. 12³·⁵ and freq.), the young king caused the destruction of the high places throughout his dominions (2 K 23⁵·⁸·¹³·¹⁹). The idolatrous priests were apparently put to death (2 K 23⁵), the priests of J″ were to be allowed to come to Jerus., but not as sacrificing priests (2 K 23⁹); the worship of J″ was henceforth to have its sole sanctuary at Jerusalem.

A reformation so radical as that just sketched had of course its losses as well as its gains. The latter were seen in the sweeping away of a system that was polluting the very life-blood of the nation, and in the quickening impulse which it must have given to political unification, and to the spread of a more spiritual conception of the national God. But the loss was very great. It was an age when the social and the religious instincts found expression through the same channels, and the abolition of the local shrines must have affected everyday life in the rural districts in a hundred ways. For instance, from time immemorial all shedding of blood had been looked upon as sacrifice; now sacrifice was to be lawful only at Jerusalem. Again, many of the older local festivals would lose their importance now that there was no sanctuary round which they could revolve (cf. 1 S 1³ 20⁶ 25², 2 S 13²³). And, lastly, the abolition of the country priesthood, whilst it deprived a large class of the means of livelihood (Jg 17⁵), removed from their position the recognized educational authorities (Mic 3¹¹, Dt 33¹⁰), and made no provision for any substitute. Still, the spontaneous religious feeling of the country districts needed outlets for their expression, and the loss of those ‘who handled *torah*’ had to be supplied. If the body ecclesiastic was to have its heart in Jerus., it needed also its main arteries throughout the country, and in time such were found for it. In the post-ex. community the synagogue (wh. see) with its worship of prayer supplied to some extent the place of the high place with its cycle of sacrifices, and the recognized teachers of the Levitical law took the place of the older provincial priests.

III. The fortunes of the local high places thus briefly sketched from the historical books may be traced through the same stages in the legal codes. In the earliest legislation high places are not actually mentioned, but they are presupposed. Cf. Ex 20²⁴ ‘An altar of earth shalt thou make unto me, and shalt sacrifice thereon thy burnt-offerings, and thy peace-offerings, thy sheep and thine oxen: in every place where I record my name I will come unto thee and I will bless thee.’

Cf. also Ex 22²⁹, which presupposes the existence of local sanctuaries. In entire agreement with this the writers of the narrative portions of JE represent the Patriarchs as erecting altars wherever occasion demanded. Thus, e.g., Abraham builds altars at Shechem (Gn 12⁷), at Bethel (12⁸ 13⁴), at Mamre (13¹⁸), and on Mount Moriah (22⁹); Jacob sacrifices on the mountain of Gilead (31⁵⁴), and builds altars at Shechem (33²⁰) and at Bethel (35¹·³·⁷); Isaac does the same at Beer-sheba (46¹); and Moses builds an altar at Rephidim (Ex 17¹⁵), and prescribes the erection of one on Mount Ebal (Dt 27⁵; cf. Jos 8³⁰).

When we reach the Great Code of the 7th cent. [D = Deuteronomy] all this is altered. True, the compiler nowhere mentions by name the high places of J″, but his zeal for their removal betrays itself in every page of his work. All the sanctuaries of Can. origin are to be destroyed (Dt 12²·³), and for the Israelites there is to be but one place of sacrifice. 'Ye shall not do so unto the Lord your God. But unto the place which the Lord your God shall choose . . . thither thou shalt come, and thither ye shall bring your burnt-offerings . . .' (12⁴⁻⁷). 'Take heed to thyself that thou offer not thy burnt-offerings in every place that thou seest' (12¹³; cf. 12²¹·²⁶ 14²³⁻²⁵ 15²⁰ 16²·⁵·⁶·¹⁵·¹⁶ 17⁸ 18⁶).

Lastly, in the latest of the Pentateuchal Codes (P = Priestly Code) the one sanctuary is not so much inculcated as tacitly assumed (cf. Wellh. Proleg. p. 34).

IV. It has been said above that בָּמָה originally signified 'high, rising ground,' and it is probable therefore that the simplest form of high place was an altar on any slight elevation. They were situated generally, it may be supposed, near a city; cf. 1 S 9²⁵ 10⁵. Close to the altar would be placed the Mazzébah and the Ashérah. Sometimes we find the high place distinguished from the altar (2 K 23¹⁵, Is 36⁷, 2 Ch 14⁸). Again, the high place is distinguished from the hill upon which it stood (Ezk 6³, 1 K 11¹⁷ 14²³). In these passages the name seems to be transferred from the actual site to the apparatus for worship which stood upon it. In the vicinity of the altar were erected buildings for various purposes, the so-called 'houses of high places' (1 K 12³¹ 13³², 2 K 23¹⁹). In the case of idolatrous high places, these sometimes contained an image of the god worshipped (2 K 17²⁹). With 'high place' in this secondary sense of 'shrine' or 'sanctuary' we may compare those passages which speak of 'high places' in valleys (Jer 7³¹ 19⁵ 32³⁵, Ezk 6³), or in cities (1 K 13³², 2 K 17⁹·²⁹ 23⁵), or 'at the entering in of the gate' (2 K 23⁸; cf. Ezk 16²⁴). Cf. also Am 7⁹, where it is synonymous with 'sanctuary' (מִקְדָּשׁ). In some of these cases it is probable that an artificial high place, with of course the necessary adjuncts, is intended. With this would agree the terms which are used of the destruction of 'high places.' So, e.g., 'destroy' (Ezk 6³, 2 K 21³; cf. Lv 26³⁰, Nu 33⁵², where a synonymous term is used), 'break down' (2 K 23⁸·¹⁵), 'burn' (2 K 23¹⁵).

In connexion with these local sanctuaries we find, in addition to the Mazzébahs and Ashérahs, also Ephods and Teraphim (wh. see). So in Jg 17⁵, 1 S 21⁹; cf. Jg 8²⁷, Hos 3⁴. That the former were images used in consultation of J″ is probable from 1 S 14¹⁸ mg. 23⁹ 30⁷. (See Moore on Jg 8²⁷). And in connexion with the Ephod we have the Urim and Thummim, or sacred lots for giving oracles, 1 S 14⁴¹ (on the reading see Driver, ad loc.). For the priests of these high places see CHEMARIM, PRIEST.

V. In four passages of OT the plur. of the word is used as a proper name. These are Nu 21¹⁹·²⁰, Nu 21²⁸ RVm 'Bamoth of Arnon,' Jos 13¹⁷ Bamoth-

baal. In this connexion it is noteworthy that the word occurs twice upon the Moabite Stone.

l. 3 'and I made this high place for Chemosh in QRHH.'

l. 27 'I built Beth Bamoth, for it was destroyed.'

LITERATURE.—Wellh. Proleg. pp. 17–51 (Eng. tr.); Driver on Deut. 12¹ and pp. xliii–li; Baudissin, Studien, ii. 256 ff.; W. R. Smith, OTJC² 236 ff., 275, 360. For a theory as to the reason for the choice of high ground as a place of worship see W. R. Smith, RS¹ p. 470.

W. C. ALLEN.

HILEN (חִילֵן), 1 Ch 6⁵⁸.—See HOLON, No. 1.

HILKIAH (חִלְקִיָּה, חִלְקִיָּהוּ, 'J″ is my portion,' or 'he whose portion is J″').—1. The father of Eliakim, who was 'over the household' under Hezekiah (2 K 18¹⁸·²⁶·³⁷ = Is 36³·²² ; cf. Is 22²⁰).

2. The high priest in the reign of Josiah. He it was who found the book of the law in the temple, whilst the building was undergoing repair in the 18th year of Josiah (B.C. 621). That this book was substantially the Bk. of Deuteronomy is generally acknowledged (see DEUTERONOMY). Hilkiah communicated the news of his discovery to Shaphan the scribe, and this latter, having first made himself acquainted with the contents of the book, then read it before the king. Josiah was greatly moved upon hearing the threats and warnings of Deuteronomy against the introduction of idolatrous cults and the unrestricted worship of J″ elsewhere than at the central sanctuary—'the place which the LORD God shall choose to put his name there' (Dt 12⁵). Immediately a deputation was formed by order of the king, consisting of Hilkiah and others, who proceeded to Huldah, the prophetess, to learn at her mouth the will of the Lord. Huldah predicted the certain fall of the kingdom of Judah, on account of the religious abuses which had been introduced under king Manasseh, but added that for Josiah's sake a respite was to be granted, that he might not see the evil which J″ would bring upon Jerusalem.* After receiving the message of the prophetess, the young king at once commenced active measures, and carried out the great religious reformation which is associated with his name (2 K 22 f. = 2 Ch 34⁸ff.).

The narrative contains no suggestion by which a charge of fraud can be fastened upon Hilkiah, as though he had deposited the book in the temple and had then professed to make discovery of it, while all the time he was acquainted with the author of it, even if he were not himself the author. On the contrary, the simple and straightforward account of the repairs which were being carried out in the temple, and which led to the discovery, makes the inference obvious that the high priest was previously unacquainted with the book, and that it must have been placed in the temple for safety some time previously, either during the troublous reign of Manasseh, or during the earlier years of Josiah.

3. The father of Jeremiah, and member of a priestly family at Anathoth (Jer 1¹). 4. The father of Gemariah, who acted as ambassador from king Zedekiah to Nebuchadrezzar (Jer 29³). 5. 6. Levites of the clan of Merari, 1 Ch 6⁴⁵ [Heb.³⁰] 26¹¹. 7. A contemporary of Ezra, who stood at his right hand when he read the book of the law publicly (Neh 8⁴). Probably the same Hilkiah is mentioned as one of the chiefs of the priests who went up to Judæa with Zerubbabel and Jeshua (Neh 12⁷·²¹).

C. F. BURNEY.

HILL, HILL-COUNTRY.—'Hill' is in AV the rendering of (1) גִּבְעָה (always), (2) הַר (sometimes), (3) in Mt 5¹⁴, Lk 4²⁹ ('the brow of the hill') 9³⁷ of

---

* Probably, Huldah's speech has been to some extent amplified by a redactor of K in exilic times. See KINGS, BOOKS OF.

ὄρος (RV in 9³⁷ 'mountain'), and (4) in Lk 3⁵ 23³⁰ of βουνός (LXX usu. for גִּבְעָה); it occurs also in 1 S 9¹¹ for מַעֲלֵה (RV 'ascent'), in Is 5¹ in 'a very fruitful hill' (the paraphr. rend. of the Heb. 'a horn, the son of fatness'—'horn' being, as in Arab., fig. for a small isolated eminence), and in Ac 17²² for πάγος (RV 'Areopagus'). *Hill* stands also in RV for עֹפֶל, a swelling or bulging place, in 2 K 5²⁴, Is 32¹⁴, Mic 4⁸.

'Hill' is thus the most characteristic rendering of גִּבְעָה, a word which, coming from a root signifying *to be convex* (cf. גָּבִיעַ 'bowl,' Aram. גְּבִינָא 'hump-backed'), no doubt denotes properly (Stanley, *Sin. and Pal.* 138, 497) the large rounded hills, mostly bare or nearly so, so conspicuous in parts of Palestine, especially in Judah. Several places situated on such hills derived their names from the circumstance, as '*Gibeah* of Saul,' '*Gibeah* of Phinehas,' '*Gibeah* of the Foreskins,' etc. (see under GIBEAH); cf. the *hill* of Moreh (or of the Teacher) Jg 7¹, the *hill* of God (Gibeah) 1 S 10⁵, the *hill* of Hakîlah 1 S 23¹⁹ 26¹·³, the *hill* of Ammah 2 S 2²⁴, the *hill* of Gareb Jer 31³⁹, also 1 S 6¹, 2 S 6³·⁴ 'the hill' (near Kiriath-jearim)—all localities so called from the same marked topographical feature. Zion, it may be noticed, though sometimes termed a 'hill' in AV, RV (as Ps 2⁶ 3⁴ 15¹), is in the Heb. regularly a 'mountain' (הַר); it is spoken of as a גִּבְעָה only Is 10³² 31⁴ (in both ‖ 'mountain'), Ezk 34²⁶; cf. Zeph 1¹⁰. Hills of the same kind were also a favourite spot for the idolatrous rites of the Canaanites, which the Israelites were sometimes only too ready to take part in: the standing phrase is 'on every high *hill*, and under every spreading tree' (1 K 14²³, 2 K 17¹⁰, Jer 2²⁰ *al.*; cf. Dt 12², Hos 4¹³, Is 65⁷, Jer 13²⁷, Ezk 20²⁸ etc.). Notice that גִּבְעָה is also the term used in Ex 17⁹·¹⁰. A recollection of what a גִּבְעָה was adds force to Isaiah's picture of every high hill being fertilized by 'streams and water-courses' in the ideal future (30²⁵). גִּבְעָה is never used for a range of mountains (like הַר); but it often stands in poet. parallelism with 'mountain.' See *e.g.* Gn 49²⁶, Is 2², 30¹⁷ 40⁴·¹² 41¹⁵.

The passages in which 'hill' stands for הַר may next be considered. הַר is a much more general term than גִּבְעָה: it may be applied to what we should call a mountain-range, to a simple 'mountain,' and also to a block of elevated country (as the central part of Palestine). It thus no doubt in particular cases may correspond to what we should term a 'hill'; but it lacks the definite and distinct characteristics of the גִּבְעָה. Its being represented by 'hill' in AV is sometimes a source of confusion. Thus the 'hill' of Ex 24⁴ is the 'mount' of vv.¹²·¹³·¹⁵ etc.; the 'hill' of Nu 14⁴⁴·⁴⁵, Dt 1⁴¹·⁴³ is the 'mountain' of Nu 14⁴⁰, Dt 1⁴⁴; 1 K 11⁷ the 'hill' in front of Jerusalem is the 'mount' of Olives; the 'hill' of Zion in Ps 2⁶, and the 'holy hill' of 3⁴ 15¹ 43³ 99⁹ (cf. 24³ 68¹⁶ᵇ), is the 'mount' Zion of other passages. Other passages in which 'mount' or 'mountain' would have been better than 'hill' are Gn 7¹⁹ (see v.²⁰), Dt 8⁷ 11¹¹, Jos 15⁹ 18¹³·¹⁴, Jg 2⁹ 16³, 1 S 25²⁰ 26¹³, 2 S 13³⁴ 16¹³ 21⁹, 1 K 16²⁴·²⁴·²⁴ (of Samaria, see Am 4¹ 6¹ AV), 20²³·²⁸ 22¹⁷, 2 K 1⁹ 4²⁷ (see v.²⁵), Ps 18⁷ 68¹⁵·¹⁶ᵃ (of the great range of Jebel Hauran) 80¹⁰ 95⁴ 97⁵ 98⁸ 104¹⁰·¹³·¹⁸·³² 121¹, Lk 9³⁷ (see v.²⁸). In the great majority of these passages the correction has been made in RV.

עֹפֶל, which is represented by 'hill' in RV of 2 K 5²⁴, Is 32¹⁴, Mic 4⁸, was also (with the art.) the name of the bulging side of Zion on the S. of the Royal Palace: this is probably alluded to in Is 32¹⁴, Mic 4⁸; in 2 K 5²⁴ the name is applied to some similarly shaped spot in Samaria (cf. Mesha's Inscr. l. 22).—'Hill' is never, it may be added, to be understood in RV in the common English sense of an *ascent*, and only twice in AV

(1 S 9¹¹, 2 S 16¹): the Heb. for this is מַעֲלֵה ('going up,' or 'ascent').

Hill-country occurs in AV 4 times, Jos 13⁶ 21¹¹ (for הַר), and Lk 1³⁹·⁶⁵ (for ἡ ὀρεινή [often in LXX for הָהָר]); also Jth 1⁶ 2²² 4⁷ 5¹ 6⁷·¹¹. In RV the term has been employed much more frequently. As was remarked above, the Heb. הַר is used not only of a single mountain, and of a range of mountains, but also often of a *mountainous tract of country*, esp. the elevated mountain tract, which forms, as it were, the backbone of Palestine, gradually rising from the plain of Jezreel on the N., sloping down on the E. and W. to the Jordan Valley and the Mediterranean Sea, respectively, and terminating (approximately) in the S. in the neighbourhood of Beersheba. In AV, הַר, in this application, is usually rendered 'mountain(s)' or 'mount,'—in neither case very suitably, 'mount' especially (as in 'Mount Ephraim,' 1 S 1¹ and frequently) suggesting a single eminence (as Mount Ararat, Mount Etna, Mount Zion, etc.), and not a tract of mountainous country. Accordingly, 'hill-country,' the phrase already used in the AV of Jos 13⁶ 21¹¹, has in RV been generally substituted in all these cases. Thus Dt 1⁷·¹⁹·²⁰ 'the hill-country of the Amorites,' and 1⁷ 'the hill-country' (both of the high central ground of Canaan): so Jos 9¹ 10⁶·⁴⁰ 11³·¹⁶ 12⁸. Two parts of this 'hill-country,' which are frequently particularized, are the 'hill-country' of Ephraim (Jos 17⁵·¹⁶·¹⁸ 19⁵⁰ 20⁷ 21²¹ 24³⁰·³³, Jg 3²⁷ 4⁵ 7²⁴ 10¹ 17¹·⁸ 18²·¹³, 1 S 1¹ 9⁴ 14²², 2 S 20²¹, 1 K 4⁸ 12²⁵, 2 K 5²² 19¹·¹⁶·¹⁸, 2 Ch 13⁴ 15⁸ 19⁴: in Jer 4¹⁵ 31⁶ 50¹⁹ 'the *hills* of Ephraim'); and the 'hill-country' of Judah (Jos 11²¹ 20⁷ 21¹¹, 2 Ch 27⁴, Lk 1⁶⁵; cf. v.³⁹, Jos 18¹², Jg 1⁹·¹⁹, 1 S 23¹⁴), the latter forming a clearly defined part of the territory of Judah (opp. to the 'lowland,' the 'Negeb,' and the 'wilderness'), the cities of which are enumerated in Jos 15⁴⁸⁻⁶⁰ (cf. Jer 32⁴⁴ 33¹³ 'the cities of the hill-country'; and see JUDAH). We also have the 'hill-country' of Naphtali (Jos 20⁷), as well as of the Ammonite territory (Dt 2³⁷), and of Gilead (3¹²), on the E. of Jordan. G. A. Smith (*HGHL* 53) objects to the rendering 'hill-country,' on the ground that the Central Range of Palestine was recognized by the Hebrews as forming a single block, which they called accordingly not by a collective name but by a singular name, *the mountain*. The observation is, no doubt, correct; but 'the mountain' would in English have been so strongly suggestive of a single eminence that it could hardly be considered a preferable rendering.

S. R. DRIVER.

HILLEL (הִלֵּל 'he hath praised'; cf. the name in New Heb. of the well-known Rabbi *Hillel*).—The father of the judge Abdon, of Pirathon in Ephraim (Jg 12¹³·¹⁵).

HIN.—See WEIGHTS AND MEASURES.

HIND.—See HART.

HINGE (צִיר *zîr*, Arab. *ṣā'ir*, a pivot).—There seems to have been anciently only one kind of hinge in Syria, the pivot and socket. Doors of houses in Lebanon are made of wood, and generally the pivots on which the doors turn are projections of a piece of wood which runs the whole length of the door, and is called the *ṣiyâr*. The pivots themselves are called by the carpenters *sûs*, and are always of wood; they turn generally in sockets of iron, but sometimes a hole is made in a stone for the lower socket, and one is bored in the lintel for the upper.

On the east of the Jordan, in the Hauran, ancient buildings have been found in which the doors are made of one slab of stone, the projecting pivots being of stone also. The sockets are holes bored in the stone lintel and threshold. In 1 K 7⁵⁰ ‍נָף‍ is the *socket*. (For a good illustration of an ancient door socket [of Sargon I.] see Hilprecht, *Recent Researches in Bible Lands*, p. 93).

DOORS OF LEBANON HOUSES, SHOWING PIVOTS AND LOCK.

The ancient Egyp. hinge consisted of a socket of metal with a projecting pivot, into which the corner of the door was inserted. This kind is not common in Syria. **W. CARSLAW.**

HINNOM, VALLEY OF, also called **Valley of the Son of H., Valley of the Children of H.** (‍גֵּי הִנֹּם‍ Jos 15⁸ 18¹⁶, Neh 11³⁰; elsewhere [except in 2 K 23¹⁰, where *Kethibh* has ‍גֵּי בְנֵי ה‍] always ‍גֵּי בֶן־ה‍ Jos 15⁸ 18¹⁶, 2 Ch 28³ 33⁶, Jer 7³¹·³² 19²·⁶ 32³⁵).— Hinnom is mentioned in the OT invariably in connexion with the term *gai* [construct *gê*] (ravine), the Kidron being called *naḥal*, and the vale of Rephaim *'ēmeḳ*. It seems probable that *gai* denotes the channel or course through which water may make its way in the hills, and thus in Palestine becomes a ravine in the mountains; but the word cannot by itself be taken to mean any particular nature of ravine. It is used, in contradistinction to mountains, to denote valleys or depressions (Is 40⁴).

Naḥal is the exact equivalent of the modern *wâdy*. See BROOK. It is used of the deep gorges of the rivers Arnon and Jabbok, and of the shallow sandy stream of the 'river of Egypt' (*Wâdy el-'Arîsh*).

'*Emeḳ* is a broad vale fit for flowers (Ca 2¹), for corn land (Ps 65¹³), for battlefields (Job 39²¹), and chariots (Is 22⁷).

It has been suggested by Birch (*PEFSt*, 1878, p. 179) that these three names represent the three valleys which encompass Jerusalem, east, centre, and west, in the order they are given in the OT, viz.:—*naḥal*, Kidron; *gai*, Tyropœon or Hinnom; *'ēmeḳ*, Rephaim; but, unfortunately, this easy solution of a very difficult question does not satisfy the conditions.

Although the same appellative is used in the OT for a particular portion of a valley, there seems no reason against the various lengths of a valley being called *naḥal*, *gai*, and *'ēmeḳ* in succession according to the requirements of the case; and it is obvious that when the branches of a valley have these different names, the portion below the junction must differ in name from one or other of them. Stanley (*SP*, Appendix, p. 482) points out that in 1 S 17² *'ēmeḳ* and *gai* seem to be used convertibly, and suggests that the *'ēmeḳ* 'of the terebinth' contracted into a *gai* in its descent towards the plain of Philistia. It is suggested that in this case the *'ēmeḳ* 'of the terebinth' (Valley of Elah) was the designation of the valley generally, while the separate portions were termed *gai*, etc., according to their character. At the present day the Arabs are in the habit of giving descriptive names to each reach of a valley, in addition to the general name for the whole valley.

Whatever view is taken of the position of the valley of Hinnom, all writers concur in its extending to the junction of the three valleys of Jerusalem below Siloam, *i.e.* there must be one spot below Siloam which all agree in making a portion of the valley of Hinnom. It is suggested that the valley of Hinnom does not end here, but is the name of the whole valley (*Wâdy en-Nâr*), extending from the north of Jerusalem to the Dead Sea. The point, then, which requires to be cleared up is whether it is the east valley or *Kidron*, the centre valley or *Tyropœon*, or the west valley or *Wâdy er-Rubâbeh*.

It is stated (Neh 11³⁰) that on the return of the children of Judah after the Captivity, they 'encamped from Beersheba unto the valley of Hinnom'—where the *gai* of Hinnom may be the *Wâdy en-Nâr*, extending from Jerusalem to the Dead Sea. The valley of H. was near the gate Harsith of Jerusalem (Jer 19²), which in AV is tr⁴ 'east gate' (AVm 'sun gate'), and in RVm 'gate of potsherds.' It is stated (1 Ch 4²³) that the potters 'dwelt with the king for his work,' possibly near the king's palace at the southern side of the temple near the water gate, above the Kidron.

The word *gai* is also used for the '*valley* gate' (2 Ch 26⁹, Neh 2¹³·¹⁵ 3¹³), which appears to have been on the west side of Jerusalem above the Tyropœon valley near the present Jaffa gate.

The valley of Hinnom is mentioned in connexion with the boundary-line between Judah and Benjamin (Jos 15⁸ 18¹⁶), but otherwise principally with reference to the abominable rites and ceremonies of the Ammonites. The high places of Tophet and Baal, where children were passed through the fire to Molech (Jer 7³¹ 32³⁵), were built in this valley. Ahaz and Manasseh burnt incense and passed their children through the fire to Molech (2 Ch 28³ 33⁶). This practice was perhaps tolerated in Jerusalem by Solomon (1 K 11⁷). Josiah defiled Tophet in order to prevent these horrible rites from being carried out there; and from the allusion to the graves of the children of the people (2 K 23⁶·¹⁰), it would appear that it was near the common burial-place. It was to receive the name of the 'Valley of Slaughter' in time to come (Jer 7³² 19¹¹).

According to Buxtorf, Lightfoot, and others (following Kimchi), there were perpetual fires kept up in this valley for consuming dead bodies of criminals and carcases of animals, and the refuse of the city; and this may be accepted (but see Robinson, *BRP* i. 274) as the most probable method of disposing of the immense masses of refuse which required to be destroyed for the sake of the health of the city (Rosenmüller, *Biblische Geogr.* II. i. pp. 156, 164).

The Talmudists place the mouth of hell in the valley of H. 'There are two palm trees in the valley of Hinnom between which a smoke ariseth —and this is the door of Gehenna' (see Barclay, *City of the Great King*, p. 90, and art. GEHENNA). In this sense it was used by our Lord (Mt 5²⁹ 10²⁸, etc.). Jerome (*Comm. in Jer.* 7³¹, and on Mt 10²⁸) describes Tophet as a pleasant spot in the valley of Hinnom, with trees and gardens watered from Siloam, lying at the foot of Moriah (*i.e.* in the gardens below Siloam at the junction of the east and west valleys).

Stanley (*Sin. and Pal.* p. 172) suggests that the ravine (*gai*) was named Ge Ben Hinnom, or Ge-Hinnom, after some ancient hero who had encamped there, and that from this was formed the word Gehenna. In the Mohammedan traditions the name *Gehenna* is applied to the valley of the Kidron (Ibn Batuteh, 124; Le Strange, *Pal. under the Moslems*, p. 218). Stanley further points out (*Recov. of Jerus.* xiv.) that the valley of H. includes, if it is not identical with, the glen of the Kidron *east* of the city. 'This appears to follow beyond question from Jer 19¹¹; and it agrees, not only with the Mussulman nomenclature, but with almost all the biblical indications on the subject, and especially with the word Ge-hinnom.'

The point which now requires clearing up is the identification of one of the three valleys which encompass Jerusalem as the valley of Hinnom. From En-rogel, 'the border went up by the valley of the son of H. unto the side of the Jebusite southward (the same is Jerusalem); and the border went up to the top of the mountain that lieth before the valley of H. westward, which is at the uttermost part of the vale of Rephaim northward' (Jos 15⁸). 'And the border went down to the uttermost part of the mountain that lieth before the valley of the son of H., which is in the vale of Rephaim northward, and it went down to the valley of H., to the side of the Jebusite southward, and went down to En-rogel' (Jos 18¹⁶). In considering the direction of the valley of Hinnom south of the city of Jebus, it must be recollected that though we know the limits of ancient Jerusalem, on east, west, and south, by the deep valleys that begirt it, we do not know for certain what portions of it comprised the city of Jebus, and there is considerable difference of opinion on the subject owing to the many very difficult points which are not yet cleared up; in fact, the only solution appears to be derived from considering the dual condition of the ancient city to which references appear constantly in OT and early writings.

The following points seem to be concurred in generally :—

(1) That the temple mount (Moriah) is the eastern hill on which the Dome of the Rock now stands.

(2) That the city of David as mentioned in the Book of Nehemiah is on the spur of Ophel south of the temple area and extending to Siloam.

(3) That the Akra of the Maccabees and Josephus is either north or north-west of the temple area.

(4) That the upper part of the city, the modern Zion, is the φρούριον or upper market-place of Josephus, taken into the city by king David, and not necessarily a part of the ancient city Jebus.

A very brief summary of the information concerning Jerusalem is necessary to clear up this question as to Hinnom. It appears to be conclusively proved by the Tel el-Amarna tablets, that as far back as the year B.C. 1400, or prior to the time of the Judges, Jerusalem or Jebus was known as Urusalim (the element *Uru* being indicated by the Sumerian ideogram *uru*='city' (Hommel, *AHT* p. 201). 'Jebus, which is Jerusalem,' is first spoken of in OT in the account of the spies (Nu 13²⁹, Jos 11³) as 'the Jebusite in the mountains,' and in the Book of Joshua (15⁶³) is allotted to Judah, and (18²⁸) also to Benjamin. It is stated that neither the children of Judah nor the children of Benjamin could drive out the Jebusites, and that they dwelt with them there. It would appear, therefore, either that Jerusalem was common to both tribes, or that a portion was allotted to each, or that different writers reckoned it differently. Lightfoot, quoting from the Talmud, states (*Prospect of Jerusalem*), 'For most part of the courts were in the portion of Judah; but the altar, porch, temple, and most holy place were in Benjamin.' It was reserved for king David to capture the stronghold of Zion, and the *Millo* or citadel. It is stated (2 S 5⁷=1 Ch 11⁵), 'Nevertheless, David took the stronghold of Zion : the same is the city of David.' The going up of Joab by the 'gutter' or watercourse, related subsequently, may have been a separate assault on another part of the city. Josephus evidently favours this view, for he says that David began the siege, and that he took the lower city (τὴν κάτω πόλιν) by force, but the citadel (ἄκρα) held out, and that it was taken by Joab (*Ant.* V. ii. 2, VII. iii. 1). If the stronghold of Zion may be accepted as the lower city of Josephus, and Millo as the Akra or citadel which Joab took, all difficulties concerning the passages appear to vanish.

The difference between the stronghold of Zion and the citadel of Millo seems to be accentuated in the following passages :—

'And David dwelt in the stronghold (*mĕzûdah*), and called it, The city of David. And David built round about Millo and inward' (2 S 5⁹). 'And he built the city round about, from Millo even round about; and Joab repaired the rest of the city' (1 Ch 11⁸). Millo is mentioned as separate from the walls of the city also in the following passages, 1 K 9¹⁵. ²⁴ 11²⁷, 2 Ch 32⁵. The meaning of *Millo* is given in *QPB* as *rampart*, and by Gesenius (*Lex.*) as a *rampart* or *mound*, built up and filled with stones or earth. Lightfoot says, 'Millo, which was an outward place and the suburb of Zion, distinguished and parted from Zion by a wall, yet a member of it and belonging to it.' Williams (*Holy City*, part ii. p. 43) says, 'It must never be forgotten that Jerusalem was originally two distinct cities united together by David.' Stanley has pointed out that the stronghold, fort or castle, of Zion, in all the passages (2 S 5⁷. ⁹. ¹⁷, 1 Ch 11⁵. ⁷. ¹⁶), represents the Hebrew words *mĕzûdah* (מְצוּדָה) or *mĕzâd* (מְצָד), the root meaning a lair whence hunters seek their prey, and to which they can flee as unto a safe retreat (Gesen.); the word itself denoting the top or summit of a mountain, or mountain castle. This word in the LXX is tr⁴ in all these instances as ἡ περιοχή. Grove has also pointed out that *Millo* is rendered in every case (except 2 Ch 32⁵) by the LXX as ἡ ἄκρα (the citadel), which they employ nowhere else in the OT. This word ἡ ἄκρα is also used both by Josephus and the Book of Maccabees for the fort or citadel overlooking the temple to the north-west, during the struggle with the Macedonian adherents of Antiochus, which was at last razed and the rocky hill levelled by Simon Maccabæus (Jos. *Ant.* XIII. vi. 7; *BJ* v. iv. 1; but cf. 1 Mac 1³⁰ᶠ· 14³⁶ᶠ·). Sayce (*PEFSt*, 1883, p. 214) also points to a 'stronghold of Zion' on the lower hill taken by David before he stormed the Jebusite citadel on the upper hill; * and states further, 'The dual form Jerushalaim, which apparently goes back to the time of the Maccabees, probably refers to the old division of Jerusalem into the lower city and the temple-hill.' The whole testimony appears, therefore, to be in favour of a Jerusalem separated into two portions—one called the lair or stronghold, which is the city of David, the other called the Millo or citadel. Now, the Book of Nehemiah clearly seems to place the city of David on the spur of Ophel south of the temple, above Siloam (Neh 3^{16} 12^{37}). Again, Josephus, while placing ἡ ἄκρα (the citadel) to the north-west of the temple, also speaks of the lower part of the city being taken by David, and places it near Ophel. The Books of Maccabees speak of the same citadel (ἡ ἄκρα) as Josephus does, and call the temple mount Sion (1 Mac 4^{37} 5^{54}). It therefore appears, that to accept the Ophel spur as the city of David or Zion, and the high ground east of the holy sepulchre as the Millo or citadel of the ancient Jerusalem, will satisfy the various data in the OT, the Books of Maccabees, and Josephus. We thus arrive at the conclusion that the boundary-line between Judah and Benjamin, which went up the valley of Hinnom, was drawn south of either the spur of Ophel or of the citadel (ἡ ἄκρα), or of both.

The next point to ascertain is the position of En-rogel; and this seems comparatively easy, as there appears to be a consensus of opinion at the present day that it corresponds to the copious Virgin's Fountain. It is the only known fountain in the vicinity of Jerusalem. The Bîr Eyûb is a *well* and not a *spring*, the water being 70 to 80 ft. below the surface of the ground in summer. In a land where there are so few springs, this alone ought to identify it. The Virgin's Fountain is close to the stone *Zehweileh*, which Ganneau has identified as the stone Zoheleth, which is close to En-rogel (1 K 1^9). This position of En-rogel satisfies the requirements of the two passages (2 S 17^{17}, 1 K 1^9). Josephus describes it in two passages (*Ant.* VII. xiv. 4, IX. x. 4) as close to the royal gardens, and the Book of Nehemiah places the king's garden near Siloam (Neh 3^{15}). The Virgin's Fountain also appears to be Gihon-in-the-valley (Siloam being Gihon). Thus Hezekiah stopped the upper outlet at the Virgin's Fountain (Gihon) and brought it through the rock to Siloam (2 Ch 32^{30}) to the west side of the city of David, the city of David being on Ophel.

The third point to ascertain is the general position of the 'mountain that lieth before the valley of H. westward.' Assuming that the fountain of Nephtoah is identified with '*Ain Lifta*, about 2½ miles to the north-west of Jerusalem, the mountain which lieth before the valley of Hinnom westward appears to be the high ground immediately north of Jerusalem, which, though not exactly a mountain, is the highest ground in the neighbourhood, from which valleys start in all directions to the Mediterranean and Dead Sea. The site of the Russian hospice may be said to occupy the position of this mountain. The line of boundary between Judah and Benjamin may now be traced from En-shemesh (east of Jerusalem) to En-rogel, thence up the valley of Kidron to a point opposite to the southern side of the temple, thence across the temple courts south of the temple, and up the valley on the south side of Akra to the Jaffa gate, and thence north by the Russian hospice to Lifta. Under this disposition the valley of Kidron becomes the

valley of Hinnom; but it is suggested, that while the Kidron is only the name for the small narrow portion of the valley east of the temple, the valley of Hinnom is the name of the whole valley reaching from near the Russian hospice to the Dead Sea, which is now called *Wâdy en-Nâr* or the Valley of Fire. 'The head of this valley of Hinnom or Kidron commences near the Jaffa road, a mile and a half north-west of Jerusalem, and runs along the northern side of the Tombs of the Kings' (*Recovery of Jerus.* p. 291). Thus the boundary-line, after leaving the valley of H. on the east of the temple, again approaches it north-west of Jerusalem at the highest point of the land, i.e. to the 'top of the mountain that lieth before the valley of Hinnom westward' (Jos 15^8).

As all writers appear to concur in considering that the position of Tophet in the valley of Hinnom was in the vicinity of Siloam, near the junction of the three valleys which are about Jerusalem, on the level ground there, it seems quite immaterial, so far as Tophet is concerned, which of those valleys was Hinnom, and the interest in this matter lies in the question, already answered, connected with the topography of Jerusalem as to the position of the city of David.

A brief description is here given of these three valleys—

(1) The Kidron Valley will alone suit the requirements of Jos 15^8 18^{16}, if En-rogel is to be accepted as identical with the Virgin's Fountain in the Kidron, as from thence the line 'went *up* by the valley of the son of Hinnom.' This identification allows of the partition of Jerusalem between Judah and Benjamin, and suits the requirements of OT, Books of Maccabees, Josephus, Talmudists, Jerome, and Jewish and Arab tradition. It also meets the requirement of Jos 15^8 and 18^{16}, under which the boundary-line twice approaches the valley of H.,—first at En-rogel, and secondly at the top of the mountain before the valley of H. eastward. Against this identification is the use of the word *gai* in connexion with the valley gate; but this objection is involved in the identification itself of the *nahal* Kidron and the *gai* Hinnom as one and the same.

(2) The centre valley (or Tyropœon of Josephus), reaching from near the Jaffa gate or the Damascus gate to Siloam, has been identified by W. R. Smith (*Encyc. Brit.*^{9} 'Jerusalem'), Sayce (*PEFSt*, 1883, p. 213), Birch (*PEFSt*, p. 179), and Schwartz (*Das H. L.* p. 190), as the valley of Hinnom. This appears to necessitate the Bîr Eyûb being identified as En-rogel, although Birch expressly states that the Virgin's Fountain is En-rogel. The line passing up the Tyropœon Valley separates the eastern mount from the western, and thus places part of the city, but none of the temple courts, in Judah. The difficulty about adopting this valley as the valley of H. is that it exists only in Jerusalem. It begins at the Damascus gate or at the Jaffa gate, and ends at the pool of Siloam. It is an important division in the city of Jerusalem, but it is very insignificant compared with the valleys to east and west of the city. It cannot fulfil either of the conditions of extending as far as the mountain that lieth before the valley of H., or as far as the '*ēmek* where Tophet was: a glance at the map or model will show that it is a geographical impossibility to consider the gardens below Siloam as part of the central valley. These gardens clearly belong to the junction of the east and west valleys. There is thus no part of the central valley where the high places of Tophet and Baal could have been built.

(3) The identification of the *Wâdy er-Rubâbeh* as the valley of H. has hitherto been generally accepted among Western writers, though Jewish

Arab tradition is against it. This valley commences as an '*ēmek* to the north-west of Jerusalem, and fulfils the condition of reaching 'the mountain which lieth over against the valley of H. to the westward'; it passes W.S.W. towards the Jaffa gate, then to south, and again trends round to the west and joins the Kidron near Siloam, thus compassing Jerusalem to the west and south. Two large reservoirs are built in it—the *Birket Mamilla* above, and the *Birket es-Sultân* below the Jaffa gate; its description in detail is given in the article JERUSALEM. At the junction of this valley with the Kidron it again forms an '*ēmek* or fields (Jer 31⁴⁰). But to identify the *Wâdy er-Rubâbeh* with the valley of H. appears to require En-rogel to be located at the *Bîr Eyûb*, and the whole of Jerusalem to be in Benjamin.

The junction of the east and west valleys cannot be considered to belong to one valley more than the other, and, so far as localizing Tophet, all will allow that the valley of H. extended to this junction. It is stated by Jeremiah (7³²) that the valley of H. in the vicinity of Tophet shall be called the 'valley of slaughter,' 'for they shall bury in Tophet till there be no more place'; later on he prophesies (31⁴⁰), 'and the whole valley ('*ēmek*) of the dead bodies, and of the ashes, and all the fields unto the brook Kidron, unto the corner of the horse gate to the east, shall be holy unto the Lord.' This seems clearly to point to the ground stretching from above the Virgin's Fountain to the Bîr Eyûb, including the mouth of Wâdy er-Rubâbeh. Now, this land is here described as '*ēmek*, although Kidron is termed a *naḥal*, and the valley of H. (wherever located) is termed a *gai*. This ground is also called fields (*shĕdēmôth*, Jer 31⁴⁰ [*Kerê*]), and the 'king's garden' by Siloam (Neh 3¹⁵), probably the same as the king's dale ('*ēmek*), where Absalom raised a pillar (2 S 18¹⁸), stated by Josephus (*Ant.* VII. x. 3) to be 2 furlongs from Jerusalem. Josephus also relates that the 'king's paradise' or 'garden' was in the vicinity of En-rogel, where Adonijah conspired against king David (1 K 1⁹; *Ant.* VII. xiv. 4, IX. x. 4). Perhaps this may be the 'king's dale' or 'vale' ('*ēmek*) of Shaveh (Gn 14¹⁷), where Melchizedek met Abraham. The garden of Uzza is not located (2 K 21¹⁸). This junction of the valleys may be the valley ('*ēmek*) of Jehoshaphat or of decision (Jl 3². ¹². ¹⁴), where all nations shall be judged in 'the day of the LORD,' thus agreeing with the tradition of Christians, Moslems, and Jews for many centuries. See JEHOSHAPHAT (VALLEY OF). The 'king's gardens' were in the immediate vicinity of the remarkable waterworks constructed by the kings of Judah. The Virgin's Fountain is identified as Gihon in the valley (2 Ch 33¹⁴), the upper outlet of which was stopped by king Hezekiah, who 'brought it straight down by an underground way on the west side of the city of David' (2 K 20²⁰, 2 Ch 32³⁰). This account exactly describes the rock-cut passage which runs through the Ophel spur to Siloam. There is, however, a still more ancient watercourse by which the Virgin's Fountain supplied the city of David with water (discovered by the present writer in 1868), and this waterduct has been identified by some as the 'gutter' by which Joab got up into the city of the Jebusites. On the outside of the Virgin's Fountain can still be seen the old conduit which led the overflow waters down the Kidron, and which may be identified as the conduit of the upper pool in the highway of the fuller's field (2 K 18¹⁷, Is 7³ 36²). It may possibly also be the 'king's pool' (Neh 2¹⁴). The pool between the two walls at Siloam is also mentioned (Is 22⁹. ¹¹, Neh 3¹⁵). But perhaps the greatest instance yet known of the magnitude of the waterworks of the past in the valley of

Hinnom is the remarkable aqueduct cut in the rock running down the *Wâdy en-Nâr* below the *Bîr Eyûb*, discovered and cleared out in 1868 for several hundred yards, and serving for no apparent purpose. This seems probably the aqueduct to carry off 'the brook that overflowed through the midst of the land,' for 'Why should the kings of Assyria come, and find much water?' (2 Ch 32⁴).

LITERATURE. — Rosenmüller, *Biblisch. Geogr.* ii. 156, 164; Robinson, *BRP*; Stanley, *SP*; Barclay, *City of the Great King*; Riehm, *HWB*; Tobler, *Topog.*; Baedeker-Socin, *Pal.*; *Recov. of Jerus.*; Williams, *Holy City*; *SWP*.

C. WARREN.

HIP.—The only occurrence of this word in AV is in the proverbial expression Jg 15⁸ 'And he smote them hip and thigh (שׁוֹק עַל־יָרֵךְ) with a great slaughter.' The Heb. is lit. 'leg upon thigh,' but the origin of the phrase is quite unknown. The phrase 'hip and thigh' comes from the Gen. Bible, which offers in the marg. 'horsemen and footmen,' the suggestion of Targ.; but that does not explain the expression. Nor is Kimchi's 'heels over head,' in reference to their flight, more likely or more lucid. Others suppose the meaning to be that they were cut in pieces, and limb piled on limb in bloody confusion. We may compare '*catch one* or *have one on the hip*,' supposed to belong to the language of wrestling, and found in Shaks. and elsewhere, as *Merch. of Venice*, I. iii. 47—

> ' If I can catch him once upon the hip,
> I will feed fat the ancient grudge I bear him.'

RV introduces 'hip' into Gn 32³²*bis* 'the sinew of the hip,' for AV 'the sinew which shrank.' See SINEW.   J. HASTINGS.

HIPPOPOTAMUS.—See BEHEMOTH.

HIRAH (חִירָה).—The Adullamite with whom Judah, according to the story of Gn 38 (J), appears to have entered into a kind of partnership in the matter of flocks (see Dillm. *ad loc.*). In vv.¹². ²⁰ he is called the 'friend' (רֵעַ) of Judah. Instead of רֵעֵהוּ, the LXX must have read רֹעֵהוּ 'his shepherd,' for in both these verses it has ποιμήν. This reading is followed also by Vulg. (*pastor, opilio*) and Luther (*Hirte*), but there can be little doubt that it is wrong. From v.¹ it is evident that Hirah's relation to Judah was an independent one, even if Judah was the more important man of the two. After Tamar had successfully carried out her stratagem, it was by the hand of his 'friend' Hirah that Judah sent the promised kid to the supposed *ḳĕdēshâh*, Gn 38²⁰ff.   J. A. SELBIE.

HIRAM (חִירָם; Χειράμ).—Some confusion exists as to the actual form of the name. In the books of Samuel and Kings the form given above is that which is usually adopted; but in 1 K 5¹⁰. ¹⁸ [Heb. 24. 32] 7⁴⁰ **Hirom** (חִירוֹם) occurs, while the Chronicler adheres to the form **Huram** (חוּרָם; in 1 Ch 14¹ *Kethîbh* חירם). The LXX invariably gives Χειράμ; Josephus Εἴρωμος (*c. Apion.* i. 17, 18) and Εἴραμος (*Ant.* VIII. ii. 6, etc.). The name further appears as Σίρωμος (Herodotus, vii. 98; Syncellus, p. 343 ff.) and Σούρων (Eupolemon cited by Eusebius, *Præp. Evang.* ix. 33, 34). The name is undoubtedly Phœnician, and is equivalent to Ahiram (אֲחִירָם Nu 26³⁸) = 'brother of the exalted one';* cf. Baethgen, *Beiträge zur Semit. Religionsgeschichte*, p. 156 (but see Gray, *Heb. Prop. Names*, 75 ff., upon whose theory the meaning is 'brother is exalted'). According to Movers (*Die Phönizier*, i. p. 505 f.), Hiram or Huram is the name of a deity = 'the coiled *or*

* Names of this type are especially common in Phœnician; cf. Abibaal, Abiram. Similar instances of the dropping of the initial א occur in Hebrew (Hiel, 1 K 16³⁴ חִיאֵל, for אֲחִיאֵל), and in Phœnician (חמלכת, חמלך = 'brother of Milk,' 'of Milkath'; חתמלכת = 'sister of Milkath').

twisted one'; but this derivation is very improbable.

1. King of Tyre, and contemporary with David and Solomon. According to 2 S 5[11], 1 Ch 14[1], H. sent an embassy to David after the conquest of Jerusalem, and provided him with artisans and materials for the building of his palace. On the accession of Solomon messengers were again sent to the Israelite court, doubtless to offer congratulations to the new king (1 K 5[1f.]). A treaty was concluded between the two kingdoms, in accordance with which H. supplied cedar trees and fir trees from Lebanon, together with skilled workmen for the building of the temple. In return, Solomon paid a yearly tribute of 20,000 cors of wheat and 20,000 baths of pure oil (after the reading of LXX, 2 Ch and Josephus; the Hebrew gives '20 cors of oil,' 1 K 5[6-11]). At the end of the twenty years 'wherein Solomon had built the two houses, the house of the LORD and the king's house,' he presented Hiram with twenty cities in the land of Galilee. The gift, however, failed to please the Phœnician king,[*] though in return he made Solomon a present of 120 talents of gold (1 K 9[10-14]). The friendly relations between the two monarchs were further strengthened by their combined trading operations: for 'the king (Solomon) had at sea a navy of Tarshish with the navy of Hiram: once every three years came the navy of Tarshish, bringing gold and silver, ivory, and apes, and peacocks' (1 K 10[22], 2 Ch 9[21]). In addition to this, we are expressly told that the sailors of Solomon's merchant vessels trading between Ezion-geber (at the top of the Gulf of Akabah) and Ophir were accompanied by Hiram's servants, 'shipmen that had knowledge of the sea' (1 K 9[26-28], 2 Ch 8[17. 18]), and were well acquainted with the route to Ophir (1 K 10[11]).

In the Chronicler's account of Solomon's dealings with Hiram (2 Ch 2[3f.]) the yearly tribute paid by the former is increased to '20,000 measures of beaten wheat, and 20,000 measures of barley, and 20,000 baths of wine, and 20,000 baths of oil,' and is applied to the maintenance of the Tyrian workpeople.

This statement seems due to some confusion on the part of the Chronicler: probably a certain quantity of wheat and pure oil was supplied to the Phœnician court, and a similar contribution of barley, wine, and oil handed over to 'the hewers that cut timber.' The Book of Kings only mentions the former payment, which the Chronicler incorrectly combines with a second statement (apparently obtained from another source) relating to the workpeople only. A more striking discrepancy between the two accounts occurs at 2 Ch 8[1. 2], where the Chronicler, who ignores the present of gold made by Hiram to Solomon (1 K 9[14]), refers to the cities of Galilee as if they had been presented to Solomon by Hiram. The omission, as well as the contradiction of the statement of 1 K 9[11f.], is probably due to the desire of the Chronicler to bring the history more into conformity with the views of his own age. According to the later conception it would be as improbable that Solomon, with his fabulous riches, should receive gold from Hiram, as that he should present Israelite cities to a foreign monarch.

A more serious difficulty, however, confronts us when we compare the biblical narrative with the information supplied by Josephus from the Tyrian historians, Menander and Dius (*Ant.* VIII. ii. 6–9, v. 3; *c. Apion.* i. 17, 18). According to the latter, Hiram was the son of Abibaal, and died at the age of 53 after a glorious reign of 34 years. Now, we have already seen that the building of David's palace followed immediately after the capture of Jerusalem (2 S 5[11]), *i.e.* in the seventh year of David's reign. It is further stated (1 K 9[10f.]) that Hiram was still alive in the twentieth year of Solomon's reign, so that, according to the biblical narrative, the total length of his reign must have exceeded 50 years. The disagreement between the two accounts is made even clearer by the statement of Josephus (*Ant.* VIII. iii. 1), that the building of the temple began in the 11th year of Hiram. For the temple was begun in the 4th year of Solomon (1 K 6[1]), so that Hiram and David could have reigned only 8 years contemporaneously. It has been conjectured by Ewald (*Gesch.* iii. p. 307) and Bertheau (on 2 Ch 2[2]) that the Hiram of David's reign was the grandfather of Solomon's contemporary. Thenius, on the other hand (on 2 S 5[11], 1 K 5[1]), supposes that Abibaal was merely an honorary title, and that both father and son were called Hiram. The most probable solution of the difficulty is that the Books of Samuel are not chronologically arranged, and that David's palace was not actually built until the end of his reign (Movers, *Die Phönizier*, ii. 1, p. 148 f.; see SAMUEL, BOOKS OF).

Josephus further recounts (*Ant.* VIII. v. 3; *c. Apion.* i. 17, 18), on the authority of Menander and Dius, that Solomon and Hiram engaged in a contest with riddles, in which the former was finally overcome by a young Tyrian named Abdemon. In another passage (*Ant.* VIII. ii. 6–7) he sets forth the letters which passed between the two kings on the subject of the building of the temple, and asserts that copies were preserved, not only in Jewish books, but in the Tyrian state-records (cf. 2 Ch 2[11]). In all probability, these letters are to be ascribed to Josephus himself; they are given at greater length by Eupolemon (Eusebius, *Præp. Evang.* ix. 33, 34), and are mentioned by Alexander Polyhistor (Clem. Alex. *Strom.* i. 21). According to Clem. Alex. (*loc. cit.*) and Tatian (*Or. c. Græcos,* § 37), Solomon married the daughter of Hiram (cf. 1 K 11[2. 5], where Zidonians are mentioned among Solomon's wives).

Among the more important events of the glorious reign of Hiram may be mentioned (1) the campaign against the inhabitants of Cyprus, who had refused to pay the customary tribute; (2) the fortification of the island of Tyre; (3) the erection of new temples to Hercules and Astarte. H. further restored many old sanctuaries and enriched one of the chief temples (that of Zeus-Baalsamin) with numerous golden ornaments, in particular with a golden pillar (mentioned by Herodotus, ii. 44). See Movers, *Die Phönizier*, II. i. 141 f.

2. The artificer procured by king Solomon from Tyre for the purpose of casting the various vessels and ornaments of brass for the temple (1 K 7[13f.]): acc. to 2 Ch 2[13], he was also 'skilful to work in gold and in silver . . . in iron, in stone, and in timber, in purple, in blue, and in fine linen, and in crimson.' The more important of his works were the two pillars of brass, the molten sea and the twelve oxen, the ten bases and the ten lavers, all of brass, besides the vessels of brass required for the temple service. According to 1 K 7 his mother was a widow woman of the tribe of Naphtali, and his father a Tyrian brassworker. The Chronicler, however, describes him as 'Huram Abi[*] (חוּרָם אָבִי;

---

[*] 1 K 9[13] 'and he called them the land of Cabul.' Cabul is usually taken as='worth nothing.' It is more probable that the LXX ὅριον represents the truer reading, viz. 'land of Galilee' (אֶרֶץ הַגָּלִיל), supposing him to have connected the word with זְבֻל 'dung.' See Klostermann *in loc.*). Buhl (*GAP* p. 221), however, considers that the territory lay somewhere near the town of that name (Jos 19[27]) in N. Galilee: in this case the LXX ὅριον is treated as a mistranslation of גְּבוּל, as if גְּבוּל.

[*] The word 'Abi' (אָבִי 'my father') is usually taken (Bertheau on 2 Ch 2[13]) in the sense of 'master,' a title of respect and distinction; cf. Gn 4[20-22] 45[8] etc.

4¹⁶ אֲבִיר חוּרָם), the son of a woman of the daughters of Dan' (2 Ch 2¹³ᶠ·). As Giesebrecht has shown (*ZATW*, 1881, p. 239 f., but see Cheyne in *Expository Times*, June 1898, p. 471ᵃ), it is probable that the Chronicler has here preserved the truer account; the latter portion of the name was omitted as unintelligible by the author of Kings (cf. LXX to 2 Ch 2¹³ τὸν πατέρα μου, παῖδα μου). He further suggests that the dislike felt by the editor of Kings to the idea of the temple being built by a half-Phœnician, caused him to insert the words 'a widow of the tribe of Naphtali' (מִמַּטֵּה נַפְתָּלִי . . . אַלְמָנָה), the alteration of מִבְּנוֹת דָּן ('of the daughters of Dan') into מִמַּטֵּה נַפְתָּלִי ('of the tribe of Naphtali') being the more permissible, since Dan lay in the territory of Naphtali. Josephus (*Ant.* VIII. iii. 4) describes him as of the tribe of Naphtali on his mother's side, his father being Ur of the stock of Israel (cf. on this later tradition Ed. König in *Expos. Times*, May 1898, p. 346ᵃ).

J. F. STENNING.

HIRE, HIRELING.—Hire in AV is equivalent always to mod. *wages*. Thus Gn 31⁸ 'The ringstraked shall be thy hire'; Is 23¹⁸ 'And her merchandise and her hire shall be holiness to the LORD' (Del. 'her gain and her wages become holy unto J''''); Mic 3¹¹ 'The heads thereof judge for reward, and the priests thereof teach for hire'; Lk 10⁷ 'the labourer is worthy of his hire.' Tindale has the word very much as in the mod. use in Mk 12¹ 'And let yt out to hyre unto husbandmen.' The plu. 'hires,' now obsolete, occurs once in AV, Mic 1⁷ 'All the hires thereof shall be burned with fire.' So Wyc. (1388) in Lv 25⁵³, Ezk 16³³, and (1380) Ro 6²³ 'Treuli the hyris of synne, deeth' (1388, 'For the wagis of synne is deth').

A hireling is a hired servant (for which see FAMILY, vol. i. p. 849ᵃ), and properly carries no suggestion of unfaithfulness. Thus Tindale, *Works*, i. 146, 'Hereby mayest thou not understand that we obtain the favour of God, and the inheritance of life, through the merits of good works, as hirelings do their wages.' So Rhem. has 'hireling' in Lk 15¹⁷· ¹⁹, where all the other VSS have 'hired servant.' And cf. Sir 7²⁰ 'Whereas thy servant worketh truly, entreat him not evil, nor the hireling that bestoweth himself wholly for thee.' But through Christ's use of the word in Jn 10¹²· ¹³ it has come to express not only one who has no interest in his work, but even one who is unfaithful in the doing of it. Gosson (*Schoole of Abuse*, Arber's ed. p. 25) says, 'Poetrie and pyping have allwaies bene so united togither, that til the time of Melanippides, Pipers were Poets hyerlings; but marke I pray you, how they are nowe both abused.' The word 'hireling' is now as greatly abused as either, being carried quite beyond our Lord's meaning and intention. Shaks. does not use the word; but Milton (*PL* iv. 193) gives us—

'So clomb this first grand Thief into God's fold; So since into his church lewd hirelings climb.'

Then South, *Sermons*, iv. No. 5—'If we consider even Judas himself, it was not his carrying the bag, while he followed his master, but his following his master only that he might carry the bag, which made him a thief and an hireling.' Finally, Cowper, *Truth*—

'But with averted eyes th' omniscient Judge Scorns the base hireling, and the slavish drudge.'

J. HASTINGS.

HIS.—Under an impression, probably, that the 's of the poss. case was a shortened form of *his* (though it is really the remains of the Anglo-Saxon genitive ending -*es*), this adj. was employed throughout a long period to indicate possession. It probably arose from a desire to avoid adding *s* to a word which already had that sound, perhaps more than once. Hence it is generally found after words ending in *s*, and especially after proper names. Thus Ridley, *Brefe Declaration* (Moule's ed.), p. 119, 'Innocentius his fantastical invention'; and p. 140, 'Duns his fantastical imagination'; Knox, *Hist.* p. 101, 'Secondarily, said he, I greatly doubt whether James his commandment or Pauls obedience, proceeded of the holy Ghost'; Fuller, *Holy Warre*, I. 3 (p. 4), 'But his Holinesse his converting facultie worketh the strongest at the greatest distance.' It is freely employed, however, where there is no need to avoid repeating *s*. Thus Cranmer, *Works* (Parker Soc.), i. 2, 'And where he had reasons for the King his party, that he was moved of God his law, which doth straitly forbid and that with many great threats, that no man shall marry his brother his wife.' And, on the other hand, old writers had not so nice an ear as we ourselves in the matter of multiplying sibilants. We find in Cranmer, *Works*, i. 18, 'the King's Grace's most honourable Council,' and p. 151, 'the King's Highness's realm'; * and in Hall (*Works*, ii. 190) even 'We are Moseses disciples.' The idiom indeed was left after a time to the caprice or taste of the writer. Tindale gives us in Mt 22³² 'I am Abrahams God, and Ysaacks God, and the God of Jacob.'

In AV 1611 *his* was used for the poss. case in 1 K 15¹⁴ 'Asa his heart was perfect with the LORD all his dayes,' and in Est 3⁴ 'to see whether Mordecai his matters would stand.' In 1762 these were changed into the usual form with '*s*. But in the heading of Dt 10 'Moses his suit' remains, and even 'Sarai her name' in Gn 17 ʰᵉᵃᵈⁱⁿᵍ, and the foll. examples of *his* are still found in the Apocr., 1 Es 1 ʰᵉᵃᵈⁱⁿᵍ 2³⁰ ³⁷· ⁸, To 1 ʰᵉᵃᵈⁱⁿᵍ, Jth 12¹⁶ 13⁹ 15¹¹. Three ʰᵉᵃᵈⁱⁿᵍ 2 Mac 1³³ᵐ 4³⁸ 12²²; and in the Translators' Preface we find, 'Doth not their Paris edition differ from the Lovaine, and Hortensius his from them both,' and 'We might be taxed peradventure with S. James his words.'

For his=its, see ITS.   J. HASTINGS.

HITHERTO was formerly an adv. of space as well as of time, as in Shaks. *I Henry IV.* III. i. 74—

'England, from Trent and Severn hitherto, By south and east, is to my part assigned.'

So in AV, Job 38¹¹ 'Hitherto shalt thou come, but no further' (עַד־פֹּה); 2 S 7¹⁸=1 Ch 17¹⁶ 'Who am I, O LORD God, and what is my house, that thou hast brought me hitherto?' (עַד־הֲלֹם, RV 'thus far'). Even when the ref. is to time, 'hitherto' was used in a sense that is now unfamiliar, expressing not only what has been up till now, but what is still going on. In Jn 16²⁴ 'Hitherto have ye asked nothing in my name,' the meaning is that that which is true up till now is no longer to be so. But in Jn 5¹⁷ 'My Father worketh hitherto, and I work,' though the Gr. (ἕως ἄρτι) is the same, the meaning is that the work still goes on (RV 'even until now'). Cf. Hamilton's *Catechism*, fol. 14ᵇ 'Quhat is the trew sence of the same bukis is ye consent and authorite of our mother the haly kirk, fra the Apostils tyme hitherto'; and Udal, *Erasmus Paraphrase*, ii. fol. 279ᵃ 'He is as yet hitherto alyve, that the hater wisheth evill unto, and yet he him selfe is al ready dead. That mans life is safe: and this hath lost everlasting lyfe, being his owne murtherour.'   J. HASTINGS.

HITTITES (חִתִּי *Ḥitti*, pl. *Ḥittim*,† Χετταῖοι).— In Jos 1⁴ the country between the Lebanon and the Euphrates is described as 'the land of the

* Cf. Lk 4³⁸ 'Simon's wife's mother.'
† The proper name חֵת Ḥeth (Gn 10¹⁵ 23³) may be an assimilation to the Bab. name Khatti which we find in contract-tablets of the age of Abraham.

Hittites,' which is more closely defined in Jg 1²⁶ as to the north of Palestine. In 2 S 24⁶ the unintelligible and corrupt 'Tahtim-hodshi' must be corrected into 'the Hittites of Kadesh,' according to a corrected reading of the LXX (Luc. εἰς γῆν Χεττιεὶμ Καδής), so that the power of David extended northward as far as Kadesh on the Orontes close to the lake of Homs. Solomon imported horses from 'the kings of the Hittites,' as well as from the kings of Aram, from Egypt, or perhaps a northern Miẓir, and (according to a suggestion of Fr. Lenormant) from Ḳue on the Gulf of Antioch, the price of a horse being 150 shekels of silver (about £25, 1 K 10²⁸·²⁹). These northern 'kings of the Hittites' were supposed by the Syrians of Damascus, when they were besieging Samaria at a later date, to have been 'hired' against them by the king of Israel (2 K 7⁶).

Besides the northern Hittites, other Hittites, or 'sons of Heth,' are mentioned in the OT as inhabiting the south of Palestine. Abraham found them at Hebron (Gn 23³ 25¹⁰); in Nu 13²⁹ the Hittites are named along with the Jebusites and Amorites as dwelling in the mountains of Canaan; and Ezk (16³) declares that the father of Jerus. was an Amorite, and its mother a Hittite. These southern Hittites are probably alone meant in Gn 10¹⁵, though, as the Hamathites are also included among the children of Canaan, it is possible that the northern Hittites may be referred to as well. 'Uriah the Hittite' (2 S 12) may have belonged to the Hittites of the south, like the two Hittite wives of Esau (Gn 26³⁴ 36²; cf. 27⁴⁶).

On the Egyp. monuments the Khata or Hittites are first mentioned in the Annals of Thothmes III. of the 18th dynasty (B.C. 1503–1449). In B.C. 1470 the Pharaoh marched to the banks of the Euphrates and received the tribute of the land of the Hittites, 'the Greater,' consisting of 8 rings of silver 400 lb. in weight, and 'a great piece of crystal.' In B.C. 1463 tribute was again sent from 'the king of the Greater Hittite land.' Thothmes IV., the grandson of Thothmes III., repulsed an attack made by the Hittites upon Tunip (now *Tennib*) in N. Syria, and his two successors, Amenôphis (Amen-hotep) III. and IV., as we learn from the Tel el-Amarna tablets, were constantly called on to oppose the Hittite 'king,' who led his forces through the passes of the Taurus into the Egyp. province of N. Syria, or intrigued with disaffected Canaanites in Palestine. We hear, finally, of Eta-gama, the native governor of Kadesh on the Orontes, joining with the king of the Hittites and the king of Mitanni or Aram-naharaim against the Egyptians.

The decay of the Egyp. power in Syria enabled the Hittites to establish themselves, not only at Carchemish on the Euphrates, but also in the Amorite city of Kadesh on the Orontes, near the lake of Homs. Seti I., the second king of the 19th dynasty, claims to have overthrown them. They were ruled at the time by Mutal, the son of Mul-sar, who had been murdered, and who was the son of Saplil. Ramses II., the successor of Seti, continued the war. In the 5th year of the Pharaoh's reign (B.C. 1343), Ramses, while besieging Kadesh, saved himself from a Hittite ambuscade only by performing prodigies of valour, which formed the subject of a sort of epic on the part of the court-poet Pentaür. In the 21st year of Ramses (B.C. 1327) a treaty, offensive and defensive, was made between him and 'the great king of the Hittites,' Khata-sar, who had succeeded his brother Mutal, which put an end to the war. Among other stipulations it was agreed that all political refugees on either side should be pardoned. The observance of the treaty was placed under the protection of the Hittite and Egyptian deities, and the Hittite text of it was engraved on a silver plate, on which

was an image of the god Sutekh embracing the Hittite king. The plate was brought to Egypt by the Hittite ambassador Tar-Tiseb. The treaty was faithfully kept, being cemented by the marriage of the daughter of the Hittite king to Ramses, and Kadesh continued to mark the southern limit of Hittite rule.

In the Aramæan districts south of the Taurus the Hittites do not seem to have been more than a conquering caste, and their power was broken by the invasion of the hordes from the islands and coasts of the Greek seas, who poured through Syria and the land of the Amorites into Egypt in the reign of Ramses III. of the 20th dynasty. When the Assyr. monuments, in the time of Tiglath-pileser I. (B.C. 1100), first begin to refer to the Khattâ (also written Khatê), in place of a single Hittite king who is able to summon allies from the distant regions of Asia Minor, we find a number of separate Hittite states. Of these Carchemish seems to have been the wealthiest and most important. The Assyrians penetrated into Kummukh (Commagênê), and compelled Sadi-Tesub (or Sadi-Anteru), son of Khattu-sar, the Hittite king, to become tributary. The name of Khattu-sar is plainly the same as that of the opponent of Ramses II.

In B.C. 880 Assur-naẓir-pal, the Assyr. king, received tribute from Sangara of Carchemish, and forced his way over the fords of the Euphrates to the west. His successor, Shalmaneser II. (B.C. 854), defeated a league of Hittites and Aramæans from Kummukh and the adjoining countries, of which Sangara was the head. The Assyrians had already extended the name of 'Hittite' from the Hittites proper to all the inhabitants of Syria and Palestine, and we find Shalmaneser II. including even the kings of Israel, of Ammon, and of the Arabs, among the 'Hittite' princes. Just as the Babylonians had given the name of 'Amorites' to all the inhabitants of Syria and Palestine, the 'Amorites' having been the dominant people of the west when the Babylonians first became acquainted with it, so the fact that the Hittites were the first and most powerful of the antagonists whom the Assyrians encountered in their Syrian campaigns, caused the name of 'Hittite' in the Assyr. period to be applied to all the nations west of the Euphrates. The capture of Carchemish by Sargon in B.C. 717, and the death of its last king, Pisiris, broke up the Hittite power in northern Syria, and threw the trade of W. Asia into Assyr. hands.

The Hittites under the name of Khatê are mentioned in the cuneiform inscriptions of Armenia or Ararat. In the 9th cent. B.C. Menuas, king of Biainas or Van, defeated the Hittite king Sada-halis, and sacked the towns of Surisilis and Tarkhi-gamas. His son and successor, Argistis I., continued the war and conquered the Hittite city of Milid (the modern Malatiyeh). The 'land of the Hittites' of the Vannic inscriptions extended along the banks of the Euphrates from Palu in the east to Malatiyeh in the west.

A study of the Hittite proper names preserved in the Egyp. and cuneiform texts goes to show that they all belonged to the same family of speech, and that they can be traced far to the westward in Asia Minor. Thus the names of the Hittite princes, Saplil, Mutal, and Khata-sar, mentioned by the Egyptians, reappear in those of Sapalulvi, Mutallu, and Khattu-sar, who, according to the Assyr. monuments, were kings of Gurgum (in the neighbourhood of Zinjerli, N. of the Gulf of Antioch) and of Kummukh or Commagênê, while Mutallu is the Motalos of certain Gr. inscriptions of Asia Minor. It is further clear from the Tel el-Amarna tablets that the Hittites were of Cappadocian origin, that they had poured down from the fastnesses of the Taurus and had occupied the Aramæan cities and fertile fields of northern Syria. We may further gather from the Egyp. records that in the 14th and 13th cent. B.C. they had not only established themselves so far to the south as Kadesh on the Orontes, but had founded a military empire, which enabled the king of Kadesh to summon allies and vassals from Asia Minor.

The Hittites, as represented on the Egyp. monuments, were an ugly race, with yellow skins, black hair and eyes, receding foreheads, and protrusive upper jaws. The type is still preserved among some of the Cappadocian peasantry, especially S.W. of Nigdeh in the neighbourhood of the ancient Tyana. They wore boots with upturned ends, originally intended for use among the snows of the Taurus mountains; but they became so characteristic a national dress that at the Ramesseum in Thebes even the Hittites of Kadesh, on the warm plains of Syria, are depicted as wearing them. Over a tunic they also wore a long robe, which was allowed to fall open on one side in walking, and they seem to have gathered the hair at the back of the head into a sort of pigtail.

A curious class of monuments has been discovered of late years in Asia Minor and northern Syria, on which all these characteristics are reproduced. The monuments consist of bas-reliefs in a peculiar style of art, and of inscriptions in an equally peculiar hieroglyphic system of writing. Both the sculptures and the inscriptions exhibit heads and figures with exactly the same features, the same pigtails, costume, and snow-shoes as those which the Egyp. artists assigned to the Hittites. As we learn from the Egyp. records that the Hittites had a script of their own, as, moreover, the monuments referred to are found in the region over which the Hittite power extended according to the Egyp. and Assyr. texts, while there is no other known power to which they can be ascribed, the conclusion is obvious that they must be the monuments of the people called Hittites by the Hebrews, Egyptians, Assyrians, and Armenians. A reminiscence of their empire is probably preserved in a passage of Solinus (ch. xli. p. 195, ed. Mommsen).

Hittite art was based on that of early Babylonia, though some of the later monuments of it are modelled on the Assyr. art of the 9th and 8th cent. B.C. But, though based on Babylonian art, the elements which had been borrowed were profoundly modified, and a new and remarkable style of art was thus developed. The Hittites seem to have had a special fancy for combining parts of different animals into strangely composite and sometimes grotesque forms. It was through the Hittites that the winged horse made its way into Europe, like the two-headed eagle, originally derived, it would seem, from the heraldic symbol of the ancient Bab. city of Lagas (Telloh), but in later days adopted by the Seljukian sultans, and borrowed from them by the Crusaders.

Hittite sculptures and inscriptions can be traced as far south in Syria as Hamah (Hamath), and as far westward in Asia Minor as Lydia. In the pass of Kara-bel, near the site of Sardis, are the figures of two Hittite warriors, one of them accompanied by Hittite hieroglyphs, and supposed by Herodotus (II. 106) to be memorials of Egyp. conquest, while other Hittite hieroglyphs have been found at the side of the so-called 'Weeping Niobê' on Mount Sipylus. From the fact that the figures in the pass are those of warriors, and that in such of the inscriptions as are legible, including one discovered by Ramsay in Phrygia, the characters which denote the grammatical affixes are always the same, we may infer that the Hittite monuments, both of Syria and of Asia

Minor, all belong to one people, and that the more distant of them imply conquest on the part of a great military power rather than artistic influence. The influence of Hittite art, which can be traced into prehistoric Greece, is of a different character.

There is a bilingual inscription, in cuneiform and Hittite characters, on the silver 'boss' of Tarkondêmos, but it has proved insufficient to furnish a key to the interpretation of the inscriptions. A brilliant attempt has been made, indeed, by Jensen (*ZDMG*, 1894, pp. 235 ff., 429 ff.), of which Hilprecht speaks very highly (*Rec. Res. in Bible Lands*, p. 178, 'correct in its principal results'; cf. *Bab. Exped. of Pennsyl.* i. 13, 'Jensen has forced the Hittite sphinx to surrender her long guarded secret'). The present writer cannot assent to Hilprecht's verdict. All we can gather with certainty is that the hieroglyphs are partly ideographic, partly phonetic; that some of them are determinatives; that the lines read alternately from right to left, and from left to right; and that the grammatical relations are marked by affixes. Most of the inscriptions are in relief. The proper names of genuine Hittite origin found in the Egyp. and Assyr. texts are non-Semitic, and a comparison of them goes to show that the nom. sing. of the noun was characterized by the suffix -s. As the Hittites ruled over an Aramaic population in N. Syria, we naturally find Aramæan by the side of Hittite names. The Hittite hieroglyphs were of native origin, and may have been selected from an older pictorial system of writing, once used in Asia Minor, of which certain characters on two seals discovered at Yuzghât, on the one side, and the Cretan pictographs recently brought to light by Evans, on the other side, may be further relics.

The primitive home of the Hittite race was probably Cappadocia. Here, at any rate, in the ruins of Boghaz Keui and Eyuk, to the east of the Halys, are the remains of two of their most important cities. Boghaz Keui seems to have been a centre of religious worship, and the figures of numerous deities are carved in relief upon its rocks. The mural crown worn by some of the goddesses passed westward into Greek art. Ramsay (*Cities and Bishoprics of Phrygia*, I. pp. xiii–xv, 1895) has pointed out that the ancient high-roads which intersected Asia Minor and led to northern Syria met at Boghaz Keui, indicating that here was the centre of an empire which once extended from Kadesh on the Orontes to the shores of the Ægean.

The relation between the Hittites of N. Syria and the Hittites of Genesis and Ezekiel who lived in S. Palestine is uncertain. We may infer, however, from the identity of name, that in the view of the biblical writers the two populations were connected in race. This is supported by the fact that, according to the Egyp. monuments, the Hittites and Amorites were interlocked in the north, just as they were, according to the OT, in the south. It is further verified by the expression, 'the land of the Hittites, the Greater,' used by Thothmes III., which implies that there was another lesser Hittite-land, as well as by a bas-relief at Karnak in which the people of Ashkelon are represented with characteristically Hittite features. This shows that a fragment of the Hittite race must have been settled in the south of Palestine (but see Gray, *Expos.* May, 1898, p. 340 f.).

LITERATURE.—Sayce, *The Monuments of the Hittites* in *TSBA*, 1881, *The Hittites*, 1888, *The Races of the OT*, 1891; W. Wright, *The Empire of the Hittites*, 1884; Perrot and Chipiez, *Histoire de l'Art dans l'Antiquité*, vol. iv. (1887); L. de Lantsheere, *De la Race et de la Langue des Hittites*, 1892; Del., *Paradies*, 269 ff.; Schrader, *KAT²* 107 ff.; Meyer, *Gesch.* i. 213 f., *ZAWT* i. 125 ff.; Stade, *Gesch.* i. 143; Budde, *Urgesch.* 346 ff.; Jensen, *Hittit. u. Armen.*, 1898; Conder, *Hittites*, 1898.

A. H. SAYCE.

HIVITES (חִוִּי, always with the art. collectively,

חִוִּי ; Εὑαῖοι).—The name of one of the petty tribes inhabiting Canaan, who were dispossessed by the Israelites. To judge from the passages which localize them most definitely, their home was in Central Palestine ; in Jos 9[7] (JE) and 11[19] (D[2]) the inhabitants of Gibeon, about 6 miles N.N.W. of Jerusalem, and (it seems to be implied in 9[17]) of certain neighbouring cities, are called Hivites ; in Gn 34[2] (P ; or [Corn.] E) the term is applied to Hamor, father of Shechem (who is here represented as an individual),* likewise a city in Central Palestine (Gn 33[18], Jg 9 etc.), 30 miles N. of Jerusalem ; 2 S 24[7] is ambiguous ; but the statement that Joab passed from Zidon, through 'all the cities of the Hivites' to Beersheba, in the S. of Judah, is evidently quite consistent with the same locality. The expression, 'all the cities of the Hivites,' in this passage is, however, peculiar, and would seem to point to a somewhat considerable group of cities, still inhabited by Hivites, and *possibly* even further to the N. than Shechem. But if such existed, we do not know more about them ; and it is remarkable that in the accounts in Jos 16[10] 17[12-13. 14-18], Jg 1 of the districts which the Israelites failed to conquer, there is no mention of Hivites. The other notices of the Hivites are (1) in the rhetorical lists of nations expelled by the Israelites (JE, D, D[2]), Ex 3[8. 17] 13[5] 23[23. 28] 33[2] 34[11], Dt 7[1] 20[17], Jos 3[10] 9[1] 11[3] 12[8] 24[11], Jg 3[5], 1 K 9[20] (=2 Ch 8[7]), from which nothing definite can be inferred respecting the place of their abode (unless their being mentioned usually before the Jebusites [of Jerusalem] may be taken as an indication that they were pictured as having lived near them) ; and (2) in Gn 10[17] (=1 Ch 1[15]), where, in accordance with the custom of Hebrew genealogists of representing the peoples inhabiting a country as the 'sons' of its eponymous ancestor, they are included among other tribes 'begotten' by Canaan.†

We do not possess the necessary data for determining with any confidence the character or racial affinities of the Hivites (see speculations in Ewald, *Hist.* i. 237 ; Sayce, *Races of the OT*, 119 f.). They were the actors in the ruse by which the Gibeonites secured themselves against the Israelite invaders ; and if the isolated notice in Gn 34[2] is to be depended upon, the people of Shechem, who take part against the Israelites in the graphic narrative of Jg 9, may have been Hivite (though they are not so termed in the narrative itself). Shechem and Gibeon are elsewhere (Gn 48[22] E ; 2 S 21[2]) spoken of as 'Amorite' ; but, in view of the manner in which the term 'Amorite' is employed (above, vol. i. p. 84 ; Driver, *Deut.* pp. 10–12), it is doubtful whether this fact authorizes the definite conclusion that the Hivites were racially 'Amorite.' In Gn 36[2] 'Zibeon the *Hivite*' is almost certainly an error for 'Zibeon the *Horite*' (see vv.[20. 24]) : in Jos 11[3] read with LXX, and in agreement with the known home of the Hittites in the N., 'the *Hittite* under Hermon' in v.[b], with 'the *Hivite*' for 'the *Hittite*' in v.[a] ; and similarly in Jg 3[3] 'the *Hittites* (for 'the *Hivites*') that dwelt in Mount Lebanon.' It has been conjectured that חִוִּי is connected with Arab. *ḥiwā'*, 'a circle of tents' (cf. HAVVOTH-JAIR), and means properly 'tent-dweller,' 'villager' (Ges. 'paganus') ; but it is extremely uncertain if this is really the case (cf. Moore on Jg 3[5]).

S. R. DRIVER.

HIZKI (חִזְקִי, possibly shortened from חִזְקִיָּהוּ, 'J" strengthened').—A Benjamite, 1 Ch 8[17], AV Hezeki. See GENEALOGY.

---

* In 33[19] 'the children of Hamor, the father of Shechem,' Shechem is clearly the place (father=founder, as 1 Ch 2[50. 51] etc.); cf. Jg 9[28] 'the men of Hamor, the father of Shechem.'
† 'Hivite' is read also by LXX, followed by Lagarde, Cheyne, Orelli, Duhm, and others, in Is 17[9] ('like the deserted places of the *Hivites* and the Amorites, which they deserted before the children of Israel').

HIZKIAH (AV Hezekiah).—A son of Neariah, a descendant of David, 1 Ch 3[23].

HO.—The oft-occurring interjection הוֹ, which is more sympathetic—has more of *grace* in it—than הוֹי Woe !, is tr[d] 'Ho !' in Is 55[1] and Zec 2[6 bis] ; to which RV adds Is 29[1]. Ho ! does little more than arrest attention, unless its occurrence in Is 55[1] has given it something of an evangelical tone. Shaks. uses it very often, expressing by its means (1) mockery or rebuke, (2) exultation, (3) pain, and (4) simply calling attention. See AH, HA.

HOBAB (חֹבָב 'beloved,' Ges. ; 'serpent,' Wellh.). —The name occurs twice (Nu 10[29], Jg 4[11]. In Jg 1[16] B inserts Ἰοβόρ [so Jos. *Ant.* v. ii. 3] ; A, Ἰωάβ). It is uncertain whether he was (1) the father-in-law (AV, RVm) or (2) brother-in-law (RV) of Moses.

The conflicting views may be tabulated thus—

(1) Reuel		(2) Reuel (Jethro)
Hobab (Jethro)		
Zipporah = Moses.		Hobab　　Zipporah = Moses.

Nu 10[29] is ambiguous, as חֹתֵן 'father-in-law' may refer either to Hobab or Reuel. In support of (1) it may be stated that (*a*) חֹתֵן is always rendered father-in-law except in RV text of Jg 1[16] 4[11]. (*b*) Mohammedan tradition, almost without exception (Lane's *Kuran*, p. 47 n.), identifies Shoaib or Sho'eib [a corruption (?) of Hobab], a prophet sent to the Midianites (*Koran*, Sur. 7. 11. 26. 29) with Moses' father-in-law Jethro. (*c*) The narrative in Ex 2 seems to preclude the idea that the priest of Midian had sons. On the other hand, (*a*) חֹתֵן possibly means any relation on the wife's side, and (*b*) Reuel (Hobab's father) and Jethro seem to be identified (Ex 2[18] 3[1], so Jos. *Ant.* v. ii. 3). However, Ewald (*HI* ii. p. 25 n.[7]) conjectures that in Ex 2[18] we should read 'Jethro the son of Reuel' (LXX ins. Ἰοθόρ in v.[16 bis], and A substitutes Ἰοθόρ for Reuel in v.[18]). 'Hobab was the man's real personal name, and Jethro, which signifies *prefect*, his title.' (*c*) In Ex 18[27] (E) Jethro, unopposed by Moses, 'went his way into his own land' ; whereas in Nu 10[29 ff.] (JE) it is implied that Hobab yielded to Moses' importunity, and remained with Israel. A parallel difficulty occurs in Nu 24[25] (JE) compared with Nu 31[8] (P). In each case we must remember that we have not all the facts before us : we are dealing, not with one consecutive narrative, but with a compilation of fragments. A difficulty, which equally affects both views, is the fact that Hobab is called a Kenite (Jg 1[16] 4[11]), whereas Exodus speaks of Moses' father-in-law as a Midianite. See, further, Dillm.-Ryssel, *Ex-Lv*, 1897, 25 ff. Whoever Hobab was, he was the human agent by whom God led His people through the wilderness. This service to Israel was long kept in grateful remembrance (1 S 15[6]).

N. J. D. WHITE.

HOBAH (חוֹבָה).—The place to which, acc. to Gn 14[15], Abraham pursued the defeated army of Chedorlaomer. It is described as 'on the left hand' (מִשְּׂמֹאל, *i.e.* 'to the north') of Damascus.' It is identified by Wetzstein (see Del. *Genesis*,[4] p. 561 ff.) with the modern *Ḥoba*, 20 hours N. of Damascus. This certainly appears to be 'etwas weit,' as Siegfried-Stade remark ; but the identification is accepted by Dillmann as more probable than one with a *Ḥoba* mentioned by von Troilo about a mile N. of Damascus.

J. A. SELBIE.

HOBAIAH.—See HABAIAH.

HOD (הוֹד 'majesty').—An Asherite, 1 Ch 7[37]. See GENEALOGY.

HODAVIAH (הוֹדַוְיָהוּ or הוֹדַוְיָהוּ; Kittel prefers to vocalize הוֹדְוָיָה, cf. LXX A Ὠδουία).—**1.** A Manassite clan, 1 Ch 5²⁴. **2.** The name of a Benjamite family, 1 Ch 9⁷. **3.** A Levitical family name, Ezr 2⁴⁰, called in Neh 7⁴³ **Hodevah** (which see). **4.** A descendant of David, 1 Ch 3²⁴ (הוֹדַוְיָהוּ; AV, following *Kethibh* הוֹדְיָיְהוּ, Hodaiah).

HODESH (חֹדֶשׁ 'new moon').—One of the wives of Shaharaim, a Benjamite, 1 Ch 8⁹. See GENEALOGY.

HODEVAH (*Kethibh* הוֹדְוָה, *Ḳerê*, followed by RVm, הוֹדְיָה Hodeiah).—A Levitical family name, Neh 7⁴³, called in Ezr 2⁴⁰ **Hodaviah** (which see).

HODIAH (הוֹדִיָּה 'my "majesty" is J"').—**1.** A man of Judah, 1 Ch 4¹⁹. AV wrongly takes it as a woman's name (see GENEALOGY, IV. 55). **2.** A Levite, Neh 8⁷ 9⁵ 10¹⁰. **3.** Another Levite, Neh 10¹³. **4.** One of those who sealed the covenant, Neh 10¹⁸.

HOGLAH (חָגְלָה 'partridge'). — Daughter of Zelophehad, Nu 26³³ 27¹ 36¹¹, Jos 17³ P.

HOHAM (הוֹהָם), king of Hebron, formed an alliance with other four kings against Gibeon, but was defeated by Joshua at Beth-horon, and put to death along with his allies at Makkedah (Jos 10³ᶠᶠ·). According to Hommel (*AHT* 223 n.), Hoham is identical with the Minæan name *Ḥauhum* (beginning with the guttural aspirate); but this combination is extremely precarious.

HOISE.—This is the older and more correct form of *hoist*, to which the *t* has probably been added from its presence in the past ptcp. It occurs Ac 27⁴⁰ 'they . . . hoised up the mainsail to the wind.' Cf. Hall, *Works*, ii. 37, 'Who can pitty the shipwracke of those marriners, which will needes put forth, and hoise sailes in a tempest?' RV gives 'hoisting up the foresail,' and introduces 'hoist' also in 27¹⁷ for the simple vb. (αἴρω) of which the compound (ἐπαίρω) is here used. Both 'hoist' and 'hoised' are found as participles. Thus Hall, *Works*, ii. 40, 'Mee thinkes, I see Christ hoysed upon the highest battlements of the Temple'; and Shaks. *Hamlet*, III. iv. 27— 'Hoist with his own petard.'   J. HASTINGS.

HOLD.—As a subst. 'hold' occurs frequently in AV for a protected place, mod. 'stronghold,' for which the Heb. is generally מְצוּדָה or מְצָד. In Jg 9⁴⁶· ⁴⁹ the word so trᵈ is צְרִיחַ, which occurs elsewhere only in 1 S 13⁶, and of which the meaning is so doubtful that Moore declines to give it any rendering. Some commentators reckon it a secret chamber. RV retains 'holds' in Jg and gives that trⁿ in 1 S, with 'holes' in marg. See Moore on Jg 9⁴⁶. The 'hold' of Ac 4³ is a general word, lit. 'keeping' (τήρησις). The same word with the adj. δημόσιος is trᵈ in 5¹⁸ 'public prison.' RV gives 'ward' and 'public ward.' In Rev 18² is found another general word (φυλακή), also originally an abstract term, 'guarding,' then a 'guard-room.' It occurs twice in this verse, being rendered in AV first 'hold' and then 'cage' (RV 'hold'). Perhaps 'dungeon' would be the best word here. For the Eng. word it will be enough to quote Bunyan, *Holy War*, p. 18, 'Wherefore into the castle he goes: it was that which Shaddai built in Mansoul for his own delight and pleasure; this now is become a Den and Hold for the Giant Diabolus.'

The verb 'to hold' is used in some obsolete or archaic senses: **1.** To *reckon*, *account*, in 'hold guiltless' Ex 20⁷, Dt 5¹¹, 1 K 2⁹, or 'not guilty' Zec 11⁵: 'hold innocent' Job 9²⁸; and 'hold con-

tented' Sir 29³. **2.** To *grip*, Job 41²⁶ 'The sword of him that layeth at him [leviathan] cannot hold' (RV 'avail'; Davidson, 'The sword does not hold or bite, but glances off his adamantine armour'); or *restrain*, *keep under restraint*, Lk 24¹⁶ 'But their eyes were holden that they should not know him' (ἐκρατοῦντο); Ro 7⁶ 'But now we are delivered from the law, that being dead wherein we were held' * (κατειχόμεθα, RV 'we were holden'); or *retain*, *keep hold of*, Job 23¹¹ 'My foot hath held his steps' (RV 'held fast to his steps'); Col 2¹⁹ 'And not holding the Head' (κρατῶν, RV 'holding fast'); or *arrest* (fig.) Ca 7⁵ 'The king is held in the galleries' (RV 'held captive'). Cf. Mk 3²¹ Tind. 'They went out to holde him. For they thought he had bene beside himselfe' (κρατῆσαι, Cran. 'to laye handes upon him,' AV 'to lay hold on him'). **3.** To *support*, *maintain*, Ps 139¹⁰ 'thy right hand shall hold me'; 1 Mac 6⁵² 'Whereupon they also made engines against their engines, and held them battle a long season' (ἐπολέμησαν ἡμέρας πολλάς, RV 'fought for many days'). Cf. Defoe, *Crusoe*, p. 366, 'The battle, they said, held two Hours, before they could guess which Party would be beaten.' **4.** Some phrases deserve attention: (1) *Hold forth*, Ph 2¹⁶ 'Holding forth the word of life' (ἐπέχοντες, Tind. 'holdinge fast,' Gen. [1557] 'putting forth,' Lightfoot 'holding out'). (2) *Hold in*, Jer 6¹¹ 'I am weary with holding in.' (3) *Hold of*, Wis 2²⁴ 'Nevertheless through envy of the devil came death into the world: and they that do hold of his side do find it' (οἱ τῆς ἐκείνου μερίδος ὄντες, RV 'they that are of his portion'). Cf. Tindale, *Pent.*, Prologue to Numbers, 'He will hold of them and be sworne unto them to be their servaunte.' (4) *Hold to*, Sir 30¹³ 'Chastise thy son and hold him to labour' (ἔργασαι ἐν αὐτῷ, RV 'take pains with him'); Mt 6²⁴ (= Lk 16¹³) 'either he will hate the one, and love the other; or else he will hold to the one, and despise the other' (ἀνθέξεται). Cf. Dt 17¹⁶ Tind. 'But in ani wyse let him not holde to many horsses, that he bringe not the people agayne to Egipte thorow the multitude of horsses' (quoted also by Latimer, *Sermons*, Arber's ed. p. 25). (5) *Hold up* = support, Ps 119¹¹⁷ 'Hold thou me up, and I shall be safe'; 17⁵ 'Hold up my goings in thy paths, that my footsteps slip not' (תָּמֹךְ אֲשֻׁרַי בְּמַעְגְּלוֹתֶיךָ, RV 'My steps have held fast to thy paths'; Wellhausen - Furness, 'My steps — they have followed close in thy footprints'); and the phrase 'hold up my face to,' 2 S 2²² 'Wherefore should I smite thee to the ground? how then should I hold up my face to Joab thy brother?' (6) *Hold with*, Dn 10²¹ 'And there is none that holdeth with me in these things but Michael your prince'; 1 Mac 3² 'And all his brethren helped him, and so did all they that held with his father' (RV 'that clave unto'); Ac 14⁴ 'But the multitude of the city was divided: and part held with the Jews, and part with the apostles.' So Hos 11¹² Cov. 'But Ephraim goeth aboute me with lies, and the house of Israel dyssembleth. Only Juda holdeth him with God, and with the true holy thinges.'   J. HASTINGS.

HOLINESS.—IN THE OLD TESTAMENT.—The notion of holiness is expressed in Heb., as in the Semitic languages generally, by the two roots קדשׁ and חרם. Of these the latter was most widely diffused amongst the Semitic peoples, but in Heb. usage it was restricted to certain extreme kinds of consecration, usually involving the total destruction of the devoted thing (see CURSE). The distinctively OT developments of the idea are connected with קֶדֶשׁ, which is the root commonly employed by the Northern Semites; and in this

---

* Cf. Lk 4³⁸ Rhem. 'And Simons wives mother was holden with a great fever.'

article the various applications of this root will alone be considered.*

The original idea conveyed by the words is altogether uncertain, neither etymology nor the analogy of the cognate dialects having as yet thrown much light on the subject.† The truth is, that the words are nowhere found save in a religious sense, and the attempt to ascertain the physical conception on which this use is based is generally abandoned by modern scholars as hopeless. There is, however, a certain probability that the primary idea is that of 'separation' or 'cutting off.'‡ Although this view is not capable of demonstration, it may be adopted provisionally as one that fits in remarkably well with OT usage. Thus the technical antithesis to שָׁדֵק is לֹח, a word which means simply 'open to common use,' 'profane' (see 1 S 21⁵, Ezk 22²⁶ etc.). At all events, it is correct to say that a holy object is one 'separated' from common use and contact by supernatural sanctions; and if we start from this negative definition of what the OT means by holiness, we shall probably not be far from the fundamental meaning of the root. It only needs to be remarked that in hardly any case does the 'separation' denoted by קרש amount to absolute removal from human use or contact (as is the case with חרם). All that is usually involved is that the use of the 'holy' is *restricted* by ceremonial rules, or confined to privileged persons or to particular times—a principle of which abundant illustration will be found in what follows. The holiness of places, things, seasons, even of persons, is thus safeguarded by a set of recognized religious usages, which sometimes, as in the Levitical ritual of OT, attain a high degree of complexity.

It is obvious from what has been said, that holiness, as a religious term, did not originate within the sphere of the revealed religion of Israel. It is one of those primitive concepts which have been taken up and purified by revelation, but which may retain some traces of their origin in a lower stage of belief. It is not surprising, therefore, if some survivals of ancient Semitic heathenism should appear amongst OT applications of the idea of holiness. One such survival is probably to be found in the conception of holiness as a quality transmissible by contact, and constituting in certain circumstances a danger to be scrupulously avoided (see Ezk 44¹⁹ 46²⁰, Ex 29³⁷ 30²⁹, Lv 6²⁷ etc.; cf. Hag 2¹²ᶠ.).§ Another peculiar case is that of the vineyard (or field) sown with different kinds of seed, which is said thereby to 'become holy'

* The two primary words in which the root appears are the abstract noun שָׁדֵק (holiness) and the adj. קָרוֹשׁ (holy); the verbal forms in use appear to be all denominatives derived from these. The simple form of the verb (קָדֵשׁ) occurs only 10 times, always with the sense of 'become holy,' or 'contract holiness'; Ex 29²¹·³⁷ 30²⁹, Lv 6¹¹·²⁰, Nu 17²·³, Dt 22⁹, 1 S 21⁶, Hag 21² (in Is 65⁵, and possibly 1 S 21⁶, the text is wrongly pointed). The secondary sense is, of course, still more obvious in the two causatives (שָׁדֵק and קִדֵּשׁ) and the two reflexives (נָקְדֵשׁ and הִתְקַדֵּשׁ). The other derivatives are מִקְדָּשׁ (sanctuary), קְרֵשׁ [f. (קְרֵשָׁה) (ἱερόδουλος), and the proper names קָדֵשׁ and קֶרֶשׁ.

† Dillmann (AT Theol. p. 254) refers to the Assyr. kuddušu (said to be a synonym for ' bright'), and is disposed to connect the root, as others have done before him, with חרש (new). Delitzsch, on the other hand (PRE², art. 'Heiligkeit Gottes'), reasoning from the Sumerian equivalent of kadištu (sacred prostitute), found a confirmation of the old theological definition of holiness as freedom from defect (omnis labis expers). But these are highly speculative constructions, which command no confidence, and, moreover, give no assurance that they reach the original sense of the word.

‡ See Baudissin, pp. 19–40; Nöldeke, LCBl, 1879, col. 361 f.

§ An Arabian parallel to the communication of holiness by clothing is given by W. R. Smith in Rel. Sem.² p. 451. 'At Mecca, in the times of heathenism, the sacred circuit of the Caaba was made by the Bedouins, either naked, or in clothes borrowed from one of the Ḥoms, or religious community of the sacred city. . . . It appears that sometimes a man did make the circuit in his own clothes, but in that case he could neither wear them again nor sell them, but had to leave them at the gate of the sanctuary.'

(Dt 22⁹; cf. Lv 19¹⁹). Again, in the pagan rites described in Is 65⁵, the bystanders are warned not to come near lest they should be 'sanctified' (the verb to be pointed as *Piel*). These phenomena, which appear to our minds to introduce an irrational element into the idea of holiness, irresistibly suggest an affinity with a custom universal amongst primitive peoples, according to which man's free use of natural objects, etc., was restrained by fear of supernatural penalties. This institution has come to be denoted by the name *taboo*, and the instances just cited seem to indicate a close analogy between taboo and the primitive associations of the word 'holiness' in Semitic religion. This would account for the remarkable points of contact between the laws of holiness and those of uncleanness; the two notions being in their origin practically identical. The first great step towards the spiritualizing of the idea of holiness was taken by OT religion when it established a distinction between things whose use is prohibited because they are appropriated to J″, and things that may not be touched because they are hateful to Him. The latter belong to the category of the UNCLEAN (see the art.), while the term 'holy' is, as a rule, reserved for the former.*

In considering OT uses of the terms for holiness, it will be convenient to arrange them in the following order: I. Holiness of places, things, and seasons; II. Holiness of God and angels; III. Holiness of man.

I. HOLINESS OF PLACES, THINGS, AND SEASONS. —The material objects classed as holy are far too numerous to be separately mentioned here. The general principle of OT religion undoubtedly is that things are holy in virtue of their connexion with the worship of J″. The sanctuary itself in all its parts, the utensils employed in the ritual, the clothing of the attendants, the sacrifices and everything dedicated to J″, are sacred in various degrees through having been brought within the sphere of J‴s worship, and so 'separated' from their natural and common relations. It is true that the cases mentioned above (Dt 22⁹, Ex 29³⁷, Lv 6²⁷ etc.) can only with some difficulty be brought completely under this principle. An attempt is made to sustain the rule by the theory that such things or persons were forfeited for the use of the priests or the service of the sanctuary, as was the case with the censers of Korah's§ company, which having become holy through being presented to God were unfit for use, and were directed to be made into plates for the altar (Nu 16³⁶⁻⁴⁰ [Heb. 17¹⁻⁵]). This is possible, although there is no clear evidence of it, and, in the case of the field (Dt 22⁹), a more likely supposition would be that the crop was simply not to be used. Even if it was confiscated, that was only a consequence of the holiness it had *already* contracted for a different reason; and it is probable that in such cases we have a survival of a conception of holiness in which a relation to J″ was not the exclusive regulating principle. But, with these unimportant exceptions, the rule holds good that holiness is an attribute of the things pertaining to the worship of J″, and is acquired by them through nearness to Him who is the source of all holiness. Holiness, in short, expresses a *relation*, which consists negatively in separation from common use, and positively in dedication to the service of J″.

An important corollary from this principle is that there is no such thing as natural or inherent holiness in any class of created objects (Baud. p. 45).

* On the analogies between taboo and the Heb. laws of uncleanness and holiness, see J. G. Frazer, Encyc. Brit.⁹ art. 'Taboo'; and W. R. Smith, Rel. Sem.² pp. 151 ff., 446–454. A good account of Taboo will be found in Jevons' Introd. to the History of Rel. chs. vi.–viii.

Things *are* clean or unclean according to their natural condition,[*] and all that man can do is to recognize the fact and regulate his attitude to them accordingly. But things *become* holy by being dedicated to J″, and for nearly every kind of holy object the law prescribes specific ceremonies of consecration. Naturally, only things inherently clean could be so dedicated; hence, to some extent, holiness and cleanness are practically identical, and in OT the terms are liable to be interchanged. Nevertheless, the ideas are radically distinct, the category of cleanness is much more comprehensive than that of holiness, and nothing but confusion of thought can result from overlooking the distinction.[†]

Of all material embodiments of the idea of holiness, the most instructive and the most fundamental is the 'holy place' or sanctuary.[‡] Without a particular place set apart for religious purposes, there could be no such thing as sacred objects or times or even persons in the OT sense (W. R. Smith, *Rel. Sem.*[2] p. 141). A holy place is in the first instance a space marked off, 'separated,' from common ground (see Ezk 42[20]), and only to be entered by those who comply with the conditions of sanctity prescribed by usage or law. These conditions may in some cases be very simple (Ex 3[5], Jos 5[15]), in others, as in the central sanctuary of Israel, they are extremely complicated; but they always exist, and compliance with them constitutes the holiness of the persons concerned. What in Israel makes the holiness of a place is the presence of J″, whose nature as the Holy One is expressed in the rules which regulate admission to His dwelling-place. Every spot where J″ appears to men is holy ground (Ex 3[5], Jos 5[15]); even the temporary camp in time of war is consecrated by the presence of the God of the armies of Israel (Dt 23[15]). The sanctuaries frequented by Israelites in pre-exilic times were the stated places where at set seasons the worshippers appeared before J″, and probably were all regarded as having been consecrated by a Theophany, in accordance with Ex 20[24]. When the sacredness of these places was abolished by the law of the one sanctuary, the temple of Jerusalem became the sole earthly dwelling-place of J″ (Ezk 43[7], Ps 132[14], Zec 2[10] etc.), and the centre from which the whole life of the people was sanctified. The symbolism of the second temple in particular, with its graduated series of sacred spaces culminating in the inmost shrine or most holy place, its different classes of ministers, and its minutely regulated ceremonial, was so designed as to form an impressive exhibition to the Israelites of the ruling idea of holiness. The quality of holiness pertains also to Mount Zion and Jerusalem (Is 11[9] 27[13], Zeph 3[11] etc.; Is 48[2] 52[1], Dn 9[24] etc.), and in a less degree to the whole land (Zec 2[10] etc.). There is but one passage dating from before the Exile (Ex 15[13]) in which holiness is directly predicated of the land of Canaan; but the idea is implied in Hos 9[3. 4] and elsewhere, and must be ancient.

Holy *seasons*, in like manner, are portions of time set apart from ordinary employments and dedicated to J″ by acts of worship (Neh 8[9-11] 10[31]). The chief of such seasons was the Sabbath (Gn 2[3], Ex 20[8. 11], Is 58[13] etc.). The relation to the cultus is less apparent in the case of the year of Jubilee (Lv 25[12]), but the separation from common time is equally obvious.

Amongst the various objects belonging to the temple ritual the term holy is applied to the *sacrifices* (Ex 28[38] etc.), the *shewbread* (1 S 21[5]), the *incense* (Ex 30[35. 37]), the *anointing oil* (which the people were expressly forbidden to compound for common use, Ex 30[25. 33] etc.), the *priestly clothing* (Ezk 42[14], Ex 28[2. 4] etc.), etc. etc. (For a complete enumeration, see Baud. p. 44 f.).

II. HOLINESS OF GOD (AND ANGELS).—From a very early time the word 'holiness' appears to have been used by the Northern Semites to express the general idea of Godhead. In this vague sense it occurs in the Phœnician inscription of Eshmunazar in the title 'holy gods,' and the same phrase is found in the mouth of heathen speakers in Dn 4[8. 9. 18] 5[11]. In that expression 'holy' is not intended to convey any information as to the character of the gods; it is a mere 'otiose epithet, "the holy gods" meaning nothing more than "the gods."'[*] It will be found that no sense less comprehensive than this suffices to explain the Hebrew usage of the term. There are, no doubt, passages where one special attribute is more immediately suggested to the mind by the context, but there are others where it is clear that no particular divine quality is meant to be predicated, and indeed there is no single attribute which will cover all the applications of the word 'holiness' to God. The plural קְדֹשִׁים (a so-called pl. of majesty formed after the analogy of אֱלֹהִים) is used of J″ almost as a proper name in Pr 9[10] 30[3] (? Hos 12[1]), and similarly the sing. קְדוֹשׁ in Is 40[25], Job 6[10], Hab 3[3]. A predicate which is thus capable of being elevated to a proper name may be presumed to be that which includes all specific attributes, viz. divinity. Again, when J″ is said to swear by His holiness (Am 4[2], Ps 89[35], cf. 60[6] 108[7]), it might be supposed that the expression signifies to swear by that special attribute which is to be exercised in the act promised, just as when He swears by His strength (Is 62[8]). But the more natural interpretation is, that to swear by His holiness is to swear by His divinity, or, as it is elsewhere expressed, by Himself (Am 6[8], Gn 22[16] etc.). It is probably in the same vague sense that the adj. is used of the divine *arm* (Is 52[10], Ps 98[1]), or the divine *word* (Jer 23[9], Ps 105[42]). So also in the numerous passages where holiness is predicated of the *name* of God (Am 2[7], Ezk 20[39], Lv 20[3] etc.), the name of J″ being the expression of His whole being as revealed in Israel. Nor is the case different in such expressions as 'there is none holy as J″' (1 S 2[2]). The meaning there is not that among divine beings J″ alone possesses the specific attribute of holiness, but that He alone is worthy to be regarded as truly divine; in other words, what is asserted is not anything about His character, but simply His supreme Godhead.[†]

It is plausible, though possibly misleading, to connect this most general sense of holiness with the assumed root-idea of the word, and to say that the aspect of divinity denoted by holiness is the

---

[*] *i.e.* from the standpoint of the law and the religion generally. There is much to be said for the view that *originally* uncleanness itself denoted a relation, viz. a relation to false deities.

[†] The antithesis of קֹדֶשׁ, as has been said, is חֹל; the opposite of טָהוֹר (clean) is טָמֵא (unclean). See Baud. p. 22 ff.

[‡] The proper designation of a sanctuary is מִקְדָּשׁ (used even of the sacred places of the heathen Is 16[12], Ezk 28[18]); but in the Law the central sanctuary (tabernacle) is more frequently described simply as קֹדֶשׁ, sometimes also as מָקוֹם קָדוֹשׁ = 'holy place' (but only in such expressions as 'eat [wash] in a holy place'). קֹדֶשׁ is also used of the temple in Ezk, Ps, Dn, Ch.

[*] Davidson, *Ezekiel* (Camb. Bible), p. xxxix.

[†] The facts adduced in this paragraph are adverse to the view held by some writers, that holiness, even when predicated of J″, is a merely relative idea, denoting His fidelity to His covenant with Israel. There are, no doubt, passages which, taken by themselves, might seem to countenance that explanation. But when we take account of all the uses of the word, and especially of the fact that it was a common epithet of heathen deities, it is abundantly clear that holiness is an essential attribute of J″, apart altogether from His special relation to Israel. All the applications of the term can be explained in harmony with this position. Thus, to take a salient instance, the phrase 'Holy One of Israel' (see below) need not be paraphrased: 'the God who is Holy in virtue of His relation to Israel.' It may equally mean, and in point of fact does mean, 'the (essentially) Holy Being, who is God of Israel.'

'separation' of God from the world, or His transcendence. There is no doubt that the term does express the sense of an awful contrast between the divine and the human (Hos 11⁹), although hardly, perhaps, between God and the universe. The opposition which is implied in its application to J″ is rather to the presumption and pride of man on the one hand, and the pretended deity of false gods on the other, than to the whole of created existence.* But whether this idea lies in the word itself, or whether it was reached through the impression caused by the multitude of inviolable things belonging to the sphere of deity, is a point which cannot be certainly determined. It has to be remembered that, in early times at least, the holiness of the gods had no definite meaning apart from the holiness of their physical surroundings.† An illustration of this mode of thinking is furnished by the exclamation of the men of Beth-shemesh after they had looked into the ark : 'Who is able to stand before J″ this holy God?' (1 S 6²⁰). There is evident that the holiness of J″ and the holiness of the ark are practically identical, J″'s holiness being the quality manifested in His vindication of the inviolability of the sacred symbol. And so it must have been to a large extent in ancient religion : the divine holiness was not so much an object of intellectual contemplation as a fact borne in upon the mind by the constant presence of things and persons that might not be touched, places that might not be entered, and times in which ordinary employments were suspended, because of their appropriation to the service or worship of God.

The question as to the contents of the idea of divine holiness thus resolves itself into the larger question of the conception of Godhead by which religious practice and devotion were ruled ; and the development of the idea in OT may be expected to proceed step by step with the progressive revelation of the character and nature of J″. Certain features of divinity, no doubt, retain a prominence due to the ancient associations of the word. The term never ceases to emphasize the awful side of the divine manifestation, and even in later writings this may sometimes be the only thought conveyed by its use. But that, after all, only means that J″ was always regarded as a Being of awful and unapproachable majesty, to be feared just because He was divine. And while the history of the idea certainly does not show any abatement of the sentiment of awe due to J″ as the Holy One, it does exhibit an advance towards the conception of Him as one to be feared, not simply because He is all-powerful, but because of His opposition to all that is impure and sinful.

There are three main aspects of deity specially associated with the term 'holiness' in different parts of the OT ; and all of these might without difficulty be derived from the fundamental sense of *unapproachableness*, which is never absent from the notion of J″'s holiness.

(1) The negative idea of unapproachableness readily passes over into the positive conceptions of *greatness*, *power*, *majesty*, and the like. Of all uses of the word this is the most widely prevalent ; and in nearly every part of the literature we find expressions where holiness conveys no other thought than the might and majesty of the God of Israel, or the awe and fear which His presence inspires in man. This appears, *e.g.*, in the words of the men of Beth-shemesh already cited (1 S 6²⁰). So in Is 8¹³ to 'sanctify J″' is to regard Him as an object of fear and dread. In Ex 15¹¹ J″ is extolled as 'glorious in holiness, fearful in praises, doing wonders.' In the Psalms He is addressed as 'terrible out of his holy places' (68³⁵) ; His name is 'holy and terrible' (111⁹) ; 'J″ is great in Zion, and exalted above all the peoples,' therefore they are exhorted to praise His 'great and terrible name ; holy is it' (99², ³). This conception is specially prominent in the Bk. of Ezekiel, where the divine holiness appears to denote no other attribute than that of majesty, exhibited in the exercise of irresistible power. J″'s 'holy name' is synonymous with His 'great name' (36²¹, cf. v.²³) ; and when He is said to 'sanctify himself' (*i.e.* show Himself to be holy), or to 'sanctify his name,' which is profaned when He is forced to conceal any of His divine attributes, the meaning always is that by a display of might He produces the recognition of His true majesty (36²⁰⁻²⁴ 38¹⁶, ²³ 20⁴¹ etc.). These illustrations, which might easily be multiplied, will serve to show how largely the usage of the words for holiness is influenced by the majestic and awe-inspiring side of the divine nature.

(2) The priestly *Torah*, being largely occupied with questions of cleanness and uncleanness, was naturally led to present divinity as opposition to all that is impure ; and hence in the legal books the idea of holiness approximates to that of *physical purity* (cf. Lv 11⁴⁴ff. 20²⁵, ²⁶, Ezk 43⁷, ⁹ etc.). It is an undue exaggeration of this fact that has led some theologians to suppose that the primary significance of holiness is purity in a physical sense, or freedom from defect, or 'normality of life' (Diestel). In reality this is but one manifestation of divinity (readily intelligible as a modification of the fundamental conception of unapproachableness) ; and although it is necessarily emphasized by priestly writers, it is altogether inadequate to explain the whole range of meaning covered by the term 'holy.' What it expresses is J″'s jealous care for the purity of His own worship, and that, again, is probably rooted in antagonism to the worship of heathen deities and other forms of superstition, especially the worship of dead ancestors (see Lv 19²⁸, Dt 14¹ etc.). The most characteristic expression of the idea is perhaps in the striking but somewhat difficult sentence, 'Be ye holy : for I am holy' (Lv 11⁴⁴ 19² 20²⁶, cf. 20⁷ 21⁶⁻⁸). Evidently, the holiness of Israel is there conceived as in some sense a reflexion of the holiness of J″, for it is hardly reasonable to take the word 'holy' in two diverse acceptations in the two members of the sentence. While there are many ways in which holiness might be predicated of J″, and many also in which it might be predicated of Israel, there are very few in which the word could be applied to both. At all events, in such a connexion the holiness of God cannot be His deity in general, nor His power or majesty, but must mean that separation from impurity which belongs to His nature, and is to be reproduced and exhibited in the life of His people. Holiness in this sense is the ruling principle of the Levitical legislation, just as ethical righteousness is the supreme idea of prophecy. Although the expression of the idea occurs chiefly in later writings (esp. Ezk and the Priestly Code), the thought itself is undoubtedly ancient, and must have exercised an influence on the development of the notion of holiness.

(3) The *ethical* sense of the divine holiness is most clearly to be discerned in some parts of the prophetical writings, particularly in those of Isaiah. To the prophets J″ was essentially a moral Being, 'of too pure eyes to behold evil' (Hab 1¹³), and swift to resent and punish the iniquity of His people. And since holiness embraced every distinctive attribute of Godhead, it was to be expected that, in the light of this ethical concep-

---

* The opinion that holiness was predicated of the gods as having their dwelling-place in heaven does not appear to be well founded.

† W. R. Smith, *Rel. Sem.*² p. 141.

tion of God, the word should take on the sense of moral perfectness, at least on its negative side of opposition to human sin. Accordingly, in Am 2⁷ we find the holiness of J″'s name set in contrast to the immoral practices of Canaanitish heathenism which had been introduced into the religion of Israel. It may be objected that in this instance the opposition to J″'s holiness lies not so much in the immorality of the custom as in its association with the worship of strange gods. But, even if that be true, the significance of the allusion is hardly diminished. The fact remains that a rite consistent with the godhead of other deities was inconsistent with the holiness of J″, and the only reason that can be assigned for the difference is that J″'s godhead or holiness included a moral element which placed a wide gulf between Him and the deities of the Semitic pantheon. In the teaching of Isaiah the thought of the divine holiness has a central importance which it possesses in that of no other prophet; and it is there also that the ethical aspect of the idea receives the fullest expression. In his inaugural vision the great fact impressed on his mind is the holiness of the God of Israel (Is 6³), and this perception awakes in him the consciousness, not merely of creaturely infirmity, but of uncleanness in a moral sense, as adhering both to himself and his nation (v.⁵). The connexion of holiness and morality is again expressed in a striking manner in the words of 5¹⁶, where we read that 'the holy God shall sanctify himself in righteousness,' i.e. He shall show Himself to be holy by the exercise of punitive righteousness. But indeed Isaiah's whole conception of national sin as rebellion against J″ and ignorance of His character, and his demand that J″ should be 'held holy' by compliance with His revealed will (1⁴ 3⁸ 8¹³ 29²³ etc.), imply a view of holiness which is profoundly ethical; and all this is embraced in the divine title which is continually on his lips, **'the Holy One of Israel.'** There is, however, no passage of the OT where it can be supposed that moral purity exhausts the idea of holiness. It never appears detached from the underlying thought of majesty and power; it is, in short, an *element* of holiness as conceived by the prophets; but neither in their writings nor in any other part of the literature does it supersede the vaguer original meaning of the word. So in a later prophet the words, 'Thou that art of too pure eyes to behold evil,' etc. (Hab 1¹³), are no doubt connected with the name 'my Holy One' in the previous verse, but at the same time they cannot be regarded as the complete equivalent of that phrase.

There are some other applications of the word which fall to be mentioned here, although they can scarcely be said to throw any additional light on its meaning. (1) The expression **Holy Spirit** (wh. see), so frequent in NT, occurs in OT only 3 times (Ps 51¹¹, Is 63¹⁰. ¹¹). In such a connexion 'holy' may mean much or little; it may be equivalent to '*divine*' Spirit' in any of the senses in which holiness is predicated of J″, or it may describe the Spirit as the source of moral purity in the life of the consecrated nation. It is, at all events, of some importance to observe that 'the divine Spirit is not called the *holy* Spirit in so far as it is the principle of cosmical life, but only in so far as it works in the Theocracy' (Oehler). (2) *Angels* are called 'holy ones' in Job 5¹ 15¹⁵, Ps 89⁶. ⁸, Dn 8¹³ etc., not on account of their superior purity (see Job 4¹⁸ 15¹⁵), but as partaking of the divine nature ('sons of God'). (3) Lastly, *heaven*, as the dwelling-place of God, is frequently spoken of as a holy place (Hab 2²⁰, Jer 25³⁰, Is 63¹⁵, Zec 2¹³, Ps 11⁴ 20⁶ etc.).

III. HOLINESS OF MEN.—The OT applications of the word 'holy' to human persons are of two kinds. There is first an external holiness, which consists merely in consecration to religious functions, and does not differ materially from the holiness of things. In this sense the term is applied to several classes of persons in Israel. The degraded beings devoted to shameful practices in the Canaanitish sanctuaries were known as קְדֵשִׁים and קְדֵשׁוֹת ('holy men' and 'holy women'), in token of their dedication to the service of the god or goddess (Dt 23¹⁸ etc.). This, of course, is a heathen usage, which has nothing to do with the specifically OT idea of sanctity. Again, *soldiers on a campaign* are consecrated persons (1 S 21⁵. ⁶), war being a religious act initiated by sacred rites (Is 13³, Jer 6⁴ 22⁷, Mic 3⁵ etc.). The *Nazirites* are holy during the period covered by their vow (Nu 6⁵ff.). An official holiness belongs to the *priests and Levites*, who are consecrated to J″ by special ceremonies (Ex 29¹ff., Lv 8¹². ³⁰ etc.), and whom Israel is enjoined to 'sanctify,' *i.e.* treat as sacrosanct persons (Lv 21⁸). In a similar sense we are probably to understand the sanctity ascribed to the *prophets* (2 K 4⁹, Jer 1⁵): when the great lady of Shunem speaks of Elisha as a 'holy man of God,' she is not thinking of the saintliness of his character; he is holy, simply as one who stands in a near relation to God. Finally, the attribute of holiness pertains to the whole people of Israel as a nation severed from the rest of mankind, and consecrated to J″ (Ex 19⁶, Nu 16³. ⁵. ⁷, Dt 7⁶ 14² etc.), and hence inviolable (Jer 2³). In this sense J″ speaks of Himself frequently as the 'sanctifier' (מְקַדֵּשׁ) of Israel (Ezk 20¹² 37²⁷ᶠ., Ex 31¹³, Lv 20⁷ᶫ. etc.).

But this outward holiness implies, in the case of persons, the observance of certain rules, compliance with which constitutes sanctification in an active and sometimes an ethical sense. No doubt, each of the classes enumerated above was subject to prescribed rules of this kind, as was notably the case with the priests and Nazirites. But the most important developments of the idea are those connected with the application of the term 'holiness' to the religious community as a whole. J″ sanctifies Israel by choosing it from other peoples to be His familiar people, and by taking up His abode in its midst; but Israel is thus bound to *sanctify itself*, by conforming to the requirements that express J″'s holy will and nature. These requirements, as we have already seen, were mainly external and ceremonial, consisting in avoidance of occasions of physical defilement. But moral precepts are also included (Lv 19, etc.), and are expressly embraced in the formula, 'Be ye holy: for I am holy.' The holiness of Israel, in fact, had to be maintained by obedience to the entire Law of God (Nu 15⁴⁰); and, in so far as the Law contains a summary of moral duty, the conception of holiness has an ethical significance. It is true that the Law recognizes no distinction between the moral and the ceremonial, and to that extent its teaching is not truly ethical in our sense of the word. Still, where holiness is presented as an ideal to be realized in conduct, and where this ideal is connected with the essential holiness of God (as in the phrase just quoted), the notion is already charged with ethical meaning; and so in the spiritual religion of the Psalms the external element disappears, the conditions of entrance into J″'s 'holy place' being described in terms which are exclusively ethical (Ps 15. 24³ᶠ.).

From a theological point of view, the chief interest of the OT doctrine of holiness lies in this progressive spiritualizing of the idea under the influence of an expanding revelation of God. Although the various steps of the process are obscure, the fact is certain that holiness did come to be conceived more and more as a moral quality. It is probable that the ethical aspect was first introduced in the application of the term to God, and thence transferred to the holiness He requires in His worshippers. In OT the development is arrested at a certain stage, because of the material associations with which the use of the word was invested. One step remained to be taken in order to reach the full Christian sense of holiness, and that was the abrogation of the ceremonial as a term of fellowship with God. When our Lord enunciated the principle that a man is defiled, not by what enters into him, but by what comes out of him, He raised religion to a new level, and made it possible to liberate the moral essence of holiness from the imperfections which clung to it throughout the older dispensation.

LITERATURE.—The modern discussion of holiness appears to start from a passage in Menken's *Anleitung zum eigenenen Unterricht in den Wahrheiten der heil. Schr.* (1805, *Schriften*, Bd. vi. pp. 46–53). His observations have little scientific value, but seem to have aroused interest by the paradoxical position, laid down with hardly an attempt at proof, that holiness means 'self-humbling love and grace' on the part of God.—Diestel's paper (in *JDTh*, 1859, pp. 3–63), though in some respects arbitrary and one-sided, is a far more adequate treatment of the subject. His chief results are these two: (1) that, *in form*, holiness is always a relative idea, Israel being holy as belonging to J″, and conversely J″ being holy as belonging to Israel, in the covenant relation; and (2) that the *content* of the notion has to be determined from the conditions of the covenant as laid down by the Law, the ruling principle of which Diestel finds to be 'normality of life.'—Baudissin's elaborate monograph (*Studien zur semitischen Religionsgeschichte*, 1878, ii. pp. 3–142) devotes considerable space to the criticism of these and other views of earlier writers. It contains an invaluable and apparently exhaustive collection of the OT material, and for thoroughness of treatment leaves nothing to be desired. The most important result, in the judgment of Nöldeke (*LCBl*, 1879, No. 12, col. 361 f.), is the conclusive demonstration that throughout the OT the ideas of holiness and purity remain distinct. See further the *OT Theologies* of Oehler, Schultz, Dillmann, Marti, and Bennett; Kuenen, *Religion of Israel* (i. 43 ff. [Eng. tr.]); Duhm, *Theol. der Propheten*, 168 ff.; Smend, *Alttest. Religionsgeschichte*, 333 ff.; W. R. Smith, *OTJC*² 228, 364, 377, *Prophets of Israel*², 224 ff., 424, *RS*² 140 ff., 151 ff., 446 ff. ; the arts. in Schenkel, *Bibellex.*, and Herzog, *PRE*² (by Delitzsch) ; Cheyne's Note in *Origin of the Psalter*, 331 f., and Davidson's in *Ezekiel* (Camb. Bible), xxxix f.   **J. SKINNER.**

HOLINESS IN NT.—The study of the NT conception of holiness must proceed mainly from a consideration of the following terms : ἅγιος, ἁγιασμός, ἁγιότης, ἁγιωσύνη. Besides this group of words denoting *holy* or *holiness*, we have in NT ἱερός, ὅσιος, σεμνός, ἁγνός, and their cognates. It is the word ἅγιος and its kindred terms which express the characteristic NT idea of holiness. In order to define and illustrate this idea it is necessary to examine the meaning and use of terms synonymous with ἅγιος, so that the significance of the latter may be set in the clearer light.

Etymologically, ἱερός is believed to signify *vigorous* or *strong*. The word thus naturally denotes, in classic usage, that which is associated with the gods, that which belongs to them, or that which is divine. It thus approaches θεῖος in meaning. The word is commonly applied, not to persons, but to things, which are ἱερά because they originate with the gods, belong to them, or are bestowed by them. The term is applied to men when it is desired to designate them as having special relation to the gods, or as being under their protection. Kings and persons who are initiated into the mysteries are sometimes called ἱεροί in this sense. The term ἱερός thus denoted an external rather than an internal and moral relation to the gods. It did not imply excellence. It meant *sacred* in the sense of inviolable, entitled to reverence, but did not bear the meaning which we attach to the terms *morally pure* and *holy*. While in NT the word has higher associations because of the circle of religious ideas with which it is there connected, it retains clear traces of its history. It emphasizes an outer rather than an inner and spiritual relation with God. The word occurs as an adjective but twice. In 1 Co 9¹³ οἱ τὰ ἱερὰ ἐργαζόμενοι is a periphrasis for the priests. Τὰ ἱερά, *res sacræ*, are the rites of the Levit. cultus. These rites are sacred because their performance is an act of divine worship. In 2 Ti 3¹⁵ (as also in Philo and Jos.) ἱερὰ γράμματα is the OT. These writings are regarded as ἱερά because divinely inspired and teaching divine truth. The use of words cognate with ἱερός in NT agrees with that of ἱερός. Thus ἱερεύς is a priest; ἱερόν designates the temple-enclosure ; ἱερόθυτον (1 Co 10²⁸) denotes something which has been offered in sacrifice ; and ἱεροπρεπής (Tit 2³) means *befitting sacred things or places*, 'reverent in demeanour' (RV). It will be seen that this whole group of words designates ideas and relations which are more distinctively characteristic of OT than of NT, ἱερός in this sense having been taken over from the LXX, where it abounds in 1 Es and the Books of Maccabees.

The word ὅσιος means *pious, godly*. It is the nearest Gr. equivalent of the Lat. *sanctus* and of the Heb. חָסִיד. In its classic use it commonly denoted what was consecrated by law or custom, whether of the gods or of men. In NT, however, it has a distinctively religious significance, and means *consecrated to God, pure, holy, pious*. The NT use of ὅσιος, ὁσιότης may be seen in such passages as He 7²⁶, where Christ, as High Priest, is described as ὅσιος, ἄκακος, ἀμίαντος, κεχωρισμένος ἀπὸ τῶν ἁμαρτωλῶν ; Lk 1⁷⁵, where the people of God are spoken of as serving Him ἐν ὁσιότητι καὶ δικαιοσύνῃ ; and Eph 4²⁴, where the new man is said to be created according to God ἐν δικαιοσύνῃ καὶ ὁσιότητι τῆς ἀληθείας. In both classic and NT usage this group of words is commonly associated with δίκαιος and its cognates. In the LXX οἱ ὅσιοι τοῦ θεοῦ is a frequent designation of God's true worshippers. It will thus be seen that holiness, in the sense of ὁσιότης, includes especially what is designated by the words *reverence, piety, Frömmigkeit*.

Σεμνός properly means *deserving of reverence or awe*, and in classic usage is applied both to the gods and to men. It is even used of things, in the sense of *grand, magnificent, impressive*. In NT σεμνός denotes *deserving of reverence, honourable*. It is once applied to deeds, Ph 4⁸ (RV 'honourable'), and three times to persons, 1 Ti 3⁸·¹¹, Tit 2², in all of which cases RV renders *grave*. In like manner RV renders σεμνότης *gravity* in all three passages in which it occurs, 1 Ti 2² ³⁴, Tit 2⁷. The word signifies something more than *gravity* ; it suggests *dignity* or *worth*. It is obvious, however, that σεμνότης designates but a secondary aspect of the NT idea of holiness.

Ἁγνός, ἁγνότης mean *pure, purity*. In LXX these words refer to ceremonial purity. In NT they refer to freedom from moral faults in general, and esp. to freedom from carnal sins. In one passage ἁγνός is applied to God (1 Jn 3³). The characteristic use of the word is seen in passages like 2 Co 11², Tit 2⁵. Ἁγνός represents an aspect of holiness, but only in a limited and negative way. Even the idea of moral purity is inadequate to represent the full content of the Christian conception of holiness.

The characteristic NT word for *holy* is, as we have seen, ἅγιος. It is the nearest Gr. equivalent of the Heb. קָדוֹשׁ, and is the common rendering of that word in the LXX. It is probably from the same root as ἁγνός (Lat. *sacer*), and the fundamental meaning of the two words is nearly the same. Ἅγιος, however, which is a rare word in classic Greek, appears to have diverged from ἁγνός in the direction of a moral and religious conception of holiness. It is generally believed that the fundamental idea which underlies the word is that of separation, and that its moral signification therefore is : separation from sin, and so, consecration to God. The Christian use of the word lifted it into accord with the highest ethical conceptions, and gave it the idea of separateness from the sinful world, harmony with God, the absolutely good Being, moral perfection. Thus ἅγιος is, above all things, a qualitative and ethical term. It refers chiefly to character, and lays emphasis upon the demands which that which is sacred (ἱερόν) in the highest sense makes upon conduct.

It is necessary briefly to refer to the LXX use of this word, and to the circle of OT ideas which it represents. We find that ἅγιος is predicated of God as the absolutely perfect One, and of men and things so far as they are devoted to Him, and, as we may say, in some way identified with Him. Israel, *e.g.*, was an ἔθνος ἅγιον because God's peculiar possession. Men are called upon to sanctify themselves, that is, to cleanse themselves from all defilement, to forsake sin, and to come into harmony of life with God. So men may sanctify things by regarding, treating, or using them as sacred, that is, by associating them with God's perfection. The basis of this demand upon men that they be holy is the obligation to be like God : 'Ye shall be holy : for I the Lord your God am holy' (Lv 19²). Now this holiness, as seen in OT, seems to wear a twofold aspect. It comprehends both 'the goodness and the severity of God.' It issues both in redemption and in judgment. These two aspects of the divine holiness appear continually in inseparable connexion and interplay. 'Holiness (in the OT) is the perfect purity of God, which in and for itself excludes all fellowship with the world, and can only establish a relationship of free, electing love, whereby it asserts itself in the sanctification of God's people, their cleansing and redemption ; therefore "the purity of God manifesting itself in atonement and redemption, and correspondingly in judgment'" (Cremer, *Bib.-Theol. Lex. s.v.*).

It is evident that ἅγιος and its kindred words are best adapted to represent the NT idea. They express something more and higher than ἱερός, *sacred, outwardly associated with God* ; something more than ὅσιος, *reverent, pious* ; something more than σεμνός, *worthy, honourable* ; something more than ἁγνός, *pure, free from defilement.* Ἅγιος is more positive, more comprehensive, more elevated, more purely ethical and spiritual. It is characteristically Godlikeness, and in the Christian system Godlikeness signifies completeness of life.

The words ἅγιος and ἁγιάζειν occur very frequently in NT. The three nouns (ἁγιασμός, ἁγιότης, ἁγιωσύνη), which are kindred to them, are not of frequent occurrence. The most common among these three nouns, ἁγιασμός, is found ten times (1 Th 4³· ⁴· ⁷, 2 Th 2¹³, Ro 6¹⁹· ²², 1 Co 1³⁰, 1 Ti 2¹⁵, He 12¹⁴, 1 P 1²). In five instances it is rendered in AV *holiness*, and in five *sanctification.* In RV it is uniformly rendered *sanctification.* Ἁγιότης occurs twice (2 Co 1¹², He 12¹⁰), and is rendered *holiness* in both AV and RV. Ἁγιωσύνη occurs three times (1 Th 3¹³, Ro 1⁴, 2 Co 7¹), and is tr. in both VSS *holiness.* Ἁγιότης (*sanctitas*), ἁγιωσύνη (*sanctitudo*), ἁγιασμός (*sanctificatio*), denote the *quality,* the *state,* the *process,* respectively (Lightfoot, *Notes,* p. 49). Ὁσιότης occurs twice (Lk 1⁷⁵, Eph 4²⁴), and is rendered *holiness* in both. AV renders εὐσέβεια (piety) in Ac 3¹² *holiness,* RV *godliness.*

Let us next illustrate the use of the group of words under review, directing special attention to the fifteen passages in which the nouns denoting *holiness* are used. There does not appear to be anything distinctive in the use of the words by the different NT writers. We shall therefore have no occasion to treat the NT books separately. We find ἅγιος applied to God in Jn 17¹¹ : 'Holy Father, keep them in thy name which thou hast given me,' etc., where God, as the One who is absolutely good—wholly separate from all that is sinful and wrong—is besought to guard from evil those whom He has given to His Son. The idea closely resembles that which is found in 17²⁵ : 'O righteous (δίκαιος) Father, the world knew thee not, but I knew thee,' etc. The idea of God's righteousness here appears to be the quality which prevents Him from passing the same judgment upon Christ's disciples as He passes upon the sinful world. It is the equitableness of God. In both cases the attribute of God which is referred to is not the forensic or retributive element in the divine nature, but God's moral self-consistency, His justice to His own equity. In Rev 4⁸ God is addressed as 'Holy, Holy, Holy,' because He is worthy of all praise and honour. His holiness is His supreme and absolute excellence.

The term *holy* is constantly applied throughout NT to the divine Spirit. As proceeding from God, as the bearer of revelation, and as the mediator of spiritual life, the Spirit is pre-eminently holy. It is the special function of the Holy Spirit to make holy the souls of those in whom He dwells. This conception of the Spirit's nature and function is not prominent in OT, where the Spirit is scarcely more than a name for the power or presence of God. There He bestows strength upon heroes, skill upon artificers, and the knowledge of the divine will upon prophets. The designation of the Spirit as Holy accords entirely with the NT idea of the sanctifying function of the Spirit, and the hallowing of the people of God by inward consecration to Him. The Holy Spirit is conceived of as revealing the inner nature and essential goodness of God, and as accomplishing the transformation of men into His moral likeness. Hence the sin against the Holy Spirit represents

the acme of wickedness. It is hatred of supreme and absolute goodness. It despises the perfect purity and unselfish love which dwelt in Him to whom God gave the Spirit without measure, and thus treats perfect goodness as if it were evil. Such a state of mind involves complete moral obduracy. In this, and not in the limitation of the divine mercy, lies the impossibility of its forgiveness. See further HOLY SPIRIT.

With special appropriateness is Christ, as the Son and Revealer of God and the Redeemer of mankind from sin, designated as *holy.* He is the fulfilment of the OT picture of the true and faithful servant of J". He is accordingly spoken of as God's 'holy servant' (ὁ ἅγιος παῖς, Ac 4³⁰), by whom He accomplishes His gracious, saving purposes. So evil spirits are represented as recognizing in Jesus 'the Holy One of God,' the long-promised Messiah, the Messenger of the divine mercy, and the Conqueror of Satan.

Christians are frequently designated as ἅγιοι, *holy ones, saints.* They are such as the elect or beloved of God, who by faith and love have entered into fellowship with Him, and who by obedience to His will and by purity of life have become conformed to the image of His Son. St. Paul speaks of believers as κλητοὶ ἅγιοι (1 Co 1²), saints by a divine call, in the same sense as he speaks of himself as a κλητὸς ἀπόστολος (Ro 1¹), an apostle who became such by having presented to him, and by accepting, a divine commission. Esp. are men represented as holy when they have been made the special instruments of the divine will and have been taken into close fellowship with God in the work of revelation and redemption. In this sense the prophets are designated (acc. to the common reading) as 'holy men of God,' οἱ ἅγιοι θεοῦ ἄνθρωποι (2 P 1²¹). In like manner, the 'holy prophets' declared the divine purpose to restore all things through the Messiah (Ac 3²¹). So the 'mystery of Christ,' viz. that the gospel was for the Gentiles, was made known to God's 'holy apostles and prophets in the Spirit' (Eph 3⁵).

In a secondary sense impersonal objects are spoken of as holy. The ways and means whereby God reveals and accomplishes His will are *holy,* because they are associated with Him who is pre-eminently holy and are instrumental in the sanctification of men. Thus the gracious call which God in the gospel addresses to men—inviting them to receive a wholly unmerited salvation—is a *holy calling,* κλῆσις ἁγία (2 Ti 1⁹). The Messianic promise given in OT times was a *holy covenant,* διαθήκη ἁγία (Lk 1⁷²). The OT Scriptures are, by reason of the sacredness of their contents and their disclosure of the divine will and purpose, *holy writings,* γραφαὶ ἅγιαι (Ro 1²).

We turn now to the group of nouns denoting *holiness.* Ἁγιασμός would properly denote the act of sanctifying, τὸ ἁγιάζειν, and something of this active meaning is preserved in 2 Th 2¹³ : 'God chose you from the beginning unto salvation in sanctification of the Spirit' (ἐν ἁγιασμῷ πνεύματος), that is, in sanctification wrought by the Spirit ; cf. 1 P 1² : 'in sanctification of the Spirit,' etc. The active force of the word may also be observed, although in a somewhat different form, in 1 Th 4³ : 'For this is the will of God, even your sanctification,' etc. The will of God is this : that He may accomplish your sanctification. In 1 Co 1³⁰ Christ is called our 'sanctification,' in the sense that He is the cause or ground of our sanctification.

In most cases in NT, however, ἁγιασμός denotes the effect or result of ἁγιάζειν. (See, however, Sanday-Headlam's note on Ro 6¹⁹). In 1 Th 4⁴· ⁷ it denotes the sphere of holy action in opposition to the sphere of lustful desire. In Ro 6¹⁹ ἁγιασμός stands opposed to ἀνομία. These terms denote the ends to which the members are devoted in the sinful and in the Christian life respectively. In the latter the members are presented as servants to righteousness unto the end of sanctification (εἰς ἁγιασμόν). Similarly, in v.[22] Christians are said to have their fruit unto sanctification (εἰς ἁγ.), that is, to attain it as the result and reward of their life. In these passages from 1 Th and Ro, sanctification is particularly set in contrast to carnal lust, although its nature is not limited by that contrast. In 1 Ti 2[15] sanctification is contemplated as a virtue, or as the Christian's normal state, and is correlated with faith and love. In He 12[14] 'the sanctification' (the definite article used only here and in 1 Th 4[3]) is the Christian character, the goal of Christian effort, the preparation for the presence of God: 'Pursue after the sanctification without which no man shall see the Lord,' that is, enter into blessed fellowship with Christ.

Ἁγιότης is used (acc. to the most probable reading) in 2 Co 1[12] in ref. to St. Paul's manner of life at Corinth, to the uprightness of which his conscience bears witness. It is here correlated with the sincerity or purity (εἰλικρίνεια) which God effects by the Holy Spirit. Here *holiness* designates the life and character which the grace of God produces. In the one other passage where the word is used (He 12[10]) it is applied to God. Earthly parents, says the author, chasten their children with wrong or imperfect motives, or to secure some temporary good, but God chastens His children for their highest final good, that they may be 'partakers of his holiness' (εἰς τὸ μεταλαβεῖν τῆς ἁγιότητος αὐτοῦ), that is, that they may be transformed into moral likeness to Himself, and become partakers in His own eternal nature (cf. 2 P 1[4]). This passage carries us to a higher point than do those previously examined, in that it represents the holy nature of God as the type and goal of all perfection in man.

Ἁγιωσύνη is twice used of the moral purity, the God-like character, which the gospel requires and imparts: 1 Th 3[13] 'To the end he may stablish your hearts in holiness before our God,' etc., that is, in the possession of that holy life which will be acceptable to Christ at His coming; and 2 Co 7[1] 'Perfecting holiness in the fear of God,' that is, perfectly illustrating in character the holy life which comports with reverence for God. In Ro 1[4] the word occurs in a description which St. Paul is giving of the Son of God, 'who,' he says, 'was born of the seed of David according to the flesh, who was declared to be the Son of God with power, according to the spirit of holiness, by the resurrection of the dead.' Here the phrase κατὰ πνεῦμα ἁγιωσύνης stands in evident contrast to the phrase κατὰ σάρκα. The phrase probably means: the spirit of Christ, that is, His inner, essential life, which is characterized by holiness. If this is the meaning, then ἁγιωσύνης expresses the quality of Christ's spiritual nature. He is *par éminence* holy. He is in absolute accord with God.

We may sum up our results thus: In the absolute sense God alone is holy, and His holiness is the ground of the requirement of holiness in His creatures (1 P 1[16]). Holiness is the attribute of God, according to which He wills and does only that which is morally good. In other words, it is the perfect harmony of His will with His perfect ethical nature. But the divine holiness is not to be thought of as a mere passive, quiescent state. It is an active impulse, a forthgoing energy. In God's holiness, that is, in the expression of His perfect ethical nature, His self-revelation is grounded. Nay, creation itself, as well as redemption, would be inconceivable apart from the divine holiness, the energizing of God's absolutely good will.

By some theologians holiness and love are identified. More commonly they are sharply distinguished—holiness being regarded as the self-preservative or retributive attribute of God, and love as His beneficent, self-imparting attribute. To discuss this subject here would carry us too far. It seems clear, at least, from our investigation, that holiness and love represent closely kindred conceptions, and that there is an inner harmony between them. They are the two words which best express God's moral perfection, and the difference between them seems rather formal than real. At any rate, in their application to men, they seem to express, better than any other words, the highest aims of human life and the most comprehensive obligation of God's perfect law. See, further, the preceding art., and art. HOLY SPIRIT.

LITERATURE.—Studies of the words in Cremer's *Bib. Theol. Lex.* and Trench *NT Syn.*; art. 'Heiligkeit' in Schenkel's *Bib. Lex.* and in Herzog's *RE*; Issel, *Der Begriff d. Heiligkeit im NT*; Sanday-Headlam, *Romans* on 1[3. 7] and the literature there cited.   G. B. STEVENS.

HOLM TREE.—The name of this tree occurs in Is 44[14] RV as the equivalent of תִּרְזָה. The holm is prob. *not* the tree there intended (see CYPRESS).

It occurs also in Sus v.[58]. Two evergreen oaks, both growing in Pal. and Syria, *Quercus Ilex*, L., and *Q. coccifera*, L., are prob. included under the LXX πρῖνος, which is the orig. for *holm tree*. The former is a low tree, growing along the coast and the foot hills of the maritime ranges. The latter is one of the stateliest trees of the East. Its comus is often quite spherical, and sometimes 40 to 50 ft. in diameter. The trunk not infrequently attains a diameter of 6 ft. The leaf of both species is smaller than that of the *holly*, but resembles it in the fact that it is evergreen, of a rich glossy green, and usually with spiny teeth, though some of the varieties have nearly entire leaves. It is from the

THE HOLM OAK, QUERCUS COCCIFERA, L.

resemblance of its leaf to the *holly* (Old English *hollen*) that it obtained its name of holm. For the play on the words πρῖνος and πρίσαι see SUSANNA.

The holm oak is the tree, *par excellence*, around which are grouped the superstitions of the Orientals. One or more grand specimens are sure to be planted over the *welys* or tombs of the Moslem saints. Abraham's Oak is of this species. The dense mass of dark foliage gives to these fine old trees an aspect of solidity possessed by no others in the East. The Druses and other sects often hang bits of rag on their lower branches as a votive offering. A tree so decorated is called *umm-esh-sheraṭíṭ*, i.e. *mother of rags*. Such trees have probably existed from time immemorial on the 'high places.' See OAK.   G. E. POST.

HOLOFERNES ('Ολοφέρνης).—The arch-enemy of the Jews, assassinated before Bethulia (*i.e.* Jerusalem) by Judith, who thus saved her nation. In Jth 2⁴ H. is called 'the chief captain of the army of Nebuchadnezzar.' In the Midrash he is called 'king of Javan,' * and takes the place of Nebuchadnezzar. It is obvious that no one in the days of the historical Nebuch. could have borne the name and played the part of H. as described in Judith. There was an Orophernes king of the Cappadocians in B.C. 158 ff., who was a friend of Demetrius Soter, and supported the latter in his unjustifiable claims as against Ariarathes V., king of the Cappadocians (Polyb. iii. 5. 2, ed. Schweighäuser). Hence the Jews might know about Orophernes as the friend of their great enemy, and might represent him as he is represented in Judith. This would make the date of the book about B.C. 150. See Hicks, *Journ. Hellen. Studies*, vi. 1885, pp. 261–274. The form 'Οροφέρνης is found on coins discovered at Pirene, and in two inscriptions found on amphora-handles (Knidos); see Dumont, *Inscriptions céramiques*, Paris, 1872, p. 329, No. 9, and p. 388, No. 7. The same form is given by late classical authors, *e.g.* Polyb. xxxii. 20. 4, xxxiii. 12. § 2, 3, 9; Aelian, *Var. Hist.* ii. 41, ed. Hercher; Diod. Sic. xxxi. cc. 32 and 34; fluctuating with 'Ολο- and 'Ολο-, *e.g.* Appian, *Bell. Syr.* p. 118, ed. Stephan. 1592; Diod. Sic. xxxi. 19. § 2, 7, ed. Müller. If 'Ολοφέρνης is the original form, ὁλο- will be Greek = 'destroying' (cf. ὁλοεργής), and -φέρνης, Persian = 'brilliance, majesty,' cf. Pherendates, Pharnacos, Artaphernes; the root *fra* = 'shine.' The form 'Οροφ. will then represent the Persian pronunciation of the Greek 'Ολοφ. The aspirated 'Ολοφ is due to confusion with compounds in ὁλο-. The Vulg. form Holofernes is aspirated as in *Hiob, Hesther, Hierusalem*, etc.

Dante introduces Holofernes in *Purgatorio* xii. 59 as one of the instances of defeated pride in the Circle of the Proud. The following famous representations of Judith and Holofernes in art may be quoted: Botticelli, in the Uffizi, Florence (see Ruskin, *Mornings in Florence*, ch. 3); Michael Angelo, in the Sistine Chapel; Cristoforo Allori, in the Pitti; Paris Bordone; Guido, in the Spada Gallery, Rome; Donatello, statue in the Loggia dei Lanzi, Florence.

LITERATURE.—Scholz, *Das Buch Judith*, Würzburg, 1896.
                                        G. A. COOKE.

HOLON (חֹלֹן).—**1.** A city of Judah in the Hebron hills, given to the Levites, Jos 15⁵¹ 21¹⁵. In the parallel passage 1 Ch 6⁵⁸ [Heb.⁴³] it is called **Hilen**. It is noticed with Debir, and probably lay W. or S.W. of Hebron. The ruin *Beit Aûla*, in the lower hills west of Hebron, would be a suitable site. See *SWP* vol. iii. sh. xxi. **2.** A city of Moab near Heshbon, Jer 48²¹. Its site has not been recovered.   C. R. CONDER.

HOLYDAY.—'That kept holyday' is the trⁿ in Ps 42⁴ of חֹגֵג, ptcp. of חָגַג 'to make a pilgrimage,' RV 'keeping holyday.' 'Holyday' also occurs in Col 2¹⁶ as the trⁿ of ἑορτή, feast, RV 'feast day.' See FEASTS.

In both places AV of 1611 has two words, 'holy day' in Ps 42⁴, 'Holy day' in Col 2¹⁶; and it would be well, owing to the mod. associations of the word 'holiday,' to keep that form still.

HOLY OF HOLIES, HOLY PLACE.—See TEMPLE.

HOLY ONE.—See GOD, vol. ii. p. 204ᵇ, and HOLINESS, vol. ii. p. 398ᵃ.

* See Jer 46¹⁶ 50¹⁶ חֶרֶב הַיּוֹנָה, LXX μάχαιρα Ἑλληνική. Scholz.

HOLY SPIRIT.—In Christian theology the Holy Spirit is the third Person or eternal distinction within the Unity of God. The following article is an attempt to trace in the progressive revelation vouchsafed to Israel and to the Church the steps which have led to this conception. Our sources are the Old and New Testaments, and the intermediate Jewish writings which illustrate the effect of the OT revelation upon the Jewish people, and prepare us to understand the fuller teaching of the Gospel of Christ.

A. Old Testament.
　　i. Use of the terms 'Spirit,' 'Spirit of God,' 'Holy Spirit.'
　　ii. Work of the Spirit of God in—
　　　　(a) Creation.
　　　　(b) Intellectual life.
　　　　(c) Prophetic inspiration.
　　　　(d) Anointing the Messiah.
　　　　(e) Moral and religious life of men.
　　iii. Relation of the Holy Spirit to the Life of God.
　　iv. Signs of progress in the teaching of the OT.

B. Apocrypha and other pre-Christian Jewish writings.
　　i. Palestinian thought.
　　ii. Alexandrian thought.

C. New Testament.
　　i. Names and titles of the Holy Spirit.
　　ii. Historical events revealing the relation of the Spirit to Christ and to the Church.
　　　　(a) Revival of prophecy at the time of the Incarnation.
　　　　(b) Work of the Spirit in reference to the Incarnate life—
　　　　　　(α) Conception.
　　　　　　(β) Baptism.
　　　　　　(γ) Ministry.
　　　　(c) Work of the Spirit in reference to the life of the Church—
　　　　　　(α) Gift to the Apostles.
　　　　　　(β) Effusion on the Church.
　　　　　　(γ) Results, temporary and permanent.
　　iii. Direct teaching on the Person and Work of the Spirit.
　　　　(a) Teaching of Christ—
　　　　　　(α) In the Synoptic narrative.
　　　　　　(β) In the Fourth Gospel.
　　　　　　(γ) In the form of baptism.
　　　　(b) Teaching of the Apostles and first Disciples—
　　　　　　(α) In the Acts and Catholic Epistles.
　　　　　　(β) In the Pauline Epistles.
　　　　　　(γ) In the Apocalypse.
Summary.
Literature.

A. THE OLD TESTAMENT.—i. The word רוּחַ, in LXX πνεῦμα, but also ἄνεμος (about 50 times), θυμός (5 times), πνοή (4 times), ψυχή (twice), etc., belongs to a root רוח *flavit, spiravit*, used only in the Hiph. הֵרִים *olfecit, e.g.* Gn 8²¹). In OT רוּחַ signifies (1) the breath of the atmosphere, wind: Gn 3⁸ לְרוּחַ הַיּוֹם = LXX τὸ δειλινόν, Aq. ἐν τῷ ἀνέμῳ τῆς ἡμέρας, Symm. διὰ πνεύματος ἡμ.), Nu 11³¹, Job 4¹⁵ 41¹⁶, Jer 2²⁴ 14⁶; (2) the breath of man. Since the human breath is at once an indication of animal life, and a vehicle of thought and passion, the word is also used to represent (3) the principle of vitality, in the phrase רוּחַ חַיִּים (Gn 6¹⁷ 7¹⁵· ²²), or absolutely, as in Gn 45²⁷, 1 K 10⁵, Job 12¹⁰ 34¹⁴, Ps 104²⁹, Ec 3¹⁹ 12⁷; (4) the life of passion (Gn 41⁸, Nu 5¹⁴, 2 S 21⁵, Pr 25²⁸), or of thought and will (Dt 34⁹, Job 15² 32⁸, Jer 51¹¹); (5) the spiritual element in human nature (Nu 27¹⁶, Ps 31⁵, Ec 12⁷); lastly, from the sphere of human nature the word (6) passes into that of the divine. In anthropomorphic descriptions of the life of God it retains its primary sense; God's displeasure is the רוּחַ אַפּוֹ (Ex 15⁸, Job 4⁹, Ps 18¹⁵), His power in operation is the רוּחַ פִּיו (Ps 33⁶, Is 11⁴; cf. 2 Th 2⁸). But the writers of the OT conceive also of a Spirit in God which bears some analogy to the higher life of man; the 'Spirit of Elohim' or 'of Jʹʹ (רוּחַ אֱלֹהִים, רוּחַ יהוה, LXX πνεῦμα θεοῦ, πν. Κυρίου) is repeatedly mentioned in every part of the OT. In a few cases, it is true, this phrase may be interpreted of the wind which God sends on the earth (Ex 15¹⁰, 1 K 18¹², 2 K 2¹⁶, Is 40⁷ 59¹⁹, Hos 13¹⁵), or of the human breath or spirit as deriving its origin from God (Job 27³; cf. Gn 2⁷). But these are exceptions; in the great majority of passages the

'Spirit of God' is the vital energy of the divine nature, corresponding to the higher vitality of man.* This energy is usually presented in one of its relations to man or to the world, *e.g.* as a creative or vitalizing force (Gn 1², Job 26¹³, Is 32¹⁵), or as propagating or sustaining created life (Job 34¹⁴, cf. 10¹², Ps 104³⁰) ; as the source of reason and intellect in man (Job 32⁸), and in particular of special gifts and endowments (Gn 41³⁸, Ex 28³ 31³· ⁶ 35³¹), such as the artistic skill of Bezalel (Ex 36¹ᶠ·), the military tact of Joshua (Dt 34⁹), the heroism of the Judges (Jg 13²⁵ 14⁶ etc.), the wisdom of Solomon (1 K 3²⁸) ; as the well-spring of inspiration in the Hebrew lawgivers, poets, and prophets (Nu 11¹⁷· ²⁵ᵗ· ²⁹, 2 S 23², 1 K 22²⁴, Ezk 11⁵, Dn 4⁸· ⁹ 5¹¹), and of moral purity and strength and penitence (Neh 9²⁰, Ps 51¹¹, Is 63¹⁰ᶠ·, Ezk 36²⁶ᶠ·, Zec 12¹⁰). Especially is the energy of the Divine Spirit connected with the mission and work of the Messiah (Is 11¹ᶠ· 61¹ᶠ·), on whom, as the prophets foresaw, it was to rest in the fulness of strength and goodness.†

ii. These aspects of the working of the Divine Spirit must be separately examined.

(*a*) *Creative and conservative Operations in Nature.*—In the cosmogony of Gn 1 the Spirit of God broods — מְרַחֶפֶת — over the formless cosmic matter, before the cosmos begins to emerge out of chaos. The Greek versions render the verb by ἐπεφέρετο or ἐπιφερόμενον (Vulg. *ferebatur*), understanding by ר׳ מְרַחֶפֶת a wind sweeping over the abyss (cf. Ac 2²). But the verb suggests another image, that of the bird brooding over her nest : see Delitzsch, *ad loc.*, and cf. Dt 32¹¹ ; *Chagigah*, ed. Streane, p. 84 ; Basil. M. *Hom. in Hexaem.* 2, τὸ ἐπεφέρετο (φησὶν [Σύρος τις]) ἐξηγοῦνται ἀντὶ τοῦ Συνέθαλπε καὶ ἐζωογόνει τὴν τῶν ὑδάτων φύσιν κατὰ τὴν εἰκόνα τῆς ἐπωαζούσης ὄρνιθος καὶ ζωτικήν τινα δύναμιν ἐνιείσης τοῖς ὑποθαλπομένοις. This metaphor suits the secondary rather than the primary meaning of רוּחַ ; it is not the wind, but the divine energy that is regarded as vitalizing the germs which the Divine Word is about to call forth. This conception of the co-operation of the Spirit and the Word is 'specially characteristic of the OT' (Cheyne, *Origin of the Psalter*, p. 322 ; cf. Ps 33⁶). It rests on the relation of the breath to the voice, but its significance is not limited by that analogy. The Breath of God vitalizes what the Word creates. Moreover, its vitalizing energy is continuous ; it conserves, renews, or withdraws life, in the ceaseless processes of nature (Job 33⁴, Ps 33⁶ 104³⁰). Thus the OT already justifies the epithet τὸ ζωοποιόν, applied to the Divine Spirit by the Church in the 'Nicene' Creed.

(*b*) *Bestowal of intellectual gifts.*—'The LORD God . . . breathed into [man's] nostrils the breath of life' (נִשְׁמַת חַיִּים, πνοὴν ζωῆς), by virtue of which he 'became a living soul' (הָיָה נֶפֶשׁ, Gn 2⁷). This ἐμφύσησις (cf. Jn 20²²) represents the Breath of God as originating the personal life of man, together with the intellectual and spiritual powers which distinguish it from the life of the mere animal (ר׳ הַבְּהֵמָה Ec 3²¹). As the sacred Books proceed, they reveal the same Force lying behind the special endowments which mark off man from man. The Divine Spirit is said to be 'in' (Gn 41³⁸, Nu 27¹⁸) or 'upon' (Nu 11¹⁷ᶠ· 24²) the man who possesses exceptional powers of any kind ; he is what he is, because he is filled with the spirit of wisdom and understanding (πνεῦμα θεῖον σοφίας, Ex 31³ ; πν. αἰσθήσεως, συνέσεως, Ex 28³ 35³¹, Dt 34⁹).

(*c*) *Inspiration of the Prophets.*—One gift stands out as pre-eminently due to the presence in man of

the Spirit of God. The 'prophet' (נָבִיא, LXX mostly προφήτης ; on the etymology of the Heb. word see W. R. Smith, *Prophets of Israel*, p. 390 f.), or 'seer' (רֹאֶה), as he was called till after the age of Samuel (1 S 9⁹), was in an especial sense the man of the Spirit (אִישׁ הָרוּחַ, ἄνθρωπος ὁ πνευματοφόρος, Hos 9⁷), Vulg. *vir spiritualis*. It has been said that 'the ideal of the OT is a dispensation in which all are prophets' (W. R. Smith, *OTJC²* p. 291, citing Nu 11²⁹) ; and the title of prophet is given to Abraham (Gn 20⁷) and Moses (Dt 18¹⁵), while it is withheld from Balaam, in whom, though 'the Spirit of God came upon' him (Nu 24²), the sacred writers recognize a diviner (τὸν μάντιν, Jos 13²²) rather than a true seer. The true prophet is one who is lifted up by the Spirit of God into communion with Him, so that he is enabled to interpret the divine will, and to act as a medium of communication between God and men. The prophetic gift belonged to the nation, as the elect people ; but it was realized in its highest degree only by those whose characters and lives fitted them for personal intercourse with God. The professional prophet seems sometimes scarcely to have risen above the level of μαντική (1 S 10⁵ᵗ· 19²⁰ᶠ·) ; the change of 'heart' promised to Saul (10⁶· ⁹) is clearly not of a moral or spiritual kind. On the other hand, the prophets who taught Israel and Judah from the 8th cent. onwards have left us the clearest evidence of a genuine inspiration in the elevation and penetration of their teaching, and the revelation of a spiritual religion which their writings contain. No other national literature presents such a phenomenon. It is attributed by the prophets themselves to the Spirit of God ; cf. *e.g.* 2 S 23² (where see Driver's note), Ezk 2² 3¹²· ¹⁴ etc., Mic 3⁸, and the frequent appeals to a divine source, such as the repeated כֹּה אָמַר יהוה of Is, and וַיְהִי דְבַר־יהוה in Jer.

(*d*) *Anointing the Messiah.*—The Davidic King, in whom the elect nation was to find its crown and consummation, must, as the first Isaiah foresaw (Is 11²), receive all the gifts of the Divine Spirit in their fulness : 'the spirit of wisdom and understanding (intellectual gifts), of counsel and power (practical powers), of the knowledge and fear of J"' (religious endowments). In the strength of this abiding presence (ἀναπαύσεται ἐπ᾽ αὐτὸν πνεῦμα θεοῦ) the Second David will show Himself to be the perfect King. It is remarkable that Deutero-Isaiah foretells a similar equipment of the 'Servant of the LORD,' the ideal Israel. 'I have put my Spirit upon him' is J"'s assurance (42¹), and the Servant answers, 'The LORD God hath sent me, and his Spirit' (48¹⁶, cf., however, Delitzsch, *ad loc.*) ; 'the Spirit of the LORD God is upon me, because the Lord hath anointed me to preach good tidings unto the meek' (61¹ᶠ·). The ideal Prophet no less than the ideal King needs the fulness of the Spirit, and, when He comes, shall receive it. If, as some think (Kirkpatrick, *Doctrine of the Prophets*, p. 400), the prophet himself and not the Servant of J" is the speaker in the last passage, the ultimate reference is still to the highest fulfilment of the prophetic office (Lk 4²¹). The Spirit is the χρίσμα which makes the Christ (מָשַׁח יהוה אֹתִי).

(*e*) *Moral and religious Elevation.*—The ethical side of the Spirit's work comes into view in the teaching of the psalmists and prophets. In Ps 51¹¹ the Spirit is described as רוּחַ־קָדְשֶׁךָ, LXX τὸ πνεῦμά σου τὸ ἅγιον, *i.e.* the energizing principle of the divine holiness (Cheyne, *Origin of the Psalter*, p. 322 ; on the idea of 'holiness,' see Kirkpatrick, *Doctrine*, etc. p. 173 f.),—a title found again in Is 63¹⁰· ¹¹. In the Psalm this Divine Spirit of holiness is apparently regarded as imparting to the individual Israelite dispositions which may bring him nearer to the character of God, the 'clean heart'

---

* 'It is, in fact, the divine working rather than the divine nature that the Hebrew Scriptures regard as spiritual' (W. R. Smith, *Prophets of Israel*, p. 61).

† 'The Holy Spirit' is not an OT expression, and '*His*' or '*Thy* Holy Spirit' occurs only in Is 63¹⁰· ¹¹, Ps 51¹¹.

and 'steadfast spirit'; in the prophetic passage it is represented as having dwelt in the elect nation from the days of the Exodus (cf. Neh 9²⁰, Hag 2⁵), and as grieved by their rebellions against its guidance. Nor was the moral guidance of the Spirit limited to Israel, if we may adopt the common interpretation of Gn 6³, which represents the Spirit of J'' as judging, ruling, and working in men before the Flood; but the sense of יְדוֹן is uncertain (*Oxf. Heb. Lex.* p. 192), and the ethical application is at least doubtful (Delitzsch, *ad loc.*). It is certain, however, that the prophets foresee a large extension of the moral operations of the Divine Spirit in the days of the Messianic kingdom (Jer 31³¹ᶠᶠ·, Ezk 36²⁶ᶠ·), and the prophecy of Joel (2²⁸) speaks of an outpouring of the Spirit 'upon all flesh,' which, although it is conceived under the image of a general bestowment of the gift of prophecy, pointed, in St. Peter's judgment (Ac 2¹⁶ᶠ·), to the Pentecostal effusion, which brought with it the setting up of the kingdom of God in the hearts of men of all nations.

A difficulty arises from the mention in the historical books of an 'evil spirit sent by or proceeding from J''' (Jg 9²³, 1 S 16¹⁴ [כְּאַח רָּע] 18¹⁰, 1 K 22²¹ᶠ· [יֵצֵא הָרוּחַ, שֶׁקֶר 'ר'], 2 Ch 18²⁰ᶠᶠ·), and even of an 'evil spirit of God' (1 S 19⁹ LXX πνεῦμα θεοῦ πονηρόν). Schultz (*OT Theol.* ii. 205, 270) contends that the Spirit is in all cases the same, the Spirit of God working good or evil according to the character of the man on whom it operates. But it is incredible that the sacred writers intend to identify the 'good Spirit' of God (Ps 143¹⁰) with the power which inspired Saul with jealousy and the prophets of Ahab with lying words. The evil spirit is *from* God and is God's, inasmuch as it is His creature and under His control; but it is not His personal energy. As Wellhausen (on 1 S 16¹⁴) points out, the expression יהוה 'ר is apparently limited to the good Spirit, which is the operative presence of J'' Himself.

iii. 'The Spirit of God' as revealed in the OT is 'God exerting power' (A. B. Davidson on Ezk 36²⁷). On this account it is invested with personal qualities, and personal acts are ascribed to it. If the truth, mercy, and light of God are partly hypostatized by the Psalmist (Ps 43³ 57³ etc.; see Cheyne, *Origin*, etc. p. 322), the Spirit of God, the principle of life which resides in the depth of the Divine Nature, and represents the Divine presence in the world and in man, is necessarily regarded as quasi-personal; it broods, rules, speaks, guides, quickens, because it is the living energy of a personal God. The Spirit of J'' is personal, inasmuch as the Spirit is God (Ps 139⁷, Is 63⁹· ¹⁰). There is, besides, a quasi-independence ascribed to the Spirit, which approaches to a recognition of distinct personality (cf. *e.g.* Is 48¹⁶), especially in passages where the Spirit and the Word are contrasted (Schultz, ii. p. 184). But the distinction applies only to the external activities of these two divine forces; the concept of a distinction of Persons within the Being of God belongs to a later revelation.

iv. It may be asked whether a progress can be observed in the OT doctrine of the Spirit. On the one hand, certain points are clear from the first: the Pentateuch in its oldest parts reveals the Spirit of God as the source and support of the higher life in man, and as endowing him with intellectual gifts, and in particular with the gift of prophecy. All this belongs to the teaching of JE, while P adds that the Spirit at the first vitalized the cosmos. Even in pre-exilic times the Spirit is revealed as the quasi-personal energy of God in man and the world. The greatest prophet of the 8th cent. already recognizes the office of the Spirit as the Anointer of the Messiah (Is 11²ᶠᶠ·). But

as the revelation proceeds, the ethical character of the Spirit's influence on man comes more distinctly into view. The higher view of prophecy, as contrasted with mere soothsaying, appears first in Deuteronomy (see Driver on Dt 18⁹⁻²²); and it is to the period of the Exile and the days that followed it that we must probably attribute the thought of the Spirit as the regenerating and directing force in human nature, and of its operations as about to be extended to men who lay beyond the circle of kings and prophets, and beyond the fold of Israel (for the date of Ps 51, cf. W. R. Smith, *OTJC²*, p. 440; Kirkpatrick, *Psalms*, ii. p. 284; and for the date of Joel, see Driver, Camb. Bible, *Joel and Amos*, p. 11 ff.).

B. THE APOCRYPHA OF OT AND OTHER JEWISH LITERATURE.—i. In the non-canonical literature of Palestine, references to the Divine Spirit are rare, and when they occur are little else than echoes—sometimes broken and imperfect echoes—of the canonical teaching. The religious man is filled with the spirit of understanding (Sir 39⁶; cf. Is 11²); on the ungodly God sends the spirit of error (Ps-Sol 8¹⁵; cf. Is 19¹⁴). The youth Daniel, seized by righteous indignation at the miscarriage of justice in the case of Susanna, is represented as having his holy spirit (τὸ πνεῦμα τὸ ἅγιον παιδαρίου) stirred within him by the act of God, or as suddenly endowed with the spirit of wisdom by the angel of the Lord (Sus ⁴⁵, Theod., LXX). The son of David is to be mighty in the Holy Spirit (δυνατὸν ἐν πνεύματι ἁγίῳ, Ps-Sol 17⁴²); but, as the Cambridge editors of the Psalms of Solomon point out, there is in this no approach to a belief in a personal Spirit of God, although the use of τὸ πνεῦμα τὸ ἅγιον and πν. ἅγιον (first in Ps 50 [51]¹³, Is 63¹¹, LXX) is interesting as an anticipation of NT phraseology. The above list nearly exhausts the references to the Holy Spirit in the Palestinian books. The growing angelology of the Pharisees (see Edersheim, *Life and Times*, ii. p. 748) may possibly have obscured the biblical conception of the Divine Spirit as the operative force in nature and in man: thus in the Book of Enoch (60¹²ᶠ·, ed. Charles, p. 156) the powers of nature are represented as wielded by created spirits, amongst whom they have been distributed; God is the 'Lord of Spirits,' but of a ruling Spirit of God no mention is made. To the later Jews the Holy Spirit was chiefly the spirit of prophecy (Cheyne, *Origin*, p. 333); they recognized that David spake by the Holy Spirit (Mk 12³⁶), while they attributed the works of Christ to the operation of a πνεῦμα ἀκάθαρτον (Mk 3³⁰). Of the inspiration of Scripture they entertained the strongest belief; although the Torah possessed unique authority, all the books of the Canon were sacred (αἱ ἱεραὶ βίβλοι, τὰ ἱερὰ βιβλία, Josephus, Philo; see the reff. in Ryle, *Canon of the OT*, p. 291); it was realized that the prophets were taught by a divine *afflatus* (Jos. c. *Ap.* i. 8, τῶν προφητῶν τὰ μὲν ἀνώτατα καὶ παλαιότατα κατὰ τὴν ἐπίπνοιαν τὴν ἀπὸ τοῦ θεοῦ μαθόντων; cf. *Ant.* IV. vi. 5, VI. viii. 2). But when prophecy ceased, it seemed as if the presence of the Divine Spirit had been suspended or withdrawn.

ii. At Alexandria, on the other hand, the old consciousness of the perpetual activity of the Spirit of God survived, associating itself with the philosophical thought of Hellenism and growing under its influence into new forms of belief. The Book of Wisdom recalls the teaching of the OT as to the omnipresence of the Spirit (1⁷, πνεῦμα Κυρίου πεπλήρωκεν τὸν κόσμον, 12¹ τὸ γὰρ ἄφθαρτόν σου πνεῦμά ἐστιν ἐν πᾶσιν), its conservating and sustaining power in nature (1⁷ τὸ συνέχον τὰ πάντα), its special relation to man, as the author of his spiritual nature (15¹¹), and of his intellectual endowments and religious knowledge (7⁷ ἐπεκαλεσάμην καὶ ἦλθέν μοι πνεῦμα σοφίας, 9¹⁷ βουλὴν δέ σου τίς ἔγνω, εἰ μὴ σὺ ἔδωκας σοφίαν καὶ ἔπεμψας τὸ ἅγιόν σου πνεῦμα ἀπὸ ὑψίστων;). This connexion of Wisdom with the Spirit appears in the canonical books, but in Alexandrian Jewish thought it is carried further. The Spirit is sometimes identified with Wisdom (1⁵ᶠ· ἅγιον γὰρ πνεῦμα παιδείας . . . φιλάνθρωπον γὰρ πνεῦμα σοφία . . . ὅτι πνεῦμα Κυρίου, where the linking of the clauses seems to leave no doubt as to the author's meaning; cf. 9¹⁷), sometimes regarded as its indwelling power (7²²ᶠ· ἔστιν γὰρ ἐν αὐτῇ πνεῦμα νοερόν, ἅγιον, μονογενές . . . παντοδύναμον, παντεπίσκοπον). The Alexandrian doctrine of the Spirit finds its completion in Philo. The Spirit of God, he says, is ἡ ἀκήρατος σοφία ἧς πᾶς ὁ σοφὸς εἰκότως μετέχει (Gig. 5 f.). Indivisible in itself, it can be distributed and communicated like fire from torch to torch. In a sense the Spirit comes to all men, since even the worst of men have their moments of inspiration, their glimpses of better and higher things; with a few, the wisest and the best, the divine afflatus abides, and they become the 'hierophants' and instructors of their kind (Gig. 12). Philo's conception of the prophet reverts largely to the Platonic ἐνθουσιασμός (Tim. 71 D). The prophet is simply the interpreter of the divine voice, and so long as he is under divine influence he cannot exercise his reason, for he has made over the citadel of his soul to the Divine Spirit, which is in full possession of it (De spec. legg. 8, καθ᾽ ὃν χρόνον ἐνθουσιᾷ . . . μετανισταμένου μὲν τοῦ λογισμοῦ καὶ παρακεχωρηκότος τὴν μὲν ψυχῆς ἀκρόπολιν, ἐπιπεφοιτηκότος δὲ καὶ ἐνῳκηκότος τοῦ θείου πνεύματος: cf. Quis rer. div. her. 53, and other passages quoted by Sanday, Inspiration, p. 74 f.). This mechanical inspiration was shared, according to Philo, even by the Alexandrian translators of the OT (Vit. Mos. ii. 7, καθάπερ ἐνθουσιῶντες προεφήτευον). Of the ethical aspect of the Spirit's work in man, Philo has little to say, except that its function is to promote clearness of mental vision and capacity for the intellectual knowledge of God, and that it fulfils this mission either by purifying and elevating, or, as in the case of the prophet, by superseding the natural faculties. Of the Spirit as restoring the moral nature of man we hear nothing; the writings of Philo contain no reference to Ps 51¹⁰ᶠ· or Ezk 36²⁶ (cf. Ryle, Philo and Holy Scripture, p. 291 ff.). The omission may be partly due to the circumstance that he employs himself chiefly about the Pentateuch, but it is more probably to be traced to the predominance of the intellectual interest in Alexandrian thought.

C. THE NEW TESTAMENT.—i. The NT adopts the phrases used in reference to the Divine Spirit by the Greek translators of the OT. Thus we find in the NT as in the OT the terms τὸ πνεῦμα τὸ ἅγιον (πνεῦμα ἅγιον), τὸ πνεῦμα τοῦ θεοῦ, or πνεῦμα θεοῦ, πν. Κυρίου, or simply τὸ πνεῦμα, or in certain contexts the anarthrous πνεῦμα. But they are used in quite different proportions: thus τὸ πνεῦμα τὸ ἅγιον (πν. ἅγ.), found in the Greek OT only in Ps 51 and Is 63, occurs in the NT between 80 and 90 times, while τὸ πνεῦμα τοῦ θεοῦ (πν. θεοῦ, Κυρίου), the normal expression in the LXX, is comparatively rare in NT. Moreover, the writers of the NT employ phrases which are unknown to the LXX; the Spirit of God is further defined as the 'Spirit of the Father' (Mt 10²⁰), 'the Spirit of his Son' (Gal 4⁶), the 'Spirit of Jesus' or 'of Christ' (Ac 16⁷, Ro 8⁹, Ph 1¹⁹, 1 P 1¹¹). In a few instances the plural is used to denote the various gifts or μερισμοί (He 2⁴) of the one Spirit; e.g. 1 Co 14³², Rev 1⁴ 4⁵ 5⁶ 22⁶. New attributes are assigned to the Spirit, corresponding to new gifts bestowed upon men; we read not only of the spirit of wisdom (Ac 6³· ¹⁰), but of the spirit of truth (Jn 14¹⁷ 15²⁶ 16¹³), of life (Ro 8²), of grace (He 10²⁹), of sonship (τῆς υἱοθεσίας, Ro 8¹⁵). Above

all, the Spirit receives a personal name, which it shares with the Son of God in His historical manifestation (Jn 14¹⁶ ἄλλον παράκλητον; 14²⁶ 15²⁶ 16⁷ ὁ παράκλητος). These facts warn us that in passing from OT to NT we may expect a fuller theology of the Spirit.

ii. The new light which is thrown upon the subject by the Christian revelation is largely historical. (a) The gospel history opens with an outburst of prophecy. As the moment of the Incarnation drew near, men and women in Israel found themselves lifted up by the Spirit into new regions of thought and endowed with new powers of expression. The movement began in the family of a priest. A child was born of whom it was foretold that he should 'be filled with the Holy Spirit from his mother's womb' (Lk 1¹⁵· ⁸⁰); and the inspiration was shared by his parents (Lk 1⁴¹· ⁶⁷). Others were touched by the same current of divine energy—Simeon, to whom there came an oracular warning from the Holy Spirit of the presence of the infant Christ (Lk 2²⁵ᶠ· πνεῦμα ἦν ἅγιον ἐπ᾽ αὐτόν, καὶ ἦν αὐτῷ κεχρηματισμένον ὑπὸ τοῦ πνεύματος, κ.τ.λ.); Hannah, the daughter of Phanuel, who was accounted a prophetess (προφῆτις, Lk 2³⁶). Such a revival of prophetic gifts had not occurred since the days of Ezra and Nehemiah; even the Maccabæan age had looked for it in vain (1 Mac 4⁴⁶ 14⁴¹).

(b) The new prophecy proclaimed the advent of the Messiah, partly preparing His way, partly welcoming and announcing Him when He came. But the chief outpouring of the Spirit was on the Messiah Himself. It fulfilled itself in two miraculous events—the Conception and the Baptism; the first introductory to the human life of the Christ, the second to His ministry and Messianic work.

(α) Two Gospels relate in independent yet not inconsistent narratives the miracle of the Conception and Virgin Birth (see Gore, Dissertations, p. 36 f.). In both it is ascribed to the Holy Spirit (Lk 1³⁵, Mt 1¹⁸· ²⁰). Both contexts are conceived in the spirit of the OT and belong to the earliest age of Christianity, when the fullest teaching of the gospel had not yet been assimilated. We shall therefore probably be right in interpreting πνεῦμα ἅγιον here in its OT sense, as the power of God in active exercise, although we may believe that the Church has rightly identified this power with the personal Holy Ghost revealed by Christ. It is not without significance that in both Gospels the power which wrought the Conception is described as πνεῦμα ἅγιον rather than as πνεῦμα θεοῦ or Κυρίου. The Holy Spirit sanctified the Flesh which it united with the Word (Lk 1³⁵ διὸ καὶ τὸ γεννώμενον ἅγιον κληθήσεται). Not only was 'the new departure in human life,' which began with the birth of the Second Adam (Gore, Diss. p. 65), fitly preceded by a directly creative act, but the new humanity was consecrated at the moment of its conception by the overshadowing of the Divine Spirit. The Conception was therefore truly 'immaculate'; that which was conceived, although true flesh, was free from the taint of human corruption. It is worth while to notice, in passing, that the Gospels do not hint at an immaculate conception of the mother of the Lord; the special illapse of the Spirit is limited, so far as we can learn, to the conception of her Son. (On the miraculous conception as an article of the Christian faith the reader may consult Pearson, On the Creed, art. iii., and, on the early history of the doctrine, the present writer's Apostles' Creed, iv.).

(β) The Holy Spirit did not leave the sacred humanity which it had sanctified in the moment of conception; the childhood of Jesus was filled with a strength and wisdom which were the marks of a special grace (Lk 2⁴⁰ τὸ δὲ παιδίον . . ἐκραταιοῦτο πληρούμενον σοφίᾳ, καὶ χάρις θεοῦ ἦν ἐπ' αὐτό; cf. v.[52]). But in or about His thirtieth year (ἦν . . ὡσεὶ ἐτῶν τριάκοντα) a stage was reached when a new illapse of the Spirit on the Second Adam became necessary. The first had sanctified His humanity, the second was to consecrate His official life. It came in connexion with the baptism of John. With the majority of the religious Israelites of His generation, Jesus went to be baptized. As He rose from the Jordan, the sign was given by which the Baptist knew Him to be the Messiah (Jn 1[33]); John saw the Spirit descend in the form of a dove and rest upon Him. Mr. F. C. Conybeare (*Expositor*, IV. ix. p. 455) cites Philo to show that the dove was the accepted symbol in Alexandrian thought of the divine reason or wisdom, and concludes that the evangelists have converted a metaphor into a fact. But the evangelists—the Synoptists in any case—were strangers to Alexandrian symbolism, and they limit themselves to what they believed to be matters of fact. In this case the fact depends on the eye-witness of the Baptist, attested by his disciple, St. John. The evangelists, however, guard against the impression that the Spirit assumed a material form (Mt ὡσεὶ περιστεράν, Mk, Lk, Jn ὡς π.); even St. Luke's σωματικῷ εἴδει does not involve this inference. The appearance, whether real or subjective, was doubtless symbolical, but the symbol rests on the OT. It carries our thoughts back to the birdlike motion attributed to the Spirit in Gn 1[2]. At the baptism of Jesus the Spirit of God brooded a second time over the waters, to vivify a new creation by resting on the new Head of mankind. If the symbolism of the dove is to be pressed, it may be taken to indicate the character of the Lord's ministry and of the kingdom of heaven (Mt 10[16]).

The illapse at the baptism was regarded by the first generation as the anointing of the Christ (Ac 10[38] ἔχρισεν αὐτὸν ὁ θεὸς πνεύματι ἁγίῳ καὶ δυνάμει). In the historical books of the OT חָשַׁם, LXX ὁ χριστός, is the title of the priest (Lv 4[3. 5. 16] 6[15]), and the king (1 S 12[3] etc.), who were admitted to their respective offices by the ceremony of unction. In the Psalms and Prophets the title is specially given to the Davidic king (Ps 2[2] 17[54] 19[6] etc.), or to a king raised up by God for a certain work (Is 45[1] τῷ χριστῷ μου Κύρῳ), or to Israel regarded as the servant of the Lord, or to a prophet who speaks in His name (Is 61[1]). But when the form of the Second David took shape in the inspired thought of the Prophet and the expectations of the Jewish people, it was to the future king of Israel that the name was usually applied. The Psalms of Solomon already speak of 'the Lord Christ' (17[36] 18[tit.], see Ryle and James, note on 17[36]), and the Gospels show that at the time of the advent the Christ was expected both by Jews (*e.g.* Jn 1[20]) and Samaritans (Jn 4[25]). The Jewish Messiah, however, was chiefly the anointed king; the conception of Messiah as the Prophet was less distinct, and that of a Christ-Priest (ἱερεὺς ὁ χριστός, Lv 4[5. 10] 6[22]) entirely wanting, until it presented itself to the writer of the Epistle to the Hebrews (Stanton, *Jewish and Christian Messiah*, p. 293 ff.). Yet the Church has rightly seen that the work to which the Messiah was anointed was sacerdotal and prophetic as well as regal. The baptism, with the descent of the Spirit, was the consecration of Jesus to the Messianic office in all the fulness of its functions and powers. Some of the Fathers find the moment of the Messianic unction in the miraculous conception (so Gregory of Nazianzus expounds Ps 45[7], and see Aug. *De Trin.* xv. 46, cited by Mason, *Baptism and Confirmation*, p. 94), but the earlier interpretation fixes upon the Baptism: see Iren. III. ix. 3, 'Verbum Dei . . qui est Jesus . . qui et assumpsit carnem et unctus est a Patre Spiritu,

Jesus Christus factus est'; cf. Jerome on Is 61.[*] The Gnostic schools exaggerated the importance of the Baptism, confusing the descending Spirit with the pre-existent Christ and ignoring the miraculous Conception. But if the Incarnate life began with the overshadowing of Mary, the official Messianic life dates from the Baptism (cf. Pearson, art. ii.). (γ) From that moment Jesus began His Christ-work (Lk 3[23] ἦν Ἰ. ἀρχόμενος), and in the oldest record of the ministry it is regarded as the ἀρχὴ εὐαγγελίου (Mk 1[1. 9]). Henceforth His life is full of the manifested workings of the Spirit, in whose energy the evangelists find the source of the teaching, miracles, and entire ministry of the Christ (Mk 1[12], Lk 4[1. 14], Mt 12[28], Ac 1[2]). Some of these revealed relations between the Holy Spirit and the ministry of Christ are of special interest. Immediately after the baptism the Spirit impelled Him to meet the Tempter in the wilderness (Mt, ἀνήχθη ὑπὸ τοῦ πνεύματος; Mk, τὸ πνεῦμα αὐτὸν ἐκβάλλει). The conquest of evil being at once the first responsibility of the Second Adam, and the first step in the redemption of the race, it was the first work of the Spirit in the Christ. The Spirit of God in man was shown to be the power by which the spirit of evil is to be overcome: 'every victory won' is 'His alone.' To the Holy Spirit also our Lord attributes His power to cast out unclean spirits from the possessed (Mt 12[28]). We may extend the saying to His other miracles (cf. Jn 14[10] ὁ δὲ πατὴρ ἐν ἐμοὶ μένων [*i.e.* by the Spirit] ποιεῖ τὰ ἔργα αὐτοῦ). When in the 5th cent. Nestorius unduly pressed this point, Cyril of Alexandria guarded the doctrine of the Incarnation by insisting that the Spirit by which Christ wrought was His own, and not an imparted power, foreign to His personal life (*Anath.* 9). Nevertheless, the truth remains that the Spirit, who is one with the Son in the Divine Unity, was imparted to His humanity, and strengthened it with supernatural power. The same is true of Christ's teaching; the Lord Himself ascribes it to the anointing Spirit (Lk 4[18f.]). As the supreme prophet He spoke in the power of the Spirit, not at intervals as other prophets, but whenever He opened His lips to teach. Yet behind the human faculties which were guided by the Spirit, was the eternal Word in personal fellowship with the Father; His formula is not that of the old prophets, 'Thus saith the Lord,' but one which expressed personal authority, 'Verily I say unto you.'

(c) The Spirit descended on the Second Adam to abide (Jn 1[32. 33]; contrast Gn 6[3] LXX). The illapse was not a momentary act, but a new departure in human life, the beginning of a permanent indwelling of the Spirit in man. The 'Gospel of the Hebrews' has rightly seized upon this point: 'descendit fons omnis spiritus sancti et requievit super eum et dixit illi: Fili mi, in omnibus prophetis expectabam te ut venires et requiescerem in te; tu es enim requies mea.' But the Baptist's testimony reaches further. The Spirit became immanent in the Sacred Humanity, that it might be communicated through the Christ to mankind. Jesus was baptized with the Spirit, that He might baptize the world therewith (Jn 1[33]; cf. Mt 3[11], Mk 1[8], Lk 3[16]). The experience of the first generation of believers showed that this hope was realized; Christians shared Christ's unction (1 Jn 2[20]), and the unction abode in them, as it abode in Christ (v.[27]). This conviction was expressed in the early use of unction in connexion with Christian baptism (Tert. *De bapt.* 7; Cypr. *Ep.* 70; Cyr. Hier. *Cat. myst.* ii.).

Two historical events mark the extension

* Pearson points out that the two views are not necessarily inconsistent, referring to the double unction received by David (1 S 16[13], 2 S 2[4], 5[3]).

of the Messianic unction to the Church. (a) On the night that followed the Resurrection Christ communicated the Spirit to the apostles (Jn 20²² ἐνεφύσησεν καὶ λέγει αὐτοῖς Λάβετε πνεῦμα ἅγιον). The act which accompanied the gift clearly looks back to Gn 2⁷; a new spirit was breathed into humanity by the risen Lord. He began with the apostles, quickening them by communicating His own Spirit, that they might be prepared to carry on His work (καθὼς ἀπέσταλκέν με ὁ πατήρ, κἀγὼ πέμπω ὑμᾶς). The gift 'answers to the power of the Resurrection' (Westcott, citing Godet): it is primarily the quickening of the spiritual life of the apostles, but it is conferred with special reference to the work which lies before them. There is therefore no necessity to interpret λάβετε as if it were λήμψεσθε (Theodore of Mopsuestia), and to refer it to the Pentecostal effusion. The apostles received on Easter night the first-fruits of the new life of the Spirit secured to the Church by the Lord's Resurrection, and were thus consecrated and endowed for their great ministry. Their successors were, potentially at least, included in the gift, and the Western Church of the Middle Ages rightly saw in the words *Accipite Spiritum sanctum* the promise of all ministerial power (Hooker, *Eccles. Pol.* v. lxxvii. 5).

(β) If the Resurrection brought the quickening power of the Spirit to the Eleven and to those who should succeed them in the ministry of the word, the Ascension was followed by the outpouring of the fulness of the Spirit on the Church (Ac 1⁵·⁸ 2¹ff·). As at the baptism of the Christ and the consecration of the apostles, the descent of the Spirit was accompanied by external signs. The dove did not reappear, nor was the breath of Christ felt, but the sound of a great gale (ἦχος ὥσπερ φερομένης πνοῆς βιαίας) fell upon the ear, and tongues of flame, darting hither and thither and finally resting on the heads of all, appealed to the eye. The symbolism of the wind had been explained by our Lord (Jn 3⁷·⁸); the fire would remind the apostles of the prediction of the Baptist (Mt 3¹¹ etc.). Every detail had its significance. The sound of the rushing wind seemed to fill the house, for the new life was to permeate the whole world. The tongues of fire were self-distributing, and none was left without his portion, for the Spirit divideth to every man as He wills (1 Co 12¹¹), and all believers are made to drink of the same Fountain (*ib.* ¹³). The gift was at once collective and individual; it was for the whole body, and for each member.

Both from the promise of Christ and from the event, it is clear that the Pentecostal gift marked the beginning of a new era in the history of the Spirit's relations to mankind. The 'dispensation of the Spirit,' which began at the Pentecost after the Crucifixion, was so great an advance on all earlier manifestations that St. John does not hesitate to deny that there had been any gift of the Spirit before it (Jn 7³⁹ οὔπω γὰρ ἦν πνεῦμα: see Westcott *ad loc.*, and cf. Ac 19²). The new manifestation differed from the old, not in degree only, but in kind; before the Incarnation the Spirit had no abiding place in man; since Pentecost the presence of the Spirit is immanent in the Church (Jn 14¹⁶; cf. Cyril. Alex. on Jn 7³⁹ τὴν ὁλοσχερῆ καὶ ὁλόκληρον κατοίκησιν ἐν ἀνθρώποις τοῦ ἁγίου πνεύματος σημαίνειν αὐτὸν ὑποτοπήσωμεν). The coming of the Spirit corresponds to the coming of the Son, *mutatis mutandis*. The Son came to unite Himself to human nature, the Spirit came to inhabit it. The Son came to tabernacle amongst men, the Spirit to dwell in them. But with each coming a divine mission began which marks a new departure in God's dealings with mankind.

(γ) The coming of the Spirit, like the coming of the Son, manifested itself at first by supernatural signs. To regard the gifts of tongues as unhistorical (Zeller, Weizsäcker), is permissible only to those who deny the possibility of the miraculous. That the fact is recorded by so careful a historian as Luke, writing within half a century of the event, and with opportunities of investigating the truth of the story which reached back at least twenty years further, may lead us to hesitate before we assent to these views. The γλωσσολαλία of Ac 2 may have been, like the wind and the fire, rather a sign of the Spirit's coming and a symbol of His work, than a gift intended to supersede the acquirement of foreign tongues, or even an actual assistance to the apostles in their subsequent preaching. But if we may trust the primitive fragment appended to St. Mark's Gospel, the Lord Himself had promised His disciples some manifestation of this kind ('Mk' 16¹⁷); and one of St. Paul's undoubted Epistles leaves no doubt that some form of the manifestation existed in the Church of Corinth (1 Co 12²⁸ 13¹·³ 14²ff·). Further, we have the witness of Irenæus (ap. Eus. *HE* v. 7) that he had himself heard the gift exercised in its Pentecostal form (πολλῶν ἀκούομεν ἀδελφῶν . . παντοδαπαῖς λαλούντων διὰ τοῦ πνεύματος γλώσσαις). The gift was, however, singularly open to abuse, and St. Paul seems to have felt that it had nearly fulfilled its purpose, and might soon disappear (1 Co 13⁸). Prophecy, another Pentecostal gift, if less novel and impressive, fills a larger place in the early history of the Church. On the day of Pentecost, St. Peter claimed that the words in which Joel foretold a great revival and extension of prophecy in the latter days had been fulfilled by the coming of the Spirit (Ac 2¹⁶ᶠ·). Prophets accordingly arose in the Apostolic Church (Ac 11²⁷ 13¹ 15³² 19⁶ 21⁹), and took rank next after apostles (1 Co 12²⁸, Eph 2²⁰ 3⁵ 4¹¹), in some localities surviving as an order into the second or third generation (*Didache*, 10–13). The new prophecy surpassed in St. Paul's esteem all other spiritual gifts, because of its ethical value (1 Co 14¹·³·⁴). The NT prophet was the inspired teacher of the first age: if he left no literary remains which can be compared with the writings of the Hebrew prophets, it is difficult to exaggerate his importance in the infancy of the Church, when the local bishops or presbyters were as yet but little qualified to instruct their congregations in the mystery of the gospel, and the apostles' writings were as yet incomplete or imperfectly circulated. But the institution, as St. Paul saw (1 Co 13⁸), lacked permanence, and it was gradually superseded, notwithstanding the Montanist reaction, by the local ministry, strengthened by the growth of the Episcopate.

One invaluable monument of the spiritual gifts of the first generation has survived to our own time. It was promised that the Holy Spirit should bring to the remembrance of the apostles the words and acts of Christ, and that He should lead them into the whole cycle of Christian truth. The Gospels witness to the fulfilment of the first of these promises; the Acts, Epistles, and Apocalypse correspond to the second. The literature of the first generation, preserved in the Canon of the NT, bears the impress of an inspiration which we miss when we pass to the Epistles of Clement and 'Barnabas.' It is a standing proof of the reality of the miracle of Pentecost that the first age of the Church should have produced a series of writings which, in the elevation of their spiritual tone and the fruitfulness of their teaching, remain absolutely alone. Side by side with this monument of the Spirit's work must be placed another—the Christian Society, or Catholic Church. As the idea of the Church rose before the mind of St. Paul, he saw in its external form a body which the Spirit of God animated and made one (1 Co 12¹³, Eph 4⁴). History has proved his words true. The vitality of the greatest and oldest community in the world witnesses to the divine power which brought it into being. The Church on her part has marked her sense of her dependence on the Spirit by the order of her creed : she believes in her own permanence and life, because she believes in the Holy Ghost. *Credo . . in Spiritum sanctum, sanctam Ecclesiam.*

iii. We turn now from the historical facts connected with the coming of the Spirit to the teaching of Christ and the apostles in reference to the nature and work of the Holy Spirit.

(*a*) (*a*) With one conspicuous exception, hereafter to be stated, the teaching of Christ upon this subject, so far as it is reported by the Synoptists, goes but a little way beyond that of the OT. He recognizes the inspiration of the OT Scriptures (Mt 22⁴³, Mk 12³⁶, Lk 24²⁵ᶠ·⁴⁴) and His own Messianic unction (Lk 4¹⁸, Mt 12²⁸) ; to ascribe His works to Beelzebul is to blaspheme the Spirit, and therefore to commit an 'eternal sin' (Mk 3²⁹). This saying, viewed in the light of its context (Mt 12³²), attributes Deity to the Holy Spirit, but does not on that account exceed the limits of the OT revelation (see above, p. 404). Occasionally, the Synoptic Gospels represent our Lord as looking forward to a fuller coming of the Spirit. The apostles will be inspired to defend themselves before the world (Mt 10²⁰) ; nay, the Holy Spirit will be given by the Father in heaven to all who ask Him for the gift (Lk 11¹³). A remarkable reading in St. Luke's recension of the Lord's Prayer gives the petition, ἐλθέτω τὸ ἅγιον πνεῦμά σου ἐφ᾽ ἡμᾶς καὶ καθαρισάτω ἡμᾶς (Chase, *The Lord's Prayer*, etc., 24 f. ; Resch, *Agrapha*, p. 398) ; but it is valuable only as showing the interpretation which the Church put upon the opening clauses of the Prayer.

(*β*) The Fourth Gospel, however, relates a series of conversations running through the course of our Lord's ministry, which reveal entirely new views of the Spirit's relation to the individual life, to the Church, and to God. The conversation with Nicodemus (Jn 3⁵⁻⁸) asserts the principle of the new birth, tracing the beginnings of the spiritual life in men to the Spirit of God, and apparently connecting the birth of the Spirit with the future sacrament of Christian baptism. Similarly, the discourse of Jn 6 speaks of the spiritual food of the new life, which was to be imparted in the mystery of Christ's body and blood. In the conversation with the woman of Samaria (Jn 4¹⁰), and the proclamation at the Feast of Tabernacles (Jn 7³⁷ᶠ·), the Lord directs attention to Himself as the Fountain of the Spirit, from which believers should continually receive, and in turn communicate, fresh supplies of the water of life. The language is mystical, but the evangelist was able after the event to find its fulfilment in the dispensation of the Spirit (Jn 7³⁹, Rev 22¹⁷). But the fullest and clearest revelation was reserved for the last discourse on the night before the Passion (Jn 14¹⁶·¹⁷·²⁶ 15²⁶ 16⁷·¹³). It opens with the promise, 'I will pray the Father, and He shall give you another Paraclete, to be with you for ever, the Spirit of truth' (cf. v.²⁶ ὁ δὲ παράκλητος, τὸ πνεῦμα τὸ ἅγιον, where the identification is complete). The Holy Spirit, then, was to be Christ's substitute and representative on earth, a *vicaria vis* (Tertullian, *Præscr.* 13) ; and the work assigned to Him is that of an advocate (on παράκλητος see Westcott's detached note, and Lightfoot's early work, *On a Fresh Revision of the NT*², p. 50 f.). No function more characteristic of personal life could have been attributed, and Christ speaks accordingly of the Spirit as ὁ παράκλητος, not as τὸ παράκλητον,—a choice of gender which is emphasized by the repeated use of the masculine pronoun (ἐκεῖνος μαρτυρήσει . . ἐκεῖνος ἐλέγξει . . . ἐκεῖνος ἐμὲ δοξάσει.) But the personality of the Deputy is in fact essential to the Lord's

reasoning ; no impersonal influence could supply the lack of personal guidance and probation which the apostles would feel when the Lord was taken from them.* It is therefore futile to compare His mode of speaking in this passage with the prosopopœia by which in the OT and Apocrypha the wisdom of God is described as a personal (female) agent. Further, it cannot be maintained that Christ is speaking in Jn 14–16 merely of a new operation of divine power in man (cf. Ps 139⁷), or of His own Spirit as perpetuating itself in the lives of His disciples. For He proceeds to distinguish the coming Paraclete both from the Father and from Himself : 'the Father will give you another Paraclete . . . the Father will send [him] in my name . . . I will send him from the Father . . . the Spirit of truth which proceedeth from the Father.' The differentiation is perfect ; the Spirit is not the Father, nor is He the Son ; as a Person, He is distinct from both. Again, we are permitted to learn something as to His relation to both. He is sent by both, but He is sent by the Son from the Father ; He proceeds from the Father (παρὰ τοῦ πατρός). Although this is scarcely equivalent to the ecclesiastical phrase ἐκ τοῦ πατρός (see Westcott, *ad loc.*, and on the origin of the later phrase, cf. Hort, *Two Dissertations*, p. 86 f.), the words used by Christ teach implicitly that the Spirit possesses an eternal relation with the Father upon which His temporal mission rests (cf. Jn 16²⁷·²⁸ with 1¹⁴, and Westcott's notes).

The Lord proceeds in the same great discourse to shadow forth the work to which the new Paraclete was about to be sent. His mission would be primarily to the disciples and the Church (Jn 14¹⁶·¹⁷), in the way of fellowship (μεθ᾽ ὑμῶν), presence (παρ᾽ ὑμῖν), and indwelling (ἐν ὑμῖν) ; and this threefold relation was to be permanent (εἰς τὸν αἰῶνα), not, as Christ's historical manifestation, transient (Westcott). His functions would be (1) to carry on the teaching work of Christ, partly by quickening the memories of Christ's immediate followers (Jn 14²⁶), partly by guiding them into new truth, till all had been learnt (Jn 14²⁶ 16¹³), and revealing the new order (Jn 16¹³ τὰ ἐρχόμενα ἀναγγελεῖ ὑμῖν) ; (2) to glorify the Son, as the Son glorifies the Father, by revealing the Son to the Church in the fulness of the divine life (Jn 16¹⁴·¹⁵). But the Spirit would also have a mission to the world, although it could not discern or recognize Him (14¹⁷ οὐ θεωρεῖ αὐτὸ οὐδὲ γινώσκει). He would co-operate with the Church in bearing witness to Christ (Jn 15²⁶·²⁷), and His witness would carry the force of an irresistible conviction (Jn 16⁸ ἐλέγξει τὸν κόσμον) concerning the great facts of human sin, divine righteousness, and the process of judgment by which, from the Advent onwards, the victory of righteousness is being determined.

(*γ*) The crowning revelation followed the Resurrection, and is recorded by St. Matthew alone (28¹⁹). The disciples had been taught that the Divine Spirit is a living Person, and that He is not to be identified with either the Father or the Son. From the formula of baptism they now learnt that the three Persons are comprehended under One Name ; the Spirit is one with the Father and the Son in the Unity of the Divine Life. The words justify the place which has been assigned to the Holy Ghost in the creeds and the worship of the universal Church (Basil, *Ep.* ii. 125, δεῖ γὰρ ἡμᾶς

* When Beyschlag (*NT Theology*, Eng. tr. ii. p. 279) writes, 'The notion of the Holy Spirit as a third Divine personality . . . is one of the most disastrous importations into the Holy Scriptures,' he assumes that this idea has been imported, and that his own construction of the Lord's words ('just a pictorial personification') is convincing and even necessary. Against these assumptions must be set (1) the plain and natural interpretation of Christ's words, and (2) the judgment of the Christian Society, in which, according to Christ's promise, the Spirit dwells.

βαπτίζεσθαι μὲν ὡς παρελάβομεν, πιστεύειν δὲ ὡς βαπτιζό-μεθα, δοξάζειν δὲ ὡς πεπιστεύκαμεν). But they also foretell the new relation which under the gospel was to subsist between the human spirit and the Spirit of God. To be baptized 'into the Name . . . of the Holy Ghost' is to be placed in a position of lifelong dependence upon the Divine Spirit, and consecration to the service which He inspires.

(b) From the moment of the Pentecostal descent the presence of the Paraclete entered as a fact into the daily life of the Christian society. (a) The apostles realized at once that the promise of Christ had been fulfilled, and that a new dispensation had begun (Ac 2³³· ³⁸ᶠ·). As the years went on, they were able to interpret from their own experience the details of Christ's teaching (Ac 5³², 1 Jn 5⁶ with Jn 15²⁶; Ac 9³¹ with Jn 14¹⁶; 1 P 4¹⁴, Ja 4⁵ with Jn 14¹⁶· ¹⁷). They realized that as apostles they were specially endowed with the Spirit of God; to practise a deception upon them in their apostolic character was to attempt to deceive the Holy Spirit, and therefore to lie to God (Ac 5³· ⁴· ⁹); when they and other officers of the Church took counsel on matters of discipline, the Holy Spirit shared their deliberations and their judgment (Ac 15²⁵); to them, as apostles, belonged the power of imparting the Holy Spirit to the baptized by the laying on of their hands (Ac 8¹⁵ᶠ· 19⁶, cf. He 6²); individually, they were conscious of receiving direct communications from the Holy Spirit (Ac 11¹² 13² 16⁶· ⁷). But they recognized also that the gift belonged to the whole Church and to every member of it (Ac 2²⁸ 10⁴⁴⁻⁴⁷ 11¹⁵· ¹⁶ 13⁵² 15⁸· ⁹). This fact was evidenced, not merely by miraculous manifestations (Ac 10⁴⁶ 19⁶), but by the new life of the Christian brotherhood. Miracles might have chiefly attracted attention in the first days, but even then the practical wisdom and joyful spirit of the common Christian life were seen to be fruits of the Spirit of Christ (Ac 6³ 13⁵²); and the maturer experience of the Apostolic Church realized that the Holy Spirit is the source of Christian holiness (1 P 1²), the inspirer of prayer (Jude ²⁰), the means of an abiding union between Christ and Christians (1 Jn 3²⁴ 4¹²), the pledge of future glory in the presence of God (1 P 4¹⁴).

(β) It is, however, to the Epistles of St. Paul that we must turn for the fullest treatment which the doctrine of the Spirit receives within the limits of the NT. Not that St. Paul sets himself to construct a philosophy of religion in which the relation of the Holy Spirit to God, to the Church, and to the human soul receives scientific treatment. He treats the whole subject incidentally and in connexion with his argument, or with the practical interests of the communities he is addressing. But he treats it with an insight, a freshness, and a precision due partly to his unique experience, partly to the intensity of his interest in the gospel and its workings upon human nature. There is a manifest progress in the apostle's handling of this subject which corresponds to the progress in his own life and work. In the earliest group of Epistles (1 and 2 Th) he scarcely exceeds the usual teaching of the first generation. He connects the gift of the Holy Spirit with spiritual power (1 Th 1⁵) and joy (v.⁶), with moral purity (1 Th 4⁸) and religious consecration (2 Th 2¹³); he offers practical guidance in reference to the miraculous χαρίσματα, warning believers against indiscriminately accepting all prophetic utterances on the one hand, and despising them all upon the other, and thus quenching the heavenly fire (1 Th 5¹⁹ᶠ·, cf. 2 Th 2²). One interesting verse shows that he recognized in human nature an element corresponding to the Divine Spirit, and fitted to be the sphere of His operations (1 Th 5²³ ὑμῶν τὸ πνεῦμα). The next group of letters (Ro, 1, 2 Co, Gal) carries us into

the heart of his teaching on this subject, and we find ourselves in the midst of what is largely a new revelation. In these Epistles, St. Paul, starting with his conception of the human spirit (Ro 1⁹, 1 Co 2¹¹, Gal 6¹⁸), sometimes places the Spirit of God in sharp contrast with the spirit of man, whilst in other places he exhibits the two in close correspondence and co-operation. Instances of the former point of view will be found in Ro 8¹⁶· ²⁶, 1 Co l.c., Gal 4⁶. In such passages the distinct personality of the Divine Spirit comes strongly into view; the Spirit of God bears witness with the spirits of men (Ro 8²⁶), helps our infirmity, and makes entreaty for us with sighs too deep for words (ὑπερεντυγχάνει στεναγμοῖς ἀλαλήτοις, Ro 8²⁶), calling from the depth of our hearts upon the Father (Gal 4⁶, cf. Ro 8¹⁵); while at the same time He abides within the life of God, searching the depths of the Divine Nature and counsels, even as the human spirit is privy to the inmost thoughts of man (1 Co 2¹¹). The Spirit of God is, from St. Paul's point of view, uncreated and divine, for it is internal to the Essence of God. Where the Spirit dwells and works, God dwells and works (1 Co 3¹⁶ 6¹⁹, 2 Co 3¹⁶); it is by the Spirit that God is immanent in men. Yet the identification is not so complete as to exclude a true distinction between the Spirit and other Persons in God. The Holy Ghost is the Spirit of Him that raised up Christ from the dead (Ro 8¹¹), i.e. the Father; He is also the Spirit of Christ (Ro 8⁷), not merely because He anointed the Messiah, but on account of His personal relation to the Son of God (Gal 4⁶); He is the Spirit of the Son. Lastly, the three Persons are named in the same sentence as distinct hypostases (2 Co 13¹⁴). In a few passages the Spirit of Christ in St. Paul appears to mean either our Lord's human spirit (Ro 1⁴ κατὰ πνεῦμα ἁγιωσύνης: see Sanday-Headlam, ad loc., and Westcott on Jn 9¹⁴), or His pre-existent nature (2 Co 3¹⁷ ὁ δὲ κύριος τὸ πνεῦμά ἐστιν), or His risen life (1 Co 15⁴⁸ ὁ ἔσχατος Ἀδὰμ [ἐγένετο] εἰς πνεῦμα ζωοποιοῦν); in other contexts the Holy Spirit is identified with Christ, because it is through the Spirit that the ascended Lord dwells in the Church and operates in believers (Ro 8⁹· ¹⁰). But the ambiguity rarely occurs; in the great majority of cases the distinctness of the Persons is clearly seen, and the reader can discriminate between the spiritual nature of Christ, and the Spirit who anointed Him and is one with Him in the unity of God.

But by far the larger number of St. Paul's references to the Spirit in these Epistles are concerned with His operations on the spirit of man. Living in an age of physical manifestations, the apostle does not ignore the miraculous gifts (Ro 12⁶ 15¹⁸· ¹⁹, 1 Co 12. 14, Gal 3⁵), and in one place (1 Co l.c.) he treats of these at length; they, too, are χαρίσματα (Ro 1¹¹ 12⁶, 1 Co 1⁷, cf. Lightfoot, Notes, etc. p. 148 f.), but not the chiefest or best (1 Co 12³¹ 13¹), or the most abiding. The permanent results of the Spirit's coming are faith, hope, and love (1 Co 13¹³); its normal fruits are the virtues which make up the fulness of the Christian life (Gal 5²²· ²³). The Holy Spirit consecrates even the human body which has received the sacramental pledges of His presence, and has thus become the temple of God (1 Co 3¹⁶ 6¹⁹); and He will hereafter raise it up in the likeness of Christ's resurrection (Ro 8¹¹), a spiritual body (1 Co 15⁴²⁻⁴⁴), not liable to corruption or death. But His special sphere is the human spirit. Here His indwelling already works a new life, answering to the life of the Risen Christ (Ro 8² 10¹³). This life of the Spirit in man is pre-eminently a life of sonship towards God; those who follow it possess the privileges of sons in the divine family (Ro 8¹⁴); they are joint heirs of the Heir of all things

(Ro 8[17], cf. Mt 21[38], He 1[2]), brethren of the First-born of God (Ro 8[29]). If the sonship is secured by the Incarnation and the Resurrection, it is manifested and sealed by the gift of the Spirit, who is the πνεῦμα υἱοθεσίας (Ro 8[15. 16], Gal 4[4-6]). He creates in the adopted sons a character corresponding to their new relation to God and to Christ (Ro 8[29. 30]), by a renewal of the mind which works a transformation in their lives (Ro 12[2] μεταμορφοῦσθε τῇ ἀνακαινώσει τοῦ νοός), and has the effect of engraving the divine will, once written on tables of stone, upon hearts of flesh which will retain the impression and translate it into human life (2 Co 3[3]). Yet all these operations of the Spirit are but the foretaste of greater things to come. The gift of the Spirit already received by the Church is the ἀπαρχή (Ro 8[23])—the first-fruits of the harvest yet to be reaped; the present indwelling of the Spirit in the heart is the ἀρραβών (2 Co 1[22] 5[5])—the first instalment of the fuller life, and the earnest that it is to follow (on the word ἀρρ. see Lightfoot, *Notes*, p. 323). Of the Spirit's future work the resurrection of the body will form a true part, for the reanimation of man's physical nature is at once a proper function of the 'Giver of life' (Ro 8[12]), and the manifestation of our adoption into the divine family (Ro 8[3]). But the resurrection itself is but a fresh departure in the history of the race; beyond it there lies an immeasurable life of progress unfettered by sin and death, 'the liberty of the glory of the sons of God' (Ro 8[21]); and of this also St. Paul regards the Holy Spirit as the motive power.

In some of these contexts it is not easy to determine whether by πνεῦμα the apostle means the Spirit of God in man, or the spirit of man under the influence of the Spirit of God. The question arises especially in passages which contrast the Spirit with the flesh (Ro 8[4f.], Gal 5[16]). The σάρξ is human nature on its weak and mortal side; is then the πνεῦμα, which is opposed to it, the same nature in its victory over death and sin? Lightfoot (on Gal 5[17]) is disposed to reject this view: 'Throughout this passage,' he writes, 'the πνεῦμα is evidently the Divine Spirit, for the human spirit in itself and unaided does not stand in direct antagonism to the flesh.' This is, of course, true; but the objection does not apply to the interpretation which regards πνεῦμα as the human spirit influenced by and so far identified with the Spirit of God. On the whole this interpretation seems preferable, although it is clear that in both places the apostle's thought passes at times from one meaning of the word to another, refusing to be bound by an absolute rule (cf. Sanday-Headlam, *Romans*, p. 196). A somewhat similar antithesis of πνευματικός and ψυχικός (1 Co 2[14], cf. 15[44]) presents the same difficulty. The ψυχικός is under the control of the ψυχή, or lower rational nature; in the πνευματικός the πνεῦμα, the higher nature, the understanding and the will guided by the Spirit of God, has the ascendant. Here, again, we cannot exclude the thought either of the Divine Spirit or the spirit of the man; the two are regarded as in their operation one, and the one term covers both, although the human spirit is in the foreground of the thought. Similarly, in the antithesis of πνεῦμα and γράμμα (Ro 2[29] 7[6], 2 Co 3[6]), the heart of the contrast lies in the opposition of the external to the spiritual; and while πνεῦμα points to the action of the personal Spirit, who is the Giver of spiritual life, its precise meaning must be determined by the context. In the two former passages the reference seems to be to the spirit of man under divine influence; in the latter, to the new life of the Spirit which characterizes the gospel as compared with a dispensation of external law. Even the law has its spiritual element, for it was written by the finger of God (Ro 7[14] ὁ νόμος

πνευματικός ἐστιν), and its righteous judgments find an echo in the life of the spiritual man (Ro 8[4]); but, considered as a mere edict, it stands in direct opposition to the Spirit (Gal 5[18]), whose sphere is in the heart of the inner man; and he who is guided by the Spirit is emancipated from the external control which he no longer needs.

When we pass from the Epistles of the third missionary journey to those of the Roman imprisonment and the later 'pastoral' Epistles, we find the apostle's point of view somewhat modified. The intensity of his interest in the individual life has now been supplemented by a new interest in the unity and catholicity of the Church (cf. Hort, *Romans and Ephesians*, p. 128 ff.; *Ecclesia*, p. 135 ff.). He touches on the relations of the Spirit to the individual with a freshness of conception which shows that he is as keenly impressed as ever with their primary importance (Eph 1[13. 14] 4[30] 6[17. 18], Ph 1[19], Col 1[7], 2 Ti 1[14]); yet it is as the Spirit of the universal Church that he now specially delights to contemplate the Holy Ghost. To some extent this position had been occupied in 1 Co, but there 'he is dealing with the Ecclesia of a single city, . . . in the Epistle to the Ephesians he is dealing with the universal Ecclesia' (Hort, p. 141). The Spirit is in these later Epistles the bond of Catholic unity (Eph 4[3. 4], cf. 2[18], Ph 2[1]), the source of ministerial gifts (Eph 4[7-12], 2 Ti 1[6. 7]) and sacramental grace (Tit 3[5]). Thus the teaching of the earlier Epistles finds its complement in that of the later, where it appears that the same divine gift which sanctifies and perfects the individual member of Christ, is the bond of corporate unity and the source and support of the common life which animates the whole body of the Church.

(γ) One book of the NT remains. *The Apocalypse* returns to the standpoint of the OT when it represents the Holy Spirit in the light of the Spirit of prophecy (Rev 1[10] 2[7] etc., 4[2] 14[13] 19[10] 22[6]). Yet incidentally it takes up St. Paul's later view. What the Spirit says, He says to the Churches (Rev 2[7. 11. 17. 29] 3[1. 6. 13. 22]). For each of the Churches He has a separate message (Rev 1[4] 3[1] 4[5] 5[6]); the sevenfold gift of God (Rev 1[4] 3[1] 4[5] 5[6]) fulfils its work in each Christian brotherhood as in each Christian soul under different conditions, and with partial and fragmentary results varying according to the measure in which it is bestowed, and the manner in which it is received. To the universal Church the Spirit bears another relation: He co-operates with it in its witness to Christ; His voice is joined with that of the bride in calling for the bridegroom's return (Rev 22[17a]). Yet in this book of world-wide and time-long interests the need of the individual is not overlooked, and the last mention of the Spirit in the Apocalypse refers to it (Rev 22[17b] ὁ διψῶν ἐρχέσθω· ὁ θέλων λαβέτω ὕδωρ ζωῆς δωρεάν).

Summary.—It may be well briefly to summarize the results of this examination of the teaching of the Old and New Testaments upon the subject of the Holy Spirit.

The first chapter of Genesis represents the Divine Spirit as co-operating with the Divine Word in the ordering of the *cosmos*; the last chapter of the Apocalypse represents Him as speaking in the Universal Church. There are few of the intermediate books which contribute nothing to the doctrine of the Spirit. In every section of the Canon He fills a prominent and important place.

If it be asked what the Bible teaches with regard to the essential nature of the Holy Spirit, the answer is on one point explicit and unanimous. The Holy Spirit is, in the strict sense of the word, divine. No biblical writer yields any support to the Arian conception of a created Intelligence above the angels but inferior to the Son, to whom the name 'Spirit of God' is improperly applied.

But to the further inquiry, whether this Divine Spirit is a person, the reply, if on the whole decisive, does not come with equal clearness from the earlier and the later books. The Old Testament attributes personality to the Spirit only in so far as it identifies the Spirit of God with God Himself, present and operative in the world or in men. But the teaching of Christ and of the apostles, whilst accentuating the personal attributes of the Spirit, distinguishes the Spirit from the Father and the Son. The baptismal formula comprehends the Father, the Son, and the Holy Spirit in the Unity of the Name which consecrates and claims for itself the whole life of man.

On the office and work of the Holy Spirit the Canon throws fuller light, for here a more precise knowledge is necessary to the well-being of the Church. But here again the revelation is progressive, corresponding in its growth to the growing needs of men. The Spirit appears first in connexion with the cosmogony of Genesis, and the writers of the Old Testament frequently refer to His work in sustaining and renewing physical life. But the Hebrew Canon attributes to Him also the endowment of human nature with intellectual and spiritual gifts, and especially regards Him as the source of the great gift of prophecy. It speaks of Him as the author of moral purity and religious consecration. Lastly, it foretells the coming of an ideal King, a perfect Servant of God, in whom the Spirit should rest in His fulness, and an extension of the Spirit's gifts in the last days to the whole nation and to the world. At this point the New Testament takes up the thread of the revelation. The Synoptic Gospels show how the ideals of the Old Testament were fulfilled in the life and ministry of Jesus Christ. The Fourth Gospel predicts the mission of the Spirit to the Church; the Acts and Epistles relate the fulfilment of His mission in the experience of the Apostolic Church. We are permitted to see how it has changed the whole spiritual order, raising a new Israel out of the old, transforming an elect nation into a Catholic Church, pouring new life into the body of the disciples, sanctifying individual wills, carrying conviction to the world, and guiding believers into the fulness of the truth. In St. Paul's writings the biblical doctrine of the operations of the Holy Spirit reaches its completion. The apostle sees in the Spirit of Christ the source of the vital unity which inspires the Church, the quickening and compacting power of the new creation. But he teaches with equal clearness that the Spirit has come to regenerate and restore the personal life of each of the baptized, dwelling in the body as His temple, identifying Himself with the human spirit in its struggle after God, until He has perfected the nature which the Son of God redeemed and has raised it to the measure of the stature of the fulness of Christ.

LITERATURE.—The following works, amongst others, may be consulted on the Biblical Theology of the Holy Spirit.
PATRISTIC AND MEDIÆVAL.—Tertullian, adv. Prax.; Origen, de principiis, i. 3; Athanasius, Epp. ad Serap.; Cyril of Jerusalem, Catech. xvi. xvii.; Didymus, de Sp. Sanct.; Basil, de Sp. Sanct. (ed. Johnston); Gregory of Nazianzus, Orat. Theol. v.; Ambrose, de Sp. Sanct.; Augustine, de Trin. iv. v. xv., in Joann. tr. xxix.; John of Damascus, de fide orth. i.; Anselm, de process. Sp. Sanct.; Thomas Aquinas, Summa, p. i. q. 36-38.
MODERN.—Petavius, de Trin. ii. iii. vii.; Pearson, Bp., Exp. of the Creed, artt. iii. vii.; Owen, J., Pneumatologia; Heber, Bp., Personality and Offices of the Comforter; Hare, J. C., Mission of the Comforter; Kahnis, C. F. A., Lehre von h. Geiste, Bd. i.; Gaume, Traité du S. Esprit; Moberly, Bp., Administration of the Holy Spirit in the Body of Christ; Hutchings, W. H., Person and Work of the Holy Ghost; Webb, Bp., Person and Office of the Holy Spirit; Buchanan, J., Office and Work of the Holy Spirit; Smeaton, G., Doctrine of the Holy Spirit; Benson, Archbp., The Seven Gifts; Wirgman, A., The Sevenfold Gifts; Koellhg, W., Pneumatologie; Candlish, J. S., Work of the Holy Spirit.
H. B. SWETE.

HOMAM.—See HEMAM.

HOMER.—See WEIGHTS AND MEASURES.

HOMICIDE.—See CRIMES AND PUNISHMENTS, vol. i. p. 521[b].

HONEST, HONESTY.—These words have greatly deteriorated in the three centuries that lie between us and the issue of AV. What they mean now we know; then they meant something nearly approaching the meaning of the Latin words from which they come. Honestus (from honos, 'honour') had two meanings in Latin: (1) 'Regarded with honour,' 'honourable'; (2) 'Bringing honour,' 'becoming,'—and those are just the meanings of 'honest' as it is used in AV. The word had at the time a special, one might almost say technical, meaning when used of women: it meant 'chaste.' Thus in his chapter in The Profane State (v. 1. p. 359) on 'The Harlot,' T. Fuller speaks of her crisping and curling and the like, and then adds, 'I must confesse some honest women may go thus, but no whit the honester for going thus.' And this is of course his meaning in The Holy Warre (ii. 46, p. 106), 'Thus Jerusalem, after it had fourscore and eight yeares been enjoyed by the Christians, by Gods just judgement was taken again by the Turks. What else could be expected? Sinne reigned in every corner; there was scarce one honest woman in the whole citie of Jerusalem.' And this meaning occurs once in AV, 2 Es 16[49] 'Like as a whore envieth a right honest and virtuous woman,' though the adj. so tr[d] is as general a one as idoneus, 'proper.' With that exception 'honest' means either (1) honourable, or (2) becoming.

Neither adj., adv., nor subst. occurs in OT, a fact not without significance in comparing the OT ethics with that of Apocr. and NT. The commonest word tr[d] 'honest' is καλός, which means 'seemly' or 'becoming,' but with an ethical content enabling it to describe such character or conduct as deserves respect or esteem. So To 5[13] 7[7], Wis 4[12], 2 Mac 6[23], Lk 8[15], Ro 12[17], 2 Co 8[21] 13[7], 1 P 2[12]. RV retains 'honest' in To 5[13] 7[7], Lk 8[15]; gives 'honourable' in Wis 4[12], Ro 12[17], 2 Co 8[21] 13[7]; 'his excellent education' for 'his most honest education' in 2 Mac 6[23]; and 'seemly behaviour' for 'honest conversation' (ἀναστροφὴ καλή) in 1 P 2[12]. In Sir 29[14] the adj. εὐσχήμων, 'decorous,' is tr[d] 'honest' (omitted in RV); and in 29[14] ἀγαθός, 'good' (as RV); while, lastly, in Ph 4[8] the word is σεμνός, for which we scarcely have an equivalent adj. (RV 'honourable,' RVm 'reverend').*

These two meanings of 'honest' may be illustrated thus: (1) Honourable, Ac 17[12] Wyc. 'And sotheli manye of hem bileveden, and of hethen wymmen honeste (some MSS 'honest heithen wymmen'), and men not fewe'; Ru 1[22] Cov. 'There was a kinsman also of the kynred of Eli Melech Naemis huszbande, whose name was Boos, which was an honest man'; North, Plutarch, p. 894, 'Now as the Rhodians were desirous to be ridde of this warre, and that Demetrius also was willing to take an honest occasion to do it, the Ambassadours of the Athenians came nappily to serve both their desires.' T. Fuller (Holy Warre, v. 7, p. 239) speaks of 'terms honest and honourable'; and Rutherford (Letters, No. 56) says, 'There is no quarrel more honest or honourable

* The best rendering, says Vincent (Intern. Crit. Com.), is 'venerable' (as AVm), if divested of its conventional implication of age. And he notices that Matthew Arnold (God and the Bible, p. xxii) suggests 'nobly serious,' as opposed to κοῦφος, 'lacking intellectual seriousness.' 'Honest' is Tindale's word, whom all the VSS follow; Wyc. has 'chaste,' Ellicott chooses 'seemly.' See also J. A. Clapperton in Preacher's Magazine, viii. 457.

than to suffer for truth.' (2) *Becoming :* Tindale, *Pent.*, Prologe, 'And beholde how righteous, howe honest and howe due a thinge it is by nature that every man love his brother unfaynedly even as him selfe, for his fathers sake.' So Is 52¹ Cov. 'Put on thine honest rayment o Ierusalem, thou citie of the holy one'; and Golding, *Calvin's Job*, p. 571 (on 32¹¹⁻²²), 'There is a certaine honest comelinesse to be kept.'

The adv. **honestly** is the trⁿ in Sir 22⁹ of ἐν ἀγαθῇ ('If children live honestly,' ἐν ἀγαθῇ ζωῇ); in 2 Mac 12⁴³ and He 13¹⁸ (Amer. RV 'honourably') of καλῶς; and in Ro 13¹³, 1 Th 4¹² of εὐσχημόνως, 'decorously (Amer. RV 'becomingly').

The subst. **honesty** occurs only in 1 Ti 2² 'that we may lead a quiet and peaceable life in all godliness and honesty' (ἐν πάσῃ εὐσεβείᾳ καὶ σεμνότητι, RV 'in all godliness and gravity'). For the Eng. word cf. Joy, *An Apology to W. Tindale* (Arber's ed. p. 19), 'Tindale shulde have goten hym more honesty and lesse shame yf he had writen once lesse to the reader'; and North, *Plutarch*, p. 852, 'The great force of Demosthenes eloquence . . . did so inflame the Thebans courage with desire of honour, that it trode under their feete all maner of considerations, and did so ravish them with the love and desire of honesty, that they cast at their heeles all feare of danger.'　　　J. HASTINGS.

HONEY.—See FOOD, vol. ii. p. 37ᵇ.

HOODS is AV trⁿ in Is 3²³ of an article of female attire, designated by the Heb. term צְנִיפוֹת. RV has **turbans**, and there can be little doubt that this is the correct rendering, and that it might have been introduced into the text of RV in Job 29¹⁴ and Is 62³ (AV, RV 'diadem'), as well as in Zec 3⁵ (AV, RV 'mitre'). The derivation from *ẓânaph* gives the meaning of something wrapped round, as the similar Arab. *liffeh*, 'turban-band,' is taken from *laff*, 'to wrap round.' In the East the head-covering is usually a protection against heat rather than against cold. The habit of keeping the head always covered makes it sensitive to cold, and during a time of severe weather Orientals cover their heads with shawls, after the manner of hoods, but it is not a permanent article of dress. See DRESS, vol. i. p. 626ᵇ.

　　　　　　　　　　　　　　　　　　G..M. MACKIE.

HOOK represents various words in both Heb. and Arab., and sometimes the meaning is very different from what is usually understood by the Eng. word *hook*. **1.** The hooks (וָוִים) used in the tabernacle (Ex 26³² etc.) are, in the Arab. VS, tr. by a word (*ruzaz*) which means a hook or ring with a spike for being driven into wood. **2.** In 2 K 19²⁸, Is 37²⁹, Job 41², Ezk 29⁴, the Arab. VS has *ring (khazâmet)* as tr. of חָח or חוֹחַ. The ring meant in these passages is one which is put in the nose of a wild animal to bring it under control. In Syria gipsies frequently lead bears about among the villages by means of ropes fastened to rings inserted in the cartilage of the nose. In Ezk 38⁴ חָח is tr. in Arab. *shakîmat*, the bit of the bridle of a horse. **3.** In Ezk 40⁴³ שְׁפַתַּיִם (gutters?) is tr. in Arab. *maâzîb*. **4.** Pruning-hooks (מַזְמֵרָה, Arab. *manâjil*), Is 2⁴ 18⁵, Mic 4³, Jl 3¹⁰. In Syria pruning-hooks are somewhat like the reaping-hooks or sickles used in England, only very much smaller. The handle is of steel, and of the same piece as the blade. It is hollow, and, when the pruning-hook is used to cut down thorns, a long sticl is thrust into the hollow handle. **5.** Fish-hooks (צִנָּה, סִיר Am 4², חַכָּה Job 41¹, Is 19⁸, Hab 1¹⁵; ἄγκιστρον, Mt 17²⁷). **6.** Flesh-hooks (מַזְלֵג or מִזְלָגָה) Ex 27³, Nu 4¹⁴, 1 S 2¹³·¹⁴; Arab. *minshal*), with two or three prongs for lifting meat out of a pot.

　　　　　　　　　　　　　　　　　　W. CARSLAW.

HOOPOE (דּוּכִיפַת *dûkhîphath*, ἔποψ, *upupa*, AV lapwing).—This bird is mentioned only in the list of unclean birds (Lv 11¹⁹, Dt 14¹⁸). It is generally admitted that the *hoopoe*, *Upupa epops*, L., is the bird intended. It migrates to Egypt and the Sahara in the winter, but returns to Pal. and Syria at the beginning of March, and spreads suddenly over the whole country. The Arabs call it *hudhud* from its cry. Its Gr. and Lat. names are derived from its habit of *inspecting* the ground. The head of the hoopoe is depicted on the Egyptian monuments. It was supposed by the ancients, as also the modern Arabs, to search the ground for hidden wells and springs. This opinion is based on its habit of bending its head downwards, and alternately erecting and depressing its crest. The Arabs say that it reveals these secrets. In reality it is seeking its food, which consists of small insects and worms. It resorts to dunghills, finding it easy to dig out the insects from the dung. But this is by no means its exclusive source of supply. Perhaps it was this habit which caused it to be regarded as unclean in the Mosaic law. It is not now considered unfit for food. It is often shot, or caught on bird-lime, and sold with other game birds. Tristram says that the Arabs call it the 'doctor bird.' Its general colour is russet, but the wings and tail are black, with white bars. The feathers of the crest are 2 in. long, and black-tipped. It is as large as a thrush.　　　G. E. POST.

HOPE.—AV trⁿ of the following Heb. and Gr. words :—

1. בָּטַח (vb.), בֶּטַח (noun), Job 6²⁰, Ps 16⁹ (לָבֶטַח correctly trᵈ by RV 'in safety'; cf. מִבְטָח Jer 17⁷, בִּטָּחוֹן Ec 9⁴ (elsewhere only 2 K 18¹⁹=Is 36⁴). The vb. בָּטַח (root perh. = 'repose oneself on') is very common in OT. AV generally tr. by 'trust.' **2.** כָּסַל (from root='thick,' 'fat') Job 8¹⁴ 31²⁴, Ps 78⁷. It is best trᵈ 'confidence' (so AV, RV in Pr 3²⁶, its only other occurrence in this sense). The form כִּסְלָה occurs Job 4⁶. **3.** מַחְסֶה Jer 17¹⁷, Jl 3¹⁶ (better RV 'refuge'; so frequently in Pss). **4.** תִּקְוָה, מִקְוֶה Ezr 10², Job 4⁶, etc. (the root קוה is the frequent 'wait for (on) J"' of OT). **5. 6.** Practically synonymous with this are יחל (vb., *Niph.*, *Pi.*, *Hiph.*), תּוֹחֶלֶת (noun), Job 6¹¹, Ezk 13⁶, Ps 31²⁴ and oft., Pr 13¹², and שָׂבַר (vb.), שֵׂבֶר (noun), Ps 119¹¹⁶·¹⁶⁶ 145⁵, Est 9¹, Is 38¹⁸ (root meaning 'look closely at,' Neh 2¹³·¹⁵). **7.** חול (root='writhe'), 'wait anxiously,' La 3²⁶ (cf. Gn 8¹⁰ [?], Jg 3²⁵, Mic 11², Job 35², Est 4⁴).

In NT the noun is ἐλπίς and the vb. ἐλπίζω, always of favourable expectation (contrast ἐλπὶς πονηρά of LXX, Is 28¹⁹). In He 10²³ 'the profession of our faith' should be 'the confession of our hope' (τὴν ὁμολογίαν τῆς ἐλπίδος).

The second in St. Paul's triumvirate of graces (1 Co 13¹³) has attracted less attention than its companions. With respect to the nature of hope in general, faith is its inseparable condition; in He 11¹ 'foundation' might almost be substituted for 'assurance.' But its distinctive feature is desire of future good. Hope may accordingly be defined as desire of future good, accompanied by faith in its realization. The object both of faith and of hope is something unseen. Faith has regard equally to past, present, or future, while no doubt in Scripture referring mainly to the future (see, however, He 11³). Hope is directed only to the future. Expectation differs from hope in referring either to good or evil things, and therefore lacks the element of desire.

In the nature of things the grace of hope is peculiarly prominent in OT. That was the time of promise and prophecy, ours is the time of fulfilment (Mt 13¹⁷). Everything then had a forward look. The Heb. golden age lay in the future. The pious Hebrew was a minor (Gal 4³). It is quite in keeping with the old economy that the element of faith or confidence which is latent in hope was especially active. In OT Luther often renders 'hope' by 'trust.' It is often hard to say whether faith or desire is most prominent (Ps 38¹⁵

78⁷ etc.). 'These all died in faith' is almost equivalent to 'These all died in hope' (He 11¹³). They 'endured as seeing him who is invisible' (v.²⁷). It is often said that the hope of OT believers was directed less to spiritual than to temporal good, such as health, riches, victory; but this is only partially true. Spiritual aspiration cannot well be purer or stronger than in passages like Ps 63¹ 17¹⁵; and temporal good is not forbidden to Christian hope (Mt 6³³). Heb. hope, no less than Christian, was set on God (Ps 33¹⁸· ²² 42¹¹ etc.). Jeremiah beautifully addresses J″ as 'the hope of Israel' (14⁸ 17¹³). If in NT St. Peter is the apostle of hope,—not so much because of frequent express references (1 P 1³· ¹³· ²¹ 3¹⁵) as from the general strain of his teaching,—in OT Jeremiah may be called the prophet of hope for the same reason (17⁷· ⁵⁰⁷); his hope was deeply spiritual in nature (31³³ᶠ·, He 10¹⁶).

In NT hope is wider in range, more definitely spiritual in contents, and is attended with greater certainty. It is a 'better hope,' because grounded on 'a better covenant which hath been enacted on better promises' (He 7¹⁹ 8⁶). The blessings it seeks are not limited to the future life, but include all that is promised to faith in the present life. Or, to speak more correctly, distinctions of present and future are often ignored in Scripture. The divine promises and Christian aspiration refer to both (1 Co 2⁹, Ph 3¹²⁻¹⁴). Still, the perfect blessings of the future life are often definitely referred to, giving peculiar magnificence to Christian hope (Ro 5² 8²¹· ²³, Tit 2¹³ etc.). If St. Peter is the apostle, St. Paul is the theologian of this grace. Very significantly, as the prophets make J″ the ground of human hope, St. Paul makes Christ the ground (1 Co 15¹⁹, 1 Ti 1¹, Col 1²⁷). More specifically, Christ's resurrection is the irrefragable seal of hope (1 Co 15, 1 P 1³); hence it is a 'living hope.' Christian hope accompanies a state of peace with God, is attested by experience, and certain of glorious fulfilment because arising out of a sense of God's fatherly love to us (Ro 5¹⁻⁵). It is equally with faith a factor in the process of salvation (Ro 8²⁴ᶠ·). It is a spring of ceaseless joy (Ro 5³ 12¹²). Its object is salvation or eternal life, or the glory of God (Tit 1² 3⁷, 1 Th 5⁸, Ro 5²). Its expression is patient doing and suffering (1 Th 1³, He 6¹¹ᶠ· 12¹). Hope is aptly called 'an anchor of the soul,' staying it amid the buffetings of earthly change (He 6¹⁹). St. Paul puts the final honour on this grace by placing it above faith, and only below love (1 Cor 13¹³). Like its sister graces, it continues in the future life, because the bliss of that life is capable of endless increase. When God is called 'the God of hope,' it must be as the author, not the subject of hope (Ro 15¹³). St. John has only one reference to hope, describing it as a motive to personal sanctification (1 Jn 3³). 'Fulness of hope' (He 6¹¹) accompanies 'fulness of faith' (10²²) and 'fulness of understanding' (Col 2²). Hope stands sometimes for its object (Eph 1¹⁸, Col 1⁵, Tit 2¹³).

                         J. S. BANKS.

HOPHNI (חָפְנִי, B Ὀφνεί, A Ὀφνί; the meaning 'fighter' suggested by Gesenius [*Thes.* p. 506] is very doubtful), and **Phinehas**, 'the two sons of Eli, priests unto the LORD at Shiloh' (1 S 1³).* They are described as 'men of Belial (*i.e.* worthless, unprincipled men) who knew not the LORD, nor the due of the priests from the people' (1 S 2¹²ᶠ· RVm, following the reading of the Versions and most moderns). The particular sin of which the sons of Eli were guilty lay in their abuse of their

---

* Possibly, the account here given is incomplete. Wellhausen (*Büch. Sam.* 35) points out that the sons of Eli are mentioned before he himself has been introduced. Thenius and Klostermann insert 'Eli and' with the LXX; more probably we should read simply 'and Eli, priest unto the LORD, was there' (Budde, *Richter u. Samuel*, p. 196).

privileges as priests, in that they claimed more than the customary share of the sacrifices, and further insisted on having it when, and as, they pleased, so that 'men abhorred the offering of the LORD' (see Driver, *Deut.* p. 216; Wellhausen, *Proleg.* pp. 68, 153 f.). The further charge of licentiousness which is brought against them (1 S 2²²ᵇ) is most probably due to a later editor; the clause is wanting in the LXX, and is omitted by Wellh., Budde, Driver, and Klostermann. The mild rebuke of their father had no effect on their evil practices, and, in consequence, a curse is pronounced against the house of Eli, first by an unknown prophet (1 S 2²⁷⁻³⁶), and afterwards by the youthful Samuel (1 S 3¹¹⁻¹⁴· ¹⁸). In accordance with the sign given in the former prophecy, Hophni and Phinehas both perished in the battle with the Philistines at Aphek, whither they had accompanied the ark of God (1 S 4¹¹; in 4⁴ read 'and the two sons of Eli, H. and P., were with the ark of the covenant of God').

The history of the house of Eli which is given in 1 S 1–4 clearly belongs to the later (E) of the two documents from which the books of Samuel (see SAMUEL, BOOKS OF) are mainly compiled; but it is probable that the narrative has in parts been expanded (esp. in 1 S 2²⁷⁻³⁶*) by a later Deuteronomistic editor.   J. F. STENNING.

HOPHRA (Heb. חָפְרַע; LXX Οὐαφρῆ; Herod. Ἀπρίης; Manetho Οὐάφρις).—The Egyptian original, whence the other forms were derived, is *W'ḥ-ib-r'* (see p. 656ᵃ note, vol. i. of this *DB*). The name of this king—the fourth of the 26th or Saite Dynasty—occurs but once in the Bible (Jer 44³⁰); yet his influence upon Jewish history was considerable. He was the son and successor of Psammetichus II, and reigned from 588 to 569. Although Hophra-Apries is mentioned on numerous Egyptian monuments, there is an almost complete dearth of native documents from which to reconstruct his history. Material, however, for the two chief episodes of his reign is supplied, on the one hand by the contemporary prophecies of Jeremiah and Ezekiel, and on the other by Herodotus, who visited Egypt not much more than a century later.

The constant ambition of the Saite Pharaohs was the recovery for Egypt of her ancient position of suzerainty in Asia. In this none of them had hitherto been more than temporarily successful; the Syrian conquests of Necho had been cancelled by the revival of Babylonian power under Nebuchadrezzar, while in the next reign—that of Psammetichus II — we hear of no campaigns except in Nubia. But, on the accession of Apries, an Asiatic policy became again the king's main interest. A favourable opportunity seemed to be offered by a return to power of the patriotic faction in Judah, and the consequent revolt of Zedekiah. The Babylonian force sent to punish this display of independence was compelled, by the appearance in the south of an Egyptian army, to desist from the siege of Jerusalem (586). The check, however, was but momentary. Apries does not appear to have ventured a battle, and the Jews once more learned the value of Egypt's friendship. While their Egyptian allies withdrew, Jerusalem fell, and the Babylonians wreaked their vengeance on

---

* The text of this section is in considerable confusion, and the meaning can be extracted only with difficulty. The two events which are foretold are: (1) the almost entire destruction of Eli's house (v.³¹, referring to the massacre of the priests at Nob, 1 S 22¹⁷⁻²⁰); (2) the raising up of a faithful priest (v.³⁵, referring to the appointment of Zadok in the place of Abiathar, the great-great-grandson of Eli, by Solomon, 1 K 2²⁷). The sign given in attestation of the prophecy (v.³⁴) is the death of Hophni and Phinehas in one day. See Wellhausen, *Der Text der Bücher Sam.* p. 48 f.; Driver, *Heb. Text of Sam.* p. 32 f.; Budde, *op. cit.* p. 199 f.

the nation. Nevertheless, the succeeding years of anarchy and bloodshed in Judah induced many of the remaining inhabitants to quit their homes and fly to Egypt for protection. Apries received them and settled them in the frontier fortress of Daphnæ (Tahpanhes, Tell Defeneh), in the eastern Delta, the station of one of the mercenary corps of Ionians and Carians who formed at the time the strength of the Egyptian armies. Certain remains of buildings on this site have been identified with the pavement, etc., referred to by Jeremiah (43⁹), who himself shared the Egyptian exile of his countrymen.

The much discussed inscription, in which some have recognized a reference to Nebuchadrezzar's punitive expedition to Egypt and to the reign of Apries, more probably relates merely the repression of some internal revolt (see *Æg. Zeitschr.* 1884, 87, 93); while the cuneiform fragment, claimed as corroborative evidence for the same event, can be so regarded only on the hypothesis —otherwise unsupported—of a temporary co-regency of Apries and Amasis, since the war it relates appears to have been directed against the latter king. It is curious, though scarcely important, that a tradition of Nebuchadrezzar's invasion should have survived even into Mohammedan times.*

The event of the reign, of which we hear most from Herodotus, is a campaign, undertaken later than those in Syria, in response to an appeal by the Libyans for help against the encroaching Greeks of Cyrene. The expedition was unsuccessful, and the consequent national resentment led to the deposition of Apries in favour of *I'ḥms*-Amasis, one of his generals, by whom he and the Greek mercenaries were defeated at Momemphis. Apries, detained for a time in captivity, was eventually given over to popular vengeance and strangled.

                                        W. E. CRUM.

HOR (MOUNT) (הֹר, Arab. *Jebel Haroun*, 'Aaron's Mount').—**1.** A mountain named as a stage in Israel's journey to Canaan (Nu 20²² 21⁴ 33³⁷, Dt 32⁵⁰), and as the place of Aaron's death (Nu 20²³·²⁵·²⁷ 33³⁸·³⁹·⁴¹, Dt 32⁵⁰) (all P). The modern *Jebel Haroun* is identified with the closing scene of Aaron's life both by situation and by tradition. Mount Hor is stated to be situated 'by the border of the land of Edom' (Nu 20²³); Eusebius states that 'Mons Hor, in quo mortuus est Aaron, erat juxta urbem Petram' (*Onomasticon*), which is the case with J. Haroun, as Petra lies at its eastern base; and Josephus affirms that Aaron's death occurred on a high mountain enclosing Petra (*Ant.* IV. iv. 7). Tradition concurs, and amongst the Arab inhabitants J. Haroun is held sacred as the sepulchre of Aaron, and a small mosque marks the site. It is fair to add that the identity of Hor with *Jebel Haroun* is disputed by Ewald, Knobel, Dillm. (on Nu 20²²), Sayce (*HCM* 265), Buhl (*Gesch. d. Edomiter*, 11f., *Lex.*, 'Ganz falsch die spätere Tradition'), and esp. Trumbull (*Kadesh-barnea*, 128 ff.).

DESCRIPTION.—On approaching the saddle, or watershed, of the Wady el-Arabah from the south, the almost unbroken range of the Edomite mountains opens out to the eastward at Wady Abu Kuseibeh, disclosing a wide valley, at the head of which is J. Haroun, standing out conspicuously amidst an assemblage of broken ridges tumultuously thrown together, and constituting the frontiers of Mount Seir. The mount rises with a bold and precipitous front facing the west, flanked by two lofty bastions of sandstone standing erect on the granitic pedestal, and from its base stretches a wide and gently sloping plain, also enclosed by lesser heights, upon which we can well picture to ourselves the Israelitish host encamped during the

* See *Abû Ṣâliḥ*, ed. Evetts (Oxf. 1895), p. 83, note.

solemn period of Aaron's ascent, and in full view of the summit of the mount which was to be his tomb; or (as it is in the narrative) 'in the eyes of all the congregation' (Nu 20²⁷). Here also we may suppose they camped while Moses sent an ambassage to the king of Edom across the intervening pass to ask permission to march through his territory (Nu 20¹⁴ff.). The summit of the mount is marked by a little white mosque supposed to cover the tomb of the high priest, and from this point the ridge descends gradually eastwards until it breaks off in the line of cliffs which enclose the quadrangle of Petra, and the channel for the Wady Musa which flows through the city (see PETRA). The mount is quite inaccessible directly from the west, owing to its precipitous face in this direction; but the summit is gained by ascending from the pass leading into Petra, called the Wady Haroun, which runs along the southern flank of the mount. The elevation of the summit is about 4780 feet above the Gulf of Akabah, or 6072 feet above the surface of the Dead Sea,* and from this point an extensive and remarkable view is obtained when the atmosphere is clear—towards the south, west, and north. In the first direction, the eye follows the range of lofty and rugged heights down along the side of the Arabah towards the Red Sea; in the second, it looks across the wide plain of the Arabah to the white cliffs which bound the Badiet et-Tih (Wilderness of Paran), and across this arid tableland itself for many miles towards the horizon; and towards the north, the deep hollow of the Ghōr may be faintly discerned, with the broken slopes of the hills of Southern Palestine bounding the view in that direction. Turning to the east, the observer marks the white crest of the Arabian Desert plateau, sloping steeply downwards into the deep hollow of the Wady Musa, in which lies, almost hidden from view amongst its red-faced cliffs and precipices, Petra, the ancient capital of Edom. Such was the scene which met the eyes of Aaron ere they closed for ever. His body is supposed to have been laid in a sepulchre immediately below the crest of the mount, and over it stands the little white mosque, conspicuous from afar: a token of the sacred character of the spot in the eyes of the wild inhabitants.

GEOLOGY.—Mount Hor is formed of reddish sandstone and conglomerate ('Nubian sandstone' of Russegger) of Cretaceous age; the beds rising in a precipitous wall of natural masonry tier above tier, and presenting a bold front towards the west. These huge beds of sandstone compose the upper part of the ridge to a depth of about a thousand feet from the summit, where they rest on a solid foundation of granite and porphyry of great geological antiquity, associated with which, in some way not very clear, are masses of agglomerate, beds of ash and dykes of igneous rock, all of volcanic origin, but of an age anterior to the Cretaceous sandstone. This latter formation dips towards the east, and gradually descends in the direction of the Wady Musa, where it forms the cliffs which surround the city of Petra. Along the flanks of the escarpment of the Arabian Desert to the eastward the sandstone formation passes below the white marls and limestones of Upper Cretaceous age, which form the surface of the plain at a level of over 5000 feet above the sea.†

2. Another mountain called by the same name (Nu 34⁷·⁸) was to be the northern limit of the inheritance of the tribes of Israel, which was to extend from the shore of the Great Sea (Mediterranean) eastward along the border of Mount Hor

* As determined by the aneroid observations of Mr. Reginald Laurence, Monday, 10th December 1893 (*Mount Seir*, p. 95).
† Hull's *Memoir on the Geology of Arabia Petræa*, with Maps and Sections (1886).

unto the entering in of Hamath (Syria and the Lebanon). If *Hôr* be an archaic form of *har*, Mt. Hor signifies some conspicuous height among lesser heights; and when we come to apply this meaning to the region of the Lebanon, we cannot remain long in doubt as to the special mount indicated. Among all the mountains on the borders of Syria and Palestine, Mount Hermon is pre-eminently the most conspicuous and important, owing to its enormous mass and great elevation, which reaches 10,000 feet above the level of the sea. On this ground we may identify this second Mount Hor with Hermon, although Porter (*Five Years in Damascus*[2], 333), followed by Neubauer (*Géog. du Talm.* 9), Furrer (*ZDPV* viii. 27), and Buhl, prefer *Jebel Akkar*, a N.E. spur of Lebanon.

LITERATURE.—Mount Hor in Arabia Petræa has been visited by Burckhardt, Léon de Laborde, the Expedition sent out by the Committee of the Palestine Exploration Fund in 1883–84, by Lartet under the Expedition of the Duc de Luynes in 1880, by Professor Palmer and Dean Stanley. The principal references to authorities are the same as those under the head of SELA or PETRA.   E. HULL.

HORAM (הֹרָם), king of Gezer, came to the relief of Lachish when it was besieged by Joshua, but was defeated and slain (Jos 10[33]).

HOREB.—See SINAI.

HOREM (חֲרֵם).—A city of Naphtali in the mountains, Jos 19[38] (see Dillm. *ad loc.*). The name means 'consecrated' (cf. Sabæan prop. names חרם, יחרמאל, Halévy, *Étud. Sab.* 471, 504). It is prob. to be identified with the modern *Ḥûrah* west of Kedesh-naphtali. See *SWP* vol. i. sh. iv.   C. R. CONDER.

HORESH.—In 1 S 23[15] (cf. [16. 18]) David is found 'in the wilderness of Ziph in a (the) wood' (בְּחֹרְשָׁה, where בְּ and ה *locale* are combined; LXX ἐν τῇ Καινῇ, implying a reading בַּחֲרָשָׁה; see Driver, *Text of Sam. ad loc.*). The word *ḥóresh* means 'wooded height' in Is 17[9], Ezk 31[3] (if the text in these two passages is correct; see *Oxf. Heb. Lex. s.v.*), 2 Ch 27[4], and this is probably its meaning in 1 S, although some would make Horesh a proper name, as in RVm (see Stade, *Gesch.* i. 245).   J. A. SELBIE.

HOR-HAGGIDGAD (הֹר הַגִּדְגָּד).—A station in the journeyings of the Israelites, mentioned only Nu 33[32. 23]. The Heb., which means the hole or cavern of Gidgad, indicates the character of the locality, and suggests the land of the Horites, or its neighbourhood. The LXX translates τὸ ὄρος Γαδγάδ, reading הַר 'a mountain.' See BEEROTH-BENE-JAAKAN, GUDGODAH, and EXODUS, § iv.   A. T. CHAPMAN.

HORI (חוֹרִי).—1. A son of Seir, Gn 36[22]=1 Ch 1[39]. As Dillmann remarks, the national name appears here as a clan name. 2. The father of Shaphat the Simeonite spy, Nu 13[5].

HORITES (חֹרִי, AV sometimes Hori, Horims).—The predecessors of the Edomites in the country of Seir. They were there as early as the time of Abraham (Gn 14[6]). J" destroyed them before the sons of Esau, and gave the latter their country (Dt 2[12. 22]). There was, however, such a mingling of the family of Esau and his Horite (in Gn 36[2] read *Horite* for *Hivite*) connexions, that the Horite name and descent was preserved (Gn 36, esp. vv.[20. 21. 29-30]). They are not explicitly said to be *rephaim*, as are the Emim and the Zamzummim, in Dt 2[10t. 20t.]; but from what is there said it is natural to infer that they were. Except in Dt 2[12], they are spoken of as 'the Horite,' using the gentilic noun in the sing., a form of speech that is never used of the other giant peoples; but this can be accounted for by the fact just mentioned, that, in their mingling

with their conquerors, the H. name and descent had been preserved, so that, in the time of Moses and later, they were properly a people, and not merely a race of subordinate men, as in the case of the Anakim and others.

The name Horite is supposed to mean 'cave-dweller' (see Driver, *Deut.* p. 38). On the theory that the Horites were *rephaim*, this fact is of interest in its bearing on the character of the *rephaite* civilization; but they did not always remain cave-dwellers. See GIANTS, REPHAIM, and cf. Hommel, *AHT* 263 f.   W. J. BEECHER.

HORMAH (חָרְמָה, Ἑρμά, Ἀνάθεμα).—After the return of the spies, an attempt to go up into the S. of Judah was repulsed by the Canaanite and Amalekite (the Amorite according to Dt), who drove the Israelites to Hormah (Nu 14[45], Dt 1[44]). In this passage of Nu, Hormah occurs with the def. art., and the rendering of Dt 1[44], preferred by critics (following LXX, Syr., Vulg.), is '*from* Seir to Hormah' (see Driver, *ad loc.*).

The Canaanite king of Arad (Nu 21[1-3]) fought against Israel when in the neighbourhood of Mt. Hor, and took some of them prisoners. Thereupon Israel vowed that if the Lord would give them victory, they would place the Canaanite cities under the ban. The place was accordingly named Hormah. According to Jg 1[17], Judah and Simeon utterly destroyed Zephath and called it Hormah. If the events of Nu 21[3] happened immediately after the attack of the king of Arad, it would seem that the Israelites conquered at that time some portion of the S. of Judah, and in that case a way would have been open for an advance northward. The generally received view seems therefore probable, that Nu 21[3] describes what took place at a later period, and Jg 1[17] supplies further details.

Hormah is mentioned, Jos 12[14], along with Arad as one of the 31 royal cities taken by Joshua, in 15[30] as 'one of the uttermost cities . . . toward the border of Edom in the South,' and in 19[4], 1 Ch 4[30] as part of the inheritance of Simeon. In 1 S 30[30] it occurs after the cities of the Kenites (cf. the same connexion in Jg 1[16. 17]).

The position of Hormah depends upon that assigned to Kadesh, and two identifications have been proposed: that of Robinson, who identifies it with es-Sufah, a pass through the mountains on one of the roads from Petra to Hebron; and that of Rowlands and Palmer, who propose Sebaita as its site, in the Wady el-Abyadh, about 25 miles in N.N.E. direction from 'Ain Kadis. Both identifications are made with Zephath, which is mentioned only Jg 1[17], and assume that the old Canaanite name has survived—an assumption not without difficulty, in face of the evidence of the OT that the place was known as Hormah. Either site is appropriate according to the theory adopted as to the position of Kadesh. If the identifications of Ziklag and Jerahmeel (1 S 30[29]) be accepted as being in the neighbourhood of Sebaita, they would increase the probability in favour of that site. Its distance from Arad may be urged as an objection, but we do not know the extent of the territory belonging to the king of Arad, nor does it state in Nu 21[2. 3] that the cities were in his territory. See Robinson, *BRP*[2] ii. 181; Palmer, *Desert of the Exodus*, 374 ff.; and art. KADESH.   A. T. CHAPMAN.

HORN (קֶרֶן, κέρας) has, besides its usual meaning, three other significations in the Bible. **1.** A kind of bugle or *cornet* (from L. *cornu*) for military purposes (Jos 6[5]), which see under TRUMPET. **2.** An emblem of strength or power derived from the offensive weapons of some animals. As the word is always used in the sing., it is very likely that the special animal from which this use of it came was the one-horned rhinoceros, or the fabulous unicorn which still appears on the insignia of British arms. This emblematical sense of *power* is the principal use made of this word in both OT and NT. Thus the horn is said to be 'exalted' (Ps 89[17]) when the figure represents the show of great power, or 'broken' (Jer 48[25]) when the idea is that of its destruction. The same metaphor is sometimes used in the sense of arrogance : 'Lift not up the horn . . . speak not with a stiff neck' (Ps 75[4. 5] RV); compare the contrary expression of *humiliation* : 'I have sewed sackcloth upon my skin, and have laid my horn in the dust' (Job 16[15] RV). Another form of the figurative sense is when it represents *kings* (in the Books of Dn and Rev), who wielded the power of a whole nation. There is no real connexion between any of these metaphoric uses and the Ashteroth - karnaim— the two-horned Astarte (Gn 14[5])—who, in Phœn. mythology, was the goddess of the Moon, and on whose head the crescent is represented in some of her statues. Alexander the Great is also called in the Koran (18. 82), and by Arab. writers, 'the two-horned,' most probably in reference to the two rams' horns seen in some of his coins curling backwards above his ears, which he adopted in honour of Ammon the Egyptian god, to whom the ram was sacred. An equally erroneous idea has been long entertained about the silver horn worn on the head by women of the Lebanon about fifty years ago, which was simply an exaggerated piece of head-dress for supporting the veil to cover the head and face, and had no reference to symbolized *power.* See DRESS in vol. i. p. 627ᵃ, where the horn is figured. **3.** The *horns of the altar* were four projecting points on its corners—sometimes seen on heathen structures of this kind. They were probably ornamental, but among the Jews they were smeared with the blood of sacrificial victims (Ex 29[12]), and may have been used for binding the animal until the time came for its slaughter (Ps 118[27], where, however, the text is corrupt). Criminals enjoyed immunity of danger to their lives from an avenger so long as they took hold of these horns (1 K 1[50]), just as in the Middle Ages Christian churches and altars were resorted to for the same purpose. See ALTAR, vol. i. p. 77ᵃ.

J. WORTABET.

HORNET (צִרְעָה *zir'áh*, σφηκία, *crabro*).—The hornet is mentioned thrice in the Hex. (Ex 23[28], Dt 7[20], Jos 24[12]). The first two passages contain the general promise that God would send the hornet before the Isr. to drive out their enemies. In the last it is said that God did send the hornet before them to drive out the two kings of the Amorites. (For *two* here we should certainly read *twelve*. So LXX, δώδεκα. See Dillm. *ad. loc.*). We have no details of a pest of hornets in Scripture. It is, however, not impossible that such a pest may have aided in the work. Other insects, as ants and locusts, have, at times, vast desolating power. The author of Wisdom (12[8-10]) takes the passage literally. Hornets multiply at times in large numbers, and there are records in profane history of plagues of them. There are four species in the Holy Land, two of which construct nests of *papier maché* in bushes and trees, and two underground or in cavities of the rocks. Their sting is exceedingly painful, and that of large numbers at once may be fatal (cf. Driver on Dt 7[20]). Many have thought that the meaning of hornets in these passages is figurative, and equivalent to the 'terror' (Ex 23[27]). They argue from the Lat. *œstrus*, a *gadfly*, which, from the *terror* and *madness* it inspired in cattle, gave its name to those mental conditions. Whether we adopt the literal or the metaphorical sense, the object is to represent that the agency of apprehension and terror prepared the way for the un-

paralleled victories of the Israelites (Gn 35[5], Dt 32[25], Jos 2[11], Ps 44[3. 6]).

G. E. POST.

HORONAIM (חֹרֹנַיִם, חֹרֹנָיִם, perh. 'the two hollows').—A city of Moab, whose site has not been recovered with certainty. It is mentioned in Is 15[5], Jer 48[3] (in both 'the way to H.,' דֶּרֶךְ ח) 48[5] ('the descent of H.,' מוֹרַד ח) 48[34]. Also on the Moabite Stone (ll. 31, 32) it occurs as חורנן, *i.e.* prob. חוֹרֹנֵן *Ḥoronên*: 'Chemosh said unto me, Go down, fight against Ḥoronên ; and I went down.' The language here, compared with that of Jer 48[5], has led some to find its site to the south of the Arnon, at some inconspicuous ruins mentioned by de Luynes in the neighbourhood of the *Wady ed-Derâ'a* (see Buhl, *GAP* 272 f.).

In Jos 10[10. 11] the LXX 'Ωρωνείν implies a reading חרנים, which ought prob. to be read also in 2 S 13[34] (see Well. and Driver, *ad loc.*). In these passages, of course, the reference is to the two Beth-horons.

J. A. SELBIE.

HORONITE (הַחֹרֹנִי, ὁ Ἀρωνεί, Neh 2[10. 19] 13[28]).—A title given to Sanballat, the opponent of Nehemiah. The name probably denotes an inhabitant of Beth-horon, a town on the borders of Ephraim, about 18 miles N.W. of Jerus. (Jos 10[10] 16[3. 5] etc.). Some scholars (so Gesen.) have derived the title from Horonaim, a town in S. Moab (Is 15[5], Jer 48[3. 5. 34]), pointing to the close connexion of Sanballat with Tobiah the Ammonite ; but see Neh 4[2].

H. A. WHITE.

HORROR has greatly strengthened its meaning since it came into the Eng. language. The Lat. word *horror* (from *horrere*, to stand on end) is used primarily of the *bristling* of hair, etc., and secondarily of the fear which causes the hair to stand on end. Now the meaning is expressed thus : 'Horror is that very strong and painful emotion which is excited by the view or contemplation of something peculiarly atrocious in the conduct of another ; by some vice which exceeds the usual extravagance of vice ; enormities that surpass the bounds of common depravity.' This intensity of meaning has been gained gradually. Even in AV of 1611 'horror' means no more than 'dread.' It occurs in Gn 15[12] 'An horror of great darkness fell upon him' (אֵימָה חֲשֵׁכָה גְדֹלָה 'a terror, a great darkness'); Ps 55[5] 119[53], Ezk 7[18], 2 Mac 3[17] 'For the man was so compassed with fear and horror of the body' (φρικασμός, RV 'a shuddering'). Cf. Melvill, *Diary*, p. 144 'Ther was na thing behind bot bitter teares and heavie lamentation, partlie for the present lose, bot mikle mair for the esteat that was till ensew upon the Kirk, quhilk everie an apprehendit in graitter and graitter missour of horrour and feirfulness.' Bp. Hall, speaking of the angel's visit to Zacharias (*Works*, ii. 3), says, 'It was the weaknesse of him that served at the Altar without horror, to be daunted with the face of his fellow servant.'

Horrible is that which causes great fear : Ps 11[6] 'Upon the wicked he shall rain snares, fire, and brimstone, and an horrible tempest' (רוּחַ זִלְעָפוֹת RV 'burning wind'; King 'scorching blast'), 40[2] 'He brought me up also out of an horrible pit' (בּוֹר שָׁאוֹן, AVm 'a pit of noise,' RVm 'a pit of tumult *or* destruction,' LXX ἐκ λάκκου ταλαιπωρίας, so Vulg. 'de lacu miseriæ,' and Dou. 'the lake of misery'); Jer 5[30] 18[13] 23[14], Hos 6[10] (all 'a horrible thing' = 'a thing to be dreaded'); 2 Es 11[45] 15[28] (both 'horribilis'), 15[34] ('horridus'); Wis 3[19] (χαλεπός, Vulg. 'dirus'), 8[15] (φρικτός, Vulg. 'horrendus'), 11[18] 'shooting horrible sparkles out of their eyes' (δεινοὺς σπινθῆρας, Vulg. 'horrendas scintillas'), 16[5] 'horrible fierceness' (δεινὸς θυμός, Vulg. 'sæva ira'), 17[5] 'that horrible night' (τὴν στυγνὴν ἐκείνην νύκτα, Vulg. 'illam noctem horrendam'), 18[17] 'visions of horrible dreams' (φαντασίαι ὀνείρων δεινῶν, Vulg. 'visus somniorum malorum'), 19[17] 'compassed about with horrible great darkness' (ἀχανεῖ σκότει, Vulg. 'subitaneis tenebris'). In every case the word means 'to be dreaded,' 'dreadful'; the element of loathing does not enter.

And so with **horribly**, Jer 2[12], Ezk 32[10] 'be horribly afraid'; Wis 6[5] 'Horribly and speedily shall he come upon you' (φρικτῶς, Vulg. 'horrende'). Cf. He 10[31] Rhem. 'It is horrible to fal into the handes of the living God'; and Defoe, *Crusoe*, p. 590, 'Never Tyrant, for such I acknowledged myself to be, was ever so universally beloved, and yet so horribly feared by his subjects.'

                            J. HASTINGS.

HORSE.—Four Heb. words are used for *horse*, and one, or perhaps two, for *mare*. 1. אַבִּיר *'abbîr*. This word means *strong* or *valiant*, and is applied metaphorically to the h. (Jer 8[16] AV, RV 'neighing of his strong ones'), 47[3] 'the stamping of the hoofs of his strong *horses*' (RV 'of his strong ones'), 50[11] 'bellow as bulls' (AVm 'neigh as steeds,' RV 'neigh as strong horses').

2. פָּרָשׁ *pârâsh*. The orig. signification of this word is *horseman* or *cavalier* (cf. Arab. *fâris*), as distinguished from the rider of an *ass* or a *camel*. It signifies, secondarily, a *riding horse*, such as is used in war. In this sense it corresponds to the Arab. *faras*, which, however, is generic for all horses. The reason why the Hebrews designated by *pârâsh* only cavalry mounts is that civilians did not use horses for riding. Only two clear instances are given in OT of any person, not of military rank, riding a horse,—that of Mordecai (Est 6[9, 10]), who rode the king's horse (סוּס, not פָּרָשׁ) as a special honour; and that of the 'posts on horseback, riding on swift steeds' (סוּסִים, Est 8[10]). In the obscure passage (Is 28[28]), so differently tr[d] in AV and RV, it is not certain whether the horses (פָּרָשָׁיו) were harnessed to the cart, or ridden or driven. When the peaceful mission of Christ is announced (Zec 9[9]), although he is heralded as a king, it is said that 'he is just, and victorious (lit. saved); lowly, and riding upon an ass,' *i.e.* is not like military conquerors, who ride horses. Then to illustrate the character of this reign it is said (v.[10]), 'I will cut off the chariot from Ephraim, and the horse (סוּס) from Jerus.,' *i.e.* where all is peace the horse is not needed any more than the chariot (see Ass). It is easy in many cases to determine from the context whether *pârâsh* is to be tr[d] *horse* or *horseman*. Thus 'twelve thousand *pârâshîm*' (1 K 4[26]) plainly refers to *cavalry horses* as distinguished from *chariot horses*, and not to 'horsemen,' as in AV and RV. It is clear that the people of the house of Togarmah (Ezk 27[14]) traded, not in 'horsemen,' as in AV, but in *cavalry horses*, 'war horses,' RV. It is the 'war horses' that run (RVm Jl 2[4]), not the 'horsemen' (text AV, RV). In the pursuit of Saul 'the chariots and the horsemen' (בַּעֲלֵי פָרָשִׁים, owners of horses) followed hard after him' (2 S 1[6]). On the other hand, *pârâsh* (2 S 8[4], Jer 4[29]) can refer only to the 'horsemen.' The '*pârâsh*' (Nah 3[3]) who 'lifteth up,' RV 'mounting,' marg. 'charging,' must be the *horseman*. Sometimes neither the *horse* nor his *rider* seems specially designated, and in these cases *pârâsh* corresponds to *cavalry* (Ex 14[9, 17, 18, 23, 26, 28], Hab 1[8]). In other cases *pârâsh* will apply to either the *horse* or his *rider*. Thus (1 S 8[11]) וּבְפָרָשָׁיו may be 'for his war horses,' as has just before been said 'for his chariots,' or 'to be his horsemen,' as in text AV, RV; and צֶמֶד פָּרָשִׁים (Is 21[7]) may mean a 'couple of horsemen,' or a *pair of horses*, or 'horsemen in pairs,' or a 'pair of horsemen,' or *horses in pairs* (cf. AV with RV text and marg.).

3. סוּס *sûs*. This word is often used for *chariot horses* (Ex 14[9] etc., Jos 11[4], 1 K 4[26], Jer 50[37], Ezk 27[14]). It is used even more freq. for *riding horses*,

esp. *war horses* (Gn 49[17], Est 6[9, 10], Job 39[19-25], Jer 6[23] 8[16], Hab 1[8], Zec 1[8] etc.). In not a few cases it seems *general* for horses (Dt 17[16], 1 K 18[5] etc.). In one it seems to refer to a *hunter* (Job 39[18]).

4. רֶכֶשׁ *rekhesh*. This word is used in three places, in all of which RV renders it by 'swift steeds' (Est 8[10, 14], AV 'mules'; 1 K 4[28], AV 'dromedaries,' marg. 'mules' or 'swift beasts'; Mic 1[13], AV 'swift beast'). In the last it clearly refers to a *chariot horse*.

5. רַמָּךְ *rammâk*. This word, rendered AV 'dromedaries' (Est 8[10], RV 'stud'), is Pers. *ramah*, 'flock' or 'herd.' See DROMEDARY.

6. סוּסָה *sûsâh*, ἡ ἵππος, *equitatus*. AV (Ca 1[9]), following Vulg., renders this word 'a company of horses,' RV 'a steed,' marg. 'the steeds.' These renderings would make the point of similarity between the bride and the horses their triumphant march. Others would make סֻסָתִי=*my mare*. It is difficult, if this rendering be adopted, to see what is the connexion between this word and the expression 'in the chariots of Pharaoh,' which immediately follows.

It may seem strange that the Isr., who certainly knew the horse well in Egypt (Gn 47[17]), and who came into a country, many of the tribes of which had large numbers of war horses, should not have adopted and used so noble an animal. The explanation is to be sought in the pastoral habits of the Isr., inherited from their patriarchal ancestors, and continued through the period of their residence in Egypt. These habits led them to seek first the conquest of the hill-country of Canaan. This country is not adapted for the movements either of cavalry or chariots, and the aborigines of these regions seem not to have had horses. But when the Isr. came into the plains of N. Pal. they at once encountered large numbers of chariots and horsemen, but, acting under the command of God, who delivered them into their hands, they houghed the horses and burned the chariots (Jos 11[4-9]). The fact that the Phil. plains had chariots and horses (Jg 1[19]) prevented the early conquest of that region. An encounter, 150 years later, in the plain of Jezreel, resulted in another overthrow of the chariots. The Isr., entrenched in their hills, were slow in adopting cavalry and chariots. The Arabs of that day do not seem to have used the horse. In the account of the great raid of Zebah and Zalmunna (Jg 7. 8) no mention is made of horses. David began their use by reserving 100 of the chariots of N. Syria, with their horses (2 S 8[4]). Solomon increased this force by importations from Egypt, at a fixed price of 150 shekels for a cavalry horse, and 600 for a chariot and its three horses (1 K 10[28, 29]). He had 12,000 of the former and 1400 chariots, which, at three horses to a chariot, would make 4200 (cf. 1 K 10[26] with 4[26], where 40,000 should read 4000). When the kingdom was divided, the ten tribes, which held the plains of N. Pal., had many chariots. When nearly all their chariots and horses were taken in the great overthrow by the Syrians (2 K 13[7]) they never recovered from the blow. The small number of chariots possessed by the Judæan kingdom led to a constant reliance on Egypt for chariots and cavalry in the encounters with Syria and Assyria. Against this the prophets inveighed (Is 31[1], Ezk 17[15] etc., cf. Dt 17[18]). The cavalry and chariots of Assyria were esteemed the most formidable in the world, and are often mentioned in the prophets (Hab 1[8], Nah 3[2] etc.). The Jews brought back 736 horses from Babylon (Neh 7[68]). Horses were regularly employed in war in Pal. down to late Roman times. There was a chariot road to Egypt in the days of the apostles (Ac 8[28]), and there are abundant evidences of the use of these formidable engines of war in the cities E. of the Jordan, in the pass by the Nahr el-Kelb near

Beirût, and in many other places in the land. It is probable that the present breed of Arabian horses are descendants of the very fine stock for which Assyria was famous. White horses (Rev 6[2] 19[11. 14]) were ridden by conquerors. Horses and chariots were dedicated to the sun by idolatrous kings (2 K 23[11]). Horses had halters (Is 30[28]) and bridles (Ps 32[9]). The bridles were decorated with bells (Zec 14[20]; Layard, *Nin.* ii. 29, 275). The horses were often not shod, hence the hardness of their hoofs (Is 5[28]). Chariots and horses had rich trappings (Ezk 27[20]). Saddles were rare (Layard, ii. 357).

G. E. Post.

HORSE GATE.—See Jerusalem.

HORSELEECH (עֲלוּקָה *ʾălûḳah*, βδέλλα, *sanguisuga*).—The obsolete Heb. root עלק corresponds to the Arab. *ʾaliḳa*, which means to *hang to*. The Arab. generic name for leeches is *ʾălaḳ*, and for an individual *ʾălaḳah*. If we regard the creature intended as one of the annelids, *ʾălûḳâh* should be rendered *leech* rather than *horseleech*. Of the annelids found in Syria and Pal. the medicinal leech, *Hirudo medicinalis*, Sav., and the horseleech, *Hæmopis sanguisorba*, Sav., are the most common. There are also species of *Bdella*, *Trochetia*, and other genera of leeches, in the stagnant waters. They cling to the feet and legs of those who wade into such waters. They also infest the fountains and pools, and the watering-troughs of cattle, and attach themselves to the throat or nostrils of beasts and men. The tenacity with which they adhere is such that they must sometimes be pulled apart in order to detach them. The pertinacity with which they suck quite justifies the expression 'the *ʾălûḳâh* hath two daughters, Give, Give' (Pr 30[15]). It is, however, possible that the allusion may be to the *ʾălûḳ* of the Arabs, the *ghûl* or *female spectre*, which they allege sucks blood like the vampire, and feeds on the flesh of the dead (see Wildeboer, *ad loc.*).

G. E. Post.

HORSELITTER.—Only 2 Mac 9[8] (φόριον [= φορεῖον], which is tr[d] 'litter' in 3[27]), RV 'litter' (which see). The word is used in Malory's *Morte Darthur* (Caxton's text) several times. Thus i. 3, 'So it was done as Merlin had devised, and they carried the king forth in a horse-litter with a great host towards his enemies'; and x. 37, 'Then came queen Morgan le Fay to Alisander, and bad him arise, and put him in a horse-litter: and gave him such a drink that in three days and three nights he waked never but slept.'

HORTICULTURE.—See Garden.

HOSAH (חֹסָה 'refuge').—A Levitical doorkeeper of the temple, whose station was by the 'gate of Shallecheth,' 1 Ch 16[38] 26[10. 11. 16]. See Genealogy, III. 39.

HOSAH (חֹסָה).—A city of Asher, apparently south of Tyre, Jos 19[29]. The site is doubtful.

HOSANNA.—An acclamation used by the people on the occasion of our Lord's triumphal entry into Jerusalem. It occurs six times in the Gospels: twice (Mk 11[9], Jn 12[13]) it stands absolutely, twice (Mt 21[9. 15]) it is followed by the dative ('to the Son of David'), and twice (Mt 21[9], Mk 11[10]) by the adjunct 'in the highest'. The circumstance that in all three Gospels the words 'Blessed *is* he that cometh in the name of the Lord,' from Ps 118[26], follow it, has given rise to the assumption that it is borrowed from the preceding verse of that psalm, which begins with *'ănnāh J'' hoshî'āh nā*, i.e. ' save, pray' (Sept. σῶσον δή). This v.[25] of the psalm, according to the ritual of the temple, is said to

have been repeated once on each of the first six days of the joyous Feast of Tabernacles during the solemn procession around the altar of burnt sacrifice and seven times on the seventh day (John Lightfoot, *The Temple Service*, etc., ch. xvi. § 2; De Sola and Raphall, *Eighteen Treatises from the Mishna*, 2nd ed., tr. Succah, ch. iv. § 5; M. Schwab, *Le Talmud de Jérus. traduit*, vol. vi. 33). This seventh day thus came to be called the 'Great Hosanna' (Buxtorf, *Lex.* 992) or 'Hosanna Day' (Zunz, *Gottesdienstliche Vorträge*, u.s.w. 2te Aufl. p. 395 n.; Dalman, *Gram. d. jüdisch-paläst. Aramäisch*, p. 198), and the name was transferred not merely to the prayers of the occasion, but also to the branches of palm trees and willows (Lv 23[40]) which were carried and waved on that festivity. Similarly, in Christian usage, Palm Sunday, to which our Lord's entry has given name, has in certain periods and regions been called 'Hosanna Sunday' or 'Day of Hosannas,' or simply 'Osanna'; and the term has been applied to the 'Sanctus,' 'Tersanctus,' or 'Triumphal Hymn' (as it is variously called) sung by the people at the conclusion of the 'Eucharistic Preface' in all liturgies (C. E. Hammond, *Liturgies Eastern and Western*, 1878, p. 381; Bingham, *Antiq.* xiv. 2, 5); and later the extended use of the word gave rise, especially in the languages of Southern Europe, to such verbs as *hosannare*, *oisisannare*, etc., together with corresponding adjectives (see Ducange, *Gloss. med. et. infim. Latin.*, ed. Favre, iii. 167 f.).

How the Hebrew term *hos(h)î'āna*—employed by Luther not only in his translation of the NT, but even in some editions of his translation of the Psalms (see Bindseil and Niemeyer's ed.), and adopted at first by Tindale in his NT of 1525 (ed. E. Arber, 1871)—became changed into *hosana* (-*anna*), those who hold this opinion are not quite agreed. Jerome, in his reply to the inquiry of Damasus about the meaning of the term (*Opp.* i. 375 ff., *Ep.* xx. in Migne, *Patrol. Lat.* xxii.), lets fall in one place the conjecture that the shorter form is an ignorant corruption (cf. Origen on *Mt. l.c.*, ed. Lommatzsch, iv. 58). The more common supposition regards it as having arisen by syncope or contraction (Jerome as above; Levita, *Tishbi, s.v.*; and the commentators generally); or as a supposed Aramaic form (there is no root ישע in Aram.) of the verb with the pronominal suffix (meaning 'Save *us*.' See Kautzsch, *Gram. des Bib.-Aram.* 1884, p. 173, and, against this, Dalm. *l.c.*).

But though the words 'Blessed is he that cometh,' etc., are indubitably borrowed from Ps 118, and though vv.[22f.] of that psalm receive express Messianic reference both from our Lord (Mt 21[42], Mk 12[11], Lk 20[17]) and St. Peter (Ac 4[11], 1 P 2[7]), it may be doubted whether the rejoicing multitudes in the evangelic story were consciously indebted to the psalm or its use at the Feast of Tabernacles either for the cry 'Hosanna' or the festive demonstration with palm and other branches. To find the explanation of either word or act in the psalm and its use, involves the NT interpreter in grave embarrassments. The language of the psalm is supplicatory, that of the Gospels is jubilant. The psalmist's petition looks towards himself and those whom he represents (the English Pr. Bk. even follows the Vulg. in inserting the object 'me': *Salvum me fac*, 'Help me'); the *Hosanna* of the Gospels finds its expressed object in 'the Son of David.' This aspect of the case makes equally against discovering the original of our term in the Aramaic אושַׁעְנָא 'Save *us*.' The obvious incongruity between the supplicatory sense and the tone of the narrative has driven expositors to jejune and far-fetched explanations: some, for example, by transposing the Greek, have extorted the rendering '(Saying) to the Son of

David, Oh save'; or, by arbitrarily changing υἱῷ to υἱέ, 'O Son of David, save.' Others, resorting to the secondary sense of *Hosanna*, have taken the shout to mean 'Triumphal palms to the Son of David' (cf. Syr. Philox.). The phrase 'in the highest' also has been made to signify 'O thou that dwelledt in the heavens,' or 'May our cry be ratified in heaven,' or 'taken up by the angels,' etc. The inappropriateness of finding an echo of the psalmist's supplication in the Hosanna of the Gospels is made only the more evident by adducing the ceremonies of the Feast of Tabernacles. For that feast occurred in the autumn ; the triumphal entry in the spring. Consequently, some critics (*e.g.* Wünsche, *Erläuterung der Evang. aus Talmud u. Midrasch*, p. 241 n.) have felt compelled to assume that the Passover and the Feast of Tabernacles have been confounded in the Gospels, or that a usage of the latter festival has been arbitrarily transferred to the former. Nor is the difficulty relieved by the fact that shouts of joy and waving of palms had become usual at the Feast of Dedication as well as at the Feast of Tabernacles (2 Mac 10[6. 7]). For as the Feast of Dedication occurred only two months later than the Feast of Tabernacles (cf. Jn 10[22]), the chronological discord is thereby only slightly abated.

This extension of the jubilant usages of the Feast of Tabernacles, however, does seem to point in the right direction, and to set us free to follow the plain contextual indications of the evangelists' narrative. According to those indications, it is most natural to regard the word *Hosanna*, as respects its form, as neither syncopated nor contracted, but the shorter Hiphil imperative with the appended enclitic (נָא-יְשַׁע ; cf. Ps 86[2], Jer 31[7]). For this form there is distinct Talmudic warrant (Dalman, *Grammatik des jüdisch-paläst. Aramäisch*, p. 198 ; Levy, *Neuhbr. u. chald. Wörterbuch*, i. 461 ; Schindler, *Lexicon Pentaglot.* ed. 1653, col. 819). As respects its force, we must, for the same contextual reasons, assume that it had already lost its primary supplicatory sense and become an ejaculation of joy or shout of welcome. As a quaint writer somewhat plumply puts the matter, 'It was a kind of *holy hurrah* '; and the 'Hosanna in the highest' corresponded roughly to our 'three times three.' Cf. the analogous Greek and Roman exclamations 'Ἰὴ παιάν,' 'Io triumphe, terque quaterque.' The waving of palms, etc., and strewing of the way with garments and branches find abundant precedents in ancient usage, including the Jewish : 2 Mac 10[6. 7] 14[4], 1 Mac 13[51], 2 K 9[13] ; Jos. *Ant.* XIII. xiii. 5 ; see Wetstein, *Nov. Test. Græc.* i. 460 f. ; Keim, *Jesu von Naz.* iii. 89 n. 4 (Eng. trans. v. 107 n. 2) ; Schoettgen, *Horæ Hebr.* etc. on Mt 21[8]. The general use of the palm among the Jews on joyous occasions is attested by extant coins: F. W. Madden, *Coins of the Jews*, Lond. 1881, p. 73.

This ejaculatory interpretation of *Hosanna* finds some confirmation in the post-biblical history of the word. Not without significance is the circumstance that down to quite modern times it was simply transliterated in versions of Scripture, not translated. The Anglo-Saxon versions seem to be the first to render it 'Hail' (see S. C. Malan, *The Gosp. of St. John trans. from the eleven oldest versions*, etc., 1862 ; J. Bosworth, *Gothic and Anglo-Saxon Gospels*, 1865). Yet Ciasca in his Latin version of the Arabic text of Tatian's Harmony renders it *Laus*, *Gloria*, and the Armenian Vulgate, *Blessing* (see Hill, *S. Ephraem's Gospel Commentary*, 1896, p. 110). The *Didaché* (10. 6) and the *Apostolic Constitutions* (8. 12, al. 13, p. 259, 17, ed. Lagarde ; cf. 7. 26, p. 209, 26) attest its early liturgical use in churches of heathen origin ; compare its doxological use, too, in the

account by Hegesippus (in Euseb. *HE* II. xxiii. 14) of the martyrdom of James the brother of the Lord. Although it is correctly interpreted (σῶσον δή) in the *Gospel of Nicodemus*, ch. i. (ed. Thilo, p. 510 ff. ; *Gesta Pilati*, A. c. i. 4, p. 210, ed. Tdf.), yet even Clement of Alex. (*Pædag.* I. v. 12) says it is equivalent in Greek to φῶς καὶ δόξα καὶ αἶνος, and the diversity of opinion on this point in intelligent Christian circles appears sufficiently in the correspondence between Damasus and Jerome referred to above. By the 10th cent. so thoroughly has its etymological meaning become obscured that Suidas or his annotator (see Gaisford's ed. vol. ii. col. 2794 *b*) can define it εἰρήνη καὶ δόξα, and add, 'Some say it signifies σῶσον δή ; *incorrectly*.' Especially instructive are the comments of Augustine (in his *Doctrina Christiana*, ii. 11, Migne, xxxiv. col. 42, and *Tract. in Johan.* li. 2, Migne, xxxv. col. 1764): he says explicitly that the word is nothing more than an interjection of admiring joy, a term expressing an emotional mood, not a connected thought ; and he contrasts it with 'Amen' and 'Hallelujah,' the intrinsic meaning of which evidently in his day still clung to them. The contrast he draws finds illustration in pseudo-Justin in the 5th cent. in his *Responsio ad Quæst.* 50 (Otto, *Corp. apol. christ.* ed. 3, vol. v. p. 74), where 'Hallelujah' is correctly interpreted 'Sing praise to the Eternal,' but 'Hosanna' is said to mean 'Transcendent majesty.' The practice of employing the phrase 'Hosanna in the highest' as a glad greeting—deprecated by Jerome on Mt 21[15] (*Opp.* vii. col. 152, Migne, *Patrol. Lat.* xxvi.)—appears as late as A.D. 570, in the *Itinerary of Antoninus* (ed. Gildemeister, Berlin, 1889, § 40).

LITERATURE.—The discussions of the term are numerous, and widely scattered in commentaries and exegetical works. Specimens of the older may be seen in the *Critici Sacri* ; in Poole's *Synopsis* ; in Lampe on Jn 12[13] ; J. C. Wolf, *Curæ*, etc., on Mt 21[9], where numerous reff. are given. Worth consulting, also, are the 7th ch. of Gabriel Groddeck's essay on the Feast of Tabernacles in Ugolini's *Thesaurus*, etc. vol. xviii. p. 534 ff., and the note in F. B. Dach's ed. (1726) of the treatise *Succah*, ch. iv. § 5, p. 331 ff. Special essays on the word (or the triumphal entry) by Bindrim (1671), Winzer (1703), Zopf (1703), Nothdurfft (1713), Bucher (1728), Wernsdorf (1765), J. C. Pfaff (1789), J. M. H. Harras, J. G. Rau, Sauerbrei, J. G. Walch, and others, are catalogued ; but they have not been accessible to the present writer.

J. H. THAYER.

HOSEA.—

i. NAME AND LIFE OF THE PROPHET. — The prophet Hosea (Heb. הוֹשֵׁעַ 'salvation,' Gr. Ὠσῆε, Lat. *Osee*, so AV Ro 9[25]), whose name is identical with the original name of Joshua (Nu 13[8]), and with that of the last king of Israel (AV Hoshea 2 K 15[30]), was certainly a native of the Northern Kingdom, the condition and destiny of which he has in view throughout his prophecy. The references in the prophecy to Judah, though pretty numerous, are more incidental, and Jerusalem is nowhere mentioned.* Israel is 'the land' (1[2]), its king is 'our king' (7[5]), and it is 'the house of Jehu' on which the blood of Jezreel shall be visited, and 'the kingdom of the house of Israel' that shall be made to cease (1[4]). It is the localities of the Northern Kingdom that are familiar to the

* References to Judah are : 1[7. 11] 3[5] 4[15] 5[5. 10. 12-14] 6[4. 11] 8[14] 10[11] 11[12] 12[2]. A number of these passages appear to disturb the connexion, and have been thought later insertions or alterations of the text.

prophet, Gilead and Tabor (5^1 6^8 12^{11}), Gibeah (5^8 9^9 10^9), Gilgal (4^{15} 9^{15} 12^{11}), Jezreel ($1^{4. 5. 11}$ 2^{22}), Ramah (5^8), Shechem (6^9), and particularly Bethel (4^{15} 5^8 $10^{5. 8. 15}$ 12^4) and Samaria (7^1 $8^{5. 6}$ $10^{5. 7}$ 13^{16}). In like manner it is the internal condition of Israel and the state of parties there to which allusion is made : the neglect and selfishness of the priests ($4^{5ff.}$ 5^1 8^{11}) ; the heathenish revelry of the people at the feasts (2^{13} 9^1), and their immoralities at the high places ($4^{13. 14}$ 6^{10}) ; and the conspiracies, bloodshed, and anarchy that followed the death of Jeroboam—'all their kings are fallen' (7^7 13^{11}).*

Little is known of the prophet's history. His father was named Beeri (1^1), and he represents himself as taking to wife a woman called Gomer, who became the mother of several children, to whom he gave symbolical names prophetical of the destiny of his country (ch. 1). The rather obscure passage 9^8 may imply that he and others were exposed to persecution—'as for the prophet, the snare of a fowler is on all his ways, and enmity in the house of his God.' Whether the words of the previous verse, 'the prophet is a fool, the man of the spirit is mad,' be contemptuous language used by the people ($2 K 9^{11}$, Jer 29^{26}), to which the prophet replies : Yes, 'because of the multitude of thine iniquity, and the great enmity' ; or whether the words be those of the prophet himself, expressing the distraction to which he was driven by the wickedness and hostility of the people (Jer $23^{9ff.}$), is rather uncertain.

There is nothing to indicate with any certainty to what rank of life the prophet belonged. Duhm (*Theol. d. Proph.* 130 f.) has argued that he was probably a member of the priestly class, on account of his frequent references to the priests ($4^{6ff.}$ 5^1 6^9), to the *Torah* of God (4^6 8^{12}), to 'unclean things' (9^3, cf. 5^3 6^{10}), to 'abominations' (9^{10}), and to persecution 'in the house of his God' ($9^{7. 8}$). He was certainly a man sufficiently educated to follow and estimate the politics of his country, whether at home or abroad (7^{1-11} $5^{13f.}$), and to pass judgment on the course the national history had taken from the beginning. If any inference could be drawn from the figures and comparisons in which the prophecy is so rich, it would be that the prophet, like Amos, belonged to the country rather than the city. Such images are : (*a*) those from wild beasts, the lion, panther, and bear (5^{14} 6^1 11^{10} $13^{7. 8}$), and other creatures of the field, as the wild ass (8^9), and birds (7^{11} 9^{11} 11^{11}), and from the snares and pits employed in trapping them ($5^{1. 2}$ 7^{12} 9^8). (*b*) Those from agricultural life, *e.g.* from stubborn cattle (4^{16} 9^{15}), the yoke and ways of easing it (11^4), harnessing, threshing, plowing, and harrowing ($10^{11ff.}$) ; from the operations of the husbandman, as sowing and reaping : 'sowing the wind' (8^7), 'sowing righteousness' ($10^{12ff.}$) ; from the corn floor (9^1 13^3), and the like. And in general (*c*) the imagery reflects country life, *e.g.* references to the vine and fig and the time when their fruit is choice (9^{10} 10^1), to the furrows of the field (10^4 12^{12}), the poppy (10^4), thorns and thistles (10^8), nettles (9^6), reeds (13^{15}, cf. the images in $2^{21ff.}$ $14^{5ff.}$) ; to the rains of the various seasons, the winter, early and latter rain (6^3 10^{12}), to the morning cloud and the early dew (6^4 13^3), to the swollen country brooks—'like a splinter on the face of the water' (10^7), and to the hot desert wind that smites the vegetation and leaves the fountains dry (13^{15}). Hosea is· the only writer before Deut. (19^{14} 27^{17}) who refers to the removal of boundary stones in the fields (5^{10}). Whether this imagery warrants any conclusion regarding the prophet's position in life or not, it is evidence of a fine poetic sensibility, of profound sympathy with nature and love of creature life. The prophet lives in the things that are around him, sympathizing with the life in everything and feeling its charm. It is characteristic of his images that they are painted in a word and never developed. Those of them that refer to human life have usually something pathetic in them : Ephraim's decadence among the nations is like grey hairs coming up on the head of one old before his time (7^9) ; in his inability to grasp the crisis now come upon him, and use it as the entrance upon a larger life, he is like the child that dies on the threshold of birth (13^{13}). In His guidance of His people God has been like one that teaches a child to go (11^3). Ephraim must bring out his children to the murderer ; more merciful would it be if God would deny them children, giving them a miscarrying womb and dry breasts (9^{11-14}). The pleasant homes of Ephraim shall be overgrown with nettles, his children shall be wanderers among the nations, and a foreign land shall bury them ($9^{6. 17}$).

Jewish writers identify Beeri the father of Hosea with Beerah, a Reubenite prince carried captive by Tiglath-pileser ($1 Ch 5^6$). According to Christian tradition the prophet was of the tribe of Issachar, and from a place called Belemoth or Belemon (Baalmoth,

Ephrem Syrus in Knobel, *Prophetismus*, ii. 154 ; the form Belemon has been compared with a place Balamon [RV], near Dothan, mentioned in Jth 8^3). A Jewish legend (in Carpzov, *Introd.*) states that the prophet died in Babylon, and was carried to Galilee and buried in Safed (Neubauer, *Géog. du Talmud*, 227). According to another tradition he was a native of Gilead, and the grave of Nebi Osha (prophet Hosea) is shown near es-Salṭ (Baedeker, *Palest.* 337).

ii. THE PROPHET'S TIME.—Chs. 1-3 contain references to events and prophecies of the time of Jeroboam II., though written later ; while much in chs. 4-14 reflects the period of disorder that followed his death. The chronology of the period is obscure. The annals of Tiglath-pileser state that Menahem paid tribute to Assyria in 738 ($2 K 15^{19}$) ; this must have been towards the end of his reign (said to have lasted about ten years, $2 K 15^{17}$) ; and as his two predecessors reigned only 7 months in all, Jeroboam's death must have occurred *c.* 746-745. Hosea's ministry therefore began some time previous to this date (1^4). The prophet's career probably closed before 735-734, the date of the Syro-Ephraimitic invasion of Judah, as he makes no allusion to this event, nor yet to the deportation of northern Israel by Tiglath-pileser in 734. Gilead is still an integral part of Israel (5^1 6^8 12^{11}), and Assyria is not spoken of as an enemy but as a delusive support (5^{13} 7^{11} 8^9 $12^{1. 2}$ 14^3). The title 'king Jareb' (LXX '$I\alpha\rho\epsilon\iota\mu$) given to the king of Assyria (5^{13} 10^6) remains obscure. (See JAREB). Not less obscure is 10^{14} 'as Shalman spoiled Beth-arbel.' If Shalman were a shorter form of Shalmaneser, reference might be to Shalmaneser III. (783-773), though the period of his reign is rather remote. Others consider that Shalmaneser IV. (727-722) is referred to, and regard the words as a later gloss. Nothing is known of any operation of Shalmaneser IV. against a place Beth-arbel, and it is by no means certain that Shalman is a contraction for Shalmaneser.* Even if the word 'Judah' be genuine in 5^{13} (which there may be some reason to doubt, as it is not repeated in the parallelism), the passage does not say that Judah had recourse to Assyria for help as Ephraim did, and contains no allusion to the appeal of Ahaz to Tiglath-pileser. The reference to the kings of Judah in the heading (1^1) is no doubt from the hand of a later editor (cf. Is 1^1, Mic 1^1). The first part of the title, 'The word of the LORD which came to Hosea, the son of Beeri,' may be older ; at any rate the name Beeri is historical. The name 'Jeroboam' may be an inference from 1^4 'the house of Jehu,' and be due to the hand which inserted the names of the kings of Judah. If this is not the case, the title must be restricted to chs. 1-3 ; but there is little probability that these chapters were put out or ever existed separately. Chs. 1-3 appear rather an introductory programme to 4-14, expressing the principle or essential conception of the prophet's teaching, and showing how it was symbolized in his personal experience. Though referring to events in the early part of the prophet's career, chs. 1-3 contain the result of reflection on his whole history and teaching, and in date of composition may be the latest part of the book. The only thing that might seem opposed to this conclusion is the fact that in chs. 1-3 there is no reference to the dynastic revolutions often alluded to in chs. 4-14. But chs. 1-3 are meant to present the prophet's fundamental conception, which is that of the conjugal tie between J$^{\prime\prime}$ and Israel, and Israel's unfaithfulness to this tie ; and this unfaithfulness, which is a state of the mind, 'a spirit of whoredom,' is most conspicuous in the cultus (though cf. 3^4 'without king,' etc.).

Hosea may have heard Amos, he must at least have heard of him and of his teaching, but there is

---

* Cf. Schrader, *KAT*² 440 ff., and the Comm. *in loc.*

hardly any trace in his book of the earlier prophet's influence. Such parallels as have been cited are entirely inconclusive, *e.g.* the following (the passages from Amos are placed second) : 4^3, 8^8 ; 5^5, 8^7 ; 5^7, 7^4 ; 9^8, 7^{17} ; 10^4, 6^{12} ; 10^8, 7^9 ; 12^8, 8^5 ; $12^{10f.}$, $2^{10f.}$. Ch. 4^{15} is certainly an echo of Am 5^5, but the verse is in disorder, and its originality doubtful. In other places Bethaven for Bethel (5^8 10^5) may be uncertain, as copyists sometimes made the change (*e.g.* LXX has Bethaven in 12^4). Ch. 8^{14} ends with a favourite refrain of Amos, but the words are suspicious.

iii. THE PROPHET'S BOOK.—The book has two divisions, chs. 1–3 and chs. 4–14. Chs. 1–3 set forth the history or parable of the prophet's marriage to a woman who became unfaithful, with the moral of the story, which is the love-relation of J″ to Israel, and Israel's unfaithfulness to this relation. The story is told in ch. 1, 3, the exposition of it is given in ch. 2. In chs. 1–3 the prophet has abstracted from his prophetic speeches and career the essential conception of his teaching and set it as a kind of programme at the head of his book. Chs. 4–14 are more a reflection of his prophetic ministry as it was actually exercised, though the chapters have also been written or redacted under the influence of his fundamental idea (cf. for evidence chs. 4–6).

A. *FIRST DIVISION.*—Chs. 1–3.—' In the beginning when J″ spake to Hosea, J″ said to Hosea, Go, take a wife of whoredoms, and children of whoredoms. And he went and took Gomer, the daughter of Diblaim.' A 'wife of whoredoms' does not mean a woman already a sinner ; nor yet a woman with a propensity to unchastity, a sense which the words could not bear. A 'wife of whoredoms' is explained by 'children of whoredoms.' The children did not yet exist ; they were born in the prophet's house, for Hosea did not marry a woman with a family ; and in like manner the woman when taken was not yet that which she afterwards became. If the events be real, the words are written from a much later period in the prophet's history. Looking back on his experiences with Gomer, and all that he had suffered and learned through them, Hosea felt that his impulse to take this woman to wife was the beginning of J‴'s speaking to him (cf. Jer 32^8). Whether the events were real or not, chs. 1–3 were probably written at a late period of Hosea's life.

Gomer bare a son, and the LORD said, ' Call his name Jezreel, for I will visit the blood of Jezreel upon the house of Jehu ' (1^4). The blood of Jezreel refers to the murder by Jehu of all the descendants of Ahab and the whole house of Omri (2 K 10). The name **Jezreel** is used merely to recall the deed of blood. It is an ominous sound, a knell rung in the ears of Jeroboam and the nation to awaken the sense of guilt and the presentiment of retribution. Again, Gomer bore a daughter, and the LORD said, ' Call her name Lo-ruhamah (' unpitied '), for I will no more have pity on the house of Israel ' (1^6). Finally, she bore a son who was called Lo-ammi (' not-my-people '), ' for ye are not my people, and I will not be your God ' (1^9). The three names suggest the three successive steps in the destruction of the inhabitants of the land : Jezreel calling to remembrance the blood that lies on the land ; **Lo-ruhamah** pointing to a condition of Israel, when, no more pitied by J″, she shall be delivered over to calamity and her enemies ; and **Lo-ammi** indicating that the people shall be driven out of Canaan, the house of J″, and go into exile. Ch. 3 attaches itself to ch. 1^{1-9}. The last symbolical word in ch. 1 was Lo-ammi, pointing to a divorce by J″ of His people, or at least a casting out of them out of His house. Ch. 3 continues the history. ' And the LORD said unto me,—

Again, go love a woman, loved of a paramour and an adulteress,

As J″ loveth the children of Israel, though they turn to other gods.'

The woman whom Hosea is bidden again go love is of course the same woman Gomer of the first chapter. She is a woman loved of a paramour and an adulteress. The word Lo-ammi (1^9) suggests the unrecorded step in the history : the woman had fled or been driven from the prophet's house and become the slave-concubine of another. He is bidden renew his love to her. So he acquired her again to himself for a small price (that of a slave, Ex 21^{32}), returning to her in mind, but deferring for a long time to return to her in union (3^3). The explanation is added : ' The children of Israel shall remain many days without king, and without sacrifice,' etc. The LORD'S love continues with His people, whom He shall keep in long restraint and discipline in exile, till their mind change and they seek Him. Ch. $2^{2ff.}$ is the exposition of this history : (1) Israel's whoredoms with the baals (the calf images, which are no God, 8^6), vv. $^{2-5}$; (2) her perplexities when ' unpitied,' vv. $^{6-13}$; (3) her exile and discipline in the wilderness, vv. $^{14-18}$; and (4) her change of mind and new espousals and obtaining of mercy for ever, vv. $^{19-23}$. Though ch. 3 be appended somewhat loosely, it supplies an essential step in the story, and its contents are drawn into the exposition ch. 2^{14-23}.

The Marriage of Hosea.—Various opinions have been held on this subject. 1. It has been supposed that Hosea allied himself with a woman already known as a sinner, with the view of reclaiming her. It is very difficult to believe either that the prophet should do such a thing, or that he should represent himself as commanded by God to do it. It is a different thing when he seeks to reclaim the woman afterwards (3^1), and represents his efforts to do so as the command of God, because she was then his wife. Moreover, the representation that the woman was already a sinner when taken to wife does not suit the symbolism. It is the view of the prophet and all the early prophets that Israel was pure in the first time of her union to J″, and only corrupted herself later. Hosea says, ' I found Israel like grapes in the wilderness,' a figure suggesting His delight in her (9^{10}) ; and in Jer 2^2 He says, ' I remember of thee the kindness of thy youth, thy bridal love, how thou didst follow me in the wilderness.' Though this view was formerly advocated, and deserves mention because supported by Pusey, it has probably few adherents now.

2. It has been maintained by many that the whole story is an allegory. Neither the arguments for this view nor those against it are of much force. (1) It is argued that prophets often represent themselves as commanded to perform actions which, from the nature of the case, could not really have been performed (Ezk $4^{2ff.}$). The actions were ideal ; their meaning was easily seen when they were described ; and they had no existence except in the idea and the description. All this is true ; but it is equally true that prophets, particularly in early times, did sometimes perform real actions having a symbolical meaning (1 K 22^{11}, Jer 28^{10}). (2) The fact that the names of the children, Jezreel, Lo-ruhamah, and Lo-ammi, are significant makes neither for nor against the allegorical interpretation. Real children might have been given symbolical names, as was the case with Isaiah's sons (7^3 8^1). On the other hand, no symbolical meaning has been discovered for the name of the mother, Gomer. (3) The argument of Ewald, and others after him, that the prophet would have made himself ridiculous if he had published such a pitiful narrative about himself all the while that his wife was virtuous and his domestic relations happy, has little force. If his hearers *understood* that he spoke a parable, they would not have given a thought either to himself or his wife, but have attended only to the moral of his tale. (4) The statement so often repeated, that there is nothing to suggest that the prophet is not narrating an actual history, will not be acquiesced in by everyone. When it is said, ' Go, take a wife of whoredoms, for the land committeth whoredom against the LORD' (1^2) ; and then, ' Again go love a woman, an adulteress, as J″ loveth the children of Israel, while they turn to other gods' (3^1), the first impression produced by the words is that the actions commanded were not real, but meant merely to clothe an idea. Cf. the exposition $2^{2ff.}$.

3. It is held by many that a certain substratum of fact underlies the prophet's narrative. The chief arguments for this view are, first, that it is more in harmony with the realism of ancient prophecy to suppose that Hosea alludes, however reservedly, to a fact, than that he is putting forth a mere literary fable ; secondly, that no symbolical meaning can be discovered in Gomer-bath-Diblaim, which must therefore be the name of an actual person ; and thirdly, that we have thus an explanation of the origin of the prophet's central conception of the love-relation of J″ to His people and their unfaithfulness. The conception was suggested by the prophet's own experiences. Some such miserable history as he narrates had befallen him. His wife

had gone astray, sharing the common corruption of morals about her. What had happened to him was not an individual case. It was not individuals that were corrupt, the corruption was general—Israel was corrupt. And meditating on his history he saw in it a reflection of the history of J″ and His people, of His love and Israel's insensibility to it. And reflecting further on it, the conviction forced itself upon him that it was not an accident or a misfortune that had brought him through such painful experiences, it was God's providential way of revealing to him His own heart towards His people—his impulse to take this woman to wife was the beginning of J″'s speaking to him (1²).

The attempt to fit this theory into the prophet's life is not without difficulty. (1) The prophet's taking Gomer to wife was due to his own natural impulse ; it was not till much later that he concluded that the impulse had been prompted by God. The same must be said of his return in love to her after she had left his house (ch. 3) : it was due to his own unchanging affection ; and it was only later reflection that led him to interpret his own act as the command of God. (2) But now, these events must have covered a good part of the prophet's life. The birth and weaning of three children, according to the habits of Heb. mothers, would occupy 6 to 10 years ; and when to this is added the time during which the woman was away from the prophet's home and under the protection of another, and the time occupied in recovering her, it will appear that not much short of the whole prophetic life of Hosea is covered. (3) It is of some consequence to ask, When did his wife's infidelity become known to the prophet? Wellhausen, who claims to have given the cue to the interpretation both of Kuenen and W. R. Smith, argues, and surely rightly, that it was not till after the birth of his first child. But if so, it was not his misfortunes that gave Hosea his prophetic word. Israel's apostasy was plain to him, and he foreshadowed her doom in Jezreel, the name of his first child, before any misfortunes overtook him. At most, his misfortunes may at a later time have given a *complexion* to his prophetic thoughts. (4) Wellh. (followed by Nowack) appears to think that Gomer's unfaithfulness was discovered before the birth of the other two children. There is really no evidence on the point. There is certainly none in the names of the children, for Lo-ruhamah and Lo-ammi are names having a purely objective reference to the impending fate of Israel ; there is not the slightest evidence that they express any feeling on the part of the father toward the children, or any dislike of them as of doubtful parentage. It is hard to believe that Hosea would have continued to retain an adulteress in his house. It is said that ' he concealed the shame of their mother and acknowledged her children as his own, hiding his bitter sorrow in his own heart' (W. R. Smith, *Prophets*, 179, cf. 183). If he concealed the shame at the time, he certainly took effectual pains to proclaim it to all the world soon afterwards. It would be more natural to suppose that it was only after all the children were born that the woman's character was revealed to the prophet, either through her desertion or in some other way, and that then for the first time he could use the bitter words, ' a wife of whoredom and children of whoredom.' Even the passage 4¹⁴ leaves any other view improbable.

It is not of much consequence for the interpretation of the prophet's book whether we suppose his marriage real or parabolical. In any case his conception of the relation of J″ to Israel is clear. If the story is a parable, it evidently helped Hosea's mind in conceiving the divine relation to imagine a human analogy to it. And many scholars have felt that it helped them to realize his idea and how he reached it to suppose the story historical :—to fancy a man of the prophet's depth and sensitiveness of nature united to a light woman, who could not even understand a mind and love like his ; his anguish and desolateness on discovering how things were ; and yet, amidst whatever inward struggles, his patience and self-forgetfulness, and the unchanging trueness of his affection, which could not let his wife go, but sought her out in order to recover her from her evil. Such a history of his own, it is thought, helps to explain the colour which he has thrown over the relation of J″ to His people—the human and moral and personal colour which he gives to the relation.

One or two general considerations may be stated. (1) Israel's unfaithfulness and declension must have been patent to Hosea apart from any history of his own, as it was to Amos and to Elijah a century earlier. And J″'s constant goodness must have been equally patent, as it was to Amos (2⁹⁻¹¹) and to Isaiah (1²). And the fatal issues of the people's ingratitude must have also been clear. These general truths needed no particular history of his own to impress them on Hosea. (2) It is not therefore these ideas of the relation of J″ to Israel

that are peculiar to Hosea, but the conception of the marriage tie under which the relation has been brought. Wellhausen considers the conclusion 'unavoidable' that something in the prophet's experience must have suggested this new idea (*Kl. Proph.* p. 105). But there was little in it new. It was customary to regard the community or land as mother of the inhabitants ; to regard the god as the ' baal,' *i.e.* lord or husband of the land ; and also to regard the inhabitants as his children (Nu 21²⁹). It therefore ' lay very near to think of the god as the husband of the worshipping nationality or mother land. It is not at all likely that the conception was in form original to Hosea or even peculiar to Israel ' (W. R. Smith, *Proph.* 171 ; cf. *RS* 92 ff.). The idea was so current that Hosea makes Israel express it, ' I will return to my first husband ' (2⁷), and again, ' Thou shalt no more call me my baal ' (2¹⁶). It did not therefore need any experiences of the prophet's own to suggest this idea to him. (3) What is strange rather is that he did not reject the idea, considering its associations. He has retained it, and what is new in him lies in this, that he lifts the conception of the marriage relation of God and people out of the nature-sphere, to which it originally belonged, into the moral sphere, and gives it developments of surprising depth and tenderness. No one will affirm that domestic experiences of his own were necessary to this, and no one need deny that they might have been helpful. Even on the latter supposition, it must have been some higher influence that enabled him to make the transition from his own history to that of God and the people, for it was not just every good man with a bad wife in Israel that perceived in his own experiences a reflection of the history of God with His people, and forthwith became a prophet. (4) The question is not without wider connexions. There may be a risk of attributing too much to circumstances and too little to mental idiosyncrasy in the prophets, and of forgetting that they had stable convictions regarding God, and were not dependent on incidents for their ideas of Him. Hosea's conception of God is very unlike that of Amos, but every line of his book proves that he was very unlike Amos in type of mind. There may also be a risk of allowing our general views of the stage of religious development reached by Israel in this age to modify our particular views of Hosea's teaching. If we suppose that Hosea is the first to reach the profound thoughts of the spirituality and love of God which he sets forth, we shall welcome any incident or occasion in his life which just at this time suggested such thoughts. But his allusions to the history of Israel do not suggest that he came with an idea of God learned from some other source which he read into the history. He does not read the love of God into the history, he reads it out of it. It is the history that has taught him what J″ is (9¹⁰ 11¹ᶠᶠ· 12⁹ᶠᶠ· 13⁴ᵗ·).

B. *SECOND DIVISION.*—Chs. 4-14.—Attempts have been made to divide these chapters into sections illustrating particular ideas, but without success. Ewald found three sections—first, the arraignment, 4¹-6¹¹ᵃ ; second, the punishment, 6¹¹ᵇ-9⁹ ; and third, retrospect of the earlier history, exhortation, and comfort, 9¹⁰-14¹⁰. Driver (*LOT*⁶ 303) finds the thought of Israel's *guilt* to predominate in 4-8 ; her *punishment* in 9¹-11¹¹ ; while both ideas are combined in chs. 12. 13, with a glance into the brighter future in ch. 14. But in truth the passage is scarcely divisible ; it consists of a multitude of variations all executed on one theme, Israel's apostasy or unfaithfulness to her God. This unfaithfulness is a condition of the mind, ' a spirit of whoredoms,' and is revealed in all the aspects of Israel's life, though particularly in three things: (1) The cultus, which, though ostensibly service of J″, is in truth worship of a being altogether different from Him; (2) the internal political disorders, the changes of dynasty, all of which have been effected with no thought of J″ in the people's minds; and (3) the foreign politics, the making of covenants with Egypt and Assyria, in the hope that they might heal the internal hurt of the people, instead of relying on J″ their God. The three things are not independent, the one leads to the other. The fundamental evil is that there is 'no knowledge of God in the land,' no true conception of Deity. He is thought of as a nature‑god, and this conception exercises no restraint on the passions or life of the people; hence the social immoralities and the furious struggles of rival factions; and these, again, lead to the appeal for foreign intervention. The prophet sometimes couples (1) and (2) together, as in 8⁴ᶠᶠ·, and sometimes (2) and (3), as in 5¹³ 12¹. Chs. 4–13 are one long indictment of Israel and threat of punishment; a few passages illustrating the unchanging love of J″ at the beginning (9¹⁰ 11¹), and all through the people's history (11³· ⁴, cf. 2⁸), only throw their unfaithfulness into deeper shadow.*

(1) *The Cultus.*—Chs. 4–6 are mainly devoted to the cultus, though it is often alluded to all through the chapters (8. 9¹ 10¹· ⁶· ⁸ 11² 13²). The term 'whoredom' is specially applied to the cultus. The idea may have been suggested by the gross immoralities practised at the sanctuaries (4¹³· ¹⁴), or it may be a corollary from the conception of the marriage relation of J″ to Israel. The cultus is whoredom or unfaithfulness, because, whatever be the name which the people give the god they serve, he is another than J″. There is 'no knowledge of God in the land'; under the name of J″ they are worshipping a *baal*. The feasts of J″ are 'the days of the *baals*' (2¹³), the local Jehovahs are *baals*. They are not the true husband of Israel, but 'her lovers' or paramours; she goes after them and forgets J″ (2⁵· ¹³). Israel is a harlot, following her 'lovers' for the hire which they give her on all the corn-floors (9¹ 2⁵). The judgment of Hosea is that the genuine Israelitish spiritual conception of J″ has been changed, and another conception substituted for it. He goes further, and asserts that the people are not unconscious of the change: 'I will return to my first husband' (2⁷, cf. 5¹⁵ 6¹ᶠᶠ·). The conception of J″ that has taken the place of the true idea of Him is that of a local nature-god, from whom nothing higher is expected than the fruits of nature (2⁵ 9¹), and who seeks nothing in return but such nature gifts (5⁶). But this is not J″. He desires piety (or goodness, חֶסֶד), not sacrifices (6⁶); He has no pleasure in the flesh which they sacrifice and eat (8¹³). His service is that of the mind and life. Such has been their God from the land of Egypt (12⁹ 13⁴), who has continuously spoken to them by His prophets, for by a prophet J″ brought up Israel from the land of Egypt, and by a prophet was he preserved; and He has multiplied visions (12⁹ᶠ· ¹³). The ritual cultus, because of the perverted notion that it is what J″ desires, is 'sin' (4⁸): Ephraim multiplies altars to sin (8¹¹ 10⁸). And it is the priests, whose office it was to instruct the people in the true knowledge of God, who are responsible for the people's ignorance. They themselves have rejected knowledge (4⁶). For interested reasons they foster the people's propensity to sensuous service: 'They feed upon the sin of my people'—the sacrificial cultus (4⁸). And it is in vain that J″ writes or might write moral *Torahs* ever so many, revealing the 'know-

ledge' of Him; they are accounted a foreign thing (8¹²). A 'spirit of whoredom' possesses the people. Their mind is wholly away from J″ as He truly is.

Hosea's judgment is that the religion of Israel has become Canaanitized; it is the old native gods that are worshipped, though under the name of J″. The Dionysiac revelry at the feasts is not Israelitish, it is that of 'the peoples,' the heathen (9¹). He hardly ascribes real existence to the *baals*, it is a distinction of conceptions of J″ which he draws. As for the 'calves,' he will not allow that they have any relation to J″—'a workman made it: it is no god' (8⁶). Its wooden kernel shall become splinters, and its gold hull shall be a present to king Jareb (8⁶ 10⁶). With mock sympathy he describes the people and priests of Samaria as 'mourning' over its fate (10⁵), and makes merry over the spectacle of human worshippers kissing calves! (13²). But though the loss of 'knowledge of God' be the worst form of Israel's declension and the source of all other forms of it,—for religion ramifies into all the channels of life, and the nature-god instead of restraining human passions is rather served by the indulgence of them (4²· ¹³· ¹⁴),—Hosea sometimes suggests a broader ground for Israel's corruption. It was due to their entrance upon the Canaanite civilization: 'according to the goodness of his land they made goodly images' (10¹ 4¹¹ 11² 13²· ⁶). In their whole mind the people has become Canaanitized: 'He is Canaan; the balances of deceit are in his hand' (12⁷ᶠ·). Not till all the forms of Canaanitish life be swept away (2³) and Israel have again to go through the wilderness will she learn to know J″ as the chief good, and respond to Him as in the days of her youth (2¹⁴· ¹⁵ 12⁹, cf. Jer 2²). See iv.

(2) *The Internal Misrule.* — Whether Hosea directly calls the internal political condition 'whoredom' is not quite certain. He does so name the external politics: making alliances abroad is 'hiring loves' (8⁹). And there was no reason why he should not have given the same name to the internal politics, for 'whoredom' is less particular actions than a state of the mind, indifference to J″. In 8⁴ 'setting up kings' and making images are coupled together, and perhaps called 'their two transgressions' (10¹⁰). The term 'to be unfaithful' (בגד) appears used both of political and religious defection (5⁷ 6⁷, possibly 10⁹ for 'stood'). The term 'adulterers' (7⁴) hardly refers to political immorality, but J″ complains of the people that 'they have departed from him' and 'speak lies against him' (7¹³), that they surround Him with lies and deceit (11¹²), and multiply lies and violence (11⁷ 12¹ 13¹⁶). They are untrue to J″; they make and unmake kings, with no regard to Him or the principles of His religion: 'They have set up kings but not by me, princes and I knew it not' (8⁴); 'all their kings are fallen, there is none among them that calleth upon me' (7⁷). The 'pride' (גאון) of Israel, *i.e.* his self-confidence and indifference to J″, testifieth to his face (5⁵ 7¹⁰).

The picture which the prophet draws of the internal condition of the kingdom in his day is a terrible one. Jeroboam, who is supposed to have died *c.* 746–5, was succeeded by his son Zechariah, who, after a reign of six months, was assassinated by Shallum. The murderer was able to maintain himself no more than a month, when he was attacked and slain in Samaria by Menahem. In all likelihood Menahem would have shared the same fate at the hand of some other conspirator but for the assistance of Pul, king of Assyria, to whom he paid 1000 talents of silver that his hand might be with him to confirm the kingdom in his

---

*How entirely threats pervade chs. 4–13 may be seen from these passages: 4 16ff. 19 5 5. 8. 9. 10 7 12. 16 8 1. 3. 5. 6. 13 9 1-6 9 7. 11. 15. 17 10 1-8 10 9-15 11 5. 6. 7 12 2. 9. 14 13 1-4 13 5-8 13 9-11 13 12f..

hand (2 K 15¹⁹). As an Assyrian vassal (5¹³ 7¹¹ 8⁹ 12¹) Menahem was able to maintain himself for some years against other factions, which probably sought the help of Egypt (7¹¹ 8¹³ 9³⋅ ⁶ 11⁵). Under the long and successful reign of Jeroboam the country had advanced greatly in material prosperity. There were ample resources in the land to nourish the various factions, and they struggled with one another with a fury which the prophet can compare to nothing but the raging heat of an oven, though the figure contains the darker trait of a long-sighted policy which suppressed the fire till the time came to let it blaze out (7⁴⁻⁷). Society appears completely dissolved : there is nothing but 'false swearing, and murder, and stealing, and committing adultery,' and one deed of blood follows on the heels of another (4²). The prophet alludes to incidents which would be understood by his hearers, though they are obscure to us. We cannot identify that scene of revelry and possibly regicide which signalized 'the day of our king' (7⁵) ; nor tell why Gilead (Gilgal ?) is said to be 'tracked with blood' (6⁸ 12¹¹) ; nor why it is said that 'all their wickedness is in Gilgal' (9¹⁵) ; nor what is meant by 'transgressing the covenant,' nor what *there* refers to (6⁷) ; nor explain the allusion, 'the company of priests murder in the way to Shechem' (6⁹) ; nor what is meant when the rulers and priests are charged with being 'a snare on Mizpah, and a net spread on Tabor' (5¹). These and other allusions, such as to 'the days of Gibeah' (9⁹ 10⁹), are obscure, but they indicate that internal convulsions were breaking the nation to pieces (5¹⁰ 7¹⋅ ⁹ 8⁸).*

When Hosea assails 'king and princes,' he is scarcely condemning monarchy in principle as a form of government incompatible with the idea of the theocracy. His judgment is practical and historical, not theoretical. As a matter of history, and particularly in the prophet's day, the monarchy has failed to secure the peace and well-being of the people : 'Where now is thy king that he may save thee, and thy princes that they may deliver thee ?' (13¹⁰). It has, on the contrary, been the constant source of faction and anarchy. It is the motives and methods of setting up and deposing dynasties that Hosea condemns, of which the revolution of Jehu is an example (1⁴). It is true that in his picture of the final condition of Israel (2¹⁸⁻²³ 14) the king finds no place ; but this is due to his personification of the community, and his thinking not of its form but of its mind. Following the Targum, some scholars interpret 'the days of Gibeah' (9⁹ 10⁹) of the election of Saul ; but though Saul belonged to Gibeah he was not made king there, but at Mizpah according to one tradition (1 S 10¹⁷ff·), or at Gilgal according to another (1 S 11¹⁵). Hosea speaks of the days of Gibeah as signalized by some *crime* (10⁹), though the story of Jg 19 ff. scarcely corresponds to his allusions. At any rate, his reprobation of 'king and princes' must not be read as merely a condemnation of the 'schism' of the North ; his idea is much wider and more general. He is weary of Politics. His ideal is already that of the Church of God.

(3) *External Politics.*—Reliance on foreign help is also 'unfaithfulness' to J" (8⁹). The love of J" elevates the subject of it into a personality. Corresponding to His mind there must be another mind, with a sense of benefit and capacity for affection. And when Israel leans on foreign powers, this reveals not only distrust of J", but alienation of mind from Him, and dissatisfaction with the whole range of affections and duties which the relation to J" imposes.

To the prophet the issue of all this is certain : J" will drive Israel out of His house (9¹⁵). Hosea

* For walking 'after the commandment' (5¹¹) the VSS read 'after vanity' ; but the reading is feeble and indefinite.

has no clear idea of the instrument or means of Israel's destruction. It is 'the sword' (7¹⁶ 11⁶), the 'enemy' (8³ 5⁸⋅ ⁹) ; or it is natural, internal decay (7⁸⋅ ⁹ 9¹⁶), the moth and rottenness (5¹²). Israel shall be made to go through the wilderness (2¹⁴) ; but they shall also eat unclean things in Assyria (9³ 8⁹) ; and again, Egypt shall gather them, Moph shall bury them (9⁶ 7¹¹ 8¹³ 9³ 11⁵) ; and again, they shall be wanderers among the nations (9¹⁷ 10¹⁰). The question sometimes put, whether it was the prospect of national overthrow that impressed upon the prophets the national sin, or the sin that led them to forecast the overthrow, receives a ready answer so far as Hosea is concerned. He perceives that apostasy from J" contains destruction in it (7¹³ 13⁹ ?), that moral law operates as infallibly as natural law : 'they have sown the wind and reap the whirlwind' (8⁷), 'ye have plowed wickedness, ye have reaped iniquity' (10¹³ ; cf. on the other hand 10¹²) ; unchastity tends not to increase but to childlessness (9¹⁰ff· 4¹⁰) ; Egypt and Assyria whose help they seek shall swallow them up.

iv. SOME GENERAL IDEAS. — (1) *God and Religion.*—J" is God : 'there is no knowledge of God' has for parallel 'they do not know J"' (5⁴, cf. 2²⁰). His nature as revealed in Israel's history is Love. It was in love that He redeemed them from Egypt : 'when Israel was a child I loved him' (11¹) ; and He has an emotional delight in the object of His love (9¹⁰). His love has followed Israel all through their history (11³⋅⁴ 7¹⁵) ; even His chastisements are not without love—'I will speak to her heart '(2¹⁴ 3) ; and their restoration and everlasting peace will be due to His love (14⁴ 2¹⁸ff· cf. 11⁸ff·). J" is spiritual, and religion is piety (6⁴⋅ ⁶) : it is a state of the mind, not external service. It is partly this feeling of the inwardness of religion that leads to the prophet's personification of the community. He thinks of the community as a personal mind, an individual soul, in its relation to God and in His relation to it, with all the mutual, mystical interchange of thoughts and affections towards each other of the two minds. And it was in the wilderness at the Exodus that this true religious relation was perfectly realized, when Israel possessed nothing, through no medium, but mind to mind. And it is in the wilderness that it shall be perfectly realized again, when Israel, destitute of all sacramental tokens of J"s favour, land, corn, and wine, shall feel that she possesses Himself, and shall respond as in the days of her youth (2¹⁵). Such a surprisingly inward conception of religion implies two things : *first*, that the commonplaces of Israel's faith must have been long familiar, such as J"s redemption of His people, His constant goodness, the freeness of His choice of them, and the moral nature of His whole relation to them (cf. reference to covenant 8¹ and fatherhood 11¹), together perhaps with the consciousness on Israel's part that it had declined to a lower stage of religious life than it once occupied (2⁷). And *secondly*, that the prophet transcends the stage of religion reached in OT times, and anticipates a more perfect future. In his day the religious unit or subject was the community, but his personification of the community as an individual soul implies that his conception of religion requires a true personal subject—that only the individual mind can be truly in religious communion with God.

(2) *The People.*—The history of the patriarchal age and of the Exodus might almost be constructed out of Hosea's allusions. This history is his Bible, where he finds the texts of his homilies. Israel is to him a moral person, and it is not so much her actions as her mind towards J" that he has regard to. He has, however, the idea that a course of conduct leads to a state of mind in which amendment is hopeless ; as, on the other hand, the state

of mind reveals itself in all manner of insensate actions—'Ephraim is joined to idols: let him alone' (4[17]); 'my people ask counsel at their stocks, for a spirit of whoredom causeth them to err' (4[12] 5[3. 4]) They have better moments when the thought of a return to J" fascinates them (6[1ff.]); but it is a passing emotion like the morning cloud, a dramatic ideal which they have not depth and earnestness to realize (7[14. 16]). J" is at His wits' end with them (6[4]). On account of his conception of Israel as a moral person, Hosea draws no distinction between classes among the people. It is Israel His spouse whom J" drives out of His house, and it is she whom He again betrothes to Himself for ever (2[19] 14). Hosea confines his eschatology to the destiny of Israel; the nations find no place in his picture of the end. It was the Assyrian empire that brought the idea of the world, the nations, before the prophets' minds, and Hosea had probably passed away before Assyria closely touched on Israel. His prophecy ends with the prediction of the restoration, the holy beauty and eternal endurance of God's people: 'they shall bloom like the lily, and cast forth their roots like Lebanon' (14[5]).

Comparisons of one prophet with another are usually unjust to one of the two compared. Amos' mind is filled with great general ethical principles, valid eternally and enforcing themselves universally whether in heaven or on earth; Hosea starts from a religious relation of J" and people, historically formed, the mutual, mystical intimacies of which engross his thoughts. It is less in ideas than in apt terms to express them that the prophets advance on one another. Am. speaks of the goodness of J", Hos. first calls it 'love'; Am. inculcates compassion, 'humanity,' Hos. first finds the right word for this (חֶסֶד 4[1]). On the other hand, while Hos. laments the want of trust in J" revealed in the foreign alliances of Israel, it is Isaiah that first uses the positive word 'faith' (7[9]). And again, though Hos. expresses the idea of the 'new covenant' when he speaks of J" betrothing Isr. again to Himself (2[19]), it is Jer. that coins the right phrase.

v. INTEGRITY AND TEXT.—Jerome already described Hosea's style as *commaticus*—consisting of short clauses. His fondness for asyndetous construction gives a monotonous, dirge-like music to his verses—'the days of visitation are come; the days of recompense are come' (9[7]); 'Egypt shall gather them, Moph shall bury them' (9[6]). He little addresses the people; rather, turning his face away from them, he speaks of them to himself in shuddering disjointed monologue. A number of passages have been regarded by recent scholars as interpolations, particularly those referring to Judah (see i. note*), and those describing the material blessings of Israel restored (2[16ff.] 14; for list of passages athetized by various scholars see Driver, LOT[6] 306). Reference to Judah in itself need not excite suspicion any more than Isaiah's references to N. Israel. The abruptness of some of the references is strange (5[10]), though the general unconnectedness of Hosea's style must be considered. Ch 1[10]–2[1] is either a later amplification of something briefer, or it is wholly late; its right place seems after 3[5]. Nowack goes to an extreme in his excision of passages: 2[6. 7] are supported by 5[6. 15] 6[1ff.]; 2[14] by 12[9], and 2[20] by 4[1] 5[4]; and in many other cases the reasons urged for excision appear inadequate.

The *Text* of Hosea has been imperfectly handed down. A multitude of passages are corrupt, some incurably, e.g. 4[4. 18] (in v.[19] read the last word *altars*), 5[2. 7. 11] (זָר), 6[7] 7[4] 8[10b] (LXX 'and they shall cease a little from anointing king and princes'—though the ironical 'a little' is unnatural), 8[13]

(הבהבי), 9[8] 9[13] 10[9] 11[3] (read אקחם and ורועתי), 11[6. 7. 12] and others.

LITERATURE.—Besides works on the Minor Prophets as a whole, such as Ewald, Hitzig-Steiner, Keil, Pusey, von Orelli, etc., particular comm. on Hosea are: Pocock, Oxf. 1685; Simson, 1851: Wünsche, 1868; Nowack, 1880, and *Kleine Propheten* (Handkom.), 1897; Scholz, 1882; Cheyne (Camb. Bible), 1884. Cf. Valeton, *Amos en Hosea*, 1894; G. A. Smith, *The Book of the Twelve Proph.* (Expositor's Bible), 1896; Wellhausen, *Die Kleinen Proph.*[2] (Skizzen v.) 1893; also W. R. Smith, *Prophets*, Lect. iv.; Billeb, *Die wichtigsten Sätze d. Altt. Kritik vom Standp. der Proph. Am. u. Hos. aus betrachtet*, 1893. On the Text, Houtsma, ThT, 1875, p. 55 ff.; Oort, *ib.* 1890, pp. 345 ff. 480 ff.; Bachmann, *Alttest. Untersuch.* 1894; Ruben, *Critical Remarks on some passages of OT*, 1896; Loftman, *Kritisk undersökning af den Masoretiska texten till prof. Hoseas bok*, 1894, and *Kommentar till prof. Hoseas bok*, 1896.

A. B. DAVIDSON.

HOSEN is AV translation in Dn 3[21] of פְּטִישִׁין,* which is probably better represented by RV 'tunics' (Siegfried-Stade and Strack [the latter doubtfully], *Rock*, RVm has 'turbans'). RV has 'hosen' in the same verse and in v.[27] as tr[n] of סַרְבָּלִין (AV both times 'coats'; Siegfried-Stade, *Unterkleider*; Strack says 'an article of dress, probably trunk-hose' (*Pluderhosen*)). See, further, art. DRESS in vol. i. p. 625[b].

The Eng. word 'hosen' is the plu. of a Teut. word 'hose' (of which the root is unknown) denoting a covering for the leg, 'breeches,' 'trousers.' Hose is also used for the plu., but the sing. occurs in Shaks. (*Taming of the Shrew*, v. i. 69, 'A silken doublet! a velvet hose! a scarlet cloak!') and elsewhere. The 'doublet' for the body, and the 'hose' or 'hosen' for the legs, were the necessary articles of male attire in Shakespeare's day; the cloak being needful for full dress or for cold weather, as *Merry Wives*, III. i. 47, 'In your doublet and hose, this raw rheumatic day!' The hosen generally covered the feet as well as the legs; and when the coverings of legs and feet were afterwards separated, they were called respectively 'upper stocks,' and 'nether stocks' or 'stockings.' By and by both 'hosen' and 'stockings' were restricted to the covering of the feet. Coverdale (from whom comes 'hosen' in Dn 3[21]) intended to denote the long Eastern trousers. J. HASTINGS.

HOSHAIAH (הוֹשַׁעְיָה 'Jah has saved').—1. A man who led half the princes of Judah in the procession at the dedication of the walls of Jerus., Neh 12[32]. 2. The father of a certain Jezaniah (Jer 42[1]), or Azariah (43[2] and LXX), who was a man of importance among the Jews after the fall of Jerus. (LXX Μαασαίου).

H. A. WHITE.

HOSHAMA (הוֹשָׁמָע, abbrev[n] or textual error for יְהוֹשָׁמָע 'J" hath heard').—A descendant of David, 1 Ch 3[18]. See GENEALOGY.

HOSHEA (הוֹשֵׁעַ 'deliverance,' represented by *Ausi* on the Assyrian monuments, LXX Ὡσῆε, Syr.

ܐܘܣܥ) was the son of Elah. The accession of this king of Israel took place in the twelfth year of king Ahaz according to the biblical chronology, 2 K 17[1]. But this scheme it is impossible to maintain in its integrity [see art. CHRONOLOGY OF OT], as it is inconsistent in some details with itself (see Stade, *GVI* 88 ff., 558 ff.; Wellhausen, *Prolegg. zur Gesch. Isr.*[2] 285 ff.). It is also inconsistent with the date of the Assyrian inscriptions, mainly established by the Eponym Canon (Schrader, *COT* ii. pp. 161–195, 320 ff.). According to the annals of Tiglath-pileser III. (3 Rawl. 10, No. 2, line 28), Pekah, king of Israel (*bît Ḫumri*), was slain, and Hoshea ascended the throne as the nominee of the Assyrian conqueror in the same year. The original passages may be found in transcribed form in Schrader, *COT* i. p. 247, *KIB* ii. p. 32. The biblical narrative describes Hoshea, the son of Elah, as a conspirator against Pekah, whom he slew. On the other hand, it seems fairly clear, from the annals of Tiglath-pileser, though the text is mutilated in many portions, that we should render 'Pekah I slew, Hoshea I appointed . . . over them.' But there is no real contradiction between this statement and that of Scripture. Hoshea was the head of an Assyrian party in Samaria,[*] whereas Peḳaḥ represented a policy of resistance to the encroachments of Assyria. This policy underlies his attack on Ahaz in concert with Rezin ; see Cheyne's remarks (*Comment. on Isaiah*), introductory to Is 7. There are significant passages in the oracles of the contemporary prophet Hosea in which Ephraim is compared to a silly dove hovering between homage to Egypt and homage to Assyria (Hos 5[13] 7[11]). This theory of Ephraim's shifting foreign policy affords a very probable explanation of the course of events. Accordingly, Hoshea made himself the facile instrument of Assyrian power, which in 733 was threatening the very gates of Samaria. It is also probable that from the commencement of his reign (B.C. 732), down to the death of Tiglath-pileser (727), he paid tribute to Assyria like Jehu and Menaḥem before him. This may be clearly inferred from the mutilated conclusion of the inscription already quoted, and it is in consonance with the statement in 2 K 17[3]. But we also learn from this verse that soon after the accession of Tiglath-pileser's successor, Shalmaneser (*Shulmânu-asharidu*) IV., the payment of the annual subsidy ceased. Probably, the Ephraimite king expected that the death of Assyria's energetic ruler, Tiglath-pileser, the combatant king (*Jareb* [?]) of Hosea's oracles, would bring the Palestinian states some respite. In our opinion, Isaiah's beautiful poem, 9[7]-10[4] 5[25-30], belongs to this time[†] (B.C. 726). The language of the opening verses which describe ' Ephraim and the inhabitants of Samaria saying in pride and exaltation of heart " bricks have fallen, but with hewn stone will we build ; sycomores have been hewn down, but with cedars we will replace them," ' clearly suggests that Ephraim at this period was beginning to recover in a material sense from the disastrous effects of the invasion of 734–732.

The new political developments that arose in Samaria were doubtless anxiously watched from the banks of the Nile. Palestine was of great strategic importance to Egypt. For the possession of Samaria, Ashdod, Jerusalem, or Lachish by the ever-encroaching Assyrian power would be a menace to security on the Nile. During the preceding decades Egypt had been weakened by intestine divisions, but now it had passed under the hands of an energetic Ethiopian ruler Shabaka[‡] (Meyer, *Gesch. des alten Ægyptens*, pp.

343 f. 346). Henceforth Egypt sought to confront Assyria by supporting the Palestinian and Hittite states. Hoshea of Israel and Hanno of Gaza were sustained in this policy of resistance to the Ninevite power by promises of aid by the Egyptian monarch. After the death of Tiglath, the Egyptian party and policy, which opposed Assyrian domination, were in the ascendant at Samaria, just as we find in later times took place in Jerusalem (comp. Is 20. 30[1-5] 31[1-3]). But bitter experience was destined in the coming years to prove that the Egyptian power was a broken reed. Within the next fifteen years Samaria, Gaza, and Ashdod were in succession fated to discover that Egypt's ' strength was to sit still,' and a terrible overthrow was to overtake them from the arms of Assyria through the procrastinating impotence of their South-western ally.

The cessation of tribute by the king of Israel, which had hitherto been paid annually, was the first serious indication to the Assyrian monarch that Ephraim was preparing to throw off his yoke. In the summer of the year B.C. 724 the armies of Assyria were directed against the Israelite capital. Hoshea at once endeavoured to avert disaster by gifts to the Assyrian monarch, but Shalmaneser had by this time discovered that Hoshea was playing a double part. Perhaps the Assyrian troops intercepted the emissaries which the latter was despatching to the king of Egypt. At this point it is by no means easy to discover the precise order of events narrated in 2 K 17[3ff.]. Fritz Hommel (*Gesch. Babyl. u. Assyr.* p. 675) thinks that a decisive battle was fought before the walls of Samaria, in which king Hoshea was taken prisoner. The biblical statements (v.[4]) would seem to warrant this view. It would somewhat simplify the chronological problem and allow nine years for the reign of Hoshea (Tiele, *Bab.-Assyr. Gesch.* i. p. 232 *ad fin.*).[*] But it is by no means certain that the capture and imprisonment of the Israelite king did not take place after the final overthrow of Samaria.

Shortly before this time the prophet Hosea uttered his last oracles. The final four chapters evidently belong to the closing years of the Northern kingdom. The shadows of the last overwhelming calamity rest on the prophet's soul. There is indescribable pathos in these closing appeals. J" pleads with Ephraim (11[7]) : ' My people are bent to backsliding from me [?] . . . How shall I give thee up, Ephraim ? how shall I abandon thee, Israel ? How shall I make thee as Admah ? how shall I set thee as Zeboim ? Mine heart is turned within me, my compassions are kindled together.' But, alas ! Israel's doom is irrevocable. ' The iniquity of Ephraim is bound up, his sin is laid up in store. . . . Samaria shall bear her guilt, because she hath rebelled against her God : they shall fall by the sword, their infants shall be dashed in pieces' (13[12] 14[1]).

At nearly the same time Isaiah delivered his oracle against Ephraim (28[1ff.]) : ' Woe to the crown of pride of the drunkards of Ephraim and to the fading flower of his glorious beauty, which is on the summit of the fertile valley of them that are overcome with wine. Behold, the LORD hath a mighty and strong one ; as a tempest of hail, a destroying storm, a tempest of mighty waters overflowing, shall he cast down to the earth

---

[*] Comp. Winckler, *Gesch. Israel's* (Theil i.), p. 180, and *Geschichte Babyloniens u. Assyr.* p. 230 ff.

[†] Cheyne, Dillmann, and Duhm would place it some nine years earlier, *i.e.* shortly before the Syro-Ephraimite war ; but it is not easy to see what substantial grounds exist for placing it so early. If we take the Assyrian invasion of 734 as the historic background, the refrain becomes doubly significant, and the graphic description of the advancing Assyrian hosts in Is 5[26-28] (forming, as Dillmann rightly considers, a natural pendant or conclusion to the poem) seems to be based on a vivid and not too remote historic experience. 9[11] remains obscure, whether we accept the earlier or later date ; and even when we regard the Hebrew text as sound (certainly doubtful in the opening part of the verse), the phrase ' enemies of Rezin' would be thoroughly intelligible under the historic conditions which we have suggested.

[‡] The ordinary identification of the אוֹס (wrongly pronounced Sô by the Massoretes) with this Ethiopian ruler can hardly be maintained. LXX Σηγωρ ; Lucian, ed. Lagarde, reads, πρὸς Ἀδραμελεχ Αἰθίοπα τὸν κατοικοῦντα ἐν Αἰγύπτῳ. In line 25 of the Khorsabad inscr. of Sargon mention is made of Sibi, *tartan* or generalissimo of the Egyptian forces who co-operated with Ḥanunu (Hanno) of Gaza in resisting the arms of Assyria. In all probability, we ought to identify this Sibi (properly *Sib'i*) with the אוֹס (as we should pronounce it) of the Hebrew text. But this personage was not the supreme king of Egypt or Pharaoh. This is clear from the same passage in Sargon's inscription, for in line 27 this monarch is referred to under his usual title *Pir'u* as quite a distinct personage from Sibi. It is this Pharaoh whom we may identify with Shabaka or Sabaco. The Assyrians were quite able to pronounce this name, as the great Rassam cylinder (Rm), col. ii. 22, testifies, where it occurs in the form

Shabakû. See Winckler, *Untersuch. zur altorient. Gesch.* p. 92 ff. On the complex text of 2 K 17[1-6] see *AT-liche Unters.* p. 15 ff.

[*] Fritz Hommel in his *Gesch. Bab. u. Ass.* pp. 964 ff. 669 ff. places the overthrow of Peḳah in 733, but in his art. ASSYRIA (wh. see) places it two years later. This appears to be too late, though exact chronological sequence in the events of Tiglath-pileser's campaigns (734 ff.) is difficult to attain. See Winckler, *Gesch. Babyl. u. Assyr.* p. 230.

violently. The crown of pride of the drunkards of Ephraim shall be trodden under foot.'

The fulfilment of these prophecies of doom followed swiftly. We know that in the year 724 Samaria was invested by the Assyrian armies. Towards the end of the siege (B.C. 722) Shalmaneser died. Meanwhile, the beleaguered inhabitants were anxiously expecting a relieving force to arrive from the banks of the Nile, which should divert the forces of Assyria and raise the siege of the hard-pressed city. But a fatal paralysis seemed to hamper the movements of Egypt. Time went on—more than two years elapsed—and no relieving force appeared. The numbers of the garrison were doubtless thinned by constant battles with the besiegers, and by the ravages of grim famine. Sargon (*Šarrukinu*), in all probability a usurper, and certainly an able Assyrian general, succeeded to the throne of Assyria in B.C. 722. The siege was pressed on with vigour under this energetic commander. Egypt's procrastination was now Israel's ruin, and the fatal end was at hand. It is summarized in barely two ruthless lines of the great Khorsabad inscription (lines 23 and 24): 'Samaria I besieged, I captured. 27,290 of her inhabitants I carried away. 50 chariots I collected from their midst. The rest of their property I caused to be taken (?). My viceroy I placed over them, and imposed the tribute of the previous king.'

From 2 K 17[6] we learn that the inhabitants were deported to Eastern localities in or near Babylonia (see Schrader, *COT* ii. p. 267 ff.), while Babylonian inhabitants were settled in the districts of Canaan vacated by the exiled Israelites (v.[24]). Illustrative passages confirming these facts may be found in the annals of Sargon.

And so the curtain falls upon the remarkable and chequered history of the kingdom of the Ten Tribes. Respecting king Hoshea, we do not know whether he survived the tragic close of the kingdom which he ruled, or suffered the barbarous tortures too frequently inflicted on Assyrian captives. About his personal character we know little. We may infer that it lacked decisive energy and lofty patriotism. Beginning his reign as a mere puppet in Assyria's hands, he shaped his career as an opportunist. He was too astute to offend any national susceptibilities by abandoning the worship of J″, too cautious and politic to play the rôle of a purist in religious practices. Indeed an accurate historic treatment of Israel's religious history may esteem it highly improbable that such a course, forestalling the reformation of the 7th cent., could ever have entered into Hoshea's thoughts. Whether amid the syncretic tendencies in the traditional religious practices which then prevailed he was at all influenced by the teachings of the contemporary Ephraimite prophet Hosea towards higher ideals, is a question suggested, but suggested only, by the clause (17[2]), that though he committed evil it was not 'as the kings of Israel who were before him.' The impartial historian will not judge this last king of Ephraim too severely, but will unhesitatingly admit that he lived in times of direst difficulty and peril, when nothing but miraculous divinely guided statesmanship, like that of Isaiah, could have saved the realm from overwhelming disaster.

OWEN C. WHITEHOUSE.

HOSPITALITY, HOST.—No customs have taken a deeper and more permanent hold on the mind and life of the Orient than those which gather round the reception and entertainment of the guest. Few legal enactments, by whatever sanctions enforced, have met with such hearty and universal obedience as the unwritten laws of hospitality. The main practices evidently originated amid nomadic conditions. When applied to the more settled order of village or town, they were of necessity more or less modified. In modern times the influence of the tourist, and the growing usages of the West, have done much to corrupt the old simplicities. Yet in [many towns and villages, remote from the annual streams of sightseers and pilgrims, and the encroachments of civilization, the traveller will find hospitable and generous welcome, and an aversion to anything like payment. Even in such centres as Safed and Tiberias, one or two wealthy men keep open house for all-comers, where friend and foe are alike free to enjoy food and shelter for the night. In the villages, where poverty reigns supreme, a **guest-chamber**, usually the best room in the place, is often attached to the sheikh's dwelling; and there the stranger is provided for at the cost of the community. The desert Arabs, however, have preserved almost unchanged through four millenniums the customs presented in the scriptural pictures of patriarchal life.

Among the nations of antiquity the virtue of hospitality was highly esteemed. In the Egyptian Book of the Dead, in the Hall of two Truths, the god who tests the spirits thus speaks in commendation of one who has passed the judgment: 'The god has welcomed him as he wished. He has given food to the hungry, drink to the thirsty, clothing to the naked.' The Greeks thought that any stranger-guest might be a god in disguise; and the hospitable entertainment of helpless strangers, not self-declared enemies or robbers, was well-pleasing to Ζεὺς ξένιος, under whose protection they were. The ties established by hospitality were hereditary on both sides. The Romans regarded any violation of the rights of hospitality as a crime and impiety; while the Sibylline books declared that the age of the Messiah, when the happiest conditions for humanity would be realized, should witness the triumph of faith, love, and hospitality.

Turning to the Arabs, among whom are best reflected the immemorial usages of the East, we find that among them a man's hospitality is largely the measure of his reputation. 'A close fist and a narrow heart,' they say; and the niggardly soul shall not hold rule over them. To be described as 'a man of much ashes,' is a coveted distinction; the heap of ashes by his tent indicating the extent of his cooking for the entertainment of guests. 'A man whose dogs bark loudly' is one held in esteem; the dogs guiding the wanderer who might not otherwise find his dwelling. The sheikh's tent always stands in the camp nearest the travelled way, to offer first welcome to the approaching stranger. His superior position must be vindicated by superior liberality. Ibn Rashîd, in Hâyil, who exercises a somewhat uncertain sway over the wandering tribes of central Arabia, entertains at least 200 guests daily; and every stranger in Hâyil is invited to his table. The name of this ruler is accordingly highly honoured. But the poorest man will not turn the needy away. The guest, indeed, is often regarded as a benefactor, whose arrival affords his host the opportunity of honourable service.

Baiti baitak, 'my house is yours,' is part of the hospitable salutation with which the guest is welcomed. The phrase survives in the towns and cities most influenced by Western civilization; only, however, as an expression of courtesy. In remote villages, and in the desert camps, it is a simple statement of fact. As the proverb has it, 'The guest while in the house is its lord.' The present writer has been frequently thus promoted to the lordship of a house of hair, the owner waiting without until the guest bade him enter, and standing up until invited to recline on his own cushions. The stores, be they small or plentiful, are equally at the guest's command. The best of everything is placed before him; and whatever he may desire will be procured if the possibility exists. No sacrifice is too great to be made for the comfort of the guest: many will not stop even at the honour of wife and daughter (cf. Gn 19[8], Jg 19[24]). No man is demeaned by any service to his guest, even by pouring water on feet and hands, and waiting on him at meat. As one said, 'I am the slave of my guest as long as he is with me, but save in this there is no trace of the slave in my nature' (Ḥamâsa, p. 727, quoted by W. R. Smith, *RS*[2] p. 68).

There are certain well-understood provisions for preserving the honour of the host, which all guests are expected to observe. No pains should be spared to reach the resting-place before sunset. The proverb runs, 'He who arrives after sundown goes supperless to bed.' The reason being that this leaves the host too little time to prepare such a repast as his own credit requires. The law may not be enforced; but, while shelter may be demanded, in such a case there is no obligation to give food. This explains the seeming lack of hospitality in the parable (Lk 11[5-9]). Again, the guest is careful not to eat all that is brought to him, especially if his host be a poor man; somewhat must be left over, as evidence that he has had enough, and more than enough. Usually, supplies are too liberal to permit of complete consumption; but when a large company settles on a man for the night there is need for care, that he be not put to shame. Clean dishes would 'blacken his face' in presence of his guests. It is his pride to furnish over and above necessities. Yet, again, it is permissible to manifest great satisfaction with the fare whilst partaking. In drinking coffee, *e.g.*, pleasure is fittingly expressed by drawing in the liquid with considerable noise, smacking of the lips, etc. Such visible tokens of appreciation greatly delight the host. But the offer of anything in payment would be taken as an insult. The Arab eats not in the morning; the guest departs with a simple 'good-bye.' He has had no more than his right; and presently his host will enjoy like treatment at his or some other brother's hands. The recognition of this obligation to the needy stranger must often have been the very condition of life to wanderers in waste lands.

That the guest is inviolable is one of the first principles of Arab hospitality. To be safe, the stranger needs but enter the tent, or only touch a tent rope; then, even if he be an enemy, no hand will be raised against him. The homicide may claim the rights of sanctuary from the slain man's next-of-kin himself, the avenger of blood, on whom lies the chief obligation of revenge. And as the duty of vengeance belongs to all the family or tribe of the murdered man, so protection granted by one is binding upon all. To slay an enemy in battle, or when meeting him in the open field, is esteemed an act of true and valorous manhood; to fall upon one seeking shelter in his tent, would stain an Arab's name with everlasting dishonour. To injure the guest is the mark of deepest depravity. The Arabs of el-Lejâ are held in reprobation as the greatest of rascals; it is said of them that 'they will even murder the guest.' An Arab tradition points to the reputed site of Sodom as the place where stones rained down from heaven upon the people who abused 'some travellers seeking hospitality there.' In Mal 3[5] the LORD is announced as a swift witness against such as turn aside the stranger in judgment.

But the ties of hospitality receive a more weighty sanction when a meal is partaken of in common.

For an Arab to injure one who has eaten with him from the same dish, would be equivalent to lifting his hand against his own flesh and blood. They are 'brothers of the bread,' pledged by this act to do each other no harm, and also actively to promote each other's safety to the full extent of their ability. This obligation, however, lasts no longer than they may be supposed to retain the food thus eaten in their bodies; and the limit usually recognized is thirty-six hours. But constant repetition of eating and drinking in common may give permanence to the bonds. W. R. Smith (*RS*[2] p. 270 f.) quotes several illustrations of the length to which these ideas are sometimes carried. Zaid al-Khail, a famous warrior in the days of Mohammed, refused to slay a vagabond who had stolen his camels because the thief had surreptitiously drunk from his father's milk-pail before the theft. In *Amthâl* of Mofaddal al-Dabbi, a man claims and obtains help of Al-Ḥârith in recovering his stolen camels, because the water which was still in their stomachs when they were taken from him had been drawn with the help of a rope borrowed from Al-Ḥârith's herdsmen. On the other hand, after the battle of Coshâwa, a captive refused to eat the food of his captor, who had slain his son, and thus kept alive his right of blood revenge.

The protection of the stranger may anticipate his arrival at the tent of his host. It is not uncommon for one in danger to shelter himself under the name of some powerful chief, whose *dakhîl* he claims to be. It is then the duty of all to assist him in reaching his protector's dwelling: any injury done to him is regarded as an outrage upon the honour of the man who, his name thus invoked, has become the stranger's patron and avenger. Thus are deliverance and safety found in 'the name of the LORD' (Pr 18[10], Jl 2[32], Ac 2[21], Ro 10[13] etc.).

The guest may claim entertainment for three days and three nights; and for so long the host may require him to stay. This latter right, although seldom exercised, is always acknowledged. Should the stranger remain beyond this period, he may be put to some useful work—a provision, probably, against idlers and hangers-on. Permanent abode in the dwelling of his host (Ps 23[6]) the guest may secure only by becoming identified with the family through marriage or adoption. See GER.

The religious significance and origin of these customs is suggested by the name universally given to the stranger entertained. He is 'the guest of God,' *daif Ullah*, that is, one for whom loyalty to God demands hospitable treatment. The Arab is himself a sojourner with God, under the blue canopy of His mighty tent. All that comes to him, whether by robber raid or natural increase of his flocks, he takes as the gift of God, the Generous and Bountiful; in the stranger whom night-fall brings to his tent, he sees a fellow-guest, to be treated according as God has dealt with himself. The spirit in which the obligation is accepted is well expressed in the proverb, 'He who has bread is debtor to him who has none'; which, in turn, suggests comparison with Ro 1[14].

The rights of asylum, associated with temples and holy places, are survivals from the times when, by retreat to the sanctuary, direct appeal was made for the protection of the deity there worshipped; and in certain temples these refugees, guests receiving the gods' hospitality, were organized for service. Ezekiel (44[7]) denounces this practice, which had obtained a hold even in Jerusalem; and the Phœnician inscription at Larnaca affords evidence of its existence among surrounding nations. With the movement of the peoples, there grew up the idea that in migrating to any country it was wise to submit to the god of the land, and to claim his protection, since only by his favour, and as his guests, might they continue to dwell there. This was the relation in which Israel stood to God. All directions for the generous treatment of the poor and the stranger are based upon recognition of this fact (Ex 22²¹ 23⁹, Lv 19³³. ³⁴ 25²³, Dt 10¹⁹ 14²⁹ 15⁷, 2 Ch 7²⁰). To use the stranger ill was to insult the god on whose hospitality he was thrown. See GER.

The ties established between host and guest by eating together carry us back to the days when all worshippers of a god were believed to partake with their deity in the sacrificial feast. Traces of this idea are found in Lv 3¹⁻⁹ with 7¹⁵ and Dt 27⁷. Admission to this meal signified acknowledgment of the bond between the one so admitted and the god, and therefore that of brotherhood in the common faith. This involved sacred obligations of mutual help and protection. And it is interesting to note that the animal killed by the Arab for the entertainment of his guest still bears the ancient name *dhabîhah*, 'sacrifice'; and to the feast thus provided every member of the tribe may come freely, uninvited, as a simple matter of right (*RS* 236, 247, 266, 439).

These considerations cast over the customs of hospitality the spell of antiquity and of religious sanction, than which nothing could more powerfully affect the mind of the Orient. This influence is seen in the practice of sealing friendship in a common meal, *e.g.* Gn 26³⁰, and esp. 31⁵⁴. Israel was thus beguiled into a covenant with the Gibeonites (Jos 9¹⁴), which held good notwithstanding discovery of their deceit. The bitterness of the Psalmist's lot is accentuated by the fact that one who had eaten of his bread lifted up the heel against him (Ps 41⁹). Old Testament illustrations of ancient hospitality are found in Gn 18¹⁻⁸ 19¹⁻³, Ex 2²⁰, Jg 13¹⁵, Ps 23⁵; Rahab received the reward of hospitality in the safety of herself and her relations (Jos 2). The outrage on hospitality committed by the inhabitants of Gibeah was terribly avenged (Jg 20).

There are two apparent violations of hospitality mentioned with approval. One is the case of Joab, who claimed asylum in the tent of the LORD, and who was slain there by Solomon's order. But Joab had put himself beyond the pale of this benign law by his own breach of its most solemn obligations (1 K 2³¹⁻³³). The other is that of Jael, who drove the tent-peg through the head of her sleeping guest. It may be taken as evidence of the fearful degeneracy and lawlessness of these times, that this dastardly action finds honourable mention in a song of praise. But, while applauded in the excitement of triumph by those whom it so largely helped, the deed was one which, in calm judgment, would be pronounced infamous.

In the NT the customs of hospitality are recognized as binding (Lk 7⁴⁴⁻⁴⁶). It is commended and enjoined as a Christian virtue (Ro 12¹³. ²⁰, 1 Ti 3², Tit 1⁸, He 13², 1 P 4⁹); and, affording a curious parallel to the passage quoted above from the Egyptian Book of the Dead, the exercise of hospitality is taken as affording the evidence on which final judgment is based (Mt 25³⁵ with 10⁴⁰ and Jn 13²⁰).

Host occurs but twice in our Eng. Bible, Lk 10³⁵ and Ro 16²³. In the former case it stands for πανδοχεύς, the keeper of an inn or place of entertainment, where all were received on an undertaking as to payment. The πανδοχεῖον or πανδοκεῖον might be a simple khân, or a place affording accommodation to travellers. From this we have the modern Arabic *funduk*, used for 'inn' or 'hotel.' ξένος in Ro 16²³ is used in classic Greek

for the 'guest-friend,' *i.e.* any citizen of a foreign State with whom one has a treaty of hospitality for self and heirs, confirmed by mutual presents and an appeal to Zeὺς ξένιος. In this sense both parties are ξένοι' (Liddell and Scott). While mostly denoting the receiver of hospitality, it was also used for the entertainer; and in that sense it is employed here. The generous hospitality of Gaius, not limited to St. Paul, but extended to 'the whole Church,' marks him out for special honour.

LITERATURE.—Robinson, *BR*² ii. 347, etc.; W. R. Smith, *RS* pp. 76, 269, etc., *Kinship*, 41, etc.; Doughty, *Arabia Deserta*; Thomson, *Land and Book*; Burckhardt, *Notes on the Bedouins and Wahâbys*; Lane, *Modern Egyptians* (Gardner, 1895), p. 296, etc.; Trumbull, *Oriental Social Life*, pp. 73–142; Conder, *Heth and Moab*, pp. 314–356 *passim*.   W. EWING.

HOST.—Hostis, in classical Lat. 'an enemy,' came to mean 'the enemy's army,' and then, in mediæval Lat., 'an army' simply. This was its meaning when taken into Eng. from Old Fr. *host*; and this is its meaning always in AV, where it occurs as tr. of all the usual Heb. words for 'army.' Tindale uses it specially for the army in camp, Lv 9¹¹ 'the flesh and the hyde he burnt with fyre without the hoste.'   J. HASTINGS.

HOST OF HEAVEN, THE (צְבָא הַשָּׁמַיִם).—An expression occurring several times in the OT, and denoting most frequently the *stars*, but sometimes *angels*. The word 'host' is the ordinary Heb. word for *army*; and its use implies that those whom it characterizes are conceived partly as numerous, and partly as forming a regularly organized body, obedient to the commands of its lord or head.

A. As applied to the *stars*, it (1) denotes them (often coupled with the sun and moon) as *objects of religious veneration*, Dt 4¹⁹ 17³, Zeph 1⁵, Jer 8² 19¹³, 2 K 17¹⁶ 21³. ⁵ 23³. ⁵ (2 Ch 33³. ⁵); so also Ac 7⁴². It appears from these passages that the idolatrous worship of the heavenly bodies—though there are traces of it previously *—first became prominent in Israel in the 7th cent. B.C.: it was patronized by Manasseh, who 'built altars for all the host of heaven in the two courts' of the Temple (2 K 21⁵); it is mentioned in Dt as a form of idolatry which might prove specially seductive to the Israelite; according to Jer 19¹³, Zeph 1⁵, it was carried on upon the roofs of houses. Josiah, in his reformation, destroyed the altars built by Manasseh in the Temple, burnt the vessels used in the rites, and put down the priests who took part in them (2 K 23³. ⁵. ¹²). From the terms of 2 K 23¹² 'the altars which were on the roof of the upper chamber of Ahaz,' taken in conjunction with what is stated in Jer 19¹³, Zeph 1⁵, it is difficult to avoid the inference that, though the 'host of heaven' itself is not expressly mentioned, the worship had in fact been introduced into Judah before Manasseh by Ahaz. This systematic worship of the heavenly bodies was in all probability imported from Assyria and Babylonia, where there was a deeply rooted popular belief in the power of the stars to rule the destinies of individuals and nations, and where from a remote antiquity the events which had been observed to follow from given celestial phenomena had been tabulated for future reference (above, vol. i. p. 194; Sayce, *Hibb. Lect.* 396–403).

* Proper names, as Beth-shemesh, En-shemesh, and (probably) Jericho imply an ancient worship of the sun and moon: see also Am 5²⁶ (*c.* 750 B.C.); and (under Ahaz) Is 17⁸ ('sun-pillars,'—though some scholars think that this and the preceding word a later addition): 2 K 23¹¹ 'the horses which the kings of Judah had given to the sun' and 'chariots of the sun' (though, the kings not being specified, the date when these were introduced is uncertain). 2 K 17¹⁶ also, attributes the worship of the 'host of heaven' to the people of the *northern* kingdom; but the statement (which occurs in a Deuteronomic passage) *may* be only a rhetorical generalization.

Ahaz and Manasseh were both addicted to heathen observances, and both were also vassals of Assyria ; * so that there is no difficulty in understanding their readiness to patronize Assyrian superstitions.†

The expression (2) denotes the stars as *witnessing, in virtue of their apparently countless numbers, and the order and regularity of their appearance, to J‴'s creative and administrative power.* So Jer 33²² (as innumerable), Is 34⁴ (as dependent for their existence upon J‴'s will, and so as mouldering away in the day of His wrath); and 'their host' in Is 40²⁶ ('that bringeth out their host by number ; he calleth them all by name . . . not one is lacking'), 45¹² ('I have stretched out the heavens, and all their host I have commanded'), Ps 33⁶, Gn 2¹ (where 'their host' is referred to 'earth' only zeugmatically), Neh 9⁶ᵃ ('thou hast made heaven, the heaven of heavens, and all their host'). The expression also denotes the stars in Dn 8¹⁰ (as audaciously assailed by the 'little horn' [Antiochus Epiphanes]), God being (v.¹¹) their 'captain' or 'prince.'

B. 'Host of heaven' denotes *celestial beings in attendance upon J‴*, in 1 K 22¹⁹ = 2 Ch 18¹⁸ (Micaiah's vision), and Neh 9⁶ᵇ ; probably in Dn 4³⁵ ⁽³²⁾ (where the Aram. חַיִל is the word which in the Targ. regularly corresponds to צָבָא in this expression): and so also in Lk 2¹³. 'All ye his hosts' in Ps 103²¹, and 'all his host' (Ḳerê, 'hosts') in Ps 148², are meant, probably, in the same sense. J‴'s celestial attendants are alluded to frequently elsewhere, though not under this name, as Ps 29¹ 89⁵⁻⁷, Is 6, Job 1⁶ 2¹ 5¹ 15¹⁵ 21²²ᵇ 38⁷, Dn 7¹⁰ (see further ANGEL, vol. i. p. 95); and the term 'host' designates them, like the stars, as an organized body. For passages in which they are spoken of in terms suggestive of an *army*, see Gn 32² (a 'camp'), Jos 5¹ᵈ˙ but others (as Oehler, *AT Theol.* § 196; Schultz, *OT Theol.* ii. 228; Baudissin, *Sem. Rel. gesch.* i. 121-123; Dillm., Duhm, Cheyne;§ cf. LXX) think the stars are intended.

The question arises, in what relation these two senses of the expression 'host of heaven' stand towards each other. Of course the connexion may be a merely verbal one: angels and stars were equally pictured by the Hebrews as forming a 'host'; both belonged to the heavens; and both were accordingly called independently by the same name. Nevertheless, it is the opinion of many scholars that the connexion between the two senses is closer than this. Ewald (*Lehre von Gott,* ii. 294 f.) suggested that the stars were regarded as the 'visible image,' or counterpart, of the host, or army, of angels, by which J″ was conceived to be surrounded. Stade (*Gesch.* ii. 236–238) supposes that the divinities, whom the heathen nations, and the unspiritual Israelites, supposed to inhabit

the heavenly bodies, and whom they venerated accordingly, were harmonized with monotheism by being incorporated into the ranks of the angels, as subjects of the supreme God: the 'host of heaven,' originally denoting these divinities, became thus the name for the countless ministers of the heavenly King. Others remind us that the stars, moving (as it seemed) in the heaven with surprising order and regularity, were regarded by the Greeks and other ancient nations as animate beings ; * and suppose that this facilitated their being called by the same name as angels. Thus Montefiore (*Hibb. Lect.* 429) writes : 'The stars, to the Jews, no less than to the Greeks, animate beings, become a portion of the heavenly host which attended Yahweh on high'; cf. Baudissin, *l.c.* p. 120 (Hebrew popular belief regarded the stars as animated beings, similar to angels). In estimating this last view, it should, however, be remembered that there is no passage in the OT which actually speaks of the stars as animated, or distinctly identifies them with angels; for the poetical passage in Jg 5²⁰ (the stars from their courses fighting against Sisera) is no evidence of the former belief; and the fact that in Job 38⁷ 'morning stars' stand in poetical parallelism with 'sons of God' does not prove that the poet treated them as identical. No doubt, in a later age, the stars were treated as conscious beings, and even sometimes identified with angels (as Enoch 18¹²⁻¹⁶ 21¹˙⁶, where seven stars are represented as bound in a prison-house of fire, for disobedience in not rising at their appointed time, just as angels themselves are in 21⁷⁻¹²; and Rev 9¹˙¹¹, where the star which falls from heaven and receives the key of the abyss, is called the 'angel' of the abyss) : but it is a question how much such passages prove for the beliefs of the 8th or 7th centuries B.C. Our knowledge of the origin and history of the expression 'host of heaven' is too imperfect to enable us to pronounce with any confidence upon these theories ; but, so far as we can judge (1 K 22¹⁹), it seems to have been first applied to denote angelic beings. Whether its application afterwards to the stars was connected merely verbally with this usage, or whether it was facilitated by one or other of the considerations just alluded to, cannot be definitely determined ; at the same time, we may at least agree (cf. above, vol. i. p. 95ᵇ) that the movements and appearance of the stars may well have suggested to the Hebrews, as they did to other ancient nations, the idea that they were animated, and that hence a tendency may have arisen—though how far it was consistently carried out we do not know—to place them in the same class, or even to identify them, with angels, who also formed an order of heavenly beings, regarded by the Hebrews as in a special degree the ministers and instruments of Divine Providence (cf. Dillm. *AT Theol.* 320).   S. R. DRIVER.

An ambiguous position is taken by Is 24²¹, where mention is made of the 'host of the height' (*sc.* of heaven), whom J″ will 'visit' (punish) in the day of judgment on the world which the (post-exilic) prophet depicts. This expression is understood by Delitzsch to refer to angels (the allusion being taken to be to a germinal form of the doctrine, which was afterwards more fully developed, of patron-angels, presiding over the different nations of the earth); ‡ but others (as Oehler, *AT Theol.* § 196; Schultz, *OT Theol.* ii. 228; Baudissin, *Sem. Rel. gesch.* i. 121-123; Dillm., Duhm, Cheyne;§ cf. LXX) think the stars are intended.

HOSTS, LORD OF.—See LORD OF HOSTS.

HOTHAM (חוֹתָם 'seal').—1. An Asherite, 1 Ch 7³². 2. Father of two of David's heroes, 1 Ch 11⁴⁴. In this latter instance AV has incorrectly **Hothan**. See GENEALOGY.

HOTHIR (הוֹתִיר).—A son of Heman, 1 Ch 25⁴. See GENEALOGY, III. 23 n.

HOUGH.—The 'hough' (mod. spelling *hock*) of a

---

* For Manasseh, see Schrader, *KAT* ² on 2 K 21¹.

† For other allusions to the worship of heavenly bodies (though not of the 'host of heaven,' as such) in the same age, see Jer 7¹⁸ 44¹⁹ (above, vol. i. p. 169ᵇ note), Ezk 8¹⁶ : cf. also (later) Job 31²⁶ᶠ˙.

‡ Cf. Smend, *ZAW*, 1884, p. 200 (gods of the heathen).

§ In *SBOT* p. 205 ('astral spirits') ; cf. *Introd. to Is.* 70, 151 (in his *Comm.* he explained, with Hitzig, of stars and angels together).

* That the stars were divine beings, says Aristotle, a traditional belief among the Greeks ; and he even accommodated it to his own philosophy (*Metaph.* XII. (Λ) viii. 26–30, 1074ᵇ, 1 ff. : cf. *Phys.* ii. 4, 196ᵃ, 33 ; *de Cœl.* i. 2, 269ᵃ, 30 ff. ; *Met.* VI. (E) i. 18, 1026ᵃ, 18, where they are called τὰ φανερὰ τῶν θείων, with Schwegler's note ; *Eth. Nic.* vi. 7, 1141ᵇ a, ἀνθρώπου πολὺ θειότερα τὴν φύσιν).

quadruped is the joint between the knee and the fetlock in the hind leg; in man the back of the knee joint, called the ham. To hough is to cut the tendon of the hough, to hamstring. The subst. occurs in 2 Es 15³⁶ 'unto the camel's hough' (usque ad suffraginem cameli, AVm 'pastern *or* litter'). The vb. is found Jos 11⁶·⁹, 2 S 8⁴, 1 Ch 18⁴ of houghing horses (עָקַר in Piel). Tind. translates Gn 49⁶ 'In their selfe-will they houghed an oxe,' which is retained in AVm, and accepted by RV for AV text 'they digged down a wall' (see Spurrell). In his *Diary* (Wodrow, p. 123), Melvill says of 'Mr Jhone Caldcleuche, a daft wousten man,' that he 'bosted that he wald houche Mr Andro [Melvill], with mikle mair daft talk,' where the word is shown in its later and more general sense of doing one a serious injury.   **J. HASTINGS.**

HOUR.—See TIME.

HOUSE (בַּיִת [etym. uncertain; Ges. derives from a root='spend the night'], οἶκος, οἰκία, *domus*).— This article deals with the fixed dwellings of man in Syria and Egypt, exclusive of tents and temporary dwellings, which are treated of under other headings (CAVE, PALACE, TEMPLE, TENT); but, in a hot climate, where life is spent in a great measure in the open air under the shade of trees, rocks, and in booths in connexion with permanent habitations, it is not practicable entirely to divide the several subjects. It will be found that the difference to be met with in the habits of the people is not so much between those who live in permanent and in temporary dwellings, as between those who live in fixed abodes and in movable habitations. The dwellers in towns and villages have fixed abodes, though often of a very frail character; while the nomadic tribes, roving over the country in quest of pasture for their herds and flocks, require habitations which, though they can be readily packed up and carried away, are often of a very permanent texture.

Permanent fixed dwellings existed from the very earliest times (Gn 4¹⁷ 10¹¹ᶠ· [both, however, prehistorical] 12¹⁵ [Hyksos period ?]), and in the days of Abraham cities of considerable antiquity were already in existence in Palestine and Egypt ('Now Hebron was built seven years before Zoan in Egypt,' Nu 13²³, which, however, may refer only to the rebuilding by Ramses II., cf. Sayce, *HCM* 190 f.). Evidence to the same effect is supplied by the Babylonian (Nippur) and Egyptian discoveries as well as by Bliss's excavations at Lachish.

Although the family of Lot, on separating from Abraham, dwelt in the cities of the plain (Gn 13¹²), yet the Hebrews throughout their sojourn in Canaan, until going down into Egypt, were dwellers in tents (Gn 13¹⁸ 26²⁵ 31³³ 35²¹): in Egypt they lived in houses (Ex 12⁷·²⁷), and on entering the Promised Land, after forty years' camping in the wilderness, took possession of the towns and cities built by the Canaanites (Dt 6¹⁰ᶠ·): they thus had no opportunity of establishing any distinctive style of architecture, as did the Egyptians, Assyrians, and Greeks, and there is no class of buildings which can be described as characteristically Hebrew, unless perhaps the synagogues, which do not appear to have been numerous in Palestine till after the time of John Hyrcanus (B.C. 135). The houses of the Hebrews, therefore, were the houses of the people of the land where they dwelt, and we have thus to seek for them in Syria and Egypt.

We have the following records for our use, viz. : The pictures on the monuments of Egypt and Assyria, the ruins remaining on the ground, the descriptions given in the Bible and by early writers, and the modern dwellings themselves.

In drawing inferences as to the arrangements of houses in ancient times from the system adopted in modern dwellings, we must make due allowance for the more jealous seclusion of Moslem women at the present day, and also for the present method of sitting with the legs tucked up, which necessitates taking off the out-door shoe. There was far more social equality of the two sexes among the Hebrews in ancient times than there is now among the Moslems. This affected all the household arrangements, and did not require the careful seclusion of the women's apartments, which complicates the construction of modern houses. Hebrew women, instead of being immured in a harem, mingled freely with the other sex in carrying out their social duties. They attended the flocks (Gn 29⁶), prepared the meal (Gn 18⁶), invited guests (Jg 4¹⁸), and even on occasion criticized the conduct of their husband (1 S 25²⁵). They conversed with strangers in a public place with propriety (Gn 24²⁴ 29⁹ᶠ·), and took part in public affairs of any special kind (1 S 18⁶, which would suggest that they sat in an *agora*). This freedom of action naturally influenced the arrangements of the apartments in the house, and caused them to differ from those of the present day. The custom of sitting on a divan with the legs tucked up instead of sitting on a chair or stool also affects greatly all household arrangements, even to ceremonials and cleanliness, as may be seen at present in the life of the Chinese, who use chairs, and the Japanese, who sit on divans or couches. Another matter not to be lost sight of in considering the nature of the houses in early days, is the patriarchal customs of the Hebrews, and the improbability of their having many wants, accustomed as they were to living so much in tents.

The houses of the poor in early days must always have been of a very primitive character. Very often they were built of clay (mud or sunburnt brick), 'whose foundation is in the dust'; 'which are ready to become heaps'; 'by slothfulness the roof sinketh in, and through idleness of the hands the house leaketh' (Job 4¹⁹ 15²⁸, Ec 10¹⁸, Is 9¹⁰). These houses, as at the present day, were of a very unstable description, and if not instantly attended to were liable to be overthrown by heavy rainfall, hailstorm, and strong winds (Ezk 13¹⁰ᶠ·). Another inconvenience of mud houses is their liability to be 'dug through' or broken into by thieves (Job 24¹⁶, Mt 6¹⁹ 24⁴³).

In other instances houses might be built of stone with plaster (Lv 14⁴⁰ᶠ·) and mortar (Ezk 13¹¹), and wood of sycomore, holm tree (but see HOLM) and the oak (Is 9¹⁰). These stone houses were also very insecurely built; the mortar, frequently made with mud and slime instead of burnt limestone, becomes as slippery as soap during heavy rains, and whole villages have been known to be overthrown in one night during bad weather (*Land and the Book*, ii. 57). In some parts of the country, however, the houses are very carefully built of squared stone throughout, owing to the total absence of wood; and those houses do not readily decay, Mt 7²⁴ (Buckingham, *Arab Tribes*, 180, 326).

In the fenced cities the houses forming the walls are necessarily built solidly, 'great, and fenced up to heaven' (Dt 1²⁸), but those within the city do not differ materially from those in villages, except that for want of space the roofs are made more use of, and there are two storeys and often a court within the house. These houses, whether of mud or stone, are also very insecurely built, and are constantly falling down.

The people congregated, as they still do, for safety in villages and towns, and did not build isolated houses in the fields. The houses of the poor are quadrangular, usually of one storey in villages, and containing but one apartment, in which in cold weather the cattle also are housed; the portion for the use of the family being raised on a dais some 2 ft. or more above that where the cattle are herded. On this raised platform are the beds, chests, cooking utensils (1 S 28²⁴ (?)). The light comes through the door, and when there are windows they are merely apertures raised some height above the ground, sometimes with wooden gratings. There is no chimney, and the smoke from the fire finds its way out through the holes in the building.

The roofs are usually flat, except where no wood is to be obtained. They are formed of rough rafters or boughs of trees with brushwood laid across, and over all a plaster of mud, rolled flat in showery weather with a stone roller. Upon the roofs are often temporary erections of straw or boughs of trees, for sleeping under, though in dry climates the roof is generally used without any covering except a quilt. It was prescribed by Dt 22⁸ that a parapet (EV '**battlement**') should be erected round the roof, for the protection of those using it for recreation or other purposes. A stairway outside the house frequently gave access to the roof without the necessity of passing through the house. This arrangement is probably alluded to in our Lord's words, 'Let him that is on the housetop not go down nor enter in to take anything out of his house' (Mk 13¹⁵). Rahab hid the spies 'with the stalks of flax which she had laid in order upon the roof' (Jos 2⁶); Peter 'went up upon the housetop to pray' (Ac 10⁹). For similar uses of the roof cf. Jg 16²⁷ (where see Moore's note), 1 S 9²⁵ᶠ·, 2 S 11² 16²², Is 22¹, Jer 19¹³, Zeph 1⁵, Neh 8¹⁶.

A considerable amount of discussion has been occasioned by the narrative of the healing of the paralytic (Mt 9²ᶠᶠ·, Mk 2³ᶠᶠ·, Lk 5¹⁸ᶠᶠ·), and the means adopted by his four friends to bring him into the presence of Jesus. Both Mark and Luke imply that the sick man's bearers first made their way to the roof, which would be readily accessible by an outside stairway or a ladder. Their further proceedings are described thus in Mk 2⁴ 'they uncovered the roof where he was, and when they had broken it up, they let down the bed whereon the sick of the palsy lay' (ἀπιστέγασαν τὴν στέγην ὅπου ἦν, καὶ ἐξορύξαντες χαλῶσι τὸν κράββατον, κ.τ.λ.); in Lk 5¹⁹ 'They let him down through the tiles with his couch into the midst before Jesus' (διὰ τῶν κεράμων καθῆκαν αὐτὸν σὺν τῷ κλινιδίῳ, κ.τ.λ.). It is not quite clear whether Jesus was teaching in the 'upper room' of a house with more than one storey, or on the ground floor of a one-storeyed house, or, as some think, in a gallery outside the house. In any case there would have been no difficulty either in getting rid of the covering of the roof or making an opening in the battlement that surrounded it. For a full discussion of the meaning of the passage the reader may refer to such works as Gould (on Mk 2⁴) and Plummer (on Lk 5¹⁹), both in *Internat. Crit. Comm.*; Bruce (on Mk 2⁴) in *Expositor's Gr. NT*; Thomson, *Land and the Book* (1880), p. 358; Tristram, *Eastern Customs*, 34 f.

In the villages there is usually a **court** attached to the house, in which the cattle, sheep, and goats are penned; and in towns they are all brought within the walls and penned in courts and cellars belonging to the houses.

The monuments of Assyria and Egypt represent the houses much as they appear at present (Layard, *Nineveh*; Wilkinson, *Ancient Egyptians*).

In examining the ruins of ancient cities east of the Jordan, one is much struck with the prominence of the temples and the complete effacement of the private dwellings, showing that the latter were built of materials that have readily decayed. This had been noticed elsewhere; and even at Athens in the time of Pericles, foreigners were struck by the contrast between the splendour of the public buildings and the mean dwellings of the common people (Thuc. ii. 14, 65; Dicaearch, *Stat. Græc.* p. 8).

The most striking peculiarity in the aspect of houses at the present day is their blank and desolate appearance from the outside: streets 8 ft. or less in width, houses 40 to 60 ft. high, with blank stone walls and little ornament of any kind,

except the door and the projecting window over it, all peeping into which is jealously guarded against by the wooden lattice which fills up the window aperture; it is pierced with holes, and often elaborately carved. The doorways and the doors are often highly ornamented (Is 54¹², Rev 21²¹) and enriched with arabesques, and have sentences from the *Korân* inscribed on them (cf. Dt 6⁹). The doors are usually of hard wood, studded with iron nails or

CARVED HOUSE-DOOR OF PEASANT'S COTTAGE
(MT. LEBANON).

sheeted with iron, opening inwards, and furnished with bars and bolts. They are fastened with wooden locks, and wooden keys are required, often of enormous size, large enough for a stout club (Is 22²²; *Land and the Book*, i. 493). There is an opening in the door to insert the hand and key from the outside, the lock being on the inside (see below, **Lock** and **Key**). On entering the gate there is usually a porch or vestibule with a long stone bench for the doorkeeper and servants, where the master of the house receives visits and transacts business (Gn 19¹ 23¹⁰ 34²⁰, Job 29⁷ may serve to illustrate this custom, although in these passages it is the gate of a city, not the door of a house, that is referred to). This porch is separated from the chambers within by a twisted passage, so that a view inside cannot be obtained from it. The house is built round one or more courts according to the wealth of the family, each room opening into the court, and seldom one into the other; there is a verandah round the court. In the larger houses at Damascus there are often several courts, all fitted up with great magnificence, the floors paved with marble, the walls lined with faïence, the ceilings have carved ornaments and tracery and are painted in gay colours, and ornamented wooden screens separate the several chambers.

In towns there are generally two or more storeys, and on each floor the chambers open on to a common balcony running round the inside of the court, with a staircase open to the sky, usually in a corner of the court.

The passage from the entrance doorway leads into the court, which is usually paved with marble or flagging, and may have in the centre a well (2 S 17¹⁸) or a fountain, with citron and orange trees around, and overhead an awning may be stretched to keep off the sun.

As it is customary for the married sons to remain under their parents' roofs and bring up families, a house may often have forty or fifty inmates exclusive of the servants and slaves.

Opening into the first court on the ground floor, in smaller houses, are the principal apartments, the women's apartments being either in an inner court or on the floor above; but in larger houses where there are several courts, the first floor of the first court is used for the reception rooms, one large chamber being specially reserved for entertaining guests, who are treated with great honour (Lk 22¹², Ac 1¹³ 9³⁷ 20⁸). In addition to the guest-chamber of the house, in every village or encampment there is a public guest-room for entertainment of strangers, kept up at the expense of the inhabitants (cf. Gn 18¹, Ex 2²⁰, Jg 13¹⁵ 19¹⁷ˡ·). In wealthy houses the principal reception chamber opening into the first court is highly ornamented, paved with marble, with a fountain, and at the farther end the floor is raised and called the *liwan*, with a divan running round the sides, formed of mattresses and cushions covered with carpets. The ceilings and walls are elaborately ornamented and brilliantly painted (Jer 22¹⁴ of a palace).

Moslems drop the slipper or shoe at the door when they enter an inner room or step on to the *liwan*. And this is necessary both for comfort and cleanliness, as they sit with their feet tucked under them; but it would not be safe to assume that this custom prevailed among the Hebrews in early days in private life, though it was their custom so far as sacred ground was concerned (Ex 3⁵, Jos 5¹⁵, Lk 7³⁸). There is no clear indication of the Hebrews before the Captivity having used a divan on a raised *liwan*, and the words signifying 'seats' in the Hebrew do not throw much light on the subject. The ancient Egyptians are shown in one picture squatting on the ground at dinner (Wilkinson, *Anc. Eg.* i. 58, 181). A bas-relief on the walls of Khorsabad represents the guests seated on high chairs at a festival (Layard, *Nineveh*, ii. 411).

The inner courts are often planted with fine trees, and the interior walls, verandahs, and staircase clothed with vines and creepers.

Ewald (*Geschichte²*, iii. 451, 602) suggests that the *'armōn*, 'keep,' of a palace was the harem or women's apartment, the most securely guarded portion of Eastern houses; but Gesenius (*Lex.*) says, 'None of the ancients rendered the word "women's apartment," as very many of late have done, after J. D. Michaelis,' and gives the meaning as 'fortress,' 'palace' (so *Oxf. Heb. Lex.*, and Siegfried-Stade). The harem of the king of Persia is spoken of in Est 2³, and also the chamberlain, keeper of the women. It is also probable that king Solomon, after his foreign marriages, kept a harem at Jerusalem; but this was not part of the life of the Hebrews. And the customs of Moslems regarding the seclusion of women can throw little light upon the customs of people among whom the sexes were on almost equal terms.

The doors of the inner court are not usually furnished with locks and bolts, and a curtain is often all that separates it from the outer court, the idea being that all is private within the outer gate or outer court (Dt 24¹⁰, Ac 10¹⁷ 12¹³).

The upper rooms of the house are called the *'ālīyah*, which is also the Hebrew word (עֲלִיָּה) for upper chamber. Thomson (*Land and the Book*, i. 235) states that in northern Syria this is the most desirable part of the establishment, is best fitted up, and is still given to guests who are to be treated with honour. The women and servants live below, and their apartment is called *'ardīyeh*,

or ground floor; in common parlance *beit*, or house. Every respectable dwelling has both winter and summer house, *beit shatawy* and *beit seify*. If these are on the same floor, then the exterior and airy apartment is the summer-house, and that for winter is the interior and more sheltered room (2 K 4¹⁰, Jer 36²², Am 3¹⁵; see Driver's note). In the Lebanon the upper rooms are used in summer and the lower rooms in winter. In some parts of the country where the cold in winter is severe, vaults under ground are used during the cold weather. With regard to the use of the roof of the house, the 'housetop,' see ROOF.

The only mention of cooking-places is in Ezk 46²³ (the temple). The kitchens would probably, as with the Romans and Greeks, have had a hearth, with stone divisions for resting the pots on. There were no other fireplaces (Jer 36²² RV). It is supposed that there were no chimneys, but a smoke-hole is spoken of (Hos 13³; see **Window**), and it is difficult to understand how the smoke could be got rid of in two-storeyed buildings without chimneys of some kind.

Leprosy of houses (Lv 14³⁴·⁵⁵) is described by Gesenius as probably a nitrous scab; Thomson (*Land and Book*, ii. 518) alludes to leprosy in garments and in buildings as phenomena not only unknown, but utterly unintelligible at this day.

In considering the household arrangements of the Hebrews, the gradual advance of civilization and luxury must not be forgotten, and the probability that even the rich in early days lived with a roughness of surroundings which would be considered as squalor in later days. The influence of the Greeks and Romans on the customs of Palestine and the East has also to be considered. In the very earliest days of the entry of the Hebrews into the Promised Land, the Philistines from Caphtor (which is generally identified with Crete) were in possession of the lowlands of Judah; from B.C. 332 to B.C. 63 Palestine was more or less directly under Greek influence, and from the latter date for many centuries it was directly under Roman influence. The customs of the people have therefore been influenced by Egypt, Assyria, Syria, Persia, Greece, and Rome; and though the dwellings of the poor may have been little affected by these influences, there can be no doubt that those of the rich would have reflected the feelings of the masters of the day. 'How apt we all are to look at the manners of ancient times through the false medium of our everyday associations! How difficult it is to strip our thoughts of their modern garb, and to escape from the thick atmosphere of prejudice in which custom and habit have enveloped us! and yet, unless we take a comprehensive and extended view of the objects of archæological speculation, unless we can look upon ancient customs with the eyes of the ancients, unless we can transport ourselves in the spirit to other lands and other times, and sun ourselves in the clear light of by-gone days, all our conception of what was done by the men who have long since ceased to be must be dim, uncertain, and unsatisfactory, and all our reproductions as soulless and uninstructive as the scattered fragments of a broken statue' (Niebuhr, *Kleine Schriften*, p. 92).

Chamber (bed-, guest-, inner, upper).—When a particular apartment of a house is alluded to, the word 'chamber,' 'parlour,' or 'closet' is generally used in AV, the word 'room' being used in a general sense, 'Is there room in thy father's house for us?' 'We have room to lodge in' (Gn 24²³), except in three instances in the NT (Mk 14¹⁵, Lk 22¹², Ac 1¹³).

The word 'closet' occurs only once in the OT (Jl 2¹⁶), where it is used for the *nuptial tent* (see Driver, *ad loc.*), as is the word 'chamber' in Ps 19⁵. It is used twice in NT, where it represents ταμεῖον, 'store-house' or 'closet' (Mt 6⁶, Lk 12³). The word 'parlour' is used only three times. In Jg 3²⁰ᶠ· the summer parlour (עֲלִיָּה) of Eglon means the roof-chamber, raised above the flat roof at one corner or upon a tower-like annexe to the building (Moore). In 1 Ch 28¹¹ RV 'the inner chambers' (חֲדָרִים) is trᵈ 'inner parlour' in AV. In 1 S 9²² 'parlour' is used for לִשְׁכָּה, which signifies a room in which the sacrificial meals were held (see Driver, ad loc.). In RV it is trᵈ 'guest-chamber.'

There are thus only three Hebrew words used in connexion with chambers of houses. **1.** חֶדֶר a chamber: Job 9⁹ 37⁹ ἀποθήκη, cubiculum; inner chamber: Gn 43³⁰, 1 K 20³⁰ 22²⁵, 2 K 9², 1 Ch 28¹¹, 2 Ch 18²⁴; bed-chamber: 2 S 4⁷ 13¹⁰, 2 K 6¹², 2 Ch 22¹¹, Ec 10²⁰; women's apartment: Ca 1⁴ 3⁴; bridal-chamber: Jg 15¹ 16⁹, Jl 2¹⁶ (chamber); store-house: Pr 24⁴.

2. עֲלִיָּה (ὑπερῷον, cœnaculum), an upper chamber on the roof of a house: Jg 3²⁰ᶠᶠ· (Eglon), 2 K 1² (Ahaziah), 4¹¹ (Elisha), 23¹² (Ahaz).

3. לִשְׁכָּה (κατάλυμα, triclinium), a sacrificial dining-room: 1 S 9²²; used in later times for the chambers in the Temple Court in which the priests lived: Jer 35²·⁴, Ezk 40¹⁷ etc.

In the smaller houses there were probably no bedrooms, and in houses generally all rooms could be used for sleeping in, as is the case at the present day; but the inner chambers appear to have been more particularly set apart for sleeping, or were used as closets in which the bedding was kept (2 S 4⁷, Ec 10²⁰; Jos. Ant. XII. iv. 11; 2 K 11²). The furniture of a chamber for sleeping in is given (2 K 4¹⁰) as 'a bed, and a table, and a stool, and a candlestick'; its position in a retired portion of the house is indicated in Ex 8³, 2 K 6¹², and other passages. Joash and his nurse were hidden in a chamber for the beds (2 K 11², 2 Ch 22¹¹), probably a closet for the bedding. In the poorer class of houses the place set apart for laying down the beds was often merely a portion of the common room devoted to daily avocations, with the floor somewhat raised, or else a room in which the family all slept together (Lk 11⁷). The constant reference to chambers for withdrawing to and inner chambers among all classes, shows that it was usual to have more than one room in the house, except with the very poor. Houses were often two storeys in height, and the upper chamber or 'ăliyah was used for withdrawing to or sleeping in (Jg 3²⁰, 2 K 4¹¹). The chamber from which Ahaziah fell through the lattice was of this nature. Altars appear to have been erected in these upper chambers on the roof (2 K 23¹²).

Doorway (פֶּתַח 'opening', 'entrance'), **Door** (דֶּלֶת).—The doorway of the house differs from the gate of the city (שַׁעַר, πύλη, porta) in that the first was for private and the latter for public purposes. When דֶּלֶת is used of the gate of a city, it appears to differ from שַׁעַר, which denotes the whole structure, including posts, open space, etc., in being restricted to the actual door which swings on its hinges (Oxf. Heb. Lex.).

The doorway consisted of three parts:—The threshold or sill (סַף, which is used in some cases for door, 2 K 12⁹ 22⁴, Jer 35⁴), the two side posts (מְזוּזוֹת), and the lintel (מַשְׁקוֹף), Ex 12⁷ᶠ·. The door itself was of wood, stone, or metal, according to circumstances. Wooden and metal doors have disappeared; but in Asia Minor, and east of the Lake of Gennesaret, stone doors exist to the present day in situ, the stone hinges resting in the sockets (Burckhardt, Syria, p. 58).

These doors were often made with two leaves, and had bolts and bars (Jg 3²³ 16³, Neh 3⁸ 7³, Ca 5⁵). See **Bar, Bolt, Key.**

The doorways were often highly ornamented and enriched with tracery (Is 54¹², Rev 21²¹), and

inscribed with sentences of Scripture in accordance with the Mosaic Law, 'Thou shalt write them upon the posts of thy house, and on thy gates' (Dt 6⁹ 11²⁰). In Moslem countries the same practice exists at the present day. The mĕzûzâh, the distinctive mark of a Hebrew habitation, is a kind of amulet like the phylacteries, and consists of a tube of vellum, inside of which are scrolls with various scriptural texts. These at the present day are hung up inside the doorway on the doorpost. Inside the doorway was a bench for the doorkeeper and servants, and there the master of the house sat and transacted business.

The door could be broken in readily. 'They pressed, and came near to break the door' (Gn 19⁹). The willing bondman was received into the household by having his ear thrust through with an awl into the door (Ex 21⁶, Dt 15¹⁷). The inner chamber in Amnon's house had a door with a bolt (2 S 13¹⁷).

Bar (בְּרִיחַ).—(1) A cross-beam, a bar which passed from one side to the other through the rings of the several boards of the holy tabernacle, which were thus held together (Ex 26²⁶ᶠ· 35¹¹ 36³¹ᶠ·, Nu 3³⁶ 4³¹). (2) A bolt or bar for shutting a door of a gate or house.

The bar was used principally at night time (Neh 7³, Rev 21²⁵), as it is at the present day, to keep the door closed. It was made of wood or iron (Is 45²), and was inserted into sockets in the gateposts or doorway of houses (Ovid, Amor. i. 6). The door could not be opened until the bar was removed. Chamber doors were sometimes barred as well as bolted (2 S 13¹⁷; Eurip. Orest. 154 b). The first mention of the use of bars with gates is in the account of the taking of the cities of Og king of Bashan by Moses (Dt 3⁵). Samson carried away the gates of Gaza, posts, bars, and all (Jg 16³). In the rebuilding of the walls of Jerusalem in the time of Artaxerxes, both bars and bolts of the gates of the city are mentioned (Neh 3³ᶠ·).

In the Bible, bars are mentioned in connexion with city gates only, and not with reference to houses. In Jon 2⁶ the term is used in a metaphorical sense.—'The bars of the earth' (pictured as a house out of which Jonah is shut—Oxf. Heb. Lex.). The gates of Damascus, Jerusalem, and other walled cities in the East are closed at night and barred.

Bolt or **lock** (מַנְעוּל, from the root נָעַל, to fasten with a bolt, or to bind sandals to the feet).—In Dt 33²⁵ this word (in the form מִנְעָל) is given as 'bars' (RV) or 'shoes' (AV, RVm), κλεῖθρον, sera. The idea of binding and loosing with a key appears in Mt 16¹⁹ 'I will give unto thee the keys of the kingdom of heaven, and whatsoever thou shalt bind on earth shall be bound in heaven; and whatsoever thou shalt loose on earth shall be loosed in heaven.'

The bolt or lock is referred to in connexion with the doors both of city gates and of houses; but in the two instances in which the Heb. word is trᵈ 'lock' in AV, it is given as 'bolt' in RV (Ca 5⁵, Neh 3³ᶠ·). It does not appear that city gates and palaces which had both bars and bolts would require the bolt to be opened with a key, both because they were not opened from the outside, and because guards were present to protect them from being opened by unauthorized persons (Neh 3³ᶠ· 7³).

The bolt was shot into a socket made to receive it in the threshold on the inside of a gate or doorway. In the Pompeian doorways two holes in the sill correspond to the two bolts of the leaves of the doors (Gell, Pompeiana, 2 ser. vol. i. p. 167); in doorways with a single leaf the bolt would shoot into a socket in the doorpost. In the Odyssey (i. 442, iv. 802, xxi. 6, 46–50) the door was drawn to with a silver ring and the bolt fastened with a thong; to open the door from the outside the thong of the ring was loosed, and the 'well bent key' (of brass with an ivory handle) was put in, and by means of it the bolt was struck back. By degrees improvements were made in bolts until locks and keys of very advanced design came into existence, among the Greeks and Romans. In Jg 3²³ᶠ· an account is given of a door which could be locked by means of a key from inside or outside. Ehud locked the doors of Eglon's summer parlour, and Eglon's servants, after waiting for their master to open the doors from the inside, took a key and opened them from the outside. In Ca 5⁴· ⁵ reference is made to the hole in the door through which the hand was put in with the key in withdrawing the bolt ; the handles of the lock (AV) or bolt (RV) are also mentioned. ' My beloved put in his hand by the hole in the door.' In Dt 33²⁵ bars or bolts are spoken of as of iron and brass. Reference to the bolting of an inner chamber is made in the account of Amnon and Tamar (2 S 13¹⁷ᶠ·). Ancient Egyptian doors, with two leaves, had central bolts and bars (Wilkinson, *Anc. Eg.* i. 15).

Key (מַפְתֵּחַ, from the root פָּתַח, 'open,' κλείς, *clavis*). This instrument to open a lock or withdraw a bolt is mentioned only once in its literal sense (Jg 3²⁵ᶠ·). In other instances the term is used figuratively (Is 22²², Lk 11⁵², Mt 16¹⁹) as a symbol to denote power and authority delegated to a steward, chamberlain, or minister, ' And the key of the house of David will I lay upon his shoulder ; and he shall open and none shall shut : and he shall shut and none shall open.' Merchants and others at the present day in Palestine and Egypt are accustomed to carry large keys of wood or iron over their shoulders, if too long to hang at the girdle. Thomson (*Land and the Book*, i. 493) mentions the enormous wooden keys used in Palestine ; in some cases almost a load to carry.

The lock or bolt for magazines, houses, and garden gates is made of wood and hollowed out, about 2 ft. long for a gate and 6 to 9 in. long for a chamber door. It slides through a groove in a piece of wood attached to the door, and shoots into a socket in the doorpost or sill. When the bolt is shot, some pins in the groove drop into corresponding holes in the bolt, and it cannot be withdrawn without an instrument to force up these pins out of the holes and pull the bolt back. This instrument is called the key, and consists of a piece of wood furnished with a number of pins in exactly the same position (reversed). It is introduced into the hollow bolt, and, raising the groove pins, it draws back the bolt. Unless these pins exactly fit, the bolt cannot be released (Lane, *Mod. Eg.* i. 42).

In some cases doors were sealed with clay. Job 38¹⁴ ' It is changed as clay under the seal.' At Athens a jealous husband sometimes sealed the door of the woman's apartment (Aristoph. *Thesm.* 422). The king sealed with his own signet the stone brought to the den of lions into which Daniel was cast (Dn 6¹⁷). The sepulchre of our Lord was made sure by sealing the stone at the door (Mt 27⁶⁶).

Hinge (צִיר).—In early days doors were poised, not hung, on hinges (Pr 26¹⁴) ; that is to say, hinges were door-pivots let into sockets in the threshold and lintel on which the door swung. Remains of stone doors with the hinges or pivots attached are found in various parts of Syria and Egypt and Asia Minor.

The Greeks and Romans used hinges for doors like those now in use in Europe ; four hinges of bronze are preserved in the British Museum.

Knock (דָּפַק).—There is no mention of a knocker having been affixed to doors, as with the Greeks and Romans. In Jg 19²² the word (מִתְדַּפְּקִים) is used of beating violently (till they were tired) against

a door. In Ca 5² we hear of the beloved knocking (דָּפַק) at the door. At the present day one stands on the outside of the house and knocks, and calls loudly (Mt 7⁷, Lk 12³⁶ 13²⁵, Ac 12¹³, Rev 3²⁰).

Window (חַלּוֹן, θυρίς).—The Hebrew word is derived from the root חָלַל ' pierce.' This word appears to be used generally where the windows of houses are referred to, which originally were but openings pierced in the walls, without shutters. The word **casement** in Pr 7⁶ (AV) appears as **lattice** in RV, being the trⁿ of 'eshnâb. The windows in Daniel's chamber, open towards Jerusalem (Dn 6¹⁰ [Heb. ¹¹], represent an Aram. word (כַּוִּין) whose derivation is quite uncertain (the root כּוא means *to burn*). The words (מְחֶזָה אֶל־מֶחֱזָה) trᵈ ' light over against light ' (1 K 7⁴· ⁵) are derived from חָזָה ' see.' The meaning of שְׁקָפִים and שֶׁקֶף in same verses trᵈ ' windows ' in AV is uncertain. There are three words signifying ' lattice-' or ' net-work ' filling up the aperture of a window. **1.** אֲרֻבָּה. It is used to denote the smoke-hole of a room (Hos 13⁸) ; the windows of a dove-cote (Is 60⁸) ; and the aperture of the window as being closed with lattice-work and not with glass. It is also used for the ' windows of heaven ' (Gn 7¹¹ 8², 2 K 7²· ¹⁹, Is 24¹⁸, Mal 3¹⁰). **2.** חֲרַכִּים (Aram.) lattice-work or net-work of a window, Ca 2⁹ (only), ' He glanceth through the windows.' **3.** אֶשְׁנָב (of doubtful etym. synonymous with חַלּוֹן), lattice through which the cold air passes (?). Jg 5²⁸ ' The mother of Sisera looked down (see Moore) through the lattice'; Pr 7⁶ ' In at the window of my house I looked forth through my casement' (' lattice ' RV) [all].

There is another word trᵈ ' lattice,'—שְׂבָכָה, lattice- or net-work, which is principally used with reference to the lattice- or net-work surrounding the capitals of the columns (1 K 7¹⁷ᶠ·), but it is also used for the lattice or balustrade in the upper chamber of Ahaziah in Samaria through which he fell ; this word has probably no connexion with window.

At the present time in Eastern towns there is usually a large window prominently projecting over the doorway into the street, and fitted with lattice-work, which is opened only upon the occasion of high ceremonies. It is probable that in early days also one or perhaps more windows of the palaces and larger houses opened into the street, as there is constant reference to windows opening into the street or into the city wall. In the houses of the poorer classes, however, it is doubtful whether any windows existed, and what did exist were only apertures to admit light and let out the smoke. At the present day in the houses in the Lebanon the walls of the rooms are perforated with small openings (in addition to the windows), which let in light and air. Where there are courts, however, there are windows opening inwards. Among the Greeks, windows were not uncommon (Aristoph. *Thesm.* 797). The Romans had few windows, the bedrooms being lighted from the principal apartments, and the rooms on the upper floor only being lighted from the street (Juv. iii. 270). In Pompeii it can be seen how very few houses have windows opening on to the streets, and even in these cases the sills of the windows are over 6 ft. above the footway, and are very small, about 3 ft. by 2 ft.

The discoveries at Pompeii prove that glass was used for windows under the early emperors, as glass windows have been found in several of the houses ; glass may therefore have been in use in Palestine in the houses of the wealthy at an earlier date. Pliny (c. 70 A.D., *HN* xxxvi. 45) states that windows were made of *mica*, from countries near Palestine, viz. Cyprus and Cappadocia.

The references in the Bible to windows to look out from are almost all in connexion with palaces.

'Abimelech king of the Philistines looked out at a window' (Gn 26⁸). The mother of Sisera looked forth through a window (Jg 5²⁸). 'Michal the daughter of Saul looked out at the window' (2 S 6¹⁶). 'Jezebel looked out at the window' (2 K 9³⁰). In the following cases, however, there are windows in houses of the less opulent classes—Rahab the harlot let the spies down through a window on the town wall of Jericho (Jos 2¹⁵); Elisha when sick in his own house directed king Joash to 'open the window eastward' (2 K 13¹⁷); St. Paul at Damascus was let down by the wall in a basket through a window (2 Co 11³³); Eutychus, asleep on the window-seat of an upper chamber at Troas, fell down from the third storey, ἀπὸ τοῦ τριστέγου (Ac 20⁹). Windows are spoken of (Jer 22¹⁴) in connexion with a wide house and spacious chambers, ceiled with cedar and painted with vermilion. It is threatened (Jl 2⁹) that locusts shall enter in at the windows like a thief. The pelican and the porcupine singing in the windows is a sign of desolation (Zeph 2¹⁴).

LITERATURE.—The Heb. Archæologies of Keil, Benzinger, and Nowack; Edersheim, Sketches of Jewish Social Life, 93–96; Erman, Life in Ancient Egypt, 167–199; Tristram, Eastern Customs in Bible Lands, 69–88; Trumbull, Threshold Covenant (Index).

C. WARREN.

HOW.—**1.** How is sometimes used for 'that,' introducing a dependent sentence which states a fact, without reference to the manner of it. Thus 1 S 2²² (RV 'how that'), 1 Ch 18⁹ 'Now when Tou king of Hamath heard how David had smitten all the host of Hadarezer king of Zobah' (RV 'that'); especially in NT (Gr. ὅτι), Lk 1⁵⁸ 21⁵ ('And as some spake of the temple, how it was adorned with goodly stones and gifts'), Jn 4¹ 12¹⁹ 14²⁸, Ac 14²⁷ ('they rehearsed all that God had done with them, and how he had opened the door of faith unto the Gentiles,' RV 'how that'), 20³⁵, Gal 4¹³, Philem ¹⁹, Ja 2²² ('Seest thou how faith wrought with his works,' RV 'Thou seest that'), Rev 2². Cf. Shaks. Tit. Andron. II. iii. 207—

'Now will I fetch the king to find them here,
That he thereby may give a likely guess
How these were they that made away his brother.'

2. Still more frequently we find 'how that' where mod. usage would use 'that' alone. Ex 9²⁹ 'that thou mayest know how that the earth is the LORD'S' (מִי, RV 'that'), 10², Dt 1³¹, Jos 9²⁴, Ru 1⁶, 1 S 24¹⁰·¹⁸, 2 S 18¹⁹, 1 K 5³, 2 K 9²⁵ etc., and esp. in NT (again for ὅτι). The older versions have this form yet oftener, as in Tindale, Gn 20¹³ 'This kyndnesse shalt thou shewe unto me in all places where we come, that thou saye of me, how that I am thy brother'; Mt 6¹⁸ 'that it appere not unto men howe that thou fastest'; Jn 9¹⁸ 'But the Jewes dyd not beleue of the felowe, how that he was blynde and receaved his syght.'

Howbeit (=nevertheless, notwithstanding) is common. In writers of the period 'howbeit' sometimes stands for 'notwithstanding that,' 'although,' as Melvill, Diary, p. 371, 'the King sattelit and dimitted us pleasandlie, with many attestations that he knew nocht of the Papist Lords' hom-coming till they war in the countrey; and whowbeit the esteates had licenced them to mak thair offers, they sould nocht be receaved till they tham selves war furthe of the countrey again.'

Howsoever is once found with its parts separated, 2 S 24³ 'how many soever they be.' Cf. Knox, Hist. p. 30, 'how suspitious and infamous so ever they were.' Howsoever means either 'in whatever way,' Zeph 3⁷ 'howsoever I punished them'; or 'come what may' (rather more than 'nevertheless') Jg 19²⁰, 2 S 18²²·²³.

J. HASTINGS.

HOZAI (חוֹזָי) is given as a prop. name in RV of

2 Ch 33¹⁹, where AV and RVm give 'the seers.' AVm has Hosai, LXX τῶν ὁρώντων. The latter may have read חוֹזִים, which appears to be supported also by the Syriac. If we retain the MT, the tr. of RV seems the only defensible one; but perhaps the original reading was חוֹזָיו 'his seers' (so Kittel in Haupt, ad loc.).

J. A. SELBIE.

HUCKSTER.—Huckster is properly the fem. of 'hawker,' but the distinction between the Anglo-Sax. fem. termination -ster and the masc. term. -er was early obliterated. The root of the word is held by Skeat to be Du. hucken, to stoop (under a load). The huckster has always been distinguished from the merchant as a retailer of small wares, a pedlar; and the word has from very early times carried a certain opprobrium. Thus Sir T. Moore, Workes, p. 1304, 'To shewe him selfe a substanciall merchaunt and not an hukster, he gently let them have it even at their owne price'; and Glanvill, Vanity of Dogmatizing, Pref., 'Therefore I seek no applause from the disgrace of others, nor will I huckster-like discredit any man's ware, to recommend mine own.' The word occurs in Sir 26²⁹ (and in the heading to the chapter) 'A merchant shall hardly keep himself from doing wrong; and an huckster shall not be freed from sin' (κάπηλος, which occurs elsewhere in LXX only Is 1²², and not at all in NT, though the vb. καπηλεύω is found in 2 Co 2¹⁷, EV 'corrupt,' RVm 'make merchandise of'). Here the κάπηλος stands parallel to the ἔμπορος, and the charge of not being without sin applies equally to both. The sentiment is in accordance with Rabbinic notions. See Edersheim's note.

J. HASTINGS.

HUKKOK (חֻקֹּק).—A place near Tabor on the west of Naphtali, Jos 19³⁴. It is the present village Yâḳûḳ (but see Dillm. Josua, ad loc.), near the edge of the plateau to the N.W. of the Sea of Galilee, between Tabor and Hannathon, marking the border of Zebulun and Naphtali, Jos 19¹⁴.

LITERATURE.—SWP vol. i. sh. vi.; Guérin, Galilée, i. 354 ff.; Robinson, BRP² iii. 81 f.; Asher, Benj. of Tudela, ii. 421, where R. Parchi locates the tomb of the prophet Habakkuk at Yâḳûḳ.

C. R. CONDER.

HUKOK (חֻקֹק) of 1 Ch 6⁷⁵ [Heb. ⁶⁰] is a textual error for **Helkath** (which see) of Jos 21³¹.

HUL (חוּל).—The eponym of an Aramæan tribe (Gn 10²³) whose location is quite uncertain. The various attempts that have been made to establish its identity will be found in Dillmann, who does not consider that any of them has been successful.

HULDAH (חֻלְדָּה 'weasel' (?); for bearing of this name on Totem theory, see Gray, Heb. Prop. Names, 90, 101, 103).—A prophetess who lived during the reign of Josiah. All we know concerning her is recorded in 2 K 22¹⁴⁻²⁰ (reproduced almost verbatim in 2 Ch 34²²⁻²⁸). She is described as the wife of Shallum 'the keeper of the wardrobe,' who dwelt in the second quarter (mishneh) of the city. See COLLEGE. In spite of our scanty information, she must have had a well-recognized standing as a prophetess, for it was to H. that the messengers of Josiah betook themselves when they were sent to 'inquire of the Lord.' The king's alarm at the contents of the book found in the temple by Hilkiah was only partially allayed by the answer of H., which was in many points far from reassuring, although Josiah on account of his personal piety was to escape the worst of the coming evils.

J. A. SELBIE.

HUMILITY (עֲנָוָה, ταπεινοφροσύνη; on the special Christian sense of the latter and on its relation to πραότης, see Trench, NT Syn.⁸ 142 ff.).—In one aspect the whole Bible may be viewed as a revelation of the character of God, and the divine love of humility is a feature of that character which is traceable throughout. In Ps 18³⁵ 113⁶ the virtue of humility is attributed to God Himself, who humbleth Himself to behold the things that are in heaven and earth ; and recent advances in our knowledge, both of the infinitely great in heaven and of the infinitely little on earth, have deepened our wonder at God's providence, at the contrast of His greatness and His minute care for the least of His works (cf. Mt 10²⁹· ³⁰). But, after all, our words 'great' and 'little' can have no direct significance to Him who is absolute and eternal ; and, while in men different qualities often stand out sharply distinct, in the transparent simplicity of the divine character we at once see through the humility to the love which underlies it ; so that on both grounds it seems unnatural to us to dwell upon 'the great God's great humbleness,' in distinction from the love that moved Him to create, and to deign to take notice of that which He created.

But when we turn to consider the Bible record of God's dealings with the moral natures of men, there is scarcely any divine characteristic so marked as that which is expressed in the words, 'Surely he scorneth the scorners, but he giveth grace to the lowly' (Pr 3³⁴=Ja 4⁶), and 'Thus saith the high and lofty One that inhabiteth eternity, whose name is Holy : I dwell in the high and holy place, with him also that is of a contrite and humble spirit, to revive the spirit of the humble, and to revive the heart of the contrite ones' (Is 57¹⁵). From Babel (Gn 11⁴) to Nebuchadnezzar (Dn 4³⁰· ³⁷), from the song of Hannah (1 S 2³) to the Magnificat (Lk 1⁵¹), the lessons of history and the insight of the prophet have taught that 'pride goeth before destruction, and an haughty spirit before a fall' (Pr 16¹⁸), while 'blessed are the meek : for they shall inherit the earth' (Ps 37¹¹ = Mt 5⁵). Especially is the duty of humility enforced in Ps and Pr and in some of the Prophets. For though God is known to bless the humble, yet the sense of His special favour is apt to beget pride, and therefore the Deuteronomist and Ezekiel are led to insist on the utter absence of merit in Israel ; and to explain that God's choice of His people was not determined by any good qualities in them on which they should pride themselves (Dt 7⁷ 8¹⁷· ¹⁸ 9⁴⁻⁷ 26⁵ 32¹⁰, Ezk 16, where Jerus. is charged with having used God's gifts to minister to her own vanity, cf. Ro 11¹⁷⁻²⁴) ; while Amos protests that other races besides the children of Israel are equally the objects of God's providence, 9⁷⁻¹⁰.

So far, the Bible idea might not seem to be very far removed from the familiar conception of Herodotus and the Greek tragedians, that God looks askance as with envy on human presumption, and even on innocent success. Yet the Bible at least dwells rather on God's love of the lowly than on His hatred of the proud, and there is no sign of His displeasure at mere prosperity. But our sense of the contrast between the Greek idea and that of the Bible will be deepened if we consider the relations of humility to other virtues.

(1) Humility towards God is based on *truth*. It is the simple recognition of facts as they really are —see Ro 12³. No man can dare to boast before God (Ps 143², 1 Co 1²⁹), and whatever of merit or success he has he owes to God's bounty (1 Co 4⁷). Hence walking humbly with God is put by Micah (6⁸) as a climax after doing justly and loving mercy. Pride comes from forgetting God and forming false judgments on oneself or others from the world's standpoint, e.g. Dt 8¹⁷· ¹⁸, Is 10¹²⁻¹⁵, Lk 17¹⁰ 18¹⁰⁻¹⁴, 2 Co 10¹². (2) From man's dependence upon God follows the principle that there can be no true advance without *readiness to receive* grace, i.e.

humility. God demands of man that he should humbly ask for help, that he should open his mouth wide that God may fill it. St. Paul attributes the Jews' failure to their not subjecting themselves to this condition (Ro 10³). Abraham is an example of the humility whose prayer God hears (Gn 18²⁷⁻³²). (3) As sons who owe all to their Father, men are bound to obey, and humility is thus closely connected with *obedience*. The command to perform acts, even those which to the natural man seem foolish, is the test of the humility and faith which God will bless : thus Naaman (2 K 5¹³). Similarly, circumcision is, in metaphor, connected with humility (Lv 26⁴¹, Dt 10¹⁶ 30⁶). (4) In 2 Ch 32²⁶ 33¹² 34²⁷ *repentance* and conversion are identified with humbling oneself. God sends chastisements to humble men and bring them to a better mind (Ps 119⁷⁵, La 3³³ הִנָּה, the same root as is commonly used for humble) ; but man can refuse to learn the lesson (Ex 10³, 2 Ch 36¹²· ¹³). Fasting as a self imposed chastisement is often connected with humility (1 K 21²⁷· ²⁹, Ezr 8²¹ etc.).

Humility as regards one's fellow-men fills a much smaller space, especially in OT, than humility towards God. It was often inculcated by Christ (Mt 18¹⁻⁴ 20²⁵⁻²⁸) ; and St. Paul connects it directly with love (1 Co 13⁴), while jealousy and envy, sins which have their root in pride, are reckoned among the manifest works of the flesh (Gal 5²⁰· ²¹). So in Ph 2³⁻⁵ he condemns faction and vainglory, and commends the 'lowliness of mind' in which each counts 'other better than himself ; not looking each of you to his own things, but each of you also to the things of others.' Such a 'mind' conforms to the pattern of the humility of the Son of God, who emptied Himself and became incarnate.

We can only touch lightly on the humility of Christ, which was shown in His earthly life from beginning to end. He abhorred not the Virgin's womb, and the lowly circumstances of His birth have ever been the theme of Christian artists and poets. The humility of the thirty years' subjection to His parents, and of the three years of unceasing toil, privation, and opposition, was crowned when He endured the cross, despising shame (He 12²). We may notice specially His praying (Lk 9¹⁸ etc.), His admitting weariness, distress, and pain (Jn 4⁶, Mk 14³⁴, Jn 19²⁸), and the solemn words and acts by which He inculcated humility (Mt 11²⁹ and Jn 13¹²⁻¹⁶). At the same time, He asserted His authority (e.g. to forgive sins, to judge men, to found an undying Church) ; He proclaimed Himself as the only way to God, etc. (Jn 14⁶) ; He claimed that He alone knew the Father of right (Mt 11²⁷). And He felt and expressed burning indignation at bigotry, hypocrisy, and blind self-complacency. St. Paul followed His example, and in him too we see that humility is compatible with righteous indignation, and even with just and true self-assertion.

It is worth observing also that St. Peter, who was at first the type of self-reliant boldness (Mt 16²² 26³³⁻³⁵), is afterwards particularly careful to dwell on the need of humility (1 P 2¹³· ¹⁷· ²⁰ 3⁴· ⁸ 5³· ⁵· ⁶).   W. O. BURROWS.

HUMTAH (חֻמְטָה).—A city of Judah, noticed next to Hebron, Jos 15⁵⁴. The site is doubtful.

HUNGER.—See FOOD.

HUNTING (צוּד, θηρεύειν, ἀγρεύειν, venor, capio, capio venatione, capio prædam, 'to hunt' ; צַיִד, צֵידָה, θήρα, θήρευμα, ἐπισιτισμός, venandi, venatio, cibaria, 'hunting,' 'venison' ; צַיָּד, θηρευτής, venator, 'hunter' ; חַיָּה, θηρίον, especially in חַיְתוֹ אֶרֶץ חַיַּת הָאָרֶץ, τὸ θηρίον τῆς γῆς, τὸ θηρίον τὸ ἄγριον, bestia terræ, agri, etc.).

When the earliest extant documents originated, the Israelites had not only passed out of, but had entirely forgotten that Israel ever passed through, that stage in the development of primitive tribes at which men's chief business and resource is hunting. Adam (Gn 3[17]) and Cain (4[2]) cultivate the soil, and Abel is a shepherd (*ib.*). Israel, in the persons of Isaac and Jacob, is contrasted with the hunting tribes, Ishmael, the 'archer' (Gn 21[20] E), and Esau, the 'cunning hunter' (Gn 25[27] J); it is Nimrod, the founder of Assyria, who is 'a mighty hunter before J"' (Gn 10[9] R). Hebrew, however, preserves a trace of the hunting stage of primitive society. צֵידָה *ẓêdâh*, by etymology 'hunting' or 'game,' and so used in *Kethîbh* of Gn 27[3], is regularly used for provision (Gn 42[25] etc.); thus suggesting a time when game was the ordinary food.

Moreover, in historic times, hunting was neither a common nor a favourite occupation in Israel. The account of Jacob and Esau shows that the Israelites were not addicted to hunting. Other references to hunting are general and casual; no actual hunt is ever mentioned. The references to lions, leopards, bears, etc. etc., and the lists of clean and unclean animals (Dt 14), show that both big and small game were abundant. But the only instances we meet with are where a shepherd or wayfarer has to defend himself or his charge; cf. the supposed fate of Joseph (Gn 37[33]), Samson (Jg 14[6] 15[4]), David (1 S 17[34-37]), Benaiah (2 S 23[20], apparently something more than an act of self-defence), the unnamed prophet of 1 K 13[24]; cf. also Is 5[29] 31[4], Am 3[12]. On the other hand, the allusions in Lv 17[13], 1 S 26[20] 'as when one doth hunt a partridge in the mountains,' Job 10[16] 38[39] 41[26], Pr 12[27] etc. etc., show that the Israelites were familiar with hunting; and the gazelle (צְבִי) and the hart (אַיָּל) are referred to as ordinary articles of diet (Dt 12[15. 22]), and are mentioned with the roebuck (יַחְמוּר 1 K 4[23]) as part of the provision made for Solomon's table. Bows and arrows (Gn 27[3]), slings (1 S 17[40]), nets (Job 19[6], Ps 9[15], Is 51[20] etc.), snares and traps (פַּח Am 3[5], מוֹקֵשׁ Am 3[5]), cf. the group of terms in Job 18[8-10], were used to catch game, especially wild birds. Also pits (פַּחַת Is 24[17], שַׁחַת Ps 35[7]) were dug as traps for larger animals; and sometimes a net was concealed (Ps 35[7]) in such a pit. The few references to hunting furnish us with names of some of the animals hunted and instruments used, but afford scarcely any data as to details in the nature of the instruments or the methods of hunting.

The comparative indifference of the Israelites to hunting is the more striking when we remember how devoted Egyptian and Assyrian kings and nobles were to the pursuit; their monuments depict many hunting scenes. It is true that our Hebrew documents probably come from the central districts at a time when they were too densely populated for much sport. We might hear more of hunting if we had earlier writings from the frontier lands south of Judah and east of Jordan.

In the Apocrypha we read in Sirach of a decoy partridge in a cage (11[30]), of a gazelle taken in a snare (27[20]), and of the use of game for food (36[19]). Jos. (*Ant.* IV. viii. 9) refers to hunting dogs, which are never mentioned in OT, and tells us that Herod the Great was a mighty hunter (*Ant.* XV. vii. 7, XVI. x. 3; *BJ* I. xxi. 13). NT only uses a few metaphors borrowed from hunting (*e.g.* Lk 11[54] θηρεῦσαι; Lk 21[35], Ro 11[9], 1 Ti 3[7] 6[9], 2 Ti 2[26], παγίς; Mt 22[15] παγιδεύειν). See, further, NET, SNARE, and the articles on animals.

LITERATURE.—Benzinger, *Heb. Arch.* 1894, p. 204 f.; Nowack, *Lehrb. der Heb. Arch.* 1894, i. 221, 222.

W. H. BENNETT.

HUPHAM (חוּפָם, LXX omits), Nu 26[39]. — See HUPPIM.

HUPPAH (הֻפָּה 'canopy,' 'chamber').—A priest of the 13th course, 1 Ch 24[13]. See GENEALOGY.

HUPPIM (חֻפִּים, perh. 'coverings').—The head of a Benjamite family, his precise parentage being obscure, Gn 46[21] P, 1 Ch 7[12. 15], Nu 26[39] (**Hupham**) P.

HUR (חוּר).—**1.** (Ὤρ) mentioned with Aaron as the companion of Moses during the battle between the Israelites under Joshua and the Amalekites (Ex 17[10. 12]). He was also with Aaron while Moses ascended Mt. Sinai (Ex 24[14]; all E). **2.** (Ὤρ) a Judahite, the grandfather of Bezalel the chief artificer of the Tabernacle (Ex 31[2]= 35[30] 38[22]; all P). The Chronicler traces back his descent through Caleb and Hezron to Perez (1 Ch 2[19. 20. 50] 4[1-4], 2 Ch 1[5]), while Josephus (*Ant.* III. ii. 4, vi. 1) makes this Hur the husband of Miriam and identical with Hur No. **1** above. **3.** (Οὑρ) one of the five kings of Midian, who, with Balaam, were slain by the Israelites under Phinehas after the 'matter of Peor' (Nu 31[8]). The incident is referred to in Jos 13[21], where the kings are described as 'chiefs' (נְשִׂיאִים) of Midian, and 'princes' (נְסִיכִים) of Sihon, king of the Amorites. **4.** According to the Hebrew, an Ephraimite, the father of one of the twelve officers of Solomon who 'provided victuals for the king and his household every month' (1 K 4[8], where RV reads BEN-HUR). Klostermann (*in loc.*) restores 'Azariah, the son of Zadok the priest (from v.[2]), in Beth-horon in the hill-country of Ephraim.' He appeals to B and Luc. Βαιώρ, which he regards as an error for Βαιθώρ=Beth-horon (בֵּית־חֹרֹן), corrupted in the Hebrew to בֶּן־חוּר; A Βὲν υἱὸς Ὤρ). The further reading of A (Βεέν) he takes as presupposing בֵּן, in itself a corruption of בֵּן־חוּר=the priest. K.'s conjectural emendation of the text is very ingenious, but can hardly be considered as probable. No doubt the text is corrupt, and it seems probable that the name of the officer in question has been lost. **5.** (LXX omits) The father of Rephaiah, who ruled over half the district of Jerusalem and assisted Nehemiah in repairing the walls (Neh 3[9]).

J. F. STENNING.

HURAI.—See HIDDAI.

HURAM (חוּרָם).—**1.** A Benjamite (1 Ch 8[5]). See GENEALOGY. **2. 3.** See HIRAM.

HURI (חוּרִי).—A Gadite, 1 Ch 5[14]. See GENEALOGY.

HUSBANDRY.—The 'husband' is originally the 'master of the house' (Icel. *hús*, a 'house,' and *búandi*, 'inhabiting'), but the word is used in AV only in the mod. sense of a married man. See FAMILY, MARRIAGE.

So a husbandman is a householder, as Mt 20[1] Wyc. 'The kyngdam of hevenes is lic to an husbond man' (Tind. and all others 'householder'), but in AV it always means a tiller of the ground, a farmer. Then 'husbandry' is first the occupation of a husbandman, 2 Ch 26[10] 'he had much cattle, both in the low country and in the plains: husbandmen also, and vinedressers in the mountains, and in Carmel: for he loved husbandry' (אֲדָמָה, lit., as AVm, 'ground'); 1 Es 4[6] 'Those that are no soldiers, and have not to do with wars, but use husbandry' (γεωργοῦσιν τὴν γῆν); Sir 7[15] 'Hate not laborious work, neither husbandry' (γεωργίαν). But, secondly, in 1 Co 3[9] 'husbandry' is used figuratively in the sense of 'that which is cultivated': 'ye are God's husbandry' (θεοῦ γεώργιον, lit., as RVm, 'God's field'). The first meaning is common. Thus Shaks. *As You Like It*, II. iii. 65—

> 'But, poor old man, thou prun'st a rotten tree,
> That cannot so much as a blossom yield,
> In lieu of all thy pains and husbandry.'

Golding, *Justine*, fol. 181, 'The women have all the doyng in houskeping and husbandrie, and the men geve themselfs to warre and robbyng.' The second meaning is rare, being in 1 Co 3⁹ an adaptation of the word to suit the Gr., as Shaks. uses 'husbandry' of the *product* of husbandry in *Henry V.* v. ii. 39—

> 'Alas! she hath from France too long been chased,
> And all her husbandry doth lie on heaps,
> Corrupting in its own fertility.'

J. HASTINGS.

HUSHAH (חֻשָׁה, Ὠσάν), the son of Ezer, the son of Hur (see HUR 2), and therefore of the tribe of Judah. Probably H. represents the name of a place, otherwise unknown, in Judah (1 Ch 4⁴). See HUSHATHITE.

HUSHAI (חוּשַׁי, Χουσεί, *Chusai*).—An Archite (2 S 15³² 17⁵·¹⁴), *i.e.* a native of 'the border of the Archites' (Jos 16²) to the W. of Bethel. See ARBITE. He is further described as 'the friend of David' (רֵעֶה דָוִד 15³⁷), while at 2 S 16¹⁶ the two titles are united. It is probable, therefore, that the LXX is right in reading 'the Archite, the friend of David,' at 2 S 15³², though its rendering ὁ ἀρχιέταιρος represents a strange combination of the gentilic name (in a Græcized form) and ἑταῖρος, the whole = 'chief companion.' At the rebellion of Absalom he was induced by David to act as if he favoured the cause of the king's son. By so doing he was enabled both to defeat the plans of Ahithophel and to keep David informed (by means of Ahimaaz and Jonathan, the sons of Zadok and Abiathar the priests) of the progress of events in Jerusalem (2 S 16¹⁶–17²³). He is probably to be identified with the father of Baana, one of Solomon's twelve commissariat officers (1 K 4¹⁶). G. Buchanan Gray (*Hebrew Proper Names*, p. 323) suggests that חוּשַׁי may be a parallel formation to אֲבִישַׁי (Abishai), the א being dropped as in חִירָם, חִיאֵל. J. F. STENNING.

HUSHAM.—A king of Edom, Gn 36³⁴·³⁵ (חֻשָׁם) = 1 Ch 1⁴⁵·⁴⁶ (חֻשָׁם).

HUSHATHITE (הַחֻשָׁתִי; B ὁ Ἀστατωθεί, Ἀνωθείτης, Αθεί, Θωσαθεί, Ἰσαθεί; A Ἀουσαστωνθεί, Ἀσωθείτης, Ἰαθεί (א ὁ Ἀσωθί), Οὐσαθι), probably = an inhabitant of Husha. This description is applied to SIBBECAI (wh. see), one of David's 'thirty' heroes (2 S 21¹⁸ = 1 Ch 20⁴, 2 S 23²⁷ = 1 Ch 11²⁹ 27¹¹). In the latter passage of 2 S the Hebrew reads מְבֻנַּי (Mebunnai), but a comparison with the parallel lists makes it clear that we must read Sibbecai as in 21¹⁸ (סִבְּכַי). B A read ἐκ τῶν υἱῶν (= מִבְּנֵי); but many MSS have Σαβουχαί, Luc. Σαβενί. In 1 Ch 11²⁹ 27¹¹ the gentilic name appears as Hushshathite (הַחֻשָׁתִי).

J. F. STENNING.

HUSHIM (חֻשִׁים).—**1.** The eponym of a Danite family, Gn 46²³, called in Nu 26⁴² **Shuham**. In 1 Ch 7¹² Hushim seems to be a Benjamite, but it is possible that for 'sons of Aher' we should read 'sons of another' (אַחֵר, not a proper name), *i.e.* Dan (so QPB, *ad loc.*). See further GENEALOGY, VIII. 6 note. **2.** The wife of Shaharaim the Benjamite, 1 Ch 8⁸ (חֻשִׁים) 8¹¹ (חֻשִׁים). J. A. SELBIE.

HUSKS (κεράτια).—These are the pods of the Carob Tree, *Ceratonia Siliqua*, L., the *kharnúb* or *kharrúb* of the Arabs. It is a fine tree with a hemispherical comus, often 40 ft. in diameter. The foliage is dark, glossy evergreen. The leaves are pinnate, of three to four pairs of oblong,

obtuse to retuse, or obovate leaflets, 2 to 3 in. long, and 1½ to 2 broad. The tree is diœcious. The flowers are in short racemes, the staminate reduced to five stamens on a top-shaped calyx. The pods are from 5 to 10 in. long, 1 to 1½ broad, and ¼ to ⅛ of an in. thick. They consist of a leathery

THE CAROB TREE, CERATONIA SILIQUA, L.
(On the left side is a hedge of Indian Fig, the plant on which the Cochineal grows.)

case, enclosing a sweet pulpy substance, in which the seeds are embedded. This pulp is edible and nutritious, and often eaten by the poorer people. The pods are ground and boiled, in order to extract the saccharine substance, which has the colour and consistence of treacle, and is used as food. The name *St. John's Bread*, applied to these pods, is from a tradition that they were the *locusts* which that prophet ate in the wilderness (Mt 3⁴, Mk 1⁶). But this tradition is contrary to the text of the Gospels. There are also no carob trees in the wilderness. There can be no doubt as to the possibility of the prodigal son eating the pods (Lk 15¹⁶).

G. E. POST.

HUZZAB (הֻצַּב).—A word of uncertain meaning, which occurs only in Nah 2⁷. It may be taken either as a verb or a noun. Gesenius adopts the former of these alternatives, connects the word with the preceding verse, and translates, ' the palace is dissolved *and made to* flow down' (הֻצַּב being Hoph. of נצב, unused in Qal = *flow*). Others make it Hoph. of יצב and tr. 'it is decreed' (RVm). Far better suited to the context is the interpretation followed in the text of both AV and RV, which finds in H. a reference to the Assyr. queen. It may be questioned, indeed, whether the Massoretic vocalization of the word is correct. Both Luther and Wellhausen content themselves with the simple rendering 'die Königin'; Kautzsch leaves the clause untranslated, holding that the text is corrupt, and that הצב represents a noun *with the article*, which is intended to be a designation of the queen of Assyria. Wellhausen (*Klein. Prophet.* 32, 158) suggests that Assyriology may yet clear up the question. The LXX ἡ ὑπόστασις gives us no help (cf. Nowack and A. B. Davidson, *ad loc.*, also the latter and Cheyne in *Expos. Times*, vii. 568, viii. 48). J. A. SELBIE.

HYACINTH.—See JACINTH.

HYÆNA (צָבוּעַ [prob. textual error for זבע *zâbhôa'*, ὕαινα]. *Zâbhûa'* is almost identical with the Arab. *dab'* [pl. *dubu'*], which signifies a *hyæna*).—This animal is quite common in all Syria and Palestine. Its den is often in a rock-hewn tomb or a cave. It freq. exhumes the bodies of the dead, and devours them. It breaks or gnaws the bones of its hideous meal to extract the marrow. It will, when pressed by hunger, attack large animals, and even men. The passage in which *zâbhûa‘* occurs (Jer 12[9]) is a part of a series of images illustrating the state of God's heritage. If it be rendered 'mine heritage is to me the ravenous hyæna (although ה in הָעַיִט is generally taken as interrogative); birds of prey are against her round about; go ye, assemble all the beasts of the field, bring them to devour,' the picture is that of a collection of the hyæna, jackals, foxes, vultures, ravens, and crows around a carcase. The meaning then would be that the chosen people have become ravenous beasts and birds, which are assembled to devour the prey they have slain. But even if ה be taken as the article, it is difficult to regard צָבוּעַ as other than predicate. Another objection to translating הָעַיִט צָבוּעַ *the ravenous hyæna*, is that עַיִט is always in OT employed for *birds of prey* (Gn 15[11], Job 28[7], Is 18[6] 46[11], Ezk 39[4]). But it *may* mean *a ravenous beast* as well as bird, the root signifying 'one that rushes' on its prey (cf. Arab. *saba'a*, to *ravin*). If we tr. the first '*ayiṭ beast* and the second *bird*, we have a play on language conformable to Oriental taste. The tr[n] 'speckled bird' (AV, RV and the majority of modern commentators) is derived from the root צָבַע 'dye' (cf. Jg 5[30] צֶבַע 'dyed stuff'). Siegfried-Stade (*s.* עַיִט) suggest the emendation מְרֻפָּא צָבוּעַ 'torn by the hyæna.'

The expression 'Valley of Zeboim' (1 S 13[18]) means *Valley of Hyænas*.   G. E. Post.

HYDASPES (Ὑδάσπης). — The name of a river mentioned along with the Euphrates and the Tigris (Jth 1[6]), and in such a context as to imply that it must be sought for on the Babylono - Median frontier. Probably, however, there is a confusion with the Hydaspes in N.W. India, a circumstance which, considering the unhistorical character of the Bk. of Judith, is not to be wondered at. *Hydaspes* (for *Vitasta*) is an assimilation to the Eranian *personal* name *Hudhâspa*, 'possessing well-equipped horses' (Diod. II. vi. 1; Heliodor. 106, 17; Pseudo - Callisth. II. x. 2; Horace, *Sat.* II. viii. 14). Of course no river could possibly be called by such a name, and it is simply a mistake of Strabo or his authorities when the Vitastâ (the modern *Bêhat* or *Jalam*) appears in his pages as the Hydaspes.   F. Hommel.

HYMENÆUS (Ὑμέναιος). — A false teacher of the time of St. Paul. His name occurs twice in the Epp. to Timothy, but there only in the NT. On the first occasion he is mentioned along with Alexander (see ALEXANDER, No. 4) as having 'made shipwreck concerning the faith,' and in consequence both have been 'delivered unto Satan, that they might be taught not to blaspheme' (1 Ti 1[19. 20]). On the second occasion he and Philetus (which see) are characterized as 'men who concerning the truth have erred, saying that the resurrection is past already, and overthrow the faith of some' (2 Ti 2[17. 18]). Mosheim, indeed, and others have held that two different persons must be referred to, on account of the milder terms of condemnation used in the second passage. But these arise naturally from the fact that in the first case it is the man's diseased moral state which is in view, a state requiring for its amendment the severest personal treatment; while in the second the apostle is thinking rather of the doctrinal error into which H. had fallen.

This error is described generally as 'saying that the resurrection is past already,' and in the absence of further particulars it is impossible to determine the full extent of the heresy. But it seems most probable that H. had yielded to what we know to have been a very prevalent Gnostic tendency, springing from an undue contempt for the body,

namely, denying the resurrection in its literal sense, and attaching to the word only a spiritual meaning. Everything in Scripture, according to this view, that referred to a future state of being, in so far as it involved a bodily resurrection, was explained or allegorized away, and stress was laid only on the resurrection of the soul from sin, regarding which it could be said that it was 'past already.' The deadly danger of this error is shown by the apostle's description of it as 'a gangrene,' which, if not at once destroyed, would spread and corrupt the whole community; and in support of this prediction, and as helping further to define the erroneous character of H.'s teaching, commentators generally adduce from the Fathers such passages as Irenæus, *Hær.* II. xxxi. 2, where certain heretics are described as holding 'that the resurrection from the dead is simply an acquaintance with that truth which they proclaim,' and Tertullian, *de Resurr.* 19, where we read of some 'who distort into some imaginary sense even the most clearly described doctrine of the resurrection of the dead, alleging that even death itself must be understood in a spiritual sense. . . . Wherefore that also must be held to be the resurrection, when a man is reanimated by access to the truth, and having dispersed the death of ignorance, and being endowed with new life by God, has burst forth from the sepulchre of the old man.'

With regard to the sentence of condemnation passed upon H., considerable difference of opinion has prevailed. By the 'delivering unto Satan,' or more literally 'the Satan' (τῷ Σατανᾷ), 'the Evil One in his most distinct personality' (Ellicott, *in loc.*), some have understood simply excommunication from the Church. But in the parallel passage 1 Co 5[5], 'delivering unto Satan' seems to be distinguished from excommunication in itself, which is denoted by 'taking away' or 'putting away from among you' (cf. v.[5] with vv.[2. 13]). Others in consequence refer the words rather to the infliction of some bodily loss or suffering, such as we find, for example, in the case of Job. But this does not meet the full and authoritative nature of the apostle's language, 'Whom I delivered (παρέδωκα) unto Satan.' It is best, therefore (with Meyer, Ellicott, and others), to combine both interpretations, and to understand by the expression the highest form of excommunication, by which the condemned person was not only cut off from all Christian privileges, but subjected besides to some bodily disease or death. It was a sentence apparently which on account of its awful nature was not pronounced by the Church, but only by an apostle (cf. the somewhat analogous cases of Ananias and Sapphira Ac 5, and Elymas Ac 13[11]), though in certain circumstances the apostle could empower others to pass sentence for him (1 Co 5[3. 4]). It is further of importance to observe that both here and in 1 Co 5[5] the *remedial* intention of the punishment is emphasized. In the latter case the flesh is destroyed, 'that the spirit may be saved in the day of the Lord Jesus'; while H. and his companion were delivered to Satan, not for their final destruction, but that 'they might be taught (παιδευ-θῶσιν in NT sense of teaching by disciplining or chastening) not to blaspheme.' [See further CHURCH, vol. i. p. 432; CURSE, p. 534[b]; and in addition to the commentators, cf. Suicer, *Thesaur.* ii. p. 940, and Bingham, *Antiq.* XVI. ii. 15].

       G. Milligan.

HYMN IN NT (for OT see POETRY and SONG). — The use of hymns among Christians was common from the first existence of the Church, both in public worship and in private life (1 Co 14[15. 26], Eph 5[19], Col 3[16], Ja 5[13], Ac 16[25]), such hymns being treated not only as the natural expression of religious emotion, but also as a method of instruction

(διδάσκοντες καὶ νουθετοῦντες ἑαυτοὺς ψαλμοῖς, Col *l.c.*).
The fullest description of them is the triple division
into ψαλμοί, ὕμνοι, ᾠδαὶ πνευματικαί (Eph-Col). Of
these ψαλμός is properly 'a song with musical
accompaniment,' and doubtless includes the OT
Psalms : ὕμνος, a song in praise of God or of
'famous men' (cf. Sir 44¹ πατέρων ὕμνος), such as
that in Ac 4²⁴⁻³⁰ ; ᾠδὴ πνευματική, any song on a
spiritual theme, such perhaps as Eph 5¹⁴. But
the distinction is not technical, and cannot be
pressed rigidly, for ὕμνος is used of the Psalms of
David (Ps 71²⁰, Jos. *Ant.* VII. xii. 3), and both ὕμνος
and ᾠδή occur frequently in the titles of those
Psalms [see Trench, *NT Syn. s.v.* ; Ltft. on Col 3¹⁶].
Such Christian hymns would naturally be either
direct importations from the services of the Jewish
Temple and Synagogue, or the fresh utterances of
Christian inspiration influenced in form by these
Jewish models (cf. He 2¹² ; Philo, *in Flacc.* 14, *de
Vit. Cont.* §§ 3. 10. 11 ; Driver, *LOT⁶* pp. 359–367 ;
Edersheim, *The Temple, its ministry and services*,
pp. 56, 143). A reference to a purely Jewish hymn
is found in Mt 26³⁰, probably the latter half of the
Hallel, Pss 115–118, used in the paschal services ;
but an entirely different hymn, professedly Christian, yet of a strong Gnostic tinge, and undoubtedly spurious, will be found attributed to
our Lord on this occasion in the Acta Johannis,
c. 11 (*Texts and Studies*, v. 1), and fragments of
it are discussed by Aug. *Ep.* iv. 237, §§ 4–8.
The fresh utterances of Christian inspiration
often fell into an exalted and poetic form of expression which make it difficult to draw the line
between prose and poetry. Thus the enthusiastic
acclamation of the crowd (Mt 21⁹=Mk 11⁹, Lk
19³⁸), the thanksgiving of the Church on the
release of the apostles (Ac 4²⁴⁻³⁰), the hymn of the
love of man (1 Co 13) and of the love of God (Ro
8³¹⁻³⁹), the praise of God's blessings in Eph 1³⁻¹⁴
with the triple refrain εἰς ἔπαινον τῆς δόξης αὐτοῦ
(⁵·¹¹·¹⁴) ; even the Lord's Prayer itself, in the more
elaborate form given by Mt 6⁹⁻¹³ 'with its invocation, its first triplet of single clauses with one
common burden expressed after the third but
implied with all, and its second triplet of double
clauses variously antithetical in form and sense'
(see WH, ii. pp. 319, 320),—all these have a quasi-
rhythmical structure which only just falls short of
the level of poetic hymn.
In other passages we have probably fragments
from hymns already in use in the Church, *e.g.*
Eph 5¹⁴ (perhaps a baptismal hymn addressed to
the new convert), 1 Ti 3¹⁶, which should be arranged
in two strophes, each containing three lines : perhaps 1 Co 2⁹, and the half-stereotyped doxologies
of 1 Ti 1¹⁷ 6¹⁶, 2 Ti 4¹⁸, Rev 4⁸·¹¹ 5⁹·¹²·¹³ 7¹⁰⁻¹² 11¹⁵·
¹⁷·¹⁸ 12¹⁰⁻¹² 15³·⁴ 19¹·²·⁵⁻⁸. Finally, the most elaborate structure is to be found in the Evangelical
Canticles given by St. Luke, viz.:—
(*a*) 1⁴⁶⁻⁵⁵. *The Magnificat*, based very largely
upon the language of the OT, especially of the
Song of Hannah (1 S 2¹⁻¹⁰), and falling naturally
into four strophes (i.) ⁴⁶⁻⁴⁸, (ii.) ⁴⁹·⁵⁰, (iii.) ⁵¹⁻⁵³, (iv.)
⁵⁴·⁵⁵ (Plummer, *ad loc.*).
(*b*) 1⁶⁸⁻⁷⁹. *The Benedictus*, modelled upon the
language of the OT prophets and upon the eighteen
Benedictions used in the Temple service. This
falls into two halves (⁶⁸⁻⁷⁵·⁷⁶⁻⁷⁹), the first half containing three strophes (⁶⁸⁻⁶⁹·⁷⁰⁻⁷²·⁷³⁻⁷⁵), and the
second only two ⁷⁶⁻⁷⁷·⁷⁸⁻⁷⁹ (Plummer, *ad loc.* ;
Edersheim, *Jesus the Messiah*, i. p. 158).
(*c*) 2¹⁴. *The Gloria in Excelsis.* In this the
clauses are carefully balanced, whether arranged
in a double or triple form. It was early used in
the Church as a morning hymn (*Apost. Const.*
vii. 47), and is found in a collection of hymns at
the end of the Psalter in Codex Alex. of the LXX.
It was also incorporated in the Latin Liturgies ;

but from very early times it existed in a double
form ; for while the morning hymn seems always
to have read εὐδοκία, the text of St. Luke and the
translation of the Latin Liturgies support εὐδοκίας
(Plummer, *ad loc.* ; WH, ii. App. 52–56).
(*d*) 2²⁹⁻³². *The Nunc Dimittis* : falling into three
strophes ²⁹· ³⁰⁻³¹· ³², and early (*Apost. Const.* vii. 48)
used as an evening hymn (Plummer, *ad loc.*).
For the later development of Christian hymns
see Pliny, *Ep.* 97 ; Ignat. *Eph.* 4, *Rom.* 2 ; *Martyr.
(Ant. Act.)* 7 ; Justin Martyr, *Apol.* i. 13 ; Tertullian, *Apol.* 39 ; Duchesne, *Origines du Culte
Chrétien*, iv. § 3 ; Kayser, *Beiträge zur ältesten
Kirchen-hymnen* ; Christ und Paranikas, *Antho-
logia Græca Carminum Christianorum* ; Daniel,
Thesaurus Hymnologicus ; Julian, *Dict. of Hymn-
ology* ; art. HYMN in *Encycl. Brit.* ; and art.
VERSE-WRITERS in Smith, *Dict. Chr. Biog.*
                       W. LOCK.

HYPOCRITE.—The ὑποκριτής is primarily 'one
who answers,' ὑποκρίνεται ; and hence (1) 'an interpreter,' and (2) 'an actor.' This is the commonest
meaning in classical Greek (Aristoph. Plat. Xen.
etc.). The use of the word for 'a pretender,'
'hypocrite,' is not classical. On the other hand,
the word is never found in biblical Gr. of an actor
on the stage. It means either 'one who acts a
false part in life,' *i.e.* one who pretends to be pious
when he is not, or (even worse than this) 'one
who is utterly bad,' whether he acts a part or not.
In Job it is twice used in the general sense of
'impious' ; βασιλεύων ἄνθρωπον ὑποκριτὴν ἀπὸ δυσκο-
λίας λαοῦ (34³⁰) ; and ὑποκριταὶ καρδίᾳ τάξουσιν θυμόν
(36¹³). In Pr 11⁹ and Is 33¹⁴ Aq. Sym. and Theod.
have ὑποκριταί, where in the LXX we have ἀσεβεῖς.
The same is true of Aq. and Theod. in Job 15³⁴,
where in the LXX we have ἀσεβής ; and Aq. has it
Job 20⁵, where παράνομος is the tr. in LXX. In
AV of OT 'hypocrite' occurs in Job 8¹³ 13¹⁶ 15³⁴ 17⁸
20⁵ 27⁸ 34³⁰ 36¹³, Pr 11⁹, Is 9¹⁷ 33¹⁴, and 'hypocritical'
in Ps 35¹⁶, Is 10⁶—in all these instances as a misrendering of חָנֵף 'godless' or 'profane,' the rendering of RV. So also 'hypocrisy' in AV of Is 32⁶ is
correctly rendered by RV 'profaneness' (חֹנֶף).
In NT, although the meaning of 'pretending
to be religious and devout' prevails (Mt 6². ⁵. ¹⁶
7⁵ 15⁷ 23¹³⁻²⁹, Mk 7⁶, Lk 6⁴² 13¹⁵), yet the more
general meaning sometimes occurs. In Mt 24⁵¹
'shall cut him asunder and appoint his portion
with the *impious*' makes better sense than 'with
the *hypocrites*' ; and here Lk has 'with the unfaithful,' μετὰ τῶν ἀπίστων (12⁴⁶), instead of μετὰ
τῶν ὑποκριτῶν. In Lk 12⁵⁶ this general meaning is
perhaps as suitable as the other. Comp. Mk
12¹⁵ with Mt 22¹⁸ and Lk 20²³ ; where Mk has
ὑπόκρισιν, Mt πονηρίαν, and Lk πανουργίαν, which
does not prove that the three terms are equivalent,
but is some evidence that ὑπόκρισις may mean
'wickedness' (Hatch, *Biblical Greek*, p. 92). The
term includes *dissimulatio* (Gal 2¹³) as well as
simulatio ; and concealment of convictions was
common among opponents of the gospel.
Hypocrites are compared to 'whited sepulchres,
outwardly beautiful, but full of uncleanness' (Mt
23²⁷) ; to 'the tombs which appear not,' and which
defile all who come in contact with them, without
their being aware of them (Lk 11⁴⁴) ; and to leaven
(Lk 12¹). And hypocrisy is condemned, not merely
as a gross form of deceit, but as folly, for it never
succeeds. Sooner or later the inevitable exposure
comes, and the hypocrite is unmasked (Lk 12². ³).
                       A. PLUMMER.

HYRCANUS, AV **HIRCANUS** ('Υρκανός).—The
son of Tobias, 'a man in very high place,' who had
money deposited at Jerus., in the temple treasury,
at the time of the visit of Heliodorus (2 Mac 3¹¹).
Jos. speaks of 'the sons of Tobias' as supporters
of Menelaus (*Ant.* XII. v. 1) ; also of H. the son of

a farmer of the revenue named Joseph, who was the son of Tobias and nephew of Onias II. But it is doubtful whether we should, with Rawlinson (*Speaker's Comm.*), identify this H. with the person mentioned in 2 Mac.

The name seems to be a local appellative. Its use among the Jews is perhaps to be explained from the fact that Artaxerxes Ochus transported a number of Jews to Hyrcania (cf. Schürer, *HJP* I. i. 273 f.).   H. A. WHITE.

HYSSOP.—The problem in regard to this plant has been much complicated by attempting its solution first in OT. The difficulties will greatly lessen if we approach the question first from the NT side. The word occurs twice in NT. Once in a recital of the ordinances of the first covenant, the author of the Ep. to the Heb. summarizes the sprinklings of blood and water by means of a wisp of scarlet wool and hyssop (He 9¹⁹), as these had been laid down in various places in the Pentateuch. Here it is clear that he adopts the rendering of the LXX ὕσσωπος. The other passage (Jn 19²⁹) says that ' they filled a sponge with vinegar, and put it upon hyssop, and put it to his mouth.' Here the evangelist alludes to a plant, known to his readers by the name by which he called it. He is not quoting a passage from the OT, but recording a new fact. What was this plant? Here again the problem has been complicated by assuming that κάλαμος, in the parallel passages (Mt 27⁴⁸, Mk 15³⁶), is the same as ὕσσωπος. In these passages it is said that, after filling the sponge with vinegar, ' they put it on a reed (καλάμῳ), and gave him to drink.' Now, the meaning of κάλαμος is indubitably a *reed* or *cane*, not a *rod* or *stick*, as some would have it. The word has in it no suggestion of *hyssop*, and would not have been so understood by the readers of Mt and Mk. It is therefore an unwarrantable assumption that reed and hyssop are the same (although it is fair to add that the present writer has against him, on this point, almost all modern commentators, who hold that Mt and Mk's περιθείς καλάμῳ and Jn's ὑσσώπῳ περιθέντες are identical in meaning). Admitting their diversity, the passages are easily harmonized by noting that St. John mentions both the articles used to mitigate the thirst of our Saviour, but omits telling how they ' put it to his mouth.' It is clear that this could not have been done by the hand alone. Mt and Mk omit the hyssop, but mention the reed by which the sponge, vinegar, and hyssop were ' put to his mouth.'

The word ὕσσωπος appears to have been used by the Greeks, with some latitude, for plants of the *Labiate Family*, much as we use the words *marjoram, thyme, mint, sage,* and *hyssop* itself. Several different genera were doubtless included. The genus *Hyssopus* is of modern creation, and none of the species grow wild in Sinai, Pal., or Syria. There are, however, several species of *marjoram* which grow wild, and are known under the Arab. name *ṣa'tar*, which according to high rabbinical authority was the *hyssop*. We are inclined to think that it was from one of these, probably *Origanum Maru*, L., that the hyssop of Jn was taken. This plant, the leaves and heads of which have a pungent, aromatic flavour, has been used from remote antiquity as a condiment. Its powder, sprinkled over bread, is eaten largely in Bible lands at the present day. Like the peppermint, it tastes at first hot, but this is followed by a cooling, refreshing feeling, and a flow of saliva which quenches thirst. The addition of this substance to the vinegar or sour wine on the sponge would be eminently suited to the purpose of moistening and cooling the mouth of the parched sufferer on the Cross. We are now in a position to ask whether the plants known to the Arabs as *ṣa'tar* suit the requirements of OT *hyssop*. Hyssop is mentioned alone in connexion with the sprinkling of the passover (Ex 12²²), ' and ye shall take a bunch of hyssop and dip it into the blood that is in the basin, and strike the lintel,' etc.). This species of *Origanum* is eminently adapted for this purpose. It has straight, slender, leafy stalks, with small heads. Several of these stalks grow from one root, so that the hand could enclose and break off, at one effort, a suitable bunch or wisp for sprinkling. In certain of the sprinklings, as in leprosy (Lv 14), there was added to the bunch some *cedar wood* (prob. a twig of *Juniperus Phœnicea*, L., or one of its congeners), scarlet, and a living bird. ' Purge me with hyssop' (Ps 51⁷) no doubt refers to such ceremonial purification, as the succeeding clause, ' wash me, and I shall be whiter than snow,' refers to the ceremonial washing which followed the cleansing of the leper. It is a gratuitous assumption here to attribute to the hyssop medicinal virtues of a detergent sort. It was not used internally, but for sprinkling. A similar bunch, with the exception of the bird, was thrown into the fire which consumed the red heifer (Nu 19⁶).

This species suits well ' the hyssop that springeth out of the wall' (1 K 4³³). It grows in clefts of rocks, in chinks of old walls, and on the terrace walls throughout the land. Thus it will be seen that it suits perfectly all the requirements of OT as well as of NT. *Thymbra spicata*, L., has been suggested, but it is a plant not found in the desert or the interior.

Royle proposed as the equivalent of אֵזוֹב '*ēzôbh*, the Heb. original of ὕσσωπος, the *caper, Capparis spinosa*, L. His argument was based on the supposed etymol. resemblance between אֵזוֹב and Arabic '*aṣaf*, one of the two Arab. names for the *caper*. It is fatal to this theory, however, that it does not explain the passage in Jn. It is improbable that St. John would have written ὕσσωπος if he had meant κάππαρις, the well-known Gr. name of the *caper*. These words are never interchangeable. Nor could St. John have been biassed, as the writer of He 9¹⁹, by a LXX rendering, for, as above pointed out, he was *narrating*, not *quoting*. In order to strengthen his etymol. theory, Royle assumes that ὕσσωπος and κάλαμος were the same, and shows how a *stick*, 3 or 4 ft. long, could be obtained from the caper, suitable for the purpose for which the *reed* was used. But, even if it were possible philologically to apply the term κάλαμος to a *rod* from the caper, any one familiar with the mode of its growth would be likely to reject this plant. The branches of the caper are slender, straggling, and usually beset with hooked prickles. They are eminently unsuitable for the purpose described. On the other hand, the *reed*, a general term for the straight, stiff, hollow stems of the larger grasses, as *Arundo Donax*, L., and *Saccharum Ægyptiacum*, L., would precisely suit the narrative, and was doubtless then as now used to tie things to, in order to hand them up. A further objection to Royle's theory is, that the caper would have been wholly unsuitable to make a *bunch*. Its branches are straggling, prickly, *noli-me-tangere*, with large, stiff leaves and flowers 3 in. broad. It is impossible for us to think that such an intractable plant should have been selected for sprinkling. Finally, the etymology is weak, even for the OT '*ēzôbh*, which is composed of the radicals *aleph, zayin,* and *beth*, while '*aṣaf* is composed of *alif, ṣod,* and *fê*. For the passage in John it has been shown above that the etymol. argument not only fails to confirm the claims of the caper, but is wholly fatal to them. The Arabic *zúfa* is etymol. much nearer to '*ēzôbh*, and *zúfa* is doubtless the same as *ṣa'tar*.   G. E. POST.

I

I AM.—See under GOD, vol. ii. p. 199[b].

IADINUS (A Ἰάδινος, B -ει-, AV Adinus), 1 Es 9[48]. —One of the Levites who taught the people the law of the Lord after the return under Ezra. The name corresponds to Jamin in Neh 8[7] (om. LXX), who with the other persons there mentioned is distinguished from the Levites.

IBHAR (יִבְחָר ; '[God] chooses' ; 2 S 5[15], B Ἐβεάρ, A Ἰεβάρ ; 1 Ch 3[6] 14[5], B Βαάρ, A Ἰεβαάρ ; Jebahar, Jebaar), one of David's sons, born at Jerusalem : his name occurs in all three lists immediately after that of Solomon and before that of Elishua. According to 1 Ch 3[6] he was the son of a wife and not of a concubine ; otherwise he is unknown alike to history and to tradition. It is noteworthy that in the Peshiṭta to 2 S 5[15] his name is given as

ܝܘܟܒܪ (Juchabar), a form which occurs elsewhere as the equivalent of Jochebed (Ex 6[20], Nu 26[59] יוֹכֶבֶד) and of Ichabod (1 S 4[21] אִי כָבוֹד) : in 1 Ch the form given (ܝܘܟܒܪ) agrees with that of the MT.   J. F. STENNING.

IBLEAM (יִבְלְעָם).—A town belonging to West Manasseh, Jos 17[11] (JE ; wanting in the LXX, see Budde, Richt. u. Sam. 13 f.), Jg 1[27]. It is mentioned also in 2 K 9[27] in connexion with the death of king Ahaziah, who fled by the way of Beth-haggan (En-gannim [?] ; 'the garden house' AV, RV), and 'the ascent of Gur, which is by Ibleam.' The biblical data seem to be well satisfied by the modern ruin Bel'ame, some 13 miles E. of N. of Samaria, more than half-way to Jezreel. Conder (SWP ii. p. 98) prefers Yebla, N.W. of Beisan, while Wilson and others favour Jelame, 3½ miles S. by W. from Zer'in (Jezreel). In 2 K 15[10] קְבָל עָם (AV, RV 'before the people') should certainly be emended to בְיִבְלְעָם ('in Ibleam' ; so Siegfried-Stade, Oxf. Heb. Lex. etc., following Luc. ἐν Ἰεβλαάμ). **Gath-rimmon** (wh. see) of Jos 21[25] is a scribal error for Ibleam. It is the same place which is called in 1 Ch 6[55] [Eng.[70]] **Bileam** (wh. see).

LITERATURE.—Dillm. on Jos 17[11] ; Moore on Jg 1[27] ; Baedeker-Socin, Pal.[3] 228 ; Schultz, ZDMG iii. 49 ; SWP ii. 47 f., 51 f. ; Guérin, Samarie, i. 339 ff.   J. A. SELBIE.

IBNEIAH (יִבְנְיָה ; 'J" buildeth up').—A Benjamite, 1 Ch 9[8]. See GENEALOGY.

IBNIJAH (יִבְנִיָּה).—A Benjamite, 1 Ch 9[8]. See GENEALOGY.

IBRI (עִבְרִי).—A Merarite Levite, 1 Ch 24[27]. See GENEALOGY.

IBSAM (יִבְשָׂם, AV Jibsam).—A descendant of Issachar, 1 Ch 7[2]. See GENEALOGY.

IBZAN (אִבְצָן, meaning doubtful, cf. אָבֵץ a town in Issachar, Jos 19[20], Ἀβεσσάν), one of the Minor Judges, following Jephthah, Jg 12[8-10]. He came from Bethlehem, probably the Bethlehem in Zebulun (Jos 19[15]), 7 miles N.W. of Nazareth. He had 30 sons and 30 daughters, an evidence of his social importance, and arranged their marriages. He judged Israel 7 years, and was buried at Bethlehem. Nothing is said of Ibzan's exploits, and his name does not occur elsewhere ;

but, on the analogy of other Minor Judges, Tola, Jair, and Elon, we may suppose that he represents a clan, with numerous branches and alliances. See Moore, Judges, p. 271 n. According to Jewish tradition, Ibzan was the same as Boaz (Talm. B. Baba Bathra, 91a and comment.; Rashi, Comment. on Jg 12[8f.]).   G. A. COOKE.

ICHABOD (אִי כָבוֹד ; B οὐαὶ βαρχαβώθ ; A οὐαὶ χαβώθ ; Ichabod), son of Phinehas and grandson of Eli. His mother died in giving him birth, overwhelmed by grief at the news of the sudden death of her husband and her father-in-law. The name is usually explained as 'inglorious' (from אִי, the ordinary negative in Ethiopic and Phœnician [cf. Job 22[30]], and כָבוֹד 'glory'), in accordance with the meaning suggested by 1 S 4[21] ('The glory is departed from Israel' ; B omits). Possibly, Ithamar (אִיתָמָר) and the Zidonian Jezebel (אִיזֶבֶל 1 K 16[31] etc.) are words of the same formation, cf. Gray, Heb. Prop. Names, p. 246 n. The rendering of the LXX points to a different interpretation (אִי being treated as=אוֹי ; in 1 S 14[3] LXX has Ἰωχαβήλ).   J. F. STENNING.

ICONIUM (Ἰκόνιον), an ancient city near the borders of Lycaonia and Phrygia, still retains its ancient name in the form Konia, and is at present the terminus of a railway that extends from the Bosphorus southwards. Its situation, amid luxuriant orchards at the western edge of the vast plains of central Asia Minor, level and uncultivated, watered by a stream which issues from the hilly region on the west, and loses itself in the plain after making this part of it a garden, is strikingly like that of Damascus (though hardly equal to it in beauty) ; and this has made the city always a centre of life and the most important in the district. It is commonly described by the ancient writers as a city of Lycaonia, e.g. Cicero, Fam. xv. iv. 2 ; cf. III. v. 4, vi. 6, xv. iii. 1 ; Att. v. xx. 2 ; Strabo, p. 568 ; Pliny, NH v. 25 (95) ; Stephanus Byzant. s.v., and many others. It is not consistent with its Lycaonian character that Ac 14[6] represents Paul and Barnabas as fleeing from Iconium into Lycaonia ; but the discrepancy is one of those unstudied touches which prove the originality and accuracy of the narrative. The author conceives that, in traversing the 18 miles separating Iconium from Lystra, the apostles crossed the frontier and entered Lycaonia. Now, Xenophon (Anab. I. ii. 19) describes Iconium as the easternmost city of Phrygia ; and immediately on leaving it, he entered Lycaonia. The evidence of other visitors or natives proves that the Iconians always considered themselves to be by race Phrygians and not Lycaonians. Stephanus quotes a legend about a king Annakos of Iconium, on whose death followed the Deluge, which destroyed the whole population ; and his subjects are called Phrygians in the legend. Pliny, NH v. 41 (145), gives a list of famous Phrygian cities, and among them is Conium : the list contains several which had disappeared in Pliny's time, and is doubtless taken from some older Greek writer. In A.D. 163, at the trial of Justin Martyr, one of his associates named Hierax described himself as a slave from Iconium of Phrygia. Firmilian, bishop of Cæsareia Capp., who attended the council of Iconium, describes it as a city of Phrygia (Cyprian, Epist. 75, 7). Iconium does not on its coin boast itself as a member of the Koinon Lycaoniæ, which was formed soon after A.D. 137. Though claiming Phrygian stock, Iconium (like most cities of Asia Minor) loved to connect itself with Greek legend, deriving its name from the image (εἰκών) of Medusa, brought there by Perseus (Eustath. *ad Dionys. Per.* 856), or from the clay images of men made by Prometheus there after the Flood to replace the drowned people (Steph. Byz.).

Iconium, as a rule, shared the fate of Lycaonia (wh. see). Ruled by the Seleucid kings of Syria in the 3rd cent., it was assigned to the Pergamenian kings in B.C. 190, but was never actually made part of their kingdom, and probably passed soon after under the power of the Galatæ, forming part of the Tetrarchy Proseilemmene, which was transferred from Lycaonia to Galatia (Pliny, *NH* 25 (95); Ptolemy, v. iv. 10), probably about 164 (*Studia Biblica*, iv. p. 46 ff.; see GALATIA, p. 87). Then, along with Galatia,* it probably passed to the Pontic kings not later than B.C. 129; but it was set free during the Mithridatic wars. Its lot is uncertain, until in B.C. 39 Antony gave it to Polemon along with Cilicia Tracheia.† In 36 Antony transferred it to Amyntas, who was at the same time made king of Galatia. At his death, in B.C. 25, it was incorporated in the Roman empire as part of the Province Galatia. Under Claudius it was honoured with the name Claudiconium (probably in compensation cn for the bestowal of the name Claudioderbe cn the frontier city Derbe). Under Hadrian it was constituted a Roman colony with the title *Colonia Aelia Hadriana Iconiensium.*‡ It seems to have remained during the 2nd and 3rd cents. part of the Province Galatia (Ptol. v. 4. 12),§ whereas Lycaonia was made part of the triple Province Cilicia-Isauria-Lycaonia, probably in 137. About 295 Diocletian constituted southern Galatia with parts of the surrounding country into a new Province Pisidia, of which the capital was Antioch, and Iconium the second metropolis (μετὰ τὴν μεγίστην ἡ πρώτη, Basil, *Epist.* 8 (137 Mi.)), while eastern Lycaonia was perhaps still united with Isauria Provincia; hence Ammianus describes Iconium as a city of Pisidia (xiv. 2). But about A.D. 372 it became the metropolis of a new Provincia Lycaonia, extending from the shores of Karalis and Trogitis (Bey-Sheher and Seidi-Sheher Lakes) to the western end of Ak-Göl near Cybistra. This arrangement lasted till the end of the Byzantine Provincial system, and is found in all *Notitiæ Episcopatuum.*

Iconium, like most of Asia Minor, was several times overrun by the Saracens, but its fate is hardly alluded to by historians. It shared in the recovered prosperity of the reviving Byzantine empire, till it was overrun by the Seljuk Turks in 1070, and passed by treaty into their hands, probably in 1072. Though John and Manuel Comnenus approached Iconium more than once (Nicet. Chon. pp. 42, 72; Cinnam. p. 42), and Frederick Barbarossa occupied it in 1190, it remained a Turkish city permanently (the Christian population being permitted to reside in the large village Tsille, 6 miles N.). Konia was the capital of the Seljuk empire, and is still capital of a vilayet.

Being an important commercial city situated on one of the great routes between Cilicia and the

west, Iconium was naturally a centre for Jewish settlers, Ac 14¹; but the only memorials of the colony are *CIG* 9270, and perhaps 3995b, 3998, 4001b (Jewish-Christian?). Lystra is only 18 miles S.S.W. from Iconium, and hence the character of an inhabitant of Lystra was naturally well known among the Iconians (Ac 16²), for Lystra, though in the same district as Derbe (Ac 14⁶ 16¹), was actually much closer to Iconium.

Christianity was introduced into Iconium by St. Paul and St. Barnabas on their first missionary journey (Ac 14¹ff.), and the city was visited on the second journey (16²ff.). St. Paul's sufferings and difficulties there are mentioned 1 Ti 3¹¹. The interesting legend of St. Thekla is connected with these visits: the legend as we have it was composed by a presbyter of Asia about the middle of the 2nd cent., but contains some details that go back to the 1st cent.; and it probably rests on a historical basis. It rightly traces St. Paul's journey from Pisidian Antioch along the 'Royal Road' (*i.e.* Imperial Highway) that connected Antioch the military centre with the garrison city Lystra, relating how on the way (probably not far from Selki-Serai) he was induced by Onesiphorus to diverge from that road and go across the hill-country to Iconium. It tells that queen Tryphaina (of Pontus) had estates somewhere in this neighbourhood; and this may well be true, as she was granddaughter of Polemon, who formerly possessed Iconium: it rightly makes her a relative of the Roman emperor (Claudius). On this legend see Lipsius, *Apokr. Apostelgesch.* ii. p. 424 ff.; Zahn, *GGA*, 1877, p. 1307 ff.; Ramsay, *Church in Rom. Emp.* pp. 31 f. 380 ff. (with many other authorities there quoted).

According to the North-Galatian theory, nothing else is recorded in NT about Iconium. On the South-Galatian view, soon after St. Paul's second journey, it was visited by Jewish emissaries (coming doubtless from Jerusalem), who persuaded the Iconians that St. Paul was not a real apostle of God, but the mere messenger of the superior apostles, and that the keeping of the whole Jewish law was incumbent on all zealous Christians (urging that St. Paul by circumcising Timothy had practically become a preacher of circumcision, Gal 5¹¹). St. Paul, learning this defection, wrote the Epistle to the Galatians, probably from Syrian Antioch (Ac 18²²; or, according to Zahn and Rendall, from Corinth), and soon afterwards visited Iconium again on his way to Ephesus. The Iconian church was evidently thoroughly reconciled to the Pauline teaching, remained in communication with St. Paul during his stay at Ephesus (1 Co 16¹), and joined in the contribution which he organized among all his churches for the benefit of the poor Christians in Jerusalem. St. Peter's first Epistle was addressed to it among others.

According to legend, Sosipater (Ro 16²¹; Sopater of Berœa, Ac 20⁴) was first bishop of Iconium; Terentius or Tertius (Ro 16²²) succeeded him. Cornutus or Coronatus, a martyr bishop (12 Sept. *sub Perennio præside*), is perhaps historical. Celsus, bishop earlier than *c.* 260, is mentioned by Eusebius (*HE* vi. 19) as permitting a qualified layman Paulinus to do church work. Nikomas, bishop about A.D. 264 and 269, is also mentioned by Euseb. (vii. 28). A council was held in Iconium about 232 (Cyprian, *Epist.* 75, 7). Numerous Christian inscriptions are found in the country round Iconium, some of which are probably of the 3rd cent., showing that Christianity spread comparatively early round the city as centre (see GALATIA, p. 88). A monastery τῶν Γαλατῶν in the neighbourhood of Iconium is mentioned by Gregorius Magn. (*Dial.* iv. 38, p. 441). St. Chariton, a native of Iconium, is said to have been

* Van Gelder, *de Gallis in Gr.* p. 277.

† Appian, *B.C.* v. 75; Strab. p. 568. Being thus summed up with Cilicia, it is occasionally mentioned as a Cilician city, Pliny, *NH* 22 (93), Jerome, *Lib. Nom. Loc. ex Actis,* vol. iii. p. 1302; there is no reason to infer that a distinct Cilician Iconium ever existed.

‡ Some writers erroneously regard the bestowal of the title Claudiconium as implying that it was made a colony by Claudius.

§ Ptolemy does not here mention Iconium (which, in v. vi. 16, he puts in Cappadocia by a pure blunder); but he gives Lystra, Antioch, and Apollonia in Galatia, and *à fortiori* Iconium must have been in that province. Firmilian, *l.c.*, mentions Galatia and (the triple Province) Cilicia as most closely connected with Iconium.

arrested under Aurelian and released, and afterwards to have founded several monasteries in Palestine.

W. M. RAMSAY.

IDALAH (יִדְאֲלָה).—A town of Zebulun, named between Shimron and Bethlehem (Jos 19[15]). The site is uncertain.

IDBASH (יִדְבָּשׁ).—One of the sons (acc. to LXX) of Etam, 1 Ch 4[3]. The MT is undoubtedly corrupt. See GENEALOGY.

IDDO.—1. אִדּוֹ (? אֲדַר 'strength') Ezr 8[17] 'The chief, at the place Casiphia,' who provided Ezra with Levites and Nethinim. The text implies that I. was himself one of the Nethinim, but it is impossible that the head of a Levitical seminary should have belonged to the lowest order of ministers. Read, with Ryle, 'unto Iddo and his brethren (i.e. Levites) and the Nethinim.' 1 Es 8[45.46] has 'Loddeus the captain who was in the place of the treasury . . . Loddeus and to his brethren and to the treasurers in that place,' connecting the name Casiphia with keseph 'silver' (so LXX ἐν ἀργυρίῳ τοῦ τόπου). It must have been near Babylon, and can have no connexion with the Caspian Mountains or Caspiæ Pylæ. **2.** (יִדּוֹ 'beloved') 1 Ch 27[21] son of Zechariah, captain of the half tribe of Manasseh in Gilead, perh. = No. **4.** **3.** Ezr 10[43] יִדּוֹ Kethib RV, יַדַּי Kerê, RVm Jaddai, AV Jadau, 1 Es 9[35] Edos) one of those who had taken strange wives. **4.** 1 K 4[14] (עִדּא 'timely,' Ges.) father of Abinadab, who was Solomon's commissariat officer at Mahanaim in Gilead (see No. 2). **5.** (עִדּוֹ) 1 Ch 6[21] a Gershonite Levite called Adaiah in v.[41]. **6.** A seer (hozeh) and prophet (nabi) cited by the Chronicler as an authority for the reigns of (a) Solomon, 2 Ch 9[29] (Kethib יֶעְרִי Jedai, Kerê יֶעְדִי Jedo, LXX Ἰωήλ) 'the visions of I. the seer concerning Jeroboam the son of Nebat'; (b) Rehoboam, 2 Ch 12[15] (עִדּוֹ) 'the history of I. the seer after the manner of (or, in reckoning the) genealogies'; and of (c) Abijah, 2 Ch 13[22] (עִדּוֹ) 'the midrash of the prophet Iddo.' The first passage cited is probably the ground of the tradition adopted by Jos. (Ant. VIII. viii. 5) and Jerome (Qu. Heb. in 2 Ch 9[29] 12[15] 15[1]) that the prophet who denounces Jeroboam in 1 K 13 was named Jadon or Jaddo. Jerome also identifies Iddo with Oded. **7.** יִדּוֹ Zec 1[1] (עִדּוֹא Zec 1[7], Ezr 5[1] 6[14]) 1 Es 6[1] Addo. Grandfather (father acc. to Ezr) of the prophet Zechariah; possibly of the same family as No. 2. **8.** עִדּוֹא Neh 12[4.16] (in v.[16] Kethib has עֲדַיִא) one of the priestly clans that went up with Zerubbabel.

N. J. D. WHITE.

IDOLATRY.—The idolatry of Israel, in ordinary usage, is held to include two forms of aberration from true religion. The more heinous type was the worship of alien or fictitious divinities, best described as heathenism (Götzendienst); the less heinous was the worship of the God of Israel by the mediation of images (Bilderdienst). The particular problems arising under these two heads being dealt with in separate articles (see ASHTORETH, BAAL, CALF, EPHOD, etc.), the main object here must be to indicate the general drift and features of the protracted conflict between the religious ideals and the popular religious tendencies which are mirrored in the OT.

Idolatry (εἰδωλολατρεία), which occurs once in AV (1 S 15[23]) as tr. of תְּרָפִים, has no exact Heb. equivalent. There are, however, nine or ten Heb. words which AV, and, in the main, RV (following LXX) render by 'idol,' and which give lively expression to the varied sentiments of contempt, loathing, and apprehension excited in the prophetical writers by idolatry. The terms are: אָוֶן nothingness (Is 66[3]), אֵימִים objects of terror (Jer 50[38]), אֱלִיל neutral expression for any divinity (Is 57[5]), אֱלִיל a cypher (often, esp. in Is), גִּלּוּלִים massy blocks (Lv 26[30]), מִפְלֶצֶת a terror (1 K 15[13]), פֶּסֶל or סֶמֶל a figure (2 Ch 33[7]), עֲצַבִּים

carvings, with perhaps a play on sorrow (Hos 4[17]), cf. עֹצֶב צִיר a figure (Is 45[16]). Image in AV is used as the equivalent of about an equal number of terms, of which the following alterations in RV may be noted : חַמָּן a sun-image (Lv 26[30]), מַצֵּבָה a pillar, תְּרָפִים untranslated. פֶּסֶל is the graven image (Ex 20[4]), but is sometimes used comprehensively (Is 40[19]), מַסֵּכָה (Ex 34[17]) and נֶסֶךְ (Is 41[29]) denote the molten image. In NT 'image' translates εἴκων and once χαρακτήρ (He 13 'express [RV 'very'] image'). See more fully under IMAGE. The common idol was an uncouth figure of clay or wood ; the more pretentious was of gold or silver, or at least plated. The process of manufacture is contemptuously described in Is 44[11ff.].

I. HEATHENISM IN ISRAEL.—Not the least interesting chapter in the history of this subject is that upon which the narrative of Genesis throws little if any light, viz. the religion of the stock from which the Hebrews sprang. The teaching of Genesis is to the effect that there was a primitive knowledge of the true God, which was handed down through Noah to the line of Shem, of which Abraham became the custodian, and which he transmitted to his posterity. It is, at the most, implied in the story of the Call of Abraham (Gn 12[1]), and first stated explicitly in Jos 24[2ff.], that the patriarchal religion had a background of idolatry. For the reconstruction of this primitive Semitic heathenism there is some material available. It is reasonable to suppose, in the first place, that vestiges of the older beliefs and customs survived to the later period illuminated by the OT. A second source, which has been closely examined in the same interest, especially by Wellhausen (Skizzen und Vorarbeiten, Heft 3) and W. R. Smith (RS[2]), is the type of heathenism which prevailed in Arabia before the rise of Islam, and which, it is assumed, had not widely diverged from that of the common ancestor of the Semitic peoples. The examination of this evidence has shaken the older view that Semitic idolatry began in the worship of the heavenly bodies (so, e.g., Maimonides, De Idololatria, who explains star-worship by an intelligible desire to honour what God had honoured, but traces the later phase of image-service to the designs of false prophets, cap. i. § 4). The suggestion of Ewald (Gesch. Isr.[3] i. p. 380), that a polytheistic system may be detected in the genealogies of Gn 4 and 5, where the gods and goddesses of an earlier age have been degraded to patriarchal rank, has not met with much favour. By other writers, esp. Stade, it is held that an important, if not the most important, element in the early religious life of the Semites was ancestor-worship—sacrifices having been offered at Hebron and Shechem to Abraham and Joseph ere they were offered to Jahweh ; and for proof stress is laid on significant features of burial and mourning (cf. Is 65[4]), the long persistence of the worship of a species of household gods known as Teraphim, and the specific designation of spirits as Elohim (1 S 28[13]). The special purpose of W. R. Smith's work in this field, on the other hand, was to draw attention to the vestiges of a primitive totemism or animal-worship both among Arabs and Hebrews ; and these he found to linger, in the case of the Hebrews, in the denomination of tribes and families after animals, birds, and reptiles ; in a vigorous animal-cult, described by Ezekiel as flourishing so recently as the eve of the Exile (Ezk 8[10]) ; and in the distinction of clean and unclean beasts, where the totem of the earlier survived as the unclean animal of the later period (Journ. of Philology, ix. 75 ff.). There are, however, reasons for regarding both ancestor-worship and animal-worship as secondary in the development of the religions of nature ; and others are of opinion that the evidence rather points to a polydæmonism as the original type of Semitic heathenism. Of this the fundamental conception is that men are in contact with a realm of spirits which take to do with their concerns, and to which they can draw near in some spot or object in which these are housed—as the well, the tree, the sacred stone (so Kayser, *Theologie des AT*, p. 21 ff.). From polytheism it is distinguished by the fact that the spirits have not yet attained to a clear-cut individuality, or to the possession of a mythology, while it tends to run down into fetishism through the adoration of the tenement in place of the tenant. In one of the most speculative regions of history a certain conclusion is, of course, unattainable, but the view in question at least harmonizes with what is known of the primeval modes of Semitic thought, while such an animistic religion formed some sort of a preparation for the introduction of the higher faith. In particular, it could offer no such opposition as a developed polytheism to the claim of one God upon the undivided allegiance of a people.

When Israel emerges into the light of history, it has broken, at least in principle, with heathenism. In the national memory the momentous step was connected with Abraham; and although the date of the patriarchal narratives makes them in large measure the vehicle of prophetic ideals, there is no reason to doubt that Mosaism reposed on and appealed to a religious past, in which the light of revelation had dawned. The work of Moses was to widen and perpetuate the breach with heathenism, and this he accomplished through the coincidence of the divine deliverance of Israel with the hour of his prophetic mission. Mosaism, whatever else it may have included, was at least a revolt from heathenism, from which it sought to protect Israel by prohibiting the worship of any divinity save J" its God (Ex 20³), and by bringing under His ban immoral acts and practices to which the genius of heathenism is at the best indifferent. From this standpoint there are two notable declensions related in the history of the period. The story of the golden calf, though its main significance belongs to the sphere of the minor idolatry, is also conceived as an apostasy to other gods than J" (Ex 32⁸). The second reported lapse is the idolatry with Moab at Peor, where Israel succumbed to the fascinations of a Baal-cult that consecrated sexual licentiousness (Nu 25). These incidents, however, even if historical,—and it may be noted that they belong in substance to our oldest capital source,—were mere episodes of temporary reaction natural to a period of intense religious fervour. The Israel which hurled itself upon Canaan was the people of J", and saw in the gods of the nations real gods indeed, but His and their enemies.

Upon the settlement in Canaan there followed a heathen revival. The history of the Book of Judges moves through a succession of cycles: the people forsake J" and serve the Baalim and the Ashtaroth; J" in anger delivers them into the hands of the spoiler; then it repents Him, and He raises up judges who save them; then once more they turn back, and deal more corruptly than their fathers (Jg 2¹¹ff.). For this relapse various causes are plausibly assigned—intermarriage with the Canaanite population, association of the Baal-cult with the agricultural year, a sense of the possession of proprietary rights by the old divinities in the land of Canaan (Smend, *AT Religionsgeschichte*, p. 50). But doubtless the strongest enticement lay in the character of the Canaanitish worship, which, in the main resting on a deification of the productive forces of nature, gathered up into religion all that is comprehended in laughter and licence. And if it had also quite another side, which revealed the divinity as cruel, and lusting for agony and blood, there was an element in the Hebrew nature to which this also appealed. The divine remedy for the backsliding was war. When Israel was attacked and spoiled, or when the hand of the oppressor was heavy upon them, they remembered that of old time J" had been their deliverer, the religious enthusiasm welled up afresh, and under a leader whom it possessed they marched to victory. Such a leader also, without doubt, was Saul, although the history lays most stress on his later defection from, and his desertion by, J". But among those who delivered Israel in the name of J" the noblest and the best character was that of David, whose piety, even if allied with the superstition of divination, and marred by sensuality and cruelty, in some respects was the model of Christian communion with God; and the final outcome of the experiences of the period of the Judges, and esp. of the career of David which established the monarchy, was to place the sovereignty of J" on as firm a basis as in the first flush of the wars of conquest. But again with an era of peace there came a heathen reaction, beginning in the seduction of Solomon to Canaanitish and cognate cults through the influence of his wives (1 K 11¹⁻⁸), and extending throughout a great portion of the history both of the Northern and the Southern Kingdoms.

In the Northern Kingdom the religious life took in the first instance an opposite direction. Antagonism to the heathenish innovations in Jerusalem may have been a factor in the power behind Jeroboam, as the setting up of the worship of the golden calves in two ancient sanctuaries may have been conceived in the interests of the ancestral religion; at all events, there is no reason to charge Jeroboam and his immediate successors with deliberate apostasy from J". The recrudescence of heathenism in the Northern Kingdom is connected with Ahab, who built a temple in Samaria to the Zidonian Baal (1 K 16³²), and supported a heathenish priesthood. How far the hostile designs of Ahab against the religion of J" extended is less certain. Many modern writers are of opinion that Ahab remained loyal to the national God — for which the names of his sons, Ahaziah and Jehoram, afford some evidence, and that the story of the persecutions is at least exaggerated (see, *e.g.*, Smend, *op. cit.* p. 154 ff.). But, while it is true that the OT annals give broad effects and neglect fine distinctions, the Elijah traditions make it impossible to doubt that we have to deal in the case of Ahab with a dangerous assault on the national religion; and this impression is confirmed by the observation that the house of Omri was shortly afterwards destroyed with all its works in the name of the God of Israel (2 K 10). At all events, the intrusion of the alien cult received an effectual check. The annalist grants that the successors of Jehu stopped short in the sin of Jeroboam the son of Nebat, however persistently the heathen leaven may have continued to work in the local sanctuaries.

The main sources for our knowledge of heathenism in this period are the writings of the 8th cent. prophets. Their testimony is, however, somewhat obscure, owing to the difficulty of distinguishing between the degraded worship of J" and the rites of heathenism proper. It appears that J" could be worshipped in name while the conception formed of Him was no higher or purer than that of the heathen. 'God has so utterly abolished the idols with whom Satan contested with Him the allegiance of His people that we have no certain knowledge what they were' (Pusey on Am 5²⁶). The final commentary on the history of the Northern Kingdom mentions as the chief forms star-worship, Baal-worship, accompanied by the most cruel rites, and magic (2 K 17). By the Baal-cult we have doubtless to understand the worship, not of a simple mighty rival of J", but of a multitude of local divinities characterized by alternating moods of prodigality and ferocity. According to Amos, the worship of the Baalim (?, see Driver, *ad loc.*) was one of the four great sins of Israel, aggravated by its association with inhumanity, fornication, and drunkenness (2⁷·⁸). As the places of worship, are mentioned hills and mountains and groves (*passim*). The central object was the altar, with which were associated the sacred pillar and post—doubtless conceived as 'houses of God.' The rites included the offering of incense (1 K 11^8) and of sacrifices, in times of crisis human sacrifices (2 K 17^{17}). In expostulating with his country-men, Hosea pleads that J″ was from of old the God of Israel who conferred on them great benefits (11$^{1\text{-}4}$), and from whose hand they receive their present blessings (2^8); while the Baalim are mere creations of their own, who, as proved by experience, are powerless to protect them (13^1).

In the Southern Kingdom we discover a more vigorous and developed type of heathenism, but also a more passionate and energetic resistance. A significant note in the record of Rehoboam's reign shows that the idolatry of Solomon left as a legacy the vilest form of consecrated prostitution (1 K 14^{24}); and of this, as well as of the seducing idols, Judah was purged by Asa (1 K 15$^{9\text{ff.}}$). A similar tribute of praise is accorded to Jehoshaphat, and especially to Hezekiah (2 K 18^4); and that the latter had to deal with a true heathenism, as well as with a debased worship of J″, may be collected from the contemporary witness of Isaiah.

'The land,' Isaiah declares, ' is become full of not-gods' (2^8). As the chief abominations he mentions the Asherahs and the sun-images (17^8), of which, however, the former is not necessarily a clue to heathenism. He also mentions the popularity of magicians, soothsayers, etc. (2^6 3^2 8^{19}). Specially noticeable is the rise to a pure monotheism in the contemptuous dismissal of the rival gods as mere human handiwork (2^8), things of naught (31^7), and his extension of J″'s sovereignty to the ends of the earth.

From the reforms of Hezekiah there is a sudden descent to the corruptions of the reign of Manasseh, who introduced the worship both of the heavenly bodies and of the Canaanitish divinities, and along with the latter their cruel and licentious rites (2 K 21). To understand such a lapse from the general tradition of the Davidic house we have to bear in mind two facts : the apparent political expediency of showing reverence for the celestial gods of the great empire in the North, and the doubts which the course of events may have aroused as to whether there was indeed in J″ power and will for effectual deliverance (cf. Smend, *AT Theologie*, p. 270 ff.). But in Josiah, another, and the greatest of the reformers, was to follow. In centralizing the worship at Jerusalem he dealt at heathenism the most effective blow possible, while he suppressed with a stern hand the innova-tions of his father, and the abominations that had crept in in their wake (2 K 23^5).

The programme of the reformation under Josiah contained in Deut. is terrible in its thoroughness. Not only does it embody the threat of destruction as the penalty of national apostasy (6^{15} 8^{19} etc.), but it prohibits the individual from practising idolatry, under pain of death (17$^{2\text{ff.}}$). Further, those who per-suade others to idolatry are to be punished with death (13^6). Nay, the subject was not even to be looked into (12^{30}). The destruction of the furniture of heathenism is a most sacred duty (7$^{5.\,25}$ 12^2). How deeply and harmfully heathenism had eaten into the life of the people may be inferred from the fierceness of these enactments, which occur in a code otherwise marked by exceptional mildness and humaneness.

How far short of fulfilling the reformation fell of fulfilling the prophetic expectations is indicated by the prophets of the Chaldæan period. It would seem that the closing decades of the monarchy were marked by yet wilder excesses, as if the nation were making a last desperate cast in a losing game with fate. 'Thy gods, O Judah,' cries Jeremiah, ' are according to the number of thy cities' (2^{28}). Specially instructive is the vision of Ezekiel (ch. 8), in which he enumerates the three main forms of heathenism by which Judah was polluted — an animal - worship embracing loath-some beasts and reptiles, the cult of Tammuz, which drew the women after it, and the adoration of the sun-god. And the last of the kings succumbed to the contagion of the times, and scouted the counsel that was delivered to them by the prophets in the name of J″.

The purification came in the discipline of the Exile. Surrounded by the emblems of foreign idolatry, the exiles became deeply conscious of the grandeur and truth of the spiritual religion taught by their prophets ; and although we know that a large number remained in Babylon, of whom many would become merged in the adjacent heathen mass, the remnant which returned brought with them the contempt of the great exilic prophet for the manufactured gods of gold and silver and wood, and the stubborn loyalty to J″ which was to become in Roman times the wonder and the hatred of the world. That even after the Exile heathen practices lingered in the community is argued by Smend (*loc. cit.* p. 39) from Ps 16$^{1\text{ff.}}$, Zec 10^2 13^2, Job 31^{26}, cf. Is 27^9; but in any case it was a rapidly vanishing quantity. And the lessons of past experience had been carefully gleaned. The dissolution of mixed marriages by Ezra excluded the most dangerous of the influences which made for heathenism, while the Law sought to guarantee the purity of religion by an uncompromising policy of national isolation.

II. Idolatrous Worship of J″. —In the age of the Judges, as we have seen, and in the middle period of the Northern Kingdom, the imminent danger had been the submersion of Jahwism under the refluent wave of heathenism. In the 8th and 7th cents. the object on which prophetism con-centrates its fervent energy is the purification or spiritualization of the worship which was rendered to the national God. Of that worship an ancient and increasingly marked feature was the use of images, and with Hosea there begins an attack upon image-service as inconsistent with the spirit of Jahwism, and virtually substituting fetishes for the living God (8$^{5.\,6}$ 10^5).

That the practice was ancient, and sanctioned by high authority, does not admit of dispute. After his victory over Midian, one of the chosen instruments of J″, Gideon, made an ephod out of the spoils—by which the context suggests that we are to understand a gold-plated image (Jg 8$^{24\text{ff.}}$). Still more instructive is the story of Micah the Ephraimite, who out of 200 shekels of silver framed a graven image and a molten image, and hired Jonathan, a descendant of Moses, to be his priest (Jg 17^3). Even David has closely associated with him emblems of idolatry ; for besides that he tolerates the probably ancestral cult of the human figures called Teraphim (1 S 19^{13}), the interroga-tion of the Ephod, here again most likely an image of J″, is a habit of his religious life (1 S 21^9 23$^{6.\,9}$ 30^7). It could not therefore, as above hinted, im-press the national mind as an impious innovation when Jeroboam associated the worship of J″ with the symbols of the golden bulls, and the absence of any polemic against the image-worship in the crusade of Elijah is generally regarded as proving that it was acquiesced in even by the enlightened conscience of the time. (On the other side König, *Hauptprobleme der altisraelitischen Religionsges-chichte*, p. 65). That the idolatrous worship of J″ had even reached back to the Mosaic age, and was sanctioned by Moses, it is not necessary to admit. Apart from the case for the originality of the second commandment, there are independent grounds for believing, on the analogy of other faiths, that primitive Mosaism embodied the con-ception of an imageless worship (Reichel, *Vor-hellenische Götterculte*). Sufficiently significant is the obvious fact that from the Judges to the 8th cent. the idols became more and more numerous and costly, and that only in the Assyrian period were they realized to be alien to the genius of the national religion.

In the prophetic campaign against the historic-ally legitimated idolatry we may distinguish three important phases. Were it made out that Ex 34 contains an older Decalogue, we might have to recognize an earlier attempt at reformation, as it is possible to hold that that code, in prohibiting 'molten gods' (Ex 34[17]), tacitly sanctioned the simpler type of the graven images (Smend, *AT Theol.* p. 195). The great effort was put forth in the Northern Kingdom, but the prophets were unable even to weaken the idolatry which was embedded in the political framework, and the kings persisted to the last in the sin of Jeroboam, the son of Nebat. In Judah the first notable contribution to a more spiritual ritual was made by Hezekiah, in whose reforming spirit may be detected a reflection of the zeal of Isaiah. In the report of some of his acts, especially of his suppression of the high places and their insignia, critics have suspected the ante-dating of later reforms; but there is at least unmistakable evidence of his active aggression against the idolatrous elements of the traditional religion (2 K 18[4]). Specially noteworthy is his removal of the brazen serpent, by which he withdrew the most sacred of sanctions, the Mosaic, from the approach to J" through figured symbol. The Reformation under Josiah is here memorable, not merely as consolidating the worship in an imageless sanctuary, but as energetically acting on the Deuteronomic prohibition of the posts and pillars (Dt 16[21ff.]), which, before there had been images to give expression to the character of a divinity, had been venerated as places of a god's abode. 'He brought out the Asherah from the house of the Lord, and burned it at the brook Kidron' (2 K 23[6]). On the whole it may be said that in Judah more energy was shown in, and more success followed on, the purification of the Jahweh-worship than was the case in Israel, but that in Judah also the purer Jahwism had its reaction in a grosser heathenism.

On two general features of the OT idolatry as exhibited by the sacred writers a remark may be made. The first feature is the astonishing strength of its fascinations. The perverse obstinacy of the chosen people in opposition to the logic of conscience, history, and heaven, can only be explained on the assumption that idolatry offered some deeply-satisfying provision for human nature. Wherein did this attraction lie? As regards the form which has been described as heathenism, the answer is obvious: it was popular because it was not ethical. There are many things which are felt to be attractive if only they were lawful, and the genius of heathenism, especially of the Canaanitish type, was to make it possible to overleap the boundaries of right and wrong with an appeased conscience. Were we confronted by a new religion which in a solemn spirit, and with a reasoned claim, threw its mantle over all which we assign to the world, the flesh, and the devil, we should realize something of the strength of the opposition with which the prophets of J" had to contend. As regards idolatrous worship of God, again, the need which it met is a universal one. The invisible God of the infinite attributes is a being whom thought with difficulty grasps, to whom the heart hardly warms—and the necessity of a more vivid and concrete manifestation of His essence is common ground of all the great religions save one. As a fact, we can approach God only through the aid of symbols—mental pictures and words are no less symbols than paintings and statues; and it is not clear that there is any difference in principle between the verbal representation of God as our Father and the more graphic representation of the same conception which can be given in His special material by the artist. The prophet did not scruple to use imagery which represented God as flying and even as roaring and ravening like a beast of the forest, and the image of the idolater was more effective than the imagery. But the justification of the prophetic attitude is that the image was too effective. Where a certain spiritual

level has been reached, the visible symbol may be a real aid to devotion; but on lower levels the worshipper stops at the outward form, and sinks back into a true heathenism. And so it worked out, against the wise opposition of the prophets, in Israel: the symbol became to the unspiritual people a fetish, and the fetish poisoned the national life.

From what has been said, we are in a better position to appreciate the scheme of retributive justice which the prophetical writers find exemplified in the history of Israel and Judah, and of their kings. Because of idolatry Israel was removed from its place, and Judah after it went into captivity. The religious reformation is followed by a prosperous reign, the backsliding is avenged by the Philistine, the Assyrian, or the Chaldæan. That, says criticism, is not history. As a fact it is, in the main outline, history, and it is besides the vehicle of the grandest and most certain of historical generalizations—viz. that the Ruler of the world is on the side of purity and righteousness. The idolatry of Israel was, as we have seen, a description from the religious side of the evil doings which God hates, and it is therefore rightly written down as the cause of His vindictive and chastening judgments upon Israel.

Idolatry in NT.—The references to idolatry in NT are naturally of much more contracted scope. With the Jews the opposition to idolatry had become since the days of Antiochus Epiphanes a fanaticism, and the subject scarcely finds a place in the sayings of our Lord. From the circumstances of his mission it occupied a considerable space in the thoughts of St. Paul. Of peculiar importance is what we may call his philosophy of heathenism expounded in Ro 1, where he traces it to its origin in a sin against the light of nature, shows that this was punished by the withdrawal of the former light, and sets forth the hideous moral corruption of the Roman world as the result of the religious apostasy. A somewhat milder judgment of the heathen world is passed in the speech at Athens (Ac 18), where ignorance of God is not insisted on as matter of guilt, and an appeal is made to men on the ground of the dignity of their origin to rise to the recognition of the true God, and hearken to His latest accredited word. A special problem arose for Christian casuistry in connexion with meats offered to idols, which the apostle resolves by referring it to the arbitrament of a conscience enlightened by the twin principles of Christian liberty and Christian sympathy (1 Co 8). To the view popularized by Milton that the idols of the heathen were in reality devils, some colour is lent by 1 Co 10[14ff.]; but, against this is to be put the emphatic protest, 'we know that no idol is anything in the world' (1 Co 8[4]). Idolatry appears in the catalogue of the works of the flesh (Gal 5[20]), and of those which exclude from eternal salvation (1 Co 6[9]); but, as is characteristic of NT thought, the apostle widens the old religious conception, and makes it include all practices which are tantamount to a dethronement of God in favour of a creature. So gluttony and covetousness, where 'non objecto sed solo acto peccatur,' are species of idolatry (Eph 5[5], Ph 3[19]). The recollection of the blessed deliverance from the darkness of heathenism is appealed to as furnishing a motive to sanctification (1 Th 1[9]). Finally, St. John predicts an idolatrous apostasy in the last days (Rev 9[20]).

LITERATURE.—The OT idolatry is naturally one of the capital topics in the histories of Israel and in the monographs on the Biblical Theology of the OT. For the presentation of the subject from the purely evolutionist point of view, see Wellhausen, *Isr. u. jüd. Geschichte*; Stade, *Geschichte des Volkes Israel*: for a more conservative treatment, Kittel, *Hist. of Hebrews*. In addition to the works on Biblical Theology above mentioned, among which Smend's *AT Religionsgeschichte* is full and suggestive, may be mentioned Duhm, *Theologie der Propheten.* See also art. 'Baal,' by Ed. Meyer, in Roscher's *Lexicon.* For the Image Controversy in the Greek Church, see in Mansi's *Councils* the decrees of the Seventh Œcumenical Council ; and for a review of the arguments, Harnack's *Dogmengeschichte,* ii. p. 460 ff. **W. P. PATERSON.**

IDUEL ('Ιδούηλος), 1 Es 8⁴³.—In Ezr 8¹⁶ ARIEL. The form is due to confusion of ר and ד.

IDUMÆA, IDUMÆANS.—See EDOM.

IEDDIAS (A 'Ιεδδίας, B 'Ιεξείας, AV Eddias), 1 Es 9²⁶.—One of those who agreed to put away their 'strange' wives. Called IZZIAH (יזִּיָה : B 'Αξειά, A 'Αξιά, א 'Αδειά) Ezr 10²⁵.

IEZER, IEZERITES (אִיעֶזֶר Nu 26³⁰ P), contracted from ABIEZER, wh. see.

IGAL (יִגְאָל '[God] redeems').—**1.** (B 'Ιλαάλ, A F 'Ιγάλ ; *Igal*) One of the twelve spies sent by Moses from the wilderness of Paran : he is described as the son of Joseph of the tribe of Issachar (Nu 13⁷).
2. (Γαάλ ; Luc. 'Ιωήλ) One of David's heroes, the son of Nathan of Zobah (2 S 23³⁶). In the parallel list (1 Ch 11³⁸) the name is given as 'JOEL (יוֹאֵל 'Ιωήλ), the brother (A ; 'the son' B) of Nathan.'
3. ('Ιωήλ ; *Jegaal* ; AV Igeal) Son of Shemaiah of the royal house of David (1 Ch 3²²). **J. F. STENNING.**

IGDALIAH (יִגְדַּלְיָהוּ 'J" is great').—A 'man of God,' father of Hanan, whose name is mentioned in connexion with Jeremiah's interview with the Rechabites (Jer 35⁴).

IGNORANCE is spoken of in Scripture mainly in connexion with sin ; it modifies to some extent the sinner's responsibility. Thus even of a sin in which the chief actors knew well that they were doing wrong—the crucifixion—St. Peter says, 'Ye did it in ignorance' (κατὰ ἄγνοιαν, Ac 3¹⁷) ; St. Paul, 'if they had known, they would not have crucified the Lord of glory' (1 Co 2⁸) ; and the Lord Himself, 'Father, forgive them : for they know not what they do' (Lk 23³⁴). They all knew something, but not everything ; not, for instance, what the apostles only grasped through the resurrection and the teaching of the Risen One, that He was the Son of God, and His death a propitiation for the whole world ; hence, according to NT, though their guilt was deep, in some cases awful, it was not unpardonable. The choice of evil, by one who knows clearly and fully what it is, removes the possibility of pardon : such a choice would be the αἰώνιον ἁμάρτημα of which Jesus speaks in Mk 3²⁹—sin, final and irretrievable.
On a broad view, the pre - Christian ages of human history, or the pre-Christian part of any one's life, may be characterized as 'times of ignorance' (Ac 17³⁰, 1 P 1¹⁴). The meaning is not that the heathen know nothing ; there is a light which lightens every man, a law written on the heart, however blurred or even misleading the writing may have become. But they do not know everything, and therefore, according to NT teaching, their sin is pardonable, and repentance and forgiveness are to be preached to them. Ignorance, such as it is, does not entirely exculpate ; but it precludes final condemnation out of hand. When those who have lived in heathen ignorance are converted, their past life will not appear guiltless ; on the contrary, they will be ashamed and confounded when they look back on it ; when it stands out before them in the light of God's eternal law, and of the life of Jesus, they will be unable to understand how they lived as they did ; they will condemn themselves, and humbly acknowledge their guilt. They were ignorant,

but not innocent ; yet, because of their ignorance, not without hope. Such guilt as theirs leaves the possibility of feeling in the moral nature ; they may yet be pricked in their hearts, and repent and be saved. It is thus St. Paul interprets his own experience : 'I was a blasphemer, etc. ; but I obtained mercy, because I did it ἀγνοῶν ἐν ἀπιστίᾳ' (1 Ti 1¹³).
The gradual enlightenment of the Christian conscience, its entrance under the teaching of experience into fuller possession of the mind of Christ, has to be considered, in applying the plea of ignorance in extenuation of guilt. Thus to keep slaves might once have been done ignorantly —κατ' ἄγνοιαν, like the crucifixion—by a Christian ; now it would be a sin against the light. Each generation is amazed at what its fathers perpetrated or tolerated or did not see ; to say they knew no better is to utter at once their excuse and their condemnation, for such is the connexion between moral integrity and moral enlightenment that we feel sure they might have, and ought to have, known better. St. Paul not only mentions 'the times of ignorance,' which God 'winked at' (Ac 17³⁰), but indicates the genesis of that ignorance in a way which makes it itself an ominous feature of non-Christian life (Ro 1¹⁸⁻²³, Eph 4¹⁷⁻¹⁹). In the last resort it is due to an immoral suppression, and even extinction, of divine light. It keeps pace with, as it is due to a πώρωσις of the heart ; though the two things, once initiated, are mutually cause and effect. Men act in the hardness of their hearts, and the light is dimmed ; they act in the darkening light, and the capacity for feeling is deadened. If this process had its perfect work in any one, so that he had lost utterly the power of distinguishing good and evil, the result would not be the ἄγνοια which mitigates guilt ; it would be that ignorance of the 'moral universal' which is itself a final condemnation.
The verb ἀγνοεῖν is used in He 5², and the subst. ἀγνοήματα in He 9⁷, to describe sin in the character of 'sin of ignorance.' For the OT conception see Nu 15, Lv 4. The main idea is that of unwitting error or inadvertence. For such sins a sacrifice was provided, more serious in proportion to the culpability of the offender. Thus more was expected—or ignorance was less of a plea—in the case of a priest or a ruler than in that of a private person. Sins of ignorance *were* sins, and therefore had to be expiated ; but they were not highhanded sins, and therefore they *could* be expiated. They were not renunciations of the covenant, which could not be purged with sacrifice or offering for ever, but had to be punished by extermination. What are commonly called 'infirmities' in Christians may be said to answer now to 'sins of ignorance.' There is a disproportion, so to speak, between our nature and our calling. We are flesh and blood, with inherited vices perhaps, and it is our calling to be holy as God is holy. In spite of faith and vigilance the Christian may be overtaken in a fault. The sudden fall, from which the heart instantly revolts, which it condemns, which it deeply mourns, is the sin of ignorance under the new covenant. If we had only known, if we had seen at the moment how it grieved God, scandalized others, hurt ourselves, we should never have done it. This leaves pardon possible, and we have a High Priest, who was Himself compassed with infirmity (though with none that issued in sin), that He might be able to bear gently with those who sin in ignorance and go astray (τοῖς ἀγνοοῦσι καὶ πλανωμένοις, He 5²). **J. DENNEY.**

IGNORANCES.—This plural form is given as the

tr[n] of ἄγνοιαι in 1 Es 8[75], Sir 23[3], and of ἀγνοήματα in To 3[8], Sir 23[2] 51[19]. It is a literal rendering of the Greek, and can scarcely be illustrated from Eng. secular literature, though other abstract words like 'impenitences' are found, and this plu. is quoted with other meanings. RV retains the form, except in 1 Es 8[75] 'errors.' For sins of ignorance see the previous article and article SIN.   J. HASTINGS.

IJON (עִיּוֹן).—A town in the north part of the mountains of Naphtali, noticed with Dan and Abel-beth-maacah in 1 K 15[20] (=2 Ch 16[4]) as taken by the captains of the armies of Benhadad. It was captured also and depopulated by Tiglath-pileser (2 K 15[29]). The name is thought to survive in the *Merj 'Ayun* or 'meadow of springs,' a plateau N.W. of Dan. The most important site in this plateau is *Tell Dibbîn*, immediately south of the Leontes ravine, which Robinson and others have suggested may be the site of Ijon.

LITERATURE.—Robinson, *BRP* iii. 375 ; Baedeker-Socin, *Pal.*[2] 349 ; Porter, *Handbook* (Index) ; Guérin, *Galilée*, ii. 280 ; Buhl, *GAP* (Index, s. 'Ijon').   C. R. CONDER.

IKKESH (עִקֵּשׁ).—The father of Ira, one of David's heroes, 2 S 23[26], 1 Ch 11[28] 27[9].

ILAI (עִילַי ; B ʿHλεί, A ʿHλί ; *Ilai*), an Ahohite, one of David's heroes (1 Ch 11[29]). In the parallel list (2 S 23[28]) the name appears as ZALMON (צַלְמוֹן ; B ʾΕλλών, A Σελλώμ, Luc. ʾΑλιμάν). It seems probable that the Chronicler has preserved the more correct text. Klostermann conjectures עַלְיָן or אֶלְיַעֲשִׂי as the original form ; Wellhausen עִלַּי : Thenius, however, adheres to the text of Samuel.
    J. F. STENNING.

ILIADUN (B Ελιαδούν, A ʾΙλ-, AV Eliadun), 1 Es 5[58] ([56] LXX).—Perhaps to be identified with HENADAD, Ezr 3[9].

ILL.—Like 'evil' (of which it is a contraction), 'ill' is used in AV as adv., adj., and subst. The only occurrence of the subst. is Ro 13[10] 'Love worketh no ill to his neighbour' (κακόν). Cf. Rhem. NT Note to Mt 3[10] 'It is not only damnable to doe il, but also not to doe good.' The adj. was formerly, with the meaning of 'bad,' applied to persons as well as things. Thus in the Rhem. NT, the Note on 'Thamar' (Mt 1[3]) is, 'Christ abhorred not to take flesh of some that were il, as he chose Judas among his Apostles : let us not disdaine to receive our spiritual birth and sustenance of such as be not alwayes good'; and in the Note on the Penitent Thief (Lk 23[43]) occurs, 'Learne only not to despaire, though thou hast been il [=wicked] to the last moment of thy life.' Again, T. Adams on 1 P 1[4] says, 'If thy words and works be ill meal, thank the miller, thy heart, for such corrupt thoughts'; and on 1[6] 'The husband told his wife that he had one ill quality, he was given to be angry without cause; she wittily replied that she would keep him from that fault, for she would give him cause enough.' The adj. occurs in Dt 15[21] 'any ill blemish'; Jl 2[20] 'his ill savour'; Jth 8[8] 'ill word'; Wis 5[23], Sir 29[7] 'ill dealing'; 9[18] 'ill tongue,' 41[11] 'ill name.' The adv. is found in Gn 43[6] 'Wherefore dealt ye so ill with me?' Job 20[26], Ps 106[32] 'go ill'; Is 3[11] 'be ill'; Jer 40[4] 'seem ill'; Mic 3[4] 'they have behaved themselves ill in their doings'; and Wis 18[10] 'an ill according cry' (ἀσύμφωνος βοή); as well as in the phrase 'ill-favoured,' Gn 41[3, 4, 19, 20, 21, 27], for which see FAVOUR, and cf. North, *Plutarch*, 889, 'He had no further leysure, but to cast an ill-favoured cloke about him, the first that came to hand, and disguising himselfe to flie for life'; Fuller, *Profane State*, v. 3, p. 365, 'The suspicion is increased if the party accused be notoriously ill-favoured; whereas

deformity alone is no more argument to make her a Witch, then handsomenesse had been evidence to prove her an Harlot.'   J. HASTINGS.

ILLUMINATE, ILLUMINATION.—Milton uses the verb to illuminate (' give light to,' ' enlighten ') literally in *PL* vii. 350—
         ' And made the stars,
  And set them in the firmament of heaven,
  To illuminate the earth.'
He has it figuratively in *Sam. Agon.* 1689, 'Though blind of sight . . . with inward eyes illuminated'; so T. Fuller, *Holy State*, iii. 12, p. 184, ' Of Naturall Fools'—' God may sometimes illuminate them, and (especially towards their death) admit them to the possession of some part of reason.' It is figuratively that the vb. occurs in AV, Bar 4[2] 'Walk in the presence of the light thereof, that thou mayest be illuminated'; and He 10[32] 'after ye were illuminated, ye endured a great fight of afflictions' (φωτισθέντες, RV ' enlightened ').

AV has followed the Rhem. NT here, which (after Vulg.) has 'illuminate' in the foll. passages in which the Gr. is φωτίζειν, Eph 1[18] 3[9], 2 Ti 1[10], He 6[4] 10[32], Rev 18[1] 21[23] 22[5], having ' lighten ' in the remaining places, viz. Lk 11[36], Jn 1[9], 1 Co 4[5]. No other version uses the word ; but in He 6[4] Wyc. (1380) has ' illumyned,' 1388 ' lightned.' It may be noted that Shaks. uses the three forms of the vb. ' illume,' ' illumine,' and ' illuminate '; Milton only ' illume ' and ' illuminate.'

Illumination occurs in AV but once, Sir 25[11] ' The love of the Lord passeth all things for illumination' (εἰς φωτισμόν ; RV after edd. omits). Cf. the Rhem. tr[n] of 2 Ti 1[10] 'But it is manifested now by the illumination (ἐπιφάνεια, Vulg. *illuminatio*) of our Saviour Jesus Christ, who hath destroied death, and illuminated (φωτίζειν, Vulg. *illuminare*) life and incorruption by the Gospel'; and the heading to Jn 9 'Our Lord . . . foretelleth by this occasion the exececation of the Jewes (because of their wilful obstinacie) and illumination of the Gentils who confesse their owne blindnes.'   J. HASTINGS.

ILLYRICUM (ʾΙλλυρικόν) was a term used in various senses ; but in the mouth of St. Paul (Ro 15[19]) it must undoubtedly be interpreted in its Roman sense, as denoting the Roman province which extended along the Adriatic from Italy and Pannonia on the north to the Macedonian province on the south. That this Roman sense was in the apostle's mind is shown, not merely by his consistent practice of using geographical terms in the Roman sense (Zahn, *Einleitung*, p. 130) and by the fact that it was natural and almost necessary in writing to a Roman church to follow the Roman usage, but also by the very form of the word. The Greek term was ʾΙλλυρίς or ʾΙλλυρία ; and the strict and regular Greek noun, used to translate the Latin *Illyricum*, was ʾΙλλυρίς (so in Strabo, pp. 323, 327 ; while Ptolemy formally gives ʾΙλλυρίς in the Greek version of 2 Ch 16 corresponding to Illyricum in the Latin version). But St. Paul simply transliterates the Roman form into Greek as ʾΙλλυρικόν ; Ro 15[19] is probably the only passage in Greek where a noun ʾΙλλυρικόν is used (showing how Roman St. Paul was in his expression of political or geographical ideas); elsewhere ʾΙλλυρικός is always an adjective.

The conquest of Illyricum had been a very slow process ; a province Illyria had been formed as early as B.C. 167, and during the following two centuries all new conquests east and north-east of the Adriatic were incorporated in Illyricum, until in A.D. 10 Augustus separated Pannonia from it, and gave a final organization to Illyricum. The province was important and warlike ; a large force of troops was required to maintain there, two legions, vii and xi, being stationed there by Augustus ; and the governor was a consular *legatus Augusti pro prœtore*. The northern half of the province was called Liburnia, and the southern, Dalmatia (wh. see). The name Dalmatia, however, gradually came into use to denote the province as a whole; and from the Flavian period onwards it became the regular and usual term. Pliny, writing before 77, uses both terms. Suetonius uses Illyricum for the time of the earlier emperors (distinguishing Dalmatia as a part of the country under Augustus), while he uses both names for the time of Otho and of Claudius. It is therefore interesting to find that St. Paul in a later epistle (2 Ti 4[10]) uses the later term Dalmatia, and not the older term Illyricum. This affords no argument for a post-Pauline date. The name Dalmatia was coming into use during his lifetime; and such changes first affect the usage of ordinary life before they affect the formal official and literary usage. If Pliny, who was so much affected by the expression of his authorities (who, being early, would all use the name Illyricum), could use the term Dalmatia before 77, St. Paul might use it ten years earlier. In fact, we may from the usage of St. Paul date the definite change in popular Roman usage from the one term to the other about A.D. 57 to 67.

In Ro 15[19] St. Paul says he has preached the gospel 'even unto Illyricum.' He is here stating the exterior limit up to which his work had extended; and there is no reason to understand (contrary to Ac) that he had actually preached in Illyricum. The doubt whether an exterior or a contained limit is meant in geographical expressions is observable in many cases, and must be determined by the context and by other evidence (see, for example, *Cities and Bishoprics of Phrygia*, i. p. 319 f.).   W. M. RAMSAY.

IMAGE, IMAGERY.—Image is loosely used in AV and RV as the tr[n] of many different Heb. words. A complete list of these words may be given for reference from other articles and for the proper interpretation of this important expression.

1. צֶלֶם *zelem*, a copy or counterpart, is translated 'image' by AV and RV in all its occurrences (Gn 1[26. 27 *bis*] 5[3] 9[6], Nu 33[52] צַלְמֵי מַשְׂכִּתָם 'their molten images'], 1 S 6[5 bis. 11], 2 K 11[18], 2 Ch 23[17], Ps 73[20], Ezk 7[20] 16[17] 23[14], Am 5[26]), except Ps 39[6] 'vain shew,' AVm 'image,' RVm (badly) 'shadow.' See next article.

2. סֶמֶל *semel*, a resemblance or likeness, is rendered 'image' in Ezk 8[3. 5] (AV and RV); but 'figure' in Dt 4[16] and 'idol' in 2 Ch 33[7. 15]. See IDOLATRY.

3. תְּמוּנָה *těmûnâh*, similitude, is rendered 'image' in Job 4[16] only; elsewhere 'likeness' (Ex 20[4], Dt 4[23. 25] 5[8], Ps 17[15]), or 'similitude' (Nu 12[8], Dt 4[12. 15. 16]). RV has 'form' everywhere except Ps 17[15] 'likeness,' m. 'form.' See FORM.

4. מַשְׂכִּית *maskîth*, representation, picture, is translated variously: Lv 26[1] (אֶבֶן מַשְׂכִּית) AV 'image of stone,' RV 'figured stone'; Nu 33[52] AV 'pictures,' RV 'figured stones'; Ps 73[7] (עָבְרוּ מַשְׂכִּיּוֹת לֵבָב) AV 'they have more than heart could wish,' AVm 'they pass the thoughts of the heart,' RVm 'the imaginations of their heart overflow'; Pr 18[11] AV 'conceit,' RV 'imagination'; 25[11] AV 'pictures,' RV 'baskets,' RVm 'filigree work'; Ezk 8[12] AV and RV 'imagery.' See PICTURE.

5. מַצֵּבָה *mazzêbhâh*, pillar, is translated simply 'pillar' by AV and RV in Gn 28[18. 22] 31[13. 45. 51. 52 bis] 35[14·20], Is 19[19]; in Dt 12[3] AV and RV 'pillar,' RVm 'obelisk'; in Ezk 26[11] AV 'garrison,' RV 'pillar,' RVm 'obelisk'; elsewhere AV has 'image' with 'statue' or 'standing image' in marg., RV always 'pillar' with 'obelisk' in marg. [Gn 23[24] 24[4] 34[13], Lv 26[1] AV 'standing image'], Dt 7[5] [AVm 'statue or pillar'] 16[22], 1 K 14[23], 2 K 3[2] 10[26. 27] 17[10] 18[4] 23[14], 2 Ch 14[3] 31[1], Jer 43[13], Hos 3[4] 10[1·2], Mic 5[13] [AV 'standing image']). See PILLAR.

6. חַמָּן] only in plu. חַמָּנִים *hammânîm*, pillars for sun-worship. AV translates by 'images' in Lv 26[30]; by 'images' with marg. 'sun images' in 2 Ch 14[5] 34[4], Is 17[8] 27[9], Ezk 6[4]·6; and by 'idols' in 2 Ch 34[7]: RV always 'sun-images.' See IDOLATRY and SUN.

7. תְּרָפִים, only plu., *těrâphîm*, is always simply transliterated in RV 'teraphim.' AV has 'teraphim' in Jg 17[5] 18[14. 17. 18. 20], Hos 3[4]; but 'images' in Gn 31[19] (m. 'teraphim') 31[34. 35], 2 K 23[24] (m. 'teraphim'), Ezk 21[21] (m. 'teraphim'), with the sing. 'image' in 1 S 19[13. 16]; 'idolatry' in 1 S 15[23]; and 'idols' with marg. 'teraphims' in Zec 10[2]. See TERAPHIM.

8. עָצָב] only in plu. עֲצַבִּים *'ăzabbîm*, is translated 'idols' almost everywhere by both AV and RV (1 S 31[9], 1 Ch 10[9], 2 Ch 24[18], Ps 106[36. 38] 115[4] 135[15], Is 10[11] 46[1], Hos 4[17] 8[4] 13[2] 14[8], Mic 1[7], Zec 13[2]); but both give 'images' in 2 S 5[21], and RV gives 'images' though AV has 'idols' in Jer 50[2]. See IDOLATRY.

9. גִּלּוּל] only in plu. גִּלּוּלִים or גִּלֻּלִים *gillûlîm*, a distinctive word, properly 'idol blocks,' or such term of disparagement, in Ezk thirty-nine times; elsewhere only nine times (Lv 26[30], Dt 29[17], 1 K 15[12] 21[26], 2 K 17[12] 21[11. 21] 23[24], Jer 50[2]). It is tr[d] 'idols' in AV and RV everywhere except Jer 50[2] in AV 'images.' See IDOLATRY.

10. אֱלִיל *'ělîl*, worthlessness, is often applied in derision to foreign gods. Its translation (when plu.) is usually 'idols' in both AV and RV, Lv 19[4] (RVm 'things of nought') 26[1], 1 Ch 16[26] (RVm 'things of nought'), Ps 96[5] (RVm 'things of nought') 97[7], Is 2[8. 18. 20 bis] 10[10. 11] 19[1. 3] 31[7], Ezk 30[13], Hab 2[18]. In Jer 14[14] both versions give 'a thing of nought'; in Job 13[4] *rôph'ê 'ělîl* is in both 'physicians of no value'; while in Zec 11[17] *hoi rô'î ha'ělîl* is translated in AV 'Woe to the idol shepherd' (where 'idol' is apparently used as an adj.), in RV 'Woe to the worthless shepherd.' See GOD, IDOLATRY.

11. פֶּסֶל *pesel* (from פָּסַל to carve) is translated 'graven image' by RV everywhere (Ex 20[4], Lv 26[1], Dt 4[16. 23. 25] 5[8] 27[15], Jg 17[3. 4] 18[14. 17. 18. 20. 30. 31], 2 K 21[7], 2 Ch 33[7], Ps 97[7], Is 40[19. 20] 42[17] 44[9. 10. 15. 17] 45[20] 48[5], Jer 10[14] 51[17], Nah 1[14], Hab 2[18]). AV has 'carved image' in Jg 18[18], 2 Ch 33[7]; elsewhere it agrees with RV.

12. פָּסִיל] from same root, only in plu. פְּסִילִים *pěsîlîm*, is also translated by RV 'graven images' in all its occurrences (Dt 7[5. 25] 12[3], 2 K 17[41], 2 Ch 33[19. 22] 34[3. 4. 7], Ps 78[58], Is 10[10] 21[9] 30[22] 42[8], Jer 8[19] 50[38] 51[47. 52], Hos 11[2], Mic 1[7] 5[13]), except Jg 3[19. 26] where both versions have 'quarries' in text, with 'graven images' in margin. AV gives 'carved images' in 2 Ch 33[22] 34[3. 4]; elsewhere as RV.

13. מַסֵּכָה *massêkâh*, lit. 'a pouring out,' is used of molten metal, and (with the word for 'calf' added) of a 'molten calf' in Ex 32[4. 8], Dt 9[16], Neh 9[18]; or 'molten gods' Ex 34[17], Lv 19[4] (with word for 'gods'); but generally it stands alone and is translated 'molten image' (Nu 33[52] [Heb. here adds *zelem*], Dt 9[12] 27[15], Jg 17[3. 4] 18[14. 17. 18], 1 K 14[9], 2 K 17[16], 2 Ch 28[2] 34[3. 4], Ps 106[19], Is 30[22] 42[17], Hos 13[2], Nah 1[14], Hab 2[18]). In Is 30[1] the words נְסֹךְ מַסֵּכָה are rendered in AV and RV 'that cover with a covering'; in RVm 'weave a web *or* pour out a drink-offering *or* make a league.'

14. נֶסֶךְ *nesek*, or נֵסֶךְ *nesek*, from the same root as the last, is the word for a 'drink-offering,' and is so translated by AV and RV in all its occurrences, except Is 41[29] 48[5], Jer 10[14] 51[17] where both versions have 'molten image,' and Nu 4[7] where קְשׂוֹת הַנָּסֶךְ is rendered in AV 'covers to cover withal,' in RV 'cups to pour out withal.'

In the Apocr. 'image' occurs in the following places: 2 Es 5[37] 8[44] (both *imago*), Wis 2[23] 7[26] 13[13. 16] 14[15] (all εἰκών), 14[17] (ἐμφανῆ εἰκόνα, AV 'an express image,' RV 'a visible image'), 15[4] (εἶδος, RV 'form'), 15[5] (εἰκών), 15[13] (γλυπτά, EV 'graven images'), 17[21] (εἰκών); 1 Mac 3[48] (εἴδωλον, RV 'idol'), 5[68] (γλυπτά, EV 'carved images'); 2 Mac 2[2] (ἀγάλματα, EV 'images').

In NT χαρακτήρ is translated 'express image' in He 1[3] (χαρακτὴρ τῆς ὑποστάσεως αὐτοῦ, 'the express image of his person,' RV 'the very image of his substance,' RVm 'the impress of his substance'; it is the only occurrence in NT of χαρακτήρ, which gives us our word 'character'). Elsewhere image is always εἰκών, and that Gr. word is always so translated in both versions.

Imagery occurs twice: Ezk 8[12] 'Son of man, hast thou seen what the ancients of the house of Israel do in the dark, every man in the chambers of his imagery?' (בְּחַדְרֵי מַשְׂכִּיתוֹ, RV 'in his chambers of imagery'); and Sir 38[27] 'give themselves to counterfeit imagery' (εἰς ὁμοιῶσαι ζωγραφίαν, RV 'to preserve likeness in his portraiture'). In the Prol. to Deut. Tindale uses the word in the sense of images or idols, 'And to beware ether of makynge imagerye or of bowinge them selves unto images.' Sir T. Elyot is very near the use in Sir when he says (*The Governour*, ii. 403), 'It is written that the great kynge Alexander on a tyme beinge (as it hapned) unoccupyed, came to the shoppe of Apelles, the excellent paynter, and standyng by hym whyles he paynted, the kynge raisoned with hym of lines, adumbrations, proportions, or other like thinges pertainyng to imagery, whiche the paynter a litle whyles sufferynge, at the last said to the kynge with the countenance all smylyng,

Seest thou, noble prince, howe the boye that gryndeth my colours dothe laughe the to scorne?' Bp. Atterbury uses the word in the same sense as Ezk, 'It might be a mere dream which he saw; the imagery of a melancholick fancy.'

J. HASTINGS.

IMAGE.—About a score of Heb. words are rendered in AV 'idol' or 'image.' See preceding art. and IDOLATRY. The terms reserved for the expression which in Christian doctrine (to which the present art. is confined) represents 'image' or 'likeness,' are צֶלֶם and דְּמוּת, to which correspond εἰκών and ὁμοίωσις in the NT. For the latter Heb. word the LXX once at least uses ἰδέα (Gn 5³). צֶלֶם sometimes (Dn 3¹⁹) signifies an aspect or expression of countenance. In biblical Greek κατ' εἰκόνα is sometimes used adverbially = 'after the manner of,' as e.g. Hos 13² κατ' εἰκόνα εἰδώλων, 'after the fashion of idols.' Wis 13¹³ εἰκόνι ἀνθρώπου, 'in the manner of a man.'

There are two main biblical doctrines which find expression under these terms, viz. that of (1) *man as made in the image of God*, and (2) that of *Christ the Son, as the image of the Father*, or *of the invisible God.*

I. The passages in which this view of man is expressly stated are: Gn 1²⁶· ²⁷ 5¹· ³ 9⁶, 1 Co 11⁷, Col 3¹⁰, Ja 3⁹. To these should be added Ps 8, which, though not containing the phrase 'image of God,' is a poetical *replica* of the creation-narrative of Gn 1 as far as it refers to man. St. Paul's address at Athens is another passage where the idea of 'likeness' between man and his Maker is fully implied, though the word is not used. A quite factitious importance has been attached to the difference between צֶלֶם and דְּמוּת in the primal passage. There is really no difference. At the utmost, it is that between an original or pattern and that which is framed according to the pattern. The double expression in Gn 1²⁶ and 5³ is simply intended to strengthen the idea. The divine image which man bears is one corresponding to the Original.

This grand assertion is the distinctive feature of the Bible doctrine concerning man. It distinguishes the revealed teaching about him from all ethnic or naturalistic views, and is the real foundation of all our ideas about the dignity of man. Although thus definite and significant, however, the phrase is not explicit. Large place is left for discussion as to whether this definition refers to something in man's own nature or mainly to his relations: and among these whether to his aspect towards the other creatures or his relation to God. This is why the doctrine of the Divine Image in man has been a topic so fruitful of differences in theology. For long the theological bent was to make the *imago Dei* distinctive of man unfallen. In the loss of the image by sin lay man's need of redemption. 'What we lost in Adam,' says Irenæus, 'to wit, the divine image and similitude, that we receive again in Christ Jesus.' But later on, it was seen that this was too sweeping. Then set in the tendency to expound the idea in a double sense. The cruder form of this was the Romish, as expressed by Bellarmin—that by the Fall man lost the 'likeness' of God, though he retained the 'image.' But Protestants held a not dissimilar view, viz. that the image had two meanings. In one sense it is essential to man's nature, and in this sense consists of his intellectual powers, his liberty of will, and his superiority among the creatures,—features which can never be wholly lost, but remain with man though fallen. In the other sense it includes those ornaments or complements of the idea—immortality, grace, holiness, righteousness—which were defaced or blotted out by man's transgres-

sion. One point of unity and consistency with Scripture holds fast amid these variations of view. For it is certain that in the passages cited above the divine image is recognized as existing in man fallen as well as unfallen. Among recent evangelical divines of a philosophical cast the tendency has been to return to the position of the early Eastern Church, and place the image mainly in that which distinguishes man among created beings, rather than in that which marks off the unfallen from the fallen condition. The Greek Christian Fathers did define it as something rather metaphysical than ethical. But to place the image mainly in the possession of 'Spirit' and 'Free Will' is to overlook the moral and religious elements essential to man's nature. Man in his ideal is a 'spirit' and 'will' under the dominion of conscience, developed freely no doubt, but in subjection and obedience to God. That this biblical notion of the divine image is a profoundly simple and consistent one, is made clear by the NT passages which speak of its renewal in grace (Col 3¹⁰, cf. Eph 4²⁴), where the moral elements are prominent and supreme. But they cannot be read as defining what the divine image was in man at the first, for they treat expressly of the 'new man.' The unity and simplicity of the idea are conserved, if we note that this description of the 'new man' presupposes corresponding outlines in the first man which were broken off by sin, and are for the first time fully realized in man redeemed and renewed.

Another suggestive point in the discussion comes out of the question, long debated, whether the divine image in man was a gift of grace added to his nature, i.e. was in a sense something 'supernatural,' or was wholly natural and concreated from the first, as Protestants have always maintained. The real point in dispute is much confused and hidden. The mediæval view is really one of dualism or divergence in man's nature. It splits his life into two. It accentuates the distinction between nature and grace, between things secular and sacred; whereas the true view is that of an original unity in the creature made after God's image, and a harmonious development of the human and divine elements in him. For there is a truth in the mediæval idea of a 'supernatural gift of righteousness' to man, though it was crudely expressed. Human nature only attains its ideal when cultivated by divine grace. The nature of man is incomplete without its Godward development, and this can take place successfully only through grace. For it is essential to man's highest to be not left to himself. Mere human nature or 'unassisted reason,' as the phrase goes, is a contradiction of the Bible idea of man. That idea is that human nature rightly and fully developed manifests the divine, and is a reflection of what it has received of God.

II. That Christ is *'the Image of the Father'* belongs to the doctrine of the Saviour's pre-existent Godhead as taught in the NT. It is one of the ways in which that truth is set forth. The precisely relevant passages are 2 Co 4⁴, Col 1¹⁵⁻¹⁷, He 1²· ³. The idea is not restricted to the term εἰκών which occurs in the first two citations, but is also expressed by two kindred phrases in He 1³ ἀπαύγασμα τῆς δόξης, 'the effulgence of his glory,' and χαρακτὴρ τῆς ὑποστάσεως αὐτοῦ, 'the very image of his substance.' It will be noted from the context of all these passages that the terms are used not so much of the incarnate Redeemer as of the eternal Son. No doubt, according to the teaching of Jesus and that of all His apostles, the 'Christ come in the flesh' is for us the mirror and reflection of God. 'He that hath seen me,' says Jesus, 'hath seen the Father' (Jn 14⁹). This is the prominent and prevailing sense of the Christian doctrine that Christ is the Revelation or Image of God. This is the central teaching of the Incarnation. But in the few places where the word 'image' or its equivalents is used in this connexion by the writers of the NT Epistles, it is employed in support of a special doctrine of Christ's essential divine personality. In this respect it stands on the same plane as the title ὁ υἱός, '*the* Son,' used so widely throughout the NT writings, and ὁ λόγος in the Johannine passages.

Notice (1) that in the Hebrews passage, where Christ as υἱός is the subject of the assertion, the other terms supplement and complete the idea of His divine Sonship. To say that He who is the Son is the 'effulgence of God's glory' and 'the very image or impress of his substance,' is not only to reassert the Sonship, but to add to it the idea of 'likeness.' It affirms community of nature with the Father in the same way as when He is called '*the* Son of God.' It thus strengthens the expression of Christ's place in the Godhead by affirming at once His likeness to God and yet His personal distinctness, for how can any one be spoken of as 'the image' of himself?

Further, note (2) how this term 'image' as used of the pre-existent Christ, echoes, like ὁ λόγος, a form of older or pre-Christian speech. Εἰκών and ἀπαύγασμα are both applied to the 'Wisdom' of Old Testament literature, e.g. in Wis 7²⁶ 'For she is the "brightness" of the everlasting light, the unspotted mirror of the power of God, and the "image" of his goodness.' Χαρακτήρ is applied by Philo to the Logos; so also εἰκών, as where he says the Logos is εἰκὼν δι' οὗ ὁ κόσμος ἐδημιουργεῖτο. It is probable, therefore, that the writer of the Fourth Gospel, the writer 'to the Hebrews,' and St. Paul were all drawing on ancient terms, common to the Jewish Alexandrian schools, which had been applied in pre-Christian thought to a personified divine attribute. The NT writers are in these passages rescuing these terms to describe their Master's Person and glory. Judaizing Gnosticism had employed some of these expressions to uphold the doctrine of a graduated hierarchy of divine manifestation, more especially that of a secondary or representative divine being alongside of the supreme and invisible God,—a notion which, when applied to the Person of Christ, became afterwards the Arian heresy. The apostolic writers apply these terms ὁ λόγος, ἡ εἰκών, and the like, to their Lord in a way fitted to bring out what is true in them and to repudiate what is false;—conspicuously, so as to repel the notion of inferiority in the second member of the divine Trinity.

Note (3) how this is clenched by the fact that in the context of the three passages Jn 1¹⁻³, Col 1¹⁵⁻¹⁷, and He 1². ³ the special function of creating and upholding the universe is ascribed to Christ under His titles of Word, Image, and Son respectively. The kind of Creatorship so predicated of Him is not that of a mere instrument or artificer in the formation of the world, but that of One 'by whom, in whom, and for whom' all things are made, and through whom they subsist. This implies the assertion of His true and absolute Godhead. It was evidently meant to be so. For there is no more direct and successful method of affirming that Christ is God than to ascribe to Him the making and governing of all things in the supreme form which the ascription takes in these passages.

Something remains to be said of a possible connexion between these two facts noted by biblical theology, viz. that 'man is made in the divine image,' and that 'Christ is,' in the supreme sense, 'the Image of God.' The older dogmatic was wont to distinguish the two, by saying that the divine image in man was *accidentalis* compared with that Godlikeness which belonged to the eternal Son as *Imago substantialis*. But what Scripture teaches of their connexion can be briefly stated. It has two distinct lines—one referring to the original creation of man, the other to his redemption.

Man is represented in Scripture as the crown or goal of that earthly creation of which the Eternal Word is the Author. He who is the 'Image of the Invisible God' is also declared to be the 'Firstborn or First-begotten of all creation' (Col 1¹⁵), i.e. the absolute heir and sovereign Lord of all things. There is thus a propriety in holding man to be a copy of the Logos. But there is no express Scripture for the assertion that man was created in the likeness of the eternal Son. On the contrary, it is always the image or likeness of God that is spoken of in this connexion. No doubt, it is implied that the Logos or Image of God is He 'in whom and for whom' man was created. But it would be a misreading of these passages to take them as affirming that man was created after the likeness of the Son, and not of the Father or of the Holy Spirit. Everywhere Scripture represents man as created after the image of the Elohim, or of the Godhead. Man is said to be 'the image and glory of God,' not of Christ alone.

On the other hand, when the new creation of man is referred to, the NT is explicit in asserting that Christ is the prototype of the redeemed or renewed humanity. The 'divine image' is restored in those who are predestinate to be 'conformed to the image of his Son.' We are 'renewed in the spirit of our mind' only as we put on 'the new man—renewed in knowledge after the image of him that created him' (Col 3¹⁰), —a new creation in which 'Christ is all in all' (Col 3¹¹). Likeness to His Image is only to be completed when the redeemed shall see their Redeemer as He is (1 Jn 3²). The likeness shall then extend even to the outward form. 'He shall fashion anew the body of our humiliation, that it may be conformed to the body of his glory' (Ph 3²¹ RV); 'As we have borne the image of the earthy, we shall also bear the image of the heavenly' (1 Co 15⁴⁹).

All this is explicit and clear. There has long been a desire and tendency among theological thinkers to complete the connexion of the two statements. It looks extremely probable to infer that man must have been created from the first in the image of Him who was afterwards to be incarnate for man's redemption, and who in redeeming men conforms them to His own likeness. It is a tempting and perhaps innocent speculation, but not an ascertainment of biblical theology.

LITERATURE.—Seb. Schmidt, *De Imagine Dei in Homine ante Lapsum*, 1659; Bp. George Bull, *State of Man before the Fall* (Works, vol. ii., Oxford edition, 1846); Keerl, *Der Mensch das Ebenbild Gottes*, 1863; Grinfield, *The Image and Likeness of God in Man* (Lond. 1837); Laidlaw, *The Bible Doctrine of Man*, 2nd ed. 1895; Cremer, art. 'Ebenbild Gottes' in *PRE*³; Driver, *Sermons on Old Test.* 173 f.   J. LAIDLAW.

IMAGINE, IMAGINATION.—The verb to 'imagine' has always in AV the obsolete meaning of purpose, scheme, contrive. Thus Gn 11⁶ 'Nothing will be restrained from them which they have imagined to do' (יָזְמוּ, RV 'they purpose'); Zec 7¹⁰ 'Let none of you imagine evil against his brother in your heart' (אַל־תַּחְשֹׁבוּ, Amer. RV 'devise'). Cf. Elyot, *The Governour*, ii. 74, 'It was reported to the noble emperour Octavius Augustus that Lucius Cinna, which was susters sonne to the great Pompei, had imagined his dethe'; and Tindale, Notes to Deut., 'Zamzumims, a kinde of geauntes and signifieth myschevous or that be all waye imagininge.' RV generally retains 'imagine,' but Amer. RV prefers 'think' in Job 6[26], 'meditate' in Ps 2[1] 38[12], and 'devise' in Ps 10[2] 21[11] 140[2], Pr 12[20], Hos 7[15], Nah 1[9. 11], Zec 7[10] 8[17].

Imagination has always the sense of evil purpose, contrivance. This is so even in Ro 1[21] 'became vain in their imaginations,' where the Gr. is διαλο-γισμός, more consistently tr[d] 'reasoning' in RV; and in 2 Co 10[5] 'casting down imaginations,' where the Gr. is λογισμός, and AVm RVm give 'reasonings'; in the only other occurrence in NT of this Gr. word (Ro 2[15]) AV and RV have 'thoughts,' RVm 'reasonings.' But 'reasoning' is plainly too colourless, the evil intent in the Gr. words here being lost. For 'imagination' in the sense of mischievous intention, cf. Is 55[7] Cov. 'Let the ungodly man forsake his wayes, and the unrightuous his ymaginacions, and turne agayne unto the LORDE.' Tindale uses the word in the sense of a visible representation of a thought, Nu 33[52] 'Se that ye dryve out all the inhabiters of the londe before you, and destroy their Ymaginacions and all their Ymages of Metall.' The Heb. subst. *shĕrîrûth* expresses *firmness* in a bad cause, and is mistranslated by 'imagination' in AV: RV gives 'stubbornness' in all its occurrences (Dt 29[19], Ps 81[12], Jer 3[17] 7[24] 9[14] 11[8] 13[10] 16[12] 18[12] 23[17]).

J. HASTINGS.

IMALCUE, AV Simalcue (Σινμαλκονή A, 'Ιμαλκονέ אV, Εἰμαλκουαί; *Simalchue, Emalchuel,* also *Malchus*), 1 Mac 11[39].—An Arab prince to whom Alexander Balas entrusted his youthful son Antiochus. After the death of Alexander, in B.C. 145, Imalcue reluctantly gave up the boy to Tryphon, who placed him on the throne of Syria as Antiochus VI. in opposition to Demetrius II. Nikator (1 Mac 11[39-54]; Jos. *Ant.* XIII. v. 1; Diodorus in Müller's *Frag. Hist. Græc.* ii. p. xvii n. 21). Elsewhere Diodorus (*op. cit.* n. 20) names Diocles, prince of Abæ in Arabia, as the guardian of the young (νήπιος) Antiochus. Josephus and the Syriac give the name as Malchus, Diodorus as Jamblichus, both representing the Heb. מלכו, a name which appears on Palmyrene inscriptions. Cf. *Speaker's Comm.* and Zöckler, *ad loc.*; also Schürer, *HJP* I. i. 247.

H. A. WHITE.

IMLA (יִמְלָ 2 Ch 18[7. 8]=IMLAH [יִמְלָה], 1 K 22[8. 9]; perhaps 'he is full,' and so 'fulness,' the first form of the name being etymologically the more correct).—The father of Micaiah, a prophet of J" in the days of Ahab.

C. F. BURNEY.

IMMANUEL (עִמָּנוּאֵל, 'Εμμανουήλ, 'God is with us,' or, as others, 'God with us').—The name of a child whose birth was predicted by Isaiah, and who was to be a sign from God to Ahaz during the Syro-Ephraimitic war (Is 7). The name does not occur again in Scripture; and much difference of opinion has prevailed on the question wherein the point of the sign lay, whether in the person of Immanuel himself, or in the meaning of his name, or in the time of his birth, or in the conditions of his life, or in several of these things together. Other things in the prophecy are also obscure. The mother of Immanuel is described as *the 'almah* (LXX ἡ παρθένος), a term which means merely 'young woman' (cf. the *masc.* 1 S 17[56] 20[22]), though in usage it appears said only of unmarried persons. Even if the more technical word for 'virgin' (בְּתוּלָה) had been employed, the term might have described the young woman merely at the moment when the prophet spoke; the idea of a virgin conception and birth could have been expressed without ambiguity only by a circumlocution. The force of the art. (הָעַלְמָה) may also be variously understood. Some take the art. as generic, referring to the class of persons called 'almah (Ec 7[26]), in which case the meaning would be that any or many of this class

would exemplify the prediction, calling their children Immanuel. But perhaps the '*almah* becomes definite to the prophet's mind just from the circumstances connected with her and the part she performs (2 S 17[17]). There is nothing in the passage to suggest that the '*almah* is of mean birth or estate; but the generality of the term is unfavourable to the idea that the wife of the prophet —called 'the prophetess' 8[3]—or the wife of king Ahaz meant. Neither is there anything in the passage to suggest that the '*almah* is a personification of the house of David or the people of Judah. The prophecy is to be explained partly from the historical circumstances, partly from the circle of thoughts which had filled the prophet's mind from the beginning (chs. 1-6), and in the light of which he interpreted the circumstances, and partly from ideas regarding the house of David that had long formed part of the national faith. It cannot be altogether without significance that it is 'the house of David' that is addressed and spoken of throughout the chapter.

The historical circumstances were these: In the days of Ahaz the kings of Syria and Ephraim formed an alliance and made war on Judah. The object of the allies was possibly to compel Judah to enter into a confederacy against Assyria, and not improbably Egypt had its hand in the game (7[18]). Ahaz being reluctant, the allies resolved to dethrone the house of David and set a tool of their own upon the throne of Judah. Amidst the terror inspired by the alliance (7[2]), the prophet was bidden go to meet the king and say to him in regard to the purpose of the allies, 'It shall not stand.' He added the solemn warning that faith in J" was the condition of deliverance. Shortly after, the prophet offered the corroboration of any sign which the king might ask. This offer Ahaz rejected, putting it away under the pretext that he would not put God to the proof. Roused to passion by the king's unbelief or obstinacy, the prophet exclaimed, 'Is it too small a thing for you to weary men, that ye weary my God also? Therefore the Lord himself shall give you a sign.'

The subject may be approached by asking: Of what is Immanuel the sign or corroboration?

1. Some answer, of the promise, 'It shall not stand'—of the failure of the northern coalition, and of the deliverance of Judah from Ephraim and Syria. In this case the sign lies partly in the meaning of the name Immanuel, 'God is with us,' and partly in the time of his birth. His mother and he are no persons in particular—they are any young woman and her son. By the time young women conceive and bear sons they will be calling their children 'God is with us,' in token of Judah's deliverance from Syria and Ephraim: 'Before the child shall know to reject evil and choose good, the land before whose two kings thou fearest shall be depopulated,' v.[16] (Duhm). This interpretation is simple, but difficult to accept. (1) It requires the excision of vv.[15. 17]. For, whoever Immanuel and his mother be, they are Judæans, and when it is said that the child shall eat thick milk and honey (v.[15]), it is implied that Judah shall be reduced by war to a pasture land no more cultivated (v.[21ff.])—a thing in direct contradiction to the supposed meaning of the sign. (2) The sign becomes virtually a duplicate of that of Mahershalal (8[1-4]), for though Assyria is not named as the destroyer of Syria and Ephraim in 7[16], it is admittedly in the prophet's mind. A duplication of the same sign is highly improbable. (3) Is it probable or possible that Isaiah should conceive Judæan mothers expressing their thankfulness for deliverance from Ephraim and Syria by using the name Immanuel? He has himself

the utmost contempt for the northern alliance
(7⁴). The danger does not seem to him to lie
there (8¹²). Further, that which will make the
northern alliance abortive is the Assyrian invasion,
but everywhere in the passage he assumes that
the Assyrian will devastate Judah also (7¹⁸. ²⁰ 8⁷. ⁸).
The Assyrian invasion will extend over Israel and
Judah in common. Immanuel cannot be a sign
of deliverance from Ephraim and Syria, for the
deliverance will be effected only through a calamity infinitely greater. (4) Though the sign first
offered to Ahaz was to be a token of deliverance
from the allies (7¹¹. ¹²), the change of tone on the
prophet's part suggests that the sign now given
will be of a different sort. It is a mistake to
suppose that the sign must be something which
Ahaz could see, in corroboration of something else.
The sign may be just the coming fact, or some aspect
of it, as it was said to Moses, 'And this is the
sign to thee that I have sent thee : when thou hast
brought forth the people out of Egypt, ye shall
serve God upon this mountain' (Ex 3¹² ; cf. Is 37³⁰).
2. Some regard the sign as lying partly in the
meaning of the name Immanuel, and partly in
the circumstances of his birth and life ; that is,
the sign is twofold, first, of deliverance from the
northern coalition (Immanuel), and second, of the
Assyrian devastation of Judah ('milk and honey
shall he eat,' vv.¹⁵. ¹⁷). But, as before, against this
is the utter uselessness of giving Ahaz a sign of
deliverance from the allies when that deliverance
is effected only by the complete desolation of his
own country at the same time.
3. It is therefore probable that the sign is of
larger significance. Several things must be taken
into account. First, that which others would call
a national crisis, the prophets, and particularly
Isaiah, consider a religious crisis. His statement
to Ahaz, 'if ye do not believe ye shall not be
established' (v.⁹), is not the enunciation of a
commonplace. It is the central thought of his
prophetic life (69ff. and often). And this faith is
wanting both in prince and people (7¹². ¹³ 8⁵ff.).
Secondly, throughout this interview the prophet's
mind is in a state of extreme exaltation, as his
offer to Ahaz of a sign anywhere in all the universe
of things shows. And this exaltation is intensified
by the king's rejection of the sign offered him—
'Will ye weary my God also' ? (7¹³). The sign
now given will not be a favourable one forced
upon Ahaz, but one of a wider kind. The prophet
casts his eye forward over the whole destiny of
the kingdom of J″. He sees his conceptions of
this destiny about to take shape in history. The
conditions and the instruments of fulfilling what
he had from the beginning foreseen to be inevitable are now present. A great judgment shall
sweep over the land, 'the Lord will bring on thee
days that have not been since Ephraim departed
from Judah' (v.¹⁷) ; 'milk and honey shall every
one eat that is left in the land' (v.²²). The
country shall be reduced to a pasture land, whose
scanty inhabitants shall live on milk and wild
honey. But this is not the end ; a remnant shall
turn : amidst the desolation and behind it there
will be those who say, 'God is with us.'* The
sign has no reference to Syria and Ephraim ; it
refers to the destiny of the people, though, of

course, to the prophet's mind or his vision this
destiny had two steps—the Assyrian devastation,
and the repentance and salvation that would follow
it. This view is supported by the fact that where
Immanuel is mentioned again it is in connexion
with the Assyrian invasion (8⁸. ¹⁰). But does not
this interpretation require the omission of v.¹⁶
'Before the child know to reject evil and choose
good, the land shall be depopulated, before whose
two kings thou art in terror' ? (so Budde). Even
if this should be the case, we must choose that
side on which there appears to lie the greater
probability. The chapter and the succeeding ones
have not escaped interpolation. V.¹⁶ might be
due to the same hand that inserted the words
'within sixty-five years Ephraim shall be broken
that it be not a people' (v.⁸, cf. 8⁷). The verse
in its present form cannot be read along with v.¹⁷.
Perhaps, however, it might be sufficient to omit
the last words of the verse, 'before whose two
kings thou art in terror.' With this omission
'the land' would be Judah as in 6¹¹, and the
whole passage v.¹⁴ff. have reference to the desolation of Judah. It is certainly very improbable
that Isaiah should have spoken of Syria and Israel
as a single 'land,' though a reader might have so
understood the word and helped out the sense by
the gloss 'before whose two kings,' etc.*
This view still leaves room for different interpretations of Immanuel. The 'almah and her son
might be considered merely examples of something
general, in which case Immanuel would represent
the new generation rising up after the desolation
(v.¹⁵), the 'holy seed' of 6¹³ (cf. the change of mind
described in 8²¹ff.). The force of the sign to Ahaz
would lie in the threat of invasion and the destruction of the order of things now existing of
which he and his house was a great part, though
the prophet's own interest would be chiefly in that
which was to follow this, the new faith in J″, expressed in the words 'God is with us.' He himself
and his children, not by their names, but by their
faith amidst the darkness already as good as fallen
on the nation, are a 'sign' of this future faith of
the people (8¹⁶⁻¹⁸). There are some things, however, which rather suggest a more precise meaning
for Immanuel. (1) The whole passage relates to
the 'house of David.' It was the design of the
allies to dethrone this house, a purpose which could
not but awaken wider thoughts in the prophet's
mind. As represented in Ahaz this house had
pronounced judgment on itself (7⁹. ¹³), and with
his assured conviction of the imminent destruction
of the nation the prophet cannot have helped forecasting also the fate of the royal family. If, as is
likely, the prophecies, chs. 9. 11, belong to this
period, they show that he contemplated its downfall (11¹). (2) The words 'thy land, O Immanuel'
(8⁸) suggest that Immanuel, in the prophet's mind,
is an individual person, to whom the land in some
way belongs. (3) The general line of the prophet's
thoughts at this time may be fairly appealed to.
In 9¹⁻⁷ the 'child born' is certainly a member of
the house of David, and he is there introduced in
such a matter of course way as to suggest that he
had been already referred to and was known.
Such a reference could only be found in ch. 7. (4)
The names given to the child in ch. 9 may all be
summed up in the name Immanuel, of which they
are an analysis. These considerations may suggest
that Immanuel is identical with the child of ch. 9
and the 'shoot' of ch. 11. If so, the sign does not
lie in the meaning of the word Immanuel, but in
the person who was the embodiment of the mean-

---

* Whether it can also be said through the, desolation, i.e.
by its discipline, will depend on whether יַדְעוֹ (v.¹⁵) is to be
rendered 'that he may know' (AV) or 'when he knows' (RV),
and on whether 'to reject evil and choose good' be a moral
act. To dispose of the sense 'that he may know' by saying
that eating milk and honey will hardly 'promote the formation
of ethical character,' is to use a pleasantry which misses the
point. Eating milk and honey is a token and synonym of desolation and hardship, and it is the teaching of all the prophets
from Hosea downward that it is just through the discipline
of such things that the people shall be brought to a right
ethical mind.

* This reading of v.¹⁶ was suggested in Expos. Times, 1894.
The same idea has occurred to others, e.g. Buhl, Jesaja oversat
og fortolket, Kjöb. 1894 ; Kittel, 'Jesaja' (Exeg. Handb.⁶), Leip.
1898).

ing, and who was 'called' Immanuel because he was Immanuel.

If Immanuel be an individual person of this significance, the question of the 'almah perhaps rises in importance. The art. 'the' 'almah would be easiest explained if in some previous prophecy she had been already mentioned. But the assumption of such prophecies may not be held admissible. The passage Mic 5³ 'until the time that she (or, one) that travaileth hath brought forth' alludes to the prophecy of Isaiah. The authenticity of the passage has been doubted, though, of course, not everything which has been doubted is doubtful. If the passage belonged to Mic, it would show how the prophecy of Is was read perhaps 20 or 30 years after it was spoken. It was held to refer to the Messiah, and to be still awaiting fulfilment; and, what is of interest in regard to the way prophecy was interpreted in those days, Isaiah's apparent expectation of the nearness of the Messiah's birth (if 7¹⁶ be original) was not held of any importance so far as the general meaning of the prophecy was concerned. All these things hold good if the passage be younger than Mic, though we should not in that case have a contemporary, but a later interpretation of the prophecy of Isaiah.

It is uncertain whether the LXX interpreters found anything mysterious in the passage, for Gr. παρθένος, like Lat. virgo, was used generally for 'girl' or 'young woman' (Gn 24¹⁴. ⁴³). Possibly to evade the technical sense put on the word by the Christians, the three newer Gr. translators (Aq., Theod., and Symm.) adopt the term νεᾶνις, a change of which Irenæus takes notice and disapproves. There is some evidence that the idea that the Messiah would be born of a virgin was to some extent prevalent both in Palestine and Alexandria. The idea may have been suggested by the somewhat mysterious language of Is, or by the LXX version, or by both. In general, it was more the actual life of Christ that suggested to NT writers the application to Him of OT passages, than a prevalent method of interpreting the passages. They saw in His life the full religious meaning of the passages, and the question of their original sense or application did not occur to them. As Bleek long ago argued (Comm. on Ep. to Heb.), historical interpreters may have to distinguish between the things which NT writers affirm and corroborate by OT passages, and the proofs or corroborations which they adduce. The things they assert we take on their authority, but the kind of confirmations by which they support them, however valid they may have seemed to those to whom they were addressed, and however well they served as evidence then, may not seem of such importance now. We believe in the resurrection of Christ because it is testified to by eye-witnesses; St. Peter's interpretation of Ps 16 is at best only a corroboration of it. And in like manner we believe in the virgin birth because it is affirmed by one 'who had traced the course of all things accurately from the first' (Lk 1³); the interpretation put on Is 7 (Mt 1²²ᶠ·) occupies but the secondary place of a confirmation of it.

LITERATURE.—Besides the Comm. on Is (see particularly the *Additional Note* of Skinner, i. 60 ff.), the following essays among others may be named:—De Lagarde, *Semitica*, 1878; Studer, 'Zur Textkritik des Jes.,' *Jhrb. f. Prot. Theol.*, 1879; Bredenkamp, *Vaticinium quod de Imm. edidit Jes.*, 1880; Budde, 'Ueber das siebente Cap. d. Buches Jes.' (in *Études dédiées à Mr. le Dr. Leemans*), 1885; Giesebrecht, *Die Immanuelweissagung*, *SK*, 1888; F. C. Porter, 'A suggestion regarding Isaiah's Immanuel' in *Jl. of Bib. Lit.*, 1895.   A. B. DAVIDSON.

IMMER (אִמֵּר).—**1.** Eponym of a priestly family, 1 Ch 9¹² 24¹⁴, Ezr 2³⁷ 10²⁰, Neh 3²⁹ 7⁴⁰ 11¹³. **2.** A priest contemp. with Jeremiah, Jer 20¹. **3.** The name of a place (?), Ezr 2⁵⁹=Neh 7⁶¹. The text is uncertain (cf. 1 Es 5³⁶, and see ADDAN).

IMMORTALITY.—See ESCHATOLOGY.

IMNA (יִמְנָע).—An Asherite chief, 1 Ch 7³⁵. See GENEALOGY.

IMNAH (יִמְנָה).—**1.** The eldest son of Asher, Nu 26⁴⁴ (AV Jimna), 1 Ch 7³⁰. **2.** A Levite in the time of Hezekiah, 2 Ch 31¹⁴. See GENEALOGY.

IMNITES (הַיִּמְנָה).—Patronymic from Imnah (No. 1), Nu 26⁴⁴ (AV Jimnites). See GENEALOGY.

IMPLEAD.—Ac 19³⁸ 'The law is open, and there are deputies: let them implead one another,' i.e. 'accuse' as RV; Gr. ἐγκαλεῖν, to summon one to answer a charge, to bring a charge against; cf. Cotgrave, *Fr. Dict.* s.v. *Emplaider*, 'to sue, to bring an action against'; and Hakluyt, *Voyages*, i. 117, 'They shall not be bound to come before the justices aforesaid, except any of the same barons doe implead any man, or if any man be impleaded.'   J. HASTINGS.

IMPORTABLE, in the sense of 'unendurable,' is used in Pr. Man, 'And thine angry threatening toward sinners is importable.' The Rhem. NT uses the word in Mt 23⁴ 'For they binde heavy burdens and importable, and put them upon men's shoulders.' Other examples are: Elyot, *The Governour*, i. 14, 'And all thoughe Hietro, Moses' father in lawe, counsailed hym to departe his importable labours, in continual jugementes, unto the wise men that was in his company, he nat withstandynge styll retayned the soveraintie by goddis commandement'; Becon, *Works*, i. 53, 'He alone shall tread down the wine-press, and take upon his back the great and importable burden of your sins all.'   J. HASTINGS.

IMPORTUNITY occurs only in the Parable of the Loaves, Lk 11⁸ 'because of his importunity he will rise and give him as many as he needeth.' The word means radically 'difficulty of access' (from *portus*, a harbour); but the Lat. adj. means 'unsuitable,' 'troublesome,' 'rude'; and the subst. *importunitas*, 'unfitness,' 'insolence,' as Cic. *De Sen.* iii. 7, 'importunitas et inhumanitas omni ætate molesta est.' In the course of its history as an Eng. word 'importunity' has lost some of its force. Even when introduced by Tindale in 1526, it was scarcely strong enough to translate the Gr. ἀναίδεια [T, WH ἀναιδία] of Lk 11⁸, since that word is literally 'shamelessness.' Christ spoke by contrast, not comparison; if shameless persistence can win a boon from one who is not a friend, surely we may offer prayer that is earnest enough to obtain our Father's blessings.   J. HASTINGS.

IMPOTENT.—Impotent is 'without strength,' 'weak,' as the Geneva trⁿ of Gal 4⁹ 'how is it, that ye are tourned backwarde unto impotent and beggerly ceremonies?' (ἀσθενής, Wyc. 'feble,' Tind. and others 'weak'). The word is applied in AV to persons who are infirm of body: Bar 6²⁸, Ac 14⁸ (ἀδύνατος); Jn 5³· ⁷ (ἀσθενεῖν, RV 'sick'); Ac 4⁹ (ἀσθενής). So Fuller, *Holy Warre*, i. 18, p. 28, 'In which compasse (i.e. in Palestine) in David's time were maintained thirteen hundred thousand men, besides women, children, and impotent persons'; and *Holy State*, ii. 19, p. 124, 'When Religion is at the stake, there must be no lookers on (except impotent people, who also help by their prayers), and every one is bound to lay his shoulders to the work.' Adams contrasts it with 'potent' in his *Exposition of II Peter* (on 1³ p. 26), 'But is there nothing that God cannot do? Yes, he cannot lie, he cannot die, he cannot deny himself. He is for potent, not for impotent works.'   J. HASTINGS.

IMRAH (יִמְרָה).—An Asherite chief, 1 Ch 7³⁶. See GENEALOGY.

IMRI (אִמְרִי).—**1.** A Judahite, 1 Ch 9⁴. **2.** Father of Zaccur, who helped to build the wall, Neh 3². See GENEALOGY.

IN.—**1.** 'In' is sometimes used in AV where we should now use *at*, as Mt 11²⁴ 'But I say unto you, That it shall be more tolerable for the land of Sodom in the day of judgment, than for thee'; but in 11²² 'But I say unto you, It shall be more tolerable for Tyre and Sidon at the day of judgment, than for you.' The Gr. is ἐν ἡμέρᾳ κρίσεως in both places, and RV has 'in the day of judgement' in both. This apparent looseness is due to two causes: (1) the wide range of meaning of the Heb. prep. בְּ, much of which was taken up in NT by ἐν; and (2) the greater freedom about 1611 and earlier in the use of the smaller Eng. prepositions. Shaks. has 'at the day of judgment' in *Merry Wives*, III. iii. 227, the only place in which that phrase occurs; but he says in *Othello*, I. ii. 93—

> 'How! the Duke in council
> In this time of the night;'

and *Merch. of Venice*, II. iv. 1—

> 'Nay, we will slink away in supper time.

So also To 2¹ 'there was a good dinner prepared me, in the which I sat down to eat' (καὶ ἀνέπεσα τοῦ φαγεῖν, RV 'and I sat down to eat').
 2. The Heb. בְּ being used for the agent and the instrument, and being often followed in this respect by the Gr. ἐν, it is not surprising to find the instrumental ἐν represented in Eng. by 'in' instead of 'by' or 'through.' So Gal 3¹⁹ 'it was ordained by angels in the hand of a mediator' (δι' ἀγγέλων ἐν χειρὶ μεσίτου, RV 'through angels by the hand of a mediator'). It is difficult to decide in many places whether the ἐν is instrumental or (spiritually) local. RV often prefers 'in' to AV 'by.' Thus He 1¹˙² 'God having of old time spoken unto the fathers in (AV 'by') the prophets by divers portions and in divers manners, hath at the end of these days spoken unto us in (AV 'by') his Son.' See the Heb. Grammars and Lexicons on בְּ, the Gr. NT Grammars and Lexicons on ἐν, and the commentaries on the various passages, as Sanday-Headlam on Ro 1¹⁹, Lightfoot on Gal 1¹⁶ and Col 1⁴˙¹⁶, Abbott on Eph 4¹⁷; also Westcott in *Expos. Times*, iii. 396; and cf. 1 P 3¹⁸ Wyc. 'made dede in fleisch, but made quyk in spirit' (so Tind. 'was kylled as pertayninge to the flesshe; but was quyckened in the sprete,' AV 'by the Spirit,' RV 'in the spirit'). In 2 P 1¹˙² Wyc., Tind., and Rhem. have 'in the righteousness,' and 'in the knowledge,' but Cran. and AV 'through,' Geneva 'by.' Aldis Wright refers to Gn 21¹⁸ where AV and RV have 'Arise, lift up the lad, and hold him in thine hand,' under the influence of Heb. בְּ, though the meaning is 'take him by the hand,' and he quotes Shaks. *Rich. III*. IV. i. 2—

> 'Who meets us here? my niece Plantagenet,
> Led in the hand of her kind aunt of Gloucester.'

 3. The Gr. prep. εἰς, which expresses movement and corresponds with mod. Eng. 'into' or 'unto,' is often translated 'in' (Clapperton in *Preacher's Magazine*, viii. 499, says 'one hundred and thirty-one times'). In that way some significant shades of meaning are lost, as in Ac 8¹⁶ 'they were baptized in the name of the Lord Jesus' (εἰς τὸ ὄνομα, RV 'into the name'; all other versions as AV); 1 Co 8⁶ 'God, the Father, of whom are all things, and we in him' (εἰς αὐτόν, AVm 'for him,' RV 'unto him'); Eph 4¹³ 'Till we all come in the unity of the faith, and of the knowledge of the Son of God, unto a perfect man' (εἰς τὴν ἑνότητα . . . εἰς ἄνδρα τέλειον, AVm 'into the unity,' RV 'unto the unity'). In mod. Eng. 'in' and 'into' are kept easily apart, 'into' being expressive of movement, 'in' of rest (though we still say 'fall in love,' 'come in question'). But in 1611 they were not so sharply distinguished. Thus Shaks. has (*Merch. of Venice*, v. i. 55)—

> 'How sweet the moonlight sleeps upon this bank !
> Here we will sit, and let the sounds of music
> Creep in our ears';

Rich. III. I. ii. 261—

> 'But first I'll turn yon fellow in his grave';

and *Sonnets* 112—

> 'In so profound abysm I throw all care.'

And so at an earlier time Coverdale translates Is 52¹ 'For from this tyme forth, there shal no uncircumcised ner uncleane person come in the.' On the other hand, but more rarely, 'into' was used for 'in,' as Lk 13²¹ Wyc. 'It is lijk to sourdough, that a womman took, and hidde it in to thre mesuris of mele, til al were sourid'; and Shaks. *Tempest*, I. ii. 361—

> 'Therefore wast thou
> Deservedly confined into this rock.'

It is not surprising therefore that we should find 'in' for 'into' frequently in AV, as Gn 42²³ 'We cannot tell who put our money in our sacks' (so RV); 50²⁶ 'he was put in a coffin' (so RV); Dt 24¹ 'Then let him write her a bill of divorcement, and give it in her hand' (so RV); Neh 2¹² 'What my God had put in my heart' (RV 'into'). Cf. Ps 73⁵, Pr. Bk. 'They come in no misfortune like other folk'; 136¹³ Pr. Bk. 'Who divided the Red Sea in two parts.'
 4. 'In' is occasionally found for 'on,' as in the familiar example, Mt 6¹⁰ 'Thy will be done in earth, as it is in heaven' (ὡς ἐν οὐρανῷ καὶ ἐπὶ γῆς, RV 'Thy will be done, as in heaven, so on earth'; 'in earth' is probably due to Vulg. 'in cælo, et in terra'; it is found in all the Eng. versions). So Gn 1²² 'let fowl multiply in the earth' (so RV); 6⁵ 'in the earth' (AV and RV), but 6⁶ 'on the earth' (AV and RV); Wis 10⁴ 'For whose cause the earth being drowned with the flood, wisdom again preserved it, and directed the course of the righteous in a piece of wood of small value' (δι' εὐτελοῦς ξύλου, Vulg. *per contemptibile lignum*, RV 'by a poor piece of wood,' Ball 'on a paltry plank': 'in' was probably used because the translator had the ark before his mind). Cf. Mt 5^heading 'The Sermon in the Mount'; Ac 13¹⁴ Wyc. (1388) 'and thei entriden in to the synagoge in the dai of sabatis' (Tind. 'on the saboth daye'); Shaks. *Othello*, I. iii. 74—

> 'What in your part can you say to this?'

and Milton, *Lycidas*, 185—

> 'Henceforth thou art the genius of the shore,
> In thy large recompense, and shalt be good
> To all that wander in that perilous flood.'

 5. 'In' is used along with a verbal subst. to signify 'in process of,' 'while,' as Gn 35¹⁸ 'as her soul was in departing'; 2 Mac 4³⁰ 'while those things were in doing'; Jn 2²⁰ 'Forty and six years was this temple in building.' Cf. Joy, *Apology to Tindale* (Arber's ed. p. ix), 'he knew yat I was in correctynge it myselfe'; Knox, *Hist.* 107, 'While these things were in doing in Scotland.'
 6. 'In that'=because, has now gone out of use. It occurs Gn 31²⁰ 'And Jacob stole away unawares to Laban the Syrian, in that he told him not,' and other places. Cf. Hooker, *Eccles. Polity*, 'Some things they do in that they are men . . . some things in that they are men misled and blinded with error.' J. HASTINGS.

INCARNATION, THE.—

Introduction.
i. Witness of OT.
    (a) The 'Son of David.'
    (b) The self-manifesting J″.
    (c) The 'Servant of J″,' etc.
ii. NT account of Jesus Christ.
    A. (a) Supernatural birth.
       (b) Sinlessness.
    B. (1) Christ's lordship.
       (2) His 'Sonship.'
       (3) God revealed in Christ.
       (4) Unique significance attached to work and death of Christ.
       (5) Tradition as to historic events of Christ's life, and acceptance of His Messianic claim presupposed by the apostolic writers.
iii. Scriptural doctrine of the purpose and results of the Incarnation.
    1. Cosmic significance of the Incarnation.
    2. A crowning disclosure of God.
    3. For the restoration of man.
    Or, otherwise, Christ's functions are distinguished as those of—
       (1) Prophet.
       (2) Priest.
       (3) King.
Literature.

This term shortly expresses the fundamental fact of Christianity, as St. John describes it in his Gospel (1¹⁴), ὁ Λόγος σὰρξ ἐγένετο. It signifies the act of condescension whereby the Son of God, Himself very God and of one substance with the Father, took to Himself human nature in order to accomplish its redemption and restoration. The NT insists upon the I. as a physical, historic fact (1 Jn 1³), but points for its true explanation to the grace, or love, of God (Jn 3¹⁶, 1 Jn 4⁹· ¹⁰). The expression of St. Paul, 'mystery of godliness' (1 Ti 3¹⁶), implies, on the other hand, that the redemptive action of God is beyond our power completely to analyze or comprehend. Such being the general aspect of the fact, we find the most comprehensive statement of it in the prologue to St. John's Gospel (1¹⁻¹⁸). St. John begins by intimating a plurality of persons within the Godhead; he describes the functions of the Logos, the objective utterance or self-expression of Deity, in His relation to the created universe of which He is the author and sustainer, and to man, whose conscience and reason owe whatever illumination they possess to His presence and operation. St. John also teaches, as a further presupposition of his doctrine of the I., the occurrence of a fall, or process of aversion from God, whereby man became subject to the power of 'darkness' or moral evil. It was to recover man from his state of alienation, and to raise him into the life of divine sonship, that the Word was finally manifested in a human form. After being heralded by the witness of creation, and by the voice of Heb. prophecy which culminated in the testimony of the Baptist, the Word finally made His appearance within the pale of an elect people of God; His manifestation, however, had a two-fold issue: the incarnate Word was rejected by the chosen nation to which, as touching His manhood (Ro 1³), He belonged; on the other hand, to those individuals who welcomed Him and recognized His true nature and claim, He communicated a due measure of the fulness of 'grace and truth' which resided in Himself, imparting to them 'power to become children of God,' and unveiling to them the glory, i.e. the essential character and life, of the Most High. St. John in this passage strikes the keynote of many varied representations of the Incarnation. It was before all else a unique exhibition of divine grace; a supreme manifestation of divine truth. The NT writers dwell now on one, now on the other, of these two aspects of the fact. Thus the Son is spoken of as 'given' (Jn 3¹⁶), or 'sent' (3¹⁷· ³⁴, 1 Jn 4⁹, Gal 4⁴), by the Father; but it was not less true that He gave Himself (Eph 5²⁵,

1 Ti 2⁶, Gal 2²⁰). That which displayed the grace of God the Father (Tit 2¹¹), 'the kindness and love of God our Saviour' towards man (ib. 3⁴), is also to be regarded as exhibiting the grace of the Son (2 Co 8⁹ 13¹⁴). The motive of the I. is, in short, the redemptive love of God. On the other hand, the I. was a signal manifestation of truth: a revelation of the divine character, supplementing and qualifying that which was revealed of God in nature, conscience, and history. St. John says expressly that 'No man hath seen God at any time; God only-begotten, which is in the bosom of the Father, he hath declared him' (1¹⁸, cf. 14⁹).

Such, then, is the dominant point of view from which NT writers regard the I.: it is an act of unmerited grace—a movement of divine love towards fallen man for his restoration and re-creation; it is also a culminating moment in a progressive and continuous self-revelation of God (He 1¹· ²); nor is there any hesitation in identifying this divine movement with the historic career of Jesus Christ. Historically, however, the recognition of His higher nature started from the acknowledgment of His Messiahship. He was first recognized as one whose advent had been foretold, and awaited with eager expectation, for a period of many centuries; as the promised seed of Abraham in whom all families of the earth were to be blessed (Gn 12³). Jesus Christ did, in fact, claim to fulfil and satisfy the hopes and anticipations to which successive prophets had given utterance. In 'the fulness of time' (Gal 4⁴) He appeared, to crown the hopes of the elect people from whom, as touching the flesh, He sprang. It is accordingly necessary to briefly summarize the testimony of OT to the fact of the Incarnation.

i. *Witness of OT.*—There are elements in the theological conceptions of OT which prepare the mind for the mystery of a divine I., e.g. the doctrine that man is made in God's image (Gn 1²⁷), and is capable of intercourse and union with God. Thus Ezk 1²⁶ implies that man's bodily structure was essentially adapted to represent the form of Deity; and the revelation of God in nature (Ps 19¹ etc.) would suggest the possibility of His self-manifestation under the form of human nature. Further, the so-called 'Theophanies' of OT— the manifestations of J‴s presence in a created 'angel'—point in the same direction. Again, the ascription by OT of various titles, functions, and relationships to the Godhead, served to prepare the Jewish mind for the Christian doctrine of a triune Deity, which is necessarily connected with that of the Incarnation. Further, the striking personification of the divine Wisdom which meets us in such passages as Pr 8²²ᶠ· (cf. Wis 7²²ᶠ· 8¹ᶠ· 18¹⁵ᶠ·) seems to anticipate St. John's doctrine of the creative Logos, or St. Paul's teaching in passages like Col 1¹⁵⁻¹⁹. Of special importance, however, is the witness of prophecy, the 'Messianic hope' being at its root an anticipation of the union of divine and human attributes in a single personality. The main points of Messianic doctrine may be summarized as follows: In its earliest stages prophecy is vague and indeterminate. Starting with the promise recorded in Gn 3¹⁵, it points to a victory of the woman's seed over the evil principle represented by the serpent, the 'seed' being afterwards more precisely described as 'the seed of Abraham,' in whom all the nations of the earth are to be blessed (Gn 12³ 18¹⁸ 22¹⁸ etc.). The tribe of Judah is indicated in Gn 49¹⁰ as the future depositary of sovereignty over the nations (cf. Nu 24¹⁷). The passage Dt 18¹⁵ contributes a further element to the Messianic idea, viz. the notion of a prophetic mediator between God and His people, probably in a comparatively late literary form giving expression to the hopes and ideas which the career and work of Moses had suggested. For it is noticeable, in regard to the Messianic hope in its earlier stages, that the actual history of Isr. itself gives birth to Messianic conceptions, e.g. the Exodus from Egypt helped to give form and colour to the national expectations of future deliverance from foes and oppressors; the rise of prophecy and of the kingdom suggested the image of an ideal prophet and a righteous king. At any rate, it is in the early period of the kingdom that the Messianic hope takes a clear and definite shape.

(a) The oracle, 2 S 7^{5-16} (cf. Pss 2. 89. 132), points to a future descendant of David whose throne is to be everlasting, and who is to stand in a unique relation to God as His 'Son.' This title, solemnly transferred from the nation (Ex 4^{22}) to the king, implies that the 'Son of David' is to be henceforth regarded as the representative of the chosen nation. This oracle is specially important as determining the scope and future direction of Heb. prophecy. In the prophets and psalmists we find successive pictures of a monarch who is extolled either as a warrior victorious over Judah's foes (Ps 2), or as a royal bridegroom taking to himself the daughter of an alien people (Ps 45), or as a monarch reigning in righteousness and peace (Ps 72), and blessed with signal marks of divine favour, length of days and perpetual communion with God (Pss 21. 61). These predictions of an ideal ruler culminate during the crisis of the struggle with Assyria. Thus Am 9^{11-15} points to the revival of David's house as Judah's last remaining hope; Hos 1^{11} 3^5 goes further, and foretells the appearance of a second David. Mic 5^{1-5} directs the thoughts of the faithful to Bethlehem, the original home of the Davidic family, and predicts its future greatness as the birthplace of the Messianic deliverer. Isaiah describes the Messiah's righteous rule, directed and inspired by the Spirit of J" (11), and dwells on the glory and peace of the city which Messiah chooses as his metropolis (4. 32, cf. Zec 9^{9ff.}). Indeed it may be said that at this period (c. 750–700) the Davidic monarch becomes the central figure of prophecy; and Ro 1^3 shows that the Davidic descent of Christ was ever regarded as an essential element in the Messianic claim (cf. Ac 2^{30}, 2 Ti 2^8), and our Lord Himself bears witness to the current belief that Christ was 'the son of David' in Mk 12^{35}.

(b) Closely connected, however, with this conception is another, viz. that of a personal advent of J" to set up His throne in Zion, as the Judge and Saviour of His people. This thought indeed (Am 4^{12} etc., Is 2. 32, etc.) is not actually combined with the picture of a Davidic king; the figure of the son of David is nowhere identified with the self-manifesting J". Both elements enter into the general current of Messianic thought, but they find fulfilment and mutual adjustment only in the person of Jesus Christ. In Ezk 34^{11. 24} we find an instance of the juxtaposition of the two ideas. In this and in other instances it is evident that there were parallel streams of prediction which, owing to necessary limitations in the prophetic faculty, were not brought into combination.

(c) New elements were added to the Messianic picture by the prophets of the pre-Chald. and exilic period (700–538). The most impressive of these is the wonderful conception of the 'servant of J",' the representative of the faithful remnant of God's chosen people, who by his vicarious sufferings makes atonement for their transgressions, and by his loyal fulfilment of the divine mission entrusted to him becomes the 'light of the Gentiles' and the missionary of the nations, so accomplishing in his own person the ideal functions of the chosen people (Is 40–66, passim). In the post-ex. period of prophecy the priestly and mediatorial

work of the coming Messiah rises into prominence (Ps 110) together with his relation to humanity at large as 'the Branch' (Zec 3^8 6^{12}, cf. Jer 23^5 and the phrase 'Son of Man,' Dn 7^{13}). At the same time is indicated his close relation to J". He is called J"'s 'fellow' (Zec 13^7), His 'angel' (Mal 3^1), one in whom J" Himself is pierced (Zec 12^{10}). Such expressions are to be compared with earlier passages which they elucidate or develope: e.g. the prophecy of Immanuel (Is 7^{14}), or of the king whose name 'shall be called J" is our righteousness' (Jer 23^{5. 6}, cf. Is 9^6). The deepest and most permanent element pervading the varied imagery of the prophets is the thought of the advent of J" Himself to judge, redeem, and govern His people, and to sanctify them by the bestowal of His Spirit (Ezk 36^{25-27} 37^{27}). The Redeemer who should come to Zion would be Himself divine (cf. Is 59^{16-20}).* See MESSIAH.

ii. *NT account of Jesus Christ.* — A. It was through experience of the *Manhood* and *human life* of Christ that men gradually arrived at the recognition of a higher nature, of which the lower was only a veil. Thus the preaching of the I. began with an appeal to facts and incidents open to ordinary observation; Jesus Christ was first known as 'a man' (Ac 2^{22}), and NT lays special stress on the verity and completeness of His manhood. The Gospels describe His birth (Mt 1^{18ff.}, Lk 2^{6ff.}), His growth 'in wisdom and stature' (Lk 2^{52}), His liability to the ordinary and innocent infirmities of human nature, e.g. hunger (Lk 4^2, Mk 11^{12}), weariness (Jn 4^6), thirst (Jn 4^7 19^{28}), pain and weakness (cf. He 5^2), death. His body was subject to ordinary conditions of nurture and development; it was the apt instrument of creaturely service and obedience to the will of God (He 10^{5-7}), and of self-sacrifice on behalf of His fellow-men (Mt 26^{28}). The soul of Christ was subject to human affections and emotions: compassion (Mt 9^{36}), love (Mk 10^{21}, Jn 11^5), grief (Jn 11^{35}, Lk 19^{41}), fear and anguish (Mk 22^{44}, cf. He 5^7), anger (Mk 3^5, Jn 2^{15ff.}). He had a true human will (Jn 6^{38}, Mt 26^{39}), which, however, is described as ever subjecting itself to the guidance of the divine will. This subjection necessarily implied the possibility of temptation, and of painful effort of will (Mt 26^{38}, Lk 22^{42}), so that 'He learned obedience by the things which he suffered' (He 5^8). Finally, Jesus Christ possessed a human spirit (Lk 2^{40} 10^{21}, Jn 11^{33}, Mk 8^{12}), which was apparently the seat or sphere of His divine personality (Ro 1^4), and which in the hour of death He commended into the hands of God (Lk 23^{46}). After death this human spirit of Christ, divinely 'quickened' (1 P 3^{18}), is found to have preached the gospel to certain of the departed (ib. 4^6).

Thus the humanity of Jesus Christ was real and complete. He was made like His brethren in all things (cf. He 2^{17}); 'in all points tempted like as we are, yet without sin' (ib. 4^{15}). On the other hand, there is nothing in Scripture to support the idea that Christ's humanity was *docetic* or unreal, or that He failed to undergo a real human experience. In all the main conditions of human life He was on a level with His fellow-men; a partaker of flesh and blood (ib. 2^{14}); submitting to a life of hard toil, poverty, suffering, moral conflict with keen and varied temptation, alternations of success and failure, honour and dishonour, favour and disrepute. Specially noteworthy is the fact that Christ's life was one of continual prayer (Mt 14^{23}, Mk 1^{35}, Lk 3^{21} 5^{16} 9^{29} 22^{41}, Jn 11^{41} etc.). It is

* The Messianic beliefs of the period between 165 and our Lord's birth do not come within the scope of this article. A brief survey of them will be found in Loofs, *Dogmengeschichte*, § 7. See also Schürer, *HJP* § 29; Drummond, *The Jewish Messiah*; Stanton, *The Jewish and the Christian Messiah*.

in virtue of a general similarity of conditions that Christ is described as the 'captain of faith' (He 12[2]), *i.e.* He exhibited those very virtues which are appropriate to man's creaturely condition : trust, reverence, submission, faith, obedience. For the same reason He is pointed to as the true pattern of manhood (Jn 13[15], 1 Jn 2[6], 1 P 2[21]). He is the great exemplar of humanity, because the circumstances of His life and probation were, speaking broadly, similar to those of ordinary men. He was found in outward guise or fashion as a man (Ph 2[7]) ; on a level with other men 'in all points' that can fall under human observation, 'yet without sin' (He 4[15], 2 Co 5[21], 1 Jn 3[5]).

This brings us to two points in which, according to NT, Jesus Christ was different from other men : (*a*) He was supernaturally born, (*b*) He was without sin.

(*a*) The *birth* of Christ is described by Mt and Lk. They tell us that He was conceived by the Holy Spirit (see p. 405[b]), without the intervention of a human father (Mt 1[20], Lk 1[32. 33]). By the operation of the 'creator Spirit' the 'Word was made flesh.' It is to be observed that this account of the birth is not contradicted, but rather suggested, by the teaching of other NT writers. Thus St. John speaks of Christ as ὁ ἄνωθεν ἐρχόμενος (Jn 3[31]), and St. Paul calls Him 'the second man from heaven' (1 Co 15[47]), a phrase which evidently describes the *origin* of the second Adam in contrast to that of the first. Further, as has been already observed, NT speaks of Christ as sinless, holy, sanctified by God (Jn 10[36]) ; 'knowing no sin' (2 Co 5[21]) ; 'holy, harmless, undefiled, and separated from sinners' (He 7[26]) ; 'a lamb without spot and blemish' (1 P 1[19]) ; 'the righteous one' (1 Jn 2[1], cf. Ac 3[14] 22[14]). True, He appeared 'in the likeness of the flesh of sin' (Ro 8[3], cf. Ph 2[7]), *i.e.* He took the very flesh which had been the instrument of human sin, but in assuming it He purified it from the sinful taint : * His flesh was, in fact, 'like' ours, inasmuch as it was flesh ; but it was only 'like,' for it was also sinless. Christ, then, was without sin, and NT suggests a close connexion between His sinlessness and His miraculous birth by constantly representing Christ as the Head or First Principle of a new race (ἀρχή, Col 1[18]), 'the firstborn among many brethren' (Ro 8[29]), the 'second Adam' (Ro 5[14], 1 Co 15[45]), the 'new man' (Eph 2[15]). Thus the tradition of the Church which first meets us in Mt and Lk is corroborated to some extent by antecedent considerations. If NT writers are correct in representing Jesus Christ as a new moral creation, it might be asked whether this new creation can have involved anything short of a new mode of generation. 'Must not the physical generation of the second Adam have been such as to involve at once His community with our nature and His exemption from it?'† If, in fact, Jesus Christ was what NT writers believed Him to be, a pre-existent being, the narrative of the virginal birth would have antecedent credibility. 'The chief ground,' says Prof. Stanton, 'on which thoughtful Christian believers are ready to accept it [the miraculous birth] is that, believing in the personal indissoluble union between God and man in Jesus Christ, the miraculous birth of Jesus seems to them the only fitting accompaniment of this union, and so to speak the natural expression of it in the order of outward facts.'‡ If it be rejoined that the 'fact of its necessity from a doctrinal point of view would tend to the formation of a legend,' it may with equal justice be urged that the evangelists' account of the birth testifies to the early prevalence of the belief in the Divinity of Christ. The ultimate reason, in fact,

for belief in this, as in all the other miraculous occurrences recorded in the Gospel, is faith in the higher nature of Jesus Christ. What Augustine says of the Gospel miracles strictly applies to the supernatural birth of Christ : *Mirum non esse debet a Deo factum miraculum . . . Magis gaudere et admirari debemus quia Dominus noster et salvator Jesus Christus homo factus est, quam quod divina inter homines fecit.** The accounts of miracles, it must be remembered, were written for those who were already Christians, *i.e.* who already believed in Christ as a superhuman person. The Gospels were not primarily intended to create such a belief ; they rather presuppose it.

(*b*) *The sinlessness of Christ* appears at first sight to conflict with the possibility of His being tempted. We have, however, already noticed that NT describes Christ as liable to temptation (Mt 4, Lk 4, esp. He 4[15], Lk 22[28]) ; but it never allows us to suppose that He suffered from any disordered affections, any inward propensity to sin. He had no illicit desires, no discord between the flesh and the spirit ; † sin could have no enticing or illusive power in His case (Ja 1[14]) ; He had no affinity for sin, no experimental knowledge of it (1 Jn 3[5], 2 Co 5[21]). On the other hand, He possessed in their perfection and integrity all those human faculties and senses to which moral temptation appeals,—all necessary and innocent affections and instincts to which some things appear naturally desirable, others naturally repugnant. Accordingly, He was capable of being tempted : for 'if the highest virtue does not exclude that instinct inseparable from humanity, to which pain is an object of dread, and pleasure of desire, which prefers ease and quiet to tumult and vexation, the regard and esteem of others to their scorn and aversion ; to which ill-requited toil or experienced unkindness are sources of corroding anguish and depression : then every conjuncture which presents but one of these objects of dread as the concomitant of doing God's will, or associates one of their desirable opposites with neglect or disobedience,—every such conjuncture must produce a conflict between duty and these necessary instincts of humanity sufficient to constitute temptation in the strictest sense.'‡ Christ, then, could be really tempted ; He felt the pressure of moral evil ; He experienced the pain of resistance to it, and He endured, He remained stedfast even under the full weight of manifold difficulties. There is nothing in the Gospels to warrant the idea suggested by John Damascene that 'He repelled the assaults of the enemy like smoke.' They rather suggest that the strength conferred on His human nature by the Divine Spirit was 'infallibly sufficient, but not more than sufficient, to sustain Him in His conflict, and bear Him through the fearful strife.'§ He verily 'suffered being tempted' ; He was made morally 'perfect through sufferings' (He 2[10. 18] 5[9]). In the power of the Divine Spirit (Lk 4[1. 14], Mk 1[12]) He was enabled to prevail over the tempter, but it was by a process of moral struggle ending in victory ; indeed the writer of Rev seems to summarily describe the human life of Christ as a continuous victory over evil (Rev 5[5] 6[2] 19[11], cf. Jn 16[33]).

With the above significant exception NT depicts Jesus Christ as one who shared in all points the nature of man. He was (to use a later theological term) 'consubstantial' with men. Accordingly, the general conditions of His human life enable Him

---

* Cf. Sanday-Headlam on *Romans*, *ad loc.*
† Gore, *Dissertations*, p. 66.
‡ *The Jewish and the Christian Messiah*, p. 376 f.

* *In Joh. Tract.* xvii.
† Aug. *Op. imperf. c. Jul.* iv. c. 57: 'Christus ergo nulla illicita concupivit, quia discordiam carnis et spiritus quæ in hominis naturam ex prævaricatione primi hominis vertit, prorsus ille non habuit, qui de spiritu et virgine non per concupiscentiam carnis est natus.'
‡ Mill, *Five Sermons on the Temptation*, p. 35.
§ Bruce, *Humiliation of Christ*, p. 269.

to be the perfect pattern of human goodness (see below, p. 466ª). And indeed there are facts recorded in the Gospels which plainly indicate that Christ underwent a real human development, moral and mental, and that He was even subject to some necessary human limitations in respect of knowledge. At this point it is necessary to touch on these points only so far as they concern the perfection of Christ's humanity. Morally, then, Christ is said to have developed; He grew in wisdom (Lk 2⁵²); He was 'made perfect'; 'He learned obedience by the things which he suffered' (He 2¹⁰ 5⁸). There were some qualifications necessary for the discharge of His high-priestly functions which He acquired through the moral discipline of actual human experience, esp. the graces of sympathy (He 2¹⁷ 4¹⁵ 5²), patience, faith (cf. Westcott on He 12²). He was perfected in the sense that He was progressively educated by His human experience; He became a consummate 'leader of salvation' (He 2¹⁰), a perfect high priest (ib. vii. 28). Further, Christ is represented as subject, at least in some degree, to ordinary laws of *mental* growth and development. ' He advanced (προέκοπτεν) in wisdom' as well as in stature (Lk 2⁵²). Occasions are mentioned on which He expresses surprise (Mt 8¹⁰, Mk 6⁶); and He also appears at times to desire information as to matters of fact (Mk 9²¹, Jn 11³⁴, cf. Mt 21¹⁹, Mk 11¹³). Finally, in regard to one special point He professes ignorance (Mk 13³²). From these phenomena it may be inferred that Christ's human faculties, supernaturally exalted and illuminated though they were by the operation of the Holy Spirit, were yet subject to limitation; and so far the impression produced by the records, that Christ lived as very man among men, is further strengthened. The Synop. Gospels especially portray a real human life and character; they present to faith as its immediate object the figure of a true man, 'the man Christ Jesus' (1 Ti 2⁵, cf. Jn 8⁴⁰).

B. Besides giving ample evidence of their belief in the real manhood of the historical person Jesus Christ, NT writers endeavour in different ways to express their sense of something transcendent and superhuman in His personality. There is no question, it may be observed, in regard to the actual belief of the apostles themselves, which may be gathered from their Epistles. The importance of the Gospels is that they describe the way in which this belief was arrived at. Speaking broadly, the apostles believed that in the historical Christ a *pre-existent being* had manifested Himself,* a being to whom belonged the dignity of a unique divine sonship. This common belief is by no means equally prominent in all the apostolic Epistles; but it is always latent, and even where not expressed it is usually implied in the attributes or functions ascribed to Christ. This belief, then, was slowly and hesitatingly reached by successive steps which can be traced with some clearness in the Gospel narrative. The Gospels record those utterances of Christ which suggested the idea of His higher nature. He Himself proposed the question to His disciples, 'Whom say men that I, the Son of Man, am?' (Mt 16¹³); He Himself ascribed to His own person a particular significance (e.g. Mt 10³⁷); He pointed men to Himself, and the Gospels record the effect on His hearers of Christ's utterances. They describe the moral authority of His teaching (Mt 7²⁹, Mk 1²⁷, Lk 4³²), the impression produced by His personality, the claim He put forward to forgive sins (Mt 9²⁻⁶, Lk 5²⁰⁻²⁴), to judge men according to their personal relation to Himself (Mt 7²³), to revise, expand, interpret the Mosaic Law (Mt 5²¹ff. 12⁸ 19⁴), to be the giver of

rest to the burdened soul (Mt 11²⁸), to be an object of devotion to the heart of man superseding all other interests (Mt 10³⁷, Lk 14²⁶). There can be no serious doubt, moreover, that Christ claimed to be the Messiah. In calling Himself 'the Son of Man' He adopted a title which indisputably involved Messianic pretensions. Further, He claimed to stand in a unique relation to God; although He very rarely applies to Himself the title 'Son of God,' He never disclaims it; on occasions of exceptional urgency He refuses to disown it (Mt 16¹⁶ 26⁶³); indeed, He habitually speaks of God as 'my Father' (Mt 23 times), and He attributes to Himself powers and prerogatives which imply coequality with God. He exercises sovereign authority over souls, claiming them as His own, and putting forward that jealous, exclusive claim which can rightfully belong only to the Creator Himself (Mt 10³⁷. ⁴⁰, Lk 10¹⁶, Mt 24³⁵ 13⁴¹, Lk 21³³). He promises to bestow the Holy Spirit (Mt 10¹⁹, Lk 12¹², cf. 21¹⁵); He speaks of Himself as having given a commission to the ancient prophets of Israel (Mt 23³⁴, cf. Lk 11⁴⁹). Finally, in one solemn passage common to Mt and Lk, He claims an exclusive knowledge of the Father (Mt 11²⁷, Lk 10²²), and an exclusive power of manifesting Him. On the other hand, the negative consideration is important, that although Christ is the preacher of humility, repentance, conversion, and the vehement rebuker of Pharisaic self-righteousness, He never betrays any consciousness of guilt, such as OT prophets frequently exhibit, nor any sense of a personal need of reconciliation with God.

But the Gospels do not merely preserve characteristic utterances of Christ, they describe the process of apostolic belief in Him. We can trace more or less distinctly the successive stages through which the faith of the apostles advanced to the point of acknowledging the higher, or preexistent personality of Christ. The Fourth Gospel seems, indeed, to serve, among other purposes, that of depicting the development of faith. To sum up briefly the gist of the evangelic testimony: it would seem that the apostles discerned in Jesus Christ first a Teacher or Rabbi sent from God, then successively the expected Messiah, the Holy One, the Lord of nature, the searcher of hearts, the revealer of God, the supreme example of suffering love, the conqueror of death, the Son of God. Faith, finally, bows before Him as 'Lord and God' (Jn 20²⁸). This point is arrived at only after a long and heart-searching discipline of suspense and hesitation; but it unquestionably represents the final answer of the apostles to a question which was morally inevitable, and which, as a matter of fact, had been repeatedly and openly raised,—the question 'who is this?' (Mt 21¹⁰, Lk 5²¹ 7⁴⁹ 9⁹; cf. Mt 8²⁷, Mk 4⁴¹, Lk 8²⁵). The ultimate answer seems to have been based on a number of convergent considerations: on the effect of Christ's personality, and the 'self-evidencing' power of His appeal to heart and conscience, on the superhuman claims which His teaching disclosed, and on the symbolic acts of power by which He at once illustrated and authenticated His teaching. For much of the evidential importance of the Gospel miracles depends on their moral character. They are in keeping with all that Christ reveals of God's nature and attributes. They are exactly such phenomena as we should expect in a universe in which physical forces are subordinated to righteous law and a purpose of grace. They reveal power, but the power is that of righteous will; and they are symbolic of the redemptive action of God which the doctrine of Christ proclaims. But what finally crowned and justified the faith of the apostles was the actual resurrection of Jesus Christ from death. Their testimony is concentrated on

* Notice the use of the vb. φανεροῦσθαι in relation to the Incarnation, e.g. 1 Ti 3¹⁶, 1 P 1²⁰, 1 Jn 3⁵. ⁸.

this fact, the real occurrence of which alone explains their spiritual transformation and the stedfastness of their belief in face of hostile opinion. The apostles seem to have recognized, some more quickly than others, but all sooner or later, that the resurrection was in fact inevitable, Christ being what He claimed to be. It afforded a key to the entire life; it was the ground of a final assurance that under the veil of mortal flesh the eternal Son of God Himself had 'tabernacled' among men (Jn 1¹⁴). It was the supreme revelation to the apostles of the glory of the Divine Word, who, as man, had lived and conversed with them on earth. It was the starting-point of a new and higher life, and of a more exalted faith. The resurrection followed by the ascension 'declared,' determined, or proved Jesus Christ (Ro 1⁴) to be, not merely the promised Messiah and 'the Lord' to whom all power was given in heaven and earth (Mt 28¹⁸), but a heavenly being who had been manifested in a human form, and had returned into the divine glory whence He originally came. Thenceforth Jesus Christ became an object of worship, and the gospel of redemption preached by the apostles had His person for its central theme (Ac 28³¹).

Such, then, seems to have been the conception of Christ to which the apostles were led by their long intercourse with Him. When, however, we turn to the apostolic teaching in regard to Christ's higher nature, we cannot fail to recognize a striking diversity of treatment. All the writers are at one in their general conception of the I. as a supreme self-manifestation of God; but we seem to trace, not only a certain advance in clearness of perception, corresponding to differences of phraseology (e.g. contrast the OT Messianic title παῖς in Ac 4²⁷ with λόγος in St. John's Gospel), but to a certain extent distinct aspects of Christ's person.* These must be recognized even though they form no sufficient basis for the idea of radically different and mutually exclusive types of NT Christology— 'adoptianist,' 'pneumatic,' etc. Thus (1) the simple objective view of Christ as fulfilling in His person and life the OT Messianic expectations is characteristic of St. James and St. Peter; (2) the earlier Epistles of St. Paul estimate Christ's person from the side of anthropology: man's yearning for reconciliation and union with God finds its satisfaction in Christ; (3) a more transcendental treatment of Christ's person marks the later Pauline and Johannine writings; they deal with cosmological and mystical aspects of the Incarnation. And it must be remembered that 'between the clear-sighted apostle of the Gentiles and the straitest of [Jewish or Ebionite] zealots there lay every conceivable gradation of intermediate positions.'† But the apostles themselves seem to have a fundamental bond of union in their belief about Christ as one who may be worshipped,‡ and whose name may be co-ordinated with that of God. It cannot be shown that St. Paul taught anything about Christ that was not implied in the belief of his fellow-apostles; but we must remember that 'what to them was the result of their belief in Christ, was to him the starting-point from which logical conclusions were seen to follow, practical applications made, in every direction.'

What, then, was the earliest conception of Christ's higher nature current in the Church? We turn to Ac, and find that the earliest preaching of Christ is naturally conditioned by conceptions of God already current among those to whom the gospel message was proclaimed. St. Peter is a Jew speaking to Jews, to whom any unqualified declaration of Christ's Deity or pre-existence would have appeared perplexing, and even blasphemous. We notice in his preaching an avoidance of the phrase υἱὸς θεοῦ (contrast Mt 16¹⁶); his starting-point is the well-known historical figure, the facts of whose life, ministry, and recent passion were notorious in Jerus. (Ac 2²² 3¹³ 4¹⁰ 5³⁰ 10³⁷ᶠ·). St. Peter dwells repeatedly on the exaltation of One who had been known as man. This man, 'approved of God' (2²²), bearing all the marks of God's commissioned 'servant' (παῖς, 3¹³, cf. Is 52¹³), manifesting clear tokens of divine unction, was 'made' by God 'both Lord and Christ' (2³⁶). The main points in St. Peter's preaching which would naturally strike a Jewish audience would be (1) his references to the fulfilment of Messianic prophecy in Christ (2²³ᶠ· 3²² 4¹¹), for we must remember that to Jewish ears the very title 'Messiah' would imply a superhuman being; (2) his insistence on the resurrection as at once the seal of Christ's divine unction and mission (2³² 3¹⁵ 4¹⁰ 5³¹, cf. 13³⁰), and a decisive manifestation of the glory of His person. The resurrection had proclaimed Him 'prince of life' (3¹⁵), source of spiritual blessing and power (3²⁶), 'prince and saviour' (5³¹), 'judge of quick and dead' (10⁴²). Speaking generally, the same point of view is characteristic of St. Peter's 1st Epistle. He regards Christ as the exalted man, enthroned at God's right hand, and bestowing the gift of the regenerating Spirit (1 P 1²³). Christ is One whose human acts and sufferings have preternatural virtue; who is destined to judge mankind (4⁵); who is the author of Messianic salvation, 'both in its negative aspect as a rescuing from the wrath under which the whole world is lying, and in its positive aspect as the imparting of eternal life.' On the other hand, it is doubtful whether the two passages 1¹¹ and ²⁰ necessarily imply the doctrine of Christ's pre-existence.† With St. Peter we may couple St. James and St. Jude, each of whom calls himself 'slave of Christ.' St. James even speaks of Christ as 'Lord of glory' (2¹), and looks for His appearance in judgment (5⁸·⁹); he also uses language (1¹⁸·²¹) implying that in Christ is revealed a principle of supernatural power which the law was unable to bestow (cf. Ro 8³).

On the whole, it may be taken for granted that St. Peter's sermons in Ac, together with his 1st Ep. and the Epp. of St. James and St. Jude, present us with the general conception of Christ current in the earliest apostolic age. By the first Christians Christ was regarded as the promised Messias, whose mission had been sealed by His resurrection and exaltation, and in whom the Jewish expectations concerning the 'kingdom of God,' and anticipations of future 'salvation,' were spiritually fulfilled. There can be little doubt that both these ideas ('the kingdom' and 'salvation') were coloured by Jewish preconceptions. There was, for instance, a widespread expectation of the speedy second coming of Christ—an idea which seems, indeed, to have been shared by the apostles themselves. But, at any rate, the conception of Christ just indicated formed the starting-point, so to speak, for the deeper conceptions of St. Paul, the writer of He, and St. John. In proceeding to gather up the

---

* Loofs, Dogmengeschichte, § 11. 3, rightly remarks, 'Wesentliche Verschiedenheiten in der religiösen Schätzung Christi . . . sint überhaupt nicht zu konstatieren . . . verschieden aber hat man diese Einzigartigkeit Jesu zu erklären versucht.'

† Robertson, Athanasius [Nicene and post-Nicene Fathers, ser. ii.], Introd. p. xxii.

‡ Loofs, l.c., 'Anrufung Christi . . . ist . . . nicht andres als das praktische Korrelat des Prädikats κύριος.'

* Sanday-Headlam on Ro 1¹⁶.

† See Harnack, Dogmengeschichte, vol. i. appendix i. Harnack believes in regard to 1 P 1¹⁸ᶠ· that the writer holds to the old Jewish conception of 'pre-existence,' i.e. predestination in the counsels of God. Christ 'was manifested in these last days for our sake, that is, He is now visibly what He already was before God. What is meant here is not an incarnation, but a revelation' [Eng. tr. vol. i. p. 322]. The passage 1¹¹ᶠ· may refer to the prophets either of the old or of the new dispensation, but according to the usual interpretation the OT prophets are meant.

main christological theses of the apostolic teaching *regarded as a whole*, we are for the most part, but not exclusively, dependent on these last-mentioned writers.

The following points appear to be of main importance: (1) The conception of Christ's *Lordship*. The name κύριος meets us in St. Peter's sermons, in Ja and Jude, in Jn and Rev, and in St. Paul's Epistles, *passim*. The word does not necessarily imply Divinity,* but in NT it meets us in contexts and connexions which, taken together, involve the ascription of Deity to Christ. The 'Lordship' of Christ means His 'sovereignty' in the sphere of nature and in that of grace. To Christ belongs a lordship which He has merited by His life of creaturely service and obedience (Ro 10⁹, 1 Co 12³, 2 Co 4⁵). He is supreme over the universe and over His Church (Col 1¹⁶⁻¹⁸, Ph 2¹⁰ᵗ.). Christians belong to Him (Ro 14⁸, 1 Co 3²³); they are 'under law to Christ' (1 Co 9²¹, Gal 6²). He is the fountainhead of all grace, authority, disciplinary and ministerial power (1 Co 5⁴, 2 Co 10⁸ 13¹⁰). He is to be awaited as judge (2 Co 5¹⁰). St. Paul applies to Christ OT Jahweh passages (*e.g.* Ro 10¹³=Jl 2³²; cf. Ro 10¹¹⁻¹³, 1 Co 2¹⁶ 10²²); he ascribes to Him the absolute title ὁ κύριος (1 Co 16²³, 2 Co 1¹⁴ 11³¹ 12⁸, Ro 14¹⁴), and in one passage, which is of the nature of a climax, he uses an even stronger expression, '*God over all blessed for evermore*' (Ro 9⁵).†

(2) Parallel to the idea of lordship is that of *Sonship*. Christ is υἱὸς θεοῦ—a recognized title of Messiah, which, like κύριος, is often illustrated by its context; often by other characteristic NT phrases with which it is closely associated. The 'Sonship' of Christ is spoken of as unique (ὁ ἴδιος υἱός, Ro 8³²; ὁ ἑαυτοῦ υἱός, *ib.* 8³; μονογενής, Jn 1¹⁸, 1 Jn 4⁹), *i.e.* it is not ascribed to Christ merely as a Messianic title, but as connoting a personal relationship to God. The phrase is used in contexts which imply a literal pre-existence; the Son of God is 'sent' (Ro 8⁸, Gal 4⁴, 1 Jn 4⁹⁻¹⁴); He 'comes' (1 Jn 4² 5⁶ 5²⁰); He was originally an inhabitant of heaven (1 Co 15⁴⁷); the I. was a change of state in the life of a pre-existent being, of the Word Himself (Jn 1¹⁸), of One who is essentially 'spirit' (2 Co 3¹⁷).‡ The 'Sonship' of Christ is thus defined, and acquires a new significance. It is not merely 'ethical,' *i.e.* such as any man may acquire by moral affinity to God; nor merely theocratic; it denotes a special, unique, incommunicable relationship (Jn 10³⁶⁻³⁸). Hence, especially in St. Paul's earlier Epistles (Th, Ro, Co, Gal), a position is habitually assigned to Christ which inevitably implies His real Deity. He is co-ordinated with God in greetings and farewells (*e.g.* 2 Th 1², 2 Co 13¹⁴). He is the source of St. Paul's apostolate (Gal 1¹); the agent or mediator in creation (1 Co 10⁴) and in redemptive history (1 Co 10⁴). The I. was, in fact, an act of self-abnegation whereby a life of creaturely limitations was accepted in exchange for the glories of heaven (2 Co 8⁹, Gal 4⁴).

In two passages of later Epp. these christological thoughts are more fully developed. In Ph 2⁵⁻¹¹ St. Paul deals with the *method* of man's redemption. Christ is set forth as the example of one who foregoes prerogatives that might be claimed, and renounces for a season a state of divine glory, bliss, and sovereignty which was His by natural right. The passage exhibits specially the original divine dignity, the unity, and the continuous action

of the person who passed voluntarily from a state of heavenly bliss to a condition of creaturely servitude and suffering. This process St. Paul speaks of as one of self-emptying (ἑαυτὸν ἐκένωσεν, 5⁷); it was an action by which a being, possessing the attributes of Deity itself, took upon Himself conditions non-natural to Deity, while continuing in a real sense to be what He was before. The reward of His self-sacrificing 'obedience' (5⁸; cf. Ro 5¹⁹) was exaltation according to an essential law of divine action. In the human nature which He vouchsafed to assume, He was raised to the throne of divine lordship as the object of universal worship. In Col 1¹⁵⁻²⁰ St. Paul deals with the cosmic significance of the I. of the Son. As the 'image of the invisible God,' He occupies a position of unique pre-eminence and sovereignty, both over the physical universe and over the new or moral creation, the Church of redeemed humanity. He is the essential mediator in nature, the 'firstborn of all creation,' *i.e.* prior to creation, and sovereign over it; in relation to history He is the inheritor of the Messianic promises (Ps 89); in relation to the Church He is the essential mediator in the sphere of grace, the firstborn from the dead, the fountainhead and principle of a new supernatural life. In this majestic statement St. Paul seems to unfold a conception essentially identical with that of the prologue to St. John's Gospel.

(3) In Christ *God reveals Himself*; in Him man is able to discern the character and nature of 'the invisible God' (Col 1¹⁵). The word εἰκών in the passage here quoted is found in an earlier Epistle (2 Co 4⁴). It may be compared both with the Johannine phrase Λόγος, and with the expression in He 1³ χαρακτὴρ τῆς ὑποστάσεως. The 'Image' of God is at once the *adequate expression* and the *essential revealer* of Deity (cf. Jn 1¹⁸ 6⁴⁰ 12⁴⁵ 17³, Gal 1¹⁶, He 1², and consider Mt 11²⁷=Lk 10²²). In Him the divine Fatherhood is manifested, not as a mere creative relationship in which God stands to mankind, but as an internal and ultimate mystery of the Godhead (Ro 8¹⁵, Eph 4⁶, Jn 14⁶·⁹ 16²⁷); in Christ the love of God (1 Jn 4⁹) and His holiness (Jn 17¹¹, Rev 4⁸ 16⁵) are alike revealed. But beyond this, the inner mystery of the divine nature is in part unfolded. An essential Fatherhood, an essential Sonship, eternal and intemporal, subsists within the sphere of Deity: a necessary relationship of communion and dependence between two divine Persons (Jn 1¹⁻⁴). St. Paul seems to recognize the perfect equality of these divine Persons, especially in such a phrase as that of Ph 2⁶ (ἐν μορφῇ θεοῦ ὑπάρχων); while in 1 Co 15²⁴⁻²⁸ he teaches the fundamental relation of dependence in which the Son stands to the Father. Thus the revelation of God 'in a Son' (He 1²) is the manifestation of the divine 'glory' in a twofold sense ; the Son manifests at once the moral perfections of the Godhead, and the internal distinctions of Person subsisting within the divine essence. In Him the whole fulness of Deity has its permanent abode (Col 1¹⁹); to faith it can be manifested (2 Co 4⁶); by human souls it can be apprehended as a source of life-giving grace (Jn 1¹⁶).

(4) All the apostles agree in attributing a unique significance to the work and death of Christ. In Him the divine purpose of 'salvation' was realized: deliverance from wrath, and the imparting of eternal life (1 Th 5⁹·¹⁰).* Jesus Christ stands in relation to human sin not merely as judge, but as 'saviour' and deliverer (1 Th 1¹⁰, Ph 3²⁰ etc.). He gives Himself a ransom (λύτρον, 1 Ti 2⁶; cf. Mt 20²⁸, Jn 11⁵¹·⁵² etc.); He dies 'for our sins' (1 Co 15³; cf. Mt 26²⁸, 1 P 2²⁴ 3¹⁸), thus inaugurating a new covenant, the distinctive features of which are remission of sins (1 Co 11²⁵), a new right of access

---

* See Sanday-Headlam on Ro 14.

† See the careful note on this passage in Sanday-Headlam, *Romans*, pp. 233-238. They adopt this rendering 'with some slight, but only slight, hesitation.'

‡ '*The Lord is the Spirit.*' . . . 'It is with this most original conception of the divine essence of Jesus Christ that we must associate the fact of His pre-existence' (Sabatier, *The Apostle Paul* [tr. by Hellier], p. 332).

* See Sanday-Headlam's note on σωτηρία, *Romans*, p. 23.

to God (He 7[19] etc., Eph 2[13-18]), life and immortality (Ro 2[7], 1 Co 15[42]), the gift of the Holy Spirit (Gal 3[2], Eph 1[13], He 6[4]; cf. Ac 2[38], 1 Jn 3[24]). The effects of the redemptive work are described under several different aspects. In Ro and Gal St. Paul connects his doctrine of justification with the Person of Christ. He is the justifier of humanity; through faith in Him the merits of His death are appropriated by men (Ro 3[25f.]), and they are brought into a new relation to God, they are treated as righteous (δικαιούμενοι, Ro 3[24]), 'accepted in the Beloved' (Eph 1[6]). The shedding of His blood was, in fact, a sacrifice which had propitiatory value (Ro 3[25f.]). It was parallel to, while it transcended, the sacrifices of the Levitical law; they were material in quality, often repeated, ineffective in result; Christ's sacrifice was spiritual, and therefore real; one only because perfect in moral quality, effectual for the entire removal of sin (He 10[1-18]). Under another aspect Christ is the High Priest of humanity (He 4[14]): its perfect representative and adequate intercessor before God; quick to sympathize and powerful to save (ib. 4[15] 5[2] 7[25]). He appears in the innermost sanctuary of the true tabernacle, there to present Himself in the presence of God on man's behalf (He 7[25] 9[23f.]). Once again, Christ is the second Adam, the Head of a new race (Ro 5[12f.], 1 Co 15[45ff.]). His influence on humanity is parallel to that of the first Adam in the extensiveness of its range, but transcendent in the beneficence and power of its effects (Ro 5[15-21]). The result of Adam's sin was death; the mediatorial work of Christ has its issue in the triumphant reign of grace in 'eternal life' (Ro 5[21] 6[23]; cf. Jn 3[15. 16. 36] 5[24] 6[40. 47] 20[31]).

In Eph, one very prominent thought is that of the extension of the life of the incarnate Redeemer, risen and glorified, in the Church. The Church is His body, the complement or fulness of His being (Eph 1[23]); Christ is her Head, infusing into her the grace and virtue of His humanity (Eph 1[22] 4[11] 5[23]); present in the manifold operations of His Spirit; uniting His people in fellowship with Himself. St. Peter teaches characteristically that the Church is the true people of God, inheriting by right of spiritual descent the titles of ancient Isr. (1 P 2[9]; cf. Gal 4[26], He 12[22]); while St. John dwells on the mystery of fellowship with God attained in Christ (1 Jn 1[3]), and on the grace of sonship vouchsafed to individual believers (Jn 1[12]). In a word, the work and passion of Christ are regarded by the apostles as the source of all spiritual blessing; as the means of bringing all Messianic promises to accomplishment.

(5) It remains to notice that all the apostolic writers seem to presuppose an authoritative tradition as to the historic events of Christ's career, and a general acceptance in the Church of His Messianic claim. In his sermons (Ac 2, etc.) St. Peter appeals, as we have seen, to the known facts of the Passion and Resurrection; while St. Paul, in spite of the fact that his starting-point is that of one who had not known Christ after the flesh, but was called to believe in a glorified Saviour, alludes in various passages to recognized incidents of Christ's human life (see Ro 1[3] 8[3], Gal 4[4], 2 Co 8[9] 5[21], 1 Co 15[3], Ph 2[5f.], and other passages). There was, in short, an apostolic 'tradition' (παράδοσις) or 'traditions' which formed the common groundwork of teaching (cf. Ro 6[17], 1 Co 11[2], 2 Th 2[15] 3[6]). The Messianic conception of Christ's person specially distinguishes St. Peter's sermons in Ac, but it is by no means absent from the earlier thought of St. Paul,* and in St. John's teaching occupies a prominent place. In Rev, for instance, the image of Christ is Messianic. He is described in terms suggestive of His human descent from the chosen people

(Rev 5[5] 11[15] 12[10] 22[16]); and His kingly dominion is Messianically conceived as a victorious conflict with enemies (6[2] 12[5] 19[11-16]), though His lordship and royalty are the fruit of humiliation (see especially 5[6]; cf. Jn 1[29. 36]). There is also a strong Messianic element in the Gospel of Jn, e.g. the titles 'Lamb of God,' 'Son of God,' 'King of Israel,' 'He that should come' (6[14]), 'sent' (9[7]), etc.*

Such are the leading points of view under which the apostles describe the higher nature of our Lord. Taken together they combine the various lines of Messianic prediction in a single conception, that of the God-man. Jesus the Messiah of prophecy is the central object of their thought and devotion. Nothing more significantly illustrates this than the use by NT writers of the designation δοῦλος Ἰησοῦ Χριστοῦ; in this case the name of Christ replaces that of J″ in an already familiar OT phrase (δοῦλος θεοῦ or κυρίου). Further, we may notice that prayer is addressed to Christ (Ac 7[59], 2 Co 12[8], Jn 9[38]); and that He is the object of universal adoration in heaven (Rev 5[8f.]); that He is, in a word, God.

It has been found convenient to survey NT teaching in regard to the person of Jesus Christ as a whole. But it is important to bear in mind the fact that the Christian idea of the God-man was one which would not be readily apprehended in all its bearings by men who, like the twelve apostles, had been educated in Jewish modes of thought, and had perhaps imbibed to a great extent the national spirit of their countrymen. It was not till after the fall of Jerus., and the beginnings at least of the movement by which the message of the gospel was extended to the heathen world, that Christians could become fully conscious of the significance of the divine fact on which their religion was based—the appearance of the God-man on earth.† When we consider that our Lord confined His own ministerial activity and that of the Twelve to the 'house of Israel' (Mt 10[6]), we shall not be surprised that there appears in NT a lower, as well as a higher, form of christological doctrine; a form which is, roughly speaking, represented by the teaching of the Synoptists, and St. James, and St. Peter, as contrasted with that of St. Paul and St. John. But, as we have pointed out, the distinct aspects under which different NT writers present the figure of Christ cannot fairly be construed as representing radically different types of belief in regard to His person. See SON OF GOD.

iii. It may be next inquired what light Scripture throws upon the purposes and results of the Incarnation. The significance assigned to the event in Scripture presupposes something much more than the mere inspiration, 'adoption,' or exaltation of a man. The I. was no mere presence of God in a man; no mere mode of mystical indwelling; no mere moral relationship such as might subsist between friends. It was a real, permanent, indissoluble union of two perfect natures, divine and human; an assumption of manhood into personal unity with a divine being, so that the Godhead employs the manhood as an organ, and wears it as a vesture; so that all the acts and sufferings of the human nature properly belong to the Godhead. This is the doctrine of the NT; it is implied in the express statement of Jn 1[14] (ὁ λόγος σὰρξ ἐγένετο); in all references to the personality of the Son of God as single and continuous (e.g. 1 Co 8[6], Eph 4[5. 10], Ph 2[5f.], He 1[3] etc.); in such 'theopaschite' language as that of Ac 20[28]; in the ascription of life-giving properties to the flesh of Christ (Jn 6[53f.]), or of cleansing efficacy to His blood (He 9[14]); in the mention of His human nature as an object of adoration (Ph 2[10]). In fact, speaking generally, the NT regards the I. not as the birth of a unique man, but as a momentous event in the eternal life of God : a manifestation, a forthcoming, a mission, a redemptive movement, a visitation, a great descent. In the I. the self-same Person who had pre-existed in the form of God, who had created and sustained in being the universe of things visible and invisible, 'descended' from heaven (Eph 4¹⁰), and submitted Himself to a fresh series of experiences in the sphere of human life and history, without ceasing to be in essence what He ever had been, the Son or Word of the Father. He and none other lay in the cradle, grew in wisdom and stature, was tempted and troubled, suffered, died and lay in the grave, rose again, and ascended to the right hand of God. He is 'the same yesterday, to-day, and for ever' (He 13⁸). It follows that in virtue of this unity of Person, subsisting in two different states, heavenly and earthly, both human and divine attributes are ascribed to Christ, and may be rightly interchanged. An instance of this 'cross and circulatory' mode of speech (technically called *communicatio idiomatum*) may be found in 1 Co 2⁸, and possibly also in Jn 3¹³.

The belief of the first Christians as to the real nature of the I. may, in fact, be gathered rather from the *significance attached to Christ's work* than from express statements in Scripture about His person. All the NT writers are at one in ascribing to the appearance and work of Jesus Christ an element of *finality*. St. Peter and St. James reflect to some extent the current Messianic belief in the nearness of Christ's return to judgment (1 P 4⁷·¹⁷, Ja 5⁸·⁹). The 'revelation' of Christ is the goal of human hope and expectation (1 P 1¹³). St. Paul teaches that Christ is the supreme object of faith; religion consists ultimately in a right relation of the soul to Him (Ro 3²⁶ etc.). Christ is a Being in whom souls are mystically incorporated by baptism. They share sacramentally the acts, experiences, and sufferings of His earthly life (Ro 6³ᶠ·, Gal 2²⁰, Col 2¹², Eph 2⁵·⁶ 5³⁰). They are 'in Christ' (Ro 8¹ 12⁵, Gal 1²² 3²⁶·²⁸, Eph 1¹ 2¹⁰, Ph 1¹ etc.) 'and Christ in them' (Ro 8¹⁰, Gal 2²⁰ etc.); their souls and bodies are His temple (2 Co 13⁵).

The writer of Hebrews regards Christianity mainly under one aspect—as the final religion. Christ as 'Son' of God brings to man a final authoritative message from God. The religion which is based on His revelation and finished work has the characteristic of 'perfection' (τελείωσις). It establishes that unimpeded fellowship between God and man which was impossible under the Levitical system (7¹¹). Christianity is 'the better hope whereby we draw near to God' (7¹⁹). In this verse we have the 'dogmatic centre' of the Epistle. To St. John Christianity is the absolute religion—the final disclosure of God, revealing the possibility of perfect fellowship between God and man. It is final because it rests on the fact of a real I. of God. 1 Jn 'is probably the final interpretation of the whole series of divine revelations. . . . It declares that in the presence of Christ there has been given and there will be given that knowledge of God for which man was made, issuing in fellowship which is realized here in the Christian society, and which reaches to the source of all life.'* The collective testimony of the apostles, viewed as a whole, irresistibly proves the power of the impression which Christ's life and personality had made. No doubt they varied in their power of analyzing that impression. But the doctrine of the true Deity of Christ is the necessary inference from all that they ascribed to Him, and taught concerning Him.

The august dignity and glory of the event corresponds to the importance of the purpose it was designed to serve: the consummation of the

* Westcott, *The Epistles of St. John*, p. viii.

universe, the disclosure of God, the restoration of humanity.

1. The cosmic significance of the I., and the view that it was eternally purposed independently of the fact of human sin, seems indeed to be implied in such passages as Eph 1⁴⁻¹⁰, and possibly He 2¹⁰— passages which seem to suggest that the I. of the Son was an event predestined before the foundation of the world. The universe may well, so far as human reason can judge, have been framed with a view to the I. of its Creator. When, however, the question is raised whether this event was predestined in view of man's foreseen fall, scriptural testimony fails us, and we are left to the consideration whether it is *a priori* probable that God would have made His highest gift to His creatures contingent on human transgression. On the other hand, the evolutionary movement, whether in physical nature or in human history, which tends towards a 'fulness of time' (Gal 4⁴, cf. Eph 1¹⁰), seems unaccountably to fail unless crowned by the appearance of One who is the flower of human kind, and whose coming marks a climax in revelation. But here, again, we have to fall back on *a priori* reasoning.

2. At least we know that the I. is a crowning disclosure of God. He who had revealed something of His nature, His 'power and Godhead,' in the works of creation (Ro 1²⁰); who had spoken to man in divers ways, through the warnings of conscience, through visions, dreams, and oracles; who had manifested His purposes in judgment, type, and inspired prophecy, finally spoke to man 'in a Son' (He 1²). In Christ the will, mind, and character of God were finally revealed. 'If we searched all space,' says Luthardt, 'we should discover only the gospel of power; if we surveyed all time, only the gospel of righteousness. Only in Jesus Christ do we learn the gospel of grace.' Christ indeed revealed the essence of God's being: fatherly love and self-imparting holiness. In the character of Christ, in His life of self-forgetful love, in His compassion for sinners, in the severity of His judgment on sin, is manifested the essential character of God: 'He that hath seen me,' He said, 'hath seen the Father' (Jn 14⁹; cf. 12⁴⁵, Col 1¹⁵, εἰκὼν τοῦ θεοῦ τοῦ ἀοράτου). Further, by His claim to stand in a unique relation to God, He manifested the distinctions of relationship existing within the divine essence. He unfolded the name of God as Triune (Mt 28¹⁹). The formula of baptism, in fact, supplements those passages in which the Son and the Spirit are represented as subordinate to God, or ministering to His will. It implies that these two blessed Persons are co-equal with the Father in nature and state, and in their claim to be, together with Him, worshipped and glorified.

3. The mystery of the I. was intended for the restoration of man, for the removal of sin and its effects (Lk 15⁴ 19¹⁰, Jn 1²⁹ 3¹⁴ᶠ·, Gal 4⁴, Ro 5²·⁶ᶠ·, 1 Co 15²¹⁻²⁶, 1 Ti 1¹⁵, 1 Jn 3⁵). The coming of Christ made all things new; it restored all things to their original unity (Eph 1¹⁰). The Redeemer gathered up into Himself elements which the Fall had disintegrated; He represents manhood to God in its initial truth and purity, corresponding to the divine thought, fulfilling its true law, attaining its ideal destiny, perfection through suffering (He 2⁸ᶠ·). In Him is exhibited the fact that sin is no true or necessary element in human nature, but a vice or corruption of it. The first step in the re-creation of humanity must be the exhibition of a true pattern of manhood in a life perfectly well-pleasing to the Father (Jn 8²⁹; cf. Lk 3²², Mt 17⁵). It is needless to illustrate the way in which NT writers constantly point to the example of Christ. He Himself bids men 'learn of him' (Mt 11²⁹) and follow His example (Jn 13¹⁵); and St. Paul tells

the Thessalonians that they themselves 'are taught of God to love one another' (1 Th 4⁹; cf. Jn 6⁴⁵). But, further, Christ removes the barrier which sin had raised between man and his Creator; He 'takes away the sin of the world' (Jn 1²⁹); He makes atonement for it (cf. He 2¹⁷); He offers a propitiatory sacrifice for it (cf. Ro 3²⁵ ἱλαστήριον, 1 Jn 2² 4¹⁰ ἱλασμός), the sacrifice of *Himself* (He 9²⁶). He assumed human nature, in its outward aspect such as the Fall had left it, with all its obligations (cf. Mt 3¹⁵), its accumulated heritage of weakness and pain, its necessary subjection to vanity (Ro 8²⁰); He 'laid hold of it' (ἐπιλαμβάνεται, He 2¹⁶) in its weakness indeed, but not in its perversion and corruption, for He was without sin, though He suffered for sin (Ro 8³ etc.); and by a continuous act of perfect obedience (Ro 5¹⁹) He discharged the debt of entire self-devotion by which alone man could satisfy the jealous love and the righteous claim of his Creator (cf. He 10¹⁻¹⁰). His death on the cross was a representative and vicarious act of submission to the just penalties of human sin (see different modes of expression: in Gal 2²⁰ ὑπὲρ ἐμοῦ, 1 Co 15³ ὑπὲρ τῶν ἁμαρτιῶν ἡμῶν, Ro 8³ περὶ ἁμαρτίας, Mt 26²⁸ περὶ πολλῶν, 20²⁸ λύτρον ἀντὶ πολλῶν, etc.); and the effects of Christ's acceptance of death are described under different metaphors: 'redemption' (*i.e.* according to OT associations, deliverance from slavery at a mighty cost), 'propitiation' (*i.e.* an act or process by which sin is neutralized), 'remission' of sins (Ro 3²⁵ etc.), 'reconciliation with God,'* 'salvation,' etc.

But the work of redemption is followed by the work of re-creation and sanctification. The resurrection, by which the seal is set on the mission and work of the Son, and the ascension, by which as High Priest He passes within the veil to appear in the presence of God in our behalf (He 9²⁴), are followed by the outpouring of the Comforter, in whose coming the presence of Christ in His Church is accomplished; He comes as a 'quickening spirit' (1 Co 15⁴⁵) to inspire, enlighten, heal, strengthen, and sanctify His members, to unite them to Himself and to God, to dwell permanently in their hearts, to impart to them 'by habitual and real infusion' His own righteousness, to make them partakers of His life, to enable them for the life of divine service and sonship, to conform them to the likeness of Himself, and raise them into the glory of the risen life (Ro 8⁹ᶠ, Gal 2²⁰ etc., Jn 6⁵⁴ᶠ.).

These three aspects of the work accomplished by the incarnate Son of God may be otherwise distinguished, according to Messianic conceptions, as prophetic, priestly, and kingly functions. Thus (1) as Prophet, Christ places Himself, so to speak, in line with the ancient prophets of Israel (Mt 23²⁹ᶠ.). Like them, He teaches, He reveals the will of God, He preaches the divine requirement; like many among them, He is dishonoured, rejected, and slain (cf. Lk 4²⁴ᶠ· 13³³ᶠ.). It is in the exercise of His prophetic office that He preaches the kingdom of God, and reveals its principles and mysteries (see Mt 13³⁵). He elucidates the moral law; He guides souls; He instructs His disciples; He denounces the hypocrisy of the Pharisees; He rebukes, threatens, predicts the future (Mt 5²⁰ 15¹³ 22²¹· ²⁹, 23¹³ᶠ· etc.). As prophet endued with power, 'the power of the Spirit' (Lk 4¹⁴; cf. Mt 12²⁸), He works miracles which are themselves emblems or symbols of the diverse operations of grace. And He exhibits the divine will for man, not merely by authoritative teaching and by deeds of power, but by a life of unbroken zeal, devotion, and fidelity to God (cf. He 3²); His example, in short, is one element in the exercise of His prophetic office. In Him, according to the prophecy of Isaiah, man is 'taught of God' (Is 54¹³; cf. Jn 6⁴⁵).

* See a note in Sanday-Headlam on *Romans*, p. 129 f.

(2) As High Priest, Christ offers a propitiatory sacrifice on behalf of man—the sacrifice of Himself. The writer of Hebrews implies that, for the discharge of His priestly function, Christ was prepared by the discipline of earthly life: He vouchsafed to 'learn' obedience, sympathy, compassion, fellow-feeling with sinners; His participation in a common nature fitted Him to be a faithful representative of mankind. He fulfils in Himself two distinct types of priesthood: He is a priest after the order of Melchizedek (He 7), *i.e.* His priesthood belongs to an order eternal and supra-national, connected with a celestial service and a 'true tabernacle' (8²), based on divine promises, and combining kingly with priestly functions (cf. Zec 3⁸⁻¹⁰ 6⁹⁻¹⁵). Further, He fulfilled all that had been prefigured by the Levitic ordinances and priesthood, by offering Himself as a spotless victim (He 7²⁷ 8³ 9¹⁴· ²⁶ 10¹⁰⁻¹²), and by entering within the veil of the true tabernacle, there to present Himself in the presence of God on behalf of His brethren, and to dedicate them in His own Person for the life of acceptable service (4¹⁴ 6²⁰ 7²⁵ 8¹· ²· ⁶ 9¹²). As the true Melchizedek, in whom the offices of king and priest are united, He bestows blessing, and feeds His people with eucharistic bread and wine (cf. Gn 14¹⁸ᶠ·). As the antitype of the Aaronic priest He cleanses the whole sphere of worship with His own blood (9²³ᶠ·); He purges the individual conscience from the defilement of sin (9¹³· ¹⁴), and 'ever liveth to make intercession for' mankind (7²⁵).

(3) Finally, as King, Christ is the personal centre of the kingdom of God. The royalty of the Messiah had been predicted by ancient prophecy, and as 'King of the Jews' Christ was proclaimed on the cross (Jn 18³⁷ 19¹⁹). As King, He assumes an absolute authority over the consciences and hearts of men as their rightful lord. In Him the ancient theocratic idea, that God was the true King of Isr., dwelling among His subjects, and residing in His temple as in a palace, was fulfilled. In Rev St. John to some extent reverts to the OT and later Jewish conception of the Messianic King as a warrior victorious over Israel's foes. The Son of God is crowned with 'many crowns'; He rides forth conquering and to conquer (Rev 6² 12⁵ 14¹⁴ 19¹¹⁻¹⁶); and the same thought of Messianic Kingship is a leading idea of Mt. As King, Christ proclaims 'with authority' the dawn of His kingdom in the Sermon on the Mount (Mt 5–7). He explains its nature and conditions in the parables of the kingdom (Mt 13), and after His resurrection He claims 'all authority' in heaven and on earth (Mt 28¹⁸). As King, He is the fountainhead of ministerial power, the Master whom His servants honour and obey, the omnipotent source of grace, power, life, and mercy (He 4¹⁶). He founds a mediatorial system whereby men attain what they seek for, union with Himself and with the Father. With authority He institutes the sacrament of baptism or incorporation (Mt 28¹⁹, Jn 3³ᶠ·), and the Eucharist or sacrament of union (Mt 26²⁶ etc., Jn 6⁴⁷ᶠ·). He bestows the Spirit; He gives 'gifts unto men'; He appoints a ministerial order, which He commissions to act, and to proclaim forgiveness in His name (Eph 4¹¹ᶠ·, Jn 20²²ᶠ·) in order that the central purpose of His coming may be accomplished, 'that repentance and remission of sins' should be preached in His name among all nations, beginning at Jerus. (Lk 24⁴⁷). Finally, He rules the universe, bearing all things onward in their appointed course (He 1³), extending His kingdom through gradual subdual of all hostile elements: 'He must reign till he hath put all enemies under his feet' (1 Co 15²⁵). He waits expectant 'till his enemies be made his footstool' (He 10¹³; cf. 1¹³); and in the last day it is He who will sit as King 'on the throne of his glory' to judge the world (Mt 25³¹ᶠ·).

Thus the I., properly understood, is a key to the history of the universe. All history, it has been said, is summed up in the three sentences, *He is coming, He has come, He will come again* (cf. Rev 22[13]); and certainly this is the fundamental teaching of Scripture. If the OT foresees (Gal 3[8]) the I., the NT develops its significance as an actual event, and persistently points to the return of the Incarnate as the goal of history. There is no reason for denying a certain advance in the intellectual apprehension and statement of the doctrine of the I. on the part of the apostles, so far as it can be clearly demonstrated. Indeed it is what we should *a priori* expect. But in this article we have been concerned with positive and definite results, with the ultimate position which the NT assigns to Christ; and it is contended that the divergent and varied testimonies of Holy Scripture can only be satisfactorily adjusted and reconciled by the belief that Jesus of Nazareth was not only the expected Messiah of prophecy, but in a unique and absolute sense divine: God of God, Light of Light, very God of very God.

LITERATURE.—Ebrard in Herzog's *RE*, 'Jesus Christus der Gottmensch'; Oehler, *Theol. of OT*; Weiss, *Bib. Theol. of NT*; Dorner, *Person of Christ*; Hooker, *Ecclesiastical Polity*, bk. v. §§ 50–57; Pearson, *On the Creed*; Browne, *Exposition of the 39 Articles*; Andrewes, *Sermons on the Nativity*; Liddon, *Bampton Lectures*; Wilberforce, *Doctrine of the Incarnation*; Dale, *The Atonement*; Fairbairn, *Christ in Modern Theology*; Bruce, *The Humiliation of Christ*; Gore, *Bampton Lectures*; Westcott, *Christus Consummator*; Kingdon, *God Incarnate*; Ottley, *Doct. of the Incarnation*; Adamson, *Studies of the Mind in Christ*. For the apostolic belief in regard to Christ's Person see also Harnack, *History of Dogma* (introductory division).

R. L. OTTLEY.

INCENSE is AV tr[n] of two Heb. words which at first were quite distinct in meaning, although latterly the second of them came to be practically synonymous with the first. **1.** לְבֹנָה, **frankincense** (wh. see), is tr[d] 'incense' by AV in Is 43[23] 60[6] 66[3], Jer 6[20] 17[26] 41[5], in all of which passages RV accurately substitutes 'frankincense.' The Gr. equivalent is λίβανος, which appears in NT in Mt 2[11] and Rev 18[13]. **2.** קְטֹרָה (in Dt 33[10] קְטוֹרָה [cf. the prop. name *Keturah*, קְטוּרָה], in Jer 44[21] קִטֵּר), generally reproduced in LXX by θυμίαμα or θυμιάματα (cf. for NT usage Lk 1[10], Rev 5[8] 8[3f.] 18[13], in the last along with λίβανος). In Ex 30[35. 37] RV substitutes 'incense' (קְטֹרֶת) for 'perfume,' in 2 Ch 2[6] 'burn incense' (הַקְטִיר) for 'burn sacrifice,' and in Rev 5[8] 18[13] 'incense' (θυμιάματα) for 'odours' of AV (cf. Rev 8[3]).

Frankincense was an ingredient of the holy incense, Ex 30[24]; it was used as incense, Jer 6[20]; it was put on the meal offering (Lv 2[1. 2. 15. 16] 6[8], cf. 5[11], Nu 5[15]); also on the shewbread, Lv 24[7]; one form of luxury was to burn it as a perfume, Ca 3[6] 4[6. 14]; along with gold it is mentioned as part of the tribute to be brought to Israel, Is 60[6] (cf. Mt 2[11] of the gifts of the Magi to the infant Jesus). Both frankincense (λίβανος) and incense (θυμίαμα) are mentioned amongst the merchandise of the apocalyptic Babylon, Rev 18[13]. On the Arabian traffic in incense see ARABIA, vol. i. p. 134[b].

The offering of incense, which bulks so largely in the later ritual, appears to have been unknown in the earlier stages of Israel's history. Wellhausen (who is followed in his conclusions more or less closely by Kuenen, Nowack, Benzinger, and many others) will have it that the first mention of offering incense is in Jer 6[20]. In the older literature קטר,* according to him, always refers to the burning of the fat or the meal and making these go up in sweet smoke (cf. Lv 3[5] [P] etc.) to J″, while the substantive קְטֹרָת in like manner has the

quite general sense of what is burnt upon the altar.* The meaning 'incense' belongs to it for the first time with certainty in Ezekiel (8[11] 16[18] 23[41]); subsequently the word occurs frequently in P, always in this sense; elsewhere only in Pr 27[9], where it is used not with a sacred but a secular application (EV 'perfume'). Even in such late passages as 1 S 2[28], Ps 66[15] 141[2] Wellhausen denies that it means anything more than *sweet smoke*, which is the sense he attributes to it in the only two certainly pre-exilic passages where it occurs, Is 1[13] and Dt 33[10] (otherwise Dillm. and Steuernagel, both of whom find the meaning 'incense' in Dt 33[10], although Steuernagel considers that this implies a pretty late date for the passage, which, however, he would make prior to P, because all Levites have according to it the prerogative of burning incense to J″, whereas in P this duty and privilege is assigned only to the seed of Aaron; cf. Nu 16[5. 10] 17[5] [Eng. 16[40]]). Again, in Am 4[4f.] 5[21ff.], Is 1[11ff.], Mic 6[6f.], where we have detailed lists of ritual acts, there is no mention of incense, and JE as well as the books of Judges, Samuel, and Kings are equally silent. לְבֹנָה, 'frankincense,' appears first in Jer 6[20] 17[26] 41[5], elsewhere only in P (Ex 30[24], Lv 2[1. 2. 15. 16] 5[11] 6[8] 24[7], Nu 5[15]), Deutero-Isaiah (Is 43[23] 60[6] 66[3]), the Chronicler (1 Ch 9[29]), and Canticles (3[6] 4[6. 14]).

From all this it may perhaps be inferred that the use of incense was introduced not long before the time of Jeremiah (in 6[20] it is referred to as rare, costly, unnecessary). It may have been connected with the gradual refinement of the cultus, the extension of commerce, and the contagion of the rites of heathen religions (cf. Jer 11[12. 17] 48[35], 2 Ch 34[25]).

In P incense has a very extensive use, and is regarded as extremely sacred. It was to be used with every meal offering (Lv 2[1. 2] etc.), as well as to be offered alone, in which latter case it safeguarded the high priest on the Day of Atonement when he entered the Holy of Holies (Lv 16[12f.]); and it made atonement for the people after the rebellion of Korah (Nu 17[11f.] [Eng. 16[46f.]]). The holy incense was to be prepared according to a special recipe (Ex 30[34f.]) from stacte, onycha, and galbanum (see sep. arts. on these words), along with pure frankincense—an equal weight of each (see Dillm. *ad loc.*). Josephus states that there were thirteen ingredients used in his day, and that a great store of these was always kept in the temple (*BJ* v. v. 5, VI. viii. 3). It was forbidden (Ex 30[37f.]) to imitate this preparation for private use; to burn it was the prerogative of the high priest; the presumption of the Korahites in taking it upon them to burn incense was punished with death (Nu 16; cf. the Chronicler's account of Uzziah's leprosy, 2 Ch 26[16ff.]); Aaron's own sons died for offering it improperly (Lv 10[1f.]).

Nothing shows more clearly the growing importance attached by P to incense than the circumstance that finally an **altar of incense** (מִזְבַּח הַקְּטֹרֶת) is introduced. Of this there is no trace in Solomon's temple (1 K 7[48] being part of what is otherwise known to be a late passage), and in the account of the Tabernacle it is generally admitted that the mention of the incense altar comes in awkwardly at the end (Ex 30[1ff.]). Hence the majority of modern critics are disposed to assign the mention of this altar to a late stratum of P. It is pointed out, for instance, that even in the ritual of the Day of Atonement (Lv 16 [P]) it is not upon an altar but with censers (wh. see) that incense is offered (v.[12]). Even Pseudo-Hecatæus (*ap.* Jos. *c. Ap.* i. 22) mentions nothing as being in the interior of the temple but the candlestick and a golden βωμός, which probably refers to the table of the shewbread (cf. Ezk 41[22] 44[16], with Davidson's

<hr/>

* The *Piel* of this verb is used by the older writers, the *Hiphil* by P and the Chronicler, while in the transition period represented by the compiler of Kings the two formations are used promiscuously.

* 'The root *katara* in Arabic signifies *to exhale an odour in roasting*' (Driver on Am 5[5]).

and Bertholet's notes). Dillmann, who does not share Wellhausen's scepticism as to the existence of an altar of incense, admits that at least Ex 30[10] is an addition to the original law, designed for the purpose of supplementing Lv 16[16b]. On this question, as well as on the position of the altar, and the difficulty occasioned by He 9[4], see **Incense Altar** under art. TABERNACLE.

According to Ex 30[7f.] incense had to be offered on the altar every morning and evening (cf. *Joma* iii. 5). The Mishnic tract *Tamid* gives a full account of the ritual of the morning service, which may possibly be fairly correct for NT times, although it is of little value for our knowledge of the ritual some centuries earlier. We are told, *inter alia*, that it was the custom to decide by lot which of the priests were to perform the various functions (cf. *Joma* ii. 4), amongst which the offering of incense was counted specially solemn, although it was no longer the exclusive prerogative of the high priest. John Hyrcanus (Jos. *Ant.* XIII. x. 3) and Zacharias (Lk 1[9.20]) are both said to have received a divine revelation while engaged in this act. In offering the incense, fire was taken from the altar of burnt-offering and carried into the temple, where it was laid upon the incense altar, and then the incense was emptied from a golden vessel upon the fire. See a full account in Schürer, *HJP* II. i. 295.

The use of incense in the temple may have been partly for antiseptic fumigation, but it is largely explained by the partiality of the Oriental for sweet odours. He enjoys these himself, and he offers them to those whom he desires to honour (cf. Dn 2[46]). In India it was customary to scent the roads when the king went out (Curt. VIII. ix. 23); when Xerxes crossed the Hellespont, incense was burnt on the bridge (Herod. vii. 54); as Alexander the Great marched against Babylon, there were altars erected to him and incense burnt (Curt. v. i. 20). It is easy to see how such customs could be transferred to the cultus, in honour of the object of worship. If this cannot be proved for some other Oriental nations, at least it is certain in the case of such neighbours of Israel as the Phœnicians (2 K 23[5], Jer 7[9] 11[13] 32[29] 44[17ff.], Hos 2[15]), the Babylonians (Herod. i. 183, possibly Is 65[3]), and the Egyptians (Plutarch, *Isid.* 81; Dioscor. i. 24). Cf., further, 1 K 11[8], 2 K 22[17], Jer 1[16] 19[13], Ezk 6[13] 23[41]. In Israel incense was supposed to be specially acceptable to J″ (Dt 33[10]), and, as we have seen, to have an atoning efficacy (Nu 17[11f.] [Eng. 16[46f.]]). See the very full and interesting note of Dillmann, *Ex–Lv*[3], p. 359 f., from which the above illustrations are taken. We may add the explanation of the religious value of frankincense suggested by W. R. Smith (*RS*[1] 406): 'frankincense was the gum of a very holy species of tree, which was collected with religious precautions . . . it appears to have owed its virtue, like the gum of the *samora* tree, to the idea that it was the blood of an animate and divine plant.'

On the symbolical meaning of incense and its ingredients much has been written both in ancient and in modern times that is pure baseless phantasy. In Rev 5[8] incense represents the prayers of the saints (cf. Ps 141[2]). The reading *al* (which is the correct text) does not in the least necessitate a reference to φιάλαι instead of θυμιάματα (see Bousset, *ad loc.*). The point of comparison is probably the ascending to heaven of the smoke of the incense (cf. Dillm. on Lv 1[9]). In Rev 8[3] there was given to the angel much incense that he should add it (ἵνα δώσῃ) to the prayers of the saints, and in v.[4] the smoke of the incense goes up (not 'with' RV, but) 'for (RVm; Bousset 'zu Gunsten') the prayers of the saints,' *i.e.* giving them an extra claim to acceptance.

LITERATURE.—*Oxf. Heb. Lex. s.* לְבוֹנָה; Siegfried-Stade, *s.* קְטֹרֶת, קְטָרָה; Dillmann, *Ex–Lv*[3], 294, 350, 359, also on Dt 33[10]; Driver on Dt 33[10], also *LOT*[6] 37, and art. 'Exodus' in Smith's *DB*[2] p. 1022 f.; Wellhausen, *Proleg.* (1895), 64 ff., *Comp.* 139 ff., *JDTh*, 1877, p. 410 ff., *Reste*[2], 114; Kuenen, *Hexateuch* (Macmillan), 74 f.; Stade, *ZATW* iii. 143 ff., 168 ff.; Nowack, *Heb. Arch.* ii. 246 f.; Benzinger, *Heb. Arch.* 401 f., 444 f.; Schürer, *HJP* II. i. 268, 281, 289, 293, 295; Delitzsch, *Studien*, 113 ff.; Hommel, *AHT* 270 f., 279. See also art. CENSER and literature there cited.   J. A. SELBIE.

INCENSE ALTAR.—See TABERNACLE.

INCEST.—See CRIMES AND PUNISHMENTS, vol. i. p. 521[b].

INCONTINENCY, INCONTINENT.

— Incontinency is the tr[n] of *incontinentia* in 2 Es 5[10], and of ἀκρασία (Vulg. *incontinentia*) in 1 Co 7[5]. In 2 Es the word has probably the general sense of 'absence of self-control,' 'lawlessness,' for so both the Lat. and the Eng. words have sometimes been used. The usual sense, however, has always been 'unchastity,' and that is the meaning in 1 Co.

The Gr. word ἀκρασία occurs also in Mt 23[25], where it is tr[d] 'excess' by both AV and RV (Vulg. *immunditia*). It describes the character of the ἀκρατής (from κρατεῖν, to control), one who wants self-restraint, its opposite being ἐγκράτεια. This ἀκρασία must be distinguished from ἀκρᾱσία, which comes from κεράννυμι, to mix, is associated with ἄκρατος, 'untempered,' and is used by Theophr. (*C.P.* III. ii. 5) of a bad (lit. 'badly mixed') climate.

The adj. 'incontinent' occurs only in 2 Ti 3[3] as tr[n] of ἀκρατής, which has probably the general meaning of 'unrestrained,' 'uncontrolled' (RV 'without self-control'). It is scarcely possible, however, to find an instance of 'incontinent' in this general sense; and it is probable that Wyc. and Rhem., from whom AV accepted the word, understood the Vulg. *incontinentes* in the sense of 'unchaste.' Tind. (whom the other versions follow) has 'ryatours.'   J. HASTINGS.

INCREDULITY.—In 2 Es 15[3] the Lat. *incredulitates dicentium* is rendered 'the incredulity of them that speak against thee.' The word means no more than 'unbelief' (as RV). The Rhem. NT, which confesses itself a translation of 'the old vulgar Latin text, not the common Greek text,' makes frequent use of the word. Thus Mt 13[58] 'And he wrought not many miracles there because of their incredulity'; 17[20] 'Then came the disciples to Jesus secretly, and said, Why could not we cast him out? Jesus said to them, Because of your incredulity'; He 3[19] 'And we see that they could not enter in, because of incredulitie.' In the same version *incredulous* occurs no less frequently, as Mk 9[19] 'O incredulous generation'; Lk 1[17]; Jn 3[36] 'he that is incredulous to the Sonne shal not see life'; 20[27] 'be not incredulous but faithful'; He 11[31] 'By faith, Rahab the harlot perished not with the incredulous.'

Incredulity is used in the same way in Preface to AV 1611, 'it is a fault of incredulitie to doubt of those things that are evident.'   J. HASTINGS.

INDIA (הֹדּוּ, ἡ Ἰνδική).—This name, which in the OT is found only in Est 1[1] 8[9] (cf. 1 Es 3[2], Ad. Est 13[1] 16[1]), represents the Old Persian *Hind'u* and the Sansk. *Sindhu* (=*sea* or *great river*), and is applied, not to the peninsula of Hindostan, but to the country immediately adjoining the Indus, *i.e.* the Punjab, and perhaps also Scinde. This is the portion of I. which was first known to the Greeks, and which is described by Herodotus (iii.|94, 98) as forming the most easterly region of the empire of Darius; Elsewhere (vii. 9) he names I. and Ethiopia as being among the most distant parts of the empire; and similarly in Est the dominions of Ahasuerus (Xerxes) are said to extend from I. to Ethiopia, comprising 127 provinces. At a later

period we have evidence of intercourse between I. and Syria, in the allusion to the Indian drivers in charge of the war elephants of Antiochus V. (1 Mac 6³⁷). In 1 Mac 8⁸, indeed, I. is said to have been a part of the dominions of Antiochus the Great, taken from him by the Romans and given to Eumenes, king of Pergamum. But neither Antiochus nor Eumenes can really have had possessions in India. The statement must therefore be due to the inaccuracy of the historian; unless, as has been conjectured, we should correct the text and read 'Ionia and Mysia' instead of 'India and Media.'

But although the name I. occurs only in the later Jewish literature, the products of the country were known to the Hebrews at a much earlier date. Many modern scholars have identified the Pison and the gold-producing Havilah of Gn 2¹¹ with the Indus and I. (so Ges. *Thes.*; but cf. Dillm. and Del. *ad loc.*). This view is as old as the Targ. Jerushalmi, which in Gn 2¹¹ 10⁷ renders Havilah by Hindeki, while in Targ. Jon. of Is 11¹¹, Jer 13²³, Hindeki represents Cush. We meet with Indian articles and Indian words in the accounts of the foreign trade of Solomon. The ships from Ophir brought *almug* trees (1 K 10¹¹ אַלְמֻגִּים, 2 Ch 2⁸ [Heb. 7] 9¹⁰ אַלְגּוּמִּים), perhaps sandalwood; and the navy of Tarshish (1 K 10²²) imported ivory (שֶׁנְהַבִּים, ? cf. Sansk. *ibhas*, elephant), apes (קֹפִים = Ind. *kapi*, cf. Halévy, *Mél. de crit.* 81), and peacocks (תֻּכִּיִּים = Malabar *tôgai*, cf. Ges. *Thes.*). See Cheyne and Hommel in *Expos. Times*, July and August, 1898, pp. 470, 524. It is probable also that Indian wares were included in the merchandise of Tyre, whose extensive caravan trade is described in Ezk 27. According to v.¹⁵ the men of Dedan brought presents of ivory and ebony, products either of I. or Ethiopia; cassia and calamus (v.¹⁹) are spoken of by the ancients as coming from I., and perhaps the 'bright iron' was imported from the same country (see Smend). Real knowledge of I. in more Western countries dates from the time of Alexander's conquests, and of the travels of Megasthenes (*c.* B.C. 300), whose works were continually quoted by later Gr. writers. But though it appears that a regular trade with I. by way of the Red Sea was carried on in the Græco-Roman period (cf. *Periplus Mar. Eryth.* 37. 44); and individual Indians, and even Indian embassies, are mentioned as visiting the Rom. Empire (cf. *Mon. Anc.* v. 50, 51; Suet. *Aug.* 21; Dio Cass. liv. 9); yet it is probable that at the beginning of our era the knowledge of that country was but slight, and it is a mistake to suppose that Indian thought can have exerted any appreciable influence upon the West by that time (cf. Schürer, *HJP* II. ii. 215 f.; Lightfoot, *Colossians*, 389 ff.). In particular, Zeller (*Phil. d. Griech.* III. ii. 223) denies that any trace of Buddhists is to be found in Gr. literature before the middle of the 2nd cent. A.D.   H. A. WHITE.

INDIFFERENT.—'It is a striking testimony,' says Trench (*Select Glossary*, p. 111), 'of the low general average which we have come to assume common to most things, that a thing which does not *differ* from others, is thereby qualified as poor; a sentence of depreciation is pronounced upon it when it is declared to be *indifferent*.' And he points out that the same feeling embodies itself in Greek 'at the other end' when διαφέρειν means *præstare* and τὰ διαφέροντα *præstantiora*. But this is a modern fault. About 1611 and earlier, to be called 'indifferent' was to be highly complimented, for it meant to be *impartial*, not making a difference where none existed. In the *Joint Attestation of Several Bishops and Learned Divines of the Church of England, avowing that her Doctrine was confirmed, and her Discipline was not impeached, by the Synod of Dort*, we read, 'As for ourselves,

in the ingenuity of our conscience, we herein do not decline the judgment of any indifferent dispassionate man; and such we hope this true and plain narration will satisfy' (M. Fuller, *Life of Bp. Davenant*, p. 107). Tindale, in *The Obedience of a Christian Man* (*Works*, i. 236), says of God, 'Neither is there any respect of persons with him; that is, he is indifferent and not partial; as great in his sight is a servant as a master.' The adj. occurs in Sir 42⁵, where 'merchants' indifferent selling' is praised (B περὶ ἀδιαφόρου πράσεως καὶ ἐμπόρων, A℧C διαφόρου and om. καί, RV 'Of indifferent selling of merchants,' so Cowley-Neubauer after Heb. text). The meaning is clearly 'impartial.' But even Tindale, in a note to Ex 12³, says, 'That I here cal a shepe, is in Ebrue a word indifferent to a shepe and a gotte both.' Then in his 'Godly Letter' (*Works*, iii. 177) Knox represents 'the haill Counsaile' as saying of Grindall, Lever, and others of the Protestant preachers, 'Thay wald heir no mo of thair sermonis: they wer but indifferent fellowis; (yea, and sum of thame eschameit not to call thame pratting knaves).' And at a later time Thomas Adams (on 2 P 1⁴) speaks of 'idle indifferents, that do neither good nor harm.'

The adv. *indifferently* occurs in the Communion Service in the Prayer (1662) for the King and his officers 'that they may truly and indifferently administer justice.' Joy, in his *Apology to Tindale* (Arber's ed. p. 4), says, 'I desier every indifferent reder to iuge indifferently.' So Tind. in *Prologe* to Deut. 'god is lorde above all lordes and loveth all his servauntes indifferently, as well the poor and feble and the straunger, as the rich and mightye'; which is a recollection of his trⁿ of Ja 1⁵ 'Yf eny of you lacke wysdome, let him axe of God which geveth to all men indifferentlie, and casteth no man in the teth.' And on the miracle of the Ten Lepers, Bp. Hall says (*Works*, ii. 154), 'The miracle indifferently wrought upon all, is differently taken.'

The subst. *indifferency* is also found in the Pr. Bk. of 1604, in the King's Proclamation for the Uniformity, etc., 'the indifferency and uprightness of our Judgment.' Cf. Knox, *Works*, iii. 271, 'I knowledge and confesse . . . the lacke of fervencye in reproving synne, the lacke of indifferency in feedyng those that were hongrye, and the lacke of diligence in the execution of mine office.' But Hall uses the word nearly in the mod. sense (*Works*, ii. 148), 'How many are there that thinke there is no wisdome but in a dull indifferency?'   J. HASTINGS.

INDITE.—To 'indite' a letter is now to write it, and even so the expression is somewhat old-fashioned; but formerly it was to dictate or at least compose, and the 'inditer' is distinguished from the writer. Thus in Pref. to AV 1611, the Translators, describing the Scriptures as 'a fountaine of most pure water springing up unto everlasting life,' add, 'And what marvaile? The originall thereof being from heaven, not from earth; the authour being God, not man; the enditer the holy spirit, not the wit of the Apostles or Prophets; the Pen-men such as were sanctified from the wombe, and endewed with a principall portion of God's spirit.' So in Ps 45¹ 'My heart is inditing a good matter,' is naturally followed by 'my tongue is the pen of a ready writer.'

word (with note 'I have received by divine inspiration in my hart and cogitation a most high Mysterie'); Bish. 'My heart is inditing of a good matter.' Mod. expositors translate more literally: Del. 'My heart bubbles over with a goodly word'; Per. 'My heart is overflowing with a goodly matter'; Cheyne, 'My heart bubbles with goodly words'; Kay, 'My heart is teeming with a good word'; Kirkp. 'My heart bubbleth over with goodly words'; Kautzsch, 'Mein Herz wallt über von lieblicher Rede'; Wellh.-Furness, 'My heart overflows with a theme that is good'; RV, 'My heart overfloweth with a goodly matter'; Driver, 'My heart is astir with a goodly matter.'

The Eng. word comes from Low Lat. *indictare* (a frequentative of *indicere*, to proclaim), and it entered the Eng. lang. at first in the French form *endicter*, 'indite' being a later spelling in imitation of the Latin, while 'dite' is a vernacular shortening. Knox has the form 'dite' (which he spells 'dyte'), as *Hist.* 214, 'those Prayers were dyted unto the people by the holy Ghost, before they came to the uttermost of trouble, to assure them, that God, by whose Spirit the Prayer was dyted, would not contemne the same in the midst of their calamities.' Thomas Fuller uses 'endite,' as in *Holy State*, iv. 5 (p. 261), 'More hold is then to be taken of a few words casually uttered, then of set solemn speeches, which rather shew men's arts then their natures, as endited rather from their brains then hearts.'

The same verb meant also to *accuse* (after the Lat.); but now a distinction is made, the verb to accuse, though pronounced the same, being spelt 'indict.' Golding, in *Calvin's Job* (on 32[1-3]), has 'so then, what remayneth, but too learne first and formoste too condemne our selves, and too bring our inditement alwayes readie made, when we come before God, and too say, that we be wretched sinners.' On the other hand, Elyot (*The Governour*, ii. 343) has 'Plato (or rather Socrates, Plato indictynge).' But Fuller, *Holy Warre*, iii. 16, p. 134, spells the word in the mod. way, 'indicted by his conscience for his cruelty.' RV has used the subst. 'indictment' in Job 31[35] 'O that I had one to hear me! . . . and that I had the indictment which mine adversary hath written' for AV 'and that mine adversary had written a book.'   J. HASTINGS.

INFIDEL, INFIDELITY.—An 'infidel' in our modern speech is one who deliberately rejects the Faith; but at one time a person might be called an 'infidel' who had never heard it. *Infidelis* in eccles. Latin simply meant 'unbelieving,' and 'infidel' carried the same purely negative meaning. Thus Tindale, in his general *Prologe* to the Pent., says, 'Behold how soberly and how circumspectly both Abraham and also Isaac behave them selves amonge the infideles'; and in Rhem. NT the tr[n] of Ro 15[31] is 'Helpe me in your praiers for me to God, that I may be delivered from the infidels that are in Jewrie'; while Hooker (*Eccles. Polity*, III. viii. 6) speaks of 'Festus, a mere natural man, an infidel, a Roman, one whose ears were unacquainted with such matters.' Hence RV changes 'infidel' of 2 Co 6[15], 1 Ti 5[8] into 'unbeliever,' which is all that the Gr. word (ἄπιστος) means.

So 'infidelity' was once no more than 'unbelief,' as the marg. note to Lv 7[5] in Matthew's Bible, 'Trespace after the order of the scrypture signifyeth somtyme all the lyffe past which we have lyved in infidelyte, being ignoraunt of the veritie, not only in doyng open synnes, but also when we have walked in oure awne rightwesnes'; and still more clearly in Fuller, *Holy State*, iv. 18, p. 335, 'After his [Gustavus Adolphus'] death, how did men struggle to keep him alive in their reports! partly out of good will, which made them kindle new hopes of his life at every spark of probability, partly out of infidelity that his death could be true.' This is all that 'infidelity' means in 2 Es 7[44] ('incredulitas').   J. HASTINGS.

INGATHERING, FEAST OF.—See TABERNACLES (FEAST OF).

INHABIT.—We do not now use 'inhabit' intransitively. Hence RV changes 1 Ch 5[9] 'And eastward he inhabited unto the entering in of the wilderness' into 'he dwelt.' Cf. Pr. Bk. 1552, Act of Uniformity (Keeling, p. vii), 'all and every person, and persons, inhabiting within this realm'; and Defoe, *Crusoe*, p. 510, 'There are many Travellers, who have wrote the History of their Voyages and Travels this way, that it would be very little Diversion to any Body, to give a long Account of the Places we went to, and the People who inhabit there.' Nor do we now speak of a single person inhabiting a place, as Jer 48[18] 'Thou daughter that dost inhabit Dibon,' though the construction may be defended on the ground that 'daughter' stands for the whole people (RV 'O thou daughter that dwellest in Dibon').

Figurative examples of the word are: (1) Ps 22[3] 'O thou that inhabitest the praises of Israel' (יוֹשֵׁב תְּהִלּוֹת, RVm 'art enthroned upon'), a bold adaptation, says Kirkpatrick, of the phrase 'that sittest enthroned upon the cherubim' (2 S 6[2], 2 K 19[15], Ps 80[1] 99[1]), the praise-songs of Israel being regarded as clouds of incense which form J"'s throne. Cheyne (*in loc.*) sees in the phrase a poetic glorifying of the 'old mythic phrase.' The cherubim were the forces of nature; but J" is not merely a God of force, He is a God of praise-producing loving-kindness. See also Cheyne in *Expos.* 3rd ser. vii. 20 ff. (2) Is 57[15] 'the high and lofty One that inhabiteth eternity, whose name is Holy' (שֹׁכֵן עַד). This tr[n] is after LXX κατοικῶν τὸν αἰῶνα and Vulg. *habitans æternitatem*, and is first used in Geneva Bible 'that inhabiteth the eternitie' (Wyc. 'wonende the everelastingte,' 1388 'that dwellith in everlastyngnesse'). Modern expositors translate more directly, as Del. 'the eternally-dwelling One'; Cheyne and Orelli, 'who dwelleth for ever'; Skinner, 'that sitteth (enthroned) for ever.'

The old and rare form **inhabitance** is found in Wis 12[7m]. 'new inhabitance' for text 'a worthy colony' (ἀξία ἀποικία). So Beaumont and Fletcher, *Sea Voyage*, iv. 1—

'Here's nothing, sir, but poverty and hunger;
No promise of inhabitance; neither track of beast.'

Inhabiter is used for 'inhabitant' in Rev 8[13] 12[12]. It occurs in Coverdale, as Is 26[9] 'For . . . the inhabitours of the earth lerne righteuousnesse'; and 40[22] 'all the inhabitours of the worlde are in comparison of him but as greshoppers'; cf. Pr. Bk. Ps 75[4] 'The earth is weak and all the inhabiters thereof.' The fem. form **inhabitress** occurs in Jer 10[17m], an attempt to show the gender of the Heb. word used in the passage. Cf. Chapman, *Hymne to Venus*—

'An inhabitresse
On this thy wood-crowned hill.'
    J. HASTINGS.

INHERITANCE. — The English word 'inheritance' represents, in the OT, the terms חֵלֶק, יְרֻשָּׁה, מוֹרָשָׁה, and נַחֲלָה. Of these, however, the first is more frequently (and properly) rendered 'portion' (LXX μερίς), and the second and third are rare. The last mentioned occurs nearly two hundred times. Although the common term for the expression of the idea of 'inheritance' proper, or estate which descends to the heir of the last holder, נַחֲלָה need not imply this, and, in ordinary biblical usage, signifies possession generally. The same remark applies to the NT (and LXX) term κληρονομία (cf. the use of 'inherit' and derivatives, *e.g.* in Shaks. . . . 'the great globe itself, yea, all which it inherit'—*Tempest*, iv. 1, also *Hamlet*, i. 1, etc.). At the same time this idea remains, though latent, in both terms, and may in certain connexions of thought become explicit.

i. *Old Testament.* — For the Hebrew law and practice regulating succession see art. HEIR. From these it is evident how true is the remark of Keil, that Israel was 'essentially a land-holding people.' In her case, however, social institutions and usages appear as charged throughout with a religious significance, arising in this instance from the fact that the possession of a national territory, on which the theocracy should be maintained, was among the most elementary and indispensable conditions for the fulfilment of her destiny. The 'land of promise' (He 11[9]), accordingly, holds a prominent place among the blessings represented as assured to her from the first. It is the burden of the patriarchal covenants (Gn 15[18-21] 26[3] 28[13]) ; a renewed pledge of its acquisition lies behind the exodus from Egypt (Ex 6[8]) ; the entrance of the people upon possession, although not effected without fierce and protracted warfare, is due rather to the interposition of their God on their behalf (Jos 21[43-45], Ps 44[1-3]) ; and the subsequent division of the land among the several tribes, clans, and families is provided for by detailed regulations bearing divine sanction (Nu 32. 34, Jos 18[4-9]), and is finally accomplished by lot (Jos 14[2]), the 'whole disposing' whereof is 'of the Lord.' Obtained thus by divine infeftment, the land is regarded as held thereafter conditionally upon fidelity on the part of the people to the covenant under which it has accrued to them, and as bound up in the closest way with their moral history. It is 'defiled' by their crimes and impieties (Lv 18[25], Jer 16[18]) ; may even, by a quasi-personification, be said to 'sin' with its sinful inhabitants (Dt 24[4]) ; and divine punishment takes the form, now of blight and famine overtaking the devoted land for the people's sake (Dt 11[8ff.]), now of their forfeiture of it outright (Dt 4[26ff.]). On the other hand, reinstatement in the divine favour is signified by restoration to the land and to its peaceful enjoyment. Also, inasmuch as the election of God is 'without repentance,' it appears as His purpose that His people should hold it 'for ever' (Gn 13[15] etc.). The portion allotted to each several tribe even is to be that tribe's inalienable possession (Nu 36[1-12])—an idea which underlies the remarkable provisions connected with the Jubilee Year, and which may have dictated the severe condemnation pronounced (Dt 19[14], Hos 5[10]) upon the removing of a neighbour's landmark (cf. Driver, *Deut. in loc.*, however, and Knobel quoted there). Yet withal J[″] remains ultimate owner or inheritor here. The land is 'the inheritance of J[″]' (Ex 15[17], 1 S 26[19]). 'The inheritance is mine, and ye are strangers and sojourners with me' (Lv 25[23]).

Thus far the land as such, and as the scene of God's fellowship with His people, constitutes the 'inheritance,' which may be regarded as pertaining either, ultimately and absolutely, to Him, or, derivatively and conditionally, to them. So concrete an idea, however, determined thus religiously, could scarcely fail in course of time to be still further spiritualized, as indeed appears in two directions. This is not the place to inquire how far the conception even as already defined may represent the reflection of subsequent modes of thought upon the conditions of an earlier time ; but in any case in certain later writings it undergoes a further development. On the one hand, OT faith learns to claim not the land but J[″] Himself, fellowship with whom within its borders lends it its significance and value, as the true and proper 'inheritance.' Probably we are to find the immediate suggestion of this way of thinking in the provision by which the priests (Nu 18[20]) and the Levites generally (Dt 18[2]) were to have no territorial inheritance allotted to them : J[″] was to be their inheritance. That is to say, their portion was to consist of the altar-dues and first-fruits (Dt 18[1-5]) offered by the Israelites to J[″], 'the service of the god of the land' being 'a burden on the land' (W. R. Smith, *RS* p. 229). From this the step was a short one to the employment of the term to signify that enjoyment of God which is the ob-

ject of religious faith and hope always (cf. Ps 16[5]). In any case by the time of Jeremiah the conception of J[″] as the 'portion' of His people was a common one (Jer 10[16] 51[19]), while in certain of the Psalms even individual faith claims Him thus (73[26] 119[57] 142[5]). From the other side, again, the original signification of the term gives way similarly. J[″]'s 'inheritance' ceases to be the land His people occupy, and becomes rather the people itself. Israel is, in a special sense, His own, brought out of Egypt 'to be unto Him a people of inheritance' (Dt 4[20]), 'chosen to be a peculiar people unto himself, above all peoples that are upon the face of the earth' (Dt 7[6])—'J[″]'s portion is His people ; Jacob is the lot of His inheritance' (Dt 32[9])—a conception which broadens out under the influence of the later universalism until it includes the Gentiles also (Is 19[25] 47[6] 63[17], Ps 2[8]). Here the idea has parted with its original associations altogether. In place of attaching to what is at most only a fundamental condition of the realization of the covenant, it now expresses that mutual appropriation and enjoyment of each other on the part of God and His people which is the essence of the covenant itself. Still, this by no means represents the ordinary usage of the term anywhere in the OT. Even when it becomes most highly volatilized, so to say, OT thinking remains charged with elements which belong to the outward conditions amid which it has arisen. The fellowship of God and His people, even in its perfect form, is always represented as to be maintained in the territory originally assured to them ; and to the last it is an essential feature in the picture of the Messianic time that the people shall then at length enter upon sure and peaceful possession of their own land (Is 60[21], Jer 23[8], Ps 37[9] etc., To 4[12]), where they shall enjoy the immediate presence of their God and serve Him in righteousness (Ezk 37[21-28] etc.).

ii. *New Testament.*—In the NT use of the term these limitations naturally disappear. Here also hope grounded on divine promises retains the central place in the religious life (Ro 8[24], cf. He 11), and its content as a fellowship with Himself into which God graciously introduces men is the same always ; but the external conditions amid which in the OT this is realized remain in the NT merely as a metaphorical colouring in the language expressive of the final spiritual good made available through Jesus Christ. Thus our Lord's saying, 'Blessed are the meek : for they shall *inherit the earth*' (Mt 5[5]), may be regarded merely as a figurative mode of signifying the fulness of life and blessedness to which faith ultimately brings men (so Meyer and others ; for a more literal interpretation see *Expositor's Greek Testament, in loc.*). Elsewhere Jesus speaks of the faithful inheriting 'the kingdom' (Mt 25[34]), which, in accordance with His general teaching, is not merely already come, but also, and even more, awaits realization in the future. And again, He represents this as synonymous with entering upon 'life eternal' (Mt 25[46], cf. Mk 10[17]), but neither term does He define more fully. In the earlier apostolic writings a similar indeterminateness of usage prevails. In Ja, for example, that which faith inherits is 'the kingdom which God hath promised to them that love Him' (2[5]), or again, 'the crown of life' which has been similarly promised (1[12]), both expressions being employed to denote generally the ultimate full possession of salvation. In 1 P the connexion of ideas is only slightly more elaborate. Here singular stress is laid upon the hope which lies at the heart of faith always. Possession of it is the distinctive note of the Christian life (1[3] 3[15]) ; it looks towards the Parousia and the 'grace' which shall be 'manifested' then (1[7, 8, 13] 5[1, 4]) ; and just as it appears to the writer that the 'people of God' has now first, through Christ's death and resurrection, been truly constituted (2^{4-10}), so also he represents their 'inheritance' as now at length fully discovered and secured (1^{3-5}). It has been suggested (by Weiss, *NT Theologie*, § 50 (c) Anm. 4) that the characterization of the 'inheritance' as 'incorruptible, undefiled, and that fadeth not away,' contains a covert allusion to various OT phrases applied to the land of Israel (Is 24^4, Jer 2^7, Is $40^{6ff.}$); and this is possible. But no closer definition of it is given. As synonyms the expressions 'life' (3^7, cf. 4^6) and 'glory' or 'crown of glory' ($5^{1.\ 4.\ 10}$) are employed, but without being explained further

In the hands of two of the NT writers, however, the idea in question receives much fuller treatment. From his peculiar point of view, the author of the Epistle to the Hebrews is naturally led to make not a little of a conception which had played so large a part in the world of OT faith (see note on κληρονομία in Westcott's *Hebrews*, p. 167 f.). That which constitutes the 'inheritance' of the believer is described variously as 'the blessing,' *i.e.* the covenant (12^{17}), 'salvation' (negatively, from death and every evil, $2^{14.\ 15}\ 5^7$; positively, as the securing of man in his eternal destiny, $2^3\ 5^9\ 9^{28}$), 'the promises' (6^{12}), and otherwise. But, in order to apprehend the idea as it presents itself to this writer's mind, it must be subsumed under and interpreted in harmony with the general conceptions and argument of the Epistle. Religion with him is regarded in the light of a covenant into which God has graciously entered with men. Essentially this has been one and the same from the beginning, but historically it has embodied itself in two forms, the Sinaitic and that made through Christ, so diverse in various respects that they may be distinguished as the 'first' and 'second' covenants (8^7), of which the earlier proved ineffective and only the later has truly realized the purposes which such an arrangement had in view. In one sense the covenant may be considered as its own end. As signifying a state of relatedness in which God becomes to men their God and they become His people, it stands for that which in itself makes great part of their blessedness, and which is only secured in the 'new covenant' (8^{13}), under the provisions of which the conscience is cleansed from dead works and the worshipper has boldness to enter into the holiest ($9^{14.\ 19}$ etc., compared with $7^{11.\ 18}$ etc.). But chiefly it is regarded as contemplating that which lies beyond itself. In its later form especially, as sealed by a 'better sacrifice' than before (9^{23}), it rests also upon 'better promises' ($8^{6.\ 10-12}$), the fulfilment of which introduces the people once for all into a sphere in which all their hopes and needs are satisfied. Through this 'eternal covenant' (13^{20}) administered by Jesus (9^{15}, where the author, through playing on the double sense of διαθήκη as meaning both 'covenant' and 'testament,' brings the idea of succession, namely on the death of 'the testator,' into view for the moment) believers receive the promise of the eternal inheritance (9^{15}); a consummation otherwise described as reaching the heavenly city (11^{16}) or the city that hath the foundations (11^{10}), or receiving the kingdom that cannot be shaken (12^{28}), or having the world to come subjected to them (2^5 etc.), or entering upon the rest of God. In such expressions the influence of OT modes of thought is obvious, and the last especially forms the subject of a remarkable passage (3. 4) in which the writer betrays almost more fully than anywhere his sense alike of the continuity of salvation under the old covenant and the new, and of the final completeness with which the latter realizes it. When Israel originally entered upon their inheritance and 'possessed the land and dwelt therein,' J″,

says the historian, 'gave them rest round about according to all that He sware unto their fathers' (Jos $21^{43.\ 44}$). But, as the author of the Epistle recognizes, it proved a delusive rest (4^8). Enemies still infesting the land, war waged from without, civil strife and manifold evils in every age disturbed the condition of peace and blessedness assured to them, and which is here (4^{3-5}) represented as a participation in the deep tranquil satisfaction with which God Himself rests in the enjoyment of the works of His hands. Nevertheless, the divine purpose cannot be defeated (4^6); it can only at most be temporarily suspended, and that which Israel through unbelief ($3^{10.\ 16.\ 17}\ 4^{11}$) came short of 'we who believe' (*i.e.* in the 'good tidings preached unto us,' 4^2) attain to (4^3). To put it otherwise, we 'inherit the promises' (6^{12}) in their full and final expression. As has been said (Davidson, *Hebrews*, p. 99), 'the mere land of Canaan was never in itself all that was understood either by those to whom it was promised or by God who promised it, when it was named as Israel's heritage. The patriarchs and people certainly looked to the possession of the land, but the idea they attached to it, or the light in which they regarded it, was that of a settled place of abode with God, where He would be fully present, and where they would find repose in His fellowship. All those religious ideas, dimly perhaps, yet in longing and imagination, clustered about it which we now attach to the heavenly world.' And all this it is, hardly to be defined more narrowly, which faith is heir to.

In the usage of St. Paul, again, the 'inheritance' often signifies the object of believing hope generally (Ac $20^{32}\ 26^{18}$, Eph $1^{11.\ 14}$, Col $1^{12}\ 3^{24}$). Also, believers are said to be heirs of 'eternal life' (Tit 3^7), or, more frequently, of 'the kingdom' (1 Co $6^{9.\ 10}\ 15^{50}$, Eph 5^5), both expressions being employed in the indeterminate manner common in the Gospels and elsewhere. When he treats of the idea more at large it is in connexion with one or other of two lines of thought. The first of these concerns his anti-Judaic polemic. Quite in the manner of the author of the Ep. to the Hebrews he insists upon the divine 'promises' as lying at the basis of all true faith and hope toward God. The possession of these differentiates the Jew from the Gentile (Ro $3^{2.\ 3}$); the covenants are essentially 'covenants of promise' (Eph 2^{12}); while the entrance of the law itself in the course of their historical fulfilment is to be regarded as a mere episode, by no means designed to supersede the promises, but rather to make more manifest the grace they contain and which bestows the inheritance (Ro 4). The import of the promise, however, is stated as being that Abraham should be 'heir of the world' ($v.^{13}$), an interpretation of the original covenant expressing in a remarkable way the universal purpose which lay within it. But in this sense the covenant is fulfilled only in Christ (Gal 3^{16}), with whom again, in St. Paul's thinking, believers are indissolubly bound up (Gal 3^9, Ro $4^{16}\ 8^{17}$); and perhaps, although it must be confessed he does not do this explicitly, it is under this point of view that we ought to bring his references to the inheriting of 'the kingdom.' It is Christ who, as Abraham's seed, has in the first instance assumed the rule of the Messianic kingdom (Gal 3^{16}), and believers, as reckoned within that seed (Gal 3^{29}) and called to His fellowship (1 Co 1^9), may be said to share in His rule (1 Co 4^8, Ro 5^{17}), in which, in accordance with Eastern modes of thought, the prerogative of judging is included (1 Co $6^{2.\ 3}$; cf. Mt 19^{28}).

More distinctive of this apostle still, however, is his attaching of the idea in question to that of the sonship of believers. For his doctrine under this head see art. ADOPTION. What is of importance here to note is, that in his view sonship carries with it an indefeasible right to the inheritance—'if sons, then heirs' (Gal 4⁷). As Weiss expresses it, 'as justification is the security for life, so its result, adoption, is the security for participation in the divine δόξα as the second chief part of Christian hope in which the whole blessedness and glory of the future eternal life is comprehended in one great view' (*Op. cit.* § 97 (c)). As Son, Christ is destined to glory, and first through His resurrection attains to it (Ro 1⁴); and so also believers, who bear 'the image of the heavenly,' are in the resurrection conformed to the 'likeness of the Son of God,' so that he becomes 'the firstborn among many brethren' (1 Co 15⁴⁹, Ro 8²⁹). The transformation of the 'body of our humiliation,' accordingly, holds an emphatic place in the inheritance which St. Paul teaches (Ph 3²¹); while along with this goes a perfect inward assimilation to the mind of the Lord, and beyond it lies that which the apostle describes as 'glory' (see art. under that title), a spiritual condition to which God's children are destined (Ro 8³⁰ 9²³), in which the mystery of their adoption is finally disclosed (Ro 8¹⁹, Col 3⁴), in the freedom and blessedness of which creation generally will share (Ro 8¹⁹ff.), and which constitutes the ultimate aim of the divine counsel (1 Co 2⁷). Of the inheritance thus conceived, the Spirit, who attests our adoption (Ro 8¹⁶), is meanwhile the seal and earnest (Eph 1¹⁴ 4³⁰).

Finally, in the Apoc. the faithful are said to 'inherit all (or 'these') things' (21⁷). What these 'things' consist of is to be gathered from the book generally. Chiefly they appear to embrace 'life'—that life 'which is life indeed' (cf. the recurring representation of the idea in such figures as the 'tree of life' 22², the 'water of life' 22¹, the 'crown of life' which the conquerors carry off 2¹⁰ 3¹¹, the 'book of life' in which their names are written 21²⁷ etc.); perfect holiness (2¹⁷ 3⁴. ⁵ 4⁴ 6¹¹ 7⁹ 19⁸); immediate fellowship with God (7¹⁵ 21³. ²² 22³), and the vision of His face (22⁴). A royal dignity (22⁵) and glory (22²⁸) also pertain to that which awaits the believer, along with deliverance from all pain and want and death (7¹⁶ 21⁴). It is a blessedness (14¹³ 19⁹ 22¹⁴) which is complete and eternal.   ALEX. MARTIN.

INIQUITY.—See SIN.

INJURIOUS.

INJURIOUS.—Like the Fr. *injurieux*, 'injurious' formerly had the meaning of 'insulting,' as well as its mod. meaning of 'hurtful.' Hence in Sir 8¹¹ and 1 Ti 1¹³ the adj. ὑβριστής which means 'insolent' is tr⁴ in AV 'injurious.' The same adj. occurs in Ro 1³⁰, where AV has 'despiteful,' RV 'insolent.' RV gives 'insolent' in Sir, but retains 'injurious' in 1 Ti. The meaning of the Eng. word may be illustrated from Shaks. *II Henry VI.* I. iv. 51—

    'Injurious duke, that threatest where's no cause

and Pope, *Iliad*, ii. 274—

    'Thus with injurious taunts attacked the throne.

The adv. was used in the same sense, as Hall, *Works*, iii. 966, 'Humane reason is apt to be injuriously saucy, in ascribing those things to an ordinary course of natural causes, which the God of nature doth by supernatural Agents.' And the subst. 'injury,' as Bacon, 'He fell to bitter invectives against the French king, and spake all the injuries he could devise of Charles.'   J. HASTINGS.

INK

INK is mentioned once in OT (Jer 36¹⁸), where Baruch says that he wrote Jeremiah's prophecies 'with ink (דְּיוֹ, perhaps from a root signifying *slowly flowing*) in the book.' W. R. Smith (*OTJC*² 71 n.) refers to Ex 32³³ and Nu 5²³ for evidence that the old Hebrew ink (derived from lamp-black [?]) could be washed off, and as the foundation of the Rabbinical prejudice against the use of a mordant in ink. From the bright colours that still survive in some papyri, it is evident that the ink used by the Egyptians must have been of a superior kind. The NT term for 'ink,' occurring three times (2 Co 3³, 2 Jn ¹², 3 Jn ¹³), is μέλαν (lit. 'black,' Lat. *atramentum*), which is also a classical term (Plato, *Phædr.* 276 C; Demos. *de Coron.* 313. 11; Plut. *Mor.* 841). See, further, under WRITING.
     J. A. SELBIE.

INKHORN.

INKHORN.—In one of Ezekiel's visions (Ezk 9². ³. ¹¹) a man appears with a scribe's inkhorn (קֶסֶת הַסֹּפֵר) by his side (lit. 'upon his loins,' בְּמָתְנָיו). The 'inkhorn' consisted of a case for the reed pens, with a cup or bulb for holding the ink, near the upper end of the case. It was carried in the girdle (hence the above expression). See illustration under art. DRESS, vol. i. p. 626ᵇ; and cf. Benzinger, *Heb. Archäol.* 290.   J. A. SELBIE.

INN.

INN.—Owing to the prevalence of hospitality in the East, down to our own times, the growth of places of public entertainment has been slow; and to this day, save in parts frequented by tourists, anything corresponding to our inn or hotel is entirely unknown (see HOSPITALITY).

The word 'inn' first occurs in our English Bible (AV) in Gn 42²⁷ as the equivalent of מָלוֹן, and is similarly employed in Gn 43²¹, Ex 4²⁴ (LXX κατάλυμα). In other passages (Jos 4³. ⁸, 2 K 19²³, Is 10²⁹, Jer 9²) מָלוֹן is rendered 'lodging-place'; and the Revisers have adopted this translation uniformly throughout. This does not imply a building of any kind, but only the place where travellers, or carriers of merchandise, were wont, with their caravans, to pass the night. לִין or לוּן appears to have been used in a sense equivalent to that of the Arab *bât*, and the corresponding participial, *mabît*, is a night-lodging. The Arabs also use the word *manzil* in a similar sense. It is 'the place of alighting,' and is now mainly employed for the house where the traveller spends the night; but it still retains its application to the spot where a company of wayfarers may have spent the hours of darkness. Occasionally one may encounter in the East a scene which probably reproduces the chief features of that mentioned in Gn 42²⁷. Near by a well or fountain, or on the bank of a stream, as the day is closing, the caravan will halt. The bales of goods are lifted from the beasts of burden, and placed so as to shelter the men from the night air. The animals, having been watered, are tethered around, and supplied with fodder which they have carried. The men draw close around a fire, where, having partaken of simple fare from their provender bags, they pass an hour in conversation or in hearing or telling tales, and then lie down under their wraps to sleep till daybreak. The place thus occupied is called *el-manzil*; the Hebrew would have called it *mālōn*.

But the development of commerce would necessitate at a very early time some better means of protecting the goods and the lives of the merchants, especially in the more remote and desolate parts, where it might be needful to rest the caravan over night. That buildings were soon erected for this purpose, we have no direct proof; but it is possible that the 'lodging-place' of wayfaring men' in the wilderness, referred to in Jer 9², may have been such an establishment. Chimham, the son of Barzillai, who returned to Jerusalem with David (2 S 19³⁷⁻⁴⁰), is supposed by some to have reared some structure near to Bethlehem, which in Jeremiah's time was known as גֵּרוּת כִּמְהָם *Gērūth chimham*. AV renders this 'habitation of Chimham'; RV 'Geruth-chimham,' but in margin 'lodging-place.'

Stanley (*S. and P.* p. 329) and others translate 'inn' or 'hostel.' It may have been such a building as offered shelter to belated merchants or travellers.[*]

Rahab, described in Jos 2[1] as אִשָּׁה זוֹנָה, is said (but see Dillm. *ad loc.*) by the Chaldee paraphrase to have been an 'innkeeper.' (See also Jos. *Ant.* v. i. 2). The instance given in *Jebamoth* xvi. 7, where the innkeeper's word is not relied on without material corroboration, cannot be quoted as showing that she was regarded with special suspicion (Smith, *DB*, art. INN), since her evidence is placed on the same level as that of the daughter of a priestly house; but it is significant that Jewish writers seem to have used פונדקית or פונדקיתא, formed from the Greek πανδοκεύτρια, as the equivalent of either 'hostess' or זוֹנָה (David Kimchi on Jos 2[1]). The idea of an 'inn' was therefore familiar to them. From *Aboda Zara* ii. 1 we gather that the פונדק, from the Gr. πανδοχεῖον, was a place where cattle might be sheltered as well as men; it seems to have corresponded in character with the modern *khân* or caravanserai. Of this order certainly was the 'inn' (πανδοχεῖον, Lk 10[34]) to which the Good Samaritan carried the victim of outrage, and which by tradition is located at *Khan Hadrûr*, on the way to Jericho. The modern building is probably only the last of a succession erected on the same spot, as in that wild district the need of some such place of retreat would always be felt. Along the great trade and pilgrimage routes in the course of time these khâns or caravanserais were raised, to which the chains of mouldering ruins that stud the sides of the main highways stand to bear testimony. Many of these buildings stood apart, and were of considerable strength, to guard against marauders. Occasionally, as at *Khân et-Tujjâr*, under the brow of Tabor, a fortress overlooked and defended the place of rest. From the days when the sea was so infested with pirates as to render navigation perilous, probably date the ruinous buildings on the caravan routes from Aleppo, Baghdâd, Damascus, and Haurân, which met on the southern border of Esdraelon, followed the common path by Antipatris to Gaza, and passed thence to Egypt. When these pests were cleared away, and transport by ship became both safe and cheap, the deserted roads were soon grassgrown, and the khâns were left to crumble (Thomson, *Land and Book*, i. 106). Those built of old by the Persian magnates on the pilgrimage roads from Baghdâd (Layard, *Nineveh and Babylon*, p. 478) probably resembled in some ways the 'castles' that mark the desert route of the Syrian haj. One great object of the latter is to preserve for the use of the pilgrims the water collected during the rainy season. Provision for pilgrims has long been made on a liberal scale by the Greek and Roman Churches; hospices for their entertainment are found near to most of the holy places the faithful are accustomed to visit. In khân and hospice alike the sojourner furnishes his own food; and he is wise to have also, if possible, his own bedding. The person in charge—the *Khânjy* (cf. πανδοχεύς of Lk 10[35])—will supply water to man and horse: nothing more is expected. For this and shelter the natives pay a trifling sum, known as *haḳ el-khân*, 'the price of the khân.'

In every town of any size in Syria more than one khân will be found, commonly resorted to by muleteers, in which the traveller's horses and native attendants are accommodated at merely nominal charges. These are often very miserable places, quite unlike the imposing buildings that once fringed the highways. There are, however, several famous khâns which represent them at

[*] Instead of זֵרוּת, however, there are weighty reasons for reading גְּדֵרוֹת 'pens or folds.' So Josephus and Aquila, followed by Hitzig and others.

their best; *e.g.* that of Antûn Beg in Beyrout, and that of As'ad Pasha in Damascus. The latter is 'one of the finest specimens of Arabian architecture in the country . . . the stone carving above the gateway and around the stalactite vaults is of the most elaborate character.' The khân is constructed of black basalt and white limestone in alternate layers, and is about two hundred feet square. The interior court is about half that size, with a large round fountain in the centre, above which is a lofty dome, resting upon four arches, each supported by four clustered pillars. These are connected with the walls by a series of similar arches and domes — eight in all. Those domes have each sixteen large windows through which light, air, and sunshine penetrate to the rooms and the court below. Around the sides are vaulted magazines of various sizes, for the disposal of merchandise of every description at wholesale.

'On either side of the main entrance a staircase leads up to an arched corridor, which extends quite around the building and communicates with the small retail shops and offices of the merchants. It forms a fine promenade, from where one can look down on the strange and truly Oriental scene in the court below, free from the noise and confusion which there characterize each commercial transaction, large or small. To Khân As'ad Pasha come caravans from Baghdâd, Mosul, Aleppo, Beyrout, and elsewhere. On entering, the muleteers and camel-drivers, with mighty din and uproar, throw down their loads of merchandise in this court, and here they must remain until the owners settle with the custom-house officials' (Thomson, *Land and Book*, iii. 373, 374). With this corresponds Lane's description of the Wakâlehs in Cairo (*Mod. Egyp.* ed. 1895, p. 325).

The ordinary khân was, however, a hollow square, open above, with arches round one or more of the sides within, and over these a series of rooms, approached by a stone stair. The rooms are for travellers; muleteers, animals, and baggage share the space and arches below. In the opinion of the present writer, this must be distinguished from the κατάλυμα or **guest chamber**,[*] in which the parents of Jesus sought shelter when they reached Bethlehem (Lk 2[7]). The meaning of this word in the NT may be gathered from a reference to Mk 14[14], Lk 22[11], taken in the light of a prevailing Jewish custom. These two passages concern a room in a private house, which the owner readily places at the disposal of Jesus and His disciples for the celebration of the Passover. This was in accordance with the ordinary practice. At the festivals of Passover, Pentecost, and Tabernacles the people were commanded to repair to Jerusalem; and it was a boast of the Rabbis, that, notwithstanding the enormous crowds, no man could truthfully say to his fellow, 'I have not found a fire where to roast my paschal lamb in Jerusalem,' or 'I have not found a bed in Jerusalem to lie in,' or 'My lodging is too strait in Jerusalem' (*Aboth R. Nathan*, cap. 34, quoted by Lightfoot, *Works*, ed. 1825, ix. p. 128). The vast numbers who came for the Passover from all parts were made free of the needed apartments, as far as the capacity of the houses permitted; and for this no payment was taken. It was, however, customary for the guests on departing to leave the skins of the paschal lambs, and the vessels which had been employed in the ceremonies, in token of gratitude for their hospitable entertainment (Talm. Bab. *Joma*, fol. 12. 1, quoted by Lightfoot, *Works*, xi. p. 325; compare also use of verb καταλύω in Lk 9[12] 19[7]). We may reasonably suppose that on such an occasion as the great enrolment, when natives of a town came from afar, the 'guest chambers' of their friends would be thrown open to receive them. Joseph, arriving late, found that in which he had purposed to stay already occupied; and no room elsewhere being available, he betook himself with his charge to the khân. Even this apparently

[*] Κατάλυμα is used, however, in Ex 4[24] to translate מָלוֹן.

was full; possibly some of the animals were moved to afford them space; and here Jesus was born.

Well-organized and equipped hotels are now to be found at the principal seaports of Egypt and Syria, and also in the chief inland towns. Along the more frequented roads the natives have learned that something may be gained by accommodating travellers; but remote from the main routes the ancient conditions prevail.

LITERATURE.—Thomson, *Land and Book*; Lane, *Modern Egyptians*; Stanley, *Sinai and Palestine*, ed. 1877, pp. 163, 529; Farrar, *Life of Christ*; Baedeker, *Palestine and Syria*, ed. 1894, pp. 163, 318, etc.; Layard, *Nineveh and Babylon*, p. 478; Doughty, *Arabia Deserta* Lightfoot, *Works*, ed. 1825, ix. p. 128, etc., xi. p. 325, etc.   W. EWING.

INNER MAN or INWARD MAN.—An expression, the exact force of which depends on the contrast intended where it occurs. In 2 Co 4[16] the contrast is between the 'outward man' (ὁ ἔξω ἡμῶν ἄνθρωπος) as mortal and perishable, and the 'inward' as spiritual and immortal; where note, that the Revisers' Greek, with WH and others, reads ὁ ἔσω ἡμῶν (instead of ὁ ἔσωθεν, TR), which exactly corresponds with the former member of the antithesis. Not very remote from this is the contrast in 1 P 3[3.4] between the 'outward adorning' (ὁ ἔξωθεν κόσμος) and 'the hidden man of the heart.'

But the two peculiarly Pauline passages are Ro 7[22] and Eph 3[16], where κατὰ τὸν ἔσω ἄνθρωπον and εἰς τὸν ἔσω ἄνθρωπον are used of something very closely akin to the 'new nature' or the 'renewed man.' The contrast in Ro 7[22] is of the 'inward man' or of the 'mind' (νοῦς, v.[23]), with 'the flesh' or 'the law of sin in the members.' In Eph 3[16] there is no direct antithesis, but a single and positive reference to the new nature, or, at least, to the seat of the Spirit's indwelling and working, to which the corresponding expression in v.[17] is 'that Christ may dwell in your hearts by faith.' It is possible in both passages to distinguish between the 'inward man' and the new or regenerate nature, but only in the sense that the former is the inner or higher self in man as acted on by divine grace, enlightened by God's law, and under preparation and discipline for salvation. Cremer holds that what is really meant by these expressions is not the mere contrast between the inward and the outward in man, between the invisible and the visible, the reality and the appearance, but the inner, spiritual, divine nature in antagonism to the flesh. 'Inward man,' upon this construction, would answer very nearly to πνεῦμα when that word is used in the special sense of (e.g.) Ro 8[10], for the 'new nature,' i.e. the spirit of man renewed and sustained by the Spirit of God. Thus the phrase must be reckoned as belonging to an entirely NT cycle of ideas—indeed to one almost exclusively Pauline.

      J. LAIDLAW.

INORDINATE.—'Inordinate love' is the clumsy tr[n] in Ezk 23[11] of עֶגְבָה, a word which occurs only there, and means 'lust' (RV 'doting'); and 'inordinate affection' in Col 3[5] of πάθος (RV 'passion'). The former tr[n] comes from Cov. (Wyc. 'lecherie'); and the latter from the Bishops' Bible (Wyc. 'leccherie,' Tind. 'unnatural lust,' Gen. 'wantounes,' Rhem. 'lust'). Inordinate is *ill-regulated*, *ungoverned*, as Bacon, *Essays*, 'Of Love' (Gold. Treas. ed. p. 36), 'the former was indeed a voluptuous Man and Inordinate, but the latter was an Austere and wise man'; and Shaks. *Othello*, II. iii. 311—'Every inordinate cup is unblessed, and the ingredient is a devil.' Wyc. uses the adv. in 2 Th 3[6] 'withdrawe you fro ech brother wandrynge unordynatly'; and Latimer, *Sermons* (Arber's ed. p. 99), 'I heare saye ye walke inordinatelye, ye talke unsemelye other wayes then it becommeth Christian subjectes.'   J. HASTINGS.

INQUISITION.—To make inquisition is to make investigation, to search, Dt 19[18], Est 2[23], Ps 9[12], 2 Es 6[19], Wis 1[9] 6[3] (RV), Sir 23[24]. In Sir 41[4] the phrase is 'There is no inquisition in the grave' (οὐκ ἔστιν ἐν ᾅδου ἐλεγμὸς ζωῆς, RV 'There is no inquisition of life in the grave,' RVm 'in Hades'), that is, no inquiry is made there how long or short a man's life has been. Coverdale uses the word in Job 10[6] 'Are thy dayes as the dayes of man, and thy yeares as mans yeares? that thou makest soch inquisicion for my wickednesse, and searchest out my synne?' and 35[15] 'Then useth he no violence in his wrath nether hath he pleasure in curious and depe inquisicions.' And Fuller (*Holy Warre*, iii. 23, p. 150), in memory of Ps 9[12], says, 'But no doubt God, when he maketh inquisition for bloud, will one day remember this bloudy Inquisition.'

     J. HASTINGS.

INSECTS.—See NATURAL HISTORY.

INSPIRE, INSPIRATION.—To 'inspire' is literally to 'breathe into,'[*] and that is the meaning of the word in its single occurrence in AV, Wis 15[11] 'Forasmuch as he knew not his Maker, and him that inspired into him an active soul, and breathed in a living spirit' (τὸν ἐμπνεύσαντα αὐτῷ ψυχὴν ἐνεργοῦσαν, καὶ ἐμφυσήσαντα πνεῦμα ζωτικόν); Vulg. 'qui inspiravit illi animam quæ operatur, et qui insufflavit ei spiritum vitalem.' Wyc. has 'enspirede' here, but in other places he uses the simple 'spire'=breathe, as Gn 2[7] 'The Lord God thanne fourmede man of the slyme of the erthe, and spiride in to the face of hym an entre [=entrance] of breth of lijf' (1388 'brethide'). All the other versions have in the passage just quoted from Wyc. 'breathed the breath,' and it is probably in memory of the Vulg. 'inspiravit in faciem ejus spiraculum vitæ' that Bacon (*Essays*, 'Of Truth,' p. 3) has 'First he breathed Light upon the Face of the Matter or Chaos; then he breathed Light into the Face of Man; and still he breatheth and inspireth Light into the Face of his Chosen'; and Milton, *PL* x. 785—

> 'Yet one doubt
> Pursues me still, lest all I cannot die;
> Lest that pure breath of life, the spirit of Man
> Which God inspired, cannot together perish
> With this corporeal clod.'

Cf. also *Judgement of the Synode at Dort*, p. 40, 'So then faith is the gift of God; not in that it is profered by God unto man's free-will, but because it is really bestowed, inspired, and infused into man.' Then the word passes into the meaning of 'fill with the spirit,' which we see in Knox, *Works*, iii. 99, 'Happie is the man whome thou wald inspyre, O Lord'; and in Tindale's tr[n] of Mk 12[36] 'for David him selfe inspyred with the holy goost, sayde.'

Inspiration occurs twice in AV: (1) Job 32[8] 'But there is a spirit in man: and the inspiration of the Almighty giveth them understanding'; Heb. נִשְׁמַת שַׁדַּי; Vulg. 'Inspiratio Omnipotentis'; Wyc. 1382 'the inbrething of the Almyghti,' 1388 'the enspiryng *ether* revelacioun of Almyghti God'; so Cov. has 'inspiration,' and is followed by all the versions except RV 'the breath of the Almighty,' which agrees with LXX πνοή, and with AV in 33[4] for the same Heb. 'The Spirit of God hath made me, and the breath of the Almighty hath given me life.' The reference is to Gn 2[7]. (2) 2 Ti 3[16] 'All scripture is given by inspiration

[*] The literal meaning is well seen in Spenser, *FQ* II. iii. 30—

> 'Her yellowe lockes, crisped like golden wyre,
> About her shoulders weren loosely shed,
> And, when the winde emongst them did inspyre,
> They waved like a penon wyde dispred,
> And low behinde her backe were scattered.'

of God, and is profitable for doctrine'; Gr. πᾶσα γραφὴ θεόπνευστος καὶ ὠφέλιμος; RV 'Every Scripture inspired of God is also profitable.' For the doctrine of the Inspiration of the Bible see under art. BIBLE, vol. i. p. 296. For this passage, reference may be made (besides the commentaries) to Perowne in *Expos. Times*, ii. 54; Warfield in *Pres. Quarterly*, July, 1889, pp. 389–406 (with *Old and New Test. Student*, Oct. 1889, ix. 245); Row, *BL* 454; Drummond, *Hib. Lect.* 77 f.; and Cremer, *s.v.* θεόπνευστος. The construction of the sentence in RV is the oldest Eng. construction : thus Wyc. 'al scripture onspired of god, is profitable,' Tind. 'al scripture geven by inspiracion of god, is profittable,' so Coverdale and the Great Bible. The Gen. Bible is the first to offer 'the whole Scripture *is* geven by spiration of God, and is profitable.' Tindale elsewhere uses the word in the same sense of a person, as Lk 2²⁷ 'And he [Simeon] came by inspiracion in to the temple.'   J. HASTINGS.

INSTANT.—Instant (*in-stare*, stand upon, press upon) is used in AV in the sense of the present immediate time, as Is 29⁵ 'it shall be at an instant suddenly'; and as an adj. in the sense of 'pressing,' 'urgent': so Lk 23²³ 'And they were instant with loud voices, requiring that he might be crucified' (ἐπέκειντο; Vulg. *instabant*, which gave Rhem. 'were instant,' whence AV; Amer. RV 'were urgent'); Ro 12¹² 'continuing instant in prayer' (again from Rhem., Vulg. *instantes*, Gr. προσκαρτεροῦντες, RV 'continuing stedfastly'); and 2 Ti 4² 'be instant in season, out of season' (ἐπίστηθι, Vulg. *insta*, Bishops 'be instant,' Rhem. 'urge'). Cf. Knox, *Hist.* 36, 'At their instant suit, more than of his own motion, was Thomas Gwilliame, a black Frier, called to bee Preacher'; and Ac 6⁴ Rhem. 'But we wil be instant in praier and the ministerie of the word.'

Instantly in AV means 'urgently,' Lk 7⁴ 'they besought him instantly' (σπουδαίως; Vulg, *sollicite*; 'instantly' is Tindale's word here; RV 'earnestly'); and Ac 26⁷ 'Unto which promise our twelve tribes, instantly serving God day and night, hope to come' (ἐν ἐκτενείᾳ, AV again from Tind., RV 'earnestly'). Cf. Tind. *Prol. to Pent.* 'It is not ynough therfore to read and talke of it only, but we must also desyre god daye and night instantly to open oure eyes, and to make us understond and feale wherfore the scripture was geven'; and his trⁿ of Mk 5¹⁰ 'And he prayd him instantly, that he wolde not sende them awaye out of the countre,' where AV follows Rhem. 'he besought him much.' So Cranmer has 'very instantly' in *Works*, i. 77, 'which prior and his brethren . . . have desired me very instantly to be a mediator for them to your Most Noble Majesty'; and Melvill, *Diary*, 171, 'In the mean tyme, the Erles of Angus and Mar, lyand at Newcastell, wryttes for me ans, and the second tyme verie instantlie, to com and pretche the Word unto tham for ther comfort.' The Rhem. NT uses 'instance' in the same sense in Eph 6¹⁸ 'watching in al instance and supplication.' Shakespeare has both adj. and adv. frequently, but always with reference to time.

J. HASTINGS.

INSTRUMENT.—In the current sense of *the means of accomplishing anything* 'instrument' frequently occurs in OT, chiefly as tr. of *kĕlî*. In NT it is found but twice, both in Ro 6¹³ and in the same sense, 'Neither yield ye your members as instruments of unrighteousness unto sin: but yield yourselves unto God, as those that are alive from the dead, and your members as instruments of righteousness unto God.' The Gr. is ὅπλα, the ordinary word for 'weapons' (as AVm and RVm), and it is very doubtful if in NT it

ever means 'instruments.' Besides, the military metaphor was more natural to St. Paul, and it reappears in v.²³ 'the wages (' your pay as soldiers' —Sanday) of sin is death.' Then the meaning is as Lightfoot expresses it (*Notes on Epistles of St. Paul*), 'Sin is regarded as a sovereign who demands the military service of subjects, levies their quota of arms, and gives them their soldiers' pay of death.' Moule hits happily on 'implements,' which is capable of either interpretation, but he also regards the metaphor as a military one.

In To 7¹⁴ and 1 Mac 13⁴² 'instrument' has the legal sense of a 'deed.' The Gr. is general, συγγραφή, a document.

For Instruments of Music see MUSIC.

J. HASTINGS.

INTELLIGENCE.—Dn 11³⁰ 'He shall even return, and have intelligence with them that forsake the holy covenant.' The meaning is more than mutual understanding, it is 'communication,' 'intercourse.' So Knox, *Hist.* 186, 'The Queene did grievously complaine, that we had intelligence with England'; and Drayton, *Pierce Gaveston*—

'From whence I found a secret means, to have
Intelligence with my kind lord the king.'

The Heb., however (וְיָבֵן), means simply 'give heed to'; RV 'have regard unto.' The Eng. word occurs also in 2 Mac 3⁹ in the ordinary sense of 'information,' which is the word preferred by RV.   J. HASTINGS.

INTEMPERANCE.—See DRUNKENNESS.

INTEND, INTENT. — To intend is used by Spenser in the lit. sense of the Lat. *intendere*, to stretch out : FQ I. xi. 38—

'The same advancing high above his head,
With sharpe intended sting so rude him smot,
That to the earth him drove, as stricken dead.'

But in AV it is used only in the sense of directing the *will* to an object. This is sometimes no more than the formation of a design, as in modern use. So Ac 5³⁵ 20¹³ (μέλλω). But sometimes it is the determination of the will, a fixed resolve, as Ac 5²⁸ 12⁴ (βούλομαι), Lk 14²⁸ (θέλω). Cf. Gal 1⁷ Tind. 'ther be some which trouble you, and intende to pervert the gospell of Christ' (θέλοντες μεταστρέψαι). The word is even used in the sense of *pursuing* a resolution (as distinguished from merely forming it). Thus in Jos 22³³ it is said that after an explanation from the eastern tribes 'the children of Israel blessed God, and did not intend to go up against them in battle,' where the meaning of AV is no doubt as explained by Davies (*Bible English*, 194), that they had intended in our sense of the word but no longer prosecuted the design. Cf. Latimer, *Sermons*, i. 342, 'The devil sleepeth not; he ever intendeth to withdraw us from prayer'; Knox, *Works*, iii. 297, 'Howe these my wordes at that tyme pleased men, the crymes and action intended agaynste me dyd declare'; and Chapman, *Homer's Iliads*, viii. 80—

'Stay, let us both intend
To drive this cruel enemy from our dear aged friend.

This verb is now rarely used with a direct object. In AV we find Ps 21¹¹ 'For they intended evil against thee' (נָטוּ 'they stretched'; Perowne, either 'they have spread against thee evil,' like a net, Lat. *tendere insidias*; or 'they have bent against thee,' etc., like a bow, Lat. *tendere arcum*; Del. 'cause evil to impend over thee,' so Cheyne; Wellh.-Furness, 'When they revolve evil against thee'; King, 'Though they plotted evil against thee'; Ad. Est 13⁴ (κατευθύνω); 2 Mac 14⁵ 'being . . . asked how the Jews stood affected and what they intended' (ἐν τίνι διαθέσει καὶ βουλῇ καθέστηκαν, RV 'what they purposed'); and 14⁸ 'even for that I intend the good of mine own countrymen' (καὶ τῶν ἰδίων πολιτῶν στοχασάμενος, RV 'I have regard also to mine own fellow-citizens'). So Knox, *Hist.* 25, 'And thus did those cruell beasts intend nothing but murther in all the quarters of this Realme.'

Intent is always *purpose, intention*, as in Tindale, *Expositions*, p. 96 (on Mt 6¹⁴⁻¹⁸), 'But and if thou think that God delighteth in the work for the work itself, the true intent away, and in thy pain for thy pain itself, thou art as far out of the way as from heaven to the earth'; and p. 147 (on 1 Jn 1³), 'To bring unto the fellowship of God and Christ, is the final intent of all the scripture.' So Jer 44²⁵ Cov. 'Purposely have ye set up youre owne good meanynges, and hastely have ye fulfilled youre owne intente'; and Knox, *Hist.* 149, 'They were minded to keep no point of the promise longer than they had obtained their intent.' The phrase in AV is usually 'to the intent that,' but the plural occurs Jer 30²⁴ 'until he have performed the intents of his heart' (מְזִמּוֹת לִבּוֹ); He 4¹² 'a discerner of the thoughts and intents of the heart' (κριτικὸς . . . ἐννοιῶν καρδίας). Fuller says of the Crusaders (*Holy Warre*, I. xii. p. 18), 'We must in charitie allow that many of them were truly zealous, and went with pious intents'; and on p. 243 (v. 9), 'Farre be it from us to condemn all their works to be drosse, because debased and alloyed with superstitious intents.'

J. HASTINGS.

INTERCESSION.—See PRAYER.

INTERMEDDLE (from Old Fr. *entre* among and *medler* to mix) meant formerly either literally to mix, as Malory, *Morte Darthur*, xvii. 15, 'Right so entered he into the chamber, and came toward the table of silver; and when he came nigh he felt a breath that him thought it was intermeddled with fire'; and Hakluyt, *Voyages*, i. 572, 'He hath intermedled in his historie certaine things contrary to the trueth'; or else figuratively to have to do with, take an interest in, which is the meaning in AV. It occurs twice, Pr 14¹⁰ 'The heart knoweth his own bitterness; and a stranger doth not intermeddle with his joy' (יִתְעָרַב, takes part in, shares, not necessarily *interferes* in; LXX ἐπιμίγνυται; Vulg. 'miscebitur'); and 18¹ 'Through desire a man, having separated himself, seeketh and intermeddleth with all wisdom' (בְּכָל־תּוּשִׁיָּה יִתְגַּלָּע), RV 'rageth against all sound wisdom,' RVm 'quarrelleth with'; Del. 'Against all that is beneficial he showeth his teeth'; *Oxf. Heb. Lex.* 'bursts out in strife against.' AV misunderstands the meaning, and takes the verb in a good sense, 'have to do with,' 'take an interest in,' after the tr. of the Gen. Bible, 'For the desire thereof he wil separate him self to seke it, and occupie him self in all wisdome,' with his margin, 'He that loveth wisdome, wil separate him self from all impediments, and give him self wholly to seke it').

J. HASTINGS.

INTERMEDIATE STATE.—See ESCHATOLOGY.

INTERPRETATION.—This subst. and its verb are used in Scripture in a variety of senses.

1. Of *dreams* (פָּתַר 'interpret,' פִּתְרוֹן 'interpretation'); the dreams of the chief butler and the chief baker, Gn 40⁵⋅⁸⋅¹²⋅¹⁶⋅¹⁸⋅²²⁴¹¹¹⋅¹²⋅¹³; Pharaoh's dream, 41⁸⋅¹⁵; Gideon's dream, Jg 7¹⁵ (where the word for 'interpretation' is the ἅπ. λεγ. שֵׁבֶר, lit. 'breaking up,' *i.e.* 'solution'). In Dn occur the Aramaic forms פְּשַׁר (verb) 'interpret' (*Qal* in Dn 5¹⁶, *Pael* ptcp. מְפַשַּׁר 5¹²), and פְּשַׁר (noun) 'interpretation'; used of the dreams of Nebuchadnezzar (Dn 2⁴ᶠᶠ⋅⁴⁵), of Daniel himself (7¹⁶); cf. the use of the same word for the interpretation to Belshazzar

of the writing on the wall (5⁷ᶠᶠ⋅), and the similar use of פְּשַׁר in Ec 8¹ (only).

Dreams being regarded as vehicles of divine communication and frequently as portending future events, it became a matter of great importance to discover their interpretation. This function was discharged at the court of Egypt by the חַרְטֻמִּים 'sacred scribes' (Gn 41⁸; cf. the complaint of the butler and the baker, *while in prison*, 'We have dreamed a dream, and there is none that can interpret it,' 40⁸). With the reply of Joseph (*ib.*), 'Do not interpretations belong to God?' compare the statement of Herodotus (ii. 83) regarding the Egyptian opinion, 'Ανθρώπων μὲν οὐδενὶ προσκέεται ἡ τέχνη, τῶν δὲ θεῶν μετεξετέροισι. The 'wise men' and 'Chaldæans' (the latter by a late conception) have similar functions attributed to them, in the Book of Daniel, at the court of Babylon.

2. Of interpreting *a foreign language*. Egyptian being, of course, the language of the court, the conversation between Joseph and his brethren was carried on by the medium of an interpreter, who was probably always expected to be in attendance at court (Gn 42²³ הַמֵּלִיץ with art. '*the* interpreter'). The interpreter being *between* (בֵּינֹתָם *ib.*) the two parties, מֵלִיץ can be used as = 'ambassador' (2 Ch 32³¹) or 'mediator' (Is 43²⁷, of prophets standing between J″ and Israel; Job 33²³, of an angel as interpreting to man God's providential treatment of him and what is right for him to do [Davidson], probably also as interceding for man to God [Dillmann, Siegfried-Stade]). הֵלִיץ and its derivatives (cf. מְלִיצָה in Hab 2⁶, 'taunt-song') have always the sense of *deriding* or *taunting* except in the four above-cited passages, Gn 42²³, 2 Ch 32³¹, Is 43²⁷, Job 33²³ (contrast 16²⁰), and in Pr 1⁶ where כְּלִיצָה (LXX σκοτεινὸς λόγος) probably means 'a dark saying' (RV 'a figure') rather than 'interpretation' (AV, RVm).

In Ezr 4⁷ the passive ptcp. מְתֻרְגָּם is used of a translation from Persian into Aramaic. From this root comes the well-known word *Targum* ('paraphrase') as well as the designation *meturgeman* applied to the official in the synagogue, who was required to translate the Hebrew (which was read to, but no longer understood by, the people) into the Aramaic vernacular. Latterly, in addition to translating the sacred text, the *meturgeman* was wont to add all manner of Haggada to it (W. R. Smith, *OTJC*² 36, 64 n., 154).

In NT we have the familiar phrase 'which is, being interpreted,' etc. (μεθερμηνευόμενος, ὃ ἑρμηνεύεται, διερμηνευόμενος, ὁ μεθερμηνεύεται), where a Heb. or Aram. expression is rendered into Greek (Mt 1²³, Mk 5⁴¹ 15²²⋅³⁴, Jn 1³⁸⋅⁴¹ etc. Ac 9³⁶ 13⁸), a symbolical force being also sometimes discovered in it (Jn 1⁴² 9⁷, Ac 4³⁶, He 7²).

Although it scarcely falls within the scope of the present article, the reference of Papias (*ap.* Eusebius, *HE* iii. 39) to St. Mark as the 'interpreter' (ἑρμηνευτής) of St. Peter may be mentioned (see MARK). Link (*SK*, 1896, Heft iii. p. 405 ff.; cf. *Expos. Times*, Aug. 1896, p. 496) contends strongly that 'interpreter' here is to be understood in its strictly literal sense, implying that the Apostle Peter, in his missionary journeys among the Jews of the Diaspora, availed himself of St. Mark's services to render Aramaic into Greek.

3. Of interpreting *the utterances of those who spoke with tongues*. This was a 'gift' (χάρισμα) which might or might not belong to the speaker with tongues himself (1 Co 12¹⁰⋅³⁰ 14⁵⋅¹³⋅²⁶⋅²⁷⋅²⁸). See CHURCH, vol. i. p. 428ᵇ, and TONGUES (GIFT OF).

4. Considerable uncertainty attaches to the meaning of the word 'interpretation' in 2 P 1²⁰ (γινώσκοντες ὅτι πᾶσα προφητεία γραφῆς ἰδίας ἐπιλύσεως οὐ γίνεται, 'knowing that no prophecy of Scripture is of private interpretation'; cf. the use of ἐπιλύειν in Mk 4³⁴ and Ac 19³⁹). All the varieties of explanation may be grouped under two heads, according as the 'interpretation' is (a) ours or (b) the prophet's own. Both the context and the very similar language of Philo (Quis rer. div. hær. p. 52) plead in favour of the second explanation. Grimm, indeed (Clavis, s. γίγνομαι), supports the first, taking the meaning to be that no one can by his own mental powers explain the prophecies of the OT, but that he requires the aid of the same spirit which originally called forth their utterance. But this true conception seems hardly in place here. See further Alford, ad loc., and Farrar (Early Days of Christianity, 119 n.), who takes the meaning to be that 'the prophets did not speak by spontaneous knowledge and spoke more than they could themselves interpret . . . If this utterance is not his own, his interpretation may also well be inadequate (cf. 1 P 1¹⁰⁻¹²).'

For interpretation of prophecy see PROPHECY.

The history of the various schemes, Jewish and Christian, for interpreting Scripture, the supposed double sense, the allegorizing method once so much in vogue, etc., lie outside the scope of this article. For details, the reader must refer to works on Rabbinical Theology and on Hermeneutics.

J. A. SELBIE.

INTREAT, ENTREAT.—In the edd. of AV since 1760 'entreat' has the meaning of 'deal with,' 'handle' (mod. 'treat'), and 'intreat' of 'beg,' 'pray.' But they are different spellings of the same verb (fr. Lat. in-tractare, through Fr. entraiter), and in 1611 the spelling was indifferently 'entreat' or 'intreat.'

In the sense of treat, 'entreat' occurs in AV 1611 eleven times, 'intreat' twelve times; in the sense of pray, 'entreat' occurs eleven times, 'intreat' twenty-eight times. In Job 19¹⁶ we find 'I intreated him with my mouth,' but in the next verse 'I entreated for the children's sake.' Again in Jer 15¹¹ we read, 'I will cause the enemie to intreat thee well in the time of evill,' while the marg. has 'Or, I will entreat the enemie for thee.' The subst. is found once 'intreaty' (Pr 18²²), once 'entreaty' (2 Co 8⁴), both meaning 'petition.'

1. To entreat is simply to 'deal with,' 'handle,' any person or thing, as Hos 6⁴ Cov., 'O Ephraim, what shal I do unto the? O Iuda, how shall I intreate the?' More, Utopia (Lumby's ed. p. 69), 'Ther com yearly to Amaurote out of every cytie iii. old men wyse and well experienced, there to entreate and debate, of the common matters of the land.' But in AV the word is used in this sense only with an adv., 'well,' 'evil,' 'spitefully,' 'shamefully,' and once in a good sense, 'courteously,' Ac 27³.

2. To intreat is to 'beseech'; but in older Eng. the word had also the meaning of 'beseech successfully,' 'persuade.' Thus Shaks. As You Like It, I. ii. 135, 'since the youth will not be entreated, his own peril on his forwardness.' In this sense 'intreat' is evidently used in AV, as Gn 25²¹ 'And Isaac intreated the LORD for his wife . . . and the LORD was intreated of him.' So 2 S 21¹⁴ 24²⁵, 1 Ch 5²⁰, 2 Ch 33¹³·¹⁹, Ezr 8²³, Is 19²². The Heb. is always the reflex. (Niph.) of עָתַר, 'āthar (as Gn 25²¹ וַיֶּעְתַּר לוֹ), which in Arabic is 'to slaughter or sacrifice' (Lane, see also Buhl s.v., and esp. We.), but in Heb. is used with the more general sense of 'supplicate' in the reflex. 'to let oneself be supplicated,' 'be persuaded,' so that 'be intreated' was an exceedingly happy rendering. In Ja 3¹⁷, 'easy to be intreated' (εὐπειθής, not elsewhere in NT), the meaning is the same. The tr. is Tindale's; Wyc. has 'able to be counceilid,' Rhem. 'suasible.'

J. HASTINGS.

INWARD, INWARDS.—Inward means: 1. Towards the inside, as 2 S 5⁹ 'And David built round about from Millo and inward' (בַּיְתָה); 2 Ch

3¹³ 'The wings of these cherubims spread themselves forth twenty cubits: and they stood on their feet, and their faces were inward' (לַבָּיִת; RV [as AVm] 'toward the house,' RVm 'inward'); Ezk 40⁹ 'the porch of the gate was inward' (מֵהַבַּיִת, RV 'toward the house'). 2. As an adj. inward has two meanings: (1) Interior, as in Bacon, Essays, 'Of Building,' p. 184, 'Beyond this Court let there be an Inward Court, of the same Square and Height'; Bunyan, Holy War, p. 133, 'The Gaoler, therefore, having received such a charge, put them all in the inward prison'; and Shaks. Cymb. III. iv. 6—

'Wherefore breaks that sigh
From the inward of thee?'

The Heb. kerebh, a subst. of frequent occurrence and variously translated (but of which the general meaning is well seen in Ps 103¹ כָּל־קְרָבַי 'all that is within me'), is rendered by 'inward part' or 'parts' in Ps 5⁹, Is 16¹¹, Jer 31³³ (see also Gn 41²¹ AVm); and by 'inward thought' in Ps 49¹¹ 64⁶, where the meaning is almost 'secret,' as in Bacon, Advancement of Learn. II. xxiii. 48, 'The government of the soul in moving the body is inward and profound.' 'Inward parts' is the trⁿ also of túḥôth (parts covered) in Job 38³⁶ (but see Davidson and RVm), Ps 51⁶; and of ḥădārîm (chambers) in Pr 20²⁷·³⁰, RV 'innermost parts.' Inward has the same meaning of 'interior' in 2 Mac 3¹⁶ 'the changing of his colour declared the inward agony of his mind' (Gr. simply ἀγωνία, RV 'distress'). And in NT there occurs 'the inward man,' Ro 7²², 2 Co 4¹⁶ (ὁ ἔσω ἄνθρωπος), i.e. the conscience or reason, as opposed to the body (ὁ ἔξω ἄνθρωπος, 2 Co 4¹⁶; see INNER MAN), a phrase used also by Shaks. in Hamlet, II. ii. 6—

'Something have you heard
Of Hamlet's transformation; so I call it,
Since not the exterior nor the inward man
Resembles that it was.'

And Pericles, II. ii. 57—

'Opinion's but a fool, that makes us scan
The outward habit by the inward man.'

We also find in 2 Co 7¹⁵ the phrase 'inward affection' as the trⁿ of σπλάγχνα, a trⁿ which comes from Tindale, and is accepted by all the Eng. VSS except Rhem. 'bowels.' Wyc. 1380 has 'entraylis,' 1388 'inwardnesse.' (2) But the adj. 'inward' means intimate in Job 19¹⁹ 'All my inward friends abhorred me' (כָּל־מְתֵי סוֹדִי, lit. as RVm 'all the men of my council'). Davidson calls the AV trⁿ 'a fine expression,' and adds, 'the reference is to such as his three friends, men whose high converse and fellowship seemed to Job, as a thoughtful godly man, something almost better than relationship, Ps 55¹⁴.' Fuller uses the word in the same sense in Holy Warre, ii. 37 (p. 92), 'the Caliph himself . . . having few of his most inward eunuchs about him'; and Evelyn, Diary, July 22, 1674, 'He was . . . so inward with my Lord Obrien that, after a few moneths of that gentleman's death, he married his widow'; and Shaks. has it not only as an adj. Rich. III. III. iv. 8, 'Who is most inward with the noble duke?' but also as a subst., Meas. for Meas. III. ii. 138, 'I was an inward of his.'

Inwards never occurs in AV or RV as an adv., but always as a subst., and the trⁿ of kerebh, bowels. See next article and SACRIFICE. In Shaks. II Henry IV. IV. iii. 115, it is used generally of the inner parts of the body, 'The second property of your excellent sherris is, the warming of the blood; which, before cold and settled, left the liver white and pale, which is the badge of pusillanimity and cowardice; but the sherris warms it, and makes it course from the inwards to the parts extreme'; but more particularly of the bowels, in *Othello*, II. i. 306—

> ' The thought whereof
> Doth like a poisonous mineral gnaw my inwards.'

J. HASTINGS.

INWARDS, INWARD PARTS. — ' Inwards,' representing קֶרֶב, is repeatedly used in AV of Ex and Lv as equivalent to ' entrails.' ' Inward parts' is used in a much wider application throughout the OT, and represents not only קֶרֶב of the original, but several other words, as מֵעִים, חֲדָרִים-בֶּטֶן, and לֵב. The phrase is used in two broadly distinct applications—(1) in the literal or corporeal, (2) in the tropical or psychical.

1. Examples of the *literal* sense are Gn 41²¹, where ' eaten them up' is rendered in AVm ' come to the inward parts' (אֶל־קִרְבֶּנָה); 1 K 17²¹, where ' let the child's soul come to him again' is on the margin ' into his inward parts' (עַל־קִרְבּוֹ).

2. Examples of the tropical application for the ' inward' or ' hidden' in character contrasted with the ' outward' or ' manifest' are Ps 5⁹ 62⁴ (Heb. ⁵), mouth or outward expression (פֶּה) contrasted with thoughts (קֶרֶב); Ps 64⁶ (Heb. ⁷), where קֶרֶב and לֵב are put for the concealed elements of character. In Is 16¹¹ both מֵעִים and קֶרֶב are used metaphorically of the divine compassions. In Jer 31³³ קֶרֶב and לֵב are used of the inward nature of man as the seat of a divine renewal.

Several familiar examples of the phrase for the ' secrets of the human soul' threaten to disappear from our Bibles under the effect of modern alterations in reading and rendering, *e.g.* Ps 49¹¹ ' Their inward thought is that their houses,' etc., by the transposition of two letters (קְבָרִם for קִרְבָּם), becomes ' Their graves are their houses,' a reading supported by Sept. Pesh. Targ. and adopted by most modern scholars (RVm); Job 38³⁶, where מֻחוֹת ' inward parts' can be rendered ' dark clouds,' and the parallel word for ' mind,' ' meteors ' (see RVm); Ps 51⁶ (Heb.⁸), where Wellhausen (following Hitzig) holds that the consonants בטחות represent, not the noun מֻחוֹת and preposition בְּ, but a derivative of the verb בטח, and accordingly renders ' Faith and trust, it is these Thou lovest (' Psalms' in *Polychrome Bible*, Lond. 1898). See, further, Cheyne in *Expositor*, Aug. 1898, p. 83 ff.

In the NT the phrase, represented by τὸ ἔσωθεν, is used only in Mt 7¹⁵ and Lk 11³⁹ in the unfavourable sense for inward wickedness. The other use of inner or inward man in relation to the renewed nature is almost wholly Pauline. See INNER MAN.

J. LAIDLAW.

IOB (יוֹב, AV Job).—The third son of Issachar, Gn 46¹³. *Job* (יוֹב) appears to be a textual error for *Jashub* (יָשׁוּב) of the parallel passages Nu 26²⁴, 1 Ch 7¹, which is read by Sam. Pent. and Pesh. even in Gn, and is supported by LXX Ἰασούφ, Luc. Ἰασούβ. So Dillmann, *Oxf. Heb. Lex.*, etc.

J. A. SELBIE.

IPHDEIAH (יִפְדְּיָה, ' J" redeems').—A Benjamite chief, 1 Ch 8²⁵. See GENEALOGY.

IPHTAH (יִפְתָּח, AV Jiphtah).—A town in the Shephelah of Judah, Jos 15⁴³. The name has not been recovered.

IPHTAH-EL (יִפְתַּח־אֵל, AV Jiphtah-el).—A ravine (גַּיְא) N.W. of Hannathon, on the north border of Zebulun, Jos 19¹⁴·²⁷. The situation of DABBESHETH (v.¹¹) seems to show that the great ravine, called *Wady el-Ḳurn*, ' valley of the horn,' west of *Kefr ʿAnân*, is intended. The word has nothing to do with the name *Jefât* (*i.e.* Jotapata of Jos. *Wars*, iii. 7), with which it has been wrongly compared (*e.g.* by Robinson, *BRP* iii. p. 107).

C. R. CONDER.

IR (עִיר, A Ὡρά, B Ῥαώμ), 1 Ch 7¹².—Shuppim and Huppim are mentioned as the sons of Ir (called in v.⁷ **Iri**) in a list of the sons of Benjamin

IRA (עִירָא, Εἶρας, Ira).—**1.** A Jairite, *i.e.* of Jair, a family of Gilead (Nu 32⁴¹ etc.). He is described as ' priest unto David' (cf. 2 S 8¹⁸, where David's sons are also called ' priests'; Driver, *Sam.* pp. 219 and 293 f.), and associated with Zadok and Abiathar (2 S 20²⁶). It may be noted in this connexion (*a*) that in the list of court officials given in 2 S 8¹⁵ff. (from which this notice [2 S 20²⁶] appears to be repeated, cf. Budde, *Richter u. Samuel*, p. 254) no mention is made of Ira, (*b*) that his name is also absent from the list in 1 Ch 18¹⁴⁻¹⁷ (which, however, is simply transcribed from 2 S 8); in both these passages a statement as to the office of David's sons is substituted (?), and (*c*) that the difficulty attaching to the word ' priest' in this passage, whether it be applied to Ira or to the sons of David (in 1 Ch 18 ' priests' is changed to ' chiefs about the king,' הָרִאשׁוֹנִים לְיַד הַמֶּלֶךְ), admits of solution if the passage is assigned to a late date (although, of course, it may be plausibly urged on the other hand that the freer use of the word ' priests' is an evidence of *antiquity*). Additional confirmation is thus given to Budde's theory that 2 S 20²³⁻²⁶ were repeated (with variations) from 2 S 8¹⁵f. by a later redactor, who wished to include the genuinely old section 2 S 9¹⁻20²² and took this means of connecting the chapters added with what preceded (see SAMUEL, BOOKS OF). Nothing further is known of this Ira, unless, following the reading of the Peshiṭta (ܐ݅ܝ݂ܬ݂ܝ݁ܪ ?) = ' of Jattir,' *i.e.* הַיַּתְרִי for הַיָּאִרִי the Jairites, Luc. ὁ Ἰεθέρ), we adopt the somewhat hazardous conjecture (Then. Klost.) that he is identical with **2.** Ira the Ithrite (הַיִּתְרִי), one of David's heroes (2 S 23³⁸ = 1 Ch 11⁴⁰). Most probably Then. and Klost. are right in pointing the text differently (הַיַּתְרִי for הַיִּתְרִי, see ITHRITE, THE), and treating Ira as a native of Jattir in the hill-country of Judah (cf. 1 S 30²⁷). **3.** (2 S 23²⁶, B Εἶρας, A *Ἰρας; 1 Ch 11²⁸ Ὡραί; 1 Ch 27⁹, B Ὀδουίας, A Εἰρά, Hira) Another of David's heroes, son of Ikkesh the Tekoite. According to 1 Ch 27⁹ he was captain of the temple guard for the sixth monthly course.

J. F. STENNING.

IRAD (עִירָד, LXX Γαιδάδ).—Son of Enoch and grandson of Cain (Gn 4¹⁸). The name perhaps means ' fugitive' (Budde, ' strong,' ' increasing,' following the Arabic *ʿarada*, which, used of plants, = ' come forth and become tall' or ' come forth hard and erect' [Lane, 1997 f.]), and may be a transformation of עִרד (Gn 5¹⁵f· = 1 Ch 1²). See Dillmann and Spurrell on Gn 4¹⁸, and Budde, *Urgeschichte*, 123 ff.

IRAM (עִירָם).—A ' duke' (אַלּוּף) of Edom, Gn 36⁴³ = 1 Ch 1⁵⁴. The precise connotation of the name in this ' geographico-statistical list' (Dillm.) is unknown. The LXX has in Gn A Ζαφωεί, DE Ζαφωείν, in 1 Ch B Ζαφωείν, A Ἡράμ.

IR-HA-HERES (עִיר הַהֶרֶם).—In Is 19¹⁸ the name to be given to one of the ' five cities in the land of Egypt that speak the language of Canaan, and swear to Jehovah of hosts'; in AV, RV, ' one shall be called The city of destruction.' The passage is difficult; and many different views have been held about it, especially in modern times.

(1) The Massoretic reading of the passage (which is supported by Aq. Theod. Pesh.) is that given above: and of this the usually accepted interpretation is that expressed in AV, RV, and adopted by Delitzsch; the name ' city of destroying'— or, more exactly, ' of *tearing down*,' the verb הָרֵם being used properly of *tearing* or *pulling* down

buildings, cities, altars, etc. (Ex 23[24], 1 K 18[30], 1 S 14[17], Ezk 13[14] etc.)—is supposed to be chosen for the sake of a punning allusion to ḥeres (חֶרֶם Job 9[7*]) 'sun,' the 'city of the sun' being a designation which might have been given in Hebrew to On, the Heliopolis of the Greeks, a city a few miles to the N.E. of the modern Cairo, in ancient times the chief centre of the sun-worship in Egypt, and full of obelisks dedicated to the sun-god, Ra. The meaning of the passage, then, is that the place which has hitherto been a 'city of the sun' will in the future be called the 'city of destroying,' i.e. a city which has devoted itself to destroying the temples and emblems of the sun ; cf. the prophecy of Jeremiah (43[13]), where it is said of Nebuchadnezzar that 'he will break in pieces the pillars (i.e. obelisks) of Beth-shemesh (the 'house, or temple, of the sun '), that is in the land of Egypt.' The objections which have been urged against this view, that it requires too much to be supplied, that חֶרֶם does not occur elsewhere, and that the expression ought rather to mean 'the destroyed city,' are not cogent : the name is, of course, meant allusively, not as a complete definition ; there are many other words which occur but once in the Hebrew Bible ; † and the sense in which the 'destroying' was meant would be determined by the context.

(2) Symm. (πόλις ἡλίου), Vulg. (civitas Solis), the Talm. (Menāḥōth, 110ᵃ), and Saadyah (10th cent.), read חֶרֶם ('sun') for הֶרֶם ('destruction'), a reading found also in 16 Heb. MSS.‡ This reading, in spite of the preference expressed for it by Ges. (Thes.) and Riehm (Einl. ii. 552 f.), cannot be deemed probable,—at least, if the words be accepted as Isaiah's : if it be adopted, be it observed, the expression used by the prophet would be, not ' one shall be the city of the sun' (in which case, no doubt, his words could be understood as a promise of the conversion of Heliopolis to the worship of Jehovah), but ' one shall be called the city of the sun,' an idiom which, according to usage (cf. 1[26] 4[3] 9[6] 61[3b. 6] 62[4], Jer 19[6], Hos 1[10]), always implies that the words following denote the character of the place or person mentioned ; and it would be very pointless to say that one of the converted cities would bear the character of a sun-city.

Ges. (Comm.), Ew., Knob., who adopt the same reading, explain it from the Arab. ḥarasa, 'the guarded or protected city'; but this is to introduce a very questionable Arabism into the text of the OT.

(3) The LXX has πόλις ασεδεκ, i.e. עִיר הַצֶּרֶק 'city of righteousness' (cf. 1[26] 61[3b]). This would yield a fair, though not a specially pertinent sense : it is open to the suspicion of being an alteration based on 1[26] (where the 'righteousness' is in pointed contrast to the unrighteousness denounced in vv.[21-23] etc.). On the other hand, that in Egypt the text of Is 19 was treated freely, and accommodated to the circumstances of a later age, is evident from the LXX rendering of v.[25], where, for 'Blessed be Egypt my people,' they substitute ' Blessed be my people that is in Egypt,' with manifest reference to the Jews settled there in the time of the Ptolemies. See further (5).

A decision on the passage is complicated by historical considerations. The high priest Onias III.,

after his deposition by Antiochus Epiphanes,—or, according to other statements, his son, Onias IV.,* — despairing of better times in Judah, sought refuge in Egypt (c. B.C. 170–160) with Ptolemy Philometor ; and conceived the idea of building there a temple, dedicated to Jehovah, in which the ancient rites of his people might be carried on without molestation, and which might form a religious centre at least for the Jews settled in Egypt. Upon his application to Ptolemy, the king granted the disused site of a sanctuary of Bubastis at Leontopolis, in the 'nome,' or district, of Heliopolis, and there Onias erected his temple.† In support of his plan he had pointed to Is 19[19] and its context,‡ as a prediction that a temple to Jehovah was to be built in Egypt.§ These facts have been supposed to have a bearing upon both the reading and the exegesis of the passage under consideration. Certainly, if the passage be Isaiah's, they will not affect either ; in that case, the first view given above is the only one which can be regarded as probable. But there are scholars whom that view fails to satisfy ; and, without going so far as to deny Isaiah's authorship of the whole of 19[16 (18)-25], it must be granted that the clause in v.[18] 'one shall be called,' etc., might well be a later addition to the original text of the prophecy : the verse would not read incompletely without it, nor does it add anything material to the main thought of the verse. Those who hold, then, that this clause (with or without the context) is not Isaiah's, adopt the following views about it.

(4) Duhm boldly translates 'shall be called Leontopolis,' explaining ḥeres from the Arab. ḥariṣ, properly the bruiser, crusher, a poet. name for a lion. But that a very special and fig. application of an Arab. root, not occurring in Heb. even in its usual Arabic sense, should be found in Heb., is most improbable.

Dillmann's suggestions are better worthy of consideration. First (5), adhering to Isaiah's authorship, but deeming (1) and (2) above both unsuitable, he thinks it possible (agreeing in this with Bredenkamp) that 'city of righteousness' was the original reading,‖ supposing that ḥeres, 'sun,' and ḥeres, 'destruction,' were alterations made intentionally after B.C. 170, for the purpose of introducing a more definite allusion to the temple of Leontopolis (which was situated, as said above, in the nome of Heliopolis), the former by those who viewed this temple with approval, the latter by those who judged it schismatic. But he goes on (6) to throw out the suggestion that, after all, the whole clause may have been added at this later date, ḥeres, 'sun,' being the original reading, which was altered afterwards by the Jews of Palestine into ḥeres, 'destruction,' in order to obtain a condemnation of the Egyptian temple,¶ and by the Jews of Egypt into ẓedek, 'righteousness,' in order to make the prophecy more distinctly favourable to it.

(7) Cheyne (Introd. to Is. pp. 102–110), followed by Skinner, rejecting the view that the passage was written in the interests of the temple of Leon-

---

* And in the pr. names מַעֲלֵה הַחֶרֶם Jg 1[35], תִּמְנַת הֶרֶם 2[9], הַר הֶרֶם 'ascent of Ḥeres' 8[13] ; 14[18] is dub., see Moore.

† The form of the word is perfectly regular and normal : cf. אֹרֶב a lying-in-wait (Job 38[40]), קֶשֶׁב an attending (Is 217), קֶטֶל a slaying (Ob 9), שֶׁבֶר a breaking, הֶרֶג a killing, חֶבֶל a destruction (Mic 2[10]), לֶכֶד a catch (Pr 3[26]), etc.

‡ The present text of the Targ. expresses a combination of both readings, (1) and (2) : קרתא בית שמש דעתירא למחרב 'the city Beth-Shemesh [see Jer 43[13], cited above], which is destined to be destroyed' (cited in the Talm. l.c. without the last clause : see Levy, NHWB ii. 112).

* See on this question Baethgen, ZATW, 1886, p. 278 ff.

† Probably at Tell el-Yahudîyeh (about 10 miles N. of Heliopolis), near which there are the remains of a Jewish necropolis (Naville, as cited below, pp. 13–15, 19 f.). The place was afterward scalled Onion.

‡ See Jos. Ant. xiii. iii. 1 end.

§ Jos. BJ i. i. 1 ; vii. x. 2–3 ; Ant. xii. V. 1, ix. 7 ; xiii. iii. 1–3, x. 4 ; xx. 10 ; Ewald, Hist. v. 355 f. ; Schürer, ii. 549–546. See also Naville, The Mound of the Jew and the City of Onias (7th Memoir of the Egyp. Expl. Fund), 1890, pp. 18–20.

‖ So Geiger, Urschrift (1857), p. 79 f. (treating the verse, however,—and indeed the whole passage, 1918-25,—as a late addition to Isaiah's prophecy, written for the express purpose of glorifying the temple of Leontopolis).

¶ Dillm. is thus far following Hitzig, Jesaia (1833), pp. 219, 233 (who indeed assigns the whole of 1916-25 to the same age, and even suggests Onias himself as its author).

topolis, and interpreting the words in v.¹⁸ ('five cities speaking the language of Canaan' [Hebrew], etc.), not as a symbolical expression for the conversion of Egyptian cities to the worship of J″, but as referring to Jewish colonies in Egypt maintaining their national language and religion, supposes vv.¹⁶⁻²⁵ to have been written in the latter years of Ptolemy Lagi (c. B.C. 290), when there were unquestionably many Jewish settlements in Egypt: the original reading was 'city of the sun,' the meaning being that one of these Jewish colonies, preserving loyally the faith of their fathers, should flourish even in Heliopolis, the city of the sun-god, the Heb. name of which should be Ir-ha-ḥereṣ; the reading was altered afterwards, when the Jews of Pal. began to show hostility towards the Egyptian temple, by the Jews of Egypt into 'city of righteousness,' and then further by the Jews of Palestine, as a counter-blow, into 'city of destruction.'

(8) König (Einl. p. 86) treats the clause as a late Palestinian gloss, written originally on the margin, in condemnation of the temple at Leontopolis ('city of destruction,' with allusion to ḥereṣ 'of the sun').

It is evident that most of these views are merely hypotheses. At the same time, the diversity of reading makes it clear that arbitrary alterations, upon one side or the other, were introduced into the text; and as positive information upon the matter fails us, it becomes necessary to resort to hypotheses in order to explain the facts. The only question is, what hypothesis explains them best? If the words are Isaiah's, the objections to 'city of the sun' being the original reading have been already stated: if the words were written after the foundation of the temple at Leontopolis, the objections to the same being the original reading are, 1. that the temple was not at Heliopolis, and 2. (as remarked by Cheyne) that a passage interpolated by an Egyptian Jew in the interests of that temple should have made its way into the Palestinian text of Isaiah. If 'city of the sun' were the original reading, the most reasonable explanation of it is Cheyne's (7), though that implies that the passage is not Isaiah's, and also involves an interpretation of vv.¹⁸⁻²⁰, which is, at least, not the obvious one. The present writer must own that the view which seems to him to be the least open to objection is (1): the difficulties which have been found in this do not (as indicated above) seem to him as serious as has been sometimes maintained; and ḥereṣ, 'sun,'—whether an intentional or accidental alteration of ḥereṣ, 'destruction,'—though unsuitable, if used in the first instance with reference to Leontopolis, could readily enough be applied to it, if found, as upon this view of the case it would be found, in the text of an ancient prophecy.*   S. R. DRIVER.

IRI.—See IR.

IRIJAH (יִרְאִיָּה 'J″ seeth').—A captain who, during the siege of Jerus., arrested Jeremiah on the charge of intending to desert to the Chaldæans (Jer 37¹³. ¹⁴).

IR-NAHASH (עִיר נָחָשׁ).—A city of Judah, 1 Ch 4¹². The site is uncertain.

---

* In connexion with the views which see in the passage an allusion to the temple at Leontopolis, it is at least remarkable that, as M. Naville observes (pp. 12, 20, 21), in the Great Harris Papyrus, which describes at length the buildings of Ramses III. (c. 1200 B.C.), mention is made of 'the abode of Ramses III., in the house of Ra (the sun-god) on the north of On,'—a name which would fairly correspond to 'city of the sun,' and which M. Naville is strongly disposed to consider was the sacred name of the city buried now under Tell el-Yahudiyeh: the close connexion of this place with On is also implied by the further statement in the Papyrus that 'all that belonged to the abode of Ramses in the house of Ra, north of On, the buildings as well as the cattle, was under the authority of the priests of On for their yearly tribute.'

IRON (יִרְאוֹן, Yir'ōn).—A city of Naphtali, in the mountains, Jos 19³⁸. It is probably the modern Yârûn. See SWP vol. i. sheet iv., and Baedeker-Socin, Pal.³ p. 261.

IRON in the English Bible almost always stands for בַּרְזֶל (in Dn Aram. פַּרְזֶל) in OT, and for σίδηρος or the adj. σιδηροῦς in Apocr. and NT [Exceptions:—In Job 41⁷ 'barbed irons' is the rendering of שְׁפוֹת, and in 1 Ti 4² 'seared (as) with a hot iron' is a paraphrase of κεκαυστηριασμένος]. Conversely, בַּרְזֶל and its Gr. equivalents are usually translated by 'iron' [Exceptions:—In Dt 19⁵, 2 K 6⁵ בַּרְזֶל is rendered '(ax-) head,' and in Is 44¹² חֲרַשׁ בַּרְזֶל is simply 'smith'; σίδηρος is trᵈ 'sword' in Jth 6⁶ 9⁸, 4 Mac 14¹⁹].

LXX is less consistent. It has σίδηρος for חֶרֶב (sword), Job 5²⁰ 15²² 39²², for גַּרְזֶן (axe), Dt 20¹⁹, for מוֹרָה (razor), Jg 13⁵ 16⁷, 1 K 1¹¹, and τέκτων σιδήρου for חָרָשׁ (smith), 1 S 13¹⁹. On the other hand, it renders בַּרְזֶל by μάχαιρα, Is 10³⁴, by σιδήριον, Dt 19⁵, 2 K 6⁵·⁶, Ec 10¹⁰, and elsewhere by σίδηρος or σιδηροῦς. Evidently both in Heb. and Gr. 'iron' was a term used somewhat generally to describe both the metal and instruments of various kinds made from it.

This well-known metal is one of the so-called elementary substances. From its abundance, the ease with which it can be separated from its ores, and its many useful properties, it is the most important of all the metals. Ordinary iron is not a pure element, but always contains a small amount of carbon, the proportion of which greatly affects its qualities. When the quantity of carbon is small (from 0·15 to 0·5 per cent.) we have wrought iron, which is extremely difficult to melt, but is tough, and can be welded at white heat. When the percentage of carbon is from 3 to 6 we have cast iron, which is brittle, and cannot be welded, but which can be melted and cast in mould. The intermediate variety, containing from 0·6 to 2 per cent. of carbon, is steel, which can be both cast and welded, and can also be tempered to various degrees of elasticity and hardness. In modern processes iron is separated from its ores in the form of cast iron, from which the other forms are obtained by removing some of the carbon. The high temperature required to melt cast iron has been urged as a difficulty in the way of understanding the use of the metal in early times. But iron can be separated from its ores without being melted. In many countries primitive processes of iron manufacture survive, and are carried on at the present day. These doubtless represent the ancient methods, and their crude product is not cast iron, but a 'bloom' or spongy mass of wrought iron or steel.

Native iron is almost unknown except in meteorites. Meteoric iron, however, contains impurities which make it brittle and exceedingly difficult to forge. For primitive methods of iron manufacture see Napier, Ancient Workers and Artificers in Metal; Day, The Prehistoric Use of Iron and Steel; Swank, Iron in all Ages (OT references in the last-named are uncritical).

In the Scripture records iron appears side by side with brass (which see) or bronze from the very earliest times, and the two metals are often mentioned together. Tubal-cain is described as an artificer in both (Gn 4²²), and similar workers are referred to in the reigns of David (2 Ch 27· ¹⁴) and Joash (2 Ch 24¹²). In Dt 8⁹ both are named among the minerals of Palestine, and in Jos 22⁸ they are among the spoils carried home by the tribe of Manasseh after the conquest of Canaan. They are mentioned in Nu 31²² in a list of incombustible materials, and in Jer 6²⁸, Ezk 22¹⁸, among the impurities of silver.

Iron is classed among the necessaries of life (Sir 39²⁶); and the Scripture allusions testify to its extensive and varied applications. Is 60¹⁷ shows that its relative value in ancient times was much the same as at present, being less than that of gold and silver, and greater than that of stone. Iron was used for *weapons of offence* (Nu 35¹⁶, Job 20²⁴, Jth 6⁶ 9⁸, 4 Mac 14¹⁹), for *war chariots* (Jos 17¹⁶·¹⁸, Jg 1¹⁹ 4³·¹³), and for *defensive armour* (2 S 23⁷, Rev 9⁹). *Saws, harrows,* and *axes* of iron were used by David in dealing (?; see Driver, *Sam.* p. 288, and cf. art. HARROW) with his Ammonite prisoners (2 S 12³¹, 1 Ch 20³). *Hands* of iron are mentioned as instruments of torture in 4 Mac 8¹² 9²⁶·²⁸. There are allusions to iron *gates* (Ac 12¹⁰), *fetters* (Ps 105¹⁸ 149⁸, 3 Mac 3²⁵, 4 Mac 11¹⁰), *prison bars* (Ps 107¹⁰·¹⁶, Is 45²), *yokes* (Dt 28⁴⁸, Jer 28¹³·¹⁴, Sir 28²⁰), and *horns* (as prophetic symbols, 1 K 22¹¹, 2 Ch 18¹⁰). *Axes* for felling trees were made of iron (Dt 19⁵, 1 K 6⁵·⁶, Is 10³⁴), and also tools for stone-quarrying (Sir 48¹⁷) and stone-hewing (Dt 27⁵, Jos 8³¹, 1 K 6⁷). There were iron * *threshing instruments* (Am 1³), *images* (Dn 5²³), *vessels* (Jos 6¹⁹·²⁴), *pans* (Ezk 4³), *nails* or bolts (1 Ch 22³, Wis 13¹⁵), *pens* or graving tools (Jer 17¹, Job 19²⁴). Iron was among the materials gathered by David for the building of the temple (1 Ch 22¹⁴·¹⁶ 29²·⁷), among the merchandise of Tyre (Ezk 27¹²·¹⁹), and of the apocalyptic Babylon (Rev 18¹²). The whetting of iron tools is referred to in Pr 27¹⁷, Ec 10¹⁰. The *heaviness* of iron is noted in Sir 22¹⁵. Its weight was reckoned by shekels (1 S 17⁷), or by talents (1 Ch 29⁷).

As to the manufacture of iron, the ore is alluded to in Job 28². The references to the 'iron furnace' (Dt 4²⁰, 1 K 8⁵¹, Jer 11⁴) may be either to the smelting furnace, in which the iron was separated from its ore, or to the blacksmith's forge, which is vividly described in Is 44¹², Sir 38²⁸.

In many of the above passages, and in a number of others, 'iron' is used metaphorically. The description of the heavens and the earth as brass and iron (Lv 26¹⁹, Dt 28²³) is a picture of drought. The iron furnace is a striking figure for the severest suffering. Iron is a symbol of strength, and as such is employed of Asher (Dt 33²⁵), of Israel (Mic 4¹³), of the fourth kingdom in Nebuchadnezzar's vision (Dn 2³³⁻⁴⁵ *passim*), and of behemoth (Job 40¹⁸ 41²⁷). Prophetic boldness is typified in Jer 1¹⁸ by an iron pillar. On the other hand, iron is an emblem of Israel's obstinacy (Is 48⁴) and corruption (Jer 6²⁸, Ezk 22¹⁸, iron being an impurity in silver). The rod of iron (Ps 2⁹, Rev 2²⁷ 12⁵ 19¹⁵) symbolizes a rule of irresistible might.

One or two passages referring to iron have been reserved for special comment.

The 'bedstead of iron,' belonging to king Og of Bashan (Dt 3¹¹), was probably a sarcophagus of basalt, the black iron-like stone of the region. This stone, and not literal iron, may possibly be intended also in Dt 8⁹. See Pliny, *Nat. Hist.* xxxvi. 11; and Driver, *Deuteronomy, in loc.*

In Jer 15¹² occurs the phrase בַּרְזֶל מִצָּפוֹן 'northern iron' (AV), 'iron from the north' (RV), of which there are two different interpretations. On the one hand, it has been supposed to refer to the iron manufactured by the Chalybians, which was reputed to be of special excellence; while, on the other hand, it has been understood simply as a figurative description of the northern invasion which Jeremiah elsewhere predicts as impending (1¹⁴ 4⁶ 6¹ 13²⁰).

In Ezk 27¹⁹ we have בַּרְזֶל עָשׁוֹת, which is rendered 'bright iron' in AV and RV, but 'wrought iron' in RVm. LXX connects the phrase with the preceding clause, and translates ἐξ Ἀσὴλ σίδηρος εἰργασμένος. The meaning is generally understood to be 'iron wares of rare workmanship' (*kunstreich verarbeitetes Eisen*—Siegfried in Kautzsch's *AT*). The Rabbis took the locality described to be in South Arabia, like Dedan, and the iron articles to

* Possibly the word in Am 1³ means hard black basalt, as in Dt 3¹¹. See Driver, *Joel and Amos*, pp. 130, 227.

be Indian swords, which were famous in that region. See Cornill and Smend, *in loc.*

The word 'iron' in Scripture is applied to articles which may have been made of wrought iron, and to others which probably were made of steel. The apparent special allusions to steel in AV are misleading (see STEEL). See also following article.

JAMES PATRICK.

IRON (*barzel*).—The use of iron was comparatively late. In the whole of the plunder of Syria about B.C. 1480 iron is never mentioned; nor is it in the cuneiform letters from Syria about B.C. 1360. No clearly dated example of it is known in Egypt before about B.C. 700. Probably it began to come into use in Syria about B.C. 900 or 1000. Beyond the generalities of iron being named among metals (Gn 4²², Nu 31²² 35¹⁶), and the phrases 'chariots of iron' (Jos 17¹⁶·¹⁸, Jg 1¹⁹ 4³·¹³) and 'bed of iron' (Dt 3¹¹[?]), the 'tool of iron' is definitely named under Solomon (1 K 6⁷), and as an axe about B.C. 850 (2 K 6⁵). Iron is mentioned under Tiglath-pileser I. (c. 1100). See *KIB* i. 39. Well-developed tools of iron (chisels, rasps, files, centre-bits, etc.) were made by Assyrians in B.C. 670, implying that such had probably been in progress for a century or two at least. It appears, then, that iron began to spread about B.C. 1000, most likely from the Chalybes in the Assyr. highlands, who still work it, and were celebrated for it anciently. This is probably quite as early as, or earlier than, it appears for any purpose in Europe. See MINES, MINING.   W. M. FLINDERS PETRIE.

IRPEEL (יִרְפְּאֵל 'El heals').—A city of Benjamin, noticed with Chephirah, Mozah, and others, Jos 18²⁷. The most probable site is the ruin *Rafât*, N. of *el-Jîb* (Gibeon). See *SWP* vol. i. sheet xvii.

IRRIGATION.—In Babylonia and Egypt, on account of the lack of rain, water was supplied to the fields and gardens by an elaborate system of irrigation. The waters of the Nile, Euphrates, and Tigris were conveyed to a distance by a network of larger and smaller canals. The water from these, or from reservoirs supplied by them, is raised by various machines, the most common of which is the *shadoof*, the essential part of which is a lever, with a weight at one end, serving to raise the full bucket at the other. Other machines are somewhat like a turbine. The water thus raised is distributed along narrow gutters. The Nile Valley is naturally fertilized by the inundations caused by the rise of the Nile; and the control and distribution of these floods was an important feature in the irrigation of Egypt. To this purpose Lake Mœris was adapted by the great engineering works of Amenemhat III. (see Herodot. i. 193; Maspero, *Dawn of Civilization*, 67 ff., 445 ff., 763 ff.; Lane, *Modern Egyptians*⁵, ii. 26 f.; Petrie, *History of Egypt*, i. 193; arts. ASSYRIA, 178ᵃ; EGYPT, ii.).

Palestine, however, is by no means a waterless country; the eastern table-lands especially are well provided with springs. In parts, however, *e.g.* on the Judæan plateau, springs are rare, moreover the rain drains away quickly; nevertheless, the earlier and the later rains suffice for the crops generally. As to need for irrigation, Palestine is expressly contrasted with Egypt in Dt 11¹⁰·¹¹ 'For the land, whither thou goest in to possess it, is not as the land of Egypt, from whence ye came out, where thou sowedst thy seed and wateredst it with thy foot, as a garden of herbs; but the land, whither ye go over to possess it, is a land of hills and valleys, *and* drinketh water of the rain of heaven.' This passage does not imply that irrigation was unknown in Palestine, but that it was only used on a small scale, for gardens, etc. Thus we read in Is 58¹¹ of a 'watered garden,' *gan râweh*; in Ec 2⁵·⁶ Solomon is made to say, 'I made me gardens and parks, and I planted trees in them of all kinds of fruit : I made me pools of water, to water therefrom the forest where trees were reared.' Cf. also Sir 24³⁰·³¹ 'I also came out as a brook from a river, and as a conduit into a garden. I said I will water my best garden, and will abundantly water my garden bed.' So G. A. Smith, *HGHL* 83, 'Vegetables thrive where summer irrigation is used.' Driver on Dt 11¹⁰ (cf. 2nd ed. p. xxi) quotes Conder, *Tent-Work*, p. 328, as stating that he had seen gardens irrigated 'by means of small ditches trodden by the foot.' Steuernagel, however, explains 'watered with the foot' in the same passage as referring to a wheel worked with the foot.

There are numerous references to *peleg* or *palgê mayîm* (Ps 1³ etc.), *i.e.* the trenches used for irrigation ; but we cannot therefore deduce a wide use of irrigation in Palestine ; some of the passages may have been written in Babylonia, or by authors familiar with the irrigation trenches of Egypt or Chaldæa ; nor is it certain that *peleg* may not sometimes mean a natural tributary.

LITERATURE.—Benzinger, *Heb. Arch.* 1894, pp. 97, 227 ff.; Driver on Dt 11¹⁰ ; Nowack, *Lehrb. der Heb. Arch.* 1894, i. 253 ff.; G. A. Smith, *HGHL* pp. 63 ff., 78 ff., 521.   W. H. BENNETT.

IR-SHEMESH (עִיר שֶׁמֶשׁ 'city of the sun,' Jos 19⁴¹).—See BETHSHEMESH 1, and HERES 1.

IRU (עִירוּ).—The eldest son of Caleb, 1 Ch 4¹⁵. The correct name is probably IR, the -u being simply the conjunction 'and' (ו) coupling it with the following name Elah. (See Kittel, *ad loc.*).

ISAAC (יִצְחָק ; in Am 7⁹·¹⁶ [where it is a poet. synonym for *Israel*], Jer 33²⁶, Ps 105⁹ יִשְׂחָק ; LXX and NT Ἰσαάκ).

1. The story of Isaac is that of the least conspicuous of the three Hebrew patriarchs. The following brief description gives all that is preserved in the Book of Genesis respecting him.

Isaac was the long promised son of Abraham and Sarah. He was born when Abraham was 100 and Sarah 91 years old (cf. Gn 17¹⁷·²⁴ 21⁵). He was circumcised on the eighth day (Gn 21⁴). He was called Isaac ('laughter') by divine command (Gn 17¹⁹), because Abraham had *laughed* at the thought of a child being 'born unto him that is an hundred years old' (Gn 17¹⁷). The jealousy of Sarah being aroused at the sight of Ishmael, Hagar's son, playing (מְצַחֵק) with Isaac, led to the expulsion of Hagar and Ishmael from the tent of Abraham (Gn 21⁸⁻²¹). See HAGAR. It would appear from this narrative (Gn 21¹⁴) that Isaac's earliest days were spent in the neighbourhood of Beersheba.

The next recorded event in the life of Isaac was the sacrifice 'in the land of Moriah,' when Abraham was bidden of God to offer his 'only son . . . Isaac' for a burnt - offering upon one of the mountains (Gn 22²). For remarks upon this trial of Abraham's faith see the article ABRAHAM. The beauty of the story is enhanced by the simple colloquy between Abraham and his son, as they went 'both of them together' to the appointed place, Isaac bearing 'the wood of the burnt-offering' (Gn 22⁶⁻⁸). The submission and obedience of Isaac are virtues as evidently intended to be emphasized in the narrative as the faith of Abraham. The life of Isaac was spared through the interposition of 'the angel of the Lord'; and 'a ram caught in the thicket by the horns' was offered up by Abraham 'for a burnt-offering in the stead of his son' (Gn 22¹³). Abraham and Isaac returned to Beersheba (Gn 22¹⁹).

The death of Sarah occurred at Hebron when Isaac was 36 years old (Gn 23¹); but Isaac is not mentioned in connexion with the purchase of the

field of Machpelah and the burial of Sarah (Gn 23). Abraham is not stated to have consulted Isaac when he despatched 'his servant, the elder of his house' (Gn 24²), to take a wife for his son from his country and kindred in Mesopotamia. Rebekah, the daughter of 'Bethuel, the son of Milcah, the wife of Nahor, Abraham's brother' (Gn 24¹⁵), is brought from Mesopotamia by Abraham's servant. Isaac, we are told (Gn 24⁶²), dwelt at that time 'in the land of the South,' near Beer-lahai-roi. Rebekah became his wife ; and Isaac 'was comforted after his mother's (or 'his father's,' reading אָבִיו for אִמּו, as his mother's name has not been mentioned in the section) death.' Isaac joined with Ishmael in committing the body of Abraham to burial in the cave of Machpelah (Gn 25⁹).

The remaining records of Isaac's life ('the generations of Isaac,' Gn 25¹²) are very meagre. Twin children are born to Rebekah after Isaac's entreaty of J″ (Gn 25²¹). In Gn 26¹⁻⁶ we are told that, in consequence of a famine, Isaac journeyed to Gerar, but was warned by God not to go down into Egypt. On the occasion of this theophany, Isaac is told of the blessing upon himself and his seed because of the obedience of his father Abraham (Gn 26⁶). In Gn 26⁷⁻¹¹ Isaac is guilty of the same cowardice and deceit in the land of the Philistines, as Abraham among the Egyptians. In order, as he thought, to save his own life, he gave out that Rebekah was his sister. Abimelech, the Philistine king, saw from a window 'Isaac . . . sporting (מְצַחֵק) with Rebekah' (Gn 26⁸), and perceived at once that she was his wife and not his sister. Abimelech justly rebuked Isaac ; and gave his people charge not to molest either him or his wife. Isaac during his sojourn in Gerar became so prosperous as a wheat-grower and herdsman as to incur the envy of the Philistines. They commenced a petty persecution of Isaac, stopping up the wells which his father Abraham had dug, and which Isaac's servants had opened again. Abimelech even counselled Isaac to withdraw from the country in the interests of peace (Gn 26¹⁶). We are then told of two wells dug by Isaac's men, and violently claimed by the Philistines ; these he called '*Esek* ('strife') and *Sitnah* ('enmity'). Moving his encampment still farther away, he dug another well, which the Philistines did not dispute, and which Isaac therefore called *Rehoboth* ('broad places'), generally identified with the modern *Ruhaibe*, a well some 25 miles S. of Beersheba.

Isaac subsequently journeyed to Beersheba (Gn 26²³), where J″ appeared to him by night and blessed him. He built an altar there to J″, and his servants digged a well. And while encamped in this spot, he received overtures for an alliance with the Philistines. Abimelech the king, Ahuzzath 'his friend,' and Phicol the captain of the host, came over from Gerar ; and Isaac made a covenant with them, and gave them a banquet. They plighted their faith to him by an oath (שְׁבֻעָה) ; and on the day of their departure Isaac heard that his servants had come upon water in the well they were digging. Accordingly he gave the well the name of *Shibah*, as if equivalent to *Shebuah* ; and thus the name Beersheba, according to one tradition (cf. for another Gn 21³¹), took its rise.

In the remaining passages in which Isaac is referred to, he is an old and feeble man. In Gn 27 he appears as a man upon his deathbed, practically blind, and desirous to bestow his last blessing upon his elder son, Esau, whom 'he loved . . . because he did eat of his venison' (Gn 25²⁸). Through Rebekah's cunning, Jacob the younger son supplants his brother. Isaac, too blind to distinguish between them by sight, is suspicious of the voice, but is reassured by Jacob's hairy garments, by their feel and smell. He pronounces upon Jacob the blessing of the birthright, in words of a high poetical strain (Gn 27[27-29]). Shortly afterwards Esau returns; and Isaac is greatly agitated when he realizes the deception practised by his younger son. But he cannot go back. He pronounces a blessing—or rather a prediction of a wild and independent destiny—upon his elder son.

Isaac's days were nearly numbered (Gn 27[41]). And Rebekah, to save Jacob from Esau's fury and revenge, induces Isaac to send Jacob away to Mesopotamia, there to obtain a wife from his own kindred, and not to imitate Esau by marriage with Canaanite women. Isaac invokes another blessing upon the head of Jacob, and sends him away to Paddan-aram unto Laban, Rebekah's brother (Gn 27[46]-28[5]).

Once more only do we hear of Isaac; and that is when we read of his death, after the return of Jacob from his 21 years' sojourn in Mesopotamia. The mention of it occurs just after the enumeration of Jacob's twelve sons; and we then read that 'Jacob came unto Isaac his father to Mamre to Kiriath‑arba (the same is Hebron), where Abraham and Isaac sojourned.' Here Isaac died, being 180 years old, and his two sons Esau and Jacob buried him (Gn 35[27-29]).

2. These somewhat disjointed notices of Isaac's life were drawn from the three main sources of tradition preserved in the Book of Genesis.

J records the promise of a son to Abraham and Sarah (Gn 18[9-15]), and the fulfilment of the promise, in Gn 21[1-7]. From the same source (Gn 21[33]) we gather that Isaac's early years were spent at Beersheba. J records the narrative of the servant's journey to Mesopotamia; and the marriage of Isaac and Rebekah (Gn 24). It mentions Isaac's inheritance from Abraham and the sojourn at Beer-lahai-roi (Gn 25[1-6. 11]). J had also the account of Isaac's dealings with the Philistines (Gn 26), and of the deception practised by Jacob upon his father (Gn 27).

E recorded the birth of Isaac and the expulsion of Hagar and Ishmael (Gn 21[6a. 8-21]); and from E we have the narrative of the sacrifice of Isaac (Gn 22[1-13]). Portions also of Gn 27 are ascribed to E, showing that this source contained the narrative of Isaac's commission to Esau to bring him the venison that he loved, and of Jacob's deception.

The Isaac narrative in P was evidently very brief. It mentions that Isaac at 40 years of age married Rebekah, the daughter of Bethuel the Syrian (Aramæan), in Paddan-aram; that his two sons were born when he was 60 years of age (Gn 25[19. 20. 26]); that Esau grieved his father and mother 40 years later by marrying two Hittite wives (Gn 26[34. 35]); that Isaac, to prevent Jacob marrying a Canaanite wife, sent him to Laban in Paddan-aram to obtain a wife from his kindred, and blessed him as he set forth (Gn 27[46]-28[9]); and that, after Jacob's return, Isaac died at Hebron 180 years old, and was buried by his sons (Gn 35[28. 29]).

3. The recognition of these different strata of tradition will enable the student to understand the cause of certain apparently contradictory statements in the narrative. Thus attention has often been called to the fact that in Gn 27 Isaac is represented as old, blind, and on his deathbed, while his death is recorded as occurring possibly 80 years later (cf. Gn 26[34] with Gn 27[1-41] and Gn 35[27]). But the narrative in Gn 27 is from the Prophetic, that in Gn 26[34] 35[27] is from the Priestly tradition. Similarly, whereas in Gn 27[41-45] Jacob is sent away to escape Esau's vengeance, which will take a murderous form as soon as Isaac dies, we find in Gn 27[46]-28[1-6] that Isaac sends Jacob away to take a wife from Paddan-aram, and blesses him, without any reference being made to the blessing obtained by guile, which has been described in the previous chapter. But the difficulty disappears when we find that Gn 27[1-45] is from the Prophetic, and Gn 27[46]-28[6] is from the Priestly source, and that the two traditions are combined, though not harmonized.

The great similarity between the story—though not harmonized—of the repudiation of Rebekah by Isaac at the court of Abimelech at Gerar, and the story of the repudiation of Sarah by Abraham, likewise at the court of Abimelech king of Gerar, will have occurred to all readers. The Abraham narrative (Gn 20) is from E; the Isaac narrative (Gn 26[8-11]) is from J. It can hardly be doubted that the two traditions are different versions of the same event.

According to the figures given in Gn 25[26], where it is stated that Isaac was 60 years old when Jacob and Esau were born, and those given in Gn 35[28], where it is stated that Isaac died at the age of 180, we should infer that Isaac's death occurred only 10 years before Jacob's descent into Egypt (Gn 47[10]). Moreover, by a comparison of the data of Joseph's age (Gn 41[46] 45[6]) with those of Jacob's age (Gn 47[9]), it would appear that Isaac was 137 years old when Jacob went to Haran.

4. The position of Isaac in the narrative is not so conspicuous or so attractive as that of Abraham or of Jacob. He impersonates, as it were, the peaceful, obedient, and submissive qualities of an equable trust in God, distinct alike from the transcendent faith of Abraham, and from that lower type which in Jacob was learned through discipline and purged from self-will. There are but a few items upon the strength of which a picture of Isaac's character can be constructed. But the submission shown at the crisis of sacrifice (Gn 22), the lonely meditation at eventide (Gn 24[63]), the intercession on his wife's behalf (Gn 25[21]), Jacob's allusion to the object of his father's fear (Gn 31[42]), are details which supply features of greater dignity and grace than are suggested by the mention of his fondness for good food in Gn 25[28] 27[4]. He is, however, a subordinate figure as compared with Abraham and Jacob; and the lower level at which he seems to stand is implied in Gn 26[5], where the covenant of blessing is granted to Isaac and his seed, not for their own sake, but for their father Abraham's sake.

It was not without significance for the Israelites that the prehistoric founders of their race were not all of heroic mould. The ordinary materials of Hebrew life, as represented in Isaac and Jacob, were selected to be the channels of special revelation no less than the more splendid and striking personality of their father Abraham. Isaac was similar to the majority in every community, yielding, easy-going, stationary, content to receive the promise without realizing the extent or nature of the privilege. The events of his life are associated with a few localities, all (except Mamre, Gn 35[27-29]) within a restricted area in S. Palestine. His encampments at Beer-lahai-roi, Gerar, and Beersheba form a sharp contrast to the varied scenes in the lives of Abraham and Jacob. The typical service of one of the patriarchs was rendered in quietness and sitting still.

5. *References in the New Testament.* — The sacrifice of Isaac is twice referred to in the NT. (1) He 11[17. 18], where the writer brings out the triumph of Abraham's faith in the conflict between the affection of a father and the duty of obedience; (2) Ja 2[21], where the apostle appeals to the great deed of sacrifice as against the perversion of the doctrine of justification by faith. In each case the submission of Isaac plays its part, but only a secondary part, in the argument of the writer.

6. The great importance attached by the Jews of the Middle Ages to the sacrifice of Isaac is

worthy of attention. 'The Jews implore the mercy of God by the sacrifice of Isaac, as Christians by the sacrifice of Christ' (Mayor, *Ep. James*, p. 97). In the submission of Isaac was seen the submission of the whole race. Cf. *Targ.* on Mic 7²⁰ 'Remember for us the binding of Isaac.' *Pesikta R. Kahana*, 'For the merit of Isaac who offered himself upon the altar, the Holy One, blessed be He, will hereafter raise the dead' (Buber).

Amongst many strange Jewish traditions respecting Isaac may be mentioned that of *Targ. Jerus.* on Gn 27¹, where Isaac's blindness is accounted for 'because when his father was binding him, he had seen the throne of glory, and from that time his eyes had begun to darken.' Even more strange is the altercation between Isaac and Ishmael, which, according to the Targum of Palestine, led to the sacrifice of Isaac : 'And it was after these things that Isaac and Ishmael contended ; and Ishmael said, It is right that I should inherit what is the father's, because I am his firstborn son. And Isaac said, It is right that I should inherit what is the father's, because I am the son of Sarah his wife, and thou art the son of Hagar the handmaid of my mother. Ishmael answered and said, I am more righteous than thou, because I was circumcised at thirteen years ; and if it had been my will to hinder, they should not have delivered me to be circumcised ; but thou wast circumcised a child of eight days ; if thou hadst had knowledge, perhaps they could not have delivered thee to be circumcised. Isaac answered and said, Behold now, to-day I am thirty and six years old ; and if the Holy One, blessed be He, were to require all my members, I would not hesitate. These words were heard before the Lord of the World, and the Word (Memra) of the Lord at once tried Abraham' (Etheridge's translation).

7. Though not employed for that purpose in the writings of the NT (yet cf. Ro 8³²), the sacrifice of Isaac was largely made use of by the Fathers as typical of the sacrifice on the cross. The earliest use of it in this connexion appears to be *Ep. Barn.* ch. 7, 'Because He was in His own person about to offer the vessel of His Spirit a sacrifice for our sins, that the type also which was given in Isaac, who was offered upon the altar, should be fulfilled' (Lightfoot's *Apostolic Fathers*, p. 251). Irenæus speaks of Abraham having yielded up his son as a sacrifice in order that God might also be pleased to give His only Son as a sacrifice for our redemption (προθύμως τῷ ἰδίῳ μονογενῆ καὶ ἀγαπητὸν παραχωρήσας θυσίαν τῷ θεῷ, ἵνα καὶ ὁ θεὸς εὐδοκήσῃ ὑπὲρ τοῦ σπέρματος αὐτοῦ πάντως τὸν ἴδιον μονογενῆ καὶ ἀγαπητὸν υἱὸν θυσίαν παρασχεῖν εἰς λύτρωσιν ἡμετέραν, ed. Stieren, i. 572). Cf. August. *De Civ. Dei*, xvi. 32.

8. The *name* 'Isaac.' It would appear that the name Isaac, derived from the root פֿחצ, and meaning 'laugh,' was connected in popular Israelite tradition with incidents preceding or attending the birth of the patriarch. It is impossible to resist the conclusion that the form of these traditions was occasioned by the stories based upon, or suggested by, the popular etymology of the name. At least three different explanations seem to have been given, in order to account for the name ; the compiler of Genesis has faithfully reproduced them all. (1) In Gn 17¹⁷ (P) 'Abram laughed' at the idea of a son being born to him in his old age; (2) in Gn 18¹² we are told that 'Sarah laughed within herself' at the prediction that she should bear a son ; (3) in Gn 21⁶ Sarah, after the birth of the child, is represented as saying, 'God hath prepared laughter (פֿחצ) for me.' The continuation of the same verse, however, suggests that there was yet another version of the same tradition, according to which the laughter was neither that of incredulity on the part of Abraham and Sarah, nor

that of joy on the part of Sarah, but that of derision on the part of those who heard the news, and who would laugh at one so old becoming a mother : 'every one will laugh at me.' It should also be noticed that the same root occurs in the sense of 'playing' in the story of Ishmael and Isaac (Gn 21⁹), and also in that of Isaac and Rebekah (Gn 26³).

A fanciful Rabbinic derivation for the name explained it to be a compound of two words יצֿאקוֹפֿ 'the out-going of statute,' as if in Isaac was to be discerned a development of the religious faith of Abraham (Hamburger, *RE*, *s.v.*).

It has been suggested that 'Isaac' may possibly be a truncated form for 'Isaac-el,' on the analogy of 'Isra-el,' 'Ishma-el,' and possibly 'Joseph-el' and 'Jacob-el' (cf. Gray's *Studies in Hebrew Proper Names*, p. 214).

See further, for several questions connected with the story of Isaac, and on the whole question of the character of the patriarchal narratives, art. JACOB.

                                         H. E. RYLE.

ISAIAH.—

Although anticipated by Amos and Hosea in many of his leading doctrines, and excelled both by Jeremiah and the great Prophet of the Exile in depth of personal experience and width of religious outlook, Isaiah was nevertheless the greatest of the Hebrew prophets — by the strength of his personality, the wisdom of his statesmanship, the length and unbroken assurance of his ministry, the almost unaided service which he rendered to Judah at the greatest crisis of her history, the purity and grandeur of his style, and the influence he exerted on subsequent prophecy.

I. NAME. — The English name *Isaiah* is an approximate transliteration of the abbreviated form *Yĕsha'yāh* יְשַׁעְיָה, which appears as the title of the prophet's book in the Hebrew Canon, and occurs besides as the name of several individuals in post-exilic writings (Ezr 8⁷· ¹⁹, Neh 11⁷, 1 Ch 3²¹). The full and older form is *Yĕsha'yāhû* יְשַׁעְיָהוּ (Gr. Ἡσαΐας, Lat. *Esaias* and *Isaias*), by which the prophet himself is always called in the text of his book (2 K 19²ᶠᶠ·, 2 Ch 26²² 32²⁰· ³²) ; also of other Jews, 1 Ch 25³· ¹⁵ 26²⁵. It means 'J″ is salvation,' and is therefore synonymous with the frequent *Joshua* or *Jeshua* (Jesus) יְהוֹשֻׁעַ or יֵשׁוּעַ, and *Hosea* הוֹשֵׁעַ, cf. the Heb. *Elisha* אֱלִישַׁע 'God is, *or* God of, Salvation'; *Elishua* אֱלִישׁוּעַ, *Ishi* יִשְׁעִי, etc., the Sabæan or Himyaritic forms אֵלְיַשַׁע and יַשַׁעְאֵל, and the Phœn. יַשַׁע.

II. PERSONAL HISTORY.—The exact limits which we are led to assign to Isaiah's career depend on the conclusions we have still to reach with regard to several disputed portions of his book. Generally speaking, however, we may say that he prophesied from the year in which king Uzziah died (B.C. 740 or 736) to the year of the sudden deliverance of Jerusalem from Sennacherib, 701, and possibly some years after this. Isaiah was therefore born about 760 (seven years before the reputed foundation of Rome), was a child when Amos appeared at Bethel (c. 755 or 750), and a youth when Hosea began to prophesy in N. Israel. Micah was his younger contemporary. Isaiah prophesied under Uzziah, Jotham, Ahaz, and Hezekiah, kings of Judah. The chief political events of his life were the ascent of the great soldier Tiglath-pileser III. to the throne of Assyria in 745, with a new policy of conquest ; the league of Aram and N. Israel in 735, and their invasion of Judah, which moved Ahaz to call Assyria to his help ; Tiglath-pileser's capture of Damascus, and the captivity of Gilead and Galilee in 734 ; the invasion of N. Palestine by Salmanassar IV. in 725, with the long siege of Samaria which fell to his successor Sargon in or about 721 ; Sargon's defeat of Egypt on her border at Raphia in 719 ; Sargon's invasion of Palestine in 711 with the reduction of Ashdod, and his defeat of Merodach-baladan and capture of Babylon in 709 ; Sennacherib's succession in 705, and invasion of Palestine in 701 ; his encounter with Egypt at Eltekeh on the borders of Philistia and Judah ; his capture of Ekron and siege of Jerusalem, with the pestilence that overtook him between Palestine and Egypt ; and his retreat from Palestine, with the consequent relief of Jerusalem—all in 701. About 695 (some say about 690 or even 685) Hezekiah was succeeded by Manasseh. Whether Isaiah lived into the reign of the latter is very doubtful. We have no prophecies from him later than Hezekiah's reign, perhaps none after 701.[*] The Mishna (*Jebamoth* 49*b* ; cf. *Sanhedr.* 103*b*) says that he was slain by Manasseh. The apocryphal work, *The Ascension of Isaiah,* which was written in the beginning of the 2nd Christian cent. (only an Ethiopic version is extant ; see Dillmann's ed. with a Latin translation, Leipzig, 1877), affirms that Isaiah's martyrdom consisted in being sawn asunder, which Justin Martyr repeats (*Dial. c. Tryph.* ch. 120, c. A.D. 150). Whether this be true, and whether it is alluded to in He 11[37], we cannot tell. See next article.

Isaiah is called the son of Amoz (אָמוֹץ 1[1] 2[1] etc.), who must not be confounded, as he has been by various Christian Fathers, with the prophet Amos (עָמוֹס). A Jewish tradition (*Megilla* 10*b*) makes Isaiah nephew of king Amaziah ; and his royal descent has been inferred from his familiarity with successive monarchs of Judah, and his general political influence. A stronger reason than these might be drawn from the presence in his name of J″, which appears to have been confined at the earlier periods of Israel's history to proper names of the royal houses. But even this is not conclusive, and one really knows nothing of either Isaiah's forefathers or his upbringing. He was married, his wife is called 'the prophetess' (8[3]), and he had two sons to whom he gave names symbolic of those aspects of the nation's history which he enforced in his prophecies : *She'ar-yashub,* 'a remnant shall return,' who was old enough in 736–735 to be taken by his father when he went to face king Ahaz (7[3]), and *Maher-shalal-hash-baz* 'spoil-speeds-booty-hastes,' who was born about a year later (8[1-4]). The legend that Isaiah was twice married has been deduced from the false inference that the 'young woman of marriageable age,' עַלְמָה of 7[14], was his wife. By this expression the prophet probably did not mean a definite individual.

The most certain and significant fact about Isaiah is that he was a citizen, if not a native, of Jerusalem,[†] and had constant access to the court and presence of the king. Jerusalem is Isaiah's 'immediate and ultimate regard, the centre and return of all his thoughts, the hinge of the history of his time, the summit of those brilliant hopes

with which he fills the future. He has traced for us the main features of her position and some of the lines of her construction, many of the great figures of her streets, the fashions of her women, the arrival of embassies, the effect of rumours. He has painted her aspect in triumph, in siege, in famine, and in earthquake : war filling her valleys with chariots, and again nature rolling tides of fruitfulness up to her very gates ; her moods of worship, panic, and profligacy. If he takes wider observation of mankind, Jerusalem is his watch-tower. It is for her defence he battles through fifty years of statesmanship, and all his prophecy may be said to travail in anguish for her new birth.'

III. STRUCTURE AND CONTENTS OF THE BOOK OF ISAIAH.—The book which bears Isaiah's name consists of 66 chapters, which fall into two very distinct collections of prophetic discourses : chs. 1–35 and chs. 40–66, which are separated by a stretch of narrative or history, chs. 36–39.

A. Chs. 1–35 are further divisible into at least five sections—(1) 1–12 a series of orations upon the religious and political state both of Judah in face of invasions by Assyria and by the confederates Syria and N. Israel, and of N. Israel in face of an invasion by Assyria ; as well as upon the Messianic future of Israel. There is also a series of narratives recounting Isaiah's call (6), his interview with king Ahaz (7), and other measures that he took (8) ; as well as a song of praise (12). This section seems composed of independent groups of oracles. Ch. 1 appears to stand by itself, and carries a title which more than covers the contents of the whole section, 'the reigns which it enumerates exhaust the range of Isaiah's career.' At the head of ch. 2 there is another title which appears to cover 2–4, which form a unity by themselves. Ch. 5 stands apart from them, and is itself composed of independent pieces. Then we have the pieces of narrative : 6 by itself on the prophet's vision in the year Uzziah died, and 7–8[4] containing more oracles and running out into others 8[5]–9[7], all of them apparently from the reign of Ahaz. 9[8]–10[4], along with 5[25-30], which obviously belongs to them, from an oracle against N. Israel. 10[5-34] is an oracle against Assyria, and ch. 11 consists of two prophecies, one of the Messiah (vv.[1-9]), the other of the restoration of all Israel (vv.[10-16]). Ch. 12 is the lyric already alluded to. (2) Chs. 13–23 contain a series of oracles upon heathen nations, with a few upon Judah, but none upon N. Israel. 13–14[23] treats of the fall of Babylon ; 14[24-27] is on Assyria, and vv.[28-32] against the Philistines, assigned by its title to the year of Ahaz' death ; 15. 16 on Moab ; 17[1-11] on the fall of Damascus and N. Israel ; vv.[12-14], the repulse of Assyria ; 18, the same in the form of an address to Ethiopia ; 19 on Egypt—vv.[16-25] appear to be separate from vv.[1-15] ; 20 on Egypt, with a bit of narrative that points to Sargon's march against her about 711 ; 21[1-10] on Babylon, 'oracle of the wilderness of the sea,' vv.[11.12] on Edom, vv.[13-17] on Arabia ; 22[1-14] against Jerusalem during a siege, and vv.[15-25] against Shebna, a statesman of Judah ; 23[1-14] on Tyre, with an appendix vv.[15-18]. (3) 24–27, an apocalyptic prophecy, describing the judgment of the whole world by supernatural convulsions, the blessedness of Israel who shall be rescued, and the resurrection of their dead. (4) 28–33, a series of oracles reflecting, apparently, the historical circumstances of Isaiah's day ; 28[1-6] predictive of the fall of Samaria, vv.[7-22] a controversy with the dissolute politicians of Jerusalem ; 29[1-8] the abasement and subsequent deliverance of Jerusalem, vv.[9-14] the spiritual stupidity of Jerusalem, vv.[15-24] exposure of a conspiracy of the court with Egypt, suddenly changing to a prediction of the future deliverance ; 30[1-17] a return to the Egyptian alliance with denun-

---

[*] Eichhorn and Möller, quoted by Vatke, *Einl.* 620, assigned chs. 40–66 to reign of Manasseh. None of the titles in the Bk. of Isaiah affirm that he prophesied under Manasseh.
[†] Some deduce from 2 K 20[4] that he lived in 'the middle' or 'lower city' (Cheyne, *Encyl. Brit.*[9] xiii. 378).

ciations, vv.[18-26] a picture of the Messianic age, vv.[27-33] apocalyptic judgment on Assyria; 31 the Egyptian alliance, with a promise for Israel and doom on Assyria; 32[1-8] a picture of the Messianic age, vv.[9-14] against the women of Jerusalem, vv.[15-20] another picture of the future; 33 denunciation of an invader of Judah, and affirmation of her deliverance. (5) Chs. 34. 35, Israel's triumph over Edom, return from exile, and blessedness.

B. Then follows the historical section 36–39, of which 36 f. narrates Sennacherib's demand for the surrender of Jerusalem; 38, Hezekiah's sickness and cure, with his hymn; and 39, Merodach-baladan's embassy to Hezekiah.

C. Chs. 40–66, the real or assumed standpoint of the bulk of which is the end of the Babylonian exile, though there are some chapters which appear to have been written in Palestine. (See below.)

IV. CRITICISM OF THE AUTHENTICITY OF THE BOOK.—The preceding analysis reveals not only that the Bk. of Isaiah is the combination of several earlier collections of oracles (ch. 1 a general preface, (a) 2–12 consisting of minor collections, (b) 13–27, (c) 28–35, (d) 36–39 (?), (e) 40–66), but also that, while many of these have obviously risen from the circumstances of Isaiah's own day, others reflect other periods, especially the Babylonian exile, and some, e.g. the apocalyptic passages, betray a style and temper very different from the oracles that belong to Isaiah's lifetime. Moreover, while some of the collections are entitled Isaiah's, others make no claim to be from his hand. Nevertheless, though Ibn Ezra hinted a few doubts and Calvin wrote as if he felt that ch. 55 at least was 'uttered during the captivity in Babylon' (on 55[3]), up to the end of last century the book was universally understood to be covered by the title in its first verse, and therefore as Isaiah's throughout. About 1780, J. B. Koppe in the Germ. ed. of Lowth's Commentary was the first to undermine this position. He was followed by Eichhorn (Introd. iii. 76), and by Döderlein (Esaias, 1789, Præf. xii), who takes it as obvious that 40 ff. are by an anonymous prophet about the end of the Exile. (Vatke refers to a more detailed proof of this by J. E. Justi). Not without opposition from the conservative school (e.g. J. V. Möller, De authentia oracc. Es. cc. 40–66), this view was developed by the great critics of the beginning of this century; and it was further perceived that if 40–66 be exilic, parts of 1–39 must also fall to the same date. In 13[1]–14[23] 21[1-10] 34. 35 Assyria is no longer as in Isaiah's day the dominant world power, nor do these oracles emphasize Jerusalem as the inviolate fortress of God. Babylon takes Assyria's place, her fall is imminent, Israel is in exile but about to be restored. To these non-Isian chapters the critics added 24–27, which, although they appear to have some reflections of the age before the Exile, and do not allude to Babylon, yet contain phrases descriptive of the Exile as actual, with promises of Israel's deliverance therefrom, and hopes of the establishment of Zion, and the repopulation of the Holy Land. To this list of exilic and post-exilic oracles some added ch. 12, and it was argued that 15–16[12] was an oracle older than Isaiah's time, to which Isaiah himself added 16[13. 14]. All the rest of the discourses in 1–39, save for some glosses, were still regarded as Isaiah's own.

Such was virtually the position of criticism down to 1890. It had been established by Gesenius, Ewald, Knobel, and Reuss, and was supported by Kuenen (in 1863), Cheyne (Is. chronol. arranged, 1870, Prophecies of Is. 1880–81, though there is little introduction in this vol., and Enc. Brit. art. 'Isaiah,' 1881; see below on 40–66), Delitzsch (who had previously argued for the unity of the book, but in 1879–80 interpreted 40–66 as from the close

of the Exile; see more fully his Comm.[4] 1889, Eng. ed. 1890), W. R. Smith (Proph. of Isr. 1882), Driver (Isaiah, Life and Times, 1888), G. A. Smith (The Expositor's Bible, 1888), Dillmann (1890). Some of these carried their doubts further than the passages described above. To the non-Isaian oracles some added 23[15-18], some the whole of 23, some 19 in whole or part, and some even 33. Others (see below) denied the unity of 40–66. Even conservative critics like Oehler, von Orelli, and Bredenkamp accepted 40–66 as from another than Isaiah, but the latter two argued for the authenticity of several of the disputed passages in 1–39, Bredenkamp and Klostermann for some in 40–66.

During the last ten years the Bk. of Isaiah, in common with all the prophetic writings, has been subjected to a still more rigorous analysis and criticism, with the result that while Kirkpatrick (Doct. of the Prophets, 1892), Driver (Introd.[6]), and Skinner (Cambridge Bible for Schools, 1896) adhere in the main to the position of the majority of critics before 1890, Duhm (in Nowack's Handkommentar, 1892), Hackmann (Die Zukunftserwartung des Jes. 1893), Cheyne (Introd. to the Bk. of Is. 1895, cf. his edition of the text and translation in Haupt's SBOT, 1898), have cast doubt upon the authenticity of many more portions of 1–39. There can be no question that the thorough analysis to which those critics have subjected the text of 1–39 has been successful in discovering a number of late glosses and other insertions in the genuine prophecies of Isaiah. In all the prophetic books the presence of such is now generally recognized. But Duhm, Hackmann, and Cheyne have cut more deeply than this, and subtracted from Isaiah long passages which were previously regarded as genuine. Their reasons are sometimes mainly subjective; they base their conclusions upon the precarious distinction between the real Isaian style and what they consider to be imitations of it, or infer them from a change of rhythm. The feature of Duhm's able essay is the relegation of a considerable number of passages to the 2nd and even to the 1st cent. before Christ. He founds this upon their apocalyptic character, but he reserves for Isaiah not a few oracles and phrases quite as apocalyptic as those he transfers to the late date. In the latter, too, there are historical allusions which are suitable to the Assyrian period; Duhm either alters the reading of these, or strains their meaning to suit the Greek period. And, finally, there is the almost indubitable fact which he fails to discredit, that the prophetic Canon was so fixed by B.C. 200 as to render impossible the inclusion within it of the prophetic Book of Daniel. Duhm, indeed, argues that the latter was excluded because of its apocalyptic character; but if he is right, the same reason should have excluded from the Bk. of Isaiah the passages which, because of their apocalyptic character, Duhm assigns to the 2nd cent. This argument therefore, for the presence in Isaiah of features of so late a date, may be said to have failed (for details see Expositor, July to Dec. 1892, and Crit. Review, 1893). Hackmann (op. cit. p. 143 ff.) denies to Isaiah the two pictures of the Messiah 9[1-6] and 11[1-9]—the former on the grounds that it starts from the ruin of the Jewish state which was not actual in Isaiah's time, and implies a rejection of the reigning king, Ahaz or Hezekiah, and a confidence in an unborn One, which it is inconceivable to associate with Isaiah. It suits better a time when there was no king in Israel and the people had not independent existence. The destruction of David's dynasty is also implied, he thinks, by 11[1-9], the picture of universal peace in which and the 'supernatural' elements are further symptoms of a late date. These reasons are anything but conclusive. Few will doubt that the delinquencies of Ahaz furnished sufficient occasion to Isaiah for his hope of the appearance of a real champion and righteous ruler of Israel. It is equally hard to believe the great prophet incapable, at that age in Israel, of a dream of universal peace ; one might as well argue that such a dream was impossible in the post-exilic period (to which Hackmann relegates it) because many of the writings of the latter, like Jl 4 and 'Zec' 10, exhibit a rude delight in war. The truth is that among all nations and in all periods of their history the hope of peace has existed along with a belief in the necessity of war, and even with a delight in it. Hackmann finds a more plausible reason (147 f.) for a late date for these passages in their language, which bears a few post-exilic features. He also denies to Isaiah the well-known passage 2^{2-5}, repeated in Mic 4^{1-5}, on the ground that its ideals of the sovereignty of J″ over foreign nations, their adoption of His law, the supremacy of the temple, and universal peace, agree better with a post-exilic than with a pre-exilic date (so, too, Mitchell, *Isaiah, a Study of Chaps.* i.–xii., New York, 1897, 108 ff.). On the last point an answer has been given above ; nor on any of the others is there anything incompatible with a date in the 8th century. (So even Duhm : on the details see the present writer's *Twelve Proph.* i. 365 f.). Cheyne, who had previously (see above) agreed with the majority of critics as to what were Isaiah's authentic prophecies, stated modifications of his views in the *JQR* for 1891 f., and in 1895 published his very able and thorough *Introd. to the Bk. of Isaiah*, in which, while accepting some of Duhm's and Hackmann's results, he went still further and withdrew nearly a third of 1–12 from Isaiah, and from the oracles hitherto regarded as genuine in 13–35 nearly a half. It is impossible to examine his argument in details. His general principle must be regarded as sound by all who have worked at the text of the prophets, viz. that to the oracles of even the greatest of the prophets later generations of Israel added supplements, in order to mitigate unqualified messages of doom, or for other purposes of edification. This is a principle, however, in the application of which there must naturally be very great difference of opinion. The conclusions do largely depend on the subjectivity of the critic ; and, speaking generally (which is all that the space of this article permits), it must be said that Cheyne's reasons for withdrawing passages from Isaiah are sometimes very hypothetical, and that, to say the least, there often exist in the periods to which he assigns these passages as many difficulties as in the age of Isaiah. There is not a little arbitrariness, as, for instance, when he says that the post-exilic origin of 2^{2-5} is 'beyond reasonable doubt' ; or in reference to 15. 16 (which he takes to be not pre- but post-Isaian) 'was Isaiah the man to use another prophet's material?' There is sometimes an undue depreciation of the literary (cf. p. 88) and spiritual abilities of the pre-exilic period in Israel, especially if one keeps in mind the wonderful composition of the constituents of JE. And one may reasonably ask whether hope and comfort were not as much required by Israel, and not as likely to be contributed by her greatest prophet, in the 8th cent. as after the Exile. These considerations detract from the conclusiveness of Cheyne's powerful and candid arguments. Some further details may be noticed. In ch. 1, vv.$^{2-4}$ and $^{27, 28}$ are taken from Isaiah, hardly with sufficient reason ; 4^{2-6} is placed after the Exile, probably correctly ; on 9^{1-6} 'Hackmann is probably right,' and better though still not conclusive reasons are offered for

a date later than Isaiah ; so with 11^{1-8}. In 13–23, 19 is all post-exilic (Skinner agrees that vv.$^{16-25}$ are probably so). 23^{15-18} is (in agreement with previous critics) a later addition. It is in 29–33 that Cheyne withdraws most from Isaiah : he gives strong reasons for the post-exilic date of 29^{16-24}, less strong for that of 30^{18-26} ; 32 is also assigned to after the Exile, but hardly with sufficient reason, though strong objections to Isaiah's authorship are not unduly stated. 33 has been suspected as not authentic since Ewald's time. Kuenen placed it under Josiah or later, Stade after the Exile, and to the latter Cheyne inclines. There are indeed several difficulties both of style and substance in assigning the ch. to Isaiah (cf. Skinner ; Driver leaves it with Isaiah).

V. The Prophecies of the Messiah in Isaiah 1–39. — In addition to the examination of the different passages given above, the Messianic element in Is 1–39 requires a more general discussion, not only because of its intrinsic importance, but on account of the tendency of recent criticism to deny that the Messiah appeared at all in the prophecy of Israel before the Exile. This thesis, stated by Marti (*Gesch. der Isr. Rel.* 190), has been elaborated by Paul Volz (*Die vorexil. Jahweprophetie u. der Messias*, Göttingen, 1897, cf. Brückner, *Komp. des B. Jes.*). Besides the evidence stated above from the language and historical allusions of the separate Messianic passages, the following are the chief reasons offered. The functions assigned to the Messiah by the disputed passages are not religious but political : to rescue Israel from her heathen tyrants and to govern her in righteousness, but neither to teach the people of God, whether as prophet or as priest, nor to convert the heathen. The rôle is national, not universal. How, it is asked, can these features be harmonized either with this fact that before the Exile the temper of prophecy is mainly threatening and judicial, or with that other, that when the pre-exilic prophets do open up the future they lay down the lines of a universal ethic? Besides, where is there room for so glorious a representative of J″ in a future which is to be filled with the manifest and all-sufficient presence of J″ Himself?

To the present writer these arguments not only appear inconclusive for a late date of the Messianic passages, but in some respects appear to support the tradition of an early date. For, that the functions of the Messiah are described in the passages as national surely suits an early, rather than the later, stages of Israel's religious development ; no detailed picture of the Messiah which was later than the second Isaiah could have omitted the duties and hopes on which the latter so brilliantly insists, of converting the heathen to the knowledge and discipline of J″. Nor is the temper of pre-exilic prophecy so exclusively judicial as is now frequently alleged. The prophets insist that a remnant of Israel shall survive the judgment. Isaiah himself not only predicted, but, during the most influential period of his career, strenuously laboured for, the continuation of the Jewish State. It is not a different dispensation which, like the later apocalyptic prophecy, he anticipates, but a continuance of the present political conditions, purified and exalted. Now among these political conditions in Judah, was the dynasty of David. In contrast with the frequent usurpations of the throne of N. Israel, David's house persisted in Judah practically unchallenged. Since David's own day the religion of J″ was closely wedded with the dynasty, and, besides, David had been successful in achieving the ideal of the unity of all Israel. By Isaiah's time, therefore, the political presuppositions of the Messianic oracles in Is 1–39 were all present. We may even affirm that it would have been passing strange if his anticipations of the religious and political future of Judah had been dissociated from the Davidic monarchy. Moreover, it ought not to be forgotten that none of these disputed passages attribute to the Messiah any of the measures for achieving the establishment of Israel which were required by the exilic or immediately post-exilic ages of the nation's history. There is no word in them of bringing back the exiles or portions of God's people scattered over the world; and no word of the post-exilic dream of a world-empire. On the contrary, in the tasks which these passages assign to the Messiah, we see exactly the two main ends upon which Isaiah's prophetic activity was bent: the deliverance of Judah from the Assyrian invasion which overthrew the kingdom of N. Israel, and the establishment of justice and a pure civic life among the people of J″.

Such considerations amply disprove Volz's contention that the conception of the Messiah was one foreign to the spirit of prophecy, and only dragged into the service of their doctrine by the later prophets, out of the popular religion of Israel. It is true that the hope of the Messiah may have been an article of the popular creed, just as, according to Amos, was the hope of the victorious day of J″. But if the prophets, and, in particular, Isaiah, did not actually create the ideal of a victorious and righteous monarch for Israel, Isaiah certainly re-created it : gave it those moral elements with which we may be sure the popular religion was incapable of investing it.

VI. THE THEOLOGY OF ISAIAH.—We are now in a position to discern the authentic doctrine of Isaiah upon God, religion, Israel, and the world. Like all the earlier prophets, Isaiah reveals his doctrine in no abstract or systematic form, but point by point in connexion with some event of contemporary history or some emergent phase of the character of his generation. Now two great facts were before him, and may be said to have formed from first to last the starting-point, if not the full premise, of his teaching. One was the moral badness of Israel's life, taken along with their stupid misunderstanding of what their God required of them. Isaiah's generation were not as a whole consciously apostate from J″; they were assiduous in His worship, lavish of sacrifice to Him, and careful to observe at all points the ritual which they believed to be His will. But they were shamelessly immoral. Luxury and the vices which spring from it sapped the national life. The administration of justice was corrupt. The rich oppressed the poor, civic duties were neglected. All this evil state of the people was contrary to the will of J″, and due to their misunderstanding of the character and demands of their God. He was a God of righteousness, and He had already made known to Israel His *torah*, as a demand for the very virtues they neglected. He loathed the assiduous worship which they combined with a life so immoral. He regarded the evil features of the latter as sin and rebellion, which required a very thorough punishment, one severe enough to destroy the bulk of the nation.*

Coincident with this state of sinfulness, in which the people were plunged, was the second fact from which Isaiah's prophecies started. The power of Assyria rose on the political horizon, threatening the destruction of all the principalities of Palestine. There had been Assyrian campaigns in N. Syria since 870. Damascus had fallen before one of them in 803, and her forces had suffered another

defeat in 773. Then came a pause of nearly thirty years. But in 745, or at least five years before Isaiah's call to prophesy, Tiglath-pileser III., a soldier of great energy, usurped the Assyrian throne, and set in motion a more vigorous policy towards Palestine. The siege of Arpad and the subjugation of Babylon detained him for nine years, but in 734–733 he overthrew Damascus and swept into captivity, besides its people, the Israelite populations of Gilead and Galilee. Isaiah had perhaps at first been uncertain whether the required punishment of Israel would proceed from Assyria or from Egypt, the only other power at that time which was capable of contesting with Syria the lordship of Palestine (cf. 7[18]). But those proofs of Assyrian power, and the novel Assyrian policy of sweeping into distant captivity the bulk of the subjugated peoples,—those proofs which came with the years 734, 733,—settled the question once for all. Assyria was the destined rod of J″'s anger, and this should accomplish itself not only in the overthrow of N. Israel, to which Isaiah holds out no hope, but in the thorough invasion of Judah. It is an interesting problem, in what proportion the moral conviction of Israel's guilt needing punishment on the one hand, and the political certainty of Assyria's advance on the other, contributed to the assurance of Isaiah's predictions. Of this we may be sure, however, that without their native convictions of J″'s righteousness and power of judgment upon Israel, the prophets could only have viewed the Assyrian advance as a perplexing, if not a paralyzing, problem. But instead of so feeling it, Isaiah is ready for Assyria, predicts the certainty of invasion while the bulk of his people still doubt the latter, and is very clear as to its meaning. That which enabled him and other prophets to see in the advance of Assyria a moral intention, which was to exhaust itself in the destruction of all the Syrian States, but stop short of the utter overthrow of Judah, was the character of Judah's God, He might above all the gods of the heathen, and His purpose of grace not to let His people be abolished. The advance of Assyria was, therefore, a secondary and subordinate factor in the inspiration of Isaiah. At the same time the appearance of the greatest empire of the age, as obviously the instrument of Israel's God, must have lent to the prophets' ideas of His government a largeness to which the religious imagination of Israel had not previously attained (see Ch. IV. of *Bk. of the Twelve Proph.* in the 'Expositor's Bible'). And so we find in Isaiah a conception of the divine providence of the world more wide and majestic than anything that had yet appeared in Israel, although several of its features had already been expressed by Amos and are implied in parts of the JE documents of the Pentateuch. All the forces of the world are subject to J″. The great empires unconsciously fulfil His will upon Israel : the heathen peoples, however they rage, break upon the limits He sets to their advance, as the sea breaks upon its shore. These limits are drawn at the utter destruction of His people. An Israel, however shortened and cut down, must survive. To this end Isaiah (though he sometimes appears to abandon the impenitent people to the destruction they court by their foolishness) insists for the most part on the inviolableness of Jerusalem. Judah may be overrun by the invader : Jerusalem cannot fall. Her security is an essential part of the providence of God.

The constant emphasis which Isaiah lays upon the inviolableness of this one spot of earth, this obscure highland fortress, not only as a settled fact of the future (10[24-34]) but as an essential article of religious faith (28[16] etc.), has been criticized as derogating from the spirituality of the religion be

---

* That Judah was equally sinful with N. Israel, in Isaiah's regard, appears not only from ch. 1, from whatever date this proceeds, but in the inaugural vision 'people of unclean lips' (6[5]), and 2[11-17] where in v.[16] at least Judah is meant.

taught. But it must be kept in mind that Jerusalem was the one spot on earth where J″ was worshipped. His shrine was there. There lived the only community which preserved for mankind the true knowledge of Him and His purposes—the little band of disciples to whom Isaiah committed His testimony and revelation. The continued existence in the world of this spiritual Israel (it is the first conception in history of the Church within the Church) is what Isaiah believes in and proclaims with such unwearied assurance against both the fears of their rulers and the arrogance of the heathen who sought their overthrow. But for their continuance the inviolableness of at least Jerusalem was necessary; otherwise they had been blotted out of history like N. Israel itself. The Assyrian policy, to judge from the case of N. Israel, did not leave room for the survival of a people of J″ among its captives, as the Babylonian did more than a century later. To interpret, therefore, Isaiah's insistence on the inviolableness of Zion as if it were derogatory to the ethical and spiritual character of his teaching, is as unjust as it would be to bring the charge of unspirituality against any of the great leaders of Christianity who have insisted in a time of persecution that the Church shall not perish, but in spite of its present tyrants survive in freedom and peace. There was no other way for a spiritual community to exist in Isaiah's day except through the security of Jerusalem. And, as we have seen above, it is also in connexion with the survival of a people of J″ that the promise of a victorious and righteous ruler comes so naturally, if not inevitably, into Isaiah's predictions.

The charge of unspirituality which is brought against the emphasis on Zion's security as a fortress might have had some justice in it if Isaiah had anywhere attempted to provide for that security by merely political means. But, on the contrary, his conviction of God's purpose to preserve Jerusalem is so profoundly spiritual that it leads him to condemn Israel's own restless attempts to save their State; and he does so with as much fierceness as he has condemned their immorality. They will not trust their God any more than they will obey His law; but, on the contrary, distrustful of His purpose and His power, they seek to effect Zion's safety by intrigues and alliances with the heathen. These, says Isaiah, will only draw them into the confusion of the world's politics, from which trust in J″ would assuredly keep them free. So, first, we find him seeking to restrain Ahaz from appealing for help to Assyria when Judah is threatened by Pekah of N. Israel and Rezin of Damascus (7): let them do their worst, they cannot harm Judah; but if Ahaz persists in calling on Assyria, J″ will punish his unbelief by summoning the heathen, either Egypt or Assyria (v.¹⁸), to overrun his land. Yet in spite of this, when Ahaz has thrown himself upon Assyria, and Judah settled down in quietness for thirty years as an Assyrian vassal, thus escaping the fate which destroyed N. Israel, Isaiah accepts the fact; and when, in 704, on the accession of Sennacherib, the nations of Palestine throw off their allegiance to the northern empire, he seeks to prevent Judah from joining them, and uses all his powers of counsel, scorn, and threatening to circumvent the political party at Jerusalem that intrigues for an alliance with Egypt (28–31). This apparent change of Isaiah's attitude to Assyria was not due to political opportunism, or only to the political experience of these thirty years, that Judah was as safe in allegiance to Assyria as in 734 he had believed she would be by abstaining from all intercourse with that heathen empire, but to the unchanging conviction that whatever Judah's political relations might be

in the providence of God, He was able to preserve her by Himself, and that her rulers' forgetfulness of this, and their anxiety to take measures of their own, would only, because of the unbelief which was their motive, end in disgrace and ruin. Besides, the intrigue with Egypt was a breach of faith with Assyria, an unhallowed and immoral thing, and this was a second proof to Isaiah that it could not succeed. He found a third in the blindness of the Jewish statesmen to the weakness of Egypt, which promised much, but never did, or could do, aught to help those who trusted in her. This gives him occasion to say that, clever as the politicians deem themselves to be, J″ is more wise. J‴'s measures for the security of Jerusalem are not mere arbitrary or supernatural exhibitions of power against her foes, but rational counsel to her statesmen, advice to keep clear of Egypt and to continue faithful to the Assyrian alliance.

The Jewish statesmen did not listen to Isaiah; and when Sennacherib invaded Palestine in 701, he found Hezekiah, like all his neighbour princes, in a state of revolt. Even then, however, Isaiah did not abate his confidence in the deliverance of Jerusalem. Once, indeed, his people seemed so corrupt, so abandoned to distrust of J″, and so incapable of the repentance to which he called them, that he announced the impossibility of their forgiveness, and condemned them to death (22¹⁻¹⁴). This, however, was momentary. Something happened to change their disposition. What it was exactly we cannot say. The most probable supposition is that Hezekiah submitted to Sennacherib, and bought the security of his city by a large tribute; but that having accepted this the Assyrian returned with heavier and more insolent demands (36. 37). Hezekiah and his statesmen were in despair (37¹), and the population, it would appear, ready to yield (36¹¹). Isaiah alone stood firm. Judah was sufficiently punished, the Assyrian in his arrogance made it clear that he expected the city to fall, because its God was no better than the gods of the States he had already overthrown. Isaiah affirmed such arrogance must be punished by J″, who would deliver His now penitent people. And the deliverance came. The hosts of Sennacherib appear to have been visited by the plague during their approach to the Egyptian border,—always in antiquity a region liable to such a visitation,—and the Assyrian corps that invested Jerusalem was suddenly withdrawn (cf. *Isaiah* 1–39 in 'Expositor's Bible'; Driver's *Isaiah* in 'Men of the Bible'; McCurdy, *HPM*, 1896, §§ 675–710). But however this may have been, Jerusalem was relieved, and Isaiah's predictions of her siege and ultimate deliverance literally fulfilled, and fulfilled, too, mainly by his own unbroken confidence and energy. It was, indeed, a victory of that faith by which the world is overcome. The people of J″, though sorely punished, were saved, the continuity of Israel's history preserved, and all the subsequent development of their religion made possible.

The above outline of Isaiah's doctrine and statesmanship makes it clear that while his long experience of the world's history, during one of its most critical periods, expanded and illustrated his belief in God, it was the latter which was the origin and root of all his convictions and his efforts on behalf of Israel. This is what Isaiah himself tells us (6). His ministry started from a vision of J″; and as his record of this vision is not placed at the beginning of his book, but after the first collection of his prophecies, and as the impressions he received from it appear (especially from vv.⁹·¹⁰) to be stated as if articulated and developed by his subsequent experience, we may see in the chapter not only the origins, but a full record, of his belief about God. J″ is the Lord or King, immeasurably exalted above everything human. His sublimity is the ruling impression on the prophet's mind, and throughout the discourses it appears again and again, in contrast both to the puny pride and ambition, 'everything high,' in Israel themselves (2), and to the overweening arrogance of the Assyrian (10, etc.). This infinite, awful sublimity is in the main what Isaiah expresses by J″'s holiness—a term whose root-meaning is probably that of separateness. But by the prophet himself this holiness is personally felt most keenly in its contrast to his own and his people's sin. The first conscience excited in Isaiah by the vision of the thrice-holy God is that he is a man of unclean lips, and dwells among a people of unclean lips (6⁵). Before he can be of use to such a Deity, his uncleanness must be purged away (6⁶ᶠ·). And so, before a people can be the people of God, their iniquity must be punished and driven out of them. The awful severity of this judgment (6⁹⁻¹² and in many other passages) is a consequence of J″'s holiness. Isaiah lived through terrible times; he predicted a fearfully rigorous judgment of God's own people by God Himself. Everywhere he betrays a burning sense of the awful earnestness of life, and the pitilessness of the divine providence in dealing with sin, with folly, and with pride. All these are consequences of the holiness of God, and another consequence is the irresistibleness of the power by which His judgments are carried through.

But though the majestic transcendence of God, and His sovereign independence of everything human and earthly, his exaltation above every entanglement and compromise of the world's life is thus the ruling article of Isaiah's creed; the prophet almost equally emphasizes the divine immanence in the world and the history of man. The correlative of J″'s holiness is His glory, of which the earth is full (6³). J″ is not only the infinitely High, but the infinitely Near. His moral interest in man's conduct extends to the minutest details. He sees and is touched by every mood and change of His people's character. He marks each fault they have, loathes each sin, feels each wound, and is swift to respond to each turn of their hearts in penitence. His passion for them, His 'zeal' or 'jealousy,' is quick and powerful. Nor is J″'s interest confined to Israel. The oracles of Isaiah on the foreign nations, and especially those on Egypt and Tyre, not only reveal that J″'s standards of righteousness are for them also, and that their sins are punished by Him as transgressions against Himself, but that He has pity for their teeming multitudes, and rejoices in their particular civilizations and destinies.

Parallel to this doctrine of the immanence and practical interest of J″ in men's life runs Isaiah's constant teaching as to His reasonableness. He is no arbitrary Deity whom Isaiah reveals, but the father and teacher of His people, who reasons and argues with them, who commends His ways to them, in opposition to their own measures, by pointing out the greater wisdom and effectiveness of the former. J″ is wonderful in counsel, and excellent in that kind of wisdom which carries things through (28²⁹). He asks their trust in His guidance, because of its reasonableness, and not simply because it is His will (29³⁴). In the most harrowing and apparently destructive processes of history He proceeds by method (28²³⁻²⁹). The politicians think themselves clever: He also is wise, and has His own righteous purposes, which He will effect in time: the destruction of evil-doers, and in the end the rescue of His people, however much He needs first to beat and break them down (31). In short, He is a God who works

in history as in nature by law—*El mishpaṭ* is His name (30¹⁸); the simplest of His moral principles effect, if violated, their own revenge (28); leave the tendencies of history, too, to Him, and they will issue right. With all this insistence on law moral and natural, is to be noted the absence of miracle and 'supernatural signs'; only once does Isaiah even seem to appeal to the latter (7¹⁰ᶠᶠ·). The divine government of the world is manifested in natural and historical processes. The unity of these processes, which all over the visible world was conspicuously illustrated by the Assyrian empire, is for Isaiah a corollary from his belief in the transcendent sovereignty of J″. Smend says truly (*AT Religionsgeschichte*, 206) that 'the idea of the *Weltgeschichte* dates from Isaiah: its oldest meaning is the glorification of the One God.'

Isaiah has received from the Christian Church the title of the Evangelical Prophet. This was given mainly in the belief that chs. 40–66 were also by him. But, even in the prophecies which criticism has left to him, we find the elements of the doctrines of Grace. God forgives sin, the most heinous and defiling (1¹⁸). Though He has passed sentence of death upon His people (22¹⁴), their penitence procures for them His pardon and deliverance (36. 37). Necessarily severe as His judgment is, cruelly as His providence bears upon sin and folly, His love and pity towards His own never fail (14³²). He is their well-beloved, and has constantly cared for them (5¹ᶠᶠ·). It is His passion for them that works their deliverance (9⁷). He longs to be gracious, and to have mercy even when His people are most given to their own destructive courses; and He waits eagerly for their prayers to Him (30¹⁸ᵗ·).

Of the future which shall follow Judah's judgment and deliverance Isaiah makes several predictions (cf. ESCHATOLOGY OF OT, vol. i. 736 ff.). First, as was to be expected, he emphasizes its ethical features. The sinners having been destroyed (1²⁸), and Jerusalem purified, the city shall be a city of righteousness (1²⁵ᶠ·), under a righteous ruler (9⁷ 11⁴ᶠᶠ·). But above all J″'s own presence and government shall be very manifest, with exceeding joy and glory. As a result, men shall abandon all their idols (2²⁰ etc.), the worship of which (as we ought to have noted above) had not wholly disappeared from Israel, in spite of the fact that the national religion was that of J″. With righteousness shall come peace (2⁴, if this be Isaiah's, 9⁷ 11³), and with peace the renewed fertility, and the free enjoyment of the fruits of the soil (1¹⁹ 4² 30²³⁻²⁶). In the last of these passages the promise is given in terms of great beauty, and suited to the needs of a people whose fields had been overrun by war for more years than one, and who have been cooped up by siege. Over all a wonderful light shall be shed: it is the symbol of the dispersion of the people's present gloom. Moreover, the nations shall willingly come to Jerusalem to be taught of Israel's God and His *torah* (2²ᶠ·; but see above, § IV., where it is pointed out that there are some objections to the authenticity of this passage). On the Messiah see above, §§ IV. V. Isaiah's Messiah is a human king, of the stock of David, and with functions that are political, both military and judicial. He is not the mediator of religious gifts to His people: forgiveness, knowledge of God, and the like. It is only in this, that he saves the people of God from destruction and reigns over them, that he can be regarded as a type of Jesus Christ.

VII. RELIGIOUS REFORMS IN ISAIAH'S TIME.— It would have been strange if a prophet so practical and statesmanlike, and so influential with the rulers of Judah, had not left his mark on legislation and ritual. We cannot believe the author of the oracles against images, the spirit that organized the city's deliverance from Assyria, to have been idle in the long opportunity of reforms afforded by the accession of Hezekiah, and by the years of peace which followed till the death of Sargon, or again during the few years, uncertain in number, of Hezekiah's lifetime after the relief of Jerusalem in 701. It is to the former of these periods that 2 K 18 assigns certain drastic reforms of worship, of which it gives the credit to Hezekiah. The list of them given in v.[4] contains the removal of the high places, the *mazzēbôth* or pillars, the *'ashērim* (see ASHERAH), and the brazen serpent called Nehushtan, to which the people burned incense; and in v.[22] the Rabshakeh is reported to have said to the Jews in 701 that Hezekiah had already removed the high places. The integrity of v.[4] has been justly doubted: the grammar is of late Hebrew. It has also been maintained (Wellhausen, *Isr. u. Jüd. Gesch.*, and Stade, *GVI* 1607 f.) that the only reform which we have any just ground for leaving with Hezekiah is the destruction of the brazen serpent and other images, which, because in 705 ff. Isaiah represents it as still future (30[22]), can only have taken place after 701.

In ascribing to Hezekiah the destruction of the high places, *mazzēbôth* and *'ashērim*, it is alleged that the hand intruded into v.[4] and the editor of v.[22] have wrongly anticipated reforms which were not effected till a century later by Josiah. But while this conclusion is undoubtedly favoured by the language of v.[4], it ignores the probabilities on the other side. It is quite true that Isaiah, while condemning images, says nothing against the high places, the *mazzēbôth* and the *'ashērim*. But to condemn images, and to do away with them, was to destroy the significance of the high places, which depended on their worship, and to concentrate the people's faith on the sanctuary in Zion, where J″ was not worshipped under any form. Besides, the Assyrian invasion, devastating as it did the whole country and yet incapable of violating Zion, worked mightily to the discredit of the high places, and the proof of Zion's unique holiness. We may also say that though Isaiah is not reported to have condemned the high places,[*] yet his fundamental principle of the oneness and spirituality of J″ must, according to the religious notions then prevalent, have logically involved the abolition of the high places, at which there was not only a half-pagan ritual, but the tendency also to think of the deity worshipped as a local deity different from J″ of Jerusalem. We are justified, then, in believing in the probability of some measures during Hezekiah's reign for the removal of the high places. But, even if we hesitate to affirm this, we may at least state with certainty that Isaiah, both by his doctrine of J″ as the one true God, who could not be worshipped under the form of an image made by man, and in his insistence upon the solitary inviolateness of Zion and in the unaided faith and energy by which he secured this, laid the indispensable foundation for the legislation of Deuteronomy and the reforms of Josiah. We may also assert that the measures in this direction which Hezekiah inaugurated under Isaiah's inspiration must have been pretty severe; otherwise they could scarcely have provoked the terrible reaction which followed under Manasseh. In this state of probability, somewhat short of certainty, we must be content, with our present data, to leave the question.

VIII. THE HISTORICAL CHAPTERS 36–39.—These

* Neither with any certainty is Micah, for the reading of Mic 1[5] is uncertain.

chapters are found also in 2 K 18[13]–20[19], where their text has been somewhat more fully and accurately preserved (for details see Driver, *LOT*[6] 226 f.; Cheyne, *Introd.* 215) than here (cf. especially 38). The passage 2 K 18[14-16] is wanting in the Book of Isaiah, and the latter's Psalm of Hezekiah is wanting in Kings. The whole section is very composite. For details we must refer to Dillmann, Duhm, Cheyne, Skinner, and to Stade's analysis in *ZATW* for 1886. Here it is only possible to give a bare outline. In 36–37 we have two narratives of Sennacherib's endeavour or endeavours to capture Jerusalem: one of them 36–37[8], the other 37[9-38].[*] Many have read these as the respective accounts of those successive attempts on Jerusalem which we saw above to be the probable course of the Assyrian campaign. But Stade and others have taken them to be variant records of one and the same assault of Sennacherib on Jerusalem, and have divided them as follows: 36[1]–37[9a] + 37-38, and 37[9b-37a].[†] Further, Cheyne believes that in these narratives the following are later insertions, 36[1. 7. 18-20] 37[4], 'to reproach the living God,' [6] 'Wherewith . . . have reviled me,' [8bc 22-32. 34]. On the question of the chronology in 36[1] and 2 K 18[10. 13] see Driver, *Isaiah*[2], 13; Cheyne, *Introd.* 216 ff.; Skinner, *Is.* 1–39, lxxvi f., 262 f. The reported message of Isaiah to Hezekiah 37[22b-35] consists of—(a) a taunt-song in the *Ḳinah* measure, vv.[22b-29], and (b) the giving of a sign to Hezekiah in another rhythm, vv.[30-32], and (c) a prediction of the relief of Jerusalem, vv.[33-35]. The taunt-song 'appears to be inserted in the narrative from some independent source . . . probably a genuine work of Isaiah'; [33-35] 'the actual message of the prophet on this occasion' (Skinner); but see Cheyne, *Introd.* 219. Chs. 38. 39 are probably from the same source as 36. 37: Duhm and Cheyne assign them to the author of the second of the two narratives in 36. 37. The 'writing of Hezekiah,' 38[9-20], was assumed even by Kuenen in the 1st ed. of his *Onderzoek*, ii. 93, and by Dillmann, to be genuine. The present writer expounded it as genuine in the 'Expositor's Bible,' *Isai.* 1–39, ch. xxv. But he now feels the force of the objections to this, drawn from the language, which has many late features (so Kuenen's later opinion, Duhm, and Cheyne).

IX. PROPHECIES CERTAINLY NOT ISAIAH'S IN CHS. 1–39.—The detailed discussion of these is hardly relevant to an article on Isaiah himself; but a few data may be given concerning the chief of them.

11[10-16].—Dillmann argues for Isaian authorship, but most think the passage implies that the Exile has taken place; the Messiah is not, as in Isaiah's own prophecies, the political ruler of Israel, but the restorer of the exiles and the resort of all nations (cf. Giesebrecht, *Beiträge*, 25 ff.; Driver, *Isaiah*[2], 214 f.). 12 is without doubt from a date after the Exile (besides the Commentaries see Francis Brown, *Jour. of Bibl. Literature*, 1890, 128 ff.). 13[1]–14[23] implies that the Jews are in exile, and in servitude to Babylon, the fall of whose king, however, is imminent; the Medes (13[17]) are already invading Babylonia. The ideas and language do not suit Isaiah's time, but do suit the exilic age. For details see Cheyne, *Introd.* 69 ff.: Driver dates it a little before B.C. 549. 15[1]–16[12] has usually been attri-

* Another division of the chapters would assign 36[1] (only with the addition 2 K 18[14-16]) to the first invasion of Sennacherib, 36[2]–37 to the second.

† Winckler (*Untersuch.* 34-36) has attempted to prove that while the first narrative refers to Sennacherib's campaign of 701, the second describes what happened on an alleged return of Sennacherib to Palestine to meet Tirhakah towards the end of his reign between 690 and 681. (Winckler makes the division between the narratives not at 37[9a] but at 37[8a].) But for this there is no conclusive evidence: cf. Cheyne, *Introd.* 234 f.

buted, on grounds of difference of style from Isaiah's, and of the suitability of its historical allusions to the time of Jeroboam II., to a prophet of that date (so among others Hitzig, Wellhausen, W. R. Smith, Dillmann, and more doubtfully Driver. Ewald, Kuenen, Baudissin, assign to at least a prophet earlier than Isaiah), Isaiah himself adding 16¹³. ¹⁴. In 1888 Schwally (*ZATW* 207 ff.) argued for the post-exilic origin of the whole section; and it forms one of those passages which Duhm would bring down to the Hasmonæan period. Cheyne thinks the most conservative theory which is possible is that a post-exilic author combined a genuine oracle on Moab, 16¹⁴, with an anonymous pre-exilic prophecy also on Moab, and filled up illegible passages in an antique style. 21¹⁻¹⁰ was assigned by some early critics (Ewald and others) to the close of the Exile, on the ground that no siege of Babylon such as the passage describes could have interested Judah before then. Then Kleinert (*SK*, 1877, 174 ff.; so also George Smith the Assyriologist) argued that the passage referred to the first of these sieges of Babylon by the Assyrians in Isaiah's time : 710, 703, 696. To this view Cheyne and Driver at first adhered ; but they have recently returned to Ewald's view (Cheyne, *Introd.* 121 ff. ; Driver, *LOT*⁶ 216). Skinner agrees. `There can be little doubt that they are right. 24–27, one of the most remarkable sections of prophecy in the OT, cannot be Isaiah's, and must be post-exilic, for the general reasons already given (to be found in greater detail in Driver, *LOT*⁶ 219 ff. ; Kirkpatrick, *Doct. of the Prophets*, 475 ff. ; Cheyne, *Introd.* 145 ff.; and Skinner, *Is.* 1–39, 204 f.). The exact date is very uncertain. Ewald and Delitzsch both placed it in the late 6th or early 5th cent.; so, too, Dillmann, Kirkpatrick, and Driver 'most plausibly.' Probably the question will ultimately lie between this date and the campaigns of Artaxerxes Ochus, *c.* 350 (see below on 63⁷–64), for which Cheyne has ably argued in detail. For an exposition of this very important prophecy see the Comm. and 'Expositor's Bible,' *Is.* 1–39. 34. 35 are two visions from the same hand, 34 of a general judgment on the Gentiles (¹⁻⁴) and a special doom upon Edom (⁵⁻¹⁷), 35 of the restoration of Israel from exile. Obviously, they must be later than the beginning of the Exile, and the great crime of Edom when the latter took place. With this their language agrees. We are quite unable to fix an exact date. Dillmann (cf. Driver, *Is.*² 131, *LOT*⁶ 226) suggests the end of the Exile. Arguing that the writer quotes late exilic and post-exilic writings, lives in Palestine, feels nothing of the Babylonian oppression, and sees imminent on Edom the same calamity as Mal 1¹⁻⁵ refers to, Cheyne suggests the end of the 5th cent. or even a later period.

X. STRUCTURE AND DATE OF CHAPTERS 40–66. —The earliest critics who assigned these chapters to the Exile believed them to be a unity. But in the first place it became obvious that after 52¹² the style changes as decisively and almost as often as in chs. 1–39, and in the second place critics who continued to support Isaiah's authorship alleged that the references are not all exilic or Babylonian, but that in the later chapters there are reflections of Palestine, and some allusions to the Exile as still to come. These facts gradually led to the perception of the composite character of 40–66. Bleek and Ewald were the first to distinguish this, the latter assigning 40¹· ² 52¹³–54¹² and 56⁹–57¹¹ to the reign of Manasseh. In 1881 Cheyne (*Enc. Brit.*⁹) adhered to the pre-exilic origin of some of these passages, but claimed also that there were others equally separable from the earlier chapters, and these he assigned partly to the early Exile and partly to after the Exile.

In 1886 Briggs (*Mess. Proph.*) sought to prove that the sections on the Servant of the Lord were in a different metre and by a different hand from the rest. In 1889 Kuenen assigned 40–49. 52¹⁻¹² and perhaps 52¹³–53¹² to one author, in the end of the Exile, the rest he considered added by this author himself, or by others, after the Return. In 1890 the present writer argued for the composite character of 40–66. In 1892 Duhm distinguished three authors : the so-called 'second Isaiah' in the Exile,* a post-exilic author of the passages on the Servant, and a 'third Isaiah' the author of the bulk of 56–66. Various articles and monographs appeared, working in the same direction. Then in 1895 Cheyne produced the most finished presentation of the theory : 40–55 from one author who combined in it a cycle of poems on the Servant of Jahweh, and the great prophecy of the restoration ;† but 56–66, a collection of ten compositions, all of them from the age of Nehemiah, except 63⁷–64¹¹, which is probably to be assigned to the reign of Artaxerxes Ochus, or about 360. Meanwhile Dillmann (1890) and Driver [both in the first and sixth (1897) editions of his *LOT*] adhered to the authorship of the great bulk of the prophecy by one prophet, mostly before but partly also after the Return. Dillmann (p. 363 ff. of his commentary) assigns 40–48 to about 545, 49–62 between 545 and the Return, and 63–66 to the very eve of the Return ; only in 66 he sees insertions from a later hand. Driver, upon the resemblance of 56⁹–57¹¹ᵃ and 59³⁻¹⁵ to passages in Jeremiah and Ezekiel, takes these to be pre-exilic prophecies incorporated by the author of 49–66 (*Isaiah*², 187 ff.). Cornill (*Einleitung in AT*) and Wildeboer (*Litteratur des AT*) admit in 49–62 many signs of composition in Palestine, which, however, do not force us to deny them to the author of 40–48. In 63–66, on the other hand, they find the marks of another and a later writer.

Chs. 40–66 have no title and make no claim to be by Isaiah. 40–48 plainly set forth the ruin of Jerusalem, and the Exile as having already taken place. Israel is addressed as if the time of their penalty in servitude to Babylon were exhausted, and their deliverance is proclaimed as immediate. Cyrus is named as their saviour, and is pointed out as already upon his career, and blessed with success by J″. Nor is it possible to argue, as some have tried to do, that the prophet is predicting these things as if they had already happened. For, as part of an argument for the unique divinity of the God of Israel, Cyrus, 'alive and irresistible, and already accredited with success, is pointed out as the unmistakable proof that *former* prophecies of a deliverance for Israel are already coming to pass. Cyrus, in short, is not presented as a prediction, but as a proof that a prediction is being fulfilled. Unless he had already appeared, and was on the point of striking at Babylon, with all the prestige of unbroken victory, a great part of 40–48 would be unintelligible' (*Isai.* 40–66, 'Expositor's Bible,' 9 ff. ; see the argument there in detail). There is thus a very clear date for these chapters ; they must have been written between 555, Cyrus' advent, and 538, Babylon's fall. If 41²⁵ implies the union of Cyrus with the Medes in 549, the possible years are reduced to eleven. Perhaps they should be confined between 545, when Cyrus took

Sardis, and 538. With this agree the thoughts, the local colour, and the language of the chapters (on the last see Cheyne, *Comm.* ii., and Driver, *Isaiah²*, 192 ff.). Nor is there any need to limit this proof to 40–48, though Babylon and Cyrus are confined to them. From 49 to 55 the circumstances are still of exile ; as A. B. Davidson remarks, 49 is parallel to 42, and takes for granted the picture of Israel's restoration in 48. The first real break occurs at 52¹³, where the prophecy of the sin-bearing Servant is introduced. Not only is this written with considerable difference of style, but, if it be left out, 54¹ follows naturally upon 52¹². Yet 52¹³–53 is an evident development from the previous sections on the Servant scattered throughout 40–52. And the whole question is raised whether these sections formed originally a poem by themselves, and if so, whether they are by a different author from the rest of 40–55. Cheyne thinks there is much which makes it impossible for any of these passages to have originally sprung, each at the place which it now occupies, from the progress of the prophet's thoughts. This is doubtful (for reasons the present writer has expressed on p. 313 ff. of *Is.* 40–66), and it would be difficult to understand why, if originally an independent poem, these sections were broken up and placed just where they are now. In any case there is nothing in them incompatible with their being from the same hand as the rest of 40–55 ; and indeed Cheyne assigns them to that hand. (For other opinions see above). 56¹⁻⁸ is assigned by Cheyne and others to Nehemiah's time ; but an earlier date is not impossible ; v.⁸, however, appears to imply that some Jews have already returned (see the linguistic analysis in Cheyne, 312 f.). 56⁹–57 is the passage which most clearly reflects the scenery of Palestine, and charges the Jews both with political sins they could commit only in their own land, and with superstitions also most natural there. Critics have been divided between a pre-exilic date, such as Manasseh's reign, when idolatry and persecution were in force (so since Ewald), and a post-exilic date (so latterly Cheyne, who, after a literary analysis of the passage, places 56⁹–57¹³ᵃ shortly before Ezra's arrival and the rest later ; the former position is by no means certain, especially after a study of Zec 1–8 and 'Malachi' ; but probably the whole prophecy is post-exilic). 58 by most critics (including the present writer) has been assigned to the Exile ; this is possible, but Cheyne gives strong reasons for a post-exilic date. 59 is very difficult to analyze and assign ; probably it is the fusion of two prophecies, one of which speaks as if Israel, in their own land, were responsible for civic justice, the other as if the great deliverance from exile were just at hand. Some argue, not very successfully, for a pre-exilic date of at least portions of this chapter, but Cheyne for a date after Ezra. 60 was previously taken by Cheyne in his *JQR* article to be by the same hand as 40 ff., but in his *Introd.* he argues for its authorship by a post-exilic imitator of that writer, on the grounds of the ideas of the chapter, its poor style, and that the author speaks as if he were a resident of Jerusalem at a time when the city had again a population, though small, and when the temple had been rebuilt, but needed expansion and ornament. These latter reflections of a historical situation are by no means certain ; there is no clear implication that the temple has been rebuilt ; on the contrary, the city itself appears to have been uninhabited for a time. It is not possible to fix a date. There is the same indefiniteness of circumstance in the poem 61–62. Cheyne affirms that it implies the land of Judah to be in part repeopled and the temple rebuilt (62⁹), but this is not evident ; one might as well argue from 62⁶ that the walls

have already been rebuilt. 61¹ proclaims liberty to the captives ; if, as Cheyne holds, this refers to the mass of Israel, the prophecy can hardly be referred, as he suggests, to a date after Cyrus, because, though numbers of Jews remained in exile in spite of that great Liberator's edict, they would not be described as in captivity. Probably, however, the reference is too general for so particular an inference from it. Besides, even after Cyrus, there must have been in various parts of the world enslaved or captive Jews. 61³ speaks of those who mourn in Zion, a phrase which appears to imply that Jerusalem is inhabited, unless we are to take it metaphorically. The language, in spite of resemblances to that of 40–55, affords a little more evidence of a later date. Nothing can be inferred from the person of the speaker in the first verses of 61 till we can conclude whether he is meant to be the Servant of the Lord, in which case we might take the passage as one of the series of oracles on that great figure, and (as some argue) from the same date as the others, or whether he is merely a representative of prophecy. But this is a question which has divided critics, and is very difficult, if not impossible, to answer (see *Isaiah* 40–66, 'Expositor's Bible,' 435 f.). On the whole, then, it is impossible to fix the date of 61. 62 ; most opinions vary between a date before the liberation under Cyrus and authorship by the writer of 40–55, and a later authorship by an imitator of that prophet.

The brilliant passage 63¹⁻⁶ stands by itself. Its description of the loneliness of J″ in achieving the overthrow of Edom (the attempts to eliminate the name of Edom from the passage cannot be said to be justified) forbids a reference to some historical defeat of that bitter people by Israel. The vision is of a purely ideal conquest of Israel's chief enemy. In 42¹³ we have a similar picture of J″ travailing for the deliverance of His people ; this, however, is not enough on which to argue for identity of authorship, while the ferocity of the passage is somewhat against it. None of the other dates suggested are sufficiently probable.

The next section is 63⁷–64, a prayer of intercession for Israel. Here, again, there is great possibility for diversity of opinion as to the date. The passage cannot well be by the author of 40–45 ; as to that, Cheyne's analysis of the ideas and language (*Introd.* 352 ff.) is very convincing. Nor is it so clear as the present writer once thought it was, that because the author appeals (63¹¹⁻¹⁵) only to the delivery from Egypt, and not to that from Babylon, the latter is still future as he writes. For Haggai and Zechariah make no mention of Cyrus' decree, or the return from Babylon, though they wrote very soon after these events. (On the objections to Kosters' theory that their silence is a proof that no return had taken place, see the present writer's *Twelve Prophets*, vol. ii. ch. 16.). What is clear is that Jerusalem has suffered desolation, that the temple has been defiled and burned by Israel's adversaries (63¹⁸ 64¹⁰ᶠ· Eng.). To what event does this refer ? Some say Nebuchadrezzar's destruction of the temple in 586, and date the passage from the early Babylonian exile. But if that were so it would be difficult to understand the Massoretic reading of 63¹⁸ 'Thy holy people possessed it but a little while' ; though this reading is uncertain. The only other similar calamities are that alleged to have taken place in the invasions of Palestine by Artaxerxes Ochus (B.C. 360 ff.) to which Cheyne refers the passage, and that by Antiochus Epiphanes in 169 to which Grotius referred it. The latter may be ruled out of consideration. Of the invasion by Artaxerxes Ochus we know extremely little (for details see W. R. Smith, *OTJC*, note D ; and Cheyne, *Introd.*

358 ff.); and that he destroyed the temple is only inferred from his cruel character, from his desecration of other shrines on that campaign, and from an ambiguous tradition in Josephus about the reign of the other Artaxerxes. Nevertheless, W. R. Smith and Cheyne have assigned to the reign of Artaxerxes Ochus Pss 74 and 79, with their references to the destruction of the temple, which others assign to Maccabæan times. And arguing from the parallels between these Pss and Is 63⁷-64 Cheyne also assigns the latter to the same date. The reasoning is strong, but not conclusive, and hampered by the uncertainty of a burning of the temple about 350. Besides, Ps 74 distinctly points to the conviction that prophecy has ceased in Israel. Not only does Is 63⁷-64 betray no such conviction, which, if it had existed, could hardly have been omitted by a writer of the mood of Is 63⁷-64, but the whole prophecy is itself an answer to the idea that the prophetic spirit had faded from the nation. Moreover, if Is 63⁷-64 has some parallels with Ps 74. 79 it has also some very striking resemblances, both of thought and of phraseology, to the prophecies of Haggai and Zechariah, and its whole tone suits the years of disillusion and despair which elapsed between the return from exile in 537 and the beginning of the rebuilding of the temple in 520. The unique phrases, 'Thy holy cities' (64¹⁰), and 'J‴s spirit in the midst of Israel' (63¹¹), find parallels in Zec 2¹⁶ [Heb.] and Hag 2⁵ respectively. There is the same sense of the people's uncleanness as in Hag 2 and Zec 3; the same sense of J‴s excessive anger as in Zechariah's first vision; the same emphasis on the Spirit of J″, and the same idea of J‴s angel, interchangeable with J″ Himself. The despair of Is 63⁷-64 is exactly that which Haggai and Zechariah appear to combat in the people, and the circumstances of the time fully explain, as already remarked, the silence of the whole prayer about the liberation from Babylon. On the whole, then, it must be regarded as more reasonable to date 63⁷-64 from about 525 than about 350.

Ch. 65, taken by the majority of critics as the divine answer to the prayer of 63⁷-64, has been assigned both to Babylonia and Palestine, both to the years before the end of the Exile and to those after the Return. Some (Dillmann, *in loco*) argue for the former, on the ground that the idolatrous practices mentioned are all suitable to Babylonia, that Israel's occupation of the Holy Land is represented as future in v.⁹, and that the phrase 'forget my holy mountain' (without reference to the rebuilt temple) recalls the exilic Ps 137⁴. To this view the present writer adhered in 1891, but he does not now feel the conclusiveness of it. For the promise of v.⁹ may be naturally interpreted, not of the first return to Zion and occupation of the surrounding district, but to the full possession of Palestine as a whole, which was still unrealized long after the first return. Besides, the idolatrous customs charged may just as easily have been prevalent in Palestine as in any other country of Western Asia, and Gad and Meni (v.¹¹) were undoubtedly Syrian deities, and worshipped in Palestine from time immemorial. In the doubt in which these allusions of the prophecy leave us as to its exact date, we are not assisted either by the ideas or by the language of the passage (for details see Cheyne, *Introd.* 320 ff.): these cannot determine between two periods so close to each other as the years just before or the century after the Return. Cheyne, who accepts the Palestinian origin, argues that the Samaritans are the people against whom the chapter is addressed, and fixes the date as that of the troubles of the Jews with the Samaritans, which Nehemiah describes. But that the charge is against superstitious and semi-pagan Jews may also plausibly be argued, and there are really no sufficient data to fix a date. On the whole, a Palestinian * and post-exilic origin is the most probable.

Equally obscure is the question of ch. 66. The chapter is probably not a unity, and the text is unusually corrupt. There are echoes of chs. 40-55, but it is quite impossible to assign the chapter to the great evangelist of the Exile. The temple either has been rebuilt or is being rebuilt (vv.¹⁻⁴. ⁶. ²⁰); the restored community has already been formed, but is not complete (v.⁹). The language points to a post-exilic date. The attacks upon the idolatrous customs reveal a close connexion between the chapter and 65. On the whole, therefore, a date soon after the Return appears probable for the bulk of the chapter; but there are probably later insertions. On this see Dillmann, Duhm, and especially Cheyne.

XI. THE THEOLOGY OF ISAIAH 40-66. — (*a*) Chapters 40-55, as we have seen, are addressed to Israel in circumstances very different from those of the generation to which Isaiah of Jerusalem spoke. Isaiah had before him a nation on their own soil: responsible for justice and social reform, for the defence of a fatherland and the conduct of a foreign policy. He appealed to kings, statesmen, and definite classes of society. But chs. 40-55 are addressed to a people in exile, without native leaders or the opportunity of developing great personalities: with no civic life and few social responsibilities; a people in the passive state, with occasion for the exercise of almost no qualities save those of penitence and faith, of memory and hope. Moreover, with Isaiah, and indeed with all prophets up to the Exile, the burden of prophesying is the people's guilt and their doom of exile. But this doom has now been fulfilled. Jeremiah limited it to 70 years. These are almost exhausted, and there are signs that the Babylonian Empire, the instrument of the doom, is approaching its fall. Cyrus, king of Anshan and Persia, having conquered the Medes (B.C. 545), and perhaps also the Lydians (542), is descending on Babylon. What is of immediate interest to Israel, therefore, is not, as formerly, the immoral state of her people and the imminence of certain events of chastisement, but the dawn of that redemption and restoration which was promised to appear after the fulfilment of God's sentence. In a word, what is now needed is not so much new predictions of the future as proofs that the fulfilment of former predictions is at hand. Consequently, while the problem before the spirit of Israel is still substantially what it was with Isaiah, viz. the survival of a people of J″, both the factors of the problem and the method of its solution are very different. Some recent critics hardly exaggerate when they say that prophecy proper ceased with the Exile. For instead of the characteristic prophet, denouncing his people upon moral grounds and predicting their doom, we have in Is 40 a commission granted to a number † of voices (whose hearers, indeed, so little feel themselves to be official prophets that they remain anonymous) to comfort Israel and proclaim that the ancient promises to her are about to be fulfilled. But the proof of this requires something more than an appeal to present facts, whether in Israel's own conduct or the general history of the world about her: the whole history and destiny of Israel are brought in, with a full and reasoned revelation of her God.

In such a scheme, it is plain, there is no need

---

* On this ground the chapter has been argued to be by Isaiah himself, or his disciples; and one scholar (Bredenkamp) dates it from the reign of Manasseh.

† Note the plural in the opening verse 40¹, 'comfort ye my people.'

for that almost exclusive insistence upon the moral attributes of J″, His demands for justice and purity, which we found in Isaiah's own teaching ; but the need is rather for emphasis upon God's intention to fulfil His word, and upon His power to bend to this end the forces of history. The change is best illustrated in the altered meaning which chs. 40-55 give to the term 'righteousness.' In the authentic prophecies of Isaiah, delivered to an unjust and immoral generation, righteousness almost exclusively means the purity and justice which God demands from His people. But in chs. 40-55, in face of a generation who are not charged with the immoralities of Isaiah's, but who are in doubt or despair about their God's power and will to fulfil His word and redeem them, righteousness signifies mainly His consistency and faithfulness. In 41²⁶ the adjective *zaddik* is applied to one whose prediction turns out to be correct.* In 41² the noun *zedek* appears to be the virtue of carrying out what one has promised ; it is associated with J‴s call to Cyrus, who has been called not in vain, but in good faith, and for a purpose which will certainly succeed. So in 41¹⁰, taken with its context, J‴s *zedek* is His trueness, the harmony of His present purpose with His ancient promise to redeem Israel—His good faith to the people He has called ; but it includes also His *power* to fulfil His word : ' the right hand of my righteousness ' is the phrase He uses. The whole chapter and other parallel passages (especially 43⁹· ¹⁰· ¹⁸f· 44⁷· ⁸ 45¹⁹⁻²⁵) imply that *zedek* or *zĕdākáh* (the forms are used indifferently) is J‴s fidelity to His calling of Israel —the quality by which He can neither forsake His own, nor for want of power fail in His promise to justify them to the world ; and so, besides being synonymous with strength, righteousness is applied to its own results, and becomes parallel to salvation—*El zaddik*, the Righteous God, is equivalent to *Mōshia'*, the Saviour (45²¹).

The chief claim, therefore, which 40 ff. make for the God of Israel is His power to direct the history of the world in conformity to a long predicted and faithfully followed purpose. This claim starts from the proof that J″ has long before predicted events now happening or about to happen, with Cyrus as their centre. But this is much more than a proof of isolated predictions, though these imply omniscience. It is a declaration of the unity of history sweeping to the high ends which have been already revealed to Israel—an exposition, in short, of the Omnipotence, Consistence, and Faithfulness of the Providence of the one true God. But with almost equal force the chapters insist upon the Creative Power of the same sovereign Deity. Alone, without counsellor or helper, He created and sustains the world, calls all things into being, and bends them to His will.† He has made and measured earth and ocean, mountains and hills (40¹²ff·). All the magnitudes and processes of nature are His : heaven, the stars, the clouds, the sea, earth, drought and floods, light and darkness, peace and calamity. Before His omnipotence, His own works and men and their works are as nothing. He is infinitely above them all, sublime and incomparable—in short, the Holy One. For holiness in these chapters is attributed to God always either in connexion with His creative power and the incomparableness to which it exalts Him (40²⁵ 41²⁰ 43¹⁵ 45¹¹), or more especially in connexion with the manifestation of that incomparable power for the redemption and glorification of His people (41¹⁴ 43³· ¹⁴ 47⁴ 48¹⁷ 49⁷ 54⁵ 55⁵). He is Jehovah, and there is none else ; God, and there is none beside Him (45⁵f· etc.).

* As the Arabic *zādik* means one who speaks truly.
† To describe this creative power the author of chs. 40 ff. is the first to use the term בָּרָא = create.

From this absolute monotheism everything else follows in chs. 40 ff. What invariably kindles the reason and style of the writer is the thought of God. The breadth and force of imagination, the assurance of hope, the daring treatment of the history of the world as a whole, may be traced to the writer's sense of God's sovereignty, and are the signs of how absolutely he was possessed by this as his principal and governing truth. But that he held it not by faith alone or a partial experience, but with the whole force of his reason, is shown, not only in the exposition of J‴s articulate, clear, reasonable and consistent revelation of Himself and His purpose (15¹⁰ff·), but also in the powerful scorn with which the author's mind sweeps down upon idolatry. If it is impossible to liken God to anything (41²⁵), then the low thoughts which Israel has of J″, the images in which the heathen figure the Godhead (41⁷ 44⁹ff·), their enchantments and divinations (47⁹· ¹²ff·), and even the chief gods of the conquering empires (46¹ff·), are all equally absurd. The ridicule which the writer pours upon these, the delight he has in exposing their futility, and the weary trouble for no end which their religions levy upon the heathen, brilliantly exhibit the intellectual assurance of this most perfect apostle of Israel's monotheism.

But though God is thus sublime He is near to men in sympathy, and full of grace and zeal for His own (40¹· ¹¹· ²⁷ff· 43² 49¹⁴ff· 51³· ¹²). Israel's maker is Israel's husband (54⁵). No prophet is more daring in his ascription of passion to the Deity. With all this writer's overpowering sense of the transcendence of J″, he does not hesitate to picture Him as an excited and furious warrior, and as a travailing woman (42¹³f·).

But as J″ is unique, so is Israel unique. Israel is His special creation, His elect, and His own. The nations are given for Israel's ransom, and the world-powers are employed as contributory to Israel's career (41⁸ 43³f· ¹⁴ 45¹⁴ etc.). Cyrus himself, in whom the power of the world is gathered up, is J‴s servant for Israel's redemption (41²ff· 44²⁸ 45¹· ⁴ etc.). Yet the creation and election of Israel are not for their own sake. ' This people I have formed for myself ; they shall show forth my praise ' (43²¹). They are to be God's revealers and witnesses to the ends of the earth (41⁸f·). They are to carry His *mishpat* and *torah* to the farthest coasts (42⁴· ⁶). Their election is an election to service—the service of mankind in the highest matters of religion and morality. In a far higher sense than Cyrus they are the servant of J″. The picture of J‴s servant fills a large part of the prophecy. Sometimes this servant is equivalent to all Israel, the seed of Abraham (41⁸ etc.). But as a whole the nation is unworthy of the high office—deaf, blind, and spoiled (42¹⁸ff·)—in need of forgiveness (43²⁵) and illumination. And so the conversion of Israel becomes part of the servant's work (49³⁻⁶). He appears to be the personification of the pious remnant of the people : the true, effective Israel ; and he is therefore obviously distinct from the nation, who are not conscious of the destiny God has for His people, or ready to carry it out. Though Israel as a whole be unready, this loyal Israel is glorious in J‴s eyes, and God is their strength (49⁵). Speaking in the first person, this Servant describes his experience as the prophet of J″, and carries it to its consequence in martyrdom (50⁴⁻⁹). Many have thought that in this passage the ideal is still more narrowly concentrated, and that we ought to see in the speaker an individual servant of J″. Many more agree that we have an individual presented to us at last in the classical passage 52¹³-53. The latter opinion the present writer feels to be correct. The nation's functions of service for God are frequently concentrated by other prophets upon an individual. The experience of the individual Jeremiah, who had, in opposition to his whole people, remained faithful to J″, and in his solitary experience suffered for the people's sins, and represented them before J″, surely afforded precedent enough for the vision of a *personal* sufferer and sin-bearer. Yet, whether we take this view, or with many eminent critics continue to see in 52[13]-53 as in 49 the personification of the righteous remnant of Israel, the religious results remain the same. The spiritual salvation of Israel is accomplished by the vicarious conscience and sufferings of the Servant. He is not merely the prophet of 49[2ff.] and 50[4. 5], nor only the martyr of 50[6ff.], who shall be ultimately vindicated by J″. His sufferings, so misunderstood by the world, have a very practical end (52[13-15]). Disregarded or misunderstood by his own people, he naturally, as they come to see, bears their transgressions and iniquity ; by his stripes they are healed (53[1ff.]). He is sinless, and therefore unjustly treated by his tyrants ; but he submits in order to offer his life as a guilt-offering ; and so wins righteousness for his people, and exerts immense influence on men (53[7-12]). Whether this figure be of the pious portion of Israel or of one holy sufferer, the Christian Church has been right in finding its fulfilment in Jesus Christ ; in His sinless suffering, in His consciousness of His solitary distinction from His people ; in His knowledge that His suffering was of God's will, and would effect the forgiveness of His people's sin, their redemption from guilt, and so His own exaltation from misunderstanding and abuse to manifest power and glory.

The equipment of Israel, then, for the religious service of mankind is the end towards which the argument and vision of chs. 40-55 are directed. But indispensable to this is the nation's redemption from Babylonian servitude, their return to the Holy Land, and the rebuilding of Jerusalem and the temple. The deliverance is to be effected by Cyrus, through his conquest of Babylonia and the humiliation of her gods (46 f.). This being certain, J″ calls upon His people to come forth from Babylon (48[20] 52[11f.]), a call that was necessary in face of the fact that numbers of Jews were unwilling to leave a home into whose life they had deeply settled, for the hard beginnings of life again upon the desolate and comparatively barren soil of Palestine. J″ promises to make easy their way across the desert (40[3ff.] 41[18f.] 43[19f.] 48[21]). Cyrus himself shall expedite their progress and arrange for the rebuilding of Jerusalem and the temple (44[28] 45[13]). The prostrate and desolate city shall rise from her ruins (40[2] 51[17ff.] 52[1f. 9]) with a full population (44[26] 49[17-19] 54[6]) : the cities of Judah shall again be inhabited (40[9] 44[26]). But even beyond these limits shall Israel break, and inherit the Gentiles (54[3]). A glory shall rest upon city and land, conscious of the presence of their God in His wonderful deeds (40[9f.] 49[18] 52[1] 54[10ff.]). The Gentiles, too, shall acknowledge this, coming to Israel with the words : Surely God is in thee (45[14] 49[7. 22f.]).

So lofty and spiritual is the prospect in chs. 40-55 ; and still so general when it descends to the details of the restoration. There is nothing priestly in the prospect, nothing warlike except in metaphor ; no directions are given for the building of the temple, nor for the institution of sacrifice ; no emphasis is laid upon the resumption of the latter, and it is not once mentioned as indispensable for the return of J″ to His people, and the renewal of His intercourse with them. To Zion J″ returns *along with* His people ; they are His Temple, He is manifest in them (45[14]). His gifts to them are spiritual : pity, grace, forgiveness,

illumination, peace ; their political restoration is but the pledge of all these. His demands upon them, too, are purely ethical and in the spirit of the older prophecy—fulfilment of His *torah* and *mishpaṭ* (51[4]). And the long argument and exhortation concludes in 55 upon the keynote of its opening chapter (40) that J″'s word is omnipotent and creative. It shall bring all these things to pass. We shall see how different this atmosphere is from that of the chapters which follow (56-66).

(b) CHS. 56-66.—In passing from chs. 40-55 into 56-66 we feel, as we have already shown (see § X.), a great difference of style. Instead of one long argument and reasoned revelation, visible in the prophecy as a whole and in the series of passages on the Servant which are scattered through it, we enter a series of detached and broken oracles, which have sometimes no relation to each other, and all of which further differ from 40-55 in their style, temper, and the religious interests that they emphasize. It is true that some of the predominant notes of 40-55 are repeated, and others are developed. The argument of the sovereignty and holiness of J″ is taken for granted, and these are asserted almost in the same phrases (57[15] 60[9. 14. 16]). 'Righteousness' is occasionally used in the same sense of the exhibition of J″'s faithfulness and burning fervour in the salvation of His people (61[10f.] 62[1ff.]). The vision of the zeal and passion of J″ is repeated and elaborated ; as before, He is the strenuous and furious warrior (59[16ff.] 63[1-6]). There is one more picture of the Servant (61[1. 3]) with his mission of comfort and restoration to the people ; and about this there is the same ambiguity as to whether it be the picture of the prophetic portion of Israel or of some individual endowed with the Spirit. The rebuilding of Jerusalem is described as more imminent, and the vision of her glory is developed in greater detail but with the same essential features of joy, beauty, fertility, an overflowing population of her returned sons and daughters, enrichment by the gifts of the Gentiles, and their acknowledgment of the God who resides in her (56[7] 60. 61[3ff.] 62. 65[18ff.] 66[6ff.]). But several new features are introduced, some of which contrast unfavourably with the lofty and spiritual tone of chs. 40-55, and some reveal the circumstances and duties of a people already re-established in civic responsibility upon their own soil. From 56 onwards the temple and its building bulk more largely (56[5ff.] 60[13] 63[18] 64[11] 66[1]) ; the sacrificial system becomes a little more prominent (56[7] 62[9] 66[20]), so do others of the institutions and ceremonies of religion ; the Sabbath (56[2. 6] 58[13f.] 66[23]), the priesthood of the people (61[6]), and the orders of priests and Levites (66[21]), the perpetual worship (58[2] 62[6] 66[23]) ; and we find, too, directions on those matters on which the returned community, effecting its reorganization, had to legislate : *e.g.* the place of eunuchs in the congregation (56[2ff.]) and the question of fasts (58[2. 3]). And there is an insistence upon civic duties and the social virtues (58[6ff.] 59[4]) ; the sins of perverting justice and equity, uttering falsehood, and committing robbery are charged upon the people in the fashion that prophecy assumed when Israel was a State (59[12ff.] 61[8]) ; and righteousness is again used in its older meaning side by side with its newer meaning (65[5]). These data confirm the conclusion reached above of a difference of authorship between 40-55 and 56-66.

LITERATURE.—Besides the general Histories of Israel and Israel's Religion, Introductions to the OT, works on OT Theology, on Prophecy, and on Messianic Prophecy, the more important special works on Isaiah are as follows :—

A. *COMMENTARIES, TRANSLATIONS, ETC., OF THE BOOK OR PARTS.*—Origen, Jerome (ed. Vallarsii, vol. iv.),Chrysostom, Cyril of Alexandria ; Gaon Sa'adya († 942), Arabic Version (with commentary, of which latter only a few fragments survive), latest edition by J. Derenbourg in *ZATW*, 1889, 1-64, 1890, 1-84; Aben Ezra, 1155, Eng. by Friedländer, London, 1877; David Kimchi (1235), Lat. ed. Florence, 1774; Ulrich Zwingli, *Complanatio Jesaiæ Latina*, Zurich, 1529, *Works*, vol. v. of ed. Schuler and Schultess; John Calvin, *Comm.*, Geneva, 1551, Eng. Edin. 1850; D. Isaaci Abrabanieli, *Comm. in Es. Proph. 30*, etc., Leyden, Elzev. 1631; Louis de Dieu, *Animadversiones in VT Libros omnes*, Leyden, 1648; Lat. trans. of Rashi's *Comm.* by Breithaupt, 1713 (not seen); Camp. Vitringa, *Comm.*, Leeuwarden, 2 vols. 1714-20, ed. Bas. 1732; Lat. trans. of Kimchi, 1774 (not seen); Robert Lowth, *Is., a New Translation with prelim. dissert. and notes*, 2 vols. London, 1778, Germ. by J. B. Koppe, 4 pts. Leipzig, 1779-81; Hensler, *Jes. übers. mit Anm.*, Hamb. 1788 (not seen); J. C. Döderlein, *Esaias*, a Latin trans. with notes, Nürn. 1789, 3rd ed. Altorf, 1789; W. Gesenius, *Comm. with trans.*, Leipzig, 1820-21; Ferd. Hitzig, *Der Proph. Jes.*, Heidelberg, 1833; Maurer, *In Jes. Comm.* 1836; Hendewerk, *Des Jes. Weiss. chronolog. geordnet*, 2 pts. Königsb. 1838, 1843 (not seen); H. Ewald, *Die Proph. des Alten Bundes*, Tüb. 1840-41, 2nd ed. 1867-68, Eng. by Fred. Smith, ii. iv. v., London, 1876-81; E. Henderson, *Bk. of Proph. Is.*[2], London, 1840; F. W. C. Umbreit, *Prakt. Comm.*, Hamburg, 1846; Ad. Knobel, *Jes. erklärt*, Leipz. 1843, 3rd ed. 1861; E. Meier, *Proph. Jes. erkl.* Pforzh. 1850 (not seen, only to ch. 23); Drechsler, *Der Proph. Jes.*, 2 vols. 1851-54; G. D. Luzzatto, *Il Profeta Isaia*, etc., Padua, 1855; J. A. Alexander, *Comm.*, Edin. 1865; Fr. Delitzsch, *Comm.* 1866, 4th ed. 1889, Eng. 1892; E. Reuss, *Les Prophètes*, 1876, cf. *Das AT*, ii., Brunswick, 1892-94; Nägelsbach in Lange's *Bibelwerk*, 1877, Eng. 1878; Birks, *Comm. on Bk. of Is.*, Lond. 1878; T. K. Cheyne, *Proph. of Is. trans. with Comm. and Appendices*, 1880, 5th ed. 1889; C. J. Bredenkamp, *Der Proph. Jes.*, Erlangen, 1887; v. Orelli, *Propheten Jes. u. Jeremia*, Nördlingen, 1887, Eng. by Banks, 1889; G. A. Smith, *Is. 1-39*, 1888, *Is. 40-66*, 1890, 'Expositor's Bible'; Aug. Dillmann, *Der Proph. Jes.*, Leipz. 1890, being 5th ed. of Knobel's work in the 'Kurzgefasstes Exeget. Handbuch z. AT' (Diestel had edited 4th ed. in 1872); Bernh. Duhm, *Das Buch Jesaia* in Nowack's *Handkommentar z. AT*, Göttingen, 1892; W. Reich, *Jes.*, vol. i. of *Das Proph. Schriftthum*, Wien, 1892; J. Skinner, *Is. 1-39*, in the *Cambr. Bible*, 1896, *40-66*, 1898; Guthe u. Ryssel in Kautzsch, *Die heil. Schrift*, 1896; H. G. Mitchell, *Is.: a Study of Chs. 1-12*, New York, 1897; T. K. Cheyne, *Is.* in *PB*, 1898; R. Kittel, 6th ed. of Dillmann's *Der Proph. Jes.*, Leipz. 1898.

B. *BOOKS AND ARTICLES OF GENERAL INTRODUCTION TO THE BK. OF ISAIAH.*—Among the Introductions to the OT in general, Kuenen's and Driver's deal with Isaiah in most detail; Special works of Introduction to Isaiah are the following:—T. K. Cheyne, *Bk. of Is. chronologically arranged*, etc., London, 1870, art. 'Isaiah' in *Encyc. Brit.*[9] 1880, *Introduction to the Bk. of Is.*, London, 1895; Klostermann, art. 'Jesaia' in Herzog-Plitt's *Real.-Encyc.* 1880; B. Stade, *ZATW*, 1881-84; Cornill, *ZATW*, 1884, 'Die Composition des B. Jes.'; C. H. H. Wright, art. 'Isaiah' in Smith's *Bible Dict.*[2] 1893; S. R. Driver, *Is., his Life and Times*, Lond. 1893; G. Douglas, *Isaiah One and his Bk. One*, London, 1895 (cf. also on same side as the last, R. P. Smith, *Authenticity and Mess. Interpr. of the Proph. of Is.*, sermons before Univ. of Oxford, 1862); Brückner, *Komposition des Buches Jes. 28-33*, Halle, 1898; Kennedy, *Argt. for Unity of Is.*, 1891.

C. *BOOKS AND ARTICLES UPON THE TEXT OF THE BK. OF ISAIAH.*—D. Kocher, *Vindiciæ text. hebr. adv. R. Lowth criticam*, Bern. 1786; T. K. Cheyne, *Notes and Criticisms on Heb. Text of Is.*, 1868, the Hebrew Text of Is. in Haupt's *SBOT*, 1899; P. de Lagarde, *Prophetæ prior. et poster. chaldaice e fide cod. Reuchlin. editi*, 1872; *Semitica*, i. 1-32; *Ztschrift für Luth. Theol.* 1876, 1 ff. on Is. 40-66 by Klostermann; 1877, 17 ff. *Zur Text-critik Jes.* by H. Strack; *Jahrb. für Prot. Theol.* 1877, 706 ff., 1879, 63 ff., 1881, 160 ff. by Studer; *ZATW*, 1881-84, K. Budde; K. Kohler in *Hebraica II.*, Chicago, 1885; *Journ. of Bib. Lit.* June 1889, 'On the metres of Is. 1,' by Francis Brown; Oort in *Theol. Tijdschr.* 1891, 461 ff. (not seen); Klostermann, *Deuterojesaja* (not seen); Bachmann, *AT Untersuch.*, 1894, 49 ff.; Perles, *Analekten zur Text-Kritik d. AT*, 1895 (not seen); Ruben, *Crit. Remarks on OT*, Lond. 1896. Also these more general works, including other matters than the text:—B. Stade, *De Is. Vatt. Aethiopicis diatribe*, Leipzig, 1873 (not seen); J. Barth, *Beiträge z. Erklärung des Jes.*, Leipzig, 1885; Giesebrecht, *Beitr. z. Jes. Kritik*, Gött. 1890. See also Geiger's *Urschrift*, Breslau, 1857.

D. *BOOKS AND ARTICLES ON THE HISTORICAL AND THEOLOGICAL CRITICISM OF IS. 1-39.*—(1) On Chronology, Assyrian history, etc.:—Hincks in *Jour. of Sacr. Lit.* Oct. 1858; J. Wellhausen, *Jahrb. für deutsche Theol.* 1875; A. Kamphausen, *Die Chronologie der Heb. Könige*, Bonn, 1883; Schrader, *KAT*[2], Giessen, 1883, Eng. by Whitehouse, *COT*[2], 2 vols. London, 1885, 1888; *RP*, both series; Duncker's and Meyer's *Histories of Antiquity*, also W. R. Smith, *Proph. of Isr.* 145 f., 402, 413 f.; Winckler, *Untersuch. zur Altorient. Gesch.*, Leipz. 1889, *AT Untersuch.* 1897, *Altorient. Forsch.* 1893; McCurdy, *HPM*, vols. i., ii., London, 1894, 1896; Tiele, *Babylon.-Assyr. Geschichte.*

(2) On the history of Isaiah's times in connexion with his teaching:—Strachey, *Jewish History and Politics*[2], 1874; Köstlin, *Jes. u. Jeremya*, Berlin, 1879; Sayce, *Life, etc. of Is.*, 1883; W. R. Smith, *Proph. of Israel*[2], London, 1896; Guthe, *Das Zukunftsbild des Jes.* (see below); J. J. P. Valeton, jun., *Viertal Voorlezingen over de Profeten des O. V.*, Utrecht, 1886; Meinhold, *Jes. u. seine Zeit*, Freiburg, 1898; Sinker, *Hezekiah and his Age*, 1898.

(3) On the theology of Isaiah in general:—Duhm, *Theol. der Proph.* Bonn, 1875; Riehm, *Messianic Prophecy*, Eng. Edinburgh, 1891; Kirkpatrick, *Doctrine of the Prophets*, 1892; Cornill, *Der Israelit. Prophetismus*, 1895, Eng. by Corkran, Chicago, 1896; A. B. Davidson, *Expository Times*, v. (1894) 296, 369, 391, 438, 488. Other manuals on the Theology of the OT and History of the religion of Israel.

(4) On the Messianic prophecies and Isaiah's view of the future:—Bredenkamp, *Vaticinium quod de Immanuele edidit Jes.* (7^1-9^6) (not seen); Giesebrecht, 'Die Immanuelweissagung' in *SK*, 1888, 217 ff.; Guthe, *Das Zukunftsbild des Jes.*, Leipz. 1885; Hackmann, *Die Zukunftserwartung des Jes.*, 1893; Porter, 'Isaiah's Immanuel' in *Journ. of Bibl. Liter.* 1895; on 2^{2-4} see comm. on Micah; G. A. Smith, *Twelve Prophets* ('Expos. Bible'), i. 365 f.; on 7, K. Budde in *Études etc. dediées à M. le Dr. Leemans*, Leyden, 1885, 121 ff.

(5) On other special subjects and chapters in Is 1-39, *e.g.* the league of Syria and N. Isr. against Judah in 734:—Caspari, *Ueber den syrisch.-ephraim. Krieg unter Jotham u. Ahaz*, Christiania, 1889; on ch. 12, F. Brown, *JBL*, 1890, 128-131; on chs. 13. 14, Hävernick, *Symbolæ ad defend. authent. Jes. xii. xiv.* 1842 (not seen); W. H. Cobb, *An Exam. of Is 13* (reprint from 'Bibl. Sacra'), 1892, cf. Cheyne in *JBL* for 1898; on $14^{24ff.}$, Stade, *ZATW*, 1883; on chs. 15. 16, Hitz. *Des Proph. Jonas Orakel über Moab* (1831, not seen); L. de Geer, *De orac. in Moabitas Jes. xv. xvi.*, T. ad Rhen. 1855 (not seen); Oort in *Theol. Tijd.* xxi. 51-64 (not seen); Baudissin in *SK*, 1888, 509 ff.; on 21^{1-10} and siege of Babylon, Kleinert, *SK*, 1879; on the question of Sargon's invasion of Palestine in 711, Hincks in *Journ. of Sacred Lit.* Oct. 1858; on Sennacherib's invasion and the relations to it of chs. 22. 23. 28-33. 36. 37, besides the relevant paragraphs in Kuenen and Cheyne, see Nowack, *SK*, 1881, 'Bemerkungen üb. das 14 Jahr des Hiskias,' and the historical works mentioned above; *Juda u. die Assyr. Weltmacht* (in the 'Programm der Technischen Staatslehranstalten zu Chemnitz,' Easter, 1885), by Asmus Sörensen; Friedr. Delitzsch, art. 'Sanherib' in Herzog-Plitt's *Real-Encyc.*; Stade, *ZATW*, 1886; Meinhold, *SK*, 1893, on c. 28; on 24-27, E. Böhl, *Vat. Jes. c. xxiv.-xxvii.*, Lips. 1861 (not seen); Hilgenfeld, *Ztsch. für Wissenschaftl. Theol.* 1866, 432 ff.; Smend, *ZATW*, 1884; Oort, *Theol. Tijd.* 1886 (not seen); on chs. 34. 35, Grätz, *JQR*, Oct. 1891; Budde, *Jahrb. für deutsche Theol.* xxiii. 428 ff., 529 ff.; on ch. 38, Dillvo, *Das Wunder an den Stufen des Ahas*, Amst. 1885; on chs. 36-39, J. Meinhold, *Die Jesajaerzählungen*, 1898.

E. *VOLUMES, ARTICLES, ETC., UPON IS. 40-66.*—(1) On general questions of Introduction:—Bunsen, *Gott in der Gesch.* i. 383 ff.; Rückert, *Heb. Propheten übers. u. erläutert*, i.; R. Stier, *Jes. nicht pseudo-Jes.*, Barmen, 1850; A. Rütgers, *De echtheid van het tweede gedeelte van Jez. aangetoond*, Leiden, 1866 (not seen); Löhr, *Zur Frage über die echtheit von Jes. 40-66*, 1876-80 (not seen); Klostermann in *Ztschr. für Luth. Theol.* 1876; *The Old Is.*, Moody Stuart, Edin. 1880; Cobb in *Biblioth. Sacra*, 1882; A. B. D[avidson], review of Del.'s *Isaiah* in *Theol. Review*, iv.; T. K. Cheyne, review of *Is. 40-66* ('Expos. Bible') in *Expositor*, 1891, i., also art. in *JQR*, 1892; Lucien Gautier in *Revue Chrétienne*, March 1893, 176 ff.; Geiger, *Jüdische Ztschr.* vi. xi. (according to Cheyne), asserts plurality of authors; on text and rhythm of several sections, K. Budde, *ZATW*, 1891; J. Ley, *Hist. Erklärung des* 2ten *Teils d. Jes.* 1893, also in *SK*, 1899, 163 ff. See also Cheyne, *Jewish Religious Life after the Exile*, 1898; and Ed. König, *The Exiles' Book of Consolation* (Edinburgh, T. & T. Clark, 1899). Both these were published too late to be taken account of in the present article.

(2) On the contemporary history (besides some of the historical works cited on Is 1-39, and general histories of Israel, Babylon, and Persia):—J. Halévy, 'Cyrus et le Retour de l'Exil' in *REJ* i. 1880; Feilchenfeld, *Die jüdischen Gegner der Heimkehr etc. unter Cyrus* (reprint from 'Jübelschrift für Dr. Hildesheimer,' Frankfort, n. d.); Sayce, *Fresh Light from the Ancient Monuments*; on the stele of Nabonidus, Scheil in *Recueil de Travaux*, etc., ed. by Maspero, xviii. 1896 (not seen); C. H. W. Johns in *Expository Times*, 1896; Messerschmidt, *Mittheilungen der Vorderasiat. Gesellschaft*, pt. i. 1896 (not seen).

(3) On the general theology of Is 40-66:—Duhm, *Theol. der Propheten*, 1875; F. Hermann Krüger, *Essai sur la théologie d'Esaie xl.-lxvi.*, Paris, 1881; A. B. Davidson, artt. in *Expositor*, 1883-84; Kirkpatrick, *Doctrine of the Prophets*, 1892.

(4) On the Servant of J″:—Schenkel, 'Krit. Versuch über den Knecht Gottes' in *SK*, 1836 (not seen); G. F. Oehler, *Der Knecht J″ im Deuterojes.*, Stuttgart, 1865 (not seen); A. Wünsche, *Leiden des Messias*; A. B. Davidson, 'The Servant of the Lord in Isaiah,' in *Brit. and For. Evang. Rev.* 1872; Tayler Lewis, 'The Purifying Messiah: Interpr. of Is. 52^{13}' in *Bibl. Sacra*, 1873, 166 ff. (not seen); *Westminster Rev.* Oct. 1875; Urwick, *The Servant of J″*, 1877; C. Taylor, 'Interpr. of יזה גוים' in *Journ. of Phil.* 1879, 62 ff.; C. H. H. Wright, 'Pre-Chr. Jewish Interpretations of Is. 53,' *Expositor*, May 1888; Briggs, *Messianic Prophecy*; John Forbes (of Aberdeen), *On the Servant of the Lord*, 1890; G. F. Dalman, *Is. 53*, 1890; Driver and Neubauer, with introduction by Pusey, *The 53rd Ch. of Is. acc. to Jewish Interpreters*, 2 vols. Oxford, 1876, 1877; M. Schian, *Die Ebed-Jahwe Lieder*, Halle, 1895; Sellin, *Serubbabel*, 1898; Laue, *Die Ebed-Jahwe Lieder*, 1898; Bertholet, *Zu Jesaja 53: ein Erklärungsversuch*, 1899. The last three appeared too late to be taken account of in the present article.

F. Besides the above there have been a number of purely practical and homiletic volumes on Isaiah. A. Marloratus, *Esai Proph. cum catholica expositione ecclesiastica*, Paris, Stephan 1564; Bullinger, *Is. Expositus Homiliis cxc.*, 1567; Sibbes' *Bruised Reed*, etc., vol. i. of his works, ed. Aberdeen, 1809; J. Smith (of Campbelton), *Summary View and Explanation of Prophets* (not seen), 1787; Macculloch (minister of

Dairsie), *Lectures on the Proph. of Is.*, 4 vols., Edin. 1791–1804 ; J. Stock, *Bk. of Proph. Is.*, Bath, 1803 ; Fraser (minister of Kirkhill), *Comm. on Proph. of Is., being a paraphr. with notes*, 1800 ; F. D. Maurice, *Prophets and Kings of OT*, xiii.-xviii. 1852 ; Perowne, *Sermons*, 1874, 'Exp. of Is 8¹⁶⁻⁹⁷' ; W. G. Elmslie's *Memoir and Sermons*, 'The Making of a Prophet,' Is 61⁻⁸, 1890 ; Driver, *Sermons on OT*, II. 'Isaiah's Vision,' III. 'Ideals of the Prophets,' 1892 ; R. Kittel, *Aus dem Leben des Proph. Jes.* (sermons), Gotha, 1894 (not seen) ; E. King, *Pract. Reflections on every Verse of Is.*, 1894 ; W. Kelly, *Exp. of Bk. of Is.*, 1897 (not seen).   G. A. SMITH.

ISAIAH, ASCENSION OF.

—i. CONTENTS OF THE ETHIOPIC BOOK.—The book falls into two parts : (A) The Martyrdom of Isaiah, (B) The Ascension of Isaiah into the Seventh Heaven. The bracketed sections are generally regarded as interpolations.

A. Hezekiah summons Manasseh, his son, to deliver to him revelations which he had received in his sickness, and writings of the prophet Isaiah. The prophet, who is present, declares that Manasseh will not regard instruction, but will cause him to be sawn asunder. After the death of Hezekiah (ch. 2), Manasseh turns to evil ways, and Isaiah retires with other prophets, first to Bethlehem, and then to the mountains beyond it. The false prophet Belkira (ch. 3) discovers his retreat, and accuses him before Manasseh on three grounds : first, that he has prophesied the destruction of Jerusalem ; secondly, that whereas Moses had said, No man can see God and live, Isaiah had said, I have seen God, and, behold, I live ; thirdly, that he had called Jerusalem and the princes and people of Judah by the names of Sodom and Gomorrah.

[3¹³–5¹ gives as a further reason for Isaiah's martyrdom the anger of Berial (or Beliar) at the visions which he had seen of the coming of the Beloved, etc. This forms an apocalyptic section in which there are many points of contact with the later part of the book, and esp. with 11²⁻²². After the return of the Beloved to the seventh heaven the twelve apostles will preach throughout the world ; but among their converts evil will multiply : and at length Berial will descend in the form of an impious king, the murderer of his mother, and will work miracles, and cause himself to be worshipped as the only God. The Lord will return and destroy him : the resurrection and judgment will follow].

While Isaiah is being martyred (ch. 5) Berial offers to release him, if he will confess that he has prophesied falsely. The prophet defies him, and is sawn asunder with a wooden saw, conversing the while with the Holy Spirit.

B. This begins with a new title : 'The vision which Isaiah the son of Amoz saw in the 20th year of the reign of Hezekiah king of Judah.' Isaiah comes from Gilgal (ch. 6), and is met by many prophets. In the presence of these, and of the king and his princes, he sits on the king's couch and prophesies. While he is speaking he falls into a trance with his eyes open. Afterwards he relates his vision to Hezekiah and the prophets, but not to the people. It is as follows :—

He is taken (ch. 7) by an angel, whose name he may not know, because he is to return to his mortal body, first up into the firmament, where he finds perpetual warfare between Satanic powers. Next he ascends into the first heaven, where he sees a throne with angels on either side ; they chant a hymn of praise, which he learns is addressed to the Glory of the seventh heaven and to His Beloved. In the second heaven he finds also a throne with angels, but more glorious ; he would fain fall down and worship, but is not permitted. In the third heaven he finds the like ; there is there no mention of the deeds of the vain world from which he has come, but he is assured that nothing escapes observation. In the fourth heaven he again sees angels on either side of a throne, the glory of those on the right being, as

before, greater than of those on the left ; and all are more glorious than those below. The same in yet greater degree is true of the fifth heaven. But in the sixth heaven (ch. 8) there is no throne, and no left hand, but all are alike in splendour : it is in close connexion with the seventh heaven, and its glory makes the glory of the five heavens below seem but darkness. At length he comes (ch. 9) to the seventh heaven, where his entry is challenged, but permitted. Here he sees the just clothed in their heavenly robes, but not yet having received their thrones and crowns. These they cannot have until the descent and return of the Beloved has been accomplished. He is shown also the books which contain the transactions of the world below, and learns that all is known in the seventh heaven. He beholds the Lord of Glory, and is bidden to worship Him. He then beholds a second most glorious one, like unto Him, and again is bidden to worship ; and then again a third, who is the angel of the Holy Spirit, the inspirer of the prophets. These two latter worship the ineffable Glory ; and the chant of praise (ch. 10) sounds up from the sixth heaven. Then the voice of the Most High is heard speaking to the Lord the Son, bidding Him descend through the heavens to the firmament, and to the world, and even to the angel of the infernal regions ; He is to assimilate Himself to those who dwell in each region in turn, so that He may not be recognized as He passes down. He will ascend at length with glory and worship from all. The prophet now beholds the descent of the Beloved. In the sixth heaven there is no change of His appearance, and the angels glorify Him. But in the fifth He is changed, and not recognized, and so in each of the lower heavens, down to the firmament, where He passes through the strife that rages there, still unrecognized. At this point the angel calls the prophet's special attention to what follows (ch. 11).

[Here follows a description of the Birth from a Virgin, and a notice of the life, death, and resurrection of the Lord, and the sending forth of the Twelve (11²⁻²²).]

Then the prophet beholds the ascent through the firmament and the six heavens : the Lord is recognized and glorified as He ascends : at length He reaches the seventh heaven, and takes His seat on the right hand of the great Glory ; and the angel of the Holy Spirit sits on the left hand. The prophet is then sent back to his mortal clothing. On his return he warns Hezekiah that these things will come to pass, but that they may not be communicated to the people of Israel.

ii. DOCUMENTS AND EDITIONS.—(a) *Ethiopic.*—This, the fullest recension, was first published in 1819 by Laurence, Regius Professor of Hebrew at Oxford, afterwards Archbishop of Cashel, from a MS which he had bought in London, and which also contained an Ethiopic version of 4 Ezra. He accompanied his edition with translations into Latin and English, and with notes and a dissertation. In 1877 this edition was superseded by Dillmann's, which was based on Laurence's MS (now in the Bodleian) and two others in the British Museum. Dillmann gave a literal translation into Latin, which remains the most satisfactory form in which those who are not Ethiopic scholars can read the book. In 1894 a French translation was issued by M. René Basset, as No. 3 of his series *Les Apocryphes Éthiopiens*; but this, though convenient, is not to be relied on for the purposes of criticism.

(b) *Latin.*—(1) A Latin version of the second part (B), the *Ascension of Isaiah* proper, was printed at Venice in 1522 from a MS not now known. It was published by Antonius de Fantis in a small volume containing the visions of the Virgin Mechtild and some other pieces. It was reprinted by Gieseler in a Göttingen programme in 1832 ; and by Dillmann, together with the two fragments next to be mentioned, in his edition of 1877. (2) Two Latin fragments were printed by Mai (1828) in his *Scriptt. Vett. Nova Collectio*, iii. p. 238 f., from a Vatican palimpsest. He found them in company with certain Arian writings, recognized them as belonging to some apocryphon of the OT, but did not identify them. They are reprinted by Dillmann, and comprise chs. 2^{14}–3^{13} and ch. 7^{1-19}. They contain enough to show that they represent a form of the book in which the bracketed section of A was present, and in which A and B were combined.

(c) *Greek.*—In 1878, the year after the appearance of Dillmann's edition, Osc. von Gebhardt published, in Hilgenfeld's *Zeitschrift f. wiss. Theol.* (p. 330 ff.), a late recension of the book in Greek from a 12th cent. MS in Paris (*Bibl. Nat.* 1534), a volume of *legenda* (Mar.–May). Under May 9 he found : προφητεία, ἀποκάλυψις καὶ μαρτύριον τοῦ ἁγίου καὶ ἐνδόξου καὶ μεγίστου τῶν προφητῶν Ἡσαΐου τοῦ προφήτου. This is not alluded to by Dr. Salmon in his excellent article in *Dict. Chr. Biogr.*, and it has also escaped the notice of M. Basset. Its importance lies in the fact that, in spite of its entire recasting of the work, it still gives us considerable portions of the original Greek. But there is little to be gained from it for the history of the tradition of the book. The object of the reviser has been to produce a lection for Church purposes ; and he has accordingly reduced the vision of the *Ascension* to small compass, and has rearranged the materials so as to put the martyrdom at the end. He appends an account of the prophet's burial, and introduces some traditions about the Pool of Siloam, which find parallels in Pseudo-Dorotheus, the Paschal Chronicle, and Pseudo-Epiphanius (see the references and citations given by v. Gebhardt).

(d) *Slavonic.*—Three versions in Old Slavonic have been published, but they have not as yet been critically investigated. For notices of them see Bonwetsch in Harnack's *Altchristliche Litteratur*, i. 916, and Basset, p. 7 n.

iii. PATRISTIC REFERENCES. — The most important of these may be noted here, grouped according to the portion of the book to which they belong.

(a) Justin Martyr (*Trypho*, 120) accuses the Jews of having obliterated from the OT the story of the death of Isaiah, ὃν πρίονι ξυλίνῳ ἐπρίσατε. Tertullian (*de Patient.* 14) says : 'His patientiæ uiribus secatur Esaias, et de domino non tacet.' The phraseology in each case suggests, though it cannot be held to prove, an acquaintance with A. Origen (*Comm. in Matth.* 23^{34} ; *Ep. ad Afric.* 9) refers to the story of the martyrdom as contained in an ἀπόκρυφον Ἡσαΐου ; moreover, he cites (*Hom. in Ies.* 5) the charge of contradicting Moses ('Moses, aiunt, non uidit ; et tu uidisti ?'). Jerome (*Comm. in Ies.* 1^{10}) gives this charge and the further one, 'quod principes Sodomorum et populum Gomorrhæ eos appellauerit,' as the two causes of the prophet's death. Ambrose (*in Ps.* 118) gives the story of the devil's offer to release Isaiah, if he would declare his prophecies to be false. The anonymous commentary printed with Chrysostom's works (Montf. t. vi.), and known as the *Opus imperfectum in Matthæum*, refers to Isaiah's prophecy of the disobedience of Manasseh and of his own death, and to Hezekiah's consequent wish to slay his son (*Hom.* i. p. xx f.).

These references do not of necessity imply more than a knowledge of a Jewish book of the Martyrdom ; some of them might be merely allusions to isolated Jewish legends (cf. Fabricius, *Cod. pseudepigr. VT*, p. 1088 ff.). But Cedrenus (Bonn ed. i. 120 f.) cites the calculation of the reign of Antichrist, with slightly changed figures ; and it is noticeable that he speaks of the book as *The Testament of Hezekiah*.

(b) Jerome, in commenting on Is 64^4, expressly mentions the 'Ascensio Esaiæ,' and says that it contained the quotation cited by St. Paul in 1 Co 2^9 'Eye hath not seen,' etc. This passage is found in *Asc.* 11^{34}, but only in the Latin version. It is probable, therefore, that Jerome knew the book in a form which contained both A and B. In the context of this last passage he implies that it was used by heretics in Spain ; and this accords with a reference in the recently recovered works of Priscillian (*Tract.* 3, p. 47, Schepss). Epiphanius twice refers to the Ἀναβατικὸν Ἡσαΐου, and says that it was used by Hieracas, an Egyptian teacher of the beginning of the 4th cent. (*Hær.* 67, 3), and by the Archontici, a sect of about the same date (*Hær.* 40, 2). The former of these references relates to the appearance of the Beloved (ὁ ἀγαπητός) on the right hand of God, and of the Holy Spirit on the left hand : the latter refers to the seven heavens.

There are two references in apocryphal writings which deserve special mention. In the *Last Words of Baruch* (ch. 9) allusion is made to the martyrdom of Isaiah in such a way as to suggest that the *Ascensio* in its Christian form was known to the writer (see Rendel Harris's edition, p. 20 ff.). In the *Actus Petri Vercellenses* (ed. Lipsius, p. 72) we have a quotation from *Asc.* 11^{14}. As both these books may have been written before the middle of the 2nd cent., their evidence is of special importance.

Two later writings of very small intrinsic worth seem to have used the *Ascensio*. One is a sermon of Potamius, printed among St. Zeno's works (Verona, 1739, p. 300) : it describes the martyrdom, and mentions Belial. The other is the apocryphal *Liber Johannis*, an Albigensian book, printed at the end of Thilo's *Codex Apocryphus NT*.

For further references the student may consult Dr. Salmon's art. in *Dict. Chr. Biogr.*, Harnack's *Altchr. Litt.* p. 854 ff., and Basset's *Introduction* : in this last he will also find a fairly complete bibliography.

iv. CRITICAL REMARKS.—In the outline given above of the Ethiopic book, Dillmann's critical dissection of it has been in the main accepted. But it may be questioned whether his theory of two separate books, A and B, as we have called them, combined and interpolated at a subsequent period, is not somewhat too rigid. It may be nearer to the truth to suppose that A does indeed reproduce a Jewish book on the Death of Isaiah, but that the whole of the remainder is due to a single Christian hand, which modified the opening section, inserted the apocalyptic vision, and added the vision of the Ascension.

There appears to be no sufficient ground for distinguishing the writer of the apocalyptic section from the author of the Ascension. The fact that the Antichrist assumes the form of a matricidal king does not of necessity take the apocalyptic section back into the 1st cent. : the reappearance of Nero as the Antichrist long haunted the imagination of the Christian apocalyptists. The calculation of the duration of his reign appears to be simply borrowed from the Book of Daniel, and gives us no guidance.

If there was a separately existing Jewish book, this may be the source of the references of Justin Martyr, of Tertullian, and even of Origen. In this case Jerome and Epiphanius (or Hieracas as quoted by the latter) would be our earliest authorities (other than anonymous) for the Christian book. Yet on internal evidence we should place it not much later than the middle of the 2nd cent. 'Elders and pastors' are the only titles applied to Christian ministers ; prophecy seems spoken of as still in exercise, though failing in influence ; and the description of Isaiah's ecstasy suggests that the writer had witnessed Christian trances.

The closest literary parallel may perhaps be found in the Testaments of the XII. Patriarchs, in which the narrative portions at the commencement of each Testament are directly taken from Jewish books, esp. from the Book of Jubilees, and the remainder, homiletical and apocalyptical, is the work of a Christian hand.

v. INTEREST FOR BIBLICAL STUDENTS.—The chief points of interest are two—(1) the conception of the firmament (as the abode of evil spirits), and of the seven heavens; (2) the use of the name 'the Beloved' as a Messianic title. If these features could be regarded as directly derived from Jewish sources, without the intervention of the NT writings, they would be important illustrations of the language of St. Paul (Eph 1² 6¹², 2 Co 12²⁻⁴, also Eph 1⁶). But on the whole it is probable that the apostle's language was familiar to the writer, and was regarded by him as giving a kind of sanction to his conceptions, if it did not actually form their starting-point.

1. For the conception of the seven heavens the student may refer to Mr. Charles' introduction to *The Book of the Secrets of Enoch*, p. xxx ff. Our author's idea of the seven heavens differs from other descriptions in that he introduces no physical phenomena (as, *e.g.*, ice and snow, sun and moon, paradise, etc.) by way of differentiating them. Tradition has supplied him with nothing but the bare number of seven, and he distinguishes one from another only by a constantly increasing glory. On the other hand, he is unwilling to place any element of evil in any of the heavens, and hence he introduces the firmament as between the earth and the first heaven, so as to find a dwelling-place for the Satanic powers of the air. Perhaps his own main interest lay in the exposition of the idea that the descent of the Beloved escaped the notice of the dwellers in the lower heavens, in the firmament, and on the earth. This idea was found in St. Paul's language in 1 Co 2⁸ 'the hidden wisdom . . . which none of the rulers of this age knew; for, if they had known it, they would not have crucified the Lord of Glory.' 'The rulers of this age' are the powers of the firmament in our book; and the title 'the Lord of Glory' also occurs in it. The same thought is found in the well-known words of Ignatius (*ad Eph.* 19): καὶ ἔλαθε τὸν ἄρχοντα τοῦ αἰῶνος τούτου ἡ παρθενία Μαρίας καὶ ὁ τοκετὸς αὐτῆς, ὁμοίως καὶ ὁ θάνατος τοῦ Κυρίου.

2. The name of the Messiah in every part of this book is 'the Beloved.' There is some ground for thinking that this was a pre-Christian Messianic title. For (1) it is used in the OT (ὁ ἠγαπημένος, LXX) as a title of Israel; *e.g.* Dt 32¹⁵ 33⁵· ²⁶, where it renders 'Jeshurun,' as it does also in Is 44²; again in Is 5, ὁ ἠγαπημένος and ὁ ἀγαπητός render יָדִיד and דּוֹד respectively. It was natural, therefore, that, like the titles 'Servant' and 'Elect,' it should be transferred from the people to the Messiah. (2) At the period when the Gospels were written 'the Beloved' and 'the Elect' were practically interchangeable terms, for Mt writes ὁ ἀγαπητός μου (12¹⁸) in citing Is 42¹, where the Heb. is בְּחִירִי (LXX ὁ ἐκλεκτός μου); and Lk (9³⁵) substitutes ὁ ἐκλελεγμένος for ὁ ἀγαπητός in the words spoken at the Transfiguration. (3) These two substitutions suggest that, whatever may have been the original meaning of the phrase ὁ υἱός μου ὁ ἀγαπητός (Mk 1¹¹ 9⁷), both Mt and Lk regarded ὁ ἀγαπητός as a separate title, and not as an epithet of υἱός; and it is interesting to note that the Old Syriac version emphasized this distinction by rendering 'My Son and My Beloved.' (4) In Eph 1⁶ St. Paul uses ἐν τῷ ἠγαπημένῳ as equivalent

to ἐν τῷ Χριστῷ in a context in which he is designedly using terms derived from Jewish sources. (5) Certain passages of the LXX where ὁ ἀγαπητός occurs were explained by Christian interpreters as Messianic (Ps 44 (45) *tit.*, Zec 12¹⁰). (6) Lastly, we have several passages in early Christian writings in which ὁ ἠγαπημένος is used as a title of Christ, *e.g.* Barn. 3⁶ 4³· ⁸; cf. Clem. Rom. 59²· ³; Ign. *Smyrn.* inscr.; Herm.*Sim.* IX. xii. 5; *Acts of Thecla*, c. 1; ὁ ἀγαπητός is also used, but usually with υἱός or παῖς (Herm. *Sim.* v. ii. 6; *Mart. Polyc.* 14; *Ep. ad Diogn.* 8; *Acts of Thecla*, c. 24; in the last three cases in a liturgical formula). It is difficult to suppose that in all these instances from Christian writings the title (esp. in the form ὁ ἠγαπημένος) has for its only source the NT. And in particular the persistent use of ὁ ἀγαπητός in the present book suggests that the writer must have thought its introduction consistent with verisimilitude in a work which sought to be regarded as an ancient Jewish prophecy of Christ.

J. ARMITAGE ROBINSON.

ISCAH (יִסְכָּה,'Ιεσχά,etym. uncertain).—A daughter of Haran and sister of Milcah, Gn 11²⁹ (J). This is the only passage in OT where she is mentioned. There is no probability (see Dillm. *ad loc.*) in the identification of Iscah with Sarai (Jos. *Ant.* I. vi. 5, Targ. Jon., Talm., Ephraem, Jerome, Rashi, etc.), and little warrant for the conjecture of Ewald (*HI* i. 313) that she was the wife of Lot.

ISCARIOT.—See JUDAS ISCARIOT.

ISDAEL ('Ισδαήλ), 1 Es 5³³.—In Ezr 2⁵⁶, Neh 7⁵⁸, GIDDEL. The form is probably due to corruption of the Greek, ΓΕΔΔΗΛ being read as ΙCΔΑΗΛ.

ISHBAH (יִשְׁבָּה).—A Judahite, the 'father' of Eshtemoa, 1 Ch 4¹⁷. See GENEALOGY.

ISHBAK (יִשְׁבָּק).—A son of Abraham by Keturah, Gn 25²=1 Ch 1³². In Gn the LXX has, A 'Ιεσβόκ (so Luc.), D 'Ιεσβούκ, E 'Ιεσόκ, in 1 Ch B Σοβάκ, A 'Ιεσβόκ. The tribe of which he is the eponym is somewhat uncertain, although Frd. Delitzsch (*ZSKF* ii. 92) identifies it with *Iasbuḳ* of the cuneiform inscriptions, where it is mentioned as a land (*māt*) whose king was allied with Sangara (Shamgar?) of Gargamis (Carchemish) and others against Assur-naẓir-pal and Shalmaneser II. (*c.* 859 B.C.). Dillmann and Delitzsch point out that the name has nothing to do with *Shanbaḳ* in the Jebel esh-Shera, which is not heard of till the time of the Crusades.

ISHBI-BENOB.—One of the four Philistines of the giant stock who were slain by the mighty men of David (2 S 21¹⁵⁻¹⁷). See, however, GOB.

ISHBOSHETH (אִישׁ־בֹּשֶׁת), who disputed the throne of Israel with David for about seven years, was the fourth son of Saul (1 Ch 8³⁴ 9³⁹). His real name as preserved by the Chronicler was Eshbaal or Ishbaal (אִישׁ־בַּעַל 'man of Baal'), but he is better known to us by the name Ishbosheth (אִישׁ־בֹּשֶׁת 'man of the shameful thing'), which he bears in 2 S 2⁸ and elsewhere. This double nomenclature is easily explained. Baal is most familiar to us as the name of a Tyrian or Phœn. divinity, but in its primary meaning of 'lord' it was the designation applied by the N. Shemites each to their own particular deity, and we know that at one time it was a frequent appellation even of the God of Israel (Hos 2¹⁶· ¹⁷). It is in this way that we must explain its use by Saul in naming his sons, for, whatever faults may be chargeable against the first king of Israel, he was certainly no idolater. In later times, when Baal had come to be regarded as a heathenish name, the words of Ex 23¹³ 'Make no mention of the name of other gods,' were interpreted so literally that in reading, and finally in writing, *Bosheth* (' the shameful thing ') was frequently substituted for *Baal*. (The text of Samuel must, according to Wildeboer, *Litt. d. AT* 82, have escaped this alteration till after B.C. 250, the date at which the Chronicler still found the original name Ishbaal written there). As Hosea apparently means to express his contempt for the impure worship of the N. kingdom by substituting (Hos 4¹⁵ 5⁸ 10⁵) *Bethaven* 'house of idolatry' for *Bethel* 'house of God,' for a similar reason the *Jerubbaal* of Jg 6³² is replaced in 2 S 11²¹ by *Jerubbesheth*. In like manner the name of Jonathan's son was not Mephibosheth but Meribbaal. In this case also it is the Chronicler that has preserved the true name (cf. 2 S 4⁴ with 1 Ch 8³⁴ 9⁴⁰). The offensive component *Baal* was occasionally got rid of in a different way. In 1 S 14⁴⁹ the name of one of Saul's sons appears as *Ishvi* (יִשְׁוִי), in which Wellhausen, followed by Budde (*Richt u. Sam.* 207), sees a corruption of *Ishjo* (אִשְׁיוֹ) or *Ishjahu*. This is supported by the LXX (Luc.) Ἰεσσιού. In this instance the word *Baal*, instead of being degraded to *Bosheth*, is transfigured into one of the forms of the name J″, and the 'man of Baal' (Ishbaal) becomes the 'man of J″' (Ishjahu). On the same principle, David's son *Beel*iada (1 Ch 14⁷) appears in 2 S 5¹⁶ as *El*iada (Benzinger, *Heb. Archäol.* 152).

According to 1 S 31², Saul's three eldest sons, Jonathan, Abinadab, and Malchi-shua fell with their father upon Mt. Gilboa. David's sovereignty was thereupon acknowledged by the men of Judah ; but Abner, who had been Saul's general, remained faithful to the cause of his master and kinsman, and under his directions Ishbosheth was proclaimed king at Mahanaim on the E. side of the Jordan. This locality was probably selected by Abner as his headquarters, because the land of Israel proper was completely overrun by the Philistines. Presently the men of David, under the command of Joab, encountered those of I., commanded by Abner, at Gibeon (2 S 2¹²f.). It was agreed to abide the issue of a combat between twelve champions selected on either side, but this proved indecisive, as all the twenty-four fell mortally wounded. A general engagement now ensued in which Abner's forces were completely routed. Some time thereafter I. had the misfortune to give deadly offence to Abner. Having detected his general in an intrigue with Rizpah, Saul's concubine, he reproached him with what, according to the usages of the time, amounted to an act of treason (2 S 3⁶⁻¹¹). Abner hotly resented such treatment, and declared his intention of transferring his allegiance to David. The full accomplishment of his purpose was, indeed, prevented by Joab, who, in order to avenge the death of his brother Asahel, treacherously murdered Abner on the occasion of his visit to David in Hebron. The cause of I., weak before, was hopelessly ruined by the defection and death of its chief supporter, and the unfortunate claimant of his father's throne was not long afterwards murdered by two of his officers (2 S 4⁵⁻⁷). The details of the crime are obscured by the rendering of AV and text of RV, although they are correctly given in the margin of the latter, which follows the Sept. That the latter is here to be preferred to the MT needs no proof (see W. R. Smith, *OTJC²* 82). Instead of the unintelligible language and meaningless repetitions of vv.⁶· ⁷, we read, 'And lo, the woman that kept the door was cleaning wheat, and she slumbered and slept, and the brothers Rechab and Baanah passed in unobserved and came into the house as Ishbosheth lay upon his bed, and they smote him and slew

him,' etc. The assassins came to David with the head of their victim ; but, instead of receiving the reward they expected, they were overwhelmed with reproaches and condemned to instant death (2 S 4⁹⁻¹²). This was the turning-point in the fortunes of David, who, although he had no complicity in the assassination, could not help profiting from the death of his rival. Seeing that he was the only possible leader against the Philistines, the whole nation of Israel now offered him their allegiance, and shortly thereafter he was able vastly to strengthen his position by wresting from the Jebusites the stronghold of Jerusalem, which city was henceforward the capital of the kingdom.

2. Ishbosheth (*i.e.* Ishbaal) should also prob. be read in 2 S 23⁸ for Josheb-basshebeth (wh. see).

J. A. SELBIE.

ISHHOD (אִישׁהוֹד 'man of majesty').—A Manassite, 1 Ch 7¹⁸ (AV **Ishod**). See GENEALOGY.

ISHI (יִשְׁעִי 'salutary').—**1.** A Jerahmeelite, 1 Ch 2³¹. **2.** A Judahite chief, 1 Ch 4²⁰. **3.** A chief of East Manasseh, 1 Ch 5²⁴. **4.** One of the captains of the 500 men of the tribe of Simeon (which see) who smote the Amalekites at Mt. Seir, 1 Ch 4⁴². See GENEALOGY, II. 5, IV. 11, 57, VII.ᵃ 8.

ISHI (אִישִׁי 'my husband,' LXX ὁ ἀνήρ μου).—The name which Hosea (2¹⁶) recommends Israel to apply to J″ instead of *Baali*, 'my lord' (see HOSEA, and cf. W. R. Smith, *Proph. of Isr.* 171, 408 f.).

ISHMA (יִשְׁמָא).—One of the sons (acc. to LXX) of Etam, 1 Ch 4³. The MT is undoubtedly corrupt. See GENEALOGY.

ISHMAEL (יִשְׁמָעֵאל 'God heareth,' or better, 'May God hear'*).—The son of Abraham, by his concubine Hagar. The history of Ishmael is contained in parts of Gn 16. 17. 21⁸⁻²¹ 25—chapters of which 16¹ᵃ· ³· ¹⁵· ¹⁶ 17. 25⁷⁻¹¹ᵃ· ¹²⁻¹⁷ belong to P, the rest (so far as it relates to Ishmael) belonging to J (ch. 16) or E (ch. 21). Sarah was barren (Gn 16¹) ; so, in accordance with the manners of the age (cf. 30³· ⁹, also 22²⁴, Ex 21⁷⁻⁸), she gives Abraham her handmaid Hagar, an Egyptian, as his concubine, in the hope that she may be 'builded up from her' (16²), *i.e.* obtain a family by her†—viz. by adopting Hagar's offspring as her own. When Hagar saw that she had conceived, a womanly feeling of superiority took possession of her, and she 'despised' Sarah (cf. 1 S 1⁶f.), who forthwith complains reproachfully to her husband, uttering the passionate wish that the indignity done to her may be visited upon him, and appealing to Jehovah to judge whether he is not to blame for permitting it. Abraham replies that Hagar is Sarah's slave, and she can do to her as she pleases. She accordingly 'deals hardly' with her, *lit.* ' humbles' her,‡ viz. by imposing upon her hard or degrading work, from which Hagar seeks refuge by flight (16⁴⁻⁶). Hagar was an Egyptian : so she naturally fled in the direction of Egypt ; and there, in the wilderness, by 'the spring on the way to Shur' — the spring known afterwards (v.¹⁴) as the well Beer-lahai-roi, and identified by many § with Muweilih, a watering-place about 25 miles W.N.W. of 'Ain Ḳadîs, on the caravan route between Hebron and

---

* The name occurs also in early Bab. as that of a slave from the land of 'Martu' or the Amorites (Thureau Dangin, *Rev. d'Assyr.*, 1897, p. 78) and in Minæan (Hommel, *Süd.-Arab. Chrestomathie*, 117, 135).

† The expression, as 30³. For the family being represented under the figure of a house, cf. Ru 4¹¹, Dt 25⁹, Ex 1²¹.

‡ See especially, on the word here used, Rahlfs, עָנָה und עִנָּה *in den Psalmen* (1892), p. 67 ff. (with numerous illustrations from Arabic) ; more briefly, Driver, *Deut.* p. 246. Cf. Gn 31⁵⁰ ('afflict').

§ See Trumbull, *Kadesh-barnea*, p. 64, and cf. Dillm.

Egypt—the angel of J″ 'found' her. He addresses to her three words (16[9-11]): firstly, bidding her return to her mistress, and 'humble herself' * under her hands; secondly, encouraging her to take this step by the promise of a numerous seed; and thirdly, fixing in anticipation the name and character of her future son: 'thou shalt call his name Ishmael, because Jehovah hath *heard* thy affliction. And he shall be a wild-ass of a man, his hand being against all, and the hand of all being against him: and in front of all his brethren he shall dwell.' The wild-ass is a wayward, intractable creature, whose home is the prairie (see the description in Job 39[5-8]; and cf. Hos 8[9] 'going alone wilfully'). Ishmael, like many of the other characters in Gn, is an impersonation of his descendants; and the narrator draws here a true and picturesque description of the Bedawis,† and of the life led by them to the present day: now, as ever, they are the free and independent sons of the desert, owning no authority save that of their own chief, reckless of life, if occasion demands it, ready to plunder the hapless traveller who ventures without permission within their domain. The tribes whom the Hebrews thus regarded as descended from Ishmael, dwelt partly, it seems, on the S. of Canaan; but in the main, as the words 'in the front of all his brethren' (so 25[18b], cf. v.[6]) imply,‡ their home was on the east of Israel and Edom (see below).

The next allusion to Ishmael is in ch. 17 (P), where, after the promise of a son to Sarah, Abraham, incredulous, and still resting his hopes upon Ishmael, utters the entreaty on his behalf (17[18]), 'Oh that Ishmael might live before thee!' § In reply, God reaffirms His promise to Sarah, but adds (with a play on his name), 'And as for Ishmael, *I have heard* thee: behold, I have blessed him, and will make him fruitful, and will multiply him exceedingly; twelve princes shall he beget, and I will make him into a great nation' (17[20]; see 25[12-16]). And at the end of the chapter, it is stated that Ishmael, being 13 years old (cf. 17[24] with 16[16], both P), was circumcised, together with the other male members of Abraham's household.

We again hear of Ishmael some three years afterwards, when Isaac was weaned ‖ (21[8-21] E). Sarah 'saw the son of Hagar, the Egyptian, whom she had borne unto Abraham, playing,' or *sporting, jesting* (19[14] 26[8], Ex 32[6], Jg 16[25]); ¶ her maternal jealousy is excited; she a second time appeals to her husband, and bids him, with some peremptoriness, 'cast out' both Ishmael and his slave-mother. Abraham, though resenting this demand,—for Ishmael was his firstborn, and had obviously also (note 'on account of his son') won his affection,—is nevertheless encouraged by God—as may be inferred from v.[14], in a nocturnal vision or dream—to yield to it: Abraham's genuine 'seed,' the inheritors of the promises, are to be in Isaac's line; and national greatness elsewhere is in store for Ishmael also. Resigned by these thoughts to the loss of his son, he sends him away with his mother, giving them a modicum of provision to support them on their journey. They wander to and fro over the dry and stony soil of the desert about Beersheba until their water is exhausted; Hagar then, faint and

desperate, flings the child down under the shade of one of the bushes, and seats herself sadly some little way off, not wishing to look upon the death of her son. But God 'heard' the voice of the crying child—the word is evidently chosen with allusion to the name Ishmael, even if it be not intended as an explanation of its origin (cf. 16[11] [J], 17[20] [P]) *,—called out to his mother, reassured her with a fresh promise (see 16[10]) of Ishmael's future greatness, and showed her a well of water, which enabled her to revive the dying lad. Ishmael grew up, made his home in the wilderness on the S. of Canaan, and became famous as an archer. His wife, it is added, like his mother, was an Egyptian.

The only other incidents of Ishmael's life which are mentioned, are that he and Isaac buried their father after his death (25[9] P), and that he himself died at the age of 137 (25[17] P).

Two expressions in ch. 21 deserve to be briefly commented upon.

(1) מְצַחֵק in v.[9] was a word which lent itself readily to Haggadistic expositions. R. Akiba (on account of its use in Gn 39[14. 17]) supposed it to refer to Ishmael's unchastity, R. Ishmael (on account of its use in Ex 32[6]) to his devotion to idolatry; other Rabbis (on account of the use of צָחַק in 2 S 2[14], Pr 26[19]) to attempts made by him to shoot his brother (*Bereshith Rabba, ad loc.*, p. 254 f. in Wünsche's translation; the second explanation also in Jer. *Quæst. ad Gen.*, and in Targ. Pseud-Jon. *ad loc.*). There were also other stories current among the later Jews respecting Ishmael's insolence towards his brother, his disputes with him concerning the birthright, etc: see Beer, *Leben Abraham's nach Auffassung der jüd. Sage*, pp. 49 ff. (where other Haggadistic expansions of the narrative of Ishmael's expulsion are also given), 57, 61. St. Paul, in Gal 4[29] (ὁ διώκων), follows some of these later traditions.

(2) 'Flung' (הִשְׁלֵךְ) in v.[15] clearly implies that hitherto Ishmael had been *carried* by his mother, although according to 16[16] 21[5. 8] he must have been 15 years old, if not more (see preced. col. and note ‖). Attempts have been made to remove the inconsistency: but it is in reality similar to the one in 12[11ff.] (as well as others occurring in other parts of Gn); 16[16] 21[5], the passages which fix the age of Ishmael, belong to P, whereas the present narrative belongs to a different writer, E, who took a different view of the chronology, and pictured Ishmael as still an infant (cf. v.[20] 'and he *grew up*').

The twelve 'princes' begotten by Ishmael (17[20]), or, in other words, the twelve eponymous ancestors of the tribes who were reputed to be descended from him, are enumerated in 25[12-16] (P): Nebaioth, Ḳedar, Adbeel, Mibsam, Mishma', Dumah, Massa, Ḥadad, Têma, Jeṭur, Naphish, and Ḳedemah. The first two of these are mentioned several times besides in the OT, chiefly as wealthy pastoral or trading tribes (Jer 49[28-32], Is 60[7], Ezk 27[21]; cf. Is 42[11], Jer 2[10], Ca 1[5], Ps 120[5]), Ḳedar also (Is 21[17]) as famous for its archers (cf. Gn 21[20]); Têma (about 250 miles S.E. of Edom) is mentioned Is 21[14], Jer 25[23], Job 6[19]: Jeṭur and Naphish appear from 1 Ch 5[19] to have been neighbours of Reuben on the E. of Jordan; the former in later days moved northwards, and are known in the Roman age as the wild and predatory mountain-tribe of Ituræans, skilled likewise in the use of the bow; for further particulars see the separate names in this Dictionary.† The home of Ishmael himself is in Gn 21[21] the wilderness of Paran, on the S. of Canaan, and no doubt there were Ishmaelites in that neighbourhood;‡ but the general situation of the tribes descended from him was unquestionably on the east of Palestine, Edom, and the Gulf of 'Aḳabah, in agreement with the expression in 16[12] and 25[18b] (cf. v.[6]) 'in the front of all his brethren': some of these tribes (25[16]) dwelt in fixed villages (חֲצֵרוֹת, cf.

* The same word (in the reflexive conj.) as in v.[9].

† Arab. *bedawi* (also *bedâwi*), a dweller in the *badw* or open plain, opp. to the *'ahl ul-ḥaḍari*, or dwellers in fixed localities (חָצֵר): see Lane *Arab. Lex.* pp. 171, 172, 589.

‡ In accordance with the general sense of the expression: see *e.g.* 1 K 11[7], Zec 14[4].

§ *i.e.* under thy eye and care; cf. Hos 6[2], Jer 30[20], Is 53[2].

‖ Which may not have been till he was two, or even three years old (2 Mac 7[27]).

¶ LXX παίζοντα (adding μετὰ Ἰσαὰκ τοῦ υἱοῦ αὐτῆς), Vulg. *ludentem*, Onk. קְחָיֵם (so 26[8], Jg 16[25]). The rend. 'mocking' is uncertain, though צָחַק has certainly this sense when followed by the prep. בְּ (*at* or *against*), 39[14. 17].

* Cf. the threefold allusion to the meaning of 'Isaac,' 17[17] (P), 18[12. 13] (J), 21[6] (E); see p. 485, No. 8.

† Cf. also Ed. Glaser, *Skizze der Gesch. u. Geogr. Arabiens* (1890), ii. 438 ff.

‡ The terms of 25[18a] 'And they dwelt from Ḥavîlah (probably north-east Arabia) unto Shur (that is in front of Egypt),' would include the wilderness of Paran. The well (and sanctuary?) of Beer-laḥai-roi may have been a common meeting-place for Ishmaelites and Israelites, at which the old traditions about Ishmael were recounted and kept alive (cf. Stade, *ZAW*, 1881, p. 348 f.).

the 'villages' of Kedar, Is 42[11]), others in חֲצֵרִים, a peculiar word, denoting, as it seems, the temporary circular encampments of nomad tribes (cf. Nu 31[10], Ezk 25[4]).* A daughter of Ishmael is also mentioned, as married by Esau, in Gn 28[9] (where she is called Mahalath) and 36[3] (where her name is given as Basemath); no doubt this statement points to the fact that certain Edomite clans (see 36[13], compared with v.[4]) had in them an admixture of Ishmaelite blood.

Ishmaelites are mentioned by J in Gn 37[25. 27. 28] 39[1] (a caravan of Ishmaelites carrying gums from Gilead to Egypt, to whom Joseph is sold by his brethren: the parallel narrative of E speaks of *Midianites*, 37[28. 36]), Jg 8[24] (where, as the term is applied to Midianites, who belonged to a different branch of the Abrahamidæ, Gn 25[4], it seems to be used in a generalized sense, 'not of race, but of mode of life,' to denote itinerant caravan-traders in general), Ps 83[6]; and individual Ishmaelites are named in 1 Ch 2[17] (Jether, 'Amasa's father: read accordingly in 2 S 17[25]), 27[30] (Obil, superintendent of David's camels).

The Hebrews classified their neighbours genealogically according to the nearer or more distant relationship in which they were regarded as standing towards themselves. The Edomites were most closely related to them: they were accordingly the descendants of Esau, the twin-brother of their own immediate ancestor, Jacob. Moab and Ammon were descended from Lot, Abraham's nephew. To Nahor, Abraham's brother, are traced twelve Aramæan tribes,—eight to a wife, Milcah, and four to a concubine, Re'umah (22[20.24]). Six tribes (one being Midian), and several sub-tribes, are the descendants of Abraham, though not by Sarah, the mother of Isaac, or by Hagar, but by a concubine, Keṭurah (25[1-4]). And here twelve tribes, spread over different parts of N. Arabia and the country E. of Israel, are traced to Abraham, through a 'handmaid,' Hagar, holding an intermediate position between Sarah and Keṭurah.† Historical recollections, similarities of language or civilization,‡ or other characteristics, the exact nature of which we cannot in every case determine, must have guided the Hebrew genealogists in thus forming ethnic groups, and defining the precise position occupied by each in relation to Israel. The Ishmaelites, being referred to Abraham himself, must have been regarded as belonging to an ancient stock, and evidently (cf. 17[20] 21[18] 'a great nation') enjoyed a reputation among the Hebrews, though at the same time some inferiority was implied in the fact that their ancestor was Abraham's son, not by his legitimate wife, but by a 'handmaid': the fact that Ishmael's mother and wife were both Egyptian shows, further, that his descendants were considered to have Egyptian blood in their veins.§ At a much later date, Ishmael was connected vaguely with Arabia in general: ‖ Moḥammed was supposed to have been

descended from him through Ḳedar;* he is mentioned several times in the Ḳor'ān, and is said to have assisted his father in the construction of the Ka'bah at Mecca.† In the OT, however, it is important to observe, Ishmael is hardly at all associated with what we term 'Arabia':‡ the 'Arabian' peninsula (including parts in the extreme South, as Ḥadramaut and Sheba) is peopled by the Joḳṭanidæ (descendants of Joḳṭan, son of Abraham's sixth ancestor, ''Eber,' and consequently much less closely connected with Israel), Gn 10[26-31]; the Ishmaelites are entirely distinct from these, and are limited to certain specified tribes, living almost entirely on the N. and N.W. of the Joḳṭanidæ.§ The circumcision of Ishmael at the age of 13 (Gn 17[25]) is in all probability intended as an explanation of the corresponding custom among the Ishmaelite tribes. Circumcision has for long been practised by the 'Arabs'; but it is commonly performed among them at a much later age than was customary with the Jews:‖ according to Eus. *Præp. Ev.* VI. xi. 49 it was performed in the 13th year by οἱ Ἰσμαηλῖται οἱ κατὰ τὴν Ἀραβίαν, and so according to Jos. *Ant.* I. xii. 2 by the Ἄραβες.

The personality of Ishmael must be estimated similarly to that of the other patriarchs (cf. vol. i. p. 15 f.; vol. ii. p. 533 ff.).¶ It is most reasonable to regard him as a historical character, but a character who at the same time was idealized, and whose biography, as told in the Book of Genesis, was coloured in some of its features by the characteristics, or historical relations, of the tribes who were considered to be his descendants. The racial affinity of these tribes to Israel is clearly indicated in the Biblical narratives; it is possible that the picture of Sarah's jealous opposition to Hagar and her son reflects to some extent old racial rivalries and conflicts, which ended in these tribes being obliged to separate from the ancestors of the Israelites, though they secured a successful independence elsewhere. The human passions and interests of Sarah and Abraham, of Hagar and Ishmael, the promptings, partly of natural affection, partly of religious feeling, under which they act, and the manner in which the hand of Providence guides and moulds the destinies of men, are all portrayed with the vividness and psychological truth which is generally characteristic of the Book of Genesis.

In Gal 4[21]-5[1] the narrative of Ishmael and Isaac is expounded allegorically. Hagar and Sarah represent the two covenants, the old and the new: Ishmael is the child after the flesh, born in bondage; Isaac is the child of promise, born in freedom: in the rivalries which arose between them, and ended in the triumph of the latter,

---

* The word for 'nations' in Gn 25[16] is also a peculiar one (אֻמּוֹת), more Arabic ('ummeh) or Aramaic (Ezr 4[10], and often in Dn; cf. in late Heb. Ps 117[1]) than Hebrew (Nu 25[15], also P, 'a head of the *peoples*, or *clans*, of a father's house [*i.e.* of a family] in Midian '), and no doubt adopted here as the technical term used properly of the Ishmaelite tribes.

† The recurrence of the numbers 6 and 12 in these tribal systems is an indication that they were to some extent formed artificially.

‡ In the case of Moab, we know, for instance, that its language differed only dialectically from Hebrew.

§ Burton (*El-Medinah and Mecca*, 1855, i. 213 f., cf. iii. 31 f.) remarks on the palpably Egyptian physiognomy of some of the Bedawi clans of Sinai, and quotes Gn 21[21]. Whether this was the case in ancient times, we do not know; but it is perhaps worth remembering that the Sinaitic peninsula was for long owned and garrisoned by the Egyptians, who worked in it mines of turquoise and copper (Maspero, *Dawn of Civil.* 349–358).

‖ Josephus (*Ant.* I. xii. 2) even calls him the κτίστης τοῦ ἔθνους τῶν Ἀράβων.

* And so, in the mediæval Jewish writers, לְשׁוֹן יִשְׁמָעֵאל and לְשׁוֹן קֵדָר both mean 'Arabic.'

† See T. P. Hughes, *Dict. of Islam, s.v.* Ishmael's tomb is shown at Mecca.

‡ In the OT 'Arab' is the name simply of a single comparatively small tribe (above, vol. i. p. 135).

§ The principal Bedawi tribes are spread also over the N. and N.W. of the Arabian Peninsula (see the *Encycl. Brit.*[9] ii. 246–9); but it should be added, to preclude misunderstanding, that we cannot identify any of them specifically with the tribes connected in the OT with Ishmael: all that can be predicated is a general resemblance in their character and mode of life to the description in Gn 16[12].

‖ Among the Bedawis of the Sinaitic Peninsula, for instance, at the age of 8 (Palmer, in the *Ordnance Survey of the Pen. of Sinai*, p. 59); among those of Arabia at the age of 5–6, but sometimes ten years later (Burton, *l.c.* iii. 81). Ibn Athir says that among the ancient Arabians the age was from 10 to 15 years (Pococke, *Spec. Hist. Arab.* 319).

¶ Kuenen (*ThT*, May 1871, p. 296 f.) and others regard Hagar and Ishmael as simply the eponymous ancestors of the tribes known as 'HAGARENES,' and 'sons of Ishmael' or 'Ishmaelites,' the narratives of Hagar's flight and expulsion being suggested by the meaning of the names (cf. Arab. *hajara*, to flee; *hejrah*, flight). Cf. p. 534, *notes.*

St. Paul sees foreshadowed the conflict in the history of the nascent Church, the defeat of the spirit which clung to carnal ordinances, and the triumph of the spirit of freedom, which had the faith and the insight to see that such ordinances must pass away. The practical conclusion follows: let the Galatian converts 'stand fast' in the freedom in which Christ had set them, and not 'be entangled again in a yoke' of Jewish ordinances.

S. R. DRIVER.

ISHMAEL.—**1.** See preceding article. **2.** One of the six sons of Azel, a descendant of Saul through Merib-baal (Mephibosheth), 1 Ch 8[38] 9[44]. **3.** The father or ancestor of the Zebadiah who was ruler (נָגִיד) of the house of Judah in the reign of Jehoshaphat, 2 Ch 19[11]. **4.** The son of Jehohanan, one of the 'captains of hundreds,' who assisted Jehoiada in restoring Jehoash to the throne of Judah, 2 Ch 23[1]. **5.** A priest of the family of Pashhur, who was forced by Ezra to put away his foreign wife, Ezr 10[22]. In 1 Es 9[22] **Ismael**.

6. Ishmael, the son of Nethaniah, the son of Elishama, a member of the royal house of David. See Jer 40–42, and the brief summary in 2 K 25[23-25]. After the fall of Jerusalem, Ishmael was a commander of one of the bodies of Jewish troops which maintained their independence in the country districts. Nebuchadnezzar had appointed **Gedaliah** (wh. see), the son of Ahikam the protector of Jeremiah (Jer 26[24]), as governor of the remnants of the Jewish state, with his residence at Mizpah; and one of his first cares was to attempt to restore confidence among the scattered inhabitants of the land, and to induce the remains of Zedekiah's army to submit to the Babylonian conquerors. At first Gedaliah's efforts met with a certain success. The captains of the Jewish forces, and Ishmael among the number, came to Mizpah, and made their submission to the new governor. Gedaliah, promising to use his influence with the Babylonians on their behalf, exhorted them to settle quietly in the cities they had occupied, and to gather in the harvest, which was then standing neglected in the fields (Jer 40[7-12]). But the restoration of peace and good order in the desolated country of Judah was not in accordance with the wishes of Baalis, the king of Ammon, who doubtless saw an opportunity of extending his territory at the expense of his neighbours on the west. He found a willing tool in Ishmael, whom he commissioned to assassinate Gedaliah. Ishmael may have been actuated by a fanatical hatred against a fellow-countryman who had consented to acknowledge the Chaldæan supremacy, or by jealousy of the preference given to Gedaliah over a member of the royal house. His designs, however, were not unknown; and Johanan the son of Kareah, and the other officers who had formerly acted with Ishmael but now supported Gedaliah, warned the latter of his danger. Gedaliah, unfortunately, would not listen to their warnings; and when Johanan, seeing how disastrous the death of Gedaliah would be for all the Jews, offered to kill Ishmael privately, the governor refused to consent to the proposal, and declared that the charges made against Ishmael were only calumnies (ib.[12-16]).

In the seventh month, that is, about three months after the fall of Jerus. and two months after the destruction of the city, Ishmael with ten confederates came to Gedaliah at Mizpah.* Here they were hospitably entertained; but during the meal rose up against their hosts, and murdered Gedaliah and all the Jewish and Chaldæan soldiers in his retinue. Ishmael must after this have gained possession of the town, for he succeeded in preventing any news of what had taken place from

being published abroad. Two days later a party of eighty pilgrims from Shechem, Shiloh, and Samaria passed by Mizpah, with offerings which they intended to present at the ruined temple in Jerusalem. On account of the destruction of the sanctuary they were attired as mourners, with beards shaven, and clothes rent, and gashes on their face and hands. With feigned grief * Ishmael went out to meet them, and invited them to visit Gedaliah at Mizpah. Once inside the city, they were put to death by Ishmael and his men. Ten of them, however, were able to ransom their lives by promising to deliver up the stores of wheat, barley, oil, and honey which they had hidden in the fields. The corpses of the seventy murdered men were thrown into a great pit or cistern, which had been made by Asa at the time of his war with Baasha (cf. 1 K 15[16-22]). The people of Mizpah, together with the royal princesses, who had been left by Nebuchadnezzar in charge of Gedaliah, Ishmael now treated as his prisoners, and attempted to carry them off to the country of the Ammonites (Jer 41[1-10]). But tidings of the events at Mizpah had reached Johanan ben-Kareah and his companions. They collected their troops and pursued after the fugitives, whom they overtook by the great pool of Gibeon, the scene of the fight between the men of Joab and of Abner (2 S 2[12-16]). The captives, among whom were the prophet Jeremiah and his scribe Baruch (cf. Jer 40[6] 42[1ff.] 43[3]), gladly went over to the pursuing forces; but Ishmael with eight of his men escaped to the Ammonites. The Jewish leaders, having failed to capture Ishmael, were now afraid of suffering the vengeance of the king of Babylon for the murder of his vassal Gedaliah. Accordingly they did not venture to return to Mizpah, but moved to the neighbourhood of Bethlehem, whence they subsequently fled to Egypt, in spite of the advice and warnings of Jeremiah (Jer 41[11]–43[13]). A reference in Jer 52[30] to 745 persons who were carried captive to Babylon in the twenty-third year of Nebuchadnezzar, i.e. four years after the fall of Jerus., is perhaps to be connected with fresh measures taken against the Jews in consequence of the outrage of Ishmael. The murder of Gedaliah was kept in memory by a fast instituted in the seventh month (Zec 7[5] 8[19]), which is celebrated on the 3rd day of Tisri (Sept.–Oct.)

H. A. WHITE.

ISHMAIAH (יִשְׁמַעְיָהוּ 'J" hears').—The 'ruler' of the tribe of Zebulun, 1 Ch 27[19].

ISHMERAI (יִשְׁמְרַי, perh. for יִשְׁמַרְיָה 'J" keeps').—A Benjamite chief, 1 Ch 8[18]. See GENEALOGY.

ISHPAH (יִשְׁפָּה). — The eponym of a Benjamite family, 1 Ch 8[16]. See GENEALOGY, VIII. 11.

ISHPAN (יִשְׁפָּן).—A Benjamite chief, 1 Ch 8[22].

ISHSECHEL, Ezr 8[18] RVm.—It is uncertain whether אִישׁ שֶׂכֶל is to be regarded as a proper name (cf. LXX ἀνὴρ σαχών A, ἀν. σαχώχ B), or should be tr⁴ 'a man of discretion,' so Luc. (ἀνὴρ συνετός) and RV; AV 'a man of understanding,' cf. 1 Es 8[47] ἄνδρα(s) ἐπιστήμονα(s). For the word שֶׂכֶל = discretion, intelligence, cf. 1 S 25[3], 1 Ch 22[12], Pr 13[15] 16[22], Ps 111[10] etc. The context leads us to expect the proper name of the representative of the sons of Mahli, and the order of the words is decidedly against the supposition that Sherebiah is meant, the conjunction having been inserted by mistake. With the name Ish-sechel we might compare Eshbaal, 1 Ch 8[33], Ishhod, ib. 7[18]. But such forms are rare,

* In 41[1] the words וְרַב הַטַּבָּחִים should be omitted; so LXX.

* In 41[6] LXX reads αὐτοὶ ἐπορεύοντο καὶ ἔκλαιον, 'they wept as they went,' which Cornill adopts; but the change does not seem to be necessary.

and it is probable that there is some corruption in the text; the proper name may have fallen out before the complimentary designation, or may have been wrongly corrected into the present form Ish-sechel. Cf. Ryssel and Ryle, *ad loc.*

H. A. WHITE.

ISHVAH (יִשְׁוָה 'resembling (his father)').— Second son of Asher, Gn 46[17] P, 1 Ch 7[30].

ISHVI (יִשְׁוִי 'resembling (his father)').—**1.** Third son of Asher, Gn 46[17], Nu 26[44] P, 1 Ch 7[30] : patron. **Ishvites**, Nu 26[44]. **2.** Second son of Saul by Abinoam, 1 S 14[49]. The orig. name may have been אִישׁ־יוֹ = אִישׁ־בַּעַל = אֶשְׁבַּעַל = אִישׁ־שָׁוֶה (Wellh. and Driver, *ad loc.*).

ISLAND, ISLE (אִי, אִיִּים, νῆσος, νησίον) is the tr. of a Heb. word which has a much wider significance. Its root-meaning is supposed to be *habitable land*, and in one passage (Is 42[15]) it means undoubtedly *dry land*, as opposed to water : 'I will make the rivers islands, and I will dry up the pools' (RV). Accordingly, some translators (Cheyne uniformly in Psalms, and in Deutero.-Isaiah frequently) render it *lands* or *countries*, with the maritime connotation entirely left out. In by far the greater number of passages, however, it signifies *coastland* —land either washed or surrounded by the sea, whether belonging to continents or islands. The idea of distance is usually contained in the word, either implicitly (Ps 97[1], Is 11[11] 42[12]) or expressly (Is 66[19], Jer 31[10]), although in Is 20[6] *this isle* plainly means *the coastland* of Canaan. The *isles that are in the sea* (Ezk 26[18]) are the *coastlands*, or *island-like countries on the seaboard*, which profited by the traffic of Tyre; and in one instance, judging by the ivory and ebony which they had to exchange, *many isles* (Ezk 27[15]) may be East Africa or India. Usually, however, they are the islands and maritime countries to the West. The *isles of the sea* on which Ahasuerus laid tribute (Est 10[1]) are the Islands and Coastlands of the Ægean, in contrast to the inland countries of Asia, as apparently also are *the isles* (Dn 11[18]) of which 'the king of the North' (11[15]), Antiochus the Great, should 'take many.' The *isles of the sea* are elsewhere the islands of the Mediterranean and the countries on the western seaboard, with which the people of Palestine traded in later times, as when Simon Maccabæus (1 Mac 14[5] RV) 'took Joppa for a haven, and made it an entrance for *the isles of the sea*.' The *isles of Elishah*—one of the sons of Javan (Gn 10[4])—which furnish blue and purple to the people of Tyre (Ezk 27[7]), may point to Elis and the Peloponnesus generally which produced those dyes. The *isles of the Gentiles* (Gn 10[5], Zeph 2[11]) are the distant coastlands of the Western Mediterranean. The *isles* are sometimes used in Ps, in Is, and in Jer to designate the West, sometimes the distant West, in contrast to the East. Tarshish and *the isles* (Ps 72[10]), and Sheba and Seba, represent respectively the western and eastern boundaries of Messiah's kingdom. The *isles and the inhabitants thereof* (Is 42[10]), and the *isles of Kittim* (Jer 2[10]) are joined with Kedar to signify all lands from west to east. There are references to individual islands both in OT and in NT. The *isles of Kittim* (Jer 2[10], Ezk 27[6]) are the coasts of Cyprus, but the name was used later for any Western maritime people, as far even as Italy (Dn 11[30], 1 Mac 1[8]); the *isle of Caphtor* (Jer 47[4] margin; comp. Am 9[7], Dt 2[23], Gn 10[14]) is held to be Crete, although some authorities identify it with the coastland of the Delta; 'the men of Dedan' (Ezk 27[15]) are in the LXX (B 'Ροδίων, A 'Αραδίων) called Rhodians (initial R being read instead of D), where the reference would be to the islanders of Rhodes, who were famous mariners; Tyre appears as an island (Is 23[2]), although *the inhabitants of the isle* may be

the dwellers on the neighbouring seacoast of Phœnicia. Cyprus (Ac 4[37] 13[4]), Crete (Ac 27, Tit 1), Cauda (Ac 27[16], AV Clauda), Melita (Ac 28[1]), Patmos (Rev 1[9]), are islands mentioned in the NT. One reference, *the island of the innocent* (Job 22[30]), which for long puzzled translators and commentators, has disappeared in RV, where the rendering is *him that is not innocent*, the mistranslation having arisen from confusing 'i, the particle *not* (found in Ichabod, Jezebel), with 'i, an island. The *wild beasts of the island* (Is 13[22] 24[14], Jer 1[39]) have also disappeared and been replaced by *wolves*, AV having mistaken the derivation of the word.

See, further, G. A. Smith's *HGHL*, pp. 135, 136, and the same author's *Isaiah*, vol. ii. pp. 109, 110.

T. NICOL.

ISMACHIAH (יִסְמַכְיָהוּ 'J" supports').—A Levite in the time of Hezekiah, 2 Ch 31[13].

ISMAEL ('Ισμάηλος), 1 Es 9[22]. — In Ezr 10[22] ISHMAEL.

ISMAERUS (A 'Ισμάηρος, B Μάηρος, AV Omaerus), —1 Es 9[34] = AMRAM (Μαρεί), Ezr 10[34].

ISRAEL, HISTORY OF.—

The object of this article is to give an outline of the political history of Israel, leaving the religious history (as far as possible) to be dealt with in the article on the Theology of the OT, to appear in a later volume of this Dictionary. A further object has been to call attention to the most important reconstructions of parts of the history, which have been offered by recent critics.

i. THE NAME.—(a) The people themselves called themselves in OT times יִשְׂרָאֵל *Yisrael* * (so also they are called by Mesha, *Moabite Stone*, lines 5, 7), or בְּנֵי יִשְׂרָאֵל *Bĕnē Yisrael*. The latter form describes the people as the descendants of an ancestor Israel (Jacob), Gn 43[6. 8. 11] (J) etc. See JACOB. In an inscription of Shalmaneser II. (c. 854 B.C.) the name *Sir'lai* occurs coupled with the mention of Ahab. For the form *Y-si-ri'l* read on the stele of Merenptah, see below, p. 509[a].

(b) Foreigners, and Israelites speaking of themselves to foreigners, used the term עִבְרִי *Ibhri*, Gn 39[14. 17] (J), Ex 1[16] 2[6] (E), 1 S 4[6. 9] 13[19] 14[11]. The name is found in Tacitus (*Hist.* v. 2, 'Hebræasque terras'; cf. Gn 40[15a] 'the land of the Hebrews') and in Jos. in referring to the language (*Ant.* I. i. 1, 2, Bekker) and to the people (*Ant.* VI. v. 3, VII. iv. 1, Bekker). No satisfactory explanation of *Ibhri* can be given. It may be connected with the *Eber* of Gn 10[21. 25]; it will then be the designation of several other peoples besides Israel. Again, it may be the adjective corresponding to the substantive עֵבֶר *'Ebher* 'other side,' 'beyond'; Is 7[20] 'beyond the river,' 9[1] [8[23] Heb.] 'beyond Jordan,' Jer 25[22] 'beyond the sea.' It would seem from these examples that *'Ibhri* (Hebrew) designated the Israelites as *not* autochthonous, but as *intruders* in Canaan from some land 'beyond'; cf. Gn 14[13] where Abram the Hebrew (the new

* The name *Israel* appears to mean 'God persists *or* perseveres' (see JACOB, p. 530[a]) rather than 'God strives' in the sense of *contends* ('es streitet Gott,' Nestle, *Eigennamen*, 60), or 'El's warrior' (Ges., Ewald, Kautzsch).

comer, τῷ περάτῃ, LXX) is distinguished from Mamre the Amorite (the old inhabitant). See HEBREW.

(c) 'Ιουδαῖος or 'Judæus' ('Jew') was the term used by classical writers, and in part by Jos. (e.g. Ant. VII. iv. 1, 'David ὁ τῶν 'Ιουδαίων βασιλεύς') in referring even to ancient times. This use is due, of course, to the great part played by the tribe of Judah and the city of Jerusalem in the post-exilic history of the people. See JEW.

ii. THE NATIONAL CHARACTERISTICS OF ISRAEL. —The character of the ancient Israelites as a nation may be gathered partly from their history, partly from a study of the facts of their history in the light of the characteristics of the modern Bedawin. The Israelites entered Canaan as nomads, and displayed, at least in the earlier period, most of the virtues and vices of tent-dwellers. They seem to have been content with the simple conditions of life under which the Bedawin live ; and to have been but little attracted by the civilization (as distinguished from the flesh-pots) of Egypt, or by the culture (as distinguished from the idolatry) of Canaan. Their ideal was that of the shepherd (Gn 46³²⁻³⁴ J), which does not in practice exclude such simple agriculture as the care of a few date palms (as among the modern Arabs), or the raising of a few scattered crops of cereals (as among the Zulus before 1878). The Israelites, as revealed in their earliest literature, appear as brave, adventurous, crafty, treacherous, and vengeful in war and enmity (the careers of Gideon, David, and Joab illustrate these characteristics) ; pure in point of sexual morality within the limits of the polygamy allowed to all Eastern peoples (cf. Gn 39⁹, 2 S 12¹⁻¹⁴ ; cf. also the laws Ex 20¹⁷, and note especially the wide scope of the language used, 21⁷⁻¹¹) ; strong in loyalty to the clan and correspondingly weak in national cohesion (see Judges and 1 and 2 Samuel, passim). The mercantile aptitude shown by Israel so much in modern times is alluded to even by Hosea (12⁷· ⁸⁼⁸· ⁹ Heb.) and Amos (8⁴· ⁵), with further allusion to cheating and fraud. Possibly Israel first learned successful trading from the Canaanites (cf. Hos 12⁷ RVm), but it is more probable that they had already practised it in their nomad period, for the nomads too were merchants, Gn 37²⁵ 'Ishmaelites' J, and ²⁸ 'Midianites' E, Ezk 27²¹.

In matters of thought the Israelites were not speculative, nor systematic. They realized, in a way the Greeks never realized, that some things were too high for them. God's government of the world (assumed as existing by all but perhaps the latest thinkers) offered the chief problems of their philosophy. 'Why do the wicked prosper?' was perhaps the chief question of the Hebrew 'philosophers.' Hebrew thought was occupied with the practical problems of religion.

And here it must be said that the Israelite (unlike the nomad) was profoundly religious. The modern Bedawy, as described, e.g., by Doughty (Arabia Deserta, passim), has little sense of the moral claims of religion, though the name of Allah is constantly on his lips. The Hebrews, on the contrary, endured (sometimes well, sometimes, indeed, ill) the yoke of a faith which made strict demands upon them for a morality higher than that of their neighbours (cf. Nowack, Heb. Archäologie, i. 101, 103).

iii. THE LAND OF ISRAEL.—Although Israel was to be 'a peculiar treasure,' סְגֻלָּה segullāh, Ex 19⁵ E, 'a special people' (עַם סְגֻלָּה 'am segullāh, RV 'a peculiar people') Dt 7⁶, the nation as a whole could not be isolated from other nations. Its home, Palestine, held an important place among the lands of the ancient Eastern world. The route

connecting Northern Syria and (through Northern Syria) the valleys of the Euphrates and Tigris with Egypt ran along the coast of Palestine ; and though this road passed for the most part through Philistine territory, its traffic must have had a great material and moral influence on Israel, whose borders lay so near it. East of Jordan ran the great road which connected Damascus with the head of the gulf of Akabah, and with the West Coast of Arabia. This road, again (if it corresponded at all with the modern Derb el-Ḥajj, i.e. the Pilgrim Road to Mecca), lay for the most part outside Israelite territory, but its nearness to Gilead for some 60 miles of its length must have exercised an important influence on the two and a half tribes east of Jordan. Towards the North the fertile plain of Esdraelon, now crossed by a railway, was traversed by a road which connected Damascus with the cities of the coast, ultimately with Tyre itself and with the Western lands beyond the Mediterranean.

With a land thus placed, Israel could not remain untouched by the movements of the great powers of Western Asia. If the Aramæans of Damascus wished to develop their trade on the Tyrian coast, or to find a new outlet for merchandise on the Red Sea, they were bound to make treaties— or war—with Israel. If the Empire of the Euphrates Valley (Assyrian, Babylonian, Persian in succession) wished to crown its conquests with the possession of the Nile, the passage of its armies must mean for Israel terror and spoiling, even if a formal submission and a seasonable payment of tribute should avert for a time worse mischief. Lastly, when Egypt desired to keep war off her own frontiers, it was Palestine which had to supply a confederacy of 'buffer states' to bear the reproach of Pharaoh's faithlessness and the main burden of his defeat.

On the other hand, two facts must be borne in mind which qualify the foregoing account of Israel's position among the nations. (1) Israel was cut off from the sea. It was Phœnicia which represented Palestine to the West. The name of Baal, not that of Jehovah, crossed the Mediterranean in early times. The civilization and religious thought which influenced the coast-lands of the West came from the Zidonians (cf. G. A. Smith, HGHL pp. 26–28). (2) Though Israel as a whole was brought into close contact with the powers of Western Asia, yet the position of the Southern kingdom was comparatively isolated. It was the Northern kingdom which sustained the perpetual conflict with the Aramæans, which maintained a close intercourse with Tyre, which finally felt first the weight of the arm of Assyria, and fell first before its armies. Judah was comparatively sheltered from the world until Samaria fell before Sargon (B.C. 722).

Indeed, the territory which fell at the disruption to the Southern kingdom was fitted not only by its geographical position, but also by its physical features, to be a nursery of free men. The Land east of Jordan, the Plain of Esdraelon, and the Maritime Plain, were open to the march of conquering armies, but the Hills of Benjamin and the Hill Country of Judah together formed a Montenegro which a resolute peasantry might defend against the forces of an empire. The ruggedness of the approaches to this district can hardly be exaggerated ; the sight of its ravines recalls at once the exploits of Jonathan (1 S 14⁴), David (23¹⁴), and Judas Maccabæus (1 Mac 3²⁴ 4²⁹⁻³⁴), and lends probability to the accounts of the victories of Asa (2 Ch 14⁹ff·) and of Jehoshaphat (20²²ff·). One circumstance only made against the isolation of Judah, viz. the mixed origin of the tribe of Judah itself, which seems to have contained a large

Edomite element, the Calebites. (See CALEB, vol. i. p. 340).

The bearing of the physical configuration of Palestine as a whole on the history of Israel has been pointed out with great force by G. A. Smith (*HGHL*, ch. ii.). 'Palestine,' he writes, 'is almost as much divided into petty provinces as Greece, and far more than those of Greece are her divisions intensified by those of soil and climate.' She has been, and always will be, a land where fragments of many races live side by side. Israel at the conquest found 'seven nations' (Dt 7[1] ['four,' Jg 3[3]]) occupying Canaan, and was content (after some slaughter) to settle down among them (Jg 3[3. 5]). These nations represented racial and not merely political divisions; see the illustrations in Sayce, *Races of the OT*, or in Nowack, *Archäologie*, i. pp. 122, 126, 365. The influence of foreigners in Israel is apparent at several periods; above all, the incorporation of a mass of the old inhabitants into Israel during the time of the Judges (see JUDGES, PERIOD OF THE) had far-reaching results. The nation always had the foreigner in its midst. We hear of a 'mixed multitude' (עֵרֶב רַב 'ērebh rabh,— read perhaps עֲרַבְרֹב 'ărabhrōbh, 'a mixed people' without reference to numbers,—Ex 12[38] E; אֲסַפְסֻף 'ăṣaphṣuph, Nu 11[4] J or E) in the wilderness with Israel, of foreign wives (Jg 3[6], 1 K 11[1], Ezr 9[1. 2], Ru 1[4]), guards (2 S 15[18], 2 K 11[4] RV; see GUARD), officers and mighty men (1 S 21[7], 2 S 23[36ff.], Is 22[15f.]), task-workers (1 K 9[20f.]), artificers (1 K 7[13f.]), Rechabites (Jer 35[2ff.]), and Gibeonites (2 S 21[1ff.], cf. Jos 9[3ff.]). The presence of the stranger (*gēr*) was recognized by law (Ex 20[10] 23[9]), and his conversion to Israel's faith was contemplated (1 K 8[41ff.], Is 56[3ff.]). In fact, in a land like Canaan, broken up into small districts, each of which was the home of a tribe, Israel could not be kept from intermixture with foreigners. See, further, FOREIGNER, GER.

In judging of the climate and fertility of the land, the true meaning of the phrase 'a land flowing with milk and honey' (Nu 13[27] JE) must be remembered. It is the nomad's praise of a pastoral country, and if we add to this description the additional advantages mentioned in Dt 6[11] ('vineyards and olive trees'), we shall arrive at a just appreciation of the nature of that part of Palestine which was permanently held by Israel. It was not (with one important exception) agricultural territory. Its rocky slopes were suited for vines and olives, its hills and uplands for pasture, but only the plain of Esdraelon deserves the description of 'a land of wheat and barley' (Dt 8[8]). The Maritime Plain testifies even now, under the hands of the German colonists, to its former fertility, but the plain was in the hands of the Philistines. Under these circumstances the Israelites never had a stock of corn, and famine is a frequent feature in their history (2 S 21[1], 1 K 17[1ff.], 2 K 4[38ff.] 8[1], Hag 1[6ff.], Neh 5[3]). We must remember, therefore, another description of Palestine as 'a land that eateth up the inhabitants thereof,' Nu 13[32] P (so *LOT*[6] p. 62, in spite of a misprint). The phrase (cf. Ezk 7[15]) describes a land subject not only to famine, but also to pestilence. The latter also played a part in the history of Israel (1 S 5[6] 6[19], 2 S 24[15], 2 K 19[35] 20[7]). The epigram quoted by Abu'l-Fida on Syria as a whole applies to Palestine, at least in part—

> 'Its atmosphere is—pestilence,
> Its dwellings are—straitness,
> Its soil is—stone,
> Its epidemics are—everlastingness.'

iv. SOURCES OF THE HISTORY.—(*a*) For the earliest period :—the narratives of J and E in the Hexateuch. (Unsupported statements in P are generally doubtful).

(*b*) For the period of the Judges :—Jg 2[6]-18[29],

apart from the editorial framework in which it is set.

(*c*) The undivided kingdom :—1 S 9–2 S 20[26]. A large part of 2 S consists of a court history of David of great historical value. 2 S 21[1]-24[25] is an appendix of less value. 1 K 1[1]-11[43] (apart from additions by the Deuteronomic editor).

(*d*) The divided kingdom, (*a*) 1 K 13–2 K 17 (mainly concerned with the Northern kingdom); the parallel passages of Chronicles add little to our information, but much illustrative matter can be obtained from Amos and Hosea. (β) 2 Ch 11–28 (mainly concerned with the Southern kingdom, and mostly treated as a romance by modern critics). (γ) 2 K 18–25 (the fall of Judah); this part of the history receives much illustration from Isaiah (first half), Micah, Jeremiah, and Ezekiel. Monuments (Moabite, Egyptian, and especially Assyrian and Babylonian) give some additional light, but the statements of classical writers, *e.g.* Herodotus, are confused for the most part and untrustworthy.

(*e*) The Persian Period. Ezra and Nehemiah are valuable in that they contain the memoirs of those two great men, but the books as a whole are ill compiled and incomplete, and it is difficult to extract a coherent story from them. Haggai and Zechariah (1–8) furnish valuable information.

(*f*) The Greek Period. Josephus (*Ant.* XI. viii.-XIII. vii.) gives some information, but his romantic stories are doubtful. For the age of the Maccabees we have a generally trustworthy guide in 1 Mac, and some hints may be gathered from 2 Mac. The Book of Daniel (written *c.* 167 B.C. ?) is generally appealed to in illustration of this age.

v. THE HISTORY.

1. *The Origins of Israel.*—The relationships of the Israelite people according to the earliest source preserved in Genesis are shown in the following table :—

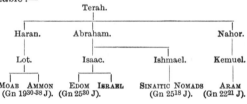

Terah.			
Haran.	Abraham.		Nahor.
Lot.	Isaac.	Ishmael.	Kemuel.
MOAB AMMON (Gn 19[30-38] J).	EDOM ISRAEL (Gn 25[30] J).	SINAITIC NOMADS (Gn 25[18] J).	ARAM (Gn 22[21] J).

That Moab, Ammon, Edom, and Israel formed together a group of tribes of kindred origin, is generally acknowledged and need not be doubted. It has, however, been questioned whether Israel was really related to Aram (the Aramæans or 'Syrians'), and Wellhausen has suggested that Israel's claim to such relationship was founded not on fact, but on an ambitious desire to be reckoned to belong to 'the mighty Aramæans' (*IJG*[3] p. 8). Yet against this we may set the fact asserted by Kittel (*Geschichte*, i. 155), that it is an unchanging trait of Israelite tradition that the origins of the Hebrew people lay beyond the Euphrates, *i.e.* in Aram-naharaim, 'Aram of the two rivers,' the country between the Euphrates and the Ḥabor. To the passages in Genesis we may add two interesting references outside it. In Dt 26[5] (D) the Israelite is told to call his ancestor 'a wandering (or 'lost') Aramæan' (cf. RVm), and in Hos 12[12] (12[13] Heb.)—an interpolation acc. to Nowack (*in loco*), but even so, probably independent of the present form of Genesis — we have mention of Jacob's flight into 'the field of Aram' (RV), an event which surely implies some previous connexion with the people of Aram.

On the other hand, the nearness of kinship between Israel and the population of the Sinai peninsula is pronounced by Wellhausen 'very probable,' and he points out that 'the real home of the Patriarchs lay between Edom and Egypt,[*] where the South of Palestine merges itself in the Desert' (*Geschichte*, p. 9). On the whole, however, it seems best to accept both relationships of Israel, for the two are equally well attested in the earliest records. Israel was no more homogeneous than any other tribe which migrates and conquers. Abraham's grand-nephew Laban was of Ḥaran (Gn 27[43] 29[4], both J), and Isaac's wife came from Aram-naharaim (so RVm Gn 24[10] J), whence Abraham himself also derived his origin (v.[4] J). (See art. ABRAHAM, vol. i. p. 15[a]). On the other hand, the genealogical table given above shows a relationship between Israel and the nomads of Sinai, and the Calebite origin of a large part of the tribe of Judah has already been alluded to. The general presentation in the earliest sources of the history of the patriarchs, viz. that Israel was a tribe from the north drawn southward, falling under the spell of Egyptian influence, and leaving behind it in the Sinaitic peninsula nomads akin to it in blood, has the strongest claims to be received as true. The historical character of the lives of the patriarchs themselves is discussed elsewhere; see especially ABRAHAM, vol. i. p. 15, and JACOB, below, p. 533 ff.

2. *Israel under the Egyptians.* — It has been denied that Israel was ever 'in Egypt'; it is therefore necessary to ascertain exactly what is asserted in the biblical accounts. The people dwelt in Goshen apart from the Egyptians (Gn 46[28]-47[4] J), as indeed the narrative of the plagues presupposes (cf. Ex 8[22] 9[26], both J). Such passages as Ex 3[22] 11[2f.] (both E) do not essentially disagree with this representation: Goshen (*if* Pithom and Rameses, Ex 1[11] J, were in Goshen, and *if* the first of these cities has been correctly identified by Naville and ancient remains near the Sweet Water Canal) bordered on Egypt proper, so that the Israelites would have Egyptian 'neighbours' north and west of them. Now the fact that we find no certain mention of the Hebrews (Israelites) on the Egyptian monuments (at present known) belonging (presumably) to the period of the Oppression and of the Exodus, does not discredit this story of Israel's sojourn and servitude in Goshen. Israel was not the only people which was impressed to work on Pharaoh's buildings; the story of Israel might very well be lost to the Egyptians amid a dozen similar memories. As a matter of fact, however, one name does meet us in the Egyptian records which recalls the name of the Chosen People. Certain foreigners called '*prw* (? '*Aperu*) were employed on task-work under Ramses II., and as late as the time of Ramses IV. This name has been compared with '*Ibhri* ('Hebrew'). The fact that the Exodus is always supposed to have taken place before the reign of the latter monarch is of small account. The name may have been passed on from the sons of Israel to their successors in the task-work. (See, however, art. EGYPT, vol. i. p. 665). If the *Ḥabiri*, so often mentioned on the Tel el-Amarna tablets as the foes of Egypt in Syria, be the Hebrews, then the Exodus must have taken place as early as the time of the Eighteenth Dynasty, and the same conclusion must be drawn if the *Y-si-r-'l* of the recently discovered stele of Merenptah (Meneptah) be Israel, for *Y-si-r-'l* appears as a Syrian people upon whom the chastisement of Pharaoh has fallen (cf. G. Steindorff, *ZATW* xvi. 330 ff.). Of the true date of the Exodus we still know nothing for certain (see CHRONOLOGY OF OLD TEST., vol. i. pp. 398, 399; and articles by Sayce, Hommel, etc., in *Expos. Times*, vols. viii. and ix.).

3. *The Exodus and the Wilderness.*—The Exodus was the natural revolt of a pastoral people against compulsory brick-making and building, against a

system which involved a reckless expenditure of the lives of the workmen; cf. Erman, *Anc. Egypt*, p. 475 ff. In the earlier sources (JE) the Israelite leader is Moses, in the later (P) his leadership is somewhat obscured by the fact that Aaron is constantly co-ordinated with him. The plagues, *eight* in number in JE (the lice כִּנִּם *kinnim* or כִּנָּם *kinnām*, Ex 8[16] [8[12] Heb.], and the boils שְׁחִין *shĕḥīn*, 9[9], being due to P), are the means of forcing Pharaoh's consent. It is noteworthy that Foreign War is not reckoned among the plagues. The theory, therefore, that the Libyan invasion in the reign of Merenptaḥ facilitated the Exodus, receives no support from the biblical accounts.

With the passage of the 'Red Sea' (see EXODUS AND JOURNEY TO CANAAN, vol. i. p. 802) we arrive at contemporary history. In Ex 15[1b-3] (Moses' Song) 'we seem,' acc. to Dillm. and Driver (*LOT*[6] 30), 'to hear Moses himself speaking'; and the latter, while pointing out certain redactional additions, writes, 'Probably the greater part of the song is Mosaic.' The Passage of the Sea must retain its place among the best attested facts of history; no argument drawn from the silence of later documents can weigh against this contemporary attestation. Moreover, as Kittel well points out (*Geschichte*, i. 206), this event lends support on the one side to the story of a sojourn in Egypt, on the other to the story of Wilderness wandering.

Early accounts (Nu 14[33] JE, cf. Am 5[25]) reckon the period of the Wandering at forty years. Of the events which marked it very little is known. One thing, however, is clear. Israel was not ready at the Exodus for the immediate conquest of Canaan (Ex 13[17] E, Nu 14[3. 40ff.] JE, Dt 1[27]).

The Mosaic Religion.—During these forty years some organization based on religion, and mainly of a religious character, was given to Israel (Ex 18[25f.]· 19[3]-24[14] E and J). A 'covenant' was made between J″ and the people, and the foundation stone of Israel's nationality was thereby laid (Ex 34[10-27] E or J). Israel professed *Islām* (resignation to God) and prepared for a *Jihād* (a war of conquest undertaken in the name of God). Moses was a pre-Christian Mohammed with a more fruitful revelation in his hand.

So far all is clear, what, however, were the exact contents of the revelation given by Moses? The two passages of Exodus referred to above (19[3]-24[14] and 34[10-27]) contain very ancient (probably Mosaic) material, but the relation between the two passages is uncertain (cf. Driver, *LOT*[6] pp. 39, 40), and the limits of what is ancient are subject to much dispute. Critics are not even agreed as to the identity of the Ten 'Commandments' (דְּבָרִים *dĕbhārīm*, 'words') which seem to be the foundation of the written Law, and Wellhausen has discovered in Ex 34 'Ten Words' of mainly ceremonial contents to dispute the title of 'The Ten Words' with Ex 20[2-17].

Two 'Words,' however, are found in both the rival Decalogues: (1) Jehovah alone is Israel's God; (2) molten images may not be made. It seems most reasonable to say that the principles of the Mosaic religion were Monotheism (a personal relation of one God to Israel), and a Repudiation of image-worship as likely to entangle the people in polytheism like that of Egypt. (See, further, Kittel, *Geschichte*, i. 246 ff.).

4. *The Conquest of Canaan.*—That Israel obtained a firm footing east of Jordan before entering Western Palestine is generally acknowledged. The war against Sihon, however (Nu 21[21-30] JE, according to some E, cf. Dt 2[26ff.]), has been questioned, and the ancient song (Nu 21[27-30]) has been referred to a war of *Israel* against Moab in the 9th cent. It is more natural, however, to find in the song early testimony to a victorious war of the Amorite against the Moabite, followed by a war of retribution waged by Israel, Moab's kinsman, against the victor. Such a war as the latter could have taken place only in very early times such as those of Moses. (See G. A. Smith, *HGHL*, Appendix III.). The war against Og, the king of Bashan (Nu 21[33ff.], Dt 3[1-4]), is not equally well attested. See also JAIR, HAVVOTH-JAIR.

Of the conquest of Western Palestine we possess two early accounts. The first of these is contained in Jos 2[1]–11[9]; it is the narrative of JE (J and E cannot be accurately separated) broken and expanded by additions from a Deuteronomic Redactor (D[2]) and from P. This narrative of JE contains all the well-known features, such as the reception of the spies by Rahab, the drying up of the waters of Jordan, the capture of Jericho, the trespass of Achan, the two attacks on Ai, the treaty with the Gibeonites, and the battles of Beth-horon and of the waters of Merom. Joshua appears as the successor of Moses and as the leader of the whole people. The conquest is represented as the work of united Israel, and its course, save for the repulse at Ai, is uniformly successful. On the other hand, generalizing passages, *e.g.* 10[28-43] ('all these kings and their land did Joshua take at one time,' v.[42]) and 11[10-23] ('So Joshua took the whole land. . . . And the land rested from war,' v.[23]) are assigned to D[2].

The second early account of the conquest of Western Palestine is found in scattered notices in the later chapters of Joshua and in ch. 1 of Judges. These notices show a similarity of style, and it is possible to make a tentative reconstruction of the narrative from which they have been taken (see Driver, *LOT*[6] pp. 162, 163). This reconstructed document gives us three glimpses of the conquest, according to which the tribes fight in groups, and not as a united Israel under one leader (Joshua). (1) We first see Judah and Simeon together with nomad tribes of the Sinaitic peninsula, such as the Kenites (Jg 1[16]), Calebites (Jos 15[13]), and Kenizzites (Jos 15[17]), conquering the hill-country of Judah, the 'south' of Arad (Jg 1[16] MT, 'Descent of Arad' LXX; cf. G. A. Smith, *HGHL* pp. 277, 278), Hebron, and Debir (Kiriath-sepher). (2) We next see the house of Joseph establishing itself on the central ridge at Bethel (Jg 1[22]), but failing to drive out the inhabitants of Gezer (v.[29]), and complaining to Joshua that progress northward was stayed by the chariots of iron which the Canaanites had in the Valley of Jezreel (Jos 17[14ff.]). Joshua advises them to make room for themselves by clearing the jungle on the central ridge. (3) The third glimpse which the reconstructed document gives is of the limitations set to the conquests of the three northern tribes, Zebulun, Asher, and Naphtali, and of the tribe of Dan, by the stiff resistance of the Canaanite and Amorite (Jg 1[30-34]). Dan seeks by conquest a new home in the north at Leshem = Laish (Jos 19[47]; cf. Jg 18[27ff.]).

In comparing these two accounts we must remember that the second is put together from fragments, and is quite incomplete. It is defective as regards Joseph and all the northern tribes, nor does it make clear to us the position of Joshua (Jos 17[14ff.]); does it treat him (as some think) as simply the leader of the House of Joseph? There is little in it, however, which clearly contradicts the account of JE in Jos 2[1]–11[9], and by piecing together the two accounts we can construct a narrative of the conquest of Western Palestine which has strong claims to be accepted.

Israel, bereaved of Moses (as Islam of Mohammed) at the beginning of a career of conquest, accepted Joshua as Moses' Khalifa (successor), and persevered on the path of conquest (JE). The Jordan was crossed (JE). Jericho, 'the city of

palm trees,' was won (JE and F *). Gibeon in a panic made terms with Israel (JE). Israel, united under Joshua, won a great victory over a southern confederacy at Beth-horon (JE). Elated by these repeated successes, Judah (perhaps a small tribe at this time) broke loose from the main body, and turned southward to join the Calebites in a division of the southern end of the central ridge (cf. F). Joshua, at the head of the strong tribe of Joseph, and followed by the tribes which afterwards settled in the north, burst in the full tide of victory across the plain of Esdraelon and defeated a northern confederacy at the Waters of Merom (JE). The Canaanites, however, after bending before the storm, recovered courage, and by their chariots and fortified cities retained control of the plain of Esdraelon and compelled the Israelites to keep to the hills (F; cf. Jg 4. 5). (On the historical probabilities considered in the light of geography, see *HGHL*, Appendix II.).

5. *The Transformation of Israel.* — This took place under the Judges (see JUDGES, PERIOD OF THE). It is clear from the earliest records of the conquest that the Canaanites were not exterminated, as the later record (D[2]) seems sometimes to assert (Jos 10[40] 11[14]). The conquerors settled down in the midst of the half-conquered majority, and the question arose which stock, which civilization, which religion, Canaanite or Israelite, would survive? The result was a compromise: a mixed stock arose, over which it was possible to set up one kingdom, the kingdom of Saul and David. The Canaanite-Israelite was not a nomad, but an agriculturalist, a city-dweller, a merchant, with a wide outlook on the world, such as became the member of an empire which touched the highway of the world of Western Asia, the Euphrates. In religion also the Canaanite-Israelite was a new production. He held his monotheism somewhat loosely, and was ready to worship at Canaanite shrines. Lastly, the new nation was much more numerous than the old invading tribes. David's armies, composed of these Canaanite-Israelites, were not inconsiderable; they enabled him to found an empire. The fusion of races which made a nation capable of winning victories like those of David took place in the period of the Judges.

6. *The Undivided Kingdom.* — We have an express statement (Gn 36[31], apparently from an early document) that Edom was governed by kings before any king reigned over Israel. It is probable that the same is true of Ammon (cf. 1 S 11[1-3]; Jg 11[12-28], however, seems to be late) and of Amalek (1 S 15[8ff.], though the passage is not early). The first movement towards the establishment of a kingdom over Israel came from the half-Canaanite Abimelech (Jg 9[1ff.]), and affected only the central tribes. In fact it was only hard experience which made the Israelites (still children of the desert in nature) willing to submit to the restraint of an organized kingdom. No doubt the Canaanite leaven in the population hastened this submission.

Of the occasion of the establishment of the kingdom we have two accounts in 1 Samuel (Driver, *LOT*[6] p. 175 ff.). According to the earlier account (1 S 9[1]–10[16] 11[1-11. 15]), J″ chooses a king (Saul) who is to save His people from the Philistines, and commands Samuel to anoint him (9[16f.]). The language used reminds us of Ex 3[7] (God charges Moses to lead Israel out of Egypt). Samuel promises Saul 'all that is desirable' in Israel (9[20] RV), and encourages him to act as king, as occasion offers, in the assurance of divine support (10[7]). The occasion for action comes in the invasion of Nahash the Ammonite, and on Saul's success the people make him king with rejoicings. According to the later account (1 S 8. 10[17-27] 12[])

* F = Fragmentary reconstructed accounts.

the Israelites, disgusted with the corrupt administration of justice by Samuel's sons, ask Samuel to make them 'a king to judge [them] like all the nations' (8⁵). Samuel (as divinely instructed) treats this demand as a rejection of J" as king, and, while granting the request, tells the people that they will have reason to repent of it, for their king will take from them all that is desirable in his eyes (8¹¹⁻¹⁷). Samuel describes Saul to the people after his election (12¹³) as 'the king whom ye have chosen,' and tells them (v.¹⁷) that their wickedness was great in asking for a king. (There may be a trace of a third account in 12¹², where, somewhat inconsistently with 8¹⁻⁵, the invasion of the Ammonites is given as the immediate occasion of the demand for a king.

The first and earliest account accords best with the known facts. Saul established his throne in the midst of a great Philistine Oppression (1 S 13⁶· ¹⁹), when the Phil. had a garrison (? צִיב) in the heart of Benjamite territory (ib. 14¹ff·), and some of the 'Hebrews' were serving by constraint in the Philistine ranks (ib. v.²¹). Saul's reign (the duration of which is quite uncertain) was an almost continuous struggle against his western neighbours (1 S 13³ 14⁵² 17¹ 18²⁵ 23¹· ²⁷ 28¹ 31¹) ; he taught Israel to face the Philistines.

The Rise of David.—Saul was the fighting chief of an infant nation, David the founder and organizer of a powerful state. Saul was the Lascaris,* but David the Vataces of Israel. The government gained vastly in intellectual power by the accession of David. Saul perhaps could not write (1 S 11⁷) ; David wrote the first letter mentioned in the Bible (2 S 11¹⁴ !), was 'prudent in speech' (1 S 16¹⁸ RV), a poet of considerable power (2 S 1¹⁷ff·), if not also a Psalmist (2 S 22¹ff·, a passage belonging to the Appendix to 2 Samuel), and a man who reflected (23¹⁻⁷). The whole history of the suppression of Absalom's rebellion stamps David as a man of the highest mental power. The king who could command and apply in the moment of his greatest need the wrathful family faithfulness of Joab and Abishai, the salt-truth of Ittai the Philistine, the friendliness of the priests Zadok and Abiathar, the allegiance of the aged counsellor Hushai, and the helpfulness of Shobi the Ammonite and Barzillai the Gileadite (2 S 17²ᵗf·), must have been a man of intellectual power far above the ordinary.

David's reign was marked by three events—(a) the choice of Jerusalem as capital ; (b) the rise of the tribe of Judah ; and (c) the foundation of an Israelite empire.

(a) Jerusalem before David's day probably consisted of a half-Israelite town grouped round the Jebusite citadel, which stood on a hill S.E. of the present Ḥaram hill, but probably separated from it by a depression now filled up. Such a town was unsuitable for the Israelite capital so long as it was dominated by the Jebusite fort. David's capture of this fort gave him a site from which he could build towards the North and West, taking in other hills ; he thus formed a capital of ample size and of great natural strength.

(b) The rise of the tribe of Judah under David is a remarkable fact. In Judges this tribe plays hardly any part save at the Conquest (ch. 1), in which it is almost overshadowed by Calebites, Kenizzites, and Kenites. It is not mentioned in the present text of the Song of Deborah (Jg 5). The earlier leaders of Israel, Moses, Aaron, Joshua, Samuel, and Saul, all belonged to other tribes, and no judge was a Judæan. Under these circumstances

* Cf. Gibbon, Decline and Fall, ch. lxii. beginning : 'In his first efforts the fugitive Lascaris commanded only 3 cities and 2000 soldiers ; his reign was the season of generous and active despair : in every military operation he staked his life and crown ; and his enemies . . . were surprised by his celerity and subdued by his boldness.'

it has been supposed (Stade, GVI i. 132) that Judah entered Canaan from the south before the rest of the tribes entered from the east, and that in ancient times Judah stood in no union with the rest of Israel. Be this as it may, from the time of David Judah played a great part in Israel's history.

(c) It may be surprising that so small a people as Israel was able to found an empire which stretched from the borders of Egypt to the Euphrates. In the south Egypt claimed a hegemony over Syria ; in the north the Hittites (1 K 10²⁹, 2 K 7⁶) and the Aramæans (Syrians) were strong, and, lastly, in the east lay the great Assyrian power. But after the reign of Tiglathpileser I. (c. 1120–1100 B.C.) Assyria was in a state of temporary decline until about the end of the 10th cent. B.C. (McCurdy, HPM i. § 181) ; and the Hittites had ceased to exercise an imperial sway (ib. § 179) ; lastly, from c. 1240 to 930 B.C., under the 20th and 21st dynasties, Egypt was weak and divided (see art. EGYPT, vol. i. 662 b). Thus room is left for an Israelite empire, c. 1017–937 B.C., the period assigned to the reigns of David and Solomon (see CHRONOLOGY OF OLD TEST. vol. i. p. 401).

The empire of David and Solomon was greater in appearance than in reality, and it was, moreover, unstable. Garrisons (or 'governors' נְצִיבִים) were placed in Damascus and in Edom (2 S 8⁶· ¹⁴), but other provinces simply paid a tribute (cf. ib. v.¹¹f·), the amount of which depended, no doubt, on the strength of their fears.

The reign of Solomon was magnificent and oppressive, the very opposite, in fact, of the ideal given in Dt 17¹⁵⁻¹⁷. He put 30,000 Israelites to task-work (1 K 5¹³f· ; 1 K 9²² is a later gloss), and alienated the northern tribes (12⁴), already dissatisfied with the House of Jesse (2 S 20¹f·) ; he filled his harem with foreign wives for the sake of prestige and policy, and patronized foreign worship (1 K 11⁵· ⁷) in order to conciliate allied or subject nations. Of twenty years given to building, he devoted seven to the erection of a temple, on which he employed foreign builders (1 K 5¹⁸), and in which he admitted foreign devices, such as the Second Commandment condemns (1 K 6²³). Whether Solomon had any strong religious feeling (such as his father had) we cannot tell ; the Prayer of Dedication in 1 K 8²³⁻⁶¹ is the work of the compiler of Kings (so Driver, LOT⁶ p. 191). On the whole, he reminds us of the typical Pharaoh, who built, oppressed, and boasted of Divine favour. The importance of the Temple must not be exaggerated ; David had already made Jerusalem a Holy City by transferring thither the ark (2 S 6¹²).

7. *The Hundred Years' War with Aram.*—The disruption of Solomon's kingdom relegated the southern half ('Judah') to a comparatively safe obscurity, and imposed upon the northern half ('Israel') the task of preventing the Aramæans (Syrians) of Damascus from advancing to the shores of the Mediterranean. From a nation like the Aramæans, eager for mercantile and material advantages, Israel invited attack in *three* directions. (1) The short route to Tyre by Dan and Abel-beth-maacah was worth seizing (1 K 15²⁰). (2) The fertile plain of Esdraelon was valuable in itself, and also because it led to the sea ; hence the fortress of Aphek in the Philistine plain became a point for Aramæan armies to march on (1 K 20²⁶, 2 K 13²², LXX, Lucian's text ; W. R. Smith, OTJC² p. 435 ; Expositor, Dec. 1895. See also APHEK). (3) Ramoth-gilead (precise site uncertain) was surrounded by good pasture-land, and commanded one of the trade routes which ran east of Jordan leading to Arabia (1 K 22³).

The kings of the house of Omri (1 K 16¹⁶–2 K 9²⁶) met the Aramæan danger with courage and skill. Alliances with Tyre (1 K 16³¹) and with

Judah (1 K 22²⁻⁴, 2 K 3⁷) secured the left flank and rear of Israel, a new capital well situated for defence was built and fortified on the hill of Samaria (1 K 16²⁴), Ahab routed Ben-hadad at Aphek (1 K 20²⁶), and Joram, it seems, recovered Ramoth-gilead from Hazael (2 K 8²⁸, cf. 9¹).

The fortune of war changed at first under the new dynasty, that of Jehu and his sons. The Aramæans under Hazael and his successor Ben-hadad began to prevail perhaps in the days of Jehu himself; they almost annihilated the armies of his successor Jehoahaz, and became masters of all the land east of Jordan (2 K 10³²ᶠ· 13³⁻⁷). On one occasion Hazael traversed the northern kingdom, reached Philistine territory, captured Gath, and threatened Jerusalem (12¹⁷). The affliction of Israel in those days was 'very bitter, for there was not . . . any helper for Israel' (14²⁶). A change came again under Joash, the third king of Jehu's line. He thrice defeated Ben-hadad, and recovered the cities taken by Hazael, presumably the cities east of Jordan (13²⁵, cf. vv.¹⁴⁻¹⁹). He even found leisure for a civil war with Amaziah of Judah, which ended in the capture of Jerusalem (14⁸⁻¹⁴). But if Joash was the deliverer, Jeroboam II., the son of Joash, was the avenger of Israel. Under him Israel recovered according to 2 K 14²⁸ 'Damascus and Hamath,' according to v.²⁵ 'from the entering in of Hamath unto the sea of the Arabah.'

The religious policy of Ahab (the true representative of the house of Omri in this) was to patronize the Baal-worship of his Tyrian allies and of his half-Canaanite subjects without actually rejecting the religion of J″ (1 K 18²¹). If he allowed Jezebel to slay the prophets of the Lord (18¹³), it was doubtless because these prophets were bold enough to protest against such toleration, and not merely because they were prophets of J″. The work of the great prophet Elijah and of the house of Jehu which embraced his cause (19¹⁷), was to inflict such blows on the worshippers of Baal that they never again hoped for any support for their religion from the heads of the Israelite state.

The Religion of the Prophets.—The reign of Jeroboam II. marked the highest point of material prosperity which Israel reached after the disruption, and perhaps the lowest point of Israel's moral degradation. Amos and Hosea, who prophesied under Jeroboam and his immediate successors, met this degradation with a revelation of God which differs in breadth and depth from the Mosaic revelation as sketched above. God, they taught, was not only Israel's God, but also the God of all the world; He would not favour Israel regardless of its moral condition, rather He would punish the sinful nation, whether that nation were Israel or another. If it be uncertain whether the Ten Commandments be Mosaic, it is at least certain that they were the code of the prophets of the 8th cent. Amos and Hosea taught Israel to worship One God, a God of Righteousness and Purity. But the manner as well as the matter of the teaching of these prophets challenges attention. Unlike Elijah and Elisha, they were 'writing prophets.' A prophet was no longer a voice only; he left a body of teaching behind him, to serve in the religious education of his people.

8. *The Tyranny of Asshur (Assyria).*—The contest between Israel and the Aramæans was ended by the interference of the Assyrians, who crushed both. We may pass over the victory of Shalmaneser II. over a confederate Aramæan-Israelite army in the days of Ahab (B.C. 854), and Jehu's payment of tribute to Shalmaneser (B.C. 842), as well as the boast of Ramman-nirārī III. (B.C. 811–783) that he exacted tribute from the 'land of

Omri.' Assyria declined while Israel flourished under Jeroboam II. (B.C. 782–741). Unfortunately Assyria revived under Tiglath-pileser III. (B.C. 745–727). We need not believe that he had anything to do with Uzziah (Azariah) of Judah* (2 K 15¹), but we have monumental references to his defeat of the allied kings Pekah of Israel and Rezin of Damascus (16⁵⁻⁹), and the monuments tell us what the Bible does not, viz. that Ausi'i' (Hoshea) was confirmed as king of Israel by Tiglath-pileser. But Hoshea succeeded to a diminished and depopulated kingdom (2 K 15²⁹); the extreme north and the land east of Jordan, after being ravaged, passed perhaps into the hands of some faithful client of Asshur. It would have been well for the kingdom of Samaria, if it had had only the open foe (Assyria) to reckon with; unfortunately, however, the false friend (Egypt) played a decisive part. From the days of Thutmosis (Thothmes) III. (B.C. 1500?) of the eighteenth dynasty and Ramses II. of the nineteenth, Egypt had looked on Canaan as within the sphere of her 'influence'; and, even when lower Egypt was divided among petty princes, one of these 'So'† (2 K 17⁴) could not resist the temptation to claim a footing in Palestine by intriguing with Hoshea of Samaria against the Assyrians (see EGYPT, vol. i. p. 663ᵃ). Shalmaneser IV. (B.C. 727–722), the successor of Tiglath-pileser, 'found conspiracy in Hoshea,' marched against Israel, and laid siege to Samaria (2 K 17⁴ᶠ·), which was taken by Sargon (Is 20¹), a usurper (B.C. 722–705) who succeeded Shalmaneser (*KIB* ii. 54, 55). Sargon tells us, 'I led forth (*aṣlula*) 27,290 of those who dwelt in the midst of it'; according to 2 K 17⁶ Israel was transported to Mesopotamia and Media. In any case the land was grievously depopulated; for even after colonists had been brought in from Babylonia and northern Syria (2 K 17²⁴), so much of the land still lay waste that lions increased and committed great ravages.

Israel having been crushed, Sargon marched against So (Sib'u) of Egypt and Hanun of Gaza, the confederates of Hoshea, and defeated them at Raphia (Rapiḥi) on the border of Egypt. The Pharaoh (Pir'u), plainly a different person from So, thereupon prudently paid 'tribute,' and Sargon retired.

Of the subsequent history of what had been the northern kingdom we know (until the time of the Return) only two facts. (1) Samaria was involved with Hamath, Arpad, and Damascus in a futile rising against Sargon (*KIB* ii. 56, 57). (2) In the decline of the Assyrian power Josiah was able to carry out his reforming measures in Bethel (2 K 23¹⁵), the 'chapel' of the northern kings (Am 7¹³), and in the cities of Samaria generally (2 K 23¹⁹).

The capture of Samaria and the march of Sargon to the Egyptian frontier revealed the danger in which Judah stood from the Assyrians.

Three policies now presented themselves to Hezekiah. (1) He might ally himself (not as Hoshea with a kinglet of lower Egypt, but) with the growing power of Ethiopia (Is 18¹ᶠ· 20⁵), under Sabakon (B.C. 707–695), who is perhaps meant, though his successor, Tirhakah (B.C. 690–664), is named in 2 K 19⁹. Thus supported, Judah might perhaps defy Assyria. (2) He might (like his father Ahaz) throw himself without any serious invitation into the arms of the king of Assyria, and accept his protection, his yoke, and his god, or at least his altar (2 K 16⁷⁻¹²). (3) He might accept the assurance of J″ given through Isaiah of the safety of Jerusalem and of those who took refuge in it (Is 28¹⁶ 29⁷ 30¹⁹ 31⁴ᶠ·). According to this

---

* *Asriya'u* of *Ja'udi* was a king in northern Syria.
† Read perhaps 'Seve' (*Sib'u* on the Assyr. monuments).

last policy, Hezekiah would not attempt to defend cities like Lachish and Libnah, which lay more or less in the great king's path to Egypt, but would withdraw his people as much as possible into the hill country and into Jerusalem itself. Judah would thus bow before the storm, and neither resist the Assyrian king nor attempt to make friends with him. Of course in a case in which three policies were possible, no one was consistently followed. In 701 Sennacherib, the son and successor of Sargon, marched into the west, having Egypt for his final objective (Herod. ii. 141). Hezekiah sent tribute (2 K 18[14]), but Libnah and Lachish, fortresses which might assist the march of the Egyptians and retard that of the Assyrians, were not surrendered to Sennacherib. The Assyrian king, in accordance with his general plan, set himself with his main army to reduce these fortresses ; but he sent 'a great host,' under the Turtan (Tartan), *i.e.* the Commander-in-chief who commanded in the absence of the king, to reduce Jerusalem (2 K 18[17]). Hezekiah was blockaded, and derided in his helplessness by the Assyrian leaders.

Thus far the Bible and the monuments agree, but the sequel is differently told. According to 2 K 19[35] the Angel of the Lord (no doubt the pestilence) slew 185,000 of the Assyrian army, and Sennacherib departed to his own land. According to Sennacherib's own account, fear fell on Hezekiah, and he acknowledged the majesty of Sennacherib by sending presents of every kind. It is hard to resist the impression that the Assyrian is escaping from the acknowledgment of failure in the long and wordy list of presents, and that the Hebrew account is based on a trustworthy tradition. In any case, Sennacherib does not claim to have taken Jerusalem, nor to have inflicted any personal chastisement on Hezekiah. The strange tradition with which Herodotus explains the retreat of 'Sanacharibus, king of the Arabians and of the Assyrians' from the frontiers of Egypt, supports as far as it goes the biblical account (ii. 141).

The retreat of Sennacherib, however,—be it remembered,—meant the escape of Jerusalem from the horrors of a sack by the Assyrians, and not the permanent deliverance of Judah from Assyrian vassalage. Esar-haddon (B.C. 681–669), continuing the work of his predecessor, conquered Egypt (B.C. 671), and we may believe him when he tells us that he demanded building materials for his palace from twenty-two kings of the west, including Manasseh, king of Judah, if *Mi-na-si-i šar (mahāzu) Ja-u-di* be he (KIB ii. 148, 149). The next king, Assur-bani-pal (the Osnappar of Ezr 4[10]), also made successful expeditions against Egypt, and it is not improbable that on one of these occasions Manasseh was carried off, as the chronicler says (2 Ch 33[11]), bound in fetters to Babylon.

Religion in Judah during the Assyrian Period. —The religious conflict was hardly less severe than the political. Under Ahaz (2 K 16[3t. 10t.]) and Manasseh (*ib.* 21[3ff.]) foreign worships and foreign superstitions were practised (cf. Is 2[6] 8[19] etc.), and against these Isaiah and Micah prophesied with fearless invective and threatening. Supported by the prophets, Hezekiah (according to 2 K 18[4. 22]) made some sweeping reforms, including the destruction of the brazen serpent, the removal of the high-places, and the centralization of the cultus in Jerusalem. Wellhausen (*IJG*[3] p. 90 f.) doubts whether the last two measures were carried out, supporting his doubt by a reference to 2 K 23[13], where, however, the *defilement* (not the *destruction*) of Solomon's high-places is ascribed to Josiah. Practical religion must have been at a very low ebb during this whole period, if we may judge from the denunciations uttered by Isaiah and Micah (esp.

Mic 3[10ff.]), and from Isaiah's favourite thought that only a remnant can survive God's judgment on Judah and Jerusalem.

9. *The Fall of Judah.*—Under Josiah (B.C. 639–608), Judah had a brief breathing space. Assurbani-pal, the last great sovereign of Assyria, died in 626, and the Assyrian power rapidly declined. Josiah took courage to repair the temple (2 K 22[3ff.]), to destroy the high-places, removing the priests attached to them, and even to extend his activity northwards to Bethel and to 'the cities of Samaria' (*ib.* 23[19]). Under him also was published 'the book of the law' (*i.e.* the Book of Deuteronomy), and the people entered into a covenant to obey its morality, and to worship J'' only in the one place which He had chosen for his sanctuary (cf. Dt 12[5f.]). Josiah himself set an example of kingly virtue (Jer 22[15f.]) as well as of Deuteronomic orthodoxy (cf. 2 K 23[21]), and the removal of the yoke of Asshur seemed to promise an era of comparative prosperity for Judah.

Unfortunately the fall of Assyria involved a contest for the spoils between Egypt under Neco(h) (AV Necho(h)) and Babylon under Nabopolassar. Necoh 'went up against the king of Assyria to the river Euphrates' (2 K 23[29]), passing through Megiddo (somewhere near Mount Carmel) on his march, and at Megiddo Josiah met his death at the hands of the Egyptian king. Of the circumstances of his death we have two accounts. According to 2 Kings (cited above), Josiah *went to meet* (Heb. not EV) Necoh, doubtless in order to come to some understanding with him, perhaps to do homage to him. Necoh, however, judging perhaps that Josiah was too strong a man to be a good vassal, had him slain at the audience ('when he saw him'). According to 2 Ch 35[20ff.] (=1 Es 1[25ff.]), on the contrary, Josiah's fate is precisely that of Ahab. He *fights* against Necoh in spite of a Divine warning, and is mortally wounded by an archer. (An obscure passage in Herodotus, ii. 159, gives no help). The sequel, however, is clear : Judah became a vassal to Egypt, and Necoh appointed the infamous Jehoiakim (2 K 23[34], Jer 22[13ff.]) to be king.

Egypt's triumph was short. Nebuchadrezzar, the son of Nabopolassar, swept Necoh out of Syria, and made Judah transfer its allegiance to Babylon. Twice Judah proved faithless to its new lord. The first revolt was punished heavily enough. Jerusalem was taken, the golden vessels of the temple were made a spoil, and Jehoiakim's son and successor Jehoiachin was carried into captivity to Babylon with his officers, his mighty men, and all the skilled artificers—10,000 captives in all (cf. Jer 24[1-7]). Nebuchadrezzar appointed as king in Judah Zedekiah (a son of Josiah), and bound him with an oath of fealty (cf. Ezk 17[12ff.]). But Zedekiah was too unstable to keep an oath, and too weak to resist the temptation of an alliance with Egypt. After a disordered reign of eleven years, during which the princes ruled rather than the king (Jer 38[5. 25]), the Babylonians took Jerusalem by blockade, blinded Zedekiah, slew his officers, burned the temple, broke down the city walls, and carried away a number of captives (Jer 52[28-30], Heb. *not* LXX B). A poor remnant of the people was left to prevent the land from relapsing into desert, and Gedaliah, son of Ahikam (the patron of Jeremiah), was appointed 'overseer' ('governor' would have been too grand a title) over them (Jer 40[5ff.]).

This—the catastrophe of Jerusalem—took place *c.* 587 B.C., but it must be remembered that Judah had been falling ever since the days of Ahaz. In fact the Southern kingdom slowly bled to death from the moment when its isolation was broken down by the dying struggles of the Northern kingdom under Pekah (2 K 15[29] 16[5], cf. Is 7[1ff.]). In particular, Judah never recovered from the brutal devastation wrought by Sennacherib, when 46 fortified towns were taken and 200,150 persons led captive (*KIB* p. 94 f. ; cf. 2 K 18¹³· ²³). We cannot form any satisfactory estimate of the numbers carried off at various times by the Chaldæans, for the passage (Jer 52²⁸⁻³⁰) which contains the most precise statements on this point is absent from LXX B𝔞A, and is in conflict with 2 K 24¹⁴ ; but it seems probable that the Chaldæan ravages were less extensive than the Assyrian, because the population had dwindled, and prosperity had diminished in the meantime. (See, further, Kosters, *ThT* xxxi. (1897) 518 ff.).

10. *The Exile and the Return.*—The captivity of Judah, reckoned from the fall of Jehoiachin (B.C. 597), lasted 59 years, or from the fall of Zedekiah (B.C. 587), 49 years, reckoning B.C. 538 as the probable *terminus ad quem*. The 'seventy' years of Jer 25¹² is a round number. Of the condition of the Jews in exile we have contradictory indications, from which we may conclude that the circumstances varied in different places and at different times. The first band of exiles were allowed to 'build houses and plant gardens' (Jer 29⁵ᶠ·), and to live in communities of their own (Ezr 8¹⁷, Ezk 1¹) under their own elders (Ezk 8¹ 14¹ 20¹). Jehoiachin, after thirty-six years of captivity, received special marks of favour from Evil-Merodach (Amil-Marduk), the successor of Nebuchadrezzar (2 K 25²⁷ᶠᶠ·). On the other hand, seditious prophets from time to time provoked the Chaldæans to cruel acts of repression (Jer 29²¹ᶠ·), and it is probable that some at least of the Jews were put to task-work, for the 'hard service' (Is 14³ᶠ·) wherein Israel was made to serve, looks like an allusion to Nebuchadrezzar's canal-works or temple-restoration, or to like undertakings of his successors, especially Nabuna'id (Nabonidus) (*KIB* iii. 2, p. 60 ff., p. 96 ff.). Yet that the lot of many Jewish families (after the first bitterness of expatriation was past) was at least tolerable in Babylonia, is clear from the fact that a considerable number of Jews (the vast majority, according to some critics) did not take part in the First Return under Sheshbazzar.

With regard to the Return a good deal has been written of late years (particularly since 1889) tending towards a reconstruction of the whole narrative. It will, however, be most convenient in this article to reproduce the account given in Ezra-Nehemiah, while pointing out from time to time how critics propose to correct and supplement it. In the first year, then, of Cyrus (Ezr 1¹), *i.e. c.* 538 B.C., the 'Persian' (see CYRUS, vol. i. p. 541 f.) king issued an edict for the rebuilding of the temple at Jerusalem, and invited the Jews to undertake the work. [We may compare with this the mutilated inscription in which Cyrus speaks of his restoration to the cities of Babylonia of gods which Nabonidus had carried off to Babylon (*KIB* iii. 2, p. 126 f.)]. The heads of Judah and Benjamin, together with the Levites, responded to the invitation, and Cyrus gave up the golden vessels of the temple, which had been carried away by Nebuchadrezzar, to Sheshbazzar (τῷ Σαβανασάρ LXX B, τῷ Σασαβασσάρῳ A, Ezr 1⁸ ; Σαναμασσάρῳ, 1 Es 2¹¹ LXX B, but Σαναβασσάρῳ, LXX Aᵃ), 'prince (א׳שׂ׳ *nāsī*) of Judah,' who brought them back to Jerusalem, together with a band of returning exiles. This—the First Return —resulted, we learn indirectly, in the laying of the foundation of the temple (Ezr 5¹⁶, but cf. 3⁹ᶠ·), but we do not know the number of those who accompanied Sheshbazzar, nor any other particulars. It is, however, negatively clear that the movement was not a success. In Babylonia the edict (in spite of the prophecies of Deutero-Isaiah) probably took the Jews by surprise, while in Judah (cf. Ezr 4⁴ᶠ·, a misplaced passage) there were 'many ad-

versaries.' The time, as the Jews said even sixteen years later (Hag 1²), was not yet come for so important an undertaking as the rebuilding of the temple. Some critics, indeed, smile altogether at the story of this 'First Return,' and reduce it to a conciliatory appointment by Cyrus of a prince of the house of David (Sanabassar) to be governor in Judæa (cf. Cheyne, *Jewish Religious Life*, pp. 5–7).

At the beginning of the reign of Darius Hystaspis (*c.* 522 B.C.), however, the Jewish exiles were prepared for a great movement, and there was, it seems, a Second Return under Zerubbabel the son of Shealtiel, a descendant of David, and Jeshua the son of Jozadak the priest (Ezr 2²). The whole 'congregation' numbered 42,360, exclusive of servants and handmaids (*ib.* 2⁶⁴ᶠ·). Of this great immigration, and of Zerubbabel and Jeshua who led it, much was expected, *imprimis* the rebuilding of the temple (Zec 6¹⁵), but the realization of the hope was delayed. The people went up 'unto Jerusalem and Judah, *every one to his own city*' (Ezr 2¹), and, after the heads had relieved their consciences by making a money-offering for the work of rebuilding, all the exiles 'dwelt in their cities' (*ib.* v.⁷⁰), or, as Haggai complained, they ran 'every man to his own house,' and allowed God's House to lie waste (Hag 1⁹). In the autumn (Ezr 3¹ᶠ·) they did indeed gather themselves as one man to Jerusalem for the erection of an altar of burnt-offering, 'but the foundation of the temple of the Lord was not yet laid' (*ib.* v.⁶).

How did the work of the temple begin at last in earnest? We have two answers, one in a 'prophetical' passage of Ezra (4²⁴ 5¹ᶠ·), written in the Aramaic tongue, and another in a 'priestly' passage, written in Hebrew by the compiler of the same book (3⁸⁻¹³). The former treats the foundation as already laid (cf. 5¹⁶), and reckons the date by the year of Darius *characteristically*, for the prophet's eye always noted political changes ; the second, on the contrary, describes in touching detail the laying of the foundation, and mentions as the date 'the second year of their coming to the House of God,' again characteristically, for the priest's eye was all for the holy place. The discrepancy between the two passages is one of words only—(1) as regards *date*, if the Return of Zerubbabel and Jeshua took place, as suggested above, at the beginning of the reign of Darius ; and (2) as regards the *nature of the work*, if we assume that after sixteen years of malice, neglect, and weather, the foundations needed some attention, which might be popularly described as relaying.

Ezr 3⁸⁻¹³, however, has a great omission, it says nothing of the activity of Haggai and Zechariah. Yet there can be no doubt that the voice of these two prophets was the deciding factor in the work ; words such as Hag 1⁴ 2⁹, Zec 4⁶⁻¹⁰ were not uttered in vain. In the second year of Darius, the second year of their return to Palestine, the exiles began to build, and in spite of an interruption by Tattenai, governor of Syria (Ezr 5³ᶠ·), the house was finished in the 6th year of Darius (6¹⁵).

This account is traversed and disputed by some modern critics. It is urged that Haggai and Zechariah never mention the Great Return of 42,000 persons, and consequently it is maintained that no considerable body of exiles (the Gōla) did return till the mission of Ezra, *c.* 432 B.C. (so Cheyne, *Introd. to Is.* p. xxxix). From this it follows that the temple which was completed *c.* 516 B.C. was built, not by the returned exiles, but by 'the people of the land,' the descendants of those left by Nebuzar-adan. But what if Haggai and Zechariah do not dwell upon the Return because they took part in it, and spoke to those who took part in it ? What if they do speak, at least once (Zec 6¹⁵), as the forerunners of a mighty host advancing from Babylon ?

One subject remains to be noticed, viz. the attitude of the builders of the temple towards the Samaritans. According to Ezr 4²ᶠ· (a passage due to the compiler of the book) Zerubbabel and Jeshua peremptorily rejected the offer of the 'adversaries (צָרִים *ẓārīm*, 'rivals') of Judah and Benjamin' to co-operate in the rebuilding. Cheyne, on the contrary, characterizes the story of rejection as 'pure imagination,' and asserts that the Samaritans maintained their connexion with the holy place 'till Nehemiah, armed with a Persian firman, interposed' (*JRL* p. 26).

After the completion of the temple a break of nearly sixty years occurs in our records, and when they speak again the Davidic line which Zerubbabel had represented has disappeared. Some critics (*e.g.* Cheyne and Sellin) partly fill the gap with a reconstruction which represents Zerubbabel as the accepted Messiah of the Jews, a rebel against Persian authority, and a martyr whose martyrdom ruined all the political prospects of the house of David. Cheyne refers Zec 6¹¹⁻¹³ (in a revised text) to the coronation and reign of Zerubbabel (*JRL* p. 14 f.), and Sellin thinks that he is meant by the Suffering Servant of Is 52¹³–53¹². The ruin of the walls of Jerusalem, which Nehemiah deplored (Neh 1³), may have been part of the vengeance taken by the Persians (or their deputies) on the Messianic kingdom of Zerubbabel.

The biblical records begin again in 'the seventh year of Artaxerxes' (Ezr 7⁸), *i.e.*, if Artaxerxes Longimanus be meant, in B.C. 458. In that year Ezra the scribe, a man of high-priestly family, went up to Jerusalem armed with a decree (given in Aramaic, *ib.* vv.¹²⁻²⁶) entrusting him with large powers, and ordering a large offering to be made in the king's name for the support of the worship of the temple. Strangely enough all that we know of the exercise of these powers is that Ezra called an assembly of the whole people in order to deal with the question of mixed marriages, that the people acknowledged the duty of putting away foreign wives, but pleaded for delay, and that a formidable list was drawn up (including the names of men of high-priestly family) of those who had taken foreign wives. Out of this list four persons (priests) actually 'gave their hands' to put away their foreign wives (Ezr 10⁶⁻⁴⁴).

In the twentieth year of Artaxerxes (Neh 2¹·⁹), *i.e.* in B.C. 445, came the mission of Nehemiah. He, unlike Ezra, was a layman and an officer at the Persian Court, and, unlike Ezra (Ezr 8²²), enjoyed the prestige of arriving with an escort of Persian officers and horsemen (Neh 2⁹). In spirit, however, Ezra and Nehemiah were one. Both aimed at reforming the religion of their people on lines stricter than any which had hitherto been laid down. To Ezra (or to the school of which he is the most conspicuous member) is probably due that rewriting with increased stringency and particularity of the earlier codes of the Hexateuch, which resulted in the formation of that which is commonly called the Priestly Code. The object which Ezra and his adherents set before themselves was the holiness of Israel (*i.e.* its separation from other peoples, and its greater strictness in the service of God).

Nehemiah worked on practical lines. He first made the separation of Israel possible by rebuilding the walls of Jerusalem 'in fifty and two days' (Neh 6¹⁵). He next removed the causes of disaffection among the poorer Jews by compelling the richer sort to restore lands and houses taken in pledge, and to forbear the exaction of usury (*ib.* 5¹⁻¹³). Ezra's edition of the book of the Law was recited and explained before an assembly of the whole people (*ib.* 8¹⁻⁸). At a great Day of Humiliation the people, headed by Nehemiah, vowed to separate themselves from the 'people of the land,' and to forbear from mixed marriages and from buying and selling on the Sabbath; they also undertook to observe the seventh year as a year of release, and to pay a third part of a shekel * for the maintenance of the sanctuary and its services (Neh 9¹ᶠ· 10¹ᶠᶠ·). Lastly, Nehemiah took measures for increasing the population of Jerusalem (Neh 11¹ᶠᶠ·).

Nehemiah's second mission to Jerusalem, 'in the two and thirtieth year of Artaxerxes' (*ib.* 13⁶), *i.e. c.* 433 B.C., apparently lasted only a short time. He found some of the old abuses still existing, and acted with his accustomed vigour against them. Some critics believe that Ezra's caravan of exiles (Ezr 8¹ᶠᶠ·) returned not in B.C. 458 (see above), but in connexion with this second mission of Nehemiah.

Of the fortunes of the Jews in the later days of the Persian empire we know next to nothing for certain, but it is probable that they took part in the rising against Artaxerxes III. 'Ochus' (B.C. 361–338), and were punished for it by a partial captivity to Hyrcania. The miseries of the times of Ochus are, it is sometimes supposed, alluded to in Is 24–27 and in several of the Psalms. On the other side, Wellhausen (*IJG*³ p. 160) believes that the Jews increased greatly in numbers under Persian rule, and that they assimilated to themselves a large element from 'the people of the land' whom Ezra and Nehemiah had tried to exclude.

11. *The Greek Period.*—The victory of Alexander the Great over Darius at Issus (B.C. 333) put an end to Persian rule in Syria. Greek influence was now brought to bear upon Palestine from two great centres, viz. Alexandria and Antioch. Moreover, the Jewish people was forced by the stress of outward events to leaven itself with foreign thoughts and foreign customs. A great dispersion took place. When at the beginning of the 3rd cent. B.C. Syria was under the rule of Egypt, Ptolemy the son of Lagus transported thousands of Jews to Egypt, to serve as colonists and as a support to his dynasty. Moreover, the Jews had learned to trade, and the openings for world-wide traffic which Alexander's conquests had made for the Greeks, attracted the Jews also. Yet the Jews who spread themselves abroad, left their hearts at home; from time to time they returned on visits to Jerusalem, themselves Hellenized, and exerting a subtle Hellenizing influence in the Holy City itself.

More than a hundred years, however, elapsed after Alexander's conquests before Greek influence drew the inhabitants of Judæa into serious political trouble. For a long time the small province, though hemmed in by Greek cities, Gaza, Joppa, Straton's Tower (*i.e.* Cæsarea), and Samaria, held out against Hellenization. But at last, at the beginning of the reign of Antiochus IV. Epiphanes (B.C. 175–164), the Greek party in Jerusalem, to which most of the ruling class belonged, felt themselves strong enough to take a decided step. A certain Jason got himself appointed high priest by Antiochus for a sum of money, with permission to set up a gymnasium in Jerusalem, and to enrol its inhabitants as citizens of Antioch, *i.e.* to confer on them the title and privileges of these citizens. A certain Menelaus in turn intrigued against Jason, and succeeded in supplanting him as high priest. The disorders consequent upon Greek innovations and scandals in the high-priesthood led to the direct interference of Antiochus, who in B.C. 168 had undertaken an expedition against Egypt. Foiled in this expedition by the *veto* of the Romans, Antiochus wrathfully determined to reduce the affairs of Judæa to order. The external means used were

* Probably equivalent to the half-shekel of Ex 30¹³ (cf. Ryle, *Ezra-Neh.* p. 274 note).

a massacre, an enslavement, and a Syrian occupation of the citadel (ἡ ἄκρα) of Jerusalem. On these followed an attempted conversion by force of the Jewish people to heathenism. The observance of the Sabbath and of circumcision was forbidden, copies of the Law were burnt, an altar was erected to Zeus in Jerusalem, and the Jews were compelled under penalty to participate in heathen sacrifices and to eat swine's flesh (1 Mac 2¹⁵ff., 2 Mac 6¹⁸ff.). A large party among the Jews were willing to fall in (at least outwardly) with the king's plans, a large party again (the חֲסִידִים ḥăsîdîm, Gr. Ἀσιδαῖοι) preferred to offer only passive resistance (1 Mac 2²⁹⁻³⁸ 7¹⁰⁻¹⁷), but there was fortunately a third party—perhaps not large in numbers at first—led by a priestly family afterwards called 'Maccabees.' Judas 'the Maccabee' was a hero of the stamp of David. Personally brave, he was also no contemptible leader, and though he died early, he had first taught the Jewish forces to face their enemies in battle with success.

The campaigns of Judas fall into three divisions. (1) Defensive, against the Syrians. By victories at Beth-horon and at Beth-zur he repulsed the enemy advancing from the West and from the South, and was not overcome until, in B.C. 162, Lysias, accompanied by the young king Antiochus V., led an army of 120,000 men and thirty-two elephants (1 Mac 6³⁰) into Judæa. (2) Offensive-defensive in Gilead and (with his brother Simon in immediate command) in Galilee. From both these districts the Jewish 'garrisons,' with their wives and children, were withdrawn and brought into Judæa. (3) Offensive, against the Edomites and Philistines, to enlarge the borders of his tiny state.

Against the immense resources of the Syrian kingdom the courage and skilful generalship of Judas would perhaps have failed had they not been seconded by the rivalries of various claimants to the Syrian throne. In the hour of victory (B.C. 162) Lysias was forced to grant to the Jews that religious freedom, the denial of which had occasioned the five years' war. In spite of further conflicts, in the course of which Judas fell, the cause of Jewish autonomy never went back, and at last, in B.C. 153, Jonathan the brother of Judas was able to put on the sacred vestments as high priest of the Jews, acknowledged by Alexander Balas, king of Syria (1 Mac 10¹⁵ff. 59ff.). In B.C. 142 Simon, the brother and successor of Jonathan, forced the Syrian garrison to evacuate the citadel of Jerusalem, and in the following year the whole nation of the Jews acknowledged the great services of the Maccabæan family by declaring Simon to be 'high priest, captain, and governor' for ever (1 Mac 14²⁷⁻⁴⁷). See, further, art. MACCABEES.

[The later history belongs rather to the Introduction to the NT. See NEW TESTAMENT TIMES, HISTORY OF].

LITERATURE.—(A) General Histories :—H. Ewald. Hist. of Isr., Eng. tr. by Martineau and Carpenter; A. P. Stanley, Jewish Church (based on Ewald); E. Renan, Histoire du Peuple d'Israël; B. Stade, GVI, 1887; J. Wellhausen, Isr. u. Jüd. Geschichte, 1894 (ed. 3, 1898), art. 'Israel' in 9th ed. of Encyc. Brit.; H. Grätz, Geschichte der Juden von den ältesten Zeiten, 1853–75 (vols. i. ii., containing the Biblical history, were written last), History of the Jews, Eng. tr. by Bella Löwy, 1891–92; R. Kittel, Geschichte der Hebräer (to B.C. 586), 1888, 1892, A History of the Hebrews, Eng. tr. by J. Taylor, Hope W. Hogg, and E. B. Spiers; A. Klostermann, GVI (to Nehemiah), 1896; C. F. Kent, History of the Hebrew People (to B.C. 586), 1897; C. H. Cornill, GVI (to A.D. 70), 1898, History of the People of Israel, Eng. tr. by W. H. Carruth, 1898; C. Piepenbring, Histoire du Peuple d'Israël (to the Maccabees), 1898; G. Maspero, Hist. Anc. des Peuples de l'Orient, vol. ii. (the Eng. tr. [under title 'Struggle of the Nations'] is not to be recommended, being in places very incorrect); H. Winckler, Gesch. des Israels in Einzeldarstellungen, i. (1895). Articles in this Dict., ASSYRIA (F. Hommel), BABYLONIA (F. Hommel), EGYPT (W. E. Crum).

(B) Historical Monographs :—Articles in this Dictionary, ABRAHAM (H. E. Ryle), DAVID (H. A. White), ISAIAH (G. A.

Smith), JACOB (Driver), JOSEPH (Driver), etc.; separate works, S. R. Driver, Life and Times of Isaiah ('Men of the Bible') [1888]; T. K. Cheyne, Jeremiah (same series).

Important works on the Return and Post-exilic Period :—Kuenen, Die Chronol. d. pers. Zeitalters, and Das Werk Esra's ('Gesam. Abhandl.,' 212 ff., 370 ff.); W. H. Kosters, Wiederherstellung Israels, Deutsch von A. Basedow; various works by v. Hoonacker, esp. Nouvelles Études sur la Restauration juive, 1896; E. Meyer, Entstehung d. Judenthums; T. K. Cheyne, Jewish Religious Life after the Exile ('JRL'), 1898 (cf. Introduction to the Book of Isaiah, p. xxxiii ff.); P. H. Hunter, After the Exile: a Hundred Years of Jewish History and Literature, 1890 : see also E. Sellin, Serubbabel (an attempted reconstruction of the career of Zerubbabel), 1898.

On the Maccabæan Period :—E. Schürer, Jewish People in the Time of Christ, Div. I. vol. i., Eng. tr. by J. Macpherson, 1890; A. W. Streane, Age of the Maccabees, 1898.

(C) Works illustrating the History of Israel from the Monuments :—E. Schrader (and other Assyriologists), Keilinschiftliche Bibliothek ('KIB,' most important historical inscriptions occur in vol. ii. and vol. iii. 2, 1890, v. 1896 [Tel el-Amarna tablets]: Assyr. text transliterated and accompanied by a Germ. trn.), Keilinschriften u. AT, ed. 2, 1883, Cuneiform Inscriptions and the OT, Eng. tr. by Owen C. Whitehouse; H. Winckler, Keilinschriftliches Textbuch zum AT (a selection from the inscriptions of those passages which illustrate passages of the OT), 1892, ATliche Untersuchungen (discussions of OT passages mainly in the light of Inscriptions), 1892; A. H. Sayce (editor), RP, 2nd ser. 1894 (translations of Assyrian and Babylonian Inscriptions and of early Egyptian documents), Higher Criticism and the Verdict of the Monuments (1894); J. F. McCurdy, History, Prophecy, and the Monuments, 1894–96; W. St. C. Boscawen, The Bible and the Monuments, 1895; Hogarth, Archæology and Authority, 1899 (OT part by S. R. Driver).

(D) Historical Geography :—G. A. Smith, HGHL; Townsend MacCoun, The Holy Land in Geography and History, New York, 1898 (excellent view-like maps).

(E) Archæology :—W. Nowack, Heb. Archäologie, 1894; J. Benzinger, Heb. Archäologie, 1894; the Publications of the PEF, particularly F. J. Bliss, Excavations at Jerusalem, 1898; Flinders Petrie, Tell-el-Hesy (Lachish); F. Buhl, Geschichte der Edomiter, 1893.

(F) Literary Histories :—Valuable hints are scattered throughout Driver, LOT; Robertson Smith, OTJC and Prophets of Israel; E. Kautzsch, Outline of the History of the Literature of the OT, Eng. tr. by J. Taylor, 1898.

(G) Histories of Religion :—A. Kuenen, Religion of Israel to the Fall of the Jewish State, Eng. tr. by A. H. May, 1874, 1875; A. Duff, OT Theology, 1891; J. Robertson, Early Religion of Israel, 1892; H. Schultz, ATliche Theologie, Aufl. 5, 1895, do. Eng. tr. of ed. 4, 1894; R. Smend, ATliche Religionsgeschichte, 1893; A. Dillmann, Handbuch der ATlichen Theol., Hrsg. v. R. Kittel, 1895. A work on this subject is expected from Prof. A. B. Davidson.

(H) Chronology. Add to the list given under CHRONOLOGY OF OLD TEST. vol. i. p. 403 :—O. Niebuhr, Chronologie der Geschichte Israels, Ægyptens, Babyloniens, und Assyriens von B.C. 2000–700.　　　　W. EMERY BARNES.

ISRAEL, KINGDOM OF.

ISRAEL, KINGDOM OF.—The tribes that had settled in the south of Pal. were from the first cut off from the northern tribes by a line of Canaanitish cities, Har-heres, Gezer, Aijalon, and Shaalbim (Jg 1²⁹·³⁵); and during the period of the judges, while there was a growing tendency among the northern tribes to coalesce under pressure of invasion, the southern tribes remained distinct. Saul never seems to have gained a paramount influence over these mountaineers of the S., who in large numbers espoused the cause of David. Though the latter, by choosing as his capital Jerus., which lay on the border-land between Benjamin and Judah, and other acts of diplomacy, succeeded in uniting for a time the northern and southern tribes, the union seems never to have been very complete, and once at least the jealousy between them nearly broke out into civil war (2 S 19⁴¹–20²). Solomon's policy was specially calculated to exasperate the northern tribes. While they were heavily taxed, and had forced labour imposed upon them, his own tribe seems to have been entirely exempt (1 K 4⁷⁻¹⁹ 5¹³⁻¹⁸). The rebellion led by Jeroboam, which was suppressed by Solomon, broke out in more formidable proportions under Rehoboam, who continued with even greater severity the oppressive policy of his father.

The separation, encouraged by the prophet Ahijah, who objected to Solomon's idolatrous practices (1 K 11²⁹⁻³⁹), took place without serious opposition, and Jeroboam became the first king of Israel (12²⁰). His aim was to counteract the centralizing effect of the great temple at Jerus. by setting up a more popular ritual at two of the many already existing local shrines, Bethel and Dan (12²⁹), where from this time J″ was worshipped under the symbol of a golden calf, probably as the God of agriculture. This cult may be regarded as a reaction from that more spiritual mode of worship which, under prophetic influence, had been established at Jerusalem. The view of the editor of the Book of Kings, that Jeroboam's act was a schismatic separation from the worship of the only legal sanctuary, is the reflexion of a post-Deut. age.

The hostility between North and South continued intermittently until the political and commercial alliance between Ahab and Jehoshaphat. While the invasions of Shishak (1 K 14²⁵) and Zerah (2 Ch 14⁹) weakened the power of Judah, Israel was already being hampered by the growing power of the Syrians of Damascus (1 K 20³⁴). Ahab, whose father Omri was the founder of the dynasty, married Jezebel, daughter of Ethbaal, king of the Zidonians (1 K 16³¹ff.), and she introduced the worship of the Tyrian Baal and Ashtaroth, with its cruel and immoral rites. In this she was opposed with varying success by the prophets Elijah and Elisha (1 K 18 ff.), through whose influence the dynasty was eventually overthrown by Jehu, and the cult exterminated by him (2 K 9. 10).

During this period the Syrians of Damascus began to take a prominent part in the history of Israel. Were the scanty records of OT our only source of information, we should have supposed the relation between Israel and Syria to have been that of practically unbroken hostility, the treaty of Benhadad II. in 1 K 20³⁴ appearing as merely a compact wrung from him in a moment of danger, and broken at the first opportunity (22¹· ²). In fact, the prophetic historian had little interest in events which lay outside the horizon of Israel, and even within it he had little in those which did not directly serve his religious purpose. We find, for example, no explanation how it was that Ramoth-gilead, after the events of 1 K 22, passed into the hands of the Israelites, as we find it in 2 K 8²⁸ 9¹. Again, from the variety of sources from which the history is drawn without the needful sifting and arrangement, there are some serious inconsistencies. It is difficult, for example, to reconcile 2 K 6²³ with 6²⁴. From the Assyr. inscriptions, however, we learn that in 854 Israel was a member of a very important alliance of small kingdoms centring in Damascus, which was summoned to his assistance by Irkhulini, king of Hamath, against the Assyr. king, Shalmaneser II. (see BABYLONIA, vol. i. p. 184ᵇ). Ahab is said to have furnished no fewer than 2000 (!) chariots and 10,000 footmen, Benhadad 1200 chariots and 10,000 footmen. Altogether 80,000 to 90,000 men were brought into the field. A great battle was fought at Ḳarḳar (Aroer). After a desperate encounter the Assyrians claim to have won the day, killing 14,000 (or according to another account 20,500), but Shalmaneser seems to have been too crippled to make any further advance. The alliance now appears to have broken up. At any rate, in the next two Assyr. campaigns against Benhadad, in 849 and 846, Ahab takes no part. Syria, from its position, was more exposed to attack than Israel, which was encouraged by this circumstance to attempt the recovery of Ramoth-gilead (1 K 22¹). During Benhadad's reign hostilities between the two kingdoms usually took the form of guerilla warfare, bands of the Syrians continually breaking into the country and carrying off spoil. Hazael, the murderer and successor of Benhadad II., proved a far more serious enemy. At first, however, he was kept in check by Assyria. In 842 Shalmaneser invaded Syria, defeated Hazael, who was now

deserted by his allies, with the loss of 1600 men, but was not successful in his attempt to take Damascus. The other small states, and Jehu among them, did not venture to resist, but sent tribute to Shalmaneser. The account of this campaign is inscribed on what is known as the Black Obelisk in the British Museum (No. 98). One of the sculptures represents Jehu paying tribute to Shalmaneser, and underneath is the following inscription :—'The tribute of Yahuah (Jehu), son of Khumri (Omri !), silver, gold, bowls of gold, vessels of gold, goblets of gold, pitchers of ·gold, lead, sceptres for the king's hand, (and) staves I received ' (see *RP* v. 41). But towards the end of Jehu's reign Hazael, left unmolested by Assyria, invaded the territory of the Transjordanic tribes with such effect as to reduce them to complete submission (2 K 10³²· ³³). He afterwards invaded the South, taking Gath, and forcing even Jerus. to capitulate. In Israel itself, during the reign of Jehoahaz, the son and successor of Jehu, Hazael's successes were so great that the fighting men were reduced to the merest minimum (2 K 13⁷). The tide of fortune began to turn in the reign of his son Jehoash, who is said to have recovered from Benhadad III. all the cities taken from his father by Hazael. He also defeated an expedition sent out by Amaziah, king of Judah, and proceeded to invest Jerus., where he broke down a large part of the wall and reduced it to submission (2 K 14¹³). It was during his reign that Ramman-nirari, the warlike grandson of Shalmaneser II., defeated the feeble Mari'a, the successor of Benhadad III., and even took Damascus ; but it is not certain whether the Israelites were affected by this campaign. The Syrians being thus temporarily crushed, and the Assyrians being at first too much engaged with Eastern affairs, and afterwards too much weakened by internal discords and the feebleness of their rulers to interfere, the kingdom of Isr. continued to gain strength, and reached the height of its power under Jeroboam II., who even ' recovered Damascus and Hamath ' (2 K 14²⁸).

With Jeroboam's death the kingdom rapidly declined. Divided by political factions, enervated by its moral corruption and social selfishness (Hos 4¹¹⁻¹⁴, Am 2⁸ 4¹ 8⁵· ⁶ etc.), it easily fell a prey to the Assyrians, who gained an accession of strength under the warlike Tiglath-pileser III. (Pul, 2 K 15¹⁹). With the exception of Pekah, none of the petty kings, who ruled for very short periods, have the least historical importance, except so far as by their folly or selfishness they advanced the ruin of their country. Twice Tiglath-pileser successfully invaded the North, and on both occasions probably Menahem paid tribute, thereby reducing his country to vassalage for the sake of securing his own rule, and in order to obtain money had to impose heavy taxes (2 K 15¹⁹ᶠ.). A spirited effort to resist Assyria was made by Pekah, who, like so many of the kings of Israel, gained his kingdom by the sword. In alliance with Rezin, king of Damascus, he invaded Judah (in 735), in order to depose Ahaz and set up the Syrian Tabeel, with a view to forming an alliance against Assyria (Is 7¹⁻⁹). But Ahaz had already submitted, and sent tribute, to Tiglath-pileser, and in the next year the latter invaded the North and utterly defeated Rezin and other Syrian members of the alliance, capturing and spoiling no fewer than 591 Syrian cities. At the same time the Israelitish cities east of Jordan fell into his hands (2 K 15²⁹), and the population was taken captive ; some of the Western cities were also taken. Pekah himself was forced to take refuge in Samaria, while the rest of the country was reduced to a desert. The final effort to throw off the Assyr. yoke made by Hoshea, who adopted the fatal policy of allying himself with So (Shabaka), king of Egypt (2 K

17⁴), brought about the invasion of Israel by Shalmaneser, and the final captivity of Israel (in 721).

The most striking feature in the history of the kingdom of Israel is its want of stability. There was no one central bond, either religious or political, to unite the people and infuse a national spirit. The seat of royalty was constantly being changed —Shechem, Tirzah, Samaria. Dynasty followed dynasty; one succeeding the other by violence. The longest, that of Jehu, lasted only five generations. The king generally held his life in his hands, and often had to maintain his authority by acts of terrorism and cruelty. There was no central religious shrine to inspire a common feeling of reverence. Religious worship, if not always absolutely revolting, as in the days of Ahab and Ahaziah, was to a large extent heathenish in its methods and conceptions (Hos 4¹³ 7¹⁴ Am 4⁵ 8¹⁴), and in the declining days of the nation's history exercised no influence on its social life. At the same time the history has its elements of interest. While the Judæans, in their isolated position on the S. hills, were developing that marked national character which has distinguished them from other nations, the Isr. were constantly coming in contact with the Can. and other foreign tribes. From these they derived not merely the evils of a bad religious influence, but also many of the advantages of a higher civilization and culture. Humanly speaking there were greater possibilities in the N. than in the S. Until almost the last page of their history, from Elijah downwards, all the great prophets came from the North, or, like Amos, carried on their work there. If in the more refined worship of Solomon's temple was the germ of the stately ritual of post-exilic Judaism, we must confess that it was in the teaching of Northern prophets, such as Elijah and Hosea, that we can trace the main growth of those spiritual truths which became the precious heritage of the Jews, and through them of the Christian world.

LITERATURE.—Apart from the historical books of OT and the works of the prophets Amos and Hosea, the most important sources of information are the monumental remains, esp. those of Assyria. Collections of these are contained in *RP*, Schrader, *COT*. The history has been thoroughly treated in Ewald's *HI* (Tr. 1883-1885), and those of Wellhausen, Kittel, and Reuss. On archæological questions, Nowack's *Heb. Arch.* 1894, is by far the best. The 'Books of Kings' in the *Speaker's Commentary*, though from a critical point of view behind the time, still contains much useful information. *A History of the Hebrew People* by Professor Kent is an excellent book, and quite up to date. The second volume appeared after this article was written.   F. H. WOODS.

ISRAELITE (Jn 1⁴⁷).—See NATHANAEL.

ISSACHAR (יִשָּׂשכָר, pointed by the Massoretes יִשָּׂשכָר* Yissākār, the second שׂ being ignored, but the true pointing should probably be יִשׂ שָׂכָר; LXX Swete Ἰσσαχάρ (but Tisch. Ἰσσάχαρ), and so NT, Treg. WH; Ἰσαχάρ TR).—**1.** The ninth son of Jacob and the fifth of Leah, Gn 30¹⁸ 35²³ etc. The meaning of the name is uncertain. Probably it means 'there is a reward' (cf. Jer 31¹⁶, 2 Ch 15⁷); if Wellhausen's suggestion (*Text der Büch. Sam.* 95), that the name should be interpreted as אִישׂ שָׂכָר, is correct, it will probably mean 'hired labourer,' though it might also be translated 'man of reward,' whatever the precise sense of that might be. In favour of the view that it means 'hired labourer' is the character given to the tribe in the Blessing of Jacob (Gn 49¹⁴·¹⁵). Kuenen (*ThT* v. 292 f.) has inferred from this passage that it is to its subject condition that the tribe owes its name. Ball (*SBOT Genesis*, on Gn 30¹⁸) thinks it may mean 'Sokar's man,' Sokar or Seker being an Egyptian god, but perhaps is a designation of the tribal totem, meaning 'The Red' and referring to the ass

* Ben-Naphtali (Baer, *Gen.* p. 84) points יִשְׂשכָר.

(cf. Gn 49¹⁴). In Genesis a double explanation of the name is given. J accounts for it by the fact that Leah hired Jacob from Rachel with the mandrakes found by Reuben (Gn 30¹⁶). E interprets it as a reward conferred by God on Leah, because she had given Zilpah to Jacob (v.¹⁸).

Our knowledge of the tribe is very meagre. Its territory in Palestine is of uncertain extent, for the delimitation of its boundaries in Jos 19¹⁷⁻²³ is from P (cf. Dillm. *ad loc.*, and Moore on Jg 5¹⁵). It lay S. of Zebulun and Naphtali, and N. of Manasseh. On the E. it was bounded by the Jordan. Whether it ever reached the sea is uncertain (see Dt 33¹⁸·¹⁹). Probably it remained an inland tribe. Its lot included nominally the very fertile plain of Esdraelon, but this was for the most part in the possession of the Canaanites. Robinson says: 'We were greatly struck with the richness and productiveness of the splendid plains, especially of Lower Galilee, including that of Esdraelon. . . . Zebulun and Issachar had the cream of Palestine' (*BRP²* iii. 160). Since the tribe is not mentioned in Jg 1, we do not know anything of the circumstances of its settlement in Palestine. Apparently both Deborah and Barak belonged to it, and in Deborah's Song (Jg 5¹⁵) it is mentioned as having taken part in the battle against Sisera. One of the judges, Tola, is said to have belonged to it (Jg 10¹·², on the text of which see Moore's note). Baasha, who conspired against, slew, and succeeded Nadab the son of Jeroboam I., also sprang from this tribe (1 K 15²⁷). In the Blessing of Jacob (Gn 49¹⁴·¹⁵) the tribe is taunted with its indolent preference of undisturbed enjoyment of its fruitful land to independence. The reference would be to a later period than the conflict with Sisera, in which it had taken a distinguished part. No reproach is uttered in the Blessing of Moses (Dt 33¹⁸·¹⁹). The latter passage is obscure (see Driver's note), but it apparently refers to the possession by Zebulun and Issachar of sanctuaries to which non-Israelites ('the peoples') resorted, and to material advantages which these tribes thus secured. 'The peoples' (v.¹⁹) would probably be Phœnicians, on account of the reference to 'the abundance of the seas.'

According to P the numbers of this tribe at the first census amounted to 54,400 (Nu 1²⁹), at the second to 64,300 (26²⁵); while the Chronicler gives the number in the time of David as 145,600. Unfortunately we can attach no weight to any of these figures.

2. Mentioned in the Chronicler's list of Korahite doorkeepers as the seventh son of Obed - edom (1 Ch 26⁵).   A. S. PEAKE.

ISSHIAH (יִשִּׁיָּה).—**1.** One of the heads of the tribe of Issachar, 1 Ch 7³ (AV Ishiah). **2.** A Korahite who joined David at Ziklag, 1 Ch 12⁶ (AV Jesiah). **3.** The son of Uzziel, 1 Ch 23²⁰ (AV Jesiah), 24²⁵. **4.** A Levite, 1 Ch 24²¹. See GENEALOGY.

ISSHIJAH (יִשִּׁיָּה).—One of those who had married a foreign wife, Ezr 10³¹ (AV Ishijah), called in 1 Es 9³² Aseas.

ISSUE.—See MEDICINE.

ISTALCURUS (A Ἰστάλκουρος, B Ἰστάκαλκος) 1 Es 8⁴⁰.—'Uthi the son of Istalcurus' here stands for 'Uthai and Zabbud' in Ezr 8¹⁴ (A καὶ Ζαβούδ, B om.). The name is apparently a corruption of the form in the Kěrê וְזַבּוּד ('and Zaccur'). See ZABBUD.

ITALA VERSION.—See VERSIONS.

ITALIAN BAND.—See AUGUSTUS' BAND.

ITALY ('Ιταλία), the geog. term for the country containing the headquarters of the Rom. empire, was originally applied only to the S. part of the peninsula round the Gulf of Tarentum. It was afterwards extended to include all the country to the foot of the Alps. Jews first attained prominence in Italy after the triumph of Pompey, B.C. 62, and, under the protection of Julius Cæsar, they rapidly increased in numbers. They seem to have characteristically appropriated a quarter of the capital, and spread to other cities. Horace (*Sat.* I. ix. 69, 'vin' tu curtis Judæis oppedere') and Juvenal (*Sat.* iii. 296 and xiv. 96, 'Judaicum ediscunt jus') speak of them as a constant element in the population. In A.D. 50 an imperial edict of Claudius banished the Jews from Rome, possibly owing to riots between the latter and the Christians (Suet. *Claud.* xxv.) as to the claims of Christ to be the Messiah. Aquila and Priscilla are mentioned among the exiles (Ac 18²) from I., which is apparently used as almost synonymous with Rome. See, further, Schürer, *HJP* II. ii. 232 ff., and the Literature cited there.

Cornelius, the first Gentile convert to Christianity, is described as a member of the Italian band or cohort (Ac 10¹), *i.e.* the regiment recruited in I., and consisting of native Italians, as distinguished from troops levied in the provinces. See AUGUSTUS' BAND.

I. is again mentioned as the destination of St. Paul (Ac 27¹) when he appealed to Cæsar. The ship on which the prisoners were embarked was on its way back to Adramyttium in Mysia, and would call at several ports on the coast of Asia, at one of which the centurion intended to transfer his charges to a vessel bound for Rome. This shows the existence of a considerable trade between that city and the Mediter. ports. The expression in He 13²⁴ 'they of I. (οἱ ἀπὸ τῆς Ἰταλίας) salute you,' is of too uncertain meaning to decide anything as to either the destination or the place of composition of this Epistle.

Christianity was introduced into I. in early times, probably on the return of the Roman Jews who are called 'strangers from Rome' (Ac 2¹⁰) to their native country after the Feast of Pentecost. The Ep. to the Romans, written about A.D. 58, points to the existence of a numerous body of Christians in that city who were partly Jews and partly Gentiles (Ro 1¹³).   C. H. PRICHARD.

ITERATE.—Sir 41²³ 'Of iterating and speaking again, that which thou hast heard' (ἀπὸ δευτερώσεως, RV 'Of repeating'). Cf. Knox, *Works*, iii. 56, 'I knaw ye will say, it [the Mass] is none uther sacrifice, but the self same, save that it is iteratit and renewit'; Boyle, *Works*, iv. 552, 'Having wiped and cleansed away the spot, I iterated the experiment.' The mod. 'reiterate' is scarcely equivalent.   J. HASTINGS.

ITHAI (אִתַּי).—A Benjamite, one of David's heroes, 1 Ch 11³¹. In the parallel passage 2 S 23²⁹, the name is אִתַּי ITTAI (wh. see).

ITHAMAR (אִיתָמָר 'island of palms' (?)*) is known to us only from P and the Chronicler. According to these writers I. was the youngest son of Aaron by Elisheba (Ex 6²³, Nu 3² 26⁶⁰, 1 Ch 6³ 24¹). Together with his three brothers, and Aaron their father, he was consecrated to the priesthood (Ex 28¹), but the two elder brothers Nadab and Abihu were slain for offering strange fire (Lv 10; cf. Nu 3⁴ 26⁶¹, 1 Ch 24²).

During the wilderness wanderings the tabernacle and its equipment, together with the Gershonites and Merarites, were under the supreme

* See Hommel, *Anc. Heb. Trad.* 116; Gray, *Heb. Proper Names*, 246 n.

direction of Ithamar (Ex 38²¹, Nu 4²⁸·³³, 7⁸). In the reign of David the families of Eleazar and I. are said to have been divided into courses in the proportion of two to one (cf. 1 Ch 24³·⁴). The compiler of the books of Chronicles represents the high priesthood as descending in unbroken succession until the captivity in the family of Eleazar (1 Ch 6³⁻¹⁴). But in the earlier historical books we find the ark under the charge of Eli and his descendants, and a comparison of 1 Ch 24³, 1 S 22⁹, 14³ would suggest that Eli belonged to the house of I. Josephus expressly states that this was the case (*Ant.* VIII. i. 3). See **High Priest** under PRIESTS AND LEVITES.   W. C. ALLEN.

ITHIEL (אִיתִיאֵל, prob. 'with me is God').—**1.** A Benjamite (Neh 11⁷). See GENEALOGY. **2.** One of two persons to whom Agur addressed his oracular sayings, the other being Ucal (Pr 30¹). Neither LXX nor Vulg. recognizes a proper name here, and most modern commentators point differently, לָאִיתִי אֵל לָאִיתִי אֵל וָאֵכָל instead of אִיתִיאֵל לְאִיתִיאֵל וָאֵכָל, and tr. 'I have wearied myself, O God, I have wearied myself, O God, and am consumed.' So RVm.   H. A. WHITE.

ITHLAH (יִתְלָה, B Σειλαθά, A Ἰεθλά, AV Jethlah). —A town of Dan, near Aijalon, Jos 19⁴². The site is unknown.

ITHMAH (יִתְמָה).—A Moabite, one of David's heroes, 1 Ch 11⁴⁶.

ITHNAN (יִתְנָן).—A city in the Negeb of Judah (Jos 15²³) whose site is uncertain. It is preceded by Hazor and followed by Ziph. In the B text of the LXX it is combined with the former of these names, Ἀσοριωνάιν, and in A with the latter Ἰθναξίφ, although Luc. has Ἰθνάν, Ζείφ.

ITHRA (יִתְרָא 'abundance' (?), Ἰοθόρ). — The father of Amasa, and husband of Abigail, David's sister. He is described as an Israelite (2 S 17²⁵), but the Chronicler undoubtedly has the better reading, 'Jether the Ishmaelite' (1 Ch 2¹⁷ יֶתֶר הַיִּשְׁמְעֵאלִי; B Ἰοθόρ, A Ἰεθέρ), which is also given by A at 2 S 17. See JETHER.

ITHRAN (יִתְרָן).—**1.** Eponym of a Horite clan, Gn 36²⁶, 1 Ch 1⁴¹. **2.** An Asherite chief, 1 Ch 7³⁷, possibly identical with Jether of the following verse. See GENEALOGY.

ITHREAM (יִתְרְעָם 2 S 3⁵; B Ἰεθεραάμ, A Ελεθεραάμ; 1 Ch 3³ Ἰθαράμ, A Ἰεθράμ, *Jethraam*), the sixth son of David by EGLAH (wh. see), born to him at Hebron.

ITHRITE, THE (הַיִּתְרִי; B ὁ Αἰθειραῖος, ὁ Ἐθθεναῖος, ὁ Ἤθηρει [א ὁ Ἰθηρεί], Ἰοθηρεί; A Ἐθραῖος, Τεθρίτης, Ἰεθερί), a gentilic adjective applied to the descendants of a family of Kiriath-jearim (1 Ch 2⁵³), amongst whom were two of David's guard (2 S 23³⁸, 1 Ch 11⁴⁰ IRA and GAREB). Possibly, however, the text of 2 S 23 and 1 Ch 11 should be pointed הַיַּתִּרִי = 'the Jattirite' (so Thenius, Klostermann, Budde), *i.e.* an inhabitant of Jattir (mentioned in 1 S 30²⁷ as one of David's haunts) in the hill-country of Judah (Jos 15⁴⁸ 21¹⁴). The Peshiṭta (2 S 23³⁸ᵃ, 1 Ch 11⁴⁰ *bis*) reads ܕܝܬܝܪ (= of Jattir), cf. its rendering 2 S 20²⁶.   J. F. STENNING.

ITS.—'Its' does not occur in AV of 1611. But in Lv 25⁵ 'it' was used where we should now use 'its' ('That which groweth of it owne accord of thy harvest, thou shalt not reape'), and in 1660 this was changed into 'its,' and is so printed in all modern editions. That is the only place in which even in modern edd. the word is found.

There is no doubt that about 1611 'its' had begun to struggle for recognition. But it is not once used by Spenser; and although it is found nine times in Shakespeare's First Folio (five of these in *Winter's Tale*), it is suspected that they were all introduced after his death. Bacon has it very rarely; Milton three times in his poetry (*PL* i. 254, iv. 813; *Ode on Nativity*, 106) and twice in his prose. By the time of Milton's death the word was established in the language.

The third pers. pron. in Anglo-Saxon was—

	Mas.	Fem.	Neut.
Nom.	he	heo	hit
Gen.	his	hire	his

The mas. forms are still in use; the fem. were both changed early; the nom. of the neut. lost its *h*, but retained *his* as the regular form for the gen. (*i.e.* possessive) up to the time we have spoken of. Consequently in AV *his* is the usual poss. case of 'it' as well as of 'he.' Thus Gn 3¹⁵ 'it shall bruise thy head, and thou shalt bruise his heel' (Tind. 'And that seed shall tread the on the heed, and thou shalt tread hit on the hele'); Lv 23³⁷ 'everything upon his day'; Nu 20⁸ 'speak ye unto the rock, and it shall give forth his water'; Pr 23³¹ 'Look not thou upon the wine when it is red, when it giveth his colour in the cup, when it moveth itself (1611 it selfe) aright'; 2 Es 4¹⁹ 'the sea also hath his place to bear his floods'; Wis 19²⁰ 'The fire had power in the water, forgetting his own virtue; and the water forgat his own quenching nature.'

But when the poss. of both genders was the same there was always the risk of some confusion. Examples that need attention are, Lv 1¹⁵ 'And the priest shall bring it unto the altar, and wring off his (RV 'its') head, and burn it on the altar'; 1 S 6⁹ 'if it goeth up by the way of his own coast to Bethshemesh' (RV 'its own border'); 2 S 6¹⁷ 'And they brought in the ark of the LORD, and set it in his place' (RV 'its'); Dn 7⁹ 'I beheld till the thrones were cast down, and the Ancient of days did sit, whose garment was white as snow, and the hair of his head like the pure wool: his (mas.) throne was like the fiery flame, and his (neut.) wheels (RV 'the wheels thereof') as burning fire'); Mt 6³³ 'But seek ye first the kingdom of God, and his righteousness' (*i.e.* 'God's righteousness; but Tind. has 'the kyngdome of heven and the rightwisnes therof,' and he is followed by Cov., Cran., and Gen.; Rhem. 'the justice of him'; Bish. as AV, which is practically the tr of Wyc. 'seke ye first the kyngdom of god and his rightfulnesse'; RV 'But seek ye first his kingdom, and his righteousness,' omitting τοῦ θεοῦ with edd.); 1 Co 15³⁸ 'But God giveth it a body as it hath pleased him, and to every seed his own body' (RV 'a body of its own').

Various methods were adopted to avoid confusion between 'his' mas. and neut. (1) The use of 'it' for the poss. is regarded as a dialectic peculiarity, belonging to the North-Western counties. Its single occurrence in AV (Lv 25⁵) comes from the Geneva version.* Its presence in Shaks. is sometimes due to imitation of the language of childhood; thus *King John II.* i. 160—

'Go to it grandam, child:
Give grandam kingdom, and it grandam will
Give it a plum, a cherry, and a fig.'

But this is not always the case; and examples

* The LXX is τὰ αὐτόματα ἀναβαίνοντα. In Ac 12¹⁰ the same Gr. word (ἥτις αὐτομάτη ἠνοίχθη [edd. ἠνοίγη] αὐτοῖς) is tr'd in AV 'the iron gate . . . which opened to them of his own accord.' In Luther's Bible Lv 25⁵ is *von ihm selber*; Ac 12¹⁰ *von ihr selbst*. The Gen. NT has in Ac 12¹⁰ 'which opened to them by it owne accorde.'

may be quoted from other authors, as *Judgement of Synode of Dort* (1619), p. 9, 'Election . . . is to bee propounded with the spirit of discretion, religiously, and holily, in it place and time.' Indeed the often occurring 'it self' in AV 1611, is an example just as good as 'it own': cf. Bp. Hall, *Works*, ii. 79 ('Contemplations,' bk. iii.), 'Why may wee not distinguish of fire, as it is it selfe, a bodily creature, and as it is an instrument of God's justice, so working, not by any materiall vertue, or power of it owne, but by a certain height of supernaturall efficacie, to which it is exalted by the omnipotence of that supreme and righteous Judge?' (2) Occasionally *the* was used for 'his,' as in Robynson's tr of More's *Utopia* (Lumby's ed. p. 101), 'They marveile also that golde, whych of the owne nature is a thing so unprofytable, is nowe amonge all people in so hyghe estimation.' (3) Sometimes the noun was personified and the fem. *her* then used. This is Milton's favourite device, as in *Hymn on Nativity*, 140—

'And Hell it self will pass away,
And leave her dolorous mansions to the peering day.'

Cf. Tindale's tr of Nu 4⁹·¹⁰ 'And they shall take a cloth of Iacyncte and cover the candelsticke of light and hir lampes and hir snoffers and fyre pannes and all hir oyle vessels which they occupye aboute it, and shall put apon her and on all hir instrumentes, a coverynge of taxus skynnes, and put it apon staves.' So in AV, Jon 1¹⁵ 'the sea ceased from her raging'; Rev 22² 'the tree of life, which . . . yielded her fruit every month.' (4) Occasionally 'of it' was adopted, as Dn 7⁵ 'it had three ribs in the mouth of it, between the teeth of it.' (5) Very often the phrase was slightly turned, and 'thereof' used, as by Fuller, *Pisgah Sight*, p. 40, 'Twice was it [Solomon's Temple] pillaged by foreign foes, and four times by her own friends before the final destruction thereof.' But 'the most curious thing of all in the history of the word "its" is the extent to which, before its recognition as a word admissible in serious composition, even the occasion for its employment was avoided or eluded. This is very remarkable in Shakespeare. The very conception which we express by "its" probably does not occur once in his works for ten times that it is to be found in any modern writer. So that we may say the invention, or adoption, of this form has changed not only our English style, but even our manner of thinking.'—Craik, *Eng. of Shaks.* p. 103.

J. HASTINGS.

ITTAI ('אִתַּי, perh. 'companionable').—1. A native of Gath, whence he was banished (?) (2 S 15¹⁹) with 600 followers, who with their families (v.²²) joined David not long (v.²⁰) before the revolt of Absalom. ('After him,' etc., in v.¹⁸ refers to Ittai, whose name has probably dropped out. So Wellhausen in Driver, *Heb. Text of Sam. ad loc.*). Ewald, following Jos. (*Ant.* VII. ix. 2), identifies this band with the 600 whom David commanded when an outlaw (1 S 23¹³ 25¹³ 27² 30⁹), and these, again, with the *gibborim* (mighty men), reading, after Thenius, in v.¹⁸ *gibborim* for *Gittim*. The LXX and Vulg. are cited as supporting this emendation; but the LXX here is at once conflated and defective. The genuine LXX (acc. to Wellhausen) and the Vulg. interpolation are merely explanatory of 'Cherethites —Gittites.' The *gibborim* of 2 S 16⁶ included the Cherethites, etc.; see also 2 S 23⁸. David's original followers were Hebrews (1 S 22²), but Ittai's 600 were Philistines (2 S 15¹⁸ 'from Gath,' ²⁰ 'thy brethren'); on the other hand they were different from the Cherethites, etc., whose captain was Benaiah. It may be added that the phrase 'the Gittith' (titles of Ps 8. 81. 84) is rendered by Hitzig and Delitzsch 'a march of the Gittite guard.'

The scene in which we first meet Ittai (2 S 15[19-22]) almost surpasses the parting of Naomi and her daughters-in-law as a portrayal of noble unselfishness, and of intense personal devotion. David, never so kingly as when in affliction, urges Ittai, as a stranger (נָכְרִי), to retire from a desperate cause, bids him either engage in the service of the new king, or return home to Gath, and dismisses him with a gracious benediction. Ittai in reply, swearing by the God of Israel, affirms an undying loyalty. In the battle with Absalom, Ittai was one of David's three generals (2 S 18[2. 5. 12]). It is possible that he fell in the engagement, as we hear of him no more. Jerome (*Qu. Heb.* on 1 Ch 20[2]) cites a tradition that it was not David but Ittai that took the crown off the head of the Ammonite idol Milcom, it being forbidden to a Hebrew to take, with his own hands, gold or silver from an idol. **2.** 2 S 23[29] (1 Ch 11[31] **Ithai** אִתַּי) one of David's heroes.   N. J. D. WHITE.

ITURÆA is the EV translation of the first term in St. Luke's description of Philip's tetrarchy (τῆς Ἰτουραίας καὶ Τραχωνίτιδος χώρας, Lk 3[1], AV 'Ituræa and the region of Trachonitis'). But Ramsay has shown (*Expositor*, 1894, ix. pp. 51 ff., 143 ff., 288 ff.) that the word is not used as a noun by any writer before Eusebius in the 4th cent. after Christ, and doubtfully even by him (so not even in Jos. *Ant.* XIII. xi. 3, where Niese reads Ἰτουραίους; nor in Appian, *Civ.* v. 7: read τὴν Ἰτουραίων). Strabo calls it τὴν Ἰτουραίων ὀρεινήν (XVI. ii. 16), and τὰ Ἀράβων μέρη καὶ τῶν Ἰτουραίων (XVI. ii. 20), and Dio Cassius, τὴν τῶν Ἰτουραίων τῶν Ἀράβων (lix. 12). Epiphanius (*adv. Hæres.* xix. 1) uses the adjective ἀπὸ τῆς Ναβατικῆς χώρας καὶ Ἰτουραίας, and Ramsay (*op. cit.* 289 n. 2) argues for the adjectival meaning of Ἰτουραῖοι even in Euseb. (*Onom.* ed. Lag. 268, 298), and more doubtfully in Jerome's translation. Elsewhere, in Greek and Latin authors, it is the name of the people which is given, Ἰτουραῖοι, *Iturœi, Ityrei,* etc. 'There remains, then, no single passage in ancient literature to justify the noun which has been forced on Luke' (Ramsay, 289), which noun, further, would render the sentence 'degenerate Greek,' 'in utter disregard of the rules of Greek expression as observed by the older classical authors' (*ib.* 144).

The Ituræans were well known to the Romans as a race of hardy archers, and they frequently appear in the pages of Latin writers. They fought with Cæsar in the African war (*Bell. Afric.* 20), and formed a bodyguard for Mark Antony when he was triumvir, rattling with their arms through the forum to the indignation of Cicero ('*Philipp.* ii. 19, 112, xiii. 18). Virgil sings them, 'Ituræos taxi torquentur in arcus' (*Georg.* ii. 448), and Lucan, 'Ituræis cursus fuit inde sagittis' (*Pharsal.* vii. 230), 'tunc et Ituræi Medique Arabesque soluto arcu turba minax' (*ib.* vii. 514). In A.D. 110 there was a 'cohors I Augusta Ituræorum sagittariorum' (*CIL* t. iii. 868). About A.D. 255 we have the statement 'habes sagittarios Ityræos trecentos' (Vopiscus, *Vita Aureliani,* c. 11), and in his Gazetteer of the geographical terms of the Latin poets, Vibius Sequester (*c.* A.D. 500) names them as 'Ithyrei, vel Itharei, Syrii usu sagittæ periti' (ed. Hesselii, 155).

The quotations given above from Strabo, Appian, and Lucan * call them or associate them with both Arabs and Syrians; and, as Schürer points out (*HJP* I. ii. App. I. 'History of Chalcis, Ituræa, and Abilene,' 326), the proper names of Ituræan soldiers, mentioned in Latin inscriptions, are Syrian (cf. Münter, *de Rebus Ituræorum,* 1824, 8-10, 40 ff.; *CIL* t. iii. n. 4371; *C. I. Rhenan.*

---

ed. Brambach, 1233 f.). This agrees with the position assigned to them on and about the skirts of the Lebanons; and considering the incessant drift upon these parts of nomad Arabs from the neighbouring deserts, we ought probably to see in the Ituræans the descendants of **Jetur** (יְטוּר) mentioned in Gn 25[15] and 1 Ch 1[31] as among the sons of Ishmael, *i.e.* as Arabian desert tribes. Eupolemus (*c.* B.C. 150), quoted by Eusebius (*Præp. Evang.* ix. 30), mentions Ituræans along with Ammonites, Moabites, Nabatæans, etc., as among the objects of David's campaigns E. of the Jordan.

Because of this semi-nomadic state and this gradual drift from the desert to the fertile parts of Syria, the exact territory of the Ituræans is difficult, if not impossible, to define. Josephus places the Ituræan kingdom in or upon the N. of Galilee in B.C. 105 (*Ant.* XIII. xi. 3), when Aristobulus having defeated them added a large part of their territory to Judæa. Upon an inscription of about A.D. 6 (*Ephemeris Epigraphica,* 1881, 537-542) Q. Æmilius Secundus relates that being sent by Quirinius 'adversus Itureos in Libano monte castellum eorum cepi.' Dio Cassius (xlix. 32) calls Lysanias, who ruled Lebanon from Damascus to the sea with his capital at Chalcis, king of the Ituræans; and the same writer (lix. 12) and Tacitus (*Ann.* xii. 23) call Soemus, who was tetrarch in Lebanon (Jos. *Vita,* 11), their governor; while Strabo places them in Anti-Lebanon with their centre at Chalcis in the Beka'. This evidence appears to prove Schürer's conclusion, that Anti-Lebanon and the valley to the east was the centre of the Ituræans just before and at the beginning of the Christian era; and Ramsay's contention, that 'the true home of such a race is *not* the long-settled and well-governed land between Lebanon and Anti-Lebanon,' conflicts not only with the data of classical writers, but with the constant proof of how rich lands in Syria were being overrun and occupied by nomadic tribes from the desert. It is probable, however, that the Ituræans extended their influence eastwards and south-eastwards from Anti-Lebanon. About B.C. 25 Zenodorus leased the domains of Lysanias, whom Dio Cassius (xlix. 32) calls king of the Ituræans, and Zenodorus' territory included Ulatha, Paneas, and the country round about. The question remains, whether the 'Ituræan region' extended so far as to include or overlap Trachonitis, the country around the Trachons, one of which is the modern Lejá. Ramsay maintains that, both according to St. Luke's statement and as a matter of fact, it did. But of the latter there is absolutely no evidence before Eusebius in the 4th cent., and in face of such silence his testimony about the east of the Jordan in the beginning of the 1st cent. cannot be allowed to prevail. In the absence of evidence, the following facts are all we have to go by. Names have been constantly in drift in that part of Syria, and as Philo extended over all Philip's tetrarchy the name of its eastern portion Trachonitis (*Legat. ad Gaium,* 41) it is possible that the adjective 'Ituræan' may likewise have been sometimes extended eastward so as to cover Trachonitis, especially as the Ituræans themselves were probably driven in that direction after the Romans took their Lebanon territory from them. At the same time, Strabo, writing after this was accomplished, still treats of Ituræa and Trachonitis as distinct. Whether, therefore, St. Luke meant by his phrase τῆς Ἰτουραίας καὶ Τραχωνίτιδος χώρας 'two distinct portions of Philip's tetrarchy or two equivalent or overlapping names for it; and whether on either of these interpretations of his words he was correct —are questions to which the geographical data of

---

* Cf. Arrian, *Al. An.* 18: οἱ πεζοὶ τοξόται οἱ τῶν Νομάδων καὶ Κυρηναίων, καὶ Βοσπορανῶν τι καὶ Ἰτουραίων.

the 1st cent. supply us with no certain answer.'* Besides the literature quoted above, see the present writer's *HGHL* 544 ff., and *Expositor*, 1894, viii. 406, ix. 51 ff., 143 ff., 231 ff., 331 f.

G. A. SMITH.

IVORY (שֵׁן *shēn*, ἐλεφάντινος).—The word *shēn* signifies a *tooth*, and is freq. employed in its orig. sense in OT (Ex 21²⁴, Lv 24²⁰ etc.). It is also freq. used in the sense of *ivory*, as being the *elephant's tooth* (AVm 1 K 10²² ; see שֶׁנְהַבִּים under ELEPHANT). Once ivory is spoken of as ' horns of teeth,' קַרְנוֹת שֵׁן (Ezk 27¹⁵). The word *horns* alludes to the shape of the tusk, but its construction with teeth shows that the Hebrews understood what ivory really was. The context always makes it clear when *shēn* should be rendered *ivory*.

In Ps 45⁸ הֵיכְלֵי שֵׁן prob. refers to *palaces* or *chambers* in them, inlaid with ivory (cf. בָּתֵּי הַשֵּׁן Am 3¹⁵, and בֵּית הַשֵּׁן 1 K 22³⁹). Chambers with elaborate panellings of ivory and ebony exist in Damascus and other cities of the East to-day. Tables, stands, screens, picture-frames, pipes, and many other articles, inlaid with ivory, mother-of-pearl, silver and gold, are found in the houses of well-to-do people in the East. Solomon imported large quantities of ivory (1 K 10²²). His throne was made of it (1 K 10¹⁸⁻²⁰). It was also used for making or inlaying couches (Am 6⁴), and the benches of galleys (Ezk 27⁶).

The Egyp. and Assyr. monuments allude to the trade in ivory, and porters bearing tusks are figured on them. Among the merchandise of Babylon (Rev 18¹²) were vessels of ivory. It was probably brought to Pal. by the caravans (' travelling companies ') of Dedanîm (Is 21¹³), as well as the ships of Tarshish (1 K 10²²). The ' tower of ivory ' (Ca 7⁴) may have been a tower richly ornamented with this substance, or a figure to illustrate the whiteness of the bride's neck, as we say ' a snowy neck,' or ' an alabaster arm.'

G. E. POST.

IVVAH (עַוָּה ; LXX variants are numerous, see Swete).—According to 2 K 18³⁴ (wanting in B of LXX), 19¹³ (=Is 37¹³ ; the name is wanting in both MT and LXX of Is 36¹⁹) a city conquered by the Assyrians, named along with Sepharvaim and Hena. It is frequently identified with **Avva** (עַוָּא), whence, according to 2 K 17²⁴, Sargon (but see Winckler, *Alttest. Untersuchungen*, 100 ff.) brought colonists to Samaria. Regarding Avva no information is to be gathered from the inscriptions (Schrader, *KAT* ² 281, 384 [*COT* ² i. 273, ii. 8]). Hommel (*Expos. Times*, April, 1898, p. 330 f.) supports the view that Hena and Ivvah (or, as he prefers, Avvah) are not places at all, but the names of the two chief gods of the three Syrian cities, Hamath, Arpad, and Sepharvaim. (For the grounds of this conclusion and the various stages through which he holds the MT to have passed before reaching its present form in 2 K 17³⁰ᶠ, see the article just cited). Winckler (*op. cit.*), on the other hand, considers that the parallelism, not to speak of other reasons, requires in 2 K 18³⁴ 19¹³ (=Is 37¹³) *one* place name, which, judging from the variety of LXX readings, has

* The identification of the name Jetur or Ituræan with the modern Jedur (*i.e.* Gedur) to the S. of Damascus, is philologically impossible.

been ill preserved, but may have been **Avvah** or **Ivvah**, and must have designated a city coming within the sphere of vision of the Jews—probably situated, like Sepharvaim, in Syria.

J. A. SELBIE.

IVY (κισσος, *hedera*).—This plant was sacred to Bacchus. The Jews were compelled, at the time of the feast of this god, to carry ivy in procession in his honour (2 Mac 6⁷). The ' corruptible crown ' (1 Co 9²⁵) of the Isthmian games was sometimes made of its leaves, at other times it was a garland of pine. The ivy, *Hedera Helix*, L., grows wild in Pal. and Syria, and climbs up the faces of the cliffs along the coast and to the middle zone of the mountain ranges.

G. E. POST.

IYE-ABARIM (עִיֵּי הָעֲבָרִים ' Iyim of the regions beyond,' distinguishing this place from the Iim of Jos 15²⁹).—The station following Oboth mentioned in Nu 21¹¹ 33⁴⁴ and described (21¹¹) as ' in the wilderness which is before Moab toward the sunrising,' and more briefly (33⁴⁴) as ' in the border of Moab.' Nothing is known , as to its position beyond these indications. The versions, though affording no geographical information, are interesting in their various renderings of the first word ; the LXX of 21¹¹ has Χαλγαει B, with a variant Ἀχελγαι in A, and (perhaps) F, and in 33⁴⁴· ⁴⁵ Γαι. The Syriac takes the word as עַיִן ' fountain,' Targ. Onk. has מגוח as its equivalent in 21¹¹ and 33⁴⁴, and in 33⁴⁵. This word is used for a ford or passage in Targ. of 1 S 13²³ 14⁴, and in Targ. Jon. of Gn 32²². See, further, Dillm. on Nu 21¹⁰.

A. T. CHAPMAN.

IYIM (עִיִּים ' heaps ' or ' ruins ').—**1.** Short form of **Iye-abarim** in Nu 33⁴⁵. See Iye-abarim for renderings of the VSS. **2.** Jos 15²⁹ (AV and RV incorrectly **Iim**), a town in Judah, one of the ' uttermost cities toward the border of Edom.' The LXX has Βακώκ B ; Αὐείμ A, reading עיים ; and Syr. reads עלין.

IYYAR (אִיָּר, Ἰάρ).—See TIME.

IZHAR (יִצְהָר ' fresh oil ' or ' shining ').—Son of Kohath the son of Levi, Ex 6¹⁸· ²¹, Nu 3¹⁹ 16¹ P, 1 Ch 6². ¹⁸· ³⁸ 23¹²· ¹⁸ ; patron. **Izharites**, Nu 3²⁷, 1 Ch 24²² 26²³· ²⁹.

IZLIAH (יִזְלִיאָה, AV Jezliah).—A Benjamite, head of a ' father's house,' 1 Ch 8¹⁸. See GENEALOGY.

IZRAHIAH (יִזְרַחְיָה ' J″ will arise *or* shine ').—A chief of the tribe of Issachar, 1 Ch 7³. See GENEALOGY.

IZRAHITES (הַיִּזְרָח).—Gentilic name in 1 Ch 27⁸, but should probably be read הַזַּרְחִי, which is possibly another form of הַזַּרְחִי **Zerahites** vv.¹¹· ¹³. See GENEALOGY.

IZRI (יִצְרִי).—Chief of one of the Levitical choirs, 1 Ch 25¹¹, called in v.³ **Zeri**. See GENEALOGY.

IZZIAH (יִזִּיָּה ' J″ will sprinkle ' ?) AV **Jeziah.**—One of those who had married a foreign wife (Ezr 10²⁵), called in 1 Es 9²⁶ **Ieddias.** See GENEALOGY.

J

J.—The symbol used by critics for the Jahwistic document. See HEXATEUCH.

JAAKAN.—See BEEROTH-BENE-JAAKAN.

JAAKOBAH (יַעֲקֹבָה).—A Simeonite prince, 1 Ch 4³⁶. See GENEALOGY.

JAALA (יַעְלָא Neh 7⁵⁸) or **JAALAH** (יַעְלָה Ezr 2⁵⁶).—The name of a family of the 'sons of Solomon's servants' who returned to Palestine with Zerubbabel. In 1 Es 5³³ Jeeli. See GENEALOGY.

JAAR (יַעַר).—Usually in OT a common noun, meaning forest or wooded height, e.g. Jos 17¹⁵, Hos 2¹⁴. Once only as proper name, RVm of Ps 132⁶ 'We found it in the field of Jaar.' Here, according to some of the best authorities, it is a poetical name for Kiriath-jearim, 'forest town,' cf. Ps 78¹² 'field of Zoan.' The name of this place appears in several forms, as Jos 15⁹·⁶⁰, 2 S 6², and in 1 Ch 13⁵ an account is given of the bringing up of the ark from Kiriath-jearim, where it had lain for twenty years after its restoration by the Philistines. The rendering of this obscure verse,—conjectured to be a fragment of antique song,—which was first suggested by Kühnöl, and has been adopted by Delitzsch, Perowne, and most moderns, would make it run thus: 'We heard of it (the ark) as being at Ephrathah, we found it in the field of Jaar (i.e. Kiriath-jearim).' Baethgen, however, understands the word as an appellative, 'auf waldigem Gefilde' (cf. LXX ἐν ταῖς δασέσι τοῦ δρυμοῦ, and Jerome 'in regione saltus'; so RV (text) 'in the field of the wood'), referring 'it' to the oath of David quoted in vv.³⁻⁵, reading 'published' (הוֹצֵאנוּה) for 'found' (מְצָאנוּה), and supposing the 'wooded field' to be a poetical designation of the country at large. Similarly Ew. (so Targ.), though he explains the 'field of the wood' of Lebanon as representing N. Palestine. However, the general drift of the reference to the ark can hardly be mistaken.
W. T. DAVISON.

JAARE-OREGIM (יַעֲרֵי אֹרְגִים; BA 'Αριωργείμ, other MSS 'Αρωρί; saltus polymitarius), according to 2 S 21¹⁹, a Beth-lehemite, the father of Elhanan, who slew Goliath the Gittite. It is, however, highly probable that the text is corrupt, the former part of the name being a mistake for JAIR (יָעִר for יָעִר), while the latter half (אֹרְגִים oregim=weavers) has been accidentally repeated from the following line. This view, which is supported by the parallel passage 1 Ch 20⁵ (Kerê יָעִר בֶּן=son of Jair; Kethibh בֶּן יָעִר), has been adopted by Thenius, Wellh., Driver, and Budde. Klostermann, following the reading of Lucian ('Ελλανὰν υἱὸς 'Ιαδδεὶν υἱοῦ τοῦ 'Ελεμί), prefers to restore 'the son of Dodai the Beth-lehemite' (בֶּן דּוֹדִי בֵּית הַלַּחְמִי, cf. 2 S 23²⁴). The rendering of the Peshiṭta (ܡܚܠܟ ܐܣܬܘ), probably points to the same text as the Hebrew (omitting Jaare), though the Arabic, which is based upon it, takes the second word (ܡܚܠܟ = doctus) as a proper name (Malaph). Similarly the Targum of Jonathan hardly presupposes a different text, since its rendering 'and David the son of Jesse, the weaver of the veils of the house of the sanctuary, who was of Bethlehem, slew Goliath the Gittite' (וקטל דוד בר ישי מחי פרוכתא בית מקדשא דמבית לחם דמן בית לחם), is an obvious attempt at harmonizing the present text with 1 S 17. Jerome seems to

have read יַעַר=saltus, instead of יָעֲרֵי (Jaare), and so far confirms the reading of 1 Ch 20⁵. For a further discussion of the relation of 1 Ch 20⁵ to 1 S 17 and to 2 S 21¹⁹, see SAMUEL (BOOKS OF), and ELHANAN.
J. F. STENNING.

JAARESHIAH (יַעֲרֶשְׁיָה, perhaps = 'J" fattens,' AV Jaresiah).—A Benjamite chief, 1 Ch 8²⁷.

JAASIEL (יַעֲשִׂיאֵל).—The 'ruler' of Benjamin, 1 Ch 27²¹, prob. = 'J. the Mezobaite' (which see) of 11⁴⁷.

JAASU (יַעְשׂוּ Ezr 10³⁷ Kethibh) or **JAASAI** (יַעֲשָׂי Kerê, so RVm), AV Jaasau.—One of those who had married foreign wives in the time of Ezra. LXX, regardless of the meaning, rendered καὶ ἐποίησαν ('and they did '), i.e. וַיַּעְשׂוּ for יַעְשׂוּ.

JAAZANIAH (יַאֲזַנְיָהוּ 2 K 25²³, Ezk 8¹¹; יַאֲזַנְיָה Jer 35³, Ezk 11¹, 'J" hears.' See also JEZANIAH. LXX 4 K 25²³, Β 'Οζονίας, A. Luc. 'Ιεζονίας, Ezk 8¹¹ 11¹, Jer 42³ [Heb. 35³], Β 'Ιεχονίας).—**1.** A Judæan, styled 'son of the Maacathite,' one of the military commanders who came to Mizpah to give in their allegiance to Gedaliah, the governor of Judah appointed by Nebuchadrezzar (2 K 25²³=Jer 40⁸ Jezaniah). After Ishmael, son of Nethaniah, had murdered Gedaliah, and carried captive the Judæans who were left at Mizpah, Jaazaniah, though not mentioned by name, appears to have joined with the other captains of the forces in giving battle to Ishmael and recovering the captives (Jer 41¹ff). Probably also he was one of those who determined, against the advice of the prophet Jeremiah, to abandon the land of Judah, and to lead the remnant of the people down into Egypt (Jer 42). **2.** A chieftain of the clan of the Rechabites, whose fidelity to the commands of his ancestor Jonadab was tested by the prophet Jeremiah as an example to the people of Judah (Jer 35³). **3.** Son of Shaphan, who appeared in Ezekiel's vision as ringleader of seventy of the elders of Israel in the practice of secret idolatry at Jerusalem (Ezk 8¹¹). **4.** Son of Azzur, one of the princes of the people at Jerusalem, against whose counsels Ezekiel was commanded by J" to prophesy (Ezk 11¹ff).
C. F. BURNEY.

JAAZIAH (יַעֲזִיָּהוּ).—A son of Merari, 1 Ch 24²⁶·²⁷. The text is hopelessly corrupt. (Cf. Berth. and Oettli, ad loc.; Kittel's proposed restoration of the text and note in Haupt's Sacred Books of OT; and Kautzsch's AT, ad loc.). See GENEALOGY.

JAAZIEL (יַעֲזִיאֵל).—A Levite skilled in the use of the psaltery, 1 Ch 15¹⁸, called in v.²⁰ Aziel. Kittel (see note, ad loc., in Haupt's SBOT) would correct the text in both instances to עֻזִּיאֵל Uzziel.

JABAL (יָבָל, LXX A 'Ιωβέλ, E 'Ιωβήδ, Luc. 'Ιωβήλ).—Son of Lamech by Adah, and originator of the nomadic form of life, Gn 4²⁰ (J). See König in Expos. Times, May, 1898, p. 347ª. The meaning of the name is quite uncertain; for conjectures see Dillm. ad loc. and Ball in SBOT.

JABBOK (יַבֹּק, 'Ιαβόκ).—One of the principal rivers of E. Palestine, now called Wady Zerḳa from the bluish colour of its water. Its course may be indicated thus: take on a map a point 18 miles E. of the Jordan on the latitude of Nâblus, and from it draw a line 18 miles long due south. On this line as diameter, and to the E. of it, draw a semicircle; and from the N. end of its diameter (the point originally taken) draw a line inclining slightly to the S. as far as the edge of the Jordan valley (here about 5 miles from the river); and from that edge draw a line in a S.W. direction to the Jordan. The figure will give approximately the course of Wady Zerka, though in its numerous windings it continually deviates from the outline figure above indicated. In its upper semicircular portion it forms a boundary between east and west; while in its lower portion it forms a boundary between north and south. These two portions are referred to in Nu 21²⁴, where the territory of Sihon is described as extending 'from Arnon unto Jabbok, even unto the children of Ammon'; *i.e.* the lower portion of the Jabbok formed the N. boundary, while the upper portion formed the E. boundary of Sihon's kingdom; and the verse may be made clear by inserting 'northwards' after Jabbok and 'eastwards' after Ammon. The upper portion is referred to in Dt 2³⁷, where the border of the children of Ammon is described as 'all the side of the river Jabbok.' The river Jabbok is also mentioned as a boundary Dt 3¹⁶, Jos 12², Jg 11¹³·²².

One remarkable incident in the patriarchal narratives is connected with this river. Jacob, after sending all that he had over the stream, was left alone to wrestle with the mysterious visitor, and to prevail (Gn 32²⁴ᶠ· referred to in Hos 12⁴). The Heb. word for wrestling (from the root אבק), which is used only here, is similar in sound to *Jabbok*, and it is intended that the name of the river should call to mind this instance of favour shown to the ancestor of the chosen race. A probable derivation of the word is from the root פקק 'pour out.' The river Jabbok is mentioned only in connexion with Jacob, and as a boundary existing at the time of Israel's appearance E. of Jordan, in the passages already noted.   A. T. CHAPMAN.

JABESH (יָבֵשׁ).—Father of Shallum, who usurped the kingdom of Israel by the assassination of king Zechariah (2 K 15¹⁰·¹³·¹⁴).

JABESH-GILEAD (יָבֵשׁ גִּלְעָד, also יָבֵשׁ or יָבֵישׁ alone in 1 S 11¹·³·⁵·⁹·¹⁰ 31¹²·¹³, 1 Ch 10¹²).—While the history of this East Jordan city as furnished in the Bible is meagre, it gives us vivid pictures of both tragic and tender scenes in ancient Hebrew life. In the early period of Jewish history it seems to have been prominent, and later to have fallen into insignificance. Its first appearance is when the Israelites are said to have made a raid upon it with a powerful force, put all the males and married women to death, destroyed the city, and carried off 400 virgins, who became wives to the Benjamites (Jg 21). Afterwards, when it had regained its position of importance, it was attacked by the Ammonites under Nahash, when Saul, to whom the inhabitants appealed for succour, came quickly with his army and utterly routed the enemy (1 S 11). Later, when Saul and his sons were slain in the disaster at Mount Gilboa, and their bodies were being ill-treated by the Philistine conquerors, the men of Jabesh-gilead rushed into the face of death, recovered the bodies, and saw that they were cared for in the kindest manner and buried with proper honours (1 S 31). David, when he was made king at Hebron, remembered this act, and sent special messengers with commendatory blessings to the men of Jabesh-gilead for their heroic devotion to Saul (2 S 2⁵). Subsequently the bones of Saul and his sons were brought thence by David and buried in the territory of Benjamin (2 S 21¹²⁻¹⁴).

No doubt the name Jabesh is preserved in the modern *Yabis*, and when on the line of this stream in the Gilead hills is one is near the site of this ancient city. Robinson (*BRP*² iii. 319 f.) suggested a place, *ed-Deir*, lying south of Wady Yabis; but this has no ancient ruins, and, besides, it is some distance off the main road. From researches made in this region by the present writer, a more appropriate place would seem to be *Miryamin*, a point north of Wady Yabis on the ancient road leading over the mountain, where there are massive ancient remains. This is about 7 miles from Pella, and corresponds to the statement of Eusebius in his *Onomasticon* (268. 81), our best authority in the absence of any special biblical indications as to its site (Merrill, *East of the Jordan*, p. 439).
S. MERRILL.

JABEZ (יַעְבֵּץ).—A descendant of Judah, who was 'more honourable than his brethren.' His name is traced to the fact that his mother bare him with *sorrow* (בְּעֹצֶב '*ōzeb*), 1 Ch 4⁹. The same play upon words recurs in his prayer or vow in the expression לְבִלְתִּי עָצְבִּי 'that it be not to my *sorrow*,' v.¹⁰. (On the correctness of MT see Kittel's note, *ad loc.*, in Haupt's *SBOT*, and on the possibility of a clause having dropped out, Kautzsch, *ad loc.*, in his *AT*).
J. A. SELBIE.

JABEZ (יַעְבֵּץ).—A place inhabited by scribes, apparently in Judah, 1 Ch 2⁵⁵. The site is unknown.

JABIN (יָבִין 'discerning,' Ἰαβείν, Ἰαβείς).—**1.** King of Hazor in N. Palestine, defeated by Joshua at the Waters of Merom [Jos 11¹⁻⁹ (JE) ¹⁰⁻¹⁵ (D²)].
2. Jabin, 'king of Canaan, that reigned in Hazor,' occurs again in Jg 4. He takes no part in the battle of the Kishon, nor is he mentioned in the ancient song (Jg 5). The introduction of Jabin and of Hazor into this narrative creates many difficulties, and the title 'king of Canaan' arouses suspicion. The probability is that two traditions relating to Jabin and Sisera have been united, and harmonized by making Sisera the captain of Jabin's host (cf. Ps 83⁹·¹⁰, which implies the union of the two traditions). The Jabin tradition probably preserved an account of the early struggles of Naphtali and Zebulun for their territory in the north. The two clans had made Kedesh their headquarters, and successfully defeated Jabin king of Hazor, who had combined with the neighbouring Canaanites to resist the intruders. This tradition forms the basis of the battle of Merom in Jos 11, which has been generalized by the Deut. redactor, and treated as the conquest of N. Palestine by Joshua and all Israel.   G. A. COOKE.

JABNEEL (יַבְנְאֵל 'El causeth to build,' B Λεμνά, A Ἰαβνήλ, for other forms see below; in Apocr. Ἰαμνεία or -*la* or -νν-, *Jebneel, Jabnia, Jamnia*).—**1.** A town on the northern border of Judah, near the sea, mentioned after Ekron, Shikkeron, and Mount Baalah (Jos 15¹¹). It is not mentioned in the lists of cities of Judah, Dan, or Simeon in the Bk. of Joshua, but in Jos 15⁴⁶ LXX substitutes Γεμνά (B) or Ἰεμναί (A), Jabneh, for MT וְיַמָּה 'even unto the sea.' It does not appear again in the OT until 2 Ch 26⁶, where under the name of **Jabneh** (יַבְנֶה, LXX B Ἀβεννήρ, A Ἰαβείς) it is captured along with Gath and Ashdod from the Philistines by king Uzziah, and its wall broken down. Josephus (*Ant.* v. i. 22) describes it as belonging to the tribe of Dan, in company with Gath and Ekron, and mentions it with the inland towns Marissa and Ashdod in contradistinction to the maritime towns Gaza, Joppa, and Dora (*Ant.* XIV. iv. 4; *BJ* I. vii. 7). It is spoken of (Jth 2²⁸) under the name of *Jemnaan* as in fear and dread of Holofernes. Under the name **Jamnia** (1 Mac 4¹⁵ 5⁵⁸ 10⁶⁹ 15⁴⁰) it is referred to as a garrison, with plains near it, Gorgias in command (*Ant.* XII. viii. 6). In 2 Mac 12⁸·⁹·⁴⁰

Judas Maccabæus set fire to the haven and navy of Jamnia, so that the light of the fire was seen at Jerusalem, 240 furlongs off. Pliny (*HN* v. 13) speaks of the two Jamnias 'Jamnes duæ, altera intus,' and places them between Azotus and Joppa. See Reland, *Pal.* p. 823. Ptolemy (v. 16) speaks of the port of the Jamnites between Azotus and Joppa, and subsequently mentions Jamnia among the cities of Judæa.

In common with Ashkelon, Azotus, and Gaza, the harbour or naval arsenal of Jamnia bore the name of *Majumas* (Reland, p. 590 f.; Raumer, Kenrick, *Phœnicia*; Le Quien, *Oriens Christ.*). Jamnia was taken from the Syrians (c. B.C. 142) by Simon Maccabæus (*Ant.* XIII. vi. 7; *BJ* I. ii. 2), and it was restored (B.C. 63) to its inhabitants by Pompey (*Ant.* XIV. iv. 4); it was repaired or rebuilt (c. B.C. 57) by Gabinius (*BJ* I. viii. 4), and was given to the Jews by Augustus (B.C. 30). Herod bequeathed (B.C. 4) Jamnia (*Ant.* XVII. viii. 1) to Salome his sister, and she left it with all its toparchy to Julia the wife of Augustus Cæsar (*Ant.* XVIII. ii. 2; *BJ* II. ix. 1). Philo Judæus (*de Legat. ad Gaium*, Opp. vol. ii. p. 575) states that in this town, the most populous of Judæa, a Roman officer named Capito raised an altar of mud for the deification of the emperor Caligula; the Jews demolished the altar, and the incensed emperor forthwith ordered an equestrian statue of himself to be erected in the Holy of Holies at Jerusalem (c. A.D. 37). Strabo (Bk. 16, 'Syria') states that *Iamneia* and the settlements around were so populous that they could furnish 40,000 soldiers. The Talmud abounds with references to the learned Rabbins who frequented the school at Jamnia. Milman (*Hist. of Jews*) states that it contained a school of Jewish learning which obtained great authority, and whether from the rank and character of its head, or from the assemblage of many of the members of the ancient Sanhedrin, who formed a sort of community in that place, it was looked upon with great respect and veneration by the Jews who remained in Palestine. This school was subsequently suppressed by the Romans, owing to the imprudent speeches of the fiery Simon ben-Jochai. Before the destruction of Jerusalem by Titus, according to Jewish tradition the Sanhedrin escaped the general wreck. Before the formation of the siege, it had followed Gamaliel, its Nasi, or Prince, to Jabneh (Jamnia; Milman, *Hist. of Jews*). According to tradition also, the great Gamaliel was buried in Jamnia, and his tomb was visited by Parchi in the 14th cent. In the time of Eusebius, Jamnia was but a small place of little importance. It gave a bishop to the Council of Nicæa, and had still a bishop in the time of the emperor Justinian (Epiph. *adv. Hær.* ii. 730).

The Crusaders found the ruins called *Ibelin* (A.D. 1144, William of Tyre), where they built the fortress Ibelin (corrupted from Jabneel), mistaking it for Gath, and it gave its name to the French family of d'Ibelin, one of whom, Jean, count of Jaffa and Ashkelon, restored (c. 1255) the famous code of the 'Assises of Jerusalem,' originally composed by Godfrey de Bouillon (Gibbon, ch. 58; Samut. l. iii. p. xii, c. 58). Benjamin of Tudela (c. A.D. 1163) identified Ibelin, three parasangs south of Jaffa, as the ancient Jabneh, and states that the site of the schools might still be traced there (*Early Travels*, p. 87). The *Itin. Ant.* places Jamnia 12 MP. from Diospolis (Lydda) and Joppa, 20 MP. from Ashkelon, and 36 MP. from Gaza. It was on the old road from Joppa to Ashkelon, through Jamnia and Azotus (*Peutinger Tables*); another road led to it from Diospolis.

The modern village of *Yebnah* stands on the ruins of the town of Jamnia. It occupies a strong site, 170 ft. above the sea, on an isolated rounded hill, south of the Wady Rûbîn, in the position assigned to it by the *Itin. Ant.*, and the old road from Jaffa to Ashkelon passes by it. The houses are of mud, but there are interesting ruins of a church and also of a mosque erected by Crusaders and Saracens. The ancient *Majumas* or harbour of Jamnia is situated immediately south of the mouth of the Wady Rûbîn. The port seems to have been double, and entered by narrow passages as at Tyre and Jaffa. The northern bay is some 400 paces across (north and south), flanked with a rocky promontory on each side. The southern bay is larger, and on the promontory south of it are the ruins of ed-Dubbeh. A large reef is visible outside, beneath the water (*SWP* vol. ii. p. 269). The port would seem to be naturally better than any along the coast of Palestine south of Cæsarea. A very little trouble in clearing a passage through the reefs would probably render the *Minet Rûbîn* a better port than Jaffa, as the reefs are farther from the beach (Conder, *PEFSt*, 1875, p. 168). The harvests about Yebnah are very abundant, and the ground is of surprising fertility (*Land and Book*). The present writer (*PEFSt*, 1875, p. 181) suggests that *Yebnah* or *Ibnah* may be the modern equivalent of **Libnah** as well as Jabneel. Libnah was given over to the priests, the sons of Aaron (Jos 21[13], 1 Ch 6[57]), within the boundary of the tribe of Judah, and has not been identified, though supposed to be near Beersheba. Both Jabneh (Jos 15[11] B) and Libnah appear as Λεμνά in the LXX.

LITERATURE.—Le Quien, *Oriens Christ.* vol. iii.; *Itin. Ant.*; *Onom. s.v.* 'Ιαμνία; Irby and Mangles, *Travels*; Lightfoot, *Opp.*; Milman, *Hist. of Jews*; Sepp, *Jer. u. das HL*; Strabo; Pliny; Philo, *de Legat. ad Gaium*; Epiphanius, *adv. Hær.* lib. ii. 730; Grätz, *Gesch. der Juden*; Neubauer, *Géog. du Talm.* 73 ff.; Schürer, *HJP* II. i. 78 f.; Guérin, *Judée*, ii. 55 ff.

2. (B Ἰεφθαμαί, A Ἰαβνήλ, *Jabnæel*). It appears in Jos 19[33] in connexion with Adami-nekeb and Lakkum as part of the northern boundary of Naphtali, Lakkum being near the Jordan. There is no clue to identifying its position. Conder (*Handbook to the Bible*, p. 269) gives the following identifications to the places in Jos 19[33]:—

Heleph is probably Beit Lîf, at the edge of the higher mountains towards the west. Adami is the ruin Adain; Nekeb (the Talmudic Tziidetha, Talm. Jerus. *Megillah* i. 1) is the ruin Seiyâdeh; Jabneel (the Caphar Yama of the Talmud) is *Yemma*, 7 miles south of Tiberias in Naphtali (*SWP* i. p. 365). The *Variorum Bible*, however, gives 'Adami-hannekeb,' *i.e.* 'Adami in the pass.' Schwarz (p. 144) places Kefr Yamah ('the village by the sea') on the southern shore of the Sea of Galilee; and Neubauer (*Géog. du Talmud*, p. 225) places it between Tabor and the Sea of Galilee, thus apparently agreeing with Conder in the identification of *Yemma* as Jabneel. Josephus speaks of 'Ιαμνεία (*Vita*, 37) or 'Ιαμνίθ (*BJ* II. xx. 6) as a rocky fastness in Upper Galilee which he fortified, together with Meroth, Achabari, and Seph (cf. *BJ* II. vi. 3).

C. WARREN.

JABNEH.—See JABNEEL.

JACAN (יַעְכָּן).—A Gadite chief, 1 Ch 5[13], AV **Jachan.** See GENEALOGY.

JACHIN (יָכִין).—**1.** Fourth son of Simeon, Gn 46[10], Ex 6[15]. In 1 Ch 4[24] he is called **Jarib** (יָרִיב), but Kittel corrects this to Jachin. In Nu 26[12] the patronymic **Jachinites** occurs. **2.** Eponym of a priestly family, 1 Ch 9[10], Neh 11[10]. See GENEALOGY.

JACHIN.—One of the brazen pillars erected in front of Solomon's temple, that on the right (looking eastward) or south of the porch, see 1 K 7[21], 2 Ch 3[17], Jer 52[21]. See for particulars BOAZ and TEMPLE.

JACINTH (ὑάκινθος, *hyacinthus*), one of the foundation stones of the New Jerusalem (Rev 21²⁰), RVm 'sapphire.' The uncertainty which surrounds the real meaning of many of the precious stones named in the Bible applies also to the jacinth; this was inevitable in an age when the principles of chemistry and crystallography were unknown. According to C. W. King (*Nat. Hist. of Gems*, p. 167), the jacinth comes to us from the Italian *giacinto*, and this from the Latin *hyacinthus*. In mediæval times the jacinth seems to have been a gem of a yellow colour, but sometimes tinged blue or purple:—characteristics which belong to varieties of quartz, such as the cairngorm and amethyst; and it was frequently employed by the Greeks for intagli in early times, and by the Romans for cameos. According to Pliny (*HN* xxi. 26), 'Hyacinthus in Gallia eximiè provenit. Hoc ibi pro cocco hysginum tingitur.' The dye *hysginum* is usually translated 'blue.'

The modern hyacinth includes the bright-red varieties of zircon; a silicate of zirconia with a little oxide of iron. It crystallizes in the form of a square prism or octahedron, and is found at Assouān on the Nile, Auvergne, Bohemia, and other volcanic countries. Large crystals have been obtained from Siberia and Ceylon.

E. HULL.

JACKAL.—This word is not found in the text of AV. It occurs in text of RV as the equivalent of *tannîm* (Is 34¹³, Jer 9¹¹ 10²² 49³³ 51³⁷, Mic 1⁸), which is tr. AV 'dragon.' We prefer in these passages the tr. *wolves* (see DRAGON 1). In one passage (Jer 14⁶) RV text tr. *tannîm*, 'jackals,' marg. 'the crocodile,' AV text 'dragons.' In two places (Is 13²² 34¹⁴) אִיִּים *'iyyîm* is wrongly trᵈ in AV 'wild beasts of the islands,' RV 'wolves.' The word *'iyyîm*, however, is etymologically equivalent to the Arab. *benât-âwa*, which means *jackals*. We think, therefore, that it should be so trᵈ here. If our views are accepted, the first passage would read 'and the jackals (*'iyyîm*) shall cry in their castles, and the wolves (*tannîm*) in their pleasant palaces,' and the second (including latter clause of v.¹³) 'an habitation for wolves (*tannîm*), a court for ostriches, and the wild beasts of the desert shall meet with the jackals (*'iyyîm*).'

Jackal also occurs in RVm as the equivalent of *shû'âl* (Jg 15⁴, Neh 4³, Ps 63¹⁰, La 5¹⁸), text AV and RV 'fox.' See Moore on Jg 15⁴, and art. FOX, p. 64ᵃ, where the meaning of *shû'âl* is more fully discussed.

G. E. POST.

JACOB (יַעֲקֹב, 'supplanter' [see below]; Ιακωβ).— **1.** Son of Isaac and Rebekah, also called *Israel*, the father of the twelve patriarchs, who were the reputed ancestors of the twelve tribes of Israel. The history of Jacob is contained in parts of Gn 25²¹–50¹³,—the narrative being chiefly JE, the passages (so far as they relate to Jacob) which belong to P being 25²⁶ᵇ 26³⁴. ³⁵ 27⁴⁶–28⁹ 29²⁴. ²⁹ 31¹⁸ᵇ (from 'and all'), 33¹⁸ᵃ 34 (partly: see below), 35⁹⁻¹³. ¹⁵. ²²ᵇ⁻²⁹ * 36 (in the main: v.⁶⁻⁷ in particular belong here), 37¹⁻²ᵃ (to 'Jacob'), 46⁶⁻²⁷ 47⁵⁻⁶ᵃ (to 'dwell'), 7⁻¹¹. ²⁷ᵇ (from 'and they'), ²⁸ 48³⁻⁶. ⁷ 49¹ᵃ (to 'sons'), ²⁸ᵇ (from 'and blessed them'), ²⁹⁻³³ 50¹². ¹³. As in most other places in Gn, P gives little more than a skeleton of the facts, the picturesque, lifelike narratives are almost entirely the work of J and E. J and E are here closely interwoven: the distinction between them will be noted where necessary; but in general these two narratives appear to have covered largely, when intact, the same ground, and, though exhibiting sometimes divergent traditions, to have been substantially similar in their contents.

The birth of Jacob is recounted in Gn 25²¹⁻²⁶.

* Perhaps also fragments in 30¹ᵃ. ⁴ᵃ. ⁹ᵇ. ²²ᵃ 35⁶.

Isaac must be pictured as still dwelling by the well Beer-lahai-roi, near Beersheba (25¹¹ᵇ); Rebekah, like Sarah before her, was barren; but in consequence of Isaac's prayer to J″, she became fruitful. The Hebrews loved to picture the characters and fortunes of the peoples with whom they were themselves acquainted, as foreshadowed in their ancestors (cf. Gn 9²⁵⁻²⁷ 16¹²): and in the case of the ancestors of Israel and Edom the rivalry which became such a marked feature in later generations, began even before their birth. The twin fathers of the two nations struggled together in the womb: their mother, concerned at such an ill-omened occurrence, went to inquire of J″,—we may suppose, at the sanctuary of Beersheba (21³³ 26²³⁻²⁵), — and received in answer the oracular declaration, couched in poetical form :—

Two nations are in thy womb,
And two peoples even from thy bowels shall be parted asunder ; *
And one people shall be stronger than the other people,
And the elder shall serve the younger.

When the time came for Rebekah to be delivered, the elder of the twins, we read, was born with the hand of the younger holding his heel,—*i.e.* endeavouring to hold him back, and to secure the first place for himself : so early did Jacob's characteristic nature display itself. From this circumstance, it is said, he was called *Jacob* (יַעֲקֹב), *i.e.* 'one who takes by the heel,' 'endeavours to trip up *or* supplant,' from עָקֵב 'a heel.'

This, at least, is the idea which the name *Jacob* suggested to the Hebrew ear. עָקַב is 'to take by the heel,' Hos 12³(4) (with allusion to the same occurrence), 'to trip up,' 'supplant,' fig. 'to defraud,' 'deceive,' Jer 9³(4), 'trust ye not in any brother, for every brother will utterly *supplant*, and every neighbour will go about with slanders'; עָקֹב Jer 17⁹ is 'deceitful,' and עֲקֻבָּה 2 K 10¹⁹ is 'subtilty.' It is another question whether this explanation expresses the actual meaning of the name. It has been supposed, for instance, that *Jacob* is really an elliptical form of *Ja‘kob'êl* : in this case *El*, 'God,' would be the subject of the verb (like *Ishmā'êl*, 'God heareth,' *Isrā'êl*, 'God persisteth,' *Yerahme'êl*, 'God is compassionate',)† and the word might be explained from the Arab. 'God follows,' or (from conj. IV.) 'God rewards.'‡ In fact there is now evidence that the name is much older than the date at which, according to the Biblical narrative, Jacob must have lived : Mr. Pinches has found on contract tablets of the age of Khammurabi (*c.* 2300 B.C.) the personal name *Ya'kub-ilu* (analogous to *Yashup-ilu, Yarbi-ilu, Yamlik-ilu, Yakbar-ilu*, etc., of the same age);§ and according to Hommel (*AHT* 203), the contracted form *Yakubu* occurs likewise. Further, in the lists of 118 places in Palestine conquered by Thothmes III. (B.C. 1503-1449, Sayce and Petrie), which are inscribed on the pylons of the temple at Karnak, there occur (Nos. 78 and 102) the names *Y-ša-p-'a-ra* and *Y-'-k-b-'â-rq*. These names (the Egyp. *r* standing, as is well known, also for *l*) can be only סְפָאל *Joseph-'êl* and עֲקֹבָאל *Jakob-'êl*; and we learn consequently that places bearing these names (cf. for the form the place-names *Jezre'el, Jabne'êl* Jos 15¹¹ [= *Jabneh* 2 Ch 26⁶], *Yiphtah'êl* Jos 19¹⁴. ²⁷, *Yekabze'êl* Neh 11²⁵, *Yirpe'êl* Jos 18²⁷) existed in Palestine, apparently in the central part, in the 15th cent. B.C.‖ What connexion, if any, exists between these names and those of the patriarchs, may never perhaps be ascertained ; but their existence at such a date in Palestine is remarkable. These facts, however, make it not improbable that (as had indeed been supposed even before their discovery ¶) names of the type *Jacob, Joseph, Jephthah*, etc., are elliptical forms of a more original *Jakob'êl, Joseph'êl*, etc. But, however that may be, to the Hebrews, as we know them, the idea which *Jacob* suggested, and in which it was supposed to have originated, was that of *supplanter*.

The boys grew up : Esau was a clever hunter, living in the open field ; Jacob was a 'plain man,' living in tents,' *i.e.* a quiet, home-loving man, pursuing the life of a shepherd among his tents

* *I.e.* shall take different courses (Gn 13¹¹) even from birth.
† Or, 'May God hear !' etc. (Gray, *Studies in Heb. Proper Names*, p. 218 ; Clermont-Ganneau, *Rev. Arch.* xxviii. (1896), p. 350.
‡ Baethgen, *Beiträge*, 158, who compares the Palmyrene name עתעקב, '‘Ate has rewarded' (or, as this sense does not appear to be found in Aramaic, '‘Ate follows,' or 'searches out'). The same root occurs also in the pr. names *'Akkub* (Ezr 2⁴² etc.), and the post-Bibl. *'Akabiah* (*Aboth*, iii. 1). 'May God supplant (our foes !)' would also be a possible explanation (Skipwith, *JQR* x. (1898), p. 667).
§ Hommel, *AHT* 61, 96, 112.
‖ See, further, Meyer, *ZATW*, 1886, p. 1 ff. ; W. M. Müller, *Asien u. Europa*, 162 ff. ; Gray, 214 f. ; Sayce, *HCM* 337 ff.
¶ Olshausen, *Lehrbuch* (1861), p. 617.

(cf. Gn 4[20]). An incident soon occurred, which displayed the contrasted characters of the two brothers. Esau returned one day exhausted from the chase : his brother was cooking pottage, and half fainting he asked to be allowed to swallow (הַלְעִיטֵנִי־נָא) a little. But Jacob saw his opportunity ; and did not scruple to make the most of it. ' Sell me first thy birthright,' he said. Esau, feeling in his exhaustion that his life depended upon it, too readily consented. Jacob, however, is still not fully satisfied ; and to make the compact more sure, obliges Esau to seal his promise with an oath. Thereupon he gives Esau the bread and pottage which he desired. The birthright, it need hardly be remarked, was a highly valued possession : it implied both a better position in the family, and also, ultimately, a larger inheritance, than fell to any of the other brothers (cf. 43[33] 48[13-20], Dt 21[17]). The narrator comments on the heedlessness with which Esau, thinking only of the moment, surrendered what would otherwise have been an inalienable right : the modern reader is more impressed by the avarice and selfishness shown by Jacob in taking such a mean advantage of his brother's need.

Gn 27[1-45] relates another characteristic incident in Jacob's life, and tells the story of the artifice by which, instigated by a designing mother, he deceives his aged father, and wrests from his brother his father's blessing. The narrative, which belongs chiefly, if not entirely, to J, is told with the picturesque detail and the psychological truth which that gifted narrator habitually displays. There is no need to repeat the details here : the vivid description of Rebekah's treacherous scheme for defeating her husband's purpose, of Jacob's too willing compliance when, with his usual caution, he has once satisfied himself that he can yield it safely, of the ready falsehood with which he allays his father's suspicions, of Isaac's dismay, and Esau's bitter cry of disappointment, when the truth is discovered, will be fresh in the memory of every reader. Only two or three points may be selected for comment. The contrasted blessings of Jacob and Esau express clearly the different geographical and political conditions of the countries owned afterwards by their respective descendants. Of Jacob, his father says :

> **27b** See, the smell of my son
>   Is as the smell of a field which Jehovah hath blessed :
> **28** And God give thee of the dew of heaven,
>   And of the fatness of the earth,
>   And plenty of corn and must :
> **29** Let peoples serve thee,
>   And nations bow down to thee :
>   Be lord over thy brethren,
>   And let thy mother's sons bow down to thee :
>   Cursed be every one that curseth thee,
>   And blessed be every one that blesseth thee.

In vv.[27b. 28] the poet thinks of the fruitful fields and vineyards of Canaan, watered by copious dews (Dt 33[28d]), and yielding in abundance ' corn and must,'—two of the three staple productions of Palestine, often mentioned together as a triad of blessings (Dt 7[13] 11[14] al. ; cf. 33[28c]) : in v.[29] he thinks further of the peoples of Canaan, subjugated under the Israelites, and of the neighbouring nations, Edomites, Moabites, and Ammonites,— all ' brothers,' or other near relations of Israel (Gn 19[37f.]),—made tributary by David (2 S 8). The ' blessing ' of Esau (vv.[39. 40]) is a very qualified one. Playing on the ambiguous sense of a Hebrew preposition,—which would more naturally mean *from* or *of* in a partitive sense (as v.[28]), but might also mean *away from*, if such a sense were favoured by the context,—the poet puts into the patriarch's mouth these words—

> **39b** Behold, (away) from the fatness of the earth shall be thy
>   dwelling,
>   And (away) from the dew of heaven above :

> **40** And by thy sword shalt thou live, and thou shalt serve thy
>   brother ;
>   And it shall come to pass, as thou roamest about at large,*
>   That thou shalt break his yoke from off thy neck.

The contrast to v.[28] is manifest. The reference is to the relatively rocky and arid territory of the Edomites, which obliged its inhabitants to find their livelihood elsewhere, by means of war and plunder. In v.[40] the doom of subjection to Jacob is not revoked ; but it is limited in duration : the time will come when, after repeated efforts,† Edom will regain its freedom. Edom revolted from Judah in the reign of Jehoram (2 K 8[20-22]) : no doubt, circumstances with which we are unacquainted,—perhaps a series of abortive efforts preceding the final success,—suggested the terms of v.[40b].

Jacob's treatment of his brother was followed by its natural consequences. Esau ' hated Jacob because of the blessing wherewith his father blessed him,' and only waited for his father's death in order to take vengeance on him. But his mother, Rebekah, ever watchful of the interests of her favourite son, urged him to flee forthwith to her brother Laban, in Ḥaran (across the Euphrates, on the Belikh, N.N.E. of Palestine), and to remain with him until Esau's resentment should have been dulled by time (27[42-45]).

At this point the compiler of the Book of Genesis has inserted a passage (27[46]–28[9]) from P, suggesting an entirely different motive for Jacob's visit—it is not here spoken of as a *flight*—to Laban. Esau, the same narrator had stated previously (26[34f.]), had, to his parents' great vexation, taken two ' Hittite ' wives ; and now Rebekah, fearful lest Jacob should do the same, mentions her apprehensions to Isaac, who thereupon charges Jacob to journey to Paddan-aram, and find there a wife among the daughters of his uncle Laban. Jacob obeys ; and departs accordingly with his father's blessing.‡ It is of course true that, *in itself*, this representation is not inconsistent with that in 27[42-45] : men notoriously act often under the influence of more motives than one ; and Rebekah may not have mentioned to Isaac her principal motive for wishing Jacob to leave his home. But presenting, as this paragraph does, all the literary marks of a hand different from the author of 27[1-45], there can be no doubt that it forms part of a different representation of the current of events.

28[10-22] § forms the true sequel of 27[1-45]. Jacob starts from Beersheba, on his journey to Haran. Travelling northwards through Canaan, he lights upon a spot where he passes the night. Even now the soil at Bethel is ' covered, as with gravestones, by large sheets of bare rocks, some few standing up here and there like cromlechs ' (Stanley, *S. and P.* 219), and the hill a little to the S.E. rises to its top in terraces of stone.‖ He dreams ; and in his dream the natural features of the locality shape themselves into a ' ladder,' or flight of stone steps, rising up to heaven ; angels are ascending and descending upon it ; and by his side ¶ (v.[13] RVm) stands J″, addressing him in words of encouragement and hope, promising him a countless posterity, who will possess the land on

---

* This, as Arabic shows, is the meaning of *rûd*, which occurs elsewhere in the OT only Jer 2[31b], Ps 55[3b] (Eng. 2[b] ; RV ' am restless '), Hos 11[12] (?) ; cf. מָרוּדִים La 17 3[19] (RVm), Is 58[7].

† Such seems to be the force of תָּרִיד כַּאֲשֶׁר : see Delitzsch.

‡ Notice, in the phrasing of 28[2. 4] the points of contact with previous promises or blessings in P : ' God Almighty,' as 17[1] al. ; ' make fruitful and multiply,' as 17[20] 48[4] (cf. 1[22. 28] 9[1. 7] 35[11]) ; ' company of peoples,' as 35[11] 48[4] ; ' land of thy sojournings,' as 17[8] (cf. 36[7] 37[1]). ' Paddan-aram,' also (for Aram-naharaim), as regularly in P (25[20] 31[18] 33[18] 35[9. 26] 46[15]).

§ 28[10. 13-16] seem to be from J ; 28[11. 12. 17-22] from E.

‖ In the *PEF Mem.* ii. 305, there is a view of a large ' gilgal, or circle of stones, near Bethel.

¶ Properly, ' (bending) over him.'

which he lies, and assuring him that He will be with him on his journeyings, and will bring him back in safety to the land he is leaving. The dream represents under a striking symbolism the thought that heaven and earth are connected, that an ever-present providence watches over the destinies of men, and also, in particular, that this was a place in which above others God was manifest upon earth, and which deserved pre-eminently to be termed His 'house.' As a mark of the sacredness of the spot, Jacob consecrates the boulder on which his head had rested, setting it up as a 'pillar,' and pouring oil upon the top of it : he also promises solemnly, if he returns home in safety, to make it a 'house of God,' and to pay J″ tithes of all his gains. Bethel became afterwards a famous and much-frequented sanctuary (Am 7¹³ etc.) ; and no doubt it was the 'pillar,' that would naturally stand beside its altar (Am 3¹⁴ : cf. Hos 10¹), and the custom of paying tithes there (Am 4⁴), the origin of both of which was thus attributed by tradition to Jacob. The Phœnicians believed in λίθοι ἔμψυχοι (Eus. *Præp. Ev.* i. 10. 18) ; and there are many traces in antiquity of stones, esteemed as sacred, being anointed with oil (λίθοι λιπαροί), and venerated as divine (Arnob. *adv. Gent.* i. 39, vi. 11 ; Is 57⁶ : cf. vol. i. p. 278ᵃ ; also W. R. Smith, *RS*¹ 109, 184–188, 214 f. [²116, 201–205, 232 f.]) ; * and the sacred 'pillar,' or monolith, of Bethel, it is difficult not to think, must in its actual origin have been regarded similarly as a shrine or abode of the deity ; but in the existing narrative the idea may possibly be that Jacob venerated it as the channel through which he received his dream.†

29¹⁻¹⁴ Jacob proceeds on his journey, reaches Ḥaran, and quickly meets with his relations. In his uncle, Laban, Jacob finds, at least for a time, his match in the art of overreaching ; and the narrative recounts first the engagement concluded by him with Laban, and then the ruse by which the latter succeeded in marrying first his elder daughter Leah, and so in securing Jacob's services as a shepherd, for 7 years more, in return for his younger daughter Rachel.‡ The section 29³¹–30²⁴ narrates the birth of 11 of Jacob's 12 sons, and of a daughter Dinah, alluding at the same time incidentally to the family jealousies which arose in consequence between his two wives. It is unnecessary to dwell here upon details : it will be sufficient to state that first Leah bears, in succession, Reuben, Simeon, Levi, and Judah : then Rachel's handmaid, Bilhah, bears two sons, Dan and Naphtali, in her mistress' name ; next Zilpah, Leah's handmaid, bears Gad and Asher ; after this, Issachar and Zebulun, as also a daughter Dinah, are born to Leah ; lastly, Rachel bears Joseph. A collateral aim of the narrative, to which evidently no small importance is attached, is to explain the names borne afterwards by the corresponding tribes : the explanations (as is constantly the case in similar cases in the OT), though apparently etymological, are, however, in reality based, not upon etymologies (in our sense of the word), but upon *assonances*, and must not, therefore, be understood as necessarily expressing the real meaning of the names. In the case of several of the names, a double explanation is given (or alluded to), — an indication of the composite

* See, further, Tylor, *Primitive Culture*³, ii. 160–167.
† It is observable that in v.²² the title, 'house of God,' is applied to the monolith itself, not to the place marked by it. Some have seen in the passage (esp. v.¹¹) an allusion to the custom of 'incubation' : cf. Smend, *AT Theol.* 39 ; Holzinger, *ad loc.*
‡ V.²⁷ 'fulfil the week of this one,' *i.e.* the week of festivities usually accompanying a marriage (Jg 14¹², To 11¹⁹) : do not break off the usual round of wedding festivities. When they were ended, Jacob received Rachel on the understanding that he was to serve Laban for 7 years more.

character of the narrative (v.¹⁶ and v.¹⁸ ; v.²⁰ᵃ and v.²⁰ᵇ ; v.²³ and v.²⁴).*

Jacob, having been in Laban's service for 14 years, was now anxious to return home to his father. He accordingly begs his uncle to let him go, together with his wives and children. Laban, however, is reluctant to part with a servant who, he is obliged to own (30²⁷ᵇ), has served him well ; and with feigned magnanimity invites him to name the terms on which he will remain with him. Jacob, in reply, professing to be very generous, declares his willingness to serve him for nothing, if he will agree to the following arrangement : Jacob will remove from the flocks all the parti-coloured animals, and having done this will take nothing but the animals so marked, which are born afterwards, as his wages. Laban, supposing that these would be few or none, closes eagerly with the offer ; and in order to make the arrangement doubly secure, removes the spotted animals from the flock himself, gives them into the hands of his sons, and places three days' journey between himself and the flocks left with Jacob (30³¹⁻³⁶). Jacob, however, is equal to the occasion ; and by means of various ingenious devices, succeeds in outwitting his not too generous uncle. (1) Jacob placed parti-coloured rods in front of the ewes at the time when they conceived, so that the latter in consequence bore parti-coloured young (vv.³⁷⁻³⁹).† (2) He arranged that the spotted lambs and kids thus produced should be in view of the rest of the flock, so that, when the ewes conceived, there should be a further tendency to bear spotted young (v.⁴⁰).‡ (3) Jacob further put up the peeled rods only when the stronger sheep were about to conceive : he thus secured all the strongest animals for himself (v.⁴²). The result was (v.⁴³) that Jacob's possessions increased immensely.

Jacob's increasing prosperity soon arouses the envy of Laban ; and he no longer views him with the same friendliness as before. Encouraged by J″ (31³), Jacob resolves accordingly, without again consulting his father-in-law, to return home : he explains his position to his wives, pointing out to them Laban's arbitrary and ungrateful treatment of him ; and they agree to accompany him (31⁴⁻¹⁶). Here it is to be observed that the description of Laban's arrangement with Jacob, and of the manner in which its consequences were evaded by Jacob, differs from that given in ch. 30 : in 31⁷⁻¹² Jacob says that Laban had been in the habit of arbitrarily changing his wages (so 31⁴¹), as seemed most likely to benefit himself, of which there is nothing in ch. 30 ; and, further, that the effect of the change had each time§ been frustrated, not by his own ingenious contrivance (as in 30³⁷⁻⁴²), but by the intervention of Providence (31⁸⁻⁹) :∥

* See, further, the articles on the several names. 29³⁴ 'be joined' ; the name 'Levi' is played on similarly in Nu 18² ⁴ (*lāwāh*, to join). 30³ 'be builded up from her' : so 16² of Hagar, the fig. being that of a house (cf. Ru 4¹¹, Dt 25⁹). 30¹⁴⁻¹⁶ 'mandrakes,' or better *love-apples*, were supposed to possess aphrodisiac properties, and to ensure conception : hence the reason why Rachel asks for them. In v.¹⁶ Leah 'hires' Jacob with the love-apples she had given to Rachel ; in v.¹⁸ Leah says that Issachar is the 'hire,' or payment, which she has received for having given Zilpah to Jacob, — manifestly two explanations of the name Issachar (*sāchār*, 'hire' or 'wages').
† The physiological principle involved is well established. According to an authority quoted by Delitzsch, cattle-breeders now, in order to secure white lambs, surround the drinking-troughs with white objects.
‡ This seems to be the meaning of v.⁴⁰ as it stands. But many modern scholars think that the words 'and set . . . of Laban' are a gloss ; in which case the verse will merely state that the parti-coloured young, produced as described in v.³⁹, were kept by themselves, not mixed with those of uniform colour (which would be Laban's).
§ Notice the imperfect tenses in 31⁸.
∥ The *dream* (31¹⁰⁻¹²) is mentioned as a notification to Jacob that the birth, by natural means (and not through Jacob's artifice), of the parti-coloured young was by God's appointment, in compensation for Laban's treatment of him (v.¹² *end*).

ch. 30 gives J's representation of the transactions, ch. 31 gives that of E.* Jacob takes flight while Laban is engaged in sheepshearing (cf. 1 S 25$^{2. 7. 11}$, 2 S 13^{23}) ; he crosses the Euphrates, and directs his steps towards Gilead (31$^{17-22}$). Rachel, at the same time, steals her father's *teraphim*, or household gods (cf. 1 S 19$^{13. 16}$), as though (Ewald) to appropriate and carry with her into Canaan the good fortune of her paternal home.

Laban, upon hearing of Jacob's departure, starts in pursuit, and overtakes him in the hill-country of Gilead. The account of the meeting is told in 31$^{26-55}$. Laban begins by expostulating with Jacob on the manner in which he has left him, and especially on the theft of his household gods, with which he charges him. Rachel, who was alone the guilty person, by a piece of woman's wit conceals the theft, and, in her turn, outwits her father : this gives Jacob the opportunity of retorting upon Laban, of reminding him of the 20 years which he had spent ungrudgingly in his service, and of reproaching him with the many attempts he had made to deprive him of his lawful earnings (vv.$^{26-42}$). Laban, smitten by his conscience (vv.$^{24. 29}$), and unable to reply, seeks to close the dispute by proposing a treaty of friendship. Up to this point the narrative has been clear ; but from v.^{46} it becomes somewhat confused, two different accounts (J and E) having, it seems, been combined together, and at the same time enlarged with additions by a redactor. The analysis is difficult, and some of the details are uncertain ; but it is clear that both a ' pillar ' and a heap of stones are described as erected as a witness ; that two distinct agreements are entered into — one (v.^{50}) that Jacob will in no way ill-treat Laban's daughters, the other (v.^{52}) that neither Jacob nor Laban will pass the boundary marked by the heap of stones with hostile intent toward the other ; that the heap of stones is the witness of the former agreement (vv.$^{48-50}$), and the pillar, therefore, presumably (v.^{52}) of the latter ; and further, that each agreement is sealed by a common meal (v.^{46} ; v.^{54}).† The narrative explains in addition the name ' Gilead,' which is derived, by a popular etymology, from *Gal-ēd*, ' Heap of witness.'‡ There must, it seems, have been somewhere on the N.E. frontier of Gilead, a cairn of stones, with a single boulder, standing up prominently beside it, the origin of which was popularly attributed to this compact between Laban and Jacob.§ The narrative, as it stands, explains also (v.^{49}) the name *Mizpah*, the ' Watch-tower,' a place of uncertain situation, but no doubt some eminence in the same neighbourhood, which overlooked the broad plain of Ḥauran, and guarded the approach from the direction of Damascus.‖ It seems that

the ancestors of the Israelites and the Syrians are here conceived as fixing the border between the territories occupied afterwards by their respective descendants, which was often, especially during the period of the Syrian wars, matter of bloody dispute between them.

The ' long game of well-matched wits ' is thus ended ; and Laban returns to Ḥaran (31^{55}), while Jacob travels on towards Canaan. As he journeys, the ' angels of God ' meet him, as if to welcome and congratulate him on his auspicious return ; and from this circumstance the name *Maḥanaim* is explained (' the double camp ').* Maḥanaim became afterwards an important place (2 S 2$^{8. 12. 29}$ the capital of Ishbosheth's kingdom ; see also 17$^{24. 27}$, 1 K 4^{14}) ; but its situation is not known : from the sequel of the present narrative, it must, however, have been N. of the Jabbok (now the *Zerḳā*), though not much N., and within sight of the Jordan (v.^{10}) : in Jos 13$^{26. 30}$ it is mentioned as a place on the border between Gad and Manasseh.†

A fresh danger now threatens Jacob, the prospect of meeting again his brother Esau, who might be supposed to have still not forgotten old grudges. Jacob sends (32$^{3-5}$) a conciliatory message to him, but learns in reply that he is coming to meet him with 400 men. He is greatly alarmed ; but his powers of resource do not desert him. He divides his party into two ' camps,' in the hope that if one should be smitten by Esau, the other at least might escape ; and besides this worldly precaution, he invokes in prayer the aid of God, reminding Him that it was He who had bidden him (31^3) return to his native land, and pleading before Him the blessings which He had already bestowed upon him (v.^{10}), and the promises which He had given him (v.^{12}).‡ (In vv.$^{7. 8}$, it is to be observed, there is clearly a second explanation, parallel to the one in v.^{2}, of the name *Maḥanaim* §). If vv.$^{13b-21}$ be the original sequel to vv.$^{3-13a}$, the passage will describe a further precaution taken by Jacob, viz. a present of cattle, consisting of 580 head, and divided into separate droves for the purpose of making a favourable impression upon Esau, who, as drove upon drove came up, would be at once gratified and surprised to learn that each was intended for himself. But the passage from v.^{13b} to v.^{21} appears to proceed from the other narrator E ;‖ so that the account of the present may be a parallel, and not a sequel, to the division into two ' camps ' in vv.$^{7. 8}$.

There follows the account of Jacob's wrestling with the angel. His party had crossed the Jabbok (the *Wādy Zerḳā*) ; and he himself was left behind ' alone,'—it is difficult to say, on which side of the stream.¶ It was the eve of the greatest crisis of his life. His future welfare hung in the balance. Long ago he had taken cruel advantage of his brother : he had had to flee before his threatened vengeance ; now Esau was on his way to meet him with a large retinue of attendants ; and what would the issue be ? In the solitude and darkness a ' strange and nameless dread ' came over him : the terrible thought that God was his antagonist took possession of him ; and so vividly did he realize it, that he seemed to himself to be engaged in an

---

* Notice the frequency with which God (אֱלֹהִים), not *Jahweh*, occurs in this narrative (vv.$^{9. 11. 16. 24. 42}$).

† The mark of amity and reconciliation, as is still the case among the Arabs. V.^{54} speaks of a sacrifice as well.

‡ Wellh. and Dillm. assign vv.$^{46-50}$ to J, and vv.$^{45. 51-54}$ to E, treating ' Behold, this heap, and' in v.^{51}, ' This heap be witness, and,' and ' and this pillar' in v.^{52}, as glosses due to the redactor. However, יָרָה (v.^{51}) is not the word that we should expect to be used of a מַצֵּבָה : perhaps (cf. LXX here and v.^{45}) we should restore, with Ball, הֲרִימֹתִי. Kautzsch and Socin assign vv.$^{51. 52}$ to J, treating the three references to the ' pillar' in these verses as glosses. The precise determination of the analysis is not important ; for, in any case, the passage describes two distinct transactions (as explained above in the text).

§ Cf. Ewald, *Hist.* i. 347 f., 356, who thinks even that the real meaning of the tradition is that the mountain-range of Gilead itself is the ' heap,' piled up by Laban and Jacob as a boundary between the two nationalities. So also Wellh. *Hist.* 325 f.

‖ It may be doubted whether the present *Kaḷʿat er-Rabad*, a height just on the N. of the Wādy 'Ajlun, with a commanding prospect (Merrill, Buhl, *Geogr.* 262), is sufficiently far to the north. It is also uncertain whether this ' Mizpah' is identical with the רָמַת הַמִּצְפֶּה of Jos 13^{26} (on the N. frontier of Gad). The abrupt way in which Mizpah is here introduced leads most critics to regard the notice respecting it as a gloss.

* The word rendered ' host' in 32^2, and ' company' in 32$^{7. 8. 10. 21}$ 33^8, properly means *camp*, and is usually so rendered. It is a pity that a different rendering has been adopted here.

† Comp. G. A. Smith, *HGHL* 586.

‡ With v.^{12} compare 28$^{14. 15}$ (the phrasing, as 22^{17} 16^{10}).

§ Vv.$^{1. 2}$ belong to E ; vv.$^{3-13a}$ to J.

‖ Notice that at v.^{21b} the narrative is at exactly the same point that it had reached at v.^{13a}.

¶ V.^{22} implies that Jacob had crossed it, v.^{23} that he had not. The two verses clearly belong to different sources. If, as most critics agree, vv.$^{24-32}$ belong to J, the scene of the wrestling will have been S. of the Jabbok.

actual struggle with a living man.* The struggle continued till the approach of daybreak.† But Jacob wrestled bravely: his mysterious antagonist saw that he could not prevail against him by the means which a wrestler would naturally employ; so, in order to escape before daylight, and at the same time to show that he was superior to Jacob, he sprained Jacob's thigh. But Jacob, though he can no longer wrestle with his antagonist, can still hold him: he perceives that he is more than an ordinary mortal; so he seizes the opportunity to win a blessing for himself, 'I will not let thee go, except thou bless me.' The blessing takes the form of a change of name. 'Thy name shall be called no more Jacob, but Israel; for thou hast *persevered* with God and with men, and hast prevailed.' The name 'Israel,' meaning (on the analogy of other names similarly formed) 'God persists (or perseveres),'‡ is interpreted as suggesting the meaning 'Perseverer with God.'§ Jacob's persevering struggle with God is just ended: of men, he has persevered against both Laban and Esau; his struggle with Laban was concluded previously; that with Esau is not yet concluded, but '*hast* prevailed' is a word full of hope for the future. At the same time, as the name was to the Hebrews the symbol or expression of the nature, the change of name is significant of a moral change in the patriarch himself: he is to be no longer the Supplanter, the Crafty one, the Overreacher, but the Perseverer with God, who is worthy also to prevail.‖ The incident serves to explain further the name *Penuel*, 'Face of God'; 'for,' said Jacob, 'I have seen God *face to face*, and yet my life is preserved.'¶ The narrator deduces also from this incident the custom of not eating in animals the muscle corresponding to the one which had been strained in Jacob's thigh: it was treated as sacred through the touch of God. The site of Penuel is uncertain; but it must have been near both the Jabbok and the Jordan. As Jacob journeys from Penuel to Succoth, so Gideon, pursuing the Midianites in the contrary direction, comes first to Succoth, and afterwards 'goes up' to Penuel (Jg 8⁵⁻⁸); it may therefore be conjectured that it was some elevated or projecting spot, near where the Jabbok descends from the uplands into the Jordan Valley: Merrill suggests Tulūl ed-Dahab, conical hills, with ruins at their top, which rise from the Jabbok Valley, with the stream flowing between them, to a height of 250 ft.**

The dreaded meeting with Esau passes off happily (33¹⁻¹⁷). Jacob prepares for the worst (vv.¹⁻³); but Esau shows a generous and magnanimous spirit: he receives his brother with all friendliness, and inquires with interest after his children (vv.⁴⁻⁷). He at first refuses Jacob's present; but Jacob by pressure induces him to

accept it, no doubt hoping thereby to purchase the continuance of his good-will in the future (vv.⁸⁻¹¹).* Esau afterwards offers Jacob his protection for the rest of the journey, or at least some of his people as an escort; but Jacob declines both these offers; he will lay himself under no obligation to his brother, nor will he incur any risk of a rupture in the cordial relations now established between them (vv.¹²⁻¹⁶). Esau accordingly returns to Edom; while Jacob moves on to Succoth (the name of which is explained from the *booths* [סֻכֹּת] built by him there for his cattle). The site of Succoth is not more certainly known than that of Penuel: it was on the E. of Jordan (Jg 8⁴·⁵), in the valley, perhaps (Dillm.) near the ford of ed-Dâmiyeh (on the road from es-Salt to Nâblus), a little S. of the point where the Jabbok enters the Jordan.† After crossing the Jordan, Jacob advanced into the heart of the country, to Shechem. There he encamped in front of the city, and bought the plot of ground on which his tent rested, of the native Shechemites for 100 *kesîṭahs*.‡ The purchase of this land is mentioned on account of the sequel: it was the place in which the bones of Joseph ultimately reposed (Jos 24³²); and it had the same interest and significance for the N. kingdom which the cave of Machpelah at Hebron (ch. 23) had for the kingdom of Judah.§

We come (ch. 34) to the somewhat remarkable narrative of the dealings of Jacob with Shechem. The chapter is plainly composite; but the criteria are in some cases ambiguous, so that critics are not fully agreed in their results. The main characteristics of the two narratives of which it is composed are, however, sufficiently clear. According to J,‖ Shechem, son of Hamor, having seduced Jacob's daughter, Dinah, desires to obtain her from her father and brothers in marriage: they agree, only imposing a condition the nature of which in the existing text of J is not specified, but which Hamor at once accedes to (vv.¹¹·¹²·¹⁹); afterwards, however, Simeon and Levi, resenting keenly Shechem's treatment of their sister, fall upon him, without their brothers' knowledge, slay him and his father, and rescue Dinah; their father blames them severely for making him and his family unpopular among the native Canaanites, and endangering their lives; they reply that the honour of their tribe is above all such considerations: 'Should he deal with our sister as with an harlot?' Here the transaction has a *personal* character: only Shechem is involved; and his aim is the personal one of securing Dinah as his wife. According to the rest of the narrative,¶ Shechem equally desires to obtain Dinah as his wife, but much wider interests are involved: the transaction assumes a *national* significance: Hamor

---

* *In the sense of the tradition,* the contest, as Dillm. remarks, is plainly an external and physical one.

† In the rare word רָבַק for *wrestle*, vv.²⁴·²⁵, there is a play on the name Jabbok (יַבֹּק), if not an explanation of its origin, as though it meant *Wrestling* (-stream).

‡ Sayce's derivation (*EHH* 73, and elsewhere) from *yāshar*, 'to be upright,' 'to direct' (!), has nothing to recommend it.

§ Cf. Arab. *shariya,* to *persist,* or *persevere;* conj. iii. (expressing the idea of *rivalry*) to *persist* or *persevere against* another (viz. in contention or wrangling). The same root is contained in *Seraiah,* 'Jah persists.' (The root means 'to *strive'* (RVm) only in the sense of *to exert oneself,* not in that of *to contend.* It has no connexion with *sar,* 'prince,' from *sārar*.)

‖ J from this point prefers, though not (in our existing texts) quite uniformly, *Israel* to *Jacob* as the designation of the patriarch.

¶ With allusion to the often expressed belief that no one could 'see God and live' (Ex 19²¹ 33²⁰, Jg 6²²f. 13²²). Notice the adversative force of the *Wāw* consecutive (Ges. § 111e).

** See Moore, *Judges,* 220f., 223; G. A. Smith, *HGHL* 585f. There was a Phœnician headland called θεοῦ πρόσωπον; and 'Penuel' may really, like this headland, have derived its name from some physical feature presented by it.

* V.¹⁰ 'forasmuch as I have seen thy face, as when one seeth the face of God' (*i.e.* I have found it *as* favourable), is manifestly, as Wellh. remarks, another explanation of the name *Penuel.* 'To see the face' is the phrase used of one admitted to the presence-chamber of a monarch, or other ruler (Gn 43³·⁵, 2 S 14²⁴·²⁸, 2 K 25¹⁹; of God, Ps 11⁷, Job 33²⁶), and, it is implied, viewed by his superior favourably. Jacob, by using this expression, pays Esau a high compliment. 'Beiden Wendungen der Sage liegt zu Grund, dass man in Peniel den unfreundlichen Gott als freundlichen erfährt' (Dillm.).

† Comp. Moore, *l.c.* p. 218 (who mentions another proposed site, at Deir 'Alla, N. of the Zerka; cf. G. A. Smith, *l.c.* p. 585).

‡ A piece of money (or metal) of uncertain value. It is mentioned besides only in Jos 24³², Job 42¹¹.

§ As Dinah, who (31⁴¹ comp. with 30²¹) must have been quite an infant when Jacob left Haran, appears of marriageable age in ch. 34, Jacob (if the narrative is to be treated as consistent) must be supposed to have passed some years at Succoth (or at Shechem, before the events mentioned in ch. 34 occurred); cf. Dillm. on 30²⁵f. 33¹⁷ 34¹.

‖ Vv.²b·³·⁵·⁷·¹¹·¹²·¹⁹·²⁶ ('two of the sons of Jacob, Simeon and Levi, Dinah's brethren, took each man his sword') ²⁶·³⁰·³¹. This narrative is naturally not quite complete, parts having been omitted when it was combined with the other narrative.

¶ P; or (Wellh., Cornill, Holzinger) E, amplified in parts by a writer of the school of P.

proposes what is virtually an amalgamation of the two communities, with full reciprocal rights of trade and inter-marriage (vv.[8-10. 21-23]) : the sons of Jacob generally (not merely Simeon and Levi) speak on their sister's behalf : they impose the condition (which is here circumcision) not on Shechem only, but on the whole people (vv.[13-18]) ; and the *entire* city experiences their vengeance (vv.[25 end. 27-29]). On the possible significance of this narrative, see p. 535.

From Shechem Jacob proceeds on his way to Bethel (about 20 miles S. of Shechem), a panic terror (35[5]) restraining the natives of the neighbourhood from pursuing him. Bethel was the spot, which, when he was starting for Ḥaran some 20 years (31[41]) previously, had been consecrated for him by his great dream (28[11-22]) ; and now, in anticipation of visiting it again, he bade his household and retainers put away all 'foreign gods' from among them : the 'God of Bethel' (31[13]) had proved Himself true to His promise (28[15]) ; He had led His servant safely through many trials and anxieties ; and at Bethel, in fulfilment of his vow (28[22]), he would now build an altar to Him. Later generations pointed to the terebinth at Shechem (cf. Jos 24[26]) as marking the spot at which the idols brought from Ḥaran (cf. Gn 31[19], Jos 24[2. 14. 23]), and the amulets,* were buried by Jacob. The erection of the altar is narrated in 35[7] (E, as also vv.[1-5. 8]). P (35[9-13. 15]) describes at this point a theophany, with a renewed promise to Jacob of a numerous and royal posterity, and of the gift of the land (vv.[11. 12]) ;† to the same occasion he also assigns (v.[10]) the change of name from *Jacob* to *Israel*, which J has narrated already at Penuel (32[28]), and the origin of the name of *Bethel*, which J had connected with Jacob's former visit to the place (28[19]). The relation of the 'pillar,' which, according to v.[14] (probably J), Jacob set up, and upon which he is said also to have poured a drink-offering and oil, to the one mentioned previously in 28[18] (E), is not clear ; the verse *may* relate to a different 'pillar,' it *may* give a different version of the origin of the same 'pillar.'‡

Leaving Bethel, Jacob continued his journey to the South. Shortly before reaching Ephrath, Rachel died in childbirth : she herself, so tradition told, called her son *Ben-oni* 'son of my sorrow,' but her father preferred a name of better omen, and called him *Ben-jamin*, 'son of the right hand.'§ On the site of her grave, Jacob erected a 'pillar,' which still bore her name in the narrator's day (35[20]). In 1 S 10[2] Rachel's grave is distinctly stated to have been on the (Northern) border of Benjamin, not far from Bethel (cf. v.[3]; and see also Jer 31[15]) : unless therefore there were different traditions respecting its site, the gloss 'the same is Beth-lehem' (in spite of its repetition in 48[7], and in spite also of its being in agreement with other statements, as Ru 4[11], Mic 5[2]) is incorrect, and there were more localities than one called *Ephrath*. Still pursuing his way, Jacob next rested beyond the 'tower of Eder' (or 'of the flock'),—a place, of which (in spite of Mic 4[8]) the situation is quite uncertain. P (35[22b-29]) brings Jacob on to Hebron (v.[27]; cf. 37[14] JE). There Isaac (who was last mentioned as

being at Beersheba *) dies ; and (according to the same source, P) Jacob and Esau meet once more for the purpose of burying him (v.[29]; cf. 25[9]).

The active period of Jacob's life is now over : the rest of his days is passed in quietude ; and Joseph becomes the moving spirit in the patriarchal family. Joseph was his father's favourite son ; his brethren envied him ; his dreams of future exaltation increased their jealousy ; but his father fondly wondered what these dreams might signify (37[12]). Jacob is still at Hebron, but his flocks are at Shechem,† tended by his other sons, and he sends Joseph thither to inquire after his brethren's welfare (37[12-14]). Deceived in his old age by his sons, as he had in his youth deceived his own aged father, he receives with inconsolable grief the evidence, as it seems to him, of Joseph's cruel death (37[31-35]). As the famine grows severe in Canaan, he sends his sons, but without Benjamin, who now naturally takes Joseph's place as his father's favourite, to buy corn in Egypt (42[1-4]): upon their inauspicious return, his distress and grief find bitter expression in the reproachful words (42[36]), 'Me have ye bereaved of my children : Joseph is not, and Simeon is not, and ye will take Benjamin away ; upon me are all these things come.' In the end, he is obliged to let Benjamin go back with his brethren into Egypt, but with characteristic prudence he sends with them a present calculated to win the favour of the great man of the land (43[11-13]). The *dénoûment* soon follows ; and ch. 45 recounts the delight with which he hears that his son is still alive, and receives the message to come and join him in Egypt (vv.[25-28]). He sets forth from Hebron, journeys to Beersheba, the home of Isaac and of his own former days (27. 28[10]), and there, when on the point of leaving for a second time the land of promise,·and taking up his abode in the land of Egypt, receives a word of encouragement and promise suitable to the occasion (46[3. 4]; cf. previously, at Bethel, 28[13-15]). Israel thus 'went down into Egypt'; and a new and momentous epoch in the history of the nation was inaugurated. The list of Jacob's sons and grandchildren who accompanied him into Egypt is given by P (46[6-27]).‡ Jacob meets his son Joseph in Goshen, and the wish of his heart is accomplished (46[29f.]). Afterwards he is honourably received by the Pharaoh, and assigned, with his sons, a residence in the pastoral district of Goshen (47[1-4. 6b] [from 'in the land '] J ; 47[5. 6a. 7-11] P). §

As the time drew near for Jacob to die, he made Joseph promise not to bury him in Egypt, but to lay him in the tomb of his fathers in Canaan

---

* This is the meaning of the 'rings' of 35[4].

† With v.[11] of. the passages cited p. 527 note ‡; and add 17[6] ('kings').

‡ Cornill conjectures that this verse originally (without 'in the place where he spake with him') stood in close connexion with v.[8]: in this case the 'pillar' would be a sepulchral stele (cf. v.[20]), and the libations would be poured out as offerings to the dead (*ZATW*, 1891, p. 15 ff.; cf. Holzinger, *Comm.* p. 217).

§ Whether this is the true explanation of the name, must remain an open question. Sayce (*EHH* 79) agrees here with Stade (*Gesch.* i. 161) in thinking that the name (the 'Southerner') has really reference to the position of the territory of Benjamin on the S. of Ephraim.

---

* 28[10] compared with 27[42-45]: according to P (35[28] compared with 25[26] 26[34]) *eighty* years previously, Jacob being now 120 years old ! (According to JE, Jacob was but 20 years in Mesopotamia, 31[41]; cf. p. 532[b]).

† The author of this passage must have pictured Jacob's flocks as roaming pretty freely over the country (cf. v.[17], Dothan being about 15 miles N. of Shechem), if he himself was at Hebron. In view of ch. 34, the mention of their being at Shechem is remarkable ; but the writer, it is possible, pictured the inhabitants of the neighbourhood as deterred by fear (cf. 35[5]) from interfering with Jacob's possessions.

‡ On difficulties connected with the enumeration, esp. in vv.[26. 27], see the Commentaries.—An interesting illustration of Jacob's descent into Egypt is afforded by the representation, on a tomb at Beni-Hassan, of 37 Asiatics (*Amu*), bringing a present of eye-paint, and led to Usertesen II., of the 12th dynasty, in his 6th year (c. B.C. 2600, Petrie). The procession is a remarkable one : it comprises men, women, and children, and two asses : the men wear long richly-coloured tunics, or in some cases coloured loin-cloths, and one is playing with a plectrum on a lyre of six strings. See Wilkinson-Birch, *Anc. Egyp.* 1878, i. 480 ; Maspero, *Dawn of Civilization*, 468–470 ; or Petrie, *Hist. of Egypt*, i. 172–174 ; also Hommel, *AHT* 52f.

‡ The sequence in vv.[5. 6] is better in the LXX ; see the Comms., or *LOT* pp. 10, 16 (6 11, 17) *n*. The situation of Goshen, fixed approximately by tradition, has been determined definitely by the researches of M. Naville ; it was the district lying between the three modern villages of Saft, Belbeis, and Tel el-Kebir, about 40 miles N.E. of Cairo.

(47^{29-31}). Ch. 48 narrates (1) how he adopted Joseph's two sons, Manasseh and Ephraim, placing them on the same level with his own children (vv.$^{3-7}$ P) ; and (2) how he blessed them, giving at the same time the first place to the younger, Ephraim, in view of the future pre-eminence of the tribe descended from him (vv.$^{1-2.\ 8-20}$ JE). There follows a special promise and gift, made to Joseph (vv.$^{21.\ 22}$ E). The terms of v.^{22} are remarkable, 'And I give thee one shoulder * (shĕkhem) above thy brethren, which I took out of the hand of the Amorite with my sword and with my bow.' There is manifestly here an allusion to Shechem, afterwards an important and central place in the territory of Ephraim (cf. G. A. Smith, HGHL 332–334), where also Joseph was buried (Jos 24^{32}) ; but nothing is said elsewhere of a conquest of Shechem by Jacob : it is evident that there is preserved here a version of Jacob's dealings with Shechem different from any which we find elsewhere.†

49$^{2-27}$ contains the more elaborate poetical Blessing, which Jacob is said to have addressed to all his sons before his death. Throughout this Blessing what the poet really has in view are the tribes ; as so often elsewhere in Genesis, the tribe is conceived as impersonated in its ancestor, and the ancestor foreshadows the character of the tribe. The poet passes the tribes in review : he singles out in each some striking feature of moral character, political state, or geographical position, for poetical amplification ; and on each he pronounces some word of praise or blame, according to its deserts. The moral instability of Reuben, the disorganized social condition of Simeon and Levi, the ideal sovereignty and vine-clad territory of Judah, the maritime advantages enjoyed by Zebulun, the ignoble indifference which led Issachar to prefer ease to independence, the quick and effective attack of Dan, the warlike bravery of Gad, the richness of Asher's soil,‡ the blessings of populousness, military efficiency, climate, and soil, which, in spite of envious assailants, are showered upon Joseph, the martial skill and success of Benjamin, —these, briefly, are the features which the poet selects, and develops one after another, in varied and effective imagery. The historical and geographical conditions reflected in the poem are those of the period of the Judges, Samuel, and David ; and this is the age in which the ancient tradition of the patriarch's Blessing must have received its present poetical form.

After this, we read, Jacob charged his sons to bury him in the family grave at Machpelah (49$^{29-32}$ P : 47$^{29-31}$ is parallel in JE), and then died (v.^{33} P). His body was embalmed, according to the Egyptian custom (50$^{1-3}$) : a great funeral procession was organized, such as was usual in Egypt (50$^{1-9}$) ; § and he was buried in the land of Canaan, in the cave at Hebron (50$^{12.\ 13}$).‖

* i.e. 'mountain-slope' or '-side' ; cf. the use of the syn. כֶּתֶף Jos 15$^{8.\ 10}$ 18$^{12.\ 12.\ 16.\ 18}$ (RV poorly, 'side ').

† In the parts of ch. 34 which belong to J, two of Jacob's sons wreak their vengeance on individual Shechemites ; but Jacob himself repudiates their deed. The present passage shows that a version must have been current according to which Jacob (i.e. Israel as a whole) conquered and took possession of Shechem. This version is allied to, and perhaps underlies, the other narrative in ch. 34, according to which the sons of Jacob (and not Simeon and Levi alone) massacred the inhabitants of Shechem ; but it is not said, or even implied, in this narrative that they retained the city as their own possession. (The statement in 33^{19} that Jacob purchased a piece of land outside the city, is of course not inconsistent with his forcible conquest of the city itself afterwards. See further, Dillm., Holzinger, and Wellh. Comp. 316 ff.

‡ The blessing on Naphtali is too uncertain in its terms to be summarized with any confidence.

§ Erman, Life in Ancient Egypt, p. 320 f.

‖ 50$^{4-11}$ (JE) is the sequel to 47$^{29-31}$ (in both Joseph alone is the prominent person) ; 50$^{12.13}$ (P) is the sequel to 49$^{29-33}$ (in both Jacob's sons in general are the actors), the détour by Atad (vv.$^{10.\ 11}$), on the East of Jordan, is manifestly made merely by the narrator, for the purpose of explaining the name 'Abel-

The chronology of Jacob's life presents serious difficulties : it is evident that the traditions (or theories) about it are inconsistent. (1) P's chronology, as often elsewhere in Gn, is entirely irreconcilable with that of JE. In ch. 27 (JE) Isaac is to all appearance upon his deathbed (cf. v.^{2}) ; yet according to P (25^{26} 26^{34} 35^{28}) he survived for eighty years, dying at the age of 180. Ussher, Keil, and others, arguing back from the dates given in 47^9 45^6 41^{46} 31^{41}, infer that Jacob's flight to Ḥaran took place in his 77th year : this reduces the 80 years to 43 years, though that is almost equally incredible ; but it involves the fresh incongruity of supposing that thirty-seven years elapsed between Esau's marrying his Hittite wives (26^{34}), and Rebekah's expressing her fear (27^{46}) that Jacob, then aged seventy-seven, should follow his brother's example ! Nor is it natural to picture Jacob seeking a wife in Haran, and tending Laban's sheep, as a man 77 years old. (2) It may be doubted whether even the chronology of JE is perfectly consistent. (a) The supposition made p. 530 note § is required, as there explained, for consistency ; but an unspecified sojourn of some years at either Succoth or Shechem is hardly consonant with the general tenor of the narrative of Jacob's return (31^{18}) from Ḥaran. It is true, in 37^2 Joseph is said to be 17 years of age ; but the years of Joseph's boyhood would be placed more naturally between 35^{22} and 37^2 than at 33^{17} or 33^{19}. (b) Joseph is called (37^3) a son of Jacob's 'old age,' as though he were appreciably younger than his brethren : yet Zebulun and Dinah could not have been more than a year or two older (30$^{20-24}$) ; for all Jacob's children (except Benjamin) must have been born, at least according to E (see 31^{41}), between the 7th and the 16–17th years of his service with Laban (leaving, say, 4–3 years for the events narrated in 30$^{25-43}$). However, 37^3 belongs very probably to the other source, J, which may have represented Joseph as born later. In P he is born when Jacob is about 90 (Gn 41^{46} [47 45^6 E] 47^9).

Allusions to Jacob in subsequent parts of Scripture.—The most important are in Hosea, who already applies his history didactically :—

(1) Hos 12$^{2-4}$ $^{(3-5)}$:—

3 In the womb he supplanted his brother ;
   And in his strength he persisted with God :
4 Yea, he persisted [יִשַׂר] with the angel, and prevailed ;
   He wept, and made supplication unto him ;
   At Bethel he found him, and there he spake with him.*

The allusions to the incidents recorded in Gn 25^{26} 32^{28} 28$^{13-15}$ are palpable. Ephraim is lax, indifferent, and frivolous : the ambition shown by its ancestor Jacob to secure pre-eminence even in the womb, the persistence with which afterwards he exerted himself to win the blessing, and the tears with which he sought it,† are held up as examples for its imitation.

(2) Hos 12$^{12f.}$ $^{(13f.)}$:—

12 And Jacob fled into the field of Aram,
   And Israel served for a wife,
   And for a wife he kept (sheep) :
13 But by a prophet did Jehovah bring Israel up out of Egypt,
   And by a prophet was he kept (preserved).

For the allusions in v.^{12}, see Gn 27^{43} (cf. 35$^{1.\ 7}$) ; 29$^{18.\ 20.\ 30}$ 31^{41}. The flight, the penury, the hardships (cf. Gn 31$^{38-41}$) undergone by Jacob are contrasted with the deliverance of his descendants under the honourable guidance of a prophet.

In Dt 26^5 'An Aramæan ready to perish‡ was my father, and he went down into Egypt, and sojourned there, few in number ; and he became there a nation, great, mighty, and populous,' the allusion is to Jacob's Aramæan connexions, and to his hard and perilous life as a shepherd in Aram-naharaim. Jacob is also most probably meant by 'thy first father ' in Is 43^{27}. In Mal 1$^{2.\ 3}$ (cited Ro 9^{13}) the reference is really national : see Gore in Studia Biblica, iii. 37 ff.; Sanday-Headlam, Romans, 245 ff.

The Character of Jacob.—Of all the characters which are sketched in any fulness in the OT, that of Jacob is the most mixed. On the one hand, he is by nature the 'supplanter' : 'is he not,' exclaims Esau, 'rightly named Jacob, for he hath supplanted me these two times'? Twice he takes a mean advantage of his brother ; he deceives his

Mizraim,' which, meaning properly Meadow of Egypt,—perhaps (cf. the so-called 'Job's Stone' [above, i. 166^b n.] as commemorating in some way the Egyptian occupation of Canaan,—is here derived, by an assonance, from 'ebel, 'mourning.'

* So Pesh., Aq., Symm., Theod. The Heb. text has with us, which must mean 'with us in the person of our ancestor.'

† A trait (v.^{4b}) not mentioned in Gn 32$^{26-29}$.

‡ Or, lost ; the word is often used of a lost sheep, as Ezk 34$^{4.\ 16}$

aged father; even where he does not directly overreach, prudence and expediency are the determining motives of his life; his thoughts centre in himself; he is ever striving to turn circumstances to his own profit, to make the most out of every opportunity. He is a striking contrast to his brother: Esau is frank, straightforward, and generous; Jacob is scheming, ambitious, and self-seeking; by fair means or foul, he sets himself to compass his ends. On the other hand, Jacob is not destitute of good qualities. He has a deeper and more stable character than Esau: Esau is governed by the impulses of the moment, is heedless of the future, has no thought for any but present and material goods: Jacob, if he is the 'Overreacher,' is also the 'Perseverer' ('Israel'); he possesses steadiness and consistency of purpose; he does not flinch from toil and exertion,—even Laban admits that he has served him well (30²⁷); he can labour and deny himself in order to attain a far-distant goal; he has cleverness, versatility, and diplomatic ability: he thus possesses qualities which, though they may be misdirected, are nevertheless adapted to form the foundation of a sound and genuine character. And one aim of the history of Jacob, as written in the Book of Genesis, is to show how, through the discipline and spiritual experiences of life, the better elements of a character may in the end prevail, and become its determining and predominant principles.

It may be asked how a character exhibiting so many doubtful qualities should have been selected by Providence as its chosen agent, and be represented as receiving so constantly the marks of God's care and approval (28¹³⁻¹⁵ 31¹²ᵇ· ¹³· ²⁴ 32¹ etc.). The answer, no doubt, is to be found in the fact that Providence does not judge by present appearances; and that Jacob possessed qualities which, in spite of the faults, and even the grave faults, by which they were accompanied, were qualities which, when purified, and elevated, and freed from purely personal aims, could be consecrated to the service of God, and made subservient to carrying out His purposes. The turning-point in his life is the struggle at Penuel. In all his dealings hitherto, whether with Esau or Laban, he has been true to his name, he has been the Supplanter or Overreacher. His treatment of Esau was without excuse: in his dealings with Laban, craft was matched against craft; though, in judging Jacob here, it is only right to remember that Laban not only takes the first dishonest step, but is throughout the chief offender. Had Laban treated Jacob honestly and generously, there is no reason to suppose that he would have sought to overreach him. But since Laban seeks, not once only, to profit at his expense, Jacob retaliates,*—and, so far as material gains are concerned, wins. But, as has just been pointed out, Jacob's character includes inconsistent elements; and the struggle at Penuel marks the triumph of the higher over the lower elements in his character. It is the critical moment of his life. He is at the point of re-entering the land which he left twenty (31⁴¹) years before; he is about to meet his brother whom he had wronged and deceived; memories of the past return upon him; his conscience smites him, and he is 'greatly afraid.' But God is his real antagonist, not Esau; it is God whom his sins have offended, and who here comes to contest His right. These thoughts and fears are, as it were, materialized in his dream. He struggles with his mysterious antagonist, and, as in his struggles with Esau and Laban, strives to win: he struggles bravely: nor can his antagonist overcome him, until by a divine touch He paralyzes his natural strength. Even then Jacob's tenacity of purpose remains unimpaired; he is conscious that he has a heavenly visitant in his embrace; and he will not let Him go until he has received from Him a blessing. The moment marks a spiritual change in Jacob's character. His carnal weapons are lamed and useless,—they fail him in his contest with God; as the result of his struggle his natural self is left behind, he rises from it an altered man. A new truth is vividly brought home to him,—the valuelessness before God of the weapons in which he has hitherto trusted. The lameness which he carries away with him is, as it were, a palpable memento of the fact. And his new name symbolizes his new nature. It is true, even before this, he has not been represented as destitute of religious feeling; his prayer in 32¹⁰ evinces humility, thankfulness, and a sense of dependence upon God. Indeed this prayer may be said to prepare psychologically for the spiritual struggle which follows. But it is the result of this struggle that henceforth the better and higher elements in his character assert themselves more strongly than they had done before. In his dealings with Esau in ch. 33 he is politic, and makes the best of the situation; but he cannot be said to treat his brother dishonourably. His rebuke of Simeon and Levi in 34³⁰, however, shows timidity and weakness, and is not prompted by any motive higher than expediency. In his old age domestic trials overtake him: he loses Rachel; for many years he is bereaved of his favourite son; the dread of losing another son weighs heavily upon him (42³⁸ 43¹⁴): his character is mellowed and softened; and the picture of his closing days is that of a just and God-fearing typical Israelite, strong in faith (48²¹), and grateful for the Providence which had 'shepherded'* him through his long course of anxieties and vicissitudes, and 'redeemed him from all evil' (48¹⁵ᶠ·).

There remains the question, *how far, and in what sense, the narratives relating to Jacob are historical.* In approaching this question there are some important things to be borne in mind. (1) Upon any view of the Book of Genesis, it was not committed to writing for many centuries after the events described in it occurred: we thus possess no guarantee whatever that it contains a *literally exact* record of the acts and sayings of the patriarchs; for it does not satisfy the primary canon of sound historical criticism, that only narratives contemporary, or nearly so, with the events narrated, and, moreover, consistent with themselves, can claim such a character. (2) It is remarkable how, in Gn, individuals and tribes seem to be placed on the same level, and to be spoken of in the same terms, and how, further, individuals seem frequently to be the impersonation of homonymous tribes. Thus Bethuel is mentioned as an individual (22²³ 24¹⁵ *al.*), but his brothers Uz and Buz are tribes (22²¹ᶠ·). Keturah, again, is described as an individual (25¹); but her sons and grandsons are tribes (25²⁻⁴). In Gn 10 nations are quite manifestly represented as individuals; and one of them, Cush, has, conversely, an individual for his son (10⁸). So elsewhere: Machir, in Gn 50²³ an individual, in Nu 26²⁹ 'begets' (the country) Gilead; in Jg 11¹ Gilead 'begets' Jephthah.† Again, Canaan, Japheth, and Shem, in Noah's blessing (Gn 9²⁵⁻²⁷), clearly represent three

---

* At least according to J (30³¹⁻⁴³). According to E (31¹⁴⁻¹⁶· ²⁶⁻⁴³), Laban arbitrarily and unfairly changes Jacob's wages; but Jacob's gains are not due to his own artifices, but to the dispositions of Providence (31⁸⁻¹²). As the two narratives are thus derived from different sources, it follows that 31⁵ᵇ· ⁷⁻⁹· ¹²· ²⁴· ²⁹ do not express, or imply, divine approval of the artifices described in 30³¹⁻⁴².

* AV, RV, entirely losing the metaphor, 'fed.'

† Comp. the curious notice of 'Ephraim' in 1 Ch 7²⁰⁻²⁴ (see art. BERIAH).

groups of nations: Ishmael (16^{12}) is in character the personification of the desert tribes whose descent is traced to him (25^{13-15}): Esau 'is Edom' (25^{30} $36^{1.~8.~19}$; cf. Jer 49^{10})), and Edom is the name of a people. More than this, 'Jacob' and 'Israel' are themselves national names, the latter a standing one, the former a poetical synonym (Gn 49^7, even in Jacob's own mouth: Nu $23^{21.~23}$, Dt 32^9 33^{28}, Hos 10^{11} 12^2, Am $7^{2.~5}$, and frequently). Heredity is undoubtedly a true principle: children inherit the qualities of their parents; they also often experience, for good or for ill, as the case may be, the consequences of their parents' acts; but it would be extending the principle altogether unduly to suppose that the character and political condition of an entire group of peoples were really determined by a father's curse upon their ancestor (Gn 9^{25}), or to imagine that the whole subsequent history of two of the Israelitish tribes was fixed in reality (49^{5-7}) by an act of their ancestors, in which, after all, they were merely maintaining, by means consistent with the manners of the age, the honour of a sister. In cases such as these, we can surely have only the explanations devised either by popular imagination, or by a poet interpreting the mind of his people, for the purpose of accounting for national character, and national conditions, as they existed at a later age.

Admitting, however, that these principles are true, how far may they be adopted in explanation of the patriarchal narratives? Are Jacob and his twelve sons, Esau, and Laban simply the personifications of corresponding peoples, Israel and the 12 tribes, Edom, and Syria (like Hellen, with his sons, Dorus and Æolus, and his grandsons, Achæus and Ion, among the Greeks), the characteristic features of each being reflections of the circumstances and relations of the age which gave them birth (cf. Wellh. *Hist.* 318–325)?* An unsubstantial figure, like Canaan, might be an example of such personification; but the abundance of personal incident and detail makes such a view improbable in the case, at least, of the principal patriarchal characters. May they then *represent* tribes and sub-tribes? in other words, may the movements, and mutual relations, of tribes and sub-tribes have been expressed in a personal and individual form? This is Ewald's view. Abraham, Isaac, and Jacob represent the successive migratory movements of Hebrew tribes from the original common home of the Hebrew and Aramæan nationalities in Aram-naharaim across the Euphrates. Jacob's father was a Hebrew already settled in Canaan: his mother was an Aramæan (Gn 25^{20}); he marries two Aramæan wives: after a long contest with his uncle (and father-in-law) Laban, 'the Aramæan' (25^{20} 28^5 $31^{20.~24}$), he ultimately comes to terms with him, returns to Canaan with great wealth, and finally gives his name to the people settled there: this means that a new and energetic branch of the Hebrew race migrated from its original home in Aram-naharaim, pushed forward into Canaan, amalgamated there with the Hebrews ('Isaac') already on the spot (becoming thereby Isaac's 'son'), and, in virtue of the superior practical abilities displayed by it, acquired ultimately supremacy over all its kin: the contest with Laban 'represents the struggle which continued, probably for centuries, between the crafty Hebrews on the opposite banks of the Euphrates, showing how in the end the southern Hebrews gained the upper hand and the northern were driven off in derision': Edom was a brother ('son') of the tribe represented by 'Isaac'; 'Jacob,' becoming fused with this tribe, is Esau's 'brother,'

but at the same time his younger brother, as arriving later in Canaan,—though, as he became afterwards the more powerful nation, he is described as having wrested from him his birthright: similarly, Jacob's wives and sons represent the existence of different elements in the original community, and the growth of tribal distinctions within it.* Ewald, however, holds at the same time that Abraham, Isaac, Jacob, and Joseph are historical characters, prominent leaders of the nation at successive stages of its history (pp. 301, 305 f., 340, 342, 345, 382).† Again, the amount of personal incident and detail in the patriarchal narratives seems to constitute an objection to this explanation of their meaning: would the movements of tribes be represented in this veiled manner on such a large scale as would be the case if this explanation were the true one? No doubt, there are elements of truth in both these explanations: each will account reasonably for *some* traits in the patriarchal narratives: the question is, whether they will account for all.

The view which on the whole may be said best to satisfy the circumstances of the case is the view that Abraham, Isaac, and Jacob are historical persons, and that the accounts which we have of them are *in outline* historically true, but that their characters are idealized, and their biographies in many respects coloured by the feelings and associations of a later age. 'J,' says Mr. Ottley,‡ and his remarks are equally true of E, 'describes the age of the patriarchs as in some essential respects so closely similar to later periods, that it can only be regarded as a picture of primitive life and religion drawn in the light of a subsequent age. We have here to do with the earliest form of history—traditional folk-lore about primitive personages and events, worked up according to some preconceived design by a devout literary artist.' The basis of the narratives in Genesis is in fact *popular oral tradition*; and that being so, we may expect them to display the characteristics which popular oral tradition does in other cases. They may well include a substantial historical nucleus: but details may be due to the involuntary action of popular invention or imagination, operating during a long period of time; characteristic anecdotes, reflecting the feelings, and explaining the relations, of a later age may thus have become attached to the patriarchs; phraseology and expression will nearly always be ascribed rightly to the narrators who cast these traditions into their present literary shape. One very conspicuous interest in these narratives is the explanation of *existing facts and institutions*—the fact, for instance, that Edom, though an older nation than Israel (36^{31}), was nevertheless politically its inferior, the sanctity of Bethel and its famous monolith, the names borne both by Israel itself and by its twelve tribes, the origin of the great border-cairn on Gilead, the names of places, as Bethel, Maḥanaim, Penuel, Succoth, Allon-ba-

---

* See the full discussion of this view in Kuenen, *ThT*, May 1871, p. 228 ff.; and cf. Smend, *AT Theol.* 12, 96 f.; Meinhold, *Wider den Kleinglauben* (1895), 19, 23.

* Ewald, *Hist.* i. 310 ff., 338, 341–344, 346, 348–350, 363, 371–374 375 ff. Cf. Stade, *Gesch.* i. 124–128 (who, however, does not allow that anything pre-Mosaic is reflected in the patriarchal narratives).

† Dillmann's view is substantially that of Ewald: recollections of tribal movements are preserved in the family histories of Genesis; Isaac and Jacob, like Lot, Ishmael, Esau, and their sons, being 'ideal personal names,' derived either from subdivisions of the nation as it existed at a later time, or from historical stages of its growth, Jacob representing a new Hebrew immigration from Mesopotamia; Abraham, however, being the personal leader of the first band of immigrants, who, according to all the Pentateuchal narrators, was the spiritual father of the entire nation (Gen.[6] 218, 219, 316 [Eng. tr. vol. ii. pp. 1–5, 190]; *AT Theol.* 77 f., 79–81). (Dillmann's remarks on these narratives of Genesis contain much that is suggestive and excellent, and deserve to be read in their entirety.) The view of Kittel (*Gesch.* i. 153 [Eng. tr. i. 168 ff.]) is similar, except that he treats the patriarchs more distinctly as personal tribal chiefs, who afterwards gave their names to the tribes led by them.

‡ *Bampton Lectures*, p. 109.

chuth, Abel-mizraim, the custom of not eating of a particular muscle (32[32]), the ethnological relations subsisting between Israel and its neighbours (Ishmaelite tribes, 25[12-17]; Edom, and the racial affinities of its inhabitants, ch. 36), the characteristics of the different tribes (48[19]; ch. 49). It may be doubted whether in all these cases we have the real historical explanations of the facts in question, and not rather explanations due to popular imagination, or suggested by current etymologies: in some cases, it will be remembered, we find duplicate and inconsistent traditions respecting the same occurrences. Wellhausen may be wrong in not allowing a more substantial historical substratum for the patriarchal narratives; but his general characterization of them is just.[*]

It must further be allowed that the characters of the patriarchs are coloured *religiously* by the feelings and beliefs of a later age. In the days of the patriarchs, religion must have been in a rudimentary stage: there are traces of this in the idea, for instance, of the revelations of deity being confined to particular spots, and in the reverence paid to sacred trees or pillars; but at the same time the patriarchs often express themselves in terms suggesting much riper spiritual capacities and experiences. Here we cannot but trace the hands of the narrators, who were men penetrated by definite moral and religious ideas, and who, writing with a didactic aim, idealized to a certain extent the characters of the patriarchs, and, while not stripping them of the distinctive features with which they were traditionally invested, so filled in the outlines supplied by tradition as to present the great figures of Hebrew antiquity as *spiritual types*, examples, for imitation or warning, as the case might be, for successive generations.

The patriarchs are, thirdly, idealized in another direction, in common with many of the other patriarchal figures in Genesis, by being invested with the characteristics which afterwards marked the tribes descended, or reputed to be descended, from them: [†] indeed it is possible that sometimes even episodes of tribal life are referred back to them in the form of incidents occurring within the limits of their own families. Ishmael, for instance, in 16[12] may be the personal son of Abraham; but if he is this, he is also something more: he impersonates the Bedawîn of the desert. So Jacob and Esau, in their contest for supremacy, are more than the twin sons of a man named Isaac: they impersonate two nations; and the later relations subsisting between these two nations plainly colour parts of the narrator's representation (esp. the terms of the Blessings). Jacob, keeping Laban's sheep, may be an individual; but when he and Laban are fixing the boundary which neither is to pass, they plainly represent two peoples. The story of Shechem and Dinah is one in which especially it may be suspected that this explanation is the correct one. Jg 9 shows how, after the conquest, Israelites and Canaanites lived in Shechem side by side; the almost complete identity of expression between Gn 33[19] 'the sons of Ḥamor, the father of Shechem,' and Jg 9[28] 'the men of Ḥamor, the father of Shechem' (where Shechem is clearly the place),[‡] raises a legitimate doubt whether in the former passage 'Shechem' does not mean the place as well, and whether therefore in ch. 34 the same name is not a personification of the inhabitants of the place: if this view be correct, ch. 34 will mean that an Israelite clan (Dinah) had

gained a footing in Shechem, and was in danger of being absorbed by the native Canaanites (the Benê Ḥamor): Simeon and Levi interposed to prevent this;[*] but their action was not supported by the Israelites at large ('Jacob,' 34[30]); cf. 49[5. 6]. Gn 49[7], it has even been conjectured, contains an allusion to the result: the Canaanites retaliated with such effect that these two tribes were broken up, and never afterwards recovered from the blow.[†] See art. SIMEON (TRIBE).

But, however that may be, it is impossible not to be impressed by the remarkable manne in which Jacob, both in the brighter and in the darker aspects of his character, is the prototype of his descendants. His doubtful qualities exactly recall that remarkable faculty of acquiring wealth and influence which the Jew possesses in such an extraordinary degree, and which, as must be admitted by his best friends, he is unfortunately apt to exercise with an exaggerated regard to self-interest. ' By Jacob's peculiar discipline of exile and suffering, a true counterpart is produced of the special faults and special gifts, known to us chiefly through his persecuted descendants in the Middle Ages. Professor Blunt has, with much ingenuity, pointed out how Jacob seems to have " learned, like maltreated animals, to have the *fear of man habitually before his eyes*." ‡ In Jacob we see the same timid, cautious watchfulness that we know so well, though under darker colours, through our great masters of fiction, in Shylock of Venice, and Isaac of York. But no less, in the nobler side of his career, do we have the germs of the unbroken endurance, the undying resolution, which keeps the nation alive still even in its present outcast condition, and which was the basis, in its brighter days, of the heroic zeal, long-suffering, and hope of Moses, of David, of Jeremiah, of the Maccabees, of the twelve Jewish apostles, and the first martyr, Stephen.' §

LITERATURE.—Comms. on Gen.; Ewald, *Hist.* i. 341-362 (who brings out well the dramatic aspects of parts of Jacob's career); Stanley, *Jewish Church*, vol. i. Lect. III.; F. W. Robertson, *Notes on Genesis*, and *Sermons*, i. 40 ff. (on the wrestling at Penuel). For post-Biblical Jewish views about Jacob, it must suffice to refer to the Targums on Gn, the Midrash *Bereshith Rabba* (tr. Wünsche, 1880), the Book of Jubilees (Dillm. in Ewald's *Jahrb.* iii.; Rönsch, 1874; Charles, 1895), the Midrashim tr[d] in Rönsch, 390 ff., and art. JACOB in Hamburger's *Real-Encyclopädie f. Bibel u. Talmud*.

2. ('Ιακώβ) The father of Joseph the husband of Mary (Mt 1[15t.]).   S. R. DRIVER.

JACOB'S WELL.—The ancient records contain no account of Jacob having dug a well. The earliest mention of it occurs in Jn 4[6] (πηγὴ τοῦ 'Ιακώβ). There, however, it is taken as matter of common belief that the well by which our Saviour conversed with the woman of Samaria was made by the patriarch. The traditions of Jew, Moslem, and Christian concur in identifying this well with that now universally known by the name *Bîr Ya'ḳûb*, or 'Jacob's well.' The Samaritans, who have dwelt in the locality for about 2300 years, have never wavered in their conviction that this was the work of Jacob. The circumstances connected with the founding of their community would lead them to make the most of all traditional associations which their neighbourhood afforded, with the fathers of Israel. That they were tempted in some cases to invent such associations, seems all too likely; but there are ele-

---

[*] *Hist.* 318-327 (cf. 464 *n.*). The contemptuous criticisms of Robertson (*Rel. of Isr.* 120-135) show little insight, and are anything but conclusive.
[†] Cf. Baethgen, *ap.* Ottley, p. 111.
[‡] 'Father'=*founder, settler*, as 1 Ch 2[21. 23] (Machir, the 'father' of Gilead), 4[2-45. 49-52] (the 'fathers' of Ziph, Hebron, and other towns), 4[3-5. 11. 12. 14. 17-21].

[*] Ewald, *Hist.* i. 359, 378 f.; cf. Dillm. pp. 369, 460.
[†] Wellh. *Comp.* 353-355, more briefly *Hist.* 324; Stade, *Gesch.* i. 147, 154; Kittel, ii. 63 (Eng. tr. ii. 70); Moore, *Judges*, p. 240 f.; who suppose that the incident referred to took place when the Israelites, after the conquest, first began to establish themselves on the W. of Jordan.
[‡] *Undesigned Coincidences*, I. viii.
[§] Stanley, *Jewish Church*[3], i. 56 f.

ments which go to confirm this tradition. It is in itself a strong presumption in favour of this site, that the Jewish belief coincides with that of the Samaritans. Considering the strenuous opposition offered to other identifications supported by the Samaritans, we may be sure this would not have escaped had there been any ground on which to attack it. The agreement indicated in the narrative between the Jews and Samaritans in the 1st cent. may be taken to prove the existence of a tradition inherited by both from a time anterior to the great quarrel. But the tradition also afforded a reasonable explanation of the presence of the well in this particular spot, in such close proximity to plentiful streams from perennial sources. These were naturally in the hands of the people of Shechem. When Jacob pitched his camp in the plain near by, being a man of peace, he would desire to avoid all occasion for the strifes so often arising from the contentions of rival herdsmen at the springs. By digging this well, he could secure the necessary supplies, make good his own independence, and enjoy an added assurance of peace. Jacob's residence here in such conditions is the one circumstance recorded in history which satisfactorily accounts for the existence of this well.

That it was here Jesus held His memorable interview with the woman of Samaria, seems beyond dispute. Going through Samaria to Galilee, Jesus must needs pass close by this place. As one journeys northward along the base of Mt. Gerizim, skirting the fertile plain of Mukhneh, almost opposite the entrance to the pass between Ebal and Gerizim, the road bifurcates, one branch bending to westward, through the vale to Shechem, and thence by way of Sebastîyeh (Samaria) and Jenîn to Galilee. The other goes northward, across the bay of the plain where it narrows between the mountains, and again divides; one limb passing downwards to Beisân and the Sea of Galilee, the other leading straight to Jenîn. Either of these roads may still be taken. While that past Sebastîyeh is naturally the more frequented to-day, the other is more direct; and it is impossible to say which was the more popular in Christ's time. But as the well in question lies in the fork between the two, it was equally easily accessible to the traveller from either.

The well is described as being close by Sychar, 'near to the parcel of ground that Jacob gave to his son Joseph' (Gn 48²²). If, as seems certain, this was the plot spoken of in Gn 33¹⁹, it lay before, *i.e.* to the east of, the city of Shechem, where, in the plain, the patriarch had chosen his residence. It became, according to St. Stephen (Ac 7¹⁶), the burying-place of those that went down to Egypt; and here the bones of Joseph were laid to rest (Jos 24³²). The modern town of Nâblus, representing the old Shechem, lies in the hollow between Ebal and Gerizim, less than 2 miles to the west, and is apparently farther distant than was the ancient city. The traditional tomb of Joseph is seen in the vale close by to the north-east; and just beyond this, to the lower slopes of Mount Ebal clings the village of 'Askar, which probably represents the town of Sychar mentioned in the narrative (see 'The Question of Sychar' in G. A. Smith's *HGHL* pp. 367–375). Eastward and southward stretches the rich plain which attracted Jacob and his flocks, whose whitening fields arrested the Saviour's eye, and where valuable crops are grown to-day.

Mount Gerizim throws its rugged crags steeply against the sky, immediately to the south, and, crowning the heights, just behind the Moslem Wely seen from the well's mouth, are the ruins of Justinian's fortress and the Samaritan place of sacrifice, enshrined in the sacred memories of

millenniums. The dark cliffs seem almost to impend over the spot, so that it would be most natural, standing at the brink of the well, to speak of it as 'this mountain.' In these respects the situation of *Bîr Ya'ḳûb* exactly meets the requirements of the history.

The mouth of the well is some feet below the present surface, in the midst of a vaulted chamber, about 15 ft. square, the roof of which has fallen in. Major Anderson made a descent into the well in 1866, an account of which he gives in the *Recovery of Jerusalem*, p. 465. 'The mouth of the well,' he says, 'has a narrow opening, just wide enough to allow the body of a man to pass through with arms uplifted, and this narrow neck, which is about 4 ft. long, opens into the well itself, which is cylindrically shaped, and about 7 ft. 6 in. in diameter. The mouth and upper part of the well is built of masonry, and the well appears to have been sunk through a mixture of alluvial soil and limestone fragments, till a compact bed of mountain limestone was reached, having horizontal strata which could easily be worked; and the interior of the well presents the appearance of having been lined throughout with rough masonry.' The estimates of depth have varied widely, from Arculfus (A.D. 670), who gives it as about 240 ft., to Maundrell (1697), who puts it at 105 ft.; and Major Anderson, who found it to be 75 ft. No doubt it was originally much deeper than it is now. In the decay of the several buildings that have stood over it, much rubbish must have fallen into it, and the habit travellers have of dropping a stone into a pit and watching how long it takes to reach the bottom, that so they may judge of the depth, contributed to the same result. This now, however, is carefully guarded against. Some years ago the well, and ground around it, were acquired by the authorities of the Greek Church in Nâblus. A dry-stone wall surrounds the plot, which has been planted out as an orchard, the keeper being accommodated in a small hovel by the gate. Over the well itself a hut has been built, the key of which is in charge of a neighbouring priest, in whose company the well may be visited.

A succession of churches stood on this spot, as we gather from the narratives of pilgrims. The last appears to have been destroyed after the crushing defeat of the Crusaders in 1187. An excellent account of the ruins of these buildings will be found in the *PEF Mem.* ii. p. 174, etc. A stone was found in 1881 (see *PEFSt*, p. 212), which may have been the original cover of the well.

The water now usually lasts until the month of May, and sometimes later. Then it disappears until the return of the rainy season. If the well were cleaned out, doubtless it would last much longer. Maundrell found 15 ft. of water in May 1697. The supply is therefore probably derived from percolation and rainfall; and apparently it has never risen near to the surface—the woman says 'the well is deep.' This possibly suggested to Jesus the phrase 'living water' as descriptive of His truth. For 'living water' is, in the language of the East, that of the fountain or stream as contrasted with that collected in cistern or well. In Jn 4⁶ the name used is indeed πηγὴ τοῦ Ἰακώβ, the well or fountain of Jacob; but in vv.¹¹·¹² the woman uses the strictly accurate term τὸ φρέαρ, the water-tank or cistern. For most purposes, living water is preferred; but where this is very 'hard' or 'heavy,' like that 'gushing from the very bowels of rocky (limestone) Mount Ebal,' the 'light' water that descends from heaven is greatly valued. Thus the water of Jacob's well is highly esteemed by the modern inhabitants of Nâblus and district (see letter from Dr. Bailey, a former missionary in Nâblus, *PEFSt*, 1897, p. 67 ; cf. also pp. 149, 196).* If the same were true in our Lord's time, apart altogether from the sacred associations which would lend it special attractions, it would be sufficient to account for the presence of the woman there, even if her home were on the lip of the rushing stream at *'Askar*.

LITERATURE.—Robinson, *BRP*² ii. 285 f. ; Thomson, *Land and Book*, ii. 146–151 ; G. A. Smith, *HGHL* pp. 367–375 ; *PEF Mem*. ii. ; Conder, *Tent-Work in Palestine*, pp. 15, 38 ; Baedeker, *Palestine and Syria*, ed. 1894, pp. 215, 216 ; *Narrative of a Mission of Inquiry to the Jews*, p. 212 ; Stanley, *Sinai and Palestine*, p. 241 ; *Expos. Times*, March 1894, p. 97 f.

W. EWING.

JACUBUS (A Ἰάκουβος, B Ἰαρσούβοος), 1 Es 9⁴⁸.— In Neh 8⁷ AKKUB.

JADA (יָדָע, perhaps 'the knowing one').—A Jerahmeelite, 1 Ch 2²⁸· ³². See GENEALOGY.

JADDUA (יַדּוּעַ).—**1.** One of those who sealed the covenant, Neh 10²¹ [Heb. ²²]. **2.** A high priest, the third in descent from Eliashib, the contemporary of Nehemiah, Neh 11¹· ²². The latter verse seems to make him contemporary with Darius the Persian, *i.e.* Darius III. Codomannus, and he is doubtless the Jaddua who is named by Josephus in connexion with Alexander the Great (Jos. *Ant*. XI. viii. 5, cf. vii. 2, viii. 7). See GENEALOGY.

H. A. WHITE.

JADDUS (B Ἰαδδούς, A Ἰοδδούς, AV Addus), 1 Es 5³⁸.—A priest whose descendants were unable to trace their genealogy at the time of the return under Zerub., and were removed from the priesthood. He is there said to have married Augia, a daughter of Zorzelleus or Barzillai, and to have been called after his name. In Ezr 2⁶¹, Neh 7⁶³ he is called by his adopted name Barzillai ; his original name Jaddus, and the name of his wife Augia, appear only in 1 Es. See BARZILLAI, No. 1.

H. ST. J. THACKERAY.

JADON (יָדוֹן, Εὐαρδών, Ἰαερείν, Ἰαρί, Ἰαρίμ, Ααρών ; ABא omit ; Neh 3⁷).—A Meronothite, who in company with the men of Gibeon and of Mizpah took part in rebuilding the wall of Jerusalem. The title Meronothite occurs again 1 Ch 27³⁰, but a place Meronoth is nowhere named. According to Jos. *Ant*. VIII. viii. 5, ix. 1, J. was the name of the man of God sent from Judah to Jeroboam (1 K 13). This tradition probably rests upon the identification of this prophet with IDDO the seer (which see).

H. A. WHITE.

JAEL (יָעֵל, 'mountain-goat' ; see on the name, Gray, *Heb. Prop. Names*, 90) is remembered on account of one famous episode in her life, of which we have two not altogether consistent accounts—one in prose (Jg 4⁴⁻²²), the other in poetry (Jg 5²⁻³¹). We shall first examine the latter, as undoubtedly the earlier version, and then consider the additional information supplied by the prose narrative.

From the Song of Deborah we learn that Deborah, a prophetess, and Barak, determined to free their countrymen from the tyranny of the kings of Canaan (5⁶· ¹⁹), which seems to have been especially felt by the tribe of Issachar (v.¹⁵). The leader of these kings was Sisera, and against his army the tribes of Ephraim, Benjamin, Manasseh (v.¹⁴), Issachar (v.¹⁵), Zebulun, and Naphtali sent troops, the latter two tribes being especially active (v.¹⁸). The decisive battle was fought 'in Taanach by the waters of Megiddo' (v.¹⁹), where a great storm came on and 'the stars in their courses fought against Sisera' (v.²⁰). The defeated leader escaped, and is described (v.²⁵) as asking for hospitality from Jael, 'the wife of Heber the Kenite' (v.²⁴). She gave the thirsty man to drink of the milk which would naturally be found in the tent of a nomad chieftain, and then 'she put her hand

* The letter is quoted in *HGHL*³ p. 676.

to the peg (יָתֵד), and her right hand to the workmen's hammer ; and with the hammer she smote Sisera, she smote through his head, yea, she pierced and struck through his temples. At her feet he bowed, he fell, he lay ; where he bowed, there he fell down dead' (vv.²⁶· ²⁷). For this exploit she is described in Deborah's triumphal ode as 'blessed above women.'

The first question to determine is, by what instrument and in what fashion is Jael here represented as having slain Sisera? Most modern critics (Cooke, Moore, Budde, etc.) hold that the words of vv.²⁶· ²⁷ indicate that Sisera was struck down as he was in the act of drinking, Jael dealing him a sudden blow, much as Saladin slew the treacherous knight in Scott's *Talisman*. And some identify the 'peg' with the handle of the 'workmen's hammer' mentioned in the parallel clause of v.²⁶. Thus W. R. Smith held that Jael's act was 'not the murder of a sleeping man, but the use of a daring stratagem. But the word "peg" suggested a tent-peg, and so the later prose story took it, and thereby misunderstood the whole thing' (*OTJC*² 132). But it is extremely doubtful whether יָתֵד can mean anything but a 'tent-pin' (Ex 27¹⁹) or 'peg' (Is 22²⁵, Ezk 15³) ; and, further, the meaning of the verbs מָחַק (ἄπ. λεγ.) and חָלַף (see Job 20²⁴) is too uncertain to entitle us to assert that there is here no hint of *piercing*, as contrasted with *crushing*, Sisera's skull. The truth is that vv.²⁶· ²⁷ of ch. 5 are too obscure to admit of dogmatism as to their meaning ; and it is by no means clear that they were misunderstood by the writer of the later prose narrative (4²²), whose account is : 'Jael took a tent-pin (יָתֵד), and took an hammer in her hand, and went softly unto him, and smote the pin into his temples, and it pierced through into the ground ; for he was in a deep sleep : so he swooned and died.'

The prose narrative, then, is not necessarily in contradiction with the Ode as to the manner of Sisera's death, though undoubtedly, if we had only the Ode to guide us, we should not be tempted to reproduce the scene described in 4²¹. The prose narrator seems to have had independent information, oral or otherwise.

There are other points of difference between chs. 4 and 5 which make it probable that the later writer has made free use of sources other than the Song. (*a*) As we have seen, 5¹⁴· ¹⁵· ¹⁸ describes the uprising of many tribes ; but in 4¹⁰ Barak collects 10,000 men from Zebulun and Naphtali only. It cannot, however, be denied that these are the tribes whose prowess is most prominent in the Song (5¹⁸). (*b*) In the poem, *kings* of Canaan are mentioned, of whom Sisera is the leader ; in 4² Sisera is the general of Jabin, king of Canaan (or [4¹⁷] of Hazor), under whose tyranny the people of Israel had been 'mightily oppressed' for twenty years (4³). (*c*) The connexion of Jabin with the Jael-Sisera story is not clear. Jabin takes no part in the action ; and it is possible that he has been introduced here through a reminiscence of Jabin, king of Hazor, the head of a Canaanite confederacy, whose army Joshua defeated at the Waters of Merom (Jos 11¹⁻¹¹). (*d*) Jabin's city, Hazor, was in Galilee, far distant from the Kishon Valley ; and Kedesh is north of Hazor. Here (4¹¹) were Heber's tents,* to which Sisera fled after his defeat, having first (4¹⁵) abandoned his chariot with the view of escaping his pursuing enemy. But (*α*) it is curious that Sisera should have passed by Jabin's stronghold when seeking shelter ;† and (*β*) it is difficult to reconcile the geographical data of the prose version with the implication that Jael's tent was not far from the battlefield.

To return to the episode of Sisera's death at the hands of Jael. The prose version makes the case against Jael blacker than the song does ; for (*a*)

* In Jg 1¹⁶ it is recorded that 'the children of the Kenite, Moses' brother-in-law,' accompanied the tribe of Judah to the north of Palestine after the conquest of the country. After some unspecified time, Heber, seemingly an important person among them, moved northward to the territory of Naphtali, and 'pitched his tent as far as the oak in Zaanannim, which is by Kedesh' (4¹¹). While living there, he seems, according to 4¹⁷, to have formed an alliance with Jabin.

† It might be urged that Sisera may have thought the tent of the women a more secure haven than Jabin's city ; a defeated and discredited general might well fear to return to his master.

in 4[18] she *invites* Sisera to her tent, (*b*) in 4[20] his trustful reliance on her loyalty is shown by his charge to her to stand at the tent door and deny, if asked, that any one lay concealed within ; and (*c*) in 4[21] she kills him when *asleep*. But, on either story, her act seems one of black and inexcusable treachery ; and difficulty has been felt in reconciling the words of approval in 5[24] with the verdict of conscience. Various expedients have been devised to evade the difficulty. It has been supposed that Jael was granted a revelation from God (cf. Jg 4[9]) bidding her slay Sisera, and that her action is to be compared to Joshua's alleged pitiless extermination of the aboriginal inhabitants of Canaan, in accordance with the command recorded in Dt 7[1. 2]. But this is to read something into the narrative for which there is no scriptural warrant ; Jael seems to have acted entirely on her own initiative. Mozley * gave a more plausible explanation. When Sisera was in Jael's power, he urges, she was in a dilemma ; she must be treacherous to him or disloyal to Israel, for, if he got away safely, no one could tell how soon he might raise another army. Now she looked on him as an outlaw, as one who had no right to life or fair dealing, for the divine command had gone forth for the destruction of him and his host ; and the idea of human personality, of the individual's private rights, was little developed in that primitive age. And thus she was justified, *relatively to the morality of her time*, in killing Sisera ; and the commendation of 5[24] is to be interpreted in like manner as expressing the natural feelings of a semi-barbarous people. This explanation, though valuable as laying stress on the rude condition of the Hebrew conscience in the early stages of Hebrew history, is not altogether satisfactory. For Jael's act was *not* in accordance with contemporary morality.† It was a violation of the duty of hospitality, conspicuously sacred among her countrymen and in her age. To such a degree did Lot regard it that he was willing to purchase the safety of his guests by the honour of his daughters (Gn 19[8]). And, according to the prose narrative, Sisera was not Jael's enemy : 'There was peace between Jabin, king of Hazor, and the house of Heber the Kenite' (Jg 4[17]). Thus she must have been in danger from the advance of Barak's army, flushed with victory, in whose track her tent lay, unless she could devise some plan for propitiating the conqueror. Self-preservation suggested the way of escape, and she adopted it. 'Come and *I* will show thee the man whom thou seekest,' she said to Barak (4[22]).

But whether her motive was patriotic or selfish, the 'moral difficulty' of the narrative is serious only to those who do not recognize the gradual education of mankind. Jael's act was not moral according even to her own standard, and thus to compare her with Judith or with Charlotte Corday is not quite apt. The approval of Deborah's Song must be ranked with those passages in the imprecatory Psalms which breathe at times the cruel and vengeful spirit of man, rather than the Spirit of God. See DEBORAH, HEBER, JABIN, SISERA.

J. H. BERNARD.

JAGUR (יָגוּר).—A town in the extreme south of Judah, Jos 15[21]. The site is unknown.

JAH (יָהּ).—An abbreviated form of *Jahweh* (יהוה), found chiefly in proper names, but occasionally also besides. The form of the abbreviation is in accordance with analogy : the apocopation of the last syllable gave rise to *yahw*, and this, by the principles of the Massoretic vocalization, became *yāhū* (cf. *tóhū* from *tohw*, and, what is even a closer parallel, *yishtaḥăweh*, shortened after the *wāw*

consecutive into *yishtāḥū*, in pause *yishtāḥū*, through an intermediate form, not recognized by the Massoretes, *yishtaḥw*) ; and *yāhū* (יהו) was afterwards shortened to *yāh* (יָהּ—with *mappiq*), and ultimately (in proper names) to *yāh* (יָה).

(1) Proper names, of which the second element is *yāh*, are very numerous in Hebrew : Mr. Gray (*Studies in Heb. Proper Names*, p. 284 ff.) enumerates 127 (*e.g.* Abijah, Uriah, Isaiah, etc.). The reader who is not conversant with Hebrew ought, however, to know that in the original the form in very many of these proper names is *yāhū* : on the whole, it may be said that the earlier form is *yāhū*, and the later form *yāh* (the *h* 'quiescing') ; but there are exceptions to this rule, and sometimes both forms occur side by side in the same context.

Thus, to take a few examples (the names, in their earlier parts are written generally in their English form), we have in 1 K 1-2 *Adoniyāhū*, except in 15[7. 18. 2]28 where we have *Adoniyāh* ; *Ahazyāhū* occurs regularly in both K and Ch, except in 2 K 1[3] 9[16. 23. 27. 29] 11[2], 2 Ch 20[35] *Ahazyāh* ; the same is the case with *Eliyāhū* (*Eliyāh* 2 K 1[3. 4. 8. 12], Mal 3[23], and, not of the prophet, 1 Ch 8[27], Ezr 10[21. 26]), *Amazyāhū* (*Amazyāh* 2 K 12[22] 13[12] 14[8] 15[1], Am 7[10. 12. 14], 1 Ch 4[34] 6[30]), *Benayāhū* (*Benayāh* 2 S 20[23], 1 Ch 4[36] 11[22. 31] 27[14], 2 Ch 20[14], Ezk 11[13] [v.[1] *Benayāhū*], Ezr 10[25. 30. 35. 43]), *Yirmĕyāhū* (the prophet), except 27[1] 28[5. 6. 10. 11. 12. 15] 29[1], Dn 9[2], Ezr 1[1] ; *Yesha'yāhū* (the prophet Isaiah) uniformly (including 2 Ch 26[22] 32[20. 32]) ; *Uzziyāhū* (the king), except 2 K 15[13. 30], Hos 1[1], Am 1[1], Zec 14[5] ; *Gedalyāhū* (in 2 K 25, Jer 39-43) uniformly, except Jer 40[5. 6. 8] 41[16] ; *Hizkiyāhū* (the king Hezekiah) uniformly, except 2 K 18[1. 10. 13. 14. 15. 16], Hos 1[1], Mic 1[1], Pr 25[1] ; *'Athalyāhū* (the queen), both K and Ch, except 2 K 11[1. 3. 13. 14], 2 Ch 22[12] ; etc. : on the other hand, *Uriyāh* occurs everywhere, except Jer 26[20. 21. 23] (*Uriyāhū*) ; *Ahiyāh* is more common than *Ahiyāhū* (only 1 K 14[4. 5. 6. 18], 2 Ch 9[29]), occurring already in 1 S 14[3. 18], *Malchiyāh* than *Malchiyāhū* (Jer 38[6]), *Micah* in Jg 17-18 than *Micāy'hū* (17[1. 4]), *Neriyāh* (Baruch's father) in Jer than *Neriyāhū* (36[14. 32] 43[6]), *Nethanyāh* in Jer 40-41 than *Nethanyāhū* (40[8] 41[9]). In Ezr-Neh proper names compounded with -*yah* are very numerous ; but the form -*yāhū* occurs but once (Ezr 10[41] *Shelemyāhū*) : on the other hand, in the parts of Ch added by the compiler many of the names of Levites and others are written with -*yāhū* (see, *e.g.*, 1 Ch 15[18. 21. 22. 24] 24[21-26] 25[12ff]. 26[2. 11. 14] 27[16ff]., 2 Ch 17[8] 29[12f].).*

(2) Outside proper names, Jah occurs only in poetry (mostly in late liturgical poetry), viz. Ex 15[2] 'My strength and a song is Jah' (cited Is 12[2], Ps 118[14]), Ex 17[16] (if the text be sound) in a poetically-worded passage of E (see RVm), Is 26[4] 'In Jah Jahweh is a rock of ages,' 38[11. 11] (Hezekiah's song), Ps 68[4. 18] 77[11] 89[8] 94[7. 12] 102[18] 115[17. 18] 118[5a. 17. 18. 19] 122[4] 130[3] 135[3. 4] 150[6a] ; in three passages in which the Massoretes treat it (questionably) as part of a compound word, Jer 2[31] (text dub.), Ca 8[6], Ps 118[5b] (read prob. as RV) ; and in 'Hallelujah' (written in MT as one word, הַלְלוּיָהּ) 23 times (see HALLELUJAH) between Ps 104[35] and 150[6b] (always as a liturgical formula at the beginning or end of a Psalm).† It would be natural to think of the abbreviated form as first arising in connexion with proper names ; but it is difficult to reconcile this view with Ex 15[2] 17[16], supposing the text of these passages to be sound, and the passages really early. The great majority of the occurrences of the word are indisputably late.

It was argued by Friedr. Delitzsch in 1881 (*Paradies*, pp. 158-166), in opposition to the generally accepted view, that *Yah* or *Yahu* was the original name of the God of Israel, and continued always to be the popular name ; *Yahweh* was a later modification of *Yahu*, designed for the purpose of establishing a connexion with *hāwāh*, to *be* (or *come to be*), and so of making the name the expression of a theological truth (above, p. 199[b]). The principal grounds alleged for this opinion were the occurrence of the shorter form in

---

* *Ruling Ideas in Early Ages*, p. 126 ff.
† See Jellett, *Moral Difficulties of the OT*, p. 61.

* When *yahw* forms the first element of a proper name, it becomes—through an intermediate *yĕhaw* (cf. יְהַב from יָהַב)— *yĕhó*, *yó* (as Jehoram, Joram) ; see Gray, p. 281 ff., who enumerates 29 names of this type ; cf. p. 300 (El-*yeho*-'enai, 'Unto Yah are my eyes').
† For Rabb. theories of the orthography in some of these cases cf. Geiger, *Urschrift*, 274-278.

all proper names, and the supposed traces of the name among Semitic nations (other than the Hebrews), who did not use the verb *hāwāh*, and could not consequently have formed a name from it. The same opinion has been adopted by Hommel (*AHT* 113 f., 115 f., 144, 145, 226), who follows Mr. Pinches * in thinking, in particular, that *Yah* is identical with *Aï* or *Ya*, found in an Arabian name *Ai-kalabu* on a contract-tablet of *c.* B.C. 2300, and in various Assyrian names (as Abu-Aï, Ashur-Aï, Samas-Aï) of 9–8 cent. B.C., and who, inferring from these indications the antiquity of the form, concludes that *Yahweh* is a later Mosaic modification of *Yah*, introduced for the purpose of imparting to it a new significance. Delitzsch's theory was criticized at the time by Philippi : † in view of the fact that Jahweh is the standing form of the name in the OT, and is attested independently for *c.* B.C. 850 by Mesha, while Jah, as shown above, is exceptional and mostly late, it is exceedingly difficult to think that the latter can be really the more original form ; while its occurrence in proper names is sufficiently accounted for by the tendency to abbreviation which would there be natural. The opinions of Pinches and Hommel have not hitherto (so far as the writer is aware) been endorsed by other Assyriologists.‡

Among the Jewish names occurring on the cuneiform tablets of the Persian period, found recently by the Pennsylvanian Expedition at Nippur, are many of the form *Gadalyāma* (or *-yāwa*), *Igdalyāma* (or *-yāwa*), *Mattanyāma* (or *-yāwa*), *i.e.* Gedaliah, Igdaliah, Mattaniah, etc.§ Mr. Pinches had noted before, from the same age (*PSBA*, *l.c.* p. 14 f.), *Gamaryāma* (or *-wa*), *i.e.* Gemariah ; *Natanayāma* (or-*wa*), *i.e.* Nethaniah ; *Shubunuyāma* (or *-wa*), *i.e.* Shebaniah ; and others. These forms would seem to show that in the Persian age the divine element in such names was pronounced as a dissyllable ; it is strange, therefore, to find them in the books Ezr-Neh (as remarked above) all but uniformly written with *-yāh.* Perhaps further investigation may explain the discrepancy.   S. R. DRIVER.

JAHATH (יַחַת, perh. for יַחְפֶּה 'he [God] will snatch up'). — **1.** A grandson of Judah, 1 Ch 4². **2.** A great-grandson of Levi, 1 Ch 6²⁰·⁴³. **3.** A son of Shimei, 1 Ch 23¹⁰. **4.** One of the 'sons' of Shelomoth, 1 Ch 24²². **5.** A Merarite Levite in the time of Josiah, 2 Ch 34¹². See GENEALOGY.

JAHAZ (יַהַץ Is 15⁴, Jer 48³⁴ ; paus. and ה *locale* יָהְצָה Nu 21²³, Dt 2³² [cf. יַהְצָה Jg 11²⁰] ; in Jos 13¹⁸ called יַהְצָה ; in 1 Ch 6⁷⁸, Jer 48²¹ יַהְצָה, RV Jahzah. The LXX renderings are :—Εἶσσα B Nu 21²³ ; Ἰάσσα BᵃAF Nu 21²³ ; B Dt 2³², A Jos 13¹⁸, Ἰάσα Jg 11²⁰ where A has Ἰηλ, Βάσαν B Jos 13¹⁸. The variations and omissions in Jos 21³⁶, 1 Ch 6⁷⁸, Is 15⁴, Jer 48²¹·³⁴ are too complicated for reproduction).—A town at which Sihon was defeated by Israel (Nu 21²³, Dt 2³², Jg 11²⁰). According to Tristram and Palmer, it was south of the Arnon on a site marked in maps as *Muhatet el-Haj.* But as Jahaz is counted among the cities of Reuben, whose southern boundary was the Arnon, a situation to the north of that river seems required. After the

---

* See *PSBA* xv. (1892) pp. 13–15 ; *Trans. Vict. Inst.* xxviii. (1895) pp. 11–13.
† See *Studia Biblica*, i. pp. 1–6 ; and comp. Gray, pp. 149–151.
‡ Comp. Jastrow in *JBLit.* xii. (1894), p. 105 f., and *Zeitsch. f. Assyr.* x. (1895), p. 222 ff. ; and Clay in the *Lutheran Church Review* (U.S.A.), 1895, p. 197. Jastrow's arguments against Pinches are forcible, though his own theory that the *ya* in the Assyr. names (as well as in many Heb. names) is an 'afformative' rests upon insufficient grounds. Delitzsch and others explain the Assyr. *ia* simply as the suffix of the first person (Clay, *l.c.* pp. 197–199).
§ Hilprecht in the *PEFSt*, Jan. 1898, p. 55 (and *Bab. Exped.* lx. 27) ; Pinches, *ib.*, Apr. 1898, p. 137 f.

crossing of the Arnon, messengers were sent to Sihon from the 'wilderness of Kedemoth,' Dt 2²⁶, and he 'went out against Israel into the wilderness and came to Jahaz,' Nu 21²³. Jahaz is mentioned in connexion with Kedemoth, Jos 13¹⁸ 21³⁶. These passages indicate a position for Jahaz in the S.E. portion of Sihon's territory. Eusebius in the *Onomasticon* (264. 94, Lagarde, p. 267) describes Jahaz as existing in his time between Medeba and Dibon (Δηβοῦς). This assigns a more central position to Jahaz, and implies that Israel, before encountering the forces of Sihon, disregarding his refusal, had advanced some distance into his land. If for Δηβοῦς we read Ἐσβοῦς, as Reland (*Pal.* tom. 2, p. 825) suggests, the position of Jahaz will be farther north. Jahaz was one of the Levite cities of Reuben belonging to the children of Merari, Jos 13¹⁸ 21³⁶ (see note in RVm), 1 Ch 6⁷⁸. According to the Moabite Stone (ll. 18–20), the king of Israel dwelt at Jahaz while at war with king Mesha, but was driven out, and the town was taken and added to Moabite territory. Isaiah (15⁴) and Jeremiah (48²¹·³⁴) refer to it as in the possession of Moab. The site has not yet been identified. See *SEP Mem.* p. 279 note, and G. A. Smith, *HGHL*, p. 559 and note.
           A. T. CHAPMAN.

JAHAZIEL (יַחֲזִיאֵל, 'El sees').—**1.** A Benjamite who joined David at Ziklag, 1 Ch 12⁴. **2.** One of the two priests who, according to 1 Ch 16⁶, blew trumpets before the ark when it was brought by David to Jerusalem. **3.** A Kohathite Levite, 1 Ch 23¹⁹ 24²³. **4.** An Asaphite Levite who is said to have encouraged Jehoshaphat and his army against an invading host, 2 Ch 20¹⁴. **5.** The ancestor of a family of exiles who returned, Ezr 8⁵, called in 1 Es 8³² **Jezalus.** On the emendation which should probably be made on the MT, see Ryle, *Ezr-Neh*, *ad loc.*, and art. SHECANIAH.

JAHDAI (the vocalization and meaning are both doubtful ; Baer points יָהְדַּי, others יֶהְדָּי ; cf. Kittel in *SBOT.* Gesenius [*Thes.*] makes the name = יהדוּ 'J'' leads ').—This name occurs in an obscure connexion (see GENEALOGY, IV. 33) in the genealogy of Caleb, 1 Ch 2⁴⁷, where Jahdai appears as the father of six sons.

JAHDIEL (יַחְדִּיאֵל 'El giveth joy ').—A Manassite chief, 1 Ch 5²⁴. See GENEALOGY, VIIᵃ. 8.

JAHDO (יַחְדּוֹ in common edd. of MT, יֶחְדּוֹ in Baer ; LXX B Ἰουραί, A Ἰεδδαί, Luc. Ἰεδδώ).—A Gadite, 1 Ch 5¹⁴. See GENEALOGY, XI. 3.

JAHLEEL (יַחְלְאֵל 'wait for God ').—Third son of Zebulun, Gn 46¹⁴, Nu 26²⁶ P : patron. **Jahleelites,** Nu 26²⁶.

JAHMAI (יַחְמַי, perh. = יַחְמְיָה 'may J'' protect,' cf. Sab. יחמאל).—A man of Issachar, 1 Ch 7².

JAHWEH.—See GOD, p. 199ᵃ, and JAH.

JAHZAH.—The form of Jahaz in 1 Ch 6⁷⁸ AV, RV, and Jer 48²¹ RV. See JAHAZ.

JAHZEEL (יַחְצְאֵל 'God divides '). — Naphtali's firstborn, Gn 46²⁴, Nu 26⁴⁸ P ; in 1 Ch 7¹³ **Jahziel** (יַחֲצִיאֵל) : patron. **Jahzeelites,** Nu 26⁴⁸.

JAHZEIAH (יַחְזְיָה = 'J'' sees,' Ἰαζίας A, Λαζειά B, Ezr 10¹⁵ ; Ἐζεκείας A, Ἐζείας B, 1 Es 9¹⁴, AV **Jahaziah**).—The son of Tikvah, one of four men who are mentioned as opposing Ezra in the matter of the foreign wives (so RV, Gesen., Bertheau, Stade, etc.). The AV regarded J. and his companions as supporters of Ezra, rendering 'were employed about this matter'; and this view is supported by LXX, 1 Es, RVm; but for the Heb. phrase here found (עָמַד עַל), cf. 1 Ch 21¹, 2 Ch 20²³, Dn 11¹⁴, in which passages *opposition* is evidently expressed.　　　　　H. A. WHITE.

JAHZERAH (יַחְזֵרָה).—A priest, 1 Ch 9¹², called in Neh 11¹³ **Ahzai**. See GENEALOGY, III. 17. Siegfried-Stade propose to emend יחזרה to אחזי=יחזיה (Ahzai). See further, Smend, *Listen*, and Ryle, *Ezr-Neh, ad loc.*

JAHZIEL.—See JAHZEEL.

JAIR (יָאִיר 'he enlightens' or 'one giving light').—**1.** A son of Manasseh and contemporary of Moses, Nu 32⁴¹, Dt 3¹⁴, Jos 13³⁰, 1 K 4¹³, 1 Ch 2²²ᶠ. **2.** One of the judges, Jg 10³ᶠᶠ. According to another tradition he was the same as **1**. A very ancient, probably the original, account of the conquest of Gilead is contained in Nu 32³⁹·⁴¹ᶠ. There can be little doubt that it describes a conquest made after the main body of Israelites were settled *west* of the Jordan. It has, however, got mixed up with the story of the Mosaic conquest of the lands east of Jordan. Even if there was a Jair contemporary with Moses, he could not have been literally the 'son' of Manasseh (see Driver on Dt 3¹⁴), hence 'son' must in any case be interpreted in the sense of *descendant*. Attempts have been made unsuccessfully by Keil and others to distinguish the Jair of the Hexateuch from the Jair of Jg, as well as to harmonize the somewhat conflicting notices about the 'tent-villages' (*havvoth-Jair*). In Jg 10³ᶠ Jair is said to have had 30 sons that rode on 30 ass colts, and to have 'judged' Israel 22 years. The 'tent-villages' are there given as 30, whereas in 1 Ch 2²³, which possibly reflects post-exilic relations (Moore), they are 23 in number. See, further, the *Comm.* of Dillm., Driver, and Moore on the above-cited passages, and the article HAVVOTH-JAIR. **3.** The father of Mordecai, Est 2⁵. **4.** עִיר *Kĕrê*,* עֵר *Kethibh*) Father of Elhanan, 1 Ch 20⁵. By a scribal error this *Jair* is called in 2 S 21¹⁹ **Jaare-oregim** (wh. see, and cf. Driver, *Text of Sam.*, and Budde, *SBOT, ad loc.*).
　　　　　　　　　　　　　　J. A. SELBIE.

JAIRITE, THE (הַיָּאִרִי; B ὁ Ἰαρείν, A ὁ Ἰαειρεί; *Jairites*), *i.e.* of the family of Jair, the son of Manasseh, whose descendants lived in Gilead (Nu 32⁴¹ etc.). The gentilic adjective occurs only in connexion with IRA (wh. see), who is further described as 'priest unto David' (2 S 20²⁶). Many scholars, however, consider that 'Jattirite' (הַיַּתִּרִי) should be read for 'Jairite' in this passage. If this reading be adopted (cf. Pesh. ܝܰܬܝܪ).

Ira might possibly be of the tribe of Levi, since Jattir was a priestly city in the hill-country of Judah (Jos 15⁴⁸ 21¹⁴, cf. 1 S 30²⁷).
　　　　　　　　　　　　　　J. F. STENNING.
JAIRUS (Ἰάειρος, the Gr. form of OT JAIR).—**1.** The father of Mordecai (Ad. Est 11²), called in Est 2⁵ **Jair**. **2.** Eponym of a family of 'temple servants' (1 Es 5³¹) (AV **Airus**, RVm **Reaiah**). **3.** The ruler of the synagogue whose daughter was restored to life by Jesus (Mk 5²², Lk 8⁴¹). See next article.

JAIRUS (RV **Jaïrus**, Ἰάειρος, probably a transcription of OT name יָאִיר), a ruler of the synagogue, who dwelt at or near Capernaum. After Jesus had returned from Gergesa (Gadara) he was approached by Jairus, a suppliant on behalf of his daughter, aged twelve, who was lying at home at

* 'So LXX, Pesh. (Jerome 'filius *saltus*,' *i.e.* יַעַר, without the *plena scriptio*).'—Driver, *Text of Sam.* 272 n¹.

the point of death, Mk 5²¹ᶠ·=Lk 8⁴⁰ᶠ·=Mt 9¹⁸ᶠ. Jesus at once set out for the house of Jairus, followed by a crowd; on the way another message came, announcing the death of the child. Having arrived, Jesus entered, taking with him Peter, James, and John, and tried to quell the noisy mourning with the words 'She is not dead, but sleepeth.' This assurance being misunderstood and ridiculed, Jesus expelled the mourners; with the parents and the three disciples went into the chamber of death; took the child's hand, and restored her with the words Talitha cumi (ταλιθὰ κούμ ܩܘܡܝ ܛܠܝܬܐ = 'maiden, arise'). So substantially the Synoptists. According, however, to Mt, Jairus comes while Jesus is at Matthew's feast, pleading for his daughter already *dead*; Mt does not give the name 'Jairus,' and calls him simply ἄρχων (of course=ἀρχισυνάγωγος). All three insert into the above narrative the incident of the woman with the Issue of Blood, which took place on the way to the house of Jairus.
　　　　　　　　　　　　　　A. GRIEVE.
JAKEH (יָקֶה (or יָקֵא; so the Vulg. *Vomentis*).—As a proper name, father of Agur, the author of the proverbs contained in Pr 30. For modes of interpreting the verse Pr 30¹, see AGUR.

JAKIM (יָקִים).—**1.** A Benjamite, 1 Ch 8¹⁹. See GENEALOGY, VIII. 12. **2.** A priest, head of the 12th course, 1 Ch 24¹². See GENEALOGY, III. 15.

JALAM (יַעְלָם).—A 'son' of Esau, Gn 36⁵·¹⁴·¹⁸, 1 Ch 1³⁵.

JALON (יָלוֹן).—A Calebite, the son of Ezrah, 1 Ch 4¹⁷. See GENEALOGY, IV. 53.

JAMBRES.—See JANNES AND JAMBRES.

JAMBRI.—Soon after the death of Judas Maccabæus (B.C. 161), Jonathan and his adherents sent their personal property, which was no longer safe in the wilderness of Judæa, to the friendly country of the Nabatæans. The convoy, which was under the charge of John, a brother of Jonathan, was attacked and captured by a robber tribe, the sons of Jambri, near Medaba, on the E. of Jordan, and John himself slain. To avenge his death, Jonathan and Simon crossed the Jordan and waylaid a large wedding party belonging to this tribe. Many were slain, and the survivors fled to the mountains (1 Mac 9³⁵⁻⁴², Jos. *Ant.* XIII. i. 2–4). There is some uncertainty as to the true reading of the proper name, which does not occur elsewhere. Ἰαμβρείν A, Ἰαμβρί ℵ*, Ἀμβρί ℵᶜ cursives; Syr. has ܐܡܒܪܝ ('Ambri), Josephus οἱ Ἀμαραίου παῖδες. 'Ambri is probably the orig. form: some have conjectured that this represents *Amorites* (so Grimm, Michaelis).　　　　H. A. WHITE.

JAMES.—This name is our Eng. equivalent for the Ἰάκωβος of the Gr. Test., from which it is derived through the Italian *Giacomo*. It is used in NT of three different persons.
　　(1) *James the son of Zebedee*, sometimes called the Great.
　　(2) *James the son of Alphæus*.
　　(3) *James the brother of the Lord*.
1. JAMES THE SON OF ZEBEDEE.—In Mk 1¹⁹ (Mt 4²¹) he and his brother John are represented as mending their nets in their boat on the Sea of Galilee, and at the call of Christ leaving the boat to their father and the hired servants. They were partners with Simon and Andrew (Lk 5¹⁰), who were fishing near them and were called at the same time in the words, 'Follow me, and I will

make you fishers of men.' This was after John the Baptist had been cast into prison by Herod. We learn from Jn 1[35ff.] that Andrew and his brother, and probably John also, were disciples of the Baptist, and had already been taught by him to see in Jesus 'the Lamb of God.' The call recorded by St. Luke (5[1-11]) is regarded by many commentators as merely another account of the call narrated by St. Mark, but there is a great difference in the circumstances. Even the words addressed to Simon, which form the chief point of contact in the two, ἀπὸ τοῦ νῦν ἀνθρώπους ἔσῃ ζωγρῶν, seem to be not so much another version of the words used by St. Mark, ποιήσω ὑμᾶς γενέσθαι ἁλιεῖς ἀνθρώπων, as a more urgent command based upon them; and there is a corresponding difference between the ἀφέντες τὰ δίκτυα, ἀφέντες τὸν πατέρα of St. Mark and the ἀφέντες τὰ πάντα of St. Luke.

The last call was that to the apostleship (Mt 10[2], Mk 3[14], Lk 6[13], Ac 1[13]). In all four lists of the apostles, Peter, Andrew, James, and John form the first group; in Mk and Ac, James and John follow Peter, and throughout the history, especially at the Transfiguration and the Agony, we find these three preferred before the others. The fact that James always precedes John (except in Lk 9[28]), and that John is sometimes described as the brother of James (Mk 5[37], Mt 17[1]), suggests that James was the elder of the two. In Ac 12[2] James is described as brother of John, to distinguish him from his greater namesake, the brother of the Lord. It is remarkable that he is never mentioned in the Fourth Gospel.

St. Mark tells us (3[17]) that Jesus surnamed the two brothers Boanerges (Sons of Thunder), alluding, perhaps, to the vehemence shown in their demand that their Master should call down fire from heaven to consume the Samaritans, who refused to receive him because he was going up to Jerusalem (Lk 9[53]); and again in their request that they might sit on his right hand and on his left hand in his kingdom (Mk 10[37]), to which our Lord replied by the prophecy that they should drink of his cup and be baptized with his baptism.

The wife of Zebedee was Salome, as we learn from a comparison of Mt 27[56] and Mk 15[40], who appears to have been a sister of the Lord's mother (see Jn 19[25] and the article on BRETHREN OF THE LORD). James and John would thus be first cousins of Jesus, which may have been one reason why their mother urged their claim to the highest position in his kingdom. We learn from Mk 15[41] (cf. Lk 8[3]) that Salome was one of the women who followed Jesus in Galilee, and ministered to him of their substance. Combined with the mention of hired servants, and with St. John's intimacy with Caiaphas the high priest, this fact makes it probable that the family of Zebedee were comparatively well off.

We hear nothing of James, as distinguished from the other apostles, for some 14 years after the Crucifixion. The fact, however, that he was the first of the Twelve to suffer martyrdom, shows that he must have attracted the attention of the Jews and of Herod Agrippa by his bold uncompromising character. This Herod was son of Aristobulus, and grandson of Herod the Great and Mariamne. Herodias, who was the cause of the murder of John the Baptist, was his sister. After reigning in splendour for three years over a kingdom larger than that of his grandfather, Agrippa sought to increase his popularity still further by putting down the new Christian heresy. Shortly before the Passover of 44, he killed James with the sword, and threw Peter into prison (Ac 12[1f.]). The sacred writer records in the same chapter the punishment which followed (v.[21ff.], cf. Jos. *Ant.* XIX. viii. 2).

Eusebius (*HE* ii. 9) gives us a quotation from the 7th book of the lost *Hypotyposes* of Clemens Alexandrinus, in which the latter mentions a tradition that the accuser of St. James was so much moved by his confession, that he declared himself to be a Christian, and was carried off with him to execution. On the way thither he asked forgiveness of the apostle, who, after a moment's hesitation, kissed him, saying, 'Peace be unto thee.' The same story is given in the *Apostolica Historia* of pseudo-Abdias (*ap.* Fabr. *Cod. Apoc. NT*), who also narrates the conversion of the magicians Hermogenes and Philetus by St. James.

The legend of Saint Iago, the patron saint of Spain, is given in Mrs. Jameson's *Sacred and Legendary Art*, vol. i. pp. 230–241. According to this, the gospel was first preached in Spain by St. James the Great, who afterwards returned to Judæa, and, after performing many miracles there, was finally put to death by Herod. His body was placed on board ship at Joppa and transported to Iria in the north-west of Spain under angelic guidance. The surrounding heathen were converted by the prodigies which witnessed to the power of the saint, and a church was built over his tomb. During the barbarian invasions all memory of the hallowed spot was lost till it was revealed by vision in the year 800. The body was then moved by order of Alphonso II. to the place now called Compostella (abbreviated from Jacomo Postolo), which became famous as a place of pilgrimage throughout Europe. The saint was believed to have appeared on many occasions mounted on a white horse, leading the Spanish armies to victory against their infidel foes.

The impossibilities of the story have been pointed out by Roman Catholic scholars. (1) It was a tradition of the early Church that the apostles, in accordance with a command of our Lord, did not leave Jerus. for twelve years after the Ascension (cf. the Κήρυγμα Πέτρου in Clem. Al. *Strom.* vi. p. 762 ; Apollonius in Euseb. *HE* v. 18 *ad fin.*). This is supported by what we read in Ac 8[1], that the apostles were still at Jerus. during the persecution in which Stephen was martyred. (2) St. Paul mentions his desire to visit Spain (Ro 15[24]) just after he had spoken of his rule not to preach the gospel on another man's foundation. The probable date of Ro is 58 [Turner,55–56], long after the martyrdom of St. James. (3) There is no certain mention of St. James in connexion with Spain till the 9th cent., when Notker, a monk of St. Gall, wrote : 'hujus Apostoli sacratissima ossa ad Hispanias translata in ultimis earum finibus condita celeberrima illarum gentium veneratione coluntur. Nec immerito, quia ejus corporali præsentia et doctrina atque signorum efficacia eidem populi ad Christi fidem conversi referuntur' (*Martyrol.* ad diem 25 Jul.). On the other hand, Innocent I. (d. 417) states that the Churches of Italy, Gaul, and Spain had all been founded by those who owed their authority to St. Peter (Ep. 25 *ad Decantium*) ; and Vincentius Fortunatus (fl. A.D. 600), speaking of the saints of different countries, makes Vincentius the chief glory of Spain ('Vincenti Hispana surgit ab arce decus,' *Carm.* vii. 3), as Alban of Britain, Hilary and Martin of Gaul, while the Jacobi are assigned to the Holy Land. (See the art. on JAMES by F. Meyrick in Smith, *DB*[2], and by R. Sinker in the *Dict. of Chr. Antiq.* ; the *Acta Sanctorum* for July 25 ; Natalis Alexander, *Hist. Eccl.* sæcl. i. § 15 ; Forbes, *Handbook of Spain*, ch. on Santiago).

2. JAMES THE SON OF ALPHÆUS.—In the four lists of the apostles we find James, son of Alphæus, standing at the head of the 3rd group, of which the other members are Thaddæus (Mk 3[18]), also called Lebbæus (Mt 10[3] cod. D and AV) or 'Ιούδας 'Ιακώβου (Lk 6[16], Ac 1[13]) ; Simon Zelotes (Lk 6[15], Ac 1[13]), also called Σ. Καναναῖος (Mt 10[4], Mk 3[18]), and Judas Iscariot. By St. Luke he is coupled with Simon, by St. Matthew and St. Mark with Thaddæus. Nothing else is told us about this James in the NT, but it is probable that he was a brother of Levi or Matthew, who is also called son of Alphæus (Mk 2[14]). The phrase 'Ιούδας 'Ιακώβου means almost certainly 'the son,' not the 'brother' of James.' He is usually identified with James the Little (AV 'the Less'), the brother of Joses and son of Mary, who is mentioned in Mk 15[40], Mt 27[56]. This Mary is apparently called ἡ τοῦ Κλωπᾶ in Jn 19[25], words which some have interpreted 'the wife of Clopas,' and have in consequence identified 'the wife of Clopas,' and have in consequence identified Clopas with Alphæus. They have also understood the clause which precedes (ἡ ἀδελφὴ τῆς μητρὸς αὐτοῦ) of this Mary, instead of understanding it of Salome, and thus have identified James, son of Alphæus, with James the brother of the Lord. The extreme improbability of this hypothesis is pointed out in the art. on the BRETHREN OF THE LORD. Hegesippus (*ap.* Euseb. *HE* iii. 11) speaks of a Clopas who was brother of

Joseph; if Mary was his wife, she would be aunt of the sons of Joseph, the brethren of the Lord. (The evidence as to the festival of James, son of Alphæus, being distinct from that of the brother of the Lord, is given in Sinker's article under this head in the *Dict. of Chr. Antiq.*).

3. JAMES THE BROTHER OF THE LORD.—See the article on the BRETHREN OF THE LORD for the proof that this James was the son of Joseph and Mary, not one of the Twelve, nor even a believer until after the Resurrection. His conversion seems to have been connected with a special appearance of the Risen Lord (1 Co 15⁷). Of his subsequent history we gather from the Acts and the Epistles of St. Paul, that, after the Ascension, he with his brothers remained at Jerusalem in the company of the eleven apostles and Mary and the other women, waiting for the descent of the Spirit (Ac 1¹⁴), and that within ten years from this time he became the head of the Church at Jerusalem. Thus in Gal 1¹⁸. ¹⁹ St. Paul says that three years after his conversion, probably about A.D. 38, he went up to Jerus. and stayed with Peter fifteen days, seeing no other apostle, but only James the Lord's brother,—a statement which is quite in accordance with Ac 12¹⁷, where Peter on his escape from prison (A.D. 44) is said to have gone to the house of Mary the mother of Mark, and desired that news of his escape might be sent to James and the brethren. In Gal 2¹⁻¹⁰ St. Paul describes a later visit to Jerus. after an interval of fourteen years, *i.e.* about A.D. 51. In this visit the leaders of the Church, James, Peter, and John (Gal 2⁹), after hearing his report of his first missionary journey, signified their approval of his work, and 'gave right hands of fellowship,' agreeing that Paul and Barnabas should preach to the Gentiles and they themselves to the circumcision. In vv.¹¹⁻¹⁴ Peter's inconsistency in regard to eating with the Gentiles at Antioch is explained by the arrival of 'certain from James.' St. Paul's second visit to Jerus. is more fully described in Ac 15⁴⁻²⁹, where James appears as president of the Council held to consider how far the Gentile Christians should be required to conform to the customs of the Jews. It is James who sums up the discussion and proposes the resolution which is carried, in the words ἐγὼ κρίνω μὴ παρενοχλεῖν τοῖς ἀπὸ τῶν ἐθνῶν ἐπιστρέφουσιν ἐπὶ τὸν θεόν, κ.τ.λ. James is seen in the same position of authority in Ac 21¹⁸, when St. Paul presents himself before him on his return from his third missionary journey (A.D. 58). After joining in praise to God for the success which had attended his labours, James and the elders who are with him warn St. Paul of the strong feeling against him, which had been excited among the 'myriads of Jewish believers who were all zealous for the law,' by the report that he had taught the Jews of the Dispersion to abandon circumcision and their other customs. To counteract this impression, they recommended him to join in a Nazirite vow, which had been undertaken by four members of their community, as a proof that the report was unfounded, and that he himself walked according to the law. From 1 Co 9⁵ μὴ οὐκ ἔχομεν ἐξουσίαν ἀδελφὴν γυναῖκα περιάγειν ὡς καὶ οἱ λοιποὶ ἀπόστολοι καὶ οἱ ἀδελφοὶ τοῦ Κυρίου, it has been inferred that St. James was a married man. On his authorship of the Epistle which goes by his name, see next article.

Further particulars are supplied by Josephus, Hegesippus, the Gospel according to the Hebrews, and other apocryphal books, including in these the *Clementine Homilies and Recognitions.*

The Gospel according to the Hebrews, which Lightfoot speaks of as one of the earliest and most respectable of the apocryphal narratives (*Gal.* p. 274), is quoted by Jerome (*de Vir. ill.* 2) to the following effect: 'The Lord after his resurrection appeared to James, who had sworn that he would not eat bread from the hour in which he had drunk the cup of the Lord till he saw him risen from the dead. Jesus, therefore, took bread and blessed and brake it, and gave it to James the Just, and said to him, My brother, eat thy bread, for the Son of Man has risen from the dead.' There are other versions of the same story, in which the vow is dated, not from the Last Supper, but from the Crucifixion (see Nicholson's ed. of the Gospel, p. 62 f., and the Introduction to Mayor's *St. James*, p. xxxvii n.). Possibly, the reference to the Last Supper may have arisen from the fact that St. James shaped his vow after the Lord's words spoken at the Supper, 'I will not drink henceforth of the fruit of the vine till the kingdom of God shall come.'

Hegesippus (c. A.D. 160) is quoted by Eusebius (*HE* ii. 23) to the following effect: 'The charge of the Church after the Ascension devolved on James the brother of the Lord in concert with the apostles. He is distinguished from others of the same name by the title "Just," which has been applied to him from the first. He was holy from his mother's womb, drank no wine or strong drink, nor ate animal food: no razor came on his head, nor did he anoint himself with oil nor use the bath. To him only was it permitted to enter the Holy of Holies. ... His knees became hard like a camel's, because he was always kneeling in the temple, asking forgiveness for the people. Through his exceeding righteousness he was called "Oblias," which, being interpreted, is "the defence of the people," and "Righteousness," as the prophet declared of him. Some of the seven sects of the Jews inquired of him, "What is the door of Jesus?" And he said that he was the Saviour; whereupon some believed that Jesus is the Christ. ... Hence arose a disturbance among the Jews, fearing that all the people would look to Jesus as the Christ. They came, therefore, and ... set James on the pinnacle of the temple and cried to him, "O thou just one to whom we all are bound to listen, tell us what is the door of Jesus." And he answered with a loud voice, "Why do ye ask me concerning Jesus the Son of Man? He is both seated in heaven on the right hand of Power, and he will come again on the clouds of heaven." And when many were convinced and gave glory at the witness of James, the same scribes and Pharisees said to each other, "We have done ill in bringing forward such a testimony to Jesus; let us go up and cast him down, that they may fear to believe him." And they cried out saying, "Alas! even the just has gone astray." And they fulfilled that which is written in Isaiah, "Let us take away the just, for he is not for our purpose." So they cast down James the Just, and they began to stone him, since he was not killed by the fall; but he kneeled down, saying, "O Lord God, my Father, I beseech thee forgive them, for they know not what they do." While they were thus stoning him, one of the priests of the sons of Rechab, of whom Jeremiah the prophet testifies, cried out, "Stop! what do ye? The just is praying for you." But one of them, who was a fuller, smote the head of the just one with his club. And so he bore his witness. And they buried him on the spot, and his monument still stands by the side of the temple with the inscription, "He hath been a true witness both to Jews and Greeks that Jesus is the Christ." And immediately Vespasian commenced the siege.'

Lightfoot has pointed out the many improbabilities in this narrative, and conjectures that it may have been taken by Hegesippus from the Ebionite Ἀναβαθμοὶ Ἰακώβου, of which we find traces in the *Clementine Recognitions.* In the *Recognitions*, as in Hegesippus, we read that James refuted the Jewish sects, and that he was hurled down from the temple by his persecutors. Lightfoot thinks that there may be truth in the statement that James was an ascetic and a Nazirite, and, we may add, in the respect entertained for him even by his unbelieving countrymen. The account of the death, however, which is given by Jos. (*Ant.* xx. ix. 1) is far more likely to be historical. 'During the interval between the death of Festus (prob. in the year 62) and the arrival of his successor Albinus, the high priest Ananus the younger, being of a rash and daring spirit, and inclined like the Sadducees in general to severity in punishing, brought to trial James the brother of Jesus, who is called the Christ, and some others before the court of the Sanhedrin, and, having charged them with breaking the laws, delivered them over to be stoned. The better class of citizens and those who were versed in the laws were indignant at this, and made complaints both to king Agrippa and to Albinus, on the ground that Ananus had no right to summon the Sanhedrin without the consent of the procurator; and Agrippa in consequence removed him from the high priesthood.' Origen (*Cels.* i. c. 47) and Euseb. (*HE* ii. 23) also cite Josephus as ascribing the miseries of the siege to the divine vengeance for the murder of James ; but this does not occur in his extant writings.

Clement of Alexandria (*ap.* Euseb. *HE* ii. 1) says that Peter and James and John, who were most honoured by the Lord, chose James the Just to be bishop of Jerus. after the Ascension, and that the Lord imparted his esoteric teaching (τὴν γνῶσιν) to James the Just and Peter and John after his resurrection, and again that this was imparted by them to the other apostles, and by the latter to the Seventy.

In the *Clementine Homilies* (written early in the 3rd cent.) James is represented, in the letter addressed to him by Clement, as the chief ruler of the Church at large, Κλήμης Ἰακώβῳ τῷ κυρίῳ καὶ ἐπισκόπων ἐπισκόπῳ, διέποντι δὲ τὴν <ἐν> Ἰερουσαλὴμ ἁγίαν Ἐβραίων ἐκκλησίαν καὶ τὰς πανταχῆ θεοῦ προνοίᾳ ἱδρυθείσας, κ.τ.λ.

Eusebius (*HE* vii. 19) reports that his episcopal chair was still shown at Jerus. at the time when he wrote.

Besides the canonical Epistle of St. James, his name is attached to the apocr. *Protevangelium Jacobi* and the so-called *Liturgy of St. James*. See *Dict. Chr. Antiq.* p. 1019 f., art. 'Liturgy,' and *Dict. of Chr. Biog.* under 'Gospels, Apocryphal,' p. 701 f.   J. B. MAYOR.

JAMES, THE GENERAL EPISTLE OF. —

i. AUTHORSHIP.—The writer describes himself (1[1]) as 'James, a servant of God and of the Lord Jesus Christ.' As the name was very common, and the description one which is applicable to all Christians, it is evident that he must have been distinguished from others who bore the same name by position or otherwise, so as to justify him in addressing the Twelve Tribes of the Dispersion with the tone of authority which is so marked a feature of the Epistle. This inference receives support from the Ep. of Jude, the writer of which styles himself 'brother of James,' evidently assuming that his brother's name would carry weight with those to whom he writes.

The Epistle itself is strongly contrasted, not only with Ro and Gal, against which some have supposed it to be directed, but also with 1 P, which, in some points, it closely resembles. In style it reminds one now of Pr, now of the stern denunciations of the prophets, now of the parables in the Gospels. It has scarcely any direct reference to Christ, who is indeed named only twice. In commending the duty of patience (5[7-11]) the writer refers to the example of the husbandman, and to Job and the prophets of the OT : if he alludes to our Lord at all, he does so only obscurely in the words ' ye killed the just ; he doth not resist you ' ; while St. Peter, on the contrary, dwells exclusively on the example of Christ (1 P 2[19-24] 4[12-14]). In urging the duty of prayer, reference is made, not (as in He 5[7]) to the promises or prayers of Christ, but to the prayer of Elijah ; the exhortation to kindness, and the warning against evil-speaking in ch. 3, are based, not on the example of Christ and the thought of our common brotherhood in him (as in 1 P 2[23], Ro 12[5], Eph 4[25]), but on the parables of nature, on the fact that man was created in the image of God, and on general reasoning ; and again (in 4[11]) speaking evil of a brother is condemned as putting a slight on the law, not as causing pain to Christ. No mention is made of the crucifixion or resurrection, or of the doctrines of the incarnation and atonement. To a careless reader the tone seems scarcely to rise above that of the OT ; Christian ideas are still clothed in Jewish forms. Thus the law, called for the sake of distinction ' the law of liberty ' or ' the royal law,' seems to stand in place of the gospel, or even of Christ himself (2[8-13] 4[11]) ;

the love of the world is condemned in the language of the OT as adultery against God. This contrast rises to its highest pitch in treating of the relation between faith and works (2[14-26]). While St. Paul writes (Ro 3[28]) 'We reckon, therefore, that a man is justified by faith without the works of the law,' the language of St. James is (2[24]) 'Ye see then that by works a man is justified, and not by faith only.' And while the case of Abraham is cited in Ro 4[3. 13. 16] in proof of the doctrine of justification by faith, and the case of Rahab is cited for the same purpose in He 11[31], St. James makes use of both to prove that man is justified by works (2[25]). Speaking generally, we may say that this Epistle has a more Jewish cast than any other writing of the NT, and that the author must have been one who would be more in sympathy with the Judaizing party, and more likely to exercise an influence over them, than any of the three great leaders, Peter, Paul, or John.

Comparing what is said of James the brother of the Lord in the preceding article, we find in him one who exactly fulfils the conditions required in the writer of the Epistle ; and if we examine the speech attributed to him in Ac 15 and the circular letter there given, which was probably drawn up by him, we find in these a remarkable similarity to the language of the Epistle. That St. Luke has recorded the actual words of the speaker, either in the original language or in a translation, seems probable from his use of the form 'Symeon' (v.[14]), which is not found elsewhere in Ac, as well as from the resemblances, noticed by Alford (vol. iv. *Prolegomena*), between 1 P and the speeches ascribed to him in the Ac. It is surely a remarkable coincidence that, out of 230 words contained in the speech and circular, so many should reappear in our Epistle, written on a totally different subject.

They are as follows : (1) the epistolary salutation χαίρειν (Ja 1[1], Ac 15[23]) found in only one other passage of the NT, the letter of Lysias to Felix (Ac 23[26]) ; (2) the curious phrase, borrowed from the LXX, which occurs in NT only in Ac 15[17] ἐφ᾽ οὓς ἐπικέκληται τὸ ὄνομά μου ἐπ᾽ αὐτούς, and Ja 2[7] τὸ καλὸν ὄνομα τὸ ἐπικληθὲν ἐφ᾽ ὑμᾶς ; (3) ἀκούσατε ἀδελφοί μου found in Ja 2[5] alone in the Epistles, compared with ἄνδρες ἀδελφοί ἀκούσατέ μου in Ac 15[13] ; (4) ἐπισκέπτεσθαι Ja 1[27], Ac 15[14] ; (5) ἐπιστρέφειν Ja 5[19. 20], Ac 15[19] ; (6) τηρεῖν and διατηρεῖν, Ja 1[27] ἄσπιλον ἑαυτὸν τηρεῖν ἀπὸ τοῦ κόσμου, Ac 15[29] ἐξ ὧν διατηροῦντες ἑαυτοὺς εὖ πράξετε ; (7) ἀγαπητός occurs in Ac only in 15[25] σὺν τοῖς ἀγαπητοῖς Βαρνάβᾳ καὶ Παύλῳ, while ἀδελφοί μου ἀγαπητοί is found three times in our Epistle ; (8) the pregnant use of the word ὄνομα in Ja 5[10] ἐλάλησαν ἐν τῷ ὀνόματι Κυρίου, v.[14] ἀλείψαντες ἐλαίῳ ἐν τῷ ὀνόματι, 2[7] τὸ καλὸν ὄνομα, and in Ac 15[14] λαβεῖν ἐξ ἐθνῶν λαὸν τῷ ὀνόματι αὐτοῦ, v.[26] ὑπὲρ τοῦ ὀνόματος τοῦ Κυρίου ἡμῶν Ἰ. Χ. ; (9) perhaps we may compare also the use of δαπανάω in Ac 21[24], probably spoken by St. James (δαπάνησον ἐπ᾽ αὐτοῖς), with our Epistle 4[3] ἵνα ἐν ταῖς ἡδοναῖς ὑμῶν δαπανήσητε, and the occurrence of ἁγνίζω in the same verse with its occurrence in Ja 4[8].

An objection may be raised to the identification of the writer of the Epistle with the brother of our Lord on the ground that no claim is made to this title in either of the Epistles which go by the name of the brothers James and Jude. If they were really brothers of the Lord, would they not have laid stress on the authority derived from this relationship, just as St. Paul lays stress on his apostleship ? But what was Christ's own teaching on the matter ? When his mother and brothers sought on one occasion to use the authority which they assumed that their kinship gave them, they were met by the words, 'Who is my mother or my brethren ?' And he stretched out his hands to his disciples and said, 'Behold my mother and my brethren.' St. Paul expresses the same idea of the disappearance of the earthly relationship in the higher spiritual union by which all the members of the body are joined to the Head, in the words 'though we have known Christ after the flesh, yet now know we him so no more' (2 Co 5[16]). Surely it is only what was to be expected that James and Jude would shrink from claiming another name than that of 'servant' to express the relation in which they stood to their risen Lord, after having failed to acknowledge him as their Master in the days of his humiliation.

So far the evidence seems to show that the writer of the Epistle was James the Just, the brother of the Lord. Let us see what further light this fact, if it be one, will throw upon the Epistle. The word 'just,' which is also used of his father Joseph, implies one who not only observes but loves the law; and we may be sure that the reverence for the law, which is so marked a feature of the Epistle, was learnt in the well-ordered home of Nazareth. There, too, he may have acquired, with the full sanction of his parents (who would gladly devote the eldest-born of Joseph in such marked way to the future service of the Messiah), those strict ascetic habits which tradition ascribes to him. But the constant intercourse with him who was full of grace and truth in childhood as in manhood, must have prepared James to find in the Ten Commandments no mere outward regulations, but an inner law of liberty and love written in the heart. That deep interest in the mysteries of the kingdom, that earnest search after truth which led the child Jesus to remain behind in the temple, must surely have had its effect upon his brother. Whatever means of instruction were within reach of the home at Nazareth would, we may feel sure, have been eagerly taken advantage of by all its inmates. While, therefore, accepting the view which seems to be best supported, that Jesus and his brothers usually spoke Aramaic, we are not bound to suppose that, with towns like Sepphoris and Tiberias in their immediate vicinity, with Ptolemais, Scythopolis, and Gadara at no great distance, they remained ignorant of Greek. In the eyes of the scribes they might 'never have learnt letters,' since they had not attended the rabbinical schools of Jerusalem; but the ordinary education of Jewish children, and the Sabbath readings in the synagogue, would give a sufficient start to enable any intelligent boy to carry on his studies for himself; while the example of Solomon and the teaching of the 'sapiential' books, with which the writer of the Epistle was intimately acquainted, held up the pursuit of knowledge and wisdom as the highest duty of man.

There are other characteristics of our Epistle which find their best explanation in the supposition that the writer was the son of Joseph and Mary. The use of parables was common among Jewish teachers, and especially common in Galilee (cf. Neubauer in *Studia Biblica*, i. p. 52); but it was carried to an unusual length by our Lord, both in his preaching to the multitude, of which it is said 'without a parable spake he not unto them,' and in his ordinary conversation, which constantly ran into a parabolic or figurative form to the great bewilderment of his disciples, as when he bid them 'Beware of the leaven of the Pharisees.' One distinctive feature of our Lord's use of parables is that there is nothing forced either in the figure or in the application: natural phenomena and the varied circumstances of human life are watched with an observant eye and a sympathetic and loving heart, and the spiritual analogies which they suggest are seen to flow naturally from them. Such a habit of mind could not have been acquired after manhood. The love of nature, the sympathy in all human interests, the readiness to find 'sermons in stones and good in everything,' must have characterized the child Jesus, and coloured all his intercourse with his fellows from his earliest years. It is interesting therefore to find the same fondness for figurative speech in the Epistles of his two brothers, St. James and St. Jude.

Another marked feature of our Epistle is the close connexion between it and the Sermon on the Mount, in which our Lord laid down the principles of the kingdom which he came to establish upon earth. It must suffice to refer here to the general harmony between the two as to the spiritual view of the law (Ja 1^{25} $2^{8.12.13}$, Mt 5^{17-44}), the blessings of adversity (Ja $1^{2.3}$ 2^5 $5^{7.8.11}$, Mt 5^{3-12}), the dangers and the uncertainty of wealth (Ja $1^{10.11}$ $2^{6.7}$ $4^{4.6.13-16}$ 5^{1-6}, Mt $6^{19-21.24-34}$), the futility of a mere profession of religion (Ja $1^{26.27}$, Mt 6^{1-7}), the contrast between saying and doing (Ja 1^{22-25} 2^{14-26} $3^{13.18}$, Mt 7^{15-27}), the true nature of prayer (Ja 1^{5-8} 4^3 $5^{13.18}$, Mt 6^{6-13}), the incompatibility between the love of the world and the love of God (Ja 2^5 3^6 4^{4-8}, Mt 6^{24}), the need to forgive others if we would be forgiven ourselves (Ja $2^{12.13}$, Mt $6^{14.15}$), the tree known by its fruits (Ja $3^{11.12}$, Mt 7^{16-20}), the interdiction of oaths (Ja 5^{12}, Mt 5^{34-37}) and of censoriousness (Ja $4^{11.12}$, Mt 7^{1-5}), the praise of singleness of aim (Ja 1^8 4^8, Mt $6^{22.23}$). Nor are these reminiscences confined to the Sermon on the Mount, or to our Lord's words as reported by St. Matthew; there is much to remind us both of St. Luke and St. John. It is worthy of note that, close as is the connexion of sentiment and even of language in many of these passages, it never amounts to actual quotation, but is rather the reminiscence of thoughts often uttered by the original speaker and sinking into the heart of the hearer, who reproduces them in his own manner.

It may be asked, if St. James was thus deeply influenced by his Brother's teaching, how are we to explain the fact that at one period of his life 'he did not believe on him'? Perhaps we may gather from the Epistle that the writer would have found a difficulty in some of the sayings of Christ. 'Before Abraham was, I am'; 'Except ye eat the flesh of the Son of Man and drink his blood, ye have no life in you,'—these must have been 'hard sayings' to the brother of Jesus even more than to strangers. This state of mind was doubtless combined with an intense love and reverence for the elder Brother, and was perhaps not incompatible with the belief in Christ's mission as a preacher of righteousness, and a willingness to accept him as the anointed King of the Jewish people; but it might easily lead to an anxious solicitude as to his sanity and the prudence of the measures which he took for extending the number of his adherents. (See the subject more fully treated in Mayor's *Introduction to St. James*, ch. i. on the Author, ch. iv. on its relation to other Books of NT).

ii. CANONICITY. — Eusebius in a well-known passage (*HE* iii. 25) distinguishes between the disputed and the undisputed books which made up the NT, and were publicly read in the church at the time when he wrote (*l.c.* iii. 31), *i.e.* in A.D. 314 (see Lightfoot in *Dict. of Chr. Biog.* ii. p. 323). Together they contain all the books included in our present Canon and no others; those which were disputed, though generally known, being the Epistle which goes under the name of James and that of Jude, as well as the 2nd of Peter and the so-called 2nd and 3rd of John. The Apoc. he had before doubtfully classed among the undisputed, but questions whether it should not rather be classed with the spurious, like the Revelation of Peter. Elsewhere he says (ii. 23), 'The first of the Epistles styled Catholic is said to be by James the Lord's brother, which is held by some to be spurious. Certainly not many old writers have mentioned it, as neither have they the Epistle of Jude.' His own practice, however, betrays no suspicion of its genuineness, as in one passage he quotes James as Scripture (*Comm. in Psalm.* p. 648, Montf.), and in another quotes Ja 5^{13} as spoken by the holy apostle (*ib.* p. 247).

The same doubt as to the canonicity of the Epistle is shown by its omission from some of the early versions and catalogues of sacred books, e.g. the Muratorian Fragment (of which Westcott says that it may be regarded as 'a summary of the opinion of the Western Church on the Canon shortly after the middle of the 2nd cent.'), and the Cheltenham list, which is supposed to have been written in Africa about the year 359. On the other hand, it was generally recognized in the East, being included in the Peshiṭta, which omits 2 P, 2 and 3 Jn, Jude, and Rev. The Pesh. used to be ascribed to the 2nd cent., and is probably not later than the 3rd, but the date is still in dispute. Ja is also found in the lists given by Origen (Hom. in Jos. vii. 1), Cyril of Jerusalem, Athanasius, Gregory of Nazianzus, and others, and was finally ratified by the Third Council of Carthage in 397. Its late reception in the West may probably be explained by the fact that it was addressed to Jews of the Eastern (?) Dispersion, that it did not profess to be written by an apostle, and that it appeared to contradict the teaching of the great Apostle to the Gentiles.

Origen (d. 253) is apparently the first who cites the Epistle as Scripture, and as written by St. James; see Comm. in Joh. xix. 6; in Rom. iv. 1, 8, ix. 24; Hom. in. Ex. iii. 3, viii. 4; in Lv. ii. 4, xiii. 3; Sel. in Ps. 31. 5, 37. 24, 118. 153; Comm. in Prov. (Mai, Nov. Bibl. vii. 51); but Clement of Alexandria (d. 220) is said by Eusebius (HE vi. 14) to have included in his Outlines (ἐν ταῖς Ὑποτυπώσεσι) short explanations of all the sacred books, μηδὲ τὰς ἀντιλεγομένας παρελθών, τὴν Ἰούδα λέγω καὶ τὰς λοιπὰς καθολικὰς ἐπιστολὰς τήν τε Βαρνάβα καὶ τὴν Πέτρου λεγομένην ἀποκάλυψιν. Cassiodorus (Inst. div. lit. 8) limits this by saying that Clement commented on the canonical Epistles, i.e. on 1 P, 1 and 2 Jn, and Ja. The notes on the first three, and on Jude, but not on Ja, are still extant in a Latin translation, and some have doubted whether the reading in Cassiodorus should not be altered accordingly; see, however, Zahn, Neutest. Kan. i. 322, Forschungen, iii. 153; Sanday in Stud. Bibl. iii. 248.

iii. DATE.—If we are right in our view of the authorship of the Epistle, it must have been written not later than A.D. 62. This view, however, although approved by the great majority of scholars and divines up to the end of last century, is regarded with suspicion by some modern scholars. We will give briefly their conclusions, and then state the reasons for believing that it was written between A.D. 40 and 50. Von Soden, in the Introduction to his Handkommentar (1890), allows that in thought and expression there is considerable resemblance between our Epistle and the writings of Clement of Rome, and especially of Hermas, but considers that there is no reason to suppose any literary connexion. They resemble one another simply because they were produced under the same conditions. No trace of our Epistle is to be found in the 2nd cent. Nothing in the letter suggests Jewish readers. The title may be genuine because Christians had learnt to regard themselves as strangers and pilgrims. It was probably written for Christians generally, in the reign of Domitian. W. Brückner, in his Chronolog. Reihenfolge d. N.T. Briefe (Haarlem, 1890), considers that it cannot be assigned to an earlier date than A.D. 150, as it borrows from 1 P, which was written during the persecution of Trajan. The Judaizing tone implies a late stage of doctrinal development, inasmuch as it attacks Paulinism as the seed of an existing Gnosticism. The true address reveals itself in the phrase 'your synagogue' (2²), by which we are to understand a little conventicle of Essene Chris-

tians at Rome. The phrase 'Diaspora' denotes similar scattered conventicles, in which alone the true Israel, the poor, are to be found. By 'the rich' is meant Christians outside the conventicle. Pfleiderer, in his Urchristenthum (1887), regards the Epistle as representing the catholicized Paulinism of the latter half of the 2nd cent. He thinks it is an abbreviation of the Shepherd of Hermas. The polemic is not directed against St. Paul, but against the later Gnostics who appealed to his authority. There is nothing Judaistic in the writer's tone; he simply enforces the truths of practical Christianity as understood by the Catholic Church. The latest writer on the subject is F. Spitta (Zur Geschichte u. Litteratur des Urchristenthums, vol. ii. 1896), who, while allowing the references to our Epistle in St. Paul's Epistle to the Romans, avoids the reproach of coming to a commonplace conclusion by starting the theory that it is a Christian adaptation of a Jewish book, written before the Christian era.* He draws this conclusion from the considerations stated in the earlier part of this article, and explains away the resemblance to the Sermon on the Mount by quoting parallels from the Apocrypha and other Jewish writings.

There is certainly much more to be said for this theory than for those which have been just described. Postponing its examination for the present, we proceed to state the grounds (independently of what has been already said under the head of authorship and canonicity) for believing that the Epistle was written before A.D. 50. In the present writer's Introduction to St. James, ch. ii., will be found proof that it was known to Irenæus, Theophilus, Justin Martyr, the writer of the Ep. to Diognetus, Ignatius, Polycarp, and, above all, Hermas, in the 2nd cent.; that it was known to Clement of Rome, to Barnabas, to the authors of the Didaché and the Testaments of the Twelve Patriarchs during the 1st cent. We can, however, afford to dispense with these witnesses, if it can be proved that it was known to more than one of the writers of the NT; and if we are not mistaken, it has been shown in the above Introduction (ch. iv.) that traces of its influence may be seen in the Epistles of St. John, in the Ep. to the Hebrews, in those to Timothy, above all in the 1st Epistle of St. Peter, and in St. Paul's Epistles to the Romans and Galatians.

Our space will not allow us to deal with more than the last two, merely premising (1) that if the Epistle of James was written by the Lord's brother, it must probably have been written before the year 51 [Turner, 49], the date of the Apostolic Council, as otherwise it must have contained some reference to the question, which was then agitating the Diaspora, as to the admission of Gentiles into the Church; (2) that if such an Epistle were in existence, containing phrases which could be turned against the doctrine of justification by faith, it was likely to be eagerly made use of by Judaizers, and would thus be brought under St. Paul's notice. It has been remarked that the words 'whosoever shall keep the law and yet offend in one point, he is guilty of all' (Ja 2¹⁰), might easily be twisted so as to represent St. James as insisting on the observance of the whole Mosaic code, and that this may possibly be alluded to in the words (Ac 15²⁴), 'We have heard that certain which went out from us troubled you, saying, Ye must be circumcised and keep the law, to whom we gave no such commandment.' On the other hand, there is less likelihood of St. Paul's

* The same view is taken by L. Massebieau in an article entitled 'L'Épitre de Jacques, est-elle l'œuvre d'un Chrétien?' which appeared in the Revue de l'histoire des religions, Paris, 1895.

Epistles, addressed to distant Churches, and dealing so much with personal questions, having been brought under the notice of St. James.

The main points of connexion between the Epistles are Ro 2^{13} οὐ γὰρ οἱ ἀκροαταὶ νόμου δίκαιοι παρὰ τῷ θεῷ, ἀλλ' οἱ ποιηταὶ νόμου δικαιωθήσονται, compared with Ja 1^{22} γίνεσθε ποιηταὶ λόγου καὶ μὴ ἀκροαταὶ μόνον, and Ja 4^{11} ποιητὴς νόμου (the only other place in NT where this phrase occurs); the phrase παραβάτης νόμου, occurring only in Ro $2^{25. 27}$ and Ja 2^{11}; Ro 7^{23} βλέπω ἕτερον νόμον ἐν τοῖς μέλεσίν μου ἀντιστρατευόμενον τῷ νόμῳ τοῦ νοός μου, compared with Ja 4^{1} πόθεν πόλεμοι; οὐκ ἐντεῦθεν ἐκ τῶν ἡδονῶν ὑμῶν τῶν στρατευομένων ἐν τοῖς μέλεσιν ὑμῶν; Ro 14^{4} σὺ τίς εἶ ὁ κρίνων ἀλλότριον οἰκέτην; τῷ ἰδίῳ κυρίῳ στήκει ἢ πίπτει, compared with Ja 4^{11} εἷς ἐστιν νομοθέτης καὶ κριτής, σὺ δὲ τίς εἶ ὁ κρίνων τὸν πλησίον; Ro 5^{3-5} καυχώμεθα ἐν ταῖς θλίψεσιν, εἰδότες ὅτι ἡ θλῖψις ὑπομονὴν κατεργάζεται, ἡ δὲ ὑπομονὴ δοκιμήν, ἡ δὲ δοκιμὴ ἐλπίδα, ἡ δὲ ἐλπὶς οὐ καταισχύνει, ὅτι ἡ ἀγάπη τοῦ θεοῦ ἐκκέχυται, compared with Ja 1^{2-4} πᾶσαν χαρὰν ἡγήσασθε ὅταν πειρασμοῖς περιπέσητε ποικίλοις, γινώσκοντες ὅτι τὸ δοκίμιον ὑμῶν τῆς πίστεως κατεργάζεται ὑπομονήν, ἡ δὲ ὑπομονὴ ἔργον τέλειον ἐχέτω ἵνα ἦτε τέλειοι; v.^{9} καυχάσθω δὲ ὁ ἀδελφὸς ὁ ταπεινός, κ.τ.λ. In these and other cases of resemblance it is easier to suppose that St. Paul works up a hint received from St. James, than that St. James omits points of interest and value which he found ready to his hand.

The crucial test, however, of the relation between the two is to be found in the controversy as to faith and works. St. James had said over and over again that 'faith without works is dead' (2^{17} etc.), his intention being (as is plain from v.^{14}, and the illustration in vv.$^{15. 16}$ of a philanthropy which is limited to words, as well as from the whole tone and argument of the Epistle), not to depreciate faith, which is with him, not less than with St. Paul, the very foundation of the Christian life (see $1^{3. 6}$ 2^{1} 5^{15}), but to insist that faith, like love, is valueless if it has no effect on the life. St. Paul himself does the same in 1 Th 1^{3}, Gal 5^{6}, 1 Co 13^{2}, Ro 2^{6-20} and elsewhere; but in arguing against his Judaizing antagonists, who denied salvation to the Gentiles unless they were circumcised, and in all other respects 'performed the works of the law,' he had maintained that it was impossible for men to be justified by these works, and that it was by faith alone that even the Jews and Abraham himself must be justified. He is therefore compelled to challenge the phrase of St. James, ἡ πίστις χωρὶς τῶν ἔργων ἀργή ἐστιν, νεκρά ἐστιν, by a direct contradiction, λογιζόμεθα γὰρ δικαιοῦσθαι πίστει ἄνθρωπον χωρὶς ἔργων νόμου, in support of which he appeals to the confession of the Psalmist (Ps 14. 143^{2}; see Ro 3^{10-20}, Gal 3^{10}) that 'by the works of the law shall no flesh be justified.' If St. James wrote after St. Paul, must he not, with these passages before him, have either attempted to meet the arguments, if he dissented; or if he agreed with them (as he certainly does in $2^{10. 11}$ 3^{2}), would he not have avoided the use of phrases such as χωρὶς τῶν ἔργων, which were liable to be misunderstood alike by the followers and the opponents of the Apostle to the Gentiles?

St. Paul goes on to argue that the blessings promised to Abraham and all the families of the earth in him, and the covenant made with Abraham and his seed, are anterior to, and irrespective of, the law; that the Scripture expressly attributes to Abraham a righteousness, not of works, but of faith, and states generally that 'the just shall live by faith.' To these arguments no reference is made by St. James, except to the familiar quotation, ἐπίστευσεν Ἀβραὰμ τῷ θεῷ καὶ ἐλογίσθη αὐτῷ εἰς δικαιοσύνην ($2^{21. 22}$), which was probably in common use among the Jews, to prove that orthodoxy of doctrine sufficed for salvation. His answer to the text so used is that Abraham's faith proved itself by action when he offered Isaac on the altar: if he had not acted thus, he would not have been accounted righteous, or called the friend of God. It is interesting to observe how St. Paul deals with this statement, to which he distinctly refers in Ro 4^{2}. St. James had said, Ἀβραὰμ ὁ πατὴρ ἡμῶν οὐκ ἐξ ἔργων ἐδικαιώθη; St. Paul replies, εἰ γὰρ ἐξ ἔργων ἐδικαιώθη, ἔχει καύχημα; but this, as he proceeds to show, is inconsistent with the phrase 'reckoned for righteousness,' which implies an act of free grace on the part of God, not a strict legal obligation of wages earned for work done. His second answer is to replace the quotation in its original context (Ro 4^{16-22}) as spoken of the birth, not the sacrifice of Isaac. Abraham's faith in the promised birth was a settled trust in God, a long-continued hoping against hope; it was this posture of mind, not any immediate action consequent upon it, which was reckoned to him for righteousness. All this is most apposite in reference to the argument of St. James, and the use which might be made of it by Judaizers. But put the case the other way: suppose St. James to have written after St. Paul; and how inconceivable is it that he should have made no attempt to guard his position against such an extremely formidable attack! Again, if St. James was really opposed to St. Paul, and desired to maintain that man was saved, not by grace, but by obedience to the law of Moses, which was incumbent alike on Gentile and on Jew, why has he never uttered a syllable on the subject, but confined himself to the task of proving that a faith which bears no fruit is a dead faith? See this more fully developed by Spitta, l.c. 202-225.

We have seen, then, (1) that the resemblance between the two Epistles is such that it can only be explained by supposing one of them to have been written with a knowledge of the other; (2) that a close comparison shows that, where there is a resemblance, the statement in St. James is in general more elementary, less exact and developed, than that in St. Paul; (3) that, in the controversy on faith and works in particular, St. Paul is evidently anxious to guard against misunderstanding by carefully defining terms which are used by St. James in a vague general sense: thus, while the latter uses πίστις indefinitely, at one time of genuine Christian trust ($1^{3. 6}$ $2^{1. 5}$ etc.), at another of an empty profession (2^{14-26}), St. Paul begins his discussion by twice defining it as 'faith in Christ' (Ro $3^{22. 26}$); while St. James had used the ambiguous word ἔργον with similar vagueness, St. Paul distinguishes between the ἔργα νόμου (Ro $3^{20. 28}$ 9^{32}) and the ἔργον πίστεως (1 Th 1^{3}, 2 Th 1^{11}), 'faith working through love' (Gal 5^{6}). There is a still more careful limitation in Gal 2^{16}, where St. James' declaration, ἐξ ἔργων δικαιοῦται ἄνθρωπος καὶ οὐκ ἐκ πίστεως μόνον, is qualified, not merely as to the principal terms ἔργον and πίστις, but also as to the extent of opposition, by the use of the hypothetical ἐὰν μή, and as to the kind of causation attributed to faith, διά being substituted for ἐκ in the words οὐ δικαιοῦται ἄνθρωπος ἐξ ἔργων νόμου, ἐὰν μὴ διὰ πίστεως Ἰησοῦ Χριστοῦ; (4) that, whereas the argument of St. James has no reference to St. Paul or to the arguments used by him, St. Paul turns aside, in the most skilful and delicate way, whatever in the argument of St. James might be made use of by Judaizers, while at the same time he reaffirms in more guarded language the truths which both apostles held in common. Nothing could be more courteous and nothing more effective. On the other hand, if we imagine St. James to be answering St. Paul, we should have to charge him with discourtesy in addition to an entire misapprehension of the situation.

It remains now to show, in opposition to Spitta, that our Epistle was written after A.D. 40. If it was written by the brother of the Lord, this is about the earliest date which would allow time for his authority to establish itself, as it evidently had done when the letter was written, and also for the growth of a Church of the Diaspora with the experiences described. The hypothesis, however, which we have to meet is that it is a Jewish writing of the 1st cent. B.C., interpolated and adopted by a Christian, in the same way as the *Didaché*, the Testaments of the Twelve Patriarchs, the Sibylline Books, and the Fourth Book of Ezra are interpolated. All that is required to restore it to its original form is, to omit the words τοῦ Κυρίου Ἰησοῦ Χριστοῦ in 1¹, and ἡμῶν Ἰησοῦ Χριστοῦ in 2¹, a change which greatly simplifies the construction of τῆς δόξης in the latter passages, leaving the familiar phrase τὴν πίστιν τοῦ Κυρίου τῆς δόξης, examples of which are quoted from the Bk. of Enoch (Spitta, p. iv).

The first thing which strikes us is that a Christian editor would not have been satisfied with such a slight revision. *We* may possibly explain the absence of any reference to Christ among the examples of patience given in 5¹⁰, ¹¹, on the ground that, before the existence of our Gospels, the Jews of the Dispersion would be less familiar with the story of our Lord, than they were with the OT Scriptures which were 'read in the synagogues every Sabbath day.' But this consideration was hardly likely to occur to a Christian (of the 1st cent.? No date is suggested by Spitta) who was desirous to adapt a Jewish book for the service of the Church. (2) We must remember that the general Judaic tone is explained and indeed required by the hypothesis that the author is the brother of the Lord, which is commended to us on so many other grounds. It is his office to interpret Christianity to the Jews. He represents and he addresses the many thousands who believe and are zealous for the law. He is the authority whom St. Paul's opponents profess to follow. Tradition even goes so far as to describe the unbelieving Jews as still doubting at the end of his life, whether they might not look to him for a declaration against Christianity (see quotation from Hegesippus in the art. on JAMES). (3) There is the fact of the resemblance of the language of the Epistle to that used by St. James in the Acts. (4) There is the fact of the extraordinary resemblance between the Epistle and our Lord's discourses, especially the Sermon on the Mount. Spitta labours to show that both borrow from older Jewish writings. Even if this were so, it would be far more probable that one of the two borrowed indirectly, taking these sayings straight from the other, than that they should both have collected them independently from a variety of obscure sources. But it is mere perversity to put forward such vague parallels as are adduced from rabbinical writings on the subject of oaths, for instance, or the perishable treasures of earth, by way of accounting for the exact resemblance existing between Ja 5¹² and Mt 5³⁴⁻³⁷, Ja 5². ³ and Mt 6¹⁹. Indeed this is true of almost all the resemblances which have been pointed out by the commentators. (5) The Epistle contains many phrases which bear a recognized Christian stamp, even though it may be possible to find some approach to them in pre-Christian documents. Such are ἀδελφοί μου ἀγαπητοί (1¹⁶, ¹⁹ 2⁵), ἡ παρουσία τοῦ κυρίου (5⁷, ⁸), τοὺς πρεσβυτέρους τῆς ἐκκλησίας (5¹⁴), προσευξάσθωσαν ἐπ᾽ αὐτὸν ἀλείψαντες ἐλαίῳ ἐν τῷ ὀνόματι (5¹⁴), κληρονόμους τῆς βασιλείας ἧς ἐπηγγείλατο (2⁵), βουληθεὶς ἀπεκύησεν ἡμᾶς λόγῳ ἀληθείας, εἰς τὸ εἶναι ἡμᾶς ἀπαρχήν τινα

τῶν αὐτοῦ κτισμάτων (1¹⁸), νόμον τέλειον τὸν τῆς ἐλευθερίας (1²⁵), suggesting a contrasted law of bondage, of the letter as opposed to the spirit. (6) But the characteristic quality, after all, is to be found, not in particular phrases or occasional reminiscences of our Lord's teaching, but in the identity of spirit between our Epistle and the Sermon on the Mount, which is so striking as to warrant the assertion that, if the former is not Christian, then neither is the latter. (7) Spitta does not suggest that the name 'James' is an addition by the supposed Christian editor. We have seen how exactly the Epistle agrees with all that we know of James the brother of the Lord; but if this is to be considered a part of the original pre-Christian document, where is the author to be found who combines in himself so many remarkable characteristics? We arrive at the same result by comparing it with the Jewish Apoc. writings, such as Ps-Sol. Where do we find an approach in any of these to the teaching of our Epistle as summed up in the section on its contents which follows?

iv. CONTENTS.—The design of the Epistle is on the one hand to encourage the believing Jews of the Dispersion, to whom it is addressed, to bear their trials patiently, and on the other hand to warn them against certain errors of doctrine and practice.

i. *Of Trial* (1¹⁻¹⁸).—(*a*) Trial is sent to perfect the Christian character. That it may have this effect wisdom is needed; and this wisdom is given in answer to believing prayer (1²⁻⁶). A warning against doublemindedness. The believer should recognize the greatness of his calling, and not allow himself to be either elated or depressed by outward circumstances (1⁷⁻¹¹). (*b*) Patient endurance of trial leads to the crown of life promised to all that love God (1¹²). (*c*) Though outward trial is appointed by God for our good, we must not imagine that the inner weakness which is brought to light by trial is from God. God is perfect goodness, and only sends what is good. The disposition to misuse God's appointments comes from man's own lusts, which, if yielded to, lead to death as their natural consequence (1¹³⁻¹⁵). (*d*) So far from God's tempting man to evil, it is only by his will, through the regenerating power of his word, that we are raised to that new and higher life which shall eventually penetrate and renew the whole creation (1¹⁶⁻¹⁸).

ii. *How we should receive the Word* (1¹⁹⁻²⁷).—(*a*) As humble listeners, not as excited speakers (1¹⁹⁻²¹). (*b*) Nor is it enough to listen to the word; we must carry it out in action (1²²⁻²⁴). (*c*) Blessing comes to him alone who patiently studies the word, and frames his life in accordance with the law of liberty embodied therein (1²⁵). (*d*) Ritual observance is of no avail unless it helps us to rule the tongue, and practise brotherly kindness and unworldliness (1²⁶⁻²⁷).

iii. *Warning against Respect of Persons* (2¹⁻¹³).—(*a*) Courtesy to the rich, if combined with discourtesy to the poor, is a sign of weakness of faith, and proves that we are not whole-hearted in the service of him who is the sole glory of believers (2¹⁻⁴). (*b*) The poor have more title to our respect than the rich, since they are more often rich in faith and heirs of the kingdom; while it is the rich who maltreat the brethren, and blaspheme the name of Christ (2⁵⁻⁷). (*c*) If it is from obedience to the royal law of love that we show courtesy to the rich, it is well; but if we do this only from respect of persons, it is a breach of the law, and a defiance of the Lawgiver, no less than murder and adultery (2⁸⁻¹¹). (*d*) Remember that we shall all be tried by the law of liberty, which looks to the heart, and not to the outward action only. It is the merciful who obtain mercy (2¹². ¹³).

iv. *Belief and Practice* (2¹⁴⁻²⁶).—(*a*) A mere profession of faith without corresponding action is of no avail (2¹⁴). As may be seen in the parallel case of benevolence, when it does not go beyond words (2¹⁵⁻¹⁷). Without action we have no evidence of the existence of faith (2¹⁸). The orthodox belief of the Jew is shared by the demons, and only increases their misery (2¹⁹). (*b*) True faith, such as that of Abraham and Rahab, necessarily embodies itself in action (2²⁰⁻²⁶).

v. *Warnings with respect to the use of the Tongue* (3¹⁻¹²).— (*a*) Great responsibility of the office of teacher (3¹). (*b*) Difficulty and importance of controlling the tongue (3²⁻⁸). (*c*) Inconsistency of supposing that we can offer acceptable praise to God as long as we speak evil of man, who is made in the image of God (3⁹⁻¹²).

vi. *True and false Wisdom* (3¹³⁻¹⁸).—(*a*) The wisdom which comes from God is simple and straightforward, full of kindness and all good fruits (3¹³. ¹⁷. ¹⁸). (*b*) If there is a wisdom which does not conduce to peace, but is accompanied by bitterness and jealousy, it is not from above, but is earthly, carnal, devilish (3¹⁴⁻¹⁶).

vii. *Warning against Quarrelsomeness and Worldliness* (4¹⁻¹⁷).— (*a*) The cause of quarrels is that each man seeks to gratify his own selfish impulses, and to snatch his neighbour's portion of worldly good (4¹. ²). (*b*) No satisfaction can be thus obtained. Even our prayers can give us no satisfaction if they are infected with this worldly spirit (4³). (c) God demands the service of the whole heart, and will reveal himself to none but those who yield up their wills to his (4¹⁻⁶). (d) Therefore resist the devil, who is the prince of this world, and turn to God in humble repentance (4⁷⁻¹⁰). (e) Cease to find fault with others. Those who condemn their neighbours condemn the law itself, and usurp the office of him, the Lord of life and death, who alone has the power and right to judge (4¹¹· ¹²). (f) Worldliness is also shown in the confident laying-out of plans of life without reference to God (4¹³⁻¹⁷).

viii. *Denunciations and Encouragements* (5¹⁻¹¹).—(a) Woe to those who have been heaping up money and living in luxury on the very eve of judgment. Woe especially to those who have ground down the poor and murdered the innocent (5¹⁻⁶). (b) Let the brethren bear their sufferings patiently, knowing that the Lord is at hand, and that he will make all things turn out for their good. Let them imitate Job and the prophets, and so inherit the blessings pronounced on those who endure (5⁶⁻¹¹).

ix. *Miscellaneous Precepts* (5¹²⁻²⁰). — (a) Swear not (5¹²). (b) Let all your feelings of joy and sorrow be sanctified and controlled by religion (5¹³). (c) In sickness let the elders be called in to pray and anoint the sick with a view to his recovery (5¹⁴· ¹⁵). (d) Confess your sins to one another, and pray for one another with all earnestness (5¹⁶⁻¹⁸). (e) The blessing on one who wins back a sinner from the error of his ways (5¹⁹· ²⁰).

The doctrinal basis of St. James' practical teaching may perhaps be stated as follows:—Man was created in the image of God (3⁹), the All-good (1¹³· ¹⁷); but he has fallen into sin by yielding to his lower impulses against his sense of right (1¹⁴· ¹⁵ ⁴¹⁻³· ¹⁷), and the natural consequence of sin is death, bodily and spiritual (1¹⁵ ⁵³· ⁵· ²⁰). Not only is man liable to sin, but as a matter of fact we all sin, and that frequently (3²). God of his free bounty has provided a means by which we may conquer sin; he has begotten us anew through his word sown in our hearts (1¹⁸· ²¹). Our salvation depends on the way in which we receive the word (1²¹). If we have a steadfast faith in God's goodness (1⁵· ⁷· ¹³ ²¹); if we read, mark, learn, and inwardly digest the word, so as to make it the guiding principle of our life, the law of liberty by which all our words and actions are regulated (1²⁵ ²¹²), bearing its natural fruit in compassion and love towards our fellow-men (1²⁷ ²⁸· ¹⁵· ¹⁶), then our souls are saved from death, we are made inheritors of the kingdom promised to those who love God (1¹²· ²⁵ ²⁵). But the training by which we are prepared for this crown of life is not pleasant to the natural man. It involves trial and endurance (1²⁻⁴· ¹²); it involves constant watchfulness and self-control and prayer for heavenly wisdom, in order that we may resist the temptations of the world, the flesh, and the devil (1²⁶ ³²⁸· ¹⁵). Thus faith is exercised; we are enabled to see things as God sees them (2¹· ⁵), to rise above the temporal to the eternal (1⁹⁻¹¹), to be not simply patient, but to rejoice in affliction (1² 5⁷· ⁸· ¹⁰· ¹¹) and exult in the hope set before us (1⁹· ¹²), until at last we grow up to the full stature of a Christian (1⁴ 3²), wise with that wisdom which comes from above, the wisdom which is steadfast, unpretending, gentle, considerate, affectionate, full of mercy and good fruits, the parent of righteousness and peace (3¹⁷· ¹⁸). But there are many who choose the friendship of the world instead of the friendship of God, so vexing his Holy Spirit and yielding themselves to the power of the devil; yet even then he does not leave them to themselves, but gives more grace, hedging in their ways in the present and warning them of judgment to come (4⁴⁻⁶ 5¹⁻⁸). If they humble themselves under his hand, and repent truly of their sins, he will lift them up; if they draw nigh to him, he will draw nigh to them (4⁷⁻¹⁰). Here, too, we may be helpful to one another by mutual confession and by prayer for one another. Great is the power of prayer prompted by the Spirit of God (5¹⁵⁻²⁰).

LITERATURE.—In addition to the works cited above, see the *Commentaries* of Cornelius a Lapide (1648), Estius (1661), Gebser (Berlin, 1828, contains extracts from the Fathers), Schneckenburger (Stuttgart, 1832), Theile (a condensed *Variorum ed.* 1833), Kern (Tübingen, 1838), Schegg (Roman Catholic), 1883, Plumptre (in *Camb. Bible*, 1878), Plummer (in *Expositor's Bible*, 1891), especially Beyschlag (Göttingen, 1888). See further B. Weiss, *Die kathol. Briefe, Text-krit. Untersuchungen u. Textherstellung*, 1892; W. Schmidt, *Lehrgehalt d. Jacobusbriefes*, 1869; R. W. Dale, *Ep. of James*, 1895; Review of Spitta's theory in *Crit. Rev.* 1896, p. 277 ff.; van Manen in *ThT*, July, 1897.

J. B. MAYOR.

JAMIN (יָמִין). — **1.** A son of Simeon, Gn 46¹⁰, Ex 6¹⁵, Nu 26¹², 1 Ch 4²⁴. The gentilic name **Jaminites** (הַיָּמִינִי) occurs in Nu 26¹². See GENEALOGY, II. 1. **2.** A Judahite, 1 Ch 2²⁷. See GENEALOGY, IV. 7. **3.** A priest (?, or Levite) who took part in the promulgating of the law, Neh 8⁷.

JAMLECH (יַמְלֵךְ).—A Simeonite chief, 1 Ch 4³⁴.

JAMNIA ('Ιαμνία, 'Ιαμνεία, 'Ιαννεία), 1 Mac 4¹⁵ 5⁵⁸ 10⁶⁹ 15⁴⁰, 2 Mac 12⁸· ⁹· ⁴⁰. — The later name of JABNEEL (wh. see). **Jamnites** (οἱ 'Ιαμνῖται, *Jamnitæ*), gentilic name, 2 Mac 12⁹; cf. οἱ ἐν 'Ιαμνίᾳ, 12⁸.

JANAI (יַעְנַי, perhaps for יַעֲנָיָה 'J" answers').—A Gadite chief, 1 Ch 5¹², AV Jaanai.

JANGLING.—In 1 Ti 1⁶ ματαιολογία is tr⁴ in AV 'vain jangling,' after Tind. and most VSS; RV 'vain talking,' which is near the Rhem. NT 'vaine talke.' This is the only occurrence of the word in bibl. Greek, but ματαιολόγος occurs in Tit 1¹⁰, EV 'vain talker.' The Eng. word 'jangle' (of Low Germ. origin; Skeat compares Lat. *gannire*, to yelp) was occasionally used in 1611 in the sense (still common) of 'quarrel,' but more frequently in the sense of 'chatter,' and that is its meaning here. Chaucer (*Persones Tale*) says, 'Jangling is whan man speketh to moche before folk, and clappeth as a mille, and taketh no kepe what he seith'; and in the same Tale, 'A philosophre seyde, whan men axed him how that men sholde plese the peple; and he answerde, "do many gode werkes, and speke few jangles."' J. HASTINGS.

JANIM (יָנִים *Kethibh*; AV Janum, following *Ḳerê* יָנוּם).—A town in the mountains of Hebron, near Beth-tappuah, Jos 15⁵³. The site is uncertain.

JANNAI (AV Janna, TR 'Ιαννά; Lach., Tisch., Treg., WH 'Ιανναί).—An ancestor of Jesus, Lk 3²⁴.

JANNES AND JAMBRES ('Ιαννῆς καὶ 'Ιαμβρῆς).— The traditional names of the two Egyp. magicians, who by their enchantments imitated the signs which Moses showed before Pharaoh. In Scripture the names occur only in 2 Ti 3⁸ 'As Jannes and Jambres withstood Moses, so do these also withstand the truth.' The allusions to them elsewhere are numerous and widespread, though full of anachronisms and contradictions. J. and J. are said to have been the sons of Balaam (*Sohar* 90. 2) or his young men (*Jerus. Targ.* Nu 22²²); and yet they were in the court of Pharaoh, and so interpreted a dream of the king as to forebode the birth of Moses, and cause the oppression (*ib.* Ex 1¹⁵). They are mentioned by name as opposing Moses (*ib.* Ex 7¹¹), but were so awed by Moses' later signs as to become proselytes, and leave Egypt with 'the mixed multitude' (*Yalkut Reubeni* 81. 2). They instigated Aaron to make the golden calf (*Tikkunim* 106. 4), and yet came with Balaam from Pethor when he visited the camp of Balak (*Jerus. Targ.* Nu 22²²). As to their death, there are diverse accounts. They were drowned in the Red Sea, or put to death after the incident of the golden calf, or during the slaughter of Phinehas. Their names occur also in the *Gospel of Nicodemus* (ch. 5), where Nicodemus warns Pilate by the example of J. and J. not to condemn Jesus; in the *Acts of Paul and Peter*, where Paul makes use of J. and J., to warn Nero against Simon's deceptions (Lipsius, *Apocr. Apostelgesch.* ii. 302), and in *Constitut. Apostol.* viii. 1, where J. and J. are paralleled with Annas and Caiaphas; while Palladius (c. A.D. 420) narrates that Macarius visited their tomb (Schürer, *HJP* II. iii. 150). In Gentile circles we find the Roman writers Pliny (*Hist. Nat.* xxx. 2) and Apuleius (*Apolog.* c. 90) mentioning Moses and Jannes among the famous magicians of antiquity; and a Gr. philosopher Numenius (2nd cent. A.D.), quoted by Eusebius (*Præp. Evang.* ix. 8), speaks of J. and J. as Egyp. ἱερογραμματεῖς. The early date of the tradition and its wide spread prove Levy in error in contending that J. and J. are John the Baptist and Jesus (*Chald. Wört.* 337).

In 2 Ti 3⁸ there is a various reading Μαμβρῆς; and it is interesting to find Mamre, מַמְרֵי or מַמְרָא in Jewish circles also. The spelling וּמַמְרֵא is found in Midrash *Vayyosha'* (i.e. from Ex 14³⁰), and also in *Yalkut Shimeoni* and the Talmudic tractate *Menachoth* 85a (quoted in Aruch). It is probable that *Jannes*, otherwise spelt יוֹנוֹס or יוֹחְנֵי, is a corruption of 'Ιωάννης = יוֹחָנָן: with a side allusion, however, to Aram. יוֹנַי 'he who misleads'; and that *Jambres* is from מָמְרֵי, ptcp. מַמְרֵי 'he who opposes.' The insertion of β into the *Yamre* and *Mamre* recalls Μαμβρή (Gn 13[18]) and 'Αμβράμ (Ex 6[18]) in LXX. Schöttgen gives other spellings of the names in Jewish writings.

LITERATURE.—Schöttgen (*Hor. Heb.*) and Wetstein (*Nov. Test.*) on 2 Ti 3[8]; Schürer *HJP* II. iii. 149 ff.; Buxtorf, *Chald. Lex. s.* יוֹחֲנָא, and the Bible Lexicons.   J. T. MARSHALL.

JANNES AND JAMBRES, BOOK OF.—An apocryphon not yet discovered. It is twice mentioned by Origen. On Mt 27[8] Origen says that St. Paul, in 2 Ti 3[8], does not quote 'from public writings, but from a sacred book, which is entitled The Book of Jannes and Mambres.' (The form Mambres is found in Codd. F G and Itala of 2 Ti 3[8], and in many Latin authors. The Jews also knew the form מַמְרֵי). On Mt 23[37] Origen adduces 2 Ti 3[8] as an instance in which an apocr. writing is quoted in Scripture. The same work is probably intended in the *Decretum Gelasii*, under the title *Pœnitentia Jamnis et Mambræ*. Whether St. Paul really read the work, or, as Theodoret opines, gathered his information from the unwritten teaching of the Jews, we can but conjecture. There are two points slightly in favour of Origen—(1) The fact that the Gentiles, Pliny, Apuleius, and Numenius knew of J. and J., seems to point to a written source; and since Pliny died A.D. 79, the work was probably in existence before 2 Ti was written. (2) The fact that Pal. Targ. gives the Gr. form of the names ינים וימברים, seems to imply that here, as in the case of Eldad and Modad (which see), the Targumist is quoting from a written source. It is probable, then, that we have here to do, not with an oral tradition, but with a definite apocryphal work.

LITERATURE.—Schürer, *HJP* II. iii. 149 ff.; Zöckler, *Apokr. d. AT*, 424; Fabricius, *Codex pseudepigr. VT*, i. 813–825.
                    J. T. MARSHALL.

JANOAH.—1. (יָנוֹחַ). A town in the northern mountains of Naphtali, near Kedesh, 2 K 15[29]. It is the modern *Yânûh*. See *SWP* vol. i. sheet ii. 2. (יָנוֹחָה, AV Janohah). A place on the border of Ephraim, east of Taanath-shiloh, Jos 16[6. 7]. In the 4th cent. A.D. (*Onomasticon, s.v.* 'Jano') it was known as lying in Akrabattine (the region of '*Akrabeh* in the hills east of Shechem), 12 Roman miles east of Neapolis (Shechem), or where the present *Yânûn* now stands, with the supposed tomb of Nun. See *SWP* vol. ii. sheet xii. (cf. Robinson, *BRP* iii. 297; Guérin, *Samarie*, ii. 6; Buhl, *GAP* 178).   C. R. CONDER.

JAPHETH (יֶפֶת, 'Ιάφεθ).—The name of one of the sons of Noah, and the ancestor of a number of tribes (esp. Gn 10[2-4]).

1. In the article HAM we have seen reasons for adopting the opinion according to which the three sons of Noah originally represented a division of the inhabitants of Palestine, but which part of the population was represented by Japheth is not clear: Wellhausen (*JDTh* xxi. 403) conjectured the Philistines; Budde (*Urgesch.* 338 ff.), the Phœnicians; but the words in the blessing of Noah (Gn 9[27]), 'God make room (so perhaps literally) for Japheth to dwell in the tents of Shem,' would seem to imply a closer relationship than that of neighbouring nations, and one more resembling that of castes of tribes forming a single state, like the Ramnes and Tities in Rome, or the Brahmins and Kshattriyas of Hindustan. Of the name 'Japheth,' however, with any such denotation there is no trace. The text of Gn offers no etymology for the name, but only an assonance with Aram. פתה 'to be wide'; and though a name derived from this root would perhaps have a parallel in the Nabatæan אפתיו,

there are other Semitic roots from which the name could with equal probability be derived; the etymology which has found most favour is from the Hebrew יפה 'to be beautiful,' whence the Arabic-speaking Jews make it the equivalent of 'Al-Hasan'; and this, though not free from grammatical difficulty, is accepted by some modern authorities.

2. As the name of one of the founders of the human race, it is natural to compare Japheth with Iapetos, a personage who appears in Homer (*Il.* viii. 479) as a giant, and in Hesiod as the father of Prometheus; while in a passage of Berosus, quoted on the very questionable authority of Moses of Chorene (ed. Florival, i. 30), a Chaldæan cosmogony makes an Iapetos joint founder of the human family with two others whom Moses not unnaturally identifies with Ham and Shem.[*] The only value of this notice is that we learn from it who first compared the Greek and Hebrew legends. The identification is etymologically possible (Lagarde, *Gesammelte Abhandlungen*, 256), but not certainly correct, since the Greek language offers a sufficiently good derivation for the name of the giant Iapetos (Ebeling, *Lexicon Homericum, s.v.*), and the original import of the biblical Japheth is not obviously connected with the giant: if the two names are in reality traceable to the same source, the latter is more probably Semitic than Greek, but it may very well be neither.

3. Many attempts have been made, both in ancient (Jos. *Ant.* I. vi. 1; Talm. Bab., *Yoma*, f. 10*a*; Talm. Jer., *Megillah*, p. 19; for other Rabbinic references see Neubauer, *Géog. du Talm.* 421 ff.) and in modern times (see Lagarde, *l.c.*, and esp. Lenormant, *Orig. de l'Hist.*[2] 1882) to identify the tribes derived from Japheth, of which Madai or Media, Javan or Ionia, and of Javan's sons Citium and Tarshish are familiar, and perhaps Meshech and Tubal may be said to be known; while the remaining names occur either in this table only (Tiras, Riphath) or chiefly besides in Ezk (esp. chs. 27. 38) and Jer (Ashkenaz). The omission of the name of Persia, which is known to Ezekiel (27[10] 38[5]), seems to give us a *terminus ad quem* for the composition of the list, while the fact that Magog occupies the second place shows that it can be little earlier than Ezekiel's time. The names of the grandsons may represent the results of more extended knowledge than that expressed in the names of the sons; but it is unlikely that the table in any form was derived from an official source; the names which it contains belong to distant nations, known to the Israelites of Ezekiel's time chiefly by hearsay, though several of them had by that date acquired some political importance. The writer who made them descendants of Japheth would seem to have already adopted the interpretation of Gn 9[27] which appears in the Targ. Onk., and Talm. Bab. *l.c.*, according to which it is God, not Japheth, who is to dwell in the tents of Shem. The first clause, 'God make room for Japheth,' when the room was no longer confined to Palestine, would be a ground for counting among Japheth's descendants the barbarians who peopled the unknown north and the islands of the unexplored sea.
                    D. S. MARGOLIOUTH.

JAPHETH ('Ιάφεθ).—A region whose identity is uncertain, mentioned in Jth 2[25]. Holofernes 'came unto the borders of Japheth, which were toward the south, over against Arabia.'

JAPHIA (יָפִיעַ; B 'Ιεφθά, A, Luc. 'Ιαφαλε;

[*] The modern Armenian poet Pakratuni (*Haig*, i. p. 17) rather ingeniously thinks of 'earthly' and 'heavenly' names. The Armenian form of the name in Moses is Japetosthé, whereon Pictet (*Origines Indo-Européennes*, i. 627) based some inferences, accepted by Lenormant, *l.c.* II. i. 191.

Japhia).—**1.** King of Lachish, who, together with the kings of Hebron, Jarmuth, and Eglon, joined Adoni-zedek, king of Jerusalem, in attacking the Gibeonites after the latter had made a treaty with the Israelites. The five 'kings of the Amorites' were routed by Joshua at Beth-horon, and fled to the cave at Makkedah, where they were slain at Joshua's command (Jos 10³ff.).

2. (B ʼΙεφίες, ʼΙανοῦε, ʼΙανουού ; A ʼΑφίε, ʼΙαφίε ; Luc. Νάφεθ, ʼΑχικάμ, ʼΙαβέγ) One of David's sons born at Jerusalem ; the list is given three times (2 S 5¹⁴b-16, 1 Ch 3⁵-8 14⁴-7).   J. F. STENNING.

JAPHIA (יָפִיעַ).—A town on the south border of Zebulun, Jos 19¹². It is probably the modern *Yâfa*, near the foot of the Nazareth hills. See *SWP* vol. i. sheet v. (cf. Robinson, *BRP*² ii. 343 f.).

JAPHLET (יַפְלֵט).—The eponym of an Asherite family, 1 Ch 7³²f. See GENEALOGY.

JAPHLETITES (יַפְלֵטִי).—The name of an unidentified tribe mentioned in stating the boundaries of the children of Joseph, Jos 16³ (see Dillmann's note).

JARAH (יַעְרָה).—A descendant of Saul, 1 Ch 9⁴². In 8³⁶ he is called **Jehoaddah**, and Kittel (in *SBOT*) would substitute יַעְרָה for יַעְרָה (so Siegfried-Stade and [doubtfully] *Oxf. Heb. Lex.*; and Gray, *Heb. Prop. Names*, 283, n. 14).

JAREB (יָרֵב, ʼΙαρείμ, ʼΙαρείβ) is twice employed by Hosea (5¹³ 10⁶) as a designation of the king of Assyria. Various opinions have been expressed as to whether it is a proper name or a descriptive epithet. AV, which, like RV, has 'king J.' in the text, offers in the marg. the alternative renderings 'the king of J.' or 'the king that should plead,' while RVm gives 'a king that should contend.' Sayce (*HCM* 417) conjectures that J. may have been the natal name of the usurper who seized the throne of Assyria after the death of Shalmaneser IV. in Dec. B.C. 723, and who is known to history as Sargon II. It was natural that he should assume the name of one of the most illustrious of the early Bab. monarchs (Sargon I.), just as his two predecessors, who were also usurpers, exchanged their original names (Pul and Ululâ) for those of earlier Assyr. kings (Tiglath-pileser and Shalmaneser). What appears to be a fatal objection to Sayce's theory, is that we seem compelled by internal evidence of the strongest character to assign the whole of Hos 4–14 to a date prior even to the deportation of the inhabitants of Gilead by Tiglath-pileser (734), whereas, if J. is to be identified with Sargon, we should have to bring down the date of some at least of these chaps. to about B.C. 722, the year when Samaria fell. Others (like AVm, RVm), connecting J. (יָרֵב) with רִיב=*strive*, render, *e.g.*, 'the warlike king' (W. R. Smith), 'a hostile king' (Gesenius), 'king Combat' (Farrar), 'Kampfhahn' (Guthe in Kautzsch's *AT*). Reuss, deriving J. from the same root רִיב, makes it = Lat. *patronus*, a title which he holds to be fairly applicable to a king whose assistance had been invoked by Ephraim and Judah (2 K 15¹⁹ 16⁷). Schrader's identification of 'the combatant king' with Assurdân (*c.* 755) lacks probability, as is pointed out by Whitehouse, who agrees with Nowack that J. is Tiglath-pileser III. (745–728). A very attractive explanation of the name is offered by McCurdy, who considers that J. is a participial adjective from the root רבב meaning 'to be great.' *Jareb* would thus answer to the familiar title of Assyr. monarchs, 'the great king' (*Hist. Proph. and Mon.* i. 415). W. Max Müller (*ZATW*, 1897, p.

334) obtains the same meaning by dividing the words מלכי רב instead of מלך ירב. So also Cheyne (*Expositor*, Nov. 1897, p. 364 ; cf. *Expos. Times*, ix. [1898] pp. 364, 428). See further, Nowack, *Kl. Proph. ad loc.*; Neubauer, *Zeitschr. f. Assyr.* iii. 103 ; Hommel, *Gesch. Bab.-Assyr.* 680 ; Schrader, *COT*² ii. 136.   J. A. SELBIE.

JARED (יֶרֶד, pausal form יָרֶד, LXX ʼΙάρεδ, NT ʼΙάρετ).—The father of Enoch, Gn 5¹⁵. ¹⁶. ¹⁸. ¹⁹. ²⁰, 1 Ch 1², Lk 3³⁷. See further, JERED.

JARHA (יַרְחָע).—An Egyptian slave who married the daughter of his master Sheshan, 1 Ch 2³⁴f. See GENEALOGY.

JARIB (יָרִיב).—**1.** The eponym of a Simeonite family, 1 Ch 4²⁴=**Jachin** of Gn 46¹⁰, Ex 6¹⁵, Nu 26¹². **2.** One of the 'chief men' who were sent by Ezra to Casiphia in search of Levites, Ezr 8¹⁶. He is called in 1 Es 8⁴⁴ Joribus. **3.** A priest who had married a foreign wife, Ezr 10¹⁸. He is called in 1 Es 9¹⁹ Joribus.

JARIMOTH (A ʼΙαριμώθ, B -ει-), 1 Es 9²⁸.—In Ezr 10²⁷ JEREMOTH.

JARMUTH (יַרְמוּת).—**1.** A town in the W. of Judah. In Jos 10 (JE) its king, Piram, joined the Canaanite league against the Gibeonites, and suffered death along with his confederates at Makkedah—all of which argues a place of considerable importance. (Cf. Jos 12¹¹ D²). According to Jos 15³⁵ (P) it was situated in the Shephelah, and belonged to the tribe of Judah, which tribe on its return re-peopled the town (Neh 11²⁹).

The site is upon the present Jebel Yarmuk, a hill, the slopes of which still show the marks of old retaining walls, and are covered with the ruins of buildings. The summit is crowned by the foundations of a wall, the early acropolis of the place. Guérin (*Judée*, ii. 371 ff.) states that the ruins lie 'three good hours from Beit Djibrin, the ancient Eleutheropolis, on the road to Jerusalem.' The town will then be identical with the ʼΙερμοῦς or Jermus of the *Onomasticon*, which Eusebius and Jerome agree in placing 10 miles from Eleutheropolis on the way to Jerusalem. And the ʼΙαβεῖς or Jarimuth of the *Onom.* may be the same place, repeated with an error in the text (see Guérin, *ad loc.*). Though the site is not within the Shephelah, it immediately commands it.

2. A city in Issachar, belonging to the Gershonite Levites (Jos 21²⁹). Probably we should read רָמָת Remeth : for (1) in the duplicate list (1 Ch 6⁷³) the name is Ramoth, in the tribal list of cities (Jos 19²¹) Remeth appears ; (2) in Jos 21²⁹ the LXX reads ʼΡεμμάθ B, ʼΙερμώθ A ; and in 19²¹ ʼΡέμμας B, ʼΡαμάθ A. The place has not been identified. Guérin (*Galilée*, i. 129 ff.) conjectures Kaukab el-Haoua, a height between Scythopolis and Tiberias, which the Crusaders named Belvoir. The only reason is that Ramah or Remeth means height (!). Conder (*PEF Mem.* 1881, p. 201) suggests Rameh N. of Samaria, near which tradition places Issachar's grave.   A. C. WELCH.

JAROAH (יָרוֹחַ).—A Gadite chief, 1 Ch 5¹⁴. The text is doubtful (cf. Kittel in *SBOT*).

JASAELUS (ʼΑσάηλος, AV Jasael), 1 Es 9³⁰.—In Ezr 10²⁹ SHEAL.

JASHAR, BOOK OF (AV Jasher, סֵפֶר הַיָּשָׁר ; LXX 2 S 1¹⁸ βιβλίου τοῦ εὐθοῦς ; Vulg. *libro justorum* ; Syr. [Syriac] ; Targ. [Aramaic]

Jos 10¹³ 'book of hymns *or* praises,' [Syriac] ;

2 S 1¹⁸ 'book of Ashir,' [Syriac] ;

'book of the law').—According to MT, this document was the source of the lines,

> 'Sun, stand thou still upon Gibeon ;
> And thou, Moon, in the valley of Aijalon.
> And the sun stood still, and the moon stayed,
> Until the nation had avenged themselves of their enemies'
> (Jos 10¹². ¹³) ;

and of David's Lament over Saul and Jonathan, 2 S 1¹⁷⁻²⁷. LXX of Jos omits the reference to the Bk. of Jashar. But probably the original text of 1 K 8¹². ¹³ stated that the lines,

> 'J" hath said that he would dwell in the thick darkness.
> I have surely built thee an house of habitation,
> A place for thee to dwell in for ever,'

were taken from this book. LXX makes our 1 K 8¹². ¹³ the close of 8⁵³, apparently following a somewhat different text, and adds οὐκ ἰδοὺ αὔτη γέγραπται ἐν βιβλίῳ τῆς ᾠδῆς. The last three words represent סֵפֶר הַשִּׁיר, which is probably a corruption, by the transposition of two letters, of סֵפֶר הַיָּשָׁר. Nothing further is known of this document. Syr. of Jos and S, and LXX of 1 K 8⁵³, suggest that יָשָׁר in Jos and S may be a corruption of שִׁיר 'song'; but this view has met with little if any support. The data are too scanty and obscure to determine either the character of the book or the meaning of its title. As the passages quoted are ancient poems on great events, especially battles, probably the book was a collection of such poems. Some other OT poems may be from this collection. The Targ. 'book of the law' represents a rabbinical theory that the Bk. of Jashar was the Pentateuch or part of it. Donaldson, in his *Jashar: fragmenta archetypa carminum Hebraicorum*, published at London in 1854, attempted a reconstruction of the book, and assigned to it a large number of passages from OT ; but his views met with no acceptance.

The date of the collection is obviously later than the time of David, and probably older than B.C. 800—the references to Jashar are assigned to J¹ (Budde, *Samuel*, etc.).

MT points שָׁר as the ordinary יָשָׁר 'upright,' and it is so understood by LXX, Vulg. etc. If so, it may be taken as 'hero,' or collectively 'heroes,' courage and warlike prowess being the virtues most admired in primitive times ; Ilgen notices the title *Hamasa*, 'warlike virtue,' 'valour,' given to a section of an Arabic anthology, containing poems in praise of heroic deeds. Or 'the hero' may be Israel, whose name is based on a root similar to שָׁר, and who is sometimes called יְשֻׁרוּן *Jeshurun* (which see), Dt 32¹⁵ 33⁵. ²⁶, Is 44². Or שָׁר may be the initial word of the book, possibly to be read as *yāshîr* 'sang,' as in יָשִׁיר אָז Ex 15¹, Nu 21¹⁷.

There are two rabbinical works with the title 'Book of Jashar,' a moral treatise by R. Shabbatai Carmuz Levita, A.D. 1394, contained in a MS in the Vatican ; and a treatise on the laws of the Jews by R. Thom, d. 1171, first printed in Italy A.D. 1544. There is also an anonymous historical narrative, with the same title, containing the Pent., Jg., and Jos with additions ; accepted by some Jews as the Bk. of Jashar ; probably the work of a Spanish Jew of the 13th cent. It is said to have first appeared at Naples, and was first printed at Venice in 1625. In 1674 a German version of this work, with additions, was published at Frankfort-on-Main by R. Jacob. In 1751 a Bristol type-founder published a forgery professing to be an English translation of the Bk. of Jashar, with a preface by Alcuin. It was reprinted in 1827 with a forged attestation by Wyclif.

LITERATURE.—Art. JASHAR in Smith's *DB*¹ ; Holzinger, *Einleitung in den Hexateuch*, 228 ff. ; Ryle, *Canon of OT*, 19 ff. : Driver, *LOT*⁶, 108, 121, 192 ; Wildeboer, *Lit. d. AT*, 73 ff. ; Kautzsch's *AT*, Beilage, 136 f. ; W. R. Smith, *OTJC*² 438 ff.

W. H. BENNETT.

JASHEN (יָשֵׁן, 'Ασάν, *Jasen*).—The sons of Jashen (בְּנֵי יָשֵׁן) are mentioned in the list of David's heroes given in 2 S 23³². In the parallel list (1 Ch 11³⁴) they appear as the sons of **Hashem** (הָשֵׁם), who is further described as the **Gizonite** (הַגִּזוֹנִי) (wh. see). The name *Gizon*, however, does not occur elsewhere, and it seems probable that the true form of the gentilic adjective has been preserved by Lucian (2 S 'Ιεσσαὶ ὁ Γουνύ ; 1 Ch Εἰρασαὶ ὁ Γουνί), viz. 'the Gunite' (הַגּוּנִי), or member of the Naphtalite family of Guni (Nu 26⁴⁸) ; so Driver, Budde, Klostermann. It is further generally admitted by most scholars that the word בְּנֵי ('sons of') has crept into the text both of 2 S and 1 Ch by dittography from the preceding הַשַּׁעַלְבֹנִי ('the **Shaalbonite**') : Lucian omits it in both passages. Hashem (1 Ch), though supported by the LXX (2 S 'Ασάν ; 1 Ch A υἱοὶ 'Ασάμ ὁ Γωννί), must, in view of Lucian's text, be rejected in favour of Jashen. For 'the sons of Jashen' (2 S 23³²) we should therefore read 'Jashen the Gunite.' See further, Driver, *Notes on the Books of Sam.* p. 283.

J. F. STENNING.

JASHOBEAM (יָשָׁבְעָם).—One of David's mighty men, 1 Ch 11¹¹ 12⁶ 27². There is reason to believe that his real name was Ishbosheth, *i.e.* Eshbaal. See JOSHEB-BASSHEBETH.

JASHUB (יָשׁוּב 'he returns ').—**1.** Issachar's fourth son, Nu 26²⁴ P, 1 Ch 7¹, called in Gn 46¹³ **Iob** (wh. see) : patron. **Jashubites**, Nu 26²⁴. **2.** A returned exile who married a foreigner, Ezr 10²⁹.

JASHUBI-LEHEM (יָשֻׁבִי לָחֶם).—The eponym of a Judahite family, 1 Ch 4²². The text is manifestly corrupt. LXX gives καὶ ἀπέστρεψεν αὐτούς, Luc. καὶ ἐπέστρεψαν ἑαυτοῖς. Kittel (in *SBOT*) reads וַיָּשֻׁבוּ בֵּית לָחֶם 'and they returned to Bethlehem,' remarking that the LXX and Vulg. (*et qui reversi sunt in Lahem*) rightly recognize the verb שׁוּב. לחם must stand for בֵּית־ל, and the last two letters of MT ישבי may be a trace of the בית. Even so, the meaning of the passage is obscure.

JASON ('Ιάσων).—A common Gr. name, not unfrequently used by Hel. Jews, or by Palestinians who were favourable to Hellenizing influences. In some cases it was adopted as the equivalent of *Joshua* or *Jesus* ('Ιησοῦς) ; cf. Jos. *Ant.* XII. v. 1.

1. J. THE SON OF ELEAZAR, one of the envoys sent by Judas Maccabæus to conclude a treaty with Rome (B.C. 161). The Greek name suggests that he belonged to the more liberal party among the Jews (Stanley), 1 Mac 8¹⁷, Jos. *Ant.* XII. x. 6.

2. J. THE FATHER OF ANTIPATER, who was sent as an ambassador by Jonathan, in B.C. 144, to renew the former treaty with the Romans (1 Mac 12¹⁶ 14²², Jos. *Ant.* XIII. v. 8). This Jason is perhaps the same as No. 1.

3. J. OF CYRENE, a Jewish writer, who composed five books on the history of the Maccabees and the wars of the Jews against Antiochus Epiphanes and his successor Eupator. Of this work our Second Book of the Maccabees is an abridgment (ἐπιτομή), and from the epitomizer's preface our whole knowledge of J. is derived. The date at which he lived can be determined only by internal evidence. Comparing the epitome with 1 Mac, which deals in the main with the same period of history, we find numerous discrepancies not only in important details, but sometimes even in the order of events ; and it cannot be doubted that on the whole the simpler narrative of 1 Mac is to be preferred. At the same time 2 Mac supplies us with many additional particulars, which there is no reason to doubt. The writer seems to have been specially well informed upon the earlier troubles which led to the Maccabæan rising. J. clearly had at his disposal valuable contemporary information; but if this was not written but oral, and frequently not received at first hand, it is easy to account for the numerous inaccuracies and legendary additions which are to be found in his work. The narrative of 2 Mac extends to B.C. 160; and J. probably wrote not long after that date. His name and place of residence imply that he was a Hellenist; the ornate and rhetorical style of the work is characteristic of the later Gr. writers; and from internal evidence it seems clear that the orig. work of J. was written in Greek. Cf. Schürer, *HJP* II. iii. 211–215; Zöckler on 2 Mac, *Einl.* 2.

4. J. THE HIGH PRIEST, the son of Simon II., and brother of Onias III., was the leader of the Hellenizing party among the Jews. His orig. name was Jesus or Joshua (Jos. *Ant.* XII. v. 1). On the accession of Antiochus Epiphanes, he induced the king, by means of a large present of money, to expel Onias from the high priesthood, and to confer the office upon himself (2 Mac 4⁴⁻¹⁷, 4 Mac 4¹⁵⁻²⁰. Josephus, *l.c.*, seems to be mistaken when he asserts that J. became high priest on the death of his brother, and also when he states that the next pretender, Menelaus, was a brother of J.). J. further procured from Antiochus permission to erect a gymnasium and 'ephebeion' in Jerus., and obtained for the inhabitants the title and privileges of 'citizens of Antioch.' Through J.'s influence Gr. customs were largely adopted among all classes of the Jews; and to the sacred games, which were celebrated at Tyre every four years in honour of Hercules, he sent a Jewish deputation with a large sum of money. This money, however, at the request of the envoys themselves, was expended on building galleys and not on sacrifices (2 Mac 4¹⁸⁻²⁰). For three years (B.C. 174–171) J. continued in power, then he was supplanted by his own envoy to Antiochus, Menelaus, who gained the office of high priest by offering a still larger bribe (*ib.* 4²³⁻²⁶). J. took refuge among the Ammonites; but the next year, on the occasion of a false report of the death of Antiochus in Egypt, he suddenly attacked Jerus. with a large force, and, becoming master of the city, drove his rival to take refuge in the citadel. On the advance of Antiochus, J. fled once more to the Ammonites, and subsequently to Egypt. Afterwards, relying on the fabled connexion between the Spartans and Jews (cf. 1 Mac 12⁷), he retired to Sparta, and there died 'in a strange land,' 'nor had he any funeral at all, or place in the sepulchre of his fathers' (2 Mac 5¹⁻¹⁰).

H. A. WHITE.

JASON ('Ἰάσων). — During St. Paul's visit to Thessalonica, he was the guest of one Jason. When the Jews caused a disturbance, they attacked Jason's house, and, failing to find the apostle, they took Jason and the brethren before the politarchs. The magistrates received security (τὸ ἱκανόν) from Jason and the others, and then dismissed them. The brethren immediately sent Paul and Silas away to Berœa (Ac 17⁵ᶠᶠ·). The nature of the security is not mentioned. According to Ramsay (*St. Paul the Traveller*, p. 231), it was a security to prevent the cause of the disturbance, Paul, from coming to Thessalonica. This put a chasm between the apostles and the Thessalonians, and hence he speaks (1 Th 2¹⁸) of Satan hindering him (διότι ἠθελήσαμεν ἐλθεῖν πρὸς ὑμᾶς, ἐγὼ μὲν Παῦλος καὶ ἅπαξ καὶ δίς, καὶ ἐνέκοψεν ἡμᾶς ὁ Σατανᾶς). This explanation is ingenious, but will perhaps hardly explain the ἅπαξ καὶ δίς.

In Ro 16²¹ the apostle sends greetings from Timothy, Lucius, Jason, and Sosipater, his kinsmen. This was very probably the same as the Jason of Thessalonica,—an identification made rather more probable by the possibility of Sosipater being the Sopater of Berœa (Ac 20⁴). He would

then be a Jew (οἱ συγγενεῖς μου). It was natural that St. Paul should lodge with a fellow-countryman, and Jason was a favourite name for Jews to assume whose Hebrew name was Joshua (Jesus); cf. Jos. *Ant.* XII. v. 1: ὁ μὲν οὖν Ἰησοῦς Ἰάσονα ἑαυτὸν μετωνόμασεν· ὁ δὲ Ὀνίας ἐκλήθη Μενέλαος. Jason did not apparently accompany St. Paul to Jerusalem (Ac 20⁴), and therefore presumably remained at Thessalonica.   A. C. HEADLAM.

JASPER.—See STONES (PRECIOUS).

JASUBUS ('Ἰασούβος), 1 Es 9³⁰.—In Esr 10²⁹ JASHUB.

JATHAN ('Ἰαθάν, AV Jonathas). — Son of Shemaiah 'the great,' and brother of Ananias the pretended father of Raphael, To 5¹³.

JATHNIEL (יַתְנִיאֵל).—The eponym of a Levitical family, 1 Ch 26². See GENEALOGY.

JATTIR (יַתִּיר and יַתִּר).—A town of Judah in the southern mountains, noticed with Socoh and Debir, a Levitical city, Jos 15⁴⁸ 21¹⁴, 1 Ch 6⁴² [Eng. ⁵⁷]. It was one of the cities to whose elders David sent of the spoil from Ziklag, 1 S 30²⁷. It appears to have been far south, since it is noticed in the latter passage with Aroer. The most probable site is the ruin 'Attir, N.E. of Beersheba, on a hill spur close to the southern desert.

LITERATURE.—*SWP* vol. iii. sheet xxiv.; Robinson, *BRP*² i. 494; Baedeker-Socin, *Pal.*², 3, 153; Buhl, *GAP* 164; Dillm. on Jos 15⁴⁸.
C. R. CONDER.

JAVAN (יָוָן, Ἰωυάν, Ἑλλάς, Ἕλληνες, *Javan, Græcia, Græci*).—A son of Japheth and father of Elishah, Tarshish, Kittim, and Dodanim (the last a textual error for Rodanim, *i.e.* Rhodes) (Gn 10²·⁴). In Is 66¹⁹ (cf. Jl 3⁶) Javan is associated with the Gr. islands, and in Ezk 27¹³ with the traders of Tubal and Meshech, while in Dn 8²¹ 10²⁰ 11² it denotes the Macedonian empire. J., in fact, is the Greek Ἰάων, 'Ionian,' and its position in Gn 10² shows that it must there mean Cyprus (in which Kition [*Kittim*] was situated), called *mat Yavnâ*, *Yânan*, and *Yânana*, 'the land of the Ionians,' in the inscriptions of Sargon and Sennacherib. In the Bab. transcripts of the inscriptions of Darius Hystaspis, *Yâvanu* represents the Ionians of Asia Minor; and when, in B.C. 711, the people of Ashdod revolted from Assyria and deposed their lawful king, they put on the throne in his place a certain Yavanu or 'Greek.' Gaza was also called Iônê, and the sea between Philistia and Egypt was known as 'Ionian' (Steph. Byz. *s.v.* Ἰόνιον). In the Egyp. hieroglyphs Ha-nibu or Ui-nivu is rendered by Uinin or 'Ionians' in demotic, and the Mediterranean is termed the 'circle of the Ha-nibu' as early as the pyramid-texts of the 6th dynasty. One of the Tel el-Amarna tablets (B.C. 1400) speaks of a Yivana or 'Ionian' in the land of Tyre, and W. Max Müller (*Asien und Europa*, p. 370) has pointed out that the name of one of the allies of the Hittites in their struggle with Ramses II. must be read Yevana, 'Ionians.'   A. H. SAYCE.

JAVAN (יָוָן), mentioned by Ezekiel (27¹⁹) among places that traded with Tyre, but distinct from Javan = Ionia, which occurs in v.¹³. See preceding article. The verse in which it is found commences וְדָן וְיָוָן מְאוּזָּל, and the third of these words is probably to be interpreted 'from Uzal,' a place in Arabia (Gn 10²⁷); but it is not clear whether Uzal is to be regarded as the factory whence 'Wĕdân and Jāvân' exported goods to Tyre, or whether 'from Uzal' is an epithet of 'Javan' intended to distinguish this Javan from the other. Of the modern authorities who regard the consonants of the text as correct, Smend thinks Javan may be the name of an Arab tribe, or of a locality in the neighbourhood of Uzal (*Ṣan'ā*); while Glaser (*Skizze*, ii. 428–436) is inclined to interpret יון as 'Greeks,' supposing a Greek colony in Arabia to be signified, but seems to prefer to identify it with *Yayn*, a place mentioned by Hamdāni (ed. Müller, p. 171, l. 10) as belonging together with *Waddān* to the territory of Juhaynah, and indeed immediately after *Ḥarrat an-Nār* in the neighbourhood of Medinah (see Doughty's map). The situation of this *Yayn* can be fixed with some accuracy from the notice in Al-Bekri (ed. Wüstenfeld, p. 859, etc.); but although the LXX rendering (οἶνον) would seem to favour the reading יין in Ezk, and the proximity of *Waddān* seems to support Glaser's identification, the fact that there is no evidence of this *Yayn* having ever been a place of importance, or connected with the trade in iron and spices, or connected with Uzal, renders it impossible to attach any scientific value to the identification.

The majority of modern critics regard the consonants as corrupt (Stade, Briggs, Cornill ; cf. *Oxf. Heb. Lex. s.* (וְדָן); and in Cornill's edition וארנב is substituted for the consonants of the text, on the authority of a wine-list of Nebuchadnezzar (Delitzsch, *Assyrische Lesestücke*, 1875, p. 63), in which a country of that name (*A-ra-na-ba-nun*) is mentioned with two others which bear some resemblances to places named in v.[18] as sending wine to Tyre. Though striking parallels to Ezekiel are found in the cuneiform inscriptions (D. H. Müller, *Ezechiel-studien*, 1895, pp. 56–62), the legitimacy of such a correction seems questionable.

D. S. MARGOLIOUTH.

JAVELIN.—See SPEAR.

JAWBONE (Jg 15[15ff.]).—See LEHI, SAMSON.

JAZER (יַעְזֵר, יַעְזֵיר, Ἰαζήρ ; AV of Nu 21[32] 32[35] **Jaazer** ; meaning of name uncertain).—A town E. of the Jordan, in Gilead, and belonging to the tribe of Gad (Jos 13[25], 1 Ch 26[31]).* The indications given in the *Onomasticon* by Eusebius and Jerome, viz. 10 (or 8) miles W. of Philadelphia and 15 N. of Heshbon, are approximately correct. It was a Levitical city (Jos 21[39]), was evidently a place of more than usual importance, and is mentioned in various connexions. The 'villages' or *daughter towns* of J. are spoken of in Nu 21[32], showing that the district was thickly inhabited, and that neighbouring places were grouped about it as their political head. It was chosen as one of the stations of David's census officers (2 S 24[5]), and, seven centuries after the conquest of the country under Moses, it was famous for its vineyards and fruitful fields (Is 16[8-10], Jer 48[32]).† Jazer is mentioned also in connexion with the wars of the Maccabees, having been, according to Josephus (*Ant.* XII. viii. 1), captured and burnt by Judas Maccabæus, after the latter had inflicted a crushing defeat upon the Ammonites under Timotheus.

When the Hebrews reached Heshbon, they discovered, lying not far to the north of it, an extensive and fertile region which they speak of as 'the land of Jazer' (Nu 32[1]). Against this a special expedition (Nu 21[32]) was fitted out by Moses (1) because of its own importance, and (2) because it lay in the line of march to the conquest of Bashan. This region at once attracted the attention of the Hebrews, and the contrast between its broad and fertile expanse and the desert which they had left made them feel that they

* In Nu 21[24] Dillm. and others read יַעְזֵר instead of MT עֵד, and tr. 'the border of the children of Ammon was Jazer.'

† In Jer 48[32] 'they reached even unto the sea of Jazer,' יָם 'sea' is a textual error, due to an accidental repetition of the יָם of the preceding clause (so Graf, Grätz, Cheyne, Giesebrecht).

had reached a paradise. 'It is not to be wondered at that the two and a half tribes were perfectly willing to stay on this side of the Jordan. Judæa has no land to compare with it, neither has Samaria, except in very limited portions. The surface of the country is slightly rolling and comparatively free from stone. Here common Arab trails broaden out into fine roads. Here are wide pasture lands and luxuriant fields of wheat and barley, and the ignorant Bedawin who own the soil point with pride to the green acres that are spread out beneath the sun.'

Jazer, now called *Khurbet Sar*, has extensive remains of antiquity, but those above ground are chiefly of the Roman period. It possesses a curious tower formed of massive blocks of unhewn stone, which could have been put into position only at the cost of immense labour. Sar is about three thousand four hundred feet above the sea-level, and in the wide view to the W. and S. the Dead Sea is embraced. On the south, Wady esh-Shita begins to descend rapidly towards the Jordan Valley, and in the opposite direction not far from the ruins are two large ponds, near to but entirely distinct from each other, peculiar and attractive objects in the landscape. The great plateau about this ancient ruin has for generations been the battle-ground of the Arab tribes in that region, and quantities of skulls are piled under the fallen arches of a once magnificent building (Merrill, *East of the Jordan*, pp. 405, 485).

S. MERRILL.

JAZIZ (יָזִיז).—A Hagrite who was 'over the flocks' of king David, 1 Ch 27[31]. See GENEALOGY.

JE.—The symbol used by biblical critics for the combination in one whole of the Jahwistic and Elohistic documents. See HEXATEUCH.

JEALOUSY.—There is no more striking example of the anthropomorphic way of speaking of God than the frequent ascription to Him of jealousy, associated as that idea is in our minds with an evil meaning. 'I am a jealous God' (אֵל קַנָּא Ex 20[5] 34[14], Dt 4[24] 5[9], Jos 24[19], Nah 1[2]). Two things may help to remove the feeling of strangeness. The phrase is probably taken from the marriage relation which is so often used in OT to describe the relation between J″ and the people of Israel (Is 54[5] 62[5], Hos 2[19] etc.). Again, although the word is now generally used in a bad sense, it has a good side, as in the case of the marriage relation in question ; and it is only in this sense, of course, that it is used in the present connexion. Just as jealousy in husband or wife is the energetic assertion of an exclusive right, so God asserts and vindicates His claim on those who belong to Him alone. The use of the figure is much bolder and more picturesque than the bare assertion of right would be. If God is the husband and Israel the wife, then idolatry and wickedness of every kind are spiritual adultery. Israel is often represented as thus provoking God to jealousy (Dt 32[16], 1 K 14[22] etc.). The phraseology occurs with special frequency in Ezk (5[13] 16[38. 42] 23[25] 36[5. 6] 38[19] 39[25]); but it is found in other prophets also (Is *passim*, Jl 2[18], Zeph 1[18], Zec 1[14] 8[2], Hos 2[2. 16]).

On the other hand, the term is used to denote passionate concern in man for God's honour, as in the case of Phinehas (Nu 25[11. 13]), Elijah (1 K 19[10]), Jehu (2 K 10[16] ; cf. Ps 119[139]). So Jn 2[17] 'The zeal (ζῆλος) of thine house' (Ps 69[9]) ; 'a zeal for God' (Ro 10[2]) ; 'I am jealous . . . with a godly jealousy' (2 Co 11[2]). Cf. ὁ κανακαῖος = ὁ ζηλωτής, Lk 6[15].

The law of the jealousy offering is found in Nu 5[11-31]. The rite was in the nature of an appeal to God, who was called upon to decide the question of the innocence or guilt of the suspected person. The subsequent practice of ordeals in the West was based on the OT institution.

The words ζηλοῦν and ζῆλος are also used in a bad sense, esp. in NT; ζῆλος is coupled with φθόνος (1 Mac 8[16]), ἔρις (Ro 13[13], 1 Co 3[3]), and ἐριθία (2 Co 12[20], Gal 5[20], Ja 3[14. 16]); cf. Ac 7[9], 1 Co 13[4], Ja 4[2].

J. S. BANKS.

JEARIM, MOUNT (הַר־יְעָרִים).—Mentioned only in Jos 15[10], where it is identified with CHESALON (wh. see).

JEATHERAI (יְאָתְרָי).—An ancestor of Asaph, 1 Ch 6[21] [Heb. 6[6]], called in v.[41] [Heb.[26]] **Ethni.**

JEBERECHIAH (יְבֶרֶכְיָהוּ; 'J" blesseth,' generally abbreviated בֶּרֶכְיָה or בֶּרֶכְיָהוּ, **Berechiah,** which see).— The father of Zechariah, a friend of Isaiah, Is 8[2].

JEBUS, JEBUSI, JEBUSITE (יְבוּס, Ιεβους; יְבוּסִי, יְבֻסִי, Ιεβουσαῖος -οι, Ιεβουσαι Jos 18[16], Ιεβουσειν Jg 19[11b]).—Jēbūs occurs only in Jg 19[10] ('Jebus, the same is Jerusalem'), v.[11], and in 1 Ch 11[4. 5], a passage which the Chronicler has so expanded from 2 S 5[6] as to introduce the name into it twice (in v.[4] adding, 'the same is Jebus,' and in v.[5] 'the inhabitants of Jebus'), each time, obviously, as an intentional archaism. On the strength of these passages, it used commonly to be said that Jebus was the old name of Jerusalem; but the Tel el-Amarna tablets have shown this view to be erroneous; the city is there called regularly *Urusalim.** It seems, that, the inhabitants being known as 'Jebusites,' it was inferred incorrectly that 'Jebus' was the name of their city; but more usually, even in early times, it is spoken of as 'Jerusalem' (Jg 1[7. 21], Jos 15[63], 2 S 5[6]).

Jebusite † was the name of the local tribe which, in the first centuries of Israel's occupation of Canaan, held Jerusalem, until its citadel, 'the stronghold of Zion,' was captured under David, being called afterwards, from this circumstance, 'the city of David' (2 S 5[6-9]; cf. 1 K 2[10] 11[43] etc.). Allusions to the Israelites' inability to expel the Jebusites from their stronghold are found in Jos 15[63], Jg 1[21]; and in Jg 19[10-12] it is described as a city of 'foreigners.' Zion was the S. part of the easternmost ‡ of the two hills, on which Jerusalem was situated; and this accordingly was the site of the old Jebusite fortress. From its position it admitted of being strongly fortified: on the E. it overhung the Kidron valley, the bottom of which was some 700–800 ft. below; on the S. its sides sloped down more gradually to even a greater depth; on the W. the Tyropœon valley—not, as now, filled up with *débris*—was some 300 ft. below it; only on the N. was the approach easier, though even here, according to Guthe's excavations, there was a natural barrier, consisting of a depression in the rock, some 30–50 yards wide, and 12 deep. The area thus indicated would include, moreover, the one natural spring in Jerusalem, Gihon.§ The situation of this stronghold thus readily explains its long resistance to the Israelites. In the end, however, in spite of the taunting words in which its inhabitants defied their assail-

ants to enter it, it was taken by David (2 S 5[6-9]), —if an addition found only in the text of 1 Ch 11[6] is to be trusted, through the prowess of Joab; and received the name which perpetuated to afterages the memory of the monarch's success. The position of the Jebusite stronghold is further alluded to in Jos 15[8] 18[16], where it is said that the (North) border of Judah and the (South) border of Benjamin passed along the valley of the son of Hinnom (whether this be the valley on the S. or the S.E. of Zion) to the south shoulder—i.e. the projecting mountain-side—of the Jebusite,—in exact agreement with the situation as defined above; it lay thus, according to these passages (P), just within the territory of Benjamin. This position of Jerusalem, so close to the border-line separating the two tribes, explains the variation observable between Jos 15[63] ('the Jebusites dwell with the children of *Judah* in Jerusalem to this day') and Jg 1[21] ('the Jebusites dwell with the children of *Benjamin* in Jerusalem to this day'); see JERUSALEM. Of the earlier history of Jerusalem, it will be sufficient here to say that its king, Adoni-zedek, is described as being defeated and slain by the Israelites (Jos 10[23. 26]; cf. 12[10]); but nothing is said here about the *city* being taken: the statement in Jg 1[8] that the children of Judah took it and burnt it, can be reconciled with v.[21] (Jos 15[63]) only by very artificial suppositions; and the verse is in all probability a gloss, due to a misunderstanding of v.[7b] (see Moore, *ad loc.*).

The only Jebusite mentioned expressly by name is ARAUNAH, the owner of the threshing-floor on the top of 'Zion,' which was bought by David for the purpose of building an altar to J" (2 S 24[16. 18. 25]; cf. 1 Ch 21[15. 18. 26. 28 22]1, 2 Ch 3[1]); but it is reasonable to suppose that Adoni-zedek (Jos 10[1] etc.), if not Adoni-bezek as well (Jg 1[5]; see v.[7 end], and cf. Moore), was Jebusite likewise. How, or when, the Jebusites obtained possession of their stronghold, we do not know: in the Tel el-Amarna letters (c. B.C. 1400), Abdichêba is ruler of 'the land (or district) of the city of Jerusalem'; but, though allusion is made to the political action taken by the 'city' and 'country' governed by Abdichêba, the name of the inhabitants is not stated. Nor do our data enable us to determine with certainty the racial affinities of the Jebusites; though their position, and the Semitic name *Adoni-zedek* ('Zedek is my lord'), would lead naturally to the inference that they were a sub-tribe of the Canaanites. In Jos 10[5] (cf. vv.[1. 3. 12]) Adoni-zedek is called a 'king of the Amorites'; but, in view of the manner in which 'Amorite' is used in E (like 'Canaanite' in J) as a general designation of the pre-Israelitish inhabitants of Canaan, no conclusion can be drawn from the statement as to the distinctive nationality of his subjects: there were at least no Amorites S. of Phœnicia in the age of the Tel el-Amarna letters.*

The Jebusites are frequently mentioned in the rhetorical enumerations of the nations of Canaan, whom the Israelites were to dispossess (or had dispossessed), as Gn 15[21], Ex 3[8. 17] 13[5], Jos 11[3] (cf. Nu 13[29]); in these lists, perhaps on account of their being numerically the smallest, they hold nearly always the last place. The buildings of David on the 'Millo' (2 S 5[9]), and still more the temple and palaces constructed by Solomon, must have greatly altered the appearance of Zion; and few of its former Jebusite possessors can have remained there. The narrative of 2 S 24 shows, however, that David treated his conquered foes with consideration. According to 1 K 9[20f.], the Jebusites, with other Canaanite races, were reduced by Solomon to serfdom, and made liable to forced service (הֶעֱלָה לְמַס עֹבֵד). In Zec 9[7], where the future

---

* Letters 180, 181, 183, 185 in Winckler's edition (Nos. 254, 234, 256, 233, in Petrie's *Syria and Egypt from the Tell el-Amarna Letters*, 1898).

† **Jebusi** in Jos 18[16. 28] (AV) is nothing but an anomalous reproduction of the form of the Heb. gentilic adj.: it is altered in RV to the usual *Jebusite.*

‡ Not, as many maps, following a tradition which does not reach back beyond the 4th cent. A.D., incorrectly exhibit, the *western* hill: see ZION; and cf. W. R. Smith, *Enc. Brit.*9 *s.v.* JERUSALEM, p. 639; Guthe, *ZDPV*, 1883, p. 271 ff.; Mühlau in Riehm's *HWB*2 i. 695, 698 f., and *s.v.* ZION; Stade, *Gesch.* i. 267, 315 f.; C. W. Wilson, *DB*2 p. 1650 f.; Ryle on Neh 3[15]. On the top of the hill (N. of the 'city of David') was built afterwards the Temple, with the royal Palace immediately contiguous to it on the S.: 'Ophel' was the bulging mountain side, S. of the 'city of David.'

§ Cf. the plan in Stade's *Geschichte*, i. p. 268.

* Petrie, *Syria and Egypt*, p. 136 f.

incorporation of the Philistines in the kingdom of God is promised, either (Wellh., Now.) *Jebusite* is an archaistic expression for Jerusalemite, or (Ew.) the allusion is to the Jebusites of old, who were incorporated into Judah by David,—'and he also shall be a remnant for our God, and he shall be as a clan-leader [or, a clan, אַלֻּף] in Judah, and Ekron *as a Jebusite.*'   S. R. DRIVER.

JECHILIAH (יְכִילְיָה *Kethîbh*, יְכָלְיָה *Ķerê* as in 2 K 15², Jecoliah; LXX, B Χααιά, A Ἰεχελιά; Vulg. *Iechelia*).—The mother of king Uzziah, 2 Ch 26³.

JECHONIAS (Ἰεχονίας).—**1.** The Gr. form of the name of king JECONIAH, employed by the English translators in the books rendered from the Greek, Ad. Est 11⁴, Bar 1³· ⁹; called in Mt 1¹¹ᶠ· **Jechoniah.** **2.** 1 Es 8⁹² (LXX ⁸⁹). In Ezr 10² SHECANIAH.

JECOLIAH.—See JECHILIAH.

JECONIAH.—See JEHOIACHIN.

JECONIAS (Ἰεχονίας).—**1.** One of the captains over thousands (χιλίαρχοι) in the time of Josiah, 1 Es 1⁹; in 2 Ch 35⁹ called CONANIAH. **2.** RVm of 1 Es 1³⁴. See JEHOAHAZ 2.

JEDAIAH.—**1.** (יְדַעְיָה) A priestly family, 1 Ch 9¹⁰ 24⁷, Ezr 2³⁶, Neh 7³⁹ 11¹⁰ 12⁶· ⁷· ¹⁹· ²¹. **2.** (same Heb.) One of the exiles sent from Babylon with gifts of gold and silver for the sanctuary at Jerusalem, Zec 6¹⁰· ¹⁴. LXX does not treat J. here as a proper name, reading τῶν (τοῖς) ἐπεγνωκότων (-κοσιν) αὐτήν. **3.** (יְדָיָה) A Simeonite chief, 1 Ch 4³⁷. **4.** (same Heb.) One of those who repaired the wall of Jerusalem, Neh 3¹⁰. See GENEALOGY.

JEDDU (B''Ιεδδος, A ''Εδδος), 1 Es 5²⁴.—In Ezr 2³⁶ JEDAIAH.

JEDEUS (Ἰεδαῖος), 1 Es 9³⁰.—In Ezr 10²⁹ ADAIAH.

JEDIAEL (יְדִיעֲאֵל).—**1.** The eponym of a Benjamite family, 1 Ch 7⁶· ¹⁰· ¹¹. **2.** One of David's heroes, 1 Ch 11⁴⁵, probably identical with the Manassite of 12²⁰. **3.** The eponym of a family of Korahite porters, 1 Ch 26². See GENEALOGY.

JEDIDAH (יְדִידָה 'darling'; B Ἰεδεία, A Ἐδιδά).—Daughter of Adaiah of Bozkath, and mother of Josiah, king of Judah (2 K 22¹).

JEDIDIAH (יְדִידְיָה 'beloved of J''; cf. Sab. ודראל; B Ἰδεδεί, A Εἰεδιδιά).—The name given to Solomon by the prophet Nathan, 2 S 12²⁵ 'for the LORD's sake' (בַּעֲבוּר יהוה). See SOLOMON.

JEDUTHUN (יְדוּתוּן [in Kethîbh of Ps 39¹ 77¹, Neh 11¹⁷, 1 Ch 16³⁸ יְדִיתוּן], LXX Ἰδιθούν, Ἰδιθώμ, etc.).—The eponym of one of the three guilds which, acc. to the Chronicler, conducted the musical service of the temple from the time of David downwards. The name does not occur in the books of Sam. or Kings or in any pre-exilic document. Not only so, but the earliest of the post-exilic writers know of only the Asaphites as singers (Neh 7⁴⁴, Ezr 2⁴¹). There is indeed mention in Neh 11¹⁷ of descendants of J. who discharged this function, but in this passage we have not the *original* memoirs of Nehemiah, and the reference is wanting in the LXX. The Chronicler makes J. like Asaph, a contemporary of David, and gives him the title of 'the king's seer' (2 Ch 35¹⁵). While in 1 Ch 16⁴¹ᶠ· 25¹ᶠ· etc. the three guilds of temple musicians are named after Heman, Asaph, and *Jeduthun*, there are other passages where the third name in the list is **Ethan** (1 Ch 6⁴⁴ 15¹⁷ etc.).

The two names are often assumed to be alternative designations of one and the same singer. It may be so, but there are circumstances which render this explanation less satisfactory than it appears at first sight. Reasonable doubts have even been expressed whether J. was originally a proper name at all. The word occurs in the title of three psalms (39. 62. 77). In the first of these (unless לִידוּתוּן be a scribal error for עַל) לִידוּתוּן may be in apposition with לַמְנַצֵּחַ (giving the sense of 'to the chief musician, namely to J.'), but in Ps 62 and 77 the reading is עַל־יְדוּתוּן (LXX ὑπὲρ Ἰδιθούν) 'upon J.' (which, after the analogy of similar expressions in the headings of the Pss, most probably means 'upon an instrument named J.'), or as in RV 'after the manner of J.' (where the last word would be the name of a tune or the opening word of a song). The whole subject of Heb. musical terms is so involved in obscurity that it is impossible to reach any certain conclusion. Seeing that the Sept. translators found many of these terms unintelligible, there is nothing improbable in the supposition that the Chronicler writing about the same date (c. B.C. 250) adopted an interpretation which took J. for a proper name, and that he transformed it, like the more familiar Heman and Ethan (which see), into the eponym of a Levitical choir. See MUSIC.

LITERATURE.—Graf, *Ges. B. d. AT* 223, 239; W. R. Smith, *OTJC*² 143 n.; Kautzsch, *Heil. Sch. d. AT* 715 n.; Cheyne, *Or. of Psalter*, 191, 111; Ewald, *Psalms*, Eng. tr. i. 44; Kuenen, *Rel. of Isr.* ii. 204; Wellhausen, *Gesch.* 152 n.; Schürer, *HJP* II. i. 225; Köberle, *Tempelsänger im AT.*   J. A. SELBIE.

JEELI (A Ἰεηλί, B Ἰειηλεί), 1 Es 5³³.—In Ezr 2⁵⁶ JAALAH, Neh 7⁵⁸ JAALA.

JEELUS (B Ἰέηλος, A Ἰεηλ), 1 Es 8⁹² (LXX ⁸⁹).—In Ezr 10² JEHIEL.

JEGAR-SAHADUTHA (יְגַר שָׂהֲדוּתָא, Aram. = 'cairn of witness,' LXX Βουνὸς μάρτυς, DE [τῆς] μαρτυρίας).—The name said to have been given by Laban to the cairn erected on the occasion of the compact between him and Jacob, Gn 31⁴⁷. See GALEED. The same Aram. root occurs in Job 16¹⁹ שָׂהֲדִי 'my witness'). On the substitution of ט for ס see Dillmann's note on this last passage.

JEHALLELEL (יְחַלֶּלְאֵל).—**1.** A Judahite, 1 Ch 4¹⁶. **2.** A Levite, 2 Ch 29¹². See GENEALOGY.

JEHDEIAH (יֶחְדְּיָהוּ 'may J'' give joy'!).—**1.** The eponym of a Levitical family, 1 Ch 24²⁰. **2.** An officer of David, 1 Ch 27³⁰. See GENEALOGY.

JEHEZKEL (יְחֶזְקֵאל 'God strengtheneth,' the same name as *Ezekiel*).—A priest, the head of the 20th (in LXX, B, the 19th) course, 1 Ch 24¹⁶.

JEHIAH (יְחִיָּה 'may J'' live'!).—The name of a Levitical family, 1 Ch 15²⁴. See GENEALOGY.

JEHIEL (יְחִיאֵל 'may El live' !).—**1.** One of David's chief musicians, 1 Ch 15¹⁸· ²⁰ 16⁵. **2.** A chief of the Levites, 1 Ch 23⁸ 29⁸. **3.** Jehiel the son of Hachmoni was 'with (= tutor of ?) the king's sons,' 1 Ch 27³². **4.** One of Jehoshaphat's sons, 2 Ch 21². **5.** One of Hezekiah's 'overseers,' 2 Ch 31¹³. **6.** A ruler of the house of God in Josiah's reign, 2 Ch 35⁸. **7.** The father of Obadiah, a returned exile, Ezr 8⁹, called in 1 Es 8³⁵ Jezelus. **8.** Father of Shecaniah, Ezr 10², called in 1 Es 8⁹² Jeelus, perhaps identical with **9.** One of those who had married foreign wives, Ezr 10²⁶, called in 1 Es 9²⁷ Jezrielus. **10.** A priest of the sons of Harim who had married a foreign wife, Ezr 10²¹, called in 1 Es 9²¹ Hiereel. See GENEALOGY.

JEHIELI (יְחִיאֵלִי). — A patronymic from JEHIEL No. 2, 1 Ch 26²¹· ²² (cf. 23⁸ 29⁸).

JEHIZKIAH (יְחִזְקִיָּהוּ, 'J″ strengtheneth'). — An Ephraimite, in the time of Ahaz and Pekah, who supported the prophet Oded in opposing the bringing of Judæan captives to Samaria, 2 Ch 28¹²ff..

JEHOADDAH (יְהוֹעַדָּה, possibly 'J″ hath deposed or hath numbered'). — A descendant of Saul, 1 Ch 8³⁶. See JARAH.

JEHOADDAN (יְהוֹעַדָּן 2 Chr 25¹ and, as vocalized, 2 K 14². The consonants of the text in 2 K 14² give the form **Jehoaddin** [so RV] יהועדין). — A lady of Jerusalem, mother of Amaziah king of Judah.

JEHOAHAZ (יְהוֹאָחָז, or **Joahaz** יוֹאָחָז 2 K 14¹, 2 Ch 34⁸ 36²· ⁴ 'J″ hath grasped'). — **1.** King of Israel, son of Jehu. His reign of seventeen years necessitates in 2 K 13¹ the reading 'one and twentieth' (Jos. *Ant.* IX. viii. 5), or in v.¹⁰ 'thirty-ninth' (Aldine LXX, and Thenius). The inroads of Hazael of Damascus, which Jehu could not resist (2 K 10³²), crushed Jehoahaz. The straits to which he was reduced by the Syrians (2 K 13⁷· ²² 14²⁶· ²⁷) led by the young prince Benhadad (13³· ²⁴) imply that the terrible anticipations of Elisha (2 K 8¹²) were being realized. These calamities were accompanied by a revival of the Asherah worship of Ahab (13⁶, cf. 1 K 16³³). Nevertheless, at the king's prayer, J″ promised Israel 'a saviour' (cf. Jg 3⁹ etc.), a promise not fulfilled in this reign (as Jos. *Ant.* IX. viii. 5, see v.²²), but in the victories of Joash and Jeroboam II. (2 K 13²⁵ 14²⁷), unless we suppose an allusion to the Assyrian king Rammân-nirâri who captured and plundered Damascus about this time (see Schrader, *COT* i. 207).

2. King of Judah (Joachaz or Jeconias, 1 Es 1³⁴; Zarakes, 1 Es 1³⁸, see *QPB*). The name Shallum, found in Jer 22¹¹, 1 Ch 3¹⁵, may possibly be significant, 'to whom it is requited' (Keil), or may contain an allusion to the unfortunate king of Israel, 2 K 15¹³ (Bertheau), but more probably it was his original name, exchanged on his accession for one of better omen. He was the third son of Josiah (2 K 23³¹· ³⁶ 24¹⁸), his position in 1 Ch 3¹⁵ being due to his insignificance. Although a bad man, ἀσεβὴς καὶ μιαρὸς τὸν τρόπον, 'impious and impure' (Jos. *Ant.* X. v. 2), he must have been a popular prince, since the people made him king in preference to his elder brother. He was anointed — a ceremony specified only in the case of a new dynasty or a disputed succession. Even the prophets Jeremiah (22¹⁰⁻¹²) and Ezekiel (19²⁻⁴) speak of him with sympathy and regret. After his victory at Megiddo it is likely that Necho resumed his march on the Euphrates, and sent a detachment to Jerusalem to bring J. to Riblah, whence he was carried a prisoner to Egypt when Necho returned, after having reduced Syria west of the Euphrates. 2 Ch 36³ might imply that Necho visited Jerusalem in person when deposing Jehoahaz. This is unlikely; but he probably did so on his return journey (see Rawlinson's note on Herodotus, ii. 159).

3. = AHAZIAH of Judah, 2 Ch 21¹⁷ 25²³.

N. J. D. WHITE.

JEHOASH or **JOASH** (יְהוֹאָשׁ, יוֹאָשׁ, אָשׁ 2 Ch 24¹ 'J″ is strong,' or 'J″ hath bestowed'*). — **1.** King of Judah (2 K 11. 12, 2 Ch 22¹⁰–24). A year-old infant when hidden by his aunt in a lumber-room of the palace (RVm, Jos. *Ant.* IX. vii. 1) from his unnatural grandmother, J. was but seven when placed on the throne of his ancestors (see ATHALIAH

* See on this name and on 'Josiah' a paper by Hommel in *Expos. Times*, viii. (1897) p. 562.

and JEHOIADA). It is sufficient here to observe that the significance of his coronation, as the revival of David's line, was emphasized, not only by the employment of David's dedicated armoury, but by a ceremonial of which there is no previous record, the investiture of the king with the royal insignia, 'the crown and the bracelets' (so Wellh. reading הָעֵדוּת instead of הָעֵדוּת 'testimony,' cf. 2 S 1¹⁰; Jerome [*Qu. Heb.* on 2 Ch 23¹¹] says 'phylacteries are meant, on which were written the ten commandments'). The covenant was renewed, not only between God and the nation, but between the people and the king (Ch omits), and, moreover, Jehoiada took steps to secure the continuance of the Davidic stock (2 Ch 24³). The death of Athaliah was followed by a reaction against the Baal worship which she had fostered; and the temple, which had been 'broken up' during her reign (2 Ch 24⁷), naturally became the object of the young king's pious care. The account in Kings of the raising of money for this purpose seems to have presented great difficulties to the Chronicler. At this period the commutation of sacrifices by a money payment appears to have been common (2 K 12¹⁶), and the money was paid to the priests directly, to each man by his patrons ('acquaintance'). The king directed that the priests should see to the necessary repairs, and should devote to this purpose (α) the money paid for the redemption of personal vows (Lv 27²), and (β) all voluntary offerings in coin. [Ch substitutes the half shekel tax of Ex 30¹³⁻¹⁶, while AV and RVm of 2 K 12⁴, supported by Targ., Rashi, etc., imply that this was a third source of revenue]. The priests [Ch 'Levites'], however, with Jehoiada at their head, ignored the king's order; possibly from poverty, as the temple was then only one of many sanctuaries (2 K 12³). At last, in the 23rd year of the reign, the business was, with their consent, taken out of their hands. Jehoiada [Ch 'the king'] placed a money chest 'beside the altar' (so Josephus) [Ch 'without at the gate'], into which the priests that kept the door (cf. 22⁴ 25¹⁸) [Ch 'all the princes and all the people'] cast the proper monies. The money was counted by the king's scribe and the high priest [Ch 'chief priest's officer'], and according to Kings was devoted solely to the repair of the fabric, whereas Ch asserts that 'of the rest were made vessels for the house of the Lord,' thus directly contradicting 2 K 12¹³. The Chronicler now records the criminal weakness of J. in yielding to the idolatrous tendencies of the princes, and his base ingratitude as shown in the murder of Zechariah, the son of those to whom he owed his life and crown. There is nothing of this in Kings. There is indeed in 2 K 12² a hint at a deterioration in J.'s character after the death of Jehoiada (denied by Ewald, who renders 'wherein' 'because,' *HI* iv. 137 n. 1); but, on the other hand, he is ranked in 2 K with Amaziah (14³), Uzziah (15³), and Jotham (15³⁴) as one who 'did right in the eyes of the Lord, yet not like David'; the shortcoming in each case being apparently that 'the high places were not taken away.' However, the reference to the murder of Zechariah in Mt 23³⁵, Lk 11⁵¹, seems to guarantee that the story is not inserted merely to give a moral reason for the calamities of Jehoash. The Syrian invasion which followed [Ch immediately] is naturally represented in Ch as a special judgment on J. and the guilty princes, whereas in Kings it is implied that Hazael (not mentioned in Ch) did not actually take Jerusalem, but was bought off by an immense bribe. In any case the invasion was a severe national humiliation, which must have caused much discontent, and this found vent in the murder of J. by two of his servants in the fortress on Mt. Zion. The Chronicler heightens the infamy of his end by adding that he was 'in great diseases,' that they 'slew him on his bed,' that he was not buried in the royal sepulchres, and that the mothers of the assassins were of the two accursed nations of Moab and Ammon (see Dt 23³). Jerome (*Qu. Heb., ad loc.*) notes that 'this is said to emphasize the wickedness of the Israelites who were unwilling to avenge God's priest.'

2. King of Israel, son of Jehoahaz. The brief epitome of his reign (2 K 13¹⁰⁻¹³) merely adds to the inevitable condemnation of his national worship an allusion to his defeat of Judah. But we derive a much more favourable impression of him from the close of the Acts of Elisha (2 K 13¹⁴⁻²⁵), and from the history of Amaziah of Judah, 2 K 14⁸⁻¹⁶ (=2 Ch 25¹⁷⁻²⁴), where the formula of conclusion is repeated from 13¹². ¹³. In J. was partially fulfilled (13²⁵) the promise (13⁴. ⁵) of a saviour from Syria, a promise repeated in the double symbolical prophecy of Elisha to the somewhat irresponsive king (13¹⁸); and when we remember the abject condition into which Israel had fallen in the previous reign, it will be evident that J. must have been one of the greatest rulers of the northern kingdom. The hiring by Amaziah of Judah of 100,000 soldiers of Israel, during this reign (2 Ch 25⁶), would indicate that all fear of Syria had been taken away. 'His might' was shown also in the thoroughness with which he followed up his victory at Bethshemesh, by breaking down the wall of Jerusalem on the weakest side. His natural disposition seems to have been good (as Jos. *Ant.* IX. viii. 6). There was a wholeheartedness in the burst of grief over the dying prophet; there was a pious recognition of the true source of Israel's strength in the words (13¹⁴) which reechoed Elisha's own apostrophe to the ascending Elijah (2¹²); and even the sarcastic fable in which he replied to Amaziah's gratuitous challenge was dictated not more by pride than by magnanimity.

N. J. D. WHITE.

JEHOHANAN (יְהוֹחָנָן 'J" hath been gracious').— **1.** 1 Ch 26³ a Korahite doorkeeper in David's time. **2.** 2 Ch 17¹⁵ one of Jehoshaphat's five captains. Possibly father of Ishmael, who held a similar post at the accession of Jehoash, 2 Ch 23¹. **3.** Ezr 10⁶ (JONAS, 1 Es 9¹; JOHANAN, Neh 12²². ²³; JONATHAN, Neh 12¹¹) high priest. He is called son of Eliashib Ezr 10⁶, Neh 12²³, but was probably his grandson, Joiada being his father (Neh 12¹¹. ²²). His high priesthood is noted as an epoch until which the heads of the Levitical families were registered in 'the book of the Chronicles' (Neh 12²³); hence presumably down to the close of the 5th cent. B.C. (H. E. Ryle, *in loc.*). **4.** Ezr 10²⁸ (=JOANNES, 1 Es 9²⁹) an Israelite, one of those who 'had taken strange wives.' **5.** Neh 6¹⁸, son of Tobiah the Ammonite, Nehemiah's adversary. **6.** Neh 12¹³ a priest, representative of the course of Amariah, in the days of Joiakim. **7.** Neh 12⁴² a priest present at the dedication of the walls.

N. J. D. WHITE.

JEHOIACHIN (יְהוֹיָכִין 8 times, יְהוֹיָכָן Jer 52³¹, יוֹיָכִין Ezk 1²; **Jeconiah** יְכָנְיָה 5 times, יְכָנְיָהוּ Jer 27²⁰ [Kethîbh],יָכָנְיָהוּ Jer 24¹; **Coniah** כָּנְיָהוּ Jer 22²⁴. ²⁸ 37¹; 'J" appointeth'; called **Joakim,** 1 Es 1⁴³; **Jechonias,** Bar 1⁸. ⁹; **Jechoniah,** Mt 1¹¹. ¹²).—King of Judah, son of Jehoiakim. Ewald conjectures that his original name was Coniah, exchanged for Jehoiachin on his accession; Keil more probably ascribes the variation to 'popular twisting and contracting of the longer name.' He reigned three months; the additional 10 days given in 2 Ch 36⁹ 1 Es 1⁴⁴ being probably due to the accidental shifting in the text of 'ten' from his age at accession, which in Ch is eight instead of eighteen. Both readings are found in 1 Es 1⁴³. Upon J., as upon Louis XVI. of France, descended the full force of the divine vengeance incurred by previous generations. In another age

he might have been 'the signet upon J"'s right hand' (Jer 22²⁴). He was scarcely on the throne when the Chaldæan forces, which had been ravaging Judæa, were joined by Nebuchadnezzar himself, and closed around Jerusalem, and J. surrendered at discretion. Jos. (*Ant.* X. vii. 1) asserts that Nebuchadnezzar had made J. king, after slaying his father; and that almost immediately afterwards, fearing that he might prove disloyal, he returned to depose him. This is both intrinsically unlikely, and is quite unsupported by the biblical narrative. From the prominent position given to the queen-mother Nehushta in 2 K 24⁸, Jer 13¹⁸ 22²⁶ 29², it is reasonable to infer that she exercised more than ordinary influence, and it was possibly at her suggestion that J. capitulated. Jos. (*Ant.* X. vii. 1) attributes it to 'his gentle and just disposition; he did not desire to see the city endangered on his account' (cf. *Ant.* X. xi. 2); and in *BJ* VI. ii. 1 he describes how at the last siege he himself appealed to John of Giscala to 'follow the example of J. who . . . did undergo a voluntary captivity . . . that he might not deliver up this sanctuary to the enemy, and see the house of God in flames; wherefore among all the Jews a sacred discourse celebrates him, and memory for ever flowing fresh hands him down immortal to posterity.' Among moderns, Ewald also takes a favourable view of his character, influenced by the theory that J. is the royal exile of Ps 84⁹, and therefore author of that Ps, as well as of Pss 42. 43. But such a view seems irreconcilable with the tone of Jer 22²⁴⁻³⁰, as well as with the unqualified condemnation in 2 K 24⁹, 2 Ch 36⁹, 1 Es 1⁴⁴. The favourable language of Jer 24⁵⁻⁷ refers to the captives generally. On the other hand, in Ezk 19⁵⁻⁹ the life of Jehoiakim and the fate of his son are fused into one ideal picture; and justly, for J. had no distinct political existence. The arm of Babylon raised to strike his father fell on him, and fulfilled the prophecy against Jehoiakim (Jer 36³⁰), 'He shall have none to sit upon the throne of David.' Conversely in Mt 1¹¹ the two reigns are included under 'Jechoniah,' the less important name being chosen as marking more distinctly the epoch of the Captivity (cf. 1 Ch 3¹⁶, 2 Ch 36¹⁰, where Zedekiah is brother of J.). It is not merely a confusion arising from the identification of the names in LXX and Josephus.

With the fall of Jerusalem, B.C. 597, the Captivity began. Captives had been taken from the country before this, Jer 13¹⁹, and possibly still earlier (Dn 1³, Berosus in Jos. *c. Apion,* i. 19), but this marks an epoch, and from it Ezekiel dates his prophecies ('our captivity,' Ezk 40¹). The flower of the nation and the treasures of the temple were carried off to Babylon. By a comparison of 2 K 24¹⁴⁻¹⁶ with Jer 52²⁸ (LXX om. Jer 52²⁸⁻³⁰) we may infer that the captives included 7000 'men of might,' 3023 of the upper classes (Jos. *Ant.* X. vi. 3), and 1000 craftsmen. The king himself is styled emphatically 'the captive' (1 Ch 3¹⁷ RV), and seems to have been kept in rigorous imprisonment for 37 years. Evil-Merodach began his reign with an act of gracious clemency by releasing J., about 55 years old. The historian (2 K 25²⁷⁻³⁰, Jer 52³¹⁻³⁴) dwells with evident pleasure on the marks of respect thenceforth shown to the captive prince, in whose person the Jewish exiles felt their nation honoured. The long imprisonment of J. proves, if that were necessary, the unhistorical character of the notices of him in Bar 1³ff. and in the History of Susanna, assuming that Hippolytus and others are right in identifying him with Joakim, Susanna's husband.

Needless difficulty has been raised over the question of J.'s children (implied 1 Ch 3¹⁷, Bar 1⁴, Mt 1¹²). Whatever be the truth as to the parentage of Shealtiel, the very prophecy which is alleged to prove his childlessness (Jer 22²⁸⁻³⁰) mentions his seed twice. Like Ezk 21²⁶, it is a declaration of the abrogation of the temporal power of David's line. It explains in what sense he was to be 'childless' (LXX ἐκκήρυκτον, 'proscribed'), 'for no man of his seed shall prosper,' words surely unmeaning if he had no seed at all. According to the Mishna (*Middôth* 2), one of the 13 gates of the court of the priests, on the north side, was called the gate of Jeconiah, because he went out by it when going into captivity.

N. J. D. WHITE.

JEHOIADA (יְהוֹיָדָע 'J" knoweth').—**1.** Father of the famous Benaiah, captain of David's bodyguard, who is scarcely ever mentioned without the addition of his father's name. J. was a native of Kabzeel (2 S 23²⁰, 1 Ch 11²²), 'a town of Judah in the South' (Jos 15²¹). In 1 Ch 27⁵ AV we read: 'Benaiah the son of J., a chief priest.' Stanley (*Jewish Ch.* Lect. 36) deduces from this that in David's time there were three rival high priests, namely, Zadok, Abiathar, and J. However, in RV ('the priest, chief') 'chief' refers to Benaiah (so Targ.) as in v.⁸, and 'the priest' may be referred directly to Benaiah (so LXX, Vulg., Jos. *Ant.* VII. xii. 4, B. ὁ ἱερεὺς τῷ γένει) or to J. (so Targ.). The latter is supported by 1 Ch 12²⁷, where, among those who came to David to Hebron, is 'J. the leader of the house of Aaron' (tribe of Levi, Jos. *Ant.* VII. ii. 2). It is not a serious objection that Kabzeel is not reckoned among the priestly cities in Jos 21. RVm of 1 Ch 27⁵ 'chief minister' is certainly wrong, being based on the Chronicler's alterations of the text in 2 S 8¹⁸ 20²⁶, where the term כֹּהֵן is applied to persons who, in his estimation, were not qualified to exercise priestly functions. In 1 Ch 27³⁴ among David's counsellors is reckoned 'J. son of Benaiah,' but we should probably read with Bertheau and Graf, 'Benaiah son of J.' **2.** High priest (the first who is so styled 2 K 12¹⁰) in the reigns of Ahaziah, Athaliah, and Jehoash. His marriage with the princess Jehosheba—the only recorded instance of such a union—possibly conferred on J. a status which enabled him the better to carry out his designs. The careful way in which the deposition of Athaliah was planned, and the promptitude and thoroughness with which it was carried out, coupled with the historical importance of the revolution thus effected, mark J. as perhaps the most eminent of Aaron's successors, not excepting Eli. Like Eli he was virtually king, for his influence, which was necessarily paramount during the minority of Jehoash, was naturally exercised (2 K 12², 2 Ch 24²) until his death, which must have been quite late in the reign (2 K 12⁶). In the time of the Captivity (Jer 29²⁶) he is alluded to as the model of a zealous ecclesiastical ruler. One circumstance there is which may seem to modify this conception of him. He was not as eager about the restoration of the temple fabric as was the king; in fact he received a rebuke for his slackness (2 K 12⁷, 2 Ch 24⁶). Josephus (*Ant.* IX. viii. 2) attributes the high priest's supineness to his consciousness of the unpopularity of the proposed tax, but more probably it was due to the impossibility of reforming a close corporation, such as that of the temple priests, even by such a chief as J.; especially when the numerous local sanctuaries, still thought legal, diminished their revenues. Acc. to 2 Ch 24¹⁵ ¹⁶ J. lived to the age of 130, and received the unique distinction of burial in the royal sepulchres, 'because he had done good in Israel, both toward God and toward his house.' See ATHALIAH, JEHOASH.   N. J. D. WHITE.

JEHOIAKIM (יְהוֹיָקִים, יוֹיָקִים, יוֹקִים 'J" raiseth up'; Joakim, 1 Es 1³⁷· ³⁸· ³⁹. See *QPB*, Bar 1³).—King of Judah, second son of Josiah (1 Ch 3¹⁵).

The circumstances under which this prince succeeded to the throne were the first and most significant indication of the long period of ignominious subjection ushered in by the defeat of Josiah by Necho at Megiddo, B.C. 609 or 610. Necho emphasized the new condition of things by deposing the popular Jehoahaz in favour of his elder brother, at the same time imposing on the latter a new name, Jehoiakim, in place of Eliakim. The substitution of the sacred title Jah for the ambiguous El was probably suggested by the young prince himself; yet the change of name was, none the less, a token of vassalage (cf. 2 K 24¹⁷). The direct history of this reign is briefly summed up in 2 K 23³⁴–25⁷, 2 Ch 36⁴⁻⁸; but considerable light is thrown upon it by the writings of the contemporary prophets Jeremiah and Habakkuk (see Jer 7–9. 10¹⁷⁻²⁵ 14–17¹⁸ 18–20. 22¹³⁻¹⁹ 25. 26. 35. 36. 45–46¹² 47. 49).

At no previous epoch was Judah in a more helpless condition of religious and moral decay. The one visible result of Josiah's reformation was that the temple and the Law were regarded as a palladium, and that the Levitical worship was accurately observed (Jer 7⁴· ²¹ 8⁸ 18¹⁸). But with the death of the good king all the old abominable idolatries returned in full force, and under the highest patronage, both of the king and the princes, who from this time forward take a large share of the government. Baal and Ashtoreth were worshipped in the very precincts of the temple; the valley of Hinnom was again hideous with the infant sacrifices to Molech; and from the city - roofs incense went up to all the host of heaven. Cruelty, corruption, and oppression flourished unchecked, for the people had 'in their viciousness grown hard.' They felt and averred 'there is no hope.' Of such a nation Jehoiakim was the representative man. In the terrible denunciation (Jer 22¹³⁻¹⁹) he is charged with covetousness, the shedding of innocent blood, oppression, and violence. All that is recorded of him bears this out. He erected by forced labour (cf. Hab 2⁹⁻¹¹) a spacious palace 'cieled with cedar and painted with vermilion,' thus (Jer 22¹⁵) vying with Ahaz (Bℵ, cf. 2 K 16¹¹) or Ahab (A, cf. 1 K 22³⁹). He relentlessly pursued and murdered, with marks of indignity, the prophet Uriah who had denounced him (Jer 26²⁰). A similar fate was well-nigh shared by Jeremiah and Baruch (Jer 36²⁶). He cut and burnt with his own hands a roll of divine words, similar to that the recitation of which caused Josiah to rend his garments (Jer 36²²); and, as an instance of his covetousness, 2 K 23³⁵ specially notes that he satisfied the demands of his suzerain (LXX, v.³³, 100 talents of gold, Syriac and Arabic 10 [so also certain Greek cursives and the Complutensian]) by a general taxation of his subjects, not, as had been customary, from the treasuries of the palace or the temple. Jos. (*Ant.* x. v. 2) well sums up his character as 'unjust and malignant; neither holy towards God nor forbearing towards man.' Ezk 19⁵⁻⁹, in which the career of Jehoiakim and the fate of his son seem combined in an ideal picture, has no reference to his moral qualities, unless we adopt the RVm of v.⁷, which implies a charge of lasciviousness, irrelevant here, though probably true in fact.

Two matters in connexion with this reign require special mention—(*a*) the invasion of Nebuchadnezzar, and (*b*) the end of Jehoiakim.

(*a*) The pretensions of Egypt to the empire of Syria were finally crushed by Nebuchadnezzar at the battle of Carchemish, B.C. 605 (2 K 24⁷). This battle took place in the *fourth* year of Jehoiakim (Jer 25¹ 46²), and opened up Syria to the Chaldæans. However, they had not yet attacked Judæa in Jehoiakim's *fifth* year (Jer 36⁹· ²⁹

'eighth' B‎ℵ, 'fifth' AQ). The fast then proclaimed by the whole nation in the 9th month was possibly in view of their approach, which yet was not so certain that one could safely predict it. Carchemish is on the Euphrates, and there were many important places, e.g. Tyre, to be reduced before the Chaldæans could reach Jerusalem. This being so, it is evident that there was no siege of Jerusalem by Nebuchadnezzar in Jehoiakim's *third* year as stated in Dn 1¹. (*Seder Olam* 25 understands this of the third year of his *rebellion*.) The date assigned in Daniel is due to a mistaken impression (Dn 9²) that Jeremiah had predicted a 70 years' duration for the captivity of Judah (2 Ch 36²¹‧²²=Jer 1¹ follows Daniel); but the 70 years of Jer 25¹¹ 29¹⁰ RV refer to the duration of Babylonian supremacy, beginning from the victory at Carchemish. Moreover, Ezekiel (1² 40¹) reckons the captivity of Judah to begin with that of Jehoiachin, B.C. 597. When Nebuchadnezzar at last appeared before Jerusalem, it is likely enough that he carried off some captives (Berosus in Jos. *Ant.* x. xi. 1; Dn 1³) and some of the temple vessels (2 Ch 36⁷, Dn 1²). It is certain that J. submitted to him, but rebelled after three years, incited by the Egyptians (Josephus). Jer 47¹ possibly refers to this. Nebuchadnezzar, who had returned to Babylon, did not at first think it necessary to quell this revolt in person, but sent (2 K 24², cf. Jer 49¹, Ezk 25³⁻⁶, Zeph 2⁸) some of his own troops, assisted by bands of the surrounding nations, to harry Judæa, not arriving himself until after the accession of Jehoiachin (2 K 24¹¹). To this interval Jer 35 probably belongs. Now J. reigned eleven years, and at least a year must be allowed to elapse between his revolt and his death, so that the *first* Chaldæan invasion may be dated in his 6th or 7th year. Jos. (*Ant.* x. vi. 1) places it in the 8th year of J., thus making Judæa independent of Egypt and Babylon alike for four years; but this is at variance with his authority Berosus, and leaves no time for the events of 2 K 24².

(*b*) The death of Jehoiakim is veiled in obscurity. According to the prophecy (Jer 22¹⁸‧¹⁹ 36³⁰), his dead body lay unburied outside the walls of Jerusalem; and this is confirmed by 2 K 24⁶, which is silent as to his burial. Jos. (*Ant.* x. vi. 3) says that Nebuchadnezzar, when admitted without resistance into Jerusalem by J., slew him, and 'commanded him to be thrown before the walls without any burial,' and took 3000 captives, including Ezekiel (cf. Jer 52²⁸); but Nebuchadnezzar did not arrive until after J.'s death. We may conjecture that J. was killed in a sally (Keil), or more probably assassinated by his indignant subjects. The LXX of 2 Ch 36⁸, which is here very strange, says that he was buried in the garden of Uzza (cf. 2 K 21¹⁸‧²⁶). The idea that he was brought captive to Babylon rests on 2 Ch 36⁶, which is either a false inference from Dn 1², or refers to an unfulfilled intention of Nebuchadnezzar's on his *first* invasion, or to Ezk 19⁸‧⁹, which, as we have seen, refers to Jehoiachin, although the preceding details refer to his father. Jerome (*Qu. Heb.* 2 Ch 36⁸) explains 'that which was found in him' (1 Es 1⁴² 'his uncleanness and impiety') to refer to heathenish marks (forbidden Lv 19²⁸) discovered on his dead body. See CUTTINGS IN THE FLESH, vol. i. p. 538ᵇ. The legend mentioned by Thenius on 2 K 24¹ (Stanley, *Jewish Ch.* 40), that the name of the demon Chodonazer was found on his skin, is merely due to a MS confusion of this note with that on 2 Ch 36¹⁰, where Jerome explains the name Nabu-chodonosor.   N. J. D. WHITE.

JEHOIARIB (יְהוֹיָרִיב 1 Ch 9¹⁰ 24⁷, elsewhere Joiarib, יוֹיָרִיב 'J'' pleadeth'; called in 1 Mac 2¹

Joarib [which see]).—The name of one of the twenty-four courses of priests; first in David's time (1 Ch 24⁷), but seventeenth in the time of Zerubbabel (Neh 12⁶) and of the high priest Joiakim (Neh 12¹⁹). The name is omitted, probably by accident, in the list of the priests that 'sealed to the covenant' (Neh 10). The clan is mentioned among those that dwelt in Jerusalem in the time of Nehemiah (11¹⁰), where read 'Jedaiah and Joiarib' as in the corresponding list 1 Ch 9¹⁰ (so Cappellus and H. E. Ryle). The Maccabees belonged to this clan (1 Mac 2¹; Jos. *Ant.* XII. vi. 1), and also Josephus (*Life* 1). The Babylonian Talmud substitutes 'Joiarib' for 'Harim' in Ezr 2³⁹=Neh 7⁴².   N. J. D. WHITE.

JEHONADAB (יְהוֹנָדָב or **Jonadab** יוֹנָדָב 'he whom J'' has impelled'; cf. *Nedabiah* and *Nadab*).—**1.** Son of Shimeah, David's brother, and the friend of Amnon the son of David. He is described as 'a very subtil man' (אִישׁ חָכָם מְאֹד), and he employed his ingenuity in aiding Amnon to carry out his intrigue against his half-sister Tamar (2 S 13³ff.). When, at the assassination of Amnon, an exaggerated report reached the ear of David to the effect that Absalom had slain all the king's sons, Jonadab was the first to grasp the true state of affairs, and to allay the king's distress by his prompt report of the safety of the royal princes (2 S 13³⁰ff.). Both AV and RV give his name uniformly as *Jonadab*, although in v.⁵ the MT has יְהוֹנָדָב *Jehonadab*. **2.** Son of Rechab, of the clan of the Kenites (1 Ch 2⁵⁵), and formulator of the rules which bound his descendants, the Rechabites, to retain a nomadic life, living in tents and abstaining from the pursuit of agriculture, and especially from the cultivation of the vine and the use of its produce (Jer 35; see RECHABITES). Jehonadab flourished at the time when Jehu, having seized the throne of the Northern Kingdom, was undertaking the extirpation from Israel of the foreign worship of Ba'al-melkart. He appears to have been thoroughly in sympathy with the measures adopted by Jehu for the vindication of the religion of J'', and he exhibited his sympathy by giving his hand to the new king, and accompanying him in his chariot to witness the final destruction of the family of Ahab at Samaria, and the ruse by which the worshippers of Ba'al were entrapped and put to death (2 K 10¹⁵‧²³). Both AV and RV have *Jonadab* in all the passages of Jer, although that is the reading of MT (יוֹנָדָב) only in 35⁶‧¹⁰‧¹⁹.   C. F. BURNEY.

JEHONATHAN (יְהוֹנָתָן 'J'' has given').—A more exact rendering of the name usually represented in English as Jonathan. In RV this form occurs twice. **1.** 2 Ch 17⁸. One of the Levites sent out by Jehoshaphat with the book of the law to teach the people in the cities of Judah. **2.** Neh 12¹⁸. The head of the priestly family of Shemaiah in the days of Joiakim the son of Jeshua. Here the longer form serves to distinguish this name from the shorter Jonathan=יוֹנָתָן in vv.¹¹‧¹⁴. In AV Jehonathan is found also in 1 Ch 27²⁵ of the son of Uzziah, who was over certain treasuries or storehouses in the time of David (RV Jonathan).   H. A. WHITE.

JEHORAM or JORAM (יְהוֹרָם, יוֹרָם 'J'' is exalted'). RV retains Joram for Jehoram, 2 K 9¹⁵⁻²⁴.

1. King of Israel. He was second son of Ahab, and succeeded his brother Ahaziah, 2 K 3¹ (on the interpolated date in 2 K 1¹⁷ see AHAZIAH, No. 1). The compiler of Kings evidently intended to refer to him all the notices of the king of Israel which occur in the Acts of Elisha; but as Elisha survived J. 43 years, it is possible that in some cases at least other kings were originally intended (so

Ewald, *HI* iv. 87). Terrified probably by his brother's fate, he began his reign by putting away the pillar of Baal that Ahab had made ; but it is evident from 2 K 9²² 10¹⁸⁻²⁷ that the foreign cult was still continued in the country, through the influence of Jezebel, and with the connivance of J. himself, whose secret disloyalty is severely exposed by Elisha (2 K 3¹³⁻¹⁴). Consistently with this, a tone of profane sarcasm, and of scarcely veiled antagonism, may be detected in his use of the sacred name J″ (2 K 3¹⁰⁻¹³ 6²⁷⁻³³, where read with Ewald 'king' מלך for 'messenger' מלאך), a tone re-echoed by his courtiers (7²). Immediately on his accession J. took steps to suppress the revolt of Mesha, which was now a matter of two years' standing. He obtained the aid of his father's ally, the compliant Jehoshaphat, who may have desired to chastise Moab for their invasion of Judah (2 Ch 20). J. was entertained at Jerusalem (Jos. *Ant.* IX. iii. 1). The route chosen at the suggestion of the king of Judah, though not the most direct from Samaria, had the triple advantage of securing the co-operation and loyalty of Edom, avoiding the hostile Syrian and Ammonite territory, and attacking Moab from an unexpected quarter. The expedition was barren of result. Before Moab was reached, the army would have perished from thirst but for the miracle wrought through Elisha in deference to Jehoshaphat. The Moabites were routed, but were not subdued. The desperate man who 'gave his firstborn for his transgression' on the wall of Kirhareseth succeeded thereby in disheartening the besiegers, who, it is obscurely hinted, felt that the wrath of God was roused against themselves, the indirect authors of so unnatural a deed, and the allies retired, having failed to realize any lasting advantage. Assuming that 2 K 4–8¹⁵ belong to this reign, the following matters of public importance may be gleaned from them. Elisha claims to have interest with the king and the captain of the host (4¹³). He gives information to the king of the secret plans of the Syrians (6⁹⁻¹²). A Syrian army penetrates to Dothan, and is led by Elisha to Samaria. He dissuades the king from an ungenerous impulse to kill them, and so procures a temporary cessation of the Syrian incursions (6¹³⁻²³). Benhadad in person besieges Samaria ; the inhabitants are reduced to the horrible straits foretold Lv 26²⁹, Dt 28⁵³, and a second time the power of J″ is vindicated by Elisha and the siege raised (6²⁴⁻⁷). This invasion may have occurred during the seven years' famine foretold by Elisha 8¹ (alluded to 4³⁸). The visit of Naaman (5⁵⁻⁸) should probably be placed after this (compare 5²⁷ 8⁴). Notwithstanding these constant attacks from Syria, J. seems to have been a vigorous monarch (δραστήριος, Jos. *Ant.* IX. ii. 2). On the death of Benhadad he deemed the opportunity a favourable one to renew the attempt to recover Ramoth-gilead at which Ahab had fallen. Ahaziah of Judah helped him (8²⁸⁻²⁹), and the town was taken (9¹⁴), but in the attack J. received arrow wounds (Jos.) which necessitated his return to Jezreel, the army remaining to hold the town (9¹⁻¹⁴). No long time elapsed when Jehu was seen approaching Jezreel. The mysterious non-return of his messengers excited the curiosity of the sick man. With all his mother's vigour he roused himself, and sallied forth eager to hear what strange news the captain of the host might be bringing. The brutal reply of Jehu to his inquiry left no doubt as to his intentions, and the king had barely time to warn his royal kinsman of his danger when he fell, pierced by the arrow of Jehu, on the fatal field of Naboth. The curse of Elijah (1 K 21¹⁹) was beginning to find fulfilment.

2. King of Judah, son of Jehoshaphat. The history of his reign is contained in 2 K 8¹⁶⁻²⁴, 2 Ch 21. It opens with a chronological difficulty. He is said in 2 K 8¹⁶ to have begun to reign in the fifth year of Jehoram of Israel. A comparison of 1 K 22⁴² and 2 K 3¹ implies that this would be two years before the death of Jehoshaphat. This accounts for the insertion 'Jehoshaphat being then king of Judah,' the spuriousness of which is strongly vouched (see *QPB*). The interpolation 2 K 1¹⁷ is discussed under AHAZIAH i. Those who maintain the genuineness of these notes of time are obliged to suppose that he was twice made viceroy by Jehoshaphat, *i.e.* in the 17th and 23rd years of that king's reign. The marriage of J. with the daughter of Ahab and Jezebel had probably seemed to Jehoshaphat a masterly stroke of conciliatory policy. In the event, however, it had the most disastrous effect on Judah. The strong character of Athaliah easily influenced for evil both her husband and son (2 K 8¹⁸⁻²⁷), and, as before in the case of Abijam (1 K 15⁴), nothing but the divine promise to David saved the favoured tribe from the ruin naturally consequent on corruption and idolatry. The most important event in this reign, and the only one recorded in Kings, is the fulfilment of Gn 27⁴⁰ in the final revolt of Edom, which had been, more or less, a dependency of Judah since David's time (2 S 8¹⁴). The narrative (8²¹) of Jehoram's attempt to recover Edom is obscure and probably corrupt. For 'to Zair' צעיר, which is otherwise unknown, Vulg. has 'to Seir,' *Seira*=שעיר (B Σειώρ, A om.). Grätz conjectured 'Zoar' צער, but Zoar is in Moab. 2 Ch 21⁹ substitutes 'with his captains' עם־שריו. The rest of the verse seems to imply that J. was surrounded by the Edomites by night, and cut his way through, but with loss and discomfiture (see *QPB*). At the same time, in a different quarter, the South-West, Libnah revolted, possibly in connexion with the Philistine invasion (2 Ch 21¹⁶⁻¹⁷). The Chronicler, mindful of the fact that Libnah was a priestly city (Jos 21¹³), assigns as the cause 'because he had forsaken the Lord, the God of his fathers.' The town was not permanently lost (see 2 K 19⁸). We learn from 2 Ch 21²⁻⁴ that on his accession J. put to death amongst others his six brethren, to whom their father had given great gifts and fenced cities (cf. 2 Ch 11²³). The defection to idolatry, which is implied in Kings, is detailed in 2 Ch 21¹¹, where he appears as a religious persecutor. This is followed by a denunciatory letter from Elijah vv.¹²⁻¹⁵, a joint invasion by the Philistines and Arabians, who, if they did not actually capture Jerusalem (so Keil), sacked the palace, and carried off all his sons but one, vv.¹⁶⁻¹⁷. The narrative concludes with his miserable and unregretted death, dishonourable burial, and exclusion from the royal sepulchres (contrast 2 K 8²⁴). A serious chronological difficulty is involved in the mention of Elijah's letter to Jehoram. But for this statement, one would naturally infer that Elijah's translation had taken place in the reign of Jehoshaphat. (*a*) It is narrated immediately after the death of Ahaziah, and so *Seder Olam*, xvii. 45, places it in the second year of Ahaziah of Israel. (*b*) Elisha began to exercise prophetical functions under Jehoshaphat, 2 K 3. He does not seem to have done so before his master's departure, 2 K 2⁹⁻¹⁵. (*c*) 2 K 3¹¹ obviously means that Elijah was no longer on earth. In reply it may be urged that there is no note of time in 2 K 2, and that it is placed in its present position merely to complete the history of Elijah. This seems more plausible than the suggestion of Kimchi, adopted by Keil, that the Lord had revealed to Elijah, before his translation, J.'s wickedness, and that then Elijah wrote this letter, which was to be sent to the king at the proper time ; just as Elijah himself anointed

Hazael and Jehu by Elisha's instrumentality (see AVm). Kennicott cuts the knot by conjecturing 'Elisha' for 'Elijah' in 2 Ch 21[12].

3. A priest, one of the commission appointed by Jehoshaphat to teach the Law, 2 Ch 17[8].

N. J. D. White.

JEHOSHABEATH.—See Jehosheba.

JEHOSHAPHAT (יְהוֹשָׁפָט 'J" hath judged'). **1.** King of Judah, son of Asa. This reign marks a new departure in the mutual relations of Judah and Israel. Hitherto there had been a standing feud between the two kingdoms (1 K 14[30] 15[7.16]), but 'J. made peace with the king of Israel' (1 K 22[44]). The immediate object of this policy was doubtless to enable the whole Hebrew race, hitherto weakened by internecine wars, to co-operate against their common enemies. Possibly, also, J. cherished a hope that the marriage of his heir Jehoram with Athaliah the daughter of Ahab, by which the political alliance was now cemented, might, in the future, lead to a peaceful re-establishment of the kingdom of David and Solomon. The actual result, however, of this alliance with the house of Omri brought to J. little credit in his relations with foreign powers; while at home, in the following reigns, it led to a recrudescence of Baal worship, and indirectly to the almost total extinction of the royal family of Judah (2 K 11[1], cf. 2 Ch 21[4.17]). There is little told directly of J. in Kings (1 K 22[41-50]). He completed the extirpation of the Canaanitish abominations begun by Asa, 1 K 15[12]. Edom was so completely subject to him that although it had a king (2 K 3 *passim*), yet he was merely a nominee ('deputy' נִצָּב) of the king of Judah. Hence, when Edom revolted in the next reign (2 K 8[20]), it is significantly said they 'made a king over themselves.' Edom being thus a vassal state, J. had access to the seaport of Ezion-geber, and attempted to revive Solomon's trade with Ophir (cf. 1 K 9[26]); but the fleet was wrecked when starting on the first voyage, and J. was so disheartened that he declined to enter into partnership with Ahaziah of Israel in order to renew the attempt. In 2 Ch 20[35ff.] the good king's misfortune is represented as a punishment for his having made a commercial alliance with Ahaziah; and the destination of the ships is not Ophir, but Tarshish. Both here and in 2 Ch 9[21] the Chronicler misunderstands the term 'ships of Tarshish.' Whatever else we know from Kings about J. is found in the history of Israel. To the strong-willed monarchs of Omri's line J. serves as a foil. They profited by the alliance with Judah. When Ahab desires to recover Ramoth-gilead, or Jehoram Moab, J. is ready with his set formula of acquiescence (1 K 22[4], 2 K 3[7]). He is extremely scrupulous to inquire of a prophet of J", and is not satisfied with an oracle which purports to come from Adonai (1 K 22[5-7], 2 K 3[11]); yet he seems quite unaffected when his ally is denounced, whether by Micaiah or Elisha. He is even persuaded to risk his own life to save that of Ahab (1 K 22[30]). From the Chronicler (2 Ch 17-20) we learn much more respecting J.'s internal administration of Judah. J. begins his reign with defensive measures against Israel (17[1.2]). His early piety is rewarded, like that of David (1 Ch 29[28]) and Solomon (2 Ch 1[12]), with 'riches and honour in abundance' (17[5] 18[1]). He then sends a commission, consisting of princes, Levites, and priests, to teach 'the book of the law of the Lord' in the cities of Judah. Godliness at home is followed by peace abroad. The Philistines and Arabians, so troublesome to Jehoram (21[16]), bring tribute. J. raises a standing army, twice as large as that of Asa (2 Ch 14[8]), of over 1,160,000 men (17[14-18]). Ewald

thinks that this incredible number refers to the entire male population, but see 17[19]. The Chronicler then (ch. 18), contrary to the plan of his work, gives a long extract from the history of Israel—Ahab's expedition to Ramoth-gilead—because of the share J. took in it. There are few variations of any interest except the needless addition in v.[31] 'and the Lord helped,' etc. It was surely by J.'s accent, when he 'cried out,' that the Syrian captains 'saw that he was not the king of Israel.' On his return, J. is rebuked for 'helping the wicked' by the prophet Jehu (cf. 2 Ch 15[2] 16[7]). He then provides for the better administration of justice by appointing local judges in every fenced city (19[5]), and two courts of appeal, ecclesiastical and civil, in Jerusalem, v.[8], consisting of Levites, priests, and leading nobles, presided over respectively by the high priest and 'the ruler of the house of Judah' (cf. Dt 1[17] 16[18] 17[8]). The Chronicler does not relate J.'s campaign with Jehoram of Israel against Moab (2 K 3, see Jehoram 1), but he gives in ch. 20 an account of a more complete deliverance from Moab, Edom, and Ammon. In this story there are two difficulties. (a) The inhabitants of Mt. Seir, vv.[10.22] (in v.[1] read with Targ. 'Edomites' for 'Ammonites,' see RVm), are here joined with Moab against Judah, whereas in 2 K 3 they not only join their suzerain J. in his attack on Moab, but are the bitterest enemies of that people (2 K 3[26]). (b) The abject terror of J. at this crisis (see esp. vv.[3.12]) is quite unaccountable, if he really possessed a tithe of the army described in 17[14ff.]. On the other hand, Ewald (*HI* iv. 56 n. 2) fairly argues that 'the valley of Jehoshaphat' (Jl 3[2.12]), which he identifies with the Wady Bereikut (=Beracah), implies some great victory of that king. He dates this event at the beginning of J.'s reign, and thereby accounts for the complete subjugation of Edom, implied in Kings. The prayer of J. on this occasion has a remarkable reference to Solomon's prayer 1 K 8[33.37], and to Dt 2[4.9.19], just as the speech of Jahaziel has to Ex 14[13.14]. **2.** The recorder or chronicler in the reigns of David (2 S 8[16] 20[24], 1 Ch 18[15]) and Solomon (1 K 4[3]). **3.** One of Solomon's twelve commissariat officers, 1 K 4[17]. **4.** Father of Jehu king of Israel, 2 K 9[2.14].

N. J. D. White.

JEHOSHAPHAT, VALLEY OF (עֵמֶק יְהוֹשָׁפָט, κοιλὰς Ἰωσαφάτ, *Vallis Josaphat*).—This valley ('*ēmek*)* is mentioned under the name of 'Jehoshaphat' only by the prophet Joel (3 [Heb. 4][2.12]). The circumstances related by the prophet concerning the 'day of the Lord' are matters of theological controversy which it would be outside the scope of this article to enter into, but the imagery rests upon a geographical basis whatever may be the symbolical import.

Some commentators have supposed that the name is only an imaginary one due to its significance, 'J" judgeth' (Orelli in Strack u. Zöckler, *Kgf. Komm. on Joel, l.c.*; Michaelis, *Bibel für Ungelehrten,* Remarks on Joel). The name may have been used with reference to the remarkable victory of king Jehoshaphat over the united forces of the heathen of several nations (2 Ch 20[16f.]), children of Ammon, Moab, and Mount Seir, which resulted to him in a bloodless victory over his enemies, and his triumphant return from the valley of Blessing.

There is no record in the Bible or Josephus as to the valley separating the temple mount from Olivet being called the valley of Jehoshaphat; but early in the 4th cent. it is called so, and the name has continued among Christians, Jews, and sub-

---

* On the possibility that this term could be applied to the valley of the *Kidron* (elsewhere always called *naḥal,* 'torrent-valley,' 'wady'), see Driver's note on Jl 3[2].

sequently Moslems, up to the present day. The unknown Pilgrim of Bordeaux (A.D. 333) says, 'For one going to the gate which is on the east, that he may ascend the Mount of Olives, there is the valley which is called Jehoshaphat' (*Itin. Hieros.*). Eusebius and Jerome (A.D. 330–400) give the same account (*OS²* 272. 89 ; 145. 13). Eucherius (427–440) says, 'Near the wall of Jerusalem, or of the temple, on the east, is Geennon or the valley of Jehoshaphat' (*Ant. Mart.* xvii. ; see also Reland, *Pal.* p. 356). Theodorus (*c.* 530), speaking of Jerusalem, says, 'There is the valley of Josaphat. There the Lord will judge the just and the sinful.' Arculf (*c.* 680) speaks of the brook Cedron in the valley of Jehoshaphat (*Early Travels*, p. 4). Willibald (721), Bernard (867), Saewulf (1102), Maundeville (1322), and Maundrell (1697) all mention the valley of Jehoshaphat as lying between Jerusalem and Olivet (*Early Travels*, p. 469). Theodoricus (1172) states that 'torrens Cedron et vallis Josaphat' lies between Moriah and Olivet. John of Würzburg (*c.* 1213) says, 'Prope juxta Jerusalem, sub Salamonis regia in accubitu in valle Josaphat natatoria Siloam.' The author of *Citez de Jherusalem* (1187) states that the valley of Josaphat is to the east, between Olivet and Mount Zion. See further, art. KIDRON (THE BROOK).

According to modern Jewish tradition, the valley between the temple mount and Olivet is the valley of Jehoshaphat, and the dearest wish of the Jew is to find a grave there (Briggs, *Heathen and Holy Lands*, p. 290). Benjamin of Tudela (A.D. 1170) calls this valley *Jehosaphat.* Some of the Rabbins have taught that it is necessary to be buried in the Holy Land to obtain a share in the resurrection preceding the Messiah's reign on earth, and that the bodies of the righteous, wherever else buried, have to roll back again under ground to Palestine (J. Nicholaus, *de Sepult. Heb.*). The 'Aven Shetyeh appears to have been a portion of rock projecting three fingers' breadth above the floor of the Holy of Holies, covering a *cavity* which was regarded as the mouth of an 'abyss,' reverenced as the centre and foundation of the world, and having the ineffable name of God inscribed upon it. Rabbi Schwartz (*Das Heilige Land*) identifies this stone with the Sakhrah. It is impossible not to suspect that these Jewish traditions are the origin of the sacredness which the Mohammedans have attached to the Sakhrah (*PEFSt*, 1875–76).

In the tract *Middôth*, Rabbi Elieser ben-Jacob said concerning the Water-gate, 'Through it the water proceeded out, and in future it will issue from under the threshold.' The Talmud teaches that there was a canal which brought water to the sanctuary from the fountain of Etam (Jerus. *Yoma*, iii. fol. 41 at *Maim Baith Hammukdash*, v. 15). Rashi thinks Etam may have been the same as Nephtoah (Jos 15⁹). The Moslems have a description of 'the day of the Lord' which was probably given by Mohammed as one of the first of his revelations, from which the following verses are extracted (*Koran*, 81) :—

'In the name of the all-merciful God a day shall come when the sun shall be shrouded and the stars shall fall from the heavens.

'When the water of the ocean shall boil, and the souls of the dead again be united to their bodies.

'When the heavens will pass away like a scroll, and hell will burn fiercely, and the joys of paradise will be made manifest.

'On that day shall every soul make known that which it hath performed.'

The day of resurrection will be preceded by signs and portents in heaven and earth, wars and tumults, a universal decay of faith, the advent of Antichrist, the issuing forth of Gog and Magog to desolate the world. Every human being will then be put upon his trial as to the manner in which he has employed his faculties, and the good and evil actions of his life. The whole assembled multitude will have to follow Mohammed across the bridge *al-Sirât*, as fine as the edge of a scimitar, which crosses the gulf of Jehennam or hell. Jehennam is a region fraught with all kinds of horrors (W. Irving, *Life of Mahomet*). The bridge *al-Sirât* that will be extended on the day of judgment between heaven and hell is to start from Jerusalem, and the pilgrim is shown a column, built horizontally into the wall [of the *Ḥaram esh-Sherîf*], which is to form its first pier. The holy rock [of the *Ḥ. esh-Sherîf*] is one of the rocks of paradise ; it stands on a palm tree, beneath which flows one of the rivers of paradise. The Sakhrah is the centre of the world, and on the day of resurrection the angel Israfîl will stand upon it to blow the last trump ; beneath it is the source of every drop of sweet water that flows on the face of the earth (Besant and Palmer, *Jerusalem*). The column called *et-Tarik* (de Saulcy) or *al-Sirât* (Ali Bey, Merj ed-Dîn, *BFS* part ii.) juts out from the east wall of the *Ḥaram esh-Sherîf*, overhanging the valley of the Kîdron (Gehennam, Jehoshaphat), and on it may be seen devout Moslems in the early morning practising the first step into paradise.

The Moslem names for the valley between the *Ḥaram esh-Sherîf* and Mount Olivet are *Wâdy Jahannum*, *W. Sitti Maryam* (from 'the tomb of the Virgin'), *W. Jûshafat* or *Shafat* (Seetzen), *W. Jehôshâfât* (Robinson), *W. el-Jos.*

In addition to this valley parting Jerusalem from Olivet being called Jehoshaphat, the name also occurs in or adjacent to the valley. In the time of Arculf (*c.* 680) the tower of Jehoshaphat was shown in the valley near the church of St. Mary. In the time of Maundrell (*c.* 1697) the present so-called tomb of Jehoshaphat went by the same name (*Early Travels*, p. 468). In *Citez de Jherusalem* (*c.* 1187) there is the street of Josafas, leading through the Josafas gate (present St. Stephen's gate) into the valley of Jehoshaphat. John of Würzburg (*c.* 1213) also speaks of the gates of Josafat leading into the valley of Jehoshaphat, and of the monument of king Josaphat 'from which the valley was named.'

LITERATURE.—In addition to the authorities cited in the article, the reader may consult Baedeker-Socin, *Pal.²* 98 ; Neubauer, *Géog. du Talmud*, 51 f. ; Robinson, *BRP²* i. 268 ff.; Driver, *Joel and Amos*, 68 f. ; Nowack, *Kl. Proph.* 108 ; Benzinger, *Heb. Arch.* 41.   C. WARREN.

JEHOSHEBA (יְהוֹשֶׁבַע 2 K 11², **Jehoshabeath**, יְהוֹשַׁבְעַת 2 Ch 22¹¹ 'J" is an oath.' Stanley, *Jewish Ch.*, Lect. 35, compares the variants Elisheba and Ἐλισαβέτ). — She was daughter of Jehoram of Judah, but not of Athaliah, according to Jos. (*Ant.* IX. vii. 1 ; Jerome, *Qu. Heb.* on 2 Ch 21¹⁷). On the death of her half-brother Ahaziah, she was instrumental in preserving the Davidic stock by concealing the infant Jehoash in a lumber-room of the palace (RVm). She seems to have had apartments in 'the house of the Lord,' *i.e.* in the temple precincts ; and, according to the Chronicler, was wife of Jehoiada. This is the only recorded instance of the intermarriage of a high priest with a princess of the royal house, but probably it was no very extraordinary distinction (cf. 1 K 4¹¹, ¹⁵). See ATHALIAH, JEHOASH, JEHOIADA.

N. J. D. WHITE.

JEHOSHUA, JEHOSHUAH.—The AV has followed the Geneva Bible in spelling Joshua's name once (Nu 13¹⁶) Jehoshua. In 1 Ch 7²⁷ the translators of AV have again followed the Gen. Bible, but have added an *h* by inadvertence, giving the unique and wrong form Jehoshuah. RV has restored Joshua in both places.

JEHOVAH.—See GOD, p. 199ᵃ.

JEHOVAH-JIREH (יהוה יִרְאֶה).—In Gn 22¹⁴ the name given to the place at which Abraham sacrificed the ram instead of his son. The name means 'J″ seeth,' *i.e.* (cf. 16¹² 'Thou art a God of *seeing*'; also Ex 3⁷, Ps 35²² etc.) *sees* the needs of His servants, and relieves them accordingly; but there is, no doubt, an allusion at the same time to the sense which the same verb has in v.⁸ 'God will *see* for himself (*i.e.* look out, provide; so 1 S 16¹·¹⁷) the lamb for a burnt-offering.' A difficulty, however, arises in connexion with the following explanatory clause, which is partly ambiguous, and partly does not correspond, as it would be expected to do, with the name to which it is attached : 'so that it is said to-day, בְּהַר יהוה יֵרָאֶה "in the mount of J″.יֵרָאֶה."' The 'mount of J″' is a designation of the Temple-hill (Is 2³ 30²⁹, Ps 24³), and the tense of 'is said' shows that the reference is to something that was said habitually (cf. Gn 10⁹ᵇ), so that there is little doubt that the clause preserves some proverb in connexion with the Temple. If the clause stood by itself, it would be most naturally rendered 'In the mount of J″' one is seen (appears),' *i.e.* men, people, appear,—the reference being to the custom of visiting the Temple at pilgrimages ('appear,' as Ex 23¹⁷, 1 S 1²², Ps 84⁷); but this rendering could only be adopted upon the supposition that the connexion with the preceding clause was of a purely verbal nature. Other renderings are 'in the mount of J″ it is seen' * (*i.e.* provided), *or* 'he [J″] is seen (appears),' *or* (Ew., Del., Keil, Dillm., Kautzsch-Socin) 'in the mount (where) J″ appears' (the sentence in this case being incomplete, as 10⁹ᵇ).† It is objected to the first of these renderings that the Niph. of רָאָה does not occur in the sense of 'be provided'; but if 'see' can be used absolutely (41³³) in the sense of 'look out,' it does not seem impossible that 'be seen' might be used similarly; still, it is true that, if the proverb had once an independent existence, this would not be a natural or obvious sense for the verb to have. In the two other renderings, the connexion of the proverb with the name 'Jehovah-jireh' depends upon the double sense of the word 'see': J″ 'sees' the needs of those who come to worship before Him on Zion, and then 'is seen,' *i.e.* reveals Himself to them by answering their prayers, and supplying their wants: His 'seeing,' in other words, takes practical effect in a 'being seen.'‡ On the whole, unless the first suggestion made above be adopted, this may be said to be the best explanation of the passage.

With changes of the punctuation, other renderings become possible, though the general sense remains the same: as 'In the mountain (בְּהַר) J″ appeareth' § (cf. LXX, *ἐν τῷ ὄρει Κύριος ὤφθη*); 'In the mountain J″ seeth *or* will see' (בְּהַר יִרְאֶה: so Pesh. and Vulg., assimilating the verb to that in clause *a*). The two clauses might also be assimilated by vocalizing the second element by

* The tense (as in 'J″ seeth') expressing what is habitual. The futures of AV, RV are (as often) misleading.

† This last rend., though of course possible formally (Ges.-K. § 155 *l*; Dav. § 25), is not, perhaps, in view of the order יהוה יראה, very probable (בהר יראה יהוה is what would be expected): see, however, though only after עַד—which is often used without a rel., and may thus have more readily expressed the sense of 'the time (when)'—Ps 48, Mic 5².

‡ Cf. Delitzsch : 'Er sah drein, in dem er sich zu sehn gab d.i. thatsächlich eingriff.'

§ So Stade, *Gesch.* i. 450, who supposes the proverb to have been framed originally with reference to mountains in general, as the places where J″ was anciently worshipped, and which were often marked by theophanies.

name יֵרָאֶה, 'is seen' (appeareth), in place of yir'eh, 'seeth' (so Strack).   S. R. DRIVER.

JEHOVAH-NISSI (יהוה נִסִּי 'J″ is my banner').—The name given by Moses to the altar he erected after the defeat of Amalek, Ex 17¹⁵ (E). The LXX (*Κύριος καταφυγή μου*) implies a derivation of the name from the root נום 'flee,' the Vulg. (*Dominus exaltatio mea*) from נשא 'lift up.' Onkelos paraphrases, 'he prayed before God who had done miracles (נִסִּין) before him'; Rashi, 'God has done us here a miracle' (נֵס). There can be little doubt, however, that נֵס here = 'banner,' God being considered the centre or rallying-point of the army of Israel, and the name of God as their battle-cry (cf. Ps 20⁷ᴸ). The interpretation of v.¹⁶ (כִּי־יָד עַל־כֵּם יָהּ) is somewhat doubtful. Many critics read נֵס for כֵּם (= כִּסֵּא 'throne'), but this appears neither to be necessary nor to yield a suitable sense. The meaning is probably either 'J″ hath sworn' (EV), or 'I (Moses) swear' (with hand uplifted to J″s throne). See Dillmann and Kalisch, *ad loc.*
                                        J. A. SELBIE.

JEHOVAH - SHALOM (יהוה שָׁלוֹם; LXX *εἰρήνη Κυρίου* and Vulg. *Domini pax* imply Heb. reading יהוה שְׁלוֹם).—The name given by Gideon to the altar he erected in Ophrah, Jg 6²⁴. The name means 'J″ is peace' (*i.e.* well-disposed), in allusion to J″s words in v.²³ 'Peace be unto thee.' There appears to be no necessity to take the second noun as genitive '(altar of) J″ of peace,' as in יהוה צְבָאוֹת. Rather is the name 'Jehovah-shalom' to be compared with such names as 'Jehovah-jireh,' 'Jehovah-nissi,' 'Jehovah-shammah,' in all of which J″ is the subject. See Moore, *Judges*, *ad loc.*
                                        J. A. SELBIE.

JEHOVAH-SHAMMAH (יהוה שָׁמָּה 'J″ is there': *Κύριος ἐκεῖ*).—The name to be given to the restored and glorified Jerusalem, Ezk 48³⁵ (cf. Is 60¹⁴⁻²² 62², Rev 21²ᵗ·). 'The prophet beheld the LORD forsake His temple (ch. 11), and he beheld Him again enter it (ch. 43); now He abides in it among His people for ever. The covenant ran that He should be their God and they His people; this is perfectly fulfilled in His presence among them. The end in view from the beginning has been reached' (Davidson).   J. A. SELBIE.

JEHOVAH - TSIDKENU (יהוה צִדְקֵנוּ 'J″ is our righteousness,' or 'J″ our righteousness,' Jer 23⁶ 33¹⁶).—In both passages (which are in fact the same prophecy repeated, the latter being not found in LXX, and perhaps the insertion of a reviser) it is the title of the Branch, the perfectly Righteous King, who is to rule over the people on their return from the Captivity. If Jer 33¹⁴⁻²⁶ is genuine, 33¹⁷ implies that the prophet has in his mind not one single king, but a succession of kings, who would fulfil the theocratic idea. If the first tr. of the words given above is right, this will mean that under the rule of the Branch men will fully realize the righteousness of J″; if the second, the title of J″ must be understood as applied to the king as God's vicegerent upon earth (cf. Is 9⁶). To suppose that either passage definitely predicts the God Incarnate is to credit the prophets with the kind of foresight which our knowledge of their writings otherwise does not justify (cf. Driver, *Sermons on OT*, 204 ff.).   F. H. WOODS.

JEHOZABAD (יְהוֹזָבָד 'J″ hath bestowed,' cf. וּבְזַרְיָה and וַבְדִּיאֵל).—**1.** One of the servants of king Joash who conspired against his master and joined in his assassination, 2 K 12²¹ = 2 Ch 24²⁶. **2.** A Benjamite chief, one of Jehoshaphat's 'men of war,' 2 Ch 17¹⁸. **3.** The eponym of a Levitical family, 1 Ch 26⁴. See GENEALOGY.

JEHOZADAK (יְהוֹצָדָק, 'J" is righteous,' cf. Zedekiah צִדְקִיָּהוּ), the father of Joshua the high priest (1 Ch 6[14. 15] [Heb. 5[40. 41]], also in RV of Hag 1[1. 12. 14] 2[2. 4], Zec 6[11], where LXX has 'Ιωσεδέκ and AV **Josedech**). The name is shortened to **Jozadak** (יוֹצָדָק) in Ezr 3[2. 8] 5[2] 10[18], Neh 12[26]. It appears as **Josedek** (AV Josedec) in 1 Es 5[5. 48. 56] 6[2] 9[19], Sir 49[12]. See GENEALOGY. H. A. WHITE.

JEHU (for form and meaning of the name see next article). — **1.** A prophet of the Northern Kingdom who predicted the downfall and destruction of the dynasty of Baasha (1 K 16[1-7. 12]). The Chronicler introduces him as denouncing Jehoshaphat for his alliance with Ahab (2 Ch 19[2]; cf. the way in which Jehu's father Hanani reproves Asa, 2 Ch 16[7]). 'The words of Jehu the son of Hanani, which are taken up into the Book of the Kings of Israel' is cited by the Chronicler (2 Ch 20[34]) as an authority for the reign of Jehoshaphat. See art. CHRONICLES, vol. i. p. 394[a] f. **2.** The king of Israel who destroyed the dynasty of Omri. See next article. **3.** A Judahite, the son of Obed (1 Ch 2[38]). **4.** A Simeonite prince (1 Ch 4[35]). While A of the LXX and Luc. have 'Ιηού, B must have [mis?] read הוא instead of יֵהוּא, for it has οὗτος. **5.** One of David's heroes (1 Ch 12[3]).

JEHU (Heb. יֵהוּא, Assyr. *Ja-u-a*, Syriac ܝܳܗܘ, Arab. *Jâhû*, LXX B Ειού, A often 'Ιηού, Luc. 'Ιού. The derivation is very uncertain. Some would regard it as an abbreviation of יְהוֹהוּא 'Jahweh is he,' just as יְשׁוּעַ = יְהוֹשׁוּעַ. As a parallel, comp. אֵלִיָּהוּ).—Jehu was son of Jehoshaphat, son of Nimshi, but he is not infrequently designated simply ben-Nimshi. From his own testimony (2 K 9[25. 26]) we learn that he witnessed, in company with Bidkar, the judicial murder of Naboth. He evidently held, in conjunction with Bidkar, an important position in Ahab's bodyguard,* and the sentence of doom pronounced by Elijah on the house of Ahab must on that memorable occasion have been carefully treasured in his memory. This raises an interesting question. Was Jehu personally known to Elijah? This seems to be suggested by 1 K 19[16]. But it is quite evident that the Elijah narrative in this chapter proceeds from a different hand from that which recorded the episodes in 2 K 8. 9, and the redactor has omitted from the Elijah section the fulfilment of the divine commands (1 K 19[15-18]), though the injunctions themselves still remain. On this subject see Thenius' remarks at the end of his commentary on 1 K 19; Stade, *Gesch.* p. 540, footnote; and Kittel, *Gesch. der Heb.* ii. 184 [Eng. tr. ii. 214].

It is not, however, our purpose to enter into the complex features of the narrative dealing with the reign of Jehu (2 K 9. 10), since this department belongs to the literary features of 1 K and 2 K (see art. KINGS (BOOKS OF)). This subject has been ably investigated by Stade in *ZATW*, 1885, p. 275 ff. It is acknowledged by critics that the section 2 K 9[1]-10[27] descriptive of Jehu's revolution comes from the same hand as 1 K 20. 22, 2 K 3 (Cornill), to which may be added 6[24]-7[20] (Driver, *LOT*[6] p. 195; Kittel, *Gesch.* ii. p. 186 [Eng. tr. ii. 216]). Kittel also agrees with Stade in attributing 10[12-16] to a later source, a view which appears to the present writer well founded. Wellhausen further endeavours to disintegrate 10[19-27] on the ground of inconsistencies (*Isr. u. Jüd.*

Gesch[2]. p. 77, footnote), but his arguments are not convincing.

Jehu ben-Nimshi rose to power on the crest of a wave of insurrectionary feeling fomented in the prophetic circles by the great personal influence of Elisha. Indeed it may even be true that he had already been designated as the earthly instrument of divine vengeance on the house of Omri by Elijah, and that Elisha had been commissioned by his illustrious predecessor to carry out the divine behest of 1 K 19[16]. The vivid and dramatic narrative in chs. 9. 10 makes it clear that the causes which led to the popular discontent against the house of Omri were not so much connected with the introduction of the Phœnician Baal and Ashtoreth worship, but rather with the highhanded judicial murder of Naboth (see AHAB, JEZEBEL, and NABOTH). Towards Phœnicia Israel had for centuries felt a traditional friendship. It began with the days of David and Solomon. In language the two were closely akin. They exchanged their commodities, and the bond which linked them was called by the 8th cent. prophet Amos 'a covenant of brethren' (Am 1[9], but see Driver's note, *ad loc.*), a fact well illustrated by the beautiful episode of Elijah and the widow of the Phœnician town of Zarephath (1 K 17[9-24]).

Jehu was the commanding officer in the army of Jehoram, which was conducting operations against the Syrian army under Hazael at the important fortress of Ramoth-gilead, a bone of contention since the days of Ahab, and now held by Israel. The severe wounds sustained by king Jehoram necessitated his retirement to Jezreel. This was the opportunity of which Elisha and the party of insurrection availed themselves. One of the 'sons of the prophets' was despatched by Elisha to Ramoth-gilead with a flask of oil and a commission to take Jehu from the group of officers which surrounded him into an inner chamber, anoint him there, and instantly withdraw in flight. These instructions were faithfully carried out. On Jehu's return to the officers' quarters, he was eagerly interrogated as to the meaning of this mysterious visit from the frenzied * prophetic messenger. On learning the truth, his fellow-officers tore their mantles from their shoulders and spread them as a carpet for their commander on the bare steps,† and proclaimed him as king with a loud flourish of trumpets. The lightning rapidity of the following movements of Jehu, and the murderous energy with which he crushed every opposition, overwhelm the reader. He immediately proceeded to Jezreel at the head of a picked cavalcade, riding with Bidkar in his chariot. The invalided king Jehoram was at that time receiving a visit from his kinsman Ahaziah king of Judah, at his royal residence. The cavalcade is descried at a distance by the watchman near the palace gates, who informs the king (cf. 2 S 18[24]). At the command of Jehoram, who feels uneasy at the news, a horseman is sent to make the inquiry, 'Is it peace?' The question was purposely ambiguous, and might be regarded as an inquiry respecting the progress of the campaign at the seat of war. But Jehu, with brutal frankness, at once makes his purpose clear, and compels the king's emissary to join his retinue. This strange proceeding is observed in Jezreel, and arouses suspicion. Both the kings at once proceed in their chariots, accompanied by their

---

* Bidkar and Jehu rode in a chariot along with others in *pairs*. So the Hebrew (רֹכְבִים צְמָדִים) should be interpreted. There was something exceptional in this. Usually *three* rode in a Hebrew chariot, as we find among the Hittites. See article CHARIOT by the present writer in Black's *Bible Encyclopædia*.

* The familiar ancient association of prophecy and madness is indicated in the Heb. מְשֻׁגָּע (cf. Jer 29[26]), but it would be an error to regard it as a scornful epithet on the basis of Hos 9[7] (cf. 1 S 21[14ff.]). In classical Arabic the verb is employed of speech or writing in the special form of prophetic rhythmic prose.

† הַמַּעֲלוֹת גֶּרֶם probably means the *bare* steps (or, perhaps, the midst of the flight of steps). The idiomatic phrase גֶּרֶם puzzled the LXX, who simply transliterate it (B γαρέμ, A γὰρ' ἵνα. Luc. combines the two, ἐφ' ἓν τῶν γαρέμ, ἐπὶ μίαν τῶν ἀναβαθμίδων).

military staff, to confront the bold insurgent. The two cavalcades met at the ill-omened spot— the field of Naboth, ever associated with Ahab's high-handed injustice consummated by treachery and murder. Jehu was quick to seize the advantage afforded him by these familiar recollections, and, as Jehoram's heart failed him and he turned, immediately discharged an arrow * with his full strength, that laid the king of Israel low. As he beheld the fallen son of Ahab, he recalled the words uttered by Elijah on that memorable spot many years before. With characteristic energy Jehu did not allow the opportunity of striking down a possible foe to escape him, and Ahaziah of Judah, who had fled at the sight of his kinsman's terrible fate, was immediately pursued on the road which he took to Beth-haggan. At a place called the Ascent of Gûr,† near Ible'am, he was overtaken and mortally wounded, and ultimately escaped to die at Megiddo.

As Jehu entered Jezreel at the head of his retinue, he was greeted by Jezebel as she sat with her attendants at the window in the stately queen's apartment in the upper storey of the royal palace. The splendid courage of the queen-dowager did not forsake her in that terrible hour of doom. Surrounded by Phœnician luxury, with elaborate head-dress and eyelids painted with stibium, she hurled her angry defiance at the victorious insurgent. To Jehu's previous reminiscence of a well-known episode she retorts with another, as she flings the taunt, 'Is it peace, O Zimri, his master's murderer?' meaning, 'Is there to be peace between me and such a traitor as you with your brief tenancy of power?' The narrator who portrays the lurid facts sheds no ray of chivalry on Jehu's relentless ferocity. The queen at his bidding is flung by the attendant eunuchs from the lofty upper window into the courtyard below, close to his chariot wheels, and suffers instant death. Jehu feasts within the palace in cold-blooded indifference until the thought of the yet unburied queen prompts the command that the ' accursed ' (הָאֲרוּרָה) should receive the rights of sepulture due to her dignity and rank. This, however, the carrion kites and scavenger dogs had by this time rendered superfluous.

But the career of assassination was not yet ended, and, without Macbeth's remorse, Jehu felt himself ' young in deed,' and could say without compunction—

'I am in blood
Stepped in so far that should I wade no more
Returning were as tedious as go o'er.'—*Macbeth*, III. iv. 137.

The seventy sons and grandsons of the royal harem of Ahab still inhabited Samaria, and they undoubtedly constituted a possible source of danger and disaffection. An artfully worded despatch to the elders in Samaria [?],‡ challenging them to set up one of these royal princes as a rival king, produced the desired effect. The palace-commander, the commander of the city, and the guardians of the sons of Ahab trembled for their own lives, and complied with Jehu's second request. They procured the death of all the royal princes, and sent their heads in baskets to Jezreel. This work of destruction was supplemented according to the section (vv.12-16)

---

* Jehu possessed the archer's skill, which Assyrian monuments almost universally attribute to their monarchs, an aptitude perfected by the exercises of the chase. Comp. the frequent hunting scenes of the Nimrud gallery of the British Museum.

† Beth-haggan is identified with Jenîn, a large village in the plain of Esdraelon, on the road between Nazareth and Nablûs. ' Ascent of Gûr' (prob. = ' whelp's hill ') was in the neighbourhood of Ible'am, identified with a spot where there is now a ruined tower called Bel'ame. See Stade, *Gesch.* p. 542, footnote, and Baedeker, *Palestine and Syria*, 2nd ed. (1894) p. 226 ff.

‡ For יזרעאל of the MT the LXX, Josephus, and Cod. Kenn. 174 read שמרון ; but the suggestion ישראל of Cleric., Mich., and Ewald is far more probable.

by a still further holocaust of 42 princes of the line of David, kinsmen of Ahaziah.* This pendant to the narrative probably belongs to a later source. Yet the following verse (v.17) clearly shows that further deeds of blood were perpetrated.

The final scene of butchery was enacted in the great temple of the Phœnician Baal, erected by Ahab in Samaria, where, under pretext of zeal for the worship of the god, a large crowd of his devotees were gathered together and then slaughtered by an armed band of eighty men who were posted at the entrance to guard the exit. The Baal 'pillars' (*mazzēbôth*) were brought forth and destroyed by fire (2 K 10²⁶).

It is not quite clear what was the religious significance of this destruction of the Baal temple in Samaria and of its devotees. Doubtless Wellhausen is right in saying (*Isr. u. Jüd. Gesch.*² p. 77) that Jehu was essentially a soldier, and his aims were political rather than religious. Yet he posed as a religious zealot, and some meaning must have been ascribed to his destruction of the Baal worshippers. It is more difficult to ascertain the precise significance of this act when we remember that Jehoram, Ahab's son (note that the name of Jahweh is expressed in this royal name), is distinctly stated to have withdrawn the specific Tyrian Baal worship from Samaria, which had been instituted by Ahab under the influence of Jezebel (2 K 3²). Yet it is quite obvious that this act of Jehoram did not touch the old local Canaanitish Baal worship which still prevailed in the high places of Israel, and too much stress should certainly not be placed on this act of suppression, which appears to have been only temporary or partial in character. This is the view taken by Prof. Peake, the writer of the article BAAL in the first volume of this Dictionary. Accordingly, we may regard the murderous policy of Jehu as simply directed to a drastic suppression of the Phœnician form of Baal worship. This view is supported by the following considerations : (1) The annihilation of Baal worship by Jehu took place in Samaria, the capital and residence of the Omri dynasty, where the Phœnician Baal had his special shrine (1 K 16³²). We nowhere read of the suppression of Baal cults generally in the high places. (2) The extinction of Canaanitish Baal worship, if it had ever taken place, could not have been effectual or permanent, since in the 8th cent. the writings of the prophet Hosea reveal the wide prevalence of local Baal cults in the Northern Kingdom. (3) The worship of the golden calf of Jeroboam I. still survived, as we infer from 2 K 10²⁹. This verse and the language of v.³¹ lead us to the conclusion that the words, ' And Jehu destroyed the Baal from Israel ' (v.²⁸), can refer only to the specific cult introduced by Jezebel perhaps characterized by gross licentiousness. (4) That Jehu wrought no real religious reformation is shown by the neutral tone of the writer of chs. 9. 10, while the strong reprobation of Hos 1⁴ faithfully reflects not only the prophetic but the popular verdict on the character and career of this monarch.

The policy pursued by Jehu towards the dynasty of Omri, and the murder of the Phœnician queen as well as the overthrow of the Phœnician worship, at once shattered the close bonds of an alliance which the dynasty of Omri had found of considerable value to Israel, and which it had taken the utmost pains to consolidate. Ahab, as we have already seen (art. AHAB), had abandoned the friendship of

---

* בֵּית עֵקֶד הָרֹעִים rendered by Targ. ' assembling house of shepherds' (cf. עָקַד ' bind' in Gn 22⁹). LXX Βαιθάκαθ, identified with Beit Ḳad about 9 miles E. of Jenîn (9²⁷) in the plain of Jezreel. See Baedeker, *Pal. and Syria*, 2nd ed. p. 242. The Βιθακάθ of Eusebius is the same spot 15 Roman miles from Legio or Lejjun.

Syria after the disastrous battle of Ḳarkar (854).
He had formed a pretty shrewd estimate of the
rising power of the Assyrian empire under Shalmaneser II., and thought it wiser to have its ruler
as his friend rather than his foe. The further
attacks made by the Assyrians upon the Aramæan
kingdom of Benhadad (Dadidri) in the years 849,
846, and 842 only made this policy of friendship
with Assyria more necessary for Israel; and Jehu,
weakened by his break with Phœnicia and by the
hostility of Judah, was driven by the force of
events to adopt the same policy of subservience to
the Assyrian monarch. The black obelisk of
Shalmaneser, in a brief statement that runs in
clearly legible characters of cuneiform between
the graphic figures of its reliefs, records the important statement: 'Tribute of Jehu, son of Omri
—objects of silver and gold—bars of silver, bars of
gold, a golden bowl, a golden ladle, golden goblets,
golden pitchers, bars of lead—a staff for the hand
of a king, shafts of spears . . . these I received.' *
    Another inscription (COT² p. 200; III. Rawl. 5,
No. 6, 40-65) places this event in a clearer light.
We there learn that the Tyrians and Sidonians
followed the same policy as Jehu. Jehu was
forced to adopt this attitude at the commencement
of his reign (842 B.C.), because in that year Shalmaneser II. made another invasion of Syria and
attacked Hazael of Damascus. It was terribly
disastrous for the young Syrian king. He lost
16,000 men and more than 1000 chariots. To save
his life he fled to Damascus, whither he was pursued and then besieged. The Assyrians ravaged
and laid his territory waste as far as the Haurân
range and even the frontiers of Lebanon. This
terrible overthrow of the year 842 was followed by
another invasion three years later, in which Syria
made little resistance. This at any rate is the
inference which may be drawn from the long
annalistic inscription taken from the obelisk of
Nimrud,† lines 102-104: 'In the 21st year of my
reign (i.e. 839) I crossed the Euphrates for the 21st
time and marched against the towns [maḥazâni]
of Hazael of Damascus. Four of his towns I
conquered, and received the tribute of the Tyrians,
Sidonians, and Byblians.'
    While the humiliations inflicted by Assyria upon
the Aramæan kingdom continued, the policy of
vassalage to Nineveh pursued by Jehu brought
him security, and Israel was safe from aggression
from his powerful northern foe, Syria. But the
tide was soon to turn. After 839 B.C. we read of
no more attacks upon the Syrian kingdom from
the shores of the Euphrates for more than 30 years.
Meanwhile Syria, with wonderful inherent energy
and recuperative power, began once more to show
itself able to take the offensive. We learn this
from the brief notice which closes the biblical
record of Jehu's reign (2 K 10³²): 'During that
time J″ began to cut off (the territories of)
Israel, and Hazael smote them in all the borders
of Israel,' and in the following verse this is explained as meaning that Israel suffered severe
losses of territory along the whole of his eastern
dominion on the other side of Jordan. Probably
Hazael annexed these territories to his own—the
harbinger of further humiliations in store for the
dynasty of Jehu, until the tide again turned in
favour of Israel under Jeroboam II.‡

                                    OWEN C. WHITEHOUSE.

* Schrader, KIB i. p. 150, COT² i. p. 199. Respecting the
phrase Jehu, 'son of Omri,' see ib. i. p. 179 and footnote **.
† Schrader, KIB i. p. 128ff.; see especially p. 142. For a
conspectus of the campaigns of Shalmaneser II., see Tiele, Bab.-
Assyr. Gesch. p. 197 ff.
‡ Here again the success of Israel was cheaply earned through
the intervention of the Assyrian arms. The terrible disaster
inflicted by Rammân-nirâri III. in 803 on the Aramæan kingdom
was a blow from which it never recovered. Rammân-nirâri III.

JEHUBBAH (יְחֻבָּה Kethîbh, but Ḳerê וְחֻבָּה = ' and
Hubbah' is to be preferred [LXX B 'Ωβάβ, A
'Οβά, Vulg. Haba]).—An Asherite, 1 Ch 7³⁴. See
GENEALOGY, XII. 5.

JEHUCAL (יְהוּכַל 'J. is able').—A courtier sent
by king Zedekiah, during the siege of Jerus., to
entreat for the prayers of Jeremiah (Jer 37³ᵗ·). He
is called in Jer 38¹ Jucal.

JEHUD (יְהֻד, LXX B 'Αζώρ, A 'Ιούθ, Luc. 'Ιούδ).—
A town of Dan, named between Baalath and
Bene-berak, Jos 19⁴⁵. It is probably the modern
el-Yehûdîyeh, 8 miles E. of Joppa. See Dillm.
Jos., ad loc.; Robinson, BRP², ii. 242; Guérin,
Judée, i. 322; Buhl, GAP 197; SWP vol. ii.
sheet iii.

JEHUDI (יְהוּדִי).—A word which generally=a
Jew, but appears to be a proper name in Jer
36¹⁴· ²¹· ²³. J. was an officer of Jehoiakim, at whose
summons Baruch read to the princes of Judah the
roll of Jeremiah's prophecies. J. was afterwards
himself employed to read the roll to the king, but
he had not proceeded far when Jehoiakim cut it in
pieces and cast it into the fire.

JEHUDIJAH (1 Ch 4¹⁸ AV).—See HAJEHUDIJAH.

JEHUEL (יְחוּאֵל Kethîbh, יְחִיאֵל Ḳerê).—A Heman-
ite in Hezekiah's reign, 2 Ch 29¹⁴. See GENE-
ALOGY.

JEIEL (יְעִיאֵל).—**1.** A Reubenite, 1 Ch 5⁷. **2.** An
ancestor of Saul, 1 Ch 8²⁹ (supplied in RV from
9³⁵). **3.** One of David's heroes, 1 Ch 11⁴⁴. **4. 5.** The
name of two Levite families: (a) 1 Ch 15¹⁸· ²¹ 16⁵· ⁵,
2 Ch 20¹⁴; (b) 2 Ch 35⁹. **6.** A scribe in the reign
of Uzziah, 2 Ch 26¹¹. **7.** One of those who had
married foreign wives, Ezr 10⁴³. In **2. 3. 6** Kethîbh
has יְעוּאֵל, Jeuel. See GENEALOGY.

JEKABZEEL, Neh 11²⁵.—See KABZEEL.

JEKAMEAM (יְקַמְעָם).—**1.** A Levite, 1 Ch 23¹⁹ 24²³.
In the former of these passages LXX has 'Ικεμιάς,
in the latter 'Ιοκόμ (B) or 'Ικεμά (A). Gray (Heb.
Prop. Names, 46 n.) points out that these LXX
readings suggest an original יקמיה, but that the
other versions on the whole support the MT.

JEKAMIAH (יְקַמְיָה 'may J″ strengthen').—**1.** A
Judahite, the son of Shallum, 1 Ch 2⁴¹. **2.** A son
of king Jeconiah, 1 Ch 3¹⁸.

JEKUTHIEL (יְקוּתִיאֵל, perh. 'preservation of God,'
possibly same as יְקַתְאֵל, see Oxf. Heb. Lex. s.v.,
and Gray, Heb. Prop. Names, 307 n 8).—A man
of Judah, 1 Ch 4¹⁸. See GENEALOGY.

JEMIMAH (יְמִימָה).—The eldest of Job's daughters
born to him after his restoration to prosperity
(Job 42¹⁴). The LXX and Vulg. render as if from
יוֹם day; most moderns connect with Arab. jemâma
=dove (see, however, Gray, Heb. Prop. Names,
p. 108).

JEMNAAN, Jth 2²⁸.—See JABNEEL.

JEMUEL (יְמוּאֵל).—A son of Simeon, Gn 46¹⁰,
Ex 6¹⁵=Nemuel of Nu 26¹², 1 Ch 4²⁴. The LXX
also exhibits both forms, having in Gn 'Ιεμουήλ, in
Ex 'Ιεμιήλ (B), in Nu and 1 Ch Ναμουήλ.

JEOPARD, JEOPARDY.—The verb to 'jeopard,'

is the 'deliverer' referred to in 2 K 13⁵, and this is a chronological datum of considerable value. See the present writer's
remarks in Schrader, COT² ii. p. 324.

that is, hazard, is derived from the subst. 'jeopardy,' peril, hazard; and that is a corruption of the Old French *jeu parti*, lit. a divided game (Low Lat. *jocus partitus*), *i.e.* a game in which the chances are even. Chaucer (*Troilus*, ii. 465) has—

'For myn estat now lyth in jupartye,
And eek myn emes [=uncle's] lyf lyth in balaunce';

and (ii. 772)—

'Sholde I now love and putte in jupartye
My sikernesse, and thrallen libertee?'

Tindale in *Prol. to Leviticus* says, 'They that be dead, yf they dyed in the faith which that sacrament preacheth, they be saffe and are past all jeopardye,' where the word has assumed its modern spelling. The verb occurs often in Tindale and other writers of that time, as Knox, *Works*, iii. 213, 'Why will ye jeoparde to loise eternall life?'; Tind. *Works*, i. 173, 'Whosoever casteth not this aforehand, I must jeopard life, goods, honour, worship (and all that there is, for Christ's sake), deceiveth himself'; Elyot, *Governour*, ii. 263, 'I name that Audacitie whiche is an excessife and inordinate truste to escape all daungers, and causeth a man to do suche actes as are nat to be jeoparded': and Dn 3²⁸ Cov. 'that have altered the kynges commaundement and joperde their bodies therupon.'

Jeopardy occurs in AV, 2 S 23¹⁷ 'is not this the blood of the men that went in jeopardy of their lives?' (הַהֹלְכִים בְּנַפְשֹׁתָם, lit., as RVm, 'that went with their lives'; but the ב is [as Driver] the *Beth pretii*, 'at the cost or risk of their lives'; W. R. Smith [*RS*² 230], 'the blood of the men that fetched it in jeopardy of their lives'); 1 Ch 11¹⁹ *bis* 'Shall I drink the blood of these men that have put their lives in jeopardy? for with the jeopardy of their lives they brought it' (AVm and RVm 'with their lives'); 12¹⁹ 'He will fall to his master Saul to the jeopardy of our heads' (בְּרָאשֵׁינוּ, AVm 'on our heads,' but it is the *Beth pretii*, as before); 1 Mac 6⁴⁴ 'Eleazar also . . . put himself in jeopardy, to the end he might deliver his people' (ἔδωκεν ἑαυτόν, RV 'gave himself'); Lk 8²³ 'there came down a storm of wind on the lake; and they were filled with water and were in jeopardy' (ἐκινδύνευον); 1 Co 15³⁰ 'And why stand we in jeopardy every hour?' (κινδυνεύομεν); and in the Preface to AV 1611, 'Yea, why did the Catholicks (meaning Popish *Romanists*) alwayes go in jeopardie for refusing to go to heare it [the English translation of the Bible]?'

The verb is rarer, Jg 5¹⁸ 'Zebulun and Naphtali were a people that jeoparded their lives unto the death in the high places of the field' (חֵרֵף נַפְשֹׁו לָמוּת), lit. 'that despised its life to death,' AVm 'exposed to reproach,' Moore, 'that recklessly exposed itself to death'); * 2 Mac 11⁷ 'Then Maccabeus himself first of all took weapons, exhorting the other that they would jeopard themselves together with him to help their brethren' (διακινδυνεύοντας); 14³⁸ 'he [Razis] did boldly jeopard his body and life with all vehemency for the religion of the Jews' (παραβεβλημένος).
                              J. HASTINGS.

JEPHTHAH (יִפְתָּח, 'he,' *i.e.* prob. J", 'will open'; cf. פְּתַחְיָה Ezr 10²³ etc.; יִפְתְּאֵל town in Zebulun, Jos 19¹⁴; יִפְתָּח also name of a town in Judah, Jos 15⁴³; Ἰεφθάέ).—Judge, and conqueror of the Ammonites (Jg 10⁶–12⁷; cf. 1 S 12¹¹). The narrative has an unusually long introduction 10⁶⁻¹⁸ (cf. 2¹¹⁻³⁶⋅ ⁷⁻¹⁰ 6⁷⁻¹⁰ [D²]); it is based, however, on what was probably a shorter introduction in the manner of E (vv.⁶ᵇ⋅ ⁸⋅ ¹⁵⋅ ¹⁶). The particulars in 10¹⁷⋅ ¹⁸ are derived from ch. 11 (cf. 8³³⁻³⁵ from ch. 9), and come from D². Apparently, this long introduction is

* See Moore *in loc.* for reff. to the use of the verb; and G. A. Smith in *Expos.* 4th Ser. vii. 168, and in *HGHL* 422, for illustration of the character described.

intended to include the Philistine as well as the Ammonite oppression (10⁷). The main interest of the story of Jephthah clearly lies, not in his personal history or defeat of the Ammonites, but in his vow and its fulfilment, and the origin of an Israelite custom.

Of the antecedents of Jephthah little is known beyond the fact that he was a Gileadite warrior, the son of a harlot. He was driven out of his home by the 'elders of Gilead' (11⁷), and became the captain of a band of freebooters in the land of Tob in E. Syria (cf. 1 S 22¹ˡ⋅, 2 S 10⁶⋅ ⁸).* The Ammonite invasion made it necessary for the Israelites east of Jordan to find a leader; and there was nothing for it but to appeal to the outlawed Jephthah to come to the rescue. The elders of Gilead begged him to be their leader; and, after expressing surprise that such a request should be made to him, Jephthah agreed, on the condition that he should become their chief when the Ammonites were defeated. A solemn compact was made accordingly, and Jephthah was appointed leader by popular acclamation (11⁴⁻¹¹ᵃ). At this moment, it would seem, when Jephthah was at Mizpah of Gilead, he went to the holy place or altar, and there, 'before J",' registered a vow to sacrifice whomsoever should be the first to meet him when he returned victorious (vv.³¹⋅ ¹¹ᵇ).† That he had a human victim in his mind is clear from the language which he used.‡

The long account of the negotiations between Jephthah and the king of the Ammonites (11¹²⁻²⁸) with regard to Israel's rights of possession in Gilead, is regarded by most critics as a late interpolation, compiled from JE's narrative in Nu 20. 21, in some places word for word; cf. vv.¹⁷⁻²²⋅ ²⁶ with Nu 20¹⁴⋅ ¹⁷ 21⁴⋅ ¹³⋅ ²¹⁻²⁴⋅ ²⁵. The remarkable thing about this section is, that although Jephthah is arguing with Ammonites, yet the language which he is made to use refers entirely to *Moabites*. The Ammonites complain that Israel had seized their land between Arnon and Jabbok; Jephthah replies that the district was taken from Sihon king of the Amorites, and not from *Moab* (!). Moab never fought against Israel (but see Jos 24⁹), why should Ammon? Even Chemosh, god of the Moabites, is referred to as having given the Ammonites their territory. An extraordinary misunderstanding thus runs through the whole passage.§

A brief description of the defeat of the Ammonites is all that is given (v.³²ᶠ⋅). The course of the battle cannot be determined exactly, but it probably went in a direction E. of Rabbah (see Jos 13²⁵ Aroer), into the territory of the Ammonites.‖ Jephthah returns in triumph to his home at Mizpah; the first person who comes to meet him is his only daughter, accompanied by a chorus of women (cf. Ex 15²⁰ᶠ⋅, 1 S 18⁶ᶠ⋅). The overwhelming grief of the father, the noble self-surrender of the daughter, and her courageous resignation to her fate, are told with admirable skill and reserve. 'He did to her what he had vowed to do.' It

* 11¹ᵇ⋅ ² are not part of the original story. V.¹ᵇ is modelled on the genealogical forms of P and Ch; v.² is best explained as due to a misunderstanding of v.⁷.

† The sequel of v.³¹ is 11ᵇ; the text has been disordered by the long interpolation, 12-28.

‡ 'Whosoever cometh forth,' 'from the doors of my house,' 'I will offer him up': these expressions are inapplicable to an animal.

§ Perhaps the interpolation was made at some moment when the Israelites wanted to assert their title to Gilead. Moore suggests such an occasion as the intrusion of the Ammonites at the beginning of the 6th cent. (Jer 49¹⁻⁵).

‖ V.²⁹ mentions various movements, the reason for which is not clear. Jephthah's object could not have been to raise the tribes; for the people are all assembled in v.11ᵃ. In 11ᵇ Jephthah is still at Mizpah; he is still there in 30, and thence sets out in due course in 32. V.29 is, in fact, an attempt to pick up the thread of the narrative after the long interpolation, 12-28 (Moore).

became henceforth a custom in Israel to celebrate the tragedy of Jephthah's daughter by four days' mourning every year.*

That such sacrifices were possible in Israel may be gathered from 1 S 14²⁴ᶠ·⁴⁵ 15³³, 2 S 21⁶·⁹; cf. Ezk 20²⁶ with Ex 22²⁸, Mic 6⁷. In times of desperation or religious degradation they became more frequent (Jer 7³¹, 2 K 16³ 17¹⁷ 21⁶, Ps 106³⁷ᶠ· etc. See Schultz, *OT Theol.* i. 191; Dillmann, *Genesis⁶*, 289 f.; Nowack, *Heb. Arch.* ii. 205 f.; Ottley, *BL*, 1897, 176 f.).

The narrative goes on to describe a severe conflict between Jephthah and the tribe of Ephraim, who, with characteristic arrogance (8¹ᶠ·), complained that they had not been invited to take part in the war. After expostulating with them, Jephthah collected his Gileadite forces, which had been dispersed when the war was ended, and went to battle. He held the Jordan fords against them; every fugitive who attempted to cross was required to pronounce the test-word *Shibboleth* ('flood'); and if he betrayed his Ephraimite origin by pronouncing it *Sibboleth*, he was put to death.†

The historical character of this narrative has been questioned by Wellh. (*Composition*, 229), who treats it as a mere replica of 8¹⁻³. His arguments, however, are not conclusive; the episode at the Jordan fords is too original to be imaginary; and the majority of modern critics support the genuineness of these verses. It is probable that the numbers in v.⁶ are exaggerated; but this does not condemn the whole story.‡ The narrative of Jephthah is brought to a close with the formula which is used of the minor judges (10²·⁵ 12¹⁰·¹²·¹⁵).§

The account of Jephthah's home and settled life at Mizpah (11³⁴ᶠᶠ·) does not seem to agree with his outlawry in 11³ᶠᶠ·. The confusion of the Ammonites and Moabites in 11¹²⁻²⁸ is also remarkable. Accordingly, Budde (*Commentary on Judges*, 1897), following an unpublished treatise by Holzinger, attempts to work out a double narrative, as in the case of Gideon. He postulates a Moabite document, and assigns it to E, and an Ammonite document, J. The suggestion is ingenious, but the data are hardly distinctive enough. The contradictions in the accounts of Jephthah's antecedents are not irreconcilable; while, with regard to the interpolation (11¹²⁻²⁸), the explanation above satisfies the case.

LITERATURE.—See, above all, Moore, *Judges*, 282 ff.; cf. also Budde, *Richter, ad loc.*, *Richt. u. Sam.* 125 ff.; Kittel, *Hist. of Hebrews*, ii. 89 f.; Wellhausen, *Comp.* 228 f.; Nöldeke, *Untersuchungen*, 195 n.; Kuenen, *Hist. Büch. d. AT*, 18 f.; Goldziher, *Der Mythos bei den Hebräern*, 113 ff.; Stade, *GVI* i. 68; Baudissin, *Stud. z. semit. Religionsgeschichte*, i. 55 ff.; Smend, *Alttest. Religionsgeschichte*, 99 ff.; Baethgen, *Beiträge*, 13 ff.; Driver, *LOT⁶* 166; Cornill, *Einleitung²*, 96 f.

G. A. COOKE.

JEPHUNNEH (יְפֻנֶּה).—**1.** The father of Caleb (Nu 13⁶). **2.** A son of Jether an Asherite (1 Ch 7³⁸).

JERAH (יֶרַח), son of Joktan, Gn 10²⁶ (1 Ch 1²⁰). The Arabic geographers knew of places named *Yurākh* and *Yarāh* in Yemen and Ḥijaz respectively (Yāḳūt and Hamdāni); and the geographer Yāḳūt quotes from Al-Ṣulaiḥi (a usurper who obtained control of Yemen in the 11th cent., and was well versed in S. Arabian geography), a verse in which *Warākh* is mentioned as a place of importance: 'What excuse have I, now I am lord of *Warākh*, for failing to meet the foe?' There are several

* See W. R. Smith, *RS* 395.
† Two historical parallels are quoted by the commentators: the 'Sicilian Vespers,' Mar. 31, 1282, when the French were made to betray themselves by their pronunciation of *ceci ei ciceri*; and again, during the revolt against the French in Flanders, May 25, 1302, when no one was allowed to pass out of the gates who could not pronounce *scilt ende friend?*
‡ In 12²ᵃ a verb must be supplied after עַמּוֹן בְּנֵי, LXX (A)ἐταπεί-νουν με, *i.e.* עִנּוּנִי 'afflicted me.' In v.⁴ the sentence from אָמְרוּ כִּי 'because they said' to the end does not make sense. The words, 'because they said, Ye are fugitives of Ephraim,' must come from v.⁵; the rest of the sentence is a gloss. The entire half-verse is om. in some MSS of LXX; in Syro-Hex. it is asterisked.
§ The closing words of 12⁷ cannot be right. LXX (A) ἐν τῇ πόλει αὐτοῦ Γαλαάδ, Vulg. *in civitate sua Galaad*. Studer conjectures בְּמִצְפֵּה גִלְעָד 11²⁹, suggested by ἐν τῇ πόλει αὐτοῦ ἐν Σεφὶ Γ', the reading of some cursive MSS; cf. Moore, *ad loc.*

references to Warākh in Hamdāni's 'Description of Arabia,' from which its site can be accurately fixed. It is possible that the name may be ancient, and that the *Jerah* of Gn may refer to it. Most commentators, however, have preferred to regard Jerah (Heb. 'moon' or 'month') as a translation of some Arabic name; but the conjectures based on this supposition by Bochart, J. D. Michaelis, and more recently Glaser (*Skizze*, ii. 425), seem devoid of probability.   D. S. MARGOLIOUTH.

JERAHMEEL (יְרַחְמְאֵל; 'may God have compassion'; B Ἰραμεήλ, Ἰερεμεήλ, Ἰερεμαήλ, Ῥαμεήλ; A Ἰερεμεήλ, Ἰερεμιήλ; *Jerameel*).—**1.** According to 1 Ch 2⁹ the firstborn son of Hezron, the son of Perez, the son of Judah. His descendants, of whom a list is given (vv.²⁵⁻³³), lived on the extreme S. border of Judah in what was technically called 'the Negeb of the Jerahmeelites' (1 S 27¹⁰ 30²⁹; see Driver, *in loc.*, and G. A. Smith, *HGHL* pp. 278–286). They appear to have been an Amalekite or Edomite clan, which was afterwards absorbed by Judah.

2. The son of Kish, a Merarite Levite of the house of Mahli. Jerahmeel appears as the only representative of this branch of the house of Merari at the time when David is said to have organized the temple service (1 Ch 23²¹ 24²⁹).

3. The king's son (RV, AVm; 'the son of Hammelech' AV, RVm) *i.e.* of the royal blood, who together with two other officers was commanded by king Jehoiakim 'to take Baruch the scribe and Jeremiah the prophet' after the burning of the roll (Jer 36²⁶).   J. F. STENNING.

JERECHU (Ἰέρεχος, Bᵃ -ειχ-, AV Jerechus), 1 Es 5²².—In Ezr 2³⁴, Neh 7³⁶ JERICHO.

JERED (יֶרֶד. It is the same name which is given in Gn 5¹⁵·¹⁶·¹⁸·²⁰, 1 Ch 1² as **Jared**).—A Judahite, the 'father' of Gedor, 1 Ch 4¹⁸.

JEREMAI (יְרֵמָי).—A Jew of the family of Hashum who had married a foreign wife (Ezr 10³³).

JEREMIAH.—Seven or eight men of this name besides the prophet (see next art.) are mentioned in OT. The Heb. is always יִרְמְיָהוּ or יִרְמְיָה. **1.** A warrior of the tribe of Gad, fifth in reputation (1 Ch 12¹⁰) of those who joined David in 'the hold in the wilderness' in the neighbourhood either of Adullam or of En-gedi, most probably of the latter. **2.** The tenth in reputation (1 Ch 12¹³) of the same Gadite band. **3.** A bowman and slinger of the tribe of Benjamin (1 Ch 12⁴), who joined David during his occupation of the frontier city of Ziklag. **4.** The head of a family in the eastern section of the tribe of Manasseh (1 Ch 5²⁴). He was probably one of the Jews carried into captivity by Tiglath-pileser, and settled by him on the Armenian frontier (1 Ch 5²⁶, 2 K 15²⁹). **5.** A Jew of Libnah, whose daughter, Hamutal or Hamital, was one of the wives of Josiah, and mother of Jehoahaz (2 K 23³¹) and Zedekiah (2 K 24¹⁸, Jer 52¹). In the last two passages the mother's name is given as Hamital, חֲמִיטַל; but a textual error is more probable than that Josiah married two sisters, both daughters of Jeremiah. The latter's place of residence (Jos 21¹³, 1 Ch 6⁵⁷), and his relations with the king, as well as the respectful way in which he is in each instance referred to as a well-known man, make it likely that he was a priest of great influence, and possibly also one of the principal instigators or agents of Josiah in the ritual restoration of his reign. **6.** The son of Habazziniah and father of Jaazaniah, who appears to have been the head of the Rechabites (Jer 35³) in the time of the prophet Jeremiah.

7. A priest who in B.C. 536 came back to Jerusalem with Zerubbabel and Jeshua (Neh 12[1]). His name was given to one of the twenty-two courses or 'fathers'-houses,' into which were divided the four families of priests (Ezr 2[36-39], Neh 7[39-42]) that returned on that occasion. It is not possible to say with certainty to which of these families Jeremiah belonged; but if the lists are parallel, he may have been a member of that of Jedaiah, with which also the high priest Jeshua was connected. The course is mentioned again (Neh 12[13]) in the priesthood (B.C. 499–463) of Joiakim, Jeshua's son and successor, when its head is said to have been Hananiah. **8.** A priest who in the name of his course, with other princes and representatives of the people, sealed in B.C. 444 Nehemiah's great covenant (Neh 10[2]). He (or his course) was also appointed to join the right-hand procession at the dedication of the wall of Jerusalem (Neh 12[34]). It is possible that in both of these cases the name is used to denote the official head of a priestly course rather than an individual in his own person. In the former, fifteen of the twenty-one names are identical with those in the lists of Neh 12[2-7] and Neh 12[11-20]; and hence there is ground for the assumption that the name is used in this instance as the official designation of a class. But in the latter the forms of expression are slightly in favour of the opposite conclusion, Neh 12[35] referring specifically to the priests' sons, whilst there is an antecedent probability that the procession would consist of selected representatives only. That, moreover, the name of Jeremiah should recur in different generations of the same family, is not forbidden by known Jewish usage. In the days of Joiakim, Hananiah was the head of the course of Jeremiah (Neh 12[12]); but Joiakim died some sixteen years before the dedication of the wall, and in the interval it is not unlikely that the headship of the course of Jeremiah had passed into the hands of a man who bore the great family name. And if this Jeremiah was a person and not a class, lapse of time is fatal to his assumed identification with the previous one (No. 7).   R. W. MOSS.

JEREMIAH THE PROPHET.—

i. LIFE OF THE PROPHET.—Jeremiah (יִרְמְיָהוּ, shorter form יִרְמְיָה 'whom J" casts,' *i.e.* possibly, as Ges. suggests, 'appoints' Dn 7[9], Ἰερεμίας, *Jeremias*) was born of a priestly family in Anathoth, now 'Anâta, a small town, an hour or an hour and a quarter N.E. of Jerusalem (Is 10[30]), and prophesied from the 13th year of Josiah till after the Captivity, a period of more than 40 years (B.C. 626–586). Though he had spoken as a prophet for five years when Josiah promulgated the Book of the Law and introduced his Reform, Jeremiah appears to have had no hand in these transactions; but from the death of Josiah till his own death in Egypt he was a prominent figure in all the history of that tragic period. Almost alone he had to expose the immoralities, the self-deception founded on superficial reforms, and the fanatical confidence in the protection of J" who dwelt in His temple, by which all classes were carried away. His conviction, constantly declared, that the Lord had determined to destroy the temple and nation, exposed him to cruel insults from the temple priests (20[2], cf. 37[13]); and he was on many occasions in danger of his life, from his townsmen of Anathoth (11[21]), the priests and prophets of the temple (26[8. 9]), the arbitrary and vindictive king Jehoiakim (36[19. 26]), and the military of the day (38[4]). The strife in which he was involved, so alien to his nature, wearied him : he longed for a lodge in the wilderness (9[2]), mourned the perpetual conflicts in which his life was passed (15[10]), cursed in despair the day of his birth (20[14]), and vowed to have done with the word of the Lord, which isolated him from all that was human,—but in vain : His word was in his heart like a fire shut up in his bones, and he must declare it (20[9]). Yet even in that degenerate day his life extorted a certain homage : the better conscience of men was on his side (26[17-19]); the Ethiopian slave was moved with pity for his distress (38[7]); king Zedekiah heard him gladly, and did what he could to mitigate his sufferings (37[20f.] 38[10]); the Chaldæans treated him with consideration (40[1ff.]), and even the wretched exiles insisted on dragging him with them as a kind of fetish to Egypt (43[5ff.]).

Jeremiah appears to have been called to the prophetic office young, though the word 'child' (נַעַר 1[6]), which he employs of himself, may chiefly express his sense of insufficiency for the task set before him. There is no reason to suppose his father Hilkiah identical with the chief priest of that name who discovered the Book of the Law in the temple (2 K 22[8]). His father may rather have been a descendant of Abiathar, whom Solomon banished to Anathoth (1 K 2[26]); and if so, traditions of the days of David and the early monarchy, and the great part their ancestor then played, would be cherished in the family and give it a sense of dignity even in its decline, and they would be the food on which the mind of the child Jeremiah was nourished. The family owned land in Anathoth (32[8]), and, though, in later times at least, living mainly in Jerusalem, the prophet continued to frequent his native village (11[18ff.] 37[11ff.], cf. 29[27] where he is contemptuously called 'the Anathothite'). His prophetic ministry was probably begun here. As he was not consulted by Josiah and the priests regarding the newly-found Book of the Law (2 K 22[12ff.]), he may have been little known in the capital, unless indeed we suppose that owing to the violence of his denunciations the authorities preferred to seek the advice of some more moderate counsellors. There is no ground for supposing the dialogue 1[4-10] coloured by the prophet's subsequent experience. No man became a prophet suddenly ; the decisive event, named his 'call,' was but the climax of many prior movements of mind leading up to it. Jeremiah felt himself 'predestinated' to be a prophet (1[4f.]). The idea may cover much belonging to the past, the godly house out of which he came with its traditions, many movements in his own mind little attended to at the time but remembered now, and the nation's whole history of which he was the child. It is no denial of the reality of the divine voice speaking to him when we look at the dialogue as a conflict in his own mind, in which thought was invalidated by opposite thought, and suggestion and resolution met by counter suggestion and irresolution. The conflict already reveals the duality in his consciousness characteristic of his whole life. God and man wrestle within him no less than they do in St. Paul. The impulses to stand forth as a prophet, awakened by the signs of the times, he calls God ; the reluctances and all the considerations that support them are himself. And when the impulses prove the stronger, it is a victory of God and a defeat of himself—' O Lord, thou didst induce me, and I was induced ; thou **art** stronger than I ' (20[7]).

The words, 'See, I have set thee over the nations,' indicate a change of view from that of the earlier prophets, though Jeremiah was perhaps not conscious of the change (28$^{7ff.}$). Israel is no more to be a people that dwells alone (Nu 23^9), the stream of its history is to flow into and colour that of the history of the nations. If prophecy now begins to concern itself with the nations, it is because J" concerns Himself with them. The consciousness of one God has created the consciousness of one world and one mankind. Jeremiah's presentiments at this time are expressed in the two symbols 1$^{11-19}$: First, the symbol of the almond tree, meaning that J" is 'wakeful' in regard to His word and purposes, and will speedily execute them; and second, the seething caldron with its mouth towards the south, indicating that the North is about to pour its desolating forces over the land. The substance of his prophetic speeches under Josiah is given in chs. 2–6. These chs. reflect chiefly his teaching before the Reform, but contain allusions to the people's mind later, and his judgment on it (2^{35} 3$^{4. 5}$ 4$^{3f.}$). The two main thoughts running through the chs. are, first, his verdict on the people's history; it has been one long course of unfaithfulness to J" (2^1–4^4); and, secondly, his unchangeable conviction that the issue of such a history must be the destruction of the nation (4^5–6^{30}). His thoughts run greatly on the same lines with those of Hosea. Israel was true to J" in the wilderness,—and with a sorrowful reminiscence J" recalls the time, 'I remember the kindness of thy youth, thy bridal love, how thou didst follow me in the wilderness' (2^2),—but apostatized and became unfaithful on entering Canaan; and this unfaithfulness has continued and become aggravated. Under the name of 'whoredom' Jeremiah includes not only the service of deities nominally different from J", but the debased service of J" at the high places, with images and other Canaanite usages. This judgment of Jeremiah has not only ideal or absolute truth, to the effect that the popular worship showed no consciousness of the true being of J", it has historical truth also; for no doubt the Canaanites absorbed into Israel carried over much of their religious practice as well as their places of worship into the nation. Even the Arabs were conscious that images were a later innovation in their religion. How profound Jeremiah's conception of the true religion of J" was, and how absolute he felt the contrast between it and the popular religion to be, appears from the figure in which he describes the one and the other: 'They have forsaken the fountain of living water, to hew out for themselves broken cisterns that can hold no water.'

The circumstances of Jeremiah's ministry at this time are not told, but some things give us a glimpse into them. The people reclaim against his judgment on their religion, saying that it is not true, and that, if there was any truth in it, the evil had been amended. That is, they claim that their service is in their intention a service of J", 'How canst thou say, I have not gone after the baals?' (2^{23}); and that such evils as the 'high places' had been done away (2^{35} 3$^{4. 5}$). Their claim that they meant to serve J" was no doubt just; it was their conception of Him that was at fault, and the modes of giving this conception expression. But both the conception and the modes of expressing it had been inherited by them, and they were unable to see that the prophet's charges were just. As to the other point, Josiah's removal of the 'high places' must have seemed good to Jeremiah, and possibly he hoped something from the Reform at first, but even in Josiah's days he had ceased to cherish any illusions in regard to it. The worship was altered, the Being worshipped remained the same; men

had changed their customs, they were unchanged in their mind. The work was superficial, a casting of seed into the old field rank with thorns; they must plough deeper—'Circumcise the foreskins of your heart' (4$^{3. 4}$). Jeremiah is not mentioned in connexion with Josiah's reform, nor indeed is he once named in the Book of Kings, but some scholars interpret Jer 11$^{1-8}$ as meaning that he undertook an itinerant mission round 'the cities of Judah' to recommend acceptance of the Book of Deuteronomy. The idea is most improbable. The prophet's 'amen' (v.^{5}) expresses acquiescence in the words of J", 'Cursed be the man that heareth not the words of this covenant,' not obedience to a command (vv.$^{2. 6}$; cf. 28^6). Jeremiah may have sought to impress on men the general idea of Dt, that of the covenant between J" and Israel, for this was his own idea in another form, but a formal championship of Dt would have been very unlike him. The expression 'cities of Judah and streets of Jerusalem' is not to be pressed to imply a circuit of the cities any more than of the streets. When Jeremiah spoke anywhere, he spoke in the cities of Judah and the streets of Jerusalem, for his words went out to all the land (26^2), just as when he spoke in Tahpanhes he addressed the dwellers in Pathros, or Upper Egypt (44^{15} etc.). The phrase 'cities of Judah and streets of Jerusalem' means the country and the capital (7^{34} 11^{13}; cf. 4^5). The other feeling prominent in the prophet's mind at this time is the imminent destruction of the people by a foe from the north (4^5–6^{30}). This 'foe' might be a creation of his moral presentiment, and assigned to the 'north' as the cloudy region of mystery where storms gather and descend upon the world of men, but such descriptions as that in 5$^{15ff.}$ seem to imply an actual people known to the time. It is usually thought that the Scythians are meant. The pathos and depth of these chs. (2–6) are not surpassed by anything in Scripture. Two things in them may be referred to—first, the prophet's profound sense of the national sin, and his presentiment of the desolations which moral evil must work in the earth. In a strange passage (4$^{23ff.}$) he fancies himself to have outlived the judgment, and to be treading on the ashes of the extinct world. He is the last man, alone amidst the silence of death: 'I beheld the earth, and, lo, it was waste and void; and the heavens, and they had no light. I beheld, and, lo, there was no man, and all the birds of the heavens were fled.' And second, his agitation at the thought of the doom hanging over his people: 'My bowels, my bowels! I am pained at my heart; my heart is disquieted in me; I cannot hold my peace, because my soul hath heard the sound of the trumpet, the alarm of war' (4$^{19ff.}$). Other passages reveal his compassion for the people, as 4^{31} 6$^{22-26}$ 10$^{19ff.}$.

Thirteen years after his reform Josiah ventured to oppose Necho the king of Egypt, and fell at Megiddo. His servants carried his body in a chariot to Jerusalem, where he was buried, and the people of the land raised his son Jehoahaz to the throne. The prince, induced or compelled to repair to Necho's headquarters at Riblah, was thrown into fetters, and after a reign of three months carried to Egypt, where he died. Jeremiah makes a pathetic reference to his father Josiah and him: 'Weep ye not for the dead, neither bemoan him; but weep sore for him that goeth away: for he shall return no more, nor see his native land' (22^{10}). In another passage he contrasts Josiah with Jehoiakim (22$^{13ff.}$), but he makes no other reference to the pious king; the statement of 2 Ch 35^{25} that Jeremiah 'lamented for Josiah' seems founded on the tradition that he was the author of Lamentations. Jehoiakim, whom Necho raised to the throne, was the ideal of a bad ruler. Frivolous and superficial in regard to the highest things of life, despotic in temper, and brutal in the measures he used to rid himself of those who crossed his humours (Jer 26[20-24]), he became the detestation of all serious-minded men. Jeremiah probably reflects the common sentiment regarding him when he says, 'They shall not lament him, saying, Ah my brother! Ah lord! or, Ah his glory! He shall be buried with the burial of an ass, dragged and cast forth beyond the gates of Jerusalem' (22[18, 19]). It was easy to be a prophet under Josiah, but in Jehoiakim Manasseh had come to life again. The early years of this reign were the period of the prophet's conflicts. The conflict was twofold : external persecution, from the priests and prophets because of his threats against the temple, for to blaspheme the temple was to blaspheme Him that dwelt therein, and was worthy of death (chs. 7. 26) ; from his townsmen of Anathoth (11[18ff.]) ; from the people (18[18]) ; and from Pashhur the overseer of the temple, who struck Jeremiah and put him in the stocks (ch. 20). But these external trials reflected themselves in a tumult of contending emotions in his own breast, forming one of the strangest episodes in religious history (11[1]-12[6] 14-20).

Meanwhile the hand of 'God who hideth himself' was operating in the north in unexpected events, which seemed again to bring the prophet's early anticipations near. These anticipations indeed seemed to have failed. The wind from the desert which was to wither up the land, whose hot breath he had already felt upon his face (4[11]), appeared to have been arrested. The storm-cloud of Scythian invasion, like other storms, followed the line of the sea, leaving Jerusalem unscathed, and was dissipated on the borders of Egypt. But in 607 Nineveh fell, and Babylon became heir of all the countries washed by the Mediterranean, the realm which had just been added by Necho to his dominions. A conflict between the rivals could not long be deferred. In 605-4 the two armies met near Carchemish, where Nebuchadnezzar inflicted a decisive defeat on Necho, and Judah exchanged the yoke of Egypt for that of Babylon. Carchemish was an epoch in Jeremiah's life. It was his justification in the eyes of others, for his foe from the north was seen to be no spectre ; perhaps it made him feel more deeply himself than ever he had felt before how truly his prophetic presentiments were of God. God had set His seal on his past, and it was this reinvigorated assurance that his prophecies were the word of God that made him commit them to writing and lay them before the people, as is told in ch. 36. Carchemish was to Jeremiah what the appeal of Ahaz to Tiglathpileser was to Isaiah : like a flash of lightning in the darkness, it lighted up to him the whole line of God's purposes on to the end. He foresaw his past anticipations passing into history. The conviction seized his mind that it was the will of J" that all nations should serve the king of Babylon ; to refuse his yoke, whether for Israel or another people, was to resist the decree of God. But the strangest and most unaccountable of all his presentiments or certainties was his reading beforehand the line of God's government of the world for two generations (ch. 25).

Jehoiakim observed his oath of allegiance to Nebuchadnezzar for three years, when he refused his yearly tribute, an act equivalent to a declaration of independence. By and by the Babylonian armies were put in motion, but, by the time they sat before Jerusalem, Jehoiakim had been removed by death, and his successor Jehoiachin, after a reign of 100 days, was compelled to surrender. He was carried to Babylon, where he lay in prison

seven and thirty years, till he was released by the son of Nebuchadnezzar (2 K 25[27ff.]) His fate awoke the liveliest sorrow in his people's minds (Jer 28[4]), and the prophet had to crush their hopes of his return in the most peremptory manner (22[24ff.] 13[18]). Zedekiah, who succeeded him on the throne, was a prince of good intentions, but weak and irresolute. He frequently consulted Jeremiah, and would have listened to his counsels had not terror of the stronger wills around him deterred him. With the first captivity under Jehoiachin and the accession of Zedekiah the period of Jeremiah's conflicts was over. God had conquered him, and he acquiesced in His will. He no more intercedes for the people, but bends his whole energies to induce them to yield to the decree of God, and subject themselves to the king of Babylon. This was his attitude both before the siege (chs. 27-29) and during it (21[1-10] 37. 38). This attitude exposed him to many hardships—he was arrested, beaten, and flung into a dungeon and left to die ; but the hardships no more, as in the days of Jehoiakim, reflect themselves in a conflict in his own heart. Like one whose vital energies have exhausted themselves in a struggle with sickness, he lies in quietness, calmly awaiting the end. He awaits it with the more composure that he sees beyond the end (chs. 30-33). After a siege of a year and a half the city fell, and the Chaldæans appointed Gedaliah as their viceroy over the people whom they left in the land. Jeremiah had been found in the city and doomed along with the rest of the inhabitants to deportation, and in company of a band of exiles had been carried north to Ramah. The part he had played in the siege, however, became known to the Chaldæans, and orders came from the highest quarters to show him consideration, and allow him his choice to go to Babylon or remain at home. He chose to remain in the land, and repaired to Gedaliah at Mizpah. When, after a rule of no more than two months, the governor was assassinated, the men of war, with Johanan, son of Kareah, at their head, resolved to flee to Egypt to escape the dreaded vengeance of the Chaldæans. Jeremiah earnestly sought to dissuade them from their purpose, but in vain, and he and Baruch were carried down with them. It was the last and the bitterest cup he had to drink. Failure was written over his life. He had preached repentance to his people, and they would not repent. He counselled submission to Babylon, and they refused to submit. He besought them to abide in the land, and become the seed of a new nation serving the Lord, and they answered by dragging him with them to Egypt. Over the people and their history, and over his hopes, the inscription might be read, 'A full end.' Nothing is known of the manner of his death, though a tradition says that he died at the hands of his own people.

Like many of the world's greatest children, Jeremiah was little esteemed in his life, but when dead his spirit breathed out upon men, and they felt its beauty and greatness. The oppressed people saw for ages in his sufferings a type of itself, and drew from his constancy courage to endure and be true. Imagery from the scenes of his life and echoes of his words fill many of the psalms, the authors of which were like him in his sorrows, and strove to be like him in his faith. From being of no account as a prophet he came to be considered the greatest of them all, and was spoken of as 'the prophet' (cf. Mt 16[14], Jn 1[21] 6[14] 7[40]) ; and it was told of him how in after-days he appeared in visions to those contending for the faith like an angel from heaven strengthening them (2 Mac 15[13ff.]).

ii. THE BOOK OF JEREMIAH.—In ch. 36 it is stated that in the 4th year of Jehoiakim (605-4), no doubt after the battle of Carchemish in which Egypt was defeated by Nebuchadnezzar, Jeremiah was commanded to write all the words which J″ had spoken to him against Israel and Judah and all the nations from the 13th year of Josiah till that time. He dictated his prophecies to Baruch, who read the roll next year in the temple in the hearing of the people assembled from all parts of the country at a fast. This roll was brought to Jehoiakim, who cut it in pieces and threw it into the grate. Jeremiah dictated the contents of the roll anew to Baruch, and added many like words (or, 'as many words more'). The added words might consist in some measure of new oracles, but in the main would be a fuller recapitulation of former prophecies. Now (1) it is natural to suppose that this second roll forms the earlier part of our present book, though how far into the book it extends is difficult to say. It was, however, only one of the elements out of which the present book was compiled, and it is not certain how far the compiler or redactor of the book maintained the original order of the roll. Some passages may have been transferred in order to unite them with later passages of a similar nature, e.g. 22^{10-12. 13ff.} with 22^{24ff.}. Some parts of ch. 25 certainly belonged to the first roll (25^{9. 10} with 36^{29}) and also to the second; the passage, however, was removed from its original place (possibly to form an introduction to a series of prophecies against the nations), and is now redactional and greatly glossed. (2) Baruch's statement, that he wrote from the prophet's mouth, need not absolutely exclude the use of some written notes by Jeremiah, though the command to 'write' his prophecies seems to imply that nothing had hitherto been published. Being dictated mainly from memory, prophecies extending over three and twenty years cannot have been reproduced exactly as they were spoken. It was the purpose of the prophet to preserve and lay before the people a compend of his ideas and teaching, his judgment upon the past history of the people and on their present condition, and his convictions regarding the inevitable issues in the future, without much regard to the circumstances in which the ideas had been originally expressed. Hence these early chapters are fragmentary and without connexion; passages in the same chapter may belong to different situations. The headings and dates are editorial, or at least secondary, and were not contained in Baruch's roll. This is evident from the indefiniteness of some of them, e.g. 3^6 'in the days of Josiah,' and from the similarity of those in the earlier to those in the later part of the book (cf. the identical forms, 7^1 34^1 35^1 40^1 44^1 and 14^1 with 46^1 47^1 49^{34}). Being dictated more than 20 years after they were spoken, the earliest passages may to some extent be coloured by later reflection. On the other hand, as it was the prophet's purpose to give a compend of the principles of his teaching, the fact that some sententious passages stand isolated, e.g. 9^{23. 24} 16^{19ff.} 17^{5ff.} 17^{12ff.}, is no evidence that they are not original. (3) The parts of the book belonging to a date subsequent to the 5th year of Jehoiakim are very confused, and the order in which they stand is in many cases inexplicable. There are passages, e.g. chs. 24. 27, which seem to come from the prophet's own hand, but most of his sayings after this time are enclosed in historical settings. These historical elements are not from the prophet's own hand, though from whose hand they come is uncertain. Naturally, there is no absolute guarantee that the prophet's words enclosed in the historical frames are exact reproductions of the language used by him. Of course Jeremiah may have preserved jottings, or some contemporary, such as Baruch, may have done so, and these may have been at the

compiler's disposal; or, in some cases the prophet's words may already have been set in the historical frame when they came into the compiler's hand; and in other instances, as it was obviously his intention to give as complete a biography of Jeremiah as possible, he may have relied on those who were contemporaries of the prophet and preserved in their memories both the scenes and the words spoken by him. There would be a number of such persons alive in the second half of the exile. At all events the histories are well informed and trustworthy, though some obscurities may suggest that they were not written till some time after the events which they describe (26^8 with 26^{16}), and that they are not all from the same hand (39^{14ff.} with 40^{1ff.}). In some cases where the narrative begins by speaking of 'Jeremiah the prophet,' and then introduces him speaking directly, there may be room for supposing that the narrator dramatizes the information at his command. The passage 42^{7-22}, both on account of its rather debased style and its other peculiarities, is probably a free construction from the hand of the historian; and in some other passages the accumulation of phrases characteristic of the prophet is in excess of what would be natural from himself, and suggests the work of a compiler very familiar with his peculiarities. Though it is impossible to say when or by whom the histories were composed, or do more than hazard very precarious conjectures in explanation of the place occupied by some of them in the book (e.g. 26. 36. 35), it is generally clear to what situations in the prophet's life they refer and what oracles they illustrate, and thus when they are disposed in their proper places the book may be read with a certain consecutiveness.

1. *The reign of Josiah.*—To Josiah's reign belong chs. 1–6, mainly to the time before its Reform. The date 1^2 belongs to ch. 1; 1^3 is a later insertion, meant probably to apply to the whole book (2 K 25^8). Chs. 2–6 are a compend of many oracles, but may be considered as two discourses, 2^1–4^4 and 4^5–6^{30}, the first giving the prophet's verdict on the people's history from the beginning, and the second announcing the inevitable issue of such a history. 3^{6ff.}, where Judah is contrasted with Israel, is rightly assigned to the reign of Josiah, for the idea that such a contrast could be of the date of chs. 30. 31 (Ew., Kuen.) is altogether improbable. 3^{14-18} appear to be later than 36^{13}; certainly vv.^{17. 18} are so, for v.^{18} implies the exile of Judah. But the reference to Zion while Judah was still there (v.^{14}) is unnatural, and mention of the 'ark' when Israel is spoken to is without meaning, and suggests that ark and temple were no more. The question whether 3^{19ff.} be the section of 3^{1-5} or of 3^{6-13} is difficult. Formally, either connexion is suitable. 3^{1-5} seems the continuation of ch. 2 and refers to 'Israel' as a whole, though Judah may be alluded to in v.^{4f.}; but Judah does not seem spoken of under the name 'Israel,' except when the general idea of the whole family is in the prophet's mind. If 3^{19ff.} follow 3^{1-5}, the passage continues as in ch. 2 to refer to the whole family of Israel. Some things are in favour of this, e.g. the gracious design of God, v.^{19}, most naturally refers to the whole family; the designation 'the lovely land' more probably describes Canaan as a whole than either half of it; and 4^{1. 2}, if original, recall the promises made to Israel in its unity. On the other hand, 'children of Israel' (v.^{21}) rather suggests Israel of the north, and 4^{3. 4}, which have no connexion with 4^{5ff.}, might be the natural conclusion to 3^{1-5}. At all events 3^{19ff.} are not spoken of Judah alone, but refer either to Israel as a whole or to Israel of the north, continuing 3^{6-13}. The words 'her sister,' vv.^{7. 8. 10}, are wanting in LXX, cf. Ezk 23^{11}. 17^{19-27} on the Sabbath, which might be after the Reform, are usually considered a later insertion.

2. *The reign of Jehoiakim.*—(1.) In ch. 7 Jeremiah threatens the temple with the fate of Shiloh. The historical commentary ch. 26, itself of later date, refers the discourse to the beginning of Jehoiakim's reign. Indeed it might naturally be placed immediately after the death of Josiah. The people's trust in the temple, which occasioned Jeremiah's threat, implies a feeling of danger, but the danger was over when Jehoiakim was raised by Necho to the throne. Neither is there any allusion to the king in ch. 26, it is the priests who arraign Jeremiah. The story of Uriah (26^{20ff.}) is an addition to illustrate the danger of Jeremiah; the incident itself may have been later, though early in the reign of Jehoiakim, for only when Egypt and Israel were friendly would extradition of the prophet have been granted. (2.) The brief oracle on Jehoahaz (Shallum) and Josiah, 22^{10-12}, is of the same period. (3.) 7^{29}–8^3 is an oracle against Tophet. Ch. 19 probably supplies the historical situation. The incidents, though before the 4th year of Jehoiakim, are later than 7^{1-28}. (4.) Chs. 7–10 as a whole (apart from 10^{1-16}) appear to belong to the same period, though there is much that is obscure in them.

The presentiment of a foe from the north (8^{16} 10^{17-22}), the vision of an invasion and siege ($8^{14\text{ff.}}$), the agitation of the prophet at the prospect of the approaching calamity ($8^{18\text{ff.}}$), and his call to the mourning women to prepare a lamentation ($9^{17\text{ff.}}$), are strange in the early years of Jehoiakim, and recall the situation in chs. 5. 6. Hence some scholars have assigned chs. 7-10 to Josiah's reign; but parts, *e.g.* $7^{1\text{ff.}}$, are certainly later. The whole at any rate appears earlier than the 4th year of Jehoiakim, for after this Jeremiah always names 'the king of Babylon.' (5.) 11^{1}–12^{6} also appear to be of this period. 11^{1-8} are very obscure. Vv.$^{9-17}$, charging Judah with 'conspiracy,' that is, defection from the Covenant, belong to the time of Jehoiakim, and the commands in vv.$^{6-8}$ are referred by Giesebrecht to the same period, though they have usually been thought to refer to Dt and Josiah's Reform. The plot of the people of Anathoth against Jeremiah's life (11^{18}–12^{6}) would hardly be occasioned by his action in connexion with Josiah's Reform, but be owing to his charge of 'conspiracy' at a later time. His complaints 12^{1-6} also suggest this period of his history. (6.) Chs. 18–20. Ch. 18 appears now connected with the historical passage 19^{1}–20^{6}. Ch. 18 teaches that God's dealing with men is moral, that He treats them as their moral conduct permits Him to do; it is only a secondary inference from this that prophecy is conditional, threats and promises being alike revocable according to men's actions. If ch. 19 gave the situation of 7^{29}–8^{3}, ch. 18 might belong to about the same time. On account of the speech in Tophet, repeated in the temple ($19^{14\text{ff.}}$), Pashhur put Jeremiah for a night in the stocks. If Jeremiah's inability to go to the temple (36^{5}) were due to Pashhur's action, the incidents and oracles 18^{1}–20^{18} would belong to the eve of the 4th year of Jehoiakim, though the narrative was not written till later. In $20^{4\text{ff.}}$, however, Pashhur is threatened with deportation to Babylon, and it would be necessary to assume (Kuen.) that the later narrator had reported Jeremiah's words somewhat generally. (7.) There is little in chs. 14–15, referring to a drought, or in 16^{1}–17^{18} to suggest a date, whether before or after the 4th year of Jehoiakim. Such passages as 15^{10} might suggest that the prophet was free to go about among the people, before he had to go into hiding for fear of arrest (36^{26}), and $16^{1\text{ff.}}$ might seem to reflect an early rather than a late date in his life. The idea that 17^{11} refers to Jehoiakim, and 17^{5-10} to his premeditated revolt (Kuen.), seems far-fetched. (15^{11-14} appear to refer to the people, and are misplaced; $16^{14.\,15}$ though in LXX is an obvious insertion). (8.) According to ch. 36, Baruch wrote a second roll in the 5th year of Jehoiakim containing additions. This roll would thus include chs. 1–6, 7–10 (except 10^{1-16}), 11^{1}–12^{6}, probably 14–15, 16^{1}–17^{18} ($22^{10\text{ff.}}$? $22^{13\text{ff.}}$?), the genuine portions of 25, and probably 45, the short promise to Baruch. Whether 18 and $20^{7\text{ff.}}$ also stood in the roll may be uncertain, as the passages are now enclosed in a historical setting of a later date. (9.) To a later time in the reign of Jehoiakim belong 12^{7-17}, which appear to reflect the situation after his revolt (2 K $24^{1\text{ff.}}$). Ch. 35 also narrates an incident in connexion with the Rechabites probably of the same time. (10.) Ch. 13, describing a symbolical action with Jeremiah's girdle, is usually assigned to the short reign of Jehoiachin, on account of the allusion to him and his mother in v.$^{18\text{f.}}$. There is nothing in the other parts of the chapter to suggest this situation; but if *Perath* (v.^{4}) be the Euphrates, the date would in any case be later than the 4th year of Jehoiakim and Carchemish.

3. *Reign of Zedekiah* (597–586).—(1.) To the beginning of the reign of Zedekiah belongs ch. 24, the vision of the two baskets of figs, the good representing the exiles of 597, the bad the people left at home. (2.) Chs. 21–23 contain a collection of fragments belonging to very different dates on the leading classes in Judah, the kings 21^{11}–23^{8}, and the prophets 23^{9-40}. Whether some of these fragments stood in the original roll may be uncertain; the present collection cannot have been made before the time of Zedekiah ($22^{24\text{ff.}}$), probably not before the Exile ($23^{3\text{ff.}}$). (3.) To the 4th year of Zedekiah (28^{1}) belong chs. 27–29 (27^{1} is a mistaken gloss, wanting in LXX), containing the prophet's opposition to the projected confederacy against Babylon (27), his conflict with Hananiah over the duration of the Exile (28), and his letter to the exiles (29). These three chapters have certain peculiarities in common: (1) The LXX text is shorter, particularly in 27; (2) certain differences of spelling appear, *e.g.* *Yirmeyah* for *Yirmeyahu*, and so in similar names, and Nebuchad*nezzar* (for *-rezzar*). The peculiarities (2) are lost in Gr.; in LXX the name Nebuch. occurs only once (27^{6}). In explanation of these peculiarities it has been suggested that chs. 27–29 may have circulated separately and been glossed; but as LXX shows that the glosses were introduced after the redaction of the book, it must also be supposed that at a late date the genuine text was collated with one of these glossed rolls of 27–29, and supplemented from it,—an intricate hypothesis. The rest of the book (except 46–51) belongs to the time of the siege and later. (4.) 21^{1-10} the prophet's reply to the message of Zedekiah at the beginning of the siege. The passage has been united to $21^{11\text{ff.}}$, the common subject being the kings of Judah. (5.) Ch. 37, containing Jeremiah's reply to another message from Zedekiah, is later, belonging to the time when the siege was raised by the appearance of the Egyptians. Ch. 34, relating to the manumission of bondservants and their reduction to slavery again, is of the same date. When the siege was raised Jeremiah attempted to go to Anathoth, but was arrested and flung into a dungeon ($37^{15\text{ff.}}$). Zedekiah released him, and placed him in the court of the guard, where he remained till the city fell (38^{28}). In this place it appears he could speak to the people ($38^{1\text{ff.}}$), and persons from the outside had access to him (ch. 32). On account of his disheartening speeches to the people and soldiery, the officers had him let down into a cistern, from which he was liberated by Ebed-melech (ch. 38), who receives the promise $39^{15\text{ff.}}$. To the time after his rescue by Ebed-melech belongs his interview with Zedekiah $38^{14\text{ff.}}$*; but whether the incident of the purchase of the field at Anathoth (ch. 32) took place before or after his rescue is uncertain. To the time of his detention in the court of the guard belongs ch. 33, somewhat later than 32 ('the second time' 33^{1}), and probably chs. 30. 31, referring to the Restoration of Judah and Israel. 33^{14-26} are not yet in LXX, and undoubtedly the chapters are otherwise greatly glossed, though much in ch. 31 is original. Possibly the chs. 30–33 formed a separate collection (30^{2}), and the subject was one that invited expansion. Usually Jeremiah employs the terms 'Israel,' 'Ephraim' (twice *house of Jacob* 2^{4} 5^{20}); it is only in these chapters that the simple name 'Jacob' occurs ($30^{7.\,10.\,18}$ $31^{7.\,11}$ 33^{26}), for 10^{16} (51^{19}) is not original, and 10^{25} is doubtful. The phrase 'my servant Jacob' $30^{10.\,11}$ ($=46^{27.\,28}$) and much else reflects the language and ideas of Is 40 ff. (6.) 38^{28b} (RV) $39^{3.\,14}$–44 narrate the events subsequent to the fall of the city, and the history of Jeremiah in Egypt ($39^{1.\,2}$ seem out of place, and vv.$^{4-13}$ are wanting in LXX).

(7.) Chs. 46–51, prophecies against the nations. There are three questions connected with these prophecies: (1) their genuineness in whole (Driver, and in the main Kuen.), or in part (Gies., Corn.), or not at all (Stade, Wellh., Smend, Schwally); (2) the time in the prophet's life to which they belong if genuine or partially so; and (3) their original position in the book. (1) Chs. 50. 51 (apart from $51^{59\text{ff.}}$) are almost universally recognized to be of a later date than Jeremiah, and by another writer. With regard to 46–49 it may be urged in favour of their genuineness, in whole or in part, (*a*) that Jeremiah was conscious of being a prophet to the nations ($1^{5.\,10}$ $18^{9\text{ff.}}$ $27^{2\text{ff.}}$); and (*b*) that he is commanded to write his prophecies 'against all the nations' (36^{2}). It is doubtful, however, if such language as 36^{2} implies the existence of prophecies formally devoted to particular nations: it might be satisfied by such passages as 1–6 $9^{24\text{f.}}$ 12^{14-17}, and particularly by $25^{9\text{ff.}}$, and the enumeration (so far as original) of nations in 25^{15-26}. Jeremiah's own statement regarding former prophets, that they prophesied against many countries and against great kingdoms (28^{8}), forbids us to press the words of 36^{2}. If a genuine nucleus existed in 46–49 this would explain the later amplification, and how though amplified the prophecies continued to be ascribed to Jeremiah. On the other hand, the figure of giving the nations to drink of the fury of J″, and the enumeration of peoples in $25^{15\text{ff.}}$, might have suggested to some writer or writers the composition of the prophecies to give body to the idea of Jeremiah (cf. the relation of $51^{59\text{ff.}}$ to chs. 50. 51). Such lengthy oracles against peoples which, with the exception of Egypt, had no significance to Jeremiah or to the time, are little probable from him. Ch. 46^{1-12} is later than Carchemish, but such an exercise on a past event is scarcely to be expected from Jeremiah. 46^{13-28} might be a prophecy by Jeremiah in Egypt, though, of course, also it might be an expansion by another writer of some of his incidental threats against that country ($43^{10\text{ff.}}$); v.^{26b} reminds of Ezk, and vv.$^{27.\,28}$ are a repetition of $30^{10.\,11}$. It is wholly improbable that Jeremiah should have excerpted Is 15. 16, as has been done in the prophecy on Moab (48^{29-38}), and equally incredible that he should have copied Obadiah, or, as the case may be, a prophecy which is the basis of Obadiah, as has been done in the prophecy on Edom ($49^{7\text{ff.}}$). If Is 15. 16 were brought down in their present form to the post-exilic time (Duhm), the problem in regard to them would perhaps be the same as that in regard to Obadiah; but such a date has not been established. And it may be said in general that the current impression that Jeremiah is accustomed to cite or use his predecessors has little evidence in its favour. A nucleus of genuine elements in 46–49 is probably the most that can be assumed; whether the expansions be due to one hand or several may be difficult to say. Some peculiarities are common to the chs., *e.g.* הִפְנָה intrans. or with obj. unexpressed, $46^{5.\,21}$ (parallel to נוּם), 47^{3}, 48^{39} (obj. expressed), 49^{24} (parallel to נוּם), cf. 49^{8}, but see particularly Nah 2^{9}; the phrase חֶרֶב הַיּוֹנָה 46^{16} 50^{16}, cf. 25^{38} (so read). The purpose of the words, 'Here endeth the judgment of Moab' 48^{47} is obscure, cf. 51^{64} (both passages are wanting in LXX). It is curious that all the promises to the nations of restitution (46^{26} 48^{47} $49^{6.\,39}$) are wanting in LXX. (2) The date of the foreign prophecies, if genuine, would be after Carchemish; whether any parts of them stood in Baruch's roll cannot be ascertained. The prophecy on Elam is assigned to the beginning of the reign of Zedekiah (49^{34}). (3) On the original place of chs. 46–49 in the book see next section (iii.). (8.) Finally, ch. 52 is a historical extract, identical with 2 K 24^{18}–25^{30}, with the omission of 2 K 25^{22-26}. Ch. 52^{28-30} are not yet in LXX.†

iii. Hebrew and Greek Texts.—The differences between the Heb. and Gr. texts are greater in the Book of Jer than they are in any other book, even Job. (1) The Gr. text is much shorter than the Heb.—according to the calculation of

* Unless the reference to the 'house of Jonathan' (38^{26}) might imply that the interview took place after his first deliverance from the dungeon (37^{18-21}).

† On chs. 50. 51 cf. Budde, *Jahrb. f. deutsche Theol.* 1878; Driver, *LOT*^{6} p. 266 ff.; Kuen., *Onderzoek*^{2}, § 57; Gies., *Handkom.* 246 ff.; Nägelsbach, *Der Proph. Jer. u. Babylon*, 1850. On chs. 25. 46–49, Schwally, *ZAW*, 1888; Smend, *Religionsges.* p. 238 ff.; Bleeker, *Jeremiah's Profetieen tegen de Volkeren.*, Groningen, 1894.

Graf by about 2700 words, or one-eighth of the book. (2) In Heb. the prophecies against the nations stand at the end of the book (chs. 46–51), in the Gr. they are inserted between 25¹³ and 25¹⁵ (v.¹⁴ being wanting), and they are given in a different order from the Hebrew. Much in (1) was due to the Heb. MS on which the translator worked, which differed materially from our present Massoretic text. The difference (2) must be spoken of with less certainty : the place given to the prophecies against the nations may have been suggested by the translator's interpretation of 25¹³, and the order in which they stand may reflect something of the political situation of the time. But (3) a multitude of differences have arisen through the defective work of the translator himself, who was anything but equal to his task. The differences between the two texts were formerly explained by the hypothesis of two recensions—a shorter one, probably from the hand of Jeremiah himself, which circulated in Egypt ; and a longer one, the work of Baruch or others, which became the basis of the MT. But the general identity of the two texts, and the fact that some of the latest elements of the book are found in LXX, show that such a hypothesis is both unnecessary and false. Both texts reflect the same archetype ; but this archetype underwent a gradual process of expansion, and the process is reflected at an earlier stage (not necessarily an earlier date) in the MS or MSS at the basis of LXX, and at a more advanced stage in those at the basis of the MT.

(1) *Comparative value of the texts.*—In estimating the relative value of the Heb. and Gr. texts, one must compare them, *first*, in those parts of the book present in both texts ; *secondly*, in regard to those parts present in Heb. but wanting in Gr. ; comparison in regard to a third class of passages, those present in Gr. but wanting in Heb., though it might be interesting, is of less importance. That is, the comparative estimate must be in regard both to quality and quantity. Speaking generally, the MT is qualitatively greatly superior to the Gr. ; but, on the other hand, quantitatively the Gr. is nearer the original text. This judgment is general, admitting many exceptions,—that is, cases where the quality of the Gr. text is better, and its readings more original than the Heb., *e.g.* 2²⁰ 4²⁸ 11¹⁵ 16⁷ 23³³ 41⁹ 46²², and many more ; and also cases where, in regard to quantity, Heb. is to be preferred, the omissions in LXX being due to faults in the translator's MS, to his own oversight, or to his tendency to scamp and abridge. Every individual case of difference must be examined before a judgment can be pronounced. In regard to such large passages as 33¹⁴⁻²⁶ 39⁴⁻¹³, and even many minor ones, *e.g.* in chs. 25. 27–29, judgment will readily be given in favour of LXX, in which they are wanting ; but there is a multitude of other cases in which a decision is difficult. Of the four synonyms for ' destroy ' 1¹⁰, LXX has only three ; and again in 18⁷, where three of the synonyms occur, LXX has only two. The exclamation, ' temple of the Lord ' 7⁴, stands in Heb. thrice, in LXX twice ; so ' O earth ' 22²⁹, only twice in LXX. The words ' of hosts ' in the divine name are said to be wanting 56 times (2¹⁹ 6⁸ etc.), the parenthetical ' saith the Lord ' 64 times, and in ' Jeremiah the prophet ' the title *prophet* is usually absent. Now, when it is considered that LXX shows an undoubted tendency to abridgment, while the ideal of later Heb. style was fulness and roundness of phraseology, the two considerations puzzle the judgment and hold it in suspense. The title *the prophet* is probably in many cases a Heb. addition, the want of the synonym a Gr. abbreviation. It would not be just to charge the LXX translator

with arbitrary omission on a large scale. There are over 30 passages which are repeated in the book (some twice), and LXX contains all the repetitions with the exception of 7, and these 7, it is safe to say, were not in the translator's MS. (For list of repeated passages see Driver, p. 276 f. ; Kuen. § 58¹¹ ; and for those wanting in LXX, Kuen. § 58¹²).

(2) *Original place of chs.* 46 ff. — It is quite evident that prophecies of the compass of chs. 46–49 as they now exist could not have been contained in Baruch's roll. If only a genuine nucleus of them existed they might have followed ch. 25 in its original form and position, though the amplification of them would be more intelligible if they had existed in a separate form. If the prophecies were extant in their present compass when the book was redacted, we might suppose that, according to the analogy of Is and Ezk, they would be placed in the middle of the book after ch. 25. And this would have been their natural place, following the symbol in 25¹⁵ᶠ· and the enumeration of nations in 25¹⁸⁻²⁶, the nations named being in the main those to which the prophecies refer. The supposition that this was the original place of 46–49 is at least plausible, if nothing more. When the extensive passage chs. 50. 51 was introduced into the book at a later time, chs. 46 ff. were connected with it and transferred to the end of the book. The place of chs. 46–51 in LXX between 25¹³ and 25¹⁵ is quite unnatural, for the chapters should certainly have followed and not preceded the enumeration of nations in 25¹⁵⁻²⁶ to which they refer. It is probable that 46–51 occupied a place at the end of the book, as in Heb., even in the MS used by the LXX translator. Simultaneously with the reception of chs. 50. 51 or in consequence of it, various glosses were introduced, *e.g.* 25¹¹ᵇ⁻¹⁴, or at least v.¹²ᶠᶠ· (50¹ᵇ ; cf. 51⁶⁰ᵇ). In 25¹³ ' even all that is written in this book, which Jeremiah prophesied against all the nations,' LXX translator took the last clause to be independent, rendering, *That which Jeremiah prophesied against the nations.* The words thus became a title, and chs. 46 ff. were transferred from their former place and made to follow it. Neither is the order of the prophecies in LXX original ; the order in Heb. corresponds in the main to that of the nations enumerated in 25¹⁵⁻²⁶, and has all the marks of originality.

The translator from Heb. had many difficulties to contend with : the text had no vowels ; the letters do not appear to have been divided (in all cases at least) into words ; the vowel letters were sparsely written, and thus the plur. and sing. forms of the verb were identical ; MSS were badly written, similar letters like *d* and *r* being often confused ; there were contractions liable to be misunderstood ; Heb. was a dead language, the living Shemitic tongue being Aramaic ; and much else. The translator of Jer shows the usual faults of the Gr. version in an aggravated form. (*a*) He divides words wrongly (56 8¹⁸ 9⁵ 20⁹ 22²⁰ 31⁸ 46¹⁵). (*b*) He vocalizes wrongly (22³· ³⁴ 31 10²⁰ 31¹³). (*c*) When letters like *d* and *r* are confused in his MS, he has not sufficient knowledge to perceive the error (21⁶ 31⁵ 15¹² 31⁵ 49²²). (*d*) He renders proper names as appellatives and *vice versâ*, 8⁷ 21¹³ 31²¹ 46¹⁶· ²⁵ 49¹³· ²⁸· ³⁰ 51²⁷ (46¹⁶ 50¹⁶ חֶרֶב, חַיֹּנָה, μάχαιρα ἑλληνική). (*e*) His knowledge of the language is very deficient : an archaic suffix puzzles him (כֻּלֹּה is read כָּלֹּה 8⁶ 15¹⁰ 20⁷) ; much in the Heb. vocabulary is unfamiliar to him (מָגוֹר מִסָּבִיב) is rendered differently each time that it occurs, and generally referred to the root *gûr*, ' to sojourn ') ; and in syntax he supposes an adj. may stand before its noun (22³⁰ 46¹⁵ ?). (*f*) He makes arbitrary changes in person and number to a greater extent than usual in LXX (23⁰ 31⁸· ²⁰ 41⁷ 67 72⁵ 81⁸ etc.). (*g*) He is loose and hasty and without a sense of responsibility, often thinking it enough to give an average or approximate rendering of the original (71ᶠᶠ·). If he has wrongly put a sense on a word which will not harmonize with the rest of the verse he modifies the other words, or, if they be wholly intractable, omits them (21⁶ 4¹¹· ¹² 52⁶ 81⁸). In 29²⁵⁻²⁹ the sense is entirely missed. (*h*) It is scarcely due to purpose, but rather to his easy-going style of operation, that when a passage is repeated *verbatim*, his rendering of it in the second instance differs much from that in the first. (*i*) He shares the curious fancy of LXX translators for rendering by a word similar in sound to the Heb. (9⁵ חָךְ בָּתוֹךְ (sic) τόχος ἰπὶ τόχῳ, 31²¹ חמרורים τιμωρίαν (48³¹ ? 51²⁷ ۴). Whether in 46¹⁵ חָף (נִסְחַף) was rendered *Aπις is rather uncertain).

LITERATURE ON THE TEXT.—Spohn, *Jeremias vates e vers. Judæorum Alex. emendatus*, 1824 ; Kueper, *Jerem. librorum ss. interpres atque vindex*, 1837 ; Movers, *De utriusque recens. vatic. Jerem. indole et origine*, 1837 ; Wichelhaus, *De Jerem. versione Alexandrina*, 1847 ; Scholz, *Der Mass. Text u. die LXX Uebers. des Buches Jer*. 1875 ; Kühl, *Das Verhältniss der Massora zur Sept. im Jeremia*, 1882 ; Workman, *The Text of Jeremiah*, 1889 ; Streane, *The Double Text of Jeremiah*, 1896 ; also the *Comm*. of Graf, p. xl ff., and Giesebrecht, p. xix ff. ; Kuen., *Onderz*. § 58 ; cf. also Cornill's critical edition of the Heb. text in Haupt's *SBOT*.

iv. REDACTION OF THE BOOK.

—In the absence of all direct information, anything better than a more or less plausible hypothesis concerning the redaction of the book is not attainable. Perhaps three stages in its history can be traced. (1) The second roll of Baruch, belonging to the 5th year of Jehoiakim. There is every reason to suppose that this roll has in the main been preserved in the early part of the book. The contents of the roll were chs. 1–6. 7–10 (except 10¹⁻¹⁶), 11¹–12⁶, probably 14. 15. 16¹–17¹⁸, 25 in its original form, possibly 45 ; whether 18. 20⁷ᶠᶠ· belonged to the roll may be uncertain ; and the same must be said of 22¹⁰ᶠᶠ· and of any parts of 46–49 that may be supposed genuine. The roll, however, was in some cases broken up, and some parts certainly belonging to it (ch. 25) are now found after elements of a much later date, while elements of a later date appear inserted before or among parts belonging to it (127ᶠᶠ·). The roll was only one of the elements used in the redaction of the book, and it was not regarded as inviolable. We should hardly be right if we regarded our present book as a growth, the roll being the fundamental writing to which other prophecies were added as they successively came into existence, or if we supposed a series of successive redactions (Kautzsch, *Abriss*, p. 75 ; cf. Driver, p. 270). The present order of the contents of the book forbids such suppositions, e.g. 21¹¹–23⁸ as a collection is later than the fall of the city, while ch. 24 is of the beginning of the reign of Zedekiah ; chs. 30–33 as a collection also belongs to the Exile, while ch. 35 is of the reign of Jehoiakim. Such a shuffling of the contents, supposing them to have had originally a historical order, is quite improbable.

(2) The second stage was the actual redaction of the book. At some time, possibly not a great many years after the prophet's death, some person or persons undertook the work of gathering together all the fragments of his oracles and furnishing as complete a biography of him as possible. The biographical interest was perhaps the predominant one. All the available materials, the original roll and other existing sources, were used, and probably the compiler himself, either from his own knowledge or by inquiry, was able also to make considerable contributions. But how much belongs to sources ready to the compiler's hand, and how much is due to himself, it is impossible to discover. As has been already said, Jeremiah may have preserved jottings of his speeches, or some contemporary such as Baruch may have done so, and these may have lain before the editor ; or, in a number of cases the prophet's words may already have been set in a historical frame when they came into the compiler's hand. There appears to be something like collections in the book, e.g. chs. 18–20. 21–23. 27–29. 30–33, and the like, and some of these may have arisen at the hands of different persons during the Exile. There is nothing more likely than that a number of the historical passages, with the prophet's words enclosed in them, may be from the hand of Baruch, who continued with the prophet after the fall of the city and accompanied him to Egypt. But some of the narratives are probably due to other persons and some to the compiler. The various headings are from the hand of the compiler, but the inference from the identity of the heading in chs. 34. 35. 40. 44, that these historical passages are the work of the compiler (Kuen.), is scarcely cogent, for the same heading has been given to chs. 7 ff., which the compiler certainly did not write. From the promiscuous way in which such historical narratives as chs. 26. 36. 35 have been placed in the book, it may perhaps be inferred that these came as distinct and complete compositions into the redactor's hand. However much in the book may be due to Baruch, everything shows that he was not the editor. The date of the redaction cannot be strictly fixed. The reverence manifested for the prophet is no criterion of date, for this reverence, beginning after his death, continued to increase. Kuenen has suggested the second half of the Exile. The passage 2 K 25²³⁻²⁶ appears to be dependent on the fuller narrative, Jer 40⁷ᶠᶠ·, and this fact would imply that the Book of Jer was in existence before the Book of Kings was closed, about the end of the Exile (on the other hand, 39¹ᵇ· ²· ⁴⁻¹³ taken from 2 K 25 is a later interpolation). There is perhaps nothing in the Book of Jer which necessitates a later date, such passages as 10¹⁻¹⁶ and chs. 50. 51 having been introduced into the book after its redaction. There is no doubt much in chs. 46–49 that might be of the post-exilic period. The complexion of chs. 30–33 might also imply a lower date than the Exile, but the want of 33¹⁴⁻²⁶ in LXX shows that the amplification of these chs. went on after the book had been compiled. The redaction took place in Babylon or Palestine, not in Egypt.

(3) This Book of Jer thus edited is the archetype both of the Heb. and Greek. But this book underwent modifications, some passages being added and some amplifications of the text being introduced. This process of enlargement forms the third stage in the history of the book. (a) Some additions and insertions penetrated into all the MSS, e.g. chs. 50. 51. 52, 10¹⁻¹⁶ (except vv.⁶⁻⁸· ¹⁰), 16¹⁴· ¹⁵ 17¹⁹⁻²⁷, and much more. (b) From others the MSS at the basis of LXX remained free, e.g. 33¹⁴⁻²⁶ 39⁴⁻¹³, and much else, particularly in chs. 25. 27–29. This latter fact does not imply with certainty that all the additions in MT are later than LXX translation, because contemporary MSS may have had different histories even in the same country (treatment of MSS being so free), and particularly if circulating in different countries. The differences between the Heb. and Gr. might certainly be easier explained if we could suppose the MS or MSS on which LXX is founded carried early to Egypt. Egyptian Jews would probably occupy themselves less with the original text than those in Babylon or Palestine, and thus the MSS, even if transcribed, would more retain their primitive form. Amplifications of the text and interpolations really reflect the moods of religious life and hope, and this life was fuller in Palestine than in Egypt.

v. LITERARY STYLE.

— The literary style of Jeremiah can scarcely be spoken of, because, strictly speaking, we have no literature from him. The narrative pieces in the book are not from his own hand ; and even when fragments of his speeches are reported in these narratives, they have in many cases passed through the narrator's mind, and may have been somewhat modified. The presence of some or many characteristic phrases of Jeremiah in the reports is not proof of their literal fidelity. And in any case such reports are mere compends, in regard to which the question of style can hardly be raised. The only parts of the book on which a judgment in respect of style can be formed are the chapters dictated to Baruch, chs. 1-17, and any other passages which appear to come directly from Jeremiah's own hand. Even the dictated passages are mere outlines and skeletons; the prophet's object was to preserve and present to others the matter, the religious contents of his oracles,—he was little solicitous about the form. No doubt something of Jeremiah's literary manner will be reflected in these fragments, but they represent very inadequately what he was capable of as a writer. We have no literature from Jeremiah in the sense in which we have literature from Isaiah. The flowers of Jeremiah's diction and thought have reached us only after being cut and pressed; the bloom and fragrance yet remaining with them suggest faintly what they were when fresh. The monotonousness and repetition, both of ideas and language, of which writers complain, are owing in good degree to the fact that, in dictating his outline, it was the prophet's purpose to impress strongly certain great ideas, and the same ideas naturally carry with them the same language, though it will always remain a question how many of the repetitions are due to himself. The literary remains of Jeremiah differ from the writings of Isaiah in being formally less perfect: the poetical rhythm is not so regular, losing itself often in elevated prose. Yet even formally there is much true poetical parallelism, and there are many examples of the *Ḳinah* or Elegy, artistically beautiful and full of pathos, *e.g.* 9²⁰. ²¹ 13¹⁸ᶠ. ²⁰ᶠ. 18¹⁴ᶠ. 22⁶ᶠ. The language of Jeremiah wants the condensed energy of that of the earlier prophets. He belonged to a later literary age, and the progress of language is always towards analysis, gaining in lucidity, but losing in compression. Much of the power of the earlier prophets arises from the fact that their age was a creative one, and they project their religious conceptions with an energy and completeness that can never again be imitated. Jeremiah is their heir, their principles already run in his blood, and what in them was intellectual power is transmuted in him into spiritual life. So far as style can be spoken of in Jeremiah, his style perfectly reflects all the articulations of thought and all the hues of emotion of his mind. He was a nature characterized by simplicity, reality, pathos, tenderness, and a strange piety, but subject to his emotions, which were liable to rise into passions. His mind was set on a minor key, and his temper elegiac. And to all this his language is true. Could sadness be expressed in sadder words than these, 'The harvest is past, the summer is ended, and we are not saved'? His phrases haunt the ear: 'Before your feet stumble on the dark mountains.' 'Is there no balm in Gilead?' 'A voice was heard in Ramah.' 'If thou hast run with the footmen and they have wearied thee.' 'Surely I have heard Ephraim bemoaning himself.' 'Return, ye backsliding children.' The quaint simplicity of his words to God provokes a smile: 'O Lord, wherefore are all they happy that deal very treacherously?' Usually his address is lofty and touching: 'O the hope of Israel, the saviour thereof in time of trouble, why shouldst thou be as a stranger in the land?' (14⁸ᶠ. 16¹⁹ 17¹²ᶠᶠ.). In sombre realism he has no match among the prophets; witness such terrible passages as 15¹ᶠ. 4²³ᶠ. (cf. the symbol 25¹⁵ᶠ., and such descriptions as 5¹⁵ᶠ. 9¹⁷⁻²²). He was sent to be the prophet of doom and death, and his soul revolted against the task. He gloats over life, its human activities (32⁴³ᶠᶠ.), its sounds and mirth and all its music (7³⁴ 16⁹); and he recoils from death, and shudders as he sees the shadow enter in at the windows, and feels the awful silence, when there is no sound of a mill and no shimmer of a candle. There is one peculiarity which gives a charm to

his style, a certain unconscious dramatizing, when, after describing a situation, he makes those involved in it speak directly, without the word 'saying,' *e.g.* 2²⁵ 3²² 4¹⁹. ³¹ 6⁴. ⁵. ²⁴ 9¹¹⁻¹⁸ 10¹⁹ 11¹⁹ 12⁴. ⁵ 14¹⁷ 15¹⁵ 17¹².

Jeremiah's language has some marks of the later style: words in *-ûth* are not infrequent, and he begins to Aramaize; cases occur of *vav cop.* with perf., and the *hê* of direction is otiose (11³). Certain phrases and expressions are often repeated: *e.g.* *to break the yoke and burst the bands* (2²⁰ 5⁵); *to turn the back and not the face* (2²⁷ 18¹⁷); *to receive correction* (2³⁰ 5³ 7²⁸); *to come into mind* (עלה על לב 3¹⁶ 7³¹ 19⁵); *the evil of your doings* (4⁴ 21¹² 23². ²²); *great destruction* (שֶׁבֶר 4⁶ 6¹ 14¹⁷); the refrain, *shall I not visit for these things?* etc. (5⁹. ²⁹ 9⁹); *heal the hurt slightly* (6¹⁴ 8¹¹); the phrase, *rising up early, and sending, speaking*, etc. (הַשְׁכֵּם 7¹³. ²⁵ 26⁵ 29¹⁹); *to incline the ear* (7²⁴. ²⁶ 11⁸ 17²³); *the voice of mirth and gladness*, etc. (7³⁴ 16⁹ 25¹⁰); *at the time that I visit them* (6¹⁵ 8¹² 11²³ 23¹²); *terror round about* (6²⁵ 20³. ¹⁰); *over which my name has been called* (7¹⁰. ¹¹. ¹⁴. ³⁰); *the sword, the famine, and the pestilence* (with a variety of order, 14¹² 15³ 21⁷); and others. See Driver's full list, p. 275. It is doubtful if *to make a full end* (כָּלָה עָשָׂה) ought to be reckoned; it seems extraneous in 4²⁷ 5¹⁰. ¹⁸ (30¹¹ = 46²⁸). Neither should the contorted syntax 14¹ 46¹ 47¹ 49³⁴ be ascribed to Jeremiah. Peculiar are חָקִיר used of God (3¹²); נוֹאָשׁ *hopeless* ! in the mouth of the people (2²⁵ 18¹²); קְצוּצֵי פֵאָה *shorn on the temples* (9²⁵ [Eng.²⁶] 25²³); יְנָאֲמוּ נְאֻם (23³¹); ' חַלְלֵי *slain of J''* (25³³); the hiph. of חלם *dream* (29⁸); the phrase הִפִּיל תְּחִנָּה *present supplication* (38²⁶ 42⁹, Qal 36⁷ 37²⁰ 42², cf. Dn 9²⁰).

vi. SOME RELIGIOUS IDEAS.—The Book of Jer does not so much teach religious truths as present a religious personality. Prophecy had already taught its truths, its last effort was to reveal itself in a life. But though the truths in Jeremiah are old, they all appear in him with an impress of personality which gives them novelty. He is not to be read for doctrines in their general form on God and the people, but for the *nuances* which his mind gives them. Though he might not be aware of it, we can perceive that all his thoughts are coloured by the religious relation to God of which he was himself conscious.

(1) *Sin.*—In his earliest time it is the sin of the people that occupies his mind, their unfaithfulness to J''. They followed Him in the wilderness, but on entering Canaan they went far away from Him. Every class became untrue to the idea of its relation to Him. It is this *change* that seems inexplicable to the prophet. He sets it in all possible lights: 'What evil did your fathers find in me?' (2⁵). He contrasts the fidelity of the nations to their gods, which yet are no gods (2¹¹). At a later time he contrasts the fidelity of men even to the injunctions of their ancestor, such as the Rechabites (35¹⁴). The instinct which guides the migrations of the stork is strangely unerring; the instinct of man's heart, which should direct it to God, as strangely errs (8⁷, cf. 2³² 18¹³ᶠᶠ.). We understand Jeremiah's wonder at the change only when we hear him say what to his mind God is: 'They have forsaken the fountain of living water.' Isaiah crushed himself and crushed created man to the ground with his awful *Ḳadosh*; his word was true, but Jeremiah's 'the fountain of living water' seems to come nearer the fulness of truth. The words at any rate suggest the immediateness of the relation of man to God in religion. And it is this that Jeremiah insists upon, as Hosea and Isaiah had done before him. His charge is the unreality of men's religion; it is not with their real selves that they serve J'', and it is not J'' in His true being that they serve. Already in Josiah's days Jeremiah perceived how illusory his Reform was. Indeed it was doubtful if it had not made the condition of things worse. Men thought that when they worshipped at Jerusalem, and multiplied offerings there, they had done what J'' desired. It was a lie which was half a truth, and therefore the harder to fight. It is not certain that Jeremiah thought the lawbook altogether a good. People prided themselves on it, it was wisdom to have it;

they thought the possession of it put them right with God (8[8. 9]). Pharisaism and Deuteronomy came into the world the same day. The lawbook little satisfied the prophetic idealism. Jeremiah seeks to draw men's minds away from all that was external—sacrifices, temple, ark, and lawbook—to that which was inward and real. People spoke much of reform; he would have used another word: 'Break up the fallow ground, and sow not among thorns'; 'Circumcise yourselves to the Lord, and take away the foreskins of your heart' (4[4]); 'O Jerusalem, wash thine heart from wickedness' (4[14]). Sin is 'the stubbornness of the evil heart' (7[24] 5[23]). It is the heart that is good or ill. Man is the heart of man. Jeremiah probably has no general doctrine of human nature or its condition, though he perhaps expresses what is technically called *habit* when he says, 'The heart is deceitful above all things, and it is desperately sick; who can know it?' (17[9]). If not from nature, by practice men become incapable of good: 'Can the Ethiopian change his skin? then may ye also do good that are inured to do evil' (13[23], cf. 7[28] 8[4ff.]). Momentarily awoke by the prophet's appeals, the people become conscious of their inability, exclaiming, 'It is hopeless' (2[25] 18[12]). And more generally, 'It is not in man that walketh to direct his steps' (10[23]). Sin is individually universal; a man cannot be found in the streets of Jerusalem (5[1], cf. 8[6. 10]). No providences in God's hand can reform them; the furnace will not purify them; they have been tried, and they are found reprobate silver (6[27ff.]). Only the creative hand of God can change them; He will give them another heart, and put His law in their inward parts (24[7] 31[31ff.]). Though Jeremiah, like Hosea, begins by considering the people as a moral personality, and never loses hold of the idea of the nation (31[16. 28. 31-34]), his thoughts just referred to are virtually individualism.

(2) *God.*—In his doctrine of God Jeremiah agrees with his predecessors, but with a significant *nuance* of his own. J" is God alone, the gods of the nations are no gods (2[11] 16[19ff.]), and the Gentiles shall yet confess it. J" rules among the nations, giving them all to drink of the wine of His cup, and putting the world and all that dwell in it into the hand of Nebuchadnezzar (25[15ff.] 27[14ff.]). Like all later prophets, Jeremiah sees His power and Godhead manifested in nature: 'Are there any among the vanities of the heathen that can cause rain? or can the heavens give showers?' (14[22] 5[24]), particularly in that perpetual wonder the restraint of the raging sea (5[22]). These are external things. It is in that which He is to His people and His servants that J" is truly revealed, *e.g.* in His gracious designs with Israel: 'I thought how I shall put thee among the children! ye shall call me my Father' (3[19]), and in the joy which His service brings: 'Thy words were found and I did eat them, they were the joy and rejoicing of mine heart' (15[16]). It is in the passages where Jeremiah intercedes for himself or the people that he realizes most fully what J" is, 14[7ff. 19ff.] 17[12ff.], or when he gives a definition of what religion is: 'Let him that glorieth glory in this, that he knoweth me, that I am the Lord which exercise loving-kindness, judgment, and righteousness in the earth, for in these things I delight' (9[24]). But the conception of God receives a new shade in Jeremiah. His definition of man as the heart of man leads to a corresponding definition of God: J" is He who trieth the heart and the reins (11[20] 17[10] 20[12]). This definition is just the reflexion of Jeremiah's own experience. He does not infer that J" searches the heart from any general doctrine he holds of the divine omniscience; he reasons the other way: Because J" tries the heart, He is omniscient, 'Can

any hide himself in secret places that I shall not see him?' (23[23. 24]). Positively, Jeremiah expresses his idea of religion when he says, 'Blessed is the man that trusteth in the Lord, whose hope the Lord is' (17[5ff.]). The principle of religion is faith.

(3) *The Future.*—Jeremiah's first and continued conviction is that the nation is doomed to destruction. There is something inexplicable to us in this certainty. It might seem mediated by his profound sense of the national sin (4[14. 22ff.]), just as he was assured that his fellow prophets were false because of their ethical shallowness, and their healing the hurt of the people slightly (23[17] 28[8]). But then this difference of ethical standard between him and other prophets is equally inexplicable. His judgment, both of the prophets and the people, seems the unconscious reflection of his own religious relation to God. But he does not analyze; he knows his consciousness, and it is given directly by God. In his earliest days Judah seems to him a mass of perdition; a man could not be found in the streets of Jerusalem (5[1]); the furnace had failed to separate silver from lead—there was no silver (6[27ff.]). Yet it was impossible that God should make a full end of His people (ch. 32); and his hopes seem for the time placed on Israel of the North. Backsliding Israel was justified above treacherous Judah. And in the name of J" he proclaims to the north, 'Return, ye backsliding children, and I will heal your backslidings' (3[14. 22]); and his prophetic ear catches a voice from the bare heights, the weeping and the supplications of the children of Israel, 'Behold, we come unto thee, thou art the Lord our God' (3[21]). With the first captivity of 597 the prophet's judgment on Judah seems softened; there was hope for the nation in the captives, and he predicts their restitution: J" will give them an heart to know Him (24[6ff.]). And, finally, during the last times of the siege, when the destruction of the nation was at hand, he embraces both Judah and Israel in his promise of restoration (chs. 30–33). All antagonisms between him and the people were now over; his human feeling had ceased to struggle against the irrevocable decree of God, and he looked forward with composure to the city's fall. His composure and certainty of the future were but the reflexion of his own experience, as in the case of all OT saints (Job 19[25ff.], Ps 73[23ff.]). The relation to God of which he is conscious is indissoluble; it outlives all forms of national existence. Indeed, from Hosea downwards the prophets become more and more indifferent to form of a state, their ideal is that of a community with a right mind towards God. Jeremiah does not place reliance on the purifying trials of the Exile; his hope is in the creative hand of God, who will give the people a heart to know Him (24[7]), and write His law in their inward parts (31[31]). The true shepherd whom He will raise up to lead them shall be called *Jehovah Ẓidḳēnu,* 'the Lord is our righteousness' (23[5ff.]).

(4) *Jeremiah's Piety.* — There were pious men before Jeremiah, but the long drawn out struggle of his life revealed piety more than ever before. Very different judgments have been passed on his natural character. The lachrymose nature traditionally ascribed to him is based partly on the idea that he was the writer of the Lamentations, and partly on his own references to his tears. A different view is expressed by Darmesteter (*Les Prophètes,* 67), who says: 'During his 40 years of prophesying he preaches, he acts, he curses: he weeps little.' The contrasts revealed in his life have been epigrammatically expressed by calling him a figure 'cast in brass, dissolving in tears.' Probably his fundamental human characteristic was weakness. In those passages where he speaks of himself as a wall of brass against his opponents,

and where J" promises him victory over them, we see not a sense of strength but a feeling of weakness. They reflect what he feels he *must* be, but is conscious he is not, what J" *will* do for him, though it is not done. Isaiah was strong in himself; the divine strength came to him unconsciously as he threw himself into action, and was not distinguishable from his own. But Jeremiah was conscious, introspective, distinguishing between himself and God. The strength he had was from without, hence it was fluctuating and convulsive. In moments of conflict he was strong. When dragged before the princes it was given him what to speak (26$^{12ff.}$). He could run with the footmen, or even like Elijah with the chariots, and not be wearied; but when the conflict was passed and he took his life and history with him into hours of stillness and solitude, the tide of divine strength receded, and he was weakness itself.

On the one hand, he had let himself be induced to be a prophet. J" had revealed His mind to him, His verdict on the people, and His purpose, and he had entered into His mind, and stood on His side. But this looking at people and things, as might be said, from the standpoint of J" isolated him; he neither borrowed nor lent, married nor was a father, rejoiced with the joyful nor sorrowed with the sorrowing (16$^{1ff.}$). Besides isolating him, it brought persecution upon him. He felt the hardness of J"'s service. Gladly would he have laid his office at His feet. He would have been thankful had he never known the truth. He cursed the day of his birth, because his fellowship with J" isolated him from all other fellowship, and crushed down all that was human in him. For, on the other hand, he profoundly sympathized with the people. He was an Israelite indeed. Israel in him struggled against its doom. The dumb mind of the people found a voice in him. He interceded for it, and his intercession was just the resistance of his human heart to the idea of the nation's destruction. He palliated its offences, saying it was misled by the prophets (14^{13}). He expressed its better self in the confessions which he put into its mouth (14$^{7-9}$ 14$^{19ff.}$ 10$^{23.24}$). He wept over it (9^1 13^{17} 14^{17}). He was told, it is enough! He was in the cruellest dilemma. If he pleaded for the people it was to be false to J", to be false to his own convictions of truth, false to what he knew to be the irrevocable will of God. On the other hand, to threaten, above all to threaten with zeal for God, was treason against his own heart and against his people. Thus both God and men seemed to reject him. But his repulse by men drove him to God, and his repulse by God made him press closer to Him. And thus his life became a fellowship with God, his thoughts and feelings a dialogue between him and God.

LITERATURE.—On the life of the prophet: Valeton, *Viertal Voorlezingen*; Cheyne, *Jer., His Life and Times*, 1888; Marti, *Der Proph. Jer. von Anatot*, 1889; Wellhausen, *Isr. u. Jüd. Gesch.*[2] p. 141 ff.; Smend, *Religionsgesch.* 234 ff.; Cornill, *Der Isr. Prophetismus*; Davidson, *The Exile and the Restoration*. Commentaries: Ewald, 1868; Hitzig, 1866; Graf, 1862; Nägelsbach (in Lange), 1868; Keil, 1872; Streane ('Camb. Bible'), 1881; Cheyne ('Pulpit Comm.'), 1883; Ball and Bennett ('Expositor's Bible'), 1890, 1895; Giesebrecht ('Hand-Komm.'), 1894.

A. B. DAVIDSON.

JEREMIAS ('Ιερεμίας), 1 Es 9^{34}.—One of the sons of Baani who put away his 'strange' wife. The name corresponds to Jeremai in Ezr 10^{33}, who is mentioned among the sons of Hashum; it has been inserted out of its right place in 1 Es.

JEREMIEL.—The name of the archangel who is introduced in 2 Es 4^{36} as answering the questions of the righteous dead. AV has *Uriel*, the same name as that of the angel who was sent to instruct Esdras, 2 Es 4^1 5^{20} 10^{28}.

JEREMOTH (יְרֵמוֹת, יְרִימוֹת).—**1. 2.** Two Benjamites, 1 Ch 7^8 8^{14}. **3. 4.** Two Levites, 1 Ch 23^{23} 25^{22}, the latter called in 24^{30} Jerimoth. **5.** A Naphtalite, 1 Ch 27^{19}. **6. 7. 8.** Three of those who had married foreign wives, Ezr 10$^{26. 27. 29}$. In the last instance *Ḳerê* has וְרָמוֹת 'and Ramoth' (so AV). See GENEALOGY.

JEREMY.—The form in which the name of the prophet *Jeremiah* appears in both AV and RV of 1 Es 1$^{28. 32. 47. 57}$ 2^1, 2 Es 2^{18}, as well as in AV of 2 Mac 2$^{1. 5. 7}$, Mt 2^{17} 27^9. In the last three passages RV has *Jeremiah*. The form *Jeremy* is used also in both AV and RV in the title of the Epistle ascribed to the prophet in Bar 6^1.

JEREMY, EPISTLE OF.—A brief apocr. composition purporting to have been written by Jeremiah to the Jews who were about to be led, or had been led (so Syr. and 7 Gr. cursives), into Babylon (cf. Jer 29 [36]^3). The author forewarns them that the captivity, which is a visitation for sin, will continue for seven generations; and his serious purpose is to secure that in exile they may not be so impressed by gorgeous idolatrous ceremonial as to fall into apostasy. To effect this, he gives, in popular style, a detailed exposure of the stupidity of idolatry, which is partly an amplification of Jer 10$^{1-16}$, Is 44$^{9-19}$, but which also manifests an intimate acquaintance with many inane and vicious heathen practices.

There is a decided lack of logical sequence in the thoughts, but the vanity of idolatry is emphasized by a sort of refrain, ten times repeated at irregular intervals, and though in every case intentionally varied as to verbal expression, yet always conveying the one meaning. 'This shows that idols are not gods, therefore fear them not.' The thoughts are decidedly forceful, and will perhaps gain in cogency if we arrange them a little more logically, thus:—I. Idols need to be manufactured. They are made by a carpenter, acc. to *his* wish (^{45}) [verses from RV throughout], covered with gold and silver (^{8}), and decked with garments (^{11}). II. They are devoid of perception. They cannot speak (^{8}), see (^{19}), hear howlings of priests (^{32}), or hear prayer (^{41}). III. They have no powers of self-conservation. They cannot wipe the dust from their face (^{13}) or eyes (^{17}), or the rust from their ornaments (^{24}), nor can they feel the smoke (^{21}). They cannot eat (^{27}). They are powerless against theft from their person ($^{10. 33. 57}$), against war ($^{48. 56}$), and fire (^{55}). They cannot rise when they have fallen, or straighten themselves when awry (^{27}). They cannot save their garments from moths (^{12}), or their wooden interior from decay (^{20}). IV. They are impotent for the discharge of their functions as gods. They bear a sceptre, but cannot rule (^{14}); a sword and axe, but cannot kill (^{15}). They cannot give wealth (^{35}), or rain (^{53}); much less can they show signs (^{67}) and restore the blind (^{37}) or the dumb (^{41}). They cannot set up one king and put down another ($^{34. 53. 56. 66}$), or deliver from injustice and death (^{38}), or even give long life to those who made them (^{46}). V. They are indifferent to ethical qualities. They requite neither good nor evil (^{34}). They punish not the perjurer (^{35}), or even the priest who robs his god to feed his lust (^{11}). They do not redress wrong (^{54}), or show mercy to the widow and the fatherless (^{38}); nay, they sanction systematic prostitution (^{43}). VI. They are thus the least useful of all things. A cup, a door, a pillar has its use (^{59}), and so have the sun and moon (^{60}), lightning and wind (^{61}), clouds (^{62}) and fire (^{63}); 'yea, even the beasts are better than they' (^{68}). Then, with rare irony, the author compares an idol to a 'scarecrow' (^{70}); impotent to protect, but deluding the imagination; and, in conclusion, says, 'Better is the man that is just and has no idols, but (adds Syr.) waits on the Lord God,' than the most sumptuous idolater.

Authorship.—The evidence that it was *not* written by Jeremiah is threefold. (1) It was manifestly composed in Greek. There are a few Hebraisms, as, *e.g.*, the imitation of infin. absol. in ἀφομοιωθέντες ἀφομοιωθῆτε (v.^{4}), and the repeated use of fut. for pres. freq., but they are such as are inseparable from Hellenistic Greek. (2) The style is quite below that of a prophet of Israel. The mind of the writer is saturated with the Bk. of Jer (cf. Jer 5^{24} with v.^{6}, 10^3 with v.^{45}, 10^8 with v.^{4}, 22^{28} with v.^{17}, 48^{37} with v.^{51}), but the style is inferior. As Ewald says, 'He only succeeds in writing like a speaker who proves and exhausts his subject from every point of view; he shows not the remotest movement towards prophetic flight.' (*HI* v. 479). (3)

The statement that the captivity should continue 'seven generations,' points away from Jeremiah towards one who deplored the long exile, and wished to believe it of divine appointment.

We believe the Ep. to have been written before 2 Mac. We cannot think as do Fritzsche, Schürer, Gifford, and others, that when 2 Mac 2² says that 'Jeremiah charged the exiles not . . . to be led astray in their minds when they saw images of gold and silver and the adornment thereof,' there is no allusion to our Epistle. The further vagaries as to the altar and the ark (2 Mac 2⁴⁻⁶) are not said to be 'in the *same* writing,' as AV (so Gifford), but ἐν τῇ γραφῇ, *i.e.* 'in' what the writer considered 'Scripture,' 'the records' of v.¹. The most probable supposition is, that the author lived in Egypt in the 1st cent. B.C., and that, deeply concerned lest his brethren should be led astray by the imposing ritual of idolatry, and feeling that additional force would be given to his warnings if he put them into the mouth of Jeremiah, he wrote his diatribe on the idolatry of Egypt as if it were intended for Babylon. He may have lived in Babylon in his youth, and there gained his acquaintance with the deification of prostitution (⁴³), to which Herodotus also testifies as occurring in the temple of Beltis (i. 199); but v.¹⁹ as clearly corresponds with Hdt.'s description (ii. 62) of the 'feast of lights' at Sais. The slightly inflated style of the Ep. is thoroughly Alexandrian. The fondness for assonance and for long compound words may be illustrated from περιάργυροι, περίχρυσοι, περιελοῦνται, περικείμενοι (⁵⁶ f.) and ἐξαποσταλέν, ἄνωθεν, ἐξαναλῶσαι (⁶⁶).

Canonicity.—Our Ep. is included in the Gr. canon, and is found in all Gr. codices of OT, except the cursives 70, 96, 229. In Syr.-Hex. it follows La, and this claims to have been tr⁴ from Origen's *Hexapla*. Indeed, Origen (inadvertently, as we think) places it in the list of the Heb. canon (cf. Eusebius, *HE* vi. 25). The uncials A B Q exhibit the same order as Syr.-Hex., as do also all the patristic lists that refer to it (see BARUCH). In Lat., Syr., and some edd. of LXX, Ep. Jer is found as Bar 6; and this is followed by Luther's Bible and other 16th cent. edd. as well as in AV and RV. Its canonicity was not called in question in the Christian Church before Jerome, who called it ψευδεπίγραφος (*Prol. in Jer.*). Theodoret passed it by; and also Hilary, though in his *Prol. in Ps.* 15 he has enumerated it in the Canon; but Tertullian quotes, as from Jer, v.⁴, about the carrying of gods on men's shoulders (*Scorp.* c. 8); and Cyprian (*On the Lord's Prayer*, c. 5) quotes v.⁶ as the suggestion of the Holy Spirit to Jeremiah, 'In the heart, O God, ought we to worship thee.'

The Text and Versions.—The Ep. is found entire in the Gr. uncials A B Q, while Γ contains 7b–24a. The differences between these MSS are comparatively unimportant. (See Swete, *OT in Gr.* 379–384; and, for description of MSS, vii.–xi.). There are about 20 Gr. cursives, some of whose various readings are given by Ceriani. Speaking generally, these cursives divide themselves into two classes. One half are thought by Field to represent the Lucianic recension (Origen's *Hex.*, Proleg. c. ix.), the other half are often found in agreement with Q.

The *Syriac* is a very free rendering of Greek. An arrangement and tr. of the VSS in στίχοι, in parallel columns, discloses that in little more than one-third of the lines does Syr. accurately represent Gr., though the last 12 verses are almost a verbatim trⁿ. Some of the more important variations are: 'Seventy years' (³) for 'seven generations'; 'An axe in his left' (¹⁵); 'As a man condemned by the king, so are their *arms* extended; [thus Walton, but Lag. 'courts'], 'Their heart is *foolish and erring*' (²⁰); 'ravens' for 'birds' (²²); 'eagerly eat' for ταριχεύουσι (²³); stones *of demons* in the mountains' (³⁸); 'before the gate,' in place of τὸν Βῆλον (⁴¹); 'They are *not* like crows which fly in the air' (⁵⁴). The only important omission is that of the 'door' and the 'pillar' in v.⁵⁹.

The *Syro-Hexaplar*, given in Ceriani's *Mon. Sacr. et Prof.* . 1, is in the main a slavishly literal trⁿ of the text of B, often in defiance of Syr. idiom; as in vv.³¹·⁴⁵. Its variations are few. We may mention, 'swallows and *other* birds' (²²), so ⁸⁸; 'weakness' for 'shame' (²⁶), so ⁸³; 'in their temples the priests *sit*' (³¹), as if καθίζουσι, with Q and its cursives; 'nor rescue the

wronged' (⁵⁴), as if ἀδικούμενον, with A and the Lucianic cursives; and 'to *devastate* the mountains' (⁶³), as if ἐξερημῶσαι, with Q and its cursives.

The *Vulg.* also adheres closely to Gr. text. Its chief deviations are in vv.⁸⁻¹¹·²⁰·⁴¹·⁵⁴, where it despairs of Gr. and makes a sense of its own. It also reads 'exquiram' (⁷) for ἐκζητῶν; 'as a dead man carried to a grave' for ὡς ἐπὶ θαν. ἀπ. (¹⁷); 'decerpentes' for ταριχεύουσι (²⁷), so Syr.: 'olive stones' for 'bran' (⁴³), and 'gloriabatur' for μιχρήσεται (⁵⁹).

LITERATURE.—Gifford in *Speaker's Apocr.* vol. ii.; Bissell in Lange's series; Zöckler, *Apokr. in Kgf. Kom.* 1891; Ewald, *Die jüngsten Propheten*, 1868; Fritzsche, *Handbuch z. d. Apokr.* 1851; Reusch, *Erklär. d. Buchs Baruch*, 1853; Reuss, *AT*, vol. vii. 1894.

J. T. MARSHALL.

JERIAH.—The chief of one of the Levitical courses, 1 Ch 23¹⁹ 24²³ (both יְרִיָּהוּ) 26³¹ יְרִיָּה, AV, RV **Jerijah**). See GENEALOGY.

JERIBAI (יְרִיבַי).—One of David's heroes, 1 Ch 11⁴⁶.

JERICHO [יְרִיחוֹ and יְרֵחוֹ, the latter uniformly (12 times) in Pent., 2 K 25⁵, and in Ezr, Neh, Ch; the former elsewhere; * the form יְרִיחֹה occurs once (1 K 16³⁴). The etym. and meaning are doubtful, although Gesenius (*Thes.*) gives the latter as 'place of fragrance,' from root רוח, while Sayce (*EHH* 250) makes it = 'city of the moon-god' (*yāreāh*). LXX Ἱεριχώ, indeclinable, both with and without fem. art.; NT Ἱεριχώ, once (Lk 19¹) with fem. art.; Vulg. *Jericho*, indecl.; Arab. *er-Riha* or *Riḥa*].—An important city in the Jordan Valley situated over against Nebo (Dt 32⁴⁹), and called the City of Palm Trees (Dt 34³). It was the first city to oppose the progress of the children of Israel after they had crossed the Jordan. It had its wall (Jos 2¹⁵), and its gate, which was closed at dusk (2⁵). Like all the Can. cities of the time, it was ruled over by a king (2³). The wealth of the place is inferred from the description of the spoil taken: vessels of brass and of iron are mentioned, and from the silver and gold Achan was able to sequester 200 shekels of silver and a wedge of gold of 50 shekels weight, as well as a goodly Babylonish garment (7²¹). We find no such rich record of spoil in the accounts of the capture of the other cities in this campaign. While the children of Israel were still encamped at Shittim on the other side of Jordan, Joshua sent two spies to investigate the state of the country as far as J. (2¹ff.). Arrived at that place, they lodged at a house on the town wall, belonging to one Rahab, a prostitute. Their errand was suspected, and news was brought to the king, who sent messengers to Rahab's house to demand that she give up the spies. In the meantime she had hidden them under the stalks of flax which were laid out on the roof to dry, and when the messengers arrived she declared that the spies had left the city at dusk, and she sent the men off on a false chase as far as the fords of the Jordan. Returning to the spies on the roof, she told them of the terror Joshua's approach had inspired, and begged that, in return for her kindness to them, they would agree to save her and her family alive in the coming troubles. This they swore to do, on condition that she preserved secrecy. That her house might be recognized she tied a scarlet thread in her window, from which she let them down with a rope, advising them to hide in the mountains. There they escaped (probably hiding in the cavern-pierced cliffs of Quarantania), and remained for three days, till their pursuers had come back. Then returning to Joshua, they gave a report which greatly encouraged the leader.

After crossing the Jordan, the Isr. encamped in the 'east border of J.' at Gilgal (Jos 4¹⁹), celebrating the passover in the 'plains of J.' This solemn ceremony was doubtless held in full view

* See Driver, *Deut.* p. lxxxix f.

of the city. While near J., Joshua saw the Captain of the Lord's Host (5[13]). From his speech before his death we gather that a preliminary skirmish preceded the siege, for he says, 'Ye came unto J., and the men of J. fought against you' (24[11]). The siege itself was extremely strict: 'none went out and none came in' (6[1ff.]). Joshua having received his commands from the Lord, delivered them to the people. They were to encompass the city once a day for six days, and on the seventh day seven times. The order of march was as follows: first came the armed men, then seven priests with trumpets of rams' horns; immediately behind the priests was borne the ark of the Covenant; and then followed the rear. The first day, having encompassed the city in silence, they returned to lodge in the camp. This was repeated for five days. On the seventh they rose very early and marched around the city seven times, but on the seventh time, when the priests blew with their trumpets, Joshua said to the people, 'Shout, for the Lord hath given you the city.' As they shouted, the wall fell down flat before them, and the people at once entered the city on every side, 'each man straight before him, and they took the city.' By special command of Joshua, Rahab and her family were saved from the general slaughter of man and beast that ensued, according to the promise she had received from the spies. Her family continued to live on in Israel, and the name Rahab occurs in the genealogy of our Lord (Mt 1[5]) as the mother of Boaz. J. was burned and everything in it, except the silver and gold, and the vessels of brass and iron, which were reserved for the treasury of the Lord's house. The disobedience of Achan to the Lord's command, that the people should reserve nothing for themselves, resulted in a terrible punishment. The defeat of the Israelites at Ai was ascribed to the fact that the accursed thing was touched. By a process of elimination the crime was traced to Achan, and he and all his family were stoned with stones and burned with fire (Jos 7[1ff.]).

Some of the Mohammedans of the country give a distorted account of the taking of J., confusing it with another scene in Joshua's life. It is said that a great Imam tried to take the city, but so difficult was the task of demolishing the walls that the work was not completed when darkness compelled the besiegers to stop. In the morning the walls had sprung up again, and the siege had to be recommenced. This went on for several days, when finally the Imam caused the sun to stand still, and thus, the day being lengthened, the destruction of the city was completed. This may not represent an early local tradition, as the plains were covered with monasteries when the Arabs took the land, and the Mohammedans very probably confused the various Biblical accounts they heard from the monks.

Not only was J. utterly destroyed, but Joshua pronounced a solemn curse on the man who should rebuild it, prophesying misfortune to his children: 'He shall lay the foundations thereof in his first-born, and in his youngest shall he set up the gates of it' (Jos 6[26]). In 1 K 16[34] we are told how this curse fell upon Hiel the Bethelite, who in the days of Ahab rebuilt the city. We infer that between these two periods the site was unoccupied, but that it continued to be known by its old name is proved by the facts that in the partition of the land J. was assigned to Benjamin (Jos 18[21]), and that David's messengers, after being maltreated by the Ammonites, were told to 'tarry in J. till your beards be grown' (2 S 10[5], 1 Ch 19[5]). Notwithstanding the fulfilment of the curse, the city became again inhabited, for, on the complaint of the 'men of the city' that the water was naught and the ground barren, Elisha healed the waters by casting salt in the spring (2 K 2[19]). There was also a settlement of the sons of the prophets at the place, who had at their command fifty strong men, whom they sent on a vain search for Elijah, when

he had been carried up into heaven from the other side of Jordan (2[16]). After this the place is mentioned several times. When Pekah, king of Israel, made his raid on the southern kingdom, taking many captives, these were released by order of the prophet Oded, and taken to J., 'the city of palm trees' (2 Ch 28[15]). Zedekiah, fleeing from Jerus. before the forces of Nebuch., was taken in the plains of J. (2 K 25[5], Jer 39[5]). In the list of returned captives (Ezr 2[34]-Neh 7[36]) the children of J. are put down at 345. These restored exiles evidently took up their abode on the old site, for in Neh 3[2] we read that the 'men of Jericho' had their share in rebuilding the walls of Jerus. Later on it was fortified by the Syrian general Bacchides (1 Mac 9[50]).

In the time of our Lord, J. had become an important place, owing to the partiality shown by the Herodian family to the city. Josephus describes the place with enthusiasm (*Wars*, IV. viii. 2–3). The city lay 150 stadia from Jerus. and 60 from the Jordan. *1 stadia = 600 ft.* It was situated in a plain, divided in the middle by the river, and flanked on either side by high mountains, of which the western range overhung the town. Palm trees abounded in the plain, those near the Jordan being the richest. In summer the climate was so hot that no one cared to come near it, but in winter the air was so mild that the inhabitants went about with linen clothing when snow covered the rest of Judea. He speaks at length of a fountain which was situated near the old city taken by Joshua, and which was healed by Elisha. He claims unusual powers of irrigation for these waters, which had only to flow lightly over the soil to make it fruitful, and which watered a plain 70 furlongs long by 20 broad, fertilizing gardens thickly set with trees, which produced balsam and myrobalanum. The palm trees were of many kinds, one yielding an excellent honey. Such was the luxuriance and rarity of the vegetation that the author declares the place might well be pronounced divine, and challenges a comparison with any other climate in the whole earth. Strabo (xvi. 2) likens the plain surrounded by mountains to a theatre, and corroborates Josephus' account of its fertility, declaring that the revenues from the balsam (from which medicine was extracted for the head and eyes) and from other plants was great.

When Pompey visited Pal. and endeavoured to clear the land of robbers, he destroyed two of their strongholds, Threx and Taurus, which commanded the approach to J. (*ib.*). After Jerus. was taken by Pompey, Gabinius, the Rom. general, divided the country into five parts, making J. one of the seats of Assembly (Jos. *Wars*, I. viii. 5). When Herod was appointed at Rome to be king of the Jews, and before he was installed in Jerus., his allies plundered J., finding the houses full of all sorts of good things (*Wars*, I. xv. 6). Later he farmed from Cleopatra the revenues of the regions about the city, which had been granted her by Antony (*Ant.* XV. iv. 2), and fortified above the town a citadel, a building fine and strong, which he called Cypros in honour of his mother, and built a city to the north of J., which he named Phasaelis after his brother (*Wars*, I. xxi. 9). J. was important enough to have its amphitheatre, for we read that from this place Salome announced to the assembled soldiers the news of the death of Herod, which had taken place in the city, though he had given orders that he should be buried at Herodium (*Wars*, I. xxxiii. 8). After his death, his ex-slave Simon, aspiring to make himself king, burned down the royal palace (*Ant.* XVII. x. 6), but this was magnificently rebuilt by Archelaus, who also accomplished important work in irrigating the plain (*Ant.* XVII. xiii. 1). In the time of Josephus (*Wars*, III. iii. 5) Judæa was divided into eleven parts, of which Jerus. was the chief, and one of which was Jericho. When Vespasian approached J. the citizens fled to the mountains (*Wars*, IV. viii. 2). He erected a citadel in the place, and set a garrison (*ib.* IV. ix. 1). Whether Josephus refers to the destruction of J. or Gerasa in this section is not clear, but we have the statement of Jerome that, at the time when Jerusalem was taken, J. was captured and destroyed on account of the perfidy of its citizens (*Onomasticon*).

J., however, still preserved its magnificence when our Lord visited it. His baptism in the Jordan occurred not far off. The hill of Quarantania, to the immediate west of the city, is pointed out as the traditional site of the Temptation. At the end of His ministry, when He was on His way from Galilee to Jerus., He passed through J., and there healed a blind man (Mk 10[46] [name given Bartimæus], Lk 18[35]), or acc. to Mt 20[29ff.] two blind men. At this same time He visited the house of Zacchæus the publican, whose eagerness to see the Lord had led him to climb a sycomore tree, as he was short of stature. The account of his conversion is one of the most graphic in the gospel history (Lk 19[1ff.]). Travellers to-day between Jerus. and J. have to be accompanied by an escort, to prevent their 'falling among thieves,' who have infested this route both before and ever since the Good Samaritan came to the relief of the man in the parable (Lk 10[30]).

We are told by Jerome (*Onom.*) that after its destruction by the Romans, J. was rebuilt a third time, but he does not say when. That the place was inhabited in the time of Origen we infer from the fact of his discovery of some valuable biblical MSS there (Eus. *Eccl. Hist.* vi. 16). This third city existed in Jerome's day as well as the ruins of the other two. It became an Episcopal See, and its bishops begin to be mentioned in A.D. 325; the last reference is to Gregorius, who was present at the Synod of Jerus. A.D. 536. The sacred sites began to be pointed out early in the 4th cent. The Bordeaux Pilgrim (A.D. 333) was shown the sycomore tree of Zacchæus on the right of the road leading to the town from the west. A mile and a half from the town was pointed out the site of the old city taken by Joshua, close to the fountain of Elisha, immediately above which was the house of Rahab. Justinian restored a hospice in J., and a church of the Mother of God (Procopius, *de Ædif.* 5. 9). Theodosius (A.D. 530) visited the fountain of Elisha, which he places 2 miles from the town, and in this latter was shown the house of Rahab, the site evidently having been shifted since the time of the Bordeaux Pilgrim. Antoninus Martyr (A.D. 570) found the walls of the town overthrown by an earthquake. The house of Rahab was still standing, and had been converted into a hospice and oratory, probably the work of Justinian referred to above. At the time of Arculf's visit (A.D. 670) the town was in ruins; only the house of Rahab was standing, but roofless. The Venerable Bede (A.D. 720) describes a similar state of things. Hence the town was in a ruinous condition for at least a century and a half, but by the end of the 6th cent. many churches and monasteries had sprung up on the surrounding plains. Besides the church at Gilgal, Arculf speaks of one on the spot where Christ was supposed to have left His garments at the time of His baptism, and of the monastery of St. John, also near the Jordan. Establishments were dedicated to St. Panteleemon, St. Calamon, St. Chrysostom, St. Eustochium, and others. At the time of the Crusaders many of these were repaired and others constructed. Under the Arabs the town again rose to importance, as is proved by the many references of the Mohammedan geographers beginning in the 9th cent. (see *Palestine under the Moslems*, by Guy Le Strange). Ya'kubi (A.D. 874) speaks of Riha as the capital of the Ghôr, the cleft of the Lower Jordan. Mukaddasi (A.D. 985) says that this city possessed many villages in the plain, which produced much indigo, and many palm and banana trees. Edrisi (A.D. 1154) mentions Ariha, Beisan, and Amta as the finest of the cities of the valley of the Ghôr. When the Crusaders conquered the land, the plain of J. was granted to the Holy Sepulchre, but in A.D. 1111 Arnulfus, the Patriarch of Jerusalem, was blamed for assigning to his niece this district, with its annual revenues, which amounted to 5000 pieces of gold (William of Tyre, xi. 15). Later it again fell into ecclesiastical hands, as it was assigned in A.D. 1138 to a convent at Bethany (*ib.* xv. 26). But by the 13th cent. the town itself had sunk to small dimensions. The square tower which may be seen to-day near the modern village of er-Riha was found by Willebrand (A.D. 1211) in a ruinous condition. Brocardus (A.D. 1230) says that the wretched town had scarcely eight houses, and that all the monuments of the sacred places were destroyed. Ricaldus, writing about the same time, calls the place 'quasi deserta.' However, the plains were at this time richly cultivated. According to the Moslem Yakut

(A.D. 1225) the finest sugar of the Ghôr was made at J.; palm trees and bananas abounded. Jaques de Vitry (cap. 53) also refers to the fields of sugar-cane. The ruins to the west of 'Ain es-Sultan, with the connecting aqueducts, appear to date from the Crusading period.

The modern er-Riha is a miserable village, containing about 300 swarthy inhabitants, possibly the descendants of the puny race called by Arculf Canaanites, who dwelt in his time on the plain. The rich patches of barley and wheat, with the gardens of the ecclesiastical establishments, give a hint of the possibilities of fertility which were so amply realized in former days. The level of the village is 900 ft. below the Mediter., and the flora and fauna of the plain differ largely from those of the rest of Pal., some species not being found nearer than the Asiatic and African tropics. A dozen isolated palms represent the splendid groves of the past. The *Zakkûm* (*Balanites Ægyptiaica*), identified by some with the *Myrobalanum* of Josephus, still abounds; also the acacia, and trees of the *Zizyphus* species, called in Arabic *Sidr* or *Dom*. A handsome Russian hospice now stands near the ruined tower mentioned by Willebrand, and there is a small Greek church. Two good hotels accommodate travellers, who may now make the journey from Jerus. by carriage-road, and continue their drive over the plain to the Jordan and the Dead Sea. J. contains only a few plots of freehold, as in recent times it has become the private property of the Sultan, together with many other parts of the Jordan Valley.

All authorities are agreed that the site of the Can. city is at Tell es-Sultan, above 'Ain es-Sultan (Elisha's fountain), one and a half miles from modern Jericho. As we have seen, Josephus places the old city near the fountain, and so does the Bordeaux Pilgrim, who gives the distance from the J. of his day as one and a half miles as above, which distance would do equally well if we identify the latter with the ruins near the pass to be mentioned later. Theodosius makes the distance 2 miles. This mound is 1200 ft. long from N. to S., and the larger part of its area is 50 ft. in height, measured above the fountain at the E., but not so high on the western side, as the original ground slopes from W. to E. Rising from the top of the mound along its edges are four superimposed mounds, the highest being some 90 ft. above the fountain. Near the base of the mound, above the spring, a hollow has been recently scooped out, revealing an ancient mud-brick wall *in situ*. The pottery found strewn over the mound belongs, as a rule, to pre-Roman times, and some pre-Israelitish ware occurs. The superimposed mounds may indicate later fortifications, but the accumulation of 50 ft. of débris below them, by analogy with the excavated mounds of Hissarlik and Tell el-Hesy (see LACHISH), probably represents the alternate growth and decay of the town for several centuries. Hence systematic excavations through the base of the mound would doubtless bring to light the remains of the pre-Israelitish city. On natural grounds, the place, with its abundant supply of water, would have been chosen by the first builders. From one and a half to two miles west of modern J., on the south bank of the Wady el-Ķelt, near the mouth of the pass, there are abundant remains of a city. An unobservant traveller might not notice them, as the houses are ruined down to the soil, but the ground-plans remain, and often the four sides of a room are quite plain. A large pool, called *Birket Mûsa*, is in the neighbourhood. The character of the pottery with which these ruins are strewn indicates the Roman site. This identification is favoured by the probable identification of the site of *Beit Jubr*, a ruined fort on the south side of the Jerus. road, commanding the ascent from the J. plain, with the fort Cypros, which Herod built *above* J.; as well as by the fact that the aqueducts in the Wady el-Kelt, two of which were constructed to bring water to this site, appear to be Rom. work (*PEF Mem.* vol. iii. p. 173). Similar ruins north of 'Ain es-Sultan suggest that Roman Jericho may have been very extensive, occupying both sites, with detached villas between, as there are signs of building at many points in the intervening fields. The settlement of the Crusaders seems to have been at the modern er-Riha, about 2 miles from the pass. In the vicinity of J. the remains of five old monastic establishments may be visited. In the precipices of Ḳuruntul (Quarantania) there are hermits' caves, with chapels adorned with frescoes. The monastery of St. John, near the traditional place of baptism, built by Justinian, and rebuilt by the Crusaders, has again been restored, but traces of the old work remain. The identification of Ḳusr el-Hajlah is not sure. Tell Mogheifir probably represents the ancient St. Eustochium, mentioned by Willibald in A.D. 721 as being in the middle of the plain. At *Khurbet el-Mifjir*, north-east of 'Ain es-Sultan, are the ruins of a splendid monastic establishment. Most picturesque of all is the convent of Ḳelt, clinging to the crags above the Wady el-Ḳelt. This has been recently restored, but some of the old frescoes remain. Further down in the valley the cliffs immediately above the stream are pierced with hermits' caves, which can be approached only by ladders. They are still inhabited, but their nicely painted wooden doors produce an incongruous effect in the midst of the wild surroundings.   F. J. BLISS.

JERIEL (יְרִיאֵל for יְרוּאֵל ' founded of El,' cf. יְרִיָּה).— A chief of Issachar, 1 Ch 7². See GENEALOGY.

JERIJAH, 1 Ch 26³¹.—See JERIAH.

JERIMOTH (יְרִימוֹת).—**1. 2.** Two Benjamites, 1 Ch 7⁷ 12⁵. **3. 4. 5.** Three Levites, 1 Ch 24³⁰ (called in 25²² **Jeremoth**) 25⁴, 2 Ch 31¹³. **6.** A son of David and father of Rehoboam's wife, 2 Ch 11¹⁸. See GENEALOGY.

JERIOTH (יְרִיעוֹת) occurs in a genealogy in 1 Ch 2¹⁸, where the only thing that is certain is that MT is corrupt (see Kittel's note in *SBOT*). It is possible that we ought to read with Wellhausen בַּת־יְרִי ' daughter of Jerioth' for אֶת־יְרִי. See, further, GENEALOGY, IV. 35 *a*, note.

JEROBOAM (יָרָבְעָם prob. 'may he plead the people's cause,' Ἱεροβοάμ).—**1.** 1 K 11²⁶⁻⁴⁰ 12¹⁻14²⁰, 2 Ch 10²ᶠᶠ· 11¹⁴⁻¹⁶ 12¹⁵ 13, son of Nebat and Zeruah, an Ephraimite of Zeredah, first king of Israel after the disruption, reigned 22 years, B.C. 937–915. Jeroboam's career began early in Solomon's reign (cf. 1 K 11²⁷ with 9¹⁵ 3¹); the king, recognizing the young man's abilities, appointed him commissioner for the house of Joseph. He used his position to plot against his master; and, when Solomon sought to kill him, was forced to flee to Egypt.* In the LXX there are two accounts of the way in which Jeroboam became king. The first agrees substantially with the Hebrew, when the contradictions of the text of 1 K 12 (cf. vv.²·³ with ²⁰) are removed.† As soon as Jeroboam heard of the

* The account of the rebellion, hinted at in 1 K 11²⁶, is not given as we should expect after v.²⁸. It is noticeable that while the compiler views this and other rebellions as punishments for Solomon's unfaithfulness (vv.⁹⁻¹³), yet they occurred early in the reign, *i.e.* before the sins which occasioned them.

† 1 K 12² is to be placed before v.¹, so that 'heard of it' refers to Solomon's death, 11⁴³; a slight change in the Heb. v.²ᵇ gives the sense 'and J. returned from Egypt'; omit v.³ᵃ and 'Jeroboam and' in v.¹²ᵃ. Thus the narrative is brought into agreement with v.²⁰.

death of Solomon, he returned from Egypt; he did not attend the conference between Rehoboam and the people at Shechem, but he kept within reach, and came when he was sent for. The other account in LXX B is inserted at 12²⁴. It covers the same ground as the first, but with considerable additions and variations. On hearing of Solomon's death, Jeroboam returned from Egypt, where he had found a patron in Shishak and an Egyptian princess for a wife, 12²⁴ᵉ,* mustered his tribe at Shechem, and so gave the immediate occasion for the revolt. The most important divergence, however, between the two Greek accounts is found in the prophecies which promise Jeroboam the leadership of the ten tribes. In the first we have the prophecy of Ahijah delivered to Jeroboam at Jerusalem in the time of Solomon; in the second a similar prophecy is put into the mouth of Shemaiah at Shechem in the time of Rehoboam. Both accounts are clearly translated from Heb. originals, which must have existed when the LXX translation was made. The Heb. text was not fixed, and the tradition was fluctuating; we cannot feel certain as to what was the actual course of events. With regard to Ahijah a similar uncertainty exists. The prophecy in 1 K 11²⁹⁻³⁹ appears to be an interpolation, for it interrupts the account of Jeroboam's rebellion, which is expected after v.²⁸ and implied by v.⁴⁰. It could not have been Ahijah's prophecy which aroused Solomon's suspicions, for it was a private communication, addressed to Jeroboam alone, as is expressly stated; no third party was aware of it.† We find, then, two different traditions of Jeroboam's accession to the sovereignty; the correct history of it must remain uncertain.

The revolt which led to the division of the kingdom and the elevation of Jeroboam was a revolt against the government of Solomon and the heavy burdens which it laid upon the people. Solomon's conception of the state was in fact alien to the national feelings. The free, democratic spirit of old Israel, which could welcome a king chosen by the people, had not become reconciled to a hereditary monarchy, especially when Solomon's heir proved to be out of sympathy with the popular demand for a less despotic government. And the tribal instinct was still strong; it had not yet surrendered to the idea of a united nation. Jealousy of the new preponderance of Judah must have been felt in the powerful tribe of Ephraim; the real strength of Israel lay in the north; neither geographical nor social conditions were in favour of Jerusalem being the centre of all Israel. Hence the revolt came to a head at Shechem, and the instigator of the democratic movement was an Ephraimite who became chieftain of the ten tribes by the free choice of the people. The historian sees in this reverse for Judah a judgment on the sins of Solomon.

But Jeroboam not merely adopted the line of democratic leader appointed by popular choice, he came forward as the patron of the popular religion and the ancient sanctuaries. He quickly realized that it was necessary for his position to establish a strong counter-attraction to the new temple at Jerusalem. Accordingly he made successful efforts to revive the popularity of the venerable holy places at Bethel and Dan, and provided them with golden images of J″ in the form of a steer or bull, in addition to the altar, asherah, and sacred stone (2 K 23¹⁵), which were there already. He also instituted a new priesthood and a popular

* LXX, Swete's edition.

† Note also that, in the Hebrew, Ahijah of the second prophecy 14¹⁻¹⁶ is clearly connected with Ahijah of the first prophecy, while the Greek introduces him as a new person. LXX B places this second prophecy in an impossible place, before the assembly at Shechem, 12²⁴ʰ⁻ⁿ. See, further, W. R. Smith, *OTJC*² 117 ff.

festival on the model of the feasts at Jerusalem.*
The popular religion saw no offence in this form of
worship (cf. Ex 32¹⁻⁶) ; and the employment of non-
Levites as priests would not have appeared so
irregular then as it would have done in later times.
But there can be no doubt that Jeroboam's action
marked a serious retrogression when compared
with the higher religious level which had been
reached at Jerusalem. For the sake of political
security Jeroboam deliberately sacrificed the higher
religious interests of Israel ; and there can be no
doubt that the sacred writer, who, whatever his
merits as a historian may be, possessed a keen
religious insight into the events of the past, was
fully justified in his unsparing verdict upon Jeroboam as the man 'who made Israel to sin' (1 K
12³⁰ 13³⁴, 2 K 17²¹ᶠ.).†

The narrative 1 K 13¹⁻³², which contains a prophetic denunciation of the altar at Bethel, belongs
to a much later time, when the names of 'the man
of God from Judah' and of 'the old prophet' were
forgotten. Some critics think that it is founded
upon 2 K 23¹⁵⁻²⁰ ; others, that the latter passage,
apparently foreign to the context where it stands,
was added by the same hand which inserted the
story here. The next narrative connected with
Jeroboam, the second prophecy of Ahijah, delivered to the queen 14¹⁻¹⁸, contains old material
which has been treated by the compiler in his
characteristic style. The language of Ahijah is
cast into much the same form as similar prophecies
delivered to Israelite kings.‡

With regard to Jeroboam's external relations, the
only information we have is that there was constant
war between him and Rehoboam and his successor
(1 K 14³⁰ § 15⁷ᵇ, cf. 2 Ch 13). At first, no doubt,
Jeroboam would have had a considerable struggle
to maintain himself against his rival. But no
decisive victory or success on Jeroboam's side is
recorded ; he seems even to have retired from
Shechem to Penuel beyond the Jordan (12²⁵).
When the Pharaoh Shishak made a plundering
expedition into Judah he certainly did not spare
the territory of his former protégé, as appears
from his triumphal inscription at Karnak ;∥ but
we are not told that Jeroboam made any attempt
at resistance. Perhaps he was more of a politician
than a warrior. He had successfully managed a
revolt, but he did not succeed in establishing a
dynasty. If the revolt was part of the divine plan
(1 K 12¹⁵), Jeroboam himself proved unequal to the
greatness of his opportunity ; and, so far from
advancing the higher interests of his people, did not
rise above the popular standards, and bequeathed
to posterity the reputation of an apostate and a
succession of endless revolutions.

2. Jeroboam II., king of Israel for 41 years, 790–
749 B.C., son of Joash, and fourth ruler of the
dynasty of Jehu. Under him N. Israel reached its
highest point of prosperity and splendour. For
years Israel had been suffering at the hands of
Syria ; but the tide turned at last, and Joash

---

* 12³¹ and 13³³ᵇ seem to have formed one sentence, of which
12³¹ has preserved the more original end. This sentence was
broken up by the insertion of 12³³. ³²ᵃ. Note tautology in
12³². ³³ ; the latter verse forms an introduction to the following
narrative. 13³³ seems to have been adapted out of older
materials to suit the preceding account, which it clearly implies.
See Lv 23³³⁻³⁶ P ; and Dillmann, Levit.² p. 583.
† The phrase is constantly repeated, 1 K 14¹⁶ 15²⁶. ³⁰. ³⁴ 16²⁶
22⁵², 2 K 3³ 10²⁹. ³¹ 13². ⁶ 14²⁴ 15⁹. ¹⁸. ²⁴. ²⁸ 23¹⁵. The compiler,
who regards past history from the point of view of Dt, looked
upon Jeroboam as the founder of a schism which violated the
first principle of the Dt. Code, the law of the one sanctuary.
‡ Cf. 1 K 16¹⁻⁴ 21²⁰ᵇ⁻²² 21²⁴, 2 K 9⁷⁻¹⁰. Note the anachronism,
14⁹ 'all that were before thee' (Jeroboam) ; Tirzah, v.¹⁷, does
not seem to have become a royal residence till later, 15²¹.
§ This is contradicted by 12²¹⁻²⁴, of doubtful authority. The
exaggeration of the numbers and the unhesitating submission
to a prophet point to later redaction.
∥ Represented in Stade, GVI i. 352.

---

recovered from Benhadad ten cities which his
father had lost (2 K 13²⁵). Syria had also been
greatly reduced by the campaigns of the Assyrian
kings, Shalmaneser III. (782–772) and Assurdan III.
(772–750) ; so that Jeroboam was able to recover
the old limits of the Davidic kingdom 'from the
entering in of Hamath unto the sea of the Arabah.'
That he was able to establish his rule in the
S.E. implies that he must have reduced the
Moabites to submission. The meagre statement
of 2 K 14²⁵ is the only definite piece of information
which the historical books give us. The complete picture of the times of Jeroboam must
be drawn from the materials furnished by the
prophecies of Amos. The nation was enjoying
the fruits of Jeroboam's successes. Confident of
J‴s patronage, Israel was at last free to devote
itself to the ease and pleasures of a period of
unwonted peace. Wealth increased, and with it
went luxury and self-indulgence (Am 3¹⁵ 5¹¹ 6⁷. ⁸. ¹¹).
Religious worship was celebrated with the greatest
splendour and popularity, both at the royal
sanctuary of Bethel (7¹³) and at Gilgal and Beersheba (4⁴ 5⁵ 8¹⁴). But along with all this material
prosperity went a deep-seated moral corruption,
which it was the prophet's chief concern to denounce. Oppression of the poorer classes by the
rich, justice sold and perverted, immorality openly
practised, rapacity and greed of gain, were the
sins which Amos marks as characteristic of the
time. He foretells the impending judgment. The
Assyrian was not far off ; the only barrier between
him and Israel, Damascus, had been removed ; J″
will summon this nation to afflict Israel, and they
will be carried captive beyond Damascus (6¹⁴ 5²⁷).

G. A. COOKE.

JEROHAM (יְרֹחָם).—**1.** The father of Elkanah and
grandfather of Samuel, 1 S 1¹. While LXX A has
Ἱεροάμ, B has Ἱερεμεήλ, i.e. Jerahmeel, and the
latter may be correct (Driver, Text of Sam. p. 3).
In the genealogy of Samuel as given by the
Chronicler, while MT has uniformly יְרֹחָם, the LXX
has in 1 Ch 6²⁷ A 'Ιεροβοάμ, B 'Ιδαέρ, and in 6³⁴ A
'Ιερεάμ, B 'Ηαδλ. **2.** A Benjamite family name,
1 Ch 8²⁷ 9⁸. **3.** A priestly family, 1 Ch 9¹², Neh
11¹². **4.** 'Sons of Jeroham' were amongst David's
heroes, 1 Ch 12⁷. **5.** A Danite chief, 1 Ch 27²².
6. The father of Azariah, a captain who helped
Jehoiada in his measures for the overthrow of
Athaliah, 2 Ch 23¹.

JERUBBAAL (יְרֻבַּעַל, 'Αρβάαλ, 'Ιαρβάλ, 'Ιεαροβάαλ,
'Ιεροβάαλ).—A name given to Gideon, Jg 6³² 7¹ 8²⁹. ³⁵
9¹. ². ⁵. ¹⁶. ¹⁹. ²⁴. ²⁸. ⁵⁷. It is = 'Baal strives,' Baal being
a name for J″, as in Ishbaal, Meribbaal ; it cannot
= 'one who strives with Baal,' as Jg 6³² would
suggest (LXX δικαστήριον τοῦ B.). Perhaps Jerubbaal should be written Jerubaal (יְרֻבַעַל from יָרֹה
not (רִיב) = 'Baal, i.e. J″, founds,' cf. Jeruel,
Jeremiah : so Wellh., Budde, Moore. This name
was altered to **Jerubbesheth** (יְרֻבֶּשֶׁת ;—besheth =
'shame') when Baal could no longer be used of
J″ without offence, 2 S 11²¹ (LXX 'Ιεροβοὰμ υἱοῦ Νήρ,
Luc. 'Ιεροβοάλ) ; cf. Ishbosheth, Mephibosheth. See
art. GIDEON.

G. A. COOKE.

JERUBBESHETH.—See JERUBBAAL.

JERUEL (יְרוּאֵל 'founded of El').—That part of
the wilderness of Judæa facing the W. shore of
the Dead Sea below En-gedi (see EN-GEDI). It was
here, according to the narrative of 2 Ch 20¹⁶, that
in the time of Jehoshaphat there assembled a great
host of the children of Moab, Ammon, and other
trans-Jordanic tribes, who had swept across the
plain at the S. of the Dead Sea, and were encamped at the foot of the lofty cliffs of Ziz (or
Haziz). This spot was near the mouth of one of

the deep ravines which descend from the table-land, along whose bed the stream, fed by perennial springs, would be available for the use of the host. The same locality was the scene of several memorable events in OT history (Gn 14[7], 1 S 24[1-4]).

E. HULL.

JERUSALEM (usually יְרוּשָׁלֵם, but יְרוּשָׁלַיְם in Est 2[6], Jer 26[18], 1 Ch 3[5], 2 Ch 25[1] 32[9]; LXX Ἰερουσαλήμ, which occurs also in NT side by side with Ἱεροσόλυμα).

I. NAMES.—The name Jerus. first occurs in Jos (10[1] 15[63]; when the inhabitants are called Jebusites, cf. Jg 19[10], 2 S 5[6]). Various trs. of the name have been proposed, some depending on the later and longer form, and on its pointing as if a dual; but these discussions are superseded by the discovery of letters from an early ruler of Jerus. (Tel el-Amarna collection), which show not only that the name existed before the Heb. conquest of Pal., but also that its meaning (as spelt U-ru-sa-lim and URU-sa-lim) is 'city of Salim,' or 'city of peace,' which agrees with the rendering by Gesenius, 'abode of peace.' The suggestion of Sayce (Academy, 7th Feb. 1891, HCM 177, EHH 28) that Salim is the name of a deity is unsupported: the sign for deity is not used as a prefix to the name, and the word Sa-lim is elsewhere found in the Tel el-Amarna letters with the meaning of 'peace.' * It is by no means improbable that the Jewish tradition, which places the Salem (properly Shalem) of Melchizedek at Jerus. (Gn 14[18], see Jos. Ant. I. x. 2; Wars, VI. x. 1), and the King's Vale (Gn 14[17], Jos. Ant. VII. xi. 3) two furlongs distant, may be correct; and the monumental spelling favours the view that the city may have been first called Salem only; but it is not doubtful that it was called Jerus. as early as the time of Joshua. It may also have been called Jebus (but see Moore on Jg 19[10. 11], cf. the Jebusite, Jos 18[28]). In Ps 76[2] we read, 'In Salem was his covert (see Jer 25[38]), and his lair (fig. of lion) in Zion.' The explanation in the Mishna (Zebaḥim xiv. 8), which connects Salem with Shiloh, together with other suggestions (see Midrash Bereshith Rabba, ch. 89), are too fanciful to need notice. In the Talm. the later and longer form of the name Jerusalem is used, and the city is also called Beth 'Olamim (בית עולמים) 'the house of Ages' (Tosephta, Tohoroth, ch. 1).

The Roman name, given by Hadrian after A.D. 135 to the restored city, was Ælia Capitolina, and this appeared on coins of the early Khalifs of Damascus in the Arab. form Ailia. Its survival to the 10th cent. is noticed by Eutychius, and it was known to Jerome, and appears in the lists of Synods as late as A.D. 536. This name was derived from that of Ælius Hadrianus himself, combined with that of Jupiter Capitolinus, whose statue Hadrian erected on the ruined site of the Temple. In the 10th to 13th cents. the city was called Beit el-Mukaddas, 'The Holy House' (see Sam. Chronicle, el-Mukaddasi, and el-Edrisi). The modern name is el-Kuds esh-Sherîf, 'The holy (city), the noble (town),' and in common speech el-Kuds only. On some of the Hasmonæan coins the longer spelling of the name Jerusalem occurs. The native Christians, as well as the Jews, still use the old name in the Arab. form Yerusalim.

II. NATURAL SITE.—Jerus. stood on the site

* Sayce's view is controverted by Zimmern (Zeitschr. f. Assyr. 1891, p. 263) and Jastrow (Journ. Bib. Lit. xi. [1892], p. 105).

occupied by the present town, though at its greatest it extended farther to N. and S. The geogr. position (taken at the Dome of the present Cathedral of the Holy Sepulchre) is 31° 46′ 45″ N. lat., 35° 13′ 25″ long. E. of Greenwich. The town stood on spurs extending S.E. from the main watershed of Pal., and still presents almost the appearance of sliding downhill towards the Kidron ravine on the S.E. This ravine (now called Wâdy en-Nâr, 'Valley of Fire') is one of the main drains of the country, and is formed by the junction of three head valleys, the longest on the E. being the Kidron proper, running due south, west of Olivet; the second, which itself had two branches, passed through the city S.E.; the third, running S. and turning E., is the Valley of Hinnom. The summit of Olivet is 2641 ft. above the Mediter., and the valleys at their junction have a level of about 2000 ft. above the same. Thus Jerus. was defended, on the E., S., and S.W., by natural fosses 500 ft. deep, and was naturally weak only on the N. and N.W., from which quarters it has always been attacked in the various sieges recorded in history. In considering the natural site it is, however, important to remember the geological character of the region, and the changes which have been due to artificial alterations—the levelling of hills and the cutting of scarps, ditches, reservoirs, and aqueducts, together with the filling up of the valleys by ruins, or with a particular purpose. The present features, though somewhat obscured by these circumstances, are, however, distinguishable in ancient accounts of the site, and the careful measurement of rock levels, in all parts of the city, now enables us to speak with certainty as to the original conditions. The strata dip down S.E. from the watershed, with an average inclination of 10° or 12°. The highest beds, called locally Nâri and Kakûli, are found on the summit and slopes of Olivet. The Nâri is identified with the nummulitic beds found on Gerizim and Carmel, which belong to the Middle Eocene period. The Kakûli is a soft white limestone with bands of flint or chert, and containing marine shells as fossils, with ammonites and other distinctive genera of the Upper Chalk. The E. cliffs of the Kidron Valley, below this white chalk, are formed by the Mezzeh—a hard silicious limestone with bands of flint and fossils. This, with the underlying beds, belongs to the period of the Lower Chalk. The Mezzeh also appears in the Sacred Rock (es-Sakhrah), on the summit of the Temple Plateau, W. of the Kidron; in the cliff of Antonia to the N.; and in the cliff of the traditional Calvary, as well as in that N. of the city at the so-called 'Jeremiah's Grotto.' Under the Mezzeh is a deep bed of fine white limestone, very suitable for building stone, and hardening by exposure. It is locally known as Meleki, and in it are excavated the great reservoirs of the Temple Area, and the ancient quarries under the city N.W. of the Temple. Beneath the Meleki again is a hard dolomitic limestone, of white colour streaked with pink, which appears on the watershed surface W. of the city, and which is called the 'Santa Croce' marble, being found near the Convent of the Cross. The alternation of these hard and soft beds accounts for the existence of cliffs and slopes, and for the water supply of the city, which is deficient on the W., the water sinking down through the Meleki bed, and only appearing in the Kidron ravine to the E., where the dolomitic limestone is near the surface. The natural drainage of the watershed is collected in this ravine, and no springs occur near the city at any higher level. The thickness of the various beds differs in different parts, the Mezzeh 'tailing off' to the N.W.

The rock is visible on the present surface on the N. and N.W., near the watershed, and in the N.W. part of the Temple Area. In the valley beds it is hidden by an accumulation of rubbish, which within the city has a depth in some cases of 40 or 50 feet. The level of the surface of the rock has in these parts been traced in mines, in wells and cisterns, and in sinking foundations for houses. About 150 such measurements have been carefully recorded, of which 40 are in the Temple Area and the rest within the ancient city, being fortunately most numerous in the most important parts. On the ridge S. of the Temple 30 such observations were made during the mining operations.* In some cases the rock is visible in great cisterns for a considerable distance, in others its absence is proved by the existence of masonry walls. Thus, although it is probable that a certain amount of earth covered the valley beds from the first, it is known that, in parts where a shingle of stones covers the rock, the filling up of the valleys has been caused by the frequent demolition of buildings during the various destructions of the city.

By the light of such observations it is easy to recover the original features now obscured by the ruins. The eastern spur, on which the Temple stood, was flanked by the Kidron on the E., and by a narrow valley on the W., having its head near the present Damascus Gate. This ridge was artificially cut across, at an early period, N. of the Temple Area, where its level was 2460 ft. above the sea; and a second scarp, facing S. and about 25 ft. high, was made, leaving a block of rock, on which the present Turkish Barracks stand, and a small flat plateau within, which rose gradually the W. valley with the Kidron at Siloam. West again natural knoll, now known as the *Sakhrah* or Sacred 'Rock.' From this point the plateau narrows into a ridge, which falls gradually S. from a level of 2440 ft. to about 2130 ft. at the junction of the W. valley with the Kidron at Siloam. West again of the narrow western valley, now filled up to a depth of some 40 ft., the main site of the city itself was cut in two by a broad, deep recess, with steep slopes to N. and S., having its head at a narrow neck of land which rises to about 2500 ft. above the sea, and divides this central valley or recess from the upper part of the Hinnom Valley W. of the city. The great recess has its bed under the modern 'Street of David' (which runs down from the W. or Jaffa Gate towards the Temple), opening out into the narrow valley already noticed W. of the Temple hill. This broad, deep recess is now also partially filled in, to a depth of 50 ft., with rubbish, and its great breadth and the steepness of its slopes were hardly suspected until proved by the examination of the rock in various large cisterns in its bed, hidden under the modern surface, and discovered about 1872 during the German excavations in the precincts of the old Hospital of the Knights of St. John.

The central recess or valley thus divides the site of Jerus. into a S. and N. quarter. The S., which is generally allowed to be the 'Upper City' of Josephus, is a flat hill, measuring about 1000 yds. N. and S. by 600 yds. E. and W. On the N. it had a very steep slope, with a precipice on the N.E.; on other sides the slopes were also steep, and the plateau, which has an average elevation of 2500 ft. above the sea, thus stands 500 ft. above the valley beds on the S.E. The N. quarter was less extensive, and for the most part lower than the S. It was formed by a spur from the main watershed, and connected with the S. by the narrow neck or isthmus already noticed, towards the W. of the city. The N. spur appears to have risen into an isolated knoll of small area,

which is now shown as the traditional site of Calvary, the summit being about 2490 ft. above the sea. In speaking of the topography of the city it will, however, be shown that the outline of the N. spur was changed in the 2nd cent. B.C. by cutting down the E. part of the N. ridge, near the narrow valley which divided it from the Temple, and which was then filled up. The later Herodian period witnessed an extension of Jerus. beyond this N. quarter, and the hill N. of the Temple (separated off by the artificial ditch as noticed above) was then occupied, and protected by another scarp 20 ft. high, running E. and W., and now supporting the modern city wall in the N.E. quarter. The part of the hill so included in the city (and which Josephus calls Bezetha) rose to about 2520 ft. above the sea close to the N. scarp, and to 2470 ft. on the S., opposite the rock of the Barracks from which the fosse separated it. The city also extended, on the N.W., over the flat ground beyond the knoll of the traditional Calvary, rising gradually to the watershed of Judæa, 2580 ft. above the sea. It would appear that from an early period the flat head of the narrow central valley was flanked by cliffs, the northern of which (at Jeremiah's Grotto outside the modern Damascus Gate) formed a remarkable isolated knoll, 2570 ft. above the sea, which is now regarded by many as the true site of Calvary. The N. ditch was probably in part natural, for in the cliff under the modern city wall, E. of the Damascus Gate, is the entrance to the great quarries under the city, where the *Meleki* beds were cut out for the Temple masonry. That these quarries existed early, and were not merely hewn for the building of Herod's Temple, has been shown by M. Clermont-Ganneau's discovery of a rudely cut sketch of a cherub, or man-bull, in the ancient Heb. or Phœn. style, attributable to a period earlier than that of Herod, and carved on the rock wall of the quarry.

The natural water supply of Jerus. is deficient, and was very early supplemented by the cutting of rain-water tanks and aqueducts. The only natural spring was in a cave on the W. side of the Kidron, S. of the Temple Area. It is remarkable for its intermittent flow, due to a natural syphon leading from a subterranean basin in the rock. The water collected by the valleys from the rocky watershed, and sinking, as above explained, down to the impervious dolomite beds beneath the hill spurs, also bursts out in winter at the junction of the three valleys, and flows in a clear rapid stream towards the Dead Sea. But this overflow is due to the sinking of a deep shaft at the well now called *Bîr Eyûb* ('Job's' or 'Joab's' [see below] well), which reaches down 125 ft. The well is connected with an ancient aqueduct, 70 to 90 ft. below the present surface, on the W. side of the Kidron Valley, and reached by stairways. Although unfinished, this aqueduct must have assisted in collecting the waters to the *Bîr Eyûb*.* The water of the upper spring was also early diverted through an aqueduct to the Pool of Siloam, as will be explained later. In the earliest period of the history of Jerus. it is possible that the bed of the Kidron, then much deeper than it now is,—in consequence of the accumulation of rubbish,—was occupied by a stream flowing on the surface from the upper cave spring, S. of the Temple. Water also found its way down the narrow ravine W. of the Temple hill, and is there still found in the subterranean cave of the *Hammâm esh-Shefa*, or 'healing-bath,' under the W. wall of the present Ḥaram enclosure. The shaft of the modern well is 86 ft. deep, the lower part having been apparently made in the

---

* This proves that no depression divides Ophel from the temple.

* This well was reopened in A.D. 1184 by the Franks, who called it 'Joab's well' (*i.e.* En-rogel).

Rom. period. The rocky chamber and passage at the bottom extend 128 ft., but no ancient notice of this reservoir has been discovered with any certainty. The water supply, both here and at the *Bîr Eyûb*, failed in the winter of 1864–1865, being dependent on the rainfall of a comparatively small area, near the watershed N. of the city. The various artificial reservoirs which supplied the city will be described later. We have no information as to any works which may have been carried out by the Jebusites before David fixed his capital in Jerusalem. The spring in the Kidron Valley existed then, and it is possible that the supply in the *Hammâm esh-Shefa* was also available, and much nearer to the surface. In Neh (as noticed later) the 'Dragon Spring' is mentioned W. of Jerus.; but if a natural supply of water is to be understood, it would seem to be now dried up, as there is no known spring on this side of the city. Jos. calls this place the 'Serpents' Pool' (*BJ* v. iii. 2).

III. HISTORY.—In accordance with Jewish tradition (Jos. *Ant.* I. x. 2, VII. xi. 3 ; *Wars*, VI. x. 1), Jerus. may be supposed to have been a city (SALEM ?) in the time of Abraham (Gn 14[18], where see the cautious note of Dillmann), whose king, Melchizedek, was priest of God Most High (*Él 'Elyôn*). The city is next noticed as the capital of a Canaanite king at the time of the Heb. conquest (Jos 10[5]). The inhabitants were Jebusites ; and although its king was killed (Jos 10[26]), yet Jerus. was not attacked until later (Jg 1[8] [?]), and remained a Jebusite town, and 'city of the stranger' (Jg 19[10-12]), in the time of the Judges. The discovery of letters from the early governor of Jerus. to Amenophis (*c.* B.C. 1480–1440), in the Tel el-Amarna collection, gives us some additional light on the history of the city. It is clear from various references that an Egyptian resident, supported by an Egyptian garrison, was there established at a time when all the Philistine towns (including Gezer) were also held by Egypt. But this garrison was withdrawn in consequence of the general rebellion of Pal. and Syria against Egypt, and the king of Jerus. reported that, in consequence, all the country had rebelled to the *Khabiri* (see HEBREWS), who had occupied Aijalon, Lachish, Gezer, Ashkelon, and Zorah, his own position being perilous in consequence. It is clear, therefore, that Jerus. was already a royal Canaanite city before the Heb. conquest under Joshua.

The boundary line of Judah was so drawn as to leave Jerus. in the lot of Benjamin (Jos 15[7], cf. 18[28], both P ; in 15[63] [JE] Jerus. belongs to Judah) ; the border ran from En-rogel (in the Kidron plain) along the Valley of Hinnom S. of Jerusalem. The city was attacked by Judah (Jos 15[63] ; in Jg 1[21] *Benjamin* has possibly been substituted for *Judah* ; Jg 1[8] is a very doubtful passage, see Moore's note), who, however, did not succeed in driving out the original Jebusites. The choice of Jerus. as a capital, in David's time, was probably due to its being already an important town, in a position more central than Hebron, and less exposed to incursion from the plains than Shechem. David's men scaled the 'gutter,'* or 'water-channel' (*zinnôr*, παραξίφιδι), and took the 'mountain fort of Zion,' or 'citadel' (Ἄκρα), which Josephus identifies with the Upper Agora of his own time (*Wars*, v. iv. 1). The mockery of David by the Jebusites shows that Jerus. was considered a strong fortress (2 S 5[6-9]). The occupation of the citadel did not lead to the expulsion of the Jebusites, for at a later period David appears to have been friendly with Araunah the Jebusite. Jerus. at the time of this conquest (about B.C. 1000) included not only the fort of the

* On the various explanations that have been offered of the very obscure passage 2 S 5[8], see Driver, *ad loc.*

upper city, but also a quarter called **Millo** (2 S 5[9]), which the LXX renders Ἄκρα. Josephus states that David joined the lower city (τὴν κάτω πόλιν) to the citadel (τὴν Ἄκραν), surrounding both with walls (see 1 Ch 11[4-8]), and established himself in the citadel, calling it (or else Jerus. generally) the city of David. The ark was soon after brought to the city of David, and 'placed in the tent that David had pitched for it' (2 S 6[12-17], 1 Ch 13[13] 15[25-16[3]]). The site of the Temple was afterwards chosen at the 'threshing-floor of Araunah the Jebusite' (2 S 24[18], 1 Ch 21[18-28]), which site was bought for fifty shekels of silver (about £9), or, according to the later account (1 Ch 21[25]), for 600 shekels of gold. Preparations for the building were made by David, and the Temple was begun by Solomon in the month of Ziv (latter part of April), in the 4th year of his reign (about B.C. 965), and finished in the month Bul (Oct.), seven years later (1 K 6[1-38]). The ark was finally removed out of the city of David into the Temple (1 K 8[1-8]), at the feast of consecration in the seventh month, Ethanim (September). The royal palace of hewn stone and cedar was not finished till later (1 K 7[1-12]), and two bronze pillars were cast for the Temple, with a 'sea' or large reservoir, and other vessels (1 K 7[13-51]). The Temple, which in plan and adornment resembled those in Babylon, described in a later age in the records of Nebuch., was provided with an altar court with walls and cedar beams (1 K 6[36]) ; but the dimensions of this court are not noticed. It is stated that the 'inner' or altar court was separated from other outer courts (2 Ch 23[5-8]). The royal palace appears (as will be shown in dealing with Topography) to have stood near the Temple on the S., and it was not in the city of David (1 K 9[24], cf. 7[8]). Solomon also built the wall of Jerus., and 'shut in the ravine [? ; RV 'repaired the breach' ; Heb. פָּנָר אֶת־פֶּרֶץ] of the city of David' (1 K 9[15] 11[27]). Jerus. was enlarged by the building of the Temple and Palace beyond the bounds of the city of David.

After the revolt of Israel from Rehoboam, Jerus. was attacked by Shishak, king of Egypt (about B.C. 935), when the gold shields made by Solomon fell a prey, with all the treasures of the Temple and of the Palace. We possess a monumental record in which Shishak (Sheshonk) gives the names of 133 cities in Pal. subdued during this campaign, and the last name *Iura . . .*, though unfortunately half-defaced, may perhaps represent Jerusalem. Another attack on the city (about B.C. 850) is recorded (2 Ch 21[16]) in the reign of Jehoram, when the Phil. and Arabs near Egypt sacked the 'king's house.' After the revolution of Jehu, and murder of Ahaziah, king of Judah, at Jezreel, Athaliah, who had usurped the throne of her grandson, was slain at the entrance of the palace, probably about B.C. 842 (2 K 11[16], 2 Ch 23[15]) ; and about B.C. 786 Jehoash of Israel marched on Jerus. from the W. plain, and broke down 400 cubits of the wall on the W., carrying off once more the treasures of the Temple and of the Palace (2 K 13[13, 14], 2 Ch 25[23]). The incursion of Ramman-nirari from Assyria (about B.C. 803) into N. Israel and to Damascus, no doubt accounts for the strengthening of Jerus. by Uzziah (2 Ch 26[9, 15]), when towers were built on the W., on that part of the wall broken down some twenty years before. The city was protected by engines of war, similar to those shown in Assyr. pictures. Jotham (about B.C. 742–736) also strengthened J. by building the 'higher gate' of the Temple, and a wall on Ophel, S. of the same (2 K 15[35], 2 Ch 27[3]). The conquests of Tiglath-pileser in Syria were then causing anxiety in Judah. Ahaz, the next king, was tributary to this Assyr. conqueror (about B.C. 734), and before that date he was attacked by the enemies of

Tiglath-pileser,—Rezin of Damascus and Pekah of Samaria,—who, however, failed to take Jerus. (2 K 16⁵). The fall of Samaria to Sargon alarmed Hezekiah, son of Ahaz, and the great improvements — from a military point of view — which were carried out in Jerus., in the water supply of SILOAM (which see), may have been begun by Ahaz at the time of the fall of Damascus in B.C. 732 (Is 8⁶). The advance of Sennacherib rendered it necessary to prepare for attack about B.C. 701 (Is 22¹¹), and the aqueduct from Gihon to Siloam was probably complete when the Assyr. came to Jerus. (2 K 20²⁰, 2 Ch 32³⁰). The account which we possess of this attack in the records of Sennacherib harmonizes with that found in the Bible (2 K 18¹³-19³⁷, 2 Ch 32⁹-²³, Is 36. 37). Sennacherib records (see Schrader, KAT²) that he invaded Philistia in B.C. 701, and defeated the Egyptians at Altaka ; that he set up new tributary rulers in Ekron and Ashdod ; and 'captured forty-six cities' of Judah, shutting up Hezekiah in Jerus., like 'a bird in a cage.' He speaks of the riches sent to Nineveh from Jerus., but is silent regarding the disaster that overtook his army on the Egyptian frontier, drove back the Assyr. beyond the Euphrates, and saved Jerus. for a century. The alliance with Egypt (see Is 36⁶) prevented any danger from Egypt to Hezekiah's capital, but that with Babylon (Is 39) was less useful, since Merodach-baladan was defeated by Sennacherib in B.C. 696. Manasseh (acceding probably about B.C. 695) was tributary to Esarhaddon and Assurbanipal, according to their inscriptions, and the former attacked Egypt in 680, and finally took Memphis (Nah 3⁸) in B.C. 670. The carrying of Manasseh to Babylon (2 Ch 33¹¹) appears to have occurred under Assurbanipal (see Jos. Ant. X. iii. 2) after B.C. 668, and this king is known to have restored Babylon as his southern capital. The further fortification of Jerus. by a wall on Ophel, outside the original city of David, and extending to the Fish Gate on the N. of Jerus., was effected apparently after his restoration. Amon, the successor of Manasseh, reigned only two years, and the rule of Josiah coincided with the last years of Assyr. empire, witnessing the terrible Scythian raid which swept down to the borders of Egypt. The Law was discovered in the Temple, and a great reformation effected in B.C. 621 (2 K 22, 2 Ch 34) ; but in B.C. 609 Necho marched to the aid of the Babylonians and Umman-manda (see Davidson, Nahum, note at end), who combined against Nineveh, and Josiah, endeavouring to stop his advance, was slain at Megiddo (2 K 23²⁹). The allies soon quarrelled over the spoils ; and the defeat of Necho at Carchemish left Pal. an easy prey to Nebuch. of Babylon, the new master of W. Asia. In B.C. 597 Jerus. was taken and despoiled (2 K 24¹-¹⁵), and Jehoiachin carried to Babylon. In B.C. 586 Nebuch. again attacked Zedekiah, who fled ' by the way to the Arabah' (2 K 25⁴), or from the S.E. side of the city. On the 7th of Ab the city was entered by the Babylonians, and on the 9th (about 1st Aug.), according to the Mishnic traditions (Taanith iv. 7), the ancient Temple of Solomon was destroyed, with the Palace and all the chief buildings of Jerusalem. The walls were broken down. The treasures of the city had already been taken in the first raid ; the sacred vessels were now carried away (2 K 25¹³, 2 Ch 36¹⁸), and the ark itself was probably removed, since Nebuchadnezzar's practice in other cases was to carry off all objects of veneration belonging to defeated peoples. Many of the chief men of Judah had followed Jehoiachin into captivity, and the rest now followed Zedekiah, leaving only the 'poor of the land as vine-dressers and husbandmen' under a Babylonian ruler of Palestine (2 K 25¹²).

The history of the ruined city remains a blank until Cyrus arose and wrested the empire from Nabonidus, the last Babylonian king. The Jews, like the Phœn., were content to remain subject to the tolerant Aryan race which ruled from India to Egypt. The Temple was refounded at Jerusalem (Ezr 3¹²), and was completed twenty years later (Ezr 6¹⁵). The return of Ezra to Jerus., and the establishment of the Law, may be referred to the reign of Artaxerxes I. (B.C. 458); see ZERUBBABEL. Acc. to Jos. (Ant. XI. vii. 1), Bagoses, a general of Artaxerxes II., profaned the Temple, and laid a tax on the sacrifices. The restoration of Jerus. by Nehemiah (Neh 3) was merely a rebuilding of the ancient wall found in ruins ; but this account is the most complete that we possess of the ancient topography of the city.

The battle of Issus and taking of Tyre laid Pal. at the feet of Alexander the Great, and about B.C. 332 he visited Jerus., according to Jos. (Ant. XI. viii. 4). The city suffered, after his death, in the long struggle between the Ptolemies in Egypt and the Seleucidæ in Antioch. Ptol. Soter, son of Lagus, entered Jerus. on the Sabbath in B.C. 305 (Ant. XII. i. 1), and Antiochus III. (called the Great) took the city from the Egyp. in B.C. 219 (Ant. XII. iii. 3). The influence of Greek art and customs began to spread over Pal. under the Seleucidæ, and when Antiochus IV. (Epiphanes) visited Jerus. in B.C. 172, there appears to have been a gymnasium (perhaps the Xystus, W. of the Temple), built by the Hellenists in the Holy City (1 Mac 1¹⁴, 2 Mac 4⁹-¹², Jos. Ant. XII. v. 1). Two years later, Antiochus, defeated in Egypt, entered Jerus. unopposed, in a Sabbatic year (1 Mac 1²⁰, Ant. XII. v. 3). The Jews, for more than three centuries and a half, had been peaceful subjects of Pers. and Gr. overlords, but the growth of Gr. influence alarmed the pious, and the tyranny of Epiphanes bred a desperate spirit of revolt. In B.C. 168 Apollonius, the Gr. general, was sent to Jerus. by Antiochus, with orders to suppress the national religion. On the 15th of Chislev he desecrated the Temple by sacrifice of swine,— probably in honour of Ashtoreth and Tammuz, to whom swine were sacrificed in this age in Cyprus and Phœnicia,—and an image of a boar is said to have been erected in Jerus. (1 Mac 1⁴⁷, Ant. XII. v. 4). The Gr. garrison was placed in a newly erected citadel on Akra, which—as will be shown later—is identified by Jos. with the Lower City. This citadel dominated the Temple, and during the revolt of Judas Maccabæus its garrison held out even after the defeat of three Gr. armies sent against the patriotic leader. In B.C. 165, after the second defeat of the Greeks, Judas and his followers restored the half-ruinous and neglected Temple, erecting a new altar in place of that desecrated by Apollonius. The 'Feast of Lights,' on the 25th of Chislev, still commemorates this restoration (1 Mac 4⁵², Ant. XII. vii. 7). Two years later, however, Antiochus V. (Eupator) retook Jerus., and overthrew the walls of the city and of the Temple (1 Mac 6⁶², Ant. XII. ix. 5). After the defeat and death of Judas at Elasa, following soon after his victory at Adasa over Bacchides the desecrator of the Temple, a period of misfortune for the Hasmonæan house followed ; but under the skilful management of Jonathan, the brother of Judas, the national cause prospered. In B.C. 143 Jonathan built a wall in the middle of Jerus. to separate the Akra citadel from the Upper Market or Agora (1 Mac 12³⁶, Ant. XIII. vi. 7). His successor Simon, the wisest and most prosperous of these famous brethren, finally took the Akra citadel on the 23rd of Ziv in B.C. 139, and partly levelled the mountain on which it had stood—a labour lasting three years (1 Mac 14³⁶, Ant. XIII. vi. 7 ; on the historical reliability of this statement see Schürer, *HJP* I. i. 262, note 14). John Hyrcanus, his son, who, being at Gazara, escaped the massacre at Dok, was besieged in B.C. 134 in Jerus. by Antiochus Sidetes, and is said by Jos. to have opened the tombs of the kings, and taken treasure thence (*Ant.* XIII. viii. 4). After his successful rule the quarrels of the Hasmonæans brought further trouble on the city, and the Romans, having under Pompey conquered Armenia to the Caucasus and to the borders of Persia, began to interfere in the affairs of Palestine. An alliance with Rome was one of the latest acts of Judas Maccabæus, and had been renewed later. The country had been at peace during the greater part of the reign of Alexander Jannæus, and the Gr. influence (as witnessed by his coins) had been steadily reasserting its power. After the death of Alexandra-Salome, the able widow of Alexander Jannæus, a war of succession broke out between her sons. Hyrcanus II., aided by Aretas (Harith) the Arab king of Petra, besieged Aristobulus II. in Jerus. in B.C. 65; but Scaurus, one of Pompey's generals, ordered him to raise the siege (*Ant.* XIV. ii. 1). In B.C. 63 Pompey himself besieged Jerus., to put an end to the increasing anarchy. Aristobulus was removed, the walls were demolished, and the bridge leading to the Temple was thrown down. Pompey is said to have entered the Holy of Holies itself. The city was made tributary to Rome (*Ant.* XIV. iv. 4; *Wars*, I. vii. 1). The subjection of Pal. was, however, not yet complete. In B.C. 55 Crassus, before his defeat in Parthia, again pillaged the Temple (*Ant.* XIV. vii. 1), and in B.C. 47 the Hasmon. rule came to an end; Antipater the Idumæan, in recognition of his services on the borders of Egypt, was made ruler of Pal. by Julius Cæsar the year after the battle of Pharsalia. Four years later his famous son, Herod the Great, became joint ruler with Phasael, and in B.C. 40 became Procurator of Judæa, by order of the Senate. He was then driven from Jerus. by the invasion of the Parthians, under their prince Pacorus, who re-established the Hasmon. Antigonus (*Wars*, I. xiii. 13). In B.C. 37 Herod, assisted by Sosius the Rom. governor of Syria, took the city from Antigonus (*Ant.* XIV. xvi. 2), and a period of strong rule and peace followed. In B.C. 24 Herod built his palace in Jerus., on the W. side of the upper city—the old Hasmonæan palace being on the E., near the Temple bridge. He also restored the citadel Baris or Antonia, N. of the Temple, and celebrated games in a new theatre in the city (*Ant.* XV. viii. 1–5, ix. 1). Later in his reign, in B.C. 19, Herod began to replace the ancient Temple enclosure by a new and much larger structure, and this work was finished in B.C. 11 (*Ant.* XV. xi. 3, 6). The death of Herod, in the year of the Nativity (B.C. 4), was signalized by the destruction of the golden eagle erected over the Temple porch (*Wars*, I. xxxiii. 3, 8). The history of Jerus. under Herod's successors, and under the procurators, is almost a blank. In A.D. 35 Pontius Pilate was recalled, in consequence of the riots caused by appropriating the Corban to the purpose of making an aqueduct from near Bethlehem to the Temple (*Ant.* XVIII. iii. 2). Agrippa the tetrarch, grandson of Herod the Great, began the building of a new wall on the N. side of the city, about ten years after the Crucifixion (A.D. 41–44), and Jerus. appears to have grown much larger during the Rom. period (*Ant.* XIX. vii. 2, viii. 2). King Agrippa, son of the last, built a palace in the upper city (*Ant.* XX. viii. 11), about A.D. 56, and the Temple courts were completed in A.D. 64 (*Ant.* XX. ix. 7). The Jewish discontent, gradually increasing since the time of Agrippa's death, led to revolt against the incompetent procurator Gessius Florus in A.D. 66, and during the riots the palaces and Antonia

were burnt (*Ant.* XX. xi. 1; *Wars*, II. xvii. 6). Cestius Gallus, president of Syria, besieged Jerus. in consequence, and took the third wall on the N., but retreated in panic (*Wars*, II. xix. 1–9), and Vespasian was called to re-establish Rom. power in Palestine. The campaign was slow and systematic, and not until all the country to the N. had been subdued, and Jericho and the plains of Joppa reconquered, did the Rom. army advance to the attack of Jerus., a task left to Titus in consequence of Vespasian's becoming emperor. The great siege in A.D. 70 was perhaps the most terrible ever undergone by the city, and the full account by Jos. illustrates the topography of Jerus. at the time of its greatest extension and strength.

The great siege lasted 143 days, from the 14th Abib, when the Romans encamped on Scopus (*Wars*, V. xiii. 7) until the final conflagration on the 8th of Elul (*Wars*, VI. viii. 5). The dates of the principal events may be briefly given.

Day of Month.		Day of Siege.	Chief Events.
Abib (Passover)	14	—	Romans arrive, John seizes the Temple (*Wars*, V. vii. 7–17).
Abib	23	1	First day of actual siege (*Wars*, V. vii. 2).
Ziv	7	15	Wall of Agrippa taken. Feast of Dedication of Temple (*Wars*, V. vii. 2).
,,	12	20	Second wall taken. Romans repulsed (*Wars*, V. viii. 1).
,,	16	24	Second wall retaken (*Wars*, V. viii. 2).
,,	21	29	Banks raised against Antonia, after three days' rest and review of troops (*Wars*, V. ix. 2).
,,	29	37	Banks against Antonia, and others commenced 12th Ziv against Hippicus, are completed (*Wars*, V. xi. 2).
Sivan	1	38	Bank at Antonia mined by the Jews (*Wars*, V. xi. 3).
,,	3	40	Banks against upper city destroyed by Jews (*Wars*, V. xi. 5).
,,	7	44	A wall of circumvallation begun and built in three days (*Wars*, V. xii. 2).
,,	10	47	New banks begun against Antonia occupying 21 days (*Wars*, VI. i. 1).
Tammuz	1	68	Antonia attacked. Romans repulsed. The wall falls during the night (*Wars*, VI. i. 3).
,,	3	70	Sabinus killed invading the Temple.
,,	5	72	Antonia surprised by night (*Wars*, VI. i. 6, 7).
,,	17	84	The daily sacrifice fails (*Taanith* iv. 4). Antonia demolished during the preceding week. Banks raised against the inner Temple (*Wars*, VI. ii. 1, 7).
,,	22	89	The Jews set fire to the N. and W. cloisters (*Wars*, VI. i. 9).
,,	24	91	The Romans fire part of cloisters (*Wars*, VI. iii. 1).
,,	27	94	The Jews destroy the W. cloister (*Wars*, VI. iii. 1).
,,	28	95	The Romans destroy the N. cloister (*Wars*, VI. iii. 2).
Ab	8	104	Engines batter the inner Temple wall for six days. Two banks being completed (*Wars*, VI. iv. 1).
,,	9	105	The gate Moked is undermined (*Taanith* iv. 9). The Rom. soldiers set fire to the Temple by night (*Wars*, VI. iv. 5). The city is plundered, the lower city burnt, the family of Izates submits (*Wars*, VI. vi. 3, 4).
,,	20	116	Banks raised against the upper city on N.W. and N.E. (*Wars*, VI. viii. 1).
Elul	7	133	Banks finished after 18 days (*Wars*, VI. viii. 4).
,,	8	134	Final conflagration and conquest of the city (*Wars*, VI. viii. 5).

The first day of the siege (23rd Abib) corresponded in A.D. 70 to the 9th April. That lunar months must be supposed is shown by Jos. (*Wars*, VI. viii. 1, 9). The final fall of Jerus. took place in the hottest part of the year, on 4th September. The terrible sufferings of the besieged from famine, thirst, and disease were thus intensified by the

season. It is unnecessary to enter into detail as to these sufferings, or as to the various factions whose conflicts added to the general misery. The Idumæans, introduced by one faction to support themselves, thought only of plunder; and concerted action against the Romans was rendered difficult. The numbers of the besieged are stated by Tacitus at 600,000 (*Hist.* v. 13); the estimate of over a million by Jos. is incredible (*Wars*, II. xiv. 3, v. vi. 1, xiii. 7, VI. ix. 3). The ordinary population cannot have exceeded 30,000 at most; but in consequence of the Passover, and of the Idumæans being admitted, the city must have been densely crowded. The Jewish system perished in blood and fire, and the few survivors were made victims of the circus games at Cæsarea, or led captive to Rome, where, on the Arch of Titus, the golden candlestick, the table of shewbread, and the silver trumpets from the Temple (but not the ark, which never stood in the Temple after the time of Nebuch.), are shown as spoils of this great victory.

In order to understand the topography of Jerus., and to distinguish its later remains, it is necessary briefly to follow the history from A.D. 70 down to the present day. After the capture of the upper city, the walls of the city and of the Temple were thrown down, with the exception of the royal towers and part of the W. wall (*Wars*, VII. i. 1), which remained as the fortress of the legion left in charge. Jerus. has no history for sixty years after its destruction, but an inscription of the time of Trajan (A.D. 117) appears to record the worship there of Serapis by a veteran who may even have been present with Titus. In A.D. 130 Hadrian visited Jerus., and in A.D. 134 occurred the desperate rebellion of the Jews under Bar Cochba and Rabbi Akiba. They were expelled from Jerus. by Julius Severus (Dion Cassius, lxix. 13), and according to later statements (Talm. Jer. *Taanith* iv. and Jerome, *Comm. on Zec* 8[19]) T. Annius Rufus ploughed up the foundations of the Temple. In the following year they were massacred at Bether (Bittîr) close to Jerus. on the W. In A.D. 136 Hadrian rebuilt the city, and called it Ælia Capitolina. He dedicated the Temple site to Jupiter Capitolinus, and decreed the exclusion of the Jews from Jerus.—a decree which, though perhaps not always enforced, was still in existence in the time of Constantine (Dion Cassius, lxix. 12; Eusebius, *Hist. Eccles.* iv. 6). The city of Hadrian appears to have been smaller than that of the time of Titus, since the S. part of the upper city was outside the wall in the 4th cent. A.D. In A.D. 130 Hadrian found only a few houses and seven synagogues (see *Biblia Sacra*, pp. 393–455). Only one of these was standing in the 4th cent. (Bordeaux Pilgrim). Hadrian appears to have repaired the walls (Orosius, *Hist.* xv., written about A.D. 416), and, according to the *Paschal Chronicle* (which is, however, a late authority), the new buildings included 'the two markets' (δημόσια), a theatre, a mint, a *tricameron*, a *tetranymphon*, and a *dodekapylon*, formerly called *anabathmoi* (*In Ann.* 3 *Æl. Hadr.*). Eusebius (*Life of Constantine*, iii. 36) speaks of a temple of Venus erected in the city, at the site of the subsequent Church of the Holy Sepulchre. This was afterwards (see Fetellus in A.D. 1151–1157) attributed to Hadrian. Jerome (*Epist.* 49) speaks of a marble statue of Venus 'on the rock of the Cross,' and Eusebius connects her worship with the dark cave (μυχόν) under this rock. A coin of Antoninus Pius represents Venus in a tetrastyle temple with the legend C.A.C., and later coins of Aurelius and Severus have the same reverse with the legend *Col. Æl. Cap.* It seems clear that either Hadrian or the Antonines erected this Venus temple in the N. quarter of Jerus., when it was rebuilt as a pagan city. A coin of Hadrian, struck in Jerus., shows a temple which may be the same. Jerome also informs us (*Comm.* Is 2[8] and Mt 24[15]) that equestrian statues of Hadrian were placed on the site of the Holy of Holies, together with an idol of Jove. These were still standing in A.D. 333 (Bordeaux Pilgrim), and an inscription on a stone now built upside down into the S. wall of the Temple enclosure bears the name of Hadrian, and probably belonged to one of these statues. The head of a small statue was picked up by a peasant, in the road N. of the Damascus Gate, in 1873. It is crowned with laurel, and the Rom. eagle appears on the front of the crown. The features resemble those of known statues of Hadrian, and the head may have belonged to one of the above statues.

A cohort was stationed at Jerus. to prevent the Jews entering the city (Sulpic. Severus, *Hist. Sac.* ii. 25), and the decree still held in A.D. 312 (Eusebius, *Theophania*). But in A.D. 333 (Bordeaux Pilgrim) we find the Jews allowed annually to visit the 'pierced stone,' which was near Hadrian's statue in the Temple. They anointed the stone, lamented over it, and tore their garments. It apparently represented the site of the Temple, over which no building is mentioned, and is usually identified with the *Sakhrah* or sacred 'rock,' still remarkable for the shaft which pierces down to the cave beneath from the surface of the rock. Jerome also speaks (*Comm.* Ezk 11[5]) of the Jews entering Jerus. to wail, in his own time. He says that for fifty years (or until A.D. 130) Jerus. remained laid even with the ground, and lost its former name (*Comm.* Ezk 5[1]);

but under Hadrian it regained the position of an ordinary provincial capital.

We hear no more of its history for nearly two centuries, until the establishment of Christianity by Constantine; but, in the tombs on Olivet, stone boxes have been found (*ost
phagi*) belonging to the 2nd, 3rd, and 4th cents. A.D., which held the bones of Jews and Jewish Christians there collected close to the Valley of Judgment. The traditional tomb of St. Pelagia (noticed from the 4th cent. down) contains also an early Gr. text—'Courage Domitela, none is immortal'—which may (as compared with others in Bashan) belong to the 2nd or 3rd cent. A.D. Pilgrimages began to be customary in the latter cent., when Alexander, a bishop of Cappadocia, visited Jerus.; and a female pilgrim is noticed by Cyprian. In A.D. 315 Eusebius speaks of pilgrims coming from all parts of the world to witness the fulfilment of prophecy, and to worship on the Mount of Olives (where the footprints of Christ were shown), which appears to have been the only sacred station then known. Our first account of the city under its new conditions is that of the Bordeaux Pilgrim, who arrived while the new cathedral of the Holy Sepulchre (or 'Church of the Anastasis') was being built by Constantine's order in A.D. 333. As regards the recognition of the site, we have no statement in earlier authors to show that the true locality was preserved by tradition. The legend of Helena's miraculous discovery of the Cross is unnoticed by contemporary writers, though in A.D. 326 the mother of Constantine visited Bethlehem and Olivet. The Cross itself is only noticed by St. Cyril twenty years after the great Basilica was built, and in A.D. 383 by Jerome (*Epit. Paulæ*, 5). Eusebius gives what purports to be Constantine's letter to Macarius (*Chron. Ann.* 339) ordering the erection of the new buildings which he elsewhere fully describes (*Life of Constantine*, bk. III. chs. 34–39). There is no doubt that the sites described are the same still shown, but the letter to Macarius speaks of them as 'long hidden under the earth'; and Eusebius says that the Venus temple was first destroyed, and 'beyond all hope' the sacred tomb was found under the mound then cleared away. There is no doubt that an ancient Jewish tomb (now called that of Nicodemus) was discovered, and that the traditional Holy Sepulchre (a tomb of the Gr. and Rom. type) is rock-cut; the surrounding rock is said to have been cut away to leave the monument isolated in the flat surrounding space.

What is lacking is any evidence that the sites are genuine. The story of the finding of the Cross is first told by Rufinus in A.D. 410, and by Theodoret about A.D. 440. The 4th cent. was an uncritical age, and many of the sites shown to pilgrims were impossible—such as that of Rephidim in Moab (St. Sylvia), of Job's Stone in Bashan, and of the Transfiguration on Olivet —a blunder of the Bordeaux Pilgrim, who also makes David to have met Goliath near Jezreel. The situation of the sites which Constantine honoured awakened apparently some suspicions from an early age. Eusebius (*Life of Constantine*, iii. 33) speaks of the new Jerus. rising round the Basilica opposite the old Jerus. in ruins; and mediæval writers all explain that the extension of the city, which in the 4th cent. A.D. surrounded the Venus temple, was due to Hadrian. A careful consideration of the topography and military considerations tend, however,— as will be seen later,—to show that these sites were equally within the city at the time of the Crucifixion. The case for the traditional sites, which have remained unchanged for fifteen centuries, is thus very weak. The buildings erected by Constantine have perished, but it is generally agreed by Willis, de Vogüé, and Prof. Hayter Lewis, that they consisted of a hemispherical building, continued eastwards by a great basilica, with a court or *atrium* on its E., and an entrance (*propylæa*) with pillars. This was, in fact, a building similar to that erected by Constantine at Bethlehem, where the original pillars of the basilica are still standing. The great leaden roof was gilded, the sacred cave was surrounded with columns, the cloisters had galleries above; the walls were adorned with sculpture (and possibly with mosaics), and, on the S. apparently, was the great tank—still traceable—in which (Cyril, *Catech. Lect.*) the neophytes were baptized at Easter, by total immersion, according to the usual rite. The details of the description are not very clear, but it is certain that the building was large and magnificent, and that it embraced not only the Holy Sepulchre in its open court surrounded by the hemisphere, but also the rock of the supposed Mount Calvary to the S.E. with the cave beneath. A site which had once been a pagan temple was thus (as in other cases at Tyre, Cæsarea, Gerasa, etc.) converted into a Christian shrine, but the strange festival of the Holy Fire (first noticed in the 9th cent.) seems to have perpetuated the pagan fire-feasts of earlier days—perhaps once celebrated at the same spot. In like manner the cave at Bethlehem had, according to Jerome, been sacred to Adonis before the grove was cut down, and the church built by Constantine over its site.

In A.D. 335 a synod was held at Jerus. and the Church of the Anastasis was consecrated (Euseb. *Life of Const.* iv. 43–47). On the temporary reversion of the state to paganism, Julian is said to have attempted to rebuild the Temple (Socrates, *Hist. Eccles.* iii. 20), but was deterred by what would seem to have been an explosion of fire-damp, in A.D. 362. About A.D. 450 the empress Eudoxia, widow of Theodosius II., retired to Jerus., where she died in A.D. 461. She built a Church of St. Stephen, of which only a few fragments have been found N. of the city, and restored the walls, enclosing the Pool of Siloam within their circuit (Evagrius, *Hist. Eccles.* i. 22). During this period the Council of Chalcedon (A.D. 451) made Jerus. a patriarchate independent of Cæsarea. Short descriptions of the city (by

Eucherius and Theodosius) belong to the 5th and 6th cents., and the number of sacred sites shown to pilgrims steadily increased; but the genuineness of these traditions is always doubtful.

About A.D. 532 Justinian erected important works in Jerus., including the Church of the Virgin—usually supposed to have stood on the site of the present Aksa Mosque, the pillars of which have Byzantine capitals which may belong to this age—together with a hospital to the W. of the Temple enclosure, and a Church of St. Sophia, which Antony of Piacenza (about A.D. 600) places at the Prætorium, distinguishing it from St. Mary. It is also placed 'in' the Prætorium by Theodosius (or Theodorus, A.D. 530), and the Prætorium was always shown by Christian tradition N. of the Temple at the site of Antonia, and near the Twin Pools in the fosse to the N. The remains of a small church in the modern barracks are believed by de Vogüé to represent St. Sophia. The Temple Area itself, as described in the 4th, 5th, and 6th cents., was in ruins, and no building stood on the site of the Holy House. The S.E. corner of the enclosure stood up as a ruined 'pinnacle' to which pilgrims refer. Even after the great Church of St. Mary was built, Antony of Piacenza speaks of the 'ruins of Solomon's Temple,' and these ruins are noticed by Eucherius (about A.D. 427–440) and by Arculf (A.D. 680). We have no account of any buildings in this area before the time of Justinian, but the description by Procopius (*de Edificiis Justiniani*, bk. v. ch. 6) shows that his work was extensive. Unfortunately, the account is not very clear: cloisters (*στοαί*) are noticed, which may have run on the outer walls of the enclosure—except, as he says, on the E. The present Golden Gate, on the E. wall of the enclosure, is architecturally Byzantine work, and may have been built in the 6th cent. (as compared with buildings in N. Syria); it is unnoticed by early writers, and apparently first mentioned by Sæwulf early in the 12th cent. The hospital attached to St. Mary is said (Antony of Piacenza) to have held from 3000 to 5000 beds. Procopius speaks of two hospices (ξενῶνες),—one for pilgrims and one for the sick,—but it is not clear where they stood.

The buildings so erected by the two great emperors, Constantine and Justinian, suffered from the attack of Chosroes II. of Persia, who, aided by 24,000 Jews, is said (*Paschal Chron.* A.D. 614) to have destroyed the Church of the Anastasis, taking the patriarch Zacharias and the Holy Cross to Persia. Immediately after, Modestus, the vice-patriarch, is said to have begun the restoration of the church (*Life of St. John Eleemon* in *Acta Sanct.* ii. p. 500). In A.D. 629 Heraclius made peace with Siroes, son of Chosroes, and entered Jerus. in triumph through the Golden Gate (*Paschal Chron.*) on the 14th Sept. This victory of Christendom was, however, shortly to be followed by the triumph of Islam. It was in the same year that Mohammed destroyed the idols of Mecca, and in A.D. 637 Khalif Omar appeared before Jerusalem. The Christians resisted for some time (four months according to Theoph., *Chronograph*, or two years according to Arab writers). The earliest accounts (including that of Eutychius, A.D. 870) are not contemporary, but all writers seem to agree that Omar's conquest was unstained by blood. He proclaimed security for life and property on payment of tribute, and allowed the existing churches to stand, though no new ones might be built. He erected a wooden mosque W. of the Sakhrah (Arculf, A.D. 680, and Jelâl ed-Dîn, A.D. 1470), and purified the Rock itself. According to Eutychius (*Annals*, written not later than A.D. 940), the Christians had built nothing on the site of the Temple thus accepted by Islam.

The Ommiyah dynasty of Khalifs being established at Damascus, 'Abd el-Melek, the 10th Khalif (according to all Arab authorities, see Guy le Strange, *Pal. under the Moslems*), erected a *Kubbeh* or 'Dome' over the Sacred Rock in A.D. 688. The small 'Dome of the Chain' to the E. is said to have been the model of this building, which originally consisted of a drum supported on arches, and on pillars torn from some earlier Byzantine building, with an outer arcade—octagonal, and adorned with glass mosaics. These still remain, and the Kufic text above this outer arcade still preserves the date of building, A.H. 72. Under these Khalifs, and under the great Abbaside dynasty of Baghdad, the relationship of Islam and Christendom was friendly, and Harûn el-Rashîd is said to have sent the keys of Jerus., with other presents, to Charlemagne, who erected in Jerus., E. of the Holy Sepulchre, chapels, and a hospice for Lat. pilgrims (Bernard, *Itin.*), towards the close of the 8th cent. A.D. The buildings on the site of Constantine's Church of the Anastasis, which Modestus erected as already noticed, and of which Arculf drew a rough plan on a wax tablet for the abbot of Iona, appear to have been small separate chapels. The Holy Sepulchre was enclosed in a round church. Calvary was covered by a separate building, and a third to the E. replaced the Basilica of Constantine. On the S. was a chapel of St. Mary, and N. of Calvary a chapel of the 'Prison of Christ.' In the early part of the 9th cent. the patriarch Thomas restored the dome over the round church (Eutychius, *Ann.* A.D. 813–833), and these buildings remained uninjured during the rule of the Abbasides.

But in A.D. 969 Jerus. fell under the power of the Shia'h Khalif of Egypt, Mue'z (see Gibbon, ch. lii.), and in A.D. 1010 Hakem, the crazy and fanatical Egyp. Khalif, ordered the destruction of the chapels by fire (Will. Tyre, i. 4). Through the influence of the Byzantine emperor, Constantine Monomachus, they were restored in A.D. 1048 by the patriarch Nicephorus, but the new buildings, which existed when the Crusaders took Jerus., were small and poor (Will. Tyre, i. 6, viii. 3). They were similar to those of Modestus, but included a chapel of St. Mary N. of the Sepulchre, and three chapels of St. John, Holy Trinity, and St. James (which still remain), to the S. The cave under the site of Constantine's Basilica, which is covered by a dome resting on clumsy Byzantine pillars, dating perhaps from the time of Modestus, was shown as the 'Chapel of St. Helena,' and as the place where the Cross was miraculously discovered.

The history of the Temple enclosure is traced during this earlier Moslem age by inscriptions, and by the later Arab histories. In A.D. 728 a cupola was erected over the Aksa Mosque (Justinian's Church of St. Mary), and this building was injured by earthquake about A.D. 758–775, but restored soon after by the Khalif el-Mahdi. In A.D. 831 the Khalif el-Mamûn restored the Dome of the Rock, and apparently enclosed it in the present octagonal outer wall. The beautiful bronze gates of this wall bear the above date (A.H. 216). The beams on the old roof resting on the wall also bear a date answering to A.D. 913. In A.D. 1016 an earthquake partly destroyed the dome, and the mosaics were repaired in A.D. 1027 as stated in their inscriptions. The present wood-work of the dome was erected in A.D. 1022. In A.D. 1060 the roof of the Aksa fell and was repaired.

The decreasing power of the Arab race, and the rise of the Seljuk Turks, led to the attack on Jerus. by Isar el-Atsis, a Turcoman general, who drove out the Egyptians in A.D. 1077, when 3000 of the inhabitants are said to have been slain (Will. of Tyre, i. 6). The cruelty of the Turkish rulers was the immediate cause of the first Crusade, when reported by Peter the Hermit after his visit to Jerus. in A.D. 1094. The number of pilgrims had been steadily increasing since about A.D. 1000, when the Amalfi merchants founded the hospice of St. John Eleemon, on the site apparently of that of Charlemagne. While the great contest raged round Antioch, the Egyptians took advantage of the absence of Turkish forces in the N., and seized Jerus. in 1098, expelling the Turcomans after a siege of 40 days. They then rebuilt the walls a few months before the army of Godfrey appeared from the plains (Will. Tyre, vii. 19). The Crusaders encamped on the N. and W., and subsequently extended on the S.W. After forty days of desperate struggle, the city fell on 15th July 1099 (Will. Tyre, viii. 5), and a terrible massacre followed. No sooner was the feudal system established in Pal. than extensive building operations began. About A.D. 1103 a new cathedral to cover the chapels of Nicephorus—already described—was commenced (Sæwulf, *Itin.*; Will. Tyre, viii. 3), and by A.D. 1140 the Church of St. Mary the Great was built S. of the cathedral. In A.D. 1136 the new buildings in the Temple Area, and the new decorations of the Dome of the Rock, then called Templum Domini, were finished after 20 years of work, a chapter of canons having been established in A.D. 1112 (Will. Tyre, viii. 3). The city increased in prosperity for half a cent., and was filled with churches and palaces, many of which remain almost intact. For eighty years it was never besieged, and its walls fell into decay, until the increasing dangers of the Lat. kingdom led to their being renewed in A.D. 1177 (Will. Tyre, xxi. 25). But, after the fatal defeat at Hattîn, the Franks in Jerus. were besieged by Saladin, and surrendered, escaping any massacre, in A.D. 1187. Saladin reconverted the Temple enclosure into a *Ḥaram* or 'sacred' Moslem sanctuary, and two years later restored and regilt the Dome of the Rock, as shown by an inscription in the dome itself. In A.D. 1192 he repaired the city walls to oppose Richard Lion Heart, and from his time downwards the Egyp. and Turkish rulers have added constantly new buildings in the area, with minarets, stained-glass windows, and other details, which it is impossible here to notice fully.

The main building periods of Jerus., after A.D. 70, have been described at some length, in order to explain the present conditions of Jerus. archæology, and to distinguish the works of later ages. In A.D. 1219 the city walls were dismantled by order of the Sultan of Damascus, and ten years later Frederic II., emperor of Germany, received Jerus. by treaty from the Sultan of Egypt. In spite of the conditions of this treaty, the Christians, in A.D. 1239, began to rebuild the walls, when Daûd Emir of Kerak fell upon them, massacred many, and demolished the walls and the citadel. Yet in 1243 Jerus. was again restored, without conditions, to Christendom by the Sultan of Damascus, and its walls repaired. In the following year the Kharezmian Tartars—foes of Islam and Christendom alike—seized Jerus., massacred the population, and rifled the tombs of the Lat. kings near the foot of Calvary. In 1247 they were driven N. by the Sultan of Egypt, and Jerus. remained subject to Egypt for 270 years, until the Ottoman Sultan Selim I. conquered Syria in A.D. 1517. Inscriptions on the walls show that the present ramparts are due to Suleimân the Magnificent in A.D. 1542. The line differs somewhat from that of the 12th cent. on the N.W. and S.

Jerus. under the Turks remained without a history, and hardly increased at all in size, until some 30 years ago. The Church of the Holy Sepulchre was partly destroyed by fire in A.D. 1808, but most of its present structures, including the bell tower, the choir, and the chapels, remain as they were in the 12th cent. In 1825 there was a revolt against Turkish rule in the city. In 1832 it was taken by Mohammed Ali from Egypt. In 1834 the peasantry entered by the drains, and shut up the garrison in the capital for a week. They were relieved by Ibrahim Pasha on the 6th of June. In 1840 Jerus. was restored to the Turks by Europe. The Anglican bishopric was founded two years later. In 1850 the riots of Gr. and Lat. clergy preceded the Crimean War. In recent years there has been a steady influx of Jewish inhabitants, so that a population of about 20,000 souls in 1872 has risen to about 50,000 at the present time. New quarters have sprung up outside the walls, on W., N., and S., and a railway from Jaffa has just recently been completed. The main cause of this rapid development, which has led to much misery and poverty in the city, was the persecution of the Jews in Russia under the late Tzar.

IV. TOPOGRAPHY.—From the preceding account of the history it will be seen that, in treating of the topography of Jerus., we have to bear in mind various changes due to human agency throughout a period of nearly 4000 years ; and that in studying the Antiquities we have to separate the work of Romans, Byzantines, Arabs, Crusaders, Egyptians, and Turks from the older remains of the semi-Greek period, of the Hebrews, or of the Canaanites. We have, in like manner, to distinguish later traditions from the true topography of the earliest writers, and monkish sites from those of the Bible. Our only real authorities are the OT for the earlier periods, and Josephus for the condition of the city just before the great destruction, which he witnessed in A.D. 70. In the Mishna we have, however (Tract *Middoth*), a valuable account of Herod's temple, written about A.D. 150 at Tiberias, by men who were able to visit the ruins, and to hear the remembrances of rabbis who had survived the siege. The accounts given by Jos. were, on the other hand, penned far away in Rome,—that in the *Wars* about A.D. 72, and the *Antiquities* as late as A.D. 93.

The long controversies which have raged as to most of the features of the ancient city have been silenced by the survey of Jerus. in 1864 by Sir C. W. Wilson, by de Vogüé's careful study of the Temple site in 1860–1863, and by the celebrated excavations of Sir C. Warren (1867–1870) ; and the differences of opinion now existing are few and comparatively unimportant. The principal discrepancies which will be found on the most recent maps concern three points only—(1) the position of the 'City of David,' (2) the position of 'Akra,' (3) the size and exact position of the Temple. The first two may here be briefly considered. The third will be noticed in treating of the Temple Area.

As regards the extent of the city at the time of David's siege, we read that 'David took the stronghold of Zion, the same is the city of David,' and 'dwelt in the fort, and called it the city of David ; and David built round about from Millo (Akra in LXX) and inwards' (2 S 5[7. 9]). Jos. (*Ant.* VII. iii. 1) explains that, having crossed the ravine, David seized the citadel ('Ἄκραν) 'and settled himself in Jerus., which he called David's own city' : he adds, 'But David having also surrounded the lower city (τὴν κάτω πόλιν) and joined the citadel (τὴν Ἄκραν), to it made them one body.' In another passage he says that the upper city of his own time was called by David the fort (φρούριον), ' but by us the Upper Agora ' (ἡ ἄνω ἀγορά), and that the other hill, called Akra ('Ἄκρα), supported the lower city (τὴν κάτω πόλιν) (*Wars*, V. iv. 1). From these passages it is clear that Jos. considered the city in David's time to have coincided with the upper and lower city of his own days ; and he describes the old wall surrounding the upper city (*Wars*, V. iv. 2) as having been built by David and Solomon. He agrees with the LXX in identifying **Millo** (that part of the city which was not the fort) with the quarter called Akra by the Greeks, though he also uses the word (with the article, however) of the fort itself. He regards the term 'city of David' as equivalent to Jerus. as it existed in David's time. He never uses the term Zion, which (see ZION) is in no part of the OT identified with any particular quarter of the city, though in the 1st cent. B.C. the author of 1 Mac appears to apply this name esp. to the Temple hill. The site of the upper city, or Upper Agora, is by general consent identified with the principal S.W. hill of Jerus., which Christian writers from the 4th cent. A.D. downwards call Zion. It is also not disputed that the lower city

lay to the N. of this hill, which commanded the whole town, and was indeed the only hill on which a strong military situation could be found. The meaning of the word Millo is doubtful (it is usually rendered 'rampart' or 'filling'), and the site is not clearly indicated in the OT, but there is no reason to doubt that Jos. is right in identifying it with the lower city of his own time. It appears clear, then, that the Temple hill was not included in Jerusalem. It was the site of a threshing-floor, and such floors are always found outside towns and villages in Palestine. When the Temple was built, and the quarter of the Nethinim arose on **Ophel** ('the swell'),—a name applied later to the lower and narrower spur of the same hill S. of the Temple,—walls were of necessity extended to include this new quarter. The 'city of David' thus became a term applying to the old main quarters of Jerus., which alone existed in David's age, or perhaps esp. to the stronghold of Zion or upper city.

It has, however, been supposed by some recent writers (*e.g.* W. R. Smith, C. Wilson, Stade, Sayce, Buhl) [*] that the term 'city of David' should be applied to the spur S. of the Temple, the name Ophel not applying to the whole spur. It is clear, however (Neh 3[26. 27], *Wars*, V. iv. 2), that Ophel was a place with houses, and the spur in question presents an area of only a few acres, the crest being lower than the summits of the other hills, and unfitted for the erection of a citadel. The theory rests partly on a passage which, as rendered in AV, would make the aqueduct from Gihon run 'to the W. side of the city of David,' under Ophel (2 Ch 32[30]). The true rendering (as given by Keil and others) may be, however, 'westwards to the city of David,' which agrees with the supposition that the latter term applies to the upper city. It is sometimes also urged that the tombs of the kings buried 'in the city of David' were on Ophel—a question to be considered later. The indications found in other passages seem to show that no part of the Temple ridge was within the city of David. In 1 K 8[1] we find the ark described as brought up to the Temple 'out of the city of David' (so 2 Ch 5[2]). In Neh 3[15] the 'stairs that go down from the city of David' are noticed with Siloam. In 2 Ch 32[5] 'the Millo' is placed 'in the city of David,' and it was not on the Temple ridge. In 2 Ch 33[14] we read that Manasseh built 'an outer wall westwards to the city of David, as far as Gihon in the ravine.' It appears therefore that the topography shown in most recent maps is correct, and that the city of David included the fortress (מְצָדָה) of the upper city, and the quarter called Millo, or the lower city to the N. Solomon also fortified 'the Millo' (1 K 9[24]), and 'shut in the ravine (? ; RV 're-paired the breach' ; Heb. סָגַר אֶת־פֶּרֶץ) of the city of David his father' (1 K 11[27]) ; and after the building of his own palace he brought his Egyp. queen to *her* palace 'out of the city of David' (1 K 9[24]). Subsequent notices of Millo (2 K 12[20], 2 Ch 32[5]) do not throw much more light on the subject, though Silla, noticed in the first of these, may be connected with the 'causeway' of another passage (1 Ch 26[16]), and with the stairs from the city of David, if the word (see SILLA) means 'steps.' The causeway in question was W. of the Temple. As regards the water supply of Jerus. at this time the Gihon spring (now called the Virgin's Fountain) was at some distance from the upper city ; but it is possible that the great reservoir (now called *Hammâm el-Batrak*, 'the Patriarch's Pool,' and by others Hezekiah's Pool), which stands immediately N. of the upper city, was already in existence within the walls. It is very probably the 'upper pool'

[*] On the question of the site of the 'city of David' and of Zion, see further art. ZION, where a different view from the above is contended for ; and cf. art. JEBUS, p. 554 n ‡.

(Is 36²) which, in Hezekiah's time, had a conduit, and was situated near a 'highway.' It was here that the Assyr. appeared before Jerus. in B.C. 701, and Jos. tells us (*Wars*, V. vii. 2) that the 'camp of the Assyr.' was on the N.W. side of the old city, which was the natural quarter whence they would have approached from Philistia. The pool in question is called by him Amygdalon, and a conduit entering the city on this side is also noticed by him. An aqueduct still leads from the Birket Mamilla outside Jerus. on the W. to the Patriarch's Pool. This upper pool may have formed the chief supply of water within Jerus. as early as David's time.

As regards the royal palace of Solomon and of the later kings, we learn that it took thirteen years to build (1 K 7¹⁻¹²). 'For he built the house of the forest of Lebanon : the length thereof was 100 cubits, and the breadth thereof 50 cubits, and the height thereof 30 cubits.' The pillars were of cedar with rafters above. It had a porch 50 cubits wide and 30 cubits long at one end, in which was the ivory throne of judgment. A *Ḥarîm* or women's house appears to have been attached ; courts existed both ·within and outside, and the 'great court' (v.¹²) seems to have been connected with the Temple itself. In later times we read of the king's high house by the court of the guard (Neh 3²⁵, see 12³⁹), as being immediately south of the Temple, and the King's Gate was in the same vicinity (1 Ch 9¹⁸), being probably the high gate of the king's house (2 Ch 23²⁰), and the gate of the guard near the king's house, which adjoined the Temple (2 K 11¹⁹). Solomon's palace was outside the city of David (1 K 9²⁴, 2 Ch 8¹¹), and the Horse Gate was by the king's house outside the Temple, being the way by which the horses came to the king's house (2 K 11¹⁶, 2 Ch 23¹⁵). This gate was on Ophel S. of the Temple (Neh 3²⁸, see Jer 31⁴⁰, Jos. *Ant.* IX. vii. 2, 3). It is clear that Ezk refers to the palace as being divided from the Temple only by a wall (Ezk 43⁸), and there is a general agreement that the palace stood south of the Temple. It seems to have still existed after the Captivity,—probably in ruins,—but disappeared when the royal cloister of Herod's enlarged Temple enclosure was built, and it is not noticed by Jos. in his account of the Jerus. cf his own time.

The fortification of the Ophel spur, south of the Temple, was begun by Jotham (2 Ch 27³), for Uzziah is only said to have strengthened the W. wall (2 Ch 26⁹· ¹⁵), and it was completed by Manasseh (33¹⁴). This wall existed no doubt, therefore, in Hezekiah's time, but was rendered more formidable by his successor. It is described in the latter passage as extending from the city of David to Gihon in the ravine, and as stretching to the Fish Gate on the N. side of the city. Ophel and the Temple were thus included, about B.C. 800, in the fortified circuit. As regards Gihon, it is to be noted that it is described as 'in the torrent-valley' (*naḥal*), a term which appears to apply exclusively to the Kidron Valley, the valley of Ben Hinnom being always denoted by another word (*gai*). Thus when Solomon was taken down to Gihon (1 K 1³³· ³⁸) he was in full view of the faction supporting Adonijah on the cliff of Zoheleth (now *Zuhweileh*) on the opposite side of the Kidron. The term Gihon ('bursting forth') indicates a natural spring, such as is found only at the so-called Virgin's Pool or '*Ain Umm ed-Deraj* ('spring of the mother of steps') under the E. slope of Ophel. In the Bk. of Jos (15⁷ 18¹⁶) this spring is called En-rogel, usually rendered 'Fuller's Spring,' and sometimes connected with the Fuller's Field (Is 36²),* but the true meaning is perhaps the

*In the Mishna, *Sheḳalim* viii. 1, it is stated that the upper market-place was occupied by pagan fullers.

'spring of the water channel.' Hezekiah was the first to connect this spring with the Pool of Siloam by the aqueduct still existing (2 K 20²⁰, Is 22¹¹, 2 Ch 32⁴· ³⁰), although it would seem that the 'ditch (or basin) between the two walls' had, according to Is, been already made for the waters of an older pool in the time of Ahaz. In the last-quoted passage Hezekiah's great work is described fully, and, as tr. more correctly than in the AV, may read 'stopped the upper spring of Gihon and brought it straight underground, westwards, to the city of David.' In 2 Ch 32⁴ we read that when preparing for the Assyr. attack Hezekiah 'stopped the watercourse that ran (or overflowed) through the midst of the land' (or 'earth'; the LXX read πόλις, 'city'), in order to prevent the Assyrians from getting water. It seems probable that the sudden flow of the Gihon spring (which occurs intermittently) had formerly made a stream, flowing down the Kidron Valley (the bed of which was then much deeper), and that by means of the aqueduct the water was diverted to the Siloam pool, close to the city walls. The Gihon spring now rises in a cave reached by a descent of many steps, but the earth in front of the cave may have been first piled up by Hezekiah, and some natural outlet must at first have existed. The actual line of the old wall near Siloam is unknown, but in the account of the flight of Zedekiah we read of the 'way of the gate between the two walls, which is by the king's garden' (2 K 25⁴, Jer 39⁴), this gate leading to the Arabah or Jordan Valley. Jos. understands a 'fortified ditch' on the side nearest to Jericho (*Ant.* X. viii. 2), and the king's garden (belonging no doubt to the palace) was close to Siloam (Neh 3¹⁵). Hence the wall of Jotham and Manasseh appears to have passed near Siloam. Gihon is called by Jos. 'Solomon's Pool' (*Wars*, v. iv. 1), and placed close to Ophel.

The general topography of Jerus., before its destruction by Nebuch., thus appears to be clear ; but the site of the tombs of the kings is still controverted. Fifteen kings are said in the OT to have been buried in the 'city of David,' though Josephus only says 'in Jerusalem.' These were David, Solomon, Rehoboam, Abijah, Asa, Jehoshaphat, Joram, Ahaziah, Joash, Amaziah, Azariah, Jotham, Ahaz, Hezekiah, and Josiah. The monument was known in the time of John Hyrcanus (*Ant.* VII. xv. 3) and of Herod (XVI. vii. 1), both of whom sought treasure in it. It appears to have been known in the time of the apostles (Ac 2²⁹), but Josephus unfortunately does not describe its position. According to the Mishna (*Parah* iii. 2, see Tosephta, *Baba Bathra*, ch. 1), the only tombs in Jerus. were those of the family of David and of the prophetess Huldah. Certain unworthy kings were, however, buried elsewhere. Manasseh was buried 'in the garden of his own house in the garden of Uzza' (2 K 21¹⁸), and Amon was buried in the same place (v.²⁶). They are not said to have been buried in the city of David (see *Ant.* IX. x. 4, X. iii. 2), and, if the garden of Uzza was the same as the king's garden, it lay not far from the palace, and near Siloam, as above explained. This may account for the notice of the 'sepulchres of David' (Neh 3¹⁶) near Siloam, if the term 'city of David' is to be strictly applied only to the older city. It is possible that all the kings were buried in this 'burying-place' (2 Ch 26²³), but it is remarkable that one ancient tomb is known in the lower city — that now called the tomb of Nicodemus immediately W. of the traditional Holy Sepulchre. Jos. gives a remarkable account of the tombs of the kings (*Ant.* VII. xv. 3) which might apply to this existing tomb, with three *Kukim* or tunnel graves at the far end, and three on each side, thus accommodating nine bodies. A hole in the floor leads to other *Kukim* below, to the left of the entrance. It might, therefore, have sufficed for the kings buried in the city of David if—which cannot now be determined on account of a wall foundation—there were six *Kukim* in the lower tier. It is not impossible that this monument may be the real tomb of the kings, but it is also possible that all were buried near Siloam within the city walls; and future excavation may reveal the 'sepulchres of David' near Siloam.

The most complete account of the topography of Jerus. in the Bible is found in the Bk. of Neh, which relates his survey of the ruined walls, and details his restoration of the ancient circuit. In the first passage (Neh 2¹³⁻¹⁵) he describes how he went out by the gate of the valley (*gai*), W. of Jerus., 'E. of the Dragon Spring,' which seems to have been the Serpents' Pool of Jos. (τῶν ὄφεων κολυμβήθρα), W. of the city (*Wars*, v. iii. 2), the site being, however, unknown; and passing S. by the Dung Gate he reached the 'Gate of the Spring,' and the King's Pool (probably Siloam). Then, going up N. by the 'torrent-valley' (Kidron), and finding the road blocked with ruins, he returned to the Valley Gate. In the second passage (Neh 3¹⁻³²) the whole course of the wall is described from N. of the Temple, W., S., E., and N., to the starting-point. The names of the gates, and other details, agree with the scattered notices of earlier passages, and must be considered in order. The **Sheep Gate**, repaired by the priests (cf. Neh 12³⁹), is generally allowed to have been on the N. of the Temple. The towers *Hananel* and *Meah* appear to have belonged to the 'fortress' (*birah*, an Aram. word, Assyr. *biratu*) of 'the house' or Temple (Neh 2⁸), which was apparently the later Baris on the site of Antonia (see 1 Ch 29¹⁹, Jos. *Ant.* XVIII. iv. 3, *Wars*, I. iii. 3, v. 4; Mishna, *Middoth* i. 9, *Tamid* iv. 1, *Zebaḥim* xii. 3). These two towers are again noticed (Neh 12³⁹) in the same position, and Hananel (Jer 31³⁸) marked the opposite extreme (on the east) of the breadth of the city measured from the Corner Gate. The **Fish Gate** (2 Ch 33¹⁴, Neh 3³ 12³⁹, Zeph 1¹⁰) was probably the entrance by which men of Tyre brought fish to Jerus. (Neh 13¹⁶), and is generally supposed to have been on the N. wall. The **Old Gate** or gate of the old (city) was probably in the city of David, the wall of Manasseh extending to the Fish Gate (2 Ch 33¹⁴), in connexion with which a place called the 'second' (city or quarter) is noticed (הַמִּשְׁנֶה, Zeph 1¹⁰); it is also noticed in the time of Josiah (2 K 22¹⁴, AV wrongly 'college'). It is not impossible that Jos. refers to this quarter, in one passage, when speaking of the 'other city' (ἄλλην πόλιν, *Ant.* XV. xi. 5). These indications would seem to place the *Fish Gate* at the head of the narrow valley which bounds the Temple on the W. E. of this valley was the 'second quarter,' walled in by Manasseh, and W. of it was the old city of David. Next to the Old Gate is noticed (Neh 3⁸ 12³⁸) the **Broad Wall**, probably in the weakest part of the city on the N.W., and in this vicinity a gate called the **Gate of Ephraim** (2 K 14¹³, 2 Ch 25²³, Neh 8¹⁶ 12³⁹) is noticed, about 400 cubits from the Corner Gate: inside this gate and the Water Gate there was a 'broad place' (Neh 8¹⁶ AV 'street'), where booths could be erected, and the Gate of Ephraim was between the Broad Wall and the Old Gate. The description applies to the flat ground immediately N. of the N.W. corner of the upper city. Beyond the Broad Wall was the **Tower of Furnaces** (Neh 3¹¹) near the Gate of the Valley which probably led out to the Valley of Hinnom, to which this term (*gai*) seems to be generally confined (see 2 Ch 26⁹, Neh 2¹³). The Tower of Furnaces may be one of those built by

Uzziah at the Valley Gate, and at the Corner Gate, and his towers thus seem to have occupied the site of the later 'Royal Towers' (*Wars*, II. xvii. 6) at the N.W. corner of the upper city. The **Corner Gate** (2 K 14¹³, 2 Ch 25²³ 26⁹, Jer 31³⁸, Zec 14¹⁰) was apparently the same as the 'first' (or 'principal') gate, and was clearly on the W. of the city, where the principal road from the plains reached Jerusalem. The **Dung Gate** was 1000 cubits from the Valley Gate (Neh 2¹³ 3¹⁴ 12³¹), and is perhaps the same as the **Harsith** Gate near the Valley of Hinnom (Jer 19²), sometimes rendered **Gate of Potsherds**. The dunghills of the city must have been in this neighbourhood. The place called Bethso by Jos. (*Wars*, v. iv. 2) is sometimes explained to mean *Beth ẓoah*, 'house of dung,' and would be in the same vicinity, on the W. side of the upper city. The **Gate of the Spring** (Neh 2¹⁴ 3¹⁵ 12³⁷) may have led to Siloam, with which it is noticed, and was apparently near the S.E. slope of the upper city. It is probably the gate by which Zedekiah fled (2 K 25⁴, Jer 39⁴), and is noticed in connexion with the wall of the Pool of Siloah, and with the king's garden, and the stairs from the city of David. The next points on the wall were 'over against' the sepulchres of David, and at the 'Tower of Heroes' (*gibborim*), and the 'turning of the wall' (Neh 3¹⁶·¹⁹). On Ophel was the 'Projecting Tower' near the **Water Gate**, and apparently close to the ancient palace by the 'Court of the Guard' (Neh 3²⁵·²⁶). The Water Gate would lead to the Gihon spring—probably by the rocky shaft which runs up to the surface of the hill, at the back of the cave in which the Gihon wells up. Between this and the Temple the ruins of a great projecting tower still exist on the old wall. The **Horse Gate** leading to the palace was close to the Temple, and from it the priests repaired the wall (2 K 11¹⁶, 2 Ch 23¹⁵, Neh 3²⁸, Jer 31⁴⁰). The palace is again noticed as the 'House of David' (Neh 12³⁷). On the E. wall of the Temple were two gates called **Gate of Benjamin** (Jer 20², Zec 14¹⁰) and **Gate of the Guard** (2 K 11⁶·¹⁹ [הַשַּׁעַר אַחַר הָרָצִים], Neh 12³⁹ [הַמַּטָּרָה 'ש']). One of these may have been the Upper Gate (2 K 15³⁵, 2 Ch 23²⁰), noticed with Ophel, and one the **Gate of Ham-miphkad** (Neh 3³¹). The description of the circuit closes at the N.E. corner of the Temple, and at the **Sheep Gate** whence it commences. There is, as shown, nothing which indicates discrepancy between this formal account and the earlier incidental notices of the city before the Captivity, or any difficulty in tracing the approximate line of the walls. The city so described occupied about 200 acres, and it is spoken of as extensive in Nehemiah's time (Neh 7⁴). The suggestion once made, that Jerus. before the Captivity occupied only the E. Temple hill, has found few supporters, and it would reduce the city to the impossible area of some 10 acres, not including the Temple. The upper city and lower city are clearly supposed by Jos. to have existed in the time of David and Solomon, and the measurements of 400 and 1000 cubits, above noticed, cannot be reconciled with a view which would make Solomon's capital smaller than any of the modern village hamlets of Palestine. Ancient cities like Tyre and Cæsarea occupied an area of more than 100 acres, as did Rabbath Ammon; and Jerus. was at least as important as any of these.*

---

* Other places in Jerus. noticed in OT include the Temple Gate Sur (2 K 11⁶; in 2 Ch 23⁵ 'gate of the foundation' [הַיְסוֹד] should prob. be 'gate Sur' [סוּר]), the New Gate—apparently the higher (or inner) Temple Gate (Jer 26¹⁰ 36¹⁰), the graves of the common people (Jer 26²³ 31⁴⁰) apparently in the Kidron Valley, the Prison or 'Guard' (Jer 37¹⁵ [בֵּית הָאֵסוּר] ²¹ 38⁶ [הַמַּטָּרָה חֲצַר]), the Baker's Street (37²¹); the Third Entry (or Chief Entry) of the Temple (38¹⁴), the King's wine-presses (probably near the king's

We must next consider the topography of the Greek age, when the Hasmonæans carried out important works at Jerus., and the position of the Gr. citadel or Akra, which threatened the Temple. The Greeks are said to have fortified the city of David for themselves to lie in wait against the Temple (1 Mac 1³³), to which the term Zion seems to be applied by this writer (1 Mac 4³⁶·⁶⁰ 7³²) : the Gr. tower was by (παρά) the Temple (1 Mac 9⁵² 13⁵²), and they issued from the city of David to the Temple (14³⁶). Since the Temple hill was not in the city of David, it would seem that the tower in question was not on the Temple hill. Josephus, in relating the history of this period, calls the tower 'the Akra,'—a term which, as before noticed, he applies to citadels both in the upper and in the lower city. He, however, places the Gr. fortress in the lower city, which was then high, overlooking (ὑπερκειμένη) the Temple (Ant. XII. v. 4). From this citadel Nicanor came down to (εἰς) the Temple (XII. x. 5), and the citadel lay over (ἐπέκειτο) the Temple (XII. ix. 3). In another place he says that the Akra was no other than the lower city (Wars, V. vi. 1), and this apparent contradiction is explained in the passage which relates how Simon, brother of Judas Maccabæus, took the Gr. citadel, and levelled the hill on which it stood, so that the Temple might be higher than it (ὑψηλότερον ᾖ τὸ ἱερόν), a work which occupied three years (Ant. XIII. vi. 6). The tower (ἡ Ἄκρα) of 1 Mac is thus identified by Jos. with Akra, afterwards the lower city. He distinctly explains this in another passage (Wars, V. iv. 1), where he says that the Temple ridge (λόφος) was naturally lower than the Akra, and separated from it by a broad valley (φάραγγι), which the Hasmonæans filled up in order to join the city to the Temple, and demolished the tower so that the Temple might be higher than it. Before the destruction of the Gr. tower Jonathan built a wall in the middle of the city (1 Mac 12³⁶, Ant. XIII. v. 11), which divided the Jews from the Greeks. It seems clear that such a wall—which may have run along the N. face of the hill of the upper city—could not have affected a citadel on the Temple hill. Some recent writers have supposed this citadel to have stood N. of the Temple, where Baris—the later Antonia—was subsequently built by the Hasmonæans (Ant. XV. xi. 4), this view being supported by the Eng. tr. (Ant. XII. ix. 3), which makes the Akra 'adjoin' the Temple,—an incorrect rendering. It is clear that if the site of the Akra was levelled it cannot have been the same high rock still existing, on which—by general consent—Baris or Antonia is held to have been built, apparently by John Hyrcanus (Ant. XVIII. iv. 3), though, as already shown, towers there probably existed in Nehemiah's time and earlier. Most modern plans (including the Ord. Surv. of Jerus., which shows Akra W. of the Temple) agree in placing the lower city N. of the upper and W. of the Temple. The valley W. of the Temple may thus conveniently be termed in future the Hasmonæan Valley, which they filled in with the soil from the Akra hill when it was lowered.

From the Hasmonæan period we pass on to consider Jerus. as it existed under Herod the Great, and at the time of the great siege by Titus ; and here the accounts given by Jos. are easily understood, and accord with the earlier topography of OT. Tacitus gives us a short de-

garden, Zec 14¹⁰), 'the suburbs' (parbarim)* close to the Temple (2 K 23¹¹), and the middle city (2 K 20⁴) or middle court (MSS and all versions). The site of the Middle Gate (Jer 39³) is unknown. The gate Shallecheth (1 Ch 26¹⁶) was by a causeway W. of the Temple.

* Perhaps 'colonnade.' The word (פַּרְבָּר) in 1 Ch 26¹⁸, פַּרְוָרִים in 2 K 23¹¹) is apparently Persian, and means properly *something lighted*, namely, by the sun.

scription (Hist. v. 11. 12), in which he states that Jerus. occupied two hills, with great walls with flanking portions, and crags with towers 60 ft. above the crags, or 120 ft. high when on the flat ground. There were other walls under the royal palace, and the tower of Antonia was particularly conspicuous. There was a fountain of water which ran perpetually, and the mountains were hollowed beneath, and pools and cisterns made for rain water. This brief notice agrees with the more detailed account by Josephus. He states (Wars, V. iv. 1, 2) that Jerus. had three walls on the only side (the N.) on which it was not defended by impassable valleys. It was founded on two hills facing (ἀντιπρόσωπος) each other, and these were divided by a valley in which the houses ended (κατέληγον) on either side (ἐπάλληλοι). The hill which supported (on the S.W.) the upper city (τὴν ἄνω πόλιν ἔχων) was by far the highest and largest. It was the fortress (φρούριον) of David, and the Upper Agora of the time of Josephus. The other hill (to the N.W.) was called Akra (not the Akra), and was gibbous (ἀμφίκυρτος) in shape. Over against (ἀντικρύ) this was a third ridge (λόφος), naturally lower than Akra, and separated from it by the broad valley filled in by the Hasmonæans. The valley dividing the upper and lower city was called Tyropœon ('of the cheesemakers'), and reached to Siloam. This is clearly the deep, broad valley, or recess, described under the head 'Natural Site,' which falls E., on the N. side of the upper city, and joining the Hasmonæan Valley runs down to meet the Kidron at Siloam. The original city stood on the two hills, and the third to the E. was the Temple ridge. In another passage (Ant. XV. xi. 5) Jos. says that the city was placed opposite the Temple like a theatre, girt with a deep valley (that of Hinnom) on the S. Opposite Antonia was a fourth hill called Bezetha (which Jos. renders 'the new city'), separated from that citadel by a deep fosse. It is not impossible that this word is the Aram. Bezatha (בזאתא [?]), 'division.' (Schürer, HJP I. ii. 239 n., thinks it is בית זיתא 'place of olives'). It was the N. part of the Temple ridge divided off by the still existing rock-cut fosse. Jos. next describes the walls, of which the first was attributed to David and Solomon, and later kings. The **First Wall** ran E. from the tower Hippicus to the Xystus, under the W. wall of the Temple, and this N. face of the wall seems to be the same wall in the middle of the city built by the Hasmonæans. Hippicus stood at the N.W. angle, and was one of three royal towers (Wars, II. xvii. 1), the other two being Phasaelus and Mariamne. They stood close to Herod's palace in the upper city (Wars, I. xxi. 1, II. xvii. 6, V. iv. 4, VI. viii. 1), and varied in height, though apparently, according to Tacitus (Hist. v. 11), the tops of the towers were on a level. This was due to the varying height of the rock basis, and these towers possibly correspond with the three main towers of the modern citadel, that which is popularly known as Hippicus being the largest, and corresponding to Phasaelus, the largest royal tower. Phasaelus had an outer 'cloister,' and the great 'Tower of David' is still distinguished by an outer walk round it, at the top of the scarp of the main ditch. From Hippicus the old wall, on the W. side of the upper city, ran S. to Bethso (already noticed as perhaps meaning the 'House of Dung'), which lay where the dunghills of the city are still placed. It passed a gate called the Gate of the Essenes, and its S. face extended to Siloam, where it bent, and evidently left the pool outside, since the Romans drew water at Siloam before the city was taken (Wars, V. ix. 4). On the E. it passed by Solomon's Pool (prob. Gihon), and reached to Ophel, where it joined the E. cloister of the Temple. The Tyropœon Valley, as already explained, was divided from the upper Hinnom Valley by a narrow neck of land, close to the royal towers. It is remarkable that in this valley of 'Cheesemakers' there is still a street where fresh cheeses are sold, and the modern features of the city generally — the fortress of Antonia, the castle at the royal towers, the Temple itself, the situation even of the dunghills outside the wall — retain to the present day the same character as in the time of Josephus. The main market of Jerus. is placed just where the Upper Agora of Herodian times, and of Nehemiah's age, must have existed. The **Second Wall** is more briefly described. It started from a gate called Gennath (prob. the 'garden' gate of the palace), which was in the first wall, and circling round (κυκλούμενον) enclosed the N. part only (τὸ προσάρκτιον κλίμα μόνον) reaching to Antonia. It thus defended Akra or the lower city. It is clearly probable that this wall was built on high ground, and more likely to have crossed the neck of high land already noticed than to have dived down into the Tyropœon, more than 100 ft. below the ground outside it. But if it went 'in a curve,' and started from this point near Phasaelus, it must have also enclosed, or run close to, the high knoll now shown as Calvary. What is known of the rock in this part indicates the existence of a broad trench, W. and N. of the knoll in question, which may have been the fosse of the second wall which, joining Antonia—the modern barracks—at its N.W. angle, was also protected by the Bezetha fosse, which is traceable W. of Antonia. The discovery of part of an ancient wall N. of the royal towers will be noticed under the heading ' Antiquities.

The **Third Wall** of Jerus. had no existence till after the Crucifixion, being that of Agrippa (*Ant.* XIX. vii. 2; *Wars,* V. iv. 2). It ran from Hippicus to a great octagonal tower called Psephinus, at its N.W. corner—a place whence a wide view was obtained, and consequently on very high ground. Thence it ran E. to the Women's Towers, opposite the tomb of Helena, widow of the king of Adiabene, which was 3 furlongs from Jerus. (*Ant.* XX. iv. 3), and acc. to Pausanias had a rolling stone at its entrance (*Greciæ Descript.* viii. 16). Jerome states that it lay E. of the great N. road (*Epit. Paulæ*), and these indications point to the conspicuous monument in Gr.-Jewish style, with a rolling stone at the door, which is now called the 'Tomb of the Kings.' If the measurement is correct, the third wall must have run farther N. than the present N. wall of Jerusalem. Some suppose it to have followed the present line throughout, placing Psephinus—in accordance with mediæval tradition —at the castle of the Pisans (Ḳal'at Jalûd), a ruined 12th cent. castle near the N.W. corner of modern Jerusalem. Robinson, however, found traces of an ancient wall running N.W., in continuation of the present wall, towards the high ground on the watershed near the present Russian cathedral, where probably Psephinus stood.

Jos. says that the third wall stretched a long way (μηκυνόμενον) by the royal caverns, after passing the point opposite Helena's monument, and here it must have stood on the same scarp occupied by the modern wall, E. of the Damascus Gate, in which scarp is the entrance to these caverns or quarries under the city. It then bent (prob. at the existing N.E. angle, which has a rock scarp and fosse), and from the corner tower (still extant), near the Monument of the Fuller (γναφέως), it ran to meet the old wall (apparently of the Temple) by the Kidron Valley. This general description offers no great difficulties, and the only points in dispute are the exact line of the second wall, and of the third wall towards the W. As regards the first point, it should be further noticed

that Jos. describes a great pool called Amygdalon, where the 10th and 15th Legions encamped in attacking the upper city on the N.W. (*Wars,* V. xi. 4). The name seems to mean 'almond pool,' but perhaps stands for *Ham-migdalon,* ' Pool of the Great Tower,' from its proximity to Phasaelus. It is usually identified with the existing *Hammâm el-Batrak,* the 'upper pool' already noticed. This pool is not mentioned till after the taking of the second wall, and seems to have lain inside its circuit, which agrees with the course of the wall generally advocated. Those who regard the traditional Calvary as the true site seek to trace the second wall on the lower ground, S. and E. of the Calvary knoll, in which case it is almost impossible so to draw its lines as to allow of its both running 'in a circle,' and also avoiding the deep broad Tyropœon, which has its head close to the E. side of the pool Amygdalon. If the second wall ran close to the knoll, the third wall cannot have coincided, on the N.W., with the present city wall, which is too close to the line so traced. The whole question is thus mainly influenced by opinion as to the site of Calvary.

In concluding this account of the topography about A.D. 70, various places noticed by Jos. may be briefly mentioned. On the N., 7 furlongs from the city, was Scopus (*Wars,* II. xix. 7, V. 3), near the present village Sha'fat, a high ridge commanding a view of Jerusalem. Close to Antonia was the pool Struthius (*Wars,* V. xi. 4), prob. the later Piscina Interior, recently discovered W. of the Church of St. Anne. E. of the Kidron, on Olivet, was a place called the Rock of the Dovecots (τῆς περιστερεῶνος), and just N. of the village of Siloam is a quarry with remains resembling a dovecot (*Wars,* V. xii. 2; see Ord. Survey Notes, p. 64). On the S. was the tomb of Ananus, which is possibly the Gr.-Jewish tomb in the cliff S. of the Hinnom Valley, close to its junction with the Kidron, now known as the 'retreat of the apostles,' and used—as is shown by remains of frescoes—as a chapel in the Middle Ages. W. of Jerus. were 'Herod's monuments,' near the Serpent Pool (*Wars,* V. iii. 2, vii. 2, xii. 3). The exact site is unknown, but a fine Gr.-Jewish masonry tomb has recently been discovered W. of the Upper Hinnom Valley, opposite the upper city. These places are noted as points on the wall of circumvallation, made by Titus after the third wall was taken. It ran along the E. slope of the Kidron, and outside the Hinnom Valley. On the N.W. it passed the camp of the Assyr., which was outside the second wall (*Wars,* V. xii. 2). Within the city there was a theatre, in an unknown position (*Ant.* XV. viii. 1), and the palace of the Hasmonæans (*Ant.* XX. viii. 11; *Wars,* II. xvi. 3) overlooked the W. cloister of the Temple, near the great bridge, and stood apparently on the cliff at the N.E. corner of the upper city. Other palaces of Agrippa, of Bernice, and of Helena are noticed (*Wars,* II. xvii. 6, IV. xix. 11, VI. vi. 1–3): the first may have been Herod's palace, but that of Helena (and of Monobasus her husband) was in the lower city, as were apparently the Council house and the archives (*Wars,* VI. vi. 3). The Xystus, or gymnasium, built by the high priest Jason (1 Mac 1[14]; *Ant.* XII. v. 1), was near the great bridge, in the valley W. of the Temple (*Wars,* II. xvi. 2, 3, V. iv. 1, VI. iii. 2, viii. 1). The Hippodrome S. of the Temple may be the same as Herod's theatre (*Wars,* I. xxxiii. 6, II. iii. 1). Jos. also speaks of secret passages near the royal towers and Herod's palace (*Wars,* VI. viii. 1), and such a passage still exists leading from the site of this palace underground towards the Temple hill. The city and Temple were supplied with water by Pilate's aqueduct, 200 furlongs long, from Etham ('*Ain 'Atân*) S. of Bethlehem, and from '*Ain*

Kueizîba still farther S. It still brings water along the S. slope of the upper city to the Temple enclosure (*Ant.* XVIII. iii. 2; see Talm. Bab. *Joma* 31*a*).

The places noticed in NT in or near Jerus.— Bethesda, Gethsemane, and Calvary—have been separately treated. Bethesda was very probably the same as Gihon. Calvary cannot be located with certainty, but is now regarded by many as the knoll N. of the Damascus Gate, which was outside the third wall, at the so-called 'Jeremiah's Grotto.' See, further, art. GOLGOTHA. The Judgment Hall of Pilate (Jn 18[28]) appears to have been distinct from Herod's palace (Lk 23[7]), and was probably in Antonia. The Pavement ($\lambda\iota\theta\acute{o}\sigma\tau\rho\omega\tau o\nu$), called Gabbatha (wh. see) in Aram., was in this hall (Jn 19[13]), and Jos. uses this term in speaking of the Temple pavement (*Wars*, VI. i. 8). The site of the high priest's palace (Mt 26[58], Mk 14[54], Lk 22[54], Jn 18[15]) was probably also near the Temple.

Talmudic notices of Jerus. (see Neubauer, *Géog. Talm. s.v.*) are of little value, unless from the Mishna. An ancient rose garden is said to have existed (Talm. Bab. *Baba Ḳamma* 82*a*). All tombs and tanneries were outside the town (Mishna, *Baba Bathra*, ii. 9), but ancient tombs were suspected to exist under the surface (*Parah* iii. 2), and foundations were consequently not dug deep (*Baba Ḳamma* vii. end). Only the royal tombs and that of Huldah were allowed within the walls (Tosephta, *Baba Bathra*, ch. i.). The upper and lower markets are noticed (Tosephta, *Sanhed.* ch. 14), and there were two places called Betzain (בצעין), an upper and a lower, in Jerusalem. The lower dated from Ezra's age, the upper was included in Jerus. by a later king, and lay on the 'weak' (that is, the N.) side (Talm. Jer. *Sanhed.* v.; Tosephta, *Sanhed.* ch. 3; Talm. Bab. *Shebuoth* 16*a*; *Megillath Taanith*, ch. 6). This word seems to mean a 'cutting' or 'fosse,' and the upper Betza may be the Bezetha fosse. A place called *Beth Mamila* is also noticed (Talm. Bab. *Erubin* 51*b*, *Sanhed.* 24*a*; *Bereshith Rabba*, ch. 51), the name of which may survive at the *Birket Mamilla*, W. of the city. The 'market of fatteners' and the 'wool market' were towards the N. (Mishna, *Erubin* x. 9; see Jos., *Wars*, v. viii. 1, where the wool, cloth, and braziers' markets are placed just inside the second wall); and the pagan fullers occupied the upper market (Mishna, *Shekalim* viii. 1). The Stone of Proclamation (Mishna, *Taanith* iii. 8), where lost property was cried, seems to have been in the lower city. The tomb of Kalba Shebuya—a rich man of the time of the great siege (Talm. Bab. *Gittin* 56*a*)—is placed by modern Jewish tradition at the tomb of Helena of Adiabene. The tomb of the Sanhedrin (popularly of the judges) and that of Simon the Just are also shown by the Jews N. of the city. They are Gr.-Jewish monuments.

Space will not allow of any account of the later Roman, Byzantine, Arab, Norman, or recent topography of Jerusalem. The important points have been noticed in speaking of the history. The obliteration of the older ruins in later times must be carefully held in view in considering existing remains, and the mediæval traditions often confuse a topography which is only to be studied in the Bible and in Josephus.

v. ANTIQUITIES.—The existing antiquities dating before A.D. 70 include the remains of the city walls, towers, pools, aqueducts, and tombs, together with the foundations of the temple walls, its bridges and gates, and the site of Antonia with its outer fosse. The extant inscriptions are few. Many of these ruins have been brought to light by excavation since 1867. They are mingled with later remains, such as the Ecce Homo Arch,—probably erected by Hadrian or his successors,—the work of

Constantine and Justinian, the wall of Eudoxia, and the numerous churches and chapels of Byzant. and 12th cent. origin; while the Temple Area is covered with the buildings of the Khalifs succeeding 'Abd el-Melek. The remains of **Walls**, as yet known, belong chiefly to the *first wall*. Its N. face followed the steep slopes and cliffs which are shown, by observations of the rock in house foundations, to have formed the N. side of the hill of the upper city. The royal towers still present, in their lower courses, the large drafted masonry of Herod's age, which occurs also in the Temple walls; but a later sloping scarp was added outside the walks which surround the so-called Tower of David (prob. Phasaelus), by the Crusaders. At the Protestant cemetery, south of the present S.W. angle of the Turkish wall, a rock scarp, with projecting rock bases for towers, was explored in 1874–5. It has recently (1894–6) been traced eastwards, and it is generally allowed to represent the S.W. angle of the ancient wall. Dr. Bliss has traced a wall thence to Siloam—where it was explored by Dr. Guthe in 1881—enclosing the pool. The character of the masonry is that distinctive of the Byzantine age, and the wall appears to be that built by Eudoxia (about B.C. 450), which enclosed Siloam. The pool, as above, was outside the walls in A.D. 70. Under this wall, however, in parts, on the S. slope of the upper city, Dr. Bliss has found remains of an older wall generally of rougher masonry. In one part the Byzantine wall is not carried to the rock, but rests on rubbish under which the old wall was hidden. A gate towards the west of the south face of the upper city wall belongs to the older period, but was renewed in the later times. This seems to answer to the gate of the Essenes noticed by Jos., and it is possibly the Dung Gate of Neh. in Bethso. The point where the old wall crossed the Tyropœon above Siloam is still unknown, but on Ophel Sir C. Warren discovered a fine rampart under the surface, running S. from the S.E. corner of the Ḥaram enclosure for 70 ft., and then S.W. for 700 ft., with a great tower near this end, 80 ft. face and 20 ft. projection. The upper part of the wall is of masonry like that of the modern S. wall of Jerus., but this appears to have been re-used. The first 20 ft. from the foundations present a rough rubble of moderate dimensions, not unlike the masonry of the old wall found by Dr. Bliss. This is founded, not on rock, but on red virgin soil. The rock was traced farther S. on Ophel by Dr. Guthe in 1881, and the masonry then found was of Byzantine character. Although the older wall thus traced in parts, from the gate of the Essenes to the E. cloister of the Temple, does not usually present *in situ* the fine masonry of the Herodian age, it is possible that the rude foundations may belong to Nehemiah's age, the wall erected on them having been used up by later builders in the present city wall and in the upper part of the Temple ramparts. As regards the *second wall*, it is impossible to trace it under the houses of the modern city; but in 1883 a wall of masonry like that of the royal towers was found, running N. on the neck of high land W. of the Amygdalon Pool. This is probably part of the second wall. The *third wall* was still traceable outside the city when Dr. Robinson visited Jerus. half a cent. ago (*BRP*[2] i. 315), but the only remains of its course now traceable are the scarp E. of the Damascus Gate, and possibly the remains of a tower on a rocky knoll N. of the gate and W. of the main N. road, where the Women's Towers appear to have marked an angle in the wall. There are some fine stones in the side of a tank farther N., which may have belonged to the third wall, but they are not apparently *in situ*. It will, however, be seen that exploration has now shown us approximately the course of the first wall, and the starting-point of the second on the W., while remains of the third can also be laid down on the map from measurements and angles taken by Dr. Robinson. The points still requiring study on the ground affect the farther course of the second wall, and the point at which the first wall crossed the Tyropœon Valley. A fine flight of broad steps discovered close to Siloam on the north may mark the position of the 'stairs from the city of David' in the Tyropœon.

The various **Pools** of ancient Jerus. have been described, and it is only necessary to add that the great pool in the Hinnom Valley, now called *Birket es-Sultân*, did not exist till the 12th cent., though called in the 14th 'The lower pool of Gihon.' The wall of its dam bears an inscription of A.D. 1537. In the 12th cent. it was built by the Germans, and is called 'the German Lake' and the 'New Cistern' (*Citez de Jherusalem* after A.D. 1187, and Theodoric A.D. 1172; Cartulary of Holy Sep. Nos. 169, 170). In addition to Pilate's *Aqueduct* on the S. there was a conduit to the royal towers (Jos. *Wars*, v. vii. 2), perhaps the older conduit of the upper pool. Such a conduit still enters the city from the Birket Mamilla on the W. An aqueduct has also been found on the W. slope of Bezetha leading to the fosse N. of Antonia. It seems to have collected rain water from the rocks N. of the city to fill the fosse. It is continued through the rock of Antonia, in a narrow passage to which Jos. alludes, in connexion with Strato's Tower and Antonia (*Ant.* XIII. xi. 2; *Wars*, I. iii. 4), and it is now closed at the end by the Ḥaram wall, inside which, not far off, is a large cistern to which the passage—if used as an aqueduct—may have led. It would seem to have been cut before the time of Herod, perhaps by the Hasmonæans, and to have existed — as did the Antonia fosse—in the time of Pompey. It may, however, have served as a secret exit from a window in the Ḥaram wall, which has been found above the passage. The oldest Jerus. aqueduct is, however, probably that of Hezekiah, leading from Gihon to Siloam. The inscription found near its mouth in 1881 is cut on the rock wall of the tunnel, and records in ancient Heb. letters the fact that the tunnel was begun from both ends, the parties meeting in the middle, and that it was 1200 cubits long. The length as chained is 1658 ft. long, giving a cubit of 16 in. The point of junction was determined by the surveyors near the centre. The course of this tunnel is very winding, and the level appears to have been lowered near the mouth to obtain a proper flow. The aqueduct branches out of a passage at the back of the Gihon pool, leading to a shaft with steps reaching up to the surface of the Ophel hill at the probable site of the Water Gate. (As to the questions that have been raised regarding the date of this inscription see the Literature cited in art. HEZEKIAH, p. 377ᵃ, footnote).

The existing **Tombs** of the city include the **monument of Helena** already noticed, in an under chamber of which de Saulcy discovered a sarcophagus bearing an Aram. inscription, with the name of 'queen Sarah,' and early Rom. coins. Sarah may have been the native name of Helena. The **monuments of Herod** have also been noticed, and the tomb of Ananus (*Wars*, v. xii. 2). On the E. side of the Kidron are four fine monuments in Gr.-Jewish style, not unlike that of the Petra tombs. The most northerly (now called **Absalom's Tomb**) has a masonry cupola, and is possibly the tomb of Alex. Jannæus (*Wars*, v. xii. 2), which lay in this direction. The so-called **Tomb of St. James** is a true Jewish chamber, with an outer Doric porch bearing, in early square Heb., the

names of priests of the Bene Hezir family, and probably cut about A.D. 50. The other two monuments to the S. are uninscribed, but of the same period. The **Tombs of the Judges** (so called) belong to the Rom. period, and near them is a broken tomb with a fragment of Aram. inscription of about the 1st cent. A.D. Immediately W. of the knoll of Jeremiah's Grotto (the possible site of Calvary) are remains of a Jewish tomb, with an additional chamber in the Gr. style. There is a large cemetery near, with Christian tombs of the Byzantine and Crusaders' ages, interspersed with some which bear mediæval Jewish texts. The tombs S. of the Hinnom Valley are also Byzantine, bearing texts which connect them with the Church of St. Sion on the hill of the upper city hard by. The so-called **Tomb of Simon the Just**, N. of Jerus., is also a Greek tomb.

Before describing the remains of the Temple and of Antonia, a word may be added as to **Inscriptions** discovered at Jerusalem. The majority of these are Byzantine Greek-Christian texts and tombstones of Crusaders. An inscription of Hadrian is built upside down into the S. wall of the Temple. Another of the time of Trajan (dating A.D. 117), found in the upper city, records the worship of Serapis at Jerusalem. The osteophagi on Olivet bear Gr. names, and in one case a Heb. text is marked with a cross, as though belonging to a Jewish Christian. They date probably from the 2nd to the 4th cent. A.D. Later Jews have also cut their names on the Temple walls, but the only Jewish texts previous to A.D. 70 are those above mentioned on the tombs, the Siloam Text, probably written about B.C. 702,* and the boundary stone of the Temple enclosure, with Gr. inscription excluding strangers.

The great Ḥaram enclosure at J. presents, at its foundations, magnificent drafted masonry of Gr. character, on the S., W., and E. The dressing of the stones is found nowhere else except at Hebron, and on the arch of the Tyropœon Bridge, but in general character this masonry resembles that of the royal towers, and of the palace of Hyrcanus, built in A.D. 176 at Tyrus in Gilead. The stones average 3½ ft. in height, but on the S. wall a 'master course' 7 ft. high runs W. for 600 ft. from the S.E. angle. The longest stones measure 24 and 39 ft. The whole of this masonry is dressed smooth on face and draft, excepting at the base of the W. wall for 20 ft., under an ancient pavement near the Tyropœon Bridge, and on the E. wall N. of the Golden Gate, where the head of a cross valley exists inside the wall. Probably, in these cases, the rough-faced stones were never visible above the surface. On the E. wall, at the base, are masons' marks in red paint, and two or three Phœn. letters which have forms of a late period. The Tyropœon Bridge, crossing to the upper city from the W. wall close to the S., consisted of two spans. Beneath the old pavement under the bridge an older voussoir has been found, lying in a rock aqueduct, and evidently belonging to an older bridge. The N. side of the Ḥaram is partly bounded by the great block of rock on which the citadel of Antonia stood, and east of this the N. wall presents none of the original masonry, but is built in the later Rom. or Byzant. style. Nor is there any angle in the old E. wall at this point. The smooth masonry which occurs above the drafted was built later than the time of Hadrian,— probably by Justinian,—and the upper part of the rampart is Arab work. The original drafted

---

* This Siloam inscription, now removed and preserved in fragments in the Stamboul Museum, must not be confused with an illegible text in Phœn. characters (now in the Brit. Mus.) found in the village of Siloam. The words *Beth Baal* have been read on the latter, and it may indicate the situation of **one of** Solomon's temples on Olivet.

masonry is attributed by de Vogüé to Herod the Great—an opinion very generally accepted; and no remains of earlier work in the Ḥaram are known. The enclosure is an oblong, with right angles on the S.W. and N.E.   The S.E. angle measures 92½°. The S. wall is 922 ft. long, the N. 1042 ft., the W. 1601 ft., and the E. 1042 ft. The area included is about 35 acres. The Tyropœon Bridge appears to be of the same age with the ancient wall, and the older broken voussoir may have belonged to the bridge broken down by Pompey (Jos. *Ant.* XIV. iv. 2; *Wars*, I. vii. 2). In the S. wall there are two ancient gates, which answer to the two Huldah Gates of the Mishna (*Middoth* i. 3): they appear to have been originally both double, with two inner passages having a total width of 40 ft. (30 cubits), the roofs supported by great columns, and presenting flat domes. The domes of the W. gate remain intact, presenting a semi-classic design of coffer pattern, intertwined with a vine in low relief. This work is attributed by Ferguson the architect to the time of Herod.   The lintels of the entrances were formed by huge blocks 18 ft. span. The E. gate (now called the Triple Gate) was altered later,—probably by Justinian,—and the passages leading N. from these gates seem probably also to belong to this later period. The vaults in the S.E. corner of the Ḥaram are also later restorations, but remains of a more ancient vaulting are found, by an ancient window, on the E. wall in these vaults.

On the W. there were four entrances to the enclosure, the S. being at the Tyropœon Bridge. The next is a subterranean gate with a passage leading up from the level of the valley. The third was connected with a causeway which appears to be ancient, but which is not noticed by Josephus. The last, to the N., is now converted into a cistern, but the original passage pierced the wall, and belonged to a gate on or near the level of the valley. These gates seem therefore to answer to the *Parbar* or 'suburb' gates of the Mishna, and to the four entrances noticed by Jos., on the W. side of the Temple (*Ant.* XV. xi. 5), of which the first led to the royal S. cloister, the second to the suburb (προάστειον), the third also to the suburb, and the fourth to the 'other city,' by a descent of steps into the valley.

Within the Ḥaram there are no known remains of the ancient Temple, except the great rock-cut vaults and cisterns, of which the largest towards the S.—called the Great Sea—is supported on rock pillars, and capable of holding three million gallons.   On the N. the scarp of Antonia rises 30 ft. above the flat rock surface of the inner court, and the block of rock measures 140 ft. N. and S. by 350 ft. E. and W. The fosse to the N. was converted later (before A.D. 333) into a 'twin pool,' by walls and vaulted roofs, and this is identified in the 4th cent. A.D. with Bethesda. In A.D. 70, however, the twin pools had probably no existence. On the W. Ḥaram wall the present writer, in 1873, discovered, close to Antonia, the existence of projecting piers of the ancient masonry above the level of the inner court, resembling those which adorn the wall of the Hebron Ḥaram, which consists of masonry like that of the Jerus. enclosure.   In other parts the wall does not reach this level, but it appears probable that the same arrangement existed, at the same level, on the other faces of the enclosure.   These remains, together with 40 observations of the level of the rock surface, visible in tanks or vaults, or at the foot of the wall, are the only antiquities known to remain which enable us to understand the area and position of the Temple enclosure, and of Antonia as restored by Herod the Great.

VI. THE TEMPLE ENCLOSURE.—Solomon's Temple

(1 K 6, 2 Ch 3; *Ant.* VIII. iii.) was 60 cubits long E. and W., 20 broad, and 30 high (the cubit, as measured at Siloam, and on the masonry of the Jerus. Ḥaram and Galilæan synagogues, being about 16 in.).   Its porch to the E. was 20 cubits broad and 10 cubits deep. The chambers, on N., S., and W., were built with a wall set back in steps, so that the interiors in the third storey were 7 cubits wide, in the second 6 cubits, in the first 5 cubits. The thickness of the walls is not stated. The roofs were of cedar, and the interior gilded with designs similar to the Bab. bas-reliefs of cherubs guarding palm trees.   The whole structure and style, in short, seems to have resembled the art of Phœnicia and Chaldæa rather than that of Egypt. The Temple appears to have had an inner priests' court, with bronze altar, and an outer court, but no measurements of these are given.* In the later account (2 Ch 3⁴) the height is given as 120 cubits (LXX 20 cubits), and Jos. believed that Solomon's Temple was 60 cubits higher than the later restoration by Zerub. (*Ant.* XV. xi. 3). It is possible that the porch may have formed a lofty pylon higher than the Holy House itself. It is not clear whether the two bronze pillars, Jachin and Boaz, each 23 cubits high (1 K 7¹⁵⁻²¹), supported the lintel of the pylon gate, or whether they stood outside as stelæ (the word 'in' may be rendered 'for,' v.²¹). Jos. gives the area of Solomon's enclosure at 4 furlongs (*Ant.* XV. xi. 3), and places the E. cloister close to a deep valley (*Ant.* XX. ix. 7), stating that Sol. built the E. wall, to which later kings added others (*Wars*, V. v. 1).   But it is not clear how these details could be known when he wrote, since he states that Herod 'took away the ancient foundations' (*Ant.* XV. xi. 3), and built the cloisters 'from the foundation,' and enclosed 'double the area' (*Wars*, I. xxi. 1). He understands the Temple itself to have had an upper storey, and gives the number of chambers as 30 in all (*Ant.* VIII. iii. 2); but these accounts of a building destroyed nearly seven centuries before his time are of less value than his description of buildings which he had himself seen.

There is, however, little doubt that the Holy House occupied the same site, and was of the same length and breadth, in the time of Herod and of Solomon. Jos. says that Zerub. placed the altar 'in the same place where it had formerly been built' (*Ant.* XI. iv. 1); and as to the situation of this building, he says that 'at first the topmost plateau (τὸ ἀνωτάτω χθαμαλόν) barely sufficed for the Holy House and the altar' (*Wars*, V. v. 1, see *Ant.* VIII. iii. 9), whence it appears that the highest part of the ridge was the site selected. Herod, though he altered the enclosure, did not touch the Temple itself, which was restored by the priests. In the Mishna it is stated that the east door of the Holy House was directly opposite the summit of Olivet (*Midd.* ii. 4; *Parah* iii. 9, iv. 2; see Ezk 43¹²).   As regards the general description of the third Temple, the account given by Jos. agrees with the careful details of the Mishna (*Middoth*), but his measurements are unreliable—as in other cases at Cæsarea, Samaria, Masada, etc.—and often contradictory. He makes the altar 20 cubits square (*c. Apion.* i. 22), or elsewhere 50 cubits (*Wars*, V. v. 6), and the valleys 300 to 400 cubits deep (*Ant.* VIII. iii. 9; *Wars*, V. v. 1), the real depth not exceeding 160 ft. He speaks of stones 40 cubits long and 6 cubits

---

* There appears to have been a 'causeway' or ascent by steps to the Temple (1 Ch 26¹⁶), perhaps the same described by Jos. (*Ant.* XV. xi. 5) towards the N. part of the W. wall; but as regards the 'ascent' (עֲלִיָּתוֹ) in the time of Sol. (1 K 10⁵, in 2 Ch 9⁴), LXX, Vulg., Pesh. render in K (according to the regular sense of עֲלִיָּה) and read in Ch, 'the burnt-offerings which he offered,' and Jos. follows this reading (*Ant.* VIII. vi. 5). See ASCENT.

high (*Ant.* XX. ix. 7; *Wars*, V. v. 1), a greatly exaggerated estimate. When, therefore, he gives the circumference of the third Temple as 4 furlongs * (*Ant.* XV. xi. 3), or, including Antonia, 6 furlongs (*Wars*, VI. v. 4), we must remember that he was writing in Rome, and merely estimated the lengths. Measured along the extant walls, the area, including Antonia, is about 8 furlongs in all.

Following the description of Jos., some authorities suppose that Herod's Temple occupied a square of 600 ft. side, in the S.W. part of the Ḥaram. The objections to this view are briefly: 1st, that in this case the Temple cannot have stood on the 'topmost plateau'; 2nd, that the area noticed in the Mishna (500 cubits square) is larger; 3rd, that there are no remains of any walls, to E. and N., at the required distances, and no break in the S. wall 600 ft. from the S.W. angle; 4th, that the Ophel wall joined the 'E. cloister,' and has been discovered abutting on the E. wall of the Ḥaram; 5th, that the existing outer gates agree with the descriptions only if the Temple Area is supposed to coincide with the present boundaries of the Ḥaram; 6th, that unless placed on the topmost plateau, the Temple—surrounded by courts at various levels—must have required foundations 30 to 100 ft. deep to reach the known levels of the rock. The masonry was too heavy to have been simply founded on earth. These objections have never been answered, and in our present state of knowledge it seems safer to depend on the general statements of Jos. than on his measurements, which are hard to reconcile with his incidental remarks.

In order to study this question by the light of recent exploration it is necessary to fix the position of **Antonia**, that of each angle of the Temple enclosure, and the position of the 'topmost plateau' opposite the summit of Olivet. Antonia is described (*Wars*, V. v. 8) as standing at the corner of the N. and W. cloisters, on a rock 50 cubits high, scarped on all sides: it had four corner towers, and a large inner space with courts, baths, and places for camps. A ditch and valley protected the towers outside in the time of Pompey (*Ant.* XIV. iv. 2). Strabo speaks of this ditch as 60 ft. deep and 250 ft. broad (see *Wars*, I. vii. 3, v. iv. 2). Cloisters joined Antonia to the Temple (*Wars*, II. xvi. 5, 6), and the rock hid the Temple on the N. (*Wars*, V. v. 8), looking down on the courts (*Wars*, V. ix. 2, VI. i. 5, ii. 5, 9): when it was taken, immediate access was obtained to the flat courts and to the inner Temple (*Wars*, VI. iii. 7). The area of Antonia seems to have formed a projection on the N.W., so that when it was destroyed the Temple enclosure itself became a quadrangle (τετράγωνον, *Wars*, VI. v. 4). There is only one existing site which answers to such a description—namely, the block of rock already described at the N.W. angle of the present Ḥaram. This rock overlooks all the interior, and rises 20 ft. higher than the Sakhrah or holy 'rock,' which is the highest point within the Ḥaram. The outer fosse is also traceable, separating this site from Bezetha. The rock thus supporting the modern barracks is therefore identified, on all recent plans, with Antonia—the older Baris or Birah of the time of the Hasmonæans and of Nehemiah. It follows that the W. wall throughout may be regarded as belonging to the enclosure of Antonia and of the Temple in the time of Herod. The S.W. angle is generally agreed to be that of Herod's Temple; and as regards the S.E., Jos. (*Wars*, V. iv. 2) clearly states that the Ophel wall joined the 'E. cloister' of the Temple, so that all the E. wall

appears also to belong to the time of Herod, since the junction with the Ophel wall has been determined by excavation. The N.E. angle remains in doubt; for, as above noticed, the N. wall, east of the Antonia rock, is not of the same masonry with the others, while the cisterns inside this part of the Ḥaram are not rock-cut, but are built of masonry very late in character. It seems probable that this part of the area is modern, and that the old N. wall of the Temple ran E. and W. on the line of the present N. wall of the platform, where remains of ancient buttresses have been found. The N.E. part of the Ḥaram is crossed by a valley, running into the Kidron, which has been filled in with earth, but which, in A.D. 70, may have bounded the Temple on the N., and the inner court of Antonia on the E. A gate called Tadi led, by an underground passage, out of the Temple on this side.

As regards the 'topmost plateau,' the rock below Antonia, on the S., is visible over a considerable area at a level about 2430 ft. above the Mediterranean. It has been artificially cut down to form a flat surface. Farther S.E. it rises, in the Sakhrah itself, to a height of 2440 ft., but under the platform which surrounds the Sakhrah its height nowhere exceeds 2432 ft. About twenty observations have been made, which concur in showing a flat plateau at this level, occupying the central part of the Ḥaram. The slope to the W. is very steep, the rock falling to an average level of 2350 ft. at the base of the W. outer wall. The slope to the E. is also steep, though not equal to that on the W. On the S. the plateau narrows to a long spur, which sinks towards Siloam. It is evident that a building surrounded by terraced courts, at various lower levels, can well be fitted to the ground only if its highest floor level is placed on the highest part of the plateau now ascertained to exist, as above described. If, moreover, a line be drawn E., at right angles to the W. wall of the Ḥaram, and through the Sakhrah rock, it will be found to cut the summit of Olivet immediately N. of the present Church of the Ascension. If, on the other hand, the Temple be placed farther to the S.W. (as proposed by those who accept the measurements given by Jos.), not only can no line be so drawn, but the Temple is made to stand on the narrower and lower part of the spur, and its foundations would rest on the steep W. slopes, here falling 90 ft. below the crest of the spur. These various considerations seem, therefore, all to point to the vicinity of the Sakhrah as marking the site of the Holy House itself.

Placed in such a position, it will be found that the levels of the courts, as described in the Mishna and by Jos., agree throughout with the actual levels. In no part does the rock rise or fall so as to render it necessary to suppose foundations of more than 2 or 3 ft. The Sakhrah itself may be that 'stone of foundation' (*Eben hash-Shĕthîyah*) which supported the Holy of Holies, and was said to be the foundation of the world (Mishna, *Joma* v. 3, *Tamid* i. 1) sealing the mouth of an abyss —a legend which still attaches to the Sakhrah and its cave. Under the altar there was no hollow place (Talm. Bab. *Zebahim* 58*a*), and its position would agree with a part of the Ḥaram where there are no vaults. The gate Tadi or 'hiding' (*Middoth* i. 3) was reached by an underground passage from the N. side of the inner cloister, and remains of such a passage exist N. of the Sakhrah. On the S. side was the Chamber of the Draw-well, and on this side there is an existing tank in the required position. The Altar Court was 6 cubits lower than the floor of the Temple (or at a level of about 2432 ft. above the Mediter.),

---

* If Herod's Temple enclosure was double that of Sol., it is manifestly impossible that both measured four furlongs in circumference (see references in text.)

and the great Court of the Women, farther E., was again 7½ cubits lower (or about 2422 ft. above the same datum), but on the S. and N. the Altar Court was only 5 cubits above the outer level, which would therefore be about 2426 ft. above the datum—these levels depending on the number of steps, each half a cubit high, noticed in the Mishna (*Middoth*) and by Jos. (*Wars*, v. v.). On applying the plan to the ground it is found that, in each case, the levels so obtained agree exactly with the actual levels, as shown by the present author in 1879 (Conder's *Handbook to the Bible*, last chapter).

The details given in the Mishna (*Middoth*) suffice to enable us to draw a block plan of Herod's Temple. The exact arrangements of the gateways and cloisters can only be conjectured, but the enclosure, which is said to have been 500 cubits square, surrounded the inner courts, which no Gentile might enter. The Priests' Court, which surrounded the Holy House, and included the great altar to its east, measured 135 cubits N. and S. by 137 E. and W. On the E. was the great gate Nicanor, leading to the 'Court of the Women,' which was 135 cubits square. Between this and the Court of the Priests a narrow platform (11 cubits wide), having beneath it (*Midd.* ii. 6) chambers opening into the 'Women's Court,' was called the 'Court of Isr.,' and reserved for men only, who formed a representative congregation of Israel. The women were confined to galleries in the Women's Court, which was the general meeting-place of the Jews. Immediately outside these courts a fence (*soreg*) surrounded the Temple, and inscriptions in Gr. (one of which has been recovered) forbade any Gentile to enter on pain of death. The Holy House itself (*hekal*) included a porch (*aula*) and the Holy of Holies. The latter was 20 cubits square, and the Holy Place 40 cubits long by 20 broad (as in Solomon's Temple). The porch was 100 cubits broad N. and S., and the total length of the building was 100 cubits E. and W., the breadth of the main part being 70 cubits, including the chambers to N., S., and E., and the outer gallery (*impluvium*) beyond them on N. and S. The height of the porch was 100 cubits, and that of the main building 45 cubits with a flat roof. A second storey appears to have existed, above the Holy Place and Holy of Holies, its roof 100 cubits from the ground. The great gate of the porch was 20 cubits broad and 40 cubits high, and over it were five oak beams to which apparently the golden vine was nailed. There were apparently two veils—one to the outer gate, one to the doorway of the Holy Place, and these were annually renewed. The surrounding chambers, in three storeys, numbered 38 in all. A stairway in the *impluvium*, on the N., led to the roofs. Twelve steps led down, on the E., to the Priests' Court. In this stood the altar, of rubble and mortar, 32 cubits square at the foundation, which was 1 cubit high. The main part above was 30 cubits square and 5 cubits high; the hearth was 28 cubits square; the total height of the altar was 10 cubits, with four 'horns' at the angles. The sloping ascent on the S. was 16 cubits broad and 32 cubits long, leading to the foot of the hearth. The Court of the Priests had three gates to the N. and three to the S. The E. gate on the N. was called Nitzotz, and had an *exhedra*, the N.W. gate Moked had four chambers at the sides, where the Temple guard of priests kept watch. An underground passage led N. to Tadi, the gate near Antonia, and also to the latrines. On the S. the W. gate was named Aptinas, or, otherwise, the Water Gate, the two others being the Gate of the Offering and the Gate of Flaming. On the E. 15 steps led down

from the great gate Nicanor to the Women's Court. These gates were flanked by chambers,— those for salt, for the high priest's bath and for washing, being on the N.; those for wood, for the drawwell and the 'Chamber of Hewn Stone' where the Sanhedrin sat, being on the S. of the Priests' Court. The four chambers of Moked were for the lamb of the daily sacrifice (on S.W.), for the shewbread (on S.E.), for the stones of the old altar taken down by Judas Maccabæus (on N.E.), and for washing, with a descent to the north passage. In the corners of the Women's Court were four chambers,—that of the Nazirites on S.E., that where the wood for the altar was kept on N.E., that of the lepers on N.W., and that for oil on the S.W. The two chambers flanking Nicanor were for the vestment keeper and the pancake maker. Musical instruments were kept in the chambers under the narrow walk called the 'Court of Isr.,' which was divided from the Priests' Court by a railing, near which was a pulpit whence they addressed the people. The Court of Isr. was apparently 2½ cubits lower than the level of the Priests' Court. The *soreg* was reached by three gates, on the N., S., and E. of the Women's Court, and was a lattice-work fence. The limit of 500 cubits square was marked by the *khel* ('rampart' or 'terrace'), which was 10 cubits wide, and reached apparently by other steps (*Wars*, v. v. 2). The gates of the outer walls (or 'Mountain of the House'), namely, the two Huldah Gates on the S., the Parbar Gates and Kipunos ('descent') on the W., with Tadi on the N., have been already noticed. On the E. was the gate Shushan, the position of which is doubtful. The outer cloisters, along the rampart walls, were double except on the S., where the royal cloister is described by Jos. as having three walks, with 162 pillars, each about 6 ft. in diameter (*Ant.* xv. xi. 5). The walks were 30 ft., 45 ft., and 30 ft. wide, and this measurement (in Gr. ft.) agrees closely with the width and position of the existing Tyropœon Bridge, which has a breadth of 50 ft., and an arch 41 ft. 6 in. span. The pillars as described are of about the size of those still standing in the vaulted chamber of the Double (or W. Huldah) Gate, and the epistylia would have been about 22 ft.—the cloister stretching to the present S.E. angle of the Ḥaram. This gives a very natural inter-columniation of 2½ diameters. The pillars were 27 ft. high according to Josephus. These details, taken—except when otherwise stated—from the Tract *Middoth* of the Mishna, agree with the more general description by Jos., except in some cases as regards measurements, where the account of the Rabbis—some of whom had seen the Temple standing, and had been able to measure its ruins— is to be preferred to one written in Italy. No difficulty is found in understanding this account, or in fitting plan and section to the ground, if the Temple is placed opposite the summit of Olivet, on the 'topmost plateau' of the hill.

VII. MODERN JERUSALEM. — Within the last twenty years Jerus. has so largely increased in size and population, on account of Jewish and European settlers building houses outside the walls, that the most recent plans give little idea of the city. The Mount of Olives is covered with houses, and a considerable suburb has sprung up N. of the Damascus Gate. On the W. the Jewish cottages stretch more than a mile from the Jaffa Gate (in the W. wall), and many villas, standing in gardens, reach from W. of the Russian hospice to the vicinity of Birket Mamilla. On the S. other houses, and a German settlement, stand on the high ground S. of the Hinnom Valley. On the S.W. is the railway station. The population has increased from 20,000 souls (including Christians, Moslems, and 8000 Jews) to between 40,000 and 50,000 souls, the Jews having increased to about 30,000 in all. In 1838 there were only 3000 Jews in the city. It is beyond the present purpose to describe the modern city (see Baedeker's *Guide*), but the above-mentioned changes are too remarkable to pass unnoticed.

LITERATURE.—The lit. of the subject would form a vol. by itself, but the progress of scientific study has rendered obsolete most of the works written before A.D. 1838. The generally accepted views as to the topography, which have been given above, are substantially in accord with the conclusions of Dr. E. Robinson (*BRP*, 1838 and 1852, 2nd ed. 3 vols. 1856). The work of Sir C. Warren, and of the present writer, down to 1883, is detailed in the Jerus. vol. of *SWP*. The later explorations, to 1898, are detailed in *PEFSt*, 1883–98, and in Bliss and Dickie's *Excavations at Jerusalem*, 1898. The Ord. Surv. Notes by Sir C. W. Wilson, 1865, give valuable accounts of the antiquities then known. The works of de Vogüé (*Églises de la Terre Sainte*, 1860, and *Le Temple de Jerus.* 1863) are standard authorities for the later periods. The Byzant. and 12th cent. topography is to be studied in the series issued by the Pal. Pilgrims Texts Soc., esp. in the valuable tract, dating after A.D. 1187, called *La Citez de Jherusalem*. It is also discussed in *SWP*. The views advocated by Sir C. W. Wilson are detailed in Smith's *DB²*. The modern city is fully described by Dr. A. Socin in Baedeker's *Handbook to Pal. and Syria.* Without reference to these leading works the student will be unable to obtain correct information as to the views of the chief authorities, and the extant buildings; but familiarity with these, and with Jos. and the Mishna, will be found sufficient, without reference to obsolete theories or to popular works. A valuable and exhaustive paper on the Talm. accounts of the Temple has been published by the *PEF* in 1886, representing the labours of Dr. T. Chaplin for many years in Jerus. itself. The architectural history of the Ḥaram, by the present author, is detailed in *Tent Work in Pal.*, and the full details of the Temple in Conder's *Handbook to the Bible*, 1879. Recent discoveries have not, in any instance, upset the conclusions therein urged, and in some cases they have afforded unexpected support to those conclusions, as shown in this brief account of the Holy City.
                                    C. R. CONDER.

JERUSHA (יְרוּשָׁא 2 K 15³³ = JERUSHAH יְרוּשָׁה 2 Ch 27¹, 'possession' or 'possessed').—Mother of Jotham king of Judah. Her father's name is given as Zadok.

JESHAIAH (יְשַׁעְיָהוּ, יְשַׁעְיָה 'salvation of J"').—1. A grandson of Zerubbabel, 1 Ch 3²¹. 2. One of the sons of Jeduthun, 1 Ch 25³·¹⁵. 3. A Levite, the ancestor of one of David's treasurers, 1 Ch 26²⁵. 4. The chief of the Bĕnê-Elam who returned with Ezra, Ezr 8⁷. 5. Chief of the Merarites in time of Ezra, Ezr 8¹⁹. 6. A Benjamite, Neh 11⁷. See GENEALOGY.

JESHANAH (יְשָׁנָה).—A town, named along with Bethel, taken from Jeroboam by Abijah, 2 Ch 13¹⁹. It is probably the modern *'Ain Sinia*, a village with a spring, about 3¼ miles north of Bethel. See *SWP* vol. ii. sheet xiv. In 1 S 7¹² we ought also (so Wellh., Driver, Klosterm., Kittel, Budde) to read *Jeshanah* for MT *Shen* (הַשֵּׁן). See SHEN. Probably the same place is meant by the *Isanas* (ἡ Ἰσάνας) of Josephus (*Ant.* XIV. xv. 12), where Herod the Great defeated the troops of Antigonus.
                                    C. R. CONDER.

JESHARELAH.—See ASHARELAH.

JESHEBEAB (יֶשֶׁבְאָב).—A Levite, the head of the 14th course, 1 Ch 24¹³. B of the LXX strangely enough omits the name, although thereby the whole number of courses is reduced to twenty-three. A has Ἰσβάαλ, Vulg. *Isbaab*. Kittel (see *SBOT, ad loc.*) thinks that aversion to a name compounded with -*baal* accounts for its elimination in B. See also Gray, *Heb. Prop. Names*, 24.

JESHER (יֵשֶׁר 'uprightness').—A son of Caleb, 1 Ch 2¹⁸. The LXX Ἰωάσαρ would lead us to expect an *o* in the first syllable (cf. notes of Kittel in *SBOT*, and Baer).

JESHIMON.—This word occurs with def. art.

(הַיְשִׁימֹן) in Nu 21²⁰ 23²⁸, 1 S 23¹⁹·²⁴ 26¹·³ 'Jeshimon' AV, 'desert' RV in all. A similar variation is found in the renderings of LXX and Vulgate. The latter translates by *desertum* and *solitudo* except in 1 S 23²⁴, where it has *Jeshimon*. The LXX renders it in Samuel by τοῦ Ἰεσσαιμού (Ελεσσ... is a variant in A), but in Numbers by ἔρημος with the def. article. The Targums have יְשׁימֹן in Numbers בֵּית יְשִׁמוֹת Nu 23²⁸ Targ. Jon.), but in Samuel יְשִׁימֹן; Syr. has אשׁימֹן throughout. The word also occurs in 7 places in parallelism with *midhbar*, which always in these passages has the def. art. (except in Dt 32¹⁰), while *jeshimon* is without it. In Dt 32¹⁰, Ps 68⁷ 78⁴⁰ 106¹⁴ the word is used of the land through which the children of Israel passed on their way to Canaan, and there may be an indirect allusion to it in the other three places, Ps 107⁴, Is 43¹⁹·²⁰. RV deviates from its uniform rendering of this word by 'desert' in Dt 32¹⁰, Ps 68⁷, where with AV it has 'wilderness.' Though in these passages no distinction between *midhbar* and *jeshimon* is drawn, yet there is a difference in meaning ; *midhbar* * is strictly a place where cattle are driven (comp. the German 'Trift' and 'treiben'), the uncultivated region where pasturage (though scanty in parts) may be found ; *jeshimon* is the desolate waste without water or vegetation.

Some particular region of this character seems indicated both in Numbers and Samuel, and, as in 1 S 23²⁴ 26² Ziph and Maon (places identified as being a few miles to the south of Hebron) are mentioned as being in its vicinity, a tract of land to the west of the Dead Sea seems here indicated. The eastern slopes of Judah are called (Jos 15⁶¹) the wilderness, and, though the cities there mentioned show that the land was not entirely uninhabited, the fewness of them (compare the number six with the numbers of cities in other parts of Judah) is evidence of its barrenness. Though containing some fertile spots (as En-gedi), the region as a whole may well be called *Jeshimon*, for to its character as a desolate waste many travellers bear witness. (For the descriptions of Robinson and other travellers, see Ritter, *Comp. Geog. of Pal.* iii. 108 ff. ; and cf. G. A. Smith, *HGHL* p. 312). The traveller descending these slopes from the cities of the hill-country first passes through the pasture ground (the *midhbar*) in the neighbourhood of Ziph and Maon (the wilderness of Maon, 1 S 23²⁴, of Ziph, 26²), and at length reaches the desolate waste (*Jeshimon*) by the Dead Sea. This tract of land may be referred to in Numbers, as it would be visible from the highlands of Eastern Palestine, but Dillmann takes Jeshimon to be that part of the Arabah to the N. of the Dead Sea and E. of the Jordan, in which Beth-jeshimoth (the only place bearing a similar name) is situate. (See his *Comm.* on Nu 21²⁰ ; and cf. art. BETH-JESHIMOTH.)

From the words of 1 S 23²⁴ 'the wilderness of Maon, in the Arabah, on the south of the desert' (Jeshimon), it seems that the term Arabah, which 'is applied to at least a portion of the great valley which stretches from the Gulf of Akabah into the Jordanic basin' (see art. ARABAH, vol. i. p. 130ᵃ), here includes that portion of the valley in which the Dead Sea is situated.
                                    A. T. CHAPMAN.

JESHISHAI (יְשִׁישָׁי 'old,' 'venerable'?). — The eponym of a Gadite family, 1 Ch 5¹⁴. See GENEALOGY.

---

* AV renders this word generally by 'wilderness,' but in 12 places has 'desert.' RV has altered these into 'wilderness' except in Dt 32¹⁰, Job 24⁵. Ex 19¹·² is an instance of AV being misleading in some words of frequent occurrence (see Revisers' Preface). The reader of AV would suppose that the original of 'desert' in v.² was different from that of 'wilderness' in vv.¹·²; but *midhbar* is the Heb. equivalent of both, which is indicated by the change to 'wilderness' in RV.

JESHOHAIAH (יְשׁוֹחָיָה).—The eponym of a Simeonite family, 1 Ch 4³⁶. See GENEALOGY.

JESHUA (יֵשׁוּעַ 'J″ is salvation' or 'J″ is opulence' [see *Oxf. Heb. Lex.*], Ἰησοῦς), another form of Joshua, is used of—**1.** Joshua the son of Nun once only (Neh 8¹⁷). **2.** The head of the ninth course of priests (1 Ch 24¹¹). AV has Jeshuah. **3.** A Levite in the time of Hezekiah, who had to do with the distribution of the free-will offerings (2 Ch 31¹⁵). **4.** A man of the house of Pahath-moab whose descendants returned with Zerubbabel (Ezr 2⁶ Ἰησοῦε, Neh 7¹¹). This J. is perhaps identical with No. 2 above. **5.** A Levitical house or its successive heads in the times of Zerub., Ezra, and Nehemiah. J. is mentioned in connexion with the building of the temple (Ezr 3⁹), the explanation of the law to the people (Neh 8⁷, cf. 9⁴ᶠ·), and the sealing of the covenant (10⁹). Cf. also Ezr 2⁴⁰ 8³³, Neh 7⁴³ 12⁸· ²⁴ Ἰησού. **6.** The high priest who along with Zerub. headed the first band of exiles that returned. In Ezr and Neh he is called Jeshua (יֵשׁוּעַ), in Hag and Zec **Joshua** (יְהוֹשֻׁעַ). His grandfather Seraiah, who was high priest at the time of the capture of Jerus., was executed at Riblah by Nebuch., and his father Jehozadak carried captive to Babylon, where J. was probably born (2 K 25¹⁸ᶠᶠ·, 1 Ch 6¹⁵; see, however, Kosters, *Het herstel v. Isr.* 48 f.). On the arrival of the caravan at Jerus., J. naturally took a leading part in the erection of the altar of burnt-offering and the laying of the foundations of the temple (Ezr 3²ᶠᶠ·), in Hag and Zec he is frequently coupled with Zerub. after these prophets had begun to stimulate the people to undertake building operations in earnest (Hag 1¹· ¹²· ¹⁴, Zec 3¹ᶠᶠ· 6¹⁰· ¹¹); he supplies a figure to the imagery of the latter prophet (Zec 3¹ᶠᶠ·), and even receives a crown at his hands (6¹⁰ᶠ·). He is eulogized in Sir 49¹². For further details see ZECHARIAH, ZERUBBABEL, and refer to the Literature at the end of the latter article. J. A. SELBIE.

JESHUA (יֵשׁוּעַ).—A town in the south of Judah, Neh 11²⁶. The site is possibly at the ruin *Sa'wi* west of *Tell 'Arad* and south of *'Attîr*, as Beersheba is mentioned with it. See *PEF Mem.* iii. 409 f. Jeshua of Neh 11²⁶ appears to correspond to **Shema** (wh. see) of Jos 15²⁶ 19⁸ (?). See Dillm. *ad loc.* C. R. CONDER.

JESHURUN (יְשֻׁרוּן) occurs four times in OT as a designation for Israel (Dt 32¹⁵ 33⁵· ²⁶, Is 44²). Gesenius at one time held that יְשֻׁרוּן was a shorter form of יִשְׂרְאֵלוּן (Cod. Gr., Ven. Ἰσραελίσκος), a dimin. of יִשְׂרָאֵל (Israel), while at the same time there might be an allusion to the idea of rectitude or uprightness contained in the root יָשַׁר. Latterly he adopted a derivation simply from this last root, making J. = *the righteous little people.* The same derivation is accepted by Reuss and Cornill, the latter of whom (with Cheyne) finds light thrown upon the meaning of J. by the references in OT to the 'Book of Jashar,' where Jashar ('the upright') may be a name for Israel. (Cf. Nu 23¹⁰ 'Let me die the death of the righteous,' in which יְשָׁרִים 'righteous' seems to allude to יִשְׂרָאֵל of the preceding clause). The Sept. in all the four passages cited above, renders J. by ἠγαπημένος ('beloved'). Jerome has *dilectus* in Dt 32¹⁵, but elsewhere *rectissimus*, corresponding to εὐθύς or εὐθύτατος of Aq. Symm. and Theod., who manifestly connect J. with the root יָשַׁר. Delitzsch (*Is.⁵* ii. 189) admits that יְשֻׁרוּן is a secondary form of יָשַׁר, but declines to regard it as a diminutive, because a 'diminutive of affection corresponds little to the language of divine love' (*sic*). In spite of this dictum, Schultz' explanation of J. as 'a pet name from יָשַׁר' seems a peculiarly happy one (*OT Theol.* ii. 29 n.). Driver

(Dt 32¹⁵) agrees with Dillmann that J. is a poetical title of Israel, pointing allusively to יִשְׂרָאֵל but derived from יָשַׁר, and accordingly designating the nation under its ideal character (cf. Ex 19⁶, Dt 14² etc.) as 'the *upright* one.' J. A. SELBIE.

JESIAS (B Ἐσίας, A Ἰεσσίας, AV Josias), 1 Es 8³³.—In Ezr 8⁷ JESHAIAH.

JESIMIEL (יְשִׂימִאֵל).—The eponym of a Simeonite family, 1 Ch 4³⁶. See GENEALOGY.

JESSE יִשַׁי (etym. and meaning doubtful; perh. 'wealthy,' √ יָשׁ, Ges., but see *Oxf. Heb. Lex.*; Ἰεσσαί).—Father of David. As grandson of the wealthy Boaz (Ru 4¹⁷· ²², 1 Ch 2¹², Mt 1⁵, Lk 3³²), it is natural to suppose that he was one of the elders of Bethlehem (1 S 16⁴); but the biblical narrative is not clear on this point. He is called 'the Bethlehemite,' 1 S 16¹· ¹⁸ 17⁵⁸, and 'the Ephrathite of Bethlehem-Judah,' 1 S 17¹². We cannot draw any safe inference as to his position from the fact that his youngest son kept the sheep, or from the simple present of farm produce which he sends, now to the king (1 S 16²⁰), now to the captain (1 S 17¹⁸). The Targ. on 2 S 21¹⁹ calls him 'a weaver of the veil of the house of the sanctuary,' but that is merely an attempt to explain 'Jaare-oregim.' When first introduced into the history (1 S 17¹², on the various explanations of which see Wellh. and Driver) he is 'an old man,' 'stricken in years among men,' and he probably did not live to witness the royal dignity of the lad whom he had once thought too insignificant to share in the sacrificial feast (1 S 16¹¹). In 1 S 20²⁹ David mentions his brother as superintending the family sacrifice. This may be due to the great age of Jesse, but it is also possible that we have here a survival of the custom according to which the eldest son was the family priest. We last hear of Jesse alive in 1 S 22³· ⁴, when David, mindful of his ancestress Ruth, entrusts his parents to the care of the king of Moab. A Jewish tradition states that the Moabites killed them, but 1 S 22⁴ implies that they rejoined David when he left the cave of Adullam.

There are two slight difficulties connected with Jesse's family. (*a*) According to 1 S 16¹⁰· ¹¹ 17¹² he had eight sons; seven only are named in the genealogy, 1 Ch 2¹³⁻¹⁵. The Syriac and Arabic versions here insert 'Elihu the seventh' from 1 Ch 27¹⁸, but there we should probably read 'Eliab,' with the LXX. Jerome (*Qu. Heb.* on 1 S 17¹², 2 S 21²¹) says that the prophet Nathan, or Jonathan son of Shammah, was reckoned as one of his sons. (β) In 2 S 17²⁵ Abigail is called the daughter of Nahash; accordingly Jewish tradition (Targ. on Ru 4²², Is 14²⁹, Jerome, *Qu. Heb. in loc.*) identifies Jesse with Nahash ('serpent'), explaining the double name on the ground that he had no other sin than that original sin which the old serpent introduced into the world. Stanley (*Jewish Ch.*, Lect. 22) suggests that the same woman was first wife of Nahash, king of Ammon, and mother by him of Abigail and Zeruiah, and subsequently wife of Jesse, and mother of his sons. This theory derives some slight support from the friendliness of Nahash and his sons to David (2 S 10² 17²⁷), and also from the genealogy (1 Ch 2¹⁶), where Abigail and Zeruiah are not called the daughters of Jesse, but the sisters of his sons. It is possible, however, that נָחָשׁ בַּת־ in 2 S 17²⁵ is, as Wellh. thinks, a textual error. See NAHASH.

It is interesting to note that while in his lifetime, and in the next generation, 'the son of Jesse' was a contemptuous epithet for David (cf. Jg 9²⁸, 1 S 22¹², Is 7⁴· ⁵· ⁶· ⁹), and is so used by Saul (1 S 20²⁷· ³⁰· ³¹ 22⁷· ⁸), by Doeg (1 S 22⁹), by Nabal (25¹⁰), by Sheba (2 S 20¹), and by the ten tribes

(1 K 12[16]), yet the prophet Isaiah (11[1. 10]) associates one of the most sublime Messianic predictions with the stock (גֵּזַע) of Jesse, 'the root (שֹׁרֶשׁ) of Jesse,' and this honorific use of the phrase passed to later writers, 1 Ch 10[14] 29[26], Ps 72[20], Ac 13[22].

N. J. D. WHITE.

JESUS, the Gr. form ('Ιησοῦς) of the name Joshua (יְהוֹשֻׁעַ) or Jeshua (יֵשׁוּעַ), is employed as a designation of—**1.** Joshua the son of Nun (AV of 1 Mac 2[55], 2 Es 7[37], Sir 46[1], Ac 7[45], He 4[8], in all of which passages RV has JOSHUA). **2.** Jeshua (Joshua), the high priest contemporary with Zerubbabel (1 Es 5[5. 8. 48. 56. 68. 70] 6[2] 9[19], Sir 49[12], where both AV and RV have in every instance JESUS). **3.** The Levite (1 Es 5[26. 58] 8[63] 9[48]) who in Ezr 2[40] 3[9] is called Jeshua. **4.** An ancestor of our Lord (Lk 3[29] RV, where AV has Jose). **5.** Jesus, son of Sirach. See SIRACH. **6. 7.** See the next two articles.

JESUS CHRIST.—

Method of this article.

I. SURVEY OF CONDITIONS.
  A. *EXTERNAL CONDITIONS: GOVERNMENT, SECTS, AND PARTIES.*
  B. *INTERNAL CONDITIONS: THE STATE OF RELIGIOUS THOUGHT AND LIFE.*
    1. General conditions : (α) the darker and (β) the brighter side of contemporary Judaism.
    2. The special seed-plot of Christianity.
    3. The Messianic expectation. Literature.

II. THE PUBLIC MINISTRY.
  A. *PRELIMINARY PERIOD: FROM THE BAPTISM TO THE CALL OF THE LEADING APOSTLES.*
    i. The Baptist and the Baptism : (α) the Baptist's hesitation, (β) the Voice from Heaven, (γ) Apocryphal details, (δ) Synoptic and Johannean versions. Literature.
    ii. The Temptation.
    iii. The first disciples and the miracle at Cana.
    iv. The first Passover.
    v. Retirement to Galilee.—The Synoptic Chronology, the Healing of the Nobleman's Son.
  B. *FIRST ACTIVE OR CONSTRUCTIVE PERIOD: THE FOUNDING OF THE KINGDOM.*
    i. The Call, Training, and Mission of the Twelve (and of the Seventy).
    ii. Differentiation of the Ministry of Jesus from that of John the Baptist.
    iii. Preaching of the Kingdom.
    iv. The Messianic Works.
    v. Effect on the Populace.
    vi. Effect upon the Pharisees.
    vii. The Self-Revelation of Jesus.

THE TEACHING OF JESUS.

  a. General Characteristics of the Teaching.
    (1) Its relation to the teaching of the Baptist and to that of the Scribes.
    (2) Its universal range.
    (3) Its method.
    (4) The Parables.
    (5) Interpretation of the Parables.
    (6) The Purpose of teaching by Parables.

  b. Contents of the Teaching.
    (1) The Fatherhood of God.
    (2) The Kingdom of God : (i.) the name ; (ii.) the meaning ; (iii.) associations ; (iv.) the nature of the Kingdom : how far supernatural? (v.) present or future? (vi.) inward or outward? (vii.) national or universal?
    (3) The Members or Subjects of the Kingdom : (i.) conditions of entrance ; (ii.) character of the members ; (iii.) paradoxes of Christianity.
    (4) The Messiah : (i.) the Christ ; (ii.) the Son of David ; (iii.) the Son of Man ; (iv.) the Son of God.
    (5) The Paraclete and the Tri-unity of God. Literature.

THE MIRACLES OF JESUS.

  (i.) Different classes of Miracles.
  (ii.) Critical expedients for eliminating miracle.
  (iii.) The evidence for the Gospel miracles in general.
  (iv.) The quality of the evidence.
  (v.) Historical necessity of miracles.
  (vi.) Natural congruity of miracles.
  (vii.) The unexplained element in miracles. Literature.
  C. *MIDDLE OR CULMINATING PERIOD OF THE ACTIVE MINISTRY.*
    i. The enthusiasm and falling-away of the Populace.
    ii. Widening breach with the Pharisees.
    iii. The climax of faith among the Twelve ; St. Peter's confession.

    iv. The culminating point in the Missionary Labours of Jesus.
    v. The Transfiguration.
    vi. The Prophecies of Death and Resurrection.
  D. *CLOSE OF THE ACTIVE PERIOD: THE MESSIANIC CRISIS IN VIEW.*
    i. The so-called Peræan Ministry.
    ii. The Johannean narrative of this period.
    iii. The general character of the teaching of this period.
    iv. The prophecies of Death and Resurrection.
    v. Significance of the Death of Jesus. Literature.
  E. *THE MESSIANIC CRISIS: THE TRIUMPHAL ENTRY, THE LAST TEACHING, PASSION, DEATH, RESURRECTION, ASCENSION.*
    i. The action and the actors : (a) the Populace ; (b) the traitor ; (c) the Pharisees ; (d) the Sadducees ; (e) Pilate. Literature.
    ii. The Chronology of the last week.
    iii. The prophetic teaching of the last week.
    iv. The Last Supper : (1) the text of Lk 22[14-20] ; (2) relation of the texts to each other ; (3) other NT evidence ; (4) significance of the Eucharist ; (5) critical theories. Literature.
    v. The Resurrection : (1) the attestation ; (2) the sequence and scene of the events ; (3) attempted explanations ; (4) the permanent significance of the Resurrection.
    vi. The Ascension : (1) its leading import ; (2) its manner ; (3) its implications. Literature.

III. SUPPLEMENTAL MATTER : THE NATIVITY AND INFANCY.
    i. The sources of the narrative.
    ii. The text of Mt 1[16].
    iii. The genealogies. Literature.
    iv. The census of Quirinius.
    v. The meaning of the Virgin-birth.

IV. CONCLUDING SURVEY : THE VERDICT OF HISTORY.
  A. *CHRIST IN HISTORY.*
    i. The Christ of the Gospels. Literature.
    ii. The Christ of the Apostles.
    iii. The Christ of the Undivided Church. Literature.
    iv. The Christ of Personal Experience.
  B. *THE PERSON OF CHRIST.*
    i. The Problem as it stands.
    ii. A pressing portion of the Problem.
  C. *THE WORK OF CHRIST.*
    i. The place in the Cosmical Order of the ethical teaching of Christ.
    ii. The significance of the personal example of Christ in regard to His ethical teaching.
    iii. The Work of Christ as redemptive.
    iv. The Work of Christ as a revelation.
    v. The founding of the Church. Lives of Christ.

Method.—What method is fittest for a Christian writer to use in approaching the Life of Christ ? There is a tendency at the present moment, on the Continent perhaps rather than in England, to approach it from the side of the consciousness of Jesus as the Messiah. A conspicuous instance of this would be Baldensperger's *Das Selbstbewusstsein Jesu* (Strassburg, 1888 ; 2nd ed. 1892), a work which attracted considerable attention when it first appeared. No doubt such a method has its advantages. It places the inquirer at once at the centre of the position, and enables him to look down the various roads by which he will have to travel. The advantage, however, is more apparent than real. It would hold good only if we could be sure of obtaining a far more adequate grasp of the consciousness to be investigated than on any hypothesis is likely to be obtained. On the Christian hypothesis, frankly held, any such grasp would seem to be excluded, and the attempt to reach it could hardly be made without irreverence. It is on all grounds a safer and sounder, as well as a more promising method, to adopt a course which is the opposite of this—not to work from within outwards, but from without inwards ; to begin with that aspect of the Life which is most external, and only when we have realized this as well as we may to seek to penetrate deeper, allowing the facts to suggest their own inner meaning. We may then take in certain sidelights which our documents also afford us, which, because they come, as it were, from the side, are not therefore less valuable. And we may finally strengthen our conclusions by following the history some little way into its sequel. In other words, we shall begin by placing ourselves at the standpoint of an observer, one of those who saw the public ministry of Jesus in its early stages, in its development, and to its close. When that has been fully unrolled before us, we can draw upon other data which are not of this public character; and we may further seek to argue backwards from effects to causes.

By pursuing this method we shall have the advantage of taking the facts in no imaginary order, but in the order of the history itself. We shall have them disclosed to us in the same sort of sequence in which they were disclosed to the first generations of Christians—a method always advisable where it can be had, and in this instance peculiarly advisable, because both the origins and the immediate sequel to the origins are of extreme interest and importance.

We shall also have the incidental advantage of following, not only the historical order, but the critical order suggested by the documents. It was natural that what was transacted in public should have the fullest and the earliest attestation: it lay in the nature of the case that some of the details which were most significant, just because of their private and intimate character, should become known only by degrees. This state of things is reflected in the Gospels as we have them. The common matter of the Synoptic Gospels is also the most public matter. It by no means follows that what is peculiar to a single Gospel is by that fact stamped as less historical: no one would think (*e.g.*) of affirming this of some of the parables peculiar to St. Luke; but it is fair to suppose that in the first instance it was less widely diffused. To this class would belong the narratives of the Nativity and of the Infancy. It will be in some ways a gain not to begin with these, but to let them enter into the story as they entered into it with the first Christians. More than one point which might otherwise perplex us will in this way suggest its own explanation.

Limits of space do not allow us to go elaborately into the question as to the trustworthiness of our materials. It may suffice to point to one undoubted fact which furnishes at least a considerable presumption in their favour. The apostolic age produced some strongly marked personalities, with well defined types of thought and phraseology. Now, broadly speaking, these types have left but little trace upon the Gospels. The special type characteristic of the Gospels themselves stands out conspicuously over against them. We need hardly do more than refer to such very significant facts as that the Gospels alone contain specimens of teaching by parables; that the idea of the 'kingdom of heaven' (or 'of God'), which is quite central in the Gospels, recedes into the background in the writings of the apostles; that the same holds good of that most significant title 'Son of Man'; that, on the other hand, such a term as 'justify' is rare and hardly technical, while 'justification,' 'sanctification,' 'reconciliation' (or 'atonement'), and a number of others are wholly absent. It may be said that the Fourth Gospel is an exception, that there we have a suspicious resemblance to the style and diction of the Epp. of St. John. Some resemblance there is, and we would not entirely reject the inference drawn from it. But even here the exception is but partial. It has often been noticed that the evangelist scrupulously confines his doctrine of the Logos to the prologue.

The writer of this art. may be allowed once more to express the conviction,[*] which he believes that continued investigation will confirm, that the great mass of the Synoptic Gospels had assumed

[*] See the *Bampton Lectures* for 1893, p. 286 ff.

its permanent shape not later than the decade 60–70 A.D., and that the changes which it underwent after the great catastrophe of the fall of Jerusalem were but small, and can without difficulty be recognized.

But the task on which we are at present engaged must in the main supply its own vindication. The picture which it is here attempted to draw will commend itself so far as it is consistent and coherent, and no further. No one, indeed, expects in these days the formal and external consistency aimed at in the older Harmonies; but the writer himself believes that in their inner essence the Gospels are consistent and coherent, and if he fails to convey the impression of this, the failure will be his own. He is conscious of something tentative in the way in which he has sought to work in data derived from the Fourth Gospel with those derived from the other three. But here, again, he is giving expression to the best opinion he can form, and the value of that opinion must be judged by the result. Where he is not satisfied with his own success, he has not hesitated to say so.

To what has been said above it should be added, that if we assume the standpoint of a spectator, a brief preface will be needed to explain what that standpoint is. In other words, we shall have at the outset to take a rapid survey of the conditions under which the Life of Christ was lived, so that we may see to what His teaching had to attach itself, and what served for it as a foil, by way of contrast and antagonism.

The main divisions of our subject will thus be—

    I. SURVEY OF CONDITIONS.
    II. THE PUBLIC MINISTRY OF JESUS, preceded by that of the Baptist.
    III. SUPPLEMENTAL MATTER, not included in the Public Ministry, and derived from special sources.
    IV. THE VERDICT OF HISTORY.

I. SURVEY OF CONDITIONS.—The picture which we form for ourselves of Palestine in the time of our Lord is apt to be wanting in play and variety. A few strong and simple colours are all that are used; we do not allow enough for their blending, or for the finer and subtler tones which mingle with them. We see the worldly ambition of the Sadducees, the self-seeking and formalism of the Pharisees; over both, the rough stern rule of the Roman; and under both, the chafing tide of popular passion, working itself up to its outburst of fury in the Great War. Perhaps we throw in somewhere in a corner the cloistered communities of the Essenes; but if so, it is rather as standing apart by themselves than as entering into the general life. It is not so much that this picture is wrong as that it needs to be supplemented, and it needs a little toning down of the light and shade. This is the case especially with the internal conditions, the state of thought and of the religious life.

A. *EXTERNAL CONDITIONS: GOVERNMENT, SECTS, AND PARTIES.*—The external conditions are so comparatively simple and so well known that a rapid glance at them will suffice.

At the time of our Lord's public ministry, Judæa and Samaria were directly subject to the Romans, and were governed by a *procurator* (**Pontius Pilate,** A.D. 26–36), who was to some extent subordinate to the *legatus* of Syria. Pilate had a character for cruelty (cf. Lk 13[1]). And the Roman rule was no doubt as a whole harsh and unfeeling: we read of wholesale executions, which took the horrible form of crucifixion. But the people whom Rome had to govern were turbulent in the extreme; and so far as the Roman authorities come before us in NT, we cannot refuse them the credit of a desire to do a sort of rough justice.

The odious duty of collecting tolls and taxes for the Romans led to the employment of a class of underlings (τελῶναι, *publicani*), who were regarded almost as outcasts by their Jewish countrymen.

The north and east of Palestine were still in the hands of sons of Herod. **Antipas** (4 B.C. to 39 A.D.) held Galilee and Peræa; and his brother Philip (4 B.C. to 34 A.D.), Ituræa and Trachonitis. The name given to the former, 'that fox' (Lk 13³²), will sufficiently describe him; he was living in open sin with Herodias, the wife of another brother, but was not wholly unvisited by remorse, and had at least curiosity in matters of religion (Mk 6²⁰ ‖, Lk 23⁸). His capital was at Tiberias, on the Sea of Galilee, and he also held possession of the strong fortress of Machærus * E. of the Dead Sea. Herod Philip governed his dominions quietly, and was the best and most popular of his father's sons.

The **Sadducees** (Zadokite priests) consisted mainly of certain aristocratic priestly families (Ac 4⁶) who held almost a monopoly of the high priesthood, and who played an influential and active part in the Sanhedrin, which under the Romans wielded considerable power. They were typical opportunists, and were bent above all things on keeping their own rights and privileges. Hence they were sensitive on the subject of popular disorder, which was likely to serve as an excuse to the Romans for displacing them (Jn 11⁴⁸). It was a coalition of Pharisees and Sadducees which procured the death of our Lord, but in the period of the Acts the Sadducees were the more active persecutors. Religion with them was secondary, but they differed somewhat both in doctrine and in practice from the Pharisees (Ac 23⁸; cf. Edersheim, *Life and Times*, i. 314–321, etc.). They did not encumber themselves with the Pharisaic traditions, but took their stand upon the Pentateuch. They were notorious for strictness in judgment.

As contrasted with the Sadducees, the **Pharisees** (lit. Separatists or Purists) were essentially the religious party. They numbered more than 6000 (*Ant.* XVII. ii. 4), and were pledged to a high standard of life and scrupulous performance of religious duties (Mt 23²³). Unfortunately, the high standard was outward rather than inward. The elaborate casuistry to which the Pharisees had recourse was used as a means of evading moral obligations (Mk 7¹⁻¹³ ‖ 12³⁸⁻⁴⁰‖, Mt 23¹³⁻³³), and resulted in a spirit hard, narrow, and self-righteous.

Not exactly coextensive with the Pharisees, though largely to be identified with them (we read of 'scribes *of* the Pharisees,' Mk 2¹⁶ RV; *i.e.* 'scribes who belonged to the party of the Pharisees'), were the **Scribes** (γραμματεῖς, νομικοί, νομοδιδάσκαλοι), or professed students of the law, who supplied the Pharisees with their principles. They had to a large extent taken the place of the priests as the preachers and teachers of Judaism. Their chief fields of action were the synagogues and the Rabbinical schools. The most highly respected of the scribes were the great religious authorities of the day. It was their successors who built up the Talmud. There were differences of opinion within the body (*e.g.* the rival schools of Hillel and Shammai, contemporaries of Herod the Great), but, without, their *dicta* were unquestioned. This veneration was, as a rule, only requited with contempt.

While the Pharisees at this date for the most part (though not entirely) held aloof from politics, on the ground that religion as they conceived it could be practised indifferently under any domination, and their own experiences under the national

line, represented by Alexander Jannæus, had been the reverse of happy, the mass of the people were burning to throw off the yoke of the stranger. The party of action, which was prepared to go all lengths, was known as the **Zealots.** One member of this party was numbered among the apostles (Mt 10⁴, Mk 3¹⁸, Lk 6¹⁵, Ac 1¹³). In the siege of Jerus. they took the lead, and were distinguished at once by heroic courage and by horrible crimes.

The dynasty of the Herods had from the first claimed alliance with Hellenic culture. The founder of the dynasty had mixed with advantage to himself in the *haute politique* of his day; and he had signalized his reign by buildings in the Greek style, but on a scale of barbaric magnificence. The courts of the Herods must always have had a tincture of Hellenism about them. But the reaction against this was strong, and its influence probably did not extend very far, though it inspired the historians Nicolaus of Damascus, Justus of Tiberias, and Josephus. More likely to affect the lower and middle strata of the population would be the 'Greek cities' founded by the Syrian kings before the Maccabæan rising, such as the cluster known as Decapolis, for the most part east of the Jordan, with later foundations like the flourishing port of Cæsarea. But more important still would be the influence of the Jews of the Diaspora, constantly coming and going to the great feasts at Jerusalem, and with synagogues for their special use permanently established there (Ac 6⁹). The greatest of the centres with which the Jews were thus brought in contact were Alexandria and Antioch. And there is reason to think that the amount of intellectual intercourse and interchange was by no means inconsiderable.

There must have been other foreign influences at work, but rather by what might be called underground channels. The connexion of Palestine with Babylonia and the East, which goes back to immemorial antiquity, had been revived and deepened by the Captivity. It was kept up by intercourse with the Jews who remained in those regions. But whether or not they had come precisely in this way, there can be no doubt that Oriental, and indeed specifically Persian influences were present in the sect of the **Essenes.** The ceremonial washings, and the reverence paid to the sun, can hardly have had any other origin. The asceticism and community of goods have a Pythagorean cast, and may have come from Greece by way of Egypt, while the rejection of sacrifice and what we know of the speculative tendencies of the Essenes may well be native to the soil of Palestine. The Essene settlements were congregated near the Dead Sea.

B. *INTERNAL CONDITIONS: THE STATE OF RELIGIOUS THOUGHT AND LIFE.*

1. *General Conditions.*—To describe justly the state of Judaism in the time of Christ is a difficult and delicate thing. It is too apt to seem like an indictment of the Judaism of nineteen centuries, which not only on general grounds, but specially in view of the attitude of some Jewish apologists of the present day, a Christian theologian will be loth to bring. He will desire to make all the allowances that can rightly be made, and to state all the evidence (so far as he knows it) for as well as against. But at the same time he must not gloss over real faults and defects, without a statement of which Christianity itself can be but imperfectly understood.

Truth does not, as a rule, lie in compromises. And its interests will be perhaps best served if we set down without reserve both the darker and the brighter sides, only asking the reader to remember while he has the one before him, that the other is also there. That we attempt this difficult task at

* In *Ant.* XVIII. v. 2 Machærus is in the possession of Antipas, in the previous § it belongs to Aretas; but the reading of this latter passage is questionable (cf. Schürer, *NTZG* i. 362 n., 365 n. [*HJP* I. ii. 23, 25]).

all is due to no wanton assumption of a right to judge, but to the unavoidable necessity that what is so intimately bound up with history should be seen in the full light which history throws upon it.

(a) *The Darker Side of the Contemporary Judaism.*—As we look broadly at the religious condition of Palestine in the time of our Lord, there can be little doubt that it was in need of a drastic reformation. This is the impression inevitably conveyed by the Gospels, and by the searching criticisms of St. Paul. Nor is it belied by the witness of Josephus, and in particular by the outbreak of untamed passion, with the horrors to which it gave rise, in the Jewish War. And although it may be easy to make a selection from the Talmud of sayings of a different character, it can hardly be questioned that the same source supplies proof enough that the denunciations of the Gospels were not without foundation. There is too evident a connexion between the inherent principles of Judaism and the defects charged against it to permit us to regard these as devoid of truth.

(i.) The idea of God was perhaps the strongest side of Judaism, but it was too exclusively transcendent. It had no adequate means of spanning the gulf between God and man. The faults of Judaism were those of Deism. It had one tender place, the love of J" for Israel. But this fell some way short of the Christian idea of the Father in heaven, the God who not only loves a single people, but whose essence is love. Judaism also largely wanted the mystical element which has played such an important part in Christianity. The Johannean allegory of the Vine and the Branches, which agrees so closely with the teaching of St. Paul, the whole conception of immanent divine forces circulating through the organism, has no true analogy in it.[*] (ii.) But the most disastrous feature of Rabbinical Judaism was its identification of morality with obedience to written law. 'Duty, goodness, piety,—all these are to the Jew equivalent terms. They are mere synonyms for the same conception—the fulfilment of the law. A man therefore is good who knows the law and obeys it; a man is wicked who is ignorant of it and transgresses it' (Montefiore, *Hibbert Lectures*, p. 479). This identification of morality with law led to a number of serious evils. (iii.) Law can deal only with overt action. Hence there was an inevitable tendency to restrict the field of morals to overt action. Motive was comparatively disregarded. It is doubtless true that the Rabbis frequently insist on rightness of motive. A religion which in its Sacred Books included the Prophets as well as the Law could not do otherwise. But the legal conception was too deeply ingrained not to tell its tale. If it had not been so, there would have been no need for the Sermon on the Mount; and the address, 'Scribes and Pharisees, hypocrites,' would have had no point. (iv.) Another consequence of the stress laid on overt acts was the development of an elaborate doctrine of salvation by works. We need not suppose that this doctrine was universally held and always consciously acted upon; but it cannot be denied that there was in Judaism a widespread opinion that might be expressed in the terms, 'so much keeping of the law, so much merit'; and the idea of a 'treasure of merit', which each man stores up for himself, is constantly met with. (v.) In one sense the keeping of the law was very hard. The labours of the scribes had added to the original and primary laws an immense mass of inferential law, which was placed on the same footing of authority. This portentous accumulation of precepts was a burden

'grievous to be borne.' (vi.) Not only so, but a great part of this additional law was bad law. It was law inferred by a faulty system of exegesis. Even where the exegesis was *bonâ fide*, it was in a large proportion of cases unreal and artificial. But there was a great temptation to dishonesty, for which the way was left open by the exaggerated stress laid on acts, and the comparative ignoring of motive. In the dead level of written law the relative degrees of obligation were disregarded. Hence there were a number of precepts which were positively immoral (*e.g.* Corban, Mk 7[11. 12] ‖). (vii.) A further defect in the legal conception of religion was its intellectualism. The Talmud bears witness to what is little less than an idolatry of learning, and that, we must remember, Rabbinical learning. With religion converted into science, and the science in great part no science, we may well say, 'If the light that is in thee be darkness, how great is the darkness!' The Scholasticism of the Middle Ages had no such unchallenged supremacy; it was not the one all-pervading ideal. (viii.) For the mass of the population the double law, traditional as well as original, could not but be a burden. The accumulation of precepts not possessed of moral value is always a thing to be deprecated. And however much we may allow for the fact that the observance of all these precepts was not expected of every one, there still remained enough to be a real incubus. And yet, on the other hand, the performance of the full Pharisaic standard was not so very difficult for persons of leisure, who deliberately made up their minds to it. It did not mean, or at least it might be understood as not meaning, more than a life mechanically regulated. But then it is easy to see that the existence of this class, consciously setting itself above its neighbours, and able, without any excessive strain, to make good its pretensions, must have inevitably engendered a feeling of self-righteousness or spiritual pride. The parable of the Pharisee and the Publican (Lk 18[11-13]) must needs have been typical. (ix.) What the Pharisee was to the ordinary Jew, that the Jew was to the rest of mankind. However politically inferior, the Jew never lost his pride of race, and with him this pride of race was a pride of religious privilege. The Zealot sought to translate this into political domination, but the Pharisee was content to retire into the fortress of his inner consciousness, from which he could look with equanimity at the rise and fall of secular powers. (x.) This particular form of pride had a tendency to aggravate itself as time went on. 'To make a fence round the law' was a fundamental principle of Judaism. And in a like spirit the privileged people was tempted to make a fence round itself, and to dwell apart among the nations. Institutions which had had for their object to keep the nation clear of idolatry, were extended when the dangers of idolatry were past, until it required a revolution to say with St. Paul, 'There is neither Jew nor Greek.' (xi.) Worst and most disastrous of all was the tendency to fall back upon national privilege as a substitute for real reformation of life. We can see alike from the Gospels and from St. Paul how constantly the Jews had upon their lips, 'We have Abraham to our father' (Lk 3[8], Jn 8[33. 39], Ro 2[17-20]). It is admitted that 'the Jews were somewhat too confident of their assured participation in the blessedness of eternal life; all Israelites, except very exceptional and determined sinners, were believed to have their share in it' (Montefiore, *Hibb. Lect.* p. 482).

(β) *The Brighter Side of the Contemporary Judaism.*—The above is a long and a serious catalogue of charges, partly resting upon the logic of the creed, but also too much borne out by positive

---

[*] The comparison of Israel to a vine is not unknown to Judaism, but in a wholly different application (see Wünsche, *Erläut. d. Evang.* on Jn 15[1]).

testimony. It seems conclusively to prove that not only reformation, but a thoroughgoing reformation, was needed.

And yet there is another side which the Christian teacher ought to emphasize more fully than it has been the custom to do.

(i.) In the first place, we have to remember that Judaism is professedly the religion of the OT. It is based upon a Book which includes the Prophets and the Psalms (to use the familiar description *a potiori parte*) as well as the Law. And however much Judaism proper gave precedence to the Law, it could not forget the other parts of the volume, or run wholly counter to their spirit. It is not too much to say that even in the Talmud we can see at every turn how the spirit of legalism was corrected by an influence which is ultimately derived from what are rightly called the evangelical portions of OT. We shall see to what an extent Christianity itself is a direct development of these.

(ii.) The evidence of NT, severe as it is upon the whole, yet is not all of one tenor. Its pages are sprinkled over with Jewish characters, who are mentioned in terms of praise : Zacharias and Elisabeth, Simeon and Anna, Nathanael, Nicodemus, and Joseph of Arimathæa, the young ruler, and the scribe who was pronounced to be 'not far from the kingdom of God' (Mk 12³⁴). We must not forget that there are parts of NT itself which in recent years have been claimed by Christian scholars as thinly veneered products of Judaism (Ep. of James, Apoc.). Whatever we may think of these particular instances, there are others (such as *Didaché* and the *Testaments of the Twelve Patriarchs*) in which it is highly probable that a Jewish original has been adapted to Christian purposes. And our present investigation will bring before us many examples in which, while Christianity corrects Jewish teaching, it nevertheless takes its start from it, and that not only from the purer original, but in its contemporary form.

(iii.) The panegyrists of the Talmud have at least right on their side to this extent, that single sayings can frequently be quoted from it in disproof of the sweeping allegations brought against it by its assailants. There are grains of fine wheat among its chaff. Some of these are referred, on what seems to be good authority, to a time anterior to the coming of Christ. The 'golden rule' is attributed to Hillel. The story is that when Shammai drove away an inquirer who desired to be taught the whole Torah while he stood on one foot, the man went to Hillel, who said : 'What is hateful to thyself do not to thy fellow ; this is the whole Torah, and the rest is commentary' (Taylor, *Pirqe Aboth*, p. 37). Another great saying is ascribed to Antigonus of Soko : 'Be not as slaves that minister to the lord with a view to receive recompense ; but be as slaves that minister to the lord without a view to receive recompense ; and let the fear of Heaven be upon you' (*ib.* p. 27). There is a fair number of such sayings. If we take the treatise from which the last is directly quoted we shall see in it what is probably not an unfair representation of the better Judaism in the time of Christ, with its weaknesses sufficiently indicated, but with something also of its strength.

(iv.) It is right also to bear in mind that the Judaism of this date had no lack of enthusiasts and martyrs. Akiba in particular, though a Jew of the Jews, cannot but command our admiration (see Taylor, *ut sup.* p. 67 ff.). And in a different category his fortitude is matched by the *mitis sapientia* of Hillel, of whom it was said that his gentleness brought men 'nigh under the wings of the Shekinah' (*ib.* p. 37).

(v.) A favourable impression on the whole is given by the numerous pseudepigraphic works, which belong in the main to the two centuries on each side of the Christian era. The oldest parts of the Book of Enoch may possibly be earlier, just as some outlying members of the Baruch literature are probably later. The most typical writings are the Book of Enoch and the Psalms of Solomon (which can be dated with tolerable certainty B.C. 70–40), the Book of Jubilees and the Assumption of Moses (which may be taken as roughly contemporary with the founding of Christianity), and the Fourth Book of Ezra (2 Es) and the Apoc. of Baruch, both after the fall of Jerusalem in A.D. 70. These writings show in varying degrees most of the characteristic infirmities of Judaism, but they also show its nobler features in a way which sometimes, and especially in the two latest works, throws the infirmities into the shade.*

It is a moot point how far the pseudepigrapha can be taken as representative of the main currents of Judaism. Montefiore, writing in 1892, says, 'It must be remembered that the apocalyptic writings lie for the most part outside the line of the purest Jewish development, and often present but the fringe or excrescence, and not the real substance of the dominating religious thought' (*Hibb. Lect.* p. 467). On the other hand, Charles has no difficulty in assigning the different portions to recognized party divisions in Judaism. Schürer in like manner describes their standpoint as that of 'correct Judaism,' adding, however, that they are 'not products of the school, but of free religious individuality' (*HJP* III. ii. 49). Similarly, Baldensperger speaks of 4 Ezra and Baruch as free from the spirit of casuistry, and not 'absorbed in the Halachic rules' (p. 35, ed. 1). This verdict would apply in some degree to this class of literature generally. It is perhaps in the main of provincial origin, or at least somewhat outside the beaten tracks of Jewish teaching. The Pss. of Solomon and Bk. of Jubilees would be nearest to these. It is very probable that 4 Ezr and Apoc. Bar were directly affected by the ferment of thought caused by the birth of Christianity.

When we endeavour to put together the impressions which we derive from these various sources, we may perhaps say that the outcome of them is that Judaism at the Christian era had all the outer framework of a sound religion if only the filling in had been different. The Jew knew better than any of his contemporaries in Greece or Rome or in the East what religion was. He had a truer conception of God, and of the duty of man towards God ; but on the first head he had much still to learn, and on the second he had many faults to be corrected in the working out of detail.

The Jew had at least a profound seriousness on the subject of religion. Where this was wanting, the man was no true Jew. And, even allowing for all the external influences which told against this, there was among the Jews probably less of professed atheism, indifference, levity, than there has ever been in any other society, ancient or modern. The Jew had also an intense feeling of loyalty to this society. His love of what we should call his Church rose to a passion. It is this which makes the apocalypses which followed the fall of Jerusalem so pathetic. The faith of men has probably seldom received a shock so severe. The authors of these apocalypses feel the shock to the uttermost. They grope about anxiously to find the meaning of God's mysterious dealings ; but their faith in Him is unshaken. They are divided between passionate grief and resignation : 'Two things vehemently constrain me : for I cannot resist thee, and my soul, moreover, cannot behold the evils of my mother' (Apoc. Bar 3³).

2. *The Special Seed-plot of Christianity.* — In general terms it may be said that when we seek for affinities to Christianity we find more of them the farther we recede from the centre of official Judaism. The one thing to which Christianity is most opposed is the hard, dry, casuistic legalism

---

* For a closer and more exact but still tentative analysis and dating, the reader may be referred to the editions by R. H. Charles of *Enoch* (1893), *Secrets of Enoch* and *Apoc. of Baruch* (1896), *Assumption of Moses* (1897) ; or for a judicious presentation of average opinion, to Schürer, *HJP* II. iii. 54 ff.

of the Pharisee. If we are right in thinking of the apocalyptic literature as in the main provincial, we shall not be surprised to find the points of contact with it become more numerous. Wherever there are traces of a fresher and deeper study of the Psalms and Prophets, there we have a natural kinship for the Christian spirit.

Now there is one class among whom this continuity with Psalms and Prophets is specially marked. It has been observed * that there is a group of Psalms (of which perhaps 9. 10. 22. 25. 35. 40. 69. 109 are the most prominent) in which the words translated in EV 'poor,' 'needy,' 'humble,' 'meek' are of specially frequent occurrence. It appears that these words have acquired a moral meaning. From meaning originally those who are 'afflicted' or 'oppressed' (by men), they have come to mean those who in their oppression have drawn nearer to God and leave their cause in His hands. They are the pious Israelites who suffer from the tyranny of the heathen or of their worldly countrymen, and who refuse to assert themselves, but accept in a humble spirit the chastening sent by God. As there were many such in every period of the history of Israel, they might be said to form a class. Now there is other evidence that this class still existed at the Christian era. They are the *mansueti et quiescentes* of 4 Ezr (2 Es) 11⁴². They are just the class indicated in Ps-Sol 5¹³ᶠ. 'Who is the hope of the needy and the poor beside thee, O Lord? And thou wilt hearken: for who is gracious and gentle but thou? Thou makest glad the heart of the humble by opening thine hand in mercy.' (Compare also the reff. in Ryle and James, p. 48, and Index, *s.v.* πτωχός). The special NT designation is πτωχοὶ τῷ πνεύματι (Mt 5³). And a better expression of the spirit in question could not easily be found than the *Magnificat* (Lk 1⁴⁶⁻⁵⁵). It is clear that the group which appears in Lk 1. 2, not only Joseph and Mary, but Zacharias and Elisabeth, Simeon and Anna, all answer to this description. They are those who look for 'the consolation of Israel,' 'the redemption of Israel' (Lk 2²⁵. ³⁸), and who looked for it rather by fasting and prayer than by any haste to grasp the sword. There was no organized party, no concerted policy; but we cannot doubt that there were many devout souls scattered throughout the country, and in just the kind of distribution which the chapters Lk 1. 2 would suggest, some for shorter or longer periods making their way to Jerusalem, but the greater number dispersed over such secluded districts as the 'highlands' (ἡ ὀρεινή, Lk 1³⁹) of Judæa and Galilee.

Here was the class which seemed, as it were, specially prepared to receive a new spiritual impulse and to take up a great movement of reformation. And other tendencies were in the air which were ready to contribute to the spread of such a movement when it came. The labours of the scribes had not been all wasted. There is a good example in Mk 12³²⁻³⁴—the happy combination of Dt 4³⁹ with Lv 19¹⁸—which shows that even among the Rabbis there were some who were feeling their way towards the more penetrating teaching of Jesus.

One great transition had been made since Ezk 18. The value of the individual soul was by this time fully realized. The old merging of the individual in the family and the clan had been fully left behind. Another germ contained in the teaching of the prophets had been developed. We can see from the case of the Essenes that men's minds were being prepared for the abolition of animal sacrifices, and along with the abolition of sacrifice for an end to the localized worship of the temple.

* See **esp.** Rahlfs, עָנִי *und* עָנָו *in d. Psalmen*, Göttingen, 1892; and Driver, *Parallel Psalter*, Oxf. 1898, Glossary, *s.v.* ' poor.'

The great extension of the synagogue services would contribute to the same result.

The proselytizing zeal which the later Judaism had displayed (Mt 23¹⁵) operated in several ways. It was a step in the direction of the ultimate evangelizing of the Gentiles. It had created a class in which the liberal influences of Græco-Roman education prevented the purer principles of OT from lapsing into Judaic narrowness and formalism, and in which it was therefore natural that Christianity should strike root. We meet with specimens of this class in the Gospels (Lk 7²⁻⁵∥, Mk 15³⁸∥) as well as in the Acts. And not only was there created a class of recipients for the gospel, but in the effort to meet the demands of these converts from paganism there was a tendency to tone down and throw into the background the more repellent features of Judaism. If it is true, as it probably is, that the so-called *Didaché* is a Christian enlargement of what was originally a Jewish manual for proselytes, it would be a good illustration of this process.

3. *The Messianic Expectation.*—But by far the most important of all the preparations for the gospel, negative as well as positive, both as demanding correction and as leading up to fulfilment, was the growth of the Messianic expectation, with the group of doctrines which went along with it.

The more the stress of the times was felt, and the more hopeless it seemed that any ordinary development of events could rescue the Jewish people from its oppressors, the more were its hopes thrown into the future and based upon the direct intervention of God. The starting-point of these hopes was the great prophecy in Dn 7. The world empires, one succeeding another, and all tyrannizing over the Chosen People, were to be judged, and Israel at last was to enter on the dominion reserved for it. The figure of the **Son of Man** who appears before the Ancient of days (Dn 7¹³ᶠ.) was not in the first instance a person: it was a collective expression, equivalent to the 'saints of the Most High' in v.¹⁸. The form of a 'man' is taken in contrast to the 'beasts,' which represent in the context the dynasties of the oppressors. In conflict with the last of these Israel is at first to be hard pressed, but God Himself will interpose by an act of divine judgment; the enemy will be crushed, and there will be given to Israel a kingdom which is universal and eternal.

This dominion is Israel's by right. It had not only been repeatedly promised from Abraham onwards, but it had been earned as a matter of desert. It was the complement of Israel's possession of the law. By its observance of the law Israel had acquired a right which no other nation could acquire. In the compact or covenant between Israel and Jehovah, Israel was doing its part, and it remained for God to do His.

The grand catastrophe by which this was to be brought about, the περιπέτεια in the tragedy of the nations, was to culminate in an act of judgment. The **day of the Lord,** conceived of by the prophets at first as a decisive battle in which God intervenes, gives place to a judicial act in which those who have oppressed His people are called to account, and the parts of oppressor and oppressed are reversed. To complete the justice of the case, those of the saints who have died in the times of distress must not be left out. There must be a resurrection. And the resurrection will usher in for them a state of lasting joy and felicity. Nature would share with man. There would be a 'new heaven and a new earth.' The tendency was to conceive of these somewhat literally and materially. Elaborate but at the same time prosaic pictures are given of the inexhaustible plenty which the saints (*i.e.* Israel as a people) are to enjoy.

Their bliss is also sometimes compared to a great feast (cf. Lk 14[15]).

In the Bk. of Daniel, and, as it would seem for some time afterwards, the reign of the saints is conceived impersonally. It is the dominion of Israel, the Chosen People. But gradually there arises a tendency to go back to a more primitive stage of prophecy, and to see the kingdom as concentrated in the person of its King: there is a personal Messiah. This is conspicuously the case in the Psalms of Solomon (17. 18), the date of which is fixed between B.C. 70–40. The righteous King who is to rule over the nations is the Davidic King of the elder prophets. A personal King is also implied in *Orac. Sibyll.* iii. 49 f., 652–656. In the middle section of the Bk. of Enoch (chs. 37–71), which is also probably pre-Christian, the title 'Son of Man' is taken up from Dn and distinctly identified with a person. Here, too, as in *Orac. Sibyll.* iii. 286, and *Apoc. Bar* 72[2-6], the Messiah is not only King but Judge (cf. Enoch 45[3] 62[8-13] 69[27]). The execution of the judgment is handed over to Him by God. There is not absolute unity of view. Sometimes judgment is carried out by the Messiah, sometimes by God Himself (*e.g.* Enoch 90[18-27], *Ass. Mos.* 10[3-10]). There is also some diversity as to the extent to which the resurrection is to be of the righteous, of Israel, or of all mankind. One view is that there are to be two resurrections, with a millennial reign between them.

The Sadducees held aloof from the Messianic expectation to which they were not clearly compelled by the few allusions in the Pentateuch, and which would have been only a disturbing element in their policy of making the best—for themselves —of things as they were. Some of the scribes must have also done what they could to discourage the belief. It is well known that Hillel is said to have asserted that the prophecies of the Messiah were fulfilled in Hezekiah. But there is abundant evidence that in spite of this the expectation was widely diffused. It must have been constantly preached in the synagogues of Palestine, and it certainly took a strong hold of the popular mind. It was differently received and understood by different hearers. With some quiet God-fearing souls, 'poor in spirit' like those who come before us at the beginning of the evangelical narrative in Lk 1. 2, it was cherished secretly with awed and wistful longing (Lk 2[25. 38]). With the mass of the population, as well teachers as taught, it took its place only too easily among the body of hard, narrow, materialized beliefs which were so characteristic of the time—a visible earthly kingdom reserved for Israel as its right, and carrying with it domination over other nations, with such unlimited command of enjoyment as a sovereign people might expect under conditions specially created for its benefit: all this introduced by supernatural means, wielded by One who is variously called 'Messiah' or 'Anointed,' 'the righteous King,' 'the Elect' or 'Son of Man,' not (if the question were pressed) in the strict sense God, though endowed by God with plenary powers, a fit Head for the Chosen People in its golden age, which was at last about to begin. And scattered among these masses there were many — some banded together under the name of Zealots, and thousands more who were ready to join them at the first signal—men not of dreams but of action, who were only waiting for the leader and the hour to put their hand to the sword and rise in revolt against the hated foreigners who oppressed them, prepared to take a fearful vengeance, and proud in the thought that in doing so they would be 'doing God service' and establishing His kingdom.

LITERATURE.—Vast stores of ordered material are contained in Schürer's great work orig. called *Neutest. Zeitgeschichte*

(*NTZG*), and now as in the Eng. tr. *Hist. of the Jewish People in the Time of Jesus Christ* (*HJP*). The Eng. tr. from the 2nd much enlarged ed. came out in 1885–90; a 3rd ed., still further enlarged, has begun to appear (vols. ii. and iii., 1898). The late Dr. Edersheim's *Life and Times of Jesus the Messiah* (revised eds. from 1886) is also full of illustrative matter. Other works by the same author may also be consulted; esp. *History of the Jewish Nation after the Destruction of Jerus. under Titus* (2nd ed. carefully revised by H. A. White, 1896). Another very useful work is Weber's *System d. altsynagog. Paläst. Theol.*, now called *Jüdische Theologie* (2nd ed., somewhat improved, 1897). As there is always a danger of confusing Jewish teaching of very different dates, this book should be checked as far as possible by comparison with the *Pseudepigrapha*, Philo, NT, and the early Talmudic work *Pirqe Aboth* (*Sayings of the Jewish Fathers*, ed. Taylor, 1877, and enlarged in 1897). To these authorities should now be added G. Dalman, *Die Worte Jesu* (Bd. i., 1898 *fin.*), the most critical and scientific examination of the leading conceptions of the Gospels that has yet appeared.

Mention may be made among older works of Drummond's *Jewish Messiah* (1877) and Stanton's *Jewish and Christian Messiah* (1887). Hausrath's *NT Times* (Eng. tr. 1878–80) is picturesquely written, but far less trustworthy than Schürer; and Wünsche's *Neue Beiträge z. Erläuterung d. Evv.* (1878) is much criticized. Montefiore's *Hibbert Lectures* (1892) and arts. in *JQR* form an attractive apology for Judaism.

II. THE PUBLIC MINISTRY.—We shall now be in a position to approach the study of the Public Ministry of our Lord in the manner indicated at the outset. We shall be able to place ourselves at the standpoint of a sympathetic spectator. We shall have some rough conception of the kind of ideas which would be in his mind, and of the kind of conditions which he would see around him. We shall thus be able to follow the course of the Public Ministry with a certain amount of intelligence. We do not as yet attempt to penetrate the whole of its secret. Broadly speaking, we suppose ourselves to see what a privileged spectator might be expected to see, and no more. We reserve until a later stage the introduction of those special details of illuminative knowledge which, as a matter of history, were not accessible to the first spectators, but were only disclosed after a time. But we hold ourselves at liberty to collect and group the facts which were not removed from the cognizance of a spectator, in any way that may be most convenient to secure clearness of presentation.

It may be well to avail ourselves of this freedom at once, before giving an outline of the ministry, to state summarily certain conclusions which seem to arise out of the study of it. We shall hold the threads in our minds more firmly if we see to what results they are tending.

The anticipated conclusions, then, are these: (i.) From the very first (*i.e.* from the Baptism) our Lord had the full consciousness of the Messiah, and the full determination to found the Kingdom of God upon earth. (ii.) From the very first He had also the deliberate intention of transforming the current idea of the Kingdom. (iii.) In order to make this transformation effective, it was necessary to begin with the idea of the Kingdom and not of the King. In other words, the personal Messianic claim had to be kept in the background. But (iv.) the transformation of the idea was only a preliminary to the permanent establishment of the Kingdom; and this establishment turned round the Person of the Messiah. So that in the end the history of the Kingdom centres in the personal history of the King.

With so much of preface we proceed to give an outline of the Public Ministry according to the periods into which it seems to fall.

A. *PRELIMINARY PERIOD: FROM THE BAPTISM TO THE CALL OF THE LEADING APOSTLES.**

Scene.—Mainly in Judæa, but in part also Galilee.
Time.—Winter A.D. 26 to a few weeks after Passover A.D. 27.
     Mt 3[1-4][11], Mk 1[1-13], Lk 3[1-4][13], Jn 1[6-4][54].

* The choice of *termini a quo* and *ad quem* is sometimes inclusive and sometimes not inclusive. The most salient points are chosen. Here the *term. ad quem* is not inclusive.

B. *First Active or Constructive Period : the Founding of the Kingdom.*

Scene.—Mainly in Galilee, but also partly in Jerusalem.
Time.—From about Pentecost A.D. 27 to shortly before Passover A.D. 28.

      Mt 4[13]–13[53], Mk 1[14]–6[13], Lk 4[14]–9[6], Jn 5.

C. *Middle or Culminating Period of the Active Ministry.*

Scene.—Galilee.
Time.—Passover to shortly before Tabernacles A.D. 28.

      Mt 14[1]–18[35], Mk 6[14]–9[50], Lk 9[7-50], Jn 6.

D. *Close of the Active Period : the Messianic Crisis in View.*

Scene.—Judæa (Jn 7[10ff.], 11[54]) and Peræa (Mk 10[1] ‖, Jn 10[40]).
Time.—Tabernacles A.D. 28 to Passover A.D. 29.

      Mt 19[1]–20[34], Mk 10[1-52], Lk 9[51]–19[28] (for the most part not in chronological order), Jn 11[1]–11[57].

E. *The Messianic Crisis : the Triumphal Entry, the Last Teaching, Passion, Death, Resurrection, Ascension.*

Scene.—Mainly in Jerusalem.
Time.—Six days before Passover to ten days before Pentecost A.D. 29.

      Mt 21[1]–28[20], Mk 11[1]–16[8] [16[9-20]], Lk 19[29]–24[52], Jn 12[1]–21[23].

The chronology adopted in this article, not as certain, but as on the whole the best of current systems, is in substantial agreement with that of the art. Chronology of the New Testament. It differs from that in the writer's first work, *The Authorship and Historical Character of the Fourth Gospel* (London, 1872), by placing the Crucifixion in the year A.D. 29 rather than A.D. 30.

A. *Preliminary Period: from the Baptism to the Call of the Leading Apostles.*

Scene.—Mainly Judæa, but in part also Galilee.
Time.—Winter A.D. 26 to a few weeks after Passover A.D. 27.

      Mt 3[1]–4[11], Mk 1[1-13], Lk 3[1]–4[13], Jn 1[6]–4[54].

The Public Ministry of our Lord begins with His Baptism. (i.) This will therefore be the first point to attract our attention, and some explanation will be needed as to the Baptist and his mission. (ii.) Along with the Baptism we must needs take the Temptation, as a glimpse vouchsafed by Jesus Himself, and early and widely published, of the principles which were to determine the nature of His Ministry. (iii.) After this will come the first preliminary gathering of a few loosely attached followers, and the first miracle at Cana in Galilee. (iv.) Then the visit to Jerusalem for the Passover of the year 27, with a short stay in the South. (v.) Then we have a return to Galilee, followed by a brief period of partial retirement, leading up to the Call of the four chief apostles.

Allusions, more or less explicit, to the Baptism and to the ministry of John, are found in all four Gospels; the other events of this period are recorded only in the fourth—unless we are to identify the Healing of the Nobleman's Son (Jn 4[46-54]) with that of the Centurion's Servant (Mt 8[5-13], Lk 7[1-10]).

i. *The Baptist and the Baptism.*—Our survey of contemporary Judaism has shown us that 'the kingdom of God' was a phrase in almost every man's mouth. It meant, in point of fact, to the majority 'a kingdom for Israel' far more than a 'kingdom of God.' But though in a more or less indefinite sense it was understood to be near, no time had as yet been actually announced for it. Men were on the watch, but rather for the signs of the coming than for the actual coming itself.

We are not surprised, therefore, to find that the news that a prophet had appeared who preached the approaching coming of the Messiah caused a widespread excitement.* The aspect of this

* Stress can hardly be laid on the form of announcement in Mt 3[2], which would make the Baptist anticipate exactly the announcement of Jesus. This would seem to be due to the editor. The oldest version describes the Baptist as 'preaching a baptism of repentance for remission of sins' (Mk 1[4]).

coming, which he put in the forefront, was the aspect of judgment. The axe was laid to the root of the trees, and the fruitless tree would be burned (Mt 3[10], Lk 3[9]).

The prophet who made this announcement bore the name of John. The scene of his preaching was the wilderness of Judæa, near the lower course of the Jordan where it fell into the Dead Sea. In this wilderness he had lived in solitude for some time before he began his prophetic mission. His whole appearance was sternly ascetic. He seems to have adopted deliberately a garb and a manner of life resembling those of Elijah, probably not so much in anticipation of the verdict which was to be afterwards passed upon him (Mt 11[14]) as because he took Elijah for his model.

His character and his mission alike were severely simple. His soul was possessed with a strong conviction, wrought in him in precisely the same manner in which such convictions were wrought in the prophets of the OT, that a great crisis was near at hand. What lay beyond was dim, and, so far as the prophet had a definite picture before him, it was probably not very different from that which presented itself to his countrymen. But he saw clearly that the crisis would take the form of a judgment, and that there would be a judge, a personal judge, with a mission vastly greater than his own. At the same time, it is also borne in upon him that the preparation required by this coming judgment is a moral reformation. This he sees intensely; and again he goes back behind the teaching of his day to that of the ancient prophets. That which is required is not merely a stricter performance of the law, but a deep inward change—a change spontaneously expressing itself in right action.

Once more, and indeed very conspicuously, he made good his resemblance to the older prophets by clothing this leading idea of his in an expressive symbolical act. The rumour of him brought the people to him in crowds; and one by one, as they confessed to him their sins and convinced him of the reality of their repentance, he took them down into the running waters of the Jordan; he made them plunge in or let the waters close over their heads, and then he led them out again with the consciousness that they had left their sinful past behind them, and that they were pledged to a new life.

The process was called 'Baptism'; and John, from the fact that it constituted the main outward expression of his mission, was called 'the Baptist.' The act bore a certain resemblance to those ceremonial washings with which the Jews were familiar enough, and which held a specially prominent place in the ritual of the Essenes. But it differed from all these in that it was an act performed once for all, and not repeated from day to day. The lesson of it was that of Jn 13[10]: he who was once bathed in this thorough and searching fashion did not need to have the act repeated; the effect was to last for life.

The movement took hold especially of the lower and what were thought to be the more abandoned classes. John was kept fully employed in the work of confessing and baptizing, but he did not allow it to be forgotten that all this pointed forward to another mission greater than his own. The presentiment grew upon him that part of his task as prophet was to name this mightier successor. And again, after the manner of the older prophets, he knew that it would be made manifest to him whom he was to name.

Presently the sign was given. Among those who came to be baptized was one who passed for a relative of his own, with whom possibly, though perhaps not probably, he may have had some intercourse in boyhood (cf. Jn 1[31]). As with others who before their baptism were called upon to confess, so also with this kinsman, John had some converse, and, if we may accept what is found only in a single narrative,* at first refused to baptize him. His scruples are set aside, but it is not until the actual baptism that the full truth bursts upon him. Still, the analogy of the older prophecy is maintained. A sign is given such as that which Isaiah offered to Ahaz (Is 7[11]). From the Fourth Gospel we should gather that it was seen in prophetic vision by the Baptist (Jn 1[32-34]); from the Synoptics we should gather that it was seen in like vision by the baptized (Mk 1[10], Mt 3[16] 'he saw'). And to prophetic sight was joined also the prophetic hearing of a voice from heaven, proclaiming in words that recalled at once Ps 2[7] and Is 42[1] 'Thou art my beloved Son, in thee I am well pleased.'

(α) *The Baptist's Hesitation.*—The incident of Mt 3[14f.] is open to some suspicion of being a product (such as might well grow up by insensible degrees in the passing of the narrative from hand to hand) of the conviction which later became general among Christians, that their Master was without sin, and of the difficulty which thence arose of associating Him with a baptism 'of repentance.' We cannot exclude this possibility. But, on the other hand, the difficulty is for us, too, a real one, and the solution given, while it has nothing under the circumstances inconsistent or improbable, is attractive by its very reserve. 'To fulfil all righteousness'= to leave undone nothing which God had shown to be His will. In a general movement which embraced all the more earnest-minded in the nation, it was right that He too should share. It would not follow that the symbolical act of Baptism should have precisely the same significance for every one who submitted to it. For the main body it denoted a break with a sinful past and a new start upon a reformed life. For the Messiah it denoted a break simply, the entrance upon a new phase in the accomplishment of His mission. It took the place with Him of the 'anointing,' which marked the assumption of the active work to which they were called by the kings and prophets of old. This 'anointing' was the 'descent of the Spirit.' The Baptism of the Messiah was Baptism 'with the Spirit,' wherewith He was to baptize. The significance of Baptism in His case was positive rather than negative.

(β) *The Voice from Heaven.*—It has been too readily assumed by some distinguished writers (*e.g.* Usener) that the oldest version of the voice from heaven was in exact agreement with Ps 2[7] 'Thou art my [beloved] Son : this day have I begotten thee.' In two of the three Synoptics the reading is undoubtedly ἐν σοὶ [ᾧ] εὐδόκησα [ηὐδ-]. It is true, however, that in Lk 3[22] an important group of authorities has ἐγὼ σήμερον γεγέννηκά σε. This is the reading of the larger branch of the Western text (D a b c *al. codd. nonnull. ap.* Aug. Juvenc. *al.*). A similar reading is found in Justin, *c. Tryph. bis* and in other writers, and both readings are combined in the Ebionite Gosp. as quoted by Epiphanius. [The evidence is collected in full by Resch, *Agrapha,* p. 347 ff.]. On the other hand, it is by no means certain that in some of these cases the Ps is not directly quoted, and in all assimilation to the text of the Ps lay very near at hand. Even the Western text of Lk is divided, a smaller but very ancient branch (including e) agreeing with the mass of the Gr. MSS. There can be little doubt that not only the Canonical Gospels, but the ground document on which they are based, had the common reading. The competing reading was a natural application of Ps 2[7], and it fell in so readily with views which in different forms circulated rather widely in the 2nd cent. that we cannot be surprised if it met with a certain amount of adoption. See, further, below.

(γ) *Apocryphal Details.*—The story of the Baptism underwent various apocryphal amplifications and adornments. One of the earliest of these is the appearance of a bright light (Codd. Vercell. *et* Sangerm. *ad* Mt 3[15] ; Ev. Ebion. *ap.* Epiph., Ephraem Syr.) or of a fire upon the Jordan (Just. *c. Tryph.* 88, *Prædicatio Pauli ap.* Ps.-Cypr. *de Rebapt.* 17 *al.*). The most elaborate working up of this kind of material is found in the Syriac *Baptismal Liturgy of Severus* (Resch, *Agrapha,* p. 361 ff.).

(δ) *The Synoptic and Johannean Versions.*—When a prophet began his prophetic career he received clear proof of the reality of his call most often through some powerful inner experience or vision (*e.g.* Is 6), but also at times through Divine revelation to another (*e.g.* 1 K 19[16]). We may regard the events of the Baptism as a Divine authentication of this kind of the Mission of Jesus. But if so, there would be nothing incongruous in supposing that this authentication was vouchsafed, both to the Messiah Himself and to the Forerunner, just as a similar authentication was vouchsafed to St. Paul and to Ananias (Ac 9[3ff. 11ff.]).

* Resch (*TU.* x. ii. 57), in his later opinion, regards this narrative as belonging to the oldest evangelical document ; but the passages which he has collected in support of this view might quite well be paraphrastic allusions to the canonical Mt. The Gosp. acc. to Heb. as used by the Ebionites (Epiph. *Hær.* xxx. 13) had a similar scene after the Baptism of Jesus (Resch, *Agrapha,* p. 345 f.).

We are therefore not in any way compelled to choose between the Synoptic and Johannean versions as to the incidence of the supernatural signs. The two versions may quite well be thought of as supplementing rather than contradicting each other.

The Baptism of Jesus undoubtedly marks the beginning of His public ministry. How much more was it than this? The Judaizing Ebionites of the 2nd century, who never rose above the conception of Christ as an inspired prophet, and some Gnostic sects which separated the Man Jesus from the Æon Christus, starting from the Synoptic narrative, and combining it with Ps 2[7], dated from the Baptism the union of the human and the Divine in Christ in such a way that they are sometimes described as making the Baptism a substitute for the supernatural Birth. We can imagine how, to those who had the story of the Baptism before them, but who had not yet been reached by the tidings of those earlier events round which the veil of a sacred privacy had been drawn, and which (as we shall see) only made their way to general knowledge by slow degrees and after some length of time had elapsed, should regard the descent of the Holy Ghost as a first endowment with Divinity. The fact that it was not till then that Jesus began to perform His 'mighty works,' would seem to give some colour to the belief. And it would be likely enough that a passing phase of Christian thought, based upon imperfect knowledge, would survive in certain limited circles. But the main body of the Church did not rest in this contracted view, which was really inconsistent with the Christology revealed to us in the earliest group of St. Paul's Epistles. It accepted, and, through such leaders as Ignatius of Antioch, emphasized strongly the earlier chapters of the canonical narrative ; and the contents of those chapters gave shape to the oldest form (which can hardly be later than Ignatius) of the Apostles' Creed. Already, before the 1st century was out, St. John had presented what was to be the Catholic interpretation of the relation of the Baptism to the Godhead of Christ. Far back at the very beginning of all beginnings the Divine Word had already been face to face with God, and was Himself God ; so that, when the same Word entered into the conditions of humanity, this did not denote any loss of Godhead which was inherent and essential. Much less could the Godhead of the incarnate Christ be supposed to date from the signs which accompanied the Baptism. The object of these signs was rather to inaugurate the public ministry of the Messiah, that He might be 'manifested to Israel' (ἵνα φανερωθῇ τῷ Ἰσρ., Jn 1[31]). Though the Greek is different the idea is the same as that in Lk 1[80], where it is said of the Baptist himself that he was in the desert 'till the day of his showing unto Israel' (ἕως ἡμέρας ἀναδείξεως αὐτοῦ πρὸς τὸν Ἰσρ.). Whether or not the signs were in the first instance seen by more than the Messiah Himself and the Baptist (and it is probable that they were not), they were made public by the Baptist's declaration (Jn 1[29-34]), so that in any case there was a real 'manifestation to Israel.'

No doubt there was more than this. Besides the outward manifestation, a new epoch opened for the Son of Man Himself. But the nature of this we can describe only by its effects. The evangelists evidently have before their minds the analogy of the prophetic call and prophetic endowment. After the events of the Baptism Jesus is 'full of the Holy Spirit' (Lk 4[1], cf. Mt 4[1], Mk 1[12]). And He applies to Himself the prophetic language of Is 61[1] 'The Spirit of the Lord is upon me ; because the Lord hath anointed me to preach good tidings unto the meek,' etc. (cf. Lk 4[18] ; it is probably this allusion to 'anointing with the Spirit' which has led to the incident in Lk being placed thus early). In the Gospel according to the Hebrews this is expressed even more emphatically than in the canonical Gospels : 'Factum est autem cum ascendisset Dominus de aqua, descendit fons omnis Spiritus sancti et requievit super eum et dixit illi : Fili mi in omnibus prophetis exspectabam te, ut venires et requiescerem in te. In eo enim requies mea, tu es filius meus primogenitus qui regnas in sempiternum' (Hieron. *ad Jes.* xi. 1).

We have only to add that from this time onwards the rôle of the Messiah is distinctly assumed. The 'mighty works' very soon begin ; disciples begin to attach themselves, at first loosely, but with increasing closeness ; and there is a tone of decisive authority both in teaching and in act.

LITERATURE.—There is a strange mixture of fine scholarship and learning, with bold, not to say wild, speculation on the subject of this section in Usener's *Religionsgeschichtliche Untersuchungen*, 1 Teil, Bonn, 1889. With this may be compared Bornemann, *Die Taufe Christi durch Johannes in d. dogmatischen Beurteilung d. Christl. Theologen d. vier ersten Jahrhunderte*, Leipzig, 1896. *John the Baptist*, by the late Dr. H. R. Reynolds (3rd ed. 1888), represents the *Congregational Lecture* of 1874, and deals more with the career of John than with the questions which arise out of the Baptism of Jesus ; but it does not leave these untouched so far as they had at that date come into view.

ii. *The Temptation.*—We decline to speculate where the data fail us. But one remarkable glimpse is afforded us into the state of the inner consciousness of the Son of Man after His Baptism. Strictly speaking, this would not as yet have been available to the spectator. It was probably not at this early date that it was disclosed, even to those nearest and dearest to Him. Still, the disclosure must have been made by the Lord Himself during His lifetime ; and the extent to which it has found its way into all the Synoptics shows that it must have had a somewhat wide diffusion among the main body of the disciples. For this reason, as well as for the advantage of introducing it at the place which it occupies in the narratives, we shall not hesitate to touch upon the Temptation here, though it might perhaps more strictly come under the head of 'Supplemental Matter.'

The narratives of the Temptation are upon the face of them symbolical. Only in the form of symbols was it possible to present to the men of that day a struggle so fought out in the deepest recesses of the soul. There are two instances of such struggle in the life of the Redeemer—one at the beginning and the other at the end of His ministry (Lk 4¹³ comp. with 22⁵³). In both, the assault comes from without, from the personal Power of Evil. It is impossible for us to understand it, in the sense of understanding how what we call temptation could affect the Son of God. It could not have touched Him at all unless He had been also, and no less really, Son of Man. He vouchsafed to be tempted in order that He might be in all points like unto His brethren (He 4¹⁵).

The Temptation clearly belongs to the beginning of the Ministry. It would have had no point before ; and the issue on which it turned had evidently been decided before the public life of Jesus began, as that life throughout its whole course followed the law which was then laid down. The Temptation implies two things. It implies that He to whom it was addressed both knew Himself to be the Messiah whom the Jews expected, and also knew Himself to be in possession of extraordinary powers. To say that He was now for the first time conscious of these powers is more than we have warrant for. But, in any case, it was the first time that the problem arose how they were to be exercised. Were they to be exercised at the prompting of the simplest of all instincts—the instinct of self-preservation ? Were they to be exercised in furtherance of what must

have seemed to be the first condition on which His mission as the Messiah could be accomplished —to convince the world that He had the mission, that it was for Him to lead and for them to follow ? And, lastly, when He came forward as the Messiah, was it to be as the Messiah of Jewish expectation ? Was His kingdom to be a kingdom of this world ? Was it to embrace all the secular kingdoms and the glory of them, to enfold them in a system more powerful and more magnificent than theirs, brought about by supernatural means, with no local limitations like even the greatest of past empires, but wide as the universe itself and indestructible ? Was it to be a real restoring of the kingdom to Israel ? Was Jerusalem to be its centre, in a new sense the 'city of the Great King' ?

All these questions Jesus answered for Himself absolutely in the negative. There did not enter into His mind even a passing shadow of the ambition which marked the best of earthly conquerors. He was determined not to minister in the least to the national pride of the Jews. Still less would He work out a new pride of His own. He did not desire in any sense *volitare per ora*. Even the most natural cravings of the nature which He had assumed He refused to satisfy so long as their satisfaction ended with Himself.

These principles are involved in the narrative of the Temptation. They are laid down once for all ; and the rest of the history shows no swerving from them. At the same time it must be remembered that although the decision had been reached by Jesus Himself, it was not yet known, except so far as He was pleased to reveal it. Partly, the revelation was made by acts and the self-imposed limits of action. The clearest revelation was the story of the Temptation itself. But neither the one nor the other was wholly understood.

iii. *The First Disciples and the Miracle at Cana.* —At this point we leave for some time the Synoptic narrative and follow rather that in the Fourth Gospel, which it must be confessed comes to us with very considerable verisimilitude. If we had only the Synoptic Gospels we should have to suppose that our Lord gathered about Him a band of disciples abruptly and suddenly, capturing them as it were by the tone of authority in His command. In St. John we have the steps given which led up to this, and which make it far more intelligible.

From this Gospel it would appear that Jesus remained for some time in the neighbourhood of the Baptist ; that the Baptist more than once indicated Him in a marked and indeed mysterious way (Jn 1²⁹ 'The Lamb of God, which taketh away the sin of the world' ; cf. v.³⁶ *) ; and that one by one several of John's disciples began to attach themselves, as yet more or less loosely, to His person. The Baptist's testimony, strengthened by first impressions, awoke in them the belief that at last the 'mightier than he' predicted by the Baptist had come (Jn 1⁴¹). Such a belief at this time and under these circumstances would need no elaborate demonstration. It would be accepted in a tentative way, awaiting verification from events, and, of course, only with those contents which accorded with current Jewish opinion.

The home of Jesus was still, as it had been for some thirty years of His life, at Nazareth ; and at the time when He began to collect followers round Him, He was already on the point of returning thither

---

* The words are remarkable, especially as coming thus at the very threshold. It is possible that the evangelist may have been led to define somewhat in view of later events and later doctrines (for the allusion seems to be to Is 53). But the context, including the deputation from Jerusalem, is so lifelike and so thoroughly in accordance with probabilities, that the saying has a presumption in its favour.

(Jn 1⁴³). He had not as yet separated Himself from the domestic life of His family. It was as an incident in this life that He went to a marriage feast at the village of Cana (prob.=*Kâna el-Jelil* rather than *Kefr Kenna*) in the company of His mother and some at least of His newly - found disciples. Here occurred the first of those 'signs' which were to be one conspicuous outcome of His mission. No wonder that it impressed itself vividly on the memory of one who was present, and that it confirmed his incipient faith (Jn 2¹¹). We shall speak of these signs in their general bearing presently.

iv. *The First Passover.*—There would seem to have been some connexion between the family at Nazareth and Capernaum,* as the whole party now spend some days there (Jn 2¹²). But the Passover was near, and Jesus, with at least some of His disciples, went up to it. In connexion with this Passover, St. John places, what has the appearance of a somewhat high-handed act, the expulsion of buyers and sellers from the outer court of the temple (Jn 2¹³⁻²²). The Synoptics place a similar act in the last week of the Ministry (Mk 11¹⁵⁻¹⁸ ‖). It is possible that such an act may have happened twice ; but if we are to choose, and if we believe the Gospel to be really by the son of Zebedee, we shall give his dating the preference—the more so as in these early chapters the dates are given with great precision, and apparently with the intention of correcting a current impression.

This act was the first definite assumption of a public mission to Israel, and its scene was fitly chosen at the centre of Israel's worship. It was the act, not as yet necessarily of one who claimed to be the Messiah, but of a religious reformer like one of the ancient prophets. It was naturally followed by a challenge as to the right of such an assumption. To this the enigmatic reply was given, ' Destroy this temple, and in three days (*i.e.* in a short time, cf. Hos 6²) I will raise it up'; which seems to be rightly glossed in Mk 14⁵⁸—the Jewish Church with its visible local centre should give place to the Christian Church with its invisible and spiritual centre (cf. Jn 4²¹ᶠ·). The saying made an impression at the time, and was brought up at the trial of Jesus to support a charge of blasphemy ; the disciples at a later date referred it to the Resurrection (Jn 2²¹ᶠ·).

A striking feature in the Johannean version of His visit to Judæa is the way in which the work of Jesus in connexion with it takes up the work of the Baptist and fills in conspicuous gaps in the narrative of the Synoptics. The cleansing of the temple is an act of reformation which follows up the call to repentance. In Jn alone of the authorities have we a distinct statement that Jesus adopted the practice of baptism (3²² 4¹), though no other account of the origin of the Christian Sacrament is so natural. We find also the necessity for baptism and the 'new birth' which went with it is made the subject of a discourse with the Sanhedrist Nicodemus. The writer of the Gospel had been himself a disciple of John the Baptist, and still kept up his connexion with him, and knew what went on in his circle (Jn 3²²ᶠᶠ·). At the same time he seems to expand the discourses which he records with matter of his own (3¹⁶ᶠᶠ· ³¹ᶠᶠ·).

v. *Retirement to Galilee.*—Soon after this John the Baptist was arrested by Herod Antipas, and Jesus retired into Galilee. On the way He passed through Samaria, and paused at Jacob's well near the village of Sychar (now generally identified

---

* The site of Capernaum is still much debated. At one time it seemed as if the suffrage would go for *Tell Ḥûm*, but of late there has been a reaction in favour of *Khân Minyeh* (see the art. in this Dictionary, HGHL p. 456 f., and von Soden, *Reisebriefe* (1898), p. 160 f., who quotes a resident, Père Biever). Buhl, however, GAP p. 224, still supports *Tell Ḥûm*.

---

with '*Askar*), where His teaching made a marked impression (Jn 4³⁹⁻⁴²). The Samaritans had a Messianic expectation of their own (Jn 4²⁵) ; and if the narrator has not defined what took place in the light of subsequent events, Jesus claimed to fulfil this expectation. This was contrary to His policy for some time to come in dealing with Israel (Mk 1⁴⁴), but He may possibly have used greater freedom among non-Israelites.

The events of Jn 2¹³–4⁴⁵ may have occupied three or four weeks, but hardly more. At the time when our Lord arrives in Galilee the impression of His public acts at the Passover was still fresh (Jn 4⁴⁵). This would lead us to explain the latter half of Jn 4³⁵ as a description of the state of things actually existing ; the cornfields were at the time 'white for the harvest,' and 'Say not ye,' etc., will be a proverb. But that being so, a difficulty would be caused if the incident of the plucking of the ears of corn (Mk 2²³ᶠᶠ·) were in its place chronologically, as the crops would still be in much the same condition as during the journey through Samaria, though the wheat harvest was going on between Passover and Pentecost, and all the events implied in Mk 1¹⁴–2²² would have intervened. The time is really too short for these. It is more probable that they were spread over some months. We must conceive of our Lord as returning to Galilee with the few disciples with Him still in the state of loose attachment characteristic of this period, and Himself remaining for a while in comparative privacy. The disciples had returned to their occupations when He takes the new and decisive step involved in the call described for us in the Synoptics.

The Synoptic Chronology.—If Mk 2²³ ‖ is to be taken as strictly consecutive with the events that precede, it would follow that the call of the leading apostles took place at least a week or two before the cutting of the ripened wheat, *i.e.*, as we might infer, before rather than some time after the Passover season. In that case the Johannean and Synoptic narratives would not be easy to combine. But the sequence of incidents in Mk (Eating with sinners, 2¹³⁻¹⁷ ; Fasting, 2¹⁸⁻²² ; Two incidents relating to the Sabbath, 2²³⁻³⁶) suggests that we have here rather a typical group of points in the controversy with the Pharisees than a chronicle of events as they happened in order of time. In that case the call of the apostles might fall in the autumn, and the plucking of the ears of corn might belong to the end rather than the beginning of the period upon which we are about to enter.

The Healing of the Nobleman's Son.—As the narratives have come down to us, there are no doubt real differences between the story of the healing of the Nobleman's Son (Jn 4⁴⁶⁻⁵⁴) and that of the Centurion's Servant (Mt 8⁵⁻¹³ ‖). We must, however, reckon with the possibility—it cannot in any case be more—that they are two versions of the same event, arising out of the ambiguity of παῖς and δοῦλος. Years ago (*Fourth Gospel*, p. 100 f.) the writer had taken this view, which has since been adopted by Weiss (*Leben Jesu*, i. 423 ff.). A similar question may be raised in connexion with the common features of the narratives Lk 5¹⁻¹¹, Jn 21¹⁻¹¹. There, too, there may have been some confusion (*Fourth Gospel*, p. 267 ; cf. Loofs, *Die Auferstehungsberichte*, p. 32). Such instances mark the limits of a laxer or stricter interpretation of the historicity of the documents, between which we are not in a position to decide with absolute certainty.

B. *First Active or Constructive Period: The Founding of the Kingdom.*

Scene. — Mainly in Galilee, but also partly in Jerusalem.

Time.—From about Pentecost A.D. 27 to shortly before Passover A.D. 28.

Mt 4¹²⁻13⁵³, Mk 1¹⁴⁻6¹³, Lk 4¹⁴⁻9⁶, Jn 5¹⁻⁴⁷.

In this period the points to notice are : (i.) The Call, Training, and Mission of the Twelve, followed perhaps by a larger number (the Seventy of St. Luke) ; (ii.) the gradual differentiation of the ministry of Jesus from that of John Bapt. and its assumption of a much larger scope ; (iii.) a full course of teaching on the true nature of the Kingdom of God (or of Heaven) ; (iv.) the performance of a number of Messianic works, chiefly of healing ; (v.) the effect of these works on the common people as seen in a great amount of superficial enthusiasm, but without as yet much intelligent apprehension of the object really in view; (vi.) the growing hostility of the scribes and Pharisees caused by a more and more declared divergence of principle; (vii.) the very gentle indirect and gradual putting forward by Jesus of His claim as the Messiah.

Up to the point which we have now reached there had been no definite 'founding' of a society; no steps had been taken towards the institution even of a new sect, much less of a new religion. The Baptism of Jesus had been attended by circumstances which marked Him out in a highly significant manner; but the general knowledge of these circumstances was vague, and even in those who were not unacquainted with them they awoke expectations rather than convictions, and these, too, were vague and left for the future to define. For the rest little as yet had occurred to define them. A certain number of disciples had gathered round Jesus in the most easy and natural manner, just as disciples had gathered round many a Rabbi before Him. These simply came and went as inclination took them; they were not as yet bound by any closer ties to His person. He had gone about quietly with some of them in His company, but nothing very startling had happened. The expulsion of the buyers and sellers from the temple was a prophetic act, and two 'signs' had occurred at a considerable interval; but this was little to what the Jews expected in their Messiah. So far Jesus had worked side by side with the Baptist, and on very similar lines. If His disciples took a share in baptizing (Jn 4²), it was in the same kind of baptizing as that of John. It was a baptism 'of repentance,' and in no sense baptism 'into the name of Christ.'

The period on which we are now entering marks a great advance. The work which Jesus came to perform now took its distinctive shape. What had gone before was of the nature of foretaste, hints, foreshadowings; now the strokes follow each other in quick succession by which the purpose of Jesus is set clearly before those who have eyes to see. We may take these one by one.

i. *The Call, Training, and Mission of the Twelve (and of the Seventy).*—The first step is one which evidently struck the imagination of the followers of Jesus, because it is placed in the forefront of the Synoptic narrative. It is, in fact, the real beginning of the Public Ministry. Among those who had been the first to seek a nearer acquaintance with the new Prophet were two pairs of brothers, both from Capernaum, and both fishermen by trade. When Jesus returned to Galilee they all went back to their ordinary occupations, and they were engaged in these when suddenly they saw Him standing by the shore of the lake and received a peremptory command to follow Him (Mk 1¹⁶⁻²⁰ ‖). This 'following' meant something more than anything they had done as yet; they were to 'be with him' (Mk 3¹⁴), so that they might receive His teaching continuously and in a manner systematically. They were encouraged to ask questions, and their questions were answered. Special and full explanations were given to them which were not given to others (Mt 13³⁴). The teaching of Jesus was not esoteric, but there was this inner circle to whom peculiar advantages were given for entering into it.

The call which was issued in the first instance to the four, Peter and Andrew, James and John, was gradually extended. The one other instance particularized in the Gospels is that of Levi, the son of Alphæus, to whom was given—possibly by Jesus Himself (Weiss, *Leben Jesu*, i. 503)—the name

of 'Matthew' (='given by God'). A like call proceeded to others, till the number was made up to twelve (lists in Mk 3¹⁶⁻¹⁹, Mt 10²⁻⁴, Lk 6¹⁴⁻¹⁶, Ac 1¹³). The persons chosen belonged to the middle and lower classes. Some must have been fairly well-to-do. Not only did the fishermen own the boats they used, but the father of James and John had 'hired servants' (Mk 1²⁰), and John was acquainted with the high priest * (*i.e.*, perhaps, with members of his household, Jn 18¹⁵). Matthew was of the despised class of 'publicans.' The second Simon belonged to the party of Zealots. One, the second Judas (like his father, Simon, Jn 6⁷¹ 13²⁶ RV), was a native of Kerioth in Judæa. They were chosen evidently for a certain moral aptitude which they showed for the mission to be entrusted to them. Judas Iscariot possessed this like the rest, but wrecked his fair chances. The choice and call of Jesus did not preclude the use of common free-will.

The course of teaching in which the Twelve were initiated covered a considerable part of that of which an outline will presently be sketched, especially its first two heads. It is summarized in the phrase 'the mystery of the Kingdom' (Mk 4¹¹ ‖). Of course it is not to be thought that the disciples at once understood all that was told them. Very far from it. They had much to unlearn as well as to learn, and they showed themselves slow of apprehension. But the form of teaching adopted by Jesus was exactly fitted for its object, which was to lodge in the mind principles that would gradually become luminous as they were interpreted by events and by prolonged if slow reflection.

Jesus Himself knew full well how unripe even the most intimate of His disciples were to carry out His designs. After a time—we may suppose early in the year 28—He sent out the Twelve on a mission to villages and country districts which He was not able to visit at once Himself (Mt 10¹ff.‖). But they were not to attempt to teach. Some of the wonderful works which Jesus did Himself they also were empowered to do; but the announcement which they were to make by word of mouth was limited to the one formula with which both John and Jesus had begun: 'The kingdom of heaven is at hand' (Mt 10⁷).

In one Gospel mention is made of a mission which seems to be supplemental to this. Lk speaks not only of the Twelve being sent out, but also of Seventy sent out like the Twelve by twos (Lk 10¹ff.). When we observe that the instructions given to them are substantially a repetition of those already given to the Twelve, the question lies near at hand whether we have not in this incident a mere doublet of the preceding, the number seventy (*var. lect.* seventy-two) representing in current symbolism the nations of the known world (cf. Gn 10)—being gradually substituted in the oral tradition of Gentile Churches for the number twelve, which seemed to point specially to Israel. We note also that Lk omits the restrictions of Mt 10⁵. But, on the other hand, Lk connects with the return of the Seventy a little group of sayings (Lk 10¹⁸⁻²⁰) which have every appearance of being genuine, and so increase the credibility of the narrative which leads up to them. And there is reason to think that one at least of the special sources to which Lk had access came from just such a quarter as that indicated by the Seventy—not the innermost, but the second circle of disciples. He may therefore have had historical foundation for his statement. Nor need it perhaps mean more than that Jesus did not draw any hard-and-fast line at the Twelve, but made use of other disciples near His person for the same purpose.

ii. *Differentiation of the Ministry of Jesus from that of John the Baptist.*—We have just seen that John, Jesus Himself, and the apostles all opened their ministry with the same announcement. They also made use of the same rite—baptism. But there the resemblance ceased. These were only the links which bound the stage of preparation to the stage of fulfilment. Looking back upon the

---

* Hugo Delff (*Gesch. d. Rabbi Jesus v. Nazareth*, p. 70 ff.), distinguishing between the Apostle John and the author of the Fourth Gospel, makes the latter a Jew of priestly family.

work of John, Jesus pronounced that the least of His own disciples was greater than he (Mt 11¹¹‖). It was the difference between one who was within the range of the Kingdom and one who was without it. The work of John was perfectly good and appropriate as far as it went. Its character was indicated by the 'preaching of repentance,' with which it stopped short. In full keeping with this was John's ascetic habit and mode of life. The abandonment of this by Jesus was the first outward sign of divergence which struck the eye of the world (Mk 2¹⁸⁻²²‖, Mt 11¹⁸ᶠ·‖). But the inward divergence was far greater. John inherited the old idea as to the nature of the Kingdom and of the Messiah. While impressed with the necessity of a moral reformation as leading up to it, there is nothing to show that in other respects John's conception of King and Kingdom differed from that of his countrymen. But Jesus came to revolutionize not only the conception but the mode of carrying it out. Hence it was that towards the end of his day, with the despondency of one whose own work seemed wrecked, and who was himself confined in a dungeon, and with the disappointment natural to one who saw or heard of but few of the signs which he had expected as in process of fulfilment, John sent to inquire if Jesus were the Messiah indeed, or, in other words, if the great hope and the great faith to which he had himself given expression had proved delusive. As yet Jesus had but in part, and that very covertly, declared Himself; it was impossible all at once to open the eyes of John to the full mysteries of the Kingdom; and therefore Jesus contented Himself with appealing from the current idea to one of the fundamental passages of ancient prophecy, the higher authority of which John would recognize (Mt 11⁵‖). At the same time He hinted that patience and insight were necessary for a true faith; anything less than this might easily stumble (Mt 11⁶‖).

iii. *Preaching of the Kingdom.* — In the meantime the crowds of Galilee, and especially the Twelve, enjoyed the privilege which John did not. They were having expounded to them in full the new doctrine of the Kingdom of God (or of heaven). This doctrine is of such far-reaching importance, and is so intimately bound up with the rest of our Lord's teaching, that it has seemed best to reserve the fuller account of it for separate and connected treatment at the end of this section. In so doing we are following the example of the First Evangelist, who has massed together a body of teaching at an early place in his Gospel (Mt 5–7), not that it was all spoken on the same occasion, but as a specimen of the general tenor of the teaching of which it formed part. We have a similar example of grouped specimens of teaching in Mt 13. It must suffice to add here (a) that the main subject of the teaching at this period would seem to have been the nature of the Kingdom and the character required in its members: such sayings as Mt 7²²ᶠ· are more in keeping with a later cycle of teaching, and were probably spoken later. (b) It must be remembered that the vast majority of those who listened to this teaching heard it only by fragments. It was like the seed-corn scattered in various kinds of ground (Mk 4¹⁻²⁰‖): it was not to be expected that even under the most favourable circumstances it should germinate and bear fruit all at once. Clearly, the Twelve themselves did not take in its full significance. But it is much that they should have remembered so much of it as they did, and that when their eyes were more fully opened they should have been able to set it down so coherently.

iv. *The Messianic Works.* — Another marked characteristic of this period is the number of mir-

aculous works of healing, etc., which are attributed to it and evidently belong to it. Once more we may follow the example of the First Evangelist by treating these works, which are so much the subject of discussion in modern times, by themselves. We assume here the result which we seem to reach in the section devoted to them. We assume that the miracles are historical; and we observe only that they bear the general character indicated in the reply of Jesus to John the Baptist. They are predominantly works of mercy; and they are a direct, and as we believe conscious, fulfilment of the most authentic of ancient prophecies, as contrasted with the mere signs and wonders for which the contemporary Jews were looking. Here, as in other things, we note at once (a) that Jesus condescends to put Himself at the level of those to whom He was sent. Miracles were to them the natural credentials of any great prophet, and especially of the Messiah. Jesus therefore did not refuse to work miracles. That He should work them was part of the conditions of the humanity which He assumed. But (b) though He condescended to work miracles, it was only miracles of a certain kind. He steadily refused to perform the mere wonders which the critics of His claims repeatedly challenged Him to perform. In other words, He made His miracles almost as much a vehicle of instruction as His teaching. Those which He did perform fell into their place as the natural accompaniment of one who as in character so novel and unexpected a King was founding so novel a Kingdom.

v. *Effect on the Populace.*—It is a confirmation of the view taken above and based on the Fourth Gospel,—that the call of the Twelve was preceded by a preliminary and more sporadic ministry—that from the first day on which the regular ministry began it attracted great attention and was attended by great, if superficial, success among the populace of Galilee (Mk 1³²⁻³⁴‖). Nor did the success of this first day stand alone; it was frequently repeated, and indeed gives the character to the whole of this period (Mk 2² ¹²‖ 3⁷⁻¹⁰‖ ³²‖ 4¹‖ 5²¹‖, Lk 7¹⁶ᶠ·). Both the miracles and the teaching of Jesus made a strong impression. The people were struck by the difference between the acts and words of Jesus and those of the teachers to whom they were accustomed. Acts and words alike implied a claim to an authority different in kind from that of the most respected of the Rabbis (Mk 1²⁷‖, Mt 7²⁸ᶠ·). The Rabbis interpreted the law as they found it; Jesus laid down a new law (Mt 5²¹· ²² etc.), and when He spoke, it was with an air of command. It must not, however, be supposed that Jesus was at once recognized as the Messiah. The testimony of the Baptist had reached but few, and was by this time generally forgotten. The construction put upon the commanding attitude of Jesus was that described in Lk 7¹⁶ 'A great prophet is arisen among us; and God hath visited his people.' Still less can it be supposed that there was any adequate recognition of the change which Jesus came to work in the current conceptions of religion.

vi. *Effect upon the Pharisees.* — The populace came to Jesus with simple and credulous minds, and they did not resist the impression made upon them, though it lacked depth and permanence (Mk 4⁵ᶠ·‖). Our documents are doubtless right in representing the first signs of opposition and hostility as coming from the religious leaders, the scribes and Pharisees. They are also clearly right in representing the growth of this opposition as gradual. At first Pharisees joined freely in social intercourse with Jesus and His disciples, and even invited them to their own tables (Lk 7³⁶ᶠᶠ· probably belongs to this early period). They could not deny the possibility of a prophet arising, and they repeatedly sought to test after their manner whether Jesus were really a prophet sent from God or no (Jn 1[19ff.], Mt 12[38ff.|| 16[1ff.] 19[3ff.||], Jn 7[47ff.]). But their suspicions were soon aroused. It was evident that the teaching and manner of the life of Jesus conflicted greatly with their own. There was a freedom and largeness of view about it which was foreign to their whole habits of thought. (a) In such matters as fasting, the practice of Jesus and His disciples was different (Mk 2[18ff.], Mt 6[16ff.] etc.). Worse than this, Jesus appealed expressly to those classes which they scrupulously avoided (Mk 2[15-17]|| etc.). (b) Not only did Jesus direct His ministry especially to those whom they regarded as outcast and irreclaimable, but He made some direct attacks upon themselves. At first these attacks may have been slightly disguised (as in Mt 6[1f.], where the Pharisees are not mentioned by name), but they constantly increased in directness and severity. (c) One of the first topics on which they came into collision was in regard to the keeping of the Sabbath. Mark has collected a little group of incidents bearing upon this (Mk 2[23]-3[6]), the first of which, from the mention of the ripe corn, appears, as we have seen, to belong to the second year of the ministry, but belongs to an early phase in the conflict. To the same effect is the incident related in Jn 5[1ff.], and Luke contributes another (Lk 13[11-17]). (d) The Pharisees were also honestly shocked at seeing Jesus adopt a tone and assume prerogatives which seemed to them to encroach upon the honour of God (Mk 2[5-11]||).

It is interesting, and throws a favourable light on the documents, to note how carefully the distinction is marked between (a) the local scribes and Pharisees such as were to be found scattered throughout Galilee (Mk 2[6.]|| 16.|| 18. 24 36||, Lk 7[36]) ; (b) the scribes who came down from Jerusalem (Mk 3[22]), apparently emissaries from the hierarchy, like the deputation of Jn 1[19] ; and (c) the Herodians (Mk 3[6]), the dynastic party of the Herods, who with quite different motives acted in alliance with the Pharisees. The Herodians are mentioned again in Mk 12[13]||. The name is otherwise almost unknown to history, though the party is known to have existed. Josephus has οἱ τὰ Ἡρώδου φρονοῦντες, but not Ἡρωδιανοί. This is a pure reflexion of the facts of the time—facts which soon passed away, and which fiction would never have recovered. See, further, art. HERODIANS.

vii. *The Self-Revelation of Jesus.* — Although Jesus assumed these high prerogatives, and although, as we have seen, He both spoke and acted with an authority which permitted no question, He showed a singular reticence in putting forward Messianic or Divine claims. It is remarkable that from the first those possessed with demons publicly confessed Him for what He was; but it is no less remarkable that He checked these confessions : ' He suffered not the demons to speak, because they knew him' (Mk 1[34]|| 3[12] [Mt 12[16]]). He imposed a like injunction of silence on one healed of leprosy (Mk 1[44]||). The farthest point to which Jesus went in the way of self-revelation at this early period was by taking to Himself the special title ' Son of Man.' There was probably some precedent for the identification of this title with Messiah, but it was at least not in common use, and therefore served well to cover a claim which was made but in no way obtruded. A fuller discussion of the title will be found below (p. 622 f).

This marked reticence of Jesus in regard to His own Person is clearly part of a deliberate plan. One of its motives was to prevent the rash and reckless violence which one who appealed to the Messianic expectation was sure to excite (Jn 6[15]). But it was in full keeping with the whole of His demeanour and with the special character which He gave to His mission. The first evangelist rightly sees in this a fulfilment (which we believe here as elsewhere to have been conscious and deliberate) of the prophecy Is 42[1-3] ' My servant . . . shall not strive, nor cry aloud ; neither shall any one hear his voice in the streets,' etc.

It is impossible for us to think of the Jesus portrayed in the Gospels as forcing His claims upon the attention of the world. He rather let them sink gently into the minds of His disciples until they won an assent which was not only free and spontaneous, but also more intelligent than it could have been if enforced simply by authority. But, apart from this, it was essential to the development of His mission that the teaching of the Kingdom should precede, and precede by a sufficient interval, the public self-manifestation and offer of the King. The first thing to be done was to change the char·acter and revolutionize the moral conceptions of men. This was to be the work of quiet teaching. The hour for the Leader to come forward was the hour when teaching was to give place to action. Hence it was well that at first and for some time to come the King should remain, as it were, in the background, until the preparation for His assuming His kingship was complete.

THE TEACHING OF JESUS.

a. General Characteristics of the Teaching.

(1) *Its Relation to the Teaching of the Baptist and to that of the Scribes.*—We have seen that Jesus began by taking up not only the announcement of the Baptist that the Kingdom of God was at hand, but also his call to reformation of life and the rite of baptism by which that call was impressed upon the conscience. We are also expressly told that the call to repentance was part of the apostolic commission (Mk 6[12]). And we find it no less insisted upon after the resurrection (Lk 24[47], Ac 2[38] 3[19] 5[31] 11[18] 17[30] 20[21] 26[20]).

This is clear proof of the continuity which bound together the teaching of Jesus with that of the Baptist. The starting-point of both was the same. And yet this starting-point was very soon left behind. The heads of the Baptist's teaching are soon told ; the teaching of Jesus expands and ramifies in a thousand directions. It is like passing from the narrow cleft of the Jordan to a Pisgah-view over the whole Land of Promise.

Although it was permitted to the Baptist to prepare the way for the teaching of Jesus, so far as even to enunciate its opening lesson, the place of the Baptist is quietly assigned to him ; and it is a place outside the threshold of the Kingdom : ' He that is but little in the kingdom of heaven is greater than he ' (Mt 11[11]||).

If Christ thus drew a line between His own teaching and that of John, still more marked was the difference between it and other contemporary teaching. John was at least a prophet, and spoke with the full authority of a prophet (Mt 11[9. 13]). The scribes had no original authority at all ; they did but interpret a law which they had not made. Jesus spoke with an authority not only above that of the scribes (Mk 1[22]||), but higher still than that of John. He is the legislator of a new law (Mt 5[22] etc.), the founder of that Kingdom which John did not enter.

(2) *Its Universal Range.*—With this commanding character of the teaching of Jesus there goes a corresponding width of outlook. We began with a rapid survey of the state of parties and opinions in Palestine at the time of Christ. But the object of this survey was not to explain the teaching of Jesus by affiliating it to any existing school. It was remarked of Him that He had had no regular training (Jn 7[15]). He was not a Pharisee, not a Sadducee, not an Essene, not an Apocalyptist. The direct affinities of the teaching of Jesus were with nothing so transitory and local, but rather with that which was most central in OT. We might call it the distilled essence of OT : that essence first clarified and then greatly enlarged, the drop became a crystal sphere.

We are speaking, of course, of the substance, and of the main part of the substance, of the teaching of Jesus. The mere fact that it was conditioned by time and space involved that it should be addressed to a given generation in a language which it understood. Nor was it wholly without definite and particular applications — sidelights, so to speak, upon that space in history within which it falls. But history itself has shown that in the main it transcends all these conditions, and is as fresh at the end of eighteen centuries as when first it was delivered.

(3) *Its Method.*—This wonderful adaptability in the teaching of Jesus is accounted for in part by its extreme simplicity. If it had been a doctrine of the schools, something of the fashion of the schools would have adhered to it. But, as it was, it was addressed chiefly to the common people— sometimes to congregations in synagogues, sometimes to the chance company collected in private houses, more often still to casual gatherings in the open air.

And the language in which the teaching was couched was such as to appeal most directly to audiences like these. As a rule it takes hold of the simplest elements in our common humanity, 'das allgemein Menschliche.' The trivial incidents of everyday life are made to yield their lessons : the sower scattering his seed, the housewife baking her cakes or sweeping the house to find a lost piece of money, the shepherd collecting his sheep, the fishermen drawing in their net. Sometimes the story which forms the vehicle for the teaching takes a higher flight : it deals with landed proprietors, and banquets, and kings with their subjects. But even then there seems to be a certain deliberate simplification. The kings, for instance, are those of the popular tale rather than as the courtier would paint them.

(4) *The Parables.* — We have been naturally drawn into describing that which is most characteristic in the outward form of the teaching of Jesus—His parables. The Greek word $\pi\alpha\rho\alpha\beta o\lambda\acute{\eta}$ is used in NT in a wider sense than that in which we are in the habit of using it. In Lk 4^{23} it = 'proverb.' In Mt 15^{15} (comp. with vv.[11. 16-20]) it = 'maxim,' a condensed moral truth, whether couched in figurative language or not. It covers as well brief aphoristic sayings (*e.g.* Mk 3^{23} 13^{28} ||, Lk 5^{36} 6^{39}) as longer discourses in which there is a real 'comparison.' But these latter are the 'parables' in our modern acceptation of the term : they are scenes or short stories taken from nature or from common life, which present in a picturesque and vivid way some leading thought or principle which is capable of being transferred to the higher spiritual life of man. The 'parable' in a somewhat similar sense to this had been employed in OT and by the Rabbis, but it had never before been employed with so high a purpose, on so large a scale, or with such varied application and unfailing perfection of form.

We may say that the parables of Jesus are of two kinds. In some the element of 'comparison' is more prominent. In these the parable moves as it were in two planes—one that of the scene or story which is made the vehicle for the lesson, and the other that of the higher truth which it is sought to convey ; the essence of the parable lies in the parallelism. In the other kind there is no parallelism, but the scene or the story is just a typical example of the broader principle which it is intended to illustrate. The parables in Mt 13, Mk 4 all belong to the one class, several of those in the later chaps. of St. Luke (the Good Samaritan, the Rich Fool, the Rich Man and Lazarus, the Pharisee and the Publican) belong rather to the other.

There is a group of sayings in the Fourth Gospel to which is given the name $\pi\alpha\rho oi\mu\iota\alpha$ rather than $\pi\alpha\rho\alpha\beta o\lambda\acute{\eta}$ (Jn 10^6, cf. $16^{25.\ 29}$), though the latter term would not have been inappropriate, in which Jesus uses the method of comparison to bring out leading features in His own character and person. In this way He speaks of Himself as the Good Shepherd, the Door of the sheep, the Vine, the Light of the World. These sayings form a class by themselves, and from the peculiar way in which they are worked out—the metaphor and the object explained by the metaphor being not kept apart but blended and fused together—are commonly classed under the head of 'allegory' rather than 'parable.' This is another instance in which we draw distinctions where the Greek of the NT would not have drawn them.

(5) *Interpretation of the Parables.*—To this day there is some difference of opinion as to the interpretation of the parables. The Patristic writers as a rule (though with some exceptions) allow themselves great latitude of interpretation. Any point of resemblance to any detail of the parable, however subordinate, justifies in their eyes a direct application of that detail. A familiar instance is the identification of the 'two pence,' which the Good Samaritan gives to the host, with the two Sacraments. An opposite modern school would restrict the application to the leading idea which the parable expresses. It is, however, fair to remember that the parables are meant to illustrate the laws of God's dealings with men ; and as the same law is capable of many particular applications, all such applications may be said with equal right to be included in the parable. For instance, the parable of the Two Sons may be as true for individuals or for classes as it is for nations or groups of nations. The parable of the Great Banquet to which the invited guests do not come, and which is then thrown open to others who were not invited, no doubt points directly to the first reception of the gospel, but it is equally appropriate to every case where religious privilege is found to give no advantage, and the absence of religious privilege proves no insuperable hindrance. Any such range of application is legitimate and interesting ; nor does the aptness of the lesson to one set of incidents make it any less apt to others where a like principle is at work. Every parable has its central idea, and whatever can be related to that idea may be fairly brought within its scope. To press mere coincidences with the picturesque accessories of a parable may be permissible as rhetoric, but can have no higher value.

(6) *The Purpose of Teaching by Parables.*—If we had before us only the fact of parabolic teaching, with the parables as they have come down to us and the actual psychological effect which they are seen to exercise, we should probably not hesitate as to the reason which we assigned for them. The parabolic form is, as it were, a barb to the arrow which carries home truth to the mind. The extreme beauty of this mode of teaching, handled as it is, has been universally acknowledged. If simplicity is an element in beauty, we have it here to perfection. But when simplicity is united to profundity, and to a profundity which comes from the touching of elemental chords of human feeling,—a touching so delicate, so sure, and so self-restrained, which reminds us of the finest Greek art with an added spiritual intensity which in that art was the one thing wanting,—we have indeed a product such as the world has never seen and will not see again. We seem to be placed for the moment at the very centre of things : on the one hand there is laid bare before us the human heart as it really is or ought to be, with all its perversities and affectations stripped away ; and on

the other hand we seem to be admitted to the secret council-chamber of the Most High, and to have revealed to us the plan by which He governs the world, the threads in all the tangled skein of being. No wonder that the parables have exercised such an attractive power, not over any one class or race of men, but over humanity wherever it is found.

Then the nature of the parable, at once presenting a picture to the mind and provoking to the search for a hidden meaning or application beneath it, would seem to be exactly suited to the pædagogic method of Jesus, which always calls for some responsive effort on the part of man, and which prefers to produce its effects not all at once, but rather with a certain suspense and delay, so that the good seed may have time to germinate and strike its roots more deeply into the soil.

This natural action of the method of teaching by parables seems so obvious that we might well be content not to seek any further. But when we turn to the Gospels, we find there stated a motive for the adoption of this method of teaching which is wholly different, and it must be confessed at first sight somewhat paradoxical. All three Synoptists agree in applying to teaching by parables the half-denunciatory passage Is 6⁹⁻¹⁰; they would make its immediate object not so much to reveal truth as to conceal it—at least to conceal it for the moment from one class while it is revealed to another, and its ulterior object to aggravate the guilt of those from whom it is concealed. And, what is still more remarkable, all three Synoptists ascribe the use of this quotation to our Lord Himself, as though it really expressed, not merely the result of His chosen method of teaching, but its deliberate purpose. What are we to make of this? One group of critics would roundly deny that the words were ever used in this manner by our Lord. Jülicher (e.g.) takes his stand on Mk 4³³ 'with many such parables spake he the word unto them, *as they were able to hear it*,' which would seem to make the method a tender concession to slowness of apprehension rather than a means of aggravating it. But, on the other hand, we observe that the quotation is attributed to our Lord in what must have been the common original of all three Gospels, i.e. in one of our best and oldest sources. And while such passages as Jn 12³⁹⁻⁴¹ (where the same quotation is applied by the evangelist) and Ac 28²⁵⁻²⁷ (where it is applied by St. Paul) would show that it was part of the common property of the apostolic age, the fact that it was so would be still more intelligible if the example had been set by our Lord Himself. Nor would it be less but rather more appropriate as coming from Him, if we regard it as summing up in a broad way what He felt was and must be for many of those among whom He moved the final outcome of His mission. The lesson is very similar to that of Jn 12⁴⁶⁻⁴⁸. The Son of Man does not need to pass judgment on those who reject Him. His word judges them by an automatic process. That which is meant for their life becomes to them an occasion of falling, when from indolence or self-will it makes no impression upon them. This was the actual course of things; it was a course rendered inevitable by the laws which God had laid down, and which in that sense might be regarded as designed by Him. And inasmuch as the Son associates Himself with the providential action of the Father, it might be also spoken of as part of His own design. It is so, however, rather in the remoter degree in which, allowing for the contrariant action of human wills, whatever is is also ordained, than as directly purposed before the appeal has been made and rejected. It belongs to that department of providential action which

is not primary and due to immediate Divine initiative, but secondary or contingent upon human failure.

There is then perhaps sufficient reason to think that the words may after all have been spoken, much as we have them, by our Lord. But granting this, we should still not be forbidden to surmise that they are somewhat out of place. Standing where they do they come to us with a shock of strange severity, which would be mitigated if they could be put later in the ministry, where they occur in St. John. The transference may have been due to the position which the original passage occupies in Isaiah, where it also serves as a sort of programme of the prophet's mission. There, too, the arrangement may conceivably represent the actual historical order, but it may also represent the result of later experience, which for didactic effect is placed at the beginning of the career rather than at the end.

b. Contents of the Teaching.—There are five distinctive and characteristic topics in the teaching of Jesus—

(1) The Fatherhood of God.
(2) The Kingdom of God.
(3) The Subjects or Members of the Kingdom.
(4) The Messiah.
(5) The Paraclete and the Tri-unity of God.

With that simplicity which we have seen to be so marked a feature in His teaching, Jesus selects two of the most familiar of all relations to be the types round which He groups His teaching in regard to God and man—the family and the organized state; God stands to man in the relation at once of Father and of King. These two types by no means exclude each other, but each helps to complete the idea derived from the other without which it might be one-sided. At the same time, in different connexions, first one and then the other becomes more prominent. Thus, when stress is laid upon the Divine attributes, God appears chiefly in the character of Father; when attention is turned to the complex relations of men to Him and to one another, they are more commonly regarded under the figure of a Kingdom.

(1) *The Fatherhood of God.*—It has just been said that the doctrine that God is Father by no means excludes the doctrine that He is also King. This idea, too, is repeatedly put forward (Mt 5³⁵ 18²³ 22² etc.). The title 'King' brings out what in modern language we are accustomed to call the 'transcendence' of God. But the recognition of this was, as we saw (p. 606ᵃ *sup.*), a strong point in the contemporary Judaism, and therefore it needed no special emphasis. It was otherwise with the idea of Fatherhood.

Not that this idea was unknown to the pagan religions, and still less to the religion of Israel. From Homer onwards Zeus had borne the name 'Father of gods and men.' But this was a superficial idea: it meant little more than 'originator.' This sense also appears in the older Jewish literature, but with further connotations added to it. God is more particularly the Father of His people Israel (cf. Dt 14¹ 32⁶, Jer 3¹⁹ 31⁹. ²⁰), in a yet deeper sense of the righteous in Israel (Is 63¹⁶), and, though not with the same wealth of meaning, of the individual (Mal 2¹⁰, Sir 23¹. ⁴).

It is the tenderest side of the teaching of OT (Ps 103¹³) which is now taken up and developed. It becomes indeed the corner-stone of the NT teaching about God. The name 'Father' becomes in NT what the name Jehovah (Jahveh) was in OT, the fullest embodiment of revelation. If it is prominent in the apostolic writings, this is traceable ultimately to the teaching of Jesus (cf. Ro 8¹⁵ and comms.). The title belongs primarily to Jesus Himself as 'the Son' (ὁ Πατήρ μου, esp. Mt 11²⁷). Through Him it descends to His followers (ὁ Πατὴρ ὑμῶν, ὁ Πατήρ σου, Mt 5¹⁶·⁴⁵·⁴⁸ 6¹·⁴·⁶·⁸·⁹·¹⁴·¹⁵ etc.). But the love of God as Father extends beyond these limits even to 'the unthankful and evil' (Lk 6³⁵, Mt 5⁴⁵). The presentation of God as Father culminates in the parable of the Prodigal Son. Older conceptions of God find their counterpart in the Elder Brother of this parable (Lk 15²⁵ff. contrasted with v.²⁰). The application which is thus made of the Fatherhood of God invests the teaching of Jesus with wonderful tenderness and beauty (Mt 6³² 7¹¹ 10²⁹·³⁰, Lk 12³² etc.).

(2) *The Kingdom of God.*—If the conception of God as Father does not exclude His majesty as King, no more does the conception of His Kingdom exclude that of children gathered together in His family. Still, the leading term to denote those active relations of God with man, with which the mission of Jesus is specially connected, is ἡ βασιλεία τοῦ θεοῦ or τῶν οὐρανῶν.

The use of these terms suggests a number of questions which are still much debated. (i.) Were both names originally used? Or if one is to be preferred, which? (ii.) What is the meaning of the phrase? Does βασιλεία='kingdom' or 'reign'? (iii.) When we have determined this, with what order of ideas is the phrase to be associated? With the later Judaism? or with the teaching of the prophets? Or does it belong to the more novel element in the teaching of our Lord? (iv.) Is the Kingdom merely conceived of from the side of man or from the side of God? Is it something which man works out or which is bestowed upon him? (v.) Is it present or future? Was it in course of realization during the lifetime of Jesus Himself, or is it mainly eschatological? (vi.) Is it inward or outward? A moral reformation or the founding of a society? (vii.) Was the conception as at first framed national or universal?

These questions are put as alternatives. And they are usually so regarded. But it may be well to say at once that in almost every case there seems to be real evidence for both sides of the proposition; so that the inference is that the conception to which they relate was in fact many-sided, and included within itself a number of different *nuances*, all more or less valid. And the reason for this appears to be, that our Lord took up a conception which He found already existing, and, although He definitely discarded certain aspects of it, left others as they were, some with and some without a more express sanction, while He added new ones. The centre or focus of the idea is thus gradually shifted; and while parts of it belong to so much of the older current conception as was not explicitly repealed, other parts of it are a direct expression of the new spirit introduced into it. The one element definitely expelled was that which associated the inauguration of the Kingdom with political violence and revolution.

(i.) *The Name.* — It is well known that the phrase ἡ βασιλεία τῶν οὐρανῶν for ἡ βασ. τ. θεοῦ is a peculiarity of the First Gospel (where it occurs thirty-two times), and that it receives no sanction from the other Synoptics. Neither can Jn 3⁵, where the reading is distinctly Western, be quoted in support of it. Hence some have thought that it was a coinage of Mt. It occurs, however, also in *Ev. sec. Heb.* (Handmann, p. 89); and the fact that βασ. τ. θ. is found in Mt 12²⁸ 21³¹·⁴³ would go to show that the evangelist had no real objection to that form, while the corresponding phrase πάτηρ ὁ ἐν τοῖς οὐρανοῖς though it disappears from Lk 11² is verified by Mk 11²⁵. Moreover, we know that 'heaven' was a common metonymy for 'God' in the language of the time (cf. also Mk 10²¹, Lk 10²⁰ 12³³), and that the particular phrase 'kingdom of

heaven' (though not exactly in the sense usually assigned to it; see below under ii.) occurs repeatedly in the Talmud. It seems, therefore, on the whole probable that both forms were used by our Lord Himself. In any case they may be regarded as equivalents.

(ii.) *Meaning.*—The phrase in both its forms is ambiguous: it may mean either 'kingdom' or 'reign,' 'sovereignty,' 'rule' of heaven, or of God. It appears that in the Talmud the latter signification is the more common (Schürer, *NT Zeitgesch.*³ ii. 539 n. [Eng. tr. II. ii. 171]; Edersheim, *Life and Times,* etc. i. 267 f.). And though the former is that more usually adopted by commentators, there seems to be no reason why recourse should not be had to the latter where it is more natural (as, *e.g.* in Lk 17²⁰·²¹). The phrase covers both senses, and the one will frequently be found to shade off into the other. The best definition known to the writer is one given incidentally by Dr. Hort (*Life and Letters,* ii. 273), 'the world of invisible laws by which God is ruling and blessing His creatures.' This is the most fundamental meaning; all others are secondary. The 'laws' in question are 'a world,' inasmuch as they have a connexion and coherence of their own; they form a system, a cosmos within the cosmos; they come direct from 'heaven,' or from God; and they are 'invisible' in their origin, though they may work their way to visibility.

(iii.) *Associations.*—The sense just assigned was that which was most fundamental in the thought of Jesus. It was that which He saw ought to be the true sense, however much it might be missed by His contemporaries. It was deeper and subtler than the conception of Psalmist and Prophet, even than the bright and exhilarating picture of Ps 145¹¹⁻¹³, because it was compatible with any kind of social condition, and because it did not turn mainly on the majestic exercise of power. And if this was true of the later and more developed conception, much more was it true of the earlier notion of the theocracy, which was simply that of the Israelite State with a Prophet or Judge at the head instead of a King (1 S 12⁷⁻¹²). The contemporaries of Jesus when they spoke of the 'Kingdom of God' thought chiefly of an empire contrasted with the great world-empires, more particularly the Roman, which galled them at the moment. And the two features which caught their imagination most were the throwing off of the hated yoke and the transference of supremacy from the heathen to Israel. This was to be brought about by a catastrophe which was to close the existing order of things, and which therefore took a shape that was eschatological.

This eschatological and catastrophic side Jesus did not repudiate, though He gave a different turn to it, but the essence of His conception was independent of all convulsions. The simplest paraphrase for 'the Kingdom of God' is the clause which follows the petition for the coming of the Kingdom in the Lord's Prayer: 'Thy will be done on earth, as it is in heaven.' The only difference is that the Prayer perhaps hints rather more at the co-operation of human wills. This is not excluded in the idea of the Kingdom, which is, however, primarily the working out of the Will of God by God Himself.

(iv.) *The Nature of the Kingdom: how far Supernatural?* — The very name of the Kingdom 'of heaven *or* of God' implies that it has its origin in the world above. It 'comes' (ἔρχεσθαι, Mt 6¹⁰, Mk 9¹, Lk 11² 17²⁰; ἐγγίζειν, Mt 3² 4¹⁷ 10⁷ etc.; φθάνειν, Mt 12²⁸=Lk 11²⁰); it is 'given' (Mt 21⁴³) and 'received' (Mk 10¹⁵=Lk 18¹⁷); it is 'prepared' by God (Mt 25³⁴); it is 'inherited' (*ib.*), and men 'enter into' it (Mt 5²⁰ 19²³, Jn 3⁵); it is an object of 'search' (Mt 6[33]=Lk 12[31], Mt 13[45]). All this means that it is not built up by the labour of man, it is not a product of development from below, but 'of the creative activity of God' (Lütgert, *Reich Gottes*, p. 26). It is a gift bestowed, not something to be done, but something to be enjoyed ('Nie eine Aufgabe, wohl aber eine Gabe,' Holtzmann, *NT Th.* p. 202, partly after Lütgert). It is a prize, the highest of all prizes (Mt 13[44-46]), corresponding to the *summum bonum* of pagan philosophy.

This part of the conception has a considerable range, according as the context points to the popular view of the Messianic Kingdom as implying outward conditions of splendour, abundance, and enjoyment, or as it points to what we have called the inner thought of Jesus, the invisible laws of God's working, taken into and welcomed by the individual soul, as in the parables of the Pearl and the Treasure in the Field.

These parables show that there is a place, though a subordinate place, left for human effort, the co-operation of the human will with the Divine. The process of 'seeking' implies both effort and renunciation. There must be a concentrating of the powers of the soul upon the Will of God, if that Will is to be really done ; but where it is done it brings its own exceeding great reward (Lk 6[38]).

From this point of view it may be said, with Holtzmann (*NT Th.* i. 202-207), that the negative side of the conception is the Forgiveness of Sins as the first condition of entrance into the Kingdom, and that the positive side of it is the active practice of Righteousness with the peace and contentment which that practice brings.

(v.) *Present or Future?*—There can be no real question that the Kingdom is presented in both lights as present and as future. Strictly speaking, the future is divided, and the notes of time are threefold—present, near future, and more distant future. Take, for instance, the following passages : Mt 12[28] (=Lk 11[20]) 'If I by the Spirit of God cast out demons, then is the Kingdom of God come (ἔφθασεν) upon you' ; Mk 1[15] (=Mt 4[17]) 'The time is fulfilled, and the Kingdom of God is at hand' (ἤγγικεν) ; Mk 9[1] ‖ 'There be some here . . . which shall in nowise taste of death till they see the Kingdom of God come (ἐληλυθυῖαν) with power.' The only one of these passages about which there can be any doubt is the second (see above, p. 610), and even that belongs to the common groundwork of the Synoptic tradition, and it is supported by Mt 10[7] ‖. If the latest of these dates still falls within the lifetime of the then generation, there is a group of parables (the Mustard Seed, the Wheat and Tares, the Drag-net) which would seem at once to bring the Kingdom into the present, and to postpone its consummation.

These apparent inconsistencies are probably to be explained in the same way as others which we meet with. The future coming, the more or less distant coming, of which the Son Himself does not know the day or the hour, is the eschatological coming of the current expectation, which, if we follow our authorities, we must believe that Jesus also shared. There was, however, a certain ambiguity even in this expectation as popularly held : it was not clear exactly in what relation of time the coming of the Messiah and the establishment of His Kingdom stood to the end of all things. And this ambiguity was necessarily heightened by the peculiar nature of the coming of Christ, and the conviction which gradually forced itself upon the minds of the disciples that there must needs be a double Coming,—one in shame, the other in triumph ; one therefore which for them was past, and another still in the future.

But, apart from all this, it will be apparent that the more distinctive conception of the Kingdom as the 'world of invisible laws' by which God works is not subject to the same limitations of time. In this sense it embraces the whole providential scheme of things from the beginning ; though, as we have said, it is really a cosmos within the cosmos, and it has its culminating periods and moments, such as was above all that which dates from the Incarnation. The most characteristic expression of this aspect of the Kingdom would be the parables of the Leaven and of the Seed growing secretly.

(vi.) *Inward or Outward?*—A like conclusion holds good for the question which we have next to ask ourselves : Are we to think of the Kingdom of God as visible or as invisible? Is it an influence, a force or collection of forces, or is it an institution? We are familiar with the very common and often quite superficial identification of the Kingdom with the Church. Is this justified? Many recent writers answer this question emphatically, No (list with reff. in Holtzmann, *NT Th.* i. 208). And it is true that there are certain passages by which it seems to be excluded.

Conspicuous among these are the verses Lk 17[20. 21.] Οὐκ ἔρχεται ἡ β. τ. θ. μετὰ παρατηρήσεως. οὐδὲ ἐροῦσιν, Ἰδοὺ ὧδε, ἤ ἐκεῖ. Ἰδοὺ γὰρ ἡ β. τ. θ. ἐντὸς ὑμῶν ἐστίν. A majority of leading German scholars, including Schürer (*Die Predigt. J. C.* p. 18) and Holtzmann (with a slight modification, 'in your reach'), take the last words as meaning 'in your midst,' the main ground being that they are addressed to the Pharisees. But Field seems to have shown (*Ot. Norv. ad. loc.*) that this interpretation is lexically untenable ('no sound example'), and that the better rendering is *in animis vestris*.

But, on the other hand, parables like the Wheat and the Tares and the Drag-net are most naturally explained of a visible community ; and there can be no doubt that the popular expectation was of a visible kingdom, such as that in which the sons of Zebedee sought for a chief place.

If we keep to the clue which we have hitherto followed, the facts will be sufficiently clear. The Kingdom in its highest and most Christian sense is the working of 'invisible laws' which penetrate below the surface and are gradually progressive and expansive in their operation. But in this as in other cases spiritual forces take to themselves an outward form ; they are enshrined in a vessel of clay, finer or coarser as the case may be, not only in men as individuals but in men as a community or communities. The society then becomes at once a vehicle and instrument of the forces by which it is animated, not a perfect vehicle or a perfect instrument,—a field of wheat mingled with tares, a net containing bad fish as well as good,—but analogous to those other visible institutions by which God accomplishes His gracious purposes amongst men.

(vii.) *National or Universal?*—The same principle holds good throughout the whole of this analysis of the idea of the Kingdom. The aptest figure to express it is that of *growth*. It is a germ, secretly and silently insinuated, and secretly and silently working until it puts forth first the blade, then the ear, then the full corn in the ear. It is a mistake to cut a section of that which is thus ceaselessly expanding, and to label it with a name which might be true at one particular moment but would not be true at the next. The Kingdom of God is not the theocracy of the OT, nor the eschatological Kingdom of the Apocalypses, nor the Christian Church of the present day, or of the Middle Ages, or of the Fathers. These are phases through which it passes ; but it outgrows one after the other. For this reason, because He foresaw this inevitable and continuous growth, the chief Founder and permanent Vicegerent of the Kingdom showed Himself, as we might think, indifferent to the precise degree of extension which it was to receive during His life on earth ; He was content to say that He 'was not sent but unto the lost sheep of the house of Israel' (Mt 15²⁴), though within a generation His gospel was about to be carried to the ends of the then known earth. It was enough that the seed was planted—planted in a soil suited to it, and under conditions that ensured its full vitality, 'like a tree by the streams of water, that bringeth forth its fruit in its season, whose leaf also doth not wither.' It is characteristic of God's processes that there is no hurry or impatience about them ; the Master was not so anxious to reap immediate fruit as the disciple (Ro 1¹³), and therefore He calmly left it to His followers to see 'greater things' than He saw Himself (Jn 14¹²) ; but these 'greater things' are none the less virtually His own.

(3) *The Members of the Kingdom.*—As the 'Reign of God,' the βασιλεία τοῦ θεοῦ denotes certain Divine forces or laws which are at work in the world ; as the Kingdom of God it was at most stages a society, but at all stages a definite sphere or area, into which men might enter, and, by entering, become partakers of the same Divine forces or subject to the same Divine laws. It was therefore a matter of much moment what were the conditions of entrance into the Kingdom, and what was the character impressed upon its members. The two things run into each other, because it was required of those who entered that they should possess at least the germs of the character to be developed in them.

(i.) *Conditions of Entrance.*—These are clearly laid down : 'Except ye turn, and become as little children, ye shall in no wise enter into the kingdom of heaven' (Mt 18³). There was to be a definite change of mind, a break with the sinful past. This was to be ratified by submission to the rite of baptism, which, in the discourse with Nicodemus, is described as a new birth of 'water and Spirit' (Jn 3⁵). The entrance into the Kingdom is something more than a deliberate act of the man himself, it is a self-surrender to Divine influences. The response on the part of God is forgiveness, which is the permanent concomitant of baptism, not only that of John, but also that in the name of Christ (Mk 1⁴ ‖, comp. with Ac 2³⁸, Lk 24⁴⁷ etc.).

(ii.) *The Character of the Members.*—The typical character of the members of the Kingdom is that of a 'little child,' in which the prominent features are innocence, simplicity of aim, absence of self-assertion, trustfulness, and openness to influences from above. A sketch of such a character is given in the Beatitudes (Mt 5³⁻⁹ ; the ‖ in Lk 6²⁰⁻²⁶ refers rather to conditions or circumstances suited to the character). The Christian ideal here depicted stands out in marked contrast to most other ideals of what is admirable in man. The qualities commended ('poor in spirit'—where the Matthæan gloss is in any case right in sense,—'meek,' 'merciful,' 'pure in heart,' 'peacemakers') are all of the gentle, submissive, retiring order. And this is fully borne out by other sayings, the cheek turned to the smiter, the litigant forestalled, the requisition of labour offered freely, and even doubled (Mt 5³⁸⁻⁴¹ ‖), enemies to be loved, persecutors to be prayed for (*ib.* vv.⁴³· ⁴⁴), the sword to be sheathed (Mt 26⁵²), the duties of charity strongly inculcated (Lk 10²⁵⁻³⁷), the duty of forgiveness of injuries (Mt 18²³ff.), service greater than authority (Lk 22²⁵ff.). And it is noticeable that the same type of character is praised by St. Paul (Ro 12²¹ 'Be not overcome of evil, but overcome evil with good' ; cf. ch. 13). The whole duty of man is summed up in love to God and love to one's neighbour (again cf. Ro 13⁸⁻¹⁰). We observe, too, that the ethical teaching of Jesus is almost confined to that side of ethics which touches upon religion. Allusions to civic and industrial duties are very few, and those negative rather than positive (Mt 18²⁷ 22²¹ = Ro 13⁷).

(iii.) *Paradoxes of Christianity.*—It is only natural that these features in the teaching of Christ should be taken hold of and made a charge against Christianity, as they have been from Suetonius onwards (*Domit.* 15, 'contemptissimæ inertiæ,' of Flavius Clemens, probably as a Christian ; cf. Tertull. *Apol.* 42, 'infructuosi in negotiis dicimur'). And it may be doubted whether even yet the full intention of our Lord has been fathomed, and the exact place of the specifically Christian ideal in relation to civic and social duties ascertained. The following suggestions may be offered.

The precepts in question were probably addressed in the first instance, not to promiscuous multitudes, but to the disciples. If certain passages (as Mt 5¹) may be quoted to the contrary, it should be remembered that these introductory notes as to the circumstances under which discourses were spoken are among the least trustworthy parts of the Gospel tradition, and are often nothing more than vague conjectures of the evangelists. The type of character described bears on its face the marks of being intended for the little community of Christians (cf. Latham, *Pastor Pastorum*, p. 253).

As such we can see that it had a very special appropriateness. It was not an accident that Christianity is the religion of the Crucified. The Cross is but the culminating expression of a spirit which was characteristic of it throughout. Its peculiar note is *Victory through Suffering*. An idea like that of Islam, making its way by the sword, was abhorrent to it from the first. Jesus came to be the Messiah of the Jews, but the narratives of the Temptation teach us that, from the very beginning of His career, He stripped off from His conception of Messiahship all that was political, all thought of propagating His claims by force. A new mode of propagating religion was deliberately chosen, and carried through with uncompromising thoroughness. The disciple was not above his Master ; and the example which Jesus set in founding His faith by dying for it, was an example which His disciples were called upon to follow into all its logical consequences. Christianity, the true Christianity, carries no arms ; it wins its way by lowly service, by patience, by self-sacrifice.

History shows that there are no instruments of religious propaganda comparable to these. It also shows that the type of character connected with them is of the very highest attractiveness and beauty. Is it a complete type, a type to which we can apply the Kantian maxim, 'So act as if your action was to be a law for all human beings'? This would seem to be more than we ought to say. It is not clear that the Christian type would be what it is if it were not built upon, and if it did not presuppose, a certain structure of society, to which other motives had contributed. The ethical ideal of Christianity is the ideal of a Church. It does not follow that it is also the ideal of the State. If we are to say the truth, we must admit that parts of it would become impracticable if they were transferred from the individual standing alone to governments or individuals representing society. It could not be intended that the officers of the law should turn the cheek to the criminal. The apostles were to bear no sword, but the judge 'beareth not the sword in vain.'

May we not say that the functions of Christian morals—specifically Christian morals—are these ? (1) At their first institution to form a vehicle, the only possible vehicle, for the Christian religion. So far as Christianity has taken a real and genuine hold upon society, it is through these means and no others. Other things may have commended it for a time, but no trust can be placed in them. (2) The Christian motive acting in the midst of other motives gradually leavens and modifies them, imparting to them something which they had not before. If we look round us at the principles which at this moment regulate the action of States, in their external or international relations as well as those which are internal, we shall see that if these principles are not wholly Christian, they are also not pagan. They have a certain coherence, and they mark a very conspicuous advance as compared with the principles of the ancient world. Christianity has shown a power of modifying what it does not altogether supplant. The world even outside Christianity is still God's world. It is a world of which the essential characteristic is that it is progressive ; and it may conduce most to this progress that it should be brought under the influence of the Christian precept, not pure but in dilution. And (3) may we not draw from this the augury that in the end, at some time which we cannot see, the social structure may be still more fully recast, under the influence of Christianity : 'Nation shall not lift up sword against nation, neither shall they learn war any more' ? We can conceive a condition of things in which the Church became coextensive with the State, and in which religion penetrated the body politic in a sense in which it has never done so yet. When that time came, conduct which now would be only quixotic might be rational, and required by the public conscience.

When the verse Mt 5^{42} 'Give to him that asketh thee,' etc., is criticized from the point of view of modern political economy, the mistake is in applying a standard which is out of place. In those days the natural and, indeed, the only outlet of the kind for benefiting the poor was almsgiving ; and our Lord's main object was to strengthen the motive, which was in itself a thoroughly right one. It would have been in vain to anticipate methods which God has evidently intended to be the result of long experience. The argument from analogy comes in here with great force. God *might* have removed many forms of human ill with a word ; but as it is, He has been pleased to let improved methods, and the wisdom to use them, grow gradually and grow together. The advance which mankind slowly makes is a solid advance, and an advance not here and there, but all along the line.

We have seen that our Lord was not careful to guard against misunderstandings. It has been a salutary exercise for His followers to find out what was the true sense of His sayings for themselves.

(4) *The Messiah.*—We are not concerned here with the very remarkable historical evolution of the claim of our Lord to be the Messiah, which will come before us in connexion with the narrative of His life. At present we have to do only with His teaching on the subject, and that mainly with reference to the deeply significant names by which His claim was conveyed.

(i.) **The Christ.**—We need not delay over the title 'Messiah,' 'Christ,' 'Anointed,' which is simply that of the current Jewish expectation. It is repeatedly applied to our Lord by others, and on three occasions, at least, expressly accepted by Himself (Jn 4^{26}, Mt 16^{17}, Mk 14$^{61. 62}$ ‖, cf. Jn 11^{27}); but only once does our Lord use the term of Himself (Jn 17^{3} '$Ἰησοῦν$ $Χριστόν$), and that in a passage where we cannot be sure that the wording is not that of the evangelist. In like manner the title 'Elect' ($ἐκλελεγμένος$, Lk 9^{35}; $ἐκλεκτός$, Lk 23^{35}), which is also current (cf. Enoch 40^{5}), is applied to our Lord, but not by Himself.

(ii.) **Son of David.**—Much the same may be said of another title which belongs to a prominent side of the expectation. 'Son of David' occurs several times (on the lips of the crowd at and before the triumphal entry, of the Syrophœnician woman, of Bartimæus, of the Pharisees), but Jesus Himself does not use it, and rather propounds a difficulty in regard to it (Mk 12^{35} ‖).

(iii.) **Son of Man.**—The really characteristic title which occurs some 80 times in the Gospels, and is without doubt the one which Jesus chose to express His own view of His office, is 'the Son of Man.' Whereas the other titles are used by others of Him, this is used only by Him and of Himself. What He desired to convey by this is a question at once of no little difficulty and of great importance ('Die Frage gehört zu den verwickeltsten ja verfahrensten der ganzen neutest. Theologie,' Holtzmann).

The starting-point for this, as well as for the idea of the kingdom, is, we may be sure, Dn 7^{13}. The 'Son of Man' in that passage, as originally written, stood for Israel. The four world-empires are represented by beasts, the dominion that falls to Israel is that of a man. But in this as in other respects the passage was interpreted Messianically. In the Similitudes of the Bk. of Enoch (chs. 37–70) the Son of Man takes a prominent place. He is a person, and a superhuman person. It is He who holds the great judgment to which the Apocalyptic writings look forward. The attributes ascribed to Him are all more or less directly connected with this judgment, which is at once to vindicate the righteous, and finally to put down the wicked. The date of this portion of the Bk. of Enoch has been much debated, but opinion at the present time is still more preponderantly in favour of the view that it is pre-Christian (between B.C. 94–64, Charles, *Enoch*, p. 29 f.). The language of the Gospels requires that the title as applied to a person and to the Messiah should be not entirely new. It also requires that it should be not perfectly understood and familiar (Mt 16^{13}, Jn 12^{34}). It is probable that its use did not go beyond a small circle, the particular circle to which the Similitudes of Enoch belonged. This, however, would be enough to give the phrase a certain currency, and to make it at least suggest association with the Messiah.

It is associated with Him, especially in His character as Judge, and as the chief actor in that series of events which marks the end of the age, and the reversal of the places of good and wicked. This sense Jesus did not discard. It appears unmistakably in a number of passages (Mt 13^{41} 16^{28} 19^{28} 24$^{30ff.}$ 25$^{31ff.}$ 26^{64} etc.). But at the same time there can be no doubt that He read into it a number of other ideas, new and original, just as He read them into the conception of the Kingdom.

What is most distinctive in this novel element in the teaching of Jesus? There is an increasing tendency amongst scholars to lay stress on the Aramaic original of the phrase. The Aramaic equivalent is said to mean and to be the only way which they had of expressing 'Man' (generically, *i.e.* 'Mankind'). Hence the attempt has been made to interpret the phrase impersonally, and to get rid more or less of its Messianic application (see Holtzmann, *NT Th.* i. 256 ff.). It is true that an impersonal sense will suit such a passage as Mk 2^{28} 'The Sabbath was made for man . . . therefore the Son of Man is Lord even of the Sabbath.' At the same time this is by no means the necessary sense. And Wellhausen, who is one of those who most emphatically maintain the equation 'Son of Man'='Man,' yet sees that the expression must have been used by our Lord to designate His own person (*Israel. u. Jüd.*

Gesch.[2] p. 381). Nor can this conclusion really be avoided by such an expedient as Holtzmann's, who calls attention to the comparative rarity of the title in the early chapters and early stages of the history (*e.g.* in Mk only 2[10. 28]), and would explain it during this period impersonally, and only after St. Peter's confession personally. Against this and against more sweeping attempts (*e.g.* by Martineau, *Seat of Authority*, p. 339) to get rid of the Messianic signification altogether, it may be enough to point out that if reasonable critics like Holtzmann allow, and a narrative such as that of the Temptation seems to prove, that Jesus from the first really assumed the character of the Messiah, and if our oldest authorities with one consent treat the title Son of Man as in the later stages Messianic, it is fair to presume that it is Messianic also in the earlier. If the Similitudes of the Bk. of Enoch are pre-Christian, this conclusion would amount almost to certainty.

It is, however, fair to argue from the natural sense of the phrase in Aramaic, that by His use of it, Jesus did place Himself in some relation to humanity as a whole. And we are led to form the same inference by the conspicuous use of the corresponding Heb. in Ps 8[4] 'What is man that thou art mindful of him? and the son of man that thou visitest him?' Here the parallelism shows that 'son of man'='man.' We also know from He 2[6-10] that the psalm was at a very early date applied to Jesus as the Messiah, and at a still earlier date (the Baptism) we have the neighbouring Ps 2[7] applied to Him. It seems to follow, or at least to be a very natural presumption, that these two psalms early became an object of close study to Jesus, and helped to give outward shape to His conceptions.

Ps 8 seems specially adapted to fall in with these, as it brings out with equal strength the two elements which we know to have entered into the consciousness of Jesus—the combination of lowliness with loftiness, the physical weakness of man as contrasted with his sublime calling and destiny. We can see here the appropriateness of the application of one and the same title to Him who, on the one hand, 'had not where to lay his head,' and who must needs 'go as it was written of him,' and who yet, on the other hand, looked to come again 'with power' in His Kingdom.

We do not like to use such very modern phraseology as the 'ideal of humanity,' 'the representative of the human race'; and yet it would seem that Jesus did deliberately connect with His own person such ideas as these: He fused them as it were into the central idea of Messiahship, and we can see how the Jewish conception of the Messiah was enlarged and enriched by them. If the Messiah comes out in the claim to forgive sins, it is the Son of Man whose mission it was 'to seek and to save that which was lost' (Lk 19[10]), 'not to be ministered unto but to minister, and to give his life a ransom for many' (Mk 10[45] ‖).

Here we have another connexion in which the name is frequently used. The prophecies of the Resurrection and of the Second Coming are closely associated with the fatal end of the First : 'The Son of Man must suffer many things, and be rejected by the elders, and the chief priests, and the scribes, and be killed, and after three days rise again' (Mk 8[31] etc.). If we ask for the OT original of this 'Saviour through suffering,' no doubt it is the Second Part of Isaiah, and especially Is 53. Still, it would be rather too much to describe this idea as embodied in the title 'Son of Man.' It is embodied in the *character* of the Son of Man as conceived by Jesus, but not exactly in the name. The name which expressed it was the 'Servant of Jehovah' (παῖς κυρίου) ; and this name was undoubtedly applied to Christ by the Church as soon as it began to reflect upon His life and mission (cf. Ac 3[13. 26] 4[27. 30], Mt 12[18]), but we have no evidence that Jesus used it of Himself. One reason for the choice of the name 'Son of Man' probably was that it admitted and favoured these associations, even if it did not directly suggest them.

This comprehensive and deeply significant title touched at the one end the Messianic and eschatological expectation through the turn which had been given to it in one section of Judaism (the Book of Enoch). At the other and opposite end it touched the idea of the Suffering Servant. But at the centre it is broadly based upon an infinite sense of brotherhood with toiling and struggling humanity, which He who most thoroughly accepted its conditions was fittest also to save. As Son of God, Jesus looked upwards to the Father ; as Son of Man, He looked outwards upon His brethren, the sheep who had no shepherd.

(iv.) **Son of God.**—Only once in Synopt. (Mt 27[43]) and in a few places in the Fourth Gospel (Jn 10[36], cf. 5[25] 9[35] *var. lec.* 11[4]) is it hinted that Jesus directly assumed this title. It is repeatedly given to Him by others—by the Baptist (Jn 1[34]), by Nathanael (Jn 1[49]), by Satan hypothetically (Mt 4[3]), as also by the crowd (Mt 27[40]), by the possessed (Mk 3[11] ‖), by the disciples (Mt 14[33]), by the centurion (Mk 15[39]=Mt 27[54]), and by evangelists (Mk 1[1] *v.l.* Jn 3[18] 20[31]).

At the same time it is abundantly clear that the title was really assumed from the indirect mode in which Jesus constantly speaks of God as 'My Father.' This is very frequent in Synoptics as well as in St. John (Mt 7[21] 10[32] 11[27] 15[13] 16[17] etc.). And although, as we have seen, the consciousness which finds expression in this phrase becomes the basis of an extended doctrine of the Divine Fatherhood ('the Father,' 'our Father,' 'thy Father,' 'your Father'), there is nevertheless a distinct interval between the sense in which God can be claimed as Father by men, even the innermost circle of the disciples, and that in which He is Father to the Son. In this respect the passage Mt 11[27]=Lk 10[22] is quite explicit (cf. also the graduated scale of being in Mk 13[32] = Mt 24[36]). Although this passage stands out somewhat conspicuously in Synoptics, the context in which it occurs is so original and so beyond the reach of invention, while it supplies so marvellously the key to that which distinguishes the history of Jesus from other histories, that doubt cannot reasonably be cast upon it. It is confirmed by the sense in which the title 'Son of God' is taken by the Jews—not merely by the populace but by the learned (Mt 27[41-43], cf. Mk 15[31. 32], Jn 19[7]). And, on the other hand, it confirms sufficiently the substantial accuracy of like passages in the Fourth Gospel (*e.g.* 10[30. 38]). We are thus prepared for the unanimity with which the Church at the earliest date fixed upon this title to convey its sense of the uniqueness of Christ's nature (Ac 9[20], Ro 1[4], Gal 2[20], Eph 4[13], He 4[14] etc., 1 Jn 4[15] etc., Rev 2[18]).

This aspect of the question will come before us more fully later. We content ourselves for the present with observing that the teaching of Jesus, reserved and reticent as it is, presupposes as its background this wholly exceptional relation of 'the Son' to 'the Father.' From that as centre radiate a number of other relationships to His immediate disciples, to the Church of which they formed the nucleus, and to mankind. The Sonship of Jesus is intimately connected with His work as Messiah (Titius, p. 116). It is in this character that 'all things are delivered' to Him (Mt 11[27] ‖), in this character that He is enabled to give to the world a revelation of the Father (*ib.*), in this character that He carries out His work of redemption even to the death (Mk 14[36] ||).

(5) *The Paraclete and the Tri-unity of God.*— In the earliest Epp. of St. Paul we find that the Son of God is placed side by side with the Father, and is associated with Him as the ground of the Church's being, the source of spiritual grace, and as co-operating with Him in the providential ordering of events (1 Th 1[1], 2 Th 1[1], 1 Th 3[11f.]). It is difficult to describe the effect of the language used in any other terms than as attributing to the Son a coequal Godhead with the Father. And it is remarkable that St. Paul does this, within some twenty-two years of the Ascension, not as though he were laying down anything new, but as something which might be assumed as part of the common body of Christian doctrine.

We observe also that throughout the earliest group of Epp. there are frequent references to the work of the Holy Spirit as the one great force which lies behind at once the missionary activity and the common life of the Church of the apostolic age (esp. 1 Co 12-14, but cf. 1 Th 1[5t.] 4[8] 5[19] etc.). This, too, it is assumed that all Christians would understand.

How are we to account for the prevalence of such teaching at so early a date, and in a region so far removed from the centre of Christianity? It would be natural if the Lord Jesus Christ Himself in His intercourse with His disciples had prepared them to expect a great activity of the Holy Spirit, and if He had hinted at relations in the Godhead which made it threefold rather than a simple monad. Apart from such hints, the common belief of the Church respecting Christ Himself and the Holy Spirit seems very difficult to understand. Certain previous tendencies in Jewish thought might lead up some way towards it, but they would leave a wide gap unspanned.

When, therefore, we find that one Gospel ascribes to our Lord rather full and detailed teaching respecting the Paraclete, which is explained to be another name for the Holy Spirit (Jn 14[16. 26] 15[26]), when there is held out a clear hope and promise of a new Divine influence to take the place of that which is being withdrawn, and when in another Gospel we are also told of the institution * of a rite associated with a new revelation of God under a threefold Name, that of Father, Son, and Holy Spirit (Mt 28[19]), these phenomena are just what we are prepared for, and just such as we should have had to assume even if we had had no definite record of them. We may, then, regard them as having received—whatever the antecedent claims of the documents in which they are found—a very considerable degree of critical verification. The single verse 2 Cor 13[14] seems to require something very like what we find in Mt and Jn.

LITERATURE.—Much material of value will be found in the works on the Biblical Theology of NT by Weiss, Beyschlag, and esp. H. J. Holtzmann (1897). Reference may also be made to Bovon, *Théol. du NT*, Lausanne, 1897. The most considerable recent work on the Teaching of Jesus as a whole is Wendt's *Lehre Jesu*, Göttingen, 1890 (Eng. tr., T. & T. Clark, Edin. 1892). Bruce, *The Kingdom of God* (1890 and later) embraces the Synopt. Gospels only. In the last few years a number of monographs have appeared on the doctrine of the Kingdom and points connected with it—all, it may be said, bringing out some real aspect in the doctrine, though in the writer's opinion too often at the expense of other aspects. The series began with two prize essays, *Die Lehre vom Reiche Gottes*, by Issel and Schmoller (both Leiden, 1891), and includes treatises with similar titles by Schnedermann (Leipzig, 1893, 1895, 1896), J. Weiss (Göttingen, 1892), Lütgert (Gütersloh, 1895), Titius (Freiburg i. B. u. Leipzig, 1895), Krop (Paris, 1897); also Bousset, *Jesu Predigt in ihrem Gegensatz zum Judentum* (Göttingen, 1892); Paul, *Die Vorstellungen vom Messias u. vom Gottesreich* (Bonn, 1895); Lietzmann, *Der Menschensohn* (Leipzig, 1896); J. Weiss, *Die Nachfolge Christi* (Göttingen, 1895); Grass, *Das Verhalten zu Jesus* (Leipzig, 1895); Ehrhardt, *Der Grund-*

---

* Not, of course, the first institution, but its confirmation as a rite and its first association with the triple formula.

---

charakter d. Ethik Jesu (Freiburg i. B. u. Leipzig, 1895); Wiesen, *Die Stellung Jesu zum irdischen Gut* (Gütersloh, 1895).

THE MIRACLES OF JESUS.—There has been a certain tendency of late to recede from the extreme position in the denial of Miracles. Harnack, for instance, writes in reference to the Gospel history as follows : 'Much that was formerly rejected has been re-established on a close investigation, and in the light of comprehensive experience. Who in these days, for example, could make such short work of the miraculous cures in the Gospels as was the custom of scholars formerly?' (*Christianity and History*, p. 63, Eng. tr.).

(i.) *Different Classes of Miracles.*—Partly this change of attitude is due to the higher estimate which would now be put on the value of the evangelical sources generally, as to which something will be said below. Partly it would be due to a change of view in regard to the supernatural, which is no longer placed in direct antagonism to the natural, but which is more reasonably explained as resulting from the operation of a higher cause in nature. And partly also it would be due to the recognition of wider possibilities in nature, 'more things in heaven and earth' than were dreamt of in the narrow philosophy of the *Aufklärung*.

(a) In particular, it may be said that medical science would have no difficulty in admitting a large class of miracles of healing. All those which have to do with what would now be called 'nervous disorders,' all those in which there was a direct action of the mind upon the body, would fall into place readily enough. Given a personality like that of Jesus, the effect which it would have upon disorders of this character would be strictly analogous to that which modern medicine would seek to produce. The peculiar combination of commanding authority with extreme gentleness and sympathy would be a healing force of which the value could not easily be exaggerated.

A question would indeed still be left as to the treatment of the cases of what was called 'demoniacal possession.' There can be no doubt that Jesus Himself shared, broadly speaking, the views of His contemporaries in regard to these cases : His methods of healing went upon the assumption that they were fundamentally what every one, including the patients themselves, supposed them to be. We can well believe that this was a necessary assumption in order to allow the healing influences to operate. We must remember that all the ideas of the patient would be adjusted to the current belief, and it would be only through them that the words and acts of Christ could take effect. In the accounts of such miracles we see that there was a mutual intelligence between Healer and patient from the first (Mk 1[24f.] || [34] || 5[6] ||). It was by means of this mutual intelligence that the word of command struck home.

We should be prepared, then, to say that this class of miracles implied accommodation to the ideas of the time. But when we speak of 'accommodation' on the part of our Lord, we do not mean a merely politic assumption of a particular belief for a particular purpose. We mean that the assumption was part of the outfit of His incarnate Manhood. There was a certain circle of ideas which Jesus accepted in becoming Man in the same way in which He accepted a particular language with its grammar and vocabulary. It would have been wholly out of keeping with the general character of His Ministry if Jesus had attacked this form of disease in any other way than through the belief in regard to it which at that time was universal. The scientific description of it has doubtless greatly changed. But it is still a question which is probably by no means so clear, whether, allowing for its temporary and local character, the language then used did not contain an important element of truth. The physical and moral spheres are perhaps more intimately connected than we suppose. And the unbridled wickedness rife in those days may have had physical effects, which were not unfitly described as the work of 'demons.' The subject is one which it is probable has not yet been fully explored.

(β) There is, as we have seen, one large class of diseases in regard to which the healing force exerted by the presence and the word of Jesus has a certain amount of analogy in the facts recognized by modern medicine. We must not, however, treat that analogy as going farther than it does. It does not hold good equally for all the forms of disease which are described as having been healed. Wherever the body is subject to the action of the mind, there we can give an account of the miracle which is to some extent—to a large extent—rational and intelligible. But in cases in which the miracle involves a purely physical process it will not be possible to explain it in the same way.

This other class of miracles will fall rather under the same head as those which were wrought, not upon man, but upon nature. In regard to these miracles, the world is probably not much nearer to a reasoned account than it was. It must always be remembered that the narratives which have come down to us are the work of those who expected that Divine action would (as we should say) run counter to natural laws and not be in harmony with them, and that the more Divine it was the more directly it would run counter to them. We may be sure that if the miracles of the first century had been wrought before trained spectators of the nineteenth, the version of them would be quite different. But to suppose this is to suppose what is impossible, because all God's dealings with men are adapted to the age to which they belong, and cannot be transferred to another age. If God intended to manifest Himself specially to the nineteenth century, we should expect Him to do so by other means. We are then compelled to take the accounts as they have come down to us. And we are aware beforehand that any attempt to translate them into our own habits of thought must be one of extreme difficulty, if not doomed to failure.

(ii.) *Critical Expedients for eliminating Miracle.*—In view of the difficulty of giving a rational (*i.e.* a nineteenth century) version of miracle, it is not surprising that recourse should be had to critical expedients for explaining away Miracle altogether; in other words, to account for the narratives of miracles without assuming that objective facts corresponding to them really occurred. The expedients most in favour are: (α) imitation of similar stories in OT; (β) exaggeration of natural occurrences; (γ) translation of what was originally parable into external fact. These are causes which have about them nothing violent or incredible, and we may believe that they were to some extent really at work. The question to *what* extent, will depend mainly upon the nature of the evidence for miracles and the length of time interposed between the evidence and the events. This will be the next subject to come before us. We may, however, anticipate so far as to say that whatever degree of verisimilitude belongs to the causes suggested in themselves, they do not appear to be adequate, either separately or in combination, to account for the whole or any large part of the narratives as we

have them. And there is the further consideration, on which more will also be said presently, that something of the nature of miracle, something which was understood as miracle, and that on no insignificant scale, must be assumed to account for the estimate certainly formed by the whole first generation of Christians of the Person of Christ.

(iii.) *The Evidence for the Gospel Miracles in general.*—Coming to the question as to the evidence for the Miracles recorded in the Gospels, there are three main observations to be made : (α) that the evidence for all these miracles, generally speaking, is strong ; (β) that the evidence for all the different classes of miracles is equally strong; (γ) that although for the best attested miracles in each class the evidence is equal, there is a difference between particular miracles in each class; some are better attested than others.

(α) It is unnecessary to repeat what has been already said (p. 604 *sup.*) about the general character of the Gospel History. The critical student must constantly have in mind the question to what state of things the different phases of that history as it has come down to us correspond. Does it reflect conditions as they existed after A.D. 70 or before? And if before, how far does it reflect the later half of that period, and how far the earlier? How far does it coincide with a section of Christian thought and Christian life (*e.g.*) taken at the height of the activity of St. Paul ; and how far does it certainly point to an earlier stage than this? In other words, how much of the description contained in the Gospels belongs to the period of consequences, and how much to the period of causes?

Every attempt to treat of the life of our Lord should contribute its quota to the answer to these questions. And it is becoming more and more possible to do this, not merely in a spirit of superficial apologetics, but with a deep sense of responsibility to the truth of history. And the writer of this article strongly believes that the tendency of the researches of recent years has been to enhance and not to diminish the estimate of the historical value of the Gospels.

(β) This applies to the Gospel records as a whole, in which miracles are included. It is natural next to ask, What is the nature of the particular evidence for Miracles? How is it distributed? Does the distribution correspond to the distinction which we have drawn between the easier and the more difficult Miracles? If it did, we might suppose that the former class had better claims to credence than the latter.

But an examination of the documents shows that this is not the case. Without committing ourselves to all the niceties of the Synoptic problem, there are at any rate broad grounds for distinguishing between the matter that is found in all the three Synoptics, in the First and Third, and in one only of the Three. Whether the ultimate groundwork is written or oral, the threefold matter represents that groundwork, and is therefore, if not necessarily the oldest, at least the most broadly based and authoritative. There is reason to think that the double matter is also very ancient. It consists largely of discourse, but some few narratives seem to belong to it. The peculiar sections of the different Gospels vary considerably in their character, and it is natural to suppose that they would have the least antecedent presumption in their favour. Some confirmatory evidence would be needed for facts which rested upon their testimony alone.

Now, if it had happened that the Nature-Miracles had been confined to sections of this last kind, while the Miracles of Healing—and especially the Healing of Nervous Diseases—had entered largely into the Double and Triple Synopsis ; or—inasmuch as discourse more often bears the stamp of unmistakable originality than narrative—if the miracles of one class had appeared only in the form of narrative, while the allusions in discourse were wholly to miracles of the other, then the inference would have lain near at hand that there was a graduated scale in the evidence corresponding to a like graduated scale in the antecedent probability of the miracle.

But this is not the case. Miracles of all the different kinds occur in all the documents or sources. The Triple Synopsis contains not only the healing of demoniacs and paralytics, but the healing of the issue of blood (Mk 5²⁵‖), the raising of Jairus' daughter (ib.³⁸‖), the stilling of the storm (ib. 4³⁷‖), the feeding of the five thousand (ib. 6³⁵‖). This last miracle is found not only in all three Synoptists, but also in Jn 6⁵ff.. And there is this further point about it, that if we regard the miracles generally as a gradual accretion of myth and not based upon fact, we should undoubtedly assume that the feeding of the four thousand (Mk 8¹, Mt 15³²) was a mere duplicate of it. But it is probable that this story also belonged to the fundamental source, in spite of its omission by Luke. In that case both the feedings of a multitude would have had a place in the oldest of all our authorities, and the first growth in the tradition would have to be pushed back a step farther still. We should thus have a nature-miracle not only embodied in our oldest source, but at its first appearance in that source already pointing back some way behind it.

(γ) It thus appears that the evidence, externally considered, is equally good for all classes of miracles. It is not, as we might expect, that the evidence for the easier miracles is better than that for the more difficult, leaving us free to accept the one and reject the others. We cannot do this, because the best testimony we have embraces alike those miracles which imply a greater deviation from the ordinary course of nature and those in which the deviation is less.

It does not, however, follow that within the different classes of miracles the evidence for particular miracles is equal. When Prof. Goldwin Smith insists that all the miracles recorded in the Gospels stand or fall together, he is going in the teeth, not so much of anything peculiar to the study of the Gospels, but of the historical method generally. And the examples which he gives are unfortunate. ' We cannot pick and choose. The evidence upon which the miraculous darkness and the apparition of the dead rest is the same as that upon which all the other miracles rest, and must be accepted or rejected in all the cases alike ' (Guesses at the Riddle of Existence, p. 160). No critical student needs to be told that the evidence for the apparitions of the dead (Mt 27⁵²ᶠ·) belongs just to that stratum which carries with it the least weight. The authority for the darkness is much higher, but its miraculous character need not be magnified. Any unusual darkening of the sky would naturally strike the imagination of the disciples; and it might be not contrary to nature and yet also not accidental.

(iv.) *The Quality of the Evidence.*—So far we have spoken of the external character of the evidence. It is speaking within the mark to say that a large part of the evidence for the Gospel miracles, including some of those that are most miraculous, is separated from the facts by an interval of not more than thirty years. We may be pretty sure that before that date, and even much before it, stories of miracles like those recorded in the Gospels circulated freely among Christians, and were a common subject of teaching by catechists and others. We now proceed to ask, What is the quality of the narratives in which these stories occur ? What features are there in the stories themselves which throw light upon their historical value ?

(a) We are met at the outset by the Temptation. If there is anything certain in history, it is that the story of the Temptation has a real foundation in fact, for the simple reason that without such a foundation it would have occurred to no one to invent it. It suits exactly and wonderfully the character of Jesus as we can now see it, but not as it was seen at the time. Men were trying to apprehend that character ; they had a glimpse here and a glimpse there ; but they cannot have had more than dim and vague surmises as to what it was as a whole. But whoever first told the story of the Temptation saw it as a whole. We have therefore already drawn the inference that it was first told by none other than Jesus Himself. And by that inference we stand. There is nothing in the Gospels that is more authentic.

But the story of the Temptation presupposes the possession of supernatural powers. It all turns on the question how those powers are to be exercised. It not only implies the possession of power to work such miracles as were actually worked, but others even more remarkable from the point of view of crude interference with the order of nature. The story of the Temptation implies that Jesus *could* have worked such miracles if He had willed to do so ; and the reason why He did not work them was only because He did not will.

The keynote which is struck by the Temptation is sustained all through the sequel of the history. We can see that the Life of Jesus was what it was by an act of deliberate renunciation. When He says, as the end draws near, 'Thinkest thou that I cannot beseech my Father, and he shall even now send me more than twelve legions of angels ?' (Mt 26⁵³), the lesson holds good, not for that moment alone, but for all that has preceded it. The Public Ministry of Jesus wears the aspect it does, not because of limitations imposed from without, but of limitations imposed from within.

Here lies the paradox of the Miracles of Christ. He seems at once to do them, and so to guard against a possible misuse that it is as if He had not done them. The common idea of miracles was as a manifestation of Divine power. Jesus gave the manifestation, and yet He seemed so to check it from producing its natural effect that it is as though it did not serve its purpose. It really serves His purpose, but not the purpose which the world both then and since has ascribed to Him.

(β) We have seen that the principles laid down at the Temptation governed the whole public life of Jesus. He steadily refused to work miracles for any purely self-regarding end. If the fact that He works miracles at all is a sympathetic adaptation to the beliefs and expectations of the time, those beliefs are schooled and criticized while they are adopted (Mt 12³⁹‖ 16¹ᶠ·, Jn 4⁴⁸), the element of mere display, the element of self-assertion, even of self-preservation, is eliminated from them. They are studiously restricted to the purposes of the mission.

Now this carefully restricted character in the miracles of Jesus is unique in history. Among all the multitude of wonders with which the faith, sometimes superstitious, but more often simply naïve, of the later Church adorned the lives of the saints, there is nothing quite like it. We may say with confidence that if the miracles of Jesus had been no more than an invention, they would not have been what they are. We can see in the evangelists a certain dim half-conscious feeling of the self-imposed limitations in the use of the supernatural by Christ. But we may be very sure that they have this feeling, because the limitations were inherent in the facts, not because they formed part from the first of a picture which they were constructing *a priori*.

(γ) There are three kinds of restriction in the miracles of our Lord. The limitation in the subject-matter of the miracles is one; the limitation in the conditions under which they are wrought is another (Mt 13[58] ∥ 15[24. 26]); and the limitation in the manner in which they are set before the world is a third. In a number of cases, after a miracle has been performed, the recipient is strictly cautioned to maintain silence about it (Mk 1[34] ∥ demoniacs, 1[44] ∥ leper, 3[12] demoniacs, cf. Mt 12[16], Mk 7[36] deaf and dumb, 8[26] blind). This hangs together with the manifest intention of Jesus to correct not only the current idea of miracles, but the current idea of the Messiah as one endowed with supernatural power. If He was so endowed, it was not that He might gather about Him crowds and establish a carnal kingdom such as the Jews expected.

This, too, is a very original feature. It is certainly not one that the popular imagination would create, because the motive to create it was wanting. It is not to be supposed that the popular imagination would first correct itself and then embody the correction in a fictitious narrative. Here again we are driven to the conclusion that the narrative truly reflects the facts.

(δ) In yet another way do the accounts of the miracles work in with the total picture of the Life of Christ. They have a didactic value, which makes them round off the cycle of the teaching. This fact perhaps leaves some opening for the possibility that here and there what was originally parable may in course of transmission have hardened into miracle. An example of such a possibility would be the withering of the Fig-tree (Mk 11[12-14 20-25] ∥ compared with Lk 13[6-9]). But, on the other hand, it is just as possible that parable and miracle may stand side by side as a double enforcement of the same lesson. The story of the Temptation is proof that Jesus would not hesitate to clothe His teaching in a form at once natural and impressive to that generation, though it is less so to ours. In this He only takes up a marked characteristic of the OT Prophets.

(v.) *Historical Necessity of Miracles.*—The truth is that the historian who tries to construct a reasoned picture of the Life of Christ finds that he cannot dispense with miracles. He is confronted with the fact that no sooner had the Life of Jesus ended in apparent failure and shame than the great body of Christians—not an individual here and there, but the mass of the Church—passed over at once to the fixed belief that He was God. By what conceivable process could the men of that day have arrived at such a conclusion, if there had been really nothing in His life to distinguish it from that of ordinary men? We have seen that He did not work the kind of miracles which they expected. The miracles in themselves in any case came short of their expectations. But this makes it all the more necessary that there must have been something about the Life, a broad and substantial element in it, which *they could recognize as* supernatural and divine—not that we can recognize, but which they could recognize with the ideas of the time. Eliminate miracles from the career of Jesus, and the belief of Christians, from the first moment that we have undoubted contemporary evidence of it (say A.D. 50), becomes an insoluble enigma.

(vi.) *Natural Congruity of Miracles.*—And now, if from the belief of the Early Church we turn to the belief of the Church in our day, there a different kind of congruity appears, but a con-

gruity that is no less stringent. If we still believe that Christ was God, not merely on the testimony of the Early Church, but on the proof afforded by nineteen centuries of Christianity, there will be nothing to surprise us in the phenomena of miracles. 'If the Incarnation was a fact, and Jesus Christ was what He claimed to be, His miracles, so far from being improbable, will appear the most natural thing in the world. . . . They are so essentially a part of the character depicted in the Gospels, that without them that character would entirely disappear. They flow naturally from a Person who, despite His obvious humanity, impresses us throughout as being at home in two worlds. . . . We cannot separate the wonderful life, or the wonderful teaching, from the wonderful works. They involve and interpenetrate and presuppose each other, and form in their indissoluble combination one harmonious picture' (Illingworth, *Divine Immanence*, pp. 88–90).

If we seek to express the *rationale* or inner congruity of miracles in Biblical language, we shall find this abundantly done for us in the Gospel of St. John. Miracles arise from the intimate association of the Son with the Father in the ordering of the universe, especially in all that relates to the redemption of man. When challenged by the Jews for healing a sick man upon the Sabbath, Jesus replied, 'My Father worketh even until now (*i.e.* since, and in spite of the institution of the Sabbatical Rest), I am working also' (Jn 5[17]); the same law holds for the actions of the Son as for the conservation of the universe. And He goes on, 'Verily, verily, I say unto you, the Son can do nothing of himself, but what he seeth the Father doing: for what things soever he doeth, these the Son also doeth in like manner. For the Father loveth the Son, and showeth him all things that himself doeth: and greater works than these will he show him, that ye may marvel' (*ib.* vv.[19. 20]). Many other passages at once suggest themselves to the same effect (Jn 3[35] 8[28f.] 14[10]). The Son is 'sent' by the Father, and He is invested with full powers for the accomplishment of that mission; or rather with reference to it and for the purpose of it, He and the Father are one (Jn 10[30]).

The sayings of this character are all from the Fourth Gospel. But there is a near approach to them in the well-known passage Mt 11[27] ∥ ('All things have been delivered unto me of my Father'); and this does but form a natural climax to others, which, without it, would seem to leave something wanting and incomplete.

(vii.) *The Unexplained Element in Miracles.*— When all the above considerations are borne in mind, some may still think that there is a residuum which is not wholly explained—not so much as to the fact of miracles, or as to their congruity with the Person of Jesus, but rather as to the method of particular miracles in the form in which they have come down to us. It is quite inevitable that there should be such a residuum, which is only another name for the irreducible interval which must, when all is done, separate the reflective science-trained intellect of the nineteenth century from the naïve chroniclers of the first. Jesus Himself would seem to have been not without a prescience that this would be the case. At any rate there is a permanent significance, unexhausted by the occasion which gave rise to it, in His reply to the disciples of the Baptist, while appealing to works which, however beneficent, would, He knew, fail to realize all the Baptist's expectations: 'Blessed is he that shall find no scandal—or stumbling-block—in me' (Mt 11[6] ∥). There was doubtless something left in the mind of John which he could not perfectly piece together with the rest of such mental outfit as he had. And so we may be sure that it will be in every age, though age after age has only helped to strengthen the conviction that the modes of thought of the *Zeitgeist* may and do continually change, but that the worth for man of the Person of Jesus does not change but is eternal.

LITERATURE.—Probably the best work in English at the present moment on the presuppositions of the Gospel Miracles would be Illingworth's *Divine Immanence* (1898), a sequel to his *Bampton Lectures* (1894). It may be worth while to compare Gore, *Bamp. Lect.* (1891). On the other hand, Mozley's lectures on the same foundation for 1865 have reference rather to a phase of the controversy which is now past. There is, of course, much on the subject in the various treatises on Apologetics ; and articles are constantly appearing in magazines, as well as shorter monographs, both British and Foreign. The present writer cannot say—or at least cannot remember—that he has gained as much from these several sources as in the case of the teaching of Jesus. He would like, however, to mention with gratitude, *Grounds of Theistic and Christian Belief*, by Dr. G. P. Fisher of Yale (New York, 1883 ; also pub. in London), a very clear and temperate statement of the evidence for the Gospel Miracles on older lines ; the chap. on Miracles in Dr. A. B. Bruce, *Chief End of Revelation* (3rd ed. 1890); and three short lectures, entitled *The Supernatural in Christianity* (by Drs. Rainy, Orr, and Marcus Dods, in reply to Pfleiderer, Edinb. 1894).

The most considerable attempt in English to construct Christianity without Miracles is Dr. Edwin A. Abbott's *The Kernel and the Husk* (1886), and *The Spirit on the Waters* (1897). With this may be compared Dr. Salmon's *Non-miraculous Christianity (and other Sermons).*

There are well-known systematic works on the Gospel Miracles by the late Abp. Trench and Dr. A. B. Bruce.

C. *MIDDLE OR CULMINATING PERIOD OF THE ACTIVE MINISTRY.*

Scene.—Galilee, with an excursion across the northern border.

Time.—Passover to shortly before Tabernacles A.D. 28.

Mt 14[1]–18[35], Mk 6[14]–9[50], Lk 9[7-50], Jn 6.

This is a period of culminations, in which the prophecy of Simeon begins to be conspicuously fulfilled : 'Behold, this child is set for the falling and rising up of many in Israel, and for a sign which is spoken against' (Lk 2[34]). The main culminations are (i.) of the zeal of the populace, followed by their disappointment and falling away ; (ii.) the still greater embitterment of the scribes and Pharisees ; (iii.) the awakening at last of a more intelligent faith in the disciples, reaching its highest point in St. Peter's confession ; (iv.) the Divine testimony to Jesus in the Transfiguration ; (v.) the consciousness of victory virtually won in Jesus Himself (Mt 11[25-30], Lk 10[17-24]); (vi.) at the same time He sees clearly, and begins to announce the seeming but transient catastrophe, the final humiliation and exaltation, in which His work is to end.

The time of this period is clearly marked by the occurrence of the Passover of the year A.D. 28 at its beginning, and the Feast of Tabernacles (in October of the same year) at the end. It is probable that within these six months all the salient events referred to below may be included. The place is, broadly speaking, Galilee, beginning with the shores of the lake (Jn 6) ; but in the course of the period there falls a wider circuit than any that had been hitherto taken. In this circuit Jesus touched on, and probably crossed, the borders of the heathen districts of Tyre and Sidon (Mk 7[24]||) ; He then turned eastwards through the neighbourhood of Cæsarea Philippi (Mk 8[27]||) ; and He finally returned to Capernaum, not directly, but after taking a round to the east of the lake and through Decapolis (Mk 7[31]). The motive was probably not so much on this occasion extended preaching as to avoid the ferment excited among the population of Central Galilee. Observe Mk 7[24] and the strict injunctions of secrecy in Mk 7[36] 8[30]|| 9[9]||. If we may follow our authorities (Mk 7[32ff.] 8[1ff. 11ff.]) there was a certain amount of active work at the end of

the circuit ; but Mt 11[20ff.] appears to mark the practical close of the Galilæan ministry.

The greater part of this circuit lay within the dominions, not of Herod Antipas, where Jesus had hitherto mainly worked, but of his brother Philip. Now we know that the hostility to Him was shared by the Pharisees with the partisans of Herod (Mk 3[6] and p. 616[a] above ; cf. also Mk 8[15]). We have also, but probably at a still later date, threats, which if not actually made by Herod Antipas were at least plausibly attributed to him (Lk 13[31]). In any case, it is likely enough that intrigues were on foot between the two allied parties of the Pharisees and Herodians ; and some writers, of whom Keim may be taken as an example, have attributed to these what they describe as a 'flight' on the part of Jesus. They may have had something to do with His retirement.

This division of our Lord's Life includes several narratives (the Feedings of the Five and Four Thousand, the Walking on the Water, the Transfiguration) which sound especially strange to modern ears. We must repeat the warning, that if a nineteenth cent. observer had been present he would have given a different account of the occurrences from that which has come down to us. But the mission of Jesus was to the first cent. and not to the nineteenth. His miracles as well as His teaching were adapted to the mental habits of those to whom they were addressed. It is wasted ingenuity to try, by rationalizing the narratives, to translate them into a language more like our own. Essential features in them are sure to escape in the process. It should be enough to notice that the narratives in question all rest on the very best historical authority. They belong to the oldest stratum of the evangelical tradition. And more than this : if we suppose, as it is not unreasonable to suppose, that the Feedings of the Five and of the Four Thousand are different versions of the same event, this would throw us back some way behind even that oldest stratum ; because we should have to allow an additional period of time for the two versions to arise out of their common original (see p. 626 *sup.*). This would carry us back to a time when numbers must have been living by whom the truth of that which is reported might be controlled. In the case of the Feeding of the Five Thousand, we have the confirmatory evidence of the Fourth Gospel, which for those who believe the author to have been an eye-witness must be little less than decisive.

i. *The Enthusiasm and Falling-away of the Populace.*—It was just before the Passover of the year 28 that the impression which Jesus made on the people of Galilee seemed to reach its climax. This was the result of what is commonly known to us as the Feeding of the Five Thousand. The fact that the Passover was so near at hand accounts for a special gathering of pilgrims, or those preparing for the journey, from the Galilæan towns. In such a mixed multitude there would doubtless be many Zealots and enthusiastic expectants of the 'deliverance of Israel.' The miracle convinces these that they have at last found the leader of whom they are in search. They are aware that hitherto He had shown no signs of encouraging the active measures which they desired : and therefore they hasten to seize the person of Jesus in order to compel Him to put Himself at their head, with or against His will. He, however, retires from them ; and their disappointment is complete when on the next day the more determined among them, after following Him at no little trouble into the synagogue at Capernaum, find themselves put off with what they would regard as a mystical and unintelligible discourse. This is a turning-point in what had been for some time a gathering movement on the part of many who were willing to see in Jesus a Messiah such as they expected, but who were baffled and drew back when they found the ideal presented to them so different from their own. And the crisis once past, every possible precaution was taken to ensure that it should not recur (Mk 7$^{24.\ 36}$ 8^{30} || 9^9 ||, as above).

Are the two Feedings of Mk 6$^{30-46}$ || and Mk 8$^{1-9}$ || to be regarded as two events or one? Besides the general resemblance between the two narratives, a weighty argument in favour of the latter hypothesis is, that in the second narrative the disciples' question appears to imply that the emergency was something new. They could hardly have put this question as they did if a similar event had happened only a few weeks before. The different numbers are just what would be found in two independent traditions. The decision will, however, depend here (as in the instances noted above) on the degree of strictness with which we interpret the narrative generally.

The discourse in the synagogue at Capernaum, Jn 6$^{26-51}$, works up to one of those profound truths which fixed themselves especially in the memory of the author of the Fourth Gospel. It is not a direct reference to the Sacrament of the Lord's Supper, but it is a preparatory statement of the deep principle of which that Sacrament is the expression. We shall have more to say on this head below (see p. 637).

ii. *Widening Breach with the Pharisees.* — More than one incident occurs in this period which points to the increasing tension of the relations between Jesus and the Pharisees (Mk 8$^{11.\ 15}$). But the decisive passage is Mk 7$^{1-13}$ ||, the severity of which anticipates the denunciations of the last Passover. In this Jesus cuts away root and branch of the Pharisaic traditions and exposes their essential immorality. From this time onwards the antagonism is open and declared.

iii. *The Climax of Faith among the Twelve; St. Peter's Confession.* — We have seen how the enthusiasm of the multitudes reached its climax after the Feeding of the Five Thousand, but did not recover from the rebuff which it then received, and from that time more or less collapsed, until it flamed up for a moment at the triumphal entry. The Twelve were in a better position to enter into the mind of their Master, and it was but natural that they should be more steadfastly attached to His person. Hence their faith survived the shocks which it was continually receiving, and St. Peter gave the highest expression which it had yet received, when, in reply to a direct question, he exclaimed, 'Thou art the Christ [the Son of the Living God]' (Mt 16$^{13-20}$ ||). Jesus marked His sense of the significance of the confession by words of warm commendation. He attributes it, indeed, to a direct inspiration from Heaven. The value of the confession stands out all the more clearly when it is compared with the doubts of the Baptist (see above, p. 615). We are not to suppose that St. Peter had by any means as yet a full conception of all that was implied in his own words. He still did not understand what manner of Messiah he was confessing; but his merit was, that in spite of the rude shocks which his faith had been receiving, and in spite of all that was paradoxical and enigmatical in the teaching and actions of his Master, he saw through his perplexities the gleams of a nature which transcended his experience, and he was willing to take upon trust what he could not comprehend.

It would be out of place to attempt here to discuss the conflicting interpretations of the blessing pronounced upon St. Peter. We can only say that although it is not adequate to explain the blessing as pronounced upon the confession and not upon St. Peter himself, it is nevertheless distinctly pronounced upon St. Peter *as confessing*. It is in the fact that there is at last one who, in the face of all difficulties, recognizes from his heart that Jesus is what He is, that the first stone, as it were, of the Church is laid: other stones will be built upon and around it, and the edifice will rise day by day, but the beginning occurs but once, and the beginning of the Christian Church occurred then. It is not to detract from the merit of St. Peter — which so far as the building up of the Church is concerned was as high as human merit could be—if we interpret the blessing upon him in the light of 1 Co 3^{11}.

The Church has but one foundation, in the strict sense, Jesus Christ. It was precisely to this that St. Peter's confession pointed. But that confession was the first of all like confessions; and in that respect might well be described as the first block of stone built into the edifice.

iv. *The Culminating Point in the Missionary Labours of Jesus.* — God seeth not as man seeth. To the average observer, even to one who was acquainted with St. Peter's confession, it would seem to be the solitary point of light in the midst of disappointment and failure. A retrospect of the Galilæan ministry seemed to show little but hard-heartedness, ingratitude, and unbelief (Jn 12$^{37-40}$). Our Lord Himself can only denounce woe upon the cities which enjoyed most of His presence (Mt 11$^{20-24}$ ||). And yet about the same time two sayings are recorded which mark a deep inward consciousness of success. The ministry which might seem to be in vain was not really in vain, but potential and in promise; to the eye which saw into the future as well as into the present, and which looked into the inmost counsels of the Father, the crisis might even be regarded as past. One of these sayings is Lk 10^{18}. The success of the disciples in casting out demons draws from Jesus the remark that the power of the prince of darkness is broken. And about the same time, as if ingratitude and opposition counted for nothing, He pours out His thanks to the Father: 'I thank thee, O Father, Lord of heaven and earth, that thou didst hide these things from the wise and understanding, and didst reveal them unto babes: yea, Father, for so it was well-pleasing in thy sight' (Mt 11$^{25f.}$ ||). The next verse in both Gospels contains the clearest expression in the Synoptics of that sense of oneness with the Father which is brought out so pointedly in Jn. And the verses which follow in Mt are that wonderful invitation: 'Come unto me,' etc. He who understands this group of sayings has found his way to the heart of Christianity.

v. *The Transfiguration.* — To the confession of the apostle and to the words of thanksgiving, which are also words of serene contentment and inward assurance, there was not wanting an outward Divine sanction. This was given in the scene which is known to us as the Transfiguration (Mk 9$^{2-8}$ ||). The narrative of the Transfiguration reminds us, in more ways than one, of those of the Baptism and Temptation. Once again the apostles hear words which seem to come from Heaven confirming the mission of their Master. At the same time they see a vision which brings out the significance of that mission in a way for which as yet they can hardly have been prepared. The appearance of Moses and Elijah by the side of, and as it were ministering to, Jesus, symbolized the Law and the Prophets as leading up to and receiving their fulfilment in the Gospel.

It is impossible not to see the appropriateness of this Divine testimony to the mission of Jesus occurring just where it does. That unique relationship of the Son to the Father, which forms the constant background of the narrative of the Fourth Gospel, and is not less the background—real, if not so apparent—of the Synoptics, could not but assert itself from time to time. And what time could be fitter for a clear pronouncement of it than this, when outward circumstances were for the most part so discouraging, and when the prospect was becoming every day nearer and more certain of the fatal and terrible end? If the Son must needs go down into the valley of the shadow of death, the Father's face will shine upon Him for a moment before He enters it with a brightness which will not be obscured.

As bearing upon the essentially historical character of the narrative, however difficult and even impossible it may be for us to reconstruct its details in such a way that we could be said to understand them, note (1) the significance of the appearance of Moses and Elijah at a time when that significance can have been but very imperfectly apprehended by the disciples, and when there was absolutely nothing to suggest such an idea to them; and (2) the Transfiguration comes within the cycle of events in regard to which a strict silence was to be observed. This striking and peculiar stamp of genuineness was not wanting to it. We may note also (3) the random speech of St. Peter (Mk 9^5 ||)

as a little graphic and authentic touch which had not been forgotten.

It might be supposed that the enlargements in Lk 9³¹f. were merely editorial, but, like not a few added details in this Gospel, they become more impressive upon reflexion. The other evangelists throw no light upon the subject of the converse between the glorified figures ; Luke alone says that they ' spake of his decease which he was about to accomplish at Jerusalem.' This was, we may be sure, the subject which deeply occupied the mind of Jesus at this time ; and it is hardly less certain that the particular aspect of it which would be most present to Him would be its relation to the prophetic Scriptures of OT (and the Law also had its prophetic side). We might expect an appearance of Isaiah rather than Elijah ; but Elijah was the typical prophet, and the Jews expected his appearing (cf. Wetstein on Mt 17³). The other peculiar detail in Lk, that ' Peter and they that were with him were heavy with sleep,' may well seem confirmatory of the view (e.g.) of Weiss and Beyschlag, that the scene was presented to the three apostles in divinely caused vision.

vi. *The Prophecies of Death and Resurrection.*— The period we are describing is a kind of watershed, which marks not only the summit of the ascent but the beginning of the descent. We have seen how this was the case with the enthusiasm of the multitude : it was also the case with Christ Himself. The confession of St. Peter was immediately followed, and the Transfiguration both preceded and followed, by distinct prophecies of the fatal end which was to close His ministry — an end fatal in the eyes of men, but soon to be cancelled by His resurrection. As these prophecies will meet us again in the next period, to which they give its dominant character, we will reserve the discussion of them till then.

D. *Close of the Active Period: the Messianic Crisis in View.*

Scene.—Judæa (Jn 7¹⁰ff. 11⁵⁴) and Peræa (Mk 10¹∥, Jn 10⁴⁰).

Time.—Tabernacles A.D. 28 to Passover A.D. 29.
    Mt 19¹-20³⁴, Mk 10, Lk 9⁵¹-19²⁸ (for the most part not in chronological order), Jn 7¹-11⁵⁷.

In this period we may note more particularly (i.) the peculiar section of St. Luke's Gospel which might on a superficial view seem to be placed in this period ; (ii.) that portion of the Johannean narrative which really belongs to it ; (iii.) the general character of our Lord's Teaching at this time ; (iv.) in particular, the prophecies of Death and Resurrection ; and (v.) the hints which are given of a special significance attaching to these events.

The time of this period extends from the Feast of Tabernacles in A.D. 28 to the Passover of A.D. 29. There is more difficulty in mapping out the distribution of its parts topographically. We have some clear landmarks if we follow the guidance of the Fourth Gospel. The events of the section Jn 7¹-10²¹ partly belong to the Feast of Tabernacles and in part follow at no great interval after it. We have again in Jn 10²² a clear indication of time and place, the Feast of Dedication at Jerusalem. This would be towards the end of December. After that, Jesus withdrew beyond Jordan to the place where ' John was at the first baptizing' (Jn 10⁴⁰). Here He made a lengthened stay, and it was from hence that He paid His visit to Bethany for the raising of Lazarus. Then He again retired to a city called Ephraim on the edge of the wilderness north-east of Jerusalem, where He remained until the Jews began to gather together to attend the Passover (Jn 11⁵⁵). We have thus a fairly connected narrative extending from the beginning of the year to the Passover of A.D. 29, the scene of which is in part Judæa and in part Peræa. We have also a fixed point covering, perhaps, about a fortnight in the latter half of October and localized at Jerusalem. But what of the seven or eight weeks which separate this

from the Feast of Dedication ? Is it probable that Jesus returned to Galilee and continued His ministry there ? It does not seem so. The solemn and deliberate leave-taking from Galilee is not likely to have been so broken. The principal objection to this view would be that the secret and unexpected visit to Jerusalem at the Feast of Tabernacles does not seem consistent with the solemnity of this leave-taking. We may, however, suppose that the Galilæan ministry was practically complete before this date, and that strong expressions like those of Lk 9⁵¹, if they are to be taken as they stand, refer to one of the later journeys.

i. *The so-called Peræan Ministry.* — There is a long section of St. Luke's Gospel, Lk 9⁵¹-18³⁴, which has been often treated as a single whole and as containing the record of a special ministry, identified with the last journey towards Jerusalem, and having for its scene the lands beyond the Jordan. This is based upon the fact that the beginning of the section coincides with Mk 10¹, Mt 19¹, and that the end of it brings us to the approach to Jericho (Lk 18³⁵). It is true that some part of the time preceding the last Passover was spent in Peræa. We know this on the joint testimony of the other Synoptists and St. John (Mk 10¹, Mt 19¹, Jn 10⁴⁰). But to suppose that the whole section must be localized there is to misunderstand the structure and character of St. Luke's Gospel. It is far more probable that he has massed together a quantity of material derived from some special source to which he had access, and which could not be easily fitted into the framework supplied to him by St. Mark.

When we come to examine these materials in detail, it would seem probable that they belong to very different periods in our Lord's ministry. Some incidents, for instance, appear to assume those easier relations to the Pharisees which we have seen to be characteristic of the earlier period (Lk 11³⁷ [but not vv.⁴²⁻⁵⁴] 14¹ff.). It would be natural also to refer to this or the middle period the three parables of ch. 15 (Weiss, Leben Jesu, i. 507). On the other hand, some of the incidents are practically dated by their coincidence with the other Gospels ; while others, like the severer denunciations of the Pharisees and eschatological sections such as Lk 13²²⁻³⁰ 17²⁰⁻18⁸, are referred to the later period by their subject-matter. It would be wrong to lay too much stress on mere symmetry ; but when a natural sequence suggests itself, it may be accepted as having such probability as can be attained. The document which St. Luke is using in this part has preserved for us discourses of the utmost value, and it is largely to them that the Gospel owes its marked individuality.

ii. *The Johannean Narrative of this Period.*— The historical value of the Fourth Gospel comes out strongly in this period. Rarely has any situation been described with the extraordinary vividness and truth to nature of ch. 7 (see esp. vv.¹¹⁻¹⁵. ²⁵⁻²⁷. ³¹. ³². ⁴⁰⁻⁵²). Not less graphic are the details of ch. 9 ; and there is marked precision in the statements of Jn 10²²f. ⁴⁰f. 11⁵⁴⁻⁵⁷. We note a special intimacy with what passes in the inner counsels of the Sanhedrin (Jn 7⁴⁷⁻⁵² 11⁴⁷⁻⁵³). This intimate knowledge might have been derived through Nicodemus or through the connexion hinted at in Jn 18¹⁵.* But, apart from the peculiar verisimilitude of these details, some such activity as that described in these chs. is required to explain the great catastrophe which followed. It is impossible that Jesus should have been so much a stranger to Judæa and Jerusalem as the Synoptic narrative would at first sight seem to make Him. For the steps which lead up to the end we must go to St. John.

iii. *The general Character of the Teaching of this Period.*—There are no doubt portions of the teaching of this period preserved in the Synoptics. But except those contained in Mk 10¹⁻⁴⁵ ∥ they are difficult to identify with certainty. For the greater

* The theory of Delff has been mentioned above (p. 614 *sup.*) ; but it turns too much upon a single set of data, and leads to an arbitrary dissection of the Gospel.

part of our knowledge of it we are indebted to St. John, and we may observe that the teaching now begins to take a new character. Hitherto it has been mainly concerned with the nature of the Kingdom; henceforward greater stress is laid on the person of the King. We have already noted the remarkable verse Mt 11[27]‖ 'All things have been delivered unto me of my Father: and no one knoweth the Son save the Father; neither doth any know the Father save the Son, and he to whomsoever the Son willeth to reveal him.' This verse may be said to represent the text which the discourses in St. John set in various lights. We have now the self-revelation of the Son as the central life - giving and light - giving force of humanity. As He is the living Bread (Jn 6), so is He the living Water (Jn 7[37f.]); He is the Light of the world (Jn 8[12] 9[5]); He is the Good Shepherd (Jn 10[11]), the Resurrection and the Life (Jn 11[25]). If we suppose that these discourses were really held, we shall understand better than we could do otherwise the state of Christian thought which meets us when we open the first surviving Epistles of St. Paul.

iv. *The Prophecies of Death and Resurrection.*— From the time of St. Peter's confession Jesus began in set terms to foretell that His mission would end in His death, soon, however, to be followed by His resurrection (Mk 8[31]‖). At the moment of His highest triumph, marked by the Transfiguration, the same solemn prediction is repeated (Mk 9[31]), and again yet a third time towards the end of the period with which we are now dealing (Mk 10[32-34]‖).

(*a*) Even an ordinary observer might have seen that the signs of the times were ominous. St. Peter's confession showed no more than one adherent whose fervid faith might be supposed capable of resisting a pressure of life or death. Herod Antipas and his faction were hostile. The Pharisees were yet more hostile, and their bitterness was growing every day. Within the period before us two deliberate attempts were made on the life of Jesus (Jn 8[59] 10[39]). And with the certainty that the course on which He was bent would include nothing to conciliate these antagonisms, it was clear where they would end.

(*b*) But the foresight of Jesus took a wider range than this. He had laid it down as a principle that it was the fate of prophets to be persecuted (Mt 5[12] 23[34. 37]). In particular, He had before Him the example of the Baptist, whose fate He associated with His own (Mk 9[12f.]‖).

(*c*) But there was a deeper necessity even than this. At the Betrayal, to him who drew sword in His defence Jesus replied calmly, 'How then should the Scriptures be fulfilled, that thus it must be?' And this is His consistent language (comp. Lk 24[25f. 44. 46] etc.). The mind of Jesus was steeped in the ancient prophecies. He had Himself, as we have seen, deliberately fused the conception of the conquering Messiah with that of the Suffering Servant of Jehovah, and He as deliberately went the way to fulfil these prophecies in His own person. There was nothing accidental about His Death. He 'set his face stead- fastly' on the road which led to it.

(*d*) When we look into its lessons we are carried even behind the fulfilment of prophecy. We shall have to speak presently of the extraordinary novelty of the turn which Christ gave to His mission. Others had conquered by the exercise of force; He was the first to set Himself to con- quer by weakness, patience, non-resistance. And the natural and inevitable consummation of this new method of conquest was Death.

(*e*) In all this He was carrying out, and knew that He was carrying out, the Will of the Father.

It was conceivable that that Will might have yet ulterior objects even beyond those, deep enough as we might think, which we have been consider- ing. That Jesus ascribed to His Death such an ulterior object we are led to believe by the way in which He speaks of it. The two places in which He does so must next engage our attention.

v. *Significance of the Death of Jesus.*—The first of the passages to which allusion has just been made is Mk 10[45]‖ 'For verily the Son of Man came not to be ministered unto, but to minister, and to give his life a ransom for many.' We observe here that Jesus brings His Death under the category of service, and regards it as the climax of a life of service. This is one way of stating the great paradox to which we have just alluded. The kings of the Gentiles exercise lord- ship over their subjects; but such was not to be the ambition of the disciples of Christ; rather the very opposite; and it was Christ Himself who set them the example. At the end of the avenue stood a cross, and the Saviour of men walked up to it as if it had been a crown. It is a question of pressing interest how much farther we may go than this: is the λύτρον ἀντὶ πολλῶν to be in- terpreted by the ἀπολύτρωσις and ἱλαστήριον of Ro 3[24f.], and by the language of other similar passages? By itself we could not say that it compelled such an interpretation; but there is nothing forced in supposing that the early Church knew and followed the mind of its Founder. In that case we should have reason to think that Jesus Himself had hinted at the sacrificial char- acter of His Death, and that He too regarded it as propitiatory.

If this passage suggests a sacrificial aspect of one kind, the other is more explicit in bringing out sacrificial associations of another. All the extant accounts of the institution of the Eucharist connect the Blood shed upon the Cross with the founding of a '[new] Covenant.' This is certainly an allusion to the inauguration of the first Covenant with sacrifice (cf. Ex 24[4-8], He 9[18-23]), and the Death of Christ is clearly regarded as the Sacrifice inaugurating the second (see below, p. 638).

In other words, the momentous question came before the mind of Jesus whether the New Dis- pensation which He was founding was or was not like the Old in including the idea of Sacrifice. He deliberately answered that it was. And He deliberately foresaw, and as deliberately accepted the consequence, that the Sacrifice of this New Dispensation could be none other than the Sacri- fice of Himself.

That which gives this particular Death a value which no other death could have had is (a) the fact that it is the Death of the Messiah, of One whose function it is to be the Saviour of His people, and whose Death like His Life must in some way enter into the purpose of the whole scheme of salvation; and (β) the further fact that although the Death is a necessity in the sense that it was required for the full development of God's gracious purpose, it was nevertheless a purely voluntary act on the part of the Son, an expression of that truly filial spirit in which He made the whole of the Father's purpose His own. 'The good Shepherd layeth down his life for the sheep. . . . Therefore doth the Father love me, because I lay down my life, that I may take it again. No one taketh it away from me, but I lay it down of myself. I have power to lay it down, and I have power to take it again. This commandment received I from my Father' (Jn 10[11. 17f.]). It follows (γ) that however much it may be right to conceive of the Death of Christ as a Sacrifice, and a sacrifice which has for its object the 'remission of sins' (Mt 26[28]), we must not in connexion with it set the justice of God against

His mercy, or think of Him as really turning away His face from the Son of His love.

LITERATURE.—The subject of these last two sections not only comes into the field of New Testament Theology in general and treatises (like Wendt's and others named above) on the Teaching of Christ, but it necessarily occupies a prominent place in discussions of the Doctrine of the Atonement. Among these may be mentioned especially Ritschl's *Rechtfertigung u. Versöhnung*, vol. ii. of which goes elaborately into the exegesis of the leading passages (ed. 2, 1882), and a recent treatise by Kähler, *Zur Lehre von der Versöhnung* (Leipzig, 1898), which gives prominence to the relation of the doctrine to the Life of Christ. A lengthy monograph by Schwartzkopff deals directly with our Lord's predictions of His Passion (*Die Weissagungen Jesu Christi von seinem Tode*, u.s.w., Göttingen, 1895); and 'Christ's Attitude to His Death' is the title of some striking articles by Dr. A. M. Fairbairn in *Expos.* 1896, ii., and 1897, i.

E. *THE MESSIANIC CRISIS: THE TRIUMPHAL ENTRY, THE LAST TEACHING, PASSION, DEATH, RESURRECTION, ASCENSION.*

Scene.—Mainly in Jerusalem.

Time.—Six days before Passover to ten days before Pentecost A.D. 29.

Mt 21¹-28²⁰, Mk 11¹-16⁸ [vv.⁹⁻²⁰ an early addition], Lk 19²⁹-24⁵², Jn 12¹-21²³.

This series of momentous events has naturally furnished much matter for discussion and controversy, some of it very recent. (i.) Our first duty will be to sketch rapidly the course of the events with special reference to the motives of the human actors in them. (ii.) We must consider the debated points in the chronology of the last week. (iii.) We shall have to discuss the eschatological teaching which the Synoptists place in this period. (iv.) A number of points, critical and doctrinal, will meet us in connexion with the Last Supper. (v.) We shall have in like manner to consider both the attestation and the significance of the crowning event of all, the Resurrection. This will include some discussion of the Appearances which followed. Lastly (vi.), as our subject is the Life of Christ and not the Gospels, we must, even though in so doing we cross the threshold of St. Luke's 'second treatise,' follow the steps of the Master to His Ascension.

i. *The Action and the Actors.* — Our four Gospels, taken together, in part convey and in part suggest a view at once clear and probable of the course of events which led to the Crucifixion, and of the motives which impelled the several actors in them. We have seen that the Fourth Gospel is needed to explain the heightened enmity which had so tragic an issue. A residence in Jerusalem and Bethany of four days would not be enough to account for the overtures to Judas. The events of the Feast of Tabernacles, the Feast of Dedication, and the Raising of Lazarus, with the knowledge that Jesus had been teaching and making disciples at no great distance from Jerusalem, supply what was wanted. And in the case of the Last Week the touches which the Fourth Gospel adds to its predecessors supplement them effectively.

(a) *The Populace.*—In the Triumphal Entry we seem to see a gleam once more of the enthusiasm which had followed the Feeding of the Five Thousand. It was probably quite as superficial. We may imagine the crowd made up in part of those who had been impressed by recent teaching beyond the Jordan or in Jerusalem itself, or by the news of the still more striking miracle wrought upon Lazarus: besides these, there would doubtless be a contingent of pilgrims from more distant Galilee, the remnant of the crowds who had at one time or another followed Jesus there. But it would be too much to expect that all, or even many of these, had acquired an intelligent insight into the character of Him whom

they were cheering. They were still in the twilight of their old Jewish expectations. They supposed that the moment had at last come when the hopes which they cherished would be realized, and when before the crowds assembled for the Passover Jesus would at last put Himself forward as the Leader for whom they were waiting. Nothing, however, came of this seeming appeal to their enthusiasm. A few discourses in the temple, partly levelled against the religious authorities they were most accustomed to reverence, but containing not a word of incitement against the Romans, and that was all. What wonder if their enthusiasm died away, and if in some of the fiercer among them it changed to bitter and angry disappointment! Doubtless some of these Zealots mingled with those who cried 'Crucify him, crucify him'; it was natural that they should prefer one of their own trade, like Barabbas; but the crowds in Jerusalem at Passover time were so great that many of these fanatics may have had no personal acquaintance with Jesus at all. The choice between Jesus and Barabbas would seem to them a choice between a mock leader, a dreamer of dreams, who offered them nothing but words, and a true son of the people who had shown himself ready to grip the sword in the good cause.

(b) *The Traitor.* — It is possible that Judas Iscariot may have shared something of these feelings. In the lists of the apostles he is usually named next to a Zealot. The long course of training which he had undergone may have failed to purge his mind of the carnal expectations of his countrymen. It may have been a sudden access of disappointment, greater than ever before, because the hopes by which it had been preceded had been greater, which impelled him to seek his interview with the members of the Sanhedrin. It has even been suggested that he did what he did in order to compel his Master to declare Himself, and with the belief that He would at last exert for the deliverance of the nation the supernatural powers with which He was endowed. For this we have no sufficient warrant; and we are told expressly (Jn 12⁶ RV text and most Comms.) that Judas was guilty of petty pilfering from the common fund, and therefore may infer that he was accessible to the temptations of avarice. Still, few men act from motives that they cannot at least make plausible to themselves: so that a mixture of obstinate and misguided patriotism is more probable than pure malignity. If Judas had not been at least capable of better things, it is not likely that he would have been chosen to be one of the Twelve.

(c) *The Pharisees.*—By this time between Jesus and the Pharisees there is open war. Insidious questions are still put to Him, but only in order to 'ensnare him in his talk' (Mt 22¹⁵ ‖). And on His side Jesus replied to their treachery by the sternest denunciations. It need not be supposed that all 'scribes and Pharisees' were equally the object of these. We know that Nicodemus and Joseph of Arimathæa were members of the Sanhedrin; we do not know that they belonged to the party of the Pharisees, but we cannot doubt that there were some Pharisees like-minded with them; just as we learn from the Acts that after the Resurrection a number of the 'priests' (Ac 6⁷) and at least some Pharisees (*ib.* 15⁵) became Christians.

(d) *The Sadducees.*—With the last week of our Lord's life, or rather, if we may trust St. John, as far back as the Feast of Tabernacles (Jn 7⁴⁵), a new party comes into prominence. The Sanhedrin begins to take official action against Jesus; and, although the Pharisees had some footing in that body, its policy was more determined by the Sadducees, to whom belonged most of the 'chief priests,' and in particular Caiaphas, the acting high priest, and his yet more influential father-in-law and predecessor Annas. As against Jesus the two parties of Pharisees and Sadducees acted together, but their motives were different. The Pharisees were jealous for their authority and traditions, which were openly assailed. The Sadducees themselves rejected these traditions,—they were selfish politicians, who played their own game. Their motto was *quieta non movere*. They dreaded any kind of disturbance which might give the Romans an excuse to take the power out of their hands (cf. Jn 11[48]). It is curious to note how from this time onwards the bitterest opposition comes from the Sadducees, while leading Pharisees are neutral or even favourable (Ac 5[34-39] 23[9]).

(*e*) *Pilate.*—The position of things is this. The Jews (*i.e.* primarily the Sanhedrin) were bent upon bringing about the death of Jesus. Now they themselves had not the power of life and death (Jn 18[31]). According to the Talmud, they lost it forty years before the destruction of Jerusalem, which would be about this very time. It is probable, however, that they did not long continue to possess it after the annexation of Judæa by the Romans. This being the case, they could only act through the instrumentality of the Roman governor. This necessitated the putting forward of different reasons from those that really weighed with themselves. Rather we should say that there were really three sets of reasons : (i.) The real motive of the Sanhedrin was jealousy of its own authority,—on the part of the Sadducees fear of disturbance, on the part of the Pharisees resentment of the attacks upon themselves and their traditions, and with some of the most patriotic among them perhaps disgust at a Messiah who was not a Messiah in any sense which they could comprehend. (ii.) The ostensible reason, which with some may have been sincere enough, was the charge of blasphemy against God. This charge they tried to bring home, but for a time could not (Mk 14[59] ‖), until at last they caught at the confession of Jesus Himself. On the strength of this He was condemned (Mk 14[62-64]). (iii.) This charge, however, was not one which they could bring before the governor, and therefore they changed their ground. St. Luke, who in all these scenes draws upon special and good information, states the accusation with more precision than the other Synoptists. 'We found this man perverting our nation, and forbidding to give tribute to Cæsar, and saying that he himself is Christ a king' (or 'an anointed king,' RVm ; Lk 23[2]).

With this charge it is that the leaders of the Sanhedrin come before Pilate. Pilate has the rough Roman sense of justice, and he feels that the charge is not proved. He sees no evidence that Jesus is really a formidable conspirator, or even a conspirator at all against the State. He therefore desires to release Him ; but the Jews insist, the leaders being backed by the clamour of the crowd. The Sanhedrists know the weak point in Pilate's armour, and they fasten upon it : 'If thou release this man, thou art not Cæsar's friend : every one that maketh himself a king speaketh against Cæsar' (Jn 19[12], a most lifelike touch). For themselves they protest their loyalty, 'We have no king but Cæsar' (Jn 19[15]). For many of the Sanhedrin, Pharisees as well as Sadducees, this would be true, and those for whom it was not would discreetly hold their peace. To this pressure Pilate in the end gives way, washing his hands of the responsibility. He might have taken a nobler course, but he felt insecure of his position ; he knew that the Jews had matter of just complaint against him ; and sooner than face their malice, with the inconveniences which it might cause, he let them have their will.

LITERATURE.—With this section may be compared two works of imagination : Dr. Edwin A. Abbott, *Philochristus*, London, 1878 ; and *As Others Saw Him*, London, 1895 (written from a Jewish point of view, but sympathetic and instructive). Also Chwolson, *Das letzte Passamahl Christi*, etc., St. Petersburg, 1892, Anhang : 'Das Verhältniss d. Pharisäer, Sadducäer u. der Juden überhaupt zu Jesus Christus' (minimizing the opposition of the Pharisees, and laying the blame upon the Sadducees [Jewish, but written with much special knowledge]).

ii. *The Chronology of the Last Week.* — A number of chronological difficulties meet us in the narrative of this Last Week. (1) The *prima facie* view would certainly be that the Anointing at Bethany was placed by Mark *two* days (Mk 14[1]) and by John *six* days (Jn 12[1]) before the Passover. (2) The common opinion is that the Crucifixion took place on a Friday, and the Last Supper on the evening of Thursday ; but it has also been argued that the two events took place on Thursday and Wednesday. (3) There is a much larger division of opinion as to the date of the Crucifixion in the Jewish calendar, and the relation of the Last Supper to the Paschal Meal. The Synoptists seem to identify the two, whereas St. John expressly places the Last Supper before the Passover, and would make the Crucifixion fall on Nisan 14. (4) The authorities also appear to differ as to the time of day occupied by the Crucifixion. According to Mk 15[25] the time of the Crucifixion itself was the 'third hour' (=9 a.m.) ; according to Jn 19[14] the trial was not quite over by the 'sixth hour' (=noon), and therefore the Crucifixion was still later.

Of these discrepancies No. 2 need not detain us. The view that the Crucifixion took place upon a Thursday is almost peculiar to Dr. Westcott (*Introd. to the Study of the Gospels*, p. 322, ed. 3). It turns upon a pressing of the phrase 'three days and three nights' in Mt 12[40], along with the probability of confusion between 'preparation *for the Passover*' and the more ordinary use of the word in the sense of 'preparation *for the Sabbath*' (*i.e.* Friday). The phrasing of Mt 27[62] is somewhat peculiar, but not really less so on this way of reckoning than the other, because the day described as the 'morrow after the Preparation' would be itself the weekly παρασκευή. And Mt 12[40] is due only to the evangelist, and is not supported by the other authorities. [On the length of the interval between the Crucifixion and the Resurrection see esp. art. CHRONOLOGY OF NT in this Dict. i. 410[b] (with Field, *Ot. Norv.* iii. p. 7, there referred to), and Wright, *NT Problems*, p. 159 ff.].

No. 1 is commonly removed by treating the note of time in Mk 14[1]‖ as referring to the events of vv.[1. 2. 10. 11] and not to the intervening narrative of vv.[3-9]. In support of this, Meyer-Weiss (ed. 8, *ad loc.*) points to analogous cases of intrusive matter in Mk 3[22-30] 4[10-25] 6[14-29] 7[25-30]. On the other hand, M'Clellan (*Gospels*, p. 472 f.) restricts the application of Jn 12[1] to the arrival at Bethany, which, according to him, was on the afternoon of Friday, Nisan 8. The Anointing he would place on the evening of Tuesday, Nisan 12. Either view is possible, and neither can be verified. If we think that the fourth evangelist deliberately corrects his predecessors, we shall probably give the preference to him. On such a point Mark is not a first-hand authority, and the connexion between his placing of the Betrayal and of the Anointing may well be loose.

As to (4) the difference in regard to the hour of the Crucifixion, attempts have been made with some persistence to prove that St. John used a different mode of reckoning time from that in common use. The writer of this was at one time inclined to look with favour on these attempts. If the premiss could be proved, the data would work out satisfactorily. But, in view of the arts. by Mr. J. A. Cross in *Class. Rev.* 1891, p. 245 ff., and by Prof. Ramsay in *Expositor*, 1893, i. 216 ff., it must definitely be said that the major premiss cannot be proved, and that the attempt to reconcile the two statements on this basis breaks down (cf. also Wright, *Problems*, p. 149 ff.).

The ancient solution of the difficulty was to suppose a corruption (F for Γ, or *vice versâ*) of the text, more often in Jn than in Mk; and rightly, because in Mk there are three several notes of time (Mk 15¹ ‖ 25. 33 ‖) which hang together. So Eus. *ad Marinum*, with a group of MSS *scholia* (*vid.* Tisch. on Jn 19¹⁴), etc. This solution is accepted by Mr. Wright (*op. cit.* p. 156 ff.), and it may conceivably hold good.

Prof. Ramsay lays stress rather on the rough and approximate way in which the ancients used the reckoning by hours. It must be remembered that an 'hour' with them was a twelfth part of daylight, and not a fixed space of 60 measured minutes, as with us. If the two statements had been inverted—if Mk 15²⁵ had described the end of the trial and Jn 19¹⁴ the raising of the cross—this elasticity might have amply covered both. As the two passages stand, it hardly does so.

We may ask ourselves whether, supposing that the slaughter of the Paschal lambs began at 3 p.m. (the time of slaughter is given as 3–5 p.m. by Jos. *BJ* vi. ix. 3), there would not be a rather strong temptation on typological grounds to fix the moment of the death of the Messiah at that hour. The other notes of time would naturally be conformed to this. But, on the other hand, St. John's 'sixth hour' seems inconveniently late for the events which have to be compressed between it and the evening. The whole question must be left open. There is a choice of possibilities, but nothing more.

Can we get beyond a similar choice on the last and most important point (3), the discrepancy as to the day of the month of the Crucifixion and of the Last Supper? Perhaps not.

It is the Last Supper which the Synoptists appear to fix by identifying it with the Passover. They say expressly that on the morning of the 'first day of unleavened bread, when they sacrificed the Passover' (Mk 14¹² ‖), the disciples asked where the Passover was to be eaten. This would be on the morning of Nisan 14. In the evening, which from twilight onwards would belong to Nisan 15, would follow the Last Supper, and on the next afternoon (still, on the Jewish reckoning, Nisan 15) the Crucifixion. St. John, on the other hand, by a number of clear indications (Jn 13¹ 18²⁸ 19¹⁴. ³¹) implies that the Last Supper was eaten before the time of the regular Passover, and that the Lord suffered on the afternoon of Nisan 14, about the time of the slaying of the Paschal lambs.

We are thus left with a conflict of testimony; and the question is, on which side the evidence is strongest. Now, if we are to believe a very competent Jewish archæologist, Dr. Chwolson, the Synoptists begin with an error. 'From the Mosaic writings down to the Book of Jubilees (cap. 49), Philo, Josephus, the Palestinian Targum ascribed to Jonathan ben Uziel, the Mishnah, the Talmud, the Rabbinical writings of the Middle Ages, indeed down to the present day, the Jews have always understood by the phrase יוֹם רִאשׁוֹן לְחַג הַמַּצּוֹת "the first day of the feast of unleavened bread," only the 15th, and not the 14th' (*Das letzte Passamahl Christi u. der Tag seines Todes*, p. 3 f.); so that it would be a contradiction in terms to say with Mk 14¹² ‖ 'on the first day of unleavened bread, when they sacrificed the Passover.' It is, however, only right to add that Chwolson's assertion is denied by another very good authority, Dr. Schürer, *ThL*, 1893, col. 182. [Schürer does not directly meet the statement that where the feast of Unleavened Bread is represented as extending over eight days, the days intended are Nisan 15–22, not 14–21.*].

* It is worth noting that the Gospel of Peter agrees with the

Waiving this point, however, for the present, we observe (after Chwolson, but cf. *Authorship of the Fourth Gospel*, 1872, p. 206 f. etc.) that the Synoptists make the Sanhedrin say beforehand that they will not arrest Jesus 'on the feast day,' and then actually arrest Him on that day; that not only the guards, but one of the disciples (Mk 14⁴⁷ ‖) carries arms, which on the feast day was not allowed; that the trial was also held on the feast day, which would be unlawful (on these points see Chwolson, *op. cit.* p. 6 ff.); that the feast day would not be called simply 'Preparation'; that the phrase 'coming from the field' (Mk 15²¹ ‖) means properly 'coming from work'; that Joseph of Arimathæa is represented as buying a linen cloth (Mk 15⁴⁶), and the women as preparing spices and ointments (Lk 23⁵⁶), all of which would be contrary to law and custom.

It follows that the Synoptists are really inconsistent with themselves, and bear unwilling witness to the chronology of St. John. We may be still reluctant to think that the contradiction is final. The Synoptists, so far as they identify the Last Supper with the Passover, look as if they were telling the truth. It is possible that there may be some way of reconciling the two accounts, which we do not know enough of the circumstances to specify.

One hypothesis, which the writer was at one time tempted to entertain,—very tentatively,—that the 'Passover' which lay before the disciples and the Sanhedrin was not the Passover proper, but the eating of the *Chăgîgāh* (so Edersheim, M'Clellan, Nösgen), he now believes to be untenable (see *Expos.* 1892, i. 17 ff., 182 f., and Wright, *Problems*, p. 173 ff.). It is more likely that, for some reason or other, the regular Passover was anticipated.

Dr. Chwolson, writing as a Jew, whose interest in the question is purely archæological, would account for such anticipation by the fact that in the year of the Passion, Nisan 15 (not 14) fell upon a Sabbath. But it must be confessed that his argument seems strained (cf. also Schürer in *ThL*, *ut sup.*).

Mr. Wright thinks that the Synoptists have combined the narrative of the Last Supper with that of some previous Paschal meal partaken of by our Lord (*Problems*, p. 179 ff.). But even if this hypothesis held good, it would hardly meet the case; because it is just the details of the Last Supper, belonging to it *qua* Last Supper (*e.g.* the 'cup of blessing'), which remind us of the Passover. And, in any case, the hypothesis deserts the documents too far to be at all capable of proof.

As the question at present stands we can only acknowledge our ignorance. [The literature will have been sufficiently given in the course of this section; cf. esp. Mr. A. Wright's *Some New Testament Problems*, London, 1898, p. 147 ff.].

iii. *The Prophetic Teaching of the Last Week.* —This, too, has raised difficulties which are not only apparent but real. It is important to bear in mind that no less than six distinct kinds of prediction are ascribed to our Lord during this week or in the period preceding. There is (1) the prediction of His own death and resurrection. There is (2) the prediction of the siege and destruction of Jerusalem. With this in the great passage (Mk 13 ‖) is directly connected (3) the prediction of the end of the world and the last judgment. (4) The discourses in Jn clearly predict the coming of the Paraclete as the substitute for Christ Himself. (5) In another leading passage (Mk 9¹) a phrase is used which may be explained, though it is not

Johannean rather than the Synoptic tradition, placing the Crucifixion not on, but before, the first day of unleavened bread (πρὸ μιᾶς τῶν ἀζύμων, *Ev. Pet.* 3).

usually explained, of the remarkable spread of the Christian Church from the Day of Pentecost onwards. Lastly (6), there is the explanation which is frequently given of the 'Coming of the Son of Man' as a so-called 'historical coming,' a coming not exhausted by a single occasion, but repeated in the great events of history.

The first three of these classes of predictions are, in any case, authentic and certain. To the believer in the genuineness of the Fourth Gospel the prophecy of the Paraclete is equally certain, and there is much which goes to confirm it in the Acts and Epp. independently of its direct attestation. The other two forms of prediction are more hypothetical. They have been introduced more or less in order to meet the difficulties, although they may have substantial grounds of their own. We will not as yet beg the question either way.

The great difficulty is that as our documents stand the second and third predictions are intimately connected with each other, and in at least one other passage it would seem as if it were expressly stated that the coming of the Son of Man (i.e. the final Coming, the Coming to Judgment) would take place within the lifetime of that generation. We know that it has not so taken place, and the great question is what we are to say to this. Is it an error in One who has never been convicted of error in anything else? We must not endeavour to explain away facts; but we may interrogate them, and interrogate them somewhat strictly, to see whether they are facts or no.

We cannot disguise from ourselves, that, whatever the precise language used by our Lord, the disciples would be exceedingly prone to attribute to Him the prediction of His own return as near at hand. The connexion of the Messiah with a world-wide judgment was no new doctrine, but was a common feature in the Jewish apocalypses. But this return would seem to them, as applied to our Lord, the necessary complement of the life of humiliation which He had led upon earth. For it was reserved the full triumph over His enemies which so far must have seemed very imperfect. Resurrection and Ascension would seem to be only foretastes of the great coming in glory on the clouds of heaven. They were steps, but only steps, towards the goal.

We might have been sure, even if we had not been told, that the disciples would naturally fix their thoughts on this Second Coming, and that it would be a natural inference for them to suppose that it was near at hand. Instances like the comparison of Mt 24²⁹=Mk 13²⁴=Lk 21²⁵ show that the expectation as to time was not fixed but variable.

On the other side, no doubt, must be set the fact that in the apostolic circle the belief in the nearness of the Second Coming was almost universal (1 Th 4¹⁴ff., 1 Co 7²⁹ff. 16²³, 2 Co 5³, Ro 13¹¹. ¹², Ph 4⁵, 1 P 4⁷, 1 Jn 2¹⁸, Rev 1³ 22¹⁰ etc.). The obvious conclusion to draw from this would be that the belief had a common root in the teaching of Christ Himself.

And in favour of that conclusion might be quoted the language of 1 Th 4¹⁵, though it may be questioned how much of this is a 'word of the Lord,' and how much the construction put upon it by St. Paul. The ease with which the apostles postponed their expectation under the teaching of events would tell against the supposition that the words of Christ had been precise on the subject; and when we come to look into the Gospels there are many hints that the time of the Second Coming could not be fixed precisely and might be distant (Mt 24³⁷⁻⁵¹ ‖ 25¹⁰⁻¹³. ¹⁴). These passages are indeed so clear that they may be fairly said to neutralize those which are quoted on the other side, and to

heighten the probability that the apparent definiteness of these other passages is due to the disciples rather than to the Master.

But another hypothesis has been put forward to remove the difficulty. It has been supposed that the Coming of the Son of Man in the places where it is spoken of as near at hand refers, not to the final coming, but to another kind of coming in the great events of history. The prologue of St. John's Gospel appears to point to such repeated comings (Jn 1⁹); and if any event deserves the name, it might well be given to the Destruction of Jerusalem, which was certainly one of the turning-points of history, and had a momentous influence upon the fortunes of Christianity. There is no doubt that our Lord directly predicted this catastrophe; and it might well seem that the passages which apparently speak of the final coming as near were due to a confusion in the minds of the disciples between the two events regarded as 'Comings.'

It is, however, a question whether this idea of repeated coming can be made good. Most recent writers are inclined to set it down as a modernism (Schwartzkopff, Weissagungen Jesu Christi, etc. p. 155; Holtzmann, Neutest. Theol. i. 315). It is also very doubtful whether it has any real support in OT. What the prophets looked forward to was 'the day of the Lord'—a single great intervention of God—not a day or succession of days.

On this point the writer is glad to be able to refer to a note which he has received from Dr. Driver: 'The usual expression is "the day of J"' ": in Is 2¹², however, it is indef. (" for there is a day for," etc., or " J" hath a day"); Zec 14¹ has also "a day"; Ezk 30³ is lit. "For near is a day, and near is a day for J"'"; Is 34⁸ "For there is a day of vengeance for J" (or "J" hath"), a year of recompense for," etc.; also "his days" in apparently the same sense, Job 24¹. But these hardly differ except formally from the usual "day of J"." I do not think that a succession of judgments is represented under this figure—except, of course, in so far as what the prophet pictured as taking place in a single day was in reality effected gradually.'

Another hypothesis, however, also appears deserving of consideration. The strongest of all the passages which would make our Lord expressly predict His own Second Coming within the apostolic age itself is Mt 16²⁸ 'Verily I say unto you, There be some of them that stand here which shall in no wise taste of death, till they see the Son of Man coming in his kingdom.' But when we compare this with the parallels, Mk 9¹=Lk 9²⁷ it is clear that the words Son of Man are intrusive, and that the clause really runs, 'till they see the kingdom of God come with power' (om. 'with power,' Lk). It is not the 'Son of Man coming in his kingdom,' but the 'kingdom' itself which comes.

What is meant by the kingdom here? Is it not a very natural interpretation to explain it of that great intervention of the Spirit of God in the world, that great influx of Divine powers and energies which dates from Pentecost? In other words, is it not natural to equate it with the promise of the Paraclete in the Fourth Gospel, where it is implied that the coming of the Paraclete is equivalent to the coming of Christ Himself? (Jn 14¹⁶⁻¹⁸).

The teaching of the Fourth Gospel respecting the Paraclete is already strongly confirmed by the part assigned to the Holy Spirit by St. Paul; and if the explanation just suggested * holds good, it would be also confirmed from another and unexpected quarter.

There has been a considerable tendency in the advanced liberal camp to get rid entirely of the apocalyptic and eschatological element in the teaching of our Lord. The chief means through which this is done has been the supposed discovery

---

* A similar view is taken by Haupt, p. 133 f., and Bruston (Holtzmann, Neutest. Theol. i. 315 n.), but commended itself to the writer of this independently. Cf. also Swete, ad loc.

that in the discourse of Mk 13 ‖ there is incorporated a 'Little Apocalypse' of Jewish (Weizsäcker) or Jewish-Christian (Colani, Pfleiderer, Weiffenbach) origin, usually regarded as a 'fly-sheet' composed in A.D. 67–68 during the troubles which immediately preceded the siege of Jerusalem, and identified with the 'oracle' which led to the flight of the Christians to Pella (Eus. *HE* III. v. 3). The first to hit upon this idea was Colani (*Jésus Christ et les Croyances Messianiques de son Temps*, ed. 2, 1864, p. 201 ff.), who was followed by Weizsäcker, Pfleiderer, and on an elaborate scale by Weiffenbach, *Der Wiederkunftsgedanke Jesu*, Leipzig, 1873. This last-named work is usually referred to as having established the position. In the final form of the theory the 'fly-sheet' in question is supposed to consist of Mk 13⁷⁻⁹ᵃ ‖ 14-20 ‖ 24-27 ‖ 30-31 ‖. And it is true that these verses are fairly detachable from the rest and make a fairly compact whole.

By thus eliminating the central passage on which the eschatological teaching of Jesus seemed to rest, it became not very difficult to explain away that teaching altogether. Weiffenbach did so by the hypothesis that the critically verified allusions to the Second Coming of the Messiah all originally referred to *His Resurrection*, the predictions of which formed the genuine nucleus out of which the rest had grown through misunderstanding of the words of Jesus and the blending with them of current apocalyptic doctrines. By this expedient, Weiffenbach, whose object was less radical than that of most of those who went with him, escaped some real difficulties; but just in this it may be doubted whether he has found any follower. It will be seen that the critical analysis of Mk 13 ‖ is the starting-point of the whole construction; and that has not perhaps as yet been brought to any final solution.

iv. The Last Supper.

— The part of the Last Supper of which it is most incumbent upon us to speak here is its culmination in the solemn acts and words which institute the second of the two great Sacraments. Besides the debates of centuries which have gathered round this subject, a number of questions have been raised in recent years which require discussion. In particular, new light has been thrown upon the text of one of our leading authorities. And our first step must be to determine as nearly as we can its exact bearing.

(1) *The Text of Lk* 22¹⁴⁻²⁰.—The importance of this section is such, and it is so desirable that the evidence should be given with completeness and precision, that we may be forgiven if in this instance we print the full text of the original (after Greek RV), and then proceed to give the more crucial variants in technical fashion.

The evidence of the leading Latin MSS is given in full; that of the two oldest forms of the Syriac Version in a retranslation, based for the Sinai MS on Mrs. Lewis and Merx, and for the Curetonian on Baethgen. For the Coptic Version the new critical edition is used (Oxford, 1898).

Lk 22¹⁴⁻²⁰. 14 Καὶ ὅτε ἐγένετο ἡ ὥρα, ἀνέπεσε, καὶ οἱ ἀπόστολοι σὺν αὐτῷ. 15 καὶ εἶπε πρὸς αὐτούς, Ἐπιθυμίᾳ ἐπεθύμησα τοῦτο τὸ πάσχα φαγεῖν μεθ᾽ ὑμῶν πρὸ τοῦ με παθεῖν· 16 λέγω γὰρ ὑμῖν, ὅτι οὐ μὴ φάγω αὐτό, ἕως ὅτου πληρωθῇ ἐν τῇ βασιλείᾳ τοῦ Θεοῦ. 17 καὶ δεξάμενος ποτήριον εὐχαριστήσας εἶπε, Λάβετε τοῦτο, καὶ διαμερίσατε εἰς ἑαυτούς· 18 λέγω γὰρ ὑμῖν, ὅτι οὐ μὴ πίω ἀπὸ τοῦ νῦν ἀπὸ τοῦ γενήματος τῆς ἀμπέλου ἕως ὅτου ἡ βασιλεία τοῦ Θεοῦ ἔλθῃ. 19 καὶ λαβὼν ἄρτον εὐχαριστήσας ἔκλασε, καὶ ἔδωκεν αὐτοῖς λέγων, Τοῦτό ἐστι τὸ σῶμά μου τὸ ὑπὲρ ὑμῶν διδόμενον· τοῦτο ποιεῖτε εἰς τὴν ἐμὴν ἀνάμνησιν. 20 καὶ τὸ ποτήριον ὡσαύτως μετὰ τὸ δειπνῆσαι λέγων, Τοῦτο τὸ ποτήριον ἡ καινὴ διαθήκη ἐν τῷ αἵματί μου, τὸ ὑπὲρ ὑμῶν ἐκχυνόμενον.

Locum integrum habent Codd. Græc. et Verss. omn., iis tantum testibus exceptis qui infra nominantur; item Latt. c f q Vulg.; *agnoscunt*, Tert. *adv. Marc.* iv. 40; Eus. *Can.*; Bas. *quæ feruntur Ethica*; Cyril. Alex. *Comm in Luc.*

Om. vv.¹⁶·¹⁷·¹⁸ Cod. Copt. ℵ (*Catena Curzoniana, excerpto ut videtur Tito [Bostrensi]*).

Om. vv.¹⁷·¹⁸ Lect. 32, Pesh. codd.

Om. v. 19b. 20 τὸ ὑπὲρ ὑμῶν διδόμ.—ἐκχυνόμενον, D a ff² i l.

Iisdem omissis transp. vv.¹⁷·¹⁸ *ita ut partem* v.19 *priorem sequantur* b e. [¹⁶ Dico enim vobis, quia ex hoc non manducabo illud, donec . . . in regno dei. ¹⁷ Et, accepto pane, gratias egit, et fregit, et dedit illis, ¹⁷dicens : Hoc est corpus meum. Et accepto calice, gratias egit; et dixit : Accipite hoc et dividite inter vos. ¹⁸ dico enim vobis, quod non bibam de generatione hac vitis hujus, donec regnum dei veniat. ²¹ Verumtamen ecce manus, etc. b ¹⁶ Dico enim vobis quia jam non manducabo illud doneque adimplear in regno di. ¹⁹et accepit panem et gratias egit et fregit et dedit eis ¹⁷dicens hoc est corpus meu. Et accepit calicē et gratias egit et dixit accipite vivite inter vos. dico enim vobis amodo non vivam (*sic*) amodo de potione vitis quoadusque regnum di veniat verum ecce manus, etc. e].

Item transp. vv.¹⁷·¹⁸ *omisso* (Cur.) *vel partim interjecto* (Sin.) v.²⁰ Syrr. (Sin.-Cur.). [¹⁶ . . . ἕως ὅτου πληρωθῇ ἐν τῇ βασ. τοῦ Θεοῦ. ¹⁹καὶ λαβὼν ἄρτον εὐχαριστήσας ἱλασεν καὶ ἔδωκεν αὐτοῖς λέγων· τοῦτό ἐστι τὸ σῶμά μου τὸ ὑπὲρ ὑμῶν διδόμενον (*om.* Cur.)· τοῦτο ποιεῖτε εἰς τὴν ἐμὴν ἀνάμνησιν. ¹⁷καὶ (ὡσαύτως μετὰ τὸ δειπνῆσαι *ins. ex* v.²⁰ Sin.) δεξάμενος ποτήριον (*vel* τὸ ποτ.) εὐχαριστήσας εἶπε· λάβετε τοῦτο διαμερίσατε εἰς ἑαυτοὺς (τοῦτό ἐστι τὸ αἷμά μου [ἡ] καινὴ διαθήκη add. Sin.). λέγω (*ins.* γάρ Sin.) ὑμῖν ὅτι ἀπὸ τοῦ νῦν οὐ μὴ πίω ἀπὸ τοῦ γενήματος τούτου τῆς ἀμπέλου (*vel om.*?) ἕως ὅτου ἡ βασ. τοῦ θιοῦ ἔλθῃ].

To the textual critic these phenomena are fairly clear. The omission of vv.¹⁹ᵇ⁻²⁰ (D a ff² i l) belongs to the oldest form of the Western text. The next step (b e) was to transpose the order of vv.¹⁷·¹⁸ and ¹⁹ᵃ, so as to make the sequence of the Bread and the Cup correspond to that in the other authorities. The next (Cur.) was to supplement the words relating to the Bread from 1 Co 11²⁴. The next (Sin.) was to supplement in like manner the part relating to the Cup by somewhat free interpolations partly suggested by Mt, Mk, but mainly from 1 Co 11²⁵. In this instance Syr.-Sin. represents a later stage than Syr.-Cur., though it is more often earlier. The omissions of vv. [¹⁶] ¹⁷·¹⁸ are probably not important.

We have then confronting each other the primitive form of the Western text, which is shorter, makes Lk transpose the order of the Bread and the Cup, and omits all mention of a second Cup, and the great mass of Gk. MSS and other authorities, which introduce a second Cup, or second mention of the Cup, and fill out the whole mainly from St. Paul. We cannot doubt that both these types of text existed early in the 2nd cent. Either may be original. And this is just one of those cases where internal evidence is strongly in favour of the text which we call Western. The temptation to expand was much stronger than to contract; and the double mention of the Cup raises real difficulties of the kind which suggest interpolation.

(2) *Relation of the Texts to each other*.—The adoption of the Western text of Lk greatly diminishes the coincidences between St. Luke and St. Paul. Indeed it reduces them to the practically equivalent εὐχαριστήσας for εὐλογήσας (in reference to the Bread; Mt, Mk use it of the Cup). The greatest loss is that of the apparent confirmation by St. Luke of the command to repeat the rite in memory of its Founder. It may be doubted, however, whether the introduction of this into the text of Lk, which—to obtain the circulation it had—must have taken place exceedingly early, and must have been carried out at the headquarters of the Church, is not even stronger testimony to the current practice of the Church than that of a single writer could be, even though that writer was an evangelist.

As to the main lines of the rite all the authorities are agreed. All note the taking of the Bread, the blessing (or 'giving thanks'), the breaking, the words, 'This is my Body.' All note the Cup, which both in the Synoptic (Mt, Mk) and Pauline tradition is related to the [new] Covenant inaugurated by the shedding of the Blood of the Messiah. In the Synoptics (Mt, Mk, Lk) there is an express mention of the giving of the Bread to the disciples, with the further command, 'Take' (Mt, Mk), 'eat' (Mt), and a like communication of the Cup (Synoptics, though with some difference of phrase). And whereas St. Paul emphasizes the redemptive value of the sacrificed Body (τὸ ὑπὲρ ὑμῶν *lectio vera*), Mt, Mk do the same for the shedding of the Blood (τὸ περὶ [ὑπὲρ] πολλῶν ἐκχυννόμενον Mt, Mk, and εἰς ἄφεσιν ἁμαρτιῶν Mt). St. Paul not only doubles the command for repetition, but also adds, 'For as often as ye eat this bread and drink this cup, ye proclaim the Lord's death till he come.'

(3) *Other NT Evidence.*—We thus have the institution of the Sacrament fully set before us. But if we look at one of the documents upon which we have been drawing, the first in order of writing, though it is only incidentally historical, 1 Co 11, we find there that the Sacrament proper is associated with something else—the common meal or *agape* (Jude [12], 2 P 2[13] *var. lect.*). We ask ourselves what can be the origin of this association? It can hardly go back to the original institution. It is more probable that the association arose out of the state of κοινωνία described in Ac 2[42. 44-46] 4[32-35] 6[1. 2].

Perhaps it goes back further still, at least to the very beginning of the period. For one of the characteristic expressions is ἡ κλάσις τοῦ ἄρτου, κλᾶν ἄρτον (Ac 2[42. 46]), of which Blass says, 'est autem κλᾶν τὸν ἄρτον sollemnis designatio cenæ dominicæ.' It must, however, be somewhat wider than that, for in the immediate context we have κλῶντες τε κατ᾽ οἶκον ἄρτον μετελάμβανον τροφῆς, κ.τ.λ., where τροφή would seem to embrace the common meal as well as the Eucharist.

We are reminded further that the same phrase κλᾶν (κατακλᾶν) ἄρτον is repeatedly used of a solemn act of our Lord independently of the Eucharist (Mk 6[41] ‖ 8[6] ‖ [19], Lk 24[30]). And we gather from the context of the last passage that there was something distinctive in this particular act by which our Lord was recognized (Lk 24[35]). We are reminded also of the many instances in which attention is specially called to the 'blessing' (εὐλογεῖν or εὐχαριστεῖν) of food by our Lord. They are the same words which are used in connexion with the sacramental Bread and the sacramental Cup.

There is something in these facts which is not quite fully explained. There are *lacunæ* in our knowledge which we would fain fill up if we could. The institution of the Eucharist appears to have connexions both backwards and forwards—backwards with other meals which our Lord ate together with His disciples, forwards with those common meals which very early came into existence in the Apostolic Church. But the exact nature and method of these connexions our materials are not sufficient to make clear to us.

(4) *Significance of the Eucharist.*—We feel these gaps in our knowledge when we pass on to consider the significance of the Sacrament. Certainly Harnack was not wholly wrong, however far we may think him from being wholly right, when he held that the primary object of Christ's blessing was the *meal as such*, in its simplest elements, not specifically bread and wine (cf. *TU* VII. ii. 137).

The prominence given to the meal and to the natural products of the earth which contribute to it, finds some support in the eucharistic prayers of the *Didaché*. 'First, as regards the cup: We give thee thanks, O our Father, for the holy vine of thy son David which thou madest known unto us through thy Son Jesus; thine is the glory for ever and ever. Then as regards the broken bread: We give thee thanks, O our Father, for the life and knowledge which thou didst make known to us through thy Son Jesus; thine is the glory for ever and ever. As this broken bread was scattered upon the mountains, and being gathered together became one, so may thy Church be gathered together from the ends of the earth into thy kingdom; for thine is the glory and the power through Jesus Christ, for ever and ever. . . . Thou, Almighty Master, didst create all things for thy name's sake, and didst give food and drink unto men for enjoyment, that they might render thanks to thee; but didst bestow upon us spiritual food and drink and eternal life through thy Son' (*Did.* ix. 2-4, x. 3).

It would, however, be doing an injustice both to the ancient and to the modern writer if we supposed that they had in view only the gifts of God in nature. Harnack writes: 'The Lord instituted a meal in commemoration of His death, or rather He described the food of the body as His Flesh and Blood, *i.e.* as the food of the soul (through the forgiveness of sins), when it was partaken of with thanksgiving, in memory of His death' (*op.*

cit. p. 139). And the *Didaché* looks beyond the physical eating and drinking to the 'spiritual food and drink,' and to the 'eternal life' bestowed through the Son; and when it speaks of the 'holy vine of David,' there is at least an allusion to the Jewish doctrine of the Messiah, if not directly to the Johannean allegory of the Vine.

We thus come round to an aspect of the Supper which has been emphasized and illustrated, especially by Spitta. There are allusions not only in the immediate context of the words of institution (Mk 14[25] ‖), but also elsewhere (Lk 14[15] 'Blessed is he that shall eat bread in the kingdom of God'; cf. Mt 8[11] 22[2ff.] 25[10]) to the language in use among the Jews respecting the great Messianic banquet. This took its start from the teaching of the Prophets (*e.g.* Is 25[6]), and has points of contact with prominent passages in the Wisdom literature. Thus in Pr 9[5] Wisdom issues her invitation, 'Come, eat ye of my bread, and drink of the wine which I have mingled'; which is taken up in Sir 24[19-21] 'They that eat me shall yet be hungry, and they that drink me shall yet be thirsty.' And in a like connexion the idea of the manna is applied in Wis 16[20f.] 'Thou gavest thy people angels' food to eat, and bread ready for their use didst thou provide from heaven without their toil. . . . For thy nature (ἡ ὑπόστασίς σου) manifested thy sweetness toward thy children.'

We are clearly upon the line of thought which links on to the discourse in the synagogue at Capernaum. Indeed we meet here with the same phenomenon that has already come before us on other sides of our Lord's teaching. The current ideas are not discarded, but taken up on to a higher plane and filled with a new content. We have seen that Wisdom was regarded as giving herself to be 'eaten' (*i.e.* spiritually appropriated and assimilated). Philo repeatedly identifies the manna with the Logos (Spitta refers to ed. Mangey, i. 120, 214, 484, 564). Hence we are not surprised to find that St. Paul speaks of the πνευματικὸν βρῶμα and πνευματικὸν πόμα, the miraculously-given meat and drink which nourished the Israelites in the wilderness being treated as typical of the Christian Sacrament. In 1 Co 10[4] it is not the water, but the stricken rock as the source of the water, which St. Paul identifies with Christ Himself. But a little further he says plainly, 'The cup of blessing which we bless, is it not a communion of the blood of Christ? The bread which we break, is it not a communion of the body of Christ?' (*ib.* v.[16]). And in Jn 6[48-51] our Lord is made to describe Himself as the 'living bread which came down out of heaven,' and it is explained that the bread which He will give is His flesh, for the life of the world.

We take the view that the discourse in question does not relate directly to the Eucharist. But it does not do so only because it expresses the larger idea of which the Eucharist is a particular concrete embodiment, the one leading embodiment which Christ has bequeathed to His Church. As there is a communion with Him which is wider than—though it culminates in—that which we call κατ᾽ ἐξοχήν, the Holy Communion, so is there a sense in which He is the Bread from heaven, which is wider than that in which He is given through the sacramental Bread, but it is that bread of which He said, 'This is my Body, which is for you.'

The parallelism between Jn 6[51] and 1 Co 11[24] (cf. Mk 14[24] ‖) is so close that we are certainly justified in interpreting the words of institution in the manner in which the Sacrament itself is interpreted by both St. Paul and St. John.

No writer has brought out this aspect of the Supper as signifying primarily the spiritual assimilation of Christ more forcibly than Spitta. But when he goes on to maintain that the Eucharist has no relation to His death, it is sheer paradox, which can be maintained only by the most arbitrary methods.

The assimilation of Christ does not exhaust the meaning of the Sacrament. If we take the words of institution as they stand, another idea is even more prominent. We have seen that there is considerable doubt as to how far the Last Supper is to be identified with the Paschal meal. St. Paul describes the Death of Christ as the Christian Passover (1 Co 5[7]), and not only he but other NT writers apply to that Death the language of Sacrifice. But the particular sacrifice with which our Lord's own words most directly connect it is the sacrifice, or group of sacrifices, which inaugurated the Covenant (Ex 24[4-8]). As the sprinkling of the blood upon the altar of God and upon the people ratified the covenant between Israel and Israel's God, so (it was implied) by partaking of the consecrated symbol of the Blood of Christ the Christian had brought home to him his share in the new Covenant—a covenant which had at once its inestimable privileges and its obligations. It was the means of admission to the state of Divine favour, and it bound over those who were admitted to that favour to a life of loyal service. Here, too, if we want a comment on the words of institution, we may seek it rightly in the later NT writings. For words could not well be more strongly attested than those which accompany the giving of the bread and of the cup, and together they converge upon a root-idea which is expanded most directly in He 9[18-28], but is also illustrated by Ro 3[24f.] 5[11]. 8[1ff.], Eph 1[7], 1 P 1[19], 1 Jn 1[7] 2[2], Rev 1[5].

If we start from the idea of the Death of Christ as a Sacrifice, then it lies near at hand to conceive of the Sacrament as the sacred meal which follows the sacrifice. In this there would be combined the universal and immemorial significance of such meals as an act of communion at once with the Deity worshipped and of the worshippers with each other. This double communion, under this aspect of the sacrificial meal, seems clearly indicated in 1 Co 10[16f. 21], but it is also suggested by the words of institution, taken with the distribution of the elements of bread and wine, and the stress which is laid upon the general participation ('Drink ye all,' 'they all drank').

(5) *Critical Theories.* — A common feature in recent critical theories respecting the Last Supper is the denial that the command, 'This do in remembrance of me,' formed part of the original institution ; or, in other words, that the particular circumstances which marked this solemn parting meal were meant to be repeated in the form of a permanent Sacrament. This view was put forward about the same time, and, it is probable, independently, in England by Dr. P. Gardner (*The Origin of the Lord's Supper*, London, 1893), and in Germany by Jülicher in the vol. of essays in honour of Weizsäcker (*Theol. Abhandl.* etc., Freiburg i. B. 1892), and by Spitta (*Zur Gesch. u. Lit. d. Urchristentums*, Göttingen, 1893). The English writer is the most thoroughgoing. Assuming the correctness of the WH text of Lk 22[19. 20], St. Paul is left as the sole authority for the express command of repetition. It is then argued from the phrasing of 1 Co 11[23] 'I received of the Lord,' that the whole account belongs to one of St. Paul's ecstatic revelations, and has not a solid historical foundation. In default of this it is thought that the apostle had been influenced during his stay at Corinth by the near proximity of the Eleusinian mysteries, the central point in which 'appears to have been a sacred repast of which the initiated partook, and by means of which they had communion with the gods' (p. 18).

How St. Paul could confuse such subtle external influences with a revelation 'from the Lord,' and how he came to deliver as authoritative instructions to the Corinthians what he had (upon the theory) only himself acquired during his stay at Corinth, are only incidental questions. We cannot tell precisely how St. Paul received his knowledge in such a sense that he could refer it to the Lord. But the solemn simplicity of phrase reads like history, and, so far as other authorities exist, it is completely verified. In any case, it is incredible that a usage which is thus treated as practically the invention of St. Paul could have spread from an outlying Gentile Church over the whole of Christendom. We cannot doubt that not only the Synoptic version of the Supper, but its repetition as a Sacrament, had their origin in the Mother Church. The κλάσις τοῦ ἄρτου of Ac 2[42. 46] is an indication of this, which is confirmed by the evidence of Ignatius, Justin, and the *Didaché.* Spitta's theory, that the repeated Sacrament was due, not to a command of Christ Himself, but to the spontaneous instinct of affectionate recollection among His disciples, is more possible, but still gratuitous and hypercritical. We may not allege the witness of St. Luke himself in confirmation of St. Paul, but, as we have already seen (p. 636 *sup.*), the familiar text of his Gospel is no less valid evidence of the common belief and practice.

Of the critical theories respecting the origin of the Eucharist, that which we have just mentioned is the most important. Harnack's contention, that it was sometimes administered with water instead of wine, not only here and there among the sects but in the main body of the Church, belongs rather to the history of the Early Church than to the Life of our Lord. It turns, however, upon a somewhat cavalier treatment of the text of Justin, and has met with strong opposition and (it is believed) practically no acceptance.

LITERATURE.—A summary may be given of the more recent special literature to most of which reference has been made. Lobstein, *La Doctrine de la Cène*, Lausanne, 1889 ; a lucid exposition dating from the time before the rise of the newer theories. A reasonable criticism may go back to it with advantage. Harnack, *TU* VII. ii., 1891 (replies by Zahn, *Brot u. Wein*, Leipzig, 1892 ; Jülicher, as below ; Headlam, *Class. Rev.* 1893, p. 63) ; Jülicher in *Theol. Abhandlungen C. von Weizsäcker gewidmet*, Freiburg i. B. 1892 ; Spitta, *Zur Gesch. u. Lit. d. Urchristentum*, Göttingen ; P. Gardner, *The Origin of the Lord's Supper*, London, 1893 (comp. also a criticism by Mr. Wright, *NT Problems*, p. 134 ff.) ; Grafe in *Z. f. Theol. u. Kirche*, 1895 (said to be an excellent summary of the controversy) ; Schultzen, *Das Abendmahl im NT*, Göttingen, 1859 (also a full review and examination) ; Schaefer, *Das Herrenmahl*, Gütersloh, 1897. Bp. Wordsworth's Visitation Addresses on *The Holy Communion* (2nd ed. 1892), though written before the controversy and dealing largely with the liturgical aspect of the question, may be specially commended to English readers.

v. **The Resurrection.** — For our present purpose the discussion of the Resurrection of our Lord will resolve itself into a consideration of (1) the evidence attesting the fact ; (2) the sequence of the events, or the appearances which followed the Resurrection ; (3) the explanations which have been put forward to account for the Resurrection without miracle ; (4) its doctrinal significance.

(1) *The Attestation.*—A fact so stupendous as the Resurrection needs to be supported by strong evidence, and very strong evidence both as regards quantity and quality is forthcoming ; but all parts of it are not of equal value, and it is well that the authorities should be compared with each other and critically estimated.

When this is done one piece of evidence drops almost entirely to the rear—the concluding verses of St. Mark. This is not invalidated merely by the fact that the verses were probably not part of the original Gospel. Since Mr. Conybeare's discovery of the Armenian MS, which appears to refer them to the 'presbyter Ariston' or 'Aristion,' it is fair to attach that name to them, because, although the authority is but slender, there is nothing at all to compete with it; and the Aristion mentioned by Eusebius (*HE* iii. 39) as one of the 'elders' consulted by Papias, would suit the conditions as well as any one else belonging to the same generation (say A.D. 100–125). Such an authority cannot be wholly without weight; if it represented a distinct line of tradition, its weight would be considerable. But when the verses Mk 16⁹⁻²⁰ are examined, it seems pretty clear that the earlier portion of them is really a summary of the narratives in the extant Gospels of St. Luke and St. John, and therefore adds nothing to these Gospels beyond such further sanction as the name of Aristion may give to them. It is proof that the statements in those Gospels were accepted as satisfactory by a prominent Church teacher, himself a depositary of tradition, in the region where St. John had been active. So much the verses contribute, but not more.

There is still some mystery hanging over the close of the Second Gospel. The most probable view appears to be that its original conclusion has been lost—it is more likely than not—by some purely mechanical accident. The fragment that remains, Mk 16¹⁻⁸, is insufficient to enable us to trace it to its source. If we could be sure that it was complete, we should have to say that St. Mark was *not* here drawing upon the Petrine tradition, because that tradition could not have failed to speak of the appearance to Peter himself. It is, however, possible that that was contained in the missing portion.

This may detract somewhat from the weight of the common Synopt. narrative, which is here disappointingly meagre. And yet, if we are to throw the absence of any mark of Petrine origin into the one scale, there is a little bit of confirmatory evidence which it is fair to throw into the other. All through the history of the Passion St. Luke has access to a special source, which we may well believe to have been oral, but which gave him some items of good information. This information relates especially to the court of Herod Antipas (Lk 23⁷⁻¹²), and it is natural to connect it with the particular mention of 'Joanna the wife of Chuza, Herod's steward' in Lk 8³. Now this very same Joanna appears again in St. Luke's account of the visit of the women to the sepulchre (Lk 24¹⁰). The rest of the paragraph appears to be based as usual upon St. Mark. But the renewed mention of Joanna is an indication of the special source, which at least goes to show that there was nothing in that source which conflicted with the Marcan document. In other words, it confirms that document by a distinct line of testimony (cf. Lk 23²¹⁻²⁴).

Is it not possible that the story of the Walk to Emmaus has a like origin? The name Cleopas (=Cleopatros) is just such as we should expect to find in the same Herodian circle. In any case, the source bears other marks of being a good one. It gives a graphic picture of the dejection through which the disciples passed; and the phrase 'we hoped that it was he which should redeem Israel' points back to a time before the dreams of national triumph had been purified of the grosser element in them. But most striking of all is the direct confirmation by St. Paul (1 Co 15⁵) of another very incidental reference, the appearance to Peter (Lk 23³⁴). Not only does St. Paul confirm the fact, but he puts it practically in the same place in the series.

We have, then, every reason to think both that the special source used by St. Luke was excellent in itself, and also that it agreed in substance with the fragmentary record of St. Mark.

If St. Luke thus reaches a hand in one direction towards St. Mark, he does so in another direction towards St. John. For the appearance of Lk 24³⁶ff. corresponds to that of Jn 20¹⁹ff.; and both alike receive the seal of authentication from St. Paul (1 Cor 15⁵). We may not, for the reason given above, use Mk 16⁹ in ratification of Jn 20¹¹ff.. We note, however, that the incident of St. Thomas is a striking concrete illustration of the disbelief on which so many of our authorities lay stress.[*] For the rest, the narrative in the Fourth Gospel must go with the problem as to that Gospel generally. It has found a vigorous recent defender in Dr. Loofs (*Die Auferstehungsberichte und ihr Wert*, Leipzig, 1898).

The peculiar element in Mt might have seemed to possess the lowest claim to acceptance, were it not for the singular convergence of proof that something like the injunction of Mt 28¹⁹ must have been given, or most probably was given, by our Lord Himself (see p. 624 *sup.*; also p. 213 ff.). We believe that for this paragraph, too, there is solid foundation.

And yet the Resurrection is a part of the evangelical narrative for which the leading witness is, after all, not the Gospels, but St. Paul— the double witness of what St. Paul says and what he implies. It is hardly possible for testimony to be stronger than this is. In the same precise and deliberate manner in which he had rehearsed the particulars of the Last Supper, St. Paul enumerates one by one the leading appearances of the Lord after the Resurrection: (1) to Peter, (2) to the Twelve (as a body), (3) to an assembly of more than five hundred, (4) to James, (5) to all the apostles (1 Co 15⁵⁻⁷).

We have spoken of these as the 'leading' appearances, because St. Paul doubtless has in view, not all who under any circumstances 'saw the Lord,' but those who were specially chosen and commissioned to be witnesses of the Resurrection (Ac 1²² 4³³, cf. 1 Co 15¹⁵), *i.e.* as we should say, to assert and preach it publicly. For this reason there would be nothing in St. Paul's list to exclude such an appearance as that to Mary Magdalene (Jn 20¹¹⁻¹⁸). It may have been on this ground—because the two disciples involved were not otherwise conspicuous as active preachers or prominent leaders—that St. Paul does not mention the scene on the road to Emmaus. But it is equally possible that the story of this had not reached him.

We have seen by what a striking coincidence this story confirms, from a wholly independent quarter, the first appearance to Peter. The next in order, that to the Twelve, may well be identical with that which is more exactly described in Lk 24³³ff., Jn 20¹⁹⁻²⁴. The appearance to James is attested by another line of tradition embodied in the Gospel according to the Hebrews. Beyond this identifications are uncertain.

St. Paul contents himself with a bare enumeration, not from lack of knowledge, but because he assumes knowledge in his readers. He reminds the Corinthians of what he had delivered unto them first of all (ἐν πρώτοις, *i.e.* at the very beginning of his ministry among them). This throws back the date of the evidence some four years— we may say from the year 55 to 51, possibly earlier, but at the latest from 57 to 53.

We are thus brought to much the same date as that of another piece of evidence, not so detailed

---

[*] This trait is not less authentic because it passed over from primary documents into secondary (such as the Coptic work discovered by Carl Schmidt and commented upon by Harnack in *Theol. Studien B. Weiss dargebracht*). It really does throw into relief, and the early disciples saw that it threw into relief, the revulsion of feeling on the part of the witnesses to the Resurrection and the strength of their conviction. Otherwise Harnack, p. 8, and Loofs, p. 21.

as that in 1 Co, but quite as explicit, so far as the fact of the Resurrection is concerned, the evidence of the first extant NT writing, 1 Th 1¹⁰ 4¹⁴. The assured tone of these passages shows, not only that the apostle is speaking from the very strongest personal conviction, but that he is confident of carrying his readers with him ; we may go further and say that the belief to which he gives this expression was unquestioned, the universal belief of Christians. We might infer this from the attitude of St. Paul in regard to it. Unfortunately, we have no evidence equally early from the Church of Palestine ; but as soon as evidence begins to appear it is all to the same effect. The early chapters of Ac no doubt represent a Palestinian tradition, perhaps a written tradition ; and they take the same line as St. Paul in making it the chief function of the apostles to bear witness to the Resurrection (Ac 1⁸, ²² etc.). We need not pursue this evidence further.

It is noticeable that although there were doubts in the Apostolic Age on the subject of resurrection (1 Co 15¹², 2 Ti 2¹⁷ᶠ·), it is not as to the resurrection of Christ, but as to that of Christians. St. Paul argues on the assumption that Christ was really raised as from a premiss common to himself and his opponents.

And it is no less noticeable that even the most rationalistic of Christian sects, those (e.g.) which denied the Virgin-Birth, nevertheless shared the belief in the Resurrection (Irenæus, adv. Hær. I. xxvi. 1, 2 [where non before similiter should be expunged] ; Hippolytus, Ref. Hær. vii. 35).

(2) *The Sequence and Scene of the Events.*—It is not an exaggeration—it is only putting in words the impression left by the facts—to say that the conviction among Christians that Christ was really raised, dates from the very morrow of the Resurrection itself. It was not a growth spread over a long period and receiving gradual accretions of strength ; but it sprang suddenly into existence, and it swept irresistibly over the whole body of disciples. Of the force and universality of the belief there can be no doubt ; but when we come to details it would seem that from the first there was a certain amount of confusion, which was never wholly cleared up. We have records of a number of appearances, not all contained in a single authority, but scattered over several distinct authorities ; and it is probable enough that even when all the recorded appearances are put together they would not exhaust all those that were experienced. Different traditions must have circulated in different quarters, and specimens of these traditions have come down to us without being digested into accordance with a single type. The list which approaches most nearly to this character, that which is given by St. Paul in 1 Co, is, as we have seen, not so much a digest as a selection. It is a selection made for purposes of preaching, and consisting of items which had already been used for this purpose. Compared with this, a story like the Walk to Emmaus is such as might have come out of private memoirs. The brief record in St. Mark is more central, but in its present condition it is too mutilated to satisfy curiosity. The narrative of St. John is no less authoritative than that of St. Paul, but it is authority of a rather different kind. St. Paul writes as the active practical missionary, who seeks to communicate the fire of his own conviction to others. St. John also wishes to spread conviction (Jn 20³¹), but he does so by bringing forth the stores of long and intense recollections from his own breast. He too selects what had taken the most personal hold upon him, and does not try to cover the whole ground.

It is as a consequence of these conditions that when we come to look into the narratives of the Resurrection we find them unassimilated and unharmonized. It is not exactly easy to fit them into each other. The most important difference is as to the chief scene of the appearances. Was it Jerusalem and the neighbourhood, or was it Galilee ? The authorities are divided. St. Paul and the Gospel according to the Hebrews make no mention of locality. Mt and Mk throw the stress upon Galilee. The latter Gospel does not indeed (in the genuine portion) record a Galilæan appearance, but the women are bidden to say that the risen Lord would meet the disciples in Galilee (Mk 16⁷). This is in fulfilment of a promise to the same effect given in the course of the Last Supper, and recorded in the same two Gospels (Mk 14²⁸, Mt 26³²). The express mention of prediction and fulfilment in both Gospels not only proves their presence in the common original, but also shows that they were no accidental feature in that original, but an essential part of the whole conception. We have besides a Galilæan appearance described in Jn 21, and clearly implied at the point where the fragment of the Gospel of Peter breaks off (Ev. Pet. § 12 [60]).

On the other hand, all the scenes of Jn 20 are laid in Jerusalem ; and Jerus. or the neighbourhood is the only locality recognized in Lk 24, which ends with a command to the disciples to wait in the city for the outpouring of the Holy Spirit (Lk 24⁴⁹).

It is not unnatural that the critical school should regard these two versions as alternatives, one of which only can be taken. The more usual course has been to follow that of Mk and Mt, with or without the supposition that the grave was really found empty (Loofs, p. 18 ff.). According as this assumption was made or not, several constructions were possible, but all equally speculative.

Dr. Loofs has, however, recently argued in favour of the other tradition represented by Lk-Jn 20. And he has certainly succeeded in showing that there is as much intrinsic probability on this side as on the other. But, in order to carry out this theory, he is obliged to treat Jn 21 as having a different origin from the rest of the Gospel, and as falling into two parts, one of which (the fishing scene=Lk 5¹⁻¹¹) has got misplaced, not having originally belonged to the period after the Resurrection, while the other (the dialogue of Jn 21¹⁵⁻²³) had originally nothing to connect it with Galilee. These are strong measures, which, however high our estimate of the tradition, Lk-Jn, are obviously not open to one who thinks that the identity of style between Jn 21 and the rest of the Gospel is too great to permit of their separation. (the argument in Expos. 1892, i. 380 ff., may easily be extended to ch. 21).

The only remaining course is to combine the traditions, much as they seem to be combined in the Fourth Gospel and the Gospel of Peter. We must not disguise from ourselves the difficulties which this solution leaves. The most serious of these are caused by the command of Lk 24⁴⁹, and the contracted space within which we shall have to compress the events in Galilee. We have only 40 days to dispose of, in all, if we accept the traditional date of the Ascension,—and even if we regarded this as a round number, the nearness of the Day of Pentecost would allow us very little more margin. From these Forty Days we should have to take off a week at the beginning on account of Jn 20²⁶. And if, as we reasonably may, we suppose that there has been some *foreshortening* in Lk 24³⁶⁻⁵³, and that two or three distinct occasions are treated as if they were continuous, we should still, to find a place for the injunction to wait in

Jerus., have to cut off another like period at the end. That would leave not much more than three weeks for the retirement to Galilee and return to Jerus.—a length of time which cannot be pronounced wholly insufficient, but which does not fit in quite naturally with the way in which the apostles are described in Jn 21³ as returning to their ordinary occupations. These difficulties would be avoided if we could regard *the* Day of Pentecost as that of the following year ; but any such hypothesis would conflict with Ac 1³, and the interval implied in Jn 21¹⁴ * is also a short one.

Whichever way we turn difficulties meet us, which the documents to which we have access do not enable us to remove. We have said enough as to the nature of these documents, and of the lines of tradition to which they give expression. It is not what we could wish, but what we have. And no difficulty of weaving the separate incidents into an orderly well-compacted narrative can impugn the unanimous belief of the Church which lies behind them, that the Lord Jesus Christ rose from the dead on the third day and appeared to the disciples.

(3) *Attempted Explanations.* — This universal belief is the root fact which has to be accounted for. It would be the natural product of a real event such as the Epistles assume and the Gospels describe. But what if the event were not real? In that case the widely held and deeply planted belief in it must needs constitute a very serious problem.

In the present century a succession of efforts have been made to account for the belief in the Resurrection without accepting it as a fact. Many of the hypotheses put forward with this object may be regarded as practically obsolete and abandoned. No one now believes that the supposed death was really only a swoon, and that the body laid in the tomb afterwards revived, and was seen more than once by the disciples (on this see a trenchant sentence by Strauss, *Leben Jesu*, 1863, p. 298, end of paragraph). Equally inadmissible is the hypothesis of fraud—that the body was really taken away by Joseph of Arimathæa or Nicodemus, and that the rumour was allowed to grow that Jesus was risen. The lingering trace of this which survives in Renan, *Les Apôtres*, ed. 13, p. 16 ('ceux qui savaient le secret de la disposition du corps') is thrown in quite by the way as a subordinate detail.

More persistent is the theory of 'visions.' This has been presented in different forms, assigning the leading part now to one and now to another of the disciples. Renan, who goes his own way among critics, sees in this part of the narrative a marked superiority of the Fourth Gospel (*Les Apôtres*, p. 9). In accordance with it he refers the beginning of the series to Mary Magdalene (cf. Strauss, *Leben Jesu*, 1863, p. 309). A woman out of whom had been cast 'seven devils' might well, he thinks, have been thrown into a state of nervous tension and excitement which would give form and substance to the creations of fancy. And when once the report had got abroad that the Lord had been seen, it would be natural for others to suppose that they saw Him. Strauss and Pfleiderer (*Giff. Lect.* pp. 112, 149) start rather from the case of St. Paul. Both lay stress upon the fact that he places the appearance to himself on a level with those to the older disciples. His own vision they would agree in explaining as due to a species of epileptic seizure, and the others they would regard

as equally subjective, though led up to by different trains of psychological preparation.

It is at this point that some of the best attested details of the Resurrection interpose difficulties. To carry through a consistent theory of visions, two conditions are necessary. (*a*) If they arose, as Strauss supposes, from affectionate dwelling upon the personality of Jesus, combined with reflexion upon certain passages of OT (Ps 16¹⁰, Is 53¹⁰⁻¹²), it follows, almost of necessity, that we must also with Strauss throw over the tradition of the 'third day,' and regard the belief as the outcome of a somewhat prolonged process—a process spread over weeks and months rather than days. (*b*) On the other hand, if we must discard the tradition as to the beginning of the appearances, we must equally discard that as to their end. The wave of feverish enthusiasm to which on this hypothesis they owed their origin, certainly would not have subsided in the interval between Passover and Pentecost. We note, as it is, an ascending scale in the appearances—they occur first to individuals (Mary Magdalene, Peter, the Emmaus disciples), then to the Ten and the Eleven, then to the Five Hundred. We can see how one appearance prepares the way for another. St. Peter (*e.g.*) must have been present at three or four. With this increasing weight of testimony, and increasing predisposition in the minds of the disciples, we should naturally expect that the appearance to the Five Hundred would contain within itself the germs of an indefinite series. We should not have been surprised if the whole body alike of Christians and of half Christians had caught the contagion. But that is not the case. There is just the single appearance to James ; and then—the vision of St. Paul standing rather by itself—with one more appearance to the assembled apostles, the list comes to what seems an abrupt end.

This description of the facts rests on excellent evidence. The 'third day' is hardly less firmly rooted in the tradition of the Church than the Resurrection itself. We have it not only in the speech ascribed to St. Peter (Ac 10⁴⁰), but in the central testimony of St. Paul, and then in the oldest form of the Apostles' Creed. It is strange that so slight a detail should have been preserved at all, and still stranger that it should hold the place it does in the standard of the Church's faith. We must needs regard it as original. And for the circumscribed area of the appearances, we have at once the positive evidence of the canonical documents, and a remarkable silence on the part of the extra-canonical.

These phenomena are difficult to reconcile with a theory of purely subjective visions. An honest inquirer like Keim felt the difficulty so strongly that, while regarding the appearances as essentially of the nature of visions, he held them to be not merely subjective, but divinely caused, for the express purpose of creating the belief in which they issued.

This is the least that must be asserted. A belief that has had such incalculably momentous results must have had an adequate cause. No apparition, no mere hallucination of the senses ever yet moved the world. But we may doubt whether the theory, even as Keim presents it, is adequate or really called for. It belongs to the process of so trimming down the elements that we call supernatural in the Gospel narratives as to bring them within the limits of everyday experience. But that process, we must needs think, has failed. The facts are too obstinate, the evidence for them is too strong ; and the measures which we apply are too narrow and bounded. It is better to keep substantially the form which a sound tradition has handed down to

---

* The numbering of this Galilæan appearance as the 'third' might seem to be at variance with St. Paul's list in 1 Co 15 ; but it is clear that the appearances which St. John enumerates were those to the body of 'the disciples' (*i.e.* primarily, to a group including the apostles). He himself does not count that to Mary Magdalene ; nor would he have counted those to St. Peter or the Emmaus travellers.

us, even though its contents in some degree pass our comprehension.

(4) *The Permanent Significance of the Resurrection.*—The innermost nature of the Resurrection is hidden from us. And if we ask why the supreme proof that God had visited His people took this particular form, the answer we can give is but partial. Some things, however, seem to stand out clearly.

(*a*) In the first place it is obvious that the idea of a resurrection was present to men's minds. Herod thought that the works of Jesus were works of the Baptist restored to life (Mk 6[14. 16]‖). Men were quite prepared to see Elijah or some other of the ancient prophets reappear upon the scene (Mk 9[11-13] ‖, Jn 1[21]). In Palestine and among the circles in which Christianity arose, no mark of special divine indwelling seemed at the time so natural. The belief had not been allowed to grow up without a reason.

For (*b*) from the very first the ideas of bodily and spiritual resurrection were closely intertwined together. Perhaps the oldest passage in which there is a hint of such an idea is the vision of Ezekiel (ch. 37); and there the revivification of the body is the symbol of a spiritual revival. This intimate connexion of bodily and spiritual is never lost sight of in Christianity.

(*c*) 'Die to live' is one of the most fundamental of Christian principles, and this principle is embodied once for all in the Resurrection. If the one side was 'placarded' before the eyes of the world (Gal 3[1]) in the Crucifixion, the Resurrection was a no less signal manifestation of the other. There is a double strain of inference and application.

(*d*) On the one hand, the Resurrection of Christ was the pledge and earnest of physical resurrection and the life beyond the grave. St. Paul founds upon it the hope of immortality (1 Th 4[14], Ro 8[34], 1 Co 6[14] 15[12ff.], 2 Co 4[14] etc.).

(*e*) But he equally founds upon it the most earnest exhortations to holiness of life. It is not only that this follows for the Christian as a duty: if his relation to Christ is a right relation, it is included in it as a necessity (Ro 6[3-6]). St. Paul can hardly think of the physical Resurrection apart from the spiritual. And there is a very similar vein in the teaching of St. John (Jn 5[24], 1 Jn 3[14]). The Resurrection is the corner-stone of Christian mysticism.

(*f*) In another aspect, as a divine act, the crowning mark of divine approval, it is a necessary complement of the Crucifixion. It supplies the proof, which the world might desiderate, that the Sacrifice of the Cross was accepted. If the death of the Cross was a dying for human sin, the rising again from the tomb was the seal of forgiveness and justification (Ro 4[25], cf. 6[7]). St. Paul saw in it an assurance that the doors of the divine mercy were thrown open wide; and to St. Peter in like manner it was through it that mankind was begotten again to a 'lively hope' (1 P 1[3]).

All this mass of biblical teaching hangs together. If the Resurrection was a reality it has a solid nucleus, which would be wanting even to the theory of objective visions. The economy which begins with a physical Incarnation, naturally and appropriately ends with a physical Resurrection. Thus much we can see, though we may feel that this is not all.

Literature.—Besides the recent literature mentioned above (among which the paper by Dr. Loofs deserves rather special attention), and besides the treatment of the subject in numerous works on the Gospel History and on Apologetics, it is well to remember two monographs in English—Dr. Westcott's *Gospel of the Resurrection* (first pub. in 1866), and the late Dr. Milligan's *The Resurrection of our Lord* (first pub. in 1881).

vi. The Ascension.—The Resurrection in itself was incomplete. It was not the goal, but the way to the goal. The goal was the return of the Son to the Father, with His mission accomplished, His work done.

(1) The apostolic writers unanimously represent this return as a triumph. The keynote is struck in the speech which is put into the mouth of St. Peter on the day of Pentecost * (Ac 2[33-36]). It would seem that the form of expression which the conception assumed was influenced largely by Ps 110[1], a passage to which attention had been drawn by our Lord Himself shortly before His departure, and which spontaneously recurred to the mind as soon as the nature of His return to the Father had declared itself. Along with this would be recalled the saying with which our Lord had answered the challenge of the high priest (Mk 14[62] ‖). Psalm and saying alike represented the Messiah as seated 'at the right hand' of the Most High. This phrase appears to have at once (in the forms ἐκ δεξιῶν and ἐν δεξιᾷ) established itself in the language of the primitive Church: it occurs repeatedly, not only in the Acts (7[55f.]) and in the Pauline Epp., but in He, 1 P, and Rev; and, like the detail of the 'third day,' it occupies a fixed place in the Apostles' Creed.

The speech of St. Peter culminates in the declaration, 'Let all the house of Israel know assuredly, that God hath made him, whom ye crucified, both Lord and Christ' (Ac 2[36]); and it is substantially a paraphrase of this when in a famous passage St. Paul, after speaking of the humiliation of the Christ, adds, 'Wherefore also God highly exalted him, and gave unto him the name which is above every name, that in the name of Jesus every knee should bow,' etc. (Ph 2[9f.]). The return of the Son to the Father was not merely the resumption of a previous state of glory (Jn 6[62] 17[5] etc.), it was the resumption of it with the added approval and recognition which His obedience unto death had called forth. We speak of these things κατὰ ἄνθρωπον; or rather, we are content to echo in regard to them the language of the apostles and of the first Christians, who themselves spoke κατὰ ἄνθρωπον. The reality lies behind the veil.

(2) How did our Lord Jesus Christ enter upon this state of exaltation? Now that we have before us corrected texts of the Gospels, it would seem to be probable that they did not give an answer to this question. The answer was reserved for the second volume which St. Luke addressed to Theophilus; it forms the opening section of the Acts of the Apostles.

Mk 16[19] belongs to the Appendix to the Gospel, which we have seen (p. 638 f. *sup.*) to have been probably composed, not by St. Mark himself, but by the presbyter Aristion in the early years of the 2nd cent. The reading of Lk 24[51] stands thus—

Καὶ ἀνεφέρετο εἰς τὸν οὐρανόν, א[c] ABCLXΔΔΑΠ, etc., c f q Vulg. Syrr. (Pesh.-Harcl.-Hier.) *rell.*, Cyr-Alex. Aug. 1/2.

Om. א*D, a b e ff[2] Syr.-Sin., Aug. 1/2.

This means that the omission of the words is a primitive Western reading, which in this case is probably right: it was a natural gloss to explain the parting of the Lord from the disciples of the Ascension; there was no similar temptation to omit the words if genuine.

In Ac 1[1-11] the final separation is described as an 'ascent unto heaven.' When the last instructions had been given, the disciples saw their Lord 'taken up (ἐπήρθη) and a cloud received him out of their sight.' The over-arching sky is a standing symbol for the abode of God; and the return of the Son to the Father was naturally represented as a retreat

* When we ask how these early discourses were transmitted to the writer of the Acts, there is a natural reluctance to use them too strictly as representing the exact words spoken. And yet, taken as a whole, they fit in singularly well to the order of development and the thought of the primitive community, which has an antecedent verisimilitude and accords well with indications in the Pauline Epistles.

within its blue recesses, the ethereal home of light and glory. It is sometimes necessary that a symbol should be acted as well as written or spoken. The disciples were aware of a vanishing, and they knew that their Lord must be where His Father was.

That the narrative in the Acts is not a myth seems proved by an authentic little touch which it contains, a veritable reminiscence of what we may be sure was their real attitude at the moment, though it soon ceased to be. When they asked, ' Lord, dost thou at this time restore the kingdom to Israel ?' their thoughts were still running in the groove of the old Jewish expectation. It is the last trace of them that we have in this naïve form.

(3) From the point of view of Christian doctrine, for those who not only accept the facts of the life of Christ but the construction put on those facts by the writers of NT, the main stress of the Ascension lies upon the state to which it forms the entrance. (a) It is the guarantee for the continued existence of Him who became incarnate for our sakes. (b) It not only guarantees His continued existence, but the continued effect of His work. It puts the seal of the divine approval upon all that the Incarnation accomplished. It is the final confirmation of the lessons of the Baptism and of the Transfiguration, 'This is my beloved Son, in whom I am well pleased.' (c) The primitive phrase 'at the right hand of God' describes as nearly and as simply as human language can describe the double truth that Christ still is and that His work still is, that the Incarnation was no transient episode, but a permanent and decisive factor in the dealing of God with man. (d) This truth is stated in other words in the doctrine of the High Priesthood of Christ, a doctrine implicitly contained in many places in the writings of St. Paul, and worked out with great clearness and fulness in Ep. to Hebrews. There is something in the relation of the exalted Son to the Father and to His Church corresponding to and that may be expressed in terms of the functions of the earthly high priest in relation to God and to Israel. The great High Priest presents the prayers of His people ; He intercedes for them ; He 'pleads' or 'presents' His own sacrifice. Only, when we use this language it should be remembered that we are not speaking of 'specific acts done or words spoken by Christ in His glory. His glorified presence is an eternal presentation ; He pleads by what He is' (Moberly, *Ministerial Priesthood*, p. 246 n.).

LITERATURE.—Dr. Milligan left a volume on the Ascension as a pendant to that on the Resurrection (*Baird Lectures* for 1891), which is the most comprehensive treatment of the subject in English.

III. SUPPLEMENTAL MATTER : THE NATIVITY AND INFANCY.—Throughout His public ministry Jesus passed for the son of Joseph and Mary, two peasants of Nazareth. Some of those who were present at the long discourse in the synagogue at Capernaum expressed their astonishment at the high pretensions which it seemed to contain, by asking, 'Is not this Jesus, the son of Joseph, whose father and mother we know ?' (Jn 6⁴ ; cf. 1⁴⁵). The inhabitants of Nazareth appear to have put a similar question when He came and preached there. The exact words are somewhat differently transmitted. Mk 6³ has (in the better attested text), 'Is not this the carpenter ?' Mt 13⁵⁵ 'Is not this the carpenter's son ?' Lk 4²³ a passage which, although divergent, contains reminiscences of the same original, has still more directly, 'Is not this Joseph's son ?' In the preliminary chapters the same evangelist speaks repeatedly of ' his parents' (γονεῖς, Lk 2²⁷·⁴¹·⁴³). And not only does he himself resolve this into ' his father and his mother' (2³³),

but he makes the mother of Jesus say, 'Thy father and I sought thee sorrowing' (2⁴⁸).

It is in keeping with this language that both the First and the Third Gospels place in their forefront genealogies of Jesus, which, in spite of many attempts to prove the contrary, must be admitted to trace His descent through Joseph and not through Mary.

Yet, on the other hand, the same two Gospels, though differing widely in the details of the narrative, assert unequivocally that Joseph had no share in the parentage of Jesus, and that the place of a human father was taken by the direct action of the Spirit of God. The differences show that the two traditions are independent of each other ; and yet both converge upon this one point. They agree not only in representing Jesus as born of a virgin, but also in representing this fact as supernaturally announced beforehand,—in the one case to Joseph, in the other case to Mary.

What account is to be given of these seeming inconsistencies ? We cannot get rid of them by assigning the opposed statements to different sources. In St. Matthew the genealogy which ends in Joseph is followed immediately by the narrative of the Annunciation and Virgin-Birth. In St. Luke the successive sections of ch. 2, which begins with the Nativity and ends with the scene of the boy Jesus in the Temple, where we have seen that such expressions as 'his parents,' 'his father and mother' occur so freely, are linked together by the recurrent note, 'Mary kept all these sayings, pondering them in her heart,' 'his mother kept all these sayings in her heart' (Lk 2¹⁹·⁵¹ ; cf. also the argument which Prof. Ramsay skilfully draws from 1⁸⁰ 2⁴⁰·⁵² *). And when we turn to St. John we cannot but remember that the Gospel which records so frankly the Jews' question, 'Is not this Jesus, the son of Joseph, whose father and mother we know ?' if it nowhere refers directly to the Virgin-Birth, yet goes further than any other Gospel in asserting the pre-existence of the Son as God with God.

What we regard as inconsistent will clear itself up best if we consider the order of events and the way in which these preliminary stages of the history were gradually brought to the consciousness of the Church.

The sources from which the knowledge of them was derived were, without doubt, private.† We shall consider presently the character of these sources. We know more about that of which use was made by St. Luke than of that used by St. Matthew, and we can rely upon it as a historical authority with greater confidence. We shall see that it is ultimately traceable to the Virgin herself, in all probability through the little circle of women who were for some time in her company.

We are told expressly that the Virgin Mary 'kept all these sayings (or things) in her heart.' She, if any one, might well say, μυστήριον ἐμὸν ἐμοί. It was only by slow degrees in the intimacy of confidential intercourse that she allowed her secret to pass beyond herself, and to become known. Even if committed to writing before it came into the hands of St. Luke, it probably did not reach any wide public until it was embodied in his Gospel. The place which the Virgin-Birth occupies in Ignatius and in the Creed seems to

* *Was Christ born at Bethlehem?* p. 87.
† 'Luke gives, from knowledge gained within the family, an account of facts known only to the family, and in part to the Mother alone' (Ramsay, *op. cit.* p. 79). Prof. Ramsay, however, seems to go too far in contrasting Mt with Lk when he says, 'Matthew gives the public account, that which was generally known during the Saviour's life and after His death.' We do not think that any account was known during the Saviour's life, and we prefer to think of the Matthæan version as parallel to rather than contrasted with the Lucan.

show that it cannot have been much later than the middle of the century before the knowledge of it made its way to the headquarters of Christianity. But before some such date as that there is no reason to think that it was generally known. It was no part of our Lord's own teaching. The neighbours among whom His early life was passed, the changing crowds who witnessed His miracles or gathered round Him to hear Him, had never had it proclaimed to them. 'Jesus son of Joseph, the prophet of Nazareth,' was the common name by which He was known. And it is a great presumption of the historical truth of the Gospels that they so simply and naturally reflect this language. We may well believe that the language was shared, as the ignorance which caused it was shared, even by the Twelve themselves. It would be very fitting if the channel through which these sacred things first came to the ears of the Church was a little group of women.*

i. *The Sources of the Narrative.*—It has often been observed that whereas the first two chapters of St. Matthew appear to be written from the point of view of Joseph, the first two chapters of St. Luke are written from the point of view of Mary. In Mt the Annunciation is made to Joseph; it is Joseph who is bidden in a dream not to fear to take to him his wife; Joseph who is told what the Son whom she is to bear is to be called. It is Joseph, again, who is warned to take the young Child and His mother into Egypt, and who, when the danger is past, receives the command to return; and it is Joseph also whose anxious care is the cause that the family settle in Galilee and not in Judæa. On the other hand, when we turn to St. Luke the prominent figures at first are the two kinswomen, Elisabeth the mother of John the Baptist, and Mary. Mary herself receives the announcement of the holy thing that is to be born of her. The *Magnificat* is her song of thanksgiving. She treasures in her heart the sayings of the shepherds and of her Divine Son. The aged Simeon points his prophecy to her, and foretells that a sword should pierce through her soul.

In regard to the Matthæan document we are in the dark. The curious gravitation of statement towards Joseph has a reason; but beyond this there is not much that we can say. It would not follow that the immediate source of the narrative was very near his person. In the case of Lk we can see farther down the vista. We have already had grounds for connecting the source from which he draws ultimately with the Mother of Jesus. Through what channel did it reach the evangelist? Probably through one of the women

* 'If we are right in this view as to Luke's authority, and as to the way in which that authority reached him, viz. by oral communication, it appears that either the Virgin was still living when Luke was in Palestine during the years 57 and 58 . . . or Luke had conversed with some one very intimate with her, who knew her heart and could give him what was almost as good as first-hand information. Beyond that we cannot safely go; but yet one may venture to state the impression—though it may be generally considered fanciful—that the intermediary, if one existed, is more likely to have been a woman than a man. There is a womanly spirit in the whole narrative, which seems inconsistent with the transmission from man to man, and which, moreover, is an indication of Luke's character; he had a marked sympathy with women' (Ramsay, *op. cit.* p. 88). In view of the close resemblance between much that appears in the text and Prof. Ramsay's admirable chapter, it is perhaps right to explain that this had not been read at the time when the text was written, and that it represents an opinion formed long ago. The question as to whether the source was written or oral is left open, because there is reason to think that St. Luke used a special (written) source which may have been connected with the women mentioned below, and through them with the Virgin Mary. The writer could not speak quite so confidently as Prof. Ramsay as to the nearness of this source to the Virgin, but he does not think that it could be more than two or three degrees removed from her. It must have been near enough to retain the fine touches which Prof. Ramsay so well brings out.

mentioned in Lk 8⁸ 24¹⁰; and as Joanna is the least known of the group, and therefore the most likely to drop out for any one not personally acquainted with her, perhaps we may say, by preference, through her (cf. p. 639 *sup.*). We learn from Jn 19²⁵ (cf. Ac 1¹⁴) that the Mother of Jesus was thrown into contact with this group,—perhaps not for any great length of time, but yet for a time that may well have been sufficiently long for the purpose. And we believe that thus the secret of what had passed came to be disclosed to a sympathetic ear.

Such an inference, if sound, would invest the contents of these chapters with high authority. Without enlarging more on this, we may perhaps be allowed to refer in confirmation to what has been already said as to the appropriateness of the picture given of the kind of circle in which Christ was born, and in which His birth was most spontaneously greeted (see p. 608 above). It was just the Symeons and Annas, the Elisabeths and Zachariahs, who were the natural adherents of such a Messiah as Jesus. And the phrases used to describe them are beautifully appropriate to the time and circumstances, 'looking for the consolation of Israel,' 'looking for the redemption of Jerusalem' (Lk 2²⁵·³⁸).

The elaborate and courageous attempt of Resch (*TU* iv. Heft 3, 1897) to reconstruct, even to the point of restoring the Hebrew original, a *Kindheits-evangelium*, which shall embrace the whole of the first two chapters of Lk and Mt with some extra-canonical parallels, is on the face of it a paradox, and, although no doubt containing useful matter, has not made converts.

ii. *The Text of Mt* 1¹⁶.—Within recent years certain phenomena have come to light in the text of the first chapter of St. Matthew which demand consideration in their bearing upon this part of our subject.

The peculiarities of the Curetonian Syriac, the (so-called) Ferrar group, and some MSS of the Old Latin, had been known for some time, but in themselves they did not seem of very great importance. A new and somewhat startling element was introduced by the publication of the Sinai-Syriac in 1894. More recently still a further authority has appeared, which contains the eccentric reading. This is the curious dialogue published by Mr. F. C. Conybeare under the names of *Timothy and Aquila* (Oxford, 1898). It professes to be a public debate between a Christian and a Jew held in the time of Cyril of Alexandria (A.D. 412-444), and it is in the main a string of *testimonia* commonly adduced in the Jewish controversy. It is a question how far some of this material comes from a work older than the date assigned. The criticism of the dialogue has been acutely treated by Mr. Conybeare, but the subject needs further examination. We will set forth the evidence at length, and then make some remarks upon it.

Mt 1¹⁶ Ἰακὼβ δὲ ἐγέννησεν τὸν Ἰωσὴφ τὸν ἄνδρα Μαρίας, ἐξ ἧς ἐγεννήθη Ἰησοῦς ὁ λεγόμενος Χριστός, Codd. Græc. unc. qui exstant omn. minusc. quamplur. Verss. (incl. f ff₂, def. l), cf. Dial. Tim. et Aq. fol. 113 r°.

'Ἰακὼβ δὲ ἐγέννησεν τὸν Ἰωσήφ, ᾧ μνηστευθεῖσα παρθένος Μαριὰμ ἐγέννησεν Ἰησοῦν τὸν λεγόμενος Χριστόν, 346-826-828 (auctore K. Lake, def. 13-69); cui desponsata virgo (om. q) Maria genuit Jesum qui dicitur (vocatur g, q), Christus a g, q, cf. Dial. Tim. et Aq. fol. 93 v°.

Similiter, cui desponsata virgo Maria genuit (peperit d) Jesum Christum (om. τὸν λεγόμ., Christum Jesum d) d k Syr.-Cur.

Jacob autem genuit Joseph, cui desponsata erat virgo Maria : virgo autem Maria genuit Jesum b (cf. c).

'Ἰακὼβ ἐγέννησεν τὸν Ἰωσὴφ τὸν ἄνδρα Μαρίας, ἐξ ἧς ἐγεννήθη Ἰησοῦς ὁ λεγόμενος Χριστός· καὶ Ἰωσὴφ ἐγέννησεν τὸν Ἰησοῦν τὸν λεγόμενον Χριστόν, Dial. Tim. et Aq. fol. 93 r°.

'Ἰακὼβ ἐγένν. τὸν Ἰωσήφ. Ἰωσήφ, ᾧ ἐμνηστεύθη παρθένος Μαριάμ, ἐγέννησεν Ἰησοῦν τὸν λεγόμενον Χριστόν, Syr.-Sin.

The eccentric readings all occur within the range of the so-called Western text, and there is no doubt that they belong to a very early stage in the history of that text. Two opposite tendencies appear to have been at work, which are most conspicuously represented in ancient forms of the Syriac Version, though the original in each case was probably Greek.

On the one hand there was a tendency to emphasize the virginity of Mary, and to remove expressions which seemed in any way to conflict with this. For the blunt phrase, 'Joseph her husband,' the Curetonian Syriac with the oldest Latin authorities substitutes, 'Joseph to whom was espoused'—not only 'Mary,' but 'the Virgin Mary.' A little lower down (with Tatian's *Diatessaron*, for 'Joseph her husband being a just man' (ὁ ἀνὴρ αὐτῆς δίκαιος ὤν) it reads 'Joseph being a just man' (ἀνὴρ δίκ. ὤν). In v.²⁰ for 'thy wife' it has 'thine espoused.' In v.²⁴, again with Tatian, it has some such softened phrase as 'he dwelt chastely with her,' and for 'took his wife' it has 'took Mary'; and in v.²⁵ (but here in agreement with אBZ al.) it has simply 'brought forth a son,'—not 'her first-born son.'

In some of these readings, or parts of them, the Sinai-Syriac agrees, but along with them it has others which seem to be of a directly opposite tendency. The most prominent is, of course, 'Joseph begat Jesus,' in v.¹⁶. We might have thought that this was an accident due to the influence on the mind of the scribe of the repeated ἐγέννησεν of the previous verses ; but in v.²¹ the same MS has 'bear thee a son,' and in v.²⁵ 'she bore him a son'; and in Lk 2⁵ there is a counter change to that of the Curetonian in v.²⁰ ('with Mary his wife' for 'Mary his espoused'); all which readings hang together, and appear to be distinctly anti-ascetic. And now the singular reading in v.¹⁶ has found a coincidence in the conflate text of one of the quotations in the *Dialogue of Timothy and Aquila*.

It is of course true that both these authorities—the Sinai-Syriac and the *Dialogue*—are very far from thoroughgoing. The Syriac text has not tampered in any way with the explicit language of vv.¹⁸·²⁰ ; and—what is especially strange—in the very act of combining Ἰωσήφ with ἐγέννησεν it inserts a large fragment of the Curetonian reading (ᾧ ἐμνηστεύθη παρθένος Μαριάμ) substituted for τὸν ἄνδρα Μαρίας. On the other hand, the peculiar reading occurs in one only out of three quotations in the dialogue, and there in the form ʼof a conflation with the common text. But is it the case that these authorities point to some form of reading older than any of those now extant, which made Joseph the father of Jesus ? There would be a further question, whether, supposing that such a reading existed, it formed any part of the text of our present Gospel ?

There would seem to be three main possibilities. (*a*) The genealogy may in the first instance have had an existence independently of the Gospel, and it may have been incorporated with it by the editor of the whole. In that case it is quite conceivable that the genealogy may have ended Ἰωσὴφ δὲ ἐγέννησεν τὸν Ἰησοῦν. Unless it were composed by someone very intimate indeed with the Holy Family, it might well reflect the current state of popular opinion in the first half of the apostolic age. (*b*) The reading might be the result of textual corruption. There would always be a natural tendency in the minds of scribes to assimilate mechanically the last links in the genealogy to preceding links. A further confusion might easily arise from the ambiguous sense of the word γεννᾶν, which was used of the mother as well as of the father (cf. Gal 4²⁴). If we suppose that the original text ran, Ἰωσὴφ τὸν ἄνδρα Μαρίας ἣ ἐγέννησεν Ἰησοῦν τὸν λεγόμενον Χριστόν, that would perhaps account for the two divergent lines of variants better than any other. A reading like this appears to lie behind the Coptic (Bohairic) Version. (*c*) It is conceivable that the reading (or group of readings) in Syr.-Sin. may be of definitely Ebionite origin. That which we call 'heresy' existed in so many shades, and was often so little consistent with itself, that it would be no decisive argument against this hypothesis that the sense of the readings is contradicted by the immediate context. It would be enough for the scribe to have had Ebionite leanings, and he may have thought of natural and supernatural generation as not mutually exclusive. We can only note these possibilities ; the data do not allow us to decide absolutely between them.

LITERATURE.—The fullest discussion of this subject took place in a lengthy correspondence in *The Academy*, towards the end of 1894 and beginning of 1895.

iii. **The Genealogies.**—At the time when it was thought necessary at all costs to bring one biblical statement into visible harmony with another, two hypotheses were in favour for reconciling the genealogy of our Lord preserved in Mt 1¹⁻¹⁷ with that in Lk 3²³⁻³⁸. These were (*a*) the hypothesis of adoption or levirate marriage, according to which the actual descent might differ at several points from the legal descent, so that there might be two equally valid genealogies running side by side ; and (*b*) the hypothesis that the one genealogy might be that of Joseph, as the reputed father of Jesus, and the other genealogy (preferably St. Luke's) that of Mary. A certain handle seemed

to be given for this latter supposition by the tradition which was said to be found in the Talmud (tr. *Chagig.* 77, col. 4, Meyer-Weiss), that Mary was the daughter of Eli. [This statement appears to be founded on a mistake, and should be given up ; see G. A. Cooke in Gore, *Dissertations*, p. 39 f.]. It was felt, however, that this view could only be maintained by straining the text of the Gospel ; and it is now generally (though not quite universally) agreed that both genealogies belong to Joseph. On the other hand, the theory of levirate marriage or adoption, though no doubt a possible explanation, left too much the impression of being coined to meet the difficulty. The criticism of to-day prefers to leave the two genealogies side by side as independent attempts to supply the desiderated proof of Davidic descent. Were they the work of our present evangelists, or do they go back beyond them ? Both genealogies appear to have in common a characteristic which may point to opposite conclusions as to their origin. That in the First Gospel bears upon its face its artificial structure. The evangelist himself points out (Mt 1¹⁷) that it is arranged on three groups of fourteen generations, though these groups are obtained by certain deliberate omissions. That would be, in his case, consistent with other peculiarities of his Gospel : he evidently shared the Jewish fondness for artificial arrangements of numbers (Sir John Hawkins, *Horæ Synopticæ*, p. 131 ff.). From this fact we might infer that the stem of descent had been drawn up by himself from the OT and perhaps some local tradition. If such tradition came to him in writing, the list might still conceivably have ended in some such way as that which is found in the Sinai-Syriac, though if the list was first committed to writing in the Gospel the probability that it did so would be considerably diminished.

It would seem that a like artificial arrangement (77 generations = 7 × 11) underlies the genealogy in Lk. But as this is not in the manner of the Third Evangelist, and as he does not appear to be conscious of this feature in his list, it would be more probable that he found it ready to his hand. In that case it would be natural that it should come from the same source as chs. 1. 2, which would invest the genealogy with the high authority of those chapters. We cannot speak too confidently, but the conclusion is at least spontaneously suggested by the facts.

iv. **The Census of Quirinius.**—Until a very short time ago the best review of the whole question of the Census of Quirinius (Lk 2¹⁻⁵) was that by Schürer in *NTZG* § 17, Anhang 1 (*HJP* I. ii. 105 ff.). This was based upon a survey of the whole previous literature of the subject, and was really judicial, if somewhat severely critical, in its tone. As distinct from the school of Baur, which was always ready to sacrifice the Christian tradition to its own reconstruction of the history, Dr. Schürer is an excellent representative of that more cautious method of inquiry which carefully collects the data and draws its conclusions with no prepossession in favour of the biblical writers if also without prejudice against them. In the present instance he summed up rather adversely to the statements in St. Luke ; and in the state of historical knowledge at the time when he wrote (1890), that he should do so was upon his principles not surprising.

According to St. Luke, our Lord was born at Bethlehem on the occasion of a general 'enrolment' (ἀπο-γραφή) ordered by the emperor Augustus and carried out in Palestine under Quirinius as governor of Syria. The date was fixed as being before the death of Herod, which took place in B.C. 4 ; and it was explained that Joseph and Mary, as belonging to the lineage of David, had gone up to enter their names at Bethlehem, David's city.

There were several points in this statement which seemed to invite criticism. (i.) In the first place, there was no other evidence that Augustus ever ordered a general census of the empire, although there was good reason to think that he took pains to collect statistics in regard to it. (ii.) Even if he had ordered such a census, it seemed doubtful whether it would be carried out in a kingdom which possessed such a degree of independence as Judæa. And (iii.) if it had been conducted in the Roman manner, there would have been no necessity for Joseph and Mary to leave their usual place of residence. Further, (iv.) while it was allowed, on the strength of a well-known inscription, that Quirinius probably twice held office in Syria, yet, as it was known that Sentius Saturninus was governor B.C. 9–7, and Quinctilius Varus at least B.C. 7–4, it was argued that Quirinius' first term of office could not be before B.C. 3–1, i.e. after the death of Herod. (v.) As there was, in any case, a census of Judæa conducted by Quirinius after its annexation by the Romans in A.D. 6, it was thought that St. Luke had a confused recollection of this, and antedated it (in the Gospel, though not in Ac 5³⁷) to the lifetime of Herod.

The chief authority for the census of A.D. 6 is Josephus; and an eminent German scholar, Dr. Th. Zahn, put forward in 1893 the view that it was Josephus who was at fault in dating from this year an event which really fell in B.C. 4–3 (*Neue Kirchliche Zeitschrift*, pp. 633–654). This brought the data more nearly, though still not entirely, into agreement with St. Luke. The theory need not, however, be more fully considered as it has not met with acceptance, and there can be little doubt that it seeks a solution of the difficulties in the wrong direction.

There was one little expression which might have given pause to the critics of St. Luke, viz. his careful insertion of the word 'first' ('the first enrolment made when Q. was governor of Syria'). It might have shown that he was in possession of special knowledge which would not permit him to confuse the earlier census with that of A.D. 6. And yet the existence of the earlier census remained without confirmation, until it suddenly received it from a quarter which might have been described as unexpected if experience did not show that there is hardly anything that may not be found there—the rubbish heaps of papyrus fragments in Egypt.

Almost at the same time, in the year when Dr. Zahn made his ingenious but unsuccessful attempt (1893), three scholars, one English and two German, made the discovery that periodical enrolments (ἀπογραφαί) were held in Egypt under the Roman empire, and that they came round in a fourteen-year cycle. The proof of this was at first produced for the enrolments of A.D. 90, 104, 118, 132, and onwards; but in rapid succession the list was carried back to A.D. 76, 62, and 20.

This gave the clue, which was almost at once seized, and the whole problem worked out afresh in masterly fashion by Prof. W. M. Ramsay, first in two articles in *Exp.* 1897, and then in his volume, *Was Christ born at Bethlehem? A Study in the Credibility of St. Luke* (London, 1898). It would be too much to say that every detail is absolutely verified. The age of Augustus as compared with that which precedes and with that which follows is strangely obscure, and the authorities for it defective. But considering this, the sequence of argument which Prof. Ramsay unfolds is remarkably clear and attractive. (i.) He shows it to be very probable that there was a series of periodical enrolments initiated by Augustus at the time when he first received the tribunician power, and his reign formally began in B.C. 23 (this is the official date usual in inscriptions,

p. 140). (ii.) He also makes it probable that this was part of a deliberate and general policy—that the census-takings were not confined to Egypt, but extended to other parts of the empire, and more particularly to Syria. Here, too, there was a tendency to periodic recurrence, though the evidence is not, and is not likely to be, so complete as in the case of Egypt. (iii.) He has shown that Palestine was regarded as part of the 'Roman world,' i.e. of the empire. Though Herod had the liberty of a *rex socius*, the Roman power and the emperor's will were always in the background; he had to see that the whole Jewish people took an oath of allegiance to the emperor; he could not make war without being called to account; he could not determine his own successor or put to death his own son without an appeal to Rome; in a moment of anger Augustus threatened that whereas he had hitherto treated him (Herod) as a friend, he would henceforth treat him as a subject (Jos. *Ant.* XVI. ix. 3). It was therefore likely enough that Herod would wish, if he was not positively ordered, to fall in with the imperial policy by taking a census of his people, as another subject king did in Cilicia in A.D. 35. (iv.) But although Herod held a census at the instance of Augustus, it would be in keeping with his whole character and conduct to temper it to Jewish tastes as much as possible; and he would do this by following the national custom of numbering the people by their tribes and families. This was the broad distinction between this enrolment of Herod's and the subsequent census of A.D. 6 or 7. The latter was carried out by Roman officials and in the Roman manner, which was the real cause of the offence which it gave, and of the armed resistance which it excited. (v.) Some uncertainty still hangs over the mention of Quirinius. Mommsen thought that he was the acting *legatus* of Syria in B.C. 3–1. Prof. Ramsay inclines to the view that he held an extraordinary command by the side of Varus some years earlier, as Corbulo did by the side of Ummidius Quadratus, and Vespasian by the side of Mucianus. Such a command might carry with it the control of foreign relations, and be included under the title ἡγεμών.

v. *The Meaning of the Virgin-Birth.*—It is but a very few years since there arose in Germany (the date was 1892) a rather sharp controversy in which many leading theologians took part over the clause of the Apostles' Creed, 'Conceived by the Holy Ghost, born of the Virgin Mary.' The echoes of that controversy reached this country, and, although not much was said in public, it is probable that some impression was made upon public opinion. This impression was strengthened by the publication soon afterwards of the Sinai-Syriac with its peculiar reading, which was not unnaturally caught at as representing a more ancient and truer text than that to which we are accustomed. But if what has been written in the preceding sections has been followed, it will have been seen that between that time and the present (end of 1898) there has been a steady reaction. The eccentric reading has found its level. As it stands, it cannot possibly be original; and however it arose, it cannot really affect the belief of the Church, as it introduces no factor which had not been already allowed for. And at the same time the historical value of the documents, especially Lk 1. 2, has been gradually rising in the estimation of scholars, until the climax has been reached in the recent treatise of Prof. Ramsay. Even those who desire to see things severely as they are must feel that the opening chapters of St. Luke are full of small indications of authenticity, that they are really not behind the rest of the Gospel, and that they form no exception to the claim made at the outset that the facts recorded have been derived from 'eye-witnesses and ministers of the word.'

Along with this process there has been growing up a better and fuller philosophy of the Incarnation. This has been due especially to some of the contributors to *Lux Mundi*, and may be seen in Canon Gore's *Bampton Lectures* (1891) and *Dissertations* (1895), in Dr. Moberly's *Lux Mundi* essay, and in Mr. Illingworth's *Bampton Lectures* (1894) and *Divine Immanence* (1898).

To those who regard primitive ideas as compounded of nothing but idle imagination, ignorance, and superstition, the evidence in folk-lore of stories of supernatural birth (such as are collected in Mr. Sidney Hartland's *Legend of Perseus*, vol. i., 1894) seems to discredit all accounts of such birth, even the Christian. They do not sufficiently consider the entire difference of the conditions under which the Christian tradition was promulgated from those which surrounded the creations of mythopoeic fancy. The Christian tradition belongs to the sphere, not of myth but of history. It is enshrined in documents near in date to the facts, and in which the line of connexion between the record and the fact is still traceable.

But, apart from this, if we believe that the course of human ideas, however mixed in their character—as all human things are mixed—is yet part of a single development, and that development presided over by a Providence which at once imparts to it unity and prescribes its goal,—those who believe this may well see in the fantastic outgrowth of myth and legend something not wholly undesigned or wholly unconnected with the Great Event which was to be, but rather a dim unconscious preparation for that Event, a groping towards it of the human spirit, a prophetic instinct gradually moulding the forms of thought in which it was to find expression.

And if we ask further what it all means,—why the Son of Man was destined to have this exceptional kind of birth, the answer is, because His appearance upon earth—His Incarnation, as we call it—was to be in its innermost nature exceptional; He was to live and move amongst men, and was to be made in all points like His brethren, with the one difference that He was to be—unlike them—without sin. But how was a sinless human nature possible? To speak of a sinless human nature is to speak of something essentially outside the continuity of the species. The growth of self-conscious experience, expressed at its finest and best in the formulæ of advancing science, has emphasized the strength of heredity. Each generation is bound to the last by indissoluble ties. To sever the bond, in any one of its colligated strands, involves a break in descent. It involves the introduction of a new factor, to which the taint of sin does not attach. If like produces like, the element of unlikeness must come from that to which it has itself affinity. Our names for the process do but largely cover our ignorance, but we may be sure that there is essential truth contained in the scriptural phrase, 'The Holy Ghost shall come upon thee, and the power of the Most High shall overshadow thee; wherefore also that which is to be born shall be called holy, the Son of God.'

[The most important literature has been mentioned in the course of this section].

IV. CONCLUDING SURVEY: THE VERDICT OF HISTORY.

A. *CHRIST IN HISTORY.*—So far we have been involved in the study of the details of the Life of Christ, mainly on the basis of the Gospels. But the Gospels alone, though the fragments which they have preserved for us of that Life are beyond all price, would yet convey an incomplete idea of the total impression left by it even upon contemporaries, still less of all that it has been in the history of the world. Especially would this be the case if, as some would have us do, we were to follow the first three Gospels only, to the exclusion of the fourth. To that point we shall return for a moment presently. But the time has now come to enlarge our view, to look back upon our subject from the vantage-ground which we occupy at the end of the 19th cent., and to endeavour to see it no longer as an episode affecting a small portion of an 'unimportant branch of the Semitic peoples,' but as it enters into the course of the great world-movement of the centuries.

If we would appreciate this, we must once more go back to the Origins, not now so much in search of details, as in order, if possible, to catch rather more of the total impression. We cannot, of course, attempt to interrogate the whole of history. For our present purpose it may be enough to consider (i.) the net result, if we may so speak, of the portraiture of Christ in the Gospels; (ii.) the impression left by a similar reading of other parts of the New Testament, especially the Epistles; (iii.) the testimony borne by the Early Church, both formulated and informal; (iv.) the appeal that may be made to the religious experience of Christians.

The last of these heads is not really so disparate as it may seem from the rest. The ultimate object that we have in view is to bring home—or to suggest lines on which it may be possible to bring home — what Christ really was and is to the individual believer. In order to do this we endeavour to collect (i.) what He was to those among whom He moved during His life on earth; (ii.) what He was to His disciples, and primarily to the apostles after His departure; (iii.) what the still undivided Church apprehended Him as being. It will thus be seen that there is no real antithesis, as though the appeal were in the one case to history and in the other to experience. For our present purpose history may be regarded as the collective experience of the past, which we are seeking to put into line with the individual or collective experience of the present. Our historical survey, so far as it goes, simply embodies so many superimposed strata of experience.

i. *The Christ of the Gospels.*—We should thus be inclined to deprecate the attempts which are from time to time made to set in contrast some one or other branch of the appeal that we are making as against the rest. In this country we are accustomed to the opposition between the Christ of the (Synoptic) Gospels and the Christ of 'Dogma' or of the Church. And in Germany of late there has been a tendency to oppose the Christ conceived and preached by the apostles to the biographical Christ of the Gospels, and the experience of faith to any external and objective standards. (See especially the works of Kähler and Herrmann mentioned below).

The disparagement of the Gospels as biographies seems to us, so far as it goes,—and neither writer is really very clear on the subject,—to rest upon a somewhat undue degree of scepticism as to the critical use that can be made of the Gospels. It does not follow that all that is doubted is really doubtful. For a more detailed testing of the historical character of the Gospels we must content ourselves with referring to the previous part of this article, only adding to it the two points which will be more appropriately introduced at the end of the next section,—the peculiar kind of confirmation which the two pictures (the evangelic and the apostolic) supply to each other, the difference between them showing that the teaching of the Epistles has not encroached upon the historical truth of the Gospels, while the less obvious likeness shows that they are in strict continuity. We shall also have to state once more in that context our reasons for believing the Fourth Gospel to be really the work of an eye-witness.

But the point that concerns us most at the present moment is that, even if we make to negative criticism larger concessions than we have any right to make, there will still remain in the Gospel picture ineffaceable features which presuppose and demand that estimate of the Person of Christ which we can alone call in the strict sense Christian.

Take, for instance, that central passage Mt 11²⁸⁻³⁸ ‘Come unto me, all ye that labour and are heavy laden, and I will give you rest. Take my yoke upon you, and learn of me; for I am meek and lowly in heart: and ye shall find rest unto your souls. For my yoke is easy, and my burden is light.’ Could we conceive such words put into any other lips, even the loftiest that the history of mankind has produced? They are full of delicate self-portraiture. They present to us a character which we may say certainly *was*, because it has been so described. No mere artist in words ever painted such a canvas without a living model before him. The portrait is of One who is ‘meek and lowly in heart,’ whose yoke is easy and His burden light; and yet He speaks of both yoke and burden as ‘His’ in the sense of being imposed by Him; He invites men to ‘come’ to Him, evidently with a deep significance read into the phrase; He addresses His invitation to weary souls wherever such are to be found; and (climax of all!) He promises what no Alexander or Napoleon ever dreamt of promising to his followers, that He would give them the truly supernatural gift of rest—the tranquillity and serenity of inward peace in spite of the friction of the world; that all this should be theirs by ‘coming’ to Him.

And then how easy is it to group round such a passage a multitude of others! ‘I say unto you, Resist not him that is evil: but whosoever smiteth thee on thy right cheek, turn to him the other also’ (Mt 5³⁹). ‘The Son of Man came not to be ministered unto, but to minister’ (Mk 10⁴⁵||). ‘Suffer the little children to come unto me; forbid them not: for of such is the kingdom of God’ (*ib.* v.¹⁴||). ‘Whosoever would save his life shall lose it: and whosoever shall lose his life for my sake and the gospel’s shall save it’ (Mk 8³⁵). ‘The Son of Man came to seek and to save that which was lost’ (Lk 19¹⁰, comp. the three parables of Lk 15). ‘Inasmuch as ye did it unto one of these my brethren, even these least, ye did it unto me’ (Mt 25⁴⁰).

Sayings like these, it is needless to add, could be multiplied almost indefinitely. Through all of them there runs, indirectly, if not directly, the same self-portraiture. And it is a self-portraiture that has the same two sides. On the one hand there is the human side, the note of meekness or lowliness, condescension that is not (though it really is!) condescension but infinite sympathy, patience, tenderness; and, on the other hand, no less firmly drawn, for all the lightness and restraint of touch, an absolute range of command and authority; all things delivered to the Son in heaven and on earth (cf. Mt 11²⁷ 28¹⁸).

That which we have called the ‘human side’ fills most of the foreground in the Gospels; the other, the transcendental side, is somewhat shaded by it; and we can see that it was deliberately shaded, that the proportions were such as mainly (though, as we shall see, not entirely) corresponded to the facts, or, in other words, to the divine method and order of presentation. But when we turn from the Gospels to the rest of the NT we shall find these proportions inverted.

We only pause upon this Gospel picture a mo-

ment more to say that, apart from any question of criticism of documents or of details in the narrative, it seems to us to be utterly beyond the reach of invention. The evangelists themselves were too near to the events to see them in all their significance. They set down, like honest men, the details one after another as they were told them. But it was not their doing that these details work in together to a singular and unsought harmony.

Literature.—The fullest account of recent discussions as to the adequacy and trustworthiness of the presentation of Christ in the Gospels will be found in the second enlarged edition of Kähler's *Der sogenannte historische Jesus und der geschichtliche, biblische Christus*, Leipzig, 1896. Another work, which lays the stress rather on personal experience of the life of Christ, and is written with great earnestness from that point of view, but seems to us too restricted in its historical basis, is Herrmann's *Der Verkehr des Christen mit Gott*, ed. 2, Stuttgart, 1892 (Eng. tr. 1895).

ii. *The Christ of the Apostles.*—In passing over from the Gospels to the rest of the NT we find ourselves hampered by critical questions. What we should most wish to ascertain is the conception of Christ held by the mass of the first disciples. And to some extent we can get at this; but, so far as we can do so, it is nearly always indirectly. The writings that have come down to us are those of the leaders, not of the followers; and many even of these are encumbered with questions as to date and origin. Some of these do not so much matter, because in any case they belong to the end rather than the beginning of the apostolic age. The one book which we should most like to use more freely than we can is the Acts, the earlier chapters of which we quite agree with the author of the article in this Dictionary in estimating highly.

We will, however, cut the knot by not attempting to summarize the teaching of all the undisputed books, but by taking a single typical example of manageable compass, the first extant NT writing, 1 Thessalonians, written probably about A.D. 51—in any case not later than 53, or within the first quarter of a century after the Ascension.

Let us suppose for a moment, with the more extreme critics, that a thick curtain falls over the Church after this event. The curtain is lifted, and what do we find? We turn to the opening verse of the Ep. (emended reading). St. Paul and his companions give solemn greeting to the ‘Church of the Thess. (which is) in God the Father and the Lord Jesus Christ.’ An elaborate process of reflexion, almost a system of theology, lies behind those familiar terms. First we note that the human name ‘Jesus’ is closely associated with the title ‘Christ’ or ‘Messiah,’ which in the Gospels had been claimed with such quiet reticence and unobtrusiveness. From this time onwards the two names are almost inseparable, or the second supersedes the first: in other words, Jesus is hardly ever thought of apart from His high Messianic dignity. This effect is pressed home by the further title ‘Lord’ (Κύριος). The disciples had been in the habit of addressing their Master as ‘Lord’ during His lifetime, in a sense not very different from that in which any Rabbi might be addressed by his pupils (Jn 13¹³ᶠ·). But that sense is no longer adequate; the word has been filled with a deeper meaning. That ‘Jesus is Lord’ has become the distinctive confession of Christians (1 Co 12³, Ro 10⁹), where ‘Lord’ certainly = ‘the exalted Lord’ of the Resurrection and Ascension (cf. Ac 2³⁶).

What is still more remarkable, the glorified Jesus is, as it were, bracketed with ‘God the Father.’ Let us think what this would mean to a strict Jewish monotheist; yet St. Paul evidently holds the juxtaposition, not as something to which he is tentatively feeling his way, but as a fundamental axiom of faith. In the appellation ‘Father’ we have already the first beginning — may we not say the first decisive step, which potentially contains the rest?—of the Christian doctrine of the Trinity. And we observe, further, that the Thessalonian Church is said to have its being ‘*in* Christ’ as well as ‘*in* God.’ This is a characteristic touch of Pauline mysticism. The striking thing about it is that in this, too, the Son already holds a place beside the Father (cf. 2¹⁴ 4¹⁶).

There is another passage in the Ep. (1 Th 3¹¹) in which there is the same intimate combination of ‘our God and Father’ and ‘our Lord Jesus.’ Here the context is not exactly mystical, but the two names are mentioned in connexion with the divine prerogative of ordering events. The apostle prays that God and Christ will together ‘direct’ (κατινθύναι, ‘make straight and unimpeded’) his way to them (the Thessalonians).

It is not by accident that the Holy Spirit is in a similar manner implicated in divine action (1⁵· ⁶ 4⁸ 5¹⁹), though it would be too much to say that the Spirit is spoken of distinctly as a Person.

The historical events of the life of Christ are hardly alluded to, except His death and resurrection (1^{10} 4^{14} 5^{10}). In the last of these verses Christ is said to have died 'for us'; and in the preceding verse 'salvation,' which is contrasted with 'death,' is said to come 'through' Him. In 1^{10} He is also spoken of as delivering Christians 'from the wrath to come.' It is assumed that Christ is in heaven, from whence He is expected to come again with impressive manifestations of power (1^{10} $4^{15f.}$; cf. also the frequent allusions to ἡ παρουσία τοῦ Κυρίου).

The Second Coming is the only point on which the Ep. can be said to contain direct and formal teaching. The other points mentioned are all assumed as something already known, not as imparted for the first time.

Not only may we say that they are known, but it is also fair to infer that they are undisputed. There is a hint of controversy with the unbelieving Jews, but no hint of controversy with the Judæan Churches, which stand in the same relation to Christ ($2^{14.16}$). This is important; and it is fully borne out by the other Epistles, which show just how far the disputed ground between St. Paul and the other apostles extended. There was a good deal of sharp debate about the terms on which Gentiles should be admitted. There is no trace of any debate as to the estimate of the Person of Christ.

We have referred to the Pauline mysticism and to the hints, slight but significant, of what is known as the doctrine of the Atonement. It is clear that St. Paul ascribed to Christ not only divine attributes but divine activities—activities in the supersensual sphere, what he elsewhere calls 'heavenly places' (τὰ ἐπουράνια). We know how these activities are enlarged upon in Epp. to Co, Gal, and Ro. It would, of course, be wrong to suppose that all Christians, or indeed any great number, had an intelligent grasp of these 'mysteries'; but we can see from the Ep. to He, 1 P, Epp. Jn, and Rev, that conceptions quite as transcendental had a wide diffusion. And a verse like 2 Co 13^{14} shows that there must have been large tracts of important teaching which are imperfectly represented in our extant documents. When we consider how occasional these documents are in their origin, the wonder is not that they have conveyed to us so little of the apostolic teaching, but that they have conveyed so much.

The summary impression that we receive is indeed that the revolution foreshadowed at the end of the last section has been accomplished. The historical facts of the Lord's life were not neglected; for Gospels were being written, of which those which we now possess are only surviving specimens. But in the whole epistolary literature of NT they have receded very much into the background, as compared with those transcendental conceptions of the Person and Work of Christ, to which the Gospels pointed forward, but which (with one exception) they did not directly expound.

No doubt this was in the main only what was to be expected. The narrative of the Gospels goes back to the period before the Resurrection; the epistolary literature dates altogether after it. Still it is remarkable how we seem to be plunged all at once into the midst of a developed theology. Nor is the wonder lessened, it is rather increased, when we remark that this theology is only in part set before us deliberately as teaching. The fact that it is more often presupposed shows how deep a hold it must have taken alike of the writer and of his readers.

Impressive contrasts are sometimes drawn (e.g. at the beginning of Dr. Hatch's *Hibbert Lecture*) between the Sermon on the Mount and the Nicene Creed; and the contrast certainly is there. But it goes back far beyond the period of the Arian controversy. It is hardly less marked between the Sermon on the Mount and the writings which have come down to us under the names of St. Peter and St. Paul. And yet these writings are practically contemporary with the composition of the Gospels. The two streams, of historical narrative on the one hand and theological inference on the other, really run side by side. They do not exclude but rather supplement, and indeed critically confirm,

each other. For if the Gospels had been really not genuine histories of the words and acts of Christ, but coloured products of the age succeeding His death, we may be sure that they would have reflected the characteristic attitude of that age far more than they do. They do not reflect it, but they do account for it by those delicate hints and subtly inwoven intimations that He who called Himself so persistently Son of Man was also Son of God.

The one Gospel which bridges the gap more unmistakably than the others is the Fourth. And the reason is obvious, if St. John was its author. He had a foot in both worlds. As the disciple whom Jesus loved, he vividly remembered His incomings and outgoings. And in the same capacity, as a disciple who was also an apostle, it fell to him to build up that theology which was the deliberate expression of what Jesus was to His Church, not in a section only of His being, the short three years which He had spent among His followers, but in His being as He had revealed it to them as a whole. It is difficult to think of either function as merely assumed by the writer at second-hand. On the contrary, we acquire a fresh understanding of the weight and solemnity of his words when we think of these as springing from direct personal contact with Christ, and intense personal conviction of what Christ really was, not to himself only, but to the world. In this respect the Fourth Gospel is unique; and the very expansion which it gives of the divine claims of Christ prepares us more completely than the other Gospels alone might have done for the transition from them to the Epistles.

It is an especial satisfaction to be able to quote, in support of this view of the first-hand character of the Fourth Gospel, Dr. Loofs in *PRE*[3] iv. 29.

iii. *The Christ of the Undivided Church.*—For the purpose which we have before us we must examine the evidence of the Undivided Church on three distinct points. (a) What was the estimate of the Person of Christ in the age immediately succeeding that of the Apostles? (b) Are there any traces of a tradition different from this? (c) What is the bearing upon the subject of the creeds and conciliar decisions?

(a) On the first head we may say broadly that the mass of Christian opinion was in strict continuity with the NT, rarely (as we might expect) rising to an apprehension of its heights and depths, and keeping rather at the average level, but steadily loyal in intention, and showing no signs of recalcitrance.

Ignatius of Antioch has the strongest grip of distinctive features of NT teaching (Virgin-Birth, pre-existence, incarnation, Logos, Trinitarian language). Clemens Romanus, though much less theological, also has pre-existence and a clearly implied Trinity (lviii. 2). In the former point Barnabas and Hermas agree, though the latter shows some confusion, not uncommon at this date, between Son and Spirit. And then we have the opening words of 2 Clement which exactly describe the general temper, 'Brethren, we ought so to think of Jesus Christ as of God, as of the Judge of quick and dead.'

These, with Polycarp and Aristides, who adopt a similar tone, are the writers. And then, when we look for evidence as to popular feeling and practice, we have the wide prevalence of baptism in the Threefold Name (*Didaché* and Justin), and the hymns sung 'to Christ as God' (Pliny, *Ep. ad Trajan.* xcvi.; cf. Eus. *HE* v. xxviii. 5). It is clear that prayer was generally offered to Christ. Origen's objection to this was a theological refinement, as he held that the proper formula was εὐχαριστεῖν τῷ θεῷ διὰ X. 'I. (de Orat. 15).

The group of Apologists which stands out so clearly in the middle of the 2nd century is characterized chiefly by the use that is made of the Logos doctrine which was identified with the Logos of philosophy. With them begins a more active spirit of reflexion and speculation. The relation of the Son to the Father, and indeed the whole problem of unity and distinctions in the Godhead (Justin and Athenagoras), is beginning to be keenly canvassed. And at the same time it is clear that the question of what were afterwards called the 'Two Natures' was causing much perplexity. It was this difficulty which really lies behind the experiments of Gnosticism. When we come to the latter half and last quarter of the century, with the theologians of Asia Minor, Irenæus, and Clement of Alexandria, the foundations have been laid of a Christian theology, which already bears the stamp that marks it throughout succeeding centuries, viz. that it is not free speculation, but reflexion upon *data* given by the Bible.

(*b*) It was natural, and could not well have been otherwise, that there was in this reflexion at first a considerable tentative element. There was no break, and no conscious divergence between it and the canonical writings. But are there no signs of such divergence? Are there no signs of a tradition differing from that embodied in these writings? Perhaps we ought to say that there are.

The Gnostics began by inventing traditions of their own, but they soon fell into the groove, and professed to base their views like the rest on the canonical Scriptures. A conspicuous example of this is Heracleon's commentary on St. John. But in these circles there was what we might call recalcitrance, as when Cerinthus and Carpocrates rejected the Virgin-Birth as impossible (Iren. *adv. Hær.* I. xxvi. 1, xxv. 1). The Gnostics, however, are outside the true development of Christianity, and their systems had a different origin.

In closer contact with Christianity proper are the heretical Ebionites. For them a better claim might be made out to represent a real divergence of tradition. It is possible that their denial of the Virgin-Birth was derived from the state of things when the canonical narratives had not yet obtained any wide circulation. And yet we should have to pass upon these Ebionites a verdict similar to that already passed upon the Gnostics. They were really Jews imperfectly Christianized. If they regarded Christ as ψιλὸς ἄνθρωπος, it was doubtless because the Jews did not expect their Messiah to have any other origin. This is a different thing from, though it may have some subordinate connexion with, the views (*e.g.*) of Paul of Samosata, whose difficulty was caused by the union of the two natures. The human nature he regarded as having an ordinary human birth, though it came to be united to the Divine Logos.

A like account would hold good of Theodotus of Byzantium and the Rationalists described in Eus. *HE* v. xxviii. At last the reader may think that he is upon the track of a genuine Rationalism; but this did not go very deep. It was consistent with belief in the Virgin-Birth and in the Resurrection (Hippolytus, *Ref. Hær.* vii. 35); in fact it probably amounted to little more than a dry literal exegesis.

The *Clementine Homilies* point out that Christ did not call Himself 'God,' but the 'Son of God,' and they emphasize this distinction somewhat after the manner of the later Arians (xvi. 15, 16). When we have said this, we shall have touched (it is believed) on all the main types of what might be thought to be a denial of Christ's full Godhead.

The more pressing danger of primitive Christianity lay in an opposite direction. Loyalty to Christ was so strong that the simpler sort of Christians were apt to look upon the humanity as swallowed up in the divinity. This is the true account of the early prevalence of Docetism (which made the deity of Christ real, the humanity phantasmal or unreal), and of the later prevalence of what is known to students as Modalistic Monarchianism, and to the general reader as Sabellianism (the doctrine that the Son and the Spirit were not distinct Persons in the Godhead, but modes or aspects of the One God). The answer of Noetus was typical of the frame of mind that gave rise to this, 'What harm do I do in glorifying Christ?' (Hippol. *c. Noet.* 1): it seemed meritorious to identify Christ with God. Both these tendencies were far stronger and more widely spread than anything that savoured of Rationalism. Docetism entered largely into the Apocryphal Gospels and Acts, which were very popular; and both Tertullian (*Prax.* 1, 3) and Hippolytus (*Ref. Hær.* ix. 6, μέγιστος ἀγών) imply that the struggle against Monarchianism was severe.

It is evident from this to which side the scales inclined. The traces of anything like Rationalism in the modern sense are extremely few and slight. For the most part, what looks like it is not pure Rationalism (or Humanitarianism) at all. More formidable was the excess of zeal which exalted the divine in Christ at the expense of the human. But the main body of the Church held an even way between both extremes,—held it at least in intention, though there were no doubt a certain number of unsuccessful experiments in the construction of reasoned theory.

(*c*) It was inevitable that in the early centuries there should be a great amount of tentative thinking. But little by little this was sifted out; and by the middle of the 5th cent. the ancient Church had practically made up its mind. It formulated its belief in the Chalcedonian definition (ὅρος τῆς ἐν Χαλκηδόνι τετάρτης συνόδου) of the year 451 (which counts as Ecumenical, though the only Westerns

present were the two legates of Pope Leo and two fugitive bishops from Africa), and in the *Quicumque vult*, a liturgical creed composed, according to a tradition which may be sound, by Dionysius [of Milan] and Eusebius [of Vercelli], (cf. the remarkable preface in the Irish *Liber Hymnorum*, i. 203, ii. 92, ed. Bernard and Atkinson, Lond. 1898).

This creed and the definitions of Chalcedon represent the end of the process; the beginning is marked by the creed known as the Apostles'. Criticism has of late been active upon this creed as well as upon the so-called Nicene and Athanasian, with a result which tends, it may be generally said, to heighten the value of all three. The date of the Apostles' Creed (in its oldest and shortest form) has been reduced within the limits A.D. 100–150; Kattenbusch, the author of the most elaborate monograph on the subject, leans to the beginning of that period, Harnack to the end. It is agreed that it was in the first instance the local baptismal creed of the Church of Rome, and that it was the parent of all the leading provincial creeds of the West. The principal open question at the present moment (1899 in.) is as to its relation to the Eastern creeds. Kattenbusch and Harnack both think that it was carried to the East in the time of Aurelian (*circa* 270), and that it became the parent of a number of Eastern creeds, including that which we know as the Nicene; but this is conjecture. Harnack thinks that the Roman creed coalesced with floating formulæ, to which he gives the name of *Kerygmata*, already circulating in the East. But these also are more or less hypothetical. And the question is whether the Eastern creeds, which resemble the Roman, were not rather offshoots, parallel to it, of a single primitive creed, perhaps originating in Asia Minor. This is substantially the view of Dr. Loofs. The main argument in favour of it is that characteristic features of the Eastern type of creed already appear in Irenæus and in a less degree in Justin. Harnack would explain these features as due to his *Kerygmata*; and from the point of view of the history of doctrine the difference is not very great, because the *Kerygmata* were in any case in harmony with the creed.

It would be difficult to overestimate the value of the existence of this fixed traditional standard of teaching at so early a date. It was the rallying and steadying centre of Catholic Christianity, which kept it straight in the midst of Gnostic extravagances and among the perils of philosophical speculation. Our so-called Nicene Creed is only the Apostles' Creed in one of its more florid Oriental forms, with clauses engrafted into it to meet the rising heresies of Arius and Macedonius; while the Chalcedonian formula and the *Quicumque* take further account of the controversies connected with the names of Apollinaris, Nestorius, and Eutyches.

The decisions in question were thus the outcome of a long evolution, every step in which was keenly debated by minds of great acumen and power, really far better equipped for such discussions than the average Anglo-American mind of to-day. If we can see that their premises were often erroneous (especially in such matters as the exegesis of the OT), we can also see that they possessed extraordinary fertility and subtlety in the handling of metaphysical problems. The disparaging estimates of the Fathers, which are often heard and seen in print, are very largely based upon the most superficial acquaintance with their writings. There are many things in these which may provoke a smile, but as a whole they certainly will not do so in any really open mind. There exists at the present time in Germany a movement, which bears the name of its author Albrecht Ritschl (1822–1889), directed against metaphysics in theology generally. No doubt Ritschl also was a thinker and writer of great ability; and the stress that he lays upon religious experience is by no means without justification. But it has not yet been proved that the negative side of his argument is equally valid, or that metaphysics can be wholly dispensed with. And so long as this is the case we certainly cannot afford to ignore these ancient decisions. Every word in them represents a battle, or succession of battles, in which the combatants were, many of them, giants.

LITERATURE.—The subject of this section brings up the whole history of 'Christology,' which may be studied in well-known works of Baur, Dorner, and Thomasius, or in Harnack's *History of Dogma*. There is an excellent survey by Loofs in *PRE*[3] iv. 16 ff., art. 'Christologie, Kirchenlehre,' marked by much independent judgment and research. In English may be mentioned Gore, *Bampton Lectures* (1891); Fairbairn, *Christ in Modern Theology* (1893); R. L. Ottley, *Doctrine of the Incarnation* (1896).

The later phases of the critical discussions on the creeds are set forth in Kattenbusch, *Das Apost. Symbol* (Leipzig, 1894, 1898, unfinished); Harnack's art. 'Apost. Symb.' in *PRE³* i. 741 ff. (this is the author's most complete and latest utterance; the Eng. reader may consult *Hist. of Dogma*, i. 157 ff.), and an important art. by Loofs in *Gött. gel. Anzeigen*, 1895.

For Ritschl's attitude it may be enough to refer to his tract, *Theologie u. Metaphysik*, Bonn, 1881. We had an English version of the opposition to metaphysics in the writings of Matthew Arnold.

iv *The Christ of Personal Experience.*—In the case of Ritschl the religious experience of the individual or of communities is directly pitted against metaphysics as the criterion of theological truth. But apart from philosophical theory it is the criterion which is practically applied by hundreds of thousands of plain men—we will not say in search of a creed, but in support of the creed which they have found or inherited. And there is an immense volume of evidence derived from this source in corroboration of the truth of Christianity, or of what amounts to the same thing, the Christian estimate of the Person of Christ. The singular attraction of this Person, the sense of what Christ has done, not only for mankind at large but for the individual believer, the sense of the love of God manifested in Him, have been so overpowering as to sweep away all need for other kinds of evidence. They create a passionate conviction that the religion which has had these effects cannot be wrong in its fundamental doctrine, the pivot of the whole.

This personal experience operates in two ways. It makes the individual believer cling to his belief in spite of all the objections that can be brought against it. But it also possesses a formative power which so fashions men in the likeness of Christ, that they in turn become a standing witness to those who have not come under the same influence. St. Paul expresses this by a forcible metaphor when he speaks of himself as in travail for his Galatian converts 'until Christ be formed' in them, as the embryo is formed in the womb (Gal 4¹⁹). The image thus formed shines through the man, like a light through glass, and so He who came to be the Light of the world has His radiance transmitted downwards through the centuries and outwards to the remotest corners of the earth.

This that we speak of is, of course, matter of common knowledge and of everyday experience. The note of the true Christian cannot help being seen wherever there is genuine Christianity. It is, however, an inestimable advantage that the process should have found expression in such classics of literature as the *Confessions of St. Augustine* and the *De Imitatione*. In these it can not only be seen but studied.

B. *THE PERSON OF CHRIST.*—It is necessary that this article should be brought to a close, and the close may seem rather abrupt. And yet the design which the writer set before himself is very nearly accomplished. It will be his duty at a later date to return to his subject on a somewhat larger scale; and for the present he would conclude, not so much by stating results as by stating problems.

i. *The Problem as it stands.*—We have seen that there are four different ways of attempting to grasp what we can of the significance of the Person of Christ. Towards these four ways the attitude of different minds will be different. For some the decisions of the Undivided Church will be absolutely authoritative and final. They will not seek to go either behind them or beyond them. Others will set the comparative simplicity of the Gospel picture against the more transcendental and metaphysical conceptions of the age that followed. To others, again, the picture traced in the Gospels will seem meagre and uncertain by the side of the exalted Christ preached by the apostles.* Yet others will take refuge in the appeal to individual experience, which will seem to give a more immediate hold on Christ and to avoid the necessity and perplexities of criticism. Others, still more radical in their procedure, will begin with the assumption that Christ was only man, and will treat all the subsequent development as reflecting the growth of the delusion by which He came to be regarded as God.

This last is a drastic method of levelling down the indications of the divine in history, against which human nature protests and will continue to protest. But, short of this, the other milder alternatives seem to us to put asunder what ought rather to be combined. They seem to us to propound antitheses, where they ought rather to find harmony. As the phases in question, distinctly as they stand out from each other, are so many phases in the history of Christianity, they ought to contribute to the elucidation of the Christianity which they have in common.

They ought to contribute to it, and we believe that they do contribute to it. There is, however, room still left for closer study, especially of the *transitions*. We have been so much in the habit of studying the Gospels by themselves and the Epistles by themselves that we have not paid sufficient attention to the transition from the one to the other. If we follow this clue, it will, we believe, show that the first three Gospels in particular need supplementing, that features which in them appear subordinate will bear greater emphasis, and that the resulting whole is more like that portrayed in the Fourth Gospel than is often supposed.

For instance, we are of opinion that much of the teaching of Jn 14–16 is *required by* the verse 2 Co 13¹⁴ and other allusive passages in the early Epp. of St. Paul; that the command of Mt 28¹⁹ (or something like it) is required by *Didaché* vii. 1, 3; Just. *Apol.* i. 61; that the teaching respecting the Paraclete is required by the whole Pauline doctrine of the Spirit; that the allegory of the Vine is required by the Pauline doctrines of the Head and the Members, and of the Mystical Union; that the full sense of Mk 10⁴⁵ ‖ is required by such passages as Ro 3²⁴· ²⁵ 4²⁵ 5⁶⁻⁸ etc., and the full sense of Mk 14²⁴ ‖ by He 9¹⁸⁻²². And observations of this kind may be very largely extended.

In like manner, while it is certainly right that the conceptions current in the early Church as to the Person and Work of Christ should be rigorously analyzed and traced to their origin, full weight should be given to the analogues for them that are to be found in NT; and where they have their roots outside the Bible, even there the efforts of the human mind to express its deepest ideas may deserve a more sympathetic judgment than they sometimes receive.

And throughout, it is highly important that the doctrinal conceptions, whether of the apostolic age or or of subsequent ages, should be brought to the test of living experience, and as far as possible expressed in the language of such experience. The mind and heart of to-day demands before all things reality. It is a right and a healthy demand; and the Churches should try with all their power to satisfy it. If they fail, the fault will not lie in their subject-matter, but in themselves.

ii. *A pressing Portion of the Problem.* — There is one portion of the problem as to the

---

* 'We know, literally speaking, with much greater certainty what Paul wrote than what Jesus spoke.' 'The centre of gravity for the understanding of the Person (of Christ) and of its significance falls upon what we are in the habit of calling His Work.' Kähler, *Jesus u. das AT*, pp. 37, 60.

Person of our Lord Jesus Christ which both in this country and in Germany has excited special interest in recent years. In its most concrete form this is the question as to our Lord's Human Knowledge, which, however, runs up directly into what is generally known as the question of the *Kenosis*. And that, again, when thoroughly examined, will be found to raise the whole question of the Two Natures. In regard to this series of connected questions there is still abroad an active spirit of inquiry.

It was started in the first instance by the argument from our Lord's use of the OT in its bearing upon the question of OT criticism. This led to a closer examination of the text, Mk 13[32] || *var. lec.* That, again, expanded into a discussion of the technical doctrine of the *Kenosis* (see the art. *s.v.*), an episode in which was a renewed study of the exegesis of Ph 2[5-11]. And that in turn, in its later phase (H. C. Powell's *Principle of the Incarnation*, 1896), has opened up the whole question of the Two Natures, which in Germany for some time past has been far more freely handled than in Great Britain.

These discussions have produced one little work of classical value, Dr. E. H. Gifford's study of Ph 2[5-11], entitled *The Incarnation*, a model of careful and scientific exegesis, which appears to leave hardly anything more to be said on that head. It is also right to note the special activity on this subject of the diocese of Salisbury, largely due to the initiative and encouragement of its bishop (Mr. W. S. Swayne's *Our Lord's Knowledge as Man*, with a preface by the Bp. of Salisbury, 1891, and Mr. Powell's elaborate work, mentioned above). Weighty contributions have been made to the subject by Dr. Bright in *Waymarks of Church History* (1894), Canon Gore (*Dissertations*, 1898), and in arts. in the *Ch. Quarterly*, Oct. 1891, and July 1897.

On the Continent special views of the *Kenosis* are connected with the names of Dorner, Thomasius, Gess, Godet, and others rather more incidentally. Tracts upon the smaller questions have recently appeared by Schwartzkopff (*Konnte Jesus irren?* 1896), and Kähler (*Jesus u. das AT*, 1896).

In spite of all this varied activity, it may be doubted whether the last word has yet quite been said (Dr. Gifford's treatment of the exegetical question seems to us to come nearest to this). The first concern of the historian is that the facts shall be taken candidly as they are. It is more probable that our inferences will be wrong than the data from which they are drawn. And for the rest, we should not be surprised if a yet further examination of the subject should result rather in a list of *tacenda* than of *prædicanda*.

C. THE WORK OF CHRIST.—In regard to the Work of Christ also it is best for us to state problems. Of these the most important are the two that meet us first; they have not been much discussed; and complete agreement upon them has not yet been attained.

i. *The Place in the Cosmical Order of the Ethical Teaching of Christ.*—It is almost a question of names when it is asked whether Christ brought into the world a new ethical ideal. The question would be what constituted a new ideal. The Christian ideal, properly so called, is a direct development of what is found in OT, esp. in Pss. and the Second Part of Isaiah. But it receives a finish and an enrichment beyond what it ever possessed before, and it is placed on deeper foundations.

The chief outstanding question in regard to it would be the relation in which it stood to the older ideals of the best pagan life and philosophy in regard to the civic virtues, and to the newer ideals put forward in modern times in the name of science, art, and industry. The Christian ideal, it must be confessed, rather leaves these on one side. That it should do so would be quite as explicable if we adopt the Christian estimate of the Person of Christ as if we do not. If we do not adopt it, then the omission (so far as there is an omission) would be one of the limitations for which we were prepared. But if we take St. John's view of the relation of the Son to the Father, and see in His action the action willed by the Father, we shall see it as part of the great

world-movement, presupposing so much of that movement as had proved itself to be of permanent value in the past, and leaving room for further developments, corresponding to altered states of society, in the future. The teaching of Christ was not intended to make a *tabula rasa* of all that had gone before in Greece or Rome any more than in Judæa; nor was it intended to absorb into itself absolutely all the threads of subsequent evolution, where those threads work back to antecedents other than its own. It was intended so to work into the course of the world-movement as ultimately to recast and reform it. Its action has about it nothing violent or revolutionary, but it is none the less searching and effective. It is a force 'gentle yet prevailing.'

Some remarks have been made above (p. 621 f.) on the way in which the Christian ethical ideal operates and has operated. It is not thought that they are really sufficient; but they represent such degree of insight as the writer has attained to at present, and he would welcome warmly any new light on the subject.

ii. *The Significance of the Personal Example of Christ in regard to His Ethical Teaching.*—When once it is realized that the root principle of the ethics of Jesus is *Life through Death*, the death of the lower self with a view to the more assured triumph of the higher, it must needs break in upon us that the Life of Christ bears to His teaching a wholly different relation from that which the lives of ordinary teachers bear to theirs. An honest man will no doubt try to practise what he preaches, but that will be just a matter of maxims of conduct. The Life of Christ, we can see, was something very much more than this. It was a systematic working out of the Christian principle on a conspicuous and transcendent scale. The Death and Resurrection of Jesus were the visible embodiment of the law of all spiritual being that death is the true road to the higher life.

When we reflect further who it was that was thus exhibiting in His own Person the working out of this law to the utmost extremity, we become aware that Christians have it indeed 'placarded' before their eyes (Gal 3[1]) in a sense in which no moral law ever was set forth before.

Add that Christ had Himself predicted and that His followers generally believed that after His Ascension He was again visiting His people through His Spirit; that Divine forces were at work in the world, all radiating from Himself—Himself at once crucified and risen; add this to the previous beliefs of which we have just spoken, —remember that Christians supposed themselves to be actually conscious of these forces impressing and moulding their own hearts and lives, and we may come gradually to understand what St. Paul meant when he spoke of 'dying' or 'being crucified' with 'Christ' and 'rising again with Him.' It seems to be a similar idea to that which St. John expresses when he puts into the mouth of Christ the claim, 'I am the Way.' Rather, perhaps, we should not narrow down this phrase to anything less than the whole content of the Life of Christ on earth. 'He supplied in Himself the fixed plan, according to which all right human action must be framed: the Spirit working with their spirit supplied the ever-varying shapes in which the one plan had to be embodied' (Hort, *Huls. Lect.* p. 30).

iii. *The Work of Christ as Redemptive.*—Here we come on to more settled ground. At a very early date Christian tradition gave to Christ the title 'Saviour' (Lk 2[11], Ac 5[31] 13[23] etc.; cf. Mt 1[21], Lk 19[10]), 'Saviour of the world' (Jn 4[42]; cf. 3[17]

12^{47}). What does this title 'Saviour' include? It doubtless includes every sense in which Christ rescued and rescues men from the power and the guilt of sin. He does this, as we have seen, both by teaching and by example—by inimitable teaching and by a consummate example. But if we follow the method indicated above (p. 651), if we take the hints in the Gospels, with the fuller light thrown upon them by the Epistles, we shall be led to the conclusion that there was something yet more in the Life and Death and Resurrection of our Lord Jesus Christ than this, that there was something in these connected acts of His which had its counterpart in the sacrifices of OT; and that the deepest meaning and purpose of sacrifice was fulfilled in Him. This is a belief which Christians have held from the first days onwards; and it is a belief which does not and will not lack careful restatement at the present time.

iv. *The Work of Christ as Revelation.*—On a similar footing is the belief that Christ came not only to give, but to be a revelation of the inmost mind and character of the Father. Such a revelation was needed. It is not contained in the 'cosmic process.' If we had that process alone before us, we could not infer that God was a Being absolutely righteous and absolutely loving. The idea that He might be so could not rise above a hypothesis. But at this point the Incarnation intervenes. And here again the Synopt. Gospels present us with one central passage (Mt 11^{27}‖) with other scattered hints which are taken up and made more explicit in the Fourth Gospel, while that again does but give the fuller ground for a belief which was certainly held in the apostolic circle (comp. *e.g.* the central passage Jn 14$^{7-10}$ with 10$^{14f.}$ 3^{16}, 1 Jn 4$^{8.\ 16}$, Ro 5^8 etc.). So we get the broad doctrine led up to by St. Paul and Ep. to the He (2 Co 4$^{4.\ 6}$, Col 1^{15}, He 1^3), and finally formulated by St. John, that the Son was the Logos or Word (which might be paraphrased 'mouthpiece,' or 'vehicle of utterance of the mind') of the Father.

v. *The Founding of the Church.*—Conventional language is too often heard as though the immediate object of the Incarnation was the founding of the full hierarchical system as it existed in the Middle Ages. This language is based on the complete identification of the Church with the 'kingdom of heaven' (see p. 620 *sup.*). On the other hand, there is a school of critics, both in Germany and in England, who deny that 'Jesus ever created, or thought of creating, an organized society.' The main ground for this latter view is the doubt that rests over the two instances—one of them ambiguous—of the use of the word 'Church' which are confined to the peculiar element of the First Gospel (Mt 16^{18} 18^{17}), and the certainty that there are some senses in which the 'kingdom' and the Church cannot be identified. In some (though not in all) of those who adopt this line of reasoning there is the further tendency to minimize or restrict all that would imply an extended outlook of Jesus over the ages.

It seems to us, however, to be going too far to say that the 'kingdom of heaven' is 'without organization and incapable of being organized.' The two parables of the Tares and the Draw-net distinctly imply the existence of a society; and that the divine laws and influences which constitute the kingdom should express themselves in a society as the vehicle for their realization is antecedently probable. But when Jesus gathered round Him the Twelve, He was practically forming the nucleus of a society; and that society has had a continuous existence ever since, so that it is difficult to think that it was not contemplated. Moreover, when we turn to the writings of St. Paul, we find that even

in his earlier Epp. he seems to think of Christians as forming a single body with differentiation of function (Ro 12$^{4-8}$, 1 Co 12$^{4-30}$), and in his later Epp. (Eph, Col, Past. Epp.) the unity of the Church with its regular forms of ministry is brought out still more emphatically.

We also find that the Day of Pentecost is described in Ac as inaugurating a state of things which agrees well with the indications in Epp. Paul, while it confirms the promise of Lk 24^{49}, Jn 14$^{16.\ 26}$.

On the assumptions made in this art. it would be extremely improbable that this series of phenomena was not fully foreseen and deliberately designed by Christ. It would seem, however, that, after the manner of the divine operations in nature, He was rather content to plant a germ with indefinite capacities of growth, than thought it necessary Himself to fix in advance the details of organization.

The exact nature of the powers conferred upon the apostles is still a subject of much discussion as these concluding lines are written.

LIVES OF CHRIST.—To write the Life of Christ ideally is impossible. And even to write such a *Life* as should justify itself either for popular use or for study, is a task of extreme difficulty. After all the learning, ability, and even genius devoted to the subject, it is a relief to turn back from the very best of modern *Lives* to the Gospels. And great as are the merits of many of these modern works, there is none (at least none known to the writer—and there are several that he ought to know but does not) which possesses such a balance and combination of qualities as to rise quite to the level of a classic. What is wanted is a Newman, with science and adequate knowledge. No one has ever touched the Gospels with so much innate kinship of spirit as he. It should be needless to say that the Life of Christ can be written only by a believer. Renan had all the literary gifts—a *curiosa felicitas* of style, an æsthetic appreciation of his subject, and a saving common-sense which tempered his criticism; but even as literature his work is spoilt by self-consciousness and condescension, and his science was not of the best.

It will be well here only to name a select list of books which may be used more or less systematically. The minor works are legion.

Among the older works that would still most repay study would probably be those of Neander (ed. 7, 1873), Hase (*Leben Jesu*, ed. 5, 1865; *Geschichte Jesu*, 1876), Ewald (vol. vi. in Eng. tr. of *Gesch. d. Volkes Israel*, 1883), Andrews (American; revised ed. Edin. 1892).

In this country the books most generally current are Farrar's *Life of Christ* (since 1874); Edersheim's *Life and Times of Jesus the Messiah* (since 1883, revised editions from 1886, abridged ed. 1890); to which should perhaps be added Cunningham Geikie, *Life and Words of Christ* (1877). Of these the best is probably Dr. Edersheim's (with very ample illustrations from Jewish sources); but none of the three can quite be said to grapple with the deeper underlying problems, critical or other. A striking attempt was made by the late Prof. J. R. Seeley to realize in modern forms the ethical and social aspect of the Life of Christ in *Ecce Homo* (ed. 6, 1866). And the imaginative works, Dr. Edwin A. Abbott's *Philochristus* (ed. 3, 1878), and the anonymous *As Others Saw Him* (1895, see p. 633^b *sup.*), may be consulted with advantage. [Dr. Abbott's later works have been mentioned above (p. 628^a)].

In French, besides Renan, E. de Pressensé (1866, Eng. tr. same date and later; Protestant) may still be read. Père Didon (1891, also translated; Roman Catholic) represents with dignity the older orthodoxy, and A. Réville (1897) the newer criticism.

The most thoughtful and searching, as well as (if we except Dr. Edersheim) the most learned work, has been done in Germany. The two writers who have tried most earnestly to combine the old with the new are Bernhard Weiss, and Beyschlag. Of these we prefer Weiss. His *Leben Jesu* (1882, Eng. tr. 1883, 1884) is a conscientious and thorough piece of work, which, however, has to be studied rather than read. Beyschlag's (1885 and later) is more flowingly written, but also exhibits rather more markedly the weaker side of a mediating theology. Keim's *Jesus von Nazara* (1867–1882, abridged ed. 1873–1883) is impressive from the evident sincerity of its author, his intellectual force and command of his materials, but the critical premises are unfortunate. A concise *Life* which has just appeared by Dr. P. W. Schmidt of Basel (*Gesch. Jesu*, 1899) seems, if a glance may be trusted, to come under the head of minor works. It gains its conciseness by omitting debatable matter.

The student may be advised to take Weiss for his principal commentary, referring to Schürer (p. 609 *sup.*) for surroundings, and using along with it Tischendorf's *Synopsis Evangelica*, or a Harmony like Stevens and Burton's. He should read *Ecce Homo*.   **W. SANDAY.**

JESUS CALLED JUSTUS ('Ἰησοῦς ὁ λεγόμενος Ἰοῦστος). —A Jewish Christian resident in Rome during St. Paul's first imprisonment. The apostle sends a greeting from him to the Colossians (4¹¹), speaking at the same time of the comfort that he had received from him as a fellow-worker unto the kingdom of God. Nothing further is known of him.

J. O. F. MURRAY.

JETHER (יֶתֶר, 'abundance,' Ἰέθερ).—**1.** Father-in-law of Moses (RVm of Ex 4¹⁸ E), prob. a mistake for Jethro, יִתְרוֹ. **2.** Eldest son of Gideon, Jg 8²⁰. When called upon by his father to avenge his uncle's death by executing the two Midianite chiefs, Zebah and Zalmunna, the lad shrank from the deed 'because he was yet a youth.' It seems surprising at first to find such a youth among Gideon's 300 tested warriors; but 8⁴ᶠᶠ· belongs to a much older source than 7⁴⁻⁸, and may be connected with 6³⁴, where Gideon's men are drawn from his own clan of Abiezer; thus the boy would be included in his father's following. **3.** An Ishmaelite, father of Amasa, 1 K 2⁵· ³², 1 Ch 2¹⁷=יֶתֶר 2 S 17²⁵ Ἰοθέρ, Luc. Ἰέθερ. **4. 5.** Two men of Judah, 1 Ch 2³² 4¹⁷. **6.** A man of Asher, 1 Ch 7³⁸=יִתְרָן v.³⁷, Ἰέθερ A. **Ithran** was the name of an Edomite clan, Gn 36²⁶ P.   G. A. COOKE.

JETHETH (יְתֵת).—The eponym of an Edomite clan, Gn 36⁴⁰=1 Ch 1⁵¹, which has not been traced. The MT is not beyond suspicion, in view of the LXX (A) reading Ἰεβέρ in Gn, (B) Ἰεθέτ (A) Ἰεθέθ in 1 Ch, and Luc. Ἰεθέρ in both passages.

JETHRO (יִתְרוֹ; in Ex 4¹⁸ᵃ יֶתֶר, i.e. **Jether** [so RVm]; LXX everywhere Ἰοθόρ. יִתְרוֹ may be for יִתְרוֹן, or, as Dillmann prefers, for יֶתֶר, a name of the same class as שְׁמַע of Neh 6⁶ and bearing the same relation to יֶתֶר that שְׁמַע bears to שֵׁם of Neh 2¹⁹).—The priest of Midian and father-in-law of Moses. It was while keeping Jethro's flocks that Moses had his vision of the burning bush and received his commission from J″ to the court of Egypt (Ex 3¹ᶠᶠ·). Shortly thereafter he went to his father-in-law and obtained his permission to return to his brethren (4¹⁸). In a previous narrative (2¹⁵ᶠᶠ·) we are told how Moses, on fleeing from Egypt, came and dwelt in the land of Midian, how he assisted the seven daughters of the priest of Midian to water their flocks, and how finally he married one of these daughters named Zipporah. In this narrative no name is given to the priest (or it has been lost; see below). An analysis of the above passages shows that Ex 3¹ and 4¹⁸, as well as all the other passages where the name Jethro occurs (viz. 18¹· ²· ⁵· ⁶· ⁹· ¹⁰· ¹²), belong to E, whereas Ex 2¹⁵ᶠᶠ· is from J. Now the question arises, What is the relation of **Hobab** of Nu 10²⁹ (also J) to Jethro? Is he identical with him, so that in the latter passage חֹתֵן מֹשֶׁה, 'Moses' father-in-law,' * applies to Hobab; or is he his son, **Reuel** being another name for Jethro, so that Hobab ben-Reuel was Moses' brother-in-law; or, as a third possibility,† are Hobab and Jethro both sons of Reuel and thus brothers? Various considerations point to the following as the most probable answer to these questions. *Jethro* is the name of Moses' father-in-law according to one tradition (E), *Hobab ben-Reuel* is the name according to another (J), which appears not only in Nu 10²⁹ but also in Jg 1¹⁶ (see Moore's note) 4¹¹. All difficulty in the way of identifying Jethro and Hobab is removed if we regard 'Reuel' of Ex 2¹⁸ as a gloss due to a misconception of Nu 10²⁹ (Driver, *LOT*⁶ p. 22f.), or

---

* It is very doubtful whether the Heb. חתן has ever the sense of *brother-in-law*; at least there is no certain example in OT of its meaning anything but *father-in-law*.

† If (with Ewald, *Gesch.* ii. 38) we read 'Jethro ben-Reuel' for 'Reuel' in Ex 2¹⁸.

---

substitute for this reading 'Hobab ben-Reuel.' It is true that some obscurity (but this is so upon any theory of the relation of the two names) still arises from the circumstance that alike in Ex 2¹⁶ᶠᶠ· (J) and 3¹ (E) Moses' father-in-law is priest of Midian, whereas in Jg 1¹⁶ 4¹¹ he is a Kenite. (See, further, Moore on Jg 1¹⁶, and Dillmann-Ryssel on Ex 2¹⁸).

A very important incident is recorded in Ex 18 (E), where Moses receives a visit from Jethro, and at his father-in-law's instigation appoints subordinates to assist him in the work of 'judging' the people. In v.²⁷ we are told how thereafter Jethro 'went his way into his own country.' In J's narrative (Nu 10²⁹ᶠᶠ·) we find Hobab in the camp of Israel, and gather the impression (cf. also Jg 1¹⁶ 4¹¹) that, though at first reluctant, he finally agreed to the proposal of Moses that he should remain and give the people the benefit of his services as guide. See, also art. HOBAB.   J. A. SELBIE.

JETUR.—See ITURÆA.

JEUEL (יְעוּאֵל).—**1.** A Judahite, son of Zerah, 1 Ch 9⁶. **2.** A Levitical family name, 2 Ch 29¹³. **3.** A contemporary of Ezra, Ezr 8¹³. In 2 and 3 Ḳerê has יְעִיאֵל, Jeiel. See GENEALOGY.

JEUSH (יְעוּשׁ; in Gn 36⁵· ¹⁴, 1 Ch 7¹⁰ the *Kethîbh* has יְעִישׁ, Jeish. The *Ḳerê* is supported by Gn 36¹⁸, the LXX Ἰεούς, Ἰαούς, Vulg. *Jehus, Jaus*, as well as by the form in which the name occurs elsewhere). —**1.** A son of Esau by Oholibamah; also the eponym of a Horite clan, Gn 36⁵· ¹⁴· ¹⁸=1 Ch 1³⁵. **2.** A Benjamite chief, 7¹⁰. **3.** A descendant of Saul, 1 Ch 8³⁹. **4.** The name of a Levitical family, 1 Ch 23¹⁰ᶠ·. **5.** A son of Rehoboam, 2 Ch 11¹⁹.

W. R. Smith (*Kinship and Marriage*, 218, *RS*², 42 n. 4) proposes to identify Jeush with the Arabian lion-god Jaghûth, of whose name he declares that it is 'the exact phonetic equivalent.' This is favoured by Wellhausen (*Reste*², 22) and Nöldeke (*ZDMG*, 1886, p. 168); but Lagarde (*Mittheil.* ii. 77, *Bildung der Nomina*, 133), followed by Dillmann (*Genesis, ad loc.*), objects on the ground, amongst others, that the LXX Ἰεούς points to ' and not *gh* in Arabic (see Gray, *Heb. Proper Names*, 109).

JEUZ (יְעוּץ).—The eponym of a Benjamite family, 1 Ch 8¹⁰. See GENEALOGY.

JEW, JEWS (Heb. יְהוּדִי, יְהוּדִים (*Kethîbh* יהודיים), Aram. יְהוּדָיֵא, יְהוּדָאִין, Ἰουδαῖος, strictly = persons belonging to *Judah*). — In Jeremiah, the earliest writer employing the term whose date is certain, it is found without (32¹²) or with implied contrast to others (40¹¹· ¹² Moabites, 38¹⁹ 41³ 52²⁸· ³⁰, cf. 2 K 25²⁵ Chaldæans, 44¹ Egyptians). Curiously (unlike the earlier phrase, 'men of Judah,' אִישׁ יְהוּדָה 1 S 11⁸ etc., or אַנְשֵׁי יʹ 2 S 2⁴) it is never found in contrast to persons of the N. Kingdom (2 K 16⁶ is a more apparent than real exception, for though the 'Jews' spoken of do, in fact, belong to the S. Kingdom (14²²), yet they are contrasted with Syrians [MT] or, rather, Edomites). It seems, therefore, to have been scarcely used until the kingdom of Judah was the one existing Heb. kingdom. This change would make it the more easy for 'Jew' to be employed as a synonym of 'Hebrew' (Jer 34⁹), and for the language common to N. and S. Pal. to be called 'Jewish' (יְהוּדִית 2 K 18²⁶· ²⁸ ‖ 2 Ch 32¹⁸, cf. Neh 13²⁴). Although those who inhabited Jerus. and Judah were still regarded for a time as having a special right to the title (Neh 1² 6⁶), yet it became the national name of the people of Israel in contrast to Gentiles (Neh 4⁶ [¹² AV] 5⁸, Zec 8²³, Dn 3⁸, Est 2⁵, and often; cf. 1 Mac 8²³· ²⁷ τὸ ἔθνος τῶν Ἰουδαίων).

Josephus is therefore not far wrong when he says, ἐκλήθησαν δὲ τὸ ὄνομα ἐξ ἧς ἡμέρας ἀνέβησαν ἐκ Βαβυλῶνος, ἀπὸ τῆς Ἰούδα φυλῆς, ἧς πρώτης ἐλθούσης εἰς ἐκείνους τοὺς τόπους, αὐτοί τε καὶ ἡ χώρα τῆς προσηγορίας αὐτῆς μετέλαβον (*Ant.* XI. v. 7). Josephus also quotes a passage from Clearchus, which speaks of his master Aristotle definitely using the word 'Jew'; but as he only says that it is derived from Judæa, the country that the Jews inhabit, it is doubtful whether he uses the term in the merely local or the national sense (*c. Ap.* i. 22). Further, though nowhere expressly applied to members of the Ten Tribes (Mordecai as belonging to Benjamin would readily be called 'Jew'), yet, in view of the wide area over which 'Jews' are said to be scattered in Est 9¹⁵⁻¹⁹, it seems impossible to believe but that when the Book of Esther was written the term included them.

In Neh 2¹⁶ (and so also, perhaps, 5¹⁷, but not 5¹, cf. 5⁸) 'the Jews' are distinguished from the priests, the nobles, the princes (*sĕgānim*), and 'the rest that did the work,' and seem to mean the middle classes, which were, perhaps, then, as in NT times, the most zealous for Judaism. The term occurs as denominative of Gentiles adopting Judaism in Est 8¹⁷.

In NT J. is generally used in contrast to Gentiles (*e.g.* Jn 2⁶ Ac 14¹), Samaritans (Jn 4⁹), or proselytes (Ac 2¹⁰), *i.e.* it = Jews both in race and religion (cf. also Jn 4²²). It is more natural in the mouth of Gentiles than Jews (Mt 2², cf. Lk 23³⁷ spoken by Roman soldiers with ‖ Mt 27⁴², Mk 15³² by the high priests). In Jn it specially denotes the typical representatives of Jewish thought contrasted with believers in Christ whatever their nationality and stage of belief, or with other Jews of less pronounced opinions (*e.g.* Jn 3²⁵ 'a Jew,' 5¹⁰ 7¹³ 9²², see more fully Westcott, *St. John*, Introd. I. 1. i. *a.* γ.). In Gal 2¹³ it refers to Christians of Jewish race (cf. St. Paul, 'a Jew, a man of Tarsus,' Ac 21³⁹). Lk 23⁵¹ ('Arimathæa, a city of the Jews') perhaps means that Ar. was in Judæa, not Samaria or Galilee. For a similar use of the adj. cf. Mk 1⁵, Jn 3²². In Ro 2²⁸· ²⁹ (cf. Rev 2⁹ 3⁹) with ref. to ideal Jews who correspond to God's call and choice. In Gal 1¹³· ¹⁴ St. Paul speaks of the 'Jews' religion,' and the same expression (Gr. Ἰουδαισμός) occurs also in 2 Mac 8¹ (cf. 2²¹ 14³⁸).

Jewess (הַיְּהֻדִיָּה 1 Ch 4¹⁸). — 'And his wife the Jewess,' RV ('Jehudijah,' AV), *i.e.* perhaps of the tribe of Judah, but perhaps in the widest sense (see above), esp. if she is contrasted with Bithiah, the daughter of Pharaoh, who was, as it seems, Mered's other wife.

In NT Timothy's mother is said to be a believing Jewess, but his father a Greek (Ac 16¹). In Ac 24²⁴ Drusilla the wife of Felix is called a Jewess. In both cases there is no thought of the tribe.

Jewish (יְהוּדִית, Ἰουδαιστί). — Of the language of the inhabitants of Jerus. in time of Hezekiah (2 K 18²⁶· ²⁸ ‖ Is 36¹¹· ¹³, cf. 2 Ch 32¹⁸) and of Nehemiah (Neh 13²⁴); in both cases contrasted with that of non-Isr. nations. In the time of Hez. this was quite, and in that of Nehem. almost, certainly Hebrew. In Tit 1¹⁴ 'Jewish fables' prob. = *Haggadôth*, by which Jewish teachers popularized their philosophical speculations.   A. LUKYN WILLIAMS.

JEWEL is EV trⁿ of **1.** חֲלִי Ca 7¹ 'The joints of thy thighs (RVm 'thy rounded thighs') are like jewels.' The word comes from a root חָלָה 'adorn.' Its only other occurrence is in Pr 25¹², where it is coupled with נֶזֶם 'nose-ring,' and where AV, RV tr. 'ornament.' From the same root comes **2.** The ἅπ. λεγ. חֶלְיָה (again coupled with נֶזֶם) in Hos 2¹³ [Heb.¹⁵], used of the jewellery worn upon the occasion of a religious festival. Festal garments and ornaments were in accordance with ancient custom, Ex 3¹⁸ff.

One who had not a special robe (Gn 35²), at least washed his ordinary garments (Ex 19¹⁰) before approaching the presence of the Deity (cf. W. R. Smith, *RS* 433 f.). After the celebration was over, the festal garment and ornaments were put off, because a certain virtue was believed to attach to them from contact with the object of worship, cf. Ezk 44¹⁹ '(The priests) shall put off their garments wherein they minister and lay them in the holy chambers, and they shall put on other garments, *that they sanctify not the people with their garments*'; cf. also the mantle of Elijah, 2 K 2⁸ff. (see the interesting note of Nowack, *Kl. Proph.* 20).

3. כְּלִי, a general term for 'article,' 'utensil,' 'vessel,' 'thing.' When coupled with כֶּסֶף 'silver,' or זָהָב 'gold,' or both of them, it is trᵈ 'jewels' in Gn 24⁵³, Ex 3²² 11² 12³⁵ 35²², Nu 31⁵⁰· ⁵¹, 1 S 6⁸· ¹⁵, Job 28¹⁷ (with פָּז), Is 61¹⁰; so with יָקָר ('preciousness') in Pr 20¹⁵; with תִּפְאֶרֶת ('fairness') in Ezk 16¹⁷· ³⁹ 23²⁶; with חֶמְדָּה ('desirableness,' 'preciousness') in 2 Ch 20²⁵ (cf. חֶמְדָּה in 32²⁷, where for AV 'jewels' RV has 'vessels').

4. נֶזֶם, which in EV is three times (Pr 11²², Is 3²¹, Ezk 16¹²) trᵈ 'jewel,' means 'nose-ring.'

5. סְגֻלָּה, Mal 3¹⁷ 'in that day when I make up my jewels.' Unfortunately, there can be no doubt that this beautiful and familiar phrase rests upon a mistranslation. The Heb. reads וְהָיוּ לִי לַיּוֹם אֲשֶׁר אֲנִי עֹשֶׂה סְגֻלָּה, which can hardly mean anything else than 'They shall be mine, in the day that I do make * (cf. v.²¹), even a peculiar treasure' (so RV and Amer. RV, except that the latter gives 'mine own possession' instead of 'a peculiar treasure'). סְגֻלָּה, applied in 1 Ch 29³, Ec 2⁸ to a private treasure (of gold, silver, etc.) belonging to kings, is repeatedly used of Israel as the special possession or prize of J", Ex 19⁵, Dt 7⁶ 14² 26¹⁸, Ps 135⁴ (see Driver on Dt 7⁶).

In Ca 1¹⁰ where AV has 'rows (of jewels)' RV gives 'plaits (of hair).' The Heb. is תֹּרִים, the meaning of which is quite uncertain. Baethgen (in Kautzsch's *AT*) gives *Gehänge*, Siegfried - Stade *Schnüre*. In the second clause of the same verse RV substitutes 'strings of jewels' for AV 'chains (of gold).' The Heb. is חֲרוּזִים, which Siegfried-Stade tr. *Perlen-, Corallenschnüre*; Baethgen, *Schnüre*; *Oxf. Heb. Lex.* 'strings of beads.' In 1 P 3³ where AV has simply 'gold' RV gives 'jewels of gold,' which is a more exact rendering of χρυσίων (gen. plur.).

In Trumbull's *Studies in Oriental Social Life* (p. 319 ff.) there is a striking chapter on the extent to which gold and silver ornaments are worn by the women of Egypt and Arabia. Oriental dress lends itself to ornamental treatment much more than the Western style. The materials may be gold, silver, and rich cloth, as well as precious stones. All the references in Scripture to jewellery imply that it was highly appreciated, and might easily become dangerous to the moral life. It caused the tragedy of Achan; and provided at once the golden calf and the furnishings of the tabernacle. Among Orientals, the same taste that enjoys rich heavy perfumes and bright dazzling colours in dress, naturally found pleasure in the gorgeous display of jewellery. Jewels took the form of armlet, anklet, bracelet, crescent, earring, nose-ring, necklace, and often had a value of amulet protection. See, further, STONES (PRECIOUS).
                        J. A. SELBIE.

JEWRY. — The Gr. name Ἰουδαία was rendered by Tindale *Jewry* (usually spelt by him 'Jury'), and this was accepted by all the VSS following, except occasionally Rhem. (*Juda*) and AV. The AV was apparently the first to use the more accurate form *Judea*, and it does so everywhere in NT, except Lk 23⁵, Jn 7¹, where the earlier

---

* Or perhaps 'in the day when I act'; Nowack, *den Tag da ich Hand anlege.*

form *Jewry* has been allowed to stand. RV has everywhere the still more accurate spelling *Judæa* (wh. see). The Apocr. was more carelessly tr^d in AV, hence *Jewry* is oftener retained, as 1 Es 1^{32} 4^{49} 5$^{7. 8. 57}$ 6^1 8^{81} 9^3, Bel ^{33}, 2 Mac 10^{24}; but still *Judea* is the more frequent form. In RV the Apocr. is not more carelessly, but it is less consistently tr^d than NT, and so *Jewry* is allowed to remain in 1 Es and Bel, but changed to *Judæa* in 1 Mac. In OT the form *Jewry* occurs but once in AV, Dn 5^{13}. The Aram. is יְהוּד, a form which in the very same verse is tr^d *Judah*, as it is rendered everywhere else except Ezr 5^8 (*Judea*). RV always *Judah*. Cf. Tindale's tr^n of Mt 2$^{5. 6}$ 'And they sayde unto hym; at Bethleem in Jury (τῆς 'Ιουδαίας). For thus it is written by the Prophet. And thou Bethleem in the londe of Jury (γῇ 'Ιούδα), art not the leest concernynge the Princes of Judah ('Ιούδα).'

J. HASTINGS.

JEZANIAH (in Jer 40 [Gr. 47]^8 יְזַנְיָהוּ, LXX 'Ιεζονίας; in 42 [Gr. 49]^1 יְזַנְיָה, BA 'Αζαρίας, Q^{mg} 'Ιεζονίας).—A Judahite military officer who joined Gedaliah at Mizpah (Jer 40^8). After the murder of Gedaliah, Jezaniah was one of those who went to the prophet Jeremiah for counsel as to their future action (42^1). He is called in 2 K 25^{23} **Jaazaniah** (which see), and is apparently to be identified also with **Azariah** (עֲזַרְיָה 'Αζαρίας) of Jer 43^2, who was prominent in rejecting the prophet's advice.

JEZEBEL (אִיזֶבֶל, perhaps * 'un-exalted,' 'un-husbanded' [see *Oxf. Heb. Lex.* p. 33^a], 'Ιεζάβελ).— The daughter of Ethbaal, and wife of Ahab. Ethbaal (Ithobaal) had, after a period of revolution and anarchy, seized (*c.* B.C. 888) the throne of Tyre, which he occupied for more than thirty years. He was the first monarch of note who had reigned in Phœnicia since the days of Hiram, and his alliance was doubtless sought by Omri and Ahab in order to counterbalance the hostility of Damascus. The marriage of J. to Ahab (1 K 16^{31}) exercised a powerful influence upon the history of religion in Israel, and indirectly also in Judah, where J.'s daughter, Athaliah, afterwards shared the throne with Jehoram the son of Jehoshaphat. The worship of the Tyrian Baal was now supported by all the court influence. We are not, indeed, to suppose that Ahab abandoned the worship of J″, whose ⵏ ophets he still consulted (1 K 22^6), and whose name he meant to honour by the names he gave to his children (*Ahaziah, Jehoram, Athaliah*, all of which are compounds containing some form of יהוה). Nay, he could have pleaded that he simply copied the example of Solomon, both in his foreign marriage and in erecting a sanctuary for Baal (cf. 1 K 11$^{1. 7}$ with 16$^{31. 33}$). But what had been tolerated in the days of Solomon now met with strenuous opposition. To the great prophet Elijah, J″ was a jealous God; there was no longer room in Israel for the worship of Baal; there must be no 'halting between two opinions,' but a definite choice of the one or the other deity. The attitude assumed by Elijah, and those like-minded with him, provoked the resentment of J., in whose hands Ahab seems to have been little more than a tool. The prophets of J″ were either put to death or driven to conceal themselves (1 K 18^4), until Elijah could exclaim, 'I, even I only, am left, and they seek my life to take it away' (1 K 19^{14}). The issue of the conflict on Mount Carmel, and the slaughter of the prophets of Baal, from which Elijah hoped so much, served only to augment the persecuting zeal of the queen (1 K 19^2).

* Hommel's theory (*AHT* 116), that the first element of the word is a divine name, is very precarious. König (*Expos. Times*, Jan. 1899, p. 190^a) suggests that the first element is אִי 'island,' and that the name may mean 'exalted isle,' which may have been originally an honorific appellation of Tyre itself.

The darkest stain, however, upon the memory of J. is left by the atrocious crime she perpetrated (1 K 21) in order to procure for her husband the vineyard of Naboth the Jezreelite (see NABOTH). The judicial murder of Naboth sent a thrill of horror through the land, and, as W. R. Smith (*Proph. Isr.* 87), following Ewald and Wellhausen, has truly remarked, this crime had far more to do than the worship of Baal with undermining the throne of Ahab and Jezebel. The popular feeling is doubtless truly reflected in the terrible sentence which (according to the Deuteronomic compiler) Elijah passed upon the actors in this tragedy (1 K 21$^{17-24}$).

J. survived her husband (who fell in battle at Ramoth-gilead, *c.* B.C. 853) some ten years, and saw her two sons, Ahaziah and Jehoram, in succession seated upon the throne. The house of Omri was at length destroyed by Jehu, a cavalry officer in the service of Jehoram, who treacherously slew both his master and Ahaziah king of Judah (2 K 9$^{24ff.}$). When tidings of the catastrophe reached J., the aged queen prepared to meet death with fortitude and dignity. Having attired herself as for a state occasion (the notion that she meant to captivate Jehu by her charms is too ridiculous to need refutation), she awaited the arrival of the usurper, whom she mockingly accosted, 'Is it well with Zimri, the murderer of his master?' * The answer of the brutal Jehu was to order her eunuchs to cast her down from the window of the palace, and, as the helpless woman lay stunned by the fall, he and his captains trampled her under their horses' feet. After a banquet held to celebrate the success of his conspiracy, the savage warrior ordered the rites of sepulture to be paid to his victim; but it was discovered that her body had been devoured by the street dogs. So perished miserably the proud daughter of Tyre, and the murder of Naboth was avenged (2 K 9$^{30-37}$).

The impression of J. that is left upon us by the narrative of the OT is that of an able, resolute woman, who, once she had formed a purpose, carried it to a conclusion, without much scruple as to the methods she employed. Whether she was guilty, in a literal sense, of the 'whoredoms and witchcrafts' of which Jehu speaks in 2 K 9^{22}, we have not sufficient evidence to decide. Her accuser is by no means an unprejudiced witness, and even he may have only meant, in his coarse fashion, to allude to her worship of the Tyrian Baal. Later traditions interpreted the accusation in its most literal sense (cf. Rev 2^{20}).† There can be little doubt that the prevailing estimate of J.'s character is far less favourable than that which was cherished by her contemporaries. Much of the obloquy that attaches to her name, and that has made 'a Jezebel' a term of reproach, is due to an inexcusable misunderstanding of 2 K 9^{30}, which records a perfectly innocent and dignified act. It is surely a singular coincidence whereby the murderer and his victim, Jehu and Jezebel, are remembered best, not for the part they played at an

* AV 'Had Zimri peace who slew his master?' is an improbable rendering, and even RV (text) 'Is it peace, thou Zimri, thy master's murderer?' seems hardly to suit the occasion. Our rendering is supported by Kautzsch's *AT*, 'Geht es Simri wohl?' and by Reuss, 'Wie geht's du Simri?' which is paraphrased by the latter, 'Ei guten Tag du Canaille!'

† The correct text is τὴν γυναῖκα. The copyist who added σου seems to have understood the 'angel' of the Church as the bishop. The name 'Jezebel' must be understood symbolically and not as the real name of the woman against whom the denunciation is uttered. She appears to have been a false prophetess (within the Christian Church, and not belonging to Judaism or heathenism) whose teaching had a licentious tendency, πορνεύειν and μοιχεύειν being probably used in a literal and not a figurative sense. Bousset (see his exhaustive note) thinks there is not sufficient evidence to warrant the interesting suggestion of Schürer, that Jezebel in this text is the priestess of the Chaldæan Sibyl, Sambethe, who is believed by Schürer to have had a sanctuary at Thyatira.

important crisis in Israel's history, but he for his 'furious driving,' and she for her painted face !

LITERATURE.—W. R. Smith, *OTJC*[2] p. 237, *Proph. Isr.* 48, 76 ; Wellhausen, *Hist. of Isr. and Jud.* 65 ; Kuenen, *Rel. Isr.* i. 355 ff. ; Reuss, *Das AT*, i. 357 ; Cornill, *Der israel. Prophetismus*, 30 f.   J. A. SELBIE.

JEZELUS ('Ιεζῆλος).—**1.** (B 'Ιέθηλος) 1 Es 8³². In Ezr 8⁵ JAHAZIEL. **2.** 1 Es 8³⁵. In Ezr 8⁹ JEHIEL.

JEZER (יֵצֶר 'form,' 'purpose' ; LXX Gn 46²⁴ 'Ισσααρ, Nu 26⁴⁹ B 'Ιέσερ, A 'Ιεσρί, 1 Ch 7¹³ B 'Ισσειήρ, A Σαάρ).—The head of the **Jezerites** (הַיִּצְרִי, B 'Ιεσερεί, A 'Ιεσρί), a family of Naphtali. See GENEALOGY.

JEZIEL (יְזִיאֵל *Kerê*, וְזוֹאל *Kethîbh* ; B'Ιωήλ, A 'Αζιήλ).—A Benjamite who joined David at Ziklag, 1 Ch 12³.

JEZRAHIAH (יְזְרַחְיָה ='J" will shine,' Luc. ℵ°·ᵃ 'Ιεζρίας, ℵ*BA omit, Neh 12⁴²).—The leader of the singers at the solemn dedication of the walls of Jerus. in the time of Nehemiah. In 1 Ch 7³ *bis* the same name is rendered **Izrahiah**.

JEZREEL (יִזְרְעֵאל 'God soweth').—**1.** A Judahite (1 Ch 4³). See GENEALOGY. **2.** The symbolical name of Hosea's eldest son (Hos 1⁴), given in token of the prophet's disapproval of the massacre of Ahab's family at J., and his expectation that divine vengeance would speedily overtake the dynasty of its perpetrator, Jehu. See HOSEA, p. 421ᵃ. **3.** J. is used in Hos 2²²·²³ as a name for Israel, with a play upon the etymology of the word.

JEZREEL (יִזְרְעֵאל 'God soweth' ; LXX A 'Ιεσραέλ, 'Ιεζραέλ, 'Ιεσραήλ, 'Εσραέ ; B 'Ιαήλ, 'Ισραήλ, 'Εζερεέλ ; Jos. *Ant.* VIII. xiii. 6, 'Ιερέζηλα ; VIII. xv. 4, 6, 'Ιεζέρηλα, var. 'Ιξάρα, etc.).—This is the Heb. name of the great plain (יְ עֵמֶק, Jos 17¹⁶, Jg 6³³, Hos 1⁵) now generally called *Esdraelon*, and by the Arabs known as *Merj ibn-'Amr*. In modern times it has been applied especially to the vale between Jebel Duhy and Gilboa, sloping E. towards Beisân (see ESDRAELON). Jezreel * is the name also of—

1. A city in the territory of Issachar (Jos 19¹⁸), the site of which is now occupied by the village of *Zer'în*. This identification is beyond question. The two names are practically identical ; the soft initial *yod* of the Heb. is dropped, and, as is not unusual, the Heb. *-el* is replaced by the Arab. *-în* in the modern word. Similar instances are found in *Beitîn* for Bethel, and *Isma'în* for Ishmael. Eusebius and Jerome (*OS*² 268. 52, 165. 14) place Jezreel in the great plain between Legio (*Khân Lejjûn*) and Scythopolis (*Beisân*), and the Bordeaux Pilgrim (A.D. 333) gives the distance from Beisân as 12 Roman miles, conditions quite met by *Zer'în*. Eusebius and Jerome speak of *Esdraela*, and the Bordeaux Pilgrim of *Stradela*, both obvious modifications of the Greek name of Jezreel. In Crusading times it was called *Parvum Gerinum* (William of Tyre, xxii. 6), and in 1173 Benjamin of Tudela mentions *Zarein* (וְרִין) as Jezreel. (The Constantinople ed. gives וְרֵין, but it is full of errors). Brocardus (c. vii. 176, 177) speaks of *Zarcin*, and notes the fine view which it commands. Sir John Maundeville says, ' 5 miles from Nain is the city of Jezreel, which was formerly called Zarim ' (*Early Travels in Palestine*, Bohn's ed. p. 184). Robinson observes that from the 14th cent. to the beginning of the 19th the identification was lost sight of. He was himself the first to put it on a secure basis (*BRP* iii. 161–163 [² ii. 318–325]).

* The plain probably derived its name from the city, and not *vice versâ* (see Budde. *Richt. u. Sam.* 46 ff.).

The beautiful and commanding situation of Jezreel amply warranted the distinction conferred upon it by Ahab and Jezebel. Mount Gilboa terminates to the N. in bold bluffs which descend steeply into the vale of Jezreel, and to the N.W. throws off a low sinking promontory, thrust like a wedge between the vale of Jezreel and the great bay of Esdraelon, which sweeps round by the base of Gilboa to Jenîn. Guarded on the N. by precipitous cliffs about 100 ft. in height, with the splendid rampart of Gilboa S. and S.E., it is a position of considerable strength, being easiest of approach from the S.W. Here, at an elevation of 200 ft. above the plain, stands the village of *Zer'în*. The hovels that form the village, some thirty in number, built on a mound of rubbish, are mean and dirty, and the general aspect is one of squalor. The inhabitants have been corrupted by travellers, and have learned to prey upon all who pass, while the street dogs here have an evil reputation for savageness.

The place contains little of interest and no antiquities. There are numerous broken cisterns among the houses ; and Guérin found a white marble sarcophagus W. of the town (*Samarie*, i. 311 ; *PEF Mem.* ii. 131). The one conspicuous building is a large square tower, of no great age, now commonly used as a *medâfeh* or place for the entertainment of guests. From the top of this structure a magnificent view is obtained, including the great plain in its whole extent, and every point of importance around it, with the single exception of Tabor. S. and S.E. runs the high barren wall of Gilboa, with its memories of humiliation and defeat for Israel. From En-gannim (*Jenîn*), its white domes and minarets glancing amid the greenery of its sheltered nook, the Samaritan mountains rising behind, the eye ranges along the edge of the plain to Megiddo (*Khân Lejjûn*), and thence to the bushy heights of Carmel, the rough crest of *el-Mahrakah*, the place of Elijah's burnt-offering showing clear against the sky. Cut off from the mountain on the north by the gorge of the Kishon, low oak-clad hills divide the plain of Acre from Esdraelon, and, sweeping round eastward in more fertile slopes, drop in precipitous cliffs upon the plain just south of Nazareth, the highest of whose white houses one may descry, with the dark uplands of Galilee beyond. Mt. Tabor is hidden by the shapely mass of *Jebel Duhy*, the hill of Moreh, crowned by its *wely*, with Shunem, Nain, and Endor clinging to its sides. Far down the broad and fertile vale of Jezreel as it slopes to the Jordan Valley, we catch a glimpse of the citadel of *Beisân* ; and across the *Ghôr* the view is barred by the steep and rugged mountains of Gilead.

Besides the cisterns mentioned above, Jezreel was well situated for water supply. *Bîr es-Suweid* lies to the N. of the town ; and at the base of the cliffs to the E. the waters of *el-'Ain el-Meiyiteh*, ' the dead spring,' form quite a considerable stream. The fountain is so named because once it dried up. After deep digging the waters flowed again ; the pit was filled with loose gravel, and since then the supply has been continuous. About a mile farther E., in a cave at the base of Gilboa, a still more copious spring bursts forth, the stream from which is strong enough to turn a mill. This is probably the **fountain** where the Israelites encamped before the disastrous battle of Gilboa (1 S 29¹). It is also with some likelihood identified with the spring of Harod (Jg 7¹). The native name, *'Ain Jalûd* or *Jalût* (Arab. for Goliath), seems due to some confusion with the scene of David's encounter with the giant. ' Here is the plain where David slew Goliath,' says the Bordeaux Pilgrim ; but beyond this, says Robinson, no trace of the tradition is to be found. The fountain which the Crusaders knew as *Tubana* was doubtless the spring *'Ain Ṭuba'ûn*, some little distance off, surrounded by marshy ground. The water is slightly reddish in colour. Conder suggests that this may represent the Talmudic *Tubnia* (Tosephta, *Sheviith*, ch. vii. ; *PEF Mem.* iii. 79). The water of all these fountains is sweet, and abounds in small fish : on this was founded the legend of the Crusading army being miraculously supplied with fish for some days (William of Tyre, xxii. 27).

Jezreel is first mentioned in marking out the lot of Issachar (Jos 19^{18}). It, with its district, remained faithful to the family of Saul, after the disaster at Gilboa (2 S 2^9). The days of its greatest prosperity dawned when Ahab and Jezebel, fascinated no doubt by the beauty of the place and its surroundings, chose it as a royal residence. The palace stood on the E. side of the city, the harem being close by the gate, with windows overlooking the road leading thither (2 K 9$^{30.31}$). A tower commanding a view of the approach from Jordan, up the vale of Jezreel, also formed part of the building (*ib.* 9^{17}). This was most necessary to guard against surprise ; as then, and until comparatively recent times, the hordes of the East came this way in making their inroads upon the fruitful land of Esdraelon. An object of special admiration was the house of ivory built by the king, an evidence also of the luxury in which the royal pair indulged (1 K 22^{39} ; cf. Am 3^{15} 6^4). The establishment of idolatrous priests must also have been large (1 K 16^{33}, 2 K 10^{11}). Hither drove Ahab from Carmel through the storm, preceded by the stern, swift-footed Tishbite (1 K 18$^{45.46}$). Here was the vineyard of Naboth the **Jezreelite** (הַיִּזְרְעֵאלִי), coveted by Ahab (*ib.* 21^1). Probably it lay E. of the town, where wine-presses cut in the rock are still to be seen (2 K 9$^{21.25}$). Whether this city or Samaria was the scene of Jezebel's outrage upon Naboth and his sons (1 K 21$^{8-14}$, 2 K 9^{26}) is in some doubt. If Ahab's blood was licked by the dogs at Samaria, that would point to the southern city as the scene of Naboth's execution (1 K 22^{38}). On the other hand, the natural sense of 1 K 21 seems to place it at Jezreel ; and with this Josephus agrees (*Ant.* VIII. xv. 6).* Joram, succeeding his father Ahab, maintained Jezreel as a royal residence ; and here he was visited by his kinsman Ahaziah king of Judah (2 K 8^{29}). These two were together when surprised by the newly anointed Jehu, who slew Joram and cast his body into the plot of Naboth : Ahaziah fled, but was wounded, and died at Megiddo (2 K 9^{27}). Here Jezebel also suffered miserably for her offences, being at the conqueror's command hurled from the window into the courtyard, where she was devoured by the pariah dogs (2 K 9$^{30-37}$). By the gateway of Jezreel were piled the heads of Ahab's 70 sons, brought hither by Jehu's orders from Samaria (2 K 10^7) ; then the town became the scene of one of those sickening massacres which so often stain the records of Oriental monarchies : all who might be suspected of sympathy with the house of Ahab, 'his great men, his familiar friends, and his priests,' were relentlessly done to death (*ib.* 10^{11}). The prosperity of Jezreel seems to have ended with the downfall of the house of Ahab, and its name is seen no more in the sacred books, save only in Hos 1$^{4.11}$, where it occurs with a symbolic significance. (See HOSEA).

The Crusaders knew Jezreel as *Parvum Gerinum*, and close by occurred in 1183 a skirmish with Saladin, after which the Saracen leader retired

* It is possible that the prediction in 1 K 21^{19} (which is from a different hand from 22) contemplates the deed of Jehu in 2 K 9^{25}, and not the death of Ahab himself (cf. 1 K 21^{29}). In any case, 22^{38} is an interpolation. See, further, Wellh. *Comp.* 284.

(William of Tyre, xxii. 26). In 1217 the Christian army passed down the vale to Beisân ; but the place has been the scene of no important event in later history ; and for many centuries it has presented, practically unchanged, the aspect of squalid poverty that meets the eye of the traveller to-day.

2. A town in the hill-country of Judæa, the site of which has not been identified. It was not far from the Judæan Carmel (Jos 15^{56}). Ahinoam (the **Jezreelitess**, הַיִּזְרְעֵאלִית or הַיִּזְרְעֵאלִית), one of David's first two wives (1 S 25^{43} 27^3 30^5, 2 S 2^2 3^2, 1 Ch 3^1), was a native of this town.

LITERATURE.—*Early Travels in Palestine*, Bohn, p. 184, etc. ; Robinson, *BRP* iii. 161–168 [2 ii. 318–325] ; Thomson, *Land and Book*, ii. 177–191 ; Stanley, *Sinai and Pal.* p. 343, *History of the Jewish Church*, ii. 244 ; Conder, *Tent-Work in Palestine*, p. 65, etc. ; *PEF Mem.* ii. pp. 79, 88, 131 ; Baedeker, *Palestine and Syria*, ed. 1894, p. 242 ; G. A. Smith, *HGHL* pp. 356, 381, etc. ; Buhl, *GAP* 204 f. ; Guérin, *Samarie*, i. 311 ff.

W. EWING.

JEZREELITE, JEZREELITESS.—See preceding article.

JEZRIELUS (A ʹΙεʒρίηλος, B ʹΙεʒόρικλος ; AV Hierielus), 1 Es 9^{27}.—In Ezr 10^{26} JEHIEL. The AV form is derived from the Aldine text.

JIDLAPH (יִדְלָף, perh. 'he weepeth,' if from root דָּלַף 'drip' ; A ʹΙελδάφ, D om., Luc. ʹΙεδλάφ).—A son of Nahor, Gn 22^{22} (J). The clan of which he is the eponym has not been identified.

JOAB (יוֹאָב ' J " is father').—**1.** (ʹΙωάβ) the son of Zeruiah and brother of Abishai and Asahel. J.'s *mother* is named because she was David's sister, and thus of more importance than his *father*, of whom all we are told is that his sepulchre was at Bethlehem (2 S 2^{32}). The first mention of J. is upon the occasion of the engagement at Gibeon between David's men and those of Ishbosheth. Abner, who commanded the latter, was completely beaten, but in the course of his retreat killed Asahel, who had overtaken him. At sunset J., at the request of Abner, recalled his men from the pursuit, and returned to David's headquarters at Hebron (2 S 2$^{12-32}$). Some time afterwards Abner, having quarrelled with Ishbosheth, offered his allegiance to David. J. was absent when Saul's general visited Hebron for this purpose, but returned shortly after his departure. Prompted by a desire to avenge the death of his brother Asahel, and perhaps also by a jealous dread that Abner might supplant him in the favour of David, J. sent messengers to recall him, and then treacherously murdered him (2 S 3$^{22-27}$). At the siege of Jerus. by David, it was J., acc. to the Chronicler, who first scaled the citadel, and thus earned the reward promised by the king, that he should be chief captain of the host (1 Ch 11^6). After the defeat of the Edomites (2 S 8$^{13t.}$, cf. title of. Ps 60) J. remained in Idumæa for six months, and sought to exterminate all the male population. The terror of his name haunted that country for long (1 K 11$^{14-21}$). In conjunction with his brother Abishai, J. waged successful war against the allied forces of Syria and Ammon ; and when at length the citadel of Rabbath-ammon was ready to fall, he displayed a combination of magnanimity and prudence in sending for David to deal the final blow, so that the king himself might have the credit of the victory (2 S 11^1 12$^{26-29}$). It was during the siege of Rabbah that David was guilty of the most heinous sin of his life. J. fell in readily with the king's plan for getting rid of Uriah the Hittite, and thus obtained a new hold upon David through sharing his guilty secret (2 S 11$^{6-27}$). After Absalom's murder of Amnon, and his flight to Geshur, it was J. who, through the medium of 'a wise woman from Tekoa,' induced David to recall his son, and who at last, but with reluctance, effected a final reconciliation between them (2 S 14¹ff·). When the rebellion of Absalom broke out, J. remained loyal, and accompanied David in his flight across the Jordan. With his brother Abishai, and Ittai the Gittite, he shared the command of the royal army in the battle which proved so disastrous to Absalom and his adherents. It was by J.'s own hand that Absalom met his death as he hung defenceless in the branches of an oak. As he had not hesitated to take the rebel's life in spite of David's strict charge to the contrary, J. did not hesitate after the battle to remonstrate with the king for giving such unrestrained vent to his grief for his son's death. The sturdy common-sense of J., although his plainness of speech must have been very displeasing to his master, availed to check the disaffection that had begun to spread among the royal troops (2 S 19). It was probably resentment at J.'s conduct on this occasion that led David to transfer the command of the army to another of his nephews, Amasa, who had been Absalom's commander-in-chief (2 S 19¹³). The deadly mistake of this appointment speedily became apparent when the standard of revolt was raised by Sheba ben-Bichri. Amasa proved himself a useless *fainéant*, and the situation became so alarming that David was compelled to send Abishai (or perhaps J. himself) * to take command of the army. At any rate J. was present with the expedition, which was ultimately joined also by Amasa. J. seized the first opportunity to rid himself of his rival, whom he despatched with as little compunction as he had shown in the case of Abner (2 S 20⁸ff·, on the text and interpretation of which see Driver, *Sam., ad loc.*). He then prosecuted the campaign with vigour, and speedily brought it to a successful issue. Sheba having taken refuge at Abel-beth-maacah, J. laid siege to the town, and only desisted when the head of the rebel was cast to him over the wall (2 S 20²²). J. offered strenuous resistance to David's proposal to number the people (2 S 24¹ff·), and, acc. to the Chronicler, did not complete the work (1 Ch 21⁶). When Adonijah took steps to have himself proclaimed king, J. attached himself to his party, probably without the slightest thought of disloyalty to David, who seems himself to have intended that Adonijah should succeed him, until the household intrigue of Bathsheba, aided by the powerful support of the prophet Nathan, led him to decide in favour of Solomon. The latter, upon his accession to the throne, considered it prudent to rid himself of J., whose influence with the army might have constituted a serious danger to the new monarch. No doubt a desire to wipe away from his house the stain of the unavenged blood of Abner and Amasa partially influenced Solomon, but State reasons must have predominated. J., on hearing that Adonijah had been put to death and Abiathar deposed, needed no further intimation that his own life was in danger, and he fled to the asylum of the altar. Refusing to leave the sacred place, by Solomon's order he was slain there by Benaiah, whose readiness to act as executioner was doubtless all the greater because he thus secured the

* In 2 S 20⁶ the MT and LXX have *Abishai*, but Syr. has *Joab*, and the latter reading is adopted by Thenius, Wellh., Driver, Kittel, Löhr. On the other hand, Budde, in his notes to the Bks. of Sam. in Haupt's *Sacred Bks. of OT* (p. 95), considers that MT is correct, and that the narrative is perfectly intelligible upon this assumption. 'As the new commander-in-chief Amasa left him in the lurch, David was obliged to make use of J.'s services, but his dignity as king would not permit the acknowledgment of this by an immediate reinstatement. By charging Abishai his brother with the commission he makes sure that J. will not remain behind, and the latter willingly joins the expedition as a volunteer, in order to put the king under new obligations to himself. The fact that he takes the leadership into his own hands is so much a matter of course that it does not need to be mentioned.'

reversion of the office of commander-in-chief for himself (1 K 2²⁸⁻³⁴). Acc. to 1 K 2¹⁻¹² Solomon, in the execution of J., acted in obedience to the dying injunction of David. Wellh. and Stade hold, however, that this passage is an unhistorical interpolation. The hand of the Deuteronomic redactor is certainly evident in v.³, but Budde (*Richt u. Sam.* 263 f.), following Kuenen, defends the *antiquity* (without committing himself to the *historicity*) of at least vv.⁵⁻⁹.

The character of J. has often been unfairly estimated, either from lack of a due regard to the spirit of the age in which he lived, or from prejudice in favour of David and Solomon. The least that can be said is that he was a man of far-seeing statesman-like views, a brave soldier, a skilful commander, and a loyal subject. Even his assassination of Abner and Amasa, so repellent to us, could plead as excuse, in the one case the supposed duty to avenge his brother's death, and in the other the gross injustice of David in depriving him of his command. The Oriental is not usually distinguished for generosity to his enemies or scrupulousness in his methods of revenge, and J. was no exception to this rule ; but his action on these two occasions must not blind us to the splendid services he rendered to his country. Without him David was like Ferdinand without Wallenstein. No doubt, like the last-named great general, J. made the most of his knowledge that he was indispensable, and thus in the end was able to obtain his own terms from his master. One thing he had resolved upon, that as he alone was fit for the post, he alone must command David's army. 'Wallenstein war Nichts wo er nicht Alles war, er muss entweder gar nicht oder mit vollkommener Freiheit handeln' (Schiller). This determination to brook no rival, combined with the low moral standard of the age, will suffice to explain the most questionable episodes in the career of the Wallenstein of Israel. J.'s conduct all through the Absalomic rebellion reflects the greatest credit upon his foresight. It is needless to offer any apology for his killing of Absalom, an act that was pardonable because necessary. Nor is it possible, as we have explained already, to convict him of treason because at first he supported Adonijah. Taking everything into account, we feel that this great man deserved a better fate, and it leaves a painful impression upon us when we learn that, after he had served his king and his country so faithfully, his grey hairs were not suffered to go down to the grave in peace.

2. ('Ιωβάβ BL, 'Ιωάβ A).—The son of Seraiah, a descendant of Judah, and father 'of the valley of Charashim' (AV), or 'of (the inhabitants of) the valley of craftsmen' (AVm), or 'of Ge-Harashim' (RV), or 'of the valley of craftsmen' (RVm), 1 Ch 4¹⁴, cf. Neh 11³⁵. See GE-HARASHIM. **3.** ('Ιωβάβ, 'Ιωάβ).—The name of a family which returned from exile with Zerubbabel and Ezra (Ezr 2⁶ = Neh 7¹¹, Ezr 8⁹, 1 Es 8³⁵).   J. A. SELBIE.

JOACHAZ (A 'Ιωχάζ, B 'Ιεχονίας), 1 Es 1³⁴ (LXX³²).—Jehoahaz the son of Josiah ; cf. 2 Ch 36¹. B and the Vulgate (*Jechonias*) are in agreement with Mt 1¹¹ in omitting the short reign of Jehoahaz.

JOADANUS (A 'Ιωάδανος, B 'Ιώδανος), 1 Es 9¹⁹.—One of the sons of Jesus, the son of Josedek, the priest. The corresponding name in Ezr 10¹⁸ is GEDALIAH.

JOAH (אֹיוֹ 'J″ is brother').—**1.** Son of Asaph, the 'recorder' at Hezekiah's court, 2 K 18¹⁸· ²⁶· ³⁷ = Is 36³· ¹¹· ²². **2.** A Levitical family name, 1 Ch 6²¹ (apparently same as Ethan of v.⁴²), 2 Ch 29¹². **3.**

A Levite, son of Obed-edom, 1 Ch 26⁴. **4.** Son of Joahaz, the 'recorder' at Josiah's court, 2 Ch 34⁸.

JOAHAZ (יוֹאָחָז). — The father of Joah, the 'recorder' in the reign of Josiah, 2 Ch 34⁸. See also JEHOAHAZ.

JOAKIM ('Ιωακίμ or -είμ, LXX form of יְהוֹיָקִים).— The name is spelt Jehoiakim in canon. books, but Joacim or Joachim in Apocr. AV, and Joakim everywhere in Apocr. RV.

In Apocr. the name belongs to *six* persons. **1.** King Jehoiakim, son of Josiah, father of Jeconiah (Bar 1³). 1 Es 1⁴⁰ follows LXX of 2 Ch 36⁶ in saying that he was carried in copper chains to Babylon. This is in apparent, but not hopeless, discrepancy with 2 K 24¹·⁶ and Jer 22¹⁸ 36³⁰. **2.** Jehoiachin, son of Jehoiakim, who is erroneously called Joakim in 1 Es 1⁴³, and is said to have reigned after his father 3 months and 10 days. **3.** A priest, son of Hilkiah, to whom the captives of B.C. 597 are said, in Bar 1⁷, to have sent money for the purchase of offerings and incense. The Gr. says that the money was 'sent to J. the priest (τὸν ἱερέα), and to the priests (πρὸς τοὺς ἱερεῖς).' Hence RV renders ἱερέα, 'the high priest.' No high priest of this name, however, is mentioned in Scripture, and it is therefore better with Zöckler to regard J. as the second priest, invested with the duties of overseer or treasurer of the temple, as Pashhur (Jer 20¹) is called chief officer in the house of J″; and as Zephaniah, a son of Hilkiah and brother of Seraiah who succeeded his father, was promised to be officer in the temple (Jer 29²⁶), and was afterwards 'second priest' (Jer 52²⁴). It is reasonable to suppose that Zephaniah was J.'s successor as *sagan*, or second priest. **4.** A high priest, who, in the days of Holofernes and Judith, when the people of Judæa were 'newly come up from captivity,' is said, as head of the Senate, to have directed military affairs, by commanding the inhabitants of Bethulia to occupy the northern passes (Jth 4⁶·⁷), and at the same time to have led the people in devout supplication in the temple, clad in sackcloth, and with ashes on his mitre (Jth 4¹⁴·¹⁵). **5.** A priest, son of Zorobabel, mentioned among the returning exiles in the reign of Darius (1 Es 5⁵). **6.** The husband of Susanna, a wealthy Jew in Babylon. The rooms of his mansion were used for the administration of justice among the Jews; and acc. to Syr. W₂, for the Synagogue. The horrid calumny concocted by the two lascivious elders came on J. as a terrible blow, and, when Daniel solved the mystery, J. joined with Susanna's relatives in singing praises that no dishonour was found in her (Sus 63). W₂ stands alone in saying that J. died shortly after marriage, and that Susanna was a pious widow when her trial came.

J. T. MARSHALL.

JOANAN ('Ιωανάν WH, 'Ιωαννᾶ TR, AV Joanna). —An ancestor of Jesus, Lk 3²⁷.

JOANNA ('Ιωάνα WH, 'Ιωάννα TR), the wife of Chuza, the steward of Herod Antipas. She was one of 'certain women which had been healed of evil spirits and infirmities' (Lk 8²). Thus bound to Jesus by the tie of gratitude, J. ministered to Him of her substance, and after the crucifixion was one of the company that went to the tomb to anoint the body of the Lord (Lk 8³ 24¹⁰).

JOANNES ('Ιωάννης, AV Johannes).—**1.** (B -άνης) 1 Es 8³⁸ son of Akatan, in Ezr 8¹² JOHANAN. **2.** 1 Es 9²⁹ son of Bebai, in Ezr 10²⁸ JEHOHANAN.

JOARIB ('Ιωαρ(ε)ίβ, 'Ιωαρ(ε)ίμ), 1 Mac 2¹ 14²⁹, Jos. *Ant.* XII. vi. 1, the head of the priestly family

from which the Maccabees were descended. Acc. to 1 Ch 24⁷ this family, there called that of JEHOIARIB (which see), was the first of the twenty-four courses of priests.

JOASH (יוֹאָשׁ).—**1.** Father of Gideon, a native of Abiezer (Jg 6¹¹ 8²). Notwithstanding Gideon's modest language (6¹⁵), J. must have been the most important person in his town ('one of the principal persons of the tribe of Manasseh,' Jos. *Ant.* v. vi. 2); he had more than ten servants (6²⁷), and he was guardian of the local sanctuary of Baal. It may be reasonably supposed that the demonstrated impotence of Baal to protect his altar and the Asherah, coupled with love for his son, revived strongly in the mind of J. a conviction of the unique power of J″, which found utterance in that sarcastic address to the Abiezrites which recalls the mockery of Elijah on a like occasion, and which received a lasting memorial in the name Jerubbaal by which Gideon was known in later times (1 S 12¹¹, 2 S 11²¹). **2.** A son of Ahab to whose custody, and that of Amon, governor of Samaria, Ahab committed Micaiah on his departure for Ramoth-gilead (1 K 22²⁶=2 Ch 18²⁵). J. was probably left behind as his father's viceroy. Rawlinson suggests that here and in 2 Ch 28⁷ 'king's son' means a state officer; cf. Jer 36²⁶ 38⁶. **3.** A descendant of Shelah, son of Judah, 1 Ch 4²². Vv.²¹⁻²³ are very obscure (see *QPB*). **4.** (יוֹעָשׁ) A Benjamite, son of Becher, 1 Ch 7⁸. **5.** A Benjamite warrior who joined David at Ziklag, 1 Ch 12³. **6.** (יוֹעָשׁ) One of the comptrollers of David's private estate. He was over 'the cellars of oil,' 1 Ch 27²⁸. **7.** See JEHOASH.

N. J. D. WHITE.

JOB, BOOK OF.—In mod. edd. of the Heb. Bible, the third in order of the books called Kĕthubim in the Jewish Canon. Its place, however, has varied; in the Talm. order it stands between Ps and Pr; Jerome places it before both. In the Greek Canon the division of books is for the most part according to subject-matter. After the historical books follow Ps, Pr, Ec, Ca, Job (this is order in B); succeeded by Wis, Sir, and other extra-canonical books. Job, together with the canonical books of Pr and Ec, and the apocr. books Sir and Wis, belongs to what is called the Ḥokhmah or Wisdom-Literature of the Old Covenant, and forms its crown and climax. This article will deal severally with the Name of the book, its Contents, its Form, its Text, its Integrity, its Scope and Purpose, its Date and Authorship, and the History of its Exegesis.

i. NAME.—Heb. אִיּוֹב, Gr. 'Ιώβ, 'Ιυγ̄ϋ̄β, misrepresented in the usual Eng. pronunciation. In a postscript to the LXX (not found in Aq. or Symm., and in Theod. only in part), Job is confused with the Idumæan king *Jobab*, mentioned in Gn 36³³. The sentence runs: 'This man is described in the Syriac book as living in the land of Ausis, on the borders of Idumæa and Arabia; and his name before was Jobab, and having taken an Arabian wife, he begot a son whose name was Ennon.' By a further confusion in the name Ζαρά (Gn 36¹³), Job's descent from Esau is inferred. The traditions embodied in this postscript are followed in the Koran, but are wholly untrustworthy. (For additional traditions concerning Job, see Koran, Suras 38, 40, also Sura 21).

The derivation of the name is doubtful, and the attempts to give to it a significance drawn from etymology are very questionable. It has been taken (Ges. and others) as a passive form from root איב, meaning 'one persecuted' by Satan, or by his friends, or by calamity. Cf. ילוֹד from ילד. But this form is never purely passive (Volck, p. 6). Others (including Ewald and Delitzsch) explain after the analogy of Arab. *awwāb*, as from root

אוב, 'the penitent one, *resipiscens*, or pious, ever turning' to God. The latter explanation is favoured by Hitzig and Cheyne (see his *Job and Solomon*, p. 62 and note).

The name of Uz (עוץ) as the country in which Job lived is not of much assistance in determining his personality. The name is given to a son of Aram in Gn 10²³, to a son of Nahor Gn 22²¹ (RV, in AV Huz), and to a grandson of Seir Gn 36²⁸. This last passage, joined with Jer 25²⁰ and the mention of Uz in connexion with Edom in La 4²¹, points to a district E. or S.E. of Palestine, N. of Arabia, and adjacent to Edom. The LXX, quoted above, probably embodies a prevalent tradition; another tradition, traced out by Wetzstein (see Delitzsch, *Comm.*, Appendix), points to the district of the Hauran. Fr. Delitzsch, judging from certain cuneiform inscriptions, fixes upon a district near Palmyra for the site of Uz, which some view the names both of place and hero as symbolical only. The names *Běnê-ḳedem*, 'children of the East' (1³), 'Temanite,' and to a less extent 'Shuhite' and 'Naamathite,' may be held to confirm the general indications of locality mentioned above. (See Uz.)

Outside this book, Job is mentioned in Scripture only in Ezk 14¹⁴·¹⁹ 'These three men, Noah, Daniel, and Job'; and in Ja 5¹¹ 'Ye have heard of the patience of Job.' Both of these passages apparently imply a belief in the actual existence of the proverbially upright and patient man of that name, but not necessarily the existence of this book, or the treatment which Job's history receives in it.

ii. CONTENTS.—The following is an outline or 'argument' of this remarkable book; its form and significance will be considered later. It may be divided into five parts. **1.** *Prologue*, written in prose, chs. 1 and 2. **2.** *Colloquies between Job and his friends*, including Job's Lament, ch. 3. First colloquy, chs. 4–14; second colloquy, chs. 15–21; third colloquy, chs. 22–31. In the first two colloquies, each friend speaks once, and Job replies to each; in the third, according to the present arrangement of the text, Zophar fails to take up his turn, and Job, after replying to Bildad (ch. 26), speaks at unusual length, partly in a kind of monologue (chs. 27–31). **3.** *Intervention of Elihu*, chs. 32–37. **4.** *A Theophany*; utterances of J″, with very brief replies of Job, chs. 38–42⁶. **5.** *Epilogue*, written in prose, ch. 42⁷⁻¹⁷.

1. The Prologue introduces us to a man named Job, living in the land of Uz, of great wealth and exceptional piety, surrounded by a large and happy family, and possessing every mark of divine favour. Upon this man there falls a series of heavy calamities, succeeding one another with startling rapidity, each more severe and trying than the last. His flocks are carried off by marauders or smitten by lightning, he is stripped of all his possessions, and bereaved at a stroke of all his children. The Prologue represents this as due to a scene in the Council of Heaven, at which there appeared among the 'sons of God' a being called 'the Satan' or 'the Adversary,' who questioned the sincerity and disinterestedness of Job's religion, and received permission to afflict him in various ways, but not to touch himself. This experiment is described as resulting in Job's complete vindication. He bowed in submission to the divine will, and in all this first stage he 'sinned not, nor charged God with folly,' *i.e.* never questioned the moral rectitude of divine providence.

Another council is represented as held in heaven, at which the Adversary accounts for Job's fidelity by saying that he has not been made to suffer in his own person. Permission is then given to

inflict the utmost bodily pain upon Job, only his life is to be spared. Job is accordingly smitten with one of the most painful and loathsome of diseases, elephantiasis, a peculiarly trying form of leprosy. But in his utmost suffering and degradation he utters no complaint, though even his wife bids him 'renounce God and die.' Having received good at God's hand, he was content patiently to 'receive evil,' and in all this Job 'sinned not with his lips.'

2. Three friends, Eliphaz, Bildad, and Zophar, now come to condole with him. They sit in silent sympathy for seven days and seven nights, and 'none spake a word unto him, for they saw that his pain was very great.' The silence is at last broken by Job himself. He had thus far borne unparalleled troubles with unparalleled resignation, but now he 'opened his mouth and cursed his day.' The long-drawn wail of the third chapter is not a direct arraignment of God's providence, but it contains a bitter, agonised complaint which virtually amounts to this. He curses the day on which he was born, wondering why the misery of birth into such a life should ever have been inflicted upon him, and passionately longing for death as a blessed release which is inexplicably denied him. This outburst from the depth of a soul in anguish forms the occasion of the debate which follows. The tone of Job's complaint appears impious in the ears of his friends, who remonstrate, each after his own fashion, whilst to each elaborate speech Job makes elaborate reply. The first stage of the discussion is chiefly occupied by an assertion on the part of the friends of the justice and goodness of God, whose government of the world must be in accordance with truth and equity, the wicked suffering for their sin and the righteous enjoying divine favour. Job meets this by a passionate assertion of his own innocence, and a bitter and often very bold arraignment of the present order of things. At the second stage, the friends dwell more upon history and experience, pointing out the calamities which attend upon evil-doing, and leaving it to be inferred that some kind of sin must lie at the root of the troubles which have overwhelmed Job. On his part, Job clings all the more tenaciously to his original position. At the third stage of discussion, the friends attack Job more directly and explicitly, charging him with definite sins which they are sure he must have committed, to be thus punished. As the friends become more violent, Job becomes more calm. He has been working his way towards a solution, though as yet it is far from clear. He cares less to debate with men, and throws his soul more and more upon God, though He be still strangely and darkly hidden from him. Job's long monologue is full of pathos and sadness, but the bitterness which marked his 'curse' and opening speeches has given place to a more equable frame of mind.

Such is a general outline of the three colloquies, but it must not be understood that the progress thus sketched is uniform and unbroken. Neither Job nor his friends speak 'by the card.' Their utterances contain reasoning of a kind, but they are for the most part the outpourings of deep and earnest feeling, which cannot be reduced to syllogisms, and which necessarily imply much repetition and occasional inconsistencies. Job travels back upon his own course, varies in his moods, speaks now to God, now to the friends, now to himself; he is sometimes inconsistent, if not self-contradictory, as a sufferer wrestling with such a problem was likely to be. The speeches form part of a poem, not of an abstract demonstration, though the poet is artist enough to preserve order in the midst of variety, and never loses the thread of his argument amidst the outpourings of speakers whose feelings are sometimes at white heat. The first speech of Eliphaz is undoubtedly the most moderate, being almost apologetic in tone, whilst the last speeches show that the argument has come to a deadlock, and the resources of the friends fail them. Beyond this it is difficult to trace any clearly defined or steadily maintained advance in the arguments on either side. The conclusion shows each speaker as only more fully confirmed in his original position.

3. Here, according to the arrangement of the book as it has come down to us, an episode occurs, in which a previously unmentioned speaker, named Elihu, intervenes, and gives at considerable length his judgment upon the question in dispute (chs. 32 to 37). After a somewhat tedious introduction (32^{6-33}), Elihu blames the friends for the insufficiency of their arguments, but still more severely condemns Job for justifying himself, and undertakes to correct his many mistakes. The address to Job may be divided into four parts, corresponding with chs. 33. 34. 35 and 36–37 respectively. The gist of the whole may, however, be described as an attempted vindication of God, as at the same time a just and a merciful ruler of the world, who is great and glorious above man's power to comprehend, and who sends afflictions upon His own people as a chastisement, or as a means of purification, or as a divine warning against sin. In the stress laid upon affliction as discipline, lies Elihu's chief contribution to the discussion.

4. In the next section of the poem, J″ intervenes and 'answers Job out of the whirlwind.' Two addresses of the Almighty are given—the first in chs. 38^1–40^2, followed by a brief reply from Job $40^{3.\ 5}$; the second in chs. 40^6–41^{34}, followed by another act of submission on Job's part, 42^{1-6}. The chief subject of the divine address is the glory of God in creation, the sublime and awe-inspiring features of which are recounted in order to impress Job with the greatness of God and the littleness of man, and the unsearchable wisdom and inconceivable power of God compared with man's utter ignorance and weakness. Sometimes the description enters into minute detail, as in the picture of Behemoth (the hippopotamus) in 40^{15-24}, and Leviathan (the crocodile) in 41^{1-34}. The description of the war-horse also in 39^{19-25} is elaborate and highly poetical. The object of the whole address, however, as indicated from time to time by a series of ironical questions, is to overwhelm Job with a sense of the irresistible majesty and resource of that God the justice of whose government he has ventured to impugn. How can one who is so utterly unable to subdue a single one of God's creatures, whose knowledge of even a corner of creation is so hopelessly inadequate, dare to arraign the procedure of Him who holds a universe of such creatures in the hollow of His hand? The effect of these addresses is immediate and complete. Job first confesses himself silenced and justly rebuked, and at last in full contrition acknowledges his sin and folly, repents of his ill-advised complaints, and bows low in submission beneath the irresistible hand of the Almighty.

5. In the epilogue, the story which was begun by a scene in heaven ends with a *dénoûment* visible on earth. The friends who had thought themselves representatives of the divine cause are rebuked, because they had not spoken of God 'the thing that is right,' as His servant Job had done. They are forgiven at Job's intercession, while on Job himself is bestowed prosperity precisely double that which he had previously enjoyed. Job lived long after all his troubles were over, saw 'four generations' of descendants, and died 'being old

and full of days'—a sure mark of divine approval and favour (42^{7-17}).

iii. FORM.—The first question which falls to be considered under this head is whether the author intended to convey the idea that he was writing literal history. His narrative begins with the matter-of-fact statement, 'There was a man in the land of Uz,' etc., and both prologue and epilogue at first sight appear to be simple statements of actual fact. This view was held by a large proportion of early Jewish interpreters, but not universally. R. Resh Lakish is quoted in the Talmud (*Baba Bathra*, § 15. 1) as having said, 'Job existed not, and was not created, but he is (only) a parable.' This was altered later into 'was not created except to be a parable.' The prevailing opinion amongst both Jews and Christians for many centuries was that the Bk. of Job was strictly historical. Luther questioned, not the existence of Job, nor the substantial accuracy of the story told in the book, but its literal interpretation throughout as a record of actual facts. Some recent critics (Reuss, Merx, Hengstenberg) have gone to the opposite extreme, and represent the book as entirely imaginative. The majority of modern interpreters, however, view the book as 'poetically treated history'; some (*e.g.* Cheyne) finding in it but a small kernel of fact; others, from Grotius and Lowth to Delitzsch, Davidson, and Driver, being content to read the poem as a free and imaginative rendering of facts handed down by tradition and here substantially reproduced. It is hardly necessary to argue at length that the book cannot be read as literal history from beginning to end. The descriptions of the heavenly council in the prologue are clearly symbolical. The numbers used in the prologue, and the exact doubling of Job's possessions in the epilogue, indicate an ideal rather than an actual picture. Job's calamities come upon him in such a sudden and dramatic form, and are described in so poetical a fashion, with a sort of refrain, 'I, even I only, am left to tell thee,' that we readily understand we are not too literally to interpret every word. And never was it known that sufferer in the extremity of his anguish delivered his soul in highly elaborated poetical phraseology. If, then, the view of the book as 'poetically treated history' be taken as the most probable hypothesis. it is clear that considerable room is left for diversity of judgment as to where the solid substance of fact ends and the drapery of the poet's imaginative treatment begins. The names of the hero and his friends, the country in which he dwelt, the afflictions which befell him, the patience with which he endured them, and his emergence out of his difficulties, may perhaps be considered a kind of irreducible minimum of history used by the inspired genius of the author in his wrestling with the age-long problem before him.

Closely akin to this is the question whether the author of 'Job' intended to represent his hero, not as an individual, but as a type of the righteous in affliction. Does imaginative treatment extend so far that the name of an historical personage is merely used to embody teaching concerning national calamities and the way to meet them? Cheyne adopts the view of Chateaubriand, that 'Job is a type of righteous men in affliction' (see his *Job and Solomon*, p. 65, and the essay in *Proph. of Isaiah*, ii. 235–244), adding, that 'the common view that the hero of the poem of Job is simply an individual must, it is clear, be abandoned.' This can only be established if emphasis upon the word 'simply' is maintained. A purely allegorical view of the poem leads to questionable and sometimes fantastic exegesis. And there is no sufficient warrant for supposing that the modern dramatic mode of treating such a theme, the historical element being so far minimized as to be hardly discernible, and a purely imaginative treatment of a religious subject adopted, was likely to have been used by a Jew at any period to which this book has been assigned. It seems most satisfactory to say, with such writers as Fairbairn (*City of God*, p. 146), that 'the national reposes on the personal sense,' and with A. B. Davidson, that 'Job is scarcely to be considered Israel, under a feigned name. He is not Israel, though Israel may see itself and its history reflected in him. It is the elements of reality in Job's history common to him with Israel in affliction, common even to him with humanity as a whole . . . it is these elements of truth that make the history of Job instructive to the people of Israel in the times of affliction when it was set before them, and to men in all ages' (see his *Job*, Introd. pp. xxvi, xxvii).

The chief reasons which incline us to this view of the poem lie, in truth, upon the surface. The references in Ezk 14[14] and Ja 5[11] suggest that Job was an actual person, known to tradition. The writer of the book conveys the impression that he is dealing with actual history, and his teaching would lose much of its force if it were supposed that the whole story lay in the mere cloudland of imagination. A majority of writers, however, include the word *dramatic*, in some form or other, in their characterization of the poem. Theodore of Mopsuestia employed the epithet in the 4th cent., and in modern times Ewald, Hupfeld, and Davidson use the word drama to describe the book. Delitzsch styles it a drama not emancipated from the lyric element, reminding us that a drama need not be scenic in its character. Volck, after Nöldeke, defines Job as 'a didactic poem, in dialogue form, with dramatic development.' Milton described it as an epic, and Godet follows in the same direction. Cheyne calls it a 'germinal character drama,' and compares Goethe's 'Iphigenia' and 'Tasso.' Driver says, 'It is of the nature of a drama, and may be termed a dramatic poem. Its principal parts are constructed in the form of a dialogue, and the action which it represents passes through the successive stages of entanglement, development, and solution. The action is, however, largely internal and mental, the successive scenes exhibiting the varying moods of a great soul struggling with the mysteries of fate, rather than trying external situations' (*Introd. to O.T. Lit.*[6] p. 411). If any technical definition of form is to be given, that of Volck, quoted above, appears to be the best, or the shorter phrase 'dramatic poem' might be admitted, for a drama in the usual sense of the word the book certainly is not. The name 'lyrical' or 'didactic-lyrical' (G. Baur, *Stud. und Krit.* 1856, p. 582) is misleading in its associations. But it is probably a mistake to attempt to stretch this highly original poem upon a Procrustes' bed, in order to make it fit in with later systems of classification. 'Soul is form, and doth the body make.' The author of Job had certain materials to use, and he kept certain religious objects in view as he wrote; he possessed a poetic genius of remarkable constructive power, and his thoughts were guided by the Divine Spirit. Under these circumstances he produced, not a drama, nor a didactic poem, nor any composition of conventional form or shape, but—the Bk. of Job, which is a law to itself, and which has influenced subsequent writers whose names stand among the highest in literature, yet who, by general consent, are, merely from the literary point of view, outsoared and outshone by their great prototype.

The intimate structure of the poem can best be understood in connexion with the general subject of the poetry of the OT (see POETRY). It may, however, be well to say that the ultimate element in Job, as in all Heb. poetry, is the couplet or distich, consisting of two parallel clauses, the length of each line being determined, not by the laws of regular metre, but by the beat of an irregular but musical rhythm. The single stones of which the poetical structure is composed may be triplets or quatrains instead of couplets, but these larger or smaller units are combined so as to form a strophe (the 'paragraph' of prose), and laws, which are none the less effective because informal and instinctively obeyed, determine the varying lengths of the line, the varying character of the parallelism, and the varying structure of the strophe. An analysis of Job's lament in ch. 3, or of any of the speeches, would illustrate in detail what can here be stated only in outline. It may be remarked, however, that the skill of the poet is especially conspicuous in the success with which he employs throughout a long poem a form of composition which is chiefly suited to the gnomic wisdom of 'Proverbs' or the comparatively brief lyrics of the Psalms.

But the poetical character of Job does not depend upon the balance of syllables or the answering beat of lines and clauses. The constructive imagination of the writer is conspicuous throughout. It reveals itself as remarkably in the bold conceptions, the free, flowing outlines of the whole poem, as in the wealth, variety, and finish of its detailed imagery. The architect of a cathedral shows his skill alike in the detailed workmanship of bosses and finials and in his conception of a majestic whole. It is hardly within the compass of this article to dwell upon the poetical grandeur of *Job* viewed as a literary composition. The sublimity and simplicity of its leading conceptions, the pictures of the august scene in the council-chamber of heaven, and of the sudden desolation and overwhelming sorrow in the earthly household, of Job lying in physical anguish and mental bewilderment upon the *mezbelê* or ash-mound outside his house, and the deep sympathetic silence of his friends broken at last by the heartrending wail of the sufferer's despair, —all indicate the hand of a poet at the outset, and prepare the way for the unfolding of the tragedy that follows. Only a close study of the book can give an idea of the richness and multiplicity of its metaphors, the concentrated vigour of its phraseology, its depth of human feeling, its portraiture of patriarchal life, and the impressiveness of the descriptions of external nature, which form throughout a majestic background to the moving picture of human pain and sorrow.

Sometimes the figurative language is closely condensed—

> 'Wilt thou harass a driven leaf,
> And chase the withered stubble?' (13[25]).

Sometimes the metaphor is elaborated with startling vigour and emphasis, as in the description of the Divine Being as a giant antagonist wrestling with the puny human frame, or making a target of the miserable man who can offer no resistance—

> 'I was at ease, but he shattered me;
> He seized me by the throat and shook me;
>> He set me up as his mark,
>> His arrows beset me.
> He cleaveth my side, and doth not spare;
> He sheddeth my gall upon the ground;
> He breaketh me with breach upon breach,
> He rusheth upon me like a giant' (16[12-14]).

The description of the lion in 4[10.11], of the eagle in ch. 39, 'where the slain are, there is she,' the comparison of deceitful friends to the brook drying up in summer and the mirage of the desert in 6[15-20], the brief but graphic succession of figures to describe the rapid flight of years—

> 'My days are swifter than a runner;
> They flit away, they see no good;
> They shoot by like skiffs of reed,
> Like an eagle that swoopeth upon its prey!' (9[25. 26])—

are only examples taken at random of a poetic vitality in the writer which seems inexhaustible. The sketches of the wild beast in the desert are as faithful in detail as the limning of the glories of the constellations in the nightly sky is impressive; but in each case the work is done by a few strokes of a masterhand. One passage only may be transcribed as an example of several of the features which have been thus summarily and inadequately sketched, and it will, at the same time, illustrate the arrangement of the poem in strophes—

> 'The Shades tremble
> Deep below the waters and their inhabitants.
>> The Unseen World is naked before him,
>> The Abyss of Destruction hath no covering,
> He stretcheth out the North over the void,
> And hangeth the earth upon nothing . . .
>> The pillars of heaven tremble,
>> And are amazed at his rebuke . . .
> Lo, these are but the outskirts of his ways;
> And how small a whisper hath been heard of him
> But the thunder of his power, who can understand?'
>> (26[5. 6. 11. 14])

iv. TEXT.—The Massoretic text of the OT, as is now generally recognized, stands in some places in great need of critical emendation, but the materials extant for the purpose are very scanty. The oldest MS of Job is separated in date from its composition by more than twelve hundred years, and few critical helps from without are forthcoming to aid in the examination and, if need be, the reconstruction of the text. Under these circumstances, textual criticism virtually resolves itself into a comparison of the Heb. with the chief ancient versions, and an examination of internal evidence and inherent probabilities of corruption. Such a process naturally leads to widely differing results, varying according to the preconceptions and methods of individual critics. In modern times Merx led the way in his *Das Gedicht von Hiob* (1871), advocating a reconstruction of the text, based partly upon the ancient versions and partly upon a metrical arrangement of his own. G. Bateson Wright in 1883 carried the work some steps further. Bickell in his *Carmina V.T.* (1882) and in a series of papers in the Vienna *Zeitsch. f. K. d. Morgenlandes* (1891-94) has propounded an elaborate and revolutionary theory for ascertaining what he considers to be the primitive text of Job. He depends partly upon the LXX, but partly also on certain metrical theories, of which more will be said shortly. This work of Bickell has been popularized in English by Dillon in his *Sceptics of the Old Testament* (1895). Finally, Siegfried has published a polychromatic ed. of the text of Job (in Haupt's *Sacred Books of OT*), in which a thoroughgoing recension is advocated, based mainly upon internal evidence such as satisfies the critic.

The chief point for consideration at this stage is the LXX version.

This probably dates from the early or middle portion of the 2nd cent. B.C. The character of the translation is too free and loose to be of much service in the detailed criticism of the text, but it has been long known to scholars that the original text of the LXX was much shorter than the Textus Receptus now found in our MSS. In the time of Origen the current Gr. version was shorter than the Heb. by some 400 lines, the omissions noted by Jerome amounting to more than 700. Origen (*Ep. ad Afric.* § 4) tells us that, in the copies he used, as many as from three or four to sixteen or nineteen verses were lacking in some places, and he remedied the deficiencies by supplying the Greek from Theodotion, obelizing all the passages thus added to the Gr. text before him. Five MSS are extant preserving Origen's marks, and in 1889 Ciasca published a Coptic tr. of the LXX version of Job which exhibits the pre-Origenian state of the text. As this version substantially agrees with the evidence furnished by the five MSS above named, omitting the passages which in them are marked with asterisks, it is clear that this text gives us the LXX version in its earliest form.

The question is, what is its relation to the Hebrew? It must not be taken for granted either that it is earlier and purer than the MT, or that it is simply a curtailed and mutilated tr. from the Heb. that has come down to us. A similar state of things exists in relation to the text of Jeremiah, and scholars are not yet agreed upon an interpretation of the facts. In the case of Job, Bickell uses this evidence to support his own very sweeping reconstruction of the text, seeking to show that the book in its present state has grown by additions, successively made, to a very much shorter poem. Hatch (*Essays in Bib. Greek*, pp. 215-245) argues in the same sense, that the early Greek translation represents the primitive form, the Hebrew a later and amplified form, of the text. Dillmann, on the other hand (*Trans. Royal Prus. Acad. of Sci.* 1890), contends that, except in a few cases, omissions from the Heb. were arbitrarily made by the Gr. translator—a view apparently held previously by Bickell himself; and Driver (*Contemp. Rev.* Feb. 1896, p. 262), though with some hesitation, pronounces the latter to be the more probable hypothesis. It is noteworthy that the omissions of the LXX do not relieve the chief difficulties which attend the text of the book as it stands, whilst, in several cases at least, it is difficult to understand the context without these omitted passages, or to explain how, if they did not form

part of the original text, the passages in the Heb. came to be added to it. Glosses and amplifications on such a scale generally declare themselves as such beyond much possibility of question. Intrinsic probability, in other words, is almost entirely against the hypothesis that the shorter Gr. form represents the primitive type of text. Budde, in his latest work on Job (see Literature below), also pronounces against the view of Bickell and Hatch.

None of the other versions are of much use in textual criticism. The Peshiṭta Syriac was made from the Heb., and its renderings are occasionally serviceable in difficulties of detail. The variations of the Targum are more curious than helpful, while the old Latin version was made from the Gr., and exhibits the same peculiarities (cf. Burkitt, *Old Lat. and Itala*, p. 8 f.). A revision of it was made by Jerome, preserving the critical marks which indicated the passages supplied from the Heb. to fill up the considerable deficiencies noted above.

v. INTEGRITY.—Obviously, this subject is closely connected with the last, and some arguments of critics concerning the text have been reserved for this section, because a discussion of the genuineness of certain passages cannot be carried on without an examination into the subject-matter of the book. Criticism has been busy in recent years with the construction of *Job*, and most modern interpreters hold that the book as it has come down to us has undergone more or less of amplification or modification. Some would reduce the volume of the book by at least one half. They hold that neither prologue nor epilogue, neither the speeches of the Almighty nor those of Elihu, formed part of the original work, and that the speeches of Job and the three friends must be both reduced in bulk and altered in character, if we would read them in their original form. Representatives of this extreme view, which lops off from the statue limbs and members till a mere torso, altered in its proportions, is left, are Bickell and Studer.

Three main reasons are assigned for this trenchant handling of the text. (1) The fact that the earliest form of the LXX version was so much shorter than the Heb. as it now stands. But we have seen that it is by no means clearly proved that the shorter form represents the primitive type, and the reconstruction proposed in many respects does not follow the lines thus indicated. (2) A metrical theory concerning the composition of Job—a hypothesis of great learning and ingenuity, in which, however, few Heb. scholars have followed Bickell—demands some such system of wholesale abbreviation as is thus proposed. This attempt to make the lines of Job 'scan' can only be carried out by the application of extreme violence. Not only must whole passages be shorn away, but the lines that remain must be read with frequent elisions and accommodations. In many cases these are so violent and unnatural as to make it clear that Bickell is trying to force into uniformity and regularity an irregular though real and impressive poetical rhythm which runs through the book. It may be added, that a metrical version of a poem which can be remembered with ease would not readily be displaced by a more cumbrous and irregular form. The whole history of Heb. poetry, moreover, is against the supposition that a poem of the length of Job, and of its probable date, was composed in regular metre with lines of almost uniform regulation length.

(3) The third chief line of argument is drawn from a view of the scope and design of 'Job' which is by no means proved. It assumes that the book in its first conception was a poem of revolt, the utterance of a genuine 'sceptic of the Old Testament,' who rebelled against the current doctrine of reward and punishment, and that it has only assumed its present shape under the hands of a number of 'orthodox' manipulators, who, by various additions and interpolations, have contrived to dress up the original product of a *Sturm und Drang* period into a shape in which it might appear in the sacred Canon. Without discussing this hypothesis in full, two remarks may be made. One is, that writers in the OT are not in the habit of disguising their moods of doubt and murmuring, and even rebellion against the will of God. The psalmists give the account of their gloomy periods of unsettled faith and positive denial; while Jeremiah from time to time 'waxes very bold,' and, like Elijah in his despondency, is driven by the pressure of the problems of life to doubt and to deny the goodness of Him who controls life. This supposed dressing up of doubt into decent orthodoxy is a device of modern days. It should be noticed, also, that this theory of the origin and history of 'Job'

is hampered with the further difficulty that these large additions were made to the original text by a poet or poets whose 'imaginative power was at least not inferior to that of the original writer' (Hatch, *op. cit.* p. 244)—a somewhat large demand to make, when the original and sublime character of the book as a whole is borne in mind.

Siegfried, without going so far as Bickell, is yet very severe in his castigation of the MT. He classifies some passages — which may be represented by ch. 28, and the Elihu speeches, chs. 32–37 —as 'polemical interpolations directed against the tendency of the poem.' Other passages found in the 12th, 27th, and other chapters, are styled 'correcting interpolations, conforming the speeches of Job to the orthodox doctrine of retribution'; while others, again, are 'parallel compositions,' amongst them being found the section 40⁶–42⁶. Some fifty separate passages are banished from the text as scattered interpolations of editors, inserted during the process of 'working over' the poem, which de Wette was the first to suggest had been freely employed. The shorn remnant of the text is, especially in chs. 13 and 14, 20 and 21, and again in 30 and 31, rearranged as regards the order of its clauses and paragraphs, according to the critic's judgment. It is, perhaps, unnecessary to say that for this wholesale reorganization there is no external evidence, the primitive form of the LXX text giving very little assistance in the places where serious difficulties in subject-matter are supposed to require radical changes in the text. Studer (1881) reconstructs the whole book, making chs. 29 and 30 the original prologue—a process which A. B. Davidson describes as leaving a mere trunk, 'so misshapen that its shoulders are found in the region of its bowels.'

Two recent monographs, representing the prevailing current of contemporary criticism, may be mentioned : Grill, *Zur Composition des B. Hiob* (1890); and Laue, *Die Composition des B. Hiob* (1896). The former rejects, as not belonging to the original book, the Elihu speeches, the descriptions of Behemoth and Leviathan, also 12⁴⁻¹³ 24⁵⁻⁹. ¹⁴⁻²¹ 26²⁻²⁷ 27⁷⁻³¹, and chs. 29 and 30. Laue holds that ch. 9⁹⁻²⁴ and ch. 12 are out of place, and that the former paragraph should be placed after ch. 25, and the latter after ch. 27. Ch. 24 is condemned in part as having been 'worked over,' only a portion of it representing the original tendency of the poem. From chs. 25–28 he admits only 26¹⁻⁴ and 27¹⁻⁶ as genuine. Laue, like many other critics, pronounces the Elihu speeches and the 'Behemoth and Leviathan episodes' to be interpolations, but he holds both prologue and epilogue to be genuine and indispensable parts of the original poem.

Merx, Bateson Wright, and Cheyne may stand as representing those who advocate less sweeping but very considerable changes. Some of the chief modifications proposed are, that as Bildad's speech in ch. 25 is very short, ch. 26⁵⁻¹⁴ might be better placed as a continuation of it. To supply the place of Zophar's third speech, which is lacking, ch. 27⁸⁻²³—very awkwardly placed where it stands —might be read as coming from him. Ch. 28 is held to be a later insertion, as well as the whole episode of Elihu. The few verses, ch. 31³⁸⁻⁴⁰, even Delitzsch considers to be misplaced, forming an anti-climax in their present connexion. He would transpose and read them between vv. ³² and ³³.

A. B. Davidson is still more moderate ; he is, in fact, one of the most conservative critics of the book. He holds that, with the exception of the speeches of Elihu, no serious objection can be brought against any of the five great divisions of the poem, but the Elihu episode he, in common with nearly all moderns, pronounces to be a later addition. Further, he entertains somewhat serious suspicions concerning ch. 27⁷⁻²³, ch. 28, and the descriptions of Behemoth and Leviathan in the speeches of the Almighty, but apparently would not, on the whole, remove these from the text. A view nearly coinciding with this will be advocated in the present article ; but the ultimate decision of such a question as this largely depends, it is clear,

upon subjective considerations. Two classes of these may be mentioned. (1) What measure of difficulty in a passage warrants conjectural emendation, and how far is a 19th cent. critic competent to reconstruct an ancient poem, without being guilty of the vice of trying it by his own preconceived ideas and standards? (2) What is the view to be taken of the scope and design of the book? Can it be viewed as a fairly harmonious whole in its present state, and what amount of apparent inconsistency warrants interference with the text as it stands? These are questions which are certain to receive different answers from different types of mind. The only satisfactory line of argument in a conservative direction lies in a justification of the book as it stands, and its success must depend upon power to show that the book can be better understood as we have it, with certain comparatively slight omissions and modifications, than in the forms proposed by more destructive and revolutionary theories.

The section most open to objection is that containing the speeches of Elihu. The chief arguments against its having formed a part of the original book are the following. (*a*) Elihu is not mentioned either in the prologue or the epilogue. In the latter, especially, it would seem unnatural that Jehovah, when referring to the speeches of the three friends and Job, should pass Elihu by in silence. (*b*) Chs. 32–37 are awkwardly placed between Job's monologue and the divine answer out of the whirlwind. The intervention of the Almighty, and the words with which He addresses Job, are much better understood if ch. 38 follows immediately upon ch. 31. The ease and advantage with which this section could be detached from the rest of the poem seems to point to a line of juncture here. (*c*) Elihu's arguments appear to consist partly of a repetition of those of the three friends, partly an anticipation of the address of Jehovah. So far as Elihu does furnish an original contribution to the discussion in the emphasis which he lays upon the purifying influence of suffering viewed as chastisement, it is not in harmony with the general teaching of the book. (*d*) The style is prolix, and, in the opinion of most, distinctly inferior to the rest of the book ; though Kuenen (for example) has pronounced that style alone would in this case be insufficient to prove a later origin. (*e*) Certain peculiarities of language are discernible, a much stronger and more decided Aramaic colouring being discernible in this section. Canon F. C. Cook (*Speaker's Com.*) argues, after Schlottman, that this is the poet's way of indicating Elihu's Aramæan origin. The subject is investigated at length in Stickel's *Das Buch Hiob* (1842), Budde's *Beiträge zur Kritik des B. H.* (1876), and in an essay of Kleinert (*Stud. u. Krit.* 1886); and the bearings of these are investigated by Cheyne (*Job and Solomon*, Appendix, etc. 291–293), who sums up in the words, 'Evidently the speeches of Elihu are later compositions.' (Budde is the most distinguished of the defenders of the genuineness of the speeches).

The force of these arguments really lies in their conjunction. It will be observed that they are of different kinds, and their cumulative force is therefore all the greater. Standing alone, each one would not be fatal. Cook, for example, points out that no person is named in the book till he begins to take part in the action, and he attaches considerable weight to the arguments adduced by Elihu. Bradley, however, in his thoughtful lectures on the Book of Job (1887), takes a different view. The concurrence of arguments drawn from different quarters appears to the present writer convincing, and perhaps the strongest evidence of all is drawn from the view taken of the book as a whole, the plan and outline of which the episode of Elihu mars, or positively disfigures.

The same must, on the whole, be said of ch. 27⁷⁻²³ and ch. 28. The former passage contains an elaborate account of the afflictions which overtake the wicked, apparently quite out of place on the lips of Job, and containing precisely such arguments as had previously been urged by his friends. Compare, e.g., the speech of Zophar in ch. 20, and observe that 27¹³ is almost identical in expression with 20²⁹. There is no real connexion between the first six verses of ch. 27, in which Job asserts his own innocence, and the strain of the verses that follow, which are quite inconsistent with Job's previous contentions. The only two modes of reconciliation possible are these. (1) Job wishes to show that he does not altogether deny the fact that the wicked are punished, and is anxious to sever himself from their perilous and friendless condition. He shrinks from the very thought of being as the wicked are. He wishes to 'avoid everything that can appear ambiguous, and to take a position upon a much higher elevation' (Ewald). Even, however, if this train of thought were appropriate in Job's mouth, it cannot be said that it fits in at all suitably with 27¹⁻⁶ which precedes, or ch. 28 which follows. Or (2) it may be urged (again with Ewald) that Job has by this time conquered his doubts as to the divine moral government, that these 'have worked their own cure,' and that he anticipates already some such issue as is described in the epilogue. But it requires only a moment's consideration to see that this disturbs the whole order of the composition, that it is quite inconsistent with the language of Job's soliloquy, especially ch. 30, and it does not harmonize with the address of the Almighty to Job, which follows.

Ch. 28, again, is of the nature of an episode, beautiful and impressive in itself, worthy of a poetic genius and a devout spirit, but exceedingly difficult to understand in the place which it occupies in the poem. The general drift of the chapter is that Wisdom—in the sense of the principles of true and righteous government which direct the course of this world's affairs—is inscrutable by man; the only possible course for man is to fear and trust Jehovah, and (by implication) to leave himself and his fortunes entirely in the hands of God. Such a train of thought is quite in harmony with the teaching of other parts of Jewish sacred books,—compare several psalms and parts of Proverbs,—but it is irreconcilable with Job's previous position and subsequent language in chs. 30, 31. If Job had already reached this stage in his education, what need of chs. 38–42, and how account for the laments of ch. 31? Again, no satisfactory connexion of thought between chs. 28 and 27²³ or 27⁶ can be established. The opening פִּי may, indeed, be variously understood. 'For there is a vein for the silver' (RVm) is the most obvious translation, the rendering 'surely' being adopted to avoid a difficulty, since the inscrutability of divine wisdom affords no reason for the fate which the end of ch. 27 describes as overtaking the wicked. It is necessary to read much between the lines in order to eke out a kind of connexion between the chapters as they stand, e.g. 'the wicked are punished, but for all that there are problems in life which that simple principle does not explain, and wisdom is really inscrutable'; or 'the wicked are overthrown, and such a fate is sure to overtake all who disobey God; for wisdom can only be attained by those who fear Jehovah.' It must be felt that these attempts are so forced and artificial that there is a strong presumption against the sequence of chapters as they stand. The difficulty of the opening פִּי

would hardly, however, be a sufficient objection, if the chapter as a whole was appropriate to the frame of mind in which the book presents Job at the moment. This is far from being the ease; the opening words of ch. 29, 'Moreover, Job continued his parable—Oh that I were as in months past,' etc., exhibit far too violent a break with 27²³ for sound exegesis to explain.

We are led, therefore, to the conclusion that the section 27⁷⁻²³ is out of place, whether or no it should form part of a speech of Bildad or a third speech of Zophar; that ch. 28 also, with all its truth and beauty, cannot be understood where it stands; and that chs. 32–37 form a subsequent addition to the original book by a pious writer who was not fully satisfied with its teaching. Ch. 31³⁹⁻⁴⁰ᵃ may perhaps also with advantage be transferred to a place between vv.³² and ³³.

The arguments urged against the genuineness of other portions of the book are not, however, convincing. Cheyne holds that prologue and epilogue do not form a part of the book, the prologue being perhaps part of a prose book of Job, and the epilogue added later by an editor whose object and views were quite distinct from those indicated in the prologue. His work is done 'in a prosaic spirit,' and he makes 'a sad concession to a low view of providential dealings' (Job and Sol. p. 69). This is a natural, but perhaps superficial, objection. Dillmann in the 4th edition of his Hiob (1891) finds these arguments unsatisfactory. The reply to those who contend that prologue or epilogue, or both, do not fit in with the rest of the poem, can only be made good when the scope of the whole book is examined. It is further urged that the speeches of the Almighty are 'inserted passages' as much as those of Elihu, while the descriptions of Behemoth and Leviathan were added later still, a 'purple patch' the removal of which would be a gain. The last objection seems to resolve itself into a question of taste, on which no critic's judgment can be final. That the speeches of the Almighty constitute the book as it stands into a consistent whole, which would lose a chief portion of its meaning, if indeed it would be intelligible, without them, is a point which may conveniently be reserved till the scope of the poem is considered. The views of those who would separate prologue, epilogue, and the speeches of Jehovah from the text of the original poem are represented in the words of Cheyne when he says that the book as it stands forms a 'confused theodicy,' that these sections constitute 'disturbing elements,' and that to attempt to weld them into one whole shows a failure to understand the position. These are only the 'conflicting thoughts' of 'earnest, warm-hearted men' on the great question of the suffering of the righteous, interesting separately, but not intelligible in combination. This is the only objection to passages which in style and diction, in force and beauty, are confessedly of a piece with the rest of this noble and remarkable poem. The prose passages also, it is admitted, are not in themselves unworthy of the place in which they stand. The main issue, therefore, with regard to the integrity of the book, so far as these great divisions of it are concerned, depends upon the view taken of its scope and teaching. A fundamental difference of opinion on this head accounts for the differing conclusions of eminent critics on questions of genuineness.

vi. SCOPE AND DESIGN.—The mode of treatment adopted in this section will be to discuss the whole book as it now stands, showing how each part is related to the whole, and inquiring what teaching it may be supposed to convey in its present form. It has been shown in the last section that in all probability certain chapters did not form part of the original design : but this is matter of opinion ; and while some critics would excise more, others object to the setting aside of any portion of the book. A picture may be surveyed as a whole, apart from the varying opinions of judges who hold that the colours in one portion or another of the canvas have been laid on by a later artist. Such a survey may aid in the decision of controverted questions.

The poem of 'Job,' so remarkable for imaginative power and literary skill, was unquestionably intended to set forth theological doctrine. Nothing abstract or technical is intended by the phrase ; it is but a way of expressing the aspect from which the deepest questions of life are here viewed. The poet can be engaged with no higher themes, with no more living and burning questions, than God, man, evil, good, suffering, hope, destiny. The thesis of the book—to translate poetry into prose—is that suffering in the present life is not precisely proportioned to ill desert ; on the contrary, the righteous suffer ; yet God is, and God is good. How can this be ? It is the object of *Job* to answer the question.

In the first place, let the presuppositions of the discussion be borne in mind. The debate is not concerning the primary truths of natural theology. God is : that is an axiom unquestioned, unquestionable. And by 'God' is meant a Ruler of the world, understood to be righteous and merciful, though the exact measure of His mercy and truth be not apprehensible by man. No atheistic theories are admissible,—that would mean to give up the problem, not to solve it. The pantheist, the materialist, have here no standing - ground. A Western mind of to-day may cut the knot presented in Job in a hundred several ways not open to the Eastern—to say nothing of the Israelite—of 2500 years ago. Further, the evidently accepted religious doctrine presupposed by the book is that in this life the wicked are punished and the righteous rewarded by a just God, each man according to his deeds and character. Against this current orthodox opinion the book is a protest, but it is a religious protest. It is not a sceptical inquiry, nor a cynical denial, nor a blasphemous denunciation, either as a whole or in any of its constituent parts. It is a plea for a wider, deeper, truer, more easily defensible orthodoxy. It represents the process by which a step was taken in the formation of religious thought, and a religious explanation of life-problems was arrived at. Even those who would reduce the book to the narrowest dimensions, and who reject certain portions as pious glosses or orthodox corrections, must admit that Job's attitude throughout is that of the man who is trying to understand God, not denying His existence or mocking at His rule. Job pleads for God as truly as the friends. The ring, if we may so speak, within which the conflict is carried on—a fight for life so far as Job is concerned—*i.e.* the recognized limits of the discussion, must be borne in mind throughout.

The colloquies form the kernel of the book : let them be taken first, especially as they are the only portions which beyond all question constitute its original elements. The exact issue between Job and his friends concerns, not the punishment of the wicked, but the suffering of the righteous. Job is not concerned to deny that the wicked as such suffer : if ch. 27$^{7\text{-}23}$ belongs to him, he explicitly asserts it. What the friends assume is that only the wicked suffer, and precisely in proportion to their wickedness ; what they at first imply and afterwards explicitly declare is, that if an apparently righteous man suffers, he cannot be so righteous as he seems ; hence that Job, who is enduring exceptional pain and calamity, must

have flagrantly offended, in secret if not openly, against the laws of righteousness and the Power which executes and vindicates them. This, Job strenuously and even passionately denies. Moreover, it is contrary to hypothesis. To draw for a moment from the prologue, Job is not only asserted by the historian, but by the Almighty, to be upright ; 'perfect,' indeed, when judged by the relative standard which alone is in question, a man of thorough integrity within and without. If this be not granted, the whole problem vanishes. Job not only denies his opponents' contention, with his own consciousness and the testimony of facts to back him, but he does so successfully. The poet represents him as victor in the contest of words. The friends are silenced, though not convinced. Without availing ourselves of the justification of Job pronounced by the Almighty in the epilogue, it is clear that the friends are worsted in the conflict, and their position is rendered untenable.

But it does not follow that Job has succeeded in settling the great point at issue. The friends are wrong, but he may not be wholly right. What is Job's position, if we consider only chs. 3-31 ? Omitting for the moment the doubtful sections 27^{7}-28, and remembering in any case that Job's state of mind is set forth, not in a series of categorical propositions, but in the fervent outpourings of a deeply troubled soul, we may say that up to this point he is absolutely certain of his own righteousness, and that his sufferings are undeserved. He is deeply convinced also in what the mystics call 'the ground of the heart,' that God is righteous and rules righteously ; but how these two convictions are to be reconciled, he does not clearly see. Some light has dawned upon him from various quarters in the course of his wrestlings with the great problem. At one moment he is disposed to hope against hope, and hold fast by what he cannot see. 'Though he slay me, yet will I wait for him,' may or may not be the meaning of ch. 13^{15},—for the readings admit of almost opposite interpretations,—but the words represent Job's attitude in certain moods. Not very different is his state of mind when he pleads that he might be allowed to come face to face with the Almighty ; he is so sure that he could 'order his cause before him, and fill his mouth with arguments.' At another time he rests in the confidence that his own vindication will come, sooner or later. Whether Job expects this in the present life, or more or less vaguely in a future life, is a very important question in its place, but may for the purpose of this exposition be passed over for the moment. The passage ch. 19$^{25.\ 26}$ remains on any translation ambiguous when we ask whether the vindication was to come on this side of the grave or beyond it, though it is glorious in its triumphant assurance that the Vindicator will speak at the last—'he will speak, and cannot lie.' This confidence, however, Job is unable continuously and permanently to preserve. It is not represented as a solution of the problem. Job's last words (ch. 31) are a pathetic lament over his vanished greatness, and a reiterated asseveration, strong, though no longer bitter, that he has not offended. If ch. 28 is to be assigned to Job, it must imply that for a time and in a certain mood he was prepared to bow before the inscrutable wisdom of the Most High ; but this is not an abiding frame of mind, and cannot be presented as Job's solution of his own difficulties.

If the Elihu section formed a part of the original book—which we cannot admit—it must be understood as a contribution towards a solution, but one not completely adequate. It forms, in any case, a kind of side-chapel in relation to the whole structure. The righteous man must remember his need of chastisement; suffering is intended to exercise an educative and purifying influence, and the wise man will not recklessly rebel or fretfully chafe against it. But in the poem no one replies to Elihu, the Almighty disregards his utterances, no reference is made to them in any other part of the book, and they can scarcely be said, on any theory of their origin, to form an intimately organic part of the whole.

On the theory advocated by many modern critics, the original poem left the problem in this undetermined condition. The book puts forward no solution, it is a prolonged note of interrogation. There is nothing constructive about the colloquies when standing alone, especially in the mutilated form to which some critics would reduce them. But as the poem now stands, what solution does it furnish of the moral difficulty which it has so powerfully raised? The solution may be said to be threefold ; or rather, three classes of considerations may be borne in mind in mitigation of the difficulties propounded. The first is found in the prologue. This lifts the curtain which hides the counsels of Heaven. It suggests that the drama of our earthly life has a significance which earth does not exhaust. The government of the Most High may contemplate issues which are at present beyond us. It may be needful to prove the existence of disinterested goodness to men, to angels, to devils ; or to satisfy that strange personality who on the stage of history represents the great Accuser or Adversary of men, a being hard to persuade that goodness means something more than a pious care for one's own possessions or due consideration for one's own skin. If it were given to the righteous man, like a greater Prometheus, to suffer for such a cause, and demonstrate for once to assembled hosts of human spectators of the great drama of human life, or to invisible principalities and powers, that goodness and truth are something more than a cunning provision for the comforts they bring in their train, a life of pain and woe might be considered well spent. The vivid picture of the heavenly tribunal is only the graphic Oriental way of propounding what would now be called a philosophical or theological thesis. The lesson of Plato's *Gorgias* is here enforced against the sophistry of his *Protagoras*. Hedonism is not ethics. With magnificent daring Job is conceived as proving this great thesis on the side of God, against the insinuations of the Satan. Utilitarians should be the first to acknowledge that whether this be or be not a tenable solution of the problem of human suffering, it is a noble one. God knows the hearts of His servants, but on some is conferred the high prerogative of suffering in order to demonstrate to a scoffing world or an incredulous Accuser of the brethren what righteousness really means. This is not, however, represented in the poem as an ultimate or complete solution. The veil that has been drawn aside to allow a glimpse into the designs of Heaven drops again, and is never relifted. Job, by hypothesis, must not know of this procedure. Unless he can hold fast by the Right unaided, unconsoled, the experiment will be a failure. The fact that he never gives in or gives up is the poet's silent way of saying that the Adversary has lost his case. With all the odds against him, Job has won. He was content to 'hold hard by truth and his great soul,' beggary and leprosy and desertion and calumny notwithstanding. If the Almighty had never spoken, Job would remain alone upon the field—unconquered, if not victorious.

The Almighty, however, does speak. It is an old complaint with students of the Bk. of Job, that He says so little, according to men's concep-

tions, of what ought to be said. But much more is said than appears upon the surface. The addresses of Jehovah out of the whirlwind are a powerful plea for the probability that God's providence is right and man's indictment of it wrong. The Creator and Preserver of such a world as we see may surely be left to conduct its affairs unchallenged by the puny creature who knows but one corner of one field in a vast universe, and knows that imperfectly and ill. So far from 'binding the cluster of Pleiades or loosing the bands of Orion,' man does not know 'when the wild goats bring forth,' nor can he even 'loose the bands of the wild ass.' Thou who complainest against Me, 'where wast thou when I laid the foundations of the earth —hast thou an arm like God?' It is replied, though not in the poem, that this is no answer to Job's questions. By such arguments the Almighty may silence, but He does not convince. The poet judges otherwise. He represents Job as not only submissive, but contrite. Job acknowledges that he has been wrong in reasoning and in temper ; he not only gives up his arguments, but repents him of his sin. And the inspired poet displays deeper insight into truth and more profound knowledge of the human heart than the self-sufficient reasoner of later days. Mozley, in his masterly study of Job (*Essays*, vol. ii. p. 219), suggests that the explanation is that 'amazing power softens him, and he feels himself within its grasp a poor and feeble creature, to be dealt with just as that Power pleases'; but this is surely only half the truth. Submission of soul is not satisfaction of mind. Job has learned to *rest* in God at last. His former attitude was wrong, and only now for the first time does he see light and find peace. Why is this, when no definite answer has been given to his passionate question, Why do the righteous suffer?

First, because he has seen and heard God Himself. What is meant by that phrase it would be hard to explain, for it can only be understood by one who has heard that Voice and seen that Vision. But the experience of mankind attests that there is a whole heaven between listening to the most convincing human arguments and receiving a message which is as the very voice of God to the soul. There is a difference between hearing of God and seeing Himself. That, Job says (42⁵), is the essential difference between his former and his later state. Further, Job is convinced of God's perfect wisdom in his own case by the spectacle of His combined wisdom, power, righteousness, and goodness in creation around. It is the argument from the analogy of nature before Butler and before Origen. An indirect argument is more cogent against some forms of scepticism than a direct dealing with the difficulty. A contemplation of all that my friend is and has done—his course, his career, his character—may convince me that he is right in a particular instance which I cannot understand, more effectively than any amount of discussion concerning the case itself. Further still, Job's attitude of penitent submission is represented as the real solution of all his difficulties. Only in that attitude of spirit can man really rest. If he could reason out all the causes of all events—he cannot, but we may suppose it possible—he would still be further from the state of mind in which best to face the problems of life than Job was in ch. 42⁶. The ultimate solution is not intellectual, but moral, since the problem is more moral than intellectual. 'I retract—and repent in dust and ashes.' The words do not mean that Job does not think, does not feel ; but that he has risen above the level of keen resentment of physical pain, above the level of quick-witted dialectic and cut-and-thrust argument, soaring into the lofty altitudes or sinking into the peaceful depths where alone the godly man finds peace—in the shelter of the everlasting arms. The reasoner and the sceptic complain that the issue has been evaded; the religious man knows that he has not shirked it, but left it behind and beneath him, when he bows his head in self-abasing prayer, after a face-to-face vision of God.

After this, the epilogue might well appear to be a bathos indeed. That a man who has borne the extremity of anguish and fought the fiercest of battles and had a vision of the Almighty and come out conqueror, should descend to the level of an unusually prosperous sheikh who owns a few thousand more sheep and oxen than he did before, seems too humiliating. The irony could hardly go further than in the words, 'every man also gave him a piece of silver, and every one a ring of gold' —as if an answer to the soul's questionings were to be expressed in terms of coins and jewellery. The writer of the postscript to the LXX Version seems dimly to have felt this, for, to the words of ch 42¹⁷ 'Job died an old man and full of days,' he adds that 'it is written that he will rise again with those whom the Lord raises up.' From a modern point of view the epilogue is impossible; it does not move on the same plane as the prologue and the speeches of the Almighty. But the interpreter of *Job* should not occupy a modern point of view. The writer of the book could not say 'he will rise again at the last day.' If the light shed upon this life's tangles by the clear prospect of a future life had been vouchsafed to him, his book would have been very different. The epilogue is the author's way of saying the same thing. Under a dispensation in which there was no clear revelation of a future state, Job's subsequent prosperity was only the outward expression of the divine judgment expressed in 42⁸ 'ye have not spoken of me the thing that is right, as my servant Job hath.' The men who had prided themselves on understanding God's methods and defending Him against aspersion were condemned, and forgiven only at Job's intercession; whereas Job, who had fought against the God of narrow tradition in defence of the God of righteousness and truth was commended. His restoration to more than his former prosperity is but the outward expression of this divine sentence—a kind of 'poetic justice' which, under the conditions of the time, was felt to be needful to the vindication of Job's character and the justification of Job's arguments. And, as Froude suggests in his impressive study of this book, Job was now for the first time prepared fully to use prosperity aright (*Short Studies*, vol. i. p. 325). But the epilogue is not necessary in order to point the chief moral lessons of the book. These are independent of circumstances, and belong to all time.

Leaving the details, and taking the book as a whole, what may be said of *Job* as to its place in the history of revelation? It can only be rightly understood if it is viewed as a stage in the history of religious thought, an advance upon all that preceded it, a step forward taken at the cost of severe suffering and mental conflict, but still only one step in advance. It was given to the author of the poem to see the shallowness and insufficiency of the theory that would make righteousness and prosperity, wickedness and calamity, vary directly in proportion to one another, in the present life. It was not given to him to obtain anything more than a passing glimpse into the prospect of a future life, in which the balance might be redressed; in all probability even this phrase is too strong to express the nature of the confidence attained in ch 19²⁵· ²⁶. The mystery and the beauty of vicarious suffering in the moral and spiritual world were hidden from him. But he had begun to see that,

even as regards the present, pain may be a privilege rather than a punishment; that the loftiest spirits may have to pass through it as a trial of their loyalty rather than a chastisement for their transgressions; and that in such a case it behoves them to bear, as the Lord's chosen ones, the burden and the mystery of life, as pregnant with a deep significance certain hereafter to be made known.

It has often been said that Job is a type of Christ. The Christian holds that throughout the OT there were hints and foreshadowings of spiritual truth more fully revealed in the NT, and the suffering of the upright man under the earlier dispensation prepared the way for and was in turn explained by the suffering of the only Sinless Man, the Mediator of a new covenant. Mozley says, 'The Crucifixion is the one consummate act of injustice to which all others are but distant approaches.' The Cross of Christ is at the same time the darkest and the brightest spot upon earth, because there is most fully seen the meaning of that world-old problem of the suffering of the righteous in an evil world. What appears 'injustice' is intended to be a part of redemption. The author of *Job* did not clearly see, perhaps never dimly guessed at that mysterious solution of a mystery. But he grappled with the moral difficulties of his own time like a giant, and left upon record some lessons concerning suffering and its significance, which neither the world nor the Church has fully learned yet.

vii. DATE AND AUTHORSHIP.—There is little or no external evidence of a trustworthy kind to enable us to determine either author or date. The reference in Ezk 14¹⁴ cannot be quoted in relation to the Bk. of Job, though it may have a bearing on the historical reality of the man. Jewish tradition as represented in the Talmud (*Sota* v. 8; *Baba Bathra* 15a) assigned it to Moses. Writers so recent as Ebrard (1858) and Rawlinson (1891) have been found to hold the same position. But the earliest date assigned by the consensus of modern scholarship is the time of Solomon (Delitzsch, Cook, Cox), whilst by far the larger majority of critics place the book somewhere between the 7th and the 4th cent. B.C. For the period after the captivity of the Northern tribes, somewhere between Isaiah and Jeremiah, may be quoted the names of Ewald, Renan, Merx, Dillmann; Davidson and Driver would date the book during or shortly after the Exile, the period which Cheyne and Margoliouth are also inclined to favour. Cornill (*Einleitung*, p. 241) places the book amongst the very latest canonical OT literature. No author's name except that of Moses, which is quite out of the question, has ever been suggested. Whenever the writer lived, he is for us a great Unknown, and it is perhaps impossible to fix the time of composition, except by stating the century within which it probably falls. The following is the principal evidence on the subject furnished by the book itself.

At first sight *Job* presents a picture of primitive non-Israelitish life. Much that we are accustomed to find in other books of OT is conspicuous by its absence. The picture drawn of the life of Job is on the whole faithful to the conditions of patriarchal life. The wealth of the patriarch consists in his flocks and herds (1³ and 42¹²); such sacrifices as are mentioned (1⁵ 42⁸) are of a primitive type, performed by the head of the household as a priest. The age to which Job finally attains is patriarchal (42¹⁶); the piece of money, קְשִׂיטָה named in 42¹¹ is uncoined and primitive, mentioned elsewhere only in Gn 33¹⁹ and Jos 24³² of Jacob's purchase from the children of Hamor; whilst the musical instruments, תֹּף, כִּנּוֹר, עֻנָב, mentioned in 21¹² 30³¹ are the primitive ones of Gn 4²¹ 31²⁷

The names of God are such as belonged to patriarchal times, *El* and *Eloah* (occurring some fifty times in Job, but rarely in OT generally) being the oldest Semitic titles of the Divine Being. The name 'Jehovah,' used in the prologue and epilogue, is not found in the body of the book except once, as if by accident, in 12⁹ (compare אֱלֹוַהּ in 28²⁸). In these and other features the colouring appropriate to the circumstances of Job's life is preserved with great fidelity and skill.

It is impossible, however, to believe that the book dates from a very early or even a moderately early period in the history of Israel. Davidson asserts that the features of a much later time may be perceived 'beneath this patriarchal disguise'; that 'the author is a true Israelite, and betrays himself to be so at every turn, however wide his sympathy be with the life of other peoples, and however great his power of reanimating the past'; and he urges that no careful reader should be deceived by the 'thin antique colour of the book.' Other critics would demur to such decided phraseology, and it is certain that the book has to be searched very carefully before any traces of the law can be discovered in it, and these are not of a pronounced kind. In 22⁶ 24⁹ we read of the taking of 'pledges' (see Ex 22²⁶), and in 22²⁷ of vows, while in 24² mention is made of the removal of 'landmarks' (see Dt 19¹⁴). The adoration of sun and moon is spoken of in 31²⁸ as an iniquity to be punished by the judge; so also adultery in 31⁹. These, however, must be considered slight and doubtful references, and it is not upon them that the case turns for holding, in Davidson's words, that the book is 'the genuine outcome of the religious thought and life of Israel, the product of a religious knowledge and experience possible among no other people.' We should rather turn to the evidence that the book presupposes an advanced state of society, a knowledge of natural history and human life, a wide and varied experience impossible to a primitive inhabitant of an unsettled country bordering on the desert, who must have lived a nomadic life. Critics have pointed out that passages such as 12¹⁷⁻²¹, with its mention of counsellors and kings, priests and princes, spoiled and overthrown and captive, implies a knowledge of the history of nations, if not actually of the political changes brought about by great military empires like Assyria and Babylon. Disorder and misery must have been familiar features in the life of the author of this book; not merely personal suffering, but such as the psalmist describes when he says, 'If the foundations be destroyed, what shall the righteous do?'

Perhaps no conclusive argument can be drawn from the language. It is true that this is peculiar and striking. The book contains an unusually large proportion of Aramaic words, and of ἅπαξ λεγόμενα explicable only by the help of Arabic. But it has been argued by some that this is a mark of early date, by others that it is a mark of the Solomonic period as one of wide culture and extended intercourse, by others that it proves a date more or less contemporary with Deutero-Isaiah (Driver), only that the author of Job was brought even more within Aramaizing influences than the prophet. Dillmann does not lay stress upon the 'Aramaisms' as a mark of date, but holds that the language generally points to the period of the later Heb. in the 7th or 6th cent. B.C. Cornill thinks the 'Aramæo-Arabic' cast of the language supports the very late date he adopts (*Einleitung*, p. xxxii). The literary form and character of the poem certainly point, at least, to the maturity of Jewish literature. It is true that a poem of genius and power often characterizes the dawn of a nation's history; and in Dante, the first great writer in the vernacular of his country, is found a master of Italian who has never since been surpassed. This illustration alone is sufficient proof that the concentrated vigour and intensity of expression characteristic of some passages in Job does not necessarily imply a late date in the history of a national literature. The originality of the author of Job is one of his most striking characteristics, but it is not the originality of an early writer. His knowledge, his illustrations, his references, and, to some extent, his style, appear to imply an advanced and not a primitive period of literature and life.

The strongest argument, however, and perhaps the only one which is really conclusive, is drawn from the subject-matter. The theme here discussed and the manner of its discussion necessitate a long previous history. The problems of human life are doubtless old, but they could not be raised in the manner displayed in Job, without a previous religious history, and one of considerable duration, in which the doctrine of the three friends had come to be the current and orthodox explanation of the facts of life. The history of the OT shows that only at a comparatively late period were these maxims questioned; and when we find them not only questioned but discussed in the thorough manner of the Bk. of Job, we may be sure that it was not composed till at least the closing period of the monarchy. Other features of religious doctrine—the doctrine of God, the way in which Satan is mentioned, and the spiritual doctrine of man, for example—point, likewise, to a comparatively late date. In saying this, we do not include the passages which have often been thought to imply a doctrine of immortality, since the meaning of these is by no means certain.

The argument as to date drawn from parallel passages is one that the best critics do not press, as it is encumbered with doubt and difficulty, and is apt to resolve itself into a matter of subjective impressions. But a comparison of some passages in Job with other books in the OT is instructive, to whatever conclusions it may lead, and a few words may be said upon the subject. The parallels are numerous, though in no case are they exceedingly close; they are chiefly found in Dt, Ps, Pr, Is, Jer, and La; the books of Hos, Am, and Zec presenting in a minor degree certain points of comparison. The chief parallels with Dt are Job 5¹⁴ compared with Dt 28²⁹, Job 5¹⁸ with Dt 32³⁹, Job 20⁴ with Dt 4³², whilst the references to the removal of landmarks and other offences in Job 24² and 31⁹. ¹¹ have been thought to imply a knowledge of Dt 19¹⁴ 22²². Davidson goes so far as to say that if Dt be understood to be a composition of the reign of Josiah, B.C. 620 is the point above which the composition of Job cannot be carried. As to the Psalms, it appears quite certain that Job 7¹⁷ implies Ps 8⁵, but the date of the latter cannot easily be fixed. The reader may further compare Job 10⁹ with Ps 138⁸ 139, Job 35¹⁴ with Ps 37⁶, Job 22¹⁹ with Ps 107⁴², and Job 13⁴ with Ps 119⁶⁹. The Books of Job and Pr, as both belonging to the class of Wisdom-literature, exhibit, as might have been expected, considerable affinity. The personification of Wisdom is found in both; the providential features of human life are dealt with in both, though from different points of view; whilst some phrases are common to both books, the coincidence of form being such as can hardly be the result of accident. The proverbial expression concerning 'the lamp of the wicked being put out' of Pr 13⁹ 24²⁰, is taken up in Job 21¹⁷ in a way which absolutely proves the priority of the former. Job 6³ may be compared with Pr 27³, and Job 3²⁵ with Pr 10²⁴, though the comparison presents nothing conclusive as to date. Much more reliance may be placed upon a general comparison of the representations of Wisdom in Pr chs. 1-9 and Job 28, with regard to which it would appear manifest that Job is the later. It has been already admitted that ch. 28 may be a later addition to Job, and the date of the opening section of Pr is not conclusively fixed; but of the general teaching of Job it is clear that it must have followed upon and not preceded the general teaching of Proverbs. For the proverbial philosophy of the latter is in the main that true but insufficient generalization from experience, embodied in prudential maxims, which forms the groundwork of the arguments of the friends. Upon this *Job* forms a searching criticism, and represents a considerably later stage of thought.

The relation between Job and Isaiah, especially Deutero-Isaiah, is exceedingly interesting. It has been discussed at length by Cheyne in the essay appended to his *Proph. of Isaiah* (ii. 235 f.). Job 14¹¹ presents coincidence in expression with Is 19⁵, the latter being probably the earlier passage. But a more extended parallel with the later chapters of Isaiah may be established by a comparison of Job 12⁹ with Is 41²⁰, Job 15³⁵ with Is 59⁴, Job 9⁸ with Is 44²⁴ and 45¹², Job 26¹²·¹³ with Is 51⁹, and Job 13²⁸ with Is 50⁹. The whole teaching of the Bk. of Job should be studied in connexion with the remarkable picture of the Servant of J″, which is one of the chief features of Deutero-Isaiah. The spectacle of the righteous servant of God suffering, desolate, mocked of men and apparently afflicted of God, yet retaining his hold upon God and ultimately justified by Him, is so far common to the two books and to these almost alone in the OT as to make the comparison full of interest. Cheyne and Davidson have discussed it in full, but the question of priority is not easily settled. Perhaps the conclusion to which most readers will be brought by a study which cannot even be outlined here, will be that announced by Davidson and Driver, acquiesced in by Cheyne, that the two writers were 'surrounded by the same atmosphere of thought' and 'worked up common conceptions into independent creations.' Most critics incline to place Job the later of the two, but the view of suffering taken in Is 53 can never have presented itself to the author of Job. Either the two were entirely independent, or Job is earlier than Deutero-Isaiah, would seem to be the inevitable verdict.

A comparison with Jer furnishes two or three parallel passages in which coincidence can hardly be accidental, though priority may not be easy to determine. One of the chief of these is the 'curse' of Job 3³·¹⁰ compared with Jer 20¹·⁴·¹⁸. Dillmann in 1869 judged that the passage in Job must have been the earlier of the two, an opinion which he modified later (Hiob⁴, p. 33); while Cheyne writes that Jer 20¹⁵ 'clearly betokens the hand of the original writer.' Other parallels are Job 6¹⁵ and Jer 15¹⁸, Job 12⁴ and Jer 20⁷, whilst Job 9¹⁸ may be compared with La 3¹⁵, Job 30⁹ with La 3¹⁴, and Job 16¹³ with La 3¹². In the latter passages opinion is likely to assign a later date to the highly wrought elegy of La than to the vigorous and forcible language of Job. Ps 37 and 88 suggest a general comparison with Job, and there are points of coincidence in expression with other psalms; but all that can be said is that the writer of Job seems to have been acquainted with some psalms, whilst other psalmists appear more or less to have imitated the greater poet.

On the whole, the use of parallel passages in this instance seems to mark out the *general* position of Job in relation to other OT literature, rather than to fix definitely its date in relation to particular books. All the signs point to a period subsequent to the 7th cent. B.C., though how much later, remains undecided. As Margoliouth has pointed out, the references to Ophir in 22²⁴ 28¹⁶ give a *terminus a quo* in the Solomonic period, and a comparison with 1 Ch 21¹, in which Satan is used as a proper name, shows that Job 1 and 2, etc., in which the article is used, must have been written earlier. This furnishes a *terminus ad quem* in the 4th cent. B.C. The alternatives lie between the 'very late date somewhere in the Persian period' favoured by Margoliouth and Cheyne, and a date somewhat, though not much, earlier than the Bab. captivity, which appears to the writer the more probable. The range of a century earlier or later than the Exile would be sufficient to include all but the most extreme of modern critics.

LITERATURE.—The following may be mentioned amongst the writers who have contributed to the elucidation of the Bk. of Job during the Christian era, but chiefly during the last century. Origen's contributions towards the study of the text, and Jerome's translation, have been already referred to. Not many of the early Christian writers commented on Job, but the *Scholia* of Ephraem Syrus may be mentioned, and the bulky commentary of Gregory the Great, *Moralia in Jobum*, in which exposition proper is overlaid by a discussion of an endless variety of doctrinal and ethical questions. Amongst the Jewish expositors of the Middle Ages, R. Sa'adya Gaon wrote brief notes in Arabic, and besides Ibn Ezra and Rashi, the two most important commentaries are those of R. Moses ben Nachman and R. Levi ben Gerson, of the 13th and 14th cents. respectively. At the time of the Reformation, Luther characteristically illustrated the new spirit of exegesis by the way in which he handled the Bk. of Job; his remarks gave offence to many by their freedom. The *Conciones* of Calvin exhibit the strength and lucidity characteristic of that prince of expositors. In the 18th cent. Alb. Schultens (1737) opened a new epoch in the study of Job by his philological notes, illustrating the meaning of words largely—some have thought too largely—from the Arabic. Reiske (1779) and Schnurrer (1781) followed in the same direction. In the present century the number of commentaries on Job has multiplied very largely. The following list of selected literature during the last half century does not profess to be exhaustive or exactly chronological, the dates affixed usually indicating the publication of the first and last editions.

Umbreit, *Das B. Hiob* (1824–1832); Ewald, *Dichter des A. B.* iii. (1836–1854); Stickel, *Das B. Hiob* (1842); Schlottmann, *Das B. Hiob* (1851); Renan, *Le Livre de Job* (1859); Frz.

Delitzsch, *Das B. Hiob* (1864–1876); Hengstenberg, *Das B. Hiob erläutert* (1870–1875); Merx, *Das Gedicht von Hiob* (1871); Zöckler in Lange's *Bibelwerk* (1872); Hitzig, *Das B. Hiob* (1874); Budde, *Beiträge zur Kritik des B. Hiob* (1876); *Hiob* (in Nowack's *Handkom.* 1896, a summary of the conclusions of which is given by Budde himself in *Expos. Times*, Dec. 1896, p. 111 ff.); Reuss, *La Sainte Bible*, pt. 6 (1878–1888); Volck in *Kurzgef. Komm.* (1889); Dillmann in *Kurzgef. Exeg. H'buch* (1891); Duhm, *Das B. Hiob erklärt* (in Mohr's *Kurzer Hand - Com.* 1897); also Beer, *Text des B. Hiob untersucht* (1895). Of these, Umbreit, Ewald, Renan, Delitzsch, and Zöckler have been translated into English. Amongst recent English writers may be named Cook in *Speaker's Com.*⁷ (1880); Cox, *Commentary and New Translation* (1880); and Bateson Wright, *Translation, with Essays, chiefly Critical* (1883). A. B. Davidson published in 1862 a full commentary based upon the Heb., but this included only chs. 1–14, and has not been completed. In 1884 his English commentary appeared (*Cambr. B. for Schools*). Cheyne, *Job and Solomon* (1887); Bradley, *Lectures on Job* (1887); R. A. Watson in *Expositor's Bible* (1892); also Rawlinson in *Pulpit Commentary* (1891). The section on the Bk. of Job found in each of the chief 'Introductions' to the OT should, of course, be consulted. The following may be mentioned as representative:—Bleek (6th edition by Wellhausen, 1893), Riehm (ed. Brandt, 1889), Driver (6th ed. 1897), and Cornill (3rd and 4th ed. 1896). Amongst separate articles some of the most noteworthy are Riehm, *Zeitschr. f. Luth. Theol.* (1866); Godet, *Études Bibliques* (1874); Budde, *Beiträge* (1876), *ZATW* (1882), 193–247; Giesebrecht, *Wendepunkt des B. H.* (1879); Kleinert, *Das specifisch Hebräische in B. H.* in *Stud. u. Krit.* (1886); C. H. Wright, *Bibl. Essays* (1886); Mozley in *Bibl. and Theol. Essays* (1878); Dillmann, *Textkritisches zum B. H.* in *Sitz. Ber. der K. Akad. d. Wis.*, Berlin (1890); as well as the monographs of Grill and Laue mentioned above. The present writer has dealt with the subject in his *Wisdom Literature of Old Test.* (1893).

W. T. DAVISON.

JOBAB (יוֹבָב).—**1.** Name of a son of Joktan, Gn 10²⁹ (1 Ch 1²³): identified by Glaser (*Skizze*, ii. 314) and others with יהירב, a place mentioned in a Sabæan inscription (*CIS* iv. p. 55; Glaser, *Mittheilungen*, 3 ff.). The author of that inscription speaks of his 'fathers and uncles' as governors of YHYBB, and further mentions a king of Saba, Karibail Wathar, whom there is reason to place in the middle of the 8th cent. B.C. The name is said to occur in another inscription also (Glaser, *Skizze*, ii. 303); but in neither is there anything which fixes its locality, though its governors would appear to have been vassals of the kings of Saba. It is variously read *Yuhaibab* and *Yuhaibib*, and is compared by J. Derenbourg with the Arab. *yabâb*, 'a desert.' Earlier commentators thought of the Ἰωβαρίται of Ptolemy (vi. 7. 24), and indeed one recension of the LXX has the form Ἰοβόρ. This name seems to correspond with the Arabic *Wabâr* (so Sprenger), which denotes a considerable portion of Yemen 'all between Najrān and Ḥaḍramaut, Mahrah and Shiḥr' (Yāḳūt). Neither of these identifications can be considered more than conjectural. **2.** A king of Edom, Gn 36³³ᶠ·=1 Ch 1⁴⁴ᶠ·, confused in LXX of Job 42¹⁷ᵇ with Job (see above, p. 660ᵇ). **3.** A king of Madon, Jos 11¹. **4. 5.** Two Benjamites, 1 Ch 8⁹·¹⁸.

D. S. MARGOLIOUTH.

JOCHEBED (יוֹכֶבֶד 'J″ is glory,' cf. the Phœn. כברמלקרת 'Melkart is glory' (?) *CIS* I. i. 364).— Known to us by name only from P, who states that J. was a sister of Kohath, who was married to Amram her nephew, and who bare to him Aaron and Moses (Ex 6²⁰) and Miriam (Nu 26⁵⁹). An earlier writer, E, in narrating the birth of Moses, speaks of his mother as a daughter of Levi, but seems to have been unacquainted with her name (Ex 2¹).

W. C. ALLEN.

JOD (י).—The tenth letter of the Hebrew alphabet, and as such used in the 119th Psalm to designate the 10th part, each verse of which begins with this letter. It is transliterated in this Dictionary by *y*. See JOT.

JODA (A Ἰωδά, B Ἰούδα[s?]), 1 Es 5⁵⁸ (⁵⁶ LXX).— **1.** The same as JUDAH the Levite in Ezr 3⁹; elsewhere called HODAVIAH, Ezr 2⁴⁰; HODEVAH, Neh 7⁴³; SUDIAS, 1 Es 5²⁶. **2.** An ancestor of Jesus, Lk 3²⁶ (Ἰωδά WH, Ἰωυδά TR, AV Juda).

JOED (יוֹעֵד, etymology uncertain, Syr. ܝܘܥܕ).
—A Benjamite, the father of Meshullam and son of Pedaiah, Neh 11⁷. In the corresponding list 1 Ch 9⁷ the name does not occur.

JOEL (יוֹאֵל).*—1. The prophet (see next article). 2. A son of Samuel, 1 S 8², 1 Ch 6²⁸ (RV, see Driver's note on 1 S 8²) 6³³. 3. An ancestor of Samuel, 1 Ch 6³⁶ (called in v.²⁴ **Shaul**). 4. A Simeonite prince,˙1 Ch 4³⁵. 5. A Reubenite, 1 Ch 5⁴˙⁸. 6. A Gadite chief, 1 Ch 5¹². 7. A chief man of Issachar, 1 Ch 7³. 8. One of David's heroes, 1 Ch 11³⁸. 9. 10. 11. Levites, 1 Ch 15⁷˙¹¹˙¹⁷ 23⁸ 26²², 2 Ch 29¹². 12. A Manassite chief, 1 Ch 27²⁰. 13. One of those who married a foreign wife, Ezr 10⁴³. 14. A Benjamite overseer after the Exile, Neh 11⁹.

JOEL (יוֹאֵל, Ἰωήλ), the son of Pethuel (LXX Βαθουήλ, Vulg. *Phatuel*), is the author of the second (LXX fourth) book of the Minor Prophets. No information has reached us regarding the prophet or his father. The name Joel probably signifies ' J'' is God,' and, on the assumption of the date proposed by Credner, may contain a reference to the re-establishment of the worship of J'' after the overthrow of Athaliah (cf. 2 K 11⁴ᶠᶠ.). This, though possible, is scarcely probable. The name is not an uncommon one (cf. 1 S 8², Ezr 10⁴³, Neh 11⁹, etc.).† The book supplies no definite information, either as to the place or the time of the prophet's labours. The date is greatly disputed, but it is generally agreed that Judah, and most probably Jerus., was the theatre of Joel's prophetic activity.

i. OCCASION.—The occasion of the prophecy was an invasion of the country by locusts, accompanied by a drought of unusual severity. A calamity of this kind was not uncommon in Pal., and, in ordinary circumstances, would not be made a subject of prophetic discourse. But the visitation described by J. was exceptionally severe. Successive swarms of locusts swept over the country (1⁴), and their devastations went on for years (2²⁵). The produce of the fields, vineyards, and orchards was destroyed (1¹⁰⁻¹²). Food failed for man and beast (1¹⁰⁻¹²˙¹⁶˙¹⁷˙ ¹⁸⁻²⁰). The daily offering to J'' was suspended from lack of the necessary materials (1⁹˙¹³ 2¹⁴). This was equivalent to an interruption of the covenant relation between J'' and His people. A calamity which led to such a result was a very serious one. No prophet would have been faithful to his mission as watchman of Israel if he had failed to warn the people of the danger with which such a visitation threatened them. Joel saw in the locust invasion a special judgment from J'', and used it as a text for one of the most interesting and instructive discourses contained in the prophetical books of the OT.

ii. CONTENTS. — The book consists of three chapters. [The Heb. text has four chapters, the last five verses of ch. 2 in AV forming ch. 3 in the MT]. It divides itself easily into two parts, in the first of which (1²–2¹⁷) the prophet, and in the second (2¹⁸ to the end) J'', is the speaker.

The first part is made up of two discourses, of which, however, the theme is the same, viz. the locust invasion. The language in which the calamity is depicted differs considerably in the two chapters. But that the army, whose movements and operations are described so graphically and rhetorically in ch. 2, must be identified with the locusts of ch. 1, appears from 2²⁵, where the

promise of the removal of the judgment and the renewal of blessings is given in the words, ' I will restore to you the years that the locust hath eaten, the cankerworm, and the caterpillar, and the palmerworm, my great army which I sent among you.' * After introducing his subject (1²⁻⁴), the prophet, in the first discourse (1⁵⁻²⁰), describes the judgment which has fallen on the country in a narrative remarkable for the vividness of the picture and the minuteness of the details. The invading host pours over the land in countless myriads, with teeth like the teeth of lions for the work of destruction before them. The vine is wasted. The fig-tree is not merely stripped of its leaves,—the very bark is torn off, and trunk and branches are left bare (1⁷). The grain and the fruit crops are alike destroyed (1¹⁰⁻¹²). The prophet lingers over the desolation which has been wrought, and pushes his description into regions which, if the visitation were not real, would scarcely be referred to. The seed perishes under the clods ; the barns are left to fall into decay because there is nothing to gather into them (1¹⁷). Such a calamity falls heavily on the beasts of the field. Under the pangs of hunger and thirst they groan and cry unto God. The instinctive appeal of these irrational creatures affects the prophet so powerfully that he associates himself with them in supplicating the Lord for relief (1¹⁸⁻²⁰). Thus the first discourse closes.

In the second discourse (2¹⁻¹⁷) the language is highly poetical and rhetorical. The figure before the prophet's mind is that of an army which marches with unbroken ranks and irresistible force to the accomplishment of its mission. This army is J'''s host, at the head of which He marches (2¹¹). The army, as we have seen, is the locusts (2²⁵) ; and, if the testimony of travellers is to be relied on, the prophet's description as a whole, and the individual illustrations, are true to nature. But no description of the calamity—however powerful and startling—can exhaust the prophet's duty in connexion with it. Such a judgment calls for humiliation and prayer on the part of the people ; and the prophet urges this in terms scarcely less striking than those employed in depicting the divine visitation (1¹⁴ 2¹²⁻¹⁷).

The second part of the book (2¹⁸ to the end), with J'' as the speaker, contains the promise of blessings—first of temporal, and secondly of spiritual, blessings. The first words of the promise show that the judgment is at an end (2¹⁹ᵇ). Famine and drought are to cease ; prosperity is to be restored. The new abundance will compensate for the losses inflicted by the ravages of the locusts, and Israel, having learned in the school of suffering that J'' alone is worthy of their trust, will acknowledge and rejoice in Him as their God (2²¹⁻²⁷). This prepares the way for the bestowal of spiritual blessings (2²⁸⁻³², Heb. 3). The outpouring of the Spirit on all the people, without distinction of age or sex, of rank or class, is to follow, in point of time, the restoration of material prosperity (2²⁸ ' it shall come to pass *afterward* that I will pour out my Spirit upon all flesh'). How long afterward is not indicated. On a matter of this kind the horizon of prophecy is undefined. Then shall come the day of the Lord, which occupies so prominent a place in the book. This day, ushered in by awe-inspiring phenomena, is a day of doom for the nations hostile to Israel. These nations are brought down to the valley of Jehoshaphat ('J'' judges'), where J'''s heavenly warriors crush them as grapes are crushed in the wine-press—cut them down as the grain is cut by the reaper. Israel, on the other hand, shall dwell securely in a land of extraordinary fertility, and J'', enthroned on Mount Zion, shall dwell among them. The situation, as between the people of J'' on the one side and the hostile powers on the other, is summed up in the pointed contrast at the close of the prophecy (vv.¹⁹˙²⁰ Egypt and Edom are to be a desolation ; Judah is to dwell under the favour of J'' for ever).†

iii. INTERPRETATION.—The interpretation of the prophecy depends on the view taken of the locusts. 1. Many of the early Fathers explained the locusts figuratively ; and in recent times this view has been supported in his usual fearless fashion by Hengstenberg (*Christ. of OT*, Eng. tr. i. 296 ff.). According to this view, the prophecy refers to future events, and the locusts, in chs. 1 and 2, represent the world-powers opposed to the Church,—such as J'' judges on His great day (3¹˙² [Heb. 4¹˙²]). 2. What may be regarded as a modification of this ancient opinion has been recently proposed. According to this view the locusts are apocalyptic,— creatures of a supernatural kind, such as may

---

* This name is generally taken to mean ' J'' is God,' and this was prob. the etymology accepted by the later Hebrews, with whom the name was popular. But it is very doubtful if this was the primary meaning. Nestle (*Eigennamen*, 86) and W. R. Smith (*Kinship*, 301) identify with the god *Wail* (*Iolaos*). See, further, *Oxf. Heb. Lex. s.v.*, and Gray, *Heb. Prop. Names*, 153.

† The name might be taken as a Hiph. Impft. from יאל, (cf. יקים), but this is not a probable derivation. (See *Oxf. Heb. Lex. s.v.*).

* The words used in this verse for the locusts are the same as in 1⁴, but the order is different ; and the prophet perhaps refers to successive swarms of locusts rather than to the same swarm in different stages of growth.

† The connexion in which Egypt and Edom are mentioned at the end of the book deserves consideration. The Phœnicians and Philistines appear (v.⁴) to have been actively hostile to Judah in the prophet's day. The Egyptians and Edomites would naturally have been mentioned along with these if they had stood in the same relation to Judah. And it is possible that, in the antithesis at the close of the book, Egypt and Edom are used typically,—the former representing hostile powers that had no family connexion with Judah, the latter those that were of common ancestry.

fitly find a place in a vision of the last things, with which the Bk. of Joel closes (cf. the locusts in NT Apocalypse). 3. The third and, in recent times, the most generally accepted opinion is that the locusts are real. The prophet describes an actual locust invasion, and makes it the occasion of his prophecy. According to the first two views, the book becomes an eschatological prediction, without any historical basis, or any direct reference to the prophet's contemporaries. Against this explanation of the book, the text, on a fair interpretation, offers serious objections. (1) It is not easy to find a satisfactory explanation of the twofold call to repentance already noticed. According to the allegorical or apocalyptic view, we have to think of the prophet as sitting, like a monk in his cell, brooding over the past history of his people, and endeavouring to forecast their future. The fruit of his meditations he records for us in this short book. He has no message to his contemporaries. Even the call to repentance is a mere ideal appeal. The ground of the appeal is the locust invasion. But to the prophet's contemporaries the appeal can have no practical value, if not a single locust is visible and no trace of locust devastation can be discovered. For the ordinary purpose of prophetic teaching the appeal vanishes into thin air. This explanation utterly fails to do justice to the text. The prophet urges repentance on his fellow-countrymen with a view to the removal of a grave calamity, and the restoration of the divine favour. This purpose was realized. The second part of the book begins, as we have seen, with the promise of the withdrawal of the judgment and the bestowal of rich blessings. The explanation may be inferred from $2^{18.\ 19a}$. J"'s anger is at an end. The way is open to the restoration of the covenant relation between Him and His people. The inference is that the people have repented and humbled themselves before Him. Now, that is the practical result for which every prophet laboured among his countrymen. And when the prophetic purpose and the result aimed at are exhibited in the proper relation, as they are in Joel, it is scarcely possible to accept the view that the prophecy has no direct reference to the circumstances of the prophet's contemporaries. (2) The language in which the locust invasion is described is strongly opposed to the allegorical and apocalyptic explanation. The details of the first chapter have been partially referred to. It is highly improbable that the narrative, in this part of the book, is a pure work of imagination, produced by some recluse of post-exilic times. The description of the second chapter is equally opposed to the figurative explanation. If the language is figurative, the locusts represent the world-powers hostile to the Church. The prophet has before his mind men, —warriors, like those led by a Sennacherib or a Nebuchadnezzar. He tells us that these invaders 'run like mighty men' (v.⁷); if they were really gallant warriors, like whom else, or what else, should they run? 'They climb the wall like men of war' (ib.); if they were human soldiers, what does the prophet mean by these words? He presents a picture of an invading horde, going steadily forward, in perfect order, to the accomplishment of their task. In their progress they reach the capital, and climb the walls; but it is not said that they make breaches in the walls or cast them down. 'They leap upon the city' (v.⁹), but there is not a hint that their purpose is to destroy it. The ravages wrought by these invaders are confined to the fields. Not a man falls before them. The people suffer grievously, but it is indirectly, through the destruction of their crops, etc. And when the prophet urges the people to repent with the view of propitiating J", the effect of the with-

drawal of the judgment is, not the sparing of the lives of the inhabitants, but the renewal of fertility to the earth, so that there should no longer be the lack of the materials required for the daily meal-offering and drink-offering (vv.¹²⁻¹⁴). The description in these verses (⁷ff·) loses its point, and raises a perplexing question as to the literary character of the book, if the locusts are not real but figurative. If the prophet has before his mind — not locusts, but — a horde of cruel men sweeping over the country and leaving ruin behind them, his language raises not the least difficult of OT problems. And there should be little hesitation in admitting a real invasion of locusts.

iv. DATE.—The date is greatly disputed, but there is general agreement that it is either very early or post-exilic. The book itself contains no distinct chronological data of the kind supplied by the superscriptions in many of the other prophetical books. In such a case the most helpful and trustworthy evidence for the fixing of the date is derived from the nations (if any) mentioned in the book. On this point the argument *e silentio* is important in Joel. No mention is made of Syria, Assyria, or Babylon. But from the days of Amos to the exile of Judah, one or other of these powers has a prominent place in prophetic literature. It may therefore be reasonably inferred that J. wrote before the Assyr. power began to threaten the chosen people, or after the Bab. power ceased to be dangerous; in other words, the date is prior to the 8th cent. B.C., or later than the overthrow of Babylon by Cyrus. If the late date is accepted, the prophecy would fall in the Pers. period. No valid objection to this date can be founded on the non-mention of Persia. For, while it is true that the Jews were in subjection to the Persians, there was a radical difference between the relation of Persia to the chosen people and that of Assyria and Babylon. The latter invaded and conquered the land of promise, and carried the people into captivity. Their relation was one of active hostility. The Persians inaugurated the period of their supremacy by the restoration of the Jewish exiles to their own land. This would sufficiently account for the Persians being placed in a different category from the Assyrians and Babylonians. And the way is clear for a pre-Assyr. or post-Bab. date. The prophet, however, mentions certain peoples as hostile to Judah: Phœnicians and Philistines (3⁴ [Heb. 4⁴]), and Egyptians and Edomites (3¹⁹ [Heb. 4¹⁹]). If the typical use of Egypt and Edom is accepted (p. 672ᵇ n.†), the mention of these countries is of no importance in the discussion as to the date. Otherwise, a date must be found comparatively near to hostile action on the part of Egypt and Edom; and the same remark applies to Phœnicia and Philistia. In the period between the invasion of Judah by Shishak (c. B.C. 930) and the war in which Josiah fell (B.C. 610), there is no report of hostile action on the part of Egypt such as would meet the requirements of the prophecy. With regard to the other countries mentioned, the case is different. The Chronicler (2 Ch 21¹⁶· ¹⁷) reports an invasion of Judah by the Philistines in the reign of Jehoram, son of Jehoshaphat and son-in-law of Ahab. The serious character of this invasion may be inferred from the statement of the Chronicler, that the palace was captured, and the royal family—wives and children, with the exception of a single son— were carried into captivity. That the Philistines were actively hostile to Judah about this period is sufficiently attested by Amos (1⁶). According to this prophet, the Philistines found a market for their Jewish slaves in Edom; and in this traffic the Phœnicians are associated with the Philistines (Am 1⁹). Further, as against Edom, which apparently had been a dependency of Judah since the time of David, the Chronicler reports that, in the days of Jehoram, it made an effort to secure its independence,—' Edom revolted from under the hand of Judah and made a king over themselves' (2 Ch 21⁸, cf. 2 K 8²⁰, where the statement of Ch is confirmed). Edom, indeed, was an inveterate enemy; but in the days of Jehoram specific acts of hostility were committed, which suffice to explain the reference in Joel. It is true that in Ch the Phœnicians are not mentioned. Amos, however, includes them in the same charge as the Philistines. The Phœnicians were the great naval power of the time. The maritime carrying-trade of the world was very largely in their hands. The Jewish slaves who were sold to the Ionians (Jl 3⁶ [Heb. 4⁶]) were, no doubt, conveyed in Phœn. vessels to the slave markets of Greece. The descendants of those whom Hiram allied to Judah broke the friendly relation, and ranged themselves with the enemies of the chosen people. And there was more than this. The Phœn. Baal-worship had been introduced into the northern kingdom through Jezebel, and into Judah through her daughter Athaliah, the wife of Jehoram. The influence of Phœnicia had been powerful enough to largely suppress the worship of J″ throughout the land of promise. When that worship was restored by Jehoiada, pious Jews would regard the friendship of Phœnicia as more dangerous than the hostility of Philistia. And a prophet of the period might be expected to assign to the Phœnicians a first place among the powers hostile to Judah. This is what Joel does (3⁴ [Heb. 4⁴]). In support of the late date, attention is directed to the fact that Joel mentions only petty peoples in the neighbourhood as enemies of Judah; whereas, in the early prophets, prominence is given to a heathen power of widely extended influence, which threatens the independence of the chosen people. It is quite true that from the time of Amos, who, if Joel is late, first raises this question in OT prophecy, a world-power aiming at universal empire has to be dealt with. But if a prophet did actually appear and write a book fifty years before Amos,—what then? At that time Assyria was beyond the prophetic horizon. Egypt since the days of Shishak—a century before —had ceased to cause anxiety. Only Phœnicians, Philistines, and Edomites troubled Judah. On the assumption of the late date, the peoples mentioned by Joel raise a serious difficulty. The date proposed by Merx, and favourably regarded by other critics, is about the middle of the 5th cent. B.C., when Nehemiah restored the wall of Jerusalem. In the historical books that deal with that period, tribes in the neighbourhood of Jerus. are spoken of as bitterly hostile to the Jewish community. Chief among these are the Samaritans and the Ammonites,—no mention is made of the Phœnicians (cf. Neh 4¹ᶠ·). It is scarcely credible that a prophet living in Jerus., while Nehemiah was struggling to put the capital in a position of security, should threaten heavy judgments against powers—some of them remote—whose hostility was scarcely felt, and not so much as mention the peoples bordering on Judah whose forces were united in active opposition of the most bitter kind against the Jewish community. And the case is strengthened by the fact that Ezekiel, from whom, according to Merx, Joel is supposed to have freely borrowed, begins his denunciation of the hostile powers with the Ammonites,—as bitter opponents as the Jews of the period had to deal with (cf. Ezk 25¹ᶠᶠ·). Accordingly, if Merx' date is accepted, the mention of the peoples referred to —a factor of the weightiest importance in the determination of the dates of prophetical books— is deprived of its historical significance.

It has been urged that the Bk. of Joel is not an original work, but a *Midrash*—a sort of eschatological compendium — founded on the books of earlier prophets. According to this view, the nations named would lose their historical value. This might be admitted of the Egyptians and the Edomites, and, in a less degree, of the Philistines. But the reference to the Phœnicians cannot be explained in this way. And, in point of fact, so far as our historical information warrants an opinion, there is no period when a prophet loyal to the theocracy would be more likely to introduce his censure of hostile powers in the words of Joel (3⁴ [Heb. 4⁴]) than the early part of the reign of Joash, when Judah had just escaped the danger of ruin through the Phœn. Baal-worship. To sum up this point— a typical reference cannot be assigned to all the nations mentioned; an exact historical reference is not consistent with the post-exilic date proposed.

In connexion with the late date, another point deserves consideration. The prophet summons the people to repentance; but he does not name any special sin of which they are guilty. How unlike this is to Amos and his successors! On this ground alone it is difficult to find a suitable place for Joel between Amos and the exile of Judah. This may appear to favour a post-exilic date. But the condition of Judah described in the post-exilic books of OT is quite unlike that suggested in Joel. If the latter half of the 5th cent. is accepted as the date, Joel and Malachi would belong to the same period. Malachi gives as melancholy a picture of the moral and religious state of his countrymen as any prophet before the Exile. And the situation, then, is this. One prophet lays bare the sins which are eating as a canker into the heart of the post-exilic Church in language as severe as that of Amos or Isaiah,—while another prophet—practically a contemporary—writes as if there were not a special sin to denounce. Further, Malachi's efforts do not appear to have been crowned with much success (see his book throughout); Joel's simple, earnest appeal led to the happiest results (cf. 2¹⁸ᶠᶠ·). It follows that, if Joel had a practical message to his contemporaries, he can scarcely be placed in the generation to which Malachi belonged. A fair interpretation of the language is opposed to the view that the book is a mere Midrash, having no reference to the circumstances of the prophet's day. If the occasion of the prophet's exhortation is found in the actual condition of Judah at the time, the proposed post-exilic date is highly improbable. If the date is pre-exilic, it is not easy to point to a time more suitable than that suggested by Credner, viz. the early part of the reign of Joash of Judah. Through the reforming zeal of Jehoiada, the worship of J″ was at that time comparatively pure. And the people would be likely to respond to the earnest and affectionate appeals of a prophet like Joel.

Other points of less importance have found a place in the discussion as to the date. No king is mentioned. The prophet appeals to the priests as if the direction of affairs was in their hands. This is held to point to the condition of Judah after the return of the exiles from Babylon, when there was no king, and the administration of affairs, under the Pers. governor, was conducted by the priests and elders. The conclusion seems reasonable. It is urged in reply that Joash was only seven years of age when he ascended the throne, and that, for a time, the affairs of the kingdom would. of necessity, be left in the hands of Jehoiada the high priest. That is an important consideration. But of greater importance is the obvious purpose of the book. The prophet makes no special reference to civil or political affairs, or to the social condition of the people. His object is to reach the heart and conscience of the nation through the calamity which has fallen on the country,—to bring his countrymen as penitent suppliants before J″. In a matter of that kind it is the priests that should take the lead. And the prophet's appeal to the priestly party is appropriate.

Again, it is urged that the prophet makes no mention of the northern kingdom. But why should he? His view is confined to the disaster which has overtaken Judah. *Negative* evidence —such as the non-mention of the northern kingdom, and of a king of Judah—cannot counterbalance the positive evidence derived from the peoples named in the book, and the practical purpose of the prophet in behalf of his contemporaries. The question is, 'Whether a judgment such as Joel depicts forms a suitable theme for a prophetic book?' If it does, the absence of references found in other books of prophecy, which cover a much wider field and deal with subjects of various kinds, cannot safely be pressed in discussing the question of the date.

The importance attached to the ritual is held to favour a late date. The question of the ritual is raised, *generally*, by the prominence assigned to the priests, and, *specifically*, by the mention of fasting, and of the daily offering. Fasting, in connexion with an unexpected calamity, was a common practice from an early period of Israel's history in Canaan (cf. 2 S 1¹² 12¹⁶, 1 K 21⁹ ¹² ²⁷). The reference to fasting in Jl is quite consistent with an early date. The arrangements for the daily offering are found in P (Ex 29³⁸⁻⁴¹). Whatever date may be assigned to P, the offering of the morning and evening sacrifice was an ancient practice, with the ritual of which the people would be familiar (cf. 2 K 16¹³⁻¹⁵). The direct references to ritual in Jl are as consistent with an early as with a late date. Moreover, devotion to ceremonial was not a peculiarity of post-exilic times. It may be doubted if any generation of Israelites was more attentive to external observances than those addressed by Amos (cf. Am 4⁴⁻⁵ 5²¹⁻²³). The same may be said of Judah in the days of Isaiah (cf. Is 1), and, later, in the time of Jeremiah (cf. Jer 7). It is urged, however, that Joel attaches quite a special importance to the ritual. The interruption of the daily offering is equivalent to a breach of the covenant between J″ and Israel. And it may be doubted whether such a view can be reasonably assigned to any period between Amos and the Exile. The question is, 'Whether it is more reasonable to assign such an estimate of the ritual to post-exilic times than to an early period of reformation like that under Jehoiada?' If Mal may be trusted, Pharisaism was as *unspiritual* in the 5th cent. B.C. as it was in the most degenerate days before the Exile. The information available for the post-exilic period is scanty ; such as it is, it can scarcely be said to support the simple, spiritual explanation of Joel.

In addition to the general character and teaching of the book, there are special expressions which are held to favour a late date. It is argued that ch. 3 [Heb. 4] ¹· ¹⁷ presuppose the exile of Judah. But the words rendered 'to bring again the captivity of Judah' do not necessarily mean that Jews are actually to be brought back from exile. If this literal interpretation is insisted on, it follows that the restoration of the exiles has not yet taken place, and a date between B.C. 586 and 536 must be found—a most unlikely period for a prophet like Joel. To say that the restoration in B.C. 536 is inadequate, in view of the brilliant promises of the pre-exilic prophets, and that a restoration of a more glorious character must lie in the future, is simply to give up the literal interpretation of the words. In these circumstances, usage must be carefully considered. The words 'to bring again the captivity' seem to be used in the sense of 'to reverse a line of procedure.' Chastisement is to have an end, and that is to be followed by proofs of the divine favour (cf. Dt 30³, Am 9¹⁴, Hos 6¹¹, Jer 29¹⁴ 30³· ¹⁸ [where the expression is applied to the *tents* of Jacob], 48⁴⁷ [where the words are applied to Moab]). Moreover, it should be noted that the turning of the captivity is to take place in the same period as the outpouring of the Spirit, and, chronologically, is associated with the final judgment of the nations hostile to the Church. The prophet emphasizes this note of time, ch. 3 [Heb. 4] ¹ᵃ :—' behold, in those days, and in that time.' If this period was ushered in on the Day of Pentecost—as St. Peter teaches (Ac 2¹⁶ff.)—the turning of the captivity and the judging of the nations are thrown into Christian times, and the reference to the Bab. exile falls to the ground. Nor does the mention of the Ionians require a date in the Pers. or Gr. period. The reference to the Phœnicians and the Philistines (3⁴ [Heb. 4¹]) connects the prophet's message with his contemporaries ; the charge against these peoples is that they sold Jews as slaves to the Ionians. The Ionians were settled on the coast of Asia Minor before the 9th cent. B.C. And the ports of Asia Minor offered the nearest marketplace for the sale of slaves conveyed in Phœn. vessels. Upon the whole, the evidence available,

if used as in the case of other books of prophecy, seems to the present writer more favourable to a pre-exilic than to a post-exilic date.

v. DOCTRINE.—Joel contains a comprehensive summary of prophetic teaching. The calamities of life are the fruit of sin. The punishment of sin cannot be escaped without repentance. Sincere repentance will secure forgiveness, and the restoration of the divine favour. Further, such a calamity as Joel describes is severe enough, and deliverance from it a great blessing ; but there is a final judgment and deliverance of which these are but types. Joel uses a grave occurrence of his own day as a basis for a prediction concerning the last times, when, on the great day of the Lord, the cycle of judgment shall close, and the deliverance of the people of J″ shall be complete. To that day of the Lord the prophet sees all things tending. The locust invasion appears to be a harbinger of that day ; hence the earnestness of the prophet's appeal to the people. Such, generally, is the teaching of the book—the day of the Lord being the most important subject.

It is quite surprising how much of the imagery and thought of Joel appears in other books of Scripture. If the date is early, later writers lie under very special obligations to the author of this short book. The most striking part of the imagery is that connected with the locusts, which appear as agents in divine judgments from the time of the exodus from Egypt down to the close of the present dispensation (cf. Ex 10⁴ff., Rev 9³ff.). For the phenomena connected with the day of the Lord, the speedy approach of which is supposed to be indicated by the locust invasion, cf. Ex 10²¹ff., Is 13⁹ff., Ezk 32⁷ʰ., Am 8⁹, Mt 24²⁹, Mk 13²⁴ʰ., Lk 21²⁵ʰ., Rev 6¹²ff.. In ch. 3 [Heb. 4] ¹³ two figures occur which appear elsewhere, especially in the Bk. of Rev. The first is that of the harvest (cf. Hos 6¹¹, Jer 51³³, Mt 13³⁹, Rev 14¹⁵ʰ.). The second is that of the wine-press (cf. Is 63³, La 1¹⁵, Rev 14¹⁹ʰ.). Noteworthy also is the figure of the fountain proceeding from the house of J″, when His people are restored to His favour, and watering the dry acacia-wady (ch. 3 [He 4] ¹⁸ ; cf. Ezk 47¹ff., Zec 13¹ 14⁸, Rev 22¹). In the promise of the outpouring of the Spirit, Joel seems to have given expression to a glimpse into NT times, with which he was specially favoured. His words have been taken up by the NT Church, and will be used, to the end of our NT dispensation, to express the sum of blessing bestowed by God on His true people (cf. Nu 11²⁶⁻²⁹, Zec 12¹⁰, Ac 2¹⁶ff., Jn 16⁷ff.).

Not less important are the two closely allied truths regarding the *remnant* and the *called* (2³²) [Heb. 3⁵]. For the former, cf. Ob ¹⁷ (where the language is the same as in Jl), Is 6¹³ (and various other passages), Mic 5³· ⁷· ⁸ [Heb. 4] ¹⁸], Jer 31⁷ff., Ro 11 5ff.. For the latter, cf. Ro 9⁷ff.. It is worthy of note that, in this OT book, the truth is distinctly laid down that (as Ewald puts it) 'no man may boast of a right to redemption' (*Prophets of OT*, Eng. tr. i. 137).

This investigation might be pushed further, but enough has been stated to show that the Bk. of Jl and other books of Scripture have a great deal in common.*

The style of Joel is clear and of a high order, and the language comparatively pure. One of his words for the locusts (פֶׁלֶק) occurs

---

* Is 13⁶ (cf. Jl 1¹⁵), Am 1² (cf. Jl 3 [Heb. 4] ¹⁶), Am 9¹³ (cf. Jl 3 [Heb. 4] ¹⁸), raise directly the question of quotations. This point has not been discussed, because, in the case of such a book as the OT, an argument founded on quotations is extremely precarious. That quotations occur in the passages just mentioned is scarcely doubtful. The question is, 'Who quotes?' The words of Jl 3¹⁶ occur quite naturally in a highly poetic passage. The same words in Am 1² seem to be chosen as a sort of text for the prophet's discourse. And the reasonable view is that, in this case, Jl is the original source.

elsewhere only in Am 4⁹. This, partly, led Bleek to the conclusion that the locust invasion described in Jl was the same as that referred to in Am, and that the two prophets belonged to the same period—Joel being the earlier. If this view is accepted, the perplexing expression הַצְּפוֹנִי (the northern, 2²⁰) admits of a comparatively easy explanation. A north wind is all that is required to bring the locusts from the northern kingdom into Judah.

LITERATURE.—Pocock, *Com. on Joel*, Oxford, 1691; Credner, *Joël übers. u. erkl.*, Halle, 1831; Wünsche, *Weissag. d. Proph. Joël*, Leipzig, 1872; Merx, *Die Prophetie d. Joël u. ihre Ausleger*, Halle, 1879 (specially valuable on account of the detailed history of the exposition); Pusey, *Minor Prophets*, 1860; Driver, *LOT⁶* 307 ff., also *Joel and Amos* in Camb. Bible, 1897; Hitzig, *Kl. Proph.⁴*, 1881; Cornill, *Einleit.²* 174 f., *Der israel. Prophetismus*, 163; Wildeboer, *AT Lit.* 345 ff.; Gustav Preuss, *Joël, unter besonderer Rücksicht der Zeitfrage*, Halle, 1889; Kirkpatrick, *Doct. of Prophets*, 46 ff.; Findlay, *Bks. of the Prophets*, i. 94 ff.; Wellhausen, *Klein. Proph.* 56 ff., 207 ff.; W. R. Smith, art. JOEL in 9th ed. of *Enc. Brit.*; Farrar, *Minor Prophets*, 113 ff.; Ewald, *Prophets*, Eng. tr. i. 107 ff.; Reuss, *AT*, ii. 47 ff.; Nowack, *Kl. Proph.* 1897; G. A. Smith, *Twelve Prophets*, vol. ii. 1898; Cheyne, *Founders of OT Crit.* 312; A. B. Davidson in *Expositor*, March 1888; Gray, *ibid.* Sept. 1893; Kuenen, *Hist.-Crit. Ond.²* ii. 68; Oort in *Th. Tijd.* (1876) 362 ff.; Matthes in *Th. Tijd.* (1885) 34–66, 129–160, (1887) 357–381; Holzinger in *ZATW* (1889) 89–131. G. G. CAMERON.

JOELAH (יוֹעֵאלָה, text doubtful, see Kittel in *SBOT*. While LXX A has Ἰωηλά, B has Ἐλιά).—A warrior who joined David at Ziklag, 1 Ch 12⁷.

JOEZER (יוֹעֶזֶר 'J" is help,' B Ἰωζάρα, A Ἰωζάαρ).—One of David's followers at Ziklag, 1 Ch 12⁶.

JOGBEHAH (יָגְבְּהָה; LXX in Nu καὶ ὕψωσαν αὐτάς, in Jg Ἰεγεβάλ, B).—A town of Gad in Gilead, Nu 32³⁵, named also in connexion with Gideon's pursuit of the Midianites, Jg 8¹¹. It is the present ruin *Jubeihah* (or *Ajbeihât*), N.W. from Rabbath-ammon, and about midway between that place and es-Salt. There are remains of a considerable Roman town, and the position is suitable for the line of Gideon's pursuit, from Succoth to Penuel and thence S.E. to Jogbehah. There are three groups of ruins, hence the plur. *Ajbeihât*.

LITERATURE.—*SEP* vol. i. under the Arabic name; Burckhardt, *Syria*, 361; Oliphant, *Land of Gilead*, 232; Baedeker-Socin, *Pal.²* 288; Ewald, *GVI* ii. 547 n.; Buhl, *GAP* 261; G. A. Smith, *HGHL* 585; Dillmann on Nu 32³⁵; Moore on Jg 8¹¹. C. R. CONDER.

JOGLI (יָגְלִי).—The Danite chief who took part in the division of the land, Nu 34²² P.

JOHA (יוֹחָא, prob. textual error for יוֹיאָח; see Gray, *Heb. Prop. Names*, 283 n. 4).—1. A Benjamite, 1 Ch 8¹⁶. 2. One of David's heroes, 1 Ch 11⁴⁵.

JOHANAN (יוֹחָנָן; LXX Ἰωνά, Ἰωανάν, Ἰωνάν, Ἰωαννάν, Ἰωάννας).—1. 2 K 25²³, Jer 40⁸–43⁵ (see AZARIAH, No. 23, and GEDALIAH), the son of Kareah, chief of 'the captains of the forces,' who after the fall of Jerusalem joined Gedaliah at Mizpah. Johanan seems to have been a shrewd man; and, foreseeing the calamities which would certainly ensue if Ishmael's plot were successful, he not only joined the other captains in warning Gedaliah, but in a secret interview pressed in vain to be himself permitted to assassinate Ishmael. When the murder of Gedaliah became known, J. pursued after Ishmael, who was carrying captive the remnant of the Jews. The murderer escaped with the loss of two men (Jer 41¹· ¹⁵); but J. recovered the captives, and brought them to a khan (?) near Bethlehem, Geruth-chimham (see 2 S 19³⁸, Lk 2⁷), whence they might start for Egypt. The politic J. foresaw that the captains would be held responsible by the Chaldæan authorities for the murder of Gedaliah and the escape of the assassin. Having thus determined, J. and all the people consulted Jeremiah, earnestly affirming their resolve to follow at all risks the revealed will of the Lord; but the answer being strongly adverse to

their leaving their own land, they accused Jeremiah of being a false prophet, under the malign influence of Baruch, and carried off to Egypt both the prophet and his scribe. 2. 1 Ch 3¹⁵ eldest son of Josiah, not the same as Jehoahaz; for (a) Jehoahaz was not the eldest son (see 2 K 23³¹· ³⁶); and (β) he is mentioned in this verse as Shallum. Johanan possibly predeceased his father. 3. 1 Ch 3²⁴ a post-exilic prince of the line of David. 4. 1 Ch 6⁹· ¹⁰ a high priest, perhaps under Rehoboam, father of Azariah, No. 5. 5. 6. 1 Ch 12⁴· ¹² two warriors who came to David to Ziklag, a Benjamite and a Gadite respectively. 7. Ezr 8¹² (JOANNES, 1 Es 8³⁸) one of those who returned with Ezra. 8. 2 Ch 28¹² an Ephraimite, father of AZARIAH, No. 17. The Heb. is יְהוֹחָנָן, Jehohanan. 9. See JONATHAN, No. 6, and JEHOHANAN, No. 3.
N. J. D. WHITE.

JOHN (Ἰωάννης).—Five persons of this name are mentioned in the Apocr. 1. The father of Mattathias, and grandfather of the five Maccabæan brothers (1 Mac 2¹). 2. J., surnamed Caddis or (RV) Gaddis (wh. see), the eldest son of Mattathias (1 Mac 2², where inferior MSS read Ἰωαννάν; Jos. *Ant.* XII. vi. 1). In B.C. 161 he was slain by the 'sons of Jambri' [JAMBRI] (1 Mac 9³⁵–⁴²; Jos. *Ant.* XIII. i. 2–4). In 2 Mac 8²², and perhaps again 10¹⁹, he is by mistake called Joseph. 3. The father of Eupolemus (1 Mac 8¹⁷, 2 Mac 4¹¹, Jos. *Ant.* XII. x. 6), who was sent by Judas Maccabæus as an ambassador to Rome. The passage in 2 Mac speaks of certain royal privileges obtained for the Jews by this J., but disregarded by Epiphanes. The privileges referred to are probably those granted by Antiochus the Great (Jos. *Ant.* XII. iii. 3), among which was the right of being governed according to their own laws. 4. An envoy, who together with another named ABSALOM (which see) was sent by the Jews to treat with Lysias (2 Mac 11¹⁷). 5. One of the elder sons of Simon the Maccabee (1 Mac 16²), commonly known as J. Hyrcanus (cf. Jos. *Ant.* XIII. vii. 4), and described as 'a (valiant) man' (1 Mac 13⁵³), was appointed by his father commander of the forces, and stationed at Gazara. In conjunction with his brother Judas he defeated CENDEBÆUS (1 Mac 16¹⁻¹⁰, cf. Jos. *Ant.* XIII. vii. 3). When his father and brothers had been murdered by Ptolemy at Dok near Jericho, J., who was then at Gazara, received warning of their fate, and, having put to death the men sent to assassinate him, secured the position of high priest, which had been made hereditary in the family of Simon B.C. 135 (1 Mac 16¹¹⁻²⁴, cf. 14⁴⁶). See MACCABEES.
H. A. WHITE.

JOHN (Ac 4⁶).—A meeting of the Sanhedrin is mentioned, at which there are said to have been gathered together 'the rulers, the elders, and the scribes, with Annas the high priest, and Caiaphas, and John, and Alexander, and all who were of the high priestly family.' Nothing further is known of either John or Alexander (wh. see), and the attempts made to connect the names with other historical characters (such as Johanan ben-Sakkai) are more than improbable. A. C. HEADLAM.

JOHN, FATHER OF SIMON PETER.—In Jn 1⁴² the true reading is Σίμων ὁ υἱὸς Ἰωάνου, in 21¹⁵· ¹⁶· ¹⁷ Σίμων Ἰωάνου. The *Vetus Interpretatio Latina* of Origen (*in Matth.* tom. xv. 14, Migne, *Pat. Gr.* xiii. 1295) quotes a passage from the *Gospel according to the Hebrews* in which the words occur, 'Simon, fili Joanne, facilius est camelum intrare per foramen acus quam divitem in regnum cælorum' (cf. Hilgenfeld, *Evang. secundum Hebræos*, pp. 16, 25), a passage, however, which has no place in the Greek text. Further, a cursive MS (Matt. Mk.) of the 9th century (Tisch. *Not. Cod. Sin.* p. 58) has

four marginal glosses, in which τὸ ἰουδαϊκόν [sc. εὐαγγέλιον] is referred to. One of these agrees with a fragment quoted by Jerome from the *Gospel according to the Hebrews*, so that it appears that these scholia reproduce matter from that Gospel. On Mt 16¹⁷ (Βαριωνᾶ) there is the note : τὸ ἰουδαικὸν υἱὲ Ἰωάννου (see Handmann, *Das Hebräerevang.*, 'Texte u. Untersuch.,' v. pp. 65, 85). There is sufficient evidence, therefore, that John was found in the *Gospel according to the Hebrews* as the name of the apostle's father.

In Mt 16¹⁷ the father's name is given as Jonas—Σίμων Βαριωνᾶ.* In the LXX we find that not only is יוֹחָנָן represented in B by Ἰωνά in 2 K 25²³ and by Ἰωνάν in Jer 47 (40)⁸, but even יְהוֹחָנָן (1 Ch 26³) is represented in A by Ἰωᾶς, in A by Ἰωνάν ; cf. 1 Ch 12¹² (Ἰωάν), Ezr 8¹², Neh 6¹⁸, 1 Es 9¹, Jer 43 (50)⁴ (א'). There is ground, therefore, for the conclusion in the case in question that Ἰωνᾶς is a contraction of Ἰωάνης (so Keim, *Geschichte Jesu von Nazara*, ii. p. 213 [iii. p. 261, Eng. tr.] ; see esp. Lightfoot, *On a Fresh Revision*, p. 159 n.).

It is possible, however, that we have here an instance of a double name. Such double names were not uncommon ; see Zunz, ' Namen der Juden,' in his *Gesammelte Schriften*, ii. p. 15, who among instances of double Hebrew or Aramaic names adduces Jochanan-Joseph (*Gittin*, f. 34*b*). More common were the cases in which to a Hebrew or Aramaic name was added a Greek or Roman name —the latter being often chosen so as to make an assonance with the former. Familiar instances are Saul-Paulus (see Deissmann, *Bibelstudien*, p. 181 ff.), Joseph-Justus (Ac 1²³). It seems therefore not impossible that the name of St. Peter's father was *Jona-Jochanan* or *Jona-Johannes*. The latter name was so common (see *e.g.* the Index to Josephus, or Pape, *Wörterbuch*) that it must have been familiar to Gentiles (cf. inscription at Ancyra, *CIG* 4045), and in intercourse with them would have something of the convenience of a Greek or Roman name.

A curious specimen of the harmonizing expedient is found in a note of the Paris MSS. Reg. 1789, 1026, Πέτρος καὶ Ἀνδρέας ἀδελφοί, ἐκ πατρὸς Ἰωνᾶ, μητρὸς Ἰωαννᾶ, or (as it is otherwise read) ἐκ πατρὸς Ἰωάννου, μητρὸς Ἰωνᾶς (see Lightfoot, *ubi supra*).

F. H. CHASE.

JOHN THE BAPTIST (Ἰωάννης ὁ Βαπτιστής).—

   i. Sources of Information.
   ii. The Facts of John's Life and Ministry.
   iii. John's Work and Teaching.
   iv. John's Relation to Christ.

i. SOURCES.—In regard to John the Baptist we have practically no sources of first-hand information outside the NT besides the passage in Josephus (*Ant.* XVIII. v. 2), referred to by Eus. (*HE* i. 11). The fullest account is that of St. Luke, with which that of St. Matthew agrees closely, so far as the time after the beginning of his public ministry is concerned. St. Mark's notices are very brief. The Fourth Gospel seems to differ from the others in recording only the ' witness ' of John the Baptist *after* our Lord's baptism, while Mt and Lk give his prophetic teaching *before* that event. The relation of the Fourth Gospel to the others, in this connexion, has been made the subject of special monographs, such as that of Boissonas, mentioned at the end of this article.

ii. LIFE AND MINISTRY.—John the Baptist was the son of Zacharias and Elisabeth. The latter was ' of the daughters of Aaron ' (Lk 1⁵), while Zacharias belonged to the course of Abiah (wh. see), one of the sons of Eleazar, who gave his name to the eighth of the twenty-four courses into which the priests were divided. His priestly descent on both

*In the LXX of Jonah the name is declined—Ἰωνᾶς, Ἰωνᾶν, Ἰωνᾶ (4⁶).

sides brings into stronger contrast the prophetic character of his work. We cannot determine exactly either the time or the place of his birth. Dates varying from B.C. 6 to B.C. 3 have been assigned to it, and Lk 1³⁶ would lead us to infer that it was three months before that of our Lord. In regard to the place, it is argued that Zacharias must have lived in one of the priestly towns ; but it is possible to prove that priests often lived elsewhere. It is still more arbitrary to pick out one of the priestly towns and fix on Hebron (Othon, *Lex. Rabbin.* 324). Nor is there sufficient evidence for reading **Juttah** in Lk 1³⁹, though this place, which lay a little S. of Hebron, is mentioned (Jos 15⁵⁵ 21¹⁶) as a priestly town. A tradition, resting on the evidence of the Russian abbot Daniel (*c.* A.D. 1113), who quotes as his authority a monk of St. Sabas (Didon, *Life of Christ*, Eng. tr. App. D), fixes the residence of Zacharias at *Ain Karim*, a village to the N.W. of Bethlehem. We cannot go behind the vague statement of St. Luke, who mentions (1³⁹) ' a city of Judah in the hill country.' Of John's early life and training St. Luke, our sole authority, tells us very little. It is summed up in the two verses which state that ' the hand of the Lord was with him ' (1⁶⁶), and that ' the child grew and waxed strong in spirit, and was in the deserts till the day of his showing unto Israel ' (1⁸⁰). To these may be added the words of the angel Gabriel (Lk 1¹⁵), ' He shall drink no wine nor strong drink, and he shall be filled with the Holy Ghost, even from his mother's womb.'

With these few details we have to pass over a period of about thirty years which preceded his ἀνάδειξις (cf. Lk 10¹, Ac 1²⁴), and can only speculate on the question (which is of some interest in reference to Jn 1³¹) whether our Lord was personally known to him (as their relationship would seem to necessitate) or not. There can be little doubt that the elaborate accumulation of dates given by St. Luke (3¹,²), combined with the expression (unique in the NT) ' the word of God came,' is meant to mark the beginning of John's ministry, and to emphasize its *prophetic* character. If (see CHRONOLOGY OF THE NT, vol. i. p. 405) we may assign the fifteenth year of Tiberius to A.D. 25–26, then this is the date of the *beginning* of John's ministry. We cannot determine how long after this beginning the incident of our Lord's baptism occurred, and the arguments used to show that this interval was long (Didon, *l.c.*) or short (Weiss) are not decisive. The only definite fact to notice is that the first passover of our Lord's ministry (see CHRONOLOGY OF NT, p. 405) is that of A.D. 27, and therefore the baptism must be fixed before that time. To the period following Christ's baptism is to be assigned the carefully defined record of Jn 1¹⁹⁻⁴², while the Synoptic account belongs to the period which precedes that event.

How long an interval elapsed between Christ's baptism and John's imprisonment is the next point to consider. Here it may be noticed (1) that Lk 3¹⁹,²⁰ mentions the imprisonment before our Lord's baptism, evidently with the intention of completing the references to John before passing to our Lord's ministry ; (2) that Mt 4¹² and Mk 1¹⁴ connect our Lord's first journey into Galilee with the imprisonment, and make it follow that event in time ; (3) that St. John mentions a short stay in Galilee and a visit to Jerusalem for the passover, and *then* makes the definite statement that ' John was not yet cast into prison ' (3²⁴). We must either assume, therefore, that Jn is at variance with Mt and Mk, or that the visit to Galilee which he records preceded our Lord's public ministry there. The latter is the more probable explanation, and in that case the visit of Mt 4¹² and Mk 1¹⁴ may be identified with that of Jn 4². At any rate, for determining the date of the imprisonment, Jn's statements are more important, for that event must have been subsequent to the passover of A.D. 27; further, if we may press the allusion in Jn 4³⁵—τετράμηνός ἐστιν καὶ ὁ θερισμὸς ἔρχεται—our Lord's journey into Galilee will have taken place not very long after the passover, and if we may also use the statements of Mt and Mk which assign the imprisonment as the reason of our Lord's going into Galilee, then we may fix the imprisonment early in A.D. 27. One incident is related during that imprisonment (Mt 11², Lk 7¹⁸), viz. the message sent by John through his disciples to ask our Lord whether He was the Messiah. This is definitely connected, in St. Matthew's account, with the plucking of the ears of corn; in St. Luke it seems to be the result of the report of Christ's ministry in Galilee, and especially of the Raising of the Widow's Son. If, therefore, we follow Mt, this incident would be some time between April and June of the same year; nor would the latter month allow too little time for the completion of the Galilæan tour required by St. Luke's narrative.

The last event to which we have to try and assign a date is the death of John the Baptist, recorded Mt 14³ᶠᶠ., Mk 6¹⁴ᶠᶠ.. Little weight can be attached to the almost universal commemoration of this event on Aug. 29 (Nilles, Kalend. Utr. Eccles.), though it certainly represents a comparatively early usage. We cannot base any argument on the context in Mt and Mk, for in both the account is inserted parenthetically to explain Herod's statement that John was 'risen from the dead'; but it may be noticed that the news of his death in Mt 14¹³ leads on at once to the miracle of the Feeding of the Five Thousand. Nor can we fix the date of John's death by its coincidence with the γενέσια of Herod Antipas. Herod's reluctance (Mt 14⁵) to put John to death may, but need not, imply a considerable interval between his imprisonment and death; thus Renan (Vie de Jésus, ch. vii.) puts the arrest in the summer of 29, and the death on the birthday of Herod Antipas in 30.* We may perhaps safely argue that his death had taken place before the unnamed feast of Jn 5¹, for during our Lord's visit to Jerusalem on that occasion he refers to John's witness as past (Jn 5³⁵ ἦν); and though it is possible to argue that his witness was closed by his imprisonment, it is more natural to refer the expression to his death. John's death therefore took place before the feast of Jn 5¹, that is, certainly before the second passover of our Lord's ministry, but how long before must depend on the interpretation given to Jn 5¹. It cannot be placed later than the beginning of A.D. 28. According to tradition (Theodt. HE iii. 3), John was buried at Samaria.

The *scene* of John's ministry will be placed partly in the desert of Judæa (Mt 3¹), in which it began, and partly in the Jordan Valley, and more definitely near the fords (Bethabara [which see] = 'place of crossing over'), either those in the neighbourhood of Bethshean or those in the neighbourhood of Jericho. Two places are mentioned in connexion with his 'baptism,' viz. Bethany or Bethabara (Jn 1²⁸), and Ænon near to Salim (Jn 3²³), probably in the neighbourhood of Bethshean. From Jn 3²⁶, and also from the fact of his coming under the jurisdiction of Herod Antipas, we infer that he probably spent some time in Peræa.

iii. JOHN'S WORK AND TEACHING.—(a) The name ὁ βαπτιστής or ὁ βαπτίζων (whether given to him to distinguish him from others of the same name or not) indicates the feature of his work which attracted special attention. It was used of him

* These dates are, of course, later than those in the article on CHRONOLOGY OF NT, which is here followed.

during his lifetime by his disciples (Lk 7²⁰), and that the term is not due to the evangelist is clear from Lk 3² 7¹⁸ etc., where John is by him called son of Zacharias, or simply John. The term is used of him also during his lifetime by our Lord (Mt 11¹¹), who, however, also uses the name John simply (e.g. Mt 11¹³), by Herodias (Mt 14⁸), by Herod after John's death (Mt 14²), and by the evangelists Mt and Mk but not Lk and Jn. In regard to his baptism, we gather that his right to perform the ceremony was questioned, inasmuch as (Jn 1²⁵) it was connected, according to Jewish ideas, only with the Messiah (cf. Ezk 36²⁵, Zec 13¹ etc.), with Elias as His forerunner, and with 'the prophet' (i.e. of Dt 18¹⁵). John speaks of himself as having received a special commission from God to baptize (Jn 1³³), though this is not spoken of in the angel's message to Zacharias, and he seems (Jn 3²⁷) to defend our Lord's baptism (Jn 3²⁶, but cf. 4²) by basing it on a similar divine commission. The *import* of the rite was early a question of discussion (Jn 3²⁵), nor does the language of the evangelists make clear what was understood by it; for while Mk 1⁴ Lk 3³ define it as 'a baptism of repentance for remission of sins,' Mt 3¹¹ speaks of it as a baptism εἰς (τὴν) μετάνοιαν; but μετάνοια can hardly have been the *object* of the rite, for it was preceded (Mt, Mk) by a confession of sin. The submission of a Jew to the rite was, so far, an act involving μετάνοια, in that it implied that he put himself in the same position towards the coming βασιλεία τῶν οὐρανῶν which the proselyte took up towards the old Jewish dispensation; it implied that he rested no longer on his privileged position as a Jew, but realized his individual responsibility in regard to sin. This comes near to Sabatier's explanation (see Lit. below) of the rite as 'consecrating a new Israel,' and would perhaps best explain the meaning of our Lord's words, in regard to Himself, that a submission to John's baptism was (Mt 3¹⁵) a fulfilment, i.e. a complete realization, of what was meant by δικαιοσύνη, as something which consisted not merely in external rites, but involved moral claims. Our Lord implies that John's baptism was from heaven (Mk 11³⁰); and the refusal of the Pharisees and lawyers to receive it is in itself a virtual rejection of God's purpose, while the acceptance of it by the publicans and the people showed a truer recognition on their part of what the righteousness of God really meant (Lk 7²⁹. ³⁰ ἐδικαίωσαν τὸν θεόν). We may notice, too (Mt 21³²), that our Lord regards John as coming ἐν ὁδῷ δικαιοσύνης. So that we may regard John's baptism as emphasizing the true nature of δικαιοσύνη.

(β) We pass from his baptism to (1) his position as a teacher; (2) the language in which that teaching was conveyed; (3) its underlying ideas.

(1) The angel Gabriel connects with him (Lk 1¹⁷) the prophecy of Malachi (4⁵. ⁶), but precludes the idea that Elias would return in person as many expected (see Geux, l.c. p. 73 ff.), by saying that John should come in 'the spirit and power' of Elias. That he was Elias come in the flesh John himself (Jn 1²¹) denied, while Christ affirmed that John the Baptist was really the Elias who was to precede the Messiah's coming (Mt 11¹⁴ 17¹¹⁻¹³). The other prophecy which was applied to John the Baptist by himself (Jn 1²³) and also by the evangelists (Mt 3³, Mk 1²) is that of Is 40³. He was then 'more than a prophet,' as himself the subject of prophecy. But he was also essentially a prophet, and as such St. Luke introduces him in the unique expression already noticed, as such Zacharias refers to him (Lk 1⁷⁶ προφήτης Ὑψίστου κληθήσῃ), as such Christ regarded him (Mt 11¹¹), and the people as a rule (but cf. Mt 11¹⁸) accepted him as a prophet (Mt 14⁵ 21²⁶). In regard to his special mission we must refer also to the words used of him in Jn 1⁶ 3²⁸

(ἀπεσταλμένος) and Mt 11¹¹ (ἐγήγερται). It is then as 'the last of the prophets' and as such closing the dispensation of 'the law and the prophets' (Mt 11¹⁴, Lk 16¹⁶) that we specially think of John the Baptist.

(2) When we pass to the language in which his teaching was conveyed, we find that it is largely based on that used by OT prophecy, especially by Isaiah. His metaphors of the burning chaff, the fan, the barren tree, are all to be found in OT. Some of the expressions are difficult to trace, and not easy to explain. Thus various interpretations have been assigned to the phrase γεννήματα ἐχιδνῶν (Mt 3⁷ etc., Lk 3⁷), which is not to be found in the OT, but is one of several expressions common to our Lord and John the Baptist; another expression of which the meaning is not quite clear is the baptism 'with fire' (Mt 3¹¹).

(3) In regard to the substance of his teaching, it must be remembered (a) that even in the fullest account of it given by St. Luke we have only an abstract (cf. 3⁷ imperfect ἔλεγεν, and 3¹⁸ πολλὰ καὶ ἕτερα); (b) that St. Luke regards the character of his teaching as a consequence (3⁷ οὖν) of his carrying out the preparatory work spoken of in Is 40³. We may amplify the abstract by noticing the words which are used to describe it. They are κηρύσσω (Mk 1⁴ etc.), εὐαγγελίζω (Lk 3¹⁸), παρακαλέω (Lk 3¹⁸), and in the case of Herod ἐλέγχω; and these imply that he announced good tidings, and also the preparation necessary for it; and in both these his prophetic character appears. The 'good tidings' he announced was the near approach of 'the kingdom.' The nature of this kingdom he does not define, nor does he state how the kingdom is to be established, nor who its members are to be. Probably, in accordance with ancient Jewish belief, he expected a visible kingdom; but he advances on that in so far as consciously or unconsciously to imply that it was spiritual, and to prepare the way for the realization that it was not to be merely Jewish but universal. These points can be seen from his insistence on the *moral* preparation for it. Repentance is a necessity, for all national privileges are useless, and the fitting mode of life requires that ordinary pursuits should be followed, but in a new spirit. Thus an individual and universal responsibility is insisted on, and an individual and universal judgment is proclaimed as imminent. Limits of space prevent an examination in detail of this teaching, but it will repay careful study. We can only summarize. It was addressed (Lk 3¹⁰; cf. Mk 1⁵, Mt 3⁵) to the ὄχλοι, who came out to him in large numbers, and included in their ranks (Mt 3⁷) many Pharisees and Sadducees. The points insisted on by John are (1) confession of sins, and repentance, which had been already enforced by the OT prophets (*e.g.* Hos 6¹, Jl 2¹² etc.); (2) the uselessness of reposing on their national privileges as 'children of Abraham' is indicated, and possibly the outburst γεννήματα ἐχιδνῶν may have been provoked by the thought that many of his hearers were relying on his baptism as of value *per se*, and teaching others to do the same (Boissonas, *l.c.* p. 40); (3) a judgment is imminent (ἤδη), which is universal (πᾶν δένδρον), and determined by the character of the individual. This judgment involves a manifestation of divine ὀργή, not only towards the political enemies of Israel (as in OT), but towards the Jews. This ὀργή is frequently mentioned in OT and NT, and a resulting purification or separation, διακαθαριεῖ, probably implies not, as Godet, the universal character of the purification, but its thoroughness; (4) St. Luke alone records the answers given to different classes who realized the need of action of some kind. John's answers show the changed requirements—not outward observ-

ances or a leaving of their ordinary duties, but a new attitude towards them; (5) finally, John removes the doubts of some as to whether he was the Messiah, by asserting the inferiority of his own person and work. His teaching as recorded in St. John will be best considered under the next heading; but it will be interesting for students to try and trace whether there is any difference between St. John's teaching before and after his baptism of our Lord.

It remains under this head to say a word as to the effect of his teaching. It is clear that very large numbers came to him, and he was generally accepted as a prophet; and of the lower classes many accepted his teaching (Lk 7³⁰), though the upper classes refused to accept his baptism, and some said of him, as of our Lord, δαιμόνιον ἔχει (Mt 11¹⁸). Besides the effect of his work and teaching on the people at large, we read also of μαθηταί who fasted (Mk 2¹⁸ etc.), who attended him in prison (Mt 11² 14¹²), and to whom he taught special forms of prayer (Lk 5³³ 11¹), some of whom left him to follow Christ (Jn 1³⁷). Their number is given in Clem. *Hom.* ii. 23 as thirty. In the Acts (18²⁵ 19³) we hear of Christians at Ephesus who accepted John's baptism. Their mention shows 'how profoundly the effect of John's preaching was felt in districts as remote as proconsular Asia, even after a lapse of a quarter of a century' (Lightfoot, *Colossians*, p. 402). Later on (and Lightfoot finds a trace of this in the argument of St. John's Gospel) the Hemerobaptists connected their beliefs and practices with John the Baptist, and Christians called after him, the Sabæans or Mandæans, are still, though in diminishing numbers, to be found in the marshy districts near the confluence of the Tigris and Euphrates (see Lightfoot, *l.c.*, and literature quoted by him p. 405; and also Renan, who finds evidence of Babylonian ideas).

iv. JOHN'S RELATION TO CHRIST.—From the narrative of St. Luke (chs. 1 and 2), and from Mt 3¹⁴, we should infer that John knew our Lord, and realized the nature of His Person; but the words of Jn 1³¹⋅³³ 'I knew him not,' imply that at any rate till the sign was given at our Lord's baptism John did not recognize Him as the Messiah; and this view is taken by Strauss, Godet, and Weiss. It is quite probable that the Synoptic narrative gives John's teaching before the baptism, and that the Fourth Gospel gives the special μαρτυρία which it was John's function, in the Divine Providence (Jn 1⁷), to bear, so soon as he realized by the sign at the baptism what our Lord's real personality was. This does not require that our Lord's divinity did not begin till His baptism and the descent of the Holy Ghost there, as held by various Gnostic and Humanitarian sects.[*] To the time of John's baptism of our Lord is to be assigned that 'anointing' with the Holy Spirit (Ac 4³⁷ 10³⁸) which was His consecration to His ministry. We assume here that the Synoptic narrative does refer to the time before our Lord's baptism, and the Fourth Gospel to the period which follows. In the former his references to our Lord's *person* are only relative to himself: He is ὁ ἰσχυρότερος—He is the master, while John is the servant who bears (Mt) or looses (Mk, Lk) the master's sandals. The unwillingness to baptize our Lord (Mt 3¹⁴) does, however, require that John had some definite grasp of who it was that came to him. John speaks of the *work* of Him for whom he was preparing as consisting in a baptism 'with the Holy Ghost and with fire.' The baptism with fire must refer

---

[*] Cf. Conybeare, *Key of Truth*, pp. xii, xiii, for the teaching of Gregory the Illuminator, esp. 'John gave priesthood, and unction, and prophecy, and kingship to our Saviour Christ, and Christ gave it to the apostles, and the apostles to the clergy of the Church.'

either to the fire of judgment (as Keim, Neander, Meyer, etc.), or to the Holy Spirit (as Godet), and its effect is either that of devouring (Dt 4²⁴) or purifying (Zec 13⁹, Mal 3² etc.). In the Fourth Gospel, though we probably must not understand the twice-repeated (Jn 1¹⁵. ³⁰) 'who was before me' as a statement of belief in the pre-existence of Christ, yet the language in which John the Baptist speaks of Christ as 'the Son of God' (1³⁴) and the 'Lamb of God' implies a much higher and more definite conception of the person of Christ than any words used by John the Baptist in the Synoptic Gospels, and is best explained by the vision referred to in these Gospels, which would account for the clearer grasp. We cannot be sure that the Baptist understood completely the term 'Lamb of God' which he applied to our Lord, but he must have had in his mind some thought of Is 53. In the other passage in which he speaks of Christ as the Bridegroom, he is using language by which the relation of Jehovah to His people is frequently described in the OT (Is 54⁵ 61¹⁰, Hos 2²⁰). It is an interesting point of coincidence between the Synoptic narrative and that of St. John that our Lord uses this same expression of Himself when disciples of John were present, Mt 9¹⁴ᵗ.

To complete our notice of John's relation to Christ, it is necessary just to refer to the message which he sent to our Lord from the prison (Mt 11): we can hardly believe, after the terms applied by him to Christ in St. John, that his own faith wavered, and must suppose that he wished some confirmation of Christ's Messiahship to be given for the sake of his disciples.

Before we leave this heading of the subject, it is worth while to notice how many of our Lord's expressions resemble those found in John the Baptist's mouth. Besides the reference to the Bridegroom just mentioned, we find a connexion in the command to repent with which our Lord begins His ministry in the language about the tree and its fruits (Mt 7¹⁶ 12³³), in the expression γεννήματα ἐχιδνῶν (Mt 3⁷) used twice by our Lord (Mt 12³⁴ 23³³), and nowhere else except by John the Baptist. We must also briefly notice here the testimony borne by our Lord to John, as the greatest born of women, as closing the older dispensation of the law and the prophets, and yet as less than the least in the kingdom of heaven, because he preceded its advent (Mt 11¹¹).

It hardly falls within the scope of this Dictionary to follow the many references connected with the name of John the Baptist in art, in liturgical use, in the dedication of churches, etc. etc.—for these reference may be made to the *Dictionary of Christian Antiquities*, articles 'John the Baptist' and 'Baptisteries,' to the index of Nilles' *Kalendarium Utriusque Ecclesiæ*, to Paciandi, *Antiquitates Christianæ*, vol. iii. ('De cultu J. Baptistæ') Romae, 1755, and to various books on sacred art, etc., such as those of Kraus, Detzel, and Wessely, or Jameson's *Sacred and Legendary Art.*

LITERATURE.—Besides the books just mentioned, and the commentaries on the Gospel narratives, the following will be found useful :—Hort, *Judaistic Christianity*, p. 22 ff. ; Lightfoot, *Colossians*, p. 400 ff. ; Sabatier, article in Lichtenberger's *Encyclopädie* ; Renan, *Vie de Jésus* (index). There are a number of monographs and articles on John the Baptist, in which the points mentioned in the preceding article are more minutely investigated. Such are H. R. Reynolds, *John the Baptist* ; Simpson, *The Last of the Prophets* ; Boissonas, *De l'attitude de Jean Baptiste* ; Bornemann, *Die Taufe Christi durch Johannes* ; Breuil, *Du culte de S. Jean Baptiste* ; Chenot, *Jean le Baptiste* ; Geux, *Jean Baptiste* ; Haupt, *Johannes der Taüfer* ; Köhler, *Johannes der Taüfer* ; articles by Loisy in *Revue de l'histoire et de littérature religieuses*, iii. 1, 3.

LL. J. M. BEBB.

JOHN MARK.—See MARK.

JOHN THE APOSTLE (LIFE AND THEOLOGY OF).—

I. THE LIFE.
(a) The Gospel narratives.
(b) Other NT references.
(c) Traditions of the Early Church.
(d) The tradition of St. John's residence at Ephesus examined.
II. THE THEOLOGY.
  A. *The Gospel and Epistles of St. John.*
  (1) The 'signs' and the 'witness' of the Fourth Gospel to the Messiahship of Jesus and His unique relation to the Father.
  (2) The *Word* of God—creative and revealing functions.
  (3) Importance attached in the Epistles to a true view of the Person of Christ.
  (4) Theology of the Father and the Son.
  (5) Scheme of salvation—meaning of the terms 'world,' 'flesh,' 'eternal life'—salvation *through* Christ, implying (a) on His part the sacrifice and death of Himself, (b) on man's part (α) a being *born again* ; (β) the exercise of *faith* in the Son ; (γ) the sustaining of the new life by participation in the *life of Christ.*
  (6) Doctrine of the Holy Spirit and the Church.
  (7) The three great statements—'God is Spirit,' 'God is Light,' 'God is Love.'
  B. *The Apocalypse.*
  (a) The Doctrine of God—(α) Eternity ; (β) Universal Sovereignty ; (γ) Relation of Father and Son.
  (b) Doctrine of the Spirit.
  (c) Doctrine of Sin and Judgment, and of Salvation and the Church.

I. THE LIFE OF ST. JOHN.—The fragmentary character of the literature relating to the earliest days of the Christian Church has deprived us of any very full or certain knowledge of the lives of the apostles. And it has happened, in the case of St. Peter and St. John conspicuously, that the discussion of the traditions of their later history has been involved in controversy. It will tend to clearness if the ordinary traditional account of St. John's life is first set out, and then the range of the controversy indicated.

(a) There are but few scenes in the Gospel story in which St. John takes a prominent place ; but enough is said to produce a strong impression of the apostle's character. He appears first, according to a very natural inference, in the opening chapter of the Gospel that bears his name. Two disciples of the Baptist, hearing the witness borne by their master to Jesus, follow the new Prophet. One is named by the author—it was Andrew, the brother of Simon Peter (Jn 1⁴⁰). The other is not named, but it has seemed obvious to infer that it was St. John. His call to be an apostle is told in the Synoptic tradition, by St. Luke, with the greatest fulness of detail (Lk 5⁸⁻¹¹, Mt 4²¹. ²², Mk 1¹⁹. ²⁰). It is from this source we learn that he was son of Zebedee (for John's possible relationship to Jesus see art. SALOME), and that he and his father were fishermen and Galilæans. It has often been pointed out that the presence of hired servants in the ship (Mk 1²⁰) with Zebedee implies a position of some degree of wealth. During the course of our Lord's ministry St. John appears only rarely in a position distinct from that of the other apostles. He is clearly one of the most prominent of the group of our Lord's followers. He, with Peter and James, is admitted to witness the raising of Jairus' daughter (Mk 5³⁷, Lk 8⁵¹) ; the same three are chosen to be present at the Transfiguration (Mt 17¹, Mk 9², Lk 9²⁸), and are nearest to the Lord at the agony in Gethsemane (Mk 14³³ and parallels). Once these three, with Andrew, are described as inquiring when our Lord's last prophecies would receive fulfilment (Mk 13³). Besides these instances, the two brothers, James and John, appear (Lk 9⁵⁴) independently, as wishing to call down fire on the Samaritan village that refused them shelter ; and are brought to the Lord by their mother with a request for a special place of dignity in the kingdom (Mk 10³⁵). John is once connected with St. Peter alone ; according to St. Luke, these two apostles were sent to prepare the passover (Lk 22⁸). Once John is described as acting alone ; it is he who asks our Lord what is to be done with the man whom they had found casting out devils in Jesus' name (Mk 9³⁸, Lk 9⁴⁹). These notices, though scattered and fragmentary, definitely suggest a particular character — the character indicated by the name given to John and his brother by our Lord : *Boanerges* (wh. see), 'sons of thunder' (Mk 3¹⁷). They were fiery in their zeal and severe in temperament ; yet, for all this, they were among the closest of our Lord's chosen band. Though He rebukes their vehemence, He sees in them a character such as an apostle needs.

When we turn to the Fourth Gospel, we find that the name of John, son of Zebedee, is never once named. But there are in the account of the Passion and Resurrection certain references to an unnamed apostle whom universal tradition has identified with St. John. At the Last Supper we read of a disciple whom Jesus loved, who was reclining at the table in a place of special nearness to our Lord. It seems from the language used (ch. 13) that the three, our Lord, St. Peter, and this un-named apostle, occupied one *triclinium*. They reclined, according to custom, on the left side, obliquely across the couch. Our Lord was in the centre, St. Peter in the place second in dignity to this, parallel to the position occupied by the Lord and behind Him ; St. John in the third place, parallel also but before Him. When the prophecy of the betrayal is made, St. Peter from behind beckons to St. John in front to ask who it is. St. John, leaning back upon the breast of Jesus as he lay (13²⁵ ἀναπεσὼν ἐκεῖνος οὕτως ἐπὶ τὸ στῆθος τοῦ Ἰησοῦ), asks the question and receives the (probably whispered) communication. This same apostle is apparently he who was known to the high priest (18¹⁶), and used his acquaintance to admit St. Peter to the court of the high priest. The disciple whom Jesus loved is at the foot of the cross, and there receives the commission to take care of the Virgin-mother after the Lord's death (19²⁶). He is again in close connexion with St. Peter on the day of the resurrection. The news is brought to Simon Peter and the disciple whom Jesus loved (20²), and the two together make a visit to the tomb. In the last chapter of all, for the only time in this Gospel 'the sons of Zebedee' are mentioned (21²), and in the scene which follows, St. Peter and the disciple whom Jesus loved are the prominent agents. It is the latter who is first to recognize the Lord. The chapter is indeed inserted in order to correct an impression that this disciple is to await the coming of the Lord without dying. And then, in words which are closely parallel to the claim (19³⁵) to have been eye-witness of the scene upon the cross, it is distinctly asserted that the disciple whom Jesus loved is he that testifieth these things and that wrote these things (21²⁴).

(*b*) In the Acts, St. John appears in two im-portant scenes in company with St. Peter ; the connexion of these two apostles (noted in Lk 22⁸ and closely in agreement with the Fourth Gospel, if the beloved disciple is indeed St. John) is car-ried out in these chapters of the Acts. These are the two who heal the lame man at the Beautiful Gate of the temple, and are brought before the Sanhedrin (Ac 3. 4). These, again, are the two who go down to Samaria to bestow the gift of the Holy Ghost on those whom Philip had converted and baptized (8¹⁵). Once more the name of John is mentioned, again in connexion with St. Peter, as having been seen at Jerusalem by St. Paul when

he went up by revelation (Gal 2¹) and saw those who seemed to be pillars (Gal 2⁹). After this, except in the Revelation, the name of John dis-appears from the New Testament.

(*c*) When we pass beyond the New Testament, we find ourselves in the region of somewhat frag-mentary tradition. We learn that at some period undefined St. John left Jerusalem and took up his residence at Ephesus. Of the intervening period between the departure from Jerusalem and the residence at Ephesus we know nothing, except that Tertullian (*de Præsc. Hær.* 36) affirms that St. John came to Rome, and was there by way of suffering martyrdom. He was placed in a cauldron of boiling oil, but was miraculously preserved from death. No date is fixed for this by Tertullian, but St. John is said to have been banished after his escape to an island ('relegatur ad insulam'). Eusebius, however, definitely connects this banish-ment with the persecution of Domitian (*HE* III. xviii.), and quotes in support of his view the statement of Irenæus that St. John saw the Revelation πρὸς τῷ τέλει τῆς Δομετιανοῦ ἀρχῆς (Iren. *adv. Hær.* v. xxx. 3). Eusebius then affirms (on the basis of ὁ τῶν παρ' ἡμῖν ἀρχαίων λόγος, *HE* III. xx.) that, on the accession of Nerva, St. John removed from Patmos to Ephesus. Here he organized the Churches in Asia, and survived till the time of Trajan (Eus. *HE* III. xxiii., quoting Iren. *adv. Hær.* II. xxii. 5, III. iii. 4).

It is to this period that most of the remaining anecdotes of St. John are assigned. Polycrates, bishop of Ephesus, in a letter to Victor of Rome, says that John was priest here, and wore the πέταλον or high-priestly headdress ; that he died, and was buried there (Eus. v. xxiv.). On the authority of Apollonius, St. John is said to have raised a man from the dead at Ephesus (Eus. v. xviii.). It was in illustration of his exercise of the episcopal office with characteristic love that Clement of Alexandria tells the story of his journey into the forest to reclaim a convert who had fallen into bad ways and joined a band of robbers (Clem. Alex. *Quis Div. Salv.* ch. 42). While at Ephesus he combats fiercely the heresy of Cerinthus, refusing even to be under the same roof with the heretic (Iren. *adv. Hær.* III. iii. 4), and being persuaded to write his Gospel, specially to confute such heretics as this (*ib.* III. xi.). The Muratorian Fragment contains a story of the origin of the Gospel somewhat akin to this. It describes a discussion in which Andrew took part, in which St. John was pressed to write down his teaching about our Lord. After deliberation, and a special intimation from the Holy Spirit, he acts upon the advice. There are two stories of his extreme old age preserved, the one by Cassian, the other by Jerome. Cassian tells how he used to play with a tame par-tridge, and when censured for such frivolity used the phrase, 'the bow cannot be always bent' (*Coll.* xxiv. 21). And Jerome describes him at a time when he had to be carried into church, and was too old to speak for any length of time ; he used then, in addressing the Church, to use simply the old commandment, 'Little children, love one another.' His disciples, weary of the continual repetition, asked why he always said this : his answer was, 'Quia præceptum Domini est, et, si solum fiat, sufficit' (Jer. *Comm. in Gal.* vi. 10). The last chapter of the Gospel did not prevent the growth of a legend that the apostle was not really dead, but only asleep. And it was confidently affirmed that the ground where he lay rose and fell with his breathing, and that the dust was moved by his breath. St. Augustine mentions this (*Tract. in Joh.* cxxiv. 2), but does not altogether accept it ('Viderint . . . qui locum sciunt, utrum hoc ibi faciat vel patiatur terra, quod dicitur :

quia et revera non a levibus hominibus id audivimus ' *).

These are the fragmentary materials out of which
is built the idea of the beloved apostle prevalent
throughout the Church. They form a consistent
picture, of a character that is vehement and
tenacious, but has been moulded in its later days
by the spirit of love. The story of the journey
after the robber is quite consistent with that of
the refusal to be under the same roof with
Cerinthus the heretic. And both are parallel
to scenes in the Gospels and Acts ascribed to St.
John.

(d) The difficulties that have been raised about
the whole question of St. John's sojourn at Ephesus
do not arise from any inconsistency in the story
itself, but from considerations of a different order
altogether. They are part of the whole question
of the authorship of the writings ascribed to St.
John. If the authorities upon which the Ephesian
tradition depends are accepted as trustworthy, it
will be difficult to explain why and how the account
of the origin of the Gospel which seems to have
been part of the Ephesian tradition can be set
aside. It is not part of our subject to consider
the question of the authorship of the Gospel,
further than is necessary in order to estimate the
evidence for the tradition, but the points now to
be raised would be scarcely intelligible apart from
this explanation. See, further, next article.

The real point at issue is comparatively small.
Irenæus, who became bishop of Lyons in South
Gaul after the persecution of A.D. 177, writes a
letter to Florinus, a presbyter of the church of
Rome who has fallen into heresy. A fragment of
this letter is preserved by Eusebius (HE v. xx.).
In it Irenæus appeals to Florinus to contrast the
doctrines he has accepted with those which he
once learnt at the feet of Polycarp, who himself
claimed to be the pupil of the Apostle John. Irenæus
refers to a former time when he, as a boy (παῖς ἔτι
ὤν), saw Florinus, then in distinguished position
at court (λαμπρῶς πράττοντα ἐν τῇ βασιλικῇ αὐλῇ),
with Polycarp. Now Polycarp was martyred, at
the age of eighty-six (Mart. Polyc. § 8), on Feb.
23, 155.† Thus he must have been born (unless
the phrase in Mart. Polyc. refers to his conversion
and not his birth) in A.D. 69. If St. John really
lived till the time of Trajan, i.e. till about A.D.
100, there is no reason why Polycarp should not
have known him.

This tradition has been assailed on various
grounds. It has been asserted that there is no
real indication of Johannine influence in the
writers who date from Ephesus and its neighbourhood; more especially that Ignatius when writing
to the Ephesians in the year 115 makes no allusion
to St. John's presence there, though he does mention
St. Paul (Ign. Eph. ch. xii.), and shows signs of the
influence of the letter 'to the Ephesians.' This
argument is used by Keim (Jesus of Nazara, Eng.
tr. vol. i. p. 211 ff.), but its value is greatly
impaired by the authority of subsequent critics.
The researches of Paul Ewald (Das Hauptproblem
der Evangelienfrage), of H. Wendt (Lehre Jesu),
and especially of von der Goltz ('Ignatius von
Antiochien,' in Texte und Untersuchungen, xii. 3),
tend to show the presence in the region required,

and in the Ignatian Epistles in particular, of that
type of teaching which is associated with St. John's
name. This line of argument may therefore be
left out of account.

Another and much more impressive method of
criticism is that pursued by Harnack in his
Chronologie der Altchristlichen Literatur bis
Eusebius, Bd. i. pp. 320–340, 656–680. It will
have been noticed already that the hinge of the
whole case is the relation of Irenæus and Polycarp.
If it seemed likely that this relation was less close
than is generally supposed, no doubt the evidence
of Polycarp to the presence of St. John in Ephesus
might be seriously weakened. This is the central
point of Harnack's argument. He lays emphasis
on the youth of Irenæus (παῖς ἔτι ὤν), and the casual
character of his relation with Polycarp. There is
no evidence, he maintains, that Irenæus was in any
strict sense a pupil of Polycarp; he merely heard
him preach, like any other member of his congregation. It is, therefore, not improbable that he
confused the Apostle John with the John quoted
by Polycarp, this other John being really the Presbyter John—a person whose existence is affirmed
by Papias. To this Presbyter John, Harnack
assigns the Fourth Gospel. It is difficult to avoid
the conviction that Harnack is greatly minimizing
the significance of the passage from the letter of
Irenæus to Florinus. It is true that we do not
know exactly the age of Irenæus at the beginning
of his episcopate, and that the year of his birth
cannot be fixed within very narrow limits. It is
true that we cannot be certain of the date of the
scene ἐν τῇ κάτω 'Ασίᾳ to which Irenæus refers. It
is true that παῖς ἔτι ὤν suggests that Irenæus refers
to a time when he was from 12–17 or 18 years old.*
But (1) the tone of the letter, especially the reference to the psychology of memory, seems to imply
an advanced age; it is usually between 60 and 70
or later that the memory begins to fail for more
recent events; and (2) Harnack greatly under-
rates the fulness of the knowledge which Irenæus
claims. If it be true that the words do not imply
any direct and personal relation with Polycarp,
they do seem to imply a careful and continuous
observation of Polycarp's habits both in act and
word.† Indeed it is difficult to know what words
would convey an account of a continued and carefully treasured experience, if these do not. And
it is hardly conceivable that an experience such as
is described should have passed, and yet that
Irenæus, with all his keenness of observation,
should have failed to discover whether Polycarp
was talking of John the Apostle or not. Again,
the Twelve were a perfectly recognizable and distinct body from a very early time in the Church,
and Polycarp's discourses must have been more
than usually confused if they left his intelligent
hearers uncertain on a fundamental point such as
this. It is an even more extravagant hypothesis
that Polycarp himself was confused. People will
always estimate such a question as this somewhat
differently, so that it will be impossible to claim
that the significance of Irenæus' words is certain
beyond all possibility of discussion. At the same
time, the interpretation here given seems the most

---

* The tradition which has so profoundly influenced art, that
St. John drank poison without being affected by it, occurs in
Isidore of Seville, De ortu et obitu Sanctorum, ch. lxxii.; and in
Acta Johannis, c. 9, ed. Bousset, 1898. It is also alluded to in
the Soliloquies, falsely ascribed to Augustine, ch. xxii. The present writer has failed to trace the origin of the tradition, if it be a
tradition, which Browning has followed in A Death in the Desert.

† This seems to be the most likely date: an alternative is
Feb. 22, 156. See Lightfoot, Ignatius and Polycarp, i. pp.
626–722; C. H. Turner, 'On the day and year of St. Polycarp's
Martyrdom,' in Studia Biblica, Oxford, vol. ii. pp. 105–155; and
Harnack, Chronologie, Bd. i. pp. 334–350, and reff.

---

* Though Lightfoot, Ign. and Polyc.¹ vol. i. p. 432, quotes
passages showing the extreme looseness with which such words
as παῖς were used.

† Μᾶλλον γὰρ τὰ τότε διαμνημονεύω τῶν ἔναγχος γινομένων· αἱ γὰρ
ἐκ παίδων μαθήσεις συναύξουσαι τῇ ψυχῇ ἑνοῦνται αὐτῇ ὥστε με
δύνασθαι εἰπεῖν καὶ τὸν τόπον ἐν ᾧ καθεζόμενος διελέγετο ὁ μακάριος
Πολύκαρπος, καὶ τὰς προόδους αὐτοῦ καὶ τὰς εἰσόδους καὶ τὸν χαρα-
κτῆρα τοῦ βίου καὶ τὴν τοῦ σώματος ἰδέαν καὶ τὰς διαλέξεις ἃς ἐποιεῖτο
πρὸς τὸ πλῆθος καὶ τὴν μετὰ 'Ιωάννου συναναστροφὴν ὡς ἀπήγγελλε καὶ
τὴν μετὰ τῶν λοιπῶν τῶν ἑωρακότων τὸν Κύριον καὶ ὡς ἀπεμνημόνευε τοὺς
λόγους αὐτῶν καὶ περὶ τοῦ κυρίου τίνα ἦν ἃ παρ' ἐκείνων ἀκηκόει, καὶ
περὶ τῶν δυναμέων αὐτοῦ καὶ περὶ τῆς διδασκαλίας ὡς παρὰ τῶν
αὐτοπτῶν τῆς ζωῆς τοῦ λόγου παρειληφὼς ὁ Πολύκαρπος ἀπήγγελλε
πάντα σύμφωνα ταῖς γραφαῖς.

natural, and it would require very considerable positive evidence to overthrow it.

Such evidence is not forthcoming. The two fragments which bear on the question are less convincing than the passage from Irenæus, but their natural meaning is consistent with the above interpretation of Irenæus. Polycrates, bishop of Ephesus, writing to Victor of Rome about A.D. 180, mentions various distinguished persons in the early history of the Church who are buried in Asia Minor. Amongst these he names the Apostle Philip, John the Apostle, and Polycarp. He is a person of importance, a bishop himself, belonging to a family which has given 7 bishops to the church, and he describes himself (probably) as 65 years old (ἑξήκοντα πέντε ἔτη γεγονὼς ἐν κυρίῳ). This would bring his birth to the year A.D. 115. He describes the work of the apostle at Ephesus in the words ἐγενήθη ἱερεὺς τὸ πέταλον πεφορηκώς. If the evidence of Irenæus is invalid, doubtless the probability is increased that Polycrates has made a similar confusion, and has mistaken John the Presbyter for John the Apostle. If, however, Irenæus may be trusted in his account of Polycarp's teaching, then Polycrates becomes an independent witness to the state of things described by Polycarp, and a witness of some importance. He bears testimony to the existence of this tradition in the ecclesiastical circles at Ephesus, and he had probably extremely good opportunities of knowing what these were.*

Lastly, we come to Papias. It is to a fragment of this author that we owe our knowledge of the existence of the Presbyter John. In a passage from the Prologue to his lost work, *Expositions of the Oracles of the Lord*, which Eusebius quotes (*HE* III. xxxix.), Papias explains his method. He has not paid attention to those who have much to say (τοῖς τὰ πολλὰ λέγουσιν), but to those who teach the truth. He has collected and examined the sayings of those who followed the elders (εἴ που καὶ παρακολουθηκώς τις τοῖς πρεσβυτέροις): endeavouring to ascertain 'what Andrew, or Peter said, or what Philip, or Thomas or James ; or what John or Matthew or any of the disciples of the Lord : and what Aristion and the Presbyter John the disciples of the Lord say.' Papias is not so good a witness as the others. Eusebius describes him as σμικρὸς τὸν νοῦν, and he certainly seems to have made statements on the authority of John and the elders which are in themselves ridiculous, and can never have come from any one who knew the Lord. The passage mentioned above does not prove that Papias was a disciple of the Apostle John ; and Papias shows himself capable of serious confusion in regard to St. John's doctrine. But, in the light of the passage in the letter to Florinus, Papias' statement that he endeavoured to ascertain in Asia Minor what John and other apostles had

* The authority of Polycrates has been assailed on another ground. It is said that, when he speaks of Philip the Apostle as being at Hierapolis, he has confused him with Philip the Evangelist ; hence that he might easily have confused John the Apostle with John the Presbyter. The question turns on the allusion to Philip's daughters. Luke (Ac 21⁸·⁹) says definitely that Philip the Evangelist, 'one of the seven,' had four daughters παρθένοι προφητεύουσαι. Polycrates affirms that Philip the Apostle had three daughters, two of whom grew old as virgins, and the other ἐν ἁγίῳ πνεύματι πολιτευσαμένη died and was buried at Ephesus. Clem. Alex. (Eus. *HE* iii. 30) quotes Philip as one of the apostles who did not forbid marriage, as he τὰς θυγατέρας ἀνδράσιν ἐξέδωκεν. Papias (Eus. *HE* III. xxxix.) speaks of Philip the Apostle among his authorities. The *Dialogue between Caius and Proclus* (Eus. *HE* iii. 31) represents Philip Evang. with four daughters—as having lived at Hierapolis. The authority of the *Dialogue* is by some adduced to prove the confusion in Polycrates' letter. This seems unnecessary. The *Dialogue* is later in time, and remote in its origin (Italy as against Ephesus), and is manifestly under the influence of the Acts. The statement of Polycrates is precise, and not identical with that in the Acts. We know there were two Philips, and it is not impossible that one had three daughters, and the other four. Cf. Lightfoot, *Colossians*, pp. 45, 46.

taught, may at least stand as an additional ground for believing that St. John had dwelt at Ephesus.

We are, fortunately, not concerned with the further and more complicated question of the authorship of the Fourth Gospel, but only with the residence of St. John at Ephesus. The evidence alleged is fragmentary. Even with the addition of the Muratorian Fragment, which confirms what has been already produced, it is less than we could wish. But in a case like this the important point is not so much the extent as the character of the evidence that is to hand. And it is to be noticed that all the three authors we have named are men who would have had the best opportunities of knowing about this matter. We have only fragments of their works, but *they* were not fragmentary. They cover a century between them — a century of vigorous and active Christian life ; and they all of them held office in their several churches. We have not pressed the evidence of the Muratorian Fragment, because of the uncertainty of its origin, and the comparative lack of a true context in which to place it. But these difficulties do not attach to the evidence of Irenæus, Polycrates, and Papias. Their relation to the age in which they lived can be denied only at the expense of the surrender of the largest portion of 2nd cent. history.*

II. The Theology of St. John.

A. *The Gospel and Epistles.*—In the writings ascribed to St. John there is more of a complete and reasoned theology than is to be found in any of the other NT writers. It is therefore a comparatively simple task to indicate the lines of the author's theological thought. It must, however, always be remembered that in the Gospel the theological positions are placed in close relation with the history. So that, in some sense, a historical evolution is traceable in the doctrine described. The prologue to the Gospel (1¹⁻¹⁸) may be regarded as summing up the doctrine of the book ; and, in like manner, many of the statements in the Epistles are of the nature of inferential doctrinal affirmations. It seems best, therefore, to describe as shortly as possible the progress in doctrine in relation to the history, and then to discuss the conclusions which result.

(1) The Gospel professes to be a selection of anecdotes, out of a large number not recorded, describing the *signs* which Jesus did before His disciples. By *signs* are meant acts which convey a certain teaching, indicate a particular truth or reality. These particular signs are recorded in order to produce a particular belief—'that ye may believe that Jesus is the Christ the Son of God' (20³⁰·³¹). The main part of the Gospel describes the growth of this idea in the minds of the apostles, and, at the same time, the growth of hostility on the part of the Jews. The mode in which the conviction is brought home to the minds of Christ's followers is called *witness* (μαρτυρία), and is characterized in various ways. The first stage in the process is the witness of John the

* It is not quite clear what is meant by Polycrates' phrase ἐγενήθη ἱερεὺς τὸ πέταλον πεφορηκώς. Πέταλον is the word used for the high-priestly mitre ; and therefore the adoption of it by St. John must have meant either that he claimed that the old exclusive high priesthood was at an end, or, more probably, that he asserted its fulfilment in the Christian priesthood. Delff (*Gesch. der Rabbi Jesus v. Nazareth*, p. 71) asserts that the phrase means that St. John was of the family of the high priest, and had actually performed high-priestly functions in Jerusalem, wearing the mitre for the purpose. This interpretation of the words of Polycrates is only part of a complicated theory as to the authorship of the Fourth Gospel with which we have nothing to do. But it should be observed (1) that this is not the natural interpretation of the passage ; (2) that it assumes a degree of ignorance and confusion on the part of Polycrates which is unjustifiable. St. James is also said to have worn the πέταλον (Epiph. *Hær*. lxxiii. c. 14, where he follows the language of Hegesippus closely ; but this particular statement is absent from the passage of Hegesippus quoted in Eus. *HE* II. xxiii.).

Baptist. He first denies to the deputation of priests and Levites that he is the Christ, and then points definitely to Jesus as the Lamb of God, the person on whom the Spirit descended and abode. In consequence of the repetition of this *witness* on the following day, two of the disciples of John—Andrew and, probably, John himself—are detached from the Baptist and follow Jesus. The result of a day's colloquy is that Andrew announces to his brother Simon, We have found the Messiah. In like manner Nathanael is attracted by the same promise, though he seems to have had a stronger and loftier view of the personality of the Messiah than we usually find (1^{49}). The newly-won disciples begin, therefore, with a conviction that Jesus is Messiah. The 'sign' at Cana of Galilee gives them new thoughts. John had done no sign (10^{41}), but in this scene at Cana the disciples perceived what St. John, in the reflective language of his later life, calls the manifestation of the glory of Christ (2^{11}). This phrase seems to mean the specially Divine powers and characteristics which the Lord displayed upon earth; and therefore the importance of the passage consists in this, that St. John marks the occasion when the previous belief in the Messiahship of Jesus began to be affected by a deeper notion of His Divine nature. Looking back upon it in later life, he sees that at that moment the thought that He was Divine was dawning in them.

This event at Cana is also described (2^{11}) as the 'beginning of signs.' It is the opening incident of a particular line of witness—the witness of the works (cf. 5^{36} 10^{38} 15^{24}). This is continued at Jerusalem at the Passover, and produces a number of adherents (2^{23}). And here, again, St. John notices an impression created by Jesus upon His apostles: they found that He exercised considerable reserve in His treatment of those who professed belief, in virtue of an insight into them which he possessed.[*] After this we come to the account of the Ministry and Preaching of our Lord. As in the Synoptic Gospels, He begins by preaching (to Nicodemus) the Kingdom of God, with this difference, that He declares the necessity of new birth as the condition of entry. It is after the record of this preaching that the witness of John is finally completed and closed, in words which imply that his preparatory mission is over (3^{30}). It is noticeable that in this passage Nicodemus is attracted to the new prophet by signs (3^{2}), and that the Lord, when He is challenged to explain the new birth, refers to the witness of an experience already growing up around Him (δ οἴδαμεν λαλοῦμεν, καὶ δ ἑωράκαμεν μαρτυροῦμεν, 3^{11}). In like manner the conversation with the woman at Sychar leads to the unequivocal declaration of Messiahship on the part of the Lord (4^{26}), and an affirmation of the greatest importance as to the nature of God (4^{24}, see below, p. 689). The impression created by these two scenes on the minds of the apostles is not marked in the same way as before (2^{11} and ^{23}). But it is obvious that their view of His character is changing and developing rapidly. They have as yet no precise and clear view as to His nature, but they are careful as to commenting on, or asking questions about, what He does. This is expressed in a marked way when the apostles return and find Him talking with a woman. They are surprised, but no one said, 'What seekest thou, or Why talkest thou with her?' (4^{27}). So again, when He says, 'I have meat to eat which ye know not,' they do not ask Him what He means; but talk among themselves

[*] The phrase used, διὰ τὸ αὐτὸν γινώσκειν πάντας, does not necessarily imply supernatural knowledge; but it records the strong impression which the Master's way of dealing with men had made upon His disciples.

(4^{33}). A feeling of reserve and reverence is growing up, which completely prevents all curious questions. Their conception is developing as their experience widens.

We now come to the period at which hostility, continually increasing in fierceness, is caused by the acts and words of the Lord. The first scene is at an unnamed feast at Jerusalem, probably occurring some time before the second Passover of our Lord's ministry. The controversy arises over the law of the Sabbath. A man who had been crippled with a disease for 38 years is cured, and told by our Lord to take up the bed on which he is lying, and carry it away. This was, of course, a breach of the Sabbath law, and it seems, from the expression used (5^{16} ταῦτα ἐποίει ἐν σαββάτῳ), to have been somewhat typical of our Lord's action. In answer to the Jews, the Lord develops at length the relation between Himself and the Father; His answer, in fact, amounts to a claim to stand in the same supreme position as the Father in regard to the law in question. 'My Father worketh up till now, and I work' (5^{17}).

The discourse which follows is of great importance for our present purpose. In it the Lord, speaking first of Himself under the title of 'the Son,' affirms the absolute and indissoluble unity of the will of the Father and the Son. The Son certainly has derived Being; but the Father has given Him to have life in Himself (5^{26}); in what He does He fulfils the Father's commission, which includes the power of giving life even to the dead, and the prerogative of judgment ($5^{21. 22. 26. 27}$). This unity of action is based on love (5^{20}), and carries with it the right on the part of the Son to honour co-ordinate with that of the Father (5^{23}). It is obvious that this claim, if substantiated, completely meets the charge of independent and self-willed defiance of a law |imposed by the Father. In 5^{30} the Lord identifies Himself with the Son, and proceeds to deal with the question of evidence. Here He uses the idea characteristic of this Gospel —*witness*. This teaching, He says, is not a bare assertion of His own; He has evidence, consentient witness to establish it (5^{32}), besides the inner certainty of His own knowledge. There is first the witness of John (5^{33-35}) temporary and limited, but bearing on the truth. Secondly, there is the witness of the *works*, done in pursuance of the Father's commission (5^{36}). Thirdly, there is the witness of the Father (5^{37}, see below, p. 686), and, lastly, the witness of the Scriptures. From them will come the really damning charges against the Jews; they have disbelieved the *writings* of Moses, how can they believe Christ's *words*? ($5^{39. 46. 47}$).

St. John does not chronicle the effect of this discourse, either upon the Jews or upon the apostles, important as it obviously is. The next scene does lead to a decisive and significant result. Here, again, it is important to recall the circumstances under which the scene took place. It occurred immediately after the miracle of the Feeding of the Five Thousand. The persons thus fed seem to have been a body of Galilæan pilgrims going up to, or returning from, the Passover (cf. 6^{4}). The result of the miracle is that the pilgrims conceive the plan of seizing Jesus and making Him a king; that is, they see in Him the fulfilment of their very uninstructed Messianic hopes. The following day the fact emerges in a dialogue with the Lord that they have compared His act with that of Moses, who fed the people in the wilderness, and that their allegiance will depend on Christ's rivalling this (6^{31}). From this point the discourse takes its start. With increasing clearness our Lord points to Himself as the fulfilment of the acted prophecy of Moses. The Jews (who appear at v.[40]) protest against the claim implied in this ; but this protest only leads the Lord to the still more startling assertions, that life in any true sense depends upon connexion with Himself, and that this connexion is established by eating His Flesh and drinking His Blood. And He ends by definitely connecting this with the type of the manna in the wilderness (6^{58}, cf. 6^{49}). The result of this discourse was to separate the Twelve sharply from other followers : these are puzzled, and walk no more with Him ; the apostles, by the mouth of St. Peter, confess Him as the Holy One of God (6^{69}).

After this scene, the development of the hostility is comparatively rapid ; there are practically only three more occasions described. The first occurs at the Feast of Tabernacles. In his account of this feast St. John has shown us a perfect turmoil of conflicting ideas and surmises as to the new prophet, with a background of firm hostility on the part of the ruling class among the Jews. With the various problems and difficulties which were raised by the various parties, we have nothing to do ; the decisive utterance from which the discourse or dialogue follows is the phrase, 'I am the Light of the world' (8^{12}). The subsequent passage is of great difficulty. Emphasis is laid again upon the witness of the Father ($8^{15.\ 16}$) and the coincidence of the *works* with the will and commission of the Father ($8^{28.\ 29}$) ; and the result was that many believed on Him (8^{30}). But an attempt made by the Lord to offer true freedom to those who had believed Him, rouses their national feelings, so that when Christ, after an agitated argument, makes a claim which they understand as coequality with God, they take up stones to cast at Him as a blasphemer.* In the second of the scenes in question, at the feast of Dedication (reading ἐγένετο τότε in 10^{22}), a similar discussion is presented to us arising out of a miracle performed upon a Sabbath-day, and involving by its method a breach of the law. The Jews definitely challenge Jesus with the question of His nature (10^{24}). He refuses to answer directly, but refers again to the *works* (10^{25}) and to the Father's will, ending with the strongest assertion yet made of His union with the Father, ἐγὼ καὶ ὁ πατὴρ ἕν ἐσμεν (10^{30}). In consequence of this He has to withdraw from Jerusalem ; but St. John notes that many believed, seeing how He fulfilled the prophecy of the Baptist (10^{40-42}). The last scene is that of the raising of Lazarus and its immediate consequences. A miracle such as this could not have failed to produce an effect ; and St. John notes that it is the decisive event which leads the authorities to determine on the death of Jesus, and produces the enthusiasm among the crowds which is expressed in the Triumphal Entry (cf. $11^{47.\ 48}$ 12^{17-19}). At the end of ch. 12 St. John solemnly sums up the result of the mission of Christ ; the evidence of signs had largely failed (12^{37}) ; there were many even of the rulers who really believed, but did not dare to express it (12^{42}), and in all this St. John sees the fulfilment of the prophecy of Isaiah, when 'he saw his glory (*i.e.* of Jesus), and spake concerning him.'

In the part of the Gospel which we have now briefly considered, the author explains the series of events through which his convictions developed. We have therefore before us the idea of one who fulfilled the national expectation of a Messiah, but who, at the same time, identified Himself with the typology of the OT, spoke mysteriously of a deeper union with the Father, and who represented union with Himself as the one necessary means of satisfying human needs. These two latter points are developed at great length in the

* It is assumed that the *Pericope Adulteræ* is out of place in this chapter.

Last Discourses (cf. $14^{10.\ 31}$ 17^4 14^{1-12} 15^{1-11} etc.). But the Discourses are delivered under a sense of immediate departure, and therefore they develop, in language mysterious at the time but explained later by events, the close union of the Father and the Son, the future work of the Paraclete, and the new commandment to the followers of Jesus. The questions of the apostles recorded from time to time in the course of these chapters show that they only partially understood then what was said to them. But the teaching is continuous with what had gone before, and could only have confirmed the opinions already held by the apostles. We shall consider it more in detail further on.

One last sign is noted by St. John in the account of the Crucifixion — the effusion of blood and water, and the bearing of prophecy on the scene. This is mentioned with great emphasis, and the presence of the author as eye-witness is deliberately asserted (19^{35}). There then follows an account of the intercourse of the Risen Lord with various of His followers, and we then return to the passage mentioned before, in which St. John declares the purpose of his Gospel ($20^{30.\ 31}$).

It will be seen that the result attained by St. John is an evolution that starts from the idea of the Messiah, and rises through the witness of signs and the teaching of Discourses to a lofty and profound notion of Jesus as the Christ, the Son of God. It is this which is the fundamental idea of all St. John's theology, and it has been necessary, therefore, to put it first.

(2) It is obvious, however, that such a view could not be maintained without involving serious consequences upon the idea of God : or, to put the same thing in somewhat different language, the development in the notion of Jesus, from that of Messiah to that of the Son of God, will be found to rest upon theological presuppositions. These are revealed in the Discourses of the Lord, and in part drawn out by the author in the Gospel and Epistles. We have passed them by so far in order to display the historic movement of St. John's thought ; but we must now turn to them.

The first passage which calls for consideration is, of course, the Prologue. This contains, in summary, St. John's theology of the Incarnation. It begins by describing the Person involved—the Word ; and of Him it asserts eternal pre-existence, eternal communion with God, and finally Divinity itself. The author then proceeds to give an account of the various functions of the Word of God.* The Word of God is the instrument of

* It is impossible to discuss at length the origin and associations of this much disputed expression—the Word of God (see art. Logos). It must suffice here to say that there seems to be a great difficulty in connecting it, as would at first sight appear natural, with Greek philosophic thought. It is true that the word λόγος in its earlier usage contained ideas which might have developed into such a conception as this of St. John. But in the history of Greek thought the development of the meaning of the word was governed by the particular interest of Greek philosophy. The idea of language or speech is complex. Speech conveys information (1) as to the mind of the speaker, (2) as to the subject spoken about. In the former case the uttered word appears as the representative of the person or character or act of the speaker ; its reference to fact may be of merely secondary importance. In the other case the word has a sort of substantive existence. It does not matter who uses it ; the important thing is what it means. The more this aspect of the relation is emphasized the more the idea of a *word* tends towards that of abstract scientific definition—it is a form conveying truth. Its ideal is to correspond as nearly as may be with the reality it describes. The Greeks found the ideal correspondence between thought and thing in universality ; and therefore, concurrently with the development in philosophic thought, the word λόγος took on more and more the associations of universality, and lost more and more those of the individual thing or person. With the Hebrews, on the other hand, the Word of God meant always God speaking or doing certain things ; the Word was the emissary and representative of God. A doctrine of Incarnation in the Johannine sense is possible on the one line of thought, and impossible on the other.

Creation (πάντα δι' αὐτοῦ ἐγένετο, not ὑπ' αὐτοῦ). The gift of life, expressed in a living world, was the object, or, if we may so say, the ruling principle of the action of God through the Word, and life was to have been a sign or suggestion to man of the presence of the Word—to have been the light of men. But, owing to the intrusion of the darkness, the light now shines in a hostile atmosphere, without, however, being overcome by it. This doctrine lies closely in connexion with that of the Old Testament. The Pentateuch (Gn 1) and the Psalter (Ps 33[6]) both ascribe creation to the word of God; they use the metaphor of speech to describe the act of God in it. And throughout the OT the presence and effect of evil is continually asserted. But St. John makes a considerable and important addition to the doctrine of the OT when he unequivocally asserts the Divinity of the Word. In the OT the idea of language was a metaphor used to describe an act; it is said that in Rabbinical thought the Word of God was beginning to take on a quasi-personal character; with St. John the Word by which the world was brought into being was a person, separate enough from God (ὁ θεός, i.e.), to be in communion with God, but yet essentially Divine in nature.

We next learn St. John's conception of that Revelation of the Word which he himself had experienced. It was heralded by John the Baptist, who was sent from God to witness concerning it. The light was already in the world, and had already a place of its own in the world, but the world rejected its appeal. New birth—birth of God—was given to those who received the light when it came—a birth that broke through and destroyed the old physical succession (1[6-13]). Having thus described the Person of the Word, and the effect of His mission, St. John proceeds to describe the mode of His manifestation. 'The Word,' he says, 'became flesh, and dwelt as in a tent among us, full of grace and truth.' As thus Incarnate, the Word manifested His Divine glory. In regard to this, St John uses a remarkable phrase. He says it was 'glory as of an only-begotten from a Father,' i.e. it was identical in nature, but different, if the phrase may be allowed, in individuality from that of the Father. It was representative in the fullest sense, not merely an irradiation from without; it was Divine glory, but the glory of an only-begotten son. For the evidence of this, St. John refers to the witness of John the Baptist (1[15]), and more particularly to the experience of himself and of the Church. 'We beheld his glory,' he says (1[14]); and again 'of his fulness,' the grace and truth which came with Him, 'have all we received' in continually increasing proportions, grace in place of grace (1[16]). Then St. John explains summarily the full height of this Revelation. It superseded the Mosaic law, which was partial and external, by means of this gift of grace and complete truth (1[17]). It did not give us the vision of God: it meant that one who was God and only-begotten, who is in the bosom of the Father, had come among men and declared the truth.*

We have already seen in brief outline the process of historical observation through which St. John obtained his view of our Lord's nature. The Prologue shows us the same ideas formulated and in some degree systematized. The central point is still the Sonship,—Christ is Son of God in a unique sense,—but the mission of the Son is clearly defined in relation to other things. He is the Word of God: Eternal and Divine: He is the Instrument of Creation: the source of the knowledge of God

which men should acquire by life and nature. His coming has superseded all previous revelation. In its earlier stages, as in the case of John, revelation was for witness of a light yet to come. The revelation of the Word was the manifestation of that Light. It was complete where the law, the highest expression of the old order, was partial: it gave final certainty about God on the authority of God only-begotten.

(3) The Epistles show how fundamental a doctrine this was in St. John's theology. He asserts in the most emphatic way (1 Jn 1[1-4]) his own experience in the matter; how the life—the eternal life—which was continually (ἦν) with the Father, was manifested in time (ἐφανερώθη) to us; we saw and heard and touched beyond possibility of error. To deny the Father and the Son is the sign of antichrist (1 Jn 2[22. 23]); it is a departure from the original message (1 Jn 2[24]). It is the test of spirits: 'Every spirit which confesses Jesus Christ come in the flesh is of God, and every spirit which confesses not Jesus, is not of God, and this is that spirit of antichrist, of which ye have heard that it cometh, and now it is already in the world' (4[2. 3]; cf. 5[1. 6-8. 12]). In the Second Epistle St. John forbids his readers even to receive into their house and salute one who makes denial of this final truth (2 Jn 7-12). There is therefore no hesitation in his mind as to the truth or the necessity of this doctrine: it is the fundamental doctrine of Christianity and the test of true membership of the Church.

(4) It is in regard to this subject that the theology of St. John is most systematic. We must now pass on to the consideration of some other points less fully systematized, but no less decisive in their character. And first we must call attention to the *Theology of the Father and the Son*. It is contained, for the most part, in incidental references in the Discourses of the Lord. The Father is supreme, and is the source of the Being and all the action of the Son (5[19. 26] etc.). He has sent the Son into the world (3[16]), and given Him commission to perform certain works there (5[36] 8[26] 10[32. 37] 14[31] 15[10] 17[4]). The relation between the Father and the Son is variously described. It is a profound and complete unity: 'I and the Father are one' (ἕν ἐσμεν) (10[30] 17[11. 21]). But this unity does not destroy the distinction between the Father and the Son. The Father loves the Son (5[19] 15[9]), and the Son loves the Father (14[31]); the Father knows the Son, and is known by Him (10[15]; cf. 8[55]). Before the world was, the Son enjoyed 'glory with the Father,' to which He returns (17[5]). The Father abides (μένει) in the Son, and the Son in the Father (8[28. 29] 14[10. 11]): so that it is said 'the Father abiding in me doeth his works' (14[10]). All that belongs to the Son belongs also to the Father, 'and thine are mine' (17[10]): yet 'the Father is greater than I' (14[28]). Hence the representation of the Father by the Son is complete: 'He that hath seen me hath seen the Father' (14[9], cf. 8[19]). So that honour given to the Son is given to the Father (5[23. 38]), and those who reject the Son reject also the Father (8[19] 15[21-24]; cf. 1 Jn 2[22-24]). This fulness of union and intercourse throws some light upon the obscure subject of the witness of the Father. In 5[31. 32] the Lord disclaims bearing witness concerning Himself, but refers instead to the witness of John, and then 5[37] to the witness of the Father. In ch. 8, in answer to the Jews, He says, 'If I do bear witness of myself, my witness is true, because I know whence I came and whither I go' (8[14]), and then again (8[18]) refers to the witness of the Father. In 3[32. 33] (probably a reflective passage by the evangelist and not part of a discourse) we read, 'He that receiveth his (i.e. the Son's) witness hath set to his seal that God is true' (ἐσφράγισεν ὅτι ὁ θεὸς ἀληθής ἐστιν); and in 1 Jn 5[10] St. John says again, 'He

---

* This interpretation depends, of course, on the reading Μονογενὴς Θεός. For further information on this head, see Hort's *Two Dissertations*.

that believeth on the Son hath the witness in himself; he that believeth not God, hath made him a liar, because he has not believed in the witness which God has witnessed concerning his Son.' Thus the most obvious sign of failure to receive the witness of the Father is to misunderstand the promises of God, and the indications of His purpose, which Christ fulfils. The witness of the Father is closely allied to the witness of Scripture, but is not quite the same. It seems to consist in that inner perception of the purpose of God resting on the love of God (5^{42}), which carries conviction in the presence of the life and works of Christ; the Jews fail ' because ye have not his word abiding in you' (5^{38}); without this, they search the Scriptures, and so fail to receive their witness also. The Son appeals to this witness against the charge of self-seeking or self-advertisement; and the certainty of His knowledge of His own nature, and of His mission ('whence I come and whither I go') justifies His witness to Himself.

(5) The next point for consideration, starting with the above-described theology of God and the Incarnation, is *the process or scheme of salvation*. To do this it is necessary to define first St. John's conception of **the world**, and of the condition requiring remedy. The word κόσμος means primarily the created order; so in $1^{9.\,10}$ we find that the world was created through the Word. Also the phrase ὁ βίος τοῦ κόσμου occurs (1 Jn 3^{17}) for this world's goods. From the idea of transitoriness (*e.g.* 1 Jn 2^{17}) the word gets a sinister sense; and we find it in its most characteristic signification of the fallen world, the world in opposition to the will of God. In this sense St. John says of it that the whole world lies in the evil one (1 Jn 5^{19}). It is the embodiment of the principle of hatred to all that God requires; by the inherent necessity of its nature it hates Christ and His Church (Jn 15^{18-23}, 1 Jn 3^{13}). Christ is alien from it (Jn 8^{23} 17^{14} 18^{36}, 1 Jn 4^5). Its hostility is represented in a ruler, ὁ ἄρχων τοῦ κόσμου τούτου (Jn 12^{31} 14^{30}), who has an 'hour' in which he apparently triumphs. The characteristic attitude of the world is sin, which is 'lawlessness,' *i.e.* self-will and rebellion (1 Jn 3^4 5^{17}). Those who live in sin are under the wrath of God (3^{36}): their life is no true life, their existence may be described as death (Jn 8^{24}, 1 Jn 3^{14}). From another slightly different point of view the principle of the world's hostility is called **the flesh,** and it is clearly declared to be impossible to pass by natural evolution out of the range of the flesh. That which is born of the flesh is flesh (Jn 3^6), and therefore there is no power in the flesh to restore or recreate itself; it can only go on reproducing itself perpetually. This is the condition of things which it is Christ's mission to redeem.

The impulse to restore the world comes from the Father, and is based on love: ' God so loved the world that he sent his only-begotten Son' to save it (Jn $3^{16.\,17}$; cf. 1 Jn 4^{10-14}). The effect of the mission of Christ is variously described; He comes that the world may be saved through His means (Jn 3^{17}; cf. 4^{42}, 1 Jn 4^{14}); that is the most general phrase. He is the Lamb of God, who takes away the sin of the world (Jn 1^{29}, 1 Jn 3^5). He comes that He may destroy the works of the devil (1 Jn 3^8). But perhaps the most frequent expression of the intended result is the phrase **eternal life** (Jn 3^{16}, 1 Jn 5^{11}). This forms the subject of many of the discourses and warnings of the Lord, and it is constantly occurring in the First Epistle. Those who believe have passed from death into life (1 Jn 3^{14}; cf. Jn 8^{24}); eternal life has been promised to mankind by God (1 Jn 2^{25}). Christ Himself is identified with it (1 Jn 1^2 $5^{11.\,20}$). He declares that He has come ' that they may have life, and have abundance'

(Jn 10^{10}); the commandment of the Father is eternal life (Jn 12^{50}). And again, ' This is life eternal, that they may know thee, the only true God, and Jesus Christ whom thou hast sent' (17^3). Thus the life which Christ brings consists in union with Christ, obedience to the Father's commandments, and knowledge of God. It is not a thing to be attained only in the future; it is actually in the possession of those who believe (Jn 6^{47}, 1 Jn 5^{11-13}). From another point of view this condition is described as light. Christ is the light of the world (Jn 8^{12}; cf. 3^{19} 12^{46}) in contradistinction to the darkness of sin (cf. 1 Jn 2^{9-11}). (See below, p. 689).

The means of salvation for the world is only through Christ. This is partly implied by the general statements of the purpose of God already cited, and partly by the series of metaphorical phrases used by Christ Himself to describe His functions. Thus He is the Bread of Life ($6^{35.\,51}$); without participation in His Flesh and Blood there is no true life at all (6^{53}). He is the true fulfilment of the type of the water in the wilderness ($7^{37.\,38}$); the light of the world (8^{12} 12^{46}). He is the Door into the true fold, to the exclusion of all others ($10^{7.\,9}$); and again, He is the good Shepherd ($10^{11.\,14}$). So, at the grave of Lazarus He proclaims Himself the Resurrection and the Life (11^{25}); in answer to the question of Thomas, He declares Himself the Way, the Truth, and the Life (14^6). Through Him alone is man's access to the Father; in Him all truth and all life are summed up. Once more, He is the True Vine, the unity and quickening force of all those who believe (15^1 etc.). Nor are His functions restricted to those whom He may be connected with during His earthly life, or to those who belong to the chosen people. His work is universal in power and validity (Jn 10^{16} 11^{52} 12^{32}, 1 Jn 2^2).

The idea of God, then, if we may so say, is the salvation of the world through His Son, Christ. We must now consider what action is necessary to achieve this purpose, both on the part of Christ and of mankind. We have already spoken of the obedience of Christ, and the exact way in which He fulfilled the commission of the Father; we have now to deal more in detail with the subject. (*a*) The method by which Christ saves the world is by the sacrifice of Himself through death. The law under which He lived is first suggested by the Baptist in his witness: Behold, the Lamb of God, who taketh away the sin of the world ($1^{29.\,36}$).* Christ Himself asserts the same truth, with greater or less distinctness. First to Nicodemus obscurely (3^{14}), and again more clearly to the Jews after the feeding of the 5000. ' I am the living Bread which came down from heaven . . . and the bread which I will give is my Flesh for the life of the world' (6^{51}). He is ' the good Shepherd that giveth his life for the sheep' ($10^{11.\,18}$; cf. 1 Jn 3^{16}); and by so doing He shows that He has the uttermost love (15^{13}). So deeply is this necessity woven into the fabric of things, that the high priest 'of that year,' speaking more wisely than he knew, prophesied that He must lay down His life for the people ($11^{51.\,52}$). It is the condition of drawing all men to Him (12^{32}). In two places in the First Epistle St. John uses the phrase ἱλασμός, or propitiation (2^2 4^{10}); once (1 Jn 1^7) St. John speaks of the blood of Jesus Christ as cleansing us from all sin. And our Lord Himself uses once the peculiar phrase, ' I sanctify myself for their sake' (Jn 17^{19}).

Thus it is by this process of sacrifice that our Lord performs His part in the plan initiated by God. (*b*) We now come to consider the function of man—the response required of the world. (1) The fundamental law under which the world is ordered

* The precise reference of this phrase is, no doubt, obscure; but there can be no doubt that the association with the lamb was one of sacrifice.

here meets us. The world can do nothing for itself. He, therefore, that will see and enter the kingdom of God must be *born again*: the old physical sequence—of blood, of the will of the flesh, and the will of man—must be broken off, and a new kinship established (3^{3-6}, cf. 1^{13}). (2) Further, there is required of necessity faith in the Son, and acceptance of His mission (Jn 3^{16} 5^{24} $6^{40. 47}$, 1 Jn 3^{23}). This faith is more than mere belief (8^{31}), which in the passage quoted fails to bear criticism. But St. John supplies no definition of it, or anything approaching a definition. It is rather trust in a person than belief in the truth of what he says: or rather, this kind of belief comes as a result of the trust. It is made impossible, as we shall shortly see, by certain moral conditions. (3) The new life which the new birth begins must be sustained by continual participation in the Life of Christ. This is the burden of the strong and startling language in the synagogue at Capernaum (Jn 6^{52-59}): 'Except he eat the flesh of the Son of Man and drink his blood, ye have not life in yourselves. He that eateth my flesh and drinketh my blood hath eternal life, and I will raise him up at the last day.' And this is said in explanation of the phrase, 'the bread which I will give is my flesh for the life of the world.' It implies that the faithful must in some way, not explained by St. John, enter into and share the sacrifice of our Lord. The sacrifice is thus not an external transaction: all men must have a part in it.

In face of these demands stands the fact that Christ was in large measure rejected. He came to His own place, and His own people received Him not (Jn 1^{11}). This, which might easily become a difficulty, is met in two ways. First, St. John presents a strong theory of predestination. The failure no less than the success falls within the sovereignty of the Father. 'No man can come to me, except the Father draw him' (6^{44}); 'I manifested thy name to the men whom thou gavest me out of the world' (17^6, cf. 10^{29}). The success and the failure are even matters of prophetic prevision (12^{37-39}): Isaiah saw what would come about, 'when he saw his glory, and spake concerning him.' And Christ administers the will of the Father in this, as in other respects. 'Ye did not choose me, but I chose you, and set you that ye should go and bring forth fruit' (15^{16}, cf. 1^9). Secondly, faith depends upon certain moral conditions. Those who are evil are, *ipso facto*, incapable of faith: they shun the light ($3^{19. 20}$). This general truth is made plainer in various discourses of the Lord's. The essential moral fault which prevents faith is self-seeking, aiming at personal distinction, seeking glory one from another ($5^{41. 44}$ 7^{18}). The Jews refuse to accept the teaching of Christ, because they do not understand the spirit in which it is given: If another comes in his own name, him ye will receive (5^{43}). They will not do the Father's will, and therefore they blind themselves. 'If any man will to do his will, he shall know concerning the teaching, whether it is of God, or I speak of myself' ($7^{17. 18}$). And the peril of this position lies just in the fact that they are so self-confident. 'If ye had been blind, ye would not have had sin: but now ye say, We see; therefore your sin remaineth' (9^{41})

Thus it is that the manifestation of Christ produces a twofold effect, corresponding to the varieties of moral condition. On the one hand, it produces faith, and so eternal life; this is its natural and proper result. On the other hand, it produces rejection, which is a declaration of affinity with evil—in St. John's language, judgment (3^{19}). 'This *is* the judgment, that the light has come into the world, and men loved the darkness rather than the light, because their deeds were evil.' As eternal life is not a future state of blessedness, but is the correlative of right faith in the Son of Man, so judgment is a condition the precise opposite of life. It consists in the revelation, in action, of hostility to Christ and all that He represents. So Christ says ($12^{47. 48}$), 'If any man hear my words and keep them not, I do not judge him: for I came not to judge the world, but to save the world. He that rejecteth me and receiveth not my words, hath one that judgeth him: the word that I spake, that will judge him in the last day.' Thus judgment follows the same course of meaning as life. The Father has given into the hands of the Son the two Divine prerogatives of life and judgment ($5^{21. 22}$). Yet Christ speaks as if life were the immediate consequence of faith, and judgment the consequence of the refusal to believe (cf. 5^{24} 6^{47}). At the same time, both in the case of life and judgment, there is a sort of consummation to be looked for at the last day ($6^{40. 54}$ $12^{47. 48}$). In neither case does the condition of life or judgment begin *after* the last day; it is a process which begins here, and is defined and completed at the last day. In the same way Christ speaks before the Passion of having already overcome the world (16^{33}), and St. John in his First Epistle uses similar language of the faith (4^4 $5^{4. 5}$), although in the same Epistle he warns against continuance in sin. So again he speaks of the sinlessness of those who are 'born of God' (3^9) in similar connexions. On the other hand, to continue the refusal to accept Christ after the opportunity is finally past is 'to die in sin' (Jn $8^{21. 24}$).

(6) It remains to consider the doctrine of the Holy Spirit and the Church as we have it in these books. The provisions made by the Lord for the future are to be found chiefly in the Last Discourses. These were uttered after the Last Supper and before the arrest. The prominent note in them is, of course, one of farewell: and the provision for the future is put in language which later experience would alone fully explain. First, our Lord promises an **Advocate** ($\pi\alpha\rho\acute{\alpha}\kappa\lambda\eta\tau o\varsigma$) who will supply His place on His departure (14^{16}). There are several noticeable points in regard to this mission. Christ speaks of it as His own return (14^{18}): He promises in relation to it, that the Father will come with Himself to those who keep His sayings, and 'we will make our abode with him' (14^{23}). The Advocate is spoken of as distinct from the Father and the Son, and yet His mission is one which reveals the Father and the Son. Again, in 14^{16} Christ says, 'I will ask the Father, and he will give you another Advocate, that he may be with you for ever—the Spirit of truth.' In 14^{26} a different phrase is used: 'The Advocate, the Holy Ghost, whom the Father will send in my name'; and once again there is a further difference (15^{26}, cf. $16^{7. 13}$), 'When the Advocate comes, whom I will send to you from the Father, the Spirit of truth, that proceedeth from the Father.' Thus there is difference of language in regard to the Spirit's mission, and it is difficult to determine precisely St. John's idea. It seems clear, however, that this is due to the close intercourse and union which we have already noticed in regard to the Father and the Son. The Spirit, though sent like the Son, is one in whom full Divinity resides; His activity is a mission, not the effusion of an impersonal influence. The mission of the Holy Spirit depends on the departure of Christ (16^7, cf. 7^{39}): the two dispensations are not to be synchronous. The nature of the mission of the Advocate is gathered from various phrases in these chapters. Like the Son, He will not speak from Himself ($16^{13. 14}$), but He will speak the things He hears. His mission continues that of Christ. 'He will glorify me, because he will take of that which is mine, and will declare it unto you' (16^{14}). He

will teach, and recall all the things which Christ had said (14[26]). He will guide into all the truth, just because He speaks not of Himself (16[13]). His Presence is described as an 'anointing' ($\chi\rho\hat{\iota}\sigma\mu\alpha$, 1 Jn 2[20. 27]) which protects those who have it from error ; and is a sign (1 Jn 3[24]) of the indwelling of Christ in us. Further, He continues the process of witness to Christ already mentioned (15[26]). This last point brings us in presence of one of the most difficult passages in St. John's writings, that of the Three witnesses.[*] It is impossible to enter into the complicated discussions which lie round this verse. The witness of the Spirit is placed on a level with that of the water and the blood, and the witness of the three is said to be consentient. It seems probable that the phrase applied to Christ ($\dot{o}$ $\dot{\epsilon}\lambda\theta\dot{\omega}\nu$ $\delta\iota'$ $\ddot{v}\delta\alpha\tau os$ $\kappa\alpha\grave{\iota}$ $\alpha\ddot{\iota}\mu\alpha\tau os$) refers directly to the event noticed by St. John —the effusion of blood and water upon the cross (19[34. 35]). But also the Spirit is connected emphatically with water in the Gospel (3[5. 6]) in the passage which gives the principle for interpreting the rite of baptism. And again in 6[63] the Spirit is appealed to when the disciples are puzzled by our Lord's language about eating His flesh and drinking His blood—a passage which contains the theology, so to say, of the other Sacrament. It is probable, therefore, that those are right who see in this passage an assertion of the witness — the evidence conveyed of the truth of the faith—which comes from the Sacraments, interpreted by the Spirit. Our uncertainty (1) as to the exact significance ascribed to the effusion (19[34]), and (2) as to the exact position assigned by St. John to the Sacraments, makes this interpretation less than certain. So far we have considered the function of the Spirit in regard to the Church. He has also a function in regard to the world. The world cannot receive Him, because it neither sees nor knows Him (14[17]) ; but His presence in the world rebukes or convicts it ($\dot{\epsilon}\lambda\dot{\epsilon}\gamma\chi\epsilon\iota$) concerning sin, and righteousness, and judgment (16[8-11]). That is, the presence of the Spirit shows up in its true character the nature of sin, in the refusal to believe in Christ : the nature of righteousness, in the triumph of Christ through humiliation and death, to which the Spirit is a perpetual witness : the nature of judgment, in the final condemnation already passed upon the ruler of this world, and reiterated so long as the faith of Christ is in the world.

The effect of this mission of the Holy Spirit upon the Church has two sides : it alters men's relations to God and to one another. As regards God, it brings them into the closest possible union. Again and again Christ speaks of abiding in them. The Father and the Son will make their abode with those who love the Son (14[23]). He is the vine, and they are the branches, depending for life on their union with Him (15[4-6. 7. 11] etc.). And the same phrase is constantly used by St. John in his First Epistle (2[5. 6. 24] 3[5. 24] 4[13] 5[20]). It results in the certainty of access to God : we have boldness (2[28] 4[17]) at the last day (3[21. 22]) in judging our own conscience ; (5[14. 15]) in prayer, knowing that He hears, and that we therefore have our requests. Six times does our Lord promise fulfilment to prayer in His name (Jn 14[13] 15[7. 16] 16[23. 24. 26]). We are Christ's friends (15[14]) ; His joy is in us, and our joy is fulfilled (15[11] 17[13]), even under persecution (16[20]) ; to us He leaves His peace (14[27]). He looks forward to a consummation in His Father's house, where His followers shall be with Him for ever (14[3]) ; and then we, who are now sons, shall be like Him, for we shall see Him as He is (1 Jn 3[2. 3]). He sets before the Church as its ideal of unity the abiding of the Father in the Son, the love of the

Father and the Son (Jn 15[9. 10]), and the unity of the Father and the Son (17[11]), including in this those who shall believe through the preaching of the apostles (17[20. 24-27]). In this true correspondence between God and man, especially in the free intercourse through prayer, the Father is glorified in the Son (14[13]).

This intimate union determines the character of the Church in its relation to the world. The apostles are sent into the world as Christ Himself was sent there (17[18]) ; they are His representatives, so that they who receive them receive Him (13[20]) ; and they will meet with the same hatred and persecution from the world as He did (15[17-21]). Among themselves, they will keep His commandments (14[15. 21. 23. 24] 15[10], cf. 1 Jn 2[3]), and especially the new commandment to love one another (13[34] 15[12. 17]). This is emphasized in the Epistles when St. John is writing to the Church already constituted and at work (1 Jn 3[11. 23] 4[21], 2 Jn 5). And St. John in his usual manner continually contrasts this principle of love, which is of God (1 Jn 4[7]), with the opposing principle of hatred. This has the essence of murder in it, as the example of Cain shows (1 Jn 3[12-15], cf. Jn 8[44], where the rising desire to kill Christ is connected with the devil, who was a murderer from the beginning) ; and this hatred is inconsistent with eternal life (1 Jn 3[15]), or with the love of God (4[20]). Their power to overcome the world, in which by Christ's wish and God's ordinance (Jn 17[15]) they are placed, is their faith that Jesus is the Son of God (1 Jn 5[4. 5])—a faith which in St. John's own case and that of his fellow-apostles rested on experience (1 Jn 1[1-4], Jn 1[14]), but belongs also to those who have not seen but yet have believed (Jn 20[29]).

At His departure, the Lord gave to His Church the power to forgive sins, saying, 'Whose soever sins ye shall remit, they are remitted unto them ; and whose soever sins ye retain, they are retained' (20[23]). To St. Peter also He gave the charge to tend and feed the flock (21[15. 16. 17]). There are signs in the Epistles of the exercise of some discipline. It is made abundantly clear that sin is inconsistent with the Church altogether (1 Jn 1[6] 2[1] 3[6. 9] 5[18]) ; to do sin is to relapse into the darkness from which the light has freed us (2[8. 9], cf. 1[6. 7]). Still if a man does commit a sin ($\dot{\epsilon}\dot{\alpha}\nu$ $\tau\iota s$ $\dot{\alpha}\mu\alpha\rho\tau\hat{\eta}$) we have an Advocate with the Father, Jesus Christ the righteous (2[1]) ; the blood of Jesus Christ cleanses us from all sin. For certain sins, not unto death, St. John enjoins the prayer of intercession (1 Jn 5[16-18]) ; for heresy, he forbids all intercourse or salutation (2 Jn 10). In one church Diotrephes $\dot{o}$ $\phi\iota\lambda o\pi\rho\omega\tau\epsilon\dot{v}\omega\nu$ requires to be deprived of his undeserved eminence, and reduced to order (3 Jn 9. 10).

(7) It would be impossible to close an account of the Theology of St. John's Gospel and Epistles without reference to the three great phrases in which the nature of God is described : 'God is Spirit' (Jn 4[24]), 'God is Light' (1 Jn 1[5]), and 'God is Love' (1 Jn 4[8. 16]). These three phrases form the crown, and, at the same time, a summary of his Theology. It is important to consider them in close connexion with their content.

The first is ascribed to our Lord Himself in His dialogue with the woman of Samaria. She, finding herself in presence of a prophet, brings before Him the question that had long been at issue between the Jews and the Samaritans. 'Our fathers worshipped in this mountain, but ye say that in Jerusalem men ought to worship.' Jesus answers her implied question comprehensively. For the past ages, the Jews were right : they worshipped with some knowledge, and not blindly, looking forward to salvation : they had so much certainty about God. But for the future, both are alike wrong ; the day of local worships is over ;

God no longer chooses a particular place where men should approach Him : 'He is *Spirit*, and must be worshipped in spirit and truth.' Thus this phrase marks the transition from the old to the new order. It excludes all limitations of space and time and matter from God, and, at the same time, the context preserves the truth which the Jewish religion had enshrined.

In the second of these phrases we go further : it bears on the moral nature of God. Throughout these books the contrast of Light and Darkness is used metaphorically to express Good and Evil. In the immediate context of this phrase an instance occurs. God is *Light*, and therefore all who walk in darkness are out of communion with Him. Darkness means hatred (1 Jn 2¹¹) and blindness (*ib.*), and is passing away (2⁸). The true light was manifested ; and 'this is the message which we have heard of Him, and report to you, that God is light.' This phrase, which cannot be altogether separated from the thought of revelation, is really the correlative of the OT doctrine of the Holiness of the Lord. It conveys the assurance of the undimmed purity of God, and the need of purity to man, if he would have fellowship with God.*

In the third we pass beyond both the two previous phrases. The doctrine that God is *Love*, asserts, in the strongest possible form, His Personality, and the possibility of personal intercourse between God and Man. This is indeed the drift of the two contexts in which it occurs. The man who is without love does not know God, for God is love. Knowledge of Him, in other words, is possible, but possible through likeness in nature. And so later the same point is more strongly emphasized : 'God is love, and he that abideth in love abideth in God, and God in him' (1 Jn 4¹⁶). The object for which Christ came to earth, that man should have this fellowship with Him and with the Father, depends on the fact that God is love. But it is possible to go a little further than this. The doctrine that God is love helps to clear up those difficult phrases (mentioned above, p. 688) in which Christ speaks of the mission of the Paraclete. The account of the work of the Father, the Son, and the Spirit is full of contradictions, if they are conceived on the analogy of three separate individuals ; but these particular difficulties are in some degree modified if we think of them as Three essential eternal modes of the Divine Life, bound together in a perfect love. Such a thought explains the peculiar language used of the Word in His relation to the Father (ἦν πρὸς τὸν θεόν, ὁ ὢν εἰς τὸν κόλπον τοῦ πατρός, 1¹·¹⁸). We cannot wonder that from this text has arisen the precise theology of the Holy Trinity.

B. *THE APOCALYPSE*.—The task of describing the theology of the Apocalypse is one of very great difficulty. There is no book more obscure, or more doubtful in its historical reference. The method of the author is to explain his ideas by means of an extremely complicated symbolism, to which it is hard to find the key. In interpreting OT prophecies, the first thing to be done is to decide, if possible, on the historical occasion from which they arose. But in the case of the Apocalypse there is great difficulty in getting any certain clue to the occasion. The majority of modern critics are of opinion that the book was written in the time of Nero ; but they are not unanimous, and the ancient tradition is unvaried in favour of the times of Domitian. It will be necessary as far as possible to ignore these difficulties in the present discussion : they are dealt with in special articles. See JOHN (GOSPEL, p. 707 ff.) and REVELATION.

The aim of the book is limited, and is defined both at the beginning and at the end : it is to describe things ἃ δεῖ γενέσθαι ἐν τάχει (cf. 1¹ 22¹⁶). The visions recorded are not set down as mere pieces of the individual history of the writer : they are events which are full of meaning for the future. But interpreters are not agreed as to whether they are to be referred to the immediate history of the time, or to the whole course of the Church's life, or to the remote future at the end of the world. It is well to remember that St. John, supposing that he is the author, is capable, as has already been noticed, of idealizing in a remarkable way ; so that he speaks of the sinlessness of the regenerate at the same time that he provides against the commission of actual sin. It is possible, therefore, that the descriptions even of the end of things are the pictorial exposition of principles permanently at work. In any case it will be sufficient to consider the working of the principles, leaving aside the question of their manifestation. The book falls into two very obvious and clear divisions. The first three chapters contain the opening vision and the Epistles to the Seven Churches : this forms the first division. The second (chs. 4-22) contains the Apocalypse proper—the vision or series of visions in which the things which must shortly come to pass are revealed.*

(*a*) *The Doctrine of God*.—There is no part of the book devoted to the exposition of this doctrine ; such doctrine, therefore, as may be gathered from it, underlies the language in which the proper subject of the book is treated. We gather much, first, from the titles used of God. (*a*) In the salutation (1⁴) we have the assertion of the *eternity* of God ἀπὸ ὁ ὢν καὶ ὁ ἦν καὶ ὁ ἐρχόμενος. The name stands undeclined in the nominative, in spite of its construction with the preposition ἀπό ; and the imperfect ἦν is treated as a participle. The phrase thus stands for a Being who is subject to no change, but is always, through all the changes which occur ; it is an expansion of the old covenant-name Jehovah. The phrase is repeated in 1⁸, and is there sanctioned by the words, used by the prophets to authorize their message, λέγει ὁ Κύριος. It is worth noticing that in 4⁸, when the same words recur in the ascription of glory by the four beasts, their order is changed. The words expressing permanence occur in the second instead of the first place : ὁ ἦν, καὶ ὁ ὤν, καὶ ὁ ἐρχόμενος. After the consummation of things (11¹⁷) ὁ ἐρχόμενος is omitted (cf. 16⁵). The same meaning is carried by the striking phrases τὸ Ἄ καὶ τὸ Ὦ (1⁸ 21⁶ 22¹³), ὁ πρῶτος καὶ ὁ ἔσχατος (1¹⁷ 22¹³), ἡ ἀρχὴ καὶ τὸ τέλος (22¹³). God is conceived as eternal : from Him all things take their origin, and to Him all things return. In 10⁶ and 15⁷ τῷ ζῶντι εἰς τοὺς αἰῶνας τῶν αἰώνων, the endless continuity of an eternal Being is declared ; in 15³ ὁ βασιλεὺς τῶν αἰώνων, the idea of rule or dominion is involved. (β) This brings us to a second idea which is frequently associated with God in this book, ὁ παντοκράτωρ—the *all-ruling* (1⁸ 4⁸ 15³ 16⁷·¹⁴ 19⁶·¹⁵ 21²²). It is noticeable that, with the exception of 1⁸ 4⁸, and possibly 21²², this title is used in connexion with some statement as to the Divine judgments ; *i.e.* with the catastrophic declaration of the principles of His rule. This should be compared with the idea of judgment already traced in the Gospel of St. John (see above, p. 688). Besides this, the phrases should be noted in which the creation of the world is ascribed to God (10⁶ 14⁷). These simply contain references to it as a fact. In 4¹¹ the Will of God is definitely assigned as cause, both for the conception and realization of the created order : διὰ τὸ θέλημά σου ἦσαν καὶ

---

*Philo (*de Somn.* I. xiii., tom. i. p. 632 Mang.) uses the same phrase, but with the association of undimmed intellectual vision.

*The question of the internal structure of this section does not come before us.

ἐκτίσθησαν.* The cry of the souls slain for the word of God and the witness which they held, contains another title still, ὁ δεσπότης ὁ ἅγιος καὶ ἀληθινός (6¹⁰). This word occurs but rarely in NT of God, and not elsewhere in St. John; it would seem to convey the idea of personal relationship, as St. Paul speaks of himself as the *slave* of Christ (δοῦλος). The word ὅσιος is used 15⁴, but the usual word for the holiness of God is, as might be supposed, ἅγιος.

The various doxologies heard in heavenly places by St. John convey the same teaching, but with some differences in expression. The Elders, in their response to the ascription of the Four Beasts, say, 'Thou art worthy, Lord and our God, to receive the glory, the honour, and the power, because thou didst create all things, and for thy will they were, and were created' (4¹¹). Later on (5¹³), when the whole of creation responds to the angels and the elders, they ascribe blessing and honour and glory and might (τὸ κράτος); the redeemed (7¹⁰) speak of salvation (ἡ σωτηρία); and the angels, in response to the great multitude from every nation under heaven (7¹²), say, 'Amen: Blessing, and glory, and wisdom, and thanksgiving, and honour, and power, and strength (ἡ ἰσχύς), be unto our God for ages of ages.' All these, in various ways, assert the supreme sovereignty of God. This is specially emphasized (11¹⁷ 15³⁴) in regard to the judgments of God: the ways of God are vindicated when, after long trial, the evil is done away with, and holiness triumphs. So the elders, when they sing the song of Moses the servant of God, and of the Lamb, say, 'Just and true are thy ways, O King of ages' (15³); and again, when the waters are turned into blood (16⁶), St. John heard 'the angel of the waters saying, Thou art just, thou which art, and which wast, the Holy, because thou hast judged these things: because they poured forth the blood of saints and prophets, and thou hast given them blood to drink: they are worthy.' And the altar responds in the same sense (16⁷, cf. 19²). The majesty of God is described symbolically at the beginning of ch. 4; the Father is 'He that sitteth on the throne' in the centre of the heavenly place. The author does not attempt any description of this supreme Presence in this, or in any other of the many passages where the phrase ὁ καθήμενος ἐπὶ τῷ θρόνῳ occurs; he uses merely metaphorical language, and implies by so doing that God is in Himself invisible. Thus we have in this book an expansion of the old Hebrew doctrine of God: He is eternal, invisible, supreme Creator, Ruler, and Judge of the world. The coherence of this with the fuller Christian doctrine of God will be obvious when we consider the functions of the Son of God.

(γ) We will consider, first, the relation of the Father and the Son. It is noticeable that these names are most frequent in the first three chapters. The incarnate Son occupies a position of subordination. Thus in the preface to Rev we find these words: 'The Revelation of Jesus Christ, which God gave him, to show his servants' (1¹). And this is borne out in the chapters which follow: 'I will give him authority over the nations . . . as I also have received from my Father' (2²⁷). So He says, 'I will confess his name before my Father' (3⁵); and in 3²¹ He draws a parallel between His own victory and triumph and that of His followers. In 3¹² He even speaks of the Father as 'My God' (ὁ θεός μου). On the other hand, when St. John in the spirit on the Lord's Day sees the opening vision, the figure ὅμοιον υἱὸν ἀνθρώπου, the Son thus manifested uses of Himself words usually applied to the Father, the first and the last (1¹⁷); referring to the Resurrection, so

that there can be no possibility of mistake, and claiming further to possess the keys of Hades and of death. Moreover, the features which St. John notes in the figure—the flaming eyes, and two-edged sword from the mouth—are, as the messages to the various Churches show, symbolic of judgment. So He is the source from whom the messages to the Seven Churches come: He holds the seven stars in His right hand (*i.e.* the angels of the Seven Churches, 2¹; cf. 1¹⁶·²⁰). These phrases imply sovereignty, and the exercise of judicial office. The same position is conveyed by the various titles used in this passage of the Son. He is 'the faithful and true witness' (1⁵ 3¹⁴, cf. 1 Ti 6¹³); 'the firstborn of the dead' (1⁵), 'the amen' (3¹⁴), 'the ruler of the kings of the earth' (1⁵). These deal with His work on earth, with His function as fulfiller of the promises of God (cf. 2 Co 1¹⁹·²⁰), and with its triumph over mankind. So, too, 2¹ 3¹. But the title 'the beginning of the Creation of God' (3¹⁴), 'the first and the last' (1¹⁷ 2⁸), and those in which the prerogatives of judgment are asserted (2¹²·¹⁸ 3⁷), emphasize the Divine attributes of the Son of God (2¹⁸). The teaching in these and similar passages precisely resembles in its ambiguity the language already noted in the Gospels. There also the Son speaks of Himself as derived and subordinate, and yet exercises functions which He also reserves for the Father. Such a phrase as Jn 5²² 'Neither doth the Father judge any man, but hath given all judgment to the Son,' expresses precisely the point of view of the Apocalypse.

In the first three chapters we find Christ dealing with the Church in the world; with the fourth we pass into the region of visions and symbolism; and the words Father and Son, as already noticed, are of rare occurrence. But the theology is the same, in spite of difference of language. Sovereign over all things is 'he that sitteth on the throne.' By His right hand is the Book written within and without, sealed with seven seals (5¹). The seer is told that the Lion of the tribe of Judah, the root of David (cf. 22¹⁶, where Jesus assumes this latter title to Himself), has overcome, so as to open the Book and its seven seals (5⁵). Then 'in the midst of the Throne of the Four Beasts and in the midst of the Elders' he sees a Lamb standing as it had been slain (5⁶). The Lamb came and took the Book from the right hand of Him that sitteth on the Throne (5⁷). 'And when he received the Book, the four Beasts and the four-and-twenty Elders fell before the Lamb, having each a harp, and golden bowls full of incense, which are the prayers of the saints. And they sing a new song, saying, Thou art worthy to receive the Book, and to open its seals; because thou wast slain, and didst buy for God with thy blood out of every tribe, and tongue, and people, and nation, and madest them to our God a kingdom and priests; and they reign upon the earth' (5⁸⁻¹⁰). The angels then respond to this new song with a doxology to the Lamb parallel in character to those addressed to the Father (5¹²). And, lastly, the whole creation responds with a similar doxology, combining in it both the Lamb and Him that sitteth on the throne (5¹³). It is obvious that this is a highly significant passage. The Lamb receives the Book from the Supreme; but He is treated with worship similar to that paid to the Supreme. (Contrast the scene in which John falls down to worship the angel, 19¹⁰ and 22⁸·⁹). Moreover, through the language used by the Elders (5⁸⁻¹⁰), the Lamb is identified with Jesus Christ: 'To him that loved us and loosed us from our sins with his blood, and made us a kingdom and priests to God and his Father—to him be glory and might for ever' (1⁵·⁶, cf. 7¹⁰). The same position is maintained throughout the book. The

---

* If ἦσαν is the true reading, it is difficult to see what it can mean but this; cf. Jn 1⁴ ὃ γέγονεν ἐν αὐτῷ ζωὴ ἦν.

Lamb is mentioned in connexion with the Supreme (7⁹·¹⁰ etc.), and He performs work in which His honour is of the same sort with that of God. The redeemed are they 'who follow the Lamb whithersoever he goeth: these were bought from among men a first-fruits to God and the Lamb' (14⁴). He appears in the judgment, and witnesses the ruin of the Beast and his worshippers (14¹⁰). He wars with the Beast, and overcomes; because He is King of kings and Lord of lords (17¹⁴), cf. 'the wrath of the Lamb' (6¹⁶). The Church, the new Jerusalem, is the Bride of the Lamb (21⁹·¹⁰), and 'the Lord the God, all-Sovereign, is the temple of it, and the Lamb' (21²²). There also stands the throne of God and the Lamb (22³). Similar teaching is found in connexion with the name of Christ (much more rare than the symbolic title 'the Lamb'). 'The kingdom of the world is become (the kingdom) of our Lord and of his Christ' (11¹⁵). 'Now is come the salvation and the power and the kingdom of our God, and the authority of his Christ' (12¹⁰). The whole scheme is bound up with the order of the world: the Lamb was slain from the foundation of the world (13⁸); and yet those whose names are among the redeemed are said to have their names in the Lamb's book of life (13⁸ 21²⁷). It is difficult to draw any conclusion from this but that St. John regarded the Lamb as a Divine Being, to whom Divine honour was paid, and who was associated in His sovereignty by God. At the same time, He takes from God the commission to perform His functions: He is not independent. Little is said of human nature in regard to Him: twice only He is described as ὅμοιον υἱὸν (var. lec. υἱῷ) ἀνθρώπου (1¹³ 14¹⁴). But the sacrifice and the blood of the Lamb are the means by which men are redeemed from their sins; and there is one definite allusion to the crucifixion (11⁸ 'the great city, which spiritually is called Sodom and Egypt where also their Lord was crucified'). With this may be compared the prophecy in 1⁷ 'Every eye shall see him, and they who pierced him' (ἐξεκέντησαν), and Jn 19³⁷ ὄψονται εἰς ὃν ἐξεκέντησαν. The profession of those who follow Christ is called (from the point of view of its manifestation in the world) 'the witness of Jesus.' St. John claims to be giving this himself (1², cf. 19¹⁰). It is, as it were, a message the contents of which are obnoxious to the world (1⁹) and to the powers of darkness (11⁷ 12¹⁷ 17⁶); it involves persecution even to death (6⁹ 17⁶ 20⁴); it is the cause of the triumph of those who have it (12¹¹); and it is the fulfilment, the significance, the *spirit* of prophecy (19¹⁰).

(b) We may speak here of the *doctrine of the Spirit*, so far as it is contained in this book. It is somewhat involved in symbolism. Thus we read of the seven spirits which are before His throne (1⁴): the seven λαμπάδες (4⁶) before the throne are identified with the seven spirits, and so also the seven eyes of the Lamb (5⁶) are the seven spirits of God, sent (ἀπεσταλμένοι) into all the earth. The number *seven* probably stands for completeness, and the phrase 'the seven spirits' probably means the Spirit in the full variety of His manifestation. It is noticeable that the salutation to the seven Churches comes from the Eternal, and from the seven spirits, and from Jesus Christ (1⁴) in that order: the seven spirits, in this case only, standing between the Father and the Son. In the Epistles themselves a peculiar use is to be observed. Each Epistle begins with an announcement from Christ, made with some symbol indicative of His authority, or His intention to exercise judgment; and each ends with the same formula: 'He that hath an ear, let him hear what the Spirit saith to the Churches' (2¹¹·¹⁷ etc.). Also in 3¹ the Ep. to Sardis begins: 'These things saith he that hath the seven spirits, and the seven stars' (i.e. the angels of the

Churches, 1²⁰). In two other places the Spirit is represented as speaking, 'I heard a voice from heaven saying, Write, Blessed are the dead that die in the Lord from henceforth: Yea, saith the Spirit, that they shall rest from their labours' (14¹³). And again at the end (22¹⁷), 'the Spirit and the Bride say, Come.' There is thus comparatively little definite allusion to the Spirit in this book. What there is, seems to involve the following points: (1) the Spirit in His various manifestations proceeds from the Father: (2) Christ *holds* the seven spirits, regulates the diverse operations of the Spirit in the Church; (3) the voice of the Spirit in the Church is, in a sense, the voice of Christ; (4) the Spirit joins in the prayer of the Bride. Though somewhat limited in character, these points imply a doctrine which, both in its clearness and obscurity, resembles the doctrine of the Last Discourses (see above).

(c) The remaining points for consideration are those connected with the facts of *sin* and *judgment*, *salvation* and *the Church*. It is better to take these together, owing to the particular form in which they come before us. In dealing with the Gospel we noted the use by the author of pairs of parallel but contrasted ideas, such as Light and Darkness, Life and Judgment, This method is carried out in the Apocalypse on a very extended scale. In the visions contained in this work we witness the warfare of two contending powers: on the one side is the Lamb, and on the other the devil. The devil is described under various names. In 12³ we read, 'And another sign was seen in heaven, and behold a great red dragon, having seven heads and ten horns,' etc. This dragon is identified (12⁹, cf. 20²) with 'the old serpent, called the devil and Satan, who deceiveth the whole world.' The 'serpent' implies, of course, a reference to the story of the Fall, and this title, therefore, implies that the source of the evil in the world is the power that was against God. In other places we hear of a synagogue of Satan (2⁹ 3⁹), a throne of Satan (2¹³), and the place where Satan dwelleth (2¹³); a doctrine of Satan, called by those who follow it 'the deep things of Satan' (2²⁴ τὰ βαθέα τοῦ Σατανᾶ). But this is not all. There is described in this book an organized kingdom of evil, claiming sovereignty over men like the kingdom of the Lamb. This introduces the most tangled of all the questions connected with this book: the interpretation of **the Beast.** We cannot enter upon the various explanations proposed (see REVELATION), but must confine ourselves to the general question of the position occupied by the Beast in the book. He is the embodiment of the power of the devil (13²): he aims at winning the homage of the world, and does so win it in a large measure (13⁴): he has a certain power to vex the saints—power which is given him (ἐδόθη αὐτῷ, 13⁷). Further, he has a representative, a second Beast, who works among men in favour of the first (13¹²), and does signs (v.¹³), and inspires an image of the first beast with life and speech: he also compels some to receive a mark in their hands or foreheads, and persecutes all others (vv.¹⁶·¹⁷). In all this there is traceable a kind of attempt to caricature the methods and the kingdom of Christ. One of his heads was ὡς ἐσφαγμένην εἰς θάνατον, and the blow of his death was healed (13⁴), as if he claimed resurrection. The second Beast has two horns, like the Lamb (13¹¹). The worshippers who are deceived say, 'Who is like unto the beast, and who is able to war with him?' (13⁴), which caricatures the meaning of the word *Michael*, —'who is like unto God?'—Michael having cast the dragon out of heaven. In 16¹³ we find three powers spoken of—the dragon, the beast, and the prophet who occupies the place of the second beast.

Then later, a woman appears seated on a beast, clothed in scarlet, named Babylon the great. Between these two war arises, in pursuance of the plans of God (17¹⁷). With all the obscurity of details the general sense of this imagery seems clear. The forces of evil in the world take their origin from Satan; and the essence of the evil consists in setting up rival claims to worship as against God. This is the force of the caricature of Divine methods. Satan claims to do for men all that God can do. As in the Gospel, the final difference between those who fall under the delusions of the Beast and those who do not is explained by means of predestination. All who dwell upon the earth shall worship him (the Beast), every one whose name has not been written in the book of life of the Lamb slain from the foundation of the world (13⁸, cf. 17⁸). This, as well as the temporary power of the Beast, his persecution and ultimate fall, are in the hands of God.

With regard to the judgments of God, it is to be noted that they are retributive in character. During the time before the end the plagues of God come upon the world, and those who follow the Beast only blaspheme the more because of them, and fail to repent (16⁹. ¹⁰. ¹¹. ²¹, cf. 9²⁰ and contrast 11¹³): pain in their case fails to convert. When the end comes, men are judged κατὰ τὰ ἔργα (20¹⁴ 22¹²). More precisely, those who have slain the saints are given blood to drink (16⁶ 13¹⁰); those who commit fornication in Thyatira are cast upon a bed (2²⁰); Babylon is punished with the cup which she mixed for others (18⁶). The time of probation passes, and then the sins themselves are their own punishment: 'He that is unjust, let him be unjust still; and he that is filthy, let him be filthy still' (22¹¹).

The evil which has thus entered upon the world affects mankind, apparently as a whole; at least there is no sign in the book that any can avoid its taint. And it therefore requires to be abolished: men need salvation. In this book there is but one means to this end: *the blood of the Lamb.* The first allusion to this is in the doxology immediately before the salutation, τῷ ἀγαπῶντι ἡμᾶς καὶ λύσαντι ἡμᾶς ἐκ τῶν ἁμαρτιῶν ἐν τῷ αἵματι αὐτοῦ (1⁵). It appears again in the doxology to the Lamb (5¹¹, cf. 14⁴). The hundred and forty and four thousand are said to have washed their robes and made them white in the blood of the Lamb (7¹⁴, cf. 22¹⁴): it is by means of it that they win victory over the Beast (12¹¹). A reference to it is made when He who is called the Word of God goes forth with His garments sprinkled with blood (19¹³). Nothing is said as to the way in which this sacrifice is applied: the fact of it is asserted.

Those who are thus redeemed are made by Christ into a kingdom, priests unto God and His Father (1⁶ 5¹⁰); that is, they are a society of men ruled over by God as King. They are sealed in their foreheads (7³). They come from the twelve tribes, but not from these alone: 'I beheld, and, lo, a great multitude, that no man could number, from every nation, and tribe, and people, and tongue, standing before the throne, and before the Lamb' (7⁹; cf. 14⁶). Moreover, the whole creation has a part in the scheme of God, and responds with a doxology to the Lamb (5¹³): the 'eternal Gospel' is based on the fact of Creation (14⁶), 'I saw another angel flying in midheaven, having an eternal gospel to preach to those that sit upon the earth, and to every nation, and tribe, and tongue, and people, saying in a loud voice, Fear God, and give him glory; because the hour of his judgment has come: and worship him that made heaven, and earth, and the sun, and the springs of waters.'

In the meantime, before the end comes, the ideal of the Church is not attained. There is sin and heresy in the seven Churches. There are false apostles (2²), false Jews (2⁹), the teaching of Balaam (2¹⁴), a false prophetess (2²⁰), impurity (3⁴), lukewarmness (3¹⁵). The devil has power to persecute, so that the men in the earth may be tested (2¹⁰ 3¹⁰). Those who are slain cry out beneath the altar, How long? (6¹⁰) but others, their fellow-servants and brethren, will have to be slain as they. This fate must befall especially the two witnesses, who prophesy against the Beast (11³⁻⁸). So for all this time emphasis is laid upon the qualities of endurance and faithfulness (cf. 3¹⁰ 2¹⁰ 13¹⁰). The cowardly, the unfaithful, those who murder, and lie, and are idolaters or impure (21⁸ 22¹⁵), have no part in the heavenly kingdom. Even a Church, that is already in existence, may lose its place: 'if not, I come to thee, and will remove thy candlestick from its place, if thou repent not' (2⁵).

In the eyes of God and of the seer the time of waiting is very short. 'Behold, I come as a thief' (16¹⁵ 22²⁰). And when the time does come the harvest of the world will be reaped (14¹⁵), and the vintage gathered (14¹⁸), and the evil will be finally separated from the good. Then comes the consummation. There will be the new heaven and new earth; the sea—symbolizing probably restlessness, and division and barrenness—will be no more. And the new Jerusalem, founded on the twelve apostles of the Lamb (21¹⁴), will appear. In this the redeemed will dwell for ever (22⁵) in perfect freedom and happiness. The actual presence of God and the Lamb will make a temple for worship unnecessary: the servants of God shall see His face. Thus the purpose for which man is created is fulfilled.

It is not, perhaps, fanciful to see a symbol of this perfect communion in the fact that it is after the renewal of the heaven and earth, that He that sitteth on the throne is said to speak (21⁵). Before, voices came from the throne and from the temple, but none from the Supreme. Now at last, when all is fulfilled, He speaks.

It is manifestly impossible to exhaust within reasonable limits the meaning of this inexhaustible book. An attempt has been made to indicate the outlines of the theology assumed in it. It must be obvious by this time how closely the thought of the Apocalypse is connected with that of the Gospel and Epistles. Perhaps the most noticeable points of difference are the comparatively small place occupied in the Apocalypse by the doctrine of the Spirit, and the emphasis laid in this book upon the catastrophe of the judgment. It cannot, however, be said that these are very significant. For, first, the doctrine of the Spirit is similar in character to that in the Gospel so far as it goes; and, secondly, the judgment expresses in its final form a warfare which continues throughout the history of the world.

Literature.—A. *John the Apostle*: F. Trench, *St. John the Evangelist* (1850); Neander, *Planting of Christianity* (Eng. tr. 1864), i. 384–413; Krenkel, *Apostel Johannes* (1871); Godet, *Studies on the NT* (Eng. tr. 1871), 277–293; Stanley, *Essays on Apost. Age* ³ (1874), 234–281; Macdonald, *Life and Writings of St. John* (1877); Niese, *Leben des heil. Johannes* (1878); Culross, *John whom Jesus Loved*, 1878; Lechler, *Apost. and Post-Apost. Times* (Eng. tr. 1886); Farrar, *Early Days of Christianity* (Pop. ed. 1891), 362 ff.; Gloag, *Life of St. John* (1891); Rankin, *First Saints* (1893), 169–182; Milligan in *Expos.* 3rd Ser. x. 321–341.

B. *The Theology of St. John*: Besides the Biblical Theologies of NT (Messner, 1856; Baur, 1864; Oosterzee, 1870; Reuss, 1872; Schmid, 1877; Immer, 1877; Weiss, 1882; Adeney, 1894; Beyschlag, 1895), and the Comm. on St. John's Gospel, Epistles, and the Apoc. (for which see Lit. at these articles); Frommann, *Johann. Lehrbegriff* (1839); Köstlin, *Lehrbegriff des Ev. u. der Briefe Joh.* (1843); Sears, *Fourth Gospel the Heart of Christ* (1872); Lias, *Doct. System of St. John* (1875); Horton, *Revelation and Bible* (1892), 369–402; Wendt, *Teaching of Jesus* (1892); Wordsworth, *Primary Witness* (1892), 182–219; Caird,

Evolution of Religion (1893), ii. 217–243; Stevens, *Johan. Theology* (1894); Alexander, *Leading Ideas of the Gospels* [3] (1898), 182–236; Burton in *Biblical World*, Jan.–March, 1899.

T. B. STRONG.

JOHN, GOSPEL OF—

The Fourth Gospel is generally admitted to be the work of one remarkably gifted man. Neither in style nor in motive can criticism break it up into different centuries or antagonistic tendencies. Editorial hands have for the most part spared its subtle beauty. There is little with which it can be compared. It stands free of fashion, and possesses throughout a strongly marked idiosyncrasy.

The problem that is forced upon the student is this : Is the so-called 'Gospel' the outline of a biography, or the artistic clothing of an ideal? Have we a true report of the impression produced on the consciousness of an intimate friend by the teaching, manner, and deeds of One whom he could not think of as less than the Eternal Word of God manifest in the flesh, or must we conclude that what we have is the speculation of some one who did not shrink from creating its material and inventing the basis of its theologoumena ?

The problem is the more puzzling because to the presumed author of the Gospel is also attributed the production of the Apocalypse. If this compound authorship can be accepted, the personality of 'John' becomes almost as perplexing to scientific history as that of the Lord Jesus Christ Himself. When the diversity of the characteristics of the two documents came into the clear consciousness of the 3rd cent. (Eus. *HE* vii. 10, 24, 25), the apostolic origin of the Apocalypse was repudiated, rather than that of the Gospel. But the preponderant belief of Christians has practically accepted the unity of the Johannine writings. The fact that St. John had the insight which enabled him to preserve discourses and sayings of the Lord Jesus, to see in His human life the fulness of grace and truth, the glory of the only-begotten Son, has seemed consonant with the fact that the same eyes might also have discerned in Him the slain Lamb, the Lion of the tribe of Judah, the Prince of the kings of the earth.

If the Son of God did say and do the things recorded in this document, then everything in the universe, every fact in the history of the world, the conclusions of all philosophy, the meaning of all scientific discovery, the future of the world, and the goal of humanity, must be affected by its disclosures. We do not, indeed, contend that the Christian faith is dependent on the Fourth Gospel, or that, should this supreme expression of its inmost spirit be banished to the realm of speculative romance,

the faith or the kingdom of Christ is relegated to the same region. The ministry of the Apostle to the Gentiles must have been completed between 30 and 40 years before this Gospel saw the light. Great historic Churches grew into importance and began to suffer disintegration from internal discord before it was possible to heal them by the Valedictory Discourse. The Churches of Judæa and of the Dispersion lived by 'the faith of the Lord of Glory' (Ja 2[1]), and 'looked for the mercy of our Lord Jesus Christ unto eternal life' (Jude [20–22]), before this document could have come into circulation.

If we read between the lines of the most authentic Epp. of St. Paul, St. Peter, or the Ep. of St. James, we see that the message of the apostles had already inaugurated a new philosophy of heaven and earth, of time and eternity, new conceptions of history and ethics, and new standards of life. The leaven had spread from Jerus. to Antioch ; from thence it had spread to Ephesus, Corinth, and Rome. All this had occurred before the Fourth Gospel had been crystallized into form, or its interpretation of the baffling mystery had been offered to mankind. Even if we were robbed of the Apoc. and of the spiritual Gospel, or deprived of all confidence in either, we should still be in indefeasible possession of a faith which unriddles the universe, which works by love, which overcomes the world. We should, therefore, mistake most obvious facts if we persisted in regarding the Fourth Gospel as the 'acropolis' or citadel of the faith.

But although this is freely conceded, the inestimable preciousness of the document must still be urged with earnestness. Those who strenuously deny its historicity and repudiate its apostolic character are ready to confess, with Baur, Schenkel, Thoma, Taylor, that the highest, and essentially the truest, revelation of the Son of Man, and interpretation of the mind and will of God, are to be found in this record. Much which it contains has long since been verified by the Christian conscience as fundamentally true, and has permanently enriched the mind of man.

We hail the teaching of the Fourth Gospel as establishing for us the inspiring persuasion that the divine and human are not separated by an impassable chasm, but are in their innermost essence *one* ; that, in the portraiture of the Logos made man, humanity at its best is nothing less than the clearest and most gracious revelation of the Eternal God, and that Divinity at its greatest has been manifested through the human.

A philosophy based on the intrinsic unknowableness of God, on the impossibility of converse being held between man and his Creator, is pledged to demonstrate the late origin of the Fourth Gospel, and to find in the Johannine teaching of St. Paul some of the materials of the pious fraud of this *falsarius* of the 2nd century. Many have struggled with the attempt to discover Alexandrine philosophy in the Fourth Gospel. Efforts have been made to show that in the speculations of Cerinthus, Valentinus, and Basilides we may find the historical antecedents of this Gospel. It was even urged by Volkmar that 'John' may have used the works of Justin Martyr, rather than Justin have quoted from 'John,' and a date was provisionally determined for the appearance of the Gospel just anterior to the time when, by general admission, it is known to have been regarded in Antioch and Lyons, Alexandria, Ephesus, and Rome as one of the four indisputable authorities for the biography of the Lord Jesus.

I. EXTERNAL EVIDENCE FOR THE EARLY EXISTENCE OF *FOUR* GOSPELS.—The strength of the argument for the historicity and the credibility of

St. John's Gospel is to be found within itself : (1) in the proof which it explicitly contains of its own authorship ; (2) in the transcendent revelation it gives of an august Personality immeasurably greater than that of the supposed author himself, who did not fully assimilate words or thoughts of his Master which yet, by some psychologic process, he was able to preserve and record for all time ; (3) in the subtle harmonies between 'St. John's' conception of the Son of God and that expressed by the Synoptists and St. Paul ; (4) in the germinant force of the uttered word of Jesus, and in the triumphant response it has found in the consciousness, the fears and hopes, of the human race. And yet there are discords as well as harmonies. These we shall presently attempt to separate, but first we must clearly apprehend what is the material of which these things can be said.

There is proof that towards the last quarter of the second cent., in every part of the Roman Empire, *four* Gospels had been selected and were regarded as authentic, and that these *four* documents were identical with those which are described as 'according to' Matthew, Mark, Luke, and JOHN. Up to that period, τὸ εὐαγγέλιον was a name for the good message, or acceptable speculation, which Christian or heretical writers were offering to their followers. Thus Hippolytus (*Ref. Hær.* vii. 27) speaks of the disciples of Basilides as possessing ' a *gospel* ' which was the knowledge (γνῶσις) of supramundane things; but Theophilus of Antioch applied the name to the four separate Gospels, and we hear henceforward not only of *the Gospel*, but of τὰ εὐαγγέλια.

(*a*) The most conspicuous of these testimonies is that of IRENÆUS, Bishop of Lyons in Gaul, who lived between A.D. 140 and 202, and who wrote his treatise *Refutation of Heresies* between A.D. 180 and 190. Other fragments of his work, and a letter to Florinus, are preserved by Eusebius (*HE* v. 20). These are of considerable interest, and show, in combination, that the 'four Gospels' are, together with the Old Testament, to be regarded as 'the Scriptures.' Irenæus specifies these four (*Hær.* iii. 1), referring them by name to their respective authors. He makes frequent reference to St. John by name, and he gives a mystic reason for there being *four* Gospels, neither more nor fewer. Though this is fanciful and carries no theological weight, it shows that the canonical 'four' must have been long in circulation among the Churches of Lyons and Vienne.* Irenæus makes no fewer than 500 citations from the *four* Gospels, 100 of these being from the *Fourth* (see Index of Ante-Nicene Library, *Works of Irenæus*, ii. 193–197).

Great stress must also be laid on the relation that subsisted between Irenæus and Polycarp, the disciple of John the Apostle. If the letter to Florinus, recalling in lifelike form the appearance and ways of Polycarp, is genuine, it is quite incredible that the Johannine Gospel from which Irenæus thus quoted 100 times was not written by the venerated teacher of Polycarp.

(*b*) THEOPHILUS, Bishop of Antioch, *c.* A.D. 180, declared in his three Books addressed to Autolycus, a heathen, that the same things were advanced by the prophets and evangelists, and he quotes John (i. 13) by *name*. He is also reported to have written commentaries on the Gospels. On the genuineness of the Lat. transl. of these comm. much controversy has prevailed between Zahn and Harnack ; but there is no question that Theophilus was acquainted with St. John's writings, and he designates him as 'spirit-bearing'—occupying the same level with the *Law* and the *Prophets*. It is, moreover, far

from improbable that he refers to Jn 12²⁴ and 20²⁷, for the resemblance to St. John's language is striking, and we know that he was acquainted with the Gospel.

(*c*) CLEMENT OF ALEXANDRIA was the head of the celebrated Catechetical School from A.D. 189, and was himself a pupil of Pantænus and the teacher of Origen, who succeeded him in his office. Irenæus and Hippolytus probably for a brief period followed his instructions. He was a *littérateur*, and diligent collector of the opinions and dicta of philosophers. He held in reverence other sacred books, in addition to the Canonical writings of the NT, such as the Gospel according to the Egyptians, and the Apoc. of Peter, a fragment of which has been recently brought to light. He was accustomed to cite and compare the testimonies of ancient writers, as well as early traditions, concerning the Evangelists and the apostles. It is unfortunate that the most interesting of these are preserved for us only by Eusebius (*HE* vi.14,iii.23), but they aver the existence and value of the four Gospels. In the *Exhortation* (προτρεπτικός, § 59) he quotes from one or other of the Gospels between 400 and 500 times, and cites *St. John's* by name. Eusebius preserves the tradition of Clement, that Peter approved of Mark's narrative, and that 'John, divinely moved by the Holy Spirit, wrote a spiritual Gospel on observing that the things obvious to the senses had been set forth in earlier Gospels.'

(*d*) TERTULLIAN, whose literary work was done in Carthage between A.D. 190 and A.D. 230, left abundant testimony to the existence and apostolic authority of each of the Gospels. He cites passages from almost every chapter of the Fourth Gospel, and from some chapters almost every verse (see Watkins, *Bampton Lectures*, p. 24). His evidence is of high value, because of the close attention he paid to the text of St. Luke's Gospel, and the detailed proof he advanced, verse by verse, that Marcion's 'gospel' was a mutilated copy of St. Luke. After long and anxious reinvestigation by Baur, Ritschl, Volkmar, the author of *Supern. Religion*, and Sanday, the contention of Tertullian has been sustained ; but it is he also who makes it highly probable that Marcion was acquainted with the Fourth Gospel (see Godet's *Introd. to Gospel of St. John*, vol. i. 221) ; and without doubt, as in his work (*adv. Praxeam*, ch. xxiii.) against the monarchianism of Praxeas, Tertullian submitted to the authority of John the beloved disciple.

No weight need be laid upon the fragments which remain, chiefly in Syriac, of the writings of Melito of Sardis, or of Claudius Apollinaris of Hierapolis, though the list of their works given by Eusebius, and the high value set upon them by Jerome and Socrates, make it probable that treatises on the *Paschal Festival* and on the *Birth of Christ* showed acquaintance with the Four Gospels.

(*e*) But a strong link in the chain of proof is found in the writings of FLAVIUS JUSTINUS, the philosopher and martyr. Critics differ as to the chronology of Justin's career and the date of his martyrdom,* but Hort (*Journal of Class. and Sac. Philol.* iii. pp. 155–193), closely approximated by Volkmar, thought it safe to say that the chief works of Justin, his two *Apologies* and his *Dialogue with Trypho*, must fall between A.D. 145 and 148. Caspari and Krüger have ventured on a still earlier date. Justin tells us that, after passing through various stages of philosophic thought, he found the satisfaction of his mind restored by men of prophetic spirit, who did not demonstrate truth, but, being filled by the Holy Spirit, speaking things they had seen and heard, gave him what he wanted : 'kindled a flame in his soul,' and convinced him that 'this philosophy

* 'Religious veneration such as that with which Irenæus regarded these books is of slow growth. They must have held a great place in the Church as far back as the memory of living men extended' (R. W. Dale, *Living Christ and Four Gospels*, p. 145).

* Credner places the limits of his activity between A.D. 130–166 Volkmar reduced the limits between A.D. 140–150.

alone was profitable and safe.' The torch of Aristotle and Plato faded when he became familiar with the Light of Christ. In the first apology he frequently cites what he styles 'Memorials composed by the Apostles and their followers.' In ch. 66 he adds 'which are called *Gospels*,' but this clause, as opponents urge, may be a marginal gloss. The term or phrase is slightly varied. Thus he sometimes, as in *Ap.* i., calls them 'Memoirs of the Apostles,' sometimes 'Memoirs' simply, as in the *Dialogue*; and when he is referring to an incident mentioned by all four Evangelists, he introduces it by 'the apostles wrote.' The names of the apostles are not mentioned, yet no phrase could more adequately denote them than 'the apostles and those that followed them.' In addressing the Roman emperors, or the bigoted Jews of Rome or Asia Minor, the obscure names, Matthew, Mark, Luke, John, would have detracted from, rather than increased, their weight. This is parallel with the reticence of Tertullian, who, when writing his *Apology* and his address *To the Nations*, makes no distinct reference to the 'Gospels' or to their authors. Cyprian, Arnobius, and Lactantius follow the same rule. In Justin's references to the events of our Lord's life, he introduces a few picturesque details not to be found in the Canonical Gospels, indicating, it may be, some additional sources of information. If he possessed any 'harmony' of the evangelical narrative, as well as the 'memorials,' it is more likely that it was formed *from* them, than that it was the parent of them. It is, moreover, simply incredible that, between the date of Justin's writing the *Apology* or *Dialogue* and Irenæus' writing his *Refutation*, the Four Gospels should have been brought into existence, and utterly displaced Justin's 'memorials,' or that they should have come into such vogue as to be read in churches and be regarded as of primary importance in Lyons and Carthage, Antioch and Alexandria. Justin refers to some details which are found, so far as we know, in St. Matthew's Gospel *only*; he also cites some of the few specialities of St. Mark's Gospel, and at least seven peculiarities to be found in St. Luke's Gospel. The deviation from the strict accuracy of quotation may be the idiosyncrasy of the author, for he shows also slight and marked divergences from the LXX, and from the text of the Dialogues of Plato (see Sanday, *Gospels in the Second Century*). The deviations from strict accuracy are, as we should expect, more numerous in quotations from the Gospels than from these other sources. Except when quoting a lengthened passage from LXX or other sources, he may have fallen back upon his memory, as other divines have done in all ages.

The contemporaneousness of Justin and Irenæus is a fact of importance when we call to mind the undoubted confidence which the latter places in the *Fourth* Gospel. Irenæus makes no fewer than 30 references to the *Apology* and *Dialogue* of Justin. Equally abundant are the references to Justin by Tertullian, Theophilus, and others, to say nothing at present of Tatian, the supposed author of the *Diatessaron*.

II. EXTERNAL EVIDENCE FOR THE EARLY EXISTENCE OF THE FOURTH GOSPEL.—(*A*) We will commence with the quotations from, or references to, the Fourth Gospel by Justin himself (see Watkins, *Bampton Lectures*, pp. 73–81, for a summary of recent investigations by Ezra Abbot, Thoma, Hilgenfeld, Drummond, Sanday, Westcott, Edwin A. Abbott, and others). The resemblances between Justin and the Fourth Gospel are undeniable, but it has been contended by some that 'John' borrowed from Justin, rather than the reverse. Such a contention, however, must be held to betray a deficiency of literary perception. Others, who accept the priority of John, urge that Justin did not regard the authority of the evangelist as apostolic; and that, if he had drawn upon the Gospel, he ought to have quoted it when endeavouring to establish the pre-existence of Christ, instead of citing words of OT prophets. This suggestion supposes that we can grasp the ethic and philosophy of citation in the 2nd century. There are seven or eight passages in the *Apology*, and several in the *Dialogue*, which turn on (1) the Johannine doctrine of the Logos, its idea of the relation of the Logos to God, as His πρῶτον γέννημα (ch. xxi.), His υἱός (chs. xxii. and lxviii.), His πρωτότοκος τῷ ἀγεννήτῳ θεῷ (ch. lviii.); (2) on the *incarnation* of the Logos, His becoming σάρξ, or ἄνθρωπος, in Jesus Christ, and the 'Teacher' or 'Saviour' of the world (*Ap.* v.; *Dial.* xlviii., cv.). Many portions of the Gospel, besides the Prologue, are referred to by Justin, *e.g.* in *Ap.* xxxv. he regards Isaiah's oracle in 48² as fulfilled by a curious text of Jn 19¹³, where ἐκάθισε is altered into transitive ἐκάθισαν, and refers to Jesus being forced to sit on the βῆμα or judgment-seat, rather than to Pilate's taking his seat on it. This supposition, that part of the gross humiliation of Jesus consisted in placing *Him* upon the seat of judgment, is confirmed by the fragment of the Gospel of Peter recently discovered. In *Dial.* lxix., Justin refers to the incidents of Jesus healing those ἐκ γενετῆς πηρούς (cf. Jn 9), the lame also and dumb, by His word. Again, Jn 4¹⁰ is referred to in *Dial.* cxiv.

The most important passage is *Ap.* lxi., which professes to be the word of Christ Himself, ἂν μὴ ἀναγεννηθῆτε οὐ μὴ εἰσέλθητε εἰς τὴν βασιλείαν τῶν οὐρανῶν. Ὅτι δε καὶ ἀδύνατον εἰς τὰς μήτρας τῶν τεκουσῶν τοὺς ἅπαξ γεννωμένους ἐμβῆναι φανερὸν πᾶσίν ἐστιν. We have only to place this by the side of Jn 3³⁻⁵ to discern the original form of the idea, although there are many differences in the expression: Ἐὰν μή τις γεννηθῇ ἄνωθεν, οὐ δύναται ἰδεῖν τὴν βασιλείαν τοῦ θεοῦ. λέγει πρὸς αὐτὸν ὁ Νικόδημος, Πῶς δύναται ἄνθρωπος γεννηθῆναι γέρων ὤν; μὴ δύναται εἰς τὴν κοιλίαν τῆς μητρὸς αὐτοῦ δεύτερον εἰσελθεῖν καὶ γεννηθῆναι. Schwegler, Baur, Zeller, *Supern. Relig.*, E. A. Abbott, have called attention to every deviation, but none of the theories by which they account for these is so free from difficulty as the suggestion that Justin, in an awkward way, has appropriated with gravity, as his own confirmation of Christ's words, the semi-humorous query of Nicodemus which was passed over by our Lord in silence and implied rebuke. There was probably also an echo of Mt 18⁶ blended by Justin with our Lord's words in Jn 3³⁻⁵. The verbal differences are conspicuous, and yet accounted for by the very common interchange of the equivalent expressions 'kingdom of God' and 'kingdom of heaven.' Justin expresses the idea of γεννηθῇ ἄνωθεν by ἀναγεννηθῆτε, which is not to be wondered at, seeing that ἄνωθεν is often interpreted by 'again,' and that numerous later writers, who quote indisputably from the Fourth Gospel, make the same modification of the text (cf. also Vulg. and AV). Another deviation, the οὐ μὴ εἰσέλθητε, in place of οὐ δύναται ἰδεῖν, may easily be the reflection of the εἰσελθεῖν of v.⁵ Ezra Abbot found 69 similar deviations from the text in 46 different English divines of modern times.

Hilgenfeld and Keim admit that while the Synoptists affirm that John the Baptist was the 'voice of one crying,' Justin might have referred the exclamation to the consciousness of the Baptist by acquaintance with Jn 1²²·²³ and 3²⁸. When, in *Apol.* i. 63, Justin declares that the Jews knew neither the Father nor the Son, he must have had Jn 8¹⁹ and 16³ in his memory.

The various uses of the Prologue in the passages referred to, led even Volkmar to declare that 'the prologue of John is the primordial revelation of the Logos in its immediate majesty, and that the writings of Justin are the first attempts at a rational analysis of the contents of the revelation.' Other and later writers derived these great truths from the Prologue of St. John's Gospel; why should not Justin be allowed to have done the same?*

Albrecht Thoma (*Die Genesis des Joh. Evang.* p. 824) has endeavoured to show that Justin found his idea of the Logos in Philo Judæus, and that he derived nothing from the Gospel, unless it be the identification of Jesus with the incarnation of the Logos. But the objection to this suggestion is, that while the Logos of Philo receives many striking designations, such as 'High Priest,' 'Son,' 'First-Begotten,' etc., Philo never hints at the Messianic idea or the Incarnation. Nothing could be less like the Father of our Lord Jesus Christ than the Philonic God who, by His λόγος, 'eternal reason,' created or sustains the universe (see Reynolds' introd. to Gospel of John in *Pulpit Comm.* p. xxviii).

(*B*) What indications do we find of the existence of the Fourth Gospel between the latest date of Justin and that of the literary activity of Irenæus? (1) HERACLEON is referred to by Irenæus and Hippolytus, by Clemens Alex., and above all by Origen, as a disciple of Valentinus, the great Gnostic of the middle of the century. He is probably referred to by Irenæus as one of the unnamed Gnostics who, with Ptolemæus, helped to divide the Valentinians into two groups (*Ref. Hær.* ii. 4, vi. 35. 29), differing on the question whether the original principle of the universe was a monad or a dyad. He did not write a formal exposition of Valentinus, but a practical exegesis of the Gospels of Luke and John, in which the doctrines of Valentinus were assumed. He writes with extreme reverence for the text of the Gospels, as if they commanded attention on the highest ground. He is one of the earliest to write a commentary on any book of the NT; and from his commentary on the Fourth Gospel, Origen quotes 50 times in his own comm., sometimes accepting Heracleon's views, more frequently contradicting them. Large extracts from the comments on the first, second, fourth, and eighth chapters are thus preserved by Origen (see 'Heracleon' in *Dict. Christ. Biog.* by Salmon). The method of comment is allegorical; and while the historical or natural sense is not rejected, the higher and truer meaning is found in forced analogies. But the point of interest here is, that before Irenæus, and reaching back by Heracleon's personal relations with the celebrated heresiarch to Valentinus himself, this Gospel was esteemed as of prime importance and authority in the view of heretics as well as orthodox. That Justin should not have known this document, becomes almost incredible.

(2) This conclusion grows more certain when we compare with it the testimony of Justin's pupil, TATIAN, who between A.D. 160 and 170 issued his *Discourse to the Greeks*, in which explicit citations are made from Jn 1³·⁵, and also from Jn 1¹ 4²⁴.† After the death of Justin, Tatian held and propagated certain heterodox opinions on the subject of marriage, which he regarded as 'corruption' and whoredom. He repudiated the OT as the record of the Demiurge, in consequence of its implied sanction of polygamy. Eusebius reports that Tatian was the founder of the sect of Encratites. All that

Irenæus states is that Encratites appear to have appealed to Tatian, as holding that Adam could not be saved, seeing that 'in Adam all die.' Eusebius (*HE* iv. 29) refers to a much more important work of Tatian's, which was a patch-work of the evangelia, compiled after a fashion he did not understand, and called τὸ διὰ τεσσάρων.* This document, said Eus., 'is in the possession of some even now.' This passing observation is the first extant reference to the *Diatessaron*, on which much additional light has been thrown in recent times by unexpected discoveries, and by documents the importance of which had been long overlooked. This is not the place to tell the romantic story of the several steps by which the *Diatessaron* to which Eusebius referred has come into our hands. We are amazed at the tenuity and tenacity of the thread of proof on which the conclusion rests that we have before us the interweaving of four distinct Gospels and no others by Tatian, and dating near the middle of the 2nd cent. Seeing that this conclusion carries with it the early and wide circulation at that date of the Fourth Gospel, it naturally excites keen criticism (see *Nineteenth Century*, April 1895). The second reference in Greek antiquity is that of Theodoret (*Hær.* i. 20), Bp. of Cyrus or Cyrrhus in E. Syria (457–8), who attributes the *Diatess.* to Tatian, but condemns it for the omission of the genealogies and the rejection of the evidence that Christ, according to the flesh, was born of the seed of David. Theodoret states that more than 200 copies of this work were found in his little diocese, and that he substituted for them copies of the Four Gospels (see calculations based on this fact in Norton's *Genuineness of Gospels*, ch. 1, touching the extensive distribution of Scripture in the 5th cent.). It appears from this that the Harmony was in all probability written in Syr., which would explain Eusebius' ignorance of its contents. This (as Fuller urges) may account for the blunder made towards the close of the fourth century by Epiphanius (*Hær.* 46), who had got the idea that this document was none other than the 'Gospel according to the Hebrews.' Evidently, neither Eusebius nor Epiphanius had any definite information or actual knowledge of Syr. literature. But Victor, Bp. of Capua (*d.* A.D. 554), came into possession of a codex of NT containing an anonymous harmony of the four Gospels, which he called *Diapente*, and which he was disposed to identify with a 'harmony' made from that of Ammonius of Alexandria, or from that to which Eusebius referred as constructed by Tatian. That which Victor published was a revision in terms of Jerome's Vulg., and is one of the earliest and most valuable MSS of the Vulgate. This codex of the NT Vulg. was conveyed by Boniface to Fulda, and has had bestowed upon it the name *Fuldensis*. As far as the Gospels are concerned, it is practically identical with the Arab. VS of Tatian's Diatessaron which has subsequently come to light. Unlike the description of Tatian's Diat., it commences with Lk 1¹⁻⁴ and contains portions of genealogies which Tatian's did not. These are found to be alterations of the original text, by a careful comparison of the index with the MS. This Latin codex was translated into the Old Saxon dialect in alliterative verse under the name *Héliand*. Another link of interest is the discovery of the Homilies of Aphraates, bishop and abbot of a convent near Mosul (A.D. 336–345). They were written in Syr., and give lengthened extracts from the Diatessaron. Another interesting fragment is a treatise, the *Doctrine of Addai*, which contains the curious Syr.

---

* Kirchhofer (*Quellensammlung*) and Charteris (*Canonicity*) quote a large number of other passages from both the *Apol.* and *Dial.* which reveal greater or less resemblance to passages from every part of the Gospel.

† See Fuller's most elaborate dissertation in *Dict. of Christ. Biog.*, as well as that of Donaldson (*Hist. of Ch. Doct. and Lit.* vol. iii. pp. 1–60). Both these writers carefully analyze the 'Discourse' and summarize its teachings; Fuller gives the remarkable passage in which the Fourth Gospel is quoted.

* Salmon (*Introd. to NT⁵*, p. 74), on the authority of Mahaffy, shows that διὰ τεσσάρων may be a musical term incorrectly transferred to literature, and means a harmony of four, as διὰ πασῶν a concord of the octave, διὰ πέντε of the first and fifth notes.

legend of the Saviour's letter to king Abgarus of Edessa; and this refers to the Harmony called Ditourion = Diatessaron, which was used and read in the Syriac churches. We learn from other Syr. documents in the 12th cent., on the authority of Dionysius Bar-Salibi, that Ephraem Syrus, a deacon of Edessa, who died A.D. 373, had written a commentary on the Diatessaron of Tatian in the last ten years of his life (see Lightfoot's discussion of this belated testimony of Bar-Salibi, *Contemp. Review*, 1877). It is an extraordinary circumstance that two forms of this commentary are found to exist in the Armenian language. These have been collated and translated into Latin by Aucher and Moesinger. Tatian is not mentioned, but Ephraem comments upon one passage after another of the Gospels, and not infrequently upon a text which is a blending of two or more Gospels.

Zahn (1881) and Wace (see *Expos.* 2nd ser. ii. 1, 128, 193; iv. 161, 294) have given a careful digest of all these passages, and the text on which Ephraem appears to have been commenting. The commentary appears to have been written in Syriac. Hamlyn Hill, assisted by Armitage Robinson, has, by comparison of Moesinger's Lat. and the Arm. text, reached a very close approximation to the words of Ephraem. Zahn has been able to arrange the text of the Diatessaron in one hundred sections, with explanatory and textual criticism, collation of the Lat., Syr., and Arm. Vulgates, and the codices A, B, etc. But a remarkable addition to the *apparatus criticus* has been romantically made by the examination of two *Arabic* MSS of the Diatessaron itself: one brought from Egypt to the Vatican Library in 1719, by Assemani, known by the title of *No. XIV.*; the other, also brought from Egypt to Ciasca, of the Vatican Library, and practically a repetition of No. XIV., but with important differences in detail. The collated text has been translated into Eng., and edited by Hamlyn Hill (*Earliest Life of Christ*, 1894; see also Hill, *Dissertation on Gosp. Harmony of S. Ephraem*, 1896; and Rendel Harris, *Fragments of Com. of Ephrem Syrus*, 1895). These translations leave no valid doubt that we have the text before us on which Ephraem commented, and which the Arab. MS avers is a translation from Syriac of the long-lost Diatessaron. A large portion of St. John's Gospel is included in the Diatessaron—a fact which establishes, if it is Tatian's collation of the four Gospels, not only the existence of the Fourth, but the esteem in which it was held between A.D. 150 and 160. The doubt cherished by many about the 'Memoirs' of Justin must therefore be abandoned. Harnack's judgment in the *Encycl. Brit.* (1888, xxiii. 81) is to the same effect. Watkins justly observes, 'the Diatessaron of Tatian is the key to the Memoirs of Justin' (*Bamp. Lect.* 71), and it certainly bridges the gulf between the literary phraseology of Justin and Irenæus.

(3) The MURATORIAN FRAGMENT, one of the earliest attempts to give a list of the books of NT, not only includes the Fourth Gospel, but, in legendary fashion, describes the circumstances under which the Apostle John was urged by Andrew and other apostles to prepare his narrative with their recognition and sanction (*recognoscentibus cunctis*). This testimony is extremely important, but its value depends on its date. The writer says, 'Hermas has very recently in our days written the "Shepherd" while Pius his brother was Bishop of Rome.' The earliest dates for the commencement and close of the episcopate of Pius I. are from A.D. 139-154, the latest from A.D. 141-156. It has been customary to say that the limit of the date (*nuperrime temporibus nostris*) cannot be put later than A.D. 170 (so Döllinger,

Lightfoot, and Westcott). But Salmon * (*Introd. to NT*, and art. in Smith, *Dict. of Biog.* vol. iii.) judges differently of this limit, on the ground that the great change in the position of the Bishops of Rome with and after Pius had so long passed as to be forgotten when the unknown author penned these words, and that we cannot assume a date earlier than about A.D. 200. One of the most weighty features of the proof that the Gospel was at that moment widely prized and regarded universally in the Church as the work of the Apostle John, is the reference to the *First Epistle*, which the writer treats as an appendix to the Gospel, adding that John 'professes that he was not only an eye-witness, but also a hearer and writer (*scriptorem . . . per ordinem* 'a historian') of all the wonderful things of the Lord.' The testimony of the Fragment thus confirms the conclusion already reached by the testimonies of Theophilus, Irenæus, Tatian, Justin, and Clement of Alexandria.

(4) Our evidence may be carried still further backwards by what remains of the words or life of PAPIAS, Bp. of Hierapolis. The fragments of the works of this early Christian writer were, for the most part, preserved by Eusebius (*HE* iii. 36, 39).† He is there said to have been bishop of the Church of Hierapolis, and a contemporary of Polycarp the disciple of John. It is more than probable that he was born between A.D. 60 and 70, and wrote his exposition in five books about A.D. 135. The estimate which Eusebius expresses of his mental character in different pages is contradictory. In one place he is called an eminently small man, in derogation, perhaps, of some extravagantly chiliastic prophecies which he is said to have referred to the lips of our Lord. Elsewhere Eusebius describes Papias as 'well skilled in all kinds of learning, and mighty in the Scriptures.' His importance to us lies in the probable source of his information and the nature of his written work. This last appears to have consisted of comments upon the words, miracles, and prophecies of Christ, such as he was eager to obtain from those who had known the Lord ('the truth'), and he mentions 'the elders Andrew, Peter, John, Philip, Thomas, and James, Matthew and other "disciples"' as authorities, whose words came to him by direct speech of friends of his who had known the apostles; and he adds 'what Aristion and the elder John say (λέγουσιν),' as though these elders had survived the rest, and were still available for information.

It is a vain wish that we had more than the few hundred words which Eusebius has preserved. With only these fragments, it is misleading and arbitrary to argue from the silence of Papias as to what he knew of the four Gospels or the Epistles of St. Paul. The passage preserved by Eusebius is taken from the fourth book of the *Expositions* of Papias,—Irenæus having informed us that Papias had written five such books,—in which he confirms his interpretations by his own reminiscences of the speech of those that had known the apostles. It is worthy of special regard that the earliest witnesses and disciples of our Lord are cited in the Eusebian fragment of Papias in the very order in which they are referred to in the Fourth Gospel. Eusebius does not cite passages from Papias in proof of the authenticity of the Fourth Gospel. He adopts this course upon the principle which he follows everywhere, viz. to mention very little concerning the entirely undisputed books, but to bring confirmation from various sources of those which had, upon any ground, been rejected or dis-

* Similarly, Zahn and Harnack.
† The only other trace of the book, 'The Exposition of the Oracles of our Lord,' is in an inventory of the books in possession of the cathedral of Nismes, dated A.D. 1218.

puted. In like manner he makes no reference to any of the quotations indisputably made by Irenæus or Origen from the Gospel. The silence here is a proof that Papias made abundant use of the Gospel rather than the reverse. The references to Papias' use of 1 Peter and 1 John support a further suggestion, that Papias was familiar with the Gospels of Mark (the interpreter of Peter) and John the Divine. Eusebius does not refrain (in his *Chronicon ad Olymp.* 220) from speaking of 'Papias the Hieropolitan, and Polycarp Bp. of Smyrna, as being known to be *hearers* of John the Divine and Apostle, as is declared by Irenæus and others.'

This particular passage raises no question about John 'the elder,' of whose existence there is no proof except this solitary comment of Eusebius upon an obscure fragment of Papias. The present writer has discussed the subject fully in Introd. to Gospel in *Pulpit Com.* ; see also Salmon, art. 'Joannes Presbyteros,' in *Dict. Chr. Biog.* ; Farrar in *Expos.* (1881) 2nd ser. ii. 321 ; Haussleiter in *Theol. Lit.-blatt*, Sept. 25, 1896 ; and Gwatkin in *Contemp. Rev.*, Feb. 1897 (cf. *Expos. Times*, viii. 1897, pp. 338, 416). Westcott, Lightfoot, and Gwatkin hold to the Eusebian suggestion. Delff advocated the existence of a disciple not John the Apostle, but possibly John the Presbyter, who is credited with the authorship of the Gospel, who was the disciple whom Jesus loved, and who knew more of the esoteric teaching than any of the Twelve. But the entire story of the second John is due, as many hold, to the inaccurate interpretation by Eusebius of the saying of Papias.

(5) In conjunction with Papias, it is well here to recount the testimony of POLYCARP, Bp. of Smyrna, who may be safely credited with carrying the evidence for the existence of the Gospel back to the lifetime of St. John. The letter of Irenæus to Florinus, preserved by Eusebius, *HE* v. 20, is charged with proof of his own personal remembrances of Polycarp. Irenæus recounts his ways, his 'personal intimacy with John and with the rest who had known the Lord.' 'The miracles and doctrine of the Lord were told by Polycarp, in consistency with the *Holy Scriptures*, as he received them from the eye-witnesses of the Doctrine of Salvation.' These 'Holy Scriptures' to which Irenæus refers were no other than the Gospels,—including the Fourth,—from which he made hundreds of citations in his great work. The historical character of Polycarp's visit to Rome, and of his martyrdom, has withstood all criticism. The memorable exclamation, 'Eighty and six years have I served Christ,' limits the interval between the martyrdom and birth of Polycarp. The painstaking researches of Waddington (independently confirmed by Lightfoot) give A.D. 155 as the date of the martyrdom, and therefore A.D. 69 as that of the birth, and possibly the baptism, of this venerable link between the apostles and the subapostolic Church. This would allow for Polycarp's having attained thirty years before the death of John. It is almost impossible to believe that Irenæus blundered so extravagantly as not to have found out, in the strength of his vigorous manhood, whether it was St. John himself, or another, of whom Polycarp spoke to him, in days so well remembered. The brief Epistle of Polycarp to the Philippians contains an unmistakable citation of 1 Jn 4[2.3] : 'For every one who does not confess that Jesus Christ has come in the flesh is Antichrist, and whoso does not confess the testimony of the Cross is of the devil.' The hypothesis of Volkmar, that the author of the 1st Ep. was quoting from Polycarp, is surely discredited by the assurance that Papias also made use of 1 Jn. The authenticity of Polycarp's letter has been placed beyond question by the researches of Lightfoot (*Contemp. Review*, 1877, and *Apost. Fathers*, pt. II. vols. i. and iii.). Dale, in his *Living Christ and Four Gospels*, developed a striking argument from the absence of mysticism and the lack of originality displayed by Polycarp, in addition to the fact that John, whom he knew, must have written the Gospel which he accepted, and taught his disciples to regard as Holy Scripture. Even the contrast between the tone, the teaching, and the chronology of the Synoptics, and the Fourth Gospel, certainly strengthens the conclusion. This contrast has been greatly exaggerated, but nothing is more likely to have prevented a widespread hesitation as to the authenticity of the Gospel, on account of this contrast, than the assurance of such a man as Polycarp.

6. The testimonies available from CLEMENS ROMANUS and BARNABAS are handicapped by their own antiquity. This is peculiarly the case with Barnabas, in the opinion of hostile critics. But Keim has urged that Barnabas is saturated with the ideas of the Fourth Gospel.* If this can be sustained, it must share, with corresponding features in the writings of St. Paul, the author of He, and others, the explanation that, *pari passu* with the Synoptic tradition, there had from the first been widely diffused a tradition of the teaching of the beloved disciple. Such diffusion must have urged the apostle in his latest years to put into fixed form his undying memories, and greatly facilitated its acceptance in the earliest years of the 2nd cent. There are, indeed, phrases which reflect the influence of Johannine teaching in the *First* Epistle of Clemens Romanus. Thus, among others, ch. xlix., 'He that hath love in Christ, let him do the commandments of Christ' (cf. Jn 14[15, 23], 1 Jn 5[1-3]), and 'Jesus Christ our Lord gave His blood for us, by the will of God, and His flesh for our flesh, and His soul for our souls' (Jn 6[51] and 15[13]).

The *Second* (so-called) *Epistle of Clement*, which may be accepted, with Lightfoot, as 'an ancient homily of an unknown author,' say about A.D. 150, betrays no certain reference to either St. Paul or St. John. Still, note the tone of ch. ix. : 'If Christ the Lord, who saved us, being first spirit became flesh (ἐγένετο σάρξ), and so called us, in like manner in this flesh, we shall receive our reward. Let us then love one another.' We are certainly reminded here of Jn 1[14] and the spirit of the first Ep., or, what seems more probable, we recognize the diffusion on all sides of those aspects of our Lord's teaching which we refer to Johannine memories.

(7) IGNATIUS.—The great controversy touching the genuineness of the Ignatian letters may be regarded as having now terminated in favour of the Vossian Shorter Gr. Text, and the triumphant refutation by Lightfoot of the hypothesis of Cureton that the three short forms of the Syr. VS of the Epp. to the Romans, to Polycarp, and to the Ephesians are the sole genuine nucleus of the entire literature. If these seven letters, vouched by the Ep. of Polycarp to the Philippians to be genuine, can be regarded as the writing of the Martyr on his way to Rome, certainly not later than A.D. 116, and more probably A.D. 109, we have indubitable traces of the Fourth Gospel having already found its way from Ephesus to Antioch when the memory of St. John must have been fragrant throughout Asia Minor.

A strongly Johannine phrase, not without a special difficulty of its own, appears in the letter to the *Magnesians*, viii. 2 : 'There is one God, who manifested Himself through Jesus Christ, His Son, who is His Logos, proceeding from σιγή, who in all

---

* Charteris, *Canonicity*, quotes twenty passages which suggest some possible familiarity with Johannine phraseology.

respects was well pleasing to Him that sent Him.' Lightfoot has shown how this difficult term σιγή was used in the 1st cent., and thinks that Ignatius had a leaning to the early pre-Valentin. Gnosis of the period. Whatever be the text, whether we should read, 'proceeding from σιγή,' or 'not proceeding from σιγή,' a reference to the Fourth Gospel is obvious. In the letter to the *Romans*, vii. 2, we read, 'the living water speaking within me (or, probably truer text, 'flowing, bubbling up'), says, "Come to the Father"; I take not delight in the nourishment of corruption, nor the pleasures of this life: I desire the bread of God, which is the flesh of Jesus Christ (of the seed of David), and desire the drink of God, which is His blood, which is incorruptible love.' In this passage we have reference to Jn 4¹⁴ and 6⁵⁵·³²·³³. In the letter to the *Philadelphians*, vii. 1, ix. 1, there are further echoes, and Jn 10⁷ is expressively referred to.

Before passing from this period, we may refer to the *Acta Martyrii Polycarpi*, the date of which shortly follows the martyrdom, and 'the letter of the Churches of Lugdunum and Vienne' preserved by Eusebius, and presumably written by Irenæus, who was the bearer of it (*HE* v. 1): 'Then were fulfilled the words spoken by the Lord, that "the period should come when he that killeth you will think that he offers service to God,"' which is almost a verbal citation from Jn 16².

(8) *The Epistle to Diognetus* was once included among the writings of Justin. Whilst by some it has even been attributed to Scaliger, it is assigned by Nitzsch to A.D. 110–125, by Westcott to A.D. 117, by Bunsen to 135, and by Hilgenfeld to a much later period in the century. It does not therefore supply any valid evidence. Its early origin cannot, however, be disproved, and we find in it the remarkable phrase, apparently from Jn 17¹⁴ 'They (Christians) are not of this world.' In ch. x. there is a nearly accurate quotation of Jn 3¹⁶, and a striking interpretation of Jn 1¹ etc. applied to the functions of the Christ. There is also a reference to 1 Jn 4¹⁷ in the same chapter.

(9) In the *Testaments of the XII Patriarchs*, a Jewish Christian puts into the mouths of the founders of the Jewish race Christian counsels and consolations. Sinker, who edits and translates it for the Ante-Nicene Lib., places it at the end of the 1st or beginning of the 2nd cent. Many now regard it as a Jewish work edited for Christian readers. The Saviour is spoken of as 'Light of the world,' 'the Son of God,' 'the only Son,' 'the Lamb of God,' and 'the Spirit of truth'; 'sin unto death' (cf. 1 Jn 5¹⁶) is referred to ; 'eating of the tree of life' (Rev 2⁷)—all phrases which reveal the presence of the Johannine thought and expression.

(10) *The Didaché of the Twelve Apostles* may prove to be the most ancient of the post-apost. literature. It is referred to by Clement of Alexandria, who cites it as 'Scripture.' The simplicity of the style and the entire absence of any reference to the Ebionite or Gnostic heresies prove that it must have been antecedent to Irenæus or Justin.

The Ep. of Barnabas, which may have been written between A.D. 100 and 120, contains a confessed expansion of the earlier portions of the *Didaché*. A comparison of these related passages (see Bryennios' ed. of the *Didaché* and Schaff's *Oldest Church Manual*, where they are placed side by side, p. 228 ff.) has convinced almost all Eng. and Amer. scholars, as well as Zahn, Funk, Langen, of the priority of the *Didaché*.

The date of Hermas' *Shepherd* is very variously estimated, but, as in the case of Barnabas, what is common to the *Didaché* and the *Shepherd* is most certainly earlier than the latter (Schaff, p. 233).

We are brought by the *Didaché* into the midst of the movements of the early Church. It contains quotations from the Gospels of Mt and Lk. Though we cannot say that the writer had the Fourth Gospel in his hands, yet Harnack admits the striking connexion between the Eucharistic prayers of chs. ix. and x. and Jn 6 and 17.

John (1¹⁴) used the remarkable word ἐσκήνωσεν to denote the dwelling in (with) us of the 'Word made flesh': see here *Did.* x. 2. Christ, '*I am the true Vine*, and my *Father* is the husbandman': cf. *Did.* ix. 2, 'We give thanks to Thee, our Father, for the Holy Vine of Thy servant David, which Thou hast made known through Thy servant Jesus.' Cf. also Jn 15¹⁵ and 17²⁶ with *Did.* ix. 2, 3 and x. 2. There are, moreover, striking resemblances between 1 Jn 2⁵·¹⁷ and *Did.* x. 5, 6. Much of this teaching obviously points to a community familiar with Johannine teaching.

(11) The use which HERMAS is supposed to have made of the *four* Gospels, and his adoption of the phraseology of the *Fourth*, have been diligently investigated by Dr. C. Taylor in his *Witness of Hermas to the Four Gospels*, 1892. The argument turns on the special style and method of Hermas. He translates into some synonymous or symbolic expression ideas differently phrased by Clemens II. *Ancient Homily*, the *Didaché*, or *ad Diognetum*. Thus in the *Shepherd* ἀγγελία ἀγαθή takes the place of εὐαγγέλιον. In *Vision* iii. and *Similit*. ix. the earliest suggestion of necessary fourfoldness of the Gospels corresponds with the fourfoldness with which all the universe is compacted [a theory found in Plato and Arist. *Nic. Eth.* I. x. 11, τετράγωνος ἄνευ ψόγου]. The four cherubic figures, the four pillars on which the Christ is seated, the Old and New Gate into the Symbolic Tower, are all supposed by Taylor to have been borrowed by Irenæus from Hermas, rather than the other way. The process by which the writer establishes scores of references by Hermas to the Fourth Gospel is a subtle one, and does not carry conviction, except perhaps as to the existence of the tetrad of Gospels a generation before Irenæus wrought out the comparison.

External evidences of the use of the Fourth Gospel *by the enemies of Christianity and by well-known leaders of Gnostic heresies* must not be passed over in this rapid recital. We will, in reviewing this evidence, commence with the later testimonies, and press upwards through the century.

(1) CELSUS was probably no other than Celsus the friend of Lucian, an Epicurean. He was the author of the λόγος ἀληθής to which Origen replied in the 3rd cent. He was a bitter enemy of the Christian faith, but from Origen's great work it appears that he was intimately acquainted with the four Gospels. He lived about A.D. 178, and thus shows not only that these works were beginning to be recognized as of paramount authority, but that they were known as such by heathen controversialists. Origen (c. *Celsum*, i. 50) tells us that Celsus accused Christians of believing that 'the Son of God is come down from heaven' (see Jn 3³¹ 8²³). In i. 67 Origen quotes from Celsus, 'Thou hast made no manifestation, although they challenged thee in the temple to exhibit some unmistakable sign that thou wert Son of God' (cf. Jn 2¹⁸ 10²⁴). In i. 70 Celsus objected that the body of a God could not be thirsting at the well of Jacob, or eating broiled fish and honeycomb (Jn 4⁶ᶠ, Lk 24⁴²). ii. 31 says that Celsus objected that Christians are in error who 'declare that the Logos is Son of God, when they present no pure and holy Logos, but a degraded man punished by scourging and crucifixion. In ii. 36 Celsus referred to the *ichor* flowing in the veins of the crucified; which is a reflection of Jn 19³⁴·³⁵. The Fourth Gospel must have been widely diffused for a heathen writer about A.D. 178 to have made this use of it.

(2) We possess only a Lat. tr. of the *Recognitiones* of the PSEUDO-CLEMENT, made by Rufinus. The *Homilies* are probably the more ancient work, and are extant in Greek. The date at which this Ebionite work was produced cannot be finally determined, but the best judgment throws it into the middle of the *second* century. Hilgenfeld in 1850 declined to see any quotation from the Fourth Gospel. Lagarde, however, gives 15 supposed references to it. Thus, *Hom.* iii. 52, 'The true

Prophet hath sworn "I am the gate (πύλη) of life," whoso entereth by me, entereth into the life'; and again, 'My sheep hear my voice' (cf. Jn 10⁹ and 27). In *Hom.* xi. 26, 'Except ye be born again of or in living water (ὕδατι ζῶντι) unto the name of the Father, Son, Holy Spirit, ye shall not enter into the kingdom of the heavens' (cf. Jn 3⁵). In 1853 Dressel discovered the xixth *Homily*, where, in ch. 22, occurs an almost verbal quotation of Jn 9². ³. Hilgenfeld yielded to this evidence, which makes Baur's date for the Gospel finally incredible. There is, doubtless, little agreement between the spirit and teaching of the Gospel and the Clementines, which makes the evidence still more remarkable.

(3) MONTANUS and Montanism also suffer as evidence by the uncertainty as to their date. The disproportionate space given to this theme in Eusebius, *HE* v., does not clearly fasten the rise of this Phrygian heresy to a distinct period, though giving the names and a sketch of the writers, Miltiades, Apollonius, etc., who contended with it in the reign of Commodus, 180 ff. Some have fixed on 140—Gieseler on 150—others 157, others 180. Salmon looks to the 3rd cent. for the origin of the heresy. If the earlier date should be finally established, the evidence becomes clear that John's Gospel must have been taken as a record of the valedictory discourse, for Montanus chose therefrom the term *Paracletus*, 'the other Comforter,' as referring to no other than to *himself*; actually claiming that our Lord prophesied his (Montanus') appearance in the fulness of time. Theodoret also says that Montanus made a similar use of the terms Λόγος and Νυμφίος.

(4) MARCION admittedly makes no reference or allusion to the Fourth Gospel, but Tertullian (*adv. Marc.* iv. 3) shows that Marcion uses Gal 2 to justify his rejection of gospels supposed to be apostolic, because they *were* apostolic, not because they were not so. Tertullian (*de Carne Christi*, ch. iii.), while arguing against the hyperspiritualism of Marcion, says, 'If thou hadst not rejected the writings opposed to thy system, the Gospel of John would be there to convince thee.' Surely the Fourth Gospel is more explicit than are the Synoptics in asserting the full humanity of the Lord Jesus. Marcion reached Rome in A.D. 140, and we are thus allowed to assume an earlier and wide diffusion of the various gospels which he rejected and mutilated to serve the purposes of his own system of philosophy.

(5) VALENTINUS, the poet-philosopher of Gnostic theosophy, with his disciples Ptolemæus and Heracleon, Theodotus and Marcus, formed an important school of thought, pervading the 2nd cent. He appeared in Rome between A.D. 135-160, having been before this in Alexandria, and is said to have died in Cyprus A.D. 160. Tertullian tells us that he made use of the whole of the *instrumentum*, *i.e.* books of NT (*de Præscr. Hær.* 38). Irenæus, about A.D. 182, wrote his great work (*adv. Hær.*) in part to meet and refute the eclectic errors of Valentinus and his school. Hippolytus wrote his *Refutation of all Heresies* in the same spirit, and they both quote from the master and his disciples, not always accurately discriminating them. Now, as we have seen (cf. p. 697ᵃ), Heracleon [said by Clem. Alex. to have been well known to Valentinus] composed a comm. upon considerable portions of John's Gospel, extracts from which are preserved by Origen. These passages show that a disciple of Valentinus treated the Fourth Gospel as of divine authority. Ptolemæus also, in a letter of his addressed to Flora and preserved by Epiphanius (*adv. Hær.* xxxiii. 3-7), quotes Jn 1¹·³ and Jn 12²⁷. Indeed, Irenæus positively assures us that Valentinus and his disciples 'abundantly make use of the Gospel'; and Hippolytus confirms this by a perverted use of Jn 10⁸, which he attributes to Valentinus himself,—with the formula φησί rather than φασίν,—and cites also, as from Valentinus, the Johannine phrase, 'the Prince of this world,' 16¹¹. But the entire system of 'Æons,' and their 'Syzygies' or couples, which make up the *Ogdoad* and the *Pleroma*, is marked by the use of such terms as Πατήρ, Λόγος, Φῶς, Ζωή, 'Αλήθεια, Μονογενής, Παράκλητος, with others; it is clear that this cannot be accidental: either 'John' built upon Valentinus, or Valentinus, finding these terms in a book believed to be of sacred authority, utilized them for his own purposes. Putting the simple, natural, and religious use of these terms in the prologue of the Gospel and elsewhere, over against the highly technical and theosophical use of them in the system of Valentinus, it becomes clear that the heresiarch himself was familiar with the Fourth Gospel. In this conclusion, Bleek, Keim, Bunsen agree, as against Davidson and *Sup. Rel.* Thoma (p. 822) admits that the dependence of the Valentinian school upon the Gospel is not chronologically or dogmatically impossible, though indemonstrable.

(6) BASILIDES and the Basilidians. Basilides, whose work and system preceded that of Valentinus, both at Alexandria and Rome, is named by numerous writers—Epiphanius, Jerome (*de Viris Ill.* ch. xxi.), Hippolytus (vii. 8), and Eusebius (*HE* iv. 7) who places his period in the days of Hadrian (117-138) and speaks with intense abhorrence of his impieties and his inventions and asceticism. He does not refer to his doctrine. Hippolytus speaks of the claim made by the followers of Basilides that he had received special instructions from Matthias, one of the disciples of our Lord (Ac 1²⁴). Whether there may or may not be any truth in this report, at any rate it gives early antiquity to their father and founder. Epiphanius (*Hær.* xxiii. 1-7, xxiv. 1-9) attributes to B. a period of activity in Antioch before his appearance in Alexandria or Rome. If Basilides quoted from the Fourth Gospel, the origin of that precious document is thrown back to the earliest days of the century, and, as has already been urged, into the lifetime of the apostle. Now it is very probable that Hippolytus, in writ-

ing his great book (*Ref. Hær.* vii. 22), had the work of Basilides open before him, and that he referred to the master and to his school by his accustomed method of citation, φησί for the former, while he used φασίν, or κατ' αὐτούς or λέγουσι for the latter. If the whole of this passage is read (see Eng. tr. in *A.N. Lib.*), little doubt can remain in any candid mind that Hippolytus was quoting two passages as cited by Basilides himself from Jn 1⁹ and 2⁴. (See also Matthew Arnold, *God and the Bible*, p. 268; Mangold-Bleek, *Einleitung*, 265; Watkins, *Bamp. Lectures*, p. 365).

(7) The Oriental Gnostics, Ophites, Naassenes, Peratæ (Bunsen's *Hippolytus and his Age*, see *Introd. to St. John*, xli. 11, by Reynolds), made, according to Hippolytus, abundant use of the Fourth Gospel. We cannot depend on his citations as representing the verbal use of the Gospel made by any specific section or leader of these extreme dualists. So great was their antagonism to the OT that they took the very name of the serpent, *nahash* (Heb.) or *ophis* (Greek), as their ideal of intelligence and emancipation. What recent investigation has shown is, not that we must carry down the Pastoral Epistles or Colossians or the Fourth Gospel till after the days of Marcion for proof of the prevalence of these dualistic ideas, but that ideas of the kind were prevalent as early as the activity of St. Paul, who combated them at Corinth and Ephesus, and that the author of the Apoc. encountered them at Thyatira and elsewhere in Asia. Godet has treated the 'Christ party' in the Corinthian Church as those who sharply separated between '*Jesus*' and 'the Christ'—who could accept the heavenly Christ, but repudiate the genuine incarnation, crucifixion, or resurrection; who could even anathematize Jesus, and claim special knowledge of, and union with, the Christ. The existence of such a party reveals the presence of these Gnostic tendencies in the middle of the 1st century. Consequently, we have no occasion to wait till the middle or end of the century to find the occasion for the protest against dualism discoverable in the Fourth Gospel.

There is one exception to the uniform result of these researches into the religious ideas of the century. A shadowy sect or people, called by Epiphanius 'Αλογοι [*i.e.* persons destitute of sound sense], *Hær.* II. i. 57, had manifested some antagonism to the Logos-Gospel. Epiph. is amused with the *pun* which he has perpetrated to their discredit, and hopes that it will stick to them. The objections which they raised were not of a philosophical or religious character, but had to do with chronological difficulties which the number of passovers suggests, the close association in which the highest dignity of Christ is placed with His presence at a wedding feast, and, further, the absurd statement that the Gospel had been produced, not by the disciple whom Jesus loved, but by *Cerinthus*. Tradition certainly has made John and Cerinthus contemporary, and this tradition is confirmed by the supposition of these 'stupid' people, that the Gospel had been written by Cerinthus. The views of Cerinthus leaned towards Ebionitism; the whole teaching of the Fourth Gospel is that the Christ came down from heaven.

It is with amazement we read in Reuss, *History of NT*, p. 233, 'The unspeakable pains that has been taken to collect external evidence only shows that there is none in the proper sense of the term.' We do not wish to accept evidence that would not be accepted elsewhere, but the proofs of the existence of the Fourth Gospel seem as cogent as those that are advanced for any books of the NT, to say nothing of the most celebrated patristic or classical masterpieces.

Our conclusion is that we discern the first indications of its appearance in the wide diffusion of Johannine ideas in the epistles of Barnabas and Clement, Ignatius and Polycarp, the Epistle to Diognetus, and the *Didaché*. We have pseudepigraphical literature like the Test. of XII Patriarchs and the Clementines, early heretics and dualists like Basilides and Valentinus quoting from its pages and falsely utilizing its authority. Nay, we actually find some of them commenting at length upon considerable portions of the Gospel. There is not only abundance of such evidence outside the pale of the Church, but the celebrated Christian philosopher, Justin Martyr, in quoting from 'The Memoirs of the Apostles and those that followed them,' has preserved a large number of the apothegms of Jesus; and that these must have been taken from the Gospel becomes almost demonstrated by the romantic discovery, not only of Tatian's *Address to the Greeks*, but also of the Diatessaron, where the largest part of the Fourth Gospel is interwoven with the other three. Within 20 years of this date we have the clear testimonies of Irenæus, Theophilus of Antioch, Clement of Alexandria, and Tertullian, and then that of Athenagoras, and the Muratorian Canon, frequently cementing the fragmentary relics of the century. Even Keim admits that the evidence is as strong as for any other of the Gospels. Not one of these reminiscences or citations was placed where it has been found for the sake of the modern apologist. It is simply *marvellous* that the elements of the testimony should thus have been drawn together from such a number of sources within the compass of a century.

III. CANONICITY OF THE FOURTH GOSPEL. —There is sufficient evidence that this Gospel is among the least disputed components of the earliest collection of documents. The Apoc., 2 P, 2 and 3 Jn, are missing from the Peshiṭta. In the Old Lat. belonging to the 2nd cent., He, 2 P, and Ja are wanting. The Mur. Canon does not contain a reference to Hebrews, unless it be identified with the Letter to the Alexandrians; and the reference to 2 and 3 Jn is dubious. The document is incomplete or mutilated, and does not contain explicit mention of the Gospels of Mt or Mk. Yet all these early indications of a list of NT books contain the Gospel of John. The same may be said of Origen's list (184–253). And Eusebius' Canon, which placed among the *antilegomena* Ja, 2 P, Jude, 2 and 3 Jn, and reckoned the Apoc. spurious (νόθην), contained the Fourth Gospel. The earliest codices of the 4th cent. (B, א), the Canon of Athanasius and all those of the ecclesiastical councils, also include it. These facts establish widespread and ancient conviction as to the sacred character and authority of this document.

IV. INTERNAL EVIDENCE FOR THE AUTHORSHIP. —The familiar process by which the question of the authorship of the Fourth Gospel is limited and decided must now be briefly recounted in the light of the fresh treatment it has received at the hands of Wendt, Ewald, Weizsäcker, Beyschlag, Cross, Delff, and Sanday.

a. The author, whoever he may have been, was essentially a Jew.—From beginning to end he is saturated with Heb. and OT ideas, though they are illumined from within by the new and heavenly light which broke upon him through direct contact with Jesus.

i. The inner sources and main tendencies of the author's thought are to be found in the OT; and his quotations from it in independent freedom, even from the current Gr. VSS, are hardly now in dispute. The whole argument of the Prologue is a prophetic foreshortening of the history of 'His own,' and their age-long refusal to admit to the full the highest revelation of the Eternal. Note also the reference to the hope of the Prophet who should make all things clear, and to the Elijah of the new dispensation (1^{21} 4^{25}), our Lord's zeal for the sanctity of the temple (2^{13-20}), his familiarity with OT history (3^{14}), the ascription to Jesus by John the Baptist of the function of the Bridegroom of the true Israel, an idea which frequently appears in ancient oracles (Jer 2^2, Ezk 16^8, Hos $2^{19.\ 20}$). The writer's references to the feasts of the Jews, the passovers (chs. 2, 6, 12, 18), the unnamed feast (ch. 5) which may or may not be a passover, the feast of tabernacles (ch. 7), the feast of dedication (ch. 10), show the region of his religious ideas. He alludes to the special ceremonial of the feast of tabernacles in the pouring of water and illumination of the temple. The same conclusion may be drawn

from his numerous references to Moses (1^{17} 5^{45} 7^{22}) and Abraham (ch. 8); from the great authority attributed to the law, and even from the verbal criticism of the Psalms (ch. 10); from the declaration that 'the Scriptures cannot be broken'; and especially from the fourteen passages quoted from OT. *Five* of these are attributed to our Lord, *seven* are made by the Evangelist, *two* by other speakers (see Turpie, *Old Test. in the New*; Westcott, Introduction in *Speaker's Comm.* p. xiii; Sanday, *Expositor*, March 1892, p. 178 ff.). Four of these agree with the accurate tr. in the LXX. Some, however, are in closer agreement with the Heb. against the LXX. Thus Jn 19^{37} 'They shall look on him whom they pierced' (=Zec 12^{10}) instead of 'insulted.' This tr. is found also in Rev 1^7, and is a curious link of linguistic correspondence between the Gospel and Apoc. It is found also in Justin, and in the versions of Theod., Symm., and Aquila. This does not necessarily imply that the author was utilizing his personal knowledge of Heb., but that more accurate translations of Zec than that of LXX existed. Cf. with this Jn 6^{45} (=Is 54^{13}); and especially 13^{18} (=Ps 41^9) 'He that eateth bread with me has lifted up *his heel* against me.' Here the Gospel stands alone, the four other extant Gr. VSS differing from each other. The passage 12^{40}, quoted accurately from LXX, where this version fairly represents Heb. in Mt and Ac, is different from both authorities in our Gospel. There is no case where this Gospel agrees with LXX against the Hebrew. These peculiarities indicate knowledge of the original Scriptures. Besides these phenomena of translation, let it be observed that the author is acquainted with a majority of the OT books, the historical books, Psalms, Proverbs, and both parts of Isaiah. He is familiar with the history of Abraham, Jacob, Moses, and David, with the brazen serpent, with circumcision, with the manna in the wilderness, and with OT similitude and doctrine.

ii. A point upon which the opponents of the Johannine authorship have laid much emphasis is the writer's use of the term 'the Jews,' as of a hostile party from whom he was separated, *e.g.* 'the purifying of the Jews' (2^6), 'the passover of the Jews' (2^{13}), 'a feast of the Jews' (5^1 6^4), 'the manner of the Jews is to bury' (19^{40}). But the writer is here conveying no reproach, but explaining to Gentiles events of his early life. Doubtless 'the Jews' are discriminated from the ὄχλος of Galilæans as hostile to Jesus, but the writer calls special attention to Nicodemus, a ruler of the Jews, to Joseph, and to those of οἱ ἴδιοι who received Him, as well as to the πολλοί who 'believed on Him.' He says that Jesus made more disciples in Judæa than John (4^1), and in a most emphatic way that Jesus recognized that σωτηρία is from the Jews. Cf. the difficult passage (4^{43-45}), where Jesus is said to regard the land of Judæa as 'his own country.' Even ch. 5, which discloses the enmity of 'the Jews' to our Lord's interpretation of the Sabbath (cf. ch. 9), is penetrated throughout with the Jewish ideas of the Sabbath, of the Scriptures, and of Moses. The dramatic episodes of chs. 7–10 reveal great antagonism on the part of the mob in Jerus. and the Jewish authorities to the teaching and mandate of Jesus, but the conversations display the author's intimate knowledge of Jewish law, alike of the Sabbath and of circumcision (7^{23}), and the Jewish idea of the διασπορά. And these three or four chapters are replete with assurances that 'many believed on him,' while 8^{31} speaks of 'the Jews that had believed him.'

Again, when Jesus speaks of '*their* law' and '*your* law,' which Pharisees and Sadducees had misinterpreted, it is as one who is bringing to their memory what they and not He had forgotten.

Moreover, not infrequently, by the term 'the Jews' the writer evidently means to denote technically the ruling powers in State and Church, the Sanhedrin in its pride, in opposition to the pilgrims from Galilee or from the 'Dispersion.'

One passage from the 'Jewish' Gospel of Mt (28[15]) shows an analogous use of the οἱ Ἰουδαῖοι. See also Lk 23[51]. St. Paul's use of the term is well known, and must have familiarized men in Ephesus, Corinth, and Thessalonica with it, without suggesting for a moment that he was not a 'Hebrew of Hebrews.'

iii. The author is by many opponents of the genuineness of the Gospel allowed to be of Jewish origin and sympathy, but not a Palestinian Jew. He is supposed to have belonged to Alexandria or Ephesus, otherwise, they contend, he would never have made so many errors of a topographical or historic kind. The most serious charge is his reference to Bethany beyond Jordan (1[28] RV). But it is clear that the author was not confounding this Bethany with that near Jerusalem. And if there were two Bethsaidas, two Canas, two Antiochs, and two Cæsareas, why not two Bethanys? Origen, it is true, had not recognized the site, and probably suggested the Bethabara of AV which is found with variants in some MSS. Caspari has located it N. of the Sea of Galilee; Conder, nearly S.E. of the Sea, far above the traditional site and much nearer to Cana of Galilee. Then the reference to the Pool of Siloam (Jn 9[7]) has been triumphantly confirmed by recent discovery. The mention of 'Ænon near Salim,' of Ephraim in the wilderness, and of 'Sychar' near Shechem, has been remarkably confirmed by recent research. In association with this may be classed the picturesque reference to the brook Kidron (18[1]); the 'gabbatha' of the Roman governor, with its Aram. name (19[13]); 'Solomon's porch' (10[23]); 'the treasury in the temple' (8[20]); the scenery and various nomenclature of the Sea of Galilee; and possibly the decoration of the temple courts by the golden vine (15[1-7]).

These indications of personal knowledge have been disputed as evidence of the author's Pal. origin, because the writer might have visited Palestine and picked up, like the author of the 'Apocr. Gospel of Matthew,' a multitude of small details. So esp. Cross (Westminster Rev., Aug. 1890, p. 177). It is enough to refer to Sanday's complete reply in Expos., March 1892, p. 163.

Frequent use is made of the supposed ignorance of the writer touching the appointment of the Jewish high priest, illustrated by the statement that Caiaphas held the office 'in that year,' as though the sacerdotium had been an annual appointment. But the evangelist speaks of Annas being high priest in the very 'same year' in which Caiaphas delivered the unconscious prophecy of the effect of the death of Jesus (11[49]). Moreover, St. Luke, both in the Gospel (3[2]) and in the Acts (4[6]), speaks of Annas and Caiaphas as 'high priests.' Annas had been deposed by the Roman procurator in favour of his son-in-law Caiaphas. His influence was great, though not officially recognized by Pilate; and therefore the evangelist, who was known to the family of the high priest, in giving the account of the preliminary examination by Annas, says that Jesus was sent bound by Annas to Caiaphas the high priest, from whom alone Pilate would have accepted the official charge of the Sanhedrin. The phrase 'that same year' reflects the absorbing interest of that year in which the highest court in the nation rejected and delivered over to the Gentiles the Incarnate Son of God. (See Pulp. Com. Introd. p. xl, and notes on 11[49] 18[13. 19. 23. 24]).

Efforts have been made to relegate some of the most characteristic teaching of the Fourth Gospel

and First Ep. of the same writer to the dominant influence of Philo Judæus of Alexandria. Lücke, Bleek, Baur, Keim, Schürer, Alb. Thoma, and many others have laid great emphasis on this filiation of ideas. But Siegfried has found the same influence abundantly evident in St. James, in Ep. to Heb., and in St. Paul. Luthardt, Godet, Pressensé, and others disclaim any relation, direct or indirect, on the part of St. John with the philosophy of Philo or his school. Even Keim and S. Davidson contend for the originality of the Fourth Gospel, pre-eminently in its teaching regarding the incarnation of the Son of God and its doctrine of the Messiah. The phraseology current in the Alex. school consists of important terms also used in the Johannine writings, i.e. not only Logos, but Light, Life, Truth, the Paraclete, the Archon, the Pleroma, the μονογενής and πρωτότοκος, 'only-begotten' and 'first-born.' These terms are used to denote the relation and mediation of the Divine Essence to the κόσμος, and part at least of the process by which all things have come into being. Philo endeavoured to utilize the speculation and phrases of both Plato and the Stoics in order to expound the teaching of the Pentateuch, but the amalgam was uncertain and really valueless. No one finally accepted these high-flown allegories of 'law,' or of 'narrative,' any more than they did the Stoic interpretation of the Homeric poems. It is, however, true that the place which, about the same time, St. Paul had in Co, Gal, and Col assigned to 'Christ' and 'the Son' and the 'Rock in the wilderness,' Philo had assigned to the 'Logos.' So, too, 'the heavenly bread' is explained by Philo as the manifestation of the Logos; and other terms in He 1[1-3], and the 'Wisdom' of the Psalms, and in the Sapiential Books, are by Philo similarly correlated with the Logos. There are, however, strong reasons for disputing either a verbal or a philosophical dependence of the author of the Fourth Gospel on the Alex. theosophy.

(a) The twofold meaning of the term 'Logos.' In Greek this represents not only, as in Philo, the Reason and Self-consciousness, the rationality of a thing or person, but also 'the word,' the expression, the process by which a revelation can be made or ratiocination carried into effect. The same ambiguous word is used for the Reason and the Word of both God and man. There are those who say that they are but the reverse and obverse sides of the same reality. At any rate, the same term is used by Philo for the archetypal reason and by 'John' for the creative energy, the divine personal nature, the source of life and light in man, which is at length incarnated in humanity, the glory of God revealed, full of grace and truth, the only-begotten and beloved of the Father, able to declare Him.[*]

(b) The Philonic Logos is in no sense personal. The Logos is often identified with the 'world,' as 'intelligible,' the 'image' of God in the universe; 'by His Logos, God is both governor and good.' True, Philo spoke of the Logos who, in place of the Angel of the Lord, brought back Hagar to Sarah (de Cher. p. 108), but by Hagar he meant not the woman Hagar, typical or historic, but 'human arts and science, brought back to the true virtue.' Numerous illustrations of the same method constantly recur. There is no personality in the Logos of Philo, such as we find adumbrated in the Books of Job or Wis, and, in another form, in 'the Son' of the Fourth Gospel, the 'Christ' of St. Paul, and the ἀπαύγασμα of God in He 1[3].

(c) The doctrine of Messiah was ignored by Philo,

[*] Schürer (HJP II. iii. 340–368) has more fully given to Philo's Logos the quality of word.

and that of the incarnation of the Logos was abhorrent to the whole Neo-Platonic school.

(*d*) To the phraseology of Philo some curious analogies are found in the Fourth Gospel, but by Siegfried (*l.c.*) many similar ones have been found in all the books of NT. Even the Ep. of Ja, the Targums, and the Synop. Gospels (*Pulp. Com.* Introd. p. xlix) are supposed to reflect Philo's influence. But this phraseology is kindled into entirely new meaning by the Word made flesh,—cf. 'love,' 'faith,' 'righteousness,' 'life eternal,' —and the use of it does not in the least degree establish a non-Pal. origin for the author of the Fourth Gospel. Thoma's eloquent enumeration of the titles and glories of Philo's Logos vanishes as an anticipation of the Fourth Gospel when it is found that these are only tropical phrases for the discipline through which souls are passing to the rest of a true philosophy.

(*e*) The true origin of the ideas and phraseology of the Fourth Gospel is to be sought in the OT. St. Paul and St. John found their material in the books which they had studied from their youth, and in the traditional interpretations of the Pal. schools. The spoken word is throughout Gn 1 the creative agency, the mediator between the Eternal and the 'cosmos.' In Ps 33^6 and 147^{15} 'the word of J″' is approximately personified for the same purpose. The personifications, moreover, of the direct activity of J″ under the form of *Memra* or *Debra* of the Lord in the Targums, though they cannot attest a literary usage answering to the Prologue of 'John,' indirectly reveal a mental tone in the Aram. schools, out of which the Johannine representation sprang. The same remark may be made touching 'the Angel of J″,' distinct from the created angels, who makes His appearance throughout the OT, and suggests awful and sublime depths in the bosom of the Divine Essence. The phrase is used as Logos is used, interchangeably with Deity and invested with all J′″s glory. Kurtz in his *Old Covenant* has criticised this, his earlier view (appx. of Eng. tr.); but see Westcott (*Introd.*), Liddon (*Divinity of our Lord*). Cf. also art. ANGEL, vol. i. p. 94.

Philo used to refer the manifestations of the Angel of J″ to the operations of the Logos and to specialized functions of the human mind; the apostles found in this mysterious phraseology an age-long witness to the possibility of an incarnation.

Perhaps nothing more than a personification of *wisdom* can be found in Pr, Job, or the Sapiential Books, but this method of presentation reappears in the Epistles of Paul to the Corinthians and in those to the Colossians and Ephesians.[*] See also He $1^{1.\ 2}$, from which it is clear that ideas of the Son, robed in phraseology of the Sapiential Books descriptive of wisdom, are independent of the treatment of the Alex. philosophy, and also of the author of the Fourth Gospel. With this may be compared the almost extreme Johannine phrases of Mt 11 and Lk 10. Where could these writers have obtained these notions except from the widely diffused traditions and holy memories of the apostles themselves? Thoma has done service in demonstrating the remarkable resemblance between the root-ideas of St. Paul and the Fourth Gospel. Beyschlag, in his *Theology of NT*, vol. i., has endeavoured with success to show the identical basis of the Synoptic and Johannine ideas of the relation between the Father and Son, the Father and Christ. Yet it is very noteworthy that 'John' uses a term from Gr. philosophy to which he attached a profoundly different sense from

[*] See Watkins in Smith's *DB²* p. 1755, who also shows the link between OT and Fourth Gospel in many other particulars of 1 P.

Philo, and to which the other sacred writers have not attained. It is almost a demonstration that he was a Palestinian, not an Alexandrian Jew.

β. *The writer claims to have been an eye-witness and ear-witness of that which he describes.* Numberless unconscious touches, without any theological bias in them, reveal the indelible impression left upon the writer of what he had seen and heard. *E.g.* observe the numerous indications of 'day' and 'hour' when that which he recorded took place ($1^{29.\ 35.\ 39.\ 43}$ 2^1 3^2 $4^{43.\ 52}$ $6^{16.\ 22}$ $12^{1.\ 12}$ $13^{1.\ 30}$ 18^{28} 20^1, and many others).

In 1^{14} and in 1 Jn 1^1 he puts himself in the position of those disciples who beheld His glory, and in 19^{35} he lays the strongest emphasis on the testimony he was personally able to bear to a great sign which accompanied the piercing of the side of the dead Christ. The fact that the author speaks of himself in the third person under the term ἐκεῖνος is in keeping with other tacit references to himself elsewhere, and with a similar usage of ἐκεῖνος, referring to the subject of the sentence, in 9^{37}. The writer indicates throughout intimate acquaintance with the secret fears, thoughts, murmurs, and questionings of the innermost circle of the disciples. He knows what they thought at the time, and how they subsequently modified their views (1. $2^{11.\ 21.\ 22}$ 12^{16}); he records the conversations with Nathanael, Andrew, Philip (chs. 1–6); the questions of Peter, Thomas, Judas Alphæi, Philip, in the valedictory discourse, together with remarks of his own; he gives indications of the blank ignorance of the disciples themselves with reference to the great utterances of their Lord (4^{33} $6^{70.\ 71}$ $11^{7.\ 8.\ 16}$ 16^{17}); the innermost mind of Peter at the feet-washing ($13^{6-11.\ 22}$); the ignorance on the part of all of the deep significance of Scripture (20^9); and the conversations with Thomas (20^{24-29}).

He is, moreover, acquainted with the very thoughts and motives of Jesus Himself ($2^{24.\ 25}$ 4^1 5^6 $7^{1.\ 6}$ $13^{1ff.}$); he gives a whole group of condensed perceptions of the blended divinity and humanity of our Lord which were flashed upon his consciousness by the Saviour's work and conduct (cf.18^4–19^{28}). He certainly suggests himself as the unnamed disciple of the Baptist and of our Lord (ch. 1); and we feel that he must have been an auditor of the conversations with Nicodemus and the Samaritan woman, and with the nobleman in chs. 3. 4. Caspari's interesting suggestion that he had a house in Jerus., connected with the fish trade between that city and the lake, would explain his presence in Jerus. (ch. 5), and his intimate knowledge of what occurred (ch. 6) in 6^{17}. There is an unconscious revelation of his presence in the words, 'Now Jesus was not yet come to them.' We do not see any animosity to Peter's prominence. He is one of the two whom Jesus loved (20^2). We owe to his constant clinging to Jesus the details of the trial before Annas, the private converse with Pilate, and the words from the Cross which intrusted the Mother to his care ($19^{25.\ 26}$).

The closing scenes of ch. 21, with the appendix by the survivors, leaves it without doubt that the writer was one of the disciples whom Jesus loved, but not Simon Peter. Those present at the Sea of Galilee ($21^{1.\ 2}$) are *Peter*, distinguished from the unnamed disciple (v.^{20}); *Thomas* and *Nathanael*, who are elsewhere mentioned by name; the two *sons of Zebedee*; and *two other* of His disciples. Now, James the brother of John was early slain (Ac $12^{1.\ 2}$). It follows that the 'beloved disciple' who, in the Epilogue, is accredited with the authorship, must either have been John the son of Zebedee, or one of the two unnamed disciples. Andrew and Philip are conceivably hinted at, but, seeing they are elsewhere mentioned by name, it is not probable;

and since the two are mentioned last, it is more in accordance with the usage of the writer to understand that they did not belong to the number of the eleven apostles.

The opinion that John, who is frequently referred to in the Synoptic Gospels and in the Acts (Ac 3[1] 4[13] 8[14]–15; cf. Gal 2[9]) in conjunction with Peter or with his brother (in Synop.) as at the very centre of the apostolic group, is not the disciple who produced this wonderful narrative, brings an anomalous circumstance to view: that the author, whoever he was, never once mentions the name of John. If he was some philosophic mystic of the 2nd cent., he must have deliberately invented the innumerable touches of the eye-witness, which he introduced with such apparent artlessness, *with the view* of suggesting that he was no other than 'the beloved disciple.' This supposition is so harsh that it cannot be accepted without more cogent reasons than those which have hitherto been advanced. Delff (*Grundzüge d. Entwick.-Gesch. d. Relig.* 1883, p. 266) has argued that the beloved disciple was a friend of Joseph and Nicodemus and the high priest, resident in Jerus., familiar with the Jerus. life of Christ, and from his education, higher than that of the Twelve, better able to appreciate and work into his matchless narrative the deeper teaching of Jesus. In that case some incongruities that have afflicted critics would be dissolved, but many fresh difficulties would be created, *e.g.* the utter disappearance of this remarkable personage from evangelic tradition; his acquaintance with Peter, Andrew, Philip and Thomas, Judas Alphæi and Judas Iscariot, Nathanael, Martha, Lazarus, and the Marys, to whom he has referred, together with his utter silence about 'John,' who took so high a place in the early development of the Church in the NT and early tradition. It is incumbent upon the student to weigh the indications which other literature supplies of the character and personality of John the son of Zebedee, and to see whether they are incompatible with the revelation which the writer has unconsciously offered of himself in the composition of the Fourth Gospel.

It must, however, be acknowledged that the self-revelation is studiously repressed. He never distinctly utters his own name, or that of his parents, or of his brother. He allows others to speak for him, and he hides himself behind the shadow of his Lord, and loses himself in the light of his Master's love. We can gather here and there what he thought of 'the Jews,' of the high priest, of Judas and Pilate. We can gather the interpretation he put upon certain perplexing sayings of the Lord, so different from their own lofty tone and fathomless depths, which he was nevertheless able to remember and record. But for the most part he conceals his own individuality.

V. THE CHARACTER AND CAREER OF JOHN AS PRESERVED IN OTHER LITERATURE. — A. The *Synoptic Gospels* tell us that a man named Zebedee (Mk 1[19. 20]) with his wife Salome had two sons, James and John, that they lived at Bethsaida, near Capernaum, on the Lake of Galilee, and were partners with Simon and Andrew the sons of Jonah (or of John, see RV and crit. notes on 1[42] and 21[15. 16]) in a fishing enterprise (Mk 1[29], Lk 5[10]). They had fishing-tackle, boats, hired servants, and a house. We gather from comparing Mt 27[56] and Mk 15[40] that Salome was the name of the mother of Zebedee's children. The Fourth Gospel makes it more than possible that she was sister of the mother of Jesus, and, if this inference is correct, she and her sons were nearly related to Jesus. Zebedee accepted, without recorded murmur, the departure of his sons and of his partners Simon and Andrew at the summons of Jesus to them.

The father thenceforth disappears from view. Salome's devotion and ministry of her substance to the wants of Jesus and His disciples, suggest the religious enthusiasm and Messianic patriotism with which the family had been brought up, and it is probable that, through friendship and kinship with the holy society of Nazareth, her expectations had been raised to fever-point. Whether John was called into close companionship with Jesus only once for all, or on two or three separate occasions, belongs to the exegesis and harmony of the Gospels. Matthew (20[20]) tells us that Salome presented a request of great compass and audacity, that her two sons might sit on the Saviour's right and left hand when He should come in His kingdom. It is most likely that she cherished ideas of a temporal and visible sovereignty, and that John at this period had not been weaned from these materialistic hopes. We gather, however, that the brothers were taught some lessons about the great tribulation, the baptism of sorrow and blood through which they would have to pass to such high fellowship with the Head of the kingdom.

For years before this, John had been in the innermost circle of Christ's disciples (Mt 10[2], Lk 6[14], Mk 3[17], Ac 1[13]). He had been in the death-chamber of the child of Jairus (Mk 5[37], Lk 8[51]). He had been taken into the cloud of transfiguration (Mt 17[1], Mk 9[2], and Lk 9[28]), though Peter was the spokesman of the feelings of the three. The two brothers James and John, with Simon and Andrew, had been permitted to hear the discourse upon the last things, which had opened John's prophetic eye to the great world-wide events with which his Master's kingdom was associated. John was sent with Peter to prepare the passover. With Peter and James, he was a witness of the agony in the garden. There is not a word or a hint in all this incompatible with the spirit of the author of the Fourth Gospel.

We do not know why James and John were called by Jesus 'Boanerges.' There must have been something special in the courage and bearing or in the character of James which signalled him out to Herod Agrippa as a victim that would 'please the Jews' (Ac 12[2f.]). It is probable that, being the elder of the two brothers, he was the more prominent petitioner for the coveted dignity of nearness to the King of Sorrows when approaching the goal of His self-sacrifice. A significant record occurs in Mk 9[38ff.] and Lk 9[49ff.], where John himself exclaims, '*Master, we saw one casting out demons in thy name, and we forbade him, because he followeth not (thee) with us.*' The question seems to invite the rebuke he received, '*Forbid him not,* etc. . . .' This was an event which revealed a jealous love for the Master, and it is paralleled by the spirit which flames forth in the treatment of those enemies of the cross with whom the author of the second and third Epistles contended. But the most striking instance of this spirit is recorded in Lk 9[54. 55], where *John* as well as James burned with indignation against certain Samaritans who refused to receive Jesus. '*Master,* said they, *willest thou that we call fire from heaven to consume them, even as Elias did?*' Here again the two brothers are rebuked. The apostle of love is traditionally accredited with a similar outburst of indignant wrath in his treatment of Cerinthus. The current mediæval representation of the author of the Fourth Gospel was that of one characterized by effeminate softness. This popular conception is not justified by the letter of the Gospel, but is due to tradition and legend. In no part of NT do we find such thrilling utterance of the wrath of God against sin as in Jn. (See 3[18. 19. 36] 5[29]). It is in Jn 6[70] that Judas is called 'a devil'; cf. also 7[34] 8[23. 24. 44] 9[39]. Even in the upper chamber, we hear terrible tones of the Judge of all the earth, and the traitor is called 'the son of perdition' (15^{25} $16^{1\text{-}3}$ 17^{12}), while the Evangelist himself ($12^{37\text{-}43}$) denounces the sin of the people in language which echoes Lk 9^{54}. There was much more for John to learn, and the occasional outbreaks of stormy wrath are of the very nature of a finite human love cherished with intensity of emotion for that wonderful Person whose grandeur of being, as well as whose human loveliness, was breaking upon his mind. There are no other special references to John in the Synoptic narrative, and, as a revelation of the personal character of the author, those mentioned are explained rather than contradicted by the tone of the Fourth Gospel.

B. *The Acts of the Apostles* hides John in the company of the Twelve, and behind the more prominent figure of Peter. Still, the promises given by the ascending Lord (ch. 1), and the preaching of Peter (chs. 2. 3. and 4), reveal the tone and matter of the closing discourse of our Lord, of which John's mind was the repertory. Compare Jn 5^{20} 7^{39} 17^5 16^7 with the substance of Peter's great sermon at Pentecost, and the defence made by Peter and John (Ac 3. 4) with the vindication in the Fourth Gospel of the Messiahship of Jesus. (See esp. Jn 20^{31}). As in the Fourth Gospel, John is a silent presence in the early Church (see Ac 8), but the mission of the two apostles to Samaria prepares us for the mighty words which 'John' was at length to reveal to the world.

C. *St. Paul's Epistle to the Galatians* makes a reference to James, Cephas, and *John* as 'pillars' of the Mother Church, to whom St. Paul was willing to refer his Gentile ministry, based on Christ's own teaching concerning the place of ceremonial in the kingdom of God. This is the only reference in the writings of St. Paul to the personality of John, and so far there is not the smallest reason for questioning, on St. Paul's authority, the widely attested conviction that the beloved disciple was the author of the Fourth Gospel.

D. *The First Epistle of John.* The Mur. Canon makes distinct reference to 1 Jn as an appendix to the Gospel. It specifies two Epistles by the same evangelist later on. Eusebius (*HE* iii. 39) tells us that Papias 'used passages from the first Epistle'; and we have an unmistakable citation of 1 Jn 4^1 in Polycarp's *Epistle to Phil.* ch. viii. The extreme significance of this quotation led the author of *Supernatural Religion*, vol. ii., to contend that 'John' quoted from Polycarp, rather than *vice versâ*. Tertullian frequently refers to, or quotes from, the Epistle. Clemens Alex., Origen, and Cyprian cite it as St. John's writing. Many who opposed the authenticity of the Gospel, like Bretschneider in his *Probabilia*, with Paulus and others, do not attempt to separate the authorship of the Gospel and Epistle; but Hilgenfeld and Davidson have advanced many reasons for believing that they belong to different writers and periods. Davidson (*Introd. to NT*) assigns some ten distinct points of difference, which hardly need more than statement for their refutation. Holtzmann (*Einleitung*, p. 463) admits identity of authorship. Haupt and Lias have shown how the original form of the teaching is referred by the apostle to the words of Jesus Himself, while in the Epistle we see the method adopted by the evangelist to apply it to the condition of the Church at the close of the century. Doubtless there are differences in style, weight, compass, between the utterances of the Lord and the application of these ideas to later days, but all the fundamental conceptions of the divine character and righteousness, of 'the word of life,' of the contrariety between 'the flesh' and 'the spirit,' between 'light' and 'darkness,' the emphasis upon the divine love, upon the Holy Spirit and the eternal life, appear in a practical form in the Epistle as well as in the Gospel. There is no necessity to invoke the shadowy form of the Presbyter John to explain the differences between the two documents. They must stand or fall together. Testimony to one becomes a witness for the coexistence of the other. They combine to give us the best insight into the mind of the author of both. What is worthy of particular attention is the conviction that we have here not only the apostle of love, but one whose wrath flamed against untruthfulness, unbelief, and the spirit of the world. Let special notice be taken of 1^{10} $2^{9\text{-}11.\ 16.\ 22}$ 3^6. $^{8.\ 12.\ 15}$ 4^3 $5^{10.\ 16}$. While there is every reason for recognizing, throughout, the disciple whom Jesus loved and the author of the Fourth Gospel, there is a striking correspondence with the disciple who was ready to call fire from heaven upon those who rejected the Lord and His truth. The first Epistle is a link between the Synoptic John and the personality of whom we are in search.

E. *The Second and Third Epistles of John*, so far as they bear on the character of the author of the Fourth Gospel. The authenticity and canonicity of the smaller Epistles have had to sustain a heavy fire of criticism. Even Eusebius hesitated to acknowledge them as St. John's own, but Clemens Alexandrinus, Irenæus, and Dionysius have little doubt about them. The small circulation of these private letters is enough to account for their non-inclusion in the Peshitta, though Ephraem Syrus quotes them. The Mur. Canon leaves it doubtful whether the compiler knew of more than two Epistles in all; Theodoret does not mention them. Theodore of Mopsuestia rejected them. Jerome, building on the view taken by Eusebius of the supposed reference to the Presbyter John by Papias, is disposed to attribute them to that shadowy personage; but he does not finally come to that conclusion, as he enumerates seven Catholic Epistles. In modern times the circumstance that the author calls himself 'the elder' has been pressed against their apostolic authority; but it should be remembered that St. Peter (1 P 5^1) calls himself συμπρεσβύτερος, and that Papias calls the apostles, including St. John, 'elders.' Irenæus gives the same title to Polycarp; and when writing to Soter, Bishop of Rome, gives no higher title to his predecessors in that see, though these are supposed to have included both St. Peter and St. Paul. These considerations show that the title is one which St. John might, consistently with much other usage, have used for himself. And that Diotrephes used malicious words about John the apostle is no reason for thinking that the author was other than the apostle, when we bear in mind the parallel experience of the greatest of the apostles. These Epistles teach the same fundamental truths, and are characterized by the same omissions as the first Epistle and the Gospel, in neither of which is there distinct reference to the Church or the Christian sacraments. The prime words are used in all three Epistles, such as ἀλήθεια, ἀγάπη, ἀντίχριστος, περιπατεῖν, etc. There is the same limpid style, aphoristic utterance, and extraordinarily simple way of saying deep, loving, and terrible things. Our conclusion is that these two Epistles do much to link together the authorship of the Gospel with their own, as well as demonstrably prove that any specially prophetic and 'thunderous' symptoms of character discovered in the Synoptic Gospels were not absent from the man who wrote with intense affection, breaking into flames of wrath, the Fourth Gospel. [On this subject see detailed treatment in *Pulp. Com.* Introduction; Ebrard's *Comm. on the Epistles of John*; Huther, Haupt, Westcott, Lücke, Alexander, and others;

as well as the art. JOHN, EPISTLES OF, in this Dictionary].

F. A general comparison between the authors of the Apocalypse and of the Fourth Gospel.—The criticism of the Apoc. begun by Vischer, with Harnack's co-operation, and the theory of a Jewish document which is said to lie at the heart of it, and to be touched up by Christian vision and interlineated with Christian doctrine, have not reached a final stage. The theory might account for some of the most difficult phenomena without taking the authorship out of the hands of the Apostle John. But this is not the place to discuss either the authorship or the date of the Apocalypse. External evidence for the later date and the apostolic origin of the book is stronger than that for any other book in NT. The chief argument on which a much earlier date is assigned turns on purely internal considerations, such as, *e.g.*, the suggestion that Jerus. is still standing when the Apoc. is written, that the succession of Roman emperors fixes the moment of its grand *dénouement*, that 'the number of the Beast' is a cryptogram of *Nero Cæsar*, whose anticipated reappearance after his supposed assassination was confidently feared by the world and the Church. These are controversial matters capable of decision only by careful exegesis, and much balancing of opposing theories. Davidson, Renan, and Farrar have argued in favour of this earlier date ; while Lücke, Hengstenberg, and many others have taken the opposite side. It is admitted by all that the longer the interval between the composition of the Apoc. and the Gospel, the easier it becomes to argue that the fiery enthusiasm and prophetic blasts, and the imaginative intensity, more Hebrew than Greek, of the young apostle, may have subsided by long meditation and reflection on the vitalizing words of the Master in the days of His flesh ; that the atmosphere of Ephesus and the wide diffusion of Hel. and Alex. culture may then have had time to purge his style and refine his tone, and direct him to a new standpoint of thought and feeling. Many scholars, from Dionysius of Alexandria, who elaborated the contrasts between the Apoc. and the Gospel almost as completely as has been done by modern critics, down to the early followers of Baur, such as Zeller and Hilgenfeld, have come to the conclusion that no ingenuity can ever show the two books to have originated from the same mind, whatever interval or change of scene may be intercalated between them. Some then, with F. C. Baur, by establishing the apostolic authorship of the Apoc., have believed that they demolished the authenticity of the Gospel ; while others, by relinquishing the Apoc. and handing it over to some Judaic zealot, have believed that they left the course open to a full acceptance of the Johannine authorship of the Fourth Gospel. But however great the contrasts of an earlier and later style,—as witness, comparatively, in our own day, those of Burke and Carlyle,—a much greater conflict and dissimilarity may be observed when a man of commanding powers distinctly sets himself to approach a different subject, or to look and write from a new standpoint. Many writers, like Swift, Cowper, Wordsworth, and Tennyson, were throughout their career able to adopt, whether by dramatic temperament or deliberate *tours de force*, glaring contrasts of form, dialect, style, tone, manner, which are enough to deceive those who cannot discern the subtle resemblances, and, moreover, have no *external* evidence of authorship to guide them in their conclusions. The different attitude and atmosphere, the modified diction and general purpose of the two books, are not sufficient (whatever be the theory of date) to divorce them from each other while the internal

and external evidences of the authenticity of each remain independently so convincing.

That John, the author of the Apoc., called himself a 'bond-slave of Jesus Christ,' and not an apostle, corresponds with the modesty of the writer of the Gospel, and with the very phrase of St. Paul in four of his Epistles. He classes himself among the '*prophets*' of the NT, and does not dissociate himself from the apostles, some of whom were undoubtedly 'prophets,' and, since our Lord built His Church and kingdom (Mt 16[18]) upon the *petra* of Peter's confession, it is not surprising that John should have seen the names of the twelve apostles upon the foundations of the new Jerusalem. The author declares that 'he bare witness to the word of God, and to the testimony of Jesus Christ' (Rev 1[2]), which ranges him among the innermost circle of Christ's disciples. The 'John' cannot, by any ingenious theory, refer to any other personage of that name mentioned in NT. Further, the references to persecution, exile, Patmos, and an Ephesian residence, correspond with a whole cycle of tradition and citation which cannot be here given. It is true that Keim (*Jesus of Nazara*, Eng. tr. i. 143, 207) discounts the citations from Irenæus (ii. 22. 5, iii. 23), Clem. Alex., Justin, Apollonius (Eus. *HE* v. 18), Jerome, Epiphanius, etc., thinking that a blunder of Irenæus is the parent of all the supposed testimony ; and Keim has been followed in this by Harnack and several other recent writers. But the arguments are unsatisfactory. On the other hand, the external testimonies to the Apocalypse are in various ways confirmatory of apostolic origin and authority, while a clear mention of it in the Mur. Canon—together with that of Peter—assigns it a sure place in the reverence of the Church early in the 2nd cent.

The arguments of Dionysius of Alexandria are based on fundamental differences between the Apocalypse and the Fourth Gospel.

(1) Differences of *designation*, such as that the author of the Apoc. calls himself 'John,' whereas the author of the Gospel withholds his name. This, as Salmon (*Introd. to NT*, 276) says, can be easily accounted for. The *historical* books of OT, with the exception of Neh, are all anonymous ; the same may be said of the Synoptic Gospels and Ac, while all the *prophetic* books, with the exception of Daniel (see ch. 7), open with the name of the prophet himself. Now, the Apocalypse is distinctly prophetic, and its style and imagery are borrowed from that source. Dionysius did not reject it as uninspired, or as written by Cerinthus, or as having insufficient external testimony. He said that he could not understand its meaning, though this was not his point of critical doubt ; but that its great dissimilarity in language, style, theme, and tone from the Gospel convinced him, that as there might be many 'Johns' in Asia during the 1st cent., one of them may have been the author. He argued, further, that the resemblance between the Gospel and the first Epistle in phrase, leading terms, and decisive teaching increases the feeling of discrepancy between the Gospel and the Apocalypse. On the hearsay that there were two tombs of 'John' at Ephesus, he raises the ghost of the shadowy 'Presbyter,' who has done such notable service in the piecing together of 2nd cent. fragments. The position occupied by Dionysius in the middle of the 3rd century may have been unconsciously adopted by this wise and candid man, owing to the strong objection he entertained for the chiliasm which he found in the Apocalypse. Nevertheless, his hypothesis was comparatively disregarded until the present century, when it was used in a contrary sense by F. C. Baur and his followers, who recognized and emphasized the

apostolic authorship of the Apoc., to the entire repudiation of that of the Gospel, which was supposed to have originated under different conditions at the close of the 2nd cent. On the other hand, Lücke, Ewald, Lutzelberger, Düsterdieck, de Wette, and Neander, holding the authenticity of the Gospel as proved, and accepting the burden of the Dionysian argument, have resigned the authorship of the Apoc. to the 'Presbyter,' to 'John the Divine,' to John Mark, or to any other who could bear the weight of the responsibility. Volkmar and Renan pressed the Judaic aspects so strongly as to suppose that it was, among other things, an early manifesto against the Pauline Churches and doctrine, under the pseudonym of Balaam or the Nicolaitans.

(2) The emphasis laid upon the Heb. and Hel. *spirit* of the two books respectively has been brought into strong relief by Vischer's *Die Offenbarung Johannis eine Jüdische Apokalypse in christlicher Bearbeitung: mit einem Nachwort von Adolph Harnack*, 1886 ; see Schoen's *Origine de l'Apocalypse*, also Bousset's *Commentary*, and A. Meyer in *Theol. Rundschau*, Nov. and Dec. 1897. Doubtless the Apocalyptic literature of the Hebrews, as seen in Dn, 2 Es, Enoch, must have been present to the mind of the author ; but that he or another re-edited a Jewish Apoc. is more than the precarious criticism which has prevailed of late can be said to have proved. Moreover, the links of connexion and the subtle resemblance between these two most wonderful testimonies to Christ have been too much slighted. The use of rare words and forms characterizing both documents, the practically identical Christology, and a certain resemblance in structure, lead to the conclusion that if John be indeed the author of the Apoc., then the author of the Gospel, notwithstanding its transparent differences, must have been his pupil and follower in the deepest motives and spirit of his utterance. Again, the supposed oppositions of style are certainly balanced by interesting correspondences, the fancied solecisms can be shown to have analogous representations in classical Greek, and certain views of the OT and of the Person of Christ are almost, if not quite, peculiar to these two works. The impression therefore grows upon many, that, notwithstanding the dicta of the Tübingen school, the two books not only may, but must, have issued from the same mind. If this be the final word of the long controversy, the authenticity of the Apoc. becomes one of the strongest arguments for the apostolic origin of the Fourth Gospel.

It is common to say that the Apoc. is strongly Heb. in its grammar, while the Gospel is written in excellent Hel. Greek. The substitution of καί in the Apoc., as representative of the Heb. ן, for the rich variety of Gr. particles, is urged as a conspicuous proof of the position. But we find also in the Gospel that, where the emotions are intense, and when every sentence becomes a heart-throb, as in chs. 15, 17, and in ch. 21 (where the succession of events constitutes the very nerve of the transcendent narrative), the author is equally content with the simple καί, and dispenses with all other particles. It is urged that πάντοτε and πώποτε and καθώς are used in the Gospel, but not in the Apocalypse. Now, the last word is used often in the Synoptics ; and though the former words occur in Jn, they are not to be found in Ac, and only very occasionally in NT, so that no conclusion can be drawn from their omission in the Apocalypse. While the Heb. forms 'Amen,' 'Abaddon,' 'Hallelujah,' are found in the Apoc., and the Heb. imagery of the 'manna,' the 'root and offspring of David,' the 'twelve tribes of Israel,' and the 'New Jerus.' are introduced, they certainly are balanced by the

long list of Heb. phrases, information, and imagery found in the Gospel (see below). The Gospel makes claim for the 'Word made flesh' that Abraham rejoiced to see the days of the Christ ; that Moses wrote of Him ; that Jesus Himself was the Heavenly 'Manna' which came down from heaven, that He was the Lamb of God, taking away sin, that He was the Bridegroom of the Church, that He was greater than the temple, able to rebuild it after its wanton destruction. The Lamb (τὸ ἀρνίον, not, however, ὁ ἀμνός) of the Apoc. is in tremendous conflict with the power of the theocracy, then with the world, then with concentrated world-powers, over which He gains the victory, and receives the acclamations of the universe. The Lamb of the Gospel narrative encounters the powers of the world, displays great 'signs' in the temple, on the land and on the sea, on the bodies and minds of men. Through meekness and submission, not through impotence, through the mystery of suffering and cruel death, and the glory of resurrection, He gains a victory over the world, over all its representatives, over the flesh and the devil. He takes His perpetual place with, among, and within His people, their Lord, their King. Doubtless there is a concrete specialism in the imagery of the Apoc. which seems to conflict with the universalism of the Gospel ; but it must not be forgotten that the Apocalyptist sees 'a multitude which no man can number, gathered from every people and kindred and tribe,' who circle the throne of God and of the Lamb, and at last the 'leaves of the tree of life are for the healing of the nations.' The Hebraism of both documents is obvious, and it is hardly more conspicuous in the one than in the other. Instead of separating them by contrast, it may be held to establish community of origin.

(3) The *grammatical peculiarities* of the Apoc. include apparently 'false apposition,' the most remarkable example being 1⁴, where ἀπό is followed by ὁ ὤν, καὶ ὁ ἦν, etc. This, however, arises from the writer having regarded the phrase as a tr. of the Eternal, as = J″, and an indeclinable noun. In 30 other places he gives ἀπό its proper regimen. Other instances of unusual apposition may easily be explained without recourse to solecism, such as the ἡ λέγουσα of 2²⁰, cf. 3¹² 8⁹ etc., which are paralleled by similar constructions in Plato (Winer, 671, Eng. tr.), Thucydides, and others. Anomalous varieties of gender and number are best explained by the fervid personifying temperament which gives masculine or feminine features to neuter nouns. The same peculiarities are found in other parts of NT, though they would scarcely be expected in the quiet, limpid prose of the Fourth Gospel. As a set-off against these curiosities, a considerable number of verbal coincidences demand attention. The verb μαρτυρεῖν and the noun μαρτυρία occur very frequently in the Gospel and the Epp. of John, very sparingly in other parts of NT, and in a different sense ; but they occur 13 times in the Apocalypse. The word νικᾶν is used in the sense of overcoming evil and the world both in Gospel and Epp., and 17 times in the Apocalypse. Τηρεῖν τὸν λόγον is a phrase peculiar to the Gospel, Epp., and Apoc., and so is τηρεῖν τὰς ἐντολάς. The idea of the tabernacling of God among or with men, σκηνοῦν, is also to be found expressed by the same word in these documents. The following words are virtually peculiar to them : σφραγίζειν in the sense of 'confirm,' Ἑβραϊστί, λαλεῖν μετά τινος, κύριε σὺ οἶδας, περιπατεῖν μετά τινος, which are characteristic of all three writings. What is still more remarkable is that words strangely absent from the Gospel and Epp., like μετάνοια, γέεννα, are not to be found in Apocalypse. The word πίστις, which occurs 340 times in NT, does not occur in the Gospel, and is

almost absent from Epp. and Apocalypse. The same Gr. tr. of Zec 12[10], different from LXX, is found in the Gospel, 19[34-37], and Apoc. 1[7]. These correspondences might be greatly multiplied. Weiss and Watkins give lists of more than 100 words or phrases common to the three documents. The impression made upon some opponents of the authenticity of the Gospel is that the 2nd cent. writer who is supposed to have written it, studied the vocabulary, etc., of the Apoc., with the intention of producing the impression of Johannine authorship. This hypothesis neutralizes the hypothesis based upon their conspicuous dissimilarity.

(4) *The plan, scope, and structure of the two books.* — Many insist on the extreme contrast between the two writings in these respects, *e.g.* the absence in the Gospel of climax, the quiet flow of the stream of narrative and discourse, the movement from Jerus. to Galilee and back to the metropolis, with nearly imperceptible chronology, the lack of imaginative background, the omission of Transfiguration and Ascension, and only the quiet gathering intensity of conviction that the victory over evil must lie for all time with the Man of infinite capacity, boundless sympathy, and measureless affliction—so that at length the most sceptical of the Twelve admits His supreme claims. On the other hand, 'the revelation of Jesus Christ to His servant John' is an impressive series of tableaux, arranged in climacteric form, and with very marked septenary arrangements. After the first visions, come the letters to the Seven Churches, a special aspect and title of the Lord being presented in each. Next we have the vision of the seven seals of the Divine Book; the separate issues of the opening of the six seals; the intermezzo of the four angels and other angel; and then the new septenary group of trumpets introduced by the loosing of the seventh seal. Further, after the twofold revelation of the temple and the beasts, come the seven last plagues following on the pouring out of the seven vials. Then appear the closing contrasts of Babylon and the New Jerus.; the victory of the Logos of God over all His foes, the destruction of the Beast, the False Prophet, and the Evil One for ever and ever; and the renewal of all things in the light of the Lord. This series of magnificent images seems strangely diverse from the meditative, gentle flow of the river of life, of which we catch lucent gleams in the Fourth Gospel.

An examination of the Gospel reveals, however, a deeply pondered plan. One thing readily appears: the septenary arrangement. Seven great signs precede the Passion. These constitute a climax, and a revelation not only of divine realities but of the mind of the writer. The first sign (Jn 2[11]) shows the mastery of the Word made flesh over the material of nature; the second (4[54]) His mastery over one of the most cruel troubles of human nature, even when the Lord was not visibly present with the sufferer; the third (5[8]) shows His power to restore the forces which have been lost by sin; the fourth and fifth (6[11, 19]) are great signs of power and pity, both on earth and sea, with mastery over the forces of nature; the sixth (9[1ff.]) is a double proof of His being the 'Light of the World'; the seventh (11[43]) is a concrete conflict with the most terrible evil of humanity, and a victory over it. In addition to this, a singular parallel to the throbbing suspense or postponement of climax in the Apoc., *e.g.* at the loosing of the seventh seal, at the sounding of the seventh trumpet, and in the intercalated scenes before the final victory and glory, may be traced also in the structure of the Gospel. Thus the 'hour' of the highest manifestation seems always at hand, but is again and again postponed. Without enumerating details,

cf. Jn 2[4] 4[21. 23] 5[25. 28] 7[30] 8[20] 12[27], followed by new and wonderful departures. In the midst of the valedictory discourse, 'Arise, let us go hence,' seems to strike the hour; but even now the moment comes for still higher teaching and the Eternal Prayer. This overlapping and renewal of suspense in striking interlineation are continued throughout the story of the Passion to the confession of Thomas and the hyperbole of the closing verses. Observe, further, the presence in both documents of prologue, rehearsal, conflict, victory, epilogue, which curiously correspond with each other and which almost bind them together. In each alike the prologue is an anticipation of the successive arguments of the visions or oracles, as the case may be. As the letters to the Seven Churches give a compendious forecast of the seals, trumpets, and vials, so Gosp. chs. ii.–iv. or v. give most vivid rehearsals of characteristic specimens of the Lord's method and teaching. The sublime key-word of the Gospel, 'The Word became flesh,' rises over the entire Gospel as 'an awful rose of dawn,' just as the vision of the Divine Christ in Rev 1 dominates every subsequent paragraph in the Apocalypse.

(5) This leads us to a brief treatment of the *religious teaching* of these two documents. Many modern critics, Strauss, Baur, Harnack, Wendt, Weiss, Ritschl, put into forcible antithesis the earlier and later Johannine teaching. There is no necessity for these distinctions. Gebhardt and others have given all the evidence needed to prove that no two books of Holy Scripture are so coincident in teaching, even to special peculiarities, as the Gospel and Apocalypse. In one, the author is calmly meditating upon the concrete facts, the peerless life, the transcendent teaching, the unique ending on earth of a ministry which was beginning to exert widespread spiritual influence upon individuals, and to produce political and even cosmic effects upon humanity and the world. In the other, the vision of the place which Jesus had taken in the sphere of providential rule flashes upon him. In the one, he is sweetly dreaming over the potent, procreant fact; in the other, fancy and even grotesque imagination forecast the future. The visions of Heb. seers, by their nature, follow one another, but do not grow from less to more—they are architectural rather than spontaneous. Remembering these different conditions, it is nothing short of unique that the ideas of the *two* documents should have been so similar, if not coincident. The same writer was able to see more deeply than any other into the heart of Jesus, and was also permitted to see more accurately than other apocalyptic writers into the ferments wrought in humanity by the leaven of the kingdom. [Gebhardt's *Doct. of the Apoc.*, Eng. tr. pp. 305, 424; Reynolds' *Introd.* in *Pulpit Comm.* pp. lxxx–lxxxv].

These considerations may be held to prove that the twofold Johannine literature, instead of breaking the evidences of unity of authorship, reveals a high probability that the two documents proceeded from the same mind. We have also seen that the strong evidence for the existence of the Gospel towards the very beginning of the 2nd cent., and the traditional attribution of authorship to the son of Zebedee, are not countermanded by the characteristics of John supposed to be given in the Synoptic Gospels, the Acts, the Pauline Epistles, and the three Epistles of John.

Some able critics, like Gebhardt, Renan in some edd. of the *Vie de Jésus*, and Matthew Arnold, are ready to admit that the external evidence for the Fourth Gospel is as copious as for the Synoptic Gospels and the Pauline Epistles. Keim has even triumphed over Baur's chronology and pressed back the date of the existence of the Gospel to a time when the son of Zebedee may have been still living. But all these hold a view of the writing which deprives it of historic value. They regard it as a Christological romance in the form of a narrative, which was not intended even by the author to be taken as a serious or historical record of what was actually said and done. The intense personality of the author pervades the whole. He has, say they, very sparingly made use of the Synoptic Gospels and the teaching of St. Paul, and freely manipulated traditional material as suited his purpose, and he never intended to convey other than the grand impression produced upon his mind by the forms of the new faith. As Jth, Enoch, 2 Es, the *Shepherd*, the *Platonic Dialogues*, the *Divina Commedia*, *Paradise Lost*, etc., used semi-narrative forms for the purpose of conveying religious ideas, so our evangelist was one of the most effective writers of didactic fiction.

Others have gone much further than this. They have questioned every mark of early origin, and have thought that they found abundant evidence of later date, *e.g.* references to the second destruction of Jerus. under Hadrian. Some have found traces of Docetism, later Gnosticism, Neoplatonism in the Gospel, and have contended that it is an attempt to trace to the words of Jesus the two types of Hel. and Heb. Christianity, the writer's deliberate aim being to bring about the healing of a schism which can be traced back to the apostles themselves. The controversy turns on the relation of the Fourth Gospel to the Synoptic narrative, and this we must now examine.

VI. THE RELATION OF THE FOURTH GOSPEL TO THE SYNOPTIC NARRATIVE.—*A. A general statement of the contrast between them.*—It is now admitted that this contrast has appeared to modern criticism more extreme than to that of previous centuries. 'Atmosphere' or climate are difficult to define, but the most conservative critics are conscious of a vital change when passing from genealogical details to the abysses of eternity, from the homely life and trade of Nazareth and Capernaum to the heated discussions of the temple courts, from the Sermon on the Mount to the valedictory discourse. The *dramatis personæ* are different. Nicodemus, Lazarus, and Nathanael, the impotent and the blind man, are introduced to us for the first time. Thomas starts into prominence and a position of high argumentative importance. The chronological elements differ. The various visits to the metropolis interfere with the simple flow of the Synoptic narrative. No *direct* mention is made of the birth in Bethlehem from the virgin mother. The story and testimonies of John the Baptist are taken up where the Synoptists drop them, and yet no direct account is given of his death. The temptation, the transfiguration, the agony in the garden, the trial before the Sanhedrin, the dereliction, the ascension, are apparently ignored. The main themes of the discourses, viz. the conditions of admission into the kingdom, are exchanged for profound hints as to the uniqueness of the Lord's own person, His pre-existence, His claim to reveal the Father and to give eternal life. The miracles of the Synoptic narrative appear to set forth His comradeship and His pity for the sorrows of the world, but the later narrative of miracles of Jesus seems mainly used to insist upon the apologetic value of His miracles—they are 'signs' of the glory of God. The little children have vanished from the scene, even from the hosannas of the triumphal entry. It is considered scarcely possible to exaggerate the contrast between the gradual development of the Synoptic Christ, and the aureole of Messianic and divine splendour which invests Him from the first in 'John's' representation.

The first three Gospels represent more than one current type of tradition. The Fourth Gospel is almost universally admitted to be the work of one thoughtful mind, which has impressed itself upon the whole work. The author *in propriâ personâ* addresses his readers with explanations of his own, and at times seems to expand by further reflections or recollections even the words of his adored Master; so that a vigorous subjective element cannot be excluded, although it may have been relatively exaggerated.

B. We have to examine these *divergences* and some others, and to decide whether the admission of their existence destroys the historical value of the Fourth Gospel. *Primâ facie*, the claim of the writer to be the most intimate friend and disciple of Jesus Christ must be held to give a weight and an authority to his autoptic representations to which none of the Synoptics can lay equal claim.

(1) Can we accept the new version of the principal *scene of the ministry* of Christ? Matthew and Mark refer to one passover feast only, for which they bring Jesus to Jerus.—while all the other incidents and teachings are confined to Galilee. It is worth while to remember that to the Romans and Hellenes, to whom Mk and Lk appeal, the difference between the two must have been very insignificant. To the introspective soul of John, who thought of days, places, hours of his intercourse with 'the Word incarnate,' it was of moment to record some of these things in sharper detail. Thus, seeing that the Synoptic narrative of the public ministry ignores the Judæan ministry of the first passover, he reveals his intimate knowledge of the facts by the use of the word πάλιν in 4³, thereby corresponding with the Synoptists as to the date of the commencement of the public ministry. In ch. 5 we have an *intermezzo* in which a visit to Jerus. brings our Lord into conflict with the Pharisees on the Sabbatic law. This explains and corresponds with the long and bitter struggle with the Pharisees detailed by the Synoptists in the early portion of the Galilæan ministry. Jesus does not appear to have been accompanied by more than a few disciples on these visits to the metropolis. Caspari (*Chron. Introd. to Life of Christ*, Eng. tr. 142) has made the acute suggestion that John, who was known to Caiaphas, and had a house in Jerus. to which he resorted at the time of the great feasts, may have been the sole auditor and witness of the conversations, and have been his Master's host as well as his biographer. But 'John' never expanded these precious memoranda into a full biography. He, like his predecessors, has given us only fragments, pregnant incidents, great words, which lifted the veil from the mystery of the Lord's consciousness. The references to special occasions are abrupt, *e.g.* to the abiding in Judæa (3²²), the walking in Galilee (7¹), the retiring to Peræa (10⁴⁰), the pause at Ephraim (11⁵⁴)—other signs and teachings are cited and summarized from first to last. It is helpful to remember that even the Synoptists are not silent about visits to Judæa, as compare the (Tisch.⁸, WH) text of Lk 4⁴⁴, where εἰς τὰς συναγωγὰς τῆς Ἰουδαίας is inserted in the text —Tregelles and RV insert it in the margin. This might be synchronous with either the first visit of Jesus to Jerus. or even the second. In Lk 5¹⁷ the presence in Galilee of Pharisees from *Jerusalem* represents the impression already produced in the temple by the great discussion on the Sabbatic law. Both Matthew (23³⁷) and Luke (13²¹·³³·³⁴) record the terrible and tender apostrophe, 'O Jerusalem . . . how *often* would I,' etc. In Lk 10³⁸ the incident of Mary and Martha is not incompatible with our Lord's presence at Bethany during

the feast of Tabernacles, described in Jn 7[10]. The Synoptic narrative implies, in the final scenes, familiarity with people and things, which is best explained by the Johannine account of these visits to Jerusalem.

(2) Is the *length of our Lord's public ministry* so different, after all, in the two accounts as hopelessly to discredit either account? Browne (*Ord. sæclorum*) has endeavoured to compress even John's account into the short space of one year, contained between the first and last Passover; and this is effected by expunging from the text (Jn 6[4]) the reference to another passover; but it has the tendency to render the whole narrative unhistorical when we consider the astounding brevity of the period during which the entire personal influence of Jesus upon friends and foes must have been produced. This becomes more striking when we compare it with the length of the teaching of Socrates, Buddha, or Mohammed. The same comparison may be made with the record of the ministry of Hosea, Jeremiah, or Ezra, or with the history of the career of Moses, David, or Solomon. The fact is that there is no positive statement in any of the four Gospels upon the subject. The only *termini* are the 15th year of Tiberius (Lk 3[1]) and the recall of Pontius Pilate (A.D. 36). There is therefore more historic probability in the whole narrative if the extended chronology of John into two years and a half be followed. There is nothing to contradict it in the Synoptic narrative. See, further, art. CHRONOLOGY OF NT, vol. i. p. 406 ff.

(3) The most perplexing and debated apparent discrepancy between the first three Gospels and the Fourth turns on *the day of our Lord's death*. As judged by critics of all schools a formidable difference emerges, which some, like Baur and Strauss, have lifted into capital importance as demonstrating the late origin of the Fourth Gospel at the hands of one who was ready from doctrinal and ecclesiastical motives to contradict the far-spread tradition of a century. It is assumed that the writer wished to make it appear that Jesus was the true Passover, in whom all the ancient symbolism of the Lamb and the system of sacrifices culminated, and that he did not hesitate to affirm by a group of incidental references that our Lord was crucified at the time when the Jews were preparing to kill and eat the paschal supper; whereas the Synop. Gospels had been unanimous in their assertion that the day preceding the agony and the crucifixion was that on which the days of unleavened bread commenced and the paschal lamb was slain and eaten, and that, the Lord Jesus having been tried and condemned on the day of the Feast and Holy Convocation, was laid in the grave on the evening of the Sabbath preparation. The difference of statement is explicit, and said, by the opponents of the authenticity of the Fourth Gospel, to be irreconcilable. This conclusion is strongly emphasized by the Tübingen writers, on the ground that the Quarto-deciman and Jewish-Christian party persisted in celebrating their 'feast of the Saviour's Passover' on the 14th day of Nisan, when the Jews slew their paschal lamb. Their festivals of rejoicing commenced after their fasting had ended, on whichever day of the week it occurred. According to Eusebius (*HE* v. 24), Polycrates of Ephesus affirmed that the Eastern Churches founded their custom in part on the practice of the Apostle John himself, '*who observed the* 14th *day according to the Gospel.*' But what Gospel? Not the Fourth, according to the critics, but the Synoptic Gospels, where *John* is mentioned with Peter as preparing the Passover on the morning of the 13th Nisan, and celebrating it with the Lord on the night of the 14th. This,

it has been alleged, runs directly counter to the representations of the Fourth Gospel.

Now, the difficulty here involved has been greatly aggravated by the twofold method in which conservative critics have endeavoured to solve it. Hengstenberg, Tholuck, Edersheim, Luthardt, M'Clellan, etc., satisfy themselves that every reference in John is compatible with the Synoptic assertion that the Lord's Supper coincided with the Jewish passover on the evening of 14th–15th of Nisan. They think that several of the proceedings of the night were exceptional, *e.g.* Judas going out, that the possible purchase of things needed for the feast or gift of alms could be justified, that 'the passover' which the chief priests were intending to hold, and for the ceremonial attendance on which they would not enter the prætorium, referred to a midday meal on the feast day called 'chagigah,' a 'thank-offering,' and sometimes termed by laxity 'passover' (2 Ch 36[22] 35[7. 9]), and that the references to the παρασκευή—and the bearing of the cross, are all compatible with the first day of convocation. It is thus thought that the two accounts are harmonized; but, on the other hand, Bleek, Greswell, Godet, Weiss, Westcott, Watkins, etc., have shown the entire incompatibility of the proceedings of the trial, of the crucifixion, the bearing of the cross by one coming from field labour, the purchase of spices, etc., with the most elastic interpretation of the letter of the law then in vogue. The violations of Sabbatic law in performing or allowing deeds of mercy would have been utterly insignificant by the side of these flagrant contradictions of both letter and spirit. These numerous details (see Reynolds' *Introd.* pp. xcii–xcv, and notes on the passages in Gosp.) cannot be discussed. The Synoptists themselves supply many confirmations of the Johannine view, especially the determination on which authorities not to apprehend Jesus 'on the feast day.' Since *Luke* reckons the 50th day after the first day following the Sabbath of Passover (see Lv 23[15], Dt 16[9]) as that on which Pentecost had fully come (Ac 2[1]), and as the universal tradition and custom of celebrating it on a *Sunday* cannot be disputed, it is evident that *Luke* must have reckoned in the year of our Lord's death that the paschal feast was held on the night following the crucifixion.

St. John, who took part in the preparation of the passover, was not purposely correcting a common tradition, but making the chronology more clear. Still there remains to be accounted for the explicit manner in which Luke and Mark refer to the celebration of the supper and the blending with it of the ancient ceremonial on the night of the betrayal. Godet and Westcott do not hesitate to imply that the Synoptic narrative shows that our Lord must have anticipated by a day the legal celebration. Haste and the imminence of the tragedy are thought to account for this departure. The fresh point made by Caspari (*Chron. Introd. to Life of Christ*, Eng. tr. pp. 195–217), is that the four evangelists are unanimous in the assertion that Jesus suffered on the 14th of Nisan, after having prepared for the paschal supper, though without the *lamb*, or the *bitter herbs*, or the *elaborate ceremonial*; that the lamb may have been reserved for the evening of the day of the crucifixion itself, for the hurry and awfulness of which they were unprepared. If this be the fact, the difficulty vanishes. In its favour may be added the *Chronicon Paschale*, which quotes Clemens Alex., who, following the chronology just set forth, implies that the disciples had learned that Jesus was Himself the Lamb, the food and the wine of the feast. The fact that Origen, Chrysostom, and others in the course of the various Easter controversies, took a different view from Clemens Alex., does not here concern us. The points at issue with the Western Church turn on other considerations not vitally connected with our present discussion. With three most plausible, if not absolutely satisfactory, methods of accounting for the difficulty, it is scarcely worthy of candid scholarship to speak of irreconcilable contradiction, or of the impossibility of St. John's being the author of the Fourth Gospel.

(4) *The omission by the Synoptic Gospels of events and discourses which constitute vital portions of the Fourth Gospel* is very startling, and difficult to explain; but it is important to observe that Matthew and Luke are also almost equally characterized by peculiarities of their own. Without enumerating them here in detail

(see *Pulp. Com.* xcvi), it may be sufficient to notice that while paragraphs of various length, peculiar to the author of the Fourth Gospel, amount to *ninety-six*, yet the specialities which we owe entirely to Lk amount to no fewer than *seventy-two*, and similar peculiarities of Mt to *sixty-two*, exceeding together by thirty-eight those of the Fourth Gospel. It is sufficient to urge that the three evangelists each found in the abundance of material what best corresponded with the supreme motive of his selection. Special emphasis has been laid upon the silence of the Synoptists on an event which definitely precipitated the tragedy. Most certainly, the death and restoration of Lazarus take so signal a place in the final working out of Jewish hostility, in John's Gospel, as to imply an extraordinary reticence on the part of the Synoptists. It is possible that amid the affluence of mighty works wrought in Galilee the sorrows and joys of Bethany did not bulk so largely as they seem to the critics to do when this one event is singled out for minute inspection.

(5) *The omission by the Fourth Gospel of events of capital importance in the Synoptic narrative.*

(*a*) The miraculous birth and infancy, the youth, the family, the genealogy of Jesus, and the early ministry of John the Baptist, are passed over in silence. Yet there are significant hints of these things which carry the reader's mind over the omission, without the suspicion of ignorance or indifference.

(*b*) The baptism of Jesus by John, with its accompaniments, is not definitely recorded, and yet it is implied in the testimony of John, and in the thrilling effect produced upon the mind of the Baptist by what he saw and heard. Similarly, no account is given of the imprisonment and death of the Baptist, yet both are hinted at.

(*c*) The omission of the temptation in the wilderness has been put down to doctrinal pre-possessions of 2nd cent., but closer study seems to show that the evangelist inserts between the great testimonies of the Baptist and his imprisonment—*i.e.* in precisely the chronological position where Synoptic teaching places the temptation—a series of events covering the matter of each of them. The creative multiplication of wine, as an act of love to *others* rather than of self-assertion or the rectification of personal need, corresponds with the temptation to dispense with the Father's providential care of His beloved Son. The sudden descent upon the temple with reforming energy, in lieu of casting Himself from the pinnacle to attract the admiration of the sign-loving multitude, is charged with effective analogies. Then, thirdly, we find an unostentatious refusal of Christ to palter with evil, or to accept the sanction of the Sanhedrin in order to accomplish the ends of even His own mission. 'Thou shalt worship the Lord thy God, and him alone shalt thou serve,' rings through Jn 2. 3 and 4 just where the Synoptists had chronologically placed the mighty struggle with the suggestions of the devil.

(*d*) The omission of the transfiguration, an event which is fully described in the Synoptic narrative. This is surprising, because the latter represents the son of Zebedee as one of the three witnesses of the incident; but the explanation may be that the eyes of the beloved disciple received more convincing evidence than the bright cloud and the heavenly visitants and a super-natural voice, to establish the divine glory and Person of the Lord. 'We saw,' he said (1¹⁴), 'his glory, the glory of the only-begotten.' It is worthy of notice in this respect that Moses and Elijah were perceived by John to have prepared the way of the Saviour and His sacrifice (1¹⁷, ²³). The whole Gospel is a continuous revelation of the

glory of the Life, a vindication of the fact that Jesus *is* the light- and sight-Giver to blinded humanity.

(*e*) A more perplexing omission is that of the institution of the Eucharist, especially as the very meal at which it took place is mentioned with some other accompaniments, such as the feet-washing of the disciples. Somewhere in the folds and parentheses of the stupendous sentence (13¹⁻⁵) we imagine that the institution of the Eucharist, which was intended for the sustenance and the responses of a transcendental love, lies concealed. On no supposition can we conceive the author to have been ignorant of the sacramental rite. We know that it had spread from Jerus. to Troas (Ac 20⁷, ¹¹) and Corinth, and was so highly esteemed as to be abused by the unwary (1 Co 11²⁰ᶠ.). The best supposition is that the apostle has spread out over the discourse contained in chs. 13–17 the deepest and most essential features of the Eucharist. The teaching of transcendent love, and mutual in-dwelling and eternal life, is thus repeated by the divine Master in these chapters. More than this, John has reported the astonishing discourses at Capernaum (ch. 6), where the Lord described deep spiritual communion with Himself as 'eating his flesh and drinking his blood.' Christ laid em-phasis on the faith which accepted the Incarna-tion, the reality and nearness of the God-man, the actual and perfect humanity of the Son of God, the divine Bread which came down from heaven, under the unique phrase 'eating his flesh,' and a deep appreciation and assimilation of His sacrificial death as nothing less than 'drinking his blood,' not only of 'the blood which is the life,' but the blood which was shed. So early in His ministry, He taught that what He also elsewhere in the Synop. narrative described as a *ransom in place of many*, was effected by the giving of His life. Thus He made it evident that *life* in Him was closely bound up with the stupendous idea of the death of the Christ of God. '*He that eateth me shall live because of me.*' Two theories have prevailed—one, that a transcendental philosopher in the middle of the 2nd cent., ignoring or re-pudiating the sacrament of the body and blood, chose this way of expressing his spiritualization of this widely prevalent usage. The other hypo-thesis is, that the beloved disciple, having heard and recorded the Lord's own interpretation of eating His body and drinking His blood, was content. This seems to us far more reasonable. But why should he have omitted the symbol which was so well calculated to preserve the teaching of the great discourse at Capernaum, 6³⁴⁻⁶⁰? We have just seen that he did not repel the historical concrete always in favour of the ideal representation. But he may reasonably have been wounded by the prevalence of heathen and superstitious adjuncts to the celebration of the Eucharist. He was not a bigoted spiritualist, as we may judge by the significance of the seven great miracles recorded by him, by the interesting feet-washing which had never become a sacra-mental usage. (See art. 'Fuss-waschung' by H. Merz in Herzog's *RE*; Smith's *Dict. of Christ. Ant.* 'Baptism,' §§ 34 and 67).

(*f*) The omission of the agony in the garden. Keim says, if St. John's account of the imperial bearing of Jesus in the garden and at the arrest be historical, then the Synoptic narrative is 'pulverized.' Renan, B. Weiss, and others are ready on the other hand to allow that we owe to this Gospel historic traits which throw much light upon the incidents of the passion. In John's account we have a more definite description of the place (κῆπος) than in Mt and Mk with their χωρίον, or Lk with the indefinite τόπος. The 'garden' was a 'place' 'to which Jesus often resorted with his disciples.' Moreover, if the Synop. narrative be historical, John must have been with His Lord in the depth of the olive shade. He must even have witnessed what Luke (22[43. 44], see below) describes of an agony insupportable, of the exceeding bitter cry, of the cup which the Father gave the Son of His love to drink, of the bloody sweat, and of the supernatural rally when, having called from the depths of a divine despair to Him who was able to save Him from death, He was heard because of His godly fear. But this apostle must have seen as no other reporter saw so distinctly, the lanterns and torches which accompanied the temple-guard as they descended into the Kidron Valley by the steep side of the hill below the city wall; he knew the *name*, Malchus, of the servant of the high priest, whose *right* ear Peter smote. Note, in addition to all this, how Jesus, according to John, rebukes Simon Peter for his rash manifestation of physical courage, in words which remind us of the bitterest experience of Gethsemane. We must admit that little trace of the prostration of that awful scene presents itself when the God-man (according to the Fourth Gospel) faces the enemy. He there appears to be a match for all the treachery of Judas, the malice of the chief priests, and even the military power of Rome. He meets the serried ranks of evil in the imperial calm of the intercessory prayer. It is the manner of this evangelist, and of other scriptural writers, to leave unexplained gaps in the midst of what seems to be continuous narrative. Such a manifest *lacuna* occurs here between the close of the valedictory discourse and the arrest of the Son of Man. But we see even from the Synoptists that the great agony was over, and that the angel had strengthened Him (Lk 22[43], whose genuineness is indeed doubtful; see WH's note). The cry, 'Thy will be done,' had linked the Father's purpose of redemption with the bleeding heart of man. He had now the energy to rebuke the rabble that gathered round Him. He drove Judas to despair with words of incomparable reproach. He moved forwards, in the face of false witness, to the assertion of the highest claims of Messiahship and divine authority. Even according to the Synoptists, the agony of the garden is compatible with the most stupendous claims.

Moreover, it should not be forgotten that the Fourth Gospel never ignores the vicarious sorrow or the sacrificial agony of the Son of God. Not only does the author show in the valedictory address and prayer the keenest appreciation of suffering (see 16[2. 3. 32] 17[12] 15[18-22 f.] and 14[30]), but he gives a parallel scene of surpassing intensity in 12[25-34], when a fearful looking for of deviation from the Father's will is surmounted by 'Father, glorify thy name!' The moral significance and the culminating intensity of the sacrifice is really placed chronologically before (not after) the experience of the upper chamber. Cf. also the strange blendings of humiliation and victory in the story of the resurrection of Lazarus. We must admit that as the temptation, the transfiguration, and the Eucharist are suggested throughout the Fourth Gospel, so also is the agony of Gethsemane, and, we may add, the bodily ascension of the Lord. The question arises: is the Synoptic narrative, which presents these themes in tableaux visions or revelations, or is the Fourth Gospel, which gives the same teaching in a group of objective facts and recorded words, the more historical?

To John's eye the grand synthesis of majesty and mercy, of divinity and humanity, of the ideal and the actual, the blending of the mystery of pain with the brightness of the glory, was present in all the word and work of the Logos incarnate.

To the Synoptic tradition, the universally diffused synthesis is gathered up into scenes and acts of a drama which readers have no power to blend without philosophical and theological hypotheses. If we are right here, much of the current anti-theological criticism of the Fourth Gospel vanishes.

C. There are numerous *correspondences* between the two documents which merit special consideration.

(a) *The broad facts*, the leading *outlines* of the life of the Only-begotten are the same. The *name* of 'Jesus,' the *place* of His early residence (Nazareth), the indisputable reference to 'father,' 'mother,' 'brethren,' and 'sisters,' the significance of this in connexion with the confession of His birth from the Spirit and of His having come down from heaven, belong to the two sources. The birth at Bethlehem (Jn 7[42]) is assumed to be true by the refusal to explain away a charge actually made. The reader knows that the Synop. tradition has already forestalled the objection which John, for special reasons, reported. Both sources of tradition agree that Capernaum was chosen by Jesus as the scene of special ministry. The different treatment of the Baptist is due to the obvious fact that the Fourth Gospel takes up his story where the Synoptics lay it down. After the wondrous manifestation in the Jordan, and the confidences between Jesus and John after the temptation, the Baptist was dazzled with a vision both of His glory and of His sacrifice. He penetrated the reality of both, and used the mighty names of 'Son of God,' 'Lamb of God,' and 'Bridegroom' of the veritable Israel. All this was perfectly compatible with the fact that the previous *knowledge* of Jesus by John—even a knowledge sufficient to justify the exclamation, 'I have need to be baptized of thee' (Mt 3[14])—was as star-light to sun-light.

Two great 'signs' of our Lord's mastery over material elements and the forces of nature are recorded in the Fourth Gospel (6[1-21]), and correspond with the Synoptic narrative in all their main features, and the two throw valuable side-lights on each other; e.g. the circumstance that Jesus *constrained* His disciples to enter the boat while *He* sent the multitude away (Mt 14[22] ‖ Mk 6[45]), is best explained by the sympathy felt by the disciples towards the desire of the multitude to take Jesus by force and hail Him as Messiah King (Jn 6[15]). The combined narrative brings out the impressive feature of the history.

Jn 12 gives new and interesting details of the anointing of the Lord by a woman (cf. Mt 26, Mk 14). It is from the Fourth Gospel that we learn her name, as well as the date, the motive, the criticism of this noteworthy deed which has filled the Church and the world with the fragrance of its perfume.

John agrees with the Synoptists in the main features of the triumphal entry into Jerusalem. The accounts of the 'supper' that preceded the passion, notwithstanding differences already discussed, have much in common, e.g. the detection and departure of Judas, and much of the matter of advice and consolation given by the departing Lord (cf. Lk 13[31-38] with the valedictory discourse).

In addition to this there are numerous identities, such as the trial scenes, the denials by Peter, the conduct of Pilate, the incident of Barabbas, the 'title' and accusation, the crucifixion, the two other victims, the death itself, with its certification —the witnesses of the resurrection. Much that John wrote would be more difficult to appreciate if we could not suppose that he had the narrative of the Synoptists before him. Thus, although John does not describe the discussion in the Sanhedrin or the decision arrived at, he implies it in Pilate's private interrogation of Jesus.

(b) Other matters of fact or teaching, given in detail by the Synoptists, are characteristically hinted at in the Fourth Gospel, e.g. John does not describe the baptism of Jesus, but he pointedly refers to the accompaniments and consequences of it. The reference in 3²⁴ to the fact that 'John was not yet cast into prison,' is best explained by the evangelist's knowing from the Synoptic narrative that the commencement of our Lord's Galilæan ministry coincided with the imprisonment of John. Further, he seems to show that the previous Judæan ministry was not incompatible with the assertion that a great *public* ministry of Christ in Galilee was apparently dependent on the arrest of John's activity. The Saviour's knowledge of Peter, and the latter's acceptance of the authority of Jesus (Lk 5⁶, Mt 4¹⁸, Mk 1¹⁶), are best understood from Jn 1⁴³ and the record of their early intercourse in the place where the Baptist was first exercising his ministry. The parable of the Children of the Bridechamber in Mt 9¹⁵ is curiously confirmed by the last recorded utterance of the Baptist, Jn 3²⁹.

Again, there are proverbial sayings found in Jn which are preserved sometimes in different connexions by the Synoptics. Comp. 4⁴⁴ with Mt 13⁵⁷, Mk 6⁴, Lk 4²⁴; and 13¹⁶ with Lk 6⁴⁰ and Mt 10²⁴; also 13²⁰ with Mt 10⁴⁰ and Lk 10¹⁶.

The identity of the character of our Lord as portrayed in the Synop. and Johan. narratives is very remarkable, though this has been sometimes disputed. Even A. B. Bruce (*Apologetics*, p. 485) thinks it difficult to reconcile the apparent motive of the great miracles of the Fourth Gospel with the philanthropic, sympathetic, and personal reasons which dictate corresponding miracles and other incidents in the Synoptics. He says that while our Lord's chief motive in the Synoptics was pitifulness over human need, on the other hand the obvious purpose of His 'signs' in the Fourth Gospel was to call attention to His own Person and claims on human love and veneration. There is serious matter for contemplation here, should this contrast be observed throughout these documents. But the case of every applicant for His mercy was severally considered and dealt with according to His wisdom. As He said to the woman who washed and anointed His feet, 'Thy sins are forgiven thee'; 'She loved much'; 'Go in peace';—so to the woman taken in adultery, and brought before Him, He said, 'Go and sin no more.' Doubtless He healed many in the affluence of His love, as detailed by the Synoptists; but He would not allow the woman with the issue of blood to steal away with a purely temporal blessing; and in like manner He 'found' the sick man of Bethesda in the temple to give him warning, and did not rest after healing the blind man until He 'found' him to confer upon him the highest benediction. The reason of the miraculous feeding of the multitude in both documents is anxiety for their secular and physical requirements; and the creation of the elements of wine at the wedding feast is an answer to the call upon His pity on behalf of the embarrassed villagers. The walking of Jesus upon the boisterous lake was a distinctly expressed concern for the peril both of mind and body to which His disciples were exposed. In all these cases our Lord undoubtedly found occasion to bring out the great assurance that He had come forth from God and down from heaven; that He was the Light of the world, the Giver of strength, and a great Prophet. So though the raising of Lazarus was conditioned by consciousness of alliance with Heaven and oneness with the Father, yet few things in the Bible are more impressive than His sympathetic weeping over that grave, and His divine condolence with Martha and Mary.

Obviously, it was the purpose of the Fourth Evangelist to record the impressive words, gestures, revelations by which the Lord unveiled both Himself and the Father. These are more impressive in St. John than in the popular tradition, but they did not conceal the humanness of His love. The ironical charge, which was transformed into a crown of glory, 'He saved others, himself he could not save,' is one of the keynotes of the Fourth as well as of the other Gospels. On the other hand, do we not find in the Sermon on the Mount as well as in the charge to the twelve disciples (Mt 10), to say nothing of the interpretation of the great parables of the Sower, of the Tares, and of the Dragnet (Mt 13), and of the Seed growing secretly (Mk 4²⁶ᶠᶠ·), stupendous claims of personal dignity, and of kinship with the supreme Revealer and Arbiter of human destiny? Does any assumption of the Fourth Gospel transcend the claims made by the great prophet of Mt 23–25? The Jesus of the Fourth Gospel felt that His own powers and claims were of supreme moment to mankind, but that the end of all He said and did was the life, light, peace, and joy of His brethren, and their victory over the world. Let the following passages be specially consulted : 5⁴⁰ 6²⁷· ⁴⁷⁻⁵⁰ 7¹⁷· ³⁷· ³⁸ 8¹²· ³¹· ³² 10⁹· ¹⁰· ²⁸ 11⁴⁰ 12²⁵· ³⁵ 13³⁴· ³⁵ 14³ᶠᶠ·, and almost every paragraph of the valedictory discourse. The same features and spirit pervade the Synoptic Gospels, establishing more of unity than diversity in their theme. They alone relate the supernatural birth of Jesus. Nothing more characteristically Johannine can be found than Mt 11²⁵⁻³⁰ and Lk 10²¹· ²², wherein the Lord's supreme self-consciousness was uttered, and is revealed in most close and gracious relations with the consolation and salvation of mankind. No words in the Fourth Gospel concerning our Lord's character and prerogatives are loftier than those in the Synoptic Gospels. We believe we are justified in saying that the Synoptists would be more difficult to expound without the light of the Fourth Evangelist than the Fourth Gospel without the aid of the Synoptists.

Other interesting and mutually corroborating elements are found in the four Gospels. There is, for example, the portraiture of certain personages in the Fourth Gospel of whom we know nothing elsewhere, not even the name—unless the name be a second name of one known to us by another.

(1) The most striking instance of this is *Nathanael* (chs. 1 and 21). A widely spread idea prevails that he is to be identified with the Bartholomew of the Synoptic lists of apostles, where he is (by his patronymic only) associated with Philip and Thomas.

(2) *Nicodemus* is thrice referred to (3. 7⁵⁰ 19³⁹), nay, he is photographed by a few phrases. The familiarity of our Lord with this distinguished personage is quite parallel with numerous scattered hints of His social relationships, especially in Lk 7³⁶ 8³ 19⁵. There is no certain identification of Nicodemus with one N. ben-Gorion, who, according to the Talmud, survived the fall of Jerusalem (see Geikie, i. 584; Winer's *Realwörterbuch*, ii. 152).

(3) The *woman of Samaria* is portrayed with inimitable vivacity, and in a few sentences she has told her own story for all time. The references to Samaria and the Samaritans in Lk and Ac are all illumined by this sketch of the early intercourse of our Lord with the inhabitants of Sychar.

(4) *Mary and Martha* have been introduced to the Synoptic history almost as ideals of the contrast between the contemplative and the active

religious life. In Jn there is a brilliant page of genuine biography and history. The time and the place are recorded; the characterization of the women is beautifully preserved along unconscious lines in Jn 11. The resemblance of their brother's name to that of the beggar of St. Luke's parable does not throw any light on this story, for all the surroundings are different, unless there be a faint adumbration in Abraham's word, 'Neither will they be persuaded,' etc., of the access of malignity in the hearts of the Pharisees, as reported in Jn 12[10], on hearing of the resurrection of Lazarus.

(5) *The Virgin Mother.* The reticence of the Synoptic account is one of the marvels of NT. We learn there that probably both she and Joseph also were the lowly heirs of the family and throne of David, that she occupied a purely OT stand-point, that she saw in the great function intrusted to her a solution of the baffling paradoxes of the theocratic kingdom. Mt and Lk combine to tell us of the gracious incidents of the infancy, while Mk sheds a very strong light on the probability that she shared with her other sons the fear that her prophetic child was 'beside himself,' and that she received from Him a severe yet filial rebuke. She would doubtless have spared Him every rough handling, and sought to restrain all undue exposure to the rising storm of mingled enthusiasm and malignity. The sublime way in which, according to Mk, the Lord baffled the de-sign of the brethren, and emancipated Himself from the control of His domestic circle, is on many grounds, both literary and doctrinal, most note-worthy. Cf. and connect Mk 3[20] with [30-35]. Mary followed Jesus to Jerus. and was present at the tragedy, but there is no statement in any of the Synoptists that she was there. Lk, however, places her with her sons among the disciples before and after the Ascension, and it may be readily inferred that she was among the women who ministered to Jesus, though Mary of Magdala and Mary the mother of James the less and of Joses hide her from view. The same picture of the Virgin Mother is preserved by the beloved disciple. Here also she allows herself to be over-shadowed by others and hidden in the glory of her Son and Lord. The author of the Fourth Gospel never breathes her name, but preserves the memory of the incident which he knew best, that he received the dying legacy of his Master, and as a son with a mother took her to his own home. The reference to the mother of our Lord frees his narrative from all Docetic taint; and the firm vindication of the truth that the Lord came in the flesh and was made flesh, seemed to him to be of the very essence of the Gospel, and the denial of it to be antichrist. At the same time, his constant reference to the supernatural, heaven-descended life of Christ gives the most vital basis for His immaculate conception. Minute touches also show at Cana the manner in which, while He delivered Himself from maternal control, Jesus obeyed her desire to meet the needs of their humble hosts. Thus, in the most subtle manner, the rare and wonderful portraiture is the same in both documents.

(6) The portrait of *John the Baptist* differs from that of the Synoptists; but if it be noted that the Fourth Gospel takes up the story where the current tradition dropped it, the chief difficulty vanishes. The strange question sent from the prison (Mt 11[2] and parallels) seems all the more strange in view of the great testimonies to Jesus borne by the Baptist as given in Jn 1 and 3 (cf. Reynolds, *John the Baptist*, 419–449). But there is nothing, after all, in the 'witness of John' which transcends the OT standpoint, and Christ declares (5[36]) that He had 'greater witness than that

of John.' Like Judaism itself, John would never have accomplished his proper work if he had not held to it too tenaciously even after it had reached its climax. But this involves exegetical considera-tions that are beyond our present scope.

(7) Of nothing are we more certain than of the historical character of *Simon Peter*. The blending of courage and weakness, the desire to suggest the courses to be followed even by his Lord, succeeded by the profound deference paid to the expression of the thought of Christ as soon as his reckless blundering was corrected, recur from first to last. This double personality appears at the earliest introduction to Jesus, amid the splendours of the transfiguration and the solemnities of Geth-semane, in his base denials and bitter tears, on the morning of the resurrection amid the visions of heavenly things, in the controversy with St. Paul over the essence of justification, and in the traditions of Church history. He is a real, not an imaginary man. If St. John had given a fundamentally different interpretation of his per-sonality, it would have been strongly adverse to the historicity of his narrative; but the fact is, that in the transactions of chs. 13. 18. 20 and 21, though handling several diverse incidents, St. John's statements exactly preserve the same com-plicated features of St. Peter's inner and outer life. He who said to the Lord of the invisible world, 'Not so, Lord,' or 'Depart from me, for I am a sinful man,' or 'That be far from thee, Lord'; who would have builded tabernacles on the slopes of Hermon, or engaged a whole band of Roman soldiers with a single sword, and then declared with curses that he knew not the man whom he had risked his life to defend,—is the same as the disciple who first cried, 'Thou shalt never wash my feet' and then, 'not my feet only, but also my hands and my head'; who rushed into the sea to reach the feet of his risen Lord, and whose new act of impulsive curiosity received anew the rebuke of the Lord. The in-delible imprint of personality is carried through-out the fourfold narrative.

(8) *Caiaphas* and *Pilate*, though portrayed at a different angle and in the midst of circumstances which though concordant with those of the Syn-optists have a different bearing on the whole narrative, are alike etched from the life, and betray no departure from the reality common to the earlier representation. Caiaphas and Pilate are described as priest and ruler of Israel during the whole of the ministry of Jesus, Lk 3[1]. The remorseless resolve of the Sadducean priest to find or make a capital charge against Jesus on the ground either of sedi-tion or blasphemy; the unprincipled endeavour to keep the Pharisees from siding with Jesus in His reformatory zeal; the demand on oath from our Lord of the loftiest claim of Messiahship and Sonship with a view to his immediate condemna-tion on a charge to which Pilate could not listen; and the delivery of Jesus to the Romans on a new charge altogether, which Pilate saw through at a glance,—all this is left intact by the Fourth Evangelist, while he casts an additional light on the main motives of both the priest and the governor. The moral confusion of the motives of Caiaphas, evinced (11[49]) in his prophetic forecast of a scapegoat to the indignant majesty of Rome, offered in the person of one absolutely innocent of the crimes alleged; the superstitious fears which blended in Pilate's mind with the abuse of his sovereign power; the uprising of his moral, at least of his political, conscience, which led to the temporary delay of the sentence,—all these ele-ments are emphasized by the Fourth Gospel from its own sources of evidence. The private interviews between Pilate and Jesus, to which the

beloved disciple was privy (18^{33-38} 19^{9-12}), as well as the private and preliminary examination before Annas, add to the general information, and have a supplementary character; still the author does not ignore, but gives the result of the action of the Sanhedrin under the leadership of Caiaphas in Pilate's own words, 'Thine own nation and the chief priests delivered thee unto me' (18^{35}). The Barabbas incident brings into pointed relief the action of the priestly party as touched on in the Synoptic narrative, telling us that there was a pause and a questioning among the $\delta\chi\lambda o\varsigma$, which was overcome by the activity of the priests, who 'persuaded' the people (Mt 27^{20}); but the Johannine narrative shows how the fact corresponds with the earlier tradition; and the extremely culpable weakness of Pilate is further shown in the delineations of the Fourth Gospel. Pilate crushed the warnings of his own conscience, and was more intent on visiting his supercilious antipathy on the priests than on carrying out his own expressed conviction that the prisoner was innocent of the charge brought against Him. He yielded at last to a clamour which might complicate his relations with Tiberius, as the most fateful expression of Jewish national degradation at length burst upon his ear. 'We have no king but Cæsar' sealed the doom, not only of Jesus, but of the theocratic nation. Jesus was sacrificed to the cowardice and meanness of Pilate. The spirit of revenge which induced him to abide by the 'title' upon the Cross is another touch of characterization which we owe, as we believe, to the special sources of information possessed by the Fourth Evangelist. We are not concerned to deny that John's silence about the sublime assumption of the Messiahship and judgment of the world, and of the divine claim He made to the highest conceivable dignity, even when it sealed His death-warrant from the Sanhedrin, is a serious perplexity, but, at all events, it reveals no mere doctrinal perversity on the part of the writer to press the apparent theme and motive of his own wonderful contribution to the history of the Word made flesh.

We have thus considered the objections drawn from the chronological and biographical details of the Synoptic Gospels, and have shown that the omissions by the Synoptics of certain facts presumed to be of historical importance, as well as the striking omissions by the Fourth Gospel of events of cardinal significance in the Synoptic narrative, have often been pressed beyond their real significance. We have traced also the general correspondences in the chief facts and minute details of manner and matter between them, and examined the biographic portraiture of the most noted characters. There remain some general objections of greater or less moment which affect the whole composition.

D. Miscellaneous Objections.—*a.* The supposed exaggeration, through the mythopœic tendency in the later writer, of the *supernatural element.* The transmutation by creative process of 'water' into 'wine' is reckoned as an exaggerated and suspicious instance of divine prerogative attributed to the incarnate Logos. But this act seems by no means a more wonderful display of the will of Christ in harmony with the Supreme Will than is the multiplication of the bread, which belongs to the entire tradition. The heightened intensity of some of the special signs selected by 'John' is sometimes cited, *e.g.* the *thirty-eight* years of the man's infirmity in ch. 5 is compared disadvantageously with the *eighteen* years of similar paralysis as mentioned by Lk; so likewise the blindness from *birth* is compared unfavourably with the temporary blindness which Jesus healed, as recorded by Mt and Mk. But the way in which

Mt tells of *two* blind men where the other evangelists, Mk and Lk, mention one, and *two* demoniacs instead of one at Gadara, and two multiplications of bread and fish instead of one in the other records, is far more open to the charge of mythical enlargement than anything that is here attributed to the Fourth Gospel. There is a deepening glory in the resurrections from the dead, which has been commented upon since the days of Augustine. The daughter of Jairus just laid upon her deathbed, and the young man at Nain being carried to his grave, might seem insufficient *per se* to prove that the Lord Jesus had the keys of death in His hands, but the fourth day of death and the assumed putridity of Lazarus' corpse are more conclusive evidence that the Lord is King, and can and will raise in some way all that are in the dust of death. He had chosen death and the sepulchre as His special battlefield,—the evangelist had ample facts from which he made selection with reference alike to blindness and death, and in both cases, as well as in the bread sign and the Bethesda 'Sabbath cure,' he apparently chose the incidents for the sake of the discourses with which they were followed, and which he remembered so well. It must not be forgotten in estimating the weight of this argument that the Fourth Gospel is parsimonious in describing specific miracles, though it records the fact of their abundance ($20^{30.\ 31}$). Further, it is the only one of the four which declares that the miraculous is a kind of evidence far inferior to that of intuition and personal recognition of the divine in Himself (Jn 14^{10-14}). The miracle arrested attention, but it was still in the region of the natural and sensuous, and appealed rather to the understanding than to the higher conscience or to the spirit. The most startling and dramatic scenes, including, as we have seen, the temptation, the transfiguration, and the portents of the crucifixion, are shorn of those mysterious accompaniments which are desired by the miracle-loving multitude, and might be described as the unhistorical accretion of years. After prolonged pondering of the problem, we are convinced it might be urged that there is more of the mythical lustre overspreading the Synoptic narrative, more of the imaginative setting, and the solitary uncorroborated event or teaching in both Mt and Lk than in the Fourth Gospel, and more of the pictorial and even dramatic presentation in the Gospel of Mk than in either of them, and still more than in the stern self-repression and spiritual recollections of the great Apostle of Love.

β. Schenkel (*Charakterbild Jesu*, § ii., and elsewhere throughout his able work), Hase, Renan, Ritschl, and others, have emphasized the absence from the Fourth Gospel of that *progressive mental and official development* of the character and Messianic claim of Jesus alleged to be discoverable in the Synoptic tradition. But if the Preacher of the Sermon on the Mount identified Himself with 'righteousness,' and declared that, by penetrating the secrets of all hearts, He could and would dispose of the final destinies of individuals; if He was hailed as the Holy One of God by the demoniacs (Mk), and in the synagogue at Nazareth (Lk) aroused inveterate hatred by a double claim to Messianic dignity and to an obnoxious universalism,—there is not much room for development after that, especially when the three Gospels emphasize the significance of the Heavenly Voice which accompanied His baptism by John, and His subsequent transfiguration, as the climax of His Galilæan ministry. We are not concerned to deny the development of Jesus from His birth to the twelfth and afterwards to the thirtieth year of His life. Enough has been told to discriminate His infancy finally from that of the later legends of Buddha, or the precocities and monstrosities of the non-canonical Gospels of the Infancy. The originality of Jesus leaves no room to think that either John the Baptist or Philo, Hillel or Gamaliel, contributed anything to His mental resources or to His Messianic rôle. He knew His own mind, and followed it throughout, allowing the voice of the Father and the foreordained unfolding of human need and inquiry to determine the successive phases of revelation. While He was waiting for God, God was working in all things to the unveiling of His own true nature and the vindication of His love to the uttermost. There appears to be quite a parallel, if not a richer, development in the Fourth Gospel than in the other three. There is a wide space between the language addressed to Nathanael (1⁴⁷) and that to Philip on the night of the passion: 'Have I been so long time with you,' etc. ; between the elementary instructions given to Nicodemus (3¹⁻¹⁶) touching the fundamental aspects of the new life, and the true nature of the kingdom of God, as consisting of regenerated men on the one hand, and on the other the sublime teaching of the 'good Shepherd,' the mutual indwelling of the Vine and its branches (ch. 15); the glorification of the Son of God, who would go unto the Father, prepare a place for them, 'come again to them' in the power and presence of the Comforter. Almost every school of criticism admits a momentous advance after the close of ch. 12. Those whom He had gathered out of the world, those who at length had come to believe in the mission of the Lord, are set forth at length as face to face with each other, under the shadow of the cross, in the coronation of sacrifice, suffering, sorrow, and death. A higher strain of instruction pervades the Fourth Gospel than that current in the Synoptic tradition—one more adapted to the solitary inquirers, or to a knot of carping and critical priests, or to the society of His own disciples at great crises of their spiritual history, or to angry sticklers for their own customs when preparing their final and deadly assault upon His life, than to the ordinary and miscellaneous groups at the lake side or on the hill slopes of Galilee. However, the contrast does not interfere with the historicity of either account. The progressive aspects of each group of revelations is obviously the result of the different susceptibilities of His audience and their power to catch the meaning of His teaching. In the case of St. John's Gospel this is heightened by the circumstance that the reporter is throughout one intense, perfervid, yet contemplative spirit, who received from the infinite fulness of the God-incarnate—knowing Him to be this—just the impression which he alone could receive, and in some degree record for after generations.

γ. The *Gnostic element* in the Fourth Gospel, as distinct from the Synoptic narratives, has been supposed to carry this document from the close of the 1st to the middle of the 2nd cent., to the great disparagement of its biographical and autoptic value. Siegfried, as we have seen, endeavours to establish an influence from Philo of Alexandria upon the entire literature of NT, upon Mt and Ja as well as on Hebrews and the Johannine writings. Thoma has maintained a similar thesis. He even fastens on Valentinus, as Baur had done on Marcion, to re-date the Pauline Epistles, and so obtain, *a fortiori*, a plunge down into the 2nd cent. for the Johannine books. This kind of criticism overshoots itself. Both the 1st cent. B.C. and the 1st and 2nd cents. A.D. were seething with the ferment produced by the blending of Hel. and Oriental ideas, of Gr. and Heb. philosophy and phrase. There is no need to come down to the middle of the 2nd cent. to understand the phraseology of Col or Hebrews, the

letters of Ignatius or Barnabas, or the Wisdom of Solomon. Specific terms, such as 'Logos,' 'Life,' and 'Light,' were ready at all times to take up a richer connotation than before. The special contrast between the Synoptists and John, to the disparagement of the latter, has been pressed, as though Jn had thus received the hall-mark of the end of 2nd cent. The question arises whether the creation of the whole world by the Logos or Son is affirmed or repudiated by the Fourth Gospel. Does it recognize the dualistic view of the source of good more than do the Synop. Gospels? Surely the latter give us more references to the malice, mischief, and kingdom of Satan, of darkness and demonism, than the Fourth Gospel, which never refers to demoniac energy. There is nothing more, on the other hand, than a vague side reference to the Creation in the Synoptics (Mk 10⁶). Such language is by no means so clear and explicit with reference to Creation as πάντα δι' αὐτοῦ ἐγένετο (Jn 1³), nor can it be pretended that matter (ἡ ὕλη) or any other element in the κόσμος is excepted from the πάντα, which owe absolutely their genesis to the Logos. The non-interpenetrating characteristics of 'light' and 'darkness' is not asserted. The power of 'darkness' is not chaotic or anarchic, but represents simply the negation of 'light.' 'Darkness' is not impenetrable to 'light.' The element of will or moral nature enters into the conditions of its permanence. The idea of ὁ πονηρός belongs rather to the Synop. than Johan. representations; see Mt 5³⁷ 6¹³ 13¹⁹, Lk 11²⁶. S. Davidson considered that Jesus (Jn 17⁹) did not 'pray for the world,' because the κόσμος was hopelessly beyond the region of conversion or the power of prayer. This interpretation seems entirely inconsistent with 1²⁹ 3¹⁶ 4⁴² 6³³. ⁵¹ 8¹² 12⁴⁷ 16⁸, and even with the context of the assertion, 'I pray not for the world,' in which the Lord prays (v.²¹) for those who should believe on Him through the word of His disciples, and looks forward to the great consummation of His own mission, 'that the *world* may believe that thou didst send me.' This is the final purpose of the Lord's intercession for His disciples. We admit that pervading the Fourth Gospel there is a class of references to an elect kingdom of susceptible souls to be found throughout the world, 'the other sheep' of 10¹⁶, cf. 3²⁰. ²¹ 18³⁷, which suggest the wideness of God's mercy, and also the inscrutable and boundless depths of the divine decrees, the extent of the invisible and omnipotent graces affecting human destiny and counteracting human perversity and corruption. This is not Gnosticism, but one of the great teachings of Divine Revelation in the God-man. A Docetic element is charged upon the Fourth Gospel, and the Gnostic Ebionitism of the 2nd cent. is referred to as its source, and the later supposed date is assigned on this ground to the whole class of representation ; but the Johan. writings, and especially the Gospel, are the most decidedly pronounced anti-Docetic documents in NT. They speak of the true humanity of the Son of Man with intentional emphasis. Thus the father, mother, brothers of Jesus are spoken of ; the weariness, thirst, tears, inward groanings, personal affections, dress, food, spittle, touch, flesh, blood, bones, wounded side, are severally mentioned. He was 'made flesh,' *i.e.* full humanity ; His dead body was partially embalmed, His raiment was divided among the soldiers. After His resurrection He was prepared to take broiled fish and honey and bread. We do not admit a treatment of the supposed phantasmic appearances or disappearances of the Lord (7³⁰ 8⁵⁹ 10³⁹ 18⁶) as Gnostic or Docetic in the Fourth, when similar events are recorded in the Synop. Gospels, *e.g.* Lk 4, as well as the walking on the water and the walk to Emmaus. Hilgenfeld has laid stress on a translation his theory has demanded, that in 8⁴³·⁴⁴ our Lord is supposed to refer to 'the father of the devil,' and so to the origination of the devil by some inferior god, like the Jehovah of OT as imagined by the Ophites. The whole of this contention has been taken up favourably by the advocates of the 2nd cent. date. It proceeds from unwillingness to recognize that the Gospel places the difference between the children of God and the children of the devil, not in primordial difference of essence, but in the will of man (see Godet's *Introd.* vol. i. 182 ff.).

δ. The phenomena of the Johan. *discourses* unquestionably introduce us to a new atmosphere, and to a place and audience different from those of the Synoptics. This is not finally explained by the frequent suggestion that the Synoptics represent our Lord as addressing the multitudes in Galilee, and that the Fourth Gospel is almost exclusively occupied with individuals, or with small groups of His disciples,—because, on the one hand, we see that the great controversy of ch. 6 was conducted in the synagogue of Capernaum, and those of chs. 5 and 10 were held with large and excited groups in the temple courts. On the other hand, the great Synoptic discourse on the last things was addressed to only four of the twelve disciples. Moreover, the comparison of Mt 5–7 with Lk 6 shows that the Sermon on the Mount was a selection of the most recondite instructions addressed at the first—and in the main—to the inner circle of the disciples. The same features are observed in the special discourse to the twelve disciples in Mt 10, and correspond with much similar instruction given to the seventy disciples in Lk 10¹⁻¹⁶. We cannot account for these differences of style and subject-matter on such easy terms. A considerable element of subjective choice is distinctly claimed by the author on two occasions. He selected his materials from copious accumulations, out of a wide range of memory and of tradition. The reporter put them together with the hope and belief that they would evoke confidence in the Messiah-functions and divine Sonship of Jesus (20³¹ and 21²⁵). Some of the most 'Johannine' utterances are likewise to be found in Mt 11²⁵ᶠᶠ·, Lk 10²⁵ᶠ·. Moreover, every great claim made by our Lord in the Fourth Gospel is anticipated by the direct or implied teaching of the reported sayings, and the miracles and parables of the Synoptics. The diction of these sayings is different from that of the earlier narratives, though it is easy to exaggerate the difference, and to ignore a very fundamental element of the problem. We have already seen how much common matter there is in these four documents. Many proverbial sayings or startling apothegms, found in the Three, are not absent from the Fourth, though they are given in fresh connexions. The strain of the self-consciousness of Jesus appears frequently in the Synoptic narrative, though given there when our Lord was concerned with the judgment of men, and foreboding the consummation of all things. Whatever may be the ultimate solution of this great problem, this at least is shown to be probable, that there was from the first a twofold, double-sided strain in our Lord's discourse, on which minds of congenial and susceptible characteristics would and did lay hold, with verbal tenacity, when brought into intimate relation with Him. This corresponds with analogous phenomena in other regions of biographical record. Only by blending these and some dissimilar elements can we obtain the approximate portraiture. We need to combine the commonplace representation of the man Socrates by the matter-of-fact Xenophon, and even the lampoon of the Sophists

in the comic satire of Aristophanes, with Plato's ideal of the great teacher, martyr, citizen, and philosopher, before we have the historic Socrates on our canvas. In like manner we are bound to take account of the Pauline Christ and that of the Ep. to the Hebrews, the 'unwritten words,' the threefold type of the Synoptists, and, above all, that representation which in this Gospel presses most near to that portion of His consciousness wherein He communes with the Father and with Himself. In these conversations and soliloquies the subjective element of the reporter is more conspicuous than elsewhere. The prince of biographers is he who is able to gather up the spirit and gist of a long conversation or discourse, and present it in the words of the Master Himself. This is exactly what John seems to have done, and thus he brings us nearer than any other to the great historic reality—'historic,' *i.e.* not, as often implied, on purely non-supernatural lines, but in the sense of objective fact.

The opponents of the authenticity of the Fourth Gospel urge that the writer, alike in his prologue and in the report of the Lord's words in the epilogue, and in the first Ep., adopts a style of expression which he puts into the mouth of Nathanael and Nicodemus, Mary and Martha, Caiaphas and Pilate, the blind man and John the Baptist, corresponding in diction so closely with the phraseology of Jesus, as to suggest that the Greek words of all the speakers, including the Lord Himself, are nothing else than St. John's own strongly characterized vocabulary and diction. Some of the most acute and learned defenders of the authenticity of the document have not hesitated practically to admit this contention. Watkins (in his *Bampton Lectures*, and in his article on the same theme in Smith's *DB*²) has maintained the possibility of which we have spoken, and has endeavoured to account for the phenomena by the simple theory of translation from an *Aramaic* original. It is probable that some of the discourses have undergone this process of translation. There is a distinct tradition to a similar effect with reference to the Gospel of *Matthew*. The same peculiarity must be held equally possible in Mk and Lk. And many of the difficulties are surmounted in the present case by the theory of the translation of words uttered in Aramaic into the Greek of Jn, which, having been built up through long years, enabled him to make use of it in representing the words of others, and then he may have adopted the same favourite terms, and a somewhat similar construction of sentences on all occasions. But we cannot admit that this hypothesis completely satisfies the facts of the case.

ε. *The diction of our Lord and of His biographer.* There are peculiarities of diction, vocabulary, and structure which are certainly adopted by this writer—Gr. words are used by him and by no other, some of which are somewhat uncommon, such as ἄντλημα, ἀποσυνάγωγος, βιβρώσκειν, γλωσσόκομον, δακρύειν, δίδυμος, ἐπιχρίειν, θήκη, θρέμματα, κέρμα, κολλυβιστής, νιπτήρ, προσαίτης. But in respect of special vocabulary Jn does not differ from other writers of NT. Again, there is a peculiar fondness manifested in Gospel and Epistle for certain special and almost technical words,—which by frequent repetition acquire a deeper meaning,— such as φῶς (23 times), δόξα (42), κόσμος (78), μαρτυρία (47), γινώσκειν (55), πιστεύειν (98), σημεῖον (17 times). It is also clear that the writer adopted a Semitic connotation for ן in the καί which he makes do ample duty for the various connective particles of the Gr. tongue. A common phenomenon in the Johannine writings is simple juxtaposition of sentences, often producing by the mere use of καί, and in fact sometimes without it, an adversative, concessive, or peculiar emphasis (1^4 15^{24} 3^{11} 5^{39}). The very common antithesis of μέν and δέ is almost dropped, and καί repeatedly made to represent δέ. It is curious that the writer, after using λόγος in ch. 1, subsequently drops it and *never* puts it into the lips of Jesus. It recurs in the 1 Ep. (ch. 1) and in the Apocalypse. It therefore becomes clear by this and many other passages and peculiarities that the author had a Greek diction somewhat peculiar to himself, which he used when following his own lines of meditation or narrative. Attention may also be called to the remarkable fact, that he puts into the lips of our Lord no fewer than 145 words which he never uses in his own person. Thirty-eight of these are found also in the Synop. account of our Lord's discourses. A similar peculiarity of expression or construction is reserved by the writer for Jesus, but never adopted by himself. There are nine peculiarities of our Lord's diction, such as the reduplicated ' Amen,' which are peculiar to Jn and never found elsewhere. There are 500 words which are freely used by him in his own portions of the Gospel or in the words of one or other of the interlocutors, which he never attributes to our Lord, so that the phenomena of translation still leave some problems to be solved by closer investigation. That there was a certain amount of translation is obvious, and some strong subjective element in the selection and arrangement of material cannot be ignored; but an effort must have been made to conserve the sacred words of the Lord Jesus in a phraseology which was supposed especially adapted to represent and enshrine the original utterances of the Master. This becomes more obvious when the evangelist frequently comes into direct communication with his reader: when he speaks *in propriâ personâ* occasionally he offers a commentary on the words of our Lord, perhaps even an expansion along certain lines of his own, of the words of Jesus which, though he caught them (and even transferred them into Gr.), he had not fully comprehended. These contrasts between the writer's memories and his explanations, both of the narrative and of the discourse, deserve far more attention than they have received.

The surpassing majesty of the Prologue (1^{1-18}) indicates that the mind of the writer was interpenetrated, overwhelmed with the effect produced by his contact with the Lord Jesus Christ. Clearly, he could think of Him as nothing less than ' the only-begotten of the Father,' as the Agent by whom the fulness of grace and truth broke upon the world,—and yet he drew a distinction between ὁ θεός and the λόγος as divine element in Jesus, although in the same breath declaring an identity between them. The Word, said he, was ' in the beginning,' and ' with God,' and yet ' was God.' It was ' the Word ' by whom ' all things ' came into being. The Word was both the source and the sphere of life, of that life which was light. All the light which had ever flashed into the darkness, and which the darkness was too gross to admit, was the beaming of His face. This conflict with the darkness resulted in most tragical issues. Nevertheless, this Word at length came into the world, and did so along fresh lines, not merely as eminent in all life and light, but as a fully constituted humanity—'flesh.' From this point onward he proceeded to show how the soliloquies and words of Jesus fell upon his sensitive and susceptible soul, as belonging rather to eternity than to time, as voices which had in them an infinity of meaning and of truth. He selected a few only of these for description and comment, and they grew in weight and wonder till he laid down the pen. At the same time, we feel that the Lord did not write, and could not

have written, the Prologue. The logical exordium, the sublime climax, were neither in our Lord's own manner nor in His own phrase, as afterwards reported by the evangelist. A full discussion of this comparison must be reserved for some other place, but a brief treatment of a few of the most salient passages may be attempted.

ζ. *The incommensurability between the writer and his theme.* We come into close contact with the writer in the following passages :—1^{25} $2^{9-11.21}$ $23-25$ $3^{18-21. 23}$, possibly $34-36$ 4^{4-6} 5^{1-6} $6^{6. 15. 17. 64. 65}$ $7^{30. 39}$ 8^9 9^{20} $9^{7. 22}$ $10^{41. 42}$ $11^{6. 13. 33-35. 51. 52}$ $12^{16. 33. 37-43}$, possibly 12^{46-50} $13^{1-6. 11. 28-30}$ 16^{17-19} 17^3 $18^{4. 9. 14. 28. 32}$ $19^{14. 24. 28. 35-37}$ $20^{30. 31}$ $21^{4. 23-25}$. These passages are independent of pure narrative, and are selected mainly because the writer essays to inform his readers of the secret sentiment of the disciples or of others, which does not appear in the narrative itself, but still more because of the way in which he attempts to make more obvious the words of the Lord Himself, when the wisdom of his interpretation, though doubtless up to a point conveying a deep or an obvious meaning, is not equal to the accuracy of his report. Only a few of these can be indicated here. 2^{21} ' *But he spake of the temple of his body,*' was doubtless a natural inference of a believer in the bodily resurrection of Jesus from the death to which the Sadducean party would in the main condemn Him. The first notes of the death-peal were sounded in the temple. The departure of Jesus from Jerus. was proof of the kind of reception which the great Prophet received from ' his own ' as soon as ' darkness ' set itself to quench the new ' light.' This was one and the nearest interpretation. But with all the subsequent history of the spiritual temple of believing men, and of the rapidity—the ' three days '—in which the new body and temple rose into spiritual splendour and sufficiency, it is difficult to believe that the evangelist sounded or grasped all the significance of the weighty words. The question whether 3^{16} or $18-21$, and again $34-36$, are expansions of the remembered and cited words of Jesus and the Baptist in the explanatory terms of the evangelist, cannot be discussed here, yet would not have arisen if criticism had not recognized in both places the subtle difference between the individuality of the evangelist and the style of each of his masters. The frequent reference to ' the hour ' of Jesus, as in 7^{30} 8^{20}, suggests the knitted, anxious brow of the evangelist as he watched the approach of crisis, and the mysterious deliverance of the Lord from the malice, the arrest, the stones of His enemies. It is curious that many of the chief puzzles of exegesis are to be found in the evangelist's own comment or narrative. By far the most difficult theological *crux* is 7^{39}, which perhaps yields its treasure up to patient inquiry ; but the statement of the passage is entirely due to ' John,' viz., that ' until Jesus was glorified ' the Holy Spirit *was* not, had not been (' given ' or ' manifested '). This assertion is apparently discordant with the teaching of Christ and his apostles, and of John himself. It was a question of ' more ' or ' less,' not a contrast between nothing and something. The fulness or splendour of the new dispensation varies with the vital truth and revelation of God wherewith He energizes in the consciousness and even below the consciousness. The contrast between the quickening of intelligence under the OT, and the descent of the Holy Spirit upon Jesus, is so great as to account for John's words, and *a fortiori* the contrast between the ministry of the synagogue and the ascended Lord. The evangelist makes a great and unintentional revelation of himself in 13^{1-5}. His mind must have been working in flights of unparalleled ecstasy when he endeavoured to convey the impression which the feet-washing had made upon him. But the style of the passage, the assumption of co-ordinate emotions in the bosom of Jesus, and the motives not verbally revealed, differ profoundly from the diction and method of thought of the Lord Himself. St. John was able to represent the tones of the 'eternal now' when recording the words of Jesus, but when he tried to reflect the motives or inner spirit of Christ he could find no adequate language.

The purport of the Gospel and the plan and classification of its subject - matter have been variously presented by successive critics and commentators from Lampe of Utrecht (1724) to the present hour under the handling of Reuss, Godet, Luthardt, Thoma, and Beyschlag. Because the structure of this very wonderful book reveals a gathering intensity of meaning, and the succession of events a climacteric force, it does not follow that the broad outline of the chronology has been tampered with in either historical or theological interests. Many of the lives of our greatest men naturally arrange themselves in epochs, great opportunities, deep sayings of historic significance, crises, tragedies—as, *e.g.*, those of Socrates, Cæsar, Buddha, Luther, William of Orange. Now, if we can accept the fundamental idea of God manifest in the flesh, we are satisfied that the most unsympathetic narrator would unconsciously sift material, and gather climax, and glow with dramatic intensity in spite of himself. The Synoptic narrative, with its most solemn and far-reaching suggestions, has prepared the way for the Fourth Gospel, which everywhere presupposes the existence of the wider and more copious detail. It lays down firmly the chronological points, between which it is not impossible to show that the vistas of miracle, parable, self-revelation open out. The non-obtruded but certain septenary arrangement, the gathering of the glory as the story moves from eternity to eternity, the poetic framework showing that from the great deep to the great deep it goes, does not disturb its true proportions of credible and realizable fact.

η. *The order of the thought due to the evangelist.* —We will make some attempt to show what is the actual order of the thought, whether intentional or not, on the part of the evangelist. As many writers show careful and subtle alliteration in their prose, rhythm and accentuation in their poetry, without any consciousness on their part, so the progress of the thought comes into view with the evolution of the life and self-revelation.

A. Proem. chs. 1–4 contain specimens of the nature and method of the Lord—first manifestations of the Logos Incarnate to His own, to Israel, and the world.—i. Prologue, 1¹⁻¹⁸. Explanation of the astonishing phenomena which Jn proceeds to record. Jesus is all that Synoptists endeavoured to prove, viz. Messiah, Son of God, Son of Man ; but to St. John He is all this, because He is the incarnation of 'the Word,' v.14, who is in the beginning 'with God' and 'God,' and has been variously manifested and active before the incarnation, in nature, prophecy, conscience, and grace.
  ii. The testimonies of the forerunner, 1¹⁹⁻³⁴.
  iii. The testimony of the first witnesses, 1³⁵⁻⁵¹.
  iv. The testimony of two great signs, 2–3².
  v. Revelation of heavenly things and the new life and redemption ; meaning of the whole revelation, 3³⁻²¹.
  vi. The final testimony of the great seer, 3²²⁻³⁶.
  vii. The ministry of the Lord beyond the limits of the theocracy, the Life-giver, the Prophet, and Saviour, 4¹⁻⁴².
  viii. The summation of the Galilæan ministry, 4⁴³⁻⁵⁴.
  B. The conflict of the Logos Incarnate with His own people, down to the signing of the death-warrant, chs. 5–11.
  i. Christ (a) the source of life and healing to body and soul, of sabbatic rest and of resurrection glory, 5¹⁻²⁹ ; (b) the witnesses to these claims, 5³⁰⁻⁴⁰.
  ii. Christ sustains the life of which He is the source, 6¹⁻⁷¹. (a) The signs (on land and sea) of creative power and love, 6¹⁻²¹. (b) The interpretation of the signs, 6²²ff. (c) Effect—increase of enmity and intensifying of faith, 6⁴¹ff. 60ff.
  iii. The truth. Dramatic scenes ; conflicting parties, with murderous designs, thwarted, including the story of the adulteress, 7–8¹¹.
  iv. The light of the world (8¹²–9⁴¹) vindicated by word and

sign. The correlative Giver of sight as well as light, with conflicting issues.
  v. The Shepherd of the flock of God, 10¹⁻²¹.
  vi. Identity of essence and function with the Father (10²²⁻⁴²) where the assumption is challenged and vindicated by word and sign.
  vii. (a) The vanquisher of death and Hades (11¹⁻⁵⁷), and the claim to be the 'Resurrection and the Life.'
  (b) The different effect produced upon different classes, especially on the ecclesiastical powers. The ban of condemnation confirmed and published.
  C. The close of the public ministry.
  i. The feast of love and gratitude, and the presage of the burial, 12¹⁻⁸.
  ii. The diverse effects of the sign, 12⁹⁻¹¹.
  iii. The challenge of the authorities, 12¹²⁻¹⁹.
  iv. The request of the Greeks and the reply of Jesus, including the glorification of the Son of Man in and through death, and the anticipation of Gethsemane, 12²⁰⁻²⁹.
  v. Last words, and the reflections of the evangelist, 12³⁰⁻⁵⁰.
  D. The final manifestation of the Word Incarnate as love unto the uttermost, chs. 13–17.
  I. The inner glorification of the perfect love to His own disciples. — i. Self-abandoning service, while simultaneously giving the highest expression of His divine commission and His God-consciousness, 13¹⁻¹⁷.
  ii. Followed by the exclusion of the faithless disciple. 'It was night,' 13¹⁸⁻³⁰.
  iii. The last conversation and discourse. (1) The glorification of the Son of Man, with its great demand on the disciples, 13³¹⁻³⁵. (2) The question of Simon Peter and its terrible response and sublime consolations (13³⁶⁻¹⁴⁴). (3) The question of Thomas—bringing out the reply, that He, by death, was their way to the Father, 14⁵⁻⁷. (4) The question of Philip, with greater revelations and the promise of the greater works, 14⁸⁻²¹. (5) The question of Judas, the conditions of His self-manifestation, 14²²⁻³¹. (6) The parable of the Vine and its branches, 15¹⁻¹⁰. (7) The results of the union of Christ and His disciples—bitter but glorious, 15¹¹⁻¹⁶⁶. (8) The promise of the Paraclete, 16⁷⁻³³. (9) The high-priestly intercession for Himself, for His disciples, for the whole Church, 17¹⁻²⁸.
  II. The more outward and public glorification in the passion, 18–19⁴².—i. The betrayal, 18¹⁻¹².
  ii. Examination before Annas, with the discomfiture and denial of Simon Peter, 18¹³⁻²⁷.
  iii. The Roman trial, presupposing the decision of the Sanhedrin, 18²⁸⁻19¹⁶.
  iv. The crucifixion. Love unto the uttermost, 19¹⁷⁻²⁴.
  v. The words from the cross, 19²⁵⁻³⁰.
  vi. The side-piercing and the burial, 19³¹⁻⁴².
  III. The final glorification and the Resurrection.
  (1) The evangelist's own personal conviction, 20¹⁻¹⁰.
  (2) The manifestation to adoring love, 20¹¹⁻¹⁸.
  (3) The manifestation to the ten disciples and others, 20¹⁹. ²⁰.
  (4) The peace, the gift of the Spirit, 20²¹⁻²³.
  (5) The manifestation to anxious scepticism, eliciting the cry, 'My Lord and my God,' 20²⁴⁻²⁹.
  (6) The evangelist's summation of His argument throughout, 20³⁰. ³¹.
  IV. The Epilogue.
  (1) The manifestation of Himself in the work of life, 21¹⁻¹⁴.
  (2) The service of love. The rehabilitation of, and solemn charge given to, Simon Peter, 21¹⁵⁻¹⁹.
  (3) Special manifestation to waiting love, 21²⁰⁻²³.
  (4) Identification of the author by subsequent editors with the disciple whom Jesus loved, 21²⁴f.

By whomsoever this marvellous document was constructed, it is unique in literature. The concentration and supernatural fulness of the subject-matter — sentence within sentence, hint within hint—reveals worlds of reality with the prodigality wherewith Nature surprises us. An immensely difficult task has been successfully finished by the simplest means ; the Divine-Human Christ of the Ep. to Hebrews and the Christ of Ro 3 and 8 and 1 Co 1–4 and 10–15, of Eph and Col, nay, the mysterious personality of Rev 1–3, is not incompatible with the preacher of the Sermon and the parables of the Sower, the Drag - net, and the Prodigal Son ; and here He lives before us, and there is no inconsistency. The Supreme Man reveals Himself, still without comparison or analogy or rival, among the sons of men. He stands absolutely alone, yet infinitely near, the one who sums up but transcends all physical and physiological law. All attempts to account for the document upon principles other than those we have contended for, every hypothesis made to bring it down to the middle of the 2nd cent., and there to find an occasion or an author, must be pronounced to have failed, and we fall back upon the memories and love of the first generation or two after this great revelation had been made. It is bound by links which cannot be broken, to the history, the geography, the religion of the day, but transcends as yet all mere human history or known ways of nature.

VII. Literature.—The translation by C. R. Gregory of Luthardt's *St. John, the Author of the Fourth Gospel*, is enriched by a voluminous list of all the works and pamphlets written on the positive and negative side of this prolonged controversy, from Evanson, an Anglican clergyman in 1792, to Beyschlag in 1875. It occupies eighty 8vo pages. Crombie in his tr. of Meyer's *Comm. on Jn* has furnished an ample catalogue of selected works, bearing more upon the interpretation and exegesis of the text than on the controversy about its origin. These lists were completed in 1875. Watkins' *Bampton Lectures* have carried critical and classified enumeration to a later date. A digest of the most noteworthy literature and epoch-making works is all that can be here appended.

Evanson (Ipswich, 1792), with insufficient evidence, gave voice to a rising spirit of free-thinking among the English Deists of an earlier part of the century touching the 'dissonance of the four evangelists,' etc., and suggested that the Fourth was the work of a Platonist of the 2nd cent. Evanson was replied to by no other than Joseph Priestley and by James Simpson, and again took arms in 1794 in defence of his thesis. In 1796 Eckermann assailed the genuineness of the Gospels on the ground of the prominence therein given to miracles. He was one of the first who endeavoured to discriminate between the apost. or Johan. nucleus of the Gospel, and that which he thought had been added by later hands. Two years later, Eckermann retracted these views, 1798. Discussions prevailed between Schmidt and Bolton as to the original language, Syriac or Greek, in which the Gospel had first been written. In 1801 Vogel wrote a vulgar book in which he gave a melodramatic turn to the controversy by bringing the author of the Gospel for trial at the judgment day. Luthardt-Gregory enumerates about fifty works before 1820, but no deep impression was produced until the celebrated theologian Bretschneider issued his *Modest Enquiries into the Genius and Origin of the Gospel and Epistle of John*, in which he gathered to a point all the doubts that had been in the air for a generation. He was ably answered by Olshausen, Lücke, and others, and admitted that his doubts were resolved. Schleiermacher after this did not hesitate to recognize the true historical character of the Christ of John, anticipating views which have long been held in suspense. For several years the positions of Bretschneider were reconsidered by positive and negative critics. Paulus, de Wette, Sartorius, Stein, E. G. Bengel, Hase's different editions of his *Leben Jesu*, 1829 and 1834, and fifty other publications, prepared the way for the four edd. of the celebrated *Life of Jesus* by Strauss, 1835–1840, with which it is well to compare *Das Leben Jesu für das Deutsche Volk*, 1864. Neander's *Life of Christ* largely contributed to the refutation of Strauss, just as the latter had reduced to ridicule the rationalistic anti-supernaturalism of Paulus. Bruno Bauer (1840) made it clear that the mythical theory could not explain the Fourth Gospel, which throughout reveals the presence of a commanding thinker, who, if not a poet of distinct romantic faculty, must have been a wilful forger. Ebrard and others handled this hypothesis with severity. De Wette, Schenkel (1840), Reuss, Schwegler, and many others, grappled with special aspects of the many-sided controversy. In 1840 the highly important *Introd. and Comm.* of Lücke of Göttingen appeared, followed in 1852 by his celebrated *Einleitung in die Offenbarung des Johannes*, in which the authenticity of the Gospel is sustained by referring the Apocalypse to the Presbyter. Cf. Luthardt, *De Compositione Evangelii Johannis*. Andrews Norton, *Genuineness of the four Gospels*, 1837–1848, made a most notable contribution to the discussion as it stood before the efforts of Baur of Tübingen. The latter epoch-making theologian commenced his assault by maintaining, in 1844, that the Gospel could not have been written before A.D. 160. In the *Th. Jahrb.* 1845, Zeller pushed the date forward another decade. Baur wrote *Krit. Untersuch. über d. Canon. Evangelien, Einleit. in d. NT. theol. Wissenschaft* (1850–51 of *Th. Jahrb.*), *Das Christenthum und d. Christl. Kirche d. drei ersten Jahrh.* (1853, 3rd ed. 1863). In 1854 he replied to Luthardt, Fr. Delitzsch, Brückner, and Hase, who had disputed his positions. Hilgenfeld, in 1854, *Die Evangelien*, does not consent to postpone the date of the origin beyond A.D. 120–140. Schneider, 1854, *Die Aechtheit des Jn. Evangeliums nach den Äusseren Zeugnissen*, made an able reply to Baur's treatment of the internal evidence. Scholten, Schürer (to some extent), Ebrard, Luthardt (with reference to the relation of the Gospel to Justin Martyr and the Clementines) fought the issues earnestly. In 1856 Jordan Bucher issued his *Des Apostels Johannes Lehre vom Logos, nach ihrem Wesen und Ursprunge*, and endeavoured to identify the *Logos* of 'John' and Philo; and in 1857 Baur again replied. The date of the last passover now took a prominent place in the debate, and Tholuck again defended the position of the Fourth Gospel. The main thesis of Baur and Hilgenfeld and others was the discovery of a system of Church organization and Christian ideas through which the Fourth Gospel could alone have seen the light. Baur supposes that the Gospel reveals the presence of the 2nd cent. Gnosis, and further, that it reflects the healing of a conjectural and violent schism between the Jerus. apostles and St. Paul, and the Churches which derived their origin and tone from these sources respectively. The two tendencies towards Judaic exclusiveness on the one hand and Pauline universalism on the other, were intensified by Marcionitic anti-Judaism on the one side and Montanistic revolt against the Episcopate on the other. In the writings of Baur the further speculation was hazarded, that towards the close of the 2nd cent. a tendency towards co-operation began; that the Epp. to Col, Eph, Ti and Tit, He, and the Bk. of Ac, were fabricated to bring about a fusion of the hostile parties; that this Gospel was a part of the system of forgeries by which the Cath. Church was originated. It is supposed that an unknown writer cunningly suggested that he was the beloved friend of Jesus and knew His inmost heart; His belief in the theocracy, that 'salvation was of the Jews,' but that God was 'a Spirit'; that among Greeks as well as Jews the buried corn of wheat would bring forth much fruit. This extraordinary writer was ready to justify the Montanistic realization of the grace of the Paraclete, and also, by a delicate series of modifications of the Synoptic tradition, to make the passover of the Jews reach its climax at the hour of the crucifixion; and he sought, moreover, to link the Christ with the ΛΟΓΟΣ of a popular philosophy. Every line of the Gospel was searched for confirmation of some portion of the hypothesis; and adverse elements were cleverly contrived to spread out the occasion for the publication of the spiritual Gospel. The strife between the Eastern and Western Churches as to the celebration of the Easter festival had broken out, and it was a masterstroke to show that one of the Jerus. apostles, who is traditionally reported to have followed the Jewish celebration on the 14th Nisan, the day preceding the crucifixion, had actually set forth the identification of the crucifixion of Jesus with the sacrifice of the paschal lamb. Baur fixed A.D. 170 as the date when this astonishing feat of forgery, concealed polemic, and spiritual manifesto, first saw the light. The question of this date was discussed with great acumen. Ebrard (Introd. to *Comm.*), Thiersch, Hilgenfeld, Lange, Steitz in numerous articles in German journals, with occasional replies from Baur, who died in 1860, kept the controversy before the world.

We have already shown reason to believe that the date assigned by Baur, viz. A.D. 170, is quite untenable, and that step by step the appearance of the Gospel must be antedated at least by forty years and pushed back to the time of Basilides or Valentinus, who must have had the ideas and phrases of the Gospel before them. It has at length become impossible to deny that Justin quoted from the Fourth Gospel, and increasingly probable that Tatian, his contemporary and disciple, actually constructed a Harmony of the Four Gospels, with a chronological basis in the Gospel of John. In 1862 H. Ewald showed that no authorship of an ancient writing is so conclusively attested as that of the Fourth Gospel (see *Die Johan. Schriften übersetzt u. erklärt*). Weiss and Weizsäcker discussed, in *Jahrb. f. deutsche Theologie*, the relation of the Logos doctrine of John to its sources. Strauss and Hilgenfeld, in 1863, made assault upon the Mur. Canon and on minor defences of the Gospel; Volkmar, Renan, A. Réville thought to rehabilitate the argument that if the Fourth Gospel had been in use in A.D. 150, Marcion would have found it more useful for his purpose than Luke's. We have elsewhere shown that Marcion could not even by mutilation have expunged from John's Gospel the humanity of Jesus, his reverence for the Old Covenant, his identification of 'the Lord' of OT, the Creator of all things, with the God and Father of Christ.

In 1863 van Oosterzee's *Life of Christ*, Hengstenberg's *Comm.* on Gospel, favoured, while Echthal's *Les Évangiles* attacked the authenticity. Martineau's review of Renan's *Vie de Jésus*, and Astié, *Explication de l'Évangile*, followed in 1864, with Nicholas' advocating of a partition theory. To this may be added Schenkel's *Charakterbild Jesu*, which suggested that the original nucleus of the Gospel appeared A.D. 110–120, and was afterwards coloured by the Gnostic speculations of Basilides and Valentinus. In 1866 Holtzmann in Bunsen's *Bibelwerk*, Pressensé in his *Jésus Christ son temps sa vie*, etc., and Sabatier, *Essai sur les sources de la vie*,—all three maintaining the authenticity,—were encountered by Keim, *Geschichte Jesu von Nazara*, etc., who argued (1867) that the Gospel was published at the beg. of 2nd cent. under the name of the Apostle John, who nevertheless had never been in Ephesus. Taylor, *An Attempt to ascertain the Character of the Fourth Gospel in relation to the three first*, was strongly opposed to the authenticity. Tobler attempted to cut out the original kernel, and later on (1870) he reduced it to 81 verses. Oosterzee and Scholten again took up opposite sides, so also Ezra Abbot, Higginson, Milligan, and S. Davidson. In 1868 Riggenbach endeavoured to show that the Presbyter John and the apostle were one and the same. In 1869 Holtzmann returned to the controversy, as did Meyer, *Introd. to the Exeg. Handb.*, Godet, *Komm. z. d. Ev. Johannis*, written also in French and translated into English. Stanley Leathes' Boyle Lecture (1870) on *The Witness of St. John to Christ* and Hilgenfeld kept up the struggle. In 1871 Krenkel, in his work, *Der Apostel Johannes*, argued that the apostle was the author of Apoc., but not of Gospel; cf. Milligan, arts. in *Contemp. Rev.* and *Brit. and For. Evang. Rev.*; and Hutton, *Essays, Theological and Literary*, who defended with great force the historicity of the Gospel against Baur and his followers. Holtzmann once more took up the claims of John the Presbyter. In 1872 appeared the important Comm. and Introd. of Schaff, being a tr. and great enlargement of Lange's Comm. in his *Bibelwerk*; and the singularly valuable *Authorship and Hist. Character of 4th Gospel*, by Sanday, followed in 1876 by *The Gospels in the 2nd Cent.* In 1874 was published *Supernatural Religion, An Inquiry into the Reality of Divine Revelation*, which created almost a literature of reply. The anonymous writer was vehemently adverse to the authenticity of this Gospel (vol. ii. 251–476) on every ground and every side issue. Lightfoot in the *Contemp. Rev.* (afterwards republished) ; Sanday in the *Gospels during the 2nd Cent.* ; Row, *The Jesus of the Evangelists* ; Luthardt, *Der Johan. Ursp. des 4ten Evang.* (tr. into Eng. by C. R. Gregory, 1875),—replied very successfully. Farrar's *Life of Christ* (1874) sustained the authenticity ; but Hilgenfeld, in 1875, in *Hist.-Krit. Einleit. in das NT.*, determined the limits of production between A.D. 132 and 140. Mangold (Bleek's *Einleit.*) was again adverse, but Matthew Arnold, *Review of Objections to Literature and Dogma,* (*Cont. Review,* afterwards republished in *God and the Bible*), defended the authenticity with high literary tact, but by falling back in part on some special partition theory of his own. In 1882 the remarkable work appeared of Albrecht Thoma, *Die Genesis des Johan. Evang. : ein Beitrag zu seiner Ausleg., Gesch., u. Kritik,* in which the author endeavoured to find an Alex.-Philonic origin for the entire Gospel, which is dealt with as Philo handled the Pent., and which, on this hypothesis, could have had no meaning save among the Neoplatonic schools, where supposed forecasts and summaries of history were only crypto-grams of philosophical theory, *e.g.* ch. 9 is regarded as a cipher of the position and career of St. Paul, and ch. 21 an outline of the history of the Acts of Apostles. With ingenuity the theory was carried through 879 pages. In 1882 (Eng. tr. 1883) appeared B. Weiss, *Life of Christ.* The chapters on the 'Johannine' sources are singularly impressive, and vindicate the historicity of the Gospel against the speculations of various offshoots of the Tübingen School. The theory of the reminiscence of one who had fathomed the deep secret of the Incarnate Logos in Jesus, interprets the author's 'ideal elevation and spiritual form, but also his historical trustworthiness. If it be regarded as the invention of a semi-Gnostic philosopher of the 2nd cent., it is a delusive will-o'-the-wisp—in truth, a gigantic lie.' In the same sense Godet's invaluable Introd. to his *Commentary* touches and illumines every part of this great subject (Eng. tr. 1887). In 1885 Salmon's *Hist. Introd. to the Study of NT* gave ample space and great freshness to the maintenance of the authenticity. Edward Reuss in his *Hist. of Sac. Scrip. of NT,* tr. into Eng. by Houghton from the 5th Germ. ed., with additional bibliographical details, minimized the value of the external evidence, and left it as only barely possible that Jn was the work of the apostle. The introductory discussions of Hengstenberg are scattered throughout his *Commentary.* Special excursuses on the Paschal and other questions are to be found in M'Clellan's great work on the Gospels. Against Edwin Abbott's view in his article 'Gospels' in *Encyc. Brit.*[9] may be put Ezra Abbot's *External Evidence of the Fourth Gospel,* and Westcott's Introd. to his invaluable Comm. on the Gospel in *Speaker's Commentary* (and published separately) ; also Milligan and Moulton, Introd. to their Comm. in Schaff's *Popular Commentary,* and Watkins' Introd. to Comm. in Ellicott's *Comm. for Eng. Readers,* as well as his very important discussion of the history of criticism in *Bampton Lectures* for 1890 ; Reynolds' Introd. to his Comm. on Jn in the *Pulpit Commentary.* Keim in his voluminous *Life of Jesus of Nazara* settled down to the date A.D. 130 and to a repudiation of St. John's residence in Ephesus. He decided that early antiquity was grievously misled by Irenæus in this and other respects, just as Riggenbach, Farrar, and others think that the very personality of 'John the Presbyter' has been created by an ill-starred guess of Eusebius. In *Handkom. z. NT* ('Joh. Evangelium'), Holtzmann, 1890, argues that the most extreme critical view which he adopts doubles the value of the Gospel. Edersheim's *Life and Times of Jesus the Messiah* (1883) throws vivid light upon the Johan. as well as other sources of the great biography by his intimate acquaintance with Heb. literature. In 1890 Hugo Delff, *Das 4 Evangelium,* and (1883) in his *Grundzüge des Entwick.-Geschichte d. Religion,* advocated a special view which creates many fresh difficulties, that 'John' was neither the son of Zebedee, nor John the Presbyter, nor the author of the Apoc., but a well-to-do philosophical disciple of Jesus, whom He loved and who was specially acquainted with the ministry in Jerus., who was subsequently confounded with the John of Acts and Apocalypse. P. Ewald, in 1890, *Das Hauptproblem der Evangelienfrage,* strove to bring out the original Johan. nucleus of the entire evangelical tradition, of which John has given the richest anthology. In 1891 Gloag issued *Introd. to the Johan. Writings.* This is one of the most complete *résumés* of the entire question in the light of modern criticism, embracing not only the Gospel but the Epp. and the Apocalypse. Harnack in his *History of Dogma,* vol. i. 96–98, admits that the origin of the Johan. writings is 'a marvellous enigma,' that therein a Christ clothes the indescribable with words, that a Pauline Christ walks on the earth 'far more human than the Christ of Paul, yet far more divine.' He seems to admit that Christ Himself is the author of ch. 17, but all is suffused in a bright cloud of the supra-historical. He repudiates the dependence on Philo and Hellenism, with which John has little in common but the word λόγος, and he regards the author as a born Jew. Important articles have appeared at various times in the *Expositor* by Lightfoot, Sanday, and others. In 1891 Willibald Beyschlag of Halle published his *NT Theol.* (Eng. tr. 1895). In vol. i. pp. 216–221 he avows his firm conviction of the genuineness of the Gospel, that it rests on historic facts and is superior to the Synoptists in many important details, that 'the Logos Romance' is a critical failure, and, notwithstanding great difficulties, he imagines that the subjective element necessary to a character formed and trained by the Master Himself may solve them.

VIII. THE TEACHING OF THE FOURTH GOSPEL.

—*A. Theology and Christology.*—The teaching of Jesus cannot be satisfactorily discriminated from that of the evangelist, except in places where the latter speaks *in propriâ personâ,* or offers his interpretation of the Master's words. Alike in the Epistle and Prol. to Gospel, the apostle sums up or generalizes the teaching of Christ or of His mighty deeds, and for the ideas, thought by thought, fact by fact, he brings out a justification in the narrative itself. As to the *Abbrechungen* and *Incongruenzen* on which Wendt insists as indicating different strains of thought and purpose, *e.g.* in the different estimate of ἔργα, σημεῖα, and ῥήματα in the great plan of the Supreme Teacher, the reconciliation is not far to seek, and is to be found in the divine-human majesty of the Lord, whose Personality gives unity to all his representation. The consciousness of the Lord Jesus, as brought out in the fourfold revelation, provides the fact upon which the constructive intelligence of later centuries has founded its doctrine of the GODHEAD. To put it in a word, the Doctrine of the Divinity is simply an endeavour to state without explanation the various elements of that unique consciousness. The most fundamental element in the entire teaching is the absolute oneness of the Deity. Christ never taught the existence of two or three Gods, though the unity or solity embraced the divine indwelling in the entire universe, an infinite transcendence involving the internal relations of Fatherhood and Sonship, and all the mighty operations of the Spirit in the world and in the minds of men. There is only one veritable God, μόνος ἀληθινὸς θεός (17[3]), although the Lord was self-conscious of the nearest possible approach of the centres of the spheres, both of His divine and human nature, to the Centre of the all-including and embracing Unity. The theophanies of the OT are outshone by the eternal knowledge of the Only-begotten (1[18] and 6[46]), and the adequate sufficing power of the human life and consciousness of Jesus to disclose the secrets of the divine bosom. This revelation differs widely from the Gnostic or Oriental or modern impersonality, 'the Absolute.' Here the ineffable is clothed in forms not incompatible with the Eternal Unity. 'Father,' 'Son,' 'Word,' 'Love,' 'Life,' 'Light,' 'Spirit' are terms which make no schism of the one Deity, but are each necessary concepts in it. This is so complete and thoroughgoing that Fairbairn has skilfully pressed the position that the Lord Jesus was in fact the first monotheist in the history of the world.

A few of the elements of this great synthesis must be specified.

(1) In 4[24ff.] the spirituality of the One who is called 'the Father' is insisted upon. The spirit of man leads the way to the most direct realization of the Eternal.

(2) He is the living and life-giving One, or even Life itself. In the Logos—who is God—there is Life. The mystery of 'life' was not solved, or a definition given, by Jesus or the evangelists ; nor is the mystery reduced, but intensified, by the widest and latest researches of science ; but St. John may at least be credited with seeing behind the inexplicable phenomena of 'life'—physical, ethical, spiritual, and eternal—nothing less than the personal activity of the Lord God, the Living One.

(3) In this *life* is *light.* In 1 Jn 1[5] God is (not *luminous,* but) '*Light,* and in him is no darkness at all,' no evil, no imperfection, absolute purity, goodness, righteousness, and illumination (Jn 17[25] 1[4, 5]).

(4) The most characteristic doctrine of God which we must attribute to the evangelist is that God is *Love* (1 Jn 4[8]), or that the most essential quality

and absolute essence of God is that which freely lavishes Himself on the objects of His love. The moral perfections which our Lord attributes to this living and loving One are truth (8[26]), righteousness (17[25]), and holiness (17[11]).

(5) But the most characteristic name and function is that of 'Father,' 'my Father,' 'your Father,' the 'living Father' who has life in Himself (5[26]), who seeks for spiritual worshippers (4[23], where the vital internal relation between God as Father and God as Spirit is made very evident). This fatherly love is, first of all, lavished on the Son and on those who are given to Him. He becomes the source of life to others, and in Him God loves the world (5[19. 26] 10[17] 17[24. 26] and 3[16]). Preparation for this revelation of Fatherhood is found in OT and Hel. thought and in the Synop. teaching, but the Fourth Gospel is peculiarly saturated with the ennobling and uplifting thought. Here we come face to face with one who could speak of the Almighty as 'my Father.' He was the 'wisdom' and the 'power' of God, not only (as St. Paul represented it) as the 'image,' but as 'the Son of His love.' The relation of Logos to Theos is warmed into the deeper relation of Son to Father, the Only-begotten to the Eternal. The Fatherhood is essential to God, and therefore eternal. If the Father be thought of as the Supreme Giver evermore lavishing upon an adequate object His own fulness of being, then the Son also is eternal, and from the relation between the giver and receiver, between the Father and Son, does the very conception of Deity emerge. From before all time and worlds, and independently of time or space, the writer saw the infinite giving and receiving of Eternal Love; and he saw in the completeness of the mutual relation the moral and spiritual $\dot{a}\rho\chi\dot{\eta}$ of the universe. This is not the monad of the Platonic schools or the Gnostic sects, but the living fulness of an infinite Personality, within which there is the reciprocal interchange of gracious and everlasting relations. St. John is alive to the primordial rank and supremacy of the Father, and tells us by the lips of the Divine Son that the Father is the source of all power, and of the self-dependence of the Son. 'He gave to the Son to have life in himself,' He is 'greater' than the Son, 'gives the Spirit' to the Son without measure, He 'sent the Son into the world' to learn and fulfil all His will (5[27] 10[31-37] 14[24]). Yet the unity and the solity of the Eternal turns upon this very relation; and so identical is the substance and will of the Father and Son, that 'all things,' $\pi\acute{a}\nu\tau a$, flow out of the mutual relation (1[1-3]), the monarchy of the Father compatible with unity of the Father and Son.

(6) The relation of Logos to Theos, as conceived by the evangelist, is sustained by the successive words and deeds of Jesus which had slowly broken on the mind of the writer. The majestic words of the Prologue which are repeated in the opening sentences of the Ep. are the necessary antecedents of the events, the twofold meaning and ambiguity of the term Logos, connoting the self-consciousness and the necessarily connected utterance of the Eternal Theos. This Logos so interpreted is both 'God' and 'with God' at once. He is the organ of divine activity and the great image of His glory. Beyschlag, in his attempt to reduce all the subsequent narrative to the ordinary human consciousness of Jesus, appears to ignore or minimize the supra-historic basis which precedes the historic narrative. Before the manifestation in the flesh of Christ, the Logos was the divine agent of creation. No element of matter, no thrill of force, no harmony or beauty of the cosmos was excluded. The life and light of God streamed forth from Him. The divine immanence in nature and man

was His function. The darkness was not in harmony with the Light, and did not apprehend it. He came age after age to His own, to those who were prepared by conscience, providence, and prophecy, and His own received Him not. The Logos even to the present hour, is working in *events*, *laws*, and *forces*, designing and forecasting and evolving the eternal purpose; yet the world and even His own know it not, nay, He is rejected and despised. An element of deep tragedy has entered into human nature which has ever resisted Omnipotence, but never exhausted the resources of divine love. Conscience, even the 'light which lighteth every man,' was reinforced by prophetic voices, of which the Baptist was the highest type, and the conflict between the Spirit and the flesh, the light and the darkness, the Logos and humanity, is always in progress. The victory over the world and the flesh has made still greater demand upon an infinite compassion, and so we are led on to believe in a higher and more convincing contact of the Logos with human nature. The indwelling of the Logos with the cosmos falls immeasurably short of the Incarnation, *i.e.* of an event which is described in the assurance (v.[14]) that the Word became flesh. The Logos did not become 'all things,' but became $\sigma\acute{a}\rho\xi$, to heal the source of human corruption, and consummate the plan of God.

(7) The entire Johannine conception turns on what is meant by these words. Is the synthesis of the divine and human such as obliterates either of the two elements in the Christ; or is it one which, while preserving both in their completeness, stretches the vinculum between them, so that it snaps, and there is left no other than a human Saviour, after all? Beyschlag objects to the ecclesiastical orthodoxy, and wisely discounts the Kenotic theories of Gess, Thomasius, Godet, Pressensé, and others, on the ground that if our Lord never adopted phraseology incompatible with 'mere humanity,' the idea of a divine consciousness and the hypothesis of a true incarnation could never have arisen. Putting aside the two extremes of Nestorian and Monophysite interpretation, and shrinking from the Catholic acceptance of what is true in both, Beyschlag falls back upon the bare human consciousness and historical surroundings of Jesus. He reviews the great sayings of our Lord which affirm a remembrance of 'the glory which he had with the Father before the world was' (17[5. 24]), or which assert a conscious existence before Abraham (8[58]), or which indicate a realization of being 'in heaven' while yet on earth (3[13]), or which refer to His descent from heaven and return thither (6[39. 51. 62]), and affirm conscious unity with the Father. In doing this the critic is content with a purely Ebionitic interpretation which leaves the mystery of the greatest fact in the history of the moral world entirely unsolved. He falls back upon a method of interpreting Christ's own pre-existence, corresponding with the Rabbin. method of regarding things of high value, such as the ark of the covenant, as 'eternally pre-existent in God.' By the use of metaphor, or fervid imagination, or intense prophetic or mystic realization of the divine indwelling, and full reconciliation with God, even absorption into the divine fulness, the expressions arose from which he supposes the Christian faith to have had its origin. A similar interpretation of the words and the consciousness of Jesus is advocated in Drummond's Hibbert Lecture, *Via Veritas Vita*, where we seem called upon to forgive our Lord the use of phrases which, after all, are only the commonplaces of the religious life.

The statement, $\acute{o}$ $\lambda\acute{o}\gamma os$ $\sigma\acute{a}\rho\xi$ $\acute{e}\gamma\acute{e}\nu\epsilon\tau o$, does not, in John's usage, mean a transubstantiation of $\lambda\acute{o}\gamma os$

into σάρξ, so that henceforth there is no longer λόγος but only σάρξ, seeing that the evangelist (2⁹) uses a precisely similar phrase to denote 'the water which had become wine.' As the water took up into itself elements not previously in it, so the eternal Logos took up human nature into Himself, and this is enough for humiliation of the Infinite Love. The method of the consciousness can only occasionally (if ever) be given its fulness, but the three axes of revolution in succession suggest the entire mystery. These are 'the Son of God,' 'the Son of Man,' and the 'Christ'; and these remarkable terms are found in the Synoptic Gospels in much the same sense as in the Fourth.

The first, SON OF GOD, is an honorific ascription when used by the disciples or by the Jews, and it is nearly if not perfectly identical with 'Messiah.' It is paralleled by the extraordinary prevalence of like terms among surrounding religions and nations. In Egypt the same king is often set forth on monuments as 'the son' and 'beloved' of many different personages of the Pantheon. God-born was the highest superlative to denote glory and authority. Nathanael (1⁵⁰, ⁵¹) identifies 'the Son of God' with the theocratic king. Martha (11²⁷) anticipates the advent of one so near to and beloved of God as to have power over death and Hades. Still, the Synoptic citation of the adjuration of Caiaphas shows that he regarded the title, not only as an honorific term for Messiah, but as one which it was blasphemy to assume. The claim to be 'Son of God' in a unique sense, a sense that associated Him with God and enthroned Him as supreme Judge, was the specific charge on which Jesus was condemned by the Sanhedrin. Not merely is He the human offspring of the eternal God, but, as He spake of Himself, pre-eminently *the Son*, the highest expression of the relation of Son to Father, the archetype of Sonship in itself. Doubtless He is 'sent into the world,' to reveal the Father because He is the eternal spectator and companion of the Father, the object of eternal love, the conscious exposition of the Father's character and grace. The entire term is chastened and exalted by the ordered sequence of events. In 3²⁸, ²⁹ 4²⁵, ²⁹ 6¹⁴ the expected 'Prophet' rather than the triumphant 'King' comes into view, and Simon Peter's confession (6⁶⁸ᶠ. RV) shows that he had grasped the richer aspect of Messiahship which Jesus now permits to become His self-revelation. 12¹²⁻¹⁹, ³⁴⁻³⁶ convey the most explicit acceptance of the term by Him, and He actually uses it in the intercessory prayer (17³). The entire progress of the thought culminating in 20³¹ shows that the evangelist blended into one the correlated ideas of 'Logos made flesh,' 'the Son of God,' and 'the Christ.'

The other term SON OF MAN is a mode of expression which, with only two exceptions (Ac 7⁵⁶, Rev 1¹³), is never used by any of the disciples, but is confined to His own self-designation. It is being more and more conceded by criticism that the expression is not a euphemism for '*man*' as in the prophecies of Ezekiel, or a translation of the Aram. 'bar-enosh,' but a reflection of the transcendent meaning assigned to it in Dn 7. The ideal man there is lifted into the highest glory, and receives an eternal kingdom. It is as Son of Man that Jesus claims to be Lord of the Sabbath, the forgiver of sin, the judge of quick and dead. In the Synoptic representations and in this Gospel He calls himself Son of Man, because of the divine nature which is the substratum and explanation of the human. In 3¹⁴ 5²⁷ and elsewhere we find in this title a revelation of the highest glory and the most perfect sympathy, not a *tertium quid*, neither God nor man, but at once both God and man. He was known to be Son of

Man, the highest, holiest man, by the experience of those who knew Him best. He did not hesitate to use the title of Himself. The inference was, and still is, that He is 'Son of God,' *i.e.* that the divine will and indwelling must be presupposed to justify such a term.

(8) The relation of the Father and the Son, or of Theos and Logos, does not exhaust the Johannine conception of 'the only true God.' Indeed the OT writers speak of *the Spirit of God* as the agent of the Eternal in creation, as the primal source of the human Ego, and as discriminating the living soul of man from that of the animal. With them Spirit is the cause of all beauty or genius, of all prophetic gift, and all sanctifying grace. The Spirit of God is by the Synoptists set forth as the occasion of the humanity and formation of the person of the Lord Jesus. The divine personal Spirit perfects the human character and completes the official equipment of the Son of Man to be the Saviour of the world. So completely is He dominated by the Spirit, that He claims to communicate the Holy Spirit to others (Mt 3¹¹, cf. Lk 11¹³), while the Pauline teaching identifies the Spirit of Christ with that of the Father (Ro 8⁹⁻¹¹). The NT yearns after the unity of the self-conscious Father and the self-conscious Son—the unity of the divine nature as self-conscious in the Christ, together with the conscience of human nature, the unity of all believers in one body by the One all co-ordinating Head. These unities find their best explanation in the Lord's own teaching concerning the Spirit. In the Synop. (Mt 12²⁹, ³² and parallel passages) the dispensation of the Son of Man is contrasted with the dispensation of the Spirit; and in the Fourth Gospel Christ claims to give the Spirit to the Church, that the *world* may be convinced 'of sin, righteousness, and judgment.' The Lord so states the relation of the Holy Spirit to His own consciousness, that He identifies the coming of the Comforter with His own return. The indwelling of the Father and of the Son in human souls is effectuated by nothing less than the Spirit, *i.e.* by the activity and personality of all the fulness of the Godhead. His advent was an incoming to souls both of the Father and of the Son, for the one cannot be without the other. Beyschlag, Reuss, and others seem anxious lest they find anything like Trinitarian doctrine in these numberless references to the Ego of the Father, of the Son, of the Spirit, of the Christ. The Unitarian development of the 4th to the 6th cent. is not homogeneous, because encumbered by the attempt to repudiate the philosophical explanations of the so-called heretics. The Gospels, and particularly the Fourth, like the greatest symbols of the faith, are content to say (*a*) that Jesus was Son of Man; to show that He was Man in body, soul, spirit, will—Man, *i.e.* in all respects, in birth, frailty, limitations, sufferings, and death; (*b*) that the mind of Jesus sounded also the depth of the divine consciousness, so that in His full personality He had dwelt in the bosom of the Father and was able to reveal Him (1¹⁸); (*c*) that in the completing and glorifying of the Son of Man, in the resurrection and ascension of the Christ, the God-man shared finally in the very glory of the Eternal.

B. The Johannine Teaching concerning the Cosmos.—(*a*) The evangelist, following his Master, discriminates the world of *things* from that of *men*. Everywhere the cosmos is created, not self-originated. It is the platform of the entire representation, and consists both of heaven and earth. It is not evil in its origin or essence, though it is the theatre of both moral perversity and divine redemption. (*b*) The Gospel and Epp. use κόσμος for humanity considered apart from grace, just as they use σάρξ for human nature apart from the spiritual life.

This may include humanity in its pride, power, civilization, and refinement. To this is not given the faculty of knowing the Eternal Father (' The world hath not known thee '), or of discerning the pre-incarnate Logos, or even of seeing the Father in the Son of His love. The world of men strangely hates the highest light and shrinks from it (3¹⁹), neither comes to it. The Father loves the world in its need (3¹⁶); Jesus comes into it to ' save,' to ' draw it,' and to be a way for it unto the Father. There is vivid contrast between those who see the light, who live the heavenly life, who are ' convinced of sin, righteousness, and judgment,' who overcome the darkness and the flesh, who follow the Good Shepherd, who feed on the bread of God, with whom the Father and Son take up their abode, who are ' of the truth ' and hear the voice of the Son of God ; and, on the other hand, those who do not come, are not drawn, nor convinced, who are in danger of perishing, are ' sons of perdition,' are veritably 'lost.' The ultimate cause of the contrast cannot be explained away, nor can any good or bad name which is assigned to it modify the issue. The intense severity of our Lord's judgment (7. 8) is not due to a Gnostic twist given by this evangelist to the teaching of Jesus, but to the historic accuracy with which the tendencies and hostility of the classes in Jerus. were known and set forth. Yet the human will, and no inexorable fate, is (throughout the Johannine theology) the critical element in the question of light or darkness. The activity of the will is not the absolute solution of the puzzle, but it is the proximate occasion of all moral issues. The dualism of the Fourth Gospel is not more explicit than the dualism of other parts of NT, such as St. Paul or the Synoptists. (c) St. John and St. Paul, and the Synoptists also, recognize a moral centre of the evil in humanity. Though St. John makes no reference to demoniacs, he refers to ' the Prince of this world ' as the source and occasion of the trials of the Lord, between whom and Christ there is irreconcilable antagonism. The designs of the enemies of Jesus are affiliated to the father of lies and manslaying, and the phrase is akin to the use by our Lord and the Baptist of the terrible term ' ye brood of vipers.' Thoma (lib. cit. 202–205) regards the circumscription of the operations of the Evil One to the mind of humanity as strongly differentiating the Fourth Gospel from the rest of NT. True, there is no reference to ' possession ' in St. John ; but neither is there to leprosy, or fever, or other forms of disease on which, as we hear (2²³ 3² 4⁴⁸ 5³⁶ 20³⁰), Jesus wrought marvellous signs. The statement that St. John ignores the visible works of the devil is excessive (see 1 Jn 3⁸ and Jn 12³¹). Thoma does not agree with Hilgenfeld in finding the Valentinian Demiurge in St. John's doctrine of the ἀρχων. It is refuted by the teaching of the Gospel and Epistle on the expulsion of the devil and the consecration of the world.

C. The Johannine Soteriology.—In grasping the Johan. ideal of salvation, Beyschlag finds the same thoughts as in the Synop. teaching concerning ' the kingdom,' which phrase, when he finds it in ch. 3, he regards as the simple equivalent of ' the life ' and ' the eternal life ' given by the great Teacher and Revealer of the Father. The kingdom and the life are closely allied in the teaching of Christ, and found in both sources ; but they must be discriminated. The kingdom of God is the region within men and communities and the world in which the will of God operates through the free powers of the individual. The methods of discovering it, of entering it, of finding in it hidden potencies and of bringing forth its countless signs, whether acts or fruits, are always in evidence. It is

originated as life is in new forms, by seed charged with its future. It has internal intensive force and extensive evolutionary energy, embracing every form of divine indwelling and spiritual growth. In St. John's Gospel, Salvation is Life, Light in its essence, and Truth and Love in method, instrument, or form. But the very idea of salvation, which was appreciated, to begin with, by John the Baptist (1²⁹) and by the Samaritans (Jn 4⁴², 1 Jn 4¹⁴), implies from OT times the great need of man and the greatest work of God. It denotes the rectification or reinstitution of all the relations which had been shattered by sin,—all that is elsewhere covered by such Pauline phrases as pardon, justification, sanctification, adoption,—all such divine experiences as faith, hope, love, life eternal,— in fine, all the work wrought for us by the Christ, the Son of God,—all the internal transformation which is effected in us, in the fabric of our being, by the Spirit of the Father and of the Son. Christ in the Fourth Gospel makes provision for abolishing the shame and curse, and indicates the hopelessness involved in dying in sins. The most damning sin is a steady refusal to admit His own claim. Faith in Him is the condition of deliverance, not merely by its remoter ethical importance or its stimulus to obedience, but by the very nature of the case ; moral surrender to the highest revelation of God is salvation and eternal life.

Christ is that in human nature, and does that in it and through it which can stanch the wound and arrest the spell of sin. He had always been coming into the world—a fact testified by the prophets (1⁵ff). The great Lawgiver spoke of Him (5⁴⁶); Abraham desired a fuller revelation (8⁵⁶); all the Scriptures testified to Him (5³⁹). Nevertheless, these operations of the Logos, so long as conducted along these lines, were insufficient to secure conviction until He came into closer contact with humanity, was more obviously manifest in human flesh, and came into actual living personal union with the disturbed and imperilled roots of our mind, heart, and will. He thus provides a tangible object of faith. He renews the eye of faith, and supplies the motive of search. He is the shield from condemnation, the deliverance from wrath, the emancipation from bondage. He can ' save ' from the malicious destruction of alien powers (10¹⁰), from the deadly pangs of unsatisfied hunger (6⁵⁰); and He can give the food of which if a man eats he shall never die. Under the three often quoted metaphors, salvation covered all the need of man and all the capacities of the Infinite—LIFE, LIGHT, and LOVE.

There is no salvation if we do not consciously possess another LIFE than this ever-vanishing, always-threatened earthly existence. The heavenly life is not menaced by the million perils of earth and the organized hate of hell, by the cruel temptations of time and sense, and will be finally emancipated from the fear which hath torment. Life in its perpetuity is independent of the conditions of death, it is veritable (answering, i.e., to its ideal and archetype), it is eternal. The purport of the Fourth Gospel was to give concrete proof that Jesus has the power to establish the indispensable conditions and execute the initial stages of this everlasting life. Jesus began by declaring that He would build up the temple of His body after men had destroyed it (ch. 2), and that those who believed in Him should receive this life at His hands (3¹⁶. ¹⁷. ³⁶). He selected the palsied man as an image of the method and need of the conferring of life, and He exercised the function along the lines of the divine Father's life-giving work (5²¹⁻²⁹). He sustained human life by creative forces against various perils of hunger and storm, with express parabolic instruction as to the deliverances of the inner life from greater peril, and that by His own imperial mandate. The whole of ch. 6 is one continuous illustration of how the Incarnate One could give eternal life, how those who would feed on Him (on His flesh and blood) should die no more for ever. The whole lesson of His unique relation to life, and His power over death, is once more given in ch. 11, where no barriers block the access of His eternal power and Godhead as the Son of the Father's love, and as working out the will of the Eternal. He unriddles death and takes away its sting. In the night of the passion He says, 'because I live, ye shall live'; and the evangelist tells us that all that has been written by himself was to make evident to us, that by believing we might have life through His name (20^31).

A second analogue and interpretation of σωτηρία pervading the Fourth Gospel is LIGHT. It is the antithesis of *darkness*, both moral and intellectual. Darkness is dependent on two conditions, absence of illumination and deficiency or destitution of the power of vision, and in both respects He fulfils the functions of *light*. He is 'the light of the world' (8^12, and cf. 9^5), the forth-streaming of the Divine Glory (12^{35. 46}), the image of His substance, 'the truth' (ἀλήθεια) concerning *God*, the full expression of the archetypal *man*, the embodiment of the normal relations between God and man ('for I do always those things that please him'; 'my meat is to do,' etc. 4^{34}); 'I knew that thou hearest me always' (11^{42}). Thus salvation and eternal life is a knowledge of this *truth* (17^3), an acceptance of the light. Moral contamination occasions mental and spiritual blindness—a doctrine inverting the Platonic dictum, which charges all moral contamination on mental incapacity. In the soteriology of St. John the subjective condition is so hopelessly imperfect, and the need of visual faculty has become so imperative, that Christ is represented as restoring a man 'blind from birth' to the exercise of sight, and as commenting on the analogy between this imperial act and what He would do for humanity (9^{37-41}). The glory into which the light of the full revelation of God has ushered His own human nature is the very same light and glory which He supplicates for all His own, and into which He will bring them.

But in close association with *Life and Light* appears the highest conception of the nature of God which has ever dawned on human intelligence. If God is love, the central essence is absolute self-surrender to the well-being of others. That 'God IS LOVE,' and *Love is of God*, are the final outcome of the irradiation of St. John's mind with 'the light of the knowledge of the glory (the essential beauty) of God in the face of Jesus Christ.'

The Prologue commences the sublime details by declaring that the incarnate and only-begotten was full of *grace* and truth. He had been 'in the bosom of the Father,' and declared that which no other had seen. He said, 'the Father loveth me, because I am laying down my life—not as if that were to be the final end, as so many seem resolved to have it, but—that I may take it again' (10^17). The revelation of the principle of sacrificial love in the eternal heart of God, as the motive of the heavenly giving, sending, and equipping of the Son, receives its triumphant expression in the human life, which adequately revealed the eternal. A large portion of the Gospel is interfused with this thought. In the conversation with Nicodemus the keynote was the eternal self-sacrificing love of God, of which He had become the expression (3^{16ff.}). To the Samaritans He made it clear that He was seeking the salvation of men, 'of the world'

(4^{32. 42}), by the sacrifice of Himself. The discourses of ch. 6 indicate the fountain of self-abnegating love, by which He was giving life to the world. The excited scenes of chs. 7 and 8 combine sternest condemnation of sin with love to sinners. Chs. 9. 10. 11 are the apotheosis of love and sacrifice. Ch. 12 is the record of the response of love to Himself, the fragrance of which has filled 'the whole world.' The evangelist himself shows in 13^{1ff.} how he had personally felt the pulsation of divine love in the breast of Jesus, and how the Lord loved His own unto the uttermost. Every paragraph of the 'Discourse' and 'Prayer' is a fresh variation of the great revelation; and the scenes of the arrest, the magnanimous self-surrender, intensify the teaching. The record of His relations with His mother, with the other Marys, with the beloved disciple, with Thomas and Simon, give a perfectly unique revelation of the fundamental essence of Deity, and the forecast of the fulfilment of the high-priestly prayer, 'that the love wherewith thou lovest me may be in them, and I in them.'

We have further to state the significance assigned in the Johannine writings to *the death of the great Sacrifice*.

In the first Epistle the author regards the blood of Christ as the propitiation for the sin of the world, and as that which cleanses from all sin, and that God 'laid down his life for us.' In the Apoc. in various ways and many degrees of intensity the saved are the purchase of the blood of a high-priestly sacrifice, are souls redeemed by 'the blood of the Lamb which was slain'; while a right to the final privileges of the saved, access to the Tree of Life, is secured by washing the robes (RV).

St. Paul had laid the greatest emphasis on the expiation of sin, the redemption, the propitiation for sin, the ransom, and the righteousness of men through faith in the blood of Christ.

The Synoptists, by the record of the institution of the Lord's Supper, refer to the lips of Jesus Himself the sublime declaration that His blood was being 'shed for the remission of sin.' Mark refers to our Lord the weighty saying, that He had come to give His life a ransom for many (ἀντὶ πολλῶν).

The way in which St. John handles this momentous teaching differs from these familiar representations, but is not incompatible with them. Reuss (*Théol. Chrét.*), Beyschlag, and others emphasize the contrast, and try to exclude from the Fourth Gospel all reference to or implication of the expiatory worth of the death of Christ. We admit, of course, that the glorious dignity of the incarnate Son of God has covered even the humiliation of His death with a mantle of lustre. The 'lifting up of the Son of Man' (12^{32}), and the bursting of abundant fruit from the dying of the corn of wheat, give a character to the awful tragedy somewhat different from that of the Synoptists. Weiss, against the whole of the Tübingen school, rightly emphasizes those elements where the same truth appears in altered form, *e.g.* where John the Baptist (1^{29}) indicates the Lord Jesus in His essential character and function as fulfilling the oracle of Is 53. The chief significance of this is, that the whole passage is frequently quoted by NT writers and speakers as descriptive of the very heart of the work of Christ. By the use thus made of it by Peter, Philip, John, Matthew, Clemens Romanus, it becomes a chapter of NT doctrine, and the quotations of portions practically cover the whole oracle. Now with these citations John the Baptist's words, 'Behold the Lamb of God,' must be placed. Continual anticipations of Calvary and the Cross occur. In the record of the first cleansing of the temple, in the prolongation of 'the hour,' and in the arrest of murderous hands in act to strike, the whole of the Saviour's holy life becomes a continuous sacrifice. The double reference by the evangelist to the prophecy of Caiaphas is specially charged with the same idea ($11^{49ff.}$ 18^{14}).

In the discourse at Capernaum (6^{51}), the eating His flesh and drinking His blood, in other words the moral surrender to His violent death, is *life*. The moral assimilation of the stupendous fact of the divine-human person of the Lord, eating of the flesh, and the acceptance of the sacrifice of that mysterious life of His for the life of the world, 'drinking his blood,' utterly transcends a purely and simply human consciousness. Beyschlag here wonders at Weiss, but does not reply to him or to thousands who have come to the same conclusion before him. A full interpretation which does not emasculate the reference by our Lord Himself to the 'brazen serpent' (3^{14}), leaves the sacrificial meaning of the conquest of sin and death by the Son of Man still glittering with meaning, and calling with undiminished force for faith, love, and obedience.

We have already drawn attention to ch. 10, where our Lord, by sacrificing Himself as the Good Shepherd for the flock, does not relinquish His saving work. Indeed He renews, by resuming His life, His power to deliver men as a shepherd of the sheep, and then His arms become identified with the everlasting arms, and His hands with the almighty hands of the Father. If the Jews had taken the Tübingen view, surely they would not have lifted stones to stone their Saviour-shepherd for His presumption and blasphemy.

The whole tone of the final discourse (14. 15. 16) is that Christ's very method of departure from this world, amid the exultation of the world and the lamentation of His disciples, unveils the nature of His heavenly work, and the fact that *His* way of returning to the Father (viz. death and resurrection) is the ground on which He calls Himself their 'way,' and says that no man cometh unto the Father but by Him. The entire method by which, in this Gospel, he conveyed the fact of the resurrection to different classes of mankind is charged with the highest order of revelation, for He bare in His risen form the signs of His fearful agony and shame, and yet wielded all authority in heaven and earth.

(*a*) The method of appropriating the great salvation. *Faith* is as explicitly pressed in the Fourth Gospel as by the Synoptists and St. Paul. Believing in His name is the condition of becoming 'sons of God.' In great variety of connexion, faith is made the foundation and condition of eternal life (3^{15-18}, cf. ^{36} and 5^{24}). Coming to Him is the physical analogue of mental and moral surrender to Him (6^{35}). This is the part of man in the synthesis, the condition which God demands. He whom God hath sent is indeed the power by which the Father draws men to Himself (6^{65}, cf. 12^{32} 14^6). Belief in His name was itself conditioned by moral willingness to do the Father's will, and was itself the indispensable antecedent of receiving the Holy Spirit (7^{37-39}).

(*b*) The following of Jesus. All progress in the divine life is a prolongation of the act of faith. The abiding of Christ in the soul, and of the soul in Christ (the chief theme of ch. 15), are essential to any conception of the efficacy of faith, and emphasize the mutual relations of the human and divine will, the growth and continuance both of grace and faith. 'Following Jesus' and 'abiding in him' are frequently identified with such organic union as to ensure final partici-

pation with Him in eternal life and glory. He who sows and they who reap rejoice together (4^{37}); 'He that eateth me shall live by me' (6^{57}); 'He that receiveth whomsoever I shall send receiveth me'; 'He that receiveth me receiveth him that sent me'; 'I am in my Father, and ye in me, and I in you'; 'My Father will love you, and we will come and make our abode with you.' Union will be life-giving; and though separation between the Lord and His disciples is an obvious matter of fact, yet in the power of the spiritual presence after His ascension His disciple may be enabled to '*touch*him' (20^{17}). The 'peace,' the 'joy,' the 'love,' the 'glory' will pass from the central heart of Jesus to 'whosoever wills' or 'comes' (14^{27} 15^{11} 16^{22} $17^{22. 26}$).

D. The Johannine Eschatology.—The teaching of the Fourth Gospel differs from the rest of NT in its bearing on the future life and eternal judgment.

If, however, the truths in the parables are stripped of their imaginative clothing, and the great arguments and implications of St. Paul deprived of their metaphor, and the nucleus of the apocalyptic visions laid bare, it is probable that we shall find nothing more than, nay, not so much as, we find in the Fourth Gospel. The latter has no festival rejoicing, no exclusion of the guest who does not wear the wedding garment, no scene of final judgment and everlasting life and punishment; yet there is *judgment* ever ripening in the 'loving of darkness,' and there is freedom from condemnation and even from death in any form; and these are shown to be essentially equivalent to the moral rupture with God on the one side, or to ethical harmony with the highest concept of God as 'Light' and 'Love' on the other. The future, like the past, is lost in an eternal now. In $5^{28. 29}$ the resurrection, the final consummation, are doubtless involved, but in 15^6 the process which burns up the fruitless prunings would seem to be eternal. The blinding of the foolish heart, the abiding of the divine wrath upon the disobedient, the judgment that is always being enacted and evolved, the terror of dying in sins, the judgment that is inevitable and just (8^{16}), and the *crisis*, the expulsion of the world and its prince, all bring the reader into more vivid realization of the objective fact of judgment than do the parables of the Rich Man, the Marriage, the Talents, or the final unveiling of the great white throne. The momentous events of Heb. history had thrown a lurid light on the prophetic metaphors of the popular discourse; but as the apostle ponders and reports the principle of the eternal judgment upon men and nations and on the entire world, we get closer to the heart and mind of Jesus than by any other medium of communication.

In 1 Jn $2^{18. 28}$ and 4^{17} the writer anticipates the consummation and the *parousia*, of which the whole NT speaks. It is the perversity of criticism which endeavours to separate the two documents on this very ground, or which cannot discern the harmony between them. The kingdom of God upon earth (ch. 3), the multitudes who are 'of the truth' and 'hear his voice,' who come to the light and yield to His control, the underlying theocracy, or Christocracy, identify the teaching of the Fourth Gospel with that of the Synoptists. 'These things are written that ye may believe that Jesus is the CHRIST, the *Son of God*, and that believing ye might have *life* through His name.' In these words the beloved disciple sums up the teaching of all the Gospels.

IX. LITERATURE.—The literature of this subject is in part contained in the foregoing list of works issued during the last hundred years. Some of those which now follow embrace the theology of the Epp. and Apoc. as well as the Gospel. Beyschlag, whose work on *NT Theol.* is the last on our previous list, has taken each separately, though he has given the theology of the Gospel and the Epistles with some deliberate estimate of their agreement as well as their alleged divergences.

The following works are occupied with the entire subject :— Neander, *Hist. of Planting, etc., of Christ. Church,* Eng. tr. vol. ii. 1–58 ; Reuss, *Hist. de la Théol. Chrét.* ii. 369–561, also his *Theol. Johan.* Baur, in his *Bib. Theol.,* emphasized the details in which the author of the Gospel rose above the Hebraic and Pauline Christianity. Schmidt and van Oosterzee, in their works on *Bib. Theol. of NT,* have separated the teaching of Christ in Synop. from that of the Prologue and the Epistles of John. Köstlin, *Der Lehrbegriff des Evangeliums und der Briefe Johannis,* moves along the lines of the Tübingen criticism. Weiss, *Bib. Theol. of NT* (Eng. tr. ii. 311–421), gives an exhaustive treatment. Wendt, *Der Inhalt der Lehre Jesu,* 1890, is largely occupied with the peculiarities and (notwithstanding difficulties) the historical value of the material which was at the disposal of the writer, and in the second part with a very elaborate examination of the teaching of Jesus as gathered from the fourfold representations. Beyschlag criticizes throughout many of the conclusions of Wendt, and everywhere minimizes the amount of approach to traditional views of the person and sacrificial work of Christ, accepted by Weiss and Wendt. They all three fundamentally differ from Hilgenfeld, *Das Evangelium und die Briefe Johannis nach ihrem Lehrbegriff dargestellt,* and Albrecht Thoma, *Genesis Joh. Evangeliums,* 1882, pp. 171–302. Marcus Dods, in the *Expositor's Bible,* on St. John's Gospel, covers much of the ground in practical and forceful manner, and the *Memorabilia of Jesus,* by Peyton, with much vivacity and mystic extravagance, yet brings out the heart of the teaching of Jesus. The same may be said of Sears, *Heart of Christ,* and of a vast number of comm. (*e.g.* Westcott in *Speak. Comm.*) on the Gospel, of which no list is here attempted.

H. R. REYNOLDS.

JOHN, EPISTLES OF—

Of the twenty-one Epp. now included in the NT Canon, three, which form a series by themselves, are associated with the name of St. John. Historical testimony shows them to have been in existence in certain parts of the Church, and to have been used by men of note in the Church, at a very early period ; in the case of the longest, at least by the middle of the 2nd cent., and, in the case of the other two, before the 3rd cent. was far advanced. Their connexion with the name of John, and their wide recognition as authoritative writings, are also things of very ancient date ; taking us, in the case of the first, as far back as to Papias and Irenæus, and, in the case of the others, perhaps to Clement of Alexandria and Origen, certainly to Dionysius, the pupil of Origen. Before the close of the 4th cent. they had become so generally accepted that they were recognized in the Canons of Councils. From time to time, though never on a large scale till our own century, their claims have been disputed, their connexion with the name of John being denied, or another John than the son of Zebedee being thought to be the writer. But it has been the prevailing belief from the oldest times that they are all three apostolic writings, and part of the legacy of the beloved disciple to the Church.

They belong to a group of Epp. which from a very early date have occupied a position of their own in the NT Canon, and have been known by a distinct title. This group, which in most ancient MSS of the NT (with occasional exceptions, as in the case of ℵ) is placed between Acts and the Pauline Epp., did not appear as a separate collection at one and the same period all over the Church, nor did it include all these three Epp. from the beginning. It had neither the same name nor the same compass at all times or in all the different sections of the Christian communion.

In the Eastern Church the Epp. embraced in it received the title of *Catholic* or *General* (καθολικαὶ). In the Western Church, in which the collection was of later formation, they were known, at least from the 6th cent., as *Canonical* (*Canonicæ*). In one important section of the Church, the Syrian, the group consisted only of three Epp., and among these only the longest of the Johannine letters found a place. In other parts of the Church, and in the Eastern division at least by the beginning of the 4th cent., it embraced seven Epistles. These included our three, the longest of the three being, along with 1 Peter, the earliest accepted of the whole collection, and the two shorter being added at a later period. (See the article CATHOLIC EPISTLES).

By their inclusion in the peculiar circle of the Catholic Epp. these three are marked off in one particular respect both from the Pauline Epp. and from other Epp. which were held in a measure of honour in the Church but not ultimately accepted as canonical. In other respects they also form a class by themselves. They have a character which cannot be mistaken. They are so obviously distinguished from the other members of the group to which they belong and from the NT Epp. generally, that the least discerning eye must recognize their apartness.

The peculiar character is most evident, of course, in the largest of the three, but it discovers itself also in the smaller two. The latter are Epp. of extremest brevity, the shortest writings in the Canon. They are writings, too, of incidental interest, and personal or ecclesiastical, not to say congregational, concern ; while the former looks more like a studied composition, and deals with the weightiest questions of doctrine and the largest concerns of practice. Yet they are so much of the same stamp that in all ages the prevailing, if not absolutely universal, opinion has been, that they come from the same mint and are by the same hand. They are writings in which the profound and the simple kiss each other, great and inexhaustible thoughts being wedded to the clearest and least ambitious terms. They combine the qualities of majesty, maturity, authority, and serenity with occasional fire and vehement utterance.

They are almost impersonal as regards the mind to which we owe them. The first gives no hint of the author beyond the fact that he classes himself in an unstudied and informal way with those who had seen Christ in the flesh, and indicates a measure of acquaintance with the circumstances of those whom he addresses. The second and third give only the intimations contained in the use of the designation of 'the presbyter,' and in the mention of certain individuals whom we have no means of identifying with any confidence. Yet, devoid as they are of tangible, personal notes, the writer's individuality makes itself felt throughout. They move within a circle of ideas which, while not without points of affinity with the thought of the other NT Epp., especially the greater Pauline letters, are for the most part their own. They have a diction which also belongs in a marked degree to themselves. Their words are words of calmest dignity, yet instinct with emotion —words which might be those of the philosopher, but yet are those of the common Christian intelligence.

A large literature has grown up around these Epp., which has always found something new to say in expounding their teaching and in grappling with the problems of their history. The affluence of their thought, the fruitfulness of their doctrine, the spell of their spirituality and their deep tranquillity, have attracted the richest and devoutest minds, the most practical and the most speculative intellects in every age. Their characteristic contents, the forms in which they present the essential message of the gospel, the expression which they give to some of the cardinal Christian doctrines, the insight which they afford into the condition of the early Christian societies, the light which they shed upon the operation and the influence of certain kinds of error, make them Epp. of singular interest. Even in the few verses of the Third Ep. disclosures are found which are of far-reaching significance for the story of the life and the theory of the constitution of the primitive Church.

Questions of various interest and of no small difficulty are connected with them. They present some problems in exegesis (I 2^{19} $3^{2. 9. 19}$ $5^{6-8. 16}$), and some curious points in textual criticism (I 3^1 2^{23} $4^{3. 20}$ 5^7, II ^{8}, III ^{2}). Most things touching their literary history have been the subject of dispute, and some of them are far from easy to determine. The old debate is prolonged as to the *where* and the *by whom* of their composition; whether they were written in Ephesus, in Patmos, or elsewhere; whether by one hand or more; whether by one John or two Johns or three. The destination of the first two; the way in which the second and the third came to rank as *Catholic* Epp. and to have a position in the Canon; the source and the explanation of their special form of doctrine; whether a place can be found within the apostolic age for the type of thought and the ecclesiastical conditions which they exhibit,—these are questions which are still under discussion.

Of these questions, that of their origin and authorship is of primary importance. The answer which comes readiest to hand when one reads them together is that all three are products of the same mind. The answer that is suggested both by historical testimony and by their contents is that that mind is the mind to which we also owe the Fourth Gospel and the Apocalypse. And in point of fact these are the views which prevailed in the ancient Church, and which have been generally acquiesced in since then. But they were not left unchallenged even in ancient times, while in modern times they have been disavowed by a succession of thinkers of distinguished rank among NT critics.

In our own century, in particular, their claims to apostolic date and worth have been strongly contested, and judgments of the most diverse kind have been pronounced upon them by the critical schools. There are those who find no difficulty in attributing all three Epp., as well as the Gospel, to the Apostle John, but discover another hand in the Apocalypse. Bleek, *e.g.*, admits the existence of clear points of contact between all the writings assigned to St. John. But he is of opinion, at the same time, that the affinity between the Epp. and Gospel on the one hand, and the Bk. of Revelation on the other, is limited and occasional, while the difference is great and pervading. That difference is held to extend not only to the diction and the style, of which in the case of the Apoc. the one is confessedly peculiar

and the other is pronounced rough and broken, but to the whole genius of the books, their attitude to the Jewish people, city, and temple, their teaching on the *Parousia*, and other things. It is thought to amount to so much that, if the Epp. are ascribed to St. John, the Apoc. must either be allowed to be a forgery by a much later hand or be explained as the work of another John, 'the presbyter,' referred to by Papias in a way interpreted by many as distinguishing him from the apostle (Euseb. *HE* iii. 39). There are others, again, who read the story of these writings in the reverse way, fixing the stigma of the spurious on the Epp. alone, or on the Epp. and the Gospel together. S. G. Lange regarded the Gospel and the Apoc. as the real writings of St. John, but took the First Ep. to be the work of an imitator a century later. The Tübingen critics agree in claiming the Apoc. for St. John, and in repudiating the other writings, though they differ with regard to the order of the latter. Baur himself (in 1857) held the First Ep. to be an imitation of the Gospel by a different hand, while Hilgenfeld places the Ep. earlier than the Gospel. Among those, too, who hold by the common Johannine authorship, certain differences appear, some regarding the First Ep. as the middle term between the Gospel and the Apoc. (Godet), others giving the Ep. a position in time between the Apoc. and the Gospel.

The historical case, as it has been understood by the great majority of students, so far as concerns the main questions, is this: that, while certain doubts overhung for a time the recognition of the shorter Epp., we find them, so far back as we can trace them, bearing the name of John and never any other, when the author's name is given; and that, while certain differences of view appeared in the early Church regarding the particular John, all three were regarded by most as writings of the apostle, and had an assured position as such before the close of the 4th cent. Whether the case can be accepted as it has thus been put, and what the probabilities are with the critical theories referred to, will best appear as the final result of a study of the writings. We shall take each Ep. therefore by itself, and shall look at its order of thought and the various questions which have been raised with respect to its occasion, its purpose, its message, etc. Having done this, we shall take up anew the problem of its origin and authorship, endeavouring to estimate the worth of the traditional view on the one hand and the counter-theories on the other.

THE FIRST EPISTLE. — 1. *Order of Thought.* — The Ep. opens with some calm and lofty sentences, not cast in the form of epistolary introduction with which we are familiar in the NT, but more in that of the Ep. to the Hebrews. In these, without indicating either himself or his readers except in an indirect and general way, the writer states at once the great fact on which all that he has to say rests, viz. the historical manifestation in Jesus Christ of the life that is behind all life, the eternal life that was with the Father. He declares at the outset, too, in this Introduction, the great object which he has in view in addressing his readers, viz. that his joy in them might be perfected by seeing them one with him in that fellowship with God in which he and the brethren with whom he classes himself are conscious of standing (1^{1-4}). He enters then at once upon his specific subject, giving as the basis of his counsel and the fundamental apostolic message the truth that 'God is light'; from which the immediate inference is that a walk in the light is indispensable on our part to this fellowship with God. This inference, however, from which there can be no escape, is declared, not in its logical directness, but in the form that to profess to be in fellowship with God and to continue to walk in darkness, is to commit ourselves to a lie and to all unreality. This walk in the light is not to be thus dealt with. Too much depends on it—not only fellowship with God, but fellowship with other members of Christ's body, and also the purgation of sin by Christ's blood. The cleansing which every Christian needs and which he also obtains coming thus into view, the explanation follows that on the one hand, if we claim to have no sin, we deceive ourselves and put God Himself to the lie, while on the other hand real confession of sin brings with it the divine forgiveness and the divine cleansing (1^{5-10}). The same thought is put in another form before the writer passes to his next subject, when he proceeds to remind his readers that all that he writes to them of the revelation of life, the fellowship with God, the pardon and purification of sin, is written with the practical purpose of instructing them not to sin, and then, recognizing the sin of which the true Christian cannot but be conscious, he points to the certainty of its forgiveness in virtue of what Christ is as Paraclete and Propitiation ($2^{1.\ 2}$).

The thought of the new *fellowship* which has come by the Gospel leads to another near akin to it—that of the *knowledge* which the same Gospel requires and makes possible. The position in which those addressed were at the time, furnishes the occasion for speaking with emphasis and decision of the knowledge with which alone the believer is concerned, and of spurious forms with lofty pretensions. So the writer declares the knowledge of God in its reality to be possible only where the humble way of practical obedience to God's commandments is followed; in which connexion he urges the necessity of walking as Christ walked. In further illustration of the kind of life which befits the Christian, he identifies the walk in the light with the walk in brotherly love, and holds before his readers the duty of loving the brethren as the commandment of commandments, one at once old and new (3^{7-11}). He warns these Christians also against the love of the world and the seductions of false teachers, which are contrary to the love of the brethren, and presses this warning with the greater insistence because the world's opportunity is now short. It is the last time with it and all things, as is witnessed by the fact that many antichrists have appeared. These antichrists are described, and the description is pointed by an exhortation to these believers to abide in that knowledge which they have by the Holy Ghost, a knowledge which cannot deceive, so that they may not be put to shame in the great day of the Lord's *Parousia* (2^{12-28}).

The thought of God as *light* passes over next into the thought of God as *righteous*. Following out this new idea, the writer proceeds to say that only he who is righteous can be the child of God; that the man who has the hope of being like God or Christ must purify himself; and that, as Christ is sinless, he who is in Christ cannot sin. But he adds, with an eye to the subtle deception of the false teachers, that to *be* righteous means to *do* righteousness, and in sharp and decisive terms distinguishes those who sin as the children of the devil, from those who do not and cannot sin as the children of God. He identifies this righteousness also, which is the note of the son of God, as he had previously done in the case of the walk in light, with the love of the brethren, and again warns his readers against the love of the world, which, as was seen in the instance of Cain, means hatred of the children of God ($2^{29}-3^{12}$). At this point he sets Christ before them again as the supreme pattern of Christian love—a love which must be in deed and truth, and which carries with

it these two blessings—the consciousness of being of the truth and the confidence that our prayers shall be heard. Touching again on God's commandment, he shows that it, too, means two things, viz. belief in Christ and love of one another, and explains that he who keeps the divine commandments not only is in fellowship with God, but has through the Spirit the consciousness of that fellowship (3^{12-24}).

Returning to the question of the immediate dangers which threatened his readers, the writer speaks again of the false prophets; and his words of warning on that subject become the occasion for taking up anew the two great themes—the law of love and the keeping of God's commandments, which are so much in his view. He repeats his cautions against the seductions of misleading teachers, and indicates the marks of distinction between the spirit of God and the spirit of Antichrist, between the spirit of truth and the spirit of error (4^{1-6}). He urges again the supreme duty of love—love to God indeed in the first instance, but also, and more particularly in this case, love to man. He reminds those for whom he is so solicitous, that the man who is of God is of love, called to love Him who Himself is love, and who has given the last proof of that in the mission and propitiatory death of His Son. To love God, he tells them, is to be in God, and to have God in them, and to be delivered from the torment of fear. It is all this, but it is also a love that gives proof of itself in the obvious practical duties of loving the brethren and keeping the divine commandments. And these commandments, he adds, whatever they may be to others, cannot be grievous to those who are begotten of God ($4^{6}-5^{3}$). The mention of this new relation to God, expressed by the term 'begotten of God,' forms a natural point of transition to the idea of the new mental attitude that goes with the new birth. So the writer comes to speak of *faith*,—of what it is as belief in Jesus as the Son of God, and of the witness which it carries with it to His being that; of the victorious might that is in that belief, and of the witness as something more than any external testimony—a witness which the believer has in himself (5^{4-12}). As the letter approaches its conclusion he states again the great object with which it has been written. He refers once more to what prayer is to the children of God, the confidence in it which is their prerogative, and the things they are entitled to ask (5^{13-17}). He brings the Epistle to an end by proclaiming anew the separation of the Christian from sin and from the wicked one; the privilege which is the Christian's both in understanding and in possession; and the necessity that is laid upon those who know the true God and have fellowship with Him to keep themselves from idols (5^{18-21}).

2. *Character.* — It appears, therefore, that the argument of the Epistle, if such a term can be applied to it, turns on a few large and simple ideas. It unfolds itself mostly in terms of certain broad antagonisms—those between Christ and Antichrist, believers and the world, the children of God and the children of the devil, the love of God and the love of the world, righteousness and unrighteousness, confidence and fear, love and hate, sins and a sin unto death, walking in the light and walking in darkness, being begotten of God and being touched by 'that wicked one.' In connexion with these fundamental and recurring antitheses we have a series of statements of what the message of the gospel is; of what fellowship with God is, how it comes, and what it implies; of what Christ is, and what His mission into this world means; of what the believer is, and what the Christian vocation involves.

The message of the gospel is that God is light; that we are to love one another; that in Christ God has given us eternal life. The fellowship with God which is in view is made possible by two things —the historical manifestation of God in Christ and the believer's faith, the former being the objective ground of this new and gracious relation, the latter its subjective condition. This fellowship brings with it the graces of joy, forgiveness, knowledge, the cleansing of the life, the liberty of intercession, the answer to prayer, the assurance and fearlessness of children. It involves a walking in the light, the doing of righteousness, the purifying of ourselves, love to God and love to the brethren, filial obedience, practical benevolence, the observance of the divine commandments, the forswearing of idols. Christ is the Son of God, the only-begotten Son, the manifestation of the Father and of that eternal life which was with the Father; pre-existent as being sent by God into the world; true man, righteous, sinless, the Paraclete with the Father, the propitiation for the sin of the world. His mission is to destroy the works of the devil, to bring us back to God, to give us eternal life, to put away our sin, and to be the Saviour of the world. And the Christian is one who has fellowship with God; who confesses his sin and is cleansed and forgiven; who is begotten of God and sins not; who has the gift of knowledge and can distinguish good from evil, the children of God from the world, truth from error, the false prophet or the false spirit from the true; who walks in the light and does the truth, loving God and the brethren, imitating Christ, and finding no grievousness in the divine commandments; who has passed out of death into life; who knows that his prayers are heard, and looks with holy confidence to the coming of his Lord and the judgment, and has the consciousness of eternal life in him.

Alike in the matter of its thought and in the way in which its ideas are expressed, this Epistle has a character wholly its own. The only Epp. of the NT which are of the same stamp are the two smaller letters which are associated with it. It differs most of all from the Epp. which bear St. Paul's name. It has nothing of the formal structure, the systematic course, the dialectical movement of these. The logical particles which abound in the Pauline writings are strange to this Epistle. Its thought moves on, but not in an obvious progress to a goal. It takes the form of a succession of ideas which seem to have no logical relation, and which fall only now and again into a connected series. They are delivered, not in the way of reasoned statements, but as a series of reflections and declarations given in meditative, aphoristic fashion. This lack of the constructive quality gives the teaching of the Epistle a peculiar directness and simplicity. But it is the directness of authority, the simplicity of truths which are felt to be self-attesting. These characteristics add to the vigour, the originality, the attractiveness of the Epistle. They have strangely been regarded by some as tokens of weakness, and have been reckoned among the things which are supposed to speak of the 'feebleness of old age' (S. G. Lange). Even Baur discovered a certain 'indefiniteness,' a tendency to repetition, a want of 'logical force,' in the tenor of the Ep. which gave it a 'tone of childlike feebleness.' But those critics show a better insight—and they are of Baur's school as well as of others—who find a peculiar beauty, richness, and originality in the Epistle, a special freshness and vividness, particularly in what it says of the 'subjective, inner life of Christianity' (Hilgenfeld).

If the characteristic ideas of the Ep. are few and simple, they are of large significance, and they are presented in new aspects and relations as often as they recur. They belong to the region of primary principles, realities of the intuition, certainties of the experience, absolute truths. And they are given in their absoluteness. The regenerate man is one who *cannot* sin; Christian faith is presented in its ideal character and completeness; the revelation of life is exhibited in its finality, not in the stages of its historical realization. They are ideas which take us into the inner and essential nature of things, into the real that is behind the phenomenal, the inward that is the heart of the outward, the permanent that is the ground of the transitory, the future that is in the bosom of the present. They are mystical in the sense that they are given as truths of immediate certitude, absolute reality, inward vision. But they are not mystical in the sense of being the pure products of intuition, things only of the subjective world, or superior to the common experience of life. They are given in practical relation to the ordinary course of Christian life and conduct. They have their roots, too, in the great facts of the objective revelation of God in Christ, in that which 'we have heard, which we have seen with our eyes, which we have looked upon, and our hands have handled of the word of life' (1^1).

3. *Ideas.*—The doctrinal and ethical ideas which meet us in the other NT Epp. appear also in this letter. But they are presented in a special light, and with distinctive notes. The *Theology* of the Ep. has its own points of interest. God is seen in this Ep., as elsewhere, in His Fatherhood, His truth, His righteousness, His forgiving grace, and in the fulness of His life as expressed in His triune Being. But, above all else, He is 'light' (1^5) and He is 'love,' loving us before we loved Him, and so imparting Himself to us that He dwells in us (4$^{8.\ 10.\ 12}$). The *Christology* also has its peculiar features. Christ is the Son, 'the Son of God,' 'the Only-begotten,' who was with the Father before He appeared in the world. He is the explanation of all things. For in Him we see the eternal life that is behind all things, and from Him we have the life that is life indeed. His divine and pre-temporal relations are not left without expression or intimation. But it is especially in His human nature and relations that He forms the great subject of this Epistle. He is never called 'the Son of Man,' it is true, yet it is the integrity of His humanity that is especially affirmed—the fact that He appeared on earth in the full reality of the 'flesh,' neither in phantasmal form nor in divided being, neither as mere spirit nor yet with the divine and the human in any loose or temporary connexion, but as at once 'Jesus' and 'the Christ,'—Jesus Christ come in the flesh, and 'not by water only, but by water and blood' (2^{22} 4$^{2.\ 3}$ 5^6). His sinlessness is asserted (3^5), as it is in the Pauline and Petrine writings, and He is said to have been 'sent' by God (4^8), as St. Paul also speaks of His appearance on earth. But His entrance into our world, and His assumption of our nature and estate, are not given, as they are in St. Paul, under the aspect of a *humiliation*. The designation **'the Paraclete,'** which occurs in the NT only in the Johannine writings, and is used in the Fourth Gospel directly of the Holy Spirit and only implicitly of Christ, is applied here to the Son Himself directly and definitely (2^2). Further, in this Ep. Christ is presented less in respect of what He was and is, and more in respect of what proceeds from Him and is done by Him. It is a question whether the term 'the Word' is used directly and personally of Him. The form which the sentence takes in which that great term is used is indirect, and its subject is neuter and im-

personal (1^{1-3}). It is specifically as 'the life' that He is set before us here, and the more general term is chosen to express His appearance on earth. It is a φανεροῦσθαι. It is not said of Him that 'the Word was made flesh'; and though the idea that His entrance into our world was a real *incarnation* is implied in the description of Him as 'come in the flesh,' that event is exhibited rather as a *manifestation*, and in particular the manifestation of life.

The *Holy Spirit*, again, is spoken of especially as given by God and as bearing witness to Christ (3^{24} 5^8). *Sin* is 'unrighteousness' (1^9 $3^{6.7}$ 5^{17}) and 'lawlessness' (3^4); but it is also 'darkness' (1^6) and 'death' (3^{14}). The *believer* is the 'child' of God (τέκνον, not υἱός, 'born' or 'begotten of God,' the special relation in which he is introduced being that of the new life rather than the new standing ($3^{1.2}$). Large expression is given also to the forces of *evil* which are opposed to Christ and the children of God. They are the devil and his works (3^8), the spirit of deceit (4^6 πνεῦμα τῆς πλάνης), seducing spirits that have to be tried (4^1), the many 'antichrists' who have separated themselves from the Church or been cast out of it, and in whom the antichrist of prophecy is seen ($2^{18.19}$ 4^3). Among these forces is mentioned also '**the world**,' an expression which in this Epistle conveys the largest and most complex conception of immediate, encircling evil (2^{15-17} 3^{13} 4^{1-5} $5^{5.19}$). *Faith*, too, has its special aspect and compass here. It is the great subjective condition of the Christian life and standing, but it is not presented here either in the broad idea of it which is expressed in the Epistle to the Hebrews (11^1), or in the definite character given to it in the great Pauline Epistles. It is neither generally 'the assurance of things hoped for, the proving of things not seen,' though it comes near to that, nor distinctively the faith that justifies and gives peace with God. It is belief in Jesus Christ, the belief that comes with regeneration, that is of the new life, that is the characteristic note of the man who is born of God. As such it is power, it is victory, it is its own witness ($5^{1-5.10}$).

The Ep. also has its doctrine of *the last things*. Its theology, indeed, is not distinctively an eschatological theology. Its fundamental idea is rather that of *life*, and that 'life' not as a thing wholly or specifically of the future. It is a 'life' that has been with the Father from the beginning, and that has been historically revealed in Christ (1^{1-3}). It is *in* Christ, and it becomes our possession *now* in virtue of our belief in Him and attitude to Him ($5^{11.12}$). It is 'eternal' life, and that not in respect of its perpetuity merely, or its changelessness, but distinctively in respect of its quality—as essential life, a new ethical order of being, not a certain duration of existence, but the kind of life that means the ideal good of life, the perfection of life, its satisfaction in God. This great conception of life as 'eternal life,' which bulks so largely in the Fourth Gospel, occurring there some seventeen times, has an equally prominent place in this Ep., meeting us here six times in the forms ζωὴ αἰώνιος (3^{15} $5^{11.13.20}$) and ἡ ζωὴ ἡ αἰώνιος (1^2 2^{25}). But while this qualitative or ethical conception of life, which lifts it above distinctions of present and future, is the prevailing idea, it does not exclude the eschatological. The 'life' which is essential, and which is ours now in Christ, also looks to a fuller completeness, a future perfection. The Ep. speaks of a manifestation of what the children of God are destined to be (3^2). It has its word of hope, its vision of a blessedness still prospective, its anticipation of a manifestation in which we shall see Christ as He is, its doctrine of an advent of Christ which it expresses, as St. Paul also expresses it, as

a *Parousia* ($3^{2.3}$ 2^{28}). There is no express mention, it is true, of the *Resurrection*. But it is implied in what is said of the *Parousia* and the *Judgment*, the fact of a great Judgment in the future being stated in express terms (4^{17}). The things of the End may occupy a smaller place in this Ep. than in the writings of St. Peter and St. Paul. But alongside the present conditions which are expressed by the same words, the 'coming' of Christ, the 'judgment,' the 'life eternal' appear also as events of the end and as final conditions. These are, in brief, the main ideas of the Epistle. They have an important bearing, as will be seen, on the question of the authorship of the writing. See also art. JOHN (LIFE AND THEOLOGY OF).

4. *Form and Structure.*—There are certain questions relating to the form and construction of the Epistle. They are matters of subordinate importance, which have had a consideration given them that is much beyond their merits. One of these is the question whether this writing is really an *Epistle* or something else. The fact that it has neither an introduction nor a conclusion, such as we find in other NT Epp., neither a greeting nor a benediction nor a doxology, such as we get in the Pauline Epp., together with the circumstance that in much of its matter it does not run in terms of direct address, has led some to deny it the character of a *letter*, and to speak of it as a homiletical essay or a pastoral (Reuss, Westcott), a *libellus* rather than an Epistle (Bengel), a manual of doctrine (Heidegger), a treatise (Michaelis), a practical or polemical composition meant to form part of the Gospel (Berger, Storr). But if it wants the usual form of superscription and greeting, it has an equivalent resembling the opening of the Ep. to the Hebrews. If it has not the kind of conclusion, or the doxology, with which we are familiar in the Pauline Epp., that is the case also with the Ep. of James. The freedom of the style, the use of such direct terms as 'I write unto you,' 'I wrote unto you,' and the footing on which writer and readers stand to each other all through its contents, show it to be no formal composition or didactic treatise, but an *Epistle* in the proper sense of the word.

Nor is anything to be gained by applying to 1 Jn such ingenious distinctions as are attempted to be drawn (*e.g.* by Deissmann, *Bibelstudien*) between 'letter' and 'epistle,' and denying it the former designation. If the term 'letter' were to be restricted, indeed, in common speech to a piece of private correspondence not meant for the public, it might be necessary to speak only of 3 Jn as a 'letter,' and to describe 1 Jn and (on a particular interpretation of its address) 2 Jn as 'Epistles.' And so some would hold St. Paul's letters to be the only 'letters' in the proper sense in the NT. But there are 'open' letters as well as closed, encyclical letters as well as personal, letters to communities as well as to individuals. What gives to a composition the character of a letter is its style and contents. And though there is not a little in 1 Jn that might suit an address or discourse, there is more that fits a letter, especially such a letter as one might write who had both age and honour on his side, and who could write both freely and authoritatively. The relations which the writing indicates between writer and readers are not distant, but familiar. They are the near relations of those who know each other well.

The question of the *structure* of the Ep. has also been much debated. Some have pronounced the writing to be wholly without a plan, and to consist simply of a number of reflections, counsels, or deliverances loosely put together, without continuity or logical connexion (Calvin, cf. his *Argumentum Epist.* 1 *Joh.*; Flacius Illyricus, *Episcopus*)

Others have regarded it as a systematic composition, on a dogmatic plan, and with a methodical arrangement of ideas in all its parts. Bengel, *e.g.*, asserted for it an elaborate contextual plan on a basis mainly Trinitarian. These are extreme opinions, and the truth lies somewhere between them. It is impossible to claim for this Ep. the strict logical sequence of thought which some imagine they find in it. But it is at the same time more than a series of unrelated ideas, a collection of unconnected maxims or aphorisms. There is a certain order in the Ep., due to the object with which it is declared to have been written. But it is an order that can be taken only in a broad and general way. Attempts have been made to carry it out in detail; but they have been only partially successful. Some have distributed the contents of the Ep. into something like *eight* groups of ideas (Lücke); others have found *five* main divisions in it, viz. 1^5–2^{11} 2^{12-27} 2^{28}–3^{24a} 3^{24b}–4^{21} 5^{1-21} (Hofmann, cf. *Schriftbeweis*; Luthardt); others *four*, viz. 1^5–2^{11} 2^{12-28} 2^{29}–3^{22} 3^{23}–5^{17}, dealing respectively with the danger of moral indifference, the love of the world and Antichrist, the necessity of a life of brotherly love, and *faith* as the foundation of the Christian life (Huther). Some, again, have arranged the matter of the Ep. on the plan of *three* great exhortations, viz. 1^5–2^{28} 2^{29}–4^6 4^7–5^{21}, with Introduction and Conclusion (de Wette). Others have regarded it as consisting of Introduction, Conclusion, and *two* great connected sections, viz. 1^5–2^{28} 2^{29}–5^5, both parts setting forth the same subject of fellowship with God the Father and the Lord Jesus Christ; but each in its own way—the former having for its special theme the proposition that God is *light*, the latter the proposition that God is *righteous* (Düsterdieck, Alford). Divisions of a somewhat different kind are also suggested, as, *e.g.*, into three main sections, each with three or four sub-sections, the subjects for these sections being taken to be the 'problem of life and those to whom it is proposed,' the 'conflict of truth and falsehood without and within,' and the 'Christian life: the victory of faith' (Westcott).

There is more or less truth in these different readings of the plan of the Ep., and there is a certain measure of agreement among them. But even the simplest schemes do not admit of precise application. One can see that there are certain primary thoughts, especially the great ideas that God is light, that God is righteous, that God is love, to which much of the matter of the Ep. naturally relates itself; and that there are certain paragraphs or series of verses that have on the whole distinct subjects. But the ideas which give a special character to some particular section of the Ep. are not confined to that section. They meet us again and again, though it may not be quite in the same form. The Ep. has its introduction, its body, and its conclusion. It has its ruling thoughts, and it passes from one thought to another by points of transition which can often, if not always, be recognized. In its main contents it has a certain order and succession of ideas. But it is an order that follows the way of suggestion, not that of logical connexion. It is not systematically carried out, neither does it show itself upon the surface. It has the freedom that is proper to a letter, the unstudied, non-constructive character that belongs to a series of meditations or practical counsels.

5. *Independence.*—This is a question of greater importance. Among the NT writings there is one, though only one, that is at once seen to be of the same character as this Epistle. That is the Fourth Gospel. The resemblance is so great and unmistakable as at once to suggest the question, how the two are related to each other. In the Epistle we get the same general style as in the Gospel, the same simplicity of language with the same profoundness and exaltation of thought, the same lofty serenity, the same peculiar structure, the same sententious or aphoristic tone, the same habit of giving a statement both in the affirmative form and in the negative, and of taking up, repeating, and extending an idea already expressed; the same way of conveying truth by the use of contrasts, like that between light and darkness, life and death, love and hate; the same methods of forming sentences and carrying the thought forward. There are the same fundamental conceptions, too, of God, Christ, the purpose of the Son's mission, the nature of His work, His relations to God and to man, the character and standing of His disciples, the world, life, death, the present and the future. Many of the terms which are characteristic of the one are characteristic of the other. Of this class are the following:—ἀληθής, ἀλήθεια, ἁμαρτίαν ἔχειν, ἀνθρωποκτόνος, γεννηθῆναι ἐκ, ἐντολὴ καινή, ζωή, ζωὴ αἰώνιος, θεᾶσθαι, κόσμος, μαρτυρεῖν, μεταβαίνειν ἐκ τοῦ θανάτου εἰς τὴν ζωήν, μονογενής (of Christ), παιδία, παράκλητος, περιπατεῖν ἐν τῇ σκοτίᾳ, πιστεύειν εἰς, παῤῥησία, τὸ πνεῦμα τῆς ἀληθείας, ποιεῖν τὴν ἀλήθειαν, ποιεῖν τὴν ἁμαρτίαν, ὁ πονηρός, σκοτία, σωτὴρ τοῦ κόσμου, τέκνα θεοῦ, τεκνία, τιθέναι τὴν ψυχὴν αὐτοῦ, φανεροῦν, φῶς, χαρὰ πεπληρωμένη. Other terms distinctive of the Gospel and the Apocalypse together meet us also in the Ep.; *e.g.* ἀγαπᾶν, ἀγάπη, ἀγνίζειν ἑαυτόν, ἀληθινός, γινώσκειν, εἶναι ἐκ, θεωρεῖν, μαρτυρία, μένειν, νικᾶν, πλανᾶν, τηρεῖν τὰς ἐντολάς, τηρεῖν τὸν λόγον, φαίνειν. Peculiar syntactical forms, or peculiar uses of familiar formulæ, which occur in the Gospel, occur also in the Ep., as in the case of ἵνα, ἀλλ' ἵνα, etc. There are also many obvious parallelisms of thought and expression. Examples of these may be seen in such passages of the Ep. as— 2^{14} 2^{17} 3^8 3^{13} 3^{22} 3^{23} 4^6 4^{15} 4^{16} 5^4 5^9 5^{20} when compared respectively with those passages of the Gospel—5^{38} 8^{35} 8^{44} 15^{18} 8^{29} 13^{34} 8^{47} 6^{56} 6^{69} 16^{33} 5^{32} 17^3.

In view of all this some have denied the character of independence to the Ep., and have spoken of it as a copy of the Gospel which shows all through the imitative hand (Baur). Others, who have not been disposed to go so far as that, have regarded it as a 'companion' to the Gospel, the second part of the Gospel (Michaelis, Storr, Eichhorn), a kind of dedicatory writing meant to go with the Gospel (Hug, Thiersch, Hausrath, Hofmann, Ebrard, Haupt), a summary or recasting and practical setting of the contents of the Gospel (Hoekstra, Holtzmann), a covering letter designed to serve as a kind of introduction to the Gospel (Lightfoot), etc.

But there are clear and significant differences between the two writings, notwithstanding this remarkable general similarity. There is no such local colouring in the Ep. as we have in the Gospel. There is no such Hebrew stamp in the Ep. as there is in the Gospel. There is not a single quotation from the OT in the former, while in the latter we have both citations from the OT and references to the OT. These differences, indeed, are not conclusive. They may be due to the natural difference between narrative and letter, or to the different circumstances and objects of the writings. But there is much more than these. The ideas which are common to both are, in not a few cases, differently put, and have a different aspect.

In the Ep., *e.g.*, Christ's appearance on earth is presented, as we have seen, in the broad light of a *manifestation*. The specific function of *advocacy* or intercession is ascribed to Him. The qualities of *faithfulness* and *righteousness* on the side of God, and the grace of *confession* on the side of man, are given in a particular connexion with the forgiveness and the cleansing of sin ; and *faith* appears in the definite character of a power of overcoming. In the case of certain ideas of the Ep., the affinities are rather with the teaching of the great Pauline Epp. than with the Fourth Gospel. This is true, not only of what is said of God or of Christ as δίκαιος (cf. 1⁹ 2² with Ro 3²⁶), but also of the description of Christ as ἱλασμός (cf. 2² 4¹⁰ with Ro 3²⁵), the designation of His Second Coming as a παρουσία (cf. 2²⁸ with 1 Co 15²³, 1 Th 2¹⁹ etc.), etc. But, besides this, the Ep. has not a few ideas which it does not share with the Gospel. Such ideas are those, *e.g.*, of a 'fellowship (κοινωνία) with the Father and with His Son Jesus Christ,' a 'love perfected' (ἀγάπη τετελειωμένη), an 'Antichrist' and 'Antichrists,' a 'sin unto death' (ἁμαρτία πρὸς θάνατον), a 'Divine seed' (σπέρμα αὐτοῦ), an 'unction from the Holy One' (χρίσμα ἀπὸ τοῦ ἁγίου). Such terms as ἀγγελία and πλάνος, such phrases as ἐπιθυμία τῶν ὀφθαλμῶν, ἐπιθυμία τῆς σαρκός, ἐν σαρκὶ ἔρχεσθαι, ἐν τῷ φωτὶ περιπατεῖν, ποιεῖν τὴν ἀνομίαν, ποιεῖν τὴν δικαιοσύνην, belong to the Ep. and not to the Gospel. Such ideas, again, as those of the 'wrath of God' (ἡ ὀργὴ τοῦ θεοῦ), to 'be from above' (εἶναι ἐκ τῶν ἄνω), 'to be from beneath' (εἶναι ἐκ τῶν κάτω), and such designations as 'the Holy Spirit' (τὸ πνεῦμα τὸ ἅγιον), which are in the Gospel (3³⁶ 8²³ 1³³ etc.), do not recur in the Epistle. And to these things others might be added. Where the Gospel, *e.g.*, declares God to be 'Spirit' (πνεῦμα, 4²⁴), the Ep. declares Him to be 'love' (ἀγάπη, 4¹⁶) ; where the Gospel speaks of the Son being 'in the Father' and the 'Father in the Son' (14¹⁰·¹¹ etc.), the Ep. speaks of us as being 'in God' and God 'in us' (ἡμεῖς ἐν τῷ θεῷ 2⁵ 4⁴, ὁ ἐν ἡμῖν 2⁵ 4⁴).

There are also certain minuter differences in usage, as in the preference of the Ep. for the preposition ἀπό after such verbs as αἰτεῖν, ἀκούειν, λαμβάνειν, where the Gospel has παρά. To which must be added the fact that no clear reference to the Gospel is discovered in the Epistle. There is enough, therefore, to show that the Ep. is not dependent on the Gospel, not a second part of it, nor a remodelling of its contents, whether for practical or for polemical purposes, but an independent composition having its own particular occasion, purpose, and character.

6. *Purpose and Occasion.*—Its purpose is that the readers may have fellowship with the writer and his associates who have been eye-witnesses of the Word of life, and whose fellowship is with the Father and with His Son Jesus Christ; that the joy which the writer and his brethren have in them may be made complete by seeing that fellowship realized in their case ; and that those addressed may have the comfortable consciousness of possessing eternal life (1²·³ 5¹³). The writer's object, therefore, is to be taken in the breadth which he himself gives it. It is not to be limited to the combating of certain errors, the refutation of certain false teachers, or the reproof of certain shortcomings. The Ep. does deal with certain faults in life, certain errorists and defective doctrines. But its primary purpose is to help these Christians to be partakers with the writer and his fellow-witnesses in the completeness and satisfaction of the Christian life. It is with a view to this that other subjects are introduced, that certain instructions are given, and that counsels are offered against certain infirmities and perils.

The Ep., nevertheless, may have had a particular occasion. That is found by some in a certain critical condition of the Church or Churches addressed (Lücke, etc.) ; and there are, no doubt, things in the Ep. which point to shortcomings,

especially in the matter of brotherly love. But there is nothing to indicate that those addressed were in a peculiarly dangerous or faulty condition, or that the moral life had sunk very low among them. The Ep. is not one of reproof. It is rather written under the sense that writer and readers are living in 'the last time,' and that the Coming of the Lord is expected. Its particular occasion, therefore, may rather be sought in what it says of the appearance of certain false teachers, in which event the writer sees the token of 'the last time.' Who were those errorists that are here spoken of as 'Antichrists'? To this question many different answers have been given. Some of them may be at once dismissed as too large and indefinite. To say, *e.g.* (with Bleek), that the men in view are *Christians*, men who had lost their faith or had practised it unworthily, or that they are men who had fallen into Antinomian licence, is inconsistent both with the fact that the 'Antichrists' are described as outside the Church, and with the kind of fault that is attributed to them here. Further, if Antinomian error had been specially in view, we should have expected (so Neander), not such a declaration as 'Every one that doeth sin, doeth also lawlessness ; and sin is lawlessness' (3⁴ RV), but rather 'Every one that doeth lawlessness, doeth also sin ; and lawlessness is sin.' To say that they were *Jews* (Löffler), or that they were *Ebionites*, is equally wide of the mark, nothing being found to imply that the error in question was merely a denial of the Messiahship of Jesus, or a reduction of Christ to the rank of a second Moses. There is as little to support the idea that the Ep. has in view more than one class of errorists, Ebionites and Sabians (Storr), or Ebionite and Docetic teachers (Sander).

It is more reasonable to identify them with Docetic teachers of the Gnostic type. They are described as denying that 'Jesus is the Christ,' as denying 'the Father and the Son' (2²²·²³), and as confessing 'not Jesus' (4³). They are contrasted with those who are of the spirit that 'confesseth that Jesus Christ is come in the flesh' (4²) ; and, toward the close of the Ep., though they are not mentioned, the note that is still insisted on is belief 'that Jesus is the Christ' (5¹). These terms do not carry us to the particular refinements of Gnosticism that are connected with the name of Basilides, as some think (Pfleiderer). There is no point of contact with the strange Basilidean theories of a tripartite sonship, the division of the world into the Ogdoad and the Hebdomad, and the destiny of Jesus to be the 'first-fruits of the sorting of the things confused.' Nor is there any real analogy between the doctrine of the Son in the Ep. and the vague speculations of these Gnostics about the descent of a light from the Hebdomad upon Jesus the Son of Mary at the Annunciation. There might seem more, perhaps, that resembles the Valentinian doctrine, in which the idea of σπέρματα has a large and prominent place. But the Christology of the Ep. is far removed from any one or all of the three views of the origin of Jesus which are ascribed to Valentinus by Irenæus (i. 11. 15, etc.). The terms point to something more specific, however, than the ordinary Docetic doctrine which bore that our Lord had only an *apparent* body all through His life on earth, and until His Ascension. They best suit the teachings of the Gnostic Cerinthus, in which Oriental, Jewish, and Christian ideas seem to have been mixed up, and which distinguished between the man 'Jesus' and 'Christ' the heavenly Being, and affirmed that 'the Christ' united Himself with 'Jesus' only at the baptism of the latter, and continued with Him only till His Passion. Beyond this the terms do not seem to warrant us to go. It is probably too much to say (*e.g.* with Holtzmann) that the error in view all through the Ep. is the dualistic form of Gnosis which was Christologically Docetic and practically Antinomian, or (with Lipsius, etc.) that both Docetism and Antinomianism are intended. It is doubtful whether we can say (*e.g.* with Weiss, Harnack, etc.) that the Ep. is directed also against men within the Church who misunderstood and perverted St. Paul's doctrine. Such statements as 'he that *doeth* righteousness is righteous' (3⁷), are not enough to bear the weight of such inferences.

7. *Authorship.*—Who, then, is the *author* of an Ep. which speaks of a form of Gnostic doctrine like that associated with the name of the traditional opponent of the Apostle John in his old age? The general answer, as has been said, has been: the Apostle John himself. This was the almost universal belief of the early Church, the exceptions being few, of small account, and easily understood. The sect of the Alogi may have rejected the Ep., as they did the Gospel and the Apocalypse. But the statement in Epiphanius (*Hær.* tom. i. c. 34) amounts only to a perhaps, and the rejection, if it was the fact, would have been, as in the case of the Gospel, for doctrinal reasons. Marcion, we know, refused it a place in his very limited Canon; but his exclusion of it and of so much else in the NT turned, not upon the question of historical testimony, but on that of harmony with his own special views. At a much later period an obscure statement is made by Cosmas Indicopleustes in the 6th cent. (*Topogr. Christ.* I. vii.), to the effect that some maintained that all the Catholic Epp. were written by presbyters, not by apostles. And Leontius of Byzantium (*contr. Nestor. et Eutych.* iii. 14) speaks of Theodore of Mopsuestia as 'abrogating' the Ep. of James and the other Catholic Epp.—'Epistolam Jacobi et alias deinceps aliorum catholicas abrogat et antiquat.' This is all. And so the case stood, as far as we know, till late in the 16th cent., when Joseph Scaliger declared all three Epp. not to be by the apostle. Then S. G. Lange, with strange taste, pronounced the first unworthy of an apostle, though he felt the force of the historical testimony for its apostolic origin. Others tried to prove it to be the work of a Jewish Christian author and a Gnostic reviser (Claudius), or ascribed it to the presbyter John (Bretschneider, Paulus). But the severest assault made upon the Ep. in ancient or in modern times is that of Baur and his school. The Tübingen criticism has not been at one in all things. Some of its adherents have held the Gospel and the Ep. to be by the same author (K. R. Köstlin, Georgii); others have held them to be by different hands (Baur, Hilgenfeld, etc.). But the school has been at one in denying the apostolic origin of the Ep., and in ascribing it to a writer of the 2nd cent.

The reasons given for this view of the Ep. are such as the following:—The circumstances, the forms of thought, and the condition of the Church which appear in it, it is said, point to a later period than the apostolic. Different critics fix on different things in support of this contention. Some fix upon the doctrine of the *Logos* as they suppose it to be expressed here (Bretschneider); of which it is enough to say that in Hebrew thought and in Greek there was a soil prepared for it before the close of the 1st cent. at any rate. Others argue from the acquaintance which it betrays with Docetic error. But it is too much to assert that that type of error does not emerge till the post-apostolic age, and the particular form in view here is, as we have seen, like the doctrine attributed to Cerinthus. Others (Hilgenfeld, etc.) reason from its reference to Gnostic doctrine. But while the riper and more complicated forms of Gnosticism belong to a later

time, it is not made historically good that there was not or could not be at the earlier date Gnostic ideas of a simpler and more rudimentary kind, and it is acknowledged (*e.g.* by Hilgenfeld) that it is only an undeveloped form that appears in this Epistle. But besides that, it has to be said that the things in the Ep. which are supposed to betray the influence of Gnostic thought are not sufficient for the purpose. Of the doctrine ascribed to the 'Antichrists' we have already spoken. But much is made of the use of the terms σπέρμα and χρίσμα, and of the idea that we should only love and not *fear* God. But the terms σπέρμα and χρίσμα have a totally different application here from what they have in the far-fetched and impracticable speculations of the Gnostic sects. Nor do we require to go to Gnostic sources for their origin. They have their explanation in the ideas of Revelation—the one in the OT idea of an *anointing*, the other in the NT idea of a *birth* or a being *begotten* of God. And that there should be, not the fear that hath torment, but pure love to God, is surely a most Christian idea.

It is further argued that the Ep. cannot be an apostolic composition, because it shows the presence of Montanistic doctrine (Planck, Baur). Traces of Montanism are thought to be found especially in what is said of the moral condition of the believer, of the *unction*, and of sins 'not unto death' and 'a sin unto death.' With respect to the first, the Ep. speaks, it is true, of the moral condition of the believer in its ideal perfection. But it is not an absolute sinlessness that it ascribes to him, nor does it speak of his perfection at all in the Montanist way. For the Montanists claimed a spiritual perfection above other Christians. The idea of the *chrism* or 'unction,' as it appears here, is as little Montanistic as it is Gnostic. It rests upon biblical ideas and biblical employments of the act of anointing with oil. Neither does the distinction between two kinds of sin necessarily bear the sense which Baur puts upon it. Even if we were to grant this, it would not carry the late date with it. Hilgenfeld has pointed out that the idea of special *mortal* sins is found in the *Periodi Petri*, a part of the pseudo-Clementine literature, and, in his opinion, it is therefore earlier than Montanism. Much more, too, would surely have been made of the doctrine of the Paraclete, if the Ep. had been written by a Montanist or under Montanistic influences. Other arguments adverse to its apostolic origin and its connexion with John the evangelist are of even less importance. The brevity of the reference to the false teachers and the limited refutation of them have been held to be inconsistent with the claims preferred on behalf of the Epistle. But this is to overlook the method of the Ep., which is to present the truth, and to do that authoritatively, rather than to expose error. The vagueness of the introduction, and the want of anything in it to identify the writer with John the apostle, are also adduced. But it is customary with St. John not to name himself directly, and the author associates himself at least with the eye-witnesses of Christ's life, and speaks all through in a tone befitting one conscious of apostolic dignity.

Once more the apostolic authorship is contested on the ground that the Ep. is so different from the Apocalypse. This is, of course, an important argument with those of the Tübingen school, and it is perhaps best put by those of that school who, like Hilgenfeld, hold the Ep. to be older than the Gospel. The Apoc. being by John the apostle, the remarkable way in which it differs from the Ep. in language and conception makes it impossible, it is argued, for the latter to be by the same hand. The differences, indeed, are great, and extend not only to vocabulary, grammar, and phraseology, but to attitude, spirit, and idea. They may be explained so far, however, by difference in circumstance, time of composition, subject, and so far also by the fact that the one writing is an Ep., while the other belongs to the peculiar order of apocalyptic literature which has a form and a method of its own. The difference in idea, too, is in important cases much less than the Tübingen critics are inclined to make it. There is no such antagonism, e.g., as they suppose between the God of wrath in the Apoc. and the God of love in the Ep., or between the view of the divine righteousness as judging evil in the Apoc. and the view of the same righteousness as forgiving sin in the Epistle. That there are many points of affinity, too, between Gospel, Ep., and Apoc., is admitted by critics like Hilgenfeld. But the question of the Apoc. is one by itself. See art. REVELATION (BOOK OF).

The arguments in favour of the non-apostolic origin of the Ep. are far from convincing. Even were they much more so than they are, they could not prevail against the historical evidence. For that is peculiarly strong. The entire witness of antiquity (with the solitary exceptions already referred to in the cases of Cosmas and Leontius) from the time of Eusebius is for the Johannine authorship. Athanasius, Cyril of Jerusalem, Epiphanius, and others attest it. Jerome, speaking of the Apostle John, in his *Catalogue of Ecclesiastical Writers* (ch. 9), says of him: 'Scripsit autem et unam epistolam, cujus exordium est, Quod fuit ab initio . . . quæ ab universis ecclesiasticis et eruditis viris probatur.' Eusebius himself places it among the *Homologoumena* (*HE* iii. 25), and ascribes it to John (*HE* iii. 24, 25). Travelling back from these declarations, we find Dionysius, the scholar of Origen, citing the words of the Ep. as those of the evangelist, and reasoning against the Johannine origin of the Apoc. from its unlikeness to the Ep. in style and language (Euseb. *HE* vii. 25). We find Origen himself repeatedly quoting it or referring to it as by John (*e.g. Ev. Joh.* tom. xiii. 21). It is in the Peshiṭta, and in the Muratorian Fragment, the latter quoting the words 'Quæ vidimus oculis nostris et auribus audivimus et manus nostræ palpaverunt hæc scripsimus vobis' as John's. Similar testimony is borne to it by Cyprian (*Ep.* 25), who quotes 2[3, 4], by Tertullian (*adv. Marc.* v. 16; *adv. Prax.* ch. 13, 28; *adv. Gnost.* 12, etc.), and by Clem. Alex. (*Strom.* ii. 15, iii. 4, 5, iv. 16). Irenæus, too, quotes the Ep. several times, and ascribes it to John, the Lord's disciple, who also wrote the Gospel (*de Hær.* iii. 16; Euseb. *HE* v. 8). Further, Papias (who is described by Irenæus as Ἰωάννου μὲν ἀκουστής, Πολυκάρπου δ' ἑταῖρος) is reported by Eusebius (*HE* iii. 39) to have 'used testimonies from John's former Ep.' (κέχρηται δ' ὁ αὐτὸς μαρτυρίαις ἀπὸ τῆς Ἰωάννου προτέρας ἐπιστολῆς). And Polycarp, the disciple of St. John (*ad Philipp.* ch. 7), has the sentence πᾶς γὰρ ὃς ἂν μὴ ὁμολογῇ Ἰησοῦν Χριστὸν ἐν σαρκὶ ἐληλυθέναι, ἀντίχριστός ἐστιν; which so closely resembles 1 Jn 4[3] that few (though Scholten is of the number) have refused to see in it an evidence of Polycarp's acquaintance with the Epistle.

Whether we can carry the chain of witness further back even than Polycarp's letter, is doubtful. It depends chiefly on the date to which the *Didaché* is referred, and on the view taken of certain sentences in it. The Ep. appears to be known, indeed, to the writer of the Ep. to Diognetus; but the date of that writing, which is placed by Lightfoot (*St. Ignatius and St. Polycarp*, i. 517) between A.D. 117 and 130, is uncertain. Traces of it have also been found by some in Justin Martyr, the Ep. of Barnabas, the Shepherd of Hermas, and the Epistles of Ignatius. But these are not definite enough to prove ac-

quaintance with the *writing*. They may indicate no more than the use of terms which were common to all Christians, or to certain circles of Christians, at the time. But in the *Didaché* we have, perhaps, something more. In chs. x., xi., *e.g.*, we find the phrase τελειῶσαι αὐτὴν ἐν τῇ ἀγάπῃ σου; παρελθέτω ὁ κόσμος οὗτος; πᾶς δὲ προφήτης δεδοκιμασμένος. These remind us of the τετελείωται ἐν ἀγάπῃ of our Ep. (4[18]) and the parallel phrases in 2[5] 4[12. 17]; of the ὁ κόσμος παράγεται of 2[17] (a very similar form occurs, however, also in St. Paul, 1 Co 7[31]); and of the δοκιμάζετε τὰ πνεύματα of 4[1]. If these are regarded as reminiscences of the words of the Ep., and not simply as proofs of acquaintance with John's teaching, it may be, in oral form, and if the *Didaché* can be referred to the closing years of the first century or the opening years of the second, we have a witness earlier even than Polycarp.

To this must be added the argument drawn from the relation in which Gospel and Ep. stand to each other. If it can be shown that the two writings are by one hand, then all that goes to prove the Gospel to be the work of the evangelist John goes to prove the Ep. to be his also. This question, whether the author of the Gospel also wrote the Ep., is answered in the negative by the Tübingen critics generally. In support of that position it is urged that the two writings differ radically in their attitude to the OT law, in their view of the person of Christ, in their doctrines of the Holy Spirit and the work of Christ, in their eschatology, and in their general mode of thought. The Ep., it is said, stands 'in a more intimate relationship' to the law than is the case with the Gospel. But in point of fact there is no mention of the νόμος in the Ep., and the passages which are supposed to have it specially in view have another application. It does not appear that in the use of the term ἀνομία in 3[4] it is the Mosaic law that is particularly in view, or that the ἀπ' ἀρχῆς in 2[7. 8] refers specially to the OT law of love. The idea of a personal Logos, again, which is found in the Prologue to the Gospel, is thought to be foreign to the Epistle. But if we have not the term ὁ λόγος, we have the phrase ὁ λόγος τῆς ζωῆς in the introduction to the Ep.; and, even if it is allowed to be a question whether the latter phrase has the same sense as the former, we have a similar conception of the superhuman, pre-temporal, personal being of Christ in the terms 'life' and 'Son of God' as they appear in the Epistle. The Holy Spirit, it is further urged, is not presented as He is in the Gospel in personal relations, of which the use of the neuter term χρίσμα is supposed to be a proof. But the term χρίσμα is an easily understood term for a particular gift or operation of the Holy One; and the 'witness' which is said to be borne by the Spirit (5[6]), which is also ascribed to the Spirit by Christ in the Fourth Gospel (15[26]), points to the harmony of the two writings on the subject of the personality of the Holy Ghost. The designation of Christ as 'Advocate' (2[2]) is also held by Baur and others of his school to be in affinity with the Ep. to the Hebrews rather than with the Fourth Gospel, and to indicate a view of Christ's relation to His disciples which 'lay far apart from the evangelist.' But the idea of Christ as Intercessor is not peculiar to any particular Ep., but is found again and again in the NT; nor can it be made out that in anything else that is said of Christ's relations to His disciples there is any difference between the Ep. and the Gospel. Nor is it the case that the Ep. has an eschatology which is not known to the Gospel. The conceptions of a present judgment and a spiritual Parousia prevail, it is true, in the Gospel, but not to the exclusion of the ideas of a future judgment and a

Parousia at the end of things ($5^{28.\ 29}$ $6^{39.\ 40}$ etc.). And the eschatological conception of the Advent and the Judgment is expressed in the Ep., but not to the absolute exclusion of the form of doctrine characteristic of the Gospel. For it speaks of a passing from death to life which is already accomplished, and of eternal life as a present possession. Further, to say, with Baur, Hilgenfeld, and others, that there is a more 'material and external' mode of thought in the Ep. than in the Gospel, is to misjudge and misinterpret the former. The designation, e.g., of God as 'light' is strangely thought to express a more material conception of God than is possible to the writer of the Gospel, and the symbols of the 'water' and the 'blood' are thought to be differently used, more materially in the Ep., more ideally in the Gospel. But these suppositions rest on mistaken interpretations of the passages.

There are differences between the two writings, as we have seen, and these differences are neither few in number nor inconsiderable in weight. They are differences which go to establish the independence of the two compositions. But they are not sufficient to prove a difference of authorship. They can be made to appear so only by forced constructions, and by overlooking the distinct purposes and circumstances of the writings. They can be explained by the differences between the Gospel and the Ep. in the occasions which produced them, the subjects with which they have to deal, and the ends which they have in view, and by the natural difference between an historical composition and a letter. On the other hand, there are similarities of the most remarkable kind in thought, style, and expression, in characteristic ideas, in imagery and symbolism, and in the special type of doctrine. They are similarities which pervade the two writings, and point strongly to identity of authorship.

No explanation of the origin of the Ep., therefore, fits the facts so well as the one that has prevailed. It is to internal considerations that those appeal who reject it; and it is largely on the ground of the supposed impossibility of two writings so different in character as the Ep. and the Apoc. proceeding from one and the same hand, that the Tübingen critics deny the apostolicity of the former. The external evidence is not seriously assailed. It is admitted even by so uncompromising a critic as the late Dr. Samuel Davidson that 'the letter is well attested by the voice of antiquity, and that, as far as external evidence reaches, its authenticity seems to be secure' (*Introduction to the NT*, ii. 302).

8. *Place and Date.*—If the Ep. is the work of John, it is most natural to suppose it to have been written in Asia Minor, most probably in Ephesus. It is true that we have no definite statement in early Christian literature to that effect, and some who regard it as intended to form a companion to the Gospel are inclined to refer it to Patmos. But it is with Ephesus that the most ancient tradition connects the composition of the Gospel. What Irenæus says of John the μαθητὴς τοῦ Κυρίου and his Gospel is this: καὶ αὐτὸς ἐξέδωκε τὸ εὐαγγέλιον, ἐν Ἐφέσῳ τῆς Ἀσίας διατρίβων (adv. Hær. iii. 1), and the same is said in effect by Jerome (*Prolog. to Matth.* vol. vii. pp. 5, 6). If the Gospel and the Ep., therefore, belong to the same period in John's life, as many things go to show, it is reasonable to suppose that the Ep. as well as the Gospel was written in Asia Minor, and most probably in Ephesus, all the more that it is with that territory and that city that ancient tradition connects the closing stage of John's career.

If there is little by which to determine the *place* where the Ep. was written, there is as little

by which to fix its *date*. Some, indeed, have thought it possible to define the time of its composition precisely, and have been bold enough even to refer it to one particular year. Ebrard ascribes it to the year 95 of the Dionysian era. But his reasoning turns upon the uncertain suppositions that the Ep. is a dedicatory companion to the Gospel, and that the Gospel was written in Patmos, John being in that island, as he holds, in the fifteenth year of Domitian. Ewald, again, puts the writing of the Gospel at 80 A.D., but thinks it was not in circulation till immediately before John's death; while the Ep., according to him, was written later, but circulated earlier. All that can be said with any measure of confidence is that the Ep. belongs to the later apostolic period. This seems the natural, if not the necessary, inference from the general cast of its contents, the condition of the Christian communities which is indicated in it, the errors which it combats, the lack of any reference to the contest between legalism and liberty, and the impression which it conveys that the questions which occupy so large a place in the great Pauline Epp. are no longer the questions of the day. It is in harmony with the traditional account of the period of John's stay in Ephesus, as it appears in Polycrates (cf. Euseb. *HE* iii. 31), Irenæus (*adv. Hær.* ii. 39, iii. 1, 3), Origen, and Clement of Alexandria (Euseb. *HE* iii. 1, 23), as well as in Jerome (*de Vir. Illustr.* c. 9). It is also in harmony with the tone of the Ep., for it reads like the calm counsel of old age and ripest experience; and with the presumption which is created by St. Paul's declared principle of action (Ro 15^{20}), and by the absence of any reference to John or any salutation to him in the Pauline Epp. addressed to Asiatic Churches, that it was written after the death of the great Apostle of the Gentiles. It is most probable, also, that it was written after the destruction of Jerusalem, though how long after that event it is impossible to say. Some, indeed (e.g. Grotius, Düsterdieck, Fritzsche), have held it to be earlier than that catastrophe, on the ground of the mention of 'the last hour' in 2^{18}, or for the broader reason that an event of so terrible moment could scarcely have passed without some notice, if it had happened. But there may be no allusion to that event, for the simple reason that there was no special call to refer to it, or because it was no longer a very recent thing. Nor can anything be made of the statement in 2^{18}. The term 'the last hour' applies, not to the destruction of Jerusalem (how could the 'antichrists' be signs of that?), but to the Parousia, in which connexion we find the phrase ἔσχατοι καιροί used even by Ignatius (*Ep. ad Ephes.* c. xi.). The Gnostic teaching which is condemned, and the external position of the errorists, combine with other things to point to a period later than 70 A.D., and towards the end of the century. This is in harmony also with the traditional date of Cerinthus, with whose doctrine the view of Christ's Person repudiated in the Ep. is most probably identified, and with the period in John's life to which tradition assigns his connexion with the heretic.

It has been sought to define the time of composition more precisely by determining the chronological relation of the Ep. to the Gospel. But the materials for doing so are far too scanty, and the arguments which have been urged for the one view or the other have little weight. Some hold the Ep. to be prior to the Gospel, on the ground that writings of 'momentary design, like letters, come naturally before writings of permanent design, like narratives or histories' (Thiersch); or on the ground that a letter of warning to particular Churches against particular errors would probably have been written earlier than a composition like the Gospel, which deals with the historical foundations, and appears to be addressed to all Christendom (Huther, al.). Others argue for the posteriority of the Ep. on the basis of certain passages which are supposed to refer to the Gospel, or to presuppose it, or on the ground that the Ep. seems to require the Gospel for its explanation. But, even if the latter were granted, it would not follow that the Ep. was later than the Gospel. Reuss, who thinks that the former needs the latter as its commentary, yet admits that 'as it once had one in the oral instruction of the author, it is not thereby proved that it is later' (Hist. of the NT, Houghton's tr., p. 237). And as to the passages appealed to in particular, the opening verses in their relation to the Prologue of the Gospel, the phrase ἐν σαρκὶ ἐληλυθότα (4²) as compared with σὰρξ ἐγένετο, etc., they are almost equally applicable or inapplicable as arguments for the priority of the Ep. and for its posteriority. There is, indeed, nothing in the Ep. that can be justly said to presuppose the existence of the Gospel as we have it, or to go beyond what is explainable by the earlier oral preaching and teaching.

9. *Destination.*—The Ep. being written, then, in the scenes of the closing stage of John's apostolic ministry, it is most reasonable to suppose it to have been written for readers belonging to those parts. It has been supposed, indeed, to have been addressed to Palestinian Christians (Benson). But there is nothing to favour such a supposition, the contents of the Ep. pointing to a Gentile-Christian audience rather than a Jewish-Christian. Some have thought it directed to a single Church, that of Ephesus (Hug), or even that of Corinth (Lightfoot). But its wide scope and encyclical character are inconsistent with that. Others have regarded it as addressed to Christians outside the scene of the life and ministry of John in his old age (Holtzmann), or as an encyclical of the widest scope (Hilgenfeld). But the terms which are said to bear this out do not meet the case. The καὶ ὑμῖν and καὶ ὑμεῖς in 1³ do not suffice to establish a distinction between the Asiatic Christians among whom John was writing and those to whom his letter is directed; and while the character of the Ep. suits its designation as a *Catholic* Ep., there are things in it, especially the references to particular forms of error, which so far limit and define its destination.

The most curious thing connected with this question of the readers that are in view, is the fact that Augustine, in quoting 3², speaks of the passage as being in John's 'Epistle to the Parthians' (quod dictum est a Joanne in epistola ad Parthos, Quæst. Evang. ii. 39). That is the only certain occurrence, indeed, of this designation in Augustine's works. It is given, however, in the Benedictine edition of his Tractates on the Ep., in the title; in the *Indiculus operum S. Augustini* of Possidius; in one or two manuscripts; in the *contra Varimadum Arianum* of Idacius Clarus or Vigilius Tapsensis; and in Bede's (if it is genuine) *Prologus super septem epistolas canonicas,* where it is said that many ecclesiastical writers, and among them the great Athanasius, affirm this Ep. to be 'written to the Parthians.' Hence it has been supposed by some (Grotius, etc.) that the Ep. was addressed to Jewish Christians living beyond the Euphrates within the limits of the Parthian empire. But we hear of no connexion between John and Parthia, and the designation *ad Parthos* appears to have been unknown to the Church of the East, and even to the Church of the West before Augustine's time. It is a pure puzzle, a curiosity on which nothing can be based. It has been

accounted for as a mistake for *ad Pathmios* (Serrarius), *ad sparsos* (Wetstein), *adpertius* (Semler), *ad Spartos* (Scholz, on the authority of a 12th century manuscript, πρὸς διασπαρσαμένους (!) (Holtzmann, Mangold), πρὸς πάντας (Paulus), πρὸς παρθένους (Gieseler, etc.). Most favour the last of these explanations. Some think that the title πρὸς παρθένους was given to express the pure condition of the Churches addressed (Whiston); others, that the inscription of the Second Ep. (πρὸς παρθένους) as found in some manuscripts was transferred as more suitable to the First (Hug). Some, again, suppose that the title ran ἐπιστολὴ τοῦ Ἰωάννου τοῦ παρθένου, John having the designation ἀποστόλου καὶ εὐαγγελιστοῦ παρθένου in the inscription borne by the Apoc. in one manuscript (*Cod. Guelpher.*); others, that Augustine misunderstood what was said by Clem. Alex. (*Frag.* 1011) about the Second Ep. being written πρὸς παρθένους, and transferred the title to the First (Huther). All is conjecture, and can in no way affect the probabilities of the case (supported as these are by the tradition bearing on John's residence and work in Asia Minor) that the Ep. had in view the Churches that would be naturally addressed from Ephesus. It is therefore with those Asiatic regions in which Gnostic speculations had become rife (Apoc. 2⁶ etc·), and with that great city in which Paul had planted a Christian Church, and in which John had lived on, according to Irenæus (*adv. Hær.* ii. 22⁵, iii. 3³), into the reign of Trajan, that this majestic Ep., with its heavenly calm and its lofty message of truth and love, is connected in respect both of readers and of writer.

LITERATURE.—Among the numerous Commentaries, special mention may be made of those of Œcumenius, Calvin, Düsterdieck, Lücke, Huther, Ebrard, Rothe (most fruitful of all), Haupt, Alford, Jelf, Westcott, Holtzmann, de Wette-Brückner, Braune, Alexander (in the *Speaker's Comm.*), Ewald, Plummer; among books on *Introduction,* especially those by Weiss, Reuss, Bleek, Hilgenfeld, Salmon, S. Davidson, Holtzmann, Jülicher, Zahn ; and among works of other kinds, the Expositions by Neander, F. D. Maurice, R. S. Candlish, Lias and Watson, Erdmann's *Primæ Ep. Joan. argumentum, nexus et consilium;* Luthardt's *de Primæ Joan. Ep. Compositione;* Flatt's *de antichristis et pseudoprophetis in Ep. Joan.* ; Grörer's *Urchristenthum;* Besser's *Bibelstunden;* Pfleiderer's *Urchristenthum* and *Hibbert Lectures;* Harnack's *Geschichte der altchrist. Literatur bis Eusebius.*

THE SECOND EPISTLE.—1. *Contents.*—This brief Ep., though it touches the First Ep. at several points, and has also something in common with the Third, has an independent value, and a distinct interest. It is unmistakably a *letter,* and is distinguished from the First Ep. by its personal and private character. It is addressed, not to a wide circle of readers, as is the case with the First, but to a particular individual or Church, and it represents a writer who speaks less with the tone of command, but with more of the earnestness that cares for individual Christians, and seeks to come into direct relations with them. As to its origin and much else belonging to it, we have little or nothing to guide us beyond what can be gathered from its own tenor. It seems to have been occasioned by the pressure of dangers arising from false teaching, and its object is to secure the individual or the Church that is addressed against these perils until the writer could visit the scene in person.

With this object in view the author begins his letter, somewhat in St. Paul's way, with a commendation of the person or persons to whom he writes, and with a large Christian greeting. Again, with a tact and courtesy such as we find in St. Paul's letters, he expresses the joy which he had in the consistent life of her (be it lady or Church) whom he addresses. From this he passes on to an exhortation, couched in terms of entreaty, to fulfil the great law of Christian love—a love explained to imply a life and walk in practical obedience to the divine commandments. His reason for writing in such a strain is, as he indicates, his fear of the possible influence of certain errorists, whom he identifies with Antichrist, because they deny that Jesus is the Christ come in the complete reality of human nature. He counsels watchfulness against the insidious teaching of such deceivers, and speaks of the loss which would follow the acceptance of it. He reminds his reader or readers further of the fact that fellowship with God cannot be enjoyed unless one abides by the true doctrine of Christ. He declares those who deny that doctrine to be men not to be received or welcomed, lest one should make himself partaker in their evil. He adds certain explanations about the shortness of his letter, and his intention to come in person. He closes with a brief salutation from certain Christians with whom he is associated at the time.

2. *Authorship.*—This Ep. has much in common with the First. It speaks, as the latter does, of 'love,' 'truth,' 'the truth,' 'the commandments,' a 'new commandment' and one 'had from the beginning,' of 'loving in truth,' and 'walking in truth,' of 'abiding in' one, of a 'joy' that may be 'fulfilled.' It speaks, too, of 'Antichrist,' and deals with the same form of error—the denial that Jesus is 'the Christ come in the flesh.' And it uses the same methods of stating a thing—first positively, and then negatively. There are some things, it is true, in which it differs from 1 Jn. It has certain phrases and grammatical forms which do not occur in the First Ep.—*e.g.* εἴ τις for ἐάν τις, περιπατεῖν κατά for περιπατεῖν ἐν, ἐρχόμενος ἐν σαρκί for ἐληλυθὼς ἐν σαρκί, θεὸν ἔχειν, διδαχῇ Χριστοῦ, διδαχὴν φέρειν, βλέπετε ἑαυτούς, etc. But little can be made of such things as these. They are not enough to establish any essential difference in idea or in style. It is admitted, even by some who dispute the apostolic origin of 2 Jn, that 'these deviations do not destroy the force of the argument contained in the resemblances' (S. Davidson's *Introd. to the NT*, ii. p. 329).

This being the case, the inference would seem to be that 2 Jn is by the same hand as 1 Jn. This has been in point of fact the general view, and even some of those who have denied the Johannine authorship of 1 Jn have admitted that the two Epp. are by the same writer (Bretschneider, Paulus). But there are some who deny that identity of authorship can be inferred from the similarities which have been noticed, even though these come to so much that more than a half of the smaller Ep. can be found in the larger. They think that these striking resemblances can be explained by the art of a forger, or as the imitative work of a writer who knew 1 Jn well. So some who have recognized 1 Jn to be by the evangelist have ascribed 2 Jn to a different hand—either to the Presbyter John (Erasmus, Grotius, etc.), or to some other John unknown to us. Baur has a somewhat elaborate and far-fetched theory of the origin of this Epistle. He holds it to be of Montanist origin, and to be addressed to the Church to which the Gaius of 3 Jn belongs. He takes it to be indeed the Ep. which is referred to in 3 Jn [9], and to be intended for one of the sections of the Roman Church, in which Church he thinks a schism had taken place. He bases this largely on the statement made by Clem. Alex. in his *Hypotyposes* as to 2 Jn being written *ad quandam Babyloniam electam*, supposing that Rome is meant by the *Babylonia*, and that the term *electa*, ἐκλεκτή, is a designation given to the Church in harmony with the Montanist idea of the Church as the pure and holy bride of Christ. But all this turns on a fanciful and inconsistent interpretation of Clement's words, and those who agree for the most part with Baur, both in his general positions and in his denial of the apostolic origin of 2 Jn, often decline to follow him here. Hilgenfeld, *e.g.*, rejects this

peculiar Montanist account of the Ep., and tries to explain it as an official condemnation, in the form of a letter, of fellowship with Gnostic teachers. That the Ep. cannot be ascribed to John the evangelist, however, is also held by some who are unable to go all the way either with Baur or with Hilgenfeld, and whose general view of it is essentially different. Ebrard, *e.g.*, following Erasmus, assigns it to the *Presbyter* John, passing lightly over the resemblances to 1 Jn as so many allusions and reminiscences, and regarding the distinctive passages as essentially different from the evangelist's style.

Although the internal evidence, therefore, is held by most to point to the author of the First Ep. as also the writer of the Second, and to the Apostle John as that writer, it is not read in that way by all. How, then, does the case stand with respect to the external evidence? The historical testimony, it must be admitted, is neither very abundant nor very clear. That it should be so need not seem strange when regard is had to the extreme brevity of the Ep. and its private character. What we have is as much as could be expected, and it is on the whole sufficient for the purpose. The Ep. seems not to have been accepted by the school of Antioch. Theodore of Mopsuestia appears to be reported by Leontius of Byzantium as rejecting James and the other Cath. Epp. The words, however, viz. *ob quam causam, ut arbitror, ipsam epistolam Jacobi et alias deinceps catholicas abrogat et antiquat*, are not very precise. Theodoret makes no reference to 2 Jn. In a homily on Mt 21[23], which is doubtfully ascribed to Chrysostom, it is said of it, as well as of 3 Jn, οἱ πατέρες ἀποκανονίζονται. Jerome (*de Vir. Illus.* c. 9) contrasts the two smaller Epp. with the First, and speaks of them as ascribed to the Presbyter John. Origen, who quotes 1 Jn, never quotes either 2 Jn or 3 Jn. He knows of the circulation, however, of the two minor Epp., but remarks that 'not all affirm them to be genuine' (Euseb. *HE* vi. 25). Neither the one nor the other seems to have been included in the Peshiṭta Version. And Eusebius classes both among the *Antilegomena*. He speaks of them as the 'so-called second and third of John,' and indicates that it was questioned whether they belonged to the evangelist, 'or possibly to another of the same name as he' (*HE* iii. 25[3]).

On the other hand, Irenæus quotes 2 Jn [10, 11] as the words of 'John, the disciple of the Lord' (*adv. Hær.* i. 16[3]), and gives the statement about the 'deceivers' and 'Antichrist' (2 Jn [7]) also as by the Lord's 'disciple,' though he refers to it as in 1 Jn instead of 2 Jn (*adv. Hær.* iii. 16[8]). Clement of Alex. speaks of John 'in his *larger* Epistle' (ἐν τῇ μείζονι ἐπιστολῇ) as seeming to teach a certain thing; from which it is clear that he knew a shorter Ep. or shorter Epp. (*Strom.* ii. 15). In a fragmentary Latin translation of the *Hypotyposes* he speaks of the same Ep. in these very definite terms: *Secunda Joannis epistola, quæ ad virgines scripta simplicissima est; scripta vero est ad quandam Babyloniam Electam nomine, significat autem electionem ecclesiæ sanctæ.* He is also reported by Eusebius (*HE* vi. 14[1]) to have commented in his *Hypotyposes* on the disputed books, viz. 'the Epistle of Jude and the other Catholic Epistles.' Dionysius of Alexandria (in a passage given in Eusebius, *HE* vii. 25) speaks of John as not naming himself, ἐν τῇ δευτέρᾳ φερομένῃ Ἰωάννου καὶ τρίτῃ, καίτοι βραχείαις οὔσαις ἐπιστολαῖς, but as writing 'anonymously as *the presbyter*.' Dionysius therefore regarded the anonymity of 2 Jn as quite in John's manner. And the school of Alexandria seems to have generally accepted the Second Ep. as John the apostle's. Alexander, *e.g.*, in quoting vv.[10, 11] says of them ὡς παρήγγειλεν ὁ μακάριος 'Ιωάννης (Socrates, HE i. 6). The Muratorian Fragment refers to at least two Epp. of John in the difficult sentence, *Epistola sane Jude et superscripti Johannis duas in catholica habentur et sapientia ab amicis Salomonis in honorem ipsius scripta* (Routh, *Reliq. Sac.* i. p. 296). But the text requires emendation, and it is differently interpreted, some (Lücke, Huther, etc.) understanding it to speak for the Johannine authorship, others (reading *ut* for *et* sapientia)* taking it to mean that, as the Book of Wisdom was not written by Solomon, so these Epp. were not written by John the apostle.

It should be added that, though the great North African Fathers, Tertullian and Cyprian, do not quote 2 Jn, it is clear that it was recognized in their Church. For Cyprian himself, in reporting the statements made by the bishops at the synod which was held at Carthage in A.D. 256, speaks of Aurelius, bishop of Chullabi, as appealing to 2 Jn [10] in these words: *Joannes Apostolus in epistola sua posuit dicens, si quis ad vos venit*, etc. In like manner, although the Ep. was not in the great Syriac Version, it appears to have been used by Ephraem in the 4th cent., and that in a way indicating that it was understood to be by John the apostle (*de Amore Paup.* iii. 52; *ad Imitat. Prov.* i. 76). And while Eusebius placed it, as we have seen, among the 'disputed' books, he expresses himself differently in his *Demonstratio Evangelica* (iii. 5), when he gives, as it appears, his own opinion. There he says of John that in his Epistles he 'either makes no mention of himself or calls himself *presbyter*, but nowhere *apostle* or *evangelist*'—ἐν μὲν ταῖς ἐπιστολαῖς αὐτοῦ οὐδὲ μνήμην τῆς οἰκείας προσηγορίας ποιεῖται, ἢ πρεσβύτερον ἑαυτὸν ὀνομάζει, οὐδαμοῦ δὲ ἀπόστολον οὐδὲ εὐαγγελιστήν). It was included, too, in the Old Latin VS.

The most ancient historical testimony, therefore, although it is of limited quantity, is in favour of the authorship by John the apostle. It is testimony that comes from sources so far apart as Gaul, Alexandria, and North Africa. It is confirmed by the resemblance of 2 Jn to 1 Jn; the considerations which go to establish the Johannine origin of the latter being so far available also for the Johannine origin of the former. Nor is any difficulty created by the designation 'the elder.' That title rather supports the apostolic origin. It is still a moot point whether we have historical ground for believing in the existence of a *Presbyter* John in Ephesus as distinct from the Apostle John. Nor is there anything in the case as regards 2 Jn to make the hypothesis of this shadowy second John either necessary or helpful. It is to the *apostle* that the earliest evidence points. It is difficult, indeed, to understand how this small private letter could have been accepted as it was, and in due time made part of the Canon, unless the general opinion of the Church had ascribed it to John. And the use of the title, 'the elder,' in the inscription tells for the ordinary view. No one wishing to pass off a writing as by the apostle would have chosen so indefinite a title. No ordinary person, writing with honest intent in his own name, would have called himself '*the* elder,' as if there were none but he; while, if the writer so styling himself had been a person of extraordinary importance, it would be strange that we should know nothing of him. There is nothing to show that the title is used to distinguish 'presbyter' from 'apostle.' Apostles could also be called *presbyters*, as we see from the NT itself (1 P 5¹), and as is the case in the very sentence from Papias on which the hypothesis of a distinct *Presbyter* John is founded. It

* *Et* is confirmed, however, by the new MS of the Fragment published in *Miscellanea Cassinese*, 1897.

may be a question in what particular sense the title is applied to the writer, whether with reference to his advanced age, as St. Paul speaks of himself as the 'aged,' ὁ πρεσβύτης (Philem [9]), or, as is rather the case, in respect of his peculiar position. But on no lips could this simple title be so fit or so intelligible as on those of the evangelist, the last of the apostles, who for long years had been overseer of the Christian community in Asia Minor. On his lips the name would explain itself, and it would mean more than 'apostle.' It would be the note of the peculiar relation, both official and fatherly, which the apostle had held to the Churches and their members in those parts, and would be at once understood wherever his superintendence had been known.

3. *Time, Place, and Destination.*—It is impossible to determine with certainty the *time* when the Ep. was written. It seems to belong to the closing years of the apostle. But whether it is earlier or later than the larger Ep. we have no means of deciding. There are those (*e.g.* Ebrard) who argue that it must be later, because there are things in it which appear to refer back to the First Epistle. But the similarities and supposed allusions are not of the kind that can be explained only by the priority of the larger Epistle. It is also probable that 2 Jn was written in the *place* where 1 Jn was written, especially as the false teachers in view are of the same order in both Epp. If the visit which is intimated in v.¹² can be taken as an intended tour of inspection, we may go further, and say that, in all probability, the letter was written in Ephesus, the centre of the Asiatic circle.

The *destination* of the Ep. is also a matter of great difficulty. The most definite statement we have on the subject in early Christian literature is in the Latin fragment (if it be authentic) of the *Hypotyposes* of Clement of Alexandria, already referred to. But it is a mixed statement, and one that does not help us much. It is to the effect that the Ep. was written *ad virgines*, and to 'a certain Babylonian, *Electa* by name' (*ad quandam Babyloniam Electam*), but that this name *Electa* signified the election of the holy Church. The question turns upon the address ἐκλεκτῇ Κυρίᾳ, and the difficulty is in determining whether that refers to an individual or to a community. These different renderings of it are proposed: (1) *to an elect lady*; (2) *to the elect lady*; (3) *to the elect Kyria*; (4) *to the lady Electa*; (5) *to Electa Kyria*. Grammatically, the first is the simplest and most natural, but it is too indefinite. It is not easy to see how a letter of such a tenor could have been addressed so vaguely. The second interpretation may also be taken as grammatically defensible (cf. ἐκλεκτοῖς παρεπιδήμοις, 1 P 1¹), and has been followed by the English Versions and by Luther's German *der auserwählten Frau*. The third, which appears to have been favoured by Athanasius, and has been accepted later by Bengel, Lücke, de Wette, Düsterdieck, Ebrard, etc., is supported so far by the fact that Κυρίᾳ occurs as a proper name (Gruter, *Inscript.* p. 1127 n. 11), and by the analogy of the address of 3 Jn. But against it is the consideration that the more natural form in that case would have been Κυρίᾳ τῇ ἐκλεκτῇ, as we have Γαΐῳ τῷ ἀγαπητῷ (3 Jn¹), 'Ρούφον τὸν ἐκλεκτὸν (Ro 16¹³), and in the Ep. itself, ἀδελφῆς σου τῆς ἐκλεκτῆς (v.¹³). The fourth rendering, though favoured by Clement, has the difficulty that, while *Electus* occurs as a personal name, *Electa* seems not to be found among the names of women. But, apart from this, there is the fact that the term ἐκλεκτή occurs again in v.¹³, and it is most unlikely that two sisters should have had the same name *Electa*. The least probable interpretation is the last.

which, in addition to other difficulties, makes the person in question the bearer of two strange names.

On the whole, there is most to favour the rendering 'to the elect lady,' and the idea that the Ep. is addressed to a Christian matron, who was held in high esteem in a wide Christian circle, and about whose children the apostle had something to write, partly in praise, partly in caution. But of this lady we know nothing beyond what is told us here. The supposition that the person addressed may have been Martha of Bethany has nothing to support it but the fanciful idea that *Kyria* in Gr. is like Martha in Heb., both being feminine forms of the word for 'Lord.' The designation in question, however, has been understood by not a few to be a figurative expression for a Christian society, rather than a literal description of an individual Christian. The reason for this is found partly in John's way of using symbolical terms, partly in the idea that the salutation would come more naturally from a Church to a Church, but chiefly in the fact that there is comparatively little in the Ep. that applies distinctly to an individual, and much that runs in plural terms — loving 'one another,' looking 'to yourselves,' etc. Hence Jerome, followed by Hilgenfeld, Lünemann, and Schmiedel, held the letter to be addressed to the Church generally. But this surely is excluded by the mention of the 'elect sister.' Others, with more probability, have supposed the Ep. to be directed to a particular Church; and some have attempted to identify the Church as that of Jerusalem (Whitby), or that of Philadelphia (Whiston), or that of Corinth (Serrarius). But it is doubtful whether any writer would naturally introduce such a symbolism into a brief private letter like this. And as it admits of no doubt that the Third Ep. is addressed to an individual, it seems more reasonable to suppose that the companion letter is also written to an individual. In this case we have another example, and a very interesting one, of the private correspondence of the apostles, and an instructive instance of John's pastoral concern for an individual believer and her children.

LITERATURE.—Among the Commentaries, especially those by Huther, Düsterdieck, Lücke, Alford, Ebrard, Westcott; among the books of Introduction, those given under the First Epistle; and in addition, Ritmeier, *de Electa Domina*; Krigele, *de Κυρία Joannis*; H. G. B. Müller, *Comm. in Sec. Ep. Joan.*; Rambonnet, *de Sec. Ep. Joannea*; Knauer, *Studien u. Kritiken*, 1833; S. Cox, *The Private Letters of St. Paul and St. John*.

THE THIRD EPISTLE.—1. *Contents.*—This Ep. is also very brief. The writer explains that it is so, not because he has little to say, but because he expects shortly to see the person addressed, and to 'speak face to face' with him (vv. [13, 14]) It is occupied mostly with things of personal and circumstantial interest, but it touches some important principles, and gives us glimpses of the condition of the early Christian societies which are of great value. It has all the marks of a *letter*, in freedom of style, and in the use of inscription, benediction, and salutation. It is written with much point and spirit, with some dramatic force, and also with singular tact. It begins with an expression of the writer's love for the friend addressed, his interest in his welfare, and his joy in the reports brought him by others of his truth and his consistent walk. It then praises him specially for the kindness which he had shown to certain 'brethren and strangers,' and commends these men further to his hospitable care. In strong terms it then condemns the action of a certain Diotrephes who had acted in a very different spirit, setting himself arrogantly against the writer, and grasping at authority, neither himself receiving such stranger brethren, nor allowing others to do so. Such ambitious and unbrotherly conduct, it says, is not to be imitated, and cannot be favoured

by one who is of God. Passing from this unwelcome subject, it speaks a good word for a certain Demetrius, with whom perhaps the letter was to go, and closes with some personal explanations, a brief benediction, and mutual greetings.

2. *Time, Place, Destination.*—This Ep. raises no doubt about its *destination*. It is addressed to an individual, and is of a private character all through. But beyond the fact that his name was **Gaius**, that he had the confidence of the writer, and that he had a large and generous sense of Christian duty to strangers, we know nothing of the recipient. There is nothing to identify him with the Gaius or Caius, one of the 'men of Macedonia' who were 'Paul's companions in travel' (Ac 19[29]); with the Gaius of Derbe who accompanied Paul into Asia (Ac 20[4]); with the Corinthian Gaius who was one of the few baptized by Paul (1 Co 1[14]), and is described as Paul's 'host' and that 'of the whole Church' (Ro 16[23]); or with another of the same name who is said to have been made bishop of Pergamos by John (*Const. Apostol.* vii. 46). The fact that the Gaius of this Ep. and the Gaius of Corinth have both the character of hospitality, is a very slender basis on which to establish the identity of the two. The name Gaius was one of the commonest personal names, and the prominent men in the Churches of Asia Minor may not have been the same in John's time as in Paul's. The Ep. itself, indeed, does not show that this Gaius was a presbyter or held any official position. He may very well have been a simple member, though one of influence and repute. Nor does the Ep. make it possible for us to identify the Church to which he belonged. Some, indeed, have thought it to be the Church of Pergamos, a Gaius being mentioned in the *Apost. Const.* as bishop of that place (Wolf, Thoma); and some have taken it to be the Church of Corinth, supposing this Gaius to be the Gaius of Corinth referred to in the Pauline Epp. (Koenen). We can only say that in all probability it was one in the Ephesian circle.

Nor have we more to guide us in determining the *date* of the Ep. and the *place* where it was written. Its general character and its likeness to 2 Jn point to the close of the apostle's ministry, if it is his composition, and to one or other of the Asiatic Churches over which his superintendence was exercised. As in the case of 2 Jn, Ephesus would most probably be the place, especially if the visit referred to in v. [14] could be understood to mean a tour of inspection. And Eusebius (*HE* iii. 23), speaking of John's administration of the Churches in Asia after the death of Domitian, quotes from Clement a statement bearing that the apostle 'coming from the isle of Patmos to Ephesus, went also, when called, to the neighbouring regions of the Gentiles; in some to appoint bishops, in some to institute entire new Churches, in others to appoint to the ministry some one of those that were pointed out by the Holy Ghost.'

3. *Occasion.*—The Ep. appears to have been occasioned by the visits of certain Christian brethren who moved about from place to place, probably as travelling preachers or missionary teachers, and by the different receptions that had been given them. Such men were dependent on the hospitality of their brethren, and deserved to enjoy it. They had visited the Church to which Gaius belonged, and had also come to John. They had received a brotherly welcome from Gaius, but had been rudely treated by another member of the Church, a man of ambitious spirit who disowned the apostle's authority. The letter is written in these circumstances to encourage Gaius in his generous attitude to such strangers, and to intimate the apostle's purpose to visit the Church in person and set matters right. We gather from it, too, that it had

been preceded by another short letter, which seems to have had no effect. That letter has been identified by some with 1 Jn (Storr, etc.), by others with 2 Jn (Besser, Ewald, etc.). But the subjects dealt with in these Epp. are so unlike those questions of hospitality to a particular class which make the main contents of 3 Jn, that little can be said for such identifications. The letter appears to be one of the lost Epp. of Apostles.

4. *Affinities and Authorship.*—It has marked affinities both with 1 Jn and 2 Jn. It has some words, φιλαρεῖν, φιλοπρωτεύειν, ὑπολαμβάνειν as = *welcome*, which are not found in these others. But they are due to the case which the Ep. has to express. It has other words and phrases, such as προπέμπειν, εὐοδοῦσθαι, ὑγιαίνειν, ἐπιδέχεσθαι, πιστὸν ποιεῖν, which are either peculiar or more after Paul's style than John's. But they are far outweighed by the general resemblance in the case of the two smaller letters, the similarity of the terms in which the closing personal explanations are made (2 Jn 12, 13, 3 Jn 13, 14); and the occurrence of such parallelisms of phrase between 3 Jn and the Johannine writings as these—ἐν ἀληθείᾳ (v. 1, 3, cf. 1 Jn 3¹⁸, 2 Jn 1, 4), ἐκ θεοῦ εἶναι (v.¹¹, cf. 1 Jn 2²⁹), θεὸν ὁρᾶν (v.¹¹, cf. 1 Jn 3⁶), μαρτυρεῖν τινι (v.¹², cf. Jn 21²⁴), οἶδας ὅτι ἡ μαρτυρία ἡμῶν ἀληθής ἐστιν (v.¹², cf. Jn 21²⁴).

In respect of historical attestation this Ep. stands much in the same position as 2 Jn. The testimony to its recognition in the Church and to its being from the hand of the Apostle John, is on the whole, however, somewhat less in amount and in definiteness. Like 2 Jn, it was omitted by the Peshiṭta, and seems not to have been accepted by the school of Antioch. Like 2 Jn, it was placed by Eusebius among the Antilegomena, and was referred to by Origen as one not admitted by all to be genuine. From the time of Eusebius it appears to have been generally received. With 2 Jn it found a place in the Apostolic Canons, the sixtieth Canon of the Council of Laodicea (A.D. 364), the Canon of Cyril of Jerusalem, the Canon of the third Council of Carthage (A.D. 397), etc. It is referred to by Jerome as among the Catholic Epp., but as said to have been written together with 2 Jn by John the *presbyter* (*de Vir. Illustr.* c. 9), to whom it was also attributed in the decree of Damasus (Charteris, *Canonicity*, p. 24), and by Cosmas Indicopleustes. It is not quoted by Tertullian, Cyprian, or Irenæus. It is not mentioned by Clement of Alexandria when he deals with the Second Epistle. Eusebius, however, speaks of Clement as having explained the Catholic Epp. in his *Hypotyposes* (*HE* vi. 14), from which it may perhaps be inferred that he used this Ep. as well as the others. There is no such evidence that this Ep. was recognized by the Church of North Africa as we have in the case of 2 Jn, notwithstanding the lack of any reference to it in the writings of the great North African Fathers. On the other hand, it has a place in the Muratorian Canon (according to the most probable interpretation); it was in the Old Latin Version; it was recognized by Dionysius of Alexandria; and it was quoted by Ephraem the Syrian. The most ancient testimony to its existence and recognition associates it not with the *presbyter*, but with the Apostle John. This association is in harmony with the Johannine touches which attract our attention in it, while the arguments that go to show this Ep. to be from the same hand as the other two Epp. ascribed to John, go also to prove it to be by the Apostle John. The doubts which overhung it for a time may have been due to its private character and the length of time which a letter of this kind would naturally take before it could become widely known in the Churches.

It has been supposed by some that v.¹² shows that the writer wished to identify himself with the disciple referred to in Jn 21²⁴ (Pfleiderer). But there is nothing to support this. Ewald (*Joh. Schriften*, p. 505) was of opinion that of a number of letters written by John to individuals or particular Churches, only 2 and 3 Jn have survived; that both these Epp. were meant for the same Church; and that the Third was written lest the Second should have been prevented by Diotrephes from getting into the hands for which it was intended. Hilgenfeld has a curious theory of 3 Jn as a letter of introduction intended to assert the rights of the Church of John against the exclusiveness of the rigorous Jewish-Christian party in the matter of letters of commendation. Baur's theory is still more curious and fine-spun. He thought that a schism had been caused in the Church to which Gaius belonged by the Montanist movement; that the exclusive party was headed by Diotrephes; and that this Ep. was written under John's name against the Roman episcopate—the Roman bishop, Soter, or Anicetus, or Eleutherus, being aimed at under the pseudonym Diotrephes.

5. *Peculiar Interest.*—The great interest of this Ep. lies in the insight which it gives us into the ordinary life of the Christian communities of those early times and this wide Asiatic territory, which had enjoyed the oversight of the last of the apostles. It helps us to see what these Churches were, not as we idealize them, but in their actual everyday condition, with their excellences and defects, their noble and their ignoble figures, their meek and their ambitious members, the errors into which they might be betrayed, their varied, mixed, and stirring life. It shows us something, too, of their independence, of the kind of ministry that was in exercise among them, and their relation to it, of their order also and administration. On these latter subjects it has so much to suggest that it seems to mark a notable stage in the growth of the Church and the history of its organization. It discloses a condition of things like that with which the *Didaché* has made us familiar. It places us at the point of transition from the apostolic age to the post-apostolic, from the primitive simplicity to a more developed constitution. Harnack thinks we can see in it the struggle between the old patriarchal, provincial order of things, with its ministry of travelling missionary preachers, and the rise of the settled, organized *Church*, with its officials, its rights, and its administration. He finds in it nothing less than the emergence of the Episcopate proper, and recognizes in Diotrephes the first bishop of the monarchical type known to us by name.

LITERATURE.—Among the *Commentaries* and the books of *Introduction*, those given for the Second Ep.; also Heumann, *Comm. in Joan.* Ep. III.; Stemler, *de Diotrephe*; Gachon, *Authenticité de la 2e et 3e Ep. de Jean*; S. Cox, *The Private Letters of St. Paul and St. John*; and especially Harnack, *Ueber den dritten Johannesbrief* (*Texte u. Unters. zur Gesch. der altchr. Literatur*, xv. 3).   S. D. F. SALMOND.

JOIADA (יֹויָדָע, Ἰοειδέ, Ἰωδά, Ἰωαδά, Ἰωδαέ).—**1.** One of the two who repaired the 'old gate' (Neh 3⁶). **2.** High priest, son of Eliashib (Neh 12¹⁰, 11, 22). He seems to have sympathized with his father's gentilizing policy, since one of his sons married the daughter of Sanballat the Horonite, and so 'defiled the priesthood' (Neh 13²⁸f·).   N. J. D. WHITE.

JOIAKIM (יוֹיָקִים), Neh 12¹⁰, 12, 26; **Joakim** (Ἰωακείμ), 1 Es 5⁵, where see *QPB.*—A high priest, son of Jeshua.

JOIARIB (יֹויָרִיב, Ἀρείβ, Ἰωρείβ, Ἰωιαρίβ, Ἰωαρείμ).—**1.** Ezr 8¹⁶, one of the two teachers sent by Ezra to Iddo to ask for ministers for the temple. **2.** Neh 11⁵, ancestor of Maaseiah a Judahite, one of 'the chiefs of the province that dwelt in Jerusalem' in Nehemiah's time. See also JEHOIARIB.

JOKDEAM (יׇקְדְעׇם).—A city of Judah, Jos 15⁵⁶, whose site has not been identified. See JORKEAM.

JOKIM (יׄקִים, Ἰωακείμ), 1 Ch 4²², a Judahite, son or descendant of Shelah.

JOKMEAM (יׇקְמְעׇם; Β'Ικάμ, A 'Ιεκμαάν).—A town in Ephraim given to the Levites, near Beth-horon, 1 Ch 6⁶⁸ [Heb. ⁵³]. In Jos 21²² it is called Kibzaim (LXX omits). No site answering to either of these names is known. Jokmeam is mentioned also in 1 K 4¹², where AV has incorrectly Jokneam (but see next art.).   C. R. CONDER.

JOKNEAM (יׇקְנְעׇם, perh. 'let the people possess' [see Gray, *Heb. Prop. Names*, 218]).—A royal city of the Canaanites, on Carmel and the S.W. border of Zebulun, with a 'torrent-valley' (apparently the gorge of the Kishon, which is dry in parts in summer) to the east, Jos 12²² 19¹¹. It was given to the Levites, according to Jos 21³⁴, where it is enumerated as belonging to Zebulun. It is possibly the same as Jokmeam of 1 K 4¹² (Β Λουκάμ, Luc. Ουκάμ), which is mentioned as on the border of one of Solomon's commissariat districts, probably at the boundary between Issachar and Zebulun. The site is found at the present *Tell Ḳeimûn*, on the E. slope of Carmel, near the Kishon—a conspicuous mound with ruins of a small town. In the 4th cent. A.D. (*Onom. s.* Camon) it was known as lying 6 Roman miles N. of Legio (*Lejjûn*), on the way to Ptolemais ('*Akka*), and in the 12th cent. A.D. it was called *Cain Mons* or 'Mt. Cain,' from a legend which made it the place where Cain died. It became the centre of a small independent Seigneurie. The ruins include those of a Byzantine building, apparently a chapel. In the Samaritan Book of Joshua it is noticed as the scene of a conflict between the Hebrews and the giants, and Joshua is said to have been here shut up in magic walls of brass, till, on sending a dove to Nabih the Hebrew king of Gilead, he was rescued.

Jokneam appears in Jth 7³ under the name **Cyamon** (Κυαμών) in connexion with the encampment of Holofernes (but see Buhl, *GAP* 210; Robinson, *BRP* iii. 339 n.).

LITERATURE.—*SWP* vol. ii. sheet v., and Volume of Special Papers under 'Samaritan Topography'; van de Velde, *Narr.* i. 330 f.; Baedeker-Socin, *Pal.²* 242; Guérin, *Samarie*, ii. 241 f.; Sepp, *Holy Land*, ii. 551; Buhl, *GAP* 210; Robinson, *BRP* iii. 114 f.; Dillmann on Gn 12²² 19¹¹.   C. R. CONDER.

JOKSHAN (יׇקְשׇׁן, 'Ιεξάν, 'Ιεκσάν, 'Ιεκτάν).—Son of Abraham and Keturah, and father of Sheba (Saba) and Dedan, Gn 25² (1 Ch 1³²). The name seems quite unknown, and the suggestion of Tuch that it is identical with Joktan seems the most plausible. The two forms might represent respectively the Hebrew and Aramaic pronunciation of the same word (cf. קְשַׁר = קְטַר, אשׁא = אטא, where the Aramaic ט is hardened from ת, as in קמל for קתל, קְמִיר for קְתִיר). The Arabic genealogists apparently have no suggestion for his identification; for Yākish (or rather Yāfish), who is mentioned by a writer quoted by Yākūt (iii. 635, Osiander in *ZDMG* x. 31), owes his existence to a conflation of the names Jokshan and Japheth.

     D. S. MARGOLIOUTH.

JOKTAN (יׇקְטׇן, 'Ιεκτάν, 'Ιουκτάς, Jos. *Ant.* I. vi. 4).—Son of Eber, and father of a number of races (Gn 10²⁶, 1 Ch 1²⁰). The races mentioned dwelt 'from Mesha to Sephar'; and though the import of these names is doubtful, the occurrence among them of Saba, Ḥaḍramaut, and Salif makes it certain that Arabia or a portion of it is intended. When the attention of the Arabic genealogists was

drawn to the Old Testament by Mohammed's ostensible acceptance of it, they noticed the names that have been quoted, and drew the same conclusion from them. Two lists of identifications made by archæologists of the early centuries of Islam are given in the miscellaneous work called *Al-Iḳd al-Farīd* (ii. 51). They had to grapple with several difficulties at the outset. The native tradition made Saba son of Yashjub, and Ḥaḍramaut son of Ḥimyar (Ḥamdani, p. 85). The genealogies were harmonized by the supposition that some links had been omitted in the Hebrew record; hence Saba is made by the Arabic historians 'son of Yashjub son of Ya'rub son of Ḳaḥtān (Yoktan)'; the insertion of the link Ya'rub being to mark the epoch at which the Hebrews (sons of Eber) became Arabs (Ibn Ḳutaibah's *Manual of History*, p. 209, ed. Cairo). Moreover, the name Joktan was itself unknown; some genealogist therefore hit on the name Ḳaḥtān, which really belonged to some tribe or region (Muḳaddasi in *Bibl. Geogr. Arab.* iii. 104), and thought it near enough to be identified with the Hebrew name; and though this identification was not universally accepted (*Tāj al-'Arūs, s.v.*), it was till recently generally adopted both in the East and the West. Mas'udi, who records another and probably more ancient pedigree for Ḳaḥtān, says that he found the biblical genealogy accepted by tribal authorities all over South Arabia. What can scarcely be determined now is whether the legend that makes Ḳaḥtān founder of the S. Arabian tribes is earlier or later than his identification with Joktan; but it seems clear that there is no connexion between the two names. The word Ḳaḥtān (of which there was a variety, Aḳbāt) probably means 'droughty,' and originally applied to some strip of territory. It might have been expected that some of the numerous inscriptions that have been discovered in S. Arabia would throw light on the passage of Gn, but the most important contribution to its interpretation which has been obtained from that source would seem to be the discovery by Glaser of the ancient name of San'ā, whence it would appear that the old identification of Uzal with that city is erroneous.

Since, therefore, both the Arabic legends and the inscriptions fail us, we are left to conjecture. The name may be an ethnological invention intended to connect the Arabs with the Hebrews, and in that case the Targum on 1 Ch (published in Lagarde's *Hagiographa Chaldaice*) is probably right in deriving it from the Hebrew, with the sense 'smaller' or 'shorter,' not, however, with reference to the length of human life, but in comparison with the other 'half' (Peleg) of the sons of Eber. If, however, the name be Arabic and geographical, probably the connexion suggested by Glaser (*Skizze*, ii. 423) between it and Ḳaṭan, the name of several mountains in Arabia (Yākūt, *s.v.*), and also of a tribe mentioned by Ptolemy (*Katanitæ*), has most in its favour. The Arabs, however, tell us that Ḳaṭan is properly an anatomical term; and if these mountains be named from their resemblance to some portion of the body, the form Yoḳtan remains unexplained. If the name met us in an Arabic genealogy, we should almost certainly have the observation that Joktan was the first who had *a fixed residence* (Arab. *ḳaṭana yaḳṭunu*).

With regard to the thirteen names of Joktan's sons, the meagreness of the list forbids us to suppose that it is the intention of the genealogist to give a description of the Arabian peninsula, or indeed of any portion of it; his purpose is rather to localize ethnologically, and to some extent geographically, the races with whose names his readers were already familiar. Hence Saba and Havilah, to which peculiar interest attached, are localized differently in the tables admitted into Gn (10⁷ 25⁸).

We learn from Ezk 27[19] that Uzal was famous in connexion with the spice trade; and it is probable that, were more of the old Hebrew literature preserved, we should be able in each case to name the *sedes glossæ*. The discovery, therefore, of places with identical names in the Arabian peninsula is not sufficient to identify the localities of the table, unless it be shown that the places discovered were of sufficient importance to have been heard of by the Israelites. Glaser's suggestion (*l.c.*), that the table proceeds geographically from S. to N., seems inconsistent with the mention of Saba near the end; for surely Saba should count as a southern or, at any rate, midland state. We cannot even be sure that all the names which occur in it are connected with Arabia; the Targ. on Chron. hints that the juxtaposition of Saba, Ophir, and Havilah is due to all three being connected with the gold industry (cf. Is 60[6]), and this fact would to an ancient ethnologist have constituted a claim to affinity independently of local considerations. The more probable suggestions that have been made for the identification of the names that occur only in this passage are quoted in the separate articles.

D. S. MARGOLIOUTH.

JOKTHEEL (יָקְתְאֵל).—This name occurs twice in OT as applied to two very different places: one a city or town of the Amorites, the other the capital of Edom. **1.** A city described (Jos 15[33.38], Βʼ Ιακαρεήλ, A and Luc. ʼΙεχθαήλ) as lying in 'the Shephelah,' along with some others, from which we gather that it was situated on the extensive plain bordering Philistia, bounded on the E. by the tableland of southern Judæa, and on the W. by the Mediterranean. In the general allotment by Joshua it came into possession of the tribe of Judah. Its site has not been recovered. **2.** The name (which Wetzstein, in Del. *Jes.*[3] 703 f., explains from the Arab., 'protection of God') given (2 K 14[7], B and Luc. Καθοήλ, A ʼΙεκθοήλ) to Sela, the ancient capital of the Edomites, after its capture by Amaziah king of Judah (see SELA). It may have been bestowed by Amaziah in recognition of the aid afforded by Jʺ in the capture of a city of such amazing strength as Sela, and the overthrow of the Edomites in the Valley of Salt. The latter was at the southern end of the Dead Sea, and thus within the territory of the kings of Judah. The name 'Joktheel' did not take permanent hold on the place, because the Edomites in the reign of Ahaz regained their sovereignty (2 Ch 28[17]), and doubtless restored to their capital its original name of Sela.

E. HULL.

JOLLITY.—1 Es 3[20] 'It [wine] turneth also every thought into jollity (εὐωχία) and mirth'; and Sir 13[8] 'Beware that thou be not deceived, and brought down in thy jollity' (ἐν εὐφροσύνῃ σου; AVm 'by thy simplicity'; RV 'in thy mirth'). The meaning is 'mirth,' which is the commonest meaning of the word. Thus Shaks., *Mid. Night's Dream*, v. i. 377—

'A fortnight hold we this solemnity,
In nightly revels and new jollity';

And Milton, *PL* xi. 714—

'And all was turned to jollity and game.'

So Latimer, *Sermons* (Arber's ed. p. 58), 'Joab and the other company beynge in theyr jolitye, and kepyng good cheare, heard it.' But in a subsequent sermon (p. 113) Latimer has it with the sense of splendour, 'He shewed him al the kyngdomes of the worlde, and all theyr jolitye.' Cf. Jth 10[3] Wyc. 1382, 'she clothide hir with the clothis of hir jolite,' 1388 'gladnesse.' The adj. 'jolly' is used by Tind., Ex 15[4] 'His jolye captaynes are drowned in the red see'; and by Coverdale, Job 40[10] 'up, decke the in thy joly araye, poure out the indignacion of thy wrath.'

J. HASTINGS.

JONADAB.—See JEHONADAB.

JONAH.—
  i. Jonah and 2 K 14[25].
  ii. Jonah and Is 15 f.
  iii. Jonah and the Book of Jonah.
    1. Contents of the book.
    2. Unity of the book.
    3. Relation between the person and the book of Jonah.
    4. Formal character of the book—*A symbol. narrative.*
    5. Date of the book.
    6. The principal other interpretations of the book.
      The *externo-historical* and the *legendary* interpretations characterized and examined.
    7. The idea of the book—Universalism of God's plan of salvation, and Israel's mission to the *goyim*.
  iv. Other occurrences of the name Jonah.
    Literature.

i. JONAH AND 2 K 14[25].—The name יוֹנָה (ʼΙωνᾶς) is found in the canon. OT only in 2 K 14[25] and Jon 1[1]-4[9] (cf. Mandelkern, *Vet. Test. Concord. Heb. et Chald.* 1896, p. 1438[a]). In the former of these passages, where it is used of 'the servant of God, Jonah the son of Amittai, the prophet, which was of Gathhepher,' the expression 'through his servant' (בְּיַד־עַבְדּוֹ) is nothing remarkable, occurring as it does also in 1 K (8[56]) 14[18] 15[29], 2 K 9[36] 10[10] in the same sense as in 2 K 14[25]. The name Amittai (אֲמִתַּי) is found nowhere in OT except in 2 K 14[25] and Jon 1[1] (Mandelkern, *loc. cit.* p. 1367[b]). Hence all that we know of the father of the prophet Jonah is this at most, that he was an inhabitant of the place called גַּת הַחֵפֶר (= 'press of Ḥepher,' proper names having elsewhere also for certain reasons the article attached to them [cf. König, *Histor.-comparat. Syntax d. Heb.* 1897, § 295]). It is the same place that is meant by גִּתָּה חֵפֶר in Jos 19[13], where the context shows that we have the so-called locative form ('to Gath-hepher,' LXX ἐπί, κ.τ.λ.). There are other instances where the locative, like *Gittáh*, is accented on the last syllable (cf. *Shalishah*, etc., in 2 K 4[42] etc.).* This accentuation may be determined by the immediately following guttural (cf. *Lehrgeb.* ii. 517). The חֵפֶר without the article in Jos 19[13] may have arisen through haplography of the ה, or חֵפֶר (2 K 14[25]) and חֵפֶר (Jos 19[13]) may be related to each other as הָעַיִן and עַיִן, etc. (König, *Syntax*, § 295d). Hence we are neither to find the place-name 'Gath-hepher' in 2 K 14[25] (G. A. Smith, *Twelve Prophets*, ii. 496) nor the place-name 'Gittah-hepher' in Jos 19[13] (*ib.* note 1). The place *Gath* (*ha*)*ḥepher* lay in the territory assigned to the tribe of Zebulun, Jos 19[10. 13].

In 2 K 14[25] it is further recorded of Jonah that in the time of Jeroboam II. (*c.* B.C. 781-741) this prophet predicted the re-conquest of the eastern boundaries of Israel. In this passage 'the sea of the Arabah' (*i.e.* the Dead Sea) fixes, of course, only *exclusively* the *terminus ad quem*. The uncertain expression 'the brook of the Arabah' (נַחַל הָעֲרָבָה) in Am 6[14] does not contradict this assumption, which is commended also by other considerations (see below, § ii.).

ii. JONAH AND Is 15 f.—We should be much better informed regarding the work of the prophet Jonah, if he were the author of the prophecy which forms at least the basis of Is 15[1]-16[12], and to which Isaiah himself added the epilogue, 'This is the word which Jʺ *in time past* spake concerning Moab, and *now* hath Jʺ spoken, saying,' etc. (16[13f.]). That earlier prophecy is, in point of fact, attributed to Jonah by Hitzig (*Des Proph. Jonah Orakel üb. Moab*, 1831), Maurer, Knobel (*Der Prophetismus der Hebräer*, ii. 124), Riehm (*Einleit. in d. AT*, ii. 62), Duhm (*Theol. d. Proph.* 71), Renan (*Hist. du peuple d'Israël*, ii. 417). But (*a*) the announcement of Jonah, which is mentioned in 2 K 14[25], had certainly a much wider scope than the oracle of Is 15[1]-16[12]. (*b*) If the author of Is 15[1]-16[12] was

* For the other exceptions see König, *Heb. Lehrgebäude*, 517[3].

an inhabitant of the Northern kingdom and a subject of Jeroboam II. (which even Cheyne, *Introd. to Bk. of Isaiah*, 1895, p. 88, regards as possible), he could only ironically have called upon the Moabites to send presents to *Zion* (16¹ᶠᶠ·). (c) In the words, 'Send *lambs* (כַּר) for the ruler of the land . . . to Zion' (16¹), such a political relation of the Moabites to Jerusalem is most naturally presupposed as we find in 2 K 3⁴ (כָּרִים). In all probability, the Moabites after the time of Mesha became tributary again to the kings of Judah, and Is 15¹-16¹² related to an attack made upon the land of Moab by the Assyrians. From this part of Isaiah, then, no information regarding Jonah ben-Amittai can be derived.

iii. JONAH AND THE BOOK OF JONAH.—1. An abundant source of information about Jonah would be opened to us, if the fifth of the twelve minor prophetical books was written by him. The essential *contents* of this book are as follows:—

(a) Jonah ben-Amittai evaded the Divine commission to go and preach against the city of Nineveh (1¹⁻³). His motive, however, was not 'indolence, sloth, fear of man' (Kleinert, 1893, *ad loc.*), but the fear that J″, on account of His compassionate disposition, would not execute the threatened judgment (4²). Many exegetes have sought to justify this motive by remarking that Jonah will have feared to prove a 'prophet of lies' (וְבִיא הַשָּׁקֶר) (cf. the Midrash in *Jalqût Shim'oni on Jonah*,[*] and the *Gesch. d. Proph. Jona* by B. Wolf [see below], 1897, p. 12). Others will have it that Jonah did not wish to save a people which threatened destruction to Israel (so the *Mechilta* to Ex 1⁴, Jerome, Rashi, Kimchi,[†] Abravanel). According to *Mikhlal Jophi, ad loc.*, Jonah was afraid that the Ninevites, if they repented at the preaching of *a single* prophet, would put to shame the Israelites, who did not repent in spite of *many* prophets (אינם שבים מרמב הרעה). Yet other interpreters suppose that Jonah was reluctant to make known to a heathen people the knowledge of the true God (Hengstenberg, *Christologie*², i. 469, 'because he grudged the exercise of compassion towards the heathen').

(b) God brought about the punishment of Jonah by means of a great storm (1⁴⁻¹⁶). Acc. to Philo (*de Jona oratio*, Op., ed. Richter, vii. 377 ff.), it was the snoring of Jonah that drew the attention of the captain of the vessel to him ('Tradebat eum vox narium stertentium, quum altius reddatur in supinis jacentibus'). On the other hand, the Arabo-Syrian *History of the Prophet Jonah* makes the latter confess his fault on his own impulse, and Jonah is thus held up as a model of noble love of the truth. Moreover, the casting of lots (וְרָלוֹת 1⁷) is not introduced till after v.¹⁴, somewhat after the example of the Midrash. (For the language of the latter see Wolf, p. 16 f.). In this way the casting of lots would be a last attempt to save the life of the prophet. Also, according to Edm. Hardy (*ZDMG*, 1896, p. 153), it is related in the Hindu *Jat*, 439 (ed. Fausböll, iv. 2), how sailors discovered the guilt of Mittavindaka by casting lots three times, and how, using almost the very language of Jon 1¹⁴, they exposed him on a raft.

(c) But a merciful God thus reduced Jonah to straits, not in order to destroy him, but ultimately to rescue him (2¹⁻¹¹).

(d) Thereupon the prophet proclaimed in Nineveh that in forty days the city would be destroyed (3¹⁻⁴). The same number 40 (אַרְבָּעִים), which is common to the MT, Targum, Pesh., and Vulg., is given also in one manuscript of the above-named *History*

of the *Prophet Jonah* (p. viii, l. 3, *'arba 'ina*). But the LXX (τρεῖς), Philo (*op. cit.* § 27, 'civitas ista tres tantum dies habet'), the Arab. (ثلاثة), and the other manuscript of the *History* (ܬܠܬܐ) have all the number 3. Perhaps this variation is simply due to the relation between מַהֲלָךְ שְׁלֹשֶׁת יָמִים (3³ᵇ) and מַהֲלַךְ יוֹם אֶחָד (v.⁴ᵃ), for it might be supposed that the catastrophe would ensue after the three days' transit through the city. It is less probable that the influence at work was the 'three' of 2¹ [Eng. 1¹⁷]. But the Midrash mentioned a fast of שלשה ימים ושלשה לילות (Wolf, p. 25¹). A symbolical sense of the number 'three' is not to be thought of, nor is an interchange of the numbers μ′ and γ′ (W. Böhme, *ZATW*, 1887, p. 239) likely. Further, the verb נֶהְפָּכָה, which is imitated by מתהפכא and in the Pesh. ܡܬܗܦܟܐ, was intended to express the sense of *outward* destruction; hence correctly καταστραφήσεται (LXX), *subvertetur* (Vulgate), تنكشف (*disparebit*), and *Mikhlal Jophi, ad loc.*, רוצה לאמר כמהפכת סדום ועמרה כי מעשיה היו כמעשיהם. Wolf, indeed (*op. cit.* p. 21 f.), contends strongly that the נֶהְפָּכָה of v.⁴ is used 'with intentional ambiguity,' it not being in the plan of an all-seeing Providence to destroy the city. But this argument would be justified only if in other prophetical threatenings also, which remained unfulfilled in consequence of man's repentance, an ambiguous expression had been used. But, *e.g.*, in 1 K 21²¹ it is positively announced to king Ahab, 'Behold, I will bring evil upon thee'; no condition is added, yet the prophet was afterwards told, 'I will not bring,' etc. (v.²⁹).

(e) Then the people, as well as the king of Nineveh, took Jonah for a messenger of the Deity; a general fast was ordained, and the inhabitants turned from their evil ways (3⁵⁻¹⁰). So universal was the fasting enjoined that even 'cattle and small cattle' were neither to eat nor drink (v.⁷). Nowack (*ad loc.*) regards the words הָאָדָם וְהַבְּהֵמָה in 3⁸ as a later gloss; but, even so, the subjects would not be altered, for in v.⁷ᵇ 'cattle and small cattle' have been mentioned. A real participation of animals in the fast has therefore been rightly recognized also, *e.g.*, by Philo (*op. cit.* § 37 f.) in the passage. His words are, 'Tantum (*sic*) humiliationem animumque compositum secundum scripturam vestiti sunt, ut pecudes quoque eorum precibus vacantes eos juvarent,' etc. Further, the author of the Arab.-Syr. *History of Jonah* put in the mouth of the Ninevites the following prayer, 'If this repentance be not accepted of God, transgressors will in future despair of the possibility of return.' He went on to tell how the Divine pardon was announced by the sending of a letter and the dispelling of a darkness which had lain over the city during the fast (Wolf, *op. cit.* p. 26).

(f) Enraged at the action of God, Jonah was brought, through his own grief at the loss of a 'gourd,'[*] to see that God had rightly pardoned the Ninevites.

---

[*] On *kikayôn* (4⁶ᶠ· ⁹ᶠ·, Targ. קיקיון) cf. Herodot. ii. 94, ἐλαίωτι δὲ χρίωνται, κ.τ.λ., τὸ καλύουσι μὲν Αἰγύπτιοι κίκι; see also especially Immanuel Löw, *Aram. Pflanzennamen*, No. 298, 'The *Ricinus communis* (Linn.), under the name *kiki*, was, for the sake of its oil, cultivated as largely in ancient Egypt as it is at the present day'; cf. Diod. Sic. i. 34; Dioscorides, iv. 164; Pliny, *HN* xv. 7. Wolf (p. 52) says, 'In the Talmud (*Shabbath* 21ᵃ ᵇˡᵉ. 6 ff.) Rêsh Laḳîsh assumes that the קיק קיק of שֶׁן of the Mishnah (*Shabbath* ii. 2) is identical with the קיקיון דיונה, and Rabbah bar bar (*sic*) Chanah said that he had seen it (חזה לי קיקיון דיונה. The *kikayôn*, according to the Talmud, resembles the צלוליבא, a tree from whose pith oil and medicines were prepared. It is the Arabic *ḥirwa'un*, 'ricinus frutex' (Freytag, *Lex. Arab.*). Kimchi had already cited this explanation, which appears also in *Mikhlal Jophi*. It was not the κολοκύνθη, شجر, 'cf.

[*] ולמה ברח . . . שלחו אל נינוה להחריבה . . . ואמר יודע אני שהנגום קרובי תשובה הם ומשלח רגני על ישראל ולא די שישראל קורין אותי נביא השקר אלא אף עובדי אלילים קורין אותי נביא השקר

[†] ולא חשש (*sollicitus est*) לכבוד אלהים חשש לכבוד ישראל!

2. *The Unity of the Book* 'Jonah.'—This book might, at least partially, be a genuine source of information about Jonah ben-Amittai, *if* it were composed of several strata. The latter position was once maintained by Müller in Paulus' *Memorabilien*, vi. p. 167 ff., and by Nachtigall in Eichhorn's *Allgemeiner Bibliothek*, ix. 221–273 (cf. Eichhorn, *Einleit.* iv. § 577*b*). According to Nachtigall (and Bunsen), among the sacred books of the Hebrews there was 'a prayer of Jonah the son of Amittai,' with the note appended, 'after God had delivered him out of the hand of the king of Assyria.' This prayer is supposed to be preserved in Jon 2³⁻¹⁰, and then chs. 3 and 4 and still later chs. 1 and 2¹ᶠ·¹¹ [Eng. 1¹⁷ 2¹⁰] to have been added to it. Nachtigall has started from a correct perception, namely, that the first part of the prayer (Jon 2³⁻¹⁰) cannot have been uttered by a man who has been swallowed by a sea-monster. Jonah could not out of the belly of the fish say to God, 'Posuisti me in securo loco' (Philo, *op. cit.* § 22). Having regard to his other experiences, and even *per se*, it was impossible that Jonah should regard his sojourn in the fish's belly as a preliminary to his complete deliverance (Kimchi on 2³ בחיותו ידע שיצא ממעי הדג בשלום). This prayer could only at best then be uttered *after* Jonah's deliverance, which is recorded in 2¹¹ [Eng. ¹⁰]. If now the author of 2¹ᶠ·¹¹ had already before him that prayer of thanksgiving (Nachtigall, Bunsen), he would have introduced it after 2¹¹, otherwise he must have placed the origin of the poem within the body of the great fish, in order by this improbability to indicate the didactic purpose of his narrative. But it is more likely that this composition has been supplemented by a later writer who missed the contents of the prayer referred to in 2² (Knobel, *Der Prophetismus der Hebräer*, ii. 377). This older assumption also appears to us the only correct element in the contentions of W. Böhme ('Die Compos. d. Buches Jona' in *ZATW*, 1887, pp. 224 ff., 234), and it is approved also by Cheyne (*Origin of the Psalter*, 1891, p. 126), Budde (*ZATW*, 1892, p. 42), and Nowack (*Handcomm.* 1897, p. 180). G. A. Smith (*Twelve Prophets*, ii. 512) opposes it, appealing to וְיְמַן ('and he arranged *or* ordered') of 2¹ [Eng. 1¹⁷], as showing that the author knew that Jonah was to be saved by means of the fish. But the man who was swallowed by the fish did *not* know this. Hence, if Jonah himself wrote the book, he ascribed to himself by *prolepsis* a prayer of thanksgiving; while, if it was a later writer who put this prayer in the mouth of the swallowed Jonah, he ascribed to the hero of the narrative an action which in the situation of Jon 2² would be a psychological enigma.

Köhler, again (*Theol. Rev.* xvi. 139 ff.), thinks to discover in the Bk. of Jonah partly signs of an earlier age and partly traces of a later revision (but see G. A. Smith, ii. 510²). Finally, W. Böhme (*op. cit.*) has started the theory that four strata can be distinguished within the Bk. of Jonah. But neither his formal arguments nor those based upon the contents can be regarded as valid. This hypothesis has already been examined by the present writer in his *Einleitung*, p. 378 f., and, as no one has since ventured to defend the assumption that the Bk. of Jonah was composed from different strata, it is unnecessary to go into the question in more detail.

3. Is there *a necessary relation between the person and the Book of Jonah?* The genetic connexion

of Jonah ben-Amittai and the Bk. of Jonah appears to be based upon this much at least: We seem compelled to assume that a tradition existed, according to which Jonah ben-Amittai journeyed beyond his own country, that he was involved in a dangerous situation, and that he was ultimately delivered from this. Without such a tradition, it seems inexplicable why it is to the name of Jonah that the book is attached. Riehm, indeed (*Introduction*, ii. 167), says, 'The reason why the author selected the name of Jonah was that the only prophet that would serve his purpose was one whose *name* was on the one hand familiar to the people, but about whom on the other hand they knew *nothing more.*' This, however, is inconclusive. There were several prophets of that kind. Only in *one* event would the choice of the name Jonah ben-Amittai (Jon 1¹) be explicable without a historical tradition, namely, if *Amittai* were meant to be a *nomen appellativum, i.e.* if 'Jonah filius *creduli*' were so designated as a representative of believers κατʼ ἐξοχήν, the so-called orthodox party. We call attention to this possibility, because in investigating so difficult a question all possibilities must be weighed. It is a fact at all events that, in the case of *this* ben-Amittai (Jon 1¹), Gath (ha)hepher is *not* specified as his birthplace (see further, below, 4 *c*, p. 747*b*).

4. *The formal character of the Book of Jonah.*—Notwithstanding that the book may rest upon a tradition about Jonah, yet the essential character of the book consists in this, that it belongs to the category of symbolical narratives.

(*a*) There *were* such narratives. For instance, in Jer 25¹⁵ᶠᶠ· it is said, 'Take this cup,' etc., and 'I took the cup at the hand of J" and made all the nations drink' (v.¹⁷). Thus actions of the prophet are recorded as if they had been outwardly performed, and yet *they cannot have really been so.* Rather is the story merely a form of representation in which a Divine message is presented in a *visible* and therefore *impressive* fashion. This being manifestly the case with Jer 25¹⁵ᶠᶠ·, there is no need in 13⁴ᶠᶠ· to take the name *Pĕrath*, which everywhere else (15 times) means the Euphrates (so also in Jer 51⁶³), to refer to a place which is not meant anywhere else in OT, nor so understood by LXX (ἐπὶ τὸν Εὐφράτην, κ.τ.λ.), etc., in Jer 13⁴ᶠᶠ· and which stood in no relation to the captivity of Israel. For the same reason it is unnecessary to suppose that the prophet Ezekiel actually lay for 390 days upon his left and for 40 days upon his right side (4⁵ᵗ· etc.). Moreover, in 24³ the words 'Set on the caldron and pour water into it,' etc., are called by Ezekiel a *māshāl* (cf. the Arab. *miṭlun*, similitudo, παραβολή; see König's art. 'Zur Deutung der symbolischen Handlungen des Propheten Hesekiel,' in the *Neue kirchliche Zeitschrift*, iii. 650 ff.). Similar to the narrative of Jer 25¹⁵ᶠ· is that of Hos 1¹ᶠᶠ· and 3¹ᶠᶠ· (so, *inter alios*, Hitzig, Simson, Keil, Wünsche, Reuss [*Gesch. d. heil. Schriften ATs*, 1890, § 223]; see, further, art. HOSEA in this Dictionary). For there it is expressly said, 'Go, *take* to thee *mulierem fornicationis*,' and, even if the latter phrase can mean only 'a wife of whoredoms' (Cheyne, *Camb. Bible, ad loc.*; G. A. Smith, i. 234, 'a wife of harlotry'), it is improperly assumed by some interpreters (*e.g.* Cheyne, Wellh., Nowack, G. A. Smith) that the woman had not beforehand 'an inclination to infidelity.' Such an interpretation runs counter to the text, according to which at the very outset Hosea was inspired with the idea of marrying a *mulier fornicationis* (*i.e. idololatriæ eorumque vitiorum quæ cum illa cohærere solebant*). Besides, an 'inclination to infidelity' was a thing by no means strange to the majority of the nation, with which J" as it were contracted a marriage in the time of Moses (cf. Ex 32⁸). Again, if the com-

cucurbita, pepo' (Brockelmann, *Lex. Syr. s.v.*), Arab. يَقْطِين

(Koran, xxxvii. 146). As Jerome replaced *cucurbita* of the old Latin by *hedera* ('ivy'), there arose 'tumultus in plebe' (Augustinus, *ad Hieron.*, Epistola 88).

mission of J″ was literally carried out, Hosea must have married an adulteress (Hos 3¹). But, with a view to the visible presentation of a truth, there is *no need* for such an *outward* performance of actions which would have been not only in themselves repugnant, but also unnatural for the prophet himself.

(*b*) The above-cited symbolic tales may be imitated in the Book of Jonah (cf. especially the parallelism between Hos 1² 3¹ and Jon 1¹ 3¹, also Ezk 3²⁵ etc.). As Ezekiel was bound, etc., as the representative of the people (3²⁵ 4⁸ff. 5¹ff. etc.), so in the Bk. of Jonah it was related how Jonah undertook a mission to the *goyîm*, etc. This might happen the all more readily that elsewhere the people of Israel and the prophetic order are identified with one another; the servant of J″, who, according to Is 41⁸ etc., is the people of Israel, is a designation in 42¹ etc. of the servant of God who is to bring, *i.e.* proclaim to the *goyîm sententiam et normam iudicii* or *lucem* (Is 42⁶ 49⁶, cf. 43¹⁰), and so also the people of Israel is called the son of God (Ex 4²², Hos 11¹). This servant of God was in many ways also blind, and deaf (Is 42¹⁹), and dumb (56¹⁰); cf. Jon 1³. Further, the captivity of Israel is several times compared to a grave from which they are to come forth again alive; Ezk 37¹¹f. 'These bones are the *whole* house of Israel' (rightly interpreted even by Hengstenberg, *Christologie*, ii. p. 588, not 'ii. p. 125' as Bertholet cites it, *Kurzer Handcom. zu Hesekiel*, 1897, p. 184); cf. Ezk 19⁵ 33¹⁰ 39²⁵. Again, the captivity of Israel is compared to being devoured, 'Nebuchadnezzar hath swallowed me up like a sea-monster (*tannîn*), and he hath filled his belly' (Jer 51³⁴; cf. v.⁴⁴ יְבִלְעָ֫נִי, and in Is 27¹ the comparison of the secular power to a *livyathan* (crocodile) and a *tannîn*; see esp. G. A. Smith, 1898, pp. 523–526). Note also that Israel's deliverance from exile is compared to a new birth (Is 66⁸) and a dream (Ps 126¹). Further, as pre-exilic Israel was wont to decline its missionary call (Jon 1³), so a part of exilic and post-exilic Israel discovered in this mission only a call to threaten the *goyîm* (cf. Jer 29¹⁰, Ezk 18²⁹ 33²⁰, Ps 137⁸, Is 34 f. 63¹ff., Ob ¹⁰ff., Mal 1⁴f. 3¹⁴, Jon 3¹ff.). But in this same exilic and post-exilic period there are also voices to be heard calling for prayer to God on behalf of the *goyîm* (Jer 29⁷) and giving expression to the universalistic tendency of the theocracy (Zec 8²³, cf. Jon 3¹⁰ 4¹¹; see below, 7 *a*). The voice of such a preacher may be heard also in the Bk. of Jonah, whose author may have selected the individualistic presentation of his idea because this was least likely to miss making an impression. This, which for shortness may be called the *symbolical* interpretation of the Bk. of Jonah, is in the main upheld by Hardt, Kleinert (*Commentary*, 1874), Bloch (*Studien zur Gesch. der Samml. d. altheb. Lit.* 1876, p. 72 ff.), Cheyne (art. in *Theol. Rev.* 1877, p. 214 ff.), C. H. H. Wright (*Biblical Essays*, T. and T. Clark, 1886, p. 45 ff.),* Ed. König (*Einleitung*, 1893, p. 380), Kleinert (*Commentary*, 1893, p. 18 ff.), G. A. Smith (1898, p. 502 ff.).†

---

* Wright cites (p. xxv) the following passages: 2 S 12¹ff. (Nathan's parable) 14⁶t. (the parabolical narrative of the wise woman of Tekoa), 1 K 20³⁹⁻⁴¹ (the parabolical tale of the prisoner who was allowed to escape). These, however, do not furnish real parallels to the Bk. of Jonah, for, like all parables, they have an unknown, general subject. Nevertheless, they show that in Israel it was customary to introduce abstract truths in the form of individualistic tales. This disposition is also a factor in the origin of narratives about real visions, like those of 1 K 22¹⁹⁻²² and of Amos and Ezekiel.

† Similar is the judgment of Augusti (*Einleitung*, 1827, § 225), Hitzig (in the Preface to his Exposition of the Book of Jonah in *Kurzgef. exeg. Hdbch.*), Bleek (*Einleitung*, 1878, § 229), Riehm (*Einleitung*, 1889, ii. § 81, 'The contents of the book are pure invention'), Reuss (*Gesch. d. h. Schr. AT*s, 1890, § 407), *et alii*, who have not recognized the analogy of the symbolical narratives of the prophets.

(*c*) The choice of the name Jonah as the subject of this symbolical narrative may also (see above, 3, p. 746ᵇ) have been favoured by the following circumstance. Jonah was an inhabitant of the kingdom of Samaria, and 'the name *Jonah* signifies a dove. Ephraim, the Northern kingdom, the kingdom of Israel as distinguished from that of Judah, is termed by Hosea, the only other prophetic writer who belonged to that kingdom, "a silly dove" (יוֹנָה Hos 7¹¹); and when that prophet predicts the Return from Captivity, he speaks of Ephraim as returning as "a dove (יוֹנָה) out of the land of Assyria" (11¹¹).' C. H. H. Wright, from whose *Biblical Essays* (1886, p. 45) these words are quoted, has not, however, recalled יוֹנַת אֵלֶם רְחֹקִים (Ps 56¹), which is most probably interpreted *columba (silentii=) silens peregrinorum locorum= inter et propter peregrinos* (on the silence of *b* after *m* see König, *Syntax*, § 330m). This expression in Ps 56¹ is already referred by the Talmud to כְּנֶ֫סֶת יִשְׂרָאֵל וג', by the LXX to ὁ λαὸς ὁ ἀπὸ τῶν ἀγίων μεμακρυμμένης, and so also by the Arabic ('*ummatun*) and the Ethiopic (*chézeb*=populus). [Wellhausen (in Haupt's *SBOT*) changes אלם into אײם, but this suggestion lacks probability]. A remarkable coincidence between Israelitish and foreign conceptions may be discovered in the analogy between the sojourn of the dove (יוֹנָה) in the fish's belly, and the descent of the 'dove' Semiramis from the fish-woman (cf. the ancient picture in Vigouroux, *Die Bibel und die neueren Entdeckungen*, iii. 355) Atargatis or Δερκετώ or Dercetis, who also had a temple at Ashkelon, cf. Ovid, *Metam.* iv. 45 ff.—

'Derceti, quam versa squamis velantibus artus
Stagna Palæstini credunt motasse figura;
An magis, ut sumptis illius filia pennis
Extremos albis in turribus egerit annos.'

I venture also to call attention to the circumstance that the name 'Nineveh' (Herodot. i. 103, 106, 193, ii. 150, iii. 155, Νῖνος) is a compound with the root נן (cf. Assyr. *nûnu*, 'fish' [Del. *Assyr. Handwörterb.* 1896, p. 454*a*], Aram. נוּנָא, ܢܘܢܐ, *e.g.* Jon 2¹· ¹¹). For the oft-recurring ideographic way of writing the name of this city characterizes it as *Ni-nu-a* or *Ni-na-a*, 'fish-dwelling.' Hence in the first element of the name we should not be disposed to find '*ni*, Fett, Fettigkeit, Ueberfluss' (Frd. Delitzsch, art. 'Ninive' in *PRE*² x. 589). It may be not impossible that *nun*, which on account of the following *nua* might be differentiated, or through *n* (cf. *Lehrgebäude*, ii. 510 f. and נן) modified to *nin*, has been combined with *nua* or *naa*, and thus arose *Ni-nu-a* or *Ni-na-a*.

5. *The Date of the Book.*—This symbolical narrative was written, not in the 8th cent., but in the post-exilic period.

(*a*) Literary arguments. The story contains no positive trace that it attributed itself to Jonah. On the contrary, the book speaks of Jonah in the *third* person everywhere except in the *oratio directa* of 1⁹ 2³ff. etc. Of course the circumstance that in any writing a name is used in the *third* person, is no sure sign that that writing proceeds from a different author (cf. König, *Einleitung*, p. 314⁴ on Is 7). But, all the same, it is not without significance that Hosea, who opens with the *third* person, in the further course of his story passes to the use of the *first* person; cf. 'Then spake J″ to *me*' (Hos 3¹⁻³) with 'Then came the word of J″ to *Jonah*' (Jon 3¹ etc.).

(*b*) Linguistic indications. The Book of Hosea shows what phase of development the Heb. language had reached in the Northern kingdom in the 8th cent. But the linguistic character of the Book of Jonah is quite different from this. In Hosea the occurrences of *anokhi* to *ani* are as 11 : 11, whereas in Jonah the ratio is 2 (1⁹ 3²) : 5

($1^9 \cdot ^{12}$ $2^{5 \cdot 10}$ 4^{11}); cf. in Malachi 1 *anokhî* (אָנֹכִי הִנֵּה 3^{23}) to 8 *anî*. In Hosea we find only אֲשֶׁר (some eight times), whereas in Jonah שׁ is found (these passages are wanting in Mandelkern's *Concordance*, 1291 ff., but are given in König's *Syntax*, § 54) three times, $1^{7 \cdot 12}$ 4^{10}, as in Ezr 8^{20}, 1 Ch 5^{20} 27^{27}, Ec 1^3 etc. But in Jonah there occurs לְ בַּאֲשֶׁר (1^8) * side by side with בְּשֶׁל ($1^{7 \cdot 12}$), while in Ec 8^{17} the secondary form אֲשֶׁר בְּשֶׁל already appears (König, *Syntax*, § 389e).——רִבּוֹ ('myriad') has not been recognized by tradition in Hos 8^{12}, probably, indeed, on the authority of MSS (see König, *Lehrgeb.* ii. 222[1]); yet in Ezekiel (16^7) we have the genuinely Hebrew word רְבָבָה, whereas רִבּוֹ occurs in Jon 4^{11}, Ps 68^{18}, Ezr $2^{64 \cdot 69}$, Neh $7^{66 \cdot 71f.}$, Dn 11^{12}, 1 Ch 29^7.——הִתְעַשֵּׁת = *cogitare* in Jon 1^6, cf. Dn 6^4 and Hos 10^{13} Targ., אִתְעַשְׁתּוּן.——'J', the God of heaven' is found in Gn $24^{3 \cdot 7}$ (overlooked by G. A. Smith, ii. 497[2]), Jon 1^9, Ezr 1^2, Neh 1^5, 2 Ch 36^{23}, and the simple 'God of heaven' in Ps 136^{26}, Ezr $5^{11f. 6 9f.}$ $7^{12 \cdot 21 \cdot 23}$, Neh 1^4 2^4, Dn $2^{18f. 37. 44}$.——The notion of 'command' (verb) does not occur at all in Hosea, but it is difficult to imagine that he would have expressed it by מִנָּה (Jon 2^1 4^{6-8}, 1 Ch 9^{29}, Dn $1^{5 \cdot 10f.}$ [Aram.], Ezr 7^{25} etc.), for he expresses 'command' (noun) by צַו (5^{11}) and not by טְעֵם (Jon 3^7 [Aram.], Ezr 4^{19} etc., Dn 3^{10} etc.). — Cf., further, חֲסָק = *consēdit*, *siluit* (Jon $1^{11f.}$, Ps 107^{30}, Pr 26^{20}) common in Aramaic (Merx, *Chrest. Targ.* 294; Nöldeke, *ZDMG*, 1868, p. 499). Taking all this into account, it is an unnatural supposition that the author of the Book of Jonah should have exhibited all the above-mentioned linguistic features to a reader of the 8th cent. B.C. He must have belonged to a period when the *written* language of the Israelites had already come into close contact with the Aramaic.

(*c*) Material indications. Nineveh, at the time when the Book of Jonah was composed, was no longer in existence. This is clear from the statement (3^3), 'Now Nineveh *was* (הָיְתָה, cf. König, *Syntax*, § 362m) a great city for God' (*i.e.* according even to a superhuman standard). Hävernick (*Einl.* ii. 2, p. 359) declined to accept this interpretation, and appealed to Gn 1^2 וָבֹהוּ תֹהוּ הָיְתָה וְהָאָרֶץ. But even this passage confirms the above as the correct explanation of Jon 3^3. For to the writer of Gn 1^2 the earth was no longer a chaos. Further, the 'three days' journey' of 3^3, taken in connexion with 'and Jonah began to *enter into* the city one day's journey' (*Syntax*, § 330e), must refer to the distance *through*, not *round*, the city (Schrader, *KAT*[2] *ad loc.*). A diameter of such proportions would, however, presuppose a circumference such as even the combination of four cities (Gn $10^{11f.}$, *Keilinsch. Bibliot.* ii. 117) could not have possessed. Then it would be strange that Jonah himself or a contemporary of his should not have given the name of the 'king of Nineveh' (3^6) in question. Besides this, Sayce (*HCM* 487, quoted by Driver, *LOT*[6] 322) is of opinion that the title 'king of Nineveh' could never have been applied to him while the Assyrian empire was still in existence.

(*d*) Arguments drawn from the history of the formation of the OT Canon. (*a*) In the so-called *prophetæ priores* of the OT there is no word of Jonah's journey to Nineveh (2 K 14^{25}). Nor in the latter passage is there any reference to *other*

* It is improbable that the words לָנוּ הַזֹּאת הָרָעָה לְמִי בַּאֲשֶׁר were originally a 'marginal gloss' (so Kautzsch, *AT*; Nowack, *Kl. Proph.*, *ad loc.*; G. A. Smith, ii. 513). For if בְּשֶׁלְּמִי (v.7) were to be explained, the marginal gloss would have been simply לְמִי בַּאֲשֶׁר, the whole sentence would not have been written on the margin. Moreover, the sentence is not absolutely superfluous in v.⁸. Rather is the question there quite intelligible psychologically as an indirect introduction to the following questions. It is equally intelligible why the question *propter quem hæc calamitas nobis acciderit*, being an *apparent* repetition, should have been omitted in cod. B of the LXX.

words of Jonah, such as is intended to the Book of Micah in 1 K 22^{28} כֻּלָּם עַמִּים שְׁמְעוּ וַיֹּאמֶר (cf. König, *Einleitung*, 330 f.).——(*β*) The order of the *prophetæ posteriores*, and especially of the Minor Prophets, was only in its general principles a fixed one. This order was not meant to be chronological (König, *Einleit.* 301). The collectors of the Canon did not intend the books which have no chronological superscription to be considered as belonging to the period mentioned in the nearest preceding book which bears a date. For, on the one hand, in the case of the Book of Amos, the chronological superscription of the Book of Hosea is repeated, and, on the other hand, it cannot be meant that Nahum and Habakkuk prophesied at the date assigned to the preceding book (Mic 1^1). Therefore it may be assumed that the Book of Jonah was inserted after the Book of Obadiah on the ground, not of its chronology, but of its contents. Might it not have been supposed that the words בַּגּוֹיִם שָׁלַח צִיר ('nuntius ad gentes missus est') found a clear illustration in the story of Jonah? Moreover, in the centuries after the Exile, it was the fate of the Edomites that formed the subject of the liveliest discussion (cf. Mal 1^4, 1 Es $4^{45 \cdot 50}$, Sir $50^{25f.}$). Hence it is probable that the question why the threats pronounced against Edom had remained unfulfilled was intended to be answered in the Book of Jonah.——(*γ*) Again, the opening words וַיְהִי יְהוָה דְּבַר וְ appear to the present writer to contain an indirect allusion (*Syntax*, § 368a) to the Book of Obadiah, and to have an adversative force (*ib.* § 369f). This introduction to the Book of Jonah appears, then, to have originated when the book attained its present position in the Heb. and Gr. OT. On the other hand, probability is lacking to the theory of Budde (*ZATW*, 1892, p. 41) that the Book of Jonah was originally an extract from the 'Midrash to the Book of Kings' (2 Ch 24^{27}). For, in the first place, the story of Jon $1^{1ff.}$ would not have fitted well on to 2 K $14^{25f.}$. In the second place, this story, whose incidents are enacted wholly outside the political history and the land of Israel, would not have been at all suitable in the הַמְּלָכִים סֵפֶר מִדְרָשׁ. Not so clear is the justice of the remark of Nowack (1897, on Jon 1^1) that the Chronicles do not breathe the spirit which the supposed Midrash would have exhibited.——(*δ*) The Book of the Twelve Minor Prophets was included among the 'prophets' or 'prophecies' which already lay before Ben-Sirach (Prologue ll. 6 and 14), for 49^{10} reads καὶ τῶν δώδεκα προφητῶν τὰ ὀστᾶ ἀναθάλοι ἐκ τοῦ τόπου αὐτῶν, or, in the recently published Heb. text of the Sirach fragments, וְ הַנְּבִיאִים עָשָׂר שְׁנֵים ב. Against the view of Jacob (*ZATW*, 1887, p. 280) that 49^{10} is an interpolation, Nöldeke (*ZATW*, 1888, p. 156), Buhl (*Kanon u. Text*, 1891, p. 11), and Wellhausen (*Skizzen*, v. 211) have declared themselves. Not without importance is also the question whether the πάππος of Ben-Sirach (to whom we owe the Greek translation of the Proverbs of Sirach) and the Prologue to the book flourished as early as *c.* B.C. 300. The present writer claims to have proved this in his *Einleitung* (1893, p. 488), and his conclusions are now accepted also by J. Halévy (*Étude sur la partie du texte hébreu de l'Ecclésiastique récemment découverte*, 1897) and Baethgen (*Hand-commentar zu den Psalmen*[2], 1897, p. xxvii). This circumstance forbids one to carry down the composition of the Book of Jonah beyond the year B.C. 300, as G. A. Smith (ii. 498) is inclined to do.

In the above sections (3–5) we have sought, from the oldest indications, to characterize the Book of Jonah *positively*. What follows will give the *negative* supplement to this.

6. *The principal other interpretations of the Book of Jonah.*

(a) The symbolical character of such a narrative, although in all probability this *is* the character of the Book of Jonah, might readily be *missed*. For it is psychologically explicable how histories which are related as concrete occurrences should preferably be understood by many as an account of real events. As a matter of fact, this has happened in not a few instances. For instance, has not the story of the dead bones (Ezk 37¹⁻¹⁴) been very frequently understood (cf. Hitzig, *Bib. Theol.* 1880, p. 109) as if we had to do with literal dead bodies? And that notwithstanding the explanation of the bones in v.¹¹ 'These bones are the *whole* house of Israel.' How often, again, are the stories of the hiding of the girdle (Jer 13³⁻⁷) and of the marrying of an adulterous wife (Hos 3¹ᶠ·) understood as real history! Accordingly, the fact that this may have happened also in the case of the Book of Jonah is no proof of the non-symbolical character of the latter.

(b) Certainly, those who collected the Canon or those who arranged the Δωδεκαπρόφητον may still have rightly regarded the Book of Jonah as a symbolical narrative, for they placed it in a class of writings containing other examples of symbolical character and prophetic tendency. But at a later period the book was frequently treated as if it contained *non-symbolical* history. At the same time, in examining the evidence on this point, one has to exercise great caution. The authors in question may simply have *expressed* themselves with a natural brevity, *as if they* considered the history of Jonah a real affair. This principle may be applied to every instance where some element in the Book of Jonah is merely cited. This may be the case where Jesus Christ (Mt 12⁴⁰) illustrated his burial by the statement that it would continue only three days, like the sojourn of Jonah in the belly of the sea-monster. But the following saying (v.⁴¹), that the men of Nineveh would, on the day of judgment, put to shame the contemporaries of Jesus, is most naturally interpreted on the presupposition that the story of Jonah was a non-symbolical one. Still, the question remains whether this presupposition was merely that of the *hearers* of Jesus (see further, below, 6 d δ, p. 751ᵇ). The history of Jonah is, however, conceived as *non-symbolical* when into the mouth of Tobit * are put the words, πέπεισμαι ὅσα ἐλάλησεν Ἰωνᾶς ὁ προφήτης περὶ Νινευή (To 14⁴), and πάντως ἔσται ἃ ἐλάλησεν ὁ προφήτης Ἰωνᾶς (v.⁸). Philo, too, regarded the story of Jonah as non-symbolical, for he took pains to explain the marvel of the fish (*Orat. de Jona*, § 16, 21). The same interpretation is followed in 3 Mac 6⁸ (cf. König, *Einleit.* p. 483) and in Jos. *Ant.* IX. x. 2. According to the latter, Ἰωνᾶς εἰς Ταρσὸν ἔπλει τῆς Κιλικίας (!), and he reproduces the whole contents of the Book of Jonah, with the exception of the displeasure of Jonah at the sparing of Nineveh. So also in the Mishna, *Ta'anit* ii. 1,† Bab. *Ta'anit* 15a, *Nedarim* 38a, where וַיִּפֶּן שְׂכָרָהּ (Jon 1³) is incorrectly understood as if Jonah had paid the price of the whole ship (שֶׁל סְפִינָה כּוּלָהּ), and had thus, in contrast to Amos, been a wealthy man. (For other passages see B. Wolf, *op. cit.* p. 6). Jewish tradition, however, contains also the information that the history contained in the Book of Jonah was enacted in the reign of Osnappar (Ezr 4¹⁰ [Assurbanipal?]), and, seeing that the date of Jeroboam II. and that of Osnappar were different, the rabbinical tradition spoke of two Jonahs, of whom the first was of the tribe of Zebulun and the second of the tribe of Asher (see, further, Fürst, *Der Kanon d. AT nach*

* This book was written before the renovation of Herod's temple (König, *Einleitung*, p. 478).

† לֹא נֶאֱמַר בְּאַנְשֵׁי נִינְוֵה וַיַּרְא אֱלֹהִים אֶת שַׂקָּם וְאֶת תַּעֲנִיתָם אֶלָּא וַיַּרְא הָאֱלֹהִים אֶת מַעֲשֵׂיהֶם וְגוֹ' (Jon 3¹⁰).

d. Ueberlief. in Talm. und Midrasch, p. 33 f.). Again, in *Numeri Rabbah*, sect. 18, the Book of Jonah is called 'a book by itself and counted separately.' This, however, was simply 'because it is exclusively occupied with the heathen, and Israel is not mentioned in it. But that its canonicity was doubted in earlier times there is no evidence' (Wildeboer-Bacon, *Origin of Canon of OT*, 1895, 70–72). The *non-symbolical* or *externo-historical* interpretation of the story of Jonah is the predominating one also among the Christians of the earlier centuries (cf., *inter alios*, Justin Martyr, *Dialog. c. Tryph.* cap. 107).

(c) But gradually questions were everywhere raised about the authenticity of the ancient tradition, and in connexion with this began also the examination of the externo-historical interpretation of the Book of Jonah. The natural clearness of Luther's way of thinking is seen in his judgment upon at least the prayer of Jon 2³⁻¹⁰ 'He was not so comfortably placed as to be able to indite so fine a poem.' Continued examination of the book did not lead all critics (see above, 4 b) to a symbolical interpretation of the story. Some reached, by means of almost ludicrous * attempts, the third of the leading explanations of the Book of Jonah. This attributes a legendary character to the story, and may therefore itself be called, for shortness, *the legendary interpretation of the Book of Jonah*. Its chief representatives are the following.

Already (in his *Einleit.*⁴ iv. § 576) Eichhorn discovered in the book the presentation of a 'folk-tale.' He pointed to the fact that in 2¹ᶠ·, as compared with ch. 1, the narrative is 'quite interrupted, short, incomplete, and unsatisfying.' Hence he held that 'under such circumstances it is no arbitrary hypothesis to assume merely that Jonah, mounted upon the sea-monster, was driven ashore by the storm, and to regard the three days' sojourn in the fish's belly as a popular clothing of this.' 'If the story of Jonah's escape upon the sea-monster . . . was handed on from mouth to mouth . . . for several centuries, how readily might it assume its present form! This is also in harmony with the spirit of the ancient world, as we may gather from the similar clothing given to similar occurrences in Greek history, *e.g.* to the history of Hercules' (see the Greek quotations in Bochart, *Hierozoicon*, ii. 5, 12). The *legendary* interpretation is accepted, further, by Rosenmüller (*Scholia in Vet. Test.*, ad Jonam); Knobel (*Der Prophetismus d. Heb.* ii. 370ff.); de Wette (*Einleit.* § 291); Winer (*RL, s.v.* 'Jona'); Vatke (*Einleit.*, 1886, § 217, 'a legend'); Nowack (*Klein. Proph.*, 1897, p. 175, 'we have before us a prophetic legend'). Essentially similar is the judgment of von Orelli (1896, p. 93 f.), who says, for instance, 'The marvel of the fish was certainly received from tradition,' but 'the story in its present form was written at the close of the Chaldæan or the opening of the Persian period.' But if the book simply contained a 'Prophetenlegende,' this would in the tradition have involuntarily and unconsciously taken its rise, and then the evident didactic tendency of the book would not be adequately explained. Hence Nowack asserts that 'the author used freedom in moulding the traditional material as suited his aim.' But in that case the contents of the

* Not Abravanel (cf. Wolf, *op. cit.* p. 6, note 4, against Hävernick, *Einleit.* ii. 2, p. 327), but H. Ad. Grimm (*Der Proph. Jona aufs neue übersetzt*, etc.), supposed that Jonah *dreamed* that he was swallowed by a great fish. Clericus, again, threw out the suggestion (*Bibliot. anc. et mod.*, tome xx. 2, p. 459) that Jonah 'was picked up by a *ship* whose figurehead was a whale' ; while Anton (in Paulus' *Neues Repertorium*, Bd. iii. p. 36 ff.) supposed that Jonah *clung* to the belly of the fish. See, for more fancies of the same kind, Eichhorn, *Einleit.*⁴ Bd. iv. § 575.

book might be called simply 'the free use of an ancient prophetic legend' (Kautzsch, *Abriss d. Gesch. d. alttest. Schriftthums*, 1897, p. 120). It is more likely, however, that the book has no ancient history for basis.

Many upholders of this *legendary* interpretation, in dealing with particular features of the Book of Jonah, have appealed to *legends and myths of antiquity*. In the first place, they have reminded us that it was in the neighbourhood of Joppa that Andromeda, too, was reduced to straits by a sea-monster (Jos. *BJ* III. ix. 3, ἔνθα τῶν Ἀνδρομέδας δεσμῶν ἔτι δεικνύμενοι τύποι πιστοῦνται τὴν ἀρχαιότητα τοῦ μύθου; cf. on Andromeda also W. R. Smith, *RS* 159, and Duhm, *Kurzer Hdcom.*, 1897, on Job 7¹²). But this tale agrees with the story of Jonah in the single point of the locality, Joppa (יָפוֹ, Ἰόππη), and the latter was the natural one to fix upon in the case of a man fleeing from Palestine to the Mediterranean. Still less can the 'legend' of Jonah be derived from the story of the Trojan princess Hesione, who was delivered by Hercules from a sea-monster (*Il.* xx. 145 ff., xxi. 441 ff.). For the features of this tale, which in some measure resemble the history of Jonah, were all produced at a much later date, and hence it is far easier to see here a modification of the story of Jonah than to suppose that the author of the latter borrowed from that foreign tale (cf. Hitzig's third 'Vorbemerkung' to his *Commentar über Jona*). Finally, F. C. Baur, above all, has connected (Ilgen's *Zeitschrift*, 1837, p. 102 ff.) the story of Jonah with the Babylono-Assyrian myth of Oannes. On this see further, below, p. 751, note *.

(*d*) But even the *externo-historical* interpretation of the Book of Jonah has found defenders down to the most recent times. Of these we may mention first, Frz. Kaulen, representing the traditionalist Roman Catholic Church (*Einleit. in d. heil. Schrift*, 1892, § 414), then C. F. Keil (*Einleit.*, 1873, § 89), and J. Kennedy (*On the Book of Jonah*, 1895). This standpoint may perhaps be best characterized in some such way as the following :—

(*a*) Features which point to the didactic character of the story of Jonah are not sufficiently taken into account even by the most recent representatives of the *externo-historical* interpretation. To begin with, the circumstance is significant that the book closes with the presentation of a general truth (against B. Wolf, *op. cit.* p. 28). Cf., further, what has been said above (p. 746ᵃ) on the interpolation of the prayer (Jon 2³⁻¹⁰). Again, the repentance of the city of Nineveh is depicted with such grotesque features that the intention of the writer to indicate the didactic tendency of the narrative appears sufficiently clear. For, not to speak of the king sitting in ashes (3⁶ᵇ), the very beasts are also mentioned as partaking in the fast and the mourning (3⁷ᶠ·). This command that 'the cattle, the oxen, and the sheep should eat nothing and should drink no water,' and that 'man and beast' (see above, p. 745ᵇ) should put on sackcloth, is not to be co-ordinated with the custom whereby at the death of Masistios the Persians cut off their own hair and that of the horses and beasts of burden (Herodot. ix. 24 ; Plutarch, *Aristides*, cap. 14, ἔκειραν ἐπὶ τῷ Μασιστίῳ καὶ ἵππους καὶ ἡμιόνους), or the custom mentioned by Chrysostom of harnessing horses with black trappings to a hearse. Further, Kleinert (*ad loc.*) refers to the mourning which, according to the myth (cf. Virgil, *Eclog.* v. 19 ff.), was held over the death of Daphnis. But by his reference Kleinert himself unconsciously concedes that the representation in Jon 3⁷ᶠ· can be compared only with an *un*real occurrence. Moreover, the complaint of Jonah about the gourd (4⁸ᵇ) is put into such hyperbolical language ('for me death is better than life'), that one is compelled

to assume that the writer did not mean the complaint to be understood as a serious one. Again, the narrator puts in the mouth of the prophet the statement that he does 'right' (הֵיטֵב) to be angry over the loss of the gourd, 'even unto death.' But is this not to depict him as an ill-natured child who sulks over the loss of a toy? Certainly, it is not without ground that Ant. Baumgarten, in his *L'humour dans l'ancien Testament* (1896, p. 27¹), has adduced 'Jonah, angry even unto death at having seen the gourd perish,' as fit to be included in the category he is dealing with.

(*β*) Elements in the story, which upon the symbolical interpretation explain themselves, are wrongly *weakened* by the adherents of the *externo-historical* interpretation. For instance, the expression 'three days and three nights' (Jon 2¹) indicates by its twofold mention of the number 'three' that the writer has in view a small 'numerus rotundus' (cf. Ex 20⁵, 2 K 11⁵ᶠ·, Ezk 5², Zec 13⁸ᶠ· etc.; specially '*three* days', Gn 40¹⁰·¹² 42¹⁷, Ex 10²² 19¹¹, Jos 1¹¹ 2¹⁶· ²², 2 S 24¹³, 1 K 12⁵, 2 K 20⁵, Hos 6², Jon 2¹, Est 4¹⁶, Mt 16²¹ ; '*three* months' or 'years,' Ex 2², Lv 19²³, Is 16¹⁴ 20³, Dn 1⁵ etc. ; cf. Röckerath, *Bib. Chronol.*, 1865, 11 ff., also Rud. Hirzel, 'Rundzahlen' in *Abhand. d. sächs. Gessell. d. Wissensch.*, Leipzig, 1885). The author would not have specified in detail '*three* days and *three* nights,' if he had meant merely one day along with part of the preceding and the following day. Hence his meaning cannot have been 'a period of 37 hours' (Kaulen, *Einleit.* § 414). Such an interpretation of the text (Jon 2¹) can by no means be built upon 1 S 30¹²ᶠ·, Est 4¹⁶ 5¹ (against Kleinert and v. Orelli, *ad loc.*), which is opposed also by the expression 'seven days and seven nights' of Job 2¹³.——The representatives of the *externo-historical* interpretation appeal, further, to narratives according to which the gigantic shark *carcharias* has been known to swallow a man or even a horse whole—nay, to have vomited up a tunny fish and the body of a sailor undecomposed (Kaulen, *Einleit.* § 414). In an occurrence of this kind, which is most correctly related by Eichhorn (*Einleit.*⁴ iv. 340 f.), a ' "Seehund," after taking a sailor in its jaws, immediately of its own accord threw him out again, and he was picked up alive and only slightly injured.' Here we miss the 'three days and three nights.' Or we read in the *Neue Luth. Kirchenzeitung* (1895, p. 303 f.), that the whale-hunter, James Bartley, was in February 1891 swallowed by a whale, and that on the following day, when the animal was killed, he was taken alive out of its stomach. ' He lay in a swoon in the belly of the whale. The sailors had much difficulty in restoring him to consciousness. It was not till after three months' nursing that James Bartley recovered his reason.' But, granting the truth of this story, the Jonah of the OT was longer in the belly of the fish than James Bartley, and, so far from there being any word of illness or subsequent nursing, he is said even in the fish's belly to have indited a song of thanksgiving. This point is overlooked also by B. Wolf, *op. cit.*——Here also, finally, comes in the following point. The text (Jon 4¹⁰) says that the gourd 'tanquam filius noctis factus est et tanquam (cf. König, *Syntax*, § 332k) filius noctis (alterius) periit (so also Pesh.). The words בִּן־לַיְלָה הָיָה necessarily imply that the gourd was the product of a single night (Targ. בְּלֵילְיָא חֲדָן הֲוָא ; LXX ἣ ὑπὸ νύκτα ἐγενήθη). But Kaulen (*Einleit.* § 414) denies this sense to the text. He says, 'The plant simply grew out of the earth overnight, and must otherwise have followed the ordinary course of development.' But in that case the *kîḳayôn* would not have a full claim to the title 'filius noctis.' Further, the verb הָיָה, as the opposite of אָבַד, must have the sense of 'factus est.' Again, the meaning of v.[6] is that the ḳiḳayôn straightway in the early morning furnished a shade for Jonah; and in any case, according to v.[7], its existence was only for a single day. For at dawn of the following day (לַעֲלוֹת הַשַּׁחַר) it was smitten to death, and, when the sun rose, Jonah was without his shade.

(γ) But even the legendary interpretation of the Book of Jonah has not been refuted by the representatives of the *externo-historical* interpretation, for they have been unable to explain away the traces of the late date at which the story of Jonah was committed to writing. Can they give an adequate explanation, *e.g.*, of why the name of the Assyrian king is not mentioned, or why he is entitled 'king of Nineveh'? Can they prove that Jonah himself could have penned the statement, 'Now Nineveh *was*,' etc., or the specification of the extent of Nineveh (3[3])? On the last-mentioned point Kaulen (*Einleit*, § 414) says, 'The greatness of the city is stated as of three days' journey, either as meaning that a length of three days' journey is attributed to it, or that three days are considered necessary to visit it thoroughly (!). Both meanings are perfectly correct, according as the application of the name "Nineveh" is taken.' But the expression used in 3[3b] can, according to v.[4], refer only to the diameter of the city (see above, p. 748[a]). But the diameter even of the fourfold city (Gn 10[11]) was not equal to a three days' journey. 'The length of the road from Kouyunjik to Nimrod is only some 20 English miles. Hence the prophet after *one* day's journey would have been exactly at the other end of the city' (Frd. Delitzsch, art. 'Ninive' in *PRE*[2] x. 598).——Instead of taking into account these indications in the text, B. Wolf (*op. cit.*) lays emphasis upon the fact that, according to the Arab.-Syr. *History of the Prophet Jonah*, God announced pardon to the Ninevites by dispersing a darkness which hung over the city. Wolf (p. 32) at once infers that this must refer to the eclipse of the sun, which, according to the Assyrian Eponym list, took place in the year B.C. 763. But that later note about the dispelling of a darkness was an addition that lay ready to hand, whereby a visible token might be given of the appeasing of the Divine wrath. In any case, there is nothing about this in the biblical Book of Jonah. Hence it is an arbitrary assertion of Wolf (p. 31) that 'in the tradition of the neighbourhood the record of the eclipse was combined with the story of Jonah.' The author of the Arab.-Syr. *History of Jonah* did not mean darkness caused by an eclipse of the sun. Wolf might have recognized this from the fact that Ephraem Syrus says (*op. cit.* p. 38) that 'the darkness overhung Nineveh during the whole period of penitential mourning.'——In 2 K 8[7ff.], which is cited by B. Wolf (*op. cit.* p. 13), it is recorded that Elisha was in Damascus. But it is not said that he went there as a missionary, and, besides, 2 K 8[7] furnishes no positive basis for the reality of the details of the Book of Jonah.——Hommel (*AHT* p. 145) says, 'One sees from names like "Father is Aï (or Ja)" that the Israelitish tradition that Jonah preached Jahweh to the Ninevites is not so absurd as according to our modern critics it appears.' But, instead of abusing the critics, it would have been well if he had read the text accurately. The Book of Jonah says not a word about Jonah's preaching 'Jahweh' to the inhabitants of Nineveh. Rather is the name 'Jahweh' avoided, and it is said, 'They believed God' (אֱלֹהִים, 3[5a], so also [8. 9a. 10a]).

(δ) The NT passages involved have also frequently an incorrect meaning and an unnecessary scope attributed to them by the upholders of the *externo-historical* interpretation. *First*, it may be assumed that Jesus, in regard to the literary history of the OT, attached Himself to the notions of His contemporaries. There are certain proofs that He did so in regard to other notions that prevailed then. Not only did He speak of the rising of the sun (Mt 13[6], Mk 16[2], cf. Ja 1[11]), not only did He call the grain of mustard seed the smallest of all seeds (Mt 13[31] ‖ Mk 4[31], Lk 13[19]), because this was then the popular opinion (Lightfoot, *Horæ* ad Mt 13[31]), but in other matters too He had regard to the inferior knowledge or positive ignorance of His contemporaries. In particular, He paid the temple tax, ἵνα μὴ σκανδαλίζωμεν αὐτούς (Mt 17[27]). That is to say, although as υἱὸς τοῦ βασιλέως (v.[25f.]) He was free from the obligation, He paid the tax because the priests would not have recognized the right reason of His refusal to pay, and He would thus have given them an occasion of stumbling. For this reason He preferred to make a concession to their opinions. Now, as Christ, in astronomical, botanical, and other matters, placed Himself on the level of His contemporaries, so might He do in regard to the literary conceptions of His age. For the fulfilment of His religious mission, He required to oppose only such opinions as directly concerned the notion of the true kingdom of God—μετάνοια, πίστις, and δικαιοσύνη τοῦ θεοῦ.——*Secondly*, it is the great εὐσεβείας μυστήριον (1 Ti 3[16]) of the Person of Christ that He was as much true man as true God. He advanced in wisdom (Lk 2[40. 52]), He learned (ἔμαθεν, He 5[8]), He did not know the date of His παρουσία (Mt 24[36], Mk 13[32]); cf. Ph 2[7f.]. These data of the NT must be taken into account, even by a believing Christian. But J. Kennedy (*op. cit.* p. 57 f.) mentions none of these actual testimonies of the NT.——*Thirdly*, we have to observe that the Evangelists differ in their report of what Jesus said about the Book of Jonah. In Mt 12[39-41] it is recorded that the Νινευῖται μετενόησαν εἰς τὸ κήρυγμα Ἰωνᾶ. It is not said in Mt that Jonah was a σημεῖον *for the Ninevites*, a statement which occurs only in Lk 11[30], ἐγένετο Ἰωνᾶς τοῖς Νινευίταις σημεῖον. Matthew's account, however, must be the original one, for Luke also adds afterwards (v.[32]) that the Ninevites repented *in consequence of the preaching* of Jonah. Matthew's report, further, corresponds exactly to the narrative in the Book of Jonah, in which all that is said is that Jonah was to *preach* (קְרָא עַל, 1[1] 3[1]), and that by his cry, 'Yet forty days,' etc. (3[4]), he awakened the faith of the Ninevites. But in the Book of Jonah there is not a word to the effect that Jonah exercised any influence upon the inhabitants of Nineveh by the strangeness of his garb or the wonderful experiences he had passed through. All this, again, is silently passed over by J. Kennedy (pp. 27, 50 f.), and yet he assumes as beyond question that Jonah did not come to Nineveh as 'an unknown stranger,' but that 'his entombment in the body of a great fish, and his deliverance from that prison, was known to the people.' If that was so, the narrator of the history of Jonah has omitted a most essential point.[*] This is not the only instance in which

---

[*] The same judgment must be passed on the learned essay of H. Clay Trumbull, *Jonah in Nineveh* (Philadelphia, 1892). He starts rightly with the question, 'Where in the OT or the NT except in the Book of Jonah is there such a seemingly unnecessary miracle as the saving of a man's life by having him swallowed in a fish, instead, say, of having the vessel that carried him driven back by contrary winds to the place of its starting?' (p. 6). But 'it is well to ask if there is anything in the modern disclosures of Assyrian life and history that would seem to render the miraculous element in the story of Jonah more reasonable and the marvellous effect of his preaching at Nineveh more explicable and natural' (p. 7). Trumbull reminds us that 'prominent among the divinities of ancient Assyria was Dagan, a creature part man part fish' (p. 7), and 'according to Berosus, the very beginning of civilization in Chaldæa was under the direction of a personage, part man and part fish, who came up out of the sea' (p. 9). Trumbull now suggests that Jonah appeared to the Ninevites as one of the 'Avatars or incarnations' of Dagan (p. 10). But this is *ab initio* improbable, for

J. Kennedy makes alterations on the contents of the Book of Jonah. According to the latter, God said to Jonah, 'Preach the preaching that I bid thee' (3[1b]), and this preaching was, 'Yet forty days and Nineveh is overthrown' (v.[4b]). But Kennedy says, 'The preaching of Jonah was not a mere wild monotone, "Yet forty days and Nineveh shall be destroyed." He could find a fresh text in every street and thoroughfare.'

7. *The idea of the book.*—Whatever view one takes of the formal character and origin of the book, the ideas embodied in it are the same.

(*a*) The *main* idea is the following. Israel has been intrusted by God with the mission to call the *goyîm* also to moral amendment, and is not to look askance or to be jealous if the *goyîm* manifest repentance and if God takes back the threatenings which He had pronounced against them. With this principal idea the book opens, whether one regards 'Jonah the son of Amittai' as the representative of his nation or as an individual, and the same idea is reflected also in the whole course of the narrative and in the closing words of the book. The story of Jonah thus gives expression to those lofty thoughts which are uttered also in Is 40–66. For the 'Servant of J"' (Is 42[1]) must be the same who in 41[8] is expressly called יִשְׂרָאֵל עַבְדִּי, and of this Servant of J" it is said, 'I have made him for a light of the *goyîm*' (42[4. 6f.] 49[1-6] etc., cf. also Zec 8[23], Sir 24[30] ἐκφανῶ αὐτὰ [the contents of the νόμος] ἕως εἰς μακράν, see above, p. 747[a]). The Book of Jonah was meant, then, to proclaim the universality of the Divine plan of salvation, and to serve as a protest against the particularist tendencies which now and then led many members of the people of Israel to strive to narrow the boundaries of the Divine kingdom of grace. The book is thus a brilliant example of the diametrical opposite of the spirit which condemned the foreign wives (Mal 2[11], Ezr 9[1ff.] 10[1ff.], Neh 13[23ff.], cf. Est 9[13]), and exhibits a lovely dawn preparing the way for the clear day of the gospel (Jn 3[16], Gal 3[28] etc.).—— Similar to the above is the idea that has before now been extracted by many from the Book of Jonah. Even Ephraem Syrus discovered the primary purpose of the book to be to bring back the Ninevites to God (cf. B. Wolf, p. 36). Eichhorn (*Einleit.* iv. 351) expressed the opinion that 'the book is a proof that God has shown his concern also for the heathen by sending them direct messengers.' Essentially the same is the view of Alb. Rebattu (1875, p. 6), 'Docet, Deum non solum Judæis sed omnibus gentibus, dummodo gratia divina dignæ sint, benevolentiam suam præbere'; of Bleek (1878, § 229); of Reuss (*Geschichte*, 1890, § 408); of Renan (*Hist.* iii. 512, 'universalist school'); of Kaulen (*Einleit.*, 1892, § 412); of v. Orelli (1896); of Strack (1898). With perfect correctness also G. A. Smith (ii. 501) remarks, 'The purpose is to illustrate the mission of prophecy to the Gentiles, God's care for them, and their susceptibility to His word.'

Jonah came to Nineveh *not* as 'a personage part man and part fish.' But the main point is the following :—If God had saved Jonah by means of a fish, in order that the inhabitants of Nineveh might take him for an incarnation of the Dagan, then God would have *strengthened* the Ninevites in their faith in the fish-god Dagan. This would have been an unjustifiable 'concession' (p. 16). Nor is it the case that God caused the star (Mt 2[2]) to shine forth on account of the Magi. Besides, Trumbull's attempt (p. 14, note 1) to connect Jonah and Oannes is scarcely possible. In the event of such a connexion, we should rather have expected the form 'Ιωᾶ to be retained. Why should the change have been made from Jonah to יוֹנָן (*Johanan*, 'Ιωανάν)? On the contrary, a more probable derivation of the name Oannes is that proposed by Lenormant (Oannes= *Éa-ḫan*) or by Tiele (= *Éa-vannu*). Finally, in his account of the place-name *Nebi Yunas* (p. 17), Trumbull appears to have turned his attention too little to the Jewish diaspora and the Syrian Christians (see, on Nahum and Habakkuk, König, *Einleitung*, pp. 333, 352).

(*b*) Others have asserted that the theme of the book is a magnifying of the compassion of God. Already we hear Philo say (*Orat. de Jona*, § 2), 'Sicut in arte medicinæ peritissimi salvare ægrotos promittentes, igne et aqua regunt eriguntque, similiter sapientissimus ille, solus salvator, deperditionem indicens ac ruinam, misericordiam construit salutis.' Cf. also § 53, 'Sicut pristina vita duram merebat prædicationem, similiter pœnitentia eorum ex adverso benignitatem.' Upon this view, the Book of Jonah would be an illustration of Jer 18[7-10], where the conditional character of predictions is explained. This was the view accepted also by the Midrash *Yalkut* on Jonah, which closed with the words, באותה שעה נפל על פניו ואמר הנהג עולמך במדת הרחמים דכתיב לה' אלק' הרחמים והסליחות, *i.e.* 'At that moment Jonah fell upon his face, and spoke [to God], Guide thy world by the norm of mercy, as it is written,' etc. [Dn 9[9]]. The *Yalkut* was followed by the above-named Arab.-Syr. *History of the Prophet Jonah* (Wolf, p. 27). Also D. Kimchi in his *Commentary* reckons it as a third aim of the book, ללמד שהאל יתברך חומל על בעלי תשובה מאיזה עם שיהיו ומוחל להם וכל שכן כשהם רבים, *i.e.* 'to teach that God should be praised for sparing the penitents to whatever nation those belong, and more especially, if they are many in number.' Essentially the same is the thought of the book, as given by Keil (*Einleit.* § 89). Hitzig (*Comment.* Vorbemerkungen, No. 4) laid special emphasis on the point that the book was intended to vindicate God in the matter of unfulfilled predictions. In like manner, Kautzsch (*Abriss*, 1897, p. 120) thinks that the narrative desired to give an illustration of the Divine question (Ezk 18[23] 33[11]), 'Have I pleasure in the death of the sinner?' So also Nowack (*Handkomm.*, 1897, p. 174). The authors just named thus fail to see that in the Book of Jonah what is pre-eminently depicted is the universality of the Divine plan of salvation, and the duty of Israel to be the missionary to the *goyîm*.

(*c*) It is not at all certain that, in addition to the principal idea, the author of the Book of Jonah desired to impress other sentiments on his readers. But Ephraem Syrus (see above, 7 *a*) found a second aim of the book in this, that it gave to the Israelites an example of the penitent disposition of other nations. This, in fact, was the primary tendency of the book, according to D. Kimchi נכתבה להיות מוסר לישראל שהרי עם נכרי שאינם מישראל היה קרוב לתשובה ונ' ועוד להודיע הפלא הגדול אשר עשה האל, *i.e.* 'The book was intended to serve for instruction to Israel, showing as it did how a foreign nation, not belonging to Israel, was ready for conversion, and how at the very *first* reprimand of the prophet it turned completely from its wickedness, whereas Israel, although reprimanded early and late by the prophets, did not turn from its evil ways'). Kimchi further attributed to the book the purpose 'to make known the great miracle which God wrought upon the prophet.' According to Eichhorn (*Einleit.* iv. 351), the story was intended also to teach that 'Jahweh rules in all places and over all elements.' Riehm (*Einleit.* ii. 166) says, 'The author wishes to teach that no prophet can evade the Divine commission.' He is followed by Volck (art. 'Jona' in *PRE*[2] vii. 85). Again, Vatke (*Einleit.*, 1886, p. 688) found pre-eminent in the book the thought also that 'the honour of the prophet is not impugned if a threatening although not fulfilled, nor inspiration called in question although many predictions are not realized.' Kaulen (*Einleit.* § 412) goes the length of maintaining that Jon 1[12] already teaches what was afterwards expressed by the high priest Caiaphas (Jn 11[50]), συμφέρει ἵνα εἷς ἄνθρωπος ἀποθάνῃ ὑπὲρ τοῦ λαοῦ. Finally, M. Vernes (*Précis d' histoire juive*, 1889, p. 810) contents himself with the words, 'Jonah is a moral tale rather than a prophecy.'

iv. OTHER OCCURRENCES OF THE NAME JONAH.
—The name Ἰωνᾶς is found in *OT Apocrypha* not only in To 14[4, 8] and 3 Mac 6[8] (see above, p. 749[a]), but also in 1 Es 9[1.] (B) [23] (see JONAS, Nos. 1. 2). In NT it occurs in Mt 12[39-41] 16[4], Lk 11[29t. 32]; Βαριωνᾶ in Mt 16[17], Ἰωνᾶ in Jn 1[43] 21[15], but in these last two passages the reading Ἰωάν(ν)ου has strong evidence in its favour. See JOHN (FATHER OF SIMON PETER).

LITERATURE.—(A) TEXTUAL CRITICISM.—The Targum on *Jonah*, with supralinear punctuation, may be found in Merx' *Chrestomathia Targumica*, 1897, pp. 132-139; Karl Vollers, *Das Dodekapropheton der Alexandriner*, 1880, and in *ZATW* iii. 219 ff., iv. 1 ff.; J. Z. Schuurmanns Stekhoven, *De Alexandrijnsche vertaling van het Dodekapropheton*, Leiden, 1887; M. Sebök, *Die Syr. Uebersetzung d. Zwölf kl. Proph.*, 1887; W. Wright, *Jonah in Chald., Syr., Æth., and Arab.*, 1857; F. Perles, *Analekten z. Textkritik d. AT*, 1895, p. 12.
(B) LITERARY CRITICISM.—W. Böhme, 'Die Compos. d. Buches Jona' in *ZATW*, 1887, pp. 224 ff.; the *Einleitungen in d. AT* of Eichhorn 1825 f., Augusti 1827, Hävernick 1844, de Wette-Schrader 1868, Keil 1873, Bleek-Wellhausen 1878, Vatke 1886, Riehm 1889, Reuss 1890, Kaulen 1892, Kuenen 1892, Ed. König 1893, Cornill 1896, Driver 1897, Strack 1898; Hamburger, *RE*; Riehm, *HWB* (art. 'Jona' by Gustav Baur); *PRE*[2] vii.; L. Herzfeld, *Gesch. Isr.* i. 278; M. Vernes, *Précis d' histoire juive*, 1881, p. 810; Renan, *Hist. du peuple d' Israël*, iii. 511 ff.; [Köhler, Kittel, Seinecke do not mention the Book of Jonah in their 'Geschichten Israels'].
(C) COMMENTARIES.—Besides the ancient versions, the Rabbinical and Church expositions, cf. Rosenmüller, *Scholia in Vet. Test.* vol. x.; Frz. Kaulen, *Liber Jonæ prophetæ expositus*, 1862; M. Kalisch, *Bible Studies*, pt. ii. 'The Book of Jonah,' 1878; Keil-Delitzsch's *Bib. Comm. z. AT*, 'Die 12 kleinen Propheten[2]'; Hitzig-Steiner, *Kgf. exeg. Hdbch. z. d. kl. Proph.*[4]; Pusey, *Minor Prophets*, 1886; H. Martin, *The Prophet Jonah*, 1891; v. Orelli in Strack-Zöckler's *Kgf. Com.* 1896; Nowack, *Handkom. z. d. 12 kl. Proph.* 1897; G. A. Smith, *The Book of the Twelve Prophets* (in the 'Expositor's Bible'), vol. ii., 1898.
(D) MONOGRAPHS especially upon the purpose of the Book of Jonah.—J. Friedrichsen, *Kritische Uebersicht über die verschiedenen Ansichten über Jona*, Leipzig, 1841; H. H. Kemink, 'Overzicht van de geschiedenis der exegese van Jonas prophetie' in *Jahrb. voor wetenschaft. Theol.* ii. 269 ff.; Jäger, 'Ueber den sittlich-religiösen Zweck des Buches Jona,' in *Zeitsch. f. Theol.*, 1840, pp. 35 ff.; Riehm in *SK*, 1862, pp. 413 ff.; Alb. Rebattu, *De libri Jonæ sententia theologica*, Jena, 1875; A. E. O'Connor, *Étude sur le livre de Jonas*, Geneva, 1883; Trumbull, *Jonah in Niveveh*, Philadelphia, 1892; John Kennedy, *On the Book of Jonah*, London, 1895; Benedict Wolf, *Die Gesch. d. Proph. Jona, nach einer Karschunischen* [Arabico-Syrischen] *Handschrift, herausgegeben u. erläutert*, Berlin, 1897. This writing was discovered at the end of the 13th cent. in the library of 'Ebedjesu (Assemani, *Bibliot. Orient.* III. i. p. 285; Wolf, p. 39).   ED. KÖNIG.

JONAM (Ἰωνάμ WH, Ἰωνάν TR, AV **Jonan**).—An ancestor of Jesus, Lk 3[30].

JONAS.—**1.** (B Ἰωνᾶς, A Ἰωανάν, AV **Joanan**), 1 Es 9[1] the son of Eliasib (B Νάσειβος), to whose chamber (παστοφόριον) Esdras betook himself to mourn over the foreign marriages contracted by the people. In Ezr 10[6] called JEHOHANAN; cf. Neh 12[23] JOHANAN. **2.** (A Ἰωνᾶς, B Ἰωανᾶς) 1 Es 9[23]. The name corresponds to ELIEZER in the parallel list of Ezr 10[23]. A link between the two forms is given by the Vulg. *Elionas*; אליעזר was perhaps read for אליעזר, as was done in 1 Es 9[32] (cf. Ezr 10[31]), the former name occurring in the previous verse of Ezr. Elionas was then corrupted to Jonas. **3.** (*Jonas*) 2 Es 1[39]. The prophet Jonah.   H. ST. J. THACKERAY.

JONATHAN (יְהוֹנָתָן, יוֹנָתָן 'J'' hath given'; comp. *Theodore*) is a proper name met with from the time of the Judges downwards.

1. A Levite mentioned in a supplement to the Book of Judges (chs. 17. 18),[*] an adventurer through whom the idolatrous worship in Dan was established, and from whom the Danite priesthood was descended. The narrative in which he figures has a threefold interest, inasmuch as it throws light on the gradual conquest of Canaan, illustrates the low state of religion in the post-Mosaic age,

---

[*] The great value and antiquity of the substance of these two chapters is generally admitted by critics. Budde's attempt to disentangle two independent narratives, of which the chief is J, is approved by Cornill, disapproved by Wellh. and Kuenen, and questioned by Driver (*LOT*[6] p. 168).

and involves the sanctuary of Dan in discredit by tracing its institution to fraud, violence, and personal ambition.

This degenerate priest is described as the son of Gershom, the son of Manasseh (18[30]). The Heb. text, however, indicates that the *n* in *Manasseh* is an interpolation (מְנַשֶּׁה), and that the ancestor's name, as remembered in the Jewish tradition, should be read *Moses*. From Bethlehem of Judah the youth went forth to push his way in the world (17[7]), and first hired himself as house priest to Micah the Ephraimite for a wage of ten pieces of silver with food and raiment (v.[10])—and this though Micah's household cult had the double taint that he made use in worship of a graven and a molten image (v.[4]), and that these images had been procured from stolen money (v.[2]). (Ewald, with support from LXX, thinks the money was originally got by trading). While living with Micah he was accosted by five Danite spies, who had been sent out by their straitened tribe to explore the northern states; and after consulting the oracle he promised the blessing of God upon their enterprise (18[1-6]). The spies discovered at Laish a large and rich land and a people secure (v.[10]), and on hearing their report an armed band of 600 Danites marched northward to the easy conquest (v.[11]). Arrived at Mount Ephraim, they halted at Micah's dwelling, and, while the troop held the priest in converse, the spies entered the 'house of God' and carried off the costly furniture of the idolatrous worship (v.[17]). It was an easy matter to induce the priest to acquiesce in the robbery, and to accompany them on their expedition. 'Go with us,' they said, 'and be to us a father and a priest: is it better for thee to be priest unto the house of one man, or to be priest unto a tribe and family in Israel'? (v.[19]). Micah pursued the predatory band, but his following was too weak to engage them (v.[26]). The expedition was successful; and the priestly line founded in Dan by J. continued 'until the captivity of the land' (v.[30]). The preservation of the story is doubtless due to the fact that it lent itself to the purposes of the prophets of the Assyr. period in their opposition to the cult practised in Dan and Bethel.

2. The eldest son of Saul (1 S 14[49]), who shared in the perils and enterprises of his father's stormy reign, and was involved in his ruin. The narratives[*] in which he figures successively celebrate his martial exploits and his romantic friendship with David, and they portray a character which combines in a unique degree the heroism of the Hebrew patriot with the spirit of Christian virtue.

As warrior-prince J. takes rank among the bravest captains of Israel's iron age. Like Saul, he was fleet of foot, and of great physical strength (2 S 1[23]), and, as became a Benjamite, a noted archer (v.[22]). In the familiar speech of the people, he may have been known for his grace and agility as the gazelle. (So Ewald, rendering v.[19], 'the gazelle is slain'). He comes upon the scene as the hero of a campaign against the Philistines, in which the bearing of Saul is little more than a foil to the bold initiative, the rapid movement, and the practical sense of his son. The Philistines, it would seem, had been in effective occupation of the Israelitish territory, and the force collected by Saul had not yet made any considerable impression, when a blow struck by J. (1 S 13[3]),[†] to whom

---

[*] Of the two main strata in the Books of Samuel distinguished by modern critics (Budde, Driver, Cornill, etc.), the older contributes the account of J.'s military career (1 S 13. 14. 31[2]), while the later develops the theme of the friendship (1 S 18[1-4] 19[1-7] 23[16-18]). The distinctness of the two contributions would be complete if Stade is right in assigning ch. 20 (against Budde) to the later source. The Davidic elegy (2 S 1) commemorates equally the prowess and friendship of Jonathan.
[†] Probably the slaying of a tyrannical officer. The uncer-

Saul had intrusted a third of his following (1 S 13²), loudly sounded the note of rebellion. The Philistines answered the challenge by invading the highlands with an overwhelming force. The Hebrews, on the other hand, did not respond to Saul's expectation of a general rising; some fled beyond Jordan, some hid themselves in caves, some were pressed into the enemy's service, and he was left to front the invasion with a band which had now dwindled from 3000 to 600 men (1 S 13¹⁵). The two armies came face to face at the passage of Michmash, and took up their positions on opposite sides of a deep ravine *—the Philistines at Michmash on the north, Saul at Gibeah on the south side. Outnumbered though Saul was, his position at the top of the steep pass was impregnable; and the Philistines, after planting an outpost on their edge of the ravine, set about harrying the surrounding district (1 S 13¹⁷). The dead-lock was ended by Jonathan. Accompanied by his armour-bearer (1 S 14¹), he hailed the Philistine garrison, and, having satisfied himself that their reply was a sign that the Omnipotent God was on his side (v.¹²),† he scaled the opposing rocky rampart and fell upon the astonished garrison. As the Philistines fled he struck down twenty men, and where they lay in a row it seemed like a furrow drawn in an acre of land (v.¹⁴, perhaps, originally, 'he went through them like a ploughshare'; on other possible interpretations see art. FURROW). The panic spread to the main camp, which, weakened as it was by the absence of the marauding bands, was unable to resist what seemed an attack in force. Seeing the enemy in confusion, and discovering in it the hand of J., Saul with his men also crossed the ravine, and soon the whole force of the Philistines was in headlong flight. That the Hebrews might reap the full fruits of the victory, Saul made proclamation that none should eat until the evening on pain of death (v.²⁴). Ignorant of the prohibition, J., as he passed in hot chase through a wooded district, refreshed himself by eating wild honey (v.²⁷); and, on learning of his father's vow, he warmly blamed the short-sighted order that had taken the vigour out of the pursuit (v.³⁰). In the evening the oracle revealed that a penalty had been incurred (v.³⁷), and the divination of the lot brought the transgression home to J. (v.⁴²). Saul declared his life forfeited, but the people intervened, and by a ransom (Ewald, by a vicarious sacrifice) saved their hero (v.⁴⁵).

If the military exploits of J. chiefly impressed his contemporaries, it is his friendship with David which has most strongly appealed to the imagination of the after-world. In truth, it gives an unrivalled example of the essential notes of friendship —namely, warmth of affection, disinterestedness, helpfulness, confidence, and constancy. The love

tainty arises from the ambiguity of נצִיב, an ambiguity which may be reproduced in English by saying that he destroyed a post, i.e. either a garrison, or a pillar erected in token of the Philistine supremacy (Gn 19²⁶), or an official of some kind. The last interpretation is supported by 1 K 4¹⁹.

* The situation may be made clearer by an extract from Robinson, Bibl. Researches², i. 441 f. 'We left Jeba' (Gibeah) for Mûkhmâs. The descent into the valley was longer and steeper than any of the preceding. The path led down obliquely, and we reached the bottom in half an hour. . . . In the valley (Wady es-Suweinit), just at the left of where we crossed, are two hills of a conical, or rather a spherical, form, having steep rocky sides with small Wadys running up behind each, so as almost to isolate them. These would seem to be the two rocks mentioned in connexion with J.'s adventure. . . . Crossing the valley obliquely, and ascending with difficulty for 15 minutes we came upon the slope on which Mûkhmâs stands.'

† The sign agreed on was that he should attack only if the Philistines invited him to come up. This, it has been pointed out, was not arbitrary, as their refusing to come down indicated want of courage. There is some force in Stade's objection to this feature, that to hail the garrison was to put them on their guard, and thus endanger the chance of success.

of J. for David is represented as of sudden growth —its birthday the day when they first met after the slaying of Goliath (1 S 18¹⁻⁴). The intensity of his love is described in the language of the strongest of passions: he loved David as his own soul (v.¹), passing the love of women (2 S 1²⁶); and in the parting scene it finds expression in an outburst of true Oriental vehemence: they kissed one another, and wept one with another until David exceeded (1 S 20⁴¹). Of its spirit, disinterestedness is the merest negative description: not only had J. nothing personally to gain from David, but he was reminded by Saul that he had everything to lose (1 S 20³¹). The friendly services of J. were his first intercession with Saul on David's behalf (1 S 19¹⁻⁷), and his later interposition, as it appeared at the risk of his own life, by which he discovered his father's settled purpose, and conveyed to David a warning to flee from the court (1 S 20). The mutual confidences are frank and full. And, to supply the crowning grace of constancy, there is recorded a last stolen interview in a wood in the wilderness of Ziph, where J., seeking out the friend from whom he had been so long parted by his father's wrath, strengthened his hand in God (1 S 23¹⁶).* The relations of J. with Saul reveal essentially the same strong and affectionate character. Of their close association in all weighty business, and of their strong mutual affection, there are various direct and indirect testimonies (1 S 19² 20²). Against this may be set Saul's later suspicion that J.'s friendship with David was of the nature of a conspiracy (22⁸)—the design being to set him aside in favour, either of David, or, as is much more likely, of J. himself. But while it is quite credible that David, in view of the danger to the realm of a half-insane king, may have spoken of the desirability of the father giving way to the son (Stade, Gesch. des Volkes Israel, i. 242), it is not probable that such a design was matured, or even communicated to Jonathan.

J. fell with Saul on Mount Gilboa in battle against the Philistines (1 S 31²). At this time the fourth brother (1 Ch 9³⁹) was 40 years old (2 S 2¹⁰), and on this basis of calculation J. may have been between 40 and 50 when he died. If 1 S 13¹⁻³ fixes the date of the battle of Michmash, and if Saul reigned nearly 40 years thereafter (Ac 13²¹), J. cannot have been less than 60 at death, i.e. 30 years older than David (2 S 5⁴). These data are, however, precarious, and it is safer to follow the general impression of the history, and regard him as a contemporary of David. His dishonoured corpse was rescued from Beth-shan by the men of Jabesh-Gilead (1 S 31¹¹). He left a son 5 years old (see MEPHIBOSHETH). 3. A nephew of David who slew a giant of Gath (2 S 21²¹), probably the same as the 'uncle' (?) spoken of as a wise scribe (1 Ch 27³²). 4. A son of Abiathar the priest, who as a courier rendered service to David during Absalom's rebellion (2 S 15²⁷⁻³⁶ 17¹⁷·²⁰), and brought to Adonijah the report of Solomon's accession (1 K 1⁴²). 5. A scribe in whose house Jeremiah was imprisoned (Jer 37¹⁵·²⁰ 38²⁶). 6. One of the line of the high priests in the 5th cent. (Neh 12¹¹)—also called Johanan (12²²), referred to in Neh as introducing a change in the keeping of the genealogical records, and in Josephus (Ant. XI. vii. 1) as bringing profanation on the temple by the murder of his brother Jesus within its precincts. 7. One of David's heroes (2 S 23³², 1 Ch 11³⁴). 8. One of David's treasurers (1 Ch 27²⁵) (AV Jehonathan). 9. A Levite (Neh 12³⁵). 10. The son of Kareah, a Judahite captain after

* The passages bearing on the friendship have been somewhat roughly handled by modern critics. Ch. 20, it is alleged, is impossible after ch. 19¹⁻⁷, the story of the parting contains contradictory elements (the signal and the interview), the last interview is unhistorical, etc. In any case, David himself vouches for the main features.

the fall of Jerus. (Jer 40⁸). **11.** Father of Ebed (Ezr 8⁶). **12.** One of those who opposed (RV) or assisted (AV) Ezra in the matter of the foreign marriages (Ezr 10¹⁵). **13.** A priest (Neh 12¹⁴). **14.** Jonathan the Maccabee. See MACCABEES.

W. P. PATERSON.

JONATH ELEM REHOKIM.—See PSALMS.

JOPPA (יָפוֹ, *i.e.* *Yāphō,** in Ezr 3⁷ אֵלִי; Ἰόππη, Ἰόπη; Arabic *Yâfa*; modern name *Jaffa*).—The town is built on a whale-back rise of rocky ground, made conspicuous by its being the only eminence of the kind along the level sandy beach which extends in a straight line from Cæsarea to Gaza. To vessels approaching from the north or south, the crest of Jaffa is the first visible object on the coast-line. On nearer approach the appearance of the town is exceedingly picturesque, the closely clustered houses, with their numerous arches and walls of blue, pink, white, and yellow ochre, rising above each other, and all sparkling in the brilliant sunlight. In the low-lying ground, part of which must have once been a marsh, immediately behind the town there are extensive irrigated gardens of orange, apricot, and peach trees, the level mass of deep green foliage being relieved by the tall stems of graceful palm trees. Beyond this, the plain of Sharon, with its rich fields of wheat and barley, stretches away to where the outline of the Judæan hills forms the background of the picture.

The whole eventful history of Joppa is explained by its connexion with the influential city of Jerusalem. Geographically, Joppa was the seaport of Jerusalem; but the distance was too great, and the line of communication too often broken, for the maintenance of established ownership. Politically, it was frequently severed altogether from Judæa; and from the religious point of view the produce of Joppa in corn, wine, and oil was considered to be contaminated by its contact with heathenism, and ceremonially unfit for use at the sacred festivals.

Joppa has owed its existence and importance to the fact that it is the only place on the coast that can offer shelter to shipping between Egypt and Mount Carmel. The harbour is formed by a low ledge of rock running out at a sharp angle in a N.W. direction from the southern end of the town. The space is very limited and the water shallow, but in moderate weather Oriental craft, usually about the size of a modern herring boat, can lie at anchor and discharge cargo near the shore. The harbour is entered either by a narrow opening in the ledge or by rounding the point; but when the sea is disturbed by the prevalent N.W. wind the gap can only be rushed on the crest of a high wave, and to round the point brings a vessel broadside-on close to the edge of the surf.

Mythology points to the rock on the southern side of the gap as the spot where Andromeda was chained when Perseus slew the sea monster and delivered the maiden. Josephus, Pliny, Strabo, Jerome, and some of the travellers in the time of the Crusades, speak of the chains still remaining visible in the rock, the earlier writers also testifying to the size of the carcase that lay or was reported to have lain there.†

---

* Both AV and RV have everywhere *Joppa*, except in Jos 19⁴⁶ where AV has *Japho*.

† The incident at Joppa finds a parallel at Beyrout, where for a similar purpose and on similar rocks a maiden is said to have been exposed as a sacrifice, and to have been rescued by St. George. This gives its name to the bay, and forms the beautiful design on the English sovereign. While the body of the slain dragon has been lost sight of, faith in the living *beast of the sea* has remained undisturbed by the lapse of centuries. A few years ago a Belgian steamer reaching Beyrout at midnight blew her siren whistle to inform the agents of her arrival. The unprecedented shriek startled the town out of sleep, and next day in the bazaars the chief topic of conversation was the visit of the sea monster during the previous night.

The antiquity of Joppa is attested by its mention as *Ye-pu* on the Karnak lists among the towns of Palestine conquered by Thothmes III. It is also referred to in the journey of the Egyptian *mohar* (see Sayce, *HCM* 347). It appears as *Ja-ap-pu-u* in Sennacherib's annal-inscription (Schrader, *KAT*² 172 [*COT*² i. 160 f.]). In the distribution of the land under Joshua it belonged to the inheritance of the tribe of Dan (Jos 19⁴⁶).

It is referred to in the Bible as the place where the timber from Lebanon was beached for transport to Jerusalem (2 Ch 2¹⁶, Ezr 3⁷). Here Jonah embarked when seeking in vain to escape from the commandment to go to Nineveh (Jon 1³). In Joppa, Dorcas laboured among the poor and was raised from the dead (Ac 9³⁶⁻⁴²). Here St. Peter, on the roof of Simon's house, was taught that expansion of the meaning of salvation which has ever since divided the synagogue and the Christian Church (Ac 10¹⁻²³). Joppa was a constant sufferer during the famous wars of the Jews with Syria, Egypt, and Rome.

In the days of Judas Maccabæus its Jewish inhabitants were invited into boats by the people of the town to join in holiday enjoyment, and about 200 of them were drowned. This treachery was speedily avenged by Judas, who attacked the harbour by night and burned the boats (2 Mac 12³⁻⁷). About B.C. 148 Joppa was captured by Jonathan, brother of Judas (1 Mac 10⁷⁵·⁷⁶), and about six years after it was again captured by Simon, the third of the heroic brothers, who put a garrison into it to ensure its fidelity (1 Mac 12³³·³⁴). Shortly afterwards the same leader had once more to occupy it by a force under his officer Jonathan, son of Absalom (1 Mac 13¹¹). Pompey, after capturing Jerusalem in the time of Aristobulus and Hyrcanus (B.C. 63), restored Joppa and joined it to Syria (Jos. *Ant.* XIV. iv. 4). Sixteen years later it was given back to the Jews, being, however, exempted from the tax to Jerusalem, except what was charged on its agricultural produce and the exports to other towns on the coast (Jos. *Ant.* XIV. x. 6).

One of the principal disasters inflicted on the town was when Cestius Gallus took it and destroyed its Jewish inhabitants to the number of 8400 (Jos. *BJ* II. xviii. 10). During the Jewish wars with the Romans Joppa became a place of retreat for the lawless and those who had been made desperate by failure and suffering and the loss of relatives and property. These turned to the sea as a means of livelihood, and by their piratical outrages endangered all commerce on the Syrian coast. The town was attacked and captured (A.D. 68) by Vespasian on his way to Jerusalem. The inhabitants who had taken refuge in their ships and boats were driven on the rocks by a northerly gale, and about 4200 of them were drowned or slain by the sword (Jos. *BJ* III. ix. 2, 3).

During the time of Christ, Joppa was one of the eleven toparchies of which Jerusalem was the chief.

Since the time of the Romans similar vicissitudes have marked the history of this unfortunate seaport. It has often changed hands, and each change of ownership has been a time of destruction and renewal. It has belonged to Saracens, Crusaders, and the Sultans of Egypt; it was conquered and severely treated by Napoleon, and has finally found rest under the Turkish Government.

The modern town of *Jaffa* has about 8000 inhabitants—Moslems, Christians, and Jews. Its main street leading from the harbour is steep, narrow, crooked, dark, and dirty, with lanes still darker and dirtier leading off among the huddle of houses on each side. As might be expected in such a seaport, many types and nationalities meet and mingle together. Europeans, Egyptians, Soudanese, Northern Syrians, fellahîn of Palestine, and Bedawîn of the desert, are seen lounging about or noisily pushing their way among the baggage animals that throng the narrow street. The thoroughfare from the harbour meets a broad sandy road skirting the landward side of the town and running parallel to the coast-line. It was fitting that a town with such a history of changes should be the starting-point of the first railway in Palestine, by which it is now in daily communication with Jerusalem.

LITERATURE.—The books of Maccabees (as above) and Josephus (*passim*); Schürer, *HJP* II. i. 79–83; Buhl, *GAP* 73 f., 82, 86, 125, 187; Thomson, *Land and Book*, i. 5 ff. etc. ; W. Max Müller, *Asien u. Europa*, 159; Tristram, *Bible Places*, 70 ff. ; Bezold, *Tel el-Amarna Tablets in Brit. Mus.* 146; G. A. Smith, *HGHL* 121, 136 ff. ; Guérin, *Judée*, i. 1 ff. ; *PEF Mem.* ii. 254 ff., 275 ff. ; Clermont-Ganneau, *Mission en Pal. et en Phénicie.*   G. M. MACKIE.

JOPPA, SEA OF (אֶל־יָם יָפוֹא, πρὸς θάλασσαν Ἰόππης, *ad mare Joppe*, Ezr 3⁷), the portion of the Mediter. near the harbour of Joppa (cf. Ryssel, *ad loc.*). But RV 'to the sea, unto Joppa,' cf 2 Ch 2¹⁶ AV.

JORAH (יוֹרָה, cf. יוֹרֶה 'autumn rain,' Οὐρά,' Ιωρά). —The name of a family which returned from exile under Zerubbabel, Ezr 2¹⁸. In Neh 7²⁴ the name appears as Hariph, which is probably the true form. 1 Es 5¹⁶ reads Arsiphurith (Ἀρσειφουρειθ B, Ἀρσιφφουρειθ A), which is probably due to the conflation of a corrupt reading and the correction ; read Ἀρειφουρειθ = חרפותה. Cf. E. Meyer, *Entstehung d. Judenthums*, p. 144. See GENEALOGY.   H. A. WHITE.

JORAI (יוֹרַי 'whom J'' teacheth').—A Gadite chief, 1 Ch 5¹³. See GENEALOGY.

JORAM.—1. (יוֹרָם) son of Toi, 2 S 8¹⁰, prob. a mistake for Hadoram, the form in 1 Ch 18¹⁰. **2.** (יֹרָם) a Levite, 1 Ch 26²⁵. **3.** (Ἰωράμ) 1 Es 1⁹ = JOZABAD, 2 Ch 35⁹. **4. 5.** See JEHORAM, Nos. 1 and 2.

JORDAN, יַרְדֵּן (*Yardēn*), in prose always with the definite article הַיַּרְדֵּן (as an appellative), so called from descending (יָרַד). The two exceptions to the use of the article are Ps 42⁶ and Job 40²³. In the latter instance this arises from the name being used as a representation of any violent rush of water. (See Davidson and Dillm. *ad loc.*). The present Arabic name of the Jordan is *esh-Sheri'ah*, 'the watering-place,' to which the epithet *el-Kebîr*, 'the great,' is sometimes annexed to distinguish it from *esh-Sheri'at el-Mandhôr* or *Jarmúk*, the ancient Hieromax, which joins it from the east about two hours below the Lake of Tiberias. The common name of the great valley through which it thus flows, below the Lake of Tiberias, is *el-Ghôr*, signifying a depressed tract or plain, usually between two mountains ; and the same name continues to be applied to the valley for the whole length of the Dead Sea, and for some distance beyond ; it thus corresponds to the *Aulon* of Eusebius and Jerome (*Onomasticon*; Robinson, *BRP*² i. p. 537) and 'the Arabah' of OT. The form *el-Urdun* was used among early Arabic writers (Abulfeda, *Tab. Syr.* ; Edrisi, ed. Jaubert; Schulten's 'Index in Vit. Saladin,' *F. Jordanes*; Reland, *Palest.*) before the time of the Crusades.

It is scarcely ever called the 'river' or 'brook' or any other name than its own, 'the Jordan' (Stanley, *Sinai and Palestine*, 284). Josephus always calls it the Jordan, except once when he calls it 'the river,' without any distinctive name, when describing the borders of Issachar (*Ant.* V. i. 22).

The derivation of the name *Jordan* from *Jor* and *Dan* has been traced back as far as Jerome (*Onomasticon, s.v.* 'Dan'), who says (*Comm. in* Mt 16¹³): 'Jordanes oritur ad radices Libani ; et habet duos fontes, unum nomine Jor, et alterum Dan ; qui simul mixti Jordanis nomen efficiunt.' This was copied by Arculf, 8; Willibald, 16; Saewulf, 47; Will. of Tyre, 13, 18; Brocardus, c. 3, p. 172; Marinus Sanutus on his map; Andrichomius, p. 109; John of Würzburg, 20. It is also current among the Christians of the country to the present day. There is no basis, however, for this etymology, for the name Jordan is merely the Greek form (Ἰορδάνης) for the Hebrew *Yardēn*, which has no relation to Dan. The Arabs near *Tell el-Kâdi* (Dan) call it there *ed-Dan* or *el-Leddân* (*BRP*² iii. 392). Jerome (*Onomast. s.v.* 'Dan') considers Jor equivalent to river; but G. Williams points out that יְאֹר is the Hebrew * form of 'river,' while the proper name (Jordan) is יַרְדֵּן, and never יַאְרְדֵּן, as the proposed etymology would require.

Up to the present century most pilgrims and travellers had visited the valley of the Jordan only at Jericho, hence we had no account of its features in the upper portions. Antoninus Martyr at the close of the 6th cent., and St. Willibald in the 8th, passed down through the whole length of the valley from Tiberias to Jericho ; and in 1100 king Baldwin I. accompanied a train of pilgrims from Jericho to Tiberias (Fulcher Carnot); but there is nothing more than a mere notice of these journeys. During the present century, Seetzen, Burckhardt, Irby and Mangles, Banks and Buckingham, Thomson, Porter, Molyneux, Lynch, J. Macgregor, Guérin, Liévin, Robinson, have visited and described portions of the Jordan ; and in later years the officers of the Palestine Exploration Fund have thoroughly examined, surveyed, and described it (*PEFSt*, 1869–97, *SWP*).

GEOLOGICAL FEATURES.—The Jordan flows from north to south in a portion of a deep fissure or crevasse on the surface of the earth, nearly parallel to the eastern coast of the Mediterranean Sea, extending from the foot of the Taurus Mountains, past Antioch, up the valley of the Orontes, through Cœle-Syria, between Lebanon and Anti-Lebanon, down the valley of the Jordan and Salt Sea, and through the *Wâdy el-Arab* to the Gulf of 'Akabah, from lat. 38° N. to 30° N. This fissure appears as the most remarkable on the face of the earth, owing to its being cut off from the sea, in so dry a climate that the excessive evaporation keeps the surface of water in the Salt Sea about 1300 ft. below the level of the Mediterranean and Red Sea. It was suggested, probably first by Burckhardt, that the river Jordan originally flowed down the whole course of the depression from the Lebanon to the Gulf of 'Akabah ; but this view has been rejected with reason by Lartet and subsequently by Hull, and the following is the theory of the formation of the valley, deduced from the observations and memoirs of the above learned geologists.

Professor Hull, in his examination of the *Wâdy el-Arâbah* over a distance of 120 miles from north to south, found that it had been hollowed out along the line of a main 'fault' ranging from the eastern shore of the Salt Sea to that of the Gulf of 'Akabah. He found numerous parallel and branch 'faults' along the Arabah Valley, but there was one main 'fault' running along the base of the Edomite mountains, to which the others are of secondary importance. This is called by him the 'Great Jordan Valley Fault.' Lartet, Tristram, and Wilson had already shown that in the Jordan Valley and *Ghôr* there was the evidence of a large

* יְאֹר is really an Egyptian loan-word (see *Oxf. Heb. Lex. s.v.*), and is the special designation in OT of the Nile.

'fault' corresponding to the line of this remarkable depression, and Hull considers that the features he observed in the *Arâbah* Valley are continuous with those of the Jordan. He considers that in this part of the world the Miocene period was one of elevation, disturbance, and denudation of strata, not of accumulation, the Miocene period not being represented by any strata throughout the district traversed by his expedition. To this epoch he refers the emergence of the whole of the Palestine, and the greater part of the Sinaitic, area from the sea, in which the cretaceo-nummulitic limestone formations were deposited. To this epoch also he considers the 'faulting' and flexuring of the strata to be chiefly referable, and notably the formation of the great Jordanic line of 'fault,' with its branches and accompanying flexures in the strata, which are very remarkable along the western side of the *Ghôr*. These phenomena were accompanied and followed by extensive denudation, and the production of many of the principal features of the region referred to.

From that epoch down to the present day these physical features appear to have changed in a comparatively small degree, as the area referred to slowly rose above from the waters of the Miocene and Pliocene oceans. For a limited time there would have necessarily been a connexion between the waters of this great gulf or valley, 200 miles in length and 10 in breadth, and the southern 'Aḳabah sea through the valley of 'Aḳabah; but, from the time that the outer waters were dissevered from those of the Jordan-Arabah lake by the uprise of the land, there is no evidence that there was any subsequent connexion by means of a stream flowing down from the north into the Gulf of 'Aḳabah. All indications appear to be against this. It would appear that, at a period coming down probably to the prehistoric, a chain of fresh-water lakes existed among the tortuous valleys and hollows of the Sinaitic peninsula. There are still fresh-water shells in the wadis *Feiran* and *es-Sheikh*, and these belong to a period when the contiguous oceans were about 200 ft. higher over the land than at present, indicating that during this later period there has been a further rise of about 200 ft. The evidence of this rise was observed also in the Gulf of 'Aḳabah. From the epoch during the Miocene period when the inland sea was dissevered from the waters of the adjoining oceans, its level would entirely depend upon the amount of rain water from rivers which poured into it, balanced against the amount abstracted by evaporation. Lartet has computed that at the present day at least 6,500,000 tons of water are evaporated daily from the Salt Sea.

The occurrence of terraces of marl, gravel, and silt, through which the ravines of existing streams have been cut at an elevation of about 100 ft. above the present level of the Mediterranean, show that the level of the inland sea at one time stood for a period without change about 1400 ft. higher than it does at present; but this can have had no connexion with the chain of lakes about Sinai, which extended to prehistoric times, as this inland sea was dissevered to the south during a remote Miocene epoch; and though there may have been a connexion for some time by way of the Mediterranean through the plain of Esdraelon, yet, as the land continued to rise, the inland sea would eventually have become entirely isolated. The lowering of the water in the inland sea from evaporation is supposed to have taken place at the commencement of the Pliocene period, so that it reached somewhere about the present level long before the prehistoric times, and there cannot have been any change in the course and character of the Jordan during historic or prehistoric times. At the present time the level of the Salt Sea is

about 1300 ft. below the Mediterranean Sea, the lower part of the floor of the Salt Sea again 1300 ft. below its surface level, and the watershed of *Wâdy Arâbah* 2000 ft. above the SALT SEA, and 700 ft. above the Mediterranean Sea. The plain of Esdraelon at the watershed is about 250 ft. above the level of the Mediterranean, so that on this side there may have been communication with the ocean to a much later period than on the south side; but this point does not seem to have been raised hitherto. Hull brings forward abundant evidence of a Pluvial period having existed through the Pliocene and post-Pliocene (or Glacial) period down to recent times. As it was known from the observations of Hooker, Tristram, and others that perennial snow and glaciers existed in the Lebanon during the Glacial epoch, it is assumed by Hull that the adjoining districts to the south of the Lebanon must have had at that epoch a climate approaching to that of the British Isles at the present day, and that in a region of which many parts were over 2000 ft. above the sea-line there must have been abundant rainfall. Even when the snows and glaciers of the Lebanon had disappeared, the effects of the colder climate which was passing away must have remained for some time, the vegetation must have been more luxuriant down to within the epoch of human habitation. It is considered that the outburst of volcanic phenomena commenced to occur when the waters of the inland sea stretched as far north as the Lake *Hûleh*, that is to say, at the time they began to be lowered by evaporation, shortly after they were dissevered from the ocean, and that the period of the volcanoes of the *Jaulân* and *Haurân* ranged through the Pliocene and post-Pliocene to the recent, when concurrently with the drying up of the waters of the inland sea the volcanic action became extinct.

It would seem, then, that during the Glacial epoch Palestine and Syria presented an aspect very different from the present. The Lebanon throughout the year was snow-clad on its higher region, while glaciers descended into some of its valleys. The region of the Haurân was the scene of some extensive volcanoes; while the district around, and the Jordan Valley itself, was invaded by floods of lava. A great inland sea, occupying the Jordan Valley, stretched from Lake *Hûleh* on the north to a southern margin near the base of *Samrat Feddân* in the *Wâdy el-Arâbah* of the present day, while numerous arms and bays stretched into the glens and valleys of Palestine and Moab on either side. Under such climatic circumstances, we may feel assured, a luxuriant vegetation decked with verdure the hills and vales to an extent far beyond that of the present; and amongst the trees, as Hooker has shown, the cedar may have spread far and wide. As will be shown hereafter, Tristram supposes that the inland sea, now represented by the Jordan Valley, was one of a chain of fresh-water lakes stretching down to Southern Africa. This is a very interesting subject in relation to the practical question as to the amount of salts now deposited in the Salt Sea, and to what extent an increased rainfall would be required to render the Salt Sea habitable by fish, as contemplated in the prophecies of Ezekiel, Zechariah, Joel, and other prophets.

PHYSICAL FEATURES.—The Jordan Valley may be divided into three portions—(*a*) The Upper Jordan, running through Cœle-Syria to Lake Hûleh. (*b*) From L. Hûleh to L. Tiberias. (*c*) From L. Tiberias to the Salt Sea.

(*a*) The Upper Jordan, although always accounted to have its sources at *Bâniâs* and Dan, has its most distant prominent source in the great fountain below *Hâsbeiya* (1700 ft.), running down into the Wady et-Teim, and becoming the turbid torrent of *Nahr Hasbâny*, receiving on its way numberless springs from the Anti-Lebanon and Hermon, and particularly the stream from *Sheb'a*, the great fountain of *Suraiyît*, at the foot of Hermon and *el-Ghujar*. After rushing through a deep gorge it has worn for itself in the basalt, it penetrates the marsh of *Hûleh* for about 5 miles, where it is joined by the united streams of the *Nahr Leddân* from *Tell el-Kâḍi* (which has been joined by the *Wâḍy Laweizâny*) and the *Nahr Bâniâs*. Of these main branches of the Jordan, the *Nahr Hasbâny* is the longest by 40 miles, the *Nahr Leddân* is the largest, and the *Nahr Bâniâs* is the most beautiful. A considerable stream comes down from the plain of Ijon, the contributions of the *Nahr Bareighit*, west of *'Abel*. Several large fountains also burst out from the hills to the west side of the marsh, and send their streams to the river or lake (*Land and Book*, ii. 320). At *Ghujar* the old road from Damascus through *Bâniâs* to the west crosses the *Hasbâny* by a bridge of three arches nearly west of *Tell el-Kâḍi*. From the foot of the mound at *Tell el-Kâḍi* (Dan or Laish) gushes out one of the largest fountains in Palestine (505 ft.), called the *Nahr Leddân*, which, joining the *Nahr Bâniâs* and the *Hasbâny*, forms the Jordan. Josephus speaks of the fountains of the lesser Jordan at Dan (*Ant.* I. x. 1; v. iii. 1; VIII. viii. 4). Speaking of Semechonitis (*Hûleh*), he says: 'Its marshes reach as far as the place Daphne, which, in other respects, is a delicious place, and hath such fountains as supply water to what is called "Little Jordan," under the temple of the golden calf, when it is sent into Great Jordan' (*BJ* IV. i. 1), thus clearly identifying Daphne with Dan.

The name *Bâniâs* is the Arab pronunciation of the ancient name Paneas, a city (Cæsarea Philippi) named from the grotto Panium, which seems to have been consecrated to the god Pan, though there is no historical mention of this deity (*BRP²* iii. 406) at this spot. Josephus states (*Ant.* XV. x. 3; *BJ* I. xxi. 3) that Herod erected to Augustus Cæsar a beautiful temple of white marble near the place called Panium. 'This is a fine cave in a mountain, under which there is a great cavity in the earth; and the cave is abrupt and very deep, and full of still water. On it hangs a vast mountain, and under the cavern rise the springs of the Jordan.' There are Greek inscriptions in the votive niches here, one of which contains the designation of the person who consecrated it as the 'priest of Pan,' implying a temple of that god. The spot is now called by the people *Mughârat Bâniâs*, or *Mughârat er-Râs en-Neba*. From beneath and through the mass of rocks and stones which fill up and hide the entrance of the cavern, gushes forth the *Nahr Bâniâs*, a full and rushing river, twice as large as the stream from the fountain near *Hâsbeiya*. The water is of the purest and finest quality, limpid, bright, and sparkling. Gathering to itself the other streams just below the village, and yet itself distributing its waters over the terrace and portions of the western plain for irrigation, it rushes onward in a ravine of its own, with swift course, towards the south-west, down to the lower plain, and so to the lower *Hûleh*. It is the most beautiful of all the streams of the Jordan (*BRP²* iii. 407). It may be assumed that this great fountain of the Jordan had some historical associations before Herod built the temple there, and it has been suggested (*BRP²* iii. 409) that it is 'Baal-gad in the valley of Lebanon under Mount Hermon (Jos 11¹⁷ 12⁷), and that the shrine of the Phœnician Baal ultimately gave place to the Grecian Pan' (but see Dillmann on Jos 11¹⁷).

The little *Birket er-Râm* (the ancient lake Phiala), which Josephus (*BJ* III. x. 7) states is the real origin of the fountain of Jordan, and is carried to Panium by an underground channel, is situated in a bowl or crater. It is supplied by surface drainage, and has no outlet; it is on the right of the road leading from Cæsarea to Trachonitis, and its waters are dark, stagnant, and slimy.

The fountain of *Bâniâs* rises at an altitude of 1100 ft. (600 ft. above that of Dan). It flows as a torrent until it joins the *Leddân*, 4½ miles below *Tell el-Kâḍi*, and half a mile farther down union is effected with the *Nahr Hasbâny*.

The morass above the lake of *Hûleh* was explored thoroughly by J. Macgregor (*Rob Roy on the Jordan*) in 1869. Starting from *Absis*, at the junction of the *Leddân* and *Bâniâs*, in his canoe, he passed the junction with the *Hasbâny* at *Tell Sheik Yusûf*. He reached a village about 2 miles farther to south. He estimated the river from 30 to 100 ft. wide, with steep banks of reddish clay, rising in places to 20 ft. The waters in flood were 7 ft. deep—turbid, and brown in colour. Beyond this he struggled with his canoe for another mile, only to get firmly entangled in a maze of bushes 8 ft. high, thick-set stumps, and reeds. He was obliged to return and have his canoe carried N.W. along the edge of the morass to the western side of the valley, and on to the *'Ain Melâhah*, on the N.W. side of the lake. Here he again launched his canoe, and, exploring the Lake *Hûleh*, found the mouth of the Jordan about midway across the northern end of the lake. He explored it to the north through a channel in the floating papyrus reeds for about 4 miles, when he came to a barrier of floating jungle, which effectually stopped further progress. It would appear that all the lower portion of the morass for 4 miles is composed of this papyrus, and it is probably encroaching on Lake Hûleh. The waters of *Hûleh* were found to be considerably less in extent than the morass, and to measure about 3 miles from east to west, and 4 miles from north to south. The surface is about 7 ft. above the Mediterranean. From the southern end of *Hûleh* to the northern end of the Lake of Tiberias is about 10 miles, and the fall is 689 ft.—a rapid descent of about 70 ft. a mile over a rocky bed.

(*b*) The Jordan on issuing from *Hûleh* is about 60 ft. broad and 15 ft. deep. About 2 miles down is the *Jisr Benat Yâkob*, the first bridge over the complete Jordan, built of black basalt and with three arches, over which the great caravan route goes from *Akka* to Damascus. It appears to be of later date than the Crusading period. The canoe was unable to follow this portion of the Jordan, as it partakes of the nature of a torrent, and flows through a rocky glen, shut in by hills, forcing its turbid waters far into the Lake Tiberias, without apparently commingling them with those of the lake for some considerable distance. This has given rise to the legend that the river Jordan passes through the lake intact. It affects the level of the lake somewhat, which stands in the wet season about 6 in. higher than in the dry season.

(*c*) *The Ghôr or lower Jordan Valley.*—The Jordan between L. Tiberias and the Salt Sea lies in a deep depression, sloping nearly uniformly from north to south, at about 9 ft. to 1 mile. On either side are the mountains of Western and Eastern Palestine, rising to heights of over 3000 to 4000 ft. (2000 to 3000 ft. above the Mediterranean), and separated by the comparatively flat Jordan Valley, called the *Ghôr* by the Arabs, the *Arabah* of the Hebrews, *Aulon* of the Greeks, which is 3 miles wide at L. Tiberias, 12 to 16 miles wide at the Salt Sea, contracting to a width of 2 miles south of the plain of *Beisan*. The *Ghôr* has a very gentle slope on either side down to the lower plain (the *Zôr*), in which the Jordan runs, of about five degrees.

The banks of the *Ghôr* leading down into the *Zôr* are not regular, but are fretted away by the fervid sun, the strong winds, and occasional heavy rains in January and February. They are very ragged, and during the rainy season are covered with lovely flowers and verdure, but during most seasons of the year are a scene of utter desolation. Towards the lower portion of the Jordan Valley, where the streams (*en-Nweimeh, Faseil, el-'Aujeh, Kelt*, and others) on the west run into the *Zôr*, the plain of the *Ghôr* is broken up into a series of valleys, the original plain being left in outline here and there isolated and forlorn. These broken valleys have very steep sides, are about 100 to 200 ft. deep, and at first sight it seems impossible that the small streams which meander through them—at the best not 3 ft. deep or 6 ft. wide—can have scooped out these banks over 150 ft. in height, whose irregularities often extend more than a mile from the stream itself. From the ruins which exist about the plain, it is obvious that this work of denudation has proceeded exceedingly slowly, the features having scarcely altered during the last 2000 years. A heavier rainfall in early days would, however, readily account for a more rapid degree of change.

The plains of the Jordan are sterile only at the southern end for a few miles north of the Salt Sea over that depressed portion, which probably in early days, when there was a greater rainfall, was covered by the Salt Sea. The soil is not impregnated with salt at a height of 200 ft. above the level of the Salt Sea, and will bear plentifully provided there is any rainfall, so much so that during the rainy season the Jordan plains for miles, as far as the eye can reach, are vast meadows, abounding in grasses and flowers. Those who see the country after the sun has burned up the pasturage may well conceive the idea that nothing will grow there, for when the hot winds spring up in May the grasses are broken up and blown away, and there is little left but a few dried stumps in a howling wilderness. During January and February and part of March, flocks are brought down from the mountains to feed on the rich pasturage on the plains of Jordan, and browse within a mile of the river. In February 1868 between Jericho and *Jisr Damieh* the country was green everywhere, the weather was chilly, flowers of every hue lay in the path, and the lower Jordan plain or *Zôr* was covered with an early crop of barley, with here and there branches of the overflowing Jordan meandering through it. The plain of *Beisan* at this time was abundantly watered and covered with verdure.

In the plain of *Beisan* three distinct levels can be seen—the *Zôr*, the *Ghôr*, and an upper plain which is about 300 ft. above the *Ghôr* at Beisan. Here the *Ghôr* is cultivated with corn and indigo, watercourses and canals irrigate the crops and supply the mills with water.

At Beisan the Jordan Valley is 8 miles wide, but immediately to the north it is only 1¼ miles wide, and to the south it contracts again to about 2 miles, the hills on the west closing right down to the river. The *Ghôr* varies in width until at Jericho it is about 16 miles across, the foot of the hills being about 400 to 500 ft. above the Salt Sea.

It is quite evident from the number of aqueducts in all directions that the Jordan Valley about Jericho was once very highly cultivated, and that with a little care and a good government it might again be brought under cultivation, and its malarious and pestilential marshes removed.

The Jordan Valley on the eastern side, between the *Zerķa* and *Nimrin*, is only barren because there are no streams or fountains led out to water it. North of the *Zerķa*, where streams are numerous the valley is clothed with wheat fields and vegetation. South of the *Zerķa* there are traces of ancient canals, showing that that portion of the valley between the *Zerķa* and the road leading from *es-Salṭ* to *Nablûs* was formerly under cultivation, though it is now a desert. Perhaps more than half the Jordan Valley on the east is now reached by irrigation canals, and in those sections not occupied by wheat fields the thistles and weeds are rank, and form such dense jungles that it is almost impossible to get through them. 'Every square mile not now under irrigation could be watered from the Jordan, and the expense for a dam and canals would be small compared with the large number of square miles of valuable land that would be made productive . . . we should have 180 square miles of land as fertile as any prairie, and which at 20 to 25 bushels of wheat per acre would produce between 2 and 3 million bushels of wheat. Give these plains and deserts water, and you can transform them into gardens' (*PEFSt*, 1877, 153). The portion of the valley between the *Zerķa* and the *Mandhôr* in February and March resembles New England (U.S.) in the month of June. The soil is then burdened with its own productions. By the last of May the weeds, thistles, and wild mustard have formed an almost impenetrable jungle.

From *Wâdy Nimrin* to the Salt Sea, a distance of 15 miles, lies the great Shittim plain, watered by three copious streams, which make it a rich and beautiful oasis. This position is assigned by some authorities for the site of the cities of the Plain.

The Zôr or depressed plain through which the Jordan flows.—The Jordan issues from the Lake Tiberias gently for a mile and then becomes more rapid; although it has a nearly uniform descent throughout its course, yet it is found to have a great number of small rapids, and its descent is not quite so great about the middle. It has through many ages worked out a passage through the floor-bed of the valley or *Ghôr* (Aulon), which passage is called by the Arabs the *Zôr*. The *Zôr* varies from ¼ mile to 2 miles in width, and is a depressed plain about 20 ft. below the *Ghôr* at the northern end, and 200 ft. below towards the Salt Sea. It appears to have been formed by the changing of the river bed from side to side, breaking down the banks of the *Ghôr* and carrying the silt into the Salt Sea. The Jordan itself varies in width from 30 to 70 yards. The level of the surface of the *Zôr* is uniform with the banks of the Jordan, so that in January and February, when the waters overflow the banks, the *Zôr* is covered, and the total width of river in flood is ½ to 2 miles. The soil is for the most part very rich (except towards the southern end, where it is full of salts), and is highly cultivated, bearing heavy barley crops and vegetables.

The *Zôr* above the *Jisr Mijâmia* is not continuous; below the bridge the *Zôr* is from 50 to 100 ft. above the *Zôr*. The cliffs of the *Zôr* are here of white soft marl, about half a mile apart below the bridge, but just above the bridge the hills close in on the west, and the *Ghôr* disappears. Near the plain of *Beisan* the crops in the *Zôr* were being reaped in April (1873). Near the river the soil was covered with gigantic thistles 10 to 15 ft. high. The whole region round about the plain of *Beisan* is volcanic, and all the rocks and stones about are black and basaltic in their character. This probably accounts for the number of fords across the river in these parts.

From *Wâdy Mahleh* south of the plain of *Beisan* to *Wâdy Fârah* the mountains on the west close in upon the Jordan, narrowing the *Zôr*, which again widens out opposite to *Wâdy Fârah*, and gradually increases to 2 miles as it approaches the Salt Sea. The river is hidden for a great portion of its course by the jungle of cane and tamarisk on either side: all rank vegetation except reeds ceases about 2 miles from the Salt Sea. On entering the sea the waters form a muddy marsh covered with driftwood, too soft to be crossed by man or beast. Although the land for a few miles above the Salt Sea is a veritable desert, having at times been covered by the Salt Sea itself, yet such is the power of the sun that immediately after heavy rain in January and February small green plants and flowers spring up at once all round, even on the edge of the Salt Sea, and flourish so long as the rainy season lasts, but wither in a few hours after the rain ceases.

From L. Tiberias to the Salt Sea the direct distance is 65 miles, and the fall is 610 ft., viz. betwixt – 682 ft. at L. Tiberias to – 1292 ft. at the Salt Sea ; a fall of 9·3 ft. per mile.

The Dee of Aberdeenshire runs 72 miles, with fall of 16·5 ft. per mile. The Tweed runs 96 miles, with fall of 16 ft. per mile. The Clyde 98 miles, with fall of 14 ft. per mile. The Thames runs 215 miles, with fall of 1½ ft. per mile. The sinuosities of the Jordan, however, are so great that in the 65 miles' direct course it travels 200 miles at least (Lynch, *Narr.* p. 265), so that the actual fall is not more than 3 ft. per mile, if this estimate can be accepted.

Molyneux surveyed the Jordan from L. Tiberias to the Salt Sea in a boat in 1847, and Lt. Lynch did the same in 1848. Molyneux found the river when not in flood upwards of 100 ft. broad and 4 to 5 ft. deep near the *Jisr Mijâmia* ; for seven hours they scarcely ever had sufficient water to float the boat for 100 yards together. In many places the river is split into a number of small streams, which consequently have not much water in any of them. Occasionally the boat had to be carried upwards of 100 yards over rocks and through thorny bushes ; and in some places they had high, steep sandy cliffs all along the banks of the river. In other places the boat had to be carried on the backs of camels, the stream being quite impracticable. Lynch met with equally difficult experiences. He states, 'we have plunged down twenty - seven threatening rapids, besides a great number of lesser magnitude.' Only one straight reach of any length was noticed. The passage of the 200 miles of twists occupied 8½ days. The width varied with the depth and current, but 70 to 80 yards seems to have been an average width, with a depth of 2 to 3 ft., and current varying from 2 to 8 knots, according to circumstances. The greatest width was 180 yards at the Jordan's mouth, with a depth of 3 ft., and a very slow current.

Almost the only description of the Jordan banks from the river itself is given by Lynch in the account which he has written of his adventurous boat journey. The following are the most important passages.

'The river . . . curved and twisted north, south, east and west, turning, in the short space of half an hour, to every quarter of the compass, seeming as if desirous to prolong its luxuriant meanderings in the calm and silent valley, and reluctant to pour its sweet and sacred waters into the accursed waters of the bitter sea. . . .

' For hours in their swift descent the boats floated down in silence, the silence of the wil·lerness. Here and there were spots of solemn beauty. The numerous birds sang with a music strange and manifold ; the willow branches were spread upon the stream like tresses, and creeping mosses and clambering weeds, with a multitude of white and silver little flowers, looked out from among them ; and the cliff swallow wheeled over the falls, or, at his own wild will, darted through the arched vistas, shadowed and shaped by the meeting foliage on the banks ; and above all, yet attuned to all, was the music of the river, gushing with a sound like that of shawms and cymbals. The stream sometimes washed the banks of the sandy hills, and at other times meandered between low banks, generally fringed with trees and fragrant with blossoms. Some points presented views exceedingly picturesque — the mad rushing of a mountain torrent, the song and sight of birds, the overhanging foliage, and glimpses of the mountains far over the plain, and here and there a gurgling rivulet pouring its tribute of crystal water into the now muddy Jordan. The western shore was peculiar from the high calcareous limestone hills, which form a barrier when swollen by the efflux of the Sea of Galilee during the winter and early spring ; while the left or eastern bank was low, fringed with tamarisk and willow, and occasionally a thicket of lofty cane, and tangled masses of shrubs and creeping plants, giving it the character of a jungle. At one place we saw the fresh track of a tiger [*nimr* or cheetah ?] on the low clayey margin, where he had come to drink. At another time as we passed his lair, a wild boar started with a savage grunt and dashed into the thicket ; but for some moments we traced his pathway by the shaking cane and the crashing sound of breaking branches. . . . Many islands, some fairy-like, and covered with a luxuriant vegetation, others mere sandbars and sedimentary deposits, intercepted the course of the river, but were beautiful features in the grand monotony of the shores—the regular and almost unvaried scene of the high-banked alluvial deposit and sandhills on the one hand, and the low swamp - like shore, covered to the water's edge with the tamarisk, the willow, and the thick high cane, would have been fatiguing without the frequent occurrence of sandbanks and verdant islands. High up in the sand bluffs the cliff swallow chattered from his nest in the hollow, or darted about in the bright sunshine in pursuit of the gnat and the water fly ' (Lynch, *Narrative*, pp. 211–215).

The Plains. — The words principally used in the OT in connexion with portions of the Jordan Valley are *'ărābāh, midbār, ciccār, gĕlîlôth, jĕshîmon, sādeh, shĕdēmôth, biḳ'ah.*

The *'Arābāh.* — Without the definite article *'Arābāh* refers to any desert or wilderness ; but with the definite article it is used only for that part of the Jordan Valley which is a desert extending from some miles above Jericho to 'Aḳabah, and including the Salt Sea, which is often called ' the Sea of the Arabah ' (Dt 3¹⁷ 4⁴⁹, Jos 3¹⁶ 12³). It is used 21 times in this extended sense, and is usually tr⁴ in AV ' the plain ' or ' the plains ' : in RV it is invariably tr⁴ ' the Arabah.' In the plural ('*ărābōth*) it occurs 19 times in the historical books, and with one exception it refers to a definite spot, viz. the uncultivated land at the northern end of the Salt Sea, the steppes of Jericho (Jos 4¹³ etc.), or the steppes of Moab (Nu 22, etc.). The exceptional case is 2 S 15²⁸, tr⁴ in AV as ' the plain of the wilderness.' It is probable, however, that RV, ' the fords of the wilderness,' is correct (reading עֲבָרַת, not עַרְבַת). See ARABAH.

Midbār, ' wilderness ' (pasture land). With the article this word is generally used for the wilderness of Arabia, but sometimes for tracts of pasture land about Palestine, particularly in respect to the wilderness or pasture country east of Jerusalem, and the passing to it is ' the way of the wilderness ' (Jos 8¹⁵. ²⁰ 16¹, Jg 11²² 20⁴², 2 S 15²³. ²⁸ 17¹⁶).

Ciccār, 'round,' 'circle,' a tract of country (when the article is generally used). The word is used for denoting—(*a*) the floor of the valley through which the Jordan runs, with reference to the cultivated parts; (*b*) the oasis which formerly existed in the lower part of the valley around the cities of the Plain. In the former sense it is used 5 times. In 2 S 18²³ it is used to denote the direction taken by Ahimaaz 'by the way of the plain.' In 1 K 7⁴⁶, 2 Ch 4¹⁷ it refers to the plain of the Jordan, where was the clay ground between Succoth and Zeredah. In Neh 3²² 12²⁸ it refers to the country about Jerusalem, 'men of the plain.' In its restricted sense it is used 8 times to denote the *oasis* where the cities of the Plain were situated, Gn 13¹⁰ 19¹⁷, Dt 34³.

Gĕlīlōth, '*circle*,' is used to denote the *borders* of Jordan in two cases. Jos 22¹⁰· ¹¹ (see GELILOTH).

Jĕshīmon, '*wilderness*,' refers to a wilderness generally, and not to any particular portion of the Jordan Valley so far as can be judged (see, however, Dillm. on Nu 33⁴⁹ and art. JESHIMON).

Sādeh, '*field*,' is generally used to denote cultivated ground. It is used for the 'field of Moab,' Gn 36³⁵, but it is not certain whether this is in the Jordan Valley or upper levels. Stanley (*SP* 491) suggests that the 'Vale of Siddim' is the 'valley of the cultivated fields.'

Shĕdēmōth, '*fields*,' is used for highly cultivated ground. The 'fields of Gomorrah,' Dt 32³²; of Kidron, 2 K 23⁴; of Heshbon, Is 16⁸.

Bik'ah, a broad plain between two mountain ranges, like that of Cœle-Syria. It is used once in apposition with *ciccār*, 'the Round, even the plain (בִּקְעַת) of Jericho' (Dt 34³). 'All the region round about Jordan' (Mt 3⁵, Lk 3³) does not appear to be capable of geographical location.

Tributaries of the Jordan.—From the west (1) the *Wâdy el-Bireh*, rising about Tabor, a mountain torrent; (2) *Nahr el-Jalûd*, which rises near Jezreel (250 ft.), and passes down the valley of Esdraelon past *Beisan* to the Jordan. This is the valley by which the inland sea in the valley of Jordan would have been connected with the Mediterranean after the connexion by the Gulf of Akabah was cut off, supposing that the rise of the ground was uniform. (3) The *Wâdy Fârah*, which rises on the east of Ebal and Gerizim, flows in a beautiful perennial stream, fringed with oleanders, to the Jordan. The springs about the plain of *Beisan* and the *Wâdy el-Mâleh*—the wâdis *Fuseil*, *el-'Aujeh*, *en-Nweimeh*, and *el-Kelt*—run for a great part of the year.

On the east are (1) the *Sheri'at el-Mandhôr*, Jarmûk, or Hieromax, which flows into the Jordan past Gadara and the hot springs of Amatha, mentioned by Pliny, Strabo, Josephus, and the Talmud, but the name does not occur in the Bible. It is a large river, running through a deep gorge into the Jordan, and has its sources in the Haurân. (2) The *Wâdy el-'Arab*, a mountain torrent, the *Nahr es-Zerka* or Jabbok, which rises at 'Amman (Philadelphia), and falls into the Jordan near *Jisr ed-Damieh*. (3) The wâdis *Nimrîn*, *Kafrein*, and *Hesbân*, the last of which rises in the hills near Heshbon.

Communication. — Roads, bridges, and fords. There is an ancient road on the western bank of the Jordan which, apparently coming from Jerusalem, passes Neby Mûsa near the north-western end of the Salt Sea, passes *'Ain es-Sultân* (Jericho) and *Fûseil* (Phasaelus), near which place one branch passes to the west up *Wâdy Kerâd* to *Nablûs* (Shechem), and the other skirts *Kurn Surâbeh* to the east, and at *Tell el-'Abied* again divides, one branch to the west going up *Wâdy Fârah* to *Nablûs*, the other passing along the *Umm ed-Deraj*, a steep and rocky ascent just above the Jordan, passes through *Beisan*, and, keeping near

to the Jordan, skirts the L. Tiberias to the village *Tabarîya* (Tiberias). At *Khan el-Kerak* there is a ruin which was a fort protecting the lake district, at *Jisr Mijâmia* a branch of this road crosses the Jordan and goes through Gadara to the *Haurân*, and another branch to *Irbed*, and probably to Jerasa. This is a Roman road, and the old foundation stones and pavement are visible in many parts.

A good road from *Akka* passes down the *Sahel el-Ahma*, and, emerging by the pass at its mouth on to the Jordan, crosses at the *Jisr es-Sidd* a little below L. Tiberias and passes east to the *Haurân*; it is used by the Bedawîn and Druses to bring barley to Akka by camel. A branch of this road also on crossing the Jordan to the east runs down along the foot of the hills bounding the *Ghôr*, and passing *Fâhil* (Pella) crosses the *Zerka* at a point where it is a foaming torrent, goes to *Nimrîn*, and thence by *Kafrein* to *Hesbân*.

The road along the coast of the lake from Tiberias also crosses the Jordan near Tarichæa, where there is a ruined bridge, and passes up the east side of the lake and also by a great Roman road to Hippos and the north-east. The *Jisr Mijâmia* is 6 miles south of L. Tiberias, the point where the old important Roman road from *Nablûs* and *Beisan* to Damascus crosses the Jordan: it has one large pointed arch and three small ones.

At *Jisr Damieh*, below the junction of the Jordan and *Zerka*, the road from Neapolis (Shechem) runs to *es-Salt*, *Amman* (Philadelphia), and the east. This bridge is still in a good state of preservation (one arch), but the Jordan has left it and now passes down another portion of the *Zôr*; here is a good illustration of the change in direction of the river in a few hundred years. This bridge is said by Conder to be Saracenic: it appears to have been originally of Roman work, with extensive repairs by Moslems or Crusaders. On the east side the bank is quite low, and the wide flat at that point is often overflowed; hence a causeway at great expense and labour has been made across the low ground. 450 ft. of this causeway on the eastern side still remains, supported on arches of which nine still exist. The bridge itself could not have been less than 100 ft. in length (*PEFSt*, 1879, 139).

No remains of bridges mark the old roads from Jerusalem and Jericho to the east of Jordan, but there are still the remains of the roads which now cross to *Nimrîn* by the *el-Mandesi* and *Umm Enkhôla* fords to *Kafrein* and *Hesbân* by the *el-Ghôraniyeh* ford, and to *Hesbân* and the east of Salt Sea by the *Makhadet Hajlah* ford. These are the principal fords in the southern 25 miles of the Jordan's course. In the 40 miles to the north there are enumerated no fewer than fifty fords: probably this difference is owing to the more stony character of the Jordan bottom in the northern portion. Molyneux says of the upper part of its course (p. 115): 'I am within the mark when I say that there are many hundreds of places where we might have walked across without wetting our feet, on the large rocks and stones.' This must have been during a very dry season.

CLIMATE: FAUNA AND FLORA. — For many years past, meteorological observations have been taken at various points in Palestine, and have been tabulated and commented on annually by Glaisher. There are three distinctive climates in Palestine: (1) that of the seashore, which corresponds to other Mediterranean climates in similar latitude; (2) that of the hill-country, which is more hot and oppressive than the hill-country in other parts of the Mediterranean, owing to the vicinity of the Arabian Desert on south and east; and (3) that of the valley of the Jordan and Salt Sea.

The climate of the hill-country, Jerusalem for example, is pleasant in the winter, but hot and trying for six months in the summer. During the heat of summer in a house in Jerusalem the temperature day after day will for two or three hours reach 104° F., and it sometimes does not go below 80° F. all night. The published returns, however, give much lower readings in the air, with a mean temperature for August of 75° F. In the Jordan Valley in summer-time the heat is intense, the temperature being 110° F. after sunset, and scarcely falling during the night when in the vicinity of rocks with a southern aspect. During the first two months of the year the temperature in the Jordan Valley is very pleasant, hot in the daytime and cool at night, often going down to 40° F. except close to the Salt Sea. Much depends, however, upon the direction of the wind. In the month of March there is often snow on the hills. The climate of the Jordan Valley is tropical; that of the region of the Salt Sea is equatorial, probably the most heated in the world, owing to the depressed character of the plain, hemmed in east and west by high mountains. There is a difference of elevation between the summit of Mount Hermon and the level of the Salt Sea of over 10,000 ft., and the difference of temperature and of climate allows of a great variety of animal life. That on the seashore generally is Mediterranean, while that in the Jordan Valley, especially in the lower parts, is principally Ethiopian or Indian, though these parts are cut off from each other by the deserts of Arabia.

The following observations concerning life in the Jordan Valley are extracted principally from *SWP, Fauna and Flora* (Tristram). Here is a patch of tropical character, containing southern forms so peculiar and unique that their presence cannot be connected with any existing causes or other transporting influences. As it has been found by Humboldt that zones of elevation on mountains correspond to parallels of latitude, so here we find a zone of depression, the only one known to us, producing similar phenomena, and exhibiting in generic correspondence the fauna and flora of much lower latitudes: an Ethiopian flora identical with that now existing in Ethiopian regions in the midst of a Mediterranean district. Tristram considers that the whole of Syria and Arabia Petræa must have emerged from the Miocene ocean while the coast of the Mediterranean was the bed of a Miocene sea, and that during this period Palestine was connected with Ethiopia; that during the Miocene and Pliocene periods the Jordan basin formed the northernmost of a long system of fresh-water lakes, extending from north to south, of which, perhaps in the earlier part of the epoch, the Red Sea and Nile basin, Nyanza, Nyassa, and Tanganyika lakes were members. During that warm period, fluviatile ichthyological fauna were developed suitable to its then conditions, consisting of representative and perhaps frequently identical species, throughout the area under consideration. The advent of the Glacial period was, like its close, gradual, and, while many species may have perished, the hardiest would have survived, and have gradually modified to meet the changed conditions. But however severe the climate may have been, that of the Lebanon with its glaciers probably corresponding to the Alps at a proportional elevation (due regard being had to latitude), the fissure of the Jordan lay, as we know, as much depressed as at present, and there must have been an exceptionally warm temperature in its waters in which the existing ichthyological fauna could survive.

According to Slater's definition of boundary lines laid before the Linnæan Society in 1858, Palestine forms an extreme southern province of the Palæarctic region. An analysis of each class of its fauna and of its phanerogamic flora shows that while an overwhelming majority of its species in all cases belong to the Palæarctic region, there is in each class a group of exceptions and peculiar forms which cannot be referred to that region, and the presence of many of which cannot be explained merely by the fact of the Palæarctic infringing on the Ethiopian region, and not very distantly on the Indian, but can be satisfactorily accounted for only by reference to the geological history of the country. These species are almost all strictly confined to the area of the Jordan Valley and Dead Sea basin.

Of the mammalia, 55 are Palæarctic, 34 Ethiopian, 16 Indian, and 13 peculiar out of 118. The Indian include 9 which are also Ethiopian, and the Ethiopian 9 which are equally Indian. Of the 13 peculiar forms, 3 are modifications of Palæarctic types and 6 are Ethiopian in their character. One species, *Lepus judœæ*, the hare of the Dead Sea basin, differs from either the European or Syrian species in the form of its skull. The *Hyrax syriacus* belongs to a strictly Ethiopian genus, and no theory of immigration or dispersion can account for its presence. Fish of small size abound in the Jordan and its tributaries down to the entrance to the Salt Sea; they bear a strong affinity to many of the species of the Nile, though with far less admixture of species than is found in other rivers of the Eastern Mediterranean. Out of 35 species, 2 are Nilotic, 1 Mediterranean, 7 common to the Tigris and Euphrates, 10 common to Syria and the Damascus lakes, and 16 peculiar to the Jordan. There is a great affinity between these fish and those of the rivers and lakes of tropical Africa. These fishes probably date from the earliest times after the elevation of the country above the Eocene ocean, and they form a group more distinct and divergent from that of the surrounding region than can be found in any other class of existing life. The affinity is very close to the forms of the rivers and fresh-water lakes of east Africa, even as far south as the Zambesi; but while the genera are the same, the species are rather representative than identical. The solution lies in the theory of the Jordan basin having been one of a system of fresh-water lakes, extending from north to south as already proposed. There are no fish in the Salt Sea.

The *Avifauna* of Palestine, out of 348 known species, present 271 Palæarctic, 40 Ethiopian (10 of these also Indian), 7 Indian, and 30 peculiar to Syria. But they are not equally diffused over the whole area. The Palæarctic species almost all belong to the coast area, and the highlands east and west of Jordan, while the Ethiopian and Indian types are almost exclusively confined to the deep depression of the Jordan and Dead Sea basin, which, with the exception of some winter migrants, affords us very few Palæarctic species. There are 11 species belonging to as many different genera peculiar to the Jordan and Dead Sea basin, and not yet traced beyond its limits. Some of these belong to genera exclusively Ethiopian, most of them common to the Ethiopian and Indian regions. The *avifauna* of the Jordan and Dead Sea basin is decidedly distinct and typical in its species, revealing sometimes Indian, more generally African affinities.

Of the 3000 species of phanerogamic plants, the larger proportion consists of the common Mediterranean forms. Sir J. Hooker has remarked that though a vast number are common to the whole country, yet there is a great and decided difference between the floras of such localities as the tops of (1) Lebanon, (2) Carmel, and (3) the hills bordering the Jordan. Of 162 species of plants in *Wâdy Zuweireh* (S.W. corner of Dead Sea), 27 are common European forms extending to Northern India, the remaining 135 are African. Although the Dead Sea flora bears a very strong general similarity to that of Arabia Petræa, yet there can be no question of its distinctness from the adjacent floras of the same latitudes east and west of it.

In the Jordan Valley the *Cyperus papyrus* is locally abundant, and covers many acres in the marshes of *Hûleh*, though long since extinct in Egypt, and not known in Africa farther north than on the White Nile, lat. 7° N. *Calotropis procera* and *Salvadora persica* are never found except close to the Dead Sea, at En-gedi, Safieh, and Seisaban, and are separated by many degrees of longitude and latitude from their other known habitats.

The flora of the Salt Sea area is remarkable for a small average number of species distributed through a large number of orders. We may infer that in this borderland of Europe, Asia, and Africa, the more hardy and accommodating plants of each area hold their own, while those more readily affected by variation of soil or climate disappear.

The following plants and trees of the Jordan Valley are most common : the *Zyzyphus Spina Christi*, or *nubk* or *dôm* tree of the Arabs (which seems to correspond to the 'wait a bit' bushes of South Africa in its power of detaining the unwary traveller). It has a small sub-acid fruit like a thorn apple, very agreeable to the taste. The *Retm* or *Genista Rœtem*, broom plant, grows freely on the plain. There is also the *Balanites Ægyptiaca*, a thorny tree with large olive-like fruit, which affords the oil called *zukkûm* or *Zuk* by the Arabs, supposed to be balm of Gilead, and sold to the pilgrims as such. It is highly prized among Arabs and pilgrims as a remedy for wounds or bruises ; the latter call it ' Zaccheus oil' (*BRP*[2] i. 560). The castor-oil plant and the oleander flourish about Jericho. Tamarisks grow everywhere, on the banks of the streams and in the dry desert ; and the *Agnus Casti*, a large flowering bamboo. The acacia tree grows in great variety, also the *Populus Euphratica* on the banks of the Jordan. The caper plant hangs down from the rocks, with its delicate white blossoms, and the *Solanum Sodomæum* or Dead Sea apple, with its bright yellow fruit, is very conspicuous. Numbers of thoroughly tropical plants and trees abound—the *Zygophyllum coccineum*, *Bœrhavia*, *Indigofira* ; also on the shore of the Salt Sea the *Calotropis procera* ('*ösher* among Arabs), a beautiful green fruit the size of a peach, with nothing inside but the silky coma of the seeds ; it reaches a height of 15 ft., and grows freely in Upper Egypt, Nubia, and Arabia Felix.

The principal larger wild animals of the Jordan Valley are the jackal, fox, hyæna, boar, ibex (*beden*), and leopard. The leopard (*nimr, felis pardus*) is found in the Jordan jungle ; the writer sent one to England from the banks of the Jordan in 1867. The cheetah (*felis jubata*) is found among the hills, and is tamed by the Moslems of Syria and used in hunting gazelles. Lions are said not to exist in Palestine, though they are found not far to the east in the desert and in the jungle of the Euphrates. They are still, however, supposed by the inhabitants of the Anti-Lebanon to pay visits periodically to the neighbourhood ; and in 1869, owing to the loss of four children, one by one, at the village of Burkush, search was made for the supposed lion by the inhabitants without avail (*PEFSt*, 1870, 226). The lion coming up from the thickets of the Jordan is spoken of in Jer 49[19] 50[44]. The birds in the Jordan Valley vary very much according to the time of year, those of the hillcountry being driven down there for a short time in the cold season. During a winter visit of Chichester Hart (*PEFSt*, 1879, 286), the following were seen at Jericho : a few sun birds, 'hopping thrush, shrikes, palm dove, collared turtle, English robins, jays, chaffinches, wheatears, blackbirds, wagtails. The larger birds, such as eagles, vultures, bustards, flamingoes, water birds of various kinds, belong to Palestine or to a larger area, and not particularly to the Jordan Valley.

A review of the botany as well as the zoology of the Jordan basin reveals the interesting fact that in this isolated spot, comprising but a few square miles, a series of forms of life are found differing decidedly from the species of the surrounding region, to which they never extend, and bearing a strong affinity to the Ethiopian region, with a trace of Indian admixture.

Cultivation.—The plains about Lake Hûleh are highly cultivated, and yield heavy crops of wheat, barley, Indian corn, sesame, and even rice. The plains about L. Tiberias wave with corn, and the plains of *Beisan* and valley of Jezreel are very productive, and stand thick with corn or indigo. Stunted palms grow wild, but no large ones now exist, except the single large date palm at Jericho. There are many cucumber and vegetable-marrow gardens at the foot of the hills, irrigated by fountains. In the *Zôr*, barley and *simsim* flourish. The olive, figs, bananas, oranges, sugar-cane, tobacco, grapes, millet (dhurah), cotton, indigo, melons, cucumbers, and marrows are cultivated at Jericho, and the soil for miles around if supplied with water is yet, as of old, capable of the highest cultivation : all that is wanted is irrigation and weeding. The harvest in the Jordan Valley is fully a month in advance of that in the highlands.

JORDAN AS A BOUNDARY. — Stanley remarks (*Sin. and Pal.* 286) : ' The tropical temperature to which its whole plain is thus exposed, whilst calling out into almost unnatural vigour whatever vegetation receives the life-giving touch of its waters, withers up every particle of verdure that is found beyond their reach. As a separation of Israel from the surrounding country, as a boundary between the two main divisions of the tribes, as an image of water in a dry and thirsty soil, it played an important part ; but not as the scene of great events or the seat of great cities. Its contact with the history of the people is exceptional, not ordinary, confined to rare and remote occasions, the more remarkable from their very rarity.' This is the general view taken at the present day, with Palestine under a feeble government and an enervated race inhabiting the Jordan Valley. The valley was, however, once ' well watered everywhere as the garden of the LORD, and like the land of Egypt,' and this may very well occur again under a stable government and a more energetic race of people. The levels about Jericho and Kafrein are about 200 ft. below that of Lake Tiberias, so that the whole of the Jordan Valley might be irrigated by the Jordan waters if the matter were taken in hand as a Syrian national enterprise.

The terms 'this side Jordan,' or 'the other side Jordan,' are of constant occurrence in the early history, denoting that the Jordan was regarded as a physical feature of demarcation or boundary. The original boundary of the Promised Land was to reach 'unto the side of the sea of Chinnereth eastward. And the boundary shall go down to Jordan, and the extremity shall be at the Salt Sea' (Nu 34[12]). But the tribes of Reuben and Gad and half Manasseh saw that the eastern side of the Jordan, as now, was good for cattle, and they acquired their inheritance there (Nu 32[19]), outside the Promised Land, on condition of going armed over Jordan and fully assisting the people of Israel to conquer the land. On the completion of this work they were permitted to return to the eastern side with a blessing, after building an altar by Jordan, 'a great altar to see,' that might be a witness between them that they were one people, and that the tribes living west of Jordan should not in the future say to those on the east, 'What have ye to do with the Lord God of Israel? for the Lord hath made Jordan a boundary between us and you, ye children of Reuben and children of Gad' (Jos 22^10f.). See ED.

THE CITIES OF THE PLAIN.—The earliest account of the Jordan Valley describes it as very different in appearance from its aspect at the present time. From the high ground near Bethel, 'Lot lifted up his eyes, and beheld all the plain (*ciccār*) of Jordan, that it was well watered everywhere, before the LORD destroyed Sodom and Gomorrah, even as the garden of the LORD, like the land of Egypt, as thou comest into Zoar. So Lot chose him all the Plain of Jordan; and Lot journeyed east' (Gn 13^10f.). This would indicate a position for the cities of the Plain at the northern end of the Salt Sea, as proposed by Sir George Grove. The Arab geographers, however, place these cities at the southern end of the Salt Sea; and recently M. Clermont-Ganneau (*PEFSt*, 1886) has taken the same view, giving identifications for the several cities (see SODOM). On the other hand, Strabo (*Judæa*) in relating that Judæa is full of fire, places these cities on the western side of the Salt Sea within a radius of 60 stadia, close to Masada, and refers to the rocks there bearing the marks of fire, with a soil like ashes, pitch falling in drops from the rocks, rivers boiling up and emitting a fetid odour to a great distance; dwellings in every direction overthrown,—a description very suitable to this spot at the present day, where there are hot sulphur springs and every appearance of volcanic energy near at hand. Strabo describes the overthrow of the cities as due to shocks of earthquake, eruptions of flames, and hot springs, containing asphaltus and sulphur, causing the lake to break its bounds and the rocks to take fire. Josephus states that the country of Sodom bordered upon the Lake Asphaltitis (Salt Sea), and that the cities were burnt by lightning, in consequence of which there are still the remainders of that divine fire, and that the traces of the five cities are still to be seen (*BJ* IV. viii. 4; v. xiii. 6; Tac. *Hist.* v. 6; Diod. ii. 48, xix. 98; Curt. v. 16). He would appear (*BJ* IV. viii. 2) to place Sodom at the western side of the Arabah, near 'the utmost limits of the Asphaltitis southward,' and to place Somorrhon (Gomorrah?) on the eastern side, on the bounds of Petra in Arabia. Sir W. Dawson (*Egypt and Syria*) supposes that the overthrow of these cities may have been due to underground reservoirs of inflammable gases, and petroleum escaping through a fissure along an old line of 'fault,' causing bitumen and sulphur to rain upon the cities. There is no indication that the overthrow of these cities was accompanied by any earthquake or displacement of the level of the Salt Sea (Gn 14^3. 8. 10), though the passage 'in the vale of Siddim, which is the Salt Sea,' would appear ambiguous. The reference to the whole land which 'is brimstone, and salt, and burning, that it is not sown, nor burneth, nor any grass groweth therein, like the overthrow of Sodom' (Dt 29^23), etc., would appear to apply more to the southern end of the Salt Sea than the generally accepted site on the northern end. Assuming, however, that there was no disturbance affecting the level of the Salt Sea, it may be questioned whether the physical effect of the substitution of arid plains in lieu of the well-watered district which existed previously may not have seriously affected the fertility of the Jordan Valley. It is known that the level of the Salt Sea varies yearly many feet, according to the rainfall in the adjacent district, as is attested by the lines of driftwood which can be seen at successive levels around the Salt Sea. A change from moisture to dryness over a large area in the valley would essentially affect the surrounding country, and reduce the rainfall, lower the surface of the sea, and expose more and more dry soil. Now, supposing the effects of the overthrow of the cities of the Plain resulted in a fall of 50 ft. in the level of the waters of the lake, it is interesting to remark that the whole of the mud flat at the south of the Salt Sea for about 10 miles (Anderson, *Official Report*, p. 182) would have been covered with water, also a considerable portion of the peninsula of Lisan and the low-lying portions of the shore on the western side, while to the north the *Zôr* would have been covered over nearly as far as the Makhadet Hajlah. If this is so, the area over which the cities of the Plain can be found is very much circumscribed (Anderson, *Official Report*, p. 182). Assuming that the cities of the Plain were situated at the N.E. end of the Salt Sea, it is suggested (*PEFSt*, 1879, 144) that the following *tells* on the Abel-shittim plain were the five cities of the Plain: (1) Tell Kafrein (Abel or Abila), (2) Tell er-Rama (Beth-ramtha or Beth-haran, Julias or Livias), (3) Suweimeh (Beth-jesimoth or Besimoth), (4) Tell el-Hamman, (5) Tell Ektanu ('the little one,' or Zoar). Ganneau (*PEFSt*, 1886), however, identifies *Jebel Usdum* as Sodom, and Gomorrah with *'Ain Ghamr*, at the entrance of *Wâdy Ghamr*, about 20 leagues south of the Salt Sea, and Zoar in *Wâdy es-Safi*. This would appear closely to agree with the traditional sites given by Josephus, already mentioned.

PASSAGES OF THE JORDAN.—It was at the northern extremity of the Jordan that Abram (Gn 14^13f.), in his pursuit of Chedorlaomer, came up with him at Laish (Dan), and rescued his kinsman Lot.

The first record of a passage of the Jordan is that by Jacob (Gn 32^10). On the return journey (Gn 33^17) he crosses on his road from Succoth to Shalem (RVm; but there can be little doubt that RV 'in peace' is the correct translation), a city of Shechem; but as Succoth has not been satisfactorily identified, the ford of passage cannot be conjectured. The passage of Elijah (2 K 2^8) and the return of Elisha (2^14) over the Jordan took place over against Jericho; but there is nothing further to indicate the position, though there is a traditional spot on the east of Jordan from which the ascent of Elijah is said to have been made. The point of the Jordan where David crossed when warring against Helam (2 S 10^17) also cannot be conjectured. Again, when a fugitive to Mahanaim (2 S 15^28 17^16 19^18), he probably escaped by the quickest route over the Jordan; but this depended upon the road he took from Jerusalem, and whether he wished to avoid Jericho. The two fords which would be most suitable would be that of el-Ghôranîyeh, which would necessitate his passing by Jericho, and the Makhadet Hajlah ford, which he could have reached by the road passing the present *M. Neby Mûsa*.

The number of fords between Jisr Damieh and Lake Tiberias exceeds 50, and it would be futile to suggest any particular one which may have been used in that portion of the Jordan, in the passings over between the east and west. There was the ford or passage of the Jordan (Jg 12^5f.), taken by the Gileadites, when the Ephraimites were discovered by the pronunciation of the word 'Shibboleth.' There was Beth-barah ('even Jordan,' RV), which the Ephraimites (Jg 7^24) took possession of when they slew the Midianites, and which may be the ford *'Abarah* discovered by Conder (*SWP* ii. 89). The occurrence probably took place near this ford, as *'Ain el-Helwah* (Abel-meholah) is on the southern end of the plain of *Beisan* (Bethshean).

Passage of the children of Israel over Jordan.— This is the most important event recorded in the Bible connected with the passage of the Jordan. The people were gathered together in the plains ('*ărăbôth*) of Moab, extending from Abel-shittim ('the meadow of the acacia'), now probably Ka‡rein, to Beth-jesimoth ('house of the wastes'), now probably 'Ain Suweimeh near the Salt Sea (Nu 33⁴⁹). And they came to Jordan and lodged there for three days. The plains of Moab, where they had been staying, were from 200 to 400 ft. above the Salt Sea, and the ground which they had occupied for the last three days was probably somewhat on a lower level, but certainly not the *Zôr* or lower terrace of the Jordan as it was in flood, 'overflowing all his banks at the time of the barley harvest' (Jos 3¹ᵗ·), probably about the month of April. The description states that the waters which came down from above stood and rose up upon a heap very far from the city of Adam, that is, beside Zaretan; and those that came down toward the sea of the Arabah, even the Salt Sea, were wholly cut off (Jos 3¹⁶). The RV has 'at Adam,' and Stanley (304 note) has 'high up the river, very far, in Adam, the city which is beside Zaretan.' The site of Adam is not sufficiently identified, but it is supposed by some to be represented by *Tell Damieh*, near the bridge of that name. Conder has pointed out (*SWP* ii. 14) that somewhat higher up, where the mountains come down and overhang the Jordan, a landslip could readily block up the Jordan for a period, and T. Drake (*PEFSt*, 1874, 182; 1875, 30) suggests that Adam ('red earth') may be *Khan el-Hamrath*, the Red Ruin, situated opposite *Fâhil* (Pella), on the west side of the Jordan in the plain of *Beisan*, and that adherents of the theory that the waters of the Jordan were suddenly dammed by a landslip might perhaps point to the present appearance of the banks at this point and the curious bends of the river here to support their idea. M. Clermont-Ganneau has brought to notice that the historical stoppage of the Jordan in A.D. 1257, while the bridge *Jisr Damieh* was being repaired, is to be found in the history of Sultan Bibars. A landslip in the narrow part of the valley, some miles above *Jisr Damieh*, kept the Jordan dammed up for several hours, allowing the bed of the river to become dry by the water below running off to the Salt Sea. Stanley (*Sin. and Pal.* 304 n. 6) mentions that the appearance of the drying up of the Jordan seems to be described by Antoninus Martyr in the 6th cent., as if it occurred yearly at the visit of the pilgrims. See also King, *Morsels of Criticism*, i. 281.

THE MOUNDS IN THE JORDAN VALLEY.—All over the Jordan Valley mounds or 'Tells' are found, of artificial formation, from 50 to 100 ft. in height. They stand at the entrance to every wâdy where there is a passage for traffic, and appear in these cases to have been placed there to guard the dwellers in the plain from marauders from the hill-country. They appear usually to be formed of remains of sun-dried bricks, probably in some cases the ruins of ancient walls and castles, and in other cases the sites where the bricks were moulded and dried. Near *Beisan* alone there are 20 of these tells, apparently of the same character as those at Jericho. They usually occur in the vicinity of water.

The mounds of Jericho were examined by the present writer in Feb. 1868. Nine mounds were cut through—two at *Wâdy Kelt*, three at '*Ain es-Sultân*, and four within a short distance of the spring head. The trenches were cut across from east to west to get shelter from the sun as much

as possible. During the daytime the sun was scorching, at night it was bitterly cold. After the trenches were cut 8 ft. deep, the work was continued by shafts 8 ft. square at intervals of 4 to 6 ft., as the clay composing the mounds would not stand the cutting of one deep trench. Very little was found except pottery jars, and stone mortars for grinding corn. The general result was that the mounds were artificial, of sunburnt brick in a very friable condition, abounding in fragments of pottery. A few solid-looking jars were found (now in the *PEF* Museum). The pottery in the upper portion of these mounds was Roman and later (*SWP* iii. 225).

SCENE OF OUR LORD'S BAPTISM.—When John the Baptist was preaching in the wilderness of Judæa, 'Then went out to him Jerusalem and all Judæa, and all the region round about Jordan, and were baptized of him in the river Jordan. Then cometh Jesus from Galilee to Jordan unto John to be baptized of him.' 'These things were done in Bethabara (RV Bethany, in some MSS Betharabah *), beyond Jordan, where John was baptizing' (Jn 1²⁸). 'Then was Jesus led up of the Spirit into the wilderness to be tempted of the devil' (Mt 4¹). 'And straightway the Spirit driveth him forth into the wilderness' (Mk 1¹²).

There is not sufficient information here to fix the position on the Jordan of the scene of the baptism, but it leads to the inference that it was on the east side of the Jordan opposite to the desert of Judæa, and not so far north as Samaria. This place, Bethabara [which see] (or Bethany), beyond Jordan, was again visited by our Lord, and He abode there (Jn 10⁴⁰). The word '*ăbārāh* occurs in the OT in connexion with the Jordan. In 2 S 19¹⁸ EV tr. it 'ferry-boat' (Gesenius 'a ferry-boat' or 'raft'); 2 S 15²⁸ 17¹⁶ AV reading (עֲרָבָה) 'in the plains,' RV reading (עֲבָרַת) 'at the fords,' Ewald, Gesenius, Grätz, 'at the fords'; Jg 7²⁴ Bethbarah, 'house of passage,' (?) Gesenius. There are also three cases in which the word *ma'bārāh* ('a ford'; Gesenius, from the root '*ābar*, 'to pass over') is tr^d 'the fords' (of the Jordan), Jg 3²⁸ 12⁵, Jos 2⁷. The inference is that *Beth-abarah* is the resting-place on the other side.

Stanley (*Sin. and Pal.* p. 311) gives 'the house of a ship' (אֳנִיָה) as the meaning of Bethania (Bethany); the meaning given by Simonis is preferred by many, viz. עֲנִיָּה 'בְ, *locus depressionis*, which seems to agree exactly with the conditions, a depressed plain beyond the fords of Jordan. The other word is Beth-arabah (the name of a town west of Jordan, Jos 15⁶ etc.). The Arabah, however, is the term used for the *desert plain* of the Jordan, extending from near Jericho to the Gulf of 'Akabah (Gesen.) and *Arabah* = desert. Conder proposes (*PEFSt*, 1876–77) to identify Bethania (Bethany) with Batanea or Bashan, and the ford of the Jordan east of Beisan called '*Abâra* with Bethabara, or at least with the place of baptism, and points out that among the fifty fords of the Jordan this is the only one retaining the ancient name.

This ford of 'Abara is north of the Samaritan border, about 16 miles south of Lake Tiberias and a day's journey from Nazareth, and 22 miles from *Kefr Kena* (Cana). It does not, however, fulfil the conditions of being near to the wilderness of Judæa, and so placed as to be accessible to the multitudes from Jerusalem and the parts about Judæa.

The line of route taken by king David in his passage from Jerusalem across Jordan to Mahanaim and back does not give much assistance, but is certainly against the '*Arabah* ford site. It appears

---

* Βηθανια אּ* ABC*EF al^pl latt syrr^pesh hcl txt hier arm me codd^pl. ap Orig: Βηθαβαρα C²KT^b (V) (Λ) Πcorr syrr^sin cu 1, 22. 33 (69), al^nonn: Βηθαραβα אּc. b syrh^cl mg.

probable, however, that he would pass over Jordan, when in flight, by the very nearest ford, viz. that over against Jericho, either the *Makhadet Hajlah* or the *Ghôraniyeh* ; in coming back he may have used any crossing most convenient, and thus have had recourse to the ferry-boat. There appears therefore to be nothing against the traditional site of our Lord's place of baptism being placed on the Jordan near Kasr el-Jehûd, and not far from the 'Ain el-Kharrar on the eastern side of the Jordan, as has been current since 4th cent. Beth-nimrah ('house of the panther'?), Nu 32³⁶, identified as *Nimrîn*, lies about 8 miles to the east of the Ghôraniyeh ford, and is supposed by some to be the site of Bethabara: in the LXX (B) it takes the form Βαιθαναβρά, and Eusebius calls it Βηθναμβρίς ; he also speaks of a town called *Nabara* (or *Abara*) as identical with Nimrah near Heshbon. Epiphanius reads Bethamara for Bethabara (Rel. *Pal.* p. 627). The Bordeaux Pilgrim (A.D. 333) places it east of Jordan, 5 miles north of the Salt Sea, close to the hill where Elijah was caught up to heaven (*Itin. Hieros.*). Jerome (*Per. S. Paulæ*) identifies the place of baptism with the spot where the priests that bare the ark of the covenant of the Lord stood firm on dry ground in the midst of Jordan (Jos 3¹⁷), and also the spot where Elijah and afterwards Elisha smote the waters and passed over dry-shod. The following also speak of the place of baptism at this spot: Theodosius, Antoninus, and Arculf.

In later years the knights of St. John built a monastery here in order to enable them to carry out one of their threefold duties, viz. escorting pilgrims down from Jerusalem to Jordan. This duty is still carried out once a year by the Turkish governor of Jerusalem, who, on Monday in Passion week, escorts thousands of pilgrims to the Jordan to bathe.

ANCIENT WRITERS ON THE JORDAN VALLEY.— The *Antiquities* and *Wars* of Josephus are full of references to this valley. (*Ant.* I. x. 1 and I. xi. 1) The spring of Jordan called Dan is spoken of, and the destruction of the cities of the Plain. (*Ant.* IV. viii. 1) Moses gathered the congregation together near Jordan where the city Abila now stands, a place full of palm trees. (*Ant.* V. i. 1) Abila to Jordan 60 furlongs. (*Ant.* V. i. 2) Joshua was in fear about their passing over, for the Jordan ran with a strong current, and could not be passed over by bridges, as there never had been any bridges laid over it hitherto, and ferry-boats they had none. (V. iv. 3) The Israelites seize the ford of the Jordan (Jg 3²⁸). (VII. xi. 2) A bridge of boats laid over Jordan to enable king David to return from Mahanaim to Jerusalem. (IX. ii. 2) Elijah disappeared from among men, and no one knows of his death to this very day. (*Ant.* XV. x. 3, V. v. 1, III. x. 7 ; *BJ* IV. i. 1, I. xxi. 3) The Jordan's sources at Dan and Panium described. The lake Semechonitis (*Hûleh*) is 30 furlongs in breadth and 60 in length ; its marshes reach as far as the plain Daphne, under the temple of the golden calf at the lesser Jordan. Jordan's stream from Panium divides the marshes and fens of the lake Semechonitis ; when it has run another 120 furlongs it first passes the city Julias, and then passes through the middle of the Lake Gennesaret, after which it runs a long way over a desert, and then makes its exit into the lake Asphaltitis. Around Gennesaret the soil is so fruitful that all sorts of trees are grown upon it, particularly walnuts ; also palm trees, fig trees, and olives ; it supplies men with figs and grapes 10 months in the year. Some have thought it to be a vein of the Nile, because it produces the coracine fish as well as that lake does which is near Alexandria. (*BJ* IV. viii. 2. 3. 4, V. xiii. 6) The Jordan and

Jericho are described. Jericho is situated on a plain, with naked and barren mountains overhanging it ; these mountains extend from Scythopolis in the north to Sodom in the south at the utmost limits of the Salt Sea. Somorrhon is also spoken of, the Great Plain, the Salt Sea, and the plantations of palm trees near the Jordan. He speaks of the fountain of Jericho being healed by Elisha ; and also of the excellent gardens of Jericho, 70 furlongs long and 20 broad, abounding in palm trees, yielding honey and bees, the balsamum, that most precious of all fruits, the cypress tree, and myrobalanum. He states that it is not easy to light on any country in the world equal to it. The lake Asphaltitis is also described. (*BJ* IV. viii. 4) He describes the aqueduct from Nerea to water the palm trees of Jericho.

Strabo (XVI. ii. 16, c. A.D. 19) gives a short account of the Jordan and Jericho. Cœle-Syria, a hollow plain between the mountains of Libanus and Antilibanus. Rivers run through it, the largest of which is the Jordan, which waters a country productive and fertile of all things. It contains also a lake, which produces the aromatic rush and reed. In it are also marshes. The name of the lake is Gennesaritis. It produces also balsamum. The Lycus and the Jordan are navigated upwards chiefly by the Aradii, with vessels of burden. At Jericho is the palm plantation, which contains various other trees of the cultivated kind producing excellent fruit, but its chief production is the palm tree ; it is 100 stadia in length ; the whole is watered with streams, and filled with dwellings. Here also is a palace and the garden of the balsamum. Strabo has not only given a confused account of the Jordan, but he has mixed up together the account of the Salt Sea with that of the Lacus Serbonis, and he places Tarichæa on the Salt Sea instead of on L. Tiberias.

Tacitus (*Hist.* v. 6, A.D. 97) sums up the Jordan in a few words : ' Nec Jordanes pelago accipitur : secundum atque alterum lacum integer perfluit : tertio retinetur.'

Galen (A.D. 164) and Pausanias (V. vii. 4, A.D. 174) speak of the disappearance of the Jordan in the bitter lake.

Pliny (*Hist. Nat.* v. 15, A.D. 74) speaks of the rise of Jordan at Panium fountain, ' qui nomen dedit Cæsareæ.'

Eusebius and Jerome (*Onomast. s.v.* ' Dan ') describe Dan as being 4 R. miles distant from Paneas on the way to Tyre ; and here, too, they say the Jordan breaks forth.

The Targum of Jerusalem writes, ' Dan of Cæsarea' (*Targ. Hieros.*, Gn 14¹⁴).

The name of the Salt Sea adopted by Josephus (*Ant.* I. ix.), viz. *Asphaltitis Lacus*, is first found in Diodorus Siculus (ii. 48, B.C. 45). He gives an account of the neighbourhood : ' It is, however, well fitted for the cultivation of palms wherever it is traversed by serviceable rivers or fountains available for the purpose of irrigation. In a neighbouring valley grows the plant called balsam, which yields an abundant income, as the plant grows in no other part of the world. It is much used by physicians as a medicine.'

Justin (XXXVI. iii. 6) and Pausanias (V. vii. 4) call it θάλασσα ἡ νεκρά, ' the Dead Sea.'

' As the Jordan in the time of harvest ' (Sir 24²⁶ ; Aristeas, *Epist. ad Philocratem*).

Josephus, *BJ* IV. vii. 6, speaks of Ἄβιλα, Ἰουλιάς (Julias), Βησιμώ, near the lake Asphaltitis.

In the LXX (B) of Jos 13²⁷ the name Beth-nimrah is given as Βαιθαναβρά, and the LXX (A) of Jos 13²⁰ gives Βηδιμούθ for Beth-jesimoth.

LITERATURE.—*SWP* i. ii. iii., 'Flora and Fauna, Geology'; *BRP*² i. ii. iii. (Index); Tristram, *Land of Israel* ; *Journal Pal. Geog. Soc.* xviii. 104, 1848 ; Molyneux, *Narrative and Official*

Reports; Lynch, *Narrative and Official Reports*; Neubauer, *Géog. du Talm.* 29 ff.; G. A. Smith, *HGHL* (Index).

C. WARREN.

JORIBUS ('Ιώριβος).—**1.** (AV Joribas) 1 Es 8⁴⁴ (⁴³ LXX)=JARIB, Ezr 8¹⁶. **2.** 1 Es 9¹⁹=JARIB, Ezr 10¹⁸.

JORIM ('Ιωρείμ).—An ancestor of Jesus, Lk 3²⁹.

JORKEAM (יָרְקְעָם).—A Judahite family name, 1 Ch 2⁴⁴. Kittel (in *SBOT*) suggests that we should perhaps read יָקְדְעָם (**Jokdeam**), the name of an unidentified place in the Negeb of Judah, Jos 15⁵⁶.

JOSABDUS ('Ιωσαβεές B, 'Ιωσάβδος A), 1 Es 8⁶³= JOZABAD, No. 6.

JOSAPHIAS ('Ιωσαφίας), 1 Es 8³⁶.—In Ezr 8¹⁰ JOSIPHIAH (wh. see).

JOSECH ('Ιωσήχ WH, 'Ιωσήφ TR, AV Joseph).— An ancestor of Jesus, Lk 3²⁶.

JOSEDEK.—See JEHOZADAK.

JOSEPH (יוֹסֵף, 'Ιωσήφ).—**1.** The patriarch. See next article, where also the meaning of the name is discussed. **2.** A man of Issachar, Nu 13⁷. **3.** A son of Asaph, 1 Ch 25². ⁹. **4.** One of the sons of Bani who had married a foreign wife, Ezr 10⁴², called in 1 Es 9³⁴ **Josephus**. **5.** A priest, Neh 12¹⁴. **6.** An ancestor of Judith, Jth 8¹. **7.** An officer of Judas Maccabæus. Along with Azarias he was defeated by Gorgias, 1 Mac 5¹⁸. ⁵⁶. ⁶⁰. **8.** In 2 Mac 8²², and probably also 10¹⁹, Joseph is read by mistake for **John**, one of the brothers of Judas Maccabæus. **9. 10.** Ancestors of our Lord, Lk 3²⁴. ³⁰. **11.** The husband of Mary the mother of Jesus. See sep. article. **12.** One of the brethren of the Lord, Mt 13⁵⁵ (RV, following WH; in Mt 27⁵⁶, Mk 6³ 15⁴⁰. ⁴⁷, both AV and RV have **Joses**). **13.** Joseph of Arimathæa (wh. see). **14.** Joseph Barsabbas (wh. see), Ac 1²³. **15.** The natal name of Barnabas (wh. see), Ac 4³⁶ (AV **Joses**).

JOSEPH (יוֹסֵף, in Ps 81⁶ יְהוֹסֵף 'May [God] add'; cf. Gn 30²⁴).*—The second youngest son of the patriarch Jacob, Rachel's firstborn, and ancestor of the two northern tribes Manasseh and Ephraim.

Sources.—The history of Joseph is contained in Gn 30²³ (E), ²⁴ (J); and in Gn 37. 39–50. In these chapters the body of the narrative is derived from J and E, the parts which belong to P being only 37¹⁻²ᵃ 41⁴⁶ 46⁶⁻²⁷ 47⁵⁻⁶ᵃ. ⁷⁻¹¹. ²⁷ᵇ⁻²⁸ 48³⁻⁶ 49¹ᵃ. ²⁸ᵇ⁻³³ 50¹²⁻¹³.

The structure of JE, in the parts where the distinction of sources is most important, will appear most clearly from the following table:—

J 37²¹	25-27	28b *	31-35	39 †
E	37²²⁻²⁵ (to *bread*)	28a (to *pit*)	28c-30	36
J		42³⁸⁻⁴⁴³⁴ ¶		46²⁸⁻⁴⁷⁴. ⁶ᵇ ††
E 40 ‡	41¹⁻⁴⁵. § 47-57 42¹⁻³⁷ ‖		45¹⁻⁴⁶⁵ **	
J	47¹³⁻²⁷ᵃ (to *Goshen*) 29-31.			
E 47¹²				

* The words, 'And they sold Joseph to the Ishmaelites for 20 pieces of silver.'

† Except in v.1 the words 'Potiphar, an officer of Pharaoh's, the captain of the guard.'

‡ Except v.8 'into the prison, the place where Joseph was bound'; v.5 'The butler and the baker of the king of Egypt, which were bound in the prison'; v.15b 'And here also have I done nothing, that they should have put me into the dungeon.'

§ Except v.14 'And they brought him hastily out of the dungeon.'

‖ Except vv.27. 28.

¶ Except 43¹⁴ (on account of the allusion to Simeon), and 43²³b 'And he brought Simeon out unto them.'

** Except 45⁴ᵇ 'whom ye sold unto Egypt,' ⁵ 'that ye sold me hither,' 10ᵃ 'and thou shalt dwell in the land of Goshen,' with perhaps one or two unimportant clauses elsewhere.

†† From 'in the land of Goshen.'

* In 30²³, from another source (E), a different etymology is given, as though the word were connected with אָסַף *to take away*.

For the grounds of this analysis, reference must be made to the Comms., or, more briefly, to *LOT* p. 16 f. (⁶17 ff.). The history of Joseph must have been told at length in J and E alike, in substantially the same form in both, but with occasional variations in details; and the method mostly followed by the compiler, esp. in chs. 39–47, has been to excerpt long passages from J and E alternately, and at the same time to incorporate in each short notices embodying the characteristic differences of the other. It may assist the reader to place here a synopsis of the principal differences between the two narratives. According to J, Joseph, when his brethren plot to kill him, is rescued by Judah, and then sold by his brethren to Ishmaelites, who in their turn sell him to an Egyptian of position, whose name is not given: after the charge brought against him by his master's wife, he is thrown into the state-prison; and the keeper of this makes him overseer of the other prisoners. In the sequel, the brethren only tell Joseph about their younger brother in answer to his inquiry (43⁷ 44¹⁹); nothing is said about Simeon being detained as a hostage in Egypt; the brethren open their sacks and discover the money in them, at the lodging-place by the way; Judah offers to be surety to his father for Benjamin's return; and Goshen is named as the district allotted to Jacob and his sons. According to E, Joseph is rescued from his other brethren by *Reuben*, and thrown into a pit, from which he is drawn up by *Midianites* without his brothers' knowledge: he is sold by them to *Potiphar*, captain of the guard, who appoints him to wait on the prisoners confined in his house: the brethren, when taxed with being spies, *volunteer* the information about their younger brother (42¹³. ³²); Simeon is left in Egypt as a hostage; the brethren open their sacks at the end of their journey home; *Reuben* offers to be surety for Benjamin's return; and there is no mention of Goshen.* Thus, while both versions bring Joseph into relation with a prison, he is a prisoner himself only in J; in E he is merely appointed to *wait on* the prisoners: further, while in J the keeper of the prison (who is distinct from Joseph's master, 39²⁰. ²¹) commits the other prisoners into his charge, in E his own master, the 'captain of the guard' (37³⁶ 40³ᵃ. ⁴), appoints him to wait upon the prisoners. In the existing (composite) narrative the two versions are harmonized (though imperfectly) by Potiphar being represented as *both* Joseph's master *and also* 'captain of the guard.'

After the account of his birth (30²³ᶠ.), the next notice of Joseph's life which occurs is when he has grown into a lad, and (according to P) is 17 years old (37²ᵃ). His father's favourite,† he excites the envy of his elder brothers, which is increased by his imprudence in communicating to them the dreams,—both too manifestly suggestive of future greatness (37³⁻¹¹),—of his brethren's sheaves bowing down to his, and of the sun, moon, and eleven stars making obeisance to him. Shortly afterwards, his brethren are keeping their father's flocks at Shechem; and Joseph is sent by his father from the broad 'vale,' in which Hebron lay (37¹⁴; cf. 35²⁷), to inquire after their welfare. He finds them at Dothan (2 K 6¹³), now *Tell Dothan*, about 15 miles N. of Shechem, where the pasturage is still even richer than it is at Shechem (Robinson, *BR* iii. 122). As they see him approaching in the distance, they plan to kill him, and so to frustrate for ever the, to them, unwelcome future portended by his dreams. At this point (37²¹ᶠ.) the composition of the narrative becomes apparent, and there are two divergent accounts of the manner in which Joseph was rescued from their hands, and came to be sold into Egypt.‡ According to J, *Judah* dissuades his other brethren from carrying out their purpose, and induces them to sell Joseph to a caravan of *Ishmaelites*, who happened at the time to be passing by, on their way from Gilead to Egypt;§ and the Ishmaelites, upon their arrival in Egypt, sell him

* This last distinction agrees with that which appears in Exodus, where similarly it is only J who describes the Israelites as living apart in Goshen (8²² 9²⁶).

† The כְּתֹנֶת פַּסִּים (also 2 S 13¹⁸ᶠ., as worn by princesses), the 'coat of many colours' of AV (so LXX ποικίλος, Vulg. *polymita*), was more probably (Pesh. Aq. Symm.; also LXX Vulg. in 2 S [χιτὼν καρπωτός ; *tunica talaris*]) a tunic having sleeves for the arms, and reaching to the feet (cf. RVm), lit. (if the Aram. sense of פַּס may be adopted, for the better known otherwise in the Heb. of the OT) *a tunic of palms* (of the hands) *and soles* (of the feet),—the tunic ordinarily worn having no sleeves, and reaching only to the knees.

‡ See, above, the parts which belong to the two narratives.

§ Dothan, it is to be observed, lies upon the caravan-route leading from Beth-shean and Jezreel to Ramleh and Egypt (Rob. *l.c.*); it was thus a natural spot for the Ishmaelite dealers, travelling from Gilead, to pass.

as a slave to an Egyptian of rank. According to E, *Reuben*,[*] Joseph's eldest brother, dissuades the others from carrying out their plan ; at his suggestion they cast Joseph into a pit, and *Midianite* merchantmen, passing by,[†] draw him up out of the pit, without his brothers' knowledge, and sell him into Egypt to Potiphar, the 'captain of the guard.'[‡] Reuben upon returning, after the meal (v.[25a]) to the pit, in the hope, no doubt, of being able now to send Joseph home secretly, is disconsolate to find it empty. His father's grief, upon receiving the blood-stained coat, which his brethren bring to him, as evidence of Joseph's death, is graphically portrayed (vv.[32-35] J).

How Joseph meanwhile fared in Egypt is recounted by J in ch. 39, and by E in ch. 40 (in each case, with the exceptions noted above). The Egyptian, to whom the Ishmaelites sold him,[§] finding him to be quick and trustworthy, appoints him 'over his house,'—*i.e.* makes him superintendent of his establishment, or his *major domo*,—and intrusts to him the whole of his domestic arrangements, so that 'with him—*i.e.* beside him —he knew not ought, save the bread that he did eat,' which, on account of religious scruples, would not in Egypt be naturally intrusted to the care of a foreigner (cf. 43[32b]). Under Joseph's administration, everything prospered in his master's house ; and the blessing of heaven rested visibly upon it (39[1-6]). But Joseph was 'comely and wellfavoured,' and attracted the notice of his master's wife : she makes advances to him, which he rejects, saying nobly that he will neither betray the trust which his master reposes in him, nor sin against God. The advances are repeated, but still meet with no response. In the end, enraged at what she considers as a slight received at Joseph's hands, she brings a false accusation against him before her husband ; and he is cast into the stateprison.[‖] There, however, J'' is still with him : he wins the favour of the keeper of the prison, who finds he can place in him implicit confidence, and even commits the other prisoners to his charge (39[7-23]).

Shortly afterwards (ch. 40 E), two of the Pharaoh's officers, the chief of his cupbearers, or butlers, and the chief of his bakers, offended the king, and they were placed in custody [¶] in the house of the 'captain of the guard,'—*i.e.* Potiphar, who, according to 37[36] (also E), had bought Joseph of the Midianites. Joseph is appointed to wait upon them (40[4]) ;[**] and, coming in to them one

morning, he hears from them about their two dreams. Unable to interpret them themselves, they recount them to him ; and he interprets them correctly. Three days after, on the Pharaoh's birthday, the chief butler, as Joseph foretold, is restored to his office, and the chief baker is hung (40[5-23]).

Ch. 41 (with the exceptions noted, E) tells the story of Joseph's elevation in Egypt. After two years, during which time his position remained unaltered (the chief butler having forgotten his promise to mention him to the king), the Pharaoh had his two dreams, of the fat and lean kine, and of the full and withered ears ; and much significance being attached in Egypt to dreams, he was disturbed to find no one able to interpret them. The chief butler, reminded by the occurrence of Joseph's skill in his own case, mentions him to the Pharaoh. He is sent for ; and, being brought before the king,[*] declares to him what his dreams signify, viz. seven years of plenty, to be succeeded immediately by seven years of famine : in view of the future, he further suggests the practical measure of making provision for the years of famine by storing up in advance a fifth of the produce of each of the years of plenty. The Pharaoh, impressed by his sagacity, and recognizing it as of God (41[38f.]), forthwith invests him with authority over the entire land of Egypt, for the purpose of giving effect to this proposal, and confers upon him other signal marks of the royal favour (41[40-44]) : he further, as a mark of his admittance into the Egyptian bureaucracy, bestows upon him an Egyptian name, Zaphnath-pa'anea'ḥ, and marries him to Asenath, a daughter of Potiphera, priest of the great national temple of the sun (Ra), at On (Heliopolis, 7 miles N.E. of the modern Cairo). A notice from P (41[46]) states that Joseph, at the time of his elevation, was 30 years of age. During the 7 years of plenty, Joseph amassed corn in the granaries of every city from the surrounding district : in the 5th of these years, we are told, Asenath bore him two sons, who were named, respectively, Manasseh in allusion to his *forgetting* now his past troubles, and Ephraim on account of his *fruitfulness* in the land of his affliction. When the years of famine began, the Egyptians all came to Joseph to buy corn (41[54-56]).

Famines in Egypt are due commonly to the failure of the annual inundation of the Nile. The famine in which Joseph is concerned is stated, however, to have extended to all the earth (41[57]) ; and this circumstance is the fact upon which the entire sequel of the story hinges. 42[1-37] (E, except vv.[27. 28]) tells how, as the famine became severe in Canaan, Jacob sends all his sons except Benjamin to buy corn in Egypt. Introduced into Joseph's presence, they prostrate themselves before him (cf. the dreams, 37[7-9]), but do not recognize him : during the years of separation [†] he has grown from a youth into a man, and his Egyptian dress and shaven face further disguise him. He receives them roughly, and accuses them of being spies, sent to discover the 'nakedness of the land.' The charge throws them off their guard ; and they seek to disarm his suspicions by volunteering information [‡] about their family, of which Joseph at once takes advantage : desirous, namely, of ascertaining the truth about Benjamin, he insists that one shall be left bound in Egypt, while the others go home, and bring back their youngest brother with

---

[*] At least, if (as most critics suppose) 'Judah' stood originally in v.[21] (J) for 'Reuben' (as the text stands, v.[21b] and v.[22a] are tautologous). But even if that be not the case, we have 'Reuben' in vv.[22. 29] (E), and 'Judah' in v.[26] (J).

[†] In v.[28] the absence of the art. before 'Midianites' shows that the reference cannot be to '*the* Ishmaelites,' mentioned specifically in v.[27].

[‡] Properly, 'captain (or superintendent, chief) of the slaughterers' (of animals [*not* 'executioners']), a Heb. title, though always, as it happens, applied to foreigners (elsewhere only, with רַב for שַׂר, of Neb.'s 'captain of the guard' Jer 39[9ff.] 41[10] 43[6] 52[12ff.], 2 K 25[8ff.], and Dn 2[14]). The royal butchers came in some way to form the royal bodyguard ; cf. W. R. Smith, *OTJC*[2] 262 f. LXX ἀρχιμάγειρος,—in itself a perfectly possible rendering (see 1 S 9[23. 24]), but not probable in view of Jer 39, etc.

[§] Identified in the existing text with Potiphar (37[36]) by the harmonizing insertion in 39[1b].

[‖] The expression is a peculiar one (not the ordinary Heb. term for 'prison'), and is found only here (39[20-23]) and 40[3. 5]. Understood as two Heb. words, it might mean 'house of roundness,' i.e. a circular tower, such as might be used as a prison ; but *ṣôhar* is perhaps the Hebraized form of an Egyp. word [cf. Ebers, *Aeg. u. die Bb. Mos.* 318 f. : the very special character of the *suḥan* at Thebes (see Maspero, *Struggle*, 271 n. 5) is an objection to Sayce's view (*EHH* 87) that it may be this word].

[¶] According to the insertions in vv.[3b. 5b. 15b] (J), in the stateprison, where Joseph was bound. In vv.[14b-15a], according to E, Joseph prays to be released, not from imprisonment, but only from servitude in a foreign land, after having been 'stolen away' from his native country (in agreement with E's representation in 37[25a. c]).

[**] Cf. 41[12] (also E). In 39[22] (J) Joseph is made *overseer* of the other prisoners ; and he receives this appointment, not from his master (as here), but from the keeper of the state-prison.

---

[*] According to the notice from J, inserted in v.[14], from the dungeon, in which J represents him as imprisoned (40[15b] 39[21-23]).

[†] According to E, more than 9 (41[1. 48]) ; taking account of the additional dates given by P (37[3] 41[46]), more than 20 (13 + the 7 of 41[48]).

[‡] 41[13], cf. v.[32]. In the parallel narrative of J, this information must have been given in answer to Joseph's express inquiry ; see 43[7] 44[19].

them. Their conscience, the narrator remarks, smites them : they recognize in their misfortunes a nemesis for their treatment of Joseph ; and Reuben—who regularly takes the lead in E—reminds them how he had sought to divert them from their purpose. Joseph understood all the time what they were saying, and was much moved by it : he adheres, however, to his terms, and retains as hostage, not indeed Reuben, his former protector, but the next eldest of his brethren, Simeon. Having secretly given orders for each man's money to be restored into his sack, and having given them provision for the way, he lets the others go, and they return to Canaan. Arrived there, they report to their father what had befallen them : the surprising discovery of the money in their sacks * adds to their and his anxiety ; and he bitterly reproaches them for their inconsiderate treatment of him. Reuben steps forward, and offers his two sons as surety for the safe return of Benjamin from Egypt.

The narrative is now continued by a long extract from J (42³⁸–44³⁴, with the exceptions noted). The famine continuing in Canaan, Jacob is obliged a second time to send to Egypt for corn : he is reluctant at first to let Benjamin go as well : but after the representations of Judah,—who takes the lead in J (cf. 37²⁶ᵗ˙), as Reuben does in E,—and his offer to be surety for his safe return (cf. the similar offer of Reuben in E, 42³⁷), he consents, sending at the same time a present, to conciliate, if possible, the favour of the great Egyptian governor. Joseph, seeing Benjamin with his other brothers, and perceiving thus that they have spoken the truth, prepares to show them friendliness, and invites them to a feast in his house. E mentions at this point that Simeon was released to them. They have ready their present for Joseph ; and as he comes in, a second time (cf. 42⁶ᵇ) fulfil unconsciously his dreams (37⁷˙⁹) : he inquires tenderly for his father, and expresses his satisfaction at seeing Benjamin. At the feast, they are surprised to find themselves seated according to their ages, and Benjamin honoured with a 'mess,'—or honorary portion (cf. 2 S 11⁸),—five times as large as any of theirs.

The *dénoûment* now approaches. The brethren depart, with their sacks filled with corn, Joseph having privately given orders for his divining-cup to be hidden in Benjamin's sack. Before they can have gone far, he sends messengers after them, who overtake them, and tax them with the theft. Their consciences are clear ; and they voluntarily offer the offender to justice. Dismay and despair seize them, when the cup is found in Benjamin's sack. With affected indignation, Joseph reproaches them with what they have done : Judah, in reply, speaking on behalf of them all, attempts no excuse ; for no excuse seems to be possible : a just retribution has overtaken them (cf. 42²¹) ; they will all remain bondmen in Egypt. But Joseph presses his advantage home : he will only retain Benjamin. Judah now steps forward, and in a speech of striking beauty, remarkable not less for grace and persuasive eloquence than for frankness and generosity, intercedes on Benjamin's behalf : explaining how all had happened from the beginning, he entreats Joseph to have compassion on the feelings of an aged father, and to allow him to remain as bondman himself in his brother's stead (44¹⁸⁻³⁴). Overcome by the pathos of Judah's appeal, and convinced at last of his brethren's

altered mind, Joseph discloses himself to them (ch. 45 E*). His first inquiry is for his father. For a while they can give no answer for amazement ; but he reassures them, and allays their fears : in what they have done, they have been, after all, the unconscious instruments of Providence, for ' God did send me before you to preserve life ' (45⁵˙⁷˙⁸). And he sends an affectionate message to his father, to come and settle in Egypt, and be supported by him there.

Upon Jacob's arrival in Egypt, Joseph hastens to meet his father in Goshen (46²⁸⁻³⁰ J). He presents five of his brethren to the Pharaoh, who upon learning from them that they are shepherds, agrees to grant them an abode in GOSHEN (wh. see), a pastoral district about Saft el-Henneh, some 40 miles N.E. of Cairo (46³¹–47⁴˙⁶ᵇ J ; cf. 47⁵⁻⁶ᵃ P).† (According to P (47⁷⁻¹¹) Jacob himself is introduced by Joseph to the Pharaoh ; and Joseph assigns him, at the Pharaoh's command, an abode in the 'land of Rameses,'—probably a name for the E. part of the Delta, which Ramses II., the Pharaoh of the oppression, beautified by many new buildings, and often made his residence.) ‡

There follows a paragraph (47¹³⁻²⁶ J), describing a permanent change in the Egyptian system of land-tenure, which was attributed to Joseph. The famine continuing in Egypt, the people first gave away all their money for corn, then they gave away their cattle, finally they offered themselves and their land. The result was that all the land in Egypt, except that of the priests (who received a fixed revenue in kind from the crown, and thus had no occasion to sell their possessions for food), became the property of the Pharaoh, the previous owners becoming tenants of the king, paying him, as it were, an annual rent of ⅕ of the produce.

According to P (47²⁷ᵇ⁻²⁸) Jacob lived with Joseph in Egypt 17 years. As the time drew near for him to die, Joseph hearing of his sickness, brought in his two sons, Manasseh and Ephraim to see him. Upon hearing that they were there, the aged patriarch blessed them, giving Ephraim, the younger, against their father's desire, the first place, in view of the future greatness of the tribe descended from him (vv.¹⁻²˙⁸⁻²⁰ JE), at the same time (vv.²¹˙²² E) conferring upon Joseph, as a special gift, 'one shoulder—or mountain-slope—above his brethren' (with allusion to Shechem ; see JACOB, p. 532). A parallel text of P (48³⁻⁷) describes Jacob's *adoption* of his two grandsons, in virtue of which he places each on the same level with his own sons.

After Jacob's death, Joseph, as was natural, made suitable provision for his burial (50¹⁻¹¹˙¹⁴ JE, probably J ; 50¹²˙¹³ P). His brethren fear now that he will exact retribution for their past treatment of him, and send accordingly to crave his forgiveness. He replies generously that he is not in God's place, viz. to exact vengeance for actions which, however intended, have been overruled by God's providence for good ('to save much people alive'), and that he will continue to make provision for their nourishment and welfare (50¹⁵⁻²¹ E).§ He lived, we read, to the age of 110, surviving even the birth of his great-grandchildren.‖ Before

* Except the clauses in vv.⁴˙⁵ referring to Joseph's having been *sold* by his brethren ; v.¹⁰ as far as *Goshen* ; and perhaps v.²⁸.

† The sequence in 47⁵˙⁶ is much better in LXX than in the Heb. text.

‡ The expression is thus proleptic, even if it be not actually an anachronism.

§ The terms of v.21ᵃ (cf. 47¹²), and the expression, 'as it is this day,' in v.²⁰, seem to show that the writer pictured the famine as still continuing (cf. 45¹¹). E must have placed Jacob's death earlier than P (47²⁸).

‖ V.²³ ' the sons of Machir, son of Manasseh,' are specified, on account of the importance attaching later to the corresponding clans of the tribe of Manasseh, on the E. of Jordan (see

* In J (see 43²¹) this discovery is made at the lodging-place by the way ; and 42²⁷˙²⁸ is an extract from J's account of it (notice הָאֶחָד '*the* one,' implying others to follow, not אֶחָד. Observe also that the unusual word אַמְתַּחַת *sack*, occurring 13 times in ch. 43–44 (J), occurs also twice in 42²⁷˙²⁸, and not elsewhere in the OT).

his death he expressed his assurance that God would ultimately bring up the children of Israel out of Egypt, and gave solemn directions for his bones to be brought up with them (50²²⁻²⁶ E). The fulfilment of this injunction is described in Ex 13¹⁹, Jos 24³² (both E); in the latter place it is added that Joseph's bones were buried finally in Shechem, in the plot of ground bought there by Jacob (Gn 33¹⁹) in the centre of the territory owned by his descendants, the 'children of Ephraim.'

The *character* of Joseph is one that is singularly amiable and free from faults. He is the true son, the true brother, the true servant. Loyal and faithful, disinterested and sincere, modest and considerate, he wins the esteem of all right-minded persons with whom he has to do. He is obedient to duty in whatever position he finds himself—whether feeding his father's sheep, or attending to his master's house, or acting for the keeper of the prison, or invested by Pharaoh with authority over Egypt. 'J″ was with him' is the significant phrase by which the narrator in-dicates the Divine approval of his conduct (39². ³. ²¹. ²³). In misfortune he is resigned, and does not complain. He resists temptation. In his eleva-tion he neither presumes upon his position nor forgets his humbler relations: in spite of their cruel treatment of him, he bears his brethren no grudge; even after his father's death he is as generous and magnanimous as before (50¹⁷⁻²¹). He has deep and true affection: his younger brother and his father are ever foremost in his thoughts.* His attitude towards his other brethren, and the humiliation which he imposes on them, are, of course, dictated by the desire to prove them, and bring them to acknowledge their sin; as soon as they have done this (cf. 42²¹· ²² 44¹⁶), and he is satisfied that they are treating his father and Benjamin with genuine affection, he discloses him-self, excuses them for what they had done (45⁵⁻⁸), and, to assure them of his forgiveness and good-will, makes provision for their residence near himself in Egypt. He has a lively sense of de-pendence upon God and of his duty towards Him (39⁹ 41¹⁶ 50²⁴). He is conscious that he is in God's hands, who overrules evil that good may come, and effects His purposes even though it may be without the knowledge and against the wishes of the actual agents (50²⁰, cf. 45⁵· ⁷· ⁸). As a righteous man, persecuted and sold by his brethren, wrong-fully accused and humiliated, but afterwards exalted, and using his position for the good of others, submissive, forgiving, and tender-hearted, it is not surprising that he should often have been regarded as a type of Christ. Only the measures adopted by Joseph for the relief of the famine might be thought to strike a discordant note in his character. To appropriate the surplus produce of the seven years of plenty, and then to compel the Egyptians to *buy back*, even to their own impoverishment, what they had themselves pre-viously given up, does not seem consistent with our ideas of justice and equity. It must, however, be remembered, that, in this respect, Joseph was not, and could not be expected to be, in advance of the public morality of his age. The economic condi-tions of Egypt are, and always have been, peculiar. The fertility of the soil is dependent upon a system of irrigation, which can only be kept in proper order by the central government; and the cultivator falls

into a state of dependency and indebtedness to it at the same time. Moreover, the Egyptian *fellah* lacks inherently the spirit of independence, and, even to the present day, is content to enrich others by his labour rather than himself. Of course such considerations as these do not justify in the abstract the oppressions to which Egypt has habitually been exposed at the hands of Oriental viceroys and pashas; but they tend to show that Joseph did not do more than was consistent with the condition of the country, with the age in which he lived, and with the position in which he found himself placed at the time.* Nevertheless, as Delitzsch observes, the remark of Niebuhr remains true: 'the history of Joseph is a dangerous precedent for designing ministers.'

Joseph was the reputed ancestor of the two tribes Manasseh and Ephraim, the latter being the most powerful and important in Northern Israel. In the blessings of Jacob (Gn 49²²⁻²⁶) and Moses (Dt 33¹³⁻¹⁶), 'Joseph' manifestly represents these two tribes, though no doubt in each the poet is thinking more particularly of Ephraim; in each he descants upon the blessings of soil and climate, of populousness and military strength, enjoyed by the tribe; and in each Joseph bears the title נְזִיר אֶחָיו 'the separate (*or* crowned)·one of his brethren,' *i.e.* the tribe distinguished from the others by the possession, in a pre-eminent degree, of such distinctions as wealth, and influence, and political and military power. The terms of these blessings, and the enthusiasm which in each the poet displays for 'Joseph,' show that both spring from the period during which Ephraim was the leading tribe in Israel.† The two tribes are also grouped together elsewhere under the same common designation: not only in the expression 'children of Joseph,' Jos 16¹ 17¹⁴· ¹⁶ (J), Nu 1¹⁰· ¹², Jos 14⁴ 18¹¹ *al.* (P), but also in 'house of Joseph,' Jos 17¹⁷ 18⁵, Jg 1²²·‡ 23·‡ ²⁵ 2 S 19²⁰ ‡ 1 K 11²⁸, and (like Ephraim in Hos) *à potiori* of Northern Israel generally, Am 5⁶, Ob ¹⁸ (‖ 'house of Jacob'), Zec 10⁶, and in 'Joseph' alone (sometimes representing N. Israel generally), Dt 27¹² 33¹³· ¹⁶, Am 5¹⁵ 6⁶, Ezk 37¹⁶· ¹⁹ 47¹³ 48³², Ps 77¹⁷ ('the sons of Jacob and Joseph') 78⁶⁷ 80¹ (‖ 'Israel'), 81⁵.

On *Joseph-el*, as the name of a place in Palestine in the 15th cent. B.C., see p. 526.

Date of Joseph.—The period of Egyptian history at which the events of Joseph's life are to be placed, cannot be determined except inferentially. As in the Book of Exodus, the name of the Pharaoh is not mentioned; and in view of the general fixity of Egyptian institutions, the allu-sions to Egyptian manners and customs, as Dillm. remarks, are not sufficiently distinctive to constitute a clue to the age in which he lived.§ The biblical dates, both of the Exodus and of the patriarchal age (which is dependent upon it, Ex 12⁴¹), are too uncertain to form a secure basis for further chronological calculations (see CHRON-OLOGY, vol. i. p. 398). There are, however, strong reasons for supposing Ramses II. of the 19th dynasty (B.C. 1275–1208, Petrie) to be the Pharaoh of the oppression (Ex 18ff·); and arguing back from this *datum*, it is probable that Joseph's

---

MACHIR and MANASSEH). 'Born upon Joseph's knees,' *i.e.* recognized by him as his descendants; cf. 30³, *Odyss.* xix. 401.
* Gn 41⁵¹ *end* is naturally not to be taken *au pied de la lettre.* It is an old difficulty that Joseph did not, immediately after his elevation, take steps to inform his father of his welfare; but perhaps separations of this kind were taken in those days more as a matter of course than they would be by us; and, certainly, if Joseph had done this, both the interest and the moral of the narrative would have been greatly impaired.

* Cf. the remarks and quotations illustrative of the economic condition of Egypt in the work of Vigouroux, cited below (p. 772 n.*), ii. 183–189; also Ebers, *Gosen*, 486–8 (ed. 2, 498 f.).
† In 2 S 19⁴³ (44) LXX ‖ (בְּכוֹר for בָּכוֹר), 'I am also the *firstborn* more than thou,' the men of Israel claim the birthright—no doubt on account of the prestige enjoyed by Ephraim; cf. 1 Ch 5¹· ²: Ew. i. 422.
‡ Including here *Benjamin* (in 2 S 19²⁰ Shimei, a Benjaminite, speaks). Cf. Stade, *Gesch.* i. 160 ff.
§ Sayce's statement (*EHH* 90, cf. 83), that the Egypt which the narrative brings before us is that of the Hyksos age, is not warranted by the facts: not one of the illustrations quoted by him is *distinctive* of the Hyksos age, and the great majority are not drawn from that period at all.

elevation in Egypt is to be placed under one of the later Hyksos kings.* The Hyksos (*i.e.* Hyk-shasu, 'prince of the Shasu,' or 'spoilers,' *i.e.* desert-hordes, or Bedawis) were a race of Asiatic invaders, who (according to Manetho) held possession of Egypt for 511 years (B.C. 2098–1587, Petrie), at first devastating and destroying, but afterwards settling down, and assimilating much of the culture of the conquered Egyptians (cf. vol. i. p. 659 f.; Maspero, *Struggle of Nations*, 50 ff., 72 ff.). Zoan (Tanis), in the N.E. of the Delta,† (as excavations have shown) was one of their chief cities. George the Syncellus speaks of a general consensus of chronographers to the effect that the Pharaoh of Joseph was Aphophis,‡ *i.e.* Apepa (II.), the last important Hyksos king.§ As it happens, if we place the Exodus at about B.C. 1204 (Petrie), this would agree with the date given in Ex 12⁴¹ (1204 + 430 = 1634 B.C.).

Historical Character of Joseph.—Taken in the abstract, it cannot be said that there are serious historical improbabilities in the *substance* of Joseph's biography. Certainly the narrative contains many dramatic situations. Both Joseph and his brethren pass through a series of crises and adventures, any one of which might readily have closed the drama, though all, in fact, lead on happily to the final *dénoûment*. Truth is, however, proverbially stranger than fiction. There have been many remarkable biographies in history, and we must beware of making probability too absolutely the test of credibility. In the general fact of a foreigner, by a happy stroke of cleverness, winning the favour of an Eastern despot, and being in consequence invested by him with high powers, there is nothing unprecedented; and in the case of Egypt, in particular, the monuments supply explicit evidence of foreigners rising there to positions of political distinction. The question assumes, however, a different aspect when account is taken (1) of the fact that the narratives about Joseph are plainly not the work of a contemporary hand,‖ but were in all probability only committed to writing 700–800 years afterwards, and (2) of the further curious fact that 'Joseph' (like many of the other patriarchal names) is also a *tribal* name, the name of that subdivision of the nation which was also called after his two sons, Manasseh and Ephraim. The first of these facts at once destroys all guarantee that we possess in the Joseph-narratives a literal record of the facts. The outline, indeed, may still be historical, but for details or particular episodes popular imagination will very probably be responsible: the improbabilities which certainly attach to some of the details connected with the famine and the measures

* So Knob., Dillm., Riehm, Ebers (in Smith, *DB*² 1792 f.), Brugsch (*Steininschrift*, 131), Wiedemann (with reserve), *Aeg. Gesch.* (1884), i. 293 f., and in his small *Gesch. von alt-Aeg.* (1891) 67 f.; and others.

† Zoan would be not more than about 35 miles from Goshen; and it is true that the court of the Pharaoh in Gn is represented as being not far from Goshen (for Joseph was near to both: 45¹⁰. ¹⁶ 46²⁹-³⁴ 477), whereas the residence of the Pharaohs, both before (12–14 dyn.) and after (18–20 dyn.) the Hyksos period, was far up the Nile, at Thebes. However, an argument in support of Joseph's Pharaoh being one of the Hyksos kings could be based upon this coincidence, only if it were already certain that the narrative was the work of a contemporary hand, which might be trusted to reproduce accurately geographical facts of this kind.

‡ P. 62 (cf. p. 69) ἐπὶ πᾶσι γὰρ συμπεφώνηται ὅτι ἐπὶ 'Αφώφεως ἤρξεν 'Ιωσὴφ τῆς Αἰγύπτου: p. 107, the 17th year of Aphophis is specified. Erman (*Z. f. Aeg. Spr.* 1881, 125–7; cf. Maspero, *Struggle of Nations*, 71) has made it probable that this date was arrived at by a combination of the 430 years of Ex 12⁴¹ with Egyptian data.

§ Petrie, *Hist. of Eg.* i. 242, ii. 17 ff.

‖ Notice incidentally in this connexion the absence of *particulars* in the narrative, *e.g.* any mention of the personal name of the Pharaoh, and of the place in Egypt where he held his court; and cf. Sayce, *HCM* 228 f. Contemporary writers—for instance, Jeremiah—are in such matters much more definite and specific.

by which it was relieved (41⁴⁷⁻⁴⁹. ⁵⁴. ⁵⁶. ⁵⁷ 47¹⁴⁻²⁶) * may thus, for example, be accounted for. The second fact raises the further question whether the figure of Joseph, in part or even as a whole, is a reflection of the history and characteristics of the tribe, projected upon the past in an individual form.

According to Ewald (cf. above, p. 534), the twelve sons of Jacob represent corresponding subdivisions of the nation : the smaller part of it, distinguished in the extant tradition by the name and fame of Joseph, and consisting essentially of the two tribes of Ephraim and Manasseh (which afterwards separated), migrated into Egypt first; Joseph, who was a real person, was a leader or distinguished member of the immigrants; he rose to power in Egypt, and conferred there great benefits both upon his own people and upon the country, and in the end also attracted the remaining and stronger part of his people to the E. frontier of Egypt. His personality was a remarkable one ; and in after ages it was transfigured in the memory of his people : under the influence of Israel's religion it became an ideal of filial and fraternal affection, a high example of goodness, devotion to duty, sincerity, and love. The fundamental idea of the story consists in the happy reunion in Egypt of the long-separated members of Jacob's family, at the call of the son and brother who has risen there to high station ; this, in the narrative of Genesis, as we possess it, has been gradually elaborated by successive writers until it attained 'the mature and attractive form in which it was worthy to become an heirloom of the human race.'† The view of Dillm. (introd. to ch. 39) and Kittel (i. 168 f.) is similar : behind the individual, Joseph, there stands the tribe (Dillm.); the tribe, migrating to Egypt, acquired there power and pre-eminence over its 'brethren,' and its leader is known to tradition by the same name, Joseph (Kittel). It is an objection to this view that it duplicates the name *at one and the same time* : 'Joseph' denotes both an individual and a tribe, not at different times, but *in Egypt itself*. Stade and others see in Joseph (as in his brethren) merely the imaginary eponymous ancestor of the tribe, in whose life and experiences are reflected the political and other relations of a later age.

Any judgment upon a question of this kind must be more or less 'subjective'; but to the present writer the amount of personal incident and detail in the narrative appears, as in the case of JACOB (p. 534ᵇ), to be an objection to both these views. It seems to him to be more probable that there was an actual person, Joseph, afterwards—rightly or wrongly—regarded as the ancestor of the tribe, whose biography, during the time that it lived only in oral tradition, may have been embellished and made more dramatic in details, but who underwent *substantially* the experiences recounted of him in Gn, and who, having risen to power in Egypt, succeeded in obtaining for his fellow-tribesmen a home in the pastoral land of Goshen. This view, amongst other things, does justice to the Egyptian colouring of the narrative (see below) This colouring, it is true, is seldom specific ; it is never of a character to prove close and personal cognizance of the facts described ;‡ nevertheless, its presence in the narrative — as indeed the entire Egyptian episode in Joseph's life — is difficult to account for, if the whole were nothing but a legend, woven by popular fancy upon the hills of Ephraim.

From 47¹³⁻²⁶, however, more cannot be inferred than that the agrarian conditions described prevailed in the age of the narrator : the details of the narrative, such as the connexion with the seven years of famine, the exhaustion of the Egyptians' money, etc., will, as Dillm. remarks, 'belong merely *der naiven Sage*.' The benefit derived in consequence by the crown must have been attributed popularly to Joseph's statesmanship ; but if it be true that he rose to power under Aphophis, at the very time when the native Theban princes were beginning the war of independence, it is difficult to think that an innovation of this kind, introduced by him, could have survived the expulsion of the Hyksos Pharaohs.

It is, moreover, important to observe, as Kittel has pointed out, that this colouring is common to both J and E : as it is improbable that *two* writers would have added it independently, it may be inferred that it was inherent in the common

* Cf. Kuenen, *ThT*, May 1871, p. 269 ff.

† Ewald, *Hist.* i. 363, 382, 405, 407–409, 412–420.

‡ Institutions, officials, etc., for instance, are described *generally*, not by their specific Egypt. names : contrast the long lists of specific titles in Brugsch, *Ægyptologie*, pp. 206–232.

tradition which both represent. This is a circumstance tending to show that in its origin the Egyptian element was considerably anterior to either J or E, and increases the probability that it rests ultimately upon a foundation in fact. At the same time, it is difficult to deny that the narrative (like those of ISHMAEL and JACOB) has been coloured in some of its details by later events, and even that particular episodes may have originated in the desire to account for the circumstances and relations of a later age. The hostility of the brethren to Joseph, the leadership in one narrative (E) of Reuben, in the other (J) of Judah, the power and pre-eminence of Joseph as compared with his father and brothers, the fact that Benjamin, afterwards the smallest tribe, is the youngest brother, the 'adoption' of his two grandsons by Jacob (i.e. their elevation to the same rank as his own sons), and the priority so pointedly bestowed by him upon the younger, are, for instance, points at which it is very possible that popular imagination has thus been at work, colouring or supplementing the historical elements of the Joseph-tradition by reference to the facts and conditions of later times. And naturally the literary form of the narrative, with its charms of style and other characteristic traits, will be due to the different writers, who, severally, cast the original tradition into a written shape.

The acquaintance shown by the authors of the Joseph narratives, esp. J and E, with Egyptian customs and institutions has been long observed ; * and the principal instances deserve to be noticed here, references being added to authorities where the subject may be more fully studied.

37²⁵ (cf. 43¹¹). There would be demand in Egypt for resinous substances, such as 'gum tragacanth,' 'balm,' and 'ladanum' (the exudation of the Cistus or Rock-rose),† partly for medicinal purposes, partly for the composition of incense to be used in religious rites, and partly for embalming ; see Ebers, Aeg. 289–293. For Syrian trade with Egypt (in the 18th dyn.), including slaves, see ib. 292 ff., Erman, Life in Ancient Egypt, 516 ff.

39⁴ 'and he appointed him over his house.'‡ Such a position can hardly be regarded as distinctively Egyptian (see note ‡) : nevertheless the monuments show that large Egyptian households were organized with superintendents of their different departments (the fields, the cattle, the kitchen, etc.), the mer-per, or 'superintendent of the house,' being in particular often mentioned.§ The 'bread which' his master 'did eat' (39⁶) would not be left in Joseph's hand, on account of the scruples which the Egyptians had against eating food prepared by foreigners (cf. 43³²). To the story of Joseph and his master's wife (39⁷ᶠᶠ·) there is a remarkable parallel (which has been often compared) in the Egyptian romance, commonly called 'The Tale of the Two Brothers,' written for Seti II. (19 dyn.), and preserved in the d'Orbiney Papyrus. Two brothers, Anpu and Bata, lived together in one house : the elder, Anpu, one day sent Bata back from the fields into the house to fetch some seed : Anpu's wife there made advances to him,

which he repelled : when Anpu returned home in the evening, his wife accused Bata to him falsely. Anpu, enraged, at first sought to slay his brother, but in the end he was convinced that he was innocent and had been accused falsely, and he thereupon slew his unfaithful wife.*

40¹ᶠᶠ. A 'butler,' or 'cupbearer' (the word in the Heb. is the same, מַשְׁקֶה, lit. the one giving to drink), was, naturally, not an institution peculiar to Egypt, being found also in Persia (Neh 1¹¹, cf. 2¹), and elsewhere (cf. οἰνοχόος) : we meet, however, with a very similar title in lists of Egyptian court officials ; Chabas, for instance (Mél. Égypt. 3rd ser. 131 ff.), publishes such a list, including 'le grand des appartements ou grand supérieur de la maison' (the major domo, mentioned above), 'le saigneur de bœufs, le boulanger, le cuiseur de mets, le conducteur des contrôleurs (abu-u), qui goûtent le vin,' etc., the last of whom is considered by Chabas and Ebers to have corresponded to the 'chief of the butlers' here.† In the tomb of Ramses III. (20 dyn.) there is a representation of a royal bakery, showing a number of figures employed in various processes of bread-making, and amongst them one carrying a tray containing rolls of bread upon his head (v.¹⁶).‡ A 'superintendent of the bakery,' corresponding to the 'chief of the bakers,' is mentioned by Erman, pp. 105, 187 (cf. Ebers, 333 bottom). The custom of squeezing grapes into a cup (v.¹¹) is illustrated by Ebers § from a text published by Naville from the temple at Edfu, where it is said that grapes squeezed into water formed a refreshing beverage, which was drunk by the king. The birthday of the Pharaoh (v.²⁰), at least in the Ptolemaic period, as we learn from the Canopus and Rosetta decrees (B.C. 239 and 195), was celebrated with a great assembly of priests of all grades, and a granting of amnesties to prisoners.‖

In ch. 41 Pharaoh's dreams, both in themselves and in their subject-matter, are appropriate to the country. In Egypt (as in Babylon, and indeed in other ancient countries) much importance was attached to dreams. Thothmes IV., while sleeping under the shadow of the great Sphinx, was commanded by Râ Harmakhis to clear away the sand by which it was encumbered. A vision of the god Ptah, appearing in a dream, encouraged Merenptah to attack the Libyans. On the 'Dream-stele' discovered among the ruins of Napata, the ancient capital of Ethiopia, it is related how the Ethiopian king, Nût Amen, saw in a dream two serpents, one on his right hand and the other on his left, which were explained to portend that he would conquer Egypt, and wear on his head the two crowns, of the north as well as of the south.¶ Strange nostrums were even in vogue for the purpose of obtaining significant dreams.** Egypt is dependent for its fertility upon the annual rising of the Nile : the cow-headed goddess Hat-hor,†† the personification of fruitfulness (with whom Isis,

---

* Hengstenberg, Aeg. u. die Bb. Mose's (1841) ; Knobel (Kgf-Comm. 1852, 1860) ; Ewald (Hist. i. 419 n.) ; Dillm.; and esp. Ebers, Aeg. u. die Bb. Mose's, 1868 (ends with Gn 41³²), and in Smith, DB² s.v. JOSEPH. See also F. Vigouroux, La Bible et les découvertes modernes⁶, 1896, tom. ii. (a full but not very critical compilation) ; and H. G. Tomkins, The Life and Times of Joseph (1891).

† Tristram, Nat. Hist. of the Bible, 393 f., 337 f., 458–460 ; on 'balm,' also, above, i. 236.

‡ Cf., of Pharaoh's house, 41⁴⁰ ; of Joseph's house, 43¹⁶· ¹⁹ 44¹· ⁴ (where 'steward of his house' is lit. 'he that was over his house') : cf. 'over the house' (i.e. the palace) in 1 K 4⁶ 16⁵ 18³, 2 K 10⁵ 15⁵ 18¹⁸· ³⁷ 19², Is 22¹⁵ (all of the major domo, or governor of the palace, in Israel or Judah)

§ Ebers, Aeg. 303–305 ; Erman, 187 f.

* The tale is translated in full by Maspero in Les Contes Pop. de l'Égypte anc.² (1889), 5–32 ; Petrie, Egyp. Tales (1895), ii. 36 ff. ; somewhat abridged, in Erman, 378 f. : the part parallel to the Bibl. narrative in Ebers, Aeg. 311 ff. ; more briefly in Brugsch, Hist. of Eg.² i. 309 ff. (new ed. 1891, 123 f.) ; Sayce, HCM, 209 ff. (from Brugsch) ; Egypt of the Hebrews, 25 ff. (from Brugsch and Erman).

† On the manufacture and use of wine in Egypt, Ebers, 322–329 ; cups and goblets, 327–329, Erman, 196–198 ; a servant offering wine to a guest in a goblet, Wilkinson-Birch, i. 430 ; several such, at a feast, in The Tomb of Paheri at El Kab (11th Memoir of Egyp. Explor. Fund), Plate vii., cf. p. 24 f.

‡ See Wilkinson-Birch, Anc. Egyptians (ed. 1878), ii. 34 ; Ebers, Aeg. 332 ; or Erman, p. 191 : the man carrying the tray, also, in Maspero, Dawn of Civil. 314.

§ Durch Gosen zum Sinai¹ (1872), 480 ; Smith, DB² p. 1796ᵃ.

‖ Ebers, 334–337.

¶ Brugsch, Hist. (ed. 1891) 200, 314, 406. Cf. Wiedemann, Relig. of the Anc. Eg. 265–267 ; Ebers, 321 f. ; Herod. ii. 141.

** Wiedemann, 267 f.

†† Budge, The Mummy, 291, 292 ; Wiedemann, 143, 219.

the goddess of the fertile soil of the Delta,* was often identified), is described in inscriptions, cited by Ebers, as 'causing the Nile to appear in its season,' 'giving life to the living with her hands,' 'pouring forth fruitfulness upon the land,' etc.† The cow being sacred to both these deities, kine emerging from the Nile would be a natural emblem of fruitful seasons. *Seven* was also a sacred (and magical) number in Egypt.‡ Among the priestly classes § in Egypt were the 'writers of sacred writings' (saχ-u neter šat : in the Greek text of the Canopus decree, πτεροφόραι,—depicted on the monuments with a feather [quill] on their heads, and a book in their hand ‖), and the 'knowers of things' (reχ χet-u), or, as we might say, 'wise men' (in the Greek, ἱερογραμματεῖς, or 'sacred scribes'), of whose superior knowledge the Egyp. king would avail himself in any difficulty.¶ To these correspond, no doubt, the *hartummim* ** and 'wise men,' summoned by Pharaoh to interpret his dreams.

Joseph's shaving himself, and changing his raiment (41¹⁴), before appearing in the presence of Pharaoh, is in agreement with Egyptian customs : all respectable Egyptians shaved themselves : on the monuments, only foreigners, and natives of inferior rank, are represented as wearing beards ; cleanliness of clothes, as well as of person, was also *de rigueur*.†† With the reference to God in 41¹⁶ (cf. v.³⁹ 40⁸), comp. Herod. ii. 83. Joseph's plan for laying up corn in storehouses (41³⁴ᶠ·) at least falls in with Egyptian institutions : in all important cities granaries were established, partly for the reception of the corn-tax (an important item in the revenue), partly to provide maintenance for soldiers and other public officials : the 'superintendent of the granaries' was one of the highest officers of the state ; it was his duty to see that they were properly filled, and to report to the king annually on the harvests.‡‡ On 41⁴⁰ ('over my house,' *i.e.* palace), cf. p. 772 note ‡, and Erman, pp. 69, 77 : the terms of 41⁴¹ suggest the important office of *T'ate*, or governor, *ib.* 69, 87–89 ('the second after the king in the court of the palace'), 473. The

signet-ring (41⁴²) was in other countries also a mark of authority (Est 3¹⁰ 8², Tob 1²², 1 Mac 6¹⁵) ; but it was notably so in Egypt, where the 'keeper of the seal' (*mer chetam*) was the king's deputy.* The golden collar put round Joseph's neck (*ib.*) was a peculiarly Egyptian form of decoration : it was called 'receiving gold' ; † Ahmes, the captain-general of the marines, who freed Egypt from the Hyksos, 'received gold,' on seven different occasions, for various acts of valour.‡ Linen was prized in Egypt as a material for dress, especially for men of rank ; § but the plural '*garments* of fine linen' makes it doubtful whether (as Ebers supposes) there is a specific reference to the *shendi-t*, or *shend'ot*, the royal apron-garment, worn under the Old Empire only by royal personages, but under the Middle and New Empires, by other dignitaries as well.‖ Horses and chariots are first represented on the Egyptian monuments under the 18th dyn.: it is probable, therefore, that they were introduced into Egypt during the Hyksos period ; the words for both chariot (*merkobt*) and waggon ('*agolt*) are palpably of Semitic (Canaanite or Hebrew) origin (עֲגָלָה, מֶרְכָּבָה).¶ The king in earlier times was carried by soldiers on a sedan-chair.** Erman (p. 64) describes a scene from a tomb at Tel el-Amarna, in which Amenôphis IV. (18 dyn.), his queen and daughters, and the ministers in attendance, appear riding in chariots of state ; but it throws no light on the expression, 'the second chariot which he had.' The monuments supply illustrations, at least in and after the 18th dyn., of foreigners (including slaves from Syria) rising to positions of political importance in Egypt, and adopting there a change of name : Mery-Rê̂ ('beloved of Rê'), the armour-bearer of Thothmes III., and the priest, User-Min ('Min is strong'), were sons of a foreigner, the judge Pa-'Emer'eu (the Amorite) ; and under Merenptah, a Canaanite, Ben-Mat'ana, son of Jupa'a, from D'arbasana,†† holds the office of 'first speaker of His Majesty' (who acted as an intermediary between the king and his attendants), and receives the name of Ramses-em-per-Ra, 'Ramses in the temple of Ra.'‡‡ In fact, 'change of name was usual with *parvenus* whom the king wished to honour' (Ebers). On (*ib.*) is well known to have been the chief centre of the worship of the sun-god (Rê or Râ), possessing a famous temple, and a large body of priests (cf. Herod. ii. 3).

Famines of long duration, due to the Nile failing to overflow, are not unknown in Egypt : not only is one attested by El-Makrizi, the Arabic historian, for A.D. 1064–1071, §§ but the sepulchral inscription of one Baba, found at El-Kab in Upper Egypt, represents the deceased, in an enumeration

---

* Maspero, *Dawn of Civiliz.* 99, 132.

† Ebers, 357 f. (the dates and sources of these citations are not given : and their relevancy is perhaps doubtful).

‡ Ebers, 339 f. ; Smith, *DB* ² 1796 (in prescriptions, *seven* drugs are often prescribed, never 6, 8, or 9 ; and in charms, *seven* objects are taken). Among the numerous forms of Hat-hor, *seven* are often in particular specified (Ebers, 359 ; *Tale of Two Brothers*, p. 51, Petrie ; Brugsch, *Rel. u. Myth. d. alt. Æg.* 318f., and *Thes. Inscr. Æg.* 800–802 [temple of the seven great Hathors at Speos Artemidos]) ; and in ch. 148 of the 'Book of the Dead,' mention is made of the *seven* sacred kine with their bull, who provide food and drink for the dead, and whose good services the deceased invokes Ra (Osiris) to secure on his behalf : see Budge's tr. (1898), p. 261 f.; and the fine vignette, representing the kine, with offerings laid before them by the deceased, in sheet 35 of the magnificent facsimile of the Papyrus of Ani, pub. by the Brit. Mus. Trustees (Vigouroux, p. 112, gives a different vignette of the same subject from the Turin Papyrus, pub. by Lepsius, *Todtenbuch*, 1842).

§ Ebers, 341 ff.   ‖ Wilk.-B. ii. 324, Nos. 8, 9.

¶ In the *Tale of Two Brothers* (p. 54, Petrie), a lock of scented hair which has been brought to the king, who summons the 'scribes and the knowers of things' to tell him who its owner is. The sister-in-law of Ramses XII. is ill, and the Pharaoh is asked to send a 'wise man' to give his advice (Brugsch, 347 ; Ebers, 347, who adds that there are numerous similar instances). On the *contents* of the 'sacred writings' (which embraced magic, charms, and other subjects, as well as ritual, etc.), see Brugsch, *Ægyptologie*, 85, 149–159, 320.

** LXX ἐξηγηταί (in Ex ἐπαοιδοί, 9¹¹ φαρμακοί), RVm 'sacred scribes.' Of uncertain derivation, but found only in connexion with Egypt (41⁸· ²⁴, Ex 7¹¹· ²² 8⁷· ¹⁸· ¹⁹ 9¹¹), and (doubtless borrowed from Gn) in Dn 1²⁰ 2²· ¹⁰· ²⁷ 4⁷· ⁹ 5¹¹ (AV 'magicians').

†† Ebers, 350 ff.; cf. Wilk.-B. ii. 330, 331, 357 ; Erman, 225, 439 ; Petrie, *Tales*, i. 125 ; Herod. ii. 36.

‡‡ Erman, 108, with illustration of Cha'emhê̂'t, superintendent of the granaries under Amenôphis III. (18 dyn.), cf. 81, 86, 89, 94, 95 ; *Records of the Past*, 2nd ser. iii. 7 f., 22. Representations of Egyptian granaries may be seen in Erman, 433, 434 ; or in Wilk.-B. i. 348, 371 : cf. also Maspero, *Dawn of Civil.* 286, 287 ; close by there were offices and weighing-rooms, in which scribes registered every sack that was brought in or taken out (Erman, p. 95).

---

* Ebers, *DB*² 1797 : cf. Petrie, *Hist.* ii. 90, 172, 198 ; Brugsch, *Hist.* 321, and *Ægyptologie* (1891), 84, 207, Ptahmoses 'into whose hand the land was given, and on whose fist was the king's seal'; Tomkins, 47.

† Erman, p. 118 f., with the illustrations on pp. 120 (Ey being decorated by Amenôphis IV.), 208 ; cf. 108 ; Wilk.-B. iii. 370 f., with the Plate (investiture of a governor with chain of office by Seti I.); Vigouroux, ii. 128 (a similar scene from a stele in the Louvre); Ebers, *ZDMG*, 1877, p. 462 f. The collars were often of massive and costly workmanship.

‡ Brugsch, *Hist.* p. 114 f. (another example, p. 163 f.); or Petrie, *Hist.* ii. 21–23.

§ Cf. Erman, 111, 448 ; Petrie, *Tales*, i. 125 ; Herod. ii. 37 (for priests), 81 ; Ezk 277.

‖ Erman, 62, 206, 210.

¶ Erman, 490 f. (Under the 18th, and esp. the 19th, dynasty, many Semitic words found their way into Egyptian ; *ib.* 516 f.; Brugsch, 98 f., 302 ff.; Petrie, *Hist.* ii. 148–150.)

** Erman, 65 (an illustration).

†† Some locality in Bashan, according to W. Max Müller, *Asien und Europa nach altägypt. Denkmälern,* 273.

‡‡ Erman, 106, 517 f., 518 n. ('many similar examples').

§§ See Smith, *DB, s.v.* FAMINE. The terrible effects of a one year's famine (A.D. 1199) are described at length by Abdollatif (ed. White, 1800, p. 210 ff. : extracts in Stanley, *Jewish Church,* i. 79 f.; Vigouroux, 174 ff.).

of his virtues, as saying, 'I collected corn, as a friend of the harvest-god. I was watchful at the time of sowing. And *when a famine arose, lasting many years, I distributed corn to the city each year of famine.*' * The age of Baba (end of the 17th dyn.) would coincide approximately with that of Joseph ; and it has even been supposed that the famine referred to may be the same. Ameni (or Amony), governor of the 'nome of the Gazelle,' under Usertesen II. (12 dyn.), tells us that he made provision for his people, very much as Joseph did : ' In my time there were no poor, and none were hungry. When the years of famine came, I ploughed all the fields of the nome, I kept the inhabitants alive, and gave them food, so that not one was hungry.'†

42⁹. The charge of being spies was a natural one : Egypt was exposed on its E. side, and liable to be invaded by Asiatics ; under the 12th dyn. fortresses had been erected along the Isthmus of Suez, and under the 19th dyn. officers were stationed there to take the names of all passing in either direction.‡ The oath 'by the life of Pharaoh' (42¹⁵) is known from Egyptian monuments : in an account of criminal proceedings (20th dyn.), a thief has administered to him an oath *by the king's life*, to prevent him speaking falsely : § in a similar document, published by Chabas, the expression ' il fit un *Vie du Seigneur royal* ' occurs more than once.∥

43¹⁶. The expression 'steward of his house' (אשר על ביתו) is explained above, on 39⁴. Every great man in Egypt had such an overseer for his establishment. On Egyptian feasts, cf. the Plates in Erman, opposite pp. 250, 255, or Wilk.-B. i. 431 : the guests did not sit round a table, as with us, but on rows of chairs, facing a sideboard ; the viands, interspersed with rich floral decorations, were arranged on this, and carried round to the guests by servants. On Egyptian houses, which were often on a large scale, Erman, 174 ff. In explanation of v.³²ᵇ, see ABOMINATION, No. 1 ; and cf. (Ebers) how it is said, after Pianchi's conquest of Egypt (B.C. 766), that the defeated kings ' did not enter the king's house, because they were unclean (*i.e.* uncircumcised), and they ate fish, which is an abomination to the king' (Brugsch, p. 404, l. 150 f.).

43²¹ 'in full weight' (lit. *in its weight*). Egyptian money consisted of rings of gold (probably unstamped), which were weighed by scribes who made this their business (Erman, 109, 464 ; Wilk.-B. i. 285, 286). However, the practice of 'weighing' money was also usual among the Hebrews, even to a late date (Jer 32⁹. ¹⁰, Zec 11¹² etc.).

45⁸ ' a father (*'āb*) to Pharaoh,' v.⁹ (cf. 42³⁰. ³³) 'lord (*'ādōn*) of all Egypt.' Brugsch has pointed out that both *'āb* and *'ādōn* were official titles in Egyptian.

Āb (or *ābū*) does not mean 'father' in Egyp., but denotes primarily the *overseer* of a kitchen, wine-cellar, bakery, etc.; then in the 19th dyn. the *ābū* of the king becomes an im-

portant person in the state, and takes part in judicial investigations, etc.: see Brugsch, *Hist.* (1891), 101, 357, *Steininschrift,* 82 ; and esp. *Dict. Hiérogl.* v. 37–39, *Aegyptologie*, p. 225 f., and Erman, who represents *ābū* by the peculiar term *Truchsess,* rendered in the Eng. tr.—as badly as possible—by ' slave,' p. 105, l. 11, 10, 7, 6, 4 from bottom, p. 106, l. 1, 11, 14, 18, by 'vassal,' pp. 131–136, 141, 143, 144 (cf. *Z. f. Aeg. Spr.* 1879, pp. 73 ff., 148 ff.), by 'serfs,' p. 187 f. (3 times), and by ' vassal' again, p. 475.

'Adōn (or *Aten*) was the title given to the *viceroy* (of the Pharaoh), or the *deputy* of a governor or other official (like the Arab. *wakīl*) : thus we read of the *'ādōn* of a city, of a district, of a regiment, of a treasury, of the grand-chancellor, etc., and even of the whole country. See Brugsch, *Rev. Égypt.* i. (1880) 28 ff. (many examples cited) ; also *Hist.* 101, 124, 125 (Hor-em-heb (18 dyn.) was ' *Adon* of the whole land' for some years before he became king : see p. 231), 281, 290, 339 bottom, 344 *bis*, 347, 348 ; and Virey in *Records*, 2nd ser. iv. 3 ff. (where the same word is spelt ' tennu ').

In view, however, of the fact that both *'āb* and *'ādōn* are common Heb. words (with 45⁸ cf. esp. Is 22²¹), it must be regarded as exceedingly doubtful whether, in using them, E had really in mind the Egyptian offices to which Brugsch has referred.

On 46³⁴ᵇ see ABOMINATION, No. 1 : there is independent evidence that cow-herds and swine-herds (Herod. ii. 47) were looked down upon by the Egyptians, but not that shepherds were. 47⁶ ' overseers of cattle over that which I have.' Much attention was paid to cattle-rearing in Egypt ; and there were many fine breeds.* The Pharaoh possessed large herds ; and the *mer*, or superintendent, of the royal cattle is often mentioned in the inscriptions.† There are parallels for parties of foreigners receiving permission to settle in Egypt : see *Z. f. Aeg. Spr.* 1889, p. 125, or Tomkins, p. 81 (*Mentiu*, or nomads, expelled from their homes, appeal to Ḥor-em-ḥeb, of the 18th dyn., and receive permission to settle in a prescribed locality) ; and the remarkable inscription cited by Brugsch, ch. v. (p. 100), from the reign of Merenptah (Shasu or Bedawis, allowed to pass a border-fortress of Egypt, and to settle on the property of the Pharaoh). In 47¹⁴ the ' house ' meant is, according to Ebers, the treasury, usually called *per-het*, the ' house of silver ' : the head-treasurer was a high officer of state, having many subordinate officials under him.‡ The peculiar system of Egyptian land-tenure, which (47²⁶) is attributed to Joseph, is so far in accordance with the evidence of the monuments, that, whereas in the Old Empire the nobility and governors of the nomes possessed large landed estates, in the New Empire (which followed the expulsion of the Hyksos) ' the old aristocracy has made way for royal officials, and the landed property has passed out of the hands of the old families into the possession of the crown and the great temples.'§ The monuments do not, however, furnish any explanation of the origin of the new system : there is a conjecture in Erman, p. 102 f. ∥

50². ²⁶. Embalming the dead is, of course, well known to have been an Egyptian custom ; for descriptions of the process, see Herod. ii. 86–89 ; Budge, *The Mummy* (1893), 160 ff. ; Wilk.-B. iii. 470 ff. Egypt was famous for its physicians (*Od.* iv. 229 ; Herod. ii. 84, iii. 1. 129), and Egyptian treatises on medicine have come down to us : ¶ but here ' physicians' seems to be used improperly

---

* Brugsch, *Hist.* ed. 2, i. 304 ; ed. 1891, p. 121. Called *Bebt* in Maspero, *Struggle*, 85.

† *Ib.* p. 61 ; or Erman, p. 94. The seven-years' famine under king Toser (?) of the 3rd dyn. (c. 4400 B.C.) is known only from the late and doubtful testimony of an inscription forged by some priests of the 3rd cent. B.C. to support their claim to an ancient tithe : Brugsch, *Steininschrift u. Bibelwort* (1891), 88–97 ; Sayce, *HCM* 217 f. Brugsch thinks that this is the famine, of which a tradition had reached the Biblical writer, but that he connected it incorrectly with Joseph.

‡ Erman, 538, 539. The words ' How art thou come, *in order to spy out* ? ' (Brugsch, 110) addressed by Seqenen-Ra in Thebes to the messengers of Apepi, and quoted as parallel to Joseph's question by Brugsch, p. 112, and Tomkins, p. 62, do not, however, appear in the translations of Maspero (*Records*, 2nd ser. ii. 43, *Contes pop.* 283) and Petrie (*Hist.* ii. 18), both of which have simply, ' Why hast thou made this journey ?'

§ *Zeitschr. f. Aeg. Spr.* 1874, p. 62.

∥ *Mélanges*, iii. 1, pp. 80, 95, 105 (cf. 91).

* Erman, 436 f.

† Ebers ; Erman, 94, 95, 108 top, 143, 475 (cf. 300).

‡ Cf. Erman, 85 f., 96 f., 108 ff.

§ Erman, p. 102. Diodorus Siculus, in a later age, says that the land in Egypt belonged to the king, the priests, and the military caste (i. 73 f.; cf. Herod. ii. 168, where it is stated that every priest and warrior in Egypt possessed 12 ἄρουραι—about 9 acres—of land tax-free).

∥ In 47³¹ Chabas (*Mél.* iii. 1. 91 f.), adopting the reading of LXX (He 11²¹), saw a reference to the Egyp. custom of doing homage, at the time of taking an oath, to the magistrate's wand of office (cf. Vigouroux, 190 ; Tomkins, 82–85).

¶ Erman, 357 ff.

for embalmers (who belonged in fact to a distinct profession). Seventy days appears to have been a more usual period for the entire process than forty; but, in point of fact, it varied.* In 50[7-9] a considerable funeral procession is described, such as are often represented on the tombs,—only (Ebers) without 'horsemen': see Plates LXVI. LXVII. LXVIII. in Wilk.-B. (iii. 444, 446, 449), or Erman, p. 320 f. The 'coffin' of 50[26] is the mummy - case, or sarcophagus: the same word (אָרוֹן) is used in Phœn. of a sarcophagus.† It is remarkable that 110 (ib.) appears to have been regarded in Egypt as the ideal age for a man, and as the most perfect age to be desired. 'In the most ancient MS we possess, the Papyrus Prisse,‡ a life of 110 years is declared to be the best; and in the Papyrus Anast. iv. (T. iv. l. 4) we read "Fulfil 110 years on the earth, whilst thy limbs are vigorous."' On a granite statue at Vienna there is a prayer to Isis to grant health and happiness for 110 years. 'Many similar passages speak of 110 years as the most perfect age to be desired, and therefore by the number 110 is inferred an especially blessed and prosperous life' (Ebers).

On the Egyptian *names* found in 41[45], see above, vol. i. 665[b]; the same explanations are accepted, and cordially approved, by Ebers (*DB*[2] 1798 f.).§ It is singular that the three types of name are otherwise not common till an age much later than that to which Joseph must be referred: those of the type Zaphenath-pa'aneaḥ appear first at the end of the 20th dyn. (one instance), and are frequent only in the 22nd (the dyn. of Shishak); of those of the type Potiphera, Mr. Tomkins cites one (though not borne by a native Egyptian)¶ in the 18th dyn., but otherwise they appear first in the 22nd, and are frequent only in the 26th dyn. (B.C. 664-525); those of the type Asenath are found now and then earlier, but are frequent only in the 21st dyn. and become common afterwards.** It is, of course, unwise to build too much upon a negative argument; but the *combination* of names, otherwise all either rare or unknown at an early period, is certainly remarkable; and Steindorff, Brugsch, and Ebers all agree in inferring from the facts mentioned that the names in question did not originate before the 9th cent. B.C.†† On ABRECH (41[43]), see vol. i. p. 18: the explanation of Renouf, there given, is likewise that of Brugsch (*Steininschrift*, 83 f.).‡‡

There are also four or five Egyptian words in this part of Gn: but they are all words which were naturalized in Hebrew; they occur in other parts of the OT, and consequently afford no clue to the date of the narratives in which they are found. They are 'Pharaoh'; יְאֹר 41[1. 2. 3. 17. 18], the common Heb. name for the Nile (Is 7[18] and frequently); אָחוּ *reed-grass*, 41[2. 18] (also Job 8[11]†); שֵׁשׁ *fine linen*, 41[42] (also Ex 26[1] etc. [P], Ezk 16[10. 13] 27[7],

* Budge, *l.c.* 179.
† *CIS* I. i. 32[3. 5]; Driver, *Notes on Samuel*, xxvi.
‡ Containing the 'Precepts of Ptah-hotep' (Maspero, *Dawn of Civiliz.* 399-401): see *RP*, 2nd ser. iii. 34.
§ Brugsch also (*Steininschrift*, 83) agrees in those of Potiphera (Potiphar), and (against his former view, *Hist.* 122) Zaphenath-pa'aneaḥ : Asenath he does not here mention.
‖ Of which 'Potiphar' is usually regarded as a merely Hebrew variant.
¶ Petu-baal, 'gift of Baal'; *Life and Times of Joseph*, p. 184: see Brugsch, *Hist.* i. 255 (ed. 1891, p. 118). The name is evidently that of a Semite (Lieblein, *Recherches sur Chronologie*, 129 ff.), and not improbably (Sayce, *EHH* 85) formed in imitation of the Phœn. *Mattanbaal* ('gift of Baal').
** See Steindorff, *Z. f. Aeg. Sprache*, xxx. (1892), 50-52.
†† Hommel (*Aufsätze*, 1892, p. 4) follows Lagarde in using the same facts as a clue to the date of the document E (*c.* 700 B.C.).
‡‡ Lieblein (*PSBA*, 1898, p. 202 ff.) proposes a different explanation of Potiphar (not of Potiphera) and Zaphenath-pa'aneaḥ: he also explains 'Abrech' as *à gauche, toi!* i.e. 'go to the left!'

Pr 31[22]); and perhaps סֹהַר (p. 773[a], note **), and חרטמים (p. 768[a], note ‖).*   S. R. DRIVER.

JOSEPH THE HUSBAND OF MARY.

I. *IN THE NEW TESTAMENT.*—(1) He is not mentioned by name in Mk,† and only indirectly in Jn 1[45] 6[42]. (2) Nor are the meagre accounts in Mt and Lk easy to reconcile. Both evangelists state that he was a descendant of David (Mt 1[20], Lk 2[4]‡), and that the Virgin Mary was already espoused to him when she became with child of the Holy Ghost (Mt 1[18], Lk 1[27. 35]), and that he lived at Nazareth after the birth of our Lord (Mt 2[23], cf. 13[55], Lk 4[22], cf. 16]); but they treat each of these details differently.

(*a*) *The Davidic Descent.*—Mt, making Joseph the son of Jacob, traces his relation to David through kings, Lk through Heli and private persons (Mt 1[1-17], Lk 3[23-38]).

(*b*) *The Conception.*§—Lk tells us of the Angelic Annunciation, and of Mary's meekness and faith (1[26-38]); Mt begins at a later period (1[18]), and lets us see Joseph's character under a sharp trial. He was a man who strove to conform to the precepts of the law (δίκαιος, cf. Lk 1[6] 2[25]), and had a keen sense of personal honour, yet was not so bound by law as to be unmoved by kindly feelings. He did not 'proclaim' Mary (δειγματίσαι), though it seemed to be his duty, but resolved to divorce her in as quiet and secret a way as possible.‖ Yet though he had already come to this decision, the appearance to him, in a dream, of an angel of the Lord, with the assurance of the true origin and the work of the Child, fully in accordance as the former was with the words of prophecy ('Quod si dubitas Isaiam audi,' Ephraem on Tatian, cf. Iren. iv. 23. 1, ed. Massuet), convinced him of his mistake. He therefore took Mary, and in full faith 'was dwelling in holiness with her' (Tatian's *Diatess.*) until she bare a son.

(*c*) *Nazareth.*—Lk tells us in 1[26f.] that Mary lived in Nazareth, and was espoused to Joseph; and in 2[4] that Joseph went up out of Nazareth to Bethlehem with her. He therefore presumably (not quite necessarily) also himself lived in Nazareth before the birth of our Lord. Yet Mt 2[22. 23] gives no hint that Joseph had had any relation with Nazareth before his return from Egypt, and implies that he

* רָבִיד *collar*, 41[42] (also Ezk 16[11]†) is not the Egyp. name of the decoration mentioned on p. 773[b]; and whether it is Egyptian at all is extremely doubtful: Harkavy (*Journ. As.* Mars-Avril, 1870, p. 182 f.) suggested 'sous toutes réserves' that it might be the Egyp. *repit*, 'image qu'on porte sur le cou, collier en forme d'image,' which occurs in ch. 162 of the *Book of the Dead*,—in Budge's tr. p. 290, '[This chapter] shall be recited over the *image* (repit) of a cow, which shall be made in fine gold, and placed at the neck of the deceased' (cf. Budge's *Vocab.* p. 194). This is slender evidence that *repit* (or *erpit*) means a 'collar.' There is a Sem. root, Arab. *rabada*, one meaning of which is *to tie*.
† TR of Mk 6[3] speaks of our Lord as 'the son of the carpenter' (= ‖ Mt 13[55]), but the true reading is 'the carpenter' (see below).
‡ ἐξ οἴκου καὶ πατριᾶς Δ. Possibly the former term is the wider, and includes even those adopted into the household, while the latter refers more strictly to those of the line of the πατριά.
§ Canon Gore (*Bampton Lects.*, 1891, p. 78) points out that Mt narrates everything from Joseph's side, Lk from Mary's, and adds that this suggests that the narrative of Mt is ultimately based on Joseph's account, Lk on Mary's. If this be true we may conjecture that Mt's was derived mediately through James the Lord's brother.
‖ Dr. G. Dalman writes to the author of the present article as follows: 'Edersheim (*Life and Times of Jesus*, i. 154) is wrong in stating that Joseph had a choice in legally divorcing her either publicly or privately. Divorce has always been a private act. No public act of divorce exists. The *gēt* (bill of divorce, which is given solely in the woman's interest), never contains reasons for the divorce. Two witnesses are only necessary that they may state that the *gēt* was really handed over by *this* man to *this* woman. *Keth.* 74[b], 75[a], quoted by Edersheim, does not refer to divorce itself, but to doubts about the formal legality of an act of divorce which arose *afterwards*, and could become a reason for hearing the decision of a court of justice. Some Rabbis believed that no husband would be likely to resort to a measure which would expose his former wife to the shame of having to do with a court of justice.'

would have settled in Judæa but for fear of Archelaus and the direct warning that he received by dream. Assuming the truth of the inference from Lk's language, we must suppose that Mt was not concerned with matters of merely private importance, and that in accordance with his scheme of showing publicly the Messianic character of Jesus, he omitted everything that did not illustrate this. The significance of the birth being at Bethlehem (in the relation of that town to David and to the prophecy of Micah, and in its nearness to Rachel's tomb, Gn 35[19] 48[7], with the *midrashic* application of Jer 31[15]), and the interest of the removal to Egypt, make it natural that Nazareth should not be mentioned until this town in its turn affected the public life of Jesus. Mt then, in reference to our Lord's familiar name ('Jesus the Nazarene') being derived from it, characteristically connects it with prophetic words (2[23], Is 11[1]).

(3) We further learn from Lk that Joseph was present when the shepherds came to Bethlehem (2[16]); that he as well as Mary brought up the Babe to present Him to the Lord, and marvelled at the things that were being said about Him (2[22, 33]); that he used to go every year to Jerusalem at the passover (2[41, 42]), certainly with Mary, and perhaps with the Child; and that when the Boy was twelve years old and stayed on after the days of the feast were over, he shared with Mary in the anxiety, and, like her, did not understand the naive wonder of Jesus at their searching for Him (2[41-50]); yet his and Mary's authority remained unquestioned in the daily life of the home at Nazareth (2[51]).

(4) We gather from the remaining references to Joseph that (*a*) our Lord was commonly known as Jesus ben-Joseph, Jn 1[46] (? at Bethsaida), Lk 4[22] at Nazareth, and Jn 6[42] at Capernaum; and (*b*) Joseph was known, or remembered, as the carpenter (Mt 13[55]).

(5) Nothing is said about Joseph's death. But the command to St. John at the Cross (Jn 19[26. 27]), and the reference to 'Mary the mother of Jesus, and His brethren' (Ac 1[14]) immediately after the Ascension, imply that his death took place at least before the Crucifixion. Further, the fact that he is not mentioned with Mary and His brethren when they sought Him (Mt 12[46] and parallels), suggests that he was already dead before the middle of our Lord's ministry. Probably the usual opinion is right, viz. that he was dead before our Lord's ministry began.

II. *THE LIFE OF JOSEPH FROM APOCRYPHAL SOURCES.**—The account of Joseph is put into our Lord's mouth as He sat on the Mt. of Olives with His disciples (*Death Jos.*, Boh. § i.). He is from Bethlehem, and marries his first wife when 40 years old, living 49 years with her in wedlock (*ib.* § xiv.). He has four sons and two daughters, his wife dying when James is still young. He and his *two* sons work as carpenters (*Death Jos.*, Boh. § ii.). They, however, and his two daughters are married, and he dwells with James his youngest son (*ib.* Boh. § xi. 1). He is one year alone before Mary is given to him (*ib.* Boh. § xiv.). The priests seek a widower to whom they may espouse Mary (who has been in the temple from the age of three to

twelve, to fourteen according to others); the heralds proclaim this through all Judæa, and Joseph, throwing away his axe, goes to meet them. The high priest takes the rods of all, enters into the temple, and prays, and returns the rods to each. There is no sign till Joseph receives his rod, the last of all, when a dove comes out of the rod and flies upon his head. The priest says, 'Thou hast been chosen by lot to take into thy keeping the virgin of the Lord.' But he refuses, saying, 'I have children; and I am an old man, and she is a young girl. I am afraid lest I become a laughing-stock to the sons of Israel.' But he receives her (*Protev.* §§ 8, 9). After two years (*Death Jos.* § xiv.), or four months (Niceph. Call. ii. 3, cf. Forbes Robinson, p. 187), the Annunciation takes place. The 'righteous old man,' coming in from his house-building in districts near the seashore (Pseudo-Matt. § 10), wishes to put her away privily, but on Mary's statement of her innocence hesitates, and is assured by the angel in a dream (*Protev.* §§ 13, 14). Yet both he and Mary are accused by Annas the scribe, and by the priest, and are tried by the ordeal of drinking water and going to the hill-country. But they return to the priest unhurt (*Protev.* §§. 15. 16) and go home.

Having heard of the order for enrolment, Joseph sets Mary upon an ass; his son leads it, and he himself follows (*Protev.* § 17). On arriving at Bethlehem he writes his name by a scribe, 'Joseph the son of David, and Mary his wife, and Jesus his son are of the tribe of Judah' (*Death Jos.*, Boh. § vii.). He brings her to a tomb (Lord Crawford's MS), an inn (*Death Jos.*, Sah. vii.), a cave (*Protev.* § 18), where he leaves her while looking for a mid-wife. He sees all nature stand still in wonder (*Protev.* § 18). He is mentioned as being present at some of the many miracles performed during the flight to Egypt and the sojourn there (Pseudo-Matt. § 19 *sqq.*; *Arab. Gosp.* §§ 10-35). Also after returning to Nazareth he is necessarily an actor in the painful tricks and precocious miracles ascribed to our Lord. He lives by his daily toil, 'never eating bread for nought, but doing according to the law of Moses' (*Death Jos.*, Boh. § ix.). When he was an hundred and eleven years old his body was that of a youth, and he works at his trade of carpenter till the last day of his life (*Hist. Jos. Carp.* § 29), yet he is told that he is to die that year.* He goes up to Jerusalem, into the temple, repents before the altar, and prays. He returns to Nazareth, and laments. He is in great fear of death, and confesses to Jesus his sin in doubting Mary at the first, and in rebuking Him for His childish behaviour. Mary pleads with Jesus that Joseph may not die. While he himself is making the same request, his soul comes up to his throat. His children come and weep over him. Death comes with devils and they depart, rebuked by Jesus. Death is afraid (in *Death Jos.*, Sah. III. § xxiii. Jesus is obliged to go out before Death will come in). Jesus prays. Angels take Joseph's soul (on Epepi 26=July 20), putting it into silk napkins of fine texture. Michael and Gabriel watch it; the angels sing before it till they give it to God. The inhabitants of Nazareth and Galilee gather together and mourn for him till the 9th hour, when they are put forth by Jesus, who pours water on the body and anoints it with oil. At Jesus' prayer two angels shroud the body. The body becomes incorrupt even until the banquet of the thousand years (*Hist. Jos. Carp.* § 26). Jesus promises blessing to those who commemorate each anniversary of Joseph's death, give bread in his name to the poor, and wine to strangers and others on the day of his commemoration; who write out the book

---

* These are especially *The Book of James* (*Protevangelium*), *The Life of the Virgin* (Sahidic Fragments, published in Forbes Robinson's *Coptic Apocryphal Gospels*, 1896), *The Death of Joseph* (Bohairic and Sahidic, do.) which = *The History of Joseph the Carpenter* (Arabic), *Liber de Infantia* (Gospel of Pseudo-Matt.), *The Gospel of the Nativity of Mary*, *The Arabic Gospel of the Childhood*, *The Gospel of Thomas*.
For the dates of these see Lipsius in *Dict. Christ. Biogr.* ii. 700. The *Protevangelium* in its present form from perhaps the latter part of the 3rd cent. The rest from perhaps the 4th to the 6th cent. Many of these narrate the same incident, but one reference seemed to be sufficient here. It did not seem necessary to mention all minute variations of the legend.

* From here onwards the *Death of Joseph* (Boh.) is almost the sole authority.

of Joseph's going-forth from the body, or, if they are too poor, call their sons by the name of Joseph (*Death Jos.*, Boh. § xxvi.). The great ones of the city coming to bury Joseph find his shroud already fastened to his body. They dig at the door of the cave to place his body there. Jesus prays and embraces Joseph, who is then buried.

III. *THE CULT OF ST. JOSEPH.*—Any notice of Joseph can in these days hardly be complete without some mention of his Cult, which has of recent years attained to such an extraordinary development.

(1) The latter part of the preceding section shows that to some writers, especially to those who lived in Egypt and occupied themselves with religious romances, Joseph's attractive personality afforded scope for religious devotion. But very little, if any, trace of this is to be seen in the Fathers.* St. Bernard of Clairvaux is the first writer to show it clearly. He says (if Mgr. Ricard's quotations may be trusted), ' Joseph alone among all men was, here below, the faithful co-worker of her who was the greatest of the works of God'; † and again, ' Remember the ancient patriarch who was sold into Egypt, and know that this man (Joseph) not only inherited his name, but possessed, moreover, his chastity, his innocency, and his grace.' ‡ Thomas Aquinas also writes strongly.§ But the Roman Church has given much credit to the writings of female mystics, who from the 14th cent. onwards have spoken much of the veneration with which St. Joseph is honoured. Thus Gertrude the Great († 1310) saw in her revelations, when the name of Joseph was pronounced ' all the saints bowed their heads with respect, as a sign of honour to that glorious patriarch, and congratulated him, and rejoiced with him on his incomparable dignity.' ‖ St. Bridget of Sweden († 1373), Marie d'Agreda († 1665), Catherine Emmerich († 1824), give innumerable details of Joseph's life seen by them in visions, which are combined in popular lives of St. Joseph for Roman Catholic use to-day. Even Gerson at the Council of Constance (1414) says of Joseph's powers of intercession, ' non impetrat sed imperat.' St. Teresa († 1582), St. Francis de Sales, and Bossuet vie in exalting him.

(2) Further, the growth of the Cult may be seen in the public honours allotted to his feast, and in the status that he holds among the saints by the express decree of the pope. ' In Western Martyrologies of the 9th cent. the name of Joseph is found, and from the same time the Greeks commemorated him along with other saints of the Old Testament on the Sunday before Christmas, and along with Mary, David, and James the Less on the Sunday in the Octave of Christmas' (*Cath. Dict. s.v.* ' Joseph '). In the breviary of Sixtus IV. (1471–1484) the feast of St. Joseph (Mar. 19) is a simple rite ; in that of Innocent VIII. (1484–1492) a double rite. Pius V. (1566–1572) ordered that the office of St. Joseph should be in that of confessors

* Roman Catholic writers (*e.g.* Mgr. Ricard, *St. Joseph, sa vie et son culte*, Lille, 1896) mention Irenæus, Origen, Eusebius, Epiphanius, Gregory of Nazianzus, Gregory of Nyssa, Hilary of Poitiers, Ephraem the Syrian, Cyril of Jerusalem, Chrysostom, Jerome, Augustine, Cyril of Alexandria, and Hilary of Arles as supporting the Cult of St. Joseph. But they seldom give references or distinguish between genuine and spurious works. Thus Augustine is quoted as saying, ' Rejoice, Joseph, that by the merit of the virtue of the angels you live so angelically as to be justly called the father of the Saviour.' This is doubtless from a spurious sermon in Migne, v. p. 2110. Irenæus says Joseph ' served Jesus with a continual joy' (*adv. Hær.* iv. 40, ed. Grabe.=23. 1, ed. Massuet) ; but Irenæus really says, ' Joseph joyfully yielded obedience [*to the angel*] in regard to all the rest of the education of Christ ' (Joseph et Mariam accepit et in reliqua universa educatione Christi gaudens obsequium præstitit).

† Ricard, p. 279.
‡ E. H. Thomson, *The Life and Glories of St. Joseph*, 1891, p. 16.
§ Ricard, p. 282.   ‖ *Ib.* p. 284.

who were not popes. Gregory XV. in 1621 made it a feast of obligation for the whole world.* Urban VIII. in 1642 renewed this order. Clement XI. (1700–1721) arranged the hymns and all the parts of the office peculiar to St. Joseph, and raised it to the double degree of the second class. Much discussion was held as to the place in the Litany of the Saints which Joseph's name ought to take ; but it was decided by Benedict XIII. in 1726 that it should precede the names of the Apostles and Martyrs, and follow immediately that of St. John the Baptist.

Two other feast days were added in honour of St. Joseph. One is the day of the Patronage of St. Joseph, which was fixed for the 3rd Sunday after Easter by the Congregation of Rites in 1680, and after being observed in a gradually increasing number of places was established throughout Roman Catholic Christendom by Pius IX. in 1847. The other is that of the betrothal or marriage of Mary and Joseph (for which an office was drawn up by Gerson), and allowed (with a different office) by Benedict XIII. in 1725 to be observed in all churches on Jan 23. ' The feast is kept in England as a greater double.' †

Lastly, Pius IX. in 1871 proclaimed St. Joseph Patron of the whole Church as follows : ' Our most Holy Lord, Pius IX., Pope, moved by recent deplorable events, was pleased to comply with the desires of the Prelates, and to commit to the most powerful patronage of the Holy Patriarch, Joseph, both Himself and all the faithful, and solemnly declared him Patron of the Catholic Church, and commanded his festival, occurring on the 19th day of March, to be celebrated for the future as a double of the first class, but without an octave, on account of Lent.' ‡

But however much we may respect the faith of Joseph, and gladly recognize, not only Paul the tent-maker and Peter the fisherman, but also Joseph the carpenter, as confessedly high examples of the dignity of work, and of the spiritual reward that it receives, we can have little sympathy with teaching that stands in such lurid contrast to the reticence of the Gospels and of the early Church.

A. LUKYN WILLIAMS.

JOSEPH OF ARIMATHÆA ('Ιωσὴφ [ὁ] ἀπὸ 'Αριμαθαίας).—A wealthy Israelite and member of the Sanhedrin (βουλευτής) ; a ' good man and a righteous ' (Lk 23⁵⁰), who ' was looking for the kingdom of God ' (Mk 15⁴³). On the situation of his native place, see ARIMATHÆA and ARUMAH. He was ' Jesus' disciple ' (Mt 27³⁵), ' but secretly, for fear of the Jews ' (Jn 19³⁸). He had not consented to the judgment of the Sanhedrin against Jesus (Lk 23⁵¹), having either absented himself from the meeting (as Mk 14⁶⁴ suggests) or refrained from giving a vote. After Christ's death, the approach of sunset made it difficult for the apostles—unprepared as they were, even if they had recovered their courage —to arrange duly for His reverent interment before the Sabbath began. Joseph, hitherto fainthearted, rose to the occasion. He appears to have been present at the crucifixion, and his possession of a tomb, new and yet unused, hewn out of a rock in a neighbouring garden, suggested to him the thought of himself obtaining and burying the body of Jesus. The spectacle of the crucified Saviour had quickened his faith and love, and combined, doubtless, with his shame for past faint-heartedness, to raise him above the fear of man. His boldness is the more notable, because, to all human appearance, he was showing

* On feasts of obligation the faithful are bound to hear mass and rest from servile work (*Cath. Dict.* art. ' Feasts ').
† *Cath. Dict.* art. ' Espousals.'
‡ The Decree may be found in Latin and English in Thompson, *loc. cit.* p. 485.

sympathy with a ruined cause, at the risk of persecution to death.* His request for the body from Pilate was successful, and he took or saw it taken down from the cross. According to the *Acts of Pilate*, Joseph sought the favour with tears and entreaties; but even if Pilate's humanity were not stimulated by a timely bribe, he would be disposed to show his sympathy with a councillor who had taken no part in constraining him to condemn Christ.† Joseph's example, presumably, moved Nicodemus to similar courage. Together they received the body and laid it in the tomb, Joseph providing the fine linen (σινδών) and grave-bands (ὀθόνια), Nicodemus the abundant spices (Mt 27⁵⁷ᶠ·, Mk 15⁴²ᶠ·, Lk 23⁵⁰ᶠ·, Jn 19³⁸ᶠ·, *Gosp. of Pet.* 3 f., 23 f., *Acts of Pil.* 11. 12).

The minuteness of the Gospel record, its preservation by all the four evangelists, and its later apocryphal expansion, are due not so much to the fulfilment of Is 53⁹, still less to the growth of a myth (Strauss, *New Life of Jesus*, ch. xcvi.) based thereon (for the parallel, obscured by the Sept., is noted by no writer either of the apostolic or of the sub-apostolic age),‡ but to the desire, probably, (1) to signalize the adherence of a member of the hostile Sanhedrin; (2) to render prominent an incident so closely connected with Christ's Resurrection. None the less the correspondence with 'They made (or appointed) his grave with the wicked, and with the rich in his death,' if not exact, is striking; and even if a different original reference be adopted, it is difficult to regard as accidental the fresh significance given to the verse by the circumstances of our Lord's burial.§

A legend, which first appears in William of Malmesbury (*de Ant. Glast. Eccl.* i.), represents Joseph as sent by St. Philip from Gaul to Britain, along with eleven other disciples, in A.D. 63; as obtaining from a British king a small island in Somersetshire (afterwards the site of Glastonbury) engirt by the river Brue; and as building there, 'with twisted twigs,' the earliest Christian oratory in the land. Malmesbury, however, introduces the narrative with an 'ut ferunt,' in marked contrast to his reference of other statements in the same chapter to earlier historians. The absence, also, of any allusion to Joseph's advent in the histories of Gildas and Bede is significant. Probably some other Joseph, who founded Glastonbury, has been confounded with Joseph of Arimathæa. The story of Joseph bringing the Holy Grail to England dates from about 1200 A.D., and was probably composed by Walter Map. Ussher (*Ant. Eccl. Brit.* c. 16) mentions a tradition that Joseph

* Similar intervention nearly cost Tobit his life (To 1¹⁹), and actually led to the martyrdom of Porphyrius, a slave of Pamphilus, in the persecution of Diocletian (Eus. *Mar. Pal.* 11). The apocryphal *Acts of Pilate* and *Narrative of Joseph* represent the latter as imprisoned with a view to his execution.

† The *Gospel of Peter* represents Pilate as first asking Herod for the body. Keim's assertion (*Jes. of Naz.* vi. p. 256) that Jn 19³⁸ contradicts 19³¹·³², is hypercritical; Joseph arrived, presumably, before the soldiers had completed their work.

‡ Justin Martyr twice quotes Is 53⁹ in connexion with the fulfilment of prophecy (1 *Ap.* 51, *Dial.* 97); but in neither case is there any reference to Joseph.

§ Gesenius and Knobel, following Jewish commentators, interpret 'rich' as=proud, ungodly, vicious (against which see Urwick, *Servant of Jehovah*, p. 145); Ewald, Cheyne (*Introd. to Is.* p. 429), and Duhm adopt, without MS authority, textual emendations, and read עָרִיץ oppressor (Ew.) or עָרֵץ defrauder (Ch. and Du.); in each case the word being referred to the Babylonians, among whom the 'Servant of the LORD' would die. The *Bible Annotée* paraphrases, 'He has been interred with criminals, but after his death he has been put by the Eternal (in Sheol) in the ranks of the most honourable.' Delitzsch⁴, Urwick, etc., retain the meaning 'rich' (literally), and emphasize the similarity between OT prophecy and NT history. The interpretation, 'his sepulchral mounds,' instead of 'in his death' (adopted by Lowth, Ew., Duhm, Ch. in *Intr.*), renders the parallel more conspicuous, but is not essential to its maintenance; 'in his death' may='when he died.'

freed Ireland from poisonous reptiles, a service usually attributed to St. Patrick.

LITERATURE.—Wuelcher's Excursus on J. of A. in *Gosp. of Nic.*; Cowper's *Apocr. Gosps.*; Skeat's *Joseph of Arimathie* (Early English Texts); Ittig, *Pat. Apost.* 13; Hearne's *Hist. and Ant. of Glastonbury*; Saurin, *Discours*, x. 451, 466.
                                                        H. COWAN.

JOSEPH BARSABBAS (AV Barsabas), surnamed Justus; one of the two disciples who had been followers of Jesus during the whole of His public ministry, and were therefore deemed suitable candidates for the apostolic office vacant by the treachery and death of Judas Iscariot (Ac 1²³). *Barsabbas* means 'son of Sabba.' It has been variously interpreted 'son of an oath,' 'son of an old man,' 'son of conversion,' 'son of quiet' (see Lightfoot, *Hor. Heb.*; Winer, *Realwörterb.*); but it was probably a patronymic, Joseph's father being named Sabba. If so, we must reject Lightfoot's suggestion, that he and **Judas Barsabbas** (Ac 15²²) were brothers of James the son of Alphæus. His Roman surname Justus was doubtless assumed after the manner frequent among the Jews at that time (cf. Ac 12¹² 13¹). We have no information concerning him beyond what is implied in the one passage where he is mentioned. He is certainly to be distinguished from Joseph Barnabas (Ac 4³⁶) and from Judas Barsabbas (Ac 15²²); though it is not improbable, from the identity of the patronymic, that he and Judas were brothers. Eusebius (*HE* i. 12) makes him to have been one of 'the Seventy' (Lk 10¹), and this is not improbable. Eusebius (3³⁹) also relates from Papias a legend that Joseph Barsabbas 'drank a deadly poison and yet, by the grace of the Lord, suffered no harm.'   G. T. PURVES.

JOSEPH, PRAYER OF.—A lost Jewish apocryphon, mentioned in several catalogues of extra-canonical books. For information as to its contents we are indebted almost exclusively to a few quotations in the writings of Origen. In all the extant passages Jacob (not Joseph) is the speaker. He narrates a conversation he held with the wrestling angel Uriel; and claims to have read the tablets of heaven, and thus to know what is about to befall mankind. The work is said by Origen to have been in use παρ' Ἐβραίοις, and his quotations show it to have had an antichristian *animus*. It is a representative of a remarkable trend in Jewish theology, which led the Jews to claim for the three great patriarchs the same sublime and supernatural characteristics which Christians claimed for the Lord Jesus. For instance, Jacob claims to be 'an angel of God and a ruling spirit'; 'the first-begotten (πρωτόγονος) of every creature animated by God'; 'an archangel of the power of the Lord'; and 'the first servant in God's presence.' The wrestling angel, whom Christians claimed to be the Messiah, is told by Jacob that he is only eighth in rank among the angels, Jacob himself being first of all; and in the same strain Abraham and Isaac are said to have been 'created before every (other) work.'

LITERATURE.—Fabricius, *Codex pseudepigr. VT* i. 761-771; Schürer, *HJP* II. iii. 128; Dillmann, art. 'Pseudepigraphen,' in *PRE²*.   J. T. MARSHALL.

JOSEPHUS (A Ἰώσηφος, B Φόσηπος), 1 Es 9³⁴= JOSEPH, Ezr 10⁴².

JOSES (Ἰωσῆς).—**1.** An ancestor of our Lord (Lk 3²⁹ AV reads **Jose**, failing to observe that Ἰωσῆ of TR is genitive. The correct text as adopted by WH and RV is Ἰησοῦ, so that this Joses gives place to Jesus). **2.** One of the 'brethren of the Lord' (Mk 6³ 15⁴⁰· ⁴⁷, Mt 27⁵⁶). In Mt 13⁵⁵ where AV has **Joses**, RV adopts WH text **Joseph** (see Dalman,

Gram. p. 75). **3.** The natal name (Ac 4³⁶ AV) of **Barnabas** (which see). RV after WH has **Joseph**.

JOSHAH (יוֹשָׁה).—A Simeonite chief, 1 Ch 4³⁴. See GENEALOGY.

JOSHAPHAT (יְהוֹשָׁפָט=יוֹשָׁפָט).—**1.** One of David's heroes, 1 Ch 11⁴³. **2.** A priest in David's time, 1 Ch 15²⁴.

JOSHAVIAH (יוֹשַׁוְיָה).—One of David's heroes, 1 Ch 11⁴⁶.

JOSHBEKASHAH (יָשְׁבְּקָשָׁה).—A son of Heman, 1 Ch 25⁴·²⁴. There is reason to believe that this and five of the names associated with it are really a fragment of a hymn or prayer (see GENEALOGY, III. 23 n.; and cf. Kittel in *SBOT*, and W. R. Smith, *OTJC²* 143 n.).

JOSHEB-BASSHEBETH (יֹשֵׁב בַּשֶּׁבֶת) occurs in RV of 2 S 23⁸ as a proper name in place of the utterly meaningless 'that sat in the seat' of the AV. It is evident that the text is corrupt, and that the original name **Jashobeam** must be restored from the parallel passage, 2 Ch 11¹¹, just as the 'Hachmonite' must be substituted for the 'Tahchemonite.' (Cf. Driver, *Heb. Text of Sam.*, *ad loc.*). Budde and others would go further. In Jashobeam itself they find a corruption of the original name, and they recover the latter by the following steps. In B we find Ἰεβόσθε, and in Luc. Ἰεσβάαλ, from which it is inferred that יֹשֵׁב בַּשֶׁבֶת=ישבעל (אשבעל), so that the name of David's commander was really Eshbaal. (See notes on 2 S 23⁸ in Haupt's *Sacred Bks. of OT*, and in Kautzsch's *AT*).   J. A. SELBIE.

JOSHIBIAH (יוֹשִׁבְיָה 'J" causeth to dwell'; *Oxf. Heb. Lex.* compares Phœn. ישבעל perhaps=ישבבעל).—A Simeonite chief, 1 Ch 4³⁵. See GENEALOGY.

JOSHUA (on forms and meaning of the name see next art.).—**1.** The successor of Moses. See next article. **2.** The Bethshemite in whose field was the stone on which the ark was set, on its return from the land of the Philistines, 1 S 6¹⁴·¹⁸. **3.** The governor (שַׂר) of Jerusalem in the time of Josiah, 2 K 23⁸. **4.** The high priest who along with Zerubbabel directed affairs at Jerusalem after the restoration, Hag 1¹·¹²·¹⁴ etc., Zec 3¹·³·⁶ etc. In the books of Hag and Zec he is called Joshua, in Ezr and Neh **Jeshua** (which see).

JOSHUA.—

  i. Name.
  ii. Contents of the Book.
  iii. Relation to the Pentateuch.
  iv. Constituent Documents.
  v. Problems of their Relation and Composition.
  vi. Separation from the Pentateuch, and Date.
  vii. Relation to the Book of Judges.
  viii. Historical Value of the Book.
  ix. The Person Joshua.
  x. His Work.
  xi. Religious Teaching of the Book.
          Literature.

i. THE NAME.—1. The English form Joshua is an abbreviation of the Heb. יְהוֹשֻׁעַ (only in Dt 3²¹, Jg 2⁷) or יְהוֹשׁוּעַ (the usual form, *e.g.* Ex 17⁹, Dt 1³⁸ etc., 1 K 16³⁴), later abbreviated to יֵשׁוּעַ (of Joshua himself, Neh 8¹⁷) in order to avoid, it is said, the sequence of the vowels ô, û (*SK*, 1892, 177, 573; *WZKM* iv. 332 ff.). In Nu 13⁸·¹⁶, Dt 32⁴⁴ the form is הוֹשֵׁעַ, the same as that of the king of N. Israel (2 K 15³⁰ etc.) and the prophet (Hos 1¹·²); but Dt 32⁴⁴ is probably a textual error for הושע, so Sam., Gr., Vulg., and Syr. (cf. Driver, *in loco*), and on Nu 13⁸·¹⁶ (P) no reliance can be placed. The LXX give it as Ἰησοῦς, and so it occurs in the NT both as

Joshua's own name (Ac 7⁴⁵) and that of our Lord (Mt 1²¹·²⁵). The name, Stade (*Gram.* 93) suggests, may be a Hiphil. More probably it is a compound 'J" is salvation.' The parallel forms אבישׁוע and אלישׁוע favour this (on this and the antiquity of the name see Gray, *Heb. Proper Names*, 155, 259). Cf. the Heb. אֱלִישָׁע, still more אֱלִישׁוע and עשׁיְ, the Phœn. ישע, and the Himyarite יהשׁע, which Derenbourg transliterates Yuhashi.

Joshua the son of Nun, the successor of Moses in the leadership of Israel, is mentioned several times outside the Book of Joshua; but as the traditions concerning him are mainly found in the latter, it will be more convenient to examine its contents and composition before treating of his life.

ii. CONTENTS OF THE BOOK. — The Book of Joshua consists of twenty-four chapters, of which the first twelve take up the history of Israel from the point reached by the end of Deuteronomy, the death of Moses, and continue it through the conquest of Western Palestine; while the next nine record the division of the land among the tribes (12–21). An appendix gives Joshua's speech to Reuben, Gad, and half-Manasseh, his dismissal of them to E. Palestine (22¹⁻⁹); the controversy about the altar of Ed (22¹⁰⁻³⁴); the last days of Joshua and his death (23–24³¹); the burial of Joseph's body (24³²), and the death of Eleazar son of Aaron (24³³).

iii. RELATION TO THE PENTATEUCH.—The Book of Joshua thus proves to be the necessary supplement and completion of the Pentateuch, of whose promises and obligations it records the fulfilment in the settlement of Abraham's descendants in Canaan (cf. Gn 12⁷ etc.); in the execution (told in Deuteronomic language) of the Deuteronomic commands to Israel to take possession of the land and extirpate the Canaanites; and even in such details as the burial of Joseph's bones, which the patriarch made Israel swear they would carry up with them from Egypt (Gn 50²⁵).*

Notwithstanding this continuity of historical material and of plan, the Heb. Canon sharply separated the Book of Joshua from the Pentateuch: the Pentateuch comprises the first and earliest part of the Canon—the Torah; the Book of Joshua heads the later Canon of the Prophets, more especially the series of historical works, concluding with the Books of Kings and known as the Former Prophets. Besides, the book in its present form is an independent whole, with a definite beginning and conclusion; its orthography differs in several important details from that of the Pentateuch (*e.g.* it does not continue the epicene הוא and נער of the Pentateuch, nor the form האל for האלה, and spells Jericho יְרִיחוֹ not as always in the Pentateuch יְרֵחוֹ); while in consequence of its later adoption into the Canon its text (cf. the numerous deviations of the LXX) is in a less certain form. For some time, therefore, the book was not brought under the methods of criticism and analysis to which the Pentateuch was subjected in the end of last and beginning of this century. But in 1792 the Scotsman, Father Geddes, in his translation of the Bible, wrote (vol. I. Preface, p. xxi): 'To the Pentateuch I have joined the Book of Joshuah (*sic*), both because I conceive it to be compiled by the same author, and because it is a necessary appendix to the history contained in the former books.'† But it was de Wette, Bleek, and Ewald who were the first to extend to Joshua the documentary theory of the composition of the Penta-

---

* Cf. Jos 11ff. with Nu 27¹⁵ff., Dt 3²⁸ 31¹·⁸. 23 ; 11² with Nu 32, Dt 3¹⁸ff. ; 8³⁰ff. with Dt 11²⁹ff. 27¹·⁸. 11-14 ; 13 ff. with Nu 34 ; 14⁶-¹⁵ with Nu 14²⁴, Dt 13⁶ ; 17¹·⁶ with Nu 27¹·¹¹ 36¹·¹² ; 20 f. with Nu 35.

† Hollenberg, in his account of the criticism of Joshua (*SK*, 1874, p. 463), is, therefore, so far wrong in naming de Wette as the first to recognize that the analysis of Joshua must follow the lines of that of the Pentateuch.

teuch. De Wette (see list of literature below), after vacillating, in successive editions of his Introduction, between the fragmentary and documentary hypotheses of the composition of the Pentateuch, finally adhered to the latter, and traced through Joshua the Elohist and Deuteronomic documents. In 1822 Bleek distinguished the basis of the book as Elohist, additions to it as by the Jahwist, and its final redaction as from the hands of the Deuteronomist. Soon after Bleek began his criticism, Ewald traced up to the end of Joshua all the documents into which he had already analysed the Pentateuch. The work was continued by other critics, the most prominent of whom have been Knobel, Schrader, Nöldeke, Hollenberg, Wellhausen, Vatke (whose merits appear in his posthumous lectures on OT Introduction), Budde, Albers, Driver, Bennett, and Addis. Amid many varieties of opinion as to details, the analyses of this long list of scholars reveal a wonderful agreement, not only as to the presence in Joshua of all the Pentateuchal documents, but even as to the approximate proportions in which they stand to each other.* It is because of these results that OT criticism prefers to speak of the *Hexateuch* rather than of the *Pentateuch*.

iv. THE CONSTITUENT DOCUMENTS. — Critics, then, agree that all the chief documents of the Pentateuch are present in Joshua, and indeed this is obvious to any reader of the original who is familiar with the characteristic style and favourite topics of these documents. But the documents are present with certain ambiguities and complications, and these present a number of problems unsolved and perhaps insoluble, which are peculiar to the criticism of Joshua, as contrasted with that of the Pentateuch.

In the following analysis we start with the Deuteronomic elements, the spirit and style of which are so readily recognized. We have seen that the book is faithful to the spirit of the Deuteronomic code—even to the extent of idealizing the facts—in so far as Deuteronomy commands Israel to take full possession of the land and extirpate the native inhabitants. But the Deuteronomic dialect is also frequently observed. The following is a list and analysis of the Deuteronomic passages. They are found chiefly in chs. 1–12, and in the Appendix, chs. 21–24.

(*a*) *The Deuteronomic Passages in Joshua.*—It is not without significance that the introduction is one of the most plainly Deuteronomic passages of the Book. Ch. 1 is not only written in manifest continuation of the end of the Bk. of Deuteronomy (as completed, critics now take for granted, by a Deuteronomic editor), but it is composed almost throughout in the Deuteronomic style. Vv.$^{3-5a}$ are expanded from Dt $11^{24.\ 25a}$; Dt 31^{23} is echoed in vv.$^{5b.\ 6.\ 17b.\ 18b}$; Dt 4^6 29^8 (Heb.) in v.^{7}; Dt $1^{29.\ 30}$ 20^3 31^6 in v.^{9}; Dt 11^{31} in v.^{11b}. Terms used only in Dt, or in the meaning in which they are employed in Dt, are scattered through the chapter (*e.g.* the intransitive עְרָן, and שֹׁטְרִים in the sense of officers who communicate the orders of the chief to the people). The appeal to the Law and the Book of the Law are also Deuteronomic, and so, too, the number of the tribes settled E. of the Jordan as $2\frac{1}{2}$ (cf. v.^{12} with Dt 3^{13-21}), while JE (Nu $32^{1-5.\ 20f.}$) states them as 2. At the same time there are complications. The phrases מְשָׁרֵת מֹשֶׁה (v.^{1}), and חֲמֻשִׁים and גִּבּוֹרֵי הַחַיִל (v.^{14}), are not phrases of the Dt style, which has other terms for the two latter; the details in v.^{11a} might have been stated by any

writer. These facts have led some to conclude that a JE narrative underlies this Dt introduction to the Book. It should be observed that the Dt parallels and echoes in the chapter are all taken from the historical and parenetic portions of the Bk. of Dt which most critics now assign to another hand than that which drew up the legal kernel of the Book, chs. 12–26. 28.

In ch. 2, vv.$^{10.\ 11}$ (and perhaps v.^{24}) are not only Deuteronomic in language, but express a favourite thought of the Deuteronomist—the fear which Israel and the wonderful deeds of J″ produced on the inhabitants of W. Palestine. Chs. 3 and 4, on the Crossing of Jordan, are obviously compiled from several sources, for they contain not only differences of style, but of substance. There are, *firstly*, clauses in the Dt dialect deducing from the events described the Dt doctrines (3^7 4^{14} the magnifying of Joshua in the eyes of Israel; $4^{21.\ 24}$ the duty of teaching future generations the meaning of the events, and the impression of these on the Canaanites); and, *secondly*, in other parts of the narrative, characteristic Dt phrases occur (3^{2-4} הַכֹּהֲנִים הַלְוִיִם, etc.); but, *thirdly* also, there are traces of an original Dt account of the monument raised to commemorate the passage ($4^{2.\ 3a.\ 8}$, cf. vv.$^{21.\ 24}$), which differs from the two JE accounts of the same (see below), in so far as it makes the monument to consist of 12 stones brought by 12 men from the bed of Jordan, and places it at Gilgal. In chs. 5 and 6 (the Taking of Jericho), 5^1, the fear of the Canaanites has an echo of Dt, as also $6^{2.\ 27}$ are supposed to have (cf. v.^{2} with Dt 2^{24} 3^2 etc., and v.^{27} with Dt 2^{7-25}). In ch. 7 (Achan's Trespass) no Dt elements can be detected with certainty (though some seem to occur in vv.$^{12b.\ 14.\ 15}$) till the obvious Dt redaction of v.$^{24f.}$, on which see below among the JE passages. In 8^{1-29} (the Taking of Ai) touches of the Dt style may be detected in vv.$^{1.\ 2.\ 27b}$.

Ch. 8^{30-35} is a passage of peculiar difficulty. The linguistic evidence proves it to be in the main from the hand of a Deuteronomist editor, but besides containing, as the Dt redaction sometimes does, a trace of the priestly writer (in the phrase כְּנֵר בָּאוּר v.^{33}), it records a fact, the building of an altar at Mt. Ebal, which conflicts with the principal law of Dt, that there shall be only one sanctuary in the land. It apparently refers to two passages in Dt ($11^{29.\ 30}$ which orders blessing to be set on Gerizim, but cursing on Ebal, and the very composite 27^{1-13}, which enjoins the erection of plastered stones, when Israel crosses Jordan, and the inscription on them of the Torah vv.$^{2.\ 3}$; that this shall be at Ebal v.^{4}, and that an altar of unhewn stones shall be raised there for sacrifice to Jehovah; and that the tribes shall be divided to bless opposite Gerizim and curse opposite Ebal), yet it does not wholly agree with either of these (for it records a *reading of the whole law* where 11^{29} speaks only of the blessing and cursing, and 27^{1-13} speaks only of the *writing* of the Law). Jos 8^{30-35} appears therefore not to have been composed with the mere view of recording the fulfilment of the aforesaid Dt injunctions (and indeed it ignores Dt 27^{14-26} altogether), but to be an independent* writing based on documents, part of which, the building of the Ebal altar, cannot be Deuteronomist, but is more likely to belong to E, whose interest in northern sanctuaries is constant.† (It is to E that the corresponding passage Dt $27^{5.\ 6}$ is assigned: on the historical questions raised by the passage, see below).

In ch. 9 (the Guile of Gibeon) the introduction

(vv.[1, 2], cf. Dt 1[7], Jos 1[4]) and the closing words (v.[27b] the Dt formula 'the place which He shall choose') are Deuteronomic; so, too, vv.[9b. 10] (the reference to Sihon *and Og*) and vv.[24. 25] (cf. Dt 20[10-18]). In ch. 10 (The Victory of Gibeon and Conquest of the South), which is covered by the Dt introduction 9[1. 2], there are many fragments of the Dt style, vv.[8. 12a. 14b] (the introduction and close of the story of J which is gathered round the quotation from the Bk. of Jashar: the phrase in v.[12a] 'in the day . . . Israel' is used 9 times in Dt, and nowhere else in the Pent.; the phrase in v.[14b] יהוה נלחם לישראל is also Dt, but there is no reason why it might not have been used by another writer), and vv.[19b] (perhaps), [25]; besides vv.[28-43], the summary of the Conquest of the South, which by other documents, Jos 15[14-19], Jg 1[10-15], is attributed to Judah and Caleb. Ch. 11 (the Conquest of the North) is also treated in the summary arrangement of the Deuteronomist, and mainly in Dt language; while ch. 12 is assigned by virtually all critics to a Deuteronomic hand on the ground that vv.[1-6] follow Dt 3[9-12. 14-17] rather than the parallel Nu 21[1-31] (Og is again joined with Sihon), and that Dt touches appear in the following verses. The list of kings vv.[9-24] might be from any source.

In the Second Section of the Book, the Division of the Land, chs. 13-21, the Dt passages are few. Here again the introduction is one of them, 13[1-14], a summary description of the land still unconquered, and a charge to divide what is conquered among the 9½ tribes; and a description of E. Palestine studded not only with phrases but facts peculiar to the Deuteronomist (*e.g.* v.[14] ‖ Dt 18[1]; v.[7] 2½ tribes; v.[12] Og; cf. also vv.[7-14] generally with the Dt passage Jos 12[1-6]). There are, too, signs of an attempt to harmonize two differing accounts of the conquest (cf. Wellh. *Comp. des Hex.* p. 129; Kuenen, *Onderz.* i. 1, § 7, n. 27). Ch. 14[6. 7] is Deuteronomic; so, too, chs. 18[7. 10b] 21[41-43], which represent the conquest of the Holy Land as in complete fulfilment of the Divine promise: a representation not consistent with other passages nor borne out by the subsequent history, but in harmony with the Deuteronomist's ideal treatment of the subject. It is remarkable that in ch. 20 the Dt additions do not occur in the LXX. In the Appendix chs. 22-24, Joshua's charge to the 2½ tribes (ch. 22[1-8]), and his last charge to the nation (23[1-16]), are in the well-known hortatory style of Dt.

(*b*) *The Priestly Writing in Joshua.*—It is most convenient to take this next. In the First Section, chs. 1-12, the passages from P are few and fragmentary, and consist either (*a*) of additions to the narrative of dates and statistics (about which, however, there is this difficulty, that, though such things are characteristic of P in the Pentateuch, they do not in Joshua always agree with other statistics given by P, and being but bare figures cannot be proved on evidence of language to belong to P); or (*b*) of the substitution of characteristic terms of P for the corresponding terms of other documents; or (*c*) of statements with regard to the ritual and enforcement of the Law. Of the first of those three classes are 3[4] (?) 4[13. 19]; of the second 5[4] הוכרים כל אנשי המלחמה (6[4]), and the evident expansion of 7[24] and 7[25] וירגמו אתו כל ישראל אבן, עד 10[27]; of the third class 5[10-12] the account of the Passover, 6[23b] 7[1] 9[17-21] 11[13].

In the Second Section, on the Division of the Land, the bulk is from P (all, in fact, except the Dt passages already cited, and a few from JE which will be cited immediately). This is clear from the presence of the characteristic marks of P's style, and the agreement of the injunctions with those laid down in the Priestly Legislation in the Pentateuch. Besides the bulk of the contents, the opening and closing formulas of the various paragraphs of this section

are from P. In short, in this section, as in the Pentateuch, P furnishes the framework. In the Appendix, ch. 22[9-34] (which emphasizes the centralization of the worship by the account of the altar that was 'by Jordan') displays many of the characteristic marks of P's style. There are, however, other features which suggest an independent author.

(*c*) *The Jahwist-Elohist Documents in Joshua.* —As in the Pentateuch, the bulk of the narrative in Joshua belongs to the double document, known to critics as JE. To the trained eye the style is easily distinguished from that of Dt or P. When, however, we seek to discriminate its two constituents, which in the Pentateuch are so often discernible from each other, we receive little or no assistance from the style or the language. It exhibits, however, another and far more decisive difference. Again and again in the JE portions of Joshua it becomes evident that two accounts of the same event have been welded together, for the statements not only repeat each other with a redundancy utterly foreign to the crisp style of either of the two documents J and E, but in details often conflict with each other. In ch 1 there are only fragments of JE. Ch 2 is all JE, except vv.[10. 11]. So, too, chs. 3. 4, the Crossing of Jordan, except the Dt fragments noted above. But when these have been put aside, the remainder reveals the presence of two narratives (as Wellhausen was the first to point out); according to one of which a monument to commemorate the Passage was built at Gilgal with stones taken from the river's bed by the people, but according to the other was set up in the river's bed, and consisted of 12 stones carried by 12 representatives of the tribes. This difference (in addition to the 3rd story of the Deuteronomist referred to above) is apparent not only from the statements in 4[8. 9], but from the fact that while 3[17] describes the people as having all passed over, 4[4. 5. 10b] treat them as still about to cross. Again, 3[12] and 4[2] cannot belong to the same narrative, for they are simply 'doublets'; yet 3[12] is presupposed by 4[4]. The two narratives may be thus distinguished — (1) 3[1. 5. 10. 11. 13-17] 4[1-3. 8]; and (2) 3[12] 4[4-7. 9-11a]. Of these two accounts it is not easy to say which is J and which E.

Ch. 5 (events between Jordan and Jericho) is one of the most complicated parts of the text of Joshua. V.[1], as we have seen, is Dt. Vv.[2. 3. 8. 9] (the record of the circumcision of the people by Joshua), are from JE. But into v.[2] words have been inserted—they are not found in the LXX— implying that Joshua did this a *second* time; and vv.[4-7] (the LXX here offers a widely different reading) interpolate an account of the reasons of the operation, which is not consistent with JE's statement in v.[9], that it was undertaken for the purpose of 'rolling away the reproach of Egypt.' These words are in themselves an obviously wrong interpretation of the term Gilgal, *i.e.* 'stone-circle,' and can only mean that in the opinion of the writer Israel had been uncircumcised in Egypt, and that this neglect, which had excited the reproach of the circumcised Egyptians, was now at last repaired. In contradiction to this, vv.[4-7] declare that the Israelites while in Egypt were circumcised, but that generation had all died, and those who were born after the Exodus had not been circumcised, which neglect Joshua now made good. The phraseology of these four verses is partly P's, but most critics take them, along with the words interpolated in v.[2], to be the addition of a later writer, who was anxious to harmonize JE's account with previous reports of P about circumcision. The end of ch. 5 (vv.[13-15]) also presents a difficulty. It is generally assigned to JE; but some critics, on the alleged ground that the phrases צבא יהוה and שר as applied to an angel are found only in late writings, take the passage to be one of the very latest additions to the Bk. of Joshua. So Kuenen. This reason is not conclusive. It was an early belief that Jehovah had a heavenly host (cf. 1 K 22[19]), the belief in individual angels with special functions was also early, and we need not take שׂר in the special sense in which it is intended when applied to angels in the Bk. of Daniel, but simply in its early signification of a military officer. Vv.[13-15] may therefore very well be left to JE.

The whole of ch. 6 (the Fall of Jericho), except vv.[2 and 27], belongs to JE, but we meet in it the same phenomenon as in chs. 3 and 4, the presence (again first detected by Wellhausen) of two differing accounts—one (vv.[3. 7a. 10. 11] partly [14. 15a] 'and it came to pass . . . manner,' [15b. 20] 'and the people shouted') which relates that Israel marched round Jericho on 7 successive days, the first 6 silently, but on the 7th they shouted *at the word of Joshua*, and the walls fell; and the other (vv.[4] partly, [5. 7b. 8. 9], parts of vv.[13. 15], vv.[16a. 20b]) which relates that a portion of the armed men marched round the city 7 times on one day, having in their midst the ark and priests with trumpets, and that at the 7th round the people shouted *at the signal of the trumpets*, and the walls fell. Cf. especially vv.[16 and 20]; in the latter the people shout both before and after the trumpets, though v.[16] enjoins them not to shout till the trumpets give the signal. As in chs. 3. 4 it is not easy to assign these double accounts, present in ch. 6, respectively to J and E.

In ch. 7 (the Defeat before Ai and Achan's Sin and Doom) all is from JE except v.[1] and parts of vv.[24. 25]. The latter verses afford so instructive an example as to how the original JE narrative has been worked upon by subsequent editors that it is worth examining their details. To begin with, the LXX omits in v.[24] the words ואת־הכסף—הזהב, and in v.[25] וירגמו־באש. Moreover, in v.[24] the term 'and all Israel' has been separated from its fellow-nominative 'Joshua' at the beginning of the verse * by the words omitted in the LXX, and by the rest of the catalogue of Achan's property, while in v.[25] not only does the phrase beginning וירגמו 'and they stoned him with stones,' which is in the language of P, form a mere doublet to the phrase introduced by ויסקלו 'and they stoned them with stones,' but when we remove the former, the latter is still preceded by the words 'and they burned them with fire,' an impossible order: we cannot conceive of Achan and his property as first burned and then stoned. Besides, while v.[26], which is JE, speaks of a cairn being raised over Achan alone, v.[24] describes *them* as brought up to the valley of Achor, and v.[25] describes *them* as being burned and stoned. Of this confusion Albers has given the following reasonable explanation. The original JE narrative recorded the punishment only of Achan, but a Deuteronomic editor, wishing to bring the process into conformity with Dt 13[16. 17], which enjoins that goods subject to the Ḥerem or Ban shall be burned, has added to v.[24] the catalogue of Achan's property, which we have already seen to be an evident intrusion, and to v.[25] the notice of the burning which we have seen to be impossible *before* that of the stoning. This editor must have also changed the 'him' of both these verses into 'them'; it is remarkable that in both the LXX has 'him.' If, now, we take out of the verses those intruded elements of Dt and P, the JE remainder reads consistently: 'And Joshua, and all Israel with him, took Achan the son of Zerah, and brought *him* (LXX A) to the valley of Achor; and Joshua said, "Why hast thou brought trouble upon us? Jehovah will bring trouble upon thee." And they stoned him (LXX BA; αὐτοὺς F) with stones.'

* Though in AV they have been brought together.

In ch. 8[1-29] (the Taking of Ai) everything except the Dt fragments already noticed is from JE. But as in chs. 3. 4. 6, two accounts appear to have been fused (though it is not certain how we are to divide them between J and E). This is clear not only from the reduplication of certain details (vv.[14. 18] etc., see below), and awkward connexions (v.[14], and v.[18] with v.[19]), but still more from a double and contradictory story of the ambush, as well as from an attempt in the Massoretic text to reconcile these, and from the omission by the LXX both of the attempt and of the contradictory data. The first of the two accounts starts with v.[3] (perhaps earlier, for though vv.[1. 2] are mainly Dt, they contain other elements). According to this, after Joshua and all the army started from Gilgal for Ai, he chose and sent forward * 30,000 (? 3000) men by night to conceal themselves on the opposite or western side of Ai, and charged them to wait there till the army should pretend to flee from Ai, and drawing its inhabitants out of it, leave it empty, when the ambush were to take possession. The men chosen go forth and effect this movement, while Joshua passes the same night in the valley (in v.[9] for עם read with Ewald עמק). At this point the second account starts from v.[10], or at least from v.[11], which relates that *all* the people (omit for grammatical reasons the words 'of war') which were with him came over against Ai,† and (v.[12]) Joshua took about 5000 men and 'set them as an ambush between Bethel and Ai, westward of Ai.' Then comes the difficult v.[13], which seems an attempt to combine and summarize the two accounts. The Greek translator, or the editor of the texts he used, feeling that the combination was impossible, has substituted for 8[11b] the word 'eastward,' and for 12b, with its contradictory data, the words 'the ambushes of the city from the sea (*i.e.* westward)'; and has omitted all v.[13]. To this explanation the only alternative is that the data in v.[12], which conflict with those of the previous account of the ambush, and v.[13] have been added to the Massoretic text *after* the LXX translation was made, which is hardly possible. V.[14] alike by its repetitions, in different words, of the same actions and the awkward grammar by which they are combined, is obviously the fusion of two accounts—one: 'And it came to pass, when the king of Ai saw, that he and all his people hastened to the . . .‡ in front of the Arabah, not knowing of the ambush against them behind (to the west of) the city'; the other: 'And the men of the city rose up early, and came forth to meet Israel in battle.' The Israelites flee, and draw the men of Ai§ after them. Here, again, in vv.[16. 17] there are small doublets, and so, in fact, to the end of v.[29] (*e.g.* in v.[20b] the people fleeing to the wilderness 'turn on their pursuers,' omitted by LXX; yet in v.[21] 'Joshua and all Israel see that the ambush have

* V.[3a]. Some scholars think that according to this first account Joshua sent his ambush ahead *from Gilgal*. This can be maintained only by denying that v.[3a] belongs to the first account. But there is no cause in the clause itself for separating it from what follows. And it is not probable that any account would have made Joshua send the ambush ahead from Gilgal, for this place is 6 or 7 hours distant from Ai, and if the main body had remained there during the night in which the ambush took up its position west of Ai, starting next morning, it would not have reached Ai till the ambush had been exposed for several hours to the daylight. Take v.[3a] with what follows it, and we find the first account imply that the ambush was not chosen and despatched till the whole army had gone up towards Ai, which does not contradict the second and more detailed account, that it started after Joshua and the army had arrived in the neighbourhood of Ai.

† This still may be, though not probably, the first account.

‡ לַמּוֹעֵד 'to the appointed place.' Dillmann's theory, that one of the two narratives had previously described this tryst, is surely impossible, for the men of Ai did not know of Israel's arrival. Bennett emends לַמּוֹרָד 'to the descent.'

§ Heb. adds 'and Bethel,' but LXX omits; it must be the addition of a late scribe inserting an allusion to Jg 1.

taken the city, and that smoke goes up, and turn and smite the men of Ai'; and in v.^{24} בשׂדה (במדבר). These are quite enough (without supposing that a different use has been imputed to Joshua's javelin in v.^{18} from that in v.^{26}) to prove the fusion of two tales of the same event. V.^{27} is of course Dt. In the Dt passage vv.$^{30-35}$ the part that must have been taken from E has been already pointed out.

In ch. 9 (the Guile of Gibeon), after the Dt introduction in vv.$^{1.2}$, the JE narrative commences independently in v.^{3}. Its style is distinguishable from the Dt portions, vv.$^{9b.10.24.25.27b}$; and both in style and substance it differs from the P account, vv.$^{15b.17-21}$. But even within JE a double account is as discernible as it was in the JE portions of chs. 3. 4. 6 and 8: cf. the doublets in vv.$^{6-9a}$.* In ch. 10$^{1-27}$ we have the JE account of the defeat by Joshua of the kings of Jerusalem, Hebron, Jarmuth, Lachish, and Debir, all with territories that afterwards became Judah's. Vv.$^{1-11.16-27}$ read continuously, and relate fully how God smote the Canaanites before Israel by a great hailstorm. Vv.$^{12-15}$ break into this with a story suggested by an ancient verse of poetry, a prayer of Joshua for a day long enough to slay his foes; they add that this prayer was answered by God commanding the sun to stand still for a whole day in the heavens, and that Joshua and his force returned to their camp; while vv.$^{16ff.}$ relate that they continued the pursuit of the 5 kings whose forces had been beaten by the hailstorm recounted in v.^{11}. Vv.$^{12-15}$ are plainly an interpolation by another, who finding in the Bk. of Jashar this poetical ejaculation of Joshua for a day sufficient for his big task, prosaically added, vv.$^{13b.14}$, that this actually happened. This account of the defeat of the southern kings is not compatible with that in ch. 15$^{13ff.}$ and in Jg 1$^{1ff.}$ (see below, § vii.). In ch. 11$^{1-10.13}$ we have the JE account of the conquest of N. Canaan.

In the Second Section, chs. 13–21, on the Division of the Land, the portions by JE are comparatively few, some of them mere fragments: in ch. 13, vv.$^{1-18}$, in ch. 15, vv.$^{14-19.63}$ (see below, § vii.), in ch. 16, vv.$^{1-3}$, the boundary of Joseph; v.^{10} the Canaanite enclaves at Gezer and in Ephraim, the latter assigned to E; in ch. 17, vv.$^{1-2}$ details on Manasseh, and vv.$^{10b-18}$ Manasseh's difficulties with the Canaanites and Joshua's treatment of the house of Joseph; in ch. 18, vv.$^{2-6.8-10}$ Joshua's allotment of land to 7 tribes, by casting lots; in ch. 19^9 a detail about Simeon, vv.$^{47.48}$ the removal of Dan to Laish (see below, § vii.), and vv.$^{49.50}$ the tribes take possession and Joshua gets Timnath-serah.

In the Appendix (chs. 22–24) the whole of ch. 24, except a few insertions from Dt and P, is assigned to E.

v. PROBLEMS OF THE RELATION AND COMPOSITION OF THE DOCUMENTS. — The evidence thus collected from the text itself of the Bk. of Joshua, may be ambiguous in this or that detail; but its cumulative force and its main direction are unmistakable. Were it only by the 'doublets' it contains on the various episodes of the conquest, and by the different degrees of completeness to which various passages describe the division of the land to have been carried, the Bk. of Joshua is amply proved to be a compilation from several sources. Of these, the oldest, which supplies the bulk of the narrative of the conquest in chs. 1–12, and gives the conclusion of Joshua's history in ch. 24, but also supplies some details concerning the division of the land, belongs by linguistic evidence to the document entitled by critics JE. This document is itself composed from two narratives; for, as we have seen, in those parts of it which run through chs. 3, 4, 6 and 8, two accounts of the

* The attempt by Budde, p. 50, to get rid of the differences by emending the text, has not convinced critics.

same episodes, the crossing of Jordan and the taking of Jericho and of Ai, have obviously been combined;* and in chs. 13–21, later passages (18$^{2-6.8-10}$ and perhaps others) have been added to it, whether by the hand that combined its constituents it is impossible to say. Alongside these written traditions in JE of the Conquest and Division of the Land, there appears to have existed, either in whole or part, at least one other written tradition, and perhaps two. The passages in chs. 1–12, which on linguistic evidence are assignable to P, seem to have been taken from a Priestly narrative of the Conquest, and there was certainly a Priestly account of the Division of the Territory from which the bulk of chs. 13–21 is taken. But there are also accounts of some events of the Conquest, notably that of the monument at Gilgal (4$^{2.3a.8}$, cf. vv.$^{21-24}$), and the summary of the Conquest of the South (9$^{28-43}$), which seem to imply that there was, in addition to the two other accounts just noted above, one independent Deuteronomic account of the Conquest.

But if the existence of an original Dt narrative of the facts of the Conquest be uncertain, there was another hand at work of the same spirit and style of language. In chs. 1–12 the great majority of the Dt passages do not give evidence of belonging to an independent account of the same events as are described in JE, but consist of introductions to the various sections, the bulk of the narrative in which is JE, and of connexions and transitions; or they point out how the events related in JE illustrate the favourite doctrines of the Deuteronomic writers and enforce the Deuteronomic legislation. All these passages are easily separable from the narratives to which they have been added, and sometimes (as in ch. 7$^{24.25}$) it is clear that their insertion has not been accomplished without the modification of the original text. And, besides, single phrases characteristic of the Dt style have been scattered over most of the chapters. All this points to one conclusion. A Deuteronomic writer has 'edited,' not only chs. 1–12, but the whole book. His is the framework of the whole, his its connexion with the Bk. of Deuteronomy, the modification of the JE narratives, and the lessons deduced from them. Who he was, whether he can be identified with the author of the original Dt law-book (which is improbable), or the author of the historical supplements to the latter, or was another writer of the same spirit and style, are questions that divide critics, and depend on the still unsettled problems as to the composition of the Bk. of Deuteronomy itself.† It would be misleading, however, to take for granted that this Deuteronomic redaction was completed by one hand at one time. The reasons for supposing that various strata (though all in the Deuteronomic spirit and style) are represented in it will appear from the next paragraph.

The question of the relation of this Deuteronomic redaction (or redactions) to the elements of P which appear in Joshua is a very difficult one. Was the Dt redaction (or redactions) completed upon JE and the independent Dt traditions (described above), and was the whole only then

* We have also seen that it is not possible to assign these, on linguistic evidence, respectively to J and E.

† See the discussions in the works, cited below, of Hollenberg, Kuenen, Dillmann, and Kittel. Hollenberg's conclusion is that not the original Deuteronomist, but the Deuteronomic editor who combined Deuteronomy with the rest of the Pentateuch and added to it chs. 1–4. 27. 29–31, is the writer of these passages in Joshua. Dillmann assigns them in the main to the author of the Bk. of Deuteronomy; Kuenen, either to a writer akin in spirit and style to the author of Dt 1–4, etc.; so virtually Kittel, to a D2 whom (not certainly but on the whole) he takes to have been different from D1. There is a curious difference between the Dt passage Jos 13$^{3-5}$ and Dt 11$^{24.25a}$; but it is not very great, and does not carry us far in the discussion of the question.

combined with the passages from P? Or did the Dt redaction take place subsequently to P? The former of these alternatives is accepted by Driver (*Introd.*[6] p. 104). But there is important evidence in favour of the latter. In the Bk. of Joshua, P does not occupy the regulative position, nor supply the framework, as it does in the Pentateuch. And in the Massoretic text of Joshua portions of P have apparently been subjected to the Dt revision; in ch. 20, for instance, the substance is from P, the additional matter is Deuteronomic (see vv.[4-6]). Again, while most of the Dt passages appear in the LXX translation, and are therefore to be regarded as prior to it, a number are not found in it. For example, in ch. 7[24, 25] we saw that the LXX reproduces only some of the Dt modifications of the JE account of Achan's punishment, and the verses ch. 20[4-6] (just cited), in which Deuteronomic additions are manifest, are not found in the LXX (B). It is also probable that ch. 22[9-34] was written subsequently to the Priestly Code (cf. W. R. Smith, *OTJC*[2] 413, and Bennett, *Primer*, 90). Throughout the book, too, we find some words from a very late stage of the language (Dillmann, p. 442). All this implies that what Bennett (*Bk. Jos.* p. 22) calls 'very probable' is a certainty: the Deuteronomic redaction of the Bk. of Joshua is from more than one hand. Some of it, according to the evidence of the LXX, must be very late. Accordingly we understand why no author's name has been assigned to the Bk. of Joshua: * it takes its title from its subject and is an anonymous work. The points upon which an early author, or even one contemporary with the events described, has been assumed, are either illusory (*e.g.* the reading of 5[1] עברנו should be עברם), or can only prove the date of one or other of the constituent documents. The final redaction affords no historical allusion by which its date might be fixed.

vi. SEPARATION FROM THE PENTATEUCH, AND DATE.—Another set of problems is raised by the relation of Joshua to the Pentateuch. Most critics have held that the Bk. of Joshua was separated from the rest of the Pentateuch after JE, D, and P had been combined, but Bennett (*A Primer of the Bible*, 1897, p. 90) thinks that the JE, D, and P portions of Jos were combined by another and later editor than the editor who combined the same documents in the Pentateuch. This is certainly borne out by the different rank, alluded to above, which is assigned to P in the Pentateuch and in Joshua. But, whatever be the answer to these questions, the reason of the separation of the Book of Joshua from the Pentateuch when the latter became canonical in Israel in Ezra's time is very intelligible. The legislation really closes with Deuteronomy and the account of Moses' death, and it was legislation which Ezra and Nehemiah were anxious to enforce. That the Bk. of Joshua was not regarded in Israel as what we call canonical till long after the Torah or Five Books of Moses had reached that rank, is clear from the difference between it and them in the LXX translation. While it is evident, from the comparatively few discrepancies between the Massoretic text and that of the LXX, that the text of the Torah had long been guarded with care before the LXX translation was made, the many discrepancies in the Bk. of Joshua, the freedom with which the Greek translator or translators allowed themselves to omit and to modify, prove that when the LXX translation of it was made Joshua was not regarded as of canonical rank. The admission to the Canon of the

Prophetical Books, to which it belongs, is generally held to have been about 200 B.C.

vii. RELATION TO THE BOOK OF JUDGES.—But the problems of the analysis of the Bk. of Joshua cannot be fully stated without some comparison of its data of the Conquest with those furnished in the opening chapters of the Bk. of Judges. We have seen that in the Bk. of Joshua there are two different conceptions of how the Conquest was achieved. One is that shared by both D and P: that the Conquest of the Land was completed and the inhabitants exterminated by Joshua, and thereupon the various territories were occupied by the tribes to which he allotted them. The other, very evident from the fragments of J, in the second half of the book, takes the Conquest to have been gradual and partial. This, the older conception, is that which is supported by the Bk. of Judges. In Jg 1-2[5] we have fragments of an account of the Conquest, which an editor has found irreconcilable with the conception that dominates the Bk. of Joshua, and has therefore, by an introductory clause, Jg 1[1a], transferred to the days after Joshua's death. This, however, is impossible: we cannot conceive that Israel having gained full possession of Western Palestine and exterminated the Canaanites, was after Joshua's death driven back upon Jericho and began a second series of campaigns which gradually restored the country to them. In itself this is impossible; and that the campaigns in Jg 1 happened in Joshua's lifetime is implied not only by the account of his death which follows them in Jg 2 ff., but proved by the fact that the same episodes (*e.g.* Hebron and Caleb, Debir and Othniel) which are related in Jg 1 as happening after Joshua's death are in the Bk. of Joshua itself related as happening while he still directed the allotment of the territories. Omit Jg 1[1a] and several other verses in the same chapter which are obvious insertions by an editor and some of which flatly contradict verses that stand next them, and what is left affords an account of the Conquest which is in harmony (as already said) with the older of the two conceptions, contained in the Bk. of Joshua.*

The relation to each other of these parallel passages in the Bk. of Joshua and in Jg 1 has been differently estimated by critics. Yet the facts appear to shut out all the alternatives but one. Not only do the parallels agree (as has just been said) in their general conception of the conquest—that it took place through the efforts of separate tribes, and with incomplete results rather than (as the view of P and D which prevails in the Bk. of Joshua conceives it) by all Israel acting together and with a complete extermination of the 'inhabitants of the land'; but in parts the parallels agree word for word, and they both contain the same characteristic terms and phrases.

The following table represents the agreements and differences :—

Jg 1[1] (except the first clause)[2. 3. 5. 6. 7]: The beginning of Judah's and Simeon's campaign, and their defeat of Adoni-bezek. Jos 10[1ff.]: After Joshua's capture of Ai and treaty with Gibeon, Adoni-zedek (LXX Adoni-bezek; the reading Adoni-zedek has perhaps arisen as some echo of another ancient king of Jerusalem, Melchi-zedek), king of Jerusalem, with the kings of Jarmuth, Lachish, and Eglon, having attacked Gibeon, is defeated by Joshua and all Israel in the battle of Beth-horon, and afterwards slain.

Jg 1[19. 20. 10-15]: After Judah receives the hill-country for an inheritance, Caleb in obedience to a command by Moses receives Hebron, and takes it, slaying its Anakite lords;

* That Joshua is the author is asserted in the Talmud, 'Baba bathra,' 14[2]. It has been maintained by a few Rom. Cath. and Protestant scholars, and even in this century by, *e.g.*, J. L. König, *AT Stud.* i. 1836. But see Calvin's sane words in his *Argt.*

* On Jg 1 f. consult Wellhausen, *Comp. d. Hex.* 213-215; E. Meyer, *ZATW* i. p. 135 ff.; but especially Budde, both in *ZATW* vii. p. 94 ff., and *Richt. u. Samuel*, pp. 2 ff., 84-89; and Moore, *Judges*, in the *Internat. Crit. Comm.* p. 3 ff. The verses to be eliminated from Jg 1-2[5] are 1[a]. 4. 8. 9. 18. 36. 21[b-5a]. 8. Of these 1[4] is redundant in face of vv.[5-7]; v.[8], intimating the capture of Jerus. is contradicted by later history and the rest of the narrative.

he offers his daughter to the conqueror of Ḳiriath-sepher. This is 'Othniel. 'Othniel receives Achsah, Caleb's daughter, and with her the 'upper and lower Guloth.' Jos 15¹³ff.: Caleb, in obedience to a divine command by Joshua, receives Hebron, slaying its Anakite lords; then from v.¹⁶ the story of Debir, 'Othniel, and Achsah follows exactly as in Jg 1¹²ff.

Jg 1¹⁶. ¹⁷: The settlement of the Kenite and conquest of Simeon's land find no parallel in Joshua.

Jg 1²¹: The continued hold of the Jebusite upon Jerusalem, the *sons of Benjamin* do not drive him out. Jos 15⁶³: The same, but it is the *sons of Judah* who are said not to *have been able* to drive out the Jebusite.

Jg 1²²⁻²⁶: The house of Joseph go up to Bethel, and with them *Jehovah* (an unusual expression, and not found in the relation of the other campaigns; for *Jehovah* LXX reads *Judah*; Budde reasonably conjectures *Joshua* as the original reading); the house of Joseph takes Bethel. To this there is no parallel in the Bk. of Joshua; but a reminiscence of the capture of Bethel crops up in the story of the taking of Ai, Jos 8¹⁷ ' Ai *and Bethel*' (but this is omitted by the best MSS of LXX).

Jg 1²⁷. ²⁸: Manasseh *did not dispossess* the inhabitants of Beth-shan, Taanach, Dor, Ibleam, Megiddo, and their subject villages. But the Canaanite *resolved to dwell in that land*. When Israel grew strong they forced Canaanites to work for them. Jos 17¹². ¹³: The Bene-Manasseh *were not able* to dispossess the inhabitants of Beth-shan, Ibleam, Dor, En-dor, Taanach, Megiddo, but the Canaanite *resolved to dwell in this land*; when the Bene-Israel grew strong they forced the Canaanites to work for them.

Jg 1²⁹: Ephraim did not dispossess the Canaanite of Gezer, but the C. dwelt in his midst in Gezer. ‖Jos 16¹⁰: And he (Ephraim) did not dispossess the Canaanite who dwelt in Gezer, but the C. dwelt in the midst of Ephraim to this day, and 'had to take up the forced service of a labourer.'

Jg 1³⁰⁻³³: Zebulun, Asher, and Naphtali did not dispossess the Canaanites of certain towns. No parallels to this in Jos.

Jg 1³⁴. ³⁵: The Amorites forced the Bene-Dan into the hill-country, and did not allow them to come down into the '*emek*. And the Amorite *resolved to* dwell in Mt. Heres in Aijalon and in Sha'albim, and the hand of the house of Joseph was heavy, and they were reduced to forced labour. Jos 19⁴⁷: And the Bene-Dan went up and fought with Leshem and took it, and smote it at the edge of the sword, and took possession of it, and dwelt in it, and called Leshem Dan after Dan their father. From these two passages Budde proposes to restore the full text of the original in this order: Jg 1³⁴, Jos 19⁴⁷ᵃ. (LXX) ⁴⁷ᵇ, Jg 1³⁵ (cf. the LXX additions to Jos 19⁴⁷ᵇ).

This comparison, besides revealing the similarity of general conception and identity of several passages and characteristic phrases, shows that the passages in Jg 1, besides being set under a wrong date (v.¹ᵃ ' after the death of Joshua'), have been ' edited ' to serve the purpose of the compiler of this part of the Bk. of Judges, which as revealed in ch. 2¹ᵇ⁻⁴ is that the failure to dispossess all the Canaanites is the reason why Jehovah proceeded now to punish Israel. For instance, the passages in Joshua generally declare that the tribes *were not able* to drive out certain Canaanite communities; in Jg 1 the words in italics are omitted.* And in v.²¹ *the Benjamites* have been substituted for *Judah*, which is given in the parallel Jos 15⁶³. From all this it is clear that in the Bk. of Joshua we have the more original text of these passages; it is impossible that the editor of that book took them from Jg 1. Nor is the converse probable; for in the Bk. of Joshua, as we have seen, these passages have been inserted in a setting, the whole tendency of which is to give a conception of the conquest different from that to which they testify. There remains possible, therefore, only this conclusion, as Budde has clearly exhibited, that the editors, both of the Bk. of Joshua and of Jg 1 f., have taken them from a common source. This source, with its conception of the conquest so different from that of D and P, must, in our ignorance of any other sources of the Hexateuch, be assigned to JE. Can we decide whether it belongs to J or E? It so happens that in ch. 24 we have a piece which, for very obvious reasons, critics are agreed in assigning to E. But its conception of the conquest approaches too nearly to that of the Deuteronomic redaction of

* In v.¹⁹ᵇ the omission of the words is very plain; the infinit. להוריש cannot be construed without them.

Joshua to allow us to assign to its author the passages in question. We have therefore no alternative but to regard them as the work of J, or at least of the series of writers designated by that letter. So, for instance, Kittel, Driver (in Smith's *Dict. of the Bible*², vol. i. pt. ii. p. 1816), and especially Budde (*ZATW* vii. 155 ff.), who assigns them, not to the original J, but to the Jahwistic redactor. And to the same hand we must assign, of course, a number of other passages in the Bk. of Joshua which, though they are not found among the parallels present in Jg 1, plainly supplement the latter, and are ruled by the same conception of the conquest, viz. that it was partial, for there were many Canaanite communities and groups of communities whom the tribes could not drive out. These are Jos 13¹³ 17¹⁴⁻¹⁸, and probably the simpler forms of the doublets in the JE portions of chs. 1–12, and among them we must also include the additional matter which ch. 19⁴⁷ contributes to the story of Dan as related in Jg 1³⁴. ³⁵. See, further, art. JUDGES (BOOK OF), where on several points a different view is maintained from that represented in the present article.

viii. THE HISTORICAL VALUE OF THE BOOK OF JOSHUA. — We have seen — upon evidence afforded by itself, philological and textual—that the final redaction of the book must be placed very late in the history of Israel: certainly after Ezra's time, perhaps not till the 3rd cent. B.C. We have seen, too, that this redaction includes widely differing accounts of how the conquest and division of the land were accomplished: a Deuteronomic writer and the Priestly writer represent it to have been thorough, and effected in one generation by the whole nation acting together; the Jahwistic document (with ch. 1 of the Bk. of Judges) represents it as the work of separate tribes, and to have been far from complete. When we accept the latter alternative, not only as that of the older record, but as the only one in harmony with the data of the subsequent history under the Judges and Kings, our difficulties are not at an end. For, *first*, the Jahwistic document cannot be proved to be earlier than the 9th cent. B.C.; and, *second*, before being used by the editor of the whole book, it has been combined with the Elohist document in a form which contains such varying accounts of the different episodes of the Conquest as were likely to arise in the many centuries of tradition between the Conquest and the dates of the two constituent documents. These present, too, other difficulties. They are defective: it is remarkable that neither says a word about the conquest of the midlands of Western Palestine, the lands afterwards occupied by Manasseh and Ephraim, although one of them (E) appears to have related the celebration of a solemn service at Shechem, the centre of that region, soon after the crossing of Jordan and in obedience to a word of Moses; while both of them appear to contain a few data that could not have been inserted till long after Israel's settlement in W. Palestine.* All these facts, presented to us, be it observed, by the biblical record itself, oblige us to subject the JE narrative to examination upon the ordinary principles of historical criticism. The first question we have to ask is: are there any signs in JE of the employment of older documents? In the early books of the OT such ancient material is usually found in the citation of poetical fragments. Of such the Bk. of Joshua contains only one (10¹². ¹³)

* *e.g.* in the history of the treaty with Gibeon, though, as we shall see, there is no reason for denying the main fact of such a treaty in the time of Joshua. The contradiction with later history, which is alleged by some to exist in Jos 6²⁶—the abandonment of the site of Jericho (cf. Jg 3¹³, which represents Jericho as an inhabited town)—may be explained by a change of site.

which may be assigned (though this is not the opinion of all critics) to J. 'Thus Joshua spake to Jehovah . . . and said in presence of all Israel—

> Sun stay upon Gibeon, and moon on the valley of Aijalon.
> And the sun stayed, and the moon stood till the people took vengeance of their enemies.

Is it not written in the Book of Jashar?' * This ancient fragment witnesses to two facts: (a) that Israel had to fight at this particular point of their advance into W. Palestine, and (b) the presence there of Joshua. But the fragment stands alone in the book; on all other points we have to argue upon considerations of a general kind.

The first point which appears to be sufficiently established is the national unity of Israel, before and when they crossed the Jordan. This, it is true, has been denied. Stade (*GVI* i. 134 ff.) and others suppose that the Israelite occupation of W. Palestine proceeded gradually and peacefully—by the drifting across Jordan, one by one, of various Israelite clans, before the pressure of their increasing numbers and in desire for room and food. But the theory of a peaceful invasion is contradicted no less by the general force of tradition than by the historic probabilities; while the national unity is certified, not only by the earliest memories of the people (Bk. of Jg, *passim*) and the unanimous voice of later tradition, but by the fact that the great cause and reason of such a unity, the possession by the tribes of a common faith and a common shrine, had already been achieved by the labours of Moses. The later unity of Israel, accomplished among the separating influences of W. Palestine, geographical, social, religious, would not have been possible unless Israel had already been united before entering these. Nor do the accounts in the Bks. of Jos and Jg relate, before the capture of Jericho, anything contradictory to the theory of such a unity; it is only from Jericho onwards that J describes the tribes as separately undertaking the conquest of their respective territories. Moreover, although J represents separate conquests after Jericho, it assumes, and even explicitly states, that these were preceded by a common understanding of how the work of conquest was to be divided and the territories assigned (Jos 15¹³ 17¹⁴ᶠᶠ., Jg 1¹). If we accept this evidence of J (as against Dt and P), that the conquest was achieved by separate tribes, we should surely receive its testimony that the direction and plan proceeded from a common centre; especially when the unity of Israel, at the time of crossing Jordan, is rendered so probable by the considerations quoted above. (See Smith, *HGHL*, Appen. II.; McCurdy, *HPM* ii. 112).

ix. THE PERSON OF JOSHUA.—We are now able to consider the person of Joshua himself. The attempt has been made to relegate, not only the deeds, but the personality of this great leader to the domain of legend and myth. Stade (*GVI* i. p. 135) and others † have fastened on the undoubted fact that in each successive stratum of the tradition Joshua is made to play a more active and regulative part in the allotment and conquest of the territory. They assert that he is not mentioned by J, and that we can trace the origin of him to E. E is an Ephraimitic document, Joshua an Ephraimitic hero. And the inference is drawn by these critics, that, to begin with, Joshua is no more a person than, say, the 'Judah and Simeon his brother' of Jg 1³; but only the personification of a Josephide clan, whose centre was Timnath-

serah (Jos 19⁵⁰ 24³⁰) or Timnath-heres (Jg 2⁹) * in the S.W. of the hill-country of Ephraim.†

But, as Kuenen says, the fact that Joshua appears with increasing importance through the later strata of tradition, so far from being a proof that he did not appear in the earliest stratum, strongly supports the presupposition that he was present there. And, as a matter of fact, Joshua does appear in J (Jos 17¹⁴⁻¹⁸), not merely as the leader of Ephraim or of a part of that tribe, as E represents him, but as the arbiter over all Israel to whom the tribes appeal when they are disappointed with the territory allotted to them. Nor is it possible to deny that Joshua appears in the simpler form of the double JE narratives of the taking of Jericho and Ai, and of the treaty with Gibeon; which form Budde has very successfully argued to belong to J (*ZATW* vii. pp. 134–146, 155–157). Budde has also proposed the restoration of Joshua's name to Jg 1²² 'And the house of Joseph went up to Bethel, and *Joshua* with them.'‡ Moreover, Joshua is the speaker in the ancient poetical fragment (ch. 10¹². ¹³). And in conformity with these descriptions of all Israel acting under one leader, at least up to the taking of Ai, ch. 10⁶ states that the army returned to Gilgal after Ai was taken, and, similarly, v.¹⁵ brings them there again after the battle of Bethhoron. These verses probably belong to E.

There is, then, no point in the development of the tradition at which we can say, Here Joshua was added for the first time to the story. So far back as we can trace it, Joshua is part of the tradition, and he appears upon that line of it, the Judæan J, in which there was no temptation to create him as a tribal hero, for he does not belong to Judah but to Ephraim. On the other hand, the rest of the data of the tradition and the historical probabilities require Israel to have been under one head. In the absence of contemporary evidence, these are all the proofs of his historical reality which it is possible to obtain. But surely they are sufficient. If, as is probable, the poetical fragment is genuine, Joshua's existence as the Captain of all Israel is put beyond doubt.

x. JOSHUA'S WORK.—Joshua, then, was the successor of Moses, and led all Israel across Jordan. All the documents appear to agree that the crossing took place opposite to Jericho,—*appear*, for even here a difficulty arises. As we have seen, one of them, E, makes a statement, found both in Dt and Jos, to the effect that Israel were summoned by Moses to celebrate their arrival in W. Palestine by setting up a monument, with the law written upon it, at Shechem. Now Shechem, besides being the centre of the land, would naturally be the first goal of any invasion of W. Palestine from the other side of Jordan. No one can doubt this who is familiar with the aspect which W. Palestine presents to an observer from the site occupied by Israel in the N. of Moab. A wall of mountain, broken only by narrow gorges, runs far N. of Jericho; the first break in it, the first invitation to invade W. Palestine, is the great pass, the Wady Fera'a, which leads up from Jordan to Shechem; and it is at its mouth that the fords across Jordan are most easy. Take this geographical fact along with the evidence furnished by E, and at first sight it is hard to resist the inference of at least the probability of an invasion

---

* The rest of v.¹³ is a prose statement that the prayer of Joshua for a long day in which to complete the rout of the enemy, was fulfilled by the literal halt of sun and moon in their courses.

† Cf. Ed. Meyer, *ZATW* i. p. 134; Wellhausen, *Comp. des Hex.* p. 116 f. n. 1.

---

* These passages are reversed by Stade, *GVI* 143, n. 2.

† Stade, p. 135; Meyer, *op. cit.*

‡ MT and B read the meaningless 'and *Jehovah* with them'; A has 'and *Judah* with them.' See Budde, *op. cit.* p. 144. The substitution of another name for Joshua's in this verse and the omission of his name elsewhere in Jg 1 was necessary to the editor, when he removed the events described in Jg 1 from their proper setting and placed them all after Joshua's death. see v.¹ᵃ.

by Israel of the midlands of W. Palestine by the fords near Tell Adami and up the Wady Fera'a. Such a conclusion, too, would fill the great gap which yawns in all the other records : the absence of all account of the conquest of Ephraim and Manasseh.

But, attractive as this conclusion appears, there are many objections to it. The crossing of all Israel opposite Jericho is not only confirmed by the earliest traditions, one of which is E itself, but is supported by historical probabilities. The centre of Israel's power in E. Palestine was immediately opposite Jericho.* Nor was the crossing in face of the one fortified city which the Jordan Valley contained south of Beth-shan so improbable as it seems. Jericho, as we shall presently see, was never able to resist a siege ; and many subsequent invaders of W. Palestine from the E. have even gone out of their way to take the city before attempting the hill-country behind her, even by the open passes to the N. Their strategy is intelligible. Once captured, Jericho became a well-stocked and well-watered base for campaigns in the comparatively barren hills to the west of her. The oldest traditions assert that Joshua made himself acquainted with the defencelessness of this single fortress on the W. bank of Jordan, by a means of espionage frequently employed by commanders of invading armies. His spies were aided by a harlot among the enemy. The same documents, and P, record that Israel were demoralised by the vicious women of the land (Nu $25^{1\text{ff.}}$) ; JE ascribes to the same frailty the land's betrayal to Israel.

Joshua, then, led Israel across Jordan opposite to Jericho. All the traditions assign the passage to a miracle, similar to that by which the people escaped from Egypt across the Red Sea. The waters of the river were stopped in a great heap, not at the place of the passage, but, as appears from a somewhat corrupt text (3^{16}), higher up, where the valley of Jordan is narrower, and where it is not without interest to remember that an Arabic chronicler records the sudden damming of the river by a landslip in A.D. 1267.† The miracle was commemorated by a stone monument, according to three lines of tradition which, however, vary as to where it was erected (see above, § iv. a, c). On the story of the Circumcision see above, § iv. c. Soon after this, Jericho became an easy prey to the invaders ; and here again, as we have seen (§ iv. c), the traditions differ as to details. But the fact on which they agree, that the city fell to the mere challenge of her besiegers, is an issue singularly in harmony with the fate of Jericho before every subsequent attack which history records, and is also very explicable by the effeminate character of her inhabitants (see *Historical Geogr.* pp. 266–268). The city was razed, the site cursed, and Israel's camp continued to be at Gilgal, which is represented as the starting-point and return of the subsequent campaigns (see above, § ix.).

The Bk. of Joshua represents these as undertaken by Joshua in person with all Israel behind him ; but, as we have seen, the oldest traditions describe the invasion as prosecuted from this point by different tribes in different directions. Jg 1 indicates these directions as two, in uniformity with the geographical position of Jericho and Gilgal, from which there are roads, S.W. into what was afterwards Judæa, N.W. into what became the territory of Manasseh and Ephraim. According to Jg 1, Judah and Simeon followed the

first of these ; and the double tribe of Joseph, still under the leadership of Joshua, the second. But the independent action of Judah and Simeon is not incompatible with Joshua's continued headship over all Israel ; for, as we have seen, the same document, J, which relates their campaign, still sees in him the arbiter of the tribes, and assigns to him the allotment of their spheres of conquest (Jos $17^{14\text{-}18}$). Ai and Bethel, both of them on the easiest road from Jericho to the backbone of the range, were taken by Joshua, and his army returned to Gilgal (10^6).

At this point, the most natural in the course of events, occurs the narrative of the service at Shechem (ch. $8^{30\text{-}35}$), founded on E, which event, however, presupposes the conquest or occupation of the hill-country of Ephraim and Manasseh ; and about this not a word, as we have seen, is said. It has been supposed that the story was missing in the documents ; and if so, this would be an argument in favour of the reliability of the later tradition and redactions, which abstained from inventing a story, even if the event had happened, when they had no materials for it. But why was this one event missing on *all* the lines of tradition ? The problem is one for which no satisfactory solution has yet been offered. It is to the same point in the course of conquest that the Bk. of Joshua assigns the treaty with Gibeon. That this treaty was made in Joshua's time has been denied by many critics on the evidence of the later history. There is, however, nothing in the latter which makes so early a treaty with Gibeon an impossible thing. Budde (*ZATW* vii. p. 135 ff.) marks the fact that in Deborah's time Judah was cut off from the tribes to the N. of her by a belt of territory in possession of the Canaanites, and argues that Gibeon's independence of Israel was necessary to make that belt continuous between Jebus and Gezer.* But the geographical data do not make this a necessary conclusion ; the northern Israelites may very well have been in alliance with Gibeon and still unable to maintain connexion with Judah ; and Kittel (*Gesch.* i. p. 272 ff.) has plausibly argued that the story of Joshua fighting the Canaanites near Gibeon, if historical, renders his treaty with Gibeon extremely probable. But, as we have seen, there is ancient evidence in the poetical piece, ch. $10^{12\text{-}14}$, for the battle of Beth-horon and Joshua's defeat of the Canaanites there. The oldest tradition, which makes him return after it to Gilgal, is of course to be preferred to the Deuteronomic summary, which follows and assigns to him the conquest of the south : this must rather be assigned, as J assigns it, to Judah and the Calebites, who undertook it independently from Jericho, while Joshua himself led the house of Joseph against Ai, Bethel and the midlands. To Joshua are also assigned by fragments of E a campaign and victory in the N. of the Jordan Valley, and against the probability of this there is no conclusive argument : the narrative as it stands, however, in ch. 11 is largely the work of the Deuteronomist. For details of the question see Dillmann's *Comm.* ; Budde, *ZATW* vii. p. 149 ff. ; and Moore's *Comm. on Jg* 4.

xi. THE RELIGIOUS TEACHING OF THE BK. OF JOSHUA.—As was to be expected, the religious teaching of the book is mainly found in its later strata—the Deuteronomic and the Priestly. We have seen how they fulfil the scheme of the destiny of Israel on the lines laid down in the Pentateuch, and how the Deuteronomist enforces the law as prescribed in the Bk. of Dt, or records instances of its execution. But it is also to the Deuteronomist sections that we owe the fervent religious exhortations to Joshua and the people, which are the

---

* Stade has indeed attempted to show that this territory opposite Jericho was Moabite, but he can do so only after transferring the song (Nu 21) which celebrates the defeat of Sihon to the 9th cent. Upon this see the present writer's *Historical Geography*, App. II. p. 661 f. ; and cf. McCurdy, *Hist. Proph. and the Monuments*, ii. p. 112, and the footnote.

† See article by Lieut.-Col. Watson in *PEFSt*, 1895, p. 253 ff.

* It was completed by Sha'albim and Aijalon and possibly Kiriath-jearim.

portions of the book most frequently employed in Christian preaching and teaching. The story of Achan, as it has passed from the hand of the latest redactor, is a lesson of great power, on the possibility of individual selfishness and avarice wrecking the enterprises of the whole community. But to one of the earlier sources, probably E (see above, § iv. c), we owe the finest religious conception in the book, that of the appearance of the Angel to Joshua (ch. 5¹³⁻¹⁵). It is a noble illustration of the truth, that, in the great causes of God upon the earth, the leaders, however supreme and solitary they seem, are themselves led. There is a rock higher than they; their shoulders, however broad, have not to bear alone the awful burden of responsibility. The sense of supernatural conduct and protection, the consequent reverence and humility which form the spirit of all Israel's history, have nowhere in the OT received a more beautiful expression than in this early fragment.

LITERATURE.—1. Commentaries, Introductions, and similar works.—St. Augustin, *Locutiones de lib. Jos.*, Opera, iii. 587 ff.; Is. Abrabanel, *Comm. in Proph. Priores*, 1511 or 1512, also at Leipz. 1686; John Calvin, *Comm. in lib. Josuæ*, 1564 (the last of C.'s works); Andreas Masius, *Josuæ Imperat. Historia Illustrata*, etc., Antverp. 1574; Bonfrère, *Comm. in Jos. Jud. et Ruth*, Paris, 1631 (not seen); Osiander, *Comm. in Jos.*, Tübingen, 1681; Seb. Schmidt, *Prælectiones Academicæ in VIII. priora lib. Jos. Capita*, Hamb. 1693 (not seen); Joh. Clericus, *Comm. in histor. histor. VT*, Amsterd. 1708; Vic. Strigelius, *Lib. Jos.* . . . 1710; Corn. a Lapide, *Comm. in Jos.*, Antverp. 1718; Alex. Geddes, *The Holy Bible, trans. with notes, crit. remarks*, etc., vol. i., London, 1792; De Wette, *Beiträge z. Einleit. in's AT*, Halle, 1806–1807; *Lehrbuch der Hist. Krit. Einl. z. den Kanon. u. Apokr. Bü. des AT*, 1st ed. 1817, 6th before his death in 1849, 7th by Stähelin in 1852, 8th by Schrader, 1869 (an Eng. trans. by Theodore Parker, 1843); Bleek, *Einige Aphorist. Beitr. z. d. Untersuchungen üb. d. Pentateuch* in the *Bib. exeg. Repertorium*, Bd. 1, Leipz. 1822, cf. his *Einl. in's AT*, 1st ed. 1860, 5th ed. 1886; Maurer, *Komm. üb. d. B. Josua*, Stuttgart, 1831 (not seen); J. L. König, *AT Studien*, 1 Hft. 1836 (not seen); Keil, *Komm. ü. d. B. Jos.*, Erlangen, 1847, then in his Bibl. Comm. with Delitzsch, *Jos. Richt. Ruth*, Leipz. 1863, 2nd ed. 1874; Knobel, *Komm. z. Nu. Dt. u. Jos.*, Leipzig, 1861; J. W. Colenso, *The Pent. and Bk. of Jos. critically examined*, London, 1862–1871; Kuenen, *Hist.-Crit. Onderzoek²*, i. 1, 1885; Wellhausen, *Die Composition des Hexateuchs*, Berlin, 1885 (*Jahrb. f. Deutsche Theol.* 1876, 1877); Dillmann, *Nu. Dt. und Josua*, 1886; Vatke, *Einl. in das AT*, 1886 (posthumous); W. R. Smith, *OTJC²*, 1892; Addis, *Documents of the Hexateuch*, London, i. 1892, ii. 1898; Driver, *Introd. to the Lit. of the OT⁴*, 1891, 6th ed. 1897; cf. art. 'Bk. of Joshua' in Smith's *DB²*, 1893; Holzinger, *Einleitung in den Hexateuch*, 1893; Briggs, *Higher Crit. of the Hexateuch*, New York, 1893, 2nd ed. 1897; Oettli, *Dt. and Josh.* (not seen) in Strack's *Kgf. Komm.* 1894; W. H. Bennett, *Primer of the Bible*, London, 1897, esp. p. 90 and Appendix A. 2. Histories of Israel in which the composition and historical value of the Bk. of Joshua are more or less discussed.—Ewald, vol. i. (first published in 1843); Stade, vol. i. 1881; Kittel, vol. i. 1888. 3. Other works chiefly on the Text, Analysis of Documents, etc. (a) More general.—König; Nöldeke, *AT Liter.* 1868, and *Untersuch. z. Kritik des AT*, 1869. (b) Special.—Hollenberg in *SK*, 1874, pp. 462–506, and *Der Charakter der Alex. Uebersetz. des B. Jos.* 1876 (not seen); Budde in *ZATW*, 1887, pp. 93–166, *Richter u. Josua*, 1888, p. 148, see also his *Richter u. Samuel*, Giessen, 1890, pp. 1–89; Albers, *Die Quellenberichte in Josua* i.–xii. 1891; W. H. Bennett, 'Bk. of Jos.,' Crit. Ed. of Heb. Text in Haupt's *SBOT*. (c) Archæological.—Clermont-Ganneau, *Arch. Researches in Pal.* 1896, ii. 23 ff., 308, 328 f., 491.

G. A. SMITH.

JOSIAH (יֹאשִׁיָּה, יֹאשִׁיָּהוּ, 'J″ supports').—**1.** A king of Judah. He was the son of Amon and grandson of Manasseh. His mother's name is given as Jedidah, the daughter of Adaiah (2 K 22¹). His father was killed by conspirators after a brief reign of two years. His murderers were brought to justice, and Josiah placed on the throne at the age of eight (2 K 21²⁴). The date of his accession was probably B.C. 639, and his reign lasted thirty-one years, till B.C. 608. During the early part of his reign matters seem to have gone on much as before, the king being too young to introduce any change, if he had been disposed to do so. It was not till the eighteenth year of his reign that the reformation took place which marked an epoch in the history of the national religion. The prophetic party, which had attained great influence under Hezekiah, had lost it under Manasseh,

who carried his fanatical attachment to lower forms of religion to the point of persecuting the pure faith. The reformers could only work for the future, and wait till their opportunity came. It is not unlikely that the Scythian invasion gave it them. Hordes of Scythians burst into Western Asia about B.C. 630. The prophets (Jer 6¹, Zeph 1¹⁴⁻¹⁸) saw in them the instruments of God's judgment on sinful Judah. They invaded Palestine, and came down the sea-coast towards Egypt. Contrary to expectation, they did not attack Judah. In the relief at so great a deliverance, the reformers found themselves once more in favour. The first sign of this was a movement for the repair of the temple (2 K 22³ff.). Money was collected from the people, and the work was begun in the eighteenth year of Josiah's reign. Very soon the high priest Hilkiah announced to Shaphan the scribe that he had found the Book of the Law in the temple. Shaphan read it, and informed the king of its discovery. On hearing it read, J. was so alarmed at the threats made against disobedience to its commands, and the knowledge that they had been so often transgressed, that he sent an influential deputation to the prophetess Huldah. As her prophecy is given in 2 K 22¹⁵⁻²⁰, she predicted that the threats against Jerus. should be fulfilled, but that the king should not live to see it, but be gathered to his grave in peace.

The next step was to bring the religious practice into conformity with the law. This could be accomplished only through a drastic reformation. The elders and people of Judah and Jerusalem were summoned to a meeting in the temple, and the law was read to them (2 K 23¹ff.). The king made a covenant to obey the law, and all the people assented to it. The reform consisted in the cleansing of the temple from idolatry, in the suppression of idolatry throughout the kingdom, and, most important of all, in the abolition of the high places or local sanctuaries. After it had been carried through, a great passover was celebrated. It is difficult to overrate the importance of this reformation. The abolition of the local sanctuaries centralized the worship. This in itself was a death-blow to idolatry. Even where J″ alone was nominally worshipped at the local shrines, heathenish elements both in belief and practice inevitably crept in. One temple implied one God. Then, as a corollary of centralization, radical changes took place throughout the cultus, while the priests of the local sanctuaries were degraded into inferior ministers, without the rights of priests. Nor was this all. The acceptance of a written code as binding law was the first step in the formation of a Canon of Scripture, which was to have such immense developments later. Then for the first time Judah became a people of the law.

Critics are agreed that the law on which the reformation was based was the Deuteronomic Code, but how much of our present Book of Deut. was discovered by Hilkiah is a question on which they are divided (see DEUTERONOMY). In one respect it was found impracticable to carry out the Deuteronomic law. The priests of the high places were not admitted to the same privileges as the priests of the temple (2 K 23⁹, contrast Dt 18⁶⁻⁸). It is probable that J. found it impossible to carry through this reform on account of the opposition of the Jerus. priesthood. It has been inferred from this that Hilkiah the priest can have had no share in the composition of the work.

We know scarcely anything of the thirteen years that followed the reformation. But it seems to have been a period of peace and prosperity. One very significant fact that comes out in the narrative of J.'s measures to enforce the new law is that they were extended to Samaria, which was not strictly part of his kingdom. The explanation is that the Assyr. empire, though not yet overthrown, was so much weakened that J. was not only practically independent himself, but could interfere in an Assyr. province. And we must probably start from this in solving the riddle why he opposed the advance of the king of Egypt against Assyria. In 608 Cyaxares and Nabopolassar joined in an attack on Assyria. This gave Egypt the opportunity of seizing Syria. J. saw in this a menace of subjection to the Egyp. yoke, and naturally was unwilling to lose his independence. He was no doubt ill-advised in taking the initiative, but he probably expected that Judah would be victorious, now that it had become a people of the law. This ill-grounded confidence cost him his life and Judah her freedom. He fell in the battle at Megiddo (2 K 23²⁹).

J.'s character is very highly estimated by the editor of the Book of Kings, on account of his earnestness in the work of reform ; and the ferocity with which it was carried through (2 K 23²⁰) need not, in that age, be urged against him. Jeremiah contrasts his equity in the administration of justice with Jehoiakim's oppression of the weak and shedding of innocent blood (Jer 22¹⁵⁻¹⁷).

The account in Chronicles (2 Ch 34. 35) varies in some respects from that of Kings. It places Josiah's religious reforms almost entirely before the discovery of the law, no doubt because it seemed strange that so good a king should have waited till the eighteenth year of his reign before rooting out idolatry. It also states that the Egyp. king warned J. not to oppose him, since God had sent him against Carchemish (2 Ch 35²¹). This was perhaps intended to account for the death of so righteous a king : he had refused to obey God's warning.

2. A son of Zephaniah (Zec 6¹⁰) living at Jerus. in the time of Zechariah. The text of this passage appears to have been tampered with and to need radical correction. See Wellh., Now., and G. A. Smith, *ad loc.*   A. S. PEAKE.

JOSIAS (B ᾽Ιωσείας, BᵇA -σίας).—JOSIAH king of Judah. 1 Es 1¹· ⁷· ¹⁸· ²¹⁻²³· ²⁵· ²⁸· ²⁹· ³²⁻³⁴, Bar 1⁸.

JOSIPHIAH (יוֹסִפְיָה ' J'' adds,' Ezr 8¹⁰).—The father of one of Ezra's companions. The name of the son is not given in MT, which reads ' and of the sons of Shelomith, the son of Josiphiah ' ; but the text may be corrected by the help of LXX (ἀπὸ υἱῶν Βααλί A ; 1 Es 8³⁶ ἐκ τῶν υἱῶν Βανί A, Βανιάς B, Βαναιάς Luc.), and we should read ' and of the sons of Bani, Shelomith,' etc., עַם having fallen out after וּכְבֵנֵי. See GENEALOGY.

JOT.—Tindale rendered the ἰῶτα ἓν of Mt 5¹⁸ ' one iott ' (perhaps under the influence of the Vulg. *iota unum*), and his rendering was accepted by all subsequent translators (Cov., Cran., ' iott ' ; Gen., Rhem., Bish., AV ' iote' ; RV ' jot,' which is the mod. spelling in AV also). The ἰῶτα is the smallest letter in the Gr. alphabet ; but the corresponding letter in Heb. (י *yod*) is more distinctly the smallest, so that an argument is found in this verse in favour of Aramaic as our Lord's tongue. (See also TITTLE). After Tind. ' jot' was used to denote any minute thing, and Shaks. uses it even of a drop of blood, *Merch. of Ven.* IV. i. 302—

> ' This bond doth give thee here no jot of blood.'

Wyclif's trⁿ (1380) is, ' oon i, *that is lest lettre.*' The Germ. trⁿ is still (Stuttgart Bible Soc. ed. 1898) that of Luther, ' der kleinste Buchstabe' ; but Weizsäcker has ' ein Jota' ; and the Fr. translators give ' un (seul) iota.'   J. HASTINGS.

JOTBAH (יָטְבָה ' pleasantness ').—Named only in

2 K 21¹⁹, where we are told that king Amon's mother was ' Meshullemeth, the daughter of Haruz of Jotbah.' It was probably in Judah, but the site is unknown.

JOTBATHAH (יָטְבָתָה, Jotbath in AV of Dt 10⁷, where the Targ. has the same form. LXX has in Nu Σετεβάθα corrected to ᾽Ετέβ- in B, ᾽Ιεταβάθαν A ; in Dt Ταιβάθα B, ᾽Ιετάβ- A, ᾽Ιτέβ- F ; Vulg. *Jetabatha*).—A station in the journeyings of the Israelites mentioned only in Nu 33³³ᶠ·, Dt 10⁷, and described as ' a land of brooks of waters.' Its position is unknown, but cf. § iv. of art. EXODUS (ROUTE OF). Whether it should be identified with Jotbah, or with ᾽Ιωτάβη, the seat of a bishopric in the 6th cent. (cf. Reland, *Pal.* p. 533) whose site is unknown, is doubtful.   A. T. CHAPMAN.

JOTHAM (יוֹתָם ' J'' is perfect,' or possibly ' solitary one,' ᾽Ιωθάμ).—**1.** The youngest son of Gideon (Jg 9⁵· ⁷· ²¹· ⁵⁷). The citizens of Shechem were met in assembly to make Abimelech king, when Jotham suddenly appeared on a spur of Gerizim, and delivered in their hearing a parable with a pointed application. The parable is not consistently applied ; the author had several points in his mind, such as these : (*a*) the contrast (though this is not fully worked out) between Gideon's refusal of the kingship (8²²ᶠ·) and the arrogant claim of the worthless son of his concubine. The other sons had qualities which might have given them the right to rule ; it was left to the mean and useless ' bramble' to claim the rank of king (cf. 2 K 14⁹). (*b*) A warning to the Shechemites of the dangerous character of their upstart chief. Not only was his protection worthless if they trusted him, but he would bring destruction on them if they did not. (*c*) A rebuke of the Shechemites for their base ingratitude towards the house of Gideon. The application of the fable is most inconsistent at vv.¹⁵· ¹⁶. The point in v.¹⁵ is the relation between the Shechemites and Abimelech, but in v.¹⁶ between the Shechemites and the family of Gideon. Such inconsistencies are not uncommon in fables of this kind ; they are found in the parables of the NT. There is no need, therefore, to suppose that Jotham's parable was borrowed from some earlier popular collection, where it had quite a different moral. Jotham's ' curse' was accomplished when Abimelech burnt down the tower of Shechem and met with a violent death himself (vv.⁵⁶· ⁵⁷ [RJE]).

It is worth noticing that there is nothing distinctively religious in Jotham's parable. Judgment is passed upon Abimelech and the Shechemites on purely moral grounds ; and the consequences of their deeds are predicted, not in the form of a prophecy or a message from God, but by the moral sense of a private individual.

2. King of Judah, son of Uzziah and Jerushah (2 K 15³²⁻³⁸, 2 Ch 27¹⁻⁹). He is said to have reigned 16 years in Jerusalem (751–735) ; but during the greater part of his ' reign' he was regent in the lifetime of his father (2 K 15⁵, 2 Ch 26²¹). He was sole king from about 737 to 735. The historians represent his character in a favourable light. In 2 K it is recorded that he built the upper gate of the temple. The formidable combination of N. Israel and Syria began to show the first signs of hostility against Judah in this reign. According to 2 Ch, Jotham waged a successful war against the Ammonites. The great prophets Hosea, Isaiah, and Micah prophesied in his days.

3. A Calebite (1 Ch 2⁴⁷).   G. A. COOKE.

JOURNEY.—See SABBATH DAY'S JOURNEY.

JOURNEYINGS OF ISRAELITES.—See EXODUS AND JOURNEY TO CANAAN.

JOY.—The following are the principal Heb. and Gr. words of which 'joy' is the tr^n in AV:—

גִּיל, גִּילָה (vb. גִּיל or גּוּל, very common), the primary meaning of which, judging from the cognate Arab. *jāl*, may be to *go round or about*, *be excited* to levity, etc. (see *Oxf. Heb. Lex.* p. 162ᵇ). It would be difficult to differentiate exactly the similar terms שָׂשׂוֹן and שָׂשׂוֹן (both from root שׂוּשׂ), רִנָּה, שִׂמְחָה. In general, it may be said that they all include not only a mental emotion but some outward expression of this, such as shouting, singing, leaping, dancing, sometimes with the accompaniment of musical instruments (*e.g.* Ps 132⁹, Is 49¹³, 2 S 6¹⁶, 1 S 18⁶, Is 24⁸).

In NT we have the verb ἀγαλλιάω (-άομαι), in LXX=גִּיל, עָלַץ, רָנָה, שׂוּשׂ, and the noun ἀγαλλίασις. The latter is unknown to classical Greek but frequent in LXX, and occurs in NT in Lk 1¹⁴·⁴⁴, Ac 2⁴⁶, Jude ²⁴, He 1⁹ (quoted from Ps 45⁸ where it renders שׂוּשׂ). This word expresses vehement joy or exultation (cf. Lk 1⁴⁴). The common NT word for 'joy' (noun) is χαρά (in LXX used for שִׂמְחָה and שָׂשׂוֹן); the verb (see next art.) is χαίρω (in LXX for שָׂמַח, גִּיל, and שׂוּשׂ).

It is important to recognize the identity as well as the difference in religious experience between OT and NT believers. The difference is in circumstantials, the identity in essentials. If joy is not as prominent in OT as in NT, it is still prominent. Its presence is implied in the numerous beatitudes of the Psalms, such as 1¹ 32¹. Such passages imply conscious possession of the blessings mentioned. But explicit references to the subject are numerous and emphatic, especially in the book of Psalms. A striking point of similarity between OT and NT piety is that, in both cases, God Himself is the object and ground of the believer's joy: 'My soul shall be joyful in the Lord, it shall rejoice in his salvation' (Ps 35⁹, see also 43⁴, Is 51¹⁶ etc.). Here religious joy reaches its highest, purest expression, With this may be compared NT passages like Ph 3¹ 'Rejoice in the Lord'; 4⁴, Ro 5¹¹ 'We also rejoice in God through our Lord Jesus Christ.' A suggestive parallel is found in Ph 3³ 'We . . . glory in Christ Jesus.' Among the subordinate aspects or grounds of joy OT significantly emphasizes the divine law or word: 'His delight is in the law of the Lord' (Ps 1² 19¹⁰ 119¹⁶² etc.). As we might expect, NT is richer in its exposition of the several aspects of religious joy. Faith is a source of joy (Ph 1²⁵, Ro 15¹³); so also hope (Ro 5² 12¹²); the testimony of a good conscience (2 Co 1¹²). Christian joy is 'in the Holy Ghost' (Ro 14¹⁷), *i.e.* 'in connexion with, under the indwelling and influence of the Holy Ghost' (Alford); the Holy Spirit is the sphere or element in which it lives and moves; see also 1 Th 1⁶. It is also a participation in Christ's own joy (Jn 15¹¹ 17¹³). Persecution and suffering for Christ's sake, instead of hindering, enhances it (Mt 5¹¹·¹², Ac 5⁴¹, Ph 1²⁹). A Christian rejoices in tribulation because of the fruit it bears (Ro 5³·⁴). For the same reason, temptation may be an occasion of joy (Ja 1²). The repentance of sinners causes joy in heaven (Lk 15⁷·¹⁰). The joy of Christians should be unbroken (1 Th 5¹⁶). The power, permanence, and exuberant fulness of a believer's joy here and hereafter are often dwelt on (Ps 4⁷ 16⁹, Is 35¹⁰ 51¹¹ 61⁷, Jn 15¹¹ 17¹³, Ac 13⁵², 1 P 1⁸, Jude ²⁴). The Redeemer's joy in the certain prospect of the success of His work is mentioned in He 12². The final reward of the Christian is participation in that joy (Mt 25²¹): 'that joy of the Lord arising from the completion of his work and labour of love, of which the sabbatical rest of the Creator was typical (Gn 1³¹ 2²), and of which his faithful ones shall in the end partake; see He 4³⁻¹¹, Rev 3²¹' (Alford). As believers rejoice in God, so God rejoices in His people (Ps 147¹¹ 149⁴, Zeph 3¹⁷)—a sentiment re-echoed by a modern Christian psalmist: 'He views His children with delight.' If the reading in RV be accepted, the same sentiment is found in Lk 2¹⁴. Rejoicing in

the good of others is mentioned as the distinctive feature of Christian sympathy (Ro 12¹⁵). The 'joy of the godless' (Job 20⁵) is 'not so.'

J. S. BANKS.

JOY.—As a verb 'joy' is used by Shaks. both transitively [=(1) *gladden*, as *Rich. III.* I. ii. 220, 'Much it joys me to see you are become so penitent'; (2) *enjoy*, as *II Henry VI.* IV. ix. 1, 'Was ever king that joyed an earthly throne?'] and intransitively; but in AV it is always intransitive, with the meaning 'rejoice.' Sometimes 'joy' and 'rejoice' come together, as Ph 2¹⁷·¹⁸ 'I joy, and rejoice with you all. For the same cause also do ye joy, and rejoice with me' (χαίρω καὶ συγχαίρω . . . χαίρετε καὶ συγχαίρετε), there being no difference in meaning.

In most places of its occurrence, Tindale translated καυχάομαι, *to boast*, by the verb to rejoice, and he was followed by AV in Ro 5², Ph 3³, Ja 1⁹ 4¹⁶. Once (Ro 5¹¹) he rendered it 'joy,' and was again followed by AV as well as by Cran. and the Bishops, though the Vulg. is *glorior* (Wyc., Rhem., and RVm 'glory,' the others having 'rejoice'). Even RV gives 'rejoice,' which is plainly inadequate. If 'boast' was felt to be unsuitable, 'exult' would have served.

J. HASTINGS.

JOZABAD (יוֹזָבָד, another form of יְהוֹזָבָד, **Jehozabad,** wh. see).—1. 2. 3. Three of David's heroes, 1 Ch 12⁴·²⁰·²⁰. **4.** The eponym of a Levitical family, 2 Ch 31¹³ 35⁹. **5.** A priest who had married a foreign wife, Ezr 10²². **6.** A Levite, Ezr 8³³ 10²³, Neh 8⁷ 11¹⁶. See GENEALOGY.

JOZABDUS (Ζάβδος B, Ὠζάβαδος A), 1 Es 9²⁹= ZABBAI, Ezr 10²⁸.

JOZACAR (AV Jozachar) is mentioned only in 2 K 12²¹, where we are told that Joash, king of Judah, was murdered by his servants 'Jozacar ben-Shimeath and Jehozabad ben-Shomer.' According to 2 Ch 25⁸ Amaziah put to death his father's murderers. MSS of MT vary between יוֹזָכָר *Jōzākhār*, יוֹזָבָר *Jōzābhādh*, יוֹזָבָר *Jōzābhār* (1 MS of Kenn. cited by de Rossi), and (one of de Rossi's) יוֹזָכָר *Jōzākhādh*; LXX, B'Ιεζειχάρ (Swete); Tisch. gives B's reading as 'Ιεζιρχάρ), A and Luc. ᴸᵃᵍ·'Ιωζαχάρ; Vulg. *Josachar*; Syr. *Jozabar*. The parallel 2 Ch 24²⁶ has 'Zabad ben-Shimeath the Ammonitess, and Jehozabad ben-Shimrith the Moabitess.' LXX, B has Ζαβέλ, A Ζαβέθ for *Zabad*. In 2 K *Oxf. Heb. Lex.*, Kautzsch (*AT*), Baer, etc., read יוֹזָכָר *Jōzākhār*, as AV. יוזבד in Ginsburg's *Heb. Bible* is stated by the editor to be a misprint for יוזבר—S. R. D.]

Kittel (on Chronicles in *SBOT*) not only reads *Jōzākhār* in Kings, but emends 2 Ch 24²⁶ to *Zakhar* on the strength of the parallel in Kings. The various readings turn upon the very slight differences between ב and כ, ד and ר, which in some MSS are practically imperceptible; especially in the case of ד and ר, where *Raphe* is not used. The proximity of the very similar *Jehozabad* would facilitate corruption of the text. But the Ch text—which here, as often elsewhere, may be based on an older reading than that in our text of Kings—suggests that, in the original, there was only one name; that this was accidentally written twice over; and that, in process of further copying, the present readings in K and Ch grew out of this doublet.

Jōzākhār='J" remembers,' *Jōzābhādh*='J" bestows gifts,' must be a simple error. See also ZABAD.

W. H. BENNETT.

JOZADAK.—See JEHOZADAK.

JUBAL (יוּבָל, 'Ιουβάλ).—A son of Lamech by Adah, and inventor of musical instruments, Gn 4²¹ (J). The name prob. contains an allusion to יוֹבֵל, 'ram's horn.' Regarding the instruments named in Gn, see Dillm. *ad loc.*, and art. MUSIC.

JUBILEE.—See SABBATICAL YEAR.

JUBILEES, BOOK OF, or **LITTLE GENESIS** (τὰ Ἰωβηλαῖα, ἡ κλεινὴ Γένεσις, ἡ λεπτὴ Γένεσις ; *Leptogenesis* ; in Ethiopic *Kufâlê*).—Under these names there is extant one of the most curious and interesting of the OT Apocrypha. It is preserved complete only in an Ethiopic translation (first edited by Dillmann in 1859), but a considerable portion of a Latin version has been published by Ceriani from an Ambrosian MS, and fragments of the Greek are contained in the Byzantine chronologists, who made large extracts.

The book contains the narrative of Genesis, rewritten from the point of view of the age of the author. It gives the narrative as a later Jew might imagine or desire that it should have happened. The chief characteristics of this rewriting of the book are—(1) the narrative is put into the mouth of the 'angel of the face,' who is represented as telling Moses on Mt. Sinai all that they (the angels) had done, and the legends of Creation, and of the Lord's dealings with mankind. (2) The narrative is arranged throughout in a chronological system of years, weeks of years, and jubilees. Every event is dated ; as, for example, 'and in the first week of the third jubilee Cain slew Abel.' (3) Many legends of the class known as *Midrashim* are added to the narrative. (4) Great stress is laid on all the Jewish feasts, and their institution in patriarchal times is asserted (the Feast of Weeks, the Feast of Tabernacles, the Day of Atonement, and the Passover). For example (ch. 16), Abraham institutes the Feast of Tabernacles, 'on this account it is ordained in the tablets of heaven concerning Israel that they shall celebrate the festival of the tabernacles seven days in joy.' (5) Great stress is laid on ordinances of the Mosaic law, which are written in the 'tablets of heaven' and connected with events in the life of the patriarchs—such are new moon and sabbath, the offerings, the laws concerning blood and fornication and war. The sun was created for the sake of enabling the feasts to be calculated. (6) Some passages very derogatory to Edom are introduced.

The date of the book may be approximately fixed by the fact that it is used in the *Testimony of the XII Patriarchs*, and makes no mention of the fall of Jerusalem. On the other hand, it apparently makes use of the Book of *Enoch*. The reference to Edom shows also that it was written after the rise of the house of Herod. Ewald placed it towards the end of the 1st cent. B.C.; but hatred of Edom could exist just as well at a later date, and other indications seem to suggest a time when troubles that preceded the fall of Jerusalem were beginning, the chief eschatological passage seeming to refer to them (ch. 23).

The author was not a Herodian, not a Sadducee (for he believes in the resurrection), not a Pharisee (for he lays no stress on the written tradition), not an Essene (for he does not condemn the sacrifices), not a Hellenist (for he attacks the laxity of Hellenism). He was a Jew who, in a time of laxity and of falling away, tries to restore the authority of the fundamental principles of his faith, and represents the evils which are crowding on his people as the punishment for disobedience. He has quite clearly in his mind a definite falling away from Jewish ordinances, 'they have deserted the ordinances which the Lord had covenanted between them and him.' These ordinances particularly which they had neglected were probably the ones on which stress is laid—the sabbath, the feasts, circumcision, avoiding fornication (*i.e.* mixed marriages). It may be suggested that 'they' are really the Christians, and that the book is written by a fervent opponent of the new faith between the years A.D. 50 and 60, when disorder is begin-

ning to break out, and the effect of the people's falling away is, as he thinks, apparent.

In any case, the book is of great value in illustrating, partly by resemblance, partly by contrast, the New Testament. We have an example of the 'Law given by angels.' The theology of the book is exactly what St. Paul protests against when he condemns 'days and months and seasons and years.' There is a curious resemblance to three out of the four points insisted upon in Ac 15, and it may be noted, as perhaps helping to throw some light on that passage, that fornication is used of 'mixed marriages.'

LITERATURE.—(*a*) *The Ethiopic text.*—Dillmann, Kiel, 1859 ; a newer edition by Charles based on a larger number of MSS, Oxford, 1895. (*b*) *Latin text.*—Ceriani in *Monumenta sacra et profana*, tom. i. fasc. 1 (1864) ; Rönsch, *Das Buch der Jubiläen*, Leipzig, 1874. (*c*) *Translations.*—German, by Dillmann in Ewald's *Jahrbücher*, ii., iii., 1850, 1851, and by Littmann in Kautzsch's *Apocryphen und Pseudepigraphen*, 1899 ; English, Schodde, *Book of Jubilees*, Oberlin, Ohio, 1888, and by Charles in *JQR*, October 1893, July 1894, January 1895. (*d*) *Treatises.*—Schürer, *HJP* II. iii. 134 ff.; W. Singer, *Das Buch der Jubiläen*, 1898 ; Rönsch, *op. cit.*, and the literature there referred to.

A. C. HEADLAM.

JUCAL.—See JEHUCAL.

JUDÆA (Ἰουδαία) was the most southern of the three districts—Galilee, Samaria, and Judæa—into which Palestine west of Jordan was divided in the time of Christ (Mt 2[1], Lk 2[4], Jn 4[3. 4. 47. 54], Ac 8[1] 9[31]). In several passages (Mt 4[25], Mk 1[5] 3[7], Lk 5[17], Jn 3[22], Ac 1[8]) Judæa is distinguished from its capital, Jerusalem, which, according to the Talmuds (Neubauer, *Géog. du Talmud*, p. 56), formed a division by itself (cf. Neh 11[3]).

After the Captivity the tribal possessions of Judah, Benjamin, Dan, and Simeon were reoccupied by Israelites. Most of the 'children of the captivity' who returned from Babylon belonged to the tribe of Judah, and the limits of the reoccupied district were almost the same as those of the old kingdom of Judah. Thence the district was called *Judah*, and the people received the name of *Jews* (Jos. *Ant.* XI. v. 7). Afterwards the two names were used in a wider sense. All Israelites were called Jews, and Judæa, or 'the land of Judah,' sometimes stood for the three districts of Western Palestine (Lk 4[44] [?] * 23[5], Ac 10[37] 26[20]. See art. CHRONOLOGY OF NT, vol. i. p. 406[b] f.).

Under the Persians, Judah was a district (OT 'province,' מְדִינָה) of the 5th satrapy of the Empire (Herod. iii. 91), administered by a governor (פֶּחָה) who was generally, at least, a Jew, and was apparently assisted by a council of Jewish elders. The governor and elders dwelt at Jerusalem, the seat of government (Hag 1[1. 14] 2[2], Ezr 5[1. 8],† Neh 11[3]). The name *Judæa* first occurs in To 1[18], where it is applied to the old kingdom of Judah. The later Judæa (1 Mac 3[34] 10[38], 2 Mac 1[10]), or 'land of Judah' (1 Mac 10[30. 33. 37], cf. Is 19[17]), extended from Samaria on the north to the desert of Arabia Petræa on the south, and from the Mediterranean on the west to the Jordan Valley on the east. Its limits, which varied at different periods, cannot be more clearly defined. In the time of Judas Maccabæus, Hebron was in the hands of the Edomites (1 Mac 5[65]) ; and in the time of his brother Jonathan, three nomes, or toparchies of Samaria—Aphærema, Lydda, and Ramathaim—were added to Judæa (1 Mac 10[30. 38] 11[34]). According to Josephus (*BJ* III. iii. 5), Judæa extended from Anuath - Borkeos (ʼAina-Berkit) on the north to Iardas, a village on the confines of Arabia (perhaps *Tell ʼArâd*) on the

* The reading Ἰουδαίας instead of Γαλιλαίας is accepted by WH (text) on the authority of אBCL, etc. (see ' Notes on Select Readings,' *ad loc.*).
† In Ezr 5[8] AV reads ' Judea,' RV correctly ' Judah.' See art. JEWRY.

south, and from Joppa to the Jordan. The sea-coast as far as Ptolemais (*Acre*), and the coast towns, with the possible exception of Cæsarea, also belonged to it. The country was divided into toparchies—a division recognized by Pliny (*HN* v. 14), though his list does not completely agree with that of Josephus. There is some authority for the view that certain districts east of Jordan were included in Judæa. Strabo describes Judæa as being 'situated above Phœnicia, in the interior between Gaza and Antilibanus, and extending to the Arabians' (XVI. ii. 21). Tacitus (*Hist.* v. 6) says the borders of Judæa on the east were formed by Arabia. Josephus (*Ant.* XII. iv. 11) countenances an extension beyond Jordan, and so does the NT in Mt 19[1] ('the borders of Judæa beyond Jordan'). In Mk 10[1], where AV (following TR) reads 'the coasts of Judæa by the further side of Jordan,' RV (following WH, etc.) has the 'borders of Judæa *and* beyond Jordan.' In the time of Ptolemy (V. xvi. 9) some places east of Jordan belonged to Judæa. Possibly the boundary included the valley, and the slopes of the hills east of Jordan. The Talmudists allude to the 'mountain,' or 'king's mountain,' the *Shephēlah*, or 'low hills,' and *Daroma*, or 'the south,' as different portions of Judæa. Daroma was divided into Upper and Lower (Neubauer, p. 62).

On the division of the country after the death of Herod the Great, Judæa was given to Archelaus with the title of ethnarch. A few years later, on the deposition of Archelaus, it was added to the province of Syria, and administered by a procurator subordinate to the governor of Syria. The procurator resided at Cæsarea (*Ant.* XVII. xiii. 5, XVIII. i. 1, ii. 1), which, according to the Talmuds, was not in Judæa. This view is said to have been held by St. Luke, but it seems doubtful whether his intention is to do more than draw a distinction between Judæa and the seat of government, Cæsarea (Ac 12[19] 21[10], cf. 'Judæa and Jerusalem,' as above). In the division of Palestine at the beginning of the 5th cent. Judæa formed part of *Palestina Prima*.

The physical features of Judæa are described in the art. on PALESTINE. It will suffice to say here that the Romans covered the country with a network of roads.

LITERATURE.—Schürer, *HJP* (Index); G. A. Smith, *HGHL* (Index); Buhl, *GAP* 81 f., 131 ff.; Guérin, *Judée*; Neubauer, *Géog. du Talm.* 53, 55, 59 ff.; Baedeker-Socin, *Pal.*[3] (Index); *PEF Mem.* vol. iii.; Literature under art. PALESTINE.

C. W. WILSON.

JUDÆA, THE WILDERNESS OF (ἡ ἔρημος τῆς Ἰουδαίας, *desertum Judææ*).—The district in which John the Baptist made his first appearance as the Forerunner of Christ (Mt 3[1]). In Mk 1[4], Lk 3[2], it is called simply 'the wilderness.' It is prob. the same as the wilderness of Judah (Jg 1[16], Ps 63, title), in which were situated En-gedi and five other cities (Jos 15[61. 62])—the Jeshimon or desert tract west of the Dead Sea. It perhaps included the western bank of the Jordan to the north of the Dead Sea (Jos. *Ant.* III. x. 7, IV. viii. 2, 3).

C. W. WILSON.

JUDAH (יְהוּדָה *yĕhûdâh*, 'praised' (?), Ἰούδας, *Juda*; in Assyr. inscriptions *Ia-u-du, Ia-u-dai*, see Jastrow, *JBL* xii. (1893) 61 ff.). — **1.** The fourth son of Jacob and Leah. He was born in Paddan-aram (Gn 29[35]). In J he is very prominent. He suggests to his brethren that they should sell Joseph to the Ishmaelites (Gn 37[26f.]), pleads for Benjamin to be sent into Egypt, and becomes surety for his safety (43[8f.]). He thus takes the place corresponding to that assumed by Reuben in E (37[21f.] 42[37]). So in Gn 44[14] we read of Judah and his brethren, and it is he who makes the impassioned appeal to Joseph for Benjamin's

release (Gn 44[18-34]). In consequence of Reuben's misconduct (Gn 35[22] 49[4]) and the treacherous violence of Simeon and Levi (34. 49[5ff.]), Judah receives the firstborn's privilege (49[8ff.]). According to Gn 38 he went to Adullam and married the daughter of a Canaanite, Shua. By her he had three sons, Er, Onan, and Shelah. Er married Tamar, but died without children, as did his brother Onan, who refused to perform the duty of raising up seed to his brother. As she was not given to Shelah, she by artifice became the mother of two children by Judah, Perez and Zerah.

This narrative reveals very clearly what is true in part at least of the others, that Judah is the eponymous ancestor of the **tribe of Judah**, and that the history of the tribe has been thrown into the form of a personal history. Gn 38 thus becomes of great value for its information on the composition of the tribe. Under the metaphors of marriage and paternity the union and origin of various stocks are expressed. The most important fact that emerges is that the tribe of Judah, as we know it in the historical period, was largely of Can. origin. After the Hebrews entered Canaan, Judah left the main body, and struck out in a southerly direction to conquer a district to settle in (Jg 1[1-20]). In consequence of its union with Hirah and Shua, and later with Tamar, clans near Adullam, five Judahite clans were in course of time formed, but the two oldest of these, Er and Onan, became extinct. But Gn 38 does not exhaust our information as to the composition of Judah. In Jg 1[16] we find that the Kenites accompanied Judah into the wilderness of Judah, and then went on and dwelt among the Amalekites (reading 'the Amalekite' for 'the people'), where at a later period we find them (1 S 15[6], cf. Nu 24[20-22]). Perhaps they were of Amalekite origin. Generally they are regarded as Midianites; but this rests on a combination of J and E. Besides the Kenites we find two Kenizzite clans, Caleb and Othniel (Jg 1[12-15. 20], Jos 14[6-15] 15[13-19]). As Kenizzite, they would appear to have been originally Edomite tribes (Gn 36[11. 15. 42]). Caleb remained a distinct tribe till the time of David (1 S 30[14]). It lived in the hill-country of Judah, and Hebron was its chief town. It seems to have been the most powerful clan of Judah. Nabal is regarded as a typical Calebite (1 S 25[3]). The chief town of Othniel was Kiriath-sepher or Debir. Closely connected with Caleb was Jerahmeel, who in the highly important lists 1 Ch 2 appears as his brother. According to Wellhausen, who investigated these lists and those in 1 Ch 4[1-23] in his |*de Gen. et Fam. Jud.*|, Jerahmeel was older than Caleb, dwelt farther south, and adopted a less settled mode of life. It will be clear that Judah not only absorbed Canaanite, but, to a still greater extent, Edomite and kindred elements. These perhaps imparted the fanaticism which was later so characteristic of the tribe.

Originally, Judah seems to have been a smaller tribe than Reuben, Simeon, and Levi. But Reuben began to dwindle at an early period, and Simeon and Levi were broken up in consequence of a treacherous attack upon the Canaanites, with whom they had made an alliance (see SIMEON). Partly as a result of this, partly through the fusion with other clans already mentioned, and probably with the remnant of Simeon, Judah obtained the premier position among the Leah tribes. After the Jordan had been crossed, J. was accompanied by Simeon alone on its invasion of its portion. A victory was gained over Adoni-bezek, and Hebron and Kiriath-sepher were captured (Jg 1[8ff.]). We are also told that Jerus. was taken (v.[8]) and burnt, and three Philistine cities captured by Judah (v.[10]). But these latter statements are inconsistent with others in the same narrative, and do not well agree with the subsequent history. Judah found it impossible to make good its claim to the 'valley' (*i.e.* probably the coast plain), since it could not cope with the war-chariots of the natives. The extent of Judah's 'lot' is given in Jos 15 (P), but this chapter teaches us much less than it seems to do, partly because a very large number of the places it mentions have not been identified, partly because the description is ideal, and at no time corresponded, even approximately, with the actual facts. According to this account, Judah was bounded on the E. by the Dead Sea, on the N. by the southern boundary of Benjamin (see BENJAMIN for details), on the W. by the Mediterranean, on the S. by a line drawn from the southern tongue of the Dead Sea to the brook of Egypt, and passing through or by the ascent of Akrabbim, Zin, Kadesh-barnea, Hezron, Addar, Karka, and Azmon. Judah never reached the Mediterranean; the Phil. lay between, and so did Simeon, till the latter tribe was exterminated. As to the southern border, apart from the difficulty of fixing some of the sites mentioned, it must be observed that the territory of ·Judah shades off imperceptibly into the desert to the south. The portion of Judah is divided into four districts, the Negeb (RV South), the Shephelah or Lowland, the Hill Country, and the Wilderness of Judah. The *Negeb* is the largest portion. It is dry and barren, except in the brief spring-time; thinly populated, chiefly by nomads. The *Shephēlah* is undulating country, fertile and beautiful, separated from the sea by the Phil. plain. It was the most valuable district; but Judah could not hold it against the Philistines, who kept it in their own hands through a great part of the history. The *Hill Country* belongs to the great Central Range of Pal., and is separated by a valley from the low hills of the Shephelah. It was, historically, the most important part of Judah— rugged and barren, but with fertile valleys, and, owing to the system of terrace-cultivation, more productive than it could be now. The *Wilderness of Judah* (Jeshimon) lies between the Hill Country and the Dead Sea, a waste of unspeakable dreari- ness and desolation, 35 miles long by 15 broad. See, further, arts. HILL COUNTRY, and JESHIMON.

Judah was far more inaccessible than the Northern tribes. Protected on the E. by the Wilderness, on the S. by the Negeb, itself more or less of a wilderness, on the W. by the low hills of the Shephelah, by the valley that divides it from the Central Range and the slopes of the Central Range itself, on the N. by Benjamin with its fortresses, it lay far less open to invasion. When it was held by real defenders, it was necessary that the invaders should first master the surrounding country, and then deliver their attack across three of its borders (G. A. Smith, *Hist. Geog.* ch. xiv.). Judah was not impregnable, indeed, for it lay comparatively open from the N., and the Negeb could be crossed from the S., while passes led up to the central tableland from both E. and W., though very difficult to force against opposi- tion. But the very poverty of the country com- bined with the natural difficulties of invasion to secure it, since it offered little prize to tempt an attack. It was a very little province. Even if it had reached ,its ideal boundaries, it would have covered no more than 2000 square miles; actually its usual extent was nearer 1300, of which about half was desert.

The isolation of the territory was reflected in that of the tribe. After it had settled in its lot, it had but little to do with the Northern tribes. It is not even mentioned in the Song of Deborah, as if it were not recognized as belonging to Israel; and it appears in the story of Samson as surrender-

ing him to the Philistines (Jg 15⁹ᶠᶠ.). It seems to have drawn more closely to Israel in the time of Saul, as we see from the history of David. But Saul's persecution of David must have strained the loyalty of the tribe, and it is not surprising that on his death a kingdom of Judah was formed with David at its head, in opposition to the kingdom of Ishbaal, Saul's son (2 S 2⁴· ⁸). Both of these king- doms seem to have been tributary to the Philis- tines. The union of the two was due to the evident fact that David was the only man who could hope to lead Israel in successful revolt from the Phil., and was only hastened by the defection of Abner and the murder of Ishbaal (2 S 3¹²ᶠᶠ· ⁴⁵ᶠᶠ.). Judah, as the king's own tribe, was more closely attached to Israel than when the king belonged to another tribe. One of David's greatest and most far-sighted acts was the selection of Jerus. as his capital and the home of the ark (5⁶ᶠᶠ· 6¹²). Jerus. did not actually lie in Judah, except possibly to a slight extent, but it was on the border, and the possession of it, with the ark and temple, guaran- teed the survival of the Southern kingdom, after the loss of the Northern tribes. But in the latter years of David it is Judah, perhaps because it profited less by its connexion with the king than it expected, that seems to have been foremost in supporting Absalom, whose rebellion broke out in Hebron, the old capital of the tribe (2 S 15⁷). After its suppression Judah hung back, till its allegiance was won by the ill-timed appeal of David to its kinship with him (19¹¹ᶠᶠ.); ill-timed because David's favouritism to Judah provoked jealousy in the Northern tribes, and the abortive rising of Sheba (19⁴¹–20²²), which anticipated the successful revolt of Jeroboam. Solomon also showed an unwise partiality to Judah, as we see from the fact that it was excluded from the division into twelve districts for purposes of taxation (1 K 4). It is, accordingly, not wonderful that Judah remained loyal to Rehoboam, while the Northern tribes rejected him (12¹⁶ ᶠ.).

The **Kingdom of Judah** seems to have consisted simply of the tribe of Judah with very little of Benjamin (see BENJAMIN), and not of Judah and Benjamin. Only a brief outline of its history is here necessary; for fuller details the articles on the individual kings may be consulted. After the disruption caused by the senseless folly of Reho- boam, war was carried on between the two king- doms (1 K 14³⁰), but not in a very energetic way. In fact the treasure which Solomon had accumu- lated was taken by Shishak of Egypt when he invaded Judah (14²⁵ ᶠ.), and the superiority in wealth of the Southern kingdom would thus be lost. War continued through the reign of Abijam (15⁶ RVm), but it seems not to have been pro- secuted with vigour till Baasha succeeded Nadab the son of Jeroboam. He pressed Judah so hard that Asa took the unhappy step, fraught with future mischief, of calling in the aid of Syria. A diversion was thus effected in his favour, and Asa employed the materials of Baasha's fortress, Ramah, in erecting fortresses of his own (15¹⁷ ᶠ.). It was possibly with the accession of Omri that the relations between the two kingdoms were changed. He perhaps formed an alliance with Judah, as with Tyre (16³¹), probably in view of the dangers that threatened from Damascus. Ahab and Jehoshaphat were certainly allies (1 K 22), and Jehoshaphat's son, Jehoram, married Athaliah the daughter of Ahab (2 K 8¹⁸· ²⁶). Jehoshaphat's reign was probably prosperous, though his trading vessels were wrecked (1 K 22⁴⁸). The relations between Judah and Edom after the reign of Solomon are obscure. Edom seems to have been subject to Judah, at any rate in Jehoshaphat's time (2 K 3⁹), but it revolted from his son Jehoram

(2 K 8[20]). The good understanding with Israel continued while Omri's dynasty was on the throne, but Jehu murdered Ahaziah, Jehoram's son, and forty-two of his brethren (9[27] 10[14]). Thereupon the queen-mother, Athaliah, massacred all that remained of the royal family, except the infant Joash, and reigned six years. She was put to death by Jehoiada the priest, who made Joash king (2 K 11). Apparently, towards the end of his reign, Hazael, king of Syria, who had severely crippled the Northern kingdom, threatened Jerus., but was bought off by Joash, who perhaps in consequence of this was murdered (12[17ff.]). His son Amaziah, after a successful war with Edom, challenged Joash of Israel, who inflicted a disastrous defeat upon him (14[1-14]). Amaziah's son Azariah, or Uzziah, had a more successful reign. Syria had been exhausted in wars with Assyria, and now Assyria itself had a half-century of inactivity, and this left both Israel and Judah time to build up powerful states. Azariah recovered the port of Elath (14[22]), and from the early chapters of Isaiah we can see how wealthy Judah had become. But the signs began to be ominous before his death. Assyria resumed her old career of conquest, and Syria and Israel formed a coalition against her. When Ahaz refused to join it, they sought to compel the adhesion of Judah; whereupon Ahaz, in a panic and against the earnest warning of Isaiah, took the fatal step of calling in Tiglath-pileser, the king of Assyria (2 K 16, Is 7). The latter suppressed the coalition, but Ahaz paid too dearly for the relief, since he became tributary to Assyria. The heavy yoke was borne till Hezekiah thought himself strong enough, in alliance with other revolting states, and on the promise of help from Egypt, to throw it off (18[7]). Although the overthrow of Sennacherib saved Jerus. from capture, and the religion of Israel from destruction, yet Judah sustained very heavy loss and had to pay an enormous tribute. The reign of Manasseh seems to have been externally prosperous, so far as this was possible after the exhaustion of Judah in the Assyr. war; but it was marked by fierce reaction against the reforms of Hezekiah and the prophetic policy as a whole, by religious syncretism, and by gloomy and superstitious fanaticism (21[1-18]). But Josiah instituted a reform on the basis of Deuteronomy, the people being prepared for it by their deliverance from the dreaded Scythian invasion. His happy reign was cut short by Pharaoh-necoh, whose invasion of Syria he had opposed, probably because it threatened the loss of the independence that the decrepitude of the Assyrian Empire gave him (2 K 22. 23). After a brief reign Jehoahaz was removed by Egypt (23[31ff.]), and Jehoiakim put in his place. He changed masters, Egypt for Babylon, but revolted (24[1]), and, in consequence of this, his son, who succeeded him, was taken captive to Babylon with the flower of the nation (24[14ff.]). His successor, Zedekiah, might have reigned in peace as the vassal of Babylon, but revolting, in defiance of Jeremiah's warning, he saw his capital besieged and captured (24[18ff.]). Jerus. and the temple were destroyed, and a large part of those who remained were taken into exile, where they remained for fifty years. So fell the kingdom of Judah, B.C. 586. Many of those who were still left went down into Egypt, in fear of vengeance for Gedaliah's murder (25[26]), and thus in Babylon and Egypt Jewish colonies were planted, which were destined to be of immeasurable importance.

As compared with the Northern kingdom, Judah was through most of its history of little account. When it held Edom in subjection its power was strengthened, yet even then the scornful fable, in which Joash set Judah against Israel as a thistle against a cedar, was not without justification. In other things than size and strength the advantage lay with Israel. Life was richer, fuller, and deeper, and that not only social but, what is more important yet less recognized, religious life. It was not in Judah but in Israel that the great prophets Elijah and Elisha did their work, the schools of the prophets flourished, and the earliest (?) history of the Hebrews was written. Amos, it is true, belonged to Judah, yet even he prophesied to Israel, and his junior contemporary, Hosea, was a Northern prophet. It was not till Israel went under that Judah attained its great significance. Yet Judah had advantages of its own. The prestige of the Davidic monarchy secured a permanence of dynasty that was of untold blessing, and saved it from the frequent revolutions and usurpations that tore Israel asunder. Further, while Judah was poorer in great religious teachers, its religion was probably simpler and less corrupt than that of Israel, though its superiority may be easily exaggerated. Its possession of the temple made for greater purity of worship. Yet it was rather the respite granted after the captivity of the Northern tribes, than any religious superiority of Judah, that left it the sole depositary of the higher religion of the prophets. This had not struck its roots deep enough into the life of Israel to survive the transplanting to Assyrian soil. But between 722 and 586, under the fostering care of Isaiah and his successors, it had grown strong enough not merely to survive, but to benefit from the shock, and thus Judah became especially the people of revelation.

On the character of the tribe little need be said. It was profoundly modified by its comparative isolation and the independence this conferred, and by the large foreign elements that it had absorbed. It was narrow and provincial, fanatical and tenacious. To slay the prophets and build monuments to them was characteristic of it, as of so many other peoples; for while it was slow to learn and hostile to new truth, yet the truth when learned was changed into hard dogma and erected as a barrier against fresh revelation. The obstinacy with which an old doctrine was insisted on, when no longer applicable, and new truth opposed for its inconsistency with the old, is shown in the opposition to Jeremiah's teaching that Jerus. would be captured and the temple destroyed, based on Isaiah's doctrine of the inviolability of Zion. Yet Judah had this qualification for its task,—it produced many who were fit vehicles of revelation; it was, in fact, surprisingly rich, especially in its later history, in religious genius, a lovely flower springing, indeed, from a dry and unattractive root.

In NT the tribe of Judah is mentioned in Lk 1[39] (?), He 7[14], Rev 7[5].

Literature.—The Histories of Israel and Judah, e.g. Ewald, Wellhausen, Kittel, Stade; Kuenen, Rel. of Israel, passim; Wellhausen, De Gentibus, etc. See also articles Genealogy, Israel, and the relevant literature cited under these.

2. Judah, an overseer at the rebuilding of the temple (Ezr 3[9]) = Hodaviah of 2[40] and Hodevah of Neh 7[43]. **3.** A Levite who had married a foreign wife (Ezr 10[23]), possibly the same as the Judah of Neh 12[8. 36]. **4.** An overseer of Jerus. (Neh 11[9]).

A. S. Peake.

JUDAH 'upon' (AV) or at (RV) Jordan' is named in Jos 19[34] in the statement of the boundaries of the tribe of Naphtali. The MT בִּיהוּדָה is unrepresented in the LXX, and Bennett (SBOT, ad loc.) remarks, 'The clause is apparently an unintelligible gloss which has crept into the text. The context implies that the tribe of Judah is referred to, and this is geographically impossible.' Ewald suggests (Gesch. ii. 380) that the passage is corrupt, and that 'Chinneroth,' or some other word, originally occupied the place of 'to Judah.' Conder (*PEFSt*, 1883, p. 183) suggests an interchange of ד and ר, and of ה and ח, so as to read הוֹרָה for הוֹרָה, when the passage would run וּבְחוֹרָה הַיַּרְדֵּן, the 'Hollow of (?) Jordan,' equivalent to the *Ghôr*, or valley of the Jordan. Thomson (*Land and Book*, i. p. 389) suggests that the tomb of Seîd Yehûda (supposed by Arabs to be son of Jacob) marks the 'Judah on Jordan, toward the sun-rising.' It is suggested in *Speaker's Comm.* that the Havvoth-jair were colonized by men of Judah, and might be called 'Judah upon Jordan.' Von Raumer (*Pal.* p. 405 ff.) had contended strongly for this identification of 'Judah' with Havvoth-jair; and Keil (*Bib. Comm.*) adopts the same theory, pointing out that, according to 1 Ch 2⁵·²¹, Jair on his father's side was descended from Judah through Hezron. It cannot be said that any of the last mentioned theories has the slightest probability. Dillm. (*ad loc.*) thinks Ewald's view is the best, but allows that it leaves the origin of the present text unexplained.

C. WARREN.

JUDAH (AV Juda), Lk 1³⁹.—See JUTAH.

JUDAISM.—See RELIGION.

JUDAS ('Ιούδας, *Judas*), the Greek equivalent of the Hebrew name יְהוּדָה JUDAH.

1. The third son of Mattathias, called Maccabæus (1 Mac 2⁴, Jos. *Ant.* XII. vi. 1). See MACCABEES.

2. The son of Chalphi, one of two captains (ἄρχοντες τῆς στρατιᾶς) who stood by Jonathan when the main part of his army had been scattered by an ambush at the beginning of a battle against the Syrians at Hazor (1 Mac 11⁷⁰, Jos. *Ant.* XIII. v. 7).

3. A Jew holding some important position at Jerusalem, who is named in the title of a letter sent from the Jews of Jerusalem and Judæa and the Jewish Senate to their brethren in Egypt and to a certain Aristobulus (2 Mac 1¹⁰). The latter, who is termed the teacher (διδάσκαλος) of king Ptolemy, is doubtless to be identified with a Peripatetic philosopher who lived at the court of Ptolemy VI. Philometor (B.C. 180–145); so Clem. Alex. *Strom.* v. xiv. 97; Euseb. *Præp. Ev.* viii. 9 *fin.* This Judas is often supposed to be Judas Maccabæus; so Grimm, Rawlinson, Zöckler. The purport of the letter (2 Mac 1¹⁰–2¹⁸), which is probably not genuine, is to invite the Egyptian Jews to keep the Feast of the Dedication. Like the preceding epistle (*ib.* 1¹⁻¹⁰ᵃ), it stands in no connexion with 2 Mac, and seems to have been prefixed to this book by a later hand. See Schürer, *HJP* II. iii. 213.

4. A son, probably the eldest, of Simon the Maccabee (1 Mac 16²). He, with his brother John Hyrcanus, took the command against the Syrian army under Cendebæus, and was wounded in the engagement (*ib.* 16¹⁻¹⁰, cf. Jos. *Ant.* XIII. vii. 3). In B.C. 135, he, with his father and another brother named Mattathias, was murdered at the little fortress of Dok by Ptolemy, the son of Abubus (*ib.* 16¹¹⁻¹⁷). According to the representation of Josephus, Judas was not murdered at the same time as his father, but made prisoner, and subsequently put to death, when Hyrcanus raised the siege of Dagon (? Dok); see Jos. *Ant.* XIII. viii. 1; *Wars*, I. ii. 3–4. 5. 1 Es 9²³=Judah of Ezr 10²³. 6. An ancestor of Jesus, Lk 3³⁰. 7. One of the brethren of the Lord, Mt 13⁵⁵, Mk 6³. See art. JUDE THE LORD'S BROTHER.

H. A. WHITE.

JUDAS BARSABBAS (AV Barsabas) is mentioned in Ac 15²²·²⁷·³²·³³ as one of the two prominent members of the Jerus. Church who were sent to Antioch with Barnabas and Saul, bearing the letter of the

apostles and elders to the Gentile Churches. The personal presence of these brethren was intended to give additional weight to the assurances of fellowship which the letter contained. Judas and Silas his companion are described as chief men among the brethren (ἡγουμένους: no doubt presbyters; see He 13⁷·¹⁷·²⁴). They were also prophets, *i.e.* men whom the Spirit inspired to communicate His truth and will to the Church. Judas, with Silas, remained in Antioch to strengthen the brethren there, and then returned to Jerusalem (v.³⁴ in AV is spurious). We hear no more of Judas Barsabbas. Barsabbas is a patronymic (see JOSEPH BARSABBAS). He may have been a brother of Joseph (Ac 1²³). He is not to be identified with Jude the author of the Epistle, because the latter's brother James (see JUDE) was either the son of Joseph, the foster-father of Jesus, or the son of Alphæus. Neither can he have been the Apostle Judas, 'not Iscariot,' both because he is in Acts clearly distinguished from the apostles, and because the Apostle Judas was 'the son of James' (Lk 6¹⁶ RV).

G. T. PURVES.

JUDAS OF DAMASCUS.—In Ac 9¹¹ Ananias is told to go to the street called 'Straight,' and seek in the house of Judas a man of the name of Saul, of Tarsus. Nothing further is known of Judas. Tradition has found a house for him in Damascus, not, however, in the street called Straight, but only a few paces out of it, in a lane to the right, as one goes from west to east.

A. C. HEADLAM.

JUDAS OF GALILEE, mentioned by Gamaliel (Ac 5³⁷) as the leader of a popular revolt 'in the days of the taxing' (RV 'enrolment'), which ended, however, in his destruction and the dispersion of his followers. The 'enrolment' was the one conducted by Quirinius (which see), when in A.D. 6 or 7 he was a second time (cf. Lk 2¹) made governor of Syria. It was intended to be a basis of Roman taxation, and excited fierce opposition among the Jews, which was quieted only by the influence of the high priest Joazar (Jos. *Ant.* XVIII. i. 1). Judas, however, with a certain Pharisee, Saddoc, called the people to defend their liberties, bidding them acknowledge no Lord but God. Josephus (*Ant.* XVIII. i. 1, 6, XX. v. 2; *BJ* II. viii. 1, xvii. 8, 9, VII. viii. 1), like Gamaliel, usually calls him a Galilæan, but in one passage (*Ant.* XVIII. i. 1) a Gaulonite from Gamala, which lay east of Galilee. It is not clear whether the insurrection broke out in Judæa and the title 'Galilæan' was given to Judas because Gaulonitis was loosely identified with Galilee, or whether it broke out in Galilee and thus the title 'Galilæan' was attached to him. That it was a considerable movement appears both from Gamaliel's notice of it and from the frequency with which Josephus refers to it. According to the latter, from it there arose 'the Zealots,' the most fanatical and patriotic of the Jewish sects, whose violence under Gessius Florus (A.D. 64–66) hastened the war with Rome. Josephus mentions them, after the Pharisees, Sadducees, and Essenes, as the fourth sect of the Jews, and as founded by Judas. He does not mention, however, the death of Judas, or the fate of his insurrection. Gamaliel agrees with Josephus in the date and in the strength assigned to the revolt; nor is there any sufficient reason to question his statement that the leader perished and his followers were dispersed.

Descendants of Judas were also conspicuous for their fanatical violence. Two of his sons, James and Simon, were crucified by Tiberius Alexander (A.D. 46?–48). Another son, Menahem, a leader of the 'Sicarii' in Jerus. shortly before the war with Rome, acquired for a time much power, but was finally slain by the high priest's party.

Still another descendant was Eleazar, who, after the fall of Jerus., defended the fortress of Masada, and persuaded his followers to die by their own hands rather than submit to Rome (*BJ* VII. viii. and ix.).

Schürer (*HJP* I. ii. 4, 80) identifies Judas with the person of the same name who, after the death of Herod the Great, raised an insurrection near Sepphoris in Galilee (Jos. *Ant.* XVII. x. 5 ; *BJ* II. iv. 1) ; but Josephus does not identify them, and the earlier Judas appears to have been simply a marauder.　　　　　　　　　　　G. T. PURVES.

JUDAS ISCARIOT.—This is his usual designation in the Synoptic Gospels : Ἰούδας Ἰσκαριώτης (Mt 26¹⁴), Ἰούδας ὁ Ἰσκαριώτης (Mt 10⁴), Ἰούδας ὁ καλούμενος Ἰσκαριώτης (Lk 22³), Ἰούδας Ἰσκαριώθ (Mk 3¹⁹ 14¹⁰, Lk 6¹⁶). St. John calls him ' the son of Simon ' (Σίμωνος), thrice giving the epithet 'Iscariot' to Judas (12⁴ 13² 14²²), and twice (according to the best texts) to Simon (6⁷¹ 13²⁶). All four stigmatize him as ὁ παραδοὺς αὐτόν (Mt 10⁴), or ὃς καὶ παρέδωκεν αὐτόν (Mk 3¹⁹), or ὃς ἐγένετο προδότης (Lk 6¹⁶), or ἔμελλεν παραδιδόναι αὐτόν (Jn 6⁷¹), when they mention him for the first time. At the actual time of the treachery they use ὁ παραδιδοὺς αὐτόν, ' who was betraying him ' (Mt 26²⁵·⁴⁶·⁴⁸, Mk 14⁴²·⁴⁴, Lk 22²¹, Jn 13¹¹ 18²·⁵). See Ac 1¹⁶.

Besides (1) his names, we are told (2) that he was called with the rest of the Twelve to be an apostle ; (3) that he was covetous and dishonest, and sold his Master to the hierarchy ; (4) that he effected the betrayal immediately after the Last Supper ; and (5) that on realizing the consequences of his act he destroyed himself.

Every one of these points has given rise to a large amount of discussion, and the real or apparent uncertainty thus produced has led some to the desperate expedient of rejecting the whole story as a myth. Judas is a Christian fiction to represent the treacherous Judaism which put Jesus to death ; and no one among the Twelve was really guilty of this enormity (Volkmar, Noack). Keim justly remarks that it is incredible that Christians should invent such a crime for an apostle. From Celsus onwards the foes of Christianity have made capital out of the sin of Judas (Orig. *c. Cels.* II. xii.) ; and to prove that he never committed it, would remove a weight from the heart of Christendom. The statements in the Gospels and Acts are inexplicable, however, if Judas, ' one of the Twelve,' never betrayed the Christ.

1. The name Ἰούδας is a common one, being the Gr. form of the Heb. name Judah. There are six persons before the time of Christ who bear this name, and six in the NT. But there is no confusion respecting the traitor. Discussion has been frequent merely as to *the meaning of* '*Iscariot,*' and this question is practically settled. All other explanations may be rejected in favour of the view that it means ' man of Karioth ' or ' Kerioth ' ; '*ish Keriyoth* becoming Ἰσκαριώτης, as '*ish Tob* becomes Ἴστοβος or Ἴστωβος (Jos. *Ant.* VII. vi. 1). This explains how both father and son have this name, Kerioth being the home of the family. This also explains the reading ἀπὸ καρυώτου which א* and some other authorities have in Jn 6⁷¹, and which D has in Jn 12⁴ 13²·²⁶ 14²². (See papers on 'Iscariot' by Nestle and Chase in *Expository Times*, December 1897, and January, February, and March 1898). Kerioth (LXX Καριώθ) in Judah (Jos 15²⁵) is commonly assumed to be the place referred to in 'Iscariot.' It is generally identified with the ruins *el-Ḳarjetein* south of Hebron. See KERIOTH-HEZRON. In any case Judas is of S. Palestine, while the other eleven were of Galilee ; and this may have been one cause of estrangement between him and the rest. Judæans had a tendency to look down on Galilæans.

The life of Judas previous to his call, like that of all the Twelve, is hidden from us ; and it is remarkable that the apocr. gospels make so little use of this attractive field of speculation. The *Arabic Gospel of the Infancy* makes the boy Judas a demoniac who *bites* (? the kiss), and the demon takes flight when Judas comes into contact with the boy Jesus (xxxv.) ; but this passage stands alone.

2. The Synoptists indicate that Judas was called with the remainder of the Twelve, and in all their lists his name stands last in the last group of four, while in Ac his place is vacant (Mt 10⁴, Mk 3¹⁹, Lk 6¹⁶, Ac 1¹³). Mt and Mk place him next to Simon the Cananæan, Lk next to the other Judas ; and it is possible that one of these was the traitor's companion when the Twelve were sent out two and two (Mk 6⁷). Like the others, he received power to cast out demons and heal diseases (Mt 10¹, Lk 9¹) ; and, like them, he seems to have been successful (Mk 6¹³, Lk 9⁶). Lange conjectures that the enthusiast who said, ' I will follow thee whithersoever thou goest ' (Lk 9⁵⁷), was Judas. But Mt calls this man ' a scribe ' (8¹⁹), and it is most improbable that he was one of the Twelve, who seem to have been chosen before this took place.

But it is in connexion with their election that the chief difficulty respecting Judas is found. *Why was such a man chosen to be an apostle ?* Unless we are prepared to throw aside the express statements of St. John, we cannot here have recourse to the limitation of Christ's knowledge. He tells us, not only that Jesus ' knew all men, and . . . himself knew what was in man ' (2²⁴), but that ' Jesus knew from the beginning . . . who it was that should betray him ' (6⁶⁴), and that a year before the Passion He said, ' Did not I choose you the Twelve, and one of you is a devil ?' (6⁷⁰) The parable of the Barren Fig-tree suggests that Christ wished to give Judas every opportunity of bearing good fruit. Or, He may have desired to prevent him from becoming even worse ; or, to lessen his powers of mischief ; or, to prove to all that no one is safe or constrained, and that even an apostle can rebel to the uttermost ; *electus enim a Christo suâ libertate et vitio corruit* (Toletus). Some maintain that Christ selected Judas *because* He knew that he would betray Him and thus fulfil the divine decrees. None of these suggestions removes the difficulty, which runs up into the insoluble problems of the origin of evil, and of divine omniscience combined with human free-will. See Westcott, Add. Note on Jn 13¹⁸.

3. We may assume that Judas had some good qualities which led to his admission to the apostolic body. Among these, practical ability and energy seem to have been found. Hence, when the company begins to have funds (Lk 8³), he is selected to administer them (Jn 13²⁹). This he did dishonestly (Jn 12⁴⁻⁶) ; and the same greed led him to betray his Master to the priests for thirty shekels (Mt 26¹⁵, Mk 14¹¹, Lk 22⁵). His pilfering from the money-box is the one thing to his discredit that is told us previous to his great crime, and the Synoptists are silent as to this preparatory course of sin. But, no doubt, he yielded to other forms of temptation ; and it has been much debated *whether covetousness was the sole or the chief cause of his treachery.*[*] It was certainly *a* cause. He sought the priests, not they him ; and his question is, ' What are ye willing to *give* me ?' But disappointed ambition probably helped. He looked, like the rest of the disciples, for an earthly kingdom with profits and honours, and he may have been the first to see that

---

[*] We must not argue that so small a sum as thirty shekels *could* not have induced him to commit such a crime. Matricide has been committed for a few shillings. Thirty shekels was the price of a slave (Ex 21³²)=about £4 according to the present value of silver, but in purchasing power perhaps double that amount. The power of avarice is almost limitless.

nothing of the kind was in store for him. Jesus had refused to be made a king (Jn 6[15]); and it was soon after this that the presence of a diabolical character among the Twelve was announced (6[70]). The triumphal entry into Jerusalem led to nothing; and then the compact with the hierarchy was made. Resentment probably contributed something, at any rate as the end drew near. During the last year Judas would feel that to some extent his conduct was suspected or known. Christ's strong warnings against avarice, and His denunciations of hypocrisy, would seem at times to be aimed at him, and no doubt were in part meant specially for him. Such passages as Mt 6[19-21] 13[22], Mk 10[25], Lk 16[11-13] acquire additional meaning when we remember that Judas was among the hearers. His hypocrisy after the pilfering began must have been conscious, and seems to have been successful; for to the last the other apostles did not suspect him (Jn 13[22. 28]). But Christ declared that hypocrisy is always exposed in the end (Lk 12[2]). It was 'to the disciples first of all,' and (we may believe) to Judas most of all, that He said, 'whatsoever ye have spoken in the ear in the inner chambers shall be proclaimed upon the housetops' (Lk 12[1. 3]). And who more than Judas needed the warning, 'Look whether the light that is in thee be not darkness'? (Lk 11[35]). His chagrin at the 'waste' of the ointment, and Christ's public rebuke of his hypocritical lament, seem to have been among the incidents which completed his determination to betray Christ. Constant contact with a goodness to which he would not yield had generated a fierce hate. See Swete on Mk 14[10].

Attempts have been made both to darken and to brighten what is told us of Judas. Was he a plotter from the first? May he not have sought admission to the inner circle of Christ's disciples in order to overthrow this revolutionary Teacher? But even St. John, whose horror of him is most clearly expressed, gives no hint of this; and, if it were true, it would be amazing that Judas should share in the general success of the Twelve as preachers and workers of miracles. On the other hand, may not his motive have been much less evil than is commonly supposed? Some would represent him as a brave man who believed that patriotism required him to deliver Jesus to the rulers. Others, with more plausibility, suggest that, like the Baptist, he may have been impatient at the slow progress of the Messiah; and he may have intended merely to precipitate a crisis. If the hierarchy were encouraged to arrest Jesus, His miraculous power would defeat them, the populace would declare for Him, and His triumph would be complete. The Passover was an opportunity which must not be allowed to pass. In arguing and acting thus, Judas was presumptuous and wrongheaded, but he was not a sordid traitor. This view also, which is advocated by De Quincey and Whately, has no support in Scripture, not even in the record of his remorse. If there was nothing worse than this, would Christ have denounced him as devilish, and called him a 'son of perdition'? And granting that διάβολος in Jn 6[70] is not much stronger than Σατανᾶ in Mt 16[23] and Mk 8[33], yet of no one but Judas did He say, 'Good were it for him if that man had not been born' (Mt 26[24]). After this it is hardly necessary to point out that both Luke and John regard Judas in the last stages of his career as becoming the abode of Satan (Lk 22[3], Jn 13[2. 27]), who then 'entered into him,' an expression which is unique in Scripture in this spiritual sense. With Keim we reject these hypotheses in defence of Judas as impossible and unworthy inventions which have nothing noble to excuse them.

The enormity of the sin of Judas consisted in its being against all bonds of discipleship and friendship; against light, against mercies, affection, trust, and warnings; against his own promises and preaching. And it was committed deliberately, not under sudden strain, like Peter's denials, but with skilful and persistent calculation. He was not surprised by a violent temptation, but he carefully sought an opportunity, which he used with unswerving pertinacity, in spite of the tenderness of the feet-washing, the solemnity of Christ's public condemnation of the traitor, and the proof given to him privately that Christ knew who the traitor was. The demonstrative kiss (κατεφίλησεν) has no parallel in history, and could hardly have been invented; all the less so, because the narrative tells us that by going forward to meet His captors, and declaring Himself to be the person whom they were seeking, Jesus rendered the signal unnecessary. But the sin of Judas is unique only in its opportunity and its form; in kind it may be repeated. It is possible to 'crucify the Son of God afresh' (He 6[6]), and therefore it is possible to betray Him afresh.

4. All the Gospels represent the traitor as effecting his purpose immediately after the Last Supper, at which he was present; but the point at which he left the upper room is much disputed. *Did he, or did he not, receive the eucharistic bread and wine?* The first two Gospels seem to imply that Judas received with the rest; but they are indefinite, for they do not mention his exit. St. John is equally indefinite; for he omits the institution of the Eucharist, and we do not know where it should be inserted. St. Luke places the words, 'But behold the hand of him that betrayeth me is with me on the table,' *after* the distribution of the eucharistic bread (22[19. 21]), and apparently after the eucharistic cup also, whether or not we accept as original the disputed words (19b. 20). It is possible to hold that Judas went out between the partaking of the eucharistic bread and that of the eucharistic cup (Westcott on Jn 13); but the view mentioned by Theophylact, that Judas partook of the cup, but concealed his portion of the bread to show to the hierarchy, need only be mentioned. The majority of patristic and mediæval commentators, with some Reformation writers, adopt the view taken in the Anglican Liturgy, that Judas partook of the Eucharist (see Bynæus, *de Morte Christi*, i. pp. 443–448, Amst. 1691; Cornelius a Lapide and Maldonatus on Mt 26[20]). The majority of modern commentators hold that he did not.

5. The perplexities respecting the career of Judas continue to the end. We have two accounts of his death in Scripture, and they differ both from one another and from a third which is obviously legendary. *Can we accept any as historical?* In Mt 27[3-10] we are told that Judas, on learning that Jesus was condemned to death, was stricken with remorse: *perfecto demum scelere magnitudo ejus intellecta est*, as Tacitus says of Nero's murder of his mother (*Ann.* XIV. x. 1). He took back the thirty shekels to his employers, saying, 'I have sinned in that I have betrayed innocent blood.' But they had no further interest in the vile instrument which they had used. 'What is that to us? See *thou* to it.' There are several remarkable words in what follows: καὶ ῥίψας τὰ ἀργύρια εἰς τὸν ναὸν ἀνεχώρησεν—he *hurled* the silver pieces into the *Holy Place* and *went into solitude*. Into the ναός the priests alone might go (Lk 1[9. 21], Mt 23[16] 27[40], Mk 14[58], Jn 2[19] etc.). It included both the Holy Place and the Holy of Holies (Mt 27[51], Mk 15[38], Lk 23[45]). It is never used like ἱερόν for the whole temple. Either this is a strange exception, or Judas in his desperation rushed into the sanctuary, or (most probably) he hurled the money from a distance. The use of ῥίπτειν εἰς and not βάλλειν ἐν points to this, but is not conclusive. Again, ἀνεχώρησεν means more than 'departed';

it is commonly used of those who shun company, retire from observation (Mt 2[14. 22] 4[12] 12[15] 14[13] 15[21], Mk 3[7], Jn 6[15], Ac 26[31]). So also in LXX (Ex 2[15], Jos 8[15], Jg 4[17] etc.). Yet it is putting a great deal of meaning into it to interpret, 'he lived as a solitary, became a hermit.' But, if this be adopted, then ἀπελθὼν ἀπήγξατο means, 'he left his place of retirement and hanged himself.'

It is from this point that we can compare Matthew's account with that put into the mouth of Peter in the Acts, and with the legend. Matthew seems to mean that Judas hung himself before his betrayed Master was hanged on the cross. He plainly states that Judas left the money, and that the priests, with characteristic scrupulosity about trifles after unscrupulous breach of the gravest commandments (cf. Jn 19[31]), would not put the polluted silver into the sacred treasury,* but bought with it the potter's field, to bury aliens in. This field was afterwards known as 'the field of blood,' because it was bought with blood-money. Thus a prophecy of Jeremiah (? Zechariah) was fulfilled.†

The narrative in the Acts (1[16-20]) is strangely different. Nothing is said about the priests or the restoration of the money. On the contrary, Judas himself is said to have 'procured a field with the reward of his iniquity.' There he fell headlong in such a way that 'his bowels gushed out'; and hence the field was called 'the field of blood.' Thus a prophecy of David (Ps 69[25] 109[8]) was fulfilled. It is *possible* to harmonize the two modes of death. Judas hung himself over a precipice, the rope broke, and he was dashed to pieces. The Vulgate of Ac 1[18] suggests this method : *suspensus crepuit medius.* But why should Matthew give only one half of the tragedy, and Luke only the other? And even so there still remain grave discrepancies between the two narratives. In the one Judas restores the money, in the other he keeps it ; in the one he procures the field, in the other the hierarchy do so ; in the one the name of the field comes from the blood-money, in the other from his bloody death. Moreover, in the one he plainly commits suicide, like Ahithophel (2 S 17[23]), in the other his death may be accidental. In the Middle Ages two different spots were pointed out, one as 'the potter's field,' and the other as *Akeldama* ; and the 'tree of Judas' is still shown.

It is better to recognize the fact that we have here two different traditions, of which that in the Gospel is nearer in time to the event, and probably nearer to the truth ; but even that may have been influenced by the desire to harmonize facts with a supposed prophecy. The tradition learned by St. Luke is later ; and popular fancy guessed at the meaning of 'the field of blood.' But it is an excess of scepticism to say that nothing is known about the end of Judas. We may safely affirm that he came to a violent end, probably by his own hand. And the story of the return of the money and of the priests' treatment of it has every appearance of truth. But it may be admitted that, in the absence of evidence, a horrible end would inevitably have been invented for Judas. We may compare the cases of Dositheus the heretic and his successor Simon Magus, both of whom are represented as perishing by a violent death, and, like Judas in the Acts, by a fall (*Clem. Hom.* II. xxiv.; *Apost. Const.* VI. ix.). The accounts of

the death of Arius exhibit a similar feeling (Socrates, *HE* I. xxxviii. ; Sozomen, II. xxx.).

This tendency is seen still more clearly in the legendary account of the end of Judas, preserved in a fragment from the fourth book of Papias (Theophylact on Ac 1[18], *Catena ad Acta S. App.*; Cramer, Oxford, 1838, p. 12 ; *Patr. Apostolic Opp.*, Gebh., Harn., Zahn, I. ii. app.; Suicer, *Thesaurus, s.v. ἀπάγχω*). This story is an amplification of ἐλάκησεν μέσος καὶ ἐξεχύθη πάντα τὰ σπλάγχνα αὐτοῦ (Ac 1[18]), with details which seem to be borrowed from the death of Antiochus (2 Mac 9[5ff.]). Papias had heard that Judas became so enlarged by inflammation that where a waggon could easily pass he could not ;—not even his head, which was so swollen that even the physician could not find his eyes. Worms and corruption proceeded from his body, and he suffered horrible torments until he died ἐν ἰδίῳ χωρίῳ. The spot was shunned by every one, and for years afterwards an offensive smell tainted the neighbourhood, intolerable to all who passed by. Another addition makes the narrative more harmonious with Ac 1[18], by stating that he was crushed by a waggon, ὥστε τὰ ἔγκατα αὐτοῦ ἐκκενωθῆναι (Oecumenius, *ad loc.*). But we can hardly say that the story without this detail shows that Papias knew the Acts. He knew a story which seems to have grown in part out of the narrative preserved in the Acts. But, in any case, here, as often, we are able to contrast the sobriety and probability of the Gospel narrative with the grotesque and revolting exaggerations in noncanonical sources.

It is not necessary to enlarge on the contrast between Peter and Judas in their fall and in their repentance. The one yielded to a sudden temptation, was at once touched by his Master's reproachful look of love, and returned to his Lord in affectionate confidence at the earliest opportunity. Judas deliberately sought and persisted in evil in defiance of all loving influences, and, in his dismay at the results of his act, tried to ease his conscience, without turning to Christ or to God for forgiveness. He thus ended, not in repentance, but in despair. See Euthymius Zigabenus on Mt 27[5].

But as early as Origen quite another view was taken of the suicide of Judas. He was hurrying to do in the other world what he failed to do in this. Knowing that Jesus would soon be in Hades, and that He was the source of salvation, he determined to be there before Him, and with bared soul to meet Him and implore His forgiveness (Origen, *Tract. in Matt.* xxxv., Migne, xiii. 1767. Suicer, *s.v. Ἰούδας*, quotes the same idea from Theophanes, *Hom.* xxvii. p. 202. See also Theophylact on Mt 27[5]).

The impious sect of the Cainites had a small composition which they called the *Gospel of Judas.* They regarded him as the true Gnostic, who with supreme insight accomplished the excellent work of overthrowing the power of the Demiurge by causing the death of Christ (Iren. I. xxxi. 1 ; Epiphan. *Hær.* I. xxxviii. 1 ; Theodoret, *Hær. Fab.* I. xv. ; Pseudo-Tert. *adv. omn. Hær.* ii.).

Representations of Judas are rare in ancient art. Kraus knows only three of the traitor's kiss. These are a sarcophagus at Verona (Maffei, *Verona illustr.* iii. 54), a sarcophagus of southern Gaul (Faillon, *Monum. de S. Madeleine,* i. 462), and a mosaic of the 6th cent. in S. Apollinare at Ravenna, of which Kraus gives a sketch. In Smith's *Dict. of Chr. Ant.* i. 891 is a drawing of Judas hanging from a tree. This is from the Syriac MS of Rabula, A.D. 586. Kraus gives another from an ivory in the British Museum, which is perhaps of the 5th cent. The crucifixion is part of the same picture, so that Judas hangs side by side with Christ (*Real-Enc. d. Christ. Alt.* ii. 74, 75).

---

* They were perhaps arguing by analogy from Dt 23[18]. The wages of sin could not be offered to God. But if Judas had sinned, how could they be guiltless?

† The difficulty about the prophecy is not solved by assuming that by a slip of memory St. Matthew has written 'Jeremiah' for 'Zechariah' (cf. 'Barachias' for 'Jehoiada,' 23[35]). Zec 11[12. 13] does not agree with the evangelist's quotation. Hebrew, LXX, and Matthew differ widely ; but there must be some connexion, and perhaps through a Targum.

LITERATURE.—Zandt, *Comment. de Juda proditore*, Lips. 1769 ; Daub, *Judas Ischarioth*, Heidelb. 1816 ; Neander, *Life of Christ*, § 264 ; S. J. Andrews, *Life of our Lord*, pp. 481-493, 524-529, ed. 1892 ; and the authorities quoted in Winer, *RWB* i. 635. For the mediæval legend, see D'Ancona, *La Leggenda di Vergogna e la leggenda di Giuda*, Bologna, 1869, and the other works cited in *Enc. Brit. s.v.*, esp. *Notes and Queries*, 2nd series, v. vi. vii. ; 3rd series, vii. ; 5th series, vi. Besides the Lives of Christ (Lange, Keim, Weiss, Edersheim, Farrar, etc.) reference may further be made to such recent studies as Bruce, *Training of the Twelve*, 371 ff. ; Fairbairn, *Studies in the Life of Christ*, 258 ff. ; Steinmeyer, *Passion and Resurrection History*, 80 ff. ; Stalker, *Trial and Death of Jesus Christ*, 110 ff. ; Boyd Carpenter, *Son of Man*, 61 ff. ; S. Cox, *Expositions*, i. 331 ff., 348 ff.

A. PLUMMER.

JUDAS ('Ιούδας), 'NOT ISCARIOT,' one of the twelve (Jn 14²²), who is also described as 'Judas of James' (Lk 6¹⁶, Ac 1¹³). His identification with the disciple who is also called **Lebbæus** (Mt 10³ AV) and **Thaddæus** (Mt 10³ RV, Mk 3¹⁸) is generally accepted, although it has been suggested that Judas really took the place of Thaddæus, who had died during the ministry of our Lord. He is not to be identified with Judas or Jude, the Lord's brother. Nothing whatever is known about him or his ultimate career, except the question recorded by St. John, who is careful to distinguish him from his namesake the traitor. See, further, JUDE, LEBBÆUS, THADDÆUS.   W. MUIR.

JUDE THE LORD'S BROTHER.—A Judas is named as one of the Lord's 'brethren' in Mt 13⁵⁵, Mk 6³. He has commonly been identified by tradition with the Apostle Judas, 'not Iscariot' (Jn 14²²). But the latter is described by St. Luke (6¹⁶, Ac 1¹³) as *the son* (AV has improperly *the brother*) of James. Those who deny that the 'brethren' included any apostles, of course reject this identification also, and regard Judas the brother of Jesus as the son of Joseph either by a former wife or by Mary (see BRETHREN OF THE LORD). Assuming the latter view, we know of Judas merely that he belonged to the Nazarene household, and, like the rest of his brethren (Jn 7⁵), did not believe in Christ till after the resurrection (Ac 1¹³). He was doubtless also the author of 'the Epistle of Jude,' styling himself in v.¹ 'a servant of Jesus Christ and brother of James' (*i.e.* James the Lord's brother, Gal 1¹⁹). This indicates that his spiritual relation to Jesus was felt to be more important than the fleshly one ; also that Jude was less known in the Churches than James was. In v.¹⁷ he apparently distinguishes himself from the apostles. The Ep. indicates that he was familiar with the OT and Jewish tradition, and specially indignant against those who introduced immorality under cover of the gospel.

The only mention of Jude in ecclesiastical history is the story related from Hegesippus by Eusebius (*HE* iii. 19, 20, 32), that Domitian, having commanded the descendants of David to be slain, certain heretics made accusation against the grandchildren of Jude,* 'said to have been the Lord's brother according to the flesh' ; but that, when they were brought to the emperor, he found them to be poor, hard-working men, who described Christ's kingdom as heavenly, and destined to appear at the end of the world ; so he dismissed them with contempt. The historian adds that they afterwards ruled the Churches, being both witnesses (*i.e.* for the faith) and relatives of the Lord ; and that they lived until the time of Trajan. Nicephorus Callisti (*c.* A.D. 1350, *Hist. Eccles.* i. 33) reports a tradition that Jude's wife was Mary the mother of James and Joses, and (*ib.* ii. 3) that his mother was Salome ; but the statements of Niceph. are inconsistent with respect to these relationships, and his testimony to them is of small value.   G. T. PURVES.

* That Jude was married may be inferred from 1 Co 9⁵. The names of his grandchildren are said to have been Zoker and James (Hegesip. *ap.* Phil. Sedet., *TU* v. 169).

JUDE, EPISTLE OF.—

1. TRANSMISSION OF THE TEXT.—The authorities are (1) MSS (*a*) Uncial : אABC ('primary' MSS, Hort, *Introduction*, p. 192) K₂L₂P₂ ; the relative character of all these MSS has been elaborately investigated by B. Weiss, *Die Kath. Briefe*, in 'Texte u. Untersuchungen,' viii. 3 ; (*b*) Cursive : the chief are 13 (=33 evv.), 40, 44 (=221 Scriv.), 137 : (2) Versions : (*a*) Latin : vg. (on Old Latin texts see below under 'Fathers') : (*b*) Syriac : Harklean ; the Syriac Vulgate (Peshiṭta) did not contain 2 P, 2 3 Jn, Jude ; in modern editions they are supplied after a text taken from a Bodleian MS printed by Pococke in 1630 : (*c*) Egyptian : Bohairic (Memphitic), Sahidic (Thebaic) : (*d*) Ethiopic : (*e*) Armenian : (3) Fathers : (*a*) Greek : the chief are Clem. Alex., Origen, Didymus (chiefly Latin trans.), Ephraem (not Syriac works), Cyril Alex., the commentators Œcumenius and Theophylact, the Fragments in Cramer, *Catena* : (*b*) Latin : Tertullian does not quote from, but refers to, Jude (*de Cult. Fem.* i. 3, 'Enoch apud Iudam apostolum testimonium possidet') : his words seem to imply that the Ep. was known to his readers, and therefore current in a Latin translation. There are important quotations in Lucifer of Calaris, *de non Conv. cum Hær.* xv. (p. 33 f. ed. Hartel)—vv.¹⁻³· ⁵⁻⁸· ¹¹⁻¹³· ¹⁷⁻¹⁹· ; in Priscillian, *Tract.* i. iii. v. (pp. 29, 32, 44, 64, ed. Schepss) — vv.¹²ᵗ· ¹⁴ᵗ· ²³ ; also in the Speculum commonly known by the symbol m (pp. 455, 647, ed. Weihrich)—vv.⁶· ⁷· ¹². These quotations supply relics of pre-Hieronymic texts. An examination of them shows (1) that Lucif. and m give substantially the same text in vv.⁶ᵗ· ¹², Lucif. being rather fuller and slightly nearer to the Greek ; (2) that Lucif. and Prisc. give different texts. Sabatier quotes also from Jerome, Augustine, Vigilius, and Fulgentius small fragments of Latin texts. The whole subject needs further investigation.

The text in several places seems uncertain, and 'primitive' errors are probable. On vv.¹· ⁵ see WH, *Introduction*, *Notes on Select Readings*, p. 106 f. In v.¹² (ούτοί είσιν οι . . . σπιλάδις συνευωχούμενοι), unless the writer himself after οι changed his construction, the οι appears to be an early insertion (see the two types of sentences in vv.¹⁶· ¹⁹). In v.²² *either* the first ιλιᾶτι is intrusive (cf. WH), *or* (in view of St. Jude's fondness for triplets) οὖς δὶ should be inserted before σόζιτι (so א). In the latter case the three clauses rise to a climax, and each has its characteristic idea—hopeful compassion, desperate effort, compassion paralyzed by fear of contamination.

2. RECEPTION IN THE CHURCH.—Little or no stress can be laid on supposed coincidences with this Ep. in sub-apostolic writings—*Ep. Barn.* 2¹⁰ (cf. 4⁹), Jude ³ᶠ· ; *Ep. Polyc.* iii. 2, iv. 2, Jude ³· ²⁰ ; *Mart. Polyc.* xx. (doxology), Jude ²⁴ᶠ·. The similarity, however, of *Didaché* ii. 7 (οὐ μισήσεις πάντα άνθρωπον, άλλά ούς μὲν ἐλέγξεις, περὶ δὲ ών προσεύξῃ, ούς δὲ ἀγαπήσεις κ.τ.λ.) to Jude ²²ᶠ· in thought and still more in form is too striking to be accidental (cf. iv. 1 ἡ κυριότης, Jude ⁸) ; it need not, however, imply direct borrowing, for on other grounds it seems likely that the two documents had their origin within the same circle of Christian thought, and it is conceivable that parts of the *Didaché* are *ultimately* the work of the author of the Epistle.

There is clear evidence that at the end of the 2nd and at the beginning of the 3rd cent. the Ep. was accepted as authoritative in three important Churches. (1) Alexandria. Clement quotes it as the work of Jude in *Pæd.* iii. 8 (p. 280, ed. Potter),

Strom. iii. 2 (p. 515) ; he cites words from it (v.²²ᶠ·) as a 'commandment' in *Strom.* vi. 8 (p. 773) ; his *Hypotyposes* contained 'short explanations' of this as of other Catholic Epistles (Eus. *HE* vi. 14. 1, Photius, *Biblioth.* 109 ; see at end of this art.). The witness of Clement is carried on by Origen. If in one place he hints at doubts about its reception (*in Matt.* tom. xvii. 30, εἰ δὲ καὶ τὴν Ἰούδα πρόσοιτό τις ἐπιστολήν), yet in another (*in Matt.* tom. x. 17), speaking of Jude as one of the Lord's brethren, he commends the Epistle as 'full of strong words of heavenly grace though it be but a few lines in length,' and he repeatedly quotes from or alludes to it (*in Joh.* tom. xiii. 37, *in Matt.* tom. xv. 27, *in Rom.* lib. iii. 6 [Scriptura sacra], *in Rom.* lib. v. 1 [J. Apostolus in epistola catholica], *in Ezek.* hom. iv. 1, *Ep. ad Alexandrinos*, xvii. p. 7 f. (ed. Lommatzsch), *de Princip.* iii. 2. 1 ; the passages marked * are extant only in a Latin translation). It was also commented on by Didymus (Migne, *Pat. Gr.* xxxix. 1811-1818). (2) Carthage. It was accepted by Tertullian (see above, under 'Text'). (3) Rome. It is included in the Muratorian Canon, not improbably the work of Hippolytus (Lightfoot, *Clement*, ii. p. 405 ff.).* The writer mentions certain writings which cannot be 'received into the Catholic Church : for gall may not be mixed with honey.' He then continues, 'Epistola sane iude et superscrictio iohannis duas in catholica habentur.' The context and the introduction of the sentence by *sane* ('to be sure') imply that doubts existed which he expressly puts aside (cf. Zahn, *Gesch. des NT Kanons*, II. i. p. 93). The evidence then justifies Zahn's verdict (*ib.* I. i. p. 321) that at the meeting-point of the 2nd and 3rd cent. the Epistle was accepted 'in the Catholic Church, the Church of all the countries round the Mediterranean,' a verdict with which Harnack (*NT um Jahr* 200, 79, 86) substantially agrees. On the other hand, the following facts must be noticed. (*a*) Though accepted by Tertullian, the Ep. does not appear to be quoted by Cyprian. Like He and Ja, it is omitted in the Canon Mommsenianus (an African list of the middle of the 4th cent.), unless we accept the somewhat precarious suggestion of Harnack (*Theol. Ltzg.* 1886, col. 173) that a reference to the Epp. of St. James and St. Jude is intended in the *una sola* which stands after the mention of the three Epp. of St. John and again after that of the two Epp. of St. Peter (see Zahn, *Gesch.* II. i. p. 155 n.; Sanday in *Studia Bibl. et Eccles.* iii. p. 243 ff.). It is not unlikely that after the time of Tertullian the Ep. fell out of use in the N. African Church. It should be added that it has no place among the Books contained in the Latin *Antiqua translatio* referred to by Cassiodorus (*de Instit. Div. Lit.* xiv.). (*b*) It was not included in the Syriac Vulgate (cf. Amphilochius, *Iambi ad Seleucum* (Migne, *Pat. Gr.* xxxvii. 1593)), nor is it quoted in the Homilies of Aphraat or in the Syriac works of Ephraem (cf. *Stud. Bibl. et Eccles.* iii. p. 138). None of the Catholic Epistles is mentioned in the *Doctrine of Addai* (ed. Phillips, p. 44) among the Books publicly read in the Syrian Church. (*c*) There is no evidence that it was accepted in the School of Antioch. The passage commonly quoted from the Letter of the bishops who condemned Paul of Samosata (τοῦ καὶ τὸν θεὸν τὸν ἑαυτοῦ [καὶ κύριον] ἀρνουμένου καὶ τὴν πίστιν, ἣν καὶ αὐτὸς πρότερον εἶχε, μὴ φυλάξαντος, Eus. *HE* vii. 30. 4) can hardly be considered as a decisive reference to Jude ³ᶠ·, especially if, according to the best MSS, the words in brackets are omitted. In later times the Ep. does not seem to be quoted in the voluminous works of Chrysostom or Theodoret, and the phrase used (τῶν

* The *de Consummatione Mundi*, in which (c. x.) Jude ¹⁸ is quoted, is not a genuine work of Hippolytus (see *Hippolyt's Kleinere Exeg. u. Hom. Schriften*, ed. Achelis, p. vii).

καθολικῶν ἐπιστολαὶ τρεῖς) in the *Synopsis* (Migne, *Pat. Gr.* lvi. 313 f.) which bears the name of the former appears to show that Jude, 2 P, 1 Jn, 2 Jn were known and deliberately excluded. Theodore of Mopsuestia (who made his view of the character of a Book a criterion of canonicity), according to Leontius of Byzantium (Migne, *Pat. Gr.* lxxxvi. 1365), rejected (ἀποκηρύττει) this Epistle, as also Ja, 2 P, 2 Jn, 3 Jn (see especially Kihn, *Theod. von Mops.* pp. 67, 75 f.). This is confirmed by the fact that Junilius (*Instit. regularia*, 6, 7), whom Kihn (p. 358 ff.) shows to represent Theodore's views as to the Canon, reckons these Epistles as *mediæ auctoritatis*.

We learn from Didymus, though his words in the Latin translation in which they reach us are somewhat obscure, that the Ep. was questioned by some on account of the strange reference to the dispute about Moses' body. We learn from Jerome (*de Vir. Illustr.* 4) that it was rejected by many ('a plerisque') because it quoted from the Book of Enoch. Eusebius (*HE* iii. 25, cf. ii. 23), reflecting the average opinion of his time, ranks it among 'the disputed Books, which yet are known and acknowledged by most.' The Ep. has a place in the list of Canonical Scriptures set forth by the Third Council of Carthage in A.D. 397. This Canon, supported by the authority of Jerome and Augustine, gained universal acceptance in the W. Church.

To sum up : considering the brevity of the Ep. and its special character, it had received, by the beginning of the 3rd cent., a remarkably wide acceptance in the Church. This early acceptance, representing the voice of tradition, supports its authenticity. From the beginning of the 3rd cent., when tradition was to some extent checked by criticism, and when (in view of the Gnostic controversies) all apocryphal writings were regarded with suspicion, the internal character of the Ep., its quotation from Enoch, and its reference to the *Assumptio Moysi*, tended to become a bar to its recognition as an authoritative document of the apostolic age. Even when the question of the NT Canon was virtually settled by the general opinion of the Church, such doubts and suspicions, based on internal evidence, found occasional expression.

3. VOCABULARY, STYLE, LITERARY INDEBTEDNESS.—In the *vocabulary* of Jude there are three elements. (*a*) There is the obvious Christian element. A Christian dialect has arisen. Certain words, *e.g.* κλητοί, σωτηρία, πίστις, have attained, largely through the teaching and the writings of St. Paul (see below), a fixed and recognized meaning among Greek-speaking Christians. (*b*) The writer is steeped in the language of the LXX. In this short Ep. occur several words and phrases derived from the LXX which are not used independently by other NT writers—ἐκπορνεύειν, ἐμπαίκτης (2 P), ἐνυπνιάζεσθαι, θαυμάζειν πρόσωπα, λαλεῖν ὑπέρογκα. Moreover, it should be noted that he uses words which do not occur in the canonical books, but are found in the Book of Wisdom, ἀΐδιος (Wis 7²⁶, cf. 4 Mac 10¹⁵ *var. lec.*), ἄλογα ζῷα (Wis 11¹⁵, cf. 4 Mac 14¹⁴· ¹⁸), σπιλοῦν (Wis 15⁴). Further, with Jude ⁶ᶠ· compare 3 Mac 2⁴ᶠ·. (*c*) He has at his command a large stock of stately, sonorous, sometimes poetical words, *e.g.* ἀποδιορίζειν (Aristot.), ἄπταιστος (Xen., adverb Plat.), ἐκχυθῆναι (Aristoph., Polyb.), ἐπαφρίζειν (Moschus), ζόφος (Hom., Hes., Pind., Polyb.), παρεισδύεσθαι (Hippocr., Plut., Philo), σπιλάδες (Hom., Anthol., Joseph.), συνευωχεῖσθαι (Aristot., Joseph., Lucian), φθινοπώρινος (Aristot., Polyb., Plut.). Moreover, such phrases as πᾶσαν σπουδὴν ποιεῖσθαι (Herod.), προκεῖσθαι δεῖγμα, δίκην ὑπέχειν (Herod., Soph., Eur.), κρίσιν ἐπιφέρειν, have a true Greek ring about them. It is interesting to note that more than once he adopts and presses into the service of Christian thought a recognized Greek phrase—ἡ κοινὴ σωτηρία ('the safety of the

state,' see Wetstein's note), οἱ προγεγραμμένοι ('the proscribed,' Polyb.).

The vocabulary then of the Ep. proves that the author, though a Jew, was yet a man of some culture and, as it would seem, not without acquaintance with Greek writers. Writers, however, of the 'common' dialect, embodying older strata of the language, would suffice to supply him with his vocabulary.

From vocabulary we turn to *style*. Here we mark an entire lack of flexibility. There is indeed in the Ep. a strong rhetorical element. But the writer is never carried away. There are no rugged, broken sentences (v.[16] is no exception to this statement) as in St. Paul's Epistles. We miss entirely the power of epigram which is so strong a weapon with St. James, and the oratorical persuasiveness of the Ep. to the Hebrews. The powerful effect of the Epistle is due entirely (on the literary side) to the writer's ability πυργῶσαι ῥήματα σεμνά. The richness of the writer's vocabulary stands in marked contrast to his poverty in ways of connecting and manipulating sentences. The general structure is characterized by a certain formality and stiffness. His fondness for triplets (vv.[2, 5-7, 8, 11, 12, 19, 22f, 25]) has often been noticed. The reiteration of οὗτοί εἰσιν (οἱ) at the beginning of sentences (vv.[12, 16, 19], cf. [8, 10, 14]) is especially marked.* As the Ep. draws towards its close, there is a twice-repeated contrast between the false and the true members of the Church; in either case over against a οὗτοι is set a ὑμεῖς δέ (vv.[16f, 19f.]), an arrangement unfortunately obscured in WH. Thus the writer's Greek is a strong and weighty weapon over which, however, he has not a ready command. The elaborate and balanced doxology (cf. also v.[4] καὶ μόνον . . . Χριστόν) recalls passages in the Epistle of the Roman Clement, and suggests that the writer's words took that liturgical form which was familiar to him in his ministrations in the Christian assembly. Indeed, the impression produced by the carefully-compacted arrangement of the whole Epistle is that in it we not improbably have a résumé of words spoken by an elder in the assembly which, often repeated and pondered over, gradually formed themselves into the elaborate denunciation and exhortation of this Epistle.

The *literary affinities* of the Ep. are important both for the light which they throw on its history and also for purposes of interpretation.

(i.) We have seen that the writer was familiar with the LXX. There are one or two indications, hardly perhaps decisive, that he was acquainted with the Hebrew OT. In v.[12] ἑαυτοὺς ποιμαίνοντες probably comes from Ezk 34[2] cf. [8], but it is closer to the Heb. (רֹעִים אוֹתָם) than to the LXX μὴ βόσκουσιν οἱ ποιμένες ἑαυτούς.† In v.[12] νεφέλαι ἄνυδροι ὑπὸ ἀνέμων παραφερόμεναι may be a reminiscence of Pr 25[14] (אַיִן וְגֶשֶׁם וְרוּחַ נְשִׂיאִים), but the LXX has no resemblance to Jude. In v.[22f.] it is not improbable that the two phrases ἐκ πυρὸς ἁρπάζοντες and τὸν ἀπὸ τῆς σαρκὸς ἐσπιλωμένον χιτῶνα are derived from Zec 3[2f.], from which passage the phrase ἐπιτιμήσαι σοι Κύριος (v.[9]) is clearly taken (perhaps through the medium of the *Assumptio Moysi*). But there are no points of contact between Jude and the LXX rendering. On the other hand, the Hebrew word (צֹאָה) used here, meaning 'filthy,' is connected with the words אָץֵ, וֹאָצ, both meaning 'excrements,' and thus Jude's phrase

alludes to the associations of the Hebrew word. The probability of these references taken together is greater than their probability when each is taken separately. So far as they go, they suggest that the writer of the Ep. was a Jew of Palestine.

(ii.) The discovery of the text of the Greek version of the Book of Enoch (1–32) among the Akhmîm fragments has supplied new and important material for the criticism of Jude. As this material does not appear as yet to have been fully utilized for this purpose, no apology is needed for the subjoined table giving coincidences of thought and language. On the quotation in v.[14f.] from Enoch (1[9]), see the art. on ENOCH IN THE NT.

JUDE.	ENOCH.
1f. τοῖς . . . τετηρημένοις κλητοῖς· ἔλεος ὑμῖν καὶ εἰρήνη καὶ ἀγάπη πληθυνθείη	1[8] μετὰ τῶν δικαίων τὴν εἰρήνην ποιήσει, καὶ ἐπὶ τοὺς ἐκλεκτοὺς ἔσται συντήρησις καὶ εἰρήνη καὶ ἐπ' αὐτοὺς γενήσεται ἔλεος. 5[6] ἔσται αὐτοῖς . . . πᾶν ἔλεος καὶ εἰρήνη.
4 οἱ πάλαι προγεγρ. εἰς τοῦτο τὸ κρίμα, ἀσεβεῖς, τὴν τοῦ θεοῦ ἡμῶν χάριτα μετατ. εἰς ἀσέλγειαν κ. τὸν μόνον δ. καὶ κ. ἡμῶν Ἰ. Χρ. ἀρνούμενοι.	67[10] 'The judgment will come upon them, because they believe in the lust of their body and have denied the Spirit of the Lord.' The reference to this denial is frequent; see Charles' note on 38[2]. The sin of impurity is constantly denounced in Enoch; on the sin of the angels see below. The words ἀσεβής, ἀσέβεια, ἀσεβεῖν are characteristic of Enoch. They occur 4 times in 1[9] (= Jude [14f.]). Cf. 5[6f.] 8[2] 10[20] 13[2] 22[13]. See below on v.[18].
5 εἰδότας ἅπαξ πάντα.	12[2] ἤκουσα παρ' αὐτῶν πάντα καὶ ἔγνων ἐγὼ θεωρῶν. 25[2] περὶ πάντων εἰδέναι θέλω. Cf. the *Book of the Secrets of Enoch* 40[1.2] 61[2] 'I know all things.' The fall of the angels through lust is one of the main subjects of Enoch; see 6 ff. 12[4] 15[3] 19[1] 69[4f.] 86[3f.] 106[14].
6 ἀγγέλους τε τοὺς μὴ τηρήσαντας τὴν ἑαυτῶν ἀρχὴν ἀλλὰ ἀπολιπόντας τὸ ἴδιον οἰκητήριον εἰς κρίσιν μεγάλης ἡμέρας δεσμοῖς ἀιδίοις ὑπὸ ζόφον τετήρηκεν.	Parallels to particular phrases: (1) 9[6f.] πάντα σὺ ὁρᾷς ἃ ἐποίησεν . . . Σεμιαζᾶς, ᾧ τὴν ἐξουσίαν ἔδωκας ἄρχειν τῶν σὺν αὐτῷ ἅμα ὄντων. (2) 12[4] ἀπολιπόντας τὸν οὐρανὸν τὸν ὑψηλόν. 15[3] διὰ τί ἀπελίπετε τὸν οὐρανὸν τὸν ὑψηλόν; (3) 15[7f.] ἐν τῷ οὐρανῷ ἡ κατοίκησις αὐτῶν . . . καὶ νῦν οἱ γίγαντες . . . ἐν τῇ γῇ ἡ κατοίκησις αὐτῶν ἔσται. 27[2] ὧδε ἔσται τὸ οἰκητήριον. Cf. 38[2]. (4) 10[4ff.] δῆσον τὸν Ἀζαὴλ ποσὶν καὶ χερσίν, καὶ βάλε αὐτὸν εἰς τὸ σκότος . . . καὶ ἐπικάλυψον αὐτῷ τὸ σκότος καὶ οἰκησάτω ἐκεῖ εἰς τοὺς αἰῶνας . . . καὶ ἐν τῇ ἡμέρᾳ τῆς μεγάλης (τῆς?) κρίσεως ἀπαχθήσεται εἰς τὸν ἐμπυρισμόν. 10[12] 16[1] μέχρις ἡμέρας τελειώσεως, τῆς κρίσεως τῆς μεγάλης. 19[1] μέχρι τῆς μεγάλης κρίσεως. 22[4.11] μέχρι τῆς μεγάλης ἡμέρας τῆς κρίσεως, 25[4] 27[4] 54[6] 84[4] 91[15] 94[9] 98[10].* (5) 10[13] εἰς τὸ δεσμωτήριον συνκλείσεως αἰῶνος. 12[6] δεηθήσονται εἰς τὸν αἰῶνα. 21[10] ὧδε συνσχεθήσονται μέχρι αἰώνων εἰς τὸν αἰῶνα. 22[11] ἐκεῖ δήσουσι μέχρις αἰῶνος. 54[3] 88[1] 103[8] 'Into darkness and chains (lit. net).' (6) 10[4f.] (see above (4)). 16[2] εἰς ζοφώδη τόπον. 62[10] 'Darkness will be piled upon their faces.' Cf. *Book of the Secrets of Enoch* 18[4] 'They [the rebellious angels] are kept in great darkness.'
6f. ὡς Σόδομα κ. Γόμορρα . . . πυρὸς αἰωνίου δίκην ὑπέχουσαι.	In 67[6] the country near the Dead Sea is connected with the punishment of the angels. 'That valley of the angels who had seduced mankind burned

* In apocalyptic literature this is a regular formula, often introducing an answer to the seer's question; see *e.g.* Zec 1[9f.], Rev 7[14] 11[4.14f.], *Enoch* 46[3], *Secrets of Enoch* 7[3] 18[3] 19[3], *Apoc. Peter* 4. 5. It is probable that Jude learned the use of the phrase from such writings, for which he clearly had a special liking.

† Symmachus has the same close rendering (οἱ ποιμαίνοντες ἑαυτούς) which St. Jude seems to have here.

* The phrase occurs in the *Book of Jubilees* 23, 'usque in diem iudicii magni.' Cf. *Book of the Secrets of Enoch* 18[6] 'They will be punished at the great day of the Lord'; 44[5] 48[9] 50[4] 52[15] 'In the day of the great judgment.'

JUDE.	ENOCH.
	continually under the earth there.'
7 πρόκεινται δεῖγμα	67¹² 'This judgment wherewith the angels are judged is a testimony for the kings,' etc.
9 ὁ ἀρχάγγελος.	20⁷ ἀρχαγγέλων ὀνόματα ἑπτά, *Secrets of Enoch* 19³ 20¹ 21³ 29⁴.
11 οὐαὶ αὐτοῖς, ὅτι τῇ ὁδῷ τοῦ Καὶν ἐπορεύθησαν.	In 22⁷ (cf. 85³f.) Cain is mentioned as the murderer of Abel. 94³ 'Walk not in the path of wickedness nor in the paths of death.' Then follows a long series of woes.
12f. νεφέλαι . . . δένδρα κύματα . . . ἀστέρες.	In 2-5 all things are represented as obeying the divine will οἱ φωστῆρες, τὰ δένδρα, ἡ θάλασσα καὶ οἱ ποταμοί. 80²ff. 'In the days of the sinners . . . their seed will be tardy on their lands and fields . . . the rain will be kept back . . . the fruits of the trees will be backward . . . many chiefs of the superior stars will err.'
13 ἀστέρες πλανῆται οἷς ὁ ζόφος τοῦ σκότους εἰς αἰῶνα τετήρηται.	18¹³ff. ἴδον ἑπτὰ ἀστέρας ὡς ὄρη μεγάλα καιόμενα . . . δεσμωτήριον τοῦτο ἐγένετο τοῖς ἄστροις. The punishment of the stars is referred to in 21³⁻⁶ 90²⁴.
18 κατὰ τὰς ἑαυτῶν ἐπιθυμίας πορευόμενοι τῶν ἀσεβειῶν.	13² περὶ πάντων τῶν ἔργων τῶν ἀσεβειῶν.
21 προσδεχόμενοι τὸ ἔλεος τοῦ κυρίου ἡμῶν Ἰ. Χρ.	1⁸ At the time of the judgment ἐπ' αὐτούς [τοὺς δικαίους] γενήσεται ἔλεος. 27⁴ ἐν ταῖς ἡμέραις τῆς κρίσεως αὐτῶν εὐλογήσουσιν ἐν ἐλέει, ὡς ἐμέρισεν αὐτούς.
24 στῆσαι κατενώπιον τῆς δόξης αὐτοῦ . . . ἐν ἀγαλλιάσει.	14²⁰ ἡ δόξα ἡ μεγάλη ἐκάθητο ἐπ' αὐτῶ. 27² περὶ τῆς δόξης αὐτοῦ σκληρὰ λαλήσουσιν (‖ κατὰ Κυρίου). 63⁵ 'Would that we had rest . . . to confess our faith before His glory.' 102³ 'All the angels . . . will seek to hide themselves from the presence of the Great Glory.' 104¹ 'The angels are mindful of you for good before the glory of the Great One : your names are written before the glory of the Great One.' 5⁹ τὰ ἔτη τῆς χαρᾶς αὐτῶν πληθυνθήσεται ἐν ἀγαλλιάσει.
25 δόξα μεγαλωσύνη κράτος καὶ ἐξουσία.	5⁴ κατὰ τῆς μεγαλοσύνης αὐτοῦ. 12³ εὐλογῶν τῷ κυρίῳ τῆς μεγαλοσύνης. 14¹⁶ ὅλος [ὁ οἶκος] διαφέρων ἐν δόξῃ καὶ ἐν τιμῇ καὶ ἐν μεγαλοσύνῃ, ὥστε μὴ δύνασθαί με ἐξειπεῖν ὑμῖν περὶ τῆς δόξης καὶ περὶ τῆς μεγαλοσύνης αὐτοῦ.

(iii.) There is every reason to believe the assertion of Clement, Origen, and other Patristic writers (see the passages conveniently collected together in Charles, *The Assumption of Moses*, p. 105 ff.), that the writer derived the legend referred to in v.⁹ from a document called *The Assumption of Moses*. This document was indeed, as Charles shows, part of a book whose true title was probably *The Testament of Moses*, a fragment of which is known to us in a Latin translation under the title of *The Assumption of Moses*; and this *Testament*, as Burkitt has shown (*Guardian*, June 1, 1898), is probably the epilogue of the *Book of Jubilees*, which claims to be the record of a revelation made to Moses on Sinai by the Angel of the Presence. In view of Jude's use of this Mosaic literature the number of allusions in so short an Epistle to matters connected with Moses is noteworthy : the deliverance and punishment of Israel (v.⁵), the murmuring (v.¹⁶, cf. 1 Co 10¹⁰), the episodes of Balaam and of Korah (v.¹¹).

Between the Latin fragment of the *Assumption* (cf. Charles, p. 62) and Jude there are coincidences in thought and (to some extent) in language. With Jude³ compare *Assump.* iv. 8, 'permanebunt in præposita fide sua.' With Jude¹² cf. *Assump.* vii. 4, 'qui erunt homines dolosi, sibi placentes,

ficti in omnibus suis et omni hora diei amantes convivia, devoratores, gulæ.' With Jude¹⁶ cf. *Assump.* vii. 9, 'et manus eorum et mentes immunda tractantes, et os eorum loquetur ingentia'; v. 5 'mirantes personas locupletum et accipientes munera.' With Jude²⁴ cf. *Assump.* i. 10, 'ut facias quemadmodum sine querellam sis Deo' [MS est ideo].

(iv.) There can be no doubt that the writer was acquainted with and influenced in language and thought by St. Paul's Epistles. In the salutation to τοῖς ἐν θεῷ πατρὶ ἠγαπημένοις we have parallels in 1 Th 1⁴ 2 Th 2¹³ ; the κλητοῖς here is precisely similar to the κλητοῖς of Ro 1⁷, 1 Co 1². In v.²⁰ the words ἐποικοδομοῦντες . . . πίστει recall Col 2⁷. To different points in the closing doxology (v.²⁴f.) we have a remarkable series of parallels in St. Paul—Ro 16²⁵ff. (τῷ δὲ δυναμένῳ ὑμᾶς στηρίξαι . . . μόνῳ σοφῷ θεῷ διὰ Ἰησοῦ Χριστοῦ), Eph 3²⁰, 1 Th 5²³, 2 Th 3³, 1 Co 1⁸, Eph 1⁴, Col 1²². Besides these verbal coincidences there is a close parallel to 1 Co 10¹⁻¹³ in the prominence given (vv.⁵. ¹¹. ¹⁶) to the deliverance and punishment of Israel regarded as a warning to the Christian body.

The investigation, then, under this head has shown that the writer was influenced in vocabulary, style, and thought by the OT (certainly by the LXX, probably also by the original Hebrew), by the Book of Enoch to a remarkable degree, by another apocryphal document embodying the history of Moses, and lastly by Epistles of St. Paul (including probably Col and Eph). His vocabulary, moreover, proves him to have had at least some acquaintance with the literature of the 'common' dialect, while at the same time his stiffness in the manipulation of sentences seems to stamp him as a man whose knowledge of Greek was acquired in later rather than in earlier life.

4. THE RELATION OF JUDE TO 2 PETER.—That there is a close literary connexion between the two Epistles is clear when the following passages are compared : Jude³ ‖ 2 P 1⁵. ¹⁵ ; ⁴ ‖ 2¹⁻³, ⁵ ‖ 1¹²f. 3¹ ; ⁶ ‖ 2⁴. ⁹ ; ⁷ ‖ 2⁶. ¹⁰, ⁸ ‖ 2¹¹f. ; ⁹ ‖ 2¹², ¹¹ ‖ 2¹⁵f. ; ¹²f. ‖ 2¹³. ¹⁷, ¹⁶ ‖ 2¹⁸ ; ¹⁷f. ‖ 3²f. The hypothesis that both writers borrowed from a third document, though it has found stray advocates, may be put aside at once, as being destitute of any shred of external evidence, and as having no support in the peculiar phenomena of the two Epistles. The direct question therefore remains—*which of the two writers is the borrower?*

The priority of 2 P has found within the last few years an intrepid and resourceful champion in F. Spitta (*Der Zweite Brief des Petrus u. der Br. des Judas*, 1885).[*] The considerations are of three kinds : (i.) The general alleged historical connexion. Spitta supposes that 2 P was written by St. Peter shortly before his death ; that according to his promise (1¹⁵) he made provision for his correspondents being reminded of his teaching ; and that St. Jude wrote his Ep. by way of carrying out St. Peter's undertaking. Accordingly, in Jude, Spitta finds direct references to 2 P. In v.⁵ πάντα, and in vv.⁴. ¹² the article (οἱ), refer respectively to facts and persons well known to St. Jude's readers through 2 P † (but on the phrase οὗτοί εἰσιν οἱ see above). Lastly, he holds that in Jude¹⁷f. there is a specific reference to 2 P 3³. In regard to this last, the crucial, point, it is incredible that St. Jude,

* Spitta (*Zur Geschichte u. Litteratur des Urchristentums*, ii. pp. 409–411 (1896)) has lately reaffirmed his position as to the relation of Jude and 2 P, and supported it by a fresh argument. He holds that the *Shepherd of Hermas* is a Christian recension of an older Jewish work. Of that Jewish work Jude and 2 P contain reminiscences. But he urges that investigation shows that the echoes of it in Jude must be derived through the medium of 2 P. On Zahn's position see footnote to *Literature*.

† In v.¹⁹ there is a similar article, but no reference to 2 P can be made out. Spitta therefore supposes that the allusion is to St. Paul's Epistles.

writing with the special purpose of reminding his readers of St. Peter's Epistle, should smother his reference to the words of that Epistle in an appeal to the habitual oral teaching (ἔλεγον) of the apostles generally (τῶν ἀποστόλων), and that he should omit the chief count of his master's indictment.

(ii.) Connexion of thought. It must suffice to apply this test to two pairs of passages :—

(a) In 2 P 2[11] (ὅπου ἄγγελοι κ.τ.λ.) we have an example of forbearance answering to that adduced in Jude[9] from the *Assumptio*. It has often been pointed out that the reference in 2 P is so general that it has no meaning until it is interpreted in the light of Jude. Spitta, however, maintains that Jude has mistaken the allusion in 2 P. Adopting the reading παρὰ Κυρίου, he supposes that 2 P refers to Enoch (10[4ff.] 124 13[1]), where God is described as sending Raphael to the fallen angel Azazel, and Raphael and his fellows as executing the commission by sending Enoch to Azazel with a message of judgment. The objections to this ingenious suggestion are many, and, it seems, insuperable. It necessitates the adoption of the inferior reading παρὰ Κυρίου.[*] Again, the allusion could not have been surmised by the original readers of 2 P. Its discovery was reserved for a scholar, who, studying 2 P with Jude, had Enoch brought prominently before him. Again, no stress is laid in Enoch on the message being sent through the patriarch ; and indeed there is something grotesque in finding an example of forbearance in the angels sending a man to do what, *ex hypothesi*, they shrank from doing themselves. Lastly, a message of judgment from God could not be described as βλάσφημος κρίσις. The passages, therefore, remain decisive witnesses against the priority of 2 P. (b) An argument of a different kind is supplied by Jude[10] ‖ 2 P 2[12]. The verse in Jude fits into the context (see v.[8]), and is itself well compacted, the μὲν . . . δὲ marking a simple and forcible contrast (cf. v.[8]). The phrase φυσικῶς ἐπίστασθαι is a very natural phrase,[†] and the word φυσικῶς is necessary to limit the kind of knowledge. The clause ὡς τὰ ἄλογα ζῷα (note art.) stands after φυσικῶς, which it further defines. Lastly, φθείρονται answers to μιαίνουσιν in v.[8], just as βλασφημοῦσιν of v.[10] to βλασφημοῦσιν in v.[8]. The Petrine verse, on the other hand, is but loosely connected with the previous context ; there is something artificial in the *paronomasia* φθορᾶν, φθορᾷ, φθαρήσονται (cf. 1[4] 2[19]), and the use of the adjective φυσικὰ is, to say the least, strange. All the expressions in Jude (except ὅσα . . . ἐπίστανται) have something corresponding to them in 2 P, and it is almost impossible to conceive that the ill-compacted and artificial sentence of the latter should have been the original of the terse, orderly, and natural sentence of the former. The investigation of other parallels would lead to the same conclusion ; see especially Jude[13] ‖ 2 P 2[17], the phrase οἷς ὁ ζόφος, κ.τ.λ. in Jude referring to the stars, and being a reminiscence (see above) of passages in Enoch.

(iii.) Vocabulary and style. (a) Positive arguments. The verdict must be arrived at not by drawing up statistics as to words, but by estimating the naturalness of the use of words and phrases in the parallel passages.

In 2 P we find elaborated expressions, containing sometimes favourite words of the author, corresponding to forcible, simple expressions, sometimes echoes of Enoch, in Jude. Thus, for example, εἰδότας ἅπαξ πάντα (cf. Enoch), Jude 5‖ καίπερ εἰδότας κ. ἐστηριγμένους (cf. 3[17] 2[14] 3[16]) ἐν τῇ παρούσῃ (1[9]) ἀληθείᾳ (2[2]), 2 P 1[12]; ὑπὸ ζόφου (cf. Enoch), v.6‖ σειροὶς ζόφου, 2[4]; ἐν ταῖς ἀγάπαις ὑμῶν σπιλάδες (the meaning ' hidden rocks ' being certified by the fact that it is followed by a series of images from the natural world), v.12‖ σπίλοι καὶ μῶμοι (cf. 3[14]) ἐντρυφῶντες (cf. τὴν . . . τρυφήν, just above) ἐν ταῖς ἀπάταις αὐτῶν (the addition of αὐτῶν confirming ἀπάταις as against the reading ἀγάπαις), 2[13].

(b) Negative arguments. It must be remembered that, on the hypothesis of the priority of 2 P, Jude had the whole of 2 P before him. St. Jude wrote, according to Spitta's theory, to St. Peter's correspondents to remind them of the apostle's teaching in his letter. It is strange, therefore, that he does not refer explicitly to St. Peter or to his letter, especially as St. Peter had in that letter referred explicitly to St. Paul's letters ; strange that, since he must have regarded the whole letter with peculiar reverence, there are large tracts of it which had no influence at all over him ; equally

strange that he does not in any way catch the strongly marked literary style of his master ; and further, that words which would fix themselves in the mind of an attentive student of 2 P are not found in his letter.

These words are such as the following :—ἄθεσμος, 2[7] 3[17]; ἀποφεύγειν, 14 2[18.20]; ἀστήρικτος, 2[14] 3[16] (cf. στηρίξαι, 1[12]; -γμός, 3[17]; διό, 1[10.12] 3[14]; εἰ γάρ, 24.[20]; ἐντολή, 2[21] 3[2]; ἐπάγγελμα, 1[4] 3[13] (ἐπαγγέλλεσθαι, 2[19]); ἐπάγειν, 2[1.5]; ἐπίγνωσις, 1[2.3.8] 2[20] (verb 2[21] bis); γνῶσις, 1[5f.] 3[18]); ἐπιχορηγεῖν, 1[5.11]; εὐσεβής, 2[9], -σέβεια, 1[3.6.7] 3[11]; ἡγεῖσθαι, 1[13] 2[13] 3[9.15]; ἥττᾶσθαι, 2[19f.]; ὑπάρχειν, 1[8] 2[19] 3[11]; οὐ φείδεσθαι, 2[4f.].

To sum up : If Jude wrote first, then the author of 2 P, with the Ep. of Jude in his mind rather than actually before him, altered the sequence of its imperfectly remembered thoughts and expressions, elaborated and, with the aid of a phraseology peculiarly his own, made variations on phrases which clung to his memory. If, on the other hand, Jude wrote with the express purpose of recalling his master's letter to his readers, we must yet suppose that with rare skill he eliminated harsh and tortuous phrases, brought together scattered ideas, infused reminiscences of Enoch, and wrought the whole into natural compact and harmonious paragraphs. It is not too much to say that to have composed under such conditions a letter so forcible, so clearly and neatly expressed, and so bound together by interdependence of thought and phrase as is St. Jude's Epistle, would have been little short of a miracle of literary skill. These various lines of argument converge and, so far as demonstration is possible in literary questions, demonstrate the priority of Jude.

5. DATE OF COMPOSITION AND AUTHORSHIP.— A convenient statement of the dates assigned to the Ep. by German critics is given in Holtzmann, *Einleitung*, p. 329. The older critics of the Tübingen school, regarding the letter as a forgery of the Judaists against the Paulinists, placed it late in the 2nd cent. More recent critics place it about the middle or in the first half of the 2nd cent. Thus Pfleiderer (*Urchristenthum*, p. 835 ff.) holds that it was written against the Carpocratians of Alexandria, and therefore not before A.D. 150. Jülicher (*Einleit.* p. 147) gives the limits as 180 and 100, and urges that, since the writer's tone of wonder and anger implies that he is dealing with a new form of error, it must not be placed very late in this period. With this verdict Harnack (*Die Chronologie*, p. 466) substantially agrees.

The *superior* limit is fixed by the evidence as to the reception of the Epistle ; the *inferior* by internal evidence. The latter turns on the following points : (1) the way in which ' the faith' is spoken of as a formulated deposit (vv.[3.20]) ; (2) the language as to the apostles (v.[17])—the apostolic period is long passed ; (3) the use of Apocryphal writings ; (4) the existence of Gnosticism, either that of the Carpocratians or, as Harnack thinks, such as Epiphanius under various names describes as infesting Syria and Palestine, and which (apparently at a later time) found expression in the Coptic Gnostic literature edited by Schmidt (' Texte u. Untersuch.' viii. 1, 2).

These points must be briefly examined. (1) The use of πίστις in Gal 1[23] 3[23] 6[10], Ro 10[8], Eph 4[5], Ph 1[27], closely approximates to that of our Ep., while the thought does not go beyond that of Gal 1[6], Ro 6[17]. (2) The language of v.[17] implies that the recipients of the Ep. had been wont to receive *oral* instruction (ἔλεγον) from the *general body* of the apostles (τῶν ἀποστ.), and that this period of intercourse was now over. It may well be that some of the apostles had been removed by death, but the requirements of the language are satisfied if we suppose that the apostles were now scattered. (3) The argument from the use of Apocryphal books is serious only when it is vaguely put, as by

---

[*] The authorities are : (1) παρὰ Κυρίῳ ℵBC K₂ L₂ P₂ curs[pl] cat Thphl Oec ; (2) παρὰ Κυρίου curs[8] m tol syr-harcl cum-ar[polyg] ; (3) om. A 13 40 137 curs[al pl] boh (=me) vg-lat syrr-bodl-harcl (text) aeth aer[p].

Spitta (p. 166) among the authorities for (2) gives ' syr[p] syr[c.]' He has mistaken Tischendorf's ' syr[p c.]*' and has evolved a new Syriac version.

[†] Cf. Xen. *Cyrop.* ii. 3. 9 (inaccurately quoted by Wetstein *in loc.*), μάχη, ἣν ἐγὼ ὁρῶ πάντας ἀνθρώπους φύσει ἐπισταμένους, ὥσπερ γε καὶ τἄλλα ζῷα κ.τ.λ.

McGiffert (*Hist. of Christianity in the Apost. Age*, p. 587), 'He makes use of two late apocryphal works.' As a matter of fact, Enoch is assigned by almost all scholars to a date B.C. (Schürer, *HJP* II. iii. p. 59 ff.). The *Assumption of Moses* was probably written within the first 30 years of our era (Charles, § 11 ; Schürer, *ib.* p. 78 f., with Ewald and others, places it within the first decade after Herod's death). (4) The Gnostic character of the persons attacked in the Ep. is deduced from three passages.

(a) In v.⁴ᵇ the words τὸν μόνον δεσπότην κ. κύριον ἡμῶν 'Ι. Χρ. ἀρνούμενοι are supposed to point to a denial of God as the Creator and Governor of the world, and to a docetic view of Christ's Person. The common article, however, together with ἡμῶν placed after κύριον, proves that Christ alone is meant—a conclusion confirmed by τοῦ θεοῦ ἡμῶν in v.⁴ᵇ. The combination δέσποτα κύρει occurs several times in the LXX (*e.g.* Gn 15². ⁸; cf. Is 12⁴). The denial is a denial in life (cf. Tit 1¹⁶) of Christ's sovereignty (1 Co 6²⁰, Ro 16¹⁸, Ph 3¹⁸). (b) The ἐνυπνιαζόμενοι of v.⁸ is thought to point to visions as the source of Gnostic speculations. The word, however, in itself connotes nothing more than the wilfulness and falseness of their principles of conduct (cf. frag. in Cramer and Bengel, *in loc.*). (c) In v.¹⁹ it is urged that Jude retorts upon Gnostic teachers their own language of disparagement; *they* are the ψυχικοί. But this is to force an elaborate meaning into simple words. A phrase in v.¹⁶ (θαυμάζοντες πρόσωπα ὠφελίας χάριν) shows that the 'distinctions' they made were largely social (cf. Ja 21ᶠᶠ., 1 Co 11¹⁸. ²²). The οἱ ἀποδιορίζοντες (which Jude interprets by his antithetical ἐποικοδομοῦντες ἑαυτούς) is equivalent to St. Paul's οἱ τὰς διχοστασίας . . . ποιοῦντες in Ro 16¹⁷ (see above). The best commentary on our passage is 1 Co 31⁻³, Gal 5¹⁹ᶠ.

The arguments therefore for assigning the Ep. to the 2nd cent. break down on examination.

Other critics place the Ep. in the latter half of the 1st cent. To this class belong most English scholars (Plumptre, Lumby, Salmon, Plummer), and among recent German writers Spitta (who places Jude shortly after St. Peter's death), von Soden (who, holding that there is nothing to show that the Ep. was not written by a younger brother of the Lord, gives 80–90 as an approximate date), Kühl (who places it 65–80).

We are brought therefore to the problem of *authorship*. The Ep. begins with the words 'Ιούδας 'Ιησοῦ Χριστοῦ δοῦλος, ἀδελφὸς δὲ 'Ιακώβου. Those who place the Ep. in the 2nd cent. either suppose that it is pseudepigraphic (so Pfleiderer, who suggests that some local traditions influenced the writer to take the name of 'Jude the brother of James'), or hold that it was written by someone bearing the name Jude,* and that (to quote Harnack's view) possibly the words 'Ιησοῦ Χρ. δοῦλος, and certainly the words ἀδελφὸς δὲ 'Ιακώβου, were added at a later time (*i.e.* 150–180) to enhance its value as a weapon against Gnosticism. If it is objected that such an interpolator would have made Jude to be the apostle, Jülicher suggests that ἀδελφὸς 'Ιακώβου is a 'synonym for the title of bishop.' Those who find in the Ep. itself no evidence to show that it could not have been written in the apostolic age need not criticise these speculations. The simplest interpretation of the salutation, which identifies the writer—not with the apostle (cf. Wordsworth), nor with Judas Barsabbas (cf. J. Lightfoot, Plumptre), but—with the brother of the Lord (Mt 13⁵⁵, Mk 6³), is the best.† It appears that the Lord's kindred had a position of authority accorded them, especially among Palestinian Christians (Eus. *HE* iii. 11. 20, 33. 6, iv. 22. 4). At a much earlier date St. Paul, writing to a Gentile Church, appeals to the case of

* Grotius, *Annotationes* (on Jude 1), gives it as his opinion that 2 P was the work of Symeon the successor of James, and that our Epistle was written by Jude, the last Jewish Bp. of Jerusalem in the reign of Hadrian (Eus. *HE* iv. 5. 3 ; Epiph. *Hær.* ii. 66. 20).

† This conclusion is confirmed by the fact that Jude uses the *Assumption of Moses*. We know that his brother James the Just had much in common with what was highest in the teaching and practice of the Pharisees. To such men the *Assumption*, the work probably of a Pharisaic Quietist (Charles, *Introd.* § 10), would naturally appeal.

'the brethren of the Lord' as having a decisive bearing on the question of his own rights (1 Co 9⁵). The name of James was influential in distant Churches (Gal 2¹², Ja 1¹). There is then every reason to believe that the words ἀδελφὸς 'Ιακώβου would win a hearing for the writer, whether St. James were living or dead, especially in churches which were in constant communication with the church at Jerusalem. That Palestinian Jews, especially those who, like St. James and St. Jude, had been brought into constant communication with Jews of the Dispersion, would be likely to have a command of Greek has been shown by Mayor, *St. James*, p. xli f., Zahn, *Einleitung in das NT*, § 2 (see especially p. 31 f.).

The limits of date are now greatly narrowed. The *superior* limit is the death of St. Jude. The language of Hegesippus (*ap.* Eus. *HE* iii. 20) shows that the interview of Domitian with St. Jude's grandsons can hardly be placed late in that Emperor's reign (μέχρι Τραιανοῦ περιμεῖναι αὐτοὺς τῷ βίῳ), and that St. Jude had been dead some time before it took place (ἔτι δὲ περιῆσαν). Hence we cannot place the letter later than 80. As to the *inferior* limit, we must allow time (a) for the apostolic college to have been broken up by the separation of its members, and probably by the death of some ; (b) for such Pauline phraseology as we find in 1 Co, Ro, Col, Eph to have become known to a Hebrew Christian probably of Jerusalem, partly perhaps through personal intercourse (Ac 15. 18²² 21¹⁵ᶠᶠ.), certainly (as the kind of evidence shows) through a study of those Epistles. We cannot then place the Ep. earlier than the composition of Col and Eph. The general tone of the Ep. harmonizes best with a date somewhat late in the apostolic age. We shall not be far wrong if we suppose that it was written within a year or two of the Pastoral Epistles (assuming their genuineness), the Apocalypse (assuming the earlier date), the First Epistle of St. Peter, and the Ep. to the Hebrews.

6. PLACE OF WRITING, DESTINATION, CIRCUMSTANCES OF COMPOSITION. — Many critics, who regard the Ep. as directed against a developed Gnosticism, hold it probable that it was written in Egypt (*e.g.* Jülicher), or even more definitely in Alexandria (Mayerhoff's conjecture, adopted by, *e.g.*, Schenkel, Holtzmann, Pfleiderer). We have already considered the ground for this conjecture. The 'brethren of the Lord' would naturally have a prominent place among 'the elders' closely connected with St. James at Jerusalem. There is no reason to doubt that the Ep. was composed either there or at least in Palestine.

As to its *destination*, the salutation is quite general. From this fact some critics have deduced the conclusion that the Ep. is a circular letter (so Ewald), others that the letter-form is purely artificial (so Jülicher, Deissmann, *Bibelstudien*, p. 244). But although the destination is not named in the salutation, the situation with which the letter deals is too concrete to be universally applicable.

A brief examination of the evidence which the letter supplies as to the condition of its intended readers will furnish a clue—probable, not certain—to their identification. (1) The doctrine of God's grace had been taught among them (v.⁴). They were probably, therefore, men among whom St. Paul had worked. (2) They had received oral instruction from the apostles generally (v.¹⁷). They probably, therefore, lived at no great distance from Jerusalem. (3) They were in danger of being leavened by certain false brethren, against whom the Ep. is designed to warn them. What was the character of these false brethren ? (a) There is nothing in the Ep. to lead to the supposition that they were teachers, or that their error was doctrinal ; (β) they were grossly immoral in life,

vv.[4. 8. 10f.] (Βαλαάμ) [13. 23]; (γ) they were essentially
ἀσεβεῖς,—wholly destitute of godly fear,—and in
particular they profaned the ἀγάπαι (v.[12]) and the
associated Eucharist by their reckless participation
(συνευωχ. ἀφόβως; cf. 1 Co 11[27ff.]) and their selfish
greed (ἑαυτοὺς ποιμαίνοντες; cf. 1 Co 11[20ff.]); (δ) in
word and deed they were insubordinate against
divinely constituted authority,* vv.[8. 10. 11] (Κορέ) [16]
(γογγυσταί); (ε) they fomented schisms, v.[19]; (ζ)
they practically perverted the doctrine of grace, v.[4]
(cf. Gal 5[13], Ro 6[1. 15]).

All these points (except the last) have parallels in
St. Paul's picture of the Corinthian Church. The
same dangers from pagan associations and surroundings are emphasized also in Ac 15[20. 28], 1 Th
4[1-8], Ro 16[17ff.], Ph 3[2. 17ff.], Eph 4[17ff.], Rev 2[14. 20] 3[4],
and again in the *Didaché* (iii. 3, 6). The men,
therefore, against whom St. Jude warns his readers
appear to have brought the vices and the unchastened selfishness of paganism within the Christian
body. The Church, accordingly, to which the letter
is addressed was, it would seem, predominantly a
Gentile Church. This is confirmed by an incidental phrase, which yet has a conspicuous place in the
Ep.—περὶ τῆς κοινῆς ἡμῶν σωτηρίας (v.[3]). Jude writes
as a Hebrew Christian to Gentile Christians. The
Church which best fulfils these conditions is *the
Church in the Syrian Antioch* (cf. Beyschlag, *Neutest. Theol.* ii. p. 484), where St. Paul taught early
and late in his missionary career, a Church in
constant communication with the Church at Jerusalem (*e.g.* Ac 15[1], Gal 2[12]), visited, as we learn
incidentally, by one of the older apostles (Gal 2[11]),
and exposed to the same dangers from heathenism
as the Church at Corinth. It is of course quite
possible that the Ep., with its general salutation,
was intended to be circulated among a group of
Churches connected with Antioch (cf. Ac 15[23]).

It is not hard to conjecture the *circumstances
under which the letter*, such being its scope and
such its probable destination, *was written*. We
may suppose that members of the Church of Antioch came to Jerusalem with news that the leaven
of heathen lawlessness was spreading there. St.
Jude, one of the original 'elders' of the mother
Church, and therefore now (especially if St. James
was dead) in a position of peculiar authority, feels
the gravity of the occasion, the danger attending a perversion of St. Paul's doctrine of grace,
as St. James had realized that involved in the
perversion of the true doctrine of faith. The
messengers are returning. St. Jude would gladly
have sent by them a letter dealing with the blessings of salvation common to Hebrew and Gentile
Christians alike. The crisis, however, of which he
has heard forces him to narrow his subject to an
earnest appeal that, in the present accentuation of
the perils which were inseparable from the position
of a Gentile Church, they would preserve the purity
of the faith in matters of life and conduct.

7. SUMMARY OF THE EPISTLE.—A necessarily
brief paraphrase will bring out the connexion of
thought.

The salutation of Jude (v.[1f.]). The treacherous
entrance into your Church of certain depravers of
God's grace in Christ and practical deniers of Jesus
as Lord, force me to make my letter a simple call
to you to contend for the one faith (v.[3f.]). I need
only remind you of the ancient examples of the
danger of faithlessness and fleshly sin—Israel (the
primary type of the Christian society), the angels
who fell, and (like these last in sin and punishment) the Cities of the Plain (vv.[5-7]). Despite

such examples, these men, ever yielding to their
own wayward fancies, are guilty both of fleshly
sin and of rebellion. They deny the principle of
authority; they malign those set to rule. Unlike
the archangel in his controversy with the devil,
they do not fear to malign even the dread realities
of authority which are too high for their comprehension, while in the low region of their own animal
instincts they corrupt themselves (vv.[8-10]). Scripture (v.[11]) and nature (v.[12f.]) prefigure their manifold sins and their doom. Nay, they are the true
subject of the ancient patriarch's prophecy (v.[14f.]).
Be not as they are. *They* are unrestful—discontented, selfish, boastful, intriguing flatterers. Do
you be calm, remembering that the apostles, when
they visited you, used to tell you that such men
would arise (vv.[16-18]). Again, *these* men, having
only natural aims, cause divisions. Do *you* build
up your society on the foundation of the faith, the
Spirit helping your prayers, the love of the Father
being your protection, the final mercy of Jesus
Christ being your hope (vv.[19-21]). Such is your
duty to yourselves. What is it to these men?
Towards some, still wavering, cherish a hopeful
compassion; others you must try to save by
desperate effort; towards others you can only feel
a compassion paralyzed by fear of contamination
(v.[22f.]). To God the Father, who can preserve you
from these snares, and finally place you in His
own presence untainted and exultant, to Him
through the mediation of Jesus Christ be glory for
ever (v.[24f.]).

LITERATURE.—(1) On the reception of the Ep. in the Church,
see Charteris, *Canonicity*, p. 331 ff. (based on the next named);
Kirchhofer, *Quellensammlung*, § xxxii.; Reuss, *Gesch. d. heil.
Schriften NT*, § 233; Westcott, *History of the Canon of the NT*;
Zahn, *Geschichte des NT Kanons*, especially i. 1, p. 319 ff.
(2) Commentaries: (*a*) Ancient.—Clement of Alex., *Hypoty-
poses* (Zahn, *Forschungen*, iii. pp. 83 ff., 95 ff.); Didymus of Alex.
(Migne, *Pat. Gr.* xxxix. 1811–1818, Latin version, with a few
Greek fragments); Oecumenius (Migne, *Pat. Gr.* cxix.); Theophy-
lact (Migne, *Pat. Gr.* cxxvi.); fragments and scholia in O. F.
Matthæi, *Nov. Test.* v., 1782, *Scholia in Ep. Cath.* p. 234 ff., and in
Cramer, *Catena*, 1840; Bede (Migne, *Pat. Lat.* xciii.). (*b*) Modern.
—The Reformation period—Luther, 1523; Calvin, 1551. The 17th
century—Grotius, *Annotationes*, 1650. The present century (in
alphabetical order)—Brückner, 1865 (ed. 3); K. Burger in Strack-
Zöckler, *Kurzgefasster Kommentar*, 1895 (ed. 2); Fronmüller in
Lange, *Bibelwerk*, 1862, 1890 (ed. 4), also Eng. tr., Edinburgh,
1870; J. C. K. Hofmann, 1875; Huther in Meyer, 1852, also
Eng. tr., Edinburgh, 1881; Laurmann, 1818; Lumby in *Speaker's
Commmentary*, 1881; O. F. Keil, 1883; E. Kühl in Weiss-
Meyer, 1897 (ed. 6); A. Plummer in Ellicott's *Comm. for English
Readers*, 1883, the same in *Expositor's Bible*, 1891; Plumptre
in *Camb. Bible for Schools*, 1880; Rampf, 1854; M. F. Sadler,
1891; Schneckenburger, 1832; Schott, 1863; von Soden in *Hand-
Commentar*, 1892 (ed. 2); Stier, 1850; G. Wandel, 1898; Wiesinger
in Olshausen, *Bibelwerk*, 1862.
(3) General.—The relevant sections in the Introductions to
the NT, especially the following:—Bleek, Davidson, Hilgenfeld,
Holtzmann, Jülicher, Salmon, B. Weiss, de Wette (ed. 1860),
Zahn *; art. 'Jude' in *Ency. Brit.* (Lumby), the arts. in
Herzog (Sieffert), Smith (ed. 1895, A. Plummer), Schenkel
(Schenkel): also the following books and articles:—E. Arnaud,
Des Citations apocr. de Jude, 1849, the same, *Recherches
critiques sur l'ép. de Jude avec commentaire*, 1851 (also
Eng. tr. in *Brit. and Foreign Evang. Review*, July 1859);
L. A. Arnaud, *Essai crit. sur l'authen.* 1835; Beyschlag, *Neu-
test. Theol.* 1892 (ii. pp. 483–486); Deissmann, *Bibelstudien*, 1895

---

* The second vol. of Zahn's *Einleitung* appeared after this
article was in print. It contains (pp. 42–110) a very full discussion of the questions connected with Jude and 2 P. The
chief conclusions at which Zahn arrives are as follows. 2 P.
was written by St. Peter before, about the autumn of A.D. 63,
he visited Rome, *i.e.* 60–63. It was addressed to Churches
mainly Jewish in or near Palestine. Ep. Jude was the work of
the Lord's brother, and was addressed to the same Churches
as 2 P. The libertines of Jude are false *teachers*, and exactly
correspond to the picture drawn by anticipation in 2 P, to
which, indeed, reference is made in Jude[4. 17]. Zahn takes
Jude[5] to refer to the deliverance of a people (anarthrous λαόν)
by 'Jesus' (best supported reading) from the spiritual Egypt of
sin, and to the subsequent judgment on the unbelieving in the
destruction of Jerusalem. The date, therefore, of the Ep. must
be after 70, and is probably about 75. It may be added that
Zahn thinks that Jude used the Hebrew or Aramaic original of
Enoch.
The writer of the article would gladly have considered Zahn's
position in greater detail. But he does not find any reason to
modify his own arguments or conclusions.

---

* In v.[8] κυριότητα (cf. *Didaché* iv. 1) is abstract: it is the
principle of authority in general which they rejected. The word
δόξας probably points to actual offices of authority in the Church
(cf. Clem. Al. *Strom.* vi. 13, p. 793, ἐγκαταταγῆναι τῷ πρισβυτερίῳ
κατὰ προκοπὴν δόξης· δόξα γὰρ δόξης διαφέρει).

(p. 189 ff.); Ewald, *Sieben Sendschreiben*, 1870; Farrar, *Early Days of Christianity*, 1882 (i. pp. 220–243); Gloag, *Introd. to the Cath. Epistles*, 1887; Harnack, *Die Lehre der zwölf Apostel* ('Texte u. Untersuch.' ii. 1, 2), 1884 (p. 105 f.), the same, *Die Chronologie*, 1897 (pp. 465–469); Jessien, *De αὐθεντίᾳ ep. Judæ*, 1821; Mansel, *Gnostic Heresies*, 1875 (p. 69 ff.); McGiffert, *Hist. of Christianity in the Apostolic Age*, 1897 (pp. 585–583); Mayerhoff, *Die Petrinischen Schriften*, 1835 (pp. 171–182); Neander, *Planting of the Christian Church* (Eng. tr. in Bohn's series, p. 391 f.); Pfleiderer, *Urchristenthum*, 1887 (pp. 835–843); Renan, *St. Paul*, 1869 (p. 300 ff.); Ritschl in *SK*, 1861 (p. 103 ff., 'Ueber die im briefe des Judas characterisirten Antinomisten'); B. Weiss in *SK*, 1866 (p. 256 ff., 'Die Petrinische Frage, Das Verhältniss zum Judasbrief'); Zöckler, *Handb. d. Theol. Wissensch.*, 1883, i. p. 419 f. (Schulze).

F. H. CHASE.

JUDGE, JUDGING.—Among the early Israelites the official organization of the administration of justice was entirely unknown. There were no courts of law, no official judges, no codified laws. Disputes were settled by the natural heads of families and tribes, in accordance with the customs that had grown up in the course of their development. These customs were connected with the *family* and with *religion*. In the earliest book of Hebrew history (JE) the pictures of patriarchal times represent the father or head of the family as possessing supreme power over his property (Gn 27), his slaves (Gn 21), and the members of his own family (Gn 22. 38²⁴). Disputes between families were settled by an appeal to force, or by an amicable covenant between the heads of the families (Gn 21 ; cf. the story of Jacob and Esau in Gn 32). But J" Himself is also represented as acting as supreme judge, and that not only in the case of peoples (Babel, Sodom), but also of individuals (Gn 20⁸). So also refractory members of a family were solemnly dedicated to God's wrath (Gn 49⁵ᶠᶠ).

The beginnings of the history of Israel as a people were dominated by the strong personality of Moses. During the nomad period, family disputes were still settled by the head of the family ; but Moses himself was the supreme judge to whom appeals were brought (Ex 18¹³), and he is represented as himself bringing the matters to J" for decision (Ex 18¹⁹), though we are not told how he gained his knowledge of the will of the Deity. Moses had no officials to execute his sentences, but seems in case of division of opinion to have appealed to those who agreed with him to carry out his punishments by force (Ex 32²⁶). This work, however, proved too much for one man, and on the advice of his father-in-law he selected a number of the heads of families—already accustomed to judging in matters pertaining to their own families—to judge the intertribal disputes, reserving for himself the right of settling the more difficult questions that arose (Ex 18²⁰ᶠᶠ·; cf. the parallel account in Nu 11¹⁶· ²⁴ᶠᶠ).

It was in accordance with this appointment that the later 'Book of the Covenant' was represented as given by Moses to these elders as a body of customs for their guidance (Ex 21¹ 24). The active participation of the Deity in judging is still prominent all through this period. To seek a judgment was to 'seek Jahweh' (Ex 33⁷ᶠᶠ). It was J" Himself who punished Miriam (Nu 12¹⁰), Dathan, and Abiram (Nu 16), and the Israelites themselves (Nu 21). Achan was detected by J" (whose will on this occasion was ascertained by the drawing of lots), and the punishment was carried out by the people (Jos 7).

The settlement in Canaan, and consequent change from nomad to settled life, led to the emphasizing of *local* rather than family and tribal authority. The ancient customs were continued, but the 'elders of the city' (זִקְנֵי הָעִיר) took the place of the elders of the tribe (Jg 8¹⁶ 11⁷, and see below for Deut.; cf. Nowack, *Arch.* i. 322, and see ELDER IN OT), though the claims of the latter were not overlooked even in the 7th cent. (cf. Dt 16¹⁸). During this period the term 'judges' was applied to the local heroes, who delivered and ruled the tribes of Israel. (For the use and meaning of שׁפֵט in the Book of Judges, see the following two articles).

The institution of a monarchy also modified the previous customs, inasmuch as the king and his officials were in a better position than most to enforce their decisions by means of the power they possessed. The administration of justice in the country naturally remained in the hands of the city elders and men who had gained a reputation for wisdom ; and the settlement of disputes was by arbitration rather than by royal justice ; but where a royal officer was stationed, there he would often be appealed to. The king was the most powerful (at any rate in the best days of the monarchy), and therefore the supreme judge. The person of the king was usually accessible to the poorest of his subjects. The men of Israel brought their troubles regularly to David (2 S 15²ᶠ·). The power of the king enabled him when present to override or overawe the local courts (1 K 21, 1 S 8²⁰, 2 S 15² etc.). It was during this period (in the 9th or 8th cent.) that a short book of 'judgments' מִשְׁפָּטִים (Ex 21–23⁹; cf. EXODUS in vol. i. p. 810) was edited to guide the decisions of men who were called upon to decide certain cases. How far it obtained any authority we cannot tell, but it is very short and incomplete. Judges are mentioned only once in this code, viz. in 21²², but the word פְּלִלִים used here is a rare word ; the sentence in which it occurs is difficult to construe as it stands, and Budde has suggested a different reading, which contains no mention of judges (*ZATW* xi. 106 ff.). In Ex 21⁶ 22⁸· ⁹ RVm reads 'judges' as a translation of הָאֱלֹהִים, but the word seems to be used here as usual with the meaning 'God' given in the RV text.*

Towards the end of the 7th cent. (in 621) another code of laws—the Deuteronomic—was proclaimed, but the unfortunate death of Josiah seems to have rendered it ineffective from 608 until after the Exile. (See DEUTERONOMY). In judicial matters it confirmed for the most part the already existing customs. Judges and officers (שֹׁפְטִים וְשֹׁטְרִים) are to be appointed in all the cities, according to the tribes (Dt 16¹⁸).† The ordinary judges are as before the 'elders of the city' (Dt 19¹² 21¹⁸ 22¹⁵ᶠᶠ. etc.). In difficult matters, where men had formerly had recourse to the more immediate judgment of the Deity, the priests the Levites are to be associated with the usual judges (Dt 17⁸ᶠᶠ. 19⁷ᶠ. etc.), and the law as a whole is represented as having been delivered by Moses to the priests the sons of Levi, and unto all the elders of Israel (Dt 31⁹). The curse of J" still remains the heaviest of punishments (Dt 28¹⁵ᶠᶠ.). The greatest fault in the administration of justice during this period was due to bribery, a sin which specially excited the indignation of the preacher of moral righteousness (Am 5¹²; cf. Mic 7³, Zeph 3³). In Am 2⁸ and Mic 5¹ the word 'judge' שֹׁפֵט seems to be used of the king (see Driver on the former passage in the 'Cambridge Bible for Schools'), but in Micah the LXX have a different reading, and in Amos Nowack refers the word to the

---

* Dillmann thinks that judges who gave judgment in a sanctuary were called אֱלֹהִים in the older Hebrew ; cf. his note on this passage in the *Kurzgefasstes exegetisches Handbuch zum AT*, but Marti refers the word to the household gods (*Geschichte der israelitischen Religion*, pp. 29, 48).

† Of the שֹׁטְרִים little is known. They first appear as Israelitish superintendents of forced labour in Egypt (Ex 5, JE), then as 'officers' associated with the elders in the wilderness (Nu 11¹⁶, JE). After this they are not mentioned until Deuteronomy. They seem to have been police officials. See note in Driver's commentary on Dt 1¹⁵.

officials of the Moabites (*Die kleinen Propheten*, p. 126).

The destruction of the monarchies and the exile of both the kingdoms limited the judicial power of the people. In their captivity they were entirely subject to their conquerors. The study of their own law increased, indeed may be said now to have seriously begun, but what little they could carry into practice was only by an act of grace on the part of their masters. The return from exile led to the constitution not of a political power, but of a religious community. The Deuteronomic code was received by it as binding (Neh 8–10), and its provisions were observed as far as was consistent with the laws of the Persians, and afterwards of the Greeks and Romans. Under the Persians the Jews were allowed to follow their own laws in purely internal matters (the elders of the city are mentioned in Ezr 7²⁵ 10¹⁴), but quarrels with neighbouring powers were submitted to the Persian court (Ezr 4 and 5). In Judæa the Priestly code was soon added to the Deuteronomic, but as this is chiefly religious it scarcely affected the ordinary administration of justice. It was probably during the time of the Greek domination that further organization led to the establishment in Jerusalem of the Sanhedrin as the supreme court of the Jewish community (see SANHEDRIN). In the small towns and villages justice was administered by a council of seven (Jos. *Ant.* IV. viii. 14 ; cf. Schürer, *Zeitalter Christi*, ii. 132 ff., 3rd ed. ii. 176 ff. [*HJP* II. i. 163 ff.]), and in larger places by one of twenty-three members (Mishna, *Sanh.* i. 4). It is to one of these councils that Christ refers in Mt 5²², and to their members in v.²⁵. For further details as to the courts in the time of Christ, see the articles ROMAN LAW and SANHEDRIN.

LITERATURE.—The works on Heb. Archæology by Nowack and Benzinger ; for the administration of justice among nomad Arabs, Jacob, *Altarabisches Beduinenleben*², 209 ff.

G. W. THATCHER.

JUDGES, PERIOD OF THE.—

i. The period extends from the death of Joshua to the anointing of Saul as king over Israel.

ii. Our main authorities are the Book of Judges (specially ch. 5, 'the Song of Deborah') and 1 S 1–10. In addition to these the blessing of Jacob (Gn 49) was formerly reckoned to belong to this period ; but the more modern view is that, while vv.⁵⁻⁷· ¹⁴ᵗ· ¹⁶ᵗ· point to the period of the Judges, other verses transplant us to a later time (Kuenen, *Hex.* p. 240, Eng. tr.; Dillmann, *Gen.* vol. ii. p. 447, Eng. tr.). The Book of Ruth has reference to this period, but its composition is referred to post-exilic times by recent critics.

iii. CHRONOLOGY.—The whole period is devoid of certain dates ; the most that can be said is that its close may be assigned with probability to within fifty years of B.C. 1000. The length of the period is also very doubtful. If we follow what seems to be the Chronology of the Book of Judges itself, we have to conclude that the Judges (exclusive of Eli and Samuel) occupied a period of more than 410 years. No critic, however, has ever accepted this high total, and there are three good reasons why it should be rejected. (1) It contradicts 1 K 6¹ (480 years from the Exodus to the building of the temple). (2) It has always appeared probable that some of the Judges were contemporaries and not successors or predecessors of the rest. (3) It is

improbable that Israel could have existed in the disorganized condition which was hers under the Judges for so long a period as 400 years without being absorbed and lost in the surrounding Canaanites. Moreover, several of the details of which the number 410 is made up do not inspire confidence; the number 40 (representing a generation) or its multiples occurs frequently, and the writer of the book seems to be giving merely a rough reckoning by generations. In the present article it is assumed that the period of the Judges was relatively short, perhaps about 200 years. See CHRONOLOGY OF OLD TEST. vol. i. p. 399.

iv. POLITICAL GEOGRAPHY.—A careful study of Jg, particularly of chs. 1 and 4, shows that the Israelites on entering Palestine did not conquer it, but only overran the inland part of it. A broad strip of land along the coast remained in the hands of the Philistines (cf. Moore on Jg 1¹⁸· ¹⁹) and of the Zidonians (Jg 1³¹). The fortresses which girdled the plain of Esdraelon (Jg 1²⁷), and consequently the plain itself, remained unconquered. Moreover, scattered over the land there were cities, *e.g.* Jerusalem (Jg 1²¹), Gezer (1²⁹), and probably Shechem (Jg 9¹⁻⁴; Kittel, ii. 74), in which apparently the Israelites had a footing, but not the supremacy. No doubt some cities came at an early date into the hands of Israel or of their allies (Hebron, Jg 1¹⁰ ; Bethlehem, Jg 12⁸⁻¹⁰ ; Bethel, Jg 1²²), but it may be said generally that the Canaanites still kept their fortified cities while the Israelites occupied the villages. It was indeed only to be expected that Israel on ceasing to be a nomadic people, would pass through a stage of free village life before they could accustom themselves to the restricted life of cities. These villages were fixed encampments, collections of tents, rather than houses ordered in streets. 'To your *tents*, O Israel,' was the earlier form of the signal for dispersion, as 'every man to his own city' (1 K 22³⁶) was the later. The heaviest blow which could fall on Israel at this period is described in the Song of Deborah in the words, 'The villages (or 'villagers') ceased in Israel' (Jg 5⁷ AV and RVm). The only refuge of the people was in dens and caves and natural strongholds (Jg 6², 1 S 13⁶). They had *destroyed* such fortresses as they had won.

Had the Canaanites possessed any real cohesion among themselves, the Israelites must have been chased out of the country as the Midianites were chased out by Gideon ; but the Canaanites were hopelessly divided. They were, in fact, a mixed population, whether we reckon them as exactly seven nations or not.

v. HISTORY.—Owing to the doubtfulness of the chronology, a formal division of the epoch of the Judges into periods is impossible. Three great crises, however, stand out in the history—(1) the union of the tribes against Sisera and the Canaanites (Jg 4. 5) ; (2) the assertion of Israel's individuality (or nationality) against the Midianites ; (3) the appearance of the Philistines.

(1) All writers recognize the importance of the Israelite rising under Deborah and Barak. Israel had been checked in its conquests by the fortresses which girdled the plain of Esdraelon and by the chariots of iron which controlled it. Once checked they sank into helplessness, and the Canaanites of the plain turned upon their former assailants. Their success was great. The Israelites of the north and of the centre would have become the helots of the Canaanites, if Deborah had not prophesied and if Barak had not fought. Nor did the battle of the Kishon give Israel freedom only ; it also gave life to the idea of national unity. Six tribes, viz. Ephraim, Benjamin, Manasseh (Machir), Zebulun, Issachar, and Naph-

tali, united to fight the battle of the God of Israel ; and four others, Reuben, Gad (Gilead), Dan, and Asher, are reminded in the Song of Deborah of their failure to realize the duties of their kinship with the rest. The sole literature of this period * (so far as we know) is this song of a people struggling to assert its freedom and its nationality.

(2) Gideon represents a crisis hardly less acute than that at which Deborah appeared. Israel was passing from nomadic to settled life ; but if the fruits of agriculture were snatched from them by the Midianites, the temptation to return to a wandering (and perhaps marauding) life, would be very great. At another time, under circumstances of stress, Jephthah and David did actually return to the condition of 'children of the East.' From any such retrograde step Israel, as a whole, was saved by Gideon, the farmer called from the threshing-flail to save his people.

The deliverance wrought by Gideon brought up the question of appointing a permanent head, to judge Israel and fight their battles (cf. 1 S 8²⁰). The Midianites invaded the land every year (Jg 6¹·³), so that the crisis demanded some permanent organization to meet the standing danger. Gideon, on the invitation of the people, established a rule which was a theocracy according to his own profession, but it was administered by himself as earthly vicegerent. He established at his home at Ophrah, in addition to the rest of his state, a golden ephod (see EPHOD) of the God whose government he (and his sons after him) professed to administer (Jg 8²²⁻²⁷· ³⁰ 9²).

(3) The appearance of the Philistines was a matter of grave importance. If, as seems probable (but see art. JUDGES [BOOK OF], p. 818ᵇ), this event was contemporaneous with the beginning of Ammonite assaults on Israel, this importance is greatly enhanced. Attacked on the east by Ammon, reduced in part to subjection on the west by the Philistines, the Israelites fell into a disorganized and helpless state, from which nothing, perhaps, but the establishment of the kingdom could rescue them.

But the period of the Judges was remarkable, not only for the three crises just mentioned, but also for a slow and silent revolution which went on during the whole of its course.

It was at this time that Israel assimilated to itself a large Canaanite population. Wellhausen (*Isr. u. Jüd. Ges.*² 46 ff.) points out that this fusion would begin in the country, since the Canaanite peasant would find more in common with the Israelite settler than with his own fellow-countrymen in the cities. This incorporation of the original population into Israel explains the striking growth of the population which took place under the Judges, which, indeed, made Jacob so much stronger than the kindred tribes, Moab, Ammon, and Edom, and rendered the empire of David and Solomon a possibility.

vi. TRUSTWORTHINESS OF THE HISTORY OF THE JUDGES.—This history is so natural a preface to the period of the Kings, that no charge of improbability can be fairly laid against it as a whole. Many details, however, have been referred with more or less probability to myth or misunderstanding, and not to history.

Cushan-rishathaim (Jg 3⁸) of Mesopotamia (Aram-naharaim) is a shadowy and uncertain figure. The Shamgar of Jg 3³¹ is supposed to be irreconcilable with the Shamgar of Jg 5⁶ ; 'he was no deliverer of Israel,' writes Kittel (ii. 66 note), 'as the context [of Jg 5⁶] shows.' The minor judges Tola and Jair (Jg 10¹·³), and Ibzan,

Elon, and Abdon (Jg 12⁸⁻¹⁵) are generally said to be merely personifications of leading families. Our present account of Jephthah is open to the objection that Jephthah's 'message to Ammon' (Jg 11¹²⁻²⁷) seems to be really a document having reference rather to *Moab* ; cf. the mention of Chemosh (v.²⁴) and of Balak (v.²⁵). On the other hand, Jephthah's vow and its fulfilment are defended as natural in Jephthah's age (and therefore as probably historical) by Kittel (ii. 81). The story of Samson, finally, has not been proved a sun-myth, but many will agree with Kittel's dictum (*ib.*) : 'Samson wavers between myth, saga, and history, belonging altogether to no one of them, but in part to each.' See, further, JUDGES (BOOK OF), p. 819.

vii. RELIGION.—In speaking of the religion of this period it is necessary to regard only the statements of the ancient part of the book, avoiding the so-called 'margin.' Inquiry was made of God (Jg 1¹), probably by means of the ephod (see EPHOD) ; war was made in the name of J" (Jg 3²⁸ 4⁶), who was regarded as the national God whose dwelling was on the Arabian peninsula (Jg 5⁴·⁵ ; cf. Moore) ; the angel of J" presented himself in human form in order to make his revelations (Jg 6¹¹ 13³·⁶·¹⁰) ; prophecy was rare (Jg 4⁴, 1 S 3¹) ; the ark was regarded as equivalent to the presence of J" Himself (1 S 4³).

Canaanite influence on religion was strong during this period, for the process of fusion of Canaanite and Israelite was going on. Israel, new to the land, was introduced to the old sanctuaries by the old inhabitants, and thus learned to worship the local Baal, the native god of corn and wine, with the corrupt and corrupting forms of that lascivious shedder of blood, the Canaanite. Of Israel's morals during this period little good can be said. A time of anarchy always impairs the vitality of virtue ; and in Israel when 'every man did that which was right in his own eyes' (Jg 17⁶), very strange things were done (Jephthah, Samson, Danites, Gibeah). There was no lack of courage in this period, and hospitality was evidently regarded by the mass of the people as inviolable. The sacredness of an oath is strangely illustrated by Jg 11³⁵ and 21⁷.

Taken as a whole the period may be characterized, in the words of Amos (8¹¹), as days in which there was 'a famine in the land ; not a famine of bread, nor a thirst for water, but of hearing the words of the Lord.' The redactor of Jg is indeed continually drawing lessons from the experiences of his people under the Judges, but it seems that at the time itself the events were left for the most part to deliver their own message uninterpreted by any prophet. We may compare the period with the years of 'silence' which preceded the coming of our Lord.

viii. PARALLEL WITH THE MACCABÆAN PERIOD.—There are several points of resemblance between the Maccabæan period and that of the Judges. (1) The form of government (if it could be called a 'form') was the same at both periods. The Maccabees were Judges * (שֹׁפְטִים *shōphĕṭim*) like Gideon, Jephthah, and the rest, *i.e.* not administrators, but champions both against the enemy and against the unfaithful of their own people (cf. 1 Mac 2⁶⁵·⁶⁶ 9²⁹⁻³¹·⁷³). If some of the Maccabees were also *priests* (Jonathan, 1 Mac 10²⁰ ; Simon, 1 Mac 14⁴⁷), so were the ancient judges, Eli and Samuel. (2) Both periods were periods of almost continual struggle (if the chronology of the Judges has been rightly understood above), and the very life of Israel as a distinct people was threatened. (3) There was the same want of unity among the

---

* The Carthaginian *sufetes* resembled the *shōphĕṭim* chiefly in name.

people at both periods (cf. 1 Mac 1⁵² 6²¹ 7⁵). (4) There was the same absence of 'open vision' (1 S 3¹; cf. 1 Mac 4⁴⁶ 14⁴¹). (5) Even the language used of the Maccabæan period recalls the time of the Judges (cf. 1 Mac 9⁷³ ἤρξατο κρίνειν; 2⁴² πᾶς ὁ ἑκουσιαζόμενος; 14⁴ ἡσύχασεν ἡ γῆ πᾶσας τὰς ἡμέρας Σίμωνος).

See, further, on the whole subject, the following article.

LITERATURE.—The proper sections of the general histories of Ewald, Renan (flippant even for Renan), Wellhausen (brief), Stade (full), Kittel (very good). See also under ISRAEL. The Commentary of G. F. Moore, 1895; and J. S. Black, *Judges*, 1892 (in the 'smaller Cambridge Bible'); also the Literature cited at the end of the following article.

W. EMERY BARNES.

JUDGES, BOOK OF.—
1. The *Name* of the Book.
2. The condition of its *Text*.
3. Its *Contents* and *Arrangement*.
4. Its inner *Harmony* or *Unity*.
5. Relation to the Pentateuch '*sources.*'
6. *Character* and *Age* of the component elements.
7. Its *Author*.
8. Its *Spirit* and its place in the history of revelation. Literature.

1. THE NAME OF THE BOOK. — The seventh component of the Hebrew Old Testament is named Book of Judges (סֵפֶר שֹׁפְטִים) in the oldest sources with which we are acquainted (cf. the Talmudic Tract *Baba bathra* 14ᵇ, edited separately by Marx-Dalman in 'Traditio rabbinorum veterrima de librorum veteris testamenti ordine atque origine,' 1884, p. 14). The same expression סֵפֶר שֹׁפְטִים is found in the *Dikdûkê ha-ṭĕ'amîm* of Aharon ben-Asher (10th cent.), ed. Baer and Strack, p. 58. The self-evident term 'Book' is also frequently dropped, and thus the simple שֹׁפְטִים employed (so the usual reading in above-cited passage from the Talmud). If one compares, for instance, הַשֹּׁפְטִים (Ru 1¹) and οἱ κριταί (Sir 46¹¹), it is remarkable that the article is dropped before שֹׁפְטִים when the latter is used as the title of the Book. But in the course of transition of a *nomen appellativum* to the force of a *nomen proprium*, the article was frequently omitted (for analogies see König's *Syntax*, § 295, h-k). The Heb. title of the Book was either simply transcribed (cf. *e.g.* ٮڡطٮں in Ephraem Syrus [acc. to Brockelmann, *Lex. Syr.* 383ᵇ] and Σωφετίμ in Origen [acc. to Euseb. *HE* vi. 25]), or it might be translated (cf. *e.g. dayyânê* in the Peshiṭta, or κριταί, *e.g.* in Melito of Sardis [acc. to Euseb. *HE* iv. 26]), or (*liber*) *iudicum, e.g.* in Hieronymus, *Prologus galeatus* (=præfatio regnorum).

2. THE CONDITION OF THE TEXT.—The history of the *Text* of a literary product needs above all to be considered, in order that a basis may thus be laid for all further investigation. In the case of the Book of Judges this rule is all the more to be observed because of the very complicated history of its text.

(*a*) The Heb. text, as one finds it, notably in the *editio Baeriana libri Josuæ et iudicum* (1891), in the excellent *Biblia hebraica* of Ch. D. Ginsburg (1894), and in the well-known collections of various readings by Kennicott and de Rossi, is, of course, in substantial agreement with the Targum, the Peshiṭta, and the Vulgate.*

* Felix Perles (*Analekten zur Textkritik des AT*, 1895) suggests the following emendations on the text of Judges: 3²³ (p. 85) הַמִּסְדְּרוֹנָה 'privy,' cf. 'posticum' of Vulg.; 3²⁸ᵇ (p. 33) וַיִּרְדְּפוּ; 5⁸ (p. 91) M. Lambert's conjectural לַחֲמָשׁ שְׁעָרִים 'to five doors' (but see König's *Syntax*, § 330 m); 11³⁷ (p. 51) וְהֵרַדְתִּי, but it is more natural to suppose that it [וְרָדְתִּי (cf. Hos 12¹, Jer 2³¹) the ו was not distinctly written, and that ו has thus arisen; 12⁶ (p. 33) from יְכ which was meant for יָכֹל may have arisen יָכִין; 13¹² (p. 85) עַת (cf. König's *Syntax*, § 385 k); 20³³ᵇ (p. 34) מִמַּעֲרָב is supposed to have been written for מִמַּעֲרֵה.

(*b*) But the Greek version of the Book of Judges is an extraordinarily manifold one. This is already shown by the number and the nature of the variants which the Alexandrian (A) and the Vatican (B) MSS of the LXX present in this book. For instance, in 1¹ᵇ A reads τὸν χαναναῖον (הַכְּנַעֲנִי) and πολεμήσεαι (*sic*) ἐν αὐτῷ (בּוֹ), but B has τοὺς χαναναίους and πρὸς αὐτούς. Further, in 1⁸ A reads καὶ πολεμήσω (to represent the plur. (וַיִּלָּחֲמוּ) ἐν τῷ χαναναίῳ (הַכְּנַעֲנִי), but B has καὶ παραταξώμεθα πρὸς τοὺς χαναναίους. In 1⁴ᵇ the respective readings confront one another, ἐπάταξε (A; cf. the plur. וַיַּכּוּ of MT) and ἔκοψαν (B). In 1¹⁶ חֹתֵן of the MT is reproduced in A by πενθερός, but in B by γαμβρός, which last is the reading also of Jos. *Ant.* v. ii. 3. But the differences in the Greek translation of the Book of Judges are above all brought to view by de Lagarde, who, in his *Septuaginta-Studien* (Bd. i. 1892, p. 1 ff.) places side by side all the most important variants occurring in the first five chapters of Jg. His judgment is completely substantiated by the thorough investigations of G. Moore in his *Commentary on the Book of Judges*, 1895, pp. xliv-xlvi. Budde (*Kurzer Handcomm. z. Richterbuch*, 1897, p. xvi) has simply reproduced Moore's results. For instance, in 1⁷ the MT as well as AB have 'seventy,' but L(ucian) ἑβδομήκοντα δύο (so Jos. *Ant.* v. ii. 2, δυοῖν καὶ ἑβδομήκοντα).* But, *e.g.*, in 8¹⁰ both AB and L offer the same reading, 15,000, as the MT, and only Josephus (*Ant.* v. vi. 5) has μύριοι καὶ ὀκτακισχίλιοι. Hence, in spite of the scepticism of A. Mez (*die Bibel des Josephus*, 1895, p. 57) it is quite possible that רו was read as ירו (=מו)=15 is found for the first time in Origen; cf. König, *Einleit.* p. 90, note 1). Regarding the two main branches of the Greek version of Jg, Moore has said very judiciously, 'It would probably be going too far to affirm that they are independent; the author of the younger of them may have known and used the older' (*Judges*, p. xliv).

(*c*) Further, A. Mez (*die Bibel des Josephus*, 1895, pp. 11-18, 56-61, 80 f.) has shown, in regard to Jg, that 'the text of Josephus belongs to the most valuable relics of the history of the text of the OT.' For in the case of Jg, Josephus follows the Lucianic text (L) *not* in the same high degree of dependence as in the Books of Samuel (with four exceptions). In Jg the bond connecting the text of Josephus and that of Lucian is weaker and in many passages even broken. For instance, in 1¹⁶ the MT has קֵינִי חֹתֵן מֹשֶׁה, L has Ἰωβὰβ τοῦ Κειναίου, but Jos. (*Ant.* v. ii. 3) Ἰέθρου τοῦ Μαδιανίτου ἀπόγονοι, Μωυσέως γὰρ ἦν γαμβρός (see above for the reading of B). Again, *e.g.*, the expression וַיִּלְבֹּד in 1¹⁸ is reproduced not only in AL, but also in B by ἐκληρονόμησεν (Itala, *hereditavit*), but Jos. v. ii. 4 offers rightly εἷλον. Finally, *e.g.*, the king כּוּשַׁן רִשְׁעָתַיִם (Jg 3⁸) is called in L Χουσανρεσαμώθ, in AB (by an easily intelligible omission of the *n*, cf. König, *Lehrgebäude*, ii. 466) Χουσαρσαθάιμ, and in Jos. V. iii. 2 Χουσαράθους, etc. What right Mez has to say in reference to this, 'L ist corrigirt,' we cannot see. Still this investigation has confirmed the present writer's view (*Einleit.* p. 114 ff.) that the traditional Massoretic text is the relatively best source from which to ascertain the words of the Old Testament. This judgment is also entirely substantiated by the investigation into the text of Samuel which Löhr has carried out in the 'Kurzgef. Exeg. Hdbch.' on *Samuel*, 1898, pp. lxix ff.

3. THE CONTENTS AND ARRANGEMENT OF THE BOOK.—(*a*) The book begins with (*a*) the enumera-

* Cf. the same variation of 70 and 72 in the number of the nations (1 Ch 1⁵·²³: 14+30+26=70; but in the *Clement. Recogn.* ii. 42 we find 72); also in the number of the disciples, Lk 10¹, where Codd. BD, etc., have ἑβδομήκοντα δύο. Moreover, the number of the Greek translators of the OT came to be reduced from 72 to 70.

tion of the districts in Palestine which at the death of Joshua had not yet been conquered, and with the description of the operations undertaken by several of the tribes of Israel, in part unsuccessfully, for the complete subjection of their territory (1^{1-36}).—(β) This partial failure is traced to the Divine requital of Israel's religious disobedience, and on the same account it was announced that the Canaanites and other enemies of Israel would continue for a time to maintain their independence, with a view to the chastisement and the probation of Israel. The messenger of J″, mentioned in 2^1, was wrongly identified with Phinehas (Jos 24^{33}) in *Jalḳuṭ Shim'ônî*, vol. ii. ch. 40: והלא פנחס היה מלאך ה'.—(γ) Once more it is told how the Israelites, soon after the death of Joshua, were guilty of religious disloyalty. The author's object was to explain why the Israelites suffered repeated defeats in conflicts also with the *surrounding* nations (2^{6-3^4}, see below 4 *b*).

(*b*) The history of the individual judges is related. They belonged for the most part to the tribe which suffered most from the particular oppression at the time (3^5-16^{31}).—(*a*) *Othni'el* of the tribe of Judah, who first came upon the scene immediately after the death of Joshua (3^{7-11}).*— (β) *Ehud*, the Benjamite (3^{12-30}), broke the yoke of the neighbouring Moabites by the assassination of their king, Eglon. According to *Nazir* 23^b Ruth was a granddaughter of Eglon: רות בת בנו של עגלון *Seder Olam rabba*, ch. 12 (ed. Meyer, p. 34), combines Jg 2^{15} with Ru 2^{13b}, cf. 1 Ch 2^{11}, Ru $4^{20f.}$—(γ) *Shamgar* (3^{31}) smote the Philistines. —(δ) In conjunction with *Deborah*, of the tribe of Ephraim, the hero *Barak*, of the northern tribe of Naphtali, defeated the Canaanites, who had again assembled a strong force in the north of Canaan (4^1-5^{31}). Sisera, the commander of the army of the enemy, was slain by the woman *Jael*. Many of the Talmudists took offence at the words ' between (AV at) her feet (בֵּין רַגְלֶיהָ) he bowed' (*Jebamoth* 103^{ab}, *Nazir* 23^b), but other Talmudists, appealing to Gn 31^{29ab}, rightly found in the expression ' between her feet' nothing to the discredit of Jael.— (ϵ) *Gideon*, of the town of ' Ophrah in Ephraim' (?), expelled the Midianites and reigned for long in peace (6^1-8^{35}; cf. Γεδεών, ὃς ἑρμηνεύεται πειρατήριον. Ὤμοσε γὰρ, κ.τ.λ., 8^9,—Philo i. 424, ed. Mangey). But his son *Abimelech*, who seized the reins of power in Shechem, was speedily overcome (9^{1-57}).— (ζ) *Tola*, a man of Issachar, defended Israel ($10^{1f.}$). —(η) After him *Jair*, a Gileadite, judged Israel (10^{3-5}).—(θ) *Jephthah*, the Gileadite, smote the children of Ammon (11^1-12^7).—(ι) *Ibzan*, of Bethlehem, judged Israel (12^{8-10}); cf. *Baba bathra* 91^a: אבצן זה בעו ' Ibzan is Boaz' (Ru 2^1).—(κ) *Elon*, a Zebulunite ($12^{11f.}$), and (λ) 'Abdon, of Pirathon in Ephraim, judged Israel (12^{13-15}). At last (μ) *Samson* ' began to deliver Israel out of the hand of the Philistines' (13^{5b}), and judged Israel twenty years (13^1-16^{31}).† It is only up to this point that Jg gives a *continuous* series of narratives. This was already noted in the *Diḳdûḳê* of Aharon ben-Asher, for in § 70 it is said, ' The Book of Judges (extends) from Othniel, the son of Kenaz, to the death of Samson, the son of Manoah, the Danite' (מעניאל) (בן קנו ער שמשון בן מנוח הדני).

(*c*) The last five chapters of Jg do not continue the preceding history, but add two *episodes* to it.

(*a*) The first episode is as follows: a part of the tribe of Dan wandered from south-western Canaan to the sources of the Jordan. There they conquered the town of Laish, and called it, after the name of their tribe, Dan. In this town they established as priest a Levite from Mt. Ephraim, whom they had persuaded to accompany them (17^1-18^{31}). (β) The second episode tells how the inhabitants of Gibeah which belonged to Benjamin (20^4) abused to death the concubine of a Levite (19^{25}), and how all the other tribes of Israel punished the tribe of Benjamin for refusing to deliver up the miscreants of Gibeah (19^1-21^{25}).

The Book of Judges does not state precisely at what parts of the period of the judges these two episodes happened. The first episode is certainly assigned to a time when there had not fallen to the tribe of the Danites anything as a possession (18^{1b}), *i.e.* they had been unable to make themselves real masters of the territory assigned to them on the S.W. coast of Canaan (Jos 19^{40-48}, Ezk 48^{1b})—even Budde (on Jg 18^{1b}) regards this as not mere theory. But it is uncertain *how long* after Joshua's death the oppressions (1^{34} 10^{11b} 14^4) continued which prevented the tribe of the Danites from completely conquering their territory. In any case, neither in $1^{34f.}$ nor elsewhere is it implied that ' the southern Dan never dwelt by the sea, not to speak of itself having possessed ships' (Budde on Jg 5^{17}), and this southern Dan was nearer to the ships than the northern. Nevertheless the date of the history narrated in chs. 17 f. can be limited. For according to 18^{30} it was a grandson of Moses that was priest in the city of Dan, מֹשֶׁה being indicated as the original reading through the *Nûn suspensum* of מְנַשֶּׁה (cf. the Talmudic statements and the discussion with L. Blau in König's *Einleitung*, pp. 34, 84^1). It is thus intelligible how the oldest author who outside the Bk. of Jg has described the period of the judges,* namely Josephus, has inserted the two episodes immediately after the narratives of the first chapter of Jg. He further transposes the order of the two narratives, introducing (*Ant.* v. ii. 8–12) the contents of chs. 19–21 as an illustration of a στάσις δεινή, and with the words ὅμοια δὲ τούτοις παθεῖν καὶ τὴν Δανιτῶν συνέβη φυλήν, he appends (*Ant.* v. iii. 1) the history contained in chs. 17 f. *Seder olam rabba* (ch. 12) says, בימי כוש רשעתים היה פסלו של מיכה וג' ובימיו היתה פילגש בגבעה, *i.e.* ' in the days of Cushanrishathaim was the graven image of Micah, etc. (cf. 18^{30}), and in his days was a concubine in Gibeah.' Moore (on chs. 17 f.) also says rightly that the migration may be assigned to a time not very long after the Israelite invasion of Canaan. Are we, then, to suppose that the two episodes stood originally after the first chapter? This is not likely. For in that case we should not expect to read, ' in those days there was no *king* in Israel, but every man did that which was right in his own eyes' (17^6 18^1 19^1 21^{25}). At all events it is not without a special aim that the two narratives are placed at the end of Jg. They are intended to show the *negative* results which during the period of the judges showed themselves in the sphere of religion and morals.

Referring again to the arrangement of the Bk. of Jg, it is interesting to note the ancient division of the *Massoretic* sections (Baer, *Josua et Jud.* p. 125). These are fourteen, and they begin with the following verses of the book: 1^1 2^7 (ויעברו) 3^{31}

* *Sanhedrin* 105^a כוש רשעתים הוא לבן הארמי ' Cushanrishathaim is Laban the Aramæan,' *i.e.* he was of the descendants of Laban.

† In ' Philonis sine præparatione in Sampson oratio' (*Philonis Opera*, ed. Lips. 1830, vol. vii. pp. 351-376) it is said, ' Sampson vires sumpsit ad monstranda opera magna' (§ 12), but also ' quum, a gurgite luxuriæ raptus, illuviem passus fuerit inque abyssum immersus cupidinis, non amplius compos erat sursum aspiciendi, sed totus voluptati deditus, ut verum diceret, tanquam a iudice, a muliere coactus fuit' (§ 1).

* ' The days of the judges' are mentioned in Ru 1^1, but passed over in silence between 1 Ch 9^{44} and 10^1, and ben-Sirach's only allusion to them is in the two verses Sir $46^{11f.}$. Cf. the words of Justin (*Hist.* xxxvi. ii. 7): ' Post Mosen etiam filius eius Aruas, sacerdos sacris Ægyptiis, mox rex creatur, semperque exinde hic mos apud Judæos fuit, ut eosdem reges et sacerdotes haberent, quorum institia religione permixta incredibile quantum coaluere.'

(ואחריו) 6^1 7^1 8^4 (ויבא גדעון וגי) 9^7 (ויגידו וגי) 10^1 (ויקם וגי) 11^{32} (וילכו וגי) 14^1 (וירד שמשון וגי) 16^4 (ויהי וגי) 18^7 (ויעבר יפתח וגי) 19^{20} (ויאמר האיש), and 20^{27} (וישאלו וגי). It will be observed that several of these beginnings (e.g. 14^1 instead of 13^1) are not without much interest.

4. THE INNER HARMONY, OR THE UNITY OF THE BOOK.—(a) In 1^8 it is recorded that the members of the tribe of Judah took Jerusalem; but according to 1^{21} this city lay in the sphere of the Benjamites, and by no means can we agree that 'doubtless the author wrote Judah' (Moore, ad loc.). For, since at a later period the Judahite David conquered the city of the Jebusites (2 S $5^{6ff.}$), and since, after the so-called disruption of the kingdom, Jerusalem was the capital of the kingdom of Judah, it was natural to reckon Jerusalem to the territory of the Judahites. Hence there must have been a reliable tradition that Jerus. originally belonged to the sphere of the Benjamites, else it would not have been in Jg 1^{21} assigned to Benjamin (this also against Budde, ad loc.). Further, it is quite an unwarranted assertion that in 1^{34} on account of its difference of form 'the continuation of the Dan history is to be found, whose beginning was still read by Josephus' (Mez, l.c. p. 11). That is to say, Josephus makes the remark, Χαναναῖοι . . . τῆς Ἰούδα φυλῆς, τὴν Ἀσκάλωνα καὶ Ἀκκάρωνα παρεσπάσαντο ἄλλας τε πολλὰς τῶν ἐν τῷ πεδίῳ καὶ Δανίτας εἰς τὸ ὅρος ἠνάγκασαν συμφυγεῖν (Ant. V. iii. 1). But Mez has not noticed that the ἅρματα and the πεδίον, κ.τ.λ., previously mentioned by Josephus, point to 1^{19b} as the source of his words quoted above.

(b) The two sections 1^1-2^5 and $2^{6ff.}$ were not written by one author as parts of one and the same work. For 1^1 begins by mentioning the death of Joshua, but 2^6 mentions something that happened while he was still alive, וַיְשַׁלַּח (καὶ ἐξαπέστειλεν; Hieron. 'dimisit ergo') referring in its present context to the assembly of the people in 2^4. Neither can we say with P. Cassel, ad loc., that the author meant to 'quote' the words of Jos 24^{28}, nor is the imperf. consec. meant as a plusquamperfect (Keil, ad loc.). (See a discussion of all the analogous instances in König's Syntax, § 142). Hence, not the original sense of the passage $2^{6ff.}$ but only its present position may be explained as follows: the first section (1^1-2^5) is meant to show why the internal enemies of Israel continued after the death of Joshua, and the second to explain why Israel during the same period was beaten by foreign foes. This intention of the section $2^{6ff.}$ appears to reveal itself especially in the expressions employed in $2^{14ff.}$ (cf. 3^3). It is not till 3^5 that the Bk. of Jg returns to the mention of internal foes of Israel, on whose account no shôphĕṭîm were raised up (2^{16}). Hence it appears to the present writer that the new section begins with 3^5 and not with 3^7 as is now generally assumed. Further, 2^{10} is not in contradiction with 3^9 (1^{13}, Jos 15^{17}), if Kenaz was the brother of Caleb; and this is not only possible but even almost probable, because in 1^{13} 'the younger,' etc., stands nearer to 'brother' and 'Kenaz' than to 'Othniel.' If so, Othniel was a nephew of Caleb and did not belong to the generation of Joshua; and the Κενίαζος ὄνομα which is read in Jos. Ant. V. iii. 3 (ed. Niese) is not 'the earliest of all the ingenious attempts that have been made to reconcile 3^9 with 2^{10}' (Mez, l.c. p. 12).

(c) There are irreconcilable differences, too, within the history of Deborah and Barak. For in 4^2 there is mention only of 'the king of Canaan,' but in 5^{19} of 'kings of Canaan.' Further, according to $4^{6.\ 10}$ Barak collected his army only from the two tribes of Naphtali and Zebulun, but according to $5^{14ff.}$ warriors joined him also from the tribes of Ephraim, Benjamin, etc. On the other hand, the sleep of Sisera (4^{21}) appears to the present writer to be

presupposed also in 5^{26} (cf. vv.$^{26b.\ 27a}$), and its express mention seems to be omitted merely owing to poetic brevity. Otherwise it would be improbable that a woman should have slain the warrior. Budde says, of course, that '5^{27} shows that Sisera was struck while standing'; but this interpretation overlooks the words, 'where he bowed there he fell' ($5^{27b}\beta$).

(d) שֶׁ used as the relative is read only in 5^7 6^{17} 7^{12} 8^{26}, and in the last three passages cannot be regarded as interpolated (Giesebrecht, ZATW, Bd. i. 280; see all the instances of this שֶׁ in König's Lehrgebäude, ii. 322).

(e) The same author would not have written both the introductions to the narrative of the invasion of the Ammonites, contained in $10^{17ff.}$ and $11^{4ff.}$.

(f) In ch. 14 a great many very important points are passed over in silence of the most unnatural kind, if all the elements of the text that have come down to us are in their original form. For instance, after v.$^{8f.}$ the statement would be wanting that this journey of Samson did not lead to the marriage intended (לְקַחְתָּהּ, v.^{8a}), and that the father of Samson had got over his initial repugnance to a Philistine daughter-in-law. Probably, then, it is a later addition that the parents of Samson were present at his marriage. Josephus also relates * that Samson presented the honey to the Philistine maid, and not that he shared it with his parents (14^{9a}).

(g) Like a so-called red thread there runs through chs. 2–16 a series of passages in which the constant interchange is described between Israel's religious and moral lapses and her punishment, between Israel's repentance and God's help; cf. especially 2^{11-19} $3^{7.\ 12a}$ 4^{1-3} 6^1 8^{33-35} 10^{6-16} 13^1.

(h) Also the two episodes which close the book (chs. 17–21) have their peculiar character (e.g. the formula 'in those days there was no king in Israel,' etc., 17^6 18^1 19^1 21^{25}), and these two narratives also are wanting in a complete inward unity. For if $17^{10f.}$ $18^{17f.}$ $21^{12.\ 19}$ proceeded from one and the same author, they would contain unnatural repetitions.

5. RELATION TO THE PENTATEUCH 'SOURCES.'—The question of the unity of the book as well as that of its date, depends upon the relation of Jg to the different strata embodied in the Pentateuch. Hence it will be of advantage for the following investigation, if we first of all make an attempt to fix this relation. Now it is well known that in the Pentateuch there are four main strata to be distinguished: the Jahwistic (J; Gn 2^{4b}–3^{24} etc.), the Elohistic (E; Gn 20, etc.), the Deuteronomic (D), and the Esoteric-Priestly (P; Gn 1^1–2^{4a} etc.; cf. König, Einleitung, p. 188 ff.); and there is the possibility in abstracto that these four works continued the post-Mosaic history of Israel. But that as a matter of fact these four sources of the Pentateuch continue to flow also into the extant Bk. of Jg, can be established only by positive proofs. This proof is all the more necessary in view of the impossibility of making true progress in critical science if a number of results are assumed as already proved, and one makes it his main object always to pile up higher storeys on the building of the literary criticism of the Old Testament. Besides, the relation of the Bk. of Jg to the 'sources' of the Pentateuch is one of those questions which are differently answered even by decided friends of criticism.

(a) Is the Jahwistic stratum (J) of the Pent. continued in Jg? To begin with, the first chapter of Jg has points of contact in several passages with expressions contained in the preceding book of the OT. For instance, Jos 15^{14-19} is substantially iden-

* Ant. V. viii. 6: Καὶ ἀντλόμενος τρία μέλιτος κηρία, σὺν τοῖς λοιποῖς δώροις, οἷς ἐκόμιζε, δίδωσι τῇ παιδί.

tical with Jg 1[10-15]; Jos 15[13] resembles Jg 1[20]; Jos 15[63] is substantially the same as Jg 1[21]; Jos 17[11-13] (cf. Nu 32[39. 41f.]) resembles Jg 1[27f.]; and Jos 16[10] is substantially the same as Jg 1[29]. The opinion of the present writer is that these postscripts in both books are drawn from a common source of earlier origin, and this judgment is based upon the following observations: (*a*) The two series of passages in Jos and Jg are in only a very few instances actually identical. (*β*) In particular the tradition (Jg 1[21]) that Jerusalem belonged to the ideal sphere of the tribe of Benjamin, is to be considered the older, in opposition to the note (Jos 15[63], Jg 1[8]) that Jerus. was the object of an attack by Judah. See above, 4 *a*; and cf. the *mât* ('land' or 'district') or *mâtât* of *Urusalim* in the Tel el-Amarna letters (*Keilinsch. Bibliothek*, Bd. v. 180[25. 63] 181[49] 183[14] 185[1f.]). (*γ*) The ancient source from which the identical sentences in the two series of passages named are drawn, was not the Jahwistic. For these sentences contain a somewhat artlessly connected series of facts, and do not possess the life and the variety of colouring which mark the Jahwistic style (cf. Gn 18 f., 24, etc.). (*δ*) Precisely in the passage, Jos 15[14-19] (substantially=Jg 1[10-15]), which in some measure shows the lifelike style of the Jahwist, there is a deviation from Gn 24[64]. In the latter the rapid descent from the beast ridden is expressed by *wattippôl* (AV 'she lighted off'), but in Jos 15[18] and Jg 1[14] by *wattiznah* (AV 'she lighted [from] off'), and this verb *zânah* occurs nowhere else but in Jg 4[21]. If one takes all this into account, it will be found what degree of certainty attaches to the position of Budde, who in the *Kurzer Hdcomm.*, 1898, p. xxii, without positive argument, assigns to the Jahwistic work the following: Jg 1[1α3β. 2f. 5-7. 19. 21 (10. 20). 11-16. 36. 17. 22-29. 30-34]. Again, the view that the passages in question in the Bk. of Jos are borrowed from Jg 1 (Bertheau, *Commentar*[2], pp. 3, 37 f., 42) is, in the first place, unnecessary. For the circumstance that those passages in Jos have an 'inorganic' position in their context is explained as well by the view contended for above, that a common source of older origin is used in both books. But the view of Bertheau labours under at least *one* positive difficulty. In Jos 13[13] we find the same formula used, and yet this remark is not drawn from Jg 1.

To the *Jahwistic* source Budde (p. xxii) would attribute also, *e.g.*, 6[12b] and 11[1a], although in these sentences the expression *gibbôr hayil* (AV 'a mighty man of valour') is read. This expression is uniformly avoided in the Pent. (cf. the simple *gibbôr* in Gn 6[4] 10[8f.] ↑), but it meets us in Jos 1[14] 6[2] 8[3] 10[7], Jg 6[12] 11[1] etc. (cf. König, *Syntax*, § 267d). Winckler (*Untersuchungen zur altorient. Geschichte*, 1893-1897) speaks of the 'Quellen-Zusammensetzung der Gideon-Erzählungen' (pp. 42 ff.), and finds, *e.g.*, 7[9-14] and 7[15]–8[3] irreconcilable, because it is impossible that Gideon could have played the spy upon the Midianites (7[9ff.]) and yet have attacked them in the beginning of the middle watch (7[19]). But all that is related in 7[9ff.] might take place in a matter of four hours. The main point, however, is that Winckler adds (p. 49), 'Having thus to assume two different sources for the two narratives, it is most natural (!) to find in these E and J.' He thinks this suggestion is commended by the use in 7[14] of *hā'ĕlōhīm* 'the God.' But he has not observed that in 7[14b] it is the words of a Midianite that are reported. — The three passages in which *š* is used as the relative (6[17b] 7[12b] 8[26b])—a notable idiom of the history of Gideon—Budde (p. xxii) assigns thus, to J 8[26], to E 6[17b], to R[P] 7[12] (see below), only in the notes to the first two passages he sets these also down, *on account of* the *š*, as additions of a glossator. Also 11[8] belongs, according to Budde, to J, and yet the

concept of 'assemble themselves' is expressed only in this passage by הִתְלַקֵּם; cf. נֶאֱסַף, etc., Gn 29[3] 34[30] (both these passages are assigned to J also in Kautzsch's *AT*), Ex 32[26] (J also according to Ryssel, *Ex-Lv*, 1897, p. 370). Further, 15[1-19] is from J, according to Budde (pp. xxii, 92). But in those portions of the Pentateuch which are attributed to J, שֵׁנֵי is used before the objects enumerated, Gn 9[22] 19[1] (27[9]) 34[25], Ex 4[9] etc. (see König, *Syntax*, § 311c), but שְׁנֵיהֶם before such objects is found nowhere but in Ex 25[18a], Dt 17[6], Jos 2[1] 6[22], Jg 11[37. 39] 15[13] etc. (see *l.c.*).

(*b*) Can the *Elohistic* stratum (E) of the Pent. be traced in the Bk. of Jg? Budde has, to begin with, assigned 2[6. 8f.] to E (also 2[7] is=Jos 24[31], but as a whole it is ascribed by Budde [p. 21] to the Deut. redactor). This is correct in so far as the verses named are substantially identical with Jos 24[28-30], and that Jos 24 has indeed marks of the source E has been acknowledged by the present writer in his *Einleitung* (pp. 203 f., 248). The words of Jg 2[6-9] attach themselves to the Elohistic narrative of Joshua's end. But this does not prove that the Elohistic source has also supplied other elements in the Bk. of Jg. Budde attributes to this source, *e.g.*, 4[4-22], appealing (p. 33) to אִשָּׁה נְבִיאָה (4[4]; see the analogous expressions in König's *Syntax*, § 306o), etc. But he himself adds the judicious remark that he does not feel certain of his inference. At all events the use of מָשַׁךְ in 4[6] (where AV offers rightly 'draw') cannot be regarded as evidence. For even if Ex 12[21] could be certainly put down to E, the מֹשְׁכִים of Jg 5[14] (active, 'grasping the staff [of the commander]'—König, *Syntax*, § 212h ex.; LXX ἕλκοντες; Targ. and Pesh. כתבין, *scribentes* !) would have been a source nearer to hand for 4[6]. Further, Budde assigns 20[37a] to E, but not v.[37b] in spite of the מֹשֶׁךְ, which is found also in Job 21[33]. To an author denominated E[2] he ascribes Jg 6[7-10]. But, *e.g.*, עַל אֹדוֹת (6[7]) is found, not only in Gn (Samarit. 20[3]) 21[11. 25] 26[32], Ex 18[8], Nu 12[1] 13[24], Jos 14[6], but also in Jer 3[8]. Here then identity of expression does not prove identity of authors.

(*c*) Is a successor of the *Deuteronomic* author who, *e.g.*, wrote Dt 1[1f.]–4[40] etc. (see König's *Einleitung*, pp. 212-214) to be admitted also for the Bk. of Jg? The passages which repeatedly refer to Israel's disloyalty and Jahweh's anger, Israel's repentance and Jahweh's help (2[11-19] 3[7. 12a] 4[1-3] 6[1] 8[33-35] 10[6-16] 13[1]), have points of contact with the passages that are attributed with probability to the Deut. author, not only in their religious and moral tendency, but even in their form. For the verb הִכְעִים ('to provoke *or* vex') is found with God as the object only in Dt 4[25] (9[18]) 31[29] (32[16. 21]), Jg 2[12], and the verb מָכַר ('to sell'='deliver') is read in Dt 28[68] (התמכר) 32[30], Jg 2[14] (3[8]) 4[2. 9] 10[7]. But the same use of הִכְעִים meets us also in 1 K 14[15] 15[30] 16[2. 7. 13. 26. 33] 21[22] 22[54], 2 K 17[11. 17] 21[6] 23[26], Is 65[3], Jer 7[18f.] 8[19] 11[17] 25[6f.] 32[29f. 32] 44[3. 8], Ezk 8[17] 16[26], Ps 78[58] 106[29], 2 Ch 28[25] 33[6] 34[25] (|| 1 K 22[54], 2 K 17[17] 22[17]). Here again, then, this use of the verb הִכְעִים is no guarantee of the identity of the author of Dt 4[25] etc. with the author of Jg 2[12]. (Compare here the words of C. Niebuhr [*Studien u. Bemerkungen z. Gesch. d. alten Orients*, 1894, p. 1], 'Die wirkliche Nothwendigkeit einer sachlichen Unterscheidung von Dt und D (oder gar D[1] und D[2]) vermögen wir bisher nicht nachzuempfinden.')

(*d*) To an R[P], *i.e.* a redactor having affinities with the *priestly* stratum of the Pent., Budde (p. xxii) assigns the following passages in Jg: 1[1a] 2[17] 7[2-8a. 12. 14*] + 23 8[10a3b. 21β2. 27a3β (30-32)] 9[16b-19a (?)] 10[1-5] 11[1b. 2] 12[7b (?). 8-15] 16[31b] 20[18 (?). 23 (?). 27b. 28aα. 87b.

† By an asterisk Budde means to indicate that he regards the passage in question as having been worked over.

39. 42b. 43. 44b-46 21⁴ᵃᵝ. **14b. 19ᵅᵝ-20ᵅ.** But regarding 1¹ᵇᵅ he remarks merely that the words 'after the death of Joshua' are in direct contradiction to 2⁶ᶠᶠ. Yet this does not prove that these words are due to a redactor (Rᴾ). As little certainty appears to attach to the attributing of 2¹⁷ to this source. For כֵן עָשׂוּ לֹא 'they did not so,' reminds us not only 'strongly of P' (namely Gn 6²² etc.), but one may compare also Gn 29²⁶ 42²⁰· ²⁵ 45²¹, Ex 7⁶ etc., 1 K 20²⁵, 2 K 15¹², Jer 39¹² 42⁵, Zec 1⁶, Neh 8¹⁷. Further, on 7²⁻⁸ᵃ Budde remarks (p. 58) that צָרַף 'try' (Jg 7⁴), comes into use for the first time from Jer 9⁶ onwards, and that the suffixless לְבַד (7⁵) has parallels only in Ex 26⁶ 36⁶ (this last should be ¹⁶), Zec 12¹²⁻¹⁴. But in Jg 7⁵ it is not the usual idea 'alone' (solus) that is meant to be expressed, but the stronger idea of 'apart' (LXX κατὰ μόνας, Hieron. seorsum). Again, 7¹², which contains שׁ used for the relative, is ascribed by Budde to Rᴾ, but in the Pent. stratum P this שׁ is not found.

One might continue to criticise the views of Budde (cf. once more König's Einleitung, pp. 253 f.).* But we cease to test these in detail, and add merely a general remark. Budde says (p. xiv) that by J and E he understands, not persons, but schools.† But this was not the sense originally intended by the terms J and E, and the earlier meaning is not quite obsolete even with Budde. For he speaks still of the 'Zeitalter der Quellen J and E,' and places these sources in relation to the Hexateuch (p. xii). But according to his new view one ought to speak in the plural of 'J's' and 'E's,' and no longer of 'J' or 'E' (Budde, p. xiii), as if there were only 'the' Jahwist; we should say 'a' J(ahwist), etc. But far more important is the circumstance that upon the theory of a plurality of Jahwists the difficulty of tracing the family likeness is very seriously increased. Who has fixed the character of each J, and who can determine it? Then, indeed, is there a danger that such a J is an imaginary quantity, and that one still speaks of J but no longer has him. In any case the judgment of the present writer is to the following effect. Since the different sources from which, according to No. 4 of this article, the present Book of Judges is drawn, cannot be with certainty identified with the main strata of the Pentateuch, nothing results from the relation of Jg to these regarding the age of the materials of which Jg appears to be composed, or regarding the date of the book itself.

6. THE CHARACTER AND AGE OF THE SOURCES OF THE BOOK OF JUDGES.—(a) If any one of the components of the present Bk. of Jg is an independent whole, and reveals itself as a source, it is the *Poem in which the victory over Sisera is celebrated* (Jg 5). Its verses go tumbling on, foaming like the waves of the Kishon (5²¹), upon whose banks that victory was gained. Like the gallop of war-horses (5²²) ring the anaphora (vv.³ᵇ· ⁷ᵇ· ¹²ᵃ· ²³ᵃ), the epizeuxis (¹²ᵃ· ²²ᵇ), and the symploke (⁷ᵃ· ²⁴ᵃᵇ, cf. 19ᵅᵅᵝ· ²⁰ᵅᵅᵝ) in this poem, towards removing whose difficulties the present writer has contributed his part, he trusts not quite unsuccessfully in his Syntax (cf. p. 645). This song gives so detailed (vv.⁶· ¹⁰ᵃ· ¹⁴⁻¹⁸· ²³) and so lively a picture of the historical situation (vv.²⁴⁻²⁷· ²⁸⁻³⁰) which is commemorated in it, that it must have been born of that situation, even if it has not come down to us quite intact. This is the judg-

*W. Frankenberg (die Composition des deuteronom. Richterbuches, 1895, p. 1) remarks, 'A deeper insight into the original contents and the historical origin of the Bk. of Jg is sufficient of itself to convince one of the futility of the attempts that are ever being made afresh to build a literary bridge between the Hexateuch and our Bk. of Jg, and to discover the sources of the Hex. in the latter.'

† 'J und E sind mir durchaus nicht Personen, sondern umfassende, neben einander herlaufende schriftstellerische Schulen.'

ment rightly passed upon it even by such free critics as, e.g., Th. Nöldeke (Untersuch. z. Kritik d. AT, p. 181), H. Steiner (die Heb. Poesie, 1873, p. 24), Ed. Meyer (Gesch. d. Alterthums, i. § 167), B. Stade (Gesch. Isr. i. 49), Aug. Müller (in Königsberger Studien, 1887, p. 7), E. Renan (Hist. du peuple d'Israel, i. 136), J. Wellhausen (Comp. d. Hex. p. 23), H. Cornill (Einleitung, § 16, 3), G. Moore (Judges, p. 132 f.), J. Marquart (Fundamente, etc., 1896, p. 2), K. Budde (Comm. p. 39), Ch. Piepenbring (Hist. du peuple d'Israel, 1898, p. 85: 'ce vieux cantique').

Nor can this judgment be shattered by the arguments which are brought forward by L. Seinecke (Gesch. d. Volkes Israel, i. 243–245). Neither (a) are the political presuppositions of the Song wanting in historical reality, nor do (β) its form or (γ) its contents render a high antiquity impossible for it. For (a) even if the northern Canaanites sustained a defeat in the time of Joshua (see below, 8 a, on Jos 11¹⁰⁻¹⁴), their strength might have recovered itself. (β) The use of שׁ for the relative (5⁷) has analogies in OT passages of a more northern Palestine origin (see further, 6 d). The plur. ending -in (5¹⁰) may have the same origin, or it may be an element in the poetical dialect as in Pr 31³ etc. (see König, Lehrgebäude, ii. 434). To the same category belong also תִּנָּה (5¹¹: (?) cf. 'im Wechselgesang vortragen,' 'repeat,' 'relate'; cf. the Aram. תְּנָא in the Targ. on Ps 9¹² etc., and the Assyr. šunnú, 'communicate' (Del. Assyr. Wörterb. 1896, p. 700ᵃ). (γ) The heights of Seir (5⁴), which lay north of the Peninsula of Sinai, are named as the starting-point of Jahweh who manifested Himself on Sinai (v.⁵). This tallies with the ancient conception that the seat of the gods was in the northern region of the earth, Lv 1¹¹ 4²⁴ etc., Is 14¹³ (Jer 1¹³), Ezk 1⁴ (28¹⁴), Ps 48³ (133³), cf. Job 26⁷. This theophany is also intended as a past one. For the temporal sphere of an infin. depends upon its context (Gn 28⁵ᵇ etc. ; see König's Syntax, § 216), and בְּצֵאתְךָ, etc. (Jg 5⁴ᵅᵅ) is followed by the perfects רָעָשָׁה, etc. Then יֵעַל (v.⁶) may, coming after פִּימֵי, have arisen from עַל (cf. [אַ אֹרַח] עַל 1 Ch 7³⁹), the name of a descendant of Asher. It is probable that, as a parallel to שָׁמְגַּר, a man is intended (cf. Bertheau, ad loc.).* But even if the words עַל פִּימֵי are a gloss (Moore, Marquart, Budde), the antiquity of the poem itself is not thereby endangered. Finally, the assertion that 'from heaven forces took part in the battle' (5²⁰), contains a religio-poetical clothing of the conception that God assisted the Israelites (cf. Ex 14²⁴, Jos 10¹¹). The assertion is not then to be called a 'gross exaggeration' of a later author.†

*Marquart (Fundamente, etc., 1896, p. 2) takes Shamgar to be 'der fremde Oberkönig,' and combines him with 'Sangara of Carchemish, in the time of Ašurnâzirabal, c. B.C. 880,' and Sisera with 'Piziri the last king of Carchemish' (c. B.C. 740). What an amount of error in the Hebrew tradition is thus assumed without any sufficient reason !

† H. Winckler in his Altorient. Forschungen (1893–1897) offers the following remarks on Jg 5: שְׂדֵה in v.⁴='height' (p. 192, cf. Assyr. šadu, 'to be high'). This is possible. But it is more probable that זֶה סִינַי in v.⁵ is an intermediate exclamation (see König, Syntax, § 414a) than that זֶה הַ has arisen from רְנוּ (p. 192). The substitution of שׁוּרֵר 'row' for שֹׁרֵר in v.¹³ (p. 291) is not probable. In v.¹⁴ᵅᵅ he reads (p. 193), בְּעֵמֶק שָׁרוּ אֶפְרַיִם מִנִּי 'from Ephraim they came down (cf. שׁוּר) into the valley,' and he deletes v.¹⁴ᵅᵇ entirely. We would rather suggest that the gibbôrîm of v.¹³ ᵉˣ· are 'heroes from Ephraim,' and that then מְשָׁרֵשִׁים is meant to signify 'eradicantes, i.e. delentes inter Amalek' (cf. LXX ἐξερίζωσεν). Also the reading בְּרַבַת עַם בִּי שָׂרוּ 'and there came down in Issachar the people of Dabrat' (p. 292), is extremely precarious. For it would be unnatural if after the princes, etc. (v.¹⁴ᵇ), the population of a single city (Jos 19¹²) should be mentioned. Finally, instead of קְדוּמִים נַחַל (v.²¹ᵃ) Winckler suggests (p. 193) the sentence, 'the stream of Kishon was [dyed, or the like] with blood' (דָּמִים). But the cir-

M. Vernes (*Précis d'histoire juive*, p. 210) holds that at the very outset (*péremptoirement*) it must be regarded as a settled point that at this epoch we cannot have to do with a campaign undertaken by the tribes of Israel in common. But why might not an extraordinary danger have brought about an extraordinary coalition of many tribes of Israel for common defence against the enemy? Some tribes, indeed, declined to be stirred up from their phlegmatic condition (5^{15-17}). Further, Vernes finds in the mention of Sinai and of Seir 'l'ignorance ou, si l'on préfère, la negligence de l'homme qui écrit librement à grande distance de son sujet.' But he has himself failed to observe that the mention of Mt. Seir had reference to a *northern* starting-point of the theophany of Jahweh (see above, regarding the idea of the northern sphere as the seat of deity). Again, the days of Shamgar, although he defeated the Philistines (3^{31}), might still be a time of oppression (4^4), and, besides, the note in 4^4 *may* be primary, and that in 3^{31} secondary. Further, *if* the Kishon is called in 5^{21} 'l'antique fleuve' (but see König's *Syntax*, § 261d), this expression could be used even in the days of Deborah. According to Vernes, the sentence 'Dan אֲנִיּוֹת יָגוּר' ($v.^{17}$) is also an unnatural one, for 'jamais les Danites n'ont touché à la mer.' But even if we are not to think, with *Mikhlal Jophi*, of אֲנִיּוֹת הַיַּרְדֵּן, the Danites might 'dwell' as strangers, *i.e.* serve on board ships. Finally, Vernes will have it that even the address to kings and princes in $v.^3$ 'indique une époque de relations internationales.' Well, such an epoch was to hand already at the date of the Tel el-Amarna letters! In the *Rev. des Études juives*, xxiv. (1892), p. 249, Vernes calls *sarai* ($v.^{15}$) an 'état construit ou (!) pluriel de forme araméenne,' and co-ordinates with it '*tsavrè*, plus exactment, *tsavrai*'! ($v.^{30}$). He denies the existence of 'marques du dialecte hébreu septentrionale' (p. 249^2); but see below, 6 *d*. He thinks 'que la terminologie familière au Cantique est celle des livres de la Bible dont on admet le plus volontiers l'origine post-exilienne.' But he has failed to notice that poetry, even in the earliest times, may have preferred expressions which, owing to their rarity or their more foreign cast, lend to the Song of Deborah a special charm. Thus, *e.g.*, the verb פרע ($v.^2$) will not have been 'emprunté aux Nombres et au Lévitique' (p. 249), even if is not to be translated with M. Lambert (p. 141), 'se dépouiller (pour Dieu), offrir généreusement (cf. en himyarite la locution פרע פרע 'faire une offrande').'

H. Winckler (*Gesch. Israels*, Bd. i. (1895), p. 34) admits first that the Song (Jg 5) goes back to the pre-Davidic era, because 'it knows nothing of Judah.' But he adds that 'the form in which the Song has come down to us is a product of a much later age, which transformed it for its own ends, and made of it something quite different from what it originally was.' On what grounds does he rest this judgment? All that he says is, '$vv.^{4f.}$ are manifestly an interpolation, and form the beginning of a hymn to Jahweh which has nothing whatever to do with the Song of Deborah. Also $v.^{31}$ belongs to the same.' It is clear, he says, that the Song is a compound from a hymn to J" which is full of mythological allusions ('the stars fought'), and from a piece intended to glorify a battle fought by the Northern tribes. It would scarcely be possible to find weaker arguments than these. Are $vv.^{4f.}$ 'manifestly' an interpolation? Was it not natural that the words 'I will sing praise to the Lord God of Israel' ($v.^3$) should be actually followed by some lines in praise of this God? Was it not natural that at the beginning of a poem meant to celebrate

cumstance that no trace of such a text has been preserved in exegetic tradition (see König's *Syntax*, § 261a) is a formidable objection.

a notable action of the Deity, there should be a recalling of a well-known manifestation by which Jahweh established His renown? Would it have been more natural if, after the mention of the determination to praise the Deity ($v.^3$), the Song had proceeded 'in the days of Shamgar,' etc.? ($v.^6$). Further, the wish 'so perish all thine enemies, J"!' ($v.^{31}$) could not, it is said, be uttered by a pre-Davidic poet. But must not a poem on a decisive defeat of the northern Canaanites quite naturally burst into such a wish? Consequently Winckler has by no means established his contention, and the poem contained in Jg 5 remains one of the most important sources for the earliest history of Israel.

(*b*) Another ancient source for the present Bk. of Jg is found springing up in the first chapter. In favour of this judgment is first of all the primary character of the tradition that 'Urusalimu' belonged to the sphere of the Benjamites (Jg 1^{21}, Dt 33^{12} contrasted with Jg 1^8, Jos 15^{63}). The following circumstance is at the same time not to be overlooked. What is the meaning of the words 'with the Benjamites' in the sentence 'and the Jebusites dwelt with the Benjamites in Jerusalem unto this day'? (1^{21b}). The meaning must be 'within the territory of the Benjamites,' *i.e.* in the sphere which was assigned to the Benjamites as object of the conquest, and was also in the main actually occupied (cf. 'the Jebusites, the inhabitants of the land,' 2 S 5^6 || 1 Ch 11^4). This sense is suggested for the words 'with the Benjamites' by several considerations, one negative and several positive. In the first place, immediately before 1^{21b} it is remarked, 'and (= but) the Benjamites did not drive out the Jebusites, the inhabitants of Jerusalem.' The direct consequence of this failure of the Benjamites in their attack on the Jebusites (1^{21a}) was that the Jebusites dwelt alongside of the Benjamites in Jerusalem ($v.^{21b}$). Further, the Jebusites are called simply 'the' inhabitants of Jerusalem (Jos 15^{63}, Jg 1^{21a}), and Jebus is simply identified with Jerusalem (יְרוּשָׁלַ͏ִם הִיא יְבוּס Jg 19^{10}, Jos 18^{28}, or conversely in 1 Ch 11^4). Again, in the remark that the Levite (Jg $19^{1ff.}$) was in the neighbourhood of Jerusalem ($v.^{10}$), the latter is called simply 'this city of the Jebusites' (19^{11b}), and it is expressly added that it was 'the city of a stranger that was not of the children of Israel' (19^{12}). In any case the author of 1^{21} did not record merely the failure of the Benjamites to conquer Jerusalem. Had this been all, he might in his account of the period of the judges have passed over in silence the victory of the Judahite David (2 S $5^{6ff.}$) and yet have written after this victory. No, he must have added that the Jebusites were the—sole—inhabitants of Jerus. down to his own day. Now, it is quite true that even after David's victory (2 S $5^{6ff.}$) Jebusites continued to live in Jerusalem ($24^{16ff.\ 24}$). But at that period the Jebusites were no longer 'the' inhabitants of Jerusalem (see above), but were oppressed (1 K 9^{20}, Zec 9^7). But also most of the other portions of Jg 1 are trustworthy reflections of an ancient situation. For it was very natural that in later times there should be a disposition to represent the success of Joshua's invasion as absolute (see below, 8 *a*, on Jos 11^{10-14}). All the more do the narratives which record the defeats sustained by Israel in their attacks upon the Canaanites, bear the stamp of antiquity. This is confirmed by the wealth of details in the first chapter regarding individual occurrences of this kind which cannot be traced to a certain or probable tendency of later times.

(*c*) Now a similar dry enumeration of particulars is found also in the passages concerning Shamgar (3^{31}), Tola ($10^{1f.}$), Jair ($vv.^{3-5}$), Ibzan (12^{8-10}), Elon (v.[11f.]), and 'Abdon (vv.[13-15]). The modern view of these passages is that they were first introduced into the Bk. of Jg at its final redaction (Budde, p. x). What is there to allege in favour of this position?

(a) It is said that this late redactor (R[P], see above, 5 d) wished to obtain the number *twelve* for the judges (Budde, p. x). For 'in the light of 10[1] the sections 10[1-5] and 12[8-15] recognize Abimelech also as a judge' (pp. ix, 19). Thus 'Abimelech, Tola, Jair, Ibzan, Elon, and 'Abdon were for R[P] the minor judges.' But was Abimelech really reckoned one of the *shôphĕṭim*? What is said in 10[1]? 'And after Abimelech there arose, to defend Israel, Tola,' etc. This implies, it is said, that Abimelech was reckoned among the 'judges' or 'saviours' of Israel. One might also say that this method of argumentation is typical of a certain modern school of historiography. The express statements of the sources are absolutely ignored, and new and extremely doubtful ones are sought out. For instance, is it not related in 8[23] and 9[2] that the kind of rule (מֹשֵׁל) which was declined by Gideon because Jahweh was the true king of Israel (Ex 15[18] יְהֹוָה יִמְלֹךְ), was desired by Abimelech? Did not the latter surround himself with a body of armed men? (9[4. 29b], cf. Absalom 2 S 15[1]). Is it not expressly said that the men of Shechem made Abimelech *king* (9[6]); and is this not confirmed by the fable of Jotham? (9[8-18] 'the trees went forth to anoint a *king*,' etc.). Again, Abimelech is further called a 'prince' (9[22] וַיָּשַׂר; cf. the corresponding 'that we should *serve* him' vv.[28. 38]), but not a 'judge.' Nor does his history contain any trace of his having sought to free (הוֹשִׁיעַ) Israel from the yoke of foreign enemies. All the less can the 'to deliver Israel' (לְהוֹשִׁיעַ אֶת־יִשְׂרָאֵל 10[1]) be referred to Abimelech. Further, it is extremely questionable whether a late redactor desired to establish *twelve* as the number of the judges. For not only is Samson, to whom 'delivering Israel' is attributed (13[5], cf. 14[4] 15[3ff.] 16[23f. 30]), counted amongst the judges (15[20] 16[31]),* but also Eli (1 S 4[18b]) and Samuel (7[15]). This could not be unknown to a later redactor of the Bk. of Jg. How then can the disposition be ascribed to him to make the number of the judges twelve? Besides, Budde himself remarks that in the Bk. of Jg thirteen 'judges' are mentioned, if Abimelech as well as Shamgar is included in the number. But he is not so much inclined to give up Abimelech as Shamgar, in order to reduce the thirteen to twelve. This is quite an arbitrary procedure, for the attribute of 'delivering Israel' which belonged to the character of a *shôphēṭ* (2[16]) is ascribed to Shamgar (3[31]) but not to Abimelech. Or is Shamgar no real historical figure because in a series of MSS of the LXX and in the Itala (cf. Mez, *die Bibel des Josephus*, p. 81 note) he is named not only in 3[31] but also after 16[31]? This vacillating of the textual tradition as to the right place for mentioning Shamgar is explicable by reason of the 'and after him' and the 'Philistines.' But it does not disprove the historicity of an Israelitish hero Shamgar who came upon the scene at a stormy period (5[6]).

(β) Another ground on which the passages 10[1f. 3-5] 12[8-10. 11f. 13-15] are assigned to a very late redactor (R[P]), is the following:—In these five sections it is not recorded that Israel was false to its religion, and on that account had to suffer oppression for a term of years, and was delivered

from this by a hero. 'The extreme attenuation of the Deuteron. formula is exhibited in 3[31]. There is mention, indeed, of an act of deliverance, but of no number of years' (Budde, p. 19). But what if those circumstances of which there is no notice did not exist, or were partly not remembered? Can their absence bring into question the historical character of the persons themselves? In the section concerning Othniel (3[9-11]), which by Budde and others is separated from the above six passages, are there any more real elements? It is quite true that something had 'faded,' but this was the recollection of those personages, and not the 'Deuteronomistic formulæ.' What could have prevented the introducing of those formulæ even at a late period into the biography of the persons named. Hence the conclusion appears more certain that it was not the 'formulæ' that were wanting, but the disposition to modify historical reminiscences in accordance with these formulæ. That has been handed down regarding those persons which was known of them, and this was not little: the name of the man himself and that of his father or his tribe, or it may be the place of his birth and his burial (10[2. 5] 12[10. 12. 15]), or the remembrance of some notable deed done by him (3[31]), etc. Why should all this be set down to invention? Not because of a wish to reach the number *twelve* for the judges, as we have seen already. Or was it, perchance, to give a judge to each tribe? The tribes of the individual judges were as follows:— *Judah* (Othniel 3[9]), *Benjamin* (Ehud 3[15];? Shamgar 3[31]), *Naphtali* (Barak 4[6]), *Ephraim* (Gideon 6[11]), *Issachar* (Tola 10[1]), *Gilead* (Jair 10[3]), ? *Gilead* (Jephthah 11[1]), *Judah* (Ibzan 12[8]), *Zebulun* (Elon 12[11]), *Ephraim* ('Abdon 12[13]), *Dan* (Samson 13[2]). One may observe that in this list some tribes occur twice, and that a few tribes are wanting altogether. If an explanation of the local origin of these judges is to be sought for, it is most natural to find it in the circumstance that the hero sprang up from the tribe which felt most the weight of the invader's oppression. Finally, how came poetic fancy and constructive historiography to distribute in their present fashion the six passages 3[31] 10[1-5] 12[8-15]? It is impossible for the present writer to consent to see in this arrangement simply an arbitrary procedure.

(d) But there are in the Bk. of Jg also such life-like and vivid narratives as cannot be set down to the ideas or tendencies of a later age.

(a) The history of Abimelech (Jg 9) even M. Vernes (*Hist. juive*, p. 218) calls 'un récit d'une précision, d'un relief étonnant.' But it is not the only one of this class in Jg, as he adds, but it is the only one that is almost wholly *secular* in its character. It is the only narrative in Jg which is true to the life—only for those critics to whom the *secular* life is the *only* real life of ancient Israel. Critics who occupy such a standpoint will not deny the attribute of antiquity to such a story as that of the Benjamite Ehud, who with his *left* hand stabbed the tyrant Eglon (Jg 3[15ff.]). Such critics will not be disposed to deny the historicity of the bold figure of Jephthah, or of the tragic end of his only child (11[L]-12[7]). As a 'héros d'aventures privées' even Samson has found grace in the eyes of M. Vernes (p. 238), according to whom the exploits of Samson belonged to the 'disputes qui devaient naître fréquemment à l'époque historique des relations établies entre populations antipathiques.' *

---

* And this not without reason, as M. Vernes (*Hist. juive*, p. 237) supposed when he said, 'Laissons de côté l'étrange prétention de nous faire voir dans Samson un juge d'Israël.' For from the words, 'the Lord raised up judges, which delivered them out of the hand of those that spoiled them' (Jg 2[16], cf. 1 S 8[5b]), it results that the term *shôphēṭ* had assumed the more general sense of 'hero,' or 'leader.'

* M. Vernes adds the following note: 'Il s'agit là, ce nous semble, d'une antipathie comme entre Anglais et Français à tant d'époques de notre histoire. On est en paix officielle, on s'unit par des mariages, etc., mais de temps en temps la haine nationale se fait jour par des explosions violentes. Il reste à remarquer que Samson ne se bat pas une seule fois avec l'épée ou la lance; jamais il n'est à la tête d'une troupe quelconque.

(β) But the *religious* life also was a real one in ancient Israel. As early as the time of Moses and during the following centuries zeal for the cause of Jahweh could burn (Ex 32²⁵ff.), and enthusiasm be aroused for the defence of His honour. For, if the flame of reverence for J″ had not been kindled by Moses, why should he and not Samuel have been named as the greatest hero of the religious development of Israel? If the fire of enthusiasm for the religion of J″ was not lighted at the great epoch of the deliverance from Egypt, how could this fire have burst out just at a period of the deepest depression (1 S 4¹⁶ff.), and why should Israel have felt convicted of impiety against Jahweh? (1 S 7⁶ᵇ). Hence there is no reasonable ground for doubt that Gideon (Jg 6¹¹ff.) contended for the cult of Jahweh in opposition to the preference for Ba'al, or that he could have taken for his battle-cry, 'For Jahweh and for Gideon (will we fight),' Jg 7¹⁸ᵇ. Besides, it is in the highest degree worthy of notice that it is precisely in the history of a hero belonging to the tribe of Ephraim, *i.e.* to central Caanan, that the use of שׁ for the relative appears (6¹⁷ 7¹² 8²⁶). For it is of the tribe of Ephraim alone that it is recorded in the OT that its dialect differed from that of other Hebrews (Jg 12⁶); cf. on the speech of Ashdod as a Hebrew dialect, etc., König, *Lehrgebäude*, ii. 349, 353. Further, it is a fact that in the narratives concerning Elijah and Elisha the following linguistic peculiarities appear: אוּת 'with,' 2 K 1¹· ¹⁵ 3¹¹ff. ²⁶ 6¹⁶· ¹⁹ 8⁸; the shorter form *Eliyya* (and *Ahazya*), 1²⁻⁴· ⁸· ¹²; אַתִּי ('*attî*, 'thou,' fem.) 4¹⁶· ²³ 8¹; the corresponding לְכִי ('to thee,' fem.) 4²; כִּי ('thy,' fem.) 4³· ⁷; שׁ, relative, 6¹¹; cf. אֵיכָה 'where'?, 6¹³, so elsewhere only in Ca 1⁷ (Kethîbh) בַּשְׂדֶה 2 K 7¹², and the same phenomenon shows itself in ancient histories like those of 1 S 13²¹, 2 S 16². Therefore it is a sufficiently well-grounded judgment that the present narratives concerning Gideon are compiled from materials which, so to say, bear a *local* colouring. This judgment is at least supported, further, by two material circumstances. For it is a fact, admitted even, *e.g.*, by Wellhausen (*Prolegom.* p. 71), that the description of the offering contained in Jg 6¹⁷f. corresponds to the earliest stage of the history of the cultus in Israel. Another point has hitherto not been emphasized, but it is of no less importance. The disinclination manifested by Gideon to accept of the offer made to him to be ruler (מָשַׁל Jg 8²³ 'the Lord shall rule over you') is perfectly in place in the period before Samuel. For it was not till his time that Israel rejected the kingship of Jahweh (Ex 15¹⁸) ('they have rejected me, that I should not reign over them,' 1 S 8⁷).

(γ) In like manner the antiquity of the narrative contained in Jg 17 f. is witnessed to. For the possession by the Ephraimite Micah of a private house of gods (17⁵ᵃ) tallies with the circumstance that in the earlier period a plurality of places of worship was allowed (Ex 20²⁴⁻²⁶). Further, we see a Levite wandering about, ready to settle down wherever he found office and bread (17⁸ff· 18¹⁹f· 19¹). This situation of the members of the tribe of Levi was an actual one as long as a number of the Levitical cities were not yet conquered, such as Gezer (Jos 21²¹ 16¹⁰, Jg 1²⁹), and those remarks of the Bk. of Jg about the Levites would have possessed no probability if they had proceeded from a period when Jeroboam selected priests from among the people at large (1 K 12³¹). For the Levite spoken

Les éléments de son histoire nous semblent, en conséquence, appartenir à une époque relativement peu ancienne.' But this is nearly the opposite of the real course of things. It is precisely in olden times that heroes signalize themselves in single combat. Recall, for instance, the giant figures of the Greek world of legend, the heroes of Homer, or the giants of the German pre-historic era.

of in Jg 17⁸ff· wandered from Judah to the territory of Ephraim, etc., but after the time of Jeroboam many members of the tribe of Levi, on the contrary, moved from the territories of the Northern tribes to the kingdom of Judah (2 Ch 11¹³ᵗ·). Finally, the note that the priests of the city of Dan were descendants of Moses (Jg 18³⁰), must be borrowed from an ancient source. Later generations were so little disposed to invent such an item, that they sought rather to convert the name of Moses in this passage into Manasseh.

(δ) But also the *moral* life of ancient Israel did not lack its characteristic aim and peculiar vigour. Even in early times Israel was conscious of a certain sum of moral principles, for we read, 'no such thing ought to be done in Israel': 'do not thou this folly,' and the like (cf. Gn 20¹¹ 34⁷ᵇ, Jg 19³⁰ 20⁶ᵇ, 2 S 13¹²). And, since these principles of morality in the most central parts of Israelitish tradition are traced back to the time of Moses, why should we seek for a different origin for them? Is it at all probable, for instance, that they originated at periods which do not give themselves out as creative, but as secondary? Now these ancient principles of the morality of Israel lived in the conscience of this nation, and when they were trodden underfoot, as in the instance of Gibeah (Jg 19²³ff·), the voice of the moral conscience of the nation spoke out loudly (20⁶⁻⁸). Hence it is quite precarious to pronounce the storm of indignation that broke loose upon the Benjamites (v.⁹ff·) fictitious. Finally, the assertion that in the time of the judges a 'common acting on the part of the twelve tribes of Israel is excluded' (Budde on chs. 19-21), is quite ungrounded. Nay, it has not yet been taken into account that the Song of 5¹ff· contains an indirect proof to the contrary effect. For if in the period of the judges one could not entertain the notion that a common danger to Israel must be warded off by the common action of all the tribes, one could not have blamed those tribes which kept aloof from the struggle against the northern Canaanites (Jg 5¹⁵⁻¹⁷).

(ε) There is a series of passages in the Bk. of Jg in which the declension of the national prosperity is brought into causal connexion with the religious and moral falling away of the people (cf. especially 2¹¹ff· 3⁷· ¹²ᵃ 4¹⁻³ 6¹ 8³³⁻³⁵ 10⁶⁻¹⁶ 13¹). It has been shown above (5 c) that these passages cannot with certainty be attributed to a definite Deuteron. author, but we now add the following observations, by way of an attempt to fix positively the character and the age of these passages. (α) There was a religious-moral consciousness on the part of Israel (cf. 6 d, δ) before the period to which the origin of Dt is traced by a large number of critics, *i.e.* the reign of king Josiah. (β) During the centuries that elapsed between Moses and Samuel, 'the knees which have not bowed unto Baal' (1 K 19¹⁸) were not quite wanting. Let us recall, for instance, Deborah and Gideon. (γ) In addition to that series of passages which now are assigned by several critics to a Deuteronomist (Budde's D²), are there not others in the Bk. of Jg in which the same causal nexus between religious unfaithfulness and national decadence is emphasized? cf. 2¹⁻⁵. (δ) May not such passages have been formulated in the guilds of *nĕbî'îm* which gathered around Samuel? (1 S 10³⁻⁷ etc.). (ε) Nor can it be denied that a kernel of farewell addresses of Moses existed before these assumed their present form in Dt (cf. König, *Einleitung*, pp. 214-216). (ζ) Those passages of Jg which are now by many scholars called Deuteronomistic, are even in relation to their *contents* not really allied to the passages of the Books of Kings which have points of contact with Dt (1 K 3²ᵗ· 11⁶ etc.; see König, *Einleitung*, p. 267). For it is extremely interesting that in Jg the covenant of J″ is mentioned only in $2^{1.\ 20}$ and the commands of J″ only in $2^{17.\ 34}$, but these things are mentioned in 1 K 2^2 $3^{3.\ 14}$ $6^{12.\ 38}$ $8^{31.\ 55.\ 58.\ 61}$ $9^{4.\ 6}$ $11^{11.\ 33f.\ 38}$ 13^{21} 14^8 18^{18} $19^{10.\ 14}$, 2 K 10^{31} 13^{23} 14^6 $17^{8.\ 13.\ 15f.\ 19.\ 34.\ 37f.}$. $18^{6.\ 12}$ 21^8 $22^{8.\ 11}$ $23^{2f.\ 21.\ 24f.}$. Further, the idea of the centralization of the cultus is not emphasized in that series of passages which it is usual to call Deuteronomistic. No word of censure is uttered against the *bāmôth* as in 1 K $3^{2f.}$ 15^{14} $22^{44.\ 47}$, 2 K 12^3 $14^{3f.}$ $15^{3f.\ 34f.}$ $18^{5.\ 22}$ $23^{5.\ 8.\ 25}$. Besides, when the remark is made that D² 'den Begriff des Richter geschaffen hat' (Budde, p. xvi), in support of which Jg 2^{16} is cited, we miss here a recollection of the words, 'since the time that I commanded judges to be over my people Israel' (2 S 7^{11}).

(*f*) There are only a few passages in Jg which possess sufficiently clear marks of a late origin.

(*a*) We do not venture to reckon among these elements those passages where the intervention of a supernatural power is described, as in the expression 'an (see König's *Syntax*, § 304 *e*) angel of the LORD' (2^1 $13^{3ff.}$), or 'the Spirit of the LORD came upon him,' etc. (3^{10} 6^{34} 11^{29} $14^{6.\ 19}$ 15^{14}). For 'there are more things in heaven and earth, Horatio, than are dreamt of in your philosophy.'

(*β*) But we find, undoubtedly, a series of so-called 'round numbers'; 'seven' ($6^{1.\ 15}$ 8^{26} 12^9 $16^{7f.\ 13.\ 19}$ 20^{15}), or 'seventy' (1^7 8^{30} [repeated in $9^{2.\ 5.\ 18.\ 24.\ 56}$] 4 12^{14}), or 'seventy-seven' (8^{14}), or 'forty' (3^{11} $5^{8.\ 31}$ 8^{28} 13^1). There are, indeed, also instances where the number 'seven' is meant in an exact sense, as in the case of the seven days of the marriage feast ($14^{12.\ 17}$); for such a feast even at the present day actually lasts, as a rule, for seven days, and is called 'the king's *week*' (Wetzstein, *Zeitschrift f. Ethnologie*, v. 291, 293). But the numbers 'seven,' 'seventy,' and 'forty' are unquestionably intended frequently in an approximate sense; cf. 'seven' in Gn 4^{15} 31^{23} 33^3, Ex 7^{25}, Lv $26^{18.\ 24.\ 28}$, Dt $28^{7.\ 25}$, 1 S 2^5 etc., Is 4^1 etc.; 'seventy' in Gn 46^{27}, Ex 1^5 15^{27} $24^{1.\ 9}$, Nu $11^{16.\ 24f.}$ 33^9, Dt 10^{22}, 2 K 10^1, Is 23^{15}, Jer 25^{11} 29^{10}, Ezk 8^{11}, Ps 90^{10}, Lk 10^1; 'seventy-seven' in Gn 4^{24}; 'forty' in Gn 6^3, Ex 7^7 16^{35} etc., Dt 34^7, 1 S 4^{18} 17^{16}, 2 S 5^4 15^7, 1 K 2^{11} 11^{42} 19^8, Ezk 4^6 29^{11-13}, Am 2^{10} 5^{25}, Jon 3^4, Ps 95^{10}, Neh 9^{21}, Mt 4^2, Ac 1^3; cf. the Egyp. and the Gr. parallels in Gn 50^3 and Herodot. ii. 29, iii. 23, iv. 73. The psychological origin of the employment of these numbers lies in this, that naturally it was only approximately and by a familiar expression that one could or would indicate a smaller or a larger quantity. Cf. Adrianos, Εἰσαγωγὴ εἰς τὰς θείας γραφάς, § 85 : 'Τὸν ἑπτὰ ἀριθμὸν ἐπὶ πλεονασμοῦ λέγει (ἡ γραφή).'

To the same category may be assigned also the numbers 'eighty' (3^{30}), 'twenty' (4^3 15^{20} 16^{31}; from 40+20 arose the 60 which in Jg 12^7 is assigned by the LXX B, etc., as the length of the sway of Jephthah), 'ten' (6^7 12^{11}, cf. Gn 31^7, Lv 26^{26}, Nu 14^{22}, 1 S 1^8 etc., Is 6^{13}, Am 5^3 etc., the ten temptations of Abraham in the *Book of Jubilees*, ch. 19), and the 'fifty' which is read by LXX A, etc., in 3^{11} (cf. Gn 18^{24}, Jos 7^{21}, 1 S 6^{19} etc.). Also the number 'three' in the three years' reign of Abimelech (Jg 9^{22}) might bear the same character; because 'three' sometimes designates an approximate quantity (Gn 30^{36} $40^{10.\ 12}$ 42^{27}, Ex 2^2 etc., Is 16^{14} 20^3, Jon 2^1, Est 4^{16}, Dn 1^5, 1 Ch 21^{12}). But then the history of Abimelech possesses in other respects many marks of exactitude (see above, 6 *d*, *a*). It is certainly, however, an unjustifiable procedure to include in this class of numbers the 'eighteen' of Jg 3^{14}, the 'twenty-three' of 10^2, or the 'twenty-two' read by a few Gr. minuscula MSS in 10^2, probably in imitation of the following number 22, the

'eighteen' of 10^8, the 'forty-two' of 12^6, the 'six' of 12^7, or the 'eight' of 12^{14}.*

This last procedure would be justifiable only upon the assumption that these numbers may be regarded as the arbitrarily chosen parts of a previously fixed total. In point of fact, the following observation has been made: the sum of the interregna ($3^{8.\ 14}$ 4^3 6^1 10^8 : $8+18+20+7+18=71$) almost exactly corresponds to the sum of the years of the so-called minor Judges ($10^{2f.}$ $12^{9.\ 11.\ 14}$: $23+22+7+10+8=70$). Wellhausen, who was the first to note this correspondence (in Bleek's *Introd.*[4] p. 185, and in *Prolegom.*[2] p. 240), afterwards confessed (*Comp. of Hex.* p. 356) that he had no longer much faith in his former attempt. But Budde, in the *Kurzer Hdcomm.* (1897, p. xviii), still regards the observation as pertinent in spite of the difference of the two totals that are said to correspond with one another. But if a redactor of Jg had any thought of this correspondence, would he not have been capable of making it an exact one?

Hence the approximate character can be emphasized only in the case of the number 40 and its actual double (80) or its half (20). This is commended further by the following three considerations. The number 40 occurs with relatively great frequency as a round number (see the series of passages cited above). Further, the 480 years which, according to 1 K 6^1, elapsed between the Exodus and the beginning of the building of the temple (in the 4th year of Solomon's reign), are probably a product of 40×12. Again, the length of a generation (דוֹר, Arab. *dârun*, lit. περίοδος) was probably, in the view of the Israelites, 40 years. For a generation, with few exceptions, was doomed to die in the wilderness (Nu $14^{22f.}$ 26^{64}), and this sojourn in the wilderness lasted for (about) 40 years (Nu $14^{33f.}$ $20^{22ff.}$ 32^{13} $33^{38f.}$, Dt 2^7 8^2 29^5, Jos 5^6 etc.).† Besides, Bertheau (*Comm.*² p. xvi) rightly observes that in 1 Ch 5^{29-34} 6^{35-38} twelve generations are counted from Aaron to Ahimaaz the contemporary of David and Solomon. Kessler (*Chronol. iudicum*, etc. p. 12) remarks that no one can prove that twelve generations actually lived in the period from Moses to Solomon. But all we need is proof that Israelitish tradition ever reckoned twelve generations between a contemporary of Moses and a contemporary of Solomon, and this tradition is actually found in 1 Ch 5^{29-34} and 6^{35-38}. Consequently, it can be maintained with sufficient certainty that the chronology of the Bk. of Jg is a product of secondary combination in so far as the approximate number 40 (3^{11} 5^{31} 8^{28} 13^1), its double (3^{30}), and its half (4^3 $15^{20}\|$ 16^{31}), are employed as factors in this chronology (so, essentially, Bertheau, p. xiii; Oettli, p. 212; Moore, p. xli f.). Further, it appears to the present writer that the chronological problem of the Bk. of Jg has to be examined in the following direction:—(*a*) The number 480 (1 K 6^1) is an uncertain total, and cannot be used as the standard in estimating the chronological data of Jg. (*β*) The round numbers of Jg are really to be treated only as approximate figures equally with the 300 years which Jephthah (Jg 11^{26}) says elapsed between

---

* Budde (p. xx): 'die beiden Zahlen 18, die 23 und die 22 stellen leichte Abweichungen von 20 dar'; but even he (p. xviii) derives 'die von der Regel so weit abweichende Zahl 6 für Jephthah (127) aus einer Vorlage.'

† The round character of the number 40 has been contested by J. C. A. Kessler (*Chronologia iudicum et primorum regum*, 1882) in the words, 'fides historica numeri 40 annorum non dubia est ; nam sæpius huius spatii partes commemorantur et in eo singuli anni vel menses numerantur: Dt 2^{14}, 2 S 5^5, 1 K 2^{11}, 1 Ch 29^{27}, Ex 19^1, Nu 10^{11} 20^1, Dt 1^3' (p. 12). But Röckerath (*Bibl. Chronologie*, 1865, p. 22) already remarks that the round numbers were partly supplied in place of numbers that had become indistinct, and in any case it is inadmissible to suppose that a period of 40 years could have emerged so frequently by accident.

Israel's entrance into Canaan and his own days. Hitherto no attempt (cf. *Seder olam rabba*, ed. Meyer, p. 384 f.) that has been made has succeeded in bringing this number 300 into harmony with the other chronological statements of Jg. (γ) Both the principles just stated appear to the present writer to be more correct than the view (Nöldeke, *Untersuch. z. Kritik d. AT*, p. 173 f.; Moore, p. xli; Budde, p. xviii) that an author of the Bk. of Jg did not count the years of foreign domination (3⁸⁻ ¹⁴ 4³ 6¹ 10⁸ : 8+18+20+7+18=71 years) in addition to the years of rest, or the years of the hero who destroyed this foreign domination. This is at least *not* the meaning of the text of 3⁸⁻¹⁰; for after it has been mentioned that the Israelites served Cushan-rishathaim 8 years (3⁸), it is added by means of an imperf. consec. 'and (hence) the Israelites cried unto the LORD, and the LORD raised up a deliverer, etc. (v.⁹), and (hence) the land had rest 40 years, and Othniel died' (v.¹⁰). The exegesis which reckons the 8 years of the foreign domination to the years of Othniel, which, it is self-evident, could begin only with the shaking off of the foreign yoke, is not in harmony with the text although it was a favourite with Jewish interpreters.* As little is it the case in 3¹⁴, for the 18 years during which Israel groaned under the yoke of the Moabites cannot be included in the 80 years of rest (3³⁰). Nor are the 20 years of oppression (4³) reckoned among the 40 years of rest (5³¹). As little are the 7 years of *invasions* by the Midianites (6¹) reckoned among the 40 years during which the Midianites could not lift up their heads, and the country was in quietness; and these forty years are expressly identified with the days of Gideon (8²⁸). And was Jephthah chosen to be leader at the beginning of the 18 years of the oppression (10⁸)? Then he must have long deferred his victory; and yet the text (11⁴ᶠᶠ· ¹²ᶠᶠ·) presents the choice, the attack, and the victory of Jephthah as a continuous succession of incidents. Budde, indeed, says (p. xviii) that 'Rᵖ has not counted the times of the foreign domination as elements in the chronology of his people.' But whence does he derive this conclusion? From the circumstance that in the case of the 'minor Judges' only the length of their office is noted; and that in 10¹· ³ 12⁸· ¹¹· ¹³ we find 'after him.' But it is by no means an unquestionable fact that this 'after him' is meant to indicate an 'unbroken' succession. In any case it is a false generalizing from the data to attribute to the author of 10¹· ³ 12⁸· ¹¹· ¹³ the opinion that 'during the whole period of the judges, judge followed judge in direct succession.' And because of this opinion is he to be supposed to have rejected the years of foreign domination and to have replaced these by the years of the

* The words 'and after him (Joshua) [was raised up] Othniel, the son of Kenaz, forty years [but] subtract from them the eight years of the oppression under Cushan-rishathaim' (*Seder olam rabba*, ch. xii.), contradict the text of OT. But it is a very interesting circumstance that *Seder o. r.* does not always adopt the same exegesis. It does so with the 18 years of 3¹⁴, and of the 40 years of 5³¹ two years are subtracted for the oppression of Jabin and Sisera (שְׁנֵי שַׁעֲבוּד לִיבִין וְסִיסְרָא ב׳ שָׁנִים); but after the mention of the 40 years of Gideon it is expressly said 'and (= but) the 7 years of Midian (6¹) are not reckoned to them' (שְׁבַע שְׁנֵי מִדְיָן לֹא עָלָיו מַתְוֹכֵן. Further, how is one to explain the statement, 'from Othniel to the death of Samson are 324 years'? (*Diḳ. ha-ṭĕʿamim*, § 70 מֵעָתְנִיאֵל עַד שָׁמֵת שָׁלֹשׁ שְׁמֹשׁוּן שָׁלֹשׁ מֵאוֹת וְעֶשְׂרִים וְאַרְבַּע שָׁנִים). The numbers 40+80+40+40+23+22+6+7+10 +8+20 (3¹¹· ³⁰ 5³¹ 8²⁸ 10²ᶠ· 12⁷ᶠ· ¹¹· ¹⁴ 15²⁰ ‖ 16²¹) make up a total of only 296 years. But if 28 be added, the number 324 is obtained. May we perhaps have recourse to the 28 years which in *Seder olam rabba* (ch. xii.) are attributed to Joshua? At the end of § 70 of *Diḳdŭḳê* comes the statement, 'from Othniel to the rise of Eli as judge were 324 years.' But this also occasions an insoluble problem. Neither of these dicta of Jewish tradition is either noticed or explained in any of the helps accessible to the present writer (*Biblia Heb. et Rabbin.*; *Seder olam rabba*; Jewish and modern commentaries).

minor judges? As the text (3⁸⁻¹⁰· ¹⁴ etc., see above) shows, he has neither rejected the one nor substituted the other, for the sum of the years of the foreign domination (71) and the sum of the years of the so-called minor Judges (70) are *different*. (δ) As little ground is there for the assumption that the Bk. of Jg meant several incidents to be *synchronistic*. The words 'he (the LORD) sold them into the hands of the Philistines and into the hands of the children of Ammon' (10⁷), give only an *appearance* of right to the view that the invasion of the Ammonites (10⁸ᶠᶠ· 11⁴ᶠᶠ·) and that of the Philistines (13¹ᶠᶠ·) occurred at the same time. But in truth it is recorded in the Bk. of Jg that the attack of the Ammonites which, following the statement of 10⁷, is described in 10⁸ᶠᶠ· 11⁴ᶠᶠ·, was warded off by Jephthah, that then came the judges Ibzan, etc. (12⁸ᶠᶠ·), and that the people of Israel on account of new unfaithfulness were oppressed by the invasion of the Philistines. For the text reads, 'and the children of Israel did evil *again* in the sight of the LORD, and the LORD delivered them into the hand of the Philistines' (13¹). Hence it is not the thought expressed in Jg itself (13¹) that is seized by Kessler, who, following Keil and others, again assigns to the same date the incidents related in 10⁸–12¹⁵ and those spoken of in 13¹ᶠᶠ· (*Chronol. iudicum*, p. 29 f.). Now, the question might still arise, whether the order of events in the period of the judges was better known to the sources of the Bk. of Jg or to M. Vernes, who (p. 199) reproaches the 'auteur du livre des Juges' with having placed 'bout à bout des évènements qui ne s'enchaînent en aucune façon.' The present writer for his part prefers the order indicated in the Bk. of Judges.

(γ) Little as the round numbers of the Bk. of Jg positively point to a very late date, this is as little the case with the expression עַד יוֹם גְּלוֹת הָאָרֶץ (18³⁰). It may indeed be somewhat bold to assume הָאָרוֹן as the original reading, and to find in this passage an allusion to the גָּלָה which indirectly is asserted of the 'aron, 'ark (of the covenant)' in 1 S 4²¹ᶠ·. It is true that it is not precisely אָרֶץ of which the verb גָּלָה is elsewhere predicated. This may, however, be accidental, for גָּלָה has for subject not only the people (Is 5¹³, Am 1⁵), or Israel (Am 7¹¹· ¹⁷, 2 K 17⁶ etc.), or persons in general (2 K 24²⁴, Mic 1⁶, Ezk 12³ etc.), but also Judah (Jer 13¹⁹, La 1³, 2 K 25²¹ ‖ Jer 52²⁷ etc.), or a city, as גָּלָה (Am 5⁵) or Jerusalem (Jer 1³) or Damascus (2 K 16⁹).—Besides the period during which the descendants of Moses officiated as priests in Dan, in v.³¹ a period is named of the worship of Micah's graven image, namely, the period of the existence of the temple in Shiloh. There is no mention of this temple after the time of Eli (1 S 14³). In Ps 78⁶⁰ the overthrow of Shiloh is placed before the choosing of Mt. Zion (v.⁶⁸), and from Jer 7¹²· ¹⁴ it cannot be inferred that it was laid waste during the Assyrian wars (Moore, p. 369). Hence there is not such a serious departure from reality when in *Diḳdŭḳê ha-ṭĕʿamim*, § 70, it is said, 'on the day when Eli died, Shiloh was laid waste' (יוֹם שָׁמֵת עֵלִי חָרְבָה שִׁלֹה).—What is now the meaning of the remark in v.³¹, and why are the two dicta of v.³⁰ and v.³¹ placed side by side? In v.³¹ it must be intended to say that the end of the cult of the graven image of Micah stood in a causal connexion with the destruction of the sanctuary of J″ at Shiloh, and the two notes of v.³⁰ᶠ· would best harmonize if there was a reference to the destruction of the Shiloh sanctuary also in the words נְלוֹת וגו (v.³⁰). Now, let it be observed that Eli died when he heard that the ark of the covenant was taken (1 S 4¹⁹⁻²²). But if, in spite of all this, it remains uncertain whether in Jg 18³⁰ a statement which raised scruples was changed into an easier reading (cf. the interpolated ן in v.[31]),* yet the expression 'until the day of the exile of the land' does not point further down than the time when Tiglath-pileser 'took Kedesh, and Hazor, etc., and Galilee, all the land of Naphtali, and carried them captive to Assyria' (2 K 15[29]), i.e. about B.C. 734. And if this is the meaning of v.[30], then from the period of time indicated in v.[30] a shorter period is selected in v.[31]. For it was desired to add how long the cult of the graven image of Micah lasted, because this image was a principal subject in the preceding narrative.

(δ) In the middle of the second episode of Jg (chs. 19–21), where, e.g., we read 'Jebus which is Jerusalem' (19[10], cf. 2 S 5[6ff.]), Wellhausen (Comp. 233 ff.) and some others discover a passage of very late origin, namely, 20[1]–21[14]. What opinion are we to form of this? Now, in any case, this section must have displaced another narrative, for between the end of ch. 19 and 21[15] there is a lacuna. But common action on the part of the Israelites was not impossible shortly after the death of Joshua. Let us consider, in addition to what has been said above (6 d, δ), the story of the building of an altar beside Jordan (Jos 22[10ff.]). Was this not a protest on the part of the Israelites settled on the east of Jordan against the idea of separation from their nation? And does the unity of the Israelites, which shows itself in 1 S 7[2ff.] 8[4ff.] 11[3] ('that we may send messengers unto all the coasts of Israel'), etc., ever appear as a new phenomenon? The present writer believes that there are more traces of the unity of ancient Israel than are wont at present to be recognized by some scholars. Were there not 'elders' in Israel before Samuel? (1 S 8[4ff.]). Could these not then assemble themselves on account of the unheard of scandal perpetrated by a Benjamite city (Jg 20[1]), as readily as in connexion with the choice of a king? (1 S 8[4a]). It is quite true the expression mishkab zakhar (cf. 'that hath not lain by man') is found only in Nu 31[17ff.] and Jg 21[11ff.]; but this is no proof of the late origin of the latter verse, for the expression in question had very probably also an earlier existence. Hence the judgment of the present writer is that not the section 20[1]–21[14] as a whole, but only single elements in it bear a secondary character. Such elements are, above all, the round numbers like 400,000 (20[17]), and there is no department where hyperbole more readily comes in than the department of numbers. We do not believe that tradition required many centuries—for Budde's R[P] wrote 'perhaps about the year 400' (p. xvi)—in order to create these figures.

(ε) Only legend, and not mythology, has played a rôle in the filling out of the history of Samson. Traces of the so-called 'Folk-lore' are probably to be found, e.g., in the thirty men (14[19]), the 300 jackals (15[4]), and the 1000 men (v.[15f.]) whom he slew with the jawbone of an ass. Nay, it is not improbable that this exploit of Samson and the name Ramath-lehi, i.e. 'height of jaw,' are connected with each other. Rather may this deed of Samson's have been simply placed here, for the localizing activity of popular tradition shows itself elsewhere, or the narrative of the deed may even have been occasioned by the name of the place. The same is probably the case with the story of 'En-hakkore (15[18f.]), in which the two homonyms kore, 'partridge,' and kore, 'caller,' appear to be mixed up. But, all the same, the Samson narratives are no product of mythology. The mythological explaining away of the person of Samson is discountenanced even by M. Vernes (Hist. juive,

---

* The sentence 'the foundations of heaven moved' (2 S 22[8]) is changed into 'the foundations of the hills moved' (Ps 18[7]). See, in general, regarding such alterations of parallel texts, König's Einleitung, pp. 76 f., 82 ff.

p. 238 f.); and as we have quoted from him several statements which appear to be unfounded, it is but right that we should quote a passage of which we can thoroughly approve. He says, 'l'interprétation mythologique de l'histoire de Samson échoue au port; sans compter qu'on ne sait trop comment y faire rentrer l'aventure du lion et de l'essaim d'abeilles, des chacals, de la mâchoire, de la porte de Gaza, c'est-à-dire ce qui précède les ruses et le succès de Dalila, le Samson du dernier épisode ne saurait être tenu pour le jeune soleil du printemps. S'il se sert, en effet, du retour de sa vigueur pour triompher de ses adversaires (les ténèbres, l'hiver ?), il succombe lui-même sous cet effort, et si les deux piliers du temple doivent être tenus pour les colonnes d'Hercule, elles sont mises à une très mauvaise place.'

7. THE AUTHOR OF THE BOOK.—The author of Jg is not named in the book itself. In the Talmud (Baba bathra 14[b]) it is said, 'Samuel wrote (or edited [the sense of the verb kāthab is examined in König's Einleitung, p. 445]) his book and the Bk. of Jg and the Bk. of Ruth' (cf. Marx-Dalman, Traditio rabbinorum veterrima, p. 14). Similarly in Dikdûkê ha-ṭĕ'amîm, p. 57, it is said, שמואל הנביא זכרו לברכה כתב ספרו וספר שופטים ורות. But the tradition which becomes fixed in Baba bathra 14 f. is of such late origin, and contains such absolutely impossible elements (see the whole passage in König's Einleitung, p. 445 f.), that on these grounds alone no weight can be attached to it. But it is further shown by the above (No. 6) discussion to be an impossible position.

8. THE SPIRIT OF THE BOOK AND ITS PLACE IN THE HISTORY OF REVELATION.—Of more importance is it to examine the spirit that pervades the Bk. of Jg, to draw the picture which, framed in this book, exhibits to us a momentous period in the development of Israel. What are the leading features of this picture?

(a) The period of the judges was a time of local settlement and physical self-assertion on the part of Israel. When this people had shaken off the Egyptian yoke—which the Israelites can never have invented as a factor in their history—and were on the point of conquering the homeland of their forefathers, they encountered a uniformly violent opposition. Nevertheless, it is unquestionable that the Israelites under Joshua's leadership gained some fundamental victories. The positive tradition to this effect (Jos 6–11) is not upset by any statement to the contrary effect.

The story of the defeat of the northern Canaanites (Jos 11[10-14]) may contain some natural hyperboles (e.g. 'neither left they any to breathe'), but when these are set aside, the narrative is not set aside. Further, the statements, 'nevertheless the children of Israel expelled not the Geshurites,' etc. (Jos 13[13] 15[13-19. 63] 16[10] 17[11-18] 18[3ff.] 23[4ff.]), and the parallel statements of Jg 1[19ff.] presuppose that the foundation was laid for the conquest of Canaan, otherwise they would have neither motive nor meaning. These statements add nothing but this, that in the time of Joshua, within the conquered kingdoms, many districts still retained their independence. The interposing of these sentences shows also in what sense the partition of the land is to be understood (Jos 13[1ff.]). The territories which were assigned to the different tribes are thought of not as places of quiet possession, but rather as meant to be completely subdued. The sense of Jos 13[1-13] etc., is not that 'la terre promise est considérée comme une table rase' (M. Vernes, Essais bibliques, p. 297). Finally, neither in Jos 14[6-15] nor in Jg 1[1ff.] is the idea contained that the different tribes of Israel only in an isolated fashion made their attacks upon Canaan (Budde, Richt. u. Sam. 1890, p. 84, Hdcomm. 1897, p. 2). Budde himself admits (*ad loc.*) 'the remote possibility' that in Jg 1²² 'a short word about Ai' has fallen out. This 'word about Ai,' however, has not fallen out, nor was it a 'short' one (cf. Jos 7⁵ᶠᶠ· 8¹⁻²⁹). It is a groundless assertion that the record of Jg 1 'excludes' the narrative of the Bk. of Jos, and that the Jg narrative is the 'older' (Budde, 1897, p. 2. Charles Piepenbring [*Hist.* 1898, p. 69] accepts but does not prove this thesis. If the narrative of Jg 1ᵃᵍᵇ· ²ᶠ· ⁵⁻⁷ etc. (Budde, 1897, p. xxii), had been the older and the only correct one (Budde, p. 2), how then could Judah speak of 'his lot'? (1³). 'The narrative, according to v.³, presupposes an earlier division by lot of the yet unconquered land,' as Budde himself (p. 1) has to notice; and Charles Piepenbring says (p. 75) on Jos 18²⁻⁶· ⁸⁻¹⁰ : 'Nous y rencontrons une nouvelle preuve qu'on assigna d'avance, par le sort, aux différentes tribus, le territoire que chacune devait conquérir'; cf. the words of Budde on Jg 18¹ 'es ist Dan wohl ein Gebiet zugefallen, aber es hat sich nicht darin behaupten können, und dass dieses *nicht blosse Theorie* ist, beweisen die danitischen Reste in den südlichen Wohnsitzen, die uns in der Samsongeschichte begegnen.' A positive representation that Canaan was thus divided is also implied in other passages of Jg 1. Finally, the 'older' narrative contained in Jg 1 is pronounced to be also the 'historically more credible' (Budde, p. 2). But is it, in point of fact, probable that the tribes of Israel, which under Joshua's lead crossed the Jordan, should not have attacked with their whole force the common foe, in order to inflict upon him some decided defeats? To what end, then, is the narrative (Nu 32²⁸ᶠᶠ·, Dt 3¹⁸⁻²⁰, Jos 1¹²⁻¹⁶ 22¹⁻⁶) invented of how the tribes of Reuben, etc., which had their settlements east of the Jordan, crossed this river with the other Israelites, and did not return until the opposition of the western Canaanites was — essentially — broken? Joshua led the host only until the conquest of Jericho (Jos ⁶; so Budde, p. 1). Did he, then, withdraw from the leadership of Israel? This is 'historically credible.' But if this was really the case, why will Budde (p. 11) substitute 'and Joshua was with them' for the traditional 'and Jahweh was with them'? (Jg 1²²). And if the existence of Joshua was assumed in the narrative of Jg 1, would he have been mentioned in this *passim* fashion?

The truth lies in the middle position, and this true relation of things is exhibited in Jos and Jg; in spite of the foundation-laying victories gained under the lead of Joshua over the inhabitants of Canaan, some centuries were still needed to make the Israelites complete masters of Canaan (Jg 1¹⁹· ²¹ etc.).

(*b*) The need for external or political conflict was coupled with the task of *spiritual* self-assertion on the part of Israel against the genius of the Canaanitish nation. The period that followed the migration to Canaan was for the Hebrews the time of the severest *struggle of ideas.* For it was then that the danger was greatest that Israel should lose the consciousness of her uniqueness, seeing that many tribes with other conceptions and ideas dwelt in her midst. Cf. on this contrast, *e.g.* Pietschmann, *Gesch. der Phön.* p. 292 f.; Niebuhr, *Gesch. des ebr. Zeitalters,* p. 317 ff.; Winckler, *Gesch. Isr.* p. 133¹; Wildeboer, *Jahvedienst en Volksreligie in Israël,* 1898, p. 10 ff. But when Piepenbring (*Hist.* etc. 1898, p. 96) remarks, 'au moment où les Hébreux s'emparèrent de la Palestine, les Cananéens leur étaient bien supérieurs sous le rapport de la culture,' he must be thinking merely of outward culture, such as the art of building cities, the art of war, etc.

During this period the great matter was to

defend the heritage of religious ideas and moral principles to which Israel had fallen heir (see above, 6 *d*, *β*, *δ*). The men who were then called to deliver the people belonged to the category of true souls by whom the most important prerogatives of the Jahweh religion were maintained. Then did Gideon defend the monolatry of Jahweh against the adoration of the Canaanite Baal (6¹¹ᶠ·). The same hero kept unimpaired the principle (8²³) that Israel was under the rule only of a heavenly king (Jahweh, Ex 15¹⁸). He pre-eminently exhibits the characteristic which ben-Sirach attributes to the judges when he says, καὶ οἱ κριταί, ἕκαστος τῷ αὐτοῦ ὀνόματι, ὅσων οὐκ ἐξεπόρνευσε ἡ καρδία, καὶ ὅσοι οὐκ ἀπεστράφησαν ἀπὸ Κυρίου, εἴη τὸ μνημόσυνον αὐτῶν ἐν εὐλογίαις, κ.τ.λ. (Sir 46¹¹ᶠ·). Then was the conscience of the nation of Israel sufficiently awake to stir them up to energy when danger threatened that the Canaanite immorality (Gn 9²³· ²⁶ᵇ 19⁵ᶠᶠ· 34²ᵇ, Lv 18²⁵ etc.) might gain a footing in Israel (Jg 19³⁰ 20⁶ᵇ).

True, indeed, all the acts of the Israel of those days cannot bear to be tried by the standard of an enlightened humanity, or the ideal of evangelical Christianity. We shudder at the cutting off of thumbs and great toes (Jg 1⁶). But not only were the Athenians once guilty of the same conduct towards Æginetan prisoners (Ælian, *Var. Hist.* ii. 9), but even the Christian Abyssinians of our own day are given to this terrible practice (cf. Flad, *Zwölf Jahre in Abessinien,* etc.). Moreover, in the pre-Christian history of Divine revelation, stages of progress are not wanting; cf. *e.g.* on the history of prophecy (1 S 9⁹), or the Divine name (Ex 6²ᶠ·, 1 S 1³, Is 1⁴, Hos 2¹⁸), or the idea of retaliation (Ex 20⁵, Jer 31²⁹, Ezk 18²⁰). Although then a Deborah had not advanced to the stage of an Isaiah, and although a Samson (cf. on the Nazirites, Am 2¹²) did not stand upon the same plane as the Sermon on the Mount (Jg 16²⁸ compared with Mt 5⁴⁴), yet the Bk. of Jg stands, not without right, in the series of the *nĕbî'îm* (*Dikdûkê*, § 70, etc.). This book is a monument of that Divine Providence which sustained the people of Israel, so that they maintained their national existence, and during a time of the strongest temptations kept safe their religious-moral ideals, which had a most important end to serve in pointing to the perfect religion and morality.

LITERATURE.—(A) *Dikdûkê ha-ṭĕ'amîm,* edd. Baer et Strack, 1879; Marx-Dalman, *Traditio rabbinorum veterrina de librorum Vet. Test. ordine et origine,* 1884.—(B) Felix Perles, *Analekten zur Textkritik des AT,* 1895; Adam Mez, *Die Bibel des Josephus untersucht für Buch* v.–vii. *der Archäologie,* 1895.—(C) On the literary criticism: S. R. Driver, *LOT⁶,* 1897; Ed. König, *Einleitung in das AT,* 1893; Wilh. Frankenberg, *Die Compos. des deuteronom. Richterbuchs* (Ri 26–16), Inaugural dissertation, Marburg, 1895.—(D) Especially on the age of the sources: G. A. Cooke, *The Hist. and Song of Deborah,* 1892; C. Niebuhr, *Versuch einer Reconstellation des Debora-Lieds,* 1894; J. Marquart, *Fundamente israel. u. jüd. Gesch.* 1896.—(E) Commentaries: Rashi, etc., in *Biblia rabbinica*; Jalkût Shim'ônî (the edition used in the above article is that pub. at Frankf.-a.-M. in 1687); Michlal Jophi, ed. Abendana, 1661; C. Bertheau in *Kgf. exeget. Hdbch.* 1883; P. Cassel in Lange's *Bibelwerk* (2nd ed. 1887); Oettli in Strack-Zöckler's *Kgf. Comm.* 1893; G. Moore in the 'Internat. Crit. Comm.' (Edinb., T. & T. Clark, 1895); Karl Budde in *Kurzer Hdcomm.* 1897.—(F) Chronology: *Seder olam rabba* (ed. Joh. Meyer, 1699), cap. xii.; J. C. A. Kessler, *Chronologia iudicum et primorum regum,* 1882.—(G) History: Rich. Pietschmann, *Gesch. der Phönizier* (in Oncken's 'Allgemeine Gesch. in Einzeldarstellungen'); L. Seinecke, *Gesch. d. Volkes Israel,* 1876–1884; Stade, do., 1887 ff.; Renan, *Hist. du peuple d'Israël,* 1889 ff.; M. Vernes, *Précis d'histoire juive,* 1889; C. Niebuhr, *Gesch. des ebräischen Zeitalters,* 1894; H. Winckler, *Gesch. Israels,* 1895; Charles Piepenbring, *Hist. du peuple d'Israël,* 1898 (follows, in answering all main questions, in the track of Budde). ED. KÖNIG.

JUDGING (Ethical).—The practice of judging, against which we have so many warnings in the NT, consists not so much in the characterizing of particular actions or modes of life, as in making these the basis for a sweeping, and, in some cases, a final verdict on the character of those to whom they are rightly or wrongly attributed. The warnings are given in the interests both of the critic and the criticized. The practice is equally hurtful to both, and therefore if it is not absolutely condemned, it is surrounded by so many safeguards and limitations as to be practically forbidden. On the one hand it is an infringement of the royal law (Ja 2¹³), on the other, it stands in the way of that self-criticism which is necessary to amendment of morals and progress in religion (Mt 7³). The chief objection to judging, however, is that it must be based on partial knowledge; we are necessarily ignorant of the inner life, the motives and principles of other men; we are not acquainted either with the antecedent conditions of their actions, or the possibilities of justification, or progress, or amendment, that their future may contain. This is the position taken up by Jesus Christ in opposition to Jewish legalists. He declared that the latter judged according to appearance (Jn 7²⁴), according to the flesh (Jn 8¹⁵). As their religion consisted in the performance of certain prescribed duties, and the avoidance of outward offences, they had a rough and ready standard by which to estimate character. Christ and St. Paul had a more righteous because more complete standard; they took into account the inner thoughts and motives, and, knowing the complexity of these, deliberately refrained from judging, even where the outward evidence seemed absolutely convincing (Jn 8¹¹, 1 Co 4⁵). One last motive in the prohibition of judging must not be overlooked. It was necessary to exercise patience and forbearance, not only in the interests of the individual, but in those of the Church. This is at least indirectly taught in the Parable of the Tares (Mt 13²⁴), which cannot be limited exclusively to ecclesiastical discipline, and it is a prominent motive with St. Paul. It appears especially in his treatment of the 'strong' and 'weak' parties in Rome (Ro 14), and of the rival possessors of gifts in Corinth (1 Co 13). In one word, while self-judgment is enjoined, the judgment of others is discountenanced throughout the NT.   J. MILLAR.

JUDGMENT.—1. The truth that God will come to the world for judgment is part of the burden of OT prophecy. The rule of God, partially realized over Israel in the days of the prophets, is destined to be made perfect, and it is to extend over all the nations of the earth. This consummation will necessitate a 'day of the Lord,' i.e. a judgment of the faithless in the chosen nation and of the heathen (Is 2¹², Jl 1¹⁵ 2¹ etc.); but Israel will be saved and enjoy the blessings of a new and everlasting covenant (Is 61⁸, Jer 31³¹ᶠᶠ· etc.). See **Day of the Lord**, under ESCHATOLOGY, vol. i. pp. 735 ff.

2. When in later times the belief in a resurrection of the dead was developed (Dn 12²), till in the time of Christ it was firmly rooted in the minds of all but the Sadducees, our Lord revealed a great universal judgment of the living and the dead, the issue, represented in figurative and therefore indeterminate speech, being now the establishment of the Messianic kingdom on earth, now the complete transformation of all that at present appears, and the advent of new heavens and a new earth. The people of Christ will be called in the judgment to an everlasting participation in the glories of His heavenly kingdom, and His enemies will have the sentence of eternal condemnation pronounced on them (Mt 13³⁶ᶠᶠ· ⁴⁷ᶠᶠ· 25, Mk 13, Lk 21).

3. In accordance with the spiritual nature of the kingdom of God, and with the fact that it is even now begun on earth, we find, especially in the Johannine writings, that the judgment in one aspect or stage of it is a present act. For judgment Christ is come into this world (Jn 9³⁹). There is an actual separation of men in progress here and now, and to a great extent they themselves may see that there is nothing arbitrary in the awards which are made; the spiritual blessings bestowed on the one hand and the mental sufferings or want endured on the other, commend themselves to the enlightened conscience as just and inevitable. Christ is as a present light in the world, discerning between the souls of men, attracting and gladdening some, those who do truth, and repelling others who do evil, multiplying for them the pains of darkness, hatred, and sin (Jn 3¹⁸ᶠ· 12³¹). The former are called even now to everlasting life (3³⁶ 6⁴⁷, 1 Jn 3¹⁴), and should know that they have it (1 Jn 5¹³); the latter know not life, but abide in death, and have an immediate experience of the wrath of God (Jn 3³⁶, 1 Jn 3¹⁴ᶠ· 5¹²).

4. This judgment, which is in progress now, is destined to be perfected, though there is necessarily obscurity as to the future existence. In the last assize Christ will be the Judge as before (Mt 25³¹ᶠᶠ·, Ac 10⁴² 17³¹, 2 Co 5¹⁰, 2 Ti 4¹). Mankind will all appear before His judgment-seat. The righteous will thus have in His presence a perfect vision and possession of the goodness they have chosen in Him (2 Ti 4⁸, 1 Jn 3²); the wicked will see with dismay into what an abyss of sin and woe they have fallen (Rev 1⁷). It may be said men will hereafter judge themselves. Those who are unlike Christ will find themselves as such to be separate from Him. The two classes of people are parted because they have acquired distinct natures like the sheep and the goats (Mt 25³¹ᶠᶠ·). The future judgment will thus be 'just,' determined by what people made of themselves when they were in the body (2 Co 5¹⁰). Or the books will be opened, and men will be judged out of those things which are written in the books, according to their works (Rev 20¹²). The character of each person is a 'book' or record, preserving, in moral and spiritual effects, all that he has been and done and loved; and in the judgment these books will be 'opened,' or each man's character will be manifested as the light of Christ falls upon it. The people of Christ themselves receive different awards at the last, according to what their life has been (Lk 19¹¹ᶠᶠ·, 1 Co 3¹²ᶠᶠ·). A test like fire will try every believer's work. Some have acquired a close likeness to Christ by their lives of true holiness and love; and the greater the likeness, the more He will be known, loved, and enjoyed, or the richer they themselves will be.   G. FERRIES.

JUDGMENT HALL is the AV translation in Jn 18²⁸· ³³ and Ac 23³⁵ of the Greek πραιτώριον, though this word contains no reference to judging. In the RV it is rendered 'palace' or 'prætorium.' See PRÆTORIUM.

JUDGMENT SEAT.—The usual word employed for this in the NT is βῆμα (Mt 27¹⁹, Jn 19¹³, Ac 18¹²· ¹⁶ᶠ· 25⁶· ¹⁰· ¹⁷, Ro 14¹⁰, 2 Co 5¹⁰), properly a 'tribune.' Two of these were provided in the law-courts of Greece, one for the accuser and one for the defendant (cf. Liddell and Scott's *Greek Lexicon* under βῆμα), but in the NT the word is used of the official seat (tribunal) of the Roman judge. The word κριτήριον used in Ja 2⁶ occurs also in 1 Co 6²· ⁴, where it is translated in RVm by 'tribunals.' See, further, art. GABBATHA.

G. W. THATCHER.

JUDITH (יְהוּדִית, ᾿Ιουδίν, ᾿Ιουδίθ, ᾿Ιουδείθ).—1. A wife of Esau, daughter of Beeri the Hittite (Gn 26³⁴) (cf. Gn 36², and see OHOLIBAMAH).

2. Heroine of the BOOK OF JUDITH; daughter of Merari, of the tribe of Simeon (8¹ [cf. Nu 1⁶] 9²); widow of Manasses of the same tribe. See following article.   F. C. PORTER.

JUDITH, BOOK OF.—**1.** Contents.—The story of the Book of Judith in the LXX is as follows :— Nebuchadnezzar, king of the Assyrians in Nineveh, in his 12th year made war against Arphaxad king of the Medes, summoning all nations to his aid ; and in his 17th year was victorious and destroyed the Median capital, Ecbatana. The next year he sent Holofernes with 132,000 men to take vengeance on the western lands which had refused to come to his help. Holof. laid waste the lands of those who resisted, and required the destruction of their sanctuaries and gods, and the sole worship of Nebuchadnezzar. The Jews feared for Jerusalem and the temple, just-reconsecrated after their recent return from exile. Joakim, the high priest, and the Sanhedrin resolved upon resistance, and ordered the fortifying of certain mountain towns of Samaria which commanded the entrance into Judæa from the north. The people gave themselves to fasting and prayer. An Ammonite general, Achior, warned Holofernes, with an appeal to history, that the God of heaven protected this people unless they sinned against him, and for his counsel was delivered to the enemy. Bethulia was the point of attack, and upon the issue of its siege depended the fate of the Jewish land and religion. The three elders of the city, Ozias, Chabris, and Charmis, yielded to the demand of the famished people and promised surrender after five days. Judith, a rich young widow of the tribe of Simeon, confident of the righteousness of her people, believed that God would deliver them by her hand. Prepared by prayer, and protected by strict observance of legal rites, she made her way to Holofernes, predicted the speedy destruction of her people because she foresaw that in their hunger they would eat unclean and consecrated food, captivated him by her deceits and by her beauty, and beheaded him as he lay in a drunken stupor after a banquet in her honour. 'Her beauty took his soul prisoner ; the scimitar passed through his neck.' She returned with the head to Bethulia. Achior recognized it, and at sight of it was converted to Judaism. Confusion and fear fell upon the leaderless army of the Assyrians, and the Jews slaughtered them in their flight and gained great spoils. Judith was richly rewarded and honoured, and in a song celebrated the deliverance. Peace reigned during her long life of 105 years, and for a long time after.

2. Texts and Versions.—The LXX text exists in three recensions, (1) B A א, etc., the ruling text ; (2) cod. 58, to which Old Lat. and Syriac are closely related ; (3) cod. 19, 108, similar to (2).

A Hebrew original is commonly accepted, not only on the ground of Hebraisms in language and ideas, but also because of errors of translation (see 1^8 2^2 $3^{1.\,8.\,9.\,10}$ 4^3 8^{21} $11^{7.\,11}$ $16^{3.\,17}$, Fritzsche, Ball). Origen, indeed, says that he learned from Jews that they did not possess Tobit and Judith even among their 'Apocrypha' (*Ep. ad Afric.* 13), and there are no allusions to Jth in the older rabbinical literature. Yet it does not follow that the later Jewish versions are retranslations from the Greek. If the story had an independent history among Jews it is historically important to trace it. Jerome is the first witness to a Heb. (Aram.) original, and his testimony deserves attention.

The Vulgate.—Jerome (*Pref. to Jth.*) says that the Hebrews had Jth among their Apocrypha, and reckoned it among histories. His Jth he affirms to be a translation of this 'Chaldee' version, which he regarded as the original. He put into Latin 'only those things which a sound understanding could find in the Chaldee words.' His work was indeed hastily done, *in one night*, and carelessly, 'aiming to give sense for sense rather than word for word.' Probably, as in the case of Tobit, an interpreter rendered the Chaldee into Hebrew, and

Jerome dictated a Latin version of the Heb. to a scribe. He, of course, had the Old Lat. before him.

Jerome's testimony is commonly set aside, and it is assumed, after Fritzsche, that his modifications of the Old Lat. were mainly arbitrary, and that we can know nothing of his Chaldee text. Is this a just verdict? The Vulg., in comparison with the Old Lat. and Greek, omits many geographical details (*e.g.* LXX 2^{28} $3^{9.\,10}$ $4^{4.\,6}$ 15^4) and many concrete incidents (*e.g.* LXX 1^{13-16} 2^{7-10} $7^{6.\,17-19.\,32}$ $10^{2b.\,3b.\,9.\,10b.\,17.\,18.\,20.\,22}$ $11^{3b.\,4}$ $12^{3b.\,15b}$ $14^{8.\,9}$ 15^{11b} 16^{24b}, and parts of $8^{2.\,3.\,6.\,29.\,31}$ 9^1 $13^{12.\,13}$ $14^{2.\,3.\,11.\,12}$ $15^{12.\,13}$). Jth.'s achievement is made less sensuous and more simply religious in character (cf. LXX 10^4 11^{17} $12^{13.\,15.\,16}$). The deceptions are less bald (LXX 11^{5-7} 13^3). Homiletical additions are made (Vulg. 4^{10-13} 5^{11-15} 9^{6-8} 5^{16-19}, parts of 6^{12-21} 7^{19-22} 8^{21-26}). Changes such as these mark a secondary form of the story. But are they due to Jerome? Against that supposition it is to be argued, (1) that it was not his way to edit, but to translate ; (2) that he did not in this case take time for such revision. It is therefore probable, apart from the confirmation of the Midrash, that even such deviations of Vulg. from LXX as these were due in the main to the Chaldee version. Still more probable is this in the few cases of additional concrete detail (Vulg. $7^{6.\,7}$ 11^{11} 14^{9-12} 16^{31}).

Further, it is probable that in Jerome's Chaldee, Bethulia was identified with Jerusalem. The Vulg. never gives a clear description of the situation of Bethulia (cf. LXX $4^{6.\,7}$ $6^{7.\,10.\,11}$ 7^3 8^3 10^{13} 11^2) ; it omits or changes all passages which clearly distinguish Bethulia and Jerusalem up to 15^9 (cf. LXX $4^{6.\,7}$ 11^{19} 11^{13} 15^5 ; and Vulg. omits LXX $8^{21.\,22.\,24}$ 9^{1b} $11^{14.\,15}$). Further, Vulg. contains some positive suggestions that Jerusalem is the besieged city (Vulg. 3^{14} [cf. LXX $3^{9.\,10}$] $7^{3.\,6.\,7.\,9}$ 15^4 ; and Ozias is 'prince of Judah,' Vulg. 8^{34} 13^{23}). Only in 15^9 and perhaps 16^{22-25} does Vulg. *require* the distinction. This suggests that the identification is not due to Jerome but to his source.

Hebrew Versions.—The story of Jth exists in several forms in Hebrew, none of them from early sources (Jellinek, Beth ha-Midrasch, i. 130–141, ii. 12 ff. [translations in Lipsius, *Zeitschr. f. wissens. Theol.* (1867), p. 337 ff. ; Ball in Wace's *Apocrypha*, i. p. 252 ff. ; Scholz, *Commentar*, 2 ed., Anhang i. and ii.] ; Gaster, 'An unknown Hebrew Version of the History of Jth' [*PSBA* (1894), p. 156 ff.]). Lipsius distinguishes two forms of the story, one of which is closely related to our book. In both the scene is Jerusalem, the time that of the Maccabæan wars. Judith is in some way related to the Hasmonæan house. It is Nicanor who is beheaded ; and the deed is celebrated in connexion with the Feast of Dedication. Names are often omitted, and details vary widely. The long Midrash (Jellinek, ii. 12–22 ; Scholz, Anhang i.) summarizes chs. 1–5 briefly, but in chs. 7–14 follows the Vulgate so closely that a relationship between them is certain.* The indications of the Chaldee original in the Vulg. pointed out above are strongly confirmed by this version. The phenomena would be explained by supposing that the Midrash is a later form of Jerome's Chaldee text, still less concrete, still more general and homiletical in character. Jerusalem entirely displaces Bethulia ; Holofernes is king of Greece, and Nebuch. disappears ; Chabris and Charmis are priests, Ozias is prince of Israel (= Vulg. 13^{23}), and Joakim is not mentioned.

The older Form.—Scholz argues for the greater originality of the Vulgate against the LXX, and

* Vulg. and Midrash agree, *i.e.*, in omissions (LXX $7^{17-19.\,32}$ $8^{21-23.\,24b}$ 9^1 $10^{9.\,10f.\,17a.\,18.\,22}$ $11^{4.\,14}$ 12^{13b} $15^{3.\,4.\,5.\,11b}$) and in additions (Vulg. 6^{16-18} $7^{6.\,10.\,11.\,19-22}$ 8^{23-25} 9^{6-8} $10^{16-18.\,20}$ $11^{12.\,14.\,15}$ 12^6 $13^{6.\,16.\,23}$ $14^{7.\,8-14}$), as well as in a multitude of lesser details.

of the short Midrash (Jellinek, i. 130 f.; Lipsius, p. 355 f.; Ball, p. 252 f.; Scholz, Anh. ii.) against the long. So Gaster confidently claims originality for his Hebrew version, and is followed with surprising unreserve by Cornill (*Einl. in d. AT* [4], p. 272). 'It seems undoubted that here lies the simplest and most original form of the story, out of which the Greek romance grew' (cf. Ginsburg). But is the simple always the original form of a story? Gaster's argument, 'If it were an abridged text, names and situations would have been retained, and only the rhetorical portions omitted,' substitutes the interests of a modern historian for those of an ancient story-teller. On the other hand, in favour of the greater originality of the LXX version, apart from the general fact of its far greater age, it is to be urged that it is more natural to suppose (1) that elaborate but not especially significant geographical and historical details, aside from the main story, should be omitted rather than added by later editors; (2) that edifying and rhetorical embellishments, speeches, prayers, etc., should be added, not omitted; (3) that references to the Maccabæan period should be added, not removed to give place to an impossible or an unknown historical setting; (4) that the scene should be changed from Bethulia to Jerusalem, not the reverse; (5) that Greeks should take the place of Assyrians as Israel's enemy; (6) that Jth.'s lineage should be changed from the tribe of Simeon to the family of the Hasmonæans, not the reverse; and perhaps that she should be first a widow, afterwards a maiden. (She is a widow in the long Midrash). The originality claimed for the LXX, or its Hebrew text, is, however, relative. The story may have had a long previous history.

3. PLACE OF THE STORY.—Bethulia (Betylua) cannot, in the LXX, mean Jerusalem. Its situation is so well described (in Northern Samaria, near Dothan, $4^{6.7}$; cf. $3^{9.10}$ 5^1 $6^{7.10.11}$ $7^{3.18}$ 8^3) that few doubt its existence, though it is not otherwise known. 'To hold it for a pure fiction belongs to the gross fictions of the learned' (Fritzsche). 'He would not have built his story geographically in the air' (Schürer). It is as clearly distinguished from Jerusalem as words permit ($4^{2.6.7}$ $8^{21.24}$ 11^{19} $15^{5.8}$ $16^{18.20.21.23}$, cf. 8^3).

4. TIME OF THE STORY.—The historical setting of the LXX is impossible. Nineveh and Assyria fell 608 B.C. Nebuch., king of the Chaldæans in Babylon, destroyed Jerusalem in his 18th year (586), and died 562. The return from exile was not before 536, and the rebuilding of the temple was in 520-516. But the confusion of these events could hardly be due to ignorance. What Jew would not know the place of Nebuch. in relation to the Assyrians and to the Exile? It is possible that a copyist or translator put familiar biblical names in the place of names strange to him (Kaulen). It is also possible that the author used Nebuch. and the Assyrians as symbols, and that he meant to tell (1) no history at all but a story ('poem,' Luther), teaching that Judah is safe from all enemies if it keeps the law; or (2) future history prophetically set forth (an apocalypse, Scholz); or (3) present or recent history disguised under significant names. Thus Volkmar (1860) elaborately defended the equations: Nebuch. = Trajan, Nineveh = Rome (or Antioch), Medes = Parthians, Ecbatana = Nisibis, Holofernes = Lusius Quietus, etc. But the parallels are forced, and 'the arguments which place the Epistle of Clem. in the 1st cent. are a hundredfold stronger than those which place the Bk. of Jth in the second' (Lightfoot). More commonly the Maccabæan history is found veiled in our story. Ball suggests (not always consistently) that Nebuch. = Antiochus IV., Assyrians = Syrians, Holofernes =

Nicanor, Arphaxad = Arsaces, Medes = Parthians, Jth = Judas, Bethulia = Jerusalem, Joakim = Alcimus, etc. He says, 'The Bk. of Jth is a free composition in the manner of the Haggada, principally based upon recollections of the facts of the heroic Judas, and more especially upon the facts related in 1 Mac 3^{27}-4^{61} 6^{1-7} 7^{26-50}, 2 Mac 9^{1-3} 10^{1-8} 15' (cf. Holtzmann, *Neutest. Zeitgeschichte*, 16). But the book does not readily yield to allegorical treatment. If it was written in the reign of Alexandra (B.C. 79-70) concerning the Maccabæan wars (Ball), why is the scene Bethulia, not Jerusalem? why are Judith and Ozias Simeonites? why should Judas and his exploits be so completely veiled in a book meant to glorify him and his house?

In fact, the indications of the Maccabæan age are of a general and doubtful character. The history 'points to a time when danger threatened not only the people but also its faith. . . . This reminds us of Daniel and the Maccabæan period' (Schürer). The ritualism of the book has some late marks (8^6). The high priest did not command Samaria (4^{4-6}; cf. $15^{5.8}$) until John Hyrcanus. Hellenistic cities were not independent after the Roman period. But, on the other hand, a writer may attempt to describe past conditions, and may make mistakes in doing so. This writer professes to tell of a time long past (14^{10} 16^{25}). That he wrote in the late Maccabæan or in the Roman period is quite probable. That he wrote primarily of the Maccabæan wars there is little sign.

Schürer now (Herzog[3], 1896) attaches importance to an early view, not mentioned in his *HJP*. 'The presupposed historical background answers more to the time of Artaxerxes Ochus. In one of his expeditions against Phœnicia and Egypt, about B.C. 350, he took also some Jewish prisoners, and among his most conspicuous generals in that campaign were the satrap (king) Holofernes of Cappadocia and the eunuch Bagoas.' Sulpicius Severus (*Chron.* ii. 14-16) first argued that Jth was an actual history of that time. Gutschmid (*Jhb. f. Klas. Phil.* 1863, p. 714) says, 'Severus seems to me to have proved as much as this, that the author of the Bk. of Jth actually meant to put her history in the time of Ochus' (so Nöldeke; Keil; W. R. Smith, *OTJC*[2] 439; Wellhausen, *Isr. u. Jüd. Gesch.*[3] 186). True, Holofernes was the title of other Cappadocian kings (Ball), but no other is known to have had anything to do with the Jews (Keil). True also that Bagoas is Persian for 'eunuch.' Yet force remains in the association of the two names in Jth and in this historical assault upon Judæa under the king of the great Eastern empire. It is possible, then, that the writer lived in the 1st cent. B.C. and wrote of an event three centuries earlier. It would be possible then to think of a century or more of peace after the deliverance (16^{25} (cf. ^{23})), and to speak of the return from exile as recent (4^3 $5^{18.19}$). There was no king (5^3), and the Joiakim of Neh $12^{10.26}$ might possibly be supposed to have been high priest. See also a Persian custom in 2^7, and compare 16^{10}.

5. HISTORICAL CHARACTER.—The early chapters of the book contain historical and geographical impossibilities, and the later chapters much self-evident romance. With the geography of Palestine, however, the writer shows great familiarity.[*] The historicity of Bethulia does not prove the actuality of Judith and her deed, though it is a serious obstacle to the allegorical interpretation of the book and also to the supposition that the story originally concerned the Maccabæan age.[†]

---

[*] Schlatter thinks Jth gives a true picture not only of the geographical, but also of the political, social, and religious conditions of the isolated Jewish hill towns of Northern Samaria before the time of the Maccabees.

[†] Cf. the part played by Bethsura in 1 Mac.

Nevertheless 'it is possible that in some Palestinian town a popular festival was celebrated in memory of the heroic deed of a woman, and that after the true occasion was forgotten and had given place to a manifoldly embellished legend, a history was composed in honour of Judith, probably before the destruction of the temple' (Zunz, *Gottesdienstliche Vorträge*, p. 124). One is reminded of the little city besieged by a great king and delivered by a poor wise man (Ec 9[14. 15]), perhaps also an incident of the Persian period.

Josephus is silent both as to the invasion of Ochus and as to Jth, and his silence speaks against the antiquity of the book and its firm place in the Greek Bible of the 1st century. The NT has no reference.* The earliest reference is in Clem. Rom. i. 55, where Judith is put before Esther as an example of womanly heroism. The book was therefore classical, probably scriptural, about A.D. 90 among Christians. That Jewish tradition should come to connect the story with the Maccabæan period is natural.

6. LITERARY CHARACTER.—The book is a work of literary skill, 'as a work of art quite perfect' (Ewald). 'The representation contains nothing diffuse, bombastic, forced, but is short, simple, natural, and betrays originality. . . . Appropriate, in part admirable, are the particular descriptions. . . . Extraordinarily successful is the song of praise at the close of the book. . . . I put it unhesitatingly by the side of the best poetical products of the Hebrew spirit' (Fritzsche, 127 f., 209).

7. RELIGIOUS AND ETHICAL TEACHINGS.—The religious ideas of the book are of the Pharisaic type, particularistic and legal. Patriotism centres in zeal for the temple (4[2. 3. 11-15] 8[21. 24] 9[8. 13]; cf. 5[19] 9[1] 11[13] 16[18-20]). Israel can suffer no harm unless it sin against God (5[17-21] 11[10-19]). The fatal sin might be the most excusable of ritual transgressions (11[12ff.]), though Judith's confidence rests chiefly on the freedom of her race from idolatry (8[18-20]). In the account of Judith's own piety the food laws (10[5] 11[12-15] 12[1-9. 19]), fasts (8[6]), washings (12[7. 9]), and prayer (9. 11[17] 12[8] 13[4. 5]) are emphasized. Her persistent widowhood is praised (16[22]; cf. 8[4-8]). Social virtues are wanting, except the freeing of her slave (16[23]).† The Pharisaic union of determinism and freedom is to be observed. Salvation comes from God, and all is in accordance with His will (8[11-27] 9[5-14] 16[13-17]). Yet it is not through angel or miracle, but through the wisdom and boldness of Judith that deliverance is wrought (cf. 8[32-34] 10[9] 15[9. 10]). But she gets her strength by prayer (9. 12[8] 13[4. 5]), and the glory of God is greater because of the weakness of the means through which so great a triumph was achieved (9[11] 16[6. 7. 11. 12]). The absence of angels and miracles (cf. Tobit) and of future life and Messianic hope is to be noted. A proselyte is welcomed (14[10]).

For history of Jth in the Canon, see APOCRYPHA.

LITERATURE.—Commentaries by Fritzsche (1853), Volkmar (1860), Wolff (1861, defends historical character), Ball (*Speaker's Com.* 1888), Scholz (2nd ed. 1896, Roman Catholic); Löhr in Kautzsch's *Apocryphen und Pseudepigraphen*, 1898. On Hebrew versions, see above. Further under APOCRYPHA. Cf. Schürer, *HJP* II. iii. 32 ff., *RE*[3] i. 644 f., *GJV*[3] iii. 167 ff. ; C. D. Ginsburg in Kitto's *Cyclop. Bibl. Lit.* ; A. Schlatter, *Zur Topographie und Geschichte Palästinas*, ch. 23 (1893).

F. C. PORTER.

JUEL.—**1.** ('Ιουνά) 1 Es 9[34]=UEL, Ezr 10[34]. **2.** (Α 'Ιουήλ, Β Ουήλ) 1 Es 9[35]=JOEL, Ezr 10[43].

JULIA ('Ιουλία).—One of those greeted by St. Paul in Ro 16[15] with Philologus, Nereus, Olympas, and others. It has been suggested that Philologus

and Julia were husband and wife, and the others members of the family. The name was the commonest of all Roman female names, commonest of all among slaves of the imperial household, and nothing can be proved by it. The following inscription is interesting (*CIL* vi. 20416): D.M | IVLIAE NEREI · F · | CLAVDIAE.

A. C. HEADLAM.

JULIUS ('Ιούλιος).—The name of the centurion in whose custody St. Paul journeyed to Rome (Ac 27[1. 3]). When it was determined that St. Paul with his companions should sail to Italy, he was delivered with his companions 'to a centurion named Julius of the Augustan cohort.' Throughout the voyage the centurion is represented as treating his prisoner with some kindness and distinction. He was allowed to go ashore and see his friends at Sidon. Although the centurion does not attend to the apostle's warnings at first (vv.[9. 11]), it is at his instigation that he orders the soldiers to cut away the boat (v.[31f.]), and it is to save him that he prevents the soldiers from killing the prisoners (v.[42f.]). On arrival at Rome, St. Paul was allowed to live by himself with the soldier who guarded him (Ac 28[16]).

Two points in this narrative demand close attention, the **Augustan cohort** and the statement last made. We will take the latter first. There is an interesting variation of text. The best of the MSS (NABI) and Vulg. Pesh. Boh. read in Ac 28[16] 'And when we entered into Rome, Paul was suffered to abide by himself with the soldier that guarded him.' This is adopted by WH and by Blass in his α text. The latter in his β text on the authority of HLP[etc.] Harcl. [cor.] *Gig*, reads, 'the centurion handed over the prisoners to the head of the camp, while Paul was allowed to remain by himself without the camp with the soldiers that guarded him.' The word translated 'head of the camp' is in Greek στρατοπεδάρχης, while the one representative of the Old Latin we have here reads *principi peregrinorum*. It must be remembered that D and most Old Latin authorities are defective in this place. A portion of this latter reading is found in the TR, and has always been interpreted as referring to the *præfectus prætorio*; stress has been laid on the singular, and it has been supposed necessarily to refer to a date before 62 while Burrhus filled the office alone. Prof. Mommsen tells us that neither the term nor the duty is consonant with Roman usage, and suggests another interpretation based primarily on the technical Latin word, which appears in the version *princeps peregrinorum*. In order to perfect the organization of the Roman army and the communications with the legions on the frontier, there was a body of troops detached from the foreign legions called *frumentarii*. At some date or other they were organized under a head of their own, and had a camp on the Cælian hill. It was called the *castra peregrinorum*, and the head of it the *princeps castrorum peregrinorum* or *princeps peregrinorum*. This is represented in the Greek apparently less correctly, or at least less technically, by στρατοπεδάρχης. To this body of messengers, constantly travelling backwards and forwards, it would be natural that prisoners should be entrusted, and there is evidence to that effect. It had been usual in the absence of evidence to refer this organization to the time of Hadrian, but Mommsen thinks it more probable that it dates from the time of Augustus, and would use the Acts for evidence to that effect.

But the question now arises—What is the authority of the text? for this may be a crucial instance of the value of the β text. How, on Blass's theory, did it come about that St. Luke substituted a vague phrase for the technical lan-

---

* Cf. 1 Co 10[9. 10] with Vulg. Jth 8[25] (Scholz).
† The question of the morality of Judith's deed should not be discussed without reference to the existing state of war, and to such examples as Jael and Esther.

guage he had previously employed? If his theory be incorrect, which reading is intrinsically likely to be altered? It has become the fashion to hint that the β reading is here correct; but it may be pointed out that the phrase which is most correct technically, that of the Latin MSS, is the work of a translator who, being a Roman, would presumably have more accurate knowledge than the original writer, giving precision in his translations by employing a technical word. Following that line of argument it might be suggested that perhaps here we have an instance in which the more precise text of β arose from the influence of the Latin version and possibly bilingual MSS. At any rate, the β text is here very definitely connected with Rome. But what is the meaning of the σπεῖρα Σεβαστή? The *cohortes* of the Roman legion had no special designation, and therefore in this case we must have a cohort of auxiliary troops; and many such were named *Augusta*. But then we should have an auxiliary used for services for which, as far as we know, they were not employed. Mommsen seems to suggest a connexion with the *cohors peregrinorum*, although confessing that this name and that of the **Italian band** are still unsolved. Ramsay, starting from this suggestion, develops it as follows: 'But when we recollect (1) that Luke regularly uses the terms of educated conversation, not the strict technical terms; and (2) that he was a Greek who was careless of Roman forms or names, we shall not seek in this case to treat the Greek name (σπεῖρα Σεβαστή) as a translation of a correct Roman name; but we shall look for a body in the Roman service which was likely to be called "the troops of the Emperor" by the persons in whose society Luke moved at the time . . . we conclude, then, that "the troops of the Emperor" was a popular colloquial means of describing the corps of officer-couriers; and we thus gather from *Acts* an interesting fact, elsewhere unattested but in perfect conformity with the known facts' (*St. Paul the Traveller*, p. 315).

The conclusions of Professors Mommsen and Ramsay, which are almost always full of interest, are given with this warning, that a superstructure, however ingenious, is built on a slight foundation when it is based on a reading which on external grounds has no claim to acceptance, and may easily be a correction of the 2nd century introducing the precise phraseology and writing of the later date. The attempt of Schürer (*HJP* I. ii. 53) to connect the Augustan band with a σπεῖρα Σεβαστηνῶν does not give any assistance to the problem, and is based on a confusion of ideas.

LITERATURE.—Mommsen and Harnack in *Sitzungsberichte d. Berl. Akad.* 1895, p. 501; Schürer, *HJP* I. ii. 53; Ramsay, *St. Paul the Traveller*, pp. 314, 315, 347, 348; Wieseler, *Chron. d. Apost.* ix. p. 391 (not seen).   A. C. HEADLAM.

JUNIAS (or **JUNIA**).—In Ro 16⁷ St. Paul greets Andronicus and Junias (or Junia); the name being in the accusative, the sex is not determined (Ἀνδρόνικον καὶ Ἰουνίαν). If masculine, the name is a shortened form of Junianus; if feminine, Junia is a common name. As has been pointed out under ANDRONICUS (wh. see), there is a little doubt as to whether the two are to be included among the apostles—probably they are to be, the word being taken in its wider signification. In that case it is hardly likely that the name is feminine, although, curiously enough, Chrysostom does not consider the idea of a female apostle impossible: 'And, indeed, to be apostles at all is a great thing. But to be even amongst those of note, just consider what a great encomium this is. But they were of note owing to their works and their achievements. Oh! how great is the devotion of this woman, that she should be even counted worthy of the appellation of apostle.'
                                         A. C. HEADLAM.

JUNIPER (רֹתֶם *rōthem*). — *Rōthem* occurs three times in the Bible. Elijah sat under a *rōthem* (1 K 19⁴). The LXX transliterates this Ῥαθμέν. The poor are said to cut up the roots of the *rōthem* for food (Job 30⁴), LXX ῥίζας ξύλων. The tongue is compared (Ps 120⁴) to coals of *rōthem*, LXX τοῖς ἄνθραξιν τοῖς ἐρημικοῖς. It is clear from these references that the LXX did not understand what was meant by *rōthem*. The Arab. happily furnishes the clue. *Ratam* is a sort of broom, *Retama Retem*, L., which grows in all the deserts of Egypt, Sinai, and the Holy Land. The tr. (AV in all, and RV ,text 1 K 19⁴, Ps 120⁴) 'juniper' is incorrect. 'Broom' (RV text Job 30⁴, and marg. in other passages) is somewhat misleading. The particular species of plant not growing in other lands had better be called by its indigenous name *ratam*.

The *ratam* is a glabrescent shrub, with a few linear leaves, 3–4 lines long, purplish white flowers, half an inch long, 1–5 together in subsessile clusters along the twigs, and obliquely ovate, 1-seeded, beaked pods, half an inch long. The shrub gives the poorest kind of shade, and yet it is often the only refuge from the blazing sun of the desert. Its roots are suitable for burning, and are used for making charcoal. They would be poor eating indeed. This has led some to suppose that שֹׁרֶשׁ *shōresh* (Job 30⁴), may mean the seeds which are said to be eaten by sheep. For this, however, there is no etymological warrant. The LXX tr. is against it.   G. E. POST.

JUPITER in 2 Mac 6² is Zeus, the supreme god in the Greek pantheon. Zeus Xenios (*ib.*), *i.e.* Zeus the god of hospitality and protector of strangers, was worshipped throughout the Greek world. Zeus Olympios (*ib.*), Olympian Zeus, was probably so called because first worshipped on Mount Olympus in North Thessaly; but owing to the influence of the Homeric poetry the epithet became familiar wherever Greek was spoken, and the god was widely worshipped under that name, *e.g.* at Athens, Chalcis, Megara, Olympia, Sparta, Corinth, Syracuse, Naxos, and Miletus (Farnell, *Cults of the Greek States*, I. iv.). The juxtaposition of the two cults by Antiochus Epiphanes, who specially honoured Zeus *Olympios* (Nestle, *Marg.* p. 42), would imply to the Greek mind that the supreme God who ruled the whole world, whether of Greeks or foreigners (*Xenios*), was not J″, but the Zeus Olympios who had been a Greek god from the earliest, *i.e.* Homeric, times.

The Jupiter of Ac 14¹². ¹³ though called Zeus, was not the Greek god, but the native god of the Lycaonian population, whose Lycaonian name was represented in Greek as Zeus. The reading of Codex Bezæ in v.¹³ is τοῦ ὄντος Διὸς πρὸ πόλεως, and is to be translated 'of Zeus, who is called Zeus Propoleôs,' *i.e.* 'Jupiter-before-the-town'—the epithet *Propoleôs* being given to the god because his temple was outside the town; cf. the inscription in Claudiopolis of Isauria to Διί Προαστίῳ (Ramsay, *The Church in the Roman Empire*, pp. 51–53). The remains of this temple have not yet been discovered; but, in the opinion of Ramsay, they might be identified with but very little excavation. In Ac 19³⁵ ('the image which fell down *from Jupiter*,' τὸ [ἄγαλμα] διοπετές) the phrase 'from Jupiter' is simply='from the clear sky' (see Ramsay, p. 604 n. of vol. i. of this Dictionary).
                                         F. B. JEVONS.

JUSHAB-HESED (יוּשָׁב חֶסֶד 'loving-kindness is returned').—A son of Zerubbabel, 1 Ch 3²⁰.

JUSTICE is in Scripture essentially identical

with Righteousness (wh. see). The same words (צַדִּיק, צֶדֶק, צְדָקָה, δίκαιος, δικαιοσύνη) are rendered now by one and now by the other term, but chiefly by 'righteous,' 'righteousness.' The tendency in RV is to replace 'just' by 'righteous'; see Ps 89[14], Pr 4[18]; in Pr 10[6. 7] the same word is rendered both 'just' and 'righteous.' Referring to the artt. on Justification and Righteousness for detailed exposition of the meaning and development of the idea, we need here refer only to general considerations.

The Eng. word 'justice,' in addition to the broad sense in which it denotes moral excellence in general and is equivalent to righteousness, has acquired the special sense of honesty, fairness to others, and then judicial righteousness, whereas 'righteousness' has kept to its original meaning. In Scripture it is the broad sense that is almost exclusively meant in reference both to God and man. Or, put in another way, the justice or righteousness of Scripture denotes almost exclusively moral and religious perfection, of which every other moral excellence is a necessary corollary. There are indeed the beginnings of a special meaning, but little more; thus 'just balances' (Lv 19[36]), 'One that ruleth over men righteously' (2 S 23[3]), 'Whatsoever is right I will give you' (Mt 20[4]). But, in the main, Scripture refers only to absolute, essential righteousness; in demanding this it demands all.

Such absolute, universal righteousness is everywhere affirmed of God: 'Just and right is he' (Dt 32[4]), 'A just God and a saviour' (Is 45[21]), 'The Lord is righteous; he loveth righteousness' (Ps 11[7]), 'That he might himself be just' (Ro 3[26]). God is indeed spoken of as a Judge, Gn 18[25], Ps 7[11], Is 33[22] (שֹׁפֵט), but it is in the general sense of ruler, sovereign. It is evident, on the principle that the greater includes the less, that every special form of justice — legislative, retributive — is included in and follows from the general idea. The justice ascribed to God is absolute, perfect. 'Thou that art of purer eyes than to behold evil, and that canst not look on perverseness' (Hab 1[13]).

The term is used in the same comprehensive sense of men. The good are the just or righteous in contrast with the wicked (Ps 37[12] etc.). The Lord Jesus is so described (Ac 3[14], 1 P 3[18]). 'Whatsoever things are just' (Ph 4[8]). 'A just man' is the comprehensive description given of individuals (Gn 6[9], Mt 1[19], Mk 6[20], Lk 2[25] 23[50], Ac 10[22], 2 P 2[7]). A bishop must be just (Tit 1[8]).

Assuming that justice and mercy are the two complementary aspects of holiness, justice is the aspect emphasized in the OT. It may be regarded as distinctively the OT attribute or virtue. Not that this aspect is superseded in NT. The entire teaching of the Sermon on the Mount goes to show that Christianity immensely deepens OT ideas. But in the gospel mercy takes the central place. This is the natural order of revelation. 'The law was given by Moses; grace and truth came by Jesus Christ' (Jn 1[17]). Justice as righteousness forms the solid substratum of moral character in God and man, and must come first; but this point being secured, mercy lifts us to a higher stage (Ro 13[10]). The revelation of righteousness is crowned by the revelation of love (1 Jn 4[8]). Thus the two testaments each play a distinct part in the revelation of moral truth.   J. S. BANKS.

JUSTIFICATION.—To 'justify' means to set right, or to put on a right footing, one whose relation, either in consequence of misunderstanding or misrepresentation, or because of misconduct, has been what it should not be. Where there has been no real wrong-doing, 'justification' is simply vindication or declaration of innocence or rectitude; where there has been real wrong-doing, it pre-

supposes the fulfilment of some condition by which the wrong-doing is made good or expiated. In both cases a relation more or less abnormal is changed into one that is normal,—in the one by means of more *light*, in the other by means of more *right*.

Neither the Heb. צדק (*Pi.* and *Hiph.*) nor the Gr. δικαιοῦν means to *make righteous*, but simply to put in a right relation. It is a question primarily of relationship, not of character or conduct; though the relationship is conceived as conditioning both character and conduct.

The fundamental meaning of δικαιόω is 'to settle or recognize as right.' In Class. Lit. it means (1) to hold or deem right, Herod. i. 100; Eurip. *Supplic.* 526; Thuc. i. 140. 2; ii. 41. 2, etc.; (2) to do a man justice, *i.e.* in general, to judge or punish, Herod. iii. 29, and so frequently in later Greek, especially Dio Cassius (cf. the Scots use of 'justify'). δικαιόω came to be a technical term in ecclesiastical Greek in sense (1), used of the decree of councils, ἐδικαίωσεν ἡ ἁγία καὶ μεγάλη σύνοδος, Can. 17, Conc. Nic.

In LXX (OT and Apoc.) it is used to translate the Piel and Hiph'il of צדק (Qal=διδικαιῶσθαι), almost always with a personal object: so Ex 23[7]. The root meaning everywhere seems to be, 'to set forth as righteous,' to justify, in a legal sense. This may signify either (1) to show one to be righteous, Ezk 16[51. 52], Jer 3[11]; or (2) to declare righteous, Dt 25[1], 1 K 8[32]. Similarly in the Pseudepigraphical Books, *e.g.* Ps.-Sol ii. 16, ix. 3, where it means to justify God.

In NT the sense is determined largely by the usage of LXX. We have (1) to show one to be righteous, 1 Co 4[4], Lk 7[35]; (2) to pronounce righteous, as a judicial act, Lk 16[15] 7[29]; (3) in Pauline usage δικαιοῦν denotes the judicial act of God whereby those who put faith in Christ are declared righteous in His eyes, free from guilt and punishment, Ro 4[5], Gal 2[16] *et passim*. (3) is thus an expansion and Christian application of (2). In Ro 8[30] δικαιοῦν is specifically mentioned as an element in the divine work of saving the individual. Cremer points out that while in Hebrew Hiph. presupposes Qal,—justification, the being just,—the converse is true in Greek (δικαιοῦν—διδικαιῶσθαι).

In general we may say that in Bibl. Lit. the word δικαιοῦν is used always, or almost always, in the forensic sense, and that its proper meaning is to pronounce righteous. Of itself it does not affirm or deny the *real* righteousness of the person so declared, or treated as, righteous, and in so far as he is not really righteous it implies forgiveness. But it may be taken as certain that it cannot mean to *make* righteous, not even in 1 Co 6[11]. Verbs in -όω, derived from adjectives of *moral* meaning, never have this *efficient* signification. Godet (*Com. on Rom.* Eng. tr. i. 157) goes so far as to say that there is not a single example in the whole of Class. Lit. where the word= to make righteous. And the usage of the NT is unmistakable. See esp. Morison, *Crit. Expos. of the Third Chap. of the Ep. to the Rom.* pp. 163–198.

A word may be added on two other terms. δικαίωμα is the declaration or decision, either (1) that a thing is δίκαιον, or (2) that a person is δίκαιος. (1) gives us the common meaning of 'ordinance' or 'precept,' Lk 1[6], Ro 8[4], He 9[1]; (2) the technical Pauline sense in Ro 5[16. 18]. δικαίωμα is the act of justification regarded as complete; δικαίωσις (a word occurring only twice in NT, elsewhere replaced by the verb δικαιοῦν) is the act as in process, which, therefore, when relating to sinners=the act of acquittal, as is especially clear from Ro 5[18].

See also under RIGHTEOUSNESS.

Put into a sentence, the point of view of this article may be stated as follows:—God has ever been seeking to establish normal personal *relations* between Himself and sinful men; and so far as men have responded to the divine movement, as befitted that movement, on the one hand, and the stage of their personal and moral development to which the movement accommodated itself, on the other, such a normal *relation* was established. That relation was *justification*. The first step was thus taken to God's being to man that without which man could not be to God, still less in himself, what he was designed to be.

I. The act of justification may affect various relations.

1. *A man's relation to himself.*—A man may seek to set himself right with himself, in other words, to justify himself to himself. Something of this kind is implied in 1 Co 4[3. 4] 'I judge not mine own self. For I know nothing against myself; yet am I not hereby justified: but He that judgeth me is the Lord'; and in 1 Jn 3[19. 20] 'Hereby shall we know that we are of the truth, and shall assure our heart before Him, wheresoever our heart condemn us;

because God is greater than our heart, and knoweth all things.' Such justification is, of course, exclusively the vindication or clearing up of one's own innocence or rectitude before or to oneself. There is such a thing as mistaken self-judgment: it may be either for the better or the worse.

2. *A man's relation to his fellow-man.*—Men set themselves right with their fellow-men, whether regarded individually or corporately. If a man have been *misrepresented*, to justify himself is to clear or vindicate himself in the particular respect in which he has been misjudged; if, on the other hand, he is *guilty of wrong* in thought or word or act, the wrong relation thence arising or thereby constituted, has to be rectified by some sort of expiation or good-making of the wrong. It may be by confession of fault, or an expression of regret, or the payment of a fine, or loss of liberty, or endurance of suffering. In the legislation of Israel, as set forth in OT, provision was made both for the vindication of innocence (Nu 5[18ff.]) and the making good of real wrong-doing (Ex 21[19-30] 22[14]).

3. *Men are sometimes set right or justified by others*; that, too, in both senses, namely, the vindication of innocence or rectitude, and atonement for wrong. The *former* is referred to in Dt 25[1] 'If there be a controversy between men, and *the judges* judge them; then they shall justify the righteous and condemn the wicked.' Justification of the wicked for a reward, on the contrary, is denounced in Is 5[23]. In Ezk 16[51. 52] Jerus. is satirically represented as justifying her sinful sisters, *i.e.* causing them to appear righteous, by her own abominations (cf. Jer 3[11]). *Amends* might also be made for evil-doing within certain limits. Elihu is represented as anxious that Job should make clear his rectitude, as, *e.g.*, in Job 33[32], where we read: 'If thou hast anything to say, answer me: speak, for I desire to justify thee'; and it is said of God in Ps 37[6], 'He shall make thy righteousness to go forth as the light, and thy judgment as the noonday' (cf. Is 54[17]).

4. *The justification of men before God* is often referred to, but only to be characterized as impossible; that, too, in *both respects*. Such failure is distinctly pronounced inevitable in Ps 143[2] 'Enter not into judgment with Thy servant: for in Thy sight shall no man living be justified.' See also Job 25[4] 'How then can man be just with God?' In NT the same thing is both everywhere implied and often expressly affirmed, as, *e.g.*, in Gal 2[16] 'because by the works of the law shall no flesh be justified' (cf. Ro 3[20]), Ac 13[39] 'by him every one is justified from all things from which ye could not be justified by the law of Moses.'

Not only is the impossibility of vindicating their righteousness before God denied to men, but also that of setting themselves right by making amends for or expiating unrighteousness. That it cannot be effected by *works*, is clear from declarations like Is 57[12] 'as for thy works, they shall not profit thee'; and especially Is 64[6] 'For we are all become as one that is unclean, and all our righteousnesses are as a polluted garment . . . and our iniquities like the wind have taken us away.' Further, to say, 'The temple of the Lord, the temple of the Lord are these,' is to 'trust in lying words' (Jer 7[4]). But equally out of the question is it to purchase the divine favour by mere *sacrifices*; for 'In sacrifice and offering He has no delight' (Ps 40[6] 51[16]); 'I desire mercy, and not sacrifice' (Hos 6[6]; cf. Ps 4[5]); a multitude of sacrifices is nothing to Him (Is 1[11]); 'the solemn meeting,' 'new moons,' 'appointed feasts,' His 'soul hateth' (Is 1[13]); yea, 'The sacrifice of the wicked is an abomination to the Lord' (Pr 15[8] 21[27]).

As to NT—the impossibility either of vindicating righteousness or making amends for sin by works

of the law and by sacrifices, is the *burden* of the Epp. of St. Paul and of that to the Hebrews, besides being everywhere else implied (cf. *e.g.* Gal 2[16], Ro 3[20], He 10[5-8] where Ps 40 is quoted: 'Sacrifice and offering thou wouldest not . . . in whole burnt-offerings and sacrifices for sin thou hadst no pleasure').

5. The impossibility of justification in the sight of God, thus explicitly affirmed in the particular cases adduced, is implicitly assumed throughout OT and NT. In point of fact, the idea that men should either vindicate their own innocence or rectitude, or that they of themselves, or any creature for them, should establish a right relation between God and themselves, by acts or sacrifices, or anything of their own, is totally alien from the spirit and life that produced the writings which constitute our Bible.

Passages, indeed, in which all manner of good deeds are required, whilst contempt is cast on sacrifices and the like, may seem and are often taken to imply that by right conduct men can set themselves right with God; but this is by no means their import. As *fruits* of a right relation, both sacrifices and right conduct are obligatory and pleasing to God; as *means of establishing a right relation*, the one is an abomination, the other utterly insufficient (cf. Ps 51[15-17] with v.[19] of the same psalm).

II. 'Justification,' however, understanding it as previously defined, is undoubtedly recognized both as possible and as a fact. Men are actually set right with God, notwithstanding their sin, and their utter inability to expiate or make amends for sin.

1. 'Justification' is in some sense ascribed even to *Gentiles*. In this respect the case of Cornelius is typical. 'Of a truth,' says St. Peter regarding him, 'I perceive that God is no respecter of persons: but in every nation he that feareth Him and worketh righteousness, is *acceptable* to Him' (Ac 10[34. 35]; cf. Ps 15[2], He 11[33], Mt 8[5-13], Ro 2[14], Ac 28[28] 15[17]). To be 'acceptable' is to be on the footing with God, in the relation to Him, which conditions the bestowal of such grace as a man is capable of receiving, *i.e.* to be justified. In a certain respect Abraham may be regarded as an example of Gentile 'justification'; for, as St. Paul emphatically affirms, his faith was 'reckoned for righteousness . . . when he was in *uncircumcision*'; 'that he might be the father of all them that *believe, though they be in uncircumcision*' (Ro 4[9-11]). When he believed, he was neither Jew nor Christian.

2. 'Justification' was, further, a common experience under the *Old Covenant*. The proof of this lies first and foremost in the fact of *forgiveness*, which St. Paul treats as constituting an integral part of justification, even if he does not, as some hold, identify the two. Forgiveness followed on the offering of appointed sacrifices, and is represented as an experience which many had, and all might have, at the hands of God. The frequent injunctions to trust in the Lord, and the many declarations that it is a good thing to trust in Him, point in the same direction. How otherwise shall we account for the consciousness of righteousness which is expressed by men who at the same time make confession of sin? And the confidence placed in God as the hearer and answerer of prayer, as a refuge and stronghold, as a support and a defence, and so forth? These are either justification itself or its fruits.

3. It scarcely needs saying that the fact of justification before God is the great theme of NT, especially of the Epistles to the Galatians, Romans, and Hebrews. Whilst, as was pointed out, the self-rectification of man's abnormal relation to God, whether by 'works of law,' *i.e.* by a self-generated righteousness, or by means of sacrifice and offerings or other religious services

(Gal 3[9-12]), is treated as almost ridiculously impracticable, the blessed news is brought that though all have sinned, all may find justification through faith in Christ, whom God has set forth as a propitiation (Ro 3[21-26]).

III. But by what right, it will be asked, can 'justification' be affirmed, not only of Israelites, but even of Gentiles? The Apostle Paul's correlation of Abraham with believers in Christ (Ro 4[20-25]), has puzzled commentators enough; how then can it be right to correlate with them those whom St. Paul is supposed to represent as having been shut up under a law which brought the knowledge of sin (Ro 3[20]), and therefore the certainty of judgment (Ro 2[5-11]); whilst the sacrifices which were offered are said to make no one perfect as pertaining to the conscience? (He 9[9]). And is it not still less admissible to extend 'justification' to those who are characterised as 'sinners of the Gentiles'? (Gal 2[15]).

The difficulty now touched upon affects all the three aspects of the subject, viz., first, *the divine action* (Ro 3[20-26] *et passim*); then, the human *faith*, which, no less than divine action, is necessary to justification; and, finally, the very nature of the *relation* itself, which is termed justification.

It can only be met by the recognition, on the one hand, of the distinction between *implicit* and *explicit* justification; and, on the other, of the fact that between implicit and explicit justification there are or may be *stages* which are not subjected to the limits of earth and time.

The three points just referred to can be represented by means of concentric spheres, the outermost of which shall stand for the Gentiles, the two inner ones respectively for the Israelites and Christian believers; though it needs to be noted that since the break-up of the Jewish system—perhaps, also, largely prior thereto—the distinction between the Israelites and the Gentiles, so far as justification is concerned, has gradually been becoming less and less; their two spheres have therefore been merging into one. For there is no nation now that can be said to have legal, sacrificial, and religious institutions to which God stands in the same relation, or which discharge the same function relatively to God, as those which are summarily designated the Jewish Dispensation or Covenant. Let us consider the three points in relation to the three classes of cases specified.

1. In the case of the *Gentiles*, the divine action consists in the opening of the human eye to the sacredness and absoluteness of the right. This takes place ordinarily in connexion with some specific duty. 'I am under a sacred or absolutely binding obligation to do this or not to do that,' the man *feels*, or possibly says to himself. His eye or ear has been opened: a revelation has been made to him. If he respond, yea, and is ready to do what he sees to be right or avoid what he sees to be wrong, he has attained to a footing which for his stage of personal development is right,—in other words, he has exercised that element of faith which is possible at that stage, and attained *implicit justification*.

If he continue faithfully to say, yea, with the same purpose of obedience, even though he have to confess many failures of execution, he is destined one day to stand face to face with Christ, and, by the exercise of full, explicit faith in Him, to become partaker of that conscious peace with God of which previously he had and could have only glimpses and foretastes.

2. Speaking generally, the purpose of the *Jewish Dispensation* was, *negatively* considered, to check the decrease in humanity of the sensitiveness which conditioned justification of the kind just described; *positively* considered, on the one hand, to develop

a moral personality that should be capable of justification at ever higher stages; and, on the other hand, prepare the way for the coming and work of the Son of God, by which justification in its highest potence was to be rendered possible.

Abraham was a morally faithful man of the type of Cornelius. The special command and promise given him by God, and his ready obedience, both taken together, rendered possible a higher relation than was open to Gentiles under the conditions previously described.

In and through Abraham, God took the principles of heredity and sociality into the service of the higher spiritual development of the race, instead of leaving them to subserve, almost exclusively, its degradation. For the positive purpose referred to, that is, of developing the moral personality, two methods were pursued; *first*, institutions were regulated or called into existence, and laws were enacted or sanctioned, by which the moral consciousness was quickened, or, as St. Paul puts it, the knowledge of sin was increased (Ro 3[20]); and, *secondly*, along therewith sacrifices were sanctioned or ordered, by which a way of forgiveness was provided. Still further, with a view to checking the too natural tendency to the conception of righteousness and sacrifice which eventually dominated the mind of the vast majority of the Jewish nation,—the protest against which, be it remarked, largely colours, not only St. Paul's two great Epp. to the Galatians and Romans, but also the Ep. to the Hebrews,—prophets were commissioned, on the one hand, gradually to develop the law and unfold its true significance; and, on the other, to denounce perfunctory sacrifices, offerings, and observances.

The Israelite who loyally recognized the 'law,' that is, the entire complex of duties arising out of his national relationship, as God's means of showing him how to be holy as He was holy (Lv 19), and who availed himself of the divinely provided means of atoning for his failures, exercised faith, so far as it was then possible and required. *Ipso facto*, he thus behaved as one who belonged to the covenant, notwithstanding the sins he might commit. As such his relation was a right one; he was justified to the degree then attainable. If he were ever condemned, it was not for sins, but for open disloyalty to the covenant, with its obligations and sacrifices, *i.e.* for defiant refusal to recognize right as right and grace as grace. But even true Israelites had to wait for the new covenant which God was to make with the house of Israel, when the law should be written in their hearts (He 8[10]); though their attitude grew to be ever more completely that which we find in Simeon, who, when Jesus was presented to him in the temple, exclaimed, 'Now lettest Thou Thy servant depart, O Lord, according to Thy word, in peace; for mine eyes have seen Thy salvation' (Lk 2[29, 30]).

3. 'Justification' reached its culmination through Christ. The realization of the idea and the adoption of the term coincided. The *Gentile* had no proper sense even of forgiveness, much less of justification; but then his sense of sin was not keen enough to cause him real despair because of the lack. The *Israelite* had a profounder sense of sin, and therefore, unless he was to despair, needed an assurance of forgiveness as objective as the command which condemned him; but he never got beyond *sins*, and therefore never realized justification, in the proper sense; nor had he the term. It was reserved for Christianity to produce the consciousness of *sin*, and to meet what would otherwise have generated despair, by opening the way to justification. The apostle who faced *sinfulness* most directly, was the one to gain the profoundest insight into justification; and it is worthy of note that whilst St. Paul stretches a bridge from forgiveness to justi-

fication by once interchanging the terms (Ro 4⁶⁻⁸), he nowhere else substitutes the one term for the other, except in Col 2¹³, where he uses, not ἀφείς, but χαρισάμενος.

First of all, the *divine action* for the rectification of man's relation to Himself culminated in Christ. Through Him, *law*, revealed alike in life and suffering, and *sacrifice* both by and to God, were presented in their supremest form. Opportunity was thus given, nay more, potential ability was also generated, to respond with a *response* in which *loyal assent* to the right, *trustful surrender* to love, and, finally,—so far as those are concerned who have not seen Christ with the fleshly eye,—*belief* that realizes the invisible, are all blended, *i.e.* a response which is what NT understands by 'faith.'

Such a response under such conditions,—what is it but 'a beginning in spirit' (ἐναρξάμενοι πνεύματι, Gal 3³⁻⁵; cf. 3² 4⁶ 5⁵ᶠᶠ, He 8⁸⁻¹²), a 'receiving of sonship' (ἵνα τὴν υἱοθεσίαν ἀπολάβωμεν, Gal 4¹⁻⁵), and therefore the ability to look up to God as a son, 'crying, Abba, Father' (Gal 4⁶·⁷); in other words, what is it but, *ipso facto*, 'justification,' that is, a rectified relation, a being put on a right footing, in a right relation? The Christian believer is related rightly to God; accordingly law ceases to be mere law, and sacrifice ceases to be a means of purchasing grace; and though he may fall into sin, he can still look up to God as one whose relation has once for all been made right in and through Christ.

(Neither the Roman Catholic and other present-day kindred doctrines which represent justification as in some sense imparting *real* righteousness; nor the traditional or 'orthodox' doctrine of an imputation of the righteousness of Christ, are true to Scripture, though each of them embodies a certain aspect of the truth.)

How Christ by His work on our behalf empowered man to fulfil the conditions devolving on him, *i.e.* to exercise faith, as well as to do that which faith of moral necessity presupposed, is a point which belongs to the doctrine of the atonement; but if justice be done to NT hints on the subject, propitiation, justification, and sanctification will be found to constitute the distinguishable though inseparable factors of one great spiritual whole.

LITERATURE.—Siegfried-Stade, *s.* צדק; Cremer and Thayer-Grimm, *s.* δίκαιος and its cognates ; Neander, *Pflanzung*, etc. (tr. by Ryland, 1851); Smith (John), *Select Discourses*, esp. 7 and 8 on 'Legal and Evangelical Righteousness,' etc., 1860; Newman, *Lectures on Justification*, 1838 ; Herzog, *RE* (art. 'Rechtfertigung,' 1st ed. Kling, 2nd ed. Schmidt); Ritschl, *Rechtfertigung und Versöhnung*, Bd. iii. 2nd ed. 1883 ; Dorner, *Christliche Glaubenslehre* (tr. by Banks and Cave, *System of Christian Doctrine*, 1880–1883); Schultz (H.), 'Gerechtigkeit aus dem Glauben im A. u. N. Test.,' in *JDTh*, and *Alttest. Theologie* (tr. by Paterson, *OT Theology*, 1893); Frank, *System der Christlichen Wahrheit*, 3rd ed. 1894 ; Beck, *Christliche Glaubenslehre*, 1886 ; Kaftan, *Das Wesen der christ. Religion*, 1888 ; Romang, 'Rechtfertigung durch den Glauben,' in *SK*, 1867 ; Sabatier, *The Apostle Paul* (tr. edited by Findlay, 1891); Bruce, *St. Paul's Conception of Christianity*, 1894 ; Simon, *Reconciliation by Incarnation*, 1898.   D. W. SIMON.

JUSTLE.—Nah 2⁴ 'The charets shall rage in the streets, they shall justle one against another in the broad wayes.' Thus the term appears in AV of 1611. In mod. edd. 'charets' is spelt 'chariots,' but 'justle' is retained (and accepted by RV) though 'jostle' is the usual spelling now. Cf. Golding, *Calvin's Job*, 580, 'if we be pinched with adversitie, the passion of sorow is so vehe-

ment, as it cannot be ruled : for then a man skirmisheth in such wise, as he justleth against God, and that is to his owne destruction in the end.' T. Fuller, *Holy Warre*, II. ii. p. 45, 'He was infected with the humour of the clergie of that age, who counted themselves to want room except they justled with Princes.'
         J. HASTINGS.

JUSTUS ('Ιοῦστος).—**1.** In Ac 1²³ we are told that two names were put forward for election to the place vacated by Judas, Joseph called Barsabbas, who was called Justus, and Matthias. Justus is, of course, the Greek name assumed by a Hebrew. See JOSEPH BARSABBAS. **2.** In Ac 18⁷ we learn that St. Paul when at Corinth lodged with one Justus, or Tit(i)us Justus, a proselyte (σεβόμενος τὸν Θεόν) whose house was near the synagogue. There is some variation in the MSS. The name is *Titius Justus* in B, the Vulgate, and Memphitic versions (in Codex Amiatinus 'Titus *nomine* Justus'), *Titus Justus* in אE, *Titus* alone in the Sahidic version and Peshitta, *Justus* alone in AD and later MSS ; two MSS omit the name altogether. According to Ramsay, 'Titius Justus was evidently a Roman or a Latin, one of the *coloni* of the colony Corinth. Like the centurion Cornelius, he had been attracted to the synagogue — his citizenship could afford Paul an opening to the more educated class of the Corinthian population' (*St. Paul the Traveller*, p. 256). In Col 4¹⁰·¹¹ St. Paul speaks of Aristarchus, his fellow-prisoner, Mark the cousin of Barnabas, and **Jesus**, which is called Justus. They were all 'of the circumcision,' and were his only fellow-workers for the kingdom who were a comfort to him. The name is a Gentile surname assumed by a Jew, as in **1**.
         A. C. HEADLAM.

JUTAH or JUTTAH (in Jos 15⁵⁵ [Hahn, followed by RV; AV has Juttah, which is the punctuation of Michaelis, יוטה], in Jos 21¹⁶ יֻטָּה [hence AV and RV both have Juttah]).—A town of Judah (Jos 15⁵⁵) mentioned in connexion with Maon, Carmel, and Ziph in the mountains, given to the priests, the sons of Aaron (Jos 21¹⁶), as a city of refuge for the man-slayer. It has been left out of the catalogue of cities of refuge in 1 Ch 6⁵⁹, but *QPB* adds note, 'Insert, Juttah with her pasture grounds.' In the time of Eusebius and Jerome (*Onomast. s.v.* Ἰεττάν) it was a large village 18 MP. from Eleutheropolis, and in Daroma-ad-australem. Reland (*Pal.* p. 870) suggests that Juttah was probably the residence of Zacharias and Elisabeth, and the birthplace of John the Baptist, the πόλις Ἰούδα ('a city of **Judah**') of Lk 1³⁹ being so written by a corruption, or from a softer pronunciation, instead of πόλις Ἰούτα (so also Robinson, *BRP* ² ii. 206). Seetzen (1807) appears to have identified the modern village of *Yutta* as Juttah, and Robinson (*BRP*² i. 495, ii. 206) corroborated the identification. It is a large Moslem village, standing high on a ridge 16 miles from *Beit Jibrin* (Eleutheropolis), and in the vicinity of Maon (*Main*), Carmel (*Kurmul*), and Ziph (*Tell ez-Zif*). It is built of stone, and the water supply is from cisterns. On the south there are rock-cut tombs, and rock wine-presses are found all about the village. The country around is stony, but the inhabitants are very rich in flocks (*SWP* iii. 310).
         C. WARREN

K

KABZEEL (קַבְצְאֵל, B Καβαισελεήλ, A Κασθεήλ).— A town in the extreme south of Judah, on the border of Edom, Jos 15²¹. It is mentioned in 2 S 23²⁰ (B Καβεσεήλ; cf. 1 Ch 11²²) as the native place of Benaiah, the son of Jehoiada. In Neh 11²⁵ it appears under the name **Jekabzeel** as reinhabited after the Captivity (LXX omits in this verse both Jekabzeel and Dibon). Its site has not been identified.

C. R. CONDER.

KADESH, KADESH-BARNEA (קָדֵשׁ Gn 14⁷ [where it is also called עֵין־מִשְׁפָּט 'well of decision'] * 16¹⁴ 20¹, Nu 13²⁶ 20¹·¹⁴ et al., קָדֵשׁ בַּרְנֵעַ in Dt 1². ¹⁹ 2¹⁴ 9²³, Nu 32⁸ 34⁴, Jos 10⁴¹ 14⁶· ⁷ 15⁸ [all]; LXX Καδής, Καδής [τοῦ] Βαρνή).—With the exception of Sinai, no spot is more memorable in the history of the wanderings of the Israelites than Kadesh-barnea. It was here that the host camped during the 38 years that intervened between the sending out of the spies and the entrance into Palestine (Nu 20¹· ¹⁶ JE). It would appear, indeed, from Dt 2¹⁴ as if the time was spent *away from* Kadesh. We may perhaps infer † that at Kadesh the tabernacle with the ark of the covenant was set up; that it was the abode of Moses and the chiefs of the tribes, and that it was the general centre to which the people resorted for worship and for judgment on disputed questions. But it by no means follows that the whole multitude with their flocks and herds congregated in the immediate neighbourhood; such a multitude of people and animals would, for the sake of pasturage alone, require a wide field in which to pitch their tents. It was at Kadesh that Miriam died (Nu 20¹); it was the scene of the rebellion of Korah and his company (Nu 16); it was from Kadesh that the spies were sent in advance to ascertain and report to Moses on the physical character and the inhabitants of Canaan (Nu 13²⁶); and it was at Kadesh that the miraculous supply of water was obtained (Nu 20¹⁻¹²), when, apparently, the fountains which had caused the spot to be selected as camping ground were dried up; caused either by a prolonged drought, or by the blocking up of the underground channels by the falling in of the limestone strata. Whatever may have been the cause, the restoration of the flow of water was clearly miraculous, as it occurred at the moment of the interposition of Moses by command of God; though in a manner at variance with precise directions, which were to 'speak unto the rock' (Nu 20⁸), not to strike it with the rod. This departure from his instructions cost Moses his doom.

The position of Kadesh-barnea has been the subject of much controversy. By a comparison of various passages the site is brought within very narrow limits. It was on the borders of the Wilderness of Zin (Nu 20¹), a tract which lay along the western margin of the valley of the Arabah; it was also near the southern boundary of the territory of Judah and of the land of the twelve tribes (Nu 34⁴). It was eleven days' journey from Horeb (Mt. Sinai) by way of Mt. Seir, or, in other words, by the route of the Arabah,—doubtless the number of days occupied by the Israelitish host in their journey between these two important camps; and it was not far distant from the border of Edom and the base of Mt. Hor, a site which has been recognized as indisputable by many competent authorities. It was from Kadesh-barnea that Moses on the expiration of the 'forty years,' and the resumption of the journeys of the Israelites, sent messengers to the king of Edom asking permission to pass through his land so as to reach the tableland of Moab on their way northwards; which request was refused (Nu 20¹⁴⁻²¹ E).* All these passages lead us to infer some position in the Badiet et-Tîh—the great expanse of treeless limestone plateau which intervenes between the valley of the Arabah, opposite Mt. Hor on the east and the coast of Philistia about Gaza on the west. These conditions appear to be fully satisfied in the site discovered by the late Rev. John Rowland in 1842, to which he was guided by some Arabs when resident at Gaza. Here he found a lofty wall of limestone, at the base of which issued forth a copious spring, or several springs, which emptied themselves into a large artificially constructed basin, then into another of smaller size; and, continuing to flow down the valley, spread fertility on either hand until the waters ultimately disappeared beneath the sands of the desert. The spring is known amongst the Arabs by the name of '*Ain Ḳadîs*, or Holy Well, a name which seems to preserve the original biblical one. It was clear from the stone troughs and the marks of cattle and sheep around that the well was a favourite resort of the tribes for water, and doubtless was so even prior to the visit of the Israelites. The presence of water is a first necessity of life in those districts, and such a copious supply pointed it out as one suitable for the camping ground of the host. This spot was afterwards visited by Dr. H. Clay Trumbull, who confirms Rowland's identification, and who is the author of the most important work yet published on the subject.† The term 'city' applied to this spot probably means a camp or village of the Midianites (Nu 20¹⁶).   E. HULL.

KADESH ON THE ORONTES.—See TAHTIM-HODSHI.

KADMIEL (קַדְמִיאֵל). — The name of a Levitical family which returned with Zerubbabel, Ezr 2⁴⁰= Neh 7⁴³ (cf. 1 Es 5²⁶). The expression which follows, namely, 'of the children of Hodaviah' (or Hodevah), is apparently meant to limit the Kadmiel family to those members who belonged to the Hodaviah branch. In Ezr 3⁹ (cf. 1 Es 5⁵⁸), in connexion with the laying of the foundation of the temple, as well as in Neh 9⁴ᶠ. (the day of humiliation) and 10⁹ (the sealing of the covenant), Kadmiel appears to be an individual. The name occurs further in Neh 12⁸· ²⁴. In the last of these passages we ought certainly to read, on the strength of parallel passages, 'Jeshua, *Bani* (or Binnui), Kadmiel' instead of 'Jeshua ben-Kadmiel.' This emendation is supported by the fact that אBA as well as Luc. have υἱοὶ Καδμιήλ, implying an original בני not בן. See, further, Smend, *Listen*, p. 10, n. 10; Ryle, *Ezra and Nehemiah, ad ll. citt.*

J. A. SELBIE.

---

* In Dt 1. 24-8 there is no mention of these negotiations with Edom (Moore on Jg 11¹⁶).

† *Kadesh Barnea* (New York, 1884); also *PEFSt* (1881) p. 210. The site discovered by Rowland is supported by Ritter, Schultz, and Palmer; objected to by Robinson, Stanley, and others. It was not visited by the expedition of the *Pal. Explor. Fund* of 1883-4, as it lay to the westward of the Arabah, beyond the line of survey by Major Kitchener, R.E., now Lord Kitchener of Khartoum.

---

* The name *Ḳadesh* implies that the place was a sanctuary; no doubt it bore this character before its occupation by Israel. See, further, Driver on Dt 33², where Wellh. would read 'from Meribath-Kadesh' (מִמְּרִיבַת קָדֵשׁ) for מֵרִבְבֹת קֹדֶשׁ 'out of holy myriads,' of MT.

† But see Driver on Dt 2¹⁴.

KADMONITES, קַדְמֹנִי, Κελμωναῖοι, 'men of the East,' only in Gn 15[19], inhabitants of the Syrian desert, possibly descendants of Kedemah, the twelfth son of Ishmael (Gn 25[15]). Mentioned after the Kenites and Kenizzites, the K. are represented as occupying the district along the eastern border of Palestine, near the Dead Sea, which was also called the East Sea, יָם הַקַּדְמֹנִי (Ezk 47[18]). Their name occurs in the longest list of the nations which originally held possession of the territories promised to Abraham. Usually seven, sometimes only six, but here ten such nations are named. Ewald and many following him regard the K. as equivalent to the Běné Ḳedem, children of the East (wh. see), descendants (? Gn 25[6]) of Abraham by Keturah (Gn 29[1], Jg 7[12], 1 K 4[30], Job 1[3], Is 11[14], Jer 49[28], Ezk 25[4. 10]). In that case, K. would be the designation of no particular tribe, but of the Keturæan Arabs, as distinguished from the Ishmaelites. The children of the East are represented in the passages referred to as occupying Paddan-aram, associated with the Midianites and Amalekites, inhabiting Kedar, neighbours and conquerors of the children of Ammon, coupled with the Egyptians in their fame for wisdom, and as Easterns contrasted with the Philistines who possessed the extreme west. Job is described as one of them. It seems better to regard the K. as a particular tribe like the other nations named in this list. Whether they are to be viewed as a branch of the Ishmaelitish or of the Keturæan Arabs is not clear.

LITERATURE.—Ewald, *History of Israel*, i. 253, 314 ff., ii. 213 ff.; Dillmann, *Genesis*, Eng. tr. 1897, pp. 66, 187; Delitzsch, *New Comm. on Genesis*, Edin. 1889, ii. 127.

J. MACPHERSON.

KAIN (קַיִן, properly **Hakkain**, AV **Cain**; A Ἀκείμ, Jos 15[57].—A town of Judah in the Hebron mountains, probably the present ruin *Yukîn*, on a high knoll S.E. of Hebron, overlooking the Jeshimon. It is visible from Minyeh (see BETHPEOR), and may be the 'nest of the Kenite' on a cliff (Nu 24[21]), visible from the top of Peor. The Kenites inhabited this region. The tomb of Cain is now shown at this spot. Near it is the village of Beni N'aim, the old name of which was *Kefr Barakah*, which is the Caphar Barucha of the fourth cent. A.D. (Jerome, *Paula*), supposed to be the place where Abraham 'blessed' God (Gn 18[22]), and whence he saw the destruction of the cities of the Ciccar. See *SWP* vol. iii. sheet xxi.

C. R. CONDER.

KAIN (קַיִן 'lance,' 'spear'). — A clan name = Kenites (wh. see), Nu 24[22], Jg 4[11]. In 1 S 15[6b] Wellh. reads קַיִן instead of קֵינִי, and the same change is proposed by Meyer (*ZATW*, i. 137, n. 3) for בְּנֵי קֵינִי in Jg 1[16] (but see Moore, *ad. loc.* and on 4[11], and cf. Budde, *Richt. u. Sam.* 9, 68).

KALLAI (קַלָּי; A Καλλαί, B om.).—The head of the priestly family of Sallai, in the time of Jeshua the high priest, Neh 12[20].

KAMON (קָמוֹן; B Ῥαμνών, A Ῥαμμώ, Luc. Καλκών). —The burial-place of Jair, Jg 10[5]. The site has not been recovered. It was probably east of the Jordan; probably identical, Moore thinks, with *Kamûn* mentioned by Polybius (v. lxx. 12) in connexion with Pella. Eusebius is certainly wrong in identifying it with *Kammôna* (modern *Tell Keimûn*), 6 miles N.W. of Legio (Lejjûn). See JOKNEAM.

KANAH (קָנָה).—**1.** A *wâdy* (נַחַל), forming the boundary between Ephraim and Manasseh, terminating on the W. at the sea and on the E. at En-tappuah (Jos 16[8] 17[9]). This eastern limit must have been near Shechem lying to the S.E., but it has not been identified with any certainty. The

modern *Wâdy Ḳanah*, the channel of a small stream rising near *Nâblus* (Shechem), is regarded by Conder as representing the ancient Ḳanah (*Handbook to the Bible*, 263); but Thomson (*Land and Book*, 'Southern Pal.,' 56) considers that this tributary of the *'Aujeh* would put the boundary too far to the south (so also Dillmann). In connexion with the brook Ḳanah a difficulty arises in locating the Me-jarkon and Rakkon (Jos 19[46] *), if these three under different names are all represented by the *'Aujeh* immediately to the north of Jaffa. The discovery of *Tell Ṛakkeit* near the mouth of the *'Aujeh* makes the supposition not impossible that Me-jarkon and Rakkon were names of that river after being joined by the brook Ḳanah. All the streams crossing the northern half of the plain of Sharon are reedy and discoloured. Thomson is in favour of the *Falik* as representing Ḳanah, and its divided mouth would account for the two names Me-jarkon and Rakkon. Farther north, on each side of Cæsarea, are two streams that suggest the Bible names mentioned, namely, *el-Akhḍar* (Yellow River) and *el-Azraḳ* (Blue River). These streams would give Dan the coast-line up to Dora, and coincide with the territory assigned to that tribe by Josephus (*Ant.* v. i. 21).

2. A town on the northern boundary of Asher (Jos 19[28]). The English reader must be careful to distinguish it from Cana of Galilee (wh. see). It is very probably the modern *Ḳana*, a considerable village lying a few miles S.E. of Tyre (cf. Robinson, *BRP* [2] ii. 456; Guérin, *Galilée*, ii. 390 f.; Baedeker-Socin, *Pal.* [3] 262 f.). In its neighbourhood there is a large Phœnician sepulchral monument known as 'Hiram's Tomb' (*PEF Mem.* i. 61). Ḳanah is possibly referred to in the journey of the Egyptian *mohar* in the time of Ramses II. under the name *Pa-Kana-na*.

G. M. MACKIE.

KAREAH (קָרֵחַ 'bald').—Father of Johanan, who was a Judæan contemporary of Jeremiah, and one of the captains of the forces in the open field who escaped the deportation to Babylon at the destruction of Jerusalem by Nebuchadrezzar (2 K 25[23], Jer 40[13. 15. 16] 42[1. 8] 43[2. 4. 5]). In Jer 40[8] MT reads 'Johanan and Jonathan, sons of Kareaḥ,' but here LXX (47[8]) makes mention only of Johanan,' as in the other passages above cited. Probably therefore יוֹנָתָן in MT is due merely to mistaken repetition of יוֹחָנָן.

C. F. BURNEY.

KARIATHIARIUS (A Καριαθιαριὸς, B Καρταθειαρειὸς; RVm 'Kiriath-arim or Kiriath-jearim'), 1 Es 5[19] for Kiriath-jearim (wh. see).

KARKA (הַקַּרְקָעָה, with ה *locale*, hence AV Karkaa).—An unknown place on the south border of Judah, apparently in the Tîh plateau, Jos 15[3]. The LXX has κατὰ δυσμὰς Καδής.

KARKOR (קַרְקֹר).—A place apparently in Gilead, Jg 8[10]. The site is unknown.

KARTAH (קַרְתָּה).—A city of Zebulun given to the Levites, Jos 21[34]. It is not mentioned in the parallel passage, 1 Ch 6[77]. The site is unknown. It might be for Ḳattath (קַטָּת) by a clerical error.

KARTAN (קַרְתָּן).—A city of Naphtali given to the Levites, Jos 21[32]. The parallel passage, 1 Ch 6[76], has Ḳiriathaim (wh. see). While Luc. reads Καρθὰν in harmony with MT, B has Θεμμών, A Νοεμμών.

* There are suspicions as to the correctness of the MT (see Dillm.'s and Bennett's notes). Rakkon (רַקּוֹן), which is omitted in LXX, may have arisen by dittography from the preceding מֵי הַיַּרְקוֹן.

KATTATH (קַטָּת, B Καταυάθ, A Καττάθ, Luc. Κοττάθ).—A city of Zebulun, Jos 19¹⁵, perhaps to be identified with Ḳartah (wh. see) or with Ḳiṭron (wh. see) of Jg 1³⁰, a place from which the Zebulunites were unable to expel the Canaanites. The site is unknown. Van de Velde suggests *Tell Ḳerdaneh*, N.E. of Ḥaifa, at the source of the Nahr Na'aman. According to the Talm. (Bab. *Megillah 6a*) Ḳiṭron is the later Sepphoris (*Seffûrieh*). This is opposed by Neubauer (*Géog. du Talm.* 191).

C. R. CONDER.

KEDAR (קֵדָר, Κηδάρ).—The name of Ishmael's second son (Gn 25¹³ = 1 Ch 1²⁹). 'The earliest reference to Kedar of which the date is certain is Jer 2¹⁰' (Cheyne, *Introd. to Isaiah*, p. 131), where Kedar is made the type of a distant and barbarous tribe, being there coupled with Citium as it is with Meshech in Ps 120⁵. The import of the name is better known to the author of Jer 49²⁹, where Kedar is identified with the Běnê-ḳedem, and their nomad life, with their sheep and camels, tents, curtains, and belongings, is described; by Ezekiel (27²¹) they are coupled with 'Arab,' and described as trading with Tyre in cattle; and the author of the second part of Isaiah couples them with Nebaioth (60⁷), alludes to their pursuit of sheep-breeding (*ib.*), and to their unwalled settlements (42¹¹). In Ca 1⁵ the tents of Kedar are made typical of blackness, with perhaps an allusion to the Hebrew sense of the root קדר, 'to be turbid or black.'

While the name *Kedar* is unknown to Arabic traditions, it is said to be preserved in some Minæan inscriptions (Glaser, *Skizze*, ii. p. 439), and is known in various forms to the Greek geographers, who, indeed, locate the tribe very differently (the passages are collected by Gesenius, *Thes. s.v.*). Our chief source of information about it is to be found in the inscriptions of Assurbanipal (George Smith, *History of Assurbanipal*, pp. 256–298; S. A. Smith, *Keilschrifttexte Assurbanipal's*, i. 58–75; *Cuneiform Inscriptions of W. Asia*, iii. plates 24–28, v. plates 7–10). The land of Ḳi-id-ri (G. Smith, p. 283), Ḳa-ad-ri (*ib.* p. 290), or Ki-id-ri (S. A. Smith, p. 60), and the people called Kid-ra-ai (G. Smith, p. 271), have been justly identified with Kedar by G. Smith and all who have commented on this king's annals (Delitzsch, *Paradies*, p. 299; Glaser, *Skizze*, ii. 267–274, etc.), as being mentioned in close proximity to A-ri-bi (the Arab) and Na-ba-ai-te (Nebaioth), and described as possessors of 'asses, camels, and sheep' (S. A. Smith, *l.c.* p. 67); moreover, some people mentioned with them are, according to one interpretation of a difficult word, described as 'dwellers in tents' (S. A. Smith, *l.c.* p. 103).

It is plain that the identification of *Kedar* with the *Arabs*, which is clearly found in Ca 1⁵, and prevails in the later Jewish literature, had already commenced in Assyrian times; thus whereas Esarhaddon calls a certain Hazael king of Aribi (*Cylinder A of the Esarhaddon Inscriptions*, ed. Harper, p. 8), Assurbanipal, who repeats this passage, calls him king of Kedar (G. Smith, p. 283);* and though U-ai-te' is ordinarily styled by Esarhaddon 'king of the Arabs' (*WAI* iii. pl. 24. l. 11, 108, etc.), the Kedarites are particularly styled 'his men' (l. 107), and likewise the Arab general A-bi-ya-te' is called a Kedarite (l. 121). Nevertheless, a special country of Kedar existed, and from the detailed account of Assurbanipal's Arabian campaign it ought to be possible to locate it accurately. This monarch's army marched 100 Kash-bu Ḳaḳ-ḳa-ru from Nineveh, crossing the Tigris and Euphrates, to the wilderness of Mas, and 6 Kash-bu Ḳaḳ-ḳa-ru from

*In the corresponding plate of *WAI* this passage is obliterated.

Azalla in Mas to Kurasiti, where they besieged the Kedarites. It is not, however, clear whether the distance from Nineveh to Azalla, or to the border of Mas, is given in the first figure; and views differ as to the length of the measure employed (Glaser, *l.c.* p. 279 n.; Delitzsch, *l.c.* p. 177). Since the captives are sent to Damascus (l. 113), it seems probable that the direction of the king's march was towards Hauran (as Delitzsch, *l.c.*, suggests) rather than Yemamah (where Glaser, *l.c.*, endeavours to locate Kedar on what seem inadequate grounds). The fact, too, that the Kedarite kings invade Syria *viâ* Moab (*WAI* v. col. vii. 112; G. Smith, p. 288), points the same way.

With regard to the history of Kedar, we learn from the inscription that the gods of Hazael, king of Kedar, had been plundered by Esarhaddon (see above), but that Hazael, having sued for them, received them back (the chief being called Adar-samain), and was made vassal-king of Arabia. His son, called by Esarhaddon Ya'il, by Assurbanipal Ya'u-ta' (*WAI* iii. 21, col. viii. 37), more frequently U-ai-te' (*ib.* 21, col. viii. 7, etc.), probably on account of the heavier tribute exacted from him (Esarhaddon, *l.c.* 8, 20–24) in the next reign joined the party of Samas-sum-ukin, and invaded Syria; but being defeated by the Assyrians, fled to the friendly tribe Nebaioth, who, however, appear to have given him up to Assurbanipal. Another king of Kedar, named Ammu-ladi, thereupon invaded Syria a second time, but was also defeated, and taken together with Adi-yah, wife of U-ai-te'. Simultaneously with the expedition into Syria, U-ai-te' had despatched a force to Babylon under the Kedarites Abiyate' and Aimu, the former of whom, after defeat, sued for pardon, and obtained the sovereignty of Arabia: this, however, he quickly resigned in favour of the cousin and namesake of the former king, who with the king of Nebaioth organized a fresh revolt, against which Assurbanipal's expedition was directed. The Kedarite nest was destroyed, and severe punishment inflicted on Arabia. The date of this invasion is probably B.C. 648 (cf. Lehmann, 'Samas-sum-ukin,' *Assyriologische Bibliothek*, viii. p. 6).

While the inscriptions of Assurbanipal thus explain the co-ordination of Kedar with 'Arab' and 'Nebaioth,' it is not probable that the blow dealt to Kedar by this monarch is that to which Is 21¹⁶. ¹⁷ refers. Cheyne (*l.c.*), who thinks this passage may be Isaianic, seems inclined to connect it with an attack on the Arabs by Sargon; but this monarch nowhere mentions Kedar, and it seems doubtful whether this oracle can have been written before the hegemony of Kedar, which may have existed before the time of Hazael and Esarhaddon, but has not been shown to have been anterior to it. After two invasions of Syria by Arabs led by Kedarite kings, the name of the tribe could be made to stand for the nation, and this suggests that the oracle is later than the events described by Assurbanipal, since its author appears to reckon the Dedanim among the sons of Kedar (vv.¹³. ¹⁷); and the oracle in which they are threatened with an attack by Nebuchadnezzar (Jer 49³. ²⁸) is similarly loose in its application of their name.

Interesting as are the Kedarite names recorded in the inscriptions, they are evidently too carelessly transcribed to render identification safe; the name *Ammuladi* (like *Amme'ta'*, S. A. Smith, *l.c.* ii. 38) is clearly Arabic, whereas *Hazael* is doubtless Aramaic. The name of the tribe itself is probably derived from the Arabic root *Ḳdr*, which gives a verb meaning 'to be able or powerful,' but derivatives of which have various senses, suitable for personal names. The name of their chief god (whence either they or a neighbouring tribe were called, Glaser, *l.c.* 278), *A-tar-sa-ma-ai-in*, seems to be either Phœnician or Aramaic הדר שמן (as it is analyzed by Delitzsch, *l.c.*) rather than a form of *Athtar* (as Glaser, *l.c.*, suggests). Further suggestions for the derivation of these names are given by E. Sachau, *ZA*, 1897 (xii.), p. 44 ff.

D. S. MARGOLIOUTH.

KEDEMAH (קֵדְמָה 'eastward').— A son of Ishmael, Gn 25¹⁵ = 1 Ch 1³¹. The clan of which he is the eponymous head has not been identified. Ball ('Genesis' in *SBOT, ad loc.*) considers that in both the above passages קֵדְמָה is a mistake for נוֹדָב (Nodab), which is read in 1 Ch 5¹⁹. He remarks that *Ḳĕdĕmah*, 'eastward,' is a singular name, that נ might be misread ף, while ב and מ are often confused. Neither the LXX (Κέδμα) nor Luc. (Κέδεμα) lend any support to Ball's proposed emendation.

KEDEMOTH (קְדֵמוֹת).—A place apparently on the upper course of the Arnon, assigned to Reuben, Jos 13¹⁸, and a Levitical city, 21³⁷ (= 1 Ch 6⁷⁹ [Heb. ⁶⁴]). The 'wilderness of Ḳedemoth' is mentioned in Dt 2²⁶ as the point from which messengers were sent by Moses to Sihon. The exact site is unknown, although it has been suggested that it may be the ruin *Umm er-Raṣâṣ*, N.E. of Dibon (*Dhibân*).

LITERATURE.—Tristram,'*Land of Moab*, 140 ff.; Baedeker-Socin, *Pal.*² 193 ; Dillm. on Nu 21¹³ ; Driver on Dt 2²⁶ ; Buhl, *GAP* 268.

C. R. CONDER.

KEDESH (קֶדֶשׁ).—**1.** A city in the south of Judah (Jos 15²³) whose site is uncertain. It is to be distinguished from Kadesh-barnea (see Dillm. *ad loc.*). **2.** A city in Issachar, 1 Ch 6⁷² [Heb.⁵⁷], where, however, Kedesh is not improbably a textual error for **Kishion** (which see) of the parallel passage Jos 21²⁸. **3.** See KEDESH-NAPHTALI.

KEDESH-NAPHTALI (קֶדֶשׁ נַפְתָּלִי Jg 4⁶, also called 'Kedesh in Galilee,' Jos 20⁷ 21³², 1 Ch 6⁷⁶; called simply 'Kedesh' in Jos 12²² 19³⁷, Jg 4⁹. ¹⁰. ¹¹, 2 K 15²⁹, 1 Mac 11⁶³. ⁷³).—A city of refuge (Jos 20⁷), and likewise a Levitical city (Jos 21³²). In early times it was fortified like a number of other cities in that region (Jos 19³⁷). Its full history would reveal, (1) a sacred city of the earliest inhabitants, (2) a stronghold of unusual importance, conquered by the Hebrews, conquered in turn by the Phœnicians, and a centre of great political influence down to the time when Titus encamped with his army before its walls. From its importance in many ways, and the wonderful fertility of the region, it could never have sunk into a condition of poverty or insignificance.

It is noted in biblical history as the residence of Barak, and here the warriors of Zebulun and Naphtali were assembled by Deborah and Barak before the battle with Sisera, and it was near the city that Sisera met his death (Jg 4⁶. ¹⁰ ; cf. Moore, *ad loc.*). During one of the many invasions of W. Asia by the Assyr. armies, K., with many neighbouring cities, was captured by Tiglath-pileser (2 K 15²⁹). This was in the reign of Pekah, king of Israel, B.C. 734. In Maccabæan times, *c.* B.C. 150, it was here that Jonathan routed Demetrius, king of Syria, with his army (1 Mac 11⁶³⁻⁷³ ; Jos. *Ant.* XIII. v. 6). At the beginning of our era it belonged to Tyre, and was hostile to the Galilæans (Jos. *Wars*, II. xviii. 1 ; IV. ii. 3).

Strong foundations and walls still surviving at the modern village called *Ḳedes*, lying to the north-west of the Lake of Ḥûleh, indicate the character of the ancient city, and among the remains several of the finest sarcophagi of the country

have been recovered, one of which is double, *i.e.* made to contain two bodies under one lid, the stone pillows in each loculus being at alternate ends. K. was situated on a small plain surrounded by gentle forest-covered hills from which there was a wide outlook, and for picturesqueness and beauty it had few equals among the cities of Upper Galilee.

LITERATURE.—Guérin, *Galilée*, ii. 355 ff. ; Baedeker-Socin, *Pal.*³ 264 ; Seetzen, *Reisen*, ii. 127 ; Robinson, *BRP*² ii. 439 ; Merrill, *East of Jordan*, 121, 306 ; van de Velde, *Narrat.* ii. 417 f.; Buhl, *GAP* 235 f.; *SWP* vol. i. sh. iii. ; Moore, *Judges*, 117.

SELAH MERRILL.

KEHELATHAH (קְהֵלָתָה, Μακελλάθ, Luc. Μακελάδ, *Ceelatha*, Nu 33²². ²³).—One of the twelve stations in the journeyings of the children of Israel which are mentioned only in Nu 33. It follows Ḥazeroth. Nothing is known about its position. The word is from the same Hebrew root (קהל) as *Maḳheloth* in v.²⁵ [note that in the LXX the two words are very similar], and means 'assembly *or* congregation.'

A. T. CHAPMAN.

KEILAH (קְעִילָה) the Garmite (1 Ch 4¹⁹). — See following art. and GENEALOGY.

KEILAH (קְעִילָה, Κεειλά, in Josephus Κίλλα, the inhabitants being Κιλλανοί or Κιλλῖται).—This city is interesting principally for its connexion with the history of David. Shortly after he began to gather men around him he defeated the Philistines, who had been raiding Keilah, and robbing the threshing-floors. In Keilah he remained for a while. Thither came to him Abiathar, the representative of the priestly house of Ithamar, bringing the ephod, after Saul had slain the priests at Nob. By consulting the ephod, David knew that Saul would come down to capture him, and that the men of Keilah, notwithstanding the service he had done them, would hand him over to Saul, and he therefore left the town (1 S 23¹⁻¹³). Apart from this incident, the OT mentions the name of Keilah in three other passages. It is in one of the groups of cities assigned to Judah in the Shephelah (Jos 15⁴⁴). The two halves of the 'district of Keilah' were represented in Nehemiah's wall-building work (Neh 3¹⁷. ¹⁸). And in a genealogical fragment (1 Ch 4¹⁹), in connexion with certain other names that connect themselves with the geography, mention is made of 'the father of Keilah the Garmite' among the kindred of Caleb the son of Jephunneh.

In the time of David, Keilah was an important place, a city of gates and bars (1 S 23⁷). Nehemiah hints at its importance in his time, by speaking of it as a double district. And it was a very important place many centuries earlier, when Ebed-tob and Su-yardata of the Tel el-Amarna tablets wrote of it (under the name *Kilta*) to the Egyptian king along with Gedor, Gath, and Rabbah (*PSBA*, June 1888, *Bab. Tab. from Tel el-Amarna*, iii.), and again along with Gezer, Gath, Rabbah, and Jerusalem (*Mittheilungen aus der Orientalischen Sammlungen*, part iii. Nos. 100, 106).

Keilah is commonly identified with *Khurbet Kila*, about 7 miles east of Eleutheropolis, and 1575 ft. above the sea. This is reconcilable with the statement in the *Onomasticon*, that it is 17 miles (perhaps it should be 7, Jerome has it 8) from Eleutheropolis, on the road to Hebron ; but it is difficult to think of so elevated a region as in the Shephelah (cf. Dillm. on Jos 15⁴⁴). The *Onomasticon* is cited, as well as later writings (Nicephorus, *Hist.* xii. 48, and Cassiodorus in Sozomen, *Hist.* vii. 29), as giving the tradition that the prophet Habakkuk was buried at Keilah, though other traditions say at Hukkok.

W. J. BEECHER.

KELAIAH (קֵלָיָה).—A Levite who had married a foreign wife, Ezr 10²³, called in 1 Es 9²³ **Colius**. In Ezr the gloss is added 'which is **Kelita**' (in 1 Es, 'who was called **Calitas**' [which see]). Kelita appears in Neh 8⁷ as one of the Levites who assisted Ezra in expounding the law (cf. 1 Es 9⁴⁸, Calitas), and his name occurs amongst the signatories to the covenant, Neh 10¹⁰. It does not follow, however, that, because Kelaiah was also called Kelita, he is to be identified with *this* Kelita. Siegfried-Stade think not.

KELITA.—See KELAIAH.

KEMUEL (קְמוּאֵל).—The son of Nahor and father of Aram, Gn 22²¹ (contrast 10²² where Aram is son of Shem, and see Dillm. *ad loc.*). Knobel proposed to connect Kemuel with *Kamula* in N. Mesopotamia, but this is pronounced by Dillmann to be out of the question. **2.** The prince (נָשִׂיא) of the tribe of Ephraim, one of the twelve commissioners for the dividing of the land, Nu 34²⁴ (P). **3.** The father of Hashabaiah the ruler (נָגִיד) of the Levites, 1 Ch 27¹⁷.

KENAN (קֵינָן). — Son of Enoch and father of Mahalalel, Gn 5⁹· ¹² (AV Cainan; but AVm, like RV, Kenan) 1 Ch 1². LXX has Καινάν, which reappears in Lk 3³⁷ᶠ· (WH read Καινάμ), giving **Cainan** (which see) of EV. The name *Kenan* is simply a variation of *Cain* (קַיִן 'spear'). 'Halévy (*Recherches Bibl.* ix. 219) calls attention to the fact that Kênân was the name of a god among the Sabæans' (cf. Baethgen, *Beiträge*, 127 f.). See Dillm. on Gn 5⁹.

KENATH (קְנָת) is mentioned (Nu 32⁴²) as having been captured by a clan of Machir, which then gave it their own name of Nobah. Their occupation was only temporary, for Geshur and Aram (1 Ch 2²³) reconquered Kenath with its daughter towns.

The *Onom.* (Lagarde, 269. 15, 296. 109) speaks of a village 'now called Καναθά, lying ἐν Τραχῶνι πλησίον Βοστρῶν'; and Jos. (*BJ* I. xix. 2) mentions a Κανατθά which in his time belonged to Coele-syria. In accordance with these indications, the site has been generally identified with *el-Ḳanawât*, a place on the western edge of the Hauran range which contains important ruins from the Roman and Christian periods. The fullest description of its present condition is found in Merrill (*East of Jordan*, 36-43). If this be correct, Kenath offers an instance of the persistence of a native name during and in spite of a temporary alien occupation. The accuracy of this identification has been recently contested by, *e.g.*, Socin (*Bäd.*² 313) and Moore (*Comm. on Judges* 8¹¹). See, further, Dillm. on Nu 32⁴².

A. C. WELCH.

KENAZ (קְנַז).—The eponym of the Kenizzite clan, variously described in OT as the son of Eliphaz and grandson of Esau (Gn 36¹¹ R), as a 'duke' of Edom (Gn 36⁴² P), as the father of Othniel (Jos 15¹⁷ JE), and as the grandson of Caleb (1 Ch 4¹⁵). The **Kenizzites** (AV Kenezites), who are named amongst the inhabitants of Canaan in patriarchal times (Gn 15¹⁹ R), had probably their original settlements in Mt. Seir (which would account for K. being called a grandson of Esau or Edom), and from thence a branch migrated to the S. of Canaan (see CALEB). The Chronicler makes K. a descendant of Judah (1 Ch 4¹³⁻¹⁵).

KENITES (קֵינִי, הַקֵּינִי; הַקֵּנִי in Nu 24²², Jg 4¹¹ קַיִן, οἱ Κεναῖοι, Κιναῖοι, *Cinæus*, *Kain*), first mentioned in Gn 15¹⁹ along with the Kenizzites and Kadmonites of Edom. Balaam 'looked upon' them from the mountains of Moab, and punning upon the likeness

of their name to the Hebrew ḳên, 'nest,' declared that though their 'nest' was 'in a rock' (Ṣela', perhaps the later Petra), they should be 'wasted'* until Asshur should carry them away captive (Nu 24²¹· ²²). Acc. to Jg 1¹⁶, Hobab, the father-in-law of Moses, was a Kenite, and his descendants 'went up out of the city of palm trees with the children of Judah into the wilderness of Judah, which is in the south of Arad; and they went and dwelt among the people.' It was in this direction that the Jewish town of Kinah stood (Jos 15²²). We find one of the Kenites, Heber, separating himself from the rest of the tribe and camping in the northern part of Israel, near Kedesh, at the time of the overthrow of Sisera (Jg 4¹¹· ¹⁷). The Chronicler includes them among the ancestors of the great houses of Judah (1 Ch 2⁵⁵); and Saul forewarned the Kenites of his intended attack on the Amalekites or Bedâwin, as they had 'showed kindness to all the children of Israel when they came up out of Egypt' (1 S 15⁶). Similarly, when David pretended to Achish of Gath that he had raided the enemies of the Philistines, he associates together the Israelites of S. Judah, the Jerahmeelites (1 Ch 2²⁵) and the Kenites (1 S 27¹⁰). Subsequently he sent presents out of the spoil which he had acquired to 'the elders of Judah' who 'were in the cities of the Kenites' (1 S 30²⁹). Hammath, the ancestor of the Rechabites, is also stated to have been a Kenite (1 Ch 2⁵⁵).

It is thus clear that the K. were regarded as closely allied to the Isr., or at all events to the tribe of Judah. As the father-in-law of Moses was priest of Midian, it would seem that they were also connected with the Midianites. Like the Bedâwin, they were nomads, and the description of the Rechabites (Jer 35⁶⁻¹⁰) shows that even under the monarchy those who lived in the land of Israel still inhabited tents and clung to all the nomadic habits of their forefathers. As was natural, they were chiefly to be found in the south of Judah, and more especially in the desert to the south of it. They thus resembled the gipsies of modern Europe, as well as the travelling tinkers or blacksmiths of the Middle Ages.

Indeed, it is not improbable that they really represent a tribe of smiths. The word Ḳênî or 'Kenite' means 'a smith' in Aramaic, from a root which has given ḳayin, 'a lance,' in Hebrew. We know that the smiths of the ancient world formed a corporation which was regarded as possessing special secrets, and whose members led wandering lives. We also know that in the time of Samuel the Israelites had no smiths of their own, all having been removed by the Philistines 'lest the Hebrews make them swords or spears' (1 S 13¹⁹· ²⁰). It would appear, therefore, that the blacksmith's art was confined to a particular corporation, and that the Israelites were unacquainted with it. Yet the art of working in iron as well as bronze was known in Canaan at an early period: in the *Travels of the Mohar*, a story written in Egypt in the time of Ramses II., the hero of the tale finds an iron-smith ready to hand when an accident happens to his chariot.

Josephus, who elsewhere calls the Kenites Κενετίδες, speaks of them as 'the race of the Shechemites' (Σικιμιτῶν) in his account of Saul's expedition (*Ant.* VI. vii. 3). The Targums transform the name into Salmaite, from Salma, 'the father of Beth-lehem,' who seems to be termed a Kenite in 1 Ch 2⁵⁴· ⁵⁵. The Sam. VS of Gn 15¹⁹ inserts the same name before 'Kenite.'

A. H. SAYCE.

* Hommel (*AHT* 245 n.) follows Klostermann in reading לָעֵבֶר for לְבָעֵר, 'Kain shall belong to the 'Eber.' The emendation is not a happy one, any more than Hommel's explanation of Ash(h)ur in the same passage.

KENIZZITE.—See KENAZ.

KENOSIS (Lat. *inanitio, exinanitio, evacuatio*; Eng. 'self-stripping,' 'self-divesting,' 'self-emptying').—This is not a biblical word, occurring neither in the LXX nor in the NT (though once in its literal sense in Theod.'s tr^n of Is 34[11]). It is a technical word of later theology found in some fragments of the κατὰ Βήρωνος καὶ Ἡλικος, wrongly attributed to Hippolytus, in Gregory of Nazianzus (*Or.* 31), Cyril of Alexandria (Ep. 2 *ad Nest.* 70A), and later writers, to express the action implied in the use of the cognate verb in Ph 2[7] ἑαυτὸν ἐκένωσεν ('semetipsum exinanivit,' Vulg.; 'exhausit semetipsum,' Tert. *adv. Marc.* v. 20; 'made himself of no reputation,' AV; 'emptied himself,' RV).

In this passage the extent of the self-emptying is explained by the following participle, μορφὴν δούλου λαβών: that of which He emptied Himself, by the preceding words, τὸ εἶναι ἴσα θεῷ: so that the meaning is 'He emptied Himself' of His position of equality with God, of 'that condition of glory and majesty which was the adequate manifestation of the divine nature' (Gifford, *ad loc.*; cf. κενώσας ἑαυτὸν ἀπὸ τοῦ εἶναι ἴσα θεῷ, Synod of Antioch, *ap.* Routh, *Rell. Sacr.* iii. p. 298) by 'taking on Himself the form of a servant.' The phrase means little more than that He accepted the limitations implied in incarnation (cf. ἐπτώχευσεν πλούσιος ὤν, 2 Co 8[9]), and was probably suggested to St. Paul as the antithesis to the conception of the fulness (πλήρωμα) of God which dwelt essentially in His Son. In correspondence with this, *kenosis* in its earliest theological use is little more than a synonym for the Incarnation, but it emphasized the Incarnation as a divine act, human nature being saved from above rather than by self-development from below, and hence it is a favourite word with Cyril in his argument against Nestorius; it emphasized also the free voluntary condescension of the preincarnate Son, and the fact that there were real limitations imposed by Himself upon Himself during the incarnate life. It is put forward by St. Paul as an example of the way in which men should not look only each to his own things, but each also to the things of others. But mediæval and Reformed theology attempted to define more exactly what these limitations were, and with this there followed a change in the exact meaning of the word *kenosis*.

(*a*) It was applied to the limitations upon the Christ in His incarnate human life; to the limitations imposed upon divine omnipotence and divine omniscience within the human sphere of action, in order to allow a real growth and action of human will and human knowledge; and the word was sometimes used widely to apply to all such limitations, sometimes (*e.g.* in the discussions of the 17th cent.) it was used, in antithesis to κρύψις, of a virtual surrender of such attributes, as opposed to a possession but conscious restraint in the use of them. On these exact points the Bible does not define, but it supplies the factors that have to be reconciled, viz. the reality of a divine oneness between the Father and the Son (Jn 1[1-18] 10[30], He 1[3]), certain limitations of perfect intercourse between the Father and the Incarnate Son (Mt 27[46] ἵνα τί με ἐγκατέλιπες;), certain statements of the Lord Himself as to the limitations of His own knowledge (Mk 13[32]) and of His own 'glory' (Jn 17[4]), and statements of NT writers as to the reality of temptation, and of growth in wisdom and learning in Him (Lk 2[40-52], He 4[15] 5[7. 8]). The analogy of the primary use of the word by St. Paul also suggests that the *kenosis* was always a self-kenosis; that as the original Incarnation was an act of voluntary self-restraint, so the whole state of the incarnate life implied a constant voluntary

limitation imposed upon a power or a knowledge that was His by right (cf. Gore, *ubi infra*, p. 218; Ottley, *Incarnation*, ii. 291), 'He willed not to use His power, not to use His knowledge,' is a surer formula than 'He could not.'

(*b*) It has been also applied to limitations imposed upon the Incarnate Christ with respect to His divine attributes as exercised within the divine sphere of action during the incarnate life; so that kenosis will imply the absolute or partial cessation of the Word's cosmic functions while He was incarnate. On this point, again, the Bible supplies no clear teaching, though the language of He 1[3] (ὤν . . . φέρων . . . ἐκάθισεν) seems to imply a permanence of cosmic functions; and such a cessation conflicts not only with the general stream of Christian theology, but with the conception of the unchangeable character of the divine nature.

LITERATURE.—The best exegesis of Ph 2[7] is to be found in Gifford, *The Incarnation* (1897), (cf. also Lightfoot, *ad loc.*). For the later theological usage, cf. Bright, *Waymarks in Church History* (1894), Appendix G; Gore, *Dissertations* (1895), pp. 71-202; Bruce, *Humiliation of Christ* (1889), Lectures ii.-iv.; Powell, *Principle of the Incarnation* (1896); Mason, *Conditions of our Lord's Life on Earth* (1896); Hall, *Kenotic Theory* (1898).
W. LOCK.

KERAS (Κηράς, AV Ceras), 1 Es 5[29].—Head of a family of temple servants who returned with Zerubbabel; called KEROS (קֵרֹס, A Κήραος, B Καδής), Ezr 2[44], Neh 7[47] (אA Κειράς, B -ρά).

KERCHIEFS (מִסְפָּחֹת, ἐπιβόλαια) are mentioned only in Ezk 13[18. 21], where a woe is pronounced upon the false prophetesses 'who sew bands (or fillets, *not* pillows as in AV, RV) upon all joints of the hands, and make kerchiefs for the head of (persons of) every stature, to hunt souls.' The passage is somewhat obscure, but the reference appears to be undoubtedly to some species of divination practised in order to obtain oracles. The מִסְפָּחֹת seem to have been large veils or coverings thrown over the head and reaching down to the feet (and this is the original meaning of the Eng. word), and were adapted to every stature. The wearer of the fillets and 'kerchiefs' was in this way introduced into the magical circle (cf. Davidson's and Bertholet's notes in their *Comm. ad loc.*). Hitzig notes the analogy of the later practice of wearing *têphillîm* and putting on the large *ṭallith* at prayer (cf. Mt 23[5]).

In the Wyclif Bible of 1382 occurs the form 'couercheues' (Is 3[23], changed in 1388 into 'kercheues'), which shows the derivation from Fr. *couvre-chef* (*couvrir* to cover, *chef* the head). The Geneva version has 'vailes upon the head' in the text, but in marg. 'kerchefes to couer their heades.' The Bishops' Bible first gives 'kerchiefes' in the text. When the derivation of the word was obscured, it came to be used more generally for any small piece of dress. In this sense the word is still familiar in 'handkerchief,' though both 'kerchief' itself and its other compound 'neckerchief' are nearly gone out (see Craik, *Eng. of Shaks.* 176).
J. HASTINGS.

KERÊ.—See TEXT OF OLD TESTAMENT.

KEREN-HAPPUCH (קֶרֶן הַפּוּךְ, literally 'horn of antimony,' so Vulg.; LXX strangely Ἀμαλθείας κέρας, 'horn of Amalthæa,' *i.e.* plenty).—The youngest daughter born to Job in his second estate of prosperity (Job 42[14]). The name is indicative of beautiful eyes, from the dye made of antimony, used to tinge the eyelashes (cf. Dillm. or Davidson, *ad loc.*; and see 2 K 9[30], Jer 4[30]).
W. T. DAVISON.

KERIOTH (קְרִיּוֹת).—A place in Moab, Jer 48[24] (in v.[41] with art. הַקְּרִיּוֹת, RVm 'the cities'), Am 2[2]. It is mentioned on the Moabite Stone, l. 13, where Mesha declares that he dragged 'the altar-hearth

of Davdoh (?) before Chemosh * in Ḳeriyyoth'. Its
site is uncertain, but weighty arguments have been
adduced in favour of identifying it with Ar (wh.
see), the capital of Moab (Is 15¹), which was probably
ably situated in the valley of the Arnon, somewhere
on the N. or N.E. border of Moab (see Driver on
Am 2² and Dt 2⁹·¹⁸, and cf. Buhl, GAP 270, who
identifies Kerioth, however, not with Ar, but with
Kir—the latter of which again he identifies with
Rabbath-moab, while he considers Ar to be the
name not of a city, but of a district, that, namely,
to the south of the Arnon).   J. A. SELBIE.

KERIOTH-HEZRON (קְרִיּוֹת חֶצְרוֹן, LXX αἱ πόλεις
Ασερών, AV ' Kerioth [and] Hezron).—A place in
the Negeb of Judah (Jos 15²⁵, where it is added,
' which is Hazor.' See HAZOR, No. 4, and HEZRON,
p. 379ᵇ). Kerioth-hezron should probably be identified with the modern Ḳarjetein, N.E. of Tell
'Arâd. In all probability this was the birthplace
of the traitor disciple Judas (wh. see), the name
Iscariot being = קְרִיּוֹת אִישׁ ' man of Kerioth.' This
is much more plausible than the conjecture which
connects Iscariot with Azkaroth of Midrash Bereshith rabba, ch. 98, which Schwarz (Das heil. Land,
p. 128) identifies with el-'Askar (Sychar?).

LITERATURE.—Guérin, Judée, iii. 180 f.; Robinson, BRP² ii.
101; Buhl, GAP 182; Neubauer, Géog. du Talm. 171, 277;
Keim, Jesus of Nazara, iii. 276 n.   J. A. SELBIE.

KEROS.—Name of a family of Nethinim who
returned with Zerub., Ezr 2⁴⁴ (קֵרֹס) = Neh 7⁴⁷ (קֵירֹס).

KESITAH.—The ḳĕsîṭāh (קְשִׂיטָה) is mentioned only
three times in the OT (Gn 33¹⁹, Jos 24³², Job 42¹¹).
In the first and primary passage—to which one of
the other passages certainly, and both probably
(cf. Budde's ' Hiob,' Einleit. p. xliii) refer—Jacob
is represented as paying a hundred ḳĕsîṭāhs for the
' parcel of ground where he had spread his tent '
at Shalem. The ḳĕsîṭāh therefore must have been
a standard of value, probably metallic (cf. Job 42¹¹).
Its meaning and value in modern currency, however, are entirely unknown. The oldest versions
(LXX, Onkelos, Vulgate) give ' lamb ' or ' sheep,'
on what grounds we do not know. In our Eng.
VSS the rendering is ' piece of money ' (AV once
' piece of silver,' Jos 24³²). Ball, in Haupt's SBOT
(Genesis, p. 91), proposes for philological reasons
to point קְשִׂיטָה ḳĕshîṭāh. Spurrell (Notes on Gen.²
p. 288) has a good note (wh. see). Cf. Madden,
Coins of the Jews, p. 11; Jacobé, ' La Kesita ' in
Rev. de l'hist. et de litt. Bibl. i. 6, pp. 515–518 (not
seen); and see art. MONEY in this Dictionary.
                                A. R. S. KENNEDY.

KETAB (Κηταβ, AV Cetab), 1 Es 5³⁰.—Head of
a family of temple servants who returned with
Zerubbabel. There is no corresponding name in
the lists of Ezr and Neh.

KETHIBH.—See TEXT OF OLD TESTAMENT.

KETTLE.—See FOOD, p. 40, V. 2.

KETURAH (קְטוּרָה ' incense ').—According to Gn
25¹ (probably J), Abraham, after the death of Sarah
(this is certainly the meaning intended by the compiler of Gn in its present form), again took (וַיֹּסֶף וַיִּקַּח)
a wife (אִשָּׁה), Keturah, who bore to him six sons,
who became the ancestors of Arab tribes. In v.⁶
(R) she bears the less honourable designation of
פִּילֶגֶשׁ ' concubine ' (cf. 1 Ch 1³²). The Keturah
episode in Abraham's life is an evidence at once
of the presence of different documents in Gn, the
hopelessness of discovering a consistent chronology
in that book, and the tendency of personal to shade

---

off into tribal history. In the light of Gn 17¹⁷
' Shall a child be born to him that is a hundred years
old ? ' it would be strange if the same writer, according to whose chronology Abraham was 137 years
old at the time of Sarah's death (Gn 23¹), should
relate, without remark, the birth of six sons to him
after that event. Of course the difficulty disappears
when we observe that a tradition independent of P
and P's chronology is preserved by J in Gn 25¹⁻⁵,
relating to Keturah. Further, as has been shown
already in art. ABRAHAM (p. 16ᵃ), it is impossible
to resist the conclusion that the Keturah story is
really an embodiment of the Israelitish belief of
the relationship of Arabian clans and tribes to the
Hebrew stock rather than the record of personal
history.
   From the meaning of the name Keturah, ' frankincense,' Sprenger (Geog. Arab. 295) suggests that
the ' sons of Keturah ' were so named because the
author of Gn 25¹ff. knew them as traders in that
commodity. A tribe Ḳatûrâ, living in the neighbourhood of Mecca, is named by the later Arab
genealogists (Ritter, Erdkunde, xii. 19 ff.). On
the various Keturah tribes of Gn 25 see sep. articles
on the names of these.   J. A. SELBIE.

KEY, LOCK.—Many of the old houses in Lebanon
have still the ancient wooden lock commonly known

OUTSIDE OF LOCK.

in England as the Egyptian lock. It is generally
fixed on the outside of the door, but in large
villages and towns it is often put on the inside,
a hole being cut in the door to allow the arm
with the key to be inserted.
   The Syrian lock consists of two pieces of wood
set at right angles to each other. The upright

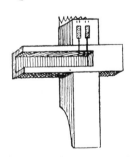

INSIDE OF LOCK, SHOWING TWO PINS.
For position of lock on door see illustration under HINGE.

piece is nailed to the door, and has in its upper
part four or five holes bored, into which headed
pins, or nails with the points cut off, are dropped;
the upper part of these holes is then plugged with
wood. When the cross-bolt is pushed rapidly into
the socket in the door-post these pins fall into
holes made in the bolt to receive them, and so
prevent its withdrawal. The bolt is hollow from
the outer end for rather more than half its length,

---

* Showing that the national god had a chief sanctuary there.
This favours the notion that Ḳerioth was the capital of Moab.

and into this hollow end the key (מַפְתֵּחַ) is inserted. The latter is a piece of wood about 9 in. long, with

KEY.

pins inserted in its upper surface at one end, to correspond with the holes in the bolt. When the pins in the key enter the holes in the bolt the key is pressed upwards, and the pins of the lock are thus raised above the bolt, which is then set free, and is withdrawn by the key. The length of the bolt is usually about 8½ in., but there are locks very much larger. The key, owing to its size, is generally stuck in the girdle, but is sometimes tied to a handkerchief and slung over the shoulder. The principle of this lock is really the same as that of Bramah's and Chubb's locks. See, further, art. HOUSE, p. 434 f.

Doors or gates are sometimes barred on the inside. The bar often extends from post to post across the door, but frequently the bar is inserted into a recess in the wall from which it is partly withdrawn, and so secures the door.

For use of 'keys' in Mt 16¹⁹ see art. POWER OF KEYS.   W. CARSLAW.

KEZIAH (קְצִיעָה, *i.e.* cassia, or 'fragrant as cinnamon').—The name of the second daughter born to Job after his restoration to prosperity (Job 42¹⁴).

KIBROTH-HATTAAVAH (קִבְרֹת הַתַּאֲוָה).—A station in the wanderings of the Israelites on the journey from Sinai to Kadesh, and within one day's journey from Sinai, Nu 11³⁴ 33¹⁶, Dt 9²². Its identification depends, therefore, on those of Sinai and Kadesh (which see). The traditional site, as early as the days of St. Sylvia of Aquitaine (*c.* A.D. 388), was a little to the north of the *Nuḳb el-Hawa*, or 'Pass of the Wind,' by which travellers are wont to reach expeditiously the plain at the foot of the traditional Sinai ('hic autem locus, ubi ss montes aperiebant, iunctus est cum eo loco quo sunt *memoriæ concupiscentiæ*'). The name, 'graves of lust,' seems to imply something of a monumental character (? cairn, cromlech).
           J. RENDEL HARRIS.

KIBZAIM.—See JOKMEAM.

KID.—See GOAT.

KIDNEYS.—The Heb. word *kĕlāyôth* (כְּלָיוֹת, LXX and Rev 2²³ νεφροί) has received two distinct renderings in our EV according as it is used literally or figuratively.

1. In the literal sense *kĕlāyôth* is used only of the kidneys of animals offered in sacrifice (except in three poetical passages, Job 16¹³, Ps 139¹³, La 3¹³, where it refers to the human organs), and is so rendered. By the law of the Priests' Code, 'the two kidneys and the fat that is upon them, which is by the flanks' (RV loins *), along with certain other parts of the viscera, were J"'s special share of all the sacrificial victims. Special instructions to this effect are given (Lv 3⁴· ¹⁰· ¹⁵) for the various victims in the case of the peace-offering—the remaining portions of the carcase being consumed by the worshippers, the blood, of course, always excepted—for the sin-offering (4⁹), the trespass-offering (7⁴), and, in narrative form, for the special consecration sacrifices (8¹⁶· ²⁵· ²⁸, Ex 29¹³· ²²). In the case of sacrificial victims burnt entire upon the altar, such instructions were unnecessary. The *raison d'être* of the peculiar sanctity attaching to these parts of the viscera is to be found in the idea, common to the Semitic and other ancient peoples, that these parts were, next to the blood, the seat of life (see esp. *RS*¹ p. 359 ff.), and accordingly, with the blood, to be given back to the Author of life. With the advance of reflexion and speculation on the mystery of life, the practice found its justification rather in the thought that the parts specified, and the kidneys in particular, were the choicest portions of the victim, and therefore appropriately devoted to J". This point of view led to the poetical figure in the comparatively late 'Song of Moses,' the 'kidney-fat of wheat' (Dt 32¹⁴, EV 'the fat of kidneys of wheat') to express the finest variety of that cereal (cf. Is 34⁶ 'the kidney-fat of rams').

2. A natural extension of the idea of the kidneys as an important seat of life led to their being regarded as one of the organs of feeling, as the seat not only of impulse and affection, but of the moral sentiments (see Delitzsch, *Biblical Psychology*, § xiii. ; Dillmann, *Handb. d. AT Theologie*, p. 359). In this, to us figurative, sense our translators have adopted the rendering 'reins' (from Lat. *renes*, 'kidneys'), as also in the three poetical passages cited above (under 1). Jeremiah in particular is fond of this use of the word *kĕlāyôth* as a synonym of *lēbh*, the heart. Thus J" is said to be 'near' in the mouth of the wicked, but far from their 'reins' (Jer 12²), a thought expressed by Isaiah (29¹³) and Ezekiel (33³¹) by the contrast of 'mouth' and 'heart.' Jeremiah also repeatedly emphasizes J"'s character as the supreme Judge who 'tries the reins and heart' of men (Jer 11²⁰, with slight variations 17¹⁰ 20¹²; cf. Ps 26², Rev 2²³). The kidneys or reins are also represented in poetry as the seat of conscience, man's moral teacher (Ps 7⁹ 'my reins instruct me'), monitor (73²¹ 'I was pricked in my reins'), and approving judge (Pr 23¹⁶ 'my reins shall rejoice, when thy lips speak right things'). With this thought may be compared the late Jewish conceit that of man's two kidneys, 'one prompts him to do good, the other to do evil' (Talmud, *Berakhoth* 61*a*; cf. Ro 7¹⁹ff·).
           A. R. S. KENNEDY.

KIDRON, THE BROOK (נַחַל קִדְרוֹן) [*i.e.* 'the torrent-valley *or* wâdy of Kidron']; LXX ὁ χειμάρρους Κεδρών, but twice (2 S 15²³ᵃ [B]ᵇ [A], 1 K 15¹³ AB) ὁ χειμάρρους τῶν Κέδρων, once (Jer 31 [Gr. 38]⁴⁰) νάχαλ [B; A χειμάρρους] K.; NT, only in Jn 18¹ ὁ χειμάρρους τῶν Κέδρων, or according to some MSS, τοῦ Κέδρου or τοῦ Κεδρών).—A deep depression in the ground on the east side of Jerusalem, which is dry not only in summer but also during the greater part of the winter season, but in which after heavy rains a torrent sometimes flows.

The generally accepted explanation of the name (קִדְרוֹן from root קָדַר 'become black') is from the dark colour of the stream or the ravine.

Baur, who has been followed by Hilgenfeld, has made this the basis of an elaborate attack on the Fourth Gospel, arguing that the writer has imagined Κέδρων to be the genitive plural of κέδρος, 'a cedar,' and therefore cannot be the Apostle John, who as a Jew would have known that the name was derived from קִדְרוֹן 'dark.' Lightfoot, who in his *Biblical Essays* discusses this objection, dwells upon the fact, already alluded to, that in two passages in the LXX (2 S 15²³, and 1 K 15¹³) the reading which has the support of AB is τῶν κέδρων ; yet the LXX translators cannot have mistaken the meaning of the word, otherwise they could not have written, as they generally do, ὁ χειμάρρους Κέδρων, which on this supposition would be a solecism. Lightfoot also calls attention to the great uncertainty as to the actual reading in Jn 18¹ ; and, though the preponderance of MS evidence is either for τῶν Κέδρων or τοῦ Κέδρου, he believes the true account to be that the original reading was τοῦ Κεδρών ; because this reading will explain the other two, whereas neither of the other two will explain either this or each other ; and also because it is much more probable that τοῦ Κεδρών would be changed into τῶν Κέδρων and τοῦ Κέδρου, than conversely, the tendency being to assimilate terminations. This solution was adopted by Griesbach and Lachmann. Westcott and Hort, however, in their 'Notes on Select Readings' defend the reading τῶν Κέδρων, and regard it as probably preserving 'the true etymology of קִדְרוֹן, which seems to be an archaic

* See the coloured illustrations in Driver and White's *Leviticus Haupt's SBOT*), facing p. 4.

(? Canaanite) plural of קָדַר, "the Dark [trees]"; for though no name from this root is applied to any tree in biblical Hebrew, some tree resembling a cedar was called by a similar name in at least the later language (see exx. in Buxtorf, *Lex. Talm.* 1976); and the Greek κέδρος is probably of Phœnician origin.' WH rightly maintain that קֶדְרון denoted not so much the stream as the ravine through which it flowed, and remark that isolated patches of cedar-forest may well have survived from prehistoric times in sheltered spots.

The Valley of Kidron (modern *Wâdy Sitti Marjam*) begins towards the north-west of Jerusalem at the foot of Mount Scopus, where the rocks appear to have been hollowed out by quarrying for stones for building tombs; afterwards it turns to the right towards the south, separating Jerusalem by a deep depression of the ground from the Mount of Olives. It is here at the east side of the city that the name *Kidron* was specially applied to it, for the descent is here much steeper than at the north side of Jerusalem; but the whole forms one continuous channel. Near the site of Gethsemane, where the ravine may have been crossed by our Lord and the eleven apostles on the evening of the betrayal, the bottom of the Kidron is about 150 ft. below Gethsemane, but nearly 380 ft. below the platform of the temple. The bed of the river becomes more perceptible as it turns towards the south, though it is only on rare occasions that water flows in it. There is, however, a curious spring which rises in a cave on the west side of the Kidron, and which appears to have originally flowed into the Kidron valley, but to have been diverted later through a tunnel cut in the rock through the ridge that forms the southern part of the Temple hill. A remarkable inscription was discovered in 1880 which records in pure Hebrew the making of this tunnel; and though it unfortunately gives no information about its date other than what can be inferred from the language and the characters in which it is written, it is conjectured with some probability that it may refer to the engineering work which was carried out by Hezekiah at the time of Sennacherib's invasion of Judæa, when 'he took counsel with his princes to stop the waters of the fountains which were without the city, and they helped him. So there was gathered much people together, and they stopped all the fountains, and the brook that flowed through the midst of the land' (2 Ch 32³·⁴). Robinson had suggested long before this discovery that the Kidron might very possibly flow beneath the present surface of the ground; and Barclay asserted that at a point in the valley about two miles below the city the murmuring of a stream could be distinctly heard, which stream on excavating he actually discovered. There may, therefore, before the time of Hezekiah, have been a flow of water in the now dry valley of the Kidron.

On leaving the city, the Kidron valley turns south-east towards the Dead Sea, and as it proceeds becomes deeper and more precipitous, its bed being more than 300 ft. deep. It passes here through a barren and desolate region, where many of the Essenes and anchorites made their homes in grottoes which have been excavated in its sides.

The name *Kidron* does not occur in the earlier books of the Bible; but after David had made Jerusalem the capital of the kingdom, the physical geography of the country in its immediate neighbourhood naturally became more closely connected with the history of Judah than it had hitherto been.

The first mention is in 2 S 15²³, where in the story of David's flight from Absalom it is recorded that he passed over the brook (*naḥal*) Kidron. The next mention is in 1 K 2³⁷, in the prohibition to Shimei against his ever crossing Kidron. This passage has been relied on by some scholars (*e.g.* Sir G. Grove) as showing that the name of Kidron was sometimes given to the ravines on the west of Jerusalem; since otherwise Solomon's prohibition would not have been transgressed by Shimei's journey to Gath, to recover his fugitive slaves; for whether Gath be identified with *Tell es-Safied* or with *Beit Jibrîn*, it would in either case be by the western or Bethlehem gate that Shimei would leave the city, and the valley on the east side would be altogether out of his way. The narrative, however, does not assert that he actually passed over Kidron; and indeed, when it is carefully examined, it rather suggests the contrary. In the prohibition Shimei is commanded, 'Go not forth thence any whither,' and then the king adds, 'For on the day thou goest out and passest over the brook Kidron, know thou for certain that thou shalt surely die.' But in the recapitulation of the prohibition made after Shimei's journey to Gath, it is the general command 'not to walk abroad any whither' which alone is dwelt on, and there is now no mention of Kidron at all. The reason for its having been expressly mentioned in the original prohibition probably was because it was on the direct road to Shimei's home at Bahurîm, and was the boundary of the city on that side.

The later references to the Kidron in the historical books of the OT all without exception occur in the accounts given of the destruction of heathen images and altars which were either burned at Kidron, or, when broken or ground to powder, were cast into its valley or on the graves which studded it. In 1 K 15¹³ and in 2 Ch 15¹⁶ it is recorded that Asa burned at Kidron the idol which his mother had set up; and in 2 Ch 29¹⁶ and 30¹⁴ that Hezekiah cast into the Kidron the pollutions which had been found in the temple, and the altars that were in Jerusalem; and in 2 K 23⁴·⁶·¹² that Josiah burned at Kidron the Asherah that had been in the house of the LORD, and stamped it small to powder, and cast the powder thereof upon the graves of the children of the people. As graves were regarded as polluting all who walked over them or came in contact with them, the intention of these reforming kings was clearly to dishonour thus the images to which worship had been paid, and the altars which had been used in that worship; but from the words of 2 Ch 34⁵ 'it would appear that in Josiah's case at least there was some intention of also dishonouring the graves,' for it is there expressly said that he strewed the dust of the images upon the graves of them that had sacrificed unto them.

The neighbourhood of Kidron would seem to be referred to in Jer 26²³; but the only place in the prophetical writings in which it is mentioned by name is in Jer 31⁴⁰. The passage is a remarkable one. 'And the whole valley of the dead bodies, and of the ashes, and all the fields unto the brook Kidron, unto the corner of the horse gate toward the east, shall be holy unto the LORD, it shall not be plucked up, nor thrown down any more for ever'.

The popular name for the Kidron valley, the **Valley of Jehoshaphat** (wh. see), is not found in the Bible or in Josephus, and cannot be traced earlier than the 4th cent. after Christ. It appears first in the *Onomasticon* of Eusebius (272, 89), and then in Jerome's *Onomasticon* (145, 13), and in his *Commentary on Joel*. It is derived from a supposed identification of the valley of the Kidron with the valley spoken of in Joel's prophecy (Jl 3²·¹²). The identification of the two is clearly an error (but see Driver, *ad loc.*). The narrow ravine of Kidron would be a most unsuitable place for the gathering of the nations; and it is to be noted that the word twice used by Joel for the Valley of Jehoshaphat is עֵמֶק, which denotes a wide spacious valley fit for cornfields and suitable for a battlefield, whereas the word habitually employed for the Kidron valley in the OT is נַחַל, denoting a narrow valley or ravine (the modern *wâdy*); and these words are never interchanged. There is, however, one passage—2 K 23[4]—in which the expression *shadmôth Ḳidrôn* (Heb. שַׁדְמוֹת קִדְרוֹן, LXX σαδημωθ [A; σαλημωθ B] Κεδρών) occurs, which is translated both in AV and RV 'fields of Kidron' (prob. a point at the junction with the Valley of Hinnom), but the usual term, *naḥal*, is again used in 2 K 23[6].

It has been suggested that the name, 'the Valley of Jehoshaphat' in Jl may be a purely imaginary name, and may represent a locality which had no existence except in the vision of the prophet. Robinson (*BRP*[2] i. 269) conjectures that it may be a metaphorical allusion to the significance of the name *Jehoshaphat*, '*J"* judgeth.' This view appears to be favoured by the trⁿ of Theodotion, χώρα κρίσεως, and by that of Targ. Jon. 'The place of the decision of judgment.' Michaelis takes this view, and supposes it to be a prediction of Maccabæan victories. It has also been suggested that the frequent mention by Joel of Mount Zion, Jerusalem, and the Temple, may have led to the belief that the valley spoken of in the same prophecy was in the immediate neighbourhood.

This characteristic of the prophet Joel may, however, suggest a somewhat different conclusion. His frequent use of the names of real localities in his prophecies may be appealed to as making it probable that the vision of the Valley of Jehoshaphat may also be connected with a real locality. It may be noted that the word used by the Chronicler (2 Ch 20[26]) to describe the valley in which Jehoshaphat assembled the people after his victory over the combined forces of the Edomites, Ammonites, and Moabites is the same word (עֵמֶק) which is twice used by Joel to describe the valley of Jehoshaphat. The author of Ch is, of course, one of the later writers of the OT, but he is more ancient than the other authorities quoted. The historical event is recorded in Kings as well as in Chronicles, though the account in Ch is fuller. The defeat of so many nations, and the great deliverance thus granted to Judah in the past, might have seemed to the prophet a not unapt type of the future gathering of the nations, and of the victory over them which he foretold. This might help to explain the transference of the title the 'Valley of Jehoshaphat' to the Kidron valley in later times: for the valley which was the scene of Jehoshaphat's victory stretches very near that part of the Kidron which turns towards the Dead Sea.

At the present time the Jewish as well as the Christian and Mohammedan population of Palestine identify the valley of Kidron with the scene of Joel's prophecy, and believe that the Last Judgment will be held there. It is the dearest wish of every Jew to obtain a grave at Kidron.

One of the four monuments by the Kidron at the foot of the Mount of Olives is associated by popular tradition with Jehoshaphat, though it is recorded in 1 K 22[50] that Jehoshaphat was buried in the city of David. This is repeated in 2 Ch 21[1].

The title given to Kidron in Jer 31[40] 'the valley of the dead bodies,' suggests that Ezekiel, who so often repeats more fully notes which had been struck by Jeremiah, may have intended to represent Kidron by the valley of dry bones to which he was carried out in the spirit of the Lord (Ezk 37). The imagery, indeed, of the vision may have been suggested by sights which he had seen in Mesopotamia, in the desert track where, as Stanley remarks, bones and skeletons of man and beast, the remnants of some vast caravan or the burial-place of some mighty host of ancient days, dry and bleaching in the yellow sands, would form a sight familiar to travellers through the wilderness; yet, as in a dream, imagery taken from one place is often transferred to another and a distant locality, so it may have been with the prophet whose spirit was so often in the land of Israel while his body was by the banks of the Chebar (cf. Ezk 40[2]), and who by the words with which ch. 37 opens seems to represent the locality to which he was carried out as a distant one.

LITERATURE.—Robinson, *BRP*[2] i. 231 f., 268 ff., 541; Buhl, *GAP* 93, 132 f.; *PEF Mem.* Jerusalem volume, 122; *ZDPV* v. 316 f., 323 f.; Benzinger, *Heb. Arch.* 41 ff.; Neubauer, *Géog. du Talm.* 51 f.; Lees, *Jerusalem Illustrated*, 129 ff.; Driver and Nowack on Jl 3[2]. See also arts. JEHOSHAPHAT (VALLEY OF) and JERUSALEM in the present volume.   J. H. KENNEDY.

KIDRON (in 1 Mac 15[39] τὴν Κεδρών [Καιδρ-] A, א om. τήν; in v.[41] τὴν Κεδρώ A, Κεδρών א*, Χεβρών א[c. a. c. b]; in 16[9] Κεδρών Aא).—A place fortified by Cendebæus (1 Mac 15[39. 41]), and the point to which he was pursued after his defeat by the sons of Simon the Maccabee (16[9]). It is named in connexion with Jamnia, and may be the modern *Ḳaṭrah* near *Yebna*. It is possibly the same town that is called Gederoth in Jos 15[41], 2 Ch 28[18].

LITERATURE.—*SWP* vol. iii. sheet xvi.; Guérin, *Judée*, ii. 35 f.; Baedeker-Socin, *Pal.*[2] 210; Buhl, *GAP* 188; Dillm. on Jos 15[36].

KILAN (A Κιλάν, B Κειλάν, AV Ceilan), 1 Es 5[15].—Sixty-seven sons of Kilan and Azetas returned with Zerub. from captivity. There are no corresponding names in the lists of Ezr 2 and Neh 7.

KINAH (קִינָה).—A town in the extreme south of Judah, Jos 15[22]. The site is unknown. The common noun *ḳinah* means 'wailing song,' 'lament for the dead'; but it is possible that the name of the above town is derived from the *Ḳenites* (קֵינִי), who settled in the Negeb (Nu 10[32]), and had several cities in that quarter (1 S 30[29]). See Dillm. *Josua*, p. 525.

KINDNESS (חֶסֶד [see careful study of this term in W. R. Smith, *Proph. of Isr.* 160 ff. 406]; χρηστότης). —1. Religion is and ought to be determinative of human life in general, and so in particular it moulds the grace of kindness. God was kind to the people of Israel, looking upon their affliction in Egypt and delivering them (Ex 3). The people were frequently reminded of this merciful intervention of J", and it was set before them as the ground of obedience and of action resembling His. Israel was not to oppress or vex a stranger, but to love him, for they knew the heart of a stranger, having been strangers in Egypt (Ex 22[21] 23[9], Lv 19[33f.]). The laws in the Book of the Covenant are specially marked by the requirement of kindness to the poor and needy, and the succeeding laws and the exhortations of the prophets continue to press the obligation. Indeed, God's pardon for sin and His rich spiritual blessings are made dependent in part on the suppliant's kindness to others in distress (Is 1[15-17] 58[6ff.]).

Christ revealed God as the Father of men, and the kindness and mercy He enjoined on His followers resemble the type of these which is manifested by God. The divine Father regards men as potentially His true sons, and yearns for the prodigal's return (Lk 15[20]). To effect His merciful purpose He uses the instruments of kindness— even His severity is kind. He makes His sun rise on the evil and the good (Mt 5[45]), and blesses even the unbelieving with rain and fruitful seasons and gladness of heart (Ac 14[17]), and He sent Christ to reveal Himself by miracles of kindness, and by opening up a way of spiritual salvation. Love to God will dispose men to view others as He does, *i.e.* as persons who are laden with suffering, but capable of the highest things, and as most likely to be influenced for good by love and kindness (Lk 6[35f.], 1 Jn 3[17]).

2. (*a*) *Intensively*, kindness is limited, or at least its form is regulated, by the condition that righteousness must be maintained and developed. A holy God cannot bestow complete happiness on the unholy. Penitence, faith, and new obedience are therefore demanded in men, and the misery endured while they are absent or deficient is but a proof of God's kindness. So, if man's brother sin against him, he must be induced to repent and turn from the wrong (Mt 18[15ff.]). He who only showers promiscuous benefits on the evil-doer shows no true kindness to the latter or to the community, but rather encourages the sinner in

sin, and so shares in it. Here kindness is manifested in reclaiming the offender from evil (which must be clearly represented as such), and in particular by the manner in which he is approached, by signs of goodwill, by patience, forbearance, timely speech, and timely silence, and all those nameless, conciliatory arts which can spring only from that love which suffereth long and is kind, and *seeketh not her own* (1 Co 13⁴ᶠ·). The ends of righteousness and of true kindness further require that man shall be just before being generous (although when a material debt is paid we still fail to give others their due if it is discharged without love, Ro 13⁷ᶠ·), and that there be no indiscriminate or injudicious bestowal of aid, such as would tend to lessen another's self-respect and reliance on self-help (2 Th 3⁷ᶠ·), not to speak of actions which are only to be described as officious (1 P 4¹⁵). So, too, it is needful to adhere to the truth, at the risk of an apparent want of kindness. The Christian should endeavour to rise to the height of Christ's example, so as to be able, on occasion given, to speak the truth to those who are in trying circumstances, with such a spirit of faith and glad confidence in the fatherly love of God that the announcement will have, not a hurtful but, as far as may be, a soothing and bracing effect (Eph 4¹⁵· ²⁵). Kindness, therefore, is based on righteous Christian love as its principle and motive ; and our Lord's golden rule (Mt 7¹²) and parable of the Good Samaritan furnish guidance for the practical application of the principle.

(*b*) *Extensively*, kindness is due to all men with whom one has to do, and even to the lower animals, the example and care of God being again our standard (Jn 4¹¹, Mt 6²⁶). People of one's own faith, as being nearer than others, and furnishing more points of contact, and yielding many services which merit gratitude, have special claims (Gal 6¹⁰). But the ungodly and sinful also call for compassionate care in view of their spiritual possibilities. Even the minor courtesies of life in general human intercourse are of value (Mt 10¹²· ⁴²).   G. FERRIES.

KINDRED (in AV 1611 nearly always *kinred*) occurs in the plur. in the sense of 'families,' 1 Ch 16²⁸, Ps 22²⁷ 96⁷ (all מִשְׁפָּחוֹת), Ac 3²⁵ (πατριαί, RV 'families'), Rev 1⁷ 7⁹ 11⁹ 13⁷ (φυλαί, RV 'tribes'). Tindale has the sing. in the same sense, Dt 29¹⁸ 'Lest there be amonge you man or woman kynred or trybe that turneth awaye in his hert this daye from the Lord oure God' (AV 'family'). Cf. Elyot, *Gouvernour*, ii. 99, 'And also for his endeavour, prowesse, and wisedome, [Moyses] was moche estemed by Pharao and the nobles of Egipte ; so that he moughte have lived there continually in moche honour and welth, if he would have preferred his singular advaile before the universall weale of his owne kynred or familie.'   J. HASTINGS.

KINE.—See Ox.

KING (THE OFFICE OF, IN ISRAEL).—I. ORIGIN. —1. Of the origin of the king (מֶלֶךְ *melek*) among Semitic peoples only uncertain inferences can be drawn from the meaning of the word and from facts more or less disputed.

MLK in Assyr. and Aram. = 'advise,' 'decree' ; Arab. = 'possess,' 'rule' ; Heb. and Eth. = 'rule.' This suggests that the term arose rather from the intellectual than the merely physical side, from counsel rather than prowess. He whose counsel was found best, eventually became king. Further, the term seems to have arisen after the purely nomadic stage of the Semitic nations (in

which the Sheikh rules)* had ceased, yet before any had gained large territories. For king seems to be closely connected with *city* life, in contrast alike to unsettled wanderings and to permanent possession of large tracts of country. Thus we find in the time of Abraham several kings in a small space round the Dead Sea, and many throughout Palestine at the time of the conquest, each ruling a town with its adjacent lands, and presumably such villages as were dependent on it. The office in such cases appears to have been normally (apparently not in Edom, Gn 36³¹ᶠᶠ·) hereditary.†

2. Side by side, however, with this there existed in each Semitic city the conception of a divine *King* who was supreme over the whole people, and from whom it had come into being. The frequency with which the gods of Semitic nations have an appellative of which *MLK* forms a part (*e.g.* Melkart of Tyre) or the whole (Milkom of Ammon), shows that this was one of their primary conceptions of Deity.

We may explain the fact of both God and ruler possessing the same title by supposing either that the root idea of *MLK* suited both alike, the term being given to the Deity as signifying Him who gives counsel (*e.g.* by oracle) ; or that the title was given to the human ruler in accordance with his claim to be descended from, or to represent, the Deity ; or (though this is very improbable) that the roots are different and the identity of the words as applied to God and to the president of a city is accidental. But, whatever the cause, the fact of the identity of titles tended to strengthen enormously the king's position.

3. Of the origin of the *office* (not the *title*) of king in Israel itself we have comparatively full particulars. We see the preparation for it and its inauguration. At the Exodus Moses supplied the place of a king,‡ centralizing in himself all the visible power. We know much less of Joshua, but the same appears to have been the case with him. But after the first flush of victory was over, when the tribes were divided by whole districts of unconquered Canaanites, and the sense even of religious unity was weakened by compliance with local religious customs, the inroads of various foes produced (at God's call) guerila chiefs who released the parts where they lived from foreign attacks. One of these, Gideon, was invited by 'the men of Israel' to 'rule' over them,§ and though he verbally refused, saying, 'The LORD shall rule over you,'‖ he appears to have ruled over his city Ophrah, for on his death his son Abimelech kills all his brothers (except Jotham) and has himself made king in Shechem (Jg 9⁶).¶ Abimelech acted as prince (שַׂר Jg 9²²) 'over

<hr>

* 'Das Königthum ist in Arabien eine fremde Pflanze,' G. Jacob (*Das Leben der vorislamischen Beduinen*, 1895, p. 164).

† Even Ebed-Tob (*c.* B.C. 1400) of Urusalim implies that this was the norm, when he contrasts his own case : 'It was not my father who installed me in this place nor my mother, but the arm of the mighty king has allowed me to enter into *my ancestral house*' (Hommel, *Ancient Heb. Trad.* p. 155). Observe that in the *MLK*, being properly the ruler merely of a city, we have perhaps the explanation of the fact that the term was not used by the Assyrian monarchs of themselves. They may have already found this title belonging to the kings of the various cities that they had conquered, and therefore they called themselves *Sar* (perhaps Is 10⁸ has a satirical allusion to this nomenclature).

‡ Dt 33⁵, however, 'and he was king in Jeshurun,' probably refers to God.

§ *Mĕshōl bānū*. From a comparison of Jg 9² with 9⁸· ¹⁰· ¹²· ¹⁴ this seems to be here synonymous with *MLK*.

‖ Jg 8²². To say that such a contrast between an earthly and the heavenly king is an anachronism, and that, therefore, these verses belong to a later date (Moore), is with our present knowledge of the sources of Jg much too drastic a treatment. See, further, art. JUDGES (BOOK), p. 816ᵃ.

¶ We do not know the relation of Ophrah to Shechem. It is possible that they were the same place, the latter representing the Canaanite part of it, which rebelled against the Israelites.

Israel' (*i.e.* apparently Shechem, and a few towns near), but his death after three years prevented a prolongation of a kingship in Israel after the Canaanite form. Jephthah had a kind of headship in Gilead (Jg 11[6-11]), but no more was done in the direction of the formal kingdom till the time of Samuel. Samuel had indeed conquered the Philistines at Ebenezer, and had recovered the district that had been formally taken over by the Philistines (1 S 7[11-14]); but, as it seems, as he became older and less energetic, the Philistines became stronger, and by their superior weapons and organization were reducing the Israelites to a condition little better than that of serfs (1 S 13[19ff.]). The danger of extinction as a nation at the hands of the Philistines was imminent, and unity in feeling and action was absolutely essential if Israel was to be preserved. It was the sense partly of this and partly of the declension of Samuel's sons from their father's uprightness in the internal administration of the district round him that led the elders of Israel to ask Samuel for a king.

The words attributed to Samuel in reply are very difficult. On the one hand, if Dt 17[14-20] (cf. 28[36]) is Mosaic, the principles that ought to guide the election of a king must, one would suppose, have been well known, and it is so far worthy of notice that in at least three out of the four points (no stranger, not multiplying horses, not multiplying wives, the study of the Law) Saul satisfied these principles. But with our present knowledge it seems impossible to reconcile Samuel's fears with a knowledge by him of the sanction given to the king in Dt. For Dt assumes that the kingdom need not be opposed to the theocratic government of the nation, but may rather become a form of it. On the other hand, Samuel's words are such as could hardly fail to suggest themselves to every far-seeing religiously-minded patriot.*

Nothing but the strongest necessity could justify (as by God's answer to Samuel it *did* justify) the commencement of a system which tended to repress the development of the free life of the individual Israelites, a life which might otherwise have attained much sooner the realization of the perfect liberty of the ideal believer in God. A king, however, was better than destruction by the Philistines or absorption by the Canaanites.

II. The Method of Appointment. — 1. *The Choice.*—(*a*) In the case of Saul. The subordination of the 'lay' to the 'religious' element in Israel is clearly seen in the action of the *elders.* Even if (as is hardly probable) any of them had an idea of a king possessing merely secular authority, no trace of such a feeling is shown, as they unite in seeking the sanction and the power of the religious authority. Further, Samuel even after consenting to their wish gives them strictly no voice in the appointment. He is guided to anoint Saul privately, and the public decision is made by lot, after which Saul is presented to the people as 'him whom the Lord hath chosen,' and they shout 'God save the king' (1 S 10[24] [E²]). Naturally, after the first success, a public assembly is called by Samuel to ensure the ratification by the people of the choice already made (1 S 11[14] [J]), he taking the opportunity of convincing the people that a visible king would not have been necessary had they served God fully, and of urging them to serve Him faithfully under the new arrangement (1 S 12 [E²]).†

(*b*) In the case of David also the appointment was from above (1 S 16[13] 'midrashic'), but effect

was not given to it until after Saul's death, when the men of Judah anointed him as their king (2 S 2[4]), and not fully until seven years later, when 'all the tribes of Israel' anointed him king over all Israel. They did this, however, only after receiving certain stipulations from David (2 S 5[3]). The virtual omission of these by Solomon, and their definite rejection by Rehoboam, caused the division of the kingdom.

(*c*) In other cases in David's line of which particulars have come down to us, the reigning king freely chose his successor from among his sons (1 K 1[33-35], but this was preferably the firstborn, 2 Ch 21[3]).* Naturally, on the restoration of Joash to his rights, Jehoiada the priest took the opportunity of obtaining from him and the people an agreement to serve the LORD, the observance of whose worship was bound up with the national constitution and national prosperity (2 K 11[17]). So again (also after conspiracies by others) the people appointed Azariah-Uzziah (2 K 14[21]), Josiah (2 K 21[24]), and, on the untimely death of Josiah, his son Jehoahaz (2 K 23[30]). The appointment of Ahaziah by the people was due solely to his being the only son left to his father, Jehoram having apparently designated another son before both his and his own death (2 Ch 21[17] 22[1]).

2. *The Anointing.*†—Besides the reference given above, see ANOINTING, §§ 8, 9. The only king of the northern dynasty whose anointing is mentioned is Jehu (2 K 9[6]), where the act is strictly private, like that of Saul and of David by Samuel. Many have thought from the absence of all mention in other cases that only those kings were anointed whose claims to the throne were disputed, but this is very unlikely. The cases of private anointing are mentioned as showing to the recipient God's choice and purpose : the public anointing is mentioned only on special occasions, just in the same way as the words 'God save the king' are recorded (1 K 1[39], 2 K 11[12]). The frequency of the term 'the LORD's anointed' confirms this (1 S 24[10] 26[9], 2 S 1[14] 19[21] [Heb. 22]). It has been suggested that kings were anointed in order that they might fulfil priestly functions (see below), but there is no hint of this. The ceremony was perhaps already purely archaic in Saul's time. The writer, however, of 1 S 16[13] ('midrashic') connects it with the gift of the spirit.‡

III. The External Marks.—(*a*) *Sceptre* (שֵׁבֶט). —This very primitive sign of supreme authority is used of the Israelitish king in Ps 45[7], and perhaps nowhere else. See SCEPTRE.

(*b*) *Spear* (חֲנִית).—This, both among pre-Mohammedan (W. R. Smith, *Kinship*, p. 171) and modern Arabs (Tristram, *Land of Israel*, p. 259), marks the presence of the sheikh. It was in the hand of Saul when David played to him (1 S 18[10] [J¹]), by his side at meal-time (20[33] [J¹]), in his hand when he sat at council (22[6] [J¹]), planted by his pillow as he slept in camp (26[7] [E¹]). He is also said by the Amalekite to have leaned on it when he was dying (2 S 1[6] [E¹]).§ These examples suggest that Saul did not use the sceptre ; but it should be noticed that in the first three passages the more offensive

---

* In the maintenance of the hereditary principle we may see, probably, the chief cause of the longer duration of the Southern kingdom.

† For the existence of this practice in Egypt at coronations, cf. T. T. Perowne in Smith's *DB²* i. 137.

‡ W. R. Smith (*RS* pp. 215, 364) conjectures (*a*) from Ps 45[8], compared with Is 61[3], that the anointing of kings was part of the ceremony of investing them in the festal dress and ornaments appropriate to their dignity (cf. Ca 3[11]) ; (*b*) from the original use of animal fat, that anointing meant the transference of the living virtues of the animal slain. He also sees in the very act of applying the ointment originally a form of homage.

§ Cf. Kirkpatrick on 1 S 18[10]. Perhaps the *javelin* (כִּידוֹן) in the hand of Joshua was as much a symbol of authority as a weapon (Jos 8[18]).

---

* It is, of course, still possible that the *form* of the objections attributed to Samuel is one 'moulded by the experiences of a later age' (Driver, *Dt.* p. 213), but the narrative as it stands probably represents his actual feelings.

† Such is the general result we appear to reach by combining all the data in 1 S ; but see *OTJC²* 135 ff.

use of the spear comes into question, and in the fourth and fifth he was engaged in war.

(c) *Crown* or *diadem* (נֵזֶר), of Saul on the battle-field (2 S 1¹⁰ [E¹]), therefore light and probably a fillet of silk ; and of Joash (2 K 11¹² ‖ 2 Ch 23¹¹, cf. Ps 89³⁹ 132¹⁸) ; with stones (Zec 9¹⁶). See, further, CROWN, §§ 3, 4, and DIADEM.

(d) *Bracelet* (אֶצְעָדָה), also of Saul (2 S 1¹⁰), and in plur. prob. (by emendation) of Joash (2 K 11¹²). See BRACELET.

(e) *Throne* (כִּסֵּא), presupposed in numerous promises and commands (*e.g.* Dt 17¹⁸, 1 S 2⁸, 2 S 3¹⁰ 7¹³. ¹⁶ 14⁹, 2 K 10³, Jer 13¹³). David's is used by Solomon (1 K 2¹²), who in audience places another throne for his mother (v.¹⁹), but afterwards has a costly new one made for himself (1 K 10¹⁸⁻²⁰), as well as a porch for it (1 K 7⁷).

(f) *A place of honour in the temple* (Ezk 46¹. ² and perhaps 2 K 23³).

(g) *Palace* (אַרְמוֹן, הֵיכָל, בַּיִת).—Solomon's (1 K 7¹⁻¹²) had apparently three chief parts, the Great Hall (or House of the Forest of Lebanon), the porch of judgment, and the porch or ordinary reception room, besides the private apartments, rich with cedar beams and pillars. So Jehoiakim's was cieled with cedar and painted with vermilion (Jer 22¹⁴). Ahab's was of ivory, *i.e.* probably panelled with it (1 K 22³⁹, cf. Ps 45⁸).

(h) *The royal chariot* (רֶכֶב).—Nowhere expressly included among the insignia of the king, but perhaps implied by the analogy of Egypt (Gn 41⁴³), and the importance that chariots held in the establishment both of the king and of the nobility (1 S 8¹¹, 1 K 9¹⁹ 10²⁶, Is 22¹⁸, Jer 17²⁵ 22⁴). Hence the fact that Absalom and Adonijah set up a chariot and attendant runners (2 S 15¹, 1 K 1⁵) indicated their claim to semi-royal state. See CHARIOT.

(i) *The royal harem* (2 S 16²¹).

(j) *The bodyguard*, primarily of Philistine mercenaries (Cherethites, Pelethites, and Gittites, 2 S 8¹⁸ [J¹] 15¹⁸ [J¹]) and perhaps Carians (2 K 11⁴. ¹⁹), who may also have been the royal butchers (see W. R. Smith, *OTJC*² pp. 260–263, and art. CHERETHITES). They were apparently identical with the 'mighty men' (1 K 1⁸. ¹⁰. ³⁸).*

IV. DUTIES OF THE KING.—1. *In war.*—As preparations of war called the kingdom into existence, so it continued to be the principal function of the king to direct warlike operations, and to see that the land was well defended by fortresses and possessed the *material* of war (*e.g.* 1 K 12²¹ᶠᶠ, 2 Ch 17² 26⁹. ¹⁵ 32²⁻⁵). Naturally the nucleus at least of a standing army was always maintained, probably the bodyguard (see above), the whole fighting force of the nation being called out only as needed (see ARMY). Sometimes also the king employed a large force of mercenaries (2 Ch 25⁶).

2. *Judicial.* — In Eastern even more than in Western lands the supreme court of appeal is the sovereign in person, and in Eastern lands more particularly each litigant, however humble, has the right of bringing his cause before the king if the latter has time to hear it (cf. 2 S 14⁵ᶠᶠ. 15², 1 K 3¹⁶ᶠᶠ.). Hence the fact that Jotham judged the people was a sign that he completely took his father's place (2 K 15⁵). So, too, right judgment is almost equivalent to a good rule (Is 16⁵). Sometimes, perhaps, the king was called 'the judge' (so of Moab, Am 2³).†

Through this concentration of the judicial functions it is probable that the powers of the 'elders' diminished, and that thus there was the more need for the royal judges whom Jehoshaphat

sent throughout Judah, whose head was 'the ruler of the house of Judah' (2 Ch 19⁵. ¹¹). They seem, however, to have become even more amenable to bribery than the elders (see below). Solomon, as stated above, built a special porch for judgment (1 K 7⁷). It is also worthy of note that the king seems to have had no power to originate laws (even Josiah's reform is based on the book that had been found, 2 K 23¹⁻³), and that he himself was under law (1 K 21⁴ᶠᶠ, Dt 17¹⁹).

3. *Religious.*—In all early Semitic nationalities, and especially in Israel, religion was bound up with the unity of the people. For a king to neglect the worship of the national god would be to alienate a large proportion of his subjects, who, believing themselves to have sprung from their god, felt that his honour was their own, and also that their own welfare depended upon the treatment he received. Hence the maintenance of the religious establishment was necessarily an important part of the king's duties.* A further question arises whether the early Semitic custom of the king being the religious head of the nation and the chief sacrificing priest obtained also in Israel. It has been asserted that this was the primary object of the anointing of the Israelitish kings, but no hint to this effect is given in the OT (see above). Yet there are certainly traces of the old custom, whether it is to be regarded as held legitimate by the Israelites themselves (till quite late times) or not.

Thus we find the following examples :—(a) Sacrifices are offered by Saul against the wish of Samuel (1 S 13⁹⁻¹¹ [J²] 14³³ᶠᶠ. [J¹]), but are evidently regarded by Saul himself as his right in Samuel's absence. Also, perhaps, by David himself (2 S 6¹³. ¹⁷ [J¹] 24²⁵ [J¹]), but in these cases the sacrifices may merely have been offered by the priests at David's order (comp., too, Ezk 45¹⁷ᵇ. ²²). (b) David wears the linen ephod (2 S 6¹⁴, cf. 1 Ch 15²⁷), which was a priestly garment (1 S 2¹⁸ 22¹⁸) (see EPHOD), and he and Solomon bless the people (2 S 6¹⁸, 1 K 8¹⁴). (c) It is more important that David and Solomon dismiss and appoint the chief priest at their pleasure (2 S 8¹⁷, 1 K 2²⁶. ²⁷. ³⁵).† This may have been due to a desire to have a royal priesthood distinct from the priests of other sanctuaries (cf. 1 Ch 6¹⁰, 1 K 4² with 1 Ch 16³⁹. ⁴⁰). It is possible that the officials manifestly not of the Levitical line who are called priests (כֹּהֲנִים), viz. David's sons (2 S 8¹⁸ [J¹]) and Ira the Jairite (2 S 20²⁶ [Rᴾ]),‡ represent those royal officials who saw to the maintenance of such royal priests, unless perhaps they were the intermediaries between the king and the whole body of the priests for certain functions, *e.g.* to supply the royal sacrifices, to superintend the royal expenditure upon the preparations for the Temple, etc.§

V. MAINTENANCE AND ESTABLISHMENT. — 1. *Taxation.*—(a) Ezk 45⁷. ⁸ 48²¹ speak of a royal

* Ezk 45¹⁷ expressly orders that the prince shall provide the sacrifices (cf. 46⁴⁻⁶ and 2 Ch 30²⁴ 35⁷).

† That David gets the choir appointed (1 Ch 15¹⁶⁻²⁴) proves nothing, for, apart from the question of the historicity of the Chronicler's narrative, even the closest sacerdotal body may depend on the laity for money. 1 Ch 16⁴⁻⁶ is more to the point, but need not imply more. So also with Solomon building the Temple, which Nowack (*Arch.* i. p. 310) strangely compares to Ahaz building the altar in wilful opposition to the type sanctioned by the nation's religious laws.

‡ *I.e.* dated by Budde 440–400 B.C., therefore (on the same principles) not much earlier than the Chronicler (see next note).

§ The Chronicler evades the difficulty by paraphrasing 'the sons of David were chief about the king' (1 Ch 18¹⁷). In 1 K 4⁵ the title is given to Zabud as well as 'the king's friend' (see below).

The word 'priests' in 2 S 8¹⁸ 20²⁶ has been explained to mean, on the one hand, spiritual counsellors, or the king's highest officials, or his daily companions (which is against usage) ; and, on the other hand, 'priest' in the fullest sense. But to believe that the sons of David and Ira the Jairite actually exercised priestly functions requires much more evidence than has yet been adduced (but see Driver on 2 S 8¹⁸). The act of Uzziah is represented by the Chronicler as monstrously illegal (2 Ch 26¹⁶⁻¹⁸), and has no parallel in Israelitish history.

* But surely not with 'the governors of the people' mentioned in 2 Ch 23²⁰, as Smith's *DB²* i. 1245, suggests.

† Not in Dt 17⁹. ¹² (Benzinger, *Arch.* p. 306), for the singular there is either generic and=plural in 19¹⁷. ¹⁸, or it refers to a president of lay judges (so Driver).

domain with which God's 'princes' will be so satisfied that they will no more oppress the people, but even with this the 'prince' is still to receive large supplies of food (45¹³⁻¹⁶). Such a royal domain is also hinted at in 1 S 8¹² (E²), and actually possessed by David (1 Ch 27²⁵⁻³¹).

(b) Presents, more or less compulsory, were given by subjects (to Saul 1 S 10²⁷ 16²⁰), and by foreigners (to David 2 S 8¹⁰, to Solomon 1 K 4²¹⁻²³ 10¹⁰⁻²⁵, and to kings of Israel from Moab 2 K 3⁴, cf. Is 16¹). The king would also certainly have his share of booty (David 2 S 8¹¹ 12³⁰, 1 Ch 26²⁷).

(c) The king had apparently the right to the first cut of the pasture land (Am 7¹) for his many horses (1 K 18⁵). The land-tax was, as it seems, unknown in Palestine. Yet there was probably a property-tax of some kind (1 S 17²⁵ [E¹]), perhaps the tenth of all produce (1 S 8¹⁵·¹⁷ [E²]). Naturally, for extraordinary needs extraordinary requisitions were levied (2 K 15²⁰ 23³⁵). Caravans paid toll (1 K 10¹⁵), and much profit must have been derived from what was in Solomon's days the royal monopoly in horses and, apparently, chariots (1 K10²⁸·²⁹), as well as from the commerce by sea (1 K 10¹¹). Apparently also the property of condemned persons (1 K 21¹·³·⁷), and of those who had left the country (2 K 8³·⁶), passed to the king. That he also sometimes seized property unjustly is implied in Ezk 45⁷·⁸.

(d) We are not told the reasons why the census was taken by David (2 S 24¹ [J¹]), but perhaps one was the desire to equalize taxation, as was evidently that of Solomon's division of the country into twelve districts (1 K 4⁷),* which were only partly named after the twelve tribes, though roughly coextensive with them.

2. Officials (שָׂרִים 2 S 8¹⁶).—Perhaps the more important of these were those 'that saw the king's face' (2 K 25¹⁹=Jer 52²⁵). It should be noticed that the details are almost confined to the time of David and Solomon (2 S 8¹⁶ff. 20²³ff., 1 K 4²ff., 1 Ch 18¹⁵ff.), and that in only a few cases can we affirm the continuance of the office throughout the monarchy.

(a) Military.—(α) The captain of the host, i.e. commander-in-chief (under the king) of the whole available fighting strength of the nation, exclusive, perhaps, of the bodyguard (see above). This position, the consolidation and concentration of an older usage (Dt 20⁹) was begun by Abner under Saul and Ishbosheth (1 S 14⁵⁰, 2 S 2⁸), by Joab (2 S 8¹⁶) and for a short time by Amasa in Judah (2 S 19¹³, 1 K 2³²), and, on Joab's removal, by Benaiah (1 K 2³⁵). In the northern kingdom the king appears to have divided the office into that of the two captains of his chariots (1 K 16⁹·¹⁶). (β) The captain of the bodyguard (see above), Benaiah (2 S 8¹⁸ 20²³).

(b) Civil.—(α) The mazkîr (מַזְכִּיר, lit.='he who brings to remembrance,' viz. Jehoshaphat in the time of David and Solomon (2 S 8¹⁶ 20²⁴, 1 Ch 18¹⁵, 1 K 4³), Joah ben-Asaph in the time of Hezekiah (2 K 18¹⁸·³⁷=Is 36³·²²), Joah ben-Joahaz in the time of Josiah (2 Ch 34⁸). This is usually rendered

---

* It is hardly accurate to say that Judah is omitted (e.g. Benzinger, p. 308), for Socoh (v.¹⁰, cf. also Jos 15³⁵·⁴⁸, 2 Ch 11⁷ 28¹⁸, 1 S 17¹) was up the vale of Elah in the Shephelah of Judah. Of the places mentioned with it in 1 K 4¹⁰ Hepher is unknown, and also Arubboth (but see Dr. C. Schick in PEFSt, Oct. 1898, p. 238. Josephus, ed. Niese, Ant. VIII. ii. 3, omits all ref. to v.¹⁰ [against Smith's DB² i. 250]), though this possibly is to be identified with Arab, mentioned in Jos 15⁵² (Socoh, v.⁴⁸ is in the next group), and also in the Shephelah, not far apparently from Dumah, which was near Eleutheropolis (see ARAB and DUMAH). But evidently Jerusalem and the part immediately round it is omitted in Solomon's twelve districts. This is explicable by the fact that being so near to the seat of government it would necessarily be more easily mulcted for provisioning troops, etc., and also may have come under the special care of one of the other officials named, e.g. the governor of the city (see below).

'recorder,' his duties being supposed to be those of chronicling the chief events; but this would hardly appear to be a sufficiently influential position. Perhaps his duty was rather that of reminding the king in matters of state, and he represented the Grand Vizier of modern times (cf. Benz. p. 310).

(β) The sôphēr (סוֹפֵר) or 'scribe' (AV, RV), apparently the writer of the royal correspondence, the Secretary of State (2 S 8¹⁷ 20²⁵, 1 Ch 18¹⁶). Solomon had two, who were apparently the sons of David's 'scribe' (1 K 4³). His duties appear to have been partly financial (2 K 12¹⁰ 22³⁻⁹), and he sometimes is mentioned before the Recorder (2 K 18¹⁸·³⁷=Is 36³·²², 2 Ch 34⁸, cf. 2 K 22³). See, further, Riehm, s.v. 'Kanzler.'

(γ) The officer over the household, אֲשֶׁר עַל הַבַּיִת (1 K 4⁶ 18³), i.e. the head of the palace, intrusted with 'the key' (Is 22²²). Apparently=סֹכֵן (Is 22¹⁵), but this may be a general term for 'official.' He perhaps stood for our High Chamberlain or Steward. Not mentioned in David's time. In the time of Hezekiah he is mentioned before both Scribe and Recorder (2 K 18¹⁸·³⁷ 19²=Is 36³·²² 37²), and certainly held a superior position to that held by the Scribe (cf. Is 22¹⁵·²⁰ with 36³).

(δ) The overseer of the forced labour (אֲשֶׁר עַל הַמַּס) first seen in the latter part of David's reign. Adoram (Adoniram) held the office from then till his murder in the revolt from Rehoboam (2 S 20²⁴, 1 K 4⁶ 5¹⁴ 12¹⁸ ‖ 2 Ch 10¹⁸).

(ε) The king's servant (עֶבֶד הַמֶּלֶךְ) is mentioned with other high officials in 2 K 22¹². The same title is on the seal of one Obadiah (figured in Nowack, Arch. i. p. 262; Benzinger, Arch. p. 258), but nothing is known of it. Perhaps it is the same as

(ζ) The king's friend (1 K 4⁵, 1 Ch 27³³, cf. 2 S 15³⁷ 16¹⁶).

(η) The king's counsellor, Ahithophel (1 Ch 27³³, 2 S 15¹², cf. ³¹ 16²⁰·²³ 17¹·⁷·¹⁴, Is 3³). Perhaps also Jonathan, David's uncle (1 Ch 27³²).

(θ) The prefect of the twelve commissariat districts (1 K 4⁵, see above).

(ι) Minor officials, e.g. the head of the wardrobe (2 K 22¹⁴, and perhaps 10²²); heads of various departments of royal properties (1 Ch 27²⁵⁻³¹); eunuchs (סָרִיסִים) or perhaps chamberlains (1 S 8¹⁵, 1 K 22⁹, 2 K 8⁶, and often; in 2 K 25¹⁹=officer); the governor of the city (שַׂר הָעִיר, 1 K 22²⁶, 2 K 23³, 2 Ch 34⁸, cf. Neh 11⁹).

(κ) Although these officials were necessary for the working of the monarchical government, which probably always tended to obliterate the old landmarks of the tribal system, with its semi-independent elders (these are still mentioned under the monarchy, 1 K 20⁷, 2 K 23¹), yet by the very severance of the ruling class from the soil it tended also to increase the difference between class and class. The Mosaic legislation, though perhaps hardly suitable for great commercial enterprises, was admirably fitted to maintain comparative equality, but the rule of the king in both N. and S. Israel produced crying injustice on the part of the rich and misery for the poor (e.g. Am 2⁶·⁷, Is 5⁸, Jer 5²⁸, Mic 3¹¹).

VI. Lastly, it may be noticed briefly that the king, both by success and by failure, played an important part in preparation for the future. His success showed the necessity for organization and concentration; his failure, in his degeneration from the nearly ideal David to the worthless Zedekiah (relieved, though the crown temporarily was, by godly representatives), showed that a kingdom as such and alone was an ineffectual protection. A wholly ideal David was hoped for (Ezk 34²³ 37²⁵), and in due time given. But before then the title of king was borne by members of the Hasmonæan dynasty from Aristobulus I. (B.C. 105–104) to Aristobulus II.

(B.C. 63), and by Herod the Great from B.C. 40 to B.C. 4. See separate articles on these names.

LITERATURE.—Besides the ordinary Histories of the Jewish People, and Dictionaries, may be mentioned Benzinger, *Hebräische Archäologie* (Leipzig, 1894); Nowack, *Lehrbuch der Hebräischen Archäologie* (Leipzig, 1894); McCurdy, *HPM* (1894–96, §§ 27–63, 511–538).   A. LUKYN WILLIAMS.

KINGDOM OF GOD, OF HEAVEN (βασιλεία τοῦ θεοῦ, τῶν οὐρανῶν).—The importance of the place which this idea of the kingdom of God holds in Scripture, and especially in the teaching of Jesus; the new prominence it has come to assume in recent years in theology (since Kant and Schleiermacher, particularly in the school of A. Ritschl, but also among theologians generally, *e.g.* Lipsius, Oosterzee, Maurice); and the attempts which have been made to find in it the supreme and controlling notion of Christian dogmatics, as well as of Christian ethics,—all render it desirable that full and careful consideration should be given to this leading thought of the Christian religion, and that the attempt should be made to present its biblical aspects in as complete a form as possible, in their relations to each other, and to the other elements of Christian truth. Little inquiry is necessary to convince us that this idea enters vitally into the whole texture of revelation, has its root in the fundamental ideas of the OT, is paramount in the earthly teaching of our Lord, receives further development—with special reference, however, to its eschatological side—in the apostolic writings, and presents points of deepest interest to students both of doctrine and morals at the present day. Our task, then, in this article will be—following the natural biblical development of the subject— to exhibit first the general features of the OT preparation for the Christian doctrine of the kingdom of God; then to set forth the teaching of Jesus on this vital topic; and, finally, to compare with this the doctrine of the Epistles and other NT writings. By pursuing this course we may hope to arrive at a notion which shall be helpful in enabling us to judge of the place and value of this doctrine in theology and ethics, and to form a correct estimate of past and current misapprehensions and mutilations of the idea.

I. OT DOCTRINE OF THE KINGDOM OF GOD.— 1. To reach the true idea of the kingdom of God in OT we must go farther back than the point from which a start is usually made—the theocratic constitution at Sinai. As in all the spheres of the Divine operation, grace invariably presupposes *nature*, so is it in this. The real basis for the idea of the kingdom of God is already laid in the Creation history. The doctrine of Scripture, in its oldest as well as in its later parts, is here entirely uniform. The one God—the God who afterwards entered into covenant with the patriarchs, and as J" brought Isr. out of Egypt, and formed it into a people for Himself—is the Almighty Maker of heaven and earth, the Creator, Lord, and Ruler of all things, animate and inanimate. The Creation narrative in Gn 1, with its delegation to man of 'dominion' over the creatures (cf. Ps 8), already lays down this doctrine, and the second history of Creation (Gn 2⁴ᶠᶠ·) is equally explicit. No limit is set in these creation histories to the absolute power of God. As H. Schultz says: 'When God, the possessor of heaven and earth (Gn 14¹⁹⁻²²), can make everything good, that is to say, finds nowhere any hindrance in anything already in existence, which, having its origin in some other being, is antagonistic to Him (Gn 1³¹); and when to His word "Be" comes the willing "And it was"; in other words, when matter obeys the Divine command like a willing servant, it is assuredly taken for granted that everything, even this chaotic matter which

obeys the creative word of God, is included within the will of God, and called forth by Him' (*OT Theol.* ii. 186, Eng. trans.). On this conception of God as Creator rests the doctrine which pervades the whole OT of *His unlimited dominion or rule in nature and providence*. The ethical or spiritual kingdom of God rests on a basis of natural dominion. This is expressed in the clearest way in psalmists and prophets. God is King of all the earth (Ps 47⁷); His kingdom ruleth over all, and angels, His hosts, and all His works in all places of His dominion, are exhorted to bless Him (Ps 103¹⁹⁻²²); natural agents are His ministers (Ps 104⁴), and continue according to His ordinances as serving Him (Ps 119⁸⁹⁻⁹¹); He is the God, even He alone, of all the kingdoms of the earth, for He made heaven and earth (Is 37¹⁶); 'all that is in the heaven and in the earth is thine: thine is the kingdom, O Lord, and thou art exalted as head above all' (1 Ch 29¹¹). This natural dominion or kingdom of God embraces all beings and events— the affairs of men as well as the agencies and powers of nature, which He disposes at His will. Nothing is withdrawn from His providential government, which takes in events great and small, remote and near, of nations and of individuals, the thoughts of men as well as their outward actions, the army of heaven as well as the inhabitants of the earth (cf. Gn 18²⁵ 45⁵⁻⁹, Ex 9¹³⁻¹⁶, Dt 32⁹, Pr 21¹, 2 Ch 16⁹, 2 K 19²⁸, Is 10¹⁵, Dn 4³⁵ etc.). The disobedience of men does not withdraw them from the range of the Divine control. If men will not serve the purposes of God willingly, they are made to serve the Divine ends unwillingly (Ex 9¹⁶). They are the clay: God is the potter; they cannot escape from the potter's hands; and if they will not be made vessels of honour, they are turned to other uses as vessels of dishonour (Jer 18⁶; cf. Ro 9²¹⁻²³). Their very wrath is made to praise Him, and the remainder of wrath He restrains (Ps 76¹⁰).

There is therefore recognized in Scripture—OT and NT alike—a natural and universal kingdom or dominion of God, embracing all objects, persons, and events, all doings of individuals and nations, all operations and changes of nature and history, absolutely without exception, which is the basis on which a higher kind of kingdom—*a moral and spiritual kingdom*—is built up. The natural creation obeys God undeviatingly by an inherent law of its constitution (Ps 119⁹¹, Is 1². ³); to man alone belongs the possibility of entering into personal relations with his Maker, and of rendering Him a free and intelligent obedience. We have seen that God's ordinary providential rule in the worlds of matter and mind is never for a moment suspended, even in the case of wicked men; but altogether higher in quality is a moral rule,—a rule in the minds and hearts of men, a rule by moral means over willing and obedient subjects. For man is not a mere natural existence; in Kant's famous phrase, he is a member of a kingdom of ends; is capable of entering into the will of his Creator, and of rendering Him a spontaneous and willing obedience. Here, then, is the idea of a kingdom of God of a higher kind—a realm of free, personal spirits, yielding voluntary obedience to the known will of their Creator,—and it lies in the nature of the case, and is already implied in the narrative of the creation of man, and of God's dealings with him, that the production of such an ethical kingdom in humanity was God's end in creation from the first (Gn 1. 2). 'How would it now look to you,' says the philosophic Saxon king Alfred, 'if there were any very powerful king, and he had no freemen in all his kingdom, but that all were slaves? Then, said I, it would not be thought by me right nor reasonable if men in such a servile condition only should attend upon him.

Then, quoth he, it would be more unnatural if God, in all His kingdom, had no free creature under His power. Therefore, He made two rational creatures, free angels and men, and gave them the great gift of freedom. Hence, they could do evil as well as good, whichever they would. He gave this very free gift, and a very fixed law to every man unto this end.' We have here, therefore, a higher type of dominion, one in which God's will is freely accepted by rational and moral intelligences ; and had this been realized on the lines originally laid down, there would have been, even on a creation basis, a kingdom of God in humanity.

2. But this brings us to the next cardinal point in the OT doctrine. The kingdom of God on the basis of creation just indicated was *not* realized. The narrative of creation is immediately succeeded in our oldest history by the record of the *Fall*—of a turning aside of man from his primitive innocence —which frustrated (speaking humanly) the original designs of the Creator, and introduced sin, death, and multiplied penal evils into the world (Gn 3). It is usual for biblical theologians to make somewhat light of this narrative, which stands at the gateway of the history of revelation, as if it did not enter deeply into the religious conceptions of the people of Israel. ' It will hardly be maintained,' says Schultz, 'that any other OT writer even hints at such an idea' as that man possessed an aboriginal dignity which was afterwards lost (*OT Theol.* ii. p. 258 ff.). It may be affirmed with some confidence, on the other hand, that, apart from explicit references to the narrative of the Fall (which, however, could not be unknown to any writer of the prophetic period), the background of the whole picture in OT is that of a world in revolt, turned aside from God, sunk, and ever sinking deeper, in unrighteousness, abandoned to idolatry and to the lusts and corruptions which are the natural fruit of apostasy from the Creator,—a world in contrariety to the divine holiness, and judged as guilty, and justly exposed to the Divine anger (Gn 6[5. 6] 8[21] 13[13] 19[20. 21], Lv 18[24-30], Dt 9[4-6], 1 K 8[46], Ps 14. 51[5] 143[2], Pr 20[9], Ec 7[20], Is 1, Hos 4, etc. Cf. Dillmann, *Alttest. Theol.* pp. 376–88). This representation of the condition of humanity as universally under sin has for its consequence a proposition of the utmost importance for the right apprehension of our subject, viz., that if God is to have a moral kingdom in the world, it must be a kingdom brought into existence through *grace*,—it must be *produced* through redemption and regeneration as the result of a divine supernatural economy of salvation. This note of grace is already struck with unmistakable clearness in the Protevangelium, where the first sin is met by the promise of a final complete victory, not without suffering, of the 'seed of the woman' over 'the seed of the serpent' (Gn 3[15]) ; and the history of revelation ever after is but the history of this developing purpose of God for the complete overthrow of evil, and the final establishment, through a mingled operation of mercy and judgment, of the kingdom of God upon earth. As entering into covenant with His people Israel for the realization of this end, God is known peculiarly by His name J″ (Ex 6[1-8]),—a name which specially denotes Him as the self-identical and changeless One, the Being who *is* eternally what He *is* (Ex 3[14]), who is and remains *one* with Himself in all He thinks, purposes, and does (Mal 3[6]), who possesses, together with immutability, the attribute of self-determining freedom and unlimited rule (Dt 4[39]) ; who, therefore, in the relation of the covenant, would display His might, demonstrate His supremacy as Moral Ruler, magnify His covenant-keeping faithfulness, and reveal Himself as the Living, Personal

God, working freely in history in pursuance of gracious purposes, and in spite of all human opposition bringing them to pass (cf. Dillmann, pp. 217, 218). The history of OT revelation, therefore, is simply, as said, the history of the developing kingdom of God in its earlier, preparatory, inchoate form, yet from the first a kingdom of grace and salvation. Herein, from the biblical point of view, lies the key to all historical developments, the explanation of all arrangements and movements of Divine providence. Israel's position brought it into contact, not only with petty neighbouring states, but with the mightiest empires of East and West. But these appear in OT only as they affect the chosen race, and it is there made manifest that the centre of God's purposes is always Israel, as, in truth, the centre of interest must always be that portion of the race with which for the time being the kingdom of God is identified. ' Just as,' in the striking words of Trench, 'in tracing the course of a stream, not the huge morasses nor the vast stagnant pools on either side would delay us ; we should not, because of their extent, count them the river, but recognize that as such, though it were the slenderest thread, in which an onward movement might be discerned ; so is it here. Egypt and Assyria and Babylon were but the vast stagnant morasses on either side of the river ; the Man in whose seed the whole earth should be blessed, he and his family were the little stream in which the life and onward movement of the world were to be treated. . . . They belong not to history, least of all to sacred history, those Babels, those cities of confusion, those huge pens into which by force and fraud the early hunters of men, the Nimrods and Sesostrises, drove and compelled their fellows . . . where no faith existed, but in the blind powers of nature, and the brute forces of the natural man' (*Hulsean Lectures*, 1845, Lect. II.).

The stadia in the development of this OT idea of the kingdom of God are those of the history of the chosen people itself. For Israel was, in the root conception of its history, a people of God, a people whom God had chosen, and called, and formed into a nation for His own praise (Ex 19[3-6], Is 43[21]). The name 'theocracy,' therefore, is properly given to its constitution, as Josephus perceived, when he framed this title for it (*c. Ap.* ii. 16). W. R. Smith, indeed, in his able work on *The Prophets of Israel* (pp. 51–53), is of opinion that so far from this title bringing out the distinctive feature of the religion of Israel, it rather denotes that which Israel had in common with all other nations of that time,—for these nations also had their supreme gods, whom they worshipped, and under whose protection they placed themselves in their national undertakings (Chemosh, *e.g.* in Moab). This, however, hardly meets the point, for certainly no other nation ever rested its whole life as Israel did on the consciousness of a redemption and covenant with God, and found the whole reason of its existence in the calling to love and serve Him, and to be a witness for Him in the midst of the earth ; nor had any other nation such a story to tell of its origin, even in legend, as Israel (Dt 4[32-38] ; cf. Schultz, *OT Theology*, i. pp. 136–138, ii. pp. 7–9). Within its national theocratic form, besides, Israel cherished, as we shall immediately see, the consciousness of a universalistic destiny, and this consciousness goes back to the very foundation of the nation's life. For the national form was not the first thing in the history of Israel. It had been preceded by an earlier form—the patriarchal—the days of the covenants with the fathers, Abraham, Isaac, and Jacob (cf. Schultz, ii. pp. 6, 7). And there already we find the clear expression of the idea that Israel was a people called with a view to the ultimate blessing of the whole world (נִבְרְכוּ in Gn 12³ 18¹⁸ 28¹⁴ ; הִתְבָּרְכוּ in Gn 22¹⁸ 26⁴).

3. It is now incumbent on us to mark the chief steps in the historical development of this idea in OT more exactly ; and here in a general view we readily distinguish as successive the *patriarchal*, the *Mosaic*, the *royal*, and the *prophetic* periods in the growth of this conception. (*a*) The early records trace for us with careful particularity the narrowing down of the line of salvation from the posterity of Seth (Gn 4²⁵⁻²⁶) to that of Shem (Gn 9²⁶⁻²⁷ ; cf. Schultz, ii. pp. 346, 347), then to the family of Terah (Gn 11²⁷⁻³²), till, finally, it concentrates itself in one world-historical figure — that of *Abraham*. Looming through the mists of the past, the personality of Abraham arrests our attention as one of the great creative origins of time. With Abraham strictly historical revelation may be said to begin. Alike on the Divine and on the human side, the transactions with him are unsurpassed in OT in interest and importance. He is the founder of the Heb. nation, — 'the religiously-elect nation of antiquity,' as Volkmar calls it ; the fountain-head of the three great monotheistic religions of the world ; to him in a special sense belonged the covenants and the promises ; out of his loins Christ came ; in him at this hour all families of the earth are being blessed. The call of Abraham—the covenants made with him — constitute, therefore, a new era in the religious history of mankind. As men multiplied and spread in the earth, they fell farther away from the true God, and there seems little doubt that, left to themselves, they would soon have lost altogether the knowledge of God which they possessed (Jos 24²). This catastrophe was averted by the choice of Abraham. Separated from his kindred, he was to be a witness for the truth which the world was suffering to be quenched in universal idolatry. The covenant was at first with the individual, but its ultimate scope was the blessing of the human race (Gn 12¹⁻³ etc.). Neither did it stop with simple declaration, but provided for the fulfilment of the promise by granting to him an heir, through whose descendants, multiplied into a great nation, the promise should be realized (Gn 15⁴⁻⁵ etc.). A special part of this promise was that kings should come out of him (Gn 17⁶). The line of promise was defined more exactly to lie through Isaac and subsequently Jacob (to the exclusion of Ishmael and Esau), with both of whom the covenant was renewed (Gn 26²⁻⁴ 28¹¹⁻¹⁵ etc.) ; then by a succession of remarkable providences the descendants of Jacob were taken down to Egypt, where, first in prosperity, afterwards under the sterner discipline of oppression, they grew to be a nation such as God required for the fulfilment of His purpose. We are aware of the boldness of the criticism which would dissipate the whole of this history into unsubstantial myth and legend. Against this revolutionary treatment we enter our respectful protest. What legend can do for the life of Abraham is sufficiently evidenced by the fables and stories in the Bk. of Jubilees, and in other Jewish, Mohammedan, and Persian accounts. The history of Abraham in the Bible stands, from internal evidence alone, on an entirely different footing from these. In its simple, coherent, divinely-elevated character, its organic unity with the rest of the history of revelation, its absolute freedom from the puerility and extravagance which mark the products of the myth-forming spirit, it approves itself as a grave, serious record of important events, the knowledge of which had been carefully preserved by family tradition, or even from an early date by written documents (cf. Dillmann, *Alttest. Theol.* pp. 77, 78 ;

and art. by Köhler on 'Abraham' in third ed. of Herzog's *RE*).

(*b*) Hitherto, while the foundations are being laid strong and deep, there has been no specific mention of a kingdom of God, such as we meet with in the *transactions of Sinai* next to be adverted to. A kingdom of God in the only form in which mankind at that time was able to apprehend it could not be created until a body of people had been called into existence out of whom it could be constituted. With the revival of the national faith under Moses, the marvellous deliverance of the Exodus, and the consolidation of the fugitive Hebrews into a nation pledged in covenant to J" at Sinai, and receiving at His hand laws and institutions for their use, the requisite conditions were fulfilled and a *kingdom of God*, or *true theocracy*, starts for the first time into visible existence. Already in the exaltation of religious feeling J" is hailed as King in Moses' Song at the crossing of the Red Sea (Ex 15¹⁸) ; but it is in the covenant at Sinai, with its attendant solemnities and sacrifices, that the theocratic constitution is formally established. There God proposes to take the people to Himself as a peculiar treasure above all people, that they may be to Him a kingdom of priests (consecrated), and a holy (separated) nation ; and the people, in accepting the terms of this covenant, and pledging themselves to obedience, enter by the sprinkling of blood into the gracious relation thus proposed (Ex 19³⁻⁶ 24⁴⁻⁸). Thenceforth they are a people of God, and J" is formally their Lawgiver and King (Is 33²²). The covenant is based on *grace*, yet the continuance of its blessings is made to depend on the fulfilment of statutory conditions (cf. Ro 10⁵) ; it is a covenant of *law*, yet God appears in it as 'merciful and gracious . . . forgiving iniquity and transgression and sin' (Ex 34⁶⁻⁷), and provision is made in sacrifices and purifications for the removal of the guilt and uncleanness by which the fellowship with God would otherwise be continually interrupted, if not entirely broken off. The people, on their part, have it set before them as an aim, to be holy because God is holy (Lv 19²), and to realize righteousness by diligent observance of all God's statutes and ordinances, from the central motive of love (Dt 4¹⁻⁵). Such, apart from doubtful details of Levitical ritual, was the general constitution under which Israel was placed, and it separated that people absolutely from their heathen neighbours (Nu 23⁹). It is easy to see, however, that notwithstanding this limitation of the covenant to a particular people, and even its obvious design to seclude this people for a time from contact with other nations, it had in it germs of universality which were certain ultimately to burst the limits of the national form, and expand into a religion for the whole world. In the words of Riehm : ' By divine revelation ideas were planted in the minds of the people of Israel, so lofty, and rich, and deep, that in the existing religious condition they could never see their perfect realization ; ideas which, with every step in the development of the religious life and knowledge, only more fully disclosed their own depth and fulness, and which must therefore necessarily have led them to look to the future for their fulfilment ' (*Mess. Prophecy*, 1867, p. 33). How much, *e.g.*, lay in the simple fact that J", the God of Isr., was yet the God of the whole earth (Ex 19⁵) ; that to Him alone belonged honour and glory ; that it was due to Him that all nations should serve Him and keep His commandments. ' On the ground of his knowledge of J" must the Israelite claim the whole earth for the kingdom of his God ' (Riehm). The ideas at the root of the covenant, in short, were larger than could be permanently embodied in an exclusively national form, and from the first these larger ideas are seen shining through, and herald-ing the wider fulfilment (*e.g.* Nu 11²⁹ 14²¹ 24¹⁷⁻¹⁹).

(*c*) The disparity between the Divine idea and the existing reality of the kingdom of God, which was manifest from the outset in the constant un-faithfulness and repeated rebellions of the people (Ex 32, Nu 11, etc.), was further accentuated in the tribal jealousies and divisions, the lawless turbulence and the gross declensions, alternating with revivals of the spirit of faith and heroism, of the periods of the Conquest and the Judges (Jos 22, Jg 2. 7. 21²⁵ etc.), and led in the time of Samuel to the demand for a king (1 S 8), and to *the establish-ment of the monarchy* under Saul (1 S 10), and then under David (1 S 16¹⁻¹⁰, 2 S 5¹⁻⁹). The sin of the people, as the event showed, did not lie simply in their desire for a king, for this it lay in the purpose of God to give them (Dt 17¹⁴⁻²⁰), but in the spirit of self-will and insubordination out of which the desire came, and the ideal of a king they had set before them—one like those of the nations around, who would judge them, and lead them to battle, and give them distinction and military glory (1 S 8⁷⁻⁹·¹⁹⁻²²). We thus arrive at another transition period in the history of the kingdom of God—the end of the judgeship and the beginning of the monarchy. It was a change which in the nature of things was bound to come. Already in Eli's days we see on every side the evidence of decay, of break-up, of failure. Under Samuel's rule there is a revival of the religion and prestige of the nation, but only for a time. The prophets do not live for ever, and the nation could not always be held together by the bond of Samuel's personality. He grew old, and his sons did not walk in his steps. Then came the clamour for a change—for a trial of a new system. Instead of the prophet, we have the royal Saul—a king after the people's hearts, but yet not after God's heart. In all this, none the less, is to be distinguished an onward move-ment,—a step to the great goal God always had in view—the bringing in of His own anointed. When Saul's reign had ended in ruin and disaster to himself and to the land (1 S 31), the way was open for God to set upon the throne *His* king—a man after His own heart, who should fulfil all His will (cf. Ac 13²²). The Davidic era thus became, despite the deep later shadows in David's personal character and career, a typical one for the history of the kingdom of God. It introduced a new abiding element into the conception of the theocracy, for we have not now simply the single, invisible Ruler, J″, but the *visible representative* of this unseen Sovereign reigning in His name on earth. The fundamental outlines of the theocratic kingdom in this new form are laid down in the promises to David (2 S 7), in whose house the kingdom is established (vv.¹². ¹⁶, Ps 89. 132); and this yields the ideal of the theocratic ruler as it henceforth appears in the history, and in the loftier strains of psalm and prophecy—one who would feel that his sole function was to be the instrument and visible representative of the great invisible King, and would rule the kingdom in strict subordination to the will and law of God; who would know that his authority was a deputed, delegated authority, and would seek at every step to be guided by God's wishes; who would have unity of will with God—would be in sympathy with God in His ends; a truly pious king, therefore, ruling the kingdom, not from worldly motives, or in a worldly spirit, or for self-aggrandizement, but for God's glory, to whom God would be a 'Father,' and he would be 'God's son' (2 S 7. 23¹⁻⁵, Ps 2. 20. 45. 72. 89. 110. 132, etc., Is 32, etc.). Only approxi-mately, and with sad defections, was this ideal realized even under David; or amidst the external splendours of the reign of Solomon; or under the

most pious of Judah's princes after the division of the kingdom; but the manifest failure of the visible theocracy only made the light of prophecy burn brighter in the hope of a future day and a greater Personage (cf. Is 7¹⁴⁻¹⁶ 9⁶·⁷ etc.), in whom, under happier conditions, the ideal *would* be realized.

(*d*) This brings us to the last stage in the OT development of the idea of the kingdom of God— the *prophetic*, with which must be conjoined the enlarged ideals and anticipations of the *psalms*. All the germs of previous revelation now blossom into an incomparable fulness of conception of the future glorious triumph of God's kingdom in Isr. and over the earth, but with a clearer apprehension, wrought by the unspeakably bitter disappointments and humiliations of the nation, of the conditions under which alone such a con-summation could be wrought out. It is a mar-vellous fact that it was not because Isr. was suc-ceeding in fulfilling its mission, but because it was failing in it, that the spirit of prophecy wrought so powerfully in the development of these germs, which lay hidden in the nation's life, to a universal form. Now at least, with unmistakable clearness, we have the full consciousness that J″ is the God of the whole earth; that His providence rules over all; that His purpose has an aspect to the Gentiles as well as to the Jews; that Isr. is His servant, with a mission to become a light to the Gentiles and a blessing to the whole of mankind (Am 4¹³ 5⁸, Mic 4¹⁻³, Is 40. 42. 60, etc.). The more evident it be-came that the existing form of the theocracy would not endure, the stronger became the con-viction that God's kingdom would not perish, but that there would be a restoration of the theocracy on a grander and more spiritual basis, accompanied with the promulgation to the nations of the world of the worship of the living God, and the pouring out of the Spirit on all flesh (Jer 31³¹⁻³⁴, Ezk 17²²⁻²⁴ 36²⁵⁻²⁷, Jl 2²⁸⁻³²). A similar development of this consciousness of the universal mission of Isr. meets us in the Psalms—the highest point, perhaps, being reached in the 87th Psalm, which foretells the future inclusion of the most distant peoples, the greatest world-powers, even the most inveterate enemies of J″, in the future city or kingdom of God (RV, cf. Ps 2. 67. 98, etc.). On no idea, accordingly, is the influence of the development in psalm and prophecy more marked than on that of the theo-cratic King—the coming Personage in whom the hopes of the spiritual part of Israel increasingly centred. The clearer it became that the restoration and perfection of the theocracy were not to be looked for from pious kings like Hezekiah and Josiah, and the higher and more spiritual the conceptions became of the 'new covenant' which God would have to make with His people, or the remnant of them, after judgment had done its work (Is 6⁹⁻¹³, Jer 31³¹⁻³⁴, Ezk 36²⁵⁻²⁷, Hos 14, etc.), the more imperative was it felt to be that the Deliverer and Ruler of the seed of David should stand in a relation of nearness and unity to J″ transcending the limits of ordinary humanity— that the perfect union between Him and J″ should be realized on the basis of an exceptional dignity of nature, raising Him to a superhuman level of character and authority (Ps 110, Is 9⁶⁻⁷, Jer 31²², Mic 5², Dn 7¹³·¹⁴, Zec 3⁸, Mal 3¹ etc.). Along another line—though not without manifest rela-tion to the former (cf. Is 52¹⁵ 53¹² 55³·⁴ etc.)—is the development of the conception of the 'Servant of J″,' which, rising from the basis of the national calling of Isr., narrowing itself after to the spiritual portion of the people (St. Paul's 'election of grace'), culminates in the majestic portraiture of the indi-vidual Suffering Servant (ch. 52¹³⁻53) whom the Church rightly identifies with her Messiah. Preludes to this representation are found in the psalms which depict the sufferings that fall upon the godly (Ps 5–14. 22, etc.), and in the historical examples which show it to be a universal law that the righteous must suffer at the hands of the wicked, as well as with and for them (*e.g.* Joseph, Moses, David); but the Isaianic conception goes beyond all others in attributing to these sufferings of the Servant an expiatory character, and connecting them with the sin-offering (Is 53$^{10-12}$; cf. Zec 13$^{1.7}$). As respects the future form of the kingdom of God, it is always represented, in characteristically OT fashion, as reaching its triumph in conjunction with a restoration of Isr. or the remnant of it (Is 6^{13}, Am 9$^{7-10}$ etc.), purified by judgment, converted and reunited (*e.g.* Ezk 37, Hos 1^{11}), and with a revival of the earlier institutions (Is 1$^{25-27}$, 4); while the nations, brought to the knowledge of the true God by the displays of His power and mercy, are either incorporated with the chosen people as sharers of their privileges (Ps 87), or become worshippers and tributaries of J″ (Ps 72$^{10. 11. 17}$, Is 60, Mal 1^{11} etc.). But the sense of the surpassing greatness of the reality constantly tends to break through the literalism of these forms, and to mould them into new shapes (Is 2$^{2. 3}$, Jl 3$^{18-21}$, Ezk 47, etc.). The one thing sure on the verge of every horizon is—'The kingdom shall be J″s' (Ob ^{21}).

There is, however, one other respect in which we can see, in this prophetic period, a distinct preparation for the NT idea of the kingdom of God. In the earlier stages of the theocracy, nation and Church—if we may so speak—were one. The Israelite was a member of the theocracy in virtue of birth and circumcision. The religious consciousness and the national consciousness were part of the same inseparable whole. But in the progress of Isr. history we observe a development which forms the necessary transition to the more spiritual idea of the kingdom in NT. It is the idea of *the Church within the Church*—of the true and spiritual Isr. in the midst of the natural Isr., who form a distinct, or at least distinguishable, body by themselves. There are earlier intimations, but in the form we have here especially in view, the growth of this idea belongs more particularly to the last dark days of the national history, when it became clear to prophetic eyes that Isr. as a people was doomed to destruction, and the efforts of the prophets were directed to gather out a remnant who might maintain the witness to God till better times came. A marked stage in this transition is seen in the ministry of Isaiah, who, when his message was rejected, gathered round him the little band of his own disciples, and sealed up the testimony in their midst (Is 8$^{16-18}$, cf. Mal 3^{16}). It is this 'ecclesia invisiblis of the Old Covenant,' as Oehler calls it,—this 'ecclesiola in ecclesia,' as Delitzsch names it,—which may be regarded as the germ of the Church-idea proper. W. R. Smith perhaps states it better than any. 'The formation of this little community,' he says, 'was a new thing in the history of religion. Till then, no one had dreamed of a fellowship of faith dissociated from all national forms, maintained without the exercise of ritual services, bound together by faith in the divine word alone. It was the birth of a new era in OT religion, for it was the birth of the conception of the Church, the first step in the emancipation of spiritual religion from the forms of political life—a step not less significant that all its consequences were not seen till centuries had passed away' (*Prophets of Israel*, pp. 274–75).

The collapse of the Jewish state in Isr. and Judah seemed to have laid the hope of the kingdom of God in ruins; but events proved that this hope was now strong enough to live on its own account,

and *the Babylonian Exile* only tended to its further enlargement and strengthening. Torn from their roots in their own land, without holy city, temple, sacrifices, the people were taught that the acceptable worship of J″ was not tied to any one place, or dependent on a fixed priesthood or ritual; brought into contact with the world, in a geographical respect, to an extent they had never been before, they gained a new view of the extension of the world in space, which carried with it an extension of their idea of the time involved in the Divine plans. A new element entered the thoughts of the Jews at this period which never afterwards left it—an enlarged sense of the scale of things in space and time, the effect of which is seen in the enlarged scale of vision of the Bk. of Daniel (whatever its date), and even of the reveries in such apocalyptic compositions as the Bk. of Enoch. More than any book of OT the prophecy of Daniel gave definite shape and direction to the conception of a kingdom of the God of heaven, granted by the Ancient of Days to one like unto a son of man, who comes to receive it with the clouds of heaven, which kingdom was an everlasting dominion that could not be destroyed (Dn 7$^{13-15}$, cf. ch. 2^{44}; 'son of man' as opposed to 'beasts'; human, not bestial). The interpretation of this symbol as referring to a kingdom 'given to the saints of the Most High' (7$^{22. 27}$) need not exclude a Messianic reference; this, at least, is most generally held to be the source of the title 'Son of Man' as used by our Lord (found also in the Bk. of Enoch 46^2 48^2 etc., both references probably of Christian origin). This kingdom of God in Dn which is to succeed the last of the four world kingdoms, and break in pieces all the others (2$^{34. 35. 44. 45}$; cf. 7$^{14. 27}$), is of supernatural origin, of holy character, strictly universal in its scope, and endures for ever. The other writings of post-ex. Judaism (Bar, Ps.-Sol, 1 Mac, pseudo-Sibyllines, etc.) never rise to the height of these older representations, and mostly fall far below them into tame generalities, borrowed from passages in psalms and prophets, without any outlook towards the saving of the Gentiles, or discernment of the need of a spiritual conversion of the people. The Messiah, so far as He is brought into view at all, appears only to destroy the wicked, and establish His kingdom with the righteous (cf. Candlish, *Kingdom of God*, pp. 88–117; Stanton, *Jewish and Christian Messiah, passim*). We are thus taken back to the return from exile under Zerub. and the outburst of genuine prophecy connected therewith (Hag, Zec), and to the strains of Mal a century later, as the period of the last great utterances on the kingdom of God in OT. These add little to the features already sketched, beyond the note of warning and expectation of the coming of the Messenger of the Covenant to His temple, preceded by the sending of Elijah, with which Malachi closes (3^1 4^5). It is difficult not to feel, though centuries intervene, in passing from OT to NT, as if the evangelist had taken up his pen precisely where Malachi laid his down. The chief phenomena of these intervening centuries—so far as they are not absolutely a blank to us—the rise of scribism, of the synagogue worship, of the Jewish sects, the Maccabæan struggle, the dispersion, the fusion of Greek and Jewish thought in Alexandria,—yield little directly for the development of the idea of the kingdom of God, though in many indirect ways their influence was profound, sometimes in narrowing and despiritualizing the conception, and giving it a Pharisaic and political complexion, and again, through the synagogues and contact with Hellenic culture, preparing the way for a freer and more universal religion. The one fact which stands out clear is that in the time of our Lord neither Pharisee, nor Sadducee, nor Essene, had any hold of a conception of the kingdom which answered to the deep, spiritual, vital import of the idea in OT. The few who cherished more worthy views were to be sought for in the private circles of the pious who talked of these things (Mal 3¹⁶), and 'looked for redemption in Jerusalem' (Lk 2²⁵·³⁸). The idea of the kingdom of God in its spiritual meaning had to be *recovered*, or more properly *discovered*, in a worldly, legalistic, Sadducean age. To bring it again, with the force of a new revelation, before the minds of men, in union with the call to repentance, was the task of John the Baptist. Then, when the time was fulfilled, Jesus came, preaching the gospel of the kingdom (Mk 1¹⁵).

II. The Teaching of Jesus on the Kingdom of God.—1. Here we may first glance at the relation of Jesus to His forerunner. St. Matthew informs us that John came preaching in the wilderness of Judæa, and saying, 'Repent ye : for the kingdom of heaven is at hand' (Mt 3²). Elsewhere this expression is not put in the mouth of the Baptist ; but there is no doubt from the tenor of his message, and from the declarations of Jesus regarding him (Mt 11¹⁰⁻¹⁴), that the kingdom was the burden of his preaching. Through him a revivification of the idea took place in the minds and consciences of the people, and the greatest commotion was created by his proclamation that the kingdom was just at hand (Mt 3⁵·⁶, Mk 1⁵). But the kingdom announced by John was something very different from the political kingdom of Pharisaic expectation. He revived the terrors, warnings, and predictions of the later OT prophecy, and gave them a forcible and immediate application to his own times. He struck at the root of the delusion that mere descent from Abraham would avail for entrance to the kingdom; proclaimed the need of repentance and changed conduct as the condition of forgiveness, declared the imminence of judgment, and a sifting of good from bad at Messiah's appearance (Mt 3⁷⁻¹⁰, Lk 3⁷⁻⁹). The kingdom he announced was ethical in its demands (Lk 3¹⁰⁻¹⁴), was connected with the person of a Coming One, who should execute the work of judgment, and also baptize with the Holy Spirit and with fire (Mt, Mk, Lk), and was immediately to be expected. John was fully conscious of his own inferiority, and of the impotence of his water-baptism to effect a real change of heart in the multitudes who resorted to him, and his hope was therefore placed in this Greater One, who had the baptism of the Spirit (Jn 1¹⁹⁻²⁷). The question, then, arises : Was Jesus from the first conscious that He was this Greater One whom John had proclaimed, or did He begin His ministry, as some have contended (*e.g.* Colani and Renan), only as a disciple and imitator of the Baptist ? That the former view is the correct one would be, of course, put beyond doubt, if the intimations of the Fourth Gospel were accepted (Jn 1³⁰⁻³⁴·⁴⁰⁻⁵¹ 3. 4²⁶ etc.) ; but the Synoptics, also, in their narratives of the relations of John and Jesus at the baptism (Mt 3¹³⁻¹⁷ and parallels), of the temptations (Mt 4¹⁻¹¹ and parallels), which would have no meaning unless Jesus was consciously entering on His work as Messiah, of the early use by Jesus of the title 'Son of Man' (Mk 2¹⁰ etc.), and by many other indications, show plainly that this is the right view to take. (Baldensperger can only get over the use of 'Son of Man,' which he also accepts as a Messianic title, by arbitrarily assuming that all the incidents in which this name occurs took place after Peter's confession—a violent and unwarrantable hypothesis, *Selbstbewusstsein Jesu*², p. 252). *How* this consciousness of His Messiahship was developed in Jesus is a question which

lies beyond our present limits. It was plainly there from the period of the baptism, and we have earlier indications of its presence (Lk 2⁴⁹, see below). We take it, therefore, as a datum to start from, that when Jesus began to preach the gospel of the kingdom He already knew His vocation to be its Founder and its Lord.

2. The relation of the Baptist to OT prophecy (Mt 11¹³·¹⁴), and the historical connexion of Jesus with John, make it evident that, in announcing the approaching advent of 'the kingdom of heaven,' Jesus had in view the very kingdom which the prophets had foretold. We have already seen that this precise expression is not met with in OT (most nearly in Dn 7¹⁴·¹⁸·²²), but Jesus in many places unmistakably takes over the OT theocratic idea (Mt 8¹¹·¹² 21⁴³ 22⁴¹⁻⁴⁶ etc.). This suggests the further question as to our Lord's own customary designation for this divine kingdom. In Mt, with but four exceptions (ch. 6³³ is an incorrect reading), the phrase employed is always 'the kingdom of heaven'; whereas the other Gospels and the remaining books of NT have uniformly 'the kingdom of God.' Which was Christ's own expression, or did He use both? (so Bruce). The contrast between Mt and the other Gospels, even in parallel passages, compels us to suppose that one is more original than the other, and the question is which. Some (as Weiss) prefer 'kingdom of God,' but preponderating reasons seem to be in favour of the form in Mt. There is reason to believe that the phrase מַלְכוּת שָׁמַיִם (rule [Dalm. *Worte Jesu*, 77 ff.] of the heavens) was a current expression in Rabbinical circles (see passages in Lightfoot and Wetstein on Mt 3²; and especially Schoettgen on Mt 11²⁹); and there is probability in the conjecture that this may have been the form employed by our Lord in His ordinary Aramaic preaching (not necessarily to the exclusion of an occasional use of the other), and that, in translating into Gr., the evangelists may either, as in our existing Mt, have retained this Heb. formula, or have (as in Mk, Lk, etc.) rendered it by its equivalent, more suitable to Gentiles — 'the kingdom of God.' This is further supported by comparison with the language of the Lord's Prayer (Mt 6⁹·¹⁰, Lk 11²). No distinction in meaning of any importance can fairly be established between the two expressions, which denote the kingdom as, on the one hand, God's, and, on the other, heavenly in its origin, aims, and end. 'The kingdom of heaven, as appears from the prophecies of Daniel, is the kingdom of the Messiah ; while the Lord's Prayer teaches us that it is the kingdom of God's Spirit, in which the will of man is made conformable to the will of God—a kingdom which comes from heaven, is heaven on earth, and ends in heaven' (Lange on Mt 3²).

3. In examining the teaching of Jesus on the nature of this kingdom, we do well to start from the point already established—*the connexion of the kingdom with His own Person*. Nothing is plainer than that, in His own view, Jesus is not simply the Founder of this kingdom, but it is *His* kingdom as well as the Father's, and He is Lord and King over it (Mt 13⁴¹ 16²⁸ 20²¹ 25³⁴·⁴⁰ etc.). The idea here is moulded by that of the OT theocracy, in which God was at once the King of the chosen nation, and exercised His functions through a visible representative. This relation, only brokenly and typically illustrated in the descendants of David, is now, in accordance with prophecy, perfectly realized in the Messianic King, whose solidarity with God in heart and will is complete (Mt 11²⁷, Jn 4³⁴ 5³⁰ 6³⁸ etc.). But the connexion of the kingdom with the Person of Jesus is more intimate even than this. Jesus is not only the

Founder and Lord of the new theocracy, but is Himself the vital germ of it,—the living embodiment and representative of its principle, — the actual type of the new relation of sonship to God into which men are invited to enter through Him, —so that the kingdom of God may truly be said to have existed on earth in His Person from the first moment of His manifestation. It is through vital relation to Him, as the Synoptics, and still more clearly the Fourth Gospel, show,—through reception of His Person and message, through faith in Him, surrender to Him, submission to His rule, keeping His commandments, which is synonymous with doing the will of the Father, through union with Him as the branches and the vine, etc.,—that the kingdom is constituted (Mt 7^{21-23} 8^{10} 11^{28-30} $16^{24. 25}$, Jn 15^{1-8} etc.). With all this goes a profoundly modified conception of the *nature* of the sovereignty in this new kingdom of God, which, as founded, not by worldly means of conquest and violence, but by humility, by service, by deeds of mercy, by suffering, by witness for the truth (Mt $11^{4-6. 29}$ 13^{19} $18^{3. 4}$ 20^{25-28}, Jn $18^{36. 37}$), is ruled in like manner, not by force or tyranny, but by the suasive influences of love over freely surrendered hearts (Mt 11^{28-30} 22^{37-40}, Jn 14^{15} 15^{15}).

4. In light of this essential relation of Jesus to His kingdom, we are now prepared to consider the *two great titles* by which this relation was expressed by Jesus Himself—'Son of Man,' and 'Son of God.' The second of these titles, to which we return below, is, in the Synoptics at least, more frequently given to Jesus by others than assumed by Jesus Himself (Mt 3^{17} $4^{3. 6}$ 14^{33} $27^{40. 54}$, Mk 3^{11} 15^{39} etc.), but it is constantly implied, even in the earlier Gospels, in His mode of speaking of His Father, and is sometimes emphatically expressed (*e.g.* Mt 11^{27} $16^{16. 17}$ $26^{63. 64}$). In Jn it is the more common. It is otherwise with the title '**Son of Man**,' which is the favourite designation of Jesus for Himself, but is never used by His disciples, or by the evangelists, in speaking of Him (only once outside the Gospels by Stephen, Ac 7^{56}). It occurs also in a singularly impressive and weighty form, with the definite article to both nouns, ὁ υἱὸς τοῦ ἀνθρώπου.* It was plainly on His own lips a Messianic title (Mk 2^{10}, Mt 16^{28} 26^{64}, Jn 5^{27} etc.), yet there is no evidence, apart from the doubtful Bk. of Enoch, that it was a current title for the Messiah in that time. The usage in the Gospels shows decisively it was not. It was not the wish of Jesus to make a public avowal of His Messiahship in His early ministry, but we find Him freely using this enigmatic title (Mk 2^{10}). The Jews evidently were perplexed as to its meaning (Jn 12^{34}). The phrase 'Son of Man' in Mt 16^{13} is manifestly not synonymous with 'Christ,' either in popular acceptation or in the minds of the disciples. We must therefore hold it for certain that the expression was one welling up from the depths of the original consciousness of Jesus, and expressing some profound conception of His mission. What precisely this is, is a point on which there is wide difference of opinion (see the various views well stated in Lietzmann's *Der Menschensohn*, 1896). Wendt will have it (*Die Lehre Jesu*, ii. pp. 442, 443) that the title is meant to designate its possessor as a weak, creaturely being—member, Messiah though He was, of the weak, creaturely race of humanity. But this theory cannot be carried through without doing violence to many passages in which this name is

* Lietzmann in his tractate, *Der Menschensohn* (1896), seeks to break the force of this by going back from the Gr. to the Aram., in which בר נשא means simply 'man' (unemphatic). But the emphatic force of the expression cannot be erased from the Gospel usage. Lietzmann stands almost alone in holding that the term was not used by Jesus, but found its way into the Gospels from a Christian misconception.

evidently used as a title of dignity; the highest functions being claimed by Jesus, not, as Wendt's argument would require, despite of His being Son of Man, but because He is Son of Man (Mk 2^{28}, Jn 5^{27} etc.). More probable is the generally accepted view which connects this title with the language of Dn 7^{13} already alluded to—'there came with the clouds of heaven one like unto a Son of Man,' etc. (cf. Mt 26^{64}). Whatever view be taken of this expression,—whether it be supposed to denote an individual (so Beyschlag), or only to symbolize the *humanness* of the new kingdom in contrast with the kingdoms of the beasts which had preceded,—there lies in it at least the notion that the kingdom of God, not resting like the others on brute force, would be the first in which the divine ideal of humanity would be realized; so that our Lord, in taking this title, may well have expressed the consciousness that there had appeared in Him the New Man of the race—the type and representative of a new humanity—one who, because of this perfection of His humanity, stood in a relation to all men, and was their natural ruler and Lord in the kingdom He had come to found. There lay thus, in the use of the title by Jesus, at once the idea of the reality and truth of His humanity, the consciousness of His unique perfection as man, the sense of His universal relation to the race, and the knowledge of His calling and function to be the Messianic King.* He was Son of Man, as embodying in Himself the divine idea of a godlike humanity—*the* Son of Man, as the unique individual of the race who sustained this character— the Son of *Man* in the universal sense, as representing in His Person, not the seed of Abraham alone, but the whole of mankind. This title, accordingly, already expresses the principle of universality of the new religion in its contrast with the national limitation of Judaism, and the current conception of the Messiah. Baldensperger is therefore only partially correct when he rejects the 'ideal man' theory of this title, and ridicules it as an attempt to carry back our nineteenth-century notions into a period to which they were quite strange (2nd ed. p. 178). There lies behind it, certainly, no such abstract conception as 'the ideal man,' yet the reality which that phrase expresses is undoubtedly present from the beginning as an element in the consciousness from which the title springs.

We return to the more particular consideration of the *second* title, '**Son of God**,' which, on the face of it, expresses the consciousness which Jesus had of His relation to God, just as the previous title expressed His consciousness of the relation He sustained to men. Those are undoubtedly right who warn us off from seeking, in the first instance, a metaphysical interpretation of this title. We shall not reach Christ's own meaning in the use of it, or the fact it represents in His consciousness, by starting with the definitions of the Nicene Creed; but must seek our clue rather in the line of the OT conceptions through which originally it came also to Him. As J″ was the Father of His nation Isr. (Ex $4^{22. 23}$, Hos 11^{1}), so was He peculiarly the Father of the theocratic King, 'I will be his Father, and he shall be my Son' (2 S 7^{14}, Ps 89^{20}). We have seen already what the relation imported in the theocratic ruler—a perfect unity with God in will and aim; such a solidarity between God and His visible representative that the purposes of the former, and those only, were perfectly executed by the latter. We saw, too, how entirely this ideal failed to be realized on the purely human basis of the OT theocracy, and

* This is, in substance, Neander's view (*Life of Christ*), and a better has not yet been found.

how manifest it became, that if ever it was to be realized, the King in whom this was done must stand in a relation of nearness and unity to J" transcending the limits of ordinary humanity—that he must possess an exceptional dignity of *nature*, raising him to a superhuman rank of character and authority (Is 9[6, 7] etc.). When, now, we turn to the Gospels, we cannot but notice that the same ideas prevail. 'Son of God' is there also a Messianic title (Mt 16[16] 26[63, 64], Jn 1[49] 10[36] etc.); and it connotes, with whatever else, a perfect oneness of thought, will, aim, sentiment, purpose, between the Father and the Son—entire moral and spiritual unity, reciprocal and exclusive knowledge, the perfect adoption by the Son of the divine ends as His own, and absolute fidelity and devotion in the execution of them (Mt 11[27], Jn 5[20] 10[15, 30] etc.). And this is not less clearly associated in Jesus with the consciousness that this unbroken oneness in spirit with God is connected with some peculiar distinction in *nature*—that His relation to God as Son is not that of other men, but that He is the Son *par excellence*—*the* Son of God in a special and solitary relation of life and affection. It is observable, accordingly, that even while He recognizes the divine affinity in every human soul, invites men to sonship in His kingdom, and teaches His disciples to address God, and to love and trust Him as their Father, He never places Himself as Son in the same category with them, but always carefully distinguishes His own relation to the Father from theirs (*e.g.* Jn 20[17]). Here, then, we come on that in the consciousness of Jesus which, while it cannot be properly spoken of as a metaphysical conception of His Person, yet legitimately lays the basis for those metaphysical, or at least transcendental, predications regarding Him which are found in the creeds, and even earlier in the Epistles, and the Johannine Prologue. What this transcendental element in the consciousness of Jesus implied, can only be inferred from His various utterances respecting Himself in the Gospels, from the claims He makes, the prerogatives He assumes, the works He does, His promise of His perpetual presence with His Church, and of His return in glory, His glimpses even into a previous state of pre-existence, etc. (Mt 7[21-23] 18[20] 25. 26[64] 28[18-20], Jn 8[58] 17[5] etc.)—all matters which we cannot discuss here. One thing, however, is at once implied in what has just been said, namely, that whereas in the OT conception the official sense of the phrase 'Son of God' overshadows the personal, in the case of Jesus it is precisely the other way—the official relation is *grounded* in the personal. He is the Son of God as Messianic King, because He is first Son of God by nature. He is 'the Son' *simpliciter*; and this consciousness of a personal peculiarity in His relation to the Father, springing as it no doubt did from His sense of entire spiritual oneness, may be presumed to go back in some form to the earliest dawn of His reflective life (cf. Lk 2[49]). There was no period of His life in which He did not know God as His Father; was not conscious of an untroubled relation of union with Him; did not find in His soul the reflection of His character; and did not yield to Him His entire love, trust, and obedience. We cannot err, therefore, in finding the root of Christ's conception of His kingdom *in His own perfect consciousness of His filial relation to His Father*, together with the new views of religion, of righteousness, of duty, and of blessedness, which this implied. The consciousness he had of Himself as Son, with the correlative idea of God as Father, leads to the designation of the kingdom as 'the kingdom of the Father' (Mt 13[43]); just as St. Paul also speaks of it as 'the kingdom of the Son of His love,' into which the Father has translated us (Col 1[12, 13]). The kingdom, in this view, is the

sphere of God's fatherly love and rule in hearts truthfully submitted to Him through His Son; of His gracious, unbounded self-communication for the blessing and enrichment of His people. This doctrine of Jesus as to the divine Fatherhood, however, is not offhand to be identified, as it so often is, with the doctrine of the paternal love of God to all men, which has for its correlate the doctrine of a universal natural sonship of man. It is surprising how little basis is found for this doctrine of a universal Fatherhood and sonship in the recorded sayings of Jesus. It is doubtful if it is to be found anywhere, except by implication in the parable of the Prodigal (Lk 15[11-32]). That Christ recognizes a natural kinship of every human soul with God (cf. Gn 1[26, 27]), and a calling and destination of every individual to be a son of God in His kingdom, is indeed most true; but Fatherhood and sonship in His ordinary speech is a relation *within* His kingdom, not a relation of mere nature, but (so throughout the whole NT) the result of a divine act of grace placing man in this relation (the Pauline υἱοθεσία; cf. Jn 1[12, 13]), and of a supernatural impartation of a new nature and life (Jn 3[5, 6]). In comparison with this higher, divine relation, the natural sinks, as it were, into the background. We gain, indeed, the right point of view for understanding this doctrine of Jesus on the divine Fatherhood, only when we observe that it takes its origin, not from the general relation of God to the world, or even from the relation of God to believers in His kingdom, but primarily from the relation of the Father to Himself. It does not begin at the circumference—the general relation of God to mankind, but at the centre—the special, unique, incomparable relation of the Father to the Son. It is in the relation to the Son that we have, so to speak, the spring of Fatherhood in the heart of God. This relation, which in its fulness none other can share, is then in its measure extended to those who are the members of His kingdom; and, finally, extends itself even as a blessed possibility to all mankind, in harmony with man's original destination (parable of Prodigal).

5. With the help of this clue afforded us by the personal consciousness of Jesus, we are able to advance to some nearer determination on the subject of His kingdom. If Jesus was indeed sure of Himself from the first as the Son of God,—if He had this perfect filial consciousness from the beginning,—there falls away every ground for assuming that His views *fluctuated* and *varied* regarding this kingdom He came to found, or that He did not clearly grasp it from the outset in its essential nature, laws, and conditions of success. The Gospels give us no warrant for supposing that such fluctuation took place; the only point which can with plausibility be raised being that discussed below: whether from the first He apprehended the necessity of His death. If the essential feature in His kingdom was the admission of men through grace into a relation of sonship akin to His own, He could not have varied in His conception of it, of its righteousness, or of the general conditions of entrance into it, unless His own self-consciousness had varied. A second weighty result we reach is, that if Jesus was fully conscious of Himself as Son of God, and Founder of this kingdom, from the first, this kingdom in His view could not have been a merely *future* thing, but must have been conceived of as *already existing*. This, again, is a point on which much discussion has been raised: whether, namely, the kingdom of God, in the teaching of Jesus, has only an eschatological significance (thus Kaftan, Schmoller, etc.), or whether it denotes an already existing reality (Ritschl, Wendt, etc.). The true view, surely, is that it is not either exclusively. It *both* has a

present being upon earth, and has a perfect, glorified form in eternity. The existence of the kingdom as a present, developing reality is implied in the parables of growth (mustard seed, leaven, seed growing secretly, Mt 13, Mk 4$^{26-32}$) ; in the representations of it, in its earthly form, as a mixture of good and bad (wheat and tares, the net of fishes, Mt 13); in the description of the righteousness of the kingdom (Sermon on the Mount) which is to be realized in the ordinary human relations ; as well as in many special sayings (e.g. Mt 12^{28}, Lk 16^{16} 17^{21}, whether ' within' or ' among ' makes no difference). But, apart from specific declarations, the truth is implied in the simple fact that Jesus Himself was present in the full consciousness of His Sonship and calling to be the Founder of the kingdom, gathering disciples to Himself as the nucleus of a future society. We have formerly observed that in the Person of Jesus, even had there been no other, the kingdom of God was already present in humanity. In Him lay the vital germ of that kingdom ; He was the bearer and representative of its principle of Sonship ; in Him its powers and grace were made manifest (Mt 12^{28}). When, as the result of His activity, a band of disciples were drawn around Him, the members of which were introduced by Him into a new fellowship with God, and in whose hearts the principle of a divine rule was manifestly established, it was more than ever evident that the kingdom of God had begun on earth.

6. Still endeavouring to keep in view the inward and essential nature of this kingdom, or reign of God among men, which Jesus came to introduce, we are led by the representations of the Gospels to form such conceptions of it as the following. In what is said under these heads, the connexion of the kingdom with its Founder, and the teaching of Jesus on God, man, righteousness, salvation, will receive further illustration.

(a) The kingdom is in its beginnings, as just stated, the introduction of a new principle of divine rule into the hearts of men, through the word (Mt 13^{19}), the truth (Jn 18^{37}), the Spirit (Jn 3$^{5, 6}$), in virtue of which, changed in disposition (Mt 18^{3}), they become doers of the will of the Father in heaven (Mt 7^{21} etc.). It is therefore, in its principle, something inward, vital, invisible (Lk 17$^{20, 21}$). It is not the idea of Jesus, however, that this kingdom should be confined solely to the inward life. It is rather a principle working from within outwards for the renewal and transformation of every department of our earthly existence (marriage, the family, the state, social life, etc., Mt 19$^{3-9}$, Jn 2$^{1-11}$, Mt 22^{21} etc.). It is thus a growing, developing thing—as it is represented in the parables (Mt 13). The kingdom is not fully come till everything in human life, and in the relations of man in society, is brought into complete harmony with the will of God (Mt 6^{10} ; cf. Neander, Life of Christ, p. 89, Eng. tr.). While, however, Jesus gives us many incidental indications of the true relation of His kingdom to society, it is the spiritual or directly religious and ethical aspect of the kingdom which alone is more prominent in His teaching. ' The whole weight is rested on the inward disposition, on the new relation to God, on the new life of the Spirit, on the new righteousness proceeding from that life, on the new hopes and privileges of the sons of God. Everything is looked at in the light of the spiritual, the eternal. We read nothing in Christ of the effects of His religion on art, on culture, on philosophy, on politics, on commerce, on education, on science, on literature, on economical or social reform ' (Christian View of God and the World, p. 406). So also with the apostles. Yet a regenerating spirit has gone forth from the gospel of the kingdom in all these departments.

(b) On the other side, the kingdom of God is viewed as a sphere of privilege and blessing into which the disciple is admitted, in which he receives the forgiveness of his sins, attains the satisfaction of his spiritual wants, is filled with righteousness, and inherits the felicity of the eternal life (Mt 5$^{3-10}$ 6^{14} 19^{29} 25$^{34. 46}$, Lk 4^{18}, Jn 6$^{27. 35. 40}$ 10^{28} etc.). It is the summum bonum for man—the good to be desired above all others, and for which everything else should be sacrificed (Mt 6^{33} 13$^{44-46}$ parables of Treasure and Pearl, 19^{29}, Lk 10^{42}, Jn 17^{3} etc.). The kingdom of God is thus emphatically with Jesus, as throughout the whole of Scripture, a kingdom of grace, the message of it ' good tidings ' (Mt 4^{23}, Lk 2$^{10. 11}$ 4^{22}). Its proclamation is a gospel, and it brings to man at once the fullest provision for his needs as a sinner, the highest satisfaction of his moral life, and the noblest end for his practical realization. God's royalty in His kingdom is shown not less by gift than by rule ; it is gracious, unstinted giving which is the foundation of the whole (Mt 7$^{7-11}$, Jn 5^{14} 6$^{32-35}$ 10$^{11. 28}$ etc.). It is thus the sphere of ' salvation,' though this term (σωτηρία) is still seldom used (Lk 19^{9}, Jn 4^{22} ; cf. Lk 1$^{69-72}$, Mt 16$^{25. 26}$ 19^{25}, Lk 19^{10}, Jn 3$^{14-17}$ 5^{34} 12^{47} etc.). The all-embracing expression for its good is ' eternal life'; yet in the Synoptics this term is always applied to the future consummation of that good (e.g. Mk 10^{30}), whereas in Jn it is used also to denote the present possession of the life of God by believers (Jn 5^{24}). Wendt justly points out, however, that even in Jn this is done only in occasional passages (Die Lehre Jesu, ii. p. 193), and the Synoptics also recognize in fact the present reception and enjoyment by believers of those blessings of the kingdom which Jn designates by ' eternal life' (Mt 5$^{3-10}$ etc.).

(c) The kingdom of God is inseparably associated with character in its members. The conditions of entrance into it are repentance and faith (Mk 1^{15}, Lk 7^{50} 13$^{3. 5}$ etc.) ; its blessings require for their reception such moral dispositions as poverty of spirit, humility, meekness, and lowliness of heart, spiritual hungering and thirsting (Mt 5$^{3. 6}$ 11$^{28. 29}$ 18$^{3. 4}$, Jn 4^{14} 6^{35}) ; as a kingdom of the truth, those only that are of the truth (Jn 18^{37}), of an honest and good heart (Lk 8^{15}), will receive it ; to know its doctrine, there must be a willingness to do the will of God (Jn 7^{17}) ; a desire for the honour of men is fatal to seeking the honour that comes from God (Jn 5^{44}). These states of mind are not the product of nature, but the result of a new spiritual birth (Jn 3$^{3. 5}$). Within the kingdom, the rule of God takes the form of the realization of a new and spiritual righteousness in the hearts of the members, and in their relations with each other and with the world. This righteousness is of the essence of the kingdom (Mt 6^{33}), and a great part of the teaching of Jesus relates to it (notably the Sermon on the Mount). It is at once part of the blessing of the kingdom (Mt 5^{6}), and a moral task set before the members for their accomplishment (Mt 5$^{13-16}$ 7^{21}). Its norm is the perfection of the Father Himself (Mt 5^{48})—the absolutely Good One (Mk 10^{18}). Like everything else in the kingdom, it is the product of a divinely given life, and develops from within outwards, from heart to conduct, as a good tree brings forth fruit (Mt 7^{17}). It differs from the righteousness of the scribes and Pharisees in motive and in aim, — being spontaneous, where theirs was formal and mechanical; spiritual, where theirs had regard only to the letter of the precept ; done with a sole respect to God, where theirs was man-pleasing (Mt 5^{17}–6^{18}). Its supreme principle is love (Mt 7^{12}, Mk 12$^{28-34}$). In relation to God, it takes the form of a spirit of dependence, and trust in His fatherly providence, which relieves from earthly care (Mt 6$^{25-34}$ 7$^{6-11}$) ; in its estimate of goods, it sets supreme store on the kingdom and its righteousness, and seeks these beyond all material blessings (Mt 6$^{19-23.\ 31-33}$) ; in its relation to man, it shows itself in mercy, forbearance, forgiveness of injuries, active beneficence, and in the bright shining of a holy example (Mt 5$^{5.\ 7.\ 38-48}$ 7^{12}). Its standards of judgment are the direct inversion of most of those which prevail in the world. It inverts, *e.g.*, the world's standards of blessedness in calling the poor in spirit, the mourning, the meek, the persecuted, etc., blessed (Mt 5$^{3-12}$; cf. Mal 3^{14}); the world's standards of greatness in pronouncing that true greatness lies in humility and service (Mt 18$^{3.\ 4}$, Mk 10^{44}, Jn 13$^{14.\ 15}$); the world's standards of wisdom in pronouncing the typical wise man of the world a fool (Lk 12$^{15-21}$) ; the world's standards of the chief good in making that consist in the kingdom and its righteousness (Mt 6^{33}), etc. Yet, in His doctrine of the righteousness of the kingdom, Jesus declares that He is not introducing anything absolutely new, but only unfolding the deepest spirit and teaching of law and prophets (Mt 5$^{17.\ 18}$ 22$^{36-39}$).

(*d*) It follows from the nature of the kingdom, as just described, that it is a kingdom entirely *spiritual* and *unworldly* in its nature (Jn 18^{36}, cf. Mk 10$^{42.\ 43}$)—supernatural and heavenly in its origin, powers, blessings, aims, and ends,—a kingdom free alike from national and ceremonial limitations, working by its own laws, and destined in the end to embrace all peoples. There is thus given us from another side what we saw to lie already in the Lord's designation of Himself as ' Son of Man '— the *universality* of the kingdom of God. Jesus already hints at this in Mt 8^{11} ' They shall come from the east and from the west, and shall sit down with Abraham,' etc. ; it is implied in His parables (Mt 13 ' the field is the world,' v.^{38} ; parable of Mustard Seed, etc.) ; is declared elsewhere (Mt 21^{43} ' The kingdom of God shall be taken from you,' etc.) ; and is announced in several sayings of Jn (*e.g.* Jn 12^{32} ' I, if I be lifted up, will draw all men unto me,' etc.). It comes out distinctly in the commission after the resurrection (Mt 28^{19}, Mk 16^{15}). It must also have been given to the consciousness of Jesus from the first by the prophecy in Dn (2$^{35.\ 44}$ 7$^{14.\ 27}$). Equally clear is it from the attitude of Jesus to mere ceremonial observances (Mt 15$^{1-20}$), and the critical, discretionary position He assumed to the whole Mosaic Law (*e.g.* the Sabbath, Mk 2^{28} ; marriage, Mt 19$^{6-9}$), that, while Himself observing the ordinances of His nation, He did not bind these on the members of His kingdom, but claimed the right as Son of Man—*i.e.* the Messiah—to alter, change, and abrogate them. His relation to the Jewish law He lays down in the principle that He came, not to destroy, but to fulfil (Mt 5^{17}). But this fulfilment was of a nature which meant in part destruction. His aim throughout was to judge the details of the law by reference to its underlying principle, and to the highest needs of men (Mk 2^{27}),—to go back at every point clearly from commands to principles, from outward conduct to dispositions of the heart, from forms of worship to spirit of worship—and this led to the dropping away of everything that was of mere provisional or temporary value. In the Sermon on the Mount, accordingly, and in all the Gospels, the whole stress is laid on the spiritual, the ethical, the eternal, and no reference is made to the ceremonial law at all. Nay, in the two similitudes of the Patch on the Old Garment, and the New Wine in Old Bottles (Mt 9$^{16.\ 17}$), Jesus indicates in the clearest way His consciousness that His kingdom was something radically new, and not simply a reformed and purified Judaism, and that the old forms were utterly inadequate to

contain the spirit of the new religion—that the latter would indeed burst and rend them, if it were put into them.

(*e*) The kingdom thus introduced into time and history has *two stadia*—an earthly and an eternal. The consideration of this point involves, finally, some investigations to which we proceed.

(*a*) A question of much importance here is as to the connexion which Jesus conceived to subsist between the founding of His kingdom and His *death*. The question is twofold : whether from the beginning of His ministry He clearly recognized the necessity of His death ; and, if He did, or even if this knowledge came later, what significance He attributed to His death for the founding of His kingdom. The first point is not to be settled on *a priori* grounds, but from an impartial consideration of the history. We cannot, however, doubt, from a review of all the circumstances, that Jesus *did*, from the commencement of His Messianic career, recognize the fate in store for Him—whether the precise *mode* of His death is another question (but cf. Jn 3$^{14.\ 16}$). It is true that it was not till after the memorable confession at Cæsarea Philippi that Jesus began to speak plainly to His disciples of His approaching sufferings and death (Mt 16^{21} etc.), but it does not follow that this was the beginning of His own knowledge on the subject. On the contrary, it is evident from the clearness, fulness, and decision with which He then announces His death and resurrection, that these topics had long occupied His own thoughts, and were already settled convictions in His mind. But we are not left entirely to conjecture. It is, on the face of it, in the highest degree improbable that one who from the outset grasped so clearly the essential nature of His kingdom in its contrast with the world, who had rejected the temptations to give it another shape (Mt 4$^{1-11}$), who predicted so accurately in His parables the stadia of its development in history (Mt 13), who forewarned His disciples of the certain persecutions which awaited them for His sake (Mt 5$^{10.\ 11}$ 10$^{16-24}$), could have been ignorant of the inevitable collision which must occur between Himself and the Jewish authorities, and which He must have foreseen could not but issue in His death. That He did anticipate it is expressly implied in His saying, ' The disciple is not above his Master,' etc. (Mt 10^{24}), and in His allusion to the bridegroom being taken away from them (Mt 9^{15}). More definitely, Jesus had deeply studied the prophecies, and in the very beginning of His ministry announced that those relating to the Servant of J" in Is were fulfilled in Himself (Lk 4^{21}). But He could not be unaware of what was written of the death of this Servant in Is 53 ; and the recorded greeting of the Baptist, ' Behold the Lamb of God,' etc. (Jn 1^{29}), would recall that passage. There are other sayings in Jn—those to Nicodemus (Jn 3$^{14.\ 16}$), and especially the enigmatic utterances about giving His flesh for the life of the world (Jn 6$^{51-56}$)— which point in the same direction. But if Jesus foresaw His death, it was impossible that He should not have regarded His temporary submission to it as in some way necessary for the ends of His kingdom—for, that His subjection to death was, and could be, *only* temporary, He never, in the strength of His Messianic consciousness, doubted. His announcement of His death is always conjoined with the declaration of His rising again (Mt 16^{21} 20^{19} etc.) ; and the shadow of the Cross never clouds for a moment His assurance of His final coming in glory to judge the world (Mt 7^{22} 10^{23} 13^{41} 16^{27}, Lk 12^{8} etc.). If, accordingly, we ask, What was the significance which Jesus attached to His death in connexion with the establishment of His kingdom ? we are driven, by the passages already cited, to see in it more than the mere illustration of a general law of sacrifice (Jn 12[24-26]), or a proof of fidelity in His vocation. We must take an incidental saying like Mk 10[45] 'For even the Son of Man came . . . to give His life a ransom for many,' not as if it stood alone, but with the depth and seriousness of meaning supplied by a context of similar utterances. The great passage on the expiatory sufferings of the Servant of J" (Is 53) must probably be our clue here also. We recall the word of the Baptist, 'The Lamb of God, that taketh away the sin of the world' (Jn 1[29]); the saying in which His death is connected with salvation in the conversation with Nicodemus ('as Moses lifted up the serpent,' etc., in Jn 3[14]; for though the 'lifting up' is a term of exaltation, we can hardly fail to associate it with His death); the 'giving his flesh for the life of the world' in Jn 6[51]; but, above all, the solemn and explicit words at the institution of the Supper, 'My blood of the covenant, which is shed for many unto the remission of sins' (Mt 26[28]; cf. Mk 14[24], Lk 22[20], 1 Co 11[25]). In keeping with this connexion of His death in the consciousness of Jesus with the remission of sins, we are told how, after the resurrection, the disciples were enjoined to make this a fundamental article of their preaching (Lk 24[47]). The death of Jesus, followed by His rising again, was evidently, in the Lord's own view, a decisive turning-point in the history of His kingdom, and in the spiritual history of the world; and not till that event had taken place, and the spirit had been given as the sequel to it, had the kingdom been fully constituted (Lk 24[49], Ac 1[5] 2[33]).

(β) It remains that we glance at *the eschatological declarations* of Jesus respecting His kingdom, for that its earthly phase is to be succeeded by a heavenly, in which the separation of good and bad shall be finally effected, and the ripened results of its long development shall be garnered up under new and glorious conditions, is a constant element in His teaching (Mt 13[40-43] 19[28. 29] 22[29. 30] 25[34. 46], Jn 14[1. 2] 17[24] etc.). This higher and eternal state, described as 'the regeneration' (παλιγγενεσία), or 'the resurrection' (*ut supra*), is introduced by the coming (παρουσία) of the Son of Man in glory, the resurrection of the dead, and a judgment which takes account of the conduct alike of the professed members of the kingdom, and of the nations of mankind (Mt 24, Jn 5[28. 29], Mt 7[21-23] 25, etc.). The principles on which this judgment proceeds are essential character, with its fruits in word and deed; faithfulness or unfaithfulness in duty; watchfulness; boldness in confessing Christ, or sin in denying Him; the presence or absence of love, etc. The separation which the judgment effects is, so far as appears, *final* (Mt 13[40-43] 25[46] etc.). In thus carrying the consummation of the kingdom into a future life, and connecting it with His personal return, Jesus goes entirely beyond OT limits; though there also the doctrines of a future life in the blessed enjoyment of God, and of a resurrection of the dead, are in process of formation (Ps 17[15] 49[14. 15] 73[23-26], Is 25[8] 26[19], Hos 6[3] 13[14], Dn 12[2] etc.). The doctrine of the resurrection was a cardinal one with the Pharisees; but it had its deep roots in the OT doctrines of man, of God, of sin, of death, and of salvation (Mt 22[29-33]), and, as connected by Jesus with the redemption and new life of His kingdom, is an essential part of His religion. The question, nevertheless, is one of some difficulty, how far the undoubtedly largely symbolical and figurative character of these discourses of Jesus on the last things entitles us to rely on them as real representations of the future? They assuredly do not give us a scientific, or perfectly objective, knowledge of the nature, the course, and relative order of these events, such as we can turn with precision into a theological system. Yet they are too definite and circumstantial to permit of our supposing that to the consciousness of Jesus they were *mere* figures, or were not intended to convey to us some real knowledge on the subjects of which they treat. This question presses especially in regard to the Parousia. Did Jesus, *e.g.*, anticipate for His kingdom a long period of development in the world before the end came; or was His Parousia regarded by Himself as immediate, or, at least, as not long to be delayed? Mt 24[29], with certain other passages (Mt 10[23] 16[28]), might seem to teach the latter, and we know that the times and the seasons were not within the human knowledge of the Son (Mk 13[32], Ac 1[6]); but a careful consideration of the whole teaching of Jesus will lead us to modify this first impression. We cannot mistake that the picture of the kingdom given us in the parables is that of a slowly developing reality, bound to a law of rhythm—'first the blade, then the ear, after that the full corn in the ear' (Mk 4[28]) —with the world and humanity as its sphere of manifestation, and good and evil growing side by side in it till both are fully ripe (Mt 13); and other passages suggest the like idea of a prolonged world-development, and a diffusion of the gospel among all nations before the end come (Mt 8[11] 21[43] 24[4-14], Lk 19[11. 12. 15]; cf. also the post-resurrection commissions, Mt 28[19. 20], Mk 16[15] etc.). Against these numerous indications the εὐθέως of Mt 24[29] (which may be variously accounted for) cannot be allowed to tell; especially as there are not wanting signs in the discourse itself of a nearer and a remoter horizon ('these things,' 'that day and hour,' vv.[34. 36]). The truth would seem to be that Jesus does not always speak of His Parousia (any more than of His kingdom) in the same sense; that it is to Him rather a process in which many elements flow together into a single image, than a single definite event, always looked at in the same light. Thus he says to the high priest, with obvious reference to the prophecy in Dn, 'Henceforth,' that is, from this time on, 'ye shall see the Son of Man sitting at the right hand of power, and coming on the clouds of heaven' (Mt 26[64]). He came in His resurrection; in the mission of the Comforter; in the power and spread of His kingdom, especially after the removal of the limitations created by the existing Jewish polity (which seems to be the meaning in Mt 16[28]); He comes in every great day of the Lord in the history of His Church; He will yet come more conspicuously in the events of the future; and, last of all, He will personally come to judge the quick and the dead. The kingdom advances to its goal, not peacefully or suddenly, but by a succession of great crises (Mt 24), and each of these is in a sense the coming of the Son of Man (cf. Reuss' *Hist. of Christ. Theol.* i. pp. 217, 218; Bruce's *Kingdom of God*, ch. 12; Orr's *Christian View of God and the World*, p. 384).

7. One topic more, of considerable importance, we must allude to before leaving this part of our subject. It is the much canvassed question of the relation of the idea of the kingdom of God to that of *the Church*. If our previous exposition is correct, these ideas are not quite identical, as they have frequently been taken to be. The kingdom of God is a wider conception than that of the Church. On the other hand, these ideas do not stand so far apart as they are sometimes represented. In some cases, *e.g.* in Mt 16[18. 19], the phrase 'kingdom of heaven' is practically synonymous with the Church. The Church is, as a society, the visible expression of this kingdom in the world; is indeed the only society which does formally profess (very

imperfectly often) to represent it. Yet the Church is not the outward embodiment of this kingdom in all its aspects, but only in its directly religious and ethical, *i.e.* in its purely spiritual, aspect. The direct business of the Church, *e.g.*, is not to take to do with art, science, politics, literature, etc., but to bear witness for God and His truth to men, to preach and spread the gospel of the kingdom, to maintain God's worship, to administer the sacraments, to provide for the self-edification and religious fellowship of believers (cf. *Christian View of God and the World*, pp. 409, 410). That Jesus contemplated the union of the members of His kingdom into such a visible society—or Church—is evident from direct statements, as in Mt 16¹⁸ ('on this rock I will build my Church'); from the institution of the apostolate (Mt 10¹⁻⁵); from the instructions about baptism (Mt 28¹⁹, ²⁰); from the rules of discipline He lays down (Mt 18¹⁵⁻¹⁸), etc.: while the important functions which He intrusts to this society are seen from the terms in which He speaks of it; the promises He gives to it (Mt 16¹⁸⁻²⁰ 18²⁰); the authority He confers upon it (Mt 16¹⁹ 18¹⁸, Jn 20²³); the sacraments He leaves with it; and the assurances of His perpetual presence, which are among His last words to it (Mt 28²⁰). In Jn the deeper root of the Church idea is manifest in the conception of the living union of the branches with the vine (Jn 15¹⁻⁷).

III. The Teaching of the Epistles and other Books of NT on the Kingdom of God.—In passing from the Gospels, and especially the Synoptics, to the remaining writings of NT, we are sensible at once of a great difference in the use made of this conception of the kingdom of God. It is no longer the central and all-comprehending notion which it was in the popular teaching of Jesus, but sinks comparatively into the background, where it does not altogether disappear, and is employed, so far as retained, in an almost exclusively eschatological sense. The difference is accounted for by the altered circumstances of the Christian community. It was no longer the Jesus of the earthly ministry, but the Risen Lord, that was the centre of the faith and hope of the Christian believers. The Christ had died, had risen again, was exalted to heaven, had poured out the Spirit, was expected speedily to return to judgment; and interest was concentrated on the meaning and bearings of these great facts on salvation. The gospel had passed over from Jews to Gentiles, and Churches were everywhere being formed and organized. Under these changed conditions it was inevitable also that nomenclature should change, and that the higher stage on which the kingdom of God had entered in history should evolve a speech, and forms of conception for itself, adapted to its new wants. And this is what actually happened. Instead of the kingdom, it is now Christ Himself who is the centre of preaching; in speaking to Gentiles, His work, the blessings of His salvation, the nature and fruits of the new life of the Spirit, the hopes connected with His appearing, are naturally dwelt on without reference to the theocratic conception; as respects the earthly form, the idea of the Church necessarily displaces every other. The one sphere which these altered conditions did not touch was the eschatological, and here accordingly we find the idea of the kingdom, as one among other forms of conception, retained.

The phenomenon which here confronts us has, of course, struck every careful student of the NT. Harnack notices it in his *Dogmengeschichte*: 'It is not wonderful,' he says, 'that in the oldest Christian preaching "Jesus Christ" meets us as frequently as, in the preaching of Jesus, the kingdom of God itself' (i. p. 70; cf. Ritschl, *Rechtferti-*

gung, ii. p. 293 ff.; Kaftan, *Das Wesen*, p. 229, etc.). In Ac there are a few references which show that 'the kingdom of God' was still the general formula for the substance of Christian preaching (8¹² 14²² 19⁸ 20²⁵ 28²³, ³¹). But in the Epistles the term recedes decidedly into the background, and, as just stated, is generally used in an eschatological sense. 1 P does not use the expression; Ja only once (βασιλεία alone, Ja 2⁵). The Pauline theology is developed from its own basis, without any systematic attempt to fit it to this conception. In He it is other ideas that rule. The term 'kingdom' occurs only once, with a future reference (12²⁸). In the Johannine writings, the only occurrences are in two places in the Gospel, and denote (on Christ's lips) the present spiritual kingdom (3³, ⁵ 18³⁶—in the latter passage '*my* kingdom'). Generally, in this Gospel, as in the Epistles, the idea of the kingdom recedes behind that of 'life.' The case of Rev requires consideration by itself. Here, clearly, the idea of the kingdom is a governing one. Believers are made a kingdom unto God, and have the hope of reigning with Christ (1⁶ 3²¹ 5¹⁰); the Lamb is 'Lord of lords, and King of kings' (17¹⁴ 19¹⁶, cf. 1⁵); and the climax of His conflict with His enemies is that 'the kingdom of the world is become the kingdom of our Lord, and of His Christ; and He shall reign for ever and ever' (11¹⁵⁻¹⁷). The peculiarity in the apocalyptic representation, however, is the interpolation before the general judgment of 1000 years' reign of Christ with His saints on earth, following upon a binding of Satan, and a first resurrection (20¹⁻⁸). The picture stands alone in NT, though the idea involved in it—that of a 'pre-eminent blossoming time' for the Church before the final consummation—'a time in which the Church shall celebrate her Sabbath eve,—the eve before the Sabbath' (Martensen)—stands in no contradiction with the teaching of Jesus, is in every way probable, and is not unfamiliar to OT prophecy (Is 11⁶ 35, etc.).

At first sight the contrast between the apostolic gospel and the teaching of Jesus in the Synoptics, as respects the use made of this idea of the kingdom, is sufficiently marked; but when we consider the subject a little more carefully—looking rather to the essence of the doctrine than to the language employed—a substantial harmony is apparent. It is plain, from the notices in the Ac above cited, and from the incidental references, that 'the kingdom of God' was still a recognized formula to cover all the contents of Christian preaching; though, for the reasons already assigned, it had no longer the same prominence as at an earlier period; and, while the prevailing tendency was to limit this title to the kingdom of the future, and to connect it with the Parousia (*e.g.* 2 Th 1⁵, 2 Ti 4¹, ⁸, where ἐπιφάνεια), there are still a few cases which show that it was also applied to the present experience and state of privilege of Christians. Such, *e.g.*, are Ro 14¹⁷, where the kingdom of God is declared to consist, not in meat and drink, but in 'righteousness, and peace, and joy in the Holy Ghost'; and Col 1¹³, where believers are spoken of as already 'translated' into 'the kingdom of the Son of his love.' Apart, however, from the mere use of the term,—which is a secondary matter, —we cannot fail to see that everything that Christ *meant* by the present being of His kingdom is fully recognized and insisted on by the apostolic writers; Christ Himself is 'the Lord' (ὁ Κύριος); He is exalted to the place of universal dominion at God's right hand (Ac 2³³⁻³⁶, 1 Co 15²⁴, ²⁵, Eph 1²⁰⁻²³, Ph 2⁹⁻¹¹, He 1⁸ 2⁹, Ja 2¹, 1 P 3²² etc.); the kingdom is that of God *and of Christ* (Eph 5⁵, Col 1¹³); He exercises, therefore, a present unlimited sway in and over His people, and over all things for their sake

(Eph 1²²). Believers, again, are 'sons of God'; are, like Isr., 'an elect race, a royal priesthood, a noly nation, a people of God's own possession,' called 'out of darkness into his marvellous light,' 'a people of God' (1 P 2⁹· ¹⁰); they are renewed and dwelt in by His Spirit, which gives them the victory over sin in their members (Ro 7²⁵ 8¹⁻⁹); grace 'reigns' in them (Ro 5²¹ 6¹²· ¹³· ¹⁹);—in short, everything that can constitute a present kingdom of God on earth is acknowledged as existing in their case. If, therefore, there is any contrast with the teaching of Christ, it is in the advance to a higher, richer conception of the spiritual life than was possible at an elementary stage of instruction.

As respects the peculiarities of the doctrine of the kingdom of God in the Pauline Epistles, it is not necessary to add much to what has been said. The kingdom, in the apostle's view, as in Christ's own teaching, is connected with 'a redemption (ἀπολύτρωσις) through his blood,' and with forgiveness of sins (Col 1¹⁴, cf. Eph 1⁷). In its form of glory it awaits the appearing of Christ (2 Th 1⁵⁻¹⁰, 2 Ti 4¹· ⁸). But as in Rev we have the millennial doctrine, so in St. Paul we have the doctrine of the development of the man of sin and of the apostasy prior to the advent (2 Th 2³⁻¹⁰, cf. Mt 24¹¹· ¹²). It is still a moot question how far this doctrine is moulded upon current representations of Antichrist, and how far it is original (cf. references in Stanton's *Jewish and Christian Messiah*, p. 310). In St. John's Epistles the idea is more generalized (1 Jn 2¹⁸· ²² 4³); while in the Apocalypse it assumes the threefold form of the Beast, the False Prophet, and the Woman (Rev 13. 17). Finally, St. Paul alone gives us the sublime idea of an ultimate rendering up of the mediatorial kingdom by the Son to the Father, 'that God may be all in all' (1 Co 15²⁸).

It lies beyond the scope of this article to discuss the various shapes which this great scriptural idea of the kingdom of God has assumed in its course down the ages. The chief are the Patristic Chiliastic idea; the Mediæval or Catholic idea (as in Augustine, who, however, has glimpses of a wider truth in his *City of God*); the Reformation idea, which still identifies the kingdom too exclusively with the Church; and the various modern forms of conception in the Church and schools from Kant downwards. A great impulse has been given to the study of this notion by the later Ritschlian theologians, who have done much to restore it to its just importance. It must however, always remain doubtful—and the diversities in the apostolic teaching give additional force to the doubt—how far this single idea of the kingdom of God is fitted to serve as the principle of an exhaustive system of theology. Its proper place would seem to be *within* the system as defining the end in the light of which God's whole purpose in Christ is to be read; and in this way it is fitted to render essential service as the bond of union between dogmatic theology and Christian ethics — two departments which have hitherto stood too far apart. It does this service by introducing the idea of an *end* which is at the same time an *aim*— in setting before the individual as his life-task the realization of that kingdom of God which is God's own end in creation and redemption. The social tendencies of our age give this idea of the kingdom of God a special value for our own time; and we may expect that its importance will be increasingly recognized,—on the one hand, in its ennobling effect on the conception of Christian work, and the higher spirit of unity it tends to engender in those engaged in it; and, on the other, in broadening the conception of Christian duty as embracing the obligation to labour for the suprem-

acy of God's will in *all* the departments of private, social, and public life. It may be that the time has come for a resuscitation of this idea of Jesus which the exigencies of the apostolic age threw somewhat into the background; and that new applications and triumphs await it in the complexities of our modern social life, which even inspired men of the first generation could not reasonably foresee.

LITERATURE.—*Biblical Theologies of Old and New Tests.*: Oehler, Dillmann, Schultz, Riehm, Reuss, Weiss, etc.; Wendt, *Die Lehre Jesu*; Ritschl, *Recht. und Ver.* ii. iii.; Schmoller, *Die Lehre vom Reiche Gottes* (1891); Issel on same subject (1891); Köstlin in *SK* (1892); Candlish, *The Kingdom of God*; Bruce, *The Kingdom of God*; Stanton, *The Jewish and Christian Messiah*; Dalman, *Worte Jesu*.　　　　　J. ORR.

KINGDOM OF ISRAEL.—See ISRAEL (KINGDOM OF).

KINGDOM OF JUDAH.—See JUDAH (KINGDOM OF).

KINGS, I. AND II.—

1. Title, Scope, and Place in Canon.
2. Purpose.
3. Method and Characteristics of the Editor.
4. Date of the Editor.
5. Later Editors.
6. Sources and Composition of *Kings* considered in detail. Literature.

1. TITLE, SCOPE, AND PLACE IN CANON.—The title in AV, RV is 'The first (second) Book of the Kings.' Heb. (ב) מלכים א 'Kings I. II.'; LXX ΒΑΣΙΛΕΙΩΝ Γ (Δ). The use of the definite article in the English Version, '*the* Kings,' is therefore unwarranted. The narrative of Kings, like those of Samuel and Chronicles, is continuous, and the division into two books is clearly a later device, and no part of the scheme of the original editor.

The division of the Hebrew text of Kings into two books is not found in the MSS or in the early printed editions. It first occurs in the great Rabbinic Bible of Daniel Bomberg, published at Venice 1516–17, where an asterisk between 1 K 22⁵⁴ and 2 K 1¹ calls attention to a note in the margin:—כאן מתחילים הלועים ספר מלכי׳ רביעי. 'Here the non-Jews (*i.e.* Christians) begin the fourth Book of Kings.' A similar note is found between 1 and 2 S. Cf. Ginsburg, *Introd. to the Massoretico-critical Edit. of the Heb. Bible*, pp. 45, 930 f. Thus the division in MT seems to have been an innovation from LXX, Vulg. While in LXX no known MS presents an undivided text of 1. 2 K, 3. 4 K, 1. 2 Ch, it is interesting to note that in B the first verse of each second book appears also at the close of each first book respectively—a fact which shows that the divider of the books was desirous of indicating the inner connexion existing between the first and second divisions in each case. Cf. the manner in which in MT Ezr 1¹⁻³ᵃ (to וְיַעַל) repeats 2 Ch 36²²· ²³, of which it originally formed the unbroken continuation.

Kings takes up the history of the kingdom of Israel at the point which has been reached by the narrative of Samuel, viz. the last days of David's reign, and the appointment of Solomon as his successor. Passing from Solomon to an account of the circumstances which led to the disruption of the kingdom, the editor from this point gives a parallel history of the divided kingdoms of Israel and Judah. The fall of the northern kingdom having been recorded (2 K 17), the narrative continues with an account of the fortunes of the southern kingdom until its destruction by Nebuchadrezzar and the final deportation of the Judæans to Babylon, B.C. 586. The concluding section of the work carries the history down to the release of king Jehoiachin from prison in the 37th year of his captivity (B.C. 561), under Evil-Merodach, the successor of Nebuchadrezzar.

Kings belongs to the second of the three divisions of the Hebrew Canon—the *Nĕbhî'îm* (נְבִיאִים) or Prophets. In this division the book forms, with Joshua, Judges, and Samuel, the earlier section, styled *Nĕbhî'îm rîshônîm* (נְבִיאִים רִאשׁוֹנִים), the Former Prophets, as distinct from the Latter Prophets—Isaiah,

Jeremiah, Ezekiel, and the Twelve minor prophets. The justification of this nomenclature as it applies to Kings is to be gathered from consideration of the purpose which the writer of the book appears to have had in view.

2. PURPOSE.—Kings may accurately be described as a *history* of the period of the monarchy of Israel and Judah; and indeed, on account of the excellence of the sources employed for the composition of the work, takes first rank among the historical documents of the OT. But the mere compilation of a history is not the sole, or main, purpose of the writer. This may rather be characterized as *religious* and *admonitory*. History is employed as the vehicle of certain special religious lessons, drawn from the past, which the writer desires to inculcate upon his own age, and upon future generations. Thus an exhaustive employment of the historical sources which lay at his disposal is no part of his plan. So far from claiming to have utilized to the full his sources of information, he definitely and repeatedly refers to them as containing further details of fact likely to be of interest to the curious (I 11⁴¹ 14¹⁹·²⁹ *al.* See below). His special purpose is consistent with a selection from his materials; and this selection he carries out with such skill that the simple narration of the facts of history generally suffices to convey the lesson which the writer has at heart, even apart from his own comment and application.

The religious standpoint of the writer of Kings is that of the Book of Deuteronomy. He is deeply imbued with the spirit of this book, and his language is strongly coloured by its phraseology (see below).

Thus his aim is to apply to the past history of his race, from the time of Solomon and onward to his own day, the Deuteronomic standard, and to exemplify the view that prosperity is to be traced to a faithful regard for this standard, failure and catastrophe to its deliberate repudiation. The leading principles of Deut. upon which the writer of Kings desires to lay stress may be said, in the main, to be two: (i.) Whole-hearted devotion to J″ as Israel's only God, an obligation based upon the fact that J″ has made choice of Israel from among the nations as His special possession. (ii.) Sacrificial worship of J″ to be conducted only at one centre, viz. at the temple at Jerusalem, the place which J″ has chosen to set His name there. Conformity to these two principles is made the test to which the deeds of individual kings are brought, and in accordance with which a verdict is pronounced upon their characters.

The writer's ideal of kingship is David, the faithful worshipper and servant of J″. The piety of David is repeatedly the norm to which the action of his descendants is referred, and, when the times are darkest and apostasy most rampant, it is for David's sake that J″ still keeps a 'lamp' alight for him at Jerusalem.

Accordingly, the marked prosperity of the earlier part of Solomon's reign is due to the fact that he 'loved J″,' walking in the statutes of David his father' (I 3³). It is true that a qualification has to be added,—' only he sacrificed and burnt incense in the high places,' a mode of action alien to the enactment of Deut. with regard to the central sanctuary (Dt 12⁵ᶠᶠ· *al.*). This, however, can be lightly passed over, in view of the fact that the temple at Jerusalem was not yet built—a point in excuse which is expressly cited (v.²), apparently by some later reviser of the text (see below on ch. 3). The building of the temple by Solomon, as the sanctuary of J‴s choice, receives specially detailed treatment (5–7); its dedication affords scope for the utmost emphasis which can be laid upon its importance as the centre of J‴s manifesta-

tion to His people (ch. 8), and is the occasion of a renewal of the promises made to Solomon upon the condition of his faithful adherence to the spirit of the Deuteronomic code (ch. 9¹ᶠᶠ·).

The decay of Solomon's power is traced (ch. 11) to his marriage alliances with foreign women in deliberate infringement of J‴s command (Dt 7¹⁻⁴, Ex 34¹²·¹⁶ J; cf. Jos 23⁷ D²), and the consequent introduction of their idolatrous cults. This leads directly to the division of the kingdom, and the irrevocable loss of ten tribes to the house of David.

Jeroboam, the first monarch of the new kingdom of Israel, though J‴s appointed agent in bringing about the disruption (ch. 11²⁹ᶠᶠ·), yet no sooner succeeds to power than he sows the seeds of the ruin of the Northern Kingdom. The introduction of the calf-worship (ch. 12²⁵ᶠᶠ·) is regarded by the writer as *the* great blot upon Israel's history; and that not only as the worship of J″ under an outward symbol in contravention of the second commandment, but also as being, so far as the kingdom of the ten tribes was concerned, a fatal blow aimed against the centralization of worship at the temple in Jerusalem. It is on account of the maintenance of this cult of the calves up to the fall of the N. Kingdom that a uniformly unfavourable verdict is passed by the writer upon every king of Israel, even upon Jehu, who was most zealous as an eradicator of the foreign cult of Ba'al-Melḳart (II 10²⁹·³¹). II 17⁷⁻¹⁸·²¹⁻²³ presents us with the writer's reflections upon the causes which brought about the destruction of the kingdom of Israel, and, among other forms of idolatry cited as instances of unfaithfulness to J″, the 'great sin' of Jeroboam occupies the crowning position (vv.²¹⁻²³).

The kingdom of Judah, as the heritage of the house of David and the seat of J‴s sanctuary at Jerusalem, is regarded by the writer with more favourable eyes. Certain of its kings—Asa, Jehoshaphat, Jehoash, Amaziah, Azariah, and Jotham—have a more or less favourable estimate taken of their characters, though in every case it is mentioned to their disadvantage that 'the high places were not removed,' *i.e.* that the sacrificial worship of J″ was conducted elsewhere than at the central sanctuary only. In the cases of Hezekiah and Josiah the writer's verdict is one of unqualified approval. This is because Hezekiah appears as the initiator of a religious reformation which aims at the removal of the high places (II 18³ᶠᶠ·)—a policy which, after the idolatrous reaction under Manasseh and his son Amon, is fully carried out by Josiah upon the lines of the Deuteronomic code, which was discovered in the temple during the 18th year of his reign (II 22³ᶠᶠ·; see DEUTERONOMY).

It is this Deuteronomic reformation which, according to Kings as it stands in its present form, avails to delay the doom pronounced upon the kingdom of Judah on account of the apostasy of Manasseh (II 21¹⁰⁻¹⁵ 22¹⁵⁻²⁰). Perhaps, in the view of the first editor of the book, it might have availed to save the kingdom and to restore it to its pristine glory. This is a question which depends mainly upon consideration of the date which is to be assigned for the editing of Kings, and the character and extent of the additions which the book has received in later times.

3. METHOD AND CHARACTERISTICS OF THE EDITOR.—The editor of Kings, in dealing with a period of about 400 years in length, naturally makes use of earlier written documents for the purpose which he has in view. These documents, which form his sources of information, are in some cases expressly named. We have mention of 'the book of the acts of Solomon' סֵפֶר דִּבְרֵי שְׁלֹמֹה; I 11⁴¹), and of 'the book of the annals' דִּבְרֵי הַיָּמִים, 'acts of days,' *i.e.* 'daily record of events') of the kings of Israel'

(I 14[19] *al.*), and also 'of the kings of Judah' (I 14[29] *al.*).*

An official 'recorder' (הַמַּזְכִּיר), lit. 'the man who brings to remembrance'; LXX ὁ ὑπομιμνήσκων, ὁ ὑπομνηματογράφος, ὁ ἐπὶ τῶν ὑπομνημάτων) is mentioned among the ministers of David (2 S 8[16] 20[25]), Solomon (1 K 4[3]), Hezekiah (2 K 18[18. 37]), and Josiah (2 Ch 34[18]), and it may be assumed that the same office existed in the northern as in the southern kingdom. Probably, the work of this 'recorder' was that of *state-annalist*, whose duty consisted in taking note in writing of the important events of his time (cf. Est 2[23] 6[1]). It is not clear whether the editor of Kings had access to the annals of both kingdoms at first-hand, or whether his 'books of the annals' were not rather continuous histories based mainly upon the annals, and thus rather of a literary than an official character. The latter view is most generally adopted (cf. especially Kuenen, *Onderzoek*, § 24[8]; Cornill, *Einleitung*, p. 111 f.).

Besides these state records, the editor employs other nameless sources, which will be noticed in dealing in detail with the composition of Kings. At this point it should be observed that, as in the cases of the Hexateuch and of Judges and Samuel, so in the case of Kings, the editor's work is rather that of a *compiler* or *redactor* than that of an author strictly so termed. In giving a summary of the events of any particular reign, he appears, it is true, often to epitomize in his own language information which was contained at greater length in the 'Annals.' In other cases, however, he incorporates whole narratives, or sections of narratives, so far as they suit his purpose, in their original form, merely welding the sources together so as to construct a continuous history.

The proof that such was the method of the editor is to be found chiefly in the variations in style and language between different portions of Kings. Lengthy prophetical narratives stand side by side with brief political and statistical notices. Different sections are marked by dialectical peculiarities. Thus the great group of narratives which, commencing with I 17 and running on into the middle of II, relate the affairs of the kingdom of Israel, shows traces of a peculiar diction (see below on I 17 ff.). Later sections, again, exhibit a decadence of style, *e.g.* the use of the perfect with weak ו in place of ו consecutive with the imperfect—II 18[4. 36] 19[18] 21[4. 6] 23[4. 5. 8. 10. 13. 14. 15]. There are variations between section and section in the form of proper names:—II 12[17a] is peculiar among the Elijah narratives in using the form אֵלִיָּה beside the ordinary אֵלִיָּהוּ; II 18[14-16] employs the form חִזְקִיָּה instead of חִזְקִיָּהוּ, which is used uniformly in II 18[13. 17-20] end. And especially, as we shall proceed to notice, the editor himself is characterized by the use of a phraseology which serves as a clear indication of the portions of his book which are to be traced to his own pen. Another mark of the composite nature of Kings is the existence of a small number of discrepancies in detail: *e.g.* I 5[13ff.] (Heb. 27ff.) 11[28] are inconsistent with I 9[22]; I 12[22-24] disagrees with I 14[30].

To the editor is due the stereotyped form into which the introduction and conclusion of a reign is thrown, and which constitutes, as it were, the *framework* upon which the narrative as a whole is built. The regularity of the editor's method in the construction of this framework is worthy of special notice. The form in which the account of a reign is *introduced* is as follows. *For kings of Judah*:—1. A synchronism of the year of accession with the corresponding reigning year of the contemporary king of Israel, probably calculated by the editor himself. This, commencing with Abijah, naturally ceases with Hezekiah, upon the fall of the N. Kingdom. 2. Age of the king at accession. 3. Length of his reign. 4. Name of the queen-mother. This, together with 2, 3, is drawn from the 'Annals.' 5. A brief verdict upon the king's character, framed in accordance with the Deuteronomic standard. *For kings of Israel*:—1. A synchronism of the year of accession with the corresponding reigning year of the contemporary king of Judah. 2. Length of the king's reign. 3.

* In speaking of the named sources of Kings, we may add the reference to 'the Book of the Upright' (Book of Jashar as in Jos 10[13], 2 S 1[18]), which is to be restored from LXX after I 8[13] (LXX I 8[53]). οὐκ ἰδοὺ αὕτη γέγραπται ἐν βιβλίῳ τῆς ᾠδῆς; represents הַיָּשָׁר being a misreading of הַשִּׁיר ... הֲלֹא הִיא כְתוּבָה עַל סֵפֶר הַשִּׁיר

A brief verdict as to his character, always unfavourable, and generally consisting of two parts: *a*. Statement of the general fact that he did evil in the sight of J"; *b*. More special mention of his following the sins of Jeroboam. The *conclusion* of the account of a reign takes the following form:—

1. An indication of the editor's principal source, containing further details as to the king in question. Usually we read—

'And the rest of the acts of M. and all that he did, are they } of the Acts of Solomon?'
not written } of the Annals of the kings of Judah?'
in the book } of the Annals of the kings of Israel?'

וְיֶתֶר דִּבְרֵי שְׁלֹמֹה
וְיֶתֶר דִּבְרֵי פ' וְכָל־אֲשֶׁר עָשָׂה חָלֹא הֵם (הֵמָּה)
דִּבְרֵי הַיָּמִים לְמַלְכֵי יְהוּדָה
דִּבְרֵי הַיָּמִים לְמַלְכֵי יִשְׂרָאֵל
כְּתוּבִים עַל סֵפֶר

When further details, general or special, are mentioned as existing in the source, these usually stand immediately after 'and all that he did,' *e.g.* I 11[41] 'and his wisdom.' An exception is I 15[23] (Asa), where 'and all his might' precedes. Slight variations of this stereotyped form are—

A. 'And the rest of all the acts,' etc. וְיֶתֶר כָּל־דִּבְרֵי וג' I 15[23] (Asa).

B. Total omission of 'and all that he did'; without further details 5 times, viz. I 14[19] (Jeroboam) 16[20] (Zimri), II 14[18] (Amaziah) 15[11] (Zechariah) 15[15] (Shallum); with further details II 20[20] (Hezekiah).

Reading 'which he did' אֲשֶׁר עָשָׂה, 5 times, viz. I 16[27] (Omri), II 1[18] (Ahaziah of Israel) 14[15] (Jehoash of Israel) 16[19] (Ahaz) 21[25] (Amon); 'and what he did' וַאֲשֶׁר עָשָׂה I 16[5] (Baasha); 'and his might which he did' וּגְבוּרָתוֹ אֲשֶׁר עָשָׂה I 22[45] (46 Heb. Jehoshaphat).

C. 'Behold, they are' הִנָּם, in place of 'are they not!' הֲלֹא הֵם 5 times, viz. I 14[19] (Jeroboam), II 15[11. 15. 26. 31] (Zechariah, Shallum, Pekahiah, Pekah).

2. Mention of the king's death and burial—
(a) 'And M. slept with his fathers,
(b) and was buried
and they buried him } (with his fathers) in X.'

וַיִּשְׁכַּב פ' עִם־אֲבֹתָיו } וַיִּקָּבֵר
וַיִּקְבְּרוּ אֹתוֹ (עִם־אֲבֹתָיו) ב' *

3. Notice of the due succession of the king's son—
'And N. his son reigned in his stead.'

וַיִּמְלֹךְ פ' בְּנוֹ תַּחְתָּיו

The following table exhibits the regularity with which this system is carried out. When any fact above mentioned as belonging to the *introduction* is omitted in that position, but added subsequently in the narrative of the reign or in the summary, this is indicated by the sign + :—

Introduction.			Conclusion.
I 3[3] 11[4-6. 42]		David 12ab	I 2[10]
		Solomon 12ab3	11[41. 43]
	Kings of Judah.		
14[21. 22. 31]	234(5)+4	Rehoboam 12ab3	14[29. 31]
15[1-3]	1345	Abijah 12ab3	15[7a. 8]
15[9-11]	1345	Asa 12ab3	15[23a. 24]
22[41-44]	12345	Jehoshaphat 12ab3	22[45. 50]
8[16. 17]	1235	Jehoram 12ab3	II 8[23. 24]
II 8[25-27] 9[29]	12345+1	Ahaziah 2b	9[28b]
11[3]	+3	Athaliah ...	...
12[1-4]	1345	Jehoash 12b3	12[20. 22]
14[1-4]	12345	Amaziah 12b(a)	14[18. 20b. (22)+]
15[1-4]	12345	Azariah 12ab3	15[6. 7]
15[32-35]	2345	Jotham 12ab3	15[36. 38]
16[1-4]	1235	Ahaz 12ab3	16[19. 20]
18[1-3]	12345	Hezekiah 12a3	20[20. 21]
21[1. 2]	2345	Manasseh 12ab3	21[17. 18]
21[19-22]	2345	Amon 12b3	21[25. 26]
22[1. 2]	2345	Josiah 12b(3)	23[29. 30]
23[31. 32]	2345	Jehoahaz ...	...
23[36. 37]	2345	Jehoiakim 12a3	24[5. 6]
24[8. 9]	2345	Jehoiachin ...	...
24[18. 19]	2345	Zedekiah ...	...
	Kings of Israel.		
I 13[33]. 14[20a]	+3b2	Jeroboam 12a3	I 14[19. 20]
15[25. 26]	123ab	Nadab 1	15[31]
15[33. 34]	123ab	Baasha 12ab3	16[5. 6]
16[8. 13]	12 +3	Elah 1	16[14]
16[15a. 19]	12 +3ab	Zimri 1	16[20]

* Once with singular active verb used impersonally: וַיִּקְבֹּר אֹתוֹ 'And (one) buried him,' II 21[26] (Amon).

In the body of the narrative there are certain formulæ which are employed for the introduction of an historical notice, to indicate that it is more or less contemporaneous with the events of the narrative immediately preceding. The frequency with which these formulæ recur, especially in the citation of brief facts from the 'Annals,' renders the inference fair that they are due to the hand of the editor, and represent his methods of piecing together the extracts derived from his sources. Of such expressions the most usual is 'Then' (אָז), I 3¹⁶ 8¹. ¹² 9¹¹ᵇ. ²⁴ᵇ 11⁷ 16²¹ 22⁴⁹ (Heb.⁵⁰); II 8²²ᵇ 12¹⁷ (Heb.¹⁸) 14⁸ 15¹⁶ 16⁵.

When greater definiteness seemed desirable, other phrases are employed. These are: ' *In those days* ' (בַּיָּמִים הָהֵם), II 10³² 15³⁷ 20¹; ' *In his days* ' (בְּיָמָיו), I 16³⁴, II 8²⁰ 23²⁹ 24¹ and 15¹⁹ (emend after LXX); ' *At that time* ' (בָּעֵת הַהִיא), I 14¹, II 16⁶ 18¹⁶ 20¹² 24¹⁰; cf. I 8⁶⁵ 11²⁹, II 8²².

Besides the construction of the framework of the book and the welding of the material, the editor is also responsible for a number of passages of greater or less length, which point and enforce the religious purpose of his composition. These passages generally take the form of a commentary upon the causes which operated in bringing about the developments of history, framed in accordance with the Deuteronomic model. Very frequently, also, the editor allows himself considerable latitude in the expansion and adaptation of the *speeches* contained in his narrative, in illustration of the same standpoint. In passages of this character the editor's hand may readily be distinguished. They exhibit a constant recurrence of strongly marked phrases, to be found elsewhere for the most part only in Deuteronomy or in books which exhibit the influence of Deuteronomy, and therefore presumably derived from that source. Other expressions stand alongside of these Deuteronomistic expressions, and are of a part with the thoughts of which they are the vehicle; and these possess an individuality of their own, and are peculiar (or nearly so) to Kings. To the former class the following phrases may be assigned: *—

1. שָׁמַר מִשְׁמֶרֶת יְהוָה *Keep the charge of J"*: I 2³, Dt 11¹; cf. Jos 22³ (D²).

2. הָלַךְ בְּדַרְכֵי יְהוָה *Walk in the ways of J"*: I 2³ 3¹⁴ 8⁵⁸ 11³³. ³⁸, Dt 8⁶ 10¹² 11²² 19⁹ 26¹⁷ 28⁹ 30¹⁶, Jos 22⁵ (D²), Zec 3⁷, 1s 42²⁴, 2 Ch 6³¹, Ps 81¹³ (¹⁴ Heb.) 119³ 128¹; cf. Hos 14⁹ (¹⁰ Heb.).

3. שָׁמַר חֻקֹּתָיו וּמִצְוֹתָיו וּמִשְׁפָּטָיו וְעֵדְוֹתָיו *Keep his statutes, and his commandments, and his judgments, and his testimonies* (generally one or more of these terms is omitted): I 2³ 3¹⁴ 6¹² 8⁵⁸. ⁶¹ 9⁴. ⁶ 11³⁴. ³⁸ 14⁸, II 17¹³. ¹⁹. ³⁷ 18⁶ 23³. The phrase is of constant occurrence in Dt 4². ⁴⁰ 5²⁹ (²⁶ Heb.) 6² al.

4. לְמַעַן תַּשְׂכִּיל אֵת כָּל־אֲשֶׁר תַּעֲשֶׂה *That thou mayest prosper in* (or *cause to prosper*) *all that thou doest*: I 2³, Dt 29⁹ (⁸ Heb.).

5. לְמַעַן יָקִים יְהוָה אֶת־דְּבָרוֹ *That J" may* (might) *establish his word*: I 2⁴ 12¹⁵ (∥ 2 Ch 10¹⁵), Dt 9⁵; cf. I 6¹², 1 S 1²³, Jer 33¹⁴, Dn 9¹².

* The sign † indicates that all occurrences of any particular phrase are cited. The sign Rᴰ denotes the Deuteronomic Redactor, *i.e.* the prime editor of Kings.

6. בְּכָל־לֵב (לְבָב) (לְבָבוֹ, לְבָבָם), וּבְכָל־נֶפֶשׁ (נַפְשׁוֹ, נַפְשָׁם) *With all the* (his, their) *heart, and with all the* (his, their) *soul*: I 2⁴ 8⁴⁸ (∥ 2 Ch 6³³), II 23²⁵ (cf. Dt 34³¹), Dt 4²⁹ 6⁵ 10¹² 11¹³ 13³ (⁴ Heb.) 26¹⁶ 30². ⁶. ¹⁰, Jos 22⁵ 23¹⁴ (both D²), 2 Ch 15¹². II 23²⁵ adds וּבְכָל־מְאֹדֶךָ *and with all his might*, a use of the substantive מְאֹד only to be paralleled by Dt 6⁵.

בְּכָל־לֵב (לְבָב) (לְבָם) *With all his* (their) *heart*: I 8²³ 14⁸, II 10³¹.

7. שָׁמַר לְ אֶת־הַבְּרִית וְאֶת־הֶחָסֶד *Keep for him* (etc.) *the covenant and the kindness* (J" as subject): I 8²³ (∥ 2 Ch 6¹⁴), Dt 7⁹. ¹², Neh 1⁵ 9³², Ps 89²⁸ (²⁹ Heb.), Dn 9⁴; cf. I 3⁶ *hast kept for him this great kindness.*

8. כַּיּוֹם הַזֶּה *As it is this day* (the phrase calls attention to the fulfilment of a promise or threat): I 3⁶ 8²⁴ (∥ 2 Ch 6¹⁵) ⁶¹, Dt 2³⁰ 4²⁰. ³⁸ 8¹⁸ 10¹⁵ 29²⁸ (²⁷ Heb.), Jer 11⁵ 25¹⁸ 32²⁰ 44⁶. ²³, 1 Ch 28⁷, Dn 9⁷. ¹⁵; כְּהַיּוֹם הַזֶּה Dt 6²⁴, Jer 44²², Ezr 9⁷. ¹⁵, Neh 9¹⁰. In pre-Deut. writings the only occurrences are Gn 50²⁰ (E), 1 S 22⁸. ¹³ †. Gn 39¹¹ (J) is different.

9. עַמְּךָ אֲשֶׁר בָּחָרְתָּ *Thy people, which thou hast chosen*: I 3⁸ a reminiscence of Dt 7⁶ 14²; cf. 4³⁷.

10. הֵנִיחַ לְ אֱלֹהַי לִי מִסָּבִיב *J" my God hath given me rest on every side*: I 5⁴ (¹⁸ Heb.), 2 S 7¹. ¹¹, Dt 12¹⁰ 25¹⁹, Jos 21⁴² 23¹ (both D²); cf. Dt 3²⁰, Jos 1¹³. ¹⁵ 22⁴ (both D²).

11. Reference to J"'s *choosing* (בָּחַר) of Jerusalem as the seat of his sanctuary: I 8¹⁶. ⁴⁴. ⁴⁸ 11¹³. ³². ³⁶ 14²¹, II 21² 23²⁷. The allusion is to Dt 12⁵. ¹¹. ¹⁸. ²¹. ²⁶ 14²³. ²⁴. ²⁵ 15²⁰ 16². ⁶. ⁷. ¹¹. ¹⁵. ¹⁶ 17⁸. ¹⁰ 18⁶ 26² 31¹¹.

12. אֱלֹהַי יִשְׂרָאֵל אֵין־כָּמוֹךָ אֱלֹהִים בַּשָּׁמַיִם מִמַּעַל וְעַל הָאָרֶץ מִתָּחַת *J" God of Israel, there is no God like thee, in heaven above, or on earth beneath*: I 8²³ a reminiscence of Dt 4³⁹; cf. Jos 2¹¹ᵇ (D²).

13. אֲשֶׁר נָתַן (נָתַן, נָתְנוּ) לַאֲבוֹתָם *Which thou gavest* (he, I gave) *to their fathers*: I 8³⁴. ⁴⁰. ⁴⁸ 14¹⁵, II 21⁸; cf. Dt 26¹⁵, and the common phrase of Dt *which J" our* (your, etc.) *God is about to give us* (you, etc.), 1²⁰. ²⁵ 2²⁹ 3²⁰ 4⁴⁰ 5¹⁶ *al.*

14. בְּאַחַד שְׁעָרָיו *In any of his gates*: I 8³⁷ (upon the authority of LXX, Pesh., in place of the impossible בְּאֶרֶץ שְׁעָרָיו, MT), Dt 15⁷ 16⁵ 17² 23¹⁶ (¹⁷ Heb.); cf. 18⁶ †.

15. כָּל־הַיָּמִים אֲשֶׁר הֵמָּה חַיִּים עַל־פְּנֵי הָאֲדָמָה *All the days that they live upon the land*: I 8⁴⁰ (∥ 2 Ch 6³¹), Dt 4¹⁰ 12¹ 31¹³ †.

16. יָדְךָ הַחֲזָקָה וּזְרֹעֲךָ הַנְּטוּיָה *Thy mighty hand and thy stretched out arm*: I 8⁴² (∥ 2 Ch 6³²), Dt 4³⁴ 5¹⁵ 7¹⁹ 11² 26⁸, Jer 21⁵ (different order) 32²¹ (אֶזְרוֹעַ), Ezk 20³³. ³⁴, Ps 136¹² †. *Mighty hand* alone: Dt 3²⁴ 6²¹ 7⁸ 9²⁶ 34¹², Ex 3¹⁹ 6¹ 32¹¹ (all JE) 13⁹ (E), Nu 20²⁰ (JE, referring to Edom), Neh 1¹⁰, Dn 9¹⁵†; cf. Jos 4²⁴ (D²). *Stretched out arm* alone, II 17³⁶, Dt 9²⁹, Jer 27⁵ 32¹⁷, Ex 6⁶ (P)†.

17. כָּל־עַמֵּי הָאָרֶץ *All the peoples of the earth*: I 8⁴³ (∥ 2 Ch 6³³) ⁵³. ⁶⁰, Dt 28¹⁰, Jos 4²⁴ (D²), Ezk 31¹², Zeph 3²⁰†.

18. נָתַן לִפְנֵי *Deliver over to* (lit. *set before*): I 8⁴⁶ (∥ 2 Ch 6³⁶), Dt 1⁸. ²¹ 2³¹. ³³. ³⁶ 7². ²³ 23¹⁴ (¹⁵ Heb.) 28⁷. ²⁵ 31⁵, Jos 10¹² 11⁶ (both D²), Jg 11⁹ Is 41², all the occurrences of the phrase in this special sense.

19. *Shall bethink themselves* (lit. *bring back to their heart* (וְהֵשִׁיבוּ אֶל־לְבָּם) *in the land whither they are carried captive*: I 8⁴⁷ a reminiscence of Dt 30ᶠ.

20. *Return unto thee with all their heart*, etc.: I 8⁴⁸, II 23²⁵, Dt 30¹⁰; cf. Jer 3¹⁰.

21. *For they be thy people and thine inheritance, which thou broughtest forth out of Egypt*: I 8⁵¹ a reminiscence of Dt 9²⁶. ²⁹.

22. כּוּר הַבַּרְזֶל *The furnace of iron*: I 8⁵¹, Dt 4²⁰, Jer 11⁴†.

23. *Hath given rest* (מְנוּחָה) *unto his people Israel*: I 8⁵⁶, probably with reference to Dt 12⁹; cf. Ps 95¹¹.

24. *There hath not failed* (lit. *fallen* נָפַל) *one word of all his good promise which he promised*: I 8⁵⁶, Jos 21⁴⁵ 23¹⁴ (both D²).

25. *That all the people of the earth may know*, etc.: I 8⁶⁰, Jos 4²⁴ (D²).

26. *That J" he is God* (lit. *the God* (הָאֱלֹהִים) ; *there is none else*: I 8⁶⁰, Dt 4³⁵· ³⁹.

27. לָשׂוּם שְׁמִי שָׁם *To put my name there*: I 9³ 11³⁶ 14²¹, II 21⁴· ⁷ (referring to I 9³), Dt 12⁵· ²¹ 14²⁴. In Dt the more ordinary phrase is *to cause his name to dwell there* לְשַׁכֵּן שְׁמוֹ שָׁם, 12¹¹ 14²³ 16²· ⁶· ¹¹ 26² ; cf. No. 64.

28. כָּל־הַיָּמִים *All the days* (*i.e. for ever*): I 9³ 11³⁶· ³⁹, II 8¹⁹ 17³⁷, Dt 4⁴⁰ 5²⁹ (26 Heb.) 6²⁴ 11¹ 14²³ 18⁵ 19⁹ 28²⁹· ³³, Jos 4²⁴ (D²), 1 S 2³²· ³⁵ (Redactor), Jer 31³⁶ (Heb.³⁵) 32³⁹ 33¹⁸ 35¹⁹. Thus the expression *used absolutely* * appears to be purely Deuteronomic. In I 8⁴⁰ Dt 4¹⁰ 12¹ 31¹³ it is defined, and to some extent limited, by the added words, *that they (ye) live upon the land*.

29. *Shall go and serve other gods, and worship them*: I 9⁶ (|| 2 Ch 7¹⁹), Jos 23¹⁶ (D²); cf. Dt 11¹⁶ 17³. The phrase עָבַד אֱלֹהִים אֲחֵרִים *serve other gods*, occurs also Dt 7⁴ 13⁶· ¹³ (⁷· ¹⁴ Heb.) 28³⁶· ⁶⁴, Jer 16¹³, Jg 10¹³ (Deut. compiler), Jos 24²· ¹⁶ (E), 1 S 8⁸ 26¹⁹ ; cf. Jer 44⁸. *Other gods*, with *serve* not preceding as governing verb, but closely following with suffix in reference, is found I 9⁹ (|| 2 Ch 7²²), II 17³⁵, Dt 8¹⁹ 13² (Heb.³) 28¹⁴ 30¹⁷ 31²⁰, Jer 11¹⁰ 13¹⁰ 16¹¹ 22⁹ 25⁶ 35¹⁵, Jg 2¹⁹ (Deut. compiler). *Other gods*, without *serve* : I 11⁴· ¹⁰ 14⁹, II 17⁷· ³⁷· ³⁸ 22¹⁷ (|| 2 Ch 34²⁵), all R^D, II 5¹⁷, Dt 5⁷ 6¹⁴ 11²⁸ 18³ 30¹⁸, Jer 1¹⁶ 7⁶· ⁹· ¹⁸ 19⁴· ¹³ 32²⁹ 44⁵· ⁸· ¹⁵, Jg 2¹²· ¹⁷ (Deut. compiler), Ex 20³ (E) 23¹³ (J), Hos 3¹, 2 Ch 28²⁵†.

30. לְמָשָׁל וְלִשְׁנִינָה *For a proverb and for a byword*: I 9⁷ (|| 2 Ch 7²⁰), Dt 28³⁷, Jer 24⁹†.

31. דָּבַק בְּ *Cleave to* ; of *strange wives*, I 11² ; of *sins of Jeroboam*, II 3³ ; of *cleaving to J"*, II 18⁶, Dt 4⁴ 10²⁰ 11²² 13⁴ (⁵ Heb.) 30²⁰, Jos 22⁵ 23⁸ (both D²)—all the occurrences in this special moral sense.

32. הָלַךְ אַחֲרֵי *Go after* ; *a false god*, I 11⁵· ¹⁰ 21²⁶, II 17¹⁵ (all R^D), I 18¹⁸· ²¹, Dt 4³ 6¹⁴ 8¹⁹ 11²⁸ 13² (³ Heb.) 28¹⁴, Jg 2¹²· ¹⁹ (Deut. compiler), Jer 2⁵· ²³ 7⁹ 11¹⁰ 13¹⁰ 16¹¹ 25⁶ 35¹⁵, Ezk 20¹⁶ ; cf. Hos 2⁵· ¹³ (⁷· ¹⁵ Heb.). Of *following J"*: I 14⁸ (R^D) 18²¹, Dt 13⁴ (⁵ Heb.), 2 Ch 34³¹, Hos 11¹⁰†.

33. עָשָׂה הָרַע בְּעֵינֵי *Do that which is evil in the sight of J"* : I 11⁶ 14²² 15²⁶· ³⁴ 16¹⁹· ²⁵· ³⁰ 21²⁰· ²⁵ 22⁵² (53 Heb.), II 3² 8¹⁸ (|| 2 Ch 21⁶) 27 (|| 2 Ch 22⁴) 13²· ¹¹ 14²⁴ 15⁹· ¹⁸· ²⁴· ²⁸ 17²· ¹⁷ 21²· ⁶ (|| 2 Ch 33²· ⁶) 15· 16· 20 (|| 2 Ch 33²²) 23²· ³⁷ (|| 2 Ch 36⁵) 24⁹· ¹⁹ (|| 2 Ch 36⁹· ¹²), 2 Ch 29⁶, Dt 4²⁵ 9¹⁸ 17² 31²⁹, Jg 2¹¹ 3⁷· ¹² 4¹ 6¹ 10⁶ 13¹ (all Deut. compiler), Nu 32¹³ (JE), 1 S 15¹⁹, Jer 52²¹†. Cf. 2 S 12⁹, Is 65¹² 66⁴, Jer 32³⁰, Ps 51⁴ (⁶ Heb.).

34. עָשָׂה הַיָּשָׁר בְּעֵינֵי *Do that which is right in the sight of J"* : I 11³³· ³⁸ 14⁸ 15⁵· ¹¹ 22⁴³ (|| 2 Ch 20³²), II 10³⁰ 12² (³ Heb.) (|| 2 Ch 24²) 14³ (|| 2 Ch 25²) 15³· ³⁴ (|| 2 Ch 26⁴ 27²) 16² (|| 2 Ch 28¹) 18³ (|| 2 Ch 29²) 22² (|| 2 Ch 34²), Dt 12²⁵ 13¹⁸ (¹⁹ Heb.) ; and with the addition of הַטּוֹב *that which is good*, 6¹⁸ 12²⁸. Elsewhere only Ex 15²⁶ (JE or D ?), Jer 34¹⁵.

35. מִלֵּא אַחֲרֵי *Go fully after J"* : I 11⁶, Dt 1³⁶, Jos 14⁸· ⁹· ¹⁴ (JE recast by D²), Nu 14¹²· ¹² (JE)†.

36. הִתְאַנֵּף *Be angry* : I 11⁹, II 17¹⁸, Dt 1⁸⁷ 4²¹ 9⁸· ²⁰†.

37. וְהָיָה אִם־תִּשְׁמַע *And it shall be, if thou wilt hearken* : I 11³⁸, Dt 28¹· ¹⁵ ; with pl. תִּשְׁמְעוּ 11¹³ ; cf. 15⁵ 11²⁸. In the same way (obedience the condition of a promise) Dt 13¹⁸ (¹⁹ Heb.) 28²· ¹³ 30¹⁰, אֲשֶׁר תִּשְׁמְעוּ 11²⁷.

38. הִשְׁמִיד מֵעַל פְּנֵי הָאֲדָמָה *Destroy from off the face of the earth* : I 13³⁴, Dt 6¹⁵, Am 9⁸ ; cf. Jos 23¹⁵ (D²). הִשְׁמִיד *destroy*, passive נִשְׁמַד, is very frequent in Dt (27 times) ; cf. Driver on Dt 1²⁷.

39. הִכְעִים *Vex* (J", by treatment wholly undeserved. RV 'provoke to anger' is inaccurate): I 14⁹· ¹⁵ 15³⁰ 16²· ⁷· ¹³· ²⁶· ³³ 21²² 22⁵³ (⁵⁴ Heb.), II 17¹¹· ¹⁷ 21⁶ (|| 2 Ch 33⁶) 15 22¹⁷ (|| 2 Ch 34²⁵) 23¹⁹· ²⁶, 2 Ch 28²⁵, Dt 4²⁵ 9¹⁸ 31²⁹ 32¹⁶, Jer 7¹⁸· ¹⁹ 8¹⁹ 11¹⁷ 25⁶· ⁷ 32²⁹· ³⁰· ³² 44³· ⁸. Elsewhere, with J" as object, only six times. With Pi'el (כְּעַסוּנִי), Dt 32²¹†.

* The same phrase כָּל־הַיָּמִים *all the days*, used in a strictly limited sense of the lifetime of an individual (for *all his, thy,* etc., *days*) is non-Deuteronomic. Cf. the writer's note on 1 K 5¹⁵.

40. מֵעַל הָאֲדָמָה הַטּוֹבָה הַזֹּאת *From upon this good land* : I 14¹⁵, Jos 23¹³· ¹⁵ (D²)†. The usual phrase in Dt of the land of Canaan is הָאָרֶץ הַטּוֹבָה *the good land* ; cf. Driver, *Deuteronomy*, p. lxxxi.

41. עַל כָּל־גִּבְעָה נְבֹהָה וְתַחַת כָּל־עֵץ רַעֲנָן *On every high hill, and under every green (or spreading) tree* : I 14²³, II 17¹⁰, Jer 2²⁰. With the variation עַל הַגְּבָעוֹת *on the hills*, II 16⁴ (|| 2 Ch 28⁴), Dt 12². Cf. Ezk 6¹³ Jer 3⁶· ¹³ 17², Is 57⁵.

42. כְּכֹל־תּוֹעֲבֹת הַגּוֹיִם (כְּתוֹעֲבֹת) *According to (all) the abominations of the nations* : I 14²⁴, II 16³ (|| 2 Ch 28³) 21² (|| 2 Ch 33²), 2 Ch 36¹⁴, Dt 18⁹.

43. הוֹרִישׁ *Drive out* (used of the expulsion of the nations of Canaan by J"): I 14²⁴ 21²⁶, II 16³ (|| 2 Ch 28³) 17⁸ 21² (|| 2 Ch 33²), Dt 4³⁸ 9⁴· ⁵ 11²³ 18¹², Jos 13⁶ 23⁵· ⁹· ¹³ (all D²), Jg 2²¹· ²³ (Deut. compiler), Ps 44² (³ Heb.). Elsewhere only Ex 34²⁴, Nu 32²¹, Jos 3¹⁰ (all JE).

44. גִּלּוּלִים *Idol-blocks* (a term of opprobrium): I 15¹² 21²⁶, II 17¹² 21¹¹· ²¹ 23²⁴, Dt 29¹⁷ (¹⁶ Heb.), Lv 26³⁰ (H), and 39 times in Ezk.†

45. כָּל־נְשָׁמָה *Anything breathing* (lit. *any breath*) : I 15²⁹, Dt 20¹⁶, Jos 11¹¹· ¹⁴ (D²), כָּל־הַנְּשָׁמָה Jos 10⁴⁰ (D²), Ps 150⁶†.

46. הֲבָלִים *Vain things* (applied to idolatrous symbols): I 16¹³· ²⁶,* Dt 32²¹ ; cf. Jer 8¹⁹ 14²². So with cognate verb, וַיֵּלְכוּ אַחֲרֵי הַהֶבֶל וַיֶּהְבָּלוּ *they followed vanity and became vain*, II 17¹⁵, Jer 2⁵.

47. (הַשְׁחִית) לֹא אָבָה *Would not destroy* : II 8¹⁹ 13²³, Dt 10¹⁰.

48. מָחָה שֵׁם מִתַּחַת הַשָּׁמַיִם *Blot out the name from under heaven* : II 14²⁷, Dt 9¹⁴ 29²⁰ (¹⁹ Heb.), the only occurrences of the exact phrase.

49. שָׁמַר לַעֲשׂוֹת *Observe to do*: II 17³⁷ 21⁸ (|| 2 Ch 33⁸), 1 Ch 22¹³ (¹² Heb.), Dt 5¹· ³² (²⁹ Heb.) 6³· ²⁵ 7¹¹ 8¹ 11²²· ³² 12¹· ³² (¹³¹ Heb.) 15⁵ 17¹⁰ 19⁹ 24⁸ 28¹· ¹⁵· ⁵⁸ 31¹² 32⁴⁶, Jos 1⁷· ⁸ 22⁵ (D²).

The following phrases, though not derived directly from Deuteronomy, are characteristic of the editor of Kings in common with Jeremiah, whose writings exhibit strong Deuteronomic affinities :—

50. כִּי שִׁמְךָ עַל הַבַּיִת הַזֶּה *That thy name is called over this house* (in token of *ownership*) : I 8⁴³ (|| 2 Ch 6³³), Jer 7¹⁰· ¹¹· ¹⁴· ³⁰ 32³⁴ 34¹⁵. The phrase is also used of the chosen people, Dt 28¹⁰, Jer 14⁹, Is 63¹⁹, 2 Ch 7¹⁴ ; of Jerusalem, Jer 25²⁹ ; of Jerusalem and the chosen people, Dn 9¹⁸· ¹⁹ ; of Jeremiah, 15¹⁶ ; of the nations, Am 9¹².

51. שִׁלַּח מֵעַל פְּנֵי (פָּנַי) *Dismiss from before my (his) face* : I 9⁷, Jer 15¹. So, but with a different verb, הִשְׁלִיךְ *cast away*, II 13²³ 17²⁰ ; מִן in place of (מֵעַל), Jer 7¹⁵ ; הֵסִיר *remove*, II 17¹⁸· ²³ 23²⁷ 24⁸, Jer 32³¹.

52. כָּל־עֹבֵר עָלָיו יִשֹּׁם וְשָׁרַק *Every one that passeth by it shall be astonished and shall hiss* : I 9⁸, Jer 19⁸ 49¹⁷ 50¹³ ; cf. Jer 18¹⁶, La 2¹⁵, Zeph 2¹⁵.

53. שָׁב מִדַּרְכּוֹ הָרָעָה *Return from his evil way* : I 13³³, Jer 18¹¹ 25⁵ 26³ 35¹⁵ 36³· ⁷. Elsewhere Jon 3⁸· ¹⁰, Ezk 13²² (מִדַּרְכּוֹ הָרַע). With pl. *their evil ways*, II 17¹³, 2 Ch 7¹⁴, Zec 1⁴†. Cf. Jer 23²², Ezk 3¹⁹ 33¹¹.

54. הִנְנִי מֵבִיא רָעָה אֶל (עַל) *Behold, I will bring evil upon* : I 14¹⁰ 21²¹, II 21¹² 22¹⁶ (|| 2 Ch 34²⁴), Jer 6¹⁹ 11¹¹ 19³· ¹⁵ 35¹⁷ 45⁵†.

55. עֲבָדַי (עֲבָדָיו) הַנְּבִיאִים *My (his) servants the prophets* : I 9⁷ 17¹³· ²³ 21¹⁰ 24², Jer 7²⁵ 25⁴ 26⁵ 29¹⁹ 35¹⁵ 44⁴. Elsewhere Am 3⁷, Zec 1⁶, Ezr 9¹¹, Dn 9¹⁰.

Other resemblances with Jeremiah, from the later chs. of 2 K, are given by Driver, *LOT* p. 193 (⁶ 203).

Phrases and modes of expression wholly or nearly peculiar to the editor of Kings are as follow :—

56. Reference to *the sins of Jeroboam, i.e. his* institution of the calf-worship. So, as causing the

* So v.², according to LXX ἐν τοῖς ματαίοις αὐτῶν, and probably

Pesh. ܒܥܒܕ ܐܝܕܝܗܘܢ 'with the work of their hands,' is place of MT בְּחַטֹּאתָם 'with their sins.'

destruction of his own house, I 14^{16} 15^{30}. In the summary of the character of kings of Israel a regular formula appears—

he did not depart from }
he walked after (*in*) } *the sins of J.* } *which he caused Israel to sin.*
he clave to }
he walked in the way of J. and in his sin (*sins*) }

So I 15$^{26.}$ (Nadab) ^{34} (Baasha) 16^{26} (Omri), II 3^{3} (Jehoram) 10^{31}, cf. ^{29} (Jehu) 13^{2} (Jehoahaz) ^{11} (Jehoash) 14^{24} (Jeroboam II.) 15^{9} (Zechariah) ^{18} (Menahem) ^{24} (Pekahiah) ^{28} (Pekah). Of the people of Israel, II 13^{6}. In all these cases the antecedent of the relative אֲשֶׁר הֶחֱטִיא is not יָרָבְעָם but חַטֹּאות יר׳; cf. II 17^{21}. I 16^{30} (Ahab), II 17^{22} חַטֹּאות יר׳ *the sins of J.* without אֲשֶׁר הֶחֱטִיא וג׳ *which he caused*, etc.: I 22^{52} ([^{53} Heb.] Ahaziah), II 23^{15} אֲשֶׁר הֶחֱטִיא אֶת־יִשְׂרָאֵל, referring not to חַטֹּאות (omitted), but to יָרָבְעָם *J., who made Israel to sin.* In I 16^{13} the sins of Baasha and Elah, and in II 21^{11} of Manasseh (אֲשֶׁר הֶחֱטִיא אֶת־יְהוּדָה), are spoken of in the same terms.

57. Reference to David as the ideal standard of a righteous king: I 3$^{3.6.14}$ 9^{4} 11$^{4.6.33.38}$ 14^{8} 15$^{3.5.11}$, II 14^{3} 16^{2} 18^{3} 22^{2}.

58. (עַבְדִּי) לְמַעַן דָּוִד אָבִיךָ *For David thy father's* (*my* or *his servant's*) *sake*: I 11$^{12.13.32.34}$, II 8^{19} 19^{34} 20^{6}; cf. I 15^{4}†.

59. A *lamp* (נִיר) for David (figurative of a lasting posterity): I 11^{36} 15^{4}, II 8^{19} (‖ 2 Ch 21^{7}); cf. Ps 132^{17}.

60. הָלַךְ לִפְנֵי י׳ *Walk before J"*: I 2^{4} 3^{6} 8$^{23.25}$ (‖ 2 Ch 6$^{14.16}$) 9^{4} (‖ 2 Ch 7^{17}). Elsewhere the Hithpa'el is used הִתְהַלֵּךְ לִפְנֵי י׳, II 20^{3} (‖ Is 38^{3}), 1 S 2^{30}, Gn 17^{1} (P) 24^{40} (J) 48^{15} (JE), Ps 56^{13} (^{14} Heb.) 116^{9}.

61. לֹא יִכָּרֵת לְךָ אִישׁ מֵעַל כִּסֵּא יִשְׂרָאֵל *There shall not fail thee* (lit. *be cut off to thee*) *a man on the throne of Israel*: I 2^{4} 8^{25} (‖ 2 Ch 6^{16}) 9^{5} (‖ 2 Ch 7^{18}); cf. Jer 33^{17}.

62. בָּנָה בַיִת לְשֵׁם י׳ *Build a house to the name of J"*: I 3^{2} 5$^{3.5}$ ($^{17.19}$ Heb.) 8$^{17.20.44.48}$. The original is 2 S 7^{13} *He shall build a house to my name*, quoted in I 5^{5} (^{19} Heb.) 8^{19}.

63. *There hath been* (*was*) *none like thee* (*him*) *before thee* (*him*), etc.: I 3^{12}, II 18^{5} 23^{25}.

64. לִהְיוֹת שְׁמִי שָׁם *That my name might be there*: I 8$^{16.29}$, II 23^{27}. Cf. No. 27.

65. *Heart perfect* (שָׁלֵם) *with J"*: I 8^{61} 11^{4} 15$^{3.14}$; cf. II 20^{3} (‖ Is 38^{3}). The adj. is thus used in application to the heart, elsewhere only eight times in Ch.

66. הֵרַע (לַעֲשׂוֹת) מִכֹּל־אֲשֶׁר (הָיוּ) לְפָנָיו *Did* (*hast done*) *evil above all that were before him* (*thee*): I 14^{9} 16$^{25.30.*33}$; cf. II 17^{2} 21^{11}.

67. מַשְׁתִּין בְּקִיר *Every man child* (lit. *mingens ad parietem*): I 14^{10} 16^{11} 21^{21}, II 9^{8}. Only besides 1 S 25$^{22.34}$.

68. עָצוּר וְעָזוּב *Shut up and left at large* (*i.e. all*; every one being supposed to fall under one of the two categories†): I 14^{10} 21^{21}, II 9^{8} 14^{26}, Dt 32^{36}†.

69. וּבִעַרְתִּי אַחֲרֵי *I will utterly sweep away*: I 14^{10} 21^{21}†; הִנְנִי מַבְעִיר אַחֲרֵי I 16^{3}†.

70. *Him that dieth to M. in the city shall the dogs eat; and him that dieth in the field shall the fowls of the air eat*: I 14^{11} 16^{4} 21^{24}†.

71. הִתְמַכֵּר לַעֲשׂוֹת הָרַע בְּעֵינֵי י׳ *Sold himself* (*themselves*) *to do that which is evil in the sight of J"*: I 21$^{20.25}$, II 17^{17}†.

72. לֹא סָר מִן־ *Turned not aside from*: I 15^{5} 22^{43}, II 3^{3} 13$^{2.6.11}$ 14^{24} 15$^{9.24.28}$ 17^{22}; with מֵאַחֲרֵי *from after*, II 10^{29} 18^{6}; with מֵעַל lit. *from upon*, II 10^{31} 15^{18}.

73. רַק הַבָּמוֹת לֹא סָרוּ עוֹד הָעָם מְזַבְּחִים וּמְקַטְּרִים בַּבָּמוֹת *Howbeit the high places were not taken away; the people still sacrificed and burnt incense in the high places*: I 22^{43} (^{44} Heb.; אַךְ for רַק), II 12^{3} (^{4} Heb.) 14^{4} 15$^{4.35}$; cf. I 3$^{2.3}$ 15^{14}, II 16^{4}.

The extent and limits of the passages which are due to the editor's hand are noticed below in dealing with the *composition* of Kings.

4. DATE OF THE EDITOR.—As Kings now stands, the earliest possible *terminus a quo* for the composition of the book is the date of the latest event related, viz. Jehoiachin's release from prison in the 37th year of his captivity, *i.e.* B.C. 561, some 25 years after the fall of Jerusalem. As, however, the writer states that the privileges granted by the Babylonian king to Jehoiachin were continued 'all the days of his life' (II 25^{30}), the strong presumption is created that the words were not penned so early as B.C. 561, but some time later, viz. subsequently to the death of Jehoiachin, whenever that may have taken place.

Agreeable to such an exilic date as is implied by the last two chs. of 2 K are certain passages in the body of the work which seem to presuppose the captivity of Judah. These are I 11^{39} II 17$^{19.20}$ 23$^{26.27}$, and perhaps, though not so clearly, I 9$^{7-9}$ II 20$^{17.18}$ 21$^{11-15}$ 22$^{15-20}$. To these we may add the reference in I 4^{24} (Heb. 5^{4}) to Solomon's dominion as extending over all the kings '*beyond the River*,' a statement which, as referring to the country W. of the Euphrates, implies that the writer is living in Babylonia on the E. side of the river.*

On the other hand, however, there are certain indications which show that the first editing of Kings must have taken place *prior to* the final decay and fall of the Judæan monarchy.

Chief among these is the use of the phrase '*unto this day*' (עַד־הַיּוֹם הַזֶּה) in the statement that the condition of affairs which the writer is describing still continues to exist up to the time of writing. If this phrase always or most frequently occurred in the course of lengthy narratives excerpted by the editor from his sources, there might then be room for the theory that a statement which was true as it stood in the old pre-exilic narratives had, through oversight on the part of an exilic editor, been allowed to stand after, through changed conditions, it had lost its force, or rather had become untrue and misleading. But, as a matter of fact, the expression is employed in connexion with terse statements of facts derived from the 'annals,' and in such cases can be due to no other hand than that of the editor himself, who, in using the phrase, either formulates his own statement, or intelligently admits a statement which he is able to verify.

The cases of the use of '*unto this day*,' which ought to be noticed as *implying the continued existence of the kingdom of Judah*, are the following:—I 8^{8} (the ends of the staves of the ark still to be seen projecting from the Adytum into the Holy place†); 9^{21} (the Canaanites still subjected by Israel to forced labour, as they had been under Solomon); 12^{19} (the division between the ten tribes and the house of David still in existence); II 8^{22} (Edom still successful in shaking off the yoke of Judah); 16^{6} (the Edomites still hold Elath, from which the Judæans were expelled by Rezin, king of Syria ‡). The other occurrences of 'unto this day' do not necessarily presuppose pre-exilic times, but may be cited to prove the frequency of the formula as employed by the editor of Kings:—I 9^{13} 10^{12}, II 14^{7} 17$^{23.34.41}$.§

* LXX (B, Luc.) prefixes (Luc. καὶ) ἐπονηρεύσατο, *i.e.* וַיָּרַע, before מכל וג׳, probably correctly.

† The most plausible explanation of the phrase is that of Ewald, *Antiquities*, 170, '*kept in* (by legal defilement) *and exempt*.' For this use of עָצוּר cf. Jer 36^{5}; Niph'al נֶעְצַר 1 S 21^{8}. Other explanations are quoted by Driver on Deut. *l.c.*

* The phrase עֵבֶר הַנָּהָר, implying an exilic standpoint, is found again in Ezr 4$^{10.11.16.17.20}$ 5$^{3.6}$ 6$^{6.8.13}$ 7$^{21.25}$ 8^{36}, Neh 2$^{7.9}$ 3^{7}. The rendering of RV text in 1 K 4^{24} 'on this side the River,' is quite impermissible, this being a direct violation of the constant meaning of עֵבֶר—country lying *across* or *on the other side of* a river.

† It is noticeable that in LXX of this passage the words 'unto this day' have disappeared, the excision being doubtless due to some later scribe who knew that in his own time their purport had ceased to be true.

‡ Reading אֱדֹם, אֲדוֹמִים, in place of ארם, ארומים.

§ In II 10^{27} עַד־הַיּוֹם, occurring in a lengthy narrative, must have been written prior to the destruction of Samaria (Kuenen, *Ond.* § 25^{14}), and is thus due to the source and not to the editor.

Again, it seems to be clear that, at the time when the editor is writing, *the Davidic dynasty still possesses a monarch reigning in Jerusalem.* David has, and is still to have, a *lamp* before J″ at Jerusalem continually (see above, No. 59 of the editor's phrases). The expression 'before J″ at Jerusalem' of I 11³⁶ implies further that *the temple is still standing intact,* a point which is also assumed in the dedication prayer of I 8¹⁵⁻⁵³ which owes its present form to the Deuteronomic editor. Throughout this prayer the leading petition is that supplication made *in* or *towards J″'s temple built by Solomon* may meet with a favourable answer (vv.²⁹· ³⁰· ³¹ᶠ· ³⁴· ³⁵· ³⁸· ⁴²· ⁴⁴· ⁴⁸). We may notice also I 9³ which likewise occurs in a section in which the editor's hand is prominent : 'I have hallowed this house which thou hast built, *to put my name there for ever ; and mine eyes and my heart shall be there perpetually.*'

Upon these grounds it may be concluded that the main editing of Kings must have taken place prior to the destruction of the Judæan kingdom, and that such sections of the book as imply an exilic standpoint are therefore of the nature of later redactional additions and interpolations.

For the work of this principal editor, influenced as we have seen him to be by the spirit and language of Deut., the *terminus a quo* is the discovery of Deut. in the year B.C. 621, the *terminus ad quem* the destruction of Jerusalem B.C. 586. And since the editor's standpoint seems to indicate that he wrote before the glamour of Josiah's reformation had wholly or nearly faded during the latter days of the Judæan monarchy, the assumption is fair that he undertook and completed his book not later than B.C. 600.*

5. LATER EDITORS. — From the preceding examination and conclusion as to the date of the main redaction of Kings it is clear that the pre-exilic book must have received certain additions at the hands of a later editor or editors before it attained the form in which we possess it. The chief of these additions is the appendix, which carries the history down to the year B.C. 561. To this appendix belongs certainly II 24¹⁰⁻25³⁰, and, presumably, 23³¹⁻ 24⁹. The conclusion of the pre-exilic book has, however, probably been worked over by the second editor, and so adapted to receive his addition that it is now impossible exactly to discover its position.

Any of the vv.²⁵· ²⁸ or even ³⁰ᵃ of ch. 23 might have formed a conclusion scarcely more abrupt than the present conclusion ch. 25³⁰. Ch. 23²⁹ᵃ, if it is not exactly imitated in style in ch. 24¹ᵃ, must be by the same hand, *i.e.*, presumably, the hand of the second editor. But, again, it is unlikely that the first editor should have appended the usual summary of a reign in v.²⁸ without mentioning the manner of the king's death. The statement of v.²⁵ᵇ seems at first sight to presuppose the writer's acquaintance with the characters of all the succeeding kings of Judah, but need not necessarily do so. Cf. the somewhat stereotyped formula of I 14⁹ᵃ with reference to Jeroboam.

Upon the other passages above mentioned as implying an exilic standpoint see below (*Composition*). It is noticeable that, apart from the difference of standpoint involved in the destruction of the Judæan kingdom and the Exile, the mould of mind of the second editor is essentially the same as that of the first editor. The same Deuteronomic mode of thought is couched in the same phraseology, while in the appendix the structural method of the first editor is faithfully imitated. Thus, if the main Deuteronomic editor or redactor be cited under the sign R^D, it is reasonable to employ the sign R^D2 in referring to the second editor of the same school of thought.†

* So Kuenen, *Onderzoek*, § 26 ; Wellhausen, *Composition*, p. 298 ff., etc. König, on the contrary, holds that the editor of Kings compiled his work not earlier than B.C. 588, *i.e.* during the Exile (*Einleitung*, § 53³).

† In speaking of a second Deuteronomic editor (R^D2) it is not, of course, intended dogmatically to assert that all passages assigned to such a writer must have flowed from *the same* pen,

Kings, as it stands in the Hebrew Bible, has, again, undergone still later revision than that of R^D2. This is clear from certain variations in form and order between the MT and the recension of the text which is represented by the LXX. While in some cases the condition of the LXX text is greatly inferior to that of MT, yet, on the other hand, it is clear that in a number of sections LXX preserves a superior arrangement in order, or a simpler form, of narrative which points to the fact that MT has suffered dislocation and interpolation at the hands of a reviser or revisers of a date later than the separation of the two recensions. As instances of this we may notice I 4²⁰⁻³⁴ (Heb. 4²⁰⁻ 5¹⁴) 5⁻7 (Heb. 5¹⁵⁻7) in the main, 8¹⁻¹³ 11¹⁻¹³, and the position of MT 21 after 19, so that 22 succeeds 20 without a break in the narrative. Consideration of such points as must here be raised is best reserved for a sectional criticism of the composition of the book.

6. SOURCES AND COMPOSITION OF KINGS CONSIDERED IN DETAIL.* — I 1¹⁻2⁴⁶. Narrative of the events which led to the establishment of Solomon as the successor of David. It is generally assumed, and with great probability, that this section originally formed part of the document 2 S 9-20, which gives a history of David. 2².³ is due to R^D (see above, *phrases of R^D*, Nos. 1-6, 60, 61).

A point of interest in connexion with the homogeneity of the narrative is the fact that after 2³⁵ᵃ LXX (B, Luc.) inserts καὶ ἡ βασιλεία κατορθοῦτο ἐν Ἱερουσαλήμ, *i.e.* MT 2⁴⁶ᵇ with the reading בירושלם for בִּיד שׁלמה. The correct position of the sentence seems to be at the end of v.³⁵, from which in MT it was separated by the insertion of the Shimei section. Solomon's establishment in the kingdom resulted from the death of his powerful adversaries, Adonijah and Joab, and could not have been much enhanced by the death of Shimei some three years later. The fact that in LXX these words precede v.³⁵ᵇ suggests that this latter may be a later insertion made to complete the information supplied by v.³⁵ᵃ.

3¹⁻11⁴³. History of Solomon's reign. The narrative follows a well-defined plan. The kernel is 5¹⁻7⁵¹ (Heb. 5¹⁵⁻7⁵¹), the description of Solomon's building operations, with its sequel, ch. 8. Around this are grouped (chs. 4. 9. 10) a series of notices, for the most part brief, illustrative of the king's wisdom, magnificence, and prosperity. Ch. 3 forms an introduction to the whole, detailing Solomon's request for wisdom, with a signal instance of its exercise : ch. 11, as a conclusion, gives a description of the circumstances which paved the way for the disruption of the kingdom.

3¹, as it stands in MT, is out of place. There can be little doubt that, together with 9¹⁶· ¹⁷ᵃ, it originally formed part of the document embodied in ch. 4²⁰ᶠᶠ·. See *ad loc.*

3². ³ expresses disapprobation of *Bāmā* worship, based upon the law of Deut. which restricts sacrifice to the central sanctuary. Similar notices by R^D are found elsewhere in Kings (see *phrases*, No. 73). The old narrative treats *Bāmā* worship as a matter of course ; cf. v.⁴ 18³⁰ 19¹⁰ etc.

Though vv.². ³ of 3 both exhibit the influence of Deut., it is scarcely possible to assign both to one author R^D. In v.³ the subject, as in vv.¹· ⁴, is Solomon, while in v.² the *people* are specified. V.³ simply places two facts side by side without any attempt at correlation :—Solomon loved J″, only he sacrificed and burned incense on the high places ; v.² supplies an explanation :—This *Bāmā* worship was a popular custom, due to the fact that the house of J″ was not yet built. Hence v.³ is the work of R^D, and opens the account of Solomon's reign by introducing the narrative of the vision at Gibeon ; v.² proceeds from a later editor, who, with a view to explaining Solomon's conduct, inserted the phrase, which he found to be frequent elsewhere, v.²ᵃ, together with the explanation which follows, v.²ᵇ, and, in order to illustrate this latter, probably moved v.¹, which

since it is obvious that more than one Deuteronomist may have had a hand in the revision of Kings. R^D2 denotes a Deuteronomic redactor *or* redactors of the Bk. of Kings who lived in exilic or post-exilic times.

* The following criticisms upon the narratives of Kings are, in the main, taken, directly or in an abridged form, from the writer's *Notes on the Hebrew Text of the Books of Kings*, which is in course of preparation by the Oxford University Press.

mentions the fact of the house of J″ being not yet built, from the position which it properly occupies in ch. 4 LXX. In LXX of ch. 3, v.¹ is wanting and v.² fragmentary.

3⁴⁻¹⁵ is an ancient narrative, to some extent revised by Rᴰ, whose hand may be traced in vv.⁶·⁸ᵃ·¹²·¹⁴ (phrases Nos. 2. 3. 8. 9. 57. 60. 63). Probably also v.¹⁵, at least in its present form, is due to Rᴰ, since if according to v.⁴ ' the great high place' was at Gibeon, it is difficult to understand why Solomon should have returned to Jerusalem to offer sacrifice, except from the Deuteronomic standpoint. The phrase 'ark of the covenant of J″' is mainly a D expression. 3¹⁶⁻²⁸ is an old narrative in its original form.

4¹⁻¹⁹, which gives a list of Solomon's officers of state, may be supposed to be derived from 'the book of the annals of Solomon.'

The list has received one later addition, viz. v.⁴ᵇ. The statement that 'Zadok and Abiathar were priests' is no part of the register in its original form as an official state document. This naturally headed the list with the name of the high priest of the time, Azariah, the son of Zadok. The insertion was made by Rᴰ or by someone still earlier, who wished, as a matter of historical interest, to notice that Zadok and Abiathar were priests at the commencement of the reign. It is noticeable that in this case only is there omission of the name of the father of any official. The sentence at the end of v.¹⁹ should be emended, after Klostermann, וְנָצִיב אֶחָד עַל כָּל־הַנִּצָּבִים אֲשֶׁר בָּאָרֶץ 'and one officer was over all the officers who were in the land,' the allusion being to Azariah of v.⁵.

4²⁰⁻³⁴ (Heb. 4²⁰⁻5¹⁴) appears in LXX (B, Luc.) in a form somewhat different from MT. 4²⁰·²¹·²⁵·²⁶ and part of v.²⁴ ('from Tiphsah . . . the river') do not appear, but are to be found in the addition at the end of ch. 2⁴⁶. At the close of 4¹⁹ the text continues in the following order:—vv.²⁷·²⁸·²²⁻²⁴·²⁹⁻³⁴, after which follow ch. 3¹, ch. 9¹⁶·¹⁷ᵃ. Thus the commencement of v.²⁷ 'And these officers provided,' etc. (וְכִלְכְּלוּ הַנִּצָּבִים הָאֵלֶּה וג׳, not, as RV, 'and those officers,' etc.), hinges directly on to the section 4⁷⁻¹⁹, which enumerates the officers and their respective districts. This explains הָאֵלֶּה 'these' of v.²⁷, which is otherwise anomalous. There can be no question that the text of the section as preserved by LXX is complete in itself, and bears the stamp of originality rather than the somewhat confused account of MT.

The disturbing factors in MT appear to have been vv.²⁰·²¹·²⁵.* These, which contain no very precise information, were added probably not from a written source, but from oral tradition, by a post-exilic scribe, who desired reference to the happy times under Solomon's golden age. The insertion led to the dislocation of vv.²⁷·²⁸, causing them to be placed after vv.²²·²³·²⁴. Probably the same hand excerpted the notice about Pharaoh's daughter and her dowry from its true position after v.³⁴, dividing it and placing part at the beginning of ch. 3 (for the reason given above, 3²·³), and part as a sequel to the mention of Gezer in ch. 9¹⁵.

5¹⁻7⁵¹ (Heb. 5¹⁵⁻7⁵¹).† The main document, represented by chs. 6. 7, appears to have been one, and was probably derived from the temple archives. 5³⁻⁵ has been amplified by Rᴰ upon the lines of 2 S 7 (phrases, Nos. 10, 62). In 5¹² the idea and phrase ' as he promised him ' (כַּאֲשֶׁר דִּבֶּר־לוֹ) are Deuteronomic,‡ and thus the first half of this verse ought probably to be assigned to Rᴰ.

In 5¹⁵⁻¹⁸ the relationship of the 70,000 + 80,000 workmen to the 30,000 of 5¹³·¹⁴ is obscure,§ and probably points to a difference of source. So Ewald and Stade; the latter noticing that הלבנן 'the Lebanon,' of v.¹⁴, is in v.¹⁵ called ההר ' the mountain.'

The narrative of 6. 7 has been much worked over in post-exilic times. In 6¹ the exact coinci-

* 4²⁶ properly belongs to ch. 10, where it occurs in LXX (B, Luc.) in connexion with v.²⁶.

† Upon the text of this section Stade's article, ' Der Text des Berichtes über Salomos Bauten,' ZATW, 1883, p. 129 ff., is most invaluable.

‡ Cf. Dt 12¹ 6³ 9³ al. Driver (Comm. on Deut. lxxxi) cites from D fifteen occurrences of (ל) דבר כאשר, besides instances from the compiler of Judges and Joshua.

§ According to 2 Ch 2¹⁶·¹⁷ the former consisted of 'the strangers that were in the land of Israel.' Of this difference, however, there is no hint in the text of Kings.

dence in length of the period of 480 years from the Exodus to the commencement of Solomon's temple, with the period which extends from this latter point to the return from the Exile, is scarcely accidental, and marks the verse as a post-exilic insertion. LXX places 6¹ between vv.¹⁶·¹⁷ᵃ of 5, into which position it has probably crept from the margin. In its place we have 6³⁷·³⁸ᵃ, which give the date of laying the foundation of the temple and of its completion. This position for these latter verses is accepted by Wellhausen (Composition, p. 267), though not by Stade. 6⁷ intrudes itself very awkwardly into the midst of the account of the side chambers, and, if forming a part of the original description, must, at any rate, be out of place. In 6⁸ᵃ read, with LXX (B, Luc.), Targ. הַתַּחְתֹּנָה 'the lowest,' in place of הַתִּיכֹנָה 'the middle.' 6⁹ (omitting נבים ושדרת, with B, Luc.) ought to follow 6¹⁰.

6¹¹⁻¹⁴, which is omitted by LXX, is not, as is generally assumed by critics, the work of Rᴰ, but is due to a post-exilic editor, who shows acquaintance with the Law of Holiness (H) and the Priestly code (P). The section contains some D phrases, such as could, and did, pass from D into P, but other expressions belong solely to P or to H. V.¹⁴ is by the same hand as vv.¹¹⁻¹³, v.⁹ᵃ being repeated in order to round off the interpolation and attach it to the preceding narrative. The following special marks of authorship should be noticed :—

V.¹² אִם־תֵּלֵךְ בְּחֻקֹּתַי If thou wilt walk in my statutes. Never in Dt; twice in Jer 44¹⁰·²³. In H, Lv 26³ (cf. 18⁴), and constantly in Ezk (whose connexion with H is well ascertained ; Driver, LOT⁶ p. 49 ff.), 5⁶·⁷ 11²⁰ 18⁹·¹⁷ 20¹³·¹⁶·¹⁹·²¹.† Cf. the phrase הָלַךְ בְּחֻקּוֹת הַגּוֹיִם walk in the statutes of the nations, Lv 18³ 20²³ (H).

וְאֶת־מִשְׁפָּטַי תַּעֲשֶׂה and wilt execute my judgments. The exact phrase (with J″ as spokesman—my judgments) belongs to H ; Lv 18⁴, Ezk 5⁷ 11¹² 18¹⁷ 20²⁴, 1 Ch 28⁷. In 1 K 11³³ᵇ the passage belongs to Rᴰ, but the words וְחֻקֹּתַי וּמִשְׁפָּטַי are an earlier insertion, as is shown by their omission in LXX. Even with מִשְׁפָּטָיו his judgments, הַמִּשְׁפָּטִים the judgments, the phrase is not specially characteristic of Dt ; * 26¹⁶ 33²¹ (blessing of Moses in Appendix) ; elsewhere Neh 10²⁹. Similar H phrases are found in Lv 18⁵, Ezk 20¹¹·¹³·²¹, Lv 19³⁷ 20²² 25¹⁸, Ezk 11²⁰ 20¹⁹ 36²⁷.

לָלֶכֶת בָּם to walk in them (the judgments). So exactly only in Lv 18⁴ (H). D's phrase is לָלֶכֶת בִּדְרָכָיו ' to walk in the ways of J″.'

V.¹³ וְשָׁכַנְתִּי בְּתוֹךְ בְּנֵי יִשְׂרָאֵל And I will dwell in the midst of the children of Israel. Very distinctive of P ; Ex 25⁸ 29⁴⁵, Nu 5³ 35³⁴, Ezk 43⁹. No occurrences in D. With the whole verse cf. Lv 26¹·¹² (H).

6¹⁵⁻²², which gives an account of the interior of the building, has been much corrupted by later glosses. Thus in v.¹⁶ לְקֹרֶשׁ הַקֳּדָשִׁים ' for the most holy place,' a phrase which belongs to P, has been added to explain לִדְבִיר ' for an adytum.' Other more serious interpolations (omitted in LXX) are הוּא הַהֵיכָל, ' that is, the temple,' in v.¹⁷, vv.¹⁸·²¹ (except last 4 words in Heb.) ²²ᵇ. In vv.¹⁵·¹⁶ emend קֹרוֹת הַסִּפֻּן ' rafters of the ceiling,' הַקֹּרוֹת ' the rafters,' with LXX (B, Luc.), Vulg., Pesh. in place of הַקִּירוֹת הַסִּפֻּן קִירוֹת. V.¹⁹ is probably due to Rᴰ (notice the phrase 'ark of the covenant of J″'). By its omission we are able, with a slight emendation, to plausibly restore the original statement of vv.¹⁷·²⁰ᵃ ' And 40 cubits was the house before the adytum. And the adytum was 20 cubits long, and 20 cubits broad, and 20 cubits high ; and he overlaid it with pure gold.' In v.²⁰ᵇ we may emend (with LXX, B, Luc.) וַיַּעַשׂ for וַיְצַף, and thus, with the last 4 words of v.²¹, we read, ' and he made an altar of cedar wood before the adytum, and overlaid it with gold.' Stade would omit all references to the use of gold-plating or gilding in Solomon's temple, but in so doing he appears to go further than is warranted by the state of the text.†

* D's usual phrases are שָׁמַר מִשְׁפָּטִים לַעֲשׂוֹת observe judgments to do them ; 5¹ 7¹¹ 11³² 12¹, 2 K 17³⁷ לִמַּד מִשְׁפָּטִים לַעֲשׂוֹת teach (someone else) judgments to do them ; 4¹·⁵·¹⁴ 6¹.

† Cf. the writer's Notes on the Hebrew Text of Kings, p. 73 f.

6²³⁻²⁸ runs smoothly when, following the clever suggestion of Stade, v.²⁶ is inserted between v.²³ᵃ and v.²³ᵇ.

6²⁹·³⁰ (omitted in LXX) is a gloss. V.²⁹ is clearly by the same hand as v.¹⁸, and v.³⁰ is redundant after ²²ᵃ, and also out of place.

6³²·³⁵ may also readily be recognized as due to the author of vv.¹⁸·²⁹. Notice the late usage of the perf. with weak ו, וְקָלַע and וְצִפָּה.

6³³ᵇ is rendered intelligible by the emendation מְזוּזוֹת רְבָעוֹת 'doorposts standing foursquare,' after LXX (B, Luc.)

7¹⁻¹², the account of Solomon's further activity as a builder, appears to be free from later interpolation, doubtless because it did not possess so great an interest for post-exilic times as did the description of the first temple.

In v.²ᵇ read 'three' (B, Luc.) for 'four,' in agreement with the statement of v.³ ; * v.⁵ᵇ פֶּתַח אֶל־פֶּתַח 'and door was over against door' (partly following B, Luc.), instead of 'and light was over against light,' a statement already made in v.⁴ᵇ ; v.⁷ᵇ עַד־הַקֹּרוֹת 'to the rafters' (Vulg., Pesh.), in place of עַד־הַקַּרְקַע ; v.⁹ᵇ וּמֵחָצֵר בֵּית 'and from the court of the house of J″' (cf. v.¹²), for וּמִחוּץ rendered by RV 'and so on the outside.'

7¹⁵⁻²² has been much mutilated and obscured by glosses. These were added for the purpose of describing the 'wreaths of chain-work' (גְּדִלִים מַעֲשֵׂה שַׁרְשְׁרוֹת) and the 'lily work' (מַעֲשֵׂה שׁוּשָׁן), of which there appears to have been no mention in the original account ; cf. the summary vv.⁴¹·⁴². The glosses are v.¹⁷ᵃ (down to שַׁרְשְׁרוֹת) in its present form, vv.¹⁹·²⁰ᵃ·²². The original description may be restored by the aid of LXX.

In 7²⁴ read שְׁלֹשִׁים בָּאַמָּה 'for 30 cubits,' in place of 'for 10 cubits.'

7²⁷⁻³⁷ is in a very disordered condition, and but little help in reconstruction can be obtained from the Versions. Stade's rearrangement and emendation is well worthy of notice. He distinguishes between two parts of the carriages of the lavers : the מְכוֹנָה the movable base 4 cubits in height, mounted upon wheels of 1½ cubits in diameter, and the מַעֲשֵׂה־כֵן the pedestal, 1½ cubits high, fitted on to the top of the מְכוֹנָה and containing the socket in which the laver was placed.

7³⁸⁻⁴⁵ is substantially correct as it stands in MT (read הַסִּירוֹת 'the pots,' in v.⁴⁰ᵃ after LXX, Vulg., in place of הַכִּיֹּרוֹת 'the lavers').

7⁴⁶⁻⁵¹ is somewhat disordered. The vv.⁴⁸ᵇ⁻⁵⁰, which describe, or rather summarize, the making of golden vessels by Ḥiram, are to be regarded as a later gloss. The remainder should take the following order : v.⁴⁷ (emending the first half verse, after LXX B, אֵין מִשְׁקָל לַנְּחֹשֶׁת אֲשֶׁר עָשָׂה אֶת־כָּל־הַכֵּלִים הָאֵלֶּה מֵרֹב מְאֹד מְאֹד 'There was no weight to the brass wherewith he made all these vessels, because it was exceeding much'), v.⁴⁶, v.⁴⁸ᵃ (emending, with LXX, Luc., 'ש וַיַּח 'and S. placed,' instead of 'ש וַיַּעַשׂ 'and S. made'), v.⁵¹.

8¹⁻¹³, the dedication of the temple, is an old narrative revised by later hands under the influence of P. In LXX vv.¹⁻⁵ appear in a much shorter form, which shows no trace of abridgment, and certainly presents substantially the original account as it left the hand of Rᴰ.

The phrases of P to be noticed are—v.¹ 'all the heads of the tribes, the princes of the fathers' ; v.⁴ᵇ the distinction between the priests and the Levites (contrast in the original account vv.³·⁶·¹⁰·¹¹ where the priests alone are mentioned) ; v.⁵ עֲדַת יִשְׂרָאֵל 'the congregation of Israel,' and the verb הַנּוֹעָדִים 'that were assembled,' used in a ceremonial connexion. Beside these we find, in LXX as in MT, v.⁴ᵃ the phrase אֹהֶל מוֹעֵד 'the tent of meeting,' mainly characteristic of P, and perhaps here substituted for an original הָאֹהֶל 'the tent' (cf. ch 1³⁹) ; v.⁶ קֹדֶשׁ

* אַרְבָּעִים וַחֲמִשָּׁה חֲמִשָּׁה עָשָׂר טוּר 'forty and five, fifteen in a row,' can refer only to הָעַמּוּדִים 'the pillars,' and not, as RV, to הַצֵּלָע (fem.).

הַקֳּדָשִׁים 'the most holy place' (cf. above on 6¹⁶) ; and vv.⁸·¹⁰ הַקֹּדֶשׁ 'the holy place,' i.e. the outer room of the temple, called הַהֵיכָל in 6¹⁷·³³ 7²¹. The hand of Rᴰ may be seen in the phrase 'ark of the covenant of J″' vv.¹·⁶, in v.⁸ᵇ (see above, date), and probably in v.⁹ᵇ.

The two vv.¹²·¹³ are found in LXX (after the section vv.¹⁴⁻⁵³) in a fuller form than in MT, which, as is shown by Wellhausen (Composition, p. 271), presupposes, after the correction of a few translator's errors, a text substantially superior to MT. The addition at the close, which points to an original text, 'is it not written in the Book of the Upright,' must also be regarded as genuine.

8¹⁴⁻⁶⁶ presents throughout clear indications that it owes its present form to Rᴰ (phrases, Nos. 2, 3, 6–8, 11–26, 28, 50, 60–62, 64, 65). The final portion (vv.⁶²⁻⁶⁶) may perhaps exhibit an older narrative into which Deuteronomic additions have been incorporated, but the remainder, and especially the central prayer of dedication, has been so thoroughly amplified by the editor that it is impossible to discover any older kernel upon which he may have based his work. The choice of subjects in the successive divisions of the prayer seems for the most part to have been suggested by the catalogue of curses contained in Dt 28¹⁵⁻⁶⁸ ;—cf. v.³³ 'When thy people Israel be smitten down before the enemy,' with Dt 28²⁵ ; v.³⁵ 'When heaven is shut up, and there is no rain,' with 28²³·²⁴ ; v.³⁷ 'pestilence,' with 28²¹ ; 'blasting, mildew,' with 28²² ; 'locust, caterpillar,' with 28³⁸·³⁹·⁴² ; 'if the enemy besiege,' etc., with 28⁴⁹ᶠ. (especially v.⁵²) ; 'whatsoever plague, whatsoever sickness,' with 28²²·²⁷·³⁵·⁵⁹⁻⁶¹ ; v.⁴⁶ 'If they sin against thee . . . and thou deliver them to the enemy, so that they carry them captive,' etc., with 28³⁶·³⁷·⁶⁴⁻⁶⁸.

The division of the prayer vv.⁴⁶⁻⁴⁹, which brings forward the possibility of a general captivity of Israel in punishment for sins, is considered by Wellhausen (Composition, p. 270), Stade (Geschichte, i. p. 74), Kamphausen (in Kautzsch, Die Heilige Schrift) to be marked by its contents as not earlier than the Exile, and therefore later than Rᴰ.* Against this view may justly be cited the vagueness of the terms of v.⁴⁶ 'so that they carry them away captive unto the land of the enemy, far off or near,' and the fact that the writer (v.⁴⁸) appears to regard the temple as still standing during the period of the Exile : 'and pray unto thee towards their land . . . the city which thou hast chosen, and the house which I have built for thy name.' But the chief argument for the pre-exilic date of the passage is to be derived from comparison of Dt 28, which, as has been noticed, forms to some extent the model of the prayer. This ch. 28 is regarded by all critics as being, if not an integral portion of D (chs. 5–26),† at least closely akin to D in standpoint and date, and thus certainly pre-exilic. Yet, notwithstanding, vv.³⁶·³⁷·⁶⁴⁻⁶⁸ threaten a captivity of the nation in language decidedly more definite than that of the passage of the prayer which has been called in question. We may therefore be content to regard these verses as containing nothing necessarily opposed to the supposition of a pre-exilic authorship, and so, as of one piece with the whole, vv.²²⁻⁵³.‡

9¹⁻⁹, the account of Solomon's second vision, is coloured throughout by the phraseology of Rᴰ (phrases, Nos. 3, 28, 29, 30, 51, 52, 57, 60, 61). Owing to the terms in which this section speaks of the exile of Israel and the destruction of the temple (vv.⁷⁻⁹ §), it is regarded by Kuenen, Wellhausen, Stade, and Kamphausen as the work of Rᴰ² in exilic times. Such a conclusion, however, is by no means inevitable. The terms of v.³ (see above, date) go quite as far to prove a pre-exilic position as do the words of vv.⁶⁻⁹ to argue a post-exilic point of view ; nor are the terms of these latter verses so definite as to preclude the opinion that they were penned by Rᴰ cir. B.C. 600 (see above on 8⁴⁶⁻⁴⁹). If vv.⁷⁻⁹ do imply an exilic stand-

* Wellhausen and Stade seem to regard these verses as determining the exilic date of the whole section, vv.¹⁹·⁶⁶. Kamphausen assigns vv.⁴⁴⁻⁵³ to D².

† Cf. Kuenen, Hexateuch, § 7²¹ ; Driver, Deuteronomy, p. 303 f.

‡ Cf. Kuenen, Onderzoek, § 26⁵.

§ Especially v.⁸, where עֶלְיוֹן must be emended to עִיִּים (cf. Mic 3¹² ‖ Jer 26¹⁸, Ps 79¹) 'and this house shall be ruinous heaps.'

point, vv.$^{6-9}$ (and not the whole section) will belong to R^{D2}, vv.$^{1-5}$ to R^{D}.

9^{10}–10^{29} consists mainly of a series of short notices drawn from the same sources as chs. 4. 5 (Heb. 4–5^{14}). The originals appear to have been cut up and pieced together with no great skill; but whether the arrangement throughout is due to R^{D}, or later hands have employed themselves in altering the sequence of the narrative, is not clear. In LXX (B, Luc.) the arrangement is somewhat different, but scarcely superior, to that of MT.

One single original document appears to be represented by 9$^{10. 17. 18. 19. 15. 20. 21. 22. 23}$, and these verses may very well have originally taken this order, the completion of Solomon's building operations being first narrated, and then followed by an account of the forced levy raised to carry out these works. After v.^{23} there probably followed in the original a list of the names of the chief officers (שָׂרֵי הַנִּצָּבִים). The statement of v.^{24b} connected by R^{D} to v.^{24b} by the particle אָז 'then,' is probably from the same document. Next to the account of the king's building activity—his most important work, there would naturally follow mention of his achievement next in importance—the provision of an efficient shipping for the increase of his wealth from external sources. This succeeds in 9$^{26-28}$ 10^{11}. But reference to the ships naturally leads up to mention of the imports introduced by their means, as we see in 9^{28} 10^{11}, and the use to which these rare and valuable materials were put. Thus there follows 10$^{12. 14-22}$. The general subject of imports suggests allusion to a specially important item—horses from Egypt, apparently first introduced into the kingdom in any considerable numbers by Solomon, 10$^{26.}$* $^{28. 29}$.

Thus the disturbing factors introduced into this main account are seen to be 9$^{11-13. 14. 16. 24a. 25}$, 10$^{1-10. 13. 23-25. 27}$. Notice in 9$^{11. 16. 24}$ the awkward pluperfects pointed by the order—subject preceding verb, פַּרְעֹה מֶלֶךְ־מִצְרַיִם עָלָה, חִירָם מֶלֶךְ־צֹר נָשָׂא אֶת־, אַךְ בַּת־פַּרְעֹה עָלְתָה, and marking the passages as mere excerpts from sources which, in describing a regular sequence of events, must have read וַתַּעַל בַּת־פַּרְעֹה, וַיַּעַל פַּרְעֹה, וַיִּשָּׂא חִירָם. In v.^{11b} אָז יִתֵּן וּ cannot represent the apodosis of v.^{10}, since אָז used in this connexion (in place of וּ consecutive) would be quite without analogy. Moreover, even if v.^{11b} could form the apodosis, the parenthesis v.^{11a} would come in with very great awkwardness. V.^{16} has already, with 3^1, been referred to its true position after 4^{34} (Heb. 5^{14}). From the same source would seem to be derived v.^{24a}, while v.^{25}, though clearly alien to its immediate context, cannot definitely be assigned to any special source. 10$^{1-10. 13}$ is an ancient narrative introduced at this point to illustrate Solomon's wealth and wisdom, much in the same way as 3$^{16-28}$ serves to depict his discernment in judgment; and the two stories may very possibly be derived from the same source. Finally, 10$^{23-25. 27}$, couched in vague and generalizing language, are probably relatively late in origin, and are here introduced to give the finishing touch to the picture of Solomon's prosperity.

11$^{1-13}$, in its present form, is coloured by the hand of R^{D} (phrases, Nos. 3, 27, 29, 31–33, 35, 36, 57, 58, 65). The view that the latter portion of this section is not earlier than the Exile (R^{D2}; so Kuenen vv.$^{9-13}$, Kamphausen, vv.$^{9. 10}$) is based upon the words of v.^{9} 'who had appeared unto him twice,' and presupposes that the narrative of the second vision, ch. 9$^{1-9}$, comes from the hand of R^{D2}; but upon this opinion see ad loc. On the other hand, the fact that vv.$^{11-13}$ speak of a division of the kingdom but make no mention of an exile, favours their pre-exilic authorship. 11$^{1-8}$ appears in LXX in a somewhat differently arranged and briefer form, which is, in the main, correct.†

11$^{14-22}$ seems, as it now stands, to be somewhat confused. Hadad, though but 'a little lad' at the time of his flight into Egypt, at once finds favour with Pharaoh, and receives from him a house, an allowance, and land. He then, in spite of his extreme youth, marries the sister of Pharaoh's queen, Tahpenes, and his son Genubath is brought up in the palace with Pharaoh's sons. The form Adad (אֲדַד) of v.^{17a}, as a variation of Hadad (הֲדַד), creates further suspicion as to the integrity of the narrative.

* This verse originally stood in combination with 4^{26} (Heb. 5^6); see on 4$^{20-34}$.

† Notice especially in v.^{8b} the text of Luc. ἰθυμία καὶ ἴθυι, i.e. in סָקְטִיר וּמְזַבֵּחַ וּ in place of מְקַטְּרוֹת וּמְזַבְּחוֹת Solomon himself burnt incense and sacrificed to the strange gods, but this fact has been toned down by some later hand into the statement of MT. Syntax, however, has suffered in the process (we should expect at least מַקְטִרוֹת וַּמְזַבְּחוֹת).

H. Winckler (Alttest. Untersuchungen, 1–6) very skilfully distinguishes and reconstructs two narratives which have been interwoven. The one speaks of an Edomite Hadad, who, as a child, is carried into Egypt by his father's servant, and brought up by Pharaoh's queen. The other makes Adad a Midianite prince, who flees with his adherents into Egypt, taking with him certain Edomites from Paran, and is well received by Pharaoh, who gives him for wife the sister of his queen. A son, Genubath, is born to him, but of his fate we are not informed.

In 11$^{23-25}$ of MT the short account of Rezon appears to have assumed its present position at the hands of a later reviser of the text. LXX (B, Luc.) omits vv.$^{23-25a}$ (down to 'all the days of Solomon'), and then, in place of the impossible MT, presupposes a text וְאֵת הָרָעָה אֲשֶׁר עָשָׂה הֲדַד וַיָּקָץ בְּיִשְׂרָאֵל וַיִּמְלֹךְ עַל־אֲדָם 'This is the evil which Hadad did; and he abhorred Israel, and reigned over Edom.' This seems to be correct both in reading and in position, referring as it does the latter part of v.^{25} to Hadad, and adding the necessary summary as to his relationship to Solomon. The definiteness, however, of the statement, 'This is the evil,' suggests that in the original narrative some explicit account of Hadad's aggressions must have intervened after v.^{22}.

The short reference to Rezon, thus omitted by LXX, has been inserted between v.^{14a} and v.^{14b}; but clearly by a later hand. So placed, it breaks the connexion of the Hadad story, and necessitates the resumption καὶ Ἀδὲρ ὁ Ἰδουμαῖος, v.^{14b}, repeated from v.^{14a}. The notice is ancient and genuine, but its original position cannot now be accurately determined.

11$^{26-40}$ seems to have originally formed part of a history of Jeroboam, and perhaps belongs to the same source as 12$^{1-19}$ 14$^{1-18}$. As the narrative stands in Kings it has probably undergone some abbreviation at the commencement, in order to fit it on to the preceding account of Solomon's 'adversaries.' Notice the summary form of the introduction v.^{26} and the phrase of R^{D} 'at that time' (בָּעֵת) v.^{29}. Vv.$^{31-39}$ show signs of expansion at the hands of the editor (phrases, Nos. 2, 3, 11, 27, 28, 34, 38, 57–59).

Not improbably the speech has received some few later additions. In v.^{33} וְחֻקֹּתַי וּמִשְׁפָּטַי 'and my statutes and my judgments,' is wanting in LXX, and the use of these terms after לַעֲשׂוֹת 'to execute' rather than לִשְׁמֹר 'to keep' being characteristic of H (see on 6^{12}), the two words may reasonably be suspected to be a later insertion. LXX also omits מִצְוֺתָי אֲשֶׁר שָׁמַר וְחֻקֹּתָי 'who kept my commandments and my statutes,' at the end of v.^{34}, and, though the phrase is Deuteronomic, yet the repeated אֲשֶׁר has something of the awkward ring of an interpolation. The omission of the close of the speech by LXX (end of v.^{33} 'and I will give thee Israel'; v.^{39}), taken in connexion with the reference of v.^{39}—the affliction of the seed of David, but not for ever—suggests that this also may be an addition of exilic or post-exilic times; though, as Kuenen points out, the statement of v.^{39} need not imply an exilic standpoint; cf. 2 S 7^{14b}. The use of the imperfect with weak וּ (וְאַעֲנֶה) is perhaps another mark of the late hand.

After the account of the disruption of the kingdom (1 K 12), the composition of the narrative takes the form indicated above in dealing with the editor's method. Into the framework of the history, constructed by the editor, are embedded—

(i.) Short notices which give an epitome of historical events. These have reference to both the N. and S. kingdoms, and were no doubt generally, if not in every case, extracted by R^{D} from the two books of 'Annals' to which he so constantly makes reference. From the character of this narrative it is to be inferred that R^{D} made use of just so much of his sources as was necessary to form an outline sketch of the history, often summarizing in a few words matter which lay before him in greater detail; cf. the recurring phrase 'and there was war between M. and N. continually,' I 14^{30} 15$^{6. 16. 32}$, and also the brief passing reference to wars in I 14^{19} 22^{45} (46 Heb.), II 13^{12} 14$^{15. 28}$.

To this epitome are to be assigned I 14^{21}–16^{34} 22$^{41-53}$, II 8$^{16-29}$ 10$^{32-36}$ 12^{17} (Heb. 18)–13^{13} 13^{22}–17^6 (except 14$^{8-14}$ 16$^{10-16}$).

(ii.) Lengthy narratives, generally incorporated in their original form, and exhibiting only here and there the marks of R^D's hand, chiefly in the expansion of speeches. These are in most cases, as is clear from their religious tone, the work of prophetical writers. In some cases, however, the narratives have to do with the affairs of the temple and its priesthood, and exhibit such a minuteness and apparent accuracy of detail that they must be regarded as due to priestly hands, and were probably derived from the temple archives. These are II 11[1-20] 12[4-16] (5-17 Heb.) 16[10-16] 22[3-23][24].

12[1-24]. In this narrative vv.[15, 17, 21-24] appear to be additions of a later hand. V.[15], with its reference to the prediction of Ahijah, probably presupposes 11[31ff.] in its present form, and must in this case be due to R^D. Vv.[21-24], standing in close connexion with v.[15] (cf. v.[15] 'for it was a thing brought about of J'', v.[24] 'for this thing is of me'), give a Judaic turn to the originally impartial narrative of vv.[1-20], and are scarcely consistent with the statement of 14[30], which is based upon the contemporary 'Annals.' Notice further, that while v.[20] speaks only of the tribe of Judah, vv.[21, 23] are careful to make reference also to the tribe of Benjamin. V.[17], which stands in an awkward position, and is absent from LXX, is probably a later gloss, though not by the same hand as vv.[15, 21-24], since it makes no reference to Benjamin.

12[26-33]. Judging by the stress which R^D lays upon Jeroboam's cult of the calves as the cause of all subsequent deflection of Israel from the pure worship of J'' (phrases, No. 56), it is probable that this narrative has obtained its present casting at his hands, though there is no reason hence to infer that any detail of fact is underived from the older source. Kuenen (Onderzoek, § 25⁴) observes justly, 'Jeroboam's measures with reference to the worship must already have been related in older narratives, but it is only natural that the Redactor, when dealing with a matter which so specially excited his interest, should not fail to set before us his own construction and his own verdict.' Vv.[32, 33] serve to introduce the story of ch. 13.

13[1-32]. The style of the language in this narrative shows traces of decadence :—cf. וְנָתַן perf. with weak ו [3], צִוָּה אֹתִי לִי vv.[9, 17], apparently first written as passives צֻוֵּיתִי לִי (cf. Wellhausen, Comp. p. 280), and perhaps כָּתֵּף v.[7]—and this fact, together with the anachronism 'in the cities of Samaria' v.[32] (cf. II 17[24, 26] 23[19]), and the non-mention of the names of the principal actors, marks the narrative as being of comparatively late origin. It may be thought to have been a story previously current in the form of oral tradition, and to have assumed a literary form shortly after the event predicted—the destruction of the altar at Bethel—had come about. Notice the precision of the statement 'Josiah by name' v.[2]. The style is about contemporary with that of the annals of Josiah's reformation, II 23[1-15, 19-24], where the perf. with weak ו is used with some frequency : vv.[5, 8, 10, 12, 14, 15].

It is, however, by no means to be hence inferred that the story is of the character of a vaticinium post eventum. Such a view presupposes that it, together with the notice of II 23[16-18], was inserted into Kings subsequently to the redaction of R^D (Wellhausen, Comp. p. 280 ; Kuenen, Ond. § 254) ; whereas, on the contrary, ch. 12[26ff.] appears to have been carefully edited by R^D so as to lead up to the story, and the resumption of the main narrative in 13[33, 34], forming a link to 14[1-20], constructs of the history a harmonious whole. If the story be merely a very late Judæan fiction, the point of the details as to the disobedience and punishment of the Judæan prophet seems to be quite inexplicable.

The narrative of 14[1-18] * exhibits very clear traces of the hand of R^D in Ahijah's prophecy vv.[7-16]

* Upon the LXX version of this narrative in its relationship to MT, see Winckler, Alttest. Untersuchungen, p. 12 ff. ; Kittel, History of the Hebrews, ii. p. 206 ff. ; and the writer's Notes on

(phrases, Nos. 3, 8, 13, 29, 32, 34, 39, 54, 56, 57, 66–70), with which should be compared the prophecies of Jehu son of Hanani against Baasha 16[1-4], of Elijah against Ahab 21[20-24], and of the young prophet against the house of Ahab II 9[6-10].

Narratives of the Northern Kingdom.—I 17-19. 20. 21. 22[1-38], II 1[2-17]‖ 2[1-18, 19-22, 23-25] 3[4-27] 4[1-7, 8-37, 38-41], 42-44 5. 6[1-7, 8-23, 24-33] 7. 8[1-6, 7-15] 9[1-10][28] 13[14-19, 20, 21] (14[8-14]). This great group consists of narratives dealing with the affairs of the kingdom of Israel. The stories are in most cases of some length, their high descriptive power and sympathetic feeling indicating that they have their origin in the kingdom to which they relate ; and this conclusion is substantiated by such touches as 'Beer-sheba which belongeth to Judah' I 19[3], 'at Beth-shemesh which belongeth to Judah' II 14[11]. No blame is anywhere attached to the calf-worship of Bethel and Dan, the efforts of Elijah and his successor being wholly directed to the rooting out of the foreign cult of the Tyrian Ba'al.

Certain peculiarities of diction probably belong to the dialect of North Palestine.

The following may be noticed :—

Suffix 2 f. sing. ־ֵ־כִי, pl. ־ֵ־יְכִי ; *Kĕthîbh* II 4[2] לֵכִי [3] שְׁכֵנְכִי, בְּנֵכִי, וְשֵׁכִי [7]. Elsewhere sing. Ca 2[3], Ps 103[3, 4], Jer 11[15] (text corrupt), pl. Ps 103[3, 4, 5] 116[7]. Cf. Syriac suff. 2 f. sing.

ـكِـ, pl. ـكِـن.

Personal pronoun 2 f. sing. *Kĕthîbh* : אַתִּי—II 4[16, 23] 8[1]. Elsewhere Jg 17[2], Jer 4[30], Ezk 36[13] †. Cf. Syriac ܐܢܬܝ. So probably *Kĕthîbh* הלכתי II 4[23] stands for הלכתּ אתי, as in Syr.

ܐܙܠܬܝ for ܐܢܬܝ ܐܙܠܬ (Duval, *Gramm. Syr.* p. 174 f.).

Demonstrative pronoun f. זה II 6[19]. Cf. Aramaic דָּא.

Infin. constr. verb ל"ה with suff. : בְּהִשְׁתַּחֲוָתִי II 5[18], perhaps presupposing form without suff. הִשְׁתַּחֲוָיה with termination as in Aram. (cf. Dalman, *Gramm. Jüd.-Pal. Aram.* p. 289 f.).

Relative שֶׁל in מִשֶּׁלָּנוּ (if not a textual error) II 6[11]. So Jg 5[7] (N. Palestine) 6[17] 7[12] 8[26] (probably Ephraimitic), and uniformly in Ca (exc. title 1[1]). Elsewhere only in exilic or post-exilic writings. In Phœnician the relative is אש with prosthetic א.

Preservation of ה of article after prep. בְ : II 7[12] בְּהַשְּׁעָרה.

Kĕthîbh אֵיכָה=*where*? II 6[13]. Elsewhere only Ca 17bis. Cf. Aram. אֵיכָא, ܐܝܟܐ.

Construction with the suff. pronoun anticipating object (akin to Syr.) : I 19[21] אֶת־נְבוֹתה . . . בְּשֵׂדֵה הַבָּשָׂר 21[13] וַיְעִרָהוּ II 9[18, 20] עִר־אֲלֵיהֶם, עַר־הֶם.

Indefinite use of אֶחָד *a certain* : I 19[4, 5] 20[13] 22[9] (cf. v.[8]) II 4[1] 8[6] ; add I 21[1] after LXX (B, Luc.). Elsewhere only I 13[11] (perhaps for אַחֵר *another*), Jg 9[53] 13[2], 1 S 1[1], 2 S 18[10], and late Ezk 1[15] 8[7, 8] etc.

To these may be added a few roots which betray the influence of Aramaic : שָׁפַק I 20[10], סְרִיּוֹת 20[14, 15, 17, 19] (elsewhere only very late), חֹרִים 21[8, 11], הֻשְׁלָה II 4[28].

There is also a fair number of ἅπαξ λεγόμενα, some of which take the place of ordinary words, and thus may be dialectical : e.g. שִׁנֵּם *gird*, I 18[46] (for אָזַר, חָגַר), אֲכִילָה *food*, 19[8] (for אָכְלָה, אֹכֶל, מַאֲכָל) ; but of others nothing can be affirmed.

The narratives are clearly not all by one author. (i.) Some are histories of Elijah and Elisha, or of movements which they initiated in the direction of religious reform. (ii.) In others the fate of the kingdom is regarded from a political standpoint, and this as determined mainly by the action of the *king* ; though here also prophets play an important part as advisers and announcers of the oracle of J''. Thus both classes have a religious colouring or motive, and may equally be regarded as the work of men of prophetic training, perhaps members of the guilds which we see coming into prominence in some of the Elisha stories.

(i.) To the former class belong I 17-19. 21,

the *Heb. Text of Kings*, where the whole question of the interrelationship of the two forms of the history of Jeroboam (11[46]–14[20]) is discussed at length, pp. 163–169.

II 1²⁻¹⁷ₐ, 2¹⁻¹⁸. ¹⁹⁻²². ²³⁻²⁵ 4¹⁻⁷. ⁸⁻³⁷. ³⁸⁻⁴¹. ⁴²⁻⁴⁴ 5. 6¹⁻⁷ 8¹⁻⁶. ⁷⁻¹⁵ 9¹⁻¹⁰²⁸ 13¹⁴⁻¹⁹. ²⁰. ²¹.

Of these I 17–19 forms a continuous narrative. From the abruptness of v.¹, no reason being assigned for Elijah's threat, and no point of connexion existing for 'hence' (מִזֶּה), v.³, it may be inferred that the commencement of the story has been omitted or abbreviated by Rᴰ, and the specification 'Elijah the Tishbite, etc.,' thus represents his summary introduction. The sequel also, in strict accordance with 19¹⁵. ¹⁶, is lacking, only one part of J'''s commission being fulfilled, vv.¹⁹⁻²¹.

I 21 is clearly out of place in MT, breaking the connexion between ch. 20 and its sequel ch. 22, and LXX is no doubt correct in placing this narrative immediately after ch. 19. The dislocation may have been due to the desire to bring the prophecy of Ahab's death (21¹⁹) nearer to the account of its occurrence (22³⁵ᶠᶠ·), and perhaps in a minor degree to the description of the king's mood as 'chafing and sullen' (סַר וְזָעֵף) in 20⁴³ as in 21⁴. Most critics (Wellhausen, Driver, Kamphausen, Kittel; but Kuenen is uncertain, *Ond.* § 25⁷) assign I 21 to the same author as I 17–19. Thus Wellhausen cites as points of contact the central position occupied by Elijah, his eagle-like swoop upon Ahab at the right moment, and the formulæ וַיְהִי אַחַר הַדְּבָרִים הָאֵלֶּה 'and it came to pass after these things' 21¹ (but cf. LXX) as 17¹⁷, וַיְהִי דְבַר י' אֶל־א' 'And the word of J'' came to E.' 21¹⁷ as וּדְבַר י' הָיָה אֶל־א' 18¹.

On the other hand, it may be maintained that Elijah is not really the central figure as in I 17–19. He does not appear upon the scene until v.¹⁷, and then takes scarcely a more conspicuous position than Micaiah in 22⁸ᶠᶠ. The king and his action form the centre of interest both at the beginning and end of the narrative. Further, Kuenen notices the absence of any reference in 21 to 17–19, and *vice versâ*, the murder of Naboth forming the single crime of Ahab and Jezebel in the one story, while in the other the sole pivot is the struggle between J'' and Ba'al. This, however, is a point of slight moment, and no definite conclusion can be reached as to the relative authorship of the two sections.

More important is the question of the connexion of I 21 with its natural sequel II 9¹⁻¹⁰²⁸. Critics generally argue or assume that the latter section is by a different author from the former, and most (Wellhausen, Driver, Kamphausen, Kittel) assign II 9 f. to the writer of I 20. 22, II 3⁴⁻²⁷ etc. (see below). The argument against identity of authorship of I 21 and II 9 f., as stated by Wellhausen, is based upon the supposed discrepancy in detail. While in I 21 it is the *vineyard* of Naboth which is mentioned, and this is described in v.¹ as 'hard by the palace of Ahab' (אֵצֶל הֵיכַל אַחְאָב), II 9²¹⁻²⁶ alludes to the חֶלְקָה, *i.e.* the *portion* or *estate* of Naboth, which lay outside the city. Again, I 21¹³ records only the death of Naboth, while II 9²⁶ speaks also of the blood of his sons as calling for vengeance.

On the other hand, the following considerations clearly make for the unity of the two narratives :—

II 9²¹ᵇ, the meeting of Joram son of Ahab with Jehu actually upon the estate of Naboth is a touch of high dramatic power which demands that the writer should not merely have *known* the story of Naboth (proved by vv.²⁵· ²⁶), but should actually have written it down himself as an introduction to the sequel II 9 f. Hence a presumption is created in favour of our Naboth narrative being the story thus written.

The parallels between the prediction I 21¹⁹· ²³ and the fulfilment II 9²⁵. ²⁶. ³⁶ cannot be insisted upon, because I 21¹⁹ᶠ. has been largely amplified by Rᴰ (*phrases*, Nos. 32, 39, 43, 44, 54, 67–71), and **it** is not now possible certainly to determine the

original kernel of Elijah's prediction. It should, however, be noticed that the usual method of Rᴰ is to expand rather than to excise, and, if this plan has here prevailed, the original speech must be contained in vv.¹⁹· ²⁰· ²³ᵇ. The disagreement in points of fact between I 21 and II 9 proves upon examination to be non-existent. Ahab's dispute with Naboth arose in the first instance about a vineyard adjoining the palace ; but this was only **a** portion of Naboth's estate (חֶלְקָה), the whole of which would lapse to the king, supposing that the family of Naboth became extinct. And I 21¹⁵, where Jezebel tells Ahab to go down and take possession of the vineyard, clearly implies the extirpation of the whole family ; in the statement 'for Naboth is not alive, but dead,' the name Naboth means Naboth *and his sons*, just as much as in v.¹⁵ 'thy blood, even thine,' means the blood of Ahab *and his son.*

More decisive, however, is the question of the supposed unity of II 9¹⁻¹⁰²⁸ with I 20. 22, II 3⁴⁻²⁷ 6⁸⁻⁷²⁰. If this be granted, the diverse authorship of I 21 and II 9 f. seems necessarily to follow, since I 21 can scarcely be regarded as of one piece with I 20. 22. The place where the dogs lick the blood of Ahab, 22³⁸, is discordant with 21¹⁹, and in general the interest of the writer of 20. 22—mainly, if not wholly, political—and his sympathetic feeling for the king of Israel, preclude the supposition that he is also the author of the Naboth story.

Wellhausen cites the following coincidences in phraseology of II 9 f. with I 20. 22, etc.:—חֶדֶר בְּחָדֶר 'a chamber within a chamber,' II 9², I 20³⁰ 22²⁵ ; חִכָּה 'tarry,' II 9³ 7⁹ ; רֶכֶב הַסּוּס 'horseman,' 9¹⁸ 7¹⁴ ; * הָפַךְ יָדָיו 'turn the hands,' II 9²³, I 22³⁴ ; תָּפַשׂ חַי 'take alive,' II 10¹⁴ 7¹², I 20¹⁸ ; and the root חרא II 10²⁷ 6²⁵. The importance of this collection is, however, open to doubt, since it contains no striking phrase, but only such as might be expected to occur in narratives nearly contemporaneous, and, having, in the main, the same subjects in common.

On the other hand, a point of phraseology, apparently hitherto overlooked, sharply separates between II 9 f. and I 20. 22, etc., and seems absolutely to preclude the theory of a common authorship. This is the title which is ordinarily applied to the *king* in the course of the narrative. I 20. 22, II 3⁴⁻²⁷ 6⁸⁻⁷²⁰ are bound together by the use of a common title. In all, the writer's phrase is '*king of Israel*,' and the proper name of the king, if it occurs at all, is in nearly every case reserved for the necessary specification at the commencement of a section.

II 9, on the other hand, agrees with I 21 in exhibiting a regular preference for the proper name simply, without further title.

The facts are as follow :—

I 20. *Ahab king of Israel*, vv.². ¹³ ; *king of Israel* 11 times, viz. vv.⁴. ⁷. ¹¹. ²¹. ²². ²⁸. ³¹. ³². ⁴⁰. ⁴¹. ⁴³ ; *the king*, vv.³⁸. ³⁹ *bis* ; *Ahab* simply, v.¹⁴.

I 22. *King of Israel* 17 times, viz. vv.². ³. ⁴. ⁵. ⁶. ⁸. ⁹. ¹⁰. ¹⁸. ²⁶. ²⁹. ³⁰ *bis*. ³¹. ³². ³³. ³⁴ ; *the king*, vv.¹⁵ *bis*. ¹⁶. ³⁵. ³⁷ᵇ.

II 3⁴⁻²⁷. *King of Israel* 8 times, viz. vv.⁴. ⁵. ⁹. ¹⁰. ¹¹. ¹². ¹³ *bis* ; *Ahab* simply, v.⁵ (probably from another source) ; *the king Joram*, v.⁶.

II 6⁸⁻⁷²⁰. *King of Israel* 7 times, viz. 6⁸. ⁹. ¹⁰. ¹¹. ¹². ²¹. ²⁶ ; *the king* 10 times, viz. 6²⁸. ³⁰ 7². ⁶. ¹². ¹⁴. ¹⁵. ¹⁷ *bis*. ¹⁸.

II 9. *Joram* or *Jehoram* simply 9 times, viz. vv.¹⁴ *bis*. ¹⁶ *bis*. ¹⁷. ²¹. ²². ²³. ²⁴ ; once *Jehoram the king*, v.¹⁵ ; and once *Jehoram king of Israel* in direct distinction from 'Ahaziah king of Judah,' v.²¹ ; never *king of Israel* simply. The double occurrence of *Joram* in v.¹⁶ is specially to be noticed, since, on account of the proximity of 'Ahaziah king of Judah,' the specification *king of Israel* might have been expected.

Similarly, in I 21 *Ahab* simply is usual ; 9 times (omitting the prophecy vv.²¹⁻²⁶), viz. 21². ³. ⁴. ⁸. ¹⁵. ¹⁶. ²⁰. ²⁷. ²⁹. *Ahab king of Samaria*, v.¹ ; *Ahab king of Israel*, v.¹⁸.

Now though this agreement in form of reference cannot be pressed to prove *identity* of authorship

---

* In 7¹⁴ MT vocalizes רֶכֶב סוּסִים, but LXX renders B ἰπιβάτας, Luc. ἀναβάτας, *i.e.* רֹכְבֵי (or רֶכֶב) for רֶכֶב.

for I 21 and II 9, any more than can the fact that I 17–19 always speaks of *Ahab* simply, be used to connect this section with I 21, because different writers may easily have employed the same obvious citation of the proper name; yet the fact of the disagreement in form of reference between I 21 and I 20. 22, etc., ought to be emphasized as demonstrating *diversity* of authorship. It is true that in I 20. 22, etc., the general use of *king of Israel* may be explained as prompted to a large extent by contrast to 'king of Syria'; but this does not sufficiently account for the almost total omission of the king's proper name, which would certainly have occurred far more frequently had the author of II 9 been the writer of these narratives. Contrast especially I 22, II 3⁴⁻²⁷, where (excepting 3⁶) the names of Ahab and Joram are never mentioned in spite of the close connexion with 'Jehoshaphat king of Judah,' with II 9, where in connexion with 'Ahaziah king of Judah' the usual form of citation is *Joram, Jehoram* simply. And, again, notice the use of *the king* simply 5 times in I 22, 10 times in II 6⁸⁻7²⁰, where the desire for distinction from 'the king of Syria' cannot have been in the writer's mind, and the occasion might have been suitable for the use of the king's proper name.

By this point, therefore, the diverse authorship of I 20. 22, etc. and II 9 seems to be proved, and this dissociation adds weight to the arguments which have been put forward above in favour of the unity of II 9¹–10²⁷ with I 21.

II 1²⁻¹⁷ᵃ is out of a different source from the preceding Elijah narratives. This fact is marked by the form of the name אֵלִיָּה vv.³, ⁴, ⁸, ¹², peculiar to this section, and generally by the inferior literary merit of the composition. The story is probably much later than I 17–19, II 21 and its sequel.

II 2¹⁻¹⁸, Elijah's translation, links itself closely on to some of the longer Elisha narratives which follow, as their introduction; but also might have formed a suitable close to the Elijah history, of which we possess a fragment in I 17–19, if this can be thought to have gone on to embody also a history of Elisha. The following coincidences between the narratives are worthy of notice, and suggest that I 17–19, II 2¹⁻¹⁸ 4¹⁻³⁷, to which we may add II 5, may be the work of one author. In the case of II 8⁷⁻¹⁵ 13¹⁴⁻¹⁹ the evidence is too slight to build upon.

	Elijah.		Elisha.
I 17⁸⁻²⁴. Miraculous provision for the widow of Zarephath during famine, and the raising of her son from death.		II 4¹⁻⁷. Miraculous provision for the wife of one of the sons of the prophets. II 4⁸⁻³⁷. Raising to life of the son of the Shunammite woman.	
I 18²⁶ וְאֵין קוֹל וְאֵין עֹנֶה 'and there was no voice, neither was there any that answered'; v.²⁹ אֵין קוֹל וְאֵין עֹנֶה וְאֵין קָשֶׁב 'but there was no voice nor any that answered, nor any attention.'		II 4³¹ וְאֵין קוֹל וְאֵין קָשֶׁב 'but there was no voice, nor any attention.'	
I 19¹³·¹⁹. Mention of Elijah's *mantle* (אַדֶּרֶת).		II 2⁸·¹³·¹⁴ *ib.*	
I 18⁴² וַיִּגְהַר אַרְצָה 'and he crouched upon the earth.'		II 4³⁴·³⁵ וַיִּגְהַר עָלָיו 'and he crouched upon him.' *	
II 2²·⁴·⁶ חַי יְיָ וְחֵי נַפְשְׁךָ אִם אֶעֶזְבֶךָ 'as J" liveth and as thy soul liveth, I will not leave thee.'		II 4³⁰ *ib.*	
II 2⁷·¹⁵ מִנֶּגֶד 'over against.'		II 4²⁵ *ib.*	
II 2¹⁷ וַיִּפְצְרוּ בוֹ עַד־בֹּשׁ 'and they urged him till he was ashamed.'		II 8¹¹ וַיָּשֶׂם עַד־בֹּשׁ 'and he set (his countenance upon him) till he was ashamed.'	
II 2¹⁷ אָבִי אָבִי רֶכֶב יִשְׂרָאֵל וּפָרָשָׁיו 'my father, my father, the chariots of Israel and the horses thereof.'		II 13¹⁴ *ib.*	

* The verb נהר is not elsewhere found.

The short Elisha stories are probably popular tales handed down orally at first, and not put into writing until some considerable time after the longer narratives.

(ii.) The second class includes I 20. 22¹⁻³⁸, II 3⁴⁻²⁷ 6⁸⁻²³. ²⁴⁻³³ 7 (14⁸⁻¹⁴).

All these, with the exception of 14⁸⁻¹⁴, deal in the same style with the same subject—Israel's relations with Syria, and may not improbably flow from one hand. Notice especially the close bond of connexion between I 22⁴·⁷ and II 3⁷·¹¹.

II 14⁸⁻¹⁴, which stands apart from the other narratives, is marked as probably N. Palestinian by its tone, and especially by the reference of v.¹¹ 'in Beth-shemesh, which belongeth unto Judah.'

It does not appear that any of the group of N. Palestinian narratives has undergone important *editorial revision*. The fact that the speech of Elijah in I 21¹⁹ᶠᶠ· has been amplified by Rᴰ has already been noticed. This is also true of the speech of the young prophet who was deputed by Elisha to anoint Jehu, II 9⁷⁻¹⁰. II 3⁴·⁵, which serves summarily to introduce the succeeding narrative, is probably not of one piece with this latter, but is rather to be assigned to the 'Annals' (cf. II 1¹). II 9²⁹ belongs to the scheme of Rᴰ.

Traces of *later interpolation* are not numerous. In I 18 the reference to the 400 prophets of the Asherah is probably to be regarded, with Wellhausen, as a later insertion. Notice the absence of אֵת before נְבִיאֵי הָאֲשֵׁרָה, and the omission of all mention of such prophets in vv.²², ⁴⁰. The insertion seems to exhibit a late confusion of the Asherah with the goddess Ashtoreth (see ASHERAH).

The statement of v.³¹ᵇ in the same narrative looks like a quotation of the exact words of P in Gn 35¹⁰; and, if this be the case, vv.³¹·³²ᵃ, which appear to describe the building of a new altar, will form a later addition to the statement of v.³⁰ᵇ which speaks merely of the *repair* (וַיְרַפֵּא) of the old altar of J". It should not, however, be overlooked that the giving of the name of Israel to Jacob is related also in J (Gn 32²⁹), and that the relationship of 1 K 18³¹ᵇ to the passage of P may be nothing more than an easy verbal coincidence. In this case vv.³¹·³²ᵃ may represent a detailed description of that which is first summarily stated in v.³⁰ᵇ, much in the same way as Gn 27²⁴⁻²⁹ stands related to Gn 27²³.

In the narrative of I 20 the grounds upon which Wellhausen regards the reference to the parts played by anonymous prophets (vv.¹³·¹⁴·²²·²⁸·³⁵⁻⁴³) as later additions are inconclusive.

I 22²⁸ᵇ, which is omitted in LXX (B, Luc.), is certainly an interpolation, derived from Mic 1¹ for the purpose of identifying Micaiah with Micah the Morashtite. The plural עַמִּים regularly denotes 'peoples,' *i.e.* foreign nations generally, and is seldom or never used of Israel.

Very possibly also vv.³⁵ᵇ⁻ (from וַיִּצֶק 'and the blood ran out,' etc.) ³⁸ may not have formed part of the original narrative of Ahab's last battle. In LXX (B, Luc.) v.³⁵ᵇᵝ precedes v.³⁵ᵇᵅ 'and he died in the evening.' V³⁸, for which v.³⁵ᵇᵝ prepares the way, hinges awkwardly on to the apparent close of the narrative in v.³⁴, and seems to be intended to satisfy the prophecy as to Ahab's death in 21¹⁹ᵇ, though the scene of the event differs from that of the prediction.

II 17⁷⁻¹⁸·²¹⁻²⁴ is the commentary of Rᴰ (*phrases*, Nos. 3, 29, 32, 33, 36, 39, 41, 43, 44, 46, 51, 53, 55, 56, 71, 72, and cf. Driver, *LOT⁶* p. 203) upon the short historical notice 17³⁻⁶.† Vv.¹⁹·²⁰ are certainly a later insertion, subsequent to the commence-

* Kuenen (*Ond.* § 25¹⁰) agrees with Wellhausen's verdict upon vv.¹³·¹⁴·²²·²⁸, but inclines to regard vv.³⁵⁻⁴³ as of much greater antiquity, and of a piece with the narrative of ch. 20.

† Possibly composite. Cf. Winckler, *AT Untersuchungen*, 15–25.

ment of the Judæan exile, and due to R[D2]. The opening of v.[21] וַיִּקְרַע 'For he rent,' etc., clearly refers immediately to the statement of v.[18] וַיִּתְאַנַּף וַיְסִרֵם ... 'was very angry ... and removed them,' but the sequence is destroyed by the interpolation, כִּי v.[21] being deprived of all point. The whole reference of the section is to the causes which brought about the rejection of the kingdom of *Israel*, no reference being elsewhere made to Judah except in v.[13], where וּבִיהוּדָה 'and unto Judah,' is probably by the same hand as vv.[19. 20].

Stade (*ZATW* vi. 163 f.) regards 17[7-17] as an exilic addition, later than R[D], upon the grounds that the writer of these verses ascribes Molech - worship (v.[17a]) and Assyrian star - worship (v.[16b]) to the Northern kingdom—the abuses which later on were rife in the Southern kingdom under Manasseh (II 21[3. 6]), and also because certain phrases appear to exhibit the influence of Jeremiah; cf. v.[13] 'Turn ye from your evil ways,' with Jer 18[11] 25[5] 35[15] 36[3. 7]; 'J'' testified,' etc., with Jer 7[25ff.], 11[7ff.]; v.[15b] 'and they followed vanity,' etc., with Jer 2[5]. The reflections embodied in these verses are, however, in strict accordance with R[D]'s plan which runs throughout his work, as the number of phrases above cited as characteristic of his hand sufficiently shows, nor is it at all unnatural that the editor who worked not many years after Josiah had removed from the kingdom of Judah the foreign abuses of Manasseh's reign, should ascribe the same kind of religious abuses to the kingdom of Israel, side by side with the worship of J'' under the form of a calf. Nor, again, need the phrases above mentioned imply dependence upon the written prophecies of Jeremiah, any more than need other phrases used by R[D] elsewhere (Nos. 50-55) in common with Jeremiah go to prove that R[D] and Jeremiah were one and the same person. All that clearly emerges from the fact of such resemblances is that the two writers were members of one prophetic school of thought, *i.e.* the Deuteronomic (cf. Driver, *LOT*[6] p. 203 at end).

The narrative of II 17[24-41] is certainly composite. Vv.[32. 41], in speaking of the races which were settled by the Assyrian king in the cities of Samaria, say that they 'feared J'',' while retaining the worship of their own national deities. In v.[34], on the contrary, it is stated with great emphasis that they 'feared not J''.' Again, while vv.[24ff.] refer exclusively to the *foreign* settlers, and only mention the introduction into their midst of a single priest of Israelitish nationality (v.[28] אֶחָד מֵהַכֹּהֲנִים), to whom was due their instruction in the worship of J''; vv.[34b-40] are couched in such terms as can refer only to *Israelites as such*, of however mixed and renegade a strain. Notice especially vv.[35. 38] the reference to the Deuteronomic covenant; v.[36] 'J'', who brought you up out of the land of Egypt.'

Thus this latter section must be regarded as a later addition to the narrative of Kings (R[D2]; *phrases*, Nos. 3, 16, 28, 29, 49), referring probably to the Samaritans of post - exilic times. V.[40b] rounds off the interpolation by the repetition of v.[34a], the statement of the older narrative to which the later writer attaches his addition. Vv.[24-34b. 41], on the other hand, form, in part at least, an ancient narrative embodied by R[D].

Stade (*ZATW* vi. 167 ff.) regards vv.[24-28. 41] as the original kernel which has received the later extension vv.[29-34a]. Possibly this latter may be assigned to R[D] himself; v.[32b] resembles I 12[31], and in v.[34a] עַד־הַיּוֹם הַזֶּה 'unto this day,' is an expression commonly employed by R[D].

II 18[1-8] is mainly the work of R[D] (*phrases*, Nos. 3, 31, 63, 72), based upon the notices of vv.[4. 7b. 8]. Vv.[7b. 8] are probably drawn in substance from the 'Annals.' With regard to v.[4] this is not so clear. The verse shows marks of a late style (perf. with weak ו, as in 21[4. 6] 23[5ff.]), and sketches the outline of a religious reformation which appears in all essentials to have resembled and anticipated the reformation of Josiah. Hence some critics regard the notice as a late and unhistorical interpolation (cf. Stade, *Geschichte*, i. 607 f., *ZATW* iii. 8 ff., vi. 170 ff.; Wellhausen, *Comp.* 291).

The occurrence of a reformation under Hezekiah is supported by 18[22] (which must, with the rejection of 18[4], be likewise branded as a later misconception), and perhaps also by the statement

of Jer 26[17-19a], which speaks of the influence exercised upon Hezekiah and all Judah by the preaching of Micah the Morashtite. Micah I[5b] MT mentions the *Bāmôth* of Jerusalem for reprobation; but this passage must not be pressed, because LXX, Pesh., Targ. presuppose a different reading.*

Certainly Isaiah does not appear to have had in view any centralization of J''s cultus, such as was prominent in Josiah's reformation, but his attacks upon the idol-worship (2[8. 18. 20] 31[7]; cf. 10[10. 11]), tree-worship (1[29]), and necromancy (8[19]), which seem to have been rife in the kingdom of Judah, are in agreement with such a movement in the direction of the pure worship of J''. Probably, therefore, as is allowed by Stade (*Ges. loc. cit.*), the statement of v.[4b] is based upon authentic information as to such a reform, and this has been later on expanded in v.[4a], under the influence of the accomplished fact of Josiah's reformation.

II 18[9-12] is a notice from the 'Annals,' introduced by the synchronism of R[D] v.[9a], and closed by his comment v.[12]. The notice is identical with 17[5. 6].

II 18[13]-20[19] = Is 36[1]-39[8].†

II 18[14-16], which is not found in Is, is distinguished from 18[13. 17ff.] by the form of the name חִזְקִיָּה Ḥizḳiyyah (instead of חִזְקִיָּהוּ Ḥizḳiyyahu), which occurs also in 18[1. 10] ('Annals'). 18[14-16] appears to be in strict agreement with the Assyrian record (Taylor Cylinder, col. iii.; cf. *COT* i. p. 286, ii. p. 1), and is probably a genuine excerpt from the 'Annals.'

It is generally agreed that the narrative of Is 36[1]-39[8] cannot be traced to Isaiah himself, but must be of a considerably later date. Notice the mention of Sennacherib's death (Is 37[38] = 2 K 19[37]), which did not happen until B.C. 681, twenty years after the campaign against Jerusalem, and certainly later than the death of Isaiah. Again, it seems to be clear that the Isaiah section (except 38[9-20] from another source) must have been extracted from our Book of Kings by the editor of Is 1-39.

Certain phrases which are due to R[D] in the Kings narrative appear also in Is; cf. 'for David my servant's sake' II 19[34] ∥ Is 37[35]; 'How I have walked before thee in truth and with a perfect heart, and have done that which is good in thy sight' II 20[3] ∥ Is 38[3]; and the redactional phrases 'In those days' II 20[1] ∥ Is 38[1], 'At that time' II 20[12] ∥ Is 39[1]. Kings is also superior to Is in the account of Hezekiah's sickness. Is 38[4-8] has been abbreviated; 38[21. 22] is misplaced.

The Kings narrative II 18[13. 17]-20[19] seems to represent a combination of three sources. Stade (*ZATW* vi. 174) notices that Isaiah's threat against Sennacherib occurs three times in similar terms: 19[7] 19[28b] 19[33]. The contents of Sennacherib's letter (19[10-13]) merely repeat in brief that which has already been said by the Rabshakeh (18[28-35]). Again, it is highly improbable that Sennacherib, after hearing the news with regard to Tirhakah (19[9a]), should have imagined that the mere dispatch of a letter would be likely to compel Hezekiah's submission, after the failure of previous verbal negotiations. The true sequel to 19[9a] seems to be 19[36f.]; upon receiving information of Tirhakah's hostile movement, Sennacherib raises the siege of Jerusalem and returns to Assyria. We have, then, two separate accounts of the Assyrian campaign, 18[13. 17]-19[9a. 36f.]; 19[9b-35] 19[9b] having probably been slightly modified by the redactor. Further, the section 19[9b-35] itself appears to be composite in character. The taunt song vv.[21-28], with its accompanying sign vv.[29-31], stands apart

* חַטָּאת 'sin,' parallel to פֶּשַׁע transgression, as in v.[4a]. The reading of MT is, however, accepted by Kittel, who regards the rendering of the Versions as merely a simplification (*History*, ii. 357).

† In addition to the authorities cited at the end of this article, cf. the Literature given under ISAIAH, especially Dillmann, *Jesaia*, 1890, p. 310 ff.; Cheyne, *Introduction to the Book of Isaiah*, 1895, p. 212 ff. (where, however, the writer proceeds upon the assumption that Kings was not compiled until after B.C. 588).

from the prosaic statement vv.[32-34]. לָכֵן, 'therefore,' of v.[32] answers, not to anything in the prophecy preceding, but to v.[20b]β אֲשֶׁר הִתְפַּלַּלְתָּ שָׁמָעְתִּי 'Whereas thou hast prayed . . . I have heard,' and, as has been noticed above, vv.[28b. 33] are duplicates of the same statement. Thus vv.[21-31], generally regarded by critics as an authentic prophecy of Isaiah, appear to have been inserted into the midst of the prophetical history 19[9b-20. 32-34], v.[21a] representing the redactor's link.

The narrative of 20[1-19] probably belongs to the author of one of the two preceding narrative sections. Cheyne, following Duhm, selects the second narrative 19[9bff]. Notice, as a point of connexion, the occurrence of a prayer of Hezekiah in each section: 19[15ff]. 20[2t]. Very possibly the chronological notice at the beginning of 18[13], 'In the 14th year of king Hezekiah,' properly refers to the events of 20[1-19], and occupies its present position upon the false assumption that Sennacherib's invasion took place in the same year as Hezekiah's sickness and recovery. This arrangement is probably due to R[D], who removed the note of time from its true position at the head of the narrative of 20[1ff], replacing it by his synchronistic phrase 'In those days.' Notice the reference to Assyria in 20[6]. The whole verse from וּמִכַּף 'and from the hand, etc.,' must be due to the author of the mistaken synchronism. Cf. the latter half with 19[34].

The 6th year of Hezekiah for the fall of Samaria, B.C. 722 (18[10]), cannot be reconciled with the 14th year for Sennacherib's campaign, B.C. 701 (18[13]), and it seems the best course to regard this latter date as true for the sickness of Hezekiah and the embassy of Merodach-Baladan, which will then fall cir. B.C. 714. Thus Hezekiah's reign may be supposed to have closed B.C. 699, i.e. some 15 years after B.C. 714 (20[6a]).

The short prophecy of 20[17. 18] has probably been worked over by R[D2] in post-exilic times, when Babylon, and not Assyria, was the oppressor.

II 21 is throughout the work of R[D] (phrases, Nos. 11, 13, 27, 42–44, 49, 54, 55, 66; and cf. Driver, LOT[6] p. 203) based upon very brief notices (vv.[3. 4a. 5. 6a. 7a. 16a]), derived, presumably, from the 'Annals.' Vv.[10-15] appear to presuppose the captivity of Judah, and must therefore, in their present form, be assigned to R[D2].

II 22[3]-23[25] is a continuous narrative, probably drawn from the temple archives. Deuteronomic phrases are found in 23[3. 19. 25] (phrases, Nos. 3, 6, 20, 39, 63), and in the speech of Huldah 22[15-20] (phrases, Nos. 29, 39, 54; and cf. Driver, LOT[6] p. 203), which seems to show signs of revision by R[D2] in exilic times. Certainly this later editor is responsible for the addition at the close of the narrative 23[26. 27] (phrases, Nos. 11, 39, 51), which strikes a note strangely alien to the enthusiasm of the pre-exilic author in view of Josiah's reformation (cf. especially vv.[22. 25]).

Upon II 23[29]-25[30] see above (Later editors). 25[22-26] is a much abbreviated account of the events described in Jer 40[7]-43[6], to which source R[D2] clearly owes his information. Jer 52, on the other hand, seems to be a later addition to the prophet's book (notice the closing words of ch. 51, 'Thus far are the words of Jeremiah'), excerpted from 2 K 24[18]-25[30], naturally with omission of 25[22-26], as having been already related in fuller detail.

LITERATURE.—O. Thenius, Die Bücher der Könige (in Kgf. Exeg. Handb.), 1e Aufl. 1849, 2e Aufl. 1873; F. Böttcher, Neue exegetisch-kritische Aerenlese zum AT, 2e Abtheilung, 1864, pp. 1-120; C. F. Keil, Die Bücher der Könige (in Bibl. Comm.), 1e Aufl. 1865, 2e Aufl. 1876 (Eng. tr. 1872); H. Ewald, The History of Israel (Eng. tr. 1871), vol. iii. p. 204 ff., vol. iv.; H. Grätz, Gesch. der Juden, vols. i. ii. 1, 1875 (frequent textual

suggestions omitted in Eng. tr. 1891); E. Schrader, COT, 1885-1888, vol. i. p. 172 ff., vol. ii.; A. Klostermann, Die Bücher Samuelis und der Könige (in Strack and Zöckler's Kgf. Komm.), 1887, p. 262 ff.; A. Kuenen, Historisch-kritisch Onderzoek, 2nd ed. 1887 (Ger. tr. 1890), §§ 24-27; I. Hooykaas, Iets over de Grieksche Vertaling van het OT, 1888; J. Wellhausen, Die Composition des Hexateuchs und der historischen Bücher des AT, 2e Druck, 1889, pp. 266-302, 359-361 (= Wellhausen-Bleek, Einleitung, 1878, p. 231 ff.), Prolegomena zur Geschichte Israels, 4e Ausg. 1895, pp. 275-299 (Eng. tr. 1885, p. 272 ff.), Israelitische und Jüdische Gesch., 2e Ausg. 1897, p. 64 ff. (enlarged from art. 'Israel' in Encyc. Brit. 1881 = History of People of Israel and Judah, 2nd ed. 1891, p. 53 ff.); B. Stade, Geschichte des Volkes Israel, 2e Aufl. 1889, 1er Band, pp. 73-79, 296 ff., ZATW iii. 129 ff. (on I 5-7), v. 178 (on I 22[48f]), v. 275 ff. (on II 10-14), vi. 156 ff. (on II 15-21); S. R. Driver, LOT[6] (1891), pp. 175-193, 6 (1897), pp. 185-203; H. Winckler, Alttest. Untersuchungen, 1892, pp. 1-54; E. König, Einleitung in das AT, 1893, pp. 263-269; A. Kamphausen (in Kautzsch's Die Heilige Schrift des AT, 1894), pp. 350-426, Beilagen, pp. 20-34; C. H. Cornill, Einleitung in das AT, 3e Aufl. 1896, pp. 108-117; R. Kittel, A History of the Hebrews (Eng. tr. 1896), vol. ii. 49 ff., 177 ff.; Piepenbring, Hist. du peuple d'Israël, 1898, p. 167 ff.

                    C. F. BURNEY.

KING'S POOL.—See POOL.

KING'S VALE, THE (עֵמֶק הַמֶּלֶךְ, AV the king's dale).—The place where the king of Sodom met Abram, Gn 14[17] (τὸ πέδιον βασιλέως). Here also the childless Absalom erected in his lifetime a monument to himself, 2 S 18[18] (ἡ κοιλὰς τοῦ βασιλέως). See HINNOM (VALLEY OF), p. 388[a]; SHAVEH (VALE OF), and JERUSALEM, p. 584[a].

KINSFOLK.—Although 'kinsfolk' is itself plural (see FOLK), and is so treated in Job 19[14] 'My kinsfolk have failed,' and Lk 2[44] 'They sought him among their kinsfolk' (ἐν τοῖς συγγενέσι [WH -εῦσιν]), it is also found with an s added, giving the irreg. plur. 'kinsfolks,' in 1 K 16[11] 'Neither of his kinsfolks, nor of his friends'; 2 K 10[11], 2 Mac 8[1] 15[18], Lk 21[16]. The NT Revisers have dropped the s in Lk 21[16], and the Apocr. Revisers in 2 Mac, but in 1 K 16[11] the OT Revisers have kept it. In 2 K 10[11] RV prefers 'familiar friends,' the Heb. expressing no reference to kinship (מְיֻדָּעִים, cf. LXX γνωστούς, the same word as is tr[d] 'acquaintance' in Lk 2[44]). For the form 'kinsfolks' cf. Strype, Life of Archbp. Whitgift, 1597, '[Geta] asked him, if those whom he had put to death had no parents, kinsfolks, nor friends'; and Bacon, Essays, 'Of Parents and Children' (Gold. Treas. ed. p. 24), 'The Italians make little difference betweene Children and Nephewes or neere Kinsfolkes.'   J. HASTINGS.

KINSMAN.—This is the proper singular form of 'kinsfolk,' with the fem. form 'kinswoman.' 'Kinsman' is the tr[n] in OT mostly of גֹּאֵל gō'ēl (see GOEL), and in NT of συγγενής. In Apocr. συγγενής is so tr[d] twice, Sir 41[21], 2 Mac 12[39], and ἀδελφός twice, To 3[15] 7[4] (RV 'brother'). In Ru 2[20] AV gives 'next kinsman' as the tr[n] of gō'ēl; RV changes this into 'near kinsman,' and gives 'near kinsman' instead of the simple 'kinsman' for all the other occurrences of gō'ēl in Ruth. In Ru 2[1] the Heb. Kethibh מְיֻדָּע means strictly no more than 'acquaintance,' but whether we adopt this reading or that of the Ḳerê מוֹדָע, 'kinsman' is plainly the meaning. Hence RV rightly retains the AV translation.

Kinswoman occurs Lv 18[12. 13. 17], Pr 7[4]; and RV adds Lk 1[36] 'Elisabeth thy kinswoman,' for AV 'thy cousin Elisabeth,' the word 'cousin' (wh. see) having become contracted in application since 1611. The Greek of TR is συγγενής, but the weight of authority is in favour of the late fem. form συγγενίς, which edd. (except Tr.) adopt.

                    J. HASTINGS.